The New GROVE® Dictionary of OPERA

Volume Four

Roe-Z
Appendices

The New GROVE® Dictionary of OPERA

Edited by

STANLEY SADIE

Managing Editor

CHRISTINA BASHFORD

Volume Four

Roe-Z
Appendices

MACMILLAN REFERENCE LIMITED, LONDON
GROVE'S DICTIONARIES OF MUSIC INC., NEW YORK, NY

The New Grove ® Dictionary of Opera

edited by STANLEY SADIE, in four volumes, 1992

First published in hardback 1992 by Macmillan Reference Limited, London. In the United States of America and Canada, Macmillan Reference has appointed Grove's Dictionaries of Music Inc., New York, NY, as sole distributor.

First published in paperback, 1998

Database creation and typesetting by Morton Word Processing Limited, Scarborough, Great Britain

Printed and bound in Hong Kong by China Translation and Printing Services Limited.

British Library Cataloguing in Publication Data

New Grove Dictionary of Opera
I.Sadie, Stanley
782.103

Library of Congress Cataloguing in Publication Data

The New Grove dictionary of opera/edited by Stanley Sadie
p. cm.
"First published in hardback 1992 by Macmillan Reference Limited, London" -
- T.p. verso
Includes bibliographical references.
ISBN 1-56159-228-5 Paperback
1. Opera - Dictionaries. I Sadie, Stanley
ML102.O6N5 1992 92-36276
782.1'03-dc20 CIP
MN

ISBN 0-333-73432-7

ISBN 1-56159-228-5

Contents

GENERAL ABBREVIATIONS vii

BIBLIOGRAPHICAL ABBREVIATIONS xi

LIBRARY SIGLA xv

THE DICTIONARY, VOLUME FOUR:

Roe — Z 1

APPENDIX A: INDEX OF ROLE NAMES 1255

APPENDIX B: INDEX OF INCIPITS OF ARIAS, ENSEMBLES ETC. 1293

APPENDIX C: LIST OF CONTRIBUTORS 1321

APPENDIX D: ILLUSTRATION ACKNOWLEDGMENTS 1331

General Abbreviations

A	alto, contralto [voice]
AB	Bachelor of Arts
ABC	American Broadcasting Company; Australian Broadcasting Commission
Abt.	Abteilung [section]
acc(s).	accompaniment(s); accompanied by
AD	anno Domini
add, addl	additional
add(s), addn(s)	addition(s)
ad lib	ad libitum
AK	Alaska (USA)
AL	Alabama (USA)
Alta.	Alberta (Canada)
AM	Master of Arts
a.m.	ante meridiem [before noon]
Amer.	American
AMS	American Musicological Society
Anh.	Anhang [appendix]
anon.	anonymous(ly)
appx	appendix
AR	Arkansas (USA)
arr(s).	arrangement(s); arranged (by/for)
ASCAP	American Society of Composers, Authors and Publishers
attrib.	attribution, attributed to
Aug	August
aut.	autumn
AZ	Arizona (USA)

B	bass [voice]
b	bass [instrument]
b	born
BA	Bachelor of Arts
bap.	baptized
Bar	baritone [voice]
bar	baritone [instrument]
BBC	British Broadcasting Corporation
BC	British Columbia (Canada)
BC	before Christ
bc	basso continuo
Bd.	Band [volume]
Berks.	Berkshire (GB)
Berwicks.	Berwickshire (GB)
BFA	Bachelor of Fine Arts
bk	book
BL	British Library
BLitt	Bachelor of Letters; Bachelor of Literature
BM	Bachelor of Music; British Museum
BME, BMEd	Bachelor of Music Education
BMI	Broadcast Music, Inc. (USA)
BMus	Bachelor of Music
bn	bassoon
Bros.	Brothers
BS, BSc	Bachelor of Science
Bucks.	Buckinghamshire (GB)
Bulg.	Bulgarian
bur.	buried

c	circa [about]
CA	California (USA)
Cambs.	Cambridgeshire (GB)
cap.	capacity
carn.	Carnival
cb	contrabass [instrument]
CBC	Canadian Broadcasting Corporation
CBE	Commander of the Order of the British Empire
CBS	Columbia Broadcasting System (USA)
CBSO	City of Birmingham Symphony Orchestra
CD	compact disc
cel	celesta
cf	confer [compare]
CG	Covent Garden, London
CH	Companion of Honour
chap.	chapter
Chin.	Chinese
Cie	Compagnie
cl	clarinet
cm	centimetre(s)
cmda	comédie mêlée d'ariettes
CNRS	Centre National de la Recherche Scientifique (F)
CO	Colorado (USA)
Co.	Company; County
col(s).	column(s)
coll.	collection, collected by
collab.	collaborator, in collaboration with
comp.	composer, composed
conc.	concerto
cond.	conductor, conducted by
cont	continuo
contrib(s).	contribution(s)
Corp.	Corporation
CRI	Composers Recordings, Inc. (USA)
CSc	Candidate of Historical Sciences
CT	Connecticut (USA)
Ct	countertenor
CUNY	City University of New York
CVO	Commander of the Royal Victorian Order
Cz.	Czech

D	Deutsch catalogue [Schubert]
d	died
d.	denarius, denarii [penny, pence]
Dan.	Danish
db	double bass
DBE	Dame Commander of the Order of the British Empire
dbn	double bassoon
DC	District of Columbia (USA)

DE	Delaware (USA)
Dec	December
ded.	dedication, dedicated (to)
Dept	Department
Derbys.	Derbyshire (GB)
DFA	Doctor of Fine Arts
dg	dramma giocoso
dir.	director, directed by
diss.	dissertation
DLitt	Doctor of Letters; Doctor of Literature
DMA	Doctor of Musical Arts
DMus	Doctor of Music
DPhil	Doctor of Philosophy
Dr	Doctor
DSc	Doctor of Science; Doctor of Historical Sciences
E.	east, eastern
EBU	European Broadcasting Union
ed(s).	editor(s); edited (by)
edn(s)	edition(s)
e.g.	exempli gratia [for example]
elec	electric, electronic
EMI	Electrical and Musical Industries
Eng.	English
eng hn	english horn
ENO	English National Opera
ens	ensemble
esp.	especially
etc.	et cetera [and so on]
ex., exx.	example, examples
f	forte
f., ff.	folio, folios
facs.	facsimile
fasc.	fascicle
Feb	February
ff	following pages
ff	fortissimo
fff	fortississimo
fig.	figure [illustration]
FL	Florida (USA)
fl	flute
fl	floruit [he/she flourished]
fp	fortepiano
Fr.	French
frag(s).	fragment(s)
GA	Georgia (USA)
Ger.	German
Gk.	Greek
Glam.	Glamorgan (GB)
glock	glockenspiel
Gloucs.	Gloucestershire (GB)
GmbH	Gesellschaft mit beschränkter Haftung [limited-liability company]
govt.	government
GSM	Guildhall School of Music and Drama, London
gui	guitar
H	Hoboken catalogue [Haydn]
Hants.	Hampshire (GB)
Heb.	Hebrew
Herts.	Hertfordshire (GB)
HI	Hawaii (USA)
HMS	His/Her Majesty's Ship
HMV	His Master's Voice
hn	horn
Hon.	Honorary; Honourable
hpd	harpsichord
HRH	His/Her Royal Highness
Hung.	Hungarian
Hunts.	Huntingdonshire (GB)
Hz	Hertz [cycle(s) per second]
IA	Iowa (USA)
IAML	International Association of Music Libraries
ibid	ibidem [in the same place]
ID	Idaho (USA)
i.e.	id est [that is]
IL	Illinois (USA)
IMS	International Musicological Society
IN	Indiana (USA)
Inc.	Incorporated
inc.	incomplete
incl.	includes, including
inst(s)	instrument(s); instrumental
int	intermezzo
IRCAM	Institut de Recherche et de Coordination Acoustique/Musique (F)
ISAM	Institute for Studies in American Music
ISCM	International Society for Contemporary Music
ISM	Incorporated Society of Musicians (GB)
It.	Italian
Jan	January
Jap.	Japanese
Jb	Jahrbuch [yearbook]
Jg.	Jahrgang [year of publication/volume]
jr	junior
K	Köchel catalogue [Mozart; no. after / is from 6th edn]
kbd	keyboard
KBE	Knight Commander of the Order of the British Empire
KCVO	Knight Commander of the Royal Victorian Order
Kgl	Königlich [royal]
kHz	kilohertz [1000 cycles per second]
km	kilometre(s)
KS	Kansas (USA)
KY	Kentucky (USA)
£	libra, librae [pounds, pounds sterling]
LA	Louisiana (USA)
Lancs.	Lancashire (GB)
Lat.	Latin
Leics.	Leicestershire (GB)
lib(s).	libretto(s)
Lincs.	Lincolnshire (GB)
LittD	Doctor of Letters; Doctor of Literature
LlB	Bachelor of Laws
LlD	Doctor of Laws
LP	long-playing record
LPO	London Philharmonic Orchestra
LSO	London Symphony Orchestra
Ltd	Limited
m	metre(s)
M.	Monsieur
MA	Master of Arts
MA	Massachusetts (USA)
mand	mandolin

mar	marimba
MBE	Member of the Order of the British Empire
MD	Maryland (USA)
ME	Maine (USA)
Met	Metropolitan Opera, New York
Mez	mezzo-soprano
mf	mezzo-forte
MFA	Master of Fine Arts
MI	Michigan (USA)
MLitt	Master of Letters; Master of Literature
Mlle(s)	Mademoiselle(s)
MM	Master of Music
M.M.	Metronome Maelzel
mm	millimetre(s)
Mme	Madame
MMus	Master of Music
MN	Minnesota (USA)
MO	Missouri (USA)
mod	modulator
Mon.	Monmouthshire (GB)
movt	movement
MP	Member of Parliament (GB)
mp	mezzo-piano
MPhil	Master of Philosophy
Mr	Mister
Mrs	Mistress
MS(S)	manuscript(s); Master of Science
MS	Mississippi (USA)
MSc	Master of Science
MT	Montana (USA)
Mt	Mount
MusB, MusBac	Bachelor of Music
MusD, MusDoc	Doctor of Music
MusM	Master of Music

N.	north, northern
nar	narrator
NBC	National Broadcasting Company (USA)
NC	North Carolina (USA)
ND	North Dakota (USA)
n.d.	no date (of publication)
NE	Nebraska (USA)
NEA	National Endowment for the Arts (USA)
NEH	National Endowment for the Humanities (USA)
NET	National Educational Television (USA)
NH	New Hampshire (USA)
NHK	Nippon Hōsō Kyōkai [Japanese national broadcasting system]
NJ	New Jersey (USA)
NM	New Mexico (USA)
no(s).	number(s)
Nor.	Norwegian
Northants.	Northamptonshire (GB)
Notts.	Nottinghamshire (GB)
Nov	November
n.p.	no place (of publication)
nr	near
NSW	New South Wales (Australia)
NV	Nevada (USA)
NY	New York State (USA)
NZ	New Zealand

ob	opera buffa; oboe
obbl	obbligato
OBE	Officer of the Order of the British Empire
OC	Opéra-Comique [company]
oc	opéra comique [genre]
Oct	October
OH	Ohio (USA)
OK	Oklahoma (USA)
OM	Order of Merit
Ont.	Ontario (Canada)
op	opera [genre]
op., opp.	opus, opera
opt.	optional
OR	Oregon (USA)
orch	orchestra, orchestral, orchestration
orchd	orchestrated (by)
org	organ
orig.	original(ly)
ORTF	Office de Radiodiffusion-Télévision Française
os	opera seria
OUP	Oxford University Press
ov(s).	overture(s)
Oxon.	Oxfordshire (GB)

P	Pincherle catalogue [Vivaldi]
p	piano
p., pp.	page, pages
PA	Pennsylvania (USA)
p.a.	per annum
PBS	Public Broadcasting Service (USA)
perc	percussion
perf(s).	performance(s); performed (by)
pf	piano(forte)
PhD	Doctor of Philosophy
pic	piccolo
pl(s).	plate(s); plural
p.m.	post meridiem [after noon]
PO	Philharmonic Orchestra
Pol.	Polish
pop.	population
Port.	Portuguese
posth.	posthumous(ly)
POW	prisoner of war
pp	pianissimo
ppp	pianississimo
pr.	printed
PRO	Public Record Office, London
prol.	prologue
PRS	Performing Right Society
Ps, ps	psalm
pseud.	pseudonym
pt(s)	part(s)
pubd	published
pubn	publication

qnt	quintet
qt	quartet

/R	(editorial) revision [in signature]
R	photographic reprint
r	recto
RAF	Royal Air Force
RAI	Radio Audizioni Italiane
RAM	Royal Academy of Music, London
RCA	Radio Corporation of America
RCM	Royal College of Music, London
rec	recorder
recit(s).	recitative(s)
red.	reduction, reduced for
repr.	reprinted
Rev.	Reverend
rev(s).	revision(s); revised (by/for)
RI	Rhode Island (USA)
RIdIM	Répertoire International d'Iconographie Musicale
RILM	Répertoire International de Littérature Musicale

RISM	Répertoire International des Sources Musicales
RMCM	Royal Manchester College of Music
RNCM	Royal Northern College of Music, Manchester
RO	Radio Orchestra
Rom.	Romanian
r.p.m.	revolution(s) per minute
RPO	Royal Philharmonic Orchestra (GB)
RSFSR	Russian Soviet Federated Socialist Republic
RSO	Radio Symphony Orchestra
RTE	Radio Telefís Éireann (Ireland)
RTF	Radiodiffusion-Télévision Française
Rt Hon.	Right Honourable
Russ.	Russian
RV	Ryom catalogue [Vivaldi]
S	San, Santa, Santo, São [Saint]; soprano [voice]
$	dollar(s)
S.	south, southern
s	soprano [instrument]
s.	solidus, solidi [shilling, shillings]
SACEM	Société d'Auteurs, Compositeurs et Editeurs de Musique (F)
Sask.	Saskatchewan (Canada)
sax	saxophone
SC	South Carolina (USA)
SD	South Dakota (USA)
Sept	September
ser.	series
Serb.	Serbian
sf, *sfz*	sforzando, sforzato
sing.	singular
SO	Symphony Orchestra
Sp.	Spanish
Spl	Singspiel
SPNM	Society for the Promotion of New Music (GB)
spr.	spring
sq	square
sr	senior
SS	Saints
Ss	Santissima, Santissimo
SSR	Soviet Socialist Republic
St	Saint, Sankt, Sint, Szent
Staffs.	Staffordshire (GB)
Ste	Sainte
str	string(s)
sum.	summer
SUNY	State University of New York (USA)
suppl(s).	supplement(s); supplementary
Swed.	Swedish
sym(s).	symphony (symphonies); symphonic
synth	synthesizer
T	tenor [voice]
t	tenor [instrument]
timp	timpani
TN	Tennessee (USA)
tpt	trumpet
Tr	treble [voice]
tr	treble [instrument]
trans.	translation, translated by
transcr.	transcription, transcribed by
trbn	trombone
TV	television
TX	Texas (USA)
U.	University
UCLA	University of California at Los Angeles (USA)
UHF	ultra-high frequency
UK	United Kingdom of Great Britain and Northern Ireland
Ukr.	Ukrainian
unacc.	unaccompanied
unattrib.	unattributed
UNESCO	United Nations Educational, Scientific and Cultural Organization
UNICEF	United Nations International Children's Emergency Fund
unperf.	unperformed
unpubd	unpublished
US	United States [adjective]
USA	United States of America
USSR	Union of Soviet Socialist Republics
UT	Utah (USA)
v, vv	voice, voices
v	verso
v., vv.	verse, verses
VA	Virginia (USA)
va	viola
vc	cello
VHF	very high frequency
vib	vibraphone
viz	videlicet [namely]
vle	violone
vn	violin
vol(s).	volume(s)
vs	vocal score, piano-vocal score
VT	Vermont (USA)
W.	west, western
WA	Washington (USA)
Warwicks.	Warwickshire (GB)
WI	Wisconsin (USA)
Wilts.	Wiltshire (GB)
wint.	winter
WNO	Welsh National Opera
WoO, WOO	Werk(e) ohne Opuszahl [work(s) without opus number]
Worcs.	Worcestershire (GB)
WV	West Virginia (USA)
ww	woodwind
WY	Wyoming (USA)
xyl	xylophone
Yorks.	Yorkshire (GB)
Z	Zimmerman catalogue [Purcell]
zar	zarzuela
*	autograph manuscript

Bibliographical Abbreviations

The bibliographical abbreviations used in this dictionary are listed below. Full bibliographical information is not normally supplied for national biographical dictionaries and general music reference works, or if details may be found elsewhere in this dictionary under the heading 'Dictionaries and guides' or 'Editions' (relevant items are indicated with D or E, respectively). General music periodicals are shown with dates only; for those in existence before 1980 full information may be found in the list forming part of the article 'Periodicals' in *The New Grove Dictionary of Music and Musicians*. Opera periodicals, listed in the present dictionary under the heading 'Periodicals', are shown here with an asterisk and serial number in brackets.

In this list, and throughout the dictionary, italic type is used for periodicals and reference works, and roman type for anthologies of music, series etc.

AcM — *Acta musicologica* (1928/9–)
ADB — *Allgemeine deutsche Biographie* (Leipzig, 1875–1912)
AllacciD — L. Allacci: *Drammaturgia* D
AMe (AMeS) — *Algemene muziekencyclopedie* (and suppl.) (Antwerp and Amsterdam, 1957–63; suppl., 1972)
AMf — *Archiv für Musikforschung* (1936–43)
AMI — L'arte musicale in Italia E
AMw — *Archiv für Musikwissenschaft* (1918/19–)
AMZ — *Allgemeine musikalische Zeitung* (1798/9–1882)
AMz — *Allgemeine Musik-Zeitung* (1874–1943)
AnM — *Anuario musical* (1946–)
AnMc — *Analecta musicologica* (some vols. in series Studien zur italienisch-deutschen Musikgeschichte), Veröffentlichungen der Musikabteilung des Deutschen historischen Instituts in Rom (Cologne, 1963–)

Baker6(–8) — *Baker's Biographical Dictionary of Musicians* (New York, 6/1978, 7/1984, 8/1992)
BAMS — *Bulletin of the American Musicological Society* (1936–48)
BDA — *A Biographical Dictionary of Actors, Actresses, Musicians, Dancers, Managers & Other Stage Personnel in London, 1660–1800* D
BeJb — *Beethoven-Jahrbuch* (1953/4–)
BMB — Bibliotheca musica bononiensis E
BMw — *Beiträge zur Musikwissenschaft* (1959–)
BNB — *Biographie nationale [belge]* (Brussels, 1866–86)
BordasD — *Dictionnaire de la musique* (Paris: Bordas, 1970–76)
Bouwsteenen: JVNM — *Bouwsteenen: jaarboek der Vereeniging voor Nederlandsche muziekgeschiedenis* (1869/72–1874/81)
BSIM — *Bulletin français de la S[ociété] I[nternationale de] M[usique]* [previously *Le Mercure musical*; also other titles] (1905–14)
BUCEM — *British Union-Catalogue of Early Music*, ed. E. Schnapper (London, 1957)
BurneyFI — C. Burney: *The Present State of Music in France and Italy* (London, 1771, 2/1773); ed. P. A. Scholes, *Dr. Burney's Musical Tours in Europe* (London, 1959)
BurneyGN — C. Burney: *The Present State of Music in Germany, the Netherlands, and United Provinces* (London, 1773, 2/1775); ed. P. A. Scholes, *Dr. Burney's Musical Tours in Europe* (London, 1959)
BurneyH — C. Burney: *A General History of Music from the Earliest Ages to the Present* (London, 1776–89) [p. nos. refer to edn of 1935]

CBY — *Current Biography Yearbook* (New York, 1940–)
CHM — *Collectanea historiae musicae* (in series Biblioteca historiae musicae cultores) (Florence, 1953–)
CMc — *Current Musicology* (1965–)
CMI — I classici musicali italiani E
ČMm — *Časopis Moravského musea* [Journal of the Moravian Museum] (*c*1915–)
CMz — *Cercetări di muzicologie* (1969–)
COJ — *Cambridge Opera Journal* [*Great Britain 27]
CroceN — B. Croce: *I teatri di Napoli* D
ČSHS — *Československý hudební slovník* (Prague, 1963–5)
CSPD — *Calendar of State Papers (Domestic)* (London, 1856–1972)

DAB — *Dictionary of American Biography* (New York, 1928–36; 8 suppls., 1944–88)
DAM — *Dansk aarbog for musikforskning* (1961–)
DBF — *Dictionnaire de biographie française* (Paris, 1933–)
DBI — *Dizionario biografico degli italiani* (Rome, 1960–)

DBL — *Dansk biografisk leksikon* (Copenhagen, 1887–1905, 2/1933–)
DBP — *Dicionário biográfico de músicos portuguezes* (Lisbon, 1900–04)
DDT — Denkmäler deutscher Tonkunst E
DEUMM — *Dizionario enciclopedico universale della musica e dei musicisti* (Turin, 1985–8)
DJbM — *Deutsches Jahrbuch der Musikwissenschaft* (1957–)
DMV — Drammaturgia musicale veneta E
DNB — *Dictionary of National Biography* (London, 1885–1901, suppls.)
DTB — Denkmäler der Tonkunst in Bayern E
DTÖ — Denkmäler der Tonkunst in Österreich E

EDM — Das Erbe deutscher Musik E
EIT — *Ezhegodnik imperatorskikh teatrov* (1892–1915)
EitnerQ — R. Eitner: *Biographisch-bibliographisches Quellen-Lexikon* (Leipzig, 1900–04, 2/1959–60)
EitnerS — R. Eitner: *Bibliographie der Musik-Sammelwerke des XVI. und XVII. Jahrhunderts* (Berlin, 1877)
EMC — *Encyclopedia of Music in Canada* (Toronto, 1981)
EMc — *Early Music* (1973–)
EMDC — *Encyclopédie de la musique et dictionnaire du Conservatoire* (Paris, 1920–31)
ERO — Early Romantic Opera E
ES — *Enciclopedia dello spettacolo* D
EwenD — D. Ewen: *American Composers: a Biographical Dictionary* (New York, 1982)

FAM — *Fontes artis musicae* (1954–)
FasquelleE — *Encyclopédie de la musique* (Paris: Fasquelle, 1958–61)
FétisB (*FétisBS*) — F.-J. Fétis: *Biographie universelle des musiciens* (and suppl.) (Brussels, 2/1860–65; suppl., 1878–80)
FlorimoN — F. Florimo: *La scuola musicale di Napoli e i suoi conservatorii* (Naples, 1880–83)
FO — French Opera in the 17th and 18th Centuries E

GänzlBMT — K. Gänzl: *The British Musical Theatre* D
GerberL — E. L. Gerber: *Historisch-biographisches Lexikon der Tonkünstler* (Leipzig, 1790–92)
GerberNL — E. L. Gerber: *Neues historisch-biographisches Lexikon der Tonkünstler* (Leipzig, 1812–14)
GfMKB — *Gesellschaft für Musikforschung Kongress-bericht* (1950–)
GiacomoC — S. Di Giacomo: *I quattro antichi conservatorii musicali di Napoli* (Milan and Naples, 1924–8)
GMB — *Geschichte der Musik in Beispielen*, ed. A. Schering (Leipzig, 1931)
GOB — German Opera 1770–1800, ed. T. Bauman E
Grove1(–5) — G. Grove, ed.: *A Dictionary of Music and Musicians* (London, 1878–90; 2/1904–10 ed. J. A. Fuller Maitland, 3/1927–8 and 4/1940 ed. H. C. Colles, 5/1954 ed. E. Blom with suppl. 1961, all as *Grove's Dictionary of Music and Musicians*)
Grove6 — S. Sadie, ed.: *The New Grove Dictionary of Music and Musicians* (London, 1980)
GroveAM — H. W. Hitchcock and S. Sadie, eds.: *The New Grove Dictionary of American Music* (New York, 1986)
GroveI — S. Sadie, ed.: *The New Grove Dictionary of Musical Instruments* (London, 1984)
GSL — *Grosses Sängerlexikon* D
GV — *Le grandi voci: Dizionario critico-biografico dei cantanti con discografia operistica* D [where two authors are separated by a semi-colon, the second one compiled the discography]

HawkinsH — J. Hawkins: *A General History of the Science and Practice of Music* (London, 1776) [p. nos. refer to edn of 1853]
HayJb — *Haydn-Jahrbuch/Yearbook* (1962–71, 1975–8, 1980–)
HiFi — *High Fidelity* (1951/2–1965)
HiFi/MusAm — *High Fidelity/Musical America* (1965–87)
HJb — *Händel-Jahrbuch* (1928–33, 1955–)
HJbMw — *Hamburger Jahrbuch für Musikwissenschaft* (1975–)
HMT — *Handwörterbuch der musikalischen Terminologie* (Wiesbaden, 1972–)
HMw — Handbuch der Musikwissenschaft, ed. E. Bücken (Potsdam, 1927–) [monograph series]
HMYB — *Hinrichsen's Musical Year Book* (1944–61)
HPM — Harvard Publications in Music E
HR — *Hudební revue* (1908–20)
HRo — *Hudební rozhledy* (1948/9–)
HS — Handel Sources E
HV — *Hudební věda* (1961–)

IIM — *Izvestiya na Instituta za muzika* (1952–)
IMa — Instituta et monumenta E
IMSCR — *International Musicological Society Congress Report* (1930–)
IMusSCR — *International Musical Society Congress Report* (1906–11)
IOB — Italian Opera 1640–1770, ed. H. M. Brown E
IOG — Italian Opera 1810–1840, ed. P. Gossett E
IRASM — *International Review of the Aesthetics and Sociology of Music* (1971–)
IRMAS — *The International Review of Music Aesthetics and Sociology* (1970–71)
IRMO — S. L. Ginzburg: *Istoriya russkoy muzïki v notnïkh obraztsakh* (Moscow, 2/1968–70)
ISAMm — Institute for Studies in American Music, monograph series

JAMS — *Journal of the American Musicological Society* (1949–)
JbMP — *Jahrbuch der Musikbibliothek Peters* (1895–1941)
JbO — *Jahrbuch für Opernforschung* [*Germany 60]
JM — *Journal of Musicology* (1983–)
JMT — *Journal of Music Theory* (1957–)
JRBM — *Journal of Renaissance and Baroque Music* (1946–7)
JRMA — *Journal of the Royal Musical Association* (1987–)
JVNM — see *Bouwsteenen: JVNM*

KJb — *Kirchenmusikalisches Jahrbuch* (1886–1911, 1930–35, 1936/8, 1950–)
KM — *Kwartalnik muzyczny* (1911/13–1913/14, 1928/9–1933, 1948–50)
Kobbé10 — G. Kobbé: *Complete Opera Book* (New York and London, 10/1987) D

LaborD — *Diccionario de la música Labor* (Barcelona, 1954)
LaMusicaD — *La musica: dizionario* (Turin, 1968–71)
LaMusicaE — *La musica: enciclopedia storica* (Turin, 1966)
LM — *Lucrări di muzicologie* (1965–)
LoewenbergA — A. Loewenberg: *Annals of Opera 1597–1940* D
LS — *The London Stage, 1660–1800* D

MA — *The Musical Antiquary* (1909/10–1912/13)
MAS — Musical Antiquarian Society [Publications] E
MB — Musica britannica E
MD — *Musica disciplina* (1948–)
ME — *Muzïkal'naya entsiklopediya* (Moscow, 1973–82)
Mf — *Die Musikforschung* (1948–)
MGG — *Die Musik in Geschichte und Gegenwart* (Kassel and Basle, 1949–68; suppl., 1973–9, index 1986)
MJb — *Mozart-Jahrbuch des Zentralinstituts für Mozartforschung* (1950–)
ML — *Music and Letters* (1920–)
MLE — Music for London Entertainment, 1660–1800 E
MM — *Modern Music* (1925–46)
MMA — *Miscellanea musicologica* [Australia] (1966–70, 1972, 1975, 1977–)
MMC — *Miscellanea musicologica* [Czechoslovakia] (1956–62, 1965–1971/3, 1975–)
MMg — *Monatshefte für Musikgeschichte* (1869–1905)
MMR — *The Monthly Musical Record* (1871–1960)
MMS — Monumenta musicae svecicae E
MO — *Musical Opinion* (1877/8–)
MQ — *The Musical Quarterly* (1915–)
MR — *The Music Review* (1940–)
MS — *Muzïkal'nïy sovremennik* (1915/16–1916/17)
MSD — Musicological Studies and Documents, ed. A. Carapetyan (Rome, 1951–)
MT — *The Musical Times* (1844/5–)
MusAm — *Musical America* (1898–1964, 1987–92)
MZ — *Muzikološki zbornik* (1965–)

NA — *Note d'archivio per la storia musicale* (1924–7, 1930–43, 1983–)
NAW — *Notable American Women* (Cambridge, MA, 1971; suppl., 1980)
NBJb — *Neues Beethoven-Jahrbuch* (1924–5, 1927, 1930, 1933, 1935, 1937–9, 1942)
NBL — *Norsk biografisk leksikon* (Oslo, 1921–)
NDB — *Neue deutsche Biographie* (Berlin, 1953–)
NicollH — A. Nicoll: *A History of English Drama, 1660–1900* (Cambridge, 1952–9)
NMA — W. A. Mozart: Neue Ausgabe sämtlicher Werke, ed. E. F. Schmid, W. Plath and W. Rehm (Kassel, 1955–91)
NNBW — *Nieuw Nederlandsch biografisch woordenboek* (Leiden, 1911–37)
NÖB — *Neue österreichische Biographie* (Vienna, 1923)
NOHM — *The New Oxford History of Music*, ed. E. Wellesz, J. A. Westrup and G. Abraham (London, 1954–)
NRMI — *Nuova rivista musicale italiana* (1967–)
NZM — *Neue Zeitschrift für Musik* (1834–1943, 1950–74, 1979–)

OC — *Opera in Canada* [*Canada 1]
OHM — *The Oxford History of Music*, ed. W. H. Hadow (Oxford, 1901–5, enlarged 2/1929–38)
OM — *Opus musicum* (1969–)
ÖMz — *Österreichische Musikzeitschrift* (1946–)
ON — *Opera News* [*USA 13]
OQ — *The Opera Quarterly* [*USA 28]
OW — *Opernwelt* [*Germany 42]

PAMS — *Papers of the American Musicological Society* (1936–8, 1940–41)
PÄMw — Publikationen älterer praktischer und theoretischer Musikwerke E
PBC — Publicaciones del departamento de música de la Biblioteca de Catalunya E
PEM — *Pipers Enzyklopädie des Musiktheaters* D
PMA — *Proceedings of the Musical Association* (1874/5–1943/4)
PNM — *Perspectives of New Music* (1962/3–)
PRM — *Polski rocznik muzykologiczny* (1935–6)
PRMA — *Proceedings of the Royal Musical Association* (1944/5–1984/5)
PSB — *Polskich słownik biograficzny* (Kraków, 1935)

QRaM — *Quaderni della Rassegna musicale* (1964–72)

Rad JAZU — *Rad Jugoslavenske akademije znanosti i umjetnosti* (Zagreb, 1867–)
RaM — *La rassegna musicale* (1928–43, 1947–62)
RBM — *Revue belge de musicologie* (1946–)
RdM — *Revue de musicologie* (1917/19–1943, 1945–)
RdMc — *Revista de musicología* (1978–)
ReM — *La revue musicale* (1920–40, 1946–)
RHCM — *Revue d'histoire et de critique musicales* (1901); *La revue musicale* (1902–11)
RicordiE — *Enciclopedia della musica* (Milan: Ricordi, 1963–4)
RiemannL 11,12 — H. Riemann: *Musik-Lexikon* (Leipzig, 1882, 11/1929 rev. A. Einstein, 12/1959–75 rev. W. Gurlitt, H. H. Eggebrecht and C. Dahlhaus)
RIM — *Rivista italiana di musicologia* (1966–)
RISM — *Répertoire international des sources musicales* (Munich and Duisburg, 1960–; Kassel, 1971–)
RMARC — *R[oyal] M[usical] A[ssociation] Research Chronicle* (1961–)
RMFC — *Recherches sur la musique française classique* (1960–)
RMG — *Russkaya muzïkal'naya gazeta* (1894–1917)
RMI — *Rivista musicale italiana* (1894–1932, 1936–43, 1946–55)
RosaM — C. de Rosa, Marchese di Villarosa: *Memorie dei compositori di musica del Regno di Napoli* (Naples, 1840)
RRAM — Recent Researches in American Music E
RRMBE — Recent Researches in the Music of the Baroque Era E
RRMCE — Recent Researches in the Music of the Classical Era E

SBL — *Svenska biografiskt leksikon* (Stockholm, 1918–)
SchmidlD (SchmidlDS) — C. Schmidl: *Dizionario universale dei musicisti* (and suppl.) (Milan, 1887–90, 2/1928–9; suppl., 1938)
SCMA — Smith College Music Archives E
SeegerL — H. Seeger: *Musiklexikon* (Leipzig, 1966)
SH — *Slovenská hudba* (1957–71)
SIMG — *Sammelbände der Internationalen Musik-Gesellschaft* (1899/1900–1913/14)

SM	*Studia musicologica Academiae scientiarum hungaricae* (1961–)
SMA	*Studies in Music* (1967–) [Australia]
SML	*Schweizer Musiker Lexikon* (Zürich, 1964)
SMN	*Studia musicologica norvegica* (1968, 1976–)
SMP	*Słownik muzyków polskich* (Kraków, 1964–7)
SMw	*Studien zur Musikwissenschaft* (1913–16, 1918–34, 1955–6, 1960–66, 1977–)
SMz	*Schweizerische Musikzeitung/Revue musicale suisse* (1861–)
SOI	*Storia dell'opera italiana*, ed. L. Bianconi and G. Pestelli (Turin, 1987–)
SouthernB	E. Southern: *Biographical Dictionary of Afro-American and African Musicians* (Westport, CT, 1982)
SovM	*Sovetskaya muzïka* (1933–41, 1946–)
StiegerO	F. Stieger: *Opernlexikon* D
STMf	*Svensk tidskrift för musikforskning* (1919–)
TVNM	*Tijdschrift van de Vereniging voor Nederlandse muziekgeschiedenis* (1885–)
VintonD	J. Vinton, ed.: *Dictionary of Contemporary Music* (New York, 1974)
VMw	*Vierteljahrsschrift für Musikwissenschaft* (1885–94)
VogelB	E. Vogel: *Bibliothek der gedruckten weltlichen Vocalmusik Italiens, aus den Jahren 1500 bis 1700* (Berlin, 1892); rev., enlarged, by A. Einstein (Hildesheim, 1962); further addns in *AnMc*, nos.4, 5, 9 and 12; further rev. by F. Lesure and C. Sartori as *Bibliografia della musica italiana vocale profana pubblicata dal 1500 al 1700* (Geneva, 1978)
WaltherML	J. G. Walther: *Musicalisches Lexicon oder Musicalische Bibliothek* (Leipzig, 1732)
WE	The Wellesley Edition E
WurzbachL	C. von Wurzbach: *Biographisches Lexikon des Kaiserthums Oesterreich* (Vienna, 1856–91)
ZfM	*Zeitschrift für Musik* (1920–55)
ZIMG	*Zeitschrift der Internationalen Musik-Gesellschaft* (1899/1900–1913/14)
ZL	*Zenei lexikon* (Budapest, 1930–31, 2/1965)
ZMw	*Zeitschrift für Musikwissenschaft* (1918/19–1935)

Library Sigla

The system of library sigla in this dictionary follows that used in its publications (Series A) by Répertoire International des Sources Musicales, Kassel, by permission. Below are listed the sigla to be found; a few of them are additional to those in the published RISM lists, but have been established in consultation with the RISM organization. Some original RISM sigla that have now been changed are retained here.

In the dictionary, sigla are always printed in *italic*. In any listing of sources a national sigillum applies without repetition until it is contradicted.

Within each national list below, entries are alphabetized by sigillum, first by capital letters (showing the city or town) and then by lower-case ones (showing the institution or collection).

A: AUSTRIA

Gk(h)	Graz, Hochschule für Musik und Darstellende Kunst und Landesmusikschule
Gmi	——, Musikwissenschaftliches Institut der Universität
HE	Heiligenkreuz, Zisterzienserstift
KR	Kremsmünster, Benediktinerstift
LA	Lambach, Benediktinerstift
LIm	Linz, Oberösterreichisches Landesmuseum
M	Melk an der Donau, Benediktinerstift
Sca	Salzburg, Museum Carolino Augusteum
Sm	——, Mozarteum (Internationale Stiftung Mozarteum)
Ssp	——, St Peter (Erzstift oder Benediktiner-Erzabtei)
Su	——, Universitätsbibliothek
SPL	St Paul, Stift
ST	Stams, Zisterzienserstift
Wdtö	Vienna, Gesellschaft zur Herausgabe von Denkmälern der Tonkunst in Österreich
Wgm	——, Gesellschaft der Musikfreunde
Wm	——, Minoritenkonvent
Wn	——, Österreichische Nationalbibliothek, Musiksammlung
Wst	——, Stadtbibliothek, Musiksammlung

ARG: ARGENTINA

BAc	Buenos Aires, Teatro Colón

AUS: AUSTRALIA

CAnl	Canberra, National Library of Australia
Msl	Melbourne, State Library of Victoria
NLwm	Nedlands, Wigmore Music Library, University of Western Australia
Scm	Sydney, New South Wales State Conservatorium of Music
Sfl	——, Fisher Library, University of Sydney

B: BELGIUM

Aa	Antwerp, Stadsarchief
Aac	——, Archief en Museum voor het Vlaamse Culturleven
Ac	——, Koninklijk Vlaams Muziekconservatorium
Ba	Brussels, Archives de la Ville
Bc	——, Conservatoire Royal de Musique
Bcdm	——, Centre Belge de Documentation Musicale [CeBeDeM]
Bmichotte	——, Michotte private collection
Br	——, Bibliothèque Royale Albert 1er/ Koninklijke Bibliotheek Albert I
Gc	Ghent, Koninklijk Muziekconservatorium
Gu	——, Rijksuniversiteit, Centrale Bibliotheek
Lc	Liège, Conservatoire Royal de Musique
Lg	——, Musée Grétry

BR: BRAZIL

Rem	Rio de Janeiro, Escola Nacional de Música, Universidade do Brasil
Rn	——, Biblioteca Nacional

C: CANADA

HNu	Hamilton, McMaster University, Mills Memorial Library
Lu	London, University of Western Ontario, Lawson Memorial Library
On	Ottawa, National Library of Canada
Qsl	Quebec, Séminaire de Québec
Tp	Toronto, Metropolitan Toronto Library, Music Department
Tu	——, University of Toronto, Edward Johnson Music Library

CH: SWITZERLAND

Bu	Basle, Öffentliche Bibliothek der Universität, Musiksammlung
BEl	Berne, Schweizerische Landesbibliothek
E	Einsiedeln, Kloster
EN	Engelberg, Stift
Gc	Geneva, Conservatoire de Musique
Lmg	Lucerne, Allgemeine Musikalische Gesellschaft

Lz ——, Zentralbibliothek
LAcu Lausanne, Bibliothèque Cantonale et Universitaire
MONbonynge Montreux, Richard Bonynge, private collection
N Neuchâtel, Bibliothèque Publique et Universitaire
Zschmitt Zürich, Schmitt private collection
Zz ——, Zentralbibliothek

CS: CZECHOSLOVAKIA

Bm Brno, Ústav Dějin Hudby Moravského Musea, Hudebněhistorické Oddělení
Bu ——, Universitní Knihovna
K Český Krumlov, Pracoviště Státního Archívu Třeboň, Hudební Sbírka
KRa Kroměříž, Státní Zámek a Zahrady, Historicko-Umělecké Fondy, Hudební Archív
KU Kutná Hora, Oblastní Muzeum
Pk Prague, Archív Státní Konservatoře v Praze
Pnd ——, Archiv Národního Divadla
Pnm ——, Národní Muzeum, Hudební Oddělení
Pr ——, Československý Rozhlas, Hudební Archív Různá Provenience
Pu ——, Národní Knihovna v Praze, Universitní Knihovna

CU: CUBA

Hin Havana, Instituto Nacional de la Música
Hn ——, Biblioteca Nacional

D: GERMANY

As Augsburg, Staats- und Stadtbibliothek
Au ——, Universitätsbibliothek
ALa Altenburg, Historisches Staatsarchiv
AN Ansbach, Regierungsbibliothek
B Berlin, Staatsbibliothek Preussischer Kulturbesitz, Musikabteilung
Ba ——, Amerika-Gedenkbibliothek (Berliner Zentralbibliothek); Deutsche Akademie der Künste
Bbb ——, Bote & Bock Archiv
Bdhm ——, Deutsche Hochschule für Musik Hanns Eisler
Bds ——, Deutsche Staatsbibliothek (formerly Königliche Bibliothek; Preussische Staatsbibliothek; Öffentliche Wissenschaftliche Bibliothek), Musikabteilung
Bdso ——, Deutsche Staatsoper
Bhbk ——, Staatliche Hochschule für Bildende Kunst
Bhm ——, Staatliche Hochschule für Musik und Darstellende Kunst
Bko ——, Komische Oper
Bmm ——, Märkisches Museum
Bp ——, Pädagogisches Zentrum
Bsommer ——, Sommer private collection
Bsp ——, Sprachkonvikt
BAs Bamberg, Staatsbibliothek
BAL Ballenstedt, Stadtbibliothek
BAR Bartenstein, Fürszt zu Hohenlohe-Bartensteinsches Archiv [in *NEhz*]
BB Benediktbeuern, Pfarrkirche
BMs Bremen, Staats- und Universitätsbibliothek
BNu Bonn, Universitätsbibliothek
BS Brunswick, Öffentliche Bücherei (Stadtarchiv und Stadtbibliothek)
Cl Coburg, Landesbibliothek
Dl Dresden, Bibliothek und Museum Löbau [in *Dlb*]
Dla ——, Staatsarchiv
Dlb ——, Sächsische Landesbibliothek
Ds ——, Staatstheater
DEl Dessau, Stadtbibliothek (formerly Universitäts- und Landesbibliothek)
DI Dillingen an der Donau, Kreis- und Studienbibliothek
DL Delitzsch, Museum und Bibliothek
DO Donaueschingen, Fürstlich Fürstenbergische Hofbibliothek
DS Darmstadt, Hessische Landes- und Hochschulbibliothek
DT Detmold, Lippische Landesbibliothek
DÜl Düsseldorf, Landes- und Stadtbibliothek
Es Eichstätt, Staats- und Seminarbibliothek [in *Eu*]
Eu ——, Universitätsbibliothek
Ew ——, Benediktinerinnen-Abtei St Walburg
EB Ebrach, Katholisches Pfarramt
F Frankfurt am Main, Stadt- und Universitätsbibliothek
FS Freising, Dombibliothek
Ga Göttingen, Staatliches Archivlager
Gs ——, Niedersächsische Staats- und Universitätsbibliothek
Hmb Hamburg, Hamburger Öffentliche Bücherhallen, Musikbibliothek
Hs ——, Staats- und Universitätsbibliothek Carl von Ossietzky
HAmi Halle an der Saale, Martin-Luther-Universität, Sektion Germanistik und Kulturwissenschaften, Fachbereich Musikwissenschaft (formerly Institut für Musikwissenschaft)
HAu ——, Universitäts- und Landesbibliothek
HG Havelberg, Prignitz-Museum
HR Harburg über Donauwörth, Fürstlich Oettingen-Wallerstein'sche Bibliothek [in *Au*]
HVl Hanover, Niedersächsische Landesbibliothek
HVs ——, Stadtbibliothek
Ju Jena, Universitätsbibliothek der Friedrich-Schiller-Universität
Kl Kassel, Landesbibliothek und Murhardsche Bibliothek der Stadt
KA Karlsruhe, Badische Landesbibliothek
KIl Kiel, Schleswig-Holsteinische Landesbibliothek
KNha Cologne, Historisches Archiv der Stadt Köln
KNu ——, Universitäts- und Stadtbibliothek
Lr Lüneburg, Ratsbücherei und Stadtarchiv
LEm Leipzig, Musikbibliothek der Stadt Leipzig
LEmi ——, Sektion Kulturwissenschaften und Germanistik der Karl-Marx-Universität, Wissenschaftsgebiet Musikwissenschaft (formerly Institut für Musikwissenschaft) [in *LEu*]
LEu ——, Universitätsbibliothek der Karl-Marx-Universität
LÜh Lübeck, Bibliothek der Hansestadt
Mbm Munich, Metropolitankapitel [in *FS*]
Mbn ——, Bayerisches Nationalmuseum
Mbs ——, Bayerische Staatsbibliothek
Mh ——, Staatliche Hochschule für Musik
Mo ——, Opernarchiv
Mth ——, Theatermuseum (Clara-Ziegler-Stiftung)
MEIr Meiningen, Staatliche Museen mit Reger-Archiv
MGmi Marburg an der Lahn, Musikwissenschaftliches Institut der Philipps-Universität
MGs ——, Staatsarchiv und Archivschule
MH Mannheim, Wissenschaftliche Stadtbibliothek und Universitätsbibliothek
MHrm ——, Städtisches Reiss-Museum
MÜp Münster, Diözesanbibliothek, Bischöfliches Priesterseminar und Santini-Sammlung
MÜs ——, Santini-Bibliothek [in *MÜp*]
MÜu ——, Universitätsbibliothek
Ngm Nuremberg, Germanisches National-Museum
Nst ——, Stadtbibliothek
NEhz Neuenstein, Hohenlohe-Zentralarchiv

OB Ottobeuren, Benediktiner-Abtei
Rp Regensburg, Bischöfliche Zentralbibliothek
Rtt ——, Fürst Thurn und Taxis Hofbibliothek
RH Rheda, Fürst zu Bentheim-Tecklenburgische Bibliothek [in *MÜu*]
ROmi Rostock, Institut für Musikwissenschaft der Universität
ROu ——, Wilhelm-Pieck-Universität, Universitätsbibliothek
RUl Rudolstadt, Staatsarchiv
Sl Stuttgart, Württembergische Landesbibliothek
SHs Sondershausen, Stadt- und Kreisbibliothek
SHsk ——, Schlosskirche [in *SHs*]
SWl Schwerin, Wissenschaftliche Allgemeinbibliothek (formerly Mecklenburgische Landesbibliothek)
SWth ——, Mecklenburgisches Staatstheater
Tu Tübingen, Eberhard-Karls-Universität, Universitätsbibliothek
W Wolfenbüttel, Herzog-August-Bibliothek
Wa ——, Niedersächsisches Staatsarchiv
WD Wiesentheid, Musiksammlung des Grafen von Schönborn-Wiesentheid
WEY Weyarn, Pfarrkirche [in *FS*]
WIbh Wiesbaden, Breitkopf & Härtel, Verlagsarchiv
WRdn Weimar, Deutsches Nationaltheater
WRl ——, Staatsarchiv (formerly Landeshauptarchiv)
WRtl ——, Thüringische Landesbibliothek, Musiksammlung [in *WRz*]
WRz ——, Zentralbibliothek der deutschen Klassik
WS Wasserburg am Inn, Chorarchiv St Jakob, Pfarramt [in *FS*]
WÜsa Würzburg, Stadtarchiv
ZI Zittau, Stadt- und Kreisbibliothek

DK: DENMARK

Kk Copenhagen, Det Kongelige Bibliotek
Kmk ——, Det Kongelige Danske Musikkonservatorium
Km(m) ——, Musikhistorisk Museum
Sa Sorø, Sorø Akademis Bibliotek

E: SPAIN

Bc Barcelona, Biblioteca de Cataluña
Bcd ——, Centro de Documentación Musical
Bim ——, Instituto Español de Musicología
Bit ——, Instituto del Teatro (formerly Museo del Arte Escénico)
Boc ——, Biblioteca Orfeó Catalá
Fbaudot El Ferrol, G. Baudot-Puentes, private collection
La León, Catedral
Mc Madrid, Conservatorio Superior de Música
Mcns ——, Congregación de Neustra Señora
Mm ——, Biblioteca Municipal
Mn ——, Biblioteca Nacional
Mp ——, Palacio Real
Msa ——, Sociedad General de Autores de España
SC Santiago de Compostela, Catedral
Zac Saragossa, Archivo de Música del Cabildo

EIRE: IRELAND

Dam Dublin, Royal Irish Academy of Music
Dtc ——, Trinity College

F: FRANCE

A Avignon, Bibliothèque Municipale Livrée Ceccano (formerly Musée Calvet)
AG Agen, Archives Départementales
AIXc Aix-en-Provence, Conservatoire
AIXm ——, Bibliothèque Municipale, Bibliothèque Méjanes
AM Amiens, Bibliothèque Municipale
BER Bernay, Bibliothèque Municipale
BO Bordeaux, Bibliothèque Municipale
BOLbrindejoint Boulogne, Y. Brindejoint, private collection
CLO Clermont-de-l'Oise, Bibliothèque
COGbuckley Cognac, W. Buckley, private collection
COM Compiègne, Bibliothèque Municipale
Dc Dijon, Bibliothèque du Conservatoire
Dm ——, Bibliothèque Municipale
Lm Lille, Bibliothèque Municipale
LYm Lyons, Bibliothèque Municipale
Mc Marseilles, Conservatoire de Musique et de Déclamation
MAC Mâcon, Bibliothèque Municipale
ML Moulins, Bibliothèque Municipale
MON Montauban, Bibliothèque Municipale
NAc Nancy, Conservatoire
NS Nîmes, Bibliothèque Municipale
Pa Paris, Bibliothèque de l'Arsenal
Pbourdon ——, M.-M. Bourdon, private collection
Pc ——, Fonds du Conservatoire National de Musique [in *Pn*]
Pcf ——, Comédie-Française, Bibliothèque
Pi ——, Bibliothèque de l'Institut de France
Pim ——, Institut de Musicologie de l'Université
Plambert ——, Lambert private collection
Pm ——, Bibliothèque Mazarine
Pmeyer ——, André Meyer, private collection
Pn ——, Bibliothèque Nationale
Po ——, Bibliothèque-Musée de l'Opéra
Poffenbach ——, P. Comte-Offenbach, private collection
Prt ——, Office de Radiodiffusion-Télévision Française
Psal ——, Editions Salabert
R(m) Rouen, Bibliothèque Municipale
Sim Strasbourg, Institut de Musicologie de l'Université
SA Salins, Bibliothèque Municipale
SMcusset St-Maud, F. Cusset, private collection
SRPalmeida St-Rémy-de-Provence, A. de Almeida, private collection
TLm Toulouse, Bibliothèque Municipale
V Versailles, Bibliothèque Municipale

GB: GREAT BRITAIN

ABu Aberystwyth, University College of Wales
ALb Aldeburgh, Britten-Pears Library
Bu Birmingham, University of Birmingham, Barber Institute of Fine Arts
BEL Belton (Lincs.), Belton House
BRu Bristol, University of Bristol Library
Ccl Cambridge, Central Library
Cfm ——, Fitzwilliam Museum
Ckc ——, King's College, Rowe Music Library
Cmc ——, Magdalene College
Cpl ——, Pendlebury Library of Music
Cu ——, University Library
CDp Cardiff, Public Libraries, Central Library [in *CDu*]
CDu ——, University of Wales College of Cardiff (formerly University College of South Wales and Monmouthshire)
DRc Durham, Cathedral
En Edinburgh, National Library of Scotland
Er ——, Reid Music Library, University of Edinburgh
Ge Glasgow, Euing Music Library
Gm ——, Mitchell Library
Gu ——, University Library
Lam London, Royal Academy of Music

Lbl	——, British Library (formerly *Lbm*, British Museum)
Lcm	——, Royal College of Music
Lfm	——, Faber Music
Lgc	——, Gresham College (Guildhall Library)
Lkc	——, University of London, King's College
Lmic	——, British Music Information Centre
Lpro	——, Public Record Office
Lst	——, Savoy Theatre Collection
Lu	——, University of London, Music Library
Lue	——, Universal Edition
Lva	——, Victoria and Albert Museum
Lwa	——, Westminster Abbey
LEbc	Leeds, University of Leeds, Brotherton Collection
LVp	Liverpool, Public Libraries, Central Library
Mp	Manchester, Central Public Library, Henry Watson Music Library
MYrees	Machynlleth, Terence Rees, private collection
NWr	Norwich, Norfolk and Norwich Record Office
Ob	Oxford, Bodleian Library
Och	——, Christ Church
Ouf	——, University, Faculty of Music
SOp	Southampton, Public Library
T	Tenbury, St Michael's College [dispersed: now principally in *F-Pn*, *V*, *GB-Ob*]
TWmacnutt	Tunbridge Wells, Richard Macnutt, private collection
WC	Winchester, Chapter Library

GR: GREECE

Aels	Athens, Ethniki Lyriki Skini
Akounadis	——, Panayis Kounadis, private collection
Aleotsakos	——, George Leotsakos, private collection
Am	——, Mousseio ke Kendro Meletis Ellinikou Theatrou
An	——, Ethniki Vivliothiki tis Ellados [National Library of Greece]

H: HUNGARY

Bn	Budapest, Országos Széchényi Könyvtára
Bo	——, Állami Operaház

HV: CROATIA

Zu	Zagreb, Nacionalna i Sveučilišna Biblioteka

I: ITALY

Ac	Assisi, Biblioteca Comunale
Af	——, S Francesco [in *Ac*]
AC	Acicatena, Biblioteca Comunale
Baf	Bologna, Accademia Filarmonica
Bas	——, Archivio di Stato
Bc	——, Civico Museo Bibliografico Musicale
Bea	——, Biblioteca Comunale dell' Arciginnasio
Bsf	——, Convento di S Francesco
Bsp	——, Basilica di S Petronio
Bu	——, Biblioteca Universitaria
BAc(n)	Bari, Biblioteca Nazionale (Consorziale)
BAn	——, Biblioteca Nazionale Sagarriga Visconti-Volpi
BGc	Bergamo, Biblioteca Civica Angelo Mai
BGi	——, Civico Istituto Musicale Gaetano Donizetti
BRc	Brescia, Conservatorio di Musica
BRq	——, Biblioteca Queriniana
BZtoggenburg	Bolzano, Count Toggenburg, private collection
CAS	Cascia, Archivio di S Rita
CATc	Catania, Biblioteche Riunite Civica e Antonio Ursino Recupero
CATm	——, Museo Belliniano
CCc	Città di Castello, Biblioteca Comunale
CF	Cividale del Friuli, Archivio Capitolare
CHf	Chioggia, Archivio dei Padri Filippini
CMbc	Casale Monferrato, Biblioteca Civica
CNM	Civitanova-Marche, Biblioteca Comunale
CORc	Correggio, Biblioteca Comunale
CR	Cremona, Biblioteca Statale
Fa	Florence, Ss Annunziata
Fas	——, Archivio di Stato
Fbecherini	——, Becherini private collection
Fc	——, Conservatorio di Musica Luigi Cherubini
Fm	——, Biblioteca Marucelliana
Fn	——, Biblioteca Nazionale Centrale
Folschki	——, Olschki private collection
FAN	Fano, Biblioteca Comunale Federiciana
FEc	Ferrara, Biblioteca Comunale Ariostea
FEd	——, Duomo
FERc	Fermo, Biblioteca Comunale
FERd	——, Duomo
FOc	Forlì, Biblioteca Civica Aurelio Saffi
FZc	Faenza, Biblioteca Comunale
Gi(l)	Genoa, Istituto (Liceo) Musicale Paganini; see *Gl*
Gl	——, Conservatorio di Musica Nicolò Paganini
Gim	——, Istituto Mazziniano
Gu	——, Biblioteca Universitaria
IBborromeo	Isola Bella, Borromeo private archive
IE	Iesi, Biblioteca Comunale
La	Lucca, Archivio di Stato
Li	——, Istituto Musicale Luigi Boccherini (incl. Bottini Collection)
Ls	——, Seminario Arcivescovile
LI	Livorno, Biblioteca Comunale Labronica Francesco Domenico Guerrazzi
Mb	Milan, Biblioteca Nazionale Braidense
Mc	——, Conservatorio di Musica Giuseppe Verdi
Mcom	——, Biblioteca Comunale
Mr	——, Archivio Storico Ricordi
Ms	——, Biblioteca Teatrale Livia Simoni
Msartori	——, Claudio Sartori, private collection
Mt	——, Biblioteca Trivulziana e Archivio Storico Civico
MAav	Mantua, Accademia Virgiliana di Scienze, Lettere ed Arti
MAC	Macerata, Biblioteca Comunale Mozzi-Borgetti
MC	Monte Cassino, Biblioteca dell'Abbazia
MOa	Modena, Accademia Nazionale di Scienze, Lettere ed Arti
MOe	——, Biblioteca Estense
MOs	——, Archivio di Stato
Na	Naples, Archivio di Stato
Nc	——, Conservatorio di Musica S Pietro a Majella
Nf	——, Biblioteca Oratoriana dei Padri Filippini
Nlp	——, Biblioteca Lucchesi-Palli [in *Nn*]
Nn	——, Biblioteca Nazionale
OS	Ostiglia, Fondazione Greggiati
Pc	Padua, Biblioteca Capitolare
Pca	——, Biblioteca Antoniana, Basilica del Santo
Pci	——, Museo Civico, Biblioteca Civica e Archivio Comunale
Pi(l)	——, Istituto Musicale (Biblioteca del Liceo Musicale); see *Pl*
Pl	——, Istituto Musicale Cesare Pollini
PAc	Parma, Conservatorio di Musica Arrigo Boito
PAi	——, Istituto di Studi Verdiani
PAt	——, Teatro Regio
PAVu	Pavia, Biblioteca Universitaria
PCcon	Piacenza, Conservatorio di Musica Giuseppe Nicolini
PEc	Perugia, Biblioteca Comunale Augusta
PEl	——, Conservatorio di Musica Francesco Morlacchi
PEsp	——, S Pietro
PEA	Pescia, Biblioteca Comunale Carlo Magnani
PESc	Pesaro, Conservatorio di Musica Gioacchino Rossini
PESr	——, Fondazione Rossini
PIv	Pisa, Teatro Verdi

PLa	Palermo, Archivio di Stato
PLcom	——, Biblioteca Comunale
PLcon	——, Conservatorio Vincenzo Bellini
PS	Pistoia, Cattedrale
PSrospigliosi	——, Rospigliosi private collection
Rasc	Rome, Archivio Storico Capitolino
Rc	——, Biblioteca Casanatense
Rdp	——, Archivio Doria-Pamphili
Ria	——, Istituto di Archeologia e Storia dell'Arte
Rli	——, Accademia Nazionale dei Lincei e Corsiniana
Rmalvezzi	——, Malvezzi private collection
Rmassimo	——, Massimo princes, private collection
Rn	——, Biblioteca Nazionale Centrale Vittorio Emanuele III
Rp	——, Biblioteca Pasqualini [in *Rsc*]
Rps	——, Archivio dei Padri Scolopi (Chiesa di S Pantaleo)
Rrai	——, Radiotelevisione Italiana
Rrostirolla	——, Giancarlo Rostirolla, private collection
Rsc	——, Conservatorio di Musica S Cecilia
Rsp	——, Santo Spirito in Sassia
Rvat	——, Biblioteca Apostolica Vaticana
REm	Reggio Emilia, Biblioteca Municipale
RIM	Rimini, Biblioteca Civica Gambalunga
RVI	Rovigo, Accademia e Biblioteca dei Concordi
Sac	Siena, Accademia Musicale Chigiana
Sc	——, Biblioteca Comunale degli Intronati
SA	Savona, Biblioteca Civica Anton Giulio Barrili
SML	Santa Margherita Ligure, Biblioteca Comunale Francesco Domenico Costa
Tci	Turin, Biblioteca Civica Musicale Andrea della Corte
Tco	——, Conservatorio Statale di Musica Giuseppe Verdi
Tf	——, Accademia Filarmonica
Tmc	——, Museo Civico
Tn	——, Biblioteca Nazionale Universitaria
Tr	——, Biblioteca Reale
TAc	Taranto, Biblioteca Civica Pietro Acclavio
TLp	Torre del Lago, Museo Puccini
TOL	Tolentino, Biblioteca Comunale Filelfica
TRc	Trent, Biblioteca Comunale
TSmt	Trieste, Civico Museo Teatrale di Fondazione Carlo Schmidl
TVco	Treviso, Biblioteca Comunale
UDc	Udine, Biblioteca Comunale Vincenzo Soppi
Vas	Venice, Archivio di Stato
Vc	——, Conservatorio di Musica Benedetto Marcello
Vcg	——, Biblioteca Casa di Goldoni
Vgc	——, Biblioteca e Istituto della Fondazione Giorgio Cini
Vlevi	——, Fondazione Ugo Levi
Vmc	——, Museo Civico Correr
Vnm	——, Biblioteca Nazionale Marciana
Vqs	——, Fondazione Querini-Stampalia
Vs	——, Seminario Patriarcale
Vsm	——, Procuratoria di S Marco
Vt	——, Teatro La Fenice
VEc	Verona, Biblioteca Civica
VEs	——, Seminario Vescovile

J: JAPAN

Tn	Tokyo, Nanki Music Library, Ohki Collection [in Tokyo College of Music Library]

N: NORWAY

Ou	Oslo, Universitetsbiblioteket

NL: THE NETHERLANDS

At	Amsterdam, Toonkunst-Bibliotheek
DHgm	The Hague, Gemeentemuseum
DHk	——, Koninklijke Bibliotheek

NZ: NEW ZEALAND

Wt	Wellington, Alexander Turnbull Library

P: PORTUGAL

Em	Elvas, Biblioteca Municipal
EVc	Évora, Arquivo da Catedral
EVp	——, Biblioteca Pública
La	Lisbon, Palácio Nacional da Ajuda
Lan	——, Arquivo Nacional de Torre do Tombo
Lc	——, Conservatorio Nacional
Ln	——, Biblioteca Nacional
Lt	——, Teatro Nacional de S Carlos
VV	Vila Viçosa, Casa da Bragança, Museu-Biblioteca

PL: POLAND

CZp	Częstochowa, Klasztor OO. Paulinów na Jasnej Górze
Kc	Kraków, Muzeum Narodowe, Biblioteka Czartoryskich
Kj	——, Biblioteka Jagiellońska
Kp	——, Biblioteka Polskiej Akademii Nauk
KA	Katowice, Biblioteka Śląska
LA	Łańcut, Muzeum
Wn	Warsaw, Biblioteka Narodowa
Wtm	——, Biblioteka Warszawskiego Towarzystwa Muzycznego
Wu	——, Biblioteka Uniwersytecka
WRol	Wrocław, Biblioteka Ossolineum Leopoldiensis; see *WRzno*
WRzno	——, Polska Akademia Nauk Zakład Narodowy imienia Ossolińskich

R: ROMANIA

Bc	Bucharest, Biblioteca Centrală de Stat

RU: RUSSIA

KAu	Kaliningrad, Universitetskaya Biblioteka
Mcl	Moscow, Gosudarstvennïy Tsentral'nïy Literaturnïy Arkhiv
Mcm	——, Gosudarstvennïy Tsentral'nïy Muzey Muzïkal'noy Kul'turï imeni M. I. Glinki
Mk	——, Gosudarstvennaya Konservatoriya imeni P. I. Chaykovskogo, Nauchnaya Muzïkal'naya Biblioteka imeni S. I. Taneyeva
Mrg	——, Rossiyskaya Gosudarstvennaya Biblioteka (formerly *Ml*, Lenin Library)
SPan	St Petersburg, Biblioteka Rossiyskoy Akademii Nauk
SPia	——, Gosudarstvennïy Tsentral'nïy Istoricheskiy Arkhiv
SPil	——, Institut Russkoy Literaturï
SPit	——, Gosudarstvennïy Institut Teatra, Muzïki i Kinematografii
SPk	——, Biblioteka Gosudarstvennoy Konservatorii imeni N. A. Rimskogo-Korsakova
SPsc	——, Gosudarstvennaya Ordena Trudovogo Krasnogo Znameni Publichnaya Biblioteka imeni M. E. Saltïkova-Shchedrina
SPtob	——, Tsentral'naya Muzïkal'naya Biblioteka Gosudarstvennogo Akademicheskogo Mariinskogo Teatra Operï i Baleta

S: SWEDEN

L Lund, Universitetsbiblioteket
Sdt Stockholm, Drottningholms Teatermuseum
Sic ——, Informationscentral för Svensk Musik
Sk ——, Kungliga Biblioteket
Skma ——, Statens Musiksamlingar (formerly Kungliga Musikaliska Akademiens Bibliotek)
Sm ——, Musikhistoriska Museet [in *Skma*]
Smf ——, Stiftelsen Musikkulturens Främjande
Ssr ——, Sveriges Radio
St ——, Kungliga Teaterns Biblioteket [in *Skma*]
Uu Uppsala, Universitetsbiblioteket

SF: FINLAND

A Turku [Åbo], Sibelius Museum Musikvetenskapliga Institutionen vid Åbo Akademi, Bibliotek & Arkiv
Hy Helsinki, Helsingin Yliopiston Kirjasto

[*SLN*]: SLOVENIA

Lf Ljubljana, Knjižnica Frančiskanškega Samostana
Lu ——, Narodna in Univerzitetna Knjižnica

UA: UKRAINE

Kan Kiev, Tsentral'na Naukova Biblioteka, Akademii Nauk
LV L'viv, Biblioteka Derzhavnoï Konservatorii imeni N. V. Lysenka

US: UNITED STATES OF AMERICA

AA Ann Arbor, University of Michigan, Music Library
AUS Austin, University of Texas
Bm Boston, University, Mugar Memorial Library
Bp ——, Public Library, Music Department
BApi Baltimore, Peabody Conservatory of Music; Peabody Institute
BAT Baton Rouge, Louisiana State University Library
BE Berkeley, University of California, Music Library
BLl Bloomington, Indiana University, Lilly Library
BLu ——, Indiana University, School of Music Library
BUu Buffalo, State University of New York at Buffalo
Chs Chicago, Chicago Historical Society
Cn ——, Newberry Library
CA Cambridge, Harvard University Music Libraries
CDs Concord, New Hampshire State Library
CHH Chapel Hill, University of North Carolina, Music Library
DM(u) Durham (NC), Duke University Library
DN Denton, North Texas State University, Music Library
Eu Evanston, Northwestern University Libraries
FAlewis Farmington (CT), Wilmarth S. Lewis, private collection
G Gainesville, University of Florida Library, Rare Book Collection
I Ithaca, Cornell University, Music Library
KBrobbin Key Biscayne (FL), Leon Robbin, private collection
KC Kansas City, University of Missouri, Kansas City Conservatory of Music
LAu Los Angeles, University of California, Walter H. Rubsamen Music Library
LAuc ——, University of California, William Andrews Clark Memorial Library
LOu Louisville, University, School of Music Library
MAhs Madison, Wisconsin Historical Society
MED Medford (MA), Tufts University Library
MSu Minneapolis, University of Minnesota, Music Library
NH New Haven (CT), Yale University, School of Music Library
NYbroude New York, Broude private collection
NYcu ——, Columbia University, Music Library
NYgs ——, G. Schirmer, Inc.
NYj ——, Juilliard School of Music
NYlibin ——, Laurence Libin, private collection
NYp ——, Public Library at Lincoln Center, Library and Museum of the Performing Arts
NYpm ——, Pierpont Morgan Library
NYwolfson ——, John Wolfson, private collection
NYyellin ——, Victor Yellin, private collection
PHci Philadelphia, Curtis Institute of Music
PHf ——, Free Library of Philadelphia
PHhs ——, Historical Society of Pennsylvania
PHlc ——, Library Company of Philadelphia
PHu ——, University of Pennsylvania Libraries (Otto E. Albrecht Music Library; Van Pelt Library; Rare Book Collection)
PRu Princeton, University, Harvey S. Firestone Memorial Library
R Rochester (NY), University, Eastman School of Music, Sibley Music Library
Su Seattle, University of Washington, Music Library
SB Santa Barbara, University of California at Santa Barbara Library
SFp San Francisco, Public Library, Fine Arts Department, Music Division
SFsc ——, San Francisco State University (formerly State College) Library, Frank V. de Bellis Collection
SLug St Louis, Washington University, Gaylord Music Library
SM San Marino (CA), Henry E. Huntington Library and Art Gallery
SPmoldenhauer Spokane (WA), Hans Moldenhauer, private collection
STu Stanford, University, Division of Humanities and Social Sciences, Music Library
U Urbana, University of Illinois, Music Library
Wc Washington, DC, Library of Congress, Music Division
Ws ——, Folger Shakespeare Library
Wsi ——, Smithsonian Institution, Music Library
WM Waltham (MA), Brandeis University Library, Music Library, Goldfarb Library
WS Winston-Salem (NC), Moravian Music Foundation

YU: YUGOSLAVIA

(for libraries in the former republic of Yugoslavia, see also under *HV*, Croatia; and [*SLN*], Slovenia)

Bn Belgrade, Narodna Biblioteka N. R. Srbije

R
CONTINUED

Roeckel, August. *See* RÖCKEL, AUGUST.

Roeckel, Joseph. *See* RÖCKEL, JOSEPH.

Rogachevsky, Joseph (*b* Mirgorod, 8/20 Nov 1891; *d* Ixelles, Belgium, May 1985). Belgian tenor of Russian birth. He left Russia in 1909, emigrating to Paris, where he studied singing at the Conservatoire. With the outbreak of World War I he joined the French army and was twice wounded. After renewed study he made his début in 1922 with the Opéra-Comique in *Tosca*. Although he returned to Paris quite frequently, the centre of his career was in Brussels at La Monnaie, which he joined in 1924, singing Werther at his début. He sang there until 1948 and was director from 1953 to 1959; afterwards he taught singing. He made guest appearances at the Vienna Staatsoper in 1929 and 1930. A fine singer, with a repertory which extended to Wagner roles such as Tannhäuser and Parsifal, he can be heard in some impressive recordings, including a complete *Manon* made in 1932. J. B. STEANE

Rogatis, Francesco Saverio de. *See* DE ROGATIS, FRANCESCO SAVERIO.

Rogatis, Pascual de (*b* Teora, 17 May 1880; *d* Buenos Aires, 2 April 1980). Argentine composer of Italian birth. He moved to Buenos Aires in 1883 and attended the Buenos Aires Conservatory of Music, studying composition under Alberto Williams. In 1901 he began teaching there, and he later taught at the National Conservatory of Music (1924–47). He was a member of the National Commission of Fine Arts and participated in composition juries at the Teatro Colón.

In his music Rogatis adopted an Americanist aesthetic, conceiving of Latin America as a single spiritual unity. He elaborated this position in his first opera, *Huemac* (1, E. Montagne; Buenos Aires, Colón, 22 July 1916), which is based on a pre-Columbian Toltec legend and relies on a pentatonic musical language. His second opera, *La novia del hereje* (4, T. Allende Iragorri; Colón, 13 June 1935), inspired by a novel by Vicente Fidel López, is set in Lima during the Spanish colonial period. It was noted for its acute sense of dramatic timing and reliance on indigenous features; it also marked one of the few known inclusions of African musical elements into the Argentine lyric theatre. This work received numerous performances at the Colón and was viewed as one of the most important Argentine operas. Rogatis also composed incidental music for the stage, including music (now lost) for the drama *Ollantay* by Ricardo Rojas, one of the leading nationalist intellectuals of the day.

M. Kuss: '*Huemac*, by Pascual de Rogatis: Native Identity in the Argentine Lyric Theatre', *Yearbook for Inter-American Musical Research*, x (1974), 68–87

——: *Nativistic Strains in Argentine Operas Premiered at the Teatro Colón (1908–1972)* (diss., UCLA, 1976)

DEBORAH SCHWARTZ

Rogel, José (*b* Orihuela, Alicante, 24 Dec 1829; *d* Cartagena, 25 Feb 1901). Spanish composer. As a child he studied the piano, flute, theory and composition with Joaquín Cascales, organist of Orihuela Cathedral. From the age of nine he was orchestrating pieces and composing waltzes and pasodobles, and in his early teens he conducted the town band. At his father's insistence he studied law in Valencia from 1845 to 1851, but simultaneously took lessons in composition, counterpoint and fugue with the cathedral organist Pascual Pérez Gascón (1802–64), supporting himself by giving flute, piano and solfège lessons. In 1852 he moved to Madrid to complete his studies, earning his living by teaching the piano and singing, arranging zarzuelas for piano and publishing dances and operatic fantasies. He also acted as conductor and composer at several theatres. Between 1854, when his zarzuela *Loa á la libertad* was first performed at the Teatro Lope de Vega, and 1881 he composed some 80 zarzuelas. By far the most successful was the two-act *El jóven Telémaco* (1866, Variedades), with which was instituted the Compañía de los Bufos Madrileños after the style of Offenbach's Bouffes-Parisiens. Rogel's style was essentially a light and facile one, and as such he was something of a precursor of the more lastingly popular Chueca.

zarzuelas in 1 act, first performed at Madrid, Teatro de la Zarzuela, unless otherwise stated

Loa á la libertad, Madrid, Lope de Vega, 1854; Soy yo, Madrid, Instituto, 1855; Las garras del diablo (E. Pérez Escrich), Madrid, Tirso de Molina, 1855/6; Don Canuto, San Sebastian, Principal, 1856; Santiaguillo, Madrid, Variedades, 1856; Recuerdos de gloria, Madrid, Principe, 1858; Las dos rosas, Barcelona, Principal, 1858, collab. Allú; El lumbra recoge, 1860; Entre Ceuta y Marruecos, 1860; Ferrando el calderero (3), 1861; Pablo y Virginia (Virto), 1861, rev. (2) *c*1868

Una tia en Indias (3), 1861; Roquelaure (3, J. Belza), 17 March 1862, collab. Caballero and C. Oudrid; Por sorpresa (2, F. Ruiz del Cerro), 20 April 1862, collab. M. Vázquez and Oudrid; El manicomio modelo (2), c1862; La casa roja, 1863; Despierta y dormida, 1863; Un hongo, 1864; Los peregrinos (Pina), 1864; Impresiones de viaje, 1864; La epístola de San Pablo (L. Correa), 1864; Las cartas de Rosalía, 1864; Soy mi hijo, 1864; La corte del rey Reuma (E. Blasco), c1864, collab. Oudrid

El que siembra, recoge, c1864; Doña Casimira, Santander, 1865; Punto y aparte (2, L. M. de Larra), 1865; Las amazonas del Tormes (2, E. Álvarez), 1865; El suplicio de un hombre (3, Bardan), 1865; El lago de las serpientes (3, Pedrosa), 1865, collab. C. Moderati; El conde y el condenado (3), 1865, collab. J. Inzenga; Revista de un muerto, Circo, 3 Feb 1866, collab. F. A. Barbieri; El jóven Telémaco (2, Blasco), Madrid, Variedades, 22 Sept 1866

Los regalos (R. de Velasco), Madrid, Variedades, 1866; Me escamo (Belza), Madrid, Variedades, 1866; Tanto corre como vuela, Madrid, Variedades, 1866; Un cuadro, un melonar y dos bodas (2), Madrid, Variedades, 1866, collab. Inzenga and L. Cepeda; El motín de las estrellas, Madrid, Variedades, 1866; Telémaco en la Abufera, Valencia, 1866; ¿Quién es el loco?, c1866; Francifredo [dux de Venecia] (2, Pina), Madrid, Variedades, 29 Jan 1867

Un muerto de buen humor (A. Llanos), Madrid, Variedades, 21 April 1867; El ajuste de una tiplo (Llanos), Madrid, Variedades, 21 April 1867; Los órganos de Móstoles (3, Larra), Madrid, Circo, 2 Oct 1867; La isla de los portentos (3), Madrid, Circo, 1868; El general Bum-Bum, Madrid, Circo, 1868; Las tres Marías, Madrid, Circo, 1868; El matrimonio (R. Puente y Brañas), Madrid, Circo, 1868; El criado de mi suegro, Madrid, Circo, c1868, collab. Caballero and I. Hernández

Los infiernos de Madrid (3, Larra), Madrid, Circo, 1869; Dos truchas en seco (Puente y Brañas), 1869; Un casamíento republicano (3), Madrid, Circo, 1869; El hábito no hace al monje (2), 1869; El rey Midas (3, Puente y Brañas), 1869; Un palomino atontado (3), 1870; Cinco semanas en globo (2), c1870; Canto de ángeles, Bufos Arderius, 1871; Un viaje de mil demonios (3), Madrid, Circo, 1871 or 1873; La Creación refundida (3), 1872; La paloma del brillante, 1873; Lola (2, Pina), 1873

El último figurín, Madrid, Circo, 1873; La vuelta al mundo (4, Larra), Madrid, Circo, 18 Aug 1875, collab. Barbieri; El commandante León (2, Pina), 1877; Vivan las Cuenas! (3, Pérez Escrich), 1878; Los dragones del rey, Lisbon, Trinidade, Oct 1880; La Pata de Cabra (3), Cartagena, 1892; Fototipias castageneros (revue, Martínez), Madrid, Circo, 22 Feb 1901, collab. G. Mateos

Adaptations from Offenbach: Genoveva de Brabante (3), Madrid, Circo, 1 May 1868; La gran duquesa (3), Madrid, Circo, Nov 1868

Other zarzuelas: Una cana al aire; Bruto; El novio; De zapatero á barón; Los barrios bajos, collab. F. Chueca and Valverde *padre*; Cuadro soldados y un cabo; Bayoneta Correo (2); Carnaval y Casta diva (2); Los estudiantes en Carnaval (2); La locura en Cartagena (2); Cuenta de hadas (3); El guape Francisco Estéban (4); Un viaje á la luna (4)

*

A. Peña y Goñi: *La ópera española y la música dramática en el siglo XIX* (Madrid, 1881; abridged E. Rincón, as *España desde la ópera a la zarzuela*, 1967), 586–93

'Rogel (José)', *Enciclopedia universal ilustrada europeo-americana* (Barcelona, 1907–30), li, 1358

E. Cotarelo y Mori: *Historia de la zarzuela, o sea el drama lírico* (Madrid, 1934)

R. Alier and others: *El libro de la zarzuela* (Barcelona, 1982, 2/1986 as *Diccionario de la zarzuela*)

ANDREW LAMB

Roger, Gustave-Hippolyte (*b* Paris, 17 Dec 1815; *d* Paris, 12 Sept 1879). French tenor. He studied at the Paris Conservatoire with Jean-Blaise Martin and in 1837 won *premiers prix* in singing and *opéra comique*. In 1838 he made his début as George in Halévy's *L'éclair* at the Opéra-Comique, where he created a number of roles written for him by Halévy, Auber and Thomas. His success rested on his considerable intelligence, fine bearing and pure tone. In 1846 he created the title role in Berlioz's *La damnation de Faust*, and in 1848 he moved from the Opéra-Comique to the Opéra, where he sang John of Leyden in the première of Meyerbeer's *Le prophète* (1849), the first of many leading tenor roles at the Opéra. In 1859 he sang there in the première of Félicien David's *Herculanum*. Shortly afterwards he lost his right arm in a shooting accident, but continued to appear on stage with a mechanical arm. His book *Le carnet d'un ténor* (Paris, 1880) contains lively memories of his career.

*

A. Lajet: *Gustave-Hippolyte Roger: notice biographique* (Paris, 1865)

O. Fouque: *Les révolutionnaires de la musique* (Paris, 1882)

HUGH MACDONALD

Roger, Victor (*b* Montpellier, 22 July 1853; *d* Paris, 2 Dec 1903). French composer. The son of a musician, he studied at the Ecole Niedermeyer and began his career as a composer of songs and operettas for the Eldorado music hall. It was with *Joséphine vendue par ses soeurs* (1866), a parody of Méhul's *Joseph*, that he made his mark, and he confirmed his success in France and abroad with the military operetta *Les vingt-huit jours de Clairette* (1892) and *L'auberge du Tohu-Bohu* (1897). Both are examples of the 'vaudeville-opérette' – more comedy-with-music than full-blown comic opera – in which he specialized. A Chevalier of the Légion d'honneur, he was critic for *La France*, edited the theatrical news in the *Petit journal* and was general secretary of the balls at the Opéra. His music shows melodic grace, charm and a flair for rhythmic effect, his compositions including, besides his songs and operettas, two ballet-pantomimes and some salon pieces.

operettas, first performed in Paris unless otherwise stated; most published in vocal score at time of production

PBP – *Bouffes-Parisiens* PFD – *Folies-Dramatiques*
PMP – *Menus-Plaisirs*

Mademoiselle Louloute (1, Péricaud and L. Delormel), Eldorado, 1882; Mademoiselle Irma (1, F. Carré), Trouville, Casino, 18 Aug 1883; Joséphine vendue par ses soeurs (3, P. Ferrier and Carré), PBP, 20 March 1886; Balazi-Boumboum (1, J.-A. Praigneau), Eldorado, 23 March 1888; Le voyage en Ecosse (1, Cottin and Lecomte), Lille, 17 May 1888; Oscarine (3, C.-L-E. Nuitter and A. Guinon), PBP, 15 Oct 1888; Cendrillonnette (4, Ferrier), PBP, 24 Jan 1890, collab. G. Serpette

La fétiche (3, Ferrier and Clairville), PMP, 13 March 1890; Mademoiselle Asmodée (3, Ferrier and Clairville), Renaissance, 23 Nov 1890, collab. P. Lacome; Samsonnet (3, Ferrier), Nouveautés, 26 Nov 1890; Les douze femmes de Japhet, Renaissance, 16 Dec 1890; Le coq (3, Ferrier and E. Depré), PMP, 30 Oct 1891; Les vingt-huit jours de Clairette (4, H. Raymond and A. Mars), PFD, 3 May 1892

Catinerette (1, Mars), Lunéville, 17 July 1893; Clary et Clara (3, Raymond and Mars), PFD, 20 March 1894; Miss Nicol-Nick (4, Raymond, Mars and A. Duru), PFD, 23 Jan 1895; La dot de Brigitte (3, Ferrier and Mars), PBP, 6 May 1895, collab. Serpette; Le voyage de Corbillon (4, Mars), Cluny, 30 Jan 1896; Sa majesté l'amour (3, M. Hennequin and Mars), Eldorado, 24 Dec 1896; L'auberge du Tohu-Bohu (3, M. Ordonneau), PFD, 10 Feb 1897

Les fêtards (3, Mars and Hennequin), Palais-Royal, 28 Dec 1897; L'agence Crook et Cie (4, Ordonneau), PFD, 22 Jan 1898; La petite tache (3, Carré), PBP, 26 March 1898; Les quatre filles Aymon (Liorat and A. Fonteny), PFD, 20 Sept 1898, collab. Lacome; La poule blanche (4, Hennequin and Mars), Cluny, 13 Jan 1899; Le jockey malgré lui (P. Gavault and Ordonneau), PBP, 4 Dec 1902

*

R. Traubner: *Operetta: a Theatrical History* (New York, 1983)

ANDREW LAMB

Roger-Ducasse, Jean (Jules Aimable) (*b* Bordeaux, 18 April 1873; *d* Taillan-Médoc, Gironde, 19 July 1954). French composer. He studied composition with Fauré at the Paris Conservatoire and later succeeded Dukas as professor of composition there. As a composer Roger-

Ducasse began in the tradition of Fauré but soon developed a more elaborate and individual style. Romantic excesses were avoided, but an exploratory spirit often led him into abstract and complex writing, strongly disciplined but always sensitive.

The 'mimodrame lyrique' *Orphée* (1913) is an ingenious combination of miming, choreography and 'pure' music in three acts or tableaux devised by the composer. Besides the orchestra, four soloists and a chorus are used in parts of Acts 2 and 3. It was first staged at the Opéra on 11 June 1926, with Ida Rubinstein dancing the part of Orpheus. Unlike Gluck's opera, the legend of Orpheus and Eurydice here takes a tragic ending: no god of love appears to bring Eurydice back to life and Orpheus is torn to pieces by the Maenads. Very different is Roger-Ducasse's other stage work, the four-act *opéra comique Cantegril* (to a libretto by Raymond Escholier), a broad comedy of life in St Gaudéric in the Pyrénées, with music of a more popular kind and with some effective ensembles. It was first produced by the Opéra-Comique (Salle Favart, 9 February 1931) with some success; it shows a well-integrated style and a genuine dramatic quality. His output also includes orchestral and other instrumental works, choral music and songs.

*

P. Landormy: 'Henri Rabaud, Max d'Ollone, Roger Ducasse', *Le théâtre lyrique en France* (Paris, 1937–9) [pubn of Poste National/Radio-Paris], iii, 158–62

DAVID COX

Rogers, Bernard (*b* New York, 4 Feb 1893; *d* Rochester, NY, 24 May 1968). American composer. He studied the piano from the age of 12, but his earliest interest was in painting and architecture; his lifelong love of art and poetry influenced his music. He attended the Cleveland Institute of Music (1922–3), then studied with Frank Bridge in England and with Nadia Boulanger in France on a Guggenheim Fellowship (1927–9). Upon his return to the USA in 1929 he taught at the Eastman School of Music where he became head of the Composition Department; his pupils included David Diamond, Dominick Argento, Robert Ward, Jack Beeson and William Bergsma. He retired in 1967.

Rogers composed four operas, each in a distinctive style. *The Marriage of Aude* (composed 1930), a lyric drama based on the *Chanson de Roland*, won a David Bispham Medal. He described his grand opera *The Warrior* (1945), after the story of Samson and Delilah, as 'a drama in which the characters speak musically'. In using declamatory recitatives and extended aria-like passages for the voice, while the orchestration was dissonant, he sought to make the music functional. *The Veil* (1948) is a horror story in which the heroine is killed by a bridal veil used in a mock marriage ceremony at an English madhouse in the early 19th century. *The Nightingale* (1954) was first performed with piano and percussion accompaniment in May 1955 by the Punch Opera Company in New York before its performance with orchestra in Rochester in 1957. The music incorporates excerpts from his 1939 orchestral suite *The Song of the Nightingale*. Rogers's style ranges from the grandly dramatic to the witty and delicate, from dissonance to melodic delicacy; his rhythmic patterns are varied and his instrumentation vivid and appropriate to the matter at hand.

The Marriage of Aude (lyric drama, 3, C. Rodda, after the *Chanson de Roland*), Rochester, NY, Eastman School, 22 May 1932

The Warrior (grand op, 4 scenes, N. Corwin, after the Bible), New York, Met, 11 Jan 1947

The Veil (tragic op, R. Lawrence), Bloomington, IN, Indiana U., 18 May 1950

The Nightingale (fairy-tale op, prol., 3 scenes, after H. C. Andersen), New York, May 1955 [with pf and perc acc.]; Rochester, NY, 6 May 1957

*

H. Hanson: 'Bernard Rogers', *MM*, xxii (1944–5), 170–75

D. Diamond: 'Bernard Rogers', *MQ*, xxxiii (1947), 207–27

R. Watanabe: 'The Nightingale', *27th Annual Eastman School Festival of American Music, 1957*, 22 [programme booklet]

——: 'The Warrior', *32nd Annual Eastman School Festival of American Music, 1962*, 8 [programme booklet]

RUTH T. WATANABE

Rogers, Nigel (David) (*b* Wellington, nr Telford, 21 March 1935). English tenor. He was a choral scholar at King's College, Cambridge, then studied singing in Italy and in Germany with Hüsch. Initially active as a concert singer, he made his operatic début in 1971 in Vienna in Monteverdi's *Il ritorno d'Ulisse in patria*; later that year he sang Nero in *L'incoronazione di Poppea* in Amsterdam. He made his Italian début in *Il combattimento di Tancredi e Clorinda* (1973, Milan) and his British début as Mosbie in Goehr's *Arden must Die* (1974, London). Other roles include Monteverdi's Orpheus (1975, Amsterdam) and Handel's Theseus (1977, Warsaw). A wide range and rigorous vocal discipline, together with clear diction, excellent intonation and a pleasing vocal astringency have made him a leading exponent of Baroque music, notable in particular for his command of early Baroque ornamentation. His recordings include the Florentine *intermedi* of 1589, Monteverdi's *Orfeo* (twice: in the second he sang the title role), *Dido and Aeneas*, *Hippolyte et Aricie* and *Billy Budd*. He wrote a chapter on the voice in the *Companion to Baroque Music*, edited by J. A. Sadie (London, 1991).

NICHOLAS ANDERSON

Rogneda. Opera in five acts by ALEXANDER NIKOLAYEVICH SEROV to a libretto by Dmitry Averkiyev based on a scenario by the composer, drawn in part from Mikhail Nikolayevich Zagoskin's novel *Askold's Grave* (1833) and Kondraty Rïleyev's narrative ballad *Rogneda* (*c*1825); St Petersburg, Mariinsky Theatre, 27 October/8 November 1865.

The title character, the abandoned wife of the Great Prince Vladimir of Kiev, made an attempt on her husband's life (so the chronicles relate), but was spared on the pleading of her son Izyaslav. Serov, abetted by a group of friends (including Dostoyevsky) who belonged to the conservative nationalist faction known as *pochvenniki* ('men of the soil'), conflated this story with that of Vladimir's baptism in AD 988, which made Byzantine Christianity the Russian state religion. The connection was provided by an episode in Zagoskin's novel in which Vladimir, threatened by a bear, is saved by a Christian named Duleb (Ruald in the opera) at the cost of his own life, thus providing the ruler with a moral example. Around this flimsy plot the composer assembled a gaudy farrago of pagan sacrifices and divinations, hunting scenes, jolly jester's songs and solemn hymnody, the last providing the opera with its climax, on words that associate Orthodox Christianity with Russian dynastic nationalism. The première was conducted by Konstantin Lyadov, with Osip Petrov (bass) as Vladimir, Fyodor Nikol'sky (tenor) as Ruald, the great contralto Dar'ya Leonova as Skulda the witch and Pavel Bulakhov (tenor) as the Jester. Though deplored by the mavericks of the nascent 'kuchka' for its

'Meyerbeerian' theatrical charlatanry and its faux nationalism à la Verstovsky, and denigrated in Soviet times for its monarchist message, the opera was a wild popular success that catapulted its composer to an ephemeral pre-eminence among Russian musicians. The revolution having put an abrupt end to its stage career, *Rogneda* survives today only through the jester's songs and especially the 'Varangian Ballad' sung by the title character (dramatic soprano) in Act 4, 'Zastonalo sinyo more' ('The Blue Sea Groaned'), which have maintained a precarious existence on the Soviet recital stage. The triumphalist mood at the end of the 'Great Patriotic War' inspired a 1945 broadcast performance, under Alexander Yurlov, that was in part preserved on records.

For a music example *see* SEROV, ALEXANDER NIKOLAYEVICH.

RICHARD TARUSKIN

Rogowski, Ludomir Michał (*b* Lublin, 3 Oct 1881; *d* Dubrovnik, 14 March 1954). Polish composer. In 1906 he graduated from the Warsaw Conservatory, where he studied composition with Noskowski and conducting with Młynarski. The following year he went to Leipzig for lessons with Arthur Nikisch. He founded the Vilnius SO in 1910, conducting it until late 1911. From 1912–14 and again from 1922 he was musical director at a Warsaw theatre, until he emigrated to Yugoslavia in 1926 to take up the post of director of the Dubrovnik Conservatory. Rogowski composed prolifically. The influence of Debussy is apparent not only in his treatment of the orchestra, highlighting the capabilities of different instruments, but in his extended tonal palette; as well as the whole-tone and pentatonic scales he made use of what he called the Slavonic scale (Lydian mode with flattened 7th: C-D-E-F♯-G-A-B♭-C) and the Persian scale (alternating semitones and tones). Folksong, particularly from Poland, France, Bosnia and Dalmatia, provided much of his material. Most of his operas are short, of 20–30 minutes' duration, with one to three soloists. Many are based on fairy-tales or are grotesque in character like *Sérénade inutile* or *Un grand chagrin de la petite Ondine*, which also includes a film fragment. He wrote one historical opera, *Królewicz Marko* ('Marko, the King's Son'). Only *Na postoju* ('During a Halt') and the operetta *Legionistka* ('The [Female] Legionary') were staged.

unperformed unless otherwise stated

Kasieńka, 1900 (fairy op, 1, J. Czekierski)
Legionistka [The Female Legionary] (operetta, 3, B. Hertz), Kraków, 29 June 1920
Tamara, 1918 (lyrical legend, F. Hellens, after a Georgian legend, trans. Rogowski)
Un grand chagrin de la petite Ondine, 1920 (Rogowski, Fr. trans.)
Sérénade inutile, 1921 (opéra-burlesque, 1, Rogowski and Hellens)
Na postoju [During a Halt] (1), Warsaw, 3 May 1923
Syrena [The Mermaid], 1924 (grotesque, 3, M. Grif)
Królewicz Marko [Marko, the King's Son], 1930 (5, Rogowski and L. Goleniszczev-Kutuzov)
Kad se mladost vratila [When Youth Came Back], 1953 (radio op)

*

M. Bristiger: 'L. M. Rogowskiego skale i idee muzyczne' [Scales and Musical Ideas in Rogowski], *Studia Hieronymo Feicht septuagenario dedicata* (Kraków, 1967), 446–56

ZOFIA CHECHLIŃSKA

Rohs, Martha (*b* Saarbrücken, 2 June 1909; *d* Vienna, 27 July 1963). German mezzo-soprano. She made her début at Aachen in 1932 and was a member of the Dresden Staatsoper from 1934, singing Octavian with the company at Covent Garden in 1936 and appearing in the première of Strauss's *Daphne* (1938). She sang in Vienna from 1937 and at Salzburg was successful as Octavian, Cherubino, and Sextus in *La clemenza di Tito* (1938–49). She made guest appearances in Paris, Brussels, Munich, Amsterdam and Rome.

DAVID CUMMINGS

Roi Arthus, Le ('King Arthur'). *Drame lyrique*, op.23, in three acts by ERNEST CHAUSSON to his own libretto; Brussels, Théâtre de la Monnaie, 30 November 1903.

Genièvre [Guinevere]	mezzo-soprano
Arthus [Arthur]	baritone
Lancelot	tenor
Mordred	baritone
Lyonnel	tenor
Allan	tenor
Merlin	baritone
A Labourer	tenor
A Knight	bass
An Equerry	baritone
Four Soldiers	two tenors, two basses

Knights, equerries, pages, bards, Guinevere's attendants

Setting Arthur's castle in Carduel and its surrounding forests and plains

Chausson's only completed opera, *Le roi Arthus*, occupied the composer for ten years, from 1885 to 1895, absorbing a major part of his creative energies until shortly before his untimely accidental death. He took great care over both the music and the libretto, showing the latter to Henri Duparc who offered detailed advice (preserved in Oulmont, 1935). Like his symphonic poem *Viviane* of 1882, it reflects the composer's deep involvement in Arthurian literature. His approach to myth and legend, like Wagner's, was one in which he allowed himself considerable freedom in the invention of detail as well as in the manipulation of the plot.

A poll of Brussels opera audiences in 1909 revealed that *Le roi Arthus* was their fourth choice as favourite opera for a revival (after *Tristan*, *Pelléas* and *Götterdämmerung*), but few performances have been given subsequently. In 1985, however, a highly acclaimed recording directed by Armin Jordan was released, providing an invaluable opportunity to reassess one of the greatest of French Wagnerian operas.

ACT 1 The principal narrative element is the adultery between Lancelot, one of the most valiant knights of the round table, and Arthur's wife Guinevere. Mordred, jealous of Lancelot's high standing and of his success with Guinevere, disturbs the lovers in Act 1 during a secret assignation, cursing them with the words 'Malheur, malheur à vous deux'. The rest of the scene, in which Chausson uses a harmonic language which is mainly diatonic but tinged with modal, quasi-medieval inflections, is concerned with Arthur's celebration of his knights' victory over the Saxons, singling out Lancelot for his bravery. There follows a love duet in the manner of a medieval *alba*, in which Lyonnel acts as a watchman during the lovers' nocturnal tryst, finally warning of the impending dawn. Here Chausson's music strongly echoes the love duet from the second act of Wagner's *Tristan*: in the same key of A♭, the lovers' vocal lines en-

'Le roi Arthus' (Chausson), Act 3 scene i (top of a hill overlooking the battlefield from which Lanceolot has retreated to meet Guinevere, followed by Lyonnel): the original production at the Théâtre de la Monnaie, 30 November 1903, with designs by Dubosq and costumes by Knopff; from 'Le théâtre' (January 1904)

twine chromatically over a throbbing accompaniment.

ACT 2 The lovers, betrayed to Arthur by Mordred, are faced with Arthur's suspicions. Guinevere lies to him but Lancelot's principles prevent him from doing likewise and he refuses Arthur's summons. Arthur turns to the wizard Merlin, who appears in an apple orchard and from the flight of 'symbolic eagles from Lomond' predicts the imminent downfall of the round table. To Arthur's annoyance he disappears before making any pronouncement about Lancelot and Guinevere. The passage is memorably set by Chausson with a recurrent motive and strikingly wandering chromatic harmonies.

ACT 3 Arthur fights Lancelot, who flees when confronted with Arthur's magic sword Excalibur. But although Lancelot is tempted to elope with Guinevere he decides that the past cannot be erased and returns to the fight. Thus bereft, Guinevere, lost for a weapon with which to end her life, strangles herself with her own long hair. Chausson's handling of this scene shows not only a masterly talent for pacing, while Guinevere slowly lights upon the idea of strangling herself, but also of dramatic contrast. He keeps the military aspect of the opera – off-stage trumpet and soldiers' choruses – alive right up to the last moment, thus highlighting Guinevere's sudden feeling of isolation. The cloying chromaticism, too, perfectly captures her slow sinking into oblivion. At the end of the opera, confronted by the dying Lancelot, Arthur, transcending mere humanity, forgives him. Out of the distance comes a boat of maidens offering eternal rest, portrayed by Chausson with a massive and luxurious double chorus, often in more than 12 parts. The opera ends with Arthur being borne, as if asleep, into the golden sunset. The C minor of the opening is resolved at last into a glowing C major.

* * *

In plot alone, the parallels with Wagner's *Tristan* are obvious. But despite the similarity of the love triangle, Chausson's resolution of the conflict is quite the opposite of Wagner's. Lancelot, unlike Tristan, is constantly remorseful for his betrayal of Arthur and of the ideals of the round table. Arthur, moreover, is a far stronger character than King Mark, and it is he who, true to his Christian principles, transcends in the final denouement, rather than the power of love as in Wagner's opera. In musical terms too, the opera is deeply infused with aspects of the Wagnerian style, as Chausson well knew. While still at work on his opera, he wrote to his friend Paul Poujaud that 'the greatest defect of my drama is without doubt the analogy of the subject with that of *Tristan*. That would still not matter, if I could only successfully de-Wagnerize myself. Wagnerian in subject and Wagnerian in music, is that not too much altogether?'.

Despite the resemblances and set aside from a host of far less successful French works displaying ill-absorbed and poorly executed Wagnerian techniques, Chausson's work has a strength of its own. For one thing, it contains many elements that are far from Wagnerian – the harmony, although chromatic, is always highly personal and throughout the opera there is an absence of any leitmotif technique. Nor are the massed choral effects, used to portray Arthur's transcendence, in any way indebted to Wagner.

On the other hand, the love duet of the second act strongly recalls the second act of *Tristan und Isolde* in dramatic situation, imagery and musical style. The half-diminished chord, so strongly associated with *Tristan*, is much in evidence, as are many of the other features of Wagner's love music: rising sequences, the chromatically intertwining voice lines of the lovers and the linear chromaticism of the accompaniment as well as the overall style of the scoring. Among the opera's most memorable moments are the entry of Merlin, prophesying the future, the scene where Guinevere strangles herself, and the chorus of women's voices accompanying Arthur as he boards the skiff and sails into oblivion. Chausson was particularly satisfied with the third act, which he considered was 'becoming clear and de-Wagnerized'.

RICHARD LANGHAM SMITH

Roi de Lahore, Le ('The King of Lahore'). *Opéra* in five acts by JULES MASSENET to a libretto by LOUIS GALLET; Paris, Opéra, 27 April 1877.

Le roi de Lahore is more significant for what it is than for what it achieves. The libretto by Louis Gallet – he also wrote the texts for Massenet's oratorios *Marie-Magdeleine* and *Eve* – re-rehearses in prolix fashion popular operatic preoccupations in 19th-century Paris: an exotic oriental setting, a virgin priestess loved by both tenor and baritone, a thundering bass High Priest, and so on. The one interesting departure from formula is the fact that the eponymous King (tenor) dies at the end of Act 2, spends Act 3 in a Hindu paradise (ballet of Blessed Spirits), and returns to earth for Acts 4 and 5 in the guise of a beggar before expiring once more with his beloved priestess Sitâ (soprano) at the final curtain, much to the chagrin of the usurping villain Scindia (baritone).

The score is similarly referential and longwinded, with obvious echoes of Auber, Bizet and Meyerbeer; the patient listener has to wade through pages of stock *grand opéra* sound and fury before being rewarded with rare and isolated examples of Massenet's characteristic word-setting, his supple melodies (the slow waltz for solo saxophone in the ballet is especially happy), or a well-crafted duet like 'Oui, je bénis la souffrance' for soprano and tenor in Act 2. *Grand opéra* was never Massenet's forte, and he was easily to improve on *Le roi de Lahore* in *Hérodiade* and *Le Cid*.

But *Le roi de Lahore*, given a première production of well-documented lavishness at the Palais Garnier (which had opened only two years previously), firmly established the 34-year-old Massenet as a successful composer of opera – luckily, in that he had composed the piece without any commission or contract. It was a two-year wonder in Paris, with 57 performances before it lapsed from the repertory, and within five years of the première it had been staged throughout Europe and in South America. It also enjoyed a marked success in Italy, where its popularity in Turin and Milan in 1879 drew comments of withering sarcasm from Verdi, whose publisher Ricordi took Massenet up with profit and indeed co-commissioned *Hérodiade* with Georges Hartmann. Massenet's influence on the *veristi* may be glimpsed every now and then in a soaring vocal phrase or a big unison string tune. Rather more surprising is the evidence of how much Tchaikovsky admired the work, which he read in score; the arioso 'Promesse de mon avenir' has, in its sudden, impulsive string repetition of a vocal line and its orchestral echoing of vocal phrase-endings, a distinctly Tchaikovskian cut.

A single, centenary revival of *Le roi de Lahore* was given by the Vancouver Opera in 1977, with Joan Sutherland; it was subsequently recorded by Decca.

RODNEY MILNES

Roi d'Ys, Le ('The King of Ys'). *Opéra* in 3 acts by EDOUARD LALO to a libretto by EDOUARD BLAU; Paris, Opéra-Comique (Salle Favart), 7 May 1888.

Ys is a legendary Breton city submerged by the sea many centuries ago. Blau fashioned the Breton folktale of a consuming tide into a libretto on the lines of *Lohengrin* with two opposing couples, good and bad. Lalo composed the opera in 1875 but it was refused by the Théâtre Lyrique in 1878 and by the Opéra in 1879. Various extracts were performed in concerts, and the whole opera was revised in 1886. It was finally staged by the Opéra-Comique in 1888, and was a long-lasting success.

In Act 1 Margared (mezzo-soprano), daughter of the King of Ys (*basse chantante*), celebrates her betrothal to Karnac (baritone), their former enemy, but confesses to her sister Rozenn (soprano) that she loves Mylio (tenor), a childhood friend who sailed away. Rozenn too loves Mylio, a love she knows is returned. This is confirmed when Mylio unexpectedly returns. During her wedding ceremony Margared learns that Mylio has arrived, and she refuses to go ahead with the marriage. Karnac curses Ys and threatens vengeance.

In Act 2 Margared realizes that Mylio loves not her but her sister. Overcome with jealousy, she overhears the King promising Rozenn's hand to Mylio when he returns victorious from combat with Karnac. In the second scene Mylio is acclaimed the victor, although he attributes his success to the support of St Corentin, the

Poster by Auguste-François Gorguet for Lalo's 'Le roi d'Ys', printed at the time of the original production at the Opéra-Comique, Paris, in 1888

city's patron saint. When the victory procession has gone Karnac appears, miserable in defeat. Margared offers to join forces with him in seeking revenge. Heedless of the statue of St Corentin (bass-baritone) warning her to repent, she plans to open the sluices that protect the city from the sea.

As the marriage of Rozenn and Mylio proceeds in Act 3, Margared's resolve wavers. But Karnac enflames her jealousy and they make for the sluices. The King is troubled that Margared is not there. When she returns, she announces that Ys is doomed: Karnac has opened the sluices. Mylio reports that he has killed Karnac but that the waves are engulfing the city. In scene ii Margared reveals to the terrified citizens that the ocean demands a sacrifice and that it must be she, since she planned the opening of the sluices with Karnac. She hurls herself into the sea from a high rock. At that moment St Corentin appears; appeased by Margared's death he calms the waves and saves the city.

The opera's central character is less the King of Ys himself, who plays little part in the action and who is never named, than Margared, a fine mezzo role written for Lalo's wife (though sung by her only in concert extracts). Reminiscent of both Ortrud and Senta, Margared redeems herself at the end by self-sacrifice and thus saves the city. Neither Rozenn nor Mylio is subject to the same emotional conflict. St Corentin acts as a benevolent supernatural force.

In the choruses Lalo used Breton folksongs he had learnt from his wife. The score is amazingly compact and forceful, for although there are ceremonial and processional scenes the music is constantly concerned with making a dramatic point or delineating character and mood. Lalo's language is chromatic (though not Wagnerian), full of augmented chords and varieties of sixth and seventh chords. He uses noisy unisons and strong rhythms for emphasis, with a particular fondness for driving 6/8 metres. His orchestration is full-blooded and imaginative, yet always subservient to the voices.

French opera is often accused of artificiality and sensationalism on the one hand and pretty sentimentality on the other. *Le roi d'Ys* is innocent of both charges. Lalo felt deeply for his subject; Brittany was not simply an exotic excuse for local colour. Many grand opera conventions are observed, it is true, but the dynamic quality of the music and its rich invention make it a truly dramatic work and – unusual for a French opera – a truly national one.

HUGH MACDONALD

Roi et le fermier, Le ('The King and the Farmer'). *Comédie mêlée de morceaux de musique* in three acts by PIERRE-ALEXANDRE MONSIGNY to a libretto by MICHEL-JEAN SEDAINE after Robert Dodsley's 'dramatic tale' *The King and the Miller of Mansfield*; Paris, Comédie-Italienne (Hôtel de Bourgogne), 22 November 1762.

The second opera on which Sedaine and Monsigny collaborated is one of the most striking works in the French *opéra comique* repertory of the second half of the 18th century. While most of the works previously performed at the Fair Theatres and the Théâtre Italien had confined themselves to comic subjects, with characters drawn from the lower social orders, *Le roi et le fermier* shows a desire on the librettist's part to ennoble his work in both the social and the theatrical sense. The idea of featuring a king on stage derives from a 'dramatic tale' by Dodsley, which had appeared in a French translation in the first volume of *Choix de petites pièces du théâtre anglois* (Paris, 1756). However, the libretto diverges considerably from its model, chiefly in the fact that its heroine, Jenny (soprano), when abducted by the villainous aristocrat Lurewel (tenor), does not succumb to his advances. At the crucial moment her conversation with Lurewel is interrupted by news that the King is coming to hunt nearby, and she escapes.

The opera opens with the distress of Richard (tenor), who suspects his fiancée of unfaithfulness. But Jenny soon enters, and the main plot, as the first reviewers pointed out, is over by the end of Act 1. The central scene of Act 2 brings the King (tenor), lost in Chéroud forest (Dodsley's Sherwood), face to face with Richard. As a gamekeeper, the latter subjects his sovereign to questioning of a kind to which he is not accustomed. In the third act the King, still incognito, takes shelter in the cottage where Richard lives with his Mother (soprano) and sister Betsy (soprano). For the first time in his life, the King sees the conditions in which his subjects live, and learns of their poor opinion of his courtiers. He also discovers how country gentlemen behave towards young peasant girls, and when Lurewel, who is also lost, enters Richard's cottage he is instantly recognized as the guilty party. Touched by the simple manners of the country folk, the King raises Richard to the nobility and gives Jenny a dowry. However, in a departure from Dodsley's play, he leaves the stage before the final chorus and vaudeville; here Sedaine was making the point that the King did not really belong in *opéra comique*, and showing the difficulty, under an absolutist regime such as that of Louis XV, of taking a monarch out of his usual social context without depriving him of dignity. The result, no doubt unintentional, is that the character of the King has less human warmth than in Dodsley's original, in keeping with the contemporary difference in status between the King of France and the King of England.

Dramatically and musically, there are considerable innovations in *Le roi et le fermier*. The new approach first reveals itself in the overture, with its two movements in different keys (E♭ and C minor), which does not reach its tonal resolution until Richard's first aria, 'Je ne sais à quoi me résoudre' (in E♭). More spectacular is the musical continuity established by Monsigny through five successive pieces: the duet at the end of the first act, interrupted several times by recitative and orchestral episodes; a descriptive entr'acte based on ideas already heard in the duet; a comic duet for two gamekeepers at the beginning of Act 2; and finally a long monologue for the King, which is itself divided into an accompanied recitative and an *ariette* with a central section picking up thematic elements of the recitative. Features such as these amply justify Monsigny's choice of the opera to appear in the portrait painted of him in 1812 by Charles Thévenin (in the Bibliothèque et Musée de l'Opéra, Paris).

MICHEL NOIRAY

Roi l'a dit, Le ('The King has Said It'). *Opéra comique* in three acts by LÉO DELIBES to a libretto by EDMOND GONDINET; Paris, Opéra-Comique (Salle Favart), 24 May 1873.

Le roi l'a dit is a lively comedy set in the reign of Louis XIV. It is remarkable in requiring a cast of 14 singers – six men and eight women – occasioned mainly by the fact that the Marquis de Moncontour (baritone), the principal figure, has four daughters and no sons to present at court. The Marquis, however, pretends to the king that he has a son and grooms his servant-girl's boyfriend, Benoit (tenor), for the role. Benoit finds himself engaged in a duel in which he conveniently feigns death, a neat solution to the Marquis's embarrassing predicament. There is a comic music lesson with ten participants, and various intrigues for the four daughters. The opera was successful both in Paris and abroad and has been revived from time to time. HUGH MACDONALD

Roi malgré lui, Le ('The King in Spite of Himself'). *Opéra comique* in three acts by EMMANUEL CHABRIER to a libretto by EMILE DE NAJAC and Paul Burani; Paris, Opéra-Comique (Salle Favart), 18 May 1887.

In his castle near Kraków, Henri de Valois (baritone), King of Poland, and his French courtiers are bored. The king wishes he was back in France; he asks Duke Fritelli (baritone), an Italian attached to the court, for his opinion on the Polish character. Fritelli replies 'Le polonais est triste et grave'. The king praises Italian women, citing an adventure he had in Venice, while Count de Nangis (tenor) admits his love for the serf Minka (soprano), who is owned by Count Laski (bass), the Polish patriot. After the king has gone, Nangis and Minka sing of their love. Minka tells the count of a ball to be given by Laski that night, and arranges to meet Nangis in the park. She reiterates her love in 'L'amour, ce divin maître'.

When Fritelli returns with his wife Alexina (soprano), the niece of Count Laski, Minka overhears their conversation. Alexina reveals that her uncle and his fellow conspirators are plotting to overthrow the king. Fritelli would prefer to talk of love, but his wife laughs at him. Realizing that she was the subject of the king's Venetian adventure, he decides to join Laski's conspiracy. The king returns and Minka, mistaking him for a courtier, reveals Laski's plot against him. Henri confronts Fritelli and insists on being taken to the ball. He pretends to lose his temper with Nangis and sends him to prison, then makes Fritelli introduce him to Alexina as Nangis, a Frenchman with a grudge against the king. Henri and Alexina recognize each other, though neither knows the other's true identity. With Fritelli they sing a trio, 'Quelle surprise, ma beauté de Venise', interrupted by Minka, waiting in the park.

In the great hall of Count Laski's palace the guests dance and sing the *Fête polonaise*. The conspirators, including the false Nangis, swear to remove Henri from the Polish throne. Minka, who knows that Henri is not Nangis but does not know that he is the king, sings a brilliant *Chanson tzigane*. The real Nangis, masked, makes a fleeting appearance and then hides. Henri, in love once more with Alexina, tries to find out from Fritelli whose wife she is; perhaps he will not leave Poland after all. Fritelli tells Laski that the king is at the ball in disguise. Laski searches the palace and finds Nangis, who admits that he is the king and is locked up. The conspirators decide that the king should be killed and choose the false Nangis to do the deed. Henri feigns agreement, intending however to kill himself, not Nangis, but Minka has already helped the count to escape.

At an inn on the Polish border, the peasants celebrate the election of a new king, the Archduke Ernest. Henri has stopped at the inn on his way back to France, Minka and Alexina arrive in search of their respective lovers. Confusion abounds until finally Henri reveals his identity. He sets off for the border, but is turned back. The Archduke Ernest has refused the Polish throne, declaring that Henri should remain king.

The brilliance of Chabrier's music, often reminiscent of Berlioz and sometimes of Bizet, rests on a superbly crafted structure. Well-known interludes such as the *Fête polonaise* and the *Chanson tzigane* become even more impressive in context, while the balance between romantic and comic episodes, a striking feature of all Chabrier's operas, is at its most perfect in *Le roi malgré lui*. If the first-act finale brings to mind Rossini, and the conspirators' chorus raises echoes of *Les Huguenots*, both ensembles display the technical wizardry of a composer whose originality of inspiration is never in doubt.

The characters, whether romantic or comic, are drawn with extreme care and are entirely convincing, especially the king, whose doubts and longings are the emotions of a real human being, however contrived the dramatic circumstances. Likewise Minka, who overhears and reveals the secrets that propel the plot is also portrayed with musical vitality. Even the Duke and Duchess Fritelli, purely comic figures in the text, emerge as interesting people through the music.

Despite its fine score, *Le roi malgré lui* was initially not very popular, with only 20 performances in more than 40 years. A new version, with the text drastically revised by ALBERT CARRÉ, was presented at the Opéra-Comique on 6 November 1929 and proved more successful, achieving 50 performances by 1946.

ELIZABETH FORBES

Poster by Jules Chéret for Chabrier's 'Le roi malgré lui', printed at the time of the original production at the Opéra-Comique, Paris, in 1887

Rokitansky, Hans Freiherr **von** (*b* Vienna, 8 March 1835; *d* Schloss Laubegg, Styria, 2 Nov 1909). Austrian bass. He studied in Bologna and Milan, making his début in 1857 at the Théâtre Italien, Paris, as Oroveso in *Norma*. He began an engagement at Prague (1862) as Cardinal Brogni in *La Juive*. From 1864 until his retirement in 1893, he was engaged at the Vienna Hofoper. He appeared at Her Majesty's Theatre, London, in 1865 and in 1866, when he sang Osmin (*Die Entführung*); he returned to London in 1876 and 1877. His roles included Leporello, Sarastro, Bertram (*Robert le diable*), Fiesco (*Simon Boccanegra*), Caspar (*Der Freischütz*), the Landgrave (*Tannhäuser*), King Henry (*Lohengrin*) and Giorgio (*I puritani*). His voice was a deep bass of great resonance.

*

V. von Rokitansky: *Über Sänger und Singen* (Vienna, 1891, 2/1896)
B. Marchesi: *The Singer's Catechism and Creed* (London, 1932)

ELIZABETH FORBES

Roland **(i).** *Tragédie en musique* in a prologue and five acts by Jean-Baptiste Lully (*see* LULLY family, (1)) to a libretto by PHILIPPE QUINAULT after LUDOVICO ARIOSTO's *Orlando furioso*; Versailles, court, 8 January 1685.

PROLOGUE

Demogorgon *king of the fairies and leader of the genies*	baritone
Fairy	soprano

TRAGEDY

Angélique *Queen of Cathay*	soprano
Roland *knight, nephew of Charlemagne*	baritone
Médor *follower of an African king*	haute-contre
Témire *confidante of Angélique*	soprano
Ziliante *prince of the eastern islands*	baritone
Astolfe *friend of Roland*	haute-contre
Belise *shepherdess, Coridon's beloved*	soprano
Coridon *shepherd, Belise's beloved*	haute-contre
Tersandre *shepherd, father of Belise*	tenor
Logistille *a wise and powerful fairy*	soprano
La Gloire [Glory]	soprano
La Renommée [Fame]	silent
La Terreur [Terror]	silent

Fairies, genies; followers of Angélique, islanders who follow Ziliante; cupids, sirens, gods of the rivers, sylvans, enchanted lovers; people of Cathay; shepherds, shepherdesses; fairies who follow Logistille, ghosts of dead heroes, followers of Glory

Setting Medieval Cathay

Lully and Quinault's penultimate tragedy was performed weekly at Versailles (in the riding-school theatre, without machinery) for two months; the production then moved to the Paris Opéra on 8 or 9 March and continued until November. The principal singers were Le Rochois (Angélique), Dumesnil (Médor) and Beaumavielle (Roland). Paris Opéra revivals occurred regularly up to 1755. Between 1686 and 1750 there were productions in Brussels (several times), Marseilles, Lyons, Rouen, Metz, Lille and Amsterdam.

Lully's dedication of the printed score to Louis XIV indicates that the king chose the subject of the story. The libretto is curiously divided. Acts 1–3 concern Angélique's internal conflict between love and 'glory' (more precisely, love and pride). Acts 4–5 concern Roland's internal struggle with unrequited love; it is resolved by a *dea ex machina* who uses magic to make Roland understand that the struggle is a heroic conflict between love and duty.

PROLOGUE *Palace of Demogorgon* Fairies and genies led by Demogorgon celebrate the return of peace after war. They prepare to amuse their hero (Louis XIV) with the story of Roland, who was led astray by love when he neglected glory.

ACT 1 *A hamlet in Cathay* Angélique, Queen of Cathay, is torn by indecision: she is loved by the great knight Roland but loves Médor, a foreigner of obscure lineage whom she nursed to health after a battle. She is ashamed and banishes Médor, then sends her confidante, Témire, to console him. The music alternates between dialogues in simple recitative and orchestrally accompanied monologues; the monologues include dramatic recitatives for Angélique and a large-scale *air* for Médor ('Ah! quel tourment'). In the *divertissement* Ziliante and his followers present Angélique with a bracelet, a gift from Roland.

ACT 2 *An enchanted forest* Angélique searches unsuccessfully for the fountain of Hatred but can find only the fountain of Love. Surrendering to her love for Médor, she is upset to see Roland approaching and uses a magic ring to make herself invisible. In a scene unified by a recurring cry of anguish ('Angélique, ingrate, inhumaine'), Roland expresses his helplessness in the face of love. After Roland has gone, Médor appears; he draws his sword to commit suicide, but Angélique stops him and offers him her love. The *divertissement* is a celebration of love by enchanted lovers and pastoral divinities.

ACT 3 *A seaport* Angélique and Médor plan to sail away to escape Roland's wrath. Unable to rid herself of Roland by being cold to him, Angélique resorts to artifice, pretending to love him and arranging a false rendezvous. Angélique and Médor are free at last; the climactic final love scene mingles pairs of adjacent *airs* over descending tetrachord ostinatos with expressive duets. Although Ariosto had allowed the lovers to steal away in secret, Quinault had to provide a *divertissement*: Angélique introduces Médor to the people of Cathay, and in an extended chaconne they pay homage to their new king and celebrate love.

ACT 4 *A grotto in the woods* Roland's friend Astolfe tries unsuccessfully to reason with him. Alone, Roland waits in vain for Angélique (*air*, 'O Nuit') and discovers verses about the happy lovers Angélique and Médor (a name he does not know) written on the grotto. A fragment of a minuet for double reeds that will soon be heard in its entirety announces the approach of a village wedding party. The group celebrates in a pastoral *divertissement*, then the bridal couple, Belise and Coridon, innocently comment on the happy love of Angélique and Médor. Roland inquires, and learns from Belise, Coridon and Belise's father Tersandre the details of the lovers' departure. The news, so terrible to Roland, is told joyously and is punctuated by the wedding party's continued happy songs and dances. The key slips to the flat side, from C major in the *divertissement*, to G minor as Angélique and Médor are mentioned and to F major and then B♭ major as the truth is gradually revealed. When Roland's pain reaches a climax, he lashes out in fury at the uncomprehending bridal group,

'Roland' (Lully), Act 4 (a grotto in the woods): wash drawing by Jean Berain showing the final scene (Roland threatens the bridal group) in the original production at Versailles, 8 January 1685; an engraving after this drawing appeared in the first edition of the libretto

who barely have time to flee before his rage gives way to insanity, expressed in a powerful mad scene.

ACT 5 The final act is dominated by ballet episodes. Responding to Astolfe's pleas, the wise fairy Logistille puts Roland to sleep so that fairies may perform mysterious ceremonies over him. She then brings forth ghosts of dead heroes who summon Roland to glory; in the chorus 'Roland courez aux armes', 'courez' is painted melismatically. Roland awakens, sane and ashamed. Urged by Glory, who is accompanied by Fame, Roland prepares to follow Terror back to his war-torn country. Terror flies before him as the fairies and ghosts of heroes celebrate.

* * *

Roland represents Lully's mature style. The use of continuous orchestral music to give structure to large-scale monologues, a development of the 1680s, reaches its most highly developed state here. In Act 4, Lully's thorough integration of drama and *divertissement*, along with his expressive use of key structure, complement Quinault's compelling presentation of Roland's psychological development; this act, especially the part involving the village wedding party, was praised throughout the 18th century. *Roland* is Lully's only *tragédie en musique* currently unavailable in modern edition.

See also ANGELICA E MEDORO. LOIS ROSOW

Roland (ii). *Tragédie lyrique* in three acts by Niccolò Piccinni (*see* PICCINNI family, (1)) to a libretto by JEAN FRANÇOIS MARMONTEL after PHILIPPE QUINAULT; Paris, Opéra, 27 January 1778.

Roland was Piccinni's first French opera; it was intended to counter the opposition during the third controversy in Paris involving French and Italian music. Given the atmosphere in Paris at the time, Piccinni expected *Roland* to fail, but it was well received and continued to be performed throughout Europe until the mid-1780s. The story, originally taken from Ariosto's *Orlando furioso*, tells of Roland's obsessive (indeed, bewitched) love for Angélique (*see* ANGELICA E MEDORO). This version begins with a scene for Angélique (soprano) and her confidante Thémire (soprano), in which Angélique is torn between her interest in the knight Roland (bass) and her love for the squire Médor (tenor), whom she nursed after he had been wounded. Thémire reminds her of her status. Angélique orders Médor to leave her, but she is grief-stricken. The first act ends with the arrival of some oriental islanders, one of whom presents her with a bracelet from Roland.

Act 2 begins in a forest, next to the fountain of love. (During the opening *divertissement* a jealous lover tries to drink at the fountain of Hatred but is persuaded to move to the fountain of Love.) Angélique reveals that she still loves Médor. She is seen by Roland but uses her magic ring to become invisible. Roland describes to Thémire his helpless love for Angélique and decides that he should return to his country to save it from ruin ('Je me reconnois, je respire'). His resolution does not last long, however, and he returns to emotional imprisonment. Thémire tries to persuade Angélique to return Roland's love, but she will not. The ladies hear Médor's voice in the forest, as he laments his fate and decides to kill himself. Angélique declares her love, and tells Médor to hide while she deals with Roland. Roland merely wants to be allowed to follow Angélique. The scene changes to a harbour, where a sailors' choral *divertissement* warns against jealousy; several dances follow. Médor sings about how love saved him from a shipwreck. Angélique and Médor plight their troth publicly, with accompanying dances.

Act 3 takes place in a grotto, where Roland's compatriot Astolfe (tenor) tries to persuade Roland to rid himself of the enchantment and return to his desperate country. Roland is not persuaded and, left alone in the forest, agonizes over whether Angélique loves Médor. He is interrupted by a group of shepherds and shepherdesses, including Bélise (soprano) and Coridon (tenor), who let him know that Angélique and Médor have left the enchanted forest. They notice Roland's misery, and bless Angélique's and Médor's love, but Roland frenziedly smashes the inscriptions that Angélique and Médor have left, uproots trees and overturns boulders. The fairy Logistille (soprano) sings an aria about the bad effects of love. The scene changes to a military camp, where a chorus of soldiers persuades Roland to return to his military calling, and the opera ends with a *marche guerrière*.

Costume for Roland in the title role of Piccinni's 'Roland' in an early production by the Académie Royale de Musique in Paris: from 'Costumes et annales des grands théâtres de Paris' (1789)

Marmontel clearly expected his audience to know Quinault's libretto, just as Quinault had expected his audience to know earlier versions of the story. This version is a somewhat capricious and fragmented drama, missing many connections. Roland's conversion back to sanity is particularly unconvincing. The core of the opera, however, is the series of long and complex scenes where Angélique, Médor and Roland explore their emotional states, and here the music tells as much as the words. The most striking scene is Roland's, as he waits in the darkening forest for Angélique (3.ii). Following the recitative, there is a short aria, beginning in F major and ending in G minor, which moves into an arioso section with unusually beautiful orchestral music that suggests both the coming of night and the darkening of Roland's soul. This gives way to an obbligato recitative in which Roland agonizes about his rival; every time Médor is mentioned the strings have a tremolo accompaniment. The scene ends with a rage aria in *ABA* form, the clarity and eloquence of which aptly round off a scene marked by flexibility of form. Although the work has many exciting and dramatic accompanied recitatives, Roland's scene alone has an extended arioso section and is thus the only one that appears to move smoothly between emotions. Piccinni's arias are often quite long – the songs of the shepherds and shepherdesses in Act 3, in charming *opéra comique* style, are the obvious exceptions – in *ABA* or italianate binary forms. Médor has an extraordinarily heroic, virtuoso piece, 'L'amour m'a sauvé du naufrage', which would be perfectly at home in Metastasian *opera seria*. Although the music rises above the dullness and incoherence of the libretto, italianate and French musical elements are not yet as fully integrated as Piccinni was later to make them. MARY HUNTER

Rolandi, Gianna (*b* New York, 16 Aug 1952). American soprano. She studied at the Curtis Institute. In 1975, three days before her scheduled début at the New York City Opera as Zerbinetta, she replaced an ailing soprano as Olympia in *Les contes d'Hoffmann*. Appearing at first as a comic coloratura, she has increasingly taken on more dramatic roles such as Gilda, Lucia (1986, San Francisco), the Queen of Night and Handel's Cleopatra (with the ENO in Geneva, 1983) and has moved into many of the roles once sung at the City Opera by Beverly Sills. She made her Metropolitan début in 1979 as Sophie in *Der Rosenkavalier*, returning as Olympia and Zerbinetta; in the latter role she made her European début at Glyndebourne (1981), where she later sang Susanna, Zdenka and Konstanze. Her roles also include Philine (*Mignon*). She sang Bianca in the North American première of *Bianca e Falliero* in Miami (1987), and has appeared as Oscar there, as Ophelia in San Diego, as Ginevra (*Ariodante*) in Geneva and Paris, as Amenaide (*Tancredi*) in Turin and as Dorinda (*Orlando*) in Chicago. She is a fluent singer, at ease in the bel canto repertory, and an accomplished actress.

MICHAEL FLEMING, ELIZABETH FORBES

Rolandi, Ulderico (*b* Rome, 23 July 1874; *d* Rome, 3 Dec 1951). Italian writer. A gynaecologist by profession, he was active as a critic and particularly as a collector of, and writer on, opera librettos. His collection, which passed to the Fondazione Cini in Venice on his death, included some 30000 librettos and 2000 scores. His writings include many studies of individual librettos and librettists, contributed to various periodicals and collective volumes from the 1920s onwards, as well as more extended studies, of which the principal one is *Il libretto per musica attraverso i tempi* (Rome, 1951).

*

V. Raeli: 'La collezione Rolandi di libretti d'opera musicali', *Accademie e biblioteche d'Italia*, i/3 (1927–8), 46–57

E. D'Arborea: *Il dottore Ulderico Rolandi nel suo regno* (Pompei, 1927)

U. Rolandi: 'Storie e vicende della collezione Rolandi di libretti per musica', *Sardegna* (Cagliari, 1930)

G. Biscottini: 'La biblioteca musical Rolandi e la sua collezione di libretti per musica', *Accademie e biblioteche d'Italia*, xvi (1941–2), 242–3

A. L. Bellini, B. Brizi and M. G. Pensa: 'La collezione di libretti d'opera della Fondazione "Cini" di Venezia', *Le fonti musicali in Italia*, i (1987), 218

Roland-Manuel [Lévy, Roland Alexis Manuel] (*b* Paris, 22 March 1891; *d* Paris, 2 Nov 1966). French composer and writer on music. He studied composition with Roussel at the Schola Cantorum. Later, on the advice of Satie, he studied with Ravel, of whom he became a lifelong devotee, and whose style is strongly reflected in his own. His only staged opera, which has been successfully revived, was *Isabelle et Pantalon*, to a witty *commedia dell'arte* libretto by Max Jacob. Isabelle is kept prisoner by Dr Pantalon, who runs a hydrotherapy centre where 'words and water' cure everything. Pierrot, her husband, tries in vain to rescue her, but it is Harlequin, her lover, who eventually succeeds. Pantalon, in a farcical scene, is subjected to a good dose of his own hydrotherapeutic medicine.

Le diable amoureux, commissioned by the Paris Opéra, was withdrawn by the composer before the première and extracts have been heard only in concert performance. Roland-Manuel also wrote incidental music for several plays as well as ballets, film music and several important books on Ravel.

Isabelle et Pantalon (opéra bouffe, 2, M. Jacob), Paris, Trianon-Lyrique, 11 Dec 1922, vs (Paris, 1922)

Le diable amoureux, 1932 (oc, R. Allard, after Cazotte), extracts perf.

Echec à Don Juan, 1941 (opéra, C. A. Puget), unperf.

La Célestine, 1942 (opéra, M. Achard, after F. de Rojas), unperf.

Jeanne d'Arc, 1955 (opéra, C. Péguy), unperf.

*

L. Aubert: 'Jean Rivier, Roland-Manuel, Manuel Rosenthal, Maurice Thiriet', *Le théâtre lyrique en France* [pubn of Poste National/Radio-Paris] (Paris, 1937–9), iii, 275–85

RICHARD LANGHAM SMITH

Rolfe Johnson, Anthony (*b* Tackley, Northants., 5 Nov 1940). English tenor. Originally a farmer, he studied at the GSM with Ellis Keeler and later with Vera Rozsa, Richard Lewis and Peter Pears. He made his début with the English Opera Group in 1973 as Count Vaudémont in *Iolanta* (Tchaikovsky), followed by Stroh (*Intermezzo*) and Lensky at Glyndebourne in 1974. His début with the ENO was in 1978 as Don Ottavio, and in 1983 he was highly successful both in Geneva and with Scottish Opera as Aschenbach (*Death in Venice*); during these years he toured widely in Europe and the USA in concerts and making recordings. In 1988 he made his Covent Garden début as Jupiter (*Semele*) and in 1989 sang an outstanding Ulysses (Monteverdi) with the ENO. He made his Metropolitan début as Idomeneus in 1991. An artist of all-round vocal quality and style, he was named Director of Singing Studies at the Britten-Pears School from 1990.

D. P. Stearns: 'Quick Study', *ON*, lii/10 (1987–8), 20–21, 46

H. Finch: 'Slings, Bows and Arrows', *The Times* (7 Nov 1989)

NOËL GOODWIN

Rolland, Romain (*b* Clamecy, 29 Jan 1866; *d* Vézelay, 30 Dec 1944). French writer on music, novelist and playwright. He took the doctorate at the Sorbonne with a dissertation on the origins of *théâtre lyrique* (1895), then taught art history in Paris. During this time he organized the first music history congress to be held in Paris (1900) and was a co-founder of the *Revue d'histoire et de critique musicales* (1901). He became director of the newly founded music school of the Ecole des Hautes Etudes Sociales (1902–11) and was appointed to the first chair of music history at the Sorbonne (1903–13).

Rolland ranged inexhaustibly over a wide field of intellectual activity. His many essays, plays and novels, several with a French historical background, including the story on which Kabalevsky's opera *Colas Breugnon* (1938) was based, expressed his philosophical idealism, and brought him the Nobel prize for literature in 1915. In his dissertation, mainly remembered for its rehabilitation of Francesco Provenzale, he subordinated analysis of form and structure to biographical sketches and plot summaries set in a scrupulously documented cultural and political context. His personal view of history, which he saw primarily in terms of the noble, superior soul, gave a distinctive flavour to his writings on Beethoven (a single-volume life and a seven-volume study) and his biography of Handel, and to his articles on a variety of musical subjects in numerous journals (later reprinted in three collections, 1908–19; Eng. trans., 1915–22). Because of its universality, its profundity and spontaneity, music, he believed, was often the first to give expression to fundamental changes in society that were then translated into words and only later into actions.

Les origines du théâtre lyrique moderne: histoire de l'opéra en Europe avant Lully et Scarlatti (diss., U. of Paris, Sorbonne, 1895; Paris, 1895, 4/1936)

'L'opéra au dix-septième siècle en Italie'; 'Les origines de l'opéra allemand'; 'L'opéra au dix-septième siècle' [in France]; 'L'opéra anglais au dix-septième siècle', *EMDC*, I/ii (1921), 685–749, 911–71; I/iii (1921), 1343, 1881

*

S. Zweig: *Romain Rolland: sa vie – son oeuvre* (Paris, 1929)

J. W. Klein: 'Romain Rolland', *ML*, xxv (1944), 13–17

M. Doisy: *Romain Rolland: 1866–1944* (Brussels, 1945)

R. Arcos: *Romain Rolland* (Paris, 1950)

Richard Strauss et Romain Rolland: correspondance, Cahiers Romain Rolland, iii (Paris, 1950; Eng. trans., 1961)

W. T. Starr: *A Critical Bibliography of the Published Writings of Romain Rolland* (Evanston, 1950)

J.-B. Barrère: *Romain Rolland par lui-même* (Paris, 1955)

H. Fähnrich: 'Romain Rolland als Musikwissenschaftler', *Mf*, ix (1956), 34–45 [with list of writings on music]

F. Raugel: 'Romain Rolland', *Revue de l'enseignement supérieur* (1956) no.2, 65–6

J. Robichez: *Romain Rolland* (Paris, 1961)

E. Bondeville: *Romain Rolland à la recherche de l'homme dans la création artistique* (Paris, 1966)

ROBERT HENDERSON

Rolle, Johann Heinrich (*b* Quedlinburg, 23 Dec 1716; *d* Magdeburg, 29 Dec 1785). German composer. He was an organist in Magdeburg from 1732 to 1736, then left for Leipzig, where he probably continued his music studies. In 1741 he was engaged as a violinist in Frederick the Great's court orchestra in Berlin. None of his compositions from this period survives, but his later works reveal the importance of his contact with the

Grauns, Bendas and C. P. E. Bach, and with the operas of Hasse and C. H. Graun. In 1747 he returned to Magdeburg to become organist at the Johanniskirche; from 1751 he was city music director, a position he held until his death.

In Magdeburg Rolle founded in 1764 a series of public concerts at which he presented his most important works, nearly 20 oratorios or 'musikalische Dramen'. He was virtually alone at this time in writing biblical-historical oratorios; composed from 1766 to 1785, they become increasingly dramatic. Like other German oratorios, they place great weight on the chorus; they also provide the chorus with a dramatic role. With their stylistic resemblance to Benda's melodramas, and occasionally their division into three 'acts', Rolle's music dramas are virtually concert operas, a lone Protestant equivalent to Jesuit school plays. Most curious (and revealing) are the stage directions in the scores, indicating scenery, costuming and gestures. While there is no evidence that these works were ever staged, nothing is left to the imagination of anyone wishing to do so. Rolle also wrote two dramatic works on non-sacred subjects. *Der Sturm, oder Die bezauberte Insel*, a one-act occasional piece based on Shakespeare's *Tempest* (J. S. Patzke, using Wieland's translation), was given in a concert performance at Magdeburg in 1782 and staged later that year at Berlin. *Melida*, a Singspiel on a tragic tale of religious bigotry by young C. J. Sucro, also appeared first in concert performance (1784, Magdeburg; vocal score Leipzig, 1785) and later on the stage. Like Rolle's sacred oratorios, both are through-composed and include powerful choruses as an essential ingredient.

J. F. Reichardt: *Briefe eines aufmerksamen Reisenden*, ii/5 (Frankfurt and Breslau, 1776)
F[riedrich] von K[öpken]: 'Ueber dem verstorbenen Musikdirektor', *Der teutsche Merkur* (Weimar, 1787), ii, 223ff
R. Kaestner: *J. H. Rolle: Untersuchungen zu Leben und Werk* (Kassel, 1932)
E. Valentin: 'J. H. Rolle: ein mitteldeutscher Musiker', *Sachsen und Anhalt: Jb der Historischen Kommission*, ix (1933), 109–60
T. Bauman: *North German Opera in the Age of Goethe* (Cambridge, 1985)
H. Smither: *A History of the Oratorio*, iii (Oxford, 1987)

THOMAS BAUMAN

Roller, Alfred (*b* Brno, 2 Oct 1864; *d* Vienna, 12 June 1935). Austrian stage designer. He was educated first by his father Joseph, a respected teacher of graphics. At Vienna University he studied law and then art history; in 1884 he enrolled at the Akademie der Bildenden Künste and studied painting and architecture under Lichtenfels and Griepenkerl. During the 1890s Roller belonged to a circle of young Viennese artists which in 1897 evolved into the *Sezession* movement, of which Roller was a co-founder. He was elected its president in 1902 and served as editor of its journal, *Ver Sacrum*. Mahler, director of the Vienna Hofoper, first met Roller in April of that year and invited him to design a new *Tristan und Isolde*; its subsequent production (21 February 1903) was a landmark in the history of stage design (*see* VIENNA, fig.8). In what was to be his fundamental style, Roller used clear, intense colour and lighting as well as architectural simplicity and clarity. He cleared the stage of excessive scenic and decorative clutter and through the unity of the arts created an atmosphere in which the audience's attention was focussed on the drama.

In May 1903 Mahler engaged Roller as director of scenic and costume design for the Hofoper, a position he retained until 1909, when he was appointed director of the Kunstgewerbeschule. Mahler and Roller's collaboration (1903–7) marked one of the high points in stage design. Roller created exemplary productions of *Fidelio* (1904), *Don Giovanni* (1905) and *Iphigénie en Aulide* (1907), the last of which Mahler considered the most satisfying production at the Vienna Opera.

Roller also designed for the spoken theatre, notably for Max Reinhardt in Berlin. He continued to design productions for the Vienna Hofoper (including *Lohengrin*, *Der fliegende Holländer* and *Parsifal*), as well as for the Burgtheater and theatres in Berlin, Dresden, Munich and Bayreuth. He created the first Viennese *Elektra* (1909), as well as the premières of *Der Rosenkavalier* in Dresden and Vienna (1911). From 1918 to 1934 he was again director of stage design at the Vienna Staatsoper, creating notable productions of *Die Frau ohne Schatten*, *Die tote Stadt*, *Die ägyptische Helena* and *Arabella*. In 1920 Roller founded the Salzburg Festival with Reinhardt, Strauss and Hofmannsthal; he designed a number of festival productions, several of which transferred to the Vienna Staatsoper.

Roller's published theoretical writings emphasize his view of stage design as a means of communication between composer, playwright and librettist as well as audience. He was the first to put into practice the ideas of the *Gesamtkunstwerk* espoused by Wagner, Adolphe Appia and, later, Edward Gordon Craig. His designs, correspondence and private library are in the Österreichisches Theatermuseum, Vienna; his designs for *Der Rosenkavalier* and *Die Frau ohne Schatten* have been published (Berlin, 1911, 1919).

For illustration *see* DRESDEN, fig.7; *FERNE KLANG, DER*; *FRAU OHNE SCHATTEN, DIE*; *ROSENKAVALIER, DER*; and STAGE DESIGN, fig.17.

'Anmerkungen zu den Dekorationsskizzen für "Elektra"', *Der Merker*, i (1909–10), 187, 200
'Bühnenreform?', *Der Merker*, i (1909–10), 193–7
Regiebemerkungen zum Rosenkavalier (Berlin, 1911)
'Bühnentechnische Bermerkungen zu der Oper "Die Frau ohne Schatten"', *Blätter der Staatsoper* (Vienna, 1919), 19
'Mahler und die Inszenierung', *Musikblätter des Anbruch*, ii (1920), 272–5 [Mahler issue]
Die Bildnisse Gustav Mahler (Leipzig, 1922)
'Die Fidelio-Bühne', *Kunst und Volk* (Vienna, 1923), 12–15
'Bühne und Bühnenhandwerk', *Thespis*, ed. R. Roessler (Berlin, 1930), 133–45

ES (F. Hadamowsky)
L. Hevesi: *Alt Kunst – Neu Kunst: Wien 1894–1908* (Vienna, 1909), 259–74
M. Mell: *Alfred Roller* (Vienna, 1922)
J. Gregor: *Wiener szenische Kunst*, i: *Die Theaterdekorationen der letzten drei Jahrhunderte nach Stilprinzipien dargestellt* (Vienna, 1924), 125–9
L. Kitzwegerer: *Alfred Roller als Bühnenbildner* (diss., U. of Vienna, 1959)
W. Schuh, ed.: *Der Rosenkavalier: Fassungen, Filmszenarium, Briefe* (Frankfurt, 1971)
D. Oenslager: *Stage Design – Four Centuries of Scenic Invention* (New York, 1975), 216–18
F. Willnauer: *Gustav Mahler und die Wiener Oper* (Vienna, 1979)
H. L. de la Grange: *Gustav Mahler, chronique d'une vie*, ii: *L'âge d'or de Vienne (1900–07)* (Paris, 1983–4)
W. Greisenegger: 'Set Designs and Costumes', *The Vienna Opera*, ed. A. Seebohm (New York, 1987), 194–200
——: 'Alfred Roller: Neubedeutung des szenischen Raumes', *SM*, xxxi (1989), 271–81
W. Greisenegger and O. Pausch: *Alfred Roller und seine Welt* (Vienna, 1991) [exhibition catalogue]
A. Hurton: 'Die Seele der Erscheinungen', *Bühne*, x (Vienna, 1991), 34–9
W. Greisenegger: *Alfred Roller* (Vienna, 1992)

E. Baker: *Alfred Roller's Production of Mozart's 'Don Giovanni': a Break in the Scenic Tradition of the Vienna Court Opera* (diss., New York U., 1993) EVAN BAKER

Rollet, Marie François Louis Gand Leblanc. *See* ROULLET, MARIE FRANÇOIS LOUIS GAND LEBLANC.

Rolli, Paolo Antonio (*b* Rome, 13 June 1687; *d* Todi, 20 March 1765). Italian librettist and poet. His father, an architect from Burgundy, may have introduced him to French literature. Like Metastasio, he was trained by Gian Vincenzo Gravina, was famed as a poetic improviser, and joined the Arcadian and Quirinian academies in Rome. He produced his first dramatic works in Rome in 1714 and 1715, the serenata *Sacrificio a Venere* and the opera *Astarto*, both set by Giovanni Bononcini.

Rolli then travelled to London, arriving there by the end of January 1716. His primary function in England was to teach Italian to the families of his noble patrons, who included the earls of Stair and Pembroke. He also established a fine literary reputation by editing Italian masterworks, by issuing his first collection of *Rime* (1717) and by translating Milton's *Paradise Lost* (1729–35). In the summer of 1719, he wrote to his friend Giuseppe Riva that he had pleased Caroline, Princess of Wales, by giving her his *Rime* and his edition of *Il pastor fido*, by reading for her part of his translation of *Paradise Lost* and by singing for her; as a result, she ordered a gold medal for him and became his most important patron. When she became queen in 1727, he was employed to teach her children, including Frederick, Prince of Wales. In the mid-1730s, his annual salary for teaching the princesses Amelia and Caroline was £73 10s. After the queen's death in 1739, he was granted an annual pension of £70 so long as he remained in England.

From 1720 until he left England in autumn 1744, Rolli wrote or rewrote opera librettos for at least 34 London productions, most of which were sponsored by three organizations. The first was the Royal Academy of Music. As its secretary during its first three seasons (1720–22), Rolli provided all texts (except *Radamisto*) and supervised all aspects of their staging for an annual salary of £200. This amount was probably augmented by a gift from each dedicatee and perhaps by a sum from the sale of each libretto. In autumn 1722 Rolli was replaced by Haym, apparently because of his unwillingness to accept a reduced salary of £150 as well as unspecified 'diminutions' and 'persecutions'. During the next decade, he was therefore asked to provide only four to six texts; since he was not responsible for staging these works, it seems unlikely that he received the 200 scudi (£50) that he claimed in a letter (1749) to Carlo Innocenzo Frugoni to be his usual fee for a libretto. In 1729 he was elected a Fellow of the Royal Society, but was greatly disappointed when the emperor named Metastasio instead of him as Zeno's successor in Vienna. His second employer was the Opera of the Nobility, formed in 1733 to rival the company managed by Handel and Heidegger. As its poet, Rolli provided at least eight operatic texts during its four seasons of existence. Since Angelo Cori, who reworked at least six texts for the company, provided all but one of those produced during its fourth season, he may have supplanted Rolli as poet during that time. With the exception of *Partenio* (1738) and the one or two texts for Handel in 1740–41, Rolli's remaining London librettos were for three seasons managed by his final employer, Charles Sackville, Lord Middlesex. During 1741–2, the librettists Rolli and Francesco Vanneschi reportedly received 300 guineas (each?) for their work. After Middlesex's financially ruinous endeavour was ended by lawsuits in mid-1744, Rolli saw no future for himself or for Italian opera in London, so he retired to Todi, the ancestral home of his mother, which had granted him a patent of nobility in 1735.

In 1744, Rolli published 12 librettos in the first of four projected volumes of *Componimenti poetici in vario genere, nuova edizione accresciuta di molte cose inedite* (*Numitore*, *Muzio Scevola*, *Floridante*, *Griselda*, *Scipione*, *Alessandro*, *Arianna in Naxo*, *Polifemo*, *Enea nel Lazio*, *Orfeo*, *Ifigenia in Aulide* and *Sabrina*). The other volumes were never published, but their contents were listed in the first volume, so we know that 11 more *drammi* (and one oratorio, *David*) were to be in the second (*Merode e Selinunte*, *Olimpia in Ebuda*, *Busiri*, *Deidamia*, *Alfonso*, *Rossane*, *Cefalo e Procri*, *Aristodemo*, *Rosalinda*, *Penelope* and *Fernando*). Rolli thus counted these librettos (as well as *Teti e Peleo*, first published in 1753) among his own creations. Yet most – and perhaps all of them, as well as those he did not include – were based upon a model, which he sometimes acknowledged on a title-page or in prefatory comments. For example, he asserted that, by virtue of his alterations, he could claim about half of *Narciso*, that he had reworked the whole and altered parts of *L'Odio e l'Amore*, that he had borrowed material for only one character in *Griselda* and that *Riccardo I* was almost entirely his. Such claims were rarely exaggerated, since he typically preserved little from his model texts. Unless aria texts had to be preserved because of borrowed music (as in *Narciso*, *Crispo* and *Griselda*), he completely rewrote them; and, since Londoners had no patience for long passages of Italian recitative, he greatly condensed them. This could be called hackwork, but Rolli was a proud poet who demanded respect for a well-wrought libretto, which he termed the 'intellectual part' of an opera. If, as he admitted, all but 3% of Italian librettos were 'a continual nonsense', it was because operatic impresarios and patrons strove to obtain the finest singers and composers, but believed that any hack could supply the necessary texts.

Rolli's librettos usually feature mythological rather than historical characters. Thus they may be considered an outgrowth of the pastoral fables favoured by the Arcadian Academy. In the preface to his final drama, *Teti e Peleo* (1749), he praised the 'fabulous' tales utilized for French operas, because, in addition to the human passions found in historical plots, they feature marvels that permit a full panoply of dramatically apt stage settings, machines and dances. His concern with such spectacle is also expressed in letters that he wrote while working on *Teti e Peleo*: he asserted that his printed librettos were merely 'dramatic skeletons', that readers were delighted by beauties that would aggravate viewers and that the composite whole was a 'new monstrosity, consisting of many unseemly, yet entirely delightful parts'.

Such sage reflections by a learned poet who was looking back on a career as a librettist that had spanned 30 years do not, of course, tell of his lack of dramatic experience when he was secretary to the Royal Academy in 1720, of the lack of success of his lyrical fables in a land that much preferred violent histories on the stage, or of the lack of clarity in many of his plots (which were further muddled by the typical need for many last-minute alterations). Commentators have sharply criticized such failings, and the first may have been Aurelio de' Giorgi Bertola (1784) and Stefano Arteaga (1785), who judged that Rolli's librettos dishonoured his fine reputation as a poet. In the 20th century, Luisi, Vallese, Knapp, Russo, Dean and others have specified the shortcomings that contribute to a lack of dramatic clarity. Only Fassini and Vallese have surveyed Rolli's entire output of librettos, but without consulting either the models he utilized or the music set to his texts. A critical study based upon such sources has yet to be done. Rolli's other texts for music include 25 cantatas and 24 canzonettas published in London in 1727.

Rolli's letters to the diplomat Riva, the castrato Senesino and the scholar Cocchi reveal an incisively intelligent mind, a haughty and caustic disdain for those in power and a ferocious opposition to any compromise. He may have been exceedingly difficult to work with, especially in a collaborative work such as opera. Yet he had significant success as a librettist in London, which means that many patrons must have greatly admired his work.

d – *drama* mel – *melodrama*

Astarto (d per musica, after A. Zeno and P. Pariati), G. Bononcini, 1715; *Numitore* (d), G Porta, 1720; *Narciso* (d, after C. S. Capece: Amor d'un ombra e gelosia d'un'aura), D. Scarlatti and T. Roseingrave, 1720; *Arsace* (tragedia, after A. Salvi: Amore e maestà), Orlandini and Amadei, 1721; *Muzio Scevola* (d, after N. Minato, as rev. by S. Stampiglia), Amadei (Act 1), Bononcini (2) and Handel (3), 1721; *L'Odio e l'Amore* [*Cyrus*] (d, after M. Noris), Bononcini, 1721; *Floridante* (d, after F. Silvani: La costanza in trionfo), Handel, 1721

Crispo (d, after G. Lemer), Bononcini, 1722; *Griselda* (d, after Zeno), Bononcini, 1722; *Erminia* (favola boschereccia, after 'un accademico quirino'), Bononcini, 1723; *Scipione* (d, after Salvi: Publio Cornelio Scipione), Handel, 1726; *Alessandro* (d, after O. Mauro: La superbia d'Alessandro), Handel, 1726; *Riccardo I, re d'Inghilterra* mel, after F. Briani: Isacio tiranno), Handel, 1727; *Arianna in Naxo* (mel), Porpora, 1733; *Fernando* (mel, after G. Gigli: La fede ne' tradimenti), C. Arrigoni, 1734

Enea nel Lazio (mel), Porpora, 1734; *Polifemo* (mel), Porpora, 1735; *Ifigenia in Aulide* (mel, after Zeno), Porpora, 1735; *Orfeo* (mel), Araia, Hasse, Vinci and Porpora, 1736; *Festa d'Imeneo*, Porpora, 1736; *Sabrina* (after J. Milton: *Comus*), pasticcio, 1737; *Partenio*, Veracini, 1738; *Merode e Selinunte, overo La maggior prova dell'amicizia* (mel, after Zeno: Meride e Selinunte), pasticcio, 1740; *Olimpia in Ebuda* (mel, after L. Ariosto: *Orlando furioso*), pasticcio, 1740; *Busiri, overo In van si fugge amore* (mel boschereccio), Pescetti, 1740, as Busiri, ovvero Il trionfo d'amore

Deidamia (mel), Handel, 1741; *Penelope* (mel), B. Galuppi, 1741; *Meraspe, ovvero L'olimpiade* (mel, after Metastasio: L'olimpiade), pasticcio, 1742; *Cefalo e Procri*, ?pasticcio, 1742 [lib. lost, possibly rev. of Narciso]; *Rossane* (mel, after Rolli: Alessandro), pasticcio, 1743; *Alfonso* (mel, after S. B. Pallavicino), Lampugnani, 1744; *Rosalinda* (mel, after W. Shakespeare: *As you Like it*), Veracini, 1744; *Aristodemo, tiranno di Cuma* (mel, after Pallavicino: Senocrita), Pescetti, 1744; *Alceste* (mel, after Metastasio: Demetrio), Lampugnani, 1744; *Teti e Peleo*, 1749 (mel, after B. de Bovier de Fontenelle), unperf.

Doubtful, all set by Handel: *Admeto, re di Tessaglia* (d), 1727 [see Strohm 1985, Dean and Knapp 1987, and Harris 1989]; *Sosarme* (d), 1732 [see Dean 1975 and Harris 1989]; *Imeneo* (d), 1740 [see Harris 1989]

*

BurneyH; *Grove6* (W. Dean); *HawkinsH*; *LS*; *NicollH*

R. Steele: *The Conscious Lovers/Gli amanti interni*, ed. and trans. P. A. Rolli (London, 1724)

P. A. Rolli: *De' poetici componimenti*, iii (Venice, 1753) [incl. *Teti e Peleo*]

A. Bertola: *Osservazioni sopra Metastasio, con alcuni versi* (Bassano, 1784)

S. Arteaga: *Le rivoluzioni del teatro musicale italiano dalla sua origine fino al presente* (Venice, 2/1785), iii, 115–16

G. Ellinger: 'Händels *Admet* und seine Quelle', *VMw*, i (1885), 201–24

E. Sola: 'Curiosità storico-artistico-letterarie tratte dal carteggio dell'inviato estense Giuseppe Riva con Lodovico Antonio Muratori', *Atti e memorie della RR. deputazioni di storia patria per le provincie modenesi e parmensi*, 3rd ser., iv (1887), 197–392

I. Luisi: 'Un poeta-editore del settecento (notizie su Paolo Rolli)', *Miscellanea di studi critici pubblicati in onore di Guido Mazzoni dai suoi discepoli* (Florence, 1907), ii, 235–59

S. Fassini: 'Gli albori del melodramma italiano a Londra', *Giornale storico della letteratura italiana*, lx (1912), 340–76

——: 'Il melodramma italiano a Londra ai tempi del Rolli', *RMI*, xix (1912), 35–74, 575–636

——: *Il melodramma italiano a Londra nella prima metà del settecento* (Turin, 1914) [incl. reprs. of Fassini 1912]

A. Salza: 'Note biografiche e bibliografiche intorno a Paolo Rolli con appendice di sei lettere sue al Muratori', *Bollettino della Regia deputazione di storia patria per l'Umbria*, xix (1915), 103–60

R. A. Streatfeild: 'Handel, Rolli and Italian Opera in London in the Eighteenth Century', *MQ*, iii (1917), 428–45

G. Bertoni: 'Giuseppe Riva e l'opera italiana a Londra', *Giornale storico della letteratura italiana*, lxxxix (1927), 317–24

L. Cellesi: 'Un poeta romano e un sopranista senese', *Bollettino senese di storia patria*, xxxvii (1930), 320–23

G. Zucchetti: 'Paolo Rolli e la sua attività letteraria negli ultimi venti anni di vita', *Convivium*, ii (1930), 519–604

L. Cellesi: 'Attorno a Händel: lettere inedite del poeta Paolo Rolli', *Musica d'oggi*, xv (1933), 7–16

T. Vallese: *Paolo Rolli in Inghilterra* (Milan, 1938)

O. E. Deutsch: *Handel: a Documentary Biography* (London, 1955)

J. M. Knapp: 'Handel, the Royal Academy of Music and its First Opera Season in London (1720)', *MQ*, xlv (1959), 145–67

A. D. McCredie: 'Domenico Scarlatti and his Opera *Narciso*', *AcM*, xxxiii (1961), 19–29

W. Dean: 'Handel's *Riccardo primo*', *MT*, cv (1964), 498–500

——: 'Handel's *Scipione*', *MT*, cviii (1967), 902–4

G. E. Dorris: *Paolo Rolli and the Italian Circle in London, 1715–1744* (The Hague, 1967)

F. Russo: *La figura e l'opera di Paolo Rolli* (Trieste, 1967)

W. Dean: *Handel and the Opera Seria* (Berkeley and Los Angeles, 1969)

M. F. Robinson: 'Porpora's Operas for London, 1733–1736', *Soundings*, ii (1971–2), 57–87

J. M. Knapp: 'The Autograph of Handel's *Riccardo primo*', *Studies in Renaissance and Baroque Music in Honor of Arthur Mendel* (Kassel and Hackensack, NJ, 1974), 331–58

W. Dean: 'Handel's *Sosarme*, a Puzzle Opera', *Essays on Opera and English Music in Honour of Sir Jack Westrup* (Oxford, 1975), 115–47; repr. in *Essays on Opera* (Oxford, 1990), 45–73

R. Strohm: 'Hasse, Scarlatti, Rolli', *AnM*, xv (1975), 220–57

W. Dean: 'An Unrecognized Handel Singer: Carlo Arrigoni', *MT*, cxviii (1977), 556–8

J. W. Hill: *The Life and Works of Francesco Maria Veracini* (Ann Arbor, 1979)

J. Milhous and R. D. Hume: 'New Light on Handel and the Royal Academy of Music in 1720', *Theatre Journal*, xxxv (1983), 149–67

C. Timms: 'Handelian and Other Librettos in Birmingham Central Library', *ML*, lxv (1984), 141–67

R. Strohm: *Essays on Handel and Italian Opera* (Cambridge, 1985)

M. Boyd: *Domenico Scarlatti: Master of Music* (London, 1986)

J. Roberts, ed.: *Materials for the Study of Handel's Borrowing*, HS, iv (New York, 1986) [incl. facs. of *Numitore* lib.]

W. Dean and J. M. Knapp: *Handel's Operas, 1704–26* (Oxford, 1987)

L. Lindgren: 'The Accomplishments of the Learned and Ingenious Nicola Francesco Haym (1678–1729)', *Studi musicali*, xvi (1987), 247–380

C. Taylor: 'Handel's Disengagement from the Italian Opera', *Handel Tercentenary Collection*, ed. S. Sadie and A. Hicks (London, 1987), 165–81

C. Caruso: 'La biblioteca di un letterato del settecento: Paolo Rolli', *Bollettino della Deputazione di storia patria per l'Umbria*, lxxxvi (1989), 141–233

E. Gibson: *The Royal Academy of Music (1719–1728): the Institution and its Directors* (New York, 1989)

E. Harris, ed.: *The Librettos of Handel's Operas: a Collection of Seventy-One Librettos Documenting Handel's Operatic Career*

(New York, 1989), vols. iii–xiii
L. Lindgren: 'Observations Concerning Musicians and Librettists in the Correspondence of Giovanni Giacomo Zamboni', *RMARC*, no.24 (1991)
L. Bianconi and G. La Face Bianconi, eds.: *I libretti italiani di Georg Friedrich Händel e le loro fonti* (Florence, 1992–)
C. Caruso, ed.: *I melodrammi del Paolo Rolli* (forthcoming)

LOWELL LINDGREN

Roman, Stella [Blasu, Florica Vierica Alma Stela] (*b* Cluj, 23 Aug 1904; *d* New York, 12 Feb 1992). Romanian soprano. She studied in Rome with Giuseppina Baldassare-Tedeschi and subsequently made her Italian début at Piacenza in 1932. After appearing successfully at the Rome Opera, she sang the role of the Empress in the La Scala première of *Die Frau ohne Schatten* in 1940. She made her Metropolitan début as Aida in 1941. For ten years (1941–50) she alternated with Zinka Milanov in such operas as *Il trovatore*, *Otello*, *Ballo*, *Cavalleria rusticana*, *La Gioconda* and *Tosca*. She appeared at San Francisco during the same period, where her roles included Donna Anna, Mimì and the Marschallin; she repeated the last at the S Carlo in Naples in 1951. An unorthodox and sometimes hectic technique prevented the singer and her warm, beautiful lirico-dramatic voice from achieving greatness, but she was a fascinating artist with easy access to high *pianissimos* and vibrant climaxes.

MAX DE SCHAUENSEE/R

Romance (Fr., Sp.; It. *romanza*; Ger. *Romanze*). A term derived from the Old French *romanz*, originally designating simply a vernacular poem or tale. Since about 1700 it has been applied most often to narrative or epic sung poetry. In Spain, *romances* developed as fragments of longer epic poems along several lines, including polyphonic settings that took on cantata-like shape in the 17th century. The French *romance* at first paralleled Spanish poetic practice. In 1718 the *Nouveau dictionnaire de l'Académie française* defined the term as 'Mot tiré de l'Espagnol, et qui signifie une sorte de Poésie en petit vers, contenant quelque ancienne histoire'. The traits of Gongora's *romances* are apparent in the genre's chief French practitioner, F.-A. Paradis de Moncrif (1687–1770).

The *romance* saw further development by Rousseau and others in the middle of the 18th century, when musical settings began to appear. In 1753 Jacques Lacombe described its desirable poetic qualities: 'One should employ a naive turn, simple expressions, cheerful lineaments, without being affected: in short, facile poetry, more unstudied than harmonious'. In his *Dictionnaire de musique* (1768) Rousseau added several further qualifications: the poem, divided into *couplets*, usually takes as its subject 'quelque histoire amoureuse et souvent tragique' and should be written 'd'un style simple, touchant, et d'un goût un peu antique'. He also outlined the typical characteristics of its *air*: 'no ornaments, nothing mannered, a sweet melody, natural, rustic', producing its effect quite apart from how it is sung; 'having no striking feature, it does not affect at first, but each couplet adds something to the effect of the preceding ones, interest grows insensibly, and at times one is moved to tears without knowing the source of the charm that produced this effect'. Instrumental accompaniment, he added, only weakens this impression.

Printed collections of *romances* frequently appeared with simple, unaccompanied melodies after 1750 in France. In *opéra comique* the genre's power to enchant found immediate use, beginning with one of the most famous examples, Rousseau's own 'Dans ma cabane obscure' in his *intermède* of 1752, *Le devin du village*. A popular ingredient in French comic opera until the Revolution, the *romance* underwent relatively few musical changes. At first the strophes (usually three or four) were all sung to the same simple tune; later, as longer *romances* became fashionable, changes of mode and strophic variation (often confined to the accompaniment) appeared. Exotic or medieval narratives figured prominently, usually underscored by modest attempts at an antique flavour in the melodies or harmonic language.

Romances often remained independent of the drama, especially those that were more expressive than narrative. For those stressing the latter, several librettists, notably M.-J. Sedaine, developed the technique of constructing the poem's narrative as a gloss on the story of the opera. This sort of *romance* could figure in the plot as an explicit onstage song, often sung as an illustrative admonition at some important juncture. In Grétry's *Richard Coeur-de-lion* (1784) the *romance* 'Une fièvre brûlante' serves to identify the faithful servant Blondel to the captive king; Grétry himself called it 'le pivot sur lequel tournoit toute la pièce'.

German opera embraced the *romance* at once, but filtered it through the native tradition of the *Bänkelsänger* or mountebanks – itinerant singers who recited tragic and often gruesome ballads at fairs and in market-places, with their episodes painted on a large piece of canvas or cloth. German poets in this tradition conceived of the *Romanze* as narrative rather than affective, and showed a decided preference for the folk-like ballad metre consisting of four-line stanzas, the first and third in iambic tetrameter, the second and fourth in iambic trimeter. After 1770 nearly all German comic operas included at least one *Romanze* and some had as many as three. Many became popular 'folksongs' on their own, such as Weisse and J. A. Hiller's 'Als ich auf meiner Bleiche' from *Die Jagd* (1770).

Although the *Romanze* is not important in Viennese popular comedy, Austrian composers set examples of it as fashionable items in German operas destined for more refined theatres. Ignaz Umlauf's 'Zu Stephan sprach in Traume' (*Das Irrlicht*, 1782) circulated widely in Germany as well as Austria. Mozart's lone operatic contribution is Pedrillo's *Romance*, 'In Mohrenland gefangen' from *Die Entführung aus dem Serail* (1782; Mozart always used the French spelling of the term), where the genre's modal uncertainty is handled with unparalleled sophistication.

During the first half of the 19th century the genre increasingly lost its distinctiveness of mood and structure. In France, about 1800, it began finding its way from comic opera into more serious works, such as Méhul's *Ariodant* (1799) and *Joseph* (1807). Although the musical structure remained essentially strophic, the *romances* in these operas show a less naive and frivolous tone. The genre's association with simple, unadorned performance was effaced as vocal ornamentation became more profuse (Mathilde's 'Sombre forêt' in Rossini's *Guillaume Tell* of 1829), the orchestra's role became more prominent and colourful, and the chorus was incorporated.

While the genre was largely foreign to Italian *opera buffa*, tragic operas in 19th-century Italy adopted the newer kind of *romance* or *romanza*. It came to designate any short slow aria such as might be entrusted to a comprimario as well as a principal singer. Sometimes the form is strophic, as in 'Cinta di fiori' from Bellini's *I puritani* (1835) and 'Non so le tetre immagini' from Verdi's *Il corsaro* (1848); sometimes it consists of a single melodic idea proceeding from minor to major, as in 'Di ladroni attorniato' from Verdi's *I masnadieri* (1847). These forms are beautifully combined and varied in 'Una furtiva lagrima', from Donizetti's *L'elisir d'amore* (1832). Later, with the disappearance of the cabaletta, the *romanza* took on greater size and importance, as in 'Cielo e mar' from Ponchielli's *La Gioconda* (1876) or 'Torna ai felici dì' from Puccini's *Le villi* (1884). In the age of *verismo* the term disappears altogether.

In German opera the *Romanze* followed a similar course. Weber included the naive type in *Der Freischütz* (1821) and a more earnest example in *Euryanthe* (1823). In the context of German traditions, the latter suggests strong generic affinities with the *Ballad*. Darker and less naive, this kind of narrative poem had appeared as early as Crugantino's *Romanze* in Goethe's *Claudine von Villa Bella* (1775–6) and culminates in Senta's Ballad in *Der fliegende Holländer*.

*

B. Lupo: 'Romanza, notturni, ariette nel primo ottocento', *RaM*, xix (1941), 81

D. Heartz: 'The Beginnings of the Operatic Romance: Rousseau, Sedaine and Monsigny', *Eighteenth-Century Studies*, xv (1981–2), 149–78

THOMAS BAUMAN (with JULIAN BUDDEN)

Romanelli, Luigi (*b* Rome, 21 July 1751; *d* Milan, 1 March 1839). Italian librettist. He was brought up in Rome and as a young man published verse in the Arcadian tradition. Having had to leave Rome towards the end of the 18th century, he embarked on a period of travel. He settled in Milan, where he became librettist at La Scala, a position he retained for nearly 30 years. During this time he produced nearly 60 librettos; except for a short period (1816–19) during which he wrote five librettos for other theatres and cities, all his works were written for La Scala. Unique among contemporary librettists, he published a collected edition containing most of his texts, eight volumes in all (1832–3). In these he added lengthy prefaces, dealing with his treatment of themes in *melodramma* and the problems he encountered. He served for many years as professor of declamation at the conservatory in Milan.

Many of Romanelli's earlier librettos are comedies and, except for *La pietra del paragone* (1812, Rossini), they tend to be heavy-handed. He responded to the demand for *semiseria* operas in the early 1820s, and in this awkward genre he was rather more successful (e.g. *Elisa e Claudio*, 1821, Mercadante). In his serious work he was typical of the post-Metastasian school in modelling his approach on his illustrious predecessor while lacking that essential clarity and elegance of style. *Fedra* (1820, Mayr) and *La vestale* (1823, Pacini) were among his most successful serious texts. A traditionalist, he inveighed against the use of Romantic plots, particularly those from abroad, but when he himself essayed librettos on such sources, as in his last libretto, *Saladino e Clotilde* (1828, Vaccai), the results were less than satisfactory. His texts are longwinded and cannot always have been gratifying to set; it is interesting that he complained vigorously about the way composers treated his verses.

mel – *melodramma*
melb – *melodramma buffo*
melg – *melodramma giocoso*
mels – *melodramma serio*
melss – *melodramma semiserio*

Il trionfo del bel sesso (dramma giocoso), Nicolini, 1799; *Il ritratto* (dramma giocoso), Zingarelli, 1799; *I baccanali di Roma* (mel), Nicolini, 1801; *Il puntiglio* (melg), Pucitta, 1802; *La fortunata combinazione* (melg), G. Mosca, 1802 (Dussek, 1810, as Il felice successo); *La capricciosa pentita* (melg), Valentino Fioravanti, 1802 (Morlacchi, 1816); *Castore e Polluce* (mels), Federici, 1803 (Radicate, 1815); *La schiava di due padroni* (mel), Valentino Fioravanti, 1803; *Le finte rivali* (melg), Mayr, 1803; *Il bevitore fortunato* (melg), Zingarelli, 1803; *L'impostore avvilito* (melg), Lavigna, 1804

Abenamet e Zoraide (mels), Nicolini, 1805; *Idomeneo* (mels), Federici, 1806; *Adelasia ed Aleramo* (mels), Mayr, 1806; *P. Emilio* (mels), C. Jannoni, 1807; *Cleopatra* (mels), J. Weigl, 1807; *La conquista del Messico* (mels), E. Paganini, 1808; *Il rivale di se stesso* (melg), J. Weigl, 1808; *Di posta in posta* (melg), Lavigna, 1808; *Coriolano* (mels), Nicolini, 1808; *Ifigenia in Aulide* (mels), Federici, 1809 (P. Parolini, 1819); *Orcamo* (mels), Lavigna, 1809; *L'amante prigioniero* (melg), C. Bigatti, 1809; *Le rivali generose* (melg), E. Paganini, 1809; *Le avventure d'una giornata* (melb), Morlacchi, 1809

Raùl di Créqui (mel), Mayr, 1810; *La contadina bizzarra* (melg), G. Farinelli, 1810; *Annibale in Capua* (mels), G. Farinelli, 1810; *Abradate e Dircea* (mels), Nicolini, 1811 (P. Bonfichi, 1817); *Chi non risica non rosica* (melg), Generali, 1811; *La casa dell'astrologo* (melg), Nicolini, 1811; *Virginia* (mels), P. Casella, 1811; *Tancredi* (mels), Pavesi, 1812; *La vedova stravagante* (melg), Generali, 1812; *La pietra del paragone* (melg), Rossini, 1812; *Tamerlano* (mels), Mayr, 1812 (Tadolini, 1824, as Moctar, gran visir d'Adrianopoli)

L'isola di Calipso (mels), P. C. Guglielmi, 1813; *Ernesto e Palmira* (melg), P. C. Guglielmi, 1813; *L'imboscata* (mels), J. Weigl, 1815; *L'eroismo in amore* (mels), Paer, 1815 (Coccia, 1821, as Mandane, regina di Persia); *Gli spensierati* (melb), P. Ray, 1816; *La difesa di Goa* (dramma per musica), R. Russo, 1818; *Adelaide di Borgona* (mels), Generali, 1819; *Fedra* (mels), F. Orlandi, 1820 [different lib. from that of Mayr 1820]; *La conquista di Granada* (mels), Nicolini, 1820; *Fedra* (mels), Mayr, 1820 [different lib. from that of Orlandi 1820]

La sciocca per astuzia (melb), G. Mosca, 1821 (G. Magagnini, 1826; Mazza, 1855); *Elvira e Lucindo* (melss), Stuntz, 1821; *Elisa e Claudio* (melss), Mercadante, 1821; *Andromaca* (mels), Pucitta, 1821; *Antigona e Lauso* (mels), Pavesi, 1822; *La dama locandiera* (melg), G. Mosca, 1822; *La vestale* (mels), Pacini, 1823; *Le finte Amazzoni* (melg), P. Raimondi, 1823; *Aspasia ed Agide* (mels), Nicolini, 1824; *Isabella ed Enrico* (melss), Pacini, 1824; *La gelosia corretta* (melss), Pacini, 1826; *Gli arabi nelle Gallie* (mels), Pacini, 1827; *Saladino e Clotilde* (mel tragico), Vaccai, 1828

*

L. Lianovosani [G. Salvioli]: *Bibliografia melodrammatica di Luigi Romanelli* (Milan, 1878)

JOHN BLACK

Romani, Felice (*b* Genoa, 31 Jan 1788; *d* Moneglia, 28 Jan 1865). Italian librettist. His childhood was not happy, his health was poor and the family fell on hard times. He grew up on the family property at Moneglia but was educated in Genoa. To please his parents he studied law at Pisa; to please himself he studied literature as well. He did not proceed with the law, but joined the faculty of letters of the University of Genoa, where he began a series of translations from the French and embarked on a large-scale collaborative venture, a comprehensive dictionary of mythology which was to appear over the period 1809–27. After travels in Europe he settled in Milan, where he came under the influence of the poet and playwright Vincenzo Monti, an influence which was to prove long-lasting.

In Milan Romani met Simon Mayr, who entrusted him with the libretto of an opera for Genoa (*La rosa bianca e la rosa rossa*, 1813) and, later that year, one for Naples (*Medea in Corinto*). On the strength of these he was engaged as librettist for La Scala, and although his contract lapsed with the return of the Austrian administration he continued to work in Milan. He quickly became the most eagerly sought-after librettist and over the next 25 years wrote over 80 texts, two-thirds of them for performance in Milan, the rest for other important Italian theatres, with one for Vienna; he resolutely refused to write for Paris, despite being pressed by several composers of standing. In 1834 he was summoned to Turin as editor of the *Gazzetta ufficiale piemontese*; he had an excellent prose style, and the appointment allowed him to further his literary and critical interests. However, the failure of the publishers Fratelli Favale and a change in the political oversight of the *Gazzetta* caused him to leave his post in 1849, and a long argument about his pension ensued. He spent the rest of his life in Moneglia, increasingly a prey to ill-health and melancholy. In 1844 he married Emilia Branca of Milan, herself a cultivated musician, and her biography of her husband, though erring on the side of hagiography, is a valuable if not always reliable source of information on his life.

It is an index of Romani's success that most of his texts were set by more than one composer – one, *Francesca da Rimini*, no fewer than 11 times. These were frequently altered to a greater or lesser extent, usually without the further involvement of the author, although in certain instances he rewrote his own texts, for instance *Giulietta e Romeo* (set by Vaccai, 1825) as *I Capuleti e i Montecchi* for Bellini in 1830, or *Rosmonda* (Coccia, 1829) as *Rosmonda d'Inghilterra* for Donizetti (1834), where the composer specified the changes he required. Sometimes the texts were mangled almost beyond recognition; *Amina* (Rastrelli, 1824) was so heavily rewritten by Tottola for Valentini in 1825 that only a few of Romani's stanzas survived, and the libretto is often attributed to Tottola.

Romani's first two librettos neatly exemplify the two sides of his literary interests. *La rosa bianca e la rosa rossa*, based on a text by Pixérécourt, was the first of a long series of raids into French literature which was to preoccupy him all his working life: of the 70 sources of his librettos that can be identified with near certainty, 48 (nearly 70%) are French. *Medea in Corinto* reflected his interest in the classics, although he drew on them only a few times. This raises the oft-debated question, whether he was a classicist or a romantic at heart. He said, replying to Cavour (quoted in Rinaldi 1965), 'I am neither a classicist nor a romantic: I love the beautiful, wherever it is to be found'; on another occasion, 'I do not like the intransigence of the classicists, but neither do I like the extreme lack of restraint of the ultra-romantics'. For Romani, the classicist–romantic antithesis is false; he used romantic source material because it was required of him, but he brought to it the sense of order and the self-discipline of his classical training. He was certainly prepared – though not perhaps always with a good grace – to plunder such ultra-romantic texts as Victor Hugo's *Lucrèce Borgia* (*Lucrezia Borgia*), Bis' *Blanche d'Aquitaine* (*Ugo conte di Parigi*) or Byron's *Parisina* (all for Donizetti, 1832–3).

From the outset of his career, Romani's texts marked him out as a superior librettist. Compared to the empty rotundities of a Romanelli, the contorted inconsequentialities of a Tottola or the crude cut-and-thrust of a Gaetano Rossi, his texts are on a different plane. He was not an innovator, nor did he write farces, but as a writer of words for musical setting he was *sui generis*. Edward Dent's summary (1955) cannot be bettered: 'Romani never wasted a word on superfluities. Never a line of his is written merely for the sake of a rhyme; not an adjective – and indeed he is very sparing of adjectives – is without significance'. His style was marked by clarity of language, unforced elegance of versification and a complete absence of 'librettist's doggerel'. His plots were usually clear, depending on the source, although some – particularly the *semiserie* – seem not properly thought through. It has to be said that one of his worst plots (*Rodrigo di Valenza*, Generali, 1817) is based on *King Lear*. Above all, he took his work very seriously.

Given that, and his vain, touchy personality, his relationship to his composers was inevitably difficult. He habitually accepted too many commissions, and consequently they found him unreliable, unpunctual and impossible to pin down. Because his work was outstanding he was bombarded with requests, which were as likely as not to be met with silence. Bellini, who needed a beautiful text to stimulate his creative processes, found him an invaluable collaborator, while Romani early recognized Bellini's genius, and that allowed him to go on rewriting 'Casta diva' until the composer was satisfied. Indeed in *Norma* we can detect an ideal partnership. On grounds of temperament they were bound to fall out sooner or later, and the bitter polemics which followed *Beatrice di Tenda* (1833, Venice) led to an estrangement which was being patched up only when Bellini died. Romani mourned him bitterly; he had written the texts of all his mature operas except *I puritani*.

Virtually all the many references to Romani as librettist in Donizetti's letters are critical, of delays in submitting texts or answering letters. Sometimes he despaired ('why has Romani refused me four times? Has he so much antipathy towards me? Is this it?') but he still sought his librettos. When Donizetti was dying, Romani travelled to Bergamo in the (vain) hope that the composer might recognize him, and came away deeply distressed. Pacini set a number of his texts, but broke with him over *Norma*, which he considered to be a recycling of *La sacerdotessa d'Irminsul*. Vaccai similarly objected to Romani's rewriting his *Giulietta e Romeo*. Romani never liked Verdi's music, presumably realizing – consciously or not – that Verdi's substitution of dramatic thrust for poetry as the stimulus for musical creativity undermined the whole ethos of his work. Yet when Romani died, it was Verdi who tried, albeit unsuccessfully, to arrange a collected edition of his work.

Romani's achievement lay in raising the libretto from the slough into which it had fallen at the beginning of the 19th century. By setting the highest possible standards, and by insisting that the words were as important as the music in opera, he was able to stimulate some of the finest works in Italian Romantic opera.

mel – *melodramma* melc – *melodramma comico*
melg – *melodramma giocoso* mels – *melodramma semiserio*
melss – *melodramma semiserio* melt – *melodramma tragico*
tl – *tragedia lirica*

La rosa bianca e la rosa rossa (dramma per musica), Mayr, 1813 (Generali, 1818; Genovés y Lapetra, 1831, as Enrique y Clotilde); *Medea in Corinto* (melt), Mayr, 1813 (P. Selli, 1839; Mercadante, 1851); *Aureliano in Palmira* (dramma semiserio per musica), Rossini, 1813; *Atar* (mels), Mayr, 1814 (Coccia, 1820; A. L. Mirò, 1836); *Il turco in Italia* (dramma buffo), Rossini, 1814; *Le due duchesse* (dramma semiserio), Mayr, 1814 (F. Celli, 1824); *L'ira d'Achille* (dramma serio per musica), G. Nicolini, 1814; *La testa di bronzo* (mel eroi-comico), Soliva, 1816 (Mercadante, 1827; D. Fontemaggi, 1835; V. Mela, 1835)

Maometto (melt), Winter, 1817, as Maometto II (F. Stabile, 1836, as Palmira); *Rodrigo di Valenza* (mels), Generali, 1817 (F. Orlandi, 1820; F. Chimeri, 1854, as Elmonda di Valenza); *La gioventù di Cesare* (mel eroicomico), Pavesi, 1817; *Le zingare delle Asturie* (melss), Soliva, 1817; *Adele di Lusignano* (melss), Carafa, 1817 (Carnicer, 1819); *I due Valdomiri* (mels), Winter, 1817; *Gianni di Parigi* (melc), Morlacchi, 1818 (Speranza, 1836; Donizetti, 1839); *Il finto Stanislao* (melg), Gyrowetz, 1818 (Verdi, 1840, as Un giorno di regno)

Il barone di Dolsheim (mel), Pacini, 1818 (Schoberlechner, 1827); *Danao* (tl), Mayr, 1819, as Le danaide (Persiani, 1827, as Danao re d'Argo); *Gl'Illinesi* (mels), F. Basili, 1819 (M. F. Sampieri, 1823; L. Viviani, 1826, as L'eroe francese; F. Strepponi, 1829; P. A. Coppola, 1835; F. Gomez, 1845, as Irza); *Clemenza d'Entragues* (azione eroica per musica), Trento, 1819; *Il falegname di Livonia* (mel), Pacini, 1819; *Il califfo e la schiava* (mel), Basili, 1819 (G. Quarquarini, 1842); *Bianca e Falliero* (mel), Rossini, 1819; *Vallace* (mels), Pacini, 1820

La sacerdotessa d'Irminsul (mel eroico), Pacini, 1820; *I due Figaro* (mel), Carafa, 1820 (G. Panizza, 1824; D. Broglialdi, 1825; Mercadante, 1835; Speranza, 1839); *Margherita d'Anjou* (melss), Meyerbeer, 1820; *Donna Aurora* (melc), Morlacchi, 1821; *La voce misteriosa* (melss), G. Mosca, 1821 (C. Mellara, 1823); *Atalia* (dramma sacro per musica), Mayr, 1822; *L'esule di Granata* (mels), Meyerbeer, 1821 (G. Tadolini, 1827, as Almanzor); *Adele ed Emerico* (melss), Mercadante, 1822; *Chiara e Serafina* (melss), Donizetti, 1822 (Mazzucato, 1840, as I corsari)

Amleto (melt), Mercadante, 1822; *Chi fa così, fa bene* (melg), F. Strepponi, 1823; *Abufar* (mel), Carafa, 1823 (M. García, 1827, as El Abufar); *Francesca da Rimini* (mel), Strepponi, 1823 (L. Carlini, 1825; M. Quilici, 1829; Mercadante, comp. *c*1830; G. Staffa, 1831; G. G. Fourier, 1832; E. Borgatta, 1837; G. Devasini and others, 1841; E. Canneti, 1843; V. Sassaroli, 1846; G. Franchini, 1857, as Francisca de Rimini); *Egilda di Provenza* (mel), Pavesi, 1823 (J. E. P. da Costa, 1827); *Amina* (melss), Rastrelli, 1824 (D'Antoni, 1825; with A. L. Tottola, C. Valentini, 1825)

Elena e Malvina (melss), Soliva, 1824 (Carnicer, 1829; Schira, 1832; Mazza, 1834; Vignozzi, 1835); *Il sonnambulo* (melss), Carafa, 1824 (L. Ricci, 1829; Valentini, 1834; Port., Mirò, 1835; Agnelli, 1842, as Il fantasma; Persiani, 1843, as Il fantasma); *Gli avventurieri* (melg), Cordella, 1825 (L. F. Rossi, 1835; Valentini, 1836; Buzzolla, 1842; Cagnoni, 1850, as Amori e trappole; Guiraud, 1861); *Giulietta e Romeo* (tragedia per musica), Vaccai, 1825 (E. Torriani, 1828; Bellini, 1830, as I Capuleti e i Montecchi); *Il Montanaro* (melc), Mercadante, 1827 (P. Campiuti, 1832, as L'incognito; G. Cagnola, 1854, as Il podestà di Gorgonzola)

La selva d'Hermanstadt (mel), F. Frasi, 1827; *Il pirata* (mel), Bellini, 1827; *Gastone di Foix* (mels), Persiani, 1827 (Mirecki, 1844, as Cornelio Bentivoglio); *Il divorzio persiano* (mel), Generali, 1828 (Strepponi, 1831, as L'Ulla di Bassora; G. Gerli, 1834, as Il pitocco); *I saraceni in Sicilia* (mels), Morlacchi, 1828 (D. Nicelli, 1829, as Il proscritto di Messina; Persiani, 1829, as Eufemio di Messina; Carnicer, 1832, as Eufemio di Messina; A. Curmy, 1843, as Il proscritto di Messina; A. Agostini, 1858, as Il rinnegato)

La regina di Golconda (mel), Donizetti, 1828, as Alina, regina di Golconda; *Colombo* (mels), Morlacchi, 1828 (L. Ricci, 1829; Carnicer, 1831, as Cristoforo Colombo; Ger., C. E. de Barbieri, 1848; Mela, 1857, as Cristoforo Colombo; F. Casella, 1865, as Cristoforo Colombo; G. Marcora, 1869, as Cristoforo Colombo); *La straniera* (mel), Bellini, 1829; *Rosmonda* (mels), Coccia, 1829 (Donizetti, 1834, as Rosmonda d'Inghilterra; A. Belisario, 1835; P. Tonassi and P. Collava, 1839, as Il castello di Woodstock; Nicolai, 1839, as Enrico II); *Saul* (tl), Vaccai, 1829 (F. Ceccherini, 1843; Speranza, 1844)

Zaira (tl), Bellini, 1829 (A. Gandini, 1829; Mercadante, 1831; A. Mami, 1845; R. Del Corona, 1863); *Giovanna Shore* (mels), C. Conti, 1829 (Lauro Rossi, 1836; E. Lacroix, 1845; V. Bonnetti, 1853); *La rappresaglia* (opera buffa), Mercadante, 1829; *Bianca di Belmonte* (mels), L. Riesck, 1829 (Genovés y Lapetra, 1838); *Annibale in Torino* (mels per musica), L. Ricci, 1830; *Anna Bolena* (tl), Donizetti, 1830; *Il romito di Provenza* (mel), Generali, 1831 (M. N. Sauli, 1846); *La sonnambula* (mel), Bellini, 1831

Il disertore svizzero (mel), Pugni, 1831 (Lauro Rossi, 1832; Pellegrini, 1841; G. B. Meiners, 1842); *La neve* (commedia lirica), L. Ricci, 1831; *Norma* (tl), Bellini, 1831 (J. Ryiken, 1889); *I normanni a Parigi* (tl), Mercadante, 1832; *Ugo conte di Parigi* (tl), Donizetti, 1832 (Mazzucato, 1843, as Luigi V re di Francia); *L'elisir d'amore* (melg), Donizetti, 1832; *Ismalia* (mel), Mercadante, 1832 (Carnicer, 1838; Cuyas, 1838, as La fattucchiera); *Il segreto* (melg), L. Maiocchi, 1833 (P. Mandanici, 1836)

Caterina di Guisa (mel), Coccia, 1833 (Mazza, 1837; L. Savi, 1838, as Caterina di Cleves; Campana, 1838; F. Chiaramonte, 1850, as Caterina di Cleves; A. Gandolfi, 1859; Paniagua y Vasques, 1859; B. Rossi, 1861; G. Nascimbene, 1868, as Enrico di Guisa); *Il conte di Essex* (mel), Mercadante, 1833; *Parisina* (mel), Donizetti, 1833 (T. Giribaldi, 1878); *Beatrice di Tenda*, Bellini, 1833 (R. Ticci, 1837; Port., F. Guimaraes, 1882, as Beatriz); *Il contrabbandiere* (mel), Pugni, 1833 (N. Perelli, 1842); *I due sergenti* (mel), L. Ricci, 1833 (Mazzucato, 1841; Sanelli, 1842)

Lucrezia Borgia (mel), Donizetti, 1833; *La figlia dell'arciere* (melt, with D. M. Andreotti), Coccia, 1834 (with G. Marini, Donizetti, 1841, as Adelia; Pedrotti, 1844; V. Barbarikine, 1877, as Adelia); *Un'avventura di Scaramuccia* (melc), L. Ricci, 1834; *Emma d'Antiochia* (tl), Mercadante, 1834 (G. Bracciolini, 1838, as Emma e Ruggero; V. Pontani, 1852, as Emma e Ruggiero; Lovati-Cozzulani, 1865, as Alda; E. Cavazza, 1877, as Emma); *Un episodio del San Michele* (melg), Pugni, 1834 (Concone, 1836; Savi, 1840, as L'avaro; E. Picchi, 1844, as Il tre di novembre; G. Lombardini, 1853, as La sartina e l'usajo; P. Repetto, 1855; G. Quarenghi, 1863, as Il dì di S Michele; C. Brizzi, 1877, as L'avaro)

Uggero il danese (mel), Mercadante, 1834; *La gioventù di Enrico V* (mel), Mercadante, 1834; *Francesca Donato* (mel), Mercadante, 1835 (P. Raimondi, 1842); Odio e amore (mel), Obiols, 1837 (A. Cosentino, 1858, as Laurina); *La solitaria delle Asturie* (mel), Coccia, 1838 (Mercadante, 1840; L. Ricci, 1845; G. Sordelli, 1846; G. Winter, 1852, as Matilde di Scozia); *La spia* (mel), Villanis, 1850; *Editta di Lorno* (mel), G. Litta, 1853; *Cristina di Svezia* (tl), Thalberg, 1855

*

L. Lianovosani [G. Salvioli]: *Saggio bibliografico relativo ai melodrammi di Felice Romani* (Milan, 1878)

E. Branca: *Felice Romani ed i più riputati maestri di musica del suo tempo* (Turin, 1882)

E. J. Dent: 'Donizetti: an Italian Romantic', *Fanfare for Ernest Newman* (London, 1955), 86–107

M. Rinaldi: *Felice Romani dal melodramma classico al melodramma romantico* (Rome, 1965)

J. Dumas: 'Felice Romani, ou le poète jugé par un musicologue', *Revue des études italiennes*, xix (1973), 35–74

W. Ashbrook: 'Donizetti and Romani', *Italica*, lxiv (1987), 606–31

A. Roccatagliati: 'Libretti d'opera: testi autonomi o testi d'uso?', *Quaderni del Dipartimento di linguistica e letterature comparate* [Bergamo], vi (1990), 7–20

J. N. Black: 'The Libretti of Felice Romani: a Bibliographical Survey', *Felice Romani: Moneglia 1988* (forthcoming)

JOHN BLACK

Romani, Pietro (*b* Rome, 29 May 1791; *d* Florence, 11 Jan 1877). Italian conductor and composer. He was a pupil of Fenaroli and was for many years singing teacher at the Reale Istituto Musicale and conductor at the Teatro della Pergola at Florence. He wrote two operas, *Il qui pro quo* (1817, Rome) and *Carlo Magno* (1823, Florence), and music for several ballets. For the performance at the Pergola of Rossini's *Il barbiere di Siviglia* in November 1816 Romani wrote a new aria for Dr Bartolo, 'Manca un foglio', to replace 'A un dottor della mia sorte'. This is still found in some modern editions of the vocal score and is sung occasionally.

Romani, Stefano (*b* Pisa, 2 Feb 1778; *d* after 1850). Italian composer. He studied composition at the Turchini conservatory, Naples, under Tritto and Sala. In Carnival 1800 his opera *Il fanatico per la musica*, a one-act *dramma giocoso* with a libretto by Cosimo Giotti, was performed at Florence, and later he composed two others, *I tre gobbi* (*c*1810, Pisa) and *L'isola incantata* (1815, Livorno). From 1812 until his retirement on 31 May 1850 he was *maestro di cappella* at the church of the Cavalieri di S Stefano, Pisa, where some of his sacred music is preserved.

FRANCO BAGGIANI

Romania [Roumania, Rumania]. In the late 18th century, Italian, French and German opera companies visited the country; in the 19th century they were joined by others, from Russia and from other Balkan countries (and some from the Near East – Egypt, Israel, Turkey), who presented performances in towns in the south and east of the country (Iaşi, Galaţi, Brăila, Constanţa, Bucharest). The repertory in the period 1770–1800 included operas by Sacchini, Paisiello, Cimarosa, Salieri, Grétry, Dittersdorf and Mozart (*Die Entführung aus dem Serail*, 1791, Sibiu; *Die Zauberflöte*, 1796, Timişoara). The main opera centres at this time were Sibiu, Cluj, Oradea, Timişoara, Arad and Bucharest.

In the first half of the 19th century, composers represented on stage included Cherubini, Méhul, Rossini, Donizetti, Bellini, Auber and Weber; one of the most active local troupes was that of Johann Gerger from Braşov. In 1818, the Cişmeaua Roşie theatre mounted significant productions of *Idomeneo*, *Die Zauberflöte*, *L'italiana in Algeri* and *La Cenerentola*. The tour of Angelica Catalani's Italian troupe to Bucharest and Braşov (1821) spurred on the establishment of the Italian opera at Bucharest, the first permanent lyric theatre in Romania (1843–88). A number of Romanian ensembles presented short operatic seasons at Bucharest, Timişoara, Cluj, Braşov, Sibiu and Iaşi (where in 1838 the students of the Dramatic and Philharmonic Conservatory performed Bellini's *Norma* in Romanian).

Later, national theatres were inaugurated at Bucharest (1852) and Iaşi (1896), as well as other theatres with excellent acoustics (e.g. at Timişoara and Cluj). Their repertories included works by Lortzing, Verdi, Wagner, Meyerbeer, Gounod, Bizet, Smetana, Mascagni and Puccini. Following the War of Independence (1877), the Romanian Opera House in Bucharest was founded, and it became a state institution in 1921. Its protagonist and the creator of the first Romanian singing-school of international status was George Stephănescu. The golden age of the Romanian Opera began in 1885, when Donizetti's *Lucia di Lammermoor* was given in Romanian, and the first generation of internationally known Romanian singers came to the fore, including Hariclea Darclée, Elena Teodorini, and Dimitrie Popovici-Bayreuth. Bruno Walter started his career at Timişoara in 1898.

In the first half of the 20th century, a number of private troupes offered complete seasons of operas, comic operas and operettas at Bucharest, Iaşi, Craiova, Timişoara, Cluj, Arad and Braşov, but none lasted long. Only after the intervention of the State were Romanian opera houses put on a firm footing: the Romanian opera houses at Cluj (1919), Bucharest (1921) and Iaşi (1942), the State Opera House at Timişoara (1946), the Hungarian Opera House at Cluj (1948) and the State Operetta Theatre at Bucharest (1950). Prominent artists included the conductors George Georgescu, George Enescu and Ionel Perlea, and the singers Florica Cristoforeanu, Viorica Ursuleac, Stella Roman, Dinu Bădescu and Maria Cebotari, many of whom also sang in opera houses throughout the world.

Operas by Romanian composers have been performed since the end of the 18th century. The comic operas *Das Freudenfest zu Tunis* (first performed in 1795), *Die Fürstengrille* (1796), *Die Einquartierung* (1796) and *Culesul viilor* ('The Vintages', 1798) were performed in German in Sibiu and Braşov. The earliest operas by a Transylvanian composer, Anton Hubacek, were staged at Sibiu (1795) and Braşov (1796). *Păstoriţa de la munte* ('The Shepherdess from the mountains') by Ioan Pátko and *Prinţul Pikko* ('Prince Pikko') by Josef Chudi were sung in Hungarian in Cluj. Ballets and intermezzos, inspired by Romanian folklore, were often added, to give local colour.

During the first half of the 19th century, there were notable operas with national and revolutionary plots by I. A. Wachmann (*Mihai Bravul în ajunul bătăliei de la Călugăreni*; 'Michael the Brave on the Eve of the Battle in Călugăreni'; 1848, Bucharest), and after the mid-century, Alexander Tache Zissus's *Magdalena* (1861, Bucharest), Carl Theodor Wagner (1866) and Julius Sulzer's (1869) operas about Michael the Brave extended the scope of 'national' opera. The establishment of the Romanian Opera in Bucharest in 1877 stimulated composers to write both serious and comic operas with more ambitious orchestration and the use of chorus; among the most productive were George Stephănescu (*Petra*, composed 1902), Mauriciu Cohen-Linaru (*Mazeppa* and *Insula florilor*) and Eduard Caudella (*Olteanca*, 1880 and *Petru Rareş, 1900*).

The first half of the 20th century saw the first full flowering of indigenous Romanian opera, dominated by works such as Dimitrie Cuclin's *Traian and Dochia* (1921) and *Agamemnon* (1922), S. V. Drăgoi's *Năpasta* ('The Calamity', 1927), Constantin Nottara's *La drumul mare* '(On the Highway', 1932), Alexandru Zirra's *Alexandru Lăpuşneanu* (composed 1930–44), Paul Constantinescu's *O noapte furtunoasă* ('A Stormy Night', 1934), Nicolae Bretan's *Horia* (1937) and, above all, Enescu's masterly *Oedipe* (1936). In the best works, a national and broader Balkan character was generated by the use of ancient and modern Romanian melodic material, with up-to-date harmony and orchestration. The melodic language includes elements from the recitation style of traditional ballads as well as micro-intervals (e.g. in *Oedipe*).

In the second half of the 20th century a much wider range of subjects was treated, with a corresponding extension of expressive means. The main composers were Gheorghe Dumitrescu, Pascal Bentoiu, Cornel Trăilescu, Aurel Stroe, Doru Popovici and Anatol Vieru. Their operas include leitmotifs, bucolic and urban humour, heroic monumentality (Dumitrescu) and drama pushed to the extremes of tragedy (Stroe), but there is a good deal of serene lyricism (Popovici, Trăilescu). The language of the most recent operas (Stroe, Vieru, Adrian Iorgulescu, Nicolae Brândus, Iiviu Glodeanu, Liana Alexandra) displays a wide range of vocal and instrumental techniques, often combined with the classical tradition of Romanian vaudeville theatre, the rhythms of popular dances and chromatic writing associated with gypsy fiddlers.

Alongside these new Romanian works the operatic repertory has expanded to include works by such composers as Britten, Bartók, Janáček, Orff, Strauss, Debussy, Ravel and Falla. Since 1950, new State opera theatres have been founded in Braşov (1955), Iaşi (1956), Galaţi (1956), Constanţa (1957) and Craiova (1979), while the conservatories at Bucharest and Cluj have set up opera studios, with permanent annual seasons. New generations of Romanian singers have won international reputations, among them Nicolae Herlea, Ileana Cotrubaş, Virginia Zeani, Viorica Cortez, Ludovic Spiess, David Ohanesian, Eugenia Moldoveanu and Maria Slătinaru. Other notable figures include the directors Jean Rinzescu, Liviu Ciulei and Lucian Pintilie and the conductors Cornel Trăilescu and Christian Badea.

An annual international opera festival was inaugurated at Constanţa in 1974, and operas were included in the International George Enescu Festival at Bucharest from 1958 and in the Timişoara Festival from 1969. The record company Electrecord of Bucharest has issued recordings of operas from the standard repertory as well as of several Romanian works.

For further information on operatic life in the country's principal centres *see* BRAŞOV; BUCHAREST; CLUJ-NAPOCA; CONSTANŢA; IAŞI; and TIMIŞOARA.

*

T. T. Burada: *Istoria teatrului în Moldova* (Iaşi, 1915–75)
R. Ghircoiaşiu: *Contribuţii la istoria muzicii româneştii* (Bucharest, 1963)
V. Cosma: 'Inceputurile teatrului muzical românesc' [The Beginnings of Romanian Musical Theatre], *Muzica*, xvii/3 (1967), 26–9
G. Breazul: *Pagini din istoria muzicii româneşti* (Bucharest, 1968–74)
A. Colfescu: 'Opereta ieri, astăzi şzi şi mîine' [Light Opera, Past, Present and Future], *Muzica*, xviii/1 (1968), 27–32
Z. Vancea: *Creaţia muzicală românească, sec. XIX–XX* (Bucharest, 1968)
P. Brâncuşi: *Istoria muzicii româneşti* (Bucharest, 1969)
V. Cosma: *Muziceni români compozitori şi muzicologi* (Bucharest, 1970)
D. Popovici: *Muzica românească contemporeana* (Bucharest, 1970)
P. Brâncuşi and N. Călinoiu: *Muzica în România socialistă* (Bucharest, 1973)
O. L. Cosma: *Hronicul muzicii româneşti* (Bucharest, 1973–5)
V. Cosma: *Două milenii de muzică pe pămîntul României* (Bucharest, 1977)
T. Moisecu: Războiul de Independenţă naţională ca tema pentru creaţia lirică românească' [The War of Independence: Theme for Romanian Lyric Theatre], *Studii de muzicologie*, xiii (1977), 99–104
V. Tomescu: *Musica Daco-Romana* (Bucharest, 1978)
G. Constantinescu: 'Unitatae şi diversitate a teatrului muzical in procesul formativ educaţional al creaţiei muzicale româneşti contemporane' [Unity and Diversity in Theatre Music: Contemporary Romanian Music and the Educational-Receptive Process], *Studii de muzicologie*, xiv (1979), 105–17
D. Popovici: 'Temi patriotică în opereta contemporană' [The Theme of Patriotism in Contemporary Operetta], *Muzica*, xxix/9 (1979), 17
T. Bratu, N. Brânduş and P. Codreanu: 'Opera românească în actualitate' [Romanian Opera Today], *Muzica*, xxx/3 (1980), 3–9
D. Popovici: 'Opera românească azi' [Romanian Opera Today], *Muzica*, xxx/8 (1980), 7–8
I. Staicovici: 'Epoca traco-dacică reflectată în creaţia românească de operă' [The Thracian-Dacian Epoch Reflected in Romanian Opera], *Muzica*, xxx/8 (1980), 24–6
G. Constantinescu: 'Aspecte ale creaţiei contemporane româneşti de operă şi balet' [Aspects of Contemporary Romanian Opera and Ballet], *Muzica*, xxxii/7 (1982), 12–21; xxxii/8 (1982), 5–11
A. Hoffman: 'Opera Română din Iaşi' [The Romanian Opera in Iaşi], *Muzica*, xxxii/1–2 (1982), 46–7
N. Sebov: *Stanovleniye moldavskogo muzïkal'nogo teatra* [The Formation and Development of Moldavian Musical Theatre] (Kishinyov, 1983)

VIOREL COSMA

Romanina, La. Name by which both VITTORIA ARCHILEI (*b* 1550; *d* 1620s or later) and BARBARA RICCIONI (*fl* 1684–1707) were known.

Roman musical (Fr.: 'musical romance'). Term used in the late 19th century for a particular kind of *opéra comique*; *see* OPÉRA COMIQUE, §6.

Romanov. The Russian imperial family. As patrons of the arts they exercised a decisive influence from about 1730 to 1800, effectively laying the foundations for the development of Russian secular music; *see* CATHERINE II and ST PETERSBURG.

Romanzini, Maria Theresa. *See* BLAND, MARIA THERESA.

Romberg, Andreas Jakob (*b* Vechta, nr Münster, 27 April 1767; *d* Gotha, 10 Nov 1821). German composer, cousin of Bernhard Heinrich Romberg. He made his début as a violinist at the age of seven. With his cousin he was a member of the electoral orchestra in Bonn (1790–93) and then joined the opera orchestra of the Ackermann theatre, Hamburg, then under the direction of the actor F. L. Schröder. He earned a favourable reputation as a soloist and composer, but left the city in 1795 for a two-year tour. After a trip to Paris in 1801, he made Hamburg his permanent home and turned his intentions increasingly towards composition. The catastrophic plight of Hamburg under the French occupation put his family into financial difficulties; he took up the post of Hofkapellmeister in Gotha, but his health soon began to fail and he died in poverty.

Romberg won European recognition as a composer, modelling his technique on Haydn and Mozart. He produced many instrumental works. A large number of his vocal works were popular, but he had little success as an opera composer; only five of his eight operas were performed. He had two sons: Heinrich Maria (*b* Paris, 4 April 1802; *d* Hamburg, 2 May 1859), who became the leader of the imperial opera in St Petersburg in 1827 and later its music director, and Ciprian Friedrich (*b* Hamburg, 28 Oct 1807; *d* Hamburg, 14 Oct 1865), the leading cellist in the orchestra of the German Opera at St Petersburg from 1835 to 1845.

Das blaue Ungeheuer, 1790–93 (3, A. W. Schwick, after C. Gozzi), unperf.
Die Macht der Musik, 1791 (3), Bonn, unperf.
Die Nebelkappen, 1793 (3), 1793, inc.
Der Rabe (Spl, 4, Schwick, after Gozzi), Hamburg, Gänsemarkt, 7 April 1794
Dom Mendoze, ou Le tuteur portugais (oc, 1), Paris, 15 Feb 1802, collab. B. H. Romberg
Point de bruit (oc), Paris, 1810
Die Ruinen von Paluzzi (romantische Oper, 3, J. F. Schink), Hamburg, 27 Dec 1811
Die Grossmut des Scipio (heroische Oper, E. Schlegel), Gotha, 1816

*

F. Rochlitz: 'Andreas Romberg', *Für Freude der Tonkunst*, i (Leipzig, 1824, 3/1868)
K. Stephenson: *Andreas Romberg: ein Beitrag zur Hamburger Musikgeschichte* (Hamburg, 1938)
E. Wulf: 'Romberg, Andreas Jakob', *Rheinische Musiker*, i, ed. K. G. Fellerer (Cologne, 1960) [with complete list of works]

KURT STEPHENSON

Romberg, Bernhard Heinrich (*b* Dinklage, Oldenburg, ?11 Nov 1767; *d* Hamburg, 13 Aug 1841). German composer, cousin of Andreas Jakob Romberg. As a cellist he played, with his cousin, in the electoral orchestra in Bonn (1790–93) and in the opera orchestra of the Ackermann theatre in Hamburg (1793–5). After teaching at the Paris Conservatoire he moved to Berlin, where he joined the royal court orchestra in 1805. Lengthy concert tours occupied his time over the next few years. In 1816 he was promoted to Hofkapellmeister in Berlin, but failed in his ambition to become the director of the opera there; after Spontini's appointment as general music director (1819), Romberg resigned his post and used his regained freedom to extend his international reputation as a solo cellist. From 1820 he lived in Hamburg (apart from returning to Berlin, 1826–31); he died a wealthy man. Like his cousin, Romberg had little success as an opera composer. All six of his operas were performed but none enjoyed acclaim.

Die wiedergefundene Statue (A. W. Schwick, after C. Gozzi), Bonn, 1790
Der Schiffbruch (operetta, J. J. Pfeiffer), Bonn, 1791
Dom Mendoze, ou Le tuteur portugais (oc, 1), Paris, 15 Feb 1802, collab. A. J. Romberg
Ulysses und Circe (3, after P. Calderón de la Barca), Berlin, Hof, 27 July 1807, vs (Leipzig, ?1807)
Rittertreue (3, F. W. Trautvetter), Berlin, Hof, 31 Jan 1817
Alma, Copenhagen, Royal, May 1824

*

StiegerO
H. Schäfer: *Bernhard Romberg: sein Leben und Wirken* (diss., U. of Bonn, 1931)
E. Wulf: 'Romberg, Bernhard Heinrich', *Rheinische Musiker*, i, ed. K. G. Fellerer (Cologne, 1960)
KURT STEPHENSON

Romberg, Sigmund (*b* Nagykanizsa, 29 July 1887; *d* New York, 10 Nov 1951). American composer and conductor of Hungarian birth. His parents planned a career in engineering for him, but when he was sent to study in Vienna he took work at the Theater an der Wien, fell in love with the musical stage, and was soon learning music and composition with the Austrian operetta composer Richard Heuberger. In 1909 he visited the USA and applied for citizenship. In a short time he found work conducting the small orchestra at Bustanoby's, a restaurant frequented by the theatrical crowd. While conducting some of his own compositions there he came to the attention of the leading New York producers, the Shubert brothers, who signed him on in 1914 as a staff composer. His task was to create melodies to embellish the lavish revues and musical comedies which the brothers presented. In 1915 they asked him to write additional music for an Edmund Eysler operetta which they were importing. Among his interpolations was his first hit, a bittersweet waltz, 'Auf Wiedersehn'. But his success was not instructive to his producers, who insisted he continue churning out ragtime ditties.

A pronounced success came with his score for the 1917 operetta *Maytime*, remembered now primarily for the waltz 'Will you remember?'. Despite the show's tremendous popularity the Shuberts demanded Romberg resume his hack composing. This time Romberg rebelled. Although he broke with the Shuberts, his next success came when he returned to their fold to revise the Franz Schubert themes employed in *Das Dreimäderlhaus*. The American version was called *Blossom Time* (1921). Its biggest hit, 'Song of love', was derived from a theme in the first movement of the 'Unfinished' Symphony. Romberg's most memorable shows all followed in the next few years. *The Student Prince* (1924) is remembered for 'Deep in my heart, dear', 'Drinking song', 'Golden days' and 'Serenade'. From *The Desert Song* (1926) came not only the title song but 'One alone', 'Riff song' and 'Romance'. *My Maryland* (1927), a musical version of the Barbara Frietchie legend, has left behind 'Mother', 'Silver moon', 'Won't you marry me?' and 'Your land and my land'. The same season saw him collaborate with George Gershwin on *Rosalie* (1928), which Broadway's most glamorous producer, Florenz Ziegfeld, mounted for Broadway's musical comedy queen, Marilyn Miller, but only Gershwin's share of the music is still heard today. *The New Moon* (1928) offered 'Lover, come back to me', 'One kiss', 'Softly, as in a morning sunrise' and 'Stouthearted men'. What little success Romberg had responding to the changing tastes of the 1930s was in a handful of melodies written for films, notably 'When I grow too old to dream' from *The Night is Young* (1935), although several of his stage pieces proved popular in screen versions during the decade. In the early 1940s he toured the USA with his own orchestra, presenting concerts of semi-classical music. The programmes included much of his own music. His last Broadway hit was *Up in Central Park* (1945), a curious attempt to mesh his middle-European style with the Americana rage of the period. Two songs from the show, 'April snow' and 'Close as pages in a book' are still heard.

Romberg wrote all or most of the music for approximately 60 shows, a record 'no other theatre composer has ever matched'. He was frequently accused of plagiarizing other men's music or themes from the classics: for example, Vincent Youmans had to be dissuaded from suing him after 'One kiss' was clearly borrowed from 'No, No, Nanette'. His music often seems less fresh and less passionate than that of his contemporary and rival, Rudolf Friml. But between them they were almost wholly responsible for the glorious, durable melodies in the final American heyday of the middle-European school of operetta.

Unless otherwise stated, all are operettas and all dates are of first New York performance. Many early revues and musicals include interpolations by other composers. Librettists and lyricists are listed in parentheses in that order; where names are separated by a comma, authors collaborated on libretto and/or lyrics.

The Whirl of the World (revue, H. Atteridge), Winter Garden, 10 Jan 1914
The Passing Show of 1914 (revue, Atteridge), Winter Garden, 10 June 1914, collab. H. Carroll
Dancing Around (revue, Atteridge), Winter Garden, 10 Oct 1914, collab. Carroll
Maid in America (revue, Atteridge), Winter Garden, 18 Feb 1915, collab. Carroll
Hands Up (revue, E. Smith, E. R. Goetz), 44th Street, 22 July 1915, collab. Goetz
The Blue Paradise (Smith; H. Reynolds), Casino, 5 Aug 1915, collab. L. Edwards, C. Lean, after E. Eysler: Ein Tag in Paradies
A World of Pleasure (revue, Atteridge), Winter Garden, 14 Oct 1915
Robinson Crusoe, Jr. (musical, Atteridge), Winter Garden, 17 Feb 1916
The Passing Show of 1916 (revue, Atteridge), Winter Garden, 22 June 1916, collab. O. Motzan
The Girl from Brazil (Smith, M. Woodward), 44th Street, 30 Aug 1916
The Show of Wonders (revue, Atteridge) Winter Garden, 26 Oct 1916, collab. Motzan, H. Timburg
Follow me (musical, R. B. Smith), Casino, 29 Nov 1916, collab. H. Tierney [mostly by Tierney]
Her Soldier Boy (R. J. Young), Astor, 6 Dec 1916, collab. E. Kálmán
The Passing Show of 1917 (revue, Atteridge), Winter Garden, 26 April 1917, collab. Motzan
My Lady's Glove (E. Smith, E. A. Paulton), after O. Straus, Lyric, 18 June 1917 [addl music by Romberg]
Maytime (Young, C. Wood), Shubert, 16 Aug 1917
Doing our Bit (revue, Atteridge), Winter Garden, 18 Oct 1917, collab. Timberg
Over the Top (revue, Atteridge, P. Bartholomae), 44th Street Roof, 1 Dec 1917
Sinbad (musical, Atteridge), Winter Garden, 14 Feb 1918
The Passing Show of 1918 (revue, Atteridge), Winter Garden, 25 July 1918, collab. J. Schwartz
The Melting of Molly (musical, M. T. Davies, E. Smith, Wood), Broadhurst, 30 Dec 1918
Monte Cristo, Jr. (musical, Atteridge), Winter Garden, 12 Feb 1919, collab. Schwartz

The Passing Show of 1919 (revue, Atteridge), Winter Garden, 23 Oct 1919, collab. Schwartz
The Magic Melody (F. A. Kummer), Winter Garden, 11 Nov 1919
Poor Little Ritz Girl (musical, G. Campbell, L. Fields; L. Hart), Central, 28 July 1920, collab. A. Gerber and R. Rodgers
Love Birds (E. A. Woolf, B. MacDonald), Apollo, 15 March 1921
Blossom Time (D. Donnelly), Ambassador, 29 Sept 1921, after Schubert
Bombo (musical, Atteridge), Jolson, 6 Oct 1921
The Blushing Bride (musical, Wood), Park, 6 Feb 1922
The Rose of Stamboul (Atteridge), Century, 7 March 1922, after L. Fall: Die Rose von Stambul [interpolations by Romberg]
Springtime of Youth (H. B. Smith, Wood), Broadhurst, 26 Oct 1922
The Dancing Girl (musical, Atteridge), Winter Garden, 24 Jan 1923
Caroline (H. B. Smith), Ambassador, 31 Jan 1923, after E. Künneke: *Der Vetter aus Dingsda*
The Passing Show of 1923 (revue, Atteridge), Winter Garden, 14 June 1923, collab. Schwartz
Innocent Eyes (musical, Atteridge, T. Seymour), Winter Garden, 20 May 1924
The Passing Show of 1924 (revue, Atteridge, Gerber), Winter Garden, 3 Sept 1924, collab. Schwartz
Artists and Models of 1924 (revue, H. W. Gribble, S. Coslow, C. Grey), Astor, 15 Oct 1924, collab. F. Coots
Annie Dear (musical, C. Kummer, Grey), Times Square, 4 Nov 1924, collab. Kummer, Tierney
The Student Prince (Donnelly), Jolson, 2 Dec 1924
Louie the 14th (musical, A. Wimperis), Cosmopolitan, 3 March 1925
Princess Flavia (H. B. Smith, after A. Hope: *The Prisoner of Zenda*), Century, 2 Nov 1925
The Desert Song (Harbach, O. Hammerstein II, F. Mandel), Casino, 30 Nov 1926
Cherry Blossoms (H. B. Smith), 44th Street, 28 March 1927
My Maryland (Donnelly), Jolson, 12 Sept 1927
My Princess (Donnelly, after E. Sheldon), Shubert, 6 Oct 1927
The Love Call (H. B. Smith, E. Locke, after A. Thomas: *Arizona*), Majestic, 24 Oct 1927
Rosalie (musical, W. A. McGuire, G. Bolton; I. Gershwin, Wodehouse), collab. G. Gershwin, New Amsterdam, 10 Jan 1928
The New Moon (Hammerstein, Mandel, L. Schwab), Imperial, 19 Sept 1928
Nina Rosa (Harbach; I. Caesar), Majestic, 20 Sept 1930
East Wind (Mandel, Hammerstein), Manhattan, 27 Oct 1931
Melody (E. C. Carpenter, Caesar), Casino, 14 Feb 1933
May Wine (Hammerstein, after Mandel and E. von Stroheim: *The Happy Alienist*), orchd D. Walker, St James, 5 Dec 1935
Forbidden Melody (Harbach), New Amsterdam, 2 Nov 1936
Sunny River (Hammerstein), St James, 4 Dec 1941
Up in Central Park (H. Fields and D. Fields), City Center, 27 Jan 1945
My Romance (R. Leigh, after Sheldon: *My Romance*), Shubert, 19 Oct 1948
The Girl in Pink Tights (J. Chodorov, J. Fields; L. Robin), 5 March 1954, completed D. Walker, Mark Hellinger

*

E. Arnold: *Deep in my Heart* (New York, 1949)
S. Green: *The World of Musical Comedy* (New York, 1960; 4/1980)
G. Bordman: *American Operetta* (New York, 1981)
——: *American Musical Comedy* (New York, 1982)
R. Traubner: *Operetta* (Garden City, NY, 1983)
J. Koegel: *The Film Operettas of Sigmund Romberg* (thesis, California State U., 1984)

GERALD BORDMAN

Rome (It. Roma). Capital of Italy. It has had a virtually unbroken operatic tradition since the early 17th century, although it has been less important as a centre for opera than Naples in the south or Venice and Milan in the north.

1. Up to 1680: (i) To 1623 (ii) The Barberini era, 1623–44 (iii) 1645–80. 2. 1680–1730. 3. Since 1730: (i) 1730–1800 (ii) The 19th century (iii) The 20th century.

1. UP TO 1680.

(i) To 1623. Throughout the 17th century musical drama in Rome shared the stage with an active tradition of non-professional spoken drama. The various Jesuit colleges gave regular public productions, and nobles and gentle literati sponsored private entertainments for invited guests. Except for the first flowering of the Teatro Tordinona from 1671 to 1674 (Rome's first attempt at subscription financing and non-local casting), operas in Rome before 1680 were almost all court entertainments. Private patrons enlisted members of their own or their peers' household establishments to provide librettos, scores and professional singers, while the furnishing of temporary stages, sets, machines, costumes and lighting was entrusted to favoured local artisans. Their custom flourished because Rome differed from all other Italian cities in its lack of a political centre of secular court life. Several prominent families there did not owe fealty to the pope, but to the emperor or to the Spanish crown. Some popes were hostile to theatrical extravagance but could not censure private life. The presence of many politically independent, wealthy patrons helps to explain the shifting sponsorship for opera in Rome and the continuing habit of private production.

The most fortunate patrons were those with access to the best singers in the city, the castratos, tenors and basses of the Sistine Chapel. The most privileged productions, large and small, drew on their services. Although some small operas given 'intra domesticos parietes' did have women, as could works staged at foreign embassies, most operas after 1630 were restricted to boys and men, a practice well known to Roman audiences from Jesuit school plays. The castratos Marc'Antonio Pasqualini and Loreto Vittori reigned in the 1630s and 40s, as did the basses Bartolomeo Nicolini and Girolamo Navarra. Giuseppe Fedi, another soprano castrato, sang his first role in 1654 and, with his brother Francesco Maria, dominated the 1670s. The lack of a future in the theatre for women forced many sopranos who had trained in Rome to leave, notably Maddalena Manelli and Anna Renzi.

The circumstances of court production also account for those Roman scores that were published. Folio-sized editions extolled the culture of the patron, honoured the event or person celebrated by the performance and often commemorated the lavishness of the staging with engravings of scenes. Eight scores appeared in print between 1600 and 1639: Cavalieri's *Rappresentatione di Anima, et di Corpo* (1600), Agazzari's *Eumelio* (1606), Filippo Vitali's *Aretusa* (1620), Domenico Mazzocchi's *Catena d'Adone* (1626), Giacinto Cornacchioli's *Diana schernita* (1629), Landi's *Sant'Alessio* (1634; *see* PRODUCTION, fig.4), Michelangelo Rossi's *Erminia sul Giordano* (1637) and Loreto Vittori's *La Galatea* (1639). The publication of Marco Marazzoli's *La Vita humana* followed in 1658 (for illustration *see* MARAZZOLI, MARCO). (Landi's *La morte d'Orfeo* (Venice, 1619) is often included in the list of Roman publications, but it is not known for whom, when or where it was performed.)

The handful of operas staged in Rome in the first quarter of the century established few precedents. Some were staged in religious institutions; some anticipated later 'allegorical' librettos in which personifications may be the main characters or act as figures representing the psychological forces that motivate humans. The *Rappresentatione di Anima, et di Corpo* and *Eumelio* were both moralizing allegories, the first produced in 1600 in an oratory, the second staged in 1606 for the edification of the adolescent students of the Roman Seminary. *David musicus*, set by Ottavio Catalani for the German College in 1613, dramatized the Hebrew story of David and King Saul's madness in Horatian

1. Set design (battle before a temple) by Giovanni Francesco Grimaldi for the performance of Angelo Cecchini's 'La Sincerità trionfante, overo L'Erculeo ardire', given by the French ambassador in Rome to celebrate the birth of Louis XIV in 1638: engraving from the libretto by Ottaviano Castelli (1640)

Latin. Further operas were produced after 1623 by the Venerable English College (1632), the boys of the Vatican Seminary (1638, 1641, 1643 and 1660), the German College (1628, 1648, 1653 and probably 1656) and the Ghislieri College (1673, 1674 and possibly 1667).

Two secular operas of 1614 and 1620 have Florentine connections, though not to the early works of Peri and Caccini. The five-part *Amor pudico*, by Jacopo Cicognini with music by several composers, celebrated an aristocratic wedding in the manner of a Florentine *veglia*; in this *festino* for a more liberal age Sistine Chapel singers performed alongside women. The Florentine Filippo Vitali set *Aretusa*, which brought Giulio Caccini's son Pompeo to Rome to paint the sets and sing the principal tenor role.

(ii) The Barberini era, 1623–44. When Cardinal Maffeo Barberini became Pope Urban VIII (ruled 1623–44) a new passion for the stage swept the city, fanned by Cardinal Maurizio of Savoy, three Barberini papal nephews, the Jesuit colleges and numerous literati eager to impress the new wealthy and influential patrons. Three very different librettists dominated this period. Ottavio Tronsarelli recalled the golden classical ages in entertainments of five short acts, well-engineered sets, vocal ensembles and dancing. The prelate Giulio Rospigliosi dramatized the psychological and moral difficulties of trusting in and following virtue. He developed multiple plots in three fairly long acts, opened the opera libretto to exotic but historically real locations from Bavaria to Palestine and increased the size and variety of the casts by including saucy young pages, *commedia dell'arte* figures, soldiers, nurses, steadfast saints and the like – all character types familiar from the contemporary spoken stage. This new kaleidoscope of devices was held together by dramaturgical convention and Rospigliosi's own thoughtful poetic style. Most of Ottaviano Castelli's exaggeratedly clever works, in contrast, mixed literary eclecticism with a strain of satire that is simple but not popular in nature. Except for *Il favorito del principe*, staged at the French Embassy in 1640, none of his texts offers naturalistic dramatic narrative.

No single composer dominated the era. Virgilio Mazzocchi set three 'school' operas for Cardinal Francesco Barberini and collaborated with Marco Marazzoli on *Chi soffre speri*, a tale by Boccaccio. Three Mazzocchi scores survive in manuscript; four operas by Angelo Cecchini are lost. Published works by four other composers have been mentioned above, but of the operas composed for Rome by Johann Kapsberger, Lorenzo Ratti, Pier Francesco Valentini, Filiberto Laurenzi and Luigi Rossi only Rossi's *Il palazzo incantato* has survived. These composers make a heterogenous group of church musicians (Ratti and Virgilio Mazzocchi), chamber performers (Marazzoli and Luigi Rossi, who both also had church positions) and instrumentalists (Kapsberger and Michelangelo Rossi); the learned, non-professional composer is represented by Domenico Mazzocchi, Valentini, and Castelli, who essayed two small experimental scores. The standard ensemble in Roman operas of this period consists of strings (two to four violins) and a sizable continuo complement of violones, two harpsichords and two or more theorbos, to which may be added harps, lutes or *lira*. Cornettos, flutes, guitars, organ or cittern were sometimes used for special music in scenes of enchantment or magic, and trumpets and drums for military or regal effect.

(iii) 1645–80. While Venetian opera developed and spread throughout Italy, opera in Rome under the Pamphili and Chigi popes became a desultory and occasional affair, little affected by changing Venetian musical styles. Apart from the anonymous and old-fashioned *Ratto di Proserpina* (1645) and Mario Savioni's *Sant'Agnese* (1651), few scores or librettos have come to light. Notable were the three operas the Barberini mounted in 1656 in honour of Queen Christina of Sweden, who converted to Catholicism and abdicated her Lutheran crown, but they did not open another Barberini era. In the 20 years to 1665 cast sizes were generally reduced and plots more tightly woven,

allowing recitative dialogue, a prominent feature of earlier works, to dominate even more. The list of known composers – Savioni, Abbatini, Marazzoli, A. F. Tenaglia, G. A. Carpano – is capped by Antonio Cesti, whose early *Orontea* was staged twice in 1661.

Two women patrons settled in Rome in the 1660s who were to vitalize a new generation of impresarios. One was Queen Christina, the other Maria Mancini Colonna, a niece of Cardinal Mazarin wedded to Lorenzo Onofrio Colonna, head of an old Roman family (the Colonna di Paliano) and grandee of Spain. Though not wealthy, Christina persuaded noblemen and rich churchmen to lend their efforts and servitors to her love of the theatre. She sponsored privately given operas in 1666, 1673 and 1678, but was most influential as one of the promoters of a Venetian-style theatre, for which Pope Clement IX (Giulio Rospigliosi) granted a licence before his death in 1669. This, the Teatro Tordinona, built by Giacomo d'Alibert, opened to a half-full house in January 1671 with a revival of Cavalli's *Scipione affricano*. Four subsequent operas given there also had librettos dedicated to the queen.

The Colonnas, who had previously gone to Venice for the opera, began in 1668 to stage large-scale operas in their Roman palace under the enthusiastic direction of Filippo Acciaiuoli. Jacopo Melani's *Il Girello* to a libretto by Acciaiuoli, which was to tour the Italian peninsula for years, was followed in 1669 by Alessandro Melani's first opera, *L'empio punito*. Two Tordinona operas were dedicated to Maria Colonna, and when the theatre was not allowed to reopen after the Holy Year (1675), Lorenzo Colonna returned to Roman tradition by giving two operas by Bernardo Pasquini and even a Sartorio opera sung by his amateur friends.

The Teatro Tordinona exposed Rome to touched-up Venetian operas for only four seasons. Pasquini in fact became the principal composer of new Roman scores. His *L'Amor per vendetta, overo L'Alcasta* was dedicated to Christina and given at the Tordinona in 1673, but at least four of his operas from the 1670s were privately produced, as were Pier Simone Agostini's *Adalinda* and Alessandro Scarlatti's first datable opera. Their librettos avoid the Venetian heroic stance and represent a stylized synthesis of crossed romances from the earlier pastorale and a new type of character, the contemporary, wordly suburban noble or *nobildama*. Locations are specified as Rome or its close environs, and topical witticisms appear. Short arias occur frequently (there are 44 in Pasquini's *La donna ancora è fedele* of 1676), often worked into the flow of the action, even with their standard two-strophe form. Arias accompanied by treble instruments steadily increase in number. Sentiment, despair and humour follow on each other's heels, but arias expressing different texts are often permeated by a similar tuneful, tonal insouciance which lends them a sophisticated unseriousness. Emotionally spontaneous within a stylized framework of language and plot, these chamber operas represent a new, almost unliterary sub-genre of musical drama that would continue to entertain the Roman élite in the next decades.

2. 1680–1730. During the 1680s operas were performed only in private palaces, mainly those of Marquis Pompeo Capranica, Prince Lorenzo Onofrio Colonna and Queen Christina. As in the 1670s the leading composer was Pasquini, but he now shared the limelight with Alessandro Scarlatti, whose first operas were written for Rome in 1678–83. The main librettists were those praised in P. J. Martello's *Della tragedia antica e moderna* (Rome, 1715): G. F. Bernini, C. S. Capece, G. D. de Totis, Silvio Stampiglia and Pietro Ottoboni (who was Venetian, but wrote his librettos in Rome). Their librettos of the 1680s are mainly playful comedies or swashbucklers *di spada e cappa* ('of sword and cloak'). In each score the 30–40 arias are brief, often in strophic form or with ostinato basses, and no more than a third are accompanied by treble instruments.

In 1690 the Arcadian Academy was formed in Rome; it is known mainly for its purifying ideals, which first took hold in Venetian librettos (e.g. those of Domenico David and Apostolo Zeno) that eliminate all comedy and feature either pastoral Arcadians or the grand heroics of historical figures. Cardinal Ottoboni, the chief patron of opera in Rome between 1690 and his death 50 years later, tried to emulate these ideals in his librettos of the 1690s, including the heroic *La Statira* (set by Scarlatti in 1690), the religious *Il martirio di S Eustachio* (F. C. Lanciani, 1690) and the pastoral *L'amore eroico fra pastori* (C. F. Cesarini, G. L. Lulier and Giovanni Bononcini, 1696). Ottoboni also supported such efforts by others; for example in 1695 he commissioned and produced *La clemenza di Salomone*, with text by Girolamo Frigimelica Roberti and music by C. F. Pollarolo. Although Stampiglia was among the founding members of Arcadia he showed little interest in reform; his most successful work was *Il trionfo di Camilla* (1697, Naples; reworked for Rome in 1698), set by Giovanni Bononcini, which includes old-fashioned comic scenes for a rowdy young manservant and a bawdy old maidservant.

Productions of the 1690s were mainly in public theatres: the Tordinona (1690–97), the Teatro Capranica (1692–8) and the Teatro Pace (1694). The favoured composer was Scarlatti; he lived in Naples in 1684–1702 but sent new scores or revisions to Rome. Other composers included two Romans, Cesarini and Lanciani (who was employed by Ottoboni), and six who had come to work in Rome: Lulier (who arrived by 1679), Severo de Luca (by 1688), Gasparini (by 1689), Bononcini (by 1692), Luigi Mancia (by 1695) and Francesco Mancini (by 1696). Most of the librettos they set had been written for other cities but were revised for Rome by Stampiglia and others. The 60–70 arias in a work were mainly exit pieces in da capo form, frequently set to foot-tapping tunes.

Opera in the public theatres became a popular attraction in Rome, so the Capranica and Tordinona were enlarged and refurbished for the carnivals of 1695 and 1696 respectively. The former, which had been a small theatre in the Capranica palace since at least 1679, was rebuilt by the architect Carlo Buratti, who fitted six tiers of 27 boxes into a richly gilt U. The latter, whose impresario was Count Giacomo d'Alibert, was rebuilt by the architect Carlo Fontane, who fitted six tiers of 35 boxes into a novel elliptical or horseshoe shape, which later became the norm for opera houses. Both were then capable of marvellous scenic effects, and Acciaiuoli was the deviser of many incredible transformations, such as those in an *intermedio* depicting Hell, which attracted many foreigners as well as native Romans to the Capranica in 1695. During the 1690s this surge in the popularity of opera among Romans was opposed by the stern Pope Innocent XII, and he halted it by ordering the destruction of the Tordinona in August 1697. The Capranica received his permission to open in 1698, but thereafter it remained shut until 1711. Indeed, with the exception of a few works produced in the palace of the exiled Queen Maria Casimira of Poland, who was in Rome in 1699–1714, there were virtually no staged dramas in Rome between 1698 and 1710, when the threat posed by the War of the Spanish Succession ended.

Surprisingly, composers of the older generation dominated the years 1710–22, when Scarlatti, Gasparini, Bononcini, Pollarolo and Caldara composed 35 of the 64 operas produced in Rome. Some of the librettos they set were likewise by older writers: Capece, Ottoboni and Stampiglia. The operas that Ottoboni produced in his Palazzo della Cancelleria in 1710–13 used texts that he or his father Antonio had written; the music was by Scarlatti, Pollarolo or Filippo Amadei and the set designs by Filippo Juvarra. All the operas sponsored by Queen Maria Casimira in 1710–14 had texts by Capece and music by Domenico Scarlatti. The productions at these two private palaces were supplemented by those at one public theatre, the Capranica (1711–47). Two other public venues, the refurbished Pace and the new Teatro Alibert, opened after the private ones had ceased operation. The Alibert was built in 1716–17 by Count d'Alibert's son in the present via Alibert, and enlarged and improved in 1720 by Francesco Galli-Bibiena, with six tiers each of 30 boxes. Its proprietors in 1726 were the Order of St John of Malta, F. de Romanis, C. M. Minucci and Marquis Maccarani. The Capranica was renovated by Juvarra in 1713, and in 1714–22 it featured works by Gasparini and Alessandro Scarlatti in an old-fashioned Baroque style. Those by Scarlatti, which interpret the text with complex motivic lines and rich textures, bring to an end the Roman late Baroque tradition.

The *galant* style overwhelmed Rome after 1720 in operas by Porpora at the Alibert in 1721–3, Vivaldi at the Capranica in 1723–4, Vinci at the Alibert in 1724–9 and Leo at the Capranica in 1726–7. The Alibert changed its name to the Teatro delle Dame after its grandiose enlargement for Carnival 1726, which featured Vinci's *Didone abbandonata*, the first Roman production of a libretto by the greatest Roman librettist, Metastasio. A new era thus began in which the music was characterized by an unobtrusive orchestra supporting (and often doubling) the vocal line – an entirely different texture from the polarized voice and continuo, with optional motivic interplay of treble instruments, that had been favoured in Rome between 1680 and 1722.

3. Since 1730.

(i) 1730–1800. In the 1730s three new theatres joined the Capranica, the Alibert and the Pace, which had been in regular use in the first decades of the 18th century; these were the Teatro Argentina, the Teatro Valle and the rebuilt Tordinona. Musical productions were also staged in the Pallacorda and, more sporadically, in the Granari, Saponari, Ornani and Pioli theatres and also in the Clementine and German colleges.

Between 1730 and the end of the century there were almost always two theatres where *opera seria* was performed, only during the carnival season as a rule; two operas, interspersed with ballets, would be presented at each of them. At the Alibert there were spring seasons only in 1731, 1732, 1738 and 1780, and between 1734 and 1737 only the Tordinona put on *opera seria*. For the rest the Capranica, Argentina and Alibert alternated in such productions until the middle of the century. An edict of 1740 ordered that the three theatres should take turns, decided by lot, and that the one remaining closed should receive compensation. In 1755 the pontifical authorities decided that only the Argentina and Alibert could stage serious works while the Capranica was being rebuilt. The Argentina was more regularly used for *opera seria*, whereas in 1760, 1765, 1772–9 and 1781 the Alibert presented *drammi giocosi* with ballets.

The Argentina belonged to the Sforza-Cesarini family. Designed by Gerolamo Theodoli, built in 1731 and in-

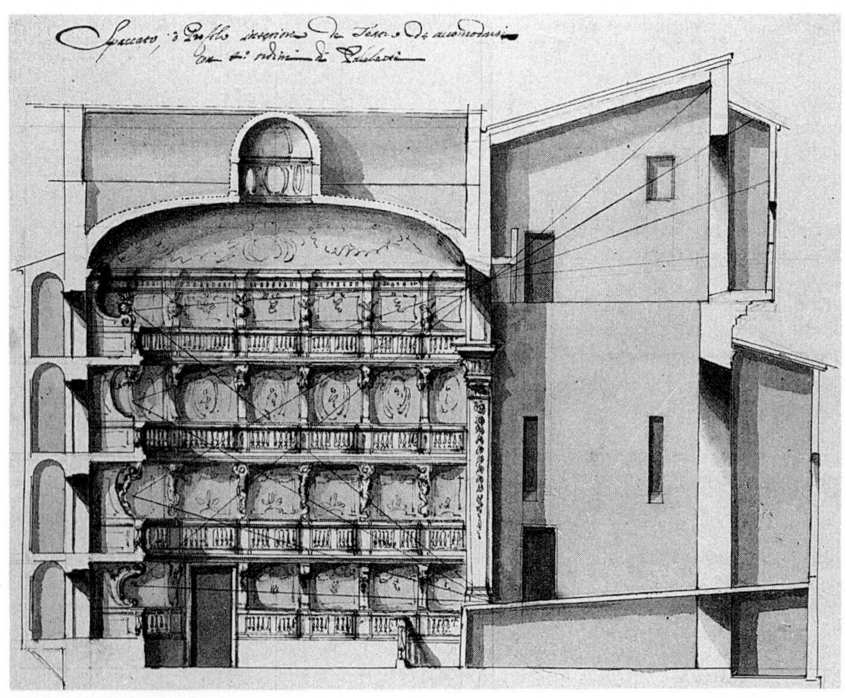

2. Design by Filippo Juvarra for the Teatro Ottoboni in the Palazzo della Cancelleria, Rome: section, showing the boxes of the auditorium

3. Performance of Leonardo Vinci's serenata 'La contesa de' numi' given in celebration of the dauphin's birth by Cardinal Melchior de Polignac in the private theatre of his palace in Rome, 26 November 1729

augurated on 13 January 1732, it had six tiers of 31 boxes. In 1741 it was renovated and improved by D. M. Vellani. The theatre was managed at first by the impresario Polvini Faliconti, then on his death in 1741 by Count Francesco Maria Alborghetti and in 1746–7 by the librettist Gaetano Roccaforte. It seems, however, that in the 1740s there was a corporate management in which several Roman nobles participated, including Marquis Angelo Gabrielli, who was lessee of the theatre in 1752–5 and in 1761 headed the Società e Compagnia di Cavalieri; composed of about 30 Roman nobles, this functioned until 1771. Thereafter the theatre was managed by professional impresarios who were also active elsewhere, such as Giuseppe Compostoff (1773–82), the choreographer Onorato Viganò (1783–8) and Andrea Campigli and his heirs (1789–95). It is possible that Roman nobles and citizens were also involved during these years. The Teatro delle Dame also experimented with a corporate management of noblemen, citizens and shareholders.

In the second half of the 18th century the Valle, Capranica, Pace, Pallacorda and Tordinona theatres all staged prose dramas interspersed with intermezzos and comic operas. The Valle belonged to the Capranica family; a season of *opera seria* was put on there in 1730, but from the late 1730s its activities were confined to spoken dramas and intermezzos. Built in 1726 to a design by Tommaso Morelli, and smaller than the Argentina and the Alibert, it was restored by Mauro Fontana in 1765 and again in 1791. It had five tiers of 27 boxes, and was the only theatre in Rome which in 1782, and regularly from 1786, offered operatic performances in the spring and autumn seasons as well as at Carnival. The Capranica (latterly a cinema), with its complicated history of ownership, underwent a number of restorations in the 18th century; in the middle of the century it had six tiers and 28 boxes. The theatre known as the Pallacorda di Firenze, which no longer exists, was designed by Nicolò Michetti and built in 1714 opposite the Palazzo Firenze in the present via Pallacorda; it was restored in 1786 by Vincenzo Mazzoneschi. The Teatro Pace, also no longer in existence, was built at the end of the 17th century in the present via del Teatro Pace and altered several times (in 1717, 1751, 1757, 1764 and 1785); another small theatre, it had five tiers of boxes.

The Teatro Tordinona, on the bank of the Tiber opposite Castel S Angelo, was rebuilt in 1732 at the instigation of Pope Clement XII to provide Rome with a government-run theatre and so put an end to the continual disputes between foreign dignitaries over the choice and use of boxes in privately owned theatres. It was designed by Domenico Gregorini and built very quickly, originally with four tiers of 26 boxes, a fifth being added in December 1734. In 1762 the theatre was strengthened and improved, and it reopened in 1764; in 1768 ten stage boxes were added, two at each level, but on the night of 29 January 1781 the theatre was destroyed by fire. It was then rebuilt to the plan of Felice Giorgi, but not completed until 1795. The new building was named the Teatro Apollo and was at first used for light opera.

The management of the many theatres operating in Rome for prose drama and comic opera still awaits study. The Valle was managed for several decades after 1757 by Marquis Gabrielli in association with Nicola De Sanctis. The smaller theatres were frequently run by cooperative companies of actors, craftsmen and musicians.

The *opera seria* repertory in 18th-century Rome centred on texts by Metastasio, some of which (*Catone in Utica*, *Semiramide riconosciuta*, *Alessandro nell'Indie*, *Artaserse*) were actually heard for the first time there. Metastasio's librettos were frequently set to new music, with the usual modifications, and librettos by Zeno, Roccaforte, Pizzi, Cigna-Santi, Sertor and others were also used. In the last quarter of the century it became more usual to stage operas that had been composed for performance elsewhere. The musicians engaged were mostly trained in Naples; some of them stayed in Rome for some time (Jommelli was there from 1749 to 1753), and so became involved in the general musical life of the city, both secular and religious. In the second half of the century, however, it was usual for well-known composers such as Piccinni, Sacchini, Anfossi, Guglielmi and Sarti to visit Rome for the opera season only. Roman composers, many of them *maestri* in the city churches, wrote mostly comic operas, *farsette*, intermezzos and the like; they included Rinaldo di Capua, G. B. Casali, P. M. Crispi, Giovanni Cavi, Giovanni Masi, Agostino Accorimboni, Girolamo Mango and Marcello Bernardini. There were also performances, especially at the Teatro Valle, of comic operas by Galuppi, Piccinni, Anfossi, Sacchini, Paisiello, Guglielmi and Cimarosa. Throughout the 18th century female singers were prohibited from appearing in public theatres in Rome, and all their roles were taken by men.

(ii) The 19th century. In the 19th century the Pace and Pallacorda theatres no longer staged opera but were confined to spoken comedies, puppet shows and other such works. At the Capranica, altered in 1802–3 and again in 1853, opera was performed only a few times in the second half of the century; the theatre was finally closed in 1881. The Alibert, which continued to stage *opera seria* and ballet in the early years of the century, was used for carnival festivities and circuses from 1811, after which date opera and ballet were rarely put on. Restored in 1827 by Gaspare Salvi, it was bought by Prince Torlonia in 1847 and rebuilt by Nicola Carnevali in 1858; in 1863 it was destroyed by fire.

Opera was regularly presented, however, at the Valle, the Argentina and the Apollo theatres. The Valle was regularly open for the carnival, spring and autumn seasons, and was rebuilt in 1821 to the design of Valadier, completed by Salvi and adorned in 1845 by a façade designed by Gaspare Servi. It was chiefly intended for *opera buffa* and *opera semiseria*, which were interspersed with prose comedies; from about 1830 serious melodrama was staged with increasing frequency. A new opera was performed there nearly every season, including Rossini's *Torvaldo e Dorliska* (1815) and *La Cenerentola* (1817), Mercadante's *Il geloso ravveduto* (1820), Donizetti's *L'ajo nell'imbarazzo* (1824), *Olivo e Pasquale* (1827), *Il furioso all'isola di San Domingo* (1833) and *Torquato Tasso* (1833), Pacini's *La gioventù di Enrico V* (1820) and Luigi Ricci's *L'orfana di Ginevra* (1829), *Il sonnambulo* (1829) and *Chi dura vince* (1834), as well as many works by relatively unknown or local composers. From the middle of the century the Valle staged only spoken drama.

In the first quarter of the 19th century the Teatro Argentina regularly presented operas and ballet during Carnival (usually *opera seria*, though in 1816 the première of Rossini's *Il barbiere di Siviglia* took place there), but between about 1825 and 1840 performances were more sporadic, the theatre being used mainly for spoken drama and concerts. Opera then reappeared; the premières of *I due Foscari* (1844) and *La battaglia di Legnano* (1849) were given there, as well as the first Roman performances of many other works by Verdi. Until the end of the century *opera buffa* and operetta were performed at the Argentina during Carnival, and in the spring and autumn seasons melodramas by Donizetti, Verdi, Meyerbeer and later Thomas and Bizet. In this period there were few premières except of works by local composers. In 1843 the theatre was bought by Prince Torlonia but was then leased (in 1861) and finally sold (1868) to the Comune of Rome. Restored by Pietro Camporese in 1837 and in 1860–61 by Carnevali, it was completely renovated in 1887 by Gioacchino Ersoch to replace the Apollo as the municipal theatre in the last decade of the century.

The Teatro Apollo (see fig.4), which in 1805 was owned by the Camera Apostolica, was bought in 1812 by Prince Francesco Santacroce and in 1820 by Giovanni Torlonia, who had it improved and renovated; it was further altered in 1830 by Valadier and in 1862 by Carnevali. Torlonia leased it to the city in 1862 and he granted a perpetual lease in 1869. It was demolished in the course of alterations to the Lungotevere in 1889. At the beginning of the 19th century the Apollo had presented opera (often comic opera) from time to time, but from 1828 its function was that of the principal theatre in the city, and regular performances of *opera seria* with ballet were given during Carnival until 1858, and then also in spring and autumn. From 1870 the carnival season was prolonged through Lent and the autumn season through Advent, but from 1874 opera occupied only the carnival-Lent season. In the course of the century the Apollo staged works mainly by Rossini, Ricci, Mercadante, Donizetti, Pacini, Verdi, Petrella, Meyerbeer, Gounod, Thomas and Massenet; premières were few but included Rossini's *Matilde di Shabran* (1821), Donizetti's *Adelia* (1841), Pacini's *Il corsaro* (1831), *Furio Camillo* (1839) and *Gianni di Nisida* (1860) and Verdi's *Il trovatore* (1853), as well as the first Italian performances of *Fidelio* and *La forza del destino*. Wagner's music was first heard in Rome at the Apollo with *Lohengrin* in 1878, and in 1883 the entire *Ring* was performed in German.

The management of Roman theatres in the first decades of the 19th century had some unusual characteristics: the involvement of several aristocratic proprietors (Sforza-Cesarini at the Argentina, Bartolomeo Capranica at the Valle, the Torlonias at the Apollo); the monopoly granted to a single impresario (alternately Cartoni and Paterni); and the lack of government subsidies, which were granted only after the 1830s and only to the Apollo for *opera seria*. For 40 years from 1840 theatrical life in Rome was dominated by Vincenzo Jacovacci, who was first impresario at the Valle and the Apollo and then also at the Argentina (1847–73). Another characteristic feature of opera in Rome in the 19th century concerns the many alterations made to librettos by the censors, especially after the 1840s.

In the last decades of the century, with the Apollo demolished and the Valle used for plays, the Argentina, as the municipal theatre, continued to be used for opera. To satisfy the new requirements of Rome, now the capital city, the Argentina was joined by new theatres built to hold larger audiences. The Teatro Drammatico Nazionale (built in 1886 and demolished in 1929), the Politeama Romano (built 1862, demolished 1883), the Teatro Manzoni (opened in 1876) and the Politeama Adriano (later the Teatro Adriano, opened in 1898) put on ballet, operetta and opera performances, often of a popular kind, as well as spoken drama. Among the theatres constructed at the end of the 19th century the

4. Interior of the Teatro Apollo, Rome, during the posthumous première of Donizetti's unfinished opera 'Le duc d'Albe' (begun 1839), given in Italian as 'Il duca d'Alba', 22 March 1882: engraving from 'Il teatro illustrato' (April 1882)

Teatro Costanzi (*see* SOCIOLOGY OF OPERA, fig.3), built by the entrepreneur Domenico Costanzi to the plans of Achille Sfondrini in the new Esquiline district, acquired particular prestige. The stalls held 1000 spectators with seating for 600, and there were three rows of boxes (108 in all), a circle with 337 numbered seats, and a gallery with a separate entrance and 800 unnumbered seats; there was also an adjoining concert hall. It was inaugurated on 27 November 1880 and until the end of the century was usually used in spring and autumn so as not to compete with the municipal theatre in the carnival-Lent season. Various impresarios worked there (including Sonzogno in 1888–90) until 1899, when, under the direction of Enrico Costanzi, the theatre's activities were expanded and regulated, the season being prolonged from the end of December to April or May. In 1887 Verdi's *Otello* was performed in the same production as that of the première at La Scala earlier in the year, and in 1890 Mascagni's *Cavalleria rusticana* received its first performance.

(iii) The 20th century. On the death of Enrico Costanzi the Teatro Costanzi was bought by a company, Stin, connected with South American theatres and directed by Walter Mocchi. From the 1911–12 season, by which time it began receiving an annual grant from the city, the theatre was directed by Emma Carelli until it was sold to the municipal administration in 1926. During this period the theatre's principal season, from the end of December to the end of April, included 12 to 15 operas; there were also occasional spring, summer and autumn seasons with popular programmes and regular seasons of spoken plays (usually in June-July and October-November) as well as operetta and ballet performances (including some by the Ballets Russes). The première of Puccini's *Tosca* took place at the Costanzi in January 1900 and the Italian première of Wagner's *Parsifal* (simultaneously with Bologna) on 1 January 1914.

The theatre was restructured in 1926–7 to plans by Marcello Piacentini and reopened in 1928 as the Teatro Reale dell'Opera, now the Teatro dell' Opera; it was then organized as a limited company and subsidized by the state. In addition to the usual operatic repertory, between the wars it staged premières of operas by Zandonai, Casella, Pizzetti, Wolf-Ferrari, Respighi, Alfano, Mulè, Malipiero and other Italians. The 1942 season was devoted entirely to contemporary works.

Opera performances have also been given in theatres used mainly for plays, such as the Eliseo, the Teatro delle Arti and the Cometa. These have included revivals of 17th- and 18th-century works, as well as new ones.

*

ES (P. M. Capponi and M. A. Ziino); *MGG* (P. Kast)

F. Clementi: *Il carnevale romano nelle cronache contemporanee* (Castello, 1899–1938)

G. Monaldi: *I teatri di Roma negli ultimi tre secoli* (Naples, 1928)

A. Cametti: *Il Teatro di Tordinona poi di Apollo* (Tivoli, 1938)

A. De Angelis: *Il Teatro Alibert o delle Dame nella Roma papale (1717–1863)* (Tivoli, 1951)

A. Rava: *I teatri di Roma* (Rome, 1953)

C. Sartori: *I libretti italiani a stampa dalle origini al 1800* (Cuneo, 1990–)

UP TO 1680

C.-F. Ménestrier: *Des représentations en musique anciennes et modernes* (Paris, 1681)

P. Mandosio: *Bibliotheca romana* (Rome, 1692)

A. Ademollo: 'Il primo melodrama a Roma', *Opinione* (1881), no.73

——: 'I primordi del teatro musicale pubblico a Roma', *Opinione* (1882), no.5

——: 'Cronaca teatrale romana del secolo XVII', *Opinione* (1882), no.20
——: *I teatri di Roma nel secolo decimosettimo* (Rome, 1888)
——: 'I primi fasti del Teatro Tor di Nona', *Fanfulla della Domenica* (1889), nos. 28–9, 31–2
H. Goldschmidt: *Studien zur Geschichte der italienischen Oper im 17. Jahrhundert* (Leipzig, 1901)
A. Solerti: *Le origini del melodramma* (Turin, 1903)
A. Cametti: 'Cristina di Svezia, l'arte musicale e gli spettacoli teatrali in Roma', *Nuova antologia*, no.155 (1911), 641–56
A. Bonaventura: *Saggio storico sul teatro musicale italiano* (Livorno, 1913), 103–31
H. Prunières: *L'opéra italien en France avant Lulli* (Paris, 1913), 1–37
F. Fuà: *L'opera di Filippo Acciaiuoli* (Fossombrone, 1921)
W. B. Squire: 'An Opera under Innocent X', *Gedenkboek aangeboden aan Dr. D. F. Scheurleer* (The Hague, 1925), 65–71
G. Pavan: 'Un dramma musicale a Roma nel 1634', *Musica d'oggi*, iii (1927), 274–77
P. Santini: 'Opera – Papal and Regal', *ML*, xx (1939), 292–8
J. E. Rotondi: *Literary and Musical Aspects of Roman Opera, 1600–1650* (diss., U. of Pennsylvania, 1959)
P. Bjurström: *Feast and Theatre in Queen Christina's Rome* (Stockholm, 1966)
F. Testi: *La musica italiana nel seicento: il melodramma* (Milan, 1970)
N. Pirrotta: *Storia dell'opera dalle origini al 1645* (Rome, 1972)
S. Gossett: 'Drama in the English College, Rome, 1591–1660', *English Literary Renaissance*, iii (1973), 60–93
S. Franchi: *Il teatro musicale a Roma: cronologia degli spettacoli, parte prima, 1600–1670* (Rome, 1974)
C. Gianturco: 'Evidence for a Late Roman School of Opera', *ML*, lvi (1975), 4–17
M. Murata: 'Il carnevale a Roma sotto Clemente IX Rospigliosi', *RIM*, xii (1977), 83–99
——: *Operas for the Papal Court, 1631–1668* (Ann Arbor, 1981)
——: 'Classical Tragedy in the Early History of Opera in Rome', *EMH*, iv (1984), 101–34
F. Hammond: 'More on Music in Casa Barberini', *Studi musicali*, xiv (1985), 235–61
V. Kapp: 'Das Barberini-Theater und die Bedeutung der römischen Kultur unter Urban VIII', *Literaturwissenschaftliches Jb*, new ser., xxvi (1985), 179–227
S. Franchi: *Drammaturgia romana: repertorio bibliografico cronologico dei testi drammatici pubblicati a Roma e nel Lazio, secolo XVII* (Rome, 1988)

1680–1730

P. Campello della Spina: 'Pontificato di Innocenzo XII: diario del Conte Gio. Battista Campello', *Studi e documenti di storia e diritto*, viii (1887), 167–98; ix (1888), 57–90; x (1889), 185–206, 449–64; xi (1890), 99–112; xii (1891), 379–91; xiv (1893), 179–89
A. Ademollo: *I teatri di Roma nel secolo decimosettimo* (Rome, 1888)
G. Pavan: 'Il Teatro Capranica: catalogo cronologico delle opere rappresentate nel secolo XVIII', *RMI*, xxix (1922), 425–44
A. Cametti: 'Roma: Teatro', *Enciclopedia italiana*, xxix (Rome, 1936)
G. Scano and G. Graglia, eds.: *Francesco Valesio: diario di Roma [1700–42]* (Milan, 1977–9)
P. Weiss: 'Pier Jacopo Martello on Opera (1715): an Annotated Translation', *MQ*, lxvi (1980), 378–403
L. Lindgren: 'Il dramma musicale a Roma durante la carriera di Alessandro Scarlatti (1660–1725)', *Le muse galanti: la musica a Roma nel settecento*, ed. B. Cagli (Rome, 1985), 35–57
S. Franchi: *Drammaturgia romana: repertorio bibliografico cronologico dei testi drammatici pubblicati a Roma e nel Lazio, secolo XVII* (Rome, 1988)
D. E. Monson: 'The Trail of Vivaldi's Singers: Vivaldi in Rome', *Nuovi studi vivaldiani: edizione e cronologia critica delle opere*, ed. A. Fanna and G. Morelli (Florence, 1988), 563–89
M. L. Volpicelli: 'Il teatro del Cardinale Ottoboni al Palazzo della Cancelleria', *Il teatro a Roma nel settecento*, ed. G. Petrocchi (Rome, 1989), 681–782
G. Staffieri: *Colligite fragmenta: la vita musicale romana negli 'Avvisi Marescotti' (1683–1707)* (Lucca, 1990)

SINCE 1730

Opere in musica rappresentate al Politeama Romano dall'anno 1871 in poi (MS, c1880, *I-Rsc*)
A. Cametti: *Un poeta melodrammatico romano: appunti e notizie in gran parte inedite sopra Jacopo Ferretti e i musicisti del suo tempo* (Milan, 1897)
——: 'Critiche e satire teatrali romane del settecento', *RMI*, ix (1902), 1–35
G. Radiciotti: *Teatro e musica in Roma nel secondo quarto del secolo XIX* (Rome, 1905)
M. Incagliati: *Il teatro Costanzi (1880–1907)* (Rome, 1907)
E. Celani: 'Musica e musicisti in Roma (1750–1850)', *RMI*, xviii (1911), 1–63; xx (1913), 33–88; xxii (1915), 1–56, 257–300
A. Cametti: *La musica teatrale a Roma cento anni fa [1816–1834]* (Rome, 1916–34)
G. Monaldi: *I miei ricordi musicali* (Rome, 1921)
G. De Dominicis: *I teatri di Roma nell'età di Pio VI* (Rome, 1922)
G. Pavan: 'Il Teatro Capranica: catalogo cronologico delle opere rappresentate nel secolo XVIII', *RMI*, xxix (1922), 425–44
V. Frajese: *Dal Costanzi all'Opera* (Rome, 1977)
P. Petrobelli: 'Don Giovanni in Italia: la fortuna dell'opera e il suo influsso', *AnMc*, no.18 (1978), 30–51
M. Rinaldi: *Due secoli di musica al Teatro Argentina* (Florence, 1978)
J. Tognelli, ed.: *Cinquant'anni del Teatro dell'Opera* (Rome, 1979)
F. Della Seta: 'Il relator sincero: cronache teatrali romane 1739–1756', *Studi musicali*, ix (1980), 93–116
M. F. Agresta: 'Il Teatro della Pace di Roma', *Studi romani*, xxxi (1983), 151–60
Sogni e favole io fingo: teatro pubblico e melodramma a Roma all'epoca di Metastasio (Rome, 1983)
J. Rosselli: *The Opera Industry in Italy from Cimarosa to Verdi* (Cambridge, 1984)
B. Cagli, ed.: *Le muse galanti: la musica a Roma nel settecento* (Rome, 1985)
B. M. Antolini: 'Attività e fortuna di Morlacchi a Roma', *Francesco Morlacchi e la musica del suo tempo (1784–1841)*, ed. B. Brumana and G. Ciliberti (Florence, 1986), 95–106
P. Pavan and M. Franceschini: 'La deputazione dei pubblici spettacoli di Roma e il suo archivio', *Architettura e archivi* (1986), 97–113
A. Bini: '*Otto mesi in due ore, o sia Gli esiliati in Siberia*: vicende di un'opera donizettiana', *RIM*, xxii (1987), 183–260
B. M. Antolini and A. Bini: *Editori e librai musicali a Roma nella prima metà dell'ottocento* (Rome, 1988)
A. Cerocchi: *I carnevali al teatro Alibert o delle Dame: analisi di un documento conservato nell'archivio del Sovrano militare Ordine di Malta in Roma* (diss., La Sapienza U., Rome, 1989)
M. G. Pastura Ruggiero: 'Fonti per la storia del teatro romano nel settecento conservate nell'Archivio di Stato di Roma', *Il teatro a Roma nel settecento*, ed. G. Petrocchi (Rome, 1989), 505–86
G. Pejrone: 'Il teatro attraverso i periodici romani del settecento', ibid, 599–615
Il teatro e la festa: lo spettacolo a Roma tra papato e rivoluzione (Rome, 1989)
L. Norci Cagiano: 'Un teatro tutto di legno: il teatro Valle e il dramma giocoso a Roma attraverso i resocoriti di viaggiatori francesi del settecento', *NRMI*, xxiv (1990), 305–34

MARGARET MURATA (1), LOWELL LINDGREN (2), BIANCA MARIA ANTOLINI (3)

Romens'ky, Mykhaylo Demyanovych (*b* Kursk, 8/20 Dec 1887; *d* Kiev, 24 Nov 1971). Ukrainian bass. He studied at the school of the Moscow Philharmonic Society, 1913–16, and began his career in 1917 at St Petersburg, Odessa and at other provincial theatres, joining the Rostov-na-Donu company in 1920, that at Kharkiv in 1934 and the Kiev company in 1942. His roles included Boris, Ivan Susanin, Lysenko's Taras Bulba, Rossini's Don Basilio and Prokofiev's Kutuzov. He retired in 1958. Such was his technique that he was able to sing to the end of his life, at the age of 83; his rich voice had a velvety smoothness that combined bel canto with powerful dramatic expression.

M. Romens'ky: *Spohady, materialy* [Recollections, Documents] (Kiev, 1982)

VIRKO BALEY

Romeo e Giulietta. Opera by N. A. Zingarelli; *see* GIULIETTA E ROMEO (i).

Roméo et Juliette (i) ('Romeo and Juliet'). *Opéra comique* in three acts by DANIEL STEIBELT to a libretto by Pierre de Ségur after WILLIAM SHAKESPEARE's play; Paris, Théâtre Feydeau, 9 October 1793.

Loosely based on Shakespeare's play but with a happy ending, the principal characters are Romeo (tenor), Juliet (soprano), Alberti (tenor), Antonio (baritone) and Cécile (soprano), with extensive writing for mixed, women's and men's choruses.

The opera enjoyed a great success; it was revived for more than 30 years after its première and translated into at least four languages. Steibelt's bold orchestration, innovative harmony and recitative-like choral writing appealed to Berlioz, who considered it the best musical setting of the story he knew (the others were by Bellini, Dalayrac, Zingarelli and Vaccai). Winton Dean (1964) called the work 'the best Shakespeare opera of the eighteenth century'.

Roméo et Juliette was originally written with sung recitative, which Steibelt removed in order to have it performed as an *opéra comique*. But because he considered it, in its original form, his best work, he restored the sung recitative in 1817 for a performance in St Petersburg. KAREN A. HAGBERG

Roméo et Juliette (ii) ('Romeo and Juliet'). *Opéra* in five acts by CHARLES-FRANÇOIS GOUNOD to a libretto by JULES BARBIER and MICHEL CARRÉ after WILLIAM SHAKESPEARE's play; Paris, Théâtre Lyrique, 27 April 1867.

Juliette [Juliet]	soprano
Roméo [Romeo] *son of Montaigu* [Montague]	tenor
Frère Laurent [Friar Laurence]	bass
Mercutio *friend to Romeo*	baritone
Stéphano *page to Romeo*	soprano
Capulet	bass
Tybalt *nephew of Lady Capulet*	tenor
Gertrude *nurse to Juliet*	mezzo-soprano
The Duke	bass
Paris *a young count*	baritone
Grégorio [Gregory] *servant to Capulet*	baritone
Benvolio *nephew of Montague*	tenor
Frère Jean [Friar John]	bass

Male and female retainers and kinsfolk of the House of Capulet and the House of Montague, masquers

Setting Renaissance Verona

Gounod first alluded to an operatic *Roméo et Juliette* in correspondence at the end of 1864, and Barbier and Carré produced a libretto in the first three months of the next year; unlike Felice Romani's book for Bellini's *I Capuleti e i Montecchi* (1830), which is only remotely connected with Shakespeare, the libretto for Gounod's opera adheres closely to the great tragedy. As in some of their previous work, Barbier and Carré borrowed from their source right down to individual expressions: most of the scenes with direct parallels to the Shakespeare play contain many metaphors drawn directly from it. Nevertheless, no single French translation of the many available in the late 1860s may be designated with confidence as the source for the choice of words in the opera.

In April 1865 Gounod began sketching and drafting *Roméo* at Saint-Raphaël in the Midi, a task he finished by July. Over the course of the next year he orchestrated the opera and in September 1866 decided to add a lavish wedding tableau to Act 4. At first, he intended the work to be performed with spoken dialogue but during rehearsals for the first production he filled the interstices between numbers with recitative. The choral prologue, for which Gounod drew on Shakespeare, as did Berlioz in his earlier dramatic symphony *Roméo et Juliette*, was not added until late in the rehearsal period, as was Juliet's *valse-ariette* 'Je veux vivre'. The latter was an obvious concession to the soprano Marie Caroline Carvalho, who was unable to perform the more dramatic fourth act *air* 'Amour ranime mon courage' at the first production.

Roméo, first performed with a cast that included Carvalho as Juliet, Pierre Michot as Romeo and Auguste Barré as Mercutio, was Gounod's most spectacular immediate success. Coming as it did during the Exposition Universelle of 1867, when Paris was invaded by visitors from the provinces and abroad, the opera drew full houses for many consecutive nights. It started its rapid conquest of foreign stages at Covent Garden on 11 July 1867 and before the end of the year had been seen at major centres in Germany and Belgium. After the demise of the Théâtre Lyrique in 1868, *Roméo* found a new Parisian home at the Opéra-Comique (Salle Favart), from 1873 to 1887; variants introduced for this production include an abbreviation of the finale to Act 1, the elimination of the Duke's role in Act 3 and extensive alterations to the finale of that act. The work was finally transferred to the Opéra in 1888, a production for which Gounod penned Romeo's imposing phrase 'Ah! jour de deuil' at the end of Act 3 and a ballet for Act 4. Though not as popular as *Faust*, *Roméo et Juliette* continues to hold the stage internationally.

PROLOGUE After a tempestuous orchestral introduction depicting the animosity between the rival Capulet and Montague houses, the curtain opens to a declaimed prologue for the soloists that summarizes the tragedy that will be enacted.

ACT 1 *A masked ball at the Capulet residence* The first number is a conventional multi-sectional *introduction* with soloists and framing chorus: in a rousing Second Empire mazurka assembled guests sing of the pleasures that await them; Tybalt assures Paris that he will become enthralled by the beautiful Juliet; Capulet escorts his daughter into the hall and jovially invites his guests to dance in adjacent rooms. When the stage is clear, the masked Romeo and his friends, Mercutio and Benvolio, come out of hiding. Romeo explains that he has recently had a dream that has filled him with foreboding about their adventure. Mercutio dismisses the dream as the work of the fairy Queen Mab, in a ternary piece coloured by delicate violin and flute filigree and many other picturesque orchestral details (ballade, 'Mab, reine des mensonges'). Romeo suddenly catches a glimpse of Juliet and falls in love instantly. He is dragged aside by his friends just as the girl and her nurse Gertrude enter the hall. In response to Gertrude's glowing praise of Paris, Juliet indicates lightheartedly, with appropriate coloratura, that she is not interested in marriage (*valse-ariette*, 'Je veux vivre'). Romeo steps out from a corner and the two realize that their destinies are one in a minuet-like duet, the restrained expression of which mirrors the formality of their first encounter in Shakespeare. Tybalt unexpectedly happens upon them and the two lovers realize their identities. Romeo and

'Roméo et Juliette' (Gounod), Act 2 (the Balcony Scene): Adelina Patti as Juliet and Giovanni Mario as Romeo in the first London performance (Covent Garden, 1867)

his friends beat a hasty retreat but, as the festive music of the opening wells up in orchestra and chorus, Capulet prevents Tybalt from pursuing them.

ACT 2 *The Capulet garden by night: to the left, Juliet's balcony* Romeo has stealthily made his way into the Capulet garden. He apostrophizes Juliet as the morning sun in the famous *cavatine*, 'Ah! lève-toi soleil!', where the fading evening star metaphor is developed musically by chromatically descending harmonies against a pedal. Shortly after she appears on the balcony, Romeo reveals his presence to her and declares his love. Their tender words are momentarily interrupted by a comic interlude in which Gregory and other Capulet servants run through the garden in search of a Montague pageboy seen in the grounds. Romeo re-emerges from hiding for a duet ('O nuit divine') in which Juliet confirms that she will marry him at any time and Romeo renews his pledge of affection. When Gertrude interrupts their tête à tête, the two lovers vainly seek to prolong their encounter in an understated *cabalette* (Ah! ne fuis pas encore!').

ACT 3.i *The cell of Friar Laurence; daybreak* After setting down a basketful of medicinal plants and flowers, Friar Laurence sings of nature's wonders (*cavatine*, 'Berceau de tous les êtres'). Romeo rushes in and reveals his love for Juliet Capulet. She soon follows and the two ask Laurence to marry them. Convinced of the strength of their attachment, he performs the ceremony (trio and quartet, 'Dieu qui fis l'homme à ton image'). The two lovers ritualistically interject a chant-like response between each stanza of his prayer and the three of them are soon joined by Gertrude for a *strette* that extols the bliss of love with an impressive crescendo and melodic sequence.

3.ii *A street in front of the Capulet house* Romeo's page Stéphano (Balthasar in Shakespeare's play) taunts the Capulets with a song about a turtle-dove held prisoner in a nest of vultures (*chanson*, 'Que fais-tu, blanche tourterelle'), and draws Gregory and other Capulet servants out of the house (finale, 'Ah voici nos gens!'). Stéphano repeats the refrain of his song in their presence and challenges Gregory to a duel. Mercutio and Benvolio come upon them, followed shortly by Tybalt and Paris. Mercutio is indignant over the fact that Gregory is duelling with a child. Tybalt warns Mercutio to mind his words and the two engage in a duel themselves. Romeo appears and asks Tybalt to forget about the hatred between the families. When Mercutio is subsequently wounded by Tybalt, Romeo seeks revenge against the latter and mortally injures his rival. A fanfare heralds the arrival of the Duke. The partisans of both houses clamour for justice and, acquainting himself with what has happened, the Duke exiles Romeo from Verona.

ACT 4.i *Juliet's room; daybreak* After an instrumental prelude in which four cellos sensuously translate the essence of the wedding night, Juliet pardons Romeo for having killed one of her relatives (duet, 'Va! je t'ai pardonné'). The two sing of their love in the slow section of the duet ('Nuit d'hyménée!') with parallel 3rds that symbolize their spiritual union. Romeo suddenly breaks away from the embrace when he hears the morning lark. Juliet at first refuses to believe him but then comes to grips with reality before a *cabalette*in which they bid each other farewell ('Il faut partir'). Capulet enters after Romeo has left, informing his daughter that she is to marry Paris that very day. Juliet is in despair at this news, and, alone with Friar Laurence, tells him that she would rather die than marry Paris. He suggests a ruse, using a potion by means of which she will appear dead; the Capulets will then transport her body to the family tomb, where Romeo will meet her. Juliet agrees to the plan and summons her courage in an *air* with a heroic melodic cast ('Amour ranime mon courage').

4.ii *A magnificent hall in the Capulet palace* Juliet is led on with a wedding march. The guests offer their best wishes and present gifts but as Capulet leads her by the arm into the chapel she collapses. Much to the dismay of all, he cries out that she is dead.

ACT 5 *The underground crypt of the Capulets* Juliet lies outstretched on a tomb. Friar Laurence learns from Friar John that Romeo has not received the letter explaining the ruse and instructs him to find another messenger. After a delicate instrumental interlude that evokes Juliet's somnolent state, Romeo appears. Believing Juliet dead, he drinks a vial of poison. At that moment she awakens and the two sing of their love with extensive thematic recollection of past moments in the opera. As he weakens, Juliet uncovers the sword she has hidden in her clothes and, with no musical preparation, abruptly stabs herself. She gives voice to her love one more time – in E♭ major, the key of Romeo's initial declaration of love in Act 2 – and with a final monumental effort the lovers ask for divine clemency before they die.

* * *

Gounod's opera has been the greatest popular success of the many founded upon Shakespeare's play. The four love duets in the work have drawn particular praise. One of the most significant tributes emerged from the pen of Verdi in the *divisi* cello scoring at the beginning of the Act 1 duet in *Otello*, which directly recalls that of the Act 4 duet in *Roméo et Juliette*. In the same duet, the dropping out of the voices during an impassioned orchestral interlude while Romeo and Juliet embrace is particularly effective. Though his famous *cavatine* in Act 2 is in the same mould as Faust's *cavatine* 'Salut! demeure', Romeo is convincing as a romantic lead, especially at such moments as 'Je te l'ai dit, je t'adore' in the Act 2 duet, where lyricism is enhanced by a metrical change from triple to common time within the prevailing tempo. That act is framed by a similar orchestral passage at beginning and end, in its later version with the voice superimposed in the sort of slow *parlante* over a lyrical strain that Gounod made his own, and of which there are several other examples in the opera. The strengths of *Roméo et Juliette* extend beyond the love music: Mercutio's Queen Mab ballade is highly evocative, and Gounod achieves (what is for him rare) dramatic verve in the great confrontation scene between the families at the end of Act 3. STEVEN HUEBNER

Romeo und Julia. Opera in two acts by HEINRICH SUTERMEISTER to his own libretto, after WILLIAM SHAKESPEARE's play; Dresden, Staatsoper, 13 April 1940.

The action takes place in Verona at the beginning of the 14th century and follows closely the plot of Shakespeare's play. There is a feud between the Montague and Capulet families, but because of an oversight Romeo (tenor), the son of Montague, receives an invitation to a ball at the Capulet palace. There he meets and falls in love with Julia [Juliet] (soprano), Capulet's daughter, though to his consternation he discovers through Juliet's Nurse (contralto) that his loved one has been promised to Count Paris (female danced role). Juliet and Romeo are wed in secret by Father Lorenzo [Friar Laurence] (bass), and even Juliet's Father (bass) is ignorant of their relationship. Friar Laurence gives Juliet a herbal drink to make her sleep deeply for 32 hours, in which time he hopes to have found a solution to the problem. Juliet's apparently lifeless body is dragged down to the Capulet family vault where she is discovered by Romeo. Believing her to be dead, he kills himself with a dagger. Juliet awakens to find Romeo's corpse next to her. She prays for redemption through death and to the accompaniment of a heavenly female chorus becomes transfigured with her loved one.

The music of *Romeo und Julia*, Sutermeister's first major opera, presents a synthesis of Romantic and impressionist elements. It marks a deliberate attempt to return to the conception of opera as a sequence of closed forms, incorporating within its scenario stylistic features related to madrigal, oratorio and pantomime. Sutermeister exploited the atmospheric background of Shakespeare's play to great effect, for example in the Nocturne of Act 1 scene iii with its offstage chorus. Commissioned by Karl Böhm and created as a vehicle for the soprano Maria Cebotari, it was enormously successful during the 1940s and 1950s but it has since fallen out of favour. ERIK LEVI

Romeo und Julia auf dem Dorfe. Opera by Frederick Delius; *see* *VILLAGE ROMEO AND JULIET, A.*

Romeo und Julie ('Romeo and Juliet'). *Ernsthafte Oper* ('serious opera') in three acts by Georg Benda (*see* BENDA family, (1)) to a libretto by FRIEDRICH WILHELM GOTTER after WILLIAM SHAKESPEARE's play and CHRISTIAN FELIX WEISSE; Gotha, Schloss Friedenstein, 25 September 1776.

Gotter's text, which begins after Romeo and Juliet have married, reflects the somewhat limited vocal resources of the Gotha court theatre. He eliminated several characters and made Juliet rather than Romeo the centre of attention; his major alteration, the substitution of a happy ending in which Juliet awakes before Romeo can poison himself, aroused controversy from the start and seriously weakens an otherwise powerful, darkling work.

Musical attention centres on Juliet and her confidante Laura (both sopranos), the latter part written for Benda's daughter Justel. The score is completely in the style of *opera seria* except that spoken dialogue replaces simple recitative, a decision Benda pointedly defended in print. Juliet's best music comes in free-flowing monologues, against which Romeo (tenor) cuts a poor figure on the whole. The capital scene, a solemn C minor funeral chorus at the beginning of Act 3, offers a northern echo of Gluck's sublime choral tableaux. The idea apparently came from David Garrick's 1750 production of Shakespeare's play.

Romeo und Julie was taken up by nearly every major theatrical company in Germany and saw performances well into the 19th century. In 1780 J. F. Reichardt praised it as 'a magnificent, ravishing work that penetrates the heart!' but added: 'If only the poet had not cut up his material so irresponsibly into well-behaved, everyday opera garb!'. THOMAS BAUMAN

Romer, Emma (*b* 1814; *d* Margate, 11 April 1868). English soprano. A pupil of Sir George Smart, she made her début at Covent Garden in 1830 in Linley's *The Duenna*. Engaged at the Lyceum Theatre, she appeared in the first performance of Barnett's *The Mountain Sylph* (1834). At Drury Lane she sang in the first performances of Barnett's *Fair Rosamond*, Balfe's *Catherine Grey* and *Joan of Arc* (1837), Benedict's *The Gypsy's Warning* and Balfe's *Diadesté* (1838), Hatton's *Queen of the Thames* (1843), Benedict's *Brides of Venice* (1844), Balfe's *The Enchantress* and Wallace's *Maritana* (1845) and Balfe's *The Bondman* (1846). She also sang in the first British performance of *La favorite* (1843, Drury Lane), which was given in English. In 1848 she took part in Bunn's autumn season of opera in English at Covent Garden, singing Adina (*L'elisir d'amore*) and also Amina (*La sonnambula*), a role for which she was particularly admired.

*

E. Fitzball: *35 Years of a Dramatic Author's Life* (London, 1859)
C. L. Kenney: *A Memoir of Michael William Balfe* (London, 1875)
W. A. Barrett: *Balfe: his Life and Work* (London, 1882)
B. Carr: 'The First All-Sung English 19th-Century Opera', *MT*, cxv (1974), 125–6 ELIZABETH FORBES

Romero (Sarachaga), Federico (*b* Oviedo, 11 Nov 1886; *d* Madrid, 30 June 1976). Spanish zarzuela librettist. From 1907 he earned his living in the Post Office in Madrid, while becoming a contributor to the journals *Nueva mundo* and *La esfera* and writing zarzuela librettos. He was instrumental in setting up the Sociedad General de Autores de España to replace the former Sociedad de Autores de España, and became the first director of the new body. His first theatrical work was a zarzuela *El árbol de Guernica*, and in all he wrote some 65 zarzuelas and other theatrical pieces, mostly in collaboration with Guillermo Fernández Shaw. These included such classics of the genre as *La canción del olvidó* (Serrano, 1916), *Doña Francisquita* (Vives, 1923), *El caserío* (Guridi, 1926), *Luisa Fernanda* (Moreno Torroba, 1932) and *La tabernera del puerto* (Sorozábal, 1936).

selective list; all zarzuelas; written with G. Fernández Shaw unless otherwise stated

La canción del olvidó, J. Serrano, 1916; *Los fanfarrones*, Eduardo Granados, 1920; *El dictador*, R. Millán, 1923; *Doña Francisquita*, Vives, 1923; *La severa* [*La morería*], Millán, 1925; *El caserío*, Guridi, 1926; *La villana*, Vives, 1927; *Las alondras*, Guerrero, 1927; *Los flamencos*, Vives, 1928; *La meiga*, Guridi, 1928; *La rosa del azafrán*, Guerrero, 1930; *Luisa Fernanda*, Moreno Torroba, 1932; *Talismán*, Vives, 1932; *La chulapona*, Moreno Torroba, 1934; *Luna de mayo*, E. Rosillo, 1934; *No me olvides*, Sorozábal, 1935; *La tabernera del puerto*, Sorozábal, 1936; *Monte Carmelo*, Moreno Torroba, 1936; *La Rosario, o La rambla de fin de siglo*, Sorozábal, 1941; *Cuidado con la pintura*, Sorozábal, 1941; *Loza, lozana*, Guerrero, 1942; *Peñamariana*, Guridi, 1944; *Mambrú se va a la guerra*, J. Dotras Vila, 1945; *Aquella conción antigua* (Romero alone), Dotras Vila, 1952

ANDREW LAMB

Romolo ed Ersilia ('Romulus and Hersilia'). Libretto by PIETRO METASTASIO, first set by Johann Adolf Hasse (1765, Innsbruck).

Requiring wives for the young men of the new settlement in Rome, Romulus organized the seizure of a number of women from the Sabini tribe while they were visiting Rome. This action angered not only the Sabines but also the inhabitants of nearby Antemnae, Caenina and Crustumium.

ACT 1 At a general nuptial celebration, Romulus assures the Sabine women of the respect of their young Roman captors, and bids them join with the youth of Rome in founding a noble race. Romulus himself is urged to take a consort and would gladly name the Sabine princess, Hersilia, whom he loves. Hersilia, daughter of Curzio [Curtius], ruler of Antemnae, is in love with him, but will not marry against her father's wishes.

ACT 2 Curtius enters Rome in search of his daughter and encounters Acronte [Acrontes], King of the Caeninenses. Acrontes, although previously rejected by Curtius as a suitor for Hersilia, bids him join his planned attack on Rome. Acrontes believes that Hersilia has already given herself to Romulus, and greatly distresses Curtius by telling him so. Curtius soon learns the truth, however, but Hersilia, fearing her inability to uphold her duty to her father, begs him take her from the city. Before she can depart, however, Ostilio [Hostilius], close friend of Romulus and unrequitedly in love with Valeria, a Roman woman of noble birth, asks Hersilia to commend Valeria to Romulus as a consort. While attempting to carry out this request, Hersilia confesses her love to the Roman king.

ACT 3 Acrontes is captured by the Romans, but he is released by Romulus and immediately leads his armies against his former captors. Faced with defeat, he calls for single combat between himself and Romulus and is slain in an attempt at further treachery. The celebrations of triumph are interrupted by a further clash of arms when Curtius and Hersilia are seized as they endeavour to leave Rome. Curtius, overcome by the magnanimity of Romulus in restoring his daughter to him unconditionally, consents to the marriage.

* * *

Classical sources that contain accounts and references to the seizure of the Sabine women include the following: Cassius Dio, *Historiarum* (book 56); Dionysius of Halicarnassus, *Antiquitatum* (book 2); Florus, *Epitomae* (book 1); Livy, *Historiarum* (book 1); and Plutarch, *Vitae* (Romulus). Hersilia is identified as possibly a married Sabine taken in error (Dionysius and Plutarch), as a Sabine mother who chose to remain with her daughter (Dio and Dionysius), as the wife of the Roman champion, Hostilius (Plutarch) and as the wife of Romulus (Livy and Plutarch). Mettius Curtius, linked by Metastasio with Antemnae, is named by all but Florus as the Sabine champion, and the slaying by Romulus of the King of Caenina is recounted by Livy and Plutarch, the latter identifying this king as Acron. Thus were Metastasio's characters provided, and the impeded love relationship between Romulus and Hersilia may well have been suggested by Antoine de Lamotte's drama *Romulus* (1722). With Hasse's music, Metastasio's drama was elaborately mounted, with stage settings by Bernardino and Fabrizio Galliari, as part of the celebrations surrounding the marriage of the future Leopold II of Austria to Maria Luisa of Spain. Anna de Amicis sang the role of Hersilia (with Gaetano Guadagni as Romulus) on that occasion. She was to play Hersilia again, this time with Gasparo Pacchierotti as Romulus, when Mysliveček set the text to honour the birthday of Maria Carolina of Austria, consort to Ferdinand IV (1773, Naples). No other settings of this drama were composed. DON NEVILLE

Roncaglia, Francesco (*b* ?Faenza, *c*1750; *d* ?Bologna, after 1812). Italian soprano castrato. A singing pupil of Gibelli in Bologna, he first sang in *opera seria* at Parma in 1767 and was then secondo uomo at Munich (1768–71), rising to primo at Mannheim (1772–6). In 1777–1803 he sang in leading Italian houses, including six years at the S Carlo, Naples, and also two seasons (1777–8, 1780–81) in London. From 1802 he was a singer in the Naples court chapel and taught singing at the Naples and Bologna conservatories. Burney described him as having an 'elegant face and figure' and a 'sweet-toned' but small voice, rising to *a''* and occasionally to *c'''*, with a 'chaste and well disciplined style of singing'. DENNIS LIBBY

Ronconi, Giorgio (*b* Milan, 6 Aug 1810; *d* Madrid, 8 Jan 1890). Italian baritone. He studied with his father, Domenico Ronconi, and made his début in 1831 at Pavia as Valdeburgo (*La straniera*). At the Teatro Valle, Rome, in 1833 he sang Cardenio in *Il furioso all'isola di San Domingo* and the title role of *Torquato Tasso*, both first performances. He also sang in five other Donizetti premières, *Il campanello di notte* (Naples, 1836), *Pia de' Tolomei* (Venice, 1837), *Maria de Rudenz* (Venice, 1838), *Maria Padilla* (Milan, 1841) and *Maria di Rohan* (Vienna, 1843), which he repeated at the Théâtre Italien, Paris. Having first sung at La Scala in 1839 as Enrico Ashton (*Lucia di Lammermoor*), he created the title role of Verdi's *Nabucco* there in 1842. The same year he made his London début at Her Majesty's Theatre, and from 1847 to 1866 he sang nearly every season at Covent Garden. His large repertory included roles by Mozart and Rossini; in 1853 he became the first London Rigoletto.

In many ways, Ronconi was the prototype of the 'modern', Verdian baritone. As the *Musical World* (11 September 1847) said: 'His voice is not particularly melodious, nor is his intonation strictly true ... nevertheless ... its power is immense, and its extent extraordinary for a barytone. In *forte* passages its volume fills the house like a thunder-peal; and in passionate phrases, when the artist comes out with an upper G, or sometimes an A, with all his power, the effect is quite electrical'. It was clearly this (as then) unprecedented power in the highest register that Verdi exploited so thoroughly, and that became a model for many baritones of the next generation. Ronconi was married to the soprano Elguerra Giannoni; his brother Sebastiano (*b* Venice, May 1814; *d* Milan, 6 Feb 1900) was a baritone who made his début at Lucca in 1836 and had a successful career in Europe and the USA.

For illustration *see* MARIA DI ROHAN.

*

H. F. Chorley: *Thirty Years' Musical Recollections* (London, 1862, 2/1926)
H. Rosenthal: *Two Centuries of Opera at Covent Garden* (London, 1958)
H. Weinstock: *Donizetti and the World of Opera in Italy, Paris and Vienna in the First Half of the Nineteenth Century* (New York, 1963)
T. Kaufman: 'Giorgio Ronconi', *Donizetti Society Journal*, v (1984), 169–206 [incl. chronology of his opera appearances]

ELIZABETH FORBES (with ROGER PARKER)

Ronconi, Luca (*b* Susah, Tunisia, 8 March 1933). Italian director. He spent his early years in Tunisia, Italy and Switzerland, and graduated in 1953 from the Accademia d'Arte Drammatica in Rome. For ten years he acted in plays by de Musset, Shaw, Wesker and several contemporary Italian authors, under such noted directors as Giorgio Strehler, Michelangelo Antonioni, Luigi Squarzina, Giorgio De Lullo and Virginio Puecher. He directed for the first time in 1963 (Goldoni's *La buona moglie* at the Teatro Valle in Rome) but his first major success was a 1966 production of Middleton and Rowley's *The Changeling* at the Palazzo Ducale, Urbino. Since then he has directed an international repertory, classical and modern, in many Italian cities and in Paris, Vienna, Zürich and Belgrade. He was the founding director of a theatre laboratory at the Teatro Metastasio, Prato, in 1977 and has been director of the Teatro Stabile, Turin, since 1989.

Ronconi's first opera production was a double bill: Honegger's *Jeanne d'Arc au bûcher* and Busoni's *Arlecchino*, at the Teatro Nuovo, Turin, in 1967. He has since produced many repertory operas, from Gluck to Berg; infrequently performed operas by Luigi Rossi, Purcell, Jommelli, Piccinni, Cimarosa, Cherubini and Rimsky-Korsakov (*The Tsar's Bride*); and recent operas by Vinko Globokar, Berio and Stockhausen. Since the mid-1970s, many of his productions have been realized for La Scala or for the Teatro Comunale, Florence, but he has also worked in other Italian houses and elsewhere in Europe. Pier Luigi Pizzi, Luciano Damiani and Gae Aulenti are among the best-known of his set and costume designers.

Ronconi is the most controversial of Italy's major producers. His work has few points of contact with Franco Zeffirelli's decorative opulence, Piero Faggioni's imaginative realism or Giorgio Strehler's text-respectful stylization. Luciano Alberti has described Ronconi's concept of theatre in general as 'both machine and dream', and of operatic theatre in particular as 'a glorious, anachronistic relic'. Ronconi's interpretations often contain an ironic commentary on the opera in question and on opera as a genre. Rather than trying to help singers to overcome or mask their weaknesses as actors, Ronconi incorporates the deficiencies into his scheme: the action, instead of being carried out *by* the characters, happens *to* them, partly as a result of intentionally cumbersome stage apparatus. He sometimes has the chorus act as spectators, rather than as participants in the action. Some observers find his approach stimulating; others find it too tenuously connected to the musical substance.

*

C. Milanese: *Luca Ronconi e la realtà del teatro* (Milan, 1973)
F. Quadri: *Il rito perduto* (Turin, 1973)
——: 'Luca Ronconi', *Drama Review*, lxxiv (1977), 103–18
——: *Il teatro degli anni settanta: tradizione e ricerca* (Turin, 1982), 159–85
A. Dossena, ed.: *Luca Ronconi, inventare l'opera* (Milan, 1986)

HARVEY SACHS

Rondine, La ('The Swallow'). *Commedia lirica* in three acts by GIACOMO PUCCINI to a text by GIUSEPPE ADAMI after a libretto by A. M. WILLNER and HEINZ REICHERT; Monte Carlo, Théâtre de l'Opéra, 27 March 1917.

Magda de Civry	soprano
Lisette *her maid*	soprano
Ruggero Lastouc	tenor
Prunier *a poet*	tenor
Rambaldo Fernandez *Magda's protector*	baritone
Périchaud	baritone/bass
Gobin	tenor
Crébillon	bass/baritone
Rabonnier	baritone
Yvette	soprano
Bianca	soprano
Suzy	mezzo-soprano
A Butler	bass
A Voice	soprano

Members of the bourgeoisie, students, painters, elegantly dressed ladies and gentlemen, *grisettes*, flower-girls and dancing girls, waiters

Setting Paris and the Riviera during the Second Empire

During a visit to Vienna in October 1913 for a performance of *La fanciulla del West* Puccini was invited by the directors of the Carltheater to compose an operetta. He agreed in principle, insisting, however, that it take the form of a through-composed comic opera 'like *Rosenkavalier* but more amusing and more organic'. Of two subjects offered successively by Willner and Reichert, Puccini chose the second and entrusted Adami with drawing up the Italian text. Work proceeded slowly over the next two years. In the meantime Italy's entry into World War I necessitated a revision of the contract, whereby the Viennese management resigned their claim to the opera's première while retaining what amounted to half the performing rights. As the younger Tito Ricordi showed no interest in the project Puccini contracted with the firm of Lorenzo Sonzogno for the publication. Because of the state of European hostilities it was decided to launch the opera on neutral territory; hence the choice of Monte Carlo. The original cast included Gilda dalla Rizza (Magda), Ina Maria

Ferraris (Lisette), Tito Schipa (Ruggero), Francesco Dominici (Prunier) and Gustave Huberdeau (Rambaldo); the conductor was Gino Marinuzzi. The first Italian performance took place at Bologna on 5 June the same year. During 1918–19 Puccini made various modifications to the score, allocating Prunier to a baritone, raising the pitch of Lisette's role and adding a *romanza* in Act 1 for Ruggero ('Parigi è la città dei desideri'). Prunier was given two appearances in Act 3, after the second of which Magda left without bidding farewell to Ruggero. In this form the opera was given in Vienna (9 October 1920) at the Volksoper, where even the conducting of Felix Weingartner failed to ensure a success. Later, Puccini prepared yet a third version in which the first two acts reverted to their original design, with Prunier once more a tenor. Act 3, however, was to be set in Ruggero's home in Montauban and introduced by a prelude with soprano voice offstage. Ruggero would be informed of Magda's past by an anonymous letter. On entering the room he would find a wallet deposited by Rambaldo. There would be a furious duet between Ruggero and Magda, interrupted by Rambaldo's return. Magda would be on stage 'alone and abandoned' as the curtain fell. There is no record of this version's having been performed, nor is there any trace of the material. All subsequent imprints of the score correspond with the original of 1917.

La rondine did not reach the Metropolitan, New York, until four years after the composer's death. It has never been seen at Covent Garden.

ACT 1 *An elegant salon in Magda's Parisian house* Prunier is holding forth to his hostess and her guests about the latest fashion for sentimental love. Lisette mocks the idea and is promptly sent about her business. Yet no one except Magda takes the poet very seriously. Prunier illustrates his theory with the story of his latest heroine, Doretta, who spurned a king's ransom for love ('Chi il bel sogno di Doretta potè indovinar'). Taking up a second verse, Magda completes the story, telling how the girl lost her heart to a student; and she repeats the refrain to her own words 'Folle amore!' In every heart, Prunier maintains, there lurks the devil of romantic love. Rambaldo claims that he knows how to exorcise it; and he gives Magda a pearl necklace. She passes it round, to general admiration, but a gentle waltz theme indicates that her thoughts are elsewhere. Rambaldo retires, having received permission to present to her the son of a childhood acquaintance. Meantime she regales her friends with her account of an innocent flirtation with a student at Bullier's Restaurant ('Ore dolci e divine'), to which his words 'Fanciulla, è sbocciato l'amore' form a waltz-like refrain. Rambaldo returns with the visitor, Ruggero Lestouc, as Magda is having her palm read by Prunier, who predicts that, like the swallow of the opera's title, she will fly south to love and happiness. The company are profuse with suggestions as to where Ruggero shall spend his first night out in Paris. The choice falls on Bullier's. As the guests leave Magda decides to remain at home, then thinks better of it and retires to her boudoir to change. Meanwhile Prunier flirts with Lisette to a sly, insinuating orchestral theme. As it is her evening off, they decide to dine out together, Lisette wearing one of her mistress's hats. When they have left Magda emerges dressed as a *grisette*, ready for an adventure at Bullier's, her mind full of Prunier's prophecy and 'Doretta's' secret.

ACT 2 *Chez Bullier* The restaurant is alive with a crowd of students, artists, flower-girls and *grisettes*. Ruggero is alone at a table. Magda appears and to the importunities of the students she replies that she is meeting somebody; whereupon they lead her to Ruggero's table. The young man fails to recognize her, but they converse amicably. Magda teases him about his probable love-affairs; to which he replies that if he should fall in love it would be for ever. He persuades her to join him in a waltz, which grows in grandeur and vivacity, incorporating reminiscences from Act 1. Prunier arrives with Lisette. The dance concluded, Magda and Ruggero return to their table and pledge their newly born love, she giving her name as Paulette. Lisette starts at the sight of her mistress; but Prunier, at a sign from Magda, convinces the girl that it is only a chance resemblance. Both couples begin a slow concertato ('Bevo al tuo fresco sorriso'), which comes to a sudden halt as Rambaldo appears at the head of the stairs. Prunier tells Lisette to keep Ruggero out of sight. Rambaldo asks Magda for an explanation and she replies that she intends to leave him; he bows ironically and retires. Ruggero returns with Magda's shawl, and the two leave to begin a new life together.

ACT 3 *The Côte d'Azur* On the terrace of a pavilion overlooking the Mediterranean Magda and Ruggero are exchanging thoughts about their first meeting and present happiness. But their money is running out. Ruggero is not unduly worried; he says that he has written to his mother for her consent to their marriage and he paints an idyllic picture of his home in the country. Magda is horrified, for Ruggero knows nothing of her past. She goes into the pavilion as Prunier and Lisette arrive. The girl is in an uncontrollable state of nerves: Prunier had tried to make her a music-hall singer, but her début had been disastrous. Magda greets them and gladly agrees to take Lisette once more into service. Prunier delivers a message from Rambaldo: he is ready to welcome her back on any terms. As Lisette goes to resume her duties Prunier leaves, but not before asking to know her evenings off. Magda is joined by Ruggero, joyfully brandishing his mother's reply: she is delighted that her son has found a virtuous bride and looks forward to meeting her. Heartbroken, Magda declares that she can never be Ruggero's wife. Their last, anguished duet ('Ma come puoi lasciarmi') takes the form of a cabaletta with orchestral peroration over a vocal 'parlante'; Ruggero collapses in tears, while Magda, supported by Lisette, makes her way slowly out of his life.

* * *

In its musical organization *La rondine* follows a characteristic Puccinian motivic pattern in which there is more room than usual for extended melodies, that are in turn often broken down into recurring motifs. Second Empire Paris is evoked by frequent waltz rhythms of the slower French rather than the Viennese variety; but there are also occasional hints of more modern dances such as the tango, one-step and even (in the lovers' duet in Act 2 'Perche mai cercate') the slow foxtrot. The large orchestral forces are delicately handled, and a number of harmonic audacities worthy of *La fanciulla del West* (unrelated parallel chords, moments of bitonality, unresolved dissonances) merely add piquancy to a score of unusual elegance. The main musical weight is thrown into Act 2, where two of the waltz themes are combined vertically, and whose concertato remains the lyrical pinnacle of the opera. In Act 3 the level of invention falls, probably because the theme of renunciation failed to fire Puccini's dramatic instinct. Hence, perhaps, the opera's virtual exclusion from the repertory.

JULIAN BUDDEN

Rondò (It.). A term that has come to signify a type of two-tempo aria that became popular in the late 18th century, and which refers both to a musical form and to its content (*see* ARIA, §2). As a form, the rondò begins with an opening slow section, often laid out in an *ABA* pattern, which gives way to a faster section, and its text, in which a new theme is established (sometimes a variation of the opening section's *A* theme). The main themes of either the fast or slow sections (or both) are usually assigned 'gavotte' rhythms, and sometimes the main theme of a rondò's slow section, and its text, will recur in the aria's second half. In the opera, these arias are generally assigned only to the prima donna or primo uomo and strategically placed close to the concluding scene or to the final number of a three-act opera's second act.

Early instances of the rondò emerged during the 1760s and 70s in the operas of such composers as J. C. Bach, Baldassare Galuppi, Niccolò Piccinni and Traetta, with later examples from composers like Cimarosa, Mozart, Paisiello and Sarti. Rondò arias from among Mozart's late works include both settings of the text, 'Non temer, amato bene', one (K490) written for the Vienna première of *Idomeneo*, the other (K505) for the independent *scena*, 'Ch'io mi scordi di te?'. Equally striking is 'Per pietà, ben mio' (*Così fan tutte*), and the two arias 'Deh, per questo istante solo' and 'Non più di fiori' (*La clemenza di Tito*).

In contemporary practice, the term 'rondò' was often used loosely, along with the designations 'rondo' and 'rondeau', terms frequently applied to what is now identified as the vocal rondo with a recurring theme in the tonic key that creates the basic pattern *ABACA*. Arias identified by any of these terms tend to express moments of high emotional intensity, unless singled out for a specific comic effect, as with Mozart's rondo 'Ha! wie will ich triumphieren' (*Die Entführung aus dem Serail*) or his rondò 'Bester Jüngling' (*Der Schauspieldirektor*). This special usage, coupled with the tendency of the theme of the slow section of the rondò to recur in a new guise in the fast section, suggests a link between the rondo and the rondò, a closeness that is strengthened by the practice of casting the episodes of the rondo in a new tempo (Mozart's 'Io ti lascio', K255) or by bringing back the main theme of the first section of a two-tempo rondò as a partial quotation in the second half, both in the tonic key and at the original slow tempo. Such is the case with Mozart's *Ah non sai qual pena* K416, an aria to which he referred both as a 'rondò' and a 'rondeau'. 18th-century usage also suggests that a two-tempo aria could attain 'rondò' (or 'rondeau') status through content alone. Both *Per pietà, non ricercate* K420 and *Aura, che intorno spiri* K431 are identified by their composer as 'rondeau' arias (the former designated a 'rondo' on the autograph), yet neither complies in all respects to the formal specifications of the rondò given above. Nor does 'Non mi dir' (*Don Giovanni*), an unquestioned rondò of profound emotional content assigned to the tragic heroine immediately before the opera's last finale.

Since 'rondò' identified an aria of special distinction, composers were not above appealing to the vanity of their singers by assigning the term to arias that were clearly not rondòs in either form, content or placement. In 19th-century opera, the form of the rondò became modified and its musical content expanded, the term itself often being applied loosely to any second-act aria for a principal singer in a two-act opera.

*

E. Arteaga: *Le rivoluzioni del teatro musicale italiano* (Bologna and Venice, 1783–8), iii, 194ff

N. E. Framery: *Encyclopédie methodique*, i (Paris, 1791)

D. Heartz: 'Mozart and his Italian Contemporaries: "La clemenza di Tito"', *MJb 1978–9*, 275–93; also in D. Heartz: *Mozart's Operas* (Berkeley, 1990), 299–317 [with T. Bauman]

H. Lühning: 'Die Rondo-Arie im späten 18. Jahrhundert: dramatischer Gehalt und musikalischer Bau', *HJbMw*, v (1981), 219–46

J. Rice: 'Rondò vocali di Salieri e Mozart per Adriana Ferraresi', *I vicini di Mozart: Florence 1987*, 185–209

S. Balthazar: 'Ritorni's *Ammaestramenti* and the Conventions of Rossinian Melodramma', *Journal of Musicological Reasearch*, viii (1988–9), 281–311

D. Neville: 'Mozart's *Scena* 'Ch'io mi scordi di te' and the Mozartian Rondò', *Mozart: Adelaide 1991*

——: 'The Rondò in Mozart's Late Operas', *Mozart: 200 Years of Research and Analysis: Hofstra University, NY, 1991*

J. Platoff: '"Non tardar amato bene" Completed – but not by Mozart', *MT*, cxxxii (1991), 557–60

DON NEVILLE

Ronga, Luigi (*b* Turin, 19 June 1901; *d* Rome, 11 Nov 1983). Italian musicologist. After taking an arts degree at the University of Turin he studied musicology at Dresden. On his return to Italy he taught music history at Palermo Conservatory and in Rome before being appointed lecturer (1938) and professor (1958) at the University of Rome, where he taught until 1971. He was president of the Istituto Italiano per la Storia della Musica and a member of several academies. His early period abroad afforded him contact with German musicology and he acquired a grounding unusual for Italian musicologists of his generation. He wrote extensively on opera.

Per la critica wagneriana (Turin, 1928)
Rossini (Florence, 1939)
Il dramma musicale di Richard Wagner (Rome, 1947)
Introduzione a 'La Diana schernita' di Cornacchioli (Rome, 1961)
La musica europea nella seconda metà dell'ottocento (Rome, 1961)

CAROLYN GIANTURCO

Ronnefeld, Peter (*b* Dresden, 26 Jan 1935; *d* Kiel, 6 Aug 1965). German composer. He studied with Blacher and others at the Berlin Musikhochschule and then with Messiaen at the Paris Conservatoire. In 1955 he won first prize in the Hilversum Conducting Competition; he taught in Salzburg and was also assistant to Dorati and Wallberg at the Salzburg festivals. Between 1958 and 1961 he was Karajan's assistant at the Vienna Staatsoper. He was then chief conductor at the Theater der Stadt, Bonn (1961–3), and finally Generalmusikdirektor in Kiel. His chamber opera *Die Nachtausgabe* ('opera piccola', 5 scenes, to his own libretto; 30 August 1956, Salzburg), the opera *Die Ameise* (4, R. Bletschacher and Ronnefeld; 21 October 1961, Düsseldorf) and two ballets are among his most notable works; they display a forceful character through advanced compositional technique and a brilliant use of stylistic parody.

MONIKA LICHTENFELD

Ronzi De Begnis [neé Ronzi], **Giuseppina** (*b* Milan, 11 Jan 1800; *d* Florence, 7 June 1853). Italian soprano. She made her début at Bologna in 1816 and in the same year married the bass Giuseppe De Begnis. The following season she appeared at Genoa, Florence and Bergamo.

In 1818 she sang Ninetta (*La gazza ladra*) at Pesaro. From 1819 to 1822 she appeared at the Théâtre Italien, Paris, where she sang Rosina in the first Paris performance of *Il barbiere di Siviglia* (1819). She made her London début at the King's Theatre in 1821 in *Il turco in Italia*. Having sung in a concert performance of *Mosè in Egitto* at Covent Garden (1822), she took part in a staged version of the work (given as *Pietro l'eremita*) at the King's later that year. During 1823 she sang in *La donna del lago* and *Matilde di Shabran*.

In 1825 Ronzi De Begnis returned to Italy, and was engaged at Naples. There she sang in the premières of Mercadante's *Zaira* (1831) and of Donizetti's *Fausta* and *Sancia di Castiglia* (1832), *Maria Stuarda* (under the title of *Buondelmonte*, 1834) and *Roberto Devereux* (1837). She also created the title role in *Gemma di Vergy* at La Scala (1834), and sang in *Anna Bolena*, *Parisina*, *Belisario* and *Pia de' Tolomei*. Having sung Giulietta in Zingarelli's *Giulietta e Romeo*, she took the role of Romeo in Bellini's *I Capuleti e i Montecchi*. Her repertory also included *Beatrice di Tenda* and *Norma*, which she sang in English at Covent Garden in 1843. She had great facility of execution and was a spirited actress. A fine Mozart singer, she excelled as Donna Anna.

ELIZABETH FORBES

Rooke [O'Rourke, Rourke]**, William Michael** (*b* Dublin, 29 Sept 1794; *d* London, 14 Oct 1847). Irish composer. He was almost completely self-taught. In 1813 he took to music as a profession, learnt counterpoint and became a violin and piano teacher; among his violin pupils was Balfe. In 1817 he was appointed chorus master and deputy leader at the theatre in Crow Street, Dublin.

Rooke composed his first opera, *Amilie, or The Love Test*, in 1818, and in 1821 he moved to England. The next year he had a musical play given at Drury Lane Theatre. In 1826 he was leading oratorios at Birmingham; that year he also sought the post of chorus master at Drury Lane under Tom Cooke. He was leader at Vauxhall Gardens (1830–33) under Bishop, and established himself as a singing teacher as well. *Amilie* was at last put on at Covent Garden on 2 December 1837, with decided success. He immediately started work on a second opera, and on 2 May 1839 Covent Garden produced *Henrique, or The Love Pilgrim*, which, though favourably received, was withdrawn after five performances because of an argument with Macready, the theatre manager, who had little patience with or respect for musicians.

Amilie, or The Love Test, 1818 (3, J. T. Haines), London, CG, 2 Dec 1837 (London, 1837)
The Pirate (musical play, W. Dimond, after W. Scott), London, Drury Lane, 15 Jan 1822
Henrique, or The Love Pilgrim (3, Haines), London, CG, 2 May 1839
Cagliostro, unperf.
The Valkyrie, ?unperf.

*

DNB (L. M. Middleton)
W. C. Macready: *Reminiscences*, ed. F. Pollock (London, 1875), i, 426–7 [5 and 7 Aug 1837]
——: *Diaries*, ed. W. Toynbee (London, 1912), i, 418ff [21–7 Dec 1837], 491 [18 Jan 1839]

Rooker, Michael Angelo (*b* London, 1743; *d* London, 3 March 1801). English scene painter. Born Michael Rooker, he was the son of Edward Rooker, a famous harlequin at Drury Lane. Paul Sandby instructed him in drawing and landscape painting. He was a scene painter at the Little Theatre in the Haymarket under George Colman the elder and later under the younger, 1779–97; when he lost his job there, reportedly because he refused to help with the manager's debts, his health was affected. Rooker's work on comic operas was confined to the music of Samuel Arnold, beginning with *Summer Amusement* (1779); the last solo work was *Auld Robin Gray* (1794), though he collaborated with Marinari on *Zorinski* (1795). For *The Battle of Hexham* (1789) he supplied nine scenes, of which one, for a camp, is in Paul Mellon's collection at Upperville, Virginia (reproduced in Rosenfeld 1981). It shows three tents and a wagon in the foreground with a range of tents in mountainous country in the background. A critic remarked (*Biographica dramatica*, 1812, ii, p.261) that one of his scenes for *Fire and Water* (1780), representing a camp in St James's Park, 'was perhaps as accurate and masterly a spectacle as ever appeared on the more extensive stages of Covent Garden and Drury Lane'. Of Arnold's *The Surrender of Calais* (1791) it was written: 'the new scenery by Rooker affords undeniable evidence of the superior powers of his pencil; particularly the view of the English camp without the walls of Calais, which forms a striking *coup d'oeil*' (*Lady's Magazine*, August 1791, pp.243–5). Rooker was praised for his attention to correctness of detail and 'distinctions of situation, time, costume and architecture' (*Thespian Magazine*, September 1793, p.214) in *The Mountaineers* (1793). He was a pioneer in the field of naturalism, and some of his scenery equalled that of Loutherbourg. The British Museum possesses a remarkable watercolour of him at work (see illustration).

*

S. Rosenfeld and E. Croft-Murray: 'A Checklist of Scene Painters Working in Great Britain and Ireland in the 18th Century (4)', *Theatre Notebook* , xix (1964–5), 133–45, esp. 144–5
S. Rosenfeld: 'A Georgian Scene-Painter at Work', *British Museum Quarterly*, xxxiv (1969–70), 33–6
——: *Georgian Scene Painters and Scene Painting* (Cambridge, 1981)

SYBIL ROSENFELD

Rooy, Anton(ius Maria Josephus) van (*b* Rotterdam, 1 Jan 1870; *d* Munich, 28 Nov 1932). Dutch bass-baritone. He studied singing in Frankfurt with Julius Stockhausen, and made his début at Bayreuth in 1897, singing Wotan at every festival until 1902, and adding the roles of Hans Sachs in 1899 and the Dutchman in 1901. His outstanding gifts were instantly recognized; and he appeared at Covent Garden in the leading Wagner roles every year but one from 1898 to 1913, and at the Metropolitan every year but one from 1898 to 1908. Having consented to sing Amfortas in the unauthorized New York *Parsifal* of 1903, he was thenceforth banned at Bayreuth. He also took part in several non-Wagner operas, and in 1907 was John the Baptist in the American première of *Salome*. For over a decade he was the unchallenged leading exponent of all the leading Wagner roles, especially Wotan, Sachs and the Dutchman. Latterly he also sang at Frankfurt. He retired in 1913, and thereafter lived in Munich. Despite primitive studio technique, brief recorded excerpts from his leading roles allow us to glimpse the noble tone and grandeur of declamation that made him a supreme Wagner interpreter.

*

L. Hevingham-Root: 'The London Red G&Ts of 1902: Anton van Rooy', *Record Collector*, xiii (1960–61), 23–8

DESMOND SHAWE-TAYLOR

Watercolour drawing by Michael Angelo Rooker depicting the artist at work on a backdrop in the scene room at the Little Theatre in the Haymarket, London: Rooker is shown working on a landscape in a scene frame, a particularly English method in which the frame was let down through a slot in the floor to enable the upper part of the cloth to be painted

Ropartz, Joseph Guy (**Marie**) [Guy-Ropartz, Joseph] (*b* Guingamp, Côtes du Nord, 15 June 1864; *d* Lanloup, Côtes du Nord, 22 Nov 1955). French composer. He studied law at Rennes, but then decided on a musical career, entering the Paris Conservatoire to study composition with Dubois and later Massenet. In 1886 he was deeply impressed by d'Indy's *Le chant de la cloche* and left the Conservatoire to study with Franck. He remained faithful to Franck and his teaching, but despite this unquestionable influence there is an individual character in Ropartz's output. In 1894 he was appointed director of the conservatory in Nancy, where he brought about a musical renaissance; he left in 1919 to undertake a similar task in Strasbourg. He retired to his native Brittany in 1929; in 1949 he was made a member of the Institut in succession to Hahn.

Ropartz's music draws upon Celtic folklore, although both his major stage works are set in Iceland. The first, *Pêcheur d'Islande* (1893), is extended incidental music, including some singing, for a play by Pierre Loti and Louis Tiercelin. Charles Le Goffic's *L'islandaise* formed the basis of his three-act opera *Le pays* (1910), first given in Nancy on 3 February 1912. It concerns Tual, a Breton sailor (tenor), shipwrecked in Iceland; he falls in love with an Icelandic girl Kaethe (soprano) but hankers both for his native land and for a girl he left behind. Passionate and Franckian, the music aptly mirrors the intense nostalgia that is at the heart of the action. There is also an unpublished comic opera, *Le diable couturier* (1, Tiercelin; 1893, Paris).

*

'Guy Ropartz, de Séverac, Canteloube', *Le théâtre lyrique en France* (Paris, 1937–9), iii, 128–37 [pubn of Poste National/Radio-Paris]
F. Lamy: *Joseph Guy-Ropartz* (Paris, 1948)
L. Kornprobst: *J. Guy Ropartz* (Strasbourg, 1949)

ARTHUR HOÉRÉE, RICHARD LANGHAM SMITH

Roqueplan, Nestor (*b* Montréal, France, 14 Sept 1805; *d* Paris, 24 April 1870). French journalist and theatre director. After law studies, he joined the staff of *Le Figaro* as a theatre critic. He wrote for a number of other papers before taking up the directorship of the Théâtre des Variétés in 1841, a post he occupied until 1847 when he became co-director of the Opéra with Charles Duponchel. Duponchel withdrew from the association in 1849, leaving Roqueplan as sole director until 1854. The two most important premières during his tenure were Verdi's *Jérusalem* (1847) and Meyerbeer's *Le prophète* (1849), though the first of these was not very successful. In 1851 Roqueplan also oversaw Gounod's début with *Sapho*. Later, as director of the Opéra-Comique from 1857 to 1860, he gave Meyerbeer's *Le pardon de Ploërmel*; the success of that work did not rescue him from severe financial troubles and, abandoning opera production, he turned to music journalism in the last decade of his life, becoming a well-known figure in fashionable boulevard society during the Second Empire. STEVEN HUEBNER

Rorem, Ned (*b* Richmond, IN, 23 Oct 1923). American composer. He first gained recognition as a song composer and, although his more recent awards have been for non-vocal symphonic works, roughly half his output consists of sung music: about three hundred early songs, a dozen cycles, profane and sacred choral pieces of every shape, and seven operas. Rorem, whose knack for limning a gracious vocal line is undeniable, contends that song specialists cannot automatically turn out good operas any more than opera composers can turn out true songs: a gift for tune and a gift for tragedy do not always join hands. Over the years he has spawned at least four mini-dramas that fall into neither camp, most recently *Anna la bonne* (1989), a scena in French written to mark the centenary of Cocteau's birth. Yet if his drive veers more towards the concert hall than the theatre, Rorem's lyric pieces for the stage are explicitly for that medium, not garlands of airs sewn together.

A Childhood Miracle, 1951 (1, E. Stein, after N. Hawthorne: *The Snow Image*), New York, 1955
The Robbers (1, Rorem, rev. M. Blitzstein, after G. Chaucer: *The Pardoner's Tale*), New York, Mannes College, 14 April 1958
Miss Julie (2, K. Elmslie, after A. Strindberg), New York, City Opera, 4 Nov 1965; rev. (1), New York, 1979
Bertha, 1968 (1, K. Koch), New York, Alice Tully Hall, 26 Nov 1973
Fables (5 very short operas, after J. de la Fontaine, trans. M. Moore), Martin, TN, 21 May 1971
Three Sisters who are Not Sisters, 1968 (3, G. Stein), Philadelphia, Temple U., 24 July 1971
Hearing (1, J. Holmes, after Koch), New York, Christ and St Stephens Church, 15 March 1977

*

E. R. Rizzo: 'Strindberg in Song', *ON*, xxx/3 (1965–6), 20–21 [Rorem's *Miss Julie*]
P. O'Connor: 'Ned Rorem at 65', *ON*, liii/4 (1988–9), 24–6, 70
JAMES HOLMES

Rosa [Rose], **Carl** [Karl] (**August Nikolaus**) (*b* Hamburg, 22 March 1842; *d* Paris, 30 April 1889). German impresario and conductor. At the age of 12 he toured England, Denmark and Germany as a violinist. After studies (from 1859) at the conservatories in Leipzig and Paris he was Konzertmeister in Hamburg (1863–5). In 1866 he went to London and appeared as a soloist, then went on a concert tour of the USA, where he met and married (1867) the soprano Euphrosyne Parepa. His wife's success in opera led to the formation of a company under Rosa's management and conductorship which in its early seasons included Wachtel, Santley, Ronconi and Formes. Early in 1871 the Rosas returned to England, then visited Egypt for reasons of health; they returned again to London, but Euphrosyne died almost immediately, on 21 January 1874. Rosa, however, was resolved to test the fortunes of opera in English in London; on 11 September 1875 the CARL ROSA OPERA COMPANY opened its first season at the Princess's Theatre with *The Marriage of Figaro*, with Rosa conducting. Between 1876 and 1882 his opera seasons in London and the provinces were noteworthy for the careful manner in which repertory was chosen, rehearsed and mounted. In addition to the premières of British works, the company staged the first performances in English of works by Wagner, Verdi and other composers. In 1883 Rosa became associated with Augustus Harris, manager of the Theatre Royal, Drury Lane, and a prosperous five years for the company followed.

Rosa bianca e la rosa rossa, La ('The White Rose and the Red Rose'). *Melodramma eroico* in two acts by SIMON MAYR to a libretto by FELICE ROMANI after RENÉ CHARLES GUILBERT DE PIXÉRÉCOURT's libretto *La rose blanche et la rose rouge*; Genoa, Teatro S Agostino, 21 February 1813.

Set at the conclusion of the War of the Roses, the opera centres on a love triangle involving Enrico (soprano), Count of Derby and a banished member of the defeated Red Roses, his beloved Clotilde (soprano) and his friend and clandestine rival Vanoldo (tenor), Count of Seymour and a partisan of the victorious White Roses. Clotilde's father, Rodolfo (bass), Sire of Mortimer, who is allied with the Red Roses, has arranged by royal decree for Vanoldo to marry Clotilde in order to unite the feuding factions. When Enrico disrupts the wedding ceremony he is jailed and sentenced to death. Guilty over his role in his friend's downfall, Vanoldo decides to help him escape by exchanging clothing with him and taking his place in prison. Their ruse delays the execution long enough for a royal pardon to be obtained, and Rodolfo allows Enrico to marry Clotilde.

La rosa was extraordinarily successful at its première and remained popular for the next 20 years, receiving performances across Italy as well as in Munich (1817), Lisbon (1822), Paris (1823), Madrid (1824) and London (1828). It demonstrates Mayr's ability to construct long, unconventional numbers, as in the enormous Act 1 finale, and his skill at exploiting unusual dramatic opportunities, as in Clotilde's 'coro e cavatina' in the same act, when Enrico appears disguised as a member of the peasant chorus and presents a bouquet to his lover during her aria. The Act 2 duet for Enrico and Vanoldo, 'E deserto il bosco intorno', published by Ricordi, became one of Mayr's most famous operatic excerpts. SCOTT L. BALTHAZAR

Rosales, Antonio (*b* Madrid, *c*1740; *d* Madrid, 1801). Spanish composer. He was chiefly a composer of *tonadillas*, of which he wrote at least 150, the first dating from 1762, the last from 1791. His first success as a zarzuela composer came on 28 November 1767, when the one-act *burlesca El tío y la tía* (Ramón de la Cruz, excerpt in *E-Mn*, score in *E-Mm*) was staged in Madrid at the Teatro de la Cruz. In 1769 he was made *músico secundario* by the Madrid theatre company manager Manuel Martínez, and on 1 July 1776 his one-act zarzuela *El licenciado Farfulla*, also to a libretto by Cruz, had its première at the Teatro del Príncipe. This popular work, which was sung everywhere in Spain until 1813, mixed Spanish folk airs with dances such as the *jácara*, *folía*, seguidilla and *coplas de caballo*. About 1787 he succeeded Rodríguez de Hita as *maestro de capilla* of the royal Encarnación convent at Madrid. 149 *tonadillas* by him are at the Biblioteca Municipal in Madrid; one, *El recitado* (*c*1775), lampooning Italian recitative, was edited by Subirá (Madrid, 1930).

According to Ramón de la Cruz, Rosales composed

with extreme speed and captured the public by incorporating street songs of the day in his stage works. The topical subject matter of his *tonadillas* was kept fresh by the dialogue's being constantly changed to stay abreast of the latest news. Rosales also composed *entremeses* and *sainetes*; 13 of the latter survive (in *E-Mm*), the earliest dated 1763.

selective list; all tonadillas and in E-Mm

El cuento de la visita, 6 April 1774; La huevera, 25 Feb 1775; Los toros, 27 April 1775; Las mañas del amor, 22 June 1775; El ponderado, 15 Sept 1775; El majo reconvenido, 6 Feb 1776; La enhorabuena, 29 April 1776; El sueño de las comparsas, 6 June 1776; El terno, 5 Aug 1776; Las pasiegas, 19 Aug 1776; La modista, 30 Sept 1776; La manchega, 10 Oct 1776; La visita, 3 Jan 1777; El mundi novo, 13 July 1777; La buena pesca, 24 April 1778; El paneque, 22 May 1778; El mayordomo y la mayordoma, 5 June 1778; La noche de San Juan, 25 June 1778; La marcialité, 5 Oct 1778

*

F. Pedrell: *Diccionario biográfico y bibliográfico de músicos y escritores de música españoles, portugueses e hispano-americanos*, i (Barcelona, 1894), 447–8 [Ramón de la Cruz's apology for the licentiousness of *El licenciado Farfulla*]
J. Subirá: *La tonadilla escénica*, iii (Madrid, 1930), 54–64, [86]–[103]
——: *Tonadillas teatrales inéditas, librettos y partituras* (Madrid, 1932), 231, 234, 253, 255, 257
E. Cotarelo y Mori: *Historia de la zarzuela* (Madrid, 1934)
F. Asenjo Barbieri: *Documentos sobre música española y epistolario (Legado Barbieri)*, ed. E. Casares (Madrid, 1988), 1158ff

ROBERT STEVENSON

Rosalie, Mlle. *See* LEVASSEUR, ROSALIE.

Rosamond. Opera in three acts by THOMAS CLAYTON to a libretto by JOSEPH ADDISON; London, Theatre Royal, Drury Lane, 4 March 1707.

Rosamond was planned as the first truly English all-sung opera, with a story drawn from English folk history linked to the current military triumphs of the Duke of Marlborough (it was 'Humbly Inscrib'd to Her Grace the Dutchess of Marlborough'). King Henry (countertenor; originally sung by Francis Hughes), returning from war, visits his mistress Rosamond (soprano; Maria Gallia) in her secret bower in Woodstock Park. The jealous Queen Eleanor (soprano; Catherine Tofts) offers Rosamond death by dagger or poison, and Rosamond drinks from the poisoned bowl. Meanwhile the sleeping king sees a vision of future British military glories (and of Marlborough's Blenheim Palace arising at Woodstock) and resolves to put honour before love. He is reconciled to the queen, who reveals that Rosamond was only drugged and is now in a nunnery. The opera ends with a celebration of conjugal love. A low-comic commentary is provided by Sir Trusty ('principal Pimp to the mighty King Harry', bass; Richard Leveridge), who squabbles with his elderly wife Grideline (contralto; Mary Lindsey) and attempts suicide by drinking from the 'poisoned' bowl.

Much was expected of the opera, and six days after the première John Walsh published *Songs in the New Opera Call'd Rosamond*. However, the work was an embarrassing failure, receiving only three subscription performances. Clayton's banal music received no praise except for a puff in the *Muses Mercury* and has since been held responsible for the failure, but Addison's rather laboured libretto must share the blame. The heroine disappears after Act 2, and the strongly pro-Marlborough sentiments antagonized the Tories in the audience.

OLIVE BALDWIN, THELMA WILSON

Rosamunde. Singspiel in three acts by ANTON SCHWEITZER to a libretto by CHRISTOPH MARTIN WIELAND after a story in JOSEPH ADDISON's *Spectator*; Mannheim, Nationaltheater, 20 January 1780.

Queen Elinor (soprano) learns that her husband Henry (tenor) is keeping a beautiful mistress, Rosamunde (soprano), in the labyrinth of the castle. In his absence the queen forces her to drink poison, but in its place a faithful servant substitutes a sleeping draught. On his return Henry banishes Elinor. At the coronation of Rosamunde, Elinor bursts in and stabs the new queen to death.

The text and music of *Rosamunde* were completed in 1777; Mozart, who was visiting Mannheim at the time, attended and even conducted rehearsals in December that year. Originally in five acts, Wieland's libretto was heavily revised under severe criticism. The death of the Elector of Bavaria in December forced the cancellation of the première, planned for January 1778. The Elector Palatine, Carl Theodor, who had commissioned the work, left for Munich and all performances for the carnival season were cancelled; the opera was not produced until two years later. Despite the passionate presence of Elinor (who owes something to Asberta in Holzbauer's *Günther von Schwarzburg*; both roles were sung by Barbara Strasser), Schweitzer's music differs little from that of his *Alceste* (1773). G. J. Vogler found it unvocal and overwrought.

THOMAS BAUMAN

Rosand, Ellen (*b* New York, 28 Feb 1940). American musicologist. She studied at Vassar College (BA 1961), Harvard (MA 1964) and New York University (PhD 1971: *Aria in the Early Operas of Francesco Cavalli*). She taught at Brooklyn and Hunter colleges, New York, between 1971 and 1977, and at Rutgers University from 1977. A prolific writer on Venetian opera, Rosand has published substantial and rigorously researched articles on aspects of Monteverdi operas, for example treating of Seneca (*L'incoronazione*) and Irus (*Ulisse*), and on such broad issues as the libretto, the scenario, the lament and madness in early Venetian opera, as well as a major study, *Opera in Seventeenth-Century Venice* (Berkeley and Los Angeles, 1991).

Rosaura [*La Rosaura*]. *Dramma per musica* in three acts by GIACOMO ANTONIO PERTI to a libretto by ANTONIO ARCOLEO; Venice, Teatro S Angelo, Carnival 1689.

Set in a vague 'Persia', the plot interweaves emotional triangles alternately in 'high' drama and comedy. The *buffo* character of the servant Gilbo (soprano) establishes a confidential relationship with the audience by innuendo and allusion, but the principal characters also contribute to the comic element. Rosaura (soprano) is in love with Gelindo (alto), eventually revealed as her lost brother Ramiro; the danger of incest remains as backdrop to the pseudo-historical framework of the comedy until the final recognition scene. In Act 2 Ersilla (soprano), daughter of the satrap Arsace (bass), welcomes to the court her lover Fidauro (soprano), disguised as a maidservant, with whom Gelindo immediately falls in love. In Act 3 Fidauro reveals the fact of his marriage to Ersilla; with Feraspe (soprano), Rosaura's unrequited lover, Arsace organizes a coup at whose height the identities of Fidauro, Feraspe (in reality Arsace's son) and Gelindo are revealed. Rosaura gives her hand to Feraspe, and the opera ends with a general reassertion of the political situation and a unison chorus praising Cupid.

The structure of the opera follows the lines usual in the period immediately preceding the Arcadian reform: there are some 50 'closed numbers', fewer than in most scores of the time; the majority are da capo arias with continuo or single-instrument obbligato, and with semi-regular versification. In general the text is not favourable to repetition, with rare exceptions (3.xiii: 'Barbaro, perfido, Amor non è'); elsewhere formal expansion is achieved by extending the ritornellos (3.xii: 'La speranza non ci tradì'). The few duets are conceived as 'arias for two voices'. Arias are frequent at the beginning of scenes, and effective use is made of two arias for the same character, separated by a short recitative, in Act 3, scene xiv; the vivid characterization of 'Mie giuste furie' (3.xi) with tremolo figures and agile passages most convincingly justifies the unrealistic coup of Act 3. Male roles other than Arsace were probably sung by castratos. Bonlini stated that *Rosaura* underwent some slight changes in arias in later editions, but a complete collation of the sources has yet to be made.

SERGIO DURANTE

Rosbaud, Hans (*b* Graz, 22 July 1895; *d* Lugano, 29 Dec 1962). Austrian conductor. He studied with Alfred Hoehn and Bernhard Sekles at the Hoch Conservatory, Frankfurt, and from his first appointment as director of the Städtische Musikschule at Mainz he showed enthusiasm for contemporary music, which he championed throughout his career. He became associated in particular with the music of Schoenberg, Berg, Webern, Bartók and Stravinsky, whose works he performed with considerable feeling and penetrating insight; he also conducted Mozart operas at Aix-en-Provence, though, some felt, with a lack of warmth and sentiment. In 1954, replacing Schmidt-Isserstedt, he conducted the première of Schoenberg's *Moses und Aron* for Hamburg radio (a performance later issued as the opera's first gramophone recording), and also its first stage production in Zürich in 1957. At the 1958 Holland Festival he conducted a highly praised double bill of Schoenberg's *Erwartung* and *Von heute auf morgen*. His performances were distinguished by intellectual strength and severe functional style, matched by a fine musicality.

GERHARD BRUNNER

Rose, Jürgen (*b* Bernburg, 25 Aug 1937). German stage designer. After studying acting and painting in Berlin, he was the principal designer for John Cranko at the Stuttgart Ballet (1962–73). He also designed ballets for the Deutsche Oper, Berlin, the National Ballet of Canada and the choreographer John Neumeier. His first important opera commission was *Don Carlos* (1970, Vienna) for Otto Schenk; other Schenk productions have included *Simon Boccanegra* (1971, Munich), *Der Rosenkavalier* (1972, Munich; 1976, La Scala), a luxuriously costumed *Così fan tutte* (1972, Deutsche Oper) and a naturalistic *Die Meistersinger* (1976, Vienna). He has also designed operas for Peter Beauvais (*Lucia di Lammermoor*, 1971, Hamburg), Boleslav Barlog (an *art nouveau Salome*, 1972, Vienna), Götz Friedrich (*Tannhäuser*, 1972, Bayreuth), August Everding (*Lohengrin*, 1977, Hamburg) and Dieter Dorn (*Die Entführung aus dem Serail*, 1979, Vienna), as well as for Günther Rennert, Rudolf Noelte and Giancarlo del Monaco. Rose is admired for his sumptuous costumes and for the painterly quality of his pictorial sets, which reveal a particular interest in *Jugendstil*; at the same time, he has designed successfully for the spare, often minimal requirements of contemporary opera. One measure of his stature is the longevity of his work, which often survives several revivals of a production.

For illustration *see* YUN, ISANG. DAVID J. HOUGH

Roselle, Anne [Gyenge, Anna] (*b* Budapest, 20 March 1894). Hungarian soprano. She grew up in the USA. Following her début in Budapest in 1915, she returned to New York, appearing first at the Strand Theatre and then in 1920 at the Metropolitan Opera, where she made her début as Musetta. Her career flourished with Antonio Scotti's touring company and when she joined the Dresden Staatsoper (1925). Her great triumph there was as Turandot in the German première of 1926; she repeated the part at Verona (1928) and with limited success at Covent Garden (1934). Her previous appearance in London had been as Donna Anna in 1929, when her performance gained strength during the course of the opera. A more substantial achievement was her singing of Marie in the first American performance of *Wozzeck* under Stokowski in 1931 at Philadelphia, where she later returned to teach. Her few recordings include two of Turandot's solos, in which her warm tone suits 'Del primo pianto' very well and 'In questa reggia' hardly at all.

J. B. STEANE

Rosen, David (*b* San Francisco, 21 Sept 1938). American musicologist. He studied at Reed College, Portland, at Columbia University and under Kerman at the University of California, Berkeley (PhD 1976). His main teaching positions have been at Brandeis University (1972–5), the University of Wisconsin, Madison (1976–89), and thereafter at Cornell. Rosen has written perceptively on Mozart, but his operatic interests centre on Verdi, whose Requiem he edited for the collected edition (1990); he has worked on the early operas and *Don Carlos* and is co-editor (with A. Porter) of *Verdi's 'Macbeth': a Sourcebook* (New York, 1984).

Rosen, Georgy Fyodorovich. *See* ROZEN, YEGOR FYODOROVICH.

Rosenberg, Hilding (Constantin) (*b* Bosjökloster, Ringsjön, Skåne, 21 June 1892; *d* Stockholm, 19 May 1985). Swedish composer. In 1915 he entered the Royal Academy of Music, Stockholm, to study composition and conducting; later he studied counterpoint with Wilhelm Stenhammar and conducting with Scherchen. In 1926 he began a long and fruitful association with the theatre director Per Lindberg, and in 1932 was appointed coach and assistant conductor at the Royal Opera, Stockholm, becoming chief conductor in 1934. Subsequently, as a result of commissions from Swedish radio, he concentrated increasingly on composition, though he continued to make guest appearances conducting his own works in Scandinavia and the USA (1948). He also exerted a great influence on Swedish musical life as a teacher, his pupils including Blomdahl and Bäck.

Rosenberg is held by many to be the leading figure in 20th-century Swedish music. During the 1920s he was a pioneer in the effort to free Swedish composition from the national Romantic tradition. His earliest works reveal the influence of Sibelius, but he was soon experimenting with various styles displaying diverse models; in Sweden he was regarded as an extreme radical. A tour of Europe in 1920 brought him into contact with the music of Schoenberg, Stravinsky and Hindemith. From early childhood he had been familiar with Lutheran chorales and Gregorian chant, and this, combined with his eager acceptance of Hindemith's principles and his studies of Bach, formed a foundation for his fine contrapuntal technique.

From 1926 Rosenberg was active in the theatre for more than 25 years, producing incidental music to over 40 plays. His work for the stage gave him the opportunity to experiment and to develop his innate dramatic sense. Several incidental scores gave rise to large-scale works, including the three major operas, *Marionetter* (composed 1938), *Lycksalighetens ö* ('The Isle of Felicity', composed 1943) and *Hus med dubbel ingång* (composed 1969). His first opera, *Resa till Amerika* (1932), was the source of an orchestral suite which incorporates the celebrated 'Railway Fugue'.

During the 1930s Rosenberg made a rapprochement with the public, simplifying his style and using clearer, essentially diatonic harmonies, chromaticism becoming more a melodic embellishment. Among the many successful works which appeared during the later 1930s are the opera *Marionetter* and the ballet *Orfeus i sta'n* ('Orpheus in Town'). The 1940s was a decade of large-scale choral works, reaching a climax in the massive opera-oratorio after Thomas Mann, *Josef och hans bröder* (1946–8), commissioned by Swedish radio; its four parts were broadcast separately, 1946–8.

Resa till Amerika (A. Henriksson), Stockholm, 24 Nov 1932
Spelet om St Örjan, 1937 (children's op); rev. 1941
Marionetter (J. Benavente), Stockholm, 14 Feb 1939
De två konungadöttrarna (children's op, Rosenberg), Stockholm, 19 Sept 1940
Lycksalighetens ö [The Isle of Felicity], 1943 (P. D. A. Atterbom), Stockholm, 1 Feb 1945
Josef och hans bröder, 1946–8 (opera-oratorio, after T. Mann), Swedish radio, Pt 1, 30 May 1946; Pt 2, 19 Dec 1946; Pt 3, 9 Sept 1947; Pt 4, 23 Jan 1948
Kaspers fettisdag [Punch's Shrove Tuesday] (A. Strindberg), Swedish radio, 28 Feb 1954
Porträttet (after N. V. Gogol), Swedish radio, 22 March 1956; rev. 1963
Hus med dubbel ingång (after P. Calderón de la Barca), Stockholm, 24 May 1970

*

H. Rosenberg: 'Lycksalighetens ö', *Musikvärlden*, i/1 (1945), 3
B. Wallner: 'Hilding Rosenberg och teatern', *Operan* (26 Oct 1956)
——: 'Komik, romantik, epik, etik, politik', *Operan 200 år* (Lund, 1973), 140
PETER H. LYNE

Rosenfeld, Gerhard (*b* Königsberg, 10 Feb 1931). German composer. He studied musicology at the Humboldt University, Berlin (1952–4), and composition with Wagner-Régeny at the Hochschule für Musik in Berlin (1954–7) and took part in the masterclasses of Hanns Eisler and Leo Spies at the Akademie der Künste (1958–61). From 1961 to 1964 he held posts in Berlin as librarian and teacher; he then moved to Berghold-Rehbrücke, near Potsdam, to work as a freelance composer. He has received various awards for his compositions, which range from operas, orchestral and chamber music to songs. Since *Das alltägliche Wunder* Rosenfeld has been increasingly concerned with combining tonal music with new methods of composition, and his operas are characterized by dramatic contrast and emotional power. The consistently high quality of his operatic works has resulted in considerable international acclaim.

all librettos by G. Hartmann
Das alltägliche Wunder (3, after J. Schwarz), Stralsund, Stadt, 29 March 1973
Der Mantel (3, after N. V. Gogol), Weimar, Deutsches National, 4 July 1978
Das Spiel von Liebe und Zufall (3, after P. Marivaux), Potsdam, Schloss, 12 Oct 1980
Die Verweigerung (1, after Gogol), Osnabrück, Städtische Bühnen, 26 Nov 1989

Unperf.: Friedrich und Montezuma (3)

*

Musik in der DDR [pubn of the Akademie der Künste], Arbeitsheft 13 (Berlin, 1973), 49–50, 147–8
DIETER HÄRTWIG

Rosenhain, Jacob [Jakob, Jacques] (*b* Mannheim, 2 Dec 1813; *d* Baden-Baden, 21 March 1894). German composer and pianist. He studied with Jakob Schmitt, Kalliwoda and Schnyder von Wartensee, making a successful début in 1832 in Frankfurt; he then took up residence there and had his one-act opera *Der Besuch im Irrenhause* performed in 1834. In 1837 he went to London, where he played in numerous concerts, and then to Paris, where he settled and became a prominent figure. His second one-act opera, *Liswenna*, was staged in 1841, and then a decade later, provided with a new libretto and renamed *Le démon de la nuit*, it was produced at the Opéra, though with limited success. His third and final opera, *Volage et jaloux*, was produced in 1863 at Baden-Baden, where he settled in 1870 and again became the centre of a distinguished artistic circle.

Der Besuch im Irrenhause, oder List um List (komische Oper, 1, J. G. Rhone, after E. Scribe), Frankfurt, 29 Dec 1834
Liswenna, 1836 (1), Paris, 1841; rev. as Le démon de la nuit (2, E. Arago and J. F. A. Bayard), Paris, Opéra, 17 March 1851, vs (Paris, 1854)
Volage et jaloux (oc, 1, T. Sauvage), Baden-Baden, 3 Aug 1863

*

StiegerO
H. R. Schäfer: 'Jakob Rosenhain', *Neue Musik-Zeitung*, xi (1890), 234–5
E. Kratt-Harveng: *Jacques Rosenhain, Komponist und Pianist: ein Lebensbild* (Baden-Baden, 1891)

Rosenkavalier, Der ('The Knight of the Rose'). *Komödie für Musik* in three acts by RICHARD STRAUSS to a libretto by HUGO VON HOFMANNSTHAL; Dresden, Königliches Opernhaus, 26 January 1911.

This might easily have been Strauss's fourth opera, instead of his fifth: even after securing Hofmannsthal's permission to set his *Elektra* play once *Salome* was composed, he worried whether he ought not to seek instead for a romantic comedy. While the *Elektra* opera took shape, composer and author discussed possible next subjects; Hofmannsthal was anxious to develop a collaboration with Strauss (who fancied a lusty Renaissance scenario). Just weeks after their *Elektra* première in early 1909, the writer announced the idea he had found to fulfil their hopes. It was the romantic-farcical plot of our *Rosenkavalier*, ardent young Octavian outwitting gross, lecherous Baron Ochs for the hand of Sophie – but with the figure of the Feldmarschallin (Field Marshal's Wife), or Marschallin, who would come to tilt the balance of the opera radically, still a mere shadow. (From first to last versions, nubile Sophie was never much more than a desirable pawn.) Much of the action was adapted from the novel *Les amours du chevalier de Faublas* by Louvet de Couvray, a contemporary of Beaumarchais; other ideas were drawn from Molière's comedy *Monsieur de Pourceaugnac*, the immediate predecessor of his *Le*

The Feldmarschallin [Marschallin], Marie Thérèse, Princess Werdenberg	soprano
Octavian, Count Rofrano ('Quinquin') *her young lover*	soprano/mezzo-soprano
Mohammed *her black page*	silent
Baron Ochs auf Lerchenau *her cousin*	bass
Sophie von Faninal	soprano
Herr von Faninal *Sophie's rich parvenu father*	baritone
Marianne *her duenna*	soprano
Valzacchi *an intriguer*	tenor
Annina *his niece and partner*	contralto
A Notary	bass
An Italian Singer	tenor
A Flautist, a Cook, a Hairdresser and his assistant, a Scholar, an Innkeeper, a Noble Widow	all silent
Three Noble Orphans	soprano, mezzo-soprano, contralto
A Milliner	soprano
A Vendor of Pets	tenor
Faninal's Major-Domo	tenor
A Police Inspector	bass
The Marschallin's Major-Domo	tenor
Four Lackeys	two tenors, two basses
Four Waiters	one tenor, three basses

Servants, hired deceivers, children, constables

Setting Mid-18th-century Vienna, in the reign of the Empress Maria Theresa

bourgeois gentilhomme which in turn would serve as the springboard for *Ariadne auf Naxos.*

Until six months before the première, the title remained the Baron's own mocking one, 'Ochs auf Lerchenau' – literally, 'ox in the lark-meadow'. (His 'auf' is now often changed without licence to a 'von', which would imply a grander status.) From the start, however, Octavian had been conceived as enjoying a liaison with an aristocratic older woman whom he would leave in order to woo Sophie; and as Hofmannsthal came to draw the Marschallin in depth, with Strauss's warm approval, she grew into one of the great soprano roles. Hofmannsthal dignified her further with the Christian names of the historical empress – as if hinting that she really is the empress, tactfully disguised – and a gracious *levée* befitting a Great Lady. The operatic centre of gravity was displaced from the farce to the *drame des sentiments.* Yet the original plot had no further use for her until the denouement, far into Act 3; and before that, as both authors admitted later, the protracted farce palls. To accommodate both strands, the opera planned as a two-and-a-half-hour light comedy had swollen to three and a quarter hours plus intervals.

The creative collaboration was of the closest – though conducted almost exclusively by correspondence, like every subsequent Strauss-Hofmannsthal project. While the composer insisted upon brisk theatrical effect, the writer stood guard over delicate details of class, propriety and feeling. For this imagined world Hofmannsthal confabulated a marvellous, untranslatable lingo out of Viennese and provincial dialects, frenchified gentility and earthy idioms, antique formal address and pure linguistic fantasy. Strauss not only rose to the prescribed great moments, but invested all the dialogue – sophisticated beyond any purpose-written libretto until then – with subtle lyrical detail. The orchestra for *Der Rosenkavalier* is nearly as opulent as that for *Elektra*; a sizable offstage band is specified too, but modern electronics make that thriftier now.

For the triumphant Dresden première under Ernst von Schuch, the first conductor of Strauss's *Feuersnot, Salome* and *Elektra*, and with Max Reinhardt as producer (it was originally to have been Georg Toller), the Marschallin was created by Margarethe Siems (Strauss's first Chrysothemis), the Baron by Karl Perron, Octavian by Eva von der Osten and Sophie by Minnie Nast; Karl Scheidemantel, the original Kunrad of *Feuersnot*, was Faninal (*see* DRESDEN, fig.8). The opera travelled quickly (at La Scala Lucrezia Bori sang Octavian, with Serafin conducting), and soon other singers established stronger titles to the roles: Richard Mayr as a peerless Ochs, the Marias Jeritza and Olczewska as Octavian, Elisabeth Rethberg and then – above all – Lotte Lehmann as the Marschallin, followed later by Viorica Ursuleac, Tiana Lemnitz, Elisabeth Schwarzkopf and Régine Crespin. Ludwig Weber and Kurt Böhme were famous Barons. Many a soprano has progressed from Octavian to Sophie (or the other way round) to the Marschallin, notably Lisa Della Casa; Sena Jurinac made an indelible mark as Octavian. She and Weber sang in Erich Kleiber's faultlessly idiomatic *Rosenkavalier* on records; Karajan's superbly engineered recording, made together with Paul Czinner's film, boasts Schwarzkopf and (as Octavian) Christa Ludwig. 35 years earlier, a silent *Rosenkavalier* film had been lavishly produced – it helped to bankrupt its producers – to a revised scenario by Hofmannsthal, with an orchestral accompaniment 'arranged' from Strauss's opera by hired hands.

ACT 1 *The Feldmarschallin's bedroom* The orchestral prelude, which notoriously represents a scene of exuberant love-making – complete with climax on whooping horns, and luxurious afterglow – also introduces much of the leading thematic material. (From the outset Octavian's thrusting horn tune suggests the virile swain of the final version, not the light-comedy travesty role that Hofmannsthal first imagined; when the theme crops up later in Octavian's vocal line, it is a rare mezzo who can match the horns in importunate fervour.) Amidst morning birdsong the rising curtain reveals the Marschallin with her 17-year-old 'Quinquin', half in and half out of bed, exchanging satisfied endearments. When little Mohammed arrives (to his own twinkling march) with the breakfast chocolate, Octavian conceals himself so hastily that she has to warn him to hide his sword too. After the page's exit she rebukes him for that ungallant gaffe; they make up over the chocolate, while the music – which has never strayed for long from basic E major – now moves into A for the first waltz of the opera (period-decorous, with a touch of Mozart).

The Marschallin alarms Octavian by recalling an occasion when her military husband came home unexpectedly. (Strauss insisted later that she is no mother-figure – the Lehmann type – but a neglected wife, still young, who has had lovers before and will have others.) They are both alarmed by a commotion and a gruff male voice outside; the youth slips into a screened alcove, while it dawns upon his mistress that the visitor is only her country cousin Ochs. Mischievous 'Quinquin' reappears disguised as a chambermaid, gormless 'Mariandel'. Now the Baron lumbers in, obsequious but

1. 'Der Rosenkavalier' (Richard Strauss): design by Alfred Roller for Act 2 (the reception hall of Faninal's town house) of the original production at the Königliches Opernhaus, 26 January 1911; it was obligatory for any theatre performing the opera to follow Roller's stage and costume designs, published by Fürstner (1911)

self-important, to declare his errand. He needs his fortunes restored, and proposes to marry young Sophie, daughter of the *nouveau riche* Faninal; since his titled status is his trump card, he wants to flash it by having some presentable, well-born emissary deliver his formal proposal with a silver rose. Relaxing in noble company, he regales his hostess with a gross conspectus (often cut, for decency's sake) of his backwoods seduction methods, all the while making crude passes at 'Mariandel'. This panting hunt-monologue in B♭ becomes a hard, bright trio as his two hearers comment in sarcastic asides. The Marschallin, who has a sense of humour, recommends her kinsman Count Rofrano as envoy, and shows Ochs his portrait in a locket. Spotting a resemblance, Ochs guesses 'Mariandel' to be a half-sister from the wrong side of the blanket (Marie Thérèse does not contradict him), and confides smugly that he keeps his own bastard son, named 'Leopold' after himself, as his body-servant.

He desires also the services of the Marschallin's notary, who arrives – as 'Mariandel' at last escapes – amid the gaggle of household staff and petitioners who gather for the morning *levée.* While Ochs and the asthmatic lawyer confer and the Marschallin's hairdresser gets to work, a trio of genteel orphans solicit alms, an eager pair of social spies (Valzacchi and Annina) find their services brusquely rejected, and an Italian tenor with flute accompaniment hopes to please with 'Di rigori armato' (a slow waltz of a curious cut, vaguely italianate but not remotely Italian). His second verse is cut short by an explosion from Ochs, enraged by the notary's scruples about writing into the marriage contract a hefty 'wedding gift', or Baron-bribe, from Faninal. Gazing sadly into a mirror, Marie Thérèse tells her *friseur* that he has made her look an old woman. The *levée* ends abruptly; but before the Baron goes off he engages the spies to procure 'Mariandel' for him, and his loutish son brings the Marschallin the silver rose.

Alone, she reflects ('Da geht er hin') that she too was married off straight from the convent, like poor Sophie, and that one day soon she will become 'old Princess Resi': a cruel mystery which has to be accepted. Octavian, returning in his own clothes, is alarmed by her sudden melancholy. She tries to make him understand that time passes inexorably ('Die Zeit, die ist ein sonderbar Ding', with magically delicate instrumentation), though sometimes at night she gets up to stop the clocks; that today or tomorrow ('Heut' oder morgen') he will leave her for a younger woman. (Rocking up and down in wide intervals, the climactic music in E recalls Electra's 'Recognition' song, and behind that a confessional passage from Act 2 of *Tristan.*) Octavian protests passionately, feels himself rebuffed, departs chastened and dejected; too late, the Marschallin realizes that she has let him go without a kiss. The lackeys she sends hot-foot after him fail to catch him, as they soon report in a mini-'hunting chorus' (which Hofmannsthal detested: it nearly reduces the tender crisis to operetta). She dispatches Mohammed with the silver rose for Octavian, and sinks into a reverie while a high, silvery violin dreams over his virile tune.

ACT 2 *The reception hall of Faninal's town house* An excited prelude sets the scene in the household which awaits the rose-bearer – and after him, the noble bridegroom-to-be. Sophie's father and her duenna Marianne are beside themselves with anticipation; she prays to be worthy of the match, reminding herself that her mother's death has left her alone in the world. Amid gleaming pomp Octavian arrives to present the rose, almost stammering over his set speech ('Mir ist die Ehre widerfahren') – from which a rapt duet blossoms: not quite knowing it, he and Sophie succumb to a *coup de foudre.* (With the presentation comes an eerie sequence of frosty chords for celesta, harps, flutes and solo violins.) Next on the formal agenda is Informal Chat, in which Sophie's unexpected mettle enchants him still further. The pockmarked Baron makes his entrance with his hayseed entourage, and proceeds to be earthily offensive and patronizing at once. Faninal and Marianne are abjectly grateful while Sophie, to her great distaste, is prodded and pawed like a prize heifer, and Ochs cajoles her with one of his waltzes, 'Mit mir ...' – 'With me, no night will be too long for you!' (his other

2. Costume designs by Alfred Roller for the original production of 'Der Rosenkavalier', published by Fürstner (1911): Herr von Faninal (left), and Marianne, the duenna (right)

one is the rollicking 'Luck of the Lerchenaus').

At last he retires with her father and the notary to settle the contract. The young pair are quickly locked in a tender duologue ('Mit Ihren Augen voll Tränen'), while the Lerchenau louts attempt rape upon the Faninal housemaids. As Octavian presses the bride to rebel, the newly hired spies, Valzacchi and Annina, hurry to alert Ochs. General uproar ensues. Octavian announces that Sophie will reject the Baron, who is first amused and then dismayed when a duel is proposed – and bawls wildly when the youth's sword scores a minor flesh wound in his arm. The horrified Faninal requests that Octavian depart forever, and threatens his daughter with relegation to the convent. Eventually calm returns and people disperse, as Ochs is mollified with bandages and wine (and his louts mutter empty threats – in a morose chorus, not at all what Hofmannsthal intended). Annina brings him further cheer: an assignation note from 'Mariandel', which she reads aloud to a waltz version of Octavian's tune. He fails to tip her – an egregious error; but the act concludes nonetheless with a swinging, exuberant reprise of 'Mit mir', and a risky low E for the complacent Baron.

ACT 3 *A candlelit private room in a cheap hotel, with a curtained alcove containing a bed* The virtuoso orchestral prelude is all hasty, conspiratorial whispers, with much fugato and intermittent punctuation by Octavian's horn motif: a snare is being laid for Ochs. The curtain rises to discover Valzacchi adjusting Annina's false widow's weeds and rehearsing the 'spectres' who are to appear from trapdoors and secret windows. Octavian looks in, wearing his 'Mariandel' dress (but his own riding boots under it), and goes out. Servants make the room ready and light the candles, many of which the Baron extinguishes when he arrives, one arm around 'Mariandel' and the other in a sling, and the unseen hotel band strikes up a new waltz.

Waltz succeeds waltz while supper is served. The solicitous innkeeper and his bustling waiters irritate Ochs, who wants to get on with the seduction. Once he is alone with his prey, it proceeds badly: 'Mariandel' is coyly backward, her face reminds him uncomfortably of the treacherous rose-knight, and at first she declines to drink any wine. (Her refusal is accompanied by an insouciant waltz in C which is later to generate the great soprano trio, much slower. That seems to make no musico-dramatic point, except on the far-fetched guess that both numbers are about 'renunciation'. More probably, Strauss's symphonic instinct demanded that the final crisis-and-resolution be developed from music already heard – not freshly tacked on, as in most Italian operas. Perhaps also he sought to fulfil Hofmannsthal's request, 'Try to think of some old-fashioned Viennese waltz, half sweet, half cheeky, which should pervade the whole Act'.) When she does imbibe, she grows maudlin and vociferous, and to the Baron's further dismay spectral faces loom out of the shadows. Annina bursts in, followed by her 'children', the hotel staff and three policemen, to denounce him as her errant husband. His lofty denial, and his claim to be blamelessly entertaining his fiancée Fräulein Faninal, do not impress the police, for 'Mariandel' loudly bewails her 'shame' – and someone has maliciously summoned Faninal himself, with Sophie in tow. Meanwhile, to high constabulary amusement, 'Mariandel' slips into the bed alcove, changes clothes and re-emerges as Count Rofrano.

Amid the confusion and mutual denunciations, the Marschallin arrives. (Often she seems to bring the real opera back with her, for by now the farce is stretched thin.) Wielding gracious authority, she soothes all the antagonists and puts them firmly in their places; no harm has been done to anyone, Ochs will of course relinquish his claims to Sophie, and the whole affair has been nothing more than a Viennese masquerade (Sophie repeats the phrase ruefully). For the Baron, the penny drops at last – 'Octavian ... Mariandel ... the Marschallin ... Octavian ...!' – but upon a caution from Marie Thérèse he swears silence: it is his moment of real, endearing dignity. Now, however, with most of the crowd rudely thrusting their bills for the soirée at him, he is reduced to ignominious flight with Leopold, while the 'Luck of the Lerchenaus' whirls merrily in the orchestra. (Strauss was determined upon a huge waltz-climax here; unfortunately, the plot-mechanics Hofmannsthal devised are really too frail to support it.)

Faninal staggers off to another room, and only the seriously involved parties remain. The Marschallin interprets Octavian's tongue-tied abashment, and Sophie's baffled distress; she recognizes that now is 'Heut' oder morgen', and comes to terms with that in a poignant, disjuncted trio with the young lovers, who are still on edge and at odds. Discreetly she allows Octavian to understand that the new situation has her blessing, and assures Sophie, after quizzing her like a careful aunt, that her cousin will know the remedy for those pale cheeks. Their great trio begins – in the ultimate Romantic key of D♭ with her 'Hab' mir's gelobt' ('I vowed to love even his love for another'); Sophie understands that something wonderful has been done for her but prefers not to inquire too far, and the obscure guilt Octavian feels melts away in the glow of new love. By a favourite Strauss sideslip, the music is wrenched into E for a full-voiced, full-hearted climax. 'In Gottes Namen', says the Marschallin, and goes off to coddle Faninal.

Alone at last for the operatic coda, the lovers carol 'Ist ein Traum?' in 3rds and in G major innocence, like babes in the wood. (Strauss hit upon this duet before there were any words ready, and sent his own dummy-verses to Hofmannsthal to ensure that the metre was faithfully copied. The inspiration was surely Hänsel and Gretel's 'Fourteen angels' duet, at night in a trackless forest, in Humperdinck's opera; Strauss had conducted its première, and later in the run his future wife sang Hänsel.) The Marschallin and the placated Faninal pass through briefly, on their ways home: he remarks philosophically that young folk just *are* like that, and she replies 'Ja, ja'. Octavian and Sophie embrace again for a reprise of their duet, this time with the end of each line iced by the 'silver rose' chords – chiming intimations of mortality, strangely touching here. After the lovers trip off little Mohammed trips on, in search of the Marschallin's dropped handkerchief, and triumphantly bears it away. Though open questions hang in the air, his modest success ends the story with a wry smile, still in the happy lovers' key of G.

* * *

The music glories in Hofmannsthal's text, which satisfied Strauss like nothing before. It was cheerful and knowing, fluent and down-to-earth, and yet made room for sumptuous effects and some elevated intensity. His 'symphonic' facility got full scope, but also his modern penchant for inserting chamber-scale music amid his opulent orchestral tapestries. In all previous operas (at least since Monteverdi's time), if there was dialogue with the quick cut-and-thrust of sophisticated conversation it was set as recitative, or else in formal ensembles; but such conversations make the very texture of *Der Rosenkavalier*, and here Strauss outdoes Wagner with dramatic music in which distinctions between recitative, arioso and formal set pieces are continuously blurred. Unaccompanied lines may have as much lyrical force – and even as much weight in the musical argument – as the big tunes, and Strauss tacks mercurially between those modes. Again and again he invests the uttered words with the poignant sense of their unspoken subtext, and in unstinting sympathy with each of Hofmannsthal's characters. With this opera, Opera itself reached a new level of endeavour. Though the score is ripely tonal it has some bold chromatic experiments, too aptly theatrical to attract much notice, but more ingeniously wrought than the bald, sensational ones in *Elektra*. DAVID MURRAY

Rosenshein, Neil (*b* New York, 27 Nov 1947). American tenor. He studied in New York, making his début in 1972 with Florida Opera as Almaviva, and then sang at Chicago, Washington DC, Dallas, Houston, Boston and Santa Fe. He first sang at the Metropolitan in 1987 as Alfredo, returning as Gounod's Faust in 1990. He made his European début in 1980 at Vaison-la-Romaine as Almaviva, and has sung in Paris, Geneva, Zürich, Amsterdam and at Covent Garden, where he made his début in 1986 as Lensky. His repertory includes Tamino, Belmonte, Oberon, Fenton, Don Carlos, Massenet's Des Grieux, Werther, Don José, Pinkerton and Števa Buryja. A fine actor, he has a strong, flexible voice and is particularly effective in roles such as Tom Rakewell, which he sang with Australian Opera (1988). ELIZABETH FORBES

Rosenstock, Joseph (*b* Kraków, 27 Jan 1895; *d* New York, 17 Oct 1985). American conductor of Polish birth. His musical studies were in Kraków and in Vienna with Schreker. He began his career in the opera houses of Darmstadt (1922–5) and Wiesbaden (1925–7). He spent one season at the Metropolitan Opera, where he made his début directing *Lohengrin* in 1929. Returning to Europe, he was music director of Mannheim Opera (1930–33) and of the Jewish Kulturbund in Berlin (1933–6) until he was compelled to flee Hitler's Germany; he then conducted in Tokyo from 1937 to 1941. In 1948 he began a long association with New York City Opera, culminating in his appointment as general manager (1952–6). After conducting in Cologne, 1958–9, he returned to the Metropolitan (1961–8), directing 175 performances of 16 operas, chiefly works of Mozart, Strauss and Wagner.

CORI ELLISON

Rosenthal, Harold D(avid) (*b* London, 30 Sept 1917; *d* London, 19 March 1987). English writer. He embarked on a teaching career, but became increasingly involved in music, principally as critic and lecturer. In 1948–9 he worked with the Earl of Harewood on the journal *Ballet and Opera* and was Harewood's assistant editor when *Opera* was founded in 1950; he was editor from 1953 to 1986. Under his guidance the journal came to provide an extensive coverage of operatic events throughout the world and exercised considerable influence on operatic life in Britain. Rosenthal was also archivist of the Royal Opera House, Covent Garden, 1950–56. He wrote extensively for other periodicals, notably in the USA, and broadcast and lectured widely on opera. His work was highly regarded for its judiciousness, based on a thorough knowledge of the human voice and the central operatic repertory.

Sopranos of Today (London, 1956)
Two Centuries of Opera at Covent Garden (London, 1958)
with J. Warrack: *Concise Oxford Dictionary of Opera* (London, 1964, 2/1979)
ed.: *The Opera Bedside Book* (London, 1965)
Great Singers of Today (London, 1956)
ed.: *The Mapleson Memoirs* (London, 1966)
Covent Garden: a Short History (London, 1967)
ed.: *A. Loewenberg: The Annals of Opera* (London, 3/1978)

*

A. Jacobs and others: 'Working with H. D. R.' *Opera*, xxviii (1987), 498–504

STANLEY SADIE

Rosenthal, Manuel (*b* Paris, 18 June 1904). French composer and conductor. At the Conservatoire he studied composition with Ravel. He later pursued a career as a conductor; he made his New York début in 1977 and appeared at the Metropolitan in 1981. In 1986 he conducted the *Ring* in Seattle. His compositions are in a noble neo-classical style.

Rayon des soieries, 1926–8 (opéra bouffe, 1, Nino), Paris, OC (Favart), 3 June 1930
Les bootleggers (operetta), Paris, 1933
La poule noire, 1934–7 (comédie musicale, 1, Nino), Paris, Champs-Elysées, 1937
Les femmes au tombeau (1, M. de Ghelderode), Paris, 1957 (1956)
Hop, signor!, 1957–61 (3, Ghelderode), Toulouse, Capitole, 24 March 1962

*

D. Saudinos: *Manuel Rosenthal: une vie* (Paris, 1992)

ANNE GIRARDOT

Roser [von Reiter], **Franz de Paula** (*b* Naarn, Upper Austria, 17 Aug 1779; *d* Budapest, 12 Aug 1830). Austrian composer and conductor. He studied under his father and may have been a pupil of Mozart in Vienna for a short time in 1789. He studied further with Georg Pasterwiz in Kremsmünster and J. G. Albrechtsberger in 1795. In 1796 he became a novice in the Cistercian monastery of Wilhering, Upper Austria, but did not take his vows; instead he became a soldier, then decided to make a career in music, probably from 1799 when he became musical director in Freiburg. Later he was a Kapellmeister of travelling opera troupes in Paris (1800) and Verona (1802), a tenor in theatres at Klagenfurt (1803) and Pest (1804), and from 1806 a composer in the service of Ignaz von Vegh at Vereb (now Székesfehérvár). After a year as a theatre Kapellmeister in Linz (1811–12) Roser settled in Vienna, where from 1812 to 1819 he was Kapellmeister at the Theater in der Josefstadt. In 1817 he founded a music lending and copying concern and in 1819 he became assistant Kapellmeister at the Kärntnertortheater; he was Kapellmeister at the Theater an der Wien from 1820 and at the German theatre at Pest from 1824. From 1826 he was a successful freelance composer for a number of farce theatres in Vienna.

Roser was one of the most prolific composers for the Vienna stage in the early 19th century. His operas, operettas, farces, ballets and other comic works written between 1800 and 1830 number at least 63; almost a third were to texts by J. A. Gleich, and most are lost.

first performed in Vienna unless otherwise stated
WJ – *Vienna, Theater in der Josefstadt*
WL – *Vienna, Theater in der Leopoldstadt*
WW – *Vienna, Theater an der Wien*

Das Waldweibchen (3), 1800
Florindo a Cordona, Vereb, Veghsches Schlosstheater, 1810
Melchyora, die Wassernixe von Mühllacken, Linz, Ständisches, 1812
Der unterirdische Gang (2, J. A. Gleich), WJ, 30 June 1812
Vierfaches Unglück (comic operetta, 1, J. Huber), WJ, 9 Sept 1812
Johann von Wieselburg (Quodlibet, 2, Gleich), WJ, 28 Nov 1812
Fritzl: der Gang nach dem Backofen (musikalisches Quodlibet, 3, K. Schorch), WJ, 23 Jan 1813
Die vornehmen Wirtinnen (musikalisches Quodlibet, 3, Gleich), WW, 6 April 1813
Fiesco, der Salamikrämer (musikalisches Quodlibet, 2, Gleich), WJ, 17 May 1813
Die kuriose Frau im Walde (musikalisches Quodlibet, 2, J. S. von Menner), WJ, 26 June 1813
Die Kosaken in Leipzig, 1813
Die Ochsenhaut (Festspiel, 3, Gleich), WL, 20 April 1814
Die Prinzessin Farakunkel (Märchen, 2, K. Wiedemann), WL, 28 May 1814
Der Kampf fürs Vaterland (militärisches Schauspiel, 3, Gleich), WL, 6 May 1815
Xaverl's Schelmereien (Posse, 2, W. Schmitt), WL, 31 May 1815
Kuno von Werningen (romantisches Schauspiel, 4, E. Stein), WL, 3 June 1815
Amor und Psyche (Parodie, 1, Wiedemann), WL, 22 July 1815
Der diebische Affe (Posse, 1, K. Meisl), WL, 27 Jan 1816
Der ästhetische Narr (komisches Quodlibet, 2, Meisl), WL, 21 Feb 1816
Abenteuer eines Haarbeutels (Faschingsspiel, 1, Rollbach), WL, 24 Feb 1816
Die Befreyung von Holland (Schauspiel, Gleich), WJ, Feb 1816
Der süsse Most (Posse, 1, Menner), WL, 6 March 1816
Das Geistergelage der sieben Brüder (romantisch-komisches Volksmärchen, 3, F. Rosenau), WL, 15 June 1816
Die verstorbene Ehefrau (Posse, 3, Gleich), WJ, 14 Nov 1816
Die Schreckensnacht am Kreuzwege (romantische Volkssage, 3, Gleich), WL, 20 Nov 1816
Die Wunderlampe (Zauberoper, Gleich), WJ, Sept/Oct 1817
Herrn von Weissvogels Witwerstand (Posse, 3, Gleich), WL, 11 Oct 1817
Fausts Narrheit, und Wagners letzter Tag (tragische Posse, J. Nissl), WJ, Feb 1818
Die Schreckensnacht im Heustadl (Posse), WL, Nov 1818
Christoph Munkel (Posse, 3), WL, 9 Jan 1819
Sultan Wampun (Quodlibet, 2), WW, 20 Feb 1819
Der Unglücksvogel (komisches Spl, 3), WW, 28 Feb 1819
Die Einsiedelei im Walde (Drama, 3, F. Biedenfeld), WW, 26 April 1819
Der vacierende Lorenz (Posse), WW, 10 May 1819
Die Geschwister auf dem Lande (Lokalsingspiel, 2, after J. F. Jünger), WW, 8 June 1819
Die Reise durch die Luft (Zauberposse, 2, Gleich), WW, 14 July 1821
Die Zigeunerin von Derneleucht (Melodrama, 3, Biedenfeld), WW, 5 Jan 1822
Der blöde Ritter (Parodie, 2, A. Bäuerle), WL, 22 March 1822
Kupfer, Silber und Gold (romantisches Feenmärchen, 3, Gleich), WW, 4 Jan 1823
Die Fee aus Frankreich (Zauberspiel, 2, Meisl), collab. W. Müller, WW, 13 Feb 1823
Die Vorstellung ohne Probe (Lustspiel, 3, Gleich), WW, 15 April 1823
Der Barbier und der Waldgeist (Zauberschwank, 2, Gleich), WL, 12 June 1823
Der alte Jüngling (Zauberposse, 2, Gleich), WW, 25 July 1823
Der Wolfsbrunnen (Zauberspiel, 2), WW, 18 Oct 1823
Die Elfeninsel (komisch-tragisches Zauberspiel, 2, Gleich), WW, 3 Jan 1824
Der Bräutigam aus Polen (Posse, 3, Gleich), WL, 16 June 1824
Die blaue Katze (grosse Feenoper, 2), WJ, 21 Aug 1824
Die Höhle Soncha (grosses melodramatisches Spektakel-Schauspiel, 3, A. Grois), WW, 16 Jan 1828
Die Hochzeit zu Pistoia (romantisch-komische Oper, 2), WW, 31 July 1828
Yelva, die russische Waise (Drama, 2, A. Prix), with Vorspiel Der Brand von Moskau, WJ, 19 Dec 1828
Die Verbannung aus dem Zauberreiche (Zauberspiel, 2, J. Nestroy), collab. A. Müller, WJ, 20 Dec 1828
Der Leopard und der Hund (romantisches Schauspiel, 3, Gleich), WL, 18 Jan 1829
Der Alpenkönig und die Mutter (romantisches Märchen, 2, Meisl), WJ, 7 March 1829
Der Tod am Hochzeitstage (Zauberspiel, 2, Nestroy), WJ, 18 Aug 1829
Adam Bünkerl und Jungfer Katherl (phantastische Posse, Meisl), WJ, 25 Oct 1829

Die Szenenreise (dramatisch-musikalisches Quodlibet, 2, K. Carl), with music by Auber and others, WW, 29 March 1830

OTHMAR WESSELY

Rose vom Liebesgarten, Die ('The Rose from the Garden of Love'). *Romantische Oper* in a prologue, two acts and an epilogue by HANS PFITZNER to a libretto by James Grun; Elberfeld, Stadttheater, 9 November 1901.

Inspired by Hans Thoma's painting *Der Wächter vom Liebesgarten* (1890), Grun may also have known of the first 'Rose+Croix' Salon (Paris, 1892), with its famous poster by Carloz Schwabe, whose *Virgin with Lilies* (1897) shares many features with the opera's scenic directions. The anti-realist, aristocratic idealism of the salon's organizer, Sâr Joséphin Péladan, might illuminate Pfitzner's interest in a nature mysticism of hierarchically arranged symbolic figures.

In the Prologue the noble inhabitants of the Garden of Love prepare for the release into the world of the forces of spring. They honour the Sun Child and the Star Maiden (mimed roles), who chooses the Guardian of the Gate of Spring by offering a red rose to Siegnot (tenor). He receives a symbolic crown after the Miracle of the Blossoms, in which white flowers fall like snow. Act 1 finds Siegnot guarding the gate. He befriends the faithful, childlike Bog-Dweller (tenor) and witnesses games in honour of Minneleide (soprano), the fairy queen of the forest. Siegnot falls in love with her, gives her his crown (in which the rose has been placed), but fails to dispel her fear of the blinding light within the garden. At her refusal to enter, darkness falls, the gate closes and the Night Sorcerer (deep bass) appears, wounds Siegnot and abducts Minneleide. Act 2, set in a subterranean cavern, revolves around Siegnot's attempts to free Minneleide. With magical assistance, he pulls down the cavern's supporting pillars and is killed along with the Night Sorcerer and his dwarfs. Minneleide and her two companions survive. The Epilogue begins with a funeral march. Siegnot's body is brought by Minneleide to the Gate of the Garden of Love, but she gains entry only after a passionate plea to the Star Maiden. The scene changes to the garden as before. The sun rises, and Siegnot is restored to life as Minneleide returns the rose to the Star Maiden.

The opera, Pfitzner's richest score, was widely successful, not least in a 1905 production in Vienna, designed by Roller and conducted by Mahler.

PETER FRANKLIN

Rosina. Comic opera afterpiece with dialogue in two acts composed and compiled by WILLIAM SHIELD to a libretto by Frances Moore Brooke after CHARLES-SIMON FAVART's *Les moissonneurs*; London, Covent Garden, 31 December 1782.

Rosina (soprano), the child of parents lost at sea, has been living with a family servant in northern England and working as a gleaner. She has fallen in love with the local squire, Mr Belville (tenor), but does not know that she has attracted not only his bashful love but also the lust of his brother, Captain Belville (tenor). Finding Rosina too sharp-witted to seduce and too moral to bribe, the Captain resorts to abduction, but two Irish labourers foil his plans and rescue Rosina. The shy Mr Belville, having hitherto believed that Rosina and his brother love each other, finally learns that Rosina's heart is free, overcomes his bashfulness, and offers her his hand in marriage. The equally important secondary plot involves the comic romantic squabbling between Rosina's fellow-gleaner, Phoebe (soprano), and her beloved rustic, William (mezzo-soprano).

Shield composed the overture and ten of the 18 songs himself. He borrowed one song each from John Garth and Stephen Paxton and from Sacchini's *Armida*(staged in London as *Rinaldo* in 1780) and found five additional melodies in Scottish, French and Irish sources. *Rosina* was one of the most popular afterpieces of the late 18th century, with the pastoral plot and Celtic songs capitalizing on the escapist interest in folk culture then prevalent in Britain as it was becoming industrialized.

LINDA V. TROOST

Rosing, Vladimir (*b* St Petersburg, 23 Jan 1890; *d* Los Angeles, 24 Nov 1963). Russian tenor and director. He studied in St Petersburg with Joachim Tartakov and in Paris with Jean de Reszke. In 1912 he made his début in *Yevgeny Onegin* at St Petersburg, and the following year went to London, where in 1915 he directed a Russian and French season at the Stoll Theatre; he introduced *The Queen of Spades* to London, 'working like a veritable Trojan' (*Musical Opinion*, July 1915) in the role of Hermann. He sang with the Carl Rosa company at Covent Garden in 1921 as Cavaradossi, and in 1923 founded a company which for six years toured the USA giving opera in English. Rosing directed, and Albert Coates conducted, the British Music Drama Opera Company, founded in 1936, and their single season at Covent Garden included the première of Coates's *Pickwick* and the first performance in England of Musorgsky's *The Fair at Sorochintsï*. His production in 1938 of George Lloyd's *The Serf* for the English Opera Society at Covent Garden was admired, but in 1939 he moved to the USA, where he organized the Southern California Opera Association and from 1950 to 1958 was director for the New York City Opera. He was one of the most determined, individualistic and enterprising figures of his day. His voice, though powerful enough, was subject to some rough usage. His insistence on intelligibility in opera was timely and influential.

J. B. STEANE

Rösler, Endre (*b* Budapest, 27 Nov 1904; *d* Budapest, 13 Dec 1963). Hungarian tenor. He made his Budapest Opera House début in 1927 as Alfredo, having studied with De Lucia and Garbin. From the outset he undertook a wide range of roles, both lyric and dramatic, favouring the Mozart repertory above all. His performances were notable not so much for beauty of voice (as a young singer he had contracted an inflammation of the vocal cords that affected his higher register) as for expressive power, great musicality, a keen sense of style, excellent acting ability and versatility in character parts such as Shuysky (*Boris Godunov*), Malatestino (Zandonai's *Francesca da Rimini*) and Loge, perhaps his greatest role. He played Florestan under Toscanini at Salzburg (1935) and appeared several times at the Florence Maggio Musicale and elsewhere. At the end of the 1950s he resigned his leading roles, playing only comprimario and character parts. He was also a leading Hungarian recitalist and concert singer.

*

P. P. Várnai: *Rösler Endre* (Budapest, 1969)

PÉTER P. VÁRNAI

Rosmer, Ernst [Bernstein-Porges, Else] (*b* Munich, 28 Oct 1866; *d* Hamburg, 1949). Austrian playwright and librettist, daughter of Heinrich Porges. She developed an interest in literary modernism after a short career on the stage. Her fairy-tale play *Königskinder* (1893) was brought to the attention of Engelbert Humperdinck, an old friend of the family, though Hugo Wolf also showed some interest in setting it. The symbolic character of the tale, which showed kinship with Gerhart Hauptmann's *Die versunkene Glocke*, inspired Humperdinck to create a musical setting which interweaves spoken dialogue and song; Rosmer also wished him only to provide incidental music. The text was criticized as obscure after the first performances of the melodrama in 1897, yet Humperdinck returned to the play in 1907 and persuaded Rosmer to let him set it as a full-scale opera.

AMANDA GLAUERT

Rospigliosi, Giulio, Pope Clement IX (*b* Pistoia, 28 Jan 1600; *d* Rome, 9 Dec 1669). Italian librettist. He studied at the Seminario Romano and the University of Pisa, and held a series of appointments in the Roman Curia, among them papal nuncio to Spain (1644–53) and Secretary of State (1655–67), before his election as pope (1667–9). He served closely with three long-term rulers of the century, Popes Urban VIII (Barberini) and Alexander VII (Chigi), as well as Philip IV of Spain. As Clement IX he granted the licence for the first public opera house in Rome, the Teatro Tordinona, which opened in 1671.

By 1624 he belonged to the inner circle of ecclesiastic courtiers and literati around Cardinal Francesco Barberini and before 1632 he had begun writing verse dramas to be set to music. 12 extant librettos can be securely attributed to him, as well as a large-scale dramatic dialogue; all but one were presented by the Barberini. The earliest group includes *Il fiume Giordano* (which became *Erminia sul Giordano* in 1633), possibly *La regina Ester, Il Sant'Alessio* and *I pastori di Bettelemme* (a dialogue for Christmas). These all show his facility with seven- and eleven-syllable rhymed verse, with which he came to depict strongly varied characters, from hungry children to suicidal lovers and adulterous assassins. His style is more discursive than lyric, dramatic in its interest in the logical development of dialogue and in the psychology rather than in the poetry of feelings.

In the librettos of 1635–43 he developed a stronger sense of action and plot and increased the atmosphere of doom around the protagonist and his or her resistance to it. A number of scenes offer melodramatic strokes: a joust suddenly halted by shocking news; an Egyptian religious ceremony disrupted by a storm and idols struck down by lightning; prison scenes; the foiling of a group of assassins intent on ambushing a prince's hunting party. The *favola* based on myth or legend yielded to the drama set at court, a trend marked in Venice by Faustini's *Ormindo* (1644), called a 'favola regia'. In *San Bonifatio* and *Chi soffre speri* characters are borrowed from ancient comedy and the *commedia dell'arte*; they speak, however, in carefully constructed rhyming verse, even when using dialect. In half the pre-1650 librettos amusing or sarcastic pages, probably played by young boys, provide contrast to the more serious characters.

While in Spain Rospigliosi reportedly wrote a 'favola' to demonstrate Italian speaking in singing to the Spanish court. Once back in Rome he offered four new librettos, three of them modelled on Spanish plays. Two are romantic comedies set in contemporary Madrid, and include the humorous servants of the original plays. No specific model has surfaced for *La Vita humana*, which resembles a type of Spanish *auto sacramental*. His only opera not produced by the Barberini, *La comica del cielo*, portrayed the sensational conversion of the Spanish actress Baltasara de los Reyes, as presented by three Spanish playwrights in 1634 about 20 years after her death. The original play's enormous success and spiritual effect in Madrid was echoed by the reaction in Rome to *La comica del cielo* in 1668.

Rospigliosi was a subtle and intellectual statesman, yet he was still able to present a churchman's difficult questions in clearly readable characters and dramatic situations. Questions of free will recur, as does the dilemma of distinguishing between reasoning in search of truth and the trap of false reasoning. Both issues give weight and focus to the individuality and self-knowledge of the principal characters. He did not write in a popular vein; rather his skills at dramatization or characterization dominate the most successful operas. His librettos were disseminated in manuscript in the second half of the century, allowing them to be given as spoken plays and read as literature.

Il Sant'Alessio, S. Landi, 1631 or 1632; *Erminia sul Giordano*, after Tasso, M. Rossi, 1633; *I santi Didimo e Teodora*, 1635; *Chi soffre speri* [*L'Egisto*; *L'Alvida*] (after Boccaccio: *Il decamerone*), V. Mazzocchi and Marazzoli, 1637; *San Bonifatio*, Mazzocchi, 1638; *L'innocenza difesa* [*La Genoinda*], Mazzocchi, 1641; *Il palazzo incantato* [*Lealtà con valore*; *La guerriera amante*; *Il palazzo d'Atlante*], after Ariosto, L. Rossi, 1642

Il Sant'Eustachio, Mazzocchi, 1643; *Dal male il bene* (with Giacomo Rospigliosi), after A. Sigler de Huerta: *No ay bien sin ageno daño*, Abbatini and Marazzoli, 1654; *Le armi e gli amori*, after P. Calderón de la Barca: *Los empeños de un acaso*, Marazzoli, 1656; *La Vita humana, ovvero Il trionfo della pietà*, Marazzoli, 1656; *La comica del cielo*, after L. Vélez de Guevara and others: *La Baltasara*, Abbatini, 1668

Doubtful: *La regina Ester*, 1632; *La Sofronia*; *La Datira* [*Rolacco, re di Svetia*]; *La costanza in amore*; *Mal ha chi mal opra*; *Teodosio* [*Eudossia*], 1692

*

L. Allacci: *Apes urbanae sive De viris illustribus ab anno MDCXXX per totum MDCXXXII* (Rome, 1633)

A. Ademollo: *I teatri di Roma nel secolo decimosettimo* (Rome, 1888)

I. Sanesi: *Poesie musicali di Giulio Rospigliosi* (Pistoia, 1894)

G. Canevazzi: *Papa Clemente IX poeta* (Modena, 1900)

A. Salza: 'Drammi inediti di Giulio Rospigliosi poi Clemente IX', *RMI*, xiv (1907), 473–508

I. Küffel: *Die Libretti G. Rospigliosis: ein Kapitel frühbarocker Operngeschichte in Rom* (diss., U. of Vienna, 1968)

M. Murata: 'Rospigliosiana overo gli Equivoci innocenti', *Studi musicali*, iv (1975), 131–43

——: 'Il carnevale a Roma sotto Clemente IX Rospigliosi', *RIM*, xii (1977), 83–99

S. Leopold: 'Das geistliche Libretto im 17. Jahrhundert: zur Gattungsgeschichte der frühen Oper', *Mf*, xxxi (1978), 245–57

M. Murata: *Operas for the Papal Court* (Ann Arbor, 1981)

V. Kapp: 'Das Barberini-Theater und die Bedeutung der römischen Kultur unter Urban VIII: Versuch einer literarhistorischen Einordnung des Schaffens von G. Rospigliosi', *Literaturwissenschaftliches Jb*, new ser., xxvi (1985), 75–100

S. Franchi: *Drammaturgia romana: repertorio bibliografico cronologico dei testi drammatici pubblicati a Roma e nel Lazio, secolo XVII* (Rome, 1988)

MARGARET MURATA

Rosquellas, Pablo (Mariano) (*b* Madrid, 15 April 1784; *d* Sucre, 12 July 1859). Spanish composer, tenor and opera administrator. He studied with his father and other family members, and continued the study of singing in Italy. He first took a post as violinist in Madrid, but then embarked on a new career as singer, actor, composer and promoter of opera, travelling to London, Paris and Brazil, where his opera *O grande califa de Bagdad* was given at Rio de Janeiro in 1819. He settled in 1823 in Buenos Aires, where he did much to introduce Italian opera, ultimately founding an opera company; he gave many Argentine premières of operas by Rossini in the late 1820s, including *Il barbiere di Siviglia*, *Otello* and *Tancredi*; in addition he presented operas by Mozart, Zingarelli and others. He also gave performances in Montevideo. In 1833 he moved to Bolivia, developing a silver mine as well as pursuing his musical career, and later he visited Chile and Peru. His works include incidental dramatic music and music for his own instrument, the violin. His son, Luis Pablo Rosquellas (1823–83), included singing and composing among his multifarious activities.

*

G. Bourligueux: *Un musicien madrilène à travers le Nouveau Monde: mélanges offerts à Paul Roche* (Nantes, 1992)

GUY BOURLIGUEUX

Ross, Elinor (*b* Tampa, FL, 1 Aug 1932). American soprano. After studying with Zinka Milanov in New York, she made her début at the Cincinnati Opera as Leonora in *Il trovatore* (1958). Appearances followed in Baltimore, Chicago, Boston and in San Francisco, where her repertory included Norma, Maddalena (*Andrea Chénier*), Elisabeth de Valois and Lady Macbeth. An appearance in the American première of Verdi's *Alzira* at Carnegie Hall in 1968 was followed by her début at the Metropolitan, as Turandot. European engagements took her to Milan (La Scala), Florence, Vienna, Venice and Budapest. Her repertory included Medea, Donna Anna, Tosca and Santuzza. She appeared as Tosca at the Metropolitan in 1973. DAVID CUMMINGS

Ross, Glynn (William) (*b* Omaha, NE, 15 Dec 1914). American administrator and director. He gained extensive experience as stage director at the Teatro S Carlo, Naples (1945–7, 1960–63), becoming the first American to direct in a major Italian house. He was stage producer at the San Francisco Opera (1948, 1950–60), Los Angeles Opera Theater (1948–60), Fort Worth Opera (1948–56), New Orleans Opera Association (1949–62), Northwest Grand Opera Association, Seattle (1953–5), and the Opera Company of Philadelphia (1960–62). In 1963 Ross founded the Seattle Opera Association to perform in the model opera house built for the World's Fair there in 1962. He served as general director until 1983 and not only staged the company's productions but also dealt with technical and administrative matters and organized tours to other western cities. Under him the company became noted for its annual *Ring* cycles with two casts, one singing in German and the other in English. In 1983 he became general director of the Arizona Opera Company.

FRANK MERKLING

Rossato, Arturo (*b* Vicenza, 27 June 1882; *d* Milan, 11 March 1942). Italian librettist and novelist. After serving in World War I, he returned to civilian life, wrote anti-war pamphlets and was active in politics. His prose works were original and challenging, but his librettos (he wrote nearly 30) were somewhat conventional. *I cavalieri di Ekebù*, based on the novel by S. Lagerlöf and set by Zandonai (1925, Milan) is his most interesting libretto. The tale is a blend of fantasy, lyricism and realism.

Giulietta e Romeo, Zandonai, 1922; *La tempesta*, Lattuada, 1922; *I cavalieri di Ekebù*, Zandonai, 1925; *Madonna Imperia*, Alfano, 1927; *Madama di Challant*, C. Guarino, 1927; *L'innocente*, Mignone, 1928; *Giuliano*, Zandonai, 1928; *Le preziose ridicole*, Lattuada, 1929; *Il gobbo nel califfo*, Casavola, 1929; *Don Giovanni*, Lattuada, 1929; *L'ultimo lord*, Alfano, 1930; *La dote di Jeannette*, Pietri, 1931

Corradino lo Svevo, P. Donati, 1931; *Il favorito del re*, Veretti, 1932; *Romanticismo*, I. Robbiani, 1932; *La farsa amorosa*, Zandonai, 1933; *Guido del popolo*, Robbiani, 1933; *Una partita*, Zandonai, 1933; *Liolà*, Mulè, 1935; *Notturno romantico*, Pick-Mangiagalli, 1936; *Astuzie d'amore*, Casavola, 1936; *Il sogno d'un mattino d'autunno*, Guarino, 1936; *Lancilotto del lago*, Donati, 1938 BARBARA REYNOLDS

Rosselli, John (*b* Florence, 8 June 1927). English writer of partly Italian descent. He studied at Swarthmore College, Pennsylvania, and was a research student in history under Herbert Butterfield at Cambridge (1948–51). He then worked for the (*Manchester*) *Guardian*, as leader writer, features editor and deputy London editor, before moving to Sussex University, 1964–89, to teach history, latterly as Reader. Rosselli has worked as a critic but is chiefly noted for his writings on the social and economic background of opera, particularly in Italy. His authoritative *The Opera Industry in Italy from Cimarosa to Verdi* (Cambridge, 1984) explored aspects of operatic history and culture unfamiliar to the music historian, as too did his *Music and Musicians in Nineteenth-Century Italy* (London, 1991) and his studies of the role, in the broadest sense, of the singer. These include an important article on the castrato (*AcM*, lx (1988), 143–79), a study of the singer's relation to his patrons (*COJ*, i (1989), 1–32) and a book on the profession itself, *Singers of Italian Opera: the History of a Profession* (Cambridge, 1992); Rosselli has also studied Italian opera in Argentina.

Rossellini, Renzo (*b* Rome, 2 Feb 1908; *d* Monte Carlo, 13 May 1982). Italian composer. He studied composition with Giacomo Setaccioli and conducting with Bernardino Molinari, and was director of the Liceo Musicale, Varese (1934–5). He taught composition at the Pesaro Conservatory from 1940 to 1942, was music critic for the Rome *messaggero* and artistic director of the Monte Carlo Opera (1972–6). A writer of chamber and orchestral music and of film scores (including those for films directed by his brother Roberto), he later turned his attention to music theatre, following the first Italian performance, in May 1955, of Menotti's *The Saint of Bleecker Street*. A conservative musician, tied to the traditions of the late 19th century and Italian realism, while also influenced by Massenet, Rossellini conformed to these musico-dramatic models in his first operas, *La guerra* (1956) and *Il vortice* (1958). From the 1960s onwards, his operatic writing, untouched by the radical stylistic developments of 20th-century music, was refined towards more slender melodies with atmospheric echoes of French impressionism.

Alcassino e Nicoletta

La guerra (1, Rossellini), Naples, S Carlo, 25 Feb 1956

Il vortice (3, Rossellini), Naples, S Carlo, 8 Feb 1958

La piovra, Naples, 1958

Le campane (television op, Rossellini), 9 May 1959, vs (Milan, 1959)

Uno sguardo dal ponte (Rossellini, after A. Miller), Rome, Opera, 11 March 1961, vs (Milan, 1961)

Il linguaggio dei fiori (Rossellini, after F. García Lorca), Milan, 1963

La leggenda del ritorno (D. Fabbri, after F. M. Dostoyevsky), Milan, 1966

L'avventuriero (Fabbri, after Dostoyevsky), Milan, 1968

L'annonce faite à Marie (P. Claudel), Paris, 1970

La reine morte (after H. de Montherlant), Monte Carlo, 1973

RAFFAELE POZZI

Rossi, Francesco. Several Italian composers of this name were active from about 1650 to about 1725. Since Rossi is such a common Italian surname, and because of a scarcity of documentary and musical evidence, it is difficult to disentangle the biographies of these composers or even to determine their number.

The most clearcut identity is that of an opera composer active in Milan, organist at S Maria presso S Celso about 1670 and *maestro di cappella* there and at S Giovanni in Conca in 1689 and 1692. His contribution typifies the evolution of Milanese opera, which in the 1660s and 70s tended to be independent of the Venetian repertory. He set to music two librettos by Carlo Torre, *La ricchezza schernita* (*dramma scenico-morale*, 2 February 1658; with three other composers) and *Arianna* (*dramma scenico*, Pavia, 15 July 1660); furnished new music for a strongly opposed performance of Cavalli's *Artemisia* (*dramma per musica*, 20 June 1663); and set to music two dramas by the impresario and singer Carlo Righenzi for Milan, *Crispo* (*dramma per musica*, 20 December 1663) and *La farsa musicale* (9 February 1664), the latter a comic opera in the Florentine manner, with prologue and comic scenes in Milanese dialect, given at the Teatro Ducale.

As frequently happened with stage works at Milan, *La regina Floridea* (a *drama musicale* on a libretto by Giulio Pancieri), whose subject matter is drawn from Spanish comedy, was composed in collaboration with other composers: Rossi composed music for Act 1, Lodovico Busca for Act 2 and P. S. Agostini for Act 3. First performed at the Teatro Ducale, Milan (? Carnival 1669), it was given four more times in the 17th century (Reggio Emilia, February 1677; Florence, Casino di S Marco, 1678; Livorno, 1679; Venice, under the title *Floridea*, given privately in November 1687 and publicly at the Teatro SS Apostoli in January 1688); it is uncertain to what extent Rossi's music was retained in these late revivals. *Bianca di Castiglia* (C. M. Maggi) was performed in October 1669 in the little theatre of Count Vitaliano Borromeo on Isola Bella, Lake Maggiore (fragments in *I-IBborromeo*), and in 1674 and 1676 at the Teatro Ducale, Milan.

Venetian theatre chronicles describe as 'abate Pugliese' the Francesco Rossi who is credited with the music for three dramas given at the Teatro S Moisè: *Il Sejano moderno della Tracia, ovvero La caduta dell'ultimo gran visire* (A. Girapoli, 1686; Bonlini reported that it opened and closed on the same night without having been heard through to its end, 'because it pleased no one'), *Corilda, ovvero L'amore trionfante della vendetta* (22 January 1688) and *La pena degl'occhi* (Carnival 1688). Though a minor figure on the Venetian operatic scene, Rossi was elected *maestro di coro* at the Ospedale dei Mendicanti on 22 July 1689 and was granted lodging there from 25 January 1694. On 8 January 1699 he was excused from his duties because of his advanced age. Bonlini attributed to 'D. Francesco Rossi', a native of the Veneto, *La ninfa Apollo* (performed by the Accademici Liberali at the Teatro S Michiel, Murano, in 1726), a greatly altered version of a pastorale by the classicist poet Francesco de Lemene, originally published in 1692 and set to music in Rome by Francesco Garbi before that date and several other times. If all these Venetian operas are supposed to be by the same composer, then the birth place and date given by Bellucci (Bari, 17 June 1627; *Rassegna pugliese*, ii, 1885, p.197) would seem to refer to a different Francesco Rossi.

Theatre chronicles do not mention a *Mitrane* of 1689, from which Fétis claimed to have taken the contralto aria 'Ah, rendimi quel core', which was performed in March 1833 at one of his historical concerts in Paris and won some popularity in the 19th century. This opera never existed. The piece is from the second half of the 18th century and doubtless came from an opera including a character named Mitrane, such as *Demetrio* (Metastasio) or *La vendetta di Nino* (Moretti), both with music by Francesco Bianchi (1774, Venice, and 1790, Naples, respectively); perhaps the character was sung by a Francesco Rossi, such as the one active at Venice in 1794–7.

AllacciD; *FétisB*
C. M. Maggi: *Rime varie* (Milan, 1700), iv, 193, 239; v, 31ff
G. C. Bonlini: *Le glorie della poesia e della musica* (Venice, 1730)
L. G. Clubb: *Italian Plays, 1500–1700, in the Folger Library* (Florence, 1968), 225–6
E. Selfridge-Field: *Venetian Instrumental Music from Gabrieli to Vivaldi* (Oxford, 1975), 302
Arte e musica all'Ospedaletto (Venice, 1978) [exhibition catalogue]

LORENZO BIANCONI, HARRIS S. SAUNDERS

Rossi, Gaetano (*b* Verona, 18 May 1774; *d* Verona, 25 January 1855). Italian librettist. His literary career began when he was 13, with the publication of religious verse. He wrote the first of his librettos in 1797, and continued writing them for nearly 60 years, until the mid-1820s mostly for Venice. Most of the early ones were farces, but there were also important texts for Mayr (*Ginevra di Scozia*), Rossini (*Tancredi* and *Semiramide*) and Meyerbeer (*Il crociato in Egitto*). Later, Milan began to predominate, with increasing numbers for Trieste and Vienna. This period included work for Pacini (*I cavalieri di Valenza*), Mercadante (*I due illustri rivali*) and Donizetti (*Maria Padilla*, of which the composer was part-author, and *Linda di Chamounix*). Rossi was also for some years stage director of the Teatro Filarmonico, Verona, and singers remembered him as intelligent, helpful and practical.

He said himself that he was not a poet but a windbag ('parolaio'); his versification was crude, often forced, marred by a fondness for *tronco* lines and for riding roughshod over the rules of scansion. Nevertheless he had an eye for dramatic situations, and his texts, if long-winded, are effective. His importance lay in his boldness in raiding foreign – primarily French – theatre for source material and for introducing strongly romantic plots to the Italian operatic stage.

His personal life was not easy and he seems to have been beset by financial worries. His importunate, even toadying, letters to Meyerbeer make pathetic reading, but he was always spoken of as genial and good-natured.

d – *dramma* dg – *dramma giocoso*
f – *farsa* fg – *farsa giocosa*
mel – *melodramma*

Carolina e Mexicow (tragedia per musica), Zingarelli, 1797; *Che originali* (f per musica), Mayr, 1798 (Schira, 1835); *Amore e paura* (f per musica), Trento, 1798; *Le quattro mogli* (dg per musica), Marinelli, 1799; *Adelaide di Guesclino* (d di sentimento), Mayr, 1799 (Gnecco, 1800); *Labino e Carlotta* (f per musica), Mayr, 1799; *Il sarto di Milano* (fg per musica), V. Fiocchi, 1799; *L'accademia in musica* (fg per musica), Mayr, 1799; *Antigona* (d per musica), F. Basili, 1799

Il ratto delle Sabine (d per musica), Zingarelli, 1799; *La pazza giornata* (d comico per musica), M. A. Portugal, 1799; *Gli sciti* (d per musica), Mayr, 1800; *La locandiera* (fg per musica), Mayr,

1800 (Farinelli, 1803, as Chi la durá la vince); *I due cognomi* (fg per musica), Trento, 1800; *Gli sposi infatuati* (fg per musica), (?) Nasolini, 1801; *Ginevra di Scozia* (d eroico per musica), Mayr, 1801 (G. Mosca, 1802; Portugal, 1805; Pucitta, 1812); *I virtuosi* (fg), Mayr, 1801

Argene (d eroico), Mayr, 1801 (Pavesi, 1807, as Aristodemo); *Adelaide e Tebaldo* (d sentimentale), Orgitano, 1801; *La Giulietta* (d semi-serio), Farinelli, 1802; *Pamela* (f in musica), Farinelli, 1802; *Il ventaglio* (f comica in musica), Farinelli, 1803; *I riti d'Efeso* (d eroico), Farinelli, 1803 ((?) Nasolini, 1812); *Arsace e Semira* (d eroico in musica), Gnecco, 1804; *Il sordo* (f comica in musica), I. Girace, 1804 (Farinelli, 1805, as Il finto sordo); *Pamela nubile* (f in musica), Generali, 1804

La calzolaia (f comica in musica), Generali, 1804; *Elisa* (d sentimentale), Mayr, 1804; *Eraldo ed Emma* (d eroico per musica), Mayr, 1805; *Trionfo d'Emilia* (d eroico per musica), Pavesi, 1805 (A. Rego, 1807; Sampieri, 1818, as Il trionfo d'Emilia); *Don Chisciotto [Chisciotte] de la Mancia* (dg), Generali, 1805; *L'Amor coniugale* (d di sentimento), Mayr, 1805; *La roccia di Frauenstein* (mel eroi-comico), Mayr, 1805; *Gli americani* (mel eroico), Mayr, 1805 (Manfroce, 1810, as Alzira; Portugal, 1816, as Il trionfo di Gusmano)

Attila (d serio per musica), Farinelli, 1806; *I cherusci* (mel eroico), Pavesi, 1807 (Mayr, 1808); *Calliroe* (mel eroico), Farinelli, 1807; *Amor soldato* (dg per musica), L. A. Calegari, 1807; *La festa della rosa* (mel comico), Pavesi, 1808 (Coccia, 1821, as La festa da rosa); *Guerre in pace* (f per musica), N. Giuliani, 1809; *Il trionfo delle belle* (d eroi-comico), Pavesi, 1809; *Zilia* (f in musica), C. Mellara, 1809; *I gauri* (mel eroico), Mellara, 1809; *Ippolita, regina delle amazzoni* (mel eroico), Pavesi, 1809

Adelina (fg per musica), Generali, 1810; *La cambiale di matrimonio* (f comica), Rossini, 1810; *Cecchina suonatrice di Ghironda* (mel comico), Generali, 1810; *L'amor figliale* (mel di sentimento), Mayr, 1811; *I solitarj* (mel di sentimento), Coccia, 1811; *Idomeneo* (mel eroico), Farinelli, 1811; *Tre mariti* (f comica in musica), Mosca, 1811 (G. Carulli, 1825; G. L. Bazzoni, 1836); *Il qui pro quo* (mel comico), F. Orlandi, 1812; *Il finto Stanislao, re di Polonia* (mel comico), Mosca, 1812

Il marito imbarazzo (f), Mellara, 1812; *Teodoro* (mel eroico), Pavesi, 1812; *Tancredi* (mel eroico), Rossini, 1813; *I baccanti* (d per musica), Paer, 1813 (Generali, 1816, as I baccanti di Roma); *Avviso al pubblico* (mel comico), G. Mosca, 1814; *Il crescendo*, Coccia, 1814; *Trajano in Dacia* (d eroico per musica), Blangini, 1814; *Evellina* (mel eroico), Coccia, 1814; *La fedeltà conjugale* (d semiserio), A. Brunetti, 1815; *La figlia dell'aria* (mel eroi-comico), F. Paini, 1815 (García, 1826)

Celanira (mel eroico), Pavesi, 1815; *Clotilde* (mel semi-serio), Coccia, 1815; *Zoraide* (mel eroico), Farinelli, 1815; *Malvina* (mel di sentimento), Vaccai, 1816; *Etelinda* (mel semiserio), Coccia, 1816 (Winter, 1818; Pellegrini, 1831); *Romilda e Costanza* (mel semi-serio), Meyerbeer, 1817; *Lanassa* (mel eroico), Mayr, 1817; *Adelaide e Comingio* (mel semi-serio), Pacini, 1817; *La sposa fedele* (mel semiserio), Pacini, 1819; *Emma di Resburgo* (mel eroico), Meyerbeer, 1819 (F. Celli, 1821; C. Uccelli, 1835, as Anna di Resburgo)

Il conte di Lenosse (mel eroico), G. Nicolini, 1820; *L'eroe di Lancastro* (mel serio), Nicolini, 1821 (Burghersh, 1829); *Maria Stuarda, regina di Scozia* (d serio per musica), Mercadante, 1821; *Valmiro e Zaida* (d per musica), F. Sampieri, 1821; *Tebaldo e Isolina* (mel eroico), Morlacchi, 1822; *Semiramide* (mel tragico), Rossini, 1823; *Ilda d'Avenel* (mel eroico), Morlacchi, 1824 (Nicolini, 1828); *Il crociato in Egitto* (mel eroico), Meyerbeer, 1824

Il paria (mel tragico), Carafa, 1826; *Mitridate* (mel eroico), Tadolini, 1826; *Giovanna d'Arco* (mel romantico), Vaccai, 1827; *I cavalieri di Valenza* (mel tragico), Pacini, 1828 (A. Gandini, 1830, as Isabella di Lara; Schira, 1836, as Os cavalleiros de Valenca; U. Fontana, 1836, as Isabella di Lara); *L'orfano della selva* (mel comico), Coccia, 1828 (N. Paoletti, 1839); *Maria di Brabante* (mel eroico), A. Guillon, 1830 (Gandini, 1833)

Amore e mistero (mel comico), F. Strepponi, 1830; *La donna bianca di Avenello* (mel comico), Pavesi, 1830 (Gallieri, 1854); *Malek-Adel* (mel eroico), Nicolini, 1830 (B. Bergonzi, 1835); *Fenella* (mel), Pavesi, 1831; *Beniowski* (mel), Generali, 1831; *Chiara di Rosembergh* (mel), L. Ricci, 1831; *Enrico di Monfort* (mel), Coccia, 1831; *Ivanhoe* (mel), Pacini, 1832; *Gli Elvezi* (mel), Pacini, 1833; *Irene* (tragedia lirica), ?Pacini, 1833; *Hernani* (mel), V. Gabussi, 1834

Carlo di Borgogna (mel romantico), Pacini, 1835; *La fidanzata delle isole* (mel romantico), P. Candio, 1835; *Chiara di Montalbano in Francia* (mel semiserio), Ricci, 1835; *Il giuramento* (mel), Mercadante, 1837; *Iginia d'Asti* (mel), S. Levy, 1837; *Il rapimento* (mel comico), P. Mandanici, 1837; *Le nozze di Figaro* (mel comico), Ricci, 1838; *Le due illustri rivali* (mel), Mercadante, 1838; *La prigione d' Edimburgo* (mel semiserio), F. Ricci, 1838; *Alisia di Rieux* (mel), Lillo, 1838

Romilda (mel), Hiller, 1839 (L. Gavazzeni, 1845; C. Boniforti, 1847, as Velleda; B. Prati, 1854, as Amilda); *Rossane* (mel), Schoberlechner, 1839; *Il bravo* (mel), Mercadante, 1839; *Giovanna II regina di Napoli* (mel), Coccia, 1840; *Ginevra degli Almieri* (mel), Levi, 1840; *Clemenza di Valois* (mel), Gabussi, 1841; *Il proscritto* (mel tragico), Nicolai, 1841; *Maria Padilla* (mel, with Donizetti), Donizetti, 1841; *Linda di Chamounix* (mel), Donizetti, 1842; *Romea di Monfort* (mel), Pedrotti, 1846

Il Lazzarone (mel comico), F. Berger, G. Rota, A. Randegger and A. Zelman, 1851; *Il perruchiere della reggenza* (mel comico), Pedrotti, 1852; *Il marito e l'amante* (d comico), F. Ricci, 1852; *Il paniere d'amore* (mel comico), F. Ricci, 1853; *Genoveffa del Brabante* (mel), Pedrotti, 1854; *I Romani in Pompejano* (mel), Rota, 1856; *Il diavolo a quattro* (mel comico), L. Ricci, 1859; *Tancreda* (dramma lirico), T. Dohler, 1880

*

A. Pighi: 'Pagina autobiografica di un librettista veronese', *Miscellanea per le nozze Biadego-Bernardinelli* (Verona, 1896), 192–7

S. Balthazar: 'Mayr, Rossini, and the Development of the Early *Concertato* Finale', *JRMA*, cxvi (1991), 236–66

JOHN BLACK

Rossi, Giacomo (*fl* 1710–31). Italian librettist. He was one of many Italians who settled in London early in the 18th century, perhaps as a language teacher. Late in 1710 he was employed by Aaron Hill to versify the scenario he had prepared from Tasso's *Gerusalemme liberata* for Handel's first London opera, *Rinaldo*. In an apologetic address to the reader of the libretto (February 1711) Rossi called it 'the delivery of but a few evenings' and complained that Handel composed the music in a fortnight and 'scarcely gave me the time to write'. Handel must have collaborated, for both libretto and score contain material from works composed in Italy. The same is true of Rossi's second libretto for Handel, *Il pastor fido* (November 1712), ruthlessly altered from Guarini's famous play. Rossi also supplied the librettos of the unsuccessful pasticcio *Ercole* (May 1712) and Handel's *Silla* (June 1713), and no doubt other operas of this period, including perhaps *Amadigi*. He showed little literary or dramatic skill. His rival Rolli satirized him in one of his epigrams after Martial. On Haym's death in August 1729 Rossi became, according to Rolli, 'Handel's accredited bard', and may have provided the librettos of *Lotario* and other operas, all adapted from earlier originals. He made revisions and additions for the revival of *Rinaldo* in April 1731. He was not the Jacopo Rossi who wrote a libretto for Lucca in 1685.

*

C. Price: 'English Traditions in Handel's *Rinaldo*', *Handel Tercentenary Collection*, ed. S. Sadie and A. Hicks (London, 1987), 120–37

W. Dean and J. M. Knapp: *Handel's Operas 1704–1726* (Oxford, 1989)

WINTON DEAN

Rossi, Giovanni (Gaetano) (*b* Borgo San Donnino, Parma, 5 Aug 1828; *d* Genoa, 31 March 1886). Italian composer. He studied music with his father, the town organist, and at the Milan Conservatory (1846–8). He was *maestro concertatore* at the Teatro Regio, Parma, in 1852 and organist at the court chapel. From that year he held posts at the conservatory (director for ten years from 1864). He was assistant conductor at the Teatro Carlo Felice, Genoa (1873), and director of the Liceo Musicale there from 1874. Rossi composed four operas, *Elena di Taranto* (1852, Parma), *Giovanni Giscala* (1855, Parma), *Nicolò de' Lapi* (1864, Ancona) and

Cuore di madre (1871, Borgo San Donnino); they were written in an up-to-date Verdian style but were not particularly successful. He also composed a few sacred works.

Elena di Taranto (3, A. Cavagnari), Parma, Ducale, 30 Oct 1852
Giovanni Giscala (3, Cavagnari), Parma, Ducale, 10 June 1855
Nicolò de' Lapi (I. Piroli), Ancona, Muse, 1864
Cuore di madre, Borgo San Donnino, 4 Oct 1871; as La contessa d'Altenberg, Genoa, 1875 MARVIN TARTAK

Rossi, Lauro (*b* Macerata, 19 Feb 1812; *d* Cremona, 5 May 1885). Italian composer. He studied at the Naples Conservatory under Zingarelli, Giovanni Furno and Crescentini, obtaining his diploma in 1829. In 1830 *Costanza e Oringaldo*, written in collaboration with Pietro Raimondi, gave him entrée to the Teatro S Carlo. Further comedies, given at the Nuovo in 1831 and all well received, brought him to the attention of Donizetti, who recommended him as assistant director of the Teatro Valle, Rome, a post he held until 1833. In 1834 his *La casa disabitata*, given at La Scala, Milan, so impressed Maria Malibran that she persuaded the impresario Barbaia to commission an opera for her. Unfortunately, she insisted that this work, *Amelia, ovvero Otto anni di costanza* (1834, Naples), include a pas de deux for herself and the dancer Mathis; but as her many accomplishments did not include ballet dancing, the opera was hissed off the stage. Embittered, it is said, and in spite of the fair success of *Leocadia* (1835, Milan), Rossi became director of a company touring Mexico, where his next opera, *Giovanna Shore*, had its première in 1836. When in 1837 the company broke up because of political unrest and the hazards of travel, Rossi set up as an impresario. In June 1840 he was in Milan to engage a company for Havana managed by a colleague with himself as musical director. Among the singers was a young Bohemian soprano, Isabella Obermeyer, who had that year made a highly successful Italian début under the name Ober. The company appeared in New York in September and opened in Havana on 27 October. In 1841 Rossi married Obermeyer, who sang thereafter as Ober-Rossi. In spring 1842 the company performed in New Orleans, returning then to Havana. In 1843 Rossi and his wife were in Europe to convalesce from yellow fever. He then settled in Milan and resumed his operatic career with a triumphant revival of *La casa disabitata*, revised as *I falsi monetari* and known for many years as 'Rossi's *Barbiere*'.

In 1846 Rossi's *La figlia di Figaro* was given at the Kärntnertor in Vienna, while in Milan *Il domino nero* was warmly received in 1849. Now a figure of some consequence, Rossi was appointed director of the Milan Conservatory. During his 20 years there his operatic output diminished considerably as he devoted himself increasingly to academic pursuits. His harmony course, published in 1858, became a standard textbook. Though in no sense a modernist, he pursued a liberal policy and his regime saw the emergence with high honours of Faccio and Boito and the founding of a chair of dramatic poetry. Rossi was among the founders of the Milan Società del Quartetto (1862) and also of the society's journal, which carried some of Boito's fieriest attacks on the state of music and literature in Italy. In 1870 the death of Mercadante led to Rossi's nomination as head of the Naples Conservatory; in 1878 he resigned his supreme position to form part of a triumvirate, appointed to carry out the government's plans for reforming the institution. In 1880 he retired to Cremona.

During his years at Naples Rossi composed two operas for Turin, *La contessa di Mons* (1874) and *Cleopatra* (1876), the first of which enjoyed a *succès d'estime*. His last opera, *Biorn*, was written to an English libretto and performed at the Queen's Theatre, London (1877). A version of *Macbeth* with the action transferred to Norway and the witches turned into Norns, it failed disastrously; none of the music, described by the critic Joseph Bennett as written at so much per yard, survives in print.

As a creative artist Rossi belonged to the generation of minor composers who achieved some individuality within the post-Rossinian tradition, but whose talent was unable to survive the tradition's collapse. Works like *I falsi monetari* and *Il domino nero* show a real invention, combined with a flair for comedy that caused Felice Romani to consider Rossi Donizetti's successor in *opera buffa*. Indeed *I falsi monetari* (in its original form), with its blunt rhythms and classical tonal schemes, would seem to have been the nearest single model for the style of Verdi's youthful *Un giorno di regno*. *Cleopatra* and *La contessa di Mons*, on the other hand, while showing an attempt to keep up with the times, offer little more than the old framework shorn of *fioriture* and cabalettas and garnished with recherchés harmonies, calculated irregularities of phrasing and an occasional excursion into local idioms (*La contessa di Mons* quotes from the famous *Jota aragonesa*). Among the later stage works exception should be made of the one-act *Il maestro e la cantante* (1867), in which Rossi shows a Sullivanesque talent for musical foolery, at one point combining a cabaletta by Bellini in the voice part with one by Donizetti in the orchestra. But Rossi was famous chiefly as an academic, and one of the first in Italy to show a genuine interest in the revival of old music.

Costanza e Oringaldo (melodramma, 1, R. Fortini), Naples, S Carlo, 30 May 1830, *I-Nc**, collab. P. Raimondi
La villana contessa (ob, A. Passaro), Naples, Nuovo, 8 May 1831; rev., Turin, 1846; *Nc* (as Le principesse villane); vs (Milan, n.d.)
La sposa al lotto (V. Torelli), Naples, Nuovo, June 1831
La casa in vendita, ovvero Il casino in campagna (Torelli), Naples, Nuovo, sum. 1831
Scomessa e matrimonio (commedia per musica, 2), Naples, Nuovo, 30 Nov 1831, *Nc**
Baldovino, tiranno di Spoleto (Servi, after A. Peracchi), Rome, Casa Contini, carn. 1832
Il maestro di scuola (Servi), Rome, Casa Contini, spr. 1832
Il disertore svizzero, ovvero La nostalgia (opera semiseria, 2, F. Romani), Rome, Valle, 9 Sept 1832, *Mr*, excerpts (Milan, n.d.)
Le fucine di Bergen (opera semiseria, 2, J. Ferretti, after B. Merelli), Rome, Valle, 16 Nov 1833
La casa disabitata, ovvero Don Eustachio di Campagna (melodramma giocoso, 2, Ferretti), Milan, Scala, 16 Aug 1834, *Mr**; rev. as I falsi monetari, Turin, 1844, *Mr*, *Nc*, vs (Milan, 1852)
Amelia, ovvero Otto anni di costanza (melodramma comico, 3, C. Bassi), Naples, S Carlo, 31 Dec 1834, *Mr*, *Nc**, excerpts (Milan, 1835; London, 1835)
Leocadia (melodramma, 2, after E. Scribe and Mélesville), Milan, Cannobiana, 30 April 1835, *Mr**
Giovanna Shore (melodramma serio, 3, Romani), Mexico City, Municipale, sum. 1836, *Nc**
Il borgomastro di Schiedam (melodramma, 3, G. Peruzzini, after Mélesville), Milan, Re, 1 June 1844, *OS*, vs (Milan, n.d.)
Dottor Bobolo, ovvero La fiera (melodramma buffo, 3, F. Rubino), Naples, Nuovo, 2 March 1845, scena e duetto (Milan, n.d.)
Cellini a Parigi (melodramma semiserio, 4, Peruzzini), Turin, d'Angennes, 2 June 1845, *Mr**, vs (Milan, n.d.)
Azema di Granata, ovvero Gli abencerragi ed i zegrini (melodramma

tragico, 2, Bassi), Milan, Scala, 21 March 1846, *Mr**, excerpts (Milan, 1846)

La figlia di Figaro (melodramma giocoso, 3, Ferretti), Vienna, Kärntnertor, 17 April 1846, *GB-Lbl*, *I-Mr**, vs (Milan, 1846)

Bianca Contarini (dramma tragico, prol., 3, F. Jannetti), Milan, Scala, 24 Feb 1847, *Mr*, *Nc*, excerpts (Milan, 1846)

Il domino nero (opera comica, 3, Rubino), Milan, Cannobiana, 1 Sept 1849, *GB-Lbl*, *I-Mr**, vs (Milan, 1849)

Le sabine (melodramma, prol., 2, Peruzzini), Milan, Scala, 21 Feb 1852, *Nc**

L'alchimista (melodramma giocoso, 3, M. D'Arienzo), Naples, Fondo, 23 Aug 1853, *Nc**, excerpts (Milan, n.d.)

La sirena (opera semiseria, 2, Peruzzini), Milan, Cannobiana, 11 Oct 1855

Lo zigaro rivale (farsa, 1, S. Cammarano), Milan, Cannobiana, spr. 1867; rev., Turin, 1867; excerpts (Turin, n.d.)

Il maestro e la cantante (scherzo comico, 1, possibly Rossi), Turin, Nota, Sept 1867, *GB-Lbl*, *I-Nn*, vs (Turin, 1868)

Gli artisti alla fiera (melodramma buffo, 3, A. Ghislanzoni), Turin, Carignano, 7 Nov 1868, *Nc*, vs (Milan, n.d.)

La contessa di Mons (melodramma, 4, D'Arienzo, after V. Sardou: *Patrie!*), Turin, Regio, 31 Jan 1874, *GB-Lbl*, *I-Nc**, vs (Turin, 1874)

Cleopatra (tragedia lirica, 4, D'Arienzo), Turin, Regio, 5 March 1876, *GB-Lbl*, *I-Nn*, vs (Turin, 1876)

Biorn (tragic op, 5, F. Marshall, after W. Shakespeare: *Macbeth*), London, Queen's, 17 Jan 1877, *Nc** (as Macbeth)

*

FlorimoN

A. Colombani: *L'opera italiana nel secolo XIX* (Milan, 1900)

G. Radiciotti: *Elenco delle opere di Lauro Rossi* (Macerata, 1910)

S. Balthazar: 'Mayr, Rossini, and the Development of the Early *Concertato* Finale', *JRMA*, cxvi (1991), 236–66

JULIAN BUDDEN

Rossi, Luigi (*b* Torremaggiore, 1597–8; *d* Rome, 20 Feb 1653). Italian composer. Born in Puglia, apparently trained in Naples, he moved to Rome some time before the end of January 1620. By August he had joined the newly formed household of Marcantonio Borghese, his junior by only a few years and the first Borghese to receive the title Prince of Sulmona from the Spanish crown. Rossi served Marcantonio for 16 years, presumably as a chamber musician and composer; he married a harpist, Costanza da Ponte, in 1627. Rossi became organist at S Luigi dei Francesi, the French church in Rome, in April 1633, the year that Cardinal Antonio Barberini the younger became Cardinal Protector of France, and in 1635 Rossi took nearly a year's leave in Florence; in November 1636 he left the Borghese in a definite move from the pro-Spanish to the pro-French orbit in Rome. In 1638 Taddeo Barberini had given a ballet miming the duel for the sword of Durindana from Ariosto's *Orlando furioso*. For the 1642 carnival season, Cardinal Antonio Barberini planned to give not only his annual spoken play, a 'comedia delli gentilhuomini', but also for the first time an opera, based on characters from *Orlando furioso* with a libretto by Giulio Rospigliosi and music by Rossi. This project, *Il palazzo incantato*, nearly foundered when Rossi became seriously ill in November 1641 with only one act set to music. But he was recovering by January, when he became the newest addition to Antonio Barberini's growing list of household musicians. The opera, in three acts, given at the Barberini palace on 22 February 1642, was unlike any musical drama Rome had seen before, even though Rossi's music was well known and *Palazzo incantato* Rospigliosi's sixth libretto. It precedes Monteverdi's *L'incoronazione di Poppea* by a year, and while comparable, the Roman work lacks the strong sense of vengeance and intrigue in Busenello's libretto for Monteverdi. The determining personality (Prunières called it 'elegiac') must have been Rossi's, because the same lyricism pervades his second and last opera, *Orfeo*. *Il palazzo incantato* survives in manuscript (*GB-Lcm*, *I-Bc*, *Rvat*/*R*1977: IOB, ii).

Rossi first went to Paris in June 1646, and with the support of the French prime minister, Cardinal Mazarin, and Rossi's patron, Cardinal Antonio Barberini, now in exile in France, *Orfeo* was produced at the Palais Royal on 2 March the following year. This three-act 'Roman' production went beyond anything that had ever been attempted in Rome, partly because its libretto, by Francesca Buti, accommodated stage machinery (designed by the Venetian Giacomo Torelli) for a grand ballet. Furthermore, Orpheus and Eurydice were played by the soprano castrato Atto Melani and Anna Francesca Costa, both from the Florentine court. Given eight times between March and May 1647, *Orfeo* achieved an undreamt-of sumptuousness in casting, staging and score. It marked the growth of all the elements of court opera since the Florentine *Euridice* settings of 1600; it also marks Rossi's surer, more experienced hand at large-scale, continuous composition.

After half a year back in Rome, Rossi returned to France to serve the queen early in 1648; he continued to receive huge sums of money from Cardinal Antonio Barberini and in autumn 1649 joined Barberini in Provence, remaining in France until at least June 1651. He thus spent at least five productive years in the north, and the sojourn is marked by the presence of his operatic arias and cantatas in contemporary and later French manuscripts and prints; an aria from *Orfeo* appears as late as 1708 in an anthology published by Ballard. Singers from *Orfeo* were also to carry Rossi's music far afield: for example, Alessandro Cecconi, who probably sang the roles of the Augur and Pluto, took Rossi's music to Sweden, where he went to serve Queen Christina. In Rome Rossi's fame was undimmed by his long absence. Though never performed in Rome, *Orfeo* was copied for the Chigi from an unknown source (MS score and libretto in *I-Rvat*; a French score has been lost since the early 19th century). Rossi's two operas and Cavalli's *Giasone* were the only ones from before 1650 to enter the Chigi's collection of 28 opera scores.

See also ORFEO (ii) and *PALAZZO INCANTATO, IL*.

*

R. Rolland: 'Notes sur l'*Orfeo* de Luigi Rossi et sur les musiciens italiens à Paris sous Mazarin', *RHCM*, i (1901), 225–36, 363–72

——: 'La représentation d'*Orfeo* à Paris et l'opposition religieuse et politique à l'opéra', *RHCM*, i (1901), 10–17

——: 'Le premier opéra joué à Paris, l'*Orfeo* de Luigi Rossi', *Musiciens d'autrefois* (Paris, 1908; Eng. trans., 1915)

H. Prunières: 'Les représentations du *Palazzo d'Atlante* à Rome', *SIMG*, xiv (1912–13), 218–26

——: *L'opéra italien en France avant Lulli* (Paris, 1913)

F. Liuzzi: 'I musicisti italiani in Francia', *L'opera del genio italiano all'estero* (Rome, 1946)

A. Ghislanzoni: *Luigi Rossi* (Milan, 1954)

P. Bjurström: *Giacomo Torelli and Baroque Stage Design* (Stockholm, 1962)

D. J. Grout: 'The Chorus in Early Opera', *Festschrift Friedrich Blume zum 70. Geburtstag* (Kassel, 1963), 151–61

G. Minghetti: 'Ricerche sul "Palagio … d'Atlante" di Luigi Rossi', *Quadrivium*, x (1969), 135–47

N. Pirrotta: *Storia dell'opera dalle origini al 1645* (Rome, 1972)

M. Murata: *Operas for the Papal Court, 1631–1668* (Ann Arbor, 1981)

MARGARET MURATA

Rossi, Michelangelo (*b* Genoa, *c*1602; *d* Rome, bur. 7 July 1656). Italian composer. Little is known of his famed violin playing, and his musical style is represented by only one volume of keyboard music, an opera and a set of polyphonic madrigals. From 1624 to 1630 Rossi was associated with the Roman household of Cardinal Maurizio of Savoy, who between 1624 and 1626 brought to Rome the theatre, ballet and other musical festivities customary to the ducal court in Turin. Rossi accompanied the cardinal to Turin at least once, performing in a lavish masque-like work in February 1628 or 1629. He was in Rome again from the end of 1629 until 1632 as organist at the church of S Luigi dei Francesi. By August 1630 he was a highly paid musician in the household of Prince Taddeo Barberini. It is tempting to attribute the setting of Taddeo's 'rappresentatione della Regina Ester' of 1632 to Rossi, for he did compose the music for Taddeo's more ambitious production, *Erminia sul Giordano*, first performed at the Palazzo Barberini alle Quattro Fontane on 30 January 1633 (for illustration *see* ERMINIA SUL GIORDANO). This three-act *dramma musicale* was a setting of a pastoral libretto by Giulio Rospigliosi, based in part on Tasso's *Gerusalemme liberata*, with supernatural scenes added to exploit the theatrical machines engineered by Francesco Guitti.

Rossi appears to have left the Barberini orbit in August 1634, abandoning the Paris-bound entourage of Giulio Mazzarini (later Cardinal Jules Mazarin), for an unknown opportunity with the Duke of Modena. Nevertheless, the score of *Erminia* was published in Rome in 1637, with Rossi's dedication to Taddeo's wife. A printed *argomento* and a letter by Rospigliosi point to a second performance shortly thereafter in Pistoia during Carnival 1638. The circumstances of Rossi's next theatrical work, the *opera-torneo Andromeda* (1638, Ferrara, Corte Vecchia), suggest a continuation of some Roman connections through its Bentivoglio sponsors and the church's governorship of Ferrara. Guitti again was engineer. Only the libretto by Ascanio Pio di Savoia and 15 engravings signed by Guitti survive (for illustration *see* GUITTI, FRANCESCO).

See also ERMINIA SUL GIORDANO.

*

R. Eitner: 'Die weitere Entwicklung der Oper', *MMg*, xiv (1882), 97–8
H. Goldschmidt: *Studien zur Geschichte der italienischen Oper im 17. Jahrhundert*, i (Leipzig, 1901), 63–70
A. Toni: 'M. A. Rossi: cenni biografici', *Bollettino bibliografico musicale*, ii/6 (1927), 1–5
U. Rolandi: 'L'*Andromeda* musicata da M. A. Rossi (1638)', *Rassegna dorica*, iii (1931–2), 48–58
I. Küffel: *Die Libretti G. Rospigliosis: ein Kapitel frühbarocken Operngeschichte in Rom* (diss., Vienna U., 1968)
O. Wessely: 'Aus römischen Bibliotheken und Archiven', *Symbolae historiae musicae: Hellmut Federhofer zum 60. Geburtstag* (Mainz, 1971), 81–102
F. Mancini, M. T. Muraro and E. Povoledo, eds.: *Illusione e pratica teatrale* (Venice, 1975) [exhibition catalogue], pl. no.18
S. Leopold: 'Quelle bazzicature poetiche, appellate ariette', *HJbMw*, iii (1978), 101–41
M. Murata: *Operas for the Papal Court, 1631–1668* (Ann Arbor, 1981)
F. Hammond: 'More on Music in Casa Barberini', *Studi musicali*, xiv (1985), 235–61, esp.244–5 MARGARET MURATA

Rossignol, Félix-Ludger. *See* JONCIÈRES, VICTORIN.

Rossignol, Le. 'Lyric tale' by Igor Stravinsky; *see* NIGHTINGALE, THE.

Rossi-Lemeni, Nicola (*b* Istanbul, 6 Nov 1920; *d* Bloomington, IN, 12 March 1991). Italian bass. A pupil of his mother, Xenia Macadon, and of Carnevali-Cusinati, he made his début at La Fenice in 1946 as Varlaam, a role he repeated in 1947 at La Scala, where he continued to appear until 1960. At first he was heard as Boris, Philip II and Mephistopheles (Gounod and Boito); he sang in all the major Italian theatres and also at Buenos Aires, San Francisco (American début, 1951), Covent Garden (1952, as Boris), the Metropolitan, Chicago and other houses. An interpreter of marked intelligence and sensitivity, he began with a smooth, mellow and well-focussed voice. Later in his career he compensated for his premature vocal decline with eloquent phrasing and vigorous declamation and specialized in modern operas such as Pizzetti's *L'assassinio nella cattedrale* (première at La Scala in 1958, and elsewhere), *Wozzeck*, Bloch's *Macbeth* and Britten's *Billy Budd* (Italian première, 1965, Florence). He had the title of Grand Officer of the Order of Merit of the Italian Republic. His second wife was the soprano Virginia Zeani.

*

GV (R. Celletti, with discography) RODOLFO CELLETTI

1. Gioachino Rossini: daguerreotype, c1850

Rossini, Gioachino (Antonio) (*b* Pesaro, 29 Feb 1792; *d* Passy, 13 Nov 1868). Italian composer. The most important Italian composer of the first half of the 19th century, Rossini transformed the form and content of Italian opera, displacing dated and dying traditions inherited from such composers as Cimarosa and Paisiello and establishing in their place a largely new set of procedures. Though best known for his comic operas – and for music that is sensuous, brilliant and rhythmically vital – Rossini's contribution to the evolution of *opera seria* and to stage works of mixed genres is equally important, making him Verdi's most significant forerunner. Rossini is also an important figure in the development of 19th-century French (and, more tangentially, German) opera. Using his enormous prestige to effect a blending of French and Italian traditions during his first residency in Paris between 1824 and 1829, Rossini created for the Paris Opéra two works – the comic *Le Comte Ory* and the political epic *Guillaume Tell* – which were to have a significant influence on composers as different as Adam and Meyerbeer, Offenbach and Wagner.

1. Early successes: up to 1813. 2. The conquest of Italy, 1813–16. 3. The Naples years, 1816–22. 4. Towards Paris. 5. Retirement and reputation.

1. EARLY SUCCESSES: UP TO 1813. Born into the closely knit community of Pesaro at a time of war and political upheaval in Europe, Rossini was brought up by parents who were both working musicians. His father, Giuseppe Antonio Rossini, was the public *trombetta* of Pesaro and a horn player of sufficient distinction eventually to acquire a teaching post at Bologna's Accademia Filarmonica. He was also an ardent and outspoken Republican (his son grew up to be politically more circumspect) whose imprisonment by the Austrians in 1799 forced his wife Anna into making more of her untrained talent as an operatic seconda donna soprano than might otherwise have been the case. From 1799 until her premature retirement in 1807, Anna sang regularly in Imola, Ravenna and elsewhere in operas by such composers as Luigi Mosca, Valentino Fioravanti and Giuseppe Gazzaniga. How frequently Gioachino travelled with his mother is not certain; yet it is clear that he heard a good deal of opera in his formative years, and also appeared on stage as a boy soprano before his precocious entry into Bologna's Accademia Filarmonica at the age of 14 in 1806. It would seem that he began composing – a *Cavatina cantata ... in vestiario* [costume] *ed azione da buffo* – as early as 1802–3, shortly before the completion of the six popular *Sonate a quattro* (*c*1804) in which the four solo strings, the double bass in particular, sometimes seem to take on the characters of players in a *buffo* opera. Though Rossini was a reluctant student of counterpoint, and the despair of his distinguished teacher Padre Stanislao Mattei, there were other respects in which he was a model student. He was exceptionally well versed in the works of Haydn and Mozart (later described by him as 'the admiration of my youth, the desperation of my mature years, and the consolation of my old age'); he was also an indefatigable répétiteur and keyboard player in local theatres.

In Bologna in 1807 Rossini heard two singers, representatives of the old order and the new, who were to have a profound impact on his life. One was the Spanish soprano Isabella Colbran, whom Rossini later married and for whom he was to write some of his most elaborate and powerful roles; the other was the great castrato Velluti. Though the castrato tradition was all but extinct as a force in contemporary operatic life, displaced in heroic roles by the contralto and the sexually unambiguous tenor, Rossini later claimed to have been deeply influenced by 'the purity, the miraculous flexibility of those voices and, above all, by their profoundly penetrating accent'. He was to write one role for Velluti, that of Arsace in the stylized and curiously old-fashioned chamber opera *Aureliano in Palmira* (1813, Milan); he also created a part for him in his cantata for the Congress of Verona in 1822, *Il vero omaggio*. And it was Rossini who oversaw the 1825 French première of Meyerbeer's *Il crociato in Egitto*, the castrato tradition's operatic swan song and one of Velluti's finest triumphs.

Rossini's creative output as a student in Bologna was limited, though he did write the music that was later to be assembled into his opera *Demetrio e Polibio*. However, it was only after his premature departure from the Accademia that Rossini began to make significant headway, beginning with a commission to set a libretto by Gaetano Rossi, *La cambiale di matrimonio*, for the Teatro S Moisè, Venice, in November 1810. As Rossini later recalled, conditions in shrewdly administered theatres such as S Moisè were ideal for an apprentice composer. Working to strictly limited budgets, a small company of singers (without chorus) would stage a one-act, 80-minute opera (or *farsa*) with minimal scenery and limited rehearsal. The cast itself usually consisted of a sextet of singers: a soprano and a tenor as the romantic leads, a seconda donna, and either a trio of comic basses (*buffi*) or a pair of basses and a tenor. Between January 1812 and January 1813 Rossini wrote no fewer than four such *farse* for the S Moisè, beginning with the hugely successful *semiseria* melodrama *L'inganno felice*, rich in sentiment and distinguished by a striking spareness in some of the vocal writing, and ending with *Il Signor Bruschino*, the most scabrous and sharp-witted one-act opera before Puccini's *Gianni Schicchi*.

What is remarkable about the *farse* produced by Rossini for the S Moisè, apart from the sheer vitality of the writing, is how an astonishingly successful structural plan appears to have formed itself in Rossini's mind at the outset; and how the structural plan becomes the Act 1 form for the longer comic operas that were to follow. In outline, the prototype consists of nine movements.

1 Overture (in *L'occasione fa il ladro* a storm is substituted);
2 *introduzione*, a tripartite structure usually involving a duettino, a short aria and a concluding trio, with two *allegro* sections framing a central *cantabile*;
3 duet (or aria);
4 aria;
5 a central ensemble, usually a trio but a quartet in *La scala di seta* and a quintet in *L'occasione fa il ladro*;
6 aria
7–8 a duet followed by an aria (reversed in *Il Signor Bruschino* and replaced by two arias in *La scala di seta*); and
9 a tripartite finale, balancing the central ensemble (no.5).

The evolution of the archetypal Rossini overture from the semi-literate efforts of the years 1808–10 is a further remarkable product of the period 1812–13. Having settled the structure – an introduction and scaled-down quick section in sonata form (with no development) – Rossini proceeded to put his personal imprint on it, with an astonishing array of opening ideas, some highly original orchestral effects and the famous crescendo. The crescendo was not itself a Rossini invention, but what he made of it is unique: an extreme control of dynamic levels and the stabilization of harmonic movement linked to a mastery of orchestral colour by which textures are progressively added to with wind and percussion instruments often deployed in extreme or unusual registers. Rossini continued to use his archetypal overture, broadening the harmonic base and enriching the orchestration, until *Semiramide* (1823) where, as in *La gazza ladra*, some of the overture's themes recur in the main body of the opera. Rossini was not, however, a slave to either the overture or its forms. *Mosè in Egitto* (1818) begins, magnificently, without one; in *Ermione* (1819) an offstage choral element is introduced; and for *Guillaume Tell* (1829) Rossini evolved an entirely new four-movement programmatic form, rich in imaginative detail.

2. THE CONQUEST OF ITALY, 1813–16. Initially, Rossini had less success away from the S Moisè. The ambitious

two-act *dramma giocoso*, *L'equivoco stravagante*, given in Bologna (October 1811), was more costly to stage and ran into trouble with the local censor. However, Rossini's precocious command of the large-scale formal structures implicit in the 80-minute *farsa* gave him the necessary confidence for the planning of his first genuinely successful two-act opera, *La pietra del paragone*, given in Milan (September 1812). Stendhal thought the opera's Act 1 finale the funniest of all Rossini's comic finales. But it was Rossini's penchant for nonsensical banter ('Ombretta sdegnosa' with its 'Mis-ipípí, pípí, pípí' refrain) and quotable jokes (the 'Sigillara' sequence in Act 1) that made him the toast of Milan and guaranteed 53 performances of 'Sigillara' in its first season. The opera also cemented some important partnerships. The role of Clarice was taken by Marietta Marcolini, the first obviously talented dramatic soprano for whom Rossini was to create bespoke roles. Even more significant, the part of the romantic lead, Count Asdrubale, was taken by a bass, Filippo Galli. Galli created many leading bass roles for Rossini, from Tarabotto in *L'inganno felice* (1812) to Assur in *Semiramide* (1823).

After his Milanese success, Rossini was not only exempted from military service; he could also designate himself a *maestro di cartello*, a composer whose name alone guarantees a public. *Tancredi*, first seen in February 1813 at the prestigious Teatro La Fenice, Venice, is a further major landmark in his career. In this two-act heroic idyll, he wrote some of his most flawlessly lyrical early music while at the same time significantly advancing his mastery of individual forms and their coordinated use in ensembles. Though the subject matter of Voltaire's original play holds the work firmly within an 18th-century aesthetic, Rossini's dynamic treatment of the once static *opera seria* forms is one of the work's most revolutionary features. Harmonic thinking is on an altogether longer time-scale. Arias and duets become multi-sectional with the option of a concluding cabaletta, while lyrical and confrontational elements can increasingly be encompassed within the confines of individual movements. At the same time, the lyrical vocal writing in *Tancredi* provides us with a distillation of Rossini's early, but ultimately far-reaching, concern for sheer beauty of vocal sound. This preoccupation not only confers on leading players in his *opere serie* a certain idealized and idealizing quality, but also establishes the aesthetic basis on which the increasingly influential Rossini would judge and advise leading singers over the next 50 years.

The Ferrara revision of March 1813, with its restoration of Voltaire's original 'tragic' ending, drafted for Rossini by the distinguished writer Luigi Lechi, is also early evidence of Rossini's possessing a stronger interest in dramatic and literary values than he has sometimes been credited with. Though there is no partnership in Rossini's career to match Mozart's with Da Ponte or Verdi's with Boito, it is now clear that Rossini took a far closer interest in the texts he set than was once assumed. Letters exist which give clear evidence of Rossini's planning new projects many months in advance of preliminary deadlines. Even where hard evidence is not available, it is possible to deduce that Rossini chose, advised on and emended the texts he set. In later years, we know that librettists were more or less domiciled with the composer – Rossi for *Semiramide* or the extensive team of writers who worked on *Guillaume Tell* at the Paris home of the banker Aguado. Equally, it is difficult to conceive that the dramatically pertinent and musically organic treatment of the final scenes of Shakespeare's *Othello* (*Otello*, 1816) was conceived and shaped by anyone other than Rossini himself. (The offstage gondolier was certainly Rossini's inspiration, freely acknowledged in later years.) The very choice of Shakespeare's play for Naples in 1816 was itself more than usually enterprising, and Rossini was to go on to select librettos from the works of Beaumarchais, the as yet unfashionable Walter Scott (read by Rossini in French translation), Racine and Schiller, as well as religious and fairy-tale sources. In 1830 he was actively considering a setting of Goethe's *Faust*. All of this suggests a musician who was both literate and moderately well read, something that can be traced back to a tolerable schooling in his native Pesaro and the influence of the literary and musical scholarship of the great families to whom, as a child, he had surprisingly easy access.

After the success of *Tancredi* (with the huge, European-wide success of 'Di tanti palpiti'), Rossini was engaged at short notice by the Teatro S Benedetto in Venice to reset a contemporary story about an Italian girl's escapades in Algiers. Few things demonstrate more clearly Rossini's emancipation from the past, his innovative genius and the purely musical basis of much of his humour than this opportunistic reworking of Angelo Anelli's libretto for *L'italiana in Algeri*, first set to music by Luigi Mosca in Milan in 1808. Despite some initial, and unfounded, charges of plagiarism, Rossini's version triumphed, with further plaudits for Galli as the lascivious Mustafà and for Marcolini as the Italian Girl. The casting of Marcolini as Isabella is of particular interest, showing as it does Rossini's willingness to introduce *opera seria* elements into *opera buffa* (Isabella's cavatina 'Cruda sorte!' and her Act 2 Rondo 'Pensa alla patria') just as surely as his intention to use some of the structures and energizing rhythms of *opera buffa* in *opera seria*. The idea that Rossini indiscriminately mixed the genres both misrepresents and over-simplifies what actually happens in specific works.

Two smaller-scale operas followed *L'italiana in Algeri*, one of them the exquisite and witty *dramma buffo*, *Il turco in Italia* (1814, Milan), notable for Rossini's increasing preoccupation with the use of ensemble-writing, the other *Aureliano in Palmira*. In December 1814 he produced *Sigismondo*: a rare box-office failure as well as an artistic one, although parts of the score were to be successfully cannibalized for later works. But if 1814 brought Rossini no runaway success, his prestige was sufficient for him to be offered a contract that was to change both the direction of his own career and the future course of Italian opera.

3. The Naples years, 1816–22. This contract was offered by the Teatro S Carlo, Naples, at the time the most lavishly financed opera house in Europe. Since 1809 its artistic director had been Domenico Barbaia, a millionaire gaming magnate and entrepreneur of genius. Already in the process of formation in Naples was a superb roster of singers, including Isabella Colbran, three distinguished tenors – Giovanni Davide, Manuel García and Andrea Nozzari – and the bass Michele Benedetti. As Barbaia was no doubt aware, Neapolitan conservatism (nurtured on the music of Cimarosa and Paisiello) had insulated the city from the Rossini phenomenon, a fact that gave Barbaia's project novelty as well as the promise of richer long-term developments.

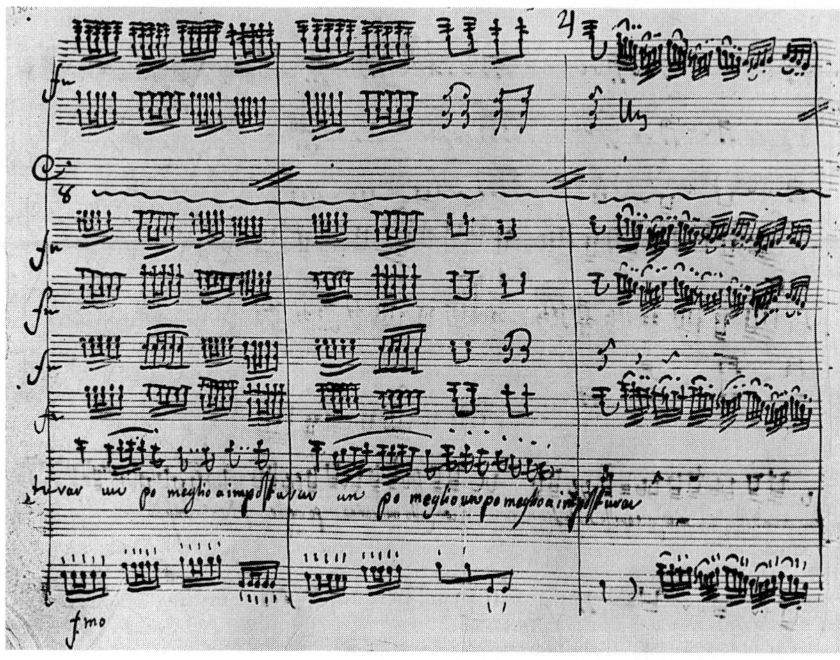

2. Page from the autograph score of Bartolo's Act 1 aria, 'A un dottor', from Rossini's 'Il barbiere di Siviglia' (1816, Rome)

Rossini's contract with the Neapolitan theatres was worth between 8000 and 12 000 francs a year. Unpaid leave to undertake commissions elsewhere was permitted, but the Neapolitan schedules were strenuous. They involved composition, administration and the musical preparation of his own as well as other people's works, a stipulation that was to expose Rossini to a significant amount of non-Italian opera in his time there. (During the composition of *Maometto II* in 1820, he oversaw the Italian *prima* of Spontini's recently revised *tragédie lyrique Fernand Cortez*.) Above all, the artistic predilections of artists like Colbran and Nozzari ensured that Rossini would now face the challenge of writing many more *opere serie* than had hitherto been the case.

Excluding the semi-pastiche *Eduardo e Cristina* (1819, Venice), Rossini wrote 18 operas between his arrival in Naples in 1815 and his departure in March 1822, nine of them for the S Carlo company. Away from Naples, he consolidated his reputation as a composer of *opera buffa*. *Il barbiere di Siviglia* (1816, Rome) is a brilliant reappropriation of Beaumarchais' play that iconoclastically outmanoeuvres Paisiello's setting at almost every point, while *La Cenerentola* (1817, Rome) is a *dramma giocoso* that mixes *buffo* antics with a degree of pathos, morbidity even, that can be seen as pointing to latent elements in Rossini's own psychological make-up. In both operas we can observe Rossini perfecting his skill in successfully bringing to *opera buffa* what Rodolfo Celletti (1991) has called 'the florid and sumptuous language' of *opera seria*. *La Cenerentola* also signals his evolving preoccupation with the *semiseria* form – comedy mixed melodramatically with potential tragedy – something that achieves its richest expression in *La gazza ladra* (1817, Milan). Despite the pastoral setting and the potential for comedy in the antics of the pilfering magpie and the (rather sinister) local mayor, the opera skirts tragedy throughout its second act, with a prison scene, a tribunal and a march to the scaffold, strangely and disturbingly scored. As with Cenerentola, so with the falsely accused Ninetta Rossini achieves a telling naturalness of musical characterization. A simple force of human emotion also permeates the portrayal of Ninetta's father, the political refugee Fernando. Relations between fathers and children in Rossini's operas can be almost as charged with emotion as they were later to be in Verdi's. After *La gazza ladra*, Rossini's non-Neapolitan Italian operas are less interesting (*Matilde di Shabran*, which Paganini helped launch in Rome in 1821, is not quite in the same league). Indeed, as David Kimbell has suggested, Rossini's relationship with emergent Romanticism became dangerously equivocal, 'his style too precariously poised between the past and the future, between high comedy, frigid formalism and flagrant melodrama' (*Italian Opera*, 1991, p.466). However, *Bianca e Falliero* (1819, Milan) is a compelling essay in the dramatic use of an openly florid style of writing (as the 1986 Pesaro Festival revival of this long-forgotten work showed).

It is in the Neapolitan operas that we can most readily trace Rossini's development as a radical, pioneering artist unselfconsciously developing techniques with which to confront an increasingly formidable array of theatrical subjects. Of particular interest are his *Otello*; the biblical *Mosè in Egitto* with its atmospheric opening Scene of the Shadows and famous Prayer; *Armida* with its Weberish (but pre-*Freischütz*) romantic allure; the dramatic and picturesque *La donna del lago*, one of the earliest Walter Scott settings; and the astonishingly powerful *Ermione*, taken from Racine's *Andromaque*. All these operas engage strong human emotions, though there is some truth in Stendhal's assertion that 'the theme of serious [erotic] love is as foreign to Rossini as it is to Walter Scott'. It is said that Rossini had no great fondness for the combination of soprano and tenor voices; if this is so, he wrote successfully against the grain in *Armida*. It is significant, though, that *Otello* lacks a central love duet, and that it is the love duet that Rossini rather obviously omitted from his reworking of Anelli's libretto for *L'italiana in Algeri*.

The virtuosity and dramatic intelligence of leading S

Carlo artists such as Colbran and Nozzari inspired Rossini during his years in Naples to fashion for them a fascinatingly varied series of bespoke roles. For Colbran alone he would range from the pathos of Desdemona's 'Willow Song' or the unvarnished beauty of Ellen's aubade at the start of *La donna del lago* to the complex webs of declamation and song, recitative and arioso for Hermione or for Anna Erisso, the tragic heroine of *Maometto II*. The power and the eloquence of Rossini's writing for solo singers in his Naples years should not, however, allow us to lose sight of the enormously increased importance of larger ensembles and, from *Mosè in Egitto* onwards, a new and increasingly individualistic use of the chorus. At one level this extension of the scale of Rossini's *opere serie* is a structural phenomenon typified by the huge first act of *Maometto II* which Rossini assembled in five monolithic blocks, with the massive 867-bar scena and terzettone itself linked by harmonic modulation into the 362-bar chorus and cavatina that follow. The organic use of rhythm and carefully crafted thematic transformations help bind the structures together. At a more basic level, we find Rossini increasingly coopting comprimario characters and the chorus into movements that would previously have functioned simply as arias or duets.

With the expansion of the chorus, physically as well as dramatically, there appears a comparable expansion of orchestral resources. In *Maometto II*, the prayer for Anna and women's chorus is most effectively accompanied by a flute, two clarinets, a bassoon, two horns and a harp; yet this is a score, written in 1820, that calls for full orchestra with substantially reinforced brass (four horns, two trumpets, three trombones and serpentone) as well as harp, extensive percussion and a stage band. There is, though, no blurring of the essential clarity and economy that is elsewhere a hallmark of Rossini's brilliantly sharp-eared orchestral writing. The finest Neapolitan operas are notable for their individual orchestral colourings: the gaunt tones of *Ermione* sit in bold contrast to the limpid beauty of *La donna del lago*. Similarly, Rossini's use (or omission) of the traditional overture is a further contribution to a growing preoccupation with the needs of serious music drama. Towards the end of Rossini's time in Naples the influence of French opera, of Spontini in particular, can be sensed in the writing for orchestra and chorus and in some of the more declamatory vocal writing. Equally, contemporaries saw evidence in *Zelmira* of a new preoccupation with German-style contrapuntalism (the opera was destined for performance in Vienna), though it must be noted that Italians had long suspected Rossini of 'Germanic' leanings. Not all Rossini's Neapolitan operas can be counted as successes. *Ricciardo e Zoraide* is not, dramatically, the kind of neglected masterpiece that *Ermione* has proved to be. Yet it was the increasing coolness of Neapolitan audiences to the best of Rossini's strikingly innovatory works of the years 1818–22 that almost certainly forced him to look to theatres and audiences beyond Italy. Even before he left Italy, Paris had become for him a necessary place of migration; though the scars of the failure of works like *Ermione* had already made him artistically wiser and more circumspect than a man barely past his 30th year might ordinarily be.

4. Towards Paris. The 1822 Viennese Rossini season had been organized by Barbaia. En route for Vienna, Rossini married Isabella Colbran. It was to be a difficult marriage to a woman nearing the end of her singing career for whom retirement was uncongenial at a time when her husband's star was increasingly in the ascendant. Though Rossini returned to his country house outside Bologna in the late summer of 1822, closeting himself with the librettist Rossi for work on *Semiramide*, his Italian career was drawing to a close. Offers of lucrative work outside Italy are said to have been made to him as early as 1818. The Viennese season of 1822 and the one at the King's Theatre, London, in the early months of 1824 no doubt raised local hopes that Rossini could be tempted their way. But he spoke neither German nor English; nor could either city match the attractions of Paris with its cosmopolitan population, its well-established Théâtre Italien and a government (unstable and unreliable, as it turned out) prepared to negotiate professionally with a man who had by now shown himself to be one of Barbaia's aptest pupils, legally astute and financially quick-witted. Rossini settled there in 1824. He was to provide the French with a sophisticated royal entertainment, *Il viaggio a Reims* (1825), as well as adaptations of two Neapolitan operas and two new works, *Le Comte Ory* and *Guillaume Tell*. But he was also, increasingly, the *éminence grise* of Franco-Italian operatic life. In addition to composing, he supervised the work of the Théâtre Italien, though by the end of 1826 he had relinquished most of his duties there in order to devote more energy to composition for the Opéra. The careers of young singers like the charismatic Maria Malibran were advanced. More importantly, Rossini took under his wing a new generation of composers, including Meyerbeer, Donizetti and the greatly admired Bellini.

If Rossini appears to have been tardy in bringing new operas before the French public, it was because a press of administrative responsibilities and social engagements joined hands with his innate shrewdness and professional circumspection. Before new works could be contemplated there was the need to master further the French language, French prosody and French theatrical practice. There was also an ensemble of singers to be built as adept in the Italian *bel canto* manner as in the French declamatory style of which Rossini was increasingly the master. In the event, he achieved his aim with a team led by the soprano Laure Cinti-Damoreau, the tenor Adolphe Nourrit, the baritone Henry-Bernard Dabadie and the bass Nicolas Levasseur. In general terms, Rossini's French operas show a process of simplification both of musical line and of dramatic structure. Floridity of utterance is banished, as is the anachronism of the coloratura contralto hero. Meanwhile, the role of the chorus continued to be developed. Of the two Paris revisions of earlier Neapolitan works, *Le siège de Corinthe* is a more stageworthy piece than the original *Maometto II*; on the other hand, it is possible to think that the French *Moïse et Pharaon* is a rather dropsical affair, a spectacular but often (in terms of key relationships) carelessly contrived inflation of an original that owes more to Haydn (the opening of *The Creation* an obvious model for the Scene of the Shadows) than it does to the spectacular pretensions of the revised version.

Of the two new works for the Paris Opéra, *Le Comte Ory* both revisits the past and anticipates the future. Outwardly, the score has something of the wit, élan and sardonic humour of *Il barbiere di Siviglia*. Yet orchestrally it inhabits a completely different world. The young Berlioz gazed openmouthed at the scoring of the exquisite, erotically sensuous nocturnal trio in Act 2. And once again there is the fact of Rossini's enormously extended formal control. On the surface, *Le Comte Ory* is light comedy, a brilliantly engaging example of the *opéra comique* genre as practised by such composers as Boieldieu, Auber and Hérold. In fact, it was written for the Paris Opéra itself, with orchestral forces not dissimilar to those later to be deployed in *Guillaume Tell*, virtuoso vocal writing that goes some way beyond the usual demands of *opéra comique*, and a structural reach (partly derived from the elaborate and sophisticated *Il viaggio a Reims*) that provides us with individual movements averaging between 300 and 400 bars in length. Once again, Rossini had created a distinctive masterpiece that critics and performers have often found difficult to 'place'.

If *Le Comte Ory* is a grand if enigmatic *jeu d'esprit*, *Guillaume Tell* is very much the great summarizing work of Rossini's career, an astonishing drawing together of the finest elements on offer in both Italian and French music theatre at the time of its composition. Here, at last, was a subject – human and political – grand enough to require the huge formal advances Rossini had made in his final years in Naples. The big italianate forms evolved by Rossini underpin much of the work – the Act 1 finale, the duet between Arnold and Mathilde in Act 2, Arnold's Act 4 aria 'Asil héréditaire', where the Italian manner itself is further transformed by the declamatory demands made on the tenor in the heroic cabaletta. But as the large forms are redeployed, so they are increasingly filled with a new, French-derived quality of dramatic declamation that is closely geared to the precise needs of a text that Rossini himself appears to have helped shape and vet down to the very last syllable. There can be little wonder that Wagner (and before him, Berlioz) so admired the score, in particular such things as the great Act 2 Trio for Walter, Tell and Arnold. Equally, many of the score's more obviously French elements can be traced back to Rossini's Naples years in works like *Armida*, *La donna del lago* and *Ermione* ('my little *Guillaume Tell*', as Rossini once described it). There are the numerous, dramatically important dance interludes and much picturesque orchestral colouring (used from the very first bars of the uniquely shaped 'programmatic' overture). Above all, there is the use of the chorus. None of Rossini's earlier works deploys the chorus on the scale of *Guillaume Tell*. Though it is also arguably the protagonist in *Le siège de Corinthe* and in *Mosè in Egitto* and its Paris revision, in *Guillaume Tell* it is a protagonist that is multi-faceted. In the dances and choral interludes of Act 1, we encounter the Swiss people in their rural habitat, harmoniously at one with Nature; and at the end of the opera it is they who hymn the sunrise and national liberation. In the inner acts, Rossini splits the chorus several ways – into three groups in Act 2 in the great oath-swearing of the men of Unterwald, Schyz and Uri, and into an abused and disruptive urban mob in the great confrontations with Gesler in Act 3.

In September 1829, shortly after the première of *Guillaume Tell*, Rossini returned to Bologna, to his wife and to his father, now a widower. (Anna Rossini had died in 1827; his father lived until 1839.) In spring 1830 he corresponded with a French government representative about a new opera on Goethe's *Faust*, but in summer 1830 the government fell. Charles X fled into exile and was replaced by the 57-year-old 'citizen king' Louis-Philippe. Committed to policies based on fairness and accountability, the new government cut the Civil List from 40 million francs a year to 12 million, invalidating Rossini's contract with the Opéra and his life annuity. After six years of lobbying and litigation, the annuity was restored; but by this time Rossini the opera composer was firmly in retirement. The thread had been broken. There had been talk of his retiring from operatic composition as early as 1816 after the wounding fiasco of the first night of *Il barbiere di Siviglia*. Clearly such talk was premature, but his father's remark in a letter written in 1827 – 'he has toiled long and wearily

3. *Commemorative fan (c1819) with a portrait of Rossini, and music and characters from his operas*

enough' – is more to the point. It was echoed by Rossini himself in 1868 when he wrote to Tito Ricordi: 'Let dear Giulio [Tito's son] study *with kindness* my first work *Demetrio e Polibio* and *Guillaume Tell.* He will see that I was not idle!'.

5. Retirement and reputation. 39 operas in 19 years, few of them failures, many of them masterpieces or works of significant imagination or innovation, is a formidable record. With *Guillaume Tell* Rossini had completed a work that was both a consummation of his career and a natural resting-point. Other composers – Donizetti, Bellini, Meyerbeer – were on hand to carry forward his revolution at a time of further dramatic change, both musical and political. Whether or not Rossini's debilitating mental and physical illnesses in the 1840s and 1850s were in any way attributable to the exhaustion and stress of earlier years is difficult to prove. They do, however, give the lie to the idea that Rossini's long retirement from operatic composition was the irresponsible whim of a born sybarite. All the available evidence suggests that the mature Rossini was a hard-working, obsessive personality, prone to anxiety and depression; and that like many great comic geniuses he wore his anxieties beneath a mask of affability and unconcern. When his health permitted, he returned to active composition, encouraged by the ministrations of the remarkable Olympe Pélissier who became his second wife after Colbran's death in 1845; he lived mainly in Bologna from 1836 until 1855, when he returned to Paris, from which time his health improved. Important works from the 1830s – the *Stabat mater* (1833) and *Les soirées musicales* (*c*1830–35) – were followed by the numerous vocal and piano pieces that make up the *Péchés de vieillesse* (1857–68) and by the *Petite messe solennelle* (1864). Significantly, none of the religious music is demonstrably operatic in character; there is virtually no music in the *Stabat mater* or the *Messe* that could be fitted naturally into one of Rossini's operas.

In the years immediately following his retirement from operatic composition, Rossini occasionally busied himself with a number of minor, largely lost, causes. These included offering public support to Vincenzo Gabussi's opera *Clemenza di Valois*, which rose and then sank without trace in Venice in 1841, and to the career of the tenor Nicola Ivanoff. In Bologna in 1840 a bizarre transformation of *Guillaume Tell*, *Rodolofo di Sterlinga*, was mounted partly for Ivanoff's benefit; Rossini also commissioned from the young Verdi a new grand aria for Ivanoff's exclusive use in Act 2 of *Ernani.* Rossini's relations with Verdi veered between the guarded and the obsequious; and though he conversed at length with Wagner during a famous meeting in Paris in 1860, his attitude to the 'music of the future' was distant and tinged with irony. Numerous young singers were taken under Rossini's wing in Paris in the 1860s, among them the young Adelina Patti, and the Marchisio sisters for whom a new production of *Semiramide* was mounted at the Paris Opéra on 9 July 1860. The work was adapted by Rossini's friend, the composer Michele Carafa, to whom the French rights had been ceded. Though the septuagenarian Rossini was now of the opinion that by the time of *Guillaume Tell* 'L'art du chant avait sombré', he seems to have found in the voices of the Marchisio singers echoes of past beauties.

Though a handful of Rossini's most popular *buffo* works remained in the repertory, the popularity of his music went into a decline in the 1840s after his retirement from operatic composition, and again, more substantially, after his death in 1868. Thereafter, changed aesthetic perspectives, the absence of good performing editions and, above all, the absence of competent singers condemned the majority of his operas, in particular the *opere serie*, to near oblivion. The neo-classicism of the 1920s benefitted his reputation, as did the arrival on the scene of the Spanish mezzo-soprano Conchita Supervia who gave classic impersonations of the Italian Girl and Cenerentola. In the 1950s, the Glyndebourne Festival Opera, led by the distinguished Rossinian Vittorio Gui, did much to stimulate interest in a range of comic operas including *Le Comte Ory*, but it was only in the mid-1960s that the *opere serie* began to be extensively re-explored. It is a counter-revolution that has owed much to the scholarship of the new *Edizione critica delle opere di Gioachino Rossini*, and to important stage revivals at the Rossini Festival in Pesaro. But perhaps it owes most to a new generation of singers of whom Marilyn Horne could be taken as a representative and historically important example. It is a generation that has developed the techniques – and shown the flair, imagination and musical responsibility – without which Rossini's legacy cannot survive as the living achievement it undoubtedly is.

See also *Adelaide di Borgogna*; *Adina*; *Armida* (vi); *Aureliano in Palmira*; *Barbiere di Siviglia, Il* (ii); *Bianca e Falliero*; *Cambiale di matrimonio, La*; *Cenerentola, La*; *Ciro in Babilonia*; *Comte Ory, Le*; *Demetrio e Polibio*; *Donna del lago, La*; *Eduardo e Cristina*; *Elisabetta, regina d'Inghilterra*; *Equivoco stravagante, L'*; *Ermione*; *Gazza ladra, La*; *Gazzetta, La*; *Guillaume Tell* (ii); *Inganno felice, L'*; *Italiana in Algeri, L'*; *Maometto II*; *Matilde di Shabran*; *Moïse et Pharaon*; *Mosè in Egitto*; *Occasione fa il ladro, L'*; *Otello* (i); *Pietra del paragone, La*; *Ricciardo e Zoraide*; *Scala di seta, La*; *Semiramide*; *Siège de Corinthe, Le*; *Sigismondo*; *Signor Bruschino, Il*; *Tancredi*; *Torvaldo e Dorliska*; *Turco in Italia, Il*; *Viaggio a Reims, Il*; and *Zelmira*.

Edition: *Edizione critica delle opere Gioachino Rossini*, ed. Fondazione Rossini (Pesaro, 1979–) [vols. in square brackets are in preparation] [EC]

BCR – *Bologna, Teatro del Corso*	NFI – *Naples, Teatro dei Fiorentini*	RAP – *Rome, Teatro Apollo*
FEC – *Ferrara, Teatro Comunale*	NFO – *Naples, Teatro del Fondo*	RV – *Rome, Teatro Valle*
LIC – *Lisbon, Teatro de S Carlos*	PI – *Paris, Théâtre Italien*	VB – *Venice, Teatro S Benedetto*
MSC – *Milan, Teatro alla Scala*	PO – *Paris, Opéra*	VF – *Venice, Teatro La Fenice*
NC – *Naples, Teatro S Carlo*	RA – *Rome, Teatro Argentina*	VM – *Venice, Teatro S Moisè*

composed shortly before first performance unless otherwise stated

title	*genre, acts*	*libretto*	*first performance*	*sources, comments*	EC
Demetrio e Polibio	dramma serio, 2	V. Viganò-Mombelli	RV, 18 May 1812, comp. before 1809	vs (Milan, 1825–6)	

title	genre, acts	libretto	first performance	sources, comments	EC
La cambiale di matrimonio	farsa comica, 1	G. Rossi, after Camillo Federici's play (1791) and G. Checcherini's lib. for Coccia: *Il matrimonio per lettera di cambio* (1807)	VM, 3 Nov 1810	vs (Milan, 1847)	
L'equivoco stravagante	dg, 2	G. Gasbarri	BCR, 26 Oct 1811	vs (Milan, 1851)	
L'inganno felice	farsa, 1	G. Foppa	VM, 8 Jan 1812	vs (Leipzig, 1819); full score (Rome, 1826)	
Ciro in Babilonia, ossia La caduta di Baldassare	dramma con cori, 2	F. Aventi	FEC, 14 March 1812	vs (Milan, 1852)	
La scala di seta	farsa comica, 1	Foppa, after F. A. E. de Planard: *L'échelle de soie*, lib. for P. Gaveaux (1808)	VM, 9 May 1812	*S-Smf**, vs (Milan, 1852)	I/vi
La pietra del paragone	melodramma giocoso, 2	L. Romanelli	MSC, 26 Sept 1812	*I-Mr**, vs (Milan, 1846)	
L'occasione fa il ladro	burletta per musica, 1	L. Prividali, after E. Scribe: *Le prétendu par hazard, ou L'occasion fait le larron* (1810)	VM, 24 Nov 1812	*F-Pc**, vs (Milan, 1853)	[I/viii]
Il Signor Bruschino, ossia Il figlio per azzardo	farsa giocosa, 1	Foppa, after A. de Chazet and E.-T. Maurice Ourry: *Le fils par hazard, ou Ruse et folie* (1809)	VM, 27 Jan 1813	*Pc**, vs (Milan, 1854)	I/ix
Tancredi	melodramma eroico, 2	Rossi and L. Lechi, after Voltaire	VF, 6 Feb 1813	*B-Bmichotte**, *I-Ms**, autograph (private collection), vs (Leipzig, 1817)	I/x
L'italiana in Algeri	dg, 2	A. Anelli, orig. for L. Mosca (1808)	VB, 22 May 1813	*Mr**, *Ms**, vs (Mainz, c1819)	I/xi
Aureliano in Palmira	dramma serio, 2	F. Romani, after G. Sertor's lib. for Anfossi: *Zenobia in Palmira* (1790)	MSC, 26 Dec 1813	frag. *B-Bmichotte**, vs (Milan, 1855)	
Il turco in Italia	dramma buffo, 2	Romani, after C. Mazzolà's lib. for F. Seydelmann (1788)	MSC, 14 Aug 1814	*I-Mr**, vs (Leipzig, 1821)	I/xiii
Sigismondo	dramma, 2	Foppa	VF, 26 Dec 1814	*Mr**, vs (Milan, 1826)	
Elisabetta, regina d'Inghilterra	dramma, 2	G. Schmidt, after Carlo Federici's play (1814) based on S. Lee: *The Recess* (novel, 1783–5)	NC, 4 Oct 1815	*PESr** (*R*1979: ERO, vii), vs (Leipzig, 1819–20)	
Torvaldo e Dorliska	dramma semiserio, 2	C. Sterbini, based on J.-B. de Coudry: *Vie et amours du chevalier de Faubles* (1790) and the Lodoiska libs. (set by Cherubini, Kreutzer, Mayr etc.) derived from it	RV, 26 Dec 1815	*F-Pc**, vs (Milan, 1855)	
Il barbiere di Siviglia [orig. title Almaviva, ossia L'inutile precauzione]	commedia, 2	Sterbini, after the play by P.-A. Beaumarchais (1775) and G. Petrosellini's lib. for Paisiello: *Il barbiere di Siviglia* (1782)	RA, 20 Feb 1816	*I-Bc**, vs (Leipzig, 1820), full score (Rome, 1828)	
La gazzetta	dramma [ob], 2	G. Palomba, after C. Goldoni: *Il matrimonio per concorso* (1763)	NFI, 26 Sept 1816	*Nc**, vs (Milan, 1854)	
Otello, ossia Il moro di Venezia	dramma, 3	F. Berio di Salsa, after W. Shakespeare	NFO, 4 Dec 1816	*PESr** (*R*1979: ERO, viii), vs (Leipzig, 1819–20)	[I/xix]
La Cenerentola, ossia La bontà in trionfo	dg, 2	J. Ferretti, after C. Perrault: *Cendrillon* (1697), C.-G. Etienne's lib. for N. Isouard (1810) and F. Fiorini's lib. for S. Pavesi: *Agatina, o La virtù premiata* (1814)	RV, 25 Jan 1817	*Baf** (*R*1968: ed. P. Gossett, BMB, xcii) [I/xx], *PESr**, vs (Paris, 1822–3)	[I/xx]
La gazza ladra	melodramma, 2	G. Gherardini, after J. M. T. Baudouin d'Aubigny and L.-C. Caigniez: *La pie voleuse* (1815)	MSC, 31 May 1817	*Mr**, vs (Bonn and Cologne, 1819–20)	I/xxi
Armida	dramma, 3	Schmidt, after T. Tasso: *Gerusalemme liberata*	NC, 11 Nov 1817	*PESr**, vs (Paris, 1823–4)	[I/xxii]
Adelaide di Borgogna	dramma, 2	Schmidt	RA, 27 Dec 1817	(Milan, 1858)	
Mosè in Egitto	azione tragico-sacra, 3	A. L. Tottola, after F. Ringhieri: *L'Osiride* (1760)	NC, 5 March 1818	with rev. Act 3, March 1819; *F-Pc** (*R*1979: ERO, ix), vs (Paris, 1822), full score (Rome, 1825); rev. as Moïse et Pharaon, 1827	
Adina, o Il califfo di Bagdad	farsa, 1	G. Bevilacqua-Aldobrandini	LIC, 22 June 1826; comp. 1818	*I-PESr**, vs (Milan, 1859)	

title	genre, acts	libretto	first performance	sources, comments	EC
Ricciardo e Zoraide	dramma, 2	Berio di Salsa, after N. Forteguerri: *Il Ricciardetto*, cantos xiv and xv	NC, 3 Dec 1818	*Nc**, vs (Mainz, 1821–2), full score (Rome, 1829/ *R*1980: ERO, x)	[I/ xxvi]
Ermione	azione tragica, 2	Tottola, after J. Racine: *Andromaque*	NC, 27 March 1819	*F-Po**, excerpt *I-PESr**, vs (Milan, 1858)	[I/ xxvii]
Eduardo e Cristina	dramma, 2	Schmidt, rev. Bevilacqua-Aldobrandini and Tottola from orig. lib. for Pavesi: *Odoardo e Cristina* (1810)	VB, 24 April 1819	vs (Paris, 1826–7)	
La donna del lago	melodramma, 2	Tottola, after W. Scott: *The Lady of the Lake* (1810)	NC, 24 Oct 1819	*PESr**, vs (Paris, 1822–3)	I/xxix
Bianca e Falliero, ossia Il consiglio dei tre	melodramma, 2	Romani, after A.-V. Arnault: *Les vénitiens, ou Blanche et Montcassin* (1798)	MSC, 26 Dec 1819	*Mr**, vs (Milan, 1828)	[I/ xxx]
Maometto II	dramma, 2	C. della Valle, after own play *Anna Erizo* (1820)	NC, 3 Dec 1820	*PAc* (*R*1981: ERO, xi), *PESr**, excerpts *GB-Lbl**, *US-NYp**, vs (Vienna, 1823); rev. as Le siège de Corinthe, 1826	[I/ xxxi]
Matilde (di) Shabran, ossia Bellezza, e cuor di ferro	melodramma giocoso, 2	Ferretti, after F.-B. Hoffmann's lib. for Méhul: *Euphrosine* (1790) and J. M. Boutet de Monvel: *Mathilde* (play, 1799)	RAP, 24 Feb 1821	*B-Bmichotte**, vs (Vienna, 1822), full score (Rome, 1833)	
Zelmira	dramma, 2	Tottola, after Dormont de Belloy (1762)	NC, 16 Feb 1822	*F-Pc** (*R*1979: ERO, xii), excerpt *B-Bmichotte*, vs (Vienna, 1822)	
Semiramide	melodramma tragico, 2	Rossi, after Voltaire	VF, 3 Feb 1823	*I-Vt** (*R*1978: ERO, xiii), vs (Vienna, 1823), full score (Rome, 1826)	[I/ xxxiv]
Il viaggio a Reims, ossia L'albergo del giglio d'oro	dg, 1	L. Balocchi, after Mme de Stael [A. L. G. Necker]: *Corinne, ou L'Italie* (1807)	PI, 19 June 1825	orig. material *A-Wn*, *F-Pc*, excerpts *I-Rc**	[I/ xxxv]
Le siège de Corinthe	tragédie lyrique, 3	Balocchi and A. Soumet, after lib. for *Maometto II*	PO, 9 Oct 1826	rev. of Maometto II, 1820; excerpts *F-Pc**, *Po**, *I-FOc** and elsewhere, vs (Paris, 1826), full score (Paris, 1826–7/*R*1980: ERO, xiv)	
Moïse et Pharaon, ou Le passage de la Mer Rouge	opéra, 4	Balocchi and E. de Jouy, after lib. for *Mosè in Egitto*	PO, 26 March 1827	rev. of Mosè in Egitto, 1818–19; excerpts *F-Pc**, *US-NYp**, *SPmoldenhauer**, *STu* and elsewhere, full score and vs (Paris, 1827/ *R*1980: ERO, xv)	
Le Comte Ory	opéra [oc], 2	E. Scribe and C.-G. Delestre-Poirson, after their own play (1817)	PO, 20 Aug 1828	excerpts *B-Bmichotte**, *F-Po**, full score and vs (Paris, 1828/ *R*1978: ERO, xvi)	
Guillaume Tell	opéra, 4	Jouy, H.-L.-F. Bis and others, after F. von Schiller (1804)	PO, 3 Aug 1829	*Pc**, full score and vs (Paris, 1829/ *R*1980: ERO, xvii)	I/ xxxix

BCRS – *Bollettino del Centro rossiniano di studi* (1955–60, 1967–)

SOURCE MATERIALS AND PRINCIPAL BIOGRAPHIES

Stendhal: *Vie de Rossini* (Paris, 1824; Eng. trans., 1956, 2/1970 with notes by R. N. Coe)

G. Mazzatinti: *Lettere inedite di Gioacchino Rossini* (Imola, 1890, 2/1892 as *Lettere inedite e rare di G. Rossini*, 3/1902 as *Lettere di G. Rossini*, with F. Manis and G. Manis)

A. Allmayer: *Undici lettere di Gioachino Rossi pubblicate per la prima volta* (Siena, 1892)

G. Biagi: 'Undici lettere inedite di G. Rossini', *Onoranze fiorentine a Gioachino Rossini* (Florence, 1902), 101

G. Radiciotti: *Gioacchino Rossini: vita documentata, opere ed influenza su l'arte* (Tivoli, 1927–9)

——: *Aneddoti rossiniani autentici* (Rome, 1929)

R. De Rensis: 'Rossini intimo: lettere all'amico Santocanale', *Musica d'oggi*, xiii (1931), 343–53

G. H. J. Derwent: *Rossini and some Forgotten Nightingales* (London, 1934)
F. Toye: *Rossini: a Study in Tragi-Comedy* (London, 1934, 2/1954)
G. Roncaglia: *Rossini l'olimpico* (Milan, 1946, 2/1953)
L. Rognoni: *Rossini* (Parma, 1956, 3/1977)
F. Schlitzer: *Rossiniana: contributo all'epistolario di G. Rossini*, Quaderni dell'Accademia chigiana, xxxv (Siena, 1956)
——: *Un piccolo carteggio inedito di Rossini con un impresario italiano a Vienna* (Florence, 1959)
F. Walker: 'Rossiniana in the Piancastelli Collection', *MMR*, xc (1960), 138–47, 203–13
V. Viviani, ed.: *I libretti di Rossini* (Milan, 1965)
P. Gossett: 'Le fonti autografe delle opere teatrali di Rossini', *NRMI*, ii (1968), 936
H. Weinstock: *Rossini: a Biography* (New York, 1968)
P. Gossett: Introduction to *La Cenerentola: riproduzione dell'autografo esistente presso l'Accademia filarmonica di Bologna*, BMB, xcii (1969)
——: *The Operas of Rossini: Problems of Textual Criticism in Nineteenth-Century Opera* (diss., Princeton U., 1970)
B. Cagli, P. Gossett and A. Zedda: 'Criteri per l'edizione critica delle opere di Gioachino Rossini', *BCRS* (1974), no.1 [whole issue]
F. Lippmann: 'Briefe Rossinis und Donizettis in der Bibliothek Massimo, Rom', *AnMc*, no.19 (1979), 330–35
J. Kallberg: 'Marketing Rossini: sei lettere di Troupenas ad Artaria', *BCRS* (1980), 41–63
R. Osborne: *Rossini* (London, 1986, 2/1987)

MEMOIRS BY CONTEMPORARIES

Stendhal: *Rome, Naples, et Florence en 1817* (Paris, 1817; Eng. trans., 1959)
Guerre aux Rossinistes (Paris, 1821)
G. Righetti-Giorgi: *Cenni di una donna già cantante sopra il maestro Rossini* (Bologna, 1823; repr. in Rognoni, 3/1977)
G. Carpani: *Le rossiniane ossia Lettere musico-teatrali* (Padua, 1824)
R. Mount Edgcumbe: *Musical Reminiscences of an Old Amateur* (London, 1824)
Stendhal: *Vie de Rossini* (Paris, 1824; Eng. trans., 1956, 2/1970 with notes by R. N. Coe)
A. Wendt: *Rossinis Leben und Treiben* (Leipzig, 1824)
H. Berton: *De la musique mécanique et de la musique philosophique* (Paris, 1826)
J. Ebers: *Seven Years of the King's Theatre* (London, 1828)
J.-L. d'Ortigue: *De la guerre des dilettanti* (Paris, 1829)
P. Brighenti: *Della musica rossiniana e del suo autore* (Bologna, 1830, 2/1833)
A. Zanolini: *Biografia di Gioachino Rossini* (Paris, 1836; Bologna, 1875)
M. Escudier and L. Escudier: *Rossini: sa vie et ses oeuvres* (Paris, 1854)
E. de Mirecourt: *Rossini, Offenbach* (Paris, 1855)
Castil-Blaze: *L'Opéra-Italien de 1548 à 1856* (Paris, 1856)
H. F. Chorley: *Thirty Years' Musical Recollections* (London, 1862, 2/1926)
E. Montazio: *Giovacchino Rossini* (Turin, 1862)
L. Escudier: *Mes souvenirs* (Paris, 1863–8)
A. Aulangier: *G. Rossini: sa vie et ses oeuvres* (Paris, 1864)
A. Azevedo: *G. Rossini: sa vie et ses oeuvres* (Paris, 1864)
G. Pacini: *Le mie memorie artistiche* (Florence, 1865, 2/1872)
F. Hiller: 'Plaudereien mit Rossini (1856)', *Aus dem Tonleben unserer Zeit*, ii (Leipzig, 1868, 2/1871)
R. Wagner: 'Eine Erinnerung an Rossini', *Allgemeine Zeitung* [Augsburg] (17 Dec 1868); repr. in *Gesammelte Schriften und Dichtungen*, viii (Leipzig, 1883); Eng. trans. in *Richard Wagner's Prose Works*, ed. W. A. Ellis (London, 1894–9), iv, 269–74
H. S. Edwards: *The Life of Rossini* (London, 1869, 2/1881 as *Rossini and his School*)
E. Hanslick: *Aus dem Concertsaal* (Vienna, 1870, 2/1896)
F. Mordani: *Della vita privata di G. Rossini: memorie inedite* (Imola, 1871)
A. Pougin: *Rossini: Notes, Impressions, Souvenirs, Commentaires* (Paris, 1871)
L. S. Silvestri: *Della vita e delle opere di Gioachino Rossini: notizie biografico-artistico-aneddotico-critiche* (Milan, 1874)
G. De Sanctis: *Gioacchino Rossini: appunti di viaggio* (Rome, 1878)
G. L. Duprez: *Souvenirs d'un chanteur* (Paris, 1880)
E. Branca: *Felice Romani ed i più riputati maestri di musica del suo tempo* (Turin, Florence and Rome, 1882)
G. Dupré: *Ricordi autobiografici* (Florence, 1895, 2/1896 as *Pensieri sull'arte e ricordi autobiografici*)
A. Cametti: *Un poeta melodrammatico romano: appunti e notizie in gran parte inedite sopra Jacopo Ferretti e i musicisti del suo tempo* (Milan, 1898)
E. Michotte: *Souvenirs personnels: la visite de R. Wagner à Rossini* [Paris, 1860] (Paris, 1906); repr. in Rognoni (3/1977); Eng. trans., ed. H. Weinstock (1968, 2/1982)
——: *Souvenirs: une soirée chez Rossini à Beau-Séjour (Passy) 1858* (Brussels, c1910; Eng. trans., 1968, 2/1982)
C. Saint-Saëns: *Ecole buissonnière* (Paris, 1913; Eng. trans. as *Musical Memories*, 1919)

GENERAL LITERATURE

Bollettino del primo centenario rossiniano (Pesaro, 1892)
G. B. Shaw: 'Rossini Centenary', *Illustrated London News* (5 and 9 March 1892)
L. Dauriac: *La psychologie dans l'opéra français: Auber, Rossini, Meyerbeer* (Paris, 1897)
——: *Rossini: biographie critique* (Paris, 1906)
A. Sandberger: 'Rossiniana', *ZIMG*, ix (1907–8), 336; repr. in *Ausgewählte Aufsätze* (Munich, 1921)
E. Istel: 'Rossiniana', *Die Musik*, x/4 (1910–11), 3–26
A. Soubies: *Le Théâtre-Italien de 1801 à 1913* (Paris, 1913)
E. Celani: 'Musica e musicisti in Roma (1750–1850)', *RMI*, xxii (1915), 257–300
G. Fara: *Genio e ingegno musicale: Gioachino Rossini* (Turin, 1915)
A. Cametti: 'La musica teatrale a Roma cento anni fa', *Regia Accademia di Santa Cecilia: annuario* (Rome, 1915–30)
F. Vatielli: *Rossini a Bologna* (Bologna, 1918)
A. Casella: 'Some Reasons why a "Futurist" may Admire Rossini', *The Chesterian*, ii (London, 1920), 321–4
H. de Curzon: *Rossini* (Paris, 1920)
V. Cavazzocca Mazzanti: 'Rossini a Verona durante il Congresso del 1822', *Atti e memorie dell'Accademia di agricoltura, scienze e lettere di Verona*, 4th ser., xxiv (Verona, 1922), 53–112
J.-G. Prod'homme: 'Rossini and his Works in France', *MQ*, xvii (1931), 110–37
H. Faller: *Die Gesangskoloratur in Rossinis Opern und ihre Ausführung* (Berlin, 1935)
Rossiniana (Bologna, 1942)
A. Capri: 'Rossini e l'estetica teatrale della vocalità', *RMI*, xlvi (1942), 353–73
A. Della Corte: 'Fra gorgheggi e melodie di Rossini', *Musica*, i (1942), 23–39
U. Rolandi: 'Librettistica rossiniana', *Musica*, i (1942), 40–66
L. Ronga: 'Vicende del gusto rossiniano nell'ottocento', *Musica*, i (1942), 6–22
——: 'Svolgimento del gusto rossiniano sino al novecento', *Musica*, ii (1943), 184–200
F. Barberio: 'La regina d'Etruria e Rossini', *RMI*, lv (1953), 64–74
S. K. Langer: *Feeling and Form* (New York and London, 1953)
Rassegna musicale, xxiv/3 (1954), 209–303 [special issue]
B. Riboli: 'Profilo medico-psicologico di Gioacchino Rossini', *RaM*, xxiv (1954), 292–303
——: 'Malattia di G. Rossini secondo una relazione medica del 1842', *Note e riviste di psichiatria*, nos.7 and 12 (1955); repr. as pamphlet (Pesaro, 1956)
H. Rosenthal: *Two Centuries of Opera at Covent Garden* (London, 1958)
F. Schlitzer: *Rossini e Siena*, Quaderni dell'Accademia chigiana, xxxix (Siena, 1958)
A. Toni and T. Serafin: *Stile, tradizioni e convenzioni del melodramma italiano del settecento e dell'ottocento* (Milan, 1958)
R. Bacchelli: *Rossini e esperienze rossiniane* (Milan, 1959)
E. N. McKay: 'Rossinis Einfluss auf Schubert', *ÖMz*, xviii (1963), 17–22
A. Porter: 'A Lost Opera by Rossini', *ML*, xlv (1964), 39–44 [*Ugo, re d'Italia*]
D. W. Schwartz: 'Rossini: a Psychoanalytic Approach to the Great Renunciation', *Journal of the American Psychoanalytic Society*, xiii (1965), 551
R. Celletti: 'Vocalità rossiniana', *L'opera* [Milan], ii/5 (1966), 3–12
G. Barblan: 'Rossini e il suo tempo', *Chigiana*, xxv (1968), 143–79
F. Bisogni: 'Rossini e Schubert', *NRMI*, ii (1968), 920–35
A. Bonaccorsi, ed.: *Gioacchino Rossini* (Florence, 1968)
R. Celletti: 'Origini e sviluppi della coloratura rossiniana', *NRMI*, ii (1968), 872–919

——: 'Il vocalismo italiano da Rossini a Donizetti: Parte I: Rossini', *AnMc*, no.5 (1968), 267–93
M. Fabbri: 'Ignoti momenti rossiniani', *Chigiana*, xxv (1968), 265–85
E. Forbes: 'Sir Walter Scott and Opera', *Opera*, xix (1968), 872–8
P. Gossett: 'Rossini and Authenticity', *MT*, cix (1968), 1006–10
P. Graves: 'Homage to Rossini', *Opera*, xix (1968), 858–64
F. Lippmann: 'Per un'esegesi dello stile rossiniano', *NRMI*, ii (1968), 813–56
M. Aspinall: 'Musica proibita', *Records and Recording*, xiv/2 (1970), 32–5
P. Gossett: 'Gioachino Rossini and the Conventions of Composition', *AcM*, xlii (1970), 48–58
J. Loschelder: 'L'infanzia di Gioacchino Rossini', *BCRS* (1972), no.1, pp.45–63; no.2, pp.33–53
R. Risaliti: 'Rossini e Liszt', *BCRS* (1972), no.3, pp.40–46
A. Storr: 'Creativity and the Obsessional Character', *The Dynamics of Creation* (London, 1972), 92–112
J. Loschelder: 'Rossinis Bild und Zerbild in der Allgemeinen musikalischen Zeitung Leipzig', *BCRS* (1973), no.1, pp.23–42; no.2, pp.23–42; (1977), no.3, pp.17–40
A. Caswell: 'Vocal Embellishment in Rossini's Paris Operas: French Style or Italian?', *BCRS* (1975), nos.1–2, pp.5–21
——: 'Mme. Cinti-Damoreau and the Embellishment of Italian Opera in Paris: 1820–1845', *JAMS*, xxviii (1975), 459–92
J. Loschelder: 'Spontini und Rossini', *BCRS* (1975), nos.1–2, pp.65–81
E. Crafts: 'A Tale of the Cats', *BCRS* (1975), no.3, pp.5–12
E. J. Dent: 'Rossini', *The Rise of Romantic Opera* (London, 1976) [lectures at Cornell U., 1937–8]
S. Alberici: 'Rossini e Pio IX', *BCRS* (1977), nos.1–2, pp.5–35
Chigiana, xxxiv (1977)
S. Alberici: 'Appunti sulle librettistica Rossiniana', *BCRS* (1978), 45–60
P. Fabbri: 'Presenze rossiniane negli archivi ravennati: due inediti, un autografo ed altro', *BCRS* (1978), 5–30
F. Lippmann, ed.: *Die stilistische Entwicklung der italienischen Musik zwischen 1770 und 1830 und ihre Beziehungen zum Norden: Rome 1978*; pubd as *AnMc*, no.21 (1982)
P. Fabbri: 'Alla scuola dei Malerbi: altri autografi rossiniani', *BCRS* (1980), 5–31
B. Cagli: 'Rossini a Londra e al Théâtre-Italien di Parigi: documenti inediti dell'impresario G. B. Benelli', *BCRS* (1981), 17–53
F. Lippmann: 'Rossini – und kein Ende', *Studi musicali*, x (1981), 279–91
W. Dean: 'Rossini's French Operas', 'Rossini's Italian Operas', *NOHM*, viii, ed. G. Abraham (London, 1982), 104–12, 403–26
G. Landini: 'Gilbert Louis Duprez ovvero l'importanza di cantar Rossini', *BCRS* (1982), 29–54
M. Viale Ferrero: 'Per Rossini: un primo tentativo di iconografia scenografica', *BCRS* (1982), 5–28
P. Gossett: 'Rossini', *The New Grove Masters of Italian Opera* (London, 1983)
P. Fabbri: 'I Rossini, una famiglia in arte', *BCRS* (1983), 125–50
S. Henze-Döhring: 'La natura nelle opere di Rossini', *BCRS* (1983), 113–23
N. Till: *Rossini: his Life and Times* (London, 1983)
J. Rosselli: *The Opera Industry from Cimarosa to Verdi: the Role of the Impresario* (London, 1984)
V. Gui: 'Scritti Rossiniani', *BCRS* (1985), 19–60
S. Castelvecchi: 'Le *Rossiniane* di Mauro Giuliani', *BCRS* (1986), 33–72
A. Gier, ed.: *Oper als Text: romantische Beiträge zur Libretto-Forschung* (Heidelberg, 1986) [incl. M. Brzoska: 'Mosè und Massimilla, Rossinis *Mosè in Egitto* und Balzacs politische Deutung', 125–45; U. Weisstein: 'Der Apfel fiel recht weit vom Stamme: Rossinis *Guillaume Tell*, ein musikalische Schweizerreise', 147–84; A. Gerhard: '"Sortire dalle vie comuni", wie Rossini einem Akademiker den *Guillaume Tell* verdarb', 185–219]
E. Neill: 'Paganini e Rossini', *BCRS* (1986), 17–32
B. Cagli and A. Ziino: *Il teatro di San Carlo, 1737–1987* (Naples, 1987), 133–68
S. L. Balthazar: 'Mayr, Rossini, and the Development of the Early *Concertato* Finale', *JRMA*, cxvi (1991), 236–66
R. Celletti: *A History of Bel Canto* (London, 1991), 135–87
D. Kimbell: *Italian Opera* (London, 1991)
F. d'Amico: *Il teatro di Gioacchino Rossini* (Bologna, 1992)
A. Gerhard: *Die Verstädterung der Oper: Rossini, Meyerbeer, Verdi und die Modernität der Pariser "Grand Opéra"* (Stuttgart, 1992)

STUDIES OF INDIVIDUAL WORKS

Overtures

P. Gossett: 'The Overtures of Rossini', *19th Century Music*, iii (1979–80), 3–31
——: 'Le sinfonie di Rossini', *BCRS* (1979), 5–123

Operas, 1810–14

G. Radiciotti: 'Il *Signor Bruschino* e il *Tancredi* di G. Rossini: leggende e storia', *RMI*, xxvii (1920), 231–66
A. Melica: 'Due operine di Rossini', *Musicisti della scuola emiliana*, Chigiana, xiii (1956), 59–66 [on *L'inganno felice* and *L'occasione fa il ladro*]
A. Damerini: 'La prima ripresa moderna di un'opera giovanile di Rossini: "L'equivoco stravagante" (1811)', *Chigiana*, xxii (1965), 229–36
P. Gossett: 'The *candeur virginale* of *Tancredi*', *MT*, cxii (1971), 326–9
F. Cacaci: 'La cambiale di matrimonio da Federici a Rossi', *BCRS* (1975), nos. 1–2, pp.22–64
P. Gallarati: 'Dramma e ludus dall'*Italiana* al *Barbiere*', *Il melodramma italiano dell'ottocento: studi e ricerche per Massimo Mila* (Turin, 1977), 237–80
P. Gossett: *The Tragic Finale of Tancredi* (Pesaro, 1977)
C. Questa: *Il ratto del serraglio: Euripide, Plauto, Mozart, Rossini* (Bologna, 1979) [on *L'italiana in Algeri*]
V. Gui: '*Il turco in Italia*', *BCRS* (1985), 38–42 [written 1969]
G. C. Ballola: 'The (A)moral of the Story', *Pesaro Festival* (1986), 16–21 [on *Il turco in Italia*; programme booklet]
M. Bent: '*Il turco in Italia.* Context and Reception: Towards an Edition', ibid, 23–9
G. C. Ballola: 'An Italian *Jeu de l'amour et du hazard*', ibid, 14–19 [*L'occasione fa il ladro*]
B. Cagli: 'The Rossini Farces: a Scheme and its Fulfilment', ibid, 31–8
F. Degrada: 'Rossini's *La scala di seta*, a Study', ibid, 29–38
A. Gazzaniga: 'From *Le fils par hasard* to *Il Signor Bruschino*', ibid, 16–21]
A. Zedda: 'A Farce to be taken very Seriously', ibid, 23–4 [on *Il Signor Bruschino*]

Operas, 1815–23

G. Romagnoli: 'Gioacchino Rossini, Giulio Perticari e *La gazza ladra*', *Vita italiana*, iii (1897), 106–9
G. M. Gatti: *Le 'Barbier de Séville' de Rossini* (Paris, 1925)
A. Della Corte: 'La drammaturgica della *Semiramide* di Rossini', *RaM*, xi (1938), no.1, pp.1–6
A. Melica: '*La gazza ladra* nella revisione di Zandonai', *BCRS* (1955–6), no.3, pp.43–51
——: 'L'aria in rondò de *La donna del lago*', *BCRS*, iii (1957–8), 101–2
A. Bonaccorsi: '*La donna del lago*', *RaM*, xxviii (1958), 135–7
G. Saponaro: '*La gazzetta* di G. Rossini', *Autumno musicale napoletano*, iii (Naples, 1960)
G. Confalonieri: 'Avventure di una partitura rossiniana: l'*Adina* ovvero *Il califfo di Bagdad*', *Le celebrazioni del 1963 e alcune nuove indagini sulla musica italiana del XVIII e XIX secolo*, Chigiana, xx (1963), 206–16
J. Klein: 'Verdi's *Otello* and Rossini's', *ML*, xlv (1964), 130–40
A. Parente: 'La *Zelmira* di G. Rossini', *Annuario del Conservatorio di musica S Pietro a Majella* (Naples, 1965)
A. Zedda: 'Appunti per una lettura filologica del *Barbiere*', *L'opera* [Milan], ii/5 (1966), 13–16
P. Gossett: Introduction to *La Cenerentola: riproduzione del autografo esistente presso l'Accademia filarmonica di Bologna*, BMB, xcii (1969)
M. Tartak: 'The Two "Barbieri"', *ML*, l (1969), 453–69
P. Isotta: '*La donna del lago* e la drammaturgica di Rossini', *BCRS*, (1970), 45–61
A. Zedda: 'Ancora sul belcanto, lo stile ed il *Barbiere*', *Rassegna musicale Curci* (1970), no.1, pp.3–10
——: 'In margine all' edizione critica del *Barbiere di Siviglia*', *BCRS*, (1970), 3–10
G. Ballola: 'Una *pièce à sauvetage* da Salvare', *BCRS* (1971), 11–27 [on *Torvaldo e Dorliska*]
A. Bonsanti: 'Appunti sullo Scott e la sua *Donna del lago*', *Annuario 1965–70 del Conservatorio di musica G. B. Martini di Bologna* (Bologna, 1971), 15–21
P. Isotta: 'Da *Mosè* a *Moïse*', *BCRS* (1971), 87–117
P. Petrobelli: 'Balzac, Stendhal, e il *Mosè* di Rossini', ibid, 205–19

A. Zedda: 'Problemi testuali della *Cenerentola*', *BCRS* (1971), 29–51
B. Cagli: 'Le fonti letterarie dei libretti di Rossini', *BCRS* (1972), no.2, pp.10–32 [on *Maometto II*]; (1973), no.1, pp.8–22 [on *Bianca e Falliero*]
G. Carli Ballola: 'Lettura dell'*Ermione*', *BCRS* (1972), no.3, pp.12–39
P. Gossett: '*La gazza ladra*: Notes towards a Critical Edition', *BCRS* (1972), no.1, pp.12–29
R. Celletti: 'La vocalità rossiniana e *La gazza ladra*', *BCRS* (1973), no.2, pp.5–21
M. Tartak: 'Matilde and her Cousins', *BCRS* (1973), no.3, pp.13–23
P. Isotta: 'I diamanti della corona: grammatica del Rossini napoletano', *Mosè in Egitto* (Turin, 1974)
L. Tozzi: 'Sulle tracce di un "péché de jeunesse": *Ricciardo e Zoraide*', *BCRS* (1974), nos.2–3, pp.9–36
——: '*Armida*, ou la couleur fantastique', *BCRS* (1975), no.3, pp.27–56
J. Mitchell: '*La donna del lago*', *The Walter Scott Operas: an Analysis of Operas based on the Works of Walter Scott* (Birmingham, AL, 1977)
F. Tammaro: 'Ambivalenza dell' *Otello* rossiniano', *Il melodramma italiano dell'ottocento: studi e ricerche per Massimo Mila* (Turin, 1977), 187–236
N. John, ed.: *La Cenerentola* (London, 1980) [ENO Opera Guide]
M. Conati: 'Between Past and Future: the Dramatic World of Rossini in *Mosè in Egitto* and *Moïse et Pharaon*', *19th Century Music*, iv (1980–81), 32–47
L'avant-scène opéra, no.37 (1981) [*Il barbiere di Siviglia* issue]
A. Lanfranchi: 'Alcune note su *Zelmira*', *BCRS* (1981), 55–84
V. Gui: '*Il barbiere di Siviglia*', *BCRS* (1985), 50–55 [written 1969]
——: '*La Cenerentola*', *BCRS* (1985), 26–8 [written 1964]
N. John, ed.: *Il barbiere di Siviglia – Moïse et Pharaon* (London, 1985) [ENO Opera Guide]
L'avant-scène opéra, no.85 (1986) [*La Cenerentola* issue]
G. Dotto: 'Rossini's Last Milanese Opera', *Pesaro Festival* (1986), 12–17 [on *Bianca e Falliero*; programme booklet]
M. Marino: 'Rossini e Pavesi: a proposito di un'aria dell' *Eduardo e Cristina*', *BCRS* (1986), 5–14
P. Gossett: '*Ermione*: Rossini's tragédie lyrique', *Pesaro Festival* (1987), 22–32 [programme booklet]
L'avant-scène opéra, no.110 (1988) [*La gazza ladra* issue]
M. Collins: 'Toward a Definitive *Otello*: Evidence from the Manuscripts', *Pesaro Festival* (1988), 35–41 [programme booklet]
F. Agostinelli and G. Gravagna: 'Ricciardo e Zoraide: from Autograph to Critical Edition', *Pesaro Festival* (1990), 31–5 [programme booklet]
P. Gossett: 'The Coarse Country Girl and the Golden Lyre', *Pesaro Festival* (1990), 17–23 [on *Ricciardo e Zoraide*; programme booklet]
M. Everist: 'Lindoro in Lyon: Rossini's *Le barbier de Séville*', *AcM*, lxiv (1992), 50–85

Operas, 1824–9

V.-J. E. de Jouy: 'Essai sur l'opéra français' (1823); ed. A. Gerhard, *BCRS* (1987), 61–91
H. Berlioz: 'Guillaume-Tell', *Gazette musicale*, i/Oct–Nov (1834), 326–7, 336–9, 341–3, 349–51; Eng. trans. in *Source Readings in Music History*, ed. O. Strunk (New York, 1950)
E. vander Straeten: *La mélodie populaire dans l'opéra 'Guillaume Tell' de Rossini* (Paris, 1879)
A. Cametti: 'Il "Guglielmo Tell" e le sue prime rappresentazioni in Italia', *RMI*, vi (1899), 580
V. Gui: 'Si naturale o la naturale a proposito del *Guglielmo Tell*', *Musica d'oggi*, xiii (1926)
E. Zanetti: '*Il Comte Ory*', *Rossiniana* (Bologna, 1942)
P. R. Kirby: 'Rossini's Overture to "William Tell"', *ML*, xxxiii (1952), 132–40
A. Porter: '*Le Comte Ory*', *Opera*, v (1954), 550–53
——: '*William Tell*', *Opera*, ix (1958), 146–50
B. Cagli: '*Guglielmo Tell*', *La guida all'opera*, ed. G. Tomasi (Milan, 1971)
M. Viale Ferrero: '*Guglielmo Tell* a Torino (1839–40), ovvero una *Procella* scenografica', *RIM*, xiv (1979), 378–94
J. Johnson: 'A Lost Rossini Opera Recovered: *Il viaggio a Reims*', *BCRS* (1983), 5–57
L'avant-scène opéra, no.81 (1985) [*Le siège de Corinthe* issue]
A. Gerhard: 'Incantesimo o specchio dei costumi: un'estetica dell'opera del librettista di *Guillaume Tell*', *BCRS* (1987), 45–60
L'avant-scène opéra, no.118 (1989) [*Guillaume Tell* issue]
H. Lacombe: 'Contributo allo studio delle fonti del *Moïse* di Rossini', *BCRS* (1989), 47–62
H. R. Cohen, ed.: *The Original Staging Manuals for Twelve Parisian Operatic Premières/Douze livrets de mise en scène lyrique datant des créations parisiennes* (Stuyvesant, NY, 1991) [incl. production book for *Guillaume Tell*]

RICHARD OSBORNE (text, bibliography), PHILIP GOSSETT (work-list)

Rössler, Tini. *See* SCHUMANN-HEINK, ERNESTINE.

Rössl-Majdan, Hilde(gard) (*b* Moosbirbaum, nr Vienna, 21 Jan 1921). Austrian contralto. She studied in Vienna, making her début in 1950 at the Staatsoper, where she was engaged for more than 20 years. At Salzburg she sang Dryad in *Ariadne auf Naxos* (1954), Lucrezia in *Palestrina* (1958), Annina in *Der Rosenkavalier* and Marcellina in *Le nozze di Figaro* (1960). She had a firm, rich-toned voice and sang a wide repertory that ranged from Handel and Mozart to Verdi, Wagner and Johann Strauss. She recorded Eduige (*Rodelinda*) and Czipra (*Der Zigeunerbaron*).

ELIZABETH FORBES

Rossoni, Giulio (*fl* 1665–81). Italian singer and composer. He was a tenor and was employed as a chamber musician at the Bavarian court at Munich from at least the beginning of 1665 to 1681. In 1667 he sang in J. C. Kerll's opera *Le pretensioni del sole* (text by the court poet Domenico Gisberti). He composed the opera *L'Adelaide regia principessa di Susa* (to a libretto by G. B. Rodoteo), performed at Munich on 31 October 1669 in celebration of the birthday of Duke Ferdinand Maria of Bavaria and given at Venice the following year by a group of amateurs at the Accademia ai Saloni. (This opera was formerly attributed to Giulio Riva (*fl* 1663–70), a physician who may have had a hand in its revision for Venice.) Rossoni also sang in operas at Milan in 1678 and at Parma in 1681.

AllacciD
F. M. Rudhart: *Geschichte der Oper am Hofe zu München* (Freising, 1865)
J. J. Maier: 'Archivalische Excerpte über die herzogliche Hof-Kapelle in München', *KJb*, ix (1894), 59–68
L. Schiedermair: 'Die Anfänge der Münchener Oper', *SIMG*, v (1903–4), 442–68, esp. 454

THOMAS WALKER (with LORENZO BIANCONI)

Rostock. City and port in north-eastern Germany. German and Italian theatrical companies visited the city from the beginning of the 17th century, and later staged Singspiels and operas in the Hoftheater (opened 1751), the Ballhaus, and, after 1786, the new Schauspielhaus. *Die Entführung* was first performed in 1786, and *Die Zauberflöte* in 1795; *Der Freischütz* was first seen in 1822, and *Tannhäuser* in 1854. Companies from Schwerin provided most of the performances until 1836, when Rostock began forming its own company. When the Schauspielhaus burnt down in 1880, productions were mounted in the converted Thaliatheater; the new Stadttheater was opened in 1895, and the orchestra reorganized. Willibald Kaehler (Kapellmeister, 1897–9) began a Wagner tradition with productions of *Die Walküre*, *Götterdämmerung* and *Die Meistersinger*, eventually drawing many famous soloists (Edyth Walker, Lilli Lehmann, Fritz Feinhals) and conductors (Nikisch, Lohse, Brecher) for festival performances. Schmidt-Isserstedt is among those who succeeded Kaehler as Kapellmeister, while guest conductors in the city included Siegfried Wagner (whose *Schmied von*

Marienburg had its première in Rostock in 1923), Strauss and Schreker. After the theatre was destroyed in an air raid in 1942, the former 'Philharmonie' building was used as a theatre and converted several times; it was renamed the Volkstheater in 1951, with 580 seats. The company gave the first performance of Wagner-Régeny's *Persische Episode* (as *Persische Spässe*) in 1963.

*

H. Ebert: *Versuch einer Geschichte des Theaters in Rostock* (Güstrow, 1872)
A. Schatz: 'Zur Vorgeschichte des Stadttheaters in Rostock', *Beiträge zur Geschichte der Stadt Rostock*, ii/3 (Rostock, 1899)
Festschrift des Rostocker Stadttheaters zum 25jährigen Jubiläum (Rostock, 1920)
W. Golther: 'Die Wagner-Überlieferung an den mecklenburgischen Theatern Schwerin und Rostock', *Mecklenburgische Monatshefte*, xii (1935), 599ff
DIETER HÄRTWIG

Rostropovich, Mstislav (Leopol'dovich) (*b* Baku, 27 March 1927). Russian conductor and cellist. While continuing a brilliant career as a cellist of exceptional mastery, he made his conducting début with *Yevgeny Onegin* at the Bol'shoy in 1968 and the next year conducted the work with the same company in Paris, both times with his wife, Galina Vishnevskaya, as Tatyana. They left the USSR in 1974. Rostropovich conducted *The Queen of Spades* at San Francisco (1975) and in 1977 became music director of the National SO in Washington, DC. His close friendship with Britten led to his becoming a joint artistic director of the Aldeburgh Festival, where in 1979 he conducted *Onegin* in a production involving student professionals from the Britten-Pears School there. His operatic performances favour extremes of tempo and dynamics in support of emotional conviction, as may be heard in recordings of the operas mentioned as well as *Lady Macbeth*, *War and Peace*, *Tosca* and *Boris Godunov*. He was made an honorary KBE in 1987. NOËL GOODWIN

Rosvaenge [Roswaenge, Rosenvinge Hansen], **Helge** (*b* Copenhagen, 29 Aug 1897; *d* Munich, 19 June 1972). Danish tenor. Engaged at Neustrelitz, he made his début as Don José in 1921. Engagements followed at Altenburg, Basle, Cologne (1927–30) and the Berlin Staatsoper, where he was leading tenor from 1930, being especially distinguished in the Italian repertory; he also sang regularly in Vienna and Munich. He appeared at Salzburg between 1933 and 1939 as Tamino, Huon (*Oberon*) and Florestan, which he also sang at Covent Garden in 1938. He sang Parsifal at Bayreuth in 1934 and 1936 but otherwise avoided the Wagnerian repertory. After World War II Rosvaenge divided his time between Berlin and Vienna, continuing to sing until the late 1960s as Calaf, Radames and Manrico. His voice showed no sign of age; it was warm and sonorous, even throughout its scale, and brilliant and lustrous in its top register. He wrote three books, an autobiography *Skratta Pajazzo* (Copenhagen, 1945; Ger. trans., 1953 as *Lache Bajazzo*), *Mach es besser, mein Sohn* (Leipzig, 1962) and *Leitfaden für Gesangbeflissene* (Munich, 1964).

*

GV (G. Gualerzi; R. Vegeto)
A. Natan: 'Roswaenge, Helge', *Primo uomo* (Basle, 1963) [with discography]
F. Tassié: *Helge Roswaenge* (Augsburg, 1975)
J. Dennis: 'Helge Rosvaenge', *Record Collector*, xxiii (1976–7), 140 [with discography]; addns, xxv (1979–80), 120–22
HAROLD ROSENTHAL/R

Rota, Nino (*b* Milan, 3 Dec 1911; *d* Rome, 10 April 1979). Italian composer. He came from a musical family – his mother, Ernesta Rinaldi, was a pianist and daughter of the composer Giovanni Rinaldi (1840–95) – and showed promise as a composer from the age of eight; his oratorio *L'infanzia di S Giovanni Battista* was performed to acclaim in 1923. He entered the Milan Conservatory the same year, where he was a pupil of Giacomo Orefice and Ildebrando Pizzetti. His first theatre piece was an opera, *Il principe porcaro* (1925–6), which remained in short score and was never performed. In the same year he moved to the Conservatorio di S Cecilia in Rome, where he was taught by Casella and gained a diploma in composition in 1929. In 1931–2 he studied at the Curtis Institute in Philadelphia, became friendly with Aaron Copland and discovered the American song tradition, the cinema and the music of Gershwin – elements that, grafted on to his passion for Italian song and operetta, were to contribute to the formation of his own expressive idiom. From 1939 he taught at the Bari Conservatory, becoming director in 1950.

Rota composed numerous orchestral and chamber works, of a naivety almost untroubled by the problems of 20th-century composition, and in 1942 began an industrious career as a writer of film music. His operatic début came also in 1942 with *Ariodante*, a 19th-century type of melodrama successfully performed in Parma. With a formidable musical instinct and unshakable belief in the immediacy of musical communication, Rota was defiantly unconcerned that his musical idiom was unfashionable. The most satisfactory approach to his work is through his film music. By putting this on the same level as his operas and concert pieces he meant to reject the widespread and presumptuous opinion that his other music was merely *divertissement*. This was particularly true of his operas. After the 19th-century melodrama of *Ariodante* and *Torquemada* (composed 1943), he reverted to one of his favourite veins, the fairy-tale world of *Il principe porcaro*, which he followed after a gap of many years with pieces such as *Lo scoiattolo in gamba* (composed 1959) and *Aladino e la lampada magica* (1968). To this fantasy genre belongs what many consider to be his most successful theatre piece, *La visita meravigliosa* (1970), an allegory on the power of innocence and ingenuousness which can easily be applied to the composer's own musical conceptions.

Rota's pieces of a more sparkling kind show a captivating directness reminiscent of 19th-century operetta and vaudeville. They comprise *I due timidi* (1950), the successful *Il cappello di paglia di Firenze* (1955) and *La notte di un nevrastenico* (1959). A contributory factor in their success is undoubtedly the characteristic 'dispatch' of Rota's music, an aptitude for lightning sketches which he considered a result of his being accustomed to the rhythm of the cinema. A feature of his mature work was the increasing tendency, in both films and operas, to borrow from his own earlier music, as if he were testing its vitality. Examples of this are *Il cappello di paglia di Firenze*, with the reworking of numerous motifs already used in sound-tracks, and the radio opera *La notte di un nevrastenico*, which quotes the blues from the film *La dolce vita*. Earlier music is even more extensively re-used in his last opera *Napoli milionaria* (1977), to a libretto by Eduardo De Filippo, a kind of musical testament in which the composer's 'napoletanità istintiva' is expressed by the re-use of material from the films *Napoli milionaria* and

Filumena Marturano (also by De Filippo), Fellini's *Le notti di Cabiria*, *La dolce vita* and *Toby Dammit* and others such as Visconti's *Rocco e i suoi fratelli* and Bondarchuk's *Waterloo*. With a libretto that was too pedestrian and naturalistic, and reflecting Rota's preference for simple melody with no intellectual pretensions, *Napoli milionaria* attracted a chorus of harsh criticism which indicated the unbridgeable gulf between the composer's poetic and musical intelligence and the academic musical world.

See also CAPPELLO DI PAGLIA DI FIRENZE, IL.

Il principe porcaro, 1925–6 (comic op, 3, N. Rota, after H. C. Andersen: *The Swineherd*), unperf.
Ariodante, 1938–41 (3, E. Trucchi, after L. Ariosto: *Orlando furioso*), Parma, Regio, 18 Nov 1942
Torquemada, 1943 (4, Trucchi, after V. Hugo), Naples, S Carlo, 24 Jan 1976
I due timidi (radio op, 1, S. Cecchi d'Amico), RAI, 15 Nov 1950; staged London, Scala (London Opera Club), 17 March 1952 (Milan, 1953)
Il cappello di paglia di Firenze (farsa musicale, 4, E. Rota and N. Rota, after E. Labiche and M. A. A. Michel: *Un chapeau de paille d'Italie*), Palermo, Massimo, 21 April 1955 (Milan, 1956)
La notte di un nevrastenico (dramma buffo, 1, R. Bacchelli), RAI, 19 Nov 1959; staged Milan, Piccola Scala, 8 Feb 1960 (Milan, 1961)
Lo scoiattolo in gamba, 1959 (favola musicale, 1, E. De Filippo, after L. Rota), Bari, Conservatorio Piccinni, 13 June 1973
Aladino e la lampada magica, 1963–5 (fiaba lirica, 3, V. Verginelli, after *The Thousand and One Nights*), Naples, S Carlo, 14 Jan 1968
La visita meravigliosa, 1965–9 (2, N. Rota, after H. G. Wells: *The Wonderful Visit*), Palermo, Massimo, 6 Feb 1970
Napoli milionaria, 1973–7 (dramma lirico, 3, De Filippo), Spoleto, Nuovo, 22 June 1977

*

S. M.: 'Un compositore quattordicenne: Nino Rota Rinaldi', *Cronache musicali*, ii/6 (1926), 2
G. Gavazzeni: 'Brevi capitoli su Nino Rota', *Musicisti d'Europa* (Milan, 1954), 255–66
G. Vigolo: 'Le sorprese del novecento', *Ricordiana*, ii/3 (Milan, 1956), 139–40
M. Mila: 'Il vaudeville di Nino Rota', *Cronache musicali 1954–59* (Turin, 1959), 207–9
A. Gentilucci: *Guida all'ascolto della musica contemporanea* (Milan, 1969), 356–7
F. d'Amico: 'Passaporto per un angelo', *L'espresso* (Rome, 1970), no.7, p.18
L. Pinzauti: 'A colloquio con Nino Rota', *NRMI*, v (1971), 74–83
G. Vigolo: 'Il cappello di paglia', *Mille e una sera all'opera e al concerto* (Florence, 1971), 282–4
F. Soprano: 'Nino Rota e l'impegno del disimpegno', *Il cappello di paglia di Firenze* (RCA TRL 2–1153, 1975) [record notes]
F. Fellini: 'L'amico magico', *Il messaggero* (13 April 1979)
P. M. De Santi, ed.: *Omaggio a Nino Rota* (Pistoia, 1981)
G. Bracco: *Fonti e destinazioni della musica di Nino Rota* (diss., U. of Naples, 1982–3)
P. M. De Santi: *La musica di Nino Rota* (Bari, 1983)
G. Bracco: 'Nino Rota: il punto della critica', *I cinquant'anni di un liceo classico*, ed. V. Bracco (Salerno, 1984), 429–38
R. Zanetti: *La musica italiana nel novecento*, ii (Busto Arsizio, 1985), 973–6, 1373–5
G. Pestelli: 'Il cappello di paglia di Firenze', *Di tanti palpiti: cronache musicali 1972–1986* (Pordenone, 1986), 209–10
D. Fabris, ed.: *Nino Rota, compositore del nostro tempo* (Bari, 1987)
J. M. Latorre: *Nino Rota: la imagen de la música* (Barcelona, 1989)
D. Fabris: 'La musica non filmica di Nino Rota: ipotesi di un catalogo', *Musica senza aggetivi: studi per Fedele D'Amico*, ii (Florence, 1991), 705–33

GIORDANO MONTECCHI

Rote Käppchen, Das [*Das rote Käppchen, oder Hilft's nicht, so schadt's nicht* ('The Red Cap, or If it helps not, at least it harms not')]. Singspiel in three acts by CARL DITTERS VON DITTERSDORF to his own libretto after FILIPPO LIVIGNI's libretto *Giannina e Bernardone*; Vienna, Kärntnertortheater, 1788.

Elderly, jealous Hans Kristoph (bass) has a run-in with the dashing young Lieutenant von Felsenberg (tenor) over his attentions to Hans's young wife Hedwig (soprano). Felsenberg is actually engaged to Caroline (soprano), niece to the hot-blooded old Hungarian hussar Emmerich (bass). After convincing them of his fidelity, he engineers a plan to cure Hans of his blind jealousy. Disguised as a Jewish pedlar, Felsenberg sells him a red cap, which, whenever it is on his head, will cause his wife to loathe all men but him.

Dittersdorf's music won popularity everywhere, and served as the justification for C. A. Vulpius's revising the work's clumsy, unpolished text for a performance at Weimar in 1791. The arias run the gamut from Hedwig's grand bravura aria to Felsenberg's burlesque of a Jewish cantor and Hans's delightful comic lieder (Beethoven wrote 13 variations on Hans's Romanze 'Es war einmal ein alter Mann', WoO 66).

THOMAS BAUMAN

Röth, Philipp (*b* Munich, 6 March 1779; *d* Munich, 27 Jan 1850). German composer. He studied the cello and other instruments with Anton Schwarz, a Bavarian court musician, and composition with Peter Winter. He was appointed a Bavarian court musician in 1796. In 1809 an opera, *Holnara*, was performed with great success at the Munich court theatre, and a second, *Pachter Robert*, followed two years later. He also wrote a number of Singspiels in the Vienna pattern for Munich (e.g. *Zemire und Azor*, a version of Bäuerle's *Der verwunschene Prinz*). Perhaps his most successful score was the *Freischütz* parody music that he and Riotte provided for *Staberl in der Löwengrube* (also known as *Alles à la Freischütz* and *Staberl als Freischütz*), mounted at the Isartortheater on 4 December 1822 by Karl Carl and performed frequently before the company (including Röth himself) took it to the Theater an der Wien during their guest season in 1826. It continued to be performed in Vienna until 1850. Röth's other successes in Vienna include *Der hölzerne Säbel* (staged successfully in all three Viennese suburban theatres between 1820 and 1822), *Der Kampf mit dem Drachen* and *Das Abenteuer im Guadarama-Gebirge* (both performed in 1825). Röth returned to Munich in 1828.

Holnara (3), Munich, court, 9 June 1809
Die Feen (Zauberspiel, 2), Munich, court, Dec 1809
Prinzessin Eselshaut (Zauberspiel, 3), Munich, court, Dec 1810
Pachter Robert (komische Oper, 1), Munich, 1811
Dichter und Tonkünstler, oder Wo nehme ich einen Plan her? (3, after L. E. Dupaty and M. G. Lambrecht), Munich, court, 24 Sept 1813
Der hölzerne Säbel (Spl, 1, F. Rosenau, after A. von Kotzebue), Vienna, Josefstadt, 23 March 1820, collab. P. J. Riotte
Der Freischütze, oder Staberl in der Löwengrube [Alles à la Freischütz; Staberl als Freischütz] (Parodie, 3, K. Carl), Munich, Isartor, 4 Dec 1822, collab. Riotte
Das neue Aschenbrödel (Spl, 1, A. Lewald), Munich, 1822
Die 12 schlafenden Jungfrauen (Spl), Munich, 1 Jan 1823
Zemire und Azor (Spl), Munich, Isartor, 22 March 1823
Der Kampf mit dem Drachen (heroisch-romantisches Schauspiel, 4, C. M. Heigel), Vienna, An der Wien, 10 Sept 1825
Das Abenteuer im Guadarama-Gebirge (Schauspiel, 2, Heigel), Vienna, An der Wien, 23 Sept 1825
Die weisse Frau, oder Ludlams Höhle (Melodram, 5, A. G. Oehlenschläger), Vienna, An der Wien, 9 Feb 1826
Der Lebensretter (Posse, 3, L. Feldmann), Munich, 14 Dec 1841

*

StiegerO
F. J. Lipowsky: *Baierisches Musik-Lexikon* (Munich, 1811)

E. Bernsdorf: *Neues Universal-Lexikon der Tonkunst*, suppl.1 (Offenbach, 1865), 307–8
H. Mendel and A. Reissmann: *Musikalisches Conversations-Lexikon*, viii (Berlin, 1877), 386 PETER BRANSCOMBE

Rothenberger, Anneliese (*b* Mannheim, 19 June 1924). German soprano. She studied in Mannheim with Erika Müller and made her début in 1943 at Koblenz, where she was soon singing such parts as Gilda and the title role in Pfitzner's *Das Christ-Elflein*. From 1946 to 1973 she was a member of the Hamburg Staatsoper, where her roles included Cherubino, Blonde, Oscar, Musetta, Olympia and the three soprano roles of *Der Prozess* in its first performance in Germany. At the 1952 Edinburgh Festival she sang Regina with the Hamburg company in the British stage première of *Mathis der Maler*. She first appeared at Salzburg in 1954, creating Telemachus in Liebermann's *Penelope*; she returned to create Agnes in the German version of his *Die Schule der Frauen* (1957) and to sing Zdenka (*Arabella*), Flaminia (Haydn's *Il mondo della luna*), Sophie and Konstanze. Her many appearances as Sophie included those at Glyndebourne (1959–60); in 1960 she made her Metropolitan début as Zdenka. She sang regularly at Munich and Vienna from the mid-1950s. Her large repertory included Mozart's Ilia, Susanna and Pamina, Berg's Lulu, Adele (*Die Fledermaus*), and the title role of Heinrich Sutermeister's *Madame Bovary*, which she created in Zürich (1967). Rothenberger had unusual acting ability and a well-schooled, if light, voice.

HAROLD ROSENTHAL/R

Rother, Artur (Martin) (*b* Stettin [now Szczecin], 12 Oct 1885; *d* Aschau, 22 Sept 1972). German conductor. He studied with Hugo Kaun in Berlin before becoming an assistant at the Bayreuth Festival in 1907, where he remained until 1914. From 1927 to 1934 he was general director of music in Dessau and from 1938 to 1958 was principal Kapellmeister at the Städtische Oper in Berlin. An accomplished musician of wide interests, Rother prepared new editions of Gluck's *La rencontre imprévue* and Mozart's *Idomeneo*. HANS CHRISTOPH WORBS

Rothier, Léon (*b* Reims, 26 Dec 1874; *d* New York, 6 Dec 1951). French bass. His early training was as a violinist, but he was persuaded to pursue singing instead. He studied at the Paris Conservatoire (1894–9) with Crosti (singing), Lhérie (*opéra comique*) and Melchissedec (opera). He made his début in 1899 as Jupiter in *Philémon et Baucis* at the Opéra-Comique, where he remained until 1903; his roles included Zuniga, the King (*Cendrillon*), Don Fernando (*Fidelio*), Maître Ramon (*Mireille*), Colline, and the junk-seller in *Louise*, which he created in 1900. He then sang with the Marseilles (1903–7), Nice (1907–9) and Lyons (1909–10) companies before going to the USA. His Metropolitan début was in 1910 as Gounod's Méphistophélès, and he remained with the company for 30 years. His roles included Ramfis, Pimen, Alvise Badoero, Raimondo, Arkel, the King (*Le roi d'Ys*) and Sparafucile. He sang Bluebeard at the American première of Dukas' *Ariane et Barbe-bleue* (1911) and created Father Time in Albert Wolff's *L'oiseau bleu* (1919) and Major Duquesnois in Deems Taylor's *Peter Ibbetson* (1931). His last appearance was as Massenet's Count des Grieux (1939). He also sang in San Francisco and with the Chicago summer opera at Ravinia.

KATHERINE K. PRESTON, ELIZABETH FORBES

Rothmüller, (Aron) Marko (*b* Trnjani, nr Brod, 31 Dec 1908). Croatian baritone. He studied in Zagreb and Vienna, making his début at Hamburg-Altona in 1932 as Ottokar (*Der Freischütz*). He returned to Zagreb for two years and in 1935 was engaged by the Zürich Opera, where he sang regularly until 1947, scoring particular successes in Verdi and Wagner and creating the Truchsess in *Mathis der Maler* (1938). In 1946 he joined the Vienna Staatsoper, singing there until 1949. Having made his London début in 1939 as Krušina (*The Bartered Bride*) at Covent Garden, in 1947 he sang Rigoletto with the New London Opera Company at the Cambridge Theatre and John the Baptist (*Salome*) during the Vienna Staatsoper's season at Covent Garden. He was a member of the Covent Garden company from 1948 to 1952, singing a wide variety of roles including Amonasro, Rigoletto, Scarpia, Gunther, Tomsky (*The Queen of Spades*) and the title role in *Wozzeck* in its first London stage performance (1952; for illustration *see* WOZZECK, fig.2). He appeared with the Glyndebourne company (1949–55) as Guglielmo, Count Almaviva, Don Carlo (*La forza del destino*), Macbeth and Nick Shadow. He made his New York début with the New York City Opera (1948) and later sang at the Metropolitan (1959–65), making his début as Kothner.

*

D. Shawe-Taylor: 'Marko Rothmüller', *Opera*, ii (1950–51), 169–74 HAROLD ROSENTHAL/R

Rothschild's Violin. Opera by V. I. Fleyshman; *see* SKRIPKA ROTSHIL'DA.

Rotterdam. Dutch city, the second largest in the Netherlands. Numerous troupes from Amsterdam, The Hague and abroad performed at the manège in the Stadsdoelen, or at the French theatre on the outskirts of the city. In 1860 the first Rotterdam-based opera company, the Hoogduitse Opera, was inaugurated under the direction of J. E. de Vries, former director of the Stadsschouwburg in Amsterdam. The performances were staged in a small theatre on the Coolsingel. In Rotterdam alone this company gave some 2093 performances in its first 25 seasons, and it also travelled to Amsterdam and The Hague. There were several premières of operas by Dutch composers: *Aleida van Holland* (W. F. Thooft) in 1866; *Eine Johannesfeier auf Amron* (Carl Dibbern) in 1880; *Imelda* and *König Arpad* (Theodor Verhey) in 1885 and 1888 respectively; and *Camela* (J. C. Visser) in 1890. In 1887 the Groote Theater (later named the Stadsschouwburg and now known as the Rotterdamse Schouwburg) opened on the Aert van Nesstraat. As in the Amsterdam Stadsschouwburg, the repertory was divided between spoken theatre and opera.

The development of an efficient rail system in such a small country diminished the need for a Rotterdam-based company, and a proposal in 1970 to have the national opera house built in Rotterdam was unsuccessful. Productions from Amsterdam and The Hague came regularly, but since the Netherlands Opera's move in 1986 to the Muziek Theater in Amsterdam few of its productions have been seen in Rotterdam. The première of Philip Glass's *Satyagraha* was staged in Rotterdam in 1980. In 1989 the Rotterdamse Schouwburg (919 seats, including two balconies) was thoroughly renovated.

*

S. A. M. Bottenheim: *Opera in Nederland* (Leiden, 1983)

MICHAEL DAVIDSON

Röttger, Heinz (*b* Herford, 6 Nov 1909; *d* Dessau, 26 Aug 1977). German composer. After studying music with Hugo Röhr and Walter Courvoisier at the Akademie der Tonkunst in Munich (1928–31), he pursued his musical studies at the University of Munich (1930–34) with Adolf Sandberger and Alfred Lorenz, obtaining the doctorate in 1937 with a thesis on formal problems in Richard Strauss's works. He began his career as Kapellmeister in Augsburg, but it was interrupted by World War II; he resumed it in 1948 at the Stralsund Stadttheater. From 1951 to 1954 he was general music director at the Rostock Volkstheater, and from then until his death was chief musical director of the Dessau Landestheater, where he organized annual Wagner festivals. His works are clearly ordered and rhythmically based. His musical style is based on 20th-century techniques, used in a personal manner, especially dodecaphony. An initial preference for brittle-sounding effects gave way in later works to distinct melodic developments.

Bellmann (1), 1946
Phaeton, 1957 (1, E. Johnn), Dessau, Landes, 8 March 1960
Der Heiratsantrag (komische Oper, 1, after A. P. Chekhov), Magdeburg, Stadt, 31 Oct 1960
Die Frauen von Troja (Johnn), Dessau, Landes, 10 Feb 1962
Der Weg nach Palermo (E. Weeber-Fried), Dessau, Landes, 2 Oct 1965
Spanisches Capriccio, Dessau, Landes, 1976 DIETER HÄRTWIG

Rouen. City and port in north-west France. It is the historic capital of Normandy; its cathedral was begun in the 13th century. In 1688 Bernard Vaultier was granted the privilege of founding an Académie Royale de Musique and took over the Théâtre des Deux Maures (built 1650), inaugurating it with a performance of Lully's *Phaëton*. The Grand Théâtre, designed by Guéroult with four galleries and 1600 seats, was opened in 1776. Its name was changed to the Théâtre des Arts during the Revolution. Boieldieu was born in Rouen and his first opera, *La fille coupable*, had its première there in 1793; *La dame blanche* was given in 1826, two months after its première by the Opéra-Comique in Paris. After the theatre's destruction by fire in 1876, a new house was built by Sauvageot behind the surviving façade and inaugurated on 30 September 1882, in the presence of Ambroise Thomas, with the overture to *La dame blanche* and *Les Huguenots*. From then on the house was usually let to an impresario, with a municipal subsidy given on condition that a certain number of new productions be mounted each season. Between 1890 and 1914 operas by Wagner, Gounod, Saint-Saëns and Massenet, as well as recent works by Albert Cahen, Lenepveu, Rubinstein, Frédéric Le Rey and Isidore de Lara, were given there. The theatre was destroyed by bombing in 1940. The present Théâtre des Arts, built beside the Seine, was opened in November 1962. A typical season runs from November to April with productions of six or seven operas and five operettas.

*

H. Geispitz and M. Vauclin: *Histoire du Théâtre des arts à Rouen 1882–1913* (Rouen, 1913)
H. Geispitz: *Histoire du Théâtre des arts à Rouen 1913–1940* (Rouen, 1951)
C. Goubault: 'Les créations lyriques au Théatre des Arts à Rouen', *Le théâtre lyrique français 1945–1985*, ed. D. Pistone (Paris, 1987), 359–82 CHARLES PITT

Rouleau, Joseph (Alfred) (*b* Matane, Quebec, 28 Feb 1929). Canadian bass. After studying in Montreal and in Italy, he made his début at Montreal in 1955. He first appeared at Covent Garden in 1957 as Colline, and at the Paris Opéra in 1960 as Raimondo (*Lucia di Lammermoor*). He sang throughout Europe, in the USSR, North and South America, and Australia. A reliable, versatile artist, his large repertory included Don Basilio, Rodolfo (*La sonnambula*), Oroveso (*Norma*), Giorgio (*I puritani*) and Sparafucile. A fine Philip II, Pope Clement (*Benvenuto Cellini*), Narbal (*Les Troyens*), Méphistophélès, Arkel, Lodovico and Don Quichotte, he also sang Boris, Pimen and Dosifey (*Khovanshchina*). In 1967 he created Bishop Tache in Harry Somers's *Louis Riel* at Toronto and in 1983 he sang Bonze in Stravinsky's *The Nightingale* at Covent Garden. Later appearances included Jacopo Loredano (*I due Foscari*) in Hamilton; Marco (*The Saint of Bleeker Street*) in Philadelphia and Trulove in Vancouver (1989); and Prince of Bouillon (*Adriana Lecouvreur*) in Montreal (1990). ELIZABETH FORBES

Roullet [Rollet, Durollet, Du Rollet], **Marie François Louis Gand Leblanc,** Bailli du (*b* Normanville, Eure, 10 April 1716; *d* Paris, 2 Aug 1786). French writer. He served with the Gardes Françaises and the Ordre de Malte, and as an attaché to the French embassy in Vienna where he met Gluck, whose first and principal propagandist in Paris he became. Supported by Marie-Antoinette, he made imperious demands on the Opéra in 1774; later, he may have acted discreditably in Gluck's interest by endeavouring to prevent improvements in the libretto of Sacchini's *Renaud*. He started the fashion for adapting 17th-century tragedies for the Opéra with *Iphigénie en Aulide* (for Gluck) in 1774, apparently the only libretto for which he was wholly responsible. He also translated the prefaces to Gluck's *Alceste* and *Paride ed Elena* for the *Gazette de littérature* (1774), wrote a *Lettre sur les drames-opéras* (1776; repr. in Lesure 1984) and probably 'ghosted' French articles signed by Gluck. He undertook the extensive alteration and translation for the French *Alceste* (1776) and collaborated with Baron Tschudi on *Les Danaïdes* (1784), taken without permission from Calzabigi and staged with Salieri's music, although advertised as being partly by Gluck. Articles by Roullet are included in a compilation entitled *Mémoires pour servir à l'histoire de la révolution opérée dans la musique par ... Gluck* (Paris and Naples, 1781). He is generally regarded as an *homme d'esprit* rather than a major literary figure.

*

G. Le Brisoys Desnoiresterres: *Gluck et Piccinni* (Paris, 1872, 2/1875)
A. Jullien: *La cour et l'Opéra sous Louis XVI* (Paris, 1878)
J. Tiersot: *Gluck* (Paris, 1910, 4/1919)
P. Howard: *Gluck and the Birth of Modern Opera* (London, 1963)
P. Smith: *The Tenth Muse: a Historical Study of the Opera Libretto* (London, 1971)
R. Angermüller: 'Reformideen von Du Roullet und Beaumarchais als Opernlibrettisten', *AcM*, xlviii (1976), 227–52
F. Lesure, ed.: *Querelle des Gluckistes et des Piccinnistes* (Geneva, 1984) JULIAN RUSHTON

Rousseau, Jean-Baptiste (*b* Paris, 6 April 1671; *d* Brussels, 16 March 1741). French librettist. He had something of a chequered career, and the success of his two opera librettos, *Jason, ou La toison d'or* (set by Collasse, 1696) and *Vénus et Adonis* (Desmarets, 1697), was meagre. Perhaps out of jealousy he circulated anonymously some malicious couplets about Danchet's *Hésione* (Campra, 1700). A second, even more scurrilous series was also ascribed to him. In 1712, at the end of a long legal process, Rousseau was banished, protesting his innocence; he died in exile. More important than Rousseau's operas are his 26 published cantata texts. Both these and his librettos show his sensitivity to the demands of the marriage of words and music; he approaches the poetic style of Quinault more closely than contemporaries such as Thomas Corneille and Campistron. CAROLINE WOOD

Rousseau, Jean-Jacques (*b* Geneva, 28 June 1712; *d* Ermenonville, 2 July 1778). Swiss philosopher, theorist and composer. His early training in music was poor and his first operatic ventures unsuccessful: in Chambéry (1739–40) he attempted to write both words and music for a serious opera, and in Lyons (1742) he composed the music for part of another opera. In 1743 he began work on an *opéra-ballet, Les muses galantes*, modelled on Rameau's *Les Indes galantes.* A sojourn in Venice (1743–4) interrupted composition, but the task was completed, with the help of Philidor, by mid-1745 and the piece presented to Rameau. Rameau heard the music with reluctance, and criticized the contributions allegedly by Rousseau as the work of a musical ignoramus. Rousseau never forgave his great contemporary.

Another task involving Rousseau's talents as a poet-musician was the hasty revision of *La princesse de Navarre* by Voltaire and Rameau as *Les fêtes de Ramire*, an occasional piece commissioned by the court to celebrate a victorious battle. The work was staged at Versailles at the end of 1745, and as a result put Rousseau on good terms with the forces of the Opéra at Paris. Revisions of *Les muses galantes* occupied another two years, when the Paris troupe put it into rehearsal. It was even brought to a general rehearsal, witnessed by a large audience, but at this point the composer withdrew the work (it was not rejected, as claimed by his enemies).

Le devin du village, given before the court at Fontainebleau in October 1752, was Rousseau's first real operatic success, and epochal in showing the way to French *opéra comique*, as it was definitively coined during the third quarter of the 18th century. The dimensions of the work are small (it lasts about an hour and has only three characters), and a folklike simplicity of tone pervades the whole; but the triumph of rustic virtue over higher-class corruption and venality contained a pertinent social message that was to be repeated in many later *opéras comiques. Le devin* held the stage for some 60 years in France and was given widely abroad.

Rousseau made several contributions to the QUERELLE DES BOUFFONS, most notably in November 1753 with his *Lettre sur la musique française.* At once the most eloquent and most extreme statement of hostility to French opera, it was all the more paradoxical following the success of *Le devin.* The philosophy of music propounded in it, and in his various articles on music for the *Encyclopédie* (later incorporated into his *Dictionnaire* of 1768), led Rousseau to conclude that opera was not possible in the French language. A consequence of this conclusion was the radical experiment represented by *Pygmalion*, a spoken monodrama sketched in the 1760s and performed at Lyons in 1770 with instrumental music by Horace Coignet (it inaugurated the genre of spoken drama with instrumental interjections later known as MELODRAMA). When the work was performed subsequently in Paris, Rousseau did not take the trouble to indicate the role of Coignet, who promptly claimed it in public. The incident provided further cause for calumny and for doubts about the musical abilities of the philosopher. Rousseau took little interest in the changes in German music during his lifetime, and seems to have been unaware that the example of *Pygmalion* set off a wave of German imitations during the 1770s. As late as 1777, the date of his essay on Gluck's *Alceste*, he believed that his example had been unheeded. Rousseau's final reconciliation with Gluck and his admiration for the operas that Gluck directed at Paris gave the lie to his earlier insults about the impossibility of opera in French. At the time of his death he was working on another pastoral opera, *Daphnis et Chloé*, the completed part of which was printed after his death. In style it is very close to *Le devin.*

See also DEVIN DU VILLAGE, LE.

texts by Rousseau unless otherwise stated

Iphis et Anaxorète, 1739–40 (tragédie lyrique)

La découverte du nouveau monde, 1742 (tragédie lyrique, 3)

Les muses galantes (opéra-ballet, 3), Paris, residence of La Pouplinière, ?1745; music to later entrée Hésiode (orig. La tasse) in Musée Chalis, nr Senlis; Musette en rondo des 'Indes galantes', ed. in *BSIM*, viii/6 (1912), 49 [see also Brook 1962]

Les fêtes de Ramire, Versailles, late 1745; rev. of Rameau's La princesse de Navarre (comédie-ballet, 3, Voltaire)

Le devin du village (intermède, 1), Fontainebleau, 18 Oct 1752 (Paris, 1753), 6 nouveaux airs (Paris, 1778)

Pygmalion (scène lyrique), Lyons, Hôtel de Ville, 1770, collab. H. Coignet, *F-Pcf*, pts *Pn*

Daphnis et Chloé (pastorale, prol., 4, P. Laujon), unperf., Act 1, with sketches of prol., Act 2, divertissement (Paris, 1779), ov. (Paris, n.d.)

WRITINGS

Only those relating to opera are included; most are reprinted in *Ecrits sur la musique*, Oeuvres complètes ... nouvelle édition, classée par ordre de matières, xix–xxii (Paris, 1788–93) and in numerous subsequent editions of the complete works.

Lettre à M. Grimm au sujet des remarques ajoutées à sa lettre sur Omphale (Paris, 1752)

Lettre d'un symphoniste de l'Académie royale de musique à ses camarades de l'orchestre, 1753, in *Théâtre et poésies* (Geneva, 1781)

Lettre sur la musique française (Paris, 1753, 2/1753); abridged Eng. trans. in O. Strunk, ed.: *Source Readings in Music History* (New York, 1950)

J. J. Rousseau ... à Mr. d'Alembert ... sur son article 'Genève' dans ... l'Encyclopédie et particulièrement sur le projet d'établir un théâtre de comédie en cette ville (Amsterdam, 1758)

Lettre à Monsieur Le Nieps ... le 5 avril 1759, in *Théâtre et poésies* (Geneva, 1781)

Essai sur l'origine des langues, où il est parlé de la mélodie et de l'imitation musicale, *c*1760 (Geneva, 1781)

*Extrait d'une lettre ... à M.*** sur les ouvrages de M. Rameau*, ii (Neuchâtel, 1764)

Dictionnaire de musique (Paris, 1768; Eng. trans., 1771)

Lettre à M. Burney sur la musique, avec fragments d'observations sur l'Alceste italien de M. le chevalier Gluck, *c*1777 (Geneva, 1781)

Extrait d'une réponse du petit faiseur à son prête-nom, sur un morceau de l'Orphée de M. le chevalier Gluck, ?1774 (Geneva, 1781)

Letters to Lesage *père*, 1754; Perdriau, 1756; Ballière, 1765; Lalande, 1768; various minor writings in Jansen (1884), appx

*

A. Jansen: *Jean-Jacques Rousseau als Musiker* (Berlin, 1884)

E. Istel: *J.-J. Rousseau als Komponist seiner lyrischen Scene Pygmalion* (Leipzig, 1901) [see also *Annales de la Société Jean-Jacques Rousseau 1905*, 141–72; rejoinders, ibid *1907*, 119–55]

A. Pougin: *Jean-Jacques Rousseau musicien* (Paris, 1901)

A. Arnheim: 'Le devin du village von J. J. Rousseau und die Parodie "Les amours de Bastien et Bastienne"', *SIMG*, iv (1902–3), 686–727

P.-M. Masson: 'Les idées de J.-J. Rousseau sur la musique', *BSIM*, viii/6 (1912), 1–17; viii/7–8 (1912), 23–32
P. P. Plan: 'Jean-Jacques Rousseau et Malesherbes: documents inédits', *Mercure de France*, xcvii (1912), 5–38
J. Tiersot: *Jean-Jacques Rousseau* (Paris, 1912, 2/1920)
J.-G. Prod'homme: 'Les dernières représentations du *Devin du village* (mai–juin 1829)', *ReM*, vii/9–11 (1926), 118–25
A. Pochon: *J.-J. Rousseau musicien et la critique* (Montreux, 1940)
A. Mooser: *Pygmalion et Le devin du village en Russie au XVIIIe siècle* (Geneva, 1946)
A. R. Oliver: *The Encyclopaedists as Critics of Music* (New York, 1947)
J. Sénelier: *Bibliographie générale des oeuvres de Jean-Jacques Rousseau* (Paris, 1949)
A. Bruyère: 'Les muses galantes: musique de Jean-Jacques Rousseau', *ReM*, no.218 (1952) [whole issue]
J. van der Veen: *Le mélodrame musical de Rousseau au Romantisme* (The Hague, 1955)
B. S. Brook: *La symphonie française dans la seconde moitié du XVIIIe siècle* (Paris, 1962), esp. i, 95ff
R. Cotte: 'Bemerkungen über das Verhältnis Jean-Jacques Rousseaus zur Musik', *BMw*, v (1963), 81–96
G. Snyders: 'Une révolution dans le goût musical au XVIIIe siècle: l'apport de Diderot et de Jean-Jacques Rousseau', *Annales, economies, sociétés, civilisations*, xviii (1963), 20–43
A. Whittall: 'Rousseau and the Scope of Opera', *ML*, xlv (1964), 369–76
E. Fubini: 'Il concetto di natura e il mito della musica italiana nel pensiero di Jean-Jacques Rousseau', *Rivista di estetica* [Turin], x (1965), 55–74
S. Sacaluga: 'Diderot, Rousseau, et la querelle musicale de 1752: nouvelle mise au point', *Diderot Studies*, x (1968), 134–73
B. Ebisawa: 'Ruso to Bani' [Rousseau and Burney], *Nomura Festschrift* (Tokyo, 1969), 50–66 [with Fr. summary]
E. Fubini, ed.: *Gli illuministi e la musica* (Milan, 1969)
S. Baud-Bovy: 'Jean-Jacques Rousseau et la musique française', *Annales de la Société Jean-Jacques Rousseau*, xxxviii (1969–71), 259–63
M.-E. Duchez: '*Principe de la mélodie* et *Origine des langues*: un brouillon inédit de Jean-Jacques Rousseau sur l'origine de la mélodie', *RdM*, lx (1974), 33–86
G. Morelli: '"Eloges rendus à un singulier mélange de philosophie, d'orgueil, de chimie, d'opéra, etc": sulle ascendenze melodrammatiche della antropologia di Jean-Jacques Rousseau', *RIM*, ix (1974), 175–228
R. Cotte: *Jean-Jacques Rousseau, le philosophe musicien* (Braine-le-Comte, 1976)
J. F. Strauss: 'Jean Jacques Rousseau: Musician', *MQ*, lxiv (1978), 474–82
H. Lagrave: 'La pantomime à la Foire, au Théâtre-Italien et aux Boulevards (1700–1789)', *Romanistische Zeitung für Literaturgeschichte*, lxxix (1980), 408–30
D. Heartz: 'The Beginnings of the Operatic Romance: Rousseau, Sedaine and Monsigny', *Eighteenth-Century Studies*, xv (1981–2), 149–78
P. Robinson: *Jean-Jacques Rousseau's Doctrine of the Arts* (Berne, 1984)

DANIEL HEARTZ

Rousseau, Marcel Samuel. *See* SAMUEL-ROUSSEAU, MARCEL.

Roussel, Albert (Charles Paul Marie) (*b* Tourcoing, 5 April 1869; *d* Royan, 23 Aug 1937). French composer. Born into a wealthy family, he was brought up by his grandfather and an aunt, his parents having died young. He set his mind upon a naval career but continued to study music while at naval school. It was the director of the Roubaix Conservatory who encouraged him to devote himself to music, having seen some of his early compositions, and Roussel resigned his naval commission in 1894. He then went to Paris, studying with Eugène Gigout and later at the Schola Cantorum where he became a professor of counterpoint, numbering Satie and Varèse among his pupils. In 1909, after his marriage, he embarked upon an extended tour of south-east Asia, an enterprise which left a profound impression upon his music. He served in the artillery during World War I but was invalided out in 1918. The remainder of his life he devoted to music.

Among Roussel's stage works there is nothing that resembles conventional opera. The highly successful *Le festin de l'araignée* (1912), a ballet-pantomime without singing, was followed by *Padmâvatî*, an *opéra-ballet*. This was the direct result of his tour to the East, followed by literary research in close collaboration with the librettist Louis Laloy. It is as much ballet as opera, bearing little relationship to the Western operatic tradition; rather it is allied to oriental traditions of music theatre where stylized characters are totally undeveloped in psychological terms, remaining as decorative symbols depicted through simple actions and dance. Roussel expressed his aims in a letter to Georges Jean-Aubry of 31 March 1903:

> For some time I had been attracted to the idea of writing a decorative work for the stage which was neither like early nor modern opera but allowed me to use the full resources of massed choirs, dances and crowd scenes, where the symphonic development was no more prominent than necessary, and clearly delineated instead of being – as so often in the theatre – a cause of boredom and of a slowing down of the action.

Pâdmavatî was followed by *La naissance de la lyre*, a project first turned down by Koechlin. It is a free adaptation by the Greek scholar Théodore Reinach of a satirical play by Sophocles discovered in 1912. Apollo has lost his herd and offers anything in the world as a reward for finding them. The thief has led them by the tail so that he will not be discovered, but the satyrs find the child Hermes who has stolen the beasts so that he can make a lyre out of their horns, and it is with music that he appeases Apollo's anger. The score consists of elaborate and extended incidental music: a fusion of ballet, choral singing and dialogue, forming a substantial work in its own right. Like *Padmâvatî* it eschews any psychological development, and employs Greek modes and refined orchestration to create the appropriate mood. Roussel wrote to Alfred Cortot expressing his aims in this work: 'seeking above all to simplify the lines' and to create 'an atmosphere of serenity and nobility'. It includes three solo parts (for Apollo, Silenus and Hermes), a silent Nymph, and choruses and dancers representing nymphs and satyrs. Striking instrumental pieces evoke the tuning and playing of the lyre.

Apart from the ballet *Bacchus et Ariane* (1931), considered by many to be his finest work for the stage, there is the ballet *Aenéas* (1935) and several suites of incidental music all infused with his highly refined chromatic harmony and delicate orchestration. *Le testament de la tante Caroline* was Roussel's final operatic work, inspired by the successes of Honegger and Ibert in the field of light operetta.

See also PADMÂVATÎ and TESTAMENT DE LA TANTE CAROLINE, LE.

Padmâvatî op.18, 1914–18 (opéra-ballet, 2, L. Laloy), Paris, Opéra, 1 June 1923
La naissance de la lyre op.24, 1923–4 (conte lyrique, 1, T. Reinach, after Sophocles), Paris, Opéra, 1 July 1925
Testament Tety Karoliny [Le testament de la tante Caroline], 1932–3 (opéra bouffe, 3, Nino [M. Veber]), Olomouc, 14 Nov 1936; in Fr., Paris, OC (Favart), 11 March 1937

*

G. Jean-Aubry: *La musique française d'aujourd'hui* (Paris, 1910, 2/1916; Eng. trans., 1919)
ReM (1937), no.178 [Roussel issue]
A. Hoérée: *Albert Roussel* (Paris, 1938)
Catalogue de l'oeuvre d'Albert Roussel (Paris, 1947)
N. Demuth: *Albert Roussel* (London, 1947)

R. Bernard: *Albert Roussel* (Paris, 1948)
B. Deane: *Albert Roussel* (London, 1961)
A. Surchamp: *Albert Roussel* (Paris, 1967)
Zodiaque, lxxx (1969) [Roussel issue]
Cahiers Albert Roussel [pubn of Amis Belges d'Albert Roussel, Brussels], ii (1979) [articles on *Padmâvatî*]
R. J. del Bontà: 'Songs of India', *OQ*, ii/1 (1984), 5–14
N. Labelle, ed.: *Albert Roussel: lettres et écrits* (Paris, 1987)
N. Labelle: *Catalogue raisonné de l'oeuvre de Albert Roussel* (Louvain-la-Neuve, 1992) RICHARD LANGHAM SMITH

Rousselière, Charles (*b* St Nazaire, 17 Jan 1875; *d* Joue-les-Tours, 11 May 1950). French tenor. Originally a blacksmith by trade, he studied with Albert Vaguet at the Paris Conservatoire and made his début at the Opéra as Samson in 1900. The following year he sang in the première of Saint-Saëns' *Les barbares*, and he remained with the company until 1905. Until 1919 he was a favourite at Monte Carlo, where he appeared first in *La damnation de Faust*; premières there included Mascagni's *Amica*, Saint-Saëns' *L'ancêtre* and Fauré's *Pénélope*. His début at the Metropolitan in *Roméo et Juliette* in 1906 coincided with that of Geraldine Farrar, who received more attention; his dramatic skill was appreciated but the power of his voice, sometimes strident, suggested that he should turn to more heroic roles. This he did on his return to France, adding Otello, Lohengrin, Siegfried and Parsifal to his repertory. He also appeared in Berlin, Buenos Aires and Milan, and in his later years sang mostly at the Opéra-Comique where in 1913 he created the title role in Charpentier's *Julien*. His varied repertory is well represented in recordings made between 1903 and 1926: his voice is strong and clearly defined, his style authoritative in declamation and well mannered in more lyrical music. J. B. STEANE

Roux, Michel (*b* Angoulême, 1 Sept 1924). French baritone. He studied at Bordeaux and Paris, and in 1948 made his début at the Opéra-Comique in *Lakmé*, becoming a company principal there and at the Opéra until 1955. His début at La Scala was in 1953 as Golaud, a role with which he became closely associated and which he recorded that year under Fournet. He sang at leading theatres in France and Italy, and in 1956 made his British début as Count Almaviva at Glyndebourne, where he returned in most years up to 1970, singing Mozart, Debussy and Rossini roles including Raimbaud, which he recorded with the Glyndebourne company under Gui (1957). His American début was at the Chicago Lyric Opera in 1959 as Athanaël (*Thaïs*). Other engagements took him to the Vienna Staatsoper and Deutsche Oper, Berlin, mainly in French and Italian roles, which he sang with intelligent style and often vivid stage character; he later taught in Paris. NOËL GOODWIN

Rovere, Agostino (*b* Monza, 1804; *d* New York, 10 Dec 1865). Italian bass. He studied in Milan, making his début in 1826 at Pavia. In 1828 he sang Clemente in Bellini's *Bianca e Fernando* (the revised version of *Bianca e Gernando*) at Genoa. Engaged at La Scala from 1831 to 1847, he created Fedrigo Locandiere in Donizetti's *Gianni di Parigi* (1839) and La Rocca in Verdi's *Un giorno di regno* (1840). He also created the Marquis in *Linda di Chamounix* (1842) at Vienna, where he sang Don Pasquale. At Covent Garden (1847–8) he sang Mozart's Bartolo and Rossini's Dr Bartolo, Haly (*L'italiana in Algeri*), Don Magnifico (*La Cenerentola*), Leporello and Dulcamara (*L'elisir d'amore*). He excelled in *buffo* roles. ELIZABETH FORBES

Rovetta, Giovanni (*b* ?Venice, 1596–7; *d* Venice, 23 Oct 1668). Italian composer. His father was a violinist associated with St Mark's, Venice, between 1614 and 1641. According to Caffi, Giovanni began his career as a boy soprano at St Mark's but the earliest known documentary evidence concerning him dates from 1614. Listed as an unsuccessful candidate for the post of *capo dei concerti* at St Mark's in March of that year, on 7 December he was one of several instrumentalists who were appointed to salaried posts there. On 2 December 1623 he became a bass singer in the choir. In spring 1627 he assumed the role of Monteverdi's vice-*maestro di cappella* and was confirmed in that position on 22 November of that year. In addition, he was *maestro di musica* at the Ospedale dei Derelitti in 1635 and at the Ospedale dei Mendicanti from 1639. Following Monteverdi's death he was appointed choirmaster of St Mark's on 21 February 1644 and held this post until his death.

Rovetta's opera *Ercole in Lidia*, to a libretto by Maiolino Bisaccioni, was first performed at the Teatro Novissimo, Venice, in 1645 (libretto in *I-Vnm*; scenario in *Rsc* and *Vcg*). John Evelyn attended a performance in June of that year and described the occasion in his diary, naming the soprano Anna Renzi as one of the singers. Rovetta was to have participated in a second operatic venture, *Argiope*. The surviving libretto by Giovanni Battista Fusconi and Pietro Michiel was dedicated to Anna Renzi in 1645 but was not published until 1649. In its preface, the musical setting was attributed jointly to Rovetta and Alessandro Leardini, but in an endnote the authors explained that unforeseen events had prevented Rovetta's participation. The music of both operas is lost, but settings of three smaller dramatic texts survive: the lament *Lagrime d'Erminia* (*Madrigali concertati ... libro primo*, 1629); a dramatic dialogue *La Gelosia placata*, to a text adapted from the work of Giulio Strozzi (*Madrigali concertati ... libro primo*, 1629; text and music in Whenham 1982); and *Il Maggio*, for Thyrsis and a chorus of nymphs (*Madrigali concertati ... libro terzo*, 1645).

J. Evelyn: *Diary* (MS, *GB-Och*); ed. E. S. De Beer (Oxford, 1955), i, 449–50
F. Caffi: *Storia della musica sacra nella già cappella ducale di S. Marco in Venezia (dal 1318 al 1797)* (Venice, 1854–5); ed. E. Surian (Florence, 1987)
G. Verardo Tieri: 'Il Theatro Novissimo: storia di "mutationi, macchine, musiche" ', *NRMI*, x (1976), 555–95; xi (1977), 3–25
J. H. Moore: *Vespers at St Mark's: Music of Alessandro Grandi, Giovanni Rovetta and Francesco Cavalli* (Ann Arbor, 1981), i, 11–18
J. Whenham: *Duet and Dialogue in the Age of Monteverdi* (Ann Arbor, 1982), i, 206–16, ii, 414–37
D. Arnold: 'Music at the *Ospedali*', *JRMA*, cxiii (1988), 156–67
P. Fabbri: *Il secolo cantante: per una storia del libretto d'opera nel seicento* (Bologna, 1990)
E. Rosand: *Opera in Seventeenth-Century Venice: the Creation of a Genre* (Berkeley, 1991) JOHN WHENHAM

Rovettino [Rovetta, Ruettino], **Giovanni Battista.** *See* VOLPE, GIOVANNI BATTISTA.

Roy, Pierre-Charles (*b* Paris, 1683; *d* Paris, 23 Oct 1764). French librettist. He received a thorough education in the classics. At some point between 1701 and 1703 he obtained a position as 'conseiller' at the Chatelet, but he rarely practised this profession and turned to writing instead. His first opera libretto, *Philomèle*, was first performed at the Paris Opéra on 20 October 1705. Between this date and 1718 he provided texts for seven *tragédies en musique*, which include some of the best of the century: *Bradamante* (1707); *Callirhoë* (1712); *Ariane* (1717); and *Sémiramis* (1718). These earned him the epithet 'successor to Quinault'. Before the time of Cahusac, only Danchet rivalled him among his contemporaries.

Apart from the story of Theseus and Ariadne, Roy generally eschewed mythological subjects, drawing instead on Euripides (*Créuse, l'Athénienne*), Ovid (*Philomèle*), Ariosto (*Bradamante*) and Pausanias (*Callirhoë, Hippodamie*); the tragic tale of the Queen of Babylon forms the subject of *Sémiramis*. His tragedies are less *galant*, less sentimental and more tragic than Quinault's; they are generally well constructed and have more dramatic force than Danchet's. Some exploit the darker side of the human psyche with an emphasis on abnormal behaviour (e.g. incest in *Philomèle* and *Sémiramis*). *Divertissements* are often skilfully linked to the dramatic action and contain original verse structures that mix three-, four- and five-syllable lines.

In the prefaces to his librettos Roy revealed a thorough knowledge of classical literature and history. He discussed his sources with admirable candour and justified alterations made to conform with the dramatic conventions of the French lyric stage. The dramatic integrity of some of his tragic librettos would have ideally suited Rameau, his exact contemporary. But in the battle between Lullistes and Ramistes, Roy sided with conservatives, mounting satirical attacks against La Pouplinière (Rameau's protector) and, in 1749, against Cahusac (Rameau's librettist for *Naïs* and *Zoroastre*); Rameau himself was the target of a vituperative allegory. According to D'Aquin de Château-Lyon, Roy had only 'antipathie pour la musique de M. Rameau'.

By 1729 Roy had won prizes from the Académie des Jeux Floreaux and the Académie Française and was elected to the Académie des Inscriptions et Belles Lettres. After his attempts to become a member of the Académie Française were repeatedly rejected, he turned to writing clandestine satires and epigrams savagely attacking the academy, thereby earning the enmity of Fontenelle, La Motte, Francine, Moncrif and Voltaire. The end result of Roy's vitriolic attacks was to harden opposition against any further consideration of his election to the academy. But he did not lack support from the aristocracy. The Duchess of Maine invited him to write for the Grandes Nuits de Sceaux in 1714 and 1715; the Duke of Luynes hailed him as 'the most famous of our lyric poets'; he was appointed a Chevalier of the Order of St Michel (1742), the first man of letters to be so honoured; and Mme de Pompadour had his works performed at her Théâtre des Petits Cabinets.

Roy never returned to *tragédie en musique* after 1718. Instead he provided librettos for several ballets that were performed at the Paris Opéra. The first version of *Les éléments* (1721) is a synthesis between court ballet and opera; the prologue and four entrées ('L'air', 'L'eau', 'Le feu', 'La terre') draw on Ovid's *Metamorphoses* and Virgil's *Eclogues* and *Aeneid*. Roy's verses were much admired: Sabatier wrote: 'Everyone knows the opening of the prologue by heart. Never did the lyric muse deploy verses of such majesty, richness, harmony' (*Les trois siècles*, 1772). Roy introduced comedy into his *ballet-héroïque Les stratagèmes de l'Amour* (written in 1726 to celebrate the marriage of Louis XV), in spite of the controversy engendered by the comic entrées in earlier *opéra-ballets* (*Les fêtes vénitiennes*, 1710, and *Les fêtes de Thalie*, 1714). In his *Avertissement* he defended his audacity as being within the bounds of good taste: 'The Public has decided that if this stage admits the Comic, it may only be a noble Comedy and must bear the character of Antiquity'.

Roy's polemical 'Lettre sur l'Opéra' (1749), reflecting his conservative point of view, may be seen as an attack on Rameau and his followers before mid-century. It contains his oft-quoted definition of *opéra-ballet*: 'This kind of Drama that assembles three or four [plots] in the same cadre, each dealt with in a single act ... pleases by its variety and sympathizes with French impatience'.

bh – *ballet-héroïque* div – *divertissement*
tm – *tragédie en musique*

Philomèle (tm), L. de Lacoste, 1705; *Bradamante* (tm), Lacoste, 1707; *Hippodamie* (tm), Campra, 1708; *Callirhoë* (tm), A. C. Destouches, 1712; *Créuse, l'Athénienne* (tm), Lacoste, 1712; *Ariane* (tm, with Lagrange-Chancel), J.-J. Mouret, 1717; *Sémiramis* (tm), Destouches, 1718; *Les éléments* (opéra-ballet), Destouches and M.-R. de Lalande, 1721; *Les stratagèmes de l'Amour* (bh), Destouches, 1726; *Le triomphe des sens* (bh), Mouret, 1732; *Les grâces* (bh), Mouret, 1735; *Le ballet de la paix* (pastorale-héroïque), Rebel and Francoeur, 1738; *Le temple de Gnide* (div, with Bellis), Mouret, 1741; *Le palais royal* (div), Mion, 1743; *Le retour du roi* (div), Rebel and Francoeur, 1744; *Les Augustales* (div), Rebel and Francoeur, 1744; *La Félicité* (bh), Rebel and Francoeur, 1746; *L'année galante* (bh), Mion, 1747; *Les fêtes de Thétis* (bh), F. Collin de Blamont and B. de Bury, 1750; *Iphise et Iante* (bh), Rebel and Francoeur, 1769; *Bacchus et la Minéïde* (bh), A. Simon, 1773

*

P.-C. Roy: 'Lettre sur l'Opéra', *Lettres sur quelques écrits de ce tems*, ed. E. C. Fréron (Geneva, 1749), ii, 7–22
E. H. Polinger: *Pierre-Charles Roy* (New York, 1930)
C. Girdlestone: *La tragédie en musique (1673–1750) considérée comme genre littéraire* (Geneva, 1972)
S. Pitou: *The Paris Opéra: an Encyclopedia of Operas, Ballets, Composers and Performers* (Westport, CT, 1983)

JAMES R. ANTHONY

Royal Academy of Music. (1) London association of noblemen, supported by the king, founded in 1719 for the promotion of Italian opera; *see* HANDEL, GEORGE FRIDERIC, §6, and LONDON, §I, 5.

(2) London conservatory (RAM) founded in 1822, which has given some notable opera performances; *see* LONDON, §II, 3.

Royal College of Music. London conservatory (RCM) founded in 1883, with a distinguished record of opera performances; *see* LONDON, §II, 3.

Royal Hunt of the Sun, The. Opera in three acts by IAIN HAMILTON to his own libretto after Peter Shaffer's play; London, Coliseum, 2 February 1977.

The opera is set in the early 16th century, at the time of the Spanish conquest of Peru. Pizarro (bass), leader of the Spanish expedition, entices men to follow him by displaying Peruvian gold. His expedition is blessed in Panama Cathedral. The Inca sovereign Atahuallpa (high baritone) welcomes the Spaniards. When he refuses to acknowledge the white God the priests authorize Pizarro to massacre the Indians. Atahuallpa is spared and is promised his freedom if a room is filled with gold, but the promise is broken. Pizarro and Atahuallpa form a strange friendship. When Atahuallpa again rejects Christianity, he is garrotted. Pizarro, half-converted to the Inca faith, waits in vain for the miracle which will restore his friend to life.

The Royal Hunt of the Sun stands as close to music theatre as to conventional opera. The music is largely illustrative, and the more vigorous and picturesque aspects of Shaffer's play are so powerfully presented that dramatic urgency is never lost. Spaniards and Peruvians are sharply characterized through the music, which however makes no use of traditional material. Similarly, the priests, the joyless villains of the opera, are given music which is ecclesiastical in tone but far removed from any known church music. There is much declamatory writing and one outstanding lyrical episode, the 'Song of the Little Finch'. HUGO COLE

Royal Italian Opera. Annual subscription seasons of Italian opera given during the 19th century in London; the name applies to the specially contracted companies that gave such a season, and to the theatres in which they sang; *see* LONDON, §II, 1.

Royal Opera House. London theatre, also known as Covent Garden; *see* LONDON, §II, 2.

Royal Swedish Opera. Company founded in 1773 in STOCKHOLM by Gustavus III, and by extension the theatre built for it in 1782 (replaced in 1898).

Royer, Alphonse (*b* Paris, 1803; *d* Paris, 11 April 1875). French theatre manager and librettist. He first made his name with historical fiction and drama of a Romantic kind and then, after making the fashionable journey to the Levant, with travel books. He subsequently devoted his energies to the theatre, writing *comédies-vaudevilles* and other plays, generally in collaboration and most often with GUSTAVE VAËZ. Royer was director of the Théâtre de l'Odéon in Paris from 1853 to 1856, and (with Vaëz as deputy for the first four years) of the Opéra from 1856 to 1862, when he was appointed Inspecteur-général des beaux-arts. As well as writing the libretto for Donizetti's *La favorite* (1840), Royer and Vaëz helped to make Italian opera accessible to the Parisian public with their French translations of Donizetti's *Lucia di Lammermoor* (1839), Rossini's *Otello* (1844) and Verdi's *I Lombardi* (as *Jérusalem*, 1847). In 1874, a few days before the opening of the new Paris Opéra, Royer brought out his brief *Histoire de l'Opéra*, a survey beginning with Lully and recounting anecdotes of 19th-century composers.

CHRISTOPHER SMITH

Royer, Joseph-Nicolas-Pancrace (*b* Turin, *c*1705; *d* Paris, 11 Jan 1755). French composer. Active in Paris by 1725, he was a brilliant and influential contemporary of Rameau through much of the latter's career. His first operatic endeavours were contributions to two *opéras comiques*, *Le fâcheux veuvage*, performed at the Foire St Laurent in September 1725, and *Crédit est mort*, presented at the Foire St Germain in February 1726. His first term as *maître de musique* at the Paris Opéra (1730–33) saw the premières of his *Pyrrhus* (1730), with sets by Servandoni, and Rameau's *Hippolyte et Aricie* (1733). Important court appointments, including *maître de musique des enfants de France*, followed the successes of two *ballets-héroïques*: *Zaïde, reine de Grenade* (1739) and *Le pouvoir de l'Amour* (1743). In 1744 he began work on Voltaire's libretto, *Pandore*, destined for the dauphin's wedding in 1745 but set aside in favour of a revival of *Zaïde*.

From 1748 until his death, Royer's energies were mainly directed to the enhancement of standards and repertory of the Concert Spirituel; included were his own revision of Gilles' *Messe de Requiem* (1750), the revival of Rameau's *In convertendo* (1751) and the first French performances of Pergolesi's *Stabat mater* (1753). In 1753 he again became *maître de musique* at the Opéra. He had returned to *Prométhée et Pandore* in 1752 (without consulting Voltaire) and by late 1754 was revising it for performances planned for winter 1756; Voltaire accused Royer of having 'sacrificed me to his semiquavers' and was only placated by the composer's sudden death in January 1755: 'God wishes to have his soul and his music'. At that time, the Duke of Luynes paid tribute to a 'very knowledgeable man, with an exceptional taste for melody' (Dufourcq).

Royer's *Pièces de clavecin* (1746) includes vivid transcriptions of movements from *Zaïde* and *Le pouvoir de L'Amour*; excerpts from both works were in the repertory of the Esterházy court ensemble by 1759.

See also ZAÏDE, REINE DE GRENADE.

Pyrrhus (tragédie, prol., 5, J. Fermelhuis), Paris, Opéra, 26 Oct 1730 (Paris,1730)

Zaïde, reine de Grenade (ballet-héroïque, prol., 3, Abbé de La Marre), Paris, Opéra, 3 Sept 1739 (Paris, 1739, 2/1745) [copy in *F-Po* includes substantial autograph revisions made before the première]; with added divertissement Momus amoureux, Paris, Opéra, 27 Oct 1739; without prol., Versailles,10 March 1745; with extended prol., Paris, 13 May 1745

Le pouvoir de l'Amour (ballet-héroïque, prol., 3, C.-H. Le Febvre de Saint-Marc), Paris, Opéra, 23 April 1743 (Paris, 1743)

Prométhée et Pandore, 1744–54 (tragédie, 5, Voltaire), private rehearsal, Paris, 5 Oct 1752

Almasis (acte de ballet, 1, F.-A. P. de Montcrif), Versailles, 26 Feb 1748 (Paris, *c*1750)

Myrtil et Zélie (pastorale-héroïque, prol., 1), Versailles, 20 June 1750 [attrib. to Royer in *MGG*]

Contribs. to: Le fâcheux veuvage (oc. 3, A. Piron), Paris, Foire St Laurent, Sept 1725; Crédit est mort (oc, 1, Piron), Paris, Foire St Germain, Feb 1726

MGG (M. Sackur, R. Cotte)

C. Parfaict and F. Parfaict: *Mémoires pour servir à l'histoire des spectacles de la foire* (Paris, 1743)

P.-L. d'Aquin de Château-Lyon: *Lettres sur les hommes célèbres … sous le règne de Louis XV* (Paris, 1752, 2/1754 as *Siècle littéraire de Louis XV*)

E. Titon du Tillet: *Le parnasse françois*, suppl.ii (Paris, 1755)

A. Piron: *Oeuvres complettes*, ed. R. de Juvigny, iv–v (Paris, 1776)

J.-G. Prod'homme: 'Une "prise de possession" de l'opéra en 1753', *RdM*, ii (1920–21), 102–5

P.-M. Masson: 'Le "Ballet héroïque"', *ReM*, ix/8 (1928), 132–54

T. Besterman, ed.: *Voltaire: Correspondence and Related Documents* (Geneva, 1968–77), D.2968 (1744), D.5914 (1754), D.6094 (1755)

N. Dufourcq, ed.: *La musique à la cour de Louis XIV et de Louis XV d'après les mémoires de Sourches et Luynes 1681–1758* (Paris, 1970)

R. S. Ridgway: 'Voltaire's operas', *Studies on Voltaire and the Eighteenth Century*, clxxxix (Oxford, 1980), 119–51

G. Sadler: 'Patrons and Pasquinades: Rameau in the 1730's', *JRMA*, cxiii (1988), 314–37

L. Sawkins: 'Classic and Baroque: Paris and the Esterházy court', *Haydn Society Newsletter*, no.10 (1990), 5–17

LIONEL SAWKINS

Roze, Marie (Hippolyte) (*b* Paris, 2 March 1846; *d* Paris, 21 June 1926). French soprano. She studied in Paris and made her début in 1865 in Hérold's *Marie* at the Opéra-Comique, where she sang in the first performances of Auber's *Le premier jour de bonheur*

(1868) and Flotow's *L'ombre* (1870). She sang Marguerite (*Faust*) at the Opéra and in 1872 made her London début at Drury Lane in the same role. She remained with Mapleson's company, first at Drury Lane, then from 1877 at Her Majesty's Theatre, until 1881. She created the Queen in Balfe's *The Talisman* (1874), and when Tietjens collapsed in mid-season (1877) Roze took over her roles of Ortrud and Donna Anna. She toured the USA in 1878–9, then joined the Carl Rosa company, with which she sang Massenet's Manon in the first British (Liverpool, January 1885) and London (Drury Lane, May 1885) performances.

ELIZABETH FORBES

Rozen [Rosen], **Yegor** [Georgy] **Fyodorovich,** Baron (*b* Revel [now Tallinn], 1800; *d* St Petersburg, 1860). Russian librettist. A poet, translator, dramatist, critic and courtier, he was originally German-speaking and learnt Russian in the military. Through his friend the poet and courtier V. A. Zhukovsky he obtained the post of secretary to the crown prince, the future Alexander II, in 1835. Zhukovsky then passed on to Rozen the task of fitting verses to Glinka's music for the opera *A Life for the Tsar*, through which Rozen won his tiny claim to immortality. Long suppressed in the Soviet Union for its monarchist sentiments, Rozen's libretto was restored to Glinka's opera in the Bol'shoy Theatre revival of 1989.

*

Poetï 1820–1830kh godov [The Poets of the 1820s and 30s] (Moscow, 1972)

V. Terras, ed.: *Handbook of Russian Literature* (New Haven, CT, and London, 1985)

RICHARD TARUSKIN

Rozhdestvensky, Gennady (Nikolayevich) (*b* Moscow, 4 May 1931). Russian conductor. He studied at the Moscow Conservatory, where his teachers included his father, Nikolay Anosov, for conducting. He made his début at the age of 20, while still a student, in Tchaikovsky's *Nutcracker* at the Bol'shoy, where he was a resident conductor from 1951 to 1961 and principal conductor from 1964 to 1970. There he conducted the first 'complete' staging of Prokofiev's *War and Peace* in 1959 and the first Russian production of Britten's *A Midsummer Night's Dream* in 1965. He made his Covent Garden début in 1970 with *Boris Godunov*, and returned there with the same work in 1991. Rozhdestvensky's repertory ranges from the classics to more recent works, such as Stravinsky's *Mavra*, Poulenc's *La voix humaine* and Fleyshman's *Rothschild's Violin* (in the version completed by Shostakovich). His recordings include his own orchestration of Musorgsky's unfinished *The Marriage*, Shostakovich's *The Nose*, and Prokofiev's *The Gambler* and *Maddalena*. A brilliant executant, he shows particular skill in relating emotional character to structural content through a mixture of intuition and logical thinking. He has held orchestral appointments in London, Stockholm and Vienna.

I. M. YAMPOL'SKY/NOËL GOODWIN

Rozkošný, Josef Richard (*b* Prague, 21 Sept 1833; *d* Prague, 3 June 1913). Czech composer. He received private music lessons with J. B. Kittl and in his youth made concert tours as a pianist; later he became an important figure in the cultural life of Prague as a choirmaster and administrator while also working as a bank clerk. Although he never held a theatrical post his main importance as a composer lies in his operatic work, but this is uneven in quality and met with mixed success in his lifetime. Of his 12 operas ten were performed, the first of them, the one-act *Ave Maria*, only privately (1855 or 1856). His first stage work to be professionally produced was the successful comic opera *Mikuláš* (1870), which received seven performances in Prague and was also staged in Plzeň and Brno. Like Smetana's *The Bartered Bride*, it is a village comedy to a text by Karel Sabina; its Czech subject matter, simple folklike musical structures and musical humour complied with the demands of the time. Rozkošný achieved popular success with his Romantic opera *Svatojanské proudy* ('The St John's Rapids', originally composed to a German text, *Die Moldaunixe*, and subsequently translated into Czech), which was given 34 times in Prague, 1871–95, and was also staged in Plzeň and Brno. The plot's hunting scenes, supernatural setting and use of national symbols, such as the River Vltava and the fairy Vltavka, enabled the composer to create a work within the genre of German Romantic opera; the effect of the opera was no doubt enhanced by the fine orchestration of Rozkošný's friend Karel Sebor.

While Rozkošný's preference for lyrical and folk music was well suited to these two operas, it was a limitation in the case of his attempt at grand historical Romantic opera, *Záviš z Falkenštejna* ('Záviš of Falkenstein', 1877), though the failure of this work was due partly to the libretto; only three performances were given. He achieved his greatest success with his comic fairy-tale opera *Popelka* ('Cinderella'), which received 70 performances in Prague, 1885–1912, and was later staged in Plzeň, Brno and Ostrava. The lyrical passages and fantastic scenes of the libretto are reflected in Rozkošný's music, which includes ballet music that became widely popular. By contrast, his fairy-tale opera *Krakonoš* (1889), based on a legend about a mountain ghost, proved a failure, ultimately because of its libretto, and received only two performances. The subject matter of the one-act opera *Stoja* (1894) concerns southern Slav peasant communities, and therefore evoked a ready response in Bohemia at the time. Here Rozkošný turned his skill in evoking local colour to the *verismo* style, and this stimulated him to make his expressive lyrical writing more pathetic. The work was staged nine times in Prague and again in Brno. The influence of contemporary naturalism appeared again in *Satanella* (1898), this time in the context of grand historical opera; four performances were given. In his last stage work, *Černé jezero* ('The Black Lake', 1906), Rozkošný returned to his most successful genre, fairy-tale Romantic opera. After nine performances in Prague, this was staged in Plzeň. For a long time Rozkošný's only work still occasionally performed was the overture to *The St John's Rapids*. Excerpts from this opera broadcast by Radio Plzeň in 1987 drew attention to the fact that Rozkošný's operatic work awaits appreciation.

first performed in Prague unless otherwise stated

Ave Maria (1, ? V. Trapp), private perf., 1855 or 1856, ?lost

Mikuláš (comic op, 2, K. Sabina), Provisional, 5 Dec 1870, *CS-Pk**

Svatojanské proudy [The St John's Rapids] (romantic op, 4, E. Rüffer: *Die Moldaunixe*), Provisional, 3 Oct 1871, *Pk**, vs (Prague, 1882); orchd K. Šebor

Záviš z Falkenštejna [Záviš of Falkenstein], 1871–7 (historical romantic op, 4, J. Böhm, after V. Hálek), Provisional, 14 Oct 1877, *Pk**, vs *Pnm**; orchd Šebor

Pytláci [The Poachers] (Böhm), excerpts, Měšťanská Beseda, May 1878, ?lost

Alchymista [The Alchemist], 1880 (Böhm), unperf., ?lost

Popelka [Cinderella] (3, O. Hostinský, after fairy-tale), National, 31 May 1885, *Pk**, vs *Pk**, excerpts, vs (Prague, n.d.)
Rusalka, 1886 (E. Mužík, after Hostinský), Act 1 only, ?lost
Krakonoš (3, J. Borecký), National, 18 Oct 1889, *Pk**, vs *Pk*, song (Prague, n.d.)
Stoja (1, O. Kučera, after J. D. Konrád), National, 6 June 1894, *Pk**, vs *Pk*
Satanella (3, K. Kádner, after J. Vrchlický), National, 5 Oct 1898, *Pk**, vs *Pk*
Černé jezero [The Black Lake], 1902, rev. 1904 (romantic op, 3, Kádner, after A. Heyduk: *Dědův odkaz* [The Grandfather's Legacy]), National, 6 Jan 1906, *Pk**, vs *Pk*; orig. title Šumavská víla [The Nymph of Šumava]

*

PEM (M. Pospíšil) [forthcoming]
L. Janáček: 'Několik slov o "Svatojanských proudech" J. R. Rozkošného [Some Words about Rozkošného's *The St John's Rapids*], *Hudební listy*, iii (1886–7), 65–6
E. Chvála: *Ein Vierteljahrhundert böhmischer Musik* (Prague, 1887)
V. A. J. Hornové [V. Horn, A. Horn and J. Horn]: *Česká zpěvohra* [Czech Opera] (Prague, 1903)
Z. Nejedlý: *Dějiny Národního divadla*, iii: *Opera Národního divadla do roku 1900* [History of the National Theatre, iii: Opera at the National Theatre up to 1900] (Prague, 1935, 2/1949)
J. Bartoš: *Prozatímní divadlo a jeho zpěvohra* [The Provisional Theatre and its Opera] (Prague, 1938)
J. Hutter and Z. Chalabala, eds.: *České umění dramatické*, ii: *Zpěvohra* [Czech Dramatic Art: Opera] (Prague, 1941), 156–8
V. Lébl: '125 let od narození Josefa Richarda Rozkošného' [125 Years since Rozkošný's Birth], *HRo*, xi (1958), 688
J. Němeček: *Opera Národního divadla v období Karla Kovařovice 1900–1920* [The Opera of the National Theatre during the Kovařovic Era, 1900–20], (Prague, 1968–9)
M. Pospíšil: 'Balada v české opeře 19. století' [The Ballad in Czech 19th-century Opera', *HV*, xvi (1979), 3–25
J. Tyrrell: *Czech Opera* (Cambridge, 1988)

MARTA OTTLOVÁ, MILAN POSPÍŠIL

Różycki, Ludomir (*b* Warsaw, 6 Nov 1884; *d* Katowice, 1 Jan 1953). Polish composer. He was a composition pupil of Noskowski at the Warsaw Conservatory and then studied with Humperdinck at the Hochschule für Musik in Berlin (1905–8). In 1907 he was appointed opera conductor and piano teacher at the Lemberg Conservatory. He spent the years 1914–20 in Berlin, then became conductor of the Warsaw Opera. In 1926 he initiated the foundation, and was first president, of the Polish Composers' Union. He was professor at the Warsaw Conservatory from 1930 to 1945, then taught at the Katowice conservatory and wrote widely on music. He received the State Prize in 1930 (for the opera *Eros i Psyche*) and again in 1952.

Różycki was a composer predominantly of dramatic works and programmatic orchestral music; he possessed a great facility, which was the cause of his early successes and of his later failures. His youthful symphonic poems on subjects from Polish history – composed in an individual and spontaneous style not lacking in fantasy – gained him many followers. Less gifted and more eclectic than his contemporary Szymanowski, he found an easier path to opera. His first such work, *Bolesław Śmiały* (1909), derived its creative impulses and thematic ideas almost directly from his symphonic poem of the same name (1906). Różycki achieved a more complete success with *Eros i Psyche*, first presented at Wrocław in 1917 and later heard in Warsaw and several German towns. The comic opera *Casanova* (1923), which contains some felicitous operetta-like arias, won notable popularity. In subsequent works for the theatre, such as the tragic opera *Beatrix Cenci* (1927), Różycki remained a fairly faithful imitator of 19th-century styles; only when he hinted at Polish themes, original or taken from folk music, did he become more individual, as in the ballet *Pan Twardowski*. Together with Szymanowski he held a leading position in Polish music for many years, but by the beginning of the 1930s he had become almost a commercial purveyor: original in expression and innovatory in technique in his early years, he became increasingly conventional.

Bolesław Śmiały (3, A. Bandrowski-Sas, after S. Wyspiański), Lemberg, 11 Feb 1909
Meduza (3, C. Jellenta), Warsaw, 26 Oct 1912
Eros i Psyche, 1914 (5, J. Żuławski), Wrocław, 10 March 1917
Casanova (comic op, 3, J. Krzewiński), Warsaw, 8 June 1923
Beatrix Cenci (4, S. Różycka, after J. Słowacki), Warsaw, 30 Jan 1927
Młyn diabelski [The Devil's Mill] (6 scenes, J. Maszyński), Poznań, 1931
Lili chce śpiewać [Lili Wants to Sing] (operetta, Krzewiński), Poznań, 1933
Pani Walewska, 1935 (3, Krzewiński and Różycki, after W. Gąsiorowski), inc.

*

J. Leszczyński: *Objaśnienia do dramatu Ludomira Różyckiego 'Bolesław Śmiały'* [Interpretation of Różycki's Drama 'Bolesław Śmiały'], ed. H. Altenberg (Lwów, 1909)
Z. Folga: '"Bolesław Śmiały" Ludomira Różyckiego jako dramat muzyczny', *Ryszard Wagner a polska kultura muzyczna* (Katowice, 1964), 105–22

BOGUSŁAW SCHÄFFER

Rübezahl. Opera by Franz Danzi; *see* BERGGEIST, DER.

Rubin, Vladimir Il'ich (*b* Moscow, 5 Aug 1924). Russian composer. In 1933 he enrolled at the Central Music School, Moscow. He served in the Army, 1941–3, then resumed his education at the Moscow Conservatory, studying the piano with A. Gol'denveyser and composition with N. Peyko. Rubin scored an early and enduring success, particularly with children's audiences, with his first opera, the comic fairy-tale *Tri tolstyaka* ('Three Fat Men'), which has been staged and televised in many cities, including Berlin.

Rubin has been especially attracted to vocal genres, including oratorio, and many of his works, including his second opera, *Iyul'skoye voskresen'ye: Sevastopol', god 1942* ('The July Resurrection: Sevastopol, the Year 1942') have been inspired by a patriotic impulse. Using a musical style which weaves together motifs from Russian folk music and soldiers' songs, *The July Resurrection* commemorates the heroism of the defenders of the city of Sevastopol; the opera was awarded the State Prize of the Russian Republic in 1972. Rubin's third opera, *Krïlatïy vsadnik* ('The Winged Horseman'), deals with the immortality of poetry, freely using the events of García Lorca's life as its basis.

Tri tolstyaka [Three Fat Men] (comic op, 4, S. Bogomazov, after Y. Olesha), concert perf., Moscow, Actors' House, 25 Nov 1956; stage, Saratov, Chernïshevsky Theatre of Opera and Ballet, 19 April 1957; rev., Moscow, Children's Music Theatre, 22 Oct 1967
Iyul'skoye voskresen'ye: Sevastopol', god 1942 [The July Resurrection: Sevastopol, the Year 1942] (tragic op, 2, Rubin), Novosibirsk, 8 May 1970
Krïlatïy vsadnik [The Winged Horseman] (prol., 2, Rubin and Bogomazov, after F. García Lorca and others), Novosibirsk, Dec 1980
Stsenï iz gusarskoy zhizni [Scenes from a Hussar's Life], 1987 (mono-opera, D. Davïdov), unperf.
Kashtanka (2, Rubin, after A. P. Chekhov, A. S. Pushkin, F. I. Tyutchev and others), Novosibirsk, 1989

*

R. Leytes: 'Talant yest' velikaya druzhestvennost' odnogo ko vsem [Talent is the Great Friendliness of the One to the Many], *SovM* (1984), no. 11, pp.35–6
A. Tevosyan: *Kompozitor Vladimir Rubin* (Moscow, 1989)

Giovanni Battista Rubini as Gualtiero (a role he created in the original production, Milan, 1827) and his wife Adelaide Comelli as Imogene in Bellini's 'Il pirata': engraving

I. Korn: 'Istoriya korotkaya i potomu grustnaya' [The History is Brief and for that Reason Sad], *SovM* (1990), no. 4, pp.39–40 [on Kashtanka]

LAUREL E. FAY

Rubinelli, Giovanni Maria (*b* Brescia, 1753; *d* Brescia, 1829). Italian alto castrato. He made his début in 1770 in Sacchini's *Calliroe* at Stuttgart, where he sang both male and female roles. In 1774 he returned to Italy and sang at Venice in Anfossi's *Lucio Silla*, at Padua in Mysliveček's *Atide*, and at Modena in Paisiello's *Alessandro nell'Indie* and Anfossi's *Demofoonte*. In 1776–8 he sang in Naples, in Paisiello's *La disfatta di Dario* and Guglielmi's *Ricimero*, then appeared in Milan at the inauguration of La Scala, singing in Salieri's *Europa riconosciuta*, Mortellari's *Troia distrutta* and, in 1779, Anfossi's *Cleopatra*. In 1784 he was in Naples, where he sang in Paisiello's *Antigone*. In 1786 he went to London, making his début at the King's Theatre in *Virginia*, a pasticcio, and also singing in Handel's *Giulio Cesare* and Bertoni's *Orfeo ed Euridice*. He continued to sing until 1800, appearing in Nasolini's *La morte di Cleopatra* at Vicenza (1791) and Andreozzi's *Agesilao* in Verona (1792). He was thought by Burney to be an admirable singer. ELIZABETH FORBES

Rubini, Giacomo. *See* LAURI-VOLPI, GIACOMO.

Rubini, Giovanni Battista (*b* Romano, nr Bergamo, 7 April 1794; *d* Romano, 3 March 1854). Italian tenor. After singing secondary roles, and touring Piedmont with a little-known troupe in 1814, he sang Lindoro in *L'italiana in Algeri* at the Teatro S Moisè, Venice, in 1815, and he attracted the attention of Domenico Barbaia, who offered him a long-term contract at the S Carlo. Rubini's Neapolitan début was in 1815 at the Teatro dei Fiorentini, again as Lindoro. He spent ten years in Naples, performing mostly at the smaller houses where comedy prevailed and benefiting from the tuition of Nozzari, a leading tenor at the S Carlo. He appeared in Rome in 1818. In 1824–5 he first sang in Vienna; world fame was in sight, with engagements in Italy and, for the first time, Paris, where he starred in *La Cenerentola*, *Otello* and *La donna del lago*. But it was in the new Romantic style of Bellini and Donizetti that he came into his own: he proved a vital influence on Bellini, creating the tenor leads in *Bianca e Gernando* (1826, Naples), *Il pirata* (1827, Milan), *La sonnambula* (1831, Milan) and *I puritani* (1835, Paris). During the composition of *Il pirata* he lodged with the composer, trying out each piece as it was written. Likewise, Bellini refused to commit to paper a note of Arturo's music in *I puritani* until Rubini was available to be consulted. The Donizetti premières in which Rubini was involved include, in Naples, *La lettera anonima* (1822), *Elvida* (1826), *Il giovedì grasso* (1828), *Gianni di Calais* (1828) and *Il paria* (1829) and, more importantly, *Anna Bolena* (1830, Milan) and *Marino Faliero* (1835, Paris).

Rubini first appeared in London in 1831. From then until 1843 he performed alternately at Her Majesty's Theatre in the Haymarket, where his parts included Don Giovanni and, on occasion, Don Ottavio, and the Théâtre Italien in Paris; there from 1839 he yielded his place in the leading quartet to the young Mario. He visited St Petersburg in 1843 and was invited by the tsar to become 'Director of Singing for the Empire'; he returned with Tamburini and others to give a season of Italian opera, 1843–4. But in 1845 he retired permanently to his villa in Romano, now a Rubini museum.

During Rubini's career the tenor, traditionally the young hero of *opera buffa*, was assuming the same role in the serious genre. In the new Romantic opera of the

1830s Rubini had at his disposal an intensity of expression that far outshone the cool heroics of the castratos and their female successors. His phenomenally high range, which induced Bellini to include a high F for him in the third act of *I puritani*, must be understood in the context of the convention of his day, when no tenor was expected to sing any note higher than *a'* with full chest resonance. The upper fifth of Rubini's range was in the less expressive falsetto register. In order to avoid ugly changes of timbre and to gather strength for high notes, he had not only to exaggerate differences between loud and soft, but to sing whole numbers in a whispering *pianissimo* instead of allowing his voice to expand naturally and easily. He is also credited with introducing Romantic mannerisms such as the 'sob'. He was neither good-looking nor a good actor; his strength lay in the beauty of his tone and the natural artistry of his phrasing.

*

A. Locatelli: *Cenni biografici sulla straordinaria carriera teatrale percossa da Giovanni Battista Rubini* (Milan, 1844)

H. F. Chorley: *Thirty Years' Musical Recollections* (London, 1862), i, 29

G. Donati-Petteni: *L'arte della musica in Bergamo* (Bergamo, 1930)

E. Gara: *Giovanni Battista Rubini nel centenario della morte* (Bergamo, 1954)

C. Traini: *Il cigno di Romano: Giovanni Battista Rubini* (Bergamo, 1954)

B. Brewer: 'Rubini – The King of Tenors', *Opera*, xxx (1979), 326–9

Donizetti Society Journal, iv (1980) [incl. B. Brewer: 'Il cigno di Romano, the King of Tenors: Giovan Battista Rubini, a Performance Study', 116–24; 'Points for the Reconstruction of the Career of G. B. Rubini', 125–59; 'Rubini's Repertory', 160–65; 'Two Nineteenth Century Accounts of Giovan Battista Rubini', 167–79

K. Huber: *Giovanni Battista Rubini: ein italienischer Opernsänger in Wien* (diss., Vienna U., 1991)

JULIAN BUDDEN

Rubinstein [Rubinshteyn], **Anton Grigor'yevich** (*b* Vïkhvatintsï on the Dnestr, nr Balta, Ukraine [Podoliya], 16/28 Nov 1829; *d* Peterhof [now Petrodvorets], nr St Petersburg, 8/20 Nov 1894). Russian composer, pianist and conductor.

1. Background. 2. Early operas. 3. Central period. 4. Later operas.

1. BACKGROUND. The greatest instrumental virtuoso Russia ever produced, Rubinstein was an enormously energetic personality who, by founding the Russian Musical Society (1859) and the St Petersburg Conservatory (1862), almost single-handedly organized professional musical activity in his country, for this purpose securing patronage at the highest levels of the aristocracy despite his Jewish ancestry. These activities and accomplishments, along with an attitude towards Russia's place in the scheme of things musical that was patriotic but decidedly not nationalistic, made Rubinstein a powerful but highly controversial figure during his lifetime, as he has remained. His enduring legacy is administrative; the institutions he founded are still active. The Russian Musical Society is now the St Petersburg (formerly Leningrad) Philharmonic, and Rubinstein's conservatory is now the State Conservatory, named after Rimsky-Korsakov.

A bewilderingly prolific composer in all media, at one time rated on a level with Brahms, Rubinstein has lost his once commanding position in the performing repertory, although his Fourth Piano Concerto remained popular with extroverted virtuosos until the middle of the 20th century and a couple of melodious salon items have won anonymous immortality as background music in countless arrangements. He wrote more operas than any of his countrymen, but only one of them, *Demon*, maintains a toehold in the Soviet repertory. Several others left individual items to the concert hall or the recital stage, but these too have by now disappeared. With the one noted exception, Rubinstein's vast operatic corpus is now a great dead mass. Perhaps that is only just: a professed adherent of 'absolute music' among other German values, Rubinstein held opera to be 'altogether a subordinate branch of our art'.

The great difference between Rubinstein's career and those of his Russian contemporaries was its cosmopolitan reach. Accepted as an international virtuoso at a time when a performing musician was still expected to compose, he was as much a fixture of European concert life (German, especially) as Russian, and the presence of his music in European and even American concert halls and opera houses was taken for granted; it was not an exotic export like the work of the more insular Russians, to be valued above all for its Russianness. It is therefore natural that, unlike the insular Russians, Rubinstein did not particularly value his Russianness as a commodity – the more so as, in the eyes of the insular Russians, his ethnicity was suspect. For him music was, by his frank profession, 'a German art'. He practised it well enough to be accepted by the Germans as an honorary German. If this made problems for the reception of his music at home, and for its treatment in romantic historiography, it also gave him a currency and a status as a representative musician of his time that no other Russian composer could equal. However he may have felt about opera, as an operatic composer he was taken very seriously in the German-speaking countries, Hanslick and Bülow (to cite only the highest authorities) regarding him as one of the viable alternatives to Wagner. That even Liszt so regarded him may be verified by a glance at the work-list below, which shows how Liszt actively propagated Rubinstein's work for the stage right alongside Wagner's during his period as Kapellmeister in Weimar.

2. EARLY OPERAS. It is sometimes noted as an irony of Rubinstein's operatic career that he appeared to start out as a 'nationalist', only to turn renegade. Such a view fails to take note of the conditions in which he came to his artistic maturity. His first opera – written at the age of 20, immediately on his return from his studies with Siegfried Dehn, Glinka's teacher, in Berlin – was composed on commission from the Russian Imperial Theatres (then the only legal theatrical organization in Russia) to a libretto prepared by two members of the theatrical management. Its subject, like that of most Russian plays and commissioned operas in the reign of Nicholas I, was patriotic: the defeat of the Mongol Golden Horde by the sainted Dmitry Donskoy at Kulikovo (1380). (At other tightly controlled periods in Russian history such subjects were again *de rigueur*: compare Yury Shaporin's oratorio on the same subject, completed on the eve of World War II.) Rubinstein next wrote a trio of one-act operas at the request of his personal patron, the German-born Grand Duchess Yelena Pavlovna, the tsar's aunt, who wanted to see depictions of various nationalities subject (some quite recently) to the Russian throne. This, too, reflected a dynastic, rather than a 'national' purport.

Sibirskiye okhotniki ('The Siberian Hunters', first given in German as *Die sibirischen Jäger*), the one survivor from this period, owing to the ministrations of Liszt, is a fairly nondescript (and musically feeble) tale of young love on the steppe threatened and, with supernatural assistance, restored. It ends with a bright (if also nondescript) orchestral ritornello labelled 'Russisches Volkslied' in the German vocal score, betraying an old-fashioned notion of national colour as a decorative tint rather than, as in Glinka and his followers, the bearer of dramatic weight. Though the national colours in Rubinstein's operas were often to change, this basic conception did not. It was one of the many factors by then driving a wedge between him and his aesthetically more intransigent musical countrymen. Yet it was not so much a function of anti-nationalism as of Rubinstein's dyed-in-the-wool aesthetic conservatism, comparable in its way to his lifelong commitment to the use of natural brass.

The wedge was hardly diminished by *Die Kinder der Heide* (1861), Rubinstein's first mature opera (and the first of many to be composed for the German stage), even though the composer transferred the action from Hungary to Ukraine precisely for the sake of local colour. Not only was the effort easily construed as a ploy to please a foreign audience with exotica, and not only was the colour applied only on the fringes; but it was also of dubious authenticity. Instead of adapting the musical idiom of real 'children of the steppes', Rubinstein imitated what he knew best – the urban romances of the day (or rather, yesterday), on the model of such fashionable popular composers as the so-called 'three Alexanders' – Alyab'yev, Varlamov and Gurilyov. 'Gypsies!', snorted Balakirev in a letter to Vladimir Stasov about the opera (which, if true, would have been a redemption, since the opera's love intrigue unfolds against a background of gypsy life). The Russian-romance style was a permanent acquisition for Rubinstein, one that he would develop into a remarkable personal idiom in *The Demon*, and for that reason worth quoting at this point. Vanya's arioso in Act 3 (ex.1) instantly betrays its stylistic debt to the salon romance by its initial leap of a 6th from the fifth scale degree to the third, and then by its chromatic ascent to the high note in what sounds like the middle section. That Rubinstein's dramatic technique had undergone considerable development since *The Siberian Hunters* is shown by the way in which, having implied a three-part form, he breaks the aria off before its completion in response to a new dramatic turn.

Ex.1 *Die Kinder der Heide*, Act 3, Vanya's arioso

['Tell me, is this hut not mine? Yet he has crept in like a wolf, he has already sunk his teeth into the breast of my white lamb, to gnaw it away! I have done what I had to do! Yes, listen and let it be said, I have slain the wolf.']

3. Central period. Rubinstein's operatic *Blütezeit* now followed, with six works (each with its own entry in this dictionary) that established him, for all his present oblivion, as one of the major European stage composers of his day. In *Feramors* (1863), after Thomas Moore's *Lalla Rookh*, Rubinstein found in musical orientalism an idiom for which he possessed enormous flair and which he thereafter exploited on every opportunity. It became a stipulated ingredient of the 'sacred opera', the genre he invented as an anti-Wagnerian alternative – for which he even contemplated building a special 'Festspielhaus' of his own – of which *Der Thurm zu Babel* was the first genuine specimen (the earlier oratorio *Das verlorene Paradies* being subsequently adapted to it). It also partly conditioned his choice as subject of Lermontov's great romantic poem *Demon*, which has a Caucasian setting (as it did the later, minor *Der Papagei*, which has a Persian one). In all, nine operas, exactly half of Rubinstein's completed output, have conspicuous oriental trappings. In practice this meant a conventionalized Islamic idiom, whatever the nominal nationality or religion involved, for adopting which Rubinstein was attacked in Russia by strict-constructing realists. The critic Herman Laroche offered

a game defence (comparing *Der Thurm zu Babel* with Serov's *Yudif'*): 'In what does Serov's masterly characterization of the extinct Assyrians consist, or Rubinstein's of the ancient Semites? Obviously in one thing only: the composers have successfully reproduced *our* subjective idea of the Assyrians and the Semites' – as Romantic composers, increasingly a rare breed in Russia, always did.

Feramors is often compared with French lyric operas on oriental subjects, but it actually predates the most familiar examples (by Bizet, Delibes or Saint-Saëns) and was written simultaneously with Félicien David's *Lalla Roukh*, before either the Russian or the French composer could have known the other's work (the earlier première of David's opera caused Rubinstein to change the name of his, and also impeded its production in Russia). It achieved phenomenal popularity in Germany and Austria, as did *Der Thurm zu Babel*, although the latter made the rounds of oratorio festivals rather than theatres (the 'sacred opera' concept meeting everywhere, but especially in Russia, with censorship).

Rubinstein finally conquered his homeland's operatic stage with *The Demon*. 'Need we speak of this opera?', wrote the theatrical chronicler Alexander Vol'f in 1884. 'Who has not heard the work of the famous pianist, which has played about 100 times in the course of nine years?' In fact it set the 19th-century record for frequency of performance of any Russian opera (excepting only *A Life for the Tsar*, the Imperial Theatres' mandatory season opener); and, as collectors of old vocal recordings know very well, it maintained its hegemony well into the 20th century, rivalled in popularity only by the Tchaikovsky operas (*Yevgeny Onegin* and *The Queen of Spades*) that were its direct stylistic progeny. Its allure lay partly in that of the literary source, perhaps the most popular poem in Russia, and partly in the exotic setting. But the chief reason lay in Rubinstein's reading of Lermontov's poem as neither fantastic nor exotic: '*The Demon*', he wrote on the 100th performance, 'belongs to all epochs, to all nations'. Treating the subject in 'universal' terms (and banishing the seductive orientalism, as was his habit, to the decorative periphery), he cast the title role, as well as that of Tamara, his inamorata, in a musical style which projected the old Russian romance idiom, with its built-in audience appeal, on to a canvas of unprecedented scale.

The combination of heroic scale, affecting lyricism and stylistic accessibility filled an evident need in Russian opera after Glinka, which up to the 1870s was either heroic but crude (Serov), sweet but fastidious (Dargomïzhsky), or doggedly anti-conventional (the young 'Mighty Kuchka'). D. S. Mirsky's sardonic if memorable comment, in his *History of Russian Literature* (1927), that Rubinstein's *Demon* is 'the most operatic of Russian operas' – a remark actually intended to belittle the literary source – is well justified. There is scarcely a role in Russian opera to compare with that of the Demon, which became one of Shalyapin's great specialities. The character's great romances, to say nothing of the veritable medley of alternating romances that make up the astounding 25-minute love–hate duet in Act 3, lifted one of the most characteristic Russian genres (though one unfamiliar and 'un-Russian' to non-Russians) to its musical zenith. It is here, not in those few relatively paltry works in which the composer quoted folk tunes or patriotic anthems, that Rubinstein showed himself a quintessentially Russian master. César Cui could rant (with scarcely veiled anti-Semitism) that 'Mr Rubinstein is no specialist in Russian declamation', and that his work 'shows a practised hand, a good knowledge of prior operas, and stubborn ignorance of the movement toward dramatic music'; but *The Demon* was not only a major contribution in its own right to the essential Russian repertory, it was a down payment on *Yevgeny Onegin*.

If *The Demon* was Rubinstein's great Russian opera, *Die Maccabäer* (1875) was the opera that brought him the most widespread success, uniquely becoming a staple of the repertory both in Germany, where it was first performed, and in Russia. Cast very much on the model of the sacred opera, but exempt from the censorship since its subject was Apocryphal, it impressed critics in both countries with its high 'Gluckian' ideals. Having taken inspiration from a pre-Wagnerian reformer, it assumed for Hanslick and his followers the aspect of an anti-Wagnerian antidote. In the words of Laroche, Hanslick's Russian disciple, 'by way of simplicity and sober restraint Mr Rubinstein apparently strives to achieve the same musical drama that Richard Wagner and other contemporaries seek to attain by means of the most unbridled over-indulgence in harmonic and instrumental detail'. (Not even Laroche, though, could condone Rubinstein's abuse of the diminished 7th chord, something that plagued all of his operas, but particularly those on stern sacred themes.)

With *Néron* (composed 1877), a monstrous grand opera commissioned and then rejected by Paris, Rubinstein overreached himself and his operatic reputation began to dip. The German theatres remained hospitable to the work, and his fellow virtuoso Bülow kept up a show of loyalty despite his Wagnerian associations ('I trust I will not lose my credence as a partisan of Bayreuth if I say that I am enraptured and overjoyed' etc.), but an entry in the diary of Rubinstein's once-loyal pupil Tchaikovsky was more typical of professional opinion: 'You feel that you are writing badly, but seeing unceremonious trash like this, which nevertheless was performed in all seriousness, your soul feels better'. For an idea of Rubinstein at his unbelievable sloppiest, consider the 'obligatory' contrapuntal juxtaposition of two themes from the Act 2 ballet (ex.2).

Ex.2 *Néron*, Act 2 ballet, *Les Mimmes*

4. LATER OPERAS. Overwork and the stubborn arrogance to which many of Rubinstein's colleagues and co-workers testified took their inevitable toll on Rubinstein's later output. As Julius Rodenberg, the composer's most constant German librettist, put it: 'Rubinstein did not know how to cross out. Tireless in work, full of seriousness and zeal while engaged in it, he did not have it in him to go over it once finished. He wanted something new, always something new'. And in the recollection of Eduard Nápravník, the chief conductor at the Mariinsky Theatre in St Petersburg (who sought any excuse to sidestep a Rubinstein première), 'he would never hear of cuts, though they be urged on him by the singers themselves, or even his own devoted disciples'.

The ill-fated *Kupets Kalashnikov* ('The Merchant Kalashnikov'), performed only twice at the Mariinsky before falling under the censor's ban, was another scrappy score. It has maintained a higher historical profile than *Néron* because of its unfortunate stage history, and because in it the composer was supposed to have made his peace with the 'nationalist' style. Actually, its national aspects were entirely conditioned by the subject, a pseudo-historical drama about Ivan the Terrible of a type fashionable in the 1870s, comparable to Tchaikovsky's *Oprichnik* or Rimsky-Korsakov's *Maid of Pskov* (both, as it happens, subjects Rubinstein had considered and rejected on the way to *The Demon*). In musical terms, the national character of *The Merchant Kalashnikov* is exactly comparable to that of Serov's *Rogneda* – a matter of trivial folksongs for the court jester, mock-ecclesiastical chanting for the monk-like *oprichniki*, dance tunes for a troupe of buffoons. The single quoted tune in it – the hackneyed 'Slava', thrice-familiar from *Boris Godunov* – is employed inappropriately (though, to be fair, no more inappropriately than in Musorgsky's opera), alongside stylizations of such patently anachronistic genres as the 'cruel' romances gypsies crooned in Moscow cabarets. A surviving letter of inquiry from Rubinstein to Stasov about the 'Slava' indicates an interest in matters of ethnographic authenticity, but the use to which Rubinstein put the melody makes one wonder whether even Stasov knew that it functioned in its natural habitat as a song to accompany maidens' yuletide fortune-telling games, not a grandiose hymn in praise of the sovereign. Given Rubinstein's aesthetic, to say all this is no particular reproach – except to the Western historians, beginning with Rosa Newmarch, who, on the basis of its superficial folklorism, have tried to make *The Merchant Kalashnikov* out as Rubinstein's 'good' opera at the expense of *The Demon*, the composer's authentic Russian masterpiece.

After *The Merchant Kalashnikov*, which though aborted was well received, Rubinstein never scored another success as an opera composer. Of his remaining six operas, the three that cost him the most effort belonged to the misbegotten sacred genre; he never lived to see the elephantine *Moses* or *Christus* staged. *Goryusha* ('The Doleful One') was based on a pseudo-historical romantic novel by Dmitry Averkiyev, the librettist of Serov's *Rogneda*. The concept was dowdy by the late 1880s, and the opera aroused little interest, despite its pretty folk choruses (one of them very similar to the bridal chorus in 5/4 from *A Life for the Tsar*, and another anticipating the 'Hops' chorus in Rimsky-Korsakov's *Tsar's Bride*). Its most curious feature was a little neo-classical *divertissement* in Act 3, with music in 'appropriate' period style, enacted by a troupe of German players before a crowd of uncomprehending boyars. *Sulamith* and *Unter Räubern*, first presented in Hamburg as a double bill, achieved only sporadic performances thereafter (and in Russia, only concert and amateur ones).

To sum up sympathetically such a motley and uneven operatic output as Rubinstein's is not easy, but his admirer Laroche came close when he averred that, at its best, 'its dramatic candour, its energy, its broad brush strokes, its noble simplicity and its unity of mood' redeemed 'its frequent absence of interesting detail, its absence of musical development, and its gaudy pomposity'. This represents a scale of values at the very opposite extreme from that of the 'Mighty Kuchka', the group whose aesthetic has dominated the historiography of Russian music both at home and abroad. If it now seems an over-generous estimate, we might remember that, as Laroche also pointed out, Rubinstein's operas absolutely needed the stage to make their effect. Except for *The Demon*, all we have now are the scores.

See also DEMON, THE; FERAMORS; KUPETS KALASHNIKOV; MACCABÄER, DIE; NÉRON; and THURM ZU BABEL, DER.

Kulikovskaya bitva [The Battle of Kulikovo], 1849–50 (3, V. Sollogub [Acts 1, 3] and V. Zotov [Act 2], after V. Ozerov: *Dmitry Donskoy*), St Petersburg, Bol'shoy, 18/30 April 1852, 1 aria *RU-SPsc*, some vocal pts, *SPtob*, ov. (Berlin, 1865); also known as Dmitry Donskoy

Sibirskiye okhotniki [The Siberian Hunters], 1852 (romantic op, 1, A. Zherebtsov), Weimar, Hof, 9 Nov 1854, as Die sibirischen Jäger, vs (Leipzig, 1893)

Sten'ka Razin, 1852 (3, M. Voskresensky), inc.

Mest' [Revenge], 1852–3 (tragic op, 1, A. Zhemchuzhnikov, after M. Lermontov: *Hajji-Abrek*), unperf., music lost but for Zulima's song

Fomka-durachok [Tom the Fool] (comic op, 1, M. Mikhaylov), St Petersburg, Alexandrinsky, 30 April/12 May 1853, lost

Das verlorene Paradies op.54, 1855–6 (sacred op, 3, A. Schlönbach, after J. Milton: *Paradise Lost*), Weimar, Hof, 1 March 1858 (concert perf.), staged Düsseldorf, 1875 (Leipzig, 1860)

Die Kinder der Heide (4, S. H. Mosenthal, after C. Beck: *Janos, Herdsman of Hungary*), Vienna, Kärntnertor, 23 Feb 1861, vs (Leipzig, 1861); perf. in Russia from 1867 as Deti stepey [Children of the Steppes] (Moscow, 1887)

Feramors, 1861–2 (lyric op, 3, J. Rodenberg, after T. Moore: *Lalla Rookh*), Dresden, Hof, 24 Feb 1863 (Leipzig, 1864)

Der Thurm zu Babel op.80, 1868–9 (sacred op, 1, Rodenberg), Königsberg, 9 Feb 1870 (concert perf.), *D-KA*; (Leipzig, 1870)

Demon, 1871 (fantastic op, prol., 3, P. A. Viskovatov and A. Maykov, after Lermontov), St Petersburg, Mariinsky, 13/25 Jan 1875, *RU-SPtob**; (St Petersburg, 1876)

Die Maccabäer, 1872–4 (3, Mosenthal, after O. Ludwig), Berlin, Königliche, 17 April 1875 (Berlin, 1876)

Néron [Nero], 1875–7 (4, J. Barbier, rev. Rubinstein), Hamburg, Dammtor, 1 Nov 1879 (Moscow, 1884)

Kupets Kalashnikov [The Merchant Kalashnikov], 1877–9 (3, N. I. Kulikov, after Lermontov), St Petersburg, Mariinsky, 22 Feb/5 March 1880 (Leipzig, n.d.)

Sulamith, 1882–3 (biblical representation, 5 scenes, Rodenberg, after the *Song of Songs*), Hamburg, Dammtor, 8 Nov 1883 (Berlin, 1884)

Unter Räubern (comic op, 1, E. Wichert, after T. Gautier: *Voyage en Espagne*), Hamburg, Dammtor, 8 Nov 1883, *PL-KA**, vs (Berlin, 1884)

Der Papagei (comic op, 1, H. Wittmann, after a Persian fairytale), Hamburg, Dammtor, 11 Nov 1884, vs (Leipzig, 1884)

Moses op.112, 1887–9 (sacred op, 8 scenes, Mosenthal), Prague, Neue Deutsches, 27–8 June 1892 (staged dress rehearsal, perf. cancelled because of bankruptcy), Riga, 20 Feb 1894 (concert perf.), vs (Leipzig, 1887–92)

Goryusha [The Doleful One], 1888 (4, D. Averkiyev, after his *Khmelevaya noch'* [Midsummer's Night]), St Petersburg, Mariinsky, 21 Nov/3 Dec 1889, vs (Moscow, 1889)

Christus op.117, 1893 (sacred op, prol., 7 episodes, epilogue, H.-A.

Bulthaupt), Stuttgart, 2 June 1894 (selections, concert perf.), staged Bremen, 25 May 1895, vs (Leipzig, 1894)

*

GENERAL

A. Vol'f: *Khronika Peterburgskikh teatrov*, ii (St Petersburg, 1884)
A. Rubinstein: *Muzïka i yego predstaviteli* (Moscow, 1891; Eng. trans., 1892, as *A Conversation on Music: Music and its Masters*)
R. Newmarch: *The Russian Opera* (London, 1914), chap. 7
L. Barenboym: *Anton Grigor'yevich Rubinshteyn: zhizn', artisticheskiy put', tvorchestvo, muzïkal'no-obshchestvennaya deyatel'nost'* [Life, Artistic Development, Creative Work, Musical and Social Activities] (Leningrad, 1957–62)
A. Rubinstein: *Literaturnoye naslediye* [Literary Legacy] (Moscow, 1983–6)

OPERAS

Feramors

E. Hanslick: *Die moderne Oper* (Berlin, 1877), 177–83
J. Rodenberg: 'Meine persönliche Erinnerungen an Anton Rubinstein', *Deutsche Rundschau*, lxxxii (1895), 246–70
C. Cui: '"Feramors" A. Rubinshteyna', *Izbrannïye stat'i* [Selected Essays], ed. Yu. V. Kremlyov (Leningrad, 1952), 488–92

The Demon

C. Cui: 'Muzïkal'nïye zametki: "Demon", fantast. opera A. G. Rubinshteyna' [Musical Notes: *The Demon*, Rubinstein's Fantastic Opera], *Sankt-peterburgskiye vedomosti* (21 Jan 1875)
P. Viskovatov: 'Moyo znakomstvo s A. G. Rubinshteynom' [My Acquaintance with Rubinstein], *Russkiy vestnik* (1896), no.4, pp.229–42
S. Sheyn: *'Demon' A. G. Rubinshteyna* (Moscow, 1953)
L. Mazel: 'Rol' sekstovosti v liricheskoy melodike (o nablyudenii B. Asaf'yeva)' [The Role of 'Sixthiness' in Lyrical Melodies: Concerning an Observation by B. Asaf'yev], *Voprosï muzïkoznaniya*, ii, ed. A. Ogolevets (Moscow, 1956), 205–25
A. Gozenpud: *Russkiy opernïy teatr XIX veka* [Russian Operatic Theatre in the 19th Century], iii (Leningrad, 1973), 125–33
A. Rubinstein: 'Po povodu sotogo predstavleniya operï "Demon"' [On the 100th Performance of the Opera *The Demon*], *Literaturnoye naslediye*, i (Moscow, 1983), 60–62

Die Maccabäer

C. Cui: 'Teatr i muzïka: kontsert g-zhi Nissen-Salomon. "Makkavei" g. Rubinshteyna' [Theatre and Music: the Nissen-Salomon Concert. Rubinstein's *Maccabäer*], *Sanktpeterburgskiye vedomosti* (29 March 1876)
——: 'Muzïkal'nïye zametki: "Makkavei," opera g. Rubinshteyna' [Musical Notes: Rubinstein's *Maccabäer*], *Sanktpeterburgskiye vedomosti* (25 Jan 1877)
E. Hanslick: *Musikalische Stationen* (Berlin, 1880), 325ff
H. Laroche: '"Die Maccabäer", opera g. Rubinshteyna', *Muzïkal'no-kriticheskiye stat'i* (St Petersburg, 1894), 57–73

Néron

G. Upton: *The Standard Operas* (Chicago, 1899), 226–30

Kupets Kalashnikov

G. Abraham: 'Anton Rubinstein: Russian Composer', *MT*, lxxxvi (1945), 361–5; repr. in *Slavonic and Romantic Music* (London, 1968), 99–106
O. Tompakova: '"Kupets Kalashnikov" A. G. Rubinshteyna', *Muzïkal'naya zhizn'* (1983), no.17, pp.16–17

Der Thurm zu Babel

H. Laroche: '"Der Thurm zu Babel" Rubinshteyna', *Muzïkal'no-kriticheskiye stat'i* (St Petersburg, 1894), 115–21

sacred operas

A. Rubinstein: 'Die geistliche Oper', in J. Lewinsky: *Vor den Coulissen*, ii (Berlin, 1882), 47–50
——: 'Die geistliche Oper', *Die Zukunft* (1894), no.10

RICHARD TARUSKIN

Rubio (y Laynez), Ángel (*b* Madrid, 12 or 27 Nov 1846; *d* Vicálvaro, Madrid, 1906). Spanish composer. He studied at the Madrid Conservatory and was for a quarter of a century one of the most prolific and successful composers of zarzuelas of the one-act *género chico*. He composed over 100 such works, of which *Dos canarios de café* (1882) and *¡Al agua, patos!* (1888) enjoyed particular success. His music is agreeably light and was eminently suited to its purpose of transient entertainment.

zarzuelas; selective list; first performed in Madrid unless otherwise stated

El teatro en 1876 (revista, R. M. Liern), collab. R. Aceves [according to Stieger, perf. 20 July 1871]; Por la tremenda (1), 1876; El fenómeno, 1877; El carbonero de Subiza (1, S. M. Granés and M. Ramos Carrión), 1878, collab. Aceves; El destierro del amor (1), Buen Retiro, 24 July 1878, collab. Aceves; La misa del gallo, 1878; El rigor de las desdichas, 1878; La salsa de aniceta (1, Liern), Apolo, March 1879; Periquito (3, Ramos Carrión), Príncipe Alfonso, Sept 1879; El pañuelo de hierbas (1, M. Pina), Zarzuela, 1879

¡Ya somos tres! (1, Pina), 1880; Mates trece (2), Zarzuela, Feb 1880, collab. C. Espino; La mejor venganza (1), Feb 1880, collab. Espino; Cibeles y Neptuno (2), Buen Retiro, Aug 1880, collab. M. Nieto; La estrella de un chino, Príncipe Alfonso, Aug 1880, collab. ?Pethengui; De verano (2, Pina), Eslava, Dec 1881, collab. M. F. Caballero; Armas al hombro (Pina), 1881; Tres pies para un banco, Variedades, 1881; Un bandido (S. Lastra), Jan 1882; Las mil y una noches (3, J. Santero), Circo de Rivas, 21 June 1882, collab. Caballero

Adios mundo amaryo, Buen Retiro, June 1882, collab. Espino; Canta hondo (1), Valencia, Nov 1882; Dos canarios de café (1, Liern), ?1882, collab. ?Espino; El grito de guerra (C. C. Navarro), Alicante, Jan 1883; La mulata y la niña, Aug 1883, collab. Espino; Dos excéntricos, Eslava, Oct 1883; Política y tauromaquia (1, F. J. de Burgos), Eslava, Nov 1883, collab. Espino; ¡Cómo está la sociedad! (1, Burgos), Dec 1883, collab. Espino; Contratos al vuelo (Mínguez), Eslava, Jan 1884, collab. Espino

La farsanta (3, Pina), Apolo, 16 April 1884, collab. Caballero; Una doncella de encargo (Flores García), Recoletes, June 1884; Los apostoles (Navarro), July 1884, collab. Espino; Viva mi tierra (2), Príncipe Alfonso, Aug 1884, collab. Espino; Baño de ola, 1884; Toros en París, 1884; La villa del oso (revista, E. Navarro Gonzalvo and F. Pérez), Felipe, June 1885, collab. Espino and Nieto; Animales y plantas, Martín, 1885, collab. Espino; El barbian de la Persia (1, Navarro Gonzalvo and Pérez), Variedades, Dec 1885

Castiellos en el aire (Pina), Eslava, Dec 1885; El año de la Nanita (L. M. de Larra), Zarzuela, Jan 1886; El testamento y la clave (2, A. Ruesga, Lastra and J. E. Prieto), Variedades, March 1886, collab. Espino; En el nombre del padre (2, Granés), Recoletes, July 1886; El país de las castañas (revista, Ruesga, Lastra and Prieto), Variedades, Nov 1886, collab. Espino; El club de las féas (M. de Palacios and G. Perrín), Variedades, Dec 1886, collab. Espino

Madrid en el año dos mil (revista, Perrín and Palacios), Variedades, 13 Jan 1887; Cuenta del año (revista, Navarro Gonzalvo), Feb 1887, collab. Espino; ¡Al agua, patos! (pasillo, 1, J. Jackson Veyán), Felipe, Nov 1888; Apuntes del natural, 1888; ¡A la Exposición!, 1890; Guasín (1, Granés), Felipe, 1891; Folies Bergère, 1892; Madrid puerto de mar, 1892; Gota serena, Barcelona, 1893; Nadar en seco (2, Navarro), Recoletes, July 1894; Números primos, 1894; Academia de hipnotismo (1, G. Merino), Romea, Jan 1895

Mujer y raina [Mariquita stoiqueardo] (1, Pérez), Romea, Feb 1895; De P. P. y W. (1, Pérez), Romea, 1895; Ensalada rusa, 1895; Las playas de Madrid, 1895; La boca del lobo (Merino), Sept 1896; Caracalla (Pérez), Sept 1896, collab. Espino; Los tenderos (A. Casanal), Eslava, Sept 1897, collab. R. Estellés; La florera sevillana (Jackson Veyán), Maravillas, 13 June 1898, collab. Estellés; El paraiso perdido (Jackson Veyán and Merino), Eldorado, 17 June 1898, collab. Estellés

El baño de Diana (Granés and Rufino), Eldorado, July 1898, collab. Estellés; La nieta de su abuelo (1, A. Caamaño), Romea, 27 Oct 1898; Niña Rosa (1, Jackson Veyán), Romea, 16 Dec 1898, collab. Estellés; A mi los reventadores (revista, Fanosa and Chivote), Romea, 28 Dec 1898; El traje de boda (1, Perrín and Palacios), 7 April 1899, collab. V. Lleó; La feria de Sevilla (1, Merino), Romea, 1 May 1899; Las buenas formas (opereta-revista, 1, Jackson Veyán), Apolo, 12 or 13 July 1899, collab. Valverde *hijo*

Cambios naturales (1, V. de la Vega), Maravillas, 19 Aug 1899, collab. Lleó; La pajarita (1, Flores García), Romea, May 1900; Don Gonzálo de Ulloa (1, Perrín and Palacios), Eslava, 26 Oct 1900; El juicio oral (revista, 1, Perrín and Palacios), Cómico, 26 Jan 1901; El chico de la portera (Caamaño), Cómico, Nov 1901, collab. Masilovet; El polo norte (juguete lírico, Varela and Pepe Saban), 24 Dec 1901, collab. ?Powel

Miscellaneous other zarzuelas: A sangre y fuego (1); Aqui, León (1);

Blanca ó negra (1), collab. Catalá; Eh, á la plaza (1); Ellos y nosotros (1); En la calle de Toledo, collab. Espino; El fantasma de la esquina (1); Flamencomanía (1); Frasquito Barbales (1), collab. Espino; Historías y cuentos (2); Lo pasado, pasado (1); Los de Cuba (juguete lírico, 1, Liern and Falgon), collab. Marín; Los Madriles; Meterse en honduras (1), collab. Espino; Una onza (1); Oro, plata, cobre y ... nada (1); Quién fuera libre (1); Los rancheros (1), collab. Estellés; La restauración (1), collab. Catalá; El teatro nuevo (1); Tio, yo no he sido (1); Tiple en puerta (1); Tuna de Alcalá (1), collab. Masilovet; El turno de los partidos (1); Viva mi niña (1)

StiegerO
Enciclopedia universal ilustrada europeo-americana (Barcelona, 1907–30), lii, 637 ANDREW LAMB

Ruddigore [*Ruddigore* (orig. *Ruddygore*); *or, The Witch's Curse*]. Operetta in two acts by ARTHUR SULLIVAN to a libretto by W. S. GILBERT; London, Savoy Theatre, 22 January 1887.

Dame Hannah (contralto) relates how a curse compels each baronet of Ruddigore to commit a daily crime. Sir Despard Murgatroyd (baritone), having fulfilled these obligations, reforms and marries Mad Margaret (mezzo-soprano) after Robin Oakapple (baritone) is exposed as the rightful heir to the title. Robin is renounced by Rose Maybud (soprano), but a twist of Gilbertian logic nullifies the curse and all ends happily.

The libretto is a burlesque of the once popular blood-and-thunder melodramas, replete with stock characters including the jolly jack tar, Richard Dauntless (tenor), with his bogus nautical jargon. Burlesque is less evident in the music, although 'I shipped, d'ye see' pokes fun at Dibdin as the entrance of Margaret does at the mad scene in *Lucia di Lammermoor*. Indeed, instead of being humorous, as Gilbert anticipated, the music of the ghost scene is dramatic, notably the brilliantly scored 'Ghosts' High Noon', sung by Sir Roderic Murgatroyd (baritone). The score is rich in fine ensembles, the pseudo-madrigal 'When the buds are blossoming' representing, perhaps, Sullivan's finest essay in that manner.

The première was not an unequivocal success, but after alterations to the second act *Ruddigore* sustained a respectable run, although it was not revived in London until 1921. Changes made then by Geoffrey Toye (including replacement of the original overture arranged by Hamilton Clarke) and later by others continue to compromise the text of one of Sullivan's most interesting scores. DAVID RUSSELL HULME

Rudel, Julius (*b* Vienna, 6 March 1921). American conductor of Austrian birth. He studied at the Vienna Academy and emigrated to the USA at the age of 17, where he continued studies at the Mannes School, New York. In 1943 he joined the music staff of the New York City Opera, making his début the next year in *Der Zigeunerbaron*. He became musical director in 1957 and remained in that post until 1979, developing the company into one of the best and most enterprising in the USA, with a strong commitment to the principles of ensemble opera and an often adventurous repertory. He obtained Ford Foundation grants for new American operas including works by Ellstein (*The Golem*) and Floyd (*Jonathan Wade*), but his success was due more to his own versatility in a repertory ranging from Monteverdi and Mozart to Janáček and Britten; he has also shown a special interest in Ginastera, conducting the premières of *Bomarzo*, *Don Rodrigo* and *Beatrix Cenci* at theatres in New York and Washington, DC. His Metropolitan Opera début was in 1978 with *Werther*. He has also appeared frequently in Europe, making his début at the Paris Opéra with *Il trovatore* and at the Vienna Staatsoper with *Die Fledermaus*, which he also conducted for his Covent Garden début in 1984. His recordings include Handel's *Giulio Cesare* (1967), *Manon* and Donizetti's *Roberto Devereux* (both 1970), *Anna Bolena* (1972), *I puritani* and *Les contes d'Hoffmann* (1973), all with Beverly Sills; in addition he has recorded Boito's *Mefistofele* (1974) and Weill's *Silbersee* (in English as *Silverlake*, 1980). A versatile conductor, Rudel is highly regarded for his professionalism; he has received numerous awards.

BERNARD JACOBSON, NOËL GOODWIN

Rudenko, Bela (Andreyevna) (*b* Bokovo-Antratsit [now Antratsit], Voroshilovgrad region, 18 Aug 1933). Ukrainian soprano. She studied with O. Blagovidova, and made her operatic début in Odessa during the 1955–6 season; from 1956 she was a soloist at the Kiev Opera. One of the leading opera singers of the Ukraine, she possesses a beautiful light soprano, with a virtuoso command of coloratura technique; on stage her performances are marked by their winning simplicity and sincerity. She is a notable Lyudmila, Rosina, Gilda, Lakmé and Natasha (*War and Peace*), and has also given fine performances in operas by Ukrainian composers: Yolan in Mayboroda's *Milana*, Yarana in his *Arsenal*.

V. Timofeyev: *Bela Andreyevna Rudenko* (Kiev, 1964)
I. M. YAMPOL'SKY

Ruders, Poul (*b* Ringsted, 27 March 1949). Danish composer. He studied under Nørholm at the conservatory in Copenhagen and has worked principally as an organist. His music draws on a variety of historical idioms; in his only opera, *Tycho Brahe*, based on the life of the Danish astronomer of the 16th century (who much influenced Johannes Kepler), he used what has been described as 'a mixture of Renaissance and atonal idioms, spiced with elements of Weill and mainstream styles' (P. E. Pind, *Opera*, xxxviii, 1987, p.1052). The work, based on a study of Brahe by Henrik Bjelke, and presented in flashback form, was first given at the Helsinore Theatre, Århus, on 16 May 1987.

Rudersdorff, Hermine (*b* Ivanovsky, Ukraine, 30 Nov/12 Dec 1822; *d* Boston, 26 Feb 1882). German soprano. She studied in Paris and Milan, making her début in 1841 at Karlsruhe. Engaged successively at Frankfurt, Breslau, Dresden and Berlin (Friedrich-Wilhelmstädtisches Theater), in 1854 she made her London début at Drury Lane. The following year she sang Donna Anna at Covent Garden, where she returned from 1860 to 1865. During the same period she also sang at the St James's Theatre (in English). Her repertory included coloratura roles such as Konstanze, Marguerite de Valois (*Les Huguenots*), Elvire (*La muette de Portici*) and Berthe (*Le prophète*), as well as more dramatic parts such as Agathe (*Der Freischütz*) and Leonore (*Fidelio*). ELIZABETH FORBES

Rudolf, Max (*b* Frankfurt, 15 June 1902). American conductor of German birth. He studied in Frankfurt and made his conducting début at the Freiburg Städtische Theater in 1923, followed by appointments at Darmstadt (Hessisches Staatstheater, 1923–9) and at the German Theatre, Prague (1929–35). After orchestral work in Sweden he left Europe in 1940 for a teaching post in Chicago. He conducted the New Opera Company in New York in 1944 and joined the Metropolitan Opera the next year, making his début in *Der Rosenkavalier* in 1946, the year he took American citizenship. He remained at the Metropolitan for 13 seasons, distinguishing himself in the Mozart repertory, and was assistant manager there from 1950 to 1958. Between 1958 and 1970 he was with the Cincinnati SO, and then became head of the opera and conducting departments at the Curtis Institute, Philadelphia, 1970–73; he returned to the Metropolitan, 1973–5, conducting mainly Mozart and Strauss. His recordings include *Hänsel und Gretel* (in English) and *Don Giovanni*. He wrote a widely used textbook, *The Grammar of Conducting* (New York, 1950, 2/1980), which testifies to a rare grasp of the mechanics of the art.

BERNARD JACOBSON, NOËL GOODWIN

Rudziński, Witold (*b* Siebież, 14 March 1913). Polish composer. A pupil of Szeligowski and others, he has been active as a musicologist and teacher. During the decade after World War II he was a strong advocate of socio-realism in music. His operas frequently reflect its influence, although most postdate that period of political involvement in Polish culture. Both *Janko muzykant* ('Janko the Musician', 1953) and *Chłopi* ('The Peasants', 1974) draw their librettos from well-known late-Romantic Polish fiction. The former is based on a familiar literary theme of the time, the persecution and suffering of the individual (Janko, a fiddler, is a mute role), while *The Peasants* is concerned with humanity's unending struggle for life on the land. *The Peasants* is perhaps Rudziński's most successful dramatic work. Its four parts (representing the four seasons, starting with autumn) provide a framework for an intricate interweaving of plots and subplots whose musical fabric embraces fragments of folk culture, secular and sacred, within a broadly lyrical language.

Rudziński's socio-political views surface most readily in *Komendant Paryża* ('The Commandant of Paris', 1960). It is set in the Paris Commune of 1871 and follows the last weeks in the life of the famous Polish General Jarosław Dąbrowski. Local colour is provided by fleeting references to the cancan from Offenbach's *Orphée aux enfers* and frequent recourse to the opening motif of the *Marseillaise*. But *The Commandant of Paris* is clearly designed as a metaphor for People's Poland: the text abounds with references to freedom, the red flag and the overriding concern of the commune. Rudziński employs some Polish folk rhythms, notably those of the fast triple-time *oberek*, but the main galvanizing force is the common-time march characteristic of Stalinist mass songs of the late 1940s and early 50s. Occasionally there are flashes of harmonic wit à la Poulenc, Prokofiev or Shostakovich, while the passacaglia at the end of Act 3 scene i and the dissonant harmonic layering at the end of the opera show a tougher side of Rudziński's musical language.

In the late 1950s and 60s Rudziński went some way towards accommodating the avant-garde trends of his younger compatriots. *Odprawa posłów greckich* ('Dismissal of the Greek Envoys', 1966; special mention in the Prince Rainier III Competition, Monaco, 1963), while maintaining that society is more important than the individual ego, moves on from Rudziński's previous approach into the world of a largely static plot, with the multiple stylistic impulses that were shortly to become a feature of Penderecki's vocal works. Chant is mixed with angular atonal lines and dissonant harmony, the instrumental forces include a harpsichord for the narrator's recitative, and the opera accumulates more avant-garde textures, including ad libitum counterpoint, as it proceeds. The same features appear in *Sulamita* ('The Shulamite', composed 1964), but both operas rarely rise to the occasion, being worthy tableaux whose time and ethos belong to a transient age.

Janko muzykant [Janko the Musician], 1948–51 (3, T. Borowski and S. Wygodzki, after H. Sienkiewicz), Bytom, Silesian Opera, 26 June 1953

Komendant Paryża [The Commandant of Paris], 1955–8 (3, T. Marek), Poznań, State Opera, 27 March 1960

Odprawa posłów greckich [Dismissal of the Greek Envoys], 1962 (1, B. Ostromęcki, after J. Kochanowski), Kraków, Municipal Music, 6 Nov 1966, vs (Kraków, 1966)

Sulamita [The Shulamite], 1964 (1, Ostromęcki), vs (Kraków, 1972)

Żółta szlafmyca [The Yellow Nightcap] (comic op, 3, E. Bonacka, after F. Zabłocki), Gdynia, Music Theatre, 25 Jan 1970, vs (pubd Warsaw)

Chłopi [The Peasants], 1970–72 (4 pts, K. Berwińska and W. Wróblewska, after W. S. Reymont), Warsaw, Wielki, 30 June 1974

Pierścień i róża [The Rose and the Ring], 1980–82 (children's op, 2, S. Karaszewski, after W. M. Thackeray), perf. Wrocław

*

Z. Hierowski: 'Nowa opera polska', *Życie literackie* (1953), no.28 [on *Janko muzykant*]

T. Marek: '"Janko muzykant" – nowa opera polska', *Przegląd kulturalny* (1953), no.27, p.6

L. Erhardt: '"Odprawa posłow greckich" w Polskim Radiu', *Ruch muzyczny* (1964), no.23, pp.12–13

Z. Mycielski: 'Nad "Odprawą" Witolda Rudzińskiego', *Ruch muzyczny* (1967), no.2, pp.3–4

T. Marek: '*The Peasants*: a New Polish Opera by Witold Rudziński', *Polish Music* (1974), no.3, pp.27–31

ADRIAN THOMAS

Rudziński, Zbigniew (*b* Czechowice, 23 Oct 1935). Polish composer. He studied composition first with Piotr Perkowski at the Warsaw Conservatory (1956–62) and later in Paris. His main contribution to opera is the one-act *Manekiny* ('Mannequins'; Rudziński, after B. Schulz), first performed at the State Opera in Wrocław on 29 October 1981. *Manekiny*'s central character, the tailor Jacob (baritone), attempts, through the creation of a wild array of mannequins – Queen Draga (mezzo-soprano), Magda Wang (soprano) and her whip, the cripple Edzio (tenor) and the anarchist Luccheni (tenor) – to surmount the anguish of the creative artist and his alienation from society. But Bruno Schulz's stories provide only humiliating defeat for Jacob at the hands of the mannequins and his maid Adela (soprano), although Rudziński invents a revelatory coda to provide a more positive, if questionable, conclusion. The strength of the opera lies in its surreal fantasy, in which Rudziński's music plays a more reticent role than the story itself. He has also composed a chamber opera, *Antygona* ('Antigone', 1979–82).

*

I. Grzenkowicz: 'Mannequins', *Polish Music* (1983), nos.1–2, pp.3–11

ADRIAN THOMAS

Ruettino [Rovetta, Rovettino], **Giovanni Battista.** *See* VOLPE, GIOVANNI BATTISTA.

Ruffini, Giovanni (*b* Genoa, 20 Sept 1807; *d* Genoa, 3 Nov 1881). Italian librettist. He embarked early on a literary career but, with his two brothers, became a close associate of Mazzini and followed him into exile after the events of 1833–4. By 1841 his friendship with Mazzini had cooled, and he found himself in Paris. Here he took up again with Michele Accursi, an old colleague and (had he known it) a double agent, who was acting as Donizetti's agent in Paris. Accursi badgered him into rewriting Anelli's libretto *Ser Marcantonio* (originally set by Stefano Pavesi in 1810) for Donizetti as *Don Pasquale* (1843, Paris). The composer altered his text to such an extent that Ruffini refused to publish it under his own name, and it was printed as by 'M. A.'; this led to a history of misattribution to Accursi, in spite of a fully documented study by Lazzari (1915). As it was at this time that Donizetti refers to having 'called in' a poet to touch up Cammarano's *Il conte di Chalais* for his *Maria di Rohan*, it is reasonable to suggest that this task may have fallen to Ruffini too, as did the preparation of the Italian translation of *Dom Sébastien*. In 1845 Donizetti discussed with him a libretto *Onore vince amore* (on a play by Iffland, rewritten by Cosenza), but this came to nothing. No other operatic activity is recorded for him. Exiled after 1848, he continued his literary career in London and Edinburgh, publishing some of his most important work in English; he returned to Italy after unification.

*

A. Lazzari: 'Giovanni Ruffini, Gaetano Donizetti e il *Don Pasquale*', *Rassegna nazionale* (1 and 16 Oct 1915)
C. B. Micca: 'Giovanni Ruffini e il libretto di Don Pasquale', *Rivista di Bergamo*, x (1931), 537–41
F. Walker: 'The Librettist of "Don Pasquale"', *MMR*, lxxxviii (1958), 219–23
P. Berri: 'Il librettista del "Don Pasquale": leggende, ingiustizie, plagi', *La Scala*, no.110 (1959), 19–24

JOHN BLACK

Ruffo, Titta [Titta, Ruffo Cafiero] (*b* Pisa, 9 June 1877; *d* Florence, 6 July 1953). Italian baritone. He studied briefly with Persichini, Sparapani and Casini. In 1898 he made his début at the Teatro Costanzi, Rome, as the Herald in *Lohengrin*, and then sang at Santiago, Chile (1900), and Buenos Aires (1902). He appeared at Covent Garden in 1903 (Enrico Ashton and Rossini's Figaro), but did not return, reputedly because of a disagreement with Melba. He made his La Scala début during the 1903–4 season as Rigoletto, and was then in demand at all the major European houses. In 1908 he sang at the Colón, where he remained a great favourite until he retired (1931). He was also very popular in the USA, where he first sang in 1912 at Philadelphia (Rigoletto); he then appeared frequently with the Chicago-Philadelphia Grand Opera Company in both cities (until 1926). His Metropolitan début (1922) was as Rossini's Figaro, and he remained with the company for eight seasons, singing Don Carlo (*Ernani*), Amonasro, Gérard (*Andrea Chénier*) and Tonio.

Ruffo's voice was outstanding for its resonance, power, range and the almost tenor-like ring of its top register, for purity and warmth, and for breath control. It also had a characteristically dark, sometimes sombre colour, particularly noticeable in Thomas' *Hamlet* and in Verdi. He was a vigorous and exuberant actor and his singing was correspondingly dramatic and forceful, if occasionally coarse and loud. His enormous success, in operas such as *L'Africaine*, *La Gioconda*, *Pagliacci* and *Il barbiere di Siviglia*, finally brought about a complete change in Italian vocal taste for baritone singing, towards an unpolished, aggressive style, and away from the refined, classical 19th-century tradition.

*

GV (R. Celletti; C. Williams)
T. Ruffo: *La mia parabola* (Milan, 1937) [with discography by W. R. Moran]
F. W. Gaisberg: *The Music Goes Round* (New York, 1943; repr. 1946 as *Music on Record*)
A. Wolf: 'Titta Ruffo', *Record Collector*, ii/5 (1947), 11–16 [with discography]
M. de Schauensee: 'Lion of Pisa', *ON*, xxxi/24 (1966–7), 26–7
A. Farkas, ed.: *Titta Ruffo: an Anthology* (Westport, CT, 1984) [with discography by W. R. Moran]

RODOLFO CELLETTI

Ruggieri [Ruggeri], **Giovanni Maria** (*fl* Venice, *c*1689–1720). Italian composer. He wrote 12 operas for four theatres in Venice, in two different periods: three from 1696 to 1699, and nine from 1707 to 1712. *Elisa* is noted as the first comic opera produced in Venice. Set in Florence, it deals with the love entanglements of private citizens of the merchant class; their servants are comic caricatures. Although none of Ruggieri's operas survive in full score, several fragments are found in aria collections. His style resembles that of his more prominent contemporaries active in Venice, such as C. F. Pollarolo and Francesco Gasparini. For Ruggieri, composition was an avocation rather than a career: the preface to his first opera, *Clotilde*, refers to him as being 'distinguished among dilettantes, the equal of the most celebrated professors of the art'. His setting of *Armida abbandonata* was presented in at least five productions between 1707 and 1715, and may have been used at least in part in others. Ruggieri himself supervised a 1715 production in Pesaro.

drammi per musica in three acts, first performed in Venice, unless otherwise stated

Clotilde (G. Neri), S Cassiano, carn. 1696; as Amar per vendetta, S Moisè, 28 Nov 1702
Mariamme (L. Burlini), SS Giovanni e Paolo, aut. 1696, arias *B-Bc*
La saggia pazzia di Giunio Bruto (L. Lotti), SS Giovanni e Paolo, 26 Nov 1698
Milziade (Lotti), SS Giovanni e Paolo, carn. 1699, arias *I-CCc*
Armida abbandonata (F. Silvani, after T. Tasso: *Gerusalemme liberata*), S Angelo, 10 Nov 1707, arias *D-MÜs* and *GB-Lbl*
Arrenione (Silvani), S Angelo, week before 10 Nov 1708, arias *Ob*, collab. others
Arato in Sparta ((?) B. Marcello), S Angelo, week before 11 Jan 1710
L'ingannator ingannato (A. Marchi), S Samuele, aut. 1710
Non son quella è la difesa (G. A. Falier), S Angelo, 1 Dec 1710
Le gare di politica e d'amore (A. Salvi), S Samuele, week before 31 Jan 1711
Elisa (commedia, D. Lalli), S Angelo, aut. 1711
Arsinoe vendicata (G. Braccioli), S Angelo, carn. 1712

HARRIS S. SAUNDERS

Ruggiero ('Rogerus'). Libretto by PIETRO METASTASIO, first set by Johann Adolf Hasse (1771, Milan) as *Il Ruggiero, ovvero L'eroica gratitudine*.

ACT 1 Rogerus, a descendant of Hector, has been captured and imprisoned by the Greeks after a heroic battle. Leone, son of Constantine and now Emperor of Byzantium, has secretly saved and freed Rogerus, whom he knows only as Erminio, and both arrive at the court of Carlo Magno [Charlemagne] in Paris. Unaware of Rogerus's return, Bradamante, his beloved, is distraught since Charlemagne has betrothed her to Leone against her wishes; Clotilde, her confidante, is also distressed, as she is in love with Leone. Leone admits to Rogerus/Erminio that he intends to marry Bradamante. Rogerus expresses support but silently laments his impending loss.

ACT 2 Upon hearing the pleas of Bradamante, Charlemagne declares that any man who can defeat her in combat may have her hand in marriage. Leone suggests to Rogerus that he disguise himself, and fight in

Leone's stead. Rogerus, reluctantly agreeing, overcomes Bradamante in combat.

ACT 3 Rogerus tells Bradamante that, to prove his devotion, he will kill himself in front of her. She prevents him, but questions his faithfulness because he had apparently given her up to Leone. Clotilde reveals to Leone Rogerus's true identity and his love for Bradamante, and tells him that Rogerus plans suicide. Leone vows to change the situation, and a resolution is reached in the presence of Charlemagne. Bradamante and Rogerus are united, as are Clotilde and Leone.

* * *

The main characters and events of this drama are drawn from LUDOVICO ARIOSTO's *Orlando furioso* (Cantos 44–6), published in 1516. In his *Bradamante* (1582), Robert Garnier followed Ariosto closely in creating what has been claimed as the first example of a French 'tragicomedy'. Two more *Bradamante* dramas followed, one by Gauthier de La Calprenède (1637) and the other by Thomas Corneille (1695), to which may be added Pierre-Charles Roy's libretto of 1707. All four have points in common with Metastasio's drama, which also reflects their Italian source and Pietro Bissari's libretto, *Bradamante* (1650), set by Cavalli. Corneille's drama was not a success; it has been suggested that combat between knights and a warrior-maiden would not have appealed to the taste of the time. This might equally apply to Metastasio's drama which, with only two settings nearly 50 years apart, was hardly a triumph. Further, the *Ruggiero* plot has several basic similarities with that of *L'olimpiade* and its female counterpart, *Nitteti*, both well known in 1771. This plot repetition, coupled with a musical setting with extensive recitative by such a veteran composer as Hasse (his last opera), may have contributed to the outmoded quality sensed by Leopold and Wolfgang Mozart. A second setting of *Ruggiero* was composed by Antonio Gandini in the 1820s, and a one-act opera by Samuel Holmes (1838) also appears to have been based on this text.

DON NEVILLE

Ruggiero [*Il Ruggiero, ovvero L'eroica gratitudine*] ('Rogerus, or Heroic Gratitude') *Opera seria* in three acts by JOHANN ADOLF HASSE to a libretto by PIETRO METASTASIO (*see* RUGGIERO above) after the last three cantos (44–6) of LUDOVICO ARIOSTO's *Orlando furioso*; Milan, Regio Ducal Teatro, 16 October 1771.

This opera, along with the youthful Mozart's *Ascanio in Alba*, was performed to celebrate the wedding of the Habsburg Archduke Ferdinand and Maria Beatrice d'Este. Its concluding *licenza*, a *recitativo stromentato* originally sung by Giovanni Manzuoli, the castrato who sang the title role, refers festively to the royal wedding. Although Metastasio had begun the libretto to mark another wedding, that of the Austrian Archduchess Marie Antoinette to the French dauphin (the future Louis XVI), he justified its use in Milan, a year later, chiefly because Ariosto, to whom he turned for his source, had served at the Este court at Ferrara. Moreover, Metastasio probably hoped the medieval setting would please the modern taste of the Milanese public.

Both librettist and composer had misgivings well before the première. Metastasio confessed in correspondence that he had strained to match his earlier successes, while Hasse complained about his advanced age (he was 72), the theatrical style currently favoured in Italy, and his aging singers. Like the primo uomo Manzuoli, the prima donna, Antonia Maria Girelli, who sang Bradamante, was nearly past her prime (the singer Hasse had wanted, Anna de Amicis, was unavailable). Charlemagne, though a minor role, was also sung by an aging singer, the tenor Giuseppe Tibaldi. Fortunately, Maria Theresa, who had commissioned Hasse and rewarded him handsomely, seemed pleased with the production. On 17 October 1771 she wrote to her future daughter-in-law that she preferred his works to those of any other composer, that he had been her music teacher in 1733, had worked hard and was now old.

The opera has only 17 arias, mostly in abridged da capo or other less symmetrical forms, and includes a relatively high proportion of *recitativo stromentato*; yet it seems old-fashioned. Rarely exhibiting the excitement and beauty of *Piramo e Tisbe* (1768) and other works of the 1760s for the Viennese court, *Ruggiero* is a historical landmark only, not a notable artistic achievement. For the only other production at the time, at the Teatro S Carlo, Naples, on 20 January 1772, Hasse adjusted the score to suit a different cast.

SVEN HANSELL

Ruggles, Carl [Charles] (**Sprague**) (*b* East Marion, MA, 11 March 1876; *d* Bennington, VT, 24 Oct 1971). American composer. As a child he was taught the violin, and he later studied composition with John Knowles Paine. After a variety of music-related jobs, in 1907 he moved to Winona, Minnesota, where he taught and founded the Winona SO. In 1917 he moved to New York, where he achieved his first successes as a composer. During the 1920s he produced his most celebrated orchestral works, such as *Men and Mountains* (1924) and *Sun-Treader* (1926–31). From the 1920s he and his family made long visits to Vermont, often as guests of the artist Rockwell Kent, a good friend of the composer. Ruggles settled there in 1924.

Predating his acknowledged compositions is an unfinished opera, *The Sunken Bell*, based on Gerhart Hauptmann's five-act 'Märchendrama' *Die versunkene Glocke* (1896). Around 1909 the New York critic and linguist Charles Henry Meltzer agreed to extract from his published translation of the play a libretto for Ruggles. The most intense period of their collaboration was between 1912 and 1923 (documented by correspondence held in *US-NH*), although the latest date on a manuscript is 1927. The opera was never performed, despite Meltzer's exhaustive efforts to promote it in New York and Chicago. Furthermore, Meltzer claimed in his unpublished memoirs that the composer was never satisfied with any version and was constantly rewriting it in a more dissonant and 'modern' form. Ruggles eventually abandoned the project, citing as reasons his disenchantment with the translated libretto, the Metropolitan Opera's refusal to consider using a real bell as a stage prop (probably a false story) and his frustration with writing opera. He destroyed the most complete copy in the early 1940s. Approximately 800 musical sketches survive, as well as Meltzer's typescript of the libretto (all in *US-NH*). Many of them are musically excellent and they reveal a stylistic evolution from Debussian and Straussian influences to Ruggles's more familiar dissonant, non-tonal language.

*

J. Kirkpatrick: 'Conversations with Carl Ruggles' (MS, 1963–71, John Kirkpatrick papers, *US-NH*)

J. Saecker: *Carl Ruggles in Winona* (diss., Winona State College, 1967)

J. Kirkpatrick: 'The Evolution of Carl Ruggles: a Chronicle Largely in his Own Words', *PNM*, vi/2 (1968), 146–66
D. Henahan: 'Carl Ruggles, Composer, is Dead at 95', *New York Times* (26 Oct 1971)
R. Y. McMahan: *'The Sunken Bell' by Carl Ruggles* (diss., Peabody Institute, Johns Hopkins U., 1990)

ROBERT YOUNG McMAHAN

Ruk-Focič, Božena (*b* Zagreb, 31 Oct 1937). Croatian soprano. She studied in Zagreb, making her début in 1961 at Basle as Micaëla. Engaged at Zagreb, she also appeared in Budapest, Belgrade, Moscow, Geneva, Zürich, Vienna and Berlin, at Covent Garden, where she made her début as Eva (1969) and at La Scala, where she sang Calypso/Penelope in the Italian première of Dallapiccola's *Ulisse* (1970). At Seattle she sang Sieglinde (1973) and Aida (1976). Her roles included Alcestis, Countess Almaviva, Agathe, Elisabeth, Elsa, Tatyana, Yaroslavna and Leonora (*Il trovatore* and *La forza del destino*). Her voice, brilliant at the top, was less secure in the middle register. ELIZABETH FORBES

Ruloffs, Bartholomeus (*b* Amsterdam, ?Oct 1741; *d* Amsterdam, 13 May 1801). Netherlands composer and librettist. His father and his brother played in the Amsterdam theatre orchestra, in which he became a violinist at the age of 16. The theatre burnt down in 1773, and Ruloffs succeeded Hendrik Chalons as conductor of the rebuilt theatre's orchestra in 1774. He also worked as a church organist and an orchestral conductor; in his last years he resigned from his conducting duties but continued to supervise the ballets at the theatre.

Though Ruloffs did not excel in a particular field, probably because of his diverse talents, he was important in the development of early musical life in Amsterdam. He translated many opera librettos (now lost) for the theatre there, including Mozart's *Die Entführung aus dem Serail* and *Die Zauberflöte*, Wranitzky's *Oberon* and Dittersdorf's *Doktor und Apotheker* and *Das rote Käppchen*. He also translated, and inserted his own music into, many French *opéras comiques*, including Grétry's *Les deux avares* (as *De twee gierigaards*, 1787) and *Richard Coeur-de-lion* (as *Richard Leeuwenhart*, 1791), Lucille Grétry's *Le mariage d'Antoine* (as *Het huwelijk van Antonio*, 1791), Monsigny's *La belle Arsène* (as *De schoone Arsène*, 1789) and Gossec's *Le tonnelier* (as *De kuiper*, 1792). In addition Ruloffs wrote the Singspiel *De bruiloft van Kloris en Roosje* (*c*1787), a stage work entitled *Komst van Willem den Eersten, Prins van Oranje, te Leyden* (1780; lost), two pantomimes, songs and instrumental music.

For illustration *see* AMSTERDAM.

*

AMZ, ii (1799–1800), 191, 396
E. G. J. Gregoir: *Biographie des artistes-musiciens néerlandais des XVIIIe et XIXe siècles* (Antwerp, 1864), 154
D. F. Scheurleer: *Het muziekleven in Nederland in de tweede helft der 18e eeuw* (The Hague, 1909)
A. N. Verveen: 'Bartholomeus Ruloffs (1741–1801)', *Amstelodamum*, xlix (1962); also in *Mens en melodie*, xvii (1962), 241–6

AREND KOOLE

Rumania. *See* ROMANIA.

Rundgren, Bengt (*b* Karlskrona, 21 April 1931). Swedish bass-baritone. After studies in Stockholm, he sang in operetta, made his début with the Swedish Royal Opera in 1962 as the Commendatore and became a principal with the company. He joined the Deutsche Oper, Berlin, in 1968 and sang small roles at Bayreuth the next year; he appeared as Fafner and Hagen in the centenary *Ring* (1976) directed by Chéreau. His American début was in 1970 with the Chicago Lyric Opera, and he sang Hagen with the Metropolitan in 1974 and for his Covent Garden début in 1976. He has sung with the Bol'shoy Opera, Moscow, in roles embracing Russian opera as well as the leading Wagner bass parts and some Verdi ones (Ramfis, Sparafucile). A *basso cantante* of vocal power and authority, he is often heard as a concert soloist. NOËL GOODWIN

Rung, Henrik (*b* Copenhagen, 31 March 1807; *d* Copenhagen, 12 Dec 1871). Danish composer. He studied in Copenhagen and played the double bass in the Royal Orchestra. His incidental music for Hertz's tragedy *Svend Dyrings Hus* (1837) won him a bursary to travel to Vienna and Rome, where he studied to be a singing teacher. Back in Copenhagen he became chorus master and then singing teacher to the soloists of the Royal Opera. He wrote several operas and *syngestykke* (Singspiels) as well as much incidental music for the theatre, but as a composer he was overshadowed by his greater contemporary, J. P. E. Hartmann.

His son, Frederik Rung (*b* Copenhagen, 14 June 1854; *d* Copenhagen, 22 Jan 1914), was also a composer. He studied with his father, then in 1872 became répétiteur and in 1884 conductor at the Royal Opera. He wrote two operas, *Det hemmelige Selskab* ('The Secret Society') in 1888 and *Den trekantede Hat* ('The Three-Cornered Hat') in 1894, both performed in Copenhagen.

all performed at Copenhagen, Royal Opera

En Bolero (2, S. Beyer, partly after E. Scribe: *La Xacarilla*), 18 March 1843
Stormen paa København (5, T. Overskou), 21 Jan 1845
Aagerkarl og Sanger (operetta, 1, H. H. Nyegaard), 18 Nov 1846
Federigo (syngestykke, 3, H. Hertz), 23 March 1848
Stella (syngestykke, 3, A. von der Recke, after Scribe: *Giralda, ou La nouvelle Psyché*), 2 Feb 1852
Flugt og Fare (syngestykke, 1, Beyer), 29 April 1852
Studenterne fra Salamanca (syngestykke, 1, Nyegaard), 21 Feb 1854
Annunciatas Fest (syngestykke, 1, von der Recke, after M. Carré and J. Loru: *Les trovatelles*), 22 May 1856 ELIZABETH FORBES

Runge, Peter-Christoph (*b* Lübeck, 12 April 1933). German baritone. He studied in Hamburg and made his début in 1958 at Flensburg as Guglielmo. After singing at Wuppertal, in 1964 he moved to Düsseldorf where he has been engaged for over 25 years. At Glyndebourne (1964–73) he sang Papageno, Amida (*Ormindo*) and Pelléas, returning in 1982 as Pantalone (*The Love for Three Oranges*). He sang Stolzius (*Die Soldaten*) at Amsterdam (1971), Edinburgh (1972) and Hamburg (1981); Otho (*L'incoronazione di Poppea*) for Scottish Opera (1973); and Count Robinson at Edinburgh and Drottningholm (1980). At Wexford he sang Romualdo in *Le astuzie femminili* (1984) and Major Max von Zastrow in *The Rising of the Moon* (1990); and at Dublin he appeared as Lord Tristan Mickleford/Bob in *Martha* (1992). His repertory includes Rossini's Figaro, Dandini, Belcore, Malatesta, Sherasmin (*Oberon*), Lortzing's Hans Sachs, Beckmesser, Golaud, Harlequin (*Ariadne auf Naxos*), the Barber (*Die schweigsame Frau*), Olivier (*Capriccio*), the title role of Lothar's *Schneider Wibbel*, Ford (*Die lustigen Weiber von Windsor*) and Wozzeck. A polished comedian, he has a light but well-projected voice. ELIZABETH FORBES

Rünger, Gertrude (*b* Posen, 1899; *d* Berlin, 10 June 1965). German mezzo-soprano and soprano. She sang at Erfurt (1924–7), then for a season at Magdeburg, and from 1928 to 1935 at Vienna, where she took part in some notable revivals such as *Don Carlos* (1931) and *Macbeth* (1933). She returned to Vienna in 1938 after a period in Berlin. Her career also expanded to include the 1933 and 1934 seasons at Covent Garden, 1937 at the Metropolitan and 1938 at La Scala, where she sang Brünnhilde in the *Ring* cycle under Krauss, and Isolde the following year under De Sabata. At Salzburg she sang Fatima (*Oberon*), the Nurse (*Die Frau ohne Schatten*), Clytemnestra (*Electra*) and Leonore (*Fidelio*). In London her most admired role was Kundry in which she 'displayed exceptional power in a wide range of dramatic expression'. Her later career included appearances as Electra under Knappertsbusch (1940) and some post-war seasons in Berlin. Her recordings are few, but solos from *Don Carlos* and *Macbeth* show fine quality, both vocal and dramatic. J. B. STEANE

Runnicles, Donald (*b* Edinburgh, 16 Nov 1954). Scottish conductor. He studied at Edinburgh and Cambridge universities, then at the London Opera Centre (1977). In 1978 he joined the Mannheim Nationaltheater as répétiteur, where he made his conducting début in *Les contes d'Hoffmann* in 1980; later he was promoted to first Kapellmeister. He spent several seasons at the Bayreuth Festival beginning in 1982, when he assisted James Levine on the centenary production of *Parsifal*. In 1987, he joined the Hanover Opera as principal conductor and began a long association with the Hamburg Staatsoper. He made his Metropolitan Opera début in 1988 with the three-act version of *Lulu*. In 1989 he was named music director of the Freiburg Opera, conducting a new production of *Lady Macbeth of the Mtsensk District* in his inaugural season. He became music director of the San Francisco Opera in 1990. NANCY MALITZ

Ruohonen, Seppo [Juhani] (*b* Turku, 25 April 1946). Finnish tenor. He studied in Turku and Vienna, making his début in 1973 at Helsinki as Don Alvaro (*Forza*); he then sang Manrico, the Duke, Don Ottavio, Hermann and Lensky with the Finnish National Opera. He sang Juhana in Kokkonen's *The Last Temptations* at Savonlinna (1977) and also Don Carlos and Erik (1983). Engaged at Frankfurt since 1978, he has sung Turiddu, Pinkerton, Luigi, Duke of Parma (*Doktor Faust*) and Radames there, and has also appeared with Scottish Opera and Opera North. His repertory includes Jeník, Faust, Don José and Cavaradossi. He has a powerful voice with particularly strong top notes. ELIZABETH FORBES

Ruprecht, (Josef) Martin [?Stephan] (*b* ?Vienna, *c*1758; *d* Vienna, 7 June 1800). Austrian composer and tenor. He was a member of Katherina Schindler's troupe that gave a guest season at the Kärntnertortheater, Vienna, in 1776. In 1778, he became a founder-member of the German National Singspiel company, appearing as Fritz in the première of Umlauf's *Die Bergknappen* and in most of the early productions, including his own *Was erhält die Männer treu?*. He sang occasionally with the Italian Opera following the closure of the Singspiel company in 1783 and joined the re-formed German company again in 1785. In 1788 he left the Opera, and shortly afterwards joined the court chapel ensemble, of which he remained a member until his death. He was considered a talented singer, though a rather ordinary actor.

Evidence for the performance of only four of Ruprecht's Singspiels can be traced; it seems likely that *Die Wette* was not performed, and that *Der Irrwisch* and *Der Derwisch*, both mentioned by Pollak-Schlaffenberg, are the product of confusion with Umlauf's *Das Irrlicht* and the Schack, Gerl and Henneberg *Der wolhltätige Derwisch* respectively. Gerber named *Die natürlichen Wunder* and *Elmire* among Ruprecht's works; the former cannot be traced, and the latter, presumably identical with Goethe's *Erwin und Elmire*, given at the Burgtheater on 20 April 1794, was not (according to Hadamowsky) set to music.

all Singspiels

Die Wette, 1777 (1), ?unperf., *A-Wgm*

Was erhält die Männer treu? (2, L. Zehnmark), Vienna, Burg, 1 May (? 30 March) 1780, *Wn*

Die Dorfhandel, oder Bunt über Eck (2, P. Weidmann), Vienna, Kärntnertor, 15 Nov 1785, *Wn*

Das wütende Heer, oder Das Mädchen im Turme (3, after C. F. Bretzner), Vienna, Kärntnertor, 1 June 1787

Der blinde Ehemann (J. F. Jünger), Vienna, Freihaus, 21 Oct 1794

Cited in Gerber: Die natürlichen Wunder, *c*1795, and Elmire

*

FétisB; *GerberNL*

I. Pollak-Schlaffenberg: 'Die Wiener Liedmusik von 1778 bis 1789', *SMw*, v (1918), 97–151

O. E. Deutsch: 'Das Freihaus-Theater auf der Wieden', *Mitteilungen des Vereins für Geschichte der Stadt Wien*, xvi (1937), 30–73

F. Hadamowsky: *Die Wiener Hoftheater (Staatstheater), 1776–1966*, i (Vienna, 1966)

O. Michtner: *Das alte Burgtheater als Opernbühne* (Vienna, 1970)

PETER BRANSCOMBE

***Rusalka* (i).** Opera by S. I. Davïdov; *see* LESTA, ILI DNEPROVSKAYA RUSALKA.

***Rusalka* (ii).** Romantic opera in four acts by ALEXANDER SERGEYEVICH DARGOMÏZHSKY to his own libretto after ALEXANDER SERGEYEVICH PUSHKIN's poem ('preserving many of his verses'); St Petersburg, Circus Theatre, 4/16 May 1856.

The outstanding Russian opera of the 1850s, its status as a standard repertory piece in its homeland dates from the Mariinsky Theatre revival of 1865. Looking back on its première – with Osip Petrov as the Miller, Dar'ya Leonova as the Princess, Pavel Bulakhov as the Prince, the latter's wife Anis'ya Bulakhova as Natasha and Konstantin Lyadov conducting – the theatrical chronicler Alexander Vol'f wrote: 'The roles of the Princess and the Miller were magisterially performed, in spite of which the new opera did not make much of an impression on the mass public ... It was hard to imagine that only a few years later Dargomïzhsky's chef d'oeuvre would become one of our favourite operas'.

Pushkin's 'dramatic romance', dating from 1832 and not quite finished, was a Singspiel libretto inspired by Ferdinand Kauer's *Das Donauweibchen*, which (both as adapted by Cavos and Davïdov and in a series of sequels by the same composers) had been for almost 30 years the showpiece of the Russian musical stage. The poet's treatment of the familiar water-nymph legend differed markedly from its prototypes: in place of Kauer's happy ending celebrating the triumph of family loyalty over supernatural blandishments, Pushkin's drama was a tragedy of expiation: a miller's daughter – unnamed in Pushkin, Natasha (soprano) in the opera – jilted by a faithless Prince (tenor), hurls herself into the Dnepr, the great river of the Ukraine; she becomes the queen of the river water nymphs (*rusalki*) and wreaks cold supernatural vengeance upon her tormentor; her father, the Miller (bass), is driven spectacularly mad by the loss of his daughter.

Despite all its supernatural trappings (and unlike its prototypes), Pushkin's play is fundamentally concerned with the human characters – with him even the water nymph was originally human – and their interaction; for this reason it has been touted by Russian critics as a benchmark of 'realism'. Dargomïzhsky's setting followed suit, and in so doing sounded a new and influential note in Russian opera. His music for the three main characters was a fecund compound of two styles, both readily identifiable (with hindsight, anyway) as characteristically Russian: an aria-cum-ensemble style modelled on the idiom of the contemporary salon romance (pointing straight to the Pushkin operas of Tchaikovsky), and a freewheeling declamatory style scrupulously modelled on the intonations and rhythms of the poetry, aimed at capturing the fugitive moods and meanings underlying the individual words of the text (and extremely influential on Musorgsky). The really epoch-making number from this point of view is the lengthy scene of accompanied recitative in Act 3, set directly to Pushkin's verses, for the Prince and the demented Miller who thinks himself 'the local raven'.

Rusalka was the opera Stravinsky praised for 'mixing the Russian popular *melos* and the prevailing Italianism with the most carefree and charming ease'. Yet the idioms are not so much mixed as juxtaposed. The 'national' idiom is largely confined to stereotyped interpolated choruses (Act 1) and dances (Act 2). It was never an aim of Dargomïzhsky's (as it was of Glinka's) to incorporate folklike traits into the fabric of the dramatic music. For him the popular style was still a 'peasant' idiom, to be distinguished from that of the main characters: the more highborn the personage, the more italianate the associated music (as, pre-eminently, in the ornate 'aria-duet' for the Prince and his princess bride in Act 2, a fully fledged sequence of three tempos with choral introduction). In the first scene of Act 3 the coordination of musical form and style with social class is especially clear: the Princess (mezzo-soprano) expresses her anxieties about her marriage in a lofty da capo aria with coda, whereupon Ol'ga [Olga] (soprano) her orphan ward, tries to console her with a four-square strophic song.

Italianate music of another sort dominates the Miller's *basso buffo* aria in Act 1 (opening the opera), and – following a tradition established in *Das Donauweibchen* and its sequels, but to vastly different purpose – Dargomïzhsky casts the role of Natasha's Loreley daughter in Act 4 for a child's speaking voice, declaiming her seductive lines in melodrama against a harp solo. In earlier treatments this had been merely an other-worldly colour. In Dargomïzhsky's opera it is the lure through which the Prince meets his doom.

RICHARD TARUSKIN

Rusalka (iii). Lyric fairy-tale in three acts by ANTONÍN DVOŘÁK to a libretto by JAROSLAV KVAPIL (i) after Friedrich de la Motte Fouqué's *Undine*; Prague, National Theatre, 31 March 1901.

Kvapil's libretto for *Rusalka* takes elements from a number of literary sources but derives principally from Fouqué's *Undine* (1811). Hans Andersen's *The Little Mermaid* and the French legend of Melusine were also cited by Kvapil as part of the background to *Rusalka*. In addition, the name if not the nature of Ježibaba is taken from the Czech translation of the play *Die versunkene Glocke* by Gerhard Hauptmann. The debt which Kvapil claimed he owed to K. J. Erben's *Kytice z pověstí* ('A Garland of National Tales') seems to have been more in its generalized national feeling than specific characterization. The libretto is suffused with a fairy-tale atmosphere which drew from Dvořák (who had used Erben as the basis for four symphonic poems in 1896) music of extraordinary poetry, particularly his evocation of the Bohemian forest. Having written his libretto in the autumn of 1899, Kvapil showed the text to Oskar Nedbal, Josef Foerster, Karel Kovařovic and Josef Suk before Dvořák, who found it entirely congenial. He began his sketch on 21 April 1900 and became absorbed with his work, producing one of his most fluent sketches. In the course of composition, he made use of material from his American sketchbooks. By 27 November 1900 the full score was completed. The National Theatre put its finest resources at his disposal, and the work was a great success.

Rusalka *a water nymph*	soprano
Prince	tenor
Foreign Princess	soprano
Vodník *a water gnome*	bass
Ježibaba *a witch*	mezzo-soprano
Hunter	baritone
Gamekeeper	tenor
Turnspit	soprano
First Wood Nymph	soprano
Second Wood Nymph	soprano
Third Wood Nymph	contralto

Wood nymphs, guests at the castle, the Prince's entourage

Setting A meadow by a lake and the grounds of a castle

In many ways, *Rusalka* stood outside the kind of operatic subject favoured by Czech composers in the 1890s and early 1900s, who were more inclined to naturalism. Nevertheless, *Rusalka* soon became Dvořák's most popular opera both in the composer's native land and in other countries. Although Mahler (who was conductor of the Vienna Hofoper at that time) took an interest in the work, the first performance in Vienna was given in 1910 by a Czech company. Its German début was on 10 March 1935 in Stuttgart, in a translation by J. Will. The first professional production in England, given at Sadler's Wells on 18 February 1959 in a translation by Christopher Hassall, had only a moderate success. A new production by David Pountney in a translation by Rodney Blumer, given by the ENO on 16 March 1983, has proved more durable.

ACT 1 *A meadow by a lake, surrounded by a forest*
In the moonlight three wood nymphs taunt the water gnome Vodník, who responds good-naturedly. Rusalka calls to him from the willow tree where she is sitting. She asks about the immortality of the human soul and confesses in a brief, exquisite aria, 'Sem často přichází' ('Often he comes here'), that she has fallen in love with a human, the Prince, who swims in the lake. Horrified that she wants to become human, Vodník sinks into the lake, telling her that she must ask the help of Ježibaba. Rusalka in 'Měsíčku na nebi hlubokém' ('Song to the

'Rusalka' (Dvořák): design by Jan Kotěra for Act 2 (the grounds of the Prince's castle) of the original production at the National Theatre, Prague, 31 March 1901

Moon') calls on the moon to tell her beloved that she waits for him. She then turns to Ježibaba, who agrees to let her walk on land but warns her that if she does not find love as a human being she will be accursed for ever. Undaunted, Rusalka begs Ježibaba to transform her, and in a humorous conjuration scene ('Čury mury fuk') Ježibaba turns her into a human, except that she cannot speak. As the warnings of Vodník fade with the night, dawn brings the sound of hunting horns. The Prince, feeling strangely drawn to the lake, sends his retinue home. He sees Rusalka; bewitched by her beauty he takes her home to the castle.

The end of this act is one of Dvořák's most effective. He circumvents the difficulty of having no opportunity for a love duet by providing the Prince with lyrical repeated phrases over a magnificently sustained accompaniment.

ACT 2 *The grounds of the Prince's castle* The Gamekeeper and the Turnspit, whose music is breathless and has affinities with the idiom of the bagpipe song, spin tales of the forest and gossip about the strangeness of the Prince since he met Rusalka in the woods. The Prince is to marry Rusalka, but he is frustrated by her silence and frigidity. During an exchange in which he tells her desperately that he must win her, a visiting Foreign Princess chides the Prince for neglecting his guest. As evening falls other guests arrive for a ballet, dominated by a graceful polonaise. As the merrymaking continues, Vodník appears in the lake, lamenting Rusalka's fate and singing about her future rejection; ironically, this is set against the bridal chorus sung by the guests. Rusalka, who has become gradually more intimidated by her surroundings, rushes into the gardens and, suddenly recovering her voice, begs Vodník to help her. Her desperate outburst takes the form of an effective though conventional aria, 'Ó, márno to je' ('Oh, useless it is'); rejected by the Prince, she can neither live nor die. The Prince, accompanied by the Foreign Princess, is dissatisfied with Rusalka; he professes his love for the Foreign Princess, whose music has a dotted, perhaps Polish rhythmic quality. Despite the passionate nature of her duet with the Prince, the music remains deliberately cold. At the climax of the duet, Rusalka intervenes and is pushed away by the Prince. Vodník pronounces his vengeance as the Prince appeals to the Foreign Princess for help. In a cruel and cutting couplet, she tells him to follow his love to hell.

ACT 3 *The meadow by the lake* Rusalka is mourning her fate. Ježibaba offers the possibility of returning to her original form if she murders the Prince. In fury and horror Rusalka refuses and sinks sadly into the lake, only to be rejected by her sisters. The Gamekeeper and the Turnspit ask Ježibaba to help the Prince, who has fallen ill since Rusalka left. Enraged by their temerity, Vodník emerges from the lake and chases them away. A *divertissement* follows for the three wood nymphs, who sing of their loveliness and tease Vodník. He responds sadly and in a passage rising to an extraordinary climax tells them of Rusalka's cursed state. The Prince, delirious, comes looking for Rusalka and asks her to return with him. She tells him of her fate resulting from his rejection and that now a kiss from her would kill him. He begs her to kiss him and give him peace. This climactic passage is relatively brief, and although the Prince and Rusalka do not sing simultaneously, the relative simplicity of the music is poignant. Rusalka asks for mercy on his soul and accepting her sad fate disappears into the lake.

* * *

The success of *Rusalka* derives from a number of factors. While much of the opera (especially the final act) is static, Dvořák provides music of extraordinarily sensual beauty. To a greater extent than in any of his previous operas, the musical texture is through-composed, although there are occasional isolated numbers which may be extracted. Apart from the delicate beauty of such motifs as Rusalka's, which occurs in the prelude and on her first appearance (ex.1),

Ex.1

and is associated with her throughout the opera, the separable numbers provide a focus for exquisite lyricism, notably in the most famous aria in the opera, 'Měsíčku na nebi hlubokém'. Dvořák's word-setting is also at its most expressive and most flexible in this work. There was also opportunity for nationally inflected passages in the more vigorous episodes with the wood nymphs at the beginning of Act 1, the first-act aria of Ježibaba, 'Čury mury fuk', and the exchanges between the Gamekeeper and the Turnspit in Acts 2 and 3. Each character has distinctive music reinforced by a consistently used series of motifs. Dvořák's debt to Wagner is apparent not only in the leitmotivic use of personal motifs but occasionally in the harmonic language. *Rusalka* represents Dvořák at the height of his maturity, exercising superb control over musical and dramatic resources. JAN SMACZNY

Rüsche-Endorf, Cäcilie (*b* Dortmund, 8 April 1873; *d* Leipzig, 13 March 1939). German soprano. She studied in Cologne and Milan, and made her début as Agathe (*Der Freischütz*) at Zürich in 1894. She was then engaged by the Cologne Opera until 1904, and was at Hanover, 1905–10. In 1906 she made her début at Bayreuth as Gutrune in *Götterdämmerung* and sang the part for the next three seasons. As her voice gathered weight she took on dramatic roles, notably Brünnhilde, and specialized in these at Leipzig from 1911 to 1919. At Covent Garden, where she sang in 1908, 1911 and 1914, she had mixed reviews ('powerful ... but shrill at the top' at her début); despite being considered 'physically unsuited to the part' (H. Rosenthal: *Two Centuries of Opera at Covent Garden*, London, 1958), she was a fine Kundry in 1914. Her few recordings suggest a voice of considerable beauty, used with taste and feeling.

J. B. STEANE

Ruse. Town in northern Bulgaria, on the Danube. In 1914 the Rusenska Operna Druzhba (Ruse Opera Society) was founded, as well as the first symphony orchestra. The opera society formed the basis of the Narodna Operna Ruse (Ruse Opera), which opened on 27 November 1949, with a performance of *La traviata*; the existing Darzhaven Simfonichen Orkestar (State SO, 1949) and an opera choir became part of the company, and Konstantin Iliev was musical director, 1949–52. The Ruse company presented opera and ballet, and over the years became one of the best in the country, with remarkable soloists and excellent conductors and directors. Besides Iliev, the conductors included Dobrin Petkov, Romeo Raichev, Dimitar Manolov and Georgi Dimitrov; the directors included Dragan Karjiev, Mikhail Hadjimishev, Stefan Trifonov and Evgeni Nemirov, as well as Tsvetana Andreeva and Vesselina Manolova, who, having studied in Czechoslovakia, contributed a different style. Fine Bulgarian singers of the calibre of Stevka Evstatieva enabled a rich repertory of Italian, German, Russian and Bulgarian operas to be established. As well as the regular season between September and July, the Martenski Muzikalni Dni (March Musical Days) festival is an additional stimulus to the high standard of performance and wide repertory. The Ruse Opera used the National Theatre until 1956, when it moved to a reconstructed building with 670 seats, where three or four performances are given each week.

R. Biks: *Bulgarski operen teatar* [Bulgarian Opera Theatre] (Sofia, 1985) MAGDALENA MANOLOVA

Rush, George (*fl* London, *c*1760–80). English composer. According to Dibdin, he travelled and studied in Italy before emerging as a theatre composer in London, where his greatest success came with two English operas performed in 1764. *The Royal Shepherd* (R. Rolt, after Metastasio's *Il re pastore*), first performed at Drury Lane on 24 February 1764, was intended as competition to Arne's *Artaxerxes*, in the Covent Garden repertory. The overture (London, *c*1764) was very popular as a concert piece, in part because of the still exceptional use of timpani. It was published both for orchestra and in harpsichord reduction, the latter reprinted as late as the end of the century. Rush's second opera, *Capricious Lovers*, was first given at Drury Lane on 28 November 1764 (vs, London, 1764; overture London, *c*1764); the libretto was devised by R. Lloyd from Favart's *La caprice amoureux ou Ninette à la cour* (a parody of Goldoni's *Bertoldo*). The work was reduced to a two-act farce and performed as an afterpiece from 2 March 1765. In 1768 Rush composed the music (now apparently lost) for *The Statesman Foiled* (R. Dossie), introduced as a two-act afterpiece at the Haymarket Theatre on 8 July 1768. Several numbers of *The Royal Shepherd* were retained and at least one song rewritten by Rush when it was re-staged as a pasticcio, *Amintas*, by G. F. Tenducci and T. E. Carter at Covent Garden on 15 December 1769 (vs, London, 1770). A harpsichordist and guitarist, Rush also composed instrumental music. He was probably in the Drury Lane orchestra at the time his operas were performed there (Roscoe). Although Dibdin and the *ABC Dario* categorized his operas as too Italian for English tastes, these works must be granted a historical niche in a period of transition from the ballad opera to the age of Dibdin.

LS
ABC Dario Musico (Bath, 1780)
C. Dibdin: *A Complete History of the Stage*, v (London, 1800), 226
P. C. Roscoe: 'George Rush: a Forgotten English Composer', *MT*, lxxxvii (1946), 297–9
R. Fiske: *English Theatre Music in the Eighteenth Century* (London, 1973, 2/1986) RONALD R. KIDD

Rushton, Julian (Gordon) (*b* Cambridge, 22 May 1941). English musicologist. He studied at Cambridge (under Leppard and Radcliffe) and Oxford (Westrup and Wellesz), where he took the DPhil. He was appointed lecturer at the University of East Anglia (1968–74) and then at Cambridge (1974–81) before becoming West Riding Professor of Music at Leeds University. His work has been primarily in French and Viennese music of the late 18th century, and in Berlioz studies; it shows a particular concern with the relationship of music and drama, as witnessed by several perceptive articles on Gluck and Piccinni, and with analytical issues, as well as with Mozart's music-dramatic methods.

Music and Drama at the Académie Royale de Musique, 1774–1789 (diss., U. of Oxford, 1970)
ed.: *W. A. Mozart: Don Giovanni* (Cambridge, 1981)
Classical Music: a Concise History (London, 1986)
'The Music' and 'Dido's Monologue and Aria', *Hector Berlioz: Les Troyens*, ed. I. Kemp (Cambridge, 1988)
ed.: *W. A. Mozart: Idomeneo* (Cambridge, 1993)

Ruslan and Lyudmila [*Ruslan i Lyudmila*]. 'Magic' opera in five acts by MIKHAIL IVANOVICH GLINKA to a libretto by Valerian Fyodorovich Shirkov (with minor contributions by Nikolay Andreyevich Markevich, Nestor Vasil'yevich Kukol'nik, Mikhail Alexandrovich Gedeonov and the composer) after ALEXANDER SERGEYEVICH PUSHKIN's narrative poem (1820), incorporating many of the original verses; St Petersburg, Bol'shoy Theatre, 27 November/9 December 1842.

Svetozar *Grand Prince of Kiev*	bass
Lyudmila *Svetozar's daughter*	soprano
Ruslan *a Kievan knight, Lyudmila's betrothed*	baritone
Ratmir *a Khazar prince*	contralto
Farlaf *a Varangian prince*	bass
Chernomor *an evil sorcerer, dwarf*	mime role
Gorislava *maiden in love with Ratmir*	soprano
Finn *a benevolent sorcerer*	tenor
Naina *an evil sorceress*	mezzo-soprano
Bayan *bard*	tenor

Sons of Svetozar, knights, nobles, immured maidens, wet-nurses and nannies, striplings, bodyguards, cupbearers, guests at table, troops, crowd; maidens of the magic castle, blackamoors, dwarfs, slaves of Chernomor, nymphs and watersprites

Setting Kiev and various fantastic locales, legendary times

Glinka conceived the plan for *Ruslan and Lyudmila* in 1836, shortly after the première of his first opera, *A Life for the Tsar*, at the suggestion of Alexander Shakhovskoy, the Intendant of the Imperial Theatres (who had written a dramatic trilogy, *Finn*, based in part on Pushkin's poem). Initially the composer had sought Pushkin's active collaboration. Before they could start work the poet was killed in a duel (29 January/10 February 1837), and Glinka began composing without a libretto. Early in 1838 a writer acquaintance named Nikolay Polevoy, to whom he had played excerpts from the score, wrote to Alexey Verstovsky (with some exaggeration) that 'the opera is almost finished, but as yet there is no text. A strange way of writing!'.

Strange or not, it was Glinka's preferred way, one that had served him well enough in his first opera. The earliest written document of *Ruslan and Lyudmila* to survive is quite in character: a detailed scenario which the composer wrote down in a notebook Kukol'nik had given him for the purpose on 6/18 November 1837. Several numbers are notated in considerable musical detail. A few – both of Lyudmila's arias, the second part of Ruslan's in Act 2, Ratmir's cavatina in Act 3, the trance-induction music in Act 4, the duet in Act 5 – are quite close to their familiar finished form. But in place of text there are only scansion marks to aid the prospective librettist (at this point Kukol'nik), as well as indications of which numbers to base on Pushkin's own words.

Shirkov, a Kharkiv landowner and amateur poet, entered the picture in the spring of 1838, when Glinka requested from him on trial a text for 'Milolika's' (Gorislava's) cavatina in Act 3 and also had him 'underlay words' to the music of Lyudmila's Act 1 cavatina, already sketched in the preliminary plan. Other numbers completed in 1838 were fairly incidental; they included the Persian chorus in Act 3 (to Pushkin's words), Chernomor's March and Finn's ballad (to Pushkin's words, somewhat adapted by Markevich). Then followed 18 months during which domestic trials and the demands of his post as head of the court chapel choir forced neglect of the project. It was upon resumption late in 1840 that Glinka composed the introduction to Act 1 and the finale to Act 5, as well as the long first part of Ruslan's Act 2 aria (the 'apostrophe to the battlefield' on Pushkin's words), and found the uniquely exalted and contemplative 'epic' tone that would eventually characterize the opera. Shirkov having left St Petersburg for his estate in 1841, finishing touches were made with the aid of Gedeonov and Kukol'nik: the former wrote the duet for Ruslan and Finn in Act 2 scene i and also patched the end of the second act; the latter rather messily rewrote the scene for Ratmir and Finn in Act 5 so as to exclude Farlaf's murder of Ruslan, and also supplied the grand finale. The composer himself seems to have been responsible for the text of Act 2 scene ii (Farlaf and Naina). The opera was submitted to the Imperial Theatres in March 1842 and first performed on the sixth anniversary of the première of *A Life for the Tsar*; it was conducted by Karl Albrecht, with Osip Petrov as Ruslan (alternating in subsequent performances with Semyon Gulak-Artemovsky), Mariya Stepanova as Lyudmila, Anfisa Petrova as Ratmir (the role was intended for Anna Vorob'yova, who sang it after the opening night) and Domenico Tosi as Farlaf.

Despite the coincidence of dates, the times were not auspicious. The very next year Rubini's Italian opera troupe set itself up in St Petersburg and Russian opera was almost immediately squeezed out of the Russian capital. In its first season *Ruslan and Lyudmila* was played 31 times; in its second, 12; in 1844–5, six; in 1845–6, two; the next season only once. In 1848 the opera was given only in Moscow, and then was dropped until after the composer's death. It has only fitfully held the stage. Denigrated by narrowminded proponents of opera-as-drama (ever since Alexander Serov, Russia's greatest music critic, called it 'not a drama, not a play, hence *not an opera*, but a randomly assembled gallery of musical scenes'), and cursed with a blessedly complicated score that prevented popular success ('not every operagoer has studied counterpoint', said Count Wielhorski, Glinka's 'friend', who cut the opera to ribbons for the première), Glinka's masterpiece was caught in a crossfire of taste. Performances during the composer's lifetime were never complete (the first such production was given not in Russia but in Prague, under Balakirev, in 1867, and there have been few since; fortunately an uncut recording was made by Bol'shoy forces under Kondrashin in the early 1950s), and as early as 1859 Vladimir Stasov lamented it – in the Lermontovish title to an article written in the aftermath of a fire that destroyed all the scenic and musical materials of the first production, including the autograph full score – as 'A Martyr of Our Time' (more commonly it was referred to as Glinka's *chose manquée*, after an early, influential review by Rafail Zotov). For most, especially in the West, *Ruslan and Lyudmila* has never meant more than a Proms overture (plus, for record collectors, Farlaf's rondo as performed by Shalyapin). But for epicures of the Russian musical stage – and especially for the generations of composers who mined it indefatigably – it has always been (as one of the miners, Tchaikovsky, put it) 'the Tsar of operas'.

It was possibly in response to his swarm of captious critics that Glinka, in his memoirs, had Pushkin vow that he would change a great deal in his youthful poem when it came to transposing it to the musical stage. The aesthetic gulf between the poet's lively, laconic *jeu d'esprit* and Glinka's opulent, slow-moving opera is extreme, going far beyond the oft-reported (and oft-decried) modifications in the plot. (Characters, including another rival suitor, Rogdai, were removed wholesale; Gorislava was added; most of Pushkin's motley anecdotal content, including a vast battle scene, was pruned away; in compensation, practically the whole *ruses d'amour* intrigue in Act 3 was freshly invented.) Pushkin's racy parody of Ariosto *à la russe* was taken seriously, treated on the one hand universally, as metaphor (the 'Slavonic liturgy of Eros,' in Asaf'yev's inspired phrase, symbolizing the life of the heart), on the other 'Ossianically', as national treasure (i.e. as a *bïlina*, a song of ancient bards such as were just then being avidly collected and published by folklorists like Ivan Sakharov, who christened the genre). The result was the quintessential Russian Romantic opera, and the only Romantic opera by a Russian worthy of comparison with the European masterpieces of the genre.

ACT 1 *The luxurious assembly hall of the Grand Prince of Kiev: a wedding feast in progress* Svetozar is giving his daughter Lyudmila to the knight Ruslan. Among the guests are Ratmir and Farlaf, Lyudmila's rejected suitors. All listen to Bayan's vatic song, foretelling sore trials followed by renewed happiness won through the strength of love. All sing the praises of the bridal pair and toast Svetozar. Bayan strikes up another song ('Yest' pustïnnïy kray': 'There is a desert land') about a young singer whose lot it is to sing the fame of Ruslan and Lyudmila (Glinka intended this song as a memorial to Pushkin). Lyudmila sings farewell to her father and to her former suitors (cavatina, 'Grustno mne, roditel' dorogoy': 'I am sad, dear father'). Svetozar blesses the nuptial pair, who are then led off to the wedding bed. The chorus sings an epithalamium to Lel', the Slavonic god of love, in the quintuple metre of traditional Russian wedding songs. All at once a thunderclap is heard and the hall is plunged in darkness; with a flash of lightning Chernomor abducts Lyudmila. When the darkness dissipates, all are frozen in a strange thraldom, about which they sing in turn over a pedal. When they come to their senses, all are dismayed at Lyudmila's disappearance. Svetozar promises her hand and half his kingdom to whomever shall rescue her. Ruslan, Ratmir and Farlaf run off in pursuit, egged on by the chorus of guests.

ACT 2.i *Finn's mountain cave* Finn greets Ruslan and reveals to him the name of Chernomor, his malefactor. In a lengthy ballad based on a Finnish melody Glinka had recorded in situ, Finn recounts the story of his unhappy courtship of Naina. He indicates to Ruslan that good fortune lies to the north.

2.ii *A thicket* Farlaf meets a gnarled old lady and is horrified to learn she is Naina. She assures him of her help in defeating Ruslan and sends him home to await her call. Farlaf exults (rondo, 'Blizok uzh chas torzhestva moyego': 'My hour of triumph is near').

2.iii *Foggy night on a deserted battlefield strewn with fragments of weaponry: lances, shields, helmets, swords; also human remains* Ruslan enters, despondent. He has lost his sword and shield in battle; the prospect of the empty field fills him with intimations of failure and mortality, about which he sings the first part of his grandiose aria ('O pole, pole, kto tebya useyal myortvïmi kostyami?': 'O field, who has bestrewn thee with dead bones?'), but gloomy thoughts give way to renewed heroic aspirations as he reaches the faster section ('Day, Perun, bulatnïy mech v ruke': 'Grant me, O Perun, a damask sword to hand'). As the morning fog dissipates, he sees before him the enormous Head of a sleeping giant. The Head (represented by a unison male chorus) awakens and tries to blow Ruslan down. Angered, Ruslan strikes the Head with his lance. The Head, beaten, gives up its sword to Ruslan, thus answering his prayer. 'But who are you, and whose sword is this?' asks Ruslan; whereupon the Head launches into its narrative ('Nas bïlo dvoye, brat moy i ya': 'We were two, my brother and I'), from which Ruslan learns that the Head's brother is none other than Chernomor, that all of Chernomor's strength is in his enormous beard and that the sword he now holds is Chernomor's own, the only weapon that can defeat him.

ACT 3 *Naina's magic castle* To distract Ratmir from his quest, Naina sets her magical slave girls singing a Persian song to enchant him ('Lozhitsya v pole mrak nochnoy': 'The dark of night settles over the plain'). Gorislava, abandoned by Ratmir, enters and bewails her fate (cavatina, 'Lyubvi roskoshnaya zvezda': 'O splendid star of love'). Ratmir enters, exhausted from his long journey (aria with english horn obbligato, 'I zhar, i znoy smenila nochi ten'': 'Sultry heat has supplanted shade of night'); the magical maidens awaken memories of his harem (tempo di valse, 'Chudnïy son zhivoy lyubvi': 'Marvellous vision of love astir'). With their dancing the magical maidens plunge Ratmir into a stupor in which he forgets Lyudmila; Gorislava, too, finds him oblivious. Ruslan now wanders in, lured by Naina. Transfixed by Gorislava he too forgets Lyudmila, to Naina's delight. But Finn appears and dispels the charms. The magical maidens disappear, the magic castle turns into a forest, Ruslan is ready to continue his quest, and Ratmir finds his true love in Gorislava.

ACT 4 *Chernomor's magic gardens; in the distance a river* Lyudmila is tormented by her bondage and by thoughts of Ruslan. She tries to throw herself in the river but the watersprites restrain her. She answers their blandishments with scorn and refuses to submit to Chernomor (aria, 'Vdali ot milogo v nevole': 'Far from my beloved and constrained'). The sorcerer's suite passes by to the strains of a grotesque march, which gives way to a trio of oriental dances – Turkish, Arabian, Caucasian (the 'Lezginka') – with which Chernomor's subjects entertain their master. Military signals announce the arrival of Ruslan. The dwarf entrances Lyudmila and goes off to do battle. The chorus narrates its progress. Ruslan emerges triumphant, accompanied by Ratmir and Gorislava; with the magic sword he has cut off Chernomor's beard. But now he finds to his horror that he cannot awaken Lyudmila. Together with his companions and the whole liberated suite of Chernomor, he speeds homeward.

ACT 5.i *Moonlit steppe* Ratmir, standing watch over the caravan by night, sings of his reawakened love for Gorislava (romance, 'Ona mne zhizn', ona mne radost'': 'She is life and joy to me'). The former slaves of Chernomor rush in with terrible news: Lyudmila has been abducted again and Ruslan has gone in pursuit. Finn materializes and explains that Farlaf has stolen her and is bringing her home to claim her from Svetozar. Finn gives Ratmir a magic ring that alone can awaken Lyudmila from her trance. (Ratmir presumably over-

'Ruslan and Lyudmila' (Glinka), Act 3 (Naina's magic castle): design by Andrey Adamovich Roller for the original production at the Bol'shoy Theatre, St Petersburg, 27 November/9 December 1842

takes Ruslan and gives him the ring; this is neither shown nor related.)

5.ii *Svetozar's assembly hall; Lyudmila is stretched out on a bridal bed at rear, surrounded by her father, Farlaf, courtiers, slave girls, nurses and wet-nurses, striplings, bodyguards, troops, crowd* There is a chorus of lamentation: 'Akh tï, svet Lyudmila, probudis', prosnisya!' ('Lovely Lyudmila, come to, awaken!'). Farlaf, unable to rouse her despite Naina's help, cowers. From the distance hoofbeats are heard. Ruslan, Ratmir and Gorislava rush in; Farlaf flees. Ruslan awakens Lyudmila with the ring. The hall resounds with rejoicing: the wedding feast is resumed as the walls fall away to reveal a panorama of ancient Kiev and a throng joins in the celebration.

* * *

The dilatory, seemingly cluttered action, which has occasioned so much critical impatience, is actually a magnificently calculated embodiment of what Mikhail Bakhtin was later to call the epic chronotope: 'closed like a circle, with everything in it totally finished and complete'. On all levels, time is rounded: the outer acts, set in Kiev, frame the magic quest with a single action (a wedding feast interrupted and resumed), in which all the music resonates thematically with Bayan's opening incantation of Pushkin's immortal first couplet: 'Dela davno minuvshikh dney/Predan'ya starinï glubokoy' ('Deeds of long since vanished days/Tales of yore profound'). The overture (written last, during rehearsals) adumbrates the music of the Act 5 finale and provides a musical frame; this cyclic effect is replicated in later acts by the use of entr'actes that quote the respective act finales. The resulting spacious, enclosed, quasi-palindromic structure became a hallmark of Russian opera, applying even to works, like *Boris Godunov*, that on the surface seem far less formal and more conventionally dramatic. (Its applicability to such avowedly 'epic' works as *Prince Igor* and *Sadko* is of course self-evident.) 'Epic time' applies on the level of single numbers as well: Glinka's forms are extremely ample, yet rarely teleological on the sonata or symphonic model (Ruslan's heroic aria being the chief exception). The preferred *modus operandi* is that of 'ostinato variations' ('Glinka variations', as they are called in Russia), in which a melody is repeated with little essential change, while harmony, tonality and tone colour conspire to work a series of 'magic transformations' around it (as in Finn's ballad, the Head's narrative, the Persian chorus, the Act 5 finale). The appropriateness of such a technique to an opera about sorcery is obvious.

Sorcery of a harmonic kind was perhaps the opera's most enduring legacy. Glinka established a convention that lasted at least to the time of *Firebird* and *Petrushka*, whereby human characters are represented by diatonic music and supernatural ones by chromatic. The nature of his chromaticism – involving what are now called interval cycles (circles of major and minor 3rds), scales formed by inserting passing notes into such cycles, and common-tone progressions – remained a potent influence on the Russian harmonic imagination for generations to come (again, up to early Stravinsky). The harmony underpinning the line in which Naina reveals herself to Farlaf, plus the harmonization of the whole-tone bass line (often called 'Chernomor's leitmotif') in the Act 4 fight chorus, will suffice to suggest its extent (ex.1). Glinka's open-voiced, primary-hued 'fantastic' orchestration was, through Rimsky-Korsakov, equally influential. Some of his textures and combinations were routinely appropriated by later composers and became generically 'Russian'. (A case in point is the use of piano and harp in tandem to represent Bayan's *gusli* in the introduction, of which the last echo was heard exactly a century later in Stravinsky's Symphony in Three Movements.)

Finally, no inventory of *Ruslan and Lyudmila* as quarry can omit its abundance of vivid national colours, particularly 'oriental' ones that were a veritable craze during the brief Russian Romantic period – a craze that was an immediate consequence of the early 19th-century military expansion into the Caucasus and 'Central Asia'. Glinka's Ratmir is the very embodiment of oriental *nega* (erotic languor – which, once established, could be as aptly expressed in a waltz as in any

Ex.1

(a) Act 2 scene ii, bars 139–42

['I am the sorceress Naina']

(b) Act 4, chorus (*Pogibnet*), orchestral part

more authentically Eastern genre), and the archetype for a host of copies culminating in Borodin's Konchakovna (*Prince Igor*) and ending in Rimsky-Korsakov's Queen of Shemakha (*The Golden Cockerel*, 1908). But like harmonic and orchestral colour, national colour in *Ruslan and Lyudmila* is prodigally variegated: besides the colours of the 'Russian orient', the score luxuriates in tunes of Persian, Turkish and Finnish extraction; and there are also powerful residual whiffs of the italianate: *buffo* in the case of Farlaf's rondo, serious in the numbers of the noble characters with their elaborate sequences of tempos – and of course in Lyudmila's coloratura, the summit of virtuosity in the Russian operatic repertory. RICHARD TARUSKIN

Russ, Giannina (*b* Lodi, 27 March 1878; *d* Milan, 26 Feb 1951). Italian soprano. She studied the piano and singing at the Milan Conservatory and appeared first in 1903 at a strikingly successful concert in Milan. Her stage début at Bologna that year was as Mimì, followed by Amelia (*Ballo*). *Semiramide*, *Nabucco* and *Les vêpres siciliennes* proved her versatility and tested her technical skill, but when she appeared at Covent Garden in 1904 as Aida she was criticized for 'persistent tremolo' and a voice 'not of sympathetic quality except when singing softly'. Her La Scala début (1905) was more successful, and she became one of Italy's leading dramatic sopranos. Her repertory now included Elisabeth (*Tannhäuser*), Donna Anna (*Don Giovanni*) and Norma. Abroad she enjoyed considerable success in Buenos Aires, though rather less with Hammerstein's Manhattan Company, where her performances were admired more for their artistry than for the voice production, which was uneven; her best singing seems to have been as Valentine in *Les Huguenots*. She retired in 1918 after she had reappeared at La Scala in Rossini's *Mosè in Egitto*. Her many recordings show why she was found more congenial in Italy than in England, but there is no mistaking the temperament, the imagination and the frequent attractiveness of her voice. J. B. STEANE

Russell, Henry (*b* London, 14 Nov 1871; *d* London, 11 Oct 1937). English singing teacher and impresario, son of the composer-singer of the same name and brother of the conductor Landon Ronald. After attempting to become a singer he succeeded as a teacher, helping Eleonora Duse, among others. At the request of the manager of the S Carlo opera house in Naples he mounted a Covent Garden season in 1904 (using the S Carlo name) for the soprano Rina Giachetti, supported by some of the finest male singers of the day; however, this failed, as did a 1905 season of operas and plays with Duse. Russell then organized gruelling 'San Carlo Opera Company' tours of the USA, first of *Don Pasquale* with his mistress, Alice Nielsen, then a more ambitious one with the failing Lillian Nordica and the tenor Florencio Constantino. This led to his being invited by a Boston backer to become the manager of the new Boston Opera House, which he ran with fair success from its opening in 1909 until its dissolution in 1914, when he returned to London.

The Times (9 and 10 Feb 1897)
Il mondo artistico [Milan] (1 April 1907), 4–5
H. Russell: *The Passing Show* (London, 1926)
Q. Eaton: *The Boston Opera Company* (New York, 1965)

JOHN ROSSELLI

Russell, Ken (*b* Southampton, 3 July 1927). British film and stage director. He began his career as a photographer, then became a director for the BBC, making several programmes on music including studies of Delius, Debussy, Elgar and Strauss and a programme with Lotte Lenya. After successes with feature films, he directed a film of The Who's rock opera *Tommy* (1974). His first stage opera direction was of *The Rake's Progress* in Florence (1982), followed by Zimmermann's *Die Soldaten* in Lyons and *Madama Butterfly* in Spoleto (both 1983), *La bohème* in Macerata, *Faust* and *L'italiana in Algeri* in Geneva (all 1984) and Boito's *Mefistofele* in Genoa (1987). Deliberately provocative and always controversial, Russell nevertheless has a wide knowledge of music and theatre which has made him one of the most influential directors of recent times. He has claimed that for him opera is 'the last believable religion'.

P. O'Connor: 'A Hot Medium', *ON*, xlix/10 (1984–5), 30, 31, 42
K. Russell: *A British Picture* (London, 1989)

PATRICK O'CONNOR

Russell, Lillian [Leonard, Helen Louise] (*b* Clinton, IA, 4 Dec 1861; *d* Pittsburgh, 5 June 1922). American soprano and actress. She studied with Leopold Damrosch, then went on to become pre-eminent in American musical theatre. She made her début in the chorus in *HMS Pinafore* in 1879, then attracted attention in other Gilbert and Sullivan productions and in Audran stagings by Tony Pastor. Between 1881 and 1899 she starred in two dozen musicals, many written expressly as vehicles for her limpid, lyrical voice. Among the shows in which she appeared were *Polly* (1885),

Pepita (1886), *Princess Nicotine* (1893) and *An American Beauty* (1896). None of the musicals written for her nor the songs she introduced are remembered today, but she remains a legend among theatre cognoscenti.

*

P. Morell: *Lillian Russell* (New York, 1940) GERALD BORDMAN

Russia. The present article covers opera in Russia itself and touches on opera in the Central Asian and the Transcaucasian republics, which had close links with Russian opera during the Soviet period. The operatic traditions of other former Soviet republics are considered separately (*see* ESTONIA, LATVIA, LITHUANIA and UKRAINE).

Except for a brief interlude between 1882 and 1917, opera in Russia has always been a state-run enterprise. Its fortunes have perhaps been more directly dependent on the vagaries of government than in any other country.

1. 18th century. 2. 19th century. 3. 20th century.

1. 18TH CENTURY. Opera was first imported to Russia as a court entertainment under the three empresses whose reigns, with minor interruptions, encompassed most of the 18th century: Anne [Anna Ioannovna] (1730–40), Elizabeth [Yelizaveta Petrovna] (1741–61) and Catherine [Yekaterina] II, known as Catherine the Great (1762–96). The first troupe to visit the newly opened, eagerly europeanizing empire to the east was a group of 24 Italian comedians and singers from the Dresden court of Friedrich August I, directed by G. A. Ristori. The latter's comic opera *Calandro*, given in Moscow on 30 November/11 December 1731, has the distinction of being the first opera performed on Russian soil. St Petersburg got its first taste of Italian music theatre two years later, in the form of several intermezzos (including *L'impresario delle Isole Canarie*, a parody of the as yet unseen *opera seria*) in the repertory of a *commedia dell'arte* troupe resident in the Russian capital from 1733 to 1735.

In the latter year Anne sent the violinist Pietro Mira to Venice to recruit an Italian opera troupe for permanent establishment in St Petersburg. The 26-year-old Francesco Araia was engaged as *maestro di capella*. The company arrived in time to stage Araia's *La forza dell'amore e dell'odio* at the Winter Palace on the empress's birthday, 29 January/9 February 1736. Over the next two decades Araia produced 11 *opere serie* for the Russian court, mostly in collaboration with Giuseppe Bonecchi, the resident librettist, but in one celebrated case – *Tsefal i Prokris* ('Cephalus and Procris'), performed by a native (serf) cast on 27 February/10 March 1755 – to a Russian text by the Empress Elizabeth's court poet Alexander Sumarokov (one aria printed in Ginzburg 1968–70, i, 446; excerpts from four others in Keldïsh and others, *Istoriya russkoy muzïki*, ii).

The other extant *opera seria* to a Russian libretto by Sumarokov is *Al'tsesta* ('Alceste') by H. F. Raupach, who briefly succeeded Araia as *maestro di capella*, serving from 1759 to 1762. Thereafter the post of court composer at St Petersburg was occupied by a distinguished succession: Vincenzo Manfredini (1762–5), Baldassare Galuppi (1765–8), Tommaso Traetta (1768–75), Giovanni Paisiello (1776–83), Giuseppe Sarti (1784–1801, with interruptions), Domenico Cimarosa (1787–91) and Vicente Martín y Soler (1790–1804, with interruptions). At its height under Catherine, the court opera rivalled the best opera theatres in Europe and saw the premières of some major works, notably Paisiello's *Il barbiere di Siviglia* (15/26 September 1782). Two native composers, Dmitry Bortnyansky and Maxim Berezovsky, were sent in the late 1760s (probably after apprenticeship with Galuppi) to complete their studies in Italy; the *opere serie* they composed there were successfully performed, making them the earliest Russian opera composers. As these operas were performed only in Italy, however, they do not properly belong to the history of opera in Russia.

Alongside the exalted court opera, visiting opera troupes of a more popular kind plied their trade in both Russian capitals, beginning with that of the impresario Giovanni Battista Locatelli, who from 1757 presented *opere buffe* (chiefly Goldoni-Galuppi, but also by Domenico Fischietti and others, some on Locatelli's own librettos) to paying audiences in a theatre near the summer palace at Peterhof, later (from 1759) in Moscow as well. In 1763, Catherine licensed him to open a private theatre called Krasnïy Kabak ('The Pretty Tavern'), which he operated for the next 20 years.

French comic opera was also imported, and was especially significant as the model for the earliest native essays in musical drama. A ukase decreeing the recruitment of a French opera troupe, dated 9/20 September 1762, was among Catherine the Great's earliest acts on her accession to the throne. The troupe, directed by Jean-Pierre Renaud, made its début on 26 September/7 October 1764 with Philidor's *Le maréchal ferrant*; by the end of their first season they had performed works by Egidio Duni, Monsigny, P. C. Gibert (*Soliman second, ou Les trois sultanes*) and others. On 3/14 January 1765 the troupe performed *Annette et Lubin*, C.-S. Favart's famous *comédie mêlée d'ariettes*, with the tunes scored by Adolfe Benoit Blaise. This piece, which became a favourite item for amateur aristocratic performance at court, was the inevitable prototype for *Anyuta*, the earliest Russian-language Singspiel. A one-act comedy of mistaken identity (peasant girl turns out to be a lady) by Mikhail Popov with little airs set by an unknown composer to popular tunes (*golosï* in Russian; cf. Fr. *timbres*), *Anyuta* was performed by members of the court opera troupe at Tsarskoye selo, Catherine's summer residence, on 26 August/6 September 1772. The music is lost. (The europeanized Bortnyansky wrote aristocratic *opéras comiques*, to actual French librettos, as entertainments for Catherine's estranged son, the future Emperor Paul.)

The line initiated by *Anyuta* was quickly taken up by the burgeoning public theatres of Moscow and St Petersburg, which sponsored the earliest Russian comic operas that have come down to us with music intact: *Pererozhdeniye* ('The Rebirth') by Dementy Alexeyevich Zorin, performed in Moscow in January 1777, and the very popular *Mel'nik – koldun, obmanshchik i svat* ('The Miller who was a Wizard, a Cheat and a Matchmaker'), to a libretto, much indebted to Rousseau's *Le devin du village*, by Alexander Ablesimov, and with the tunes scored by Mikhail Matveyevich Sokolovsky, a violinist at Michael Maddox's theatre in Moscow, where it was first performed in January 1779. In keeping with the subject, the score included a depiction of the *devichnik*, the Russian bridal party, which remained a ubiquitous and distinguishing feature of Russian comic operas and Singspiels right up to the time of Glinka, who gave the old stereotype an inspired tragic twist in *A*

Life for the Tsar.

Also very influential on the rise of Russian opera were the *comédies larmoyantes* of Michel-Jean Sedaine, imitated by the famous poet and tragedian Yakov Knyazhnin in three librettos which were set to music between 1779 and 1781 by Vasily Alexeyevich Pashkevich, an apprentice of Manfredini's who was active both at Catherine's court and in the public theatres of St Petersburg. Pashkevich gave evidence of his Italian training in *Skupoy* ('The Miser', 1781), which contains a lengthy accompanied recitative for the title character, virtually unique for its time and place. His most ambitious score, *Sanktpeterburgskiy gostinnïy dvor* ('The St Petersburg Bazaar', 1782, revised 1792), to a libretto by Mikhail Matinsky, contains an especially celebrated *devichnik* scene, a suite of seven folksongs arranged for women's chorus and an orchestra that cleverly imitates the sounds of peasant instruments.

Two of the most characteristic Russian Singspiels of the late 18th century were composed by visiting foreigners. Raupach, the former *maestro di capella*, returned to Russia after a long absence and scored a hit with *Dobrïye soldatï* ('The Good Soldiers'), which held the stage for close to 50 years beginning in 1779. The record for longevity, however, was set by *Sbiten'shchik* ('The Hot-Mead Vendor'), a kind of *Figaro*-à-la-russe by Knyazhnin, with music by the French bassoonist Antoine Bullant. First performed at court in 1784, it was still current in provincial repertory past the middle of the 19th century.

A special court genre was the Russian fairy-tale opera, created by Catherine the Great herself as moral instruction for her grandsons, the future Tsars Alexander I and Nicholas I. Three of her librettos were set by Pashkevich (two in collaboration with the Italian maestros); the remaining pair were respectively assigned to a Czech charlatan named Arnošt Vančura and to the Italian-trained Yevstigney Fomin, arguably the finest Russian composer of dramatic music in the 18th century. Another opera by Fomin, the one-act *Yamshchiki na podstave* ('Postal Coachmen at the Relay Station', 1787) in which Catherine herself is invoked as *deus ex machina* (though of course she does not appear), begins with a pair of extraordinarily developed choruses based on melismatic folksongs supplied to the composer by his librettist, the outstanding folklore connoisseur Nikolay L'vov. Fomin's most successful work, *Amerikantsï* ('The Americans', composed 1788), was written to a libretto modelled on Sedaine's *Le déserteur*.

It is important to emphasize the French roots of early Russian comic opera, because the humble social milieu the genre often depicted (very much in accordance with the imported model) entailed a reliance on peasant dialect and vernacular music that has been widely misinterpreted by historians as evidence of the 'nationalism' one expects to find in anything Russian. Only the folksong choruses by Pashkevich and Fomin, which did sound a new and distinctive note in European musical theatre, can be so regarded; but as cultural historians have demonstrated, Russia's consciousness of 'national character' itself arose in the first instance as a by-product of westernization. Otherwise, the genre reflected Russia's brief flicker of Enlightenment.

2. 19TH CENTURY. Early in the reign of Alexander I, in 1803, the public theatres of Russia were reorganized under a crown monopoly that endured until 1882. Four public theatres were established in St Petersburg: Italian, Russian, French and German, of which only the Italian, housed in a newly built theatre, the Novïy Malïy Teatr (New Little Theatre), was to be exclusively for operas. Catterino Cavos (1775–1840), a Venetian who had been on the staff of the Imperial Theatres since 1798, was named its director, and also put in charge of opera and ballet spectacles at the Bol'shoy Kamennïy Teatr (Great Stone Theatre), the Russian-language house. The French company, which performed for the public at the Bol'shoy Kamennïy, and for the court at the Hermitage and at Peterhof, was the most fashionable of the four, with a repertory of *opéras comiques*, 'rescue operas', and vaudevilles by Dalayrac, Grétry, Isouard, Méhul, Catel and Cherubini (and one Russian, Alexey Nikolayevich Titov). At its helm were luminaries like Boieldieu, Didelot and Daniel Steibelt. It lasted only until the outbreak of war with Napoleon. The Italian theatre, with a superannuated repertory of *opera buffa*, folded as early as 1807, but Cavos stayed on at the Russian, where he formed a fruitful creative partnership with Alexander Shakhovskoy, the Intendant, and became to all intents and purposes a Russian composer. Between 1805 and 1825 he turned out some 18 operas on subjects – historical, magical, oriental – that reflected the brief and belated high tide of Romanticism in Russia. Meanwhile, the Moscow Bol'shoy Theatre became the centre of a furious output of so-called 'opera-vaudevilles' – situation comedies, often borrowed from the French, with elaborate overtures and simple vocal numbers meant for actors rather than real singers to perform. Alexander Alyab'yev and Alexey Verstovsky were the most prolific practitioners of this genre. Verstovsky, who worked his way up to the post of 'inspector of theatres' in Moscow, eventually turned his hand to romantic opera. *Askol'dova mogila* ('Askold's Grave', 1835), the most successful of his six essays in the genre, remained a popular repertory item throughhout the century.

The bulk of the repertory of the Russian theatres remained non-Russian throughout this period. Russian composers were few, for the simple reason that there was no professional training in composition to be had in Russia. And they were officially despised. A schedule of payments instituted under Nicholas I in 1827 shows an outrageous discrimination against the work of indigenous composers. Despite the sporadic efforts of visiting Italian troupes – including the one directed by Luigi Zamboni, the first Figaro, which brought a massive dose of Rossini to Moscow and St Petersburg between 1829 and 1831 – the Russian public remained loyal to the French repertory and its slavish Russian imitations. (For Italian opera one had to go to the Black Sea port of Odessa, where a house devoted exclusively to it operated from 1809 to 1855.)

The year 1836 was a doubly critical one for opera in Russia. The more familiar reason for its importance, celebrated in all histories of Russian music, was the première of Glinka's *A Life for the Tsar*, hailed immediately by contemporaries like Gogol as 'a wonderful beginning', and by historians, in the apt words of Yury Keldïsh, as 'the boundary between the past and the future'. What so distinguished Glinka's opera from all its predecessors was, in the first instance, its technical command. This was the first grandly scaled opera with continuous music ever written by a Russian to a Russian text. It was sonorously scored, boasted a sophisticated thematic structure, and showed a mastery of contemporary international operatic styles and con-

'A Life for the Tsar' (Glinka), Act 4: engraving by L. Seryakov (after K. Brozh) showing the final scene in a production of c1850

ventions that would reach the level of real virtuosity in Glinka's second opera, *Ruslan and Lyudmila* (1842). At the same time, *A Life for the Tsar* managed to integrate the Russian national idiom into the stuff of the drama to an extent that amazed contemporaries, Prince Vladimir Odoyevsky writing that Glinka had proved that 'Russian melody ... may be raised to the level of tragedy' – a condition to which no previous Russian opera, whatever its quotient of Russianness, had ever aspired.

The other outstanding event of 1836, far less celebrated in nationalistic history, was the triumphant production of Rossini's *Semiramide* by the Russian troupe under Cavos's baton, and with the contralto Anna Vorob'yova scoring a sensational success as Arsace. The Russian artists accomplished what the Italians themselves had failed to do since the beginning of the century: they created a rage for contemporary Italian opera in Russia. The tsar was quick to exploit it, to the dire detriment of Russian opera, by establishing a permanent Italian opera troupe in St Petersburg (from 1843, at first under the direction of Giovanni Battista Rubini). The Russian opera company was ousted from the Bol'shoy, and the Italian company moved in. For several years in the middle of the 19th century, the Russian capital had no Russian opera company, only an Italian one.

At a stroke, Tsar Nicholas I had made his capital one of the operatic centres of Europe, on a par with Paris, Vienna and London; and he had identified himself in the eyes of the world as an enlightened despot. These must be understood as his objectives. Much has been made, especially by Soviet historians, of the tyrant's scorn for all things Russian; and it is true that, among the 'enlightened' aristocracy of the period (and not only in Russia), a 'national' style could only mean an uncultivated style. Yet mere snobbery or (to use a Soviet term) 'anti-populism' cannot explain so hugely expensive an enterprise. It was first and foremost a diplomatic move. And, in a way that can only look perverse if approached (as it usually is) from anachronistic vantage points, it was a patriotic venture as well.

In any case, for two decades and more the Imperial Italian opera in St Petersburg was unmatched anywhere for opulence and prestige. Viardot, Castellan, Tamburini, Erminia Frezzolini, Lorenzo Salvi, G. M. Mario and Giulia Grisi were St Petersburg regulars. Tamberlik first tried out his high C♯ before the Russian audience. There were even Italian virtuosos whose entire careers were made in Russia, notably the soprano Angiolina Bosio and the tenor Enrico Calzolari. The peak was reached with the première of *La forza del destino* in 1862; but that much-heralded event unexpectedly became the pinprick that burst the bubble. Not only did the opera disappoint, but widespread public outcry at the extravagance of the production at a difficult time for the nation (then recovering from the Crimean War and coming to grips with the consequences of Tsar Alexander II's emancipation of the serfs) undermined the Italian opera's prestige. While the phenomenon of Adelina Patti vouchsafed it a brief resurgence in the 1870s, the company went into a decline, closing its doors in 1885. The Bol'shoy Theatre was razed and rebuilt as the St Petersburg (Leningrad) Conservatory.

Meanwhile, the fortunes of the Russian opera

company had been on an upswing exactly corresponding to the Italian company's decline. During the dark period from 1843 to 1859 only one Russian opera of importance, Dargomïzhsky's *Rusalka*, had been produced (1856). A fire that destroyed the Circus Theatre in St Petersburg, to which the company had been consigned after a four-year 'exile' in Moscow, was a blessing in disguise. A marvellous theatre (the Mariinsky, called the Kirov during the Soviet era) was constructed on the same site in 1860, and Alexander II was interested in fostering native talent. The ensuing decade saw a great wave of new opportunities for Russian musicians, including the means of their education and professional recognition. The rehabilitation of the Russian opera was part of this wave.

By then, treatment as second-class citizens had led many Russian autodidact composers, notably Dargomïzhsky and the emergent circle around Balakirev, into a militantly maverick, 'reformist' stance, which achieved most extreme expression in Dargomïzhsky's notorious 'anti-opera', *The Stone Guest*, as well as such early declamatory works of Musorgsky as the unfinished *Marriage* and the first version of *Boris Godunov*. The dominant figure on the Russian operatic scene in the 1860s was Alexander Serov, a high-minded critic who modelled his principles, if not his actual musical style, on Wagner's example. The huge success he enjoyed with *Yudif'* ('Judith') (1863) and especially *Rogneda* (1865) proved that Russian opera could command a wide and appreciative audience in Russia. Anton Rubinstein, meanwhile, was proving that Russian composers could compete successfully on the world stage. His *Feramors* (1863), after Thomas Moore's *Lalla Rookh*, was a German repertory piece, and his *Die Maccabäer* (1875) achieved repertory status both at home and abroad. The Balakirev circle, by then known as the Mighty Kuchka ('little heap'), made its operatic début in 1869 with César Cui's *William Ratcliff*, after Heine.

By the 1870s, the invidious pay scale that discriminated against native composers was revoked and the composers whose works now form the backbone of the 'classical' Russian repertory were active. During that decade, interest focussed primarily on two genres: historical costume drama (Musorgsky's *Boris Godunov* and *Khovanshchina*, Rimsky-Korsakov's *Maid of Pskov*, Tchaikovsky's *Oprichnik*) and 'Little-Russian' (Ukrainian) peasant comedy after Gogol (Musorgsky's *Fair at Sorochintsï*, Rimsky-Korsakov's *May Night*, Tchaikovsky's *Vakula the Smith*, later revised as *Cherevichki*). The historical genre foundered, in part because of the censorship. In the following decades Rimsky-Korsakov came to specialize in folk-fantastic subjects (*The Snow Maiden*, *Mlada*, *Sadko*, *The Tale of Tsar Saltan*, *The Legend of the Invisible City of Kitezh*), culminating in the parodistic *Golden Cockerel*, which revived the social criticism of his civic-minded youth in the form of a parable (the censor was alert, however, and the opera was produced only posthumously). Tchaikovsky, both in operas and ballets, cultivated and helped define the lavish imperial style of the Alexander III period (*Maid of Orléans*, *Mazepa*, *The Enchantress*). He reached his creative peak in his essays in psychological realism (*Yevgeny Onegin*) and surrealism (*The Queen of Spades*). The epic line of *Ruslan and Lyudmila* was revived by Borodin in *Prince Igor*, completed after his death by Rimsky-Korsakov and Glazunov.

Native composers, particularly Rimsky-Korsakov, were much benefited by Alexander III's abrogation of the crown monopoly on theatres in 1882. Private enterprises, especially that of the railway tycoon Savva Mamontov (who patronized all the arts) sponsored adventurous new operas and also encouraged leading painters to collaborate in their productions, paving the way toward the 'Slavonic *Gesamtkunstwerk*' ideal that sparked the Dyagilev enterprise. Fyodor Shalyapin, the first Russian opera singer to make a stellar international career, had his start in Mamontov's company, and made his Western début in Dyagilev's sensational production of *Boris Godunov* at the Paris Opéra in 1908, for which Musorgsky's opera was specially refurbished by Rimsky-Korsakov. (In 1913 Dyagilev presented *Khovanshchina*, refurbished by Ravel and Stravinsky.)

Ironically, it was another merchant patron, Mitrofan Belyayev, who through his lavish maecenas activities put something of a brake on Russian opera in the last decade of the 19th century and the first decade of the 20th. He favoured instrumental music over vocal, and was able to offer such magnificent emoluments to the composers he sponsored as to almost singlehandedly bring about what was jocularly known as the 'Brahms phase' of Russian music. Several Belyayev-sponsored composers (Lyadov, Glazunov, Skryabin) wrote no operas at all. Opera was also a relatively minor portion of Rakhmaninov's output (three one-act works), as it was of Taneyev's (one opera, admittedly grand: *Oresteya*, 'The Oresteia').

3. 20TH CENTURY. As in the case of literature, the wave of emigration that followed the Revolution and the Bolshevik coup in 1917 divided Russian musical culture into 'Russia at home' and 'Russia abroad'. Yet it is obvious that the émigré community could hardly support opera, which demands major institutional backing, the way it could support literature; and so Russian composers abroad found it necessary to assimilate into their host communities far more than the writers did, or else come home. There were prominent examples of both manoeuvres.

The greatest figure in Russia abroad was Stravinsky, who, although the son of an opera star, was relatively cool to the lyric stage. In part this was because of his commitment to ballet, the genre through which he made his extraordinary early impact as a 'Dyagilev composer'. Later it was because of a professed distaste for the Wagnerian 'music drama', the lapsed opera of modernity, which he saw as incompatible with the ideals of neo-classicism he espoused between the world wars. With the exception of *Oedipus Rex* (1928), a very static opera-oratorio, all the little operas and quasi-operas Stravinsky wrote before his emigration to America in 1939 count as minor works. *The Rake's Progress*, to a libretto by W. H. Auden and Chester Kallman, on the other hand, is not only a major Stravinsky opus but one of the very few major repertory operas to have appeared since the death of Puccini. By the time he wrote it, however, Stravinsky was so remote from his Russian background that, like the *opere serie* of Bortnyansky and Berezovsky, *The Rake* falls into the category of 'opera by a Russian' rather than 'Russian opera'.

The only other composer in 'Russia abroad' to write any operas of significance was Sergey Prokofiev, who, unlike Stravinsky, kept faith with the genre throughout his career, trying to modernize it rather than abandon it as outmoded. His idea of modernization was rather old-fashioned, deriving from the radical realism of

Dargomïzhsky and Musorgsky, especially as regards the nature of the libretto, for which he insisted on prose texts and a fast action that precluded a great deal of lyric soliloquy. It was a recipe for failure, as far as the public was concerned, and with two exceptions (or one and a half, to be precise) Prokofiev's operatic career was a career of frustration. The exceptions were *The Love for Three Oranges*, after Gozzi's *commedia dell'arte* scenario as mediated by V. Meyerhold, composed in New York to a Russian text but first performed in Chicago to a French one, and *War and Peace*, composed after his return to Russia (a return motivated in part by the fiasco of *The Fiery Angel*, an opera Prokofiev could not get produced), which was presented in complete form only posthumously, after a tremendous amount of bureaucratic interference that finally culminated in a ban.

The vicissitudes of *War and Peace* epitomize the problems faced by the composers of 'Russia at home', the composers of the Soviet Union. Opera became for them a somewhat risky undertaking. It was for an opera, *Lady Macbeth of the Mtsensk District*, that Shostakovich was denounced and mortally threatened in 1936 by *Pravda*, the chief organ of Soviet power (an experience that put a premature end to what would have surely been one of the great operatic careers). It was an opera, Vano Muradeli's *The Great Friendship*, that provided the pretext for the musical show trials of 1948 that led to the promulgation of the infamous Resolution on Music by the Central Committee of the Soviet Communist Party. It is not surprising, then, that a number of major Soviet composers (Myaskovsky and Khachaturyan among them) steered clear of the genre.

The most characteristic Soviet operas of the Stalinist period were those that somewhat anachronistically exploited the monumental resources of 19th-century theatres, like the Moscow Bol'shoy or the Kirov, on approved historical subjects, for example Yury Shaporin's *Decembrists* and Kostyantyn Dan'kevych's *Bohdan Khmel'nits'ky* (*Bogdan Khmelnitsky*), and those that, seemingly at the opposite extreme, cultivated petty forms in a populist spirit, playing for the most part in smaller houses like the Malïy Theatre in Leningrad and the Stanislavsky-Nemirovich-Danchenko Music Theatre in Moscow. In keeping with the principle (inherited not so much from Marxist as from Tolstoyan aesthetics) that accessibility vouchsafed authenticity, a genre known as 'song opera' (*pesennaya opera*) was developed in the 1930s, of which the best known representatives were *Quiet Flows the Don* by Ivan Dzerzhinsky and *V buryu* ('Into the Storm') by Tikhon Khrennikov. In these operas, which embodied the glorified portrayal of revolutionary events and Soviet society demanded by the doctrine of socialist realism, the musical idiom approximated to that of contemporary popular music and stylized folklore as epitomized in 'mass songs', march-like vehicles for the dissemination of proletarian ideology.

Another typical Soviet project involved the exportation of the Russian classical tradition to the newly formed Central Asian republics of the USSR. Typically, a Soviet composer of the older generation, steeped in the 19th-century heritage, would be commissioned to 'found' the operatic tradition of a Union republic, sometimes in collaboration with an indigenous composer, more often singlehandedly. Thus Sergey Nikiforovich Vasilenko (1872–1956), a Moscow composer who studied with Taneyev, created the first Uzbek opera (*Buran*, 1939) in collaboration with his own pupil Mukhtar Ashrafi (1912–75), a native of Bukhara. Yevgeny Grigor'yevich Brusilovsky (1905–81) was the founder of Kazakh opera, with *Kïz-Zhibek*, which inaugurated the Alma-Ata opera house in 1934. He was a pupil of Maximilian Shteynberg, Rimsky-Korsakov's son-in-law. For Tajik opera a somewhat younger composer was recruited: Sergey Artem'yevich Balasanian (1902–82), a pupil of Kabalevsky, whose *Vosstaniye Vose* ('Vose's Uprising'; *Shurishe Vose* in Tajik), to a Tajik libretto by A. Dekhoti and M. Tursun-zade inaugurated the opera house in Stalinabad (now Dushanbe) in 1939. The founder of Kirghiz opera was Alexander Moiseyevich Veprik (1899–1958), a pupil of Myaskovsky; his opera *Toktogul* (1940) inaugurated the opera house in Frunze (now Bishkek). Finally, the opera house in Ashkhabad, the capital of the Turkmen republic, opened in 1941 with the opera *Zokhre i Takhir* by Adrian Grigor'yevich Shaposhnikov (1887/8–1967), a pupil of Glazunov. Probably the best-known examples of this sort of musical colonialism are the operas *Shakh-Senem* (1927, Baku, in Russian; revised to an Azerbaijani libretto in 1934), *Gyul'sara* (1937, Tashkent) and *Leyli i Mejnun* (1940, Tashkent) by Reyngol'd Glier, for which the composer picked up the title of People's Artist from both the Azerbaijani and Uzbek republics. (Glier was a nearly exact contemporary of Vasilenko and, like him, a Taneyev pupil.) The Soviet Transcaucasian republics, unlike the Central Asian ones, had traditional links with Russian music extending to pre-revolutionary times; therefore their earliest operas were the work of native musicians (Hajibeyov, Paliashvili, Tigranyan, Spendiaryan) trained by Russians, in most cases in Moscow or St Petersburg.

In a country where, until very recently, all the theatres have been state theatres, experimental or nonconformist opera could hardly exist; Soviet opera in consequence was increasingly isolated and (until very recently) creatively sterile. Among Soviet composers who attracted interest in the late years of the Union, some, for example Sofiya Gubaydulina, have been conspicuously indifferent to opera. Al'fred Shnitke (*b* 1934) began his operatic career only after his *de facto* emigration to Germany (*Life with an Idiot*, 1992, Amsterdam). The main practitioners of the genre at home have been establishmentarian figures (e.g. Rodion Shchedrin or Alexander Kholminov) who have clung to safe subjects from canonical literature (for example *Dead Souls* by the former) or celebrations of political and military heroism (such as *Optimisticheskaya tragediya*, 'An Optimistic Tragedy', by the latter). On the rare occasions when post-Stalinist Soviet operas have been presented abroad (such as Kirill Molchanov's *Zori zdes' tikhiye*, 'The Dawns are Quiet Here', on a World War II theme, performed by the Bol'shoy in New York in 1975), they have tended to confound audiences and critics by their blatancy and dramatic naivety. The same isolation, however, has worked to the advantage of the Soviet operatic establishment's museum functions. As one Western critic put it of the same Bol'shoy tour, it showed that 'the troupe had preserved, in socialist aspic, the conventions and some of the power of grand opera performed in a big way, by a disciplined repertory company of serious operatic voices'.

Many of the fresher Soviet operas of the post-Stalin period have been written for chamber media, among them *Kentervil'skoye privedeniye* 'The Canterville

Ghost' (composed 1965–6), after Wilde, by Alexander Knayfel' (*b* 1943), which revives the satirical tradition of Shostakovich's *The Nose*. The breakdown of boundaries between traditional musical categories is apparent in a new brand of 'song opera', distinguished from its Stalinist predecessor both terminologically (*zong-opera* as opposed to *pesennaya opera*) and in its sonic and stylistic derivations from rock, a newer form of mass popular music. The best known examples of the genre are the two-act *Orfey i Evridika* by Alexander Zhurbin (libretto by Yury Dmitrin), performed at the Leningrad Maliy Theatre in 1976, and *'Yunona' i 'Avos'* ('The Juno and the Avos', 1979), a two-act 'opera-mysterium' by Alexey Ribnikov, to a libretto by the popular Soviet poet Andrey Voznesensky concerning the 18th-century trading voyages of Nikolay Rezanov to the New World.

It remains to be seen whether the 'restructuring' (*perestroyka*) instigated by Mikhail Gorbachev in the final years of the Soviet period, to say nothing of the catastrophic collapse of the Soviet empire, will revive Russian opera at home. There have been signs of life in some of the regional houses and in the new cooperative theatres that have sprung up in the wake of economic reform. The recent operas of Edison Denisov (*b* 1929), for example, have been presented at Perm' (*L'écume des jours*, first performed in Paris in 1986) and at the peripatetic Forum Theatre in Moscow (*Chetïre devushki*, 'Four Girls', 1990). *Muzïka dlya zhivïkh* ('Music for the Living', 1984), an allegorical opera with a polyglot libretto and an unconventional narrative structure by the Georgian composer Giya Kancheli (*b* 1935), was acclaimed not only in Tbilisi but in Germany in 1990. Among the youngest generation of Soviet-trained composers to achieve prominence, Dmitry Smirnov (*b* 1948), a pupil of Denisov, stands out for his eclectic visionary operas *Tiriel* (composed 1985; 1989, Freiburg) and *The Lamentations of Thel* (composed 1986; 1989, London), both after Blake. Smirnov's theatrical works have thus far been performed only outside Russia; like Shnitke, he may be inclining toward a resurgence of 'Russia abroad'.

For further information on operatic life in the country's principal centres *see* CHELYABINSK; GATCHINA; MOSCOW; NIZHNIY NOVGOROD; NOVOSIBIRSK; PERM'; ST PETERSBURG; SAMARA; SARATOV; TSARSKOYE SELO; UFA; ULAN-UDE; VORONEZH; and YEKATERINBURG. For information on opera in other former Soviet republics referred to in this article *see* ALMA-ATA; ASHKHABAD; BAKU; BISHKEK; DUSHANBE; EREVAN; KISHINEU; MINSK; TASHKENT; and TBILISI.

*

GENERAL

V. Cheshikhin: *Istoriya russkoy operï (s 1674 po 1903 g.)* (Moscow, 1905)
R. Newmarch: *The Russian Opera* (London, 1914)
G. Abraham: *Studies in Russian Music* (London, 1935)
——: *On Russian Music* (London, 1939)
E. Stark: *Peterburgskaya opera i yeyo mastera* (Leningrad, 1940)
R. Hofmann: *Un siècle d'opéra russe* (Paris, 1946)
M. Cooper: *Russian Opera* (London, 1951)
M. Druskin: *Voprosï muzïkal'noy dramaturgii operï* [Problems of Musical Dramaturgy in Opera] (Leningrad, 1952)
B. Yarustovsky: *Dramaturgiya russkoy opernoy klassiki* [The Dramaturgy of the Russian Opera Classics] (Moscow, 2/1953; Ger. trans., 1957)
B. Asaf'yev: *Izbrannïye trudï* [Selected Works], ed. T. N. Livanova and others (Moscow, 1953–7)
B. Kremnev, ed.: *Opernïye libretto* (Moscow, 1954)
A. A. Gozenpud: *Muzïkal'nïy teatr v Rossii ot istokov do Glinki* [Musical Theatre in Russia from its Origins up to Glinka] (Leningrad, 1959)
A. Solovtsov: *Kniga o russkoy opere* [The Book of Russian Opera] (Moscow, 1960)
G. B. Bernandt: *Slovar' oper* [Dictionary of Opera] (Moscow, 1962)
G. Abraham: *Slavonic and Romantic Music* (London, 1967)
G. Seaman: *History of Russian Music*, i (Oxford, 1967)
S. Ginzburg: *Istoriya russkoy muzïki v notnïkh obraztsakh* [History of Russian Music in Examples] (Moscow, 1968–70)
B. V. Asaf'yev: *Simfonicheskiye etyudï* (Moscow, 1970)
V. A. Pankratova and L. V. Polyakova: *Opernïye libretto: russkaya opera i opera narodov SSSR* [Opera Librettos: Russian Opera and Opera of the Peoples of the USSR] (Moscow, 2/1970)
A. Swan: *Russian Music and its Sources in Chant and Folk-Song* (New York, 1973)
B. V. Asaf'yev: *Ob opere: izbrannïye stat'i* [On Opera: Selected Essays] (Leningrad, 1976)
Yu. Keldïsh and others: *Istoriya russkoy muzïki* (Moscow, 1983–) [6 of 10 vols. pubd by 1991]
G. Abraham: *Essays on Russian and East European Music* (Oxford, 1985)
S. Neef: *Handbuch der russischen und sowjetischen Oper* (Kassel and Berlin, 1989)

18TH CENTURY

A. Finagin and others: *Muzïka i muzïkal'nïy bït staroy Rossii* [Music and Musical Life in Old Russia] (Leningrad, 1927)
N. F. Findeyzen: *Ocherki po istorii muzïki v Rossii s drevneyshikh vremyon do kontsa XVIII veka* [Studies in the History of Music in Russia from Ancient Times to the End of the 18th Century], ii (Moscow and Leningrad, 1929)
A. S. Rabinovich: *Russkaya opera do Glinki* [Russian Opera Before Glinka] (Moscow, 1948)
R.-A. Mooser: *Annales de la musique et des musiciens en Russie au XVIIIme siècle* (Geneva, 1948–51)
T. N. Livanova: *Russkaya muzïkal'naya kul'tura XVIII veka v yeyo svyazyakh s literaturoy, teatrom i bïtom* [Russian Musical Culture of the 18th Century and its Relations with Literature, Theatre and Daily Life] (Moscow, 1952–3)
D. Lehmann: *Russlands Oper und Singspiel in der zweiten Hälfte des 18 Jahrhunderts* (Leipzig, 1958)
A. A. Gozenpud: *Muzïkal'nïy teatr v Rossii ot istokov do Glinki* [Musical Theatre in Russia from its Origins up to Glinka] (Leningrad, 1959)
H. Rogger: *National Consciousness in Eighteenth-Century Russia* (Cambridge, MA, 1959)
Yu. Keldïsh: *Russkaya muzïka XVIII veka* [Russian Music of the 18th Century] (Moscow, 1965)
S. Karlinsky: *Russian Drama from its Beginnings to the Age of Pushkin* (Berkeley and Los Angeles, 1985)
M. Rïtsareva: *Russkaya muzïka XVIII veka* [Russian Music of the 18th Century] (Moscow, 1987)
P. Stolyansky: *Muzïka i muzitsirovaniye v starom Peterburge* [Music and Music-Making in Old Petersburg] (Leningrad, 1989)

19TH CENTURY

A. Vol'f: *Khronika peterburgskikh teatrov* (St Petersburg, 1877–84)
A. Serov: *Kriticheskiye stat'i* [Critical Essays], ed. N. Stoyanovsky, V. Stasov and others (St Petersburg, 1892–5)
H. Laroche [G. Larosh]: *Muzïkal'no-kriticheskiy stat'i* [Critical Essays on Music] (St Petersburg, 1894)
H. Laroche: *Sobraniye muzïkal'no-kriticheskikh statey* [Collected Critical Essays on Music], ed. N. D. Kashkin and V. Yakovlev, i (Moscow, 1913)
A. N. Serov: *Izbrannïye stat'i* [Selected Essays], ed. G. Khubov (Moscow, 1950, and Leningrad, 1957)
C. Cui: *Izbrannïye stat'i*, ed. Yu. A. Kremlyov (Leningrad, 1952)
V. Stasov: *Izbrannïye sochineniya* [Selected Works], ed. E. D. Stasova and others (Moscow, 1952)
A. Ogolevets: *Materialï i dokumentï po istorii russkoy realisticheskoy muzïkal'noy estetiki* [Material and Documents on the History of Russian Realistic and Musical Aesthetics] (Moscow, 1954–6)
E. M. Gordeyeva, ed.: *Kompozitorï moguchey kuchki ob opere* [The 'Mighty Kuchka' Composers on Opera] (Moscow, 1955)
T. Livanova: *Stasov i russkaya klassicheskaya opera* (Moscow, 1956)
V. Odoyevsky: *Muzïkal'no-literaturnoye naslediye* [Musical-Literary Legacy] (Moscow, 1956)
A. Ogolevets: *Slovo i muzïka v vokal'no-dramaticheskikh zhanrakh* [Words and Music in Vocal-Dramatic Genres] (Moscow, 1960)
B. Shteynpress, ed.: *Iz muzïkal'nogo proshlogo* [From the Musical Past] (Moscow, 1960)

T. Livanova and V. Protopopov: *Opernaya kritika v Rossii* [Opera Criticism in Russia], i/1 (Moscow, 1966)
T. Livanova: *Opernaya kritika v Rossii* [Opera Criticism in Russia], i/2-iv (Moscow, 1967–73)
B. V. Asaf'yev: *Russkaya muzïka XIX i nachala XX veka* [Russian Music of the 19th and Early 20th Centuries], ed. E. M. Orlova (Leningrad, 1968)
V. Stasov: *Selected Essays on Music*, trans. F. Jonas (New York, 1968)
A. A. Gozenpud: *Russkiy opernïy teatr XIX veka (1836–1856)* [Russian Operatic Theatre in the 19th Century, 1836–56] (Leningrad, 1969)
G. Abramovsky: *Russkaya opera pervoy treti XIX veka* [Russian Opera in the First Third of the 19th Century] (Moscow, 1971)
A. A. Gozenpud: *Russkiy opernïy teatr XIX veka (1857–1872)* (Leningrad, 1971)
M. Kopshitser: *Savva Mamontov* (Moscow, 1972)
A. A. Gozenpud: *Russkiy opernïy teatr XIX veka (1873–1889)* (Leningrad, 1973)
——: *Russkiy opernïy teatr na rubezhe XIX–XX vekov i F. I. Shalyapin (1890–1904)* [Russian Operatic Theatre at the Turn of the 20th Century and Shalyapin, 1890–1904] (Leningrad, 1974)
V. Stasov: *Stat'i o muzïke*, ed. V. Protopopov [Essays on Music] (Moscow, 1975–80)
H. Laroche [G. Larosh]: *Izbrannïye stat'i* [Selected Essays], iii (Leningrad, 1976)
V. Borovsky: *Moskovskaya opera S. I. Zimina* [Zimin's Moscow Opera] (Moscow, 1977)
R. Ridenour: *Nationalism, Modernism, and Personal Rivalry in 19th-Century Russian Music* (Ann Arbor, 1981)
R. Taruskin: *Opera and Drama in Russia* (Ann Arbor, 1981)
A. Serov: *Stat'i o muzïke* [Essays on Music], ed. V. Protopopov and others (Moscow, 1984–)

20TH CENTURY

K. London: *The Seven Soviet Arts* (New Haven, CT, 1938)
V. Bogdanov-Berezovsky: *Sovetskaya opera* (Leningrad, 1940)
A. Benois: *Reminiscences of the Russian Ballet* (London, 1941)
Sovetskiy teatr: k tridtsatiletiyu sovetskogo gosudarstva [Soviet Theatre: on the 30th Anniversary of the Soviet State] (Moscow, 1947)
J. Jelagin: *Taming of the Arts* (New York, 1951)
S. Grigoriev: *The Diaghilev Ballet 1909–29* (London, 1953)
M. Grinberg and N. Polyakova, ed.: *Sovetskaya opera: sbornik kriticheskikh statey* [Soviet Opera: Collection of Critical Essays] (Moscow, 1953)
A. Olkhovsky: *Music under the Soviets* (London, 1955)
B. Yarustovsky: *Nekotorïye problemï sovetskogo muzïkal'nogo teatra* [Some Problems of the Soviet Musical Theatre] (Moscow, 1957)
A. A. Gozenpud: *Russkiy sovetskiy opernïy teatr (1917–1941)* [Russian Soviet Opera Theatre] (Leningrad, 1963)
B. Kochno: *Diaghilev and the Ballets Russes* (New York, 1970)
A. A. Gozenpud: *Russkiy opernïy teatr mezhdu dvukh revolyutsiy (1905–1917)* [Russian Opera Theatre Between the Two Revolutions] (Leningrad, 1975)
R. Taruskin: 'Current Chronicle', *MQ*, lxii (1976), 105–15
A. Lunacharsky: *O muzïke i muzïkal'nom teatre* [On Music and Music Theatre] (Moscow, 1981)
B. Schwarz: *Music and Musical Life in Soviet Russia 1917–1981* (Bloomington, IN, 1983)
B. S. Shteynpress: *Opernïye prem'yerï XX veka 1901–1940: slovar'* [Dictionary of 20th-century Opera Premières] (Moscow, 1983)
H. Gerlach: *Fünfzig sowjetische Komponisten der Gegenwart* (Leipzig and Dresden, 1984)
G. Vishnevskaya: *Galina* (New York, 1984)

RICHARD TARUSKIN

Russo, William (*b* Chicago, IL, 25 June 1928). American composer. He studied with Lee Konitz (1941–5) and Lennie Tristano (1943–7), playing the trombone in jazz bands. From 1950 to 1954 he was associated with the Stan Kenton Orchestra as a trombonist and composer-arranger. He studied English literature at Roosevelt College, Chicago, where he took private composition lessons with John J. Becker (1953–5) and Karal Jirák (1955–7). In 1958 he won a grant from the Koussevitsky Foundation and moved to New York where he formed and conducted the Russo Orchestra. He taught at the School of Jazz at Lenox, Massachusetts, (1957–60), the Manhattan School (1959–61) and, after a sojourn in Europe, at Columbia College, Chicago (1965–7), and Antioch College (1971–2). He also founded and directed several new-music and theatre programmes including the Center for New Music and Free Theater at Columbia College (1965–75) and the Rock Theater at the Peabody Institute (1969–71); in 1979 he resumed teaching at Columbia College.

Russo's extensive and varied background as a composer, ranging from jazz to works that combine blues with the classical orchestra to rock cantatas, has left its mark on his operatic efforts. His diverse musical activities share a common denominator: a love of the human voice and of the theatre. The successful blending of these attributes gives him the ability to humanize his music, direct it outward and make it accessible.

Early operatic works are jazz-based. *John Hooten* (1961) is a modern-day adaptation of Shakespeare's *Othello*, while *Land of Milk and Honey* (1964) focusses on a Jamaican in London whose dreams are obstructed by prejudice. *The Island* (1963), a one-act opera commissioned by the BBC for its experiments in stereophony, centres on the impact of civilization on primitive islanders. Scored for double jazz orchestra, the music combines recitative (representing law and order) and blues (representing the feelings of the islanders), contrasted with sections in Dixieland style. New musical and extra-musical devices are explored, including echo effects, tape delay and the lowering and raising of pitch. Multi-track tape techniques create opportunities for soloists to sing all parts of ensemble sections.

Russo's rock cantatas show a successful fusion of rock, opera, dance, jazz, lightshow and mime in a highly improvisatory style. *The Civil War* (1968) focusses on the American war between the states and the assassinations of Martin Luther King and John and Robert Kennedy. His most ambitious cantata is *Liberation* (1969) whose principal characters are Che Guevara, Thomas Paine and Socrates. The later operatic works exhibit qualities of the earlier pieces coupled with techniques explored in the rock cantatas. His one-act operas *Isabella's Fortune* (1974) and *Pedrolino's Revenge* (1974) are based on 17th-century plays and conceived in a *commedia dell'arte* form. The musical style combines Broadway, blues and soft-rock idioms, employing a combination of modal and jazz-influenced harmonies. The librettos, though well crafted, are not particularly successful at establishing contemporary equivalents for the risqué, low-brow comic plots favoured in the *commedia dell'arte*.

John Hooten, 1961 (1, Russo), London, BBC, Jan 1963; stage, Chicago, Crane High School, 12 Jan 1967
The Island (1, A. Mitchell), London, BBC, 13 July 1963
Land of Milk and Honey, 1964 (1, S. Douglass), Chicago, St James Methodist Church, 29 Jan 1967
Antigone (A. A. Hoge), Chicago, 1967
A Cabaret Opera (chamber op, E. E. Cummings, G. Stein, W. H. Auden, E. Pound and others), New York, 1970; also as: The Alice B. Toklas Hashish Fudge Review, New York, 8 Dec 1977; Paris Lights, New York, 24 Jan 1980; Boulevard, Chicago; Americans in Paris
Aesop's Fables (J. Swan), Chicago, 1971; rev. version, Chicago 1972
The Shepherds' Christmas, 1971 (chamber op, Swan), Chicago, Dec 1979
Isabella's Fortune (comic op, 1, A. Williams), New York, Commedia Company of Chicago, 11 Sept 1974
Pedrolino's Revenge (comic op, 1, J. Abarbanel), New York, Commedia Company of Chicago, 11 Sept 1974

A General Opera (chamber op, A. Weinstein), Chicago 1976
The Pay Off (cabaret op, D. Declue), Chicago, 16 Feb 1984
Talking to the Sun (multimedia musical event, K. Farrell and K. Koch), Chicago, Columbia College, 5 March 1989

*

C. Barnes: 'Two Ears for Opera', *Music and Musicians*, xii/1 (1963), 18 [on *The Island*]
J. Burks: 'Liberation', *Rolling Stone*, xxxix/11 (1969), 11
J. Balleras: 'William Russo', *Downbeat*, xlix/5 (1982), 26–7

JAMES P. CASSARO

Rust, Friedrich Wilhelm (*b* Wörlitz, nr Dessau, 6 July 1739; *d* Dessau, 28 Feb 1796). German composer. He studied law at Halle, where he was a pupil of W. F. Bach, and entered the service of Prince Leopold III of Anhalt-Dessau. In 1763–4 he lived in Potsdam, studying the violin with Franz Benda and composition with C. P. E. Bach. He visited Italy in the retinue of Prince Leopold in 1765. In 1774 he founded a theatre for opera and drama in Dessau where his own operatic works and incidental music were given; he was made court music director in 1775. He also wrote chamber and keyboard music, choral works and songs.

all MSS in D-Bds

Inkle und Yariko (duodrama, 2, Schink), Dessau, 28 July 1777
Der blaue Montag (operetta, T. Berger), Dessau, 1777
Colma (monodrama, after Ossian), *c*1780
Korylas und Lalage (pastoral), ?1786

*

F. W. Hosaeus: *Friedrich Wilhelm Rust und das Dessauer Musikleben 1766–1796* (Dessau, 1882)
R. Czach: *Friedrich Wilhelm Rust* (Essen, 1927)

RICHARD JONES

Rust [Rusti], **Giacomo** (*b* Rome, 1741; *d* Barcelona, 1786). Italian composer. He was perhaps of German descent, but was not related to F. W. Rust. He studied in Naples at the Turchini Conservatory and later in Rome under Rinaldo di Capua. From 1763 to 1777 he worked in Venice, where he brought out his first opera, *La contadina in corte* (1763; for a discussion of Rust's setting *see* Sacchini's LA CONTADINA IN CORTE). Between 1772 and 1776 he produced 12 more (two in collaboration). It was probably the popularity of these works in Italy that led the Archbishop of Salzburg to engage him for his court *cappella*, offering him 1000 gulden, an unusually high salary for Salzburg. Rust was appointed court Kapellmeister on 12 June 1777, but at the end of the year he asked to be relieved of his post because the bad weather had affected his health. His plea was granted, but his ill-health allowed him to leave only in February 1778. Just before his departure he set Metastasio's *Il Parnaso confuso* for the consecration of the Archbishop of Olmütz. In Rust's absence the performance was conducted by Michael Haydn. Although Rust had been offered the post of *maestro di cappella* at Orvieto Cathedral, he returned to Venice and resumed his operatic career. In 1783 he became *maestro de capilla* at Barcelona Cathedral, where he remained until his death.

VM – *Venice, Teatro S Moisè* VS – *Venice, Teatro S Samuele*
dgm – *dramma giocoso per musica* dm – *dramma per musica*

La contadina in corte (dgm, 3, N. Tassi), VM, 1763, *P-La*
La finta semplice (dgm, 3, P. Mililotti), Bologna, Formagliari, spr. 1772, collab. G. Insanguine
L'idolo cinese (dgm, 3, G. B. Lorenzi), VS, 28 Dec 1773, *I-MOe*, *P-La*
Il conte Baccellone (dgm, 3, M. Coltellini, after C. Goldoni: *La contessina*), VM, aut. 1774
I cavalieri lunatici (farsa, 3), Venice, S Cassiano, aut. 1774
L'amor bizzaro (dgm, 3, Bertati), VM, carn. 1775
Li due amanti in inganno [Acts 1 and 3] (dgm, 3), Venice, S Cassiano, carn. 1775 [Act 2 by M. Rauzzini]
Alessandro nelle Indie (dm, 3, P. Metastasio), VS, Ascension 1775
Il Baron di terra asciuta (dgm, 8 scenes), VS, 26 Dec 1775
Il Socrate immaginario (dgm, 15 scenes, Lorenzi), VS, carn. 1776
Calliroe (dm, 3, M. Verazi), Padua, Nuovo, June 1776, 1 aria *I-Pca*
Il Giove di Creta (dgm, 3), Venice, S Cassiano, aut. 1776, *Gl*
Li due protetti (dgm, 2, P. A. Bagliacca), VM, 26 Dec 1776
Il Parnaso confuso (festa teatrale, 1, Metastasio), Salzburg, Hof, 17 May 1778
Vologeso re de' Parti (dm, 2, A. Zeno), Venice, S Benedetto, 28 Dec 1778, *P-La*
Il talismano [Acts 2 and 3] (dgm, 3, Goldoni), Milan, Canobbiana, 21 Aug 1779, *I-Fc* [Act 1 by Salieri]
L'isola capricciosa (dgm, 2, C. Mazzolà), VS, carn. 1780, *F-Pc*
Gli antiquari in Palmira (commedia per musica, 3, G. Carpani), Milan, Scala, aut. 1780, *Pc*
Demofoonte (dm, 3, Metastasio), Florence, Pergola, aut. 1780, 1 aria *Gl*
Il castellano deluso, Parma, Ducale, carn. 1781
Artaserse (dm, 3, Metastasio), Perugia, Civico, aut. 1781
Adriano in Siria (dm, 3, Metastasio), Turin, Regio, 26 Dec 1781, *P-La*
L'incognita fortunata (farsa, 1, G. Ciliberti), Naples, Fondo, sum. 1782
L'incontri inaspettati, Rome, Capranica, Feb 1783
La caccia di Enrico IV (dgm, 2, A. Dian), VM, aut. 1783
Il marito indolente (dgm, 2, Mazzolà), Vienna, Hof, 1784
Berenice (dm, 3, J. Durandi), Parma, carn. 1786, scena and aria pubd

Arias in: L'isola di Alcina, 1772; L'avaro deluso, 1773

Miscellaneous arias and ovs.: *A-Wgm*, *B-Br*, *D-Bds*, *Dlb*, *Mbs*, *E-Mn*, *I-Bc*, *Mc*, *MOe*

THOMAS BAUMAN, ERNST HINTERMAIER

Ruth. Opera in three scenes, op.50, by LENNOX BERKELEY to a libretto by ERIC CROZIER; London, Scala Theatre, 2 October 1956.

The libretto follows the biblical story and the language of the Authorized Version fairly closely. It begins after Naomi (soprano) has returned from Moab to Bethlehem with her daughters-in-law Orpah (soprano) and Ruth (mezzo-soprano). She persuades Orpah to go back to Moab, but Ruth insists on staying with her ('Whither thou goest, I will go'). A chorus of local women comment on how Naomi has aged.

The scene changes to the fields where the reapers are at work and (a dramatic insertion by Crozier) object to the presence of Ruth, the foreigner. Berkeley may not be entirely happy with the heartiness of the reapers, but his depiction of race hatred is suitably vicious. The reapers' angry cries are interrupted by the appearance of their master, Boaz (tenor). The part was played at the première by Peter Pears, and it has to be said that Berkeley's habit of punctuating the ensemble with piano chords, together with lines like Ruth's 'they fear what they do not know, hate what they cannot understand', invite unfortunate comparisons with Britten. Ruth introduces herself to Boaz, and he promises to protect her.

Naomi brings Ruth at night to the threshing-floor, where the harvest home is to be celebrated. The reapers sing choruses of hope and rejoicing, in which Berkeley's contrapuntal abilities and strong rhythmic sense are happily displayed, and in contrast to which Boaz's unaccompanied solo 'O clap your hands all ye people!' serves to invest this kindly character with the dominance that might otherwise be lacking. Ruth and Boaz sing a subdued but intense love duet, and the chorus bless their union with praises to God. ROGER NICHOLS

Rutini, Ferdinando (*b* Florence, Nov or Dec 1763; *d* Terracina, 13 Nov 1827). Italian composer, son of Giovanni Marco Rutini. Lexicographers have given various dates and places for his birth; however, it is reasonable to assume that the son whose birth his father announced to Padre Martini in a letter of 3 December 1763 was Ferdinando. His first entry into comic writing was to add 'a much approved and pleasing' trio to Cimarosa's *Italiana in Londra*, performed by dilettantes at the theatre in the Corso de' Tintori in March 1786. In the same year he first performed as the cembalist (and therefore director) at the theatre in the via S Maria in a production of *Il barone per forza* with music by Marcello da Capua. In this capacity he worked in the various Florentine theatres, the Cocomero, Intrepidi, Borgo Ognissanti, Piazza Vecchia and Tintori, establishing a reputation as director and cembalist exclusively for comic operas, intermezzos and farces.

His most successful comic opera was the two-act *dramma giocoso Il matrimonio per industria*, performed at the Pergola, Florence's theatre of highest prestige, in June 1792. It was later presented in Varese, Cremona and Milan. Otherwise, in spite of occasional performances elsewhere, his success was limited to Florence. At the height of his productivity there, from Carnival 1796 until the same season in 1800, he composed 19 comic works while at the same time directing other such pieces at the Cocomero. For unknown reasons, Rutini left Florence in 1804 to take the post of *maestro di cappella* in Ancona (clearly a demotion), moving to Macerata in the same position, 1812–16. In an attempt to return to the theatre, he wrote three comic works for Roman productions in 1816 and 1817, apparently without success; he worked again as *maestro di cappella* in Aquapendente, 1820–25, and in Terracina until his death. After the Roman comedies he seems to have abandoned composition altogether.

Ferdinando Rutini may be regarded as the culmination and termination of the Florentine comic operatic tradition extending from Jacopo Melani in the 17th century to the Napoleonic era. Of all Florentine composers he was the most prolific and possibly the most popular, but as with his compatriots, his legacy is small: only four scores out of 44 identified comic stage works exist today. This material has yet to be fully examined. The opera *I vendemmiatori, ovvero I due sindaci*, performed at the Cocomero in 1789, is commonly misattributed to Rutini; according to the *Gazzetta toscana* and the score (*I-Fc*), it was written by Michele Neri Bondi.

first performed in Florence unless otherwise stated
FC – *Teatro del Cocomero*
FI – *Regio Teatro degl'Intrepidi*
dg – *dramma giocoso* f – *farsa*
int – *intermezzo*

L'avaro (dg, G. Bertati), Rome, Valle, spr. 1789
Amor non ha riguardi (int), FC, 13 Nov 1789; lib. not by G. Palomba
La pianella perduta nella neve (?f, G. Foppa), Parma, Ducale, aut. 1790
La baronessa giardiniera (f, D. Somigli), Piazza Vecchia, 15 Feb 1791
Il tutore ridicolo (op buffa), Gubbio, spr. 1791
L'equivoco della somiglianza [simiglianza], ovvero La giovinezza bizzarra (dg), Genoa, Falcone, and Gorizia, Bandeu, carn. 1792
Il matrimonio per industria (dg, 2), Pergola, 7 June 1792; also as Amor per industria
Amore vuol gioventù, ossia Le astuzie fortunate (dg, 2), Rome, Alibert, aut. 1792
La molinara di Gentilly (dg, 1, G. Squilloni), S Maria, 26 Dec 1793
Bellezza, ed onestà, ossia La villanella nobile [La giardiniera nobile] (f or int), S Maria, 8 Feb 1794
Zemira e Azor (int), S Maria, carn. 1794
Rosina, e Lubino (?int), Siena, sum. 1794
Le finte pazzie, o sia La pupilla bizzarra (int, 2), FC, 7 Sept 1794
Il locandiere deluso [Il locandiere burlato] (int, 1), FC, 26 Dec 1794
I tre desideri, o sia Il taglialegno (f, 1, Somigli, after J.-F. Guichard: *Le bûcheron, ou Les trois souhaits*), Borgo Ognissanti, 26 Dec 1794
La semplice (dg, Somigli), Borgo Ognissanti, carn. 1795
Balestruccio medico (dg, 1), FC, aut. 1795
Il finto medico per amore (int, 1, Somigli), Piazza Vecchia, 27 Dec 1795, *I-Fc*
Il tempo scuopre la verità [I raggiri amorosi, ossia Il tempo scuopre la verità] (f, 1, Palomba), Rome, Capranica, 24 Jan 1796; the lib. is an enlarged version of Il locandiere deluso
Cecco da Verlungo (int), Borgo Ognissanti, carn. 1796
Lo sposo per oracolo (f, 2), Piazza Vecchia, carn. 1796, *Fc*
L'accademia a Viareggio (int), FI, 26 Dec 1796
Il maestro di cappella (int), FI, 26 Dec 1796
I tre sposalizi, ossia Il paese della Cuccagna (?dg, ? after C. Goldoni), Borgo Ognissanti, 26 Dec 1796
La prova del dramma serio (dg, 1), FC, 12 Jan 1797
Il gazzettiere olandese (int, 1), FI, 23 Jan 1797
Il malato imaginario (dg, 1), FC, 13 Feb 1797
La pescatrice fortunata (int or dg, 1), Borgo Ognissanti, carn. 1797; as La principessa pescatrice, *PAc*
Chi è minchion suo danno, o sia Pasquino e Marforio (dg, 1, Somigli), FC, 26 Dec 1797
Il finto armeno, ossia L'avarizia delusa (int, 1), Borgo Ognissanti, 26 Dec 1797
Il padre fanatico, o sia L'amante volubile (dg, 1, Somigli), FI, *c*29 Jan 1798
Adelina, o sia L'incostanza vinta (dg, 1, Somigli), FC, *c*31 Jan 1798
Le donne s'attaccano sempre al peggio, o sia Il ganzatore burlato (dg, 1, Somigli), FC, 26 Dec 1798
L'erede pescatrice (int), Borgo Ognissanti, 26 Dec 1799
La locandiera (dg, 1 [? Artusi da Goldoni]), FC, 27 Jan 1800
Il tesoro del Mufti (int), S Maria, carn. 1800
Gli amanti in collera (dg, 1, Goldoni), FC, carn. 1801
Il segreto (dg, 1, G. Foppa), FC, carn. 1802
La contadina contrastata (dg, 1), FC, carn. 1803
La casa in vendita (f, 1, 'Deiafebo Milone'), FC, carn. 1804
La pianella perduta (f, 1), FC, carn. 1806
La dama soldato, ossia Il campo militare (int, 2), Rome, Apollo, 26 Dec 1816
Polissena (J. Ferretti), Rome, Argentina, 11 Feb 1817
Pulcinella maestro di cappella a' Redicofoni (f, 1, Ferretti), Rome, Apollo, carn. 1817

Terzetto in Cimarosa: L'italiana in Londra, 1786; 3 arias in Cimarosa: I due baroni, *GB-Lbl* (*c*1814)

*

StiegerO
Indice de'spettacoli teatrale (Milan, Venice and Rome, 1764–1823)
C. Gervasoni: *Nuova teoria di musica* (Parma, 1812)
A. Cametti: 'Un poeta melodrammatico romano: appunti e notizie in gran parte inedite sopra Jacopo Ferretti', *Gazzetta musicale di Milano*, lii (1897), esp.341–2
M. Fabbri: 'Incontro con Ferdinando Rutini, il dimenticato figlio musicista del "primo maestro di Mozart"', *Le celebrazioni del 1963 e alcune nuove indagini sulla musica italiana del XVIII e XIX secolo*, Chigiana, xx (1963), 195–205
C. Sartori: *Primo tentativo di catalogo unico dei libretti italiani a stampa fino all'anno 1800* (Milan, n.d.)
R. Zanetti: *La musica italiana nel settecento* (Milan, 1978)
R. L. Weaver and N. Weaver: *A Chronology of Music in the Florentine Theater*, ii: *1751–1800* (Warren, MI, 1993)

ROBERT LAMAR WEAVER

Rutini, Giovanni Marco [Giovanni Maria; Giovanni Placido] (*b* Florence, 25 April 1723; *d* Florence, 22 Dec 1797). Italian composer. From an early age he demonstrated a remarkable inclination towards music. His elder brother undertook his education, sending him to Naples in 1737. Beginning in 1739 he studied for five years at the Conservatorio della Pietà dei Turchini with Leo and Fago.

In 1748 Rutini signed the dedication of his *Sonate per cembalo* op.1, stating that he had been in Prague for some time. Together with the composer Francesco Zoppis, he was engaged for the G. B. Locatelli company.

His first and second operas, *Alessandro nell'Indie* (1750) and *Semiramide* (1752), were performed by the company at the Nuovo Teatro, Prague. Perhaps while travelling with the company, he was in Dresden in 1754 and Berlin about 1756. According to a letter to Padre Martini in 1772, at the time he lived in Prague he was under the protection of Maria Antonia Walpurgis, Electress of Saxony, who wrote the text of his cantata, *Lavinia e Turno* (1756).

The Locatelli company failed financially in 1757, but Locatelli obtained a new contract with Empress Elizabeth of Russia as impresario of the court theatre in St Petersburg. Rutini moved there and composed *Il retiro degli dei* (1757), and in the summer of 1758 the company mounted his first comic opera, *Il negligente*. He also became the conductor of the private orchestra of Count Pyotr Borisovich Sheremet'yev. In February 1761 Locatelli's second company failed and was dispersed. Rutini returned to Florence and married on 2 April. In the next two years he was concerned principally with the study of counterpoint. Although he often wrote of his desire to go to Bologna to study with Martini, he never found time for extended study with him, except for a brief period in early 1762 around the time of the première of his comic opera *Il caffè di campagna*. Instead, he pursued his study of counterpoint by correspondence. At Martini's suggestion, he began a translation of Marpurg's *Abhandlung von der Fuge* (as *Traité de la fugue*, MS, *I-Bc*). In March 1762 he was admitted to the Accademia Filarmonica of Bologna.

The earliest recorded performance of an opera by Rutini in Florence is that of *Gli sposi in maschera* – previously produced in Cremona and Bologna – at S Maria on 3 October 1763. In May 1764 he was in Livorno for the première there of *Ezio* and in Genoa during the following summer for the investiture of Francesco Maria della Rovere for which he wrote a cantata. In the next decade he travelled throughout Italy to direct performances of his music, but maintained his home and his principal activity in Florence. With his intermezzo *Le contese domestiche* (1766), Rutini was recognized in the *Gazzetta toscana* as the city's most internationally eminent composer. But a position at the Tuscan court never materialized, despite the acclaimed brilliance of his music for *L'amor per rigiro* (1773), which was mounted in the grand duke's summer palace at Poggio a Caiano. However, performances in Modena in 1769 of *L'olandese in Italia* and of the première in the following carnival season of *La Nitteti* won him the title of *Maestro di cappella al Principe ereditario di Modena* (probably the position was honorary; his Florentine obligations allowed him only brief periods elsewhere).

The climax of Rutini's Florentine productions came with *Vologeso, re de' Parti*, which the *Notizie del mondo* praised extravagantly, naming Rutini rather oddly as 'nostro abilissimo, e pur troppo noto Maestro'. His next Florentine performance, *Zulima* (1777), a revision of *Sicotencal* (1776), was reviewed with condescension and Rutini's music was not mentioned. *Zulima* was his last operatic work for Florence and his last anywhere, save one revival of *L'amor per rigiro* in Pontremoli in 1779. He continued to direct performances at the Intrepidi up to 1784, but composed mainly oratorio and keyboard sonatas. As a teacher, he was one of the founders of the Leopoldian school of Florentine composers, which included his son Ferdinando, and fostered the flowering of late 18th-century Florentine opera singers, among them the tenor Bernardo Mengozzi. Only Della Corte has commented on his operas, citing the grace of the arias and the skill in capturing a variety of moods found in his *I matrimoni in maschera*.

first performed in Florence unless otherwise stated

Alessandro nell'Indie (dramma per musica, 3, P. Metastasio), Prague, Nuovo, carn. 1750

Semiramide (dramma per musica, 3, Metastasio), Prague, Nuovo, 1752; rev. version, Dresden, Hoftheater, 1780, *D-Dlb*

Il retiro degli dei (composizione dramatica, 1 scene, G. B. Locatelli), St Petersburg, 2/13 Dec 1757, ?*RU-SPk* (as 'Pastorale'), according to Mooser

Il negligente (dg, 3, C. Goldoni), St Petersburg, sum. 1758

Il caffè di campagna (dg, 3, P. Chiari), Bologna, Formigliari, carn. 1762

I matrimoni in maschera [Gli sposi in maschera; Il tutore burlato] (dg, 3, F. Casorri), Cremona, Nuovo, Jan 1763, *D-Dlb*, *F-Pc*, *I-Fc*, *P-La* (Acts 1 and 3)

Ezio (dramma per musica, 3, Metastasio), Pergola, 30 Jan 1763, *I-Gl*

L'olandese in Italia (dg, 3, N. Tassi), Cocomero, spr. 1765, *Bc*, *Fc*

L'amore industrioso (dg, 3, G. Casorri), Venice, S Cassiano, aut. 1765, *P-La*

Il contadino incivilito (dg, 3, O. Goretti), Cocomero, 31 March 1766

Le contese domestiche [Le contese deluse] (int, 2 pts), Cocomero, 26 Dec 1766, *I-Fc*

L'amor tra l'armi (Tassi), Siena, Erranti, 3 July 1768

Faloppa mercante [Gli sponsali di Faloppa] (farsa or int, 2 pts), S Maria, 26 Dec 1769, *Fc*

La Nitteti (dramma per musica, 3, Metastasio), Modena, Corte, carn. 1770, arias in *Fc* and *Rsc*

L'amor per rigiro (farsa, 2 pts, Tassi), Poggio a Caiano, 5 Oct 1773, *Fc*

Vologeso re de' Parti (dramma per musica, 3, A. Zeno), Pergola, 22 Jan 1775, *Nc*, *P-La*

Sicotencal (dramma per musica, 3, C. Olivieri, after Voltaire), Turin, Regio, carn. 1776; rev. version, Pergola, 25 Jan 1777, as Zulima; *La*

Il finto amante (farsa, 2 pts), Pistoia, Risvegliati, sum. 1776

Gli stravaganti, *Gb-Lbl* (finale only)

*

ES (L. F. Tagliavini)

Indice de'spettacoli teatrale (Milan, Venice and Rome, 1764–1823)

C. Gervasoni: *Nuova teoria di musica* (Parma, 1812)

A. Della Corte: *L'opera comica italiana nel '700* (Bari, 1923)

M. Pedemonte: 'Un soggiorno genovese di G. M. Rutini', *Rassegna dorica*, ix (1937–8), 3

R.-A. Mooser: *Annales de la musique et des musiciens en Russie au XVIIIme siècle* (Geneva, 1948–51)

G. Balducci: *La figura e l'opera di G. M. Rutini* (diss., U. of Florence, 1964)

G. Pestelli: 'Mozart e Rutini', *AnMc*, no.18 (1978), 290–307

R. Zanetti: *La musica italiana nel settecento* (Milan, 1978)

A. Schnoebelen: *Padre Martini's Collection of Letters in the Civico Museo Bibliografico Musicale in Bologna* (New York, 1979)

M. de Angelis: *La felicità in Etruria* (Florence, 1990)

R. L. Weaver and N. W. Weaver: *Chronology of Music in the Florentine Theater*, ii: *1751–1800* (Warren, MI, 1993)

ROBERT LAMAR WEAVER

Ruvinetti Bon [née Ruvinetti], **Rosa** (*b* Bologna, *fl* 1730–62). Italian soprano. She first appeared in Bologna, in *commedie per musica* by G. M. Buini (*Il podestà di Colognole* and *La maschera levata al vizio*) and also in *opera seria*, but she soon began to specialize in comic intermezzos, especially those by Hasse, and almost always with the bass Domenico Cricchi. In 1735 she married Girolamo Bon, a painter, scenographer, librettist and leader of a troupe of actors; with him and Cricchi she performed in Russia (St Petersburg, 1745–7), Germany (1748–62) and then Hungary, in the service of Prince Paul Anton at Eszterháza from 1762. There she met Haydn and influenced the work he produced during those years (*La canterina*, *Lo speziale*, *Le pescatrici* and *L'infedeltà delusa*).

G. Lazarevich: 'Haydn and the Italian Comic Intermezzo Tradition', *Joseph Haydn: Vienna 1982*, 376–86
F. Piperno: 'Note sulla diffusione degli intermezzi di J. A. Hasse', *AnMc*, no.25 (1987), 287–303
FRANCO PIPERNO

Ruy Blas. *Dramma lirico* in four acts by FILIPPO MARCHETTI to a libretto by CARLO D'ORMEVILLE, after VICTOR HUGO's historical drama *Ruy Blas* (1838); Milan, Teatro alla Scala, 3 April 1869.

The plot deals with the villainous Don Sallustio (baritone) and his plan to revenge himself against the Queen of Spain (soprano), who has exiled him from court for his refusal to marry a lady-in-waiting whom he seduced. His revenge takes the form of presenting his valet, Ruy Blas (tenor), already in love with the Queen, as a noble (Don Cesare), who wins her favour and is made prime minister, dubbed a duke and admitted to the Order of the Golden Fleece. At this point Don Sallustio returns and reveals to the Queen that she has dishonoured herself by giving her heart to a servant. Repudiated by his beloved, Ruy Blas kills his enemy in a duel and drinks poison, an act that earns him the Queen's forgiveness. The plot features a typical Hugoesque antithesis – an ignoble aristocrat and a high-minded plebeian.

D'Ormeville's prolix libretto confronted Marchetti with a formidable task: long passages of explanatory material are set to nondescript vocal lines supported by tiresomely repeated little motifs. The big numbers of the score rarely attain genuine elevation, but the love-duet 'O dolce voluttà' (Act 3) approaches conviction, and the tenor's death scene sounds a sincere note of pathos. A sprawling work, reminiscent of Meyerbeer and replete with a jiggling *divertissement* (Act 3), it seriously overtaxed Marchetti's limited powers of inventiveness.

WILLIAM ASHBROOK

Ruzdjak, Vladimir (*b* Zagreb, 21 Sept 1922; *d* Zagreb, 9 Oct 1987). Croatian baritone. He studied in Zagreb, where he made his début in 1947 as Yeletsky (*The Queen of Spades*). Engaged at Hamburg (1955–72), he created the title role in Henze's *Der Prinz von Homburg* (1960), then sang in the British première (1962, Sadler's Wells). He sang Tarquinius at Aldeburgh (1960); Enrico Ashton, Sharpless and Rigoletto at San Francisco (1961); Amonasro at the Metropolitan (1962); and Count Almaviva at Covent Garden (1966). He also appeared in Vienna, Munich and Brussels. His repertory included Papageno, Wolfram, Yevgeny Onegin, Golaud, Nabucco, Don Carlo (*La forza del destino*), Creon (Honegger's *Antigone*), Mr Gedge (*Albert Herring*) and the King in Tal's *Ashmedai*, which he created (1971, Hamburg). An excellent actor, he had a beautiful, warm-toned voice of considerable power.

For illustration *see* PRINZ VON HOMBURG, DER.

ELIZABETH FORBES

Ruzitska, György (*b* Vienna, 1789; *d* Kolozsvár [now Cluj-Napoca, Romania], 2 Dec 1869). Hungarian composer of Austrian birth. He studied composition with Josef Gelinek in Vienna. In 1810 he travelled to Transylvania as a music teacher to the family of Baron János Bánffy, but in 1819 he moved to Kolozsvár. He soon became prominent in the town's musical life: he taught the piano and conducted the New Society of Music, and from 1835 until his death was director of the conservatory. In the 1830s he became friendly with Ferenc Erkel. Ruzitska's three-act opera *Alonso* (1829, Pest), to a libretto by Christian Heyser, is one of his most notable works. In this early composition Ruzitska still adhered to the traditions of the Viennese Classical masters; the influence of Hungarian national music, significant in his later works, is not yet found in this score.

FERENC BÓNIS

Ruzitska, József (*b* ?Pápa, *c*1775; *d* after 1823). Hungarian conductor and composer. About 1820 he was Kapellmeister of the Josephregiment in Nagyenyed. In 1821 he composed the music to the second part of the Singspiel *Arany idők* ('Golden Ages'; 2, M. Wándza) for the theatre in Debrecen. He lived in Nagyvárad (now Oradea, Romania) as a theatre musician (1821) and in Kolozsvár (now Cluj-Napoca, Romania) as Kapellmeister of the Hungarian theatre (1822–3). In the Christmas season of 1822 his two operas, *Béla futása* ('Béla's Escape'; 2, J. Kótsi Patkó, after A. von Kotzebue) and *Kemény Simon, avagy dicsőség a hazáért meghalni* ('Simon Kemény, or It is Glorious to Die for the Fatherland'; 2, K. Kisfaludy), were performed for the first time at the theatre in Kolozsvár. After 1823 no details about his life are known.

Despite the apparent brevity of his career, Ruzitska is a significant figure in Hungarian music history. His two operas were among the earliest attempts at original operatic art in Hungary. In these works he used elements of contemporary Italian and German opera, as well as those of popular national Hungarian dance music (*verbunkos*). The Hungarian parts of his operas show the influence of the music of János Bihari, a gypsy violinist and composer. With his topical historical themes and his endeavour to combine current international with popular national forms of musical expression, Ruzitska paved the way for Hungarian opera in the 19th century.

I. Bartalus: 'Az első magyar dalmű költője' [The Composer of the First Hungarian Opera], *Hölgyfutár*, xiii (1861)
Z. Ferenczi: *A kolozsvári színészet és színház története* [History of Theatrical Art and the Theatre in Kolozsvár] (Kolozsvár, 1897)
I. Lakatos: 'Az első magyar dalmű' [The First Hungarian Opera], *Erdélyi helikon*, xii (1939), 344–50
B. Szabolcsi: *A magyar zenetörténet kézikönyve* (Budapest, 1947, 3/1979; Eng. trans., 1964, as *A Concise History of Hungarian Music*)
——: *A XIX. század magyar romantikus zenéje* [Hungarian Romantic Music of the 19th Century] (Budapest, 1951)

FERENC BÓNIS

Ryba [Poisson, Peace, Ryballandini, Rybaville], **Jakub (Šimon) Jan** (*b* Přeštice, nr Klatovy, 26 Oct 1765; *d* Rožmitál pod Třemšínem, 8 April 1815). Czech composer. He attended the Piarist Gymnasium in Prague (1781–4) and from 1786 was a teacher at Mníšek. From 1788 he was a teacher and church choirmaster at Rožmitál. He held these posts until his death by suicide.

Ryba was one of the most prominent 18th-century Czech cantors and an assiduous teacher. His six stage works, for which he probably wrote the librettos, all date from before 1801. They include the Singspiel *Veselé živobytí neb vandrovní muzikanti* ('A Merry Life, or Wandering Musicians', the only one for which the libretto survives), an argument against drinking (1794); and the operetta *Das Denkmal in Arkadien* (1800) from which only one number remains. The rest of Ryba's output consists of a large number of sacred and instrumental pieces, the earlier ones written under various pseudonyms.

ČSHS
G. J. Dlabacž: *Allgemeines historisches Künstler-Lexikon*, ii (Prague, 1815), 610ff
I. Janáčková: *J. J. Ryba o svém hudebním životě* (Prague, 1946) [incl. list of works to 1801 compiled by Ryba for Dlabacž]
J. Němeček: *Jakub Jan Ryba: Život a dílo* [Ryba: Life and Works] (Prague, 1963) [with thematic catalogue, list of writings and bibliography] MILAN POŠTOLKA

Rysanek, Leonie (*b* Vienna, 14 Nov 1926). Austrian soprano. She studied at the Vienna Academy with Alfred Jerger and later with Rudolf Grossmann. She made her début at Innsbruck in 1949 as Agathe (*Der Freischütz*) and then sang at Saarbrücken, where her roles included Arabella, Donna Anna, Senta, Sieglinde and Leonora (*La forza del destino*). At the first postwar Bayreuth Festival in 1951 her Sieglinde created a sensation, and the following year she joined the Staatsoper in Munich. Her opulent voice, with its thrilling upper register, and her dramatic temperament were heard and seen to advantage in the title roles of *Der Liebe der Danae*, *Die ägyptische Helena* and *Salome*, as the Empress in *Die Frau ohne Schatten* and Chrysothemis, and as Lady Macbeth, Turandot, Tosca, Santuzza and Medea.

Rysanek was first heard in London as Danae during the Munich company's season at Covent Garden in 1953; later she appeared there as Chrysothemis, Sieglinde, Tosca and Elsa. She made her American début in 1956 at San Francisco, where she sang Senta and Sieglinde. She returned to Bayreuth as Elsa (1958), Elisabeth (1964) and Kundry (1982). In 1959 she made her début at the Metropolitan, replacing Callas as Lady Macbeth. She then appeared there regularly in the Italian and the German repertories, sharing most of her time between New York and the Vienna Staatsoper, with guest appearances in other leading European houses. In 1986 she celebrated the 30th anniversary of her American début by singing the Kostelnička at San Francisco, and also sang Ortrud at the Metropolitan. In 1988 she sang Kabanicha at Los Angeles, in 1989 Herodias (*Salome*) at Stuttgart and in 1990 Clytemnestra at Geneva.

*

GV (G. Gualerzi; R. Vegeto)
H. Rosenthal: *Great Singers of Today* (London, 1966)
HAROLD ROSENTHAL/R

Rytel, Piotr (*b* Vilnius, 20 Sept 1884; *d* Warsaw, 2 Jan 1970). Polish composer. He studied composition with Noskowski at the Warsaw Conservatory where he returned in 1918 as a professor, numbering among his pupils Andrzej Panufnik and Tadeusz Baird. As a critic, he was noted for his strident views on colleagues. Though he did not finish the second of his inter-war operas, *Koniec Mesjasza* ('The End of the Messiah'), *Krzyżowcy* ('The Crusaders') was one of the few operas written during the Nazi occupation of Poland. Rytel's primary musical language ranges from *Lohengrin* and *Tannhäuser* to *Tristan*, although dramatically his work is much tamer than Wagner's. In his last opera, *Andrzej z Chełmna* ('Andrew from Chełmno'), he demonstrates his interest in a broad dramatic sweep, but his inability to weld disparate elements, such as swathes of whole-tone harmony and extensive sections in *kujawiak* and polonaise rhythms, into a unified style illustrates why none of his operas has succeeded in becoming part of the standard Polish repertory.

*

Ijola, 1924–7 (4, Rytel, after J. Żuławski), Warsaw, Wielki, 14 Dec 1929

Koniec Mesjasza, [The End of the Messiah], 1935–6 (Rytel, after Żuławski), inc.

Krzyżowcy [The Crusaders], 1942 (Rytel)

Andrzej z Chełmna [Andrew from Chełmno], 1942–3 (4, epilogue, Rytel, after V. Hugo: *Angelo Malipiero*); rev. 1947, Warsaw, 12 March 1962 ADRIAN THOMAS

S

Saarbrücken (Fr. Sarrebruck). Capital of Saarland, in south-west Germany. Intensive theatrical activity, including opera performances, took place in the 18th century. Count Ludwig had a theatre built in the city in 1787, but it was completely destroyed in the Revolutionary Wars. Not until 1897 was the Neues Theater built. It opened with a performance of *Mignon* and was renamed the Thalia-Theater in 1899; the city took over its management in 1922. A new, grandly designed theatre was built by Paul Baumgarten under the Nazi regime. Called the Gautheater Saarpfalz, it opened in 1938 with *Der fliegende Holländer* in the presence of Hitler, Himmler and Goebbels; a year later it was closed. Performances began again after the French campaign, with the theatre then known as the Gautheater Westmark, but the building was damaged by air raids in 1942 and 1944. After the war performances resumed in 1948 with *Die Zauberflöte*, at what was called the Stadttheater Saarbrücken. A particularly interesting period was that of the administration of Herman Wedekind (1960–76), who set up contacts with Tbilisi in the USSR and with Nantes. In the early 1970s the Saarbrücken theatre became the Saarländische Staatstheater. When the city withdrew its financial support in 1988, the *Land* of Saarland gave the theatre the status of a limited company. Constant renovation went on throughout the 1980s, and the theatre reopened with *Siegfried* on 29 April 1989. The Grosses Haus holds almost 880 spectators. In its ten-month season the theatre gives about 150 evenings of opera, with five new productions in the Grosses Haus and one in an alternative venue. The annual repertory generally includes one modern work and two comic operas.

*

F. Klövekorn: *Chronik des Saarbrücker Theaters und Theaterspiels* (Saarbrücken, 1932)

GÁBOR HALÁSZ

Sabadini [Sabatini], **Bernardo** (*b* ?Venice; *d* Parma, 26 Nov 1718). Italian composer. He was a member of the clergy. According to the libretto of his oratorio *I disegni della divina sapienza*, as quoted by the revisers of Allacci, he was a Venetian. From 1 July 1681 he was organist at the Farnese court at Parma and on 1 March 1689 became *maestro di cappella* there; he was organist and 'resident' of the ducal church from February 1689 and *maestro di cappella* from 1692. As court composer he was, from 1686 to 1700, responsible for the musical preparation of operas performed at the Novissimo Teatro Ducale, Parma, and the Nuovo Teatro Ducale, Piacenza (the second capital of the state), in collaboration with the court poets: Lotto Lotti until 1687, then Aurelio Aureli until 1694 and finally Giovanni Tamagni. Ferdinando Galli-Bibiena designed the scenography, Federico Crivelli the dances and Gasparo Torelli the costumes. With this team Ranuccio II Farnese raised the court operatic spectacles, until then episodic and somewhat provincial, to a level comparable with that of the major Italian theatre cities – Venice, Bologna, Milan, Rome and Naples. Aureli supplied a repertory consisting largely of Venetian imports; later, operas of Neapolitan origin appeared. Sabadini, 'heroic composer of our times', often supplied only new arias. In the later years the success of the Farnese theatrical policy gained him some productions outside the duchy, at Turin, Rome, Genoa and Pavia. The high point of his output, however, was for the marriage festivities of Odoardo II Farnese and Dorothea Sophia of Neuburg-Pfalz in 1690 (*La gloria d'Amore* and *Il favore degli dei*). These Olympian and sumptuous spectacles reaped European fame for the Bibiena family but even at the time provoked criticism from Italian intellectuals for the degradation that the dignity of the drama and the music supposedly underwent.

Parma performances at the Novissimo Teatro Ducale, and Piacenza performances at the Nuovo Teatro Ducale, unless otherwise stated

dm – *dramma per musica*

Furio Camillo (L. Lotti), Piacenza, 1686

Didio Giuliano (Lotti, after a Sp. orig.), Piacenza, 1687

Zenone il tiranno (Lotti), Piacenza, 1687, arias *I-MOe*

Olimpia placata (dm, A. Aureli, after L. Ariosto), Parma, 1687, arias *MOe* [rev. of D. Freschi: Olimpia vendicata]

L'Ercole trionfante (dm, Aureli, after G. A. Moniglia), Piacenza, 1688, arias *MOe* [rev. of G. A. Boretti: Ercole in Tebe]

Teseo in Atene (dm, Aureli), Parma, 1688, arias *MOe* [rev. of A. Giannettini: Medea in Atene]

Hierone tiranno di Siracusa (dramma, Aureli), Piacenza, 1688, arias *MOe*

Amor spesso inganna (dm, Aureli), Piacenza, 1689, arias *Rvat* [rev. of A. Sartorio: Orfeo]

Teodora clemente (dm, A. Morselli and Aureli), Piacenza, 1689, arias *MOe* [rev. of D. Gabrielli: Teodora Augusta]

Il Vespasiano (dm, Aureli, after G. C. Corradi), Parma, 26 Dec 1689 [rev. of C. Pallavicino]

La gloria d'Amore (spettacolo festivo, Aureli), Parma, garden of Palazzo Ducale, 24 May 1690

Il favore degli dei (dramma fantastico musicale, Aureli), Parma, 25 May 1690

Pompeo continente (dramma, Aureli), Piacenza, 1690, arias ?by Sabadini *MOe*
Diomede punito da Alcide (dramma, Aureli), Piacenza, 1691, arias ?by Sabadini *MOe*
La pace fra Tolomeo e Seleuco (dm, Aureli, after Morselli), Piacenza, 1691, arias ?by Sabadini *MOe* [rev. of C. F. Pollarolo]
Circe abbandonata da Ulisse (dramma, Aureli), Piacenza, 1692, arias *MOe*
Il Massiminio (dm, Aureli), Parma, 1692, arias ?by Sabadini *MOe* [rev. of Pallavicino: Massimo Puppieno]
Talestri innamorata d'Alessandro Magno (dramma, Aureli), Piacenza, 1693
Il riso nato fra il pianto (dm, Aureli), Turin, Regio, carn. 1694, *F-Pn*
Demetrio tiranno (Aureli), Piacenza, 1694
Furio Camillo (dm, M. Noris), Parma, 1697 [rev. of G. A. Perti]
La virtù trionfante dell'inganno (G. C. Godi), Piacenza, 1697 [rev. of Eraclea, Venice, Feb 1696, possibly by Sabadini himself]
L'Aiace (A. d'Averara), Rome, Capranica, Jan 1697, arias *D-Müs*, *F-Pn*, *GB-Lbl*, *Ob*, *I-Bc*, *Rli*, *Rvat* [?rev. of C. A. Lonati, P. Magni and F. Ballarotti]
L'Eusonia, overo La dama stravagante ('Signori M. N. P. C.'), Rome, Capranica, Feb 1697, arias *D-MÜs*, *GB-Lbl*, *Lwa*, *Ob*, *I-Bc*, *Rli*, *Rvat* [?rev. of Pallavicino: Licinio imperatore; 'M. N.' is M. Noris; 'P. C.' may stand for Crateo Pradolini, pseud. of P. Ottoboni]
L'Alarico, Genoa, aut. 1698
Il Domizio (dm, Corradi), Genoa, aut. 1698 [rev. of M. A. Ziani]
Il Ruggiero (G. Tamagni, after Ariosto), Parma, 1699
L'Eraclea (dm, S. Stampiglia), Parma, 1700 [rev. of A. Scarlatti]
Il Meleagro, Pavia, 1705, collab. A. F. Martinenghi and Magni
Alessandro amante eroe, Genoa, Falcone, Jan 1706, arias *E-Mn*
Annibale, Genoa, Falcone, aut. 1706, arias *Mn*
La virtù coronata, o sia Il Fernando, Parma, Teatrino di corte, 2 Sept 1714 [attrib. Sabadini by Balestrieri]

*

AllacciD; *ES* (B. Becherini)
L. Balestrieri: *Feste e spettacoli alla corte dei Farnesi: contributo alla storia del melodramma* (Parma, 1909)
N. Pelicelli: 'Musicisti in Parma nel secolo XVII', *NA*, ix (1932), 221, 245; x (1933), 44, 122, 316
A. Yorke-Long: *Music at Court* (London, 1954), 8ff
C. Molinari: *Le nozze degli dei: un saggio sul grande spettacolo italiano nel seicento* (Rome, 1968), 202–211
L. Bianconi: 'L'Ercole in Rialto', *Venezia e il melodramma nel seicento: Venice 1972*, 259–68
C. Sartori: 'Bernardo Sabadini smascherato', *NRMI*, xi (1977), 44–9
M. Viale Ferrero: *La scenografia dalle origini al 1936* (Turin, 1980), 57, 59–61, 69
A. Chiarelli: *I codici di musica della raccolta estense* (Florence, 1987), items 518, 534, 554–5, 560, 564, 569–72 [pp.122, 126, 131–7]
F. Carboni, T. M. Gialdroni and A. Ziino: 'Cantate ed arie romane del tardo seicento nel fondo Caetani della Biblioteca Corsiniana: repertorio, forme e strutture', *Studi musicali*, xviii (1989), 49–192, esp.117–22

LORENZO BIANCONI

Sabata, Victor de. *See* DE SABATA, VICTOR.

Sabatino [Sabbatino, Sabatini], **Nicola** (*b* Naples, *c*1708; *d* Naples, 4 April 1796). Italian composer. After studying with Francesco Feo and Ignazio Prota at the Conservatorio di S Onofrio in Naples, he established himself as a composer of sacred and secular vocal music whose works were in demand in Naples and beyond. In autumn 1735 he reportedly composed the second part of the serenata *Il tempo felice* (music lost) that Pergolesi was unable to complete for the wedding of Raimondo di Sangro, Prince of Sansevero (December 1735) because of ill-health. During the 1750s he tried his hand at *opera seria*, writing *Cleante* (Rome, Argentina, February 1752; arias in *F-Pc*, *GB-Lbl*) and *Arsace* (A. Salvi; Naples, S Carlo, 30 May 1754). In 1758, it is said, he had a serenata, *Endimione*, staged in Dublin. He served as a *maestro di cappella* of various churches in Naples, and was considered a worthy composer by his contemporaries. When Naples mourned the death of Niccolò Jommelli in August 1774, Sabatino was chosen from among the musicians of the city to compose the music for the public funeral ceremonies.

*

BurneyH; *RosaM*; *StiegerO*
G. Sorge: *I teatri di Palermo* (Palermo, 1926)
U. Prota-Giurleo: *La grande orchestra del R. Teatro San Carlo nel settecento* (Naples, 1927)
——: *Il teatro di corte del palazzo reale di Napoli* (Naples, 1952)
A.-E. Cherbuliez: *G. B. Pergolesi: Leben und Werk* (Zürich and Stuttgart, 1954), 68–71
F. De Filipis and R. Arnese: *Cronache del Teatro di San Carlo* (Naples, 1961)

HANNS-BERTOLD DIETZ

Sabbatini, Giuseppe (*b* Rome, 11 May 1957). Italian tenor. At first a double bass player, he studied with Silvana Ferraro and made his début in 1987 at Spoleto as Edgardo (*Lucia di Lammermoor*), then sang Rodolfo at Trieste, returning in 1989 as Carlo/Viscount de Sirval (*Linda di Chamounix*). He has appeared at La Scala and the Vienna Staatsoper, in Paris, Berlin, Hamburg, Zürich, Florence, Parma and Bologna. His roles include Faust, Werther, Lensky and Gabriele Adorno (which he has recorded). He made his Covent Garden début in 1991 as the Duke, then sang Arturo (*I puritani*) in 1992. An effective actor and a fine musician, he has a soft-grained and flexible voice with a strong top register.

ELIZABETH FORBES

Sabina, Karel (*b* Prague, 29 Dec 1813; *d* Prague, 9 Nov 1877). Czech librettist. He studied law in Prague and Vienna, returning to Prague when his political activities attracted the attention of the police. He was sentenced to death for his part in the 1848 Revolution but the sentence was commuted and he was released in 1857. He made a living through voluminous journalistic and literary activity, including several novels and plays. From 1859 he also served as an important police informer; his double life was uncovered by Czech patriots in 1872 and he was disgraced and died in poverty.

Sabina wrote librettos for all the leading Czech composers of the day. His historical librettos for Smetana (*The Brandenburgers in Bohemia*) and Šebor (*The Templars in Moravia*) attained special status as texts for the first newly composed Czech operas in the Czech Provisional Theatre. They were, however, his weakest librettos: that for *The Brandenburgers* was particularly castigated in the 1861 opera competition as 'slátanina na kvap' ('a hastily cobbled-up job'). He was happiest in a comic mode, especially in his best-known libretto, for Smetana's *The Bartered Bride*, and in the comic librettos he wrote for Blodek, Rozkošný and Bendl. He considered his librettos more as a means of earning money than as carefully crafted patriotic products, but their rough and ready nature resulted in a refreshing, more down-to-earth diction. Furthermore their predominance of trochees (when he managed verse at all) suited sung Czech better than the more contrived metres that librettists such as Krásnohorská attempted.

selective list

Templáři na Moravě [The Templars in Moravia], Šebor, 1865; *Braniboři v Čechách* [The Brandenburgers in Bohemia], Smetana, 1866; *Prodaná nevěsta* [The Bartered Bride], Smetana, 1866, rev. version, 1870; *V studni* [In the Well], Blodek, 1867; *Vodník* [The Water Goblin], Vinář, comp. ?1867, inc.; *Zítek*, Blodek, comp. 1868–9, inc.; *Mikuláš*, Rozkošný, 1870; *Bukovín*, Fibich, 1874; *Starý ženich* [The Elderly Suitor], Bendl, 1882

*

ČSHS [lists further libs. and bibliography]

Z. Nejedlý, ed.: *Karel Sabina: Braniboři v Čechách* [The Brandenburgers in Bohemia] (Prague, 1918) [critical edn with biographical introduction]
——: *Karel Sabina: Prodaná nevěsta* [The Bartered Bride] (Prague, 1930) [critical edn with biographical introduction]
G. Abraham: 'The Genesis of *The Bartered Bride*', *ML*, xxviii (1947), 36–49
M. Očadlík: *Smetanovi libretisté* [Smetana's Librettists] (Prague, 1948), 36–43
J. Bartoš: 'K genesi Smetanovy Prodané nevěsty' [The Genesis of Smetana's The Bartered Bride], *Musikologie*, iv (1955), 7–31
J. Purš: *K případu Karla Sabiny* [The Case of Karel Sabina] (Prague, 1959)
M. Brod: *Die verkaufte Braut: der abenteuerliche Lebensroman des Textdichters Karel Sabina* (Munich, 1962)
R. Šťastný: *Čeští spisovatelé deseti století* [Czech Writers of Ten Centuries] (Prague, 1974)
P. Daněk and J. Vyšohlídová: 'Dokumenty k operní soutěži o cenu hraběte' [Documents Concerning Count Harrach's Operatic Prize Competition], *MMA*, xxx (1983), 147–75
J. Tyrrell: *Czech Opera* (Cambridge, 1988) JOHN TYRRELL

Sabini [Sabino], **Nicola** (*b* ?Naples, *c*1675; *d* Naples, 1705). Italian composer. After studying with Angelo Durante at the Conservatorio di S Onofrio, he succeeded him in May 1699 as first *maestro di cappella* there. He left this position in 1702, perhaps because of illness; he died of tuberculosis.

Sabini's historically most interesting work was his *scherzo drammatico Il mondo abbatuto* (text by S. de Falco), written in 1701 for the feast of S Casimiro and performed for the Congregazione de Musici, of which he was a member. This comedy, of which the music is lost, adumbrates later developments of the Neapolitan commercial comic theatre, with its mixture of Tuscan and Neapolitan dialect, and confirms Sabini's importance for the early development of Neapolitan *opera buffa*. He also wrote a sacred opera, *Innocenza trionfale* (S. Stampiglia; 1704).

*

GiacomoC
U. Prota-Giurleo: 'L'eco del Parnasso', *Francesco Durante* (Naples, 1955), 17 JAMES L. JACKMAN

Sablières, Jean Granouilhet [Grenouillet], **Sieur de** (*b* Languedoc, 1627; *d* Paris, *c*1700). French composer. In 1652 he entered the service of Philippe, Duke of Orléans, whose *maître et intendant de la musique de chambre* he became in 1669. He composed a pastoral opera, *Les amours de Diane et d'Endymion*, to a libretto by Henry Guichard, for the wedding of the duke. The work was staged on 13 November 1671 and performed before the king at St Germain-en-Laye the following year under the title *Le triomphe de l'amour*; the music is lost. In 1671 Sablières bought from Pierre Perrin, who was in grave financial difficulties, the royal patent to perform operas (which he aimed to do in collaboration with Guichard). Others, however, claimed rights to the licence, and when in 1672 Lully acquired the entire privilege, Sablières was forced to abandon his plan. In 1679 he was summoned to Languedoc to direct the music for the festivities organized at Pézenas and Montpellier to mark the signing of the peace treaty with Spain. He produced there 'a very pleasing sort of opera', an aristocratic *divertissement* celebrating the two nations, to a text by M. de Bray, given under the auspices of Cardinal de Bonsy, Archbishop of Narbonne. The music for this also is lost.

*

A. Pougin: *Les vrais créateurs de l'opéra français* (Paris, 1881)
C. Nuitter and E. Thoinan: *Les origines de l'opéra français* (Paris, 1886)
S. Pitou: *The Paris Opéra: an Encyclopedia of Operas, Ballets, Composers, and Performers*, i: *Genesis and Glory, 1671–1715* (Westport, CT, 1983)
MARCELLE BENOIT, CHRISTINA BASHFORD

Sacchèro, Giacomo (*b* probably Catania; *d* Catania, Oct 1875). Italian librettist. Giovanni Pacini referred to him as a fellow-citizen of Catania. As a young man Sacchèro attracted the attention and encouragement of Mercadante, but his first commission was to complete the libretto of Nini's *Cristina di Svezia*, which Cammarano had failed to submit in time, for Genoa in 1840. Subsequently he wrote principally for Milan, where he was on the roster of poets at La Scala, producing librettos for, among others, Federico Ricci, Pacini and Donizetti (*Caterina Cornaro*, the last opera to be produced in the composer's lifetime). Sacchèro's most widely performed text was his early *Corrado di Altamura*. A comparison of his Act 3 of *Cristina di Svezia* with Cammarano's own later version shows Sacchèro's deficiencies: his dramatic sense was crude, though theatrically effective, and his language coarse and violent, lacking any sense of poetry or style.

Cristina di Svezia (tragedia lirica), Nini, 1840 (Acts 1 and 2 by Cammarano); *La cantante* (melodramma giocoso), Sanelli, 1841; *Margarita di Yorck* (tragedia lirica), Nini, 1841; *Corrado di Altamura* (dramma lirico), F. Ricci, 1841; *Odalisa* (dramma lirico), Nini, 1842; *Vallombra* (dramma lirico), F. Ricci, 1842; *Caterina Cornaro* (tragedia lirica), Donizetti, 1844; *L'ebrea* (dramma lirico), G. Pacini, 1844; *I Luna e i Perollo* (dramma lirico), P. Bona, 1844; *I Burgravi* (dramma lirico), M. Salvi, 1845; *Il profeta velato* (dramma lirico), R. Manna, 1846; *I baccanti* (dramma lirico), U. Fontana, 1847; *Il corsaro* (dramma lirico), Nini, 1847; *Ariele* (melodramma lirico), A. Leoni, 1855; *Clarissa Harlowe* (dramma lirico), N. Perelli, 1858; *La martire* (dramma lirico), E. Perelli, 1869; *Costanza di Francavilla* (dramma lirico), S. Coppa, 1869; *Asraele degli Albenceraggi* (tragedia lirica), C. Angeloni, 1871

*

W. Ashbrook: *Donizetti and his Operas* (Cambridge, 1982; It. trans., as *Donizetti: le opere*, 1987) JOHN BLACK

Sacchetti, Lorenzo (*b* Padua, 4 June 1759; *d* Plzeń, after 1834). Italian scene painter, decorator and designer. He studied in Padua, where frescoes by him survive in the Pisani (1782) and da Rio (1794) palaces in via Dante. In 1784 he moved to Venice, where he worked on scenery for the S Giovanni Grisostomo and S Luca theatres. He was scene designer for the opera and ballet repertory at the S Samuele and S Moisè theatres, and for the private theatre in Casa Pepoli, until 1794 (for a list of his productions see *ES*). From 1790 he taught perspective painting at the Accademia di Belle Arti, but in 1794 he went to Vienna, introduced to the court theatres by the dancer and choreographer Salvatore Viganò. At first he was assistant to the stage designer Joseph Platzer, and then architect to the court until 1810; in 1821 he published a series of six lithographs of scenes for the Kärtnertortheater production of Nicolini's *Coriolano*.

In 1817 Sacchetti was in Prague working for the Ständetheater, and in 1830 he published there his manual of scene design, in Italian with a German translation on facing pages: *Quanto sia facile l'inventare decorazioni teatrali: guida elementare* (Prague, 1830), followed by an appendix (Vienna, 1834). At that period there is evidence for his being in Plzeń, but nothing further is known of him.

For illustration *see* STAGE DESIGN, fig.8.

*

M. Agghazy: 'Scenografie di Lorenzo Sacchetti', *La critica d'arte*, iv (1950), 69–76 [with bibliography]

D. Oenslager: *Stage Design: Four Centuries of Scenic Invention* (New York, 1975), 124–9 MARINELLA PIGOZZI

Sacchini, Antonio (Maria Gasparo Gioacchino) (*b* Florence, 14 June 1730; *d* Paris, 6 Oct 1786). Italian composer, a leading figure in serious opera of the late 18th century.

1. LIFE. When Antonio was four, his father Gaetano, a cook, attached himself to the retinue of the Infante Don Carlos and accompanied them to Naples. At the age of ten Antonio entered the Conservatorio S Maria di Loreto to study the violin with Nicola Fiorenza. He also studied singing with Gennaro Manna, and composition with Francesco Durante, who esteemed him highly and predicted that he would be 'the composer of the century'. He was asked to serve as *mastricello* in 1756, the same year that his first theatrical work, the intermezzo *Fra Donato*, was performed by the students at the conservatory and in various houses throughout the city and province. The success of *Fra Donato* and of *Il giocatore*, a second intermezzo written for the conservatory in 1757, brought invitations to compose comic works for two Neapolitan theatres – the Teatro Nuovo and the Teatro dei Fiorentini. In January 1758 he was nominated *maestro di cappella straordinario* at the conservatory, an unpaid post in which he assisted Manna, the *primo maestro*, and Pierantonio Gallo, the *secondo maestro*. When Manna retired in May 1761, Gallo became *primo maestro* and Sacchini *secondo maestro*. In the same month *Andromaca*, his first *opera seria*, was performed at the Teatro S Carlo, Naples. On 12 October 1762 he was granted leave to go to Venice, where he composed *Alessandro Severo* for the Teatro S Benedetto and *Alessandro nell'Indie* for the Teatro S Salvatore. Neglecting to return to his duties in Naples, he proceeded to Padua, where on 9 July 1763 his *Olimpiade* was such an overwhelming success that it was performed throughout Italy. Further triumphs in Rome, Naples and Florence led him to abandon his post at the conservatory for a career as an opera composer.

For the next few years Sacchini lived in Rome, where he composed for the Teatro Valle a number of comic works which achieved fame throughout Europe, including *Il finto pazzo per amore* (1765), *La contadina in corte* (1765) and *L'isola d'amore* (1766). In 1768 he moved to Venice, where he became director of the Conservatorio dell'Ospedaletto. He quickly gained a reputation as an excellent singing teacher (Nancy Storace and Adriana Gabrieli were among his pupils). He composed several oratorios for the conservatory and numerous pieces for Venetian churches. In early 1770 he visited Germany for productions in Munich and Stuttgart, and then returned to his post in Venice, where for the next two years he combined his teaching with the composition of successful operas for the major Italian theatres.

In 1772 Sacchini moved to London, where he remained for nearly ten years. Burney described *Il Cid* (January 1773) and *Tamerlano* (May 1773), his first operas for the English capital, as

> equal, if not superior, to any musical dramas I had heard in any part of Europe. The airs of Millico, the first man, were wholly written in the delicate and pathetic style of that singer; as the first woman's part was in the spirited and nervous style of Girelli. And he cherished the talents of the inferior singers in so judicious a manner, that all their defects were constantly disguised or concealed.

When Traetta arrived in London in 1776 his opera failed miserably because, according to Burney, 'Sacchini had already taken possession of our hearts, and so firmly established himself in the public favour, that he was not to be supplanted by a composer in the same style'. But Sacchini's dissolute life created many enemies and eventually brought financial ruin. His former friend, the singer Venanzio Rauzzini, went so far as to claim many of the composer's most famous arias as his own.

Faced with the threat of imprisonment, Sacchini left England in 1781 and went to Paris. He was already famous there because of performances of his *La colonie* (*L'isola d'amore*) in 1775 and *L'olympiade* (*Olimpiade*) in 1777, in adaptations by Framery. The success of these works had delighted the Piccinni supporters, who attempted to draw Sacchini to Paris as an ally in their struggle with the Gluck supporters. In autumn 1781 the composer appeared at Versailles, where he was presented to Marie Antoinette and received with enthusiasm. Joseph II was also visiting the French court at that time and, being particularly fond of Italian opera, recommended Sacchini to his sister's protection. Determined to keep the composer in France, the queen persuaded the directors of the Opéra to accept his demand for 10 000 francs for each of three operas.

From the very first, Sacchini found himself the object of intrigue and ill-will. M. de la Ferté, the *intendant des Menus-Plaisirs*, contrived to stall the performance of his first opera for Paris, *Renaud*, and to draw attention to the queen's preference for foreign composers, while the Gluckistes attempted to estrange the composer from his Piccinnist supporters. When *Renaud* was finally performed on 28 February 1783 it was not well received. The Piccinni faction asserted that the score (an adaptation of his *Armida* of 1772) was influenced by Gluck, while the Gluck supporters condemned the work for lacking dramatic power and originality. Sacchini's next opera, *Chimène*, was performed at Fontainebleau on 18 November 1783 in an atmosphere of open rivalry with Piccinni, whose *Didon* had been given a month and two days earlier and proclaimed a masterpiece. Although *Chimène* suffered in comparison, receiving only one performance while *Didon* received three, both composers were presented to the king (Sacchini by the queen herself) and given a large pension. *Chimène* was first performed at the Opéra on 9 February 1784 and received 16 performances. The *Mercure de France* found the work full of musical beauty but dramatically weak because of unnecessary arias and ritornellos.

The music for Sacchini's next opera, *Dardanus*, was completely original, and with this and the operas that followed, he attempted to create works that conformed to the ideals of French music drama. The failure of *Dardanus* can be attributed in part to an undramatic libretto and an inadequate staging brought about by his enemies at the Opéra. In autumn 1785 the queen had *Dardanus* given at Fontainebleau in a revised version, which proved a success. In the same year Sacchini completed his *Oedipe à Colone*, which the queen had promised would be the first opera to be performed at Fontainebleau during the court's forthcoming stay there, but mounting criticism of her preference for foreigners forced her to revoke her pledge and to cede the honoured place to the French composer Lemoyne. Sacchini's beloved pupil, Henri Berton, asserted that this disappointment contributed greatly to the composer's death, which occurred shortly afterwards on 6 October 1786, although Sacchini had been suffering many years from gout and the effects of dissipation. *Oedipe* was performed at the Opéra on 1 February 1787 and hailed as his masterpiece. The work formed a standard part of the repertory until 1830 with 583 performances. *Arvire et Evelina*, Sacchini's last opera, was completed by Rey, the conductor of the Opéra orchestra, and given its première in Paris on 29 April 1788. Although it did not gain the popularity of *Oedipe*, it was heard in Paris until 1827 and had 95 performances.

2. WORKS. The high esteem that Sacchini enjoyed in the judgment of his contemporaries must certainly be modified and put into perspective from a present-day vantage point. In 1770 Burney considered him one of the four greatest composers of Italy, along with Jommelli, Galuppi and Piccinni. While he placed Piccinni supreme in the comic style, he nominated Sacchini 'the most promising composer in the serious'. He described *Il Cid* and *Tamerlano* as 'so entire, so masterly, yet so new and natural, that there was nothing left for criticism to censure, though innumerable beauties to point out and admire'. A critic of the next generation, Giuseppe Carpani, hailed Sacchini as the world's greatest melodist. Indeed, his serious operas display an exceptional gift for melody, and although these melodies are not strikingly original, they are immediately appealing and encompass a wide range of emotional expression. On the other hand, the melodies in his comic works are often similar in character and tend to be monotonous. In general, his style is typical of the late Classical era with its simplicity of texture and balanced phrase structure. At times, however, the Mozartian melodic line gives way to expansive phrases that bring to mind the lyric style of the 19th century. Sacchini's harmony tends to be richer than that of most of his contemporary Italian opera composers, and especially effective is his judicious use of diminished seventh chords, dominants of degrees of the scale other than the tonic and augmented sixth chords. He often achieved dramatic tension through the use of changing harmonies over a tonic pedal point or with a sudden change from major to minor. The instrumental accompaniment is employed in such a way that it enhances but never detracts from the vocal line. As Burney observed, 'his accompaniments, though always rich and ingenious, never call off attention from the voice, but, by a constant transparency, the principal melody is rendered distinguishable through all the contrivances of imitative and picturesque design in the instruments'. The virtuoso character of the violin parts in many of the ritornellos and the care with which he notated the accompanimental figures reflect a thorough mastery of this instrument.

Sacchini employed a variety of aria forms. Only rarely did he adhere to the complete da capo form, but he often made use of altered versions of this basic plan. He also made frequent use of a cavatina-like two-part aria that approximates to the *A* portion of the da capo form, and of the vocal rondò, in both comic and serious works. Through-composed arias are occasionally found in his comic operas, while in the French works one finds the cavatina-cabaletta combination that was to become popular in the 19th century. Sacchini's accompanied recitatives are characterized by exceptional dramatic power and often combine with the following aria to form a unified musical scene through the use of common motivic material. Transitional portions of the aria itself are frequently written in the manner of accompanied recitative.

In his ensembles Sacchini was only partly successful in his attempt to define musically the various characters. In the comic works the action continues through the ensemble and is reflected by quick changes of tempo and musical character, although the key centre is generally constant. The chorus remained insignificant in his operas until his London period. Burney reported that Sacchini,

> finding how fond the English were of Handel's oratorio choruses, introduced solemn and elaborate choruses into some of his operas; but though excellent in their kind, they never had a good effect: the mixture of English singers with the Italian, as well as the awkward figure they cut, as actors, joined to the difficulty of getting their parts by heart, rendered those compositions ridiculous, which in still life would have been admirable.

Especially effective, however, are the impressive choral scenes in the French operas in which the chorus alternates with soloists in rondo fashion. Indeed, the many choruses and scenes of spectacle in his last operas not only show the strong influence of Gluck but also point the way to the grand opera of Spontini. *Dardanus* and *Oedipe* emerge as true lyric dramas from which all unnecessary ritornellos and airs have been shorn. The great fluidity in combining accompanied recitative, arioso and aria and the variety and attention to detail in the orchestration are used to excellent effect to mirror the changing emotions of the text. With his masterpiece, *Oedipe*, Sacchini admirably achieved a synthesis of Italian melodic style and Gluckian principles within a French dramatic framework.

See also ARMIDA (iii); CALLIROE (i); CONTADINA IN CORTE, LA; CRESO; DARDANUS (ii); and OEDIPE À COLONE; for a discussion of Sacchini's three *Cid* operas, *see* CID, EL.

Fra Donato (int, 2, ? P. Trinchera), Naples, Conservatorio S Maria di Loreto, 1756

Il giocatore (int), Naples, Conservatorio S Maria di Loreto, 1757, *I-Nc*, *Rrai*

Olimpia tradita (commedia, after L. Ariosto: *Orlando furioso*), Naples, Fiorentini, 1758

Il copista burlato (commedia, G. A. Federico), Naples, Nuovo, aut. 1759

La vendemmia (int, 1, C. Goldoni), Rome, Capranica, carn. 1760; as La vendimia, Barcelona, 1767

I due fratelli beffati (commedia), Naples, Nuovo, aut. 1760

Il testaccio (ob), Rome, Capranica, 1760

Andromaca (os, A. Salvi), Naples, S Carlo, 30 May 1761, *P-La*

Il curioso imprudente (A. Palomba), Naples, Fiorentini, aut. 1761, collab. N. Piccinni

La finta contessa (farsetta), Rome, Capranica, 1761

Li due bari (ob), Naples, Fiorentini, 1762

L'amore in campo (dg, 2), Rome, Valle, 1762

Alessandro Severo (os, 3, A. Zeno), Venice, S Benedetto, carn. 1763, *La*

Alessandro nell'Indie (os, P. Metastasio), Venice, S Salvatore, Ascension 1763; rev., Naples, 1768; *F-Pn*, *I-Tf*, *P-La*, *US-Wc*

Olimpiade (os, 3, Metastasio), Padua, Nuovo, 9 July 1763; adapted N. E. Framery in Fr. as L'olympiade, Paris, 2 Oct 1777 (Paris, 1777); *F-Pn*, *P-La*

Eumene (os, Zeno), Florence, Pergola, carn. 1764, *I-Rc**, *Rdp*

Semiramide riconosciuta (os, 3, Metastasio), Rome, Argentina, carn. 1764, *Rdp*, *P-La*

Lucio Vero (os, Zeno), Naples, S Carlo, 4 Nov 1764; as pasticcio, London, 1773, Favourite Songs (London, 1773); *B-Bc*, *F-Pn*, *GB-Lbl*, *I-Nc*, *P-La*, *US-Bp*, *Wc*

Il finto pazzo per amore (int, 2, T. Mariani), Rome, Valle, spr. 1765, *A-Wn*, *D-Dlb*, *Rtt*, *F-Pn*, *I-Fc*, *Mc*

La contadina in corte (ob, 2, N. Tassi), Rome, Valle, carn. 1765; Favourite Songs (London, 1782); *A-Wn*, *B-Bc*, *D-Dlb*, *MÜs*, *Rtt*, *Wa*, *F-Pn*, *I-Bc*, *Fc*, *Gl*, *MOe*, *Nc*, *Rc*, *Rdp*, *US-Wc*

Il Creso (os, 3, G. Pizzi), Naples, S Carlo, 4 Nov 1765; rev., London, King's, 1774, Favourite Songs (London, 1774); as Euriso, London, 1781; *D-Mbs*, *F-Pn*, *I-Nc*, *Rc*, *P-La*

L'isola d'amore (dg, 2, A. Gori), Rome, Valle, carn. 1766; rev., London, King's, 1776 (London, 1776); adapted Framery in Fr. as La colonie, Paris, Comédie-Italienne (Bourgogne), 16 Aug 1775

(Paris, 1776); *A-Wn, B-Lc, D-BAR, Dlb, Hs, Rtt, F-Pn, H-Bn, I-BDG, Mc, US-Bp*
Artaserse (os, 3, Metastasio), Rome, Argentina, carn. 1768, *I-Rc**, *Rdp, Rvat*
Il Cidde (os, 3, Pizzi, after P. Corneille: *Le Cid*), Rome, Argentina, carn. 1769, *I-Rsc, Rvat, P-La*
Nicoraste (os, 3, B. Vitturi), Venice, S Benedetto, Ascension 1769, *A-Wgm, P-La* (inc., attrib. C. F. Pollarolo)
Scipione in Cartagena (os, E. Giunti), Munich, Residenz, 8 Jan 1770, *B-Bc, D-Mbs, F-Pn, I-Bc, P-La*
Calliroe (os, M. Verazi), Ludwigsburg, Schloss, 11 Feb 1770, *D-Sl*
L'eroe cinese (os, Metastasio), Munich, Residenz, 27 April 1770, *DS, Mbs* (*R*1982: IOB, xc), *US-Wc*
Adriano in Siria (os, Metastasio), Venice, S Benedetto, Ascension 1771, *I-Gl, US-Wc*
Ezio (os, Metastasio), Naples, S Carlo, 4 Nov 1771, *F-Pn, I-Nc, P-La, US-Wc*
Armida (os, 3, J. Durandi, after T. Tasso: *Gerusalemme liberata*), Milan, Regio Ducal, carn. 1772, *D-Mbs, F-Pn, P-La*; rev. as Rinaldo, London, King's, 22 April 1780, Favourite Songs (London, 1780), *I-Fc*
Vologeso (os, Zeno), Parma, Ducale, 1772, *F-Pn, I-Nc, P-La*
Il Cid (os, G. Bottarelli, after Corneille: *Le Cid*), London, King's, 19 Jan 1773, Favourite Songs (London, 1773)
Tamerlano (os, A. Piovene), London, King's, 6 May 1773, Favourite Songs (London, 1773)
Perseo (os, 3, A. Aureli), London, King's, 29 Jan 1774, Favourite Songs (London, 1774)
Nitteti (os, 3, Metastasio), London, King's, 19 April 1774, Favourite Songs (London, 1774), *F-Pn**
Montezuma (os, 3, Bottarelli), London, King's, 7 Feb 1775, Favourite Songs (London, 1775)
Erifile (os, 3, G. De Gamerra), London, King's, 7 Feb 1778, Favourite Songs (London, 1778)
L'amore soldato (dg, 3, Tassi), London, King's, 4 May 1778 (London, 1778), *A-Wn, F-Pn, Po, GB-Lbl, I-Fc, US-Wc*
L'avaro deluso, o Don Calandrino (dg, 3, G. Bertati), London, King's, 24 Nov 1778
Enea e Lavinia (os, 3, Bottarelli), London, King's, 25 March 1779, Favourite Songs (London, 1779)
Mitridate (os, Zeno), London, King's, 23 Jan 1781, Favourite Songs (London, 1781)
Renaud (3, J. Leboeuf and S.-J. Pellegrin, after Tasso: *Gerusalemme liberata*), Paris, Opéra, 28 Feb 1783 (Paris, 1783); *F-Pn, Po**
Chimène (tragédie lyrique, 3, N.-F. Guillard, after Corneille: *Le Cid*), Fontainebleau, 18 Nov 1783 (Paris, *c*1784), *F-Pn**, *Po* (score and parts)
Dardanus (tragédie, 4, Guillard, after C.-A. Le Clerc de La Bruère), Versailles, Trianon, 18 Sept 1784 (Paris, 1784); rev. (3), Fontainebleau, 1785; *D-Rtt, F-Po**, *Prt, US-Wc*
Oedipe à Colone (tragédie lyrique, 3, Guillard, after Sophocles), Versailles, 4 Jan 1786, (Paris, 1787), *D-Mo, F-Pn**, *Po, I-Nc, US-Wc*
Arvire et Evelina (tragédie lyrique, 3, Guillard, after W. Mason: *Caractacus*), Paris, Opéra, 29 April 1788, completed by J.-B. Rey (Paris, 1788), *F-Po* (part autograph), *US-Wc*
Ester (int, 2), *I-Rc* (frag.)

Arias in: Ciro, *I-Nc*; La clemenza di Tito, *MAav*; Le finte gemelle, *Rdp*; Oreste, *Gl*; Il re pastore, *Rvat*; Ricimiero, *MAav*; Siroe, *Nc*

Music in: Le vicende della sorte, or The Turns of Fortune, 1770; Didone abbandonata, 1775

*

BurneyFI; *BurneyH*; *FlorimoN*
F. de Villars: 'Oedipe à Colone et Sacchini', *Art musical*, iii (1862–3), 345–8, 361–3
A. Jullien: *La cour et l'opéra sous Louis XVI: Marie Antoinette et Sacchini; Salieri et Favart* (Paris, 1878)
J. G. Prod'homme: 'L'héritage di Sacchini', *RMI*, xv (1908), 23–41
——: *Ecrits de musiciens* (Paris, 1912)
——: 'Un musicien napolitain à la cour de Louis XVI: les dernières années de Gasparo Sacchini', *Le ménestrel*, lxxxvii (1925), 505–7, 517–20
V. Morelli: 'Antonio Sacchini fra i Gluckisti e i briganti di Londra', *Vita musicale italiana*, vii–viii (1926)
A. Pompeati: 'Il Parini e la musica', *RMI*, xxxvi (1929), 556–74
U. Prota-Giurleo: *Sacchini non nacque a Pozzuoli* (Naples, 1952)
F. Schlitzer: *Antonio Sacchini: schede e appunti per una sua storia teatrale* (Siena, 1955)
U. Prota-Giurleo: *Sacchini a Napoli* (Naples, 1956)
——: *Sacchini fra Piccinnisti e Gluckisti* (Naples, 1957)
J. Rushton: *Music and Drama at the Académie Royale de Musique, Paris, 1774–1789* (diss., U. of Oxford, 1970)
E. A. Thierstein: *Five French Operas of Sacchini* (diss., U. of Cincinnati, 1974)
M. McClymonds: 'Mattia Verazi and the Opera at Mannheim, Stuttgart and Ludwigsburg', *Studies in Music from the University of Western Ontario*, vii/2 (1982), 99–136
K. J. Wilson: *L'olimpiade: Selected Eighteenth-Century Settings of Metastasio's Libretto* (diss., Harvard U., 1982) DAVID DiCHIERA

Saccomani, Lorenzo (*b* Milan, 9 June 1938). Italian baritone. He studied in Milan, making his début in 1964 at Avignon as Silvio, then singing the Herald (*Lohengrin*) at Venice. He has sung throughout Italy; at La Scala his roles include Sharpless, Marcello, Valentin and Albert (*Werther*). In 1972 he made his American début at Dallas as Enrico Ashton. He has also sung at Frankfurt, Geneva, Chicago, Brussels and Buenos Aires. His repertory includes Alphonse (*La favorite*), Riccardo (*I puritani*), Filippo (*Beatrice di Tenda*), Zurga, Escamillo and Lescaut (Massenet and Puccini). His rich-toned voice and forthright style are best displayed in Verdi: as Luna, Renato, Posa, Germont, Nabucco, Montfort, Ezio (*Attila*), Amonasro and Don Carlo (*Forza*). ELIZABETH FORBES

Sack, Erna (*b* Spandau, Berlin, 6 Feb 1898; *d* Mainz, 2 March 1972). German soprano. She studied in Prague and with Oscar Daniel in Berlin. She sang at the Berlin Staatsoper from 1928 and appeared in Bielefeld, Breslau and Wiesbaden before joining the Dresden Staatsoper in 1933. She created Isotta in *Die schweigsame Frau* and sang Zerbinetta at Covent Garden with the Dresden company under Strauss's direction; her agile coloratura encouraged the composer to write cadenzas for Zerbinetta's aria. She toured North America in 1936 and sang Rosina and Lucia at Chicago the following year. She appeared in both occupied and neutral Europe during the war, and after 1945 toured America and Germany as a concert singer. DAVID CUMMINGS

Sacramento. American city, the capital of California. Founded in 1839, it expanded dramatically in the Gold Rush of 1848. The first theatre in California, the Eagle (a wooden structure with canvas walls, seating about 70), opened on 18 October 1849; it was destroyed shortly afterwards in a flood, but other theatres sprang up, and plays and concerts were soon being presented. In 1850 Fanny Manten and her company from Milan presented the first ballet in the city, *Gasperone*. The soprano Eliza Biscaccianti was the first opera singer to visit the goldfields, giving 35 concerts in 1852 in Sacramento and the surrounding area. Others followed in 1853 and 1854, including Catherine Hayes and Anna Bishop, who presented 10 operatic 'seasons' in San Francisco and four in Sacramento; the programmes included the 'Mad Scene' from *Lucia di Lammermoor* and were sung with several changes of costume.

Selections from *Lucia* were the first documented operatic performances in Sacramento, presented in 1850 by a Spanish company. Opera in subsequent decades was provided by touring companies, some from Europe, some headed by stars like Hayes and Bishop. The leading theatre was the Metropolitan, built in 1856, with seats for 1200 and a stage big enough for a circus ring. Early performances included circuses, Shakespeare, *The Black Crook* and what was described as a 'full-length' production of *Lucia*, although operas in those days were sometimes 'cut most dreadfully', as one critic put it.

In spite of a rich musical life, it is only in recent times that Sacramento has had its own opera company. In the early years of this century travelling troupes performed there, but it was the San Francisco Opera, organized in 1923, that brought grand opera with great singers to the capital. A 33-year series of annual visits began in 1938 in the Memorial Auditorium, a horseshoe-shaped, general-purpose auditorium with 4400 seats; singers included Pons, Pinza, Baccaloni, Sutherland, Flagstad, Dorothy Kirsten, Tebaldi, Leontyne Price, Alfredo Kraus, Raoul Jobin, Giulietta Simionato and Jon Vickers. When the San Francisco company ceased touring, the Sacramento Opera Guild began working towards a permanently organized local company. The Sacramento Opera Association was formed in 1980 with Marianne Oaks as general director of the new professional company. After a trial start on a modest scale – a double bill of *The Medium* and *Gianni Schicchi* staged in April 1981 in a high school with two-piano accompaniment – operations were moved to the Sacramento Community Center Theater, which had opened in 1974. With a capacity of 2350 for opera and excellent acoustics, it has remained the company's home. By 1985–6 the company had reached its goal of three productions a season with *Bohème*, *Fledermaus* and *Lucia*. All productions were performed twice, and by 1990–91 *Tosca*, *Der Zigeunerbaron* and *Les contes d'Hoffmann* were each given three times. 25 works from the standard repertory have been produced, with singers drawn from the Metropolitan, New York City and San Francisco operas as well as European companies. Monroe Kanouse, a Czech-born resident of San Francisco, has conducted most of the productions. WILLIAM GLACKIN

Sacra rappresentazione di Abram e d'Isaac, La ('The Miracle Play of Abraham and Isaac'). Opera in one act (expanded from incidental music) by ILDEBRANDO PIZZETTI to a libretto adapted by Onorato Castellino from Feo Belcari's 15th-century miracle play of the same name; Perugia, Teatro Morlacchi, 2 October 1937.

Feo Belcari presents the familiar *Genesis* story with disarming simplicity, yet with several telling additional touches. Particularly effective is the way in which short scenes depicting the journey of Abraham and Isaac (baritone and soprano) to the place of sacrifice alternate with others showing Sarra [Sarah] (mezzo-soprano) at home, desperately wondering where they have gone and why they are away for so long. There are two angels (both sopranos), one to announce and round off the proceedings, the other to play a crucial part in the drama: both had already sung in the original incidental music, whereas the other characters' vocal lines date from the final revision. There were also choruses in the score from the very start.

Because of the unusual way in which the work gradually developed into an opera – the original incidental music was given at the Politeama Fiorentina, Florence, on 9 June 1917, further incidental music was composed in 1926, and the remainder of the text set in 1928 – the final result departs markedly from Pizzetti's usual practice by including several self-contained 'numbers' (some of them purely orchestral). This helps to make *La sacra rappresentazione di Abram e d'Isaac* into perhaps the most immediately approachable of all Pizzetti's stage works. The music has a winsome directness and charm; but this does not exclude intensely dramatic moments, especially when Abraham's hand is abruptly stayed (as he is about to sacrifice Isaac) not only by the solo voice of an angel but also by a chorus from heaven. The general musical style, though much simpler than that of Pizzetti's larger biblical opera *Dèbora e Jaéle*, evokes the Old Testament atmosphere in ways that are sometimes comparable. JOHN C. G. WATERHOUSE

Sacrati, Francesco (*b* Parma, bap. 17 Sept 1605; *d* ?Modena, 20 May 1650). Italian composer. He was active in Venice as an opera composer during the early 1640s, always in collaboration with the scenographer Giacomo Torelli. He may subsequently have belonged to the Accademici Discordati, an itinerant troupe which performed one of his operas in Bologna and possibly elsewhere. He was *maestro di cappella* of the 'musici di Bologna' who in March 1648 were invited to perform his opera *La finta pazza* in Reggio Emilia. Sacrati spent part of that year at the Villa Malvasia at Panzano near Bologna, where he composed *L'isola di Alcina*. In 1649 he became *maestro di cappella* of Modena Cathedral. Sacrati was highly esteemed by his contemporaries, including Prince Mattias de' Medici, a close acquaintance, and the librettist Giacomo Badoaro in *L'Ulisse errante* likened him to Monteverdi as the moon to the sun. *La finta pazza*, taken to Paris in December 1645 by Torelli and the ballet-master G. B. Balbi, was the first Italian opera to be performed publicly in France; how much of Sacrati's music remained in this version, which was only partly sung, and in the touring version given in several Italian cities from 1644, is not certain. Of Sacrati's works, only the latter version of *La finta pazza* is known to survive. He may have had a hand in the score of Monteverdi's *L'incoronazione di Poppea* (see Curtis 1989).

See also FINTA PAZZA, LA. For illustration *see* BALBI, GIOVAN BATTISTA; STAGE DESIGN, fig.2; and TORELLI, GIACOMO.

known only from librettos unless otherwise stated

La finta pazza (drama, prol., 3, G. Strozzi), Venice, Novissimo, ded. 14 Jan 1641; rev. version, Piacenza, Palazzo Grande, May 1644, *I-IBborromeo* (*R*: DMV, forthcoming); 4 arias ed. in Rosand (1991); lib. in Della Corte (1958)

Il Bellerofonte (drama musicale, V. Nolfi), Venice, Novissimo, carn. 1642

Venere gelosa (drama, N. E. Bartolini), Venice, Novissimo, ded. 28 Jan 1643 [attrib. Sacrati in Ivanovich 1681]

L'Ulisse errante (op musicale, G. Badoaro), Venice, SS Giovanni e Paolo, carn. 1644 [Reprezentação del Ulisse errante ... a 1 & 2, in the library of John IV of Portugal, may have been a printed version or excerpts]

La Semiramide in India (dramma, M. Bisaccioni), Venice, S Cassiano, ded. 4 Jan 1648 [attrib. Sacrati in Ivanovich]

L'isola di Alcina (tragedia, F. Testi, after L. Ariosto), Bologna, 1648

*

EitnerQ; *ES* (N. Pirrotta); *FétisB*; *WaltherML*

Indice di tutte le opere di musica che si trovano nella Stampa della Pigna di Alessandro Vincenti in Venetia (Venice, 1649–62); repr. in O. Mischiati: *Indici, cataloghi e avvisi degli editori e librai musicali italiani dal 1591 al 1798* (Florence, 1984)

Primeira parte do index da livraria de musica do muyto alto, e poderoso Rey Dom João o IV. nosso senhor (Lisbon, 1649); ed. J. de Vasconcellos (Oporto, 1874–6)

C. Ivanovich: *Minerva al tavolino* (Venice, 1681)

A. Ademollo: *I primi fasti della musica italiana a Parigi* (Milan, 1884)

H. Prunières: *L'opéra italien en France avant Lully* (Paris, 1913)

O. Rombaldi: 'Profilo della storia del teatro in Reggio Emilia, dal 1568 al 1857', *Il teatro a Reggio Emilia* (Reggio Emilia, 1957), 57–97

A. Della Corte: *Drammi per musica dal Rinuccini allo Zeno* (Turin, 1958), i, 333–430

P. Bjurström: *Giacomo Torelli and Baroque Stage Design* (Stockholm, 1962), 53–89, 95–6, 134–43

W. Osthoff: 'Maske und Musik: die Gestaltwerdung der Oper in Venedig', *Castrum Peregrini*, lxv (Amsterdam, 1964), 10–49; repr. in *The Garland Library of the History of Western Music*, xi: *Opera I: Up to Mozart* (New York, 1985), 102–41

C. Sartori: 'La prima diva della lirica italiana: Anna Renzi', *NRMI*, ii (1968), 430–52

——: 'Un fantomatico compositore per un'opera che forse non era un'opera', *NRMI*, v, (1971), 788–98

L. Bianconi and T. Walker: 'Dalla *Finta pazza* alla *Veremonda*: storie di Febiarmonici', *RIM*, x (1975), 379–454; Eng. trans. with addns in DMV (forthcoming)

C. Sartori: 'Ancora della *Finta pazza* di Strozzi e Sacrati', *NRMI*, xi (1977), 335–8

L'opera tra Venezia e Parigi: Venice 1986 [conference on *La finta pazza*; vol. ii incl. edn of Paris lib.]

A. Curtis: '*La Poppea impasticciata* or, Who Wrote the Music to *L'incoronazione* (1643)?', *JAMS*, xlii (1989), 23–54

P. Fabbri: *Il secolo cantante: per una storia del libretto d'opera nel seicento* (Bologna, 1990)

E. Rosand: *Opera in Seventeenth-Century Venice: the Creation of a Genre* (Berkeley, 1991)

——: 'Operatic Madness: a Challenge to Convention', *Music and Text: Critical Enquiries*, ed. S. P. Scher (Cambridge, 1992), 241–87

THOMAS WALKER, LORENZO BIANCONI

Sacred opera. Opera with sacred or religious connotations has existed at most periods in the history of the genre. The term 'sacred opera' has no standard usage: it may be applied to dramatic works written for, or performed in, an ecclesiastical or other religious context, but equally to operas designed for normal theatrical performance and involving a religious theme or bearing some moral or spiritual statement, or even ones that involve a deity, in the form of a god or an oracle. The present article outlines its manifestations in different social, religious and intellectual climates over the 400 years of the history of opera.

1. 17th century. 2. 18th century. 3. 19th century: (i) General trends (ii) Rubinstein's sacred operas. 4. 20th century.

1. 17TH CENTURY. The first regular production of opera concentrated mainly on works in which a spiritual content was dominant. In Rome during the 17th century patrons encouraged composers and librettists away from secular texts towards those with a sacred or moral message. Though Cavalieri's *Rappresentatione di Anima, et di Corpo* (1600) was performed under the auspices of the Oratorians in 1600, it set the scene – in its text, its music and its staging – for the incipient Roman sacred opera under the patronage of the leading families. Neither Agostino Agazzari's *Eumelio* (1606) nor Cavalieri's work presents biblical personages, yet action is expected and the high moral tone calculated to move the audience to renounce the world in favour of the joys of heaven. *Eumelio*, written for the Jesuit Roman Seminary, was the first of many musical dramas commissioned by the order. In Paris the Jesuits mounted Marc-Antoine Charpentier's *David et Jonathas* (1688); these tableaux were performed as *intermèdes* by the pupils of the Collège St Louis-le-Grand, and were intended to give the youths confidence in rhetoric and declamation besides presenting the biblical story. It belongs to a long dramatic tradition at the college, in which sacred subjects were actually in the minority. Viennese oratorios belonging to the category of Jesuit drama increasingly developed in the direction of opera: the best-known example, *Pia et fortis mulier* (1677) by J. K. Kerll, includes all the elements of contemporary Venetian opera, as well as spoken sections. (For a fuller discussion, *see* JESUIT DRAMA.) A further use of operatic procedures in a sacred context in Vienna is seen in the SEPOLCRO.

The Jesuits were quick to see opera as an educational tool, and the Barberini family in Rome were only slightly slower in realizing its potential as an improving source of recreation – a grandiose successor to the spiritual madrigal. From 1632, when the theatre in the Palazzo Barberini opened with Stefano Landi's *Sant'Alessio*, Roman opera was dominated by the patronage of the Barberini, the family of Pope Urban VIII, and by the librettos of Giulio Rospigliosi. Not all Rospigliosi's texts were sacred, though his libretto for the pastoral opera *Erminia sul Giordano* (1633) to music by Michelangelo Rossi is based on the epic of Christian chivalry, Tasso's *Gerusalemme liberata*. Marco Marazzoli's *La vita humana* (1656) celebrated Queen Christina of Sweden's arrival in Rome and her conversion: the moral text tells of the triumph of divine grace. References exist to other occasional pieces, including an 'operina sacra' performed when the Princess Chigi entered a convent in 1686. Rospigliosi's final libretto was staged in 1668, by which time he had become Pope Clement IX: *La comica del cielo, ovvero La Baltasara*, to music by Antonio Maria Abbatini, was a sumptuous production on the favourite Roman subject of religious conversion.

Although his role was central, Rospigliosi had no monopoly on operatic texts. Domenico Mazzocchi's lost operatic account of the lives of four Roman martyrs set a libretto by Ottavio Tronsarelli, *Il martirio de' Santi Abundio prete, Abundantio diacono, Marciano, e Giovanni suo figliuolo cavalieri romani* (1641). In telling the lives of Roman saints it follows the tradition of *Sant'Alessio*. As the century progressed Roman opera became detached from ecclesiastical patronage and became increasingly secular in character, a foil to the oratorio; as elsewhere in Italy, pastoral imagery and mythological subject matter came to dominate operatic production.

In northern Europe, the Protestant tradition also gave rise to sacred operas. At its foundation in 1678 the public opera house in Hamburg was viewed with suspicion by the church authorities; to quieten the objections the repertory during the early years included many operas on biblical and other sacred themes, among them Adam and Eve and the birth of Christ (Theile, 1678, 1681), the Maccabees and David (Franck, 1678, 1679), Esther (Strungk, 1680) and Cain and Abel (Förtsch, 1689).

2. 18TH CENTURY. Although, during the more secular 18th century, the central operatic tradition – that of the Metastasian serious opera, which long dominated Italy, the Habsburg empire and parts of Germany – carried a strong moral and religious undertone, sacred subjects were rarely used for opera, and when they were it was more for their intrinsic qualities, as good stories, rather than for any specifically religious purpose. That would seem to be the case with Montéclair's *Jephté*, a 'tragedy from holy scripture' given at the Paris Opéra in 1732, which drew a condemnation from the Archbishop of Paris as well as considerable public acclaim. The church authorities, regarding themselves as arbiters of the 'sacred', saw this as a misappropriation of it for theatrical entertainment.

A similar attitude informed the London church authorities when, in the same year, Handel planned to perform his *Esther* (originally written for performance at Cannons, about 1718) in a theatrical version. After a private performance, probably with some kind of action, it had been described by Viscount Percival as a

The Holy Communion enacted during the Grail scene at the end of Act 3 of Wagner's 'Parsifal': Paul von Joukowsky's design for the original production at the Festspielhaus, Bayreuth, in 1882

'religious opera'; but the Bishop of London objected to the representation of sacred subjects on stage, even if the performers held books, and when *Esther* was performed in May at the King's Theatre Handel had to comply with the ecclesiastical ruling and noted in the announcement 'There will be no Action on the Stage, but the House will be fitted up in a decent manner for the Audience'. This modification of Handel's original initiative to produce vernacular 'sacred opera' led to the oratorios, in some of which stage directions in the librettos set the scene.

During the Classical era the line between opera and oratorio was clearly drawn, and sacred subjects were not normally admissible on the theatrical stage. Non-Christian, exotic rites could however sometimes find a place, for example in Mozart's *Die Zauberflöte* (which Bernard Shaw was to describe as 'the music of my own church').

3. 19TH CENTURY.

(i) General trends. In the Romantic era no consistent patterns of sacred opera – the influences upon it, patterns of patronage or choice of subject matter – are to be found. Some composers used biblical or other sacred themes for their operas; others used historical religious controversies or other topics as their basis; and in many works the action, or part of it, takes place in an ecclesiastical setting. The French religious revival of the post-Revolution period gave rise to a number of operas on biblical topics, of which Méhul's *Joseph* (1807) is an example. Rossini wrote two operas on biblical themes, *Ciro in Babilonia* (1812), considered sufficiently sacred to be performed during Lent, when operas were normally prohibited, and *Mosè in Egitto* (1818, Naples; later adapted for Paris).

Historical religious disputes provided the subject matter for much French *grand opéra* in the early and middle 19th century, for example Meyerbeer's *Les Huguenots* (1836) and *Le prophète* (1849); Saint-Saëns' *Samson et Dalila* (1877) extends that tradition to biblical events. Religious overtones were strong too in such a work as Donizetti's *Maria Stuarda* (1835), where the story of the murder of a Catholic queen by Protestant usurpers held a particular fascination for the Italians. Verdi, himself a non-believer, drew on biblical sources for his *Nabucco* (1842), with its text treating the Babylonian exile (long supposed to conceal a protest against Austrian oppression in Italy), and in the strongly anti-clerical *Don Carlos* (1867) he depicts the pious atmosphere at the Spanish court and the ruthlessness of the Inquisition.

Wagner treated sacred themes in several works, notably *Tannhäuser* (1845), with its pilgrimage to Rome, *Lohengrin* (1850), where the protagonist is a knight of the Grail, and above all the 'Bühnenweihfestspiel' *Parsifal* (1882) with its stage enactment of Holy Communion. There is a church scene in *Die Meistersinger* (1868), as indeed in very many operas of the 19th century. Puccini's *Tosca* (1900) opens with one in which sacred and secular emotion are set in sharp contrast; his *Suor Angelica* (1918), set in a convent, has as its climax a vision of the Virgin. Many French operas, for example Gounod's *Faust* and Massenet's *Manon*, embody church scenes. Musorgsky's *Khovanshchina* (composed 1873–81) treats the religious disputes surrounding the 'Old Believers' in 17th-century Russia. The Romantics' love of exoticism occasionally finds vent in the depiction of distant or ancient religious rites, particularly on the theme of the vestal virgin, as seen in Spontini's *La vestale* (1807), Bellini's *Norma* (1831) and Bizet's *Les pêcheurs de perles* (1863); Verdi's *Aida* (1871) also depicts religious rites.

(ii) Rubinstein's sacred operas. The term 'sacred opera' (Ger. *geistliche Oper*; Russ. *dukhovnaya opera*) was used by Anton Rubinstein beginning in the late 1860s to denote a genre of his own invention amounting in essence to a staged hybrid between opera and oratorio on a biblical subject. His own contribution consisted of four works (*Der Thurm zu Babel*, *Sulamith*, *Moses* and *Christus*, 1870–95), to which may be added his early oratorio *Das verlorene Paradies* (1856), which he

adapted for the stage in 1875. They were all written to German librettos and performed almost exclusively in German-speaking countries, never in Russia, where sacred representations on the secular stage were prohibited. Although himself agnostic, Rubinstein had dreams of building in Germany an alternative to Bayreuth where oratorios by Handel, Mendelssohn and Spohr would be given theatrically alongside his own works. His sacred operas resembled oratorios in their use of polyphonic choruses and a sober, edifying style relying on 'exalted declamation'. The subjects and treatment, however, could be distinctly 'operatic': *Sulamith*, based on the *Song of Songs*, turns on an erotic love-triangle, and *Moses* includes an orgiastic dance around the Golden Calf.

4. 20TH CENTURY. Operas of the 20th century treating sacred themes include Pfitzner's *Palestrina* (1917) and Pizzetti's *Assassinio nella cattedrale* (1958, after T. S. Eliot, on the murder of Thomas à Becket). Those on biblical themes include Pizzetti's *Dèbora e Jaéle* (1922) and Honegger's *Judith* (1926); legends of the saints are also drawn on, for example in d'Indy's political, anti-semitic *La légende de Saint Christophe* (1920); there are surrealistic appearances of saints in Virgil Thomson's *Four Saints in Three Acts* (1934). Gian Carlo Menotti's *Amahl and the Night Visitors* (1951) is a tender story of a child wishing to join the Magi honouring Christ; other sacred operas by Menotti include *Martin's Lie* (1964) and *The Egg* (1976, first performed in the cathedral at Washington, DC). Poulenc's *Dialogues des Carmélites* is in no sense a sacred opera although it treats very movingly the fate of a community of nuns condemned to death during the French Revolution. Britten's *The Rape of Lucretia* (1946), on a Roman topic, ends with the drawing of a Christian message; his three church parables of 1964–8 are designed for performance in a church, in a context indebted to the medieval mystery play. Peter Maxwell Davies's *Taverner* (1972) treats the topic of a composer's religious dilemma at the time of the Reformation; but the most substantial of modern sacred operas must be Messiaen's *Saint François d'Assise* (1983), a major spiritual statement.

Among non-Christian operas, Schoenberg's *Moses und Aron* (composed 1930–32) is a clear profession of Jewish faith, expressing his longing for unity with God. From the same tradition comes Milhaud's *David* (1954), written for the 3000th anniversary of the founding of Jerusalem. Holst showed his interest in Hindu philosophy in the chamber opera *Sāvitri* (composed 1908) as well as the less-known *Sita* (1900–06).

See also BIBLE and ORATORIO.

*

S. Leopold: 'Das geistliche Libretto im 17. Jahrhundert: zur Gattungsgeschichte der frühen Oper', *Mf*, xxxi (1978), 245–57

H. E. Smither: 'Oratorio and Sacred Opera, 1700–1825: Terminology and Genre Distinction', *PRMA*, cvi (1979–80), 88–104

R. Taruskin: 'Christian Themes in Russian Opera: a Millennial Study', *COJ*, ii (1990), 83–91

GRAHAM DIXON (1, 2, 3(i), 4), RICHARD TARUSKIN (3(ii))

Saddumene, Bernardo (*fl* 1721–34). Italian librettist. Although he was prolific in Neapolitan comic opera, details of his life are known only from the librettos themselves. The earliest extant text is *Bajazete, imperador de' Turchi* (1722); *La marina de Chiaja*, in a revision by Federico (1734), refers to 'il morto Autore'. The use of Tuscan, or Tuscanized dialect, is seen in the early *Don Ciccio* and *Lo finto laccheo* (1725), and it distinguishes the eponymous protagonist of *La Carlotta* (1726). From 1729 Tuscan roles begin to predominate, with only two characters speaking Neapolitan. Of the five comedies from that year (two of which were written for Rome) only *La costanza* and *La sorella amante* are set in Naples – a marked departure from Saddumene's earlier practice. Scherillo has argued that Saddumene's comic operas represent the decadence of the genre, but this claim has been opposed by the more balanced views of Mondolfi.

Don Ciccio (commeddeja), Vinci, 1721; *Bajazete, imperador de' Turchi* (dramma traggico), Leo and others, 1722; *Ermosilla e Bacocco* (int), 1722; *Venturina e Sciarappa* (int), Leo, 1722; *Li zite ngalera* (commeddeja), Vinci, 1722; *Lo labborinto* (commeddeja), Vinci, 1723; *Lo simmele* (commeddeja), A. Orefice ? and Leo, 1724; *Lo finto laccheo* (commeddeja), G. de Majo, 1725; *La vecchia sorda* (commeddeja), Broschi, 1725; *La Carlotta* (commeddeja), Auletta, 1726; *Lo paglietta geluso* (commeddeja), 1726; *La contadina* (int), Hasse, 1728; *La baronessa o vero Gli equivoci* (commedia), Majo, 1729; *La costanza* (commedia per musica), G. Fischietti, 1729; *L'Erminia* (comedia), Majo, 1729

La fantesca (int), Hasse, 1729; *La somiglianza* (commedia per musica), G. Fischietti, 1729; *La sorella amante* (commedia per musica), Hasse, 1729; *L'Oronte, overo Il custode de se stesso* (commedia), Sellitto, 1730; *La Rosmene* (commedia per musica), Leo, 1730; *La marina de Chiaja* (chelleta napolitana pe museca), Pulli, 1731; *La Rina* (chelleta pe museca), N. Pisano, 1731, (Comes, 1740, as La taverna de Mostaccio); *Le zitelle de lo Vommaro* (chelleta pe museca), Pulli, 1731; *Li marite a forza* (commeddeja), Latilla, 1732, rev. 1735; *Amore mette sinno* (commeddia pe mmuseca), Leo and anon., 1733

*

ES (A. Mondolfi)

M. Scherillo: *L'opera buffa napoletana durante il settecento: storia letteraria* (Naples, 1883, 2/1917), 150–75

C. Troy: *The Comic Intermezzo: a Study in Eighteenth-Century Opera* (Ann Arbor, 1979)

GRAHAM HARDIE

Sadko. *Opera-bïlina* (operatically treated heroic ballad) in three or five acts (seven scenes, to be grouped 1–2/3–4/5–6–7 or 1/2–3/4/5–6/7) by NIKOLAY ANDREYEVICH RIMSKY-KORSAKOV to his own libretto, compiled from the *bïlina* 'Sadko, bogatïy gost'' ('Sadko, the Rich Trader') and other ancient ballads and tales with the assistance of VLADIMIR VASIL'YEVICH STASOV, Vasily Yastrebtsev, Nikolay Shtrup, Nikolay Findeyzen and VLADIMIR NIKOLAYEVICH BEL'SKY; Moscow, Solodovnikov Theatre, 26 December 1897/7 January 1898 (Savva Mamontov's Private Russian Opera).

Sadko was a historical figure, a wealthy member of a seafaring commercial guild of old republican Novgorod, who in 1167 dedicated a church to St Boris and St Gleb, the first martyrs of the Orthodox Church. He became a legendary figure in the great Novgorod cycle of bardic narratives (*bïlinï*) recovered and recorded by folklorists in the far north of Russia in the 18th and 19th centuries. In most versions, Sadko starts out as a humble *guslyar*, one who entertains the nobility by singing *bïlinï* to the accompaniment of his psaltery. He conceives an ambition to compete with the hereditary merchants of Novgorod, for which he is reviled and exiled. He achieves his ambition by captivating the Sea King with his playing, for which he is rewarded with golden fish, and with the hand of the Sea King's daughter. One way of reading this Slavonic Orpheus tale is as a parable of free enterprise, capitalism *avant le mot*. Such an interpretation resonates wryly with the stage history of Rimsky's opera, his first to be given its première by Savva Mamontov, the Moscow railway tycoon.

The *bïlina* also embodies an interesting metaphor for the collision of Christianity and the older pantheistic

Sadko *psaltery player and singer in Novgorod*	tenor
Volkhova *beautiful princess, the Sea King's favourite young daughter*	soprano
Okean-More *the Sea King*	bass
Lyubava Buslayevna *Sadko's young wife*	mezzo-soprano
Nezhata *young psaltery player from Kiev*	contralto
Viking } *foreign traders*	bass
Hindu } *foreign traders*	tenor
Venetian } *foreign traders*	baritone
Duda } *town entertainers*	bass
Sopel' } *town entertainers*	tenor
First and Second } *town entertainers*	mezzo-sopranos
First and Second Wizards	tenors
Apparition *ancient heroic warrior in the guise of a mendicant pilgrim*	baritone
Foma Nazar'ich *elder and commander, town father of Novgorod*	tenor
Luka Zinov'ich *town father of Novgorod*	bass
Tsaritsa-Vodyanitsa *the Sea King's mermaid wife*	ballerina

Men and women of Novgorod from every walk of life, foreign traders from Novgorod and overseas; seamen, Sadko's retinue, minstrel entertainers (merry lads), blind mendicant pilgrims (stern old men); mermaids, beautiful maidens, white swans and wonders of the sea

Corps de ballet

The Sea Queen's 12 older daughters, married to the blue seas; her little grandchildren, the small streams; fish with silver scales and golden feathers and other wonders of the sea

Setting In Novgorod and on the open sea, in half-legendary, half-historical times

pagan religion of the Slavs, when St Nicholas of Mozhaysk (converted into a nameless pilgrim elder in the opera for reasons of censorship) intervenes to end Sadko's sojourn in the Sea Kingdom and sends him back to Novgorod with his bride, who through her metamorphosis miraculously provides the city with an outlet to the sea.

With its musician protagonist and its opposition of 'real' and fantastic worlds, the story was rich material for operatic treatment, a fact recognized by the historian Nikolay Kostomarov as early as 1861. Credit for realizing its potential goes to the musical journalist and historian Nikolay Findeyzen (1868–1928), who prepared the basic scenario in 1894 and sent it to Rimsky-Korsakov, whose tone poem *Sadko* (1867) was by then a concert classic in Russia. (The tone poem's most characteristic passages all went into the opera, the celebrated opening music with its magnificent evocation of the calmly swelling sea furnishing the introduction, acting as a leitmotif in Scene 5 and crowning the brilliant finale.) Thereupon a great many cooks got to work on the broth (Stasov furnishing the opening feast scene with its depiction of Novgorod society, as well as the tenor-bass pair of entertainers so obviously copied from Skula and Yeroshka in *Prince Igor*; and Bel'sky supplying the poignant figure of Sadko's human wife Lyubava, abandoned and then reclaimed). The première was conducted by Eugenio Esposito, with choreography by Loie Fuller; Anton Sekar-Rozhansky sang the title role.

Nadeshda Zabela as Volkhova, the Sea Princess, a role she created in the original production of Rimsky-Korsakov's 'Sadko' at the Solodovnikov Theatre, Moscow, 1897/8: portrait by her husband Mikhail Vrubel

SCENE 1 The merchant brotherhood of Novgorod is feasting. Nezhata, a visiting psaltery player from Kiev, entertains them with a *bïlina* celebrating the exploits of the hero Volkh. This inspires the company to a paroxysm of self-congratulation (chorus, in 11/4 metre). Sadko enters, declines the command to sing, challenges the merchants in a recitative (on an authentic *bïlina* formula) and an aria, 'Kabï bïla u menya zolota kazna' ('If I had a hoard of gold'). His stubborn audacity when cajoled finally insults the company, who banish him from their midst; after he has gone, the entertainers mock him in a dance-song (based on a prototype in Rimsky-Korsakov's folksong collection).

SCENE 2 *The shore of Lake Ilmen* Sadko wanders disconsolately, singing to his psaltery. Suddenly the water stirs, and he beholds a wonder: a flock of white swans swimming on the lake turn into lovely long-necked maidens, daughters of the Sea King, with Volkhova, the beautiful Sea Princess, at their head. Sadko strikes up a joyous *khorovod*, the maidens form circles and disperse into the woods; Princess Volkhova alone remains on the bank. She tells Sadko that her sisters are betrothed to the blue seas, but that she is destined to marry a mortal. Sadko immediately forgets his wife and pledges his love to Volkhova; but as dawn breaks the Sea King rises up from the lake and calls his daughters back. Volkhova gives Sadko the golden fish that make his fortune.

SCENE 3 *Sadko's house* Lyubava worries that she has lost Sadko's love. Sadko enters, tells her of his plan to make his fortune on the banks of Lake Ilmen, and abandons her.

SCENE 4 *The shores of Lake Ilmen* All of Novgorod has assembled (the lines of the blind pilgrims are set to the melody of a spiritual verse imparted to Rimsky-Korsakov by Terty Filippov, Minister of the Imperial Court). The merchants taunt Sadko's latest boast, and wager their fortune against his head that he cannot harvest golden fish from the lake. He casts his net and, with the help of the unseen Volkhova, wins the bet. Now Novgorod's champion, he is celebrated in a narrative tale by the psalterist Nezhata and the entertainer Duda ('Kak na ozere na Ilmene': "Twas on the Ilmen Lake'). Sadko collects a crew and prepares to set sail for distant seas, asking the foreign traders to describe their homelands so that he will know where to go. The Viking trader sings of his country's foggy, gloomy cliffs (Song of the Varangian Trader). The Hindu trader sings of his country's natural wealth (Song of the Indian Trader). Finally the Venetian trader praises his island city's lusty songs (Song of the Venetian Trader). Sadko thanks the singers, takes leave of Lyubava and sets off for parts unknown.

SCENE 5 *On Sadko's ship* 12 years later, Sadko and his crew are becalmed. Sadko divines that the Sea King is angry because he has not been paid proper tribute. After casting their cargo overboard to placate the king, to no avail, the crew cast lots to choose a sacrificial victim. Sadko is of course chosen. He takes leave of his crew and is set adrift on a plank, from which he descends with his psaltery to the ocean floor. As he disappears beneath the waves, the wind blows up and the ship sails off.

SCENE 6 In the intermezzo between scenes Sadko hears familiar voices (and the audience familiar harmonies). He is greeted by the Sea King with full retinue, angrily. Volkhova intercedes, and persuades her father to ask Sadko to sing. He sings the praises of his host. Delighted, the Sea King grants his daughter's hand in marriage. All the wonders and monsters of the sea assemble for the wedding feast (Procession of the Sea Creatures); they hail the nuptial pair (Wedding Song). All dance: first, a Dance of the Streams and Rivulets, then a Dance of the Gold and Silver Fish and finally a general dance to Sadko's psaltery. A storm blows up overhead as the result of the dancing. The ghost of an ancient warrior appears in the guise of a pilgrim: he seizes the psaltery from Sadko's hands; the dancing comes to a halt; the ghost commands the Sea King to release his daughter to Sadko and proclaims the end of the reign of nature gods. Sadko and Volkhova seat themselves in a giant sea shell and depart.

SCENE 7 *On the green bank of Lake Ilmen* Sadko sleeps. Volkhova sings him a tender lullaby, but when dawn breaks amid the red morning fog Volkhova dissolves and turns into a swiftly running river. Sadko awakes and hears Lyubava's grievous lament; he calls joyfully to her and they are reunited. A fleet of ships now appears on the river Volkhova. All Novgorod gathers and sings the praises of Sadko, the river, the blue sea, the saintly apparition and the Lord (finale, based in part on an authentic *bïlina* tune).

* * *

This miscellany of highly coloured scenes – a consequence of the way the opera was put together – though open to criticism in terms of dramatic construction, nevertheless conforms to the episodic character of the old epic genre, and Rimsky did all he could to lend his opera an authentic *bïlina* atmosphere. The most imaginative touch was to set Sadko's recitatives to a lection tone reminiscent of the tune to which 'Sadko, the Rich Trader' was actually sung by Leonty Bogdanov, a 70-year-old peasant from the village of Seredka in Karelia, from whom it had been collected by the ethnographer Pavel Nikolayevich Rïbnikov in 1862 (ex.1).

Ex.1
(a) 'Sadko', transcr. P. Rïbnikov, from B. M. Dobrovol'sky and V. V. Korguzalov: *Bïlinï: Russkiy muzïkal'nïy epos* (Moscow, 1981), 71

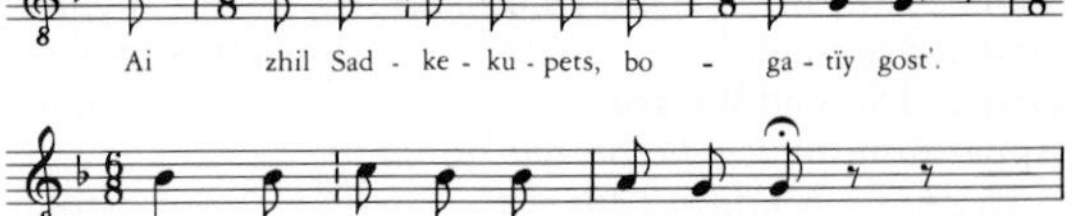

['Oh there lived Sadko the rich merchant trader. He lay down to sleep at dark of night . . .']

(b) Scene i, Sadko's recitative

['If I had a hoard of gold, if I had a brave crew.']

Sadko's *gusli* (psaltery), and Nezhata's too, is represented in the opera by the inevitable tandem, inherited from Glinka, of harp and piano.

The best-known music in *Sadko* is in the fourth scene, when the foreign traders address the Novgorod crowd at the nouveau-riche Sadko's request. The Viking (or Varangian) Trader's song became a recital favourite second to none in the USSR, while the Indian Trader's – known as 'Chanson Indoue' or 'A Song of India' – has long been a staple of 'semi-classical' background music the world over. It is curious that both are paraphrases (knowing paraphrases, one has to think) of popular items from the operas of Alexander Serov (*Rogneda* and *Yudif'*, respectively). Also Serovian (after the folksong dialogues in *Vrazh'ya sila*) are many of the recitatives. It seems Rimsky-Korsakov was belatedly paying back the long-deceased Serov for his unwontedly warm review of the old *Sadko* tone poem 30 years before.

RICHARD TARUSKIN

Sadler's Wells. Theatre in London. Originally, from 1684 to about 1879, it was a pleasure garden. Entertainment was provided at the Music House there, later converted into Sadler's Wells Theatre, opened in 1753. The theatre was reconstructed in 1931, partly for the performance of opera. The Sadler's Wells Opera company, developed from earlier operatic performances at the Old Vic, became firmly established there in 1935. It moved to the Coliseum in 1968 and became the English National Opera in 1974. *See* LONDON, §II, 1 and 2.

Saedén, Erik (*b* Vänersborg, Stockholm, 3 Sept 1924). Swedish baritone. Educated in Stockholm, he joined the Royal Opera there in 1952. He appeared at Bayreuth (1958), Edinburgh (1959 and 1974), Covent Garden (1960), Montreal (1967), Munich and Berlin, where he created the title role in Dallapiccola's *Ulisse* (1968), but his career was centred on Stockholm, where he sang in the repertory operas of Mozart, Verdi, Wagner, Strauss and Puccini. His roles also included Wozzeck, Nick Shadow, the title role of Dallapiccola's *Il prigioniero*, Yevgeny Onegin, Busoni's Faust, Baron Prus (*The Makropulos Affair*), Mr Gedge (*Albert Herring*) and Tovey (*The Mines of Sulphur*). He created the Mimaroben in Blomdahl's *Aniara* (1959), Julien in Lars Johan Werle's *Drömmen om Thérèse* (1964) and Saint Phar in Berwald's *Drottningen av Golconda* (1968) and sang in the premières of Hilding Rosenberg's *Hus med dubbel ingång* (1970) and Ligeti's *Le Grand Macabre* (1978). He sang Schigolch in *Lulu* at Covent Garden (1981) and the Royal Father in Sandström's *Slottet det vita* in Stockholm (1987). Although his voice has no special beauty of timbre, his outstanding musicality and dramatic conviction combine to make him an artist of exceptional interest.

For illustration *see* ULISSE. ELIZABETH FORBES

Saffo ('Sappho'). *Tragedia lirica* in three parts by GIOVANNI PACINI to a libretto by SALVADORE CAMMARANO after Pietro Beltrame's play of the same name; Naples, Teatro S Carlo, 29 November 1840.

The first of six collaborations between Pacini and Cammarano, *Saffo* is the most innovatory opera of the composer's second creative period, in which he self-consciously attempted to strike off in new directions after having adhered closely to Rossini's practices during the first 25 years of his career. In his memoirs Pacini recalled that he had prepared for composing the work by immersing himself in a study of Greek history and philosophy of music in an effort to find a characteristic *tinta* for depicting Greek culture. However, after completing two numbers, he apparently lost his nerve and needed Cammarano's encouragement to complete the opera that was to be universally acclaimed as his masterpiece. *Saffo* was an immense success at its première, with a cast that included Francilla Pixis as Sappho (soprano) and Gaetano Fraschini as Faone [Phaon] (tenor).

Part 1 of the opera, 'The Olympic Crown', is set in Olympia, after Sappho has won the Olympic singing contest with a passionate hymn objecting to the sacrificial suicide leap from the rock of Leucas into the sea. In doing so she has made an enemy of the Leucadian priest Alcandros [Alcander] (bass) and has alienated herself from her beloved husband Phaon, who doubts that she cherishes him as much as her new fame. Seeking revenge, Alcander convinces Phaon that Sappho has another lover and promises to give him his daughter Clymene (mezzo-soprano) in marriage. Part 2 is entitled 'Phaon's Marriage'. After searching throughout Greece for her departed husband, Sappho arrives accidentally in Leucas on the day of his wedding to Clymene, befriends Clymene, and agrees to sing at the ceremony. Enraged when she finds that Phaon is the groom, she overturns the altar, angering all those assembled. In Part 3, 'The Leucadian Leap', Sappho, contrite over her blasphemy, promises to perform the Leucadian leap as an act of penitence. She and Alcander then discover that she is his second daughter, lost long ago in a storm at sea. However, neither Sappho nor the priests are willing to rescind her commitment, and she throws herself from the rock.

Saffo is important for its integration of scenes into extended musical tableaux, for the complexity of its ensembles and for the relatively minor role played by solo numbers, all of which include chorus, secondary soloists or both. Its great Part 1 finale may have been the source of techniques later associated with Verdi's concertato slow movements. Pacini achieved a remarkable expressive intensity not only in cantabile movements but also in lyric dialogues by largely abandoning the florid bel canto that had marked his earlier works and moving closer to Bellini's impassioned melodic style.

SCOTT L. BALTHAZAR

Saggione, Joseph. *See* FEDELI, GIUSEPPE.

Sagi-Barba, Emilio (*b* Barcelona, 26 March 1876; *d* Bolop de la Marina, Alicante, 7 Aug 1949). Spanish bass-baritone. Possessing a fine voice and acting ability, he dedicated himself to the *zarzuela grande* and became one of its most distinguished exponents. He appeared most notably with his wife, the soprano Luisa Vela, with whom he created leading roles in Usandizaga's *Las golondrinas* (1914) and Millán's *La dogaresa* (1920). His later successes included Soutullo and Vert's *La del Soto del Paral* (1927), Guerrero's *La rosa del azafrán* (1930) and Moreno Torroba's *Luisa Fernanda* (1932). He then retired to concentrate on the composition of songs and theatrical works, leaving the stage to his son, the baritone Luis Sagi-Vela. He made a large number of recordings for HMV and Victor. ANDREW LAMB

Sagi-Vela (Barba), Luis (*b* Madrid, 17 Feb 1914). Spanish baritone. The son of the bass-baritone Emilio Sagi-Barba and the soprano Luisa Vela, he was educated in Madrid, studying solfège and piano with Enrique Brú and composition and harmony with Juan Bautista Lambert. He made his stage début in 1932 in Guerrero's *La rosa del azafrán* and pursued a highly successful career in theatre, concert and films in both Spain and South America. Among his major stage successes were Sorozábal's *La del manojo de rosas* (1934), Alonso's *Me llaman la presumida* (1935) and Moreno Torroba's *Monte Carmelo* (1939) and *Maravilla* (1941). During the 1960s he appeared in television productions of major zarzuelas, issued on recordings by EMI and revealing a slightly constricted but expressive voice. He was also a composer of songs and piano music.

ANDREW LAMB

Saguer, Louis (*b* Charlottenburg, 26 March 1907). French composer of German birth. Of Italian parentage, he first studied the piano and composition in Venice with two pupils of Busoni, then later studied in both Paris and Berlin. His subsequent career has similarly been shared between France and Germany. While Milhaud and Honegger advised him in France he also took a course of study with Hindemith and was an assistant to Eisler. Apart from composition, he taught analysis at Darmstadt and engaged in concert activities as pianist, harpsichordist and conductor.

Saguer has written two operas. The subject of *Mariana Pineda*, written between 1952 and 1953, is historical but its main themes are political. Based on a story by Federico García Lorca, it deals with a revolution which took place against the governor of Grenada in 1831. Mariana Pineda is assassinated for her part in the insurrection. Saguer incorporated modal folk elements and the *cante jondo* style of flamenco music into the score. The opera was first performed at Marseilles on 16 January 1970.

His second opera *Lili Merveille*, to a libretto by J. L. Bory, is the story of a film star, blended with elements from classical antiquity. Telemachus and the Mentor are in the audience at a spectacle entitled 'Lili Merveille' in which Lili Merveille is the star. They agree that the film is worthless but are captivated by Lili. The opera examines the power of this captivation, using images which hover between dream and reality. Real or not, the power of the star's image has had a profound effect on those who witness her: it is thus the power of the cinema which is the opera's central theme. The work was first given by Radio-France in June 1964.

RICHARD LANGHAM SMITH

Sahl, Michael (*b* Boston, 2 Sept 1934). American composer. He studied composition at Princeton University with Sessions and Babbitt. His other teachers included Foss, Copland and Dallapiccola. After a year as creative associate at SUNY, Buffalo (1965), he worked as pianist and music director for the singer Judy Collins (1968–9). Although his early career was devoted almost entirely to atonal music, his background was in commercial music and he began to write, compose and direct music theatre works, some in collaboration with Eric Salzman. The most notable were *Stauf* (1976), and *Civilization and its Discontents* (1977) for which Sahl received the Prix Italia in 1980.

Stauf, an anagram of 'Faust', uses elements from the Gounod opera, updating them for contemporary audiences. The action, told in flashback, shows the rise of Henry Stauf, a nuclear scientist, as he chooses between power and righteousness, ending up not in hell but in Washington, DC. His nemesis is divided between two characters, Dr Jove and Kali, while his potential redemption is in the hands of Margarita, a corporate secretary. The work's musical style ranges from rock to traditional operatic textures. *Civilization and its Discontents* takes its inspiration from 18th-century *opera buffa*. Focussing on sexual and social relationships in a singles bar, it portrays the ways in which people fill or ignore the emptiness in their lives. Structurally, the work is conventional, consisting of a series of set pieces, duets, ballads and ensembles, interspersed with aleatory material. Jazz, blues and popular music find their way into the musical style, with contemporary dance rhythms dominating several sections. The vocal ranges for the four singers are extreme, but optional parts with more limited ranges have been written by the composer.

Sahl's recent theatre works continue to stress social issues and are in an eclectic musical style. *Noah*, a morality play based on the biblical story, reveals a facile idiom, ranging from Baroque arias to jazz and rock; several numbers, especially those cast in a pop idiom, show the influence of Berg and Weill. Critics found his next work, *The Passion of Simple Simon*, less pleasing, which trivalizes the issue it attempts to consider. Focussing on the story of a sniper who kills joggers in Central Park but later becomes a punk-rock star, it is much less adventurous in style and is unevenly constructed. The choral textures are, however, cleverly handled. *Dream Beach*, which concerns an encounter between a woman on a beach and a man on a train, reveals a simplification of Sahl's earlier techniques.

librettos by the composer and Eric Salzman, and first performed in New York, unless otherwise stated

Biograffiti (collective music-theatre work, 1), workshop perfs., Space for Innovative Development, 1973; final version, Washington Square Methodist Church, 14 Dec 1974; collab. E. Salzman and QUOG Music Theatre Ensemble

The Conjuror (pop op, 2), Public, 1 June 1975, collab. Salzman

Stauf, an American Faust (moral entertainment, 2), Cubiculo, 25 May 1976, collab. Salzman; rev. version, workshop perf., Philadelphia, Prince, 1 Oct 1986; final version, Philadelphia, Play and Players, 20 Sept 1987

Civilization and its Discontents (music-theater comedy, 1), American Musical and Dramatic Academy, 19 May 1977; rev. as radio op, NPR, 1980, vs (New York, 1985); collab. Salzman

An Old-Fashioned Girl (dance drama, Sahl and A. Sahl, after T. Dreiser: *Sister Carrie*), American Musical and Dramatic Academy, 19 May 1977

Noah (musical pageant, 2), Brooklyn, Pratt Institute, 10 Feb 1978, collab. Salzman

The Passion of Simple Simon (theatre op, 3), Theatre for the New City, 1 Feb 1979; rev. as radio op, NPR, 1980; collab. Salzman

Boxes (radio op, 2 parts, Sahl and Salzman; Salzman), KCRW, 1981–2

Dream Beach (3, H. Pflanzer), Green Auditorium, 20 March 1988

*

P. G. Davis: 'QUOG Music Theater Twin Bill Limns City Life Then and Now', *New York Times* (24 May 1977) [review of *Civilization and its Discontents*]

E. Salzman and M. Sahl: *Making Changes: a Practical Guide to Vernacular Harmony* (New York, 1977)

T. Johnson: 'Music Returns to Normal', *Village Voice* (15 Jan 1979)

J. Rockwell: '*Simple Simon*: a Theater Opera', *New York Times* (6 Feb 1979)

T. Page: 'Stage: *Noah*, a Flood Story', *New York Times* (12 March 1987)

Hari: 'Stauf', *Variety* (14 Oct 1987) [review]

R. Osborne: 'Civilization and its Discontents', *Notes*, xlv (1988–9), 164–6

R. H. Kornick: *Recent American Opera: a Production Guide* (New York, 1991), 261–8

JAMES P. CASSARO

Saifiddinov, Sharofiddin Sanginovich (*b* Khodzhent [now Khundzhan], 24 Aug 1929). Tajik composer. In 1952 he completed studies in composition at the national division of the Moscow Conservatory, where his teacher was B. G. Fere. He subsequently studied composition with B. I. Zeydman at the Tashkent Conservatory, from which he graduated in 1962. From 1962 until 1986 he served as chairman of the Tajik Composers' Union. He has taught at the Institute of Arts since 1979, becoming a professor there in 1986. Among other honours, he received the Tajik State Prize in 1970.

Inspiration for many of Saifiddinov's works came from his Tajik heritage; his first opera, *Pulot va Gulru* ('Pulat and Gulru'), composed in 1956, was the first national opera by a Tajik composer. With a libretto by S. Severtsev based on the novel *Odamoni chovid* ('Eternal Souls') by Rakhim Dzhalil, the four-act opera was orchestrated by Edison Denisov, A. Nikolayev and A. Pirumov and first staged in Dushanbe on 19 March 1957. The story of the blossoming love between a village girl Gulru (dramatic soprano) and a Red Commissar Pulat (baritone) amidst the tribulations of civil war, *Pulat and Gulru* preserves the style and flavour of Tajik folk music in an opera unified through a system of leitmotifs. Saifiddinov's subsequent operas, *Rudaki* and *Ayni*, were staged in Dushanbe in 1976 and 1978 respectively.

LAUREL E. FAY

Sainctonge, Louise-Geneviève Gillot. *See* SAINTONGE, LOUISE-GENEVIÈVE GILLOT.

Sainete (Sp.: 'farce', 'titbit'; Fr. *saynète*). A short Spanish theatrical piece, which at first was an equivalent of the *entremés* (intermezzo), a little play between acts, but came to be called *sainete* when it was intended for the end of a performance after the main play of the day rather than in the middle of it. In the 17th century the *sainete* was usually a little spoken piece which could also include musical numbers, usually only one or two.

In the 18th century, however, musical numbers came to be deemed essential to a properly written *sainete*. Since the greatest quantity of extant *sainetes* belong to the second half of the 18th century (some 500 were given in Madrid alone during that period), the musical numbers found in them are mostly seguidillas (then in popular favour), but there are also choruses, quartets, minuets, jotas, fandangos, French- and Italian-style songs, marches and even short instrumental pieces, especially overtures. Many late 18th-century *sainetes* were written by the composers of the main *tonadillas* or zarzuelas, from Luis Misón to Blas de Laserna. Most were comic and quite popular in character, drawing on incidents and situations of everyday life.

In the 19th century the *sainete* lost its hold on the stage, but when after 1870 the *género chico* type of zarzuela developed, many composers called their pieces *sainete* or its diminutive *sainetillo*. Tomás Bretón's *género chico* piece *La verbena de la paloma* (1894) and Ruperto Chapí's *La revoltosa* (1897), for instance, were described by their publishers as *sainetes*, but during the period dozens of words were used to describe theatrical pieces with no specific significance. In the late 19th century the words *sainete* and *sainetillo* were also used to describe short, comic theatrical pieces without music, with a highly farcical plot bearing little relation to reality. In France, composers such as Hervé and Planquette, among others, wrote lightweight *saynètes*. Massenet used the Spanish term for his one-act *Bérangère et Anatole* (1876, Paris). ROGER ALIER

Saint-Amans [Saint-Aman, Saint-Amand, Saint-Amant], **Louis Joseph (Claude)** (*b* Marseilles, 26 June 1749; *d* Paris, *c*1820). French composer. He abandoned law studies to travel around southern France with an Italian troupe performing *opere buffe*, and then spent three years in Italy as tutor to the children of a Swiss baron. Having studied the music of several Italian composers, he decided to pursue a career as an opera composer in Paris, arriving in 1769 and making his début the following year with an *opéra comique*, *Dom Alvar et Mincia*. As neither this, nor two other works for the Comédie-Italienne, was particularly successful, Saint-Amans turned to the Opéra and composed a number of ballets and *tragédies*. Most of these remained unperformed, although he was invited to write French recitative and ballets for Sacchini's *L'olympiade* (1777). He moved to Brussels in 1778 and, during a six-year period as conductor of the Théâtre de la Monnaie, composed further works that were well received. After returning to Paris he was appointed professor of singing at the Ecole Royale de Chant and, later, the Conservatoire. He continued to write *opéras comiques* until the early years of the 19th century, but lack of critical acclaim and a move to Brest (following the loss of his position at the Conservatoire) may have led him to abandon composing for the stage during his last 15 years.

The span of Saint-Amans' career coincides exactly with that of the leading *opéra comique* composer of the period, Grétry. That Saint-Amans was overshadowed by more successful contemporaries is evident from reviews criticizing the lack of melodic invention and harmonic design in his music, although Burney commented favourably on the overture to *Dom Alvar et Mincia*. His reworking of operas by earlier composers – *Le poirier* (Vadé), *Ninette à la cour* and *La fée Urgèle* (Duni) – met with greater success, but the charming simplicity of such works had, by the late 18th century, become distinctly outmoded.

BRM – *Brussels, Théâtre de la Monnaie*
PCI – *Paris, Comédie-Italienne (Hôtel de Bourgogne)*

Dom Alvar et Mincia, ou Le captif de retour (oc, 3, A. G. Cailly, after A.-R. Le Sage), PCI, 13 June 1770
La coquette du village, ou Le baiser pris et rendu (oc, 2, L. Anseaume), PCI, 19 Sept 1771
Le poirier (oc, Anseaume), PCI, 20 June 1772 (Paris, 1772) [based on oc by J.-J. Vadé]
La mort de Didon (ballet, 3, M. Gardel), Fontainebleau, 1776
Oroès, 1776 (tragédie lyrique, 5), unperf., *F-Po*
Daphnis et Thémire (pastorale), BRM, 1778
La fausse veuve (oc, 2), BRM, 1778
Psyché et l'Amour (pastorale, 1, C. H. F. de Voisenon), BRM, 1778
La rosière de Salency (opéra, 3, ?Masson de Pézay or C.-S. Favart), BRM, 1778
L'occasion (oc, 1, ?P. F. Biancolleli), Brussels, 1778 or 1780
Le médecin de l'amour (oc, 1, Anseaume), PCI (Favart), 30 July 1783 [doubtful attrib.]
La fête de Flore (pastorale, 1, J. P. A. R. de Saint-Marc), Paris, Opéra, 1784
Le prix de l'arc (oc, 1, A. N. P. La Salle d'Offémont), Fontainebleau, 1785
Laurence (opéra, 1), Strasbourg, 1790, MS score cited by Eitner
L'isle déserte (oc, 2, ?d'Aumale), 1791
Ninette à la cour, ou Le caprice amoureux (cmda, 2, Favart), 1791 [based on oc by Duni]
L'heureux démenti (oc, 2), ?Tours, 1794
Aspasie (opéra, 2), 1795
Le pauvre homme (oc, 1), Paris, Jeunes Artistes, 1797
La tireuse de cartes (oc, 1), Paris, Jeunes Artistes, 1799
Chacun à son plan (oc, 1), Paris, Porte-Saint-Martin, 1802
La fée Urgèle (oc, ? after Favart), ? Brest, 1803 or 1804 [based on oc by Duni]

Lost, unperf.: Le faux vieillard, 1774; La forêt enchantée, 1774; Emirène, ? 1774; Scène d'Alcyone, 1789; La leçon littéraire, 1807

*

EitnerQ; *FétisB*; *MGG* (M. Briquet)
L. Petit de Bachaumont: *Mémoires secrets* (London, 1780–89)
A. d'Origny: *Annales du Théâtre-Italien depuis son origine jusqu'à ce jour* (Paris, 1788)
A. Choron and F. Fayolle: *Dictionnaire historique des musiciens* (Paris, 1810–11)
Correspondance littéraire, philosophique et critique par Grimm, Diderot, Raynal, Meister, etc., ed. M. Tourneux (Paris, 1877–82)
U. Manferrari: *Dizionario universale delle opere melodrammatiche* (Florence, 1954–5) ELISABETH COOK

Saint-Aubin [Schroeder], **Jeanne Charlotte** (*b* Paris, 9 Dec 1760; *d* Paris, 11 Sept 1850). French soprano. Having appeared on stage as a child, she was engaged at the Paris Opéra in 1786, making her début as Rosine in Grétry's *La double épreuve, ou Colinette à la cour*. She made her farewell in 1808 in the same work, this time as Mme Belmont, with her younger daughter, Alexandrine Saint-Aubin (*b* 1793), as Rosine. In 1818 she made a comeback in Dalayrac's *Une heure de mariage* at the Opéra-Comique (Théâtre Feydeau), with her elder daughter, Cécile Saint-Aubin-Duret (1785–1862), in the cast. As Cécile Duret, the latter sang at the Opéra-Comique from 1805 to 1820, making her début in Berton's *Le concert interrompu* and singing in the first performances of several operas by Isouard, including *Cendrillon* (1810), in which Alexandrine also sang, *Le billet de loterie* (1811) and *Jeannot et Colin* (1814); she also created Lorezza in Boieldieu's *Jean de Paris* (1812). Cécile's voice, a high mezzo-soprano, was extremely flexible, as the roles written for her demonstrate.

ELIZABETH FORBES

St Céré. Town in south-west France. A festival, founded in 1960, is held each July and early August. It combines some 60 concerts given in various churches of the region with, since 1976, operatic productions in the courtyard of the medieval Château de Castelnau which overlooks the Dordogne valley. At the beginning of the century the castle was acquired by the tenor Jean Mouliérat, born locally, who left it to the nation. There are usually two new productions of standard operas each year (in 1989 *Il barbiere di Siviglia* and *Lucia*), cast principally from young French singers. After the festival the company, Opéra Eclaté, takes adaptations of the productions to towns in western France where opera has rarely if ever been shown; about a hundred performances are given. Productions of chamber operas have been mounted at the Château de Montal: the double bill of Dalayrac's *Maison à vendre* and *L'amant-statue*, given in 1985, was successfully transferred to Paris. CHARLES PITT

Saint-Christophle [Saint-Christophe], Mlle de (*d* after 1682). French soprano. She was originally a member of the *musique du roi*, and is recorded as a 'musicienne de Sa Majesté' in Lully's *Ballet des arts* (8 January 1663). She joined Lully's Opéra in 1674 and sang the title role in *Alceste* (1674), Cybele (*Atys*, 1676), Juno (*Isis*, 1677), the Queen (*Psyché*, 1680) and Night (*Le triomphe de l'amour*, 1681). She was occasionally replaced by Marie Verdier, who normally took secondary roles. In 1682 Saint-Christophle sang Cassiopeia in Lully's *Persée*, and not long after retired to a convent. She was succeeded by Le Rochois. François and Claude Parfaict (MS, *F-Pn*) described her as 'grande, bien faite, belle et vertueuse', and as having nobility and taste in deportment, gesture and action, in addition to great beauty of voice. PHILIP WELLER

Saint-Evremond, Charles de Saint-Denis, Seigneur de (bap. St Denis-le-Gast, Manche, 5 Jan 1614; *d* London, 29 Sept 1703). French man of letters. After studies at the Jesuit college in Paris, he entered military service, rising to the rank of *maréchal de camp* in 1652. During the Fronde he was disgraced by his *Lettre sur la Paix des Pyrénées* (1661) and was obliged to seek exile outside France. He fled to the Netherlands and in 1670 to England, where he was appointed Charles II's Keeper of the Ducks in the Decoy at St James's Park. A keen music lover and amateur, Saint-Evremond frequented the Chelsea *académie* of Hortensia Mancini, the Duchess of Mazarin (the niece of Mazarin and mistress of the king), where French music was performed and discussed. His own home in London also became a centre of intellectual and social activity as well as of court amusements, all of which is reflected in his literary production. He is said never to have learnt to speak English.

Saint-Evremond wrote about music in letters (1674–5), essays, dialogues, poems and a farcical play about the current obsession with Lullian opera entitled *Sur les opéra*. Having left France during the era of the *ballet de cour*, his actual experience of it was limited to the performances of excerpts from Lully's *Cadmus et Hermione*, *Thésée*, *Alceste* and *Atys*, given by three male singers sent by Louis XIV in 1676 to entertain Charles II, and of music by his fellow expatriate Cambert (*Ariane*, 1674), as well as performances of such works as Shadwell's *Psyche* (1675), which employed incidental music by Locke. His views on opera were expressed at greatest length in a letter to the Duke of Buckingham, probably written in 1677–8 and first published in the February 1683 issue of *Le mercure galant*; unauthorized English translations appeared in 1685 and 1686. Like his compatriots Boileau and La Fontaine, he considered opera a flawed genre of tragedy, lacking verisimilitude, adherence to the unities (time, place and action) and – unlike the Greeks – a proper sense of proportion with regard to the place of music within drama. With few exceptions he found it boring and banal. He was generally opposed to dramatic works sung entirely from beginning to end. To him, music was a useful ornament to spoken drama, of which only certain features, such as prayers, oaths and expressions of love or sorrow, were suitable for musical setting. He excepted the works of Lully, whom he felt better understood 'the Passions' and entered 'farther into the heart of man than the Authors themselves'. Elsewhere he showed a clear preference for French style over Italian in matters of taste and vocal performance. Even so, he deplored the use of machines and reliance upon supernatural elements. In spite of the limitations of his experience, Saint-Evremond's musical writings consitute a notable contribution to the development of aesthetics and a philosophy of opera during the late 17th and early 18th centuries.

Mixt Essays upon Tragedies, Comedies, Italian Comedies, English Comedies and Opera's to his Grace the Duke of Buckingham (London, 1685)

Miscellanea: or Various Discources upon 1. Tragedy. 2. Comedy. 3. The Italian. 4. The English Comedy. 5. And Operas, to his Grace, the D. of Buckingham. Together with Epicurus his Morals, trans. F. Spence (London, 1686)

Essays and letters on music, some first appearing in *Oeuvres meslées* and others added to later edns by P. des Maizeaux: *Sur les opéra*; *Les opéra, comédie*, ed. R. Finck and E. Joliat (Geneva, 1979); *Idylle en musique*; *Observations sur le goût et le discernement des françois*; *Parodie d'une scène de l'opéra de Roland*; *Eclaircissement sur ce qu'on a dit de la musique des italiens*; *A M. Lully*; also 2 short dramatic scenes in verse and a verse/prol., all intended for musical setting.

Oeuvres meslées, vii, xi (Paris, 1684); enlarged P. des Maizeaux (Paris 1705–; Eng. trans., 1928)

Nouvelles oeuvres meslées de Saint-Evremond, ed. F. Raguenet (Paris, 1700)

Oeuvres en prose de Saint-Evremond, ed. R. Ternois (Paris, 1962–6)

*

J. L. Le Cerf de la Viéville: *Comparaison de la musique italienne et de la musique françoise* (Brussels, 1704–6)

C. Gildon: *The Life of Mr. Thomas Betterton ... With the Judgment of de St. Evremond, upon the Italian and French Music and Opera's* (London, 1710)

E. Titon du Tillet: *Le Parnasse françois* (Paris, 1732), 498–501

I. Lowens: 'St. Evremond, Dryden, and the Theory of Opera', *Criticism*, i (1959), 226–48

R. Ternois: 'Saint-Evremond, gentilhomme normand', *Annales de Normandie*, x (1960), 229–40

R. M. Isherwood: *Music in the Service of the King* (Ithaca, 1973), 244–6 ALBERT COHEN, JULIE ANNE SADIE

Saint François d'Assise ('St Francis of Assisi') [*Scènes franciscains* ('Franciscan Scenes')]. Opera in three acts by OLIVIER MESSIAEN to his own libretto; Paris, Opéra, 28 November 1983.

The work is in eight self-contained scenes, each further subdivided into small units, often placed in repetitive patterns. The solo vocal writing suggests plainchant (though the modes are Messiaen's own), and the sense of a liturgy is enhanced by a monumental chorus of 150 voices. The orchestra is on a similar scale (120 players), and includes large woodwind and tuned-percussion sections as well as three ondes martenot, all providing resources for the vivid amplified birdsongs that underline and punctuate the score. Each scene is the exposition of a single moment in the saint's life, omitting the conflicts of his early years to centre on his faith

'Saint François d'Assise' (Messiaen), Act 3 scene i, from the original production at the Opéra, Paris, 28 November 1983

and attainment of grace: there is no dramatic continuity either within the scenes or from one to another; rather they are single, static and separate, like a cycle of stained-glass windows.

There are three scenes in Act 1. In the first, 'La croix', Francis (baritone) is travelling with one of his monks, Brother Leo (baritone), and teaching him the meaning of 'perfect joy', which in a long monologue he says is to be found in the acceptance of suffering while thinking of the crucified Christ. Then in 'Les laudes' Francis and his community are discovered at prayer, and the saint sings verses from his *Lodì delle creature*. Finally, in 'Le baiser au lépreux', he meets a Leper (tenor) in great physical and spiritual distress. He tries to teach him acceptance, but is rejected, until an Angel (soprano) appears and sings that God is love. Francis, realizing that he has not loved the leper sufficiently, embraces him and brings about a miraculous cure: the ragged, raging victim is transformed back into a medieval gentleman, and he executes a dance of triumph, after which he can learn patience and penitence. The act ends with a choral epilogue.

Act 2 again is in three scenes. In 'L'ange voyageur' the Angel returns to knock emphatically at the monastery door and question the monks about predestination. One responds angrily; another gives answer, and the Angel leaves. He appears, in 'L'ange musicien', to Francis, who is at prayer. On his viol he plays a celestial melody (it is heard in fact from the ondes martenot) at which Francis faints. Three brothers come to find him, and he awakens, saying that if the music had continued longer his soul would have parted from his body. In scene vi, 'Le prêche aux oiseaux', he is with Brother Masseo (tenor), identifying the birds, to whom he preaches, praising their gifts of flight, of freedom, and of being able to sing wordless music, like the angels. He blesses them, and after a moment of silence there begins a great bird concert, with different instruments and ensembles playing different songs out of synchrony. The birds then fly off, making a great cross in the sky.

'Les stigmates', the first scene of Act 3, is set at night, and the orchestra becomes sombre, falling to owl calls and severe 12-note patterns. Francis prays that before his death he may feel in his body and heart the anguish of the crucified Christ, and the chorus responds with Christ's words of acceptance of his sacrifice. An enormous black cross is projected at the back of the stage, and from it come rays of light to pierce the saint's hands, feet and side, to an immense outburst from chorus and orchestra. The final scene is 'La mort et la nouvelle vie': Francis bids farewell to the birds, to the city and to the community. He hears the nightingale singing in the darkness, which suddenly becomes light with the appearance once more of the Angel and the Leper, both come to assist him at his death. He prays for the blinding light of divine illumination, and he dies. Brother Leo remarks on the silence of his going, and the monks depart, taking the saint's body. But the opera ends fortissimo with a huge chorale of resurrection, sung and played while intense light shines from the place where Francis's body lay.

The composition of the opera occupied Messiaen from 1975 to 1983, and, like other works of this late period, it came to encompass many of the techniques he had evolved since the beginning of his creative life. If, nevertheless, the work has an imposing identity, that comes perhaps from the block structuring and from the allied use of modes to link the elements, however disparate, so that any musical object can find a place in the divine order. PAUL GRIFFITHS

St Gall [St Gallen]. Town in north-eastern Switzerland. Opera was first performed in 1806 by a French opera ensemble, the Célicourt. The Theater am Karlstor, situated outside the city limits, held occasional opera performances until the Theater am Bohl in the city centre was inaugurated in 1857 with a production of *Don Giovanni*. This building was replaced in 1968 by the new Stadttheater (capacity 855) on Museumstrasse, which opened with *Fidelio*. There is also a studio theatre. The Stadttheater maintains a small ensemble and has become known mainly for its productions of Italian opera, often with famous guest singers. The season runs from September to June; typically there are seven opera performances a month, as well as operettas and musicals. ANDREW CLARK

Saint-Georges [Saint-George], **Joseph Boulogne,** Chevalier de (*b* nr Basse Terre, Guadeloupe, *c*1739; *d* Paris, 9 or 10 June 1799). French composer. He settled in Paris around 1749 and became renowned as a violinist and as an extremely talented athlete before writing *opéras comiques* for the Comédie-Italienne. These were preceded by a number of chamber and orchestral works, including violin concertos which Saint-Georges performed with the Concert des Amateurs under their musical director Gossec (who may also have given him early lessons in composition).

Saint-Georges made his début as a stage composer in 1777 with *Ernestine* and followed this, one year later, with *La chasse*. Although neither remained long in the repertory – the former was withdrawn after the first night and the latter was performed only four times – both were favourably received by critics who acknowledged Saint-Georges' talents as an orchestral composer and recognized his potential in opera. *Ernestine*, performed before Marie Antoinette, suffered from an implausible libretto but was redeemed by the fluency and grace of its music, the stylish design of several arias and ensembles receiving particular praise. *La chasse* was considered a superior work, containing much natural charm and vivaciousness. Nine years passed, however, before another work by Saint-Georges was staged at the Comédie-Italienne: *La fille-garçon* again received good reviews but only two performances. (*Aline et Dupré*, performed at the Théâtre de Beaujolais in 1788 and previously attributed to Saint-Georges, is actually by H.-J. Rigel.)

Saint-Georges developed the comic and lightly sentimental style of *opéra comique* established by his predecessors Duni, Monsigny and Philidor. Yet despite his obvious talents he is less well remembered than contemporaries such as Martini, Dezède and Champein, since his stage works were few, representing only one of the many interests he pursued during a colourful life.

PCI – *Paris, Comédie-Italienne*

Ernestine (oc, 3, P. Choderlos de Laclos, after Mme Riccoboni), PCI (Bourgogne), 19 July 1777, excerpts pubd

La chasse (oc, 3, Desfontaines [F. G. Fouques]), PCI (Bourgogne), 12 Oct 1778

L'amant anonyme (comédie with ballets, 2, ?after Mme de Genlis), Paris, 8 March 1780, *F-Pc*

La fille-garçon (oc, 2, Desmaillor [A. F. Eve]), PCI (Favart), 18 Aug 1787

Doubtful and spurious works: Le droit de seigneur (?Saint-Georges, ?after Beaumarchais), ?perf. privately, 1 aria pubd as no.3 in Journal de harpe, 1784; Aline et Dupré, ou Le marchand de marrons, 1788; Guillaume tout coeur, 1790 (mentioned by La Laurencie)

EitnerQ; *FétisB*; *GerberNL*; *MGG* (B. S. Brook)

A. d'Origny: *Annales du Théâtre italien depuis son origine jusqu'à ce jour* (Paris, 1788)

L. Petit de Bachaumont: *Mémoires secrets* (London, 1780–89)

A. E. Grétry: *Mémoires, ou Essais sur la musique* (Paris, 1789, 2/1797)

La Boëssière: 'Notice historique sur Saint-Georges', *Traité de l'art des armes* (Paris, 1818)

M. Tourneux, ed.: *Correspondance littéraire, philosophique et critique par Grimm, Diderot, Raynal, Meister, etc.* (Paris, 1877–82)

L. de La Laurencie: 'The Chevalier de Saint-George: Violinist', *MQ*, v (1919), 74–85

E. Derr: *Joseph Boulogne, Chevalier de Saint-Georges: Black Musician and Athlete in Galant Paris* (Ann Arbor, 1972)

ELISABETH COOK

Saint-Georges, Jules-Henri Vernoy de (*b* Paris, 7 Nov 1799; *d* Paris, 23 Dec 1875). French librettist. For nearly half a century he wrote plays, ballet scenarios and opera librettos for the Parisian stage, usually in collaboration (in many cases with Adolphe de Leuven), and in his early years he was director of the Opéra-Comique. Nothing in his large output has lasted better than the two-act ballet *Giselle, ou Les Wilis* (1841), which he and Théophile Gautier based on an idea from Heinrich Heine's *De l'Allemagne* (1835) and which was set to music by Adolphe Adam and by Friedrich Burgmüller. Among opera composers for whom Saint-Georges helped devise librettos were Flotow, Halévy, Adam, Auber and Balfe. His most significant contribution to opera was the libretto for *La jolie fille de Perth* (1867), after Sir Walter Scott, which he and Jules Adenis fashioned for Bizet. CHRISTOPHER SMITH

Saint-Huberty [Huberti], Mme de [Clavel, Antoinette Cécile] (*b* Strasbourg, 15 Dec 1756; *d* London, 22 July 1812). French soprano. She studied in Warsaw with J. B. Lemoyne and, after a period in Strasbourg, reached Paris, where she created Mélisse in Gluck's *Armide* in 1777. A fine actress, she was the mistress of the Opéra for a short time, in such roles as Gluck's Alcestis and Piccinni's Angélique (*Roland*) and Sangaride (*Atys*, 1783). Her greatest triumph was in Piccinni's *Didon* (1783); she also created Hypermestra in Salieri's *Les Danaïdes* and the title roles in Sacchini's *Chimène*, Edelmann's *Ariane* and Lemoyne's *Phèdre*. During the Revolution she emigrated with the Count of Antraigues; they were married in 1790, but the marriage was not announced until 1797, when he was imprisoned by Napoleon; she assisted in his rescue. They ended their lives in London, assassinated by a servant.

For illustration *see* DIDON (ii).

ES (F. Serpa)

E. de Goncourt: *La Saint-Huberty d'après sa correspondence et ses papiers de famille* (Paris, 1882, 2/1885) JULIAN RUSHTON

Saint-Léon [Michel], **(Charles Victor) Arthur** (*b* Paris, 17 Sept 1821; *d* Paris, 2 Sept 1870). French choreographer. The inventor of a serviceable method of dance notation, he dominated both French and Russian ballet in the 1860s. He is best known for his work at the Paris Opéra, where he was *premier maître de ballet* in the early 1850s and guest choreographer, 1863–70. Among the opera *divertissements* he arranged there were 'Le berger Aristée et les abeilles' in Halévy's *Le Juif errant* (1852) and the dances in Meyerbeer's *L'Africaine* (1865). Saint-Léon was ballet-master of the Russian Imperial Theatres from 1859 until his death.

ES (M.-F. Christout)

I. Guest: *The Ballet of the Second Empire* (London, 1974)

——: *Letters from a Ballet-master* (London, 1981) IVOR GUEST

St Louis. American city in Missouri, on the Mississippi River. Samuel Arnold's ballad opera *The Agreeable Surprise* was the first musical play performed there in 1817, and Arnold's *The Children in the Wood* was given in the following year. A production by a local stock company of Auber's *Masaniello* in 1830 was the earliest performance of grand opera. Throughout the 19th century visiting troupes, including the Maurice Strakosch (1859), Grand Italian (1865), Grover (1865), Freyer German and New Orleans French opera companies, presented a wide variety of operas. In 1886 J. H. Mapleson launched a season in St Louis. Among the venues for these early performances were the Varieties Theatre, DeBar Opera House, Guy Golterman's Municipal Theater, his Garden Theater, the Apollo Theater and the Municipal Auditorium Opera House (renamed Kiel Opera House and later Kiel Auditorium). The German Grand Opera Company presented the complete *Ring* cycle, conducted by Anton Seidl, at the Exposition Building in 1889. In addition to the New York Metropolitan, companies from Boston, Chicago and Philadelphia visited during the early 20th century. In 1914 a 'Pageant and Masque of St Louis' celebrating the city's 150th anniversary was produced in Forest Park with a cast of 7000 and an audience of 500 000. This led to the formation of the St Louis Municipal Opera Association (MUNY), which has given summer seasons of operettas, musical comedies and (occasionally) operas in the Park since 1919, when the St Louis Municipal Opera Theatre (capacity 11 475) opened. The MUNY has also given winter productions at the Fox Theater (capacity 4503), built in 1929 (closed in 1978 for renovation; reopened in 1982).

The Opera Theatre of St Louis was founded in 1976 with Richard Gaddes as general director; Charles MacKay followed, with Colin Graham as artistic director (both from 1985). The Loretto Hilton Center at Webster University has been its primary base of operations, and since 1978 the St Louis SO has served as the orchestra. Notable performances have been the world premières of seven operas, all commissioned, including *The Village Singer* (1979), *The Postman Always Rings Twice* (1982) and *The Woodlanders* (1985), all by Stephen Paulus, *Jōruri* (1985) by Minoru Miki and *Under the Double Moon* (1989) by Anthony Davis, as well as several American premières. Though considered a regional company, the Opera Theatre of St Louis has gained an international reputation. In 1983 it became the first American opera company to appear at the Edinburgh Festival, and in 1988 it was the first American regional company to appear in Japan and the first foreign one to perform a Japanese opera (*Jōruri*).

*

W. G. B. Carson: *St Louis Goes to the Opera: 1837–1941* (St Louis, 1946)

C. V. Clifford: *St Louis' Fabulous Municipal Theater: Fifty Seasons of Summer Musicals* (Louisiana, MO, 1970)

H. Jennings: 'Grand Opera in St Louis, in 1886: a Championship Season?', *Missouri Historical Review*, lxxxv/3 (1991), 304–20

JAMES M. BURK

Saint of Bleecker Street, The. Musical drama in three acts by GIAN CARLO MENOTTI to his own libretto; New York, Broadway Theatre, 27 December 1954.

The action takes place in 'the present' in the section of New York known as Little Italy. The story centres on the conflict between a religious mystic, the sickly Annina (soprano), and her agnostic brother Michele (tenor). In Act 1 scene i Annina is awaited by her neighbours, who deem her a saint who can work miracles. She is carried out from her room and sings an aria describing the crucifixion ('Oh, sweet Jesus, spare me this agony') at the end of which the stigmata appear on her hands, as has happened on previous Good Fridays. The people try to touch her but Michele arrives and drives them away. In scene ii Annina's friend Carmela (soprano) tells of her impending wedding and Annina expresses her desire to become a nun. Michele enters, angrily as usual, and denounces her religiosity. The hatred that people generally feel towards him is vividly expressed when a crowd ties him to a fence as a Catholic procession passes by.

In Act 2 the wedding of Carmela takes place a few months later. It is marred by an argument between Michele and his mistress Desideria (mezzo-soprano), who accuses him of being in love with his sister. As their anger rises he stabs her to death. In Act 3 scene i the fugitive Michele meets Annina by a subway station. Tender and loving at first, Michele becomes angry as Annina insists that she will become a nun. He curses her and rushes off. In the final scene Annina is dying when the message comes that the Church has given permission for her to become a nun. Wearing Carmela's wedding dress she dies after taking her vows, with final protestations from Michele.

While not as great a public success as *The Consul*, possibly because of the ambiguity of the subject matter (religious faith or superstition?) or the nastiness of Michele's character, *The Saint of Bleecker Street* is equally large in concept and has far more extended choral writing than Menotti's previous operas. Again the music powerfully conveys the drama, but with even more parallel chordal motion. It was later performed at La Scala, Milan, and at the Vienna Volksoper, and was broadcast on BBC television in 1957. Many of the performances, including the première, were conducted by Thomas Schippers. BRUCE ARCHIBALD

Saintonge [Sainctonge, Xaintonge], **Louise-Geneviève Gillot**, Dame de (*b* Paris, 1650; *d* Paris, 24 March 1718). French librettist. Her full-length *tragédies en musique*, *Didon* (1693) and *Circé* (1694), were set by Desmarets. At Dijon in 1714 she published a number of dramatic poems with such titles as *Idylle chantée à Versailles devant Sa Majesté*. Titon du Tillet, who adopts a particularly deferential tone in writing about her, also lists comedies, a *pastorale-héroïque, Diane et Endymion*, and a ballet, *Le charme des saisons*. She was defensive about the last, claiming that it had been written before Pic's *Ballet des saisons* (set by Collasse, 1695) and that she had been harshly treated by the cabals.

*

E. Titon du Tillet: *Le Parnasse françois* (Paris, 1732); suppl. i (Paris, 1743)

CAROLINE WOOD

St Paul. *See* MINNEAPOLIS AND ST PAUL.

St Petersburg (Russ. Sankt-Peterburg). City in Russia. Founded in 1703, it was the national capital until 1918; it has been known as Petrograd (1914–23), Peterburg (1923–4) and Leningrad (1924–91). After Moscow it is the chief cultural centre of the present-day Russian republic.

1. 18th century. 2. 1800–60. 3. 1860–1918. 4. After 1918.

1. 18TH CENTURY. The operatic history of the city began in 1735, when the Empress Anne imported a troupe of Italian singers under Francesco Araia to adorn her court with exotic and irrational entertainments. The first was an *opera seria* by Araia, *La forza dell'amore e dell'odio*, performed at the Winter Palace on the empress's birthday (29 January/9 February 1736). Araia served as *maestro di cappella*, with interruptions, until 1759. In 1755 he set a Russian libretto, *Tsefal i Prokris* ('Cephalus and Procris'), by Alexander Sumarokov, court poet to the Empress Elizabeth. Araia's successors included some famous names: Vincenzo Manfredini

(1762–5), Baldassare Galuppi (1765–8), Tommaso Traetta (1768–75), Giovanni Paisiello (1776–83), Giuseppe Sarti (1784–1801, with interruptions), Domenico Cimarosa (1787–91) and Vicente Martín y Soler (1790–1804, with interruptions). At its height under Catherine the Great, the court opera at St Petersburg rivalled the best opera theatres in Europe and staged the premières of some important works, including Paisiello's *Il barbiere di Siviglia* (15/26 September 1782). Catherine also maintained a French theatre, whose *comédies mêlées d'ariettes* provided the immediate model for the earliest efforts by Russian composers.

By the 1780s opera had become a court craze. Two theatres were specially constructed or refurbished for it: the Hermitage Theatre in the Winter Palace (renovated in 1783; see fig.1) and the Bol'shoy Kamennïy Teatr (Great Stone Theatre; see fig.3 below), built in 1783, which was to remain the principal opera house for a century (it was to suffer a major fire in 1818 which necessitated significant rebuilding). Operas in Italian, French and Russian were also performed at all the imperial residences in the outlying territory (Gatchina, Tsarskoye Selo, fig.2, Peterhof, Oranienbaum). Pavlovsk palace, built by Catherine for her estranged son Paul, was the venue for the *opéras comiques* of Bortnyansky, whose serious operas were performed only in Italy.

Public theatrical enterprises flourished from the late 1750s. The first was an *opera buffa* troupe under the direction of G. B. Locatelli which occupied the so-called Malïy (or Derevyannïy) Teatr (Little or Wooden Theatre) on Tsaritsïn Lug, St Petersburg's central park. In 1777 the theatre was acquired by Karl Knipper, a German impresario, originally to provide entertainment for the city's German population. Two years later Knipper broadened his repertory to include Singspiels in Russian, renamed his establishment the Vol'nïy Teatr (Free Theatre) and engaged the court violinist Vasily Pashkevich as his music director. The first Russian Singspiel to be presented to a paying audience in the capital was *Neschast'ye ot karetï* ('Misfortune from a Coach') by the court poet Yakov Knyazhnin and Pashkevich. It was performed at the Free Theatre on 20/31 December 1779, only six weeks after its première at court. Pashkevich wrote four more Singspiels expressly for Knipper's theatre. The last and the most ambitious, *Sanktpeterburgskiy gostinnïy dvor* ('The St Petersburg Bazaar', 1782), was revised and augmented as a court spectacle ten years later, becoming the first Russian opera (that is, one composed by a Russian to a Russian text) to have its first performance at the Bol'shoy (2/13 February 1792).

2. 1800–60. The Imperial Theatres were reorganized under a crown monopoly in the early years of the 19th century, following the accession of Tsar Alexander I. Prince Alexander Shakhovskoy, a prolific playwright, was put in charge of the theatrical bureaucracy with the title of intendant. The chief musician, with the title of inspector (later director), was the Polish composer and conductor Józef Kozłowski, who had been in Russia since the 1780s, serving various noble clans (Narïshkin, Potyomkin) before entering the service of Tsar Paul in 1799. (His main job was composing incidental music for Shakhovskoy's dramas.) St Petersburg was provided with four theatre companies, each performing in a different language – Italian, French, German and Russian. Only the Italian company, for which a new Malïy Derevyannïy Teatr (Little Wooden Theatre) was built in 1801, was reserved exclusively for opera. Public taste had changed, however, and the Italian company was disbanded in 1804. The French theatre, originally the most popular (and boasting international celebrities like Steibelt and Boieldieu at the helm), was a casualty of the war with Napoleon. From 1812, then, St Petersburg

1. The Hermitage Theatre in the Winter Palace, St Petersburg, designed by the Italian architect Quarenghi (1783–5)

2. Interior of the theatre in the imperial residence Tsarskoye Selo, near St Petersburg, during a danced entertainment: engraving from 'L'illustration' (12 December 1846)

had only the German and the Russian theatres, each performing operas in its respective language. Italian and French operas continued to dominate their repertories.

The Russian troupe, housed at the Bol'shoy, gradually came to the fore, thanks at first to a series of wildly successful adaptations of and sequels to Ferdinand Kauer's Singspiel *Das Donauweibchen* under the title *Lesta, Dneprovskaya rusalka* ('Lesta, the Dnepr Mermaid'), produced over a period of four years (1803–7). Most of the music for these spectacles was furnished by Stepan Davïdov, a pupil of Sarti, who served under Kozłowski as staff composer. One of the *Lesta* Singspiels also contained additional numbers by Catterino Cavos, a Venetian composer who had been engaged for the Italian theatre. When it closed Cavos was transferred to the Russian theatre and quickly consolidated his position as the leading composer in St Petersburg, collaborating (chiefly with Shakhovskoy) on a series of comic, magic and patriotic spectacles, including *Ivan Susanin* (1815), on a legend of civic self-sacrifice for the sake of the Romanov dynasty that later served as the subject for Glinka's first opera, *A Life for the Tsar*. Cavos trained the artists and conducted the troupe until his death in 1840 (although he stopped composing operas in 1825), initially concentrating on the French repertory which retained its favoured status even after the demise of its own theatre (Boieldieu, Dalayrac, Méhul and Grétry). Paer's frenchified *opere semiserie* – chiefly *Agnese*, which played in Russia as *Otets i doch'* ('Father and Daughter') – represented the Italian repertory, along with occasional performances of Rossini (*Il barbiere* and *La gazza ladra* only), Spontini (*La vestale*, *Fernand Cortez*) and Cherubini (*Les deux journées*, known in Russia as *Vodovoz*, 'The Water-Carrier'), with Cimarosa's *Il matrimonio segreto* the sole survivor from the old court repertory. *Der Freischütz* was introduced in 1823, in a translation by Rafail Mikhaylovich Zotov, a celebrated staff librettist then beginning a 50-year career of translating (and often replacing) the texts of foreign operas in accordance with the exceptionally stringent Russian censorship. *Don Giovanni*, with the title role a tenor, was not done until 1828 (before that only *Die Zauberflöte* and something called *Vavilonskiye razvalinï*, 'The Ruins of Babylon', presumably an adaptation, represented Mozart to the St Petersburgers). The prima donna was Nimfodora Semyonova (1788–1876), the sister of a famous tragédienne; the primo uomo was Vasily Mikhaylovich Samoylov (1782–1839). All operas were performed with spoken dialogue in place of recitative. Though its audience was enthusiastic enough, it is evident that, for the first third of the century, the St Petersburg Opera was a quite mediocre provincial company – and the German theatre, which continued until 1845 to give operas 'of every kind but German' (according to one sarcastic chronicler), was worse. (Its zenith came in 1834 with *La muette de Portici* – camouflaged as *Fenella* – which the censor would not countenance in Russian even in disguise and which by the end of 1836 had reached its 100th performance.)

Italian opera tried to stage a comeback in St Petersburg in 1829. A troupe under the direction of Luigi Zamboni, Rossini's first Figaro, was engaged at the Bol'shoy and stayed for two seasons, performing no fewer than 19 Rossini operas (along with a smattering of Mercadante, Morlacchi, Valentino Fioravanti and Schoberlechner, the prima donna's husband) in the original, and with recitatives intact. The public remained obdurate.

By the mid-1830s the Russian troupe had improved dramatically, thanks largely to two new singers. The Ukrainian-born bass Osip Petrov made a sensational début at the beginning of the decade as Sarastro, establishing the grand succession of basses that so distinguished the St Petersburg operatic stage, leading up – through Mikhail Sariotti and Fyodor Stravinsky – to Shalyapin. Even more remarkable was the début in 1833 (as Pippo in *La gazza ladra*) of Cavos's teenage protégée, the contralto Anna Vorob'yova, who eventually married Petrov. Thanks to their presence, the Russian Opera was able to mount first-class productions of *Zampa*, *Robert le diable* and other up-to-date fare, culminating in an epoch-making *Semiramide* (1836) with Vorob'yova as Arsace and Petrov as Assur. Later that year the pair repeated their triumph – Petrov as Susanin, Vorob'yova as Vanya – in Glinka's long-

3. The Bol'shoy Theatre, St Petersburg: watercolour by an unknown artist

heralded *A Life for the Tsar*, chosen by the court to inaugurate the newly refurbished Bol'shoy (Sobinin was sung by Lev Ivanovich Leonov, the natural son of the pianist John Field, making his début). The music was greeted with a certain amount of social snobbery ('on entend cela dans tous les cabarets' etc.), but a bridge had obviously been crossed. Russian opera – not only domestic singers but domestic repertory – had reached a new level of artistic competence.

Of the two sibylline premières it was *Semiramide* that bore immediate fruit – and to the dire disadvantage of Russian opera. Whereas the company could continue to develop the Italian repertory, for which their triumph had created a new audience (much to everyone's surprise), there was no domestic repertory to develop. Except for Cavos's work, which Glinka's had obviously superseded, there were only the operas of Verstovsky, so far the property of Moscow (*Askold's Grave* was not to conquer the capital until 1841), and the production of dilettantes and hacks like Feofil Tolstoy (1810–81), later one of the targets in Musorgsky's wicked song *Rayok* ('Peepshow'), whose little comic opera *Doktor v khlopotakh* ('The Doctor Came Running') had been given a couple of performances at the end of the previous season. There was not to be a major new Russian opera until Glinka's own *Ruslan and Lyudmila* in 1842; meanwhile, although Glinka's first opera remained the undisputed showpiece of the theatre, the Russian Opera pursued its Italian course with a will. Over the next six seasons it introduced Bellini and Donizetti to Russian audiences, and achieved a peak of 87 performances in 1842–3 (48 of them Glinka or Verstovsky, 26 Bellini or Donizetti). The 43-year-old Giuditta Pasta made a guest appearance with the Russian company in 1841, for which all learnt their parts in Italian. Her voice was all but gone, but she did give St Petersburg a fatal taste of international stardom, a taste confirmed by the concert appearances of the similarly worn but elegant Rubini during Lent in 1843.

Tsar Nicholas I felt that the time was now ripe to establish his capital as a world-class diplomatic and cultural centre, for which a major Italian opera house was a pre-requisite. He offered Rubini the post of 'Director of Singing for the Empire', charging him with the task of recruiting a company of celebrities to which he proposed to turn over the Bol'shoy lock, stock and barrel. Rubini returned in the autumn of 1843 with Tamburini and the young Viardot for a season of Rossini, Bellini, Donizetti and Mozart (*Don Giovanni*), and it was all over for the Russian Opera in the Russian capital. Petrov was allowed to sing second parts with the Italians, as was the young baritone Gulak-Artemovsky. They gave 51 performances to packed houses, while the Russian company, consigned to the smaller Alexandrinsky Theatre (till then used mainly for spoken drama), gave only 28 (the German company was squeezed down to 14). The next season the Italians (whose ranks now included Castellan and excluded all Russians) filled the Bol'shoy 76 times; the Russians gave 30 performances (of German, French and Russian operas only, needless to add); the German company closed its doors for ever. In 1845 Lorenzo Salvi joined the Italian company; Verdi was performed for the first time in Russia (*Lombardi*); the Russians were down to 20 performances. And thereafter, none. From 1846 to 1851 the Russian troupe was 'banished' to Moscow (returning only for tiny guest runs after the Italians had gone home). When they were allowed back, in the autumn of 1852, it was to the Teatr-tsirk (Circus Theatre), where they performed intermittently, between spoken dramas and variety shows.

The Italian Opera's appeal was invincible, and not only for the obvious reasons of state or of vocal prowess. Because its offerings were performed in foreign languages, the librettos were not subject to censorship. Therefore (as Prince Kropotkin's memoirs testify, along with the tracts and novels of Nikolay Chernïshevsky, the great proto-revolutionary writer) the Italian Opera quickly became the rallying-point not only of the uniformed and titled aristocracy but of the radical youth, who congregated in the only place they could legally assemble to hear Enrico Tamberlik (as Arnold in *Guillaume Tell*) shout 'Cercar la libertà!' (they always made him repeat it). Thus the St Petersburg Italian

Opera unexpectedly became the great unifier of the Russian social fabric.

3. 1860–1918. The absolute hegemony of Italian opera lasted to the end of the 1850s (during which decade only one Russian opera of any importance, Dargomïzhsky's *Rusalka*, was produced). In 1859 the Circus Theatre suddenly burnt down. This was salvation in disguise for the Russian troupe. On the same site in 1860 the sumptuous Mariinsky Theatre (fig.4) was erected to a plan by the court architect, none other than Catterino Cavos's son Alberto. Here the Russian company was to make a gradual comeback as the Italian gradually declined (a decline at first concealed by Adelina Patti's fabulous if ephemeral triumphs in the 1870s). The Italian company's famous peak was of course the world première of *La forza del destino* (29 October/10 November 1862). The temper of the times had so changed since the palmy days of Nicholas I that there was a public outcry over the production's extravagance (and over the fee paid to Verdi in the face of punishing limits on what a Russian artist or composer could collect). The somewhat puritanical mood engendered by the Crimean War and the aftermath of Emancipation worked in favour of operas celebrating Russian national pride: such was Serov's *Rogneda* (1865), the first Russian opera since the Italians' invasion to enjoy a success commensurate with theirs. The new popularity of the Russian Opera was vouchsafed by a new generation of singing talent: Yelizaveta Lavrovskaya, Fyodor Komissarzhevsky, Ivan Mel'nikov, Dar'ya Leonova, Fyodor Nikol'sky and, above all, the prima donna Yul'ya Platonova.

Over the 1870s, as Russian nationalism and panslavism mounted with the Balkan campaigns against the Ottoman Turks, and as (in connection with this) the prejudicial schedule of emoluments was ameliorated by the government of Alexander II, an indigenous classical repertory began to accumulate. It was largely the work of a new generation of professionally skilled composers who were to displace gradually the maverick autodidacts of the leisured class. Musorgsky was the last major representative of the older group. His *Boris Godunov*, produced at the Mariinsky in January 1874, marked the end of the era represented by Glinka, Dargomïzhsky and Serov. Before the end of the decade Tchaikovsky and Rimsky-Korsakov, both academically trained (the latter by intrepid self-instruction) and actively engaged in training their successors, had laid the cornerstone of an enduring – and exportable – repertory.

This repertory waged an uphill battle at first even within the Mariinsky: in the 1871–2 season Serov's *Vrazh'ya sila* ('The Power of the Fiend') and Dargomïzhsky's posthumously produced *Stone Guest* flopped miserably on their premières (two performances each), while *Les Huguenots*, *Le prophète* (given in Russia as 'Jan of Leyden'), *Guillaume Tell* (as 'Charles the Bold') and *Fra Diavolo* were revived to rapturous receptions. During the decade 1870–80 Russian opera also faced an additional competitor in operetta (Offenbach, Lecocq etc.), for which a craze suddenly developed in St Petersburg, leading to the one exception ever made to the crown monopoly on theatres: two private stages were authorized for operetta, the larger being the so-called Teatr-buff (Théâtre Bouffe), where Offenbach's shows were imported direct from Paris with original casts (Musorgsky, of all unlikely prospects, was a secret fan).

Despite everything, by 1879–80 Rimsky-Korsakov's *May Night* succeeded at the Mariinsky where *Rienzi* failed, and *Vrazh'ya sila* was successfully revived, reaching a total of 50 performances in the spring of 1881. By 1890 the indigenous repertory had achieved incontestable dominance at the Mariinsky and had been expanded to include works of Musorgsky and Borodin made performable by Rimsky-Korsakov, one of the two heroic paladins of Russian operatic culture.

The other was Eduard Nápravník, the much-maligned Czech conductor who took over from Konstantin Lyadov (the composer's father) as chief conductor at the Mariinsky in 1869 and held the post until 1914 (the Englishman Albert Coates briefly succeeding

4. Auditorium of the Mariinsky Theatre, St Petersburg (1860)

him). Nápravník's long, supremely competent tenure ensured the stability it took to mould a cohesive company with a strong sense of tradition. In the process he supervised the premières of some three dozen operas, including characteristic work of Dargomïzhsky, Serov, Cui, Rimsky-Korsakov, Tchaikovsky, Musorgsky and Rubinstein, as well as his own. Musorgsky's admiring letters to Nápravník have been discounted by the modernist critics who have made the composer's unprofessionalism a cause, but the same admiration (tempered by a certain irritation at the conductor's well-intentioned and often well-justified editorial interventions) can also be read in the letters and memoirs of Rimsky-Korsakov and Tchaikovsky. The latter's *Maid of Orleans* was dedicated to Nápravník.

After the Italian company was finally disbanded in 1885 (under Alexander III, the 'bourgeois tsar'), vast state funds were committed to the Mariinsky, even as the archaic crown monopoly on theatres was abrogated. (The Bol'shoy was razed and rebuilt as the St Petersburg Conservatory). For the next 30 years opera in the Russian capital experienced a golden age, during which the lavish, somewhat retrospective 'imperial style' came into its own, epitomized by Tchaikovsky's *Queen of Spades*, the St Petersburg opera *par excellence*, and by Nápravník's own *Dubrovsky*. Singers of the period included the tenor Nikolay Nikolayevich Figner and his Italian-born wife Medea Mei-Figner, dependable romantic leads in many new and newly imported works, including both of those just cited. In the tenor Ivan Vasil'yevich Yershov the Russian stage had its one great Heldentenor, indispensable for Siegmund, Siegfried, Tannhäuser, Lohengrin and Tristan, as the Wagner operas belatedly joined the Mariinsky repertory (the first St Petersburg *Ring* was given by Angelo Neumann's tour company in 1889–90); for Yershov Rimsky-Korsakov created the role of Grishka Kuter'ma in *Kitezh* (1907), the Russian *Parsifal*. Fyodor Stravinsky, the composer's father, was Osip Petrov's successor as the Mariinsky *primo basso*; his pre-eminence as singing actor was the reason Shalyapin had to remove himself strategically to Moscow (and to the privately subsidized theatre of Savva Mamontov) to gain a foothold. After Stravinsky's death in 1902 Shalyapin not only dominated the Mariinsky stage, he also functioned (from 1911) as co-director.

Unlike Moscow, the merchant-class stronghold, St Petersburg did not have any important private opera theatres in the brief period (after 1882) when such enterprises were legal, although there were adventurous and well-funded amateur organizations such as the one that gave the first performance of Musorgsky's *Khovanshchina* (in Rimsky-Korsakov's redaction) in 1886. In 1909 a temperance society sought to raise funds by sponsoring standard repertory performances in a new theatre, the huge Narodnïy Dom (Public Opera House); a similar enterprise, Iosif Lapitsky's Teatr Muzïkal'noy Dramï, functioned in the St Petersburg Conservatory's Great Hall (on the former site of the Bol'shoy) from 1912.

4. AFTER 1918. The Revolution and Bolshevik coup of 1917 – and particularly the transfer, the next year, of the seat of Soviet government to Moscow – had a profound effect on the musical life of the old capital. The new capital now assumed the role of national showcase. The Mariinsky, nationalized in December 1917 and renamed the Gosudarstvennïy Akademicheskiy Teatr Operï i Baleta (State Academic Theatre of Opera and Ballet), became the country's second theatre. In 1935 it was to be renamed again, as Teatr imeni S. M. Kirova (Kirov Theatre), in honour of Sergey Mironovich Kirov, the recently assassinated Communist Party chief of Leningrad; it reverted to the name Mariinsky in 1991. For a while its repertory was adventurous: Stravinsky's *Solovey* (1918), then-émigré Prokofiev's *Love for Three Oranges* (1926), Berg's *Wozzeck* (1927), the unretouched *Boris Godunov* in both its versions (1928). Russian classics were given radical stagings, the most famous being Vsevolod Meyerhold's 're-Pushkinized' *Queen of Spades* (1935).

From the mid-1930s, however, the Kirov was a glorified regional house (seating 1621) with an increasingly hackneyed and insular repertory of dependable standard works, Russian classics and local ephemerae such as Andrey Petrov's much-touted but tawdry *Pyotr I* ('Peter I', 1975). Two less prestigious houses became the site of innovatory work in opera: the Opernaya Studiya Konservatorii (Opera Studio of the Conservatory; seating 1718), organized by Yershov (retired as a singer but active as a professor) in 1923; and the Malïy Opernïy Teatr (Small Opera Theatre), organized in 1918 in what till then was known as the Mikhaylovsky Theatre (built 1833; seating 1212), formerly used for French drama, vaudevilles and operetta. Under the energetic direction of Samuil Samosud (1918–36) and Boris Khaikin (1936–44; he then led the Kirov till 1954), the Malïy Theatre staged the first performances of both of Shostakovich's operas – *The Nose* (1930) and *Lady Macbeth of the Mtsensk District* (1934) – as well as such early Soviet experiments in proletarian culture as *Za krasnïy Petrograd* ('For Red Petrograd', 1925) by Arseny Gladkovsky and E. V. Prussak, the first opera on a Soviet historical theme. Even after his denunciation by *Pravda* in 1936, which effectively ended his operatic career, Shostakovich maintained a special relationship with the opera houses of Leningrad, his native city. Both of his Musorgsky instrumentations (*Boris Godunov*, 1938–40; *Khovanshchina*, 1952–8, originally for a film produced in Leningrad) were given their stage premières by the Kirov Theatre around 1960 and have remained in its repertory. Since the 1960s the leading St Petersburg opera composer has been Sergey Slonimsky (*Virineya*, 1967; *Master i Margarita*, completed 1972; *Mariya Styuart*, 1981). Under Valery Gergiyev, its principal conductor from 1988, the Kirov/Mariinsky Opera has had some exciting new productions of a kind that earlier could not have reached the stage. Two have been joint ventures with the Royal Opera House, Covent Garden: *Boris Godunov*, directed by Andrey Tarkovsky (1983, London; 1990, Leningrad) and Prokofiev's *Fiery Angel* (1991, St Petersburg; 1992, London). In summer 1992 the company made its first American tour.

*

A. Vol'f: *Khronika peterburgskikh teatrov* (St Petersburg, 1877–84)

S. Sviridenko: 'Russkaya opera v Mariinskom teatre za 25 let', *RMG* (1912), nos.1–2, 4–5

P. Stolpyansky: *Muzïka i muzitsirovaniye v starom Peterburge* [Music and Music-making in early St Petersburg] (Leningrad, 1926, 2/1989)

V. Shkafer: *Sorok let na stsene russkoy operï vospominaniya 1890–1930 gg.* [40 years on the Russian Operatic stage: Reminiscences 1890–1930] (Leningrad, 1936)

20 let Gosudarstvennogo akademicheskogo Malogo opernogo teatra 1918–1938 [20th Anniversary of the State Academic Malïy Opera Theatre, 1918–38] (Leningrad, 1939)

E. Stark: *Peterburgskaya opera i yeyo mastera* [The St Petersburg Opera and its Masters] (Leningrad, 1940)

Leningradskiy gosudarstvenniy ordena Lenina akademicheskiy teatr operï i baleta [The Leningrad State Academic Theatre of Opera and Ballet] (Leningrad, 1940)
Leningradskiye teatrï v godï Velikoy Otechestvennoy voynï [The Leningrad Theatres during World War II] (Leningrad and Moscow, 1948)
D. Pokhitonov: *Iz proshlogo russkoy operï* [From the Bygone Period of Russian Opera] (Leningrad, 1949)
N. Bogolyubov: *Polveka na opernoy stsene* [Half a Century on the Operatic Stage] (Moscow, 1957)
I. Golubovsky, ed.: *Muzïkal'nïy Leningrad* (Leningrad, 1958)
V. Bogdanov-Berezovsky: *Leningradskiy gosudarstvenniy akademicheskiy ordena Lenina teatr operï i baleta im. S. M. Kirova* [The Kirov Opera and Ballet Theatre] (Leningrad, 1959)
V. Bogdanov-Berezovsky, ed.: *V godï velikoy otechestvennoy voynï* [During World War II] (Leningrad, 1959)
M. Druskin: 'Muzïkal'naya kul'tura Peterburga – Petrograda – Leningrada', *Istoriya i sovremennost'* [History and the Present] (Leningrad, 1960)
V. Bogdanov-Berezovsky: *Muzïkal'naya kul'tura Leningrada za 50 let* [Musical Culture in Leningrad during the Past 50 Years] (Leningrad, 1967)
L. Entelis, ed.: *Leningradskiy gosudarstvenniy ordena Lenina akademicheskiy teatr operï i baleta imeni S. M. Kirova 1917–1967* [The Kirov Opera and Ballet Theatre, 1917–67] (Leningrad, 1968)
Leningradskiy Malïy teatr operï i baleta [The Malïy Theatre] (Leningrad, 1968)
Teatr operï i baleta im. S. M. Kirova [The Kirov Theatre] (Leningrad, 1973)
A. Yusfin, ed.: *Muzïkal'naya panorama Leningrada* (Leningrad and Moscow, 1977)

RICHARD TARUSKIN

St Petersburg Bazaar, The. Opera by V. A. Pashkevich; *see* SANKTPETERBURGSKIY GOSTINNÏY DVOR.

Saint-Saëns, (Charles) Camille (*b* Paris, 9 Oct 1835; *d* Algiers, 16 Dec 1921). French composer. He was prolific in all spheres of music, performed in France as pianist, organist and conductor, cultivated many intellectual pursuits and left extensive writings. Within this vast range of activity lay an abiding interest in opera. He composed 12 operas, along with ballets, incidental music, dramatic choral works and even a film score, and acted as his own librettist when required. Although most of his operas were performed and revived in his lifetime, only one, *Samson et Dalila*, has retained a permanent place in the 20th-century repertory.

His early musical experience directed him towards a career as a virtuoso pianist and organist, and his tastes ranged from Bach and Rameau to Wagner and Liszt. At the Paris Conservatoire (1848–52) his success as a virtuoso impeded his reputation as a composer and he did not win the Prix de Rome; in contrast with most French composers he composed symphonies and chamber music rather than operas, although his interest in opera was aroused by his teacher Halévy, by the early support of the singer Pauline Viardot and by Gounod. As early as 1854 he began an *opéra comique* on a Persian subject but quickly abandoned it. He also composed an overture for a nameless opera proposed by Jules Barbier but never written. There exist unpublished dramatic scenes dating from the late 1850s, one entitled *La toilette de la marquise de Présalé*, one on the sleepwalking scene from *Macbeth*. From 1858 for 20 years his duties as organist of the Madeleine in Paris and his career as a pianist occupied his main energies, and a great number of his compositions were religious works (despite his professed lack of faith).

But his interest in the theatre was keen; he wrote a comic drama in three acts and sustained a number of literary friendships. During Wagner's stay in Paris in 1860–61 he had the opportunity to play *Lohengrin*, *Tristan* and *Rheingold* on the piano in the composer's presence. His enthusiasm for Wagner took him to Munich in 1869 to hear *Rheingold* and to Bayreuth in 1876 to hear the *Ring*.

After Saint-Saëns again failed to win the Prix de Rome in 1864, Auber, director of the Conservatoire, persuaded Carvalho, director of the Théâtre Lyrique, to find him an opera libretto, perhaps as consolation. Carvalho offered him Barbier and Carré's *Le timbre d'argent*, a fantastic tale in the manner of Hoffmann which might have been expected to enjoy the same success as Gounod's recent *Faust.* Although Saint-Saëns composed the opera within a year or two, it was over 12 years before *Le timbre d'argent* was staged, many mishaps and misunderstandings coming in its way, chief of which was the prejudiced belief of critics and managements that a pianist and organist who wrote symphonies could not be entrusted with an opera.

His next opera, *Samson et Dalila*, was almost equally delayed; indeed if Liszt had not displayed his legendary faith in younger composers by having it mounted in Weimar in 1877, the work might have had to wait even longer than it did. Thus his third opera, *La princesse jaune*, was the first to be staged. An unambitious *opéra comique* for only two singers on a Dutch-Japanese subject, it was played by the Opéra-Comique in 1872, without much success. It was the first of many collaborations with Louis Gallet, who provided librettos for many other composers of the day. Saint-Saëns remained a close friend until Gallet's death in 1898.

The next years were more concerned with symphonic poems, choral works and the running of the Société Nationale de Musique which Saint-Saëns had founded during the political turmoil of 1870–71. But the eventual staging of *Le timbre d'argent* at the Théâtre Lyrique in February 1877 and of *Samson et Dalila* in Weimar at the end of the same year gave Saint-Saëns the reassurance and confidence he needed to devote himself regularly to opera. Every three or four years thereafter he produced a new work, each one immediately performed, until the series closed with *Déjanire* in 1911.

His profound patriotism after the experience of the Franco-Prussian war led him to favour themes drawn from French history. He accepted the standard model of grand opera with ballets and scenes of pageantry, and he adopted Gounod's lyrical style. He opposed modernism for its own sake and liked to use historical and regional pastiche to evoke scenes from distant times and places. The most extreme case of this was his attempt to recreate the music of the Greeks for his incidental music to Sophocles' *Antigone* at the Comédie-Française in 1894.

Saint-Saëns' first historical opera was *Etienne Marcel*, staged in Lyons in 1879 and based on events in Paris in 1358. Gallet provided the libretto. Its success was only moderate and it never reached the stage of the Paris Opéra. *Henry VIII*, the next, was more successful. Commissioned by the Opéra, it was the first Saint-Saëns work to be played there; neither its libretto nor its librettists were of Saint-Saëns' choosing, yet he threw himself into the work with ardour and took considerable pains to find the correct English tone for the music. Its merits place it perhaps second to *Samson et Dalila* in quality and invention. Before his next opera, *Proserpine* (performed in 1887), he considered an *opéra comique* entitled *Guillery* based on a story by Edmond About but soon abandoned the idea. *Proserpine* was a Gallet

Open-air performance of Gallet's play 'Déjanire' (with incidental music by Saint-Saëns, a quotation from which can be seen below) at Béziers, 25 August 1898; the première of Saint-Saëns' opera on the same subject took place at Monte Carlo in 1911

libretto based on a play by Auguste Vacquerie, a story of intrigue and jealousy set in 16th-century Florence: Proserpina kills herself since the man she loves is to marry her rival Angiola. The Opéra-Comique, where it was staged, had begun to raise the dramatic level of its repertory; this is a through-composed *drame lyrique*, no lighthearted comedy with dialogue. But the theatre burnt down two months after its opening, curtailing its success.

Gallet next proposed a *Brunehilda* and an Arthurian story named *Drougha*, both of which Saint-Saëns perhaps wisely rejected. *Agnès de Méranie*, set in 1196 in the reign of Philippe-Auguste, was also spurned. He decided finally on *Ascanio*, based on Paul Meurice's play *Benvenuto Cellini*, which elaborates an incident during Cellini's stay in France at the court of François I. Saint-Saëns added an elaborate *divertissement* in an imagined Renaissance style, and the work was played at the Opéra in 1890 only a few days after *Samson et Dalila* finally reached French soil with a performance in Rouen. Saint-Saëns, who now spent more and more time abroad following the death of his mother, attended neither. *Phryné*, a comedy set in 4th-century BC Athens, was next. Sibyl Sanderson sang in the title role when it appeared at the Opéra-Comique in 1893, and its light, witty style made of it a considerable success.

Frédégonde, though, the opera started by Guiraud on Gallet's *Brunehild* libretto and dutifully completed by Saint-Saëns, was a failure at the Opéra in 1895. At that point he spoke gloomily of giving up the theatre. But he found a renewed enthusiasm thanks to three very different theatres in the south of France where his music was welcomed: at Béziers, where an open-air space intended as a bull-ring was converted into a theatre, Saint-Saëns was invited in 1898 to act as musical adviser, planning a grand work with Gallet on the story of Hercules and Dejanira. *Déjanire* was a play with text declaimed in what was thought to be a Greek manner and incidental music for a very large orchestra and chorus. *Les barbares*, another large-scale work on an ancient, this time a Roman, subject, was similarly intended for the open-air theatre at Orange. Although that project did not come off, *Les barbares*, to a bloodthirsty story by Sardou, was played at the Paris Opéra in 1901 and remained in the repertory until 1913 despite – or perhaps because of – its inflated old-fashioned staginess. *Parysatis* (incidental music), set in Persia in the reign of Artaxerxes, was his second work for Béziers, consisting of choruses and dances again requiring immense forces. It was played in 1902.

The richly decorated Garnier opera house in Monte Carlo was the stage for Saint-Saëns' last three operas. Prince Albert of Monaco's patronage and Raoul Gunsbourg's direction offered the most enticing stage for French composers at that time. Still entranced by the ancient world, Saint-Saëns composed his one-act opera *Hélène* for production in Monte Carlo in 1904, followed by *L'ancêtre* two years later. This tale of a Corsican vendetta set in Napoleonic times was too strong for Saint-Saëns' restrained musical language, although individual numbers such as the evocation of bees and Margarita's long vocalise are effective. Saint-Saëns closed his operatic career with an adaptation of *Déjanire* as an opera, played in Monte Carlo in 1911.

Despite Saint-Saëns' early admiration for Wagner, he later came to see him as a malaise to be avoided, both on stylistic and on national grounds. Eschewing modern tendencies, his style remained essentially unchanged and was consequently too pale to be successful in the era of Puccini and Strauss. Saint-Saëns was jealous of

Massenet's greater operatic gift and outspokenly hostile to Debussy. Except perhaps in *Phryné*, his admiration for Mozart had little occasion to show itself since he was never afraid of huge operatic canvases in which he could paint episodes from French history or scenes from the ancient world. The legacy of Meyerbeer and Gounod remained strong.

His operas are fluent and well crafted and his word-setting is always impeccable. He used a straightforward framework of motifs in all his operas. *Samson et Dalila* owes its success to the emotional intensity of the second act, the exotic colour of the Philistines' music and the fine choral writing, derived from its original purpose as an oratorio; an indebtedness to Wagner and Berlioz is more evident here than in his other operas.

See also ASCANIO; DÉJANIRE; ETIENNE MARCEL; HÉLÈNE; HENRY VIII; PRINCESSE JAUNE, LA; SAMSON ET DALILA; and TIMBRE D'ARGENT, LE.

all published in Paris

title	*genre, acts*	*libretto*	*composed*	*first performance*	*publication details; remarks*
Le timbre d'argent	opéra fantastique, 4	J. Barbier and M. Carré	1864–5	Paris, Lyrique, 23 Feb 1877	1877
Samson et Dalila	opéra, 3	F. Lemaire	1867–8, 1873–77	Weimar, Grossherzogliches, 2 Dec 1877	1877
La princesse jaune	opéra comique, 1	L. Gallet	1872	Paris, OC (Favart), 12 June 1872	1872
Etienne Marcel	opéra, 4	Gallet	1877–8	Lyons, Grand, 8 Feb 1879	1879
Henry VIII	opéra, 4	L. Détroyat and A. Silvestre	1881–2	Paris, Opéra, 5 March 1883	1883
Proserpine	drame lyrique, 4	Gallet, after A. Vacquerie	1886, rev. 1891	Paris, OC (Favart), 14 March 1887	1887
Ascanio	opéra, 5	Gallet, after P. Meurice: *Benvenuto Cellini*	1887–8	Paris, Opéra, 21 March 1890	1890
Phryné	opéra comique, 2	L. Augé de Lassus	1892	Paris, OC (Lyrique), 24 May 1893	1893
Frédégonde	drame lyrique, 5	Gallet	1894–5	Paris, Opéra, 18 Dec 1895	1895; completion of Guiraud's opera
Les barbares	tragédie lyrique, prol., 3	V. Sardou and P. B. Gheusi	1900–01	Paris, Opéra, 23 Oct 1901	1901
Hélène	poème lyrique, 1	Saint-Saëns	1903	Monte Carlo, 18 Feb 1904	1903
L'ancêtre	drame lyrique, 3	Augé de Lassus	1905	Monte Carlo, 24 Feb 1906	1905
Déjanire	tragédie lyrique, 4	Gallet and Saint-Saëns, after Sophocles: *Trachiniae*	1909–10	Monte Carlo, 14 March 1911	1911; orig. version incidental music, perf. 1898

WRITINGS

Harmonie et mélodie (Paris, 1885, 9/1923)
Problèmes et mystères (Paris, 1894; enlarged 1922 as *Divagations sérieuses*)
Portraits et souvenirs (Paris, 1899, 3/1909)
Quelques mots sur 'Proserpine' (Alexandria, 1902)
Ecole buissonnière: notes et souvenirs (Paris, 1913; Eng. trans., abridged, 1919)
Notice sur Le timbre d'argent (Brussels, 1914)
Regards sur mes contemporains, ed. Y. Gérard (Arles, 1990)

*

E. Hippeau: '*Henry VIII* et l'opéra français', *La renaissance musicale* (Paris, 1883)
C. Bellaigue: *M. Camille Saint-Saëns* (Paris, 1889)
E. Destranges: *Samson et Dalila: étude analytique* (Paris, 1893)
O. Neitzel: *Camille Saint-Saëns* (Berlin, 1899)
E. Baumann: *Les grandes formes de la musique: l'oeuvre de Camille Saint-Saëns* (Paris, 1905, 2/1923)
O. Séré [J. Poueigh]: 'Camille Saint-Saëns', *Musiciens français d'aujourd'hui* (Paris, 1911, 2/1921)
L. Augé de Lassus: *Saint-Saëns* (Paris, 1914)
J. Bonnerot: *C. Saint-Saëns: sa vie et son oeuvre* (Paris, 1914, 2/1922)
J. Montargis: *Camille Saint-Saëns: l'oeuvre, l'artiste* (Paris, 1919)
C. Debussy: 'Entretien sur le Prix de Rome et M. Saint-Saëns', *Monsieur Croche antidilettante* (Paris, 1921; Eng. trans., 1927)
A. Hervey: *Saint-Saëns* (London, 1921)
G. Fauré: 'Camille Saint-Saëns', *ReM*, iii/4 (1922), 97–100
H. Collet: *Samson et Dalila de C. Saint-Saëns* (Paris, ?1922)
W. Lyle: *Camille Saint-Saëns: his Life and Art* (London, 1923)
G. Servières: *Saint-Saëns* (Paris, 1923, 2/1930)
——: *Le 'wagnérisme' de Camille Saint-Saëns* (Turin, 1923)
A. Dandelot: *La vie et l'oeuvre de Saint-Saëns* (Paris, 1930)
J. Handschin: *Camille Saint-Saëns* (Zürich, 1930)
P. Aguétant: *Saint-Saëns par lui-même d'après des lettres reçues* (Paris, 1938)
A. Boschot: 'Saint-Saëns', *Portraits de musiciens*, ii (Paris, 1947), 88–102
J. Chantavoine: *Camille Saint-Saëns* (Paris, 1947)
P. Lalo: 'Camille Saint-Saëns', *De Rameau à Ravel* (Paris, 1947), 94–101
Mélanges d'histoire littéraire et de bibliographie offerts à Jean Bonnerot (Paris, 1954)
J. Harding: *Saint-Saëns and his Circle* (London, 1965)
J. M. Nectoux, ed.: *Camille Saint-Saëns et Gabriel Fauré: correspondance: soixante ans d'amitié* (Paris, 1973)
T. J. Walsh: *Monte Carlo Opera 1879–1909* (Dublin, 1975)
L'avant-scène opéra, no.15 (1978) [*Samson et Dalila* issue]
E. Bondeville, ed.: *Camille Saint-Saëns 1835–1921: correspondance inédite* (Paris, 1983) [facs. of 83 letters]
M. Faure: *Musique et société du second empire aux années vingt* (Paris, 1985)
M. Stegemann: *Camille Saint-Saëns* (Reinbek bei Hamburg, 1988)
R. Locke: 'Constructing the Oriental "Other": Saint-Saëns's *Samson et Dalila*', *COJ*, iii/3 (1991), 261–302 HUGH MACDONALD

Sakellaridis, Theofrastos (*b* Athens, 7 Sept ?1883; *d* Athens, 2 Jan 1950). Greek composer and conductor. He probably began his studies with his father Ioannis

Sakellaridis, a scholar and composer of church music in the Byzantine style, and is reported to have studied in Germany and Italy. In Athens, he built his reputation on the composition of incidental music, operas and revues, but mainly operettas, sometimes producing original ideas from his research of cabaret tunes (in his revues) and from songs he heard in gypsy encampments (in the opera *Perouzé*). For seven years, 1907–13, he adapted, composed and conducted the music of the popular yearly *Panathenaea* revues, which pungently satirized Greek society. His influence, as conductor (1908–21) of the Elliniki (Hellenic) Operetta company, which staged most of his operettas, may be compared with that of Kalomiris in serious Greek music. The decline in the popularity of operetta in Athens by the late 1930s prompted him to return to writing revues. He died in poverty. Although he emerged as a leading Greek operetta composer (airs from *O vaftistikos*, 1918, are still beloved in Greece today), Sakellaridis, who had a natural gift for stage melody, may prove equally important as a composer of serious opera between the late Ionian and new National schools.

performed in Athens unless otherwise stated

Ymenaeos [Hymenaeus], 1901 (I. Franghias), unperf., lost

O piratis [The Pirate] (1, P. Dimitrakopoulos), Arniotis (now Olympia), ?29 Sept 1907, lost

Perouze (2, G. Tsokopoulos), Arniotis, 9 Aug 1911, *GR-Aleotsakos**, vs *Aels*

To stichiomeno yefyri i i Kori tis neraidas [The Haunted Bridge, or The Fairy's Daughter] (3, Tsokopoulos), 1912

To kastro tis Orias [The Castle of Oria] (dramatic legend, Tsokopoulos), Vassilikon, aut. 1917, lost

Operettas (selected): Sia ki araxame [Touching Bottom] (Dimitrakopoulos and S. Granitsas), 1909; Sta parapigmata [At the Encampment] (3, N. Laskaris), Municipal, 9 May 1914, vs *Aels* and *Am*; Pic-nic [The Picnic] (3, Laskaris), Panellinion, 7 or 8 July 1915, vs *Aels* and *Am*; Prothymi hira [The Willing Widow] (3, Laskaris), Papaioannou, 20 June 1916; Despinis Tip-Top [Miss Tip-Top] (3, Laskaris, after Fr. operetta), Papaioannou, 5 Aug 1916, vs *Aels*; O hypnovatis [The Sleepwalker] (3, Sakellaridis), 1917, vs *Aels*, lib. *Akounadis*; I garsoniera [The Bachelor's Flat] (1), 1917

O vaftistikos [The Godson] (3, Sakellaridis, after C. M. Hennequin, P. Véber and H. de Gorsse), Papaioannou, 18 July 1918, *Aels*; I demonismeni [The Possessed] (3), Papaioannou, 27 June 1919, vs *Aels**; Arlekinos [Harlequin] (3, ?M. Lidorikis), Papaioannou, 23 June 1920, vs *Am*; Thelo na ido ton Papa [I Want to See the Pope], Papaioannou, 6 July 1920; O kyrios Seraphim [Mr Seraphim], ?1920; Ke ti mia ke tin alli [I Want Both Ladies] (3), 10 June 1922; To diavolopedo [The Mischievous Lad] (3), 1922; Glykia Nana [Sweet Nana], ?1922; Tohapse o thios [The Uncle Bought It] (1), Apollo, carn. ?1923

Alla gegonota [Other Events] (1), Apollo, carn. ?1923; I kori tis kataegidos [The Daughter of the Tempest] (3), 1923; Miss Sorolop [Miss Happy-go-Lucky] (3, ?D. Zattas), 28 July 1924; Rosita (3, S. Potamianos), 19 Jan 1925; Makris, Kondos ke Sia [Long, Short and Company] (3), ? March 1925, vs *Am*; Enas kleftis ston Paradisso [A Thief in Paradise] (3, Potamianos), 1926; Halima (3, Potamianos), ? 1926 or 1929, vs *Aels*; Kryfo romantso [Secret Romance], 19 May 1927; I kori tis maimous [The Monkey's Daughter], 1 July 1927; Miss Charleston (3, D. S. Devaris), 7 Sept 1927, vs *Aels**

Iro ke Leandros [Hero and Leander] (3), 9 Dec 1927, vs *Aels**; Ya n'kou aressi ston andra tis [To Attract Her Husband], 1927 or earlier; I agapi tis Renas [Rena's Love], 1927 or earlier; Pif-paf, 1927 or earlier; Christina (3, G. Dramalis), 24 April 1928; Xanthi-melachrini [Blonde, Brunette] (after Fr. play), 6 Nov 1928; To romantso tis Bebas [To romantso tis Bebis; Biba; Bimba] [Beba's Romance] (3), 1928, vs, lib., pts *Akounadis*; Lohagos Lili [Captain Lily], 1929; Skra, 1929; Satanerie (3), 16 Jan or June 1930; To exofreniko spiti [The Outrageous Household] (3, M. Filippidis), *c*1930, vs, lib., pts *Akounadis*

Agapate allilous [Love Each Other], *c*1930; I gyneka tou nomarchi [The Prefect's Wife], *c*1930; Kapetan Tsanakas [Captain Tsanakas], *c*1930; Lola mou lefki [O Lola, bianca...], *c*1930; Maskaralikia [Follies], *c*1930; Sacra familia (1, N. Laskaria), *c*1930; Gyneka delirio [The Irresistible Woman], 28 Nov 1931; Ioannis o protos [John the First], 1931; Pende bouboukia [Five Flower-Buds], 1932; I Loussi ke ta koroida tis [Lucy and her Dupes], 1932; To tsinganiko aema [Gypsy Blood] (prol., 2), 11 Jan 1933, vs, lib., pts *Akounadis*; Simia ke terata [Signs and Wonders], 1935; Moderna koritsia [Modern Girls] (3), 13 March 1935; Ta griza niata [Grey youth] (A. Sakellarios), *c*1936–8; Fernanda, 1948

*

Y. Sideris: 'I. Papaioannou', *Actor's Day: Athens, 29 September 1958* [programme for a study day on the Hellenic Operetta Company]

S. Petras: *Vassiliko Theatro - Elliniki Operetta* [The Royal Theatre and the Hellenic Operetta Company] (Athens, 1960)

L. I. Bratsiotis: 'Ioannis Th. Sakellaridis', *Nea Estia*, lxxx (1966), 1058–63

T. Karalivanos: *Erga Throfrastou Sakellaridi* [Works of Theofrastos Sakellaridis], unpubd MS, *GR-Aleotsakos* GEORGE LEOTSAKOS

Sakùntala [*La leggenda di Sakùntala* ('The Legend of Sakùntala')]. Opera in three acts by FRANCO ALFANO to his own libretto, after the drama *Abhijñanasakuntala* by Kalidasa (*c*400 BC); as *La leggenda di Sakùntala*, Bologna, Teatro Comunale, 10 December 1921; revised as *Sakùntala*, Rome, Teatro dell'Opera, 9 January 1952.

The opera opens to the sounds of an offstage chorus as three maidens, Sakùntala (soprano), Priyàmvada (mezzo-soprano) and Anùsuya (soprano), are serving in an Indian sanctuary. The king (tenor) arrives with a hunting party and, left alone with Sakùntala, falls in love with her. He gives her a ring as a token of his love. Later, in the same sanctuary, while lost in thoughts of love, Sakùntala forgets to open the door for the old hermit Durvàsas (bass). The hermit places a curse on the king to make him forget his bride. Sakùntala's father, Kanva (bass), returns home and announces that Sakùntala is pregnant and will be sent to the king's palace as his bride. However, when she arrives at the palace the king does not remember her, and as she has lost the ring she has no proof of his former love. She returns home in despair; meanwhile a fisherman has been found with the ring and is brought before the king. The ring causes Sakùntala's image to return to the king, who thus realizes his error. Meanwhile the distraught Sakùntala has tried to drown herself. A cloud of fire engulfs her, and the newborn heir of the kingdom is rescued by hermits from the water.

Sakùntala is certainly Alfano's best work and his only opera likely to survive in the repertory; it is also an early example of an Italian opera on a prose libretto (by Alfano himself). The choice of an Indian text is not surprising, as Alfano had previously set a number of poems by Rabindranath Tagore. The impressionistic score shows a masterly treatment of the orchestra and a compelling melodic invention. The orchestration owes much to Debussy and Ravel, although the richness of the orchestral textures sometimes appears less balanced than in contemporary French scores. On the other hand Alfano's vocal lines display an emotional intensity that recalls his earlier operas. On the whole *Sakùntala* represents a notable achievement in both harmonic and rhythmic complexity, comparable to early 20th-century music by other European composers. Alfano's gift for lyrical expression is evident in the closing scene of Act 1 and in Sakùntala's extended arias of Act 2 ('O nuvola leggera che vaghi pei cieli' and 'Padre! Padre! Solleva la fronte'). The close correlation between text and music throughout is particularly striking. The opera's initial success and its exotic subject matter might well have contributed to Alfano's being chosen by Toscanini to complete Puccini's *Turandot*. JÜRGEN MAEHDER

Sala, Nicola (*b* Tocco-Caudio, nr Benevento, 7 April 1713; *d* Naples, 31 Aug 1801). Italian composer. He studied at the Pietà dei Turchini Conservatory, Naples, with Nicola Fago and Leo, and apparently taught there for most of his life, becoming *primo maestro* in 1793. While still a *maestrino*, he seems to have composed the opera *Vologeso* (Fétis claimed to have seen a score of it with an indication, otherwise unconfirmed, that it was performed in Rome in 1737). In the 1760s he had three operas as well as several prologues and other occasional works performed at the S Carlo. He also wrote sacred music, but was most important as a teacher, influencing many Neapolitan composers through his monumental *Regole del contrappunto pratico* (Naples, 1794).

Sala's compositions, though inconsequential and mostly pedestrian, have been unjustly treated by some modern writers. In particular, Mondolfi's harsh judgment on his operas is almost entirely directed at characteristics of the contemporary *opera seria* as a genre, not of Sala's operas exclusively. His greatest weakness was in lyrical melody; some of his arias in an *agitato* or declamatory style are not ineffective.

Vologeso (os, A. Zeno), Rome, Argentina, 1737, or Lisbon, Condes, 1739
La Zenobia (os, P. Metastasio), Naples, S Carlo, 12 Jan 1761, arias in *Gb-Lbl*, *I-Mc*, *Nc* and *P-La*
Demetrio (os, Metastasio), Naples, S Carlo, 12 Dec 1762, *La*
Il giudizio d'Apollo (serenata, G. Fenizia), Naples, S Carlo, 1768
La bella eroina (prol.), Naples, S Carlo, 13 Aug 1769, *La*
Merope (os, Zeno), Naples, S Carlo, 13 Aug 1769, *I-Nc*, *P-La*

Arias in: Jommelli: Attilio Regolo, 1761
Miscellaneous arias in *B-Bc*, *D-Bds*, *DS*, *E-Mn*, *I-Mc* and *Nc*

*

ES (A. Mondolfi); *FétisB*; *FlorimoN*; *RosaM*
G. Leo: 'Nicola Sala', *Rivista storica del Sannio*, no.5 (1918)
U. Prota-Giurleo: 'Musicisti sanniti', *Samnium*, no.1 (1928)
DENNIS LIBBY (text), JAMES L. JACKMAN (work-list)

***Salammbô* (i)** [*Liviyets* ('The Libyan')]. Projected grand opera in four acts by MODEST PETROVICH MUSORGSKY to his own libretto after Gustave Flaubert's novel; concert performance of fragments, Milan (RAI), 10 November 1980.

Three major scenes and three additional numbers were composed between autumn 1863 and spring 1866. The plot, set in Carthage during the Punic Wars, in many ways parallels that of Serov's opera *Yudif'* ('Judith', 1863), which may have excited Musorgsky's interest in it. The title character (dramatic soprano), a Carthaginian priestess, seduces Mathô (baritone), a Libyan warrior (the alternative title character), so as to regain the sacred veil of the Goddess Tanit which Mathô has stolen from the temple. He is captured and tortured to death, while she, defiled by her exploit, dies in horror immediately thereafter.

Musorgsky never wrote the central dramatic scenes; opulent choral pageantry seems to have been his first interest. Two of the extant scenes represent magnificent temple rites: Act 2 scene ii (temple of Tanit, for women's voices, including the theft of the veil) and Act 3 scene i (sacrifice to Moloch, for men's voices, in hopes of regaining it). The short score of the somewhat sugary Tanit scene promises lavish obbligatos for harp, piano and glockenspiel. The remaining large number, a declamatory *scena* for the imprisoned Mathô (Act 4 scene i), exists in full score, as does a chorus of Libyan warriors, later reworked into the concert chorus *Iisus Navin*. (The remaining items are a Balearic Islander's song for the opening feast scene and a chorus of priestesses for the concluding scene of Act 4.) A good deal of thematic material from *Salammbô* eventually wound up in *Boris Godunov*; most of the literature on the work is devoted to detailing these correspondences. The *Salammbô* fragments, orchestrated and conducted by Zoltán Peskó, were first performed in 1980; a recording was issued. RICHARD TARUSKIN

***Salammbô* (ii)**. *Opéra* in five acts by ERNEST REYER to a libretto by CAMILLE DU LOCLE after Gustave Flaubert's novel; Brussels, Théâtre de la Monnaie, 10 February 1890.

Flaubert originally had Verdi in mind as the composer of an opera on *Salammbô*. He himself planned the main lines of the libretto and accepted Reyer's suggestion that Du Locle, librettist of his *Sigurd*, should write it. Some work was done in the late 1870s, but with Flaubert's death in 1880 and no prospect of a performance of *Sigurd* Reyer put the project aside. The success of *Sigurd* in 1884 brought *Salammbô* back to life. The title role was written for Rose Caron, who had sung Brunehild in *Sigurd*. The opera was in the repertory of the Paris Opéra for some years and was revived there in 1938.

The opera, set in Carthage in 240 BC, concerns the love of Salammbô (soprano), daughter of the Carthaginian leader Hamilcar (baritone), for Mathô (tenor), chief of the mercenaries in revolt against Carthage. Mathô steals the city's sacred veil, and Salammbô, knowing Mathô's passion for her, steals it back. But Mathô is condemned to die by Salammbô's hand. Instead she kills herself, and Mathô does likewise with the same sword.

Although never quite as successful as *Sigurd*, *Salammbô* was judged by many to be the superior opera. It is constructed with an eye to continuity, and it defies any simple division into conventional numbers. Reyer uses two motifs to considerable effect: one for the goddess Tanit and one for the 'Zaïmph', the sacred veil of Carthage. Although not as brilliantly colourful as the novel, the opera successfully evokes the barbaric splendour of Carthage. There are many scenes of ritual and ceremony, but the climax of the opera is the scene in Mathô's tent in Act 4 where the tensions and passions of the lovers reach breaking-point.

For illustration *see* CARON, ROSE. HUGH MACDONALD

Salamoni [Salomon, Salomone, Salomoni]. Italian family of dancers and choreographers.

(1) Giuseppe Salamoni (i) [Giuseppetto di Vienna; Salamoncino] (*b* Venice, ?1710; *d* Vienna, 22 Sept 1777). He established his reputation in Vienna in the 1730s and was identified as 'detto di Vienna' in the librettos for his first appearances in Venice (1742–4, in operas by Bernasconi, Jommelli, Hasse and others). In his early career, he also worked in Padua (1743, Jommelli's *Demofoonte*) and in London, at Drury Lane (1746–7 and 1748–9). During the 1750s he choreographed ballets for opera productions in Rome (1751–2), Venice (1753, 1757) and Milan (1751, 1753–4, 1756–7), where he worked in several Galuppi operas. On the death of his wife, the dancer Costanza Tinti Salamoni, he cancelled his 1764–5 contract in Turin and worked instead at Stuttgart with his son

Giuseppe. Throughout his career he returned to Vienna for engagements (1747–8, 1754–5, 1757, 1762–4).

(2) **Giuseppe Salamoni** (ii) (*b* Venice, *c*1730; *d* ?Moscow, ?1805). Son of (1) Giuseppe Salamoni (i). He danced with his father in London at Drury Lane (1746–7) and the following season was hired to dance at S Moisè, Venice (1747–8). In 1755 he performed in the inaugural opera at the new court theatre in Lisbon, where he remained for three years (and added 'detto di Portogallo' to his name to distinguish himself from his father). In the 1760s and 70s he worked in opera houses throughout Italy, appearing in Reggio Emilia (1757, 1761, 1764; operas by Traetta and others), Turin (1759–60), Venice (1761–2, 1763–4, 1765, 1771–2, notably in operas by Galuppi and Piccinni), Padua (1765), Trieste (1768, 1775), Rome (1763, in G. F. de Majo's *Demofoonte*, 1765–6, 1770, 1774), Milan (1766–7, 1772–3, in Mozart's *Lucio Silla* and Paisiello's *Sismano nel Mogol*) and Naples (1767–8). He danced one season in Stuttgart with his father (1764–5), and spent the final part of his career in Moscow as a dancer and choreographer for the Petrovsky Theatre.

(3) **Francesco Salamoni** (*b* Vienna, *c*1738). Son of (1) Giuseppe Salamoni (i). He danced with his father in Vienna (1754–5), Milan (1753–4) and Padua (1758). Somewhat less active than his father and brother, he worked for opera houses in Reggio Emilia, Rome, Verona, Venice and Bologna, replaced his father in Turin for the 1764–5 season and subsequently moved to Berlin.

*

J. Sasportes: *História da dança em Portugal* (Lisbon, 1970)
K. K. Hansell: 'Il ballo teatrale e l'opera italiana', *Storia dell'opera italiana*, v (Turin, 1988), 175–306
M. C. de Brito: *Opera in Portugal in the Eighteenth Century* (Cambridge, 1989) IRENE ALM

Salari, Francesco (*b* Bergamo, 1751; *d* Bergamo, 27 Dec 1828). Italian composer. He studied with, among others, Niccolò Piccinni in Naples and G. A. Fioroni in Milan. He then went to Venice, where he gave singing instruction and composed for the theatre. In 1805 he returned to Bergamo to teach singing (notably to Donizetti) and to serve as a second *maestro di cappella*. Only one of his four known operas is extant; arias also survive from what may have been a fifth opera, *Antigono* (*I-BGc*).

Ifigenia in Aulide, Casale Monferrato, 1776
Il marchese carbonaro (dg, F. Livigni), Venice, S Moisè, carn. 1776
L'amor ramingo (A. Piazza), Venice, S Samuele, carn. 1777, *I-Fc*
Le teste deboli (dg, G. Bertati), Venice, S Moisè, carn. 1780

*

A. Geddo: *Bergamo e la musica* (Bergamo, 1958)
SIEGFRIED GMEINWIESER

Salazar, Manuel (*b* San José, 3 Jan 1887; *d* San José, 6 Aug 1950). Costa Rican tenor. At the age of 19 he went to Italy to study, and later he also studied in New York. His successful début in Vicenza in 1913 as Edgardo (*Lucia di Lammermoor*) led to engagements in Catania, Fiume, Padua and Palermo. He performed in Havana with Ruffo in 1917 and from 1917 to 1921 he toured North America with Gallo's San Carlo Opera Company. He made his Metropolitan Opera début in 1921 as Don Alvaro in *La forza del destino* opposite Ponselle and remained there for two seasons, singing such roles as Canio, Chénier and Radames. After 1923 he toured the USA with small companies and later returned to Costa Rica. He made several recordings.

CORI ELLISON

Saldoni (y Remendo), Baltasar (*b* Barcelona, 4 Jan 1807; *d* Madrid, 3 Dec 1889). Spanish composer and musicologist. A choirboy successively at S María del Mar in Barcelona, the chapel of S María del Pino and the Escolanía at Montserrat, Saldoni studied the piano and organ in his native city with Mateo Ferrer and composition with Francisco Queralt. His early compositions included short religious pieces and an operetta, *El triunfo del amor*. In 1829 he moved to Madrid where he was encouraged by a fellow Catalan, Ramón Carnicer, who secured his appointment as a teacher at the Royal Conservatory on its foundation in 1830. He wrote several works on vocal technique which were praised in Spain and France. Among his operas in the Italian tradition, his greatest success was with *Ipermestra*. His creative career declined after 1840, but in 1848 he was appointed musical director of the Teatro del Príncipe and encouraged Barbieri, Gaztambide, Inzenga and Oudrid at the beginning of their careers. Disappointed by public indifference to his work, he finally abandoned the theatre and devoted his last years to the compilation of his *Diccionario biográfico-bibliográfico de efemérides de músicos españoles* (Madrid, 1868–81; facs. with indexes, 1986), which in spite of its defects is enormously important for the history of Spanish music.

El triunfo del amor (opereta, 1, J. Alegre), private perf., Barcelona, 1826
Los enredos de un curioso (melodrama lírico, 1), Madrid, Conservatorio, 6 May 1832, collab. Carnicer, M. A. P. Albéniz and Piermarini
Saladino e Clotilde (os, 2), excerpts, Madrid, Cruz, 1833
Ipermestra (os, 2, ?Pasini, after P. Metastasio), Madrid, Cruz, 20 Jan 1838
Cleonice, regina di Siria (os, 2, after Metastasio: *Demetrio*) Madrid, Cruz, 24 Jan 1840
Boabdil, último rey moro de Granada, 1844 (os, 3, M. González Aurioles)
El rey y la costurera, 1853 (zar, 3, V. Brusola)
Guzmán el Bueno, 1855 (os, 3, O. Aracri)
La corte de Mónaco (zar, 1, R. Navarrete), Madrid, Zarzuela, 16 Feb 1857
Los maridos en las máscaras (zar, 2, W. Ayguals de Izco), Barcelona, Campos Elíesos, 26 Aug 1864

*

J. Parada y Barreto: *Diccionario técnico, histórico y biográfico de la música* (Madrid, 1868)
A. Peña y Goñi: *La ópera española y la música dramática en España en el siglo XIX* (Madrid, 1881; abridged E. Rincón, as *España desde la ópera a la zarzuela*, 1967)
E. Cotarelo y Mori: *Historia de la zarzuela, o sea el drama lírico* (Madrid, 1934)
J. Subirá: *Historia de la música española e hispanoamericana* (Barcelona, 1953)
C. Gómez Amat: *Historia de la música española: el siglo XIX* (Madrid, 1984, 2/1988) CARLOS GÓMEZ AMAT

Sales [de Sala], **Pietro Pompeo** (*b* Brescia, *c*1729; *d* Hanau, 21 Nov 1797). Italian composer. After studies at Innsbruck University, he became conductor of an Italian opera troupe, with which he visited Cologne, Brussels, Lille and other cities. In 1756 he took charge of the court chapel of Prince Bishop Joseph Landgrave of Hessen-Darmstadt in Augsburg and Dillingen an der Donau. He travelled widely as a performer and composer, becoming a member of the Bologna Accademia Filarmonica and composing an oratorio for Mannheim (1762) and operas for Munich (1765) and Padua (1767). After the landgrave's death in 1768, Sales directed the court chapel of the Elector of Trier at Ehrenbreitstein am Rhein and from 1786 at Koblenz; he maintained his connection with the Munich court with new operas in 1769 and 1774. Sales was a versatile composer in the current Italian style who wrote sacred and chamber music as well as operas; he was considered a great master by his contemporaries.

Le cinesi (componimento drammatico, 1, P. Metastasio), Augsburg, carn. 1757
L'isola disabitata (azione teatrale, 1, Metastasio), Augsburg, 1758, *D-Rtt*, *US-WC*
Le nozze di Amore di Norizia (Giunti), Munich, 1765, *D-Mbs*
L'Antigona in Tebe (os), Padua, Nuovo, 1767, *P-La*
Antigono (os, 3, Metastasio), Munich, Residenz, carn. 1769, *D-Mbs**, *F-Pc*
Achille in Sciro (os, 3, Metastasio), Munich, Residenz, carn. 1774, *D-Mbs*, *F-Pc*
Il re pastore (os, 3, Metastasio), *D-Dlb*

*

F. Collignon: *Pietro Pompeo Sales* (diss., U. of Bonn, 1923)

ADOLF LAYER

Saléza, Albert (*b* Bruges, Pyrénées, 28 Oct 1867; *d* Paris, 26 Nov 1916). French tenor. He studied with Bax and Obin at the Paris Conservatoire, and made his début at the Opéra-Comique in 1888 as Mylio (Lalo's *Le roi d'Ys*). He sang first at the Paris Opéra in 1892 as Mathô (Reyer's *Salammbô*; for illustration *see* CARON, ROSE). At Monte Carlo in 1894 he sang in the première of Franck's posthumous *Hulda* and in Berlioz's *La damnation de Faust*. At the Opéra that year he sang in the première of C. E. Lefebvre's *Djelma* and the first Paris performance of Verdi's *Otello*. He made his Covent Garden and Metropolitan débuts in 1898 in Gounod's *Roméo et Juliette*, and sang Rodolfo at the first Metropolitan performance of *La bohème* (1900). His repertory included Siegmund, Tannhäuser, Gounod's Faust, Raoul (*Les Huguenots*), Edgardo (*Lucia di Lammermoor*), John of Leyden (*Le prophète*), Masaniello (*La muette de Portici*) and the Duke (*Rigoletto*). He made a final appearance at the Opéra-Comique in 1910 as Don José. He had a mellow voice with elegant diction and phrasing.

*

H. E. Krehbiel: *Chapters of Opera* (New York, 1909)
W. J. Henderson: *The Art of Singing* (New York, 1938)
I. Kolodin: *The Story of the Metropolitan Opera* (New York, 1953)
S. Wolff: *L'opéra au Palais Garnier (1875–1962)* (Paris, 1962)

ELIZABETH FORBES

Salicola [Salicoli, Selicoli], **Angiola** (*b* ?Bologna; *fl* 1681–93). Italian singer. She often performed with her more celebrated sister, Margherita; her name first appeared in 1681, when she sang Erisbe in G. F. Tosi's *Erismonda* in Bologna. She then sang in Giovanni Legrenzi's *Ottaviano Cesare Augusto* (1682, Mantua) and *Lisimaco riamato da Alessandro* (1682, Venice), P. A. Ziani's *Il talamo preservato dalla fedeltà di Eudossa* (1683, Reggio Emilia), Carlo Pallavicino's *Amore inamorato* (1686, Venice), *I due germani rivali* (composer unknown; 1686, Modena) and in Pallavicino's *L'amazone corsara, ovvero L'Alvilda regina de' Goti* and Legrenzi's *Lisimaco riamato da Alessandro* in Bologna in 1688. On 10 November 1688 she received the designation 'virtuosa and personal servant' from Duke Ferdinando Carlo Gonzaga of Mantua, with special privileges for her father, mother and family. The title was confirmed on 19 March 1690, although no document mentions a salary. The last information concerning her dates from 1693, when she sang in Ferrara in *Più timor che danno* (composer unknown), still calling herself 'virtuosa of the Duke of Mantua'.

Little is known of the career of her sister Margherita, except that she was at the Mantuan court in 1685, was heard by the Elector of Saxony in Venice and went to Dresden, enjoying a successful career in German theatres and appearing in Vienna in 1693.

*

P. Besutti: *La corte musicale di Ferdinando Carlo Gonzaga ultimo duca di Mantova: musici, cantanti e teatro d'opera tra il 1665 e il 1707* (Mantua, 1989)

PAOLA BESUTTI

Salieri, Antonio (*b* Legnago, 18 Aug 1750; *d* Vienna, 7 May 1825). Italian composer, mainly resident in Vienna. A major contributor to and shaper of Viennese operatic life from 1770 to the beginning of the 19th century, he also composed successful operas in Italy and Paris, and won much admiration from German operagoers as a composer who, in the words of one contemporary critic, 'could bind all the power of German music to the sweet Italian style'.

1. LIFE. Salieri was born in the Venetian town of Legnago, near Vicenza. He studied the violin and harpsichord with his brother Francesco and with a local organist, Giuseppe Simoni. He was orphaned in 1765 and taken to Venice; in 1766 his musical talent and ambition attracted the attention of the Viennese composer F. L. Gassmann, in Venice to oversee the production of his opera *Achille in Sciro*. Gassmann took Salieri back to Vienna as his assistant and pupil; they arrived in June 1766, and soon thereafter Salieri began a carefully planned programme of musical training. Also at about this time he began a lasting friendship with Gluck. Opportunities to write operas soon offered themselves to him. When Gassmann was in Italy composing and directing an opera in celebration of a visit by Joseph II to Rome (1770), Salieri set a libretto originally intended for Gassmann, the comedy *Le donne letterate*. Having proved himself a talented composer of comic opera, he turned to serious opera. His *Armida*, on a libretto by the innovatory poet Marco Coltellini, was successfully performed in June 1771; with its choral tableaux and spectacular scenic effects it is in the tradition of Gluck's reform operas. Salieri's ability to deal effectively with this kind of music drama would later, in the 1780s, make him a leading successor to Gluck as a composer of *tragédie lyrique* for the Paris stage.

Salieri's success in Vienna owed much to the support of Joseph II, who was also helpful to Salieri in Paris through his influence with his sister Marie Antoinette. As early as 1771 Joseph II sent a copy of Salieri's *Armida* to his brother Leopold, Grand Duke of Tuscany, reporting that it had been performed with great success in Vienna. When Gassmann died in 1774 Salieri was appointed composer and music director of the Italian opera in Vienna. Soon afterwards he collaborated with the poet and dramatist Giovanni De Gamerra on *La calamita de' cuori* (1774) and on two more operas during the next two years.

Joseph's reorganization of the court theatres in 1776, with its shift of emphasis to spoken drama, left Salieri with little opportunity to compose operas in Vienna, and he turned his attention to Italy. Between 1778 and 1780 he wrote five operas for theatres in Milan, Venice and Rome: these were comic operas, except for *L'Europa riconosciuta*, commissioned to celebrate the opening of La Scala, Milan (3 August 1778; *see* MILAN, fig.3). Here, as with *Armida*, Salieri responded to an adventurous libretto by Mattia Verazi with vivid, dramatic music. Of the comic operas that Salieri wrote for Italy, by far the most successful was *La scuola de' gelosi*, on a libretto by Caterino Mazzolà (1778, Venice), a work that did more than any other to spread Salieri's fame throughout Europe. In 1780 Joseph II commissioned him to write a Singspiel to be performed by the emperor's newly formed Nationaltheater: *Der Rauchfangkehrer* exemplifies the cosmopolitan qualities of German opera during the short life of the Nationaltheater's German opera troupe, combining elements of *opera buffa*, *opéra comique* and Singspiel. One of only two operas in German completed by Salieri, *Der Rauchfangkehrer* enjoyed considerable success until it was overshadowed by Mozart's *Die Entführung aus dem Serail*.

In 1783 Joseph replaced his German troupe with one specializing in Italian *opera buffa*. The new company made its début on 22 April with Salieri's *La scuola de' gelosi*. At about the same time Gluck, too weak to undertake the composition of a work commissioned by the Paris Opéra, handed the commission over to Salieri, and during the rest of the decade Salieri divided his time and energy between composing *tragédie lyrique* in Paris and *opera buffa* in Vienna. He went to Paris for the first time to oversee the première of his *Les Danaïdes* (1784). A violent and colourful *tragédie lyrique*, it shows him a worthy successor of Gluck. Its success led to commissions for two more French operas. The first, *Les Horaces*, failed when it was given in 1786, but the following year Salieri achieved one of his greatest operatic triumphs with *Tarare*, on a libretto by Beaumarchais.

Returning to Vienna in 1784 after the successful performance of *Les Danaïdes*, Salieri busied himself with composing and directing Italian comic operas at the Burgtheater. Joseph's practice of commissioning operas from some of Europe's leading composers, Paisiello and Martín y Soler as well as Mozart, meant that Salieri faced competition that must have threatened and inspired him. Lorenzo da Ponte, recently engaged as court theatre librettist, was his principal collaborator; he also worked with G. B. Casti, a poet under the protection of Count Rosenberg, who supervised the court opera. Salieri insisted on extensive revisions of Da Ponte's first libretto, *Il ricco d'un giorno*, including the introduction of several ensembles, the reduction of recitative and the alteration of poetic metres within aria texts. By working so closely with this inexperienced poet, Salieri probably contributed to the strength of the librettos that Da Ponte later wrote for Mozart. Salieri's collaboration with Casti resulted in two successful works: the two-act comedy *La grotta di Trofonio* (1785) and a one-act satire *Prima la musica e poi le parole* (1786).

When Salieri returned to Vienna from Paris after the success of *Tarare* in 1787, Joseph commissioned him to prepare an Italian version of the opera for Vienna. *Axur, re d'Ormus*, with a libretto by Da Ponte, follows the general outline of *Tarare* but beyond that constitutes a completely new text. Much of the political allegory of Beaumarchais' libretto was omitted, and Salieri's music is almost completely new. Performed in 1788 to celebrate the marriage of Archduke Franz to Princess Elisabeth of Württemberg, *Axur* was repeated no fewer than 100 times in the Viennese court theatres between 1788 and 1805.

After the death of Joseph II (20 February 1790) and with the accession of Leopold II, rumours circulated that Salieri was to be dismissed or had asked to be dismissed. What Salieri seems to have asked for, and received, was relief from the daily chores of rehearsing and conducting operatic productions, in exchange for which he agreed to compose a new opera each year for the court theatres. Salieri's duties in the opera house were assigned to his pupil and protégé Joseph Weigl. But Salieri did not follow the terms of his agreement. Between 1790 and 1793 he seems to have composed only one opera, *Catalina* (1792), and that was never performed. In 1795 he renewed his contact with De Gamerra and together they wrote three operas for the court theatres: *Eraclito e Democrito*, *Palmira, regina di Persia* and *Il moro*. The first and third were only moderately successful (with fewer than 20 performances in the court theatres), but *Palmira* achieved the greatest success of any of Salieri's late operas. His last major collaborator, C. P. Defranceschi, provided him with librettos for three operas performed in 1799 and 1800, including *Falstaff* (1799). Salieri's last complete opera, *Die Neger*, was given in 1804.

Salieri, who benefited so much from his teachers and mentors, devoted much of his energy to teaching, especially after he retired from operatic composition. Many of his pupils, including Beethoven, Schubert, Weigl, Winter, Herold and Meyerbeer, went on to make significant contributions to 19th-century opera.

2. Operas. Salieri's operas, the product of over 30 years' work in Vienna, Italy and Paris, are extraordinarily rich and varied, revealing him as a composer of great versatility, vivid theatricality and considerable musical talent. As might be expected of a pupil of Gassmann and a protégé of Gluck, most of his early Italian operas fall into two categories: light, comic operas along the lines of Gassmann's *La contessina* and serious operas strongly influenced by *tragédie lyrique*. In the latter group the young Salieri made his most important contributions to the history of opera in the 1770s. In *Armida* and *L'Europa riconosciuta* he responded to adventurous librettos with lively, dramatic music and followed Gluck's precept (expressed in the preface to *Alceste*) that the overture should anticipate the drama; in both operas he gave a significant dramatic role to the chorus and demonstrated skill in composing accompanied recitative.

Salieri's two most important French operas, *Les Danaïdes* and *Tarare*, are very different from one another. *Les Danaïdes*, to a libretto inspired by one by Calzabigi, is a gothic tale of horror and violence; *Tarare* is a mixture of exoticism, comedy, political allegory and romance. His music for *Les Danaïdes* is suitably dark, coloured with diminished 7th chords, tremolo and the sound of trombones; that for *Tarare*, humorous, sentimental and tragic by turn, captures the exotic spirit of Beaumarchais' libretto. Salieri handled the demands of *tragédie lyrique* with equal skill and craftsmanship in both operas, moving fluently between recitatives, choruses, arias, ensembles and instrumental numbers. The love scenes for Hypermnestra and Lynceus in *Les Danaïdes* are suffused with a lyricism as intense and moving as that which depicts the love of Astasie and Tarare. The brutal rage of Danaus is evoked as vividly as that of Atar, the tyrannical king in *Tarare*. With *Les Danaïdes* Salieri established himself as a leading successor to Gluck in the genre of *tragédie lyrique*; with *Tarare* he helped to transform the genre.

Salieri's Viennese comic operas of the 1780s show that he was inspired by the same conditions that inspired Mozart during the same decade. In *La grotta di Trofonio* and *La cifra* Salieri expertly manipulated *opera buffa* conventions, using many of the singers who shaped Mozart's vocal writing in *Le nozze di Figaro* and *Così fan tutte*. Like Mozart, Salieri also made good use of the Burgtheater orchestra: the colourful and expressive solo parts for clarinets, english horns and other instruments in *La grotta di Trofonio* add much to its musical and dramatic content. And again like Mozart, he skilfully combined serious and comic elements, endowing Eurilla in *La cifra*, for example, with a nobility of character and musical style that enhances the richness and complexity of the entire opera.

Among the most successful of Salieri's Viennese operas is *Axur, re d'Ormus*. To this five-act *dramma tragicomico* Salieri brought all that he had learnt as a composer of *tragédie lyrique*, *opera seria* and *opera buffa*. *Axur* has the fluidity of form characteristic of French opera, with extensive use of accompanied recitative and short, arioso vocal numbers. The music of the hero Atar and the heroine Aspasia has the kind of splendid vocal displays that we might expect to find in Italian serious opera; and the charming *commedia dell'arte* scene staged in Act 4 has the lightness and wit of *opera buffa*. Like *Tarare*, this is an opera *sui generis*, rendering useless the conventional genre distinctions of 18th-century opera. An admirable synthesis of styles, *Axur* represents the culmination of Salieri's career as an opera composer.

The 1790s left Salieri without the steadfast patronage of Joseph II, who had supported him in the 1770s and 1780s; without the opportunity to write operas for Paris, where he had been so successful in the previous decade; without the theatrical talent of Da Ponte, who had been dismissed in 1791 by Joseph's successor Leopold II; and without the stimulating rivalry of Mozart. Salieri's late operas are uneven in quality; some of the most successful, such as *Palmira*, look to the past, as if he were trying, near the end of his operatic career, to recapture his earlier triumphs. Much in the spirit of *Axur*, *Palmira* mixes exoticism with comedy, spectacle with sentiment; its tender love duets, stirring marches and solemn choruses of priests delighted audiences in Vienna and throughout Germany for several years.

See also Armida (ii); Axur, re d'Ormus; Cifra, La; Danaïdes, Les; Europa riconosciuta; Falstaff (i); Fiera di Venezia, La; Grotta di Trofonio, La; Horaces, Les; Palmira, regina di Persia; Prima la musica e poi le parole; Rauchfangkehrer, Der; Scuola de' gelosi, La; and Tarare.

WB – *Vienna, Burgtheater* WK – *Vienna, Kärntnertortheater*

Le donne letterate (commedia per musica, 3, G. G. Boccherini), WB, 10 Jan 1770, *A-Wn*

L'amore innocente (pastorale, 2, Boccherini), WB, carn. 1770, *Wn**, *D-Dlb*

Don Chisciotte alle nozze di Gamace (divertimento teatrale, 2, Boccherini, after M. de Cervantes), WB, aut. 1770, *A-Wn*

La moda, ossia I scompigli domestici (2, P. Cipretti), Vienna, 1771, *Wn** (only pt of Act 2), *D-B*

Armida (dramma per musica, 3, M. Coltellini, after T. Tasso: *Gerusalemme liberata*), WB, 2 June 1771, *A-Wn**, *Wst*, *B-Bc*, *CH-Zz*, *D-B*, *Wa*, *F-Pn*; (Leipzig, 1783)

La fiera di Venezia (commedia per musica, 3, Boccherini), WB, 29 Jan 1772, *A-Wn**, *B-Bc*, *D-B*, *Dlb*, *Mbs*, *MÜs*, *Rp*, *F-Pn*, *Po*, *H-Bn*, *I-Bc*, *Fc*, *MOe*, *Tf*, *US-Bp*

Il barone di Rocca antica (dg, 1, G. Petrosellini), WB, 12 May 1772, *A-Wn**, *I-Fc*

La secchia rapita (dramma eroicomico, 3, Boccherini), WB, 21 Oct 1772, *A-Wn**, *D-Dlb*, *Mbs*, *Wa*, *GB-Lbl*, *H-Bn*, *I-Bc*, *Fc*, *Gl*, *MOe*, *Nc*

La locandiera (dg, 3, D. Poggi, after C. Goldoni), WB, 8 June 1773, *A-Wn**, *D-Rtt*, *F-Pn*

La calamita de' cuori (dg, 3, G. De Gamerra, after Goldoni), WB, 11 Oct 1774, *A-Wn**, *D-B*, *US-Wc*

La finta scema (commedia per musica, 2, De Gamerra), WB, 9 Sept 1775, *A-Wn**, *Ssp*

Daliso e Delmita (azione pastorale, 3, De Gamerra), WB, 29 July 1776, *Wn**

L'Europa riconosciuta (dramma per musica, 2, M. Verazi), Milan, Scala, 3 Aug 1778, *Wn** (inc.), *D-B*, *F-Pn*, *I-Mc*, *P-La*

La scuola de' gelosi (dg, 2, C. Mazzolà), Venice, S Moisè, 27 Dec 1778, *A-Wn**, *D-Dlb*, *Rp*, *Rtt*, *F-Pn*, *H-Bn*, *I-Fc*, *MOe*

Il talismano [Act 1] (dg, 3, Goldoni), Milan, Cannobiana, 21 Aug 1779 [Acts 2 and 3 by G. Rust]; rev. (L. da Ponte), WB, 10 Sept 1788; *A-Wn**, *Wgm*, *B-Bc*, *Dlb*, *F*, *Mbs*, *Rp*, *Wa*, *F-Pn*, *I-Fc*, *MOe*, *US-Wc*

La partenza inaspettate (int, 2, Petrosellini), Rome, Valle, 22 Dec 1779, *A-Wn**, *D-Dlb*, *F-Pn*

La dama pastorella (int, 1, Petrosellini), Rome, Valle, 1780, *A-Wn**

Der Rauchfangkehrer, oder Die unentbehrlichen Verräther ihrer Herrschaften aus Eigennutz (musikalisches Lustspiel, 3, J. L. Auenbrugger), WB, 30 April 1781, *A-Wn**(R1986: GOB, xiv), *D-DS*

Semiramide (dramma per musica, 3, P. Metastasio), Munich, Residenz, carn. 1782, *A-Wn**, *D-Mbs*

Les Danaïdes (tragédie lyrique, 5, Du Roullet and Tschudi, after R. de' Calzabigi), Paris, Opéra, 26 April 1784, *A-Wn**, *F-Po*; (Paris, 1784)

Il ricco d'un giorno (dg, 3, Da Ponte, after G. Bertati), WB, 6 Dec 1784, *A-Wn**, *I-MOe*

La grotta di Trofonio (opera comica, 2, G. B. Casti), WB, 12 Oct 1785, *A-Wgm*, *Wn**, *D-B*, *CS-Bm*, *H-Bn*, *I-Fc*, *MOe*; (Vienna, *c*1786)

Prima la musica e poi le parole (divertimento teatrale, 1, Casti) Vienna, Schönbrunn Orangerie, 7 Feb 1786, *A-Wn**, *I-PEsc*

Les Horaces (tragédie lyrique, 3, N. F. Guillard, after P. Corneille), Versailles, 2 Dec 1786, *A-Wn**, *CS-Bm*, *F-Po*, *US-Wc*

Tarare (opéra, prol., 5, P.-A. Beaumarchais), Paris, Opéra, 8 June 1787, *A-Wn** (inc.), *F-Lm*, *Po*, *US-NYp*, *Wc*; ed. R. Angermüller (Munich, 1987)

Axur, re d'Ormus, (dramma tragicomico, 5, Da Ponte, after Beaumarchais: *Tarare*), WB, 8 Jan 1788, *A-Wn**, *Wst*, *CS-Bm*, *D-B*, *Dlb*, *DT*, *F*, *Hs*, *HR*, *LEm*, *Mbs*, *MÜs*, *Wa*, *E-Mc*, *Mn*, *F-Pn*, *GB-Lbl*, *H-Bn*, *I-Fc*, *Mc*, *Nc*, *PAc*, *Rsc*, *US-Wc*

Cublai, gran kan de Tartari, 1788 (dramma eroicomico, 2, Casti), unperf., *A-Wn**

Il pastor fido (dramma tragicomico, 4, Da Ponte, after B. Guarini), WB, 11 Feb 1789, *Wn**, *CH-Bu*, *D-Dlb*

La cifra (dg, 2, Da Ponte, after Petrosellini: *La dama pastorella*), WB, 11 Dec 1789, *A-Wn**, *B-Bc*, *D-B*, *Dlb*, *F*, *Mbs*, *F-Pn*, *I-Fc*

Catalina, 1792 (2, Casti), unperf., *A-Wn**

Il mondo alla rovescia (dg, 2, Mazzolà), WB, 13 Jan 1795, *Wn**, *D-B*

Eraclito e Democrito (commedia per musica, 2, De Gamerra), WB, 13 Aug 1795, *A-Wn**, *D-DS*, *I-Fc*

Palmira, regina di Persia (dramma eroicomico, 2, De Gamerra), WK, 14 Oct 1795, *A-Wn**, *CS-Bm*, *D-B*, *Dlb*, *F*, *Hs*, *Mbs*, *GB-Lbl*, *I-BGc*, *Fc*, *PAc*, *Tf*, *US-Wc*

Il moro (commedia per musica, 2, De Gamerra), WB, 7 Aug 1796, *A-Wn**, *I-Fc*

I tre filosofi (2, De Gamerra), 1797, inc., *A-Wn**

Falstaff, ossia Le tre burle (dg, 2, C. P. Defranceschi, after W. Shakespeare: *The Merry Wives of Windsor*), WK, 3 Jan 1799, *Wn**, *D-B*, *F*, *I-Fc*

Cesare in Farmacusa (dramma eroicomico, 2, Defranceschi), WK, 2 June 1800, *A-Wn**, *B-Bc*, *Br*, *CS-Bm*, *D-B*, *Dlb*, *F*, *Rtt*, *I-Fc*, *PAc*

L'Angiolina, ossia Il matrimonio per sussurro (ob, 2, Defranceschi, after B. Jonson: *Epicoene*), WK, 22 Oct 1800, *A-Wgm*, *Wn**, *D-B*, *F*, *F-Pn*, *I-Fc*, *PAc*, *US-Wc*

Annibale in Capua (dramma per musica, 3, A. S. Sografi), Trieste, Nuovo, April 1801, *A-Wn*, *I-Fc*

La bella selvaggia, 1802 (ob, 2, G. Bertati), unperf., *A-Wn**

Die Neger (Spl, 2, F. Treitschke), Vienna, An der Wien, 10 Nov 1804, *Wn**, *F-Pn*

Die Generalprobe, frag.

Das Posthaus, frag.

Doubtful: La vestale, Vienna, 1768

L. da Ponte: *Memorie* (New York, 1823–7, 2/1829–30)
F. Rochlitz: 'Antonio Salieri', *Nekrolog: allgemeine Theaterzeitung und Unterhaltungsblatt für Freunde der Kunst, Literatur and des geseligen Lebens*, xviii/99 (1825), 405–7
M. Kelly: *Reminiscences of the King's Theatre* (London, 1826, 2/1826); ed. R. Fiske (London, 1975)
I. F. E. von Mosel: *Über das Leben und die Werke des Antonio Salieri* (Vienna, 1827)
W. Neumann: *Antonio Salieri* (Kassel, 1855)
A. W. Thayer: 'Half a dozen of Beethoven's Contemporaries, II: Antonio Salieri', *Dwight's Journal of Music*, xxiii (1863–4), 185–202 passim; xxiv (1864–5), 209–347 passim; ed. T. Albrecht (Kansas City, 1989)
A. Jullien: *La cour et l'opéra sous Louis XVI* (Paris, 1878), 151–322
A. von Hermann: *Antonio Salieri: eine Studie zur Geschichte seines künstlerischen Lebens* (Vienna, 1897)
C. Serini: 'Antonio Salieri', *RIM*, xxxii (1925), 412–33
G. Magnani: *Antonio Salieri: musicista legnaghese* (Legnago, 1934)
A. Della Corte: *Un italiano all'estero: Antonio Salieri* (Turin, 1937)
E. Anderson, ed.: *Letters of Mozart and his Family* (London, 1938, 3/1985)
W. Bollert: 'Antonio Salieri und die italienische Oper', *Aufsätze zur Musikgeschichte* (Bottrop, 1938), 43–128
A. Damerini and G. Roncaglia: 'Volti musicali di Falstaff', *Chigiana*, xviii (1961), 23–31
R. Angermüller: 'Antonio Salieri und seine "Scuola di Canto" ', *Beethoven-Studien*, ed. E. Schenk (Vienna, 1970), 37–50
——: 'Beaumarchais und Salieri', *GfMKB: Bonn 1970*, 325–7
O. Michtner: *Das alte Burgtheater als Opernbühne von der Einführung des deutschen Singspiels (1778) bis zum Tod Kaiser Leopolds II. (1792)* (Vienna, 1970)
E. E. Swenson: ' "Prima la musica e poi le parole": an Eighteenth-Century Satire', *AnMc*, no. 9 (1970), 112–29
R. Angermüller: *Antonio Salieri: sein Leben und seine weltliche Werke unter besondere Berücksichtigung seiner 'grossen' Opern* (Munich, 1971) [incl. further source information and bibliography]
J. Heinzelmann: ' "Prima la musica, poi le parole": zu Salieris Wiener Opernparodie', *ÖMz*, xxviii (1973), 19–28
E. E. Swenson: *Antonio Salieri: a Documentary Biography* (diss., Cornell U., 1974)
J. Rushton: 'Salieri's *Les Horaces*: a Study of an Operatic Failure', *MR*, xxxvii (1976), 266–82
R. Angermüller: 'Salieris Vorbemerkungen zu seinen Opern', *Mitteilungen der Internationalen Stiftung Mozarteum*, xxv/3–4 (1977), 15–33
E. Walton-Myers: *Antonio Salieri's 'La cifra'* (diss., Northwestern U., 1977)
R. Angermüller: 'Salieris *Tarare* (1787) und *Axur re d'Ormus* (1788): Vertonung eines Sujets für Paris und Wien', *HJbM*, v (1981), 211–27
——: *Antonio Salieri: fatti e documenti* (Vicenza and Belluno, 1985)
J. A. Rice: *Emperor and Impresario: Leopold II and the Transformation of Viennese Musical Theater, 1790–1792* (diss., U. of California, Berkeley, 1987)
I vicini di Mozart: *Florence 1987* [incl. J. A. Rice: 'Rondò vocali di Salieri e Mozart per Adriana Ferrarese', 185–209; J. Joly: 'Riscrittura di melodrama per Salieri e Cherubini: Tarare/Axur e Demofoonte/Démophoon', 242–72; S. Martinotti: ' "Falstaff": per un altro ritratto di Salieri', 273–96; F. Claudon: 'A propos di "Falstaff": Shakespeare, Salieri et le renouveau du théâtre européen à la fin du XVIII siècle', 297–310]
V. Braunbehrens: *Salieri: ein Musiker im Schatten Mozarts* (Munich, 1989) JOHN A. RICE

Salignac, (Eustace) Thomas (*b* Générac, Nîmes, 19 March 1867; *d* Paris, 1945). French tenor. He studied in Paris and made his début in 1893 singing small roles at the Opéra-Comique. He sang at the Metropolitan from 1896 to 1903, making his début as Don José and later singing Almaviva, Don Ottavio, Alfredo, Faust, Edgardo, Ernesto (*Don Pasquale*), Romeo, Canio and Tonio (*La fille du régiment*). He sang at Covent Garden between 1897 and 1904, the year he appeared at Monte Carlo as Hoffmann. Returning to the Opéra-Comique in 1905, he sang Turiddu, Jean (*Le jongleur de Notre-Dame*), Julien (*Louise*), Des Grieux (*Manon*), Mârouf, Werther and Cavaradossi. He created roles in several operas, including Leroux's *Chemineau* (1907) and Milhaud's *La brebis égarée* (1923) and sang the title role in the first staged performance of Falla's *El retablo de Maese Pedro* in the Princesse de Polignac's private theatre (1923). He formed an *opéra comique* company which toured the USA and Canada in 1926.

ELIZABETH FORBES

Salimbeni, Felice (*b* Milan, *c*1712; *d* Laibach [now Ljubljana], Aug 1751). Italian soprano castrato. A pupil of Porpora, he made his first recorded appearance in Hasse's *Caio Fabrizio* (12 January 1732, Rome). In 1733 he joined the Hofkapelle and the Hofoper in Vienna, where he stayed until 1737 while still appearing repeatedly in Venice. His Vienna years saw the launching of some of Metastasio's most influential librettos, in which the poet tailored leading parts (e.g. Megacles in *L'Olimpiade*) to Salimbeni's gifts and even to his stiff demeanour on stage; his faithfulness to the author's intentions, Metastasio declared, ensured the success of *Achille in Sciro*, where the singer 'bore the whole weight of the work'. Salimbeni then appeared to great acclaim in Italy and in Berlin (1744–50), leaving only when Frederick the Great blamed him for the failure of the latest of the 14 operas by C. H. Graun in which he had performed. His next engagement, in Dresden, was cut short by illness, probably tubercular, and he died on his way to seek treatment in Italy. He was reckoned one of the greatest singers of his age, with a voice not large but penetrating, notable for wide range, expressiveness, pure intonation, beauty of timbre, and technical mastery.

L. Schneider: *Geschichte der Oper und der Königlichen Opernhauses in Berlin* (Berlin, 1852), 96
M. Fürstenau: *Zur Geschichte der Musik und des Theaters am Hofe der Kurfürsten von Sachsen* (Dresden, 1861–2), ii, 262–6
B. Brunelli, ed.: *Tutte le opere di Pietro Metastasio*, iii (Milan, 1953), 135–6 [incl. letter of 10 March 1736 to L. Trapassi]
H. Fetting: *Geschichte der Deutschen Staatsoper* (Berlin, 1955), 35–6 JOHN ROSSELLI

Sallé, Marie (*b* Paris, 1707; *d* Paris, 27 July 1756). French dancer. A pupil of François Prévost, she made her Paris début at the Foire St Laurent in 1718, in *La princesse de Carisme* (Lesage and Lafont); on 10 July 1721 she appeared at the Opéra in Campra's *Les fêtes vénitiennes*. In 1725 John Rich engaged five dancers, including Sallé and her brother, for the Lincoln's Inn Fields Theatre in London: the programme included Rebel's *Les caractères de la danse* (25 November). Sallé made her official Opéra début on 14 September 1727 in *Les amours des dieux* (Mouret). The *Mercure* reported that she danced (as a shepherdess) and was 'fort goûtée'. In June 1728 she danced with her great rival La Camargo and Mlle Petit in *Hypermnestre* (Gervais); she and Camargo subsequently appeared together in numerous performances. On 17 February 1729 she created a sensation by partnering Antoine Laval in *Les caractères de la danse* 'en habits de ville et sans masque'. The abandonment of the mask was the first of her technical and stylistic innovations, making her one of the most important figures in 18th-century dance.

Her early career at the Opéra was interrupted by seasons in England, where she was much impressed by Garrick. On 14 February 1734 the *Mercure* reported on the ballet *Pigmalion* at Covent Garden, in which Sallé 'dared to appear ... without a pannier, skirt or bodice, and with her hair down; she did not wear a single ornament on her head. Apart from her corset and petticoat, she wore only a simple muslin robe, draped round her after the fashion of a Greek statue'. Her triumph in *Pigmalion* was followed on 26 February by *Bacchus and Ariadne*, in which she effectively portrayed, through her attitudes and gestures, 'the sentiments of the most profound sorrow, despair, fury and weakness' (*Mercure*). In *Pigmalion* she abandoned the cumbersome regalia of Baroque stage costume for a simpler style, allowing greater freedom; in *Bacchus* she demonstrated her talent for expressive mime through gesture and facial expression, an important step towards the *ballet en action*. On 9 November 1734 Sallé appeared at Covent Garden as Terpsichore in the prologue to Handel's *Il pastor fido*, another role that afforded opportunity for expression. She subsequently danced in Handel's *Oreste* (18 December 1734), *Ariodante* (8 January 1735) and *Alcina* (16 April 1735); in the last she dressed as a man, to the audience's disapproval. After hostile press notices she returned to France. Between then and her retirement in 1740 she created three of the four examples of early 18th-century *ballets en action* cited by Noverre: the entrée 'Les fleurs' in Rameau's *Les Indes galantes* (1735); the Turkish *divertissement* in the fifth entrée of *L'Europe galante* (1736) and Hébé's entrée in Act 2 of Rameau's *Castor et Pollux* (1737). Her last important creation before her retirement on 15 June 1740 was the third entrée of Rameau's *Les fêtes d'Hébé*, in which she played Terpsichore.

Unlike Camargo, Sallé never exploited virtuosity for its own sake, but developed an expressive style of dancing appropriate to the *ballet en action*. Noverre, who admired her and many of whose ideas she anticipated by nearly 30 years, wrote:

> I was enchanted by her dancing; she possessed neither the brilliance nor the technical feats common to dancing nowadays; but for glitter she substituted simple and touching grace; free from affectation, her face was noble, expressive and intelligent. Her voluptuous dance was conceived with as much finesse as lightness, it was not by leaps and frolics that she went to your heart.

For illustration *see* DANCE, fig.2.

*

ES (M.-F. Christout)
J.-G. Noverre: *Lettres sur la danse et sur les ballets* (Lyons, 1760)
E. Dacier: *Une danseuse de l'Opéra sous Louis XV: Mademoiselle Sallé* (Paris, 1909)
C. W. Beaumont: *Three French Dancers of the XVIIIth Century* (London, 1934)
WENDY THOMPSON

Sallinen, Aulis (*b* Salmi, 9 April 1935). Finnish composer. After studying composition at the Sibelius Academy in Helsinki under Aarre Merikanto and Joonas Kokkonen, he worked in Finnish Radio (1960–70) and held a teaching post at the Sibelius Academy (1963–76). His first opera, *Ratsumies* ('The Horseman'), to a libretto by Paavo Haavikko, was completed in 1974 for the Savonlinna Opera Festival. On one level it is a historical allegory for the small Finnish nation struggling to survive under the constant pressures exerted by powerful neighbours. It traces the fortunes of a small group of people, whose relationships and interactions form the second major theme. The music matches the vivid yet dream-like quality of the libretto: it is 'modern', but at the same time very approachable. The opera reveals Sallinen's strong natural talent as a musical dramatist.

The success enjoyed by *The Horseman* encouraged the Finnish National Opera to commission another opera from Sallinen. This was *Punainen viiva* ('The Red Line'), to the composer's own libretto. It too met with great success and led to Sallinen's next challenge: the joint commission by the Savonlinna Festival, the Royal Opera, Covent Garden, and the BBC of his third opera, *Kuningas lähtee Ranskaan* ('The King Goes Forth to France'). Late in 1988 Sallinen completed his fourth opera, *Kullervo*, based on a play by Aleksis Kivi. It was commissioned by the Finnish National Opera to celebrate the completion of their new house in Helsinki in the early 1990s, but in fact the world première was in Los Angeles in 1992.

Although Sallinen's operas differ in subject and style, his musical handwriting is clearly recognizable in each one. Influences from various directions are discernible: Prokofiev and Britten, as well as Shostakovich and Weill. Yet whatever influences Sallinen may unconsciously have absorbed, the voice is unmistakably his own. In fact, he is individual enough for his music to be tantalizingly difficult to put in any straitjacket of classification. His scores combine deep compassion with a wryly ironic sense of humour and an unerring sense of dramatic pacing. He has the ability to use fairly conventional tonal materials to build strongly original orchestral and vocal counterpoint; he is a master at creating atmosphere. Sallinen has sometimes been criticized for not being avant-garde enough, yet the very approachability of his scores, combined with his seemingly inexhaustible inventiveness and his highly developed feeling for drama, is his greatest strength.

See also KING GOES FORTH TO FRANCE, THE; KULLERVO; and RED LINE, THE.

Ratsumies [The Horseman] (3, P. Haavikko), Savonlinna Festival, 17 July 1975
Punainen viiva [The Red Line] (2, Sallinen, after I. Kianto), Helsinki, Finnish National Opera, 30 Nov 1978
Kuningas lähtee Ranskaan [The King Goes Forth to France] (3, Haavikko), Savonlinna Festival, 7 July 1984
Kullervo, 1988 (2, Sallinen, after A. Kivi), Los Angeles, Music Center, 25 Feb 1992

*

R. Milnes: 'Exciting New Opera', *Opera*, xxx (1979), 226–9 [on *Punainen viiva*]
J. Parsons: 'Aulis Sallinen', *MT*, cxxi (1980), 693–5
R. Milnes: 'The King Goes Forth to France', *Opera*, xxxviii (1987), 575–80
H. F. Lewin: 'Northern Exposure', *ON*, lvi/10 (1991–2), 34–5
J. Allison: 'The Kalevala, Sallinen and "Kullervo"', *Opera*, xliii (1992), 163–70
ERKKI ARNI

Salmhofer, Franz (*b* Vienna, 22 Jan 1900; *d* Vienna, 22 Sept 1975). Austrian composer. A pupil of Schreker and Franz Schmidt at the Vienna Academy, he was conductor at the Vienna Burgtheater (1929–39), then director of the Staatsoper (1945–55) and of the Volksoper (1955–63). He composed operas and ballets, and incidental music for about 300 plays for these and other theatres. His music is firmly rooted in the tradition of the Viennese Romantics; it shows a vigorous invention and a sure instinct for dramatic effect undoubtedly resulting from his long connection with the theatre.

Dame in Traum (3, E. Decsey and G. Holm), Vienna, Staats, 25 Dec 1935 [comprises 3 one-act ops: Das allmächtige Gold, Harba and Dame in Traum]
Iwan [Ivan Sergejewitsch] Tarassenko (prol., 1, Salmhofer), Vienna, Staats, 9 March 1938
Das Werbekleid (4, Salmhofer), Salzburg, Landes, 5 Dec 1943
Dreikönig, 1945 (4, Salmhofer), Vienna, Volks, 13 April 1970

*

H. Ullrich: *Fortschritt und Tradition* (Vienna, 1956), 156ff, 328ff

Salminen, Matti (*b* Turku, 7 July 1945). Finnish bass. He studied in Helsinki and made his début there in 1966, singing small parts. After further study in Rome, he sang Philip II (*Don Carlos*) with the Finnish National Opera in 1969. He was engaged at Cologne (1972–9), and has also sung at Düsseldorf, Hamburg, Berlin, Stuttgart, Munich, Paris, Savonlinna, Salzburg and La Scala. He sang Ivan Susanin at Wexford (1973), then made his Covent Garden début (1974) as Fasolt and his Bayreuth début (1976) as Hunding, returning as Daland, the Landgrave, Titurel and King Mark. He made his Metropolitan début (1981) as King Mark, later singing Sarastro, Rocco and Hagen there. His repertory ranges from Seneca (*L'incoronazione di Poppea*), Osmin and the Commendatore to many Wagner and Verdi roles. His magnificently resonant voice, huge stature and impressive acting ability are particularly effective in the title role of *Boris Godunov*, which he first sang in 1984 at Zürich and has repeated at Barcelona (1986) and other theatres. He is also a fine Prince Gremin. ELIZABETH FORBES

Salmon [Salomon], **Karel** [Karl] (*b* Heidelberg, 13 Nov 1897; *d* Beit Zayit, nr Jerusalem, 15 Jan 1974). Israeli composer and conductor of German birth. A pupil of Richard Strauss at the Berlin Academy of Arts, he became a répétiteur at the Berlin Staatsoper, sang at the Hamburg Opera and conducted in Baden-Baden. After settling in Jerusalem in 1933, he became the first music director of the Jerusalem Broadcasting Service in 1936. In 1938 he founded the Israel Radio SO (now Jerusalem SO), and from 1957 to 1962 he was director of the Israel Broadcasting Authority's Transcription Service. In Germany he was active in reviving Handel's *Rodelinda* and in 1944 he organized the first Bach and Handel festival in Jerusalem.

On his arrival in Israel, Salmon became influenced by the folk music of the region, which resulted in such works as the *Symphonic Suite on Greek Themes* (1943) and the *Sephardic Suite* (1947). He occasionally made use of the Arab māqām combinations (though without microtones), augmented 2nds, highly embellished and improvisatory passages, as well as Arab folk instruments.

Salmon's first opera, *David and Goliath* (1930, Berlin; revised version, 1956, Jerusalem), is for marionettes; in three scenes and lasting just over half an hour, to a libretto by A. Baer after the biblical theme, it uses three singers accompanied by a chamber ensemble. *Nedarim* ('Vows'), to his own libretto, is based on a legendary episode from the life of the medieval Andalusian Jewish poet Yehuda Halevy and was composed in 1954–5 (concert performance, 1955, Kibbuz Ein Gev). Salmon also wrote the libretto to his radio *opera buffa* in two scenes, *Four Times Methuselah*, composed in 1965–6 for soloists, choir and symphony orchestra (1968, Heidelberg). In his works Salmon demonstrated his ability as an orchestrator, and successfully combined Eastern tunes and Western technique. WILLIAM Y. ELIAS

Salome. *Musikdrama* in one act by RICHARD STRAUSS to HEDWIG LACHMANN's German translation of OSCAR WILDE's play; Dresden, Hofoper, 9 December 1905.

After the mildly scandalous success of his second opera, *Feuersnot*, Strauss needed a new subject. Wolzogen, his collaborator on *Feuersnot*, worked hopefully at another raffish one-act comedy, drawn this time from Cervantes, but Strauss did nothing with it. Then a young Viennese poet sent him Wilde's *Salomé*, proposing to adapt a libretto from it; the composer was cautiously interested (he imagined it, incredibly, as a possible pendant to *Feuersnot*). Though Wilde's French original had been a failure in Paris, and in England the play was banned by the Lord Chamberlain, a German version had been well received in Breslau in 1901. Using a new translation, Max Reinhardt staged the play in Berlin the following year with spectacular success. Strauss saw it early in 1903 and swiftly decided to set this Lachmann version of the text as it stood, except for judicious trimming (mostly of subordinate clauses, though also of some marginal dialogue and one or two small roles). He began in earnest as he put the last touches to his *Symphonia domestica*, and in little more than a year the entire opera was sketched but for the Dance of the Seven Veils. During the latter months of 1904 he undertook the full score, for a very large orchestra – while he also finished his expanded modern edition of Berlioz's 60-year-old *Grand traité d'instrumentation et d'orchestration modernes* – and completed *Salome* in June 1905.

Herodes [Herod] *Tetrarch of Judaea*	tenor
Herodias *his wife*	mezzo-soprano
Salome *his stepdaughter*	soprano
Jochanaan [Jokanaan] (*the prophet John the Baptist*)	baritone
Narraboth *Captain of the Guard*	tenor
The Page of Herodias	alto
Five Jews	4 tenors, 1 bass
Two Nazarenes	bass, tenor
Two Soldiers	basses
A Cappadocian	bass
A Slave	soprano/tenor

Royal guests – Egyptians, Romans – and entourage, servants, soldiers (all silent)

Setting A great terrace in Herod's palace on Lake Galilee

Though Strauss and the Dresden conductor Ernst von Schuch had to contend with fractious singers, dismayed by the extreme vocal demands (and in the case of the respectable Marie Wittich as Wilde's perverse heroine, by what the producer Willi Wirk expected her to do on stage), the première earned 38 curtain calls. The Czech tenor Carl Burrian sang Herod, and the baritone Karl Perron was Jokanaan. *Salome* was rapidly taken up by opera houses in many countries, despite ecclesiastical disapproval in Vienna which defeated Mahler's hopes of conducting it, and sustained opposition from moralists in England and the USA. Strauss himself conducted the first Austrian and Italian performances, in Graz and Turin, and Toscanini introduced it to La Scala. When at last the opera was permitted at Covent Garden, it was ornamented by the first soprano with the natural gifts for an all-singing, all-dancing Salome, Aïno Ackté; Strauss had imagined 'a 16-year-old princess with the voice of an Isolde', a wildly optimistic formula, and many another Salome has preferred (like Frau Wittich in the première) to let a supple stand-in discard the seven veils.

In fact the multiple facets of the role – always conceived by the composer in terms of vivid dramatic presence, but not necessarily choreographic – can be made to gleam by approaches from quite various angles. There have been many famous Salomes, dancing or not, from Emmy Destinn and Mary Garden to Maria Cebotari, Ljuba Welitsch (whose recording of the final monologue set an inspired standard), Birgit Nilsson and Anja Silja. When Strauss decided that the role should be feasible for lighter lyric sopranos, and not only Isoldes, he was hoping that Elisabeth Schumann might undertake it; she never did, but for a Silver Jubilee production in 1930 he effected reductions in the orchestral weight at all the more threatening places. That version is frequently used now. There is also a French-language version – distinct from the 'official' French translation from Lachmann's German – which Strauss himself adapted from Wilde's own idiosyncratic French, with advice from Romain Rolland; he also made a few striking changes in the vocal lines. It has been reconstructed from its parts and recorded by Kent Nagano with the Lyon Opéra (released 1991).

Salome has no prelude; or rather, the whole first scene is the prelude to the action proper, which begins with Salome's entry and ends with her execution. The curtain rises in silence on the terrace of Herod's banqueting-hall – some soldiers at the parapet, a grand staircase at one side, a bronze cistern-lid visible on the other. A clarinet springs up with the first of Salome's motifs, and there is a *pianissimo* thrill of flutes and divided strings (with harps, celesta and harmonium) in C♯. The lovelorn Narraboth sings 'Wie schön ist die Prinzessin Salome heute Nacht!', while the boy Page who worships him has fearful premonitions, and a pair of common soldiers discuss the noisy banquet – where Herod's Jewish guests are arguing theology – and their prisoner Jokanaan, whose prophetic voice is heard from the cistern along with three hortatory motifs in the orchestra.

This opera is a continuous 'stage tone-poem', without separate numbers, and Strauss has now presented his symphonic mini-exposition. Most of the main thematic cells have been laid down, if not yet connected up nor developed; and a crucial polarity has been fixed between the febrile chromaticism of Salome's world – veering from one sharp key to another momentarily, but magnetized towards a vibrant C♯ tonic – and the prophet's austerely diatonic realm. He began in plain C major, though his music (which will become the vehicle of suprahuman judgment) tends towards the flat-key modulations of Romantic surrender, without the robust tonic-to-dominant thrust of Classical tonality; the opera will end in stern C minor. Now young Salome herself enters petulantly to her own waltz-music, fleeing the feast and Herod's greedy gaze. The invisible prophet's oratory excites her; the soldiers tell her as much as they know about him, but will not let her see him – they have their orders. She turns her wiles upon Captain Narraboth, who to the Page's dismay succumbs and commands that Jokanaan be brought out.

A long, turbulent interlude (all the heavy brass, for the first time, but none of the glittering percussion) tracks Jokanaan's ascent. Then, with sonorous authority, he denounces not only the monstrous sins of Salome's stepfather but those of her mother – which excites her the more. To his horror she responds by hymning his own attractions, in three rapturous 'verses'. First she praises his ivory body, and he recoils; then she disparages his body but extols his black mane; rebuffed again, she reviles his hair and sings a paean to his red mouth, which she demands to kiss. (Here poor Narraboth stabs himself in despair, virtually unnoticed.) Refusing to look at the princess, the outraged prophet curses her and retreats to his cistern. A still longer and wilder orchestral postlude mingles the prophet's themes and Salome's – notably a flickering triadic figure to which she first sang, prettily, 'Er ist schrecklich' ('He is frightful'), a passionate melody which is to crown her final monologue, and a menacing four-note motif which has carried Jokanaan's final curse and will mark Salome's demands for his head. The music accelerates to a frenzy and then freezes on a C♯ tremolo, while snapping brass chords and a winding double bassoon follow the prophet down to the depths.

There is a sudden clatter of woodwind (the Tetrarch's disputatious guests resemble the critics in *Ein Heldenleben*) and Herod enters in distracted pursuit of the princess, with his sour consort on his heels. Like Narraboth and Salome earlier, he remarks a special eeriness in the moon tonight; Herodias denies it. He summons torches and wine for his guests, and slips on the blood around Narraboth's corpse: a cold wind springs up and passes away (chromatic swirls over a prophetic motif), like a rustling of great wings, heard only by Herod. He presses wine and fruit upon the princess and implores her to sit by him. To her mother's grim satisfaction, Salome evades his blandishings. From the cistern the prophet's voice is heard again, prompting a cross theological debate among Herod's Jewish guests, and a pair of Nazarenes report what they know of the Messiah. The voice goes on to prophesy shame and death for 'the daughter of Babylon', to the great annoyance of Herodias.

Here a linking portion of Wilde's text was deleted. Abruptly, then, the Tetrarch invites his stepdaughter to dance for him. Her mother disapproves, and Salome flatly declines – until the tantalized, overwrought Herod swears solemnly to give her whatever she chooses. The cold wind rises again, and also for the last time the prophet's warning voice; Salome agrees to perform the Dance of the Seven Veils. (Strauss composed it after the rest of the score. Its Hollywood-exotic contours, bedizened with motifs from the opera proper, sometimes tempt directors to make it an elaborate production-number, far beyond the rather chaste little scenario that the composer sketched to guide himself.) When the dance is concluded, more or less brazenly according to the whims of director and soprano, Salome demands her prize from the appalled Herod: the head of Jokanaan, on a silver salver. She is implacable, and Herodias fiercely delighted. In lyrical desperation the Tetrarch proposes the most extravagant alternatives: fabulous jewels, half his kingdom, even the veil of the temple. The elaborate arioso monologue with luscious orchestral illustration, punctuated by Salome's increasingly vehement refusals, parallels her own amorous assault on the prophet earlier, against his stony rebuffs. At last, defeated and full of forebodings, Herod gives the fatal order.

Herodias snatches the death-ring from his finger, and it is passed to the executioner, who descends into the cistern. Above, Salome listens with anxious impatience. Over long *pianissimo* tremolos and a bass drumroll, a solo double bass emits high, choked whimpers (like a woman's stifled groans, says the score). As she begins to doubt the executioner's resolve and cries for the soldiers to go down too, there is a confused orchestral eruption, and then hammering timpani. Everything stops but the drumroll. From the cistern a gigantic black arm holds up

'Salome' (Richard Strauss): scene from the original production at the Dresden Hofoper, 9 December 1905, with Marie Wittich as Salome and Carl Burrian as Herod

a salver which bears the prophet's head, and the princess seizes it.

The whole orchestra bursts out in a dissonant roar. In fact, the 'recapitulation' has arrived: violins and woodwinds scream the opening motif of the opera, skewed now over a C pedal. This climactic monologue is itself virtually a self-contained tone-poem-with-voice, planned in long paragraphs and constantly reviewing the motifs of the opera. 'Ah! du wolltest mich nicht deinen Mund küssen lassen', Salome sings ('You would not let me kiss your mouth, Jokanaan, but now I will') – here is where Strauss originally supposed that nothing less than an Isolde-voice would do – and with her second 'küssen' the music settles uneasily upon a C♯ tonic. After those first exultant cries, she falls to contemplating Jokanaan's dead eyes (he would not see her, and now he cannot) and his now silent tongue, while the tonality shifts restlessly through the sharp keys. His oracular motifs return in C and related flat keys; but when she recalls his beauty it is in tenderest F♯ major, and at last she persuades herself in C♯ that he *would* have loved her, had he looked at her – 'The mystery of love is greater than the mystery of death'. Aghast, Herod calls for the lights to be put out as the princess bends towards the dead lips, a cloud covers the moon and the music is suspended on a long, breathless trill. The flickering figure is reiterated again and again by oboe and piccolo, answered by a low, dark chord (a backstage organ makes it denser) like a prolonged shudder: the effect of utter derangement is palpable. In the obscurity and in atonal chromatics, Salome sings softly that she has kissed Jokanaan's mouth, and that the taste of love is bitter. The moon re-emerges to illuminate her, the music collects itself into a final radiant C♯ and the voice soars in a brief, heroic *Liebestod*. The orchestra echoes her phrase, adding one gross dissonance like an obscene jeer – and then breaks off in frantic alarums as Herod shrieks for his soldiers to kill her. They crush their princess beneath their shields, amid C minor poundings which suggest a brutal, retributive rape.

* * *

If his two previous operas had earned him some parochial renown, it was *Salome* that established Strauss as a major operatic composer. His tone poems had already made him an international reputation, but by now he had exhausted that vein; indeed, though he was to enjoy almost another half-century of creative life he would write nothing more ambitious for orchestra than the Disney-esque *Alpine Symphony*. For large-scale composition he needed the guidance of a text. Neither his own verse-libretto for *Guntram* nor Wolzogen's purpose-built one for *Feuersnot*, however, had offered him more than broad-brush sentiments – enough to hang neo-Wagnerian leitmotifs on, but nothing to prompt the febrile élan of *Don Juan*, still less the mercurial symphonic fluency of *Till Eulenspiegel* or *Ein Heldenleben*.

Wilde's *Salomé* was the happiest possible find. As a pre-existing text it had already proved itself in performance, so there were no dramaturgical problems to solve; furthermore its single act already suggested the shape of a tone poem, and it was in prose – which gave Strauss's symphonic imagination far greater liberty than regular verse – and yet florid enough to invite lyrical setting. It provided a wealth of excuses for orchestral illustration, as did its pervasively sultry atmosphere. The composer indulged himself in a huge band with quadruple woodwind, including heckelphone, while reducing it frequently to chamber scale. The real drama lay in extreme psychological conflicts, which eminently suited Strauss (he was never comfortable with strenuous stage action, as distinct from set-piece theatrical coups), and it was fraught with currently fashionable decadence. It is unlikely that he pondered over the 'morality' of the piece; he simply turned it into an opera, with acute faithfulness and all the professional resource which had been awaiting such an opportunity. Fundamentally tonal, if spiced with bitonal passages, *Salome* does administer some calculated shocks – in the words of Gabriel Fauré, who admired the score as a whole, 'cruel dissonances which defy all explanation'. Strictly musical explanation, that is: their theatrical impact, apt and alarming, embodies the decent reactions of any *homme moyen sensuel* like the composer himself to these indecent goings-on. Necrophilia is not among the more popular perversions, and Strauss was less concerned to fathom any 'deeper meaning' it might have than to exploit its operatic potential in terms of unbridled invention, lurid but cogent, and also tender – and profoundly effective.

For an illustration of Strauss's working copy of the libretto, *see* STRAUSS, RICHARD, fig.2. DAVID MURRAY

Salomon, Johann Peter (*b* Bonn, bap. 20 Feb 1745; *d* London, 25 Nov 1815). German impresario and composer, later resident in England. He first served at the Bonn court, and by 1764 was at Rheinsberg as musical director to Prince Heinrich of Prussia, for whom he wrote several French operas. According to *The Harmonicon*, his sister Anna Salomon, a contralto, frequently performed in them. In 1780–81 Salomon settled in England, where he made his name as a brilliant violinist; he then turned to promoting and conducting concerts. He is best known for securing Haydn's visits to London in 1790–91 and 1794–5, for which the two sets of six 'Salomon' or 'London' symphonies were written. One of the founder-members of the Philharmonic Society, he led the orchestra at its first concert on 8 March 1813. He died as a result of a riding accident and was buried in the cloisters of Westminster Abbey.

Besides theatrical works, Salomon wrote songs and instrumental pieces. Despite his gift for imaginative and attractive tunes, however, he is virtually forgotten as a composer, perhaps because of his limited ability in developing his material. An overture specially written by Haydn was given with the initial run of performances of *Windsor Castle* (1795); it was replaced with one of Salomon's own compositions in 1796.

Les recruteurs (comédie lyrique, 1), Rheinsberg, 1771
Le séjour du bonheur (comédie, 1), Berlin, 5 March 1773
Titus, Rheinsberg, 1774
La reine de Golconde, Rheinsberg, 1776, 1 aria (Leipzig, 1790)
Windsor Castle, or The Fair Maid of Kent (grand masque, 2, W. Pearce), London, CG, 6 April 1795, vs (London, 1795), collab. R. Spofforth

*

F. Rochlitz: 'Johann Peter Salomon', *AMZ*, xviii (1816), 132
[W. Ayrton]: 'Memoir of Johann Peter Salomon', *The Harmonicon*, viii (1830), 45–7
H. C. R. Landon: *The Collected Correspondence and London Notebooks of Joseph Haydn* (London, 1959)
A. Tyson: 'Salomon's Will', *Studien zur Musikgeschichte des Rheinlandes III*, ed. U. Eckart-Backer (Cologne, 1965), 43–5
H. Unverricht: 'Die Kompositionen Johann Peter Salomons: ein Überblick', ibid, 35–42
H. C. R. Landon: *Haydn: Chronicle and Works* (London, 1976–80), esp. iii HUBERT UNVERRICHT

Salomon, Joseph-François (*b* Toulon, bap. 3 April 1649; *d* Versailles, 5 March 1732). French composer. He apparently arrived in Paris at an early age, but the first documented evidence of his activities, as organist and harpsichordist for Queen Marie Thérèse at Versailles, dates from 1679. Later he acquired a reputation as a gamba player, serving until 1720 or 1727 as *ordinaire de la musique de la chambre*. Titon du Tillet regarded Salomon as a minor musician who abruptly emerged as a reputable opera composer with the positive reception of the *tragédie en musique*, *Médée et Jason* (prol., 5, S.-J. Pellegrin, after Ovid: *Metamorphoses*; Paris, Opéra, 24 April 1713; *F-Pn/R* 1990: FO, xvii). Salomon's attempt to repeat this achievement with a second *tragédie en musique*, *Théonoé* (prol., 5, La Roque [Pellegrin]; Paris, Opéra, 3 Dec 1715), was however unsuccessful. As an opera composer he was soon overshadowed by his more illustrious contemporaries; Titon du Tillet was evidently unaware that Salomon had composed a second *tragédie*. Both works were published in Paris in the year of their premières.

See also MÉDÉE ET JASON.

*

FétisB; *MGG* (H.-A. Durand)
E. Titon du Tillet: *La Parnasse françois* (Paris, 1732)
J.-B. Durey de Noinville and L. Travenol: *Histoire du théâtre de l'Opéra en France*, ii (Paris, 1753)
J.-B. de La Borde: *Essai sur la musique ancienne et moderne*, iii (Paris, 1780) LESLIE ELLEN BROWN

Salomon, (Naphtali) Siegfried (*b* Copenhagen, 3 Aug 1885; *d* Copenhagen, 29 Oct 1962). Danish composer. He studied at the Copenhagen Conservatory (1899–1902), in Leipzig and with Le Flem in Paris. From 1903 he worked as an orchestral cellist and appeared as a soloist in Copenhagen, Paris and Stockholm; he also played the viol. His greatest success as a composer and conductor was with the opera *Leonora Christina* (4, A. Barfoed; Copenhagen, Kongelige, 1926), a success owing to the work's popular style and to the performance of the soprano Tenna Frederiksen Kraft in the title role. His output includes two other operas, *Duen og slangen* ('Doves and Serpents'; 1925) and *Dronning Dagmar* ('Queen Dagmar'; 1928), neither of them performed.

TORBEN SCHOUSBOE

Salonica (Gk. Thessaloniki). City in Greece. Operatic activity began in the early 20th century with performances by touring Greek companies (primarily the Elliniko Melodrama) in various buildings adapted for the purpose. Between 1905 and 1989, 76 operas (including eight by Greek composers) were performed, either by the National Opera established in Athens in 1940 (see Kyrtsani) or by important foreign companies appearing annually between October and November at the Demetria Festival (established in 1966); in addition 43 operettas were performed between 1940 and 1983.

Attempts by Salonica's own institutions to produce opera have been sporadic. In 1930 the Salonica State Conservatory presented Georgios Sklavos's *Kyra Frossyni* and in 1932 *Cavalleria rusticana*, and it has more recently given fine performances of Mozart's *Apollo et Hyacinthus* (1981), Weber's *Abu Hassan* (1990) and Offenbach's *La belle Hélène*. In 1977 Spyros Evanghelatos established the Opera Thessalonikis, affiliated to the Northern Greece State Theatre, the drama company of which he was head; performances took place in the company's theatre (cap. 1050). Its first production, *Fidelio*, was given in January 1978 with players from the Salonica State Orchestra, but after four years it had to abandon its activities for lack of funding. Among other ventures have been those of the Opera Dhomatiou Thessalonikis (Salonica

Chamber Opera) and the Opera Dhomatiou Voriou Ellados (Chamber Opera of Northern Greece). On 21 January 1992 the Salonica Friends of Music Society announced the construction of the Salonica Concert Hall (capacity 1418), to be inaugurated in 1996.

*

G. Leotsakos: *Elliniko lyriko théatro, 100 chronia, 1888–1988* [100 Years of Greek Lyric Theatre, 1888–1988] (Ypourgheio Politismou, YP 4–6, A/A 14564, 1988) [record notes]

M. Kyrtsani: *Parastassis operas sti Thessaloniki* [Opera Performances in Salonica] (diss., Aristotelian U. of Thessaloniki, 1990)

GEORGE LEOTSAKOS

Salter, Lionel (Paul) (*b* London, 8 Sept 1914). English writer on music and administrator. He studied at the RCM, London, and at Cambridge with Dent. He became known as a keyboard player, especially on the radio, and worked as a music assistant in BBC television. Returning to the BBC after war service, he held various posts, and in 1956 became head of music (television), where he did much to stimulate the presentation of opera, ballet and concerts and was widely influential in establishing techniques for music programmes. He was head of opera (for both sound and television), 1963–7, and opera coordinator and producer for the European Broadcasting Union, 1972–6. His special fields of interest include Hispanic music, Baroque opera (he has prepared performing editions of Lully's *Alceste* and Cavalli's *Erismena*) and keyboard music. His book *Going to the Opera* was published in London in 1955.

Salt Lake City. American city, in Utah, home of Utah Opera. The company began with *La bohème* on the university campus in 1978; a year later it moved to its present home in the restored Capitol Theatre with *Otello*. Three productions are staged each season, and the company has engaged such artists as Giorgio Tozzi, Martina Arroyo and Roberta Peters. The introduction of surtitles in 1985 increased subscription rates from 39% to 51% and resulted in a fifth performance of each production. Utah Opera is a regional company that takes special pride in an outreach programme providing concerts, lectures and symposia for schools and other interested organizations throughout a five-state region. Its performances reach 110 000 people a season.

WES BLOMSTER

Saltzmann-Stevens, Minnie (*b* Bloomington, IL, 17 March 1874; *d* Milan, 25 Jan 1950). American soprano. She studied in Paris with Jean De Reszke, who recommended her to Covent Garden, where she made her début in 1909 as Brünnhilde in the English *Ring*. Her intelligence of gesture, her declamation and the general smoothness and finish of her singing created a most favourable impression. She sang at Covent Garden (1910–13) as Sieglinde, Brünnhilde and Isolde; at Bayreuth in 1911 and 1913 as Kundry and Sieglinde; and in Chicago (1911–14). Her highly promising career ended prematurely through illness.

Salva, Tadeáš (*b* Lúčky pri Ružomberku, 22 Oct 1937). Slovak composer. He studied composition with Alexander Moyzes and Ján Cikker, and then with Bolesław Szabelski and Witold Lutosławski in Poland. He was the head of music broadcasting for Kosiče radio (1965) before becoming a producer for Slovak television in Bratislava in 1968 and later the Dramaturg for SL'UK (Slovak Folk Art Group). Although distinctly influenced by his Polish studies, his musical language has its origins in the characteristic elements of older Slovak folksong. *Margita a Besná*, the first Slovak television opera (1971), was written to a libretto by Veronika Vrbková after a ballad by Ján Botto. It makes use of spoken, sung and shouted words combined with expressive dance and stage action. *Plač* (1978) is based on a montage of poems by Vojtech Mihálik, Franǒ Kráĺ, Vladimir Roy, Milan Rúfus and Marcel Herz, and combines live and pre-recorded voices. His children's opera, *Mechúrik Koščúrik s kamarátmi* (1983–4), is based on a poem by M. Rúfus and scored for a small chamber orchestra, and is among the most original and most demanding Slovak operas for children.

Margita a Besná [Margita and Besná], 1971 (television op, V. Vrbková, after Ján Botto), ČST Bratislava, 24 Sept 1976

Plač [Tears], 1978 (radio op, Salva, after poems by V. Mihálik, F. Kráĺ, V. Roy, M. Rúfus and M. Herz), Devin Radio, 29 Sept 1980; also known as Plač matiek a otcov [The Tears of Mothers and Fathers]

Mechúrik Koščúrik s kamarátmi [Mechúrik Koščúrik and his Friends], 1983–4 (children's op, after M. Rúfus), unperf.

*

I. Vajda: *Slovenská opera* (Bratislava, 1988), 178–81, 225–7, 241–2

IGOR VAJDA

Salvador [Bahia]. Brazilian city, capital of the state of Bahia. Officially named Salvador da Bahia de todos os Santos, but commonly known as Bahia, it was founded in 1549, and remained the capital of colonial Brazil until 1763. In its second theatre, the Casa da Opera da Praia, the municipality paid for the mounting of three of Perez's operas in 1760, *Didone abbandonata*, *Artaserse* and *Alessandro nelle Indie*, to celebrate the marriage on 6 June of the Portuguese royal couple. The Salvador historian Guilherme de Melo credited Damião Barbosa de Araújo (*b* Itaparica, nr Salvador, 27 Sept 1778; *d* Salvador, 20 April 1856) with having been the first native of Bahia to compose an *opera buffa*, *A intriga amorosa*, presented in the Salvador Teatro do Guadelupe where he was leader of the orchestra. During the 19th century visiting Italian companies performed in the Teatro São João (60 boxes, 340 orchestra and 400 gallery seats), which was inaugurated on 13 May 1812 and burnt down in 1922. In 1845 the Clemente Mugnai company brought only a few instrumentalists, relying on local players for orchestral accompaniment, as did the Cezar Carrena company in 1846 (announced in the *Correio mercantil* as performing *Lucia*, *Il barbiere* and Nicolai's *Il templario*), the Paccini, the Bassi Galuppi and other troupes. Choruses in these productions were sung by local singers trained by Giuseppe Fachinetti, resident in Salvador after 1839. Robert Avé-Lallemant, visiting Salvador the next year, was surprised that nearly all the choristers were blacks or mulattos (he was unaware that as early as 1790 Jommelli's *Ezio in Roma* had been sung at the gold-rush town of Cuyabá by an all-male mulatto company). In 1867 José Amat brought Offenbach operettas to the São João in a season that lasted 40 nights. Gomes conducted his *Il Guarany* on 15 June 1879, returning on 6 April 1880 to conduct *Salvator Rosa*. In 1881 a street was named in his honour and on 12 October 1882 he was apostrophized in a solemn ceremony.

*

L. H. Corrêa de Azevedo: *Relação das óperas de autores brasileiros* (Rio de Janeiro, 1938)

G. de Melo: *A música no Brasil* (Rio de Janeiro, 1947)

A. R. de Souza: *História do teatro na Bahia* (Salvador, 1959)

H. Machado Brasil: *A música na cidade do Salvador 1549–1900* (Salvador, 1969)

P. Verger: *Notícias da Bahia-1850* (Salvador, 1981)
ROBERT L. STEVENSON

Salvador, Matilde (*b* Castellón de la Plana, Valencia, 23 March 1918). Spanish composer. A pupil of Vicente Asencio, whom she later married, she is predominantly a composer of vocal music. In 1943 her opera *La filla del rei Barbut* was at first prohibited by the Franco regime because the libretto (by M. S. Ribes) was in Valencian. Since the composer was young and a woman, the ban aroused strong feelings, and the work was first performed at the Teatro Principal, Castellón, on 31 March that year. The subject of *Vinatea*, set in the year 1333, was the rebellion of Vinatea, a Valencian nobleman, executed for opposing the concessions made to Castile by King Alfonso the Good. Orchestrated by Asencio, the opera was first staged at the Liceo, Barcelona, on 24 January 1974; it uses a number of voices in lower registers, and the striking purity of the vocal line shows concern for the dramatic quality of X. Casp's text. Aesthetically it follows Falla; the key political ideas are linked with references to traditional Valencian music with a sensitivity characteristic of Salvador. She has also composed two ballets and a dramatic cantata.

*

A. Fernández-Cid: *Cien años de teatro musical en España (1875–1975)* (Madrid, 1975)

J. Climent: *Historia de la música contemporánea valenciana* (Valencia, 1978)

J. Doménech i Part: 'Presentació', *Matilde Salvador: Cançons per a veu i piano* (Valencia, 1984)
XOÁN M. CARREIRA

Salvai, Maria Maddalena (*b* Florence; *fl* 1716–31). Italian soprano. In 1716 she was in the service of the Landgrave of Kassel; she sang at Darmstadt between 1718 and 1719, and then at Dresden. Recommended by Senesino for her 'most beautiful voice', she joined the Royal Academy in London in 1720 at the same time as Senesino and remained for two seasons, making her début as Polissena in Handel's *Radamisto*. She sang in *Arsace* (Orlandini-Amadei), and the first performances of the composite *Muzio Scevola* (Fidalma), Handel's *Floridante* (Rossane) and Giovanni Bononcini's *L'odio e l'amore*, *Crispo* and *Griselda*. She had a high tessitura and a compass of *e'* to *b♭''*, but seems not to have been an exceptional singer. She sang at Milan in 1725 and appeared in two operas at Venice in 1722–3, three at Naples (including Vinci's *Ernelinda* and Hasse's *Sesostrate*) in 1726–7, two at Florence in 1727–8, and three more there in 1730–31.
WINTON DEAN

Salvatori, Celestino (*b c*1798; *d* 1836 or later). Italian bass. In 1830 he sang Ernesto in Bellini's *Il pirata* at Trieste. In 1832 he sang Rodolfo (*La sonnambula*) at the Teatro della Pergola, Florence, and took part in Donizetti's *Otto mesi in due ore* at the Teatro Valle, Rome. He sang Cardenio in Donizetti's *Il furioso all'isola di San Domingo* at Turin (1833), Oroveso in *Norma* (1834) and Enrico Ashton in *Lucia di Lammermoor* (1836) at Bologna. He created the title role of Donizetti's *Belisario* at La Fenice in 1836 and repeated the part in several theatres, including La Scala, Milan. He had a powerful voice with a wide range.
ELIZABETH FORBES

Salvator Rosa. *Opera seria* in four acts by CARLOS GOMES to a libretto by ANTONIO GHISLANZONI, after Eugène de Méricourt's novel *Masaniello*; Genoa, Teatro Carlo Felice, 21 March 1874.

The action takes place in Naples on the occasion of the 1647 insurrection against the Spanish rulers. The painter Salvator Rosa (tenor) supports his friend Masaniello (baritone), a fisherman, in starting the revolt against the Spanish viceroy, the Duke of Arcos (bass-baritone). The Duke's soldiers arrest Rosa at his studio. In the ducal palace, Rosa recognizes the Duke's daughter, Isabella (soprano), as the woman of his dreams (whom he had seen frequently in the city); she is promised, however, to the commander Fernandez (tenor). In front of the insurgents, Masaniello declares the people of Naples free. After some debate the Duke finally signs a settlement with the Neapolitans. Rosa arrives, as Masaniello's messenger, and meets Isabella; they declare their love. The Duke, however, overhears, and threatens to send Isabella to a convent and Rosa to the gallows.

Masaniello, invited to the palace, is given drugged wine and becomes delirious. Rosa enters, preoccupied with Isabella's absence; he observes Masaniello's strange behaviour and accuses the Duke, who has him arrested. In the convent, the Duke proposes to Isabella that she marry Fernandez in return for Rosa's freedom; reluctantly, she agrees. Meanwhile, the Count of Badajoz (baritone) and his assassins conspire against Masaniello. Rosa is told that he is free, but Isabella then appears in a wedding gown; as they embrace, she reveals her father's scheme and says that she has poisoned herself. As he asks her to run away with him, a shot is heard inside the church where Masaniello was praying. The Duke and Badajoz appear at the entrance of the palace. Rosa, with a dagger in his hand, threatens the Duke, who attempts to have him arrested, but Isabella interposes herself, takes the dagger and stabs herself. She dies forgiving her father and urging Rosa to dedicate himself to his art.

The première was a huge success, probably because Gomes made a great deal of concession to prevailing taste. *Salvator Rosa* is generally recognized as the least inspired of his works, as a result of the haste with which he wrote it and the dramatic imbalance of the libretto which lacks coherence between scenes and conviction in the characterization of the principals. Gomes and Ghislanzoni are said to have had difficulty in their collaboration. To be sure, the opera contains well-known passages, such as the Duke's aria in Act 2, 'Di sposo ... di padre', and the serenade 'O mia pêccêrella', sung at the beginning of the opera and at the beginning of Act 4, which became quite popular. The overall melodic and harmonic content and the musical structure of the work, however, lack the care and imagination of Gomes's other operas.
GERARD BÉHAGUE

Salvayre, (Gervais Bernard) Gaston (*b* Toulouse, 24 June 1847; *d* St Ague, nr Toulouse, 17 May 1916). French composer. He studied at the Toulouse Conservatory and later with Bazin and Thomas at the Paris Conservatoire. In 1872 he won the Prix de Rome for *Calypso*. His subsequent stay in Rome was quite productive; on his return to Paris he presented ballet music for the revival of Grisar's *Les amours du diable* (1874) as well as orchestral music. In 1877 he was appointed chorus master of the Opéra-Populaire at the Théâtre du Châtelet and in the same year made an inauspicious operatic début with *Le bravo*, an opera of intrigue set in 15th-century Venice. Later stage works included *Richard III* (1883), *Egmont* (1886; an adaptation of Goethe's work in a 16th-century Belgian setting) and *La dame de Monsoreau* (commissioned by the Opéra, 1888); although these did little to advance his reputation as an opera composer, he composed several more dramatic pieces. Of these the only one to be staged was *Solange*, set in Lorraine in the aftermath of the French Revolution. Salvayre's other works include large-scale choral pieces, songs and chamber music. He was also a music critic for many years, contributing to *Gil Blas* and other reviews.

first performed in Paris unless otherwise stated; all published in Paris

Calypso (scène dramatique, V. Roussy), 1872 (1872)
Le bravo (4, E. R. Blavet), Lyrique, 18 April 1877, vs (1877)
Richard III (4, Blavet, after W. Shakespeare), St Petersburg, Mariinsky, 9/21 Dec 1883, in It. as Riccardo III; orig. Fr., Nice, 29 Jan 1891 (1883)
Egmont (drame lyrique, 4, A. Wolff and A. Millaud, after J. W. von Goethe), OC (Favart), 6 Dec 1886, vs (1886)
La dame de Monsoreau (5, A. Maquet, after A. Dumas *père*), Opéra, 30 Jan 1888, vs (1888)
Solange (oc, 3, A. Aderer), OC (Favart), 10 March 1909 (1909)
Salah-ed-Din (4, H. Bocage and P. Ferrier), ?unperf., unpubd
Myrto (comédie musicale, 3, L. Gallet), ?unperf., unpubd

RICHARD LANGHAM SMITH

Salvi, Antonio (*b* Lucignano, 17 Jan 1664; *d* Florence, 21 May 1724). Italian librettist. He was a physician in the service of the ducal court in Florence and the favourite librettist of Prince Ferdinand de' Medici. Between 1701 and 1710 he wrote seven *drammi per musica* for the entertainments the prince gave in his villa at Pratolino, and he wrote others for the public theatres of Livorno and Florence from 1694 to 1718, the year in which his *Scanderbeg* was performed to music by Vivaldi for the re-opening of the Teatro della Pergola. After the death of Ferdinand (1713) he accepted commissions outside Tuscany and wrote for theatres in Rome, Reggio Emilia, Turin, Munich and Venice. His librettos were set by the greatest composers of the day, including Perti, Alessandro Scarlatti, Gasparini and Vivaldi. Some of them were successful and were revived many times, mostly with other music; in particular *Astianatte* (also known with the title *Andromaca*) and *Amore e maestà* (or *Arsace*). Handel often used them for his operas. In the context of the so-called Arcadian reform, Salvi's work is distinguished for its simplicity of style, regularity of formal structure and above all for the prevalence of emotional content. These modern characteristics reflect to some extent the influence of French classical theatre, from which a few of his intermezzos also derive: *L'artigiano gentiluomo*, *Il malato immaginario* and *L'avaro* are after works of Molière. *Il marito giocatore e la moglie bacchettona* (or *Serpilla e Bacocco*) is one of the most famous examples of the 18th-century intermezzo.

drammi per musica in three acts unless otherwise stated

La forza compassionevole, 1694; *Astianatte*, G. A. Perti, 1701 (A. M. Bononcini, 1718; F. Gasparini, 1719; L. Vinci, 1727; G. Bononcini, 1727; N. Jommelli, 1741; as Andromaca: L. Leo, 1742; G. B. Lampugnani, 1749; D. Perez, 1750); *Arminio*, A. Scarlatti, 1703 (A. Caldara, 1705; C. F. Pollarolo, 1722; J. A. Hasse, 1730; G. F. Handel, 1737; B. Galuppi, 1747; G. Cocchi); *Publio Cornelio Scipione*, 1704 (Handel, 1726); *Il gran Tamerlano*, A. Scarlatti, 1706 (F. Gasparini and others, 1717, as Il trace in catena; G. Porta, 1720, as Teodorico)
Dionisio re di Portogallo, Perti, 1707 (Handel, 1732, as Sosarme); *Stratonica*, 1707; *Ginerva principessa di Scozia*, Perti, 1708 (D. Sarro, 1720; G. Sellitto, 1733; Vivaldi, 1736; F. Bertoni, 1753; as Ariodante: Pollarolo, 1716; Handel, 1735; Wagenseil, 1745); *Berenice regina d'Egitto*, Perti, 1709 (G. M. Ruggieri, 1711, as Le gare di politica e d'amore; D. Scarlatti and N. Porpora, 1718; F. Araia, 1734; Handel, 1737); *Rodelinda regina de Longobardi*, Perti, 1710 (Handel, 1725; G. Boniventi, 1727, as Brertarido re de' Longobardi; C. H. Graun, 1741)
Lucio Papirio, F. Gasparini, 1714 (L. A. Predieri, 1715; G. M. Orlandi, 1718; L. Leo, 1735; N. Porpora, 1737); *Amor vince l'odio overo Timocrate*, Gasparini, 1715; *Il Tartaro nella Cina*, Gasparini, 1715; *Amore e maesta'* (tragedia per musica), G. M. Orlandini, 1715 (Gasparini, 1720; G. M. Buini, 1722; as Arsace: Gasparini, 1718; D. Sarro, 1718; G. F. Brusa, 1725; G. Giacomelli, 1737; F. Feo, 1741; G. B. Lampugnani, 1741)
Il pazzo per politica, L. A. Predieri, 1717 (T. Albinoni, 1717, as Eumene); *L'amazoni vinte da Ercole*, G. M. Orlandini, 1718; *Scanderbeg*, Vivaldi, 1718; *Il carceriero di se stesso*, Orlandini, 1720; *Adelaide*, P. Torri, 1722 (Porpora, 1723; Buini, 1725; Orlandini, 1729; Handel, 1729, as Lotario; Vivaldi, 1735; G. Cocchi, 1743); *Gl'equivoci d'amore e d'innocenza*, Gasparini, 1723; *Ipermestra*, Giacomelli, 1724 (Vivaldi, 1727; Feo, 1728)

*

'Necrologio', *Giornale de' letterati d'Italia*, xxxvi (1724), 283–8
R. L. Weaver and N. W. Weaver: *A Chronology of Music in the Florentine Theater, 1590–1750* (Detroit, 1978)
R. Strohm: '"Tragedie" into "Dramma per musica"', *Informazioni e studi vivaldiani*, xi (1990), 11–25
L. Bianconi and G. La Face Bianconi: *I libretti italiani di Georg Friedrich Händel e loro fonti* (Florence, 1992–)

FRANCESCO GIUNTINI

Salvi, Lorenzo (*b* Ancona, 4 May 1810; *d* Bologna, 16 Jan 1879). Italian tenor. He studied in Naples, making his début in 1830 at S Carlo as Cam in the first performance of Donizetti's *Diluvio universale*. At the Teatro Valle, Rome, he created Fernando in *Il furioso all'isola di San Domingo* (1833) and at the Teatro Nuovo, Naples, he sang in the first performance of *Betly* (1836). At Genoa he sang Gennaro (*Lucrezia Borgia*), Edgardo and Rossini's Otello. He made his début at La Scala in Federico Ricci's *Un duello sotto Richelieu*, created the title role of Donizetti's *Gianni di Parigi*, Riccardo in Verdi's *Oberto* (1839) and Edoardo in Verdi's *Un giorno di regno* (1840). At the Teatro Apollo, Rome, he created Olivero in Donizetti's *Adelia* (1841). He was a member of the Italian Opera in St Petersburg from 1845, and from 1847 to 1849 he sang at Covent Garden, as Edgardo, Nemorino, Almaviva, Don Ramiro, Lindoro (*L'italiana in Algeri*), Ernani, Pollione, Masaniello (Auber's *La muette de Portici*) and Robert le diable.

ELIZABETH FORBES

Salvi, Margherita (*b* Madrid, 1894; *d* Santiago de Chile, 13 March 1981). South American soprano of Spanish birth. She studied with Avelina Carrera in Barcelona and Torati in Milan, and in 1925 she made her début as Gilda at the Teatro della Pergola, Florence. After a successful début in Buenos Aires in 1926, she sang Italian opera in the Netherlands (1926–8, 1933), and as a guest at the principal Italian theatres (1927) and in Monte Carlo (1929). Her Chicago Opera début was in 1929 as Rosina; she remained with the company until 1931 and returned in 1937 as Violetta. She was married to the composer and conductor Federico Longas. Both her reputation and her recordings attest to her sensitive musicianship and coloratura facility.

CORI ELLISON

Salvini-Donatelli, Fanny [Lucchi, Francesca] (*b* Florence, ?1815; *d* Milan, June 1891). Italian soprano. She made her début at the Teatro Apollo, Venice, in 1839 as Rosina. Engaged in Vienna (1842–3), she sang Abigaille (*Nabucco*) under Verdi's supervision. She created Violetta in *La traviata* at La Fenice in 1853 and was blamed indirectly for the work's failure, supposedly because she weighed 'precisely 130 kilograms'. Other Verdi roles included Lady Macbeth, Lucrezia (*I due foscari*) and Elvira (*Ernani*). After engagements throughout Europe, she sang in Paris and at Drury Lane in 1858. She retired the following year but made further appearances in 1865. Berlioz and the London critics esteemed her voice, which was expressive, flexible and lyrical, and well suited to dramatic roles.

*

N. Bazzetta di Vemenia: *Le cantanti italiane dell'ottocento* (Novara, 1945), 120 CHARLES JAHANT

Salway, Thomas (*b* *c*1706; *d* London, 6 April 1743). English tenor and actor. Salway was a treble at Cannons and then a popular singer on the London stage from 1724 until shortly before his death. He played the heroes in Carey's *The Honest Yorkshireman* and *Nancy, or The Parting Lovers* and was the dragon-killing Moore of Moore Hall in Lampe's *The Dragon of Wantley*. In Gay's *Achilles* the hero is disguised as a woman; this was one of Salway's petticoat roles. He was Damon in the first public performance of Handel's *Acis and Galatea* (1731).

*

BDA; *LS* OLIVE BALDWIN, THELMA WILSON

Salzburg. Austrian city. From the 8th century until 1806 it was the seat of a series of prince-archbishops, whose court became the centre of the city's musical life; it is specially noted in the 20th century for its festival.

1. History. 2. Festival.

1. HISTORY. The archbishop Marcus Sitticus von Hohenems, who reigned from 1612 to 1619, was half-Italian and cultivated economic and cultural links with Italy, especially with the court at Mantua. During his reign Salzburg enjoyed the first flowering of the Baroque: monody and opera were introduced, their earliest appearance north of the Alps, and in 1612 the famous exponent of the monodic style, Francesco Rasi, pupil of Giulio Caccini and a leading opera singer (he was probably Monteverdi's original Orpheus), visited Salzburg and dedicated a manuscript collection of monody to the archbishop. In 1614 a stage was erected in the archbishop's residence and inaugurated on 27 January with an Italian 'Hoftragicomedia', the first opera performance outside Italy. On 10 February the pastoral *Orfeo* was given, probably with music by Monteverdi.

The archbishop also created another remarkable setting for musical theatre, the Steintheater in the park at Hellbrunn (his summer residence outside Salzburg), the oldest surviving garden theatre in the German-speaking world. Guest performers from Italy probably joined local artists for Salzburg opera performances (the monodist Camillo Orlandi, for instance, was there in 1616). In 1617 the Benedictine Gymnasium was founded and with the university (1622) formed an important centre for drama and music. The Benedictine drama performed there developed during the 17th century and increasingly came to resemble opera.

Under succeeding prince-archbishops, music in Salzburg prospered; among composers active in the city were the Alsatian Georg Muffat (1678–90), the Bohemian H. I. F. von Biber (1670–1704) and the local composer Andreas Hofer (from 1653). All three composed dramatic music, which enjoyed new prominence, principally during the rule of Johann Ernst von Thun, for whose enthronement (1687) Muffat's opera *La fatale felicità di Plutone* was performed. Only the librettos of this and of Biber's *Alessandro in Pietra* (1689) have survived. The single surviving opera score from this period is that of Biber's *Chi la dura la vince*. Hofer, Muffat and particularly Biber also set to music a large number of Benedictine *Schuldramen*. At the beginning of the 18th century the most prolific composer of Benedictine drama was Matthias Sigismund Biechteler von Greiffenthal, in court service from 1688. Later, the Viennese deputy Hofkapellmeister Antonio Caldara came to Salzburg to compose operas and between 1716 and 1728 at least 16 of his operas and staged oratorios were performed there. His *dramma pastorale Dafne* probably opened the Heckentheater in the present Mirabellgarten in 1719.

The transition to the Rococo took place under J. E. Eberlin, who became court organist (1726) and Kapellmeister (1749); his compositions influenced a series of Salzburg court musicians, among them Leopold Mozart (court violinist from 1743 and deputy Hofkapellmeister from 1763), Michael Haydn (from 1763), A. C. Adlgasser (court organist from 1750) and Joseph Meissner (a court bass from 1747). W. A. Mozart was Konzertmeister (1769–77) and court organist (1779–81); his dramatic works given in Salzburg include the Latin intermezzo *Apollo et Hyacinthus* (1767, at the university), *La finta semplice* (1769), the serenata *Il sogno di Scipione* (written in 1771, probably performed on the inauguration of Archbishop Colloredo in 1772) and the *dramma per musica Il re pastore* (1775, these last three all at the archbishop's palace). In 1775, on the initiative of the archbishop but at the city's expense, the Ballhaus was converted into the prince-archbishops' Hoftheater, where for the most part travelling companies played, including those of Wahr, Schikaneder, Böhm and Weber. In 1803 the spiritual princedoms of Passau and Eichstädt had come under Salzburg's rule and their court musicians swelled the ranks of the musical establishment; the court was abolished in 1806.

In 1816 Salzburg changed from an episcopal seat to a provincial town, resulting in a stagnant cultural life. The former Hoftheater survived, as the Kaiserliche Königliche Nationaltheater, thanks to the public's love of the theatre. Singspiels by Weigl, Dittersdorf and Wenzel Müller and operas by Rossini, Cherubini, Mozart and Weber (*Der Freischütz*, 1825) offered a varied musical fare, but with the departure from Salzburg of Michael Haydn's most gifted pupils – Weber, Neukomm and Wölfl – the city and its theatre lost an important source of musical impulse. Alois Taux's directorship (from 1839) coincided with the theatre's heyday. The Dommusikverein und Mozarteum was founded in 1841, for 'the promotion of all branches of music, but especially church music', and in 1870 the Internationale Mozart-Stiftung was established, with a broad programme for encouraging musical activity. The Nationaltheater was replaced in 1893 by the larger Stadttheater (inaugurated with Mozart's *La clemenza di Tito*), which after extensive exterior alterations was renamed the Landestheater in 1938; operas and operettas are given there during the winter months. A much-loved local institution is the Marionetten-Theater, founded in 1913, which with its accomplished performances (mainly of Mozart) to recordings has toured abroad many times.

In the 20th century, however, it is chiefly for the

Stage of the Felsenreitschule, Salzburg, during a performance of the Jean-Pierre Ponnelle production of Mozart's 'La clemenza di Tito', 1976

annual summer festival, held from the end of July to the end of August, that Salzburg is known (see §2). In 1967 Herbert von Karajan initiated an Easter Festival (Osterfestspiele), at which a new opera production is usually given; these have included the *Ring* (1967–70), *Fidelio* (1971), *Tristan und Isolde* (1972), *Die Meistersinger von Nürnberg* (1974), *La bohème* (1975, produced by Zeffirelli), *Lohengrin* (1976), *Il trovatore* (1977), *Don Carlos* (1979), *Parsifal* (1980), *Der fliegende Holländer* (1982), *Carmen* (1985), *Don Giovanni* (1987), *Tosca* (1988) and, after the death of Karajan, *Fidelio* (1990), directed by Peter Brenner and conducted by Kurt Masur. Georg Solti was appointed artistic director from 1992.

2. FESTIVAL. In some ways the Salzburg Festival is the premier European opera festival, with its emphasis on the central opera repertory, especially Mozart but also Strauss and Verdi in particular. The first important predecessor of the present-day festival was the 1877 music festival held by the Mozart-Stiftung. Subsequent festivals under Richter (1879; 1887, the centenary of *Don Giovanni*), Jahn (1891, the centenary of Mozart's death), Joseph Hellmesberger (1901), Mottl (1904), Strauss and Mahler (1906, including a performance of *Le nozze di Figaro* by the Vienna Hofoper personally subsidized by Emperor Franz Joseph), Nikisch, Schalk and Weingartner (1910) led to the idea of a regular festival. One was planned for summer 1914 but cancelled on the outbreak of war. In 1917 Friedrich Gehmacher and Heinrich Damisch founded the Salzburger Festspielhaus-Gemeinde in Vienna with a branch in Salzburg for the purpose of establishing an annual festival of drama and music with special emphasis on the works of Mozart; the first festival took place in 1920 with Reinhardt's production of Hofmannsthal's *Jedermann* in the cathedral square, a traditional festival event ever since. Reinhardt, Hofmannsthal, Franz Schalk, Richard Strauss and Alfred Roller set the high artistic standards of the festival. Operas were first given at the 1922 festival in the small Stadttheater: *Don Giovanni* and *Così fan tutte* conducted by Strauss and *Le nozze di Figaro* and *Die Entführung aus dem Serail* conducted by Schalk. There was no opera in 1923 and the festival was cancelled in 1924 because of the economic crisis. 1925 was an important year, with the opening of the Festspielhaus (the Winterreitschule, converted into a theatre in 1924 by Eduard Hütter) and the first radio broadcast of a festival event (*Don Giovanni*, 24 August). The Festspielhaus was rebuilt in 1926 by Clemens Holzmeister to seat 1200; it was first used for opera in 1927 (*Fidelio*) and was altered in 1937 and 1939. Open-air performances have been given in the Felsenreitschule since 1926; in the same year a contemporary opera, Strauss's *Ariadne auf Naxos*, was included for the first time.

The festivals reached a peak in the 1930s when Bruno Walter, Krauss, Toscanini, Furtwängler and Knappertsbusch were the leading conductors and Herbert Graf the director of many of the operas; during this period the festival's repertory expanded greatly. But many conductors left as a result of the Anschluss in 1938 (Walter, Toscanini, Kleiber, Busch and Klemperer); events were curtailed during World War II and the 1944 festival was curtailed. The festival, renamed the Salzburger Theater- und Musik-Sommer in 1943, resumed in 1945. A number of premières have been given at the festival, notably Gottfried von Einem's *Dantons Tod* (1947) and *Der Prozess* (1953), Strauss's *Die Liebe der Danae* (1952), Henze's *The Bassarids* (1966), Berio's *Un re in ascolto* (1984) and Penderecki's *Die schwarze Maske* (1986), and also productions of rediscovered early Baroque operas such as Cavalieri's *Rappresentatione di Anima, et di Corpo* (1968).

The three principal halls used for festival events are on the site of the former court stables: the Felsenreitschule, where the stage is set against the rocks, radically altered in 1968–70 by Holzmeister (cap. 1568); the Kleines Festspielhaus (known as the Festspielhaus until 1960), redesigned in 1963 (cap. 1343) by Hans Hofmann and Erich Engels as a theatre intended principally for the performance of plays and small-scale operas; and the Grosses Festspielhaus (cap. 2371; *see* THEATRE ARCHITECTURE, fig.9), designed by Holzmeister, retaining the original façade of the stables, which opened in 1960 with *Der Rosenkavalier* conducted by Karajan. Opera performances are also sometimes given in the Residenz courtyard and the Landestheater. The Vienna PO has long been the musical backbone of the festival, playing for concerts as well as the opera. Furtwängler, Karajan (artistic director of the festival, 1956–60) and Böhm dominated the postwar era. In 1964 Karajan rejoined the directorate; in August 1989 Gerard Mortier was announced to succeed him, taking up the director's post officially in 1992.

*

R. von Freisauff: *Zur 100jährigen Jubelfeier des kaiserlich-königlichen Theaters in Salzburg* (Salzburg, 1875)

H. F. Wagner: 'Theaterwesen in Salzburg', *Mitteilungen der Gesellschaft für Salzburger Landeskunde*, xxxiii (1893), 247–329

K. O. Wagner: 'Das Salzburger Hoftheater 1775–1805', *Mitteilungen der Gesellschaft für Salzburger Landeskunde*, l (1910), 285–328

A. Kutscher: *Das Salzburger Barocktheater* (Vienna, 1924)

H. von Hofmannsthal: *Festspiele in Salzburg* (Vienna, 1938, 3/1952)

A. Kutscher: *Vom Salzburger Barocktheater zu den Salzburger Festspielen* (Düsseldorf, 1939)

L. Schmidt: 'Die Stoffe der Salzburger Schuldramatik', *Mitteilungen der Gesellschaft für Salzburger Landeskunde*, lxxix (1939), 133–42

F. Martin: 'Das erste Salzburger Musikfest', *Mitteilungen der Gesellschaft für Salzburger Landeskunde*, lxxxii–lxxxiii (1942–3), 89–94

R. Tenschert: *Salzburg und seine Festspiele* (Vienna, 1947)

H. C. Fischer: *Die Idee der Salzburger Festspiele und ihre Verwirklichung* (diss., U. of Munich, 1954)

F. J. Fischer: 'Das Salzburger Theater vom Barock zum Rokoko', *Mitteilungen der Gesellschaft für Salzburger Landeskunde*, xcv (1955), 141–88

——: 'Englische Komödianten in Salzburg', *Mitteilungen der Gesellschaft für Salzburger Landeskunde*, xcix (1959), 159–67

——: 'Wandertruppen des 17. Jahrhunderts in Salzburg', *Mitteilungen der Gesellschaft für Salzburger Landeskunde*, c (1960), 431–70

F. Hadamowsky and G. Rech, eds.: *Die Salzburger Festspiele, ihre Vorgeschichte und Entwicklung, 1842–1960* (Salzburg, 1960)

L. Welti: 'Die Prechtin, die erste deutsche Opernsängerin', *Theater in Österreich* (Vienna, 1965), 69–72

J. Kaut: *Festspiele in Salzburg: eine Dokumentation* (Salzburg, 1969)

M. Kaindl-Hönig: *Resonanz: 50 Jahre Kritik der Salzburger Festspiele* (Salzburg, 1971)

S. Dahms: *Das Musiktheater des Salzburger Hochbarocks*, i: *Das Benediktinerdrama* (diss., U. of Salzburg, 1974)

E. Hintermaier: 'Das Fürsterzbischöfliche Hoftheater zu Salzburg (1775–1803)', *ÖMz*, xxx (1975), 351–63

S. Dahms: 'Das musikalische Repertoire des Salzburger Fürsterzbischöflichen Hoftheaters (1775–1803)', *ÖMz*, xxxi (1976), 340–55

H. Boberski: *Das Theater der Benediktiner an der alten Universität Salzburg (1617–1778)* (Vienna, 1978)

J. Kaut: *Die Salzburger Festspiele 1920–1981, mit einem Verzeichnis der Werke und der Künstler, zusammengestellt von H. Jaklitsch* (Salzburg, 1982)

W. Kirkendale: 'Zur Biographie des ersten Orfeo, Francesco Rasi', *Claudio Monteverdi: Festschrift Reinhold Hammerstein zum 70. Geburtstag* (Laaber, 1986), 297–335

S. Gallup: *A History of the Salzburg Festival* (London, 1987)

J. Senigl: *Johann Michael Haydns Beiträge zum Salzburger Theaterleben* (diss., U. of Salzburg, 1987)

H. Seifert: 'Beiträge zur Frage nach den Komponisten der ersten Opern ausserhalb Italiens', *Musicologica austriaca*, viii (1988), 7–26

E. Fuhrich and G. Prossnitz: *Die Salzburger Festspiele: ihre Geschichte in Daten, Zeitzeugnissen und Bildern*, i: *1920–45* (Salzburg, 1990)

GERHARD CROLL

Salzman, Eric (*b* New York, 8 Sept 1933). American composer and festival director. His composition teachers included Babbitt, Sessions, Petrassi, Stockhausen and Nono. Salzman's activities have included writing, teaching and record producing. He has been music director of WBAI-FM in New York and editor of *The Musical Quarterly*, and has translated operas (*Pelléas et Mélisande* and *Salome*) and adapted operettas (*La fille de Mme Angot* and *Strike up the Band*). His book *Making Changes* (with Michael Sahl) constitutes an important presentation of the principles and development of the harmony of popular music.

Salzman has contributed to opera both as a composer and as a leader in the music-theatre movement in the USA. His interest in mixed media and the possibilities of music theatre as a vehicle for the expression of social and artistic concerns led to a series of works in this genre, beginning with *Foxes and Hedgehogs* (1967). They have included creations for electronic media; *Lazarus*, a 12th-century Latin drama, with its original music followed immediately by Salzman's modern analogue; and experimental presentations partly composed and partly improvised. Many were produced in association, and sometimes in collaboration (*Saying Something* and *Biograffiti*), with QUOG Music Theatre, which Salzman founded in 1970; five were written in collaboration with Michael Sahl (*The Conjurer*, *Stauf*, *Civilization and its Discontents*, *Noah* and *The Passion of Simple Simon*; Salzman also collaborated with Sahl on the book for Sahl's radio opera *Boxes*). They are musically and dramatically diverse. A characteristic component is a pop-derived style (also evident in the choice of instruments and the vocal writing) used with considerable sophistication, with the aim of reaching audiences in a more direct way than through the opera house or the commercial musical.

As co-founder (with Marjorie Samoff) and artistic director of the American Music Theater Festival in Philadelphia, Salzman presided over 25 presentations between 1983 and 1989, including 16 world premières and two American premières, of which 14 have subsequently been produced elsewhere. The works involved include operas, music theatre, historical reconstructions and mixed-genre pieces. This annual festival has developed into one of the most important American venues for new or rediscovered work for the musical stage, regardless of genre.

first performed in New York unless otherwise stated

Foxes and Hedgehogs (verses and cantos, J. Ashbery), Hunter College Playhouse, 30 Nov 1967

The Nude Paper Sermon (tropes, Ashbery and S. Wade), recorded 1969; stage, Hunter College Playhouse, 20 March 1969

Ecolog (music-theatre piece), WNET-TV, 1971

Saying Something (compilation workshop perfs., The Kitchen), 1972, collab. QUOG Music Theatre Ensemble

Biograffiti (collective music-theatre work, 1, Salzman and M. Sahl), workshop perfs., Space for Innovative Development, 1973; final version, Washington Square Methodist Church, 14 Dec 1974; collab. QUOG Music Theatre Ensemble

Lazarus (music drama, Salzman and Master of Fleury), workshop perfs., Washington Square Methodist Church, 1973; final version, LaMama, 24 April 1975

The Conjurer (pop op, 2, Salzman and Sahl), Public, 1 June 1975, collab. M. Sahl

Stauf, an American Faust (moral entertainment, 2, Salzman and Sahl), Cubiculo, 25 May 1976, collab. Sahl; rev. version, workshop perf., Philadelphia, Prince, 1 Oct 1986; final version, Philadelphia, Play and Players, 20 Sept 1987

Civilization and its Discontents (music-theatre comedy, 1, Salzman and Sahl), American Musical and Dramatic Academy, 19 May 1977; rev. as radio op, NPR, 1980, vs (New York, 1985); collab. Sahl

Noah (musical pageant, 2, Salzman and Sahl), Brooklyn, Pratt Institute, 10 Feb 1978, collab. Sahl

The Passion of Simple Simon (theatre op, 3, Salzman and Sahl),

Theatre for the New City, 1 Feb 1979; rev. as radio op, NPR, 1980; collab. Sahl
Big Jim and the Small-Time Investors, 1984–5 (music-theatre piece, N. Jackson)

*

EwenD
E. Salzman and M. Sahl: *Making Changes: a Practical Guide to Vernacular Harmony* (New York, 1977)
E. Salzman: 'Whither American Music Theater?', *MQ*, lxv (1979), 230–44
L. Valdes: 'A Nuclear-age Version of Faust Opens Tonight', *Philadelphia Inquirer* (18 Sept 1987)
M. Swed: 'A Festival without Boundaries', *New York Times* (2 April 1989)
R. H. Kornick: *Recent American Opera: a Production Guide* (New York, 1991), 261–8 JON ALAN CONRAD

Samara. City on the Volga, in Tatarstan. Between 1935 and 1991 it was known as Kuybïshev (Kuibyshev). An opera company organized in 1919 in the Olympic Theatre and appearances by touring companies preceded the founding of the Srednevolzhskaya Krayevaya Opera (Central Volga Regional Opera), which opened on 1 July 1931 with a performance of *Boris Godunov*. After the city was renamed in 1935, the company became Kuybïshevskiy Teatr Operï i Baleta (the Kuybïshev Opera and Ballet Theatre) in 1936, and performed at the local Philharmonic and in numerous theatres until it moved to the Kuybïshevskiy Dvorets Kul'turï (Kuybïshev Palace of Culture) in October 1938. It was reorganized in 1941 as the Teatr Operï, Operettï i Muzïkal'noy Komedii. The company and the city played host to the evacuated troupe from the Moscow Bol'shoy Theatre (1941–5); reorganization in 1948 restored to the theatre its 1936 name. Premières have included Shebalin's *Ukroshcheniye stroptivoy* ('The Taming of the Shrew', 1957), and works by Knipper and Slonimsky.

*

ME ('Kuybïshevskiy teatr operï i baleta'; V. A. Rabikin)
N. P. Sadkovoy: *20-letiye Kuybïshevskogo gosudarstvennogo teatra operï i baleta* [20 years of the Kuybïshev State Theatre of Opera and Ballet] (Kuybïshev, 1952)
E. Varvatsi: 'Zametki o Kuybïshevskom muzïkal'nom teatre' [Notes about Kuybïshev Musical Theatre], *SovM* (1956), no.4, pp.155–7
Muzïkal'naya kul'tura Sovetskoy Tatarii (Moscow, 1959)
G. Bernandt: *Slovar' oper vperviye postavlennïkh ili izdannïkh v dorevolyutsionnoy Rossii i v SSSR 1736–1959* [Dictionary of Operas First Performed or Published in Pre-revolutionary Russian and in the USSR 1736–1959] (Moscow, 1962), 538
Yu. V. Keldïsh, ed.: *Istoriya muzïki narodov SSSR* [History of the Music of the Soviet Peoples], i–v (Moscow, 1970–74)
G. Kantor: 'Rol' russkogo teatra v formirovanii tatarskoy operÿ' [The Role of the Russian Theatre in the Development of Tatar Opera], *Muzïka i muzïkantï bratskikh narodov Sovetskovgo Soyuza* [The Music and Musicians of the Fraternal Nations of the USSR] (Leningrad, 1972)
V. I. Zhdanova and L. E. Gol'dshteyn: *Kuybïshevskiy opernïy* (Kuybïshev, 1981)
M. Manuilov: 'Putyami neprotoryonnïmi' [Along Unexplored Paths], *SovM* (1982), no.2, pp.36–41
Samara/Kuybïshev: khronika sobïtiy 1586–1986 [Samara/Kuybïshev: a Chronicle of Events 1586–1986] (Kuybïshev, 1985)
S. I. Raymova: *Istoriya tatarskoy muzïki* (Kazan, 1986)
GREGORY SALMON

Samaras [Samara], **Spyridon** [Spyros] **(Filiskos)** (*b* Corfu, 29 Nov 1861; *d* Athens, 25 March 1917). Greek composer. He studied in Corfu with Spyridon Xyndas (perhaps his natural father), at the Athens Conservatory (probably 1873–82) with Friderikos Voloninis senior, Angelo Mascheroni and Enrico Stancapiano, and at the Paris Conservatoire (from 1882), where he was highly praised by his teachers Delibes and Massenet. Despite early success in Paris, in 1885 he shifted his activities to Italy. 1886 saw the première of his *Flora mirabilis* in Milan and in 1888 *Medgé* was impressively staged at the Teatro Costanzi, Rome, with Calvé in the title role. Samaras was closely associated with the Milanese publisher Edoardo Sonzogno whose Teatro Lirico Internazionale opened on 22 September 1894 with Samaras's *La martire*. Carefully handling his career abroad – his operas were staged also in Paris, Monte Carlo, Cologne, Vienna, Bucharest, Constantinople (now Istanbul), Smyrna (now Izmir), Alexandria and Cairo – Samaras never severed his links with Greece, where he was idolized by the press. He returned there in 1911, later earning his living by composing operettas to librettos that served national propaganda.

Samaras has been described as a pioneer of *verismo*, but analysis of his extant works reveals generally a general adherence to number-style forms, though with an early penchant for continuously flowing music. He later adopted techniques of leitmotif and 'unending melody', incorporated into a structure of separate sections (as in *Rhea*, of which the intermezzo represents one of his greatest melodic achievements). His melodic gifts were complemented by 'inventive' rather than chromatic harmonies, and the overall delicacy of his orchestration could still encompass a highly dramatic, full-blooded tutti of Mediterranean sensuousness.

A composer of the later Ionian school, Samaras in some respects can be seen as an important herald of the Puccinian style. He and Puccini unquestionably knew each other and shared librettists; even from *Flora mirabilis* (1886), of which the subject foreshadows *Turandot* (1926), Samaras seems often to have paved the way for Puccini. *La martire* (composed 1893) anticipates *La bohème*, *Tosca* and *Madama Butterfly* not only in the vocal writing and melodic design but also in the contrasting tempos and rhythmical figures, connected with changes of mood and atmosphere. Dramatically, *La martire* is effectively constructed, offering psychological insight in the portrayal of the two couples and their respective lovers, depicting for both an escape from harsh social reality. Its second act may have served as a model for Act 2 of Puccini's *La bohème*.

Olas [Olao; Olaf] (4, A. Fravassilis), ?inc., lost, collab. E. Stancapiano
Flora mirabilis (3, F. Fontana), Milan, Carcano, 16 May 1886, vs (Milan, n.d.); reorchd version, Athens, Olympia, 29 April 1979
Medgé (4, P. Elzéar), Rome, Costanzi, 11 Dec 1888, vs (Milan, 1888)
Lionella (3, Fontana), Milan, Scala, 4 April 1891, lost
La martire (novella scenica, 3, L. Illica), Naples, Mercadante, 23 May 1894, vs (Milan, 1894)
La furia domata (3, E. A. Butti and G. Macchi, after W. Shakespeare: *The Taming of the Shrew*), Milan, Lirico Internazionale, 19 Nov 1895, lost
Storia d'amore (commedia lirica, 3, P. Milliet), Milan, Lirico Internazionale, 17 Nov 1903, vs (Milan, 1903); rev. as La biondinetta (3), Gotha, Ducal, 1 April 1906, vs (Leipzig, 1905)
Mademoiselle de Belle-Isle (4, Milliet, after A. Dumas *père*), Genoa, Politeama Genovese, 9 Nov 1905, vs (Milan, 1905)
Rhea (3, Milliet), Florence, Verdi, 11 April 1908 (Milan, 1908)
Pólemos en polémo [War in War] (operetta, 3, G. Tsokopoulos and I. Delikaterinis), Athens, Municipal, 10 April 1914
I pringípissa tis Sassónos [The Princess of Sasson] (operetta, 3, N. I. Laskaris and P. Dimitrakopoulos), Athens, Municipal, 21 Jan 1915
I Kritikopoúla [The Cretan Girl] (operetta, 3, Laskaris and Dimitrakopoulos), Athens, Municipal, 30 March 1916
La Tigre (3, R. Simoni)

*

K. F. Skokos: 'O Ellin moussourgós Spyrídon Samáras, skiagrafía'

[The Greek Composer Spyridon Samaras, a Biographical Sketch], *Etíssion Imerologion ... 1887* (Athens, 1887), 154–60
M. Kyriakidis: 'Agnosta érga tou Sp. Samára' [Unknown Works of Sp. Samaras], *Eléftheron Vima* (3 Feb 1938)
A. Hadjiapostolou: *Istoría tou Ellinikou Melodrámatos* [History of the Hellenic Opera Company] (Athens, 1949)
S. G. Motsenigos: *Neoellinikí moussikí, symvolí is tin istorían tis* [Modern Greek Music: a Contribution to its History] (Athens, 1958), 233–7
M. Vassilákis: 'Mía megáli morfí tis Neoell. Moussikís: Spýros Samáras' [A Great Figure of Modern Greek Music: Spyros Samaras], *Istoría ikonografiméni*, xxxvi (1971), 57–63
V. Fidetzis: 'Chroniko' [Chronicle], *Rhea* (YP 1–3, 1985) [record notes]
G. Leotsakos: 'Spyrídon-Filiskos Samáras (1861–1917): Viografiká (Protássis ya parapéra érevna)' [Biographical Data (Proposals for Further Research)]; '"Rhea" ke Samáras' ["Rhea" and Samaras], *Rhea* (YP 1–3, 1985) [record notes, with list of works]
——: 'Samáras, Spyrídon-Filískos', *Pangósmio Viografikó Lexikó*, ixa (1988), 171–2
GEORGE LEOTSAKOS

Samarkand. City in Uzbekistan, 300 km south-west of TASHKENT. The Uzbekskiy Muzïkal'nïy Teatr (Uzbek Musical Theatre) was founded there in 1929, the Samarkandskiy Teatr Operï i Baleta (Samarkand Opera and Ballet Theatre) in 1964.

Sammarco, (Giuseppe) Mario (*b* Palermo, 13 Dec 1868; *d* Milan, 24 Jan 1930). Italian baritone. He made his début in 1888 at Palermo as Valentin. In 1894 he appeared in Naples at the S Carlo in *La damnation de Faust* and in 1895 at the Teatro Real, Madrid, as Thomas' Hamlet, a role he repeated in 1895–6 at La Scala, where he created Gérard in *Andrea Chénier*, returning there in 1902, 1905 and 1913, and singing at Buenos Aires in 1897. His Covent Garden début was in 1904 as Scarpia; he continued to appear in London until 1914, and again in 1919. He sang at the Manhattan Opera, New York (1907–10), and at Boston, Philadelphia and Chicago (1909–13). He retired from the stage in 1919. Sammarco's voice was clear but resonant, rounded and of extensive range. A stylish singer, he at first specialized in operas such as *La favorite*, *Ernani*, *Rigoletto*, *Un ballo in maschera*, *Hamlet* and *La Gioconda*, but his theatrical ability later led him to prefer *verismo* roles, particularly Tonio, Gérard, Scarpia, Wolf-Ferrari's Rafaele, and the parts he created in Leoncavallo's *Zazà* (1900) and Franchetti's *Germania* (1902).

*

GV (R. Celletti; T. Kaufmann)
J. Freestone: 'Giuseppe Maria [*sic*] Sammarco', *The Gramophone*, xxix (1951), 96 [with discography]
G. Lauri-Volpi: *Voci parallele* (Milan, 1955), 171–2
RODOLFO CELLETTI

Sammartini [St Martini, San Martini, San Martino, Martini, Martino], **Giovanni Battista** (*b* 1700/01; *d* Milan, 15 Jan 1775). Italian composer, brother of Giuseppe Sammartini (1695–1750); he was a leading figure in the development of the Classical style. He had a long connection with the Regio Ducal Teatro (precursor of La Scala) in Milan, beginning in 1720, when he and his brother were oboists in the orchestra, and lasting until 1773, when he supplied the theatre with the ballet *Il trionfo d'Amore* (now lost). Sammartini is thought to have written only three operas; he was better known as a symphonist and was prolific in the production of chamber music and church works. His pupils included Gluck, as well as a number of local composers. Boccherini played under his direction; the Mozarts, father and son, J. C. Bach and Padre Martini were his associates. In 1768 he became *maestro di cappella* to the ducal court.

In style, Sammartini's first opera, *Memet*, is more Baroque than early Classical. The music is marked by a powerful and urgent rhythmic drive; melodically it is indebted to Vivaldi and the earlier Venetian school. As in all his operas, arias are mainly in *da capo* form; accompanied recitative is reserved for dramatic situations. The work is scored for strings, with two trumpets added for colour in warlike arias and in the last-act finale. Contrast is achieved through carefully calculated diversity of tempo. His special gift is in capturing the emotional quality of dramatic situations, typified by Demetrius's 'Venite o furie' and Irene's 'Misero amante core' in Act 2. *L'ambitione superata dalla virtù*– of which the overture, the choruses of Acts 1 and 3, two arias and all the recitatives are missing – represents a departure in style: rhythmic patterns are more complex and of a *galant* nature, the vocal lines contain larger and more numerous leaps, the string texture is richer and the orchestra includes oboes and horns (used however in only two arias).

L'Agrippina shows the same mature and individual style as Sammartini's middle period symphonies. The rhythmic patterns are richer and more varied, the melodic lines are more fluent and dictate the harmonies, and the germ-cell technique of Sammartini's instrumental music is fully apparent. The instrumentation is even richer, with more extensive use of the brass (sometimes for harmonic support), though oboes are still indicated only in the opening chorus. In the manuscript the arias are all in Sammartini's hand but the recitatives are in a copyist's; the overture is missing.

Sammartini wrote a number of other dramatic works: *La gara dei geni* (one aria in *F-Pn*), a *componimento drammatico*, given at the Regio Ducal Teatro in 1747, a pair of cantatas that may have been staged at the Collegio Longone (*Paride riconosciuto*, 1750, and *Iride*, 1772; both lost), and two more written in collaboration with Jommelli in 1753, *La reggia de' fati* (two arias in *F-Pn*) and *La pastorale offerta* (one aria in *F-Pn*), of which the former was given in costume in Bologna in 1753.

Memet (tragedia, 3), Lodi, 1732, *A-HE*
L'ambitione superata dalla virtù (drama, 3), Milan, Regio Ducal, 26 Dec 1734, *B-Bc*
L'Agrippina, moglie di Tiberio (dramma per musica, 3, G. Riviera), Milan, Regio Ducal, Jan 1743, *F-Pn*

*

G. de Saint-Foix: 'Sammartini et les chanteurs de son temps', *RMI*, xliii (1939), 357–63
N. Jenkins and B. Churgin: *Thematic Catalogue of the Works of Giovanni Battista Sammartini: Orchestral and Vocal Music* (Cambridge, MA, 1976)
N. Jenkins: 'The Vocal Music of Giovanni Battista Sammartini', *Chigiana*, xxiv (1977), 277–309
M. McClymonds: *Niccolo Jommelli: the Last Years, 1769–1774* (Ann Arbor, 1980), 5
NEWELL JENKINS

Samori. *Heroisch-komische Oper* in two acts by GEORG JOSEPH VOGLER to a libretto by FRANZ XAVER HUBER; Vienna, Theater an der Wien, 17 May 1804.

Samori involves a young Indian prince, Pando (tenor), who returns from exile with his sister, Naga (soprano), to claim the throne now occupied by the benevolent despot Tamburan (bass). The action revolves around the competition of Pando and Tamburan for political control; they are also rivals for the hand of the beautiful Maha (soprano). In the end Tamburan falls in love with

Naga and relinquishes his power. A rich harmonic vocabulary and colourful orchestration give *Samori* an up-to-date Romantic flavour; Vogler's sudden shifts between the major and minor modes foreshadow Schubert's. Throughout the opera he establishes a polarity between D major and B♭ major (and other keys closely related to these) to depict contrasting sentiments.

PAUL CORNEILSON

Samosud, Samuil Abramovich (*b* Tbilisi, 2/14 May 1884; *d* Moscow, 6 Nov 1964). Georgian conductor. After studying at the Tbilisi Conservatory he conducted at the Mariinsky Theatre, Petrograd from 1917 to 1919. He was artistic director of the Malïy Theatre, Leningrad (1918–36), and of the Bol'shoy Theatre (1936–43), and the Stanislavsky–Nemirovich-Danchenko Music Theatre in Moscow (1943–50). As artistic director at the Malïy and Bol'shoy theatres, his broad artistic perspective, creative initiative and inventiveness, his organizational ability and purposeful determination were given free rein. He championed many new operas by Soviet composers, confirming the Malïy as the 'laboratory of Soviet opera'. Samosud was responsible for the premières there of Shostakovich's *The Nose* (1930), Dzerzhinsky's *Quiet Flows the Don* (1935), and the first eight scenes of Prokofiev's *War and Peace* (1946). At the Bol'shoy Theatre in 1937 he conducted the première of Dzerzhinsky's *Podnyataya tselina* ('Virgin Soil Upturned'), and at the Stanislavsky–Nemirovich-Danchenko Music Theatre gave the original (1947) version of Kabalevsky's *Sem'ya Tarasa* ('The Taras Family'), conducting the local première of the second (1950) version at the same theatre in 1951.

I. M. YAMPOL'SKY

Samponi, Gioseffo. *See* ZAMPONI, GIOSEFFO.

Samson et Dalila ('Samson and Delilah'). *Opéra* in three acts and four tableaux by CAMILLE SAINT-SAËNS to a libretto by FERDINAND LEMAIRE; Weimar, Grossherzogliches Theater, 2 December 1877.

Samson	tenor
Abimélech [Abimelech] *satrap of Gaza*	bass
The High Priest of Dagon	baritone
First Philistine	tenor
Second Philistine	bass
A Philistine Messenger	tenor
Dalila [Delilah]	mezzo-soprano
An Old Hebrew	bass

Hebrews, Philistines

Setting Gaza in biblical times

In 1867, two years after composing his first opera, *Le timbre d'argent*, and with no clear prospect of seeing it staged, Saint-Saëns embarked on an oratorio on the biblical story of Samson and Delilah. The subject was suggested by Voltaire's libretto *Samson* for Rameau. He admired Handel and Mendelssohn and was an enthusiastic supporter of the newly flourishing French choral movement. Saint-Saëns later wrote:

> A young relative of mine had married a charming young man who wrote verse on the side. I realized that he was gifted and had in fact a real talent. I asked him to work with me on an oratorio on a biblical subject. 'An oratorio!', he said, 'no, let's make it an opera!', and he began to dig through the Bible while I outlined the plan of the work, even sketching scenes, and leaving him only the versification to do. For some reason I began the music with Act 2, and I played it at home to a select audience who could make nothing of it at all.

Despite many precedents, most people expressed alarm at a biblical subject on the stage. After one more hearing of Act 2 Saint-Saëns abandoned his opera. Only after the appearance in 1872 of his third opera, *La princesse jaune*, did he feel sufficiently encouraged to resume *Samson et Dalila*. Act 1 was given a concert performance in Paris in 1875, but it aroused little interest and was severely treated by the critics. The score was finished in 1876, and although no French theatre showed any interest the opera was taken up enthusiastically by Liszt and mounted in Weimar in 1877 with Ferenczy as Samson and von Müller as Delilah; Eduard Lassen conducted.

There was still a long gap before the opera was heard in Paris. A second production in German took place in Hamburg in 1882, and it finally reached France in 1890 when it was given first in Rouen, then soon after in Bordeaux, Geneva, Toulouse, Nantes, Dijon, Montpellier and Monte Carlo, finally reaching the stage of the Paris Opéra in 1892. None of Saint-Saëns' later operas suffered the tribulations endured by *Samson et Dalila*, but none ever enjoyed the same enduring success. It has remained regularly in the repertory ever since and has been a vehicle for such singers as Caruso, Vinay, Vickers and Chauvet in the role of Samson, and Kirkby Lunn, Claussen, Gorr, Bumbry and Obraztsova in the role of Delilah.

ACT 1 *Gaza city square with the temple of Dagon to the left, at night* While the rest of the Hebrews are bewailing their fate, Samson alone has faith in God's promise of liberty. This first scene gives the clearest signs of the work's origins as an oratorio, with a fine sombre opening for the chorus leading to a fugue on the words 'Nous avons vu nos cités renversées'. Samson steps forward and sings rousingly against a constant choral prayer. The entry of Abimelech, the Philistine satrap, is marked by gross instrumentation (two ophicleides) which Bernard Shaw deplored as too Meyerbeerian, 'with his brusque measures and his grim orchestral clinkings and whistlings'. Abimelech mocks the Hebrews' God, proclaiming the superiority of Dagon, and the Hebrews cower in terror. But Samson's fervour, supported by the sound of the harp, arouses them to defy Abimelech, whereupon the latter attacks Samson with his sword. Samson seizes the sword and strikes him dead. The Hebrews scatter and the High Priest appears, cursing the Hebrews and their leader. When a messenger reports that the Hebrews are ravaging the harvest, the High Priest utters a curse that hints at his plan to use Delilah to overcome Samson's strength: 'Qu'enfin une compagne infâme trahisse son amour!'.

Dawn breaks. The Hebrews return offering a prayer to the Almighty, now in a humble unison, suggesting plainchant. Down the temple steps comes Delilah, supported by her women, who sing of the delights of spring in the delicate style of Gounod. She declares that Samson has conquered her heart and invites him to join her in her retreat in the valley of Sorek. Samson prays for protection from her charms, and an old Hebrew warns him of danger, forming an effective trio. The priestesses dance a voluptuous dance, with a tambourine to give exotic colour and some dark premonition at the end. Delilah sings her charming song

'Samson et Dalila' (Saint-Saëns): Samson (sung by Jean-Alexandre Talazac) bringing down the Temple of Dagon at the end of Act 3 of the first Paris production at the Eden-Théâtre, 31 October 1890: engraving from 'L'illustration' (8 November 1890)

'Printemps qui commence' and the old Hebrew repeats his warning. Samson wrestles with his desire to meet Delilah's glance, a desire to which she knows he will succumb.

ACT 2 *The Valley of Sorek* The introduction paints a musical picture of the luxuriant foliage that decks Delilah's retreat. She sits on a rock outside the entrance, rejoicing in her power over Samson and certain that he will fall for her malevolent enticement ('Amour! viens aider ma faiblesse!'). Distant lightning is seen. The High Priest arrives, to the accompaniment of his energetic motif in the bass. He reports that Samson and the Hebrews have defeated the Philistines. He offers her gold for Samson's capture, but she refuses it, being inspired purely by hatred and by loyalty to her gods. They sing an energetic duet of hatred, propelled by a strong symphonic accompaniment, and she promises to unlock the secret of Samson's strength.

Left alone, Delilah wonders if she can succeed, against a highly imaginative orchestral background. Samson soon appears. Distant lightning is still seen. He has come to say his last farewell, knowing that duty calls him to lead the Hebrews to victory. Inevitably he is drawn by Delilah's protestations of love to acknowledge that he loves her too. His admission 'Je t'aime!' introduces her main aria 'Mon coeur s'ouvre à ta voix', the best-known piece in the opera. At the end of the second verse Samson joins in to make it a duet. There follows a scene of tremendous power in which Delilah pretends to doubt his love and begs him to reveal the secret of his strength, but he refuses. The thunder seems to Samson to be God's wrath. She scorns him and runs into her dwelling. Samson hesitates, but soon follows her. At that moment some Philistine soldiers emerge from hiding. Delilah gives them the signal, and Samson cries out that he has been betrayed.

ACT 3.i *A prison in Gaza* Samson, blinded and bound, his hair shorn, turns a mill-wheel, graphically portrayed by the orchestra. Echoes of the Hebrews' lament from Act 1 are heard. Overcome with remorse, Samson offers his life in sacrifice, while the Hebrews are heard in the distance bewailing his fall.

3.ii *Inside the Temple of Dagon* Music covers the scene-change to the temple, where the Philistines are preparing a sacrifice to celebrate their triumph. At first they sing in the gentle tones of their song to spring from Act 1, but when the Bacchanale begins a more savage atmosphere develops. This well-known ballet sequence is a fine specimen of the kind of *divertissement* favoured by Meyerbeer and most French opera composers, with prominent augmented 2nds to suggest a Near-Eastern locale and much use of percussion to evoke the barbarism of the Philistines; there is a voluptuous episode also. After the dance Samson is led in, guided by a boy, to be mocked by the High Priest and the crowd, and also, to a trivialized variant of her love song, by Delilah, who reveals that she had sold his secret in advance and had pretended to love him out of hatred and a desire for vengeance. Samson is remorseful. Her treachery is now plain. The crowd's mockery is enhanced by more and more trivial music, with a tinkling triangle and bells, the Philistines' vacuous frivolity laid bare. Samson prays to recover his strength. The Philistines pour sacrificial libations in honour of Dagon. The High Priest tells the boy to lead Samson to the middle of the temple where all can see him; Samson whispers to the boy to guide him to the two marble pillars that support the building. As the festivities reach their climax Samson calls on God for vengeance, and with a supreme effort 'bows himself with all his might', bringing down the pillars and the whole temple upon the assembled Philistines and upon himself. The score allows little more than five seconds between Samson's mighty exertion and the descent of the curtain.

* * *

The libretto of *Samson et Dalila*, based on Chapter 16 of the *Book of Judges*, omits Samson's mighty deeds such as the slaughter of a lion and the slaying of one thousand Philistines with the jawbone of an ass which earned his fame and his leadership of the Hebrews. It concentrates instead on the story of Delilah, presenting Samson as an inspiring leader whose heart can be touched by love of a woman and Delilah as a scheming, merciless avenger. The death of Abimelech in Act 1 is an invention. Although the chorus are prominent at the beginning the Hebrews are not seen on stage again, and Saint-Saëns was right not to make an oratorio of this material.

His technique is unmistakably operatic, both in the skilful deployment of a large orchestra and in the application of motifs. At the time of *Samson et Dalila* Saint-Saëns still admired Wagner enormously, and the influence of *Der fliegende Holländer* and *Lohengrin* can be heard in the strong closing scene of Act 2. Echoes of Berlioz's *L'enfance du Christ* and *Les Troyens* are also to be heard, and the work treads paths marked out by

Meyerbeer and Gounod too. The French were wrong to believe that Saint-Saëns was an 'algébriste', since this score is far from the calculated contrivance that this implies. It is certainly his most imaginative opera score, and it reveals an instinct for theatrical emotion that any opera composer would be proud of. It allows us to savour some of the brilliance and intellectual vigour that even his enemies admired. HUGH MACDONALD

Samstag aus Licht ('Saturday from Light'). Opera in a greeting and four scenes by KARLHEINZ STOCKHAUSEN to his own libretto; Milan, Palazzo dello Sport (La Scala production), 25 May 1984.

Composed from 1981 to 1983, *Samstag* is planned as the penultimate opera in Stockhausen's seven-part cycle *LICHT*; it was the second to be completed. *Samstag* is 'Lucifer's Day' ('Saturnsday'), and Lucifer (bass) is the only solo vocalist in the opera (even so he is present only in the first and third scenes) whereas there are ten solo instrumentalists and two dancers. The theme of the opera is death, but death as illusion: as the necessary ritual act of purification preceding the attainment of Light on Sunday. The four scenes also expand gradually from small to large forces.

Whereas *Donnerstag's* 'Thursday Greeting' is performed in the foyer of the theatre, the 'Saturday Greeting' is performed at the four cardinal points of the auditorium itself, by performers dressed in 'Lucifer costumes' of black and blue-grey.

In Scene 1 ('Lucifer's Dream') Lucifer summons up a 'dream player', Majella, to perform a piano piece. The stage is 'bathed in misty grey' into which are projected five bands of colour, symbolizing the five temporal levels of the piano piece. From time to time, Lucifer soars across the stage on a hydraulic chair, and the podium on which the piano is placed also rises, falls and rotates. Lucifer invokes the elements of air, water, earth, fire and light; finally, against his will, he finds himself entranced by 'a simple melody', and sinks slowly into apparent death.

The setting for Scene 2 ('Kathinka's Chant as Lucifer's Requiem') is a cemetery dominated by a huge stylized grand piano, laid legless on its side: this is Lucifer's grave. Kathinka, a flute player in a black cat costume, performs a requiem for Lucifer which 'protects the soul of the deceased from temptation ... for 49 days after physical death, and by which it is guided to clear consciousness'. Placed around the auditorium are six percussionists representing the 'six mortal senses' – sight, hearing, smell, taste, touch and thinking; all kinds of small 'magical instruments' are built into their costumes. Kathinka leads the soul through a sequence of 22 spiritual exercises, inscribed on two huge mandala-boards. Then the 'six senses' are released, and exit, after which Kathinka, still playing, climbs into the grave. After a single, piercing scream, four figures in black stretch a 'Lucifer Flag' across the coffin.

Lucifer, however, is far from dead. At the start of Scene 3 ('Lucifer's Dance') he suddenly rises from his grave and strides through the auditorium as a towering figure portrayed by a stilt dancer. At the same time, on another side of the auditorium, 'Lucifer causes an orchestra to appear in the form of a giant human face' (for illustration *see* ORCHESTRA, fig.17): the orchestra is a symphonic wind band whose players are located at six different levels, representing eye-brows, eyes etc. There follows a sequence of dances, in many of which the parts of the face act against one another. Towards the end Michael, the main figure of *Donnerstag*, represented as a solo trumpeter, protests against this wilful distortion of the human face; but he is kicked away to seven tam-tam strokes, and the black cat from 'Kathinka's Chant' reappears to mock him further. There follows a débâcle not inappropriate to Italian opera houses – the orchestra goes on strike, and the scene ends in disarray.

For the final scene ('Lucifer's Farewell'), the audience moves to a church near the opera house. The scene is played out as a monastic ritual, with St Francis of Assisi's 'Hymn to the Virtues' as text. Everything is based on the number 13: there are 13 tenors and 2 × 13 basses, 13 sections, 13 verses, and after a sequence of 13 trombone chords the monks release a wild black bird and move outside the church. There, each of them ritually dashes a coconut against the stone slab in the courtyard, after which they move away in procession.

Clearly *Samstag* stretches conventional notions of opera to the limits: instead of opera as predominantly vocal drama, it presents a sequence of four ritual actions, in three of which the voice is entirely subservient to instrumental music. At the same time, even though most of the music can also be performed in what Stockhausen calls 'quasi concertante' versions, it would be inappropriate to regard *Samstag* merely as a sequence of concert pieces transplanted into the opera house. Each scene is, above all, theatre and serves to remind us of the extent to which, in many of the world's cultural traditions, religious ritual is also theatre (and often instrumental theatre, as in many Tibetan ceremonies). Stylistically, *Samstag* continues the path established in *Donnerstag*. However, it does mark Stockhausen's first substantial exploration of microtones, most notably in 'Kathinka's Chant'; this feature is pursued much further in *Montag*, the next opera to be composed.

For illustration *see* MILAN, fig.7. RICHARD TOOP

Samuel, Adolphe(-Abraham) (*b* Liège, 11 July 1824; *d* Ghent, 11 Sept 1898). Belgian composer. He first studied painting in Liège, then decided to specialize in music. In 1840 he went with his family to Brussels, where he studied at the conservatory with Fétis. He won the Prix de Rome with his cantata *Vendetta* and later continued his studies with Mendelssohn and Meyerbeer. In 1850 he became a professor at the Brussels Conservatory. He met Berlioz in London in 1853, and thereafter maintained a correspondence with him. He was active as a music critic, and was made director of the Ghent Conservatory in 1871. His seven symphonies clearly show the influence of Berlioz.

all first performed in Brussels

Il a rêvé (oc, 3), 1845
Giovanni da Procida (4), 1848 [in It.]
Madeleine (oc, 1, Vaez), Monnaie, 8 Dec 1849
Les deux prétendants (3), 1851
L'heure de la retraite (oc, 2), 1854 ANNE-MARIE RIESSAUW

Samuel, Léopold (*b* Saint-Gilles, Brussels, 5 May 1883; *d* Uccle, Brussels, 10 March 1975). Belgian composer. After studying at the Brussels Conservatory, he went to Berlin to complete his education. In 1911 he won the Belgian Prix de Rome. He was inspector of state musical education from 1920 to 1945, and was elected to the Belgian Royal Academy in 1958. His music is in the tradition of Franck, although there are sometimes impressionist details. He composed two operas, both in a Wagnerian style. The *drame lyrique Ilka* (3, P. Demeny) had its première at Antwerp on 25 October

1924. Samuel wrote his own libretto for *La sirène au pays des hommes*, a *légende dramatique* in five scenes based on Hans Christian Andersen's story; it was first performed at La Monnaie in Brussels on 30 March 1946.

*

R. Bernier: 'Notice sur Léopold Samuel', *Annuaire de l'Académie royale de Belgique*, cxlv (1979), 159–72 HENRI VANHULST

Samuel-Rousseau [Rousseau], **Marcel (Louis Auguste)** (*b* Paris, 18 Aug 1882; *d* Paris, 11 June 1955). French composer. He studied at the Paris Conservatoire, taking the Prix de Rome in 1905, and was later professor of harmony there; his other appointments include organist at St Sévérin (1919–22) and director of the Opéra (1941–4). His compositions, influenced by Franck and Fauré, include four operas, two ballets, orchestral and piano music and songs. While *Le roi Arthur* is set in Brittany, Samuel-Rousseau's later operas tend to the exotic. In *Tarass Boulba*, based on the legend of a cossack warrior, striking scenes in a cathedral employ plainsong as the background to dramatic action. *Le Hulla* and *Kerkeb* are oriental in setting; the latter takes place in a harem, its title role a Berber dancer.

Le roi Arthur (drame lyrique, 3, F. Beissier), concert perf., Paris, Conservatoire, 8 Nov 1903, vs (Paris, 1903)
Tarass Boulba (drame musical, 3, L. de Gramont, after N. V. Gogol), Paris, Vaudeville, 22 Nov 1919, vs (Paris, 1919)
Le Hulla, 1920 (conte lyrique oriental, 4, A. Rivoire), Paris, OC (Favart), 9 March 1923 (Paris, 1922)
Le bon roi Dagobert, 1924 (comédie musicale, 4, Rivoire), Paris, OC (Favart), 5 Dec 1927, vs (Paris, 1927)
Kerkeb, 1931 (drame musical, 1, M. Carré, after E. Rhaïs), Paris, Opéra, 6 April 1951

*

P. de Flem: 'G. Dupont, R. Laparra, F. Casadesus, Marcel Samuel-Rousseau', *Le théâtre lyrique en France* (Paris, 1937–9) [pubn of Poste National/Radio-Paris], ii, 119–30
P. Landormy: *La musique française après Debussy* (Paris, 1943)
P. Bertrand: *Le monde de la musique* (Geneva, 1947)
PAUL GRIFFITHS, RICHARD LANGHAM SMITH

S Angelo. Theatre in Venice, opened in 1677 and closed in 1803; *see* VENICE, §§3–6.

S Bartolomeo. Principal public theatre of Naples, built about 1620 and demolished in 1737; it was replaced by the Teatro S Carlo. *See* NAPLES, §1.

S Benedetto. Theatre in Venice, built by the Grimani in the early 1750s; burnt down and rebuilt in 1774, it was bought by G. Gallo in 1821, renamed after Rossini in 1868 and finally became a cinema. *See* VENICE, §§5–6 and 8.

S Carlo. Theatre in NAPLES, erected in 1737 by King Charles III of the Two Sicilies; it was enlarged in 1811 and restored after a fire in 1816, and continues as the city's main opera house.

San Carlo Opera Company. Name used first by an opera group organized by HENRY RUSSELL for tours in the USA in 1905, and then by a company founded by FORTUNE T. GALLO that toured North America from 1913 to 1951.

S Cassiano. Theatre in Venice opened in 1637, the first opera house opened to the public; it closed in 1804. *See* VENICE, §§2–6.

Sances [Sancies, Sanci, Sanes], **Giovanni Felice** (*b* Rome, *c*1600; *d* Vienna, bur. 12 Nov 1679). Italian composer and singer. He was the son of Orazio and brother of Lorenzo Sances, a singer. He was a boy soprano at the Collegio Germanico in Rome, under Catalani and Orgas, 1609–14, participating in 1614 as a 'virtuoso of Cardinal Montalto' in the opera *L'amor pudico* at the Palazzo della Cancelleria. In December 1618 he wrote from Padua to the rector of the Collegio Germanico stating that he had been travelling in the service of a patron (unnamed). In 1633 he dedicated two books of cantatas to Pio Enea degli Obizzi, who also employed him as composer of *Ermiona*, an 'introduction to a tournament', given at Padua, probably on 11 April 1636, to stage designs by Alfonso Rivarola, and with Sances singing the role of Cadmus. The company also included singers from Rome and Venice who in the following year were to participate in the first Venetian public opera. The suggestion that Sances worked for a time at S Petronio, Bologna, seems to be unfounded.

On 1 December 1636 he was appointed a singer in the chapel of the Emperor Ferdinand III in Vienna, where his many occasional works include the opera *I trionfi d'Amore*, written for the emperor's second marriage in 1648. On 1 October 1649 he was appointed assistant Kapellmeister at the imperial court and on 16 April 1669 succeeded Antonio Bertali as Kapellmeister, a position he held until his death in spite of severe illnesses. Throughout this period he continued to be very active as a composer, notably of operas and *sepolcri*.

Sances's career as a composer spans a crucial period in the development of Italian opera, both within and outside Italy. The songbooks he published in 1633 already reveal a composer of great talent, and one who was in the vanguard of musical style; they include variations on ostinato basses and songs which contrast recitative-like passages with suave triple-metre aria writing – the styles which characterize early Venetian opera. His opera *Aristomene Messenio*, composed at the end of his career, includes fully-fledged da capo arias. Sances's operas for the Austrian court stand slightly apart from the mainstream of Italian opera by virtue of their largely mythological subject matter and use of chorus; but all his later operas conform to the three-act model characteristic of mid-17th-century public opera.

For illustration *see* RIVAROLA, ALFONSO.

Ermiona (P. E. degli Obizzi), Padua, ? 11 April 1636, lib. *A-Wn* [introduction to a tournament]
I trionfi d'Amore, 1648 (dramma imperfetta, 5, licenza), lib. *Wn*, ?unperf. [for the second marriage of Emperor Ferdinand III]
La Roselmina fatta canara (3, A. Amalteo), Vienna, ? 20 Feb 1662, lib. *Wn*
Mercurio esploratore (Amalteo), Vienna, 21 Feb 1662, *Wn* [prol. and int for G. A. Cicognini: Mariana]
Apollo deluso (dramma, 3, licenza, A. Draghi), Vienna, 13 June 1669, *Wn*, collab. Leopold I
Aristomene Messenio (dramma, 3, licenza, N. Minato), Vienna, 22 Dec 1670, *Wn* [2 arias by Leopold I]

Sepolcri: Le lachrime di S Pietro (F. Sbarra), Vienna, 23 April 1666, *Wn*; La morte debellata (Draghi), Vienna, 19 April 1669, lib. *Gu*; Le sette consolationi di Maria vergine (Minato), Vienna, 4 April 1670, *Wn*; Il trionfo della croce (Minato), Vienna, 27 March 1671, *Wn*, collab. Leopold I; Il paradiso aperto per la morte di Christo (Minato), Vienna, 15 April 1672, *Wn*, collab. Leopold I; L'ingiustitia della sentenza di Pilato (Minato), Vienna, 3 April 1676, lib. *Wn*

*

AllacciD; *Grove6* (R. Schnitzler, J. Whenham)

L. von Köchel: *Die kaiserliche Hof-Musikkapelle in Wien von 1543 bis 1867* (Vienna, 1869)
P. Petrobelli: '"L'Ermiona" di Pio Enea degli Obizzi ed i primi spettacoli d'opera veneziani', *Quaderni della RaM*, iii (1965), 125–41
P. Webhofer: *Giovanni Felice Sances (ca. 1600–1679): biographisch-bibliographische Untersuchung und Studie über sein Motettenwerk* (Innsbruck, 1965)
E. Raschl: *Die weltlichen Vokalwerke des Giovanni Felice Sances* (diss., U. of Graz, 1968)
T. D. Culley: *Jesuits and Music*, i: *a Study of the Musicians Connected with the German College in Rome during the 17th Century and of their Activities in Northern Europe* (Rome, 1970)
H. Seifert: *Die Oper am Wiener Kaiserhof im 17. Jahrhundert* (Tutzing, 1985)
J. Chater: 'Musical Patronage in Rome at the Turn of the Seventeenth Century: the Case of Cardinal Montalto', *Studi musicali*, xvi (1987), 179–227
C. di Lucca: *Pio Enea II Obizzi e lo spettacolo nel '600* (diss., U. of Ferrara, 1989)

JOHN WHENHAM

Sánchez de Fuentes, Eduardo (*b* Havana, 3 April 1874; *d* Havana, 7 Sept 1944). Cuban composer. Trained as both a lawyer and a musician, he studied at the Hubert de Blanck Conservatory (1885) and later took lessons with the Cuban composer Ignacio Cervantes and others. In 1930 he became president of the National Academy of Arts and Letters.

At the age of 18 Sánchez de Feuntes won worldwide recognition for his first work, the habanera *Tú* ('You', 1892). Thereafter he wrote chiefly operas, operettas, orchestral works and songs, all infused with the idioms of Cuban music. His early operas show the influence of the *verismo* movement, but his last opera, *Kabelia* (1942), was influenced by Ravel; *Doreya* (1918) won first prize in a competition sponsored by the impresario Adolfo Bracale.

all first performed in Havana; MSS in CU-Hin

Yumuri (2, R. Fernández de Castro), Albisu, 26 Oct 1898
Il naufragio (2, Eugenio Sánchez de Fuentes, after A. Tennyson: *Enoch Arden*), It. version (S. Biaggi), Tacón, 11 Jan 1901
Dolorosa (prol., 2, F. Uhrbach), Nacional, 23 April 1910; It. version (G. Macchi), Turin, Balbo, 8 Aug 1911
Doreya (1, H. Cabrisas), Nacional, 7 Feb 1918
El caminante (1, F. Villaespesa), Nacional, 7 July 1921
Kabelia (prol., 2, Eduardo Sánchez de Fuentes, after Hindu legend), Nacional, 22 June 1942

*

J. Ardévol: *Introducción a Cuba: la música* (Havana, 1969)
A. Carpentier: *La música en Cuba* (Havana, 1979)
J. A. González: *La composición operística en Cuba* (Havana, 1987)

JORGE ANTONIO GONZÁLEZ

Sanchez Ferrer, Roberto (*b* Havana, 31 Dec 1927). Cuban composer. He attended the Alfred Levy Conservatory and studied composition with Felix Guerrero and Enrique Bellver. He served as director of the National Chamber Orchestra, and in 1961 he went to Paris as orchestral director of the Cuban Modern Dance Group. In 1962 he studied at the music conservatory in Leipzig, and after his return to Cuba he became director and conductor of the Cuban National Opera. His first opera, *Van Troy*, in three acts, to his own libretto after Phan Thi Quyen's book *Vivir como El*, was written in 1968 but has not been performed. *Ecue-Yamba-O*, again in three acts and to his own libretto, after Alejo Carpentier's tale, had its première at the Gran Teatro, Havana, on 25 December 1986.

*

J. A. González: *La composición operística en Cuba* (Havana, 1987)

JORGE ANTONIO GONZÁLEZ

Sancia di Castiglia ('Sancia of Castile'). *Tragedia lirica* in two acts by GAETANO DONIZETTI to a libretto by Pietro Salatino after an unidentified source; Naples, Teatro S Carlo, 4 November 1832.

The opera is set in the 10th century. A Moorish prince, Ircano (bass), hopes to gain the throne of Castile by disposing of the heir and marrying the widowed queen, Sancia (soprano); opposed to him is the courtier Rodrigo (tenor). When Sancia's son Garzia (mezzo-soprano) returns from the wars, he demands the throne. Ircano seeks to persuade Sancia to poison her own son; but when the cup is presented to Garzia she snatches it from him, drains it, and dies.

Sancia di Castiglia combines the tradition of *spagnuolismo*, popular at the Bourbon court in Naples, with the emphasis on pathos and suffering that was a Donizettian speciality. Although afflicted with an awkward libretto and using the already old-fashioned *musico* convention for the role of Garzia, the score contains an eloquent and elaborate aria-finale for Sancia, a role written for Ronzi de Begnis. WILLIAM ASHBROOK

Sancta Susanna ('Saint Susanna'). Opera in one act, op.21, by PAUL HINDEMITH to a libretto by August Stramm; Frankfurt, Opernhaus, 26 March 1922.

Stramm subtitled his expressionist drama 'Song of a May Night'. While omitting this, Hindemith reflected its implications in his impressionistic music. Susanna (soprano), a nun first seen in prayer before a crucifix, is overcome by the scents and sounds coming through the chapel window; then by the sight of a maid-servant and her lover (speaking roles); and finally by a warning tale told by Sister Clementia (contralto) of a former nun bricked up behind the altar for succumbing to her erotic desires. Reminded thus of her own sexuality, Susanna flings off her veils and snatches the loincloth from the crucifix, demanding from the assembled nuns to be similarly punished. The work caused a scandal in Frankfurt in 1922. GEOFFREY SKELTON

Sandberger, Adolf (*b* Würzburg, 19 Dec 1864; *d* Munich, 14 Jan 1943). German musicologist and composer. He studied in Würzburg, Munich and Berlin, his teachers including Rheinberger. After study trips abroad he became curator of the music department of the Bayerische Staatsbibliothek. He became reader in musicology at the University of Munich in 1900 and full professor in 1904, and came to exert broad influence through the work of his many famous pupils. Sandberger's primary areas of interest were 16th-century music and the Viennese Classicists, but he also published writings on 17th- and 19th-century opera, including a book on Chabrier's *Gwendoline* (1898). As a composer he tried with some success to emulate the styles of his contemporaries Cornelius (the subject of his dissertation, 1887), Reger and Strauss; among his works are the operas *Ludwig der Springer* op.12 (1894, Munich) and *Der Tod des Kaisers* op.23 (1935, Munich), both to his own librettos.

HORST LEUCHTMANN

Sanderson, Sibyl (*b* Sacramento, CA, 7 Dec 1865; *d* Paris, 15 May 1903). American soprano. She studied with Sbriglia and Mathilde Marchesi in Paris and made her début (under the name of Ada Palmer) as Massenet's Manon at The Hague in 1888. Massenet, impressed by her beauty and her voice with its range of three octaves, wrote the title roles in two operas for her: *Esclarmonde*, in which she made her Paris début at the Opéra-Comique in 1889; and *Thaïs*, in which she made her Opéra début in 1894. She appeared in Brussels (1890–01) and at Covent Garden (1891), where she sang Manon. She created the title role in Saint-Saëns' *Phryné* (1893, Opéra-Comique) and also sang Gounod's Juliet and Gilda. She sang in St Petersburg, Moscow and New York, making her Metropolitan début in 1895 as Manon. She did not have an outstandingly large or beautiful voice, but its phenomenal range compensated for any lack of size and warmth.

For illustration *see* THAÏS.

*

O. Thompson: *The American Singer* (New York, 1937), 313
J. Harding: *Massenet* (London, 1970) ELIZABETH FORBES

Sandi (Meneses), Luis (*b* Mexico City, 22 Feb 1905). Mexican composer. He studied the violin and composition at the Mexico City Conservatory and at 19 played in an opera company that toured Cuba. In 1932 he became sub-director of the National Institute of Fine Arts, with which he was closely associated for many years, becoming general director of opera in 1959. In 1938 he founded the Coro de Madrigalistas which for two decades was the foremost Mexican chorus. He retired from Mexican administrative posts in 1965 but continued to work as a writer and critic.

His unpublished one-act opera, *Carlota* ('Charlotte'; Mexico City, Palacio de Bellas Artes, 23 Oct 1948), to a libretto by the essayist and dramatist Francisco Zendejas Gómez, is set in the last days of the Mexican Second Empire. Two interlocutors serving as chorus – Patria [Native Land] and Destino [Destiny] – comment on the catastrophe awaiting Charlotte and her husband, Emperor Maximilian. Their recitations are relieved by period dances (waltz and mazurka), during which courtiers revel although on the brink of doom. Sandi's other one-act opera, *La señora en su balcón* (1964), remains unpublished and unperformed.

*

L. Herrera de la Fuente: 'La Opera de Bellas Artes', *México en el arte*, no.3 (1948), [70ff]
C. Chávez: 'La ópera como forma', *México en el arte*, no.4 (1948), [66, 72]
'Operas mexicanas', *México en el arte*, no.6 (1948), [92]
G. Carmona: 'En los ochenta años de Sandi', *Pauta*, iv/Oct–Dec (1985), 48–54 ROBERT STEVENSON

San Diego. American town, in California. Performances of Gilbert and Sullivan operettas were given by local amateurs in the 1870s and 80s. The San Diego Grand Opera Association, formed in 1919, drew on local talent to give over 40 performances of French and Italian operas during the next 13 years.

The professional San Diego Opera Company opened in 1964 with *La bohème*; it gave the first performances in the USA of *Der junge Lord* (1967) and Zandonai's *Giulietta e Romeo* (1982). Until the 1985–6 season English translations (usually those of Andrew Porter) were the rule. Walter Herbert, general director and conductor from 1969 until his death in 1975, established a split season (October–November, February–March) consisting of four performances each of four to six operas at the Civic Auditorium (3000 seats); he was succeeded as artistic director by Tito Capobianco, who was replaced by Ian D. Campbell after the 1983–4 season.

Notable productions under Capobianco included Thomas' *Hamlet* with Sherrill Milnes and Ashley Putnam (1978); the world première of Menotti's *La loca* with Beverly Sills (1979); Chabrier's *Gwendoline* (1982) and Saint-Saëns' *Henry VIII* (1983). Among the works given at the Summer Verdi Festivals held between 1978 and 1982 were *Giovanna d'Arco*, *Un giorno di regno* and *Il corsaro*; the festival expired through inadequate funding, with a final isolated production of *Oberto* in 1985. Campbell's reversion to a more conservative repertory, sung in original languages with surtitles, drew increased support from private organizations. Later notable productions included *Boris Godunov* (1989), *Dialogues des Carmélites* (1990), *Albert Herring* (1991) and Opera America's west coast première of Floyd's *The Passion of Jonathan Wade* (1991).

*

A. Porter: 'Thomas's Hamlet', *Opera*, xxxi (1980), 639–44
M. Bernheimer: 'Verdi Early and Late', *Opera* (1982), 115–18 [festival issue] ROBERT STEVENSON

Sandoni, Pietro Giuseppe (*b* Bologna, 1 Aug 1685; *d* Bologna, 16 Aug 1748). Italian composer and singing teacher. Trained by Angelo Predieri and Giovanni Bononcini in counterpoint and by Francesco Salardi on the harpsichord, he became the organist at S Giacomo in Bologna at the age of 13. Two years later he was elected to the Accademia Filarmonica; he composed oratorios and held various offices, including that of *principe* in 1713, 1714, 1739 and 1745. In 1709, he composed a *dramma per musica*, *Artaserse*, for production in Verona, and the libretto terms him a virtuoso of Prince Antonio of Parma.

He left Bologna about May 1715, and arrived in London before 26 May 1716; there he apparently worked mainly as a singing teacher, and probably contributed music to *Pyrrhus and Demetrius*, given at a benefit performance in 1716 for Diana Vico. The librettist Rolli, in letters of 1719 to Riva, gossiped about Sandoni's amorous relationships with his female students and on why he could not be proposed to the Court of Directors for the Royal Academy of Music. The singer Gaetano Berenstadt wrote to Francesco Pistocchi on 19 May 1724:

> Sandoni wants to give the impression of having taught her [Cuzzoni] ... When she has tried to follow his written passage work one smells the gigue and the sarabande ... Pretentions, clothes, pleasures, food, wines, bastards, debts, lovers are the delights of this poor fool, who claims to be the equal of Bononcini.

Sandoni's relationship with Francesca Cuzzoni before this date is uncertain; nevertheless, the two were married on 12 January 1725, and a daughter was born before 22 August 1725. Sandoni's main function may well have been to serve as Cuzzoni's 'basso continuo and treasurer', the role he is given in the scurrilous *Contre Temps; or, Rival Queans: A Small Farce* (1727).

After the Royal Academy of Music gave its last performance on 1 June 1728 and Cuzzoni had given birth to a son (*Daily Post*, 11 July 1728), the couple left for Vienna via Paris and Munich; although the faction against them was strong, they performed for the emperor. They then spent three years in Venice and one in Genoa, where Sandoni seems to have gathered rather than composed music for a version of *Olimpiade* in 1733; he did compose *Adriano in Siria* there in 1734. They returned to London in April 1734. There Sandoni composed *Issipile* (1735) for the Opera of the Nobility. He may have served as the arranger for three more Nobility operas: *Artaserse* (1734), *Onorio* (1736) and *Siroe* (1736). All three had been produced at S Giovanni Grisostomo in Venice in 1729–31, and Cuzzoni had sung in the first two. Sandoni may also have assembled the *Olimpiade* produced at Florence in June 1737 with Cuzzoni in the cast. His letters of 1738 to 1748 complain of ill-health; he is not known to have engaged in operatic activities during these years.

Sandoni is known for certain to have composed only three operas and to have arranged only one, and all but the earliest of them were undoubtedly commissioned because of his tie with Cuzzoni. Although she represented the 'old style' of singing (while Faustina Bordoni represented the new), Berenstadt placed him among the 'heroes of modern music' who opposed the old style of Bononcini. No music from his three operas is known to be extant, but pre-Classical traits abound in his only printed vocal works, his *Cantate da camera e sonate per il cembalo* (London, *c*1727/*R*1983). The vocal ornamentation that he taught may likewise have been the newest fashion, rather than the 'old style' of Tosi and Pistocchi.

Artaserse (dramma per musica, 3, A. Zeno ?and P. Pariati), Verona, Temperati, 1709
Adriano in Siria (dramma per musica, 3, P. Metastasio), Genoa, S Agostino, carn. 1734
Issipile (dramma per musica, 3, A. Cori, after Metastasio), London, King's, 8 April 1735

Pasticcio: Olimpiade (dramma per musica), Genoa, S Agostino, 1733

*

LS
Contre Temps; or, Rival Queans (London, 1727); repr. 1777 in C. Cibber: *The Dramatic Works*, iv, 371–81 [wrongly attrib.]
M. Delany: *The Autobiography and Correspondence*, ed. Lady Llanover, i (London, 1861), 117–18
G. Bertoni: 'Giuseppe Riva e l'opera italiana a Londra', *Giornale storico della letteratura italiana*, lxxxix (1927), 317–24
G. Gaspari and U. Sesini: *Catalogo della Biblioteca del liceo musicale di Bologna*, v: *Libretti d'opera in musica* (Bologna, 1943), 486–7
O. E. Deutsch: *Handel: a Documentary Biography* (London, 1955)
G. Martini [O. Penna]: *Catalogo degli aggregati della Accademia filarmonica di Bologna* (Bologna, 1973), no.357 [MS facs.]
L. Lindgren: 'La carriera di Gaetano Berenstadt, contralto evirato (*c*1690–1735)', *RIM*, xix (1984), 45, 66–7
W. Dean and J. M. Knapp: *Handel's Operas, 1704–1726* (Oxford, 1987) LOWELL LINDGREN

Sandri, Francesco (*fl* 1693–1718). Italian singer. He is first mentioned in 1693, when he took the part of Sergio in Carlo Pallavicino's *Vespasiano* in Rome. He was then active in Naples, where he sang in Giovanni Bononcini's *Il trionfo di Camilla, regina de' Volsci* (1696) and *Muzio Scevola* (1698); C. A. Lonati, P. Magni and F. Ballarotti's *Aiace* (1697); A. Scarlatti's *Emireno, overo Il consiglio dell'ombra* (1697), *Il prigioniero fortunato* (1698), *Gl'inganni felici* (1699) and *Eraclea* (1700); C. F. Pollarolo's *Tito Manlio* (1698); G. A. Aldrovandini's *Cesare in Alessandria* (1699); L. Mancia's *Partenope* (1699); and in M. A. Ziani's *Odoardo* (1700). In the last he appeared with the designation 'virtuoso of the imperial ambassador in Rome'. He is last mentioned in 1718, when he sang Nicander in Alessandro Scarlatti's *Telemaco*.

*

U. Prota-Giurleo: 'Breve storia del teatro di corte e della musica a Napoli nei secoli XVII e XVIII', *Il teatro di corte del Palazzo reale di Napoli* (Naples, 1952), 19–146 PAOLA BESUTTI

Sandrina's Secret. Opera by W. A. Mozart; *see* FINTA GIARDINIERA, LA (ii).

Sandunova [née Fyodorova], **Elizaveta Semyonovna** ['Uranova'] (*b* St Petersburg, 1772 or 30 Aug/10 Sept 1777; *d* Moscow, 21 Nov/3 Dec 1826). Russian mezzo-soprano. Her professional name, Uranova, was adopted by command of Catherine II, after the planet Uranus, discovered in 1781. She studied in St Petersburg with Paisiello, Sarti and Martín y Soler, in whose opera *L'arbore di Diana* she made her début at the Hermitage Theatre in 1790. In 1791 she was engaged as a singer at the Imperial Theatres, where she was extremely popular. With her husband, the actor Sila Nikolayevich Sandunov, she worked from 1794 in the Petrovsky Theatre, Moscow; but they were divorced in 1810 and in 1813 Sandunova returned to St Petersburg, where she performed frequently until her retirement in 1823. Renowned for her wide-ranging and expressive voice, she was one of the finest operatic singers of the early 19th century and took leading roles in numerous operas.

GEOFFREY NORRIS

Sanelli, Gualtiero (*b* Parma, 14 May 1816; *d* Maranhão, Brazil, 15 Dec 1861). Italian composer. At a very early age he joined the chorus of the ducal theatre in Parma, then became chorus master and prompter in the opera at Mantua (1835–9). As a member of a touring opera company he visited Milan and other Italian cities, then Mexico (1841) and probably other Central American countries. On his return to Europe he studied music in Paris; later he was conductor of opera seasons in England organized by Italian impresarios. By 1858 he was resident conductor in Pernambuco, Brazil, where he had gone with an opera company organized by the impresario Mariangeli. Sanelli composed 11 operas, all first performed in Italy between 1838 and 1855 and conducted by him on his tours. Vocal scores of three of them were published by Ricordi, who also possessed the autograph scores.

Le nozze improvvise (farsa, 1), Padua, Sociale, Nov 1838
La cantante (melodramma, 3, G. Sacchèro), Milan, Re, 2 Feb 1841
I due sergenti (melodramma, 2, F. Romani), Turin, Regio, carn. 1842
Ermengarda (melodramma, 3, P. Martini), Milan, Scala, 10 Nov 1844
Luiza Strozzi (dramma tragico, 3, Martini), Parma, Regio, 27 May 1846, vs (Milan, 1847)
Gennaro Annese (melodramma giocoso, 3), Florence, Pergola, 5 April 1848
Il fornaretto [Piero di Vasco] (dramma, 3, A. Codebò), Parma, Regio, 24 March 1851, vs (Milan, n.d.)
La Tradita (melodramma, 4, Codebò), Venice, Fenice, 2 March 1852, vs (Milan, 1852)
Camoëns (dramma, 3, Codebò), Turin, Regio, 25 Dec 1852
Ottavia (melodramma, 3, G. Peruzzini), Milan, Scala, 11 Feb 1854
Gusmano il buono [Gusmano il prode] (melodramma, 3, Peruzzini), Mantua, Sociale, 10 Feb 1855; rev. version, Parma, Regio, 14 Feb 1857

*

DEUMM; ES GIOVANNI CARLI BALLOLA

San Francisco. American city, in California. Opera was introduced in 1851, only three years after gold was discovered in California, as San Francisco sprang from a seaside village to a boom town. The frontier conditions rapidly created an active musical life in the town, which had become the main supply point for the mining activities. The largely male population of the new state (in 1850 more than 92%) craved not only the entertainment of the saloons, theatres and cafés that had sprung up, but also opportunities to hear the female voice and the music of their own now-distant cultures. This was particularly true of the European (chiefly German and Italian) immigrants, many of them refugees from the revolutions of 1848.

Lured by high wages, musicians found work in San Francisco. The first opera singers to arrive were the soprano Eliza Biscaccianti and the mezzo-soprano Catherine Hayes, both of whom were idolized by their audiences and earned fortunes. The first opera heard in San Francisco was *La sonnambula*, performed on 24 January 1851 by the Pellegrini opera troupe. Between that date and the great earthquake and fire of 18 April 1906, well over 5000 performances of opera and light opera were given by more than 20 troupes in 26 different theatres. The largest of these was the elaborately equipped Metropolitan (cap. 2000), built in 1853 and destroyed by fire four years later. The principal resident opera companies in the 1850s were headed by Anna Thillon, Anna Bishop and Eugenio and Giovanna Bianchi.

The intense musical activity was reported, reviewed and stimulated by local newspapers and journals (over 130 in the 1850s, of which more than a third were still being printed in 1860); many of these covered the theatrical and musical life in considerable detail, and were later supplemented by numerous publications of the 1860s and 70s that specialized in music.

In 1869, when the Central and Union Pacific railways joined the east and west coasts, San Francisco entered a new era. Dominating the west coast in importance and wealth, which flowed into the city from the Nevada silver mines, San Francisco took on the socio-economic character of the eastern cities and, accordingly, their musical tastes. As opera became increasingly pretentious in scale and aspiration, the term 'grand' was frequently used in the names of opera companies and applied to the form itself, to distinguish it from the new and popular operetta.

The most famous of the theatres built in the second half of the century was the Tivoli, which between 1879 and 1906 changed location three times and was closed for only 40 nights. Almost 10 000 performances of grand opera, light opera and operetta are estimated to have been given there, including 42 consecutive nights of Gounod's *Faust*, 41 performances of Verdi's *Otello* (between 1899 and 1906) and 84 sold-out performances of Gilbert and Sullivan's *HMS Pinafore*, which was new when it opened the second Tivoli in 1879. Alice Nielsen, who later enjoyed popularity at Covent Garden and became one of the most recorded of the early opera stars, started out in the Tivoli chorus, making her début in that theatre in the title role of *Lucia di Lammermoor*. Nielsen was a pupil of Ida Valerga, a San Franciscan and leading soprano at the Tivoli, who earlier had toured in Europe with Adelina Patti as her alternate or cover. Luisa Tetrazzini, discovered while on tour in Mexico and brought to the Tivoli Theater by its manager William Leahy, launched her career there in *Rigoletto* on 11 January 1905. In 1903 Mascagni conducted eight performances of his *Cavalleria rusticana* and *Zanetto* at the third Tivoli, a well-appointed house seating 1700.

The largest theatre in San Francisco, Wade's Opera House (1876), was renamed the Grand Opera House. When its seating was expanded from an initial 2300 to 2700, it became one of the five largest in the USA. Yet only a few resident companies played there, notably that of the soprano Inez Fabbri, who arrived in San Francisco in 1872; she became a leading figure in the city's musical life as a producer and impresario. Performances were also given by the touring companies of Max Strakosch, Clara Louise Kellogg (1877), J. H. Mapleson (1884–6) and Maurice Grau (1890, 1900–06), and by the American National Opera Company conducted by Theodore Thomas (1887). The performance of *Carmen* on 17 April 1906 by Grau's Metropolitan Opera Company, with Caruso and Fremstad in the leading roles, can be considered the end of an era; the earthquake occurred early the following morning.

The renewal of opera performances after the earthquake depended initially on the visits of such touring companies as W. A. Edwards's International Grand Opera Company in 1909 and, between 1919 and 1955, the Chicago, Scotti and San Carlo companies. Gaetano Merola visited San Francisco in 1909 as conductor of the Edwards troupe and again from 1919 to 1921 with the San Carlo company. In 1922, with funds largely provided by the city's Italian community, Merola produced *Pagliacci*, *Carmen* and *Faust* at the football stadium of Stanford University in nearby Palo Alto, which led to the formation of the San Francisco Opera in 1923. Beniamino Gigli, Giovanni Martinelli, Giuseppe de Luca, Bianca Saroya and Queena Mario were among the leading artists who appeared at the Civic Auditorium during the company's first season. In 1924 Merola initiated a week's opera performances in Los Angeles; these continued on an irregular basis until 1967.

During the San Francisco Opera's first decade Merola engaged international artists for productions of well-known works drawn from a predominantly Italian and French repertory. Exceptions were *Fay-en-Fah* (1926) by Joseph D. Redding, a local composer; Massenet's *La Navarraise* and Giordano's *La cena delle beffe* (1927); *Tristan und Isolde* (1928), led by Alfred Hertz, the conductor of the San Francisco SO; and the American première of Ravel's *L'enfant et les sortilèges* (1930).

Efforts to raise funds for a hall to accommodate the opera and the symphony orchestra were started as early as 1911 by the Musical Association of San Francisco and other groups. The War Memorial Opera House (cap. 3252) and Veterans Building (which included a concert hall) were eventually built at a total cost of $5 500 000. The opera house was inaugurated in 1932 with a performance of *Tosca*, with Claudia Muzio, Dino Borgioli, Alfred Gandolfi and others in a cast conducted by Merola (see illustration overleaf). Merola's 30 seasons as general manager were distinguished less for the standard of production than for the musical aspects and the quality of the stars engaged. The autumn season, which consisted of up to 30 performances of as many as 14 operas, was concentrated in only two months (September and October), not only because the space was also required by the symphony orchestra (whose members largely made up the opera orchestra) but also because the Metropolitan Opera's season began in November, when many of the principal singers were obliged to be in New York.

Merola died in 1953; he was succeeded by Kurt Herbert Adler, whom he had appointed chorus master in 1943 and had later promoted to assistant general manager. Adler greatly expanded the seasons (up to about 60 performances of 10 operas in the main 12-week season each autumn) and included unusual works in the repertory. Before he retired in June 1982, he had produced the American premières (some in English) of numerous works, including a staged production of

Scene from Act 1 of Puccini's 'Tosca', performed for the inauguration of the War Memorial Opera House, San Francisco, 15 October 1934

Honegger's oratorio *Jeanne d'Arc au bûcher* (1954), Orff's *Carmina burana* and *Die Kluge* (both 1958), Walton's *Troilus and Cressida* (1955), Poulenc's *Dialogues des Carmélites* (1957), Strauss's *Die Frau ohne Schatten* (1959), Britten's *A Midsummer Night's Dream* (1961), Shostakovich's *Katerina Izmaylova* (1964), Janáček's *The Makropulos Affair* (1966), Schuller's *The Visitation* (1967), Gottfried von Einem's *Der Besuch der alten Dame* (1972), and the world premières of Dello Joio's *Blood Moon* (1961) and Imbrie's *Angle of Repose* (1976). Severing the company's dependence on the Metropolitan's roster, Adler discovered many distinguished artists. He presented in their operatic débuts Leontyne Price, Marilyn Horne, Jess Thomas and Leona Mitchell and arranged the American opera débuts of, among others, Boris Christoff, Geraint Evans, Sena Jurinac, Pilar Lorengar, Birgit Nilsson, Luciano Pavarotti, Margaret Price, Leonie Rysanek and Elisabeth Schwarzkopf; Rostropovich's first appearance in the USA as an operatic conductor and Jean-Pierre Ponnelle's first American production were also at Adler's instigation.

Adler broadened the company's activities with innovative programmes for young American performers: the San Francisco Opera Auditions (initiated in 1954), the Merola Opera training programme, the Spring Opera Theater (1961), the Western Opera Theater (a small touring branch, 1966), the Brown Bag Opera (a series of informal daytime performances at various venues around the city, 1974), the San Francisco/Affiliate Artists Opera Program (1977), the American Opera Project (1979), and the Summer Opera Festival (1981), a season of 15 performances of five works using international casts.

Until 1980 the San Francisco Opera's orchestra had consisted largely of musicians from the San Francisco SO; in September 1980, when the Louise M. Davies Symphony Hall was opened, the opera company formed its own orchestra, independent of the symphony orchestra.

Adler's successor in 1982 was the Canadian-born Terence A. McEwen, a former executive of London Records. Maintaining the standards in casting, production and musical performance Adler had achieved, McEwen initiated a new production of *Der Ring des Nibelungen* (performed serially in the 1983–4 summer festivals and as a cycle in 1985) and in 1983 produced the American première of Tippett's *The Midsummer Marriage*. He reorganized the company's artists' training and development programme under one administrative branch, the San Francisco Opera Center, and, citing financial reasons, discontinued both the Spring Opera Theater, in its 21st year, and the Summer Opera Festival, following the 1985 *Ring* cycle.

McEwen resigned on 9 February 1988 because of ill-health. The noteworthy initiatives and successes of his final two seasons, 1986 and 1987, included new productions of *Don Carlos*, in a complete five-act version (in French) by John Copley (director) and John Conklin (designer), *Khovanshchina* and *Die Zauberflöte* (designed by David Hockney). He commissioned Hugo Weisgall to compose an opera, *Esther*, for performance in 1991 or later. In January 1986 he appointed Sir John Pritchard as the company's first Music Director; already a regular on the company's podium, Sir John conducted 18 productions of 14 different operas for the San Francisco Opera from 1970 until his death on 5 December 1989.

Lotfi Mansouri, general director of Canadian Opera for ten years, was appointed the company's fourth director on 12 March 1988, having already directed 31 operas for the San Francisco company since 1963. He implemented the season McEwen had planned; among its offerings were *The Rake's Progress*, the American première of Rossini's *Maometto II*, *Lady Macbeth of the Mtsensk District* and a new production of *Parsifal*. In June 1989, in a separate project of Mansouri's, the San Francisco Opera presented five performances of Philip Glass's *Satyagraha*, using the Houston Grand Opera production.

The notably successful 1989 autumn season, again planned previously by McEwen, began with an impressive new production of *Lulu* (with the reconstructed third act), directed by Mansouri and designed by Günther Schneider-Siemssen. Ann Panagulias (*b* 1964), a student of the Opera Center programme, made an impressive début in the title role (for illustration *see* COSTUME, fig.26). Other significant offerings of the season were new productions of Boito's *Mefistofele* (Robert Carsen, director; Michael Levine, designer), *Idomeneo* (John Copley, John Conklin) and Vivaldi's *Orlando furioso* (by Pier Luigi Pizzi).

In June 1990 the *Ring* cycle was revived and performed four times. The regular autumn season included new productions of *Wozzeck* (Mansouri directing), *Suor Angelica*, *Die Entführung* and *Fledermaus*; there were also three works new to San Francisco – Massenet's *Don Quichotte*, Strauss's *Capriccio* and Monteverdi's *Il ritorno d'Ulisse in patria* – and four revivals.

Regional companies in the surrounding Bay Area, each presenting four or five operas annually, include the West Bay Opera of Palo Alto (founded 1955), Oakland Opera, Marin Opera of San Rafael, Novato Opera, Cinnabar Opera of Petaluma, Berkeley Opera and San José Opera Theater. A long tradition of cabaret opera in San Francisco is maintained in Pocket Opera, a small company that gives concert and semi-staged performances of nine or more operas each season, mostly unusual works in the lively English translations of its director, Donald Pippin. The Lamplighters (1952), a Gilbert and Sullivan company, has also developed a large following.

*

F. Soule, J. Nisbet and J. H. Gihon: *Annals of San Francisco* (New York, 1885)

J. H. Mapleson: *The Mapleson Memoirs* (London, 1888); ed. H. Rosenthal (London, 1966)

San Francisco Theatre Research (San Francisco, 1938–42)

C. Lengyel, ed.: *History of Music in San Francisco* (San Francisco, 1939–42)

G. MacMinn: *The Theater of the Golden Era in California* (Caldwell, ID, 1941)

E. M. Gagey: *The San Francisco Stage* (New York, 1950)

A. Bloomfield: *Fifty Years of San Francisco Opera* (San Francisco, 1972, 2/1978)

D. Muscatine: *Old San Francisco* (New York, 1975)

K. Lockhart, ed.: *The Adler Years* (San Francisco, 1981)

R. Jacobson: 'Dream Come True', *ON*, xlvii/4 (1982–3), 8–12; xlvii/5 (1982–3), 30–35, 59 [interview with McEwen]

ROBERT COMMANDAY

S Giovanni Grisostomo. Theatre in Venice, built by the Grimani in 1678. The largest and most exclusive opera house in the city, it was renamed after Malibran in 1834, then used for all kinds of popular entertainment; it was restructured in 1919 but soon became a cinema. *See* VENICE, §§3–5 and 8.

San Jose. American city, in California. Despite performances of *Lucia di Lammermoor* and *Carmen* by the Lambardi Grand Opera in 1911, opera only began to gain momentum in 1937, when the San Carlo Opera from New York City presented *Aida* as a prelude to many tours. In the 1940s the San Francisco Opera also visited, with Pons, Albanese, Tibbett, Peerce and Pinza. During the period 1958–74 Edwin C. Dunning at San Jose State University presented 149 performances by his collegiate Opera Workshop, with 35 complete operas including Wolf-Ferrari's *Il segreto di Susanna*, Hindemith's *The Long Christmas Dinner* and Robert Ward's *The Crucible*. A graduate of that school, the San Jose mezzo-soprano Irene (formerly Yvonne) Dalis returned in 1977 after an illustrious Wagnerian career to start a professional company, which in 1984 evolved into Opera San José. By 1990, performing in the city's 529-seat Montgomery Theater, the company had presented 41 operas by 26 composers, including two world premières by local composers: Alva Henderson's *West of Washington Square* (1988) and Henry Mollicone's *Hotel Eden* (1989). Other unusual works were Mollicone's *Star Bird* and *The Face on the Barroom Floor*, Kirke Mechem's *Tartuffe* and Cimarosa's *Il matrimonio segreto* and *Il barone deluso*. Including its heavy schedule for school-children, the company gave 157 performances to 139 000 people in 1990–91, with Dalis as artistic director, and with two resident singers on season contract for the first time. The four productions received 39 public performances.

PAUL HERTELENDY

San Juan. Capital of Puerto Rico. Founded in 1521, it developed as a base for ships travelling the gold route between Spain and Central and South America. From the early 19th century, it was a regular stop for European opera companies and singers on tour from the USA via Cuba to South America. The Teatro Municipal (officially named the Teatro Tapia in 1937) opened in 1832 with recitals of opera airs offered in costume by the English tenor William Pearman, although *tonadillas* had been given as early as 1823 at the Teatro de Amigos del Pais. *Il barbiere di Siviglia*, presented in 1835 by a visiting Italian company, was probably the first complete opera seen in San Juan. In 1842 the visiting company of Stefano Busatti mounted a long season; besides repeating *Il barbiere* they offered *Lucrezia Borgia*, *Belisario*, concerts of opera excerpts and, almost a year before its New York début, *Lucia di Lammermoor*. From 1823 the Sociedad Filarmónica and its successors contributed greatly to the establishment of a local opera tradition by producing native zarzuelas and operas. The composer Felipe Gutiérrez Espinosa (1825–99), whose *Guarionex* was produced in about 1876 by the Sociedad Filarmónica, was especially important. His *Macías* (composed *c*1871) is the only extant opera written in Puerto Rico in the 19th century.

After a lapse following the island's transfer to American sovereignty in 1898, San Juan again began to receive the visits of travelling companies in 1910, when an Italian company presented *Tosca*, *Rigoletto*, *Aida*, *Fedora*, *Lucia di Lammermoor*, *Un ballo in maschera*, *Otello* and *Mefistofele*. Local activity was revived with Spanish zarzuelas, and with a production of *Cavalleria rusticana* organized by the retired tenor Antonio Paoli in 1935. Following brief seasons given by companies formed in New York but using the choral forces of the University of Puerto Rico (1954–8), San Juan fostered the rise of stable local companies. The first of these was Opera 68 (founded 1968), which changed its name to Opera de San Juan with its production of Gutiérrez's *Macías* in 1977. Other opera companies active in San Juan include Opera de Puerto Rico (1971), Teatro de la Opera (1981) and Opera de Cámara (1977). The first two concentrate on large-scale productions of the standard Italian repertory. Opera de Cámara has a more experimental approach, presenting for example the première of the only 20th-century Puerto Rican opera to date: Roberto Sierra's *El mensajero de plata* (1986). Opera production in San Juan is now based in the state-supported Centro de Bellas Artes, inaugurated in 1981, whose three halls provide modern facilities for opera, theatre, ballet, concerts and recitals.

F. Callejo: *Música y músicos portorriqueños* (San Juan, 1915; 2/1971, ed. A. Veray)
A. de Hostos: *Historia de San Juan, ciudad murada* (Havana, 1948, 2/1966)
E. Pasarell: *Orígenes de la afición teatral en Puerto Rico* (Río Piedras, 1951–67, 2/1970)
M. Casas: *Theatrical Production in Puerto Rico from 1700–1824: the Role of the Government and of the Roman Catholic Church* (diss., New York U., 1974)
D. Thompson: 'Nineteenth-Century Musical Life in Puerto Rico', *Die Musikkulturen Lateinamerikas im 19. Jahrhundert*, ed. Robert Günther (Regensburg, 1982), 327–32
——: 'Notes on the Inauguration of the San Juan (Puerto Rico) Municipal Theater', *Revista de música latinoamerica/Latin American Music Review*, xi/1 (1990), 84–91

DONALD THOMPSON

Sanjust, Filippo (*b* Rome, 9 Sept 1925). Italian director and stage designer. After studying architecture in Rome and at Princeton University, he was led by a natural aptitude for drawing to a career in stage design. In 1958 he designed 200 costumes in two weeks for Luchino Visconti's 1958 production of *Don Carlos* at Covent Garden. This successful collaboration continued with a doom-laden *Trovatore* (1964, Covent Garden) that was still being revived in 1986 and a mordant *Figaro* (1964, Rome) that was also seen at the Metropolitan Opera in 1968. He was then invited by Henze to design the premières of *Der junge Lord* (1965, Berlin) and *The Bassarids* (1966, Salzburg), both directed by G. R. Sellner. Other successful productions in Berlin by Sanjust and Sellner included an austere black and white setting, with luxurious costumes, of *Lulu* (1967), seen in Brussels in 1973 and at the Edinburgh Festival in 1975, and an opulent *Nabucco* (1979).

Sanjust has generally undertaken four or five productions each year in major European cities. Since 1969 he has preferred to combine direction with design, though not always to critical acclaim, beginning with *La Cenerentola* in Berlin. Notable successes include *Ariadne auf Naxos* (1976, Vienna), *L'incoronazione di Poppea* (1979, Brussels) and *Falstaff* (1980, Vienna). He returned to Covent Garden to design and produce *Luisa Miller* (1978), *Simon Boccanegra* (1980) and *La sonnambula* (1981). His approach to design is to build productions around a visual ground-plan, as in *Simon Boccanegra*. He is also noted for his good taste, his expert use of colour and his experiments with projected lighting, as, for example, in his Frankfurt productions of *Orfeo* (1971) and *Parsifal* (1973).

For illustration *see* *BASSARIDS, THE* and *JUNGE LORD, DER*.

DAVID J. HOUGH

Sanktpeterburgskiy gostinnïy dvor ('The St Petersburg Bazaar'). Comic opera in three acts by VASILY ALEXEYEVICH PASHKEVICH to a libretto by Mikhail Alexeyevich Matinsky; St Petersburg, Karl Knipper's Theatre, autumn 1782.

All surviving musical sources of this opera pertain to the revised version, subtitled 'Kak pozhivyosh', tak i proslïvyosh' ('You'll be Known by the Way you Live'), first given at the Bol'shoy Theatre for Catherine II on 2/13 February 1792; it was exceedingly popular from that time (provincial performances have been traced up to 1876). Because printed librettos of 18th-century musical plays with spoken dialogue ordinarily did not carry the composer's name, and because Matinsky's preface to the second version specifically (and gratefully) mentioned Pashkevich, a false impression was created in the minds of musicians unfamiliar with the earlier convention that Matinsky (an emancipated serf who was professor of geometry and geography at the élite Smol'nïy Institute in St Petersburg) had been responsible for both the words and the music of the original version, the court composer Pashkevich having been called in later as an assistant. Since 1927 a number of studies by Soviet literary and musical historians have gradually disproved the existence of Matinsky as a composer.

The libretto, especially in its earlier version, has become a classic of Russian drama. Unlike most plays of its kind it does not concern relations between social classes, nor is there a love interest. The title refers to the famous sprawling covered market in St Petersburg, and the plot is accordingly drawn from the everyday commercial life of the Russian capital. It depicts the antics of the swindler Skvalïgin ('Mr Tightwad'; bass) who conspires with his prospective son-in-law Kryuchkodey ('Mr Hook-or-Crook'; tenor) to commit a variety of frauds before being finally exposed and disgraced. So casual and anecdotal is the action that the main difference between the two versions involves the interchange of the first and third acts around the second.

That central act shows the engagement party for Kryuchkodey and Skvalïgin's daughter Khavronya (spoken), eventually invaded by the swindler's victims seeking redress. Pashkevich's music here consists of a remarkable series of seven traditional wedding songs – or, more accurately, bride's party (*devichnik*) songs – arranged for three-part women's chorus. The orchestration deftly imitates the sound of folk instruments, including the shepherd's pipe (*svirel'*) and the psaltery (*gusli*), the latter actually being named in one of the songs. The score is otherwise distinguished by its naturalistic ensembles of merchants at the bazaar, haggling customers and so forth: of the 27 musical numbers, 12 are ensemble pieces ranging from duet to octet.

RICHARD TARUSKIN

Sanmartini [San Martino, Sammartini], **Pietro** (*b* Florence, 18 Sept 1636; *d* Florence, 1 Jan 1701). Italian composer. He was not related to G. B. Sammartini. A priest, he worked as a musician in several places, among them Rome, Bologna and Arezzo. From 1659 he lived in Florence, as vice-*maestro di cappella* of the cathedral and from 1686 as *maestro*. He also served the Medici court, principally as a keyboard player. From 1692 he was a member of the Accademia Filarmonica of Bologna. Very little of his output survives: of the seven operas that he wrote, all are lost except for the printed libretto of one, *Le rivalità favorevoli* (Florence, 1688).

ARGIA BERTINI

S Moisè. Theatre in Venice, opened in 1640 and closed in 1818; *see* VENICE, §§2–6.

Sanquirico, Alessandro (*b* Milan, 27 July 1777; *d* Milan, 12 March 1849). Italian scene painter and designer. He began his career designing scenery and decorating new theatres in conjunction with other leading artists such as Paolo Landriani, Giovanni Pedroni, Giovanni Perego and Giorgio Fuentes. From 1817 to 1832 he was sole designer and chief scene painter for La Scala. From this powerful position during a rich period of operatic output, he influenced design standards for the works of Bellini, Donizetti, Mozart, Meyerbeer, Rossini and many other later composers until well into

Design by Alessandro Sanquirico for an imaginary classical scene, showing a landscape with Vesuvius behind an architectural foreground: pen, ink and wash

the 20th century. Among the hundreds of operas and ballets he designed at La Scala were the premières of Rossini's *La gazza ladra* (1817), Bellini's *Norma* (1831) and Donizetti's *Lucrezia Borgia* (1833).

Sanquirico's designs were the foundation of the style commonly associated with 19th-century grand opera. They combined the restrained neo-classicism of his early training with the romantic trait of basing stage fantasy on historical accuracy and sensibility. Vast enough in scale to accommodate the epic quality of lyric drama, they were intimate enough and sufficiently 'realistic' to render human passions credible and reasonably natural. He tended to prefer spacious settings with single perspective, unlike the more intricate plans of the late Baroque period. A typical Sanquirico formula, widely copied and still theoretically valid, was to set a scene in a richly decorated architectural foreground which opened out on to a broad landscape view painted on a backdrop, profound in its simplicity (see illustration). This solved many technical problems of scale and, at the same time, satisfied the aesthetic needs of romantic audiences for spectacle. The end of his career saw the introduction of gas lighting in theatres, and his painted scenery showed a sensitivity to the nuances of light which later scene painters lost because of advances in lighting control. One reason for Sanquirico's international influence was that portfolios of hand-coloured engravings based on his theatrical and architectural drawings were published and extensively circulated and copied (*Raccolta di scene teatrali eseguite o disegnate dai più celebri pittori scenici di Milano*, 1819–24; *Raccolta di varie decorazioni sceniche inventate ed eseguite per il R. Teatro alla Scala di Milano da Alessandro Sanquirico*, *c*1827).

For further illustration *see* CROCIATO IN EGITTO, IL; MILAN, fig.5; PIRATA, IL; SEMIRAMIDE; and SONNAMBULA, LA. PAUL SHEREN

S Samuele. Theatre in Venice, opened for opera by the Grimani family in 1710; after a fire it was rebuilt in 1747, and restored in 1853, but it reverted to more popular entertainments and was demolished in 1894. *See* VENICE, §§3–5 and 8.

Santa Cruz. American city, in western California. The Cabrillo Music Festival is held just outside the city each summer. Conceived in the early 1960s, the festival grew out of a series of concerts, initiated by the composer Robert Hughes, at the Sticky Wicket restaurant and theatre in Aptos. Several fully staged open-air performances followed, notably Gluck's *Orfeo ed Euridice* (in English), before the festival was officially inaugurated in 1963 under the sponsorship of Cabrillo College. Events are now held throughout the county of Santa Cruz. Festival music directors have included its founder, Gerhard Samuel, Carlos Chávez, Dennis Russell Davies and Marin Alsop (appointed 1992).

Although it is not primarily an opera festival, a number of innovatory productions have been given: the American première of Frank Martin's *Le vin herbé* (1968), Lou Harrison's chamber opera with puppets *Young Caesar* (1971), Henze's 'community opera' *Pollicino, or The New Adventures of Tom Thumb* (1983), and the American premières of the 'Aria of the Falling Body' and the 'Bird Aria' from John Adams's *The Death of Klinghoffer* (1991). Other outstanding performances have been Rameau's *Hippolyte et Aricie*, *La clemenza di Tito*, *Die Dreigroschenoper* and Harrison's *Rapunzel*. In 1965 Haydn's *L'anima del filosofo, ossia Orfeo ed Euridice* (composed 1791) was given its west-coast première in a concert performance directed by Samuel. J. P. NEFF

Santa Cruz de Tenerife. Capital of Tenerife, in the Canary Islands. The Teatro de la Calle de la Marina was built in 1835 and became the island's principal theatre. The first opera to be performed there was *Constantino*, an *opera seria* in three acts by Carlos Guigou to a libretto by José Placido Sansón, followed shortly by the same composer's *El templario*. The present house was built in 1851 by Manuel de Oràa as the Teatro Isabel II; since 1924 it has been known as the Teatro Guimera, in honour of a local writer. The first opera presented, by the impresario and conductor Mariano Courtier, was *Ernani* (1861), followed by *Il trovatore* and *Norma*. In 1911 the architect Antonio Pintor completely remodelled the interior, reducing the seating from 1400

The Santa Fe Opera Theater

to 870. Miguel Fleta sang there in 1928, Hipólito Lázaro in 1930. The season is traditionally during October and November, when one performance of each of three or four operas is given, usually with an international cast. Alfredo Kraus, born in the Canary Islands, has been a frequent guest. Performances are given with the Tenerife SO, which during the rest of the year gives symphony concerts in the theatre.

F. M. Viera: *Anales del teatro en Tenerife* (Santa Cruz de Tenerife, 1968) CHARLES PITT

Santa Fe. American city, capital of New Mexico. Founded in 1610, it is one of the oldest cities in the USA. The Spanish conquistadors suppressed most of the area's pre-Colombian indigenous music, but the sacred *albados* and the secular *bailes* retained elements from Native American musical forms during the 19th century. When Mexico achieved independence from Spain in 1821, New Mexico was included, but was declared American territory during the Mexican-American War in 1846. In 1912 it became the 47th state.

Although artists and writers had settled in and around Santa Fe from the end of the 19th century, very little musical activity is recorded until the foundation in 1956 of the Santa Fe Opera by John Crosby, who had become familiar with the area by attending school there. The Opera Association of New Mexico, as it was first called, was conceived as a summer festival that might provide work for young musicians of Crosby's acquaintance in New York. The first opera, *Madama Butterfly*, was given on 3 July 1957, and was followed that year by *Così fan tutte*, *The Rake's Progress*, *Ariadne auf Naxos*, *Il barbiere di Siviglia* and the world première of Marvin David Levy's *The Tower*, given in a double-bill with Pergolesi's *La serva padrona*. The original, purpose-built theatre had benches providing seating for 480 spectators, and the company consisted of 29 orchestral musicians, 11 soloists, 10 chorus members and 'just a handful of people'. The choice of operas for the first season set a pattern of mixing established repertory operas with lesser-known early 20th-century works and always included either a world or American première. Stravinsky attended the performances of *The Rake's Progress* in 1957 and returned several times, including the four seasons 1959–62, during which he participated as a conductor. In 1962 he wrote, 'I have the feeling that John Crosby's zeal really deserves special reward and special treatment'.

Many other composers have enjoyed residencies with the Santa Fe Opera, among them Hindemith, who conducted the American première of his *Neues vom Tage* in 1961, Douglas Moore, Berio, Floyd, Henze and Penderecki. The company has given the world premières of operas by Floyd (*Wuthering Heights*, 1958), Berio (*Opera*, 1970), Villa-Lobos (*Yerma*, 1971), Rochberg (*The Confidence Man*, 1982) and Eaton (*The Tempest*, 1985), as well as the first American performances of operas by Berg (*Lulu*, in both the two-act and three-act versions, 1963, 1979), H.-J. von Bose, Britten, Cavalli, Henze, Hindemith, Siegfried Matthus, Menotti, Stephen Oliver, Penderecki, Reimann, Nino Rota, Schoenberg, Shostakovich, Richard Strauss, Stravinsky and Judith Weir. Two thirds of the repertory has been made up of 20th-century works, with the remaining emphasis on the five most popular Mozart operas and an occasional excursion into the 19th-century repertory, such as *Anna Bolena* in 1959. This concentration on a contemporary repertory has proved successful with the company's benefactors; although the company receives support from the federal and state governments and the city of Santa Fe, the largest part of its budget comes from private funding. The festival season, which takes place in July and August, usually includes five operas, introduced one by one during the first month and performed in repertory for the second. Among the singers who have appeared at Santa Fe are Marilyn Horne, Frederica von Stade, Alessandra Marc, Sheri Greenawald, James Bowman, Tatiana Troyanos, Pauline Tinsley, Kiri te Kanawa, Stuart Burrows, Huguette Tourangeau, Richard Stilwell, James Morris, Donald Gramm, Benita Valente and Elisabeth Söderström. An apprentice programme for singers was begun in 1957, followed by one for technicians in 1965.

The original theatre building, on the city's outskirts, was destroyed by fire in 1967, but the following year a new, open-air theatre was inaugurated, with seating capacity increased to 1773. From the outside, the two-tiered amphitheatre has something of the feel of a bull-ring, with wooden columns and numerous doorways. Inside, the overhanging canopies act as an acoustic shell and shelter approximately half the audience from the frequent rainstorms. The stage can be left open at the back, with the night sky and the desert beyond providing a particularly atmospheric natural backdrop. A steep flight of steps leads from the backstage working areas, and some spectacular stage effects have been achieved by using this as an entrance. Among memorable productions have been those by Göran Järvefelt (*Le nozze di Figaro*, *Die schweigsame Frau*), Nikolaus Lehnhoff (*Der fliegende Holländer*, the only work by Wagner to have been performed at Santa Fe during the first 35 years), Colin Graham (*Daphne* and *Die Liebe der Danae*), Alfred Kirchner (*We Come to the River*) and Charles Ludlam (*The English Cat* and *Die Fledermaus*). Like Glyndebourne and Aldeburgh, the locality and its traditions add considerably to the allure of Santa Fe, so that many performers and spectators are drawn to return often.

*

C. Kenny: 'Opera Traffic, Keep Left', *Opera* (1972), 118–26 [festival issue]
E. Scott: *The First Twenty Years of the Santa Fe Opera* (Santa Fe, 1976)
P. O'Connor: 'Desert Culture', *Departures* (Nov–Dec 1989), 49–50
PATRICK O'CONNOR

Sant'Alessio ('St Alexis'). *Dramma musicale* in three acts by STEFANO LANDI to a libretto by GIULIO ROSPIGLIOSI; Rome, ? Palazzo Barberini ai Giubbonari, 2 March 1631, or Palazzo Barberini alle Quattro Fontane, 18 February 1632.

Choosing to remain an impoverished holy man, Alexis (soprano) has returned after many years from Palestine to the patrician house of his father Eufemiano (tenor) in Rome, unbeknown to him, his mother (soprano) or his wife (soprano). Hearing that he has been seen in the Holy Land, Alexis's wife and mother decide to search for him. Alexis tries to dissuade them, while struggling with the temptation to reveal himself and end their despair; temptation is made manifest in a hermit, the Devil (bass) in disguise, who is resolved to lure Alexis back into the secular world. At the height of his uncertainty, Alexis turns to Heaven, who instantly sends him a guardian Angel (soprano). Reassured, he prepares for a peaceful death. The family discovers Alexis's corpse in his dwelling-place under a stairway, a letter in his hand revealing his identity. Their doubt, distress and grief are finally dispelled by their dim understanding that the death marks a miraculous life, and that Christianity and Rome have gained by Alexis's sacrifices.

Rospigliosi's drama is basically moral and psychological, a test of human frailty. His main elaboration of the traditional biography of Alexis, a well-known Roman saint, lay in creating a visible antagonist in the Devil; Landi's musical characterization is entirely in powerful recitative, ranging over two and a half octaves, from C to *f'*. In 1632 J. J. Bouchard described the singer – most probably Bartolomeo Nicolini – as a 'basso di cappella [Sistina] stupendissimo'. Another addition to the basic cast was the palace page, Martio (soprano), who mocks Alexis and offers humorous commentary on palace events. When the opera was restaged in 1634 Martio shared his original lines with another page, Curtio (soprano). The two introduce themselves (1.ii) with the insouciant strophic duet 'Poca voglia di far bene', and Landi's rapid recitative captures well their youthful capriciousness. Martio is also given a comic encounter with the hermit: after exchanging sarcasms, he scuffles with the old man, who escapes by turning into a bear (2.viii).

Neither mythological nor pastoral, *Sant'Alessio* departed from the ambiance of most of its operatic precursors. Some of its importance lies in its abandonment of the short tableaux, multiplicity of characters with small parts and excuses for song and dance that opera had inherited from the *intermedio*. Jesuit school plays set within imperial courts (e.g. B. Stefonio's *Crispus* and A. Donati's *La Svevia* of 1629) offered Rospigliosi dramatic models with moral dilemmas and tragic seriousness. *Sant'Alessio* was also the product of Cardinal Francesco Barberini's interests in Roman antiquity and ancient theatre. The costumes were designed after ancient statues and medals, and the restrained use of arias and the predominantly unlyrical recitative show the influence of the antiquarian G. B. Doni, who believed that dialogue was spoken in ancient tragedy and who admitted songs in tragicomedies like *Sant'Alessio* 'as long as they were not too frequent'. In 1635 the savant N. Peiresc sent his copy of the opera to Marin Mersenne with ecstatic praise, as an example of the modern revival of ancient theatre. Another Roman feature was the cast, which consisted entirely of men and boys who were the cream of the newest generation of singers in the city. Theatrical performances in gentlemen's academies and Jesuit school plays, as well as most earlier operas given in Rome, were executed with all-male casts. More than half the soloists for *Sant'Alessio* came from the papal chapel, and several had been in operas before (F. Bianchi, A. Ferrotti, B. Nicolini, M. A. Pasqualini). At least three of the sopranos were castratos.

Scene from the revival by Alan Curtis of Landi's 'Sant'Alessio' (Tiroler Landestheater, Innsbruck, 1981) with reconstructions of the sets of 1634 by Pietro da Cortona

In representing the story of a saint, the Barberini contributed to another contemporary trend. Earlier examples of saints' lives as subjects of musical drama include Jacopo Cicognini's libretto on St Agatha (1614; performed with music by Francesca Caccini and G. B. da Gagliano, 1622), Andrea Salvadori's on St Ursula (1620; Marco da Gagliano, 1624) and L. San Martino d'Aglie's on St Eustace (d'India, reportedly 1625, Rome). Certainly, such saints were models of Counter-Reformation heroics and steadfastness, but their stories were equally sources of believable feelings, of tragic pathos and human problems uncircumscribed by classical treatments and not restricted to the romantic artifices of Arcadia.

Each of the three acts in *Sant'Alessio* has at least one scene of expressive pathos, well set off by scenes of contrasting mood. The last scene of Act 1 is the first to give vent musically to the family's unhappiness over the missing Alexis. Landi's harmony, refrain-like cadential phrases and wide-ranging melodic lines create a whole scene of lament, which is punctuated by impertinent comments from the pages. This is preceded by the gleeful malevolence of the demons in hell and is followed by a graceful, hymn-like closing chorus asking for heavenly protection for Alexis. The expressive peak of Act 2 is Alexis's central recitative soliloquy ('Alessio, che farai?'), which alternates between his conflicting feelings. In Act 3 the grief-stricken trio of his family ('Ohimé, ch'un'hora sola') concentrates the pathos for the last time, before it is gradually dissipated by the long choral finale.

All these intensely personal moments were enacted against impassive architectural settings, the conventional Renaissance *scena tragica* or 'city-set' (Acts 1 and 2; *see* PRODUCTION, fig.4), and in front of the stairs and courtyard where the saint dies (3.iii and iv). The two other animated and astonishing sets illustrate that behind the world where men are trapped lie the real realms of hell (1.iv; 3.i) and of paradise (3.v). After the performance of 1634 *Sant'Alessio* was restaged in Reggio Emilia (1645) and in Bologna (1647, omitting the closing choruses of each act and presenting the hell scene of Act 3 as the finale of Act 2). Among several modern revivals, the sets of 1634 were reconstructed in 1981 for the Teatro dell'Opera in Rome and the Tiroler Landestheater in Innsbruck (see illustration), and in 1988 for the E. Nakamichi Baroque Festival in Los Angeles. MARGARET MURATA

Santana, Huc. *See* HUC-SANTANA.

Sante, Sophia (Maria Christina) van (*b* Zaandam, 11 Aug 1925). Dutch mezzo-soprano. After studying in Amsterdam and in Italy, she appeared with Nederlandse Operastichting (1961–75), singing Eurycleia (*Il ritorno d'Ulisse*), Diana (*Iphigénie en Tauride*), Mary (*Der fliegende Holländer*), the Hostess, which she created in Ton de Leeuw's *De droom* (1965, Holland Festival), Margret (*Wozzeck*), the Mother (*Il prigioniero*), Diana (*La fedeltà premiata*), Maddalena, Meg Page (*Falstaff*), the Woman (*Erwartung*) and Larina. She had a sturdy voice, great capacity for singing difficult contemporary music and a strongly dramatic temperament.

TRUUS DE LEUR/ELIZABETH FORBES

Santi, Nello (*b* Adria, Rovigo, 22 Sept 1931). Italian conductor. He studied at the Liceo Musicale, Padua, and made his début at the Teatro Verdi there in 1951 with *Rigoletto*. Since 1958 he has conducted regularly at the Zürich Opera, and has made his home in the city. He made his Covent Garden début in 1960 with *La traviata*, and the same year appeared at the Vienna Staatsoper and at Salzburg; he has since conducted at all the major international houses, making his Metropolitan début in 1962 with *Un ballo in maschera*. In 1988 he conducted *Aida* at Earl's Court as London's first 'arena opera'. Santi has worked almost exclusively in the Italian operatic mainstream from Rossini to Puccini; his performances are distinguished by grace, propulsion and the ability to obtain fine artistic responses from singers and orchestra. His recordings include all the Verdi arias for tenor (with Bergonzi), *Pagliacci* and Montemezzi's *L'amore dei tre re*, as well as several videos. NOËL GOODWIN

Santiago. Capital of Chile. An Italian 'Compañía Lírica' headed by Domenico Pezzoni played at the Teatro Principal from June 1830 to February 1831, presenting operas by Rossini, Paer, Ferdinando Paini and Mercadante. Bellini's *I Capuleti e i Montecchi* was given in the Teatro de la Universidad in April 1844, and in 1850 both an Italian company, led by Antonio Neumane, and a French one 'direct from Paris' alternately occupied the same theatre, giving works by Donizetti, Nicolai, Verdi, Adam and Auber. The first Teatro Municipal (2700 seats) opened on 17 September 1857 with *Ernani*; it burnt down in 1870. The present Teatro Municipal was inaugurated in July 1873 with *La forza del destino*. The 1880 season included the first Chilean performance of Gomes's *Il Guarany*; in 1883 the local premières of *Don Carlos* and *Le prophète* were given, and in 1885 the first performance of a Wagner opera in Chile, *Lohengrin*. On 2 November 1895 the first opera by a Chilean had its première at the Municipal, *La florista de Lugano* by Eliodoro Ortiz de Zárate. At its première on 12 August 1902 his *Lautaro* evoked controversy. On the other hand, *Salinara* by the Italian-born Domenico Brescia (1866–1939), resident in Chile, had great success with both public and press.

Mascagni conducted *Lohengrin* and Boito's *Mefistofele* in 1911. The vassalage to Italy throughout the 1920s finally provoked an outburst from Domingo Santa Cruz in 1929, when *El mercurio* published his 'Los funerales de la ópera'. To assuage a growing outcry, a visiting company that same year gave the première of *Sayeda* by the Chilean Próspero Bisquertt. In 1932 Chilean singers tried organizing their own season, but without winning public support. *Mauricio* by the Chilean Carlos Melo Cruz was favourably reviewed in *La nación* (3 October 1939) but did not outlive its first performance. Pablo Garrido's *La sugestión* arrived at the Municipal in 1961, and *Ardid el amor*, composed in 1956 by Roberto Puelma (1893–1976), in 1972, with Chilean performers. Despite continued opposition to international repertory and singers voiced by Santa Cruz and others, international seasons were continued after 1950. In 1967 Capobianco produced a five-opera season with Domingo and Milnes in *Andrea Chénier*, Domingo in *Carmen* and the Chilean tenor Ramón Vinay (from 1969 to 1971 artistic director of the Santiago opera) in *Falstaff*, *Carmen* and *La bohème*. To appease critics, a Santiago Municipal Chamber Opera offered in 1966 unpretentious programmes with national singers. In the 1980s, operas sung by foreigners were frequently repeated with Chilean casts. The 1982 season, celebrating the 125th anniversary of the Teatro

Municipal, opened with *Otello*, followed by *Don Pasquale*, *La bohème*, *I due Foscari* and *Die Zauberflöte*, and closed with *Carmen*. In 1986 *Tristan und Isolde* was sung there for the first time in German, as was *Der Rosenkavalier* in 1987. Spanish surtitles began appearing for the first time during the 1987 season.

*

E. Pereira Salas: *Historia de la música en Chile, 1850–1900* (Santiago, 1957)
M. Canepa Guzmán: *La ópera en Chile (1839–1930)* (Santiago, 1976)
ROBERT STEVENSON

SS Giovanni e Paolo. Theatre in Venice, adapted for opera in 1639 by the Grimani family and abandoned in 1699. *See* VENICE, §§2–3.

Santina [Santini], **La.** *See* STELLA, SANTA.

Santini, Gabriele (*b* Perugia, 20 Jan 1886; *d* Rome, 13 Nov 1964). Italian conductor. After studying at Perugia and the Bologna Conservatory he began his career at the Costanzi theatre, Rome. He subsequently conducted at the Teatro Colón, Buenos Aires, for eight seasons and at the Municipal theatre, Rio de Janeiro, and from 1925 to 1929 he assisted Toscanini at La Scala. From Milan he returned to the Rome Opera, where he remained until 1933 and of which he later became artistic director, 1944–7. He conducted at leading Italian theatres, and in Paris with the Naples S Carlo company in 1951. Santini kept the lyric tradition alive both by his much-admired performances of the standard repertory and by introducing new works such as Giordano's *Il re* (1930, Milan and Rome) and Alfano's *Dottor Antonio* (1949, Rome). He also conducted the Italian premières of Ravel's *L'heure espagnole* (1929, Milan) and Milhaud's *Christophe Colomb* (1954, Rome). His recordings include *La traviata* (with Callas) and a much-praised *Gianni Schicchi* (with Gobbi). CLAUDIO CASINI

Santini, Vincenzo-Felice (*b* Parma, ?1798; *d* Munich, Oct 1836). Italian bass-baritone. He made his début in Venice in 1818 in Rossini's *L'inganno felice*. After hearing him there, Francesco Morlacchi recruited him for the Dresden Hofoper, where he enjoyed considerable success in the Italian repertory. From 1828 to 1834 Santini was associated with the Théâtre Italien in Paris. He made his Parisian début as Rossini's Figaro and established a fine reputation in *buffo* roles, especially Leporello; he was famous for his spirited delivery of the Catalogue Aria. He participated in the Parisian premières of Bellini's *La sonnambula* (1831) and *Il pirata* (1832). During the season of 1834–5 he left Paris for the Munich Hofoper, and he died less than two years later. Santini was noted for his low range and his *buffo* talents, although he had a tendency to exaggerate. He also acquitted himself creditably in serious roles; Fétis said that no one sang the bass aria in Rossini's *Zelmira* better than Santini.

For illustration *see* BARBIERE DI SIVIGLIA, IL (ii).

LAURIE C. SHULMAN

Santis, Luigi de. *See* DE SANTIS, LUIGI.

Santley, Sir **Charles** (*b* Liverpool, 28 Feb 1834; *d* London, 22 Sept 1922). English baritone. He studied in Milan and made his début at Pavia in 1857 as Dr Grenvil, then returned to England for further study with the younger Manuel Garcia. In 1859 he made his English début as Hoël (*Le pardon de Ploërmel*) with the Pyne-Harrison company at Covent Garden. He remained with the company until 1863, creating the Rhineberg in Wallace's *Lurline* (1860), Clifford in Balfe's *The Puritan's Daughter* (1861), Don Sallustio in Glover's *Ruy Blas* (1861), Danny Mann in Benedict's *The Lily of Killarney* (1862) and Fabio in Balfe's *The Armourer of Nantes* (1863).

In 1862 Santley sang Count di Luna with the Royal Italian Opera, Covent Garden, and then joined Mapleson's company at Her Majesty's Theatre, appearing as Count Almaviva and Nevers. In 1863 he sang Valentin with huge success in the first performance of *Faust* in England. He remained with Mapleson's company until 1870, singing the Dutchman (in Italian) in the first production of a Wagner opera in England. In 1875 he joined the newly formed Carl Rosa company, singing Mozart's Figaro on the opening night of its first London season. He retired from the stage in 1877 and was knighted in 1907. Although his voice was not naturally beautiful, he sang with great expression and was a particularly dramatic actor. He wrote three books on singing (1892, 1900 and 1908) and *Reminiscences of my Life* (London, 1909).

*

J. Mewburn Levien: *Sir Charles Santley* (London, 1930)
HAROLD ROSENTHAL/R

Santoliquido, Francesco (*b* San Giorgio a Cremano, Naples, 6 Aug 1883; *d* Anacapri, 26 Aug 1971). Italian composer. He studied with Giacomo Setaccioli and G. Falchi at the Conservatorio di S Cecilia, Rome, graduating in 1908. In 1912 he moved to Tunisia, founding a concert society in Tunis and, in 1927, a music school that later became a conservatory. Before returning to Italy in 1928, he was appointed Accademico di S Cecilia; from 1933 until his death he lived at Anacapri. A writer of chamber and orchestral music, Santoliquido also composed a number of operas that reflect the dominant characteristics of his style. His music displays a taste for exotic settings – and with these hints of Arab music – and a liking for effects that are impressionistic in their timbres and harmonies.

La favola di Helga (os, 1, Santoliquido), Milan, Dal Verme, 23 Nov 1910
Ferhuda (os, 3, Santoliquido), Tunis, Rossini, 1919, vs (Rome, 1920)
L'ignota, 1921 (Santoliquido), unperf.
La bajadera dalla maschera gialla (mimodramma), Rome, Indipendenti, 1923
La porta verde (4), Bergamo, Novità, 1953

*

F. Bonura and others: *Cronistoria della prima rappresentazione dell'opera 'Ferhuda'* (Rome, 1936)
RAFFAELE POZZI

Santos, (José Manuel) Joly Braga (*b* Lisbon, 14 May 1924; *d* Lisbon, 18 July 1988). Portuguese composer and conductor. He studied the violin and composition at the Lisbon Conservatory (1934–43) but abandoned his studies before graduating. He continued to study composition privately with Luis de Freitas Branco until 1945. In 1947 he joined the music studies department of Portuguese radio, for which he wrote a great deal of music. In addition he studied conducting in Venice with Hermann Scherchen in 1948 on a scholarship from the Portuguese government and, later, composition in Rome with Mortari (1959–60). He was conductor of the Oporto SO, 1955–9, assistant conductor of the

Portuguese National RSO, 1961–88, and lecturer in analysis and composition at the Lisbon Conservatory from 1972 until his death. He was also music critic for a Lisbon daily newspaper.

Braga Santos's work is mainly instrumental and may be divided into three phases. His early compositions are clearly indebted to his studies with Freitas Branco. In the 1940s and 50s he was influenced by Portuguese Renaissance polyphony: modality, repetition of rhythmic patterns and a preference for classical forms are discernible as significant features. His first opera, *Viver ou morrer* (1956), belongs to this period; it was performed only in concert form. Towards the end of the 1950s, after his wider contacts with the European mainstream, he began to experiment with free chromaticism and atonality. *Mérope* (1959), his second opera, may be considered the beginning of this new period in which harmony and form are freer and subtler, and orchestral colour becomes an essential component. In his next opera, *Trilogia das barcas* (1970), based on three 16th-century Portuguese plays, he tried to associate these new features with the madrigal forms contemporary with the text. *Mérope* and *Trilogia das barcas* are among the most significant music dramas in Portuguese 20th-century music. Braga Santos's other dramatic works include incidental and ballet music and many film scores.

See also TRILOGIA DAS BARCAS.

Viver ou morrer op.19, 1952 (1, J. de Freitas Branco, after I. Shaw), concert perf., Lisbon, S Carlos, 14 June 1956
Mérope op.28 (3, M. J. B. Santos, after F. S. Maffei, V. Alfieri and J. B. da S. L. de Almeida Garrett), Lisbon, S Carlos, 15 May 1959
Trilogia das barcas op.43 (2, M. J. B. Santos, after G. Vicente), Lisbon, Fundação Calouste Gulbenkian, 8 May 1970

*

J. de Freitas Branco: *História da música portuguesa* (Lisbon, 1959)
Catálogo geral da música portuguesa: repertório contemporâneo (Lisbon, 1978)
J. de Freitas Branco: 'Homenagem à memória de Joly Braga Santos', *São Carlos*, ix (1989), 21–41

ADRIANA LATINO

Santos, Luciano Xavier (*b* Lisbon, 1734; *d* Lisbon, 2 Feb 1808). Portuguese composer. He studied with the Venetian composer Giovanni Giorgi in the school of religious music established by João V at S Catarina de Ribamar and was admitted to the Irmandade de S Cecília, the musicians' union of Lisbon, on 20 May 1756. From then until his death he served as first organist and *mestre* of the royal chapel of the Bemposta in Lisbon. Besides a large quantity of sacred music, he composed several operas and serenatas for the court. His works have not generally been revived in modern times.

first performed in Lisbon, Queluz Palace, and MSS in P-La, unless otherwise stated

dmc – *dramma per musica da cantarsi*

Le grazie vendicate (azione teatrale, P. Metastasio), place of perf. unknown, 1762
Gli orti esperidi (dmc, 2, Metastasio), 1764, only lib. extant
Ercole sul Tago (dmc, 1, V. A. Cigna-Santi), 29 June 1765
Il natal di Giove (dmc, 1, Metastasio), 29 June 1766, only lib. extant
Il sogno di Scipione (dmc, 1, Metastasio), 1768, only lib. extant
Il Palladio conservato (dmc, 1, Metastasio), 1771
Alcide al bivio (dmc, 1, Metastasio), 5 July 1778
Ati, e Sangaride (serenata, G. Martinelli), 25 July 1779
Palmira di Tebe (serenata, Martinelli), 21 Aug 1781
Esione (dmc, 1, Martinelli), Lisbon, Ajuda, 17 Dec 1784
Il re pastore (dramma per musica, 3, Metastasio), place of perf. unknown, 1797
La Galatea (serenata, Metastasio), ?unperf.
1 aria, *P-EVc*

Doubtful: La clemenza di Tito (dramma per musica, 2, Metastasio)

*

M. C. de Brito: *Opera in Portugal in the Eighteenth Century* (Cambridge, 1989)

MANUEL CARLOS DE BRITO

Santunione, Orianna (*b* Sassolo, nr Modena, 1 Sept 1934). Italian soprano. She studied in Milan and in 1960 sang in the first performance of Donizetti's first opera, *Il Pigmalione*, at Bergamo. She made her American début in 1962 at Dallas as Nedda and her Covent Garden début in 1965 as Amelia (*Simon Boccanegra*). She sang at all the principal Italian theatres, including La Scala, where in 1967 she took the title role of Giordano's *Madame Sans-Gêne*. Her repertory included Medea, Elsa, Amelia (*Un ballo in maschera*), Leonora (*Il trovatore* and *La forza del destino*), Desdemona, Aida, Santuzza, Madelon (*Andrea Chénier*), Fedora, La Gioconda, Francesca da Rimini and Tosca. She had a warm personality and a generous, vibrant voice; perhaps her finest role was Minnie, which she sang in Naples, Florence and other cities.

ELIZABETH FORBES

Santurini, Francesco (i) ['Il Baviera'] (*b* Venice, 1627; *d* ?Venice, ?after 1688). Italian stage designer. The son of Stefano Santurini and possibly a cousin of Francesco Santurini (ii), he worked in Venice in collaboration with Gaspare Mauro at the Teatro S Apollinare in 1657 for P. A. Ziani's *Le fortune di Rodope e Damira* and at the S Cassiano in 1658 for Ziani's *L'incostanza trionfante*. He had already been active in Bavaria: engravings of his scenery for J. K. Kerll's *Oronte* (1657) and *Erinto* (1661) survive. Santurini was in the service of the Munich court from 1662 to 1669, and from 1662 to 1665 was designated 'Welscher [Italian] Engineer'; with this title came the responsibility for devising and directing machinery for the spectacular entertainments of 1662 on the occasion of the birth of the heir to the throne, who became Maximilian II Emanuel. Included in the festivities were the opera *Fedra incoronata*, Kerll's mounted tourney-ballet *Antiopa giustificata* and his water spectacle *Medea vendicativa*; these were recorded in engravings by Matthäus Küssel. After 1665 Santurini held the title 'Maestro Navale'. He also designed the scenery for Kerll's *Amor della patria*, performed in Munich in 1665.

In 1667–8 Santurini seems to have paid a brief visit to Venice, since his name appears in the libretto of Boretti's *Alessandro amante*, performed at S Moisè, but his activities on his return to Italy are difficult to trace. The architectural plan of the Teatro S Angelo (managed by Francesco Santurini (ii)) has been attributed to him but is more probably the work of Tommaso Giusti (see Mangini). There is perhaps evidence of his work at the Teatro S Salvador in 1676 in the designs for Legrenzi's *Germanico sul Reno* (for illustration *see* MACHINERY, fig.7) and *Adone in Cipro* in the Bibliothèque de l'Opéra, Paris. The attribution of these drawings to Santurini (see Molinari) has not been universally accepted, in spite of their close stylistic and compositional affinity to the sets for Freschi's *Berenice vendicativa* (1680), performed in the Teatro Grande of the Villa Contarini at Piazzola sul Brenta. Santurini was the stage designer for many entertainments there, and a complete set of engravings of scenes for *Berenice* survives.

The artistic personality and biography of Santurini remain problematic, but even if only the certain attribu-

Stage design by Francesco Santurini for the triumph scene from Freschi's 'Berenice vendicativa' performed in the Teatro Grande of the Villa Contarini at Piazzola sul Brenta, 1680: engraving

tions are taken into account he must be considered one of the great stage designers of the 17th century. Although his early work may be close to examples by Giacomo Torelli (for instance, the throne room for *Oronte*), he soon invented an extraordinary series of models and spectacular effects, such as the palace of Neptune at the bottom of the sea in *Fedra incoronata*, the hunting, stables and triumph scenes in *Berenice vendicativa* (see illustration) and the stage over the Isar river in *Medea vendicativa*.

For further illustration *see* MUNICH, fig.1.

C. Ivanovich: *Minerva al tavolino* (Venice, 1681) [appx: 'Memorie teatrali di Venezia', 400, 452]
H. Tintelnot: *Barocktheater und barocke Kunst* (Berlin, 1939), 59ff
C. Molinari: *Le nozze degli dei: un saggio sul grande spettacolo italiano nel seicento* (Rome, 1968)
M. T. Muraro: 'Teatro di San Luca o di San Salvador', and 'Teatro Grande nella Villa Contarini a Piazzola sul Brenta', *I teatri pubblici di Venezia (secoli XVII–XVIII)* (Venice, 1971), 99, 124–5 [exhibition catalogue]
N. Mangini: *I teatri di Venezia* (Milan, 1974)
Illusione e pratica teatrale (Venice, 1975), 63–6 [exhibition catalogue]
MERCEDES VIALE FERRERO

Santurini [Santorini], **Francesco (ii)** (*fl* 1674–85). Italian impresario. The son of Antonio Santurini according to Ivanovich, who thus distinguished him from Francesco Santurini (i). Santurini acted as impresario of the smallest of the Venetian opera houses, the S Moisè, from 1674 to summer 1675. During this period, Ivanovich notes, he reduced the entrance charge from four lire (the standard charge for entrance to Venetian opera houses since 1637) to a quarter of a ducat (a little more than one and a half lire), forcing the other Venetian houses to follow suit. On 15 August 1676 he entered into a contract with members of the Marcello and Capello families to build and manage for seven years a theatre for comedies and operas in a property in the Corte dell'Albero overlooking the Grand Canal. This, the Teatro S Angelo (the sixth opera house to be opened in Venice), boasted five tiers of 29 boxes. It opened in Carnival 1677 with the opera *Helena rapita da Paride*, with libretto by Aurelio Aureli and music by Domenico Freschi. The theatre ran into financial problems after its first season, and Santurini was forced to seek financial aid from his patrons. His contract was renewed for two further years in 1683. Little is known of his career after 1685. Giazotto suggested that he was associated with the Teatro S Angelo until 1717, and that he worked in partnership with Vivaldi. Mangini stated that the relevant document of 1717 is now untraceable.

C. Ivanovich: *Minerva al tavolino* (Venice, 1681) [appx: 'Memorie teatrali di Venezia', 400, 453]
L. N. Galvani: *I teatri musicali di Venezia nel secolo XVII* (Milan, 1878)
S. T. Worsthorne: *Venetian Opera in the Seventeenth Century* (Oxford, 1954)
R. Giazotto: 'La guerra dei palchi (seconda serie)', *NRMI*, i (1967), 476–87
N. Mangini: *I teatri di Venezia* (Venice, 1974)
M. Talbot: *Vivaldi* (London, 1978)
JOHN WHENHAM

Sanzogno, Nino (*b* Venice, 13 April 1911; *d* Milan, 4 May 1983). Italian conductor and composer. He studied at the Venice Liceo Musicale, and then with Gian Francesco Malipiero in Venice and Scherchen in Brussels. In 1937 he became resident conductor at La Fenice; he first conducted at La Scala in 1939. He inaugurated the Piccola Scala with Cimarosa's *Il matrimonio segreto* in 1955 and took the production to the 1957 Edinburgh Festival along with Donizetti's *L'elisir d'amore*. During these years he was responsible for many premières, including Malipiero's *L'allegra brigata* (1950), the stage première of Milhaud's *David* (1955) and Poulenc's *Dialogue des Carmélites* at La Scala (1957). He also conducted the first Italian productions of Walton's *Troilus and Cressida* (1956, La Scala) and of *Lulu*, *A Midsummer Night's Dream*, *The Fiery Angel* (world stage première) and *Lady Macbeth of the Mtsensk District*, mainly at successive Venice Festivals. As a guest conductor he introduced to Britain Dallapiccola's *Job* with the BBC SO, and conducted a double bill of Dallapiccola and Malipiero operas from the Maggio Musicale Fiorentino at the 1969 Edinburgh Festival. At the Piccola Scala and elsewhere his extensive repertory was widened by a developing interest in Classical and early music, and he was resident conductor at La Scala, 1962–5. British audiences were impressed by his quiet, subtle control, Latin precision and deep musical knowledge, and by his firm discipline masked by outward elegance and charm.

LEONARDO PINZAUTI

S Carlos. Theatre in LISBON (Teatro de São Carlos), opened in 1793; productions ceased in 1910 but began again in 1940.

São Paulo. City in Brazil, the largest in South America. The building of a Casa da Opera in rua de S Bento was approved in 1763; accounts by early 19th-century visitors attest that a performance in translation of Monsigny's *Le déserteur* by blacks and mulattos was representative of the São Paulo repertory.

The Teatro Provisório was inaugurated on 23 August 1873; its earliest seasons depended heavily on Italian operas, particularly Verdi (including *Attila*, *Poliuto* and *Luisa Miller*), as was also the case with the rebuilt Teatro S José (originally inaugurated in 1864), which opened on 11 March 1876 with *Lucia di Lammermoor*. Among the lesser-known offerings at the S José were

Marchetti's *Ruy Blas* and Petrella's *Ione*. In 1880 the S José season was presented by the Angelo Ferrari company; opening with *Les Huguenots* in Italian, it continued with Gomes's *Il Guarany* and *Fosca*.

In 1881 Maurice Grau brought the first French-language performances of Thomas' *Mignon* and of *Carmen*, and the Ferrari company returned with ten operas (including five São Paulo premières: *L'Africaine*, *Robert le diable*, *Dinorah*, *Guillaume Tell* and *Mefistofele*). Ferrari's company presented only six operas in its aborted 1882–3 season, which opened with *Ernani* and closed with *La sonnambula*, attendance having dropped for lack of internationally acclaimed stars. Reorganized under João Barbero's management, the company appealed to local pride by presenting Gomes's *Salvator Rosa*; of his later operas *Lo schiavo*, performed at the S José six weeks after its première in 1889, proved the most popular. World premières of operas by Brazilian composers include Campos's *A bela adormecida* (1924) and Araújo's *Maria Petrowna* (1929), both at the Teatro Municipal.

Lohengrin, São Paulo's first exposure to Wagner, was sung in 1892 in Italian at the S José; *Tristan und Isolde*, also in Italian, reached the Municipal in its inaugural season (which opened on 12 September 1911 with Titta Ruffo in Thomas' *Hamlet*, sung in Italian). *Parsifal* and *Die Walküre* were given there in Italian two years later; by 1922 *Die Meistersinger*, *Siegfried* and *Götterdämmerung* had been presented, in German.

Boris Godunov was the first Russian opera performed in São Paulo (1910, in Italian at the Politeama, inaugurated on 3 March 1894 with *Aida*; the theatre burnt down in 1914). *Prince Igor* followed in 1919 at the Municipal; during the 1920s *Boris* was sung there in Russian, as were *The Tale of Tsar Saltan*, *The Snow Maiden*, *The Legend of the Invisible City of Kitezh* and *The Fair at Sorochintsï*.

The golden age of São Paulo opera came to an end in 1930. A 1932 season at the Teatro Sant'Ana and the Casino Antárctico consisted of 12 operas from the Italian standard repertory. In the 1960 season at the Marcana Stadium, in which Brazilian singers were joined by foreign ones, including Virginia Zeani and Aldo Protti, a similar repertory was offered.

*

P. de Oliveira Castro Cerqueira: *Um século de ópera em São Paulo* (São Paulo, 1954)

A. Barreto do Amaral: *História dos velhos teatros de São Paulo* (São Paulo, 1979)

ROBERT STEVENSON

Sapho (i) ('Sappho'). *Opéra* in three acts by CHARLES-FRANÇOIS GOUNOD to a libretto by Emile Augier; Paris, Opéra, 16 April 1851.

The opera opens on Olympus just before a contest of poetic recitation. Phaon (tenor) loves the poet Sappho (mezzo-soprano) and is loved by the courtesan Glycère (soprano); his friend Pythéas (bass) loves Glycère. Sappho and the poet Alcée [Alcaeus] (tenor) compete, he singing of liberty and injustice and she of love; she is victorious. Having returned to the Isle of Lesbos, Phaon, Pythéas and Alcée plot to oust the tyrant Pittacus. Glycère extracts details about the conspiracy from Pythéas and forces Sappho to repudiate Phaon by threatening to reveal the plot to the tyrant. Phaon in turn takes up with Glycère. The coup is unsuccessful and, after Phaon and his co-conspirators leave the island, Sappho casts herself into the sea.

The only well-known number in the opera is Sappho's final *stances*, 'O ma lyre immortelle', a reworking of Gounod's earlier *mélodie* 'Chanson du pêcheur'. Gounod also used previous music, his setting of Lamartine's *Le soir*, for Sappho's Act 1 ode 'Héro sur la tour solitaire'. At its first appearance, the opera was a box-office failure but a *succès d'estime* for Gounod, the third act in particular attracting critical acclaim. The work failed at a revival in two acts in 1858, for which Gounod revised the Act 1 quartet and compressed events at the beginning of the original second act. In 1884 another version, this time greatly expanded to four acts and including a singing part for Pittacus (bass), was unsuccessful; that version remains unpublished.

STEVEN HUEBNER

Sapho (ii). *Pièce lyrique* in five acts by JULES MASSENET to a libretto by HENRI CAIN and Arthur Bernède after the novel by Alphonse Daudet (1884); Paris, Opéra-Comique (Théâtre Lyrique), 27 November 1897.

The heroine of this middle-period Massenet opera is not the Greek poet hymned by Gounod in 1851, but the protagonist of Daudet's overtly autobiographical novel, which was considered rather daring in its day. The plot carries echoes of *La dame aux camélias* (and indeed of *La traviata*) as well as *Carmen* and *L'arlésienne*. Fanny Legrand (soprano), known as Sapho, is an artist's model of a certain age who has lived life to the full. At a bohemian gathering in the first act she meets the young, callow Jean Gaussin (tenor) from Provence, and they run away together. In Act 2 Jean's parents visit him in Paris with Irène, the orphan girl they have adopted (the Micaëla figure), but do not encounter Fanny herself. In Act 3 the bohemians chance upon Jean in the rustic retreat where he and Fanny are living together, and tell him of her lurid past. He is shattered. In the best scene in the opera he forces her to burn all the letters from her past lovers (but reads them first), hears of her sordid childhood, learns of an illegitimate child fathered by a convicted forger, refuses to believe that he is her first and only true love, and brutally rejects her. In Act 4 Fanny visits Jean's home in Provence to try to win him back, but is defeated in an encounter with his mother (mezzo-soprano). In the last act the positions are reversed: Jean finally admits he cannot live without Fanny and comes to the rustic love-nest they once shared. It is her turn to be cool, at first; though convinced of his sincerity, she makes the supreme operatic sacrifice and, as he falls asleep after his journey, tiptoes out of his life.

Sapho was performed incomplete at the première, which was hastily prepared owing to the limited availability of Emma Calvé, for whom the title role was written, and the approaching death of Massenet's old friend Daudet, who was suffering from the syphilitic infection contracted at the time of the events depicted in the novel. The tenor Julien Leprestre was no actor, and so the brilliant, crucial Letter Scene was omitted. It was of course played at the successful revivals of 1909 and 1916, and is included in the only recording (1977).

The official designation 'pièce lyrique', or 'musical play', is significant: *Sapho* is for the most part sparely scored, often – particularly in arioso – with only one or two instruments in counterpoint to the vocal lines, so the focus is squarely on the singers and their success in declaiming language that is at times salty and direct. This, together with the contemporary setting still comparatively rare in French opera, makes *Sapho*

Massenet's sole successful contribution to the *verismo* movement rather than the more obvious and crude *La Navarraise* (1894). The structure, though, is not veristic; the short opening act has an almost cinematic fragmentation of form. The main difference from the basic *Dame aux camélias* plot lies in the depiction of the family: instead of a cold, authoritarian father there is a loving, basically sympathetic mother, a far more formidable rival to an Older Woman with a Past and one that considerably sharpens the conflict.

Revivals of *Sapho* have been rare. It depends, of course, on the presence of an old-fashioned star singer. Marguerite Carré carried the 1909 revival, and Renée Doria came out of retirement, not altogether wisely, to make the recording. But the work deserves further investigation, if only for its moments of startling modernity. RODNEY MILNES

Saporiti [Codecasa], **Teresa** (*b* 1763; *d* Milan, 17 March 1869). Italian soprano. As a member of Pasquale Bondini's company she sang, with her sister Antonia (*d* 1787), in Leipzig, Dresden and Prague. A report in the *Litteratur und Theater Zeitung* (summer 1782) refers to 'both Demoiselles Saporiti' being engaged for Bondini's company:

> The elder, Antonia, had been a concert singer in Leipzig. She sings the most difficult passages with considerable ease; it is a pity that her voice is somewhat small and that she neglects expression in recitatives. Her younger sister is half a beginner as an actress and singer, and is acclaimed only because of her figure ... the younger Demoiselle Saporiti often appears in man's costume and takes over the role of a castrato, which she does poorly and with a bad grace.

Mozart thought well enough of Saporiti, however, to write elaborate and demanding music for her as Donna Anna in *Don Giovanni* (1787, Prague). She appeared in Venice in P. A. Guglielmi's *Arsace* (1788) and his *Rinaldo* (1789), and in Francesco Bianchi's *Nitteti* at La Scala (1789), and she sang in Bologna, Parma and Modena. In 1795 she was designated *prima buffa assoluta* in a company at St Petersburg, where she achieved a personal success in Cimarosa's *L'italiana in Londra* and Paisiello's *Il barbiere di Siviglia* (1796).

*

K. H. Trögen: *Freie Bemerkungen über Berlin, Leipzig und Prag* (Copenhagen, 1785)

Bohemia, no.304 (1887) CHRISTOPHER RAEBURN

Sarabia, Guillermo (*b* Mazatlán, 1937; *d* Amsterdam, 19 Sept 1985). Mexican baritone. He studied in Zürich, making his début in 1965 at Detmold in Busoni's *Doktor Faust*, and was engaged at Düsseldorf in 1967. He made his Metropolitan début in 1973 as Amonasro, returning as Enrico Ashton, Escamillo and John the Baptist. In 1979 he sang Wozzeck at La Scala, Falstaff in Vienna and Iago in Paris. He also sang in Stuttgart, Munich, Hamburg, San Francisco and Washington DC; he made his British début in 1980 with Scottish Opera as Scarpia and sang Telramund with the Royal Opera at Manchester in 1981. His repertory included Don Giovanni, Pizarro, the Dutchman, Nélusko, Macbeth, Rigoletto, Boccanegra and Simone in Zemlinsky's *Eine florentinische Tragödie*. ELIZABETH FORBES

Saraceni, Adelaide (*b* Rosario, Argentina, 25 Nov 1895). Argentine soprano. She trained in Pesaro and in 1920 made her début at Lugo di Ramagna in *Il barbiere di Siviglia*. In the following years she appeared throughout Italy in lyric coloratura roles, such as Lucia and Violetta, and in the *soprano leggero* repertory, including Susanna (*Le nozze di Figaro*) and Norina (*Don Pasquale*). Susanna was her début role at La Scala in 1928, and she repeated it the following season when she also sang in the La Scala première of Respighi's *La campana sommersa*. Wolf-Ferrari's *La vedova scaltra* (1931) was another première. Her other roles at La Scala included Gilda, Liù and Adina (*L'elisir d'amore*). Later she added heavier parts such as Butterfly, Manon Lescaut and Adriana Lecouvreur. In 1933 she sang Marguerite de Valois in *Les Huguenots* at the Verona Arena. She also appeared at the Colón, Buenos Aires, and as a guest artist in the Netherlands. She is best remembered as Tito Schipa's charming partner in the first complete recording of *Don Pasquale* (1932).

J. B. STEANE

Saracinelli, Ferdinando (*b* Orvieto; *d* ? Florence, 26 Feb 1640). Italian poet. He was a composer and the bailiff in charge of payments and logistics for special musical events at the Medici court from 1610. He wrote *poesia per musica* and librettos for three *balletti* (Lorenzine Tedesco, 1614; Francesca Caccini, 1615; and Peri, 1616) before adapting an episode from *Orlando furioso* into *La liberazione di Ruggiero dall'isola d'Alcina*, set by Francesca Caccini in 1625. Saracinelli's gynocentric libretto portrays Ruggiero's liberation from Alcina's love spell as depending on a power struggle between Alcina and the androgynous *maga* Melissa. Alcina's role draws from Tasso's characterization of Armida (*Gerusalemme liberata*, xvi) and from two feminist poets, Moderata Fonte (*Tredici canti di Floridoro*, 1588) and Lucrezia Marinelli (*La nobiltà e l'eccelenza delle donne*, 1600, and *Amore innamorato*, 1617), to criticize late Renaissance 'courtly love' as disguised misogyny. Melissa's role presents an image of female rule designed to reflect flatteringly on the work's patron, the then-Regent Archduchess Maria Maddalena of Austria.

*

A. Solerti: *Musica, ballo e drammatica alla corte medicea, 1600–1637* (Florence, 1905)

R. Döring: *Ariostos 'Orlando Furioso' im italienischen Theater des Seicento und Settecento* (Hamburg, 1973)

S. G. Cusick: 'Of Women, Music and Power: a Model from *Seicento* Florence', *Musicology and Difference*, ed. R. Solie (Berkeley, CA, forthcoming) SUZANNE G. CUSICK

Sarajevo. Capital city of Bosnia and Hercegovina. It was incorporated into the Austro-Hungarian Empire in 1878. The first opera to be staged was Flotow's *Alessandro Stradella*, given by the Deutsches Sommer-Theater in 1882. Regular performances by visiting companies continued, although no proper theatre building existed before the foundation of the Narodno Pozorište (National Theatre) in 1921. An attempt in 1928 to found a resident opera company was short-lived, but permanent opera and ballet companies were added to the drama company in 1946. All three companies have shared the building, with operas performed three or four times a week during the season (October to June). The auditorium and stage were enlarged in 1952 and 1981 (present cap. 500). The opera established a solid local and a modest international reputation mainly on the standard Italian, German and local Romantic repertory, not neglecting 20th-century classics; it has been prominent in giving premières of contemporary operas by composers of the region. The economic and political crises of the 1980s and 90s had an adverse effect on its activity.

V. Ubavić and J. Lešić, eds.: *Spomenica povodom 50-godišnjice rada Narodnog pozorišta Sarajevo, 1921–1971* [Memoir on the 50th Anniversary of the National Theatre, Sarajevo] (Sarajevo, 1971)

BOJAN BUJIĆ

Sarasota. American town, in south-west Florida. It is a winter resort on Sarasota Bay. Opera had its origins there in 1951, when the Ringling Museum bought an 18th-century Baroque theatre in the Italian town of Asolo, shipped it to Florida and reassembled it as an annexe to the museum. The opening was celebrated in 1952 with performances of *Bastien et Bastienne* and *La serva padrona* by the New York City Center Opera. In 1958 the City Center brought its production of *Die Entführung aus dem Serail* to the Asolo. The performance was seen by Joseph Turnau, director of an opera company in Woodstock, New York, whose principal goal was taking opera to small communities; for 14 years the Turnau Opera Company played in Woodstock in the summer and at the Asolo Theatre (cap. 320), Sarasota, in the winter.

In 1974 the Turnau company ceased operations and a local organization for opera was formed. Productions were generally of modest scale, suitable for a small auditorium, with minimal scenery and costumes, and usually with two-piano accompaniment. The repertory ranged from *Orfeo ed Euridice* (Gluck) and *Don Pasquale* to *Bluebeard's Castle* and Orff's *Die Kluge*. In 1979 the company took the name Sarasota Opera and acquired the A. B. Edwards Theater at 61 North Pineapple Avenue (built 1926). In 1982 Victor DeRenzi became artistic director and conductor, and Deane Carroll Allyn, president of the previous community organization since 1977, became executive director. From then, productions were fully costumed and staged and were accompanied by an orchestra.

Renovation of the theatre was completed for the 1990 season, and the Sarasota Opera House (cap. 1033), as it is now known, has sparked a city centre redevelopment project. The company presents a ten-week season, from early January to mid-March. Five performances each of four operas are presented, usually three from the standard repertory and one more unusual work: in recent years the repertory has included *The Rake's Progress*, *Fidelio*, *Falstaff*, Catalani's *La Wally* and Verdi's *Aroldo*. These are demanding works for a small company serving a relatively conservative audience, but they have been remarkably successful, both artistically and financially. CHARLES MICHAEL CARROLL

Saratov. City in western central Russia, on the Volga river. It has one of the longest operatic histories in Russia, with performances of works by Grétry, Paisiello and Fomin documented at the homes of several nobles in specially built theatres as early as 1810. The theatre run by the local governor A. D. Panchulidzev operated well after most others had fallen out of use, presenting recent works from St Petersburg and eventually becoming independent; the old wooden building was replaced with a new stone theatre in 1865. P. M. Medvedev's troupe appeared each year in several theatres from August 1875, even despite the fire which interrupted his second season. A permanent opera troupe was established under the direction of I. O. Palitsïn in 1890, making its début on 3 October with *A Life for the Tsar*; the following season (September 1891–March 1892, shared with a dramatic troupe) was so successful financially that the city theatre directorship attempted to restrict the theatre to opera alone. The Kazansko-Saratovskoye Operno-Dramaticheskoye Tovarishchestvo (Kazan'-Saratov Opera-Dramatic Company), under M. M. Boroday and later N. I. Sobol'shchikov-Samarin, gave regular performances from 1894 in a variety of theatres. From 1908 to 1917 several private associations shared stages with touring companies; only the Saratovskaya Opera imeni N. A. Rimskogo-Korsakova (Rimsky-Korsakov Saratov Opera; 1918–20) lasted more than a single season. A permanent company was achieved in 1933 with the foundation of the Saratovskiy Teatr Operï i Baleta in the stone theatre dating from 1865; the theatre was later renamed the Saratovskiy Teatr Operï i Baleta imeni N. G. Chernïshevskogo (Chernïshevsky Saratov Theatre of Opera and Ballet). Premières there have included works by B. A. Mokrousov, G. L. Zhukovsky, G. G. Kreitner and A. S. Lensky. In 1962 the company moved to a new 1200-seat theatre. In 1986 the city was the site of the first L. V. Sobinov All-Russian Festival of Operatic Art.

*

ME (M. F. Geyli; also 'Saratovskiy teatr operï i baleta', V. V. Zlatorunsky)

L. Zakom: 'Iz istorii opernogo iskusstva v Saratove' [From the History of Opera in Saratov], *Literaturnïy Saratov (al'manakh)*, ix (Saratov, 1948)

Ya. Yevdokimov: 'Muzïkal'noye proshloye Saratova (do 1917 goda)' [Musical Past of Saratov (up to 1917)], *Iz muzïkal'nogo proshlogo* [From the Musical Past], ed. B. S. Shteynpress, i (Moscow, 1960), 143–225

N. N. Bogolyubov: *60 let v opernom teatre* [60 Years in Opera Theatre] (Moscow, 1967) GREGORY SALMON

Sardelli, Anna Maria ['La Campaspe'] (*b* Rome; *fl* 1649–59). Italian singer. One of the most celebrated of the singer-courtesans who were a feature of the Italian operatic world in the 17th and 18th centuries, she was a protégée of Prince Matthias de' Medici. The earliest mention of her refers to an episode during December 1649 and January 1650; while her protector was Francesco Guicciardini and she was engaged at the Teatro SS Giovanni e Paolo in Venice, she revealed her intention of becoming a nun. The project came to nothing, and in Carnival 1651 in Venice, after she had left Guicciardini, she sang Campaspe in Antonio Cesti's *Alessandro vincitor di se stesso*, whence her nickname. In the 1652 carnival in Venice she sang Cleopatra in *Il Cesare amante*, also by Cesti, who was probably her lover. She had to leave Venice in that year as a result of stormy love affairs, and she returned to Florence, where she sang again in Cesti's *Alessandro* (1654), signing the libretto. Thereafter, although there are references to her until 1659, little is known of her career.

*

L. Bianconi and T. Walker: 'Dalla *Finta pazza* alla *Veremonda*: storie di Febiarmonici', *RIM*, x (1975), 379–454

S. Durante: 'Il cantante', *Il sistema produttivo e le sue competenze*, *SOI*, iv, ed. L. Bianconi and G. Pestelli (Turin, 1987), 347–410

PAOLA BESUTTI

Sardinero, Vicente [Vincenzo] (*b* Barcelona, 12 Jan 1937). Spanish baritone. He studied at Barcelona and made his début there in 1964 as Escamillo. In 1966 he won the international Verdi contest at Busseto, and the following year sang Enrico Ashton at La Scala. He has sung at the major opera houses of Europe and North and South America, and his repertory includes Mozart's and Rossini's Figaro, Riccardo (*I puritani*), Alphonse (*La favorite*), Nottingham (*Roberto Devereux*) and several Verdi roles – Luna, Germont, Renato and Posa. He also sings Valentin (*Faust*), Albert (*Werther*), Tonio (*Pagliacci*) and Marcello (*La bohème*), his début role at Covent Garden (1976), though his smoothly produced, lightweight baritone is better suited to the music of Bellini and Donizetti. ELIZABETH FORBES

Sardou, Victorien (*b* Paris, 5 Sept 1831; *d* Paris, 8 Nov 1908). French dramatist and librettist. The son of an impoverished schoolmaster, he abandoned a medical training to devote himself to writing. His first success was *Les premières armes de Figaro* (1859), a *comédie-vaudeville* with a typically sprightly trouser role for Virginie Déjazet that owed as much to Scribe as to Beaumarchais. Continuing in Scribe's footsteps, Sardou made his reputation with 'well-made' plays such as *Pattes de mouche* (1860) and wrote gay, satirical comedies such as *Famille Benoîton* (1865) and, in collaboration with Najac, *Divorçons* (1880). A staunch conservative in outlook, he attacked social attitudes in *Les femmes fortes* (1860), and in *Rabagas* (1872) he pilloried political leaders of the day. It was almost certainly the successful revival of some of Victor Hugo's plays that led Sardou in middle age to write historical melodramas such as *Patrie!* (1869), *La haine* (1874), *Théodora* (1884) and *La Tosca* (1887) – tense, tragic tales of human passion, usually against a background of war or popular rebellion. The spectacle was extravagant and lavish, but Sardou, a keen amateur historian, insisted on archaeological accuracy. He took pains to devise roles for such celebrities as Gabrielle Réjane and Sarah Bernhardt, and *Robespierre* (1899) and *Dante* (1903) were written for Irving to perform in London, where, despite G. B. Shaw's fulminations, Sardou's plays were as popular as in Paris.

Sardou may fairly be regarded as Scribe's natural successor, although he achieved no real success as a librettist except in *Le roi Carotte* (1872), which he wrote for Offenbach. Most of Sardou's plays require either songs or incidental music, sometimes on a lavish scale, which was provided by numerous composers. Others were immediately attracted by the possibilities of making operas out of Sardou's melodramas, but his most significant contribution was his collaboration with Illica and Giacosa on the highly successful rewriting of *La Tosca* for Puccini's opera (1900). Popular and remarkably prolific in his day, his reputation waned rapidly after his death. Like Scribe he is remembered primarily for his highly emotional, lavishly theatrical contribution to opera.

Piccolino (comedy, 1861): Mme Grandval, 1869; J. Strauss, 1873, as Carneval in Rom; Guiraud, 1876
Les prés St-Gervais (vaudeville, 1862): Lecocq, 1874
Patrie! (drama, 1869): Lauro Rossi, 1874, as La contessa di Mons; Paladilhe, 1886
Rabagas (comedy, 1872): N. de Giosa, 1882
La haine (drama, 1874): N. F. Solov'yov, 1885, as Kordeliya
Fédora (drama, 1882): Giordano, 1898
La Tosca (drama, 1887): Puccini, 1900
Madame Sans-Gêne (comedy, 1893): E. Dłuski, 1896; Giordano, 1915
Gismonda (drama, 1894): Février, 1919
La sorcière (drama, 1903): C. Erlanger, 1912

Librettos: *La bataille d'amour* (oc, with K. Daclin), Vaucorbeil, 1863; *Le capitaine Henriot* (oc, with G. Vaëz), Gevaert, 1864; *Grisélidis* (oc), Bizet, inc., 1870–71; *Le roi Carotte* (opéra bouffe), Offenbach, 1872; *Les noces de Fernande* (oc, with E. de Najac), L. Deffès, 1878; *Don Quichotte* (with C. Nuitter), A. Renaud, 1895; *La fille de Tabarin* (comédie lyrique, with Ferrier), Pierné, 1901

J. A. Hart: *Sardou and the Sardou Plays* (Philadelphia, 1913)
G. Mouly: *La vie prodigieuse de Sardou* (Paris, 1931)
G. Mouly, ed.: *Les papiers de V. Sardou: notes et souvenirs* (Paris, 1934)
P. Smith: *The Tenth Muse* (New York, 1970)

CHRISTOPHER SMITH

Sarfaty, Regina (*b* Rochester, NY, 1932). American mezzo-soprano. She studied at the Juilliard School and made her début at Santa Fe in 1957, then sang with the New York City Opera in 1958. She appeared in many contemporary works, including Stravinsky's *The Rake's Progress* and *Oedipus Rex*, Menotti's *The Consul* and *Maria Golovin*, Floyd's *Wuthering Heights*, Robert Ward's *He who gets Slapped* and Moore's *The Wings of the Dove*. She also sang Cherubino, Dorabella, Jane Seymour (*Anna Bolena*), Clairon (*Capriccio*) and Carmen. In 1960 she made her European début at Glyndebourne as Octavian. She then joined the Zürich Opera, where her roles included Countess Geschwitz (*Lulu*) and Ismene, which she sang in the première of Kelterborn's *Die Errettung Thebens* (1963). In 1968 she returned to Santa Fe as Agave in Henze's *The Bassarids* and in 1969 sang Carmen at the Paris Opéra. In 1981 she sang Mrs Herring (*Albert Herring*) in Geneva and in 1984 Madame de Croissy (*Dialogues des Carmélites*) at Baltimore. Her full-toned, flexible voice and powerful dramatic presence made her equally successful as Preziosilla and Delilah as in the modern repertory.

ELIZABETH FORBES

Sargent, Sir **(Harold) Malcolm (Watts)** (*b* Ashford, Kent, 29 April 1895; *d* London, 3 Oct 1967). English conductor. He came to prominence in 1921 when he was invited to conduct a work of his own at a Promenade concert. He joined the RCM teaching staff in 1923. From 1939 he was principal conductor of the Hallé Orchestra and then of the Liverpool PO and the BBC SO; he was in charge of the BBC Promenade Concerts from 1948 until his death. He was also an outstanding choral conductor. Sargent's operatic experience, sporadic but varied, included the first performances of three Vaughan Williams operas: *Hugh the Drover* (1924) for the British National Opera Company, and *Sir John in Love* (1929) and *Riders to the Sea* (1937), both for the RCM. He also conducted the première of Holst's *At the Boar's Head* (1925) and the first public stage performance of Falla's *El retablo de Maese Pedro*, in Bristol (1924). At Covent Garden in 1954 he gave the première of Walton's *Troilus and Cressida*. His longest and probably deepest theatrical attachment was to Gilbert and Sullivan operettas and the D'Oyly Carte Opera Company, which he conducted on several occasions from 1923. Sargent's spruce, extrovert personality stood him in equally good stead for the Proms and for his many visits abroad. He was a popular member of the wartime BBC Brains Trust, and was knighted in 1947.

*

C. Reid: *Malcolm Sargent: a Biography* (London, 1968)

RONALD CRICHTON

Sari, Ada [Szajerówna, Jadwiga] (*b* Wadowice, 29 June 1886; *d* Ciechocinek, 12 July 1968). Polish soprano. She studied in Vienna and Milan with Antonio Rupnick. Her début, as Marguerite in *Faust* at the Costanzi, Rome, in 1909 led to engagements throughout Italy, where she sang in a lyric-dramatic repertory that included Santuzza in *Cavalleria rusticana* and Elisabeth in *Tannhäuser*. From 1912 onwards she specialized in coloratura parts such as Lucia, Rosina and Lakmé. She toured Russia with an Italian company, and in 1917 appeared as a guest artist in *Die Entführung* at Warsaw. In 1923 she sang the Queen of Night at La Scala under Toscanini. She was also heard in South America and the USA, and in later years concentrated largely on concert work, continuing to sing in Poland (with increasingly distressing results) even after 1945. Her later recordings show how the voice loosened, though the fluency remains impressive; in youth the tone was sweet and steady, the style often remarkably expressive.

J. B. STEANE

Šárka. Opera in three acts, op.51, by ZDENĚK FIBICH to a libretto by Anežka Schulzová; Prague, National Theatre, 28 December 1897.

Vlasta	*Maidens from Libuše's council*	mezzo-soprano
Šárka		soprano
Libyna		soprano
Svatava		soprano
Mlada		soprano
Radka		mezzo-soprano
Častava		contralto
Hosta		contralto
Duke Přemysl		baritone
Vitoraz *high priest*		bass
Ctirad *a chieftain*		tenor

Elders, chieftains, knights, priests, girls, women prisoners, ghosts of the dead girls

Setting Bohemia in pagan times, after the death of Libuše

'Šárka' (Fibich): costume design by Mikoláš Aleš for the title role in the original production at the National Theatre, Prague, 28 December 1897

Fibich's penultimate opera was the second of his three operas written to librettos by Anežka Schulzová, its subject matter based on an incident from the 'maidens' war' in the mythic history of Bohemia. The incident was first referred to in the 14th-century Czech verse chronicle by Dalimil, and in the 19th century it became a favourite subject in Czech art and literature. In music it is also known through Smetana's tone poem *Má vlast* and Janáček's first opera, *Šárka*.

Fibich's piano sketch, representing a near-definitive version of the work, is dated 21 January 1896–11 June 1896 (Act 1) and 17 September (beginning of Act 2); Act 3 is undated. The orchestral score, written simultaneously with the latter part of the piano sketch, is dated 15 September 1896–10 March 1897. The première followed later that year under Adolf Čech and a distinguished cast which included Růžena Maturová (Šárka), Anna Kettnerová (Vlasta), Václav Viktorin (Přemysl), Bohumil Pták (Ctirad) and Václav Kliment (Vitoraz). Partly because of its familiar Czech subject, the work became Fibich's most popular and frequently performed opera, and the title role has attracted some of the most distinguished Czech sopranos. It is represented in complete recordings made in 1953 (under Chalabala) and 1978 (Štych).

ACT 1 *The place of sacrifice near Vyšehrad* Vlasta grieves over the death of Libuše, which has brought to an end the power of the women. Libuše's consort Přemysl has assumed power and excluded women from his councils. Vlasta's reflections are interrupted by the energetic Šárka, who is not prepared to settle for reduced status. The women assemble to an elegiac ensemble for female chorus and soloists ('S teskným srdcem': 'With heavy heart'). Šárka interrupts this. She insists, to warm approval, that the women demand their rights, and this sentiment is crowned by Vlasta's march theme, 'Slyšte, věční, prosby hlas' ('Hear, eternal spirits, the voice of our plea, and return to us our sacred rights!'). The women echo this in chorus; at the end their voices mingle with those of the approaching men. The men enter to a long orchestral march, an important theme already heard in the overture. Přemysl's solo 'Přízeň bohů všem!' ('The favour of the Gods to all!') is in many sections, some based on pieces from Fibich's piano 'diary'. Přemysl then calls on the men to begin their sacrifice to the gods, an invocation to the Slav sky-god Svaroh in which the high priest Vitoraz leads the chorus antiphonally ('Bože věčný': 'Eternal God'). Once more Šárka intervenes, offending the men by interrupting their rites. Přemysl urges peace, as does Vlasta, but her plea for the women's rights is gently refused by Přemysl. Šárka and the women vow revenge and war, particularly on Ctirad, whom they feel to be especially hostile.

ACT 2 *A wild, dense forest* A bloody war between the men and the women has broken out. The women assemble, calling to one another from the distance with Valkyrie-like cries. Each new group brings news of fresh successes in the war. Libyna and Svatava lead on a group of women captives, part of the bridal train of Ctirad's friend. Ctirad is said to have gone out alone, vowing a terrible revenge. Šárka, who has taken no part so far, sees her chance. She begs Vlasta to allow her to deal with him and when the rest of the women go off to Děvín, their fortress, Šárka remains with a small band. She ruminates darkly on the approaching fight ('Jako temný stín': 'Like a dark shadow this hate crawls through my being'). 'Am I beautiful?' she asks her followers. In an ensemble ('Krásná, krásná jsi') they assure her she is. She orders them to tie her to an oak tree in Ctirad's path and to leave her until they hear the sound of her horn. The orchestra depicts the going down of the sun. In the twilight of the dense forest Šárka reflects on the horror of her task. But it is too late: Ctirad is heard approaching, singing an ancient folksong, 'Měsíc bílý' ('White moon'). He is surprised to see Šárka tied up, and at once cuts her bonds. His magnanimity overwhelms her; her hatred turns to love. A long dialogue skilfully portrays the dawning love on both sides, until climactically the two voices are heard together. This is followed by a gentle antiphonal Andante ('Viz tu krásnou noc': 'See here the beautiful night') as she sinks into his arms. In a sudden change of mood Šárka then begs Ctirad to flee – to escape the death that she had plotted. Instead, Ctirad fearlessly sounds Šárka's horn. When the women run on, it is Šárka who insists that Ctirad is hers, and she has the right to his life.

ACT 3 *A deserted, rocky valley* Přemysl and his warriors are advancing on Děvín, guided by Šárka. She has left the women in order to save Ctirad (whom the women have seized and plan to kill that evening). The men are to hide and wait for Šárka's sign. The women enter with the bound Ctirad. Ctirad sings of his threatened death ('Já nelekám se, smrti chladná': 'I do not fear you, cold death'), and in an ensemble the women invoke Morana, goddess of death ('Morano svatá! Morano hrozná!': 'Sacred Morana! Terrible Morana!'). Šárka suddenly appears and pleads for Ctirad's life. When Vlasta refuses and pronounces death for her also, Šárka gives the signal for the men to appear. In a short battle the women are overcome and forced out into the narrow pass. A storm gathers; in the clouds the dead women appear as bloody spirits, calling to Šárka. Ctirad's love cannot save her, and Šárka plunges from the rocks to her death.

* * *

Šárka has always been Fibich's most popular opera, the only one to be regularly revived in Czechoslovakia. One of his few operas to be based on Czech subject matter – a subject, moreover, that combines Bohemian mythical history and erotic passion – it is also Fibich's artistically most successful opera. In it his lyrical and dramatic gifts are seen at their best, with a well-constructed, if somewhat old-fashioned libretto that allowed melodic breadth without the longueurs of *Hedy*, or the declamatory curtnesses of *Nevěsta messinská* ('The Bride of Messina') or *Pád Arkuna* ('The Fall of Arkona'). There are many memorable moments but, as in Janáček's opera of the same name, it is the central love–hate relationship of Šárka and Ctirad that seems most to have stirred Fibich's imagination, leading to the incandescent music of their confrontation in Act 2.

JOHN TYRRELL

Sarrebruck (Fr.). SAARBRÜCKEN.

Sarro [Sarri], **Domenico Natale** (*b* Trani, Apulia, 24 Dec 1679; *d* Naples, 25 Jan 1744). Italian composer. His marriage contract, dated 6 February 1705, states that he came to Naples between the ages of six and seven, that he had studied at the Neapolitan conservatory of S Onofrio, and that he had not been outside the city since. His first known composition is a sacred opera, *L'opera d'amore*, performed in 1702 at the Arciconfraternità della Ss Trinità de' Pellegrini. In 1703 he took part in a public competition (the other competitors being Gaetano Veneziano, Cristoforo Caresana and Francesco Mancini) for the vacant post of court *maestro di cappella*. Veneziano obtained the post, but on 26 December 1704 Sarro was appointed vice-*maestro di cappella*.

During 1706 and 1707 Sarro composed several operas for the Neapolitan public theatres. Between 1708 and 1718, however, he wrote few works of this kind: this may partly have been because of changed circumstances at court. In mid-1707 the Austrians captured Naples and drove out the Spanish regime to which Sarro had pledged allegiance. Both he and Veneziano lost their court appointments on 31 August 1707. There is no evidence from Neapolitan sources that the new Austrian government put Sarro back on its payroll before 1720, so the statement in the Venetian libretto of his intermezzo *Barillotto*, performed in Venice in 1712, that he was 'Maestro nella Real Cappella di Napoli' is almost certainly false.

Sarro's promise as a dramatic composer began fully to materialize in 1718. Between this date and 1741 he composed many operas, of which the earlier ones (i.e. those produced between 1718 and 1725) constitute perhaps his most significant contribution to music. *Didone abbandonata* (1724, Naples) is particularly important because it is the first setting of Metastasio's first major libretto. In 1720 Sarro was promised two important musical posts when they became vacant. The first was that of *maestro di cappella* to the city of Naples, which he obtained in 1728 on the death of the holder, Gaetano Greco. The second was that of vice-*maestro di cappella* to the court; to help the composer until he actually occupied this post, the viceroy awarded him a salary of 22½ ducats a month. He became vice-*maestro*, with a stipend of 30 ducats a month, in late October 1725, and he remained in the service of the court for the rest of his life. In 1735 he took over the duties, though not the title, of *maestro di cappella* at court when the holder of the post, Mancini, fell ill. When Mancini died in September 1737, Sarro was appointed his successor with a monthly salary of 35 ducats. One of his first tasks was to compose the opera for the official opening of the Teatro S Carlo, newly erected by order of Charles III. The opera was *Achille in Sciro*, given on 4 November 1737, Charles's name-day.

Sarro was one of the first prominent composers to emerge from the Neapolitan conservatories during the 18th century. By choosing to confine his activities largely to Naples, he acquired only moderate fame abroad during his lifetime. Commentators have since tended to regard him as a transitional composer in between more important generations of Neapolitans represented on the one hand by the much older Alessandro Scarlatti and on the other by Porpora, Vinci, Leo, and other composers slightly younger than himself. His personal contribution to the important changes in musical style and technique that became apparent in Italian vocal music about 1720 has usually been underrated. Describing these changes in his *General History of Music*, Burney gave credit for them to Vinci, mentioning Sarro only briefly in this context. J. J. Quantz, after hearing Sarro's opera *Tito Sempronio Gracco* in Naples in 1725, declared that the composer was copying Vinci's style. Because of statements like these, Sarro has usually been considered an imitator rather than innovator.

Sarro's earliest music is in the quasi-contrapuntal style associated with Alessandro Scarlatti, though it lacks the nervous energy characteristic of Scarlatti's best work. By 1718, however, Sarro's musical textures had become less contrapuntal and his melodies more shapely as regards phrase structure and pitch. By about the time of his *Valdemaro* (1726) he had developed a style in which all the musical interest is in the top melodic part and the lower parts of the texture are reduced to mere accompaniment. These are the changes in compositional method with which Burney credited Vinci. Sarro's relationship to Vinci has yet to be fully examined, but there is no present evidence that Vinci was more progressive than Sarro during the period 1718–23 when Sarro was the fashionable composer in Naples. By about 1726, however, Vinci had become prominent, and Sarro's period of greatest success was over. Very few of his works written after 1730 survive. Those that do lack signs of major technical advance; they lack too the freshness that had made some of his earlier music attractive. Charles de Brosses, who heard the 1739 Neapolitan revival of his opera *Partenope* (1722), called him 'knowledgeable but cold and sad'. The minister Ulloa, responsible for recommending the revival of *Partenope* to the king, who did not like the work, afterwards had to excuse himself: 'The composer Sarro has always been a most celebrated man. It is true however that he flourished in a bygone age'. He promised the king to see to it that the composer's next work, a *festa teatrale* called *Le nozze di Teti e di Peleo* (1739), had music better suited 'to the grandeur of the joyous day and to good modern taste'.

See also ARSACE.

drammi per musica in three acts, first performed in Naples, unless otherwise stated

Candaule re di Lidia (A. Morselli), Fiorentini, Oct 1706
Le gare generose tra Cesare e Pompeo, S Bartolomeo, ?1706, *I-Mc, Nc, US-Wc*
Il Vespasiano (G. C. Corradi, rev. C. de Petris), S Bartolomeo, 1707, *I-Mc, Nc*
Amore fra gli impossibili (G. Gigli), Fiorentini, 1707
Barillotto (int, F. Salvi), Venice, S Angelo, aut. 1712
I gemelli rivali (N. Serino), Fiorentini, 13 Feb 1713; perf. with Batto e Lisetta (int)
Spilletta e Frullo (int, N. Giuvo), Fiorentini, 15 May 1713; perf. with Il comando non inteso, et ubbidito [probably Lotti's opera of 1710, and possibly with new arias by Sarro]
Armida al campo (F. Silvani, after T. Tasso: *Gerusalemme liberata*), S Bartolomeo, 13 Feb 1718, *D-ROu*
La fede ne' tradimenti (Gigli and G. Papis), S Bartolomeo, 15 May 1718; perf. with Padiglio e Rosicca (int)
Arsace (A. Salvi, after T. Corneille: *Le comte d'Essex*), S Bartolomeo, 10 Dec 1718 [probably perf. earlier in the royal palace], perf. with Merilla e Morante (int), *I-Mc, Nc**
Alessandro Severo (A. Zeno), S Bartolomeo, 14 May 1719; perf. with Eurinda e Curio (int)
Ginevra principessa di Scozia (A. Salvi, after L. Ariosto), S Bartolomeo, 20 Jan 1720, *Nc, F-Pc* (attrib. Vinci), perf. with Brunetta e Burlotto (int), *D-Dlb*
Endimione (serenata, P. Metastasio), 30 May 1721 [for wedding of Prince of Belmonte]
Lucio Vero (after Zeno), S Bartolomeo, Jan 1722, perf. with Sestilia e Quinzio (int), *I-Nc**
La Partenope (after S. Stampiglia), S Bartolomeo, 16 Dec 1722, perf. with Eurillo e Beltrammo (int), *A-Wgm*; rev., S Bartolomeo, 23 Jan 1723, *I-Nc*; int rev., Rome, Pace, carn. 1724, arias in *F-Pc, GB-Lbl* and *I-Rc*
Didone abbandonata (Metastasio), S Bartolomeo, 1 Feb 1724; perf. with L'impresario delle isole Canarie [Dorina e Nibbio] (int), *Nc; D-MEIr, WD* (arias), *I-Nc*; rev., Venice, S Giovanni Grisostomo, aut. 1730, *Nc*
Tito Sempronio Gracco (Stampiglia), S Bartolomeo, Jan 1725, *Nc*
Il Valdemaro (Zeno: *L'amor generoso*), Rome, Dame, carn. 1726, *Nc*, arias in *A-Wn, D-Dlb* and *LEm*
Siroe re di Persia (Metastasio), S Bartolomeo, 25 Jan 1727, perf. with Moschetta e Grullo (int), *I-Nc*
Artemisia (G. Migliavacca), S Bartolomeo, 7 Jan 1731, perf. with La furba e lo sciocco [Madama Sofia e Conte Barlacco] (int), *Nc*
Berenice (Papis, after Silvani: *La virtu trionfante dell'odio e dell'amore*), Rome, Argentina, carn. 1732, perf. with Ombrone e Giletta (int), *Nc*
La finta pellegrina (ob, F. A. Tullio), Nuovo, carn. 1734, collab. A. Orefice
Demofoonte (Metastasio), S Bartolomeo, 20 Jan 1735; music in Act 1 only, collab. F. Mancini and Leo, ints by Sellitto
Gli amanti generosi (ob, T. Mariani), Fiorentini, 15 May 1735
Fingere per godere (ob, Mariani), Nuovo, spr. 1736
La Rosaura (ob, G. A. Federico), Fiorentini, wint. 1736
Achille in Sciro (Metastasio), S Carlo, 4 Nov 1737 [inauguration of Teatro S Carlo], *Nc*
Le nozze di Teti e di Peleo (int), Palazzo Reale, 2 Dec 1739 [for wedding of Don Felipe, Infante of Spain, and Elisabeth]
Ezio (Metastasio), S Carlo, 4 Nov 1741, arias in *F-Pn* and *I-Mc*
Alessandro nell'Indie (Metastasio), S Carlo, carn. 1743

Arias in T. Albinoni: Griselda, 1706

*

BurneyH; *CroceN*; *FlorimoN*; *RosaM*
U. Prota-Giurleo: *Breve storia del teatro di corte e della musica a Napoli nel secoli XVII–XVIII* (Naples, 1952)
H. Hucke: 'La "Didone abbandonata" di Domenico Sarri nella stesura del 1724 e nella revisione del 1730', *Gazzetta musicale di Napoli*, ii (1956), 180–89; Ger. trans., 'Die beiden Fassungen der Oper "Didone abbandonata" von Domenico Sarri', *GfMKB, Hamburg 1956*, 113–17
U. Prota-Giurleo: 'Domenico Sarro', *Archivi*, new ser., xxvi (1959), 73–85
H. Hucke: 'Die neapolitanische Tradition in der Oper', *IMSCR*, viii *New York 1961*, 253–76
M. F. Robinson: *Naples and Neapolitan Opera* (Oxford, 1972)
R. Strohm: *Italienische Opernarien des frühen Settecento (1720–1730)*, *AnMc*, no.16 (1976) [whole issue]

MICHAEL F. ROBINSON (text), DALE E. MONSON (work-list)

Sarroca, Suzanne (*b* Carcassonne, 21 April 1927). French soprano. She studied in Toulouse, making her début in 1949 at Carcassonne as Charlotte (*Werther*). In 1951 she sang Carmen in Brussels, then made her début with the Opéra-Comique as Tosca and at the Paris Opéra in Rameau's *Les Indes galantes* (1952). She created Lyra in Barraud's *Numance* (1955). Her repertory included Senta, Reiza (*Oberon*), Elisabeth (*Tannhäuser*), Elisabeth de Valois (*Don Carlos*), Aida, Octavian, Marina (*Boris Godunov*), Marguerite (*Faust* and *La damnation de Faust*), Donna Anna and Leonore in *Fidelio*. She sang in most of the major European opera houses. At Salzburg she took part in Cavalieri's *Rappresentatione di Anima, et di Corpo* (1968). A reliable singer, she was also a fine actress.

ELIZABETH FORBES

Sarti [Sardi], **Giuseppe** (*b* Faenza, bap. 1 Dec 1729; *d* Berlin, 28 July 1802). Italian composer. He was a leading figure in late 18th-century opera.

1. LIFE. Sarti was the seventh of 11 children of a jeweller who was also a violinist. He began his musical education with F. A. Vallotti in Padua and at the age of ten went to study with Padre Martini in Bologna. He was organist of Faenza Cathedral from 1748 to 1752, when he accepted the directorship of the theatre in Faenza, for

which he wrote his first opera, *Pompeo in Armenia*. In December 1752 he became music director of Pietro Mingotti's opera troupe, which visited Copenhagen late in 1753. His talent and personality won him the admiration of King Frederik V, who in 1755 nominated him to succeed Scalabrini as court Kapellmeister. Later he became director of the Italian opera company at Copenhagen. He continued to compose *opere serie* and may also have written a Danish opera (*Gram og Signe*, 1756). When in 1763 the Italian opera was closed Sarti became director of court music; in this position he had the opportunity to compose instrumental works. In 1765 the king sent him back to Italy to engage singers for the proposed reopening of the opera; but the king died, and Sarti remained in Italy for the next three years. From 19 May 1766 to 11 September 1767 he was *maestro di coro* at the Pietà Conservatory in Venice. During this time he composed several serious works, as well as his first comic piece for the stage, the intermezzo *La giardiniera brillante*. On his return to Copenhagen in 1768 he resumed the post of director of the royal chapel and became the king's singing teacher. From 1770 to 20 May 1775 he directed the court theatre, for which he wrote both Italian and Danish works. While in Copenhagen he married Camilla Passi, by whom he had two daughters. In 1775 he was dismissed after siding with the wrong party in a series of political intrigues, and returned to Italy.

In 1779 Sarti entered a competition to become *maestro di cappella* of Milan Cathedral. His victory and the successful revival of his *Le gelosie villane* at La Scala greatly increased his reputation and won him many pupils, including Cherubini. During these years Sarti created a series of works that were extremely popular throughout Europe and brought his fame to its zenith; these included, besides *Le gelosie villane* (1776), the comic opera *Fra i due litiganti* (1782) and the serious operas *Medonte* (1777) and *Giulio Sabino* (1781). In 1782 Grand Duke Paul of Russia heard his *Alessandro e Timoteo* at Parma and suggested to Catherine II that Sarti might succeed Paisiello as director of the imperial chapel. The empress extended the invitation, and in 1784 he left Italy for St Petersburg, stopping in Vienna where he was graciously received by Joseph II and given the proceeds of a performance of *Fra i due litiganti*, which had gained great favour there. He met Mozart who played to him and spoke of him as an honest, good man. Mozart later quoted the theme of 'Come un agnello' from *Fra i due litiganti* in *Don Giovanni*.

In St Petersburg Sarti was showered with honours, and under his direction the Italian opera reached an artistic peak. His outstanding works of this period were the comic opera *I finti eredi* (1785) and the *opera seria Armida e Rinaldo* (1786). He also wrote French and German works and even collaborated with Pashkevich and Canobbio on a Russian opera, *Nachal'noye upravleniye Olega* ('The Early Reign of Oleg', 1790). This work, which was the sensational event of the season and remained in the repertory for the next five years, was based on a libretto by Catherine II, who supervised the production herself. Court intrigue involving the mezzo-soprano Luisa Todi sent Sarti into seclusion in a village in Ukraine given him by Prince Potemkin. There he founded a singing-school which later produced some important singers. In 1793 the empress restored him to favour and appointed him director of a conservatory modelled on those in Italy, a position he retained for the rest of his stay in Russia. While there he invented a machine for counting the vibrations of sounds, and thereafter he established a pitch standard for the St Petersburg orchestras (a' = 436). In 1801, after the death of the emperor, he decided to return to Italy. He broke his journey in Berlin to visit one of his daughters who was married to the queen mother's Kapellmeister, Natale Mussini. He died there and was buried in the Hedwigkirche.

2. Works. During a time when *opere serie* were seldom revived, and three productions of a single work were rare, Sarti's serious operas reached an astonishing level of popularity. 19 had at least two productions and eight of these were revived three or more times. *Giulio Sabino* had more than 20 productions and *Medonte* more than 30, numbers that rival exceptionally popular comic operas. Among his comic operas *I contrattempi* and *I finti eredi* achieved moderate success, and *Fra i due litiganti* and *Le gelosie villane* had between 30 and 40 productions. Among his admirers Sarti could count Haydn, who directed six of his operas at Eszterháza over a nine-year period. Sarti's almost immediate acclaim in Italy seems all the more remarkable because he had spent ten years writing traditional *opera seria* at the Danish court. On his return to Italy he had an opportunity to compose works to librettos by Giovanni de Gamerra (*Medonte*), Pietro Giovannini (*Giulio Sabino*) and Ferdinando Moretti (*Idalide*). These three operas represent some of the most traditional work of these innovatory librettists (though *Idalide* has an exotic Peruvian setting, a temple scene incorporating dance and a volcanic eruption).

Sarti also became involved in the newly revived opera in Florence during the reign of Archduke Leopold, who had been in Vienna at the time of Gluck's activity there. Sarti's first *Olimpiade* (1778) suggests an acquaintance with Paisiello's pioneering version of *Nitteti* for St Petersburg in 1777. Like Paisiello's *Nitteti*, *Olimpiade* includes not only the choruses of Metastasio's original, but also, in the middle of Act 1, a sacrificial scene with a *giuramento* for antiphonal chorus, and a dance of celebration. As in the heavily revised version of Traetta's *Nitteti* given in St Petersburg in 1769, a chorus follows the duet at the end of Act 1 and introduces a ballet related to the subject of the opera. In the sextet that concludes Act 2, three-part counterpoint and contrasting tempos and textures heighten the dramatic intensity of the 'horrible tempest' in the poetry. Sarti's setting of *Achille in Sciro* for Florence in 1779 also includes the choruses that most Italian productions omitted, and his *Mitridate a Sinope* of the same year begins with an introductory ensemble, rare in *opera seria* at that time.

In St Petersburg Sarti found himself at a court with strong ties to French culture. As in Parma and Vienna, Italian operas were frequently based on French-inspired texts and incorporated spectacular elements such as dance, pantomime, chorus, supernatural appearances and scene complexes in which the formal convention of the exit aria is suspended to admit fluent sequences of recitative, ensemble, chorus and cavatina. Sarti's *Alessandro e Timoteo* for Parma clearly demonstrates his ability to write a French-inspired opera, and similar works followed in Russia – *Armida e Rinaldo* and *Castore e Polluce*. His *festa teatrale Astrea placata* and the pastorales *Narciso* and *Il naufragio di Cipro* for Copenhagen in the 1760s have similar characteristics, as well as many ensembles. *Il naufragio* opens with an extensive, programmatic scene complex to accompany a shipwreck, and later a dragon appears. (Mozart's *Idomeneo* shares these memorable elements.) In the most curious of Sarti's works, his Russian opera *The Early Reign of Oleg*, he attempted to imitate the style of the ancient Greeks; the use of Russian subject matter and folk music foreshadows later Russian national opera.

Most of Sarti's comic operas conform to Goldoni's plan: an introductory ensemble with multi-sectional, action-ensemble finales closing Acts 1 and 2 and a simpler ensemble finale to conclude Act 3. The rest of the opera consists of recitatives and arias, with a duet for the principal *buffo* couple. His two greatest successes closely follow this pattern: *Fra i due litiganti* has a large quartet in Act 2 and a fashionable aria with interjections by a second character; *Le gelosie villane* has several trios, one of which dwindles to a solo when two of the characters depart. Beside these works, *Il militare bizzarro* (1778, Venice) and *I finti eredi* (1785, St Petersburg) stand out as notable exceptions. The first has a large action ensemble in each act (a quartet and a sextet respectively), and the second has a quintet leading to a sextet in Act 2 and incorporates chorus and dance, notably in the last finale, set at a ball.

The multiple ensembles and choruses that were to invade both serious and comic opera in the 1790s were only beginning to come into vogue during Sarti's most active period of composition. Thus his celebrated reputation must have rested almost solely on his arias. His aria forms progress from the *da capo al segno* (with the sign marked at the entrance of the voice) in the early 1760s, through the modified *dal segno* (with the sign in the second statement of the first section) of the late 1760s, to the variety of forms found in the 1770s and 80s, when through-composed ternary and abbreviated binary forms (*AA'* or *AB*) predominated, interspersed with the occasional da capo minuet and various rondo forms (particularly two-tempo rondòs for the principals). Shortened rondo forms (*ABA'B'*) predominate in his comic operas. Contrasting tempos reflect changes of mood in the poetry, and Sarti was quick to exploit opportunities to end with a fast section. Some time during the late 1760s he stopped composing the words of his ensembles twice over and wrote dynamic multi-sectional pieces in several tempos, concluding with a fast tutti. In his *opere serie*, bravura arias with lavish melismatic sections alternate with charmingly ornamented, decorative pieces, and in the dramatic works of great emotional intensity the musical style moves abruptly, contrasting the declamatory with the tender and lyrical, as the text demands. Tonality and modality range widely, expressing violently contrasting emotions or events. Chromaticism is also used with particularly striking effect.

Historians have been unduly harsh in assessing Sarti. While he was certainly sometimes guilty of producing good effects at the expense of musical nuance, he stands head and shoulders above his contemporaries in the richness and variety of his orchestral effects. Strong contrasts in dynamics, tonality and tempo, use of wind colour and varied orchestral accompaniment enhance the meaning of the words. He might detach the bassoons, cellos and violas from the continuo to double a singer's part or to take solo or obbligato roles; he used wind instruments during the vocal parts and in *B* sections, places where few of his contemporaries did so. When given the opportunity he exploited the more unusual wind instruments: clarinets at Naples and Milan, the serpent at St Petersburg and the english horn at Mestre. Marches are common in his operas, and in *Vologeso* he even provided the battle music, a task often left to someone else. He also composed ballet music for *Castore* and *Alessandro*. Sarti's meticulous and expressive orchestration produced powerfully dramatic obbligato recitatives, combining sustained accompaniment with string tremolo or measured arioso for deeply emotional expression.

See also *DIDONE ABBANDONATA* (ii); *FRA I DUE LITIGANTI IL TERZO GODE*; *GELOSIE VILLANE, LE*; *GIULIO SABINO*; and *MEDONTE, RE DI EPIRO*. For illustration *see* GONZAGA, PIETRO.

CK – *Copenhagen, Theatre on Kongens Nytorv, later Kongelige Teater (1770)*
VS – *Venice, S Samuele*

cmda – *comédie mêlée d'ariettes*
dg – *dramma giocoso*
dm – *dramma per musica*

Pompeo in Armenia (dm, 3, ? B. Vitturi), Faenza, Accademia dei Rimoti, carn. 1752
Il re pastore (dm, 3, P. Metastasio), Pesaro, Sole, carn. 1752
Vologeso (dm, 3, A. Zeno: *Lucio Vero*), CK, carn. 1754, *B-Bc*, *F-Pn*, *US-Wc*; rev., Venice, 1765, *P-La*
Antigono (dm, 3, Metastasio), CK, 14 Oct 1754, collab. others; rev., Verona, 1765, *La*
Ciro riconosciuto (dm, 3, Metastasio), CK, 21 Dec 1754, *B-Bc*, *F-Pn*, *US-Wc*; (Copenhagen, 1756) [without recits.]
Demofoonte [1st version] (dm, 3, Metastasio), CK, carn. 1755, *DK-Kk*
Sesostri (dm, 3, P. Pariati), CK, 1755
Arianna e Teseo (dm, Pariati), CK, carn. 1756
Anagilda (dm, G. Gigli), CK, aut. 1758, *S-Skma*
Achille in Sciro (dm, 3, Metastasio), CK, 1759
Armida abbandonata (dm, L. de Villati), CK, 1759
Artaserse (dm, 3, Metastasio), CK, carn. 1760, arias in *I-Fc*, *Gl*, *Nc* and *Tn*
Astrea placata (festa teatrale, 1, Metastasio), CK, 17 Oct 1760
Andromaca (dm, 3, Zeno), CK, aut. 1760
Filindo (pastorale eroica, 3, P. d'Averara), CK, 1760
Issipile (dm, 3, Metastasio), CK, spr. 1761
Nitteti (dm, 3, Metastasio), CK, 12 Oct 1761; rev., Venice, 1765, *A-Wn*, *P-La*, excerpts *GB-Lbl*
Alessandro nell'Indie (dm, 3, Metastasio), CK, aut. 1761; rev., Padua, 1766, *P-La* (2 copies)
La figlia ricuperata (dramma pastorale, P. A. Timido), CK, Feb 1762, *D-Bds*, aria *DK-Sa*
Semiramide (dm, 3, Metastasio), CK, aut. 1762; rev. Venice, 1768, *P-La* (2 copies)
Didone abbandonata [1st version] (dm, 3, Metastasio), CK, wint. 1762, *DK-Kk* (*R*1982: IOB, lxxxiv), *H-Bn*
Narciso (dramma pastorale, 3, Zeno), CK, carn. 1763
Cesare in Egitto (dm, 3, G. F. Bussani), CK, aut. 1763, *D-Bds*, *Sl*
Il naufragio di Cipro (dramma pastorale, 3, P. A. Ziani), CK, Jan or spr. 1764
Il gran Tamerlano (tragedia per musica, 3, A. Piovene), CK, early 1764
Ipermestra (dm, 3, Metastasio), Rome, Argentina, carn. 1766, *GB-Lbl*, *I-Rdp*, *Rvat*
La giardiniera brillante (int, 2), Rome, Valle, 3 Jan 1768, *Gl*
L'asile de l'amour (dramatic cantata, Deschamps, after Metastasio), Copenhagen, Christiansborg court, 22 July 1769
La double méprise, ou Carlile et Fany (cmda, 1, Deschamps), Copenhagen, Christiansborg court, 22 July 1769
Soliman den Anden [Soliman II] (syngespil, 3, C. D. Biehl, after C.-S. Favart), CK, 8 Oct 1770, *DK-Kk* (2 copies)
Le bal (oc, Deschamps), Copenhagen, Christiansborg court, 1770
Demofoonte [2nd version] (dm, 3, Metastasio), CK, 30 Jan 1771, *Kk*
Tronfølgen i Sidon [The Succession to the Throne in Sidon] (lyrisk tragi-comedia [syngespil], 2, N. K. Bredal, after Metastasio: *Il re pastore*), CK, 4 April 1771; rev., not by Sarti, 1778, *Kk*
La clemenza di Tito (dm, 3, Metastasio), Padua, Obizzi, June 1771
Il re pastore (dm, 3, Metastasio), CK, 1771
Il tempio d'eternità (festa teatrale, 1, Metastasio), CK, 1771
Deucalion og Pyrrha (syngespil, 1, C. A. Thielo and Bredal, after G. F. Pouillain de Saint Foix), CK, 19 March 1772

Aglae, eller Støtten [Aglae, or The Column] (syngespil, 1, C. Fasting and A. G. Carstens, after L. Poinsinet de Sivry), Copenhagen, Christiansborg court, 16 Feb 1774
Kierlighedsbrevene [Love Letters] (syngespil, 3, Biehl, after Boissy), Copenhagen, Christiansborg court, 22 March 1775
Farnace (dm, 3, A. M. Lucchini), VS, Ascension 1776
Le gelosie villane [Il feudatorio] (dg, 3, T. Grandi), VS, Nov 1776, *A-Wgm, D-Bds, Hs, HR, Rtt, F-Pn* (2 copies), *GB-Lcm, H-Bn, I-Fc, Pl, Vnm, US-Bp*; rev. (2), St Petersburg, 1785, *RU-SPtob*
Ifigenia [in Aulide] (dm, 3), Rome, Argentina, carn. 1777, *B-Bc, D-MÜs, F-Pn, I-Bc, P-La, US-Wc*
Medonte, re di Epiro (dm, G. De Gamerra), Florence, Pergola, 8 Sept 1777, *GB-Lbl, P-La*; Naples, 1783, *F-Pn, I-Nc, P-La, US-Bp*; Naples, 1792, *GB-Lcm*; *A-Wgm* (2 acts), *I-Fc* (2 acts), *Mc*
Il militare bizzarro (dg, 2, Grandi), VS, 27 Dec 1777, *F-Pn, US-Wc*
Scipione (dm, E. Giunti), Mestre, Casa Balbi, aut. 1778, *F-Pn, I-Fc, P-La* (2 different settings)
I contrattempi (dg, N. Porta), VS, Nov 1778, *F-Pn, H-Bn, I-Fc, Tf, US-Wc*; rev., not by Sarti, as Die Zwischenfälle, Dresden, 1782; as Gli equivoci svelati, Vicenza, 1786
Adriano in Siria (dm, 3, Metastasio), Rome, Argentina, 26 Dec 1778, *F-Pn* (Act 1), *I-Rc, RU-SPtob*
Olimpiade [1st version] (dm, 3, Metastasio), Florence, 1778, *P-La*
L'ambizione delusa (int, 2), Rome, Capranica, Feb 1779; *I-Tf* (1780, Turin)
Achille in Sciro (dm, 3, Metastasio), Florence, Pergola, aut. 1779, *Fc* (2 acts)
Mitridate a Sinope (dm, 3), Florence, Palla a Corda, aut. 1779, *F-Pn, I-Tf* (Acts 2 and 3)
Siroe (dm, 3, Metastasio), Turin, Regio, 26 Dec 1779, *GB-Lbl* (duet, 3 arias), *I-Tf* (Acts 2 and 3), *P-La* [attrib. 'Siri']
Giulio Sabino (dm, 3, P. Giovannini: *Epponina*), Venice, S Benedetto, Jan 1781 (Vienna, *c*1781); also perf. as Epponina and as Tito nelle Gallie; *CH-Zz, D-Bds, Dlb, F-Pn, H-Bn, I-Bc, BGc, Fc, Nc, OS, PESc, Vnm, P-La, US-Bp*
Demofoonte [3rd version] (dm, 3, Metastasio), Rome, Argentina, carn. 1782, *I-Rmassimo*
Alessandro e Timoteo (dm, 3, G. della Torre di Rezzonico), Parma, court, 6 April 1782, *A-Wn, B-Bc, D-SWl, F-Pn* (2 copies), *I-Fc, Nc, PAc*
Didone abbandonata [2nd version] (dm, 3, Metastasio), Padua, Obizzi, June 1782, *F-Pn, I-Gl, Pl, P-La*
Fra i due litiganti il terzo gode (dg, 2, Goldoni: *Le nozze*), Milan, Scala, 14 Sept 1782, *A-Wn, CH-Zz, D-DO, Mbs, MÜs, Rtt, DK-Kk, F-Pn*, H-Bn, I-Bc, Fc, PAc, Tf, P-La* (2 acts); also as I pretendi delusi (2), Venice, 1782, *D-Wa, I-FOc, Tf, RU-SPtob*; as Im Trüben ist gut fischen, Hamburg, 1785, *D-Bds*; as Le nozze di Dorina, Naples, 1784, *F-Pn, US-Wc*; as I rivali delusi, London, 1784; as Dorina contrastata, *I-Nc*; as Les noces de Dorine, ou Hélène et Francisque (Paris, *c*1789)
Attalo, re di Bitinia (dm, 3), Venice, S Benedetto, 26 Dec 1782, *P-La* (attrib. Bianchi)
Idalide (dm, 3, F. Moretti), Milan, Scala, 8 Jan 1783, *D-SWl, F-Pn* (inc.), *H-Bn, RU-SPtob*; also as La vergine del sole, Trieste, 1787
Erifile (dm, 2, De Gamerra), Pavia, carn. 1783, *F-Pn*
Il trionfo della pace (dm, 2, C. Olivieri), Mantua, Ducale, 10 May 1783
Olimpiade [2nd version] (dm, 3, Metastasio), Rome, Dame, 1783, *GB-Lbl* (Acts 1 and 2), *RU-SPtob, US-Wc*
Gli amanti consolati (dg, 2), St Petersburg, 1784, *D-SWl, F-Pn, GB-Lbl, I-Fc, FZc*, RU-SPtob*
I finti eredi (opera comica, 2, G. Bertati: *Il villano geloso*), St Petersburg, Kamennïy, 19/30 Oct 1785, *A-Wn, ?D-Dlb, F-Pn, H-Bn, I-Mr, Pl, RU-SPtob**
Armida e Rinaldo (dm, 2, M. Coltellini), St Petersburg, Hermitage, 15/26 Jan 1786, *A-Wgm, Wn, B-Bc* (Act 2), *F-Pn* (2 copies), *D-SWl, I-Fc* (score and pts), *FZc, Nc, S-Skma, RU-SPtob* (?autograph), *US-Wc*
Castore e Polluce (dm, 2, Moretti, after P.-J. Bernard), St Petersburg, Hermitage, 22 Sept/3 Oct 1786, *D-Hs, F-Pn, I-Fc, Mc, Nc, RU-SPtob* (pts only)
Zenoclea (azione teatrale, 2, Moretti), 1786, unperf.
Alessandro nell'Indie (dm, Metastasio), Palermo, S Cecilia, wint. 1787
Cleomene [Erifile] (dm, 3, De Gamerra), Bologna, Zagnoni, 27 Dec 1788, *I-Bc*
Nachal'noye upravleniye Olega [The Early Reign of Oleg] (5, Catherine II), St Petersburg, Hermitage, 15/26 Oct 1790, collab. Pashkevich and Canobbio
Andromeda (dm, Moretti), St Petersburg, Hermitage, 24 Oct/4 Nov 1798, *A-Wn, I-Fc* (score and pts), *FZc** (Act 1, frag.)
Enea nel Lazio (dm, 2, Moretti), St Petersburg, Kamennïy, 15/26 Oct 1799, *FZc**
La famille indienne en Angleterre (3, Marchese di Castelnau, after A. von Kotzebue), St Petersburg, Kamennïy, 1799, *FZc*, RU-SPtob*
Les amours de Flore et de Zéphire (ballet anacréontique, 2, P. Chevalier), Gatchina, 7/19 Sept 1800

Doubtful: Gram og Signe (Bredal), Copenhagen, 1756 [uses arias by Sarti]; Mitridate, Parma, 1765 [cited only in Fétis]; La calzolaia di Strasburgo, ?Modena, 1769; L'avaro, Faenza, 1777, or Mantua, 1791; Amore e matrimonio, ?1786 [unknown to Mooser]; Lo stravagante inglese, Ancona, Fenice, carn. 1792 (lib. in *I-Bc*); Les indiens et l'anglaise, 1794 [not by Sarti, a confusion with La famille indienne en Angleterre, 1799]; Palmyra, 1797, *D-Sl* [probably by Salieri]; Cesare in Farmacusa, *Sl*; Der Hypochondrist, *DS*; Isola disabitata, selections *I-FZc**; Piramo e Tisbe, duet *Fc*

*

BurneyH; *FétisB*
G. Pasolini: *Giuseppe Sarti* (Faenza, 1883)
C. Thrane: 'Sarti in Kopenhagen', *SIMG*, iii (1901–2), 528–38
A. Untersteiner: 'Giuseppe Sarti', *Gazzetta musicale di Milano*, lvii (1902), 490
A. Della Corte: *L'opera comica italiana nel '700* (Bari, 1923), ii, 69
C. Rivalta: *Giuseppe Sarti, musicista faentino del sec. XVIII* (Faenza, 1928)
F. Samory: *A Giuseppe Sarti nel 2° centenario di sua nascita* (Faenza, 1929)
R.-A. Mooser: *Annales de la musique et des musiciens en Russie au XVIIIme siècle*, ii (Geneva, 1951)
D. Lehmann: 'Zwischen Sarti und Rasumowski: Mozart im russischen Musikleben des 18. Jahrhunderts', *Acta mozartiana*, ii/2–3 (1955), 43–9
H. O'Douwes: 'De russische jaren van Giuseppe Sarti', *Mens en melodie*, xii (1957), 146
E. O. D. Downes: *The Operas of Johann Christian Bach as a Reflection of the Dominant Trends in Opera Seria 1750–1780* (diss., Harvard U., 1958)
M. S. Selden: 'Laurels for Catherine the Great (The Early Reign of Oleg)', *ON*, xxiii/20 (1958–9), 14, 30
F. Mompellio: 'La cappella del duomo dal 1714 ai primi decenni del '900', *Storia di Milano*, xvi (Milan, 1962), 553–88
M. Baroni and M. G. Tavoni, eds.: *Giuseppe Sarti, musicista faentino: Modena 1983*
Giuseppe Sarti, musicista del '700: una mostra documentaria (Faenza, 1983) [pubn of the Biblioteca Comunale, Faenza]
J. Rice: 'Sarti's *Giulio Sabino*, Haydn's *Armida*, and the Arrival of Opera Seria at Eszterháza', *HayJb 1984*, 181–98

DAVID DICHIERA (1), MARITA P. McCLYMONDS (2)

Sartori, Claudio (*b* Brescia, 1 April 1913). Italian musicologist and bibliographer. He studied at the universities of Pavia and Strasbourg and became professor of Italian literature at the Bologna Conservatory (1943), a post he held later at the Milan Conservatory (1967). Sartori is an outstanding bibliographer in the tradition of Eitner, Vogel and Einstein, and has done equally important work. His first publication in this field appeared in *Chigiana* in 1940 in the form of additions to a Scarlatti opera catalogue. In 1965 he obtained financial support for his bibliographical work and established the Ufficio Ricerche Fondi Musicali, which aims to catalogue all manuscripts and printed music in Italy up to 1900, all printed Italian librettos up to 1800 (including operas, oratorios, serenatas, cantatas and *balli*) and all literature on music in Italy. The catalogue of librettos, a fundamental resource for opera research, began to be published in 1990. A companion tool, the list of Italian music publishers, had appeared in 1958. Sartori has written on Monteverdi, Alessandro Scarlatti, Lully, Galuppi, Cherubini, Verdi and Puccini.

Monteverdi (Brescia, 1953)
Casa Ricordi 1808–1958: profilo storico (Milan, 1958)
Dizionario degli editori musicali italiani (Florence, 1958)

Giacomo Puccini a Monza (Monza, 1958)
Puccini (Milan, 1958)
ed.: *Puccini Symposium* (Milan, 1959)
with F. Lesure: 'Tentativo di un catalogo della produzione di Luigi Cherubini', *Luigi Cherubini nel II centenario della nascita* (Florence, 1962), 135–87
Quartetto milanese ottocentesco (Rome, 1974) [letters of Verdi, C. Maffei, G. Strepponi and C. Tenca]
I libretti italiani a stampa dalle origini al 1800: catalogo analitico con 16 indici (Cuneo, 1990–) CAROLYN GIANTURCO

Sartorio [Sertorio], **Antonio** (*b* Venice, 1630; *d* Venice, 30 Dec 1680). Italian composer. Gasparo Sartorio was his brother; another brother, Girolamo [Hieronymo], also had connections with the theatre, as an architect. He was a leading composer of operas for Venice in the 1660s and 70s.

1. LIFE. Antonio Sartorio is first heard of with the production of his first opera, *Gl'amori infruttuosi di Pirro*, at the Teatro SS Giovanni e Paolo, Venice, in January 1661. His next opera, *Seleuco*, was first performed in January 1666 in the Teatro S Salvatore, popularly called S Luca, where most of his later operas were also produced. By then he had been named Kapellmeister to Duke Johann Friedrich of Brunswick-Lüneburg, who reigned from 1665 and resided at Hanover. Sartorio took up his duties on Trinity Sunday 1666. During his Hanover years, 1666–75, he often travelled to Venice in the winter, both to compose operas for carnival and to enlist musicians for service at court. During his first such journey, in 1666–7, his remarkable double opera, *La prosperità di Elio Seiano* and *La caduta di Elio Seiano*, was produced in January and February 1667; the librettist, Nicolò Minato, originally intended the two operas to be given on successive nights, but it appears that composer and singers overruled him. Sartorio was in Venice again for Carnival 1670, during which his opera *Ermengarda regina de' longobardi* was performed. The librettist, Pietro Dolfin, a friend of both Sartorio and Duke Johann Friedrich, administered the duke's theatre loges and corresponded regularly with him between 1669 and 1678; his letters (in *D-HVsa*) are a valuable source of information about Venetian opera performances. Sartorio's next stay in Venice lasted from January or February 1672 to Carnival 1673. In February 1672 his best-known opera, *Adelaide*, was given for the first time. The libretto is again by Dolfin, who reworked Gissilla's arias into a cantata by adding recitatives; it was apparently conceived for a pupil of Dolfin's named Lucretia, who had sung a role (probably Gissilla) in the opera.

Poor health, but also the invitation to write one of two operas for S Luca in the coming carnival, prevented Sartorio from returning to Hanover that spring. Dolfin finally persuaded the duke to let Sartorio remain because of both the peril of the journey and the honour of having been asked to write the opera, the other being by no less a composer than Cavalli. In the event Sartorio wrote both operas. *Orfeo* was first given in December 1672. Although the Florentine emissary, Marco Antonio Altoviti, reported on 14 January (document in *I-Fas*) that Carnival was 'proceeding ... with not much applause for these first operas', and Dolfin found the scenery and costumes merely ordinary and Aureli's libretto 'very bad', both Sartorio's music and the singing of Tonina Coresi, who came specially from Rome to sing the part of Eurydice, were highly praised. The other opera was to have been Cavalli's *Massenzio*. It went into rehearsal, but there it was decided that it would not do, 'for lack of spirited ariettas' (Dolfin). Brusquely, the theatre managers turned the entire project over to Sartorio, who wrote his *Massenzio* in only 13 days; it was first performed in January 1673.

Sartorio spent the following two years at Hanover and then left Duke Johann Friedrich's employ for good in April 1675, receiving a parting gift of 50 thalers and a golden chain. He remained on good terms with the duke, corresponded regularly with him, and continued to call himself a court composer in his remaining operas. He settled in Venice, in the quarter of S Giovanni Grisostomo. On 7 May 1676 he was appointed vice-*maestro di cappella* of St Mark's, defeating Carlo Grossi by three votes. In December that year his *Giulio Cesare in Egitto* received its first performance and was particularly successful. Four further operas succeeded it in 1677–9. Towards the end of 1680 he began to compose another opera, *La Flora*, but he died before he could finish it, after seven months of illness; it was finished by M. A. Ziani and performed at the Teatro S Angelo as the first opera of the carnival season. Sartorio was succeeded at St Mark's by Legrenzi.

2. WORKS. Sartorio's operas, like those of his Venetian contemporaries, deal with heroic themes. In some of them – *La caduta di Elio Seiano*, *Massenzio* and *Antonino e Pompeiano* – true Senecan tragedy is evoked as a tyrant meets his death. Seianus commits suicide, seeking to plunge the universe into chaos, and Antoninus is assassinated on stage by the liberators of Rome. Like other composers of the post-Cavalli era Sartorio had to take account of the new tendencies of Venetian *dramma per musica*, especially the increasing primacy of aria over recitative. The growing number of arias, from about 50 in the 1660s to over 70 in the next decade, led him to develop a slightly simpler and more fluent style. Intriguing features such as the music scenes and dance scenes of *Seleuco* (1666), which had their genesis in the accumulation of closed forms, became rare in the later operas on librettos by Bussani, where the organization of scenes and distribution of arias changed, foreshadowing the entrance- and exit-aria convention of the end of the century. Sartori's treatment of strophic arias and aria texts with refrain or *intercalare*, the forerunners of da capo arias, initially shows individual solutions (e.g. *Seleuco*, Act 1 scene xii, 'Riposo non ha'), which become more conventionalized in his late operas.

Some stylistic peculiarities, like the melodic formula marked with an asterisk in ex.1, make Sartorio's music

Ex.1 *Seleuco*, Act 1 scene i

easily recognizable. Although he was interested in motif exchange between voice and bass in his arias with basso continuo, and although his bass parts might elaborate the affect of the text, he made less use of contrapuntal imitation than did some of his contemporaries (e.g. Legrenzi). About a fifth of the arias are accompanied by a four- or five-part string orchestra, which usually alternates with the voice in an echo-like manner but often turns into pure accompaniment towards the end of the aria. Following the conventions of Venetian opera Sartorio effected changes in timbre by the occasional use of viols instead of violins, as in *Adelaide* (Act 2 scene xviii 'Antri oscuri') and *Anacreonte tiranno* (Act 2 scene v 'Nell'inferno'). Although many earlier operas mention the trumpet in their texts and even feature imitations of trumpet fanfares in their string writing, *Adelaide* (1672) appears to be the first in a long line of Venetian operas to call for trumpets (two in D in the sinfonia). Sartorio wrote for a solo trumpet in one aria in *Massenzio*, and in all his subsequent surviving operas. In these arias the trumpet alternates with the voice, just as the strings do in arias with strings. He is most effective in scenes requiring great expressiveness, making occasional use of *recitativo accompagnato* or the traditional lament (on descending tetrachords) as in Orestes' 'Hermiona, qual sventura' from *Gl'amori infruttuosi di Pirro* (Act 3 scene vi).

Sartorio's greatness lay in his conveying in music the variety and, more important, the depth of the passions expressed by his librettists. His contemporaries considered him one of the most outstanding and experienced composers, a judgment doubtless grounded in admiration of his gift for writing many kinds of arias answering the demands of different scenes, affects and roles.

See also ADELAIDE; GIULIO CESARE IN EGITTO (i); and ORFEO (iii).

all drammi per musica in 3 acts; first performed in Venice unless otherwise stated

VSV – *Teatro S Salvatore*

Gl'amori infruttuosi di Pirro (A. Aureli), SS Giovanni e Paolo, lib. ded. 4 Jan 1661, 30 arias *I-Vmc* Martinengo 49–70, no.53B

Il Seleuco (N. Minato), VSV, lib. ded. 16 Jan 1666, arias *GB-Lbl* Harley 1267, *I-Vnm* It.IV–454 (=9978); 2 arias ed. in Rosand (1991)

La prosperità di Elio Seiano (Minato), VSV, lib. ded. 15 Jan 1667, *Nc* 32.3.19, *Rps* Reg.M.21a (as L'Elio Seiano), *Rvat* Chigi Q.V.63 (as Il Seiano), arias *Vmc* Martinengo 16.48 n.47 and 48

La caduta di Elio Seiano (Minato), VSV, lib. ded. 3 Feb 1667, *Vnm* It.IV–397 (=9921)

L'Ermengarda regina de' longobardi (P. Dolfin), SS Giovanni e Paolo, lib. ded. 26 Dec 1669

L'Adelaide (Dolfin), VSV, lib. ded. 19 Feb 1672, *D-HVl** IV.410, *I-Vnm* It.IV–380 (=9904) (*R*1978: IOB, viii); 2 arias ed. in Rosand (1991)

L'Orfeo (Aureli), VSV, lib. ded. 14 Dec 1672, *A-Wn* 17940 (with autograph corrections), *I-Nc* 32.2.25, *Vnm* It.IV–443 (=9967) (*R*1983: DMV, vi); 4 arias ed. in Rosand (1991)

Massenzio (G. F. Bussani), VSV, lib. ded. 25 Jan 1673, arias in *F-Pn* Vm^7.8, 9 and *I-Nc* 33.5.17, *S-Uu** vok.mus.i 165 (inc.)

Alcina (Dolfin), intended for Venice, carn. 1674–5, unperf.

Giulio Cesare in Egitto (Bussani), VSV, lib. ded. 17 Dec 1676, 4 arias *I-MOe* Mus.G.310, *Nc* 33.6.29, arias 33.5.36, 3 arias *Rvat* Barb.Lat. 4147, 43 arias *Vqs* Cl.VIII Cod.IV, ed. C. Monson, Collegium Musicum: Yale U., xii (1991)

Antonino e Pompeiano (Bussani), VSV, Jan 1677, *D-HVl* IV.414 (with autograph corrections), arias in *I-Nc* 33.5.36 and *Vqs* Cl.VIII Cod.IV, XI, XII, XIII, XVIII

L'Anacreonte tiranno (Bussani), VSV, 9 Dec 1677, *D-MÜs* Sant HS 3954 (erroneously attrib. A. Scarlatti), arias in *I-Nc* 33.5.36 and *Vlevi*, 23 arias *Vqs* Cl.VIII Cod.V

Ercole sul Termodonte (Bussani), VSV, Jan/Feb 1678, 13 arias *Vqs* Cl.VIII Cod.V

I duo tiranni al soglio (M. Noris), VSV, lib. ded. 15 Jan 1679, arias in *I-Nc* 33.5.32, and *Vqs* Cl.VIII Cod.XIX

La Flora (N. Bonis), S Angelo, carn. 1681 [completed by M. A. Ziani], 12 arias *Bca* A.462, arias in *Rvat* Barb.Lat.4137 and *Vnm* It.IV–423 (=9947)

*

ES (M. Messinis)

G. C. Bonlini: *Le glorie della poesia e della musica contenute nell'estatta notizia de' teatri della città di Venezia* (Venice, 1730)

E. Bodemann: *Die Handschriften der königlichen öffentlichen Bibliothek zu Hannover* (Hanover, 1867)

L. N. Galvani [pseud. of G. Salvioli]: *I teatri musicali di Venezia nel secolo xvii* (Milan, 1878)

H. Kretzschmar: 'Die venezianische Oper und die Werke Cavalli's und Cesti's', *VMw*, viii (1892), 1–76

B. G. Dolfin: *I Dolfin (Delfino), patrizi veneziani sulla storia di Venezia dall'anno 452 al 1910* (Belluno, 1912)

H. C. Wolff: *Die venezianische Oper in der zweiten Hälfte des 17. Jahrhunderts* (Berlin, 1937)

S. T. Worsthorne: *Venetian Opera in the Seventeenth Century* (Oxford, 1954)

L. Schrade: *Tragedy in the Art of Music* (Cambridge, MA, 1964)

A. Davidsson: 'En "Christina-opera" på Carolina rediviva', *Nordisk tidskrift för bok- och biblioteksväsen*, liv (1967), 9–19

E. Tarr and T. Walker: '"Bellici carmi, festivo fragor": die Verwendung der Trompete in der italienischen Oper des 17. Jahrhunderts', *HJbMw* iii (1978), 143–203

E. Rosand: 'L'Orfeo: the Metamorphosis of a Musical Myth', *Israel Studies in Musicology*, ii (1980), 101–20

C. Sartori: 'I ricuperi dell'Ufficio Ricerche Fondi Musicali', *NRMI*, xiv (1980), 548–54

H. Becker, ed.: *Quellentexte zur Konzeption der europäischen Oper im 17. Jahrhundert* (Kassel, 1981)

E. Rosand: 'L'Ovidio trasformato', introduction to A. Sartorio: *L'Orfeo*, DMV, vi (1983), pp.ix–lvii

C. Monson: 'Giulio Cesare in Egitto: from Sartorio (1677) to Handel (1724)', *ML*, lxvi (1985), 313–43

E. Selfridge-Field: *Pallade veneta: Writings on Music in Venetian Society 1650–1750* (Venice, 1985)

P. Fabbri: *Il secolo cantante: per una storia del libretto d'opera nel seicento* (Bologna, 1990)

N. Dubowy: *Arie und Konzert: zur Entwicklung der Ritornellanlage im 17. und frühen 18. Jahrhundert* (Munich, 1991)

E. Rosand: *Opera in Seventeenth-Century Venice: the Creation of a Genre* (Berkeley, 1991)

EDWARD H. TARR, NORBERT DUBOWY

Sartorio [Sertorio], **Gasparo** (*b* Venice, between 18 Oct 1625 and 17 Oct 1626; *d* Venice, 17 Oct 1680). Italian composer, brother of Antonio Sartorio. In 1650 his opera *Orithia*, to a libretto by Count Maiolino Bisaccioni, was performed at the Teatro Ss Apostoli, and his *L'Erginda*, to the first libretto written by Aurelio Aureli, was given at the same theatre in 1652. He composed the third act of *Iphide greca* (1671, Venice; *I-Vnm*), the music for Acts 1 and 2 being by Gian Domenico Partenio and Domenico Freschi respectively. *Armidoro*, performed at the Teatro S Cassiano on 20 January 1651, is attributed to Sartorio by Ivanovich, but to Cavalli in other sources; the music is now lost. According to his epitaph in S Fosca, Venice, he died at the age of 54.

*

C. Ivanovich: *Minerva al tavolino* (Venice, 1681, 2/1688)

T. Walker: 'Gli errori di "Minerva al tavolino": osservazioni sulla cronologia delle prime opere veneziane', *Venezia e il melodramma nel seicento: Venice 1972*, 7–20

EDWARD H. TARR

Sass, Sylvia (*b* Budapest, 12 July 1951). Hungarian soprano. She studied in Budapest, making her début there in 1971 as Frasquita. She sang Violetta in Sofia (1972) and at Aix-en-Provence (1976); Giselda (*I Lombardi*) in Budapest (1973) and at Covent Garden (1976), having made her British début in 1975 with Scottish Opera as Desdemona. In 1977 she sang Tosca at the Metropolitan; she has also appeared in Paris, Vienna, Germany, Rio, New Orleans and Toronto. Her roles include Poppaea, Donna Anna, Fiordiligi, Norma, Lady Macbeth, Elisabeth de Valois, Salome, Turandot and the Mother in Durko's *Moses*, which she created. She has a refined *pianissimo*, but in *forte* passages her tone becomes strident.

ALAN BLYTH

Sassano [Sassani], **Matteo** ['Matteuccio'] (*b* Sansevero, *c*1667; *d* Naples, 15 Oct 1737). Italian soprano castrato. He was brought up in the Conservatorio dei Poveri di Gesù Cristo in Naples, where he was a pupil of Giovanni Salvatore. The extraordinary beauty of his voice made him celebrated in the city, and his services were sought by both the archbishop and the viceroy. He left the conservatory in February 1693 for Rome, where he sang in Holy Week. In 1695 he sang to great acclaim at the court of Vienna. He returned to Naples in July 1696 and sang two serenatas by Alessandro Scarlatti. According to Prota-Giurleo, his success encouraged him to perform in the theatre, considered a defiant act for a conservatory student. In 1697 he sang in C. F. Pollarolo's *Amor e dovere* and *Tito Manlio* in Venice, the title role in the pasticcio *Perseo* in Bologna, and Sabadini's *La virtù trionfante dell'inganno* in Piacenza. At the end of the year he was at the Teatro S Bartolomeo in Naples in Gasparini's *Ajace* and Scarlatti's *La caduta de' Decemviri*. The music written in the latter for Sassano, extending from *e'* to *g''*, exploits the individual qualities of his voice. In Appio's first-act aria 'Ma il ben mio' the vocal line begins unaccompanied in long note values, and there is much use of *messe di voce*. The third-act aria 'Larve, fremiti, terrore' includes 'parlanti' passages.

Sassano's particular art must, however, have lain largely in improvisation, of which scores give only a vague idea. In 1698 he performed in Naples in Cavalli's *Mutio Scevola*, but the opera was not well received and was replaced by Pasquini's *La donna ancora è fedele* as reworked by Scarlatti. That year Sassano returned to Piacenza in Giovanni Bononcini's *Il trionfo di Camilla* and sang in Reggio Emilia in C. F. Pollarollo's *L'Ulisse sconosciuto*, where he was described as a virtuoso 'of His Catholic Majesty'. Shortly thereafter he was at the court of Spain and, after the death of Carlo II, at that of Vienna. In 1706 he was in Venice in C. F. Pollarolo's *Flavio Bertarido* and *Filippo re della Grecia*. His last performances on the stage were in 1708 in Bologna and Venice; in 1709 he returned to Naples with a considerable fortune and the title of Marquis. He continued to sing in religious functions and non-dramatic entertainment until late in life. In 1774 Giambattista Mancini recalled the freshness of his voice even in the last years. 'Matteuccio', the form of his name used by Mancini, was used again at the end of the century in a famous print depicting *Il Parnaso dei cantanti*.

*

G. Mancini: *Riflessioni pratiche sul canto figurato* (Milan, 1777)
U. Prota-Giurleo: 'Matteo Sassano detto "Matteuccio" (Documenti napolitani)', *RIM*, i (1966), 97–119
O. Termini: 'Singers at San Marco in Venice: the Competition between Church and Theatre (ca. 1675–ca. 1725), *RMARC*, no.17 (1981), 65–96
J. Rosselli: 'The Castrati as a Professional Group and a Social Phenomenon, 1550–1850', *AcM*, lx (1987), 143–79
F. Marri: 'Muratori, la musica e il melodramma negli anni milanesi (1695–1700)', *Muratoriana*, xvi (1988), 19–124

SERGIO DURANTE

Sasse [Sax, Saxe, Sass], **Marie** (**Constance**) (*b* Oudenaarde, 26 Jan 1834; *d* Auteuil, nr Paris, 8 Nov 1907). Belgian soprano. She studied in Ghent, Paris and Milan and made her début at Venice as Gilda in 1852. At the outset of her career she changed her name to Sax, then to Saxe when the instrument maker Adolphe sued her; when he sued again, she reverted to Sasse and was later known as Sass. While working in Paris as a café-concert singer she came to the notice of Carvalho, director of the Théâtre Lyrique, where she appeared as Countess Almaviva in *Figaro* in 1859. In the same year, she sang Eurydice in the historic revival of Gluck's *Orphée et Eurydice*, in Berlioz's version, with Viardot as Orpheus. She sang Elisabeth in the revised *Tannhäuser* (1861), and created Sélika in *L'Africaine* (1865) and Elisabeth de Valois in *Don Carlos* (1867), at the Opéra and Cecilia in Gomes's *Il Guarany* at La Scala (1870). Her repertory also included Valentine (*Les Huguenots*), Alice (*Robert le diable*) and Leonora (*Il trovatore*).

Wagner was pleased with her Elisabeth in *Tannhäuser*; Verdi, who disliked her attitude to colleagues at rehearsal, less so with her heroine in *Don Carlos*. When she was recommended for Amneris in *Aida*, he refused. Sasse was married, briefly, to the bass Armand Castelmary; she retired in 1877 and died in poverty. Her memoirs, *Souvenirs d'une artiste*, were published in Paris in 1902.

*

H. Blaze de Bury: *Meyerbeer: sa vie, ses oeuvres et son temps* (Paris, 1865)
C. Malherbe: *Auber* (Paris, 1911)
M. Curtiss: *Bizet and his World* (London, 1959)
A. Porter: 'The Making of "Don Carlos"', *PRMA*, xcviii (1971–2), 73–88
J. Budden: *The Operas of Verdi*, iii: *From 'Don Carlos' to 'Falstaff'* (London, 1981)
T. Walsh: *Second Empire Opera: the Théâtre-Lyrique, Paris 1851–1870* (London and New York, 1981)

RONALD CRICHTON, ELIZABETH FORBES

Satie, Erik (**Alfred Leslie**) (*b* Honfleur, 17 May 1866; *d* Paris, 1 July 1925). French composer. His father was a music publisher who, although dismayed by his son's lack of academic success (Satie was dismissed from the Paris Conservatoire in 1882), published some of his songs in 1887. At first influenced by Chabrier, Satie received scant attention from critics or public during the next two decades, and his association with the stage was slow to begin. An early work, *Geneviève de Brabant* (composed 1899–1900), probably written for a Montmartre 'shadow theatre', was only performed posthumously; it has been staged as a marionette opera, as well as with singers and actors. However, Satie's first successes were songs composed for the soprano Paulette Darty, among them 'La diva de l'Empire', performed in the revue *Dévidons la bobine* (Berck, 26 July 1904). This led to his first operetta, *Pousse l'amour* (1907), and to two revues.

Satie was a lifelong friend of Debussy, and the experience of hearing *Pelléas et Mélisande* threw him into a sort of reverential depression. 'I must think up something else or I'm done for', he wrote, apparently sensing, in Volta's words, 'the emergence of an aesthetic to whose formulation he had contributed'. Satie went back to study at the Schola Cantorum and at the age of 42 received his first diploma. Only after Debussy's death did Satie begin to consider his 'symphonic drama', *Socrate* (1920), which is the nearest thing to an opera that survives and his most influential work. In three parts, 'Portrait de Socrate', 'Bords de l'Ilissus' and 'Mort de Socrate', written for six female voices and orchestra, its calm progression and dream-like quality set it apart from any other work. The early, private performances, in a version for piano and solo voice, were given by Jane Bathori and Suzanne Balguerie; Satie was shocked that the elegant audiences in Paris salons laughed at Plato's text. When *Socrate* began its life on stage, it was in a

'Satyagraha' (Glass): scene from Achim Freyer's production for the Stuttgart Opera, 3 October 1981

famous production designed by Alexander Calder, with Eva Gauthier and Colin O'More, at Hartford, Connecticut, in 1936. The work has influenced many opera composers, notably Thomson, Poulenc, Rorem and Cage. In his lifetime Satie had a great influence over Les Six, but a collaboration involving him, Cocteau and Radiguet on a light opera, *Paul et Virginie*, intended for Dyagilev's company ended in disagreements, and the score, said to be finished, is now lost. Satie's most enduring stage works were ballets, *Parade* and *Mercure*, both designed by Picasso, and *Relache* by Picabia.

Geneviève de Brabant, 1899–1900 (marionette op, 3, C. de Latour), Paris, Champs-Elysées, 17 May 1926 (Vienna and Leipzig, 1930)
Pousse l'amour (fantaisie, 1, M. de Féraudy and J. Kolb), Paris, Comédie Royale, 22 Nov 1907; rev. as Coco chéri, Monte Carlo, Beaux-Arts, 28 Feb 1913; frag. *US-CA*
Le dîner de Pierrot (revue, 1, J. Dépaquit), Arcueil, Ecole Maternelle, 17 Sept 1909, lost
La chemise (fantaisie, Dépaquit), Arceuil, Gymnase Municipale, ?24 Oct 1909, frag.
Le piège de Méduse (comédie lyrique, 1, Satie), private perf., Paris, late 1913 or early 1914; stage, Paris, Michel, 24 May 1921; *F-Pn*; (Paris, 1929)
Socrate (drame symphonique, 3 pts, after Plato, trans. V. Cousin), concert perfs., Paris, Salle de l'Ancien Conservatoire, 14 Feb 1920 (with pf) and Salle Erard, 7 June 1920 (with orch); stage, Hartford, CT, 1936; *Pn*; (Paris, 1920)
Paul et Virginie, 1920–23 (oc, 3, J. Cocteau and R. Radiguet), unperf., frag. in *Pn* and *US-NYpm*

Recits. in Gounod: Le médecin malgré lui, Monte Carlo, 5 Jan 1924, *F-Pn*

*

R. Myers: *Erik Satie* (London, 1948)
P. Gowers: *Erik Satie: his Studies, Notebooks and Critics* (diss., U. of Cambridge, 1966)
A. Rey: *Erik Satie* (Paris, 1974)
N. Wilkins, ed. and trans.: *The Writings of Erik Satie* (London, 1980)
A. M. Gillmor: *Erik Satie* (Boston, 1988)
O. Volta, ed.: *Erik Satie et la tradition populaire* (Paris, 1988)
——: 'A la recherche d'un fantôme: Paul et Virginie d'Erik Satie', *Revue internationale de la musique française*, x/29 (1989), 47–70
——: *Satie Seen through his Letters* (London, 1989)
R. Orledge: *Satie the Composer* (Cambridge, 1990)

PATRICK O'CONNOR

Satyagraha. Opera in three acts by PHILIP GLASS to a libretto by the composer and Constance DeJong after the *Bhagavad Gita*; Rotterdam, Netherlands Opera, 5 September 1980.

Shortly after a 1976 performance of *Einstein on the Beach* in Amsterdam, Glass was asked by Hans de Roo, the director of the Netherlands Opera, to write a 'real' opera, meaning one for orchestra and chorus with soloists trained and practised in the singing of traditional operas. Glass responded with the two-hour *Satyagraha*, his second opera about an important historical figure. Taking as its central character Gandhi (tenor), it concerns the period he spent in South Africa (1893–1914) and his fight to repeal the so-called 'Black Act' – a law that restricted the movement of non-Europeans from place to place and virtually enslaved the substantial Indian community in South Africa. Gandhi developed the concept of *satyagraha* (roughly, 'truth-force') and fought the act with hunger strikes and peaceful demonstrations, eventually achieving a partial triumph, however imperfect, over the hated law. It marked the beginning of Gandhi's political career.

Each act of *Satyagraha* employs a historical figure (silent) as a sort of spiritual guardian, watching the earthly action from above. In Act 1, which has three scenes, the symbol is Leo Tolstoy; the author was one of Gandhi's inspirations throughout his life, and the two men corresponded until the Russian's death in 1910. Glass believes that the same combination of the political and the spiritual is found in the writings of both men. In Act 2, also in three scenes, Rabindranath Tagore, the poet and scholar who was the only living moral authority acknowledged by Gandhi, serves as the guardian. The symbol in the long, continuous third act is Martin Luther King, whom Glass has described as a sort of 'American Gandhi', going on to say that, together, 'Tolstoy, Tagore and King represent the past, present and future of *satyagraha*' (Glass 1987).

Although the opera has a clearly defined plot, it is not presented chronologically. After the timeless, purely philosophical opening, in which Gandhi is advised by Prince Arjuna (baritone) and Lord Krishna (bass) from the *Bhagavad Gita*, the scenes are set in 1910, 1906, 1896, 1906, 1908 and 1913 respectively. Every scene is a self-sufficient drama in miniature; connections between each one are established mainly through musical and cumulative means, rather than through a continuity of stage action.

DeJong's selections from the *Bhagavad Gita* are heard in the original Sanskrit, in an attempt to avoid upsetting the rhythm of what is, after all, a sacred text. As Glass has said:

> I liked the idea of *further* separating the vocal text from the action. In this way, without an understandable text to contend with, the listener could let the words go altogether. The weight of 'meaning' would then be thrown onto the music, the designs and the stage action. Secondly, since none of the national languages was going to be used, Sanskrit could then serve as a kind of international language for this opera.

Vastly different from traditional music drama, *Satyagraha* is designed on a moral, indeed religious, plane, and as such is closer to ritual than entertainment, to mystery play than standard opera. Few were prepared for its beauty and spiritual propulsion. In scoring it for strings, triple woodwind and organ, Glass used only what he calls 'international' instruments (i.e. those that can be found, in one form or another, in both the West and India). *Satyagraha* nevertheless uses more conventional forces (six solo voices and a chorus of 40) than the spartan *Einstein*. While *Einstein* challenges ideas about what an opera, even an avant-garde opera, should be, *Satyagraha* fits Glass neatly into the operatic continuum. *Einstein* attempted to break the rules with Modernist zeal; *Satyagraha* adapts the rules to the composer's own aesthetic. It is difficult to find any historical precedent for *Einstein*, but in *Satyagraha* one may find references to many of the composer's forerunners.

For example, in the opening scene, entitled 'The Kuru Field of Justice', an aria becomes a duet, then a trio, set down with a rich, declamatory, near-Verdian directness, over an elaborate chaconne. Other scenes seem to have been written under the spell of Wagner, Berlioz, or Glass's beloved Rossini. But at no point does the music descend to parody; the hearer is never in doubt about the identity of the composer. The closing aria is masterly: an unadorned rising scale in Phrygian mode seeming an eloquent melody in itself, repeated as it is some 30 times over shifting musical sands. The rocket-point anxiety of *Einstein* seems far away, with a serene, impelling power in its stead. While the opera was considered a step backwards by some members of the avant garde, which had lionized Glass after *Einstein*, *Satyagraha* won him new listeners, many of whom consider it his most personal and affecting score to date.

TIM PAGE

Satyricon. Opera by BRUNO MADERNA to a libretto by Maderna and Ian Strasfogel after Petronius's narrative; Holland Festival, Scheveningen, 16 March 1973.

Satyricon was composed during the period when Maderna's terminal illness was becoming increasingly apparent. The text on which it was based was Petronius's *Satyricon*, the classic work describing the decadence of late Roman society, centring on the scene of the dinner at the house of Trimalchio and his wife Fortunata. It is not easy to decide to what extent the 'open' nature of the dramatic and musical elements of the opera were due to the hurried circumstances of its composition, to what extent to the composer's desire to create a work of partly improvisational music theatre: it is in 16 unsequenced sections, with the possibility of placing taped numbers between them. The work contains a variety of pastiche elements: quotations from popular classics, and passages written in particular styles from the musical past, evoke the decadent world portrayed on stage. The musical language of the opera is thus deliberately one of collage, with little or no attempt at an 'operatic' unity of musical conception, but is capable of a powerful and stimulating effect with the imaginative collaboration of its performers and producer.

RAYMOND FEARN

Sauguet [Poupard], **Henri(-Pierre)** (*b* Bordeaux, 18 May 1901; *d* Paris, 22 June 1989). French composer. He first worked as a church organist and studied composition with Joseph Canteloube. An admirer of Bizet, Schumann and Debussy, he was also intensely interested in the music of Stravinsky and Satie; following the example of Les Six, he founded a Bordeaux counterpart, 'Les Trois', and exchanged letters with Milhaud, who encouraged him to move to Paris. From 1923 Sauguet associated with Desormière and others in forming the Ecole d'Arcueil; their inaugural concert at the Sorbonne was presided over by Cocteau. This first success brought Sauguet a commission from Mme Bériza for a stage piece, and he wrote both text and music for *Le plumet du colonel*, an impulsive, sometimes comic piece which contains a worthwhile 'Berceuse créole'. A second commission opened up the field in which Sauguet was to excel: the ballet. In the ensuing years he composed over 20 ballets in all.

Among his operatic works, Sauguet's best piece is *La chartreuse de Parme*, an opera in number form including a ballet, although some passages are closer in conception to Wagnerian music drama. Set in the mountains between Como and Milan, at La Scala and in Parma, it is Sauguet's grandest opera, and although it has been criticized as somewhat featureless, it is direct in style and freely melodic, and closes with a moving farewell scene. *La gageure imprévue* is a farcical tale of a bored Marquis and Marquess. The former has a girl secreted in his room while the latter invites in a passing officer. Set pieces, dialogue and ensembles are woven into a continous piece, mostly set in a lighthearted, clearly rhythmic style. *Les caprices de Marianne*, set in Naples, is the tale of a magistrate Claudio (bass) and his young wife Marianne (soprano). Coelio (tenor) and his ambassador Octave (baritone) pursue Marianne, who spurns the attentions of the former. A trap is set and Coelio is killed. Sauguet responded to the tale in a neo-classical language, with frequent ironic pastiche. His children's opera *Tistou, les pouces verts*, has been compared to Britten's *Let's Make an Opera* and, like that work, makes a game of the creation of an operatic show.

Sauget also composed music for films, television and radio programmes and plays, and made experiments in *musique concrète*. He remained opposed to particular systems: for him the essentials were melody, harmony and rhythm, and he developed his tonal or modal ideas in smooth curves, producing an art of clarity, simplicity and restraint. He was elected to the Académie des Beaux-Arts in 1975.

Le plumet du colonel, (opéra bouffe militaire, 1, Sauguet), Paris, Champs-Elysées, 27 Feb 1924
La contrebasse (opéra bouffe, 2, H. Troyat, after A. P. Chekhov: *Romance with a Double Bass*), Paris, Madeleine, 1930
La chartreuse de Parme, 1927–36 (4, A. Lunel, after Stendhal [M. H. Beyle]), Paris, Opéra, 6 March 1939; rev. 1968
La gageure imprévue, 1942 (oc, 1, P. Bertin, after M. J. Sedaine), Paris, OC (Favart), 4 July 1944
Les caprices de Marianne (2, J.-P. Grédy, after A. de Musset), Aix-en-Provence, 1954
Le pain des autres, 1967–74 (comédie lyrique, 2, E. Kinds, after I. S. Turgenev: *The Bread of Others*)
Boule de suif (comédie musicale, A. Husson and J. Meyer, after G. de Maupassant), Lyons, Célestins, Dec 1978
Tistou, les pouces verts, 1980 (conte lyrique, 1, J. L. Tardieu, after M. Druon), Paris, Jardin d'Acclimatation [children's op]

*

M. Schneider: *Henri Sauguet* (Paris, 1959)
J. Roy: *Présences contemporaines* (Paris, 1962)
F.-Y. Bril: *Henri Sauguet* (Paris, 1967)

ARTHUR HOÉRÉE/RICHARD LANGHAM SMITH

Saul og David ('Saul and David'). Opera in four acts by CARL NIELSEN to a libretto by Einar Christiansen; Copenhagen, Royal Theatre, 28 November 1902.

Nielsen made preliminary studies for an opera on the Old Testament story of Saul and David in 1896, and he approached Einar Christiansen with his ideas in 1898. Christiansen, a playwright, newspaper editor and from 1899 to 1909 director of the Royal Theatre, drew his libretto mainly from 1 Samuel xiii–xxxi (the final scene also incorporates material from 2 Samuel i, and fragments of the Psalms and the Song of Songs appear in David's lyrical scenes). The composition was carried out while Nielsen was a second violinist in the Royal Theatre orchestra, and it was finished in late 1901. Nielsen himself conducted the première. *Saul and David* has been an established part of the Danish repertory ever since and has been recorded three times; productions outside Denmark have been infrequent, however.

The drama centres on the dilemma of Saul, King of Israel, a magnificent bass-baritone role. In exercising his own judgment for the benefit of his people, Saul knowingly infringes divine law. Thus, despite all attempts at repentance, he ensures his own downfall and Israel's eventual defeat at the hands of the Philistines. Saul's swings of mood from proud defiance to wrath and depression define the broad sweep of the drama, while David's high tenor lyricism provides moments of repose. The dubious morality of the divine will, which effectively pre-empts significant freedom of action, and the rivalry of superstitions old and new are undercurrents to the events on stage; Nielsen focusses the attention less on these, however, than on the contrast between acceptance (as represented by the young David and the elderly prophet Samuel) and defiance (Saul, a man in his prime).

Threatened by the invading Philistines and impatient with the non-arrival of Samuel, Saul goes ahead with a sacrifice which only the prophet is entitled to perform – whereupon Samuel arrives and in a grave bass denounces Saul's disobedience and prophesies his downfall. Saul sings in defiance of Jehovah (an arioso modelled on Iago's Creed from Verdi's *Otello*). His son Jonathan (tenor) introduces his friend, the shepherd David. Comforted by David's singing, Saul leaves to march on the Philistines. David remains behind, and he and the king's daughter Mikal (Michal; soprano) declare their love for one another in a rapturous duet.

After a festive prelude Act 2 begins with David again singing to Saul. A messenger interrupts with news that the defeated Philistines have regrouped, now with the giant Goliath at their head. David volunteers to take up Goliath's challenge on behalf of Israel, and Saul promises him Michal's hand should he be victorious. The fight takes place offstage; Michal and her handmaidens are seen anxiously awaiting the outcome. Jonathan brings news of the victory and the people sing in praise of David. Saul is angered by the comparison, 'Saul has slain his thousands, David his ten thousands'. This time David's singing fails to mollify him and he throws his spear at the young hero, who escapes, swearing vengeance.

Saul is now in pursuit of the outlawed David. The third act is set in Saul's camp in the wilderness. Jonathan and Michal sing of the beauty of the night before retiring to sleep. David ascends with his companion Abisaj (Abishai; soprano) and steals Saul's sword from his side, then wakens the camp and shows that he could have killed the king had he wished. Moved by this display of loyalty Saul repents, and all sing a celebratory fugue. Samuel arrives to anoint David as the new chosen King of Israel; having confirmed Jehovah's displeasure with Saul, Samuel dies. David and Michal flee from the wrathful Saul; the people dare not lay hold of the Lord's anointed.

The fourth act opens with a stormy prelude. The curtain goes up on the house of the Witch of Endor (contralto). Saul, accompanied by his captain, Abner (bass), overcomes the witch's reluctance (Saul himself had previously forbidden the practice of witchcraft) and persuades her to summon the dead Samuel. The Shade informs him that the Philistines will sack his camp and that Saul himself will die. An interlude depicts the battle. On the deserted battlefield the wounded Jonathan declares his allegiance to David and dies. Saul, also wounded, sees his son's body and in a final act of defiance falls on his sword. David mourns both Saul and Jonathan, and the people hail him as their new king.

The twin influences of Wagner and late Verdi are evident in the continuity and pacing of *Saul and David*. Nielsen's early enthusiasm for Wagner did not extend to the leitmotif technique, however. His musical characterization is founded instead on a very personal repertory of gestures, many of them associated with the four temperaments depicted in the Second Symphony (1901–2). These ideas and the large-scale deployment of tonal regions were to be worked out in more concentrated form in the later symphonies: there are many echoes in the *Sinfonia espansiva* of 1911. *Saul and David* was to remain Nielsen's only tragic opera.

DAVID FANNING

Saunders, Arlene (*b* Cleveland, 5 Oct 1935). American soprano. After studying in Cleveland and Milan, she made her début in 1961 as Mimì at the Teatro Nuovo, Milan, and appeared with the New York City Opera. Engaged at the Hamburg Staatsoper from 1964, she sang in the première of Klebe's *Jacobowsky und der Oberst* (1965). In 1966 she sang Pamina at Glyndebourne, and the following year made her first appearances at San Francisco as Louise and Gounod's Marguerite. She created Mme Euterpova in Menotti's *Help, Help, the Globolinks!* at Hamburg (1968) and the title role in Ginastera's *Beatrix Cenci* at Washington (1971). She made her Metropolitan début as Eva in 1971. In Boston she sang Natasha (Prokofiev's *War and Peace*, 1974) and Nadia (Tippett's *The Ice Break*, 1979). She made her Covent Garden début as Minnie (*La fanciulla del West*) in 1980 and has also sung in Berlin, Munich, Milan, Vienna, Paris and Buenos Aires. Her wide repertory includes Fiordiligi, Donna Elvira, Senta, Sieglinde, Desdemona, Santuzza, Nedda, Tosca, the Marschallin and the Countess (*Capriccio*). Her voice, originally a lyric soprano, has grown more powerful, enabling her to take on the heavier Wagner and Puccini roles. ELIZABETH FORBES

Sauveterre [Sauterre, Sauter, Souter, Sovuterre], **François** [Francesco] (*d* Lisbon, 18 Jan 1775). French choreographer and dancer. His name first appears as 'Mons. Soutter', ballet-master for the 1738–9 opera season at the S Giovanni Grisostomo, Venice: his first opera was Rinaldo di Capua's *Farnace*. Except for a three-year period in Stuttgart (1758–61), where he immediately preceded Noverre and choreographed three Jommelli operas, Sauveterre worked in Italy until 1766, creating ballets for operas in Padua (1740), Turin (1740–41, 1749–50), Florence (1743–4, 1746–7), Milan (1746, 1748, 1752–3, 1755–6, 1763, 1765), Reggio Emilia (1741, 1750–51, 1753, 1755), Naples (1742, Leo's *Andromaca*), Rome (1749), Bologna (1756) and Venice (1749, 1740–51, 1763–6). Sacchini, Paisiello and Guglielmi are among the composers with whom he worked. In 1766 Sauveterre accompanied his student, Pietro Colonna, to Lisbon, and was recommended as dancing-master to the prince and choreographer for the court theatres, replacing Andrea Alberti, 'Il Tedeschino'; there he choreographed many operas by Jommelli, as well as works by Perez, Piccinni and others. A contemporary writer in Florence described his ballets as superb. He emphasized dramatic and mimetic content in the style of *ballets d'action*, giving the ballets some degree of independence within the framework of the opera.

*

J. Sasportes: *História da dança em Portugal* (Lisbon, 1970)
K. K. Hansell: 'Il ballo teatrale e l'opera italiana', *SOI*, v (1988), 175–306
M. C. de Brito: *Opera in Portugal in the Eighteenth Century* (Cambridge, 1989) IRENE ALM

Savage, Henry W(ilson) (*b* New Durham, NH, 21 March 1859; *d* Boston, 29 Nov 1927). American impresario. He had a successful career in the real-estate business in Boston, where in 1894 a default forced him to assume control of the Castle Square Opera House. He organized a company there which opened on 6 May 1895; its modestly priced productions of opera in English were immensely successful. Over the next decade Savage's activities included productions in Chicago, New York and elsewhere; in autumn 1900, with Maurice Grau, he presented a season of opera in English at the Metropolitan Opera House, New York, to great critical acclaim. The Henry Savage Grand Opera Company's English production of *Parsifal* in 1904 was a sensation and toured throughout the country for nearly a year. In 1906 a lavish production of *Madama Butterfly* (its American première) toured widely; the tour of *La fanciulla del West* in 1911 following its première at the Metropolitan was equally impressive. Savage also staged over 40 light operas, musical comedies and plays. His greatest success was Lehár's *Die lustige Witwe* (1907); other important productions included Gustav Luders's *The Prince of Pilsen* (1903) and *The Sho-Gun* (1904), and Emmerich Kalman's *Sari* (1914).

Savage was America's most successful presenter of opera in English, and his wide-ranging, accessible productions played a major part in popularizing opera and operetta outside the major urban centres. He was opposed to the promotion of particular singers as stars (particularly on financial grounds) and his exceptionally strong, reliable companies were the starting-points for many careers. Savage directed his operations efficiently but without flamboyance; his businesslike approach to some extent obscured the depth of his contribution to the musical stage.

*

DAB (A. F. Harlow)
Obituary, *New York Times* (30 Nov 1927) WILLIAM BROOKS

Savage, William (*b* ?London, 1720; *d* London, 27 July 1789). English bass. He first appeared as a boy soprano in *Alcina* (1735), then as an alto in *Giustino* (1737) and *Faramondo* (1738). From 1740 he sang as a bass, in *Imeneo* (1740) and *Deidamia* (1741) as well as in English works. He held posts in the Chapel Royal and St Paul's and was active as a teacher and composer. Burney called Savage 'a powerful and not unpleasant bass', but his pupil R. J. S. Stevens wrote that he had 'a pleasant voice of two octaves' and had 'a clear articulation, perfect intonation, great volubility of voice, and chaste and good expression' (*Life of Mr William Savage*, MS, *GB-Ge*; memoirs, *GB-Cpl*).

Savagnone, Giuseppe (*b* Palermo, 27 Nov 1902; *d* Palermo, 28 Oct 1984). Italian conductor and composer. He began his conducting career as chorus master at the Teatro Greco, Syracuse, in 1925, continuing as orchestral conductor with special responsibility for the operatic repertory. He was deputy conductor at the Teatro dell'Opera, Rome (1928–35), during which time his interest in composition gave rise to various orchestral works and the unperformed opera *Il carro di Dioniso* (1930), to a libretto by E. Romagnoli. A second opera, *Millesima seconda* (libretto by C. Meano), was given at Palermo in 1949. His theatrical output remains essentially in the Italian realist tradition, though his last opera, the comedy *Né tempo, né luogo* (to his own libretto and staged at Palermo in 1961) makes use of his ideas on harmonic theory which, involving the use of 12-note series in harmonic cycles based on the alternation of intervals, are described in his book *Prismatismo musicale* (Palermo, 1956, 2/1966) RAFFAELE POZZI

Savard, (Marie-Emmanuel-)Augustin (*b* Paris, 15 May 1861; *d* Lyons, 6 Dec 1942). French composer. He was a pupil of Massenet at the Paris Conservatoire and won the Prix de Rome in 1886. His single opera, *La forêt* (féerie lyrique, 2, L. Tailhade; Paris, Opéra, 13 Feb 1910), is a drama, rather than a descriptive fantasy, about a woodcutter who is forced to cut down a wood he has known since his childhood. Woodland creatures appear as he destroys their last refuge. A beautiful forest-maiden leads him to his death as his wife cries desperately from a passing religious procession. The well-crafted music combines modality, extreme chromaticism and experiments in whole-tone harmony.

RICHARD LANGHAM SMITH

Savary, Jerome (*b* Buenos Aires, 27 June 1942). French director. He studied in Paris, then in 1966 founded his own travelling company, 'Le Grand Magic Circus'. As an opera director he has worked at Geneva (1982–91), where he staged Offenbach's *La Périchole* and *La voyage dans la lune*, and *Die Fledermaus*; in Paris at the Opéra-Comique (1983), where he staged *La belle Hélène*; at La Scala (1983–92), where he directed Cherubini's *Anacréon*, the première of Azio Corghi's *Blimunda*, *Attila* and *Fra Diavolo*; in Rome (1984), where he staged *Don Giovanni*; at Bregenz (1985–91), where his productions of *Die Zauberflöte* (in 1989, adapted for the Vienna Volksoper), *Les contes d'Hoffmann* and *Carmen* were very popular; at Lyons (1988), where he directed *Le comte Ory*. Although Savary stages operetta with particular style, he also directs serious, large-scale operas with great imagination, as his production of *War and Peace* demonstrated at San Francisco in 1991.

ELIZABETH FORBES

Savin, Risto [Širca, Friderik] (*b* Žalec, Slovenia, 11 July 1859; *d* Zagreb, Croatia, 11 Dec 1948). Slovene composer. A high-ranking Austrian army officer by profession, he studied composition privately in Vienna (1892–6) and Prague (1897–9). He began to write in a late Romantic style, which soon developed into neo-Romanticism, incorporating elements of impressionism, and was the first Slovene to adopt wholeheartedly the principles of Wagnerian music drama. Of his three operas, *Lepa Vida* ('The Fair Vida') and *Matija Gubec* are the most popular. *The Fair Vida* can be described as the first neo-Romantic Slovene opera, and is thus of historical significance. However, it was with *Matija Gubec* that Savin reached his creative peak; here the Romantic principles are expressed in a consistently symphonic form, and the work is also his best opera in terms of expression and originality. Based on Igo Gruden's *The History of the Slovene Nation*, the opera presents events that occurred in 1573, when Matija Gubec led the Slovene and Croatian peasant uprisings. Although echoes of European music such as that of Wagner and Strauss can be heard in Savin's works, his operas are not of a cosmopolitan character, but are marked by the southern Slav spirit.

Poslednja straža [The Last Watch], 1898 (dramatic scene, 1, Savin, after A. Aškerc), Zagreb, 19 March 1906

Lepa Vida [The Fair Vida], 1907 (4, R. Batka, after J. Jurčič), Ljubljana, 18 Dec 1909

Gosposvetski sen [Gospa Sveta's Dream] (2, F. Roš), Ljubljana, 1 Dec 1923

Matija Gubec, 1922–3 (5, Savin, trans. Roš), Ljubljana, 30 Sept 1936

MANICA ŠPENDAL

Savinio, Alberto [Chirico, Andrea de] (*b* Athens, 25 Aug 1891; *d* Rome, 6 May 1952). Italian composer, writer and painter. A brother of the painter Giorgio de Chirico, he studied the piano in Athens and then privately with Max Reger in Munich. In 1910 he moved to Paris, where he made friends with members of the Parisian avant garde, including Apollinaire, Breton, Cocteau and Picasso. At the outbreak of war he returned to Italy and in 1917 helped establish Dadaism, contributing to Tristan Tzara's review *Dada*. In the 1920s and 30s his output of writing and painting broadened. He settled in Rome in 1935, and from 1946 contributed articles on music and other subjects to the *Corriere della sera* and *Corriere d'informazione*. Savinio composed most of his music during an early period to 1915, and then in his last years from 1948 to 1952. He first engaged in music theatre with the *melodrammi Carmela* (1908) and *Poema fantastico* (1909), later destroyed, probably by the composer. The first extant, though incomplete, theatrical work was *Le trésor de Rampsénit* (1912), inspired by the story of the rich Egyptian Pharaoh Rampsen, followed in the next two years by the one-act works *La mort de Niobé*, orchestrated in 1925, and *Les chants de la mi-mort*. These works explore the conflict between drama and music with recourse to bitonality, collage and prefigurings of brutalism, converging with the literary and visual avant garde of the time. The final period of Savinio's musical creativity includes two one-act works, *Agenzia Fix* and *Orfeo vedovo* (both 1950), as well as *Cristoforo Colombo* (1952). With the weight of Savinio's literary experience behind them, these operas tend to bridge the gulf between music and word, shunning the influence of painting and returning to tonality and a new smoothness, thus realizing, with the assistance of surreal settings, the ideal of a metaphysical theatre.

Carmela, 1908 (melodramma, Savinio), unperf., lost

Poema fantastico, 1909 (melodramma, Savinio), lost

Le trésor de Rampsénit, 1912 (ob, 3, M. D. Calvocoressi), Paris, 24 May 1914, inc.

La mort de Niobé, 1913 (tragedia mimica, 1, Savinio), Rome, Arti, 1925

Les chants de la mi-mort, 1914 (scene drammatiche, 1, Savinio), Milan, 1976

Agenzia Fix, 1949 (radio op, 16 episodes, Savinio), RAI, 1950

Orfeo vedovo (1, Savinio), Rome, Eliseo, 24 Oct 1950

Cristoforo Colombo (radio op, 3, Savinio), RAI, 1952

*

G. Apollinaire: 'Musique nouvelle', *Paris Journal* (21 May 1914)

E. Montale: 'Savinio e la musica', *Corriere d'informazione* (4–5 July 1955)

M. Porzio: *Savinio musicista: il suono metafisico* (Venice, 1988)

RAFFAELE POZZI

Savio, Johann Baptist (*fl* 1760s). Austro-Bohemian composer. He became music director to Joseph von Brunian's theatre company some time before Brunian took over the Kotce Theatre, Prague, in 1764. Savio's name does not occur after 1768, though his inclusion in J. J. Stankovský's novel *Vlastencové Bondy* ('Patriots at the Bonda Theatre'; 1878), where he figures as Brunian's second in a duel, shows that he was not entirely forgotten. The earliest record of Savio as a composer names him as author of the music to the arias of *Le diable à quatre, ou La double métamorphose* (*Der Teufel in allen Ecken, oder Die zweyfache Verwandlung*), an *opéra comique* translated from the French by C. L. Reuling and performed by Brunian's company (libretto, Prague, 1760, in *CS-Pu*). This work may have been performed in Vienna in the previous year. Garnier also named Savio as the composer of *Die Zigeuner, oder Der von List und Liebe besiegte Geiz* (libretto, Graz, 1766), Erdmann's *Philint und Cleone*, Nuth's *Die doppelte Ehe*, Unger's *Der nach sieben Jahren beglückte Bräutigam*, Kurz-Bernardon's *Der vergötterte Bernardon* (1764) and F. W. Weiskern's version of *Bastien und Bastienne*, first performed at the Kärntnertor, Vienna, on 5 May 1764. Felix Berner's company included all these works in its repertory in the early 70s. Although Savio's Singspiels were quite widely performed in the 1760s and 70s (Prague, Vienna, Brno, Graz and probably elsewhere), no score is known to survive. Despite his italianate name, it is more likely that his music was Austro-German in style, since Brunian strove to regenerate the Prague theatre and Berner also put the emphasis on native works.

F. X. Garnier: *Nachricht von der im Jahre 1758 von Herrn Felix Berner errichteten jungen Schauspieler-Gesellschaft* (Vienna, 1786)

O. Teuber: *Geschichte des Prager Theaters*, ii (Prague, 1885), 475–6

F. Bischoff: 'Zur Geschichte des Theaters in Graz', *Mitteilungen des Historischen Vereins für Steiermark* (Graz, 1892), 132

A. Loewenberg: '"Bastien and Bastienne" Once More', *ML*, xxv (1944), 176–81

W. Senn: 'Mozarts "Zaide" und der Verfasser der vermutlichen Textvorlage', *Festschrift Alfred Orel* (Vienna, 1960), 172–85

PETER BRANSCOMBE

Savioni, Mario (*b* Rome, 1606–8; *d* Rome, 22 April 1685). Italian alto and composer. He received the traditional training of a choirboy under Vincenzo Ugolini in Rome and was employed in the Cappella Giulia and at S Luigi dei Francesi until he entered the Sistine Chapel at the age of 34 as an alto. He sang his first opera as a child, appearing as Dorino in Vitali's *Aretusa* in 1620. His next known roles were the secondary part of Alceste in Luigi Rossi's *Il palazzo incantato* (1642) and an unknown part in *Amore e fede* (librettist and composer unknown) given in Rome by Queen Christina of Sweden in 1666.

Savioni was an important composer of Italian cantatas, in which he developed a style both lyric and rhythmically crisp that he carried into the larger forms of oratorio and opera. He composed *Sant'Agnese* (1651, *I-Rdp*), an opera in a prologue and three acts, in hasty collaboration with the librettist Domenico Benigni for the papal family of the Pamphili. The opera dramatizes the martyrdom of St Agnes, which occurred at the site of the Palazzo Pamphili and its adjacent chapel dedicated to her at the Piazza Navona; the saint's Christian resoluteness is counterpoised to the dismay and instability of the Roman Flavio (tenor) who loves her. Notable are the complexes of arias, choral music and dancing that close the first and last acts, set respectively in a garden of temptations and with Agnes in glory. Lucifer (bass) in hell makes a brief appearance (1.iv), reinforcing the opera's connections with the earlier Barberini models of opera in Rome.

P. Kast: 'Biographische Notizen zu römischen Musikern des 17. Jahrhunderts', *AnMc*, no.1 (1963), 63–4

C. Annibaldi: 'L'archivio musicale Doria-Pamphilj: saggio sulla cultura aristocratica a Roma fra 16° e 19° secolo', pt 2, *Studi musicali*, xi (1982), 298–300

MARGARET MURATA

Sāvitri. Chamber opera in one act by GUSTAV HOLST to his own libretto adapted from an incident in the Mahābharata; London, London School of Opera, 5 December 1916.

Holst became interested in Hindu literature and philosophy towards the end of the 1890s. What appealed to him, according to his daughter and biographer Imogen, was that 'here was a rational religion'. He was enthralled by the *Rig Veda* and the *Bhagavad Gita* and wanted to set to music some of the hymns these books contain, but he could not discover an English translation that satisfied him. He determined, therefore, to learn Sanskrit at the School of Oriental Languages. Although he never became fluent and had to look up every word in the dictionary and compose each sentence with a crib, he nevertheless translated 20 hymns from the *Rig Veda* and the long poem by Kalidasa on which he based his splendid and ambitious choral work *The Cloud Messenger* (1909–10). He also wrote librettos for two operas on Hindu subjects, *Sita* (1900–06) and *Sāvitri* (1908–9).

Holst began to compose *Sāvitri* after returning from a holiday in Algeria. He gave up one of his teaching posts in order to concentrate on it. Much of it was written in a small rented cottage on the Isle of Sheppey where Holst and his wife spent weekends. It is the antithesis of *Sita*, a three-act work composed on a grandiose scale and with little regard for the practicalities of staging. Holst later described it, with more than a little exaggeration, as 'good old Wagnerian bawling'. *Sāvitri* benefited from the paring of his style during his composition of the *Hymns from the Rig Veda* op.24 of 1907–8, in which full-blown Romanticism gave way to bare 4ths and 5ths over held pedals. Instead of a vast orchestra, only two string quartets, a double bass, two flutes and an english horn are required in *Sāvitri.* The offstage chorus of women's voices sings to the sound of the 'u' in 'sun'. (A mixed chorus was specified in Holst's original score, but when the opera was in rehearsal for its first performance the conductor, Hermann Grunebaum, suggested that women's voices would serve better and Holst rewrote the choral parts almost overnight.) The opera, 30 minutes long, was intended for performance in the open air, 'or else in a small building'.

The opera is set in a wood at evening. The voice of Death (bass) is heard calling to Sāvitri: 'I draw nigh to fulfil my work. I come for thy husband'. Sāvitri (soprano) has been hearing this voice day and night and has come to dread it. Her husband Satyavān (tenor), a woodman – in the original story he was au prince – returns from his work singing of his love for Sāvitri ('What wife in all the world is like to Sāvitri?'). He finds her pale and trembling and thinks she is under the sway of Māyā (the illusion of the physical world). But Sāvitri says she has forgotten Māyā; there is someone else.

Satyavān thinks he hears someone lurking in the forest and raises his axe to fell him; but as he does so the axe falls from his grasp and he collapses on the ground. Death has arrived. Sāvitri welcomes him as 'the Just One' and, because she has not shrunk from him, Death grants her a boon, but 'naught for Satyavān; my breath hath chilled his heart'. Sāvitri asks for life in all its fullness. This is granted to her, but she then claims that she cannot have this full life without Satyavān. Death, outwitted, retreats. Satyavān awakes in Sāvitri's arms. She tells him a Holy One has blessed her. Death is heard admitting that he has been conquered by 'one having Life, one free from Māyā ... for even Death is Māyā'. She is left in quiet ecstasy with Satyavān.

Sāvitri is a remarkable achievement, anticipating many of the stylistic features – particularly polytonality – of Holst's later works. Neither here nor in the Vedic Hymns does he attempt to write in a mock-oriental manner, yet there is something of Indian music about it. This can have been achieved only by instinct, for Holst had heard no Indian music at this time. The economy of the scoring does not preclude richness of texture; and although the scale of the piece is at the opposite pole to the contemporary works of Strauss, Mahler and others, there is richness and colour in Sāvitri's aria about Life that anchors the work to its period and still carries distant echoes of Wagner. Satyavān's unaccompanied song as he returns home is imbued with the spirit of English folksong and there are passages at this point in the work where the sound and shape of the music come close to Vaughan Williams's *On Wenlock Edge*, written at the same time.

Much of the vocal writing is in an effortless conversational recitative that follows the rise and fall of natural speech; in this respect *Sāvitri* strikingly anticipates the church parables of Britten of over half a century later, for there, too, the music suggests orientalism while remaining rooted in the English countryside. Perhaps the most dramatic moment in *Sāvitri* is its opening, where Death's voice is heard unaccompanied. Later, the chorus is used with the utmost poetic discretion and certain solo instruments – viola and flute, for example – take on the importance of extra characters.

MICHAEL KENNEDY

Savoi, Gaspero (*b* ?Siena; *fl* 1758–92). Italian soprano castrato. He first appeared in *opera seria* in 1758 as a secondo uomo, then sang serious parts in *opera buffa*, and female roles at Rome, both in *opera buffa* (1760–61) and as prima donna in *opera seria* (1762–5). He was then for many years secondo uomo in London, singing in Italy in 1779–80 and 1786–92. He had considerable natural gifts, including a fine voice, but in London was sometimes criticized for not making adequate use of them. DENNIS LIBBY

Savonese, Il. *See* CHIABRERA, GABRIELLO.

Savonlinna. City in south-east Finland. The soprano Aino Ackté organized some opera festivals in the medieval Olavinlinna Castle before and during World War I, and once more in 1930, but they remained isolated and occasional events. In 1967 a new festival grew out of a series of summer courses for young singers. It was originally a fairly small-scale local event, plagued by difficulties; in 1972 it was reorganized on a national footing, with the bass Martti Talvela as artistic director. He held the post until 1979, and under him the festival reached the highest international standards. His judicious choice of works, as well as his insistence upon dramatically coherent productions and the use of the Finnish language, also resulted in a startling and lasting growth in the popularity of opera in Finland. The première of Heininen's *Veitsi* ('The Knife') was given during the 1989 festival.

The Savonlinna Festival takes place every summer for four weeks. Three to five operas – some by visiting companies from the abroad – are given to audiences of 2200 each evening in the open courtyard of Olavinlinna Castle, which is protected and acoustically enhanced by a great awning. Until the new opera house in Helsinki is completed (after 1992), Savonlinna is the only venue in Finland capable of offering opera on the grand scale. In addition to standard works, the festival has consistently staged Finnish operas and commissioned new ones. Its programme also includes concerts, recitals and masterclasses by internationally renowned musicians.

ERKKI ARNI

Savova, Galina (*b* Varna, Bulgaria, 1940). Bulgarian soprano. She made her début in Sofia and was engaged there for some years. She made her Metropolitan début in 1982 as Amelia (*Un ballo in maschera*), and has also sung at Karlsruhe, New Orleans, Rome, Naples and Bologna. Her repertory includes Yaroslavna (*Prince Igor*), Leonore, Chrysothemis, Leonora (*La forza del destino*), Aida, Amelia (*Simon Boccanegra*), La Gioconda, Tosca, Minnie and Turandot, the role of her Covent Garden début in 1990. She has a powerful, lustrous voice, and although her acting ability is limited, she is a very dramatic singer. ELIZABETH FORBES

Savoy. London theatre built in 1881 by Richard D'Oyly Carte for Gilbert and Sullivan operettas; *see* LONDON, §II, 2.

Sawallisch, Wolfgang (*b* Munich, 26 Aug 1923). German conductor. He studied at the Munich Academy and in 1947 became répétiteur at Augsburg, where he made his début in *Hänsel und Gretel* that year. He was appointed Generalmusikdirektor at Aachen (1953–8), Wiesbaden (1958–60) and Cologne (1960–63), where he also directed the conductors' class at the academy. He was the youngest conductor engaged at Bayreuth when he opened the 1957 festival with *Tristan und Isolde*. After orchestral appointments in Vienna and Hamburg he became Generalmusikdirektor at the Staatsoper in Munich in 1971. In 1982 he succeeded Everding as Intendant, in which post he occasioned sharp controversy over his artistic policy as distinct from his generally admired conducting. Although widely travelled as an orchestral conductor, Sawallisch has conducted little opera outside Munich except for regular visits to La Scala. He conducted the Munich company on a visit to Covent Garden in 1972 (*Ariadne auf Naxos* and *Die schweigsame Frau*) and on a tour to Japan in 1989 while the Munich house underwent renovation. In Munich he has confined himself mostly to Wagner and Strauss, of whose operas he completed a full cycle at the 1988 festival with a concert performance of *Friedenstag* (also recorded). His other favoured operas are Hindemith's *Mathis der Maler* and Einem's *Dantons Tod*. His conducting is distinguished by a concentration on integral musical qualities, sometimes at the expense of feeling, though he balances restraint of expression with vitality of spirit. His recordings include many Strauss operas and live performances from Bayreuth.

W. Sawallisch: *Im Interesse der Deutlichkeit: mein Leben mit der Musik* (Hamburg, 1988)

A. Blyth: 'Wolfgang Sawallisch', *Opera*, xl (1989), festival issue, 16–20

NOËL GOODWIN

Sax, Adolphe [Antoine-Joseph] (*b* Dinant, 6 Nov 1814; *d* Paris, 4 Feb 1894). Belgian instrument maker. Born into a family of musical instrument makers at Dinant, he studied the flute and clarinet at the Brussels Conservatory. In 1838 he patented a bass clarinet, which was introduced in the orchestra of the Paris Opéra in 1839 by the conductor Habeneck. In *Dom Sébastien* (1843) Donizetti wrote a duo for two bass clarinets. Sax's other musical instruments included the saxhorn (now principally a brass band instrument), which Berlioz used in *Les Troyens*, the saxtuba, invented for Halévy's *Le Juif errant* (1852) and the saxophone. Saxophones were first used in opera by Georges Kastner (*Le dernier roi de Juda*, 1844), then by Limnander (*Barbe-bleue*), Thomas (*Françoise de Rimini* and *Hamlet*) and Saint-Saëns (*Henri VIII*), and later in operas by

Meyerbeer, Bizet, Massenet and d'Indy. Although the saxophone never gained a permanent place in the opera orchestra, it has since been used by Hindemith (*Hin und zurück*), Falla, Berg (*Lulu*), Britten (*Billy Budd*) and by contemporary composers such as Tippett and Birtwistle.

In 1847 Sax became director of the Fanfare (the 20-strong stage band) at the Paris Opéra. It was first employed in Verdi's *Jérusalem* (when Verdi wrote for saxhorns), then in Meyerbeer's *Le prophète*, *Robert le diable*, and even Wagner's *Tannhäuser* and the Opéra's 1860 production of Rossini's *Semiramide* (for which Sax probably composed the stage music). Sax tried to persuade Verdi to allow him to make the trumpets for the triumphal scene in *Aida* for the Cairo première, but Verdi preferred the Italian maker, Pelitti. Sax did, however, make the trumpets for the Paris première in 1880; they were still in use when *Aida* was performed at the Opéra in 1968. Sax's work on sound reflection and theatre and concert hall architecture almost certainly influenced Wagner during the construction of the Festspielhaus at Bayreuth. CHARLES PITT

Sax [Saxe]**, Marie.** *See* SASSE, MARIE.

Saxton, Robert (*b* London, 8 Oct 1953). English composer. His interest in composition began at an early age, and he was only 12 when he wrote his first opera, a two-act setting of the Cinderella fairy-tale. He had private composition lessons with Elisabeth Lutyens (1970–74), later studying with Robin Holloway at Cambridge, Robert Sherlaw Johnson at Oxford and Luciano Berio. He received a Fulbright grant to Princeton (1985–6), where he was a Visiting Fellow. On his return to Britain he taught composition at Goldsmiths' College and Bristol University, and became head of composition at the GSM in June 1990.

Many of Saxton's compositions have had literary inspirations, often concerned with eternity and ring images, as well as darkness and light. When commissioned by Opera North and the Huddersfield Contemporary Music Festival to write a chamber opera he turned to a dramatic source that explored similar concepts, Arnold Wesker's *Caritas*. Wesker's libretto, set in 14th-century Norfolk, juxtaposes two true stories to depict how adherence to ideals through dogma destroys the human spirit. In scenes evoking the unsuccessful Peasants' Revolt of 1381, injustice arouses political ideals which lead to further injustice and bloodshed; this political conflict is contrasted with the personal story of Christine Carpenter. Sealed in a cell to pursue religious ideals, Christine eventually realizes that she is not suited to immurement and becomes imprisoned in mad visions of what her life might have been. Set in two continuous acts for nine singers, children's chorus and a chamber ensemble of 13 players, the musical structure is tightly conceived, with the gradual distortion of recurring themes and motifs paralleling the characters' disillusionment. In the brief but climactic second act, a passacaglia with variations builds to a powerful finish. The opera was first performed at the Wakefield Opera House on 21 November 1991. JENNIFER R. DOCTOR

Sayão, Bidú [Balduina] **(de Oliveira)** (*b* Rio de Janeiro, 11 May 1902). Brazilian soprano. She studied with Jean De Reszke in Nice; returning to Rio de Janeiro in 1925 she sang Rosina at the Teatro Municipal in 1926, repeating the role at the Teatro Costanzi, Rome, and subsequently appeared at both Paris houses (1931), at the Colón and in Italy. In 1937 she enjoyed a tremendous success as Massenet's Manon on her début at the Metropolitan (1937), initiating a New York career that lasted until 1951, in lyric and coloratura soprano roles such as Gilda, Rosina, Gounod's Juliet, Mélisande, Violetta, Mimì, Norina, Adina, Zerlina and – perhaps most memorably – Susanna. She exuded feminine charm, warmth and refinement on stage, singing with pure, silvery tone and enlivening soubrette roles without recourse to soubrette mannerisms. She retired from the stage in 1958.

*

GV (R. Celletti; J. P. Kenyon)

J. A. Léon and A. Ribeiro Guimaries: 'Bidú Sayão', *Record Collector*, xiii (1960–61), 125 [with discography]

MARTIN BERNHEIMER

Saygun, Ahmed [Ahmet] **Adnan** (*b* Izmir, 7 Sept 1907; *d* Istanbul, 6 Jan 1991). Turkish composer. He studied in Paris with Eugène Borrel and Vincent d'Indy from 1928 to 1931, and later taught in Istanbul and Ankara. Active as conductor, musicologist and writer, he collaborated with Bartók on research into Turkish folk music, which in turn influenced his own composition. A prolific composer, Saygun was the first Turkish musician to write operas after the foundation of the republic; he also produced five symphonies, several concertos, an oratorio which brought international fame (*Yunus Emre*, 1946) and many chamber pieces. His best-known opera is *Köroğlu* (1973), often performed by the Istanbul State Opera; like the earlier *Kerem* (1948), it draws on Turkish legend and is named after its hero. Saygun's music reflects a blend of Romanticism and impressionism, but in his later works he tried to apply more recent developments.

See also KEREM and KÖROĞLU.

*

Özsoy [Feridun] (1, M. H. Egeli), Ankara, 19 June 1934
Taş bebek (1, Egeli), Ankara, 27 Dec 1934
Kerem (3, S. Batu, after Turk. legend), Ankara, 2 April 1948 [Act 1 only]; Ankara, State Opera, 22 March 1953 [complete]
Köroğlu (3, Batu), Istanbul, 23 June 1973
Gilgameş, 1976 (musical legend), unperf. FARUK YENER

Saylor, Bruce (Stuart) (*b* Philadelphia, 24 April 1946). American composer. He studied composition with Weisgall and Sessions at the Juilliard School, with Petrassi in Rome and with Perle at CUNY; he has taught at a number of colleges in the New York area. He wrote an opera, set in Revolutionary times, *My Kinsman, Major Molineux* (1, C. Plotkin, after N. Hawthorne), which was performed by the Pittsburgh Opera Society on 28 August 1976, and won praise for its atmosphere and for its management of lyrical numbers. Saylor was appointed resident composer to the Chicago Lyric Opera in 1992.

Saynète. *See* SAINETE.

Sbarra, Francesco (*b* Lucca, 19 Feb 1611; *d* Vienna, 20 March 1668). Italian librettist. His family belonged to the aristocracy of Lucca. From 1633 he was a member of the Accademia degli Oscuri at Lucca and later of the Accademia degli Accesi, for which he directed the opera *Psiche* (text by F. di Poggio; music by Tomaso Breni) at the Palazzo de' Borghi in 1645. He entered the priesthood later that year. On several occasions from 1636 he composed poetry for musical celebrations of government ceremonies.

Sbarra's most original works were a series of musical dramas and *intermedi*, tragic as well as comic, with moralizing intent and using symbolic figures; these include *La verità raminga* (1650), *La moda* (1652), *La corte* (1657) and *La tirannide dell'Interesse* (1653). In the last of these, a five-act 'tragedia politicomorale', Interest kills Intellect, enslaves Desire and with the help of Hypocrisy and Adulation makes himself absolute tyrant of the Isle of Free Will. Although performed only locally, these works saw many editions, were in wide circulation and weathered anti-seicento Italian literary criticism unusually well. Sbarra's most performed work, *Alessandro vincitor di se stesso*, with music by Cesti, owes much to G. A. Cicognini in its verse forms and handling of comedy and even in some details of plot, but has declared allegorical intent as well.

From 1659 Sbarra was in residence as counsellor and court poet at the court of Ferdinand Karl at Innsbruck, where he produced librettos and eulogistic poetry to set to music, such as the idyll *Il tributo degli elementi* for the new sovereign, Siegmund Franz, in 1663. After the extinction of the Tyrolese line in 1665 he obtained a similar position at the Viennese court, where his compositions included texts for *sepolcri*, further moralizing entertainments, ballets and the large-scale festive drama *Il pomo d'oro*, intended for the marriage celebration of Emperor Leopold I.

Alessandro vincitor di se stesso, Cesti, 1651; *Venere cacciatrice*, ? Cesti, 1659; *La magnanimità d'Alessandro*, Cesti, 1662; *L'amor della patria superiore ad ogni altro*, ? J. K. Kerll, 1665; *Nettuno e Flora festeggianti*, Cesti, 1666; *La contesa dell'aria e dell'acqua*, Bertali, 1667; *Le disgrazie d'Amore*, Cesti, 1667; *Il pomo d'oro*, Cesti, 1668

*

AllacciD
G. Malatesta Garuffi: *L'Italia accademica* (Rimini, 1688)
C. Lucchesini: *Della storia letteraria del ducato lucchese*, ii (Lucca, 1831) [incl. extensive list of writings]
G. Sforza: *F. M. Fiorentini ed i suoi contemporanei lucchesi* (Florence, 1879), 398
A. Bertacchi: *Storia dell'Accademia lucchese*, i (Lucca, 1881)
G. Sforza: 'Francesco Sbarra ed i suoi melodrammi per musica', *Gazzetta letteraria*, xiv (1890), 34
U. Rolandi: *Spettacoli musicali per la funzione delle 'Tasche' in Lucca* (Milan, 1932)
F. Hadamowsky: *Il libretto per musica attraverso i tempi* (Rome, 1951)
——: 'Barocktheater am Wiener Kaiserhof, mit einem Spielplan (1625–1740)', *Jb der Gesellschaft für Wiener Theaterforschung 1951-2*, 7-117
W. Senn: *Musik und Theater am Hof zu Innsbruck* (Innsbruck, 1954)
W. Osthoff: 'Antonio Cestis "Alessandro vincitor di se stesso"', *SMw*, xxiv (1960), 13–43
H. Seifert: 'Die Festlichkeiten zur ersten Hochzeit Kaiser Leopolds I.', *ÖMz*, xxix (1974), 6–16
C. B. Schmidt: 'Antonio Cesti's *Il pomo d'oro*: a Reexamination of a Famous Hapsburg Court Spectacle', *JAMS*, xxix (1976), 381–412
THOMAS WALKER

Sbriglia, Giovanni (*b* Naples, 23 June 1829; *d* Paris, 20 Feb 1916). Italian tenor. He studied in Naples and made his début in 1853 at S Carlo. After appearing in various Italian theatres he went to New York (1859–60) and sang at the Academy of Music with Adelina Patti in operas including *Lucia di Lammermoor*, *La sonnambula* and *Rigoletto*. In the 1860s he toured North and South America with the Teresa Parodi Opera Company. In 1875 he settled as a teacher in Paris, where his pupils included Nordica, Edouard and Jean de Reszke, Sibyl Sanderson and Pol Plançon. He had a light, flexible voice. ELIZABETH FORBES

Scacchi, Marco (*b* Gallese, nr Viterbo, *c*1600; *d* Gallese, 1681–7). Italian composer and theorist. He was a protégé and disciple of G. F. Anerio, who probably took him to Warsaw when he became choirmaster to the court of King Sigismund in the mid-1620s. By 1626 he was a royal musician and in 1628 he was appointed choirmaster, a position he retained throughout the reign of Władisław IV (1632–48) and the first months of that of Jan Kazimierz II. He retired to Gallese in 1649.

Scacchi is chiefly remembered for his violent theoretical controversy with the German composer Paul Siefert. As a composer, he is known now only for his sacred works and madrigals, but he probably composed a number of dramatic works, possibly as many as ten, to words by Virgilio Puccitelli, performed at the Polish court in Vilnius and Warsaw. *Il ratto di Helena* (4 September 1634, Vilnius) is commonly attributed to him, as is the *favola pastorale Narciso trasformato* (3 May 1638, Warsaw). The librettos survive but all the music is lost. (See A. Szweykowska: *Dramma per musica w teatrze Wazów 1635–1648*, Kraków, 1976.)

For a list of possible works and further bibliography *see* PUCCITELLI, VIRGILIO.

Scaccia [Scatia], **Giuseppe** (*b* ? Parma, Mantua or Milan; *fl* 1669–1716). Italian tenor. In a long and active career, his first recorded role was Anastasio in Antonio del Gaudio's *L'Eudosia* at Mantua in 1669. The following year, in Milan, he sang Androgeo in *Ippolita reina delle amazzoni* (a collaborative work, with music by P. S. Agostini, Lodovico Busca and P. A. Ziani). In 1675 he was at court in Turin, and from 31 August 1677 to 4 August 1698 he was in the service of the court in Parma, where he also sang in the cathedral from 3 May 1709 to 22 June 1716, and in the Steccata chapel from July 1690 to September 1694. Between 1679 and 1709 he sang in many Italian cities and during the period 1699 to 1701 he is recorded as 'virtuoso' of the Duke of Mantua. From 1697 he usually sang with Alessandra Scaccia, who was in the service of the dukes of Mantua between 1698 and 1703.

*

S. Durante: 'Alcune considerazioni sui cantanti di teatro del primo settecento e la loro formazione', *Antonio Vivaldi: teatro musicale, cultura e società: Venice 1981*, ii, 427–81
P. Besutti: *La corte musicale di Ferdinando Carlo Gonzaga ultimo duca di Mantova: musici, cantanti e teatro d'opera tra il 1665 e il 1707* (Mantua, 1989)
PAOLA BESUTTI

Scala, La. Opera house, the most famous in Italy, opened in 1778 in MILAN.

Scalabrini, Grazia Mellini. *See* MELLINI SCALABRINI, GRAZIA.

Scalabrini, Paolo (*b* 1713; *d* Lucca, 1803 or 28 Feb 1806). Italian composer. He was music director for the Mingotti opera company from 1742 at the latest, when it was at Graz. He travelled with it through Germany and parts of the Austrian empire, composing and arranging many operas and going in 1747 to Copenhagen, where the company performed every year until 1756. In 1748 he married the soprano Grazia Mellini. The same year J. A. Scheibe was dismissed as court *maestro di cappella* in Copenhagen and Scalabrini given his place, which he held until 1753; he was replaced by Sarti. Scalabrini remained there, composing several intermezzos and Danish Singspiels. He then travelled for some years, but returned to Copenhagen in 1768 as music director of an opera company he had assembled in Italy. When Sarti left in 1775, Scalabrini again became court *maestro di cappella* until, after the death of his first wife in 1781, he returned finally to Italy. According to Schmidl he died on 28 February 1806.

dm – *dramma per musica*

Sirbace (dm), Graz, Tumel, carn. 1742
Artaserse (dm, P. Metastasio), Hamburg, 1742
Oronte re de sciti (op seria, 3, C. Goldoni), 1742; with addns by Jommelli and Hasse, Hamburg, Jan 1745
Cajo Fabricio (dm), Graz, Tumel, carn. 1743
Siroe re di Persia (dm, 3, Metastasio), carn. 1744
Adelaide (dm, ? A. Salvi), Hamburg, 1744, collab. F. Finazzi
Antigono (dm, Metastasio), Prague, Nuovo, 1744
Catone in Utica, Hamburg, 1744
Venceslao (dm), Copenhagen, 1744
Angelica e Medoro (dm, Metastasio), Hamburg, 1746
Didone (dm), Hamburg, 1746
Adriano (dm, Metastasio), Copenhagen, 1749
Alessandro nell'Indie (dm, Metastasio), Copenhagen, 1749
Il marito vizioso (intermezzo, F. Darbes), Copenhagen, 1750
Den forliebte skildrer, 1756, *DK-Kk*
Koerlighed uden strømper, 1773, *Kk*, *F-Pn*
Oraklet, 1776, *DK-Kk*

Arias in *A-Wn*, *B-Bc*, *DK-Kk* and *I-PAc*

Music in: Semiramide riconosciuta (dm), Graz, Turnel, carn. 1743; Demetrio (dm), Hamburg, 1744

Doubtful: Lucio Vero (A. Zeno), Brunswick, ducal, 1756

*

SchmidlD
E. H. Müller von Asow: *Die Mingottischen Opernunternehmungen 1732–1756* (Dresden, 1915) [incl. thematic catalogue of works]
T. Krogh: *Zur Geschichte des dänischen Singspiels im 18. Jahrhundert* (Copenhagen, 1924)

Scala di seta, La ('The Silken Ladder'). *Farsa comica* in one act by GIOACHINO ROSSINI to a libretto by GIUSEPPE MARIA FOPPA after F.-A.-E. de Planard's libretto for Pierre Gaveaux's *L'échelle de soie* (1808, Paris); Venice, Teatro S Moisè, 9 May 1812.

La scala di seta is a freshly and fluently written diversion, memorable more for Rossini's youthful rhythmic flair than for anything especially striking in thematic invention or harmonic colouring. As such it is a plausible response to Planard's entertainment which offers some simple variations on the familiar theme of the secret marriage. Giulia (soprano) is secretly married to Dorvil (tenor) in spite of the wish of her guardian Dormont (tenor) that she should marry Dorvil's friend, a young army officer, Blansac (bass). The only way out of Giulia's dilemma is for her to encourage Blansac and her cousin Lucilla (mezzo-soprano) to fall in love, a plot that is brought to fruition after a bevy of overheard conversations, whispered meetings, and the elaborate use of closets, screens and the eponymous silken ladder. As befits farce, the characters in the opera have minimal inner lives. There is little that is remarkable or revealing about the delayed cavatinas of Giulia or Dorvil; Lucilla's blithe, folksy 'Sento talor nell'anima' is the more attractive and representative piece. If Rossini is interested in anyone, it is the woozy old retainer Germano (bass). His duet with Giulia effectively launches the plot, and in a memorable scene, 'Amore dolcemente', it is Germano, baffled, tired and a little drunk, who drifts the music into somnolence before Blansac arrives to trigger the elaborately plotted denouement. RICHARD OSBORNE

Scala Theatre. London theatre opened in 1905 and demolished in 1970; *see* LONDON, §II, 2.

Scalchi, Sofia (*b* Turin, 29 Nov 1850; *d* Rome, 22 Aug 1922). Italian contralto. She studied with Boccabadati and made her début in 1866 at Mantua as Ulrica (*Ballo*). In 1868 she sang Azucena (*Il trovatore*) at Covent Garden, where she returned virtually every year until 1889; she also sang in St Petersburg (1872–81 and 1889–90). Her repertory included many travesty roles as well as Maddalena (*Rigoletto*), Amneris, Léonor (*La favorite*), Fidès (*Le prophète*) and Ortrud. In 1882 she sang in New York, making her début at the Academy of Music as Arsace (*Semiramide*). At the opening night of the Metropolitan (1883) she sang Siébel in *Faust*; after singing Cenerentola at Florence (1886) and Vanya in the first London performance of Glinka's *A Life for the Tsar* (1887), she returned to New York to sing Emilia in the first American performance of Verdi's *Otello* (1888, Academy of Music). During her last seasons at the Metropolitan she sang Gluck's Orpheus (1893), Beppe in *L'amico Fritz* (1894) and Mistress Quickly in the American première of *Falstaff* (1895). She retired in 1896. She had a flexible, full-toned voice.

*

W. H. Seltsam: *Metropolitan Opera Annals* (New York, 1949)
H. Rosenthal: *Two Centuries of Opera at Covent Garden* (London, 1958) ELIZABETH FORBES

Carlo Scalzi: portrait by Charles Joseph Flipart (1721–93)

Scalzi, Carlo [Cichion] (*b* Voghera, Lombardy; *fl* 1718–38). Italian soprano castrato. He is first heard of in Rome in 1718–19, singing in three operas (two by Alessandro Scarlatti), twice playing female roles. From 1719 to 1722 he was in Venice, in five operas by Antonio Pollarolo, Giovanni Porta and Orlandini, returning in 1724–5 in operas by Vinci and others. He appeared at Reggio and Modena in 1720, Rome again in 1722, Genoa in 1722–3 and 1733, Florence in 1723 and 1729, Milan in 1724, Parma in 1725, Naples in 1726–7 (Vinci's *Ernelinda*, Hasse's *Sesostrate* and other operas) and 1730 (when he created the title role in Hasse's *Ezio*), and Rome in 1728–9 and 1731–2. Handel engaged him for the London season of 1733–4; he made his début in the pasticcio *Semiramide riconosciuta*, and subsequently sang in revivals of *Ottone* (Adalberto), *Sosarme* (Argone) and *Il pastor fido* (1734, Silvio) and in the first production of *Arianna in Creta* (Alcestes, strictly Handel's only new part for him). The numerous transpositions and alterations made by Handel give us a clear idea of Scalzi's voice, a high soprano with a compass from *c'* to *b♭''*. He made little impression in London but was placed in the front rank on the Continent. Metastasio bracketed him with Farinelli as 'incomparable'. He sang in four more operas at Venice in 1737–8, including Porpora's *Rosbale* and Hasse's *Alessandro nell'Indie*. WINTON DEAN

Scanderberg ('Skanderbeg'). *Tragédie en musique* in a prologue and five acts by FRANÇOIS FRANCOEUR and François Rebel to a libretto by ANTOINE HOUDAR DE LAMOTTE and JEAN-LOUIS-IGNACE DE LA SERRE; Paris, Opéra, 27 October 1735.

The third and last *tragédie* by Francoeur and Rebel, *Scanderberg* was successful at its première but was not revived for nearly 30 years. Lamotte began writing the libretto in 1711 but left it incomplete at his death; La Serre wrote the prologue and fifth act. The inspiration for the libretto was a historical figure, the 15th-century Albanian prince George Kastriote, called Skanderbeg, who led a successful insurrection against the ruling Turks. The plot itself, however, is a love intrigue typical of the genre, set in a Turkish sultan's palace. Skanderbeg's Act 1 monologue, 'Que ce jour est charmant', and the scenery representing the mosque in Act 5 (by Servandoni) were particularly praised. A lavish court production was mounted at Fontainebleau in 1763. LOIS ROSOW

Scannamusa, Giovanni. Pseudonym of ANELLI, ANGELO.

Scapigliatura (It.: 'bohemianism'). A term used to identify a period (1860–80) of renewal in Italian culture and a literary trend that opened the way to *verismo* while anticipating some features of the *fin-de-siècle* decadent movement. The terms *scapigliatura*, and *scapigliati*, meaning 'dishevelled young men' with reference to Murger's *Scènes de la vie de bohème*, were used in the novel *La scapigliatura e il 6 febbraio* (Milan, 1862) by Cletto Arrighi, who first gave them wide currency.

Anti-bourgeois selfconsciousness and disorderly lifestyle characterized a group of artists and intellectuals in Milan in the 1860s who adopted the name *scapigliati*. The poets Emilio Praga (1839–75) and Arrigo Boito (1842–1918) were the central figures of the group, which included the musician Franco Faccio (1840–91) and the painter Tranquillo Cremona. Rather than a movement, *scapigliatura* was a free brotherhood of dissatisfied, high-minded young men with a strong commitment towards a rejuvenation of Italian culture and the promotion of a close interrelation between poetry and its 'sister arts', music and painting. The literary trend was characterized by a reaction against Manzoni and his epigones and the adoption of themes and stylistic features from French and German authors (Baudelaire, the Parnassians, Heine, Hoffmann). Defined as a 'post-Romantic avant garde', the *scapigliati* exhibited a taste for morbid and macabre subjects, an acute perception of evil and a sense of inadequacy to achieve their ideals. Linguistic and metrical experimentation was a constant feature of their poetry.

In music, *scapigliatura* is relevant for the influence it had on the language of librettos and for the critical writings in Milanese periodicals (e.g. Boito's articles in *La perseveranza* and *Figaro*). Only three operas were produced by the *scapigliati*: Faccio's *I profughi fiamminghi* (1863) to a libretto by Praga, *Amleto* (1865) by Faccio and Boito, and Boito's emblematic *Mefistofele* (1868). Boito's obsession with the pathology of evil can be detected in his libretto for Ponchielli's *La Gioconda* (1876), where the character of Barnaba anticipates the un-Shakespearean Iago of Boito's *Otello* for Verdi.

G. Marangoni: 'Emilio Praga pittore', *Nuova antologia* (16 July 1913), 218–30
P. Nardi: *Scapigliatura: da Giuseppe Rovani a Carlo Dossi* (Bologna, 1924)
A. Boito: *Tutti gli scritti*, ed. P. Nardi (Milan, 1942)
G. Mariani: *Storia della scapigliatura* (Rome, 1967)
M. Petrucciani, ed.: *E. Praga: Poesie* (Bari, 1969)
G. Salvetti: 'La scapigliatura milanese e il teatro d'opera', *Il melodramma italiano dell'ottocento: studi e ricerche per Massimo Mila* (Turin, 1977), 566–604 MATTEO SANSONE

Scarabelli, Adelina (*b* Milan, 25 Sept 1953). Italian soprano. After studying in Brescia, in 1977 she was engaged at the Piccola Scala, where she sang in Soliva's *Testa di bronzo* (1980). She first appeared at La Scala in 1981 as Barbarina (*Le nozze di Figaro*). At Salzburg she sang Despina (1984) and the Italian Singer in *Capriccio* (1985). She has appeared at many Italian theatres, including Florence, where she sang Lauretta (1988). Her roles range from Zerlina, Susanna, Ismene (*Mitridate*) and Servilia (*La clemenza di Tito*), to Carolina (*Il matrimonio segreto*), Norina, Adina, Oscar, Nannetta, Micaëla, Liù and Musetta. Much admired as a Mozart singer, she has a flexible voice and a delightful personality. ELIZABETH FORBES

Scarabelli, Diamante Maria (*b* Bologna; *fl* 1695–1718). Italian soprano. She is first heard of at Venice in 1695 in two operas by C. F. Pollarolo, and reappeared there in 1703, 1707–12 and 1714–16, in at least 23 operas, most of them by C. F. Pollarolo, Lotti and Caldara, but including Handel's *Agrippina* (1709), in which she played Poppaea. She sang frequently in Bologna (1696–7, 1699, 1700, 1708–9, 1718), winning a spectacular success in the pasticcio *Perseo* in 1697. She also appeared in Milan (1699, 1713), Mantua (1703), Pavia (1705), Genoa (1705), Ferrara (1715) and Padua (including Orlandini's *Lucio Papirio*, 1718). She was in the service of the Duke of Mantua (1697–1708), Cardinal Grimani, Viceroy of Naples (1709) and the Duke of Modena (1715). Scarabelli was one of the most celebrated sopranos of her age; the part of Poppaea requires a flexible virtuoso technique and a compass of *c'* to *b♭''*. WINTON DEAN

Scaria, Emil (*b* Graz, 18 Sept 1838; *d* Blasewitz, nr Dresden, 22 July 1886). Austrian bass. He studied in Vienna and made his début in 1860 at Budapest as Saint-Bris (*Les Huguenots*). After further study with Garcia in London, he sang at Dessau; in 1863 he was engaged at Leipzig and in 1865 at Dresden. His repertory then included Dulcamara, Nicolai's Falstaff and Peter the Great (*Zar und Zimmermann*). Although his powerful voice had the dark colouring of a true bass, its enormous range allowed him to sing baritone roles with equal success. From 1873 until his death Scaria was engaged at the Vienna Hofoper. He sang Wotan in the first Berlin *Ring* cycle, at the Viktoria Theater (1881), and also in the first London cycle, at Her Majesty's Theatre (1882), where during *Die Walküre* he suffered a breakdown; although he sang in *Siegfried* two nights later, he did not appear in the second and third cycles. Scaria sang Gurnemanz in the first performance of *Parsifal* at Bayreuth (1882) and joined Angelo Neumann's touring company in Germany, Belgium, the Netherlands and Italy, singing Wotan and Rocco (*Fidelio*). During 1883 he sang King Mark at both Berlin and Vienna, and returned to Bayreuth as Gurnemanz, which he sang in the first concert performance of *Parsifal* in London, at the Albert Hall (1884). In 1886 he again suffered a mental breakdown and soon after died insane.

*

H. Klein: *Thirty Years of Musical Life in London* (London, 1903)
A. Neumann: *Erinnerungen an Richard Wagner* (Leipzig, 1907; Eng. trans., 1908)
E. Newman: *The Life of Richard Wagner* (London, 1933–47)
W. Beetz: *Das Wiener Opernhaus 1869 bis 1945* (Vienna, 1949)
E. Pirchan, A. Witeschnik and O. Fritz: *300 Jahre Wiener Operntheater* (Vienna, 1953)
G. Skelton: *Wagner at Bayreuth* (London, 1965, enlarged 2/1976)

ELIZABETH FORBES

Scarlatti. Italian family of composers and singers.

(1) (Pietro) Alessandro (Gaspare) Scarlatti (*b* Palermo, 2 May 1660; *d* Naples, 22 Oct 1725). Composer, especially of vocal music. He was the most important opera composer of his generation in Italy.

There are good reasons for abandoning such epithets as 'founder of the Neapolitan school of 18th-century opera' which were regularly attached to Scarlatti's name until fairly recent times. A considerable part of his working life was spent in Rome, and of the 66 operas he is known to have written (three of them in collaboration with other composers), over a third received their first performances in localities other than Naples, principally Rome and Florence. As far as both music and libretto are concerned, only one of his operas, *Il trionfo dell'onore* (1718), might be considered truly Neapolitan in character; the others are more representative of a pan-Italian style with its roots in 17th-century Venetian opera. Moreover, although J. A. Hasse probably studied with Scarlatti for a time, there is little in his operatic style, or for that matter in the style of native Neapolitans such as Leo, Vinci and Porpora (who might with some justification be said to represent a Neapolitan school), that can be shown to stem directly from the earlier composer.

Scarlatti was the second of eight children, four others of whom were also musicians. His sister Anna Maria Scarlatti (*b* Palermo, 8 Dec 1661; *d* Naples, 14 Dec 1703) sang in Agostini's *Il ratto delle Sabine* in Venice in 1680; she was also active in Rome and later in Naples, where she married the shipowner Nicolo Barbapiccola, who became impresario at the Teatro S Bartolomeo, 1703–4. She and her sister, Melchiorra Brigida Scarlatti (*b* Palermo, 5 Oct 1663; *d* Naples, 2 Dec 1736), both had scandalous reputations; Melchiorra's liaison with a court official may have influenced Alessandro's appointment as royal *maestro di cappella* in 1684. She sang in Rome and Naples and was married to a double bass player, Nicola Pagano, who was impresario at the Teatro dei Fiorentini, 1708–9. Their brother Francesco (Antonio Nicola) Scarlatti (*b* Palermo, 5 Dec 1666; *d* ?after 1741), a violinist in Naples and Palermo, composed a dialect comedy, *Lo Petracchio*, possibly in collaboration with his brother-in-law Pagano, given at Aversa in 1711, and was in London in the 1720s and possibly later in Dublin; his works include cantatas and oratorios. Another brother, Tommaso Scarlatti (*b* 1669–72; *d* Naples, 1 Aug 1760), was a tenor, trained at the Neapolitan conservatory S Onofrio; he sang in his nephew Domenico's *Giustino* in 1703, was appointed to the royal chapel in 1722 and later sang in *buffo* operas (appearances are recorded in 1736 and 1740). The opera singer Rosa Scarlatti may have been his daughter (*b* Naples, 5 May 1716).

Alessandro's son Pietro Filippo Scarlatti (*b* Rome, 5 Jan 1679; *d* Naples, 22 Feb 1750), a composer, worked in Urbino and at the royal chapel in Naples; his opera *Clitarco* (now apparently lost) was given at the Teatro S Bartolomeo there in 1728.

The relationship of (3) Giuseppe Scarlatti to others of the family remains uncertain.

1. Palermo and Rome, 1660–83. 2. Naples, 1684–1702. 3. Florence, Venice and Rome, 1702–8. 4. Naples and Rome, 1709–25.

1. PALERMO AND ROME, 1660–83. It used to be thought that Scarlatti's musical talent came from his mother's side of the family, but the researches of Umberto D'Arpa have shown that the composer's father, Pietro, was a professional musician (see Pagano 1988, p.11). Alessandro's parents moved in musical circles: one of the witnesses to their marriage was the singer and composer Marc'Antonio Sportonio (*c*1631–after 1680), a pupil of Carissimi who took part in the earliest known operatic performance in Sicily (of Cavalli's *Giasone* in 1655) and was himself the composer of several operas; and Scarlatti's uncle (his mother's brother), Vincenzo Amato (1629–70), was *maestro di cappella* at Palermo Cathedral and composed at least one opera, *L'Isaura* (1664), according to Gerber. These two musicians were probably Scarlatti's first teachers.

It may have been the prevailing conditions of famine and social unrest in Sicily, and perhaps also the relative poverty of the Scarlatti family, that led Alessandro's parents to send him and his two sisters, Anna Maria and Melchiorra Brigida, to Rome in 1672. The tradition that the young Scarlatti had lessons there from Carissimi lacks confirmation, but in any case he must have found as much to learn from the example of other composers whose music was sung and played in Rome, including Stradella, Bernardo Pasquini and Pietro Agostini. In April 1678 Scarlatti married Antonia Anzalone. He probably met her at the palace of Monsignor Pietro Filippo Bernini, where she lived, while he was making preparations for the performance there of his first opera earlier in the year. The performance, however, was cancelled at the last minute when Pope Innocent XI placed a ban on stage entertainments during Carnival, and the only surviving score, which bears neither title nor composer's name, remained unrecognized in the Vatican Library until 1986 (see Lionnet). Scarlatti must have found the opera's plot of particular significance, since it concerns the fortunes (and particularly the love affairs) of a brother and sister forced to leave Sicily during troublous times and to start a new life in Tuscolo (present-day Frascati).

For about four years from December 1678 Scarlatti was employed as *maestro di cappella* at the church of S Giacomo degli Incurabili, and from November 1682 he occupied a similar position at S Girolamo della

Carità, but he continued to compose for private patrons in Rome. In January 1679 he was commissioned to write an oratorio for the Arciconfraternita del Ss Crocifisso, and the following month his second opera, *Gli equivoci nel sembiante*, was given in the private theatre of its librettist, Domenico Filippo Contini. Like the first opera, this is an intimate pastoral comedy well suited to a private theatre, with a single outdoor set and a small cast accompanied by a few string instruments and continuo (*see* ORCHESTRA, fig.2). Helped no doubt by certain scandals attending its performances, *Gli equivoci* enjoyed an enormous success which spread Scarlatti's reputation as a promising opera composer far beyond Rome. The first audiences seem to have admired above all the tunefulness of the arias. These are mostly in the ternary form that was to predominate even more in the later operas, but Scarlatti frequently varies or extends the repeat of the first section – a practice he was to abandon as the length of each section, and the number of arias he was called upon to write, gradually increased.

Gli equivoci attracted the attention of Queen Christina of Sweden, who promptly made Scarlatti her *maestro di cappella*. His third opera, *L'honestà negli amori*, was performed at her palace in February 1680. This and *Tutto il mal non vien per nuocere* (1681) are in much the same vein as the earlier pieces, but with *Il Pompeo* (1683), written for the private theatre of another Roman patron, Lorenzo Onofrio Colonna, grand constable of Naples, Scarlatti produced the first of many heroic dramas based on episodes in Roman history. If the music appears somewhat archaic in style, and especially in structure, this is probably because Minato's libretto was originally written for Cavalli almost 20 years earlier.

The chronicle of Scarlatti's activity as an opera composer during this first Roman period is completed with *La guerriera costante* (also 1683). Of the six operas he is known to have composed during these years, only one was produced in Rome's public theatre, the Capranica. To further his career in opera he needed to free himself from the restrictions that made public opera such a risky (and for much of the time impossible) enterprise in Rome. The opportunity came when the new viceroy of Naples, the Marquis del Carpio (no doubt prompted by his friend the Duke of Maddaloni, who had already introduced *Gli equivoci* to the Neapolitans and was shortly to do the same for *Il Pompeo*) called on Scarlatti to take charge of the forthcoming opera season at the Teatro di S Bartolomeo at Naples. Del Carpio, as Spanish Ambassador to the Vatican, had witnessed Scarlatti's early operatic successes in Rome, and in 1684 he made him his *maestro di cappella* – a preferment which, it was said, was brought about by the intrigues of one of his sisters. It certainly aroused the resentment of Francesco Provenzale, the acting *maestro*, who had expected to succeed the aged P. A. Ziani in the post; Provenzale, along with other members of the *cappella*, immediately resigned.

2. NAPLES, 1684–1702. Even before this new scandal had flared up, Scarlatti had embarked on the busy life of an opera composer that was to occupy him at Naples for the next 18 years. The normal practice was for a new opera to be seen first in the viceroy's private theatre and then to transfer to the adjacent public theatre, the S Bartolomeo, in which the viceroy took a controlling interest. Scarlatti is known to have written at least 32 operas for these theatres during his first period at Naples, of which fewer than half have survived complete; the others are known only from aria collections or from their librettos. In addition, his duties at Naples included the revision of at least some of the Venetian operas that continued to provide the staple operatic diet at Naples, as they had done before his arrival. The extent of Scarlatti's involvement in the process of *rifacimento* (the adapting of imported works to the prevailing Neapolitan taste) is difficult to gauge. It has been argued that it was minimal (see Strohm 1975; Eng. trans. 1985, p.18), but it is difficult to account for the claims made in contemporary librettos or in the scores themselves that, for example, *Penelope la casta* (1696) was Scarlatti's 60th opera or *Lucio Manlio l'imperioso* (1705) his 88th unless we assume the total to include collaborative ventures such as *La santa Dinna* (Rome, 1687) as well as *rifacimenti* that involved an appreciable amount of new composition.

Scarlatti does, however, seem to have been concerned above all with the composition of completely new operas during this period, and especially after 1696, when his admirer and patron, the Duke of Medinaceli, succeeded Del Carpio as viceroy and took personal control of the Teatro di S Bartolomeo. Works like *Pirro e Demetrio* (1694), which enjoyed an international success comparable with that of *Gli equivoci nel sembiante* and was the only Scarlatti opera to be seen in London during the composer's lifetime, and *La caduta de' Decemviri* (1697), which marked the beginning of a collaboration with one of his most important librettists, Silvio Stampiglia, show the composer at the pinnacle of his fame in the theatre (*see* LIBRETTO (i), fig.1). In the opinion of Lorenz (1927) *La caduta de' Decemviri*, also marks a new departure in the development of Scarlatti's operatic style, a view not shared by Grout (1979). While much in *La caduta*, and particularly the regular alternation of simple recitative and da capo aria, can be shown to be a continuation of stylistic trends to be observed in earlier works, the opera does break with tradition in one respect: the older type of Venetian prelude, consisting typically of a slow, homophonic section in duple or quadruple metre followed by a quick, dance-like movement in triple time and perhaps a second fast movement, is here replaced by the so-called Italian form which soon became the norm in Scarlatti's operas and those of other composers. In this a fast, homophonic section, usually with rushing scales or trumpet-like figures, is succeeded by a short, slow chordal section which is often no more than a link between the opening Allegro and the final binary dance movement, again in quick tempo.

Other stylistic developments to be observed during Scarlatti's first Naples period (though not specifically in *La caduta*) include a sharper distinction than before between recitative and aria, the former adopting an even more parlando style and developing several standard harmonic and melodic formulae, particularly at cadences. The arias remain as numerous as in the earlier operas, and many of them are still very short, but second strophes are abandoned and there is greater diversity in the instrumentation. Other changes reflect those taking place in music as a whole during the period: an enrichment of the harmonic vocabulary (for example in the expressive use of the diminished seventh chord) and a vogue for 12/8 siciliana rhythms. During these years Scarlatti remained in close contact with his Roman patrons, especially the cardinals Pamphili and Ottoboni, and the same stylistic features can be observed in the operas he wrote for them. These include *La Statira*, composed for the reopening of the Tordinona theatre in 1690 to a libretto by Ottoboni himself.

In December 1701 Medinaceli, censured (and soon afterwards replaced) by Madrid for his bloody quelling of a pro-Austrian conspiracy among the nobility of Naples, withdrew the usual subvention of 4000 ducats for the coming season at the S Bartolomeo. Scarlatti, Stampiglia and the former impresario, Nicola Serino, were forced to rely on public support, and this dwindled after Aldrovandini's *Semiramide* was accorded a cool reception at the S Bartolomeo in December; the season was saved only by the success of Scarlatti's *Tito Sempronio Gracco* the following February. The uncertain future of opera at Naples must have been one of the factors influencing Scarlatti's decision to absent himself from the city in order to try his luck elsewhere.

3. Florence, Venice and Rome, 1702–8. A visit to Naples by King Philip V of Spain, and the necessity of composing a new opera (*Tiberio imperatore d'Oriente*) in his honour, forced Scarlatti to postpone his departure until June 1702. Travelling by way of Rome, where he renewed contacts with his former patrons, he arrived, uninvited and with his entire family and servants, in Florence, probably in early August. *Il Flavio Cuniberto* was staged the following month in the private theatre of Prince Ferdinando de' Medici at nearby Pratolino. Ferdinando had already promoted Scarlatti's operas in several north Italian cities and had commissioned at least one new one from him, probably *La serva favorita* (1689), but the permanent position that Scarlatti hoped to obtain for himself (and possibly also for his son Domenico) was not forthcoming, Ferdinando being financially dependent on his father, Grand Duke Cosimo III.

Scarlatti returned first to Rome and then, before the end of the year, to Naples. The Florence visit did at least result in further commissions from the prince, and a new opera by Scarlatti was given at Pratolino each September until 1706. These were all heroic works, with librettos based on incidents from Roman history. The scores, however, have not survived, and all that remains of this period in Scarlatti's career as an opera composer are a few isolated arias and an exchange of letters with the prince which throws valuable light on the composer's working method and the nature of an opera's gestation.

Scarlatti seems to have returned to Naples only to wind up his affairs there, at least for the time being. Leaving his son Domenico to continue in employment with the viceroy, he was soon back with his family in Rome, where Cardinal Ottoboni secured for him the post of vice-*maestro* at the basilica of S Maria Maggiore; he was to succeed Antonio Foggia as *maestro* there in June 1707. The possibilities that Rome offered for the composition of church music and chamber cantatas failed to satisfy Scarlatti's compositional urges and to provide the means to support his family as he would have liked. Opera was impossible, and after the earthquake of 1703 the pope turned even Carnival into a season of penitence. The annual commission from Prince Ferdinando provided Scarlatti with his only opportunities for opera during these years, but these also ceased after 1706, when the prince found the Bolognese composer G. A. Perti more ready to provide the undemanding kind of music that suited the taste of his audiences at Pratolino. In 1705 Scarlatti had sent his son Domenico off to Venice 'to take whatever opportunities arise to make a name for himself' (as he wrote in a famous letter to Prince Ferdinando), and it was to Venice that he himself now turned.

Scarlatti was obviously determined that the city that had seen the opening of the first opera house 70 years earlier, and had set the style for Italian opera ever since, should now sample his own gifts as an opera composer at their best. The two works he composed for the carnival season at the Teatro S Giovanni Grisostomo in 1707, *Mitridate Eupatore* and *Il trionfo della libertà*, stand apart from all his others in several respects. Their librettos, by Girolamo Frigimelica Roberti, include ballets but no comic scenes; unlike the other librettos Scarlatti set, they are designated as *tragedie*, and, like the classical French tragedies by which Frigimelica Roberti was strongly influenced, they are in five acts instead of the more usual three. Moreover, *Mitridate* differs from Scarlatti's other heroic operas in having neither involved love intrigues nor a magnanimous tyrant. Dent (1905) drew attention to the libretto's architectural qualities, Grout (1979) to its obsession with political doctrines.

It has been suggested that it was, at least in part, the nature of their librettos that caused both of these operas to flop in 1707, but this is unlikely in view of the fact that Frigimelica's other 'reform' librettos, set by C. F. Pollarolo, Caldara and Mancia, seem to have been successful in Venice. The failure of Scarlatti's two operas there may be attributed to other causes: a certain xenophobia on the part of the Venetians; the composer's own arrogant and condescending attitude towards the theatre management; and (most important, perhaps) those qualities in the music that we most admire today – its high seriousness, inventive instrumentation and contrapuntal textures. The Venetian operagoers might have preferred less demanding music, with more tuneful melodies and more transparent accompaniments. *Mitridate*, in short, like Mozart's *Die Entführung aus dem Serail*, was perhaps found to contain 'too many notes'. This, at any rate, was a reaction strongly expressed in a malicious satire by Bartolomeo Dotti which, among other even more damaging observations, referred to the soporific effect that the music of *Mitridate* had on the audiences at the Teatro S Giovanni Grisostomo.

After what must have been for him a humiliating defeat in Venice, Scarlatti retreated in April 1707 to Urbino, where his eldest son, Pietro, was employed as *maestro di cappella* at the cathedral. A few months later he returned to Rome, having somewhat reluctantly accepted advancement at S Maria Maggiore on the death of the *maestro*, Antonio Foggia. For the next year he was forced to resume the career of a church musician, occasionally furnishing his powerful Roman patrons with serenatas for special occasions and cantatas for their weekly *accademie*. Opera was still impossible, even in the private theatres. Under such conditions the new Austrian viceroy, Cardinal Grimani, needed to exert little pressure (though he did have to exert some) to persuade Scarlatti to return to his former post as *maestro di cappella* to the Naples court. Scarlatti's first appointment at Naples had been made over the head of Provenzale; his reappointment there brought about the demotion of Francesco Mancini. He undoubtedly had a way of making enemies!

Design by Filippo Juvarra (forest sacred to Apollo, with throne and temple) for the original production of Alessandro Scarlatti's 'Il Ciro' at the Palazzo Cancelleria, Rome, 1712

4. Naples and Rome, 1709–25. While Dotti's Venetian satire was certainly motivated by malice, it also reflected the fact that popular tastes in opera were moving against Scarlatti. *Il Teodosio*, produced in Naples only a few weeks after his reappointment there, earned the censure of Francesco Maria Zambeccari, who in a letter of 16 April spoke of Scarlatti as

> a great man, so good indeed that he succeeds ill because his compositions are extremely difficult and in the chamber style, and so do not succeed in the theatre. *In primis*, those who understand counterpoint will admire him, but in a theatre audience of a thousand people there are not twenty who do understand it, and the rest, not hearing cheerful and theatrical things, are bored. Also, the music being so difficult, the singer has to be extremely careful not to make a slip, and is therefore unable to make the gestures he is used to making and becomes too tired. Thus, [Scarlatti's] theatre style is not pleasing to most audiences, who want cheerful things and *saltarelli* such as they get at Venice.

Although Zambeccari's criticisms of Scarlatti's operatic style, like Dotti's, sprang from motives which were not entirely disinterested, there is certainly much truth in what he says. Scarlatti's style was beginning to run against the tide of popular taste, and none of the serious operas he composed after 1708 enjoyed anything like the success of his early Roman operas or some of those he produced during his first, prolific Neapolitan period. One of the most successful of the late operas was *Il Tigrane* (1715), described by Grout (1979) as 'one of the greatest, if not the very greatest, of Scarlatti's operas', but only the comedy *Il trionfo dell'onore*, given 18 times at the Teatro dei Fiorentini in 1718, can be said to have been a hit; even this was not revived during Scarlatti's lifetime. It is surely significant that, except for *Il Cambise* (1719), all the serious operas that Scarlatti composed after 1716 were intended for performance in Rome, where conservative patrons and audiences were more sympathetic to a style already becoming outmoded in Naples. These include his last known opera, *La Griselda* (1721), as well as extensive *rifacimenti* of two others originally written for Prince Ferdinando's theatre at Pratolino, *Tito Sempronio Gracco* and *Turno Aricino*.

The operas of Scarlatti's final period are not essentially different from those he was writing in the 1690s; the 'Italian' overture and the arias and duets remain the main formal components. There is no attempt to create a musical span more extended than that of a da capo aria, although a desire for greater continuity does lead to a more extensive use than hitherto of accompanied recitative. The proportions of the lyrical items do, however, show a gradual expansion, which is paralleled by an ever greater richness and variety in their instrumentation; continuo arias are quite rare in the late operas. This expansion leads, of course, to a reduction in the number of arias and duets. *La caduta de' Decemviri* (1697), for example, contained no fewer than 62; *La Griselda* has 41.

In the final analysis, Scarlatti occupies an equivocal position in the history of opera. No-one did more than he to establish Naples as a leading operatic centre during the last two decades of the 17th century; no Italian during his lifetime wrote operatic music of such quality and depth; and few composers of any age have enjoyed greater respect from their patrons (as evidence of which may be mentioned Scarlatti's election to the Arcadian Academy in 1706, the conferment of knighthood on him by Pope Clement XI, probably in 1715, and the epitaph that Cardinal Ottoboni wrote for his tomb in the church of Montesanto, Naples, lauding him as 'dear to princes and kings'). And yet Scarlatti seems hardly to have influenced the course of operatic history. Most of the 'innovations' with which he has sometimes been credited – the da capo aria, the accompanied recitative, the introduction of french horns into the opera pit, the creation of the 'Italian' overture – can be shown to predate him, while the music itself emerges more as a refinement of 17th-century styles than as a harbinger of the Classical period. As his art developed, so it became more remote from the audiences whose approval he sought to win. Possibly Zambeccari spoke truer than he intended when he said that by composing so well Scarlatti succeeded ill. Certainly those of his compositions that have been most admired by posterity do not belong in the opera house.

See also *Dafni* (i); *Equivoci nel sembiante, gli*; *Eraclea*; *Griselda* (ii); *Marco Attilio Regolo*; *Mitridate Eupatore*; *Pompeo*; *Principessa fedele, la*; *Statira* (i); *Tigrane*; and *Trionfo dell'onore, il*.

Edition: *The Operas of Alessandro Scarlatti*, ed. D. J. Grout, Harvard Publications in Music (Cambridge, MA, 1974–85) [G]

NB – *Naples, Teatro di S Bartolomeo*
NR – *Naples, Palazzo Reale*
RC – *Rome, Teatro Capranica*
VGG – *Venice, Teatro S Giovanni Grisostomo*
dm – *dramma per musica*
mel – *melodramma*

title	*genre, acts*	*libretto*	*first performance*	*sources, remarks, editions*
[untitled]	3			comp. wint. 1677–8; intended for perf. at palace of P. F. Bernini, 1678
Gli equivoci nel sembiante	dm, 3	D. F. Contini	Rome, Contini's private theatre, Feb 1679	as L'errore innocente, Bologna, 1679; as Amor non vuole inganni, Vienna, aut. 1690; *A-Wn* (Act 1 only), *B-Bc*, *I-Bc*, *MOe*, *Rsc*, *Vnm*; G vii
L'honestà negli amori	dm, 3	D. F. Bernini [? or Contini, according to D'Accone 1985]	Rome, palace of Queen Christina, 3 Feb 1680	*MOe*, *Rc* * (Act 1)
Tutto il mal non vien per nuocere	commedia per musica, 3	G. D. de Totis	RC, Jan 1681	as Dal male il bene, Naples, 1687; *D-Bds*, *I-MC* (partly autograph), *Nc*
Il Pompeo	dm, 3	N. Minato	Rome, Teatro Colonna, 25 Jan 1683	*B-Br* (*R*1986: HS, vi)
La guerriera costante	3	F. Orsini	Rome, palace of Duchess of Bracciano, carn. 1683	*I-Rvat*
L'Aldimiro, o vero Favor per favore	dm, 3	De Totis	NR, 6 Nov 1683	arias in *GB-Lbl*, *Och*, *I-Bc* and *Rvat*
La Psiche, o vero Amore innamorato	dm, 3	De Totis	NR, 21 Dec 1683	recit. and aria *PAVu*
Olimpia vendicata	dm, 3	A. Aureli	NR, 23 Dec 1685	*F-Pn*, *GB-Lbl*, *I-Vnm*; as Amor vince lo sdegno, o vero L'Olimpia placata, RC, 9 Feb 1692, with new music by Scarlatti and F. Gasparini, arias in *D-Mbs* and *I-Rvat*
La Rosmene, o vero L'infideltà fedele	mel, 3	De Totis	Rome, Palazzo Doria Pamphili, carn. 1686	*D-BD*, *MÜs*, *F-Pn*, *I-Fc* (Acts 1 and 2)
Clearco in Negroponte	dm, 3	A. Arcoleo	NR, 21 Dec 1686	*MOe*
La santa Dinna [Act 3]	commedia per musica, 3	B. Pamphili	Rome, Palazzo Doria Pamphili, carn. 1687	arias *Rvat*; Act 1 by A. Melani, Act 2 by B. Pasquini
Il Flavio	dm, 3	after M. Noris	NR, ?14 Nov 1688	arias in *GB-Och*, *I-Fc*, *MOe* and *Nc*
L'Amazzone corsara [guerriera], o vero L'Alvilda	dm, 3	G. C. Corradi	NR, 6 Nov 1689	*D-Mbs*, *I-MC*
La Statira	dm, 3	P. Ottoboni	Rome, Teatro Tordinona, 5 Jan 1690	*D-Mbs*, *GB-CDp*, *Lbl*, *I-MOe*; G ix
Gli equivoci in amore, o vero La Rosaura	mel, 3	G. B. Lucini	Rome, Palazzo della Cancelleria, Dec 1690	as La Rosaura, Florence, Borgo Ognissanti, 18 July 1692; *A-Wn*, *D-WD*, *F-Pc* (Acts 1 and 2), *GB-Lbl*; facs. of Acts 1 and 2 ed. in PÄMw, xiv, Jg.xiii–xiv (*R*1966)
L'humanità nelle fiere, o vero Il Lucullo	dm, 3		NB, 25 Feb 1691	
La Teodora augusta	dm, 3	A. Morselli	NR, 6 Nov 1692	*Och*, *I-Fc*, *Rvat*
Gerone tiranno di Siracusa	dm, 3	Aureli	NR, 22 Dec 1692	*GB-Och*
Il nemico di se stesso			RC, 24 Jan 1693	arias in *I-Bc* and *Rvat*
L'amante doppio, o vero Il Ceccobimbi	mel, 3		NR, April 1693	
Il Pirro e Demetrio	dm, 3	Morselli	NB, 28 Jan 1694	as La forza della fedeltà, Florence, carn. 1712; *B-Br*, *I-Nc*
Il Bassiano, o vero Il maggior impossibile	mel, 3	Noris	NB, spr. 1694	
La santa Genuinda, o vero L'innocenza difesa dall'inganno [Act 2]	dramma sacro per musica, 3	?Ottoboni	Rome, Palazzo Doria Pamphili, Dec 1694	*D-Mbs*, *F-Pc*, *GB-Lbl*; Act 1 by G. L. Lulier, Act 3 by C. F. Pollarolo
Le nozze con l'inimico, o vero L'Analinda	mel, 3		NB, 1695	as L'Analinda, o vero Le nozze col nemico, Florence, carn. 1702; *F-Pn*
Nerone fatto Cesare	mel, 3	Noris	NR, 6 Nov 1695	arias and duets *I-Nc*
Massimo Puppieno	mel, 3	Aureli	NB, 26 Dec 1695	*MC*; G v
Penelope la casta	dm, 3	Noris	NB, ?23 Feb 1696, ? or Palermo, 1694	arias *Nc*
La Didone delirante	opera drammatica, 3	F. M. Paglia, after A. Franceschi	NB, 28 May 1696	arias in *Bc*, *Bsp*, *Nc*, *OS* and *Rvat*
Comodo Antonino	dm, 3	Paglia, after G. F. Bussani	NB, 18 Nov 1696	arias *F-Pn*

title	*genre, acts*	*libretto*	*first performance*	*sources, remarks, editions*
L'Emireno, o vero Il consiglio dell'ombra	opera drammatica, 3	Paglia	NB, 2 Feb 1697	*A-Wn*, *I-Nc*, comic scenes *D-Dlb*
La caduta de' Decemviri	dm, 3	S. Stampiglia	NB, 15 Dec 1697	*B-Br*, *C-Mc*, *GB-Lbl*, *I-Nc*, *US-I*, *PO*, comic scenes *D-Dlb*; G vi
Il prigioniero fortunato	dm, 3	Paglia	NB, 14 Dec 1698	*GB-Lbl*, *I-Nc*, comic scenes *D-Dlb*
Anacreonte	dm, 3	Bussani	Pratolino, Villa Medicea, 1698	collab. M. Bitti and F. de Castris
La donna ancora è fedele	dm, 3	after Contini	NB, 1698	*I-Nc*, comic scenes *D-Dlb*
Gl'inganni felici	dm, 3	A. Zeno (except for comic scenes)	NR, 6 Nov 1699	arias *I-Nc*, comic scenes *D-Dlb*; as L'Agarista, o vero Gl'inganni felici, with int Brenno e Tisbe, Florence, carn. 1706
L'Eraclea	dm, 3	Stampiglia	NB, 30 Jan 1700	items in *A-Wn*, *B-Br*, *D-Dlb*, *F-Pn*, *GB-Cmc*, *Lbl* and *I-Nc*; G i
Odoardo (with int Adolfo e Lesbina)	dm, 3	?Zeno	NB, 5 May 1700	arias in *F-Pc*, *I-Nc* and *GB-BEL*, comic scenes *D-Dlb*
Dafni	favola boschereccia, 3	Paglia, ?after E. Manfredi	Naples, viceroy's villa at Posillipo, 5 Aug 1700	as L'amore non viene dal caso, Iesi, carn. 1715; *GB-Cfm* (*R*1986: HS, vii), comic scenes *D-Dlb*
Laodicea e Berenice	dm, 3	after Noris	NB, April 1701	*F-Pn*
Il pastor[e] di Corinto	favola boschereccia, 3	Paglia	Naples, viceroy's villa at Posillipo, 5 Aug 1701	*B-Br*, comic scenes *D-Dlb*
Tito Sempronio Gracco (with int Bireno e Dorilla)	dm, 3	Stampiglia	NB, Feb 1702	arias in *MÜs*, *F-Pc* and *I-Nc*, comic scenes *D-Dlb*
Tiberio imperatore d'Oriente	dm, 3	G. D. Pallavicino	NR, 8 or 17 May 1702	arias in *F-Pc*, *I-Fc* and *Nc*
Il Flavio Cuniberto	dm, 3	Noris	Pratolino, Villa Medicea, Sept 1702 (? not 1st perf.)	*GB-Och*
Arminio	dm, 3	A. Salvi	Pratolino, Villa Medicea, Sept 1703	
Turno Aricino	dm, 3	Stampiglia	Pratolino, Villa Medicea, Sept 1704	arias in *D-MÜs* and *F-Pc*
Lucio Manlio l'imperioso	dm, 3	Stampiglia	Pratolino, Villa Medicea, Sept 1706	
Il gran Tamerlano	dm, 3	Salvi, after J. Pradon	Pratolino, Villa Medicea, Sept 1706	
Il Mitridate Eupatore	tragedia in musica, 5	G. Frigimelica Roberti	VGG, 5 Jan 1707	*B-Br*, *D-Bds*, *F-Pn*
Il trionfo della libertà	tragedia in musica, 5	Frigimelica Roberti	VGG, 11 Feb 1707	arias in *A-Wn*, *B-Br* and *I-Rvat*
Il Teodosio	dm, 3	? V. Grimani	NB, 27 Jan 1709	
L'amor volubile e tiranno	dm, 3	G. D. Pioli and G. Papis	NB, 25 May 1709	as La Dorisbe, ò L'amor volubile e tiranno, Rome, 8 Feb 1711; as La Dorisbe, Genoa, aut. 1713; *B-Bc*, *D-Dlb*
La principessa fedele	dm, 3	A. Piovene (rev. ? D. A. Parrino)	NB, 8 Feb 1710	frag. *B-Br*, arias *D-MÜs*; G iv
La fede riconosciuta	dramma pastorale, 3	? B. Marcello	NB, 14 Oct 1710	*GB-Cfm**
Giunio Bruto, o vero La caduta dei Tarquini [Act 3]	dm, 3	?Sinibaldi	planned for Vienna, 1711; perf. cancelled	*A-Wn*; Act 1 by Cesarini, Act 2 by A. Caldara
Il Ciro	dm, 3	Ottoboni	Rome, Palazzo della Cancelleria, carn. 1712	*B-Bc**, *US-Wc*
Scipione nelle Spagne (with int Pericca e Varrone)	dm, 3	Zeno and N. Serino	NB, 21 Jan 1714	*B-Br*, *GB-Lbl*, *I-Bu*, *MC* (Act 1 and int); int perf. as La dama spagnola ed il cavalier romano, Bologna, carn. 1730
L'amor generoso (with int Despina e Niso)	dm, 3	Papis and Stampiglia	NR, 1 Oct 1714	*GB-Lbl*, *US-Wc*
Il Tigrane, o vero L'egual impegno d'amore e di fede	dm, 3	D. Lalli	NB, 16 Feb 1715	*GB-Bu*, *Lbl*, *I-Fc*, *Nc*; G viii
Carlo re d'Allemagna (with int Palandrana e Zamberlucco)	dm, 3	F. Silvani	NB, ?26 Jan 1716	*GB-Bu*
La virtù trionfante dell'odio e dell'amore	dm, 3	Silvani	NR, 3 May 1716	
Telemaco	dm, 3	C. S. Capece	RC, carn. 1718	*A-Wn** (*R*1978: IOB, xxiii), *D-MÜs*, *F-Pc*
Il trionfo dell'onore	commedia, 3	F. A. Tullio	Naples, Fiorentini, 26 Nov 1718	*GB-Lbl*, *US-Wc*; ed. H. Williams (New York, 1982)
Il Cambise	dm, 3	Lalli	NB, 4 Feb 1719	*I-Nc*

title	genre, acts	libretto	first performance	sources, remarks, editions
Marco Attilio Regolo (with int Leonzio e Eurilla)	dm, 3		RC, carn. 1719	*GB-Lbl*, *US-Wc*; G ii
La Griselda	dm, 3	? F. M. Rusponi, after Zeno	RC, Jan 1721	*B-Bc*, *D-Bds*, *MÜs*, *GB-Lbl** (Acts 1 and 3); G iii; ed. D. Drechsler (Kassel, 1960)

Doubtful: L'Arsate (3, ?Orsini), Rome, palace of Duchess of Bracciano, Feb 1683, arias in *I-Nc* and *Rsc*; Il Fetonte (dm, 3, De Totis), NR, 22 Nov 1685; L'Etio (dm, 3, Morselli), NR, carn. 1686, aria in *MC* and *Nc*; La Dori (dm, 3, A. Apolloni), NR, 18 Jan 1689, arias in *MOe* and *Nc*; L'Anacreonte tiranno (mel, 3, Bussani), NB, 9 Feb 1689, aria *Nc*; La serva favorita (dm, 3, C. Villifranchi), Pratolino, Villa Medicea, 1689

CONTRIBUTIONS TO OTHER COMPOSERS' OPERAS

NB – *Naples, Teatro di S Bartolomeo* NR – *Naples, Palazzo Reale*

dm – *dramma per musica*

title	genre, acts	libretto	composer(s)	first performance	Scarlatti's contribution, sources
L'Idalma, o vero Chi la dura la vince	dm, 3	G. D. de Totis	B. Pasquini	Rome, Palazzo Doria Pamphili, 1682	?reworking of Act 1
Il Giustino	dm, 3	N. Beregan	Legrenzi	NR, 6 Nov 1684	?prol.
L'amico dell'amico, e nemico di se stesso	3			?Naples, 1693	arias in *I-Bc* and *Rvat*
L'Odoacre	dm, 3	N. Bonis	Varischino	NB, 5 Jan 1694	arias
L'Arione	dm, 3	O. d'Arles	C. Valtoline, D. Erba and 25 others	Milan, 9 June 1694	
La Semiramide	dm, 3	F. M. Paglia	Aldrovandini	NR, 19 Dec 1701	?prol., arias *Nc*
L'Ariovisto	dm, 3		Perti, Magni and Ballarotti	Florence, aut. 1702	arias *D-MÜs*
Amore eroico tra i pastori	opera pastorale for puppets, 3	P. Ottoboni	Cesarini, Lulier and G. Bononcini	as La pastorella, Rome, Palazzo Venezia, 5 Feb 1705; as Love's Triumph, London, 1708	arias *GB-Lbl* (London, 1708)
Thomyris, Queen of Scythia	3	P. A. Motteux	[pasticcio]	London, Drury Lane, 1 April 1707	arias *Lbl* (London, 1707)
La Clotilda	dm, 3		F. B. Conti	London, Queen's, 2 March 1709	arias *Lbl* (London, 1709)
Lo Petracchio scremmetore	opera comica, 3	A. Capis	F. Scarlatti	Aversa, 1711	?15 arias
Il Porsenna	dm, 3	A. Piovene	Lotti	NB, 19 Nov 1713	arias in *Lbl* and *I-MC* (Act 2)
Giove in Argo		A. M. Luchini	Lotti	Dresden, Schlosstheater, 25 Oct 1717	ints: Vespetta e Milo (2 by Scarlatti, 1 by Conti)

Doubtful: arias in La forza della virtù (dm, 3, D. David), before 1699; rev. as Creonte tiranno di Tebe, spr. 1699; collab. C. F. Pollarolo and others

GerberNL

E. J. Dent: 'The Operas of Alessandro Scarlatti', *SIMG*, iv (1902–3), 143–56

——: *Alessandro Scarlatti: his Life and Works* (London, 1905, 2/1960 with addns by F. Walker)

H. Junker: 'Zwei *Griselda* Opern', *Festschrift zum 50. Geburtstag Adolf Sandberger* (Munich, 1918), 51–64

C. van den Borren: *Alessandro Scarlatti et l'esthéthique de l'opéra napolitain* (Brussels and Paris, 1921)

A. Lorenz: 'Alessandro Scarlattis Opern und Wien', *ZMw*, ix (1926–7), 86–9

——: *Alessandro Scarlattis Jugendoper* (Augsburg, 1927)

A. Cametti: 'Carlo Sigismondo Capeci (1652–1728), Alessandro e Domenico Scarlatti e la Regina di Polonia a Roma', *Musica d'oggi*, xiii (1931), 55–64

Gli Scarlatti (Alessandro – Francesco – Pietro – Domenico – Giuseppe): note e documenti sulla vita e sulle opere, Chigiana, ii (1940)

C. Sartori: 'Il *Dafni* di Alessandro Scarlatti', *RMI*, xlv (1941), 176–83

——: '*Dori* e *Arione*, due opere ignorate di Alessandro Scarlatti', *NA*, xviii (1941), 35–42

E. Zanetti: '*Gli inganni felici* in una sconosciuta raccolta di arie di Alessandro Scarlatti', *RaM*, xiv (1941), 416–30

E. J. Dent: 'A Pastoral Opera by Alessandro Scarlatti', *MR*, xii (1951), 7–14

U. Prota-Giurleo: 'Breve storia del teatro di corte e della musica a Napoli nei secoli XVII e XVIII', *Il teatro di corte del palazzo reale di Napoli* (Naples, 1952), 19–146

R. G. Pauly: 'Alessandro Scarlatti's *Tigrane*', *ML*, xxxv (1954), 339–46

C. Sartori: 'Una Arianna misconosciuta: La Laodice di A. Scarlatti', *La Scala* (1956), no.79, p.4

G. Confalonieri: 'Nota su *Varrone e Pericca* di Alessandro Scarlatti', *Immagini esotiche nella musica italiana*, Chigiana, xiv (1957), 39–49

M. Fabbri: *Alessandro Scarlatti e il Principe Ferdinando de' Medici* (Florence, 1961)

A. Garbelotto: 'Contributo per un catalogo aggiornato delle opere di Alessandro Scarlatti', *Archivio storico siciliano*, 3rd ser., xiii (1963), 239–344

C. R. Morey: *The Late Operas of Alessandro Scarlatti* (diss., Indiana U., 1965)

D. J. Grout: 'La 'Griselda' di Zeno e il libretto dell'opera di

Scarlatti', *NRMI*, ii (1968), 207–25
B. Trowell: 'Scarlatti and Griselda', *MT*, cix (1968), 527–9
J. A. Westrup: 'Alessandro Scarlatti's *Il Mitridate Eupatore* (1707)', *New Looks at Italian Opera: Essays in Honor of Donald J. Grout* (Ithaca, 1968), 133–50
R. Pagano, L. Bianchi and G. Rostirolla: *Alessandro Scarlatti* (Turin, 1972) [reviewed by R. Strohm, *RIM*, xi (1976)]
M. F. Robinson: *Naples and Neapolitan Opera* (London, 1972)
G. Rose: 'Two Operas by Scarlatti Recovered', *MQ*, lviii (1972), 420–35
L. Bianconi: 'Funktionen des Operntheaters in Neapel bis 1700 und die Rolle Alessandro Scarlattis', *Colloquium Alessandro Scarlatti: Würzburg 1975*, 13–116
D. J. Grout: 'The Original Version of Alessandro Scarlatti's *Griselda*', *Essays on Opera and English Music in Honour of Sir Jack Westrup* (Oxford, 1975), 103–14
R. Strohm: 'Alessandro Scarlatti und das Settecento', *Colloquium Alessandro Scarlatti: Würzburg 1975*, 153–76; Eng. trans. as 'Alessandro Scarlatti and the Eighteenth Century', *Essays on Handel and Italian Opera* (Cambridge, 1985), 15–33
H. C. Wolff: 'Die Buffoszenen in den Opern Alessandro Scarlattis', *Colloquium Alessandro Scarlatti: Würzburg 1975*, 191–204
R. Strohm: 'Hasse, Scarlatti, Rolle', *AnMc*, no.15 (1975), 221–57
——: 'Italienische Opernarien des frühen Settecento (1720–1730)', *AnMc*, no.16 (1976) [whole issue]
G. Jones: 'Alessandro Scarlatti's *Il Ciro*', *HJbMw*, iii (1978), 225–37
L. Lindgren: 'Le opere drammatiche "romane" di Francesco Gasparini (1689–1699)', *Francesco Gasparini (1661–1727): Camaiore 1978*, 167–82
D. J. Grout: *Alessandro Scarlatti: an Introduction to his Operas* (Berkeley, 1979)
R. Strohm: *Die italienische Oper im 18. Jahrhundert* (Wilhelmshaven, 1979)
C. Troy: *The Comic Intermezzo: a Study in the History of Eighteenth-Century Italian Opera* (Ann Arbor, 1979)
W. C. Holmes: *'La Statira' by Pietro Ottoboni and Alessandro Scarlatti: the Textual Sources, with a Documentary Postscript* (New York, 1983)
F. D'Accone: *The History of a Baroque Opera: Alessandro Scarlatti's 'Gli equivoci nel sembiante'* (New York, 1985)
L. Lindgren: 'Il dramma musicale a Roma durante la carriera di Alessandro Scarlatti (1660–1725)', *Le muse galanti: la musica a Roma nel settecento*, ed. B. Cagli (Rome, 1985), 35–57
R. Pagano: *Scarlatti, Alessandro e Domenico: due vite in una* (Milan, 1985)
W. C. Holmes: 'Lettere inedite su Alessandro Scarlatti', *La musica a Napoli durante il seicento*, ed. D. A. D'Alessandro and A. Ziino (Rome, 1987), 369–78
J. Lionnet: 'A Newly Found Opera by Alessandro Scarlatti', *MT*, cxxviii (1987), 80–81
R. Pagano: 'Giasone in Oreto: considerazioni sull'introduzione del melodramma a Palermo', *Musica ed attività musicali in Sicilia nei secoli XVII e XVIII*, I quaderni del conservatorio, i (Palermo, 1988), 11–18

(2) (Giuseppe) Domenico Scarlatti (*b* Naples, 26 Oct 1685; *d* Madrid, 23 July 1757). Composer, remembered chiefly for his keyboard sonatas. He was the sixth child of Alessandro Scarlatti. Before he was 16 he was appointed organist and composer of the viceregal chapel at Naples, where his father was *maestro*. His first opportunity to engage in opera came with the appointment of his uncle, Nicola Barbapiccola, as impresario of the S Bartolomeo theatre for the 1703–4 season in Naples. Scarlatti provided three operas for the season, one of them an extensive revision of C. F. Pollarolo's *L'Irene* (1694). The years 1708–19 were spent in Rome, mainly as a church musician, and in 1714 he was appointed *maestro* of the Cappella Giulia at St Peter's. It was during these years that he composed his other operas, seven of them for the dowager Queen of Poland, Maria Casimira, who had settled in Rome and built a small theatre in her residence, the Palazzo Zuccari, in the Piazza della Trinità de' Monti. Only two of these, *Tolomeo et Alessandro* (1711) and *Tetide in Sciro* (1712), have survived complete in their original form; the last of them, *Amor d'un ombra e gelosia d'un aura*, is known in the version produced (as *Narciso*) in London in 1720.

Maria Casimira's departure in June 1714 brought Scarlatti's most fruitful years as an opera composer to an end. He is known to have written only two after this date; both were for the Teatro Capranica in Rome, and one was composed in collaboration with Porpora. For reasons which are still not clear, Scarlatti suddenly resigned his post at St Peter's in 1719 and made a hasty retreat from Rome, arriving in Lisbon on 29 November. There he entered the service of King João V of Portugal and became music master to the king's daughter, Maria Barbara de Bragança, in whose service he remained for the rest of his life. Despite being a colleague of the renowned castrato Farinelli in Spain, he is not known to have been involved in any way in operas produced for the Spanish court.

As an opera composer Scarlatti has too often been dismissed as a pale epigone of his famous father. Yet the operas he wrote for Maria Casimira, in competition with such composers as Caldara and Pollarolo, were often judged to be the best in Rome, and if they were seldom revived elsewhere, this is hardly surprising at a time when operatic tastes were beginning to change in other cities; the same could be said even of Alessandro Scarlatti's late operas. The father's example is, of course, apparent in many features of the younger man's vocal writing, but Domenico's individuality often asserts itself in ways that betoken a keen dramatic sense. In ensembles, for example, he can distribute the individual lines in an entirely naturalistic way (sometimes jettisoning the prescribed da capo repeat in order to do so), and in arias he frequently portrays indecision or conflicting emotions by mercurial changes of tempo and dynamics. Some arias are designated *alla francese*, and in others the voice is doubled throughout at the unison or octave without any other accompaniment (common also in Handel's operas, but rarely, if ever, to be found in Alessandro Scarlatti's). Finally, the elder Scarlatti never attempted anything like the satirical farce *La Dirindina* (composed 1715), which occupies an important position in the history of the comic intermezzo.

See also DIRINDINA; NARCISO; and TETIDE IN SCIRO.

NB – *Naples, Teatro di S Bartolomeo* RC – *Rome, Teatro Capranica*
NR – *Naples, Palazzo Reale* RZ – *Rome, Palazzo Zuccari*
dm – *dramma per musica*

title	*genre, acts*	*libretto*	*first performance*	*sources, remarks*
L'Ottavia ristituita al trono	melodramma, 3	G. Convò	NB, ?Nov 1703	32 arias, 2 duets *I-Nc*
Il Giustino	dm, 3	Convò, after N. Beregan	NR, 19 Dec 1703	10 arias *F-Pn*, 21 arias, 3 duets *I-Nc*

title	genre, acts	libretto	first performance	sources, remarks
L'Irene	dm, 3	?Convò, after G. Frigimelica Roberti	NB, carn. 1704	10 arias *F-Pn*, 32 arias, 1 duet *I-Nc*; rev. of C. F. Pollarolo's setting (1694)
La Silvia	dramma pastorale, 3	C. S. Capece	RZ, 27 Jan 1710	
Tolomeo et Alessandro, ovvero La corona disprezzata	dm, 3	Capece	RZ, 19 Jan 1711	*GB-BEL*, Act 1 MS (private collection, Arrigo Perrone)
L'Orlando, ovvero La gelosa pazzia	dm, 3	Capece, after L. Ariosto	RZ, Feb 1711	
Tetide in Sciro	dm, 3	Capece	RZ, ?10 Jan 1712	*I-Vsf*, 8 arias, 2 trios *Nc*; extracts ed. T. Ochlewski (Kraków, n.d.)
Ifigenia in Aulide	dm, 3	Capece	RZ, 11 Jan 1713	aria *D-Dlb*
Ifigenia in Tauri	dm, 3	Capece	RZ, ?15 Feb 1713	3 arias *Dlb*
Amor d'un ombra e gelosia d'un aura	dm, 3	Capece	RZ, 15 Jan 1714	as Narciso, London, King's, 30 May 1720, rev. P. A. Rolli and T. Roseingrave; *Hs*, ov. and arias (London, 1720)
Ambleto	dm, 3	A. Zeno and P. Pariati	RC, carn. 1715	aria *I-Bc*
La Dirindina	farsetta per musica, 2 pts	G. Gigli		*Vlevi*; ints for Ambleto, perf. cancelled; ed. F. Degrada (Milan, 1985)
Berenice, regina d'Egitto, ovvero Le gare d'amore e di politica	dm, 3	A. Salvi	RC, carn. 1718	5 arias *D-MÜs*, collab. N. Porpora

A. Cametti: 'Carlo Sigismondo Capeci (1652–1728), Alessandro e Domenico Scarlatti e la Regina di Polonia a Roma', *Musica d'oggi*, xiii (1931), 55–64

S. A. Luciani: 'Un'opera inedita di Domenico Scarlatti', *RMI*, xlviii (1946), 433–5

R. Kirkpatrick: *Domenico Scarlatti* (Princeton, 1953)

A. Della Corte: '*Tetide in Sciro*: l'opera di Domenico Scarlatti ritrovata', *RaM*, xxvii (1957), 281–9

A. D. McCredie: 'Domenico Scarlatti and his Opera "Narcisso"', *AcM*, xxxiii (1961), 19–29

M. Viale Ferrero: *Filippo Juvarra scenografo e architetto teatrale* (Turin, 1970)

F. Degrada: 'Una sconosciuta esperienza teatrale di Domenico Scarlatti: *La Dirindina*', *Quadrivium*, xii (1971), 229–65 [Ghisi Festschrift]

W. Malinowski and M. Bristiger: 'O teatre Królowej Marii Kazimiery Domenico Scarlattim i kilku innych sprawach' [Concerning the Opera Theatre of Maria Casimira, Domenico Scarlatti and Several Other Matters], *Ruch muzyczny*, xx/13 (1976), 2–6

F. Valesio: *Diario di Roma*, ed. G. Scano (Milan, 1977–9)

R. Pagano: *Scarlatti, Alessandro e Domenico: due vite in una* (Milan, 1985)

M. Boyd: *Domenico Scarlatti – Master of Music* (London, 1986)

O. Termini: '*L'Irene* in Venice and Naples: Tyrant and Victim, or the Rifacimento Process Examined', *Antonio Caldara: Essays on his Life and Times*, ed. B. W. Pritchard (Aldershot, 1987), 365–407

G. Doderer: Preface to *D. Scarlatti: Libro di tocate per cembalo* (Lisbon, 1991), 7–53

(3) **Giuseppe Scarlatti** (*b* Naples, ?1718, or 18 June 1723; *d* Vienna, 17 Aug 1777). Composer. He came from a dynasty of musicians that included Alessandro and Domenico Scarlatti, and after those two he was the most important composer among them. His date of birth and precise relationship to the Scarlatti clan are uncertain. A Giuseppe was born in Naples in June 1723 to Alessandro's brother Tommaso; another Giuseppe, born in 1718, was possibly a nephew of Domenico, according to Burney. Since one of Giuseppe Scarlatti's earliest works, the oratorio *La Ss Vergine annunziata*, was performed in Rome in 1739, 1718 would seem to be the more likely date. Although in the libretto of the oratorio he is called 'Maestro di Cappella Napolitano', there is no record of his holding such an appointment and the title is presumably honorific.

According to the locations of his opera premières, Scarlatti seemed to have been active in a number of different cities. He composed for Rome (1739–41); for Florence, Pisa, Lucca and Turin (1741–9); for Venice (1752–4); for Naples (1755); for Venice again (1756–9, and in 1756 for Milan); and for Vienna (1759–72, with performances at Turin in 1763 and at Verona in 1765). Since *L'impostore*, on which he collaborated with Gioacchino Cocchi, was performed at Barcelona in 1752, it is possible that the performance was connected with Domenico Scarlatti's sojourn in Spain.

Between 1757 (or 1759) and his death Scarlatti seems to have been active in Vienna as composer, harpsichordist, and music teacher to members of Prince Schwarzenberg's family. Up to 1772 a number of his stage works were performed at the Burgtheater, including a *festa teatrale*, *Armida*, to a libretto by Marco Coltellini, whose intermezzo *Dove è amore è gelosia* was also set to music by Scarlatti in 1768, and the opera *Amiti e Ontario*, to a libretto by Calzabigi. Up to 1764 Scarlatti enjoyed the protection of Count Durazzo and Gluck, both very influential figures at the Viennese court.

Scarlatti composed over 30 operas, 21 of which were of the *seria* type and 11 of the *buffo* type. He set at least nine librettos by Metastasio and several by Goldoni. It is doubtful whether he composed the music for a fifth Goldoni libretto, *Il mercato di Malmantile*, which is attributed to him in the libretto for a performance of the opera in Venice in Carnival 1758. Another libretto citing the same performance date, location, cast and printer attributes the music to Fischietti (*see* MERCATO DI MALMANTILE, IL).

Giuseppe Scarlatti carried on the lyrical melodic tradition established by Alessandro and Domenico Scarlatti before him, creating in the process a charming but simple style in which the orchestra for the most part functioned as accompaniment to the vocal parts. Judging by the few repeat performances of some of his operas (such as *I portentosi effetti della Madre Natura*) very few achieved much success. He had a talent, however, for depicting slapstick elements in his comic operas, as evidenced in the mock Chinese scene in Act 2 of *L'isola disabitata*. Since so few of his *opere serie* survive, it is difficult to identify his achievements in that genre.

See also ISOLA DISABITATA, L' (i).

dm – *dramma per musica*

Merope (dm, 3, A. Zeno), Rome, Capranica, 23 Jan 1740, *I-Nc* (according to Eitner and Florimo), *P-La* (1755, Naples)
Dario (dm, 3, G. Baldanza), Rome, Argentina, carn. 1741
Arminio in Germania (dm, 3, C. Pasquini), Florence, Pergola, 24 June 1741
Siroe (dm, 3, P. Metastasio), Florence, Pergola, June 1742
Pompeo in Armenia (dm, 3, B. Vitturi), Pisa, Pubblico, carn. 1744
Ezio (dm, 3, Metastasio), Lucca, Civico, aut. 1744
Olimpiade (dm, 3, Metastasio), Lucca, Pubblico, aut. 1745
Il giocatore (commedia per musica, 2), Florence, Cocomero, carn. 1747
Artaserse (dm, 3, Metastasio), Lucca, 26 Aug 1747, *A-Wn*, *B-Bc*; in Ger., with dances by J. Starzer, Vienna, Burg, Shrove Tuesday 1763
Partenope (dm, 3, S. Stampiglia), Turin, Regio, carn. 1749, *I-Tf* (1754, Livorno)
Semiramide riconosciuta (dm, 3, Metastasio), Livorno, S Sebastiano, carn. 1751
Adriano in Siria (dm, 3, Metastasio), Venice, S Cassiano, carn. 1752
Demetrio (dm, 3, Metastasio), Padua, Nuovo, 11 June 1752, lib. *US-Wc*
I portentosi effetti della Madre Natura (dramma giocoso per musica, 3, C. Goldoni), Venice, S Samuele, 11 Nov 1752, *A-Wgm*
L'impostore (opera buffa), Barcelona, Santa Cruz, 1752, collab. ? G. Cocchi
Alessandro nell'Indie (dm, 3, Metastasio), Reggio Emilia, Pubblico, 12 May 1753, *Wgm*
De gustibus non est disputandum (dramma giocoso per musica, 3, Goldoni), Venice, S Cassiano, carn. 1754, *B-Bc*
Caio Mario (dm, 3, G. Roccaforte), Naples, S Carlo, 20 Jan 1755, *P-La*
Antigona (dm, 3, Roccaforte), Milan, Ducale, carn. 1756
L'isola disabitata (dramma giocoso per musica, 3, Goldoni), Venice, S Samuele, aut. 1757; Vienna, Burg, 1773, *A-Wgm*, *D-Dlb*; as La cinese smarrita, Genoa, Falcone, sum. 1760
La serva scaltra (dramma giocoso per musica, 3), Venice, S Moisè, aut. 1759; Vienna, Burg, 1759, *A-Wn*
La clemenza di Tito (dm, 3, Metastasio), Venice, S Benedetto, carn. 1760, *D-Bsp, F-Pn, P-La*
L'Issipile (dm, 3, Metastasio), Vienna, Burg, aut. 1760, *D-Bds, I-Tn*
Pelopida (dm, 3, Roccaforte), Turin, Regio, carn. 1763, *I-Tci* (Act 2), *P-La*
Bajazet (dm, 3, A. Piovene), Verona, Accademia Filarmonica, carn. 1765
Gli stravaganti (dramma musicale, 2, 'Alcindo Isaurense'), Vienna, Burg, 11 Feb 1765, *A-Wn*; as La moglie padrona, Vienna, Burg, 1768
Armida (festa teatrale, M. Coltellini), Vienna, Burg, *c*1766
Dove è amore è gelosia (intermezzo giocoso, Coltellini), Vienna, Burg, 1768, *A-Wn*
L'amor geloso, Vienna, Schönbrunn, 5 July 1770
Amiti e Ontario, o I selvaggi (dm, R. de' Calzabigi), Vienna, Burg, 1772

Doubtful: La madamigella (A. Palomba), Naples, Fiorentini, spr. 1755

*

BurneyH; *EitnerQ*; *FlorimoN*
H. Springer: 'Das Partiturautograph von Giuseppe Scarlattis bisher verschollener "Clemenza di Tito"', *Beiträge zum Bibliotheks- und Buchwesen: Paul Schenke ... gewidmet* (Berlin, 1913), 257–60
R. Haas: *Gluck und Durazzo* (Vienna, 1925)
P. Fienga: 'Giuseppe Scarlatti et son incertaine ascendance directe', *ReM*, no.123 (1932), 113–20

MALCOLM BOYD (1–2), GORDANA LAZAREVICH (3)

Scatia, Giuseppe. *See* SCACCIA, GIUSEPPE.

Scattola, Carlo (*b* ?1878; *d* Milan, 1947). Italian bass. He came to be associated almost entirely with comic parts, but sang in a wider repertory in his early years, as in recorded excerpts from *Mefistofele*, *Faust* and *Ernani*. He first appeared at La Scala in 1922, scoring a notable success in Wolf-Ferrari's *I quatro rusteghi* and in the première of Rocca's *Il dibuk*. From 1926 to 1935 he appeared frequently with Conchita Supervia in the Rossini revival of those years. They sang together in Rome and Turin, at the Florence Festival of 1933, at both the Opéra and the Opéra-Comique in Paris (1930) and in the 1936 season at Covent Garden, where Scattola's roles were Taddeo in *L'italiana in Algeri* and Dr Bartolo in *Il barbiere di Siviglia*, the latter with Lily Pons. He toured North America with the Columbia Grand Opera Company in 1930 and remained active in Italy throughout the war years. His partnership with Supervia is preserved on recordings in excerpts from *L'italiana* and his skill in comic vignettes by his doubling of the roles of Benoit and Alcindoro in *La bohème* with Gigli.

J. B. STEANE

Scena (It.: 'scene'). A 19th-century term for a dramatic episode, a complex of recitative (conversational, declamatory and arioso), orchestral figuration and *parlante* preparatory to a formal number, as in 'scena ed aria' or 'scena e duetto', a typical unit in opera of the Rossini period and after. The opening of Act 3 of Verdi's *Ernani* (1844) is described as 'Preludio, Scena e Cavatina'; at the beginning of an act, an orchestral *preludio* sometimes precedes a scena and provides some of its material, as in 'Dormono entrambi' (*Norma*, 1831) or 'Annina? ... Commandate?' (*La traviata*, 1853). An early example of an independent *scena* is the sleepwalking scene in Verdi's *Macbeth* (1847).

See also SCENE.

*

G. Buschmeier: *Die Entwicklung von Arie und Szene in der französischen Oper von Gluck bis Spontini* (Tutzing, 1991)

Scene. The word derives from the Greek *skene*, through the Latin *scaena*, meaning 'tent', 'hut' or 'booth', and hence 'stage' or 'decor'.

(1) The visible part of the stage (Fr. *scène*; Ger. *Szene*; It. *scena*); thus 'sulla scena', on the stage, 'derrière la scène', behind the stage. A band 'dietro la scena' is on the stage but unseen by the audience in a 'shallow' scene (*scena corta*, as opposed to *scena lunga*).

(2) The location of an opera, or an act or part of an act of an opera (Fr. *tableau*; Ger. *Bild*; It. *quadro*). By extension, the term is used for any part of an opera in a single location; thus an act may be described as 'in three scenes'. Until the mid-19th century scenes (in this sense) normally came to a clear conclusion and were followed by a pause to allow for a change of scenery, except where a *cambiamento a vista* is indicated, as in Act 1 of Verdi's *Simon Boccanegra* (1857); this was generally effected by the raising or lowering of a backdrop or by the sliding in or out of flats from the wings, while extras removed unwanted props and brought in any new ones. Later, scenes were often linked by instrumental interludes, a practice initiated by Wagner, as in *Das Rheingold* (1869, composed 1854), *Die Meistersinger* (1868), *Götterdämmerung* (1876) and *Parsifal* (1882). Wagner himself favoured a smokescreen to obscure the scene-changes. For *Pelléas et Mélisande* (1902) Debussy was content with a lowered curtain, as was Strauss in *Die Frau ohne Schatten* (1919) and Britten in *Peter Grimes* (1945) and *The Rape of Lucretia* (1946).

(3) A portion of an act during which the characters on the stage remain unchanged. In this sense, a new scene begins whenever a new character enters or when one who was present departs; it is not uncommon for an early opera to have 20 or 30 scenes in an act. In much 18th-century opera each scene would normally

culminate in an aria or an ensemble, although in *tragédie lyrique* the formal number would generally occur at the beginning of a scene. This usage, which also applies to classical theatre (Shakespeare, Racine etc.), was followed in opera up to the early 1890s; it is present in Leoncavallo's *Pagliacci* (1892) but not in Catalani's *La Wally* (also 1892) or later operas.

(4) The Italian *scena*, less often its counterparts in other languages, is used for the free mixture of recitative, arioso and orchestral music that may precede a formal number: *see* SCENA. JULIAN BUDDEN

Scènes franciscains. Opera by Olivier Messiaen; *see* *SAINT FRANÇOIS D'ASSISE*.

Scenography. The art of scenic design for theatrical and cinematic productions, embracing all visual elements from makeup to set design. *See* STAGE DESIGN.

Schaaf, Johannes (*b* Bad Cannstatt, 7 April 1933). German director. He studied medicine before joining the Stuttgart Staatstheater, where he established his reputation in spoken theatre before moving to opera. He came to prominence with his staging of *Capriccio* at the Salzburg Festival in 1985, where he blended the 18th century with elements of the 1920s. He was invited to produce Mozart operas at Covent Garden, beginning with *Le nozze di Figaro* in 1987, followed by *Così fan tutte* (1988) and *Idomeneo* (1989), and finishing with *Don Giovanni* (1992). These proved, like all his work, perceptive, idiosyncratic and controversial. His *Fidelio* (1989) in Geneva was much admired for its imaginative concept as a study of tyranny in a modern setting.

ALAN BLYTH

Schacht, Theodor, Freiherr von (*b* Strasbourg, 1748; *d* Regensburg, 20 June 1823). German composer. From 1766 to 1771 he was a pupil of Jommelli at Stuttgart. In 1771 he became a *Hofkavalier* to Prince Carl Anselm of Thurn and Taxis, who in 1773 appointed him Intendant of the court's music and commissioned him to set up an Italian Opera, which flourished from 1774 to 1778. After the building of a German theatre in 1778 Schacht dedicated himself more to the service of the court. Between 1784 and 1786 he again established an Italian Opera at the court, and was its leader and Kapellmeister. From 1786 he was the administrator and musical director of the court orchestra. In 1805 he travelled via Salzburg to Vienna, where he won respect as a composer of sacred music. He returned to Germany in 1812, lived in the castle of Scheer (in Württemberg) until 1819 and spent his last years in Regensburg. Schacht's output includes about 200 works, the strongest of which are the theatre pieces in which he cultivated the Italian style of opera.

unless otherwise stated, first performed in Regensburg, Hochfürstliches Thurn und Taxissches Hoftheater; MSS in D-Rtt

Baccocco e Serpilla (int, A. Salvi), spr. 1775
Il marito Giogatore e la moglie Bacchettona, 1775
Der betrogene Tormund, 1780
La rosière de Salency (3, A. F. J. Masson de Poézay), 1780
Das unterbrochene Fest, 1780
Der Ritter in Gefahr (Spl), 1781
Rosamund (Spl, C. M. Wieland), 1782
Amalie von Thurn und Taxis, *c*1784
Calypso abbandonata, 1784
Artaserse (3, P. Metastasio), carn. 1785
Il tutore deluso (int, 2, D. Friggieri), 1786
I rotti delle tre nazioni, 1789, collab. J. Touchemoulin
Gagliarda of a Merry Plague (opera-ballet), New York, spr. 1825 [mentioned in Manferrari]
Semiramide riconosciuta, aria *Rp*

arr. G. Benda: Romeo und Julie, Feb 1779

*

FétisB; *StiegerO*
D. Mettenleiter: *Musikgeschichte der Stadt Regensburg* (Regensburg, 1866)
S. Färber: *Das Regensburger fürstlich Thurn und Taxissche Hoftheater und seine Oper 1760–1786* (Regensburg, 1936)
U. Manferrari: *Dizionario universale delle opere melodrammatiche* (Florence, 1954–5)
S. Färber: 'Der fürstlich Thurn und Taxissche Hofkomponist Theodor von Schacht und seine Opernwerke', *Studien zur Musikgeschichte der Stadt Regensburg*, i (Regensburg, 1979), 11–122

AUGUST SCHARNAGL

Schack [Cziak, Schak, Žák, Ziak], **Benedikt (Emanuel)** (*b* Mirotice, 7 Feb 1758; *d* Munich, 10 Dec 1826). Austrian composer and tenor of Bohemian origin. After early musical training from his father, a schoolteacher, he became a pupil and singer at the Jesuit monastery in Przbram-Birkenberg at the age of 11. He later studied at Staré Sedlo and Svatá Hora and, from 1773, in Prague, where he was also a chorister at St Vitus's Cathedral. In 1775 he moved to Vienna to study medicine and took singing lessons with Karl Frieberth. After several years as Kapellmeister to Prince Heinrich von Schönaich-Carolath in Silesia (from 1780), he joined Emanuel Schikaneder's travelling troupe in 1786 as a tenor and composer. The company made visits to Augsburg and Regensburg and shorter stops in other southern cities, including Salzburg. Leopold Mozart commented in a letter to his daughter (26 May 1786) that Schack 'sings excellently, has a beautiful voice, an effortlessly smooth throat and a beautiful method'. Schikaneder and his troupe settled in Vienna, in the Freihaus-Theater auf der Wieden, in 1789. During his four-year stay in Vienna, Schack composed numerous operas for the Wieden stage and sang principal tenor roles in many of the theatre's productions. He became well acquainted with Mozart, who composed the role of Tamino for him (Schack perhaps played the flute parts himself) and also wrote the duet 'Nun liebes Weibchen' (K625/592*a*) for Schack's opera *Der Stein der Weisen*. In 1793 Schack secured an appointment in Graz. Three years later, in 1796, he moved to Munich to become a member of the ensemble of the Hoftheater. He seems to have composed no operas there. Around 1813 he was pensioned off because of his declining voice.

Schack composed almost all his operas for suburban theatres and travelling troupes. He was best known for the series of 'Anton' Singspiels that he composed with F. X. Gerl to librettos by Schikaneder. Anton, like the character Kasperl at the rival Theater in der Leopoldstadt, was a descendant of Hanswurst and Bernardon from Viennese comedies of the early and mid-18th century. In the 'Anton' Singspiels and others like them – in contrast to the scenically and musically elaborate heroic-comic operas like *Die Zauberflöte* – the serious portions of the plot were played down, the central comic character became the focus of the story, and the music consisted most often of short numbers based on a popular folk style. Schack's *Der dumme Gärtner*, the first and most successful of the 'Anton' works, serves as a representative example. Several of the solos are strophic lieder with square-cut phrasing and simple melodies, while others depend on two- and three-part forms and a few have a two-tempo (slow-fast) format. The ensembles are the most extended numbers of the work; several changes of tempo, conversational interaction between characters and *buffo*-style patter set them apart from the solos and choruses. There is little or no use in the work of recitative, coloratura or complex orchestral writing.

Der dumme Gärtner, along with numerous other Viennese suburban Singspiels, found favour on stages throughout Germany. In some northern cities the texts of many of these works were revised while the music was retained. In the foreword to a revised libretto of *Der dumme Gärtner* (Leipzig, 1797) the editor explains that

> The work's provincial veneer was always such an obstacle, that one could not perform it outside its fatherland; many connoisseurs and friends of comic opera often wished for an arrangement for other stages. Here is an attempt, in which the originality of this piece was retained as much as possible.

This type of treatment contrasted with the frequent practice in southern theatres (both national and suburban) of adopting librettos from the north but having them set to new music. Schack's regular collaboration with Gerl in composing operas was of a sort not unusual for the Theater auf der Wieden in the 1790s. Schikaneder regularly commissioned compositional 'teams' (another prominent duo was Ignaz von Seyfried and Matthäus Stegmayr) to set librettos written by himself or others: the most likely reason for this was the heavy production schedule, which demanded new Singspiels every month. Schack's recognition as an opera composer, resting mostly on the 'Anton' Singspiels and *Der Stein der Weisen*, declined rapidly after the 1790s, with the number of performances of his works steadily decreasing.

See also DUMME GÄRTNER AUS DEM GEBIRGE, DER and STEIN DER WEISEN, DER.

Die Wilden und die Gesitteten, oder Fernando und Yarico (Spl, 3, K. von Ekartshausen, after J. Addison and R. Steele: *Inkle and Yarico*), Vienna, Leopoldstadt, 3 Dec 1784, *D-Mbs*

Don Quixote, Vienna, *c*1785, collab. others

Die drei Ringe, oder Kaspar der lächerliche Mundkoch (Spl, 3, E. Schikaneder), ? Salzburg, 1786; Regensburg, 25 March 1788

Der Luftballon (Operette, 3, Schikaneder), Kempten, Sept 1786 [? same as Die Luftbälle, oder Man ertappt ihm nicht, Vienna, Leopoldstadt, 8 June 1784]

Lorenz und Suschen (Spl, Schikaneder), Regensburg, ?18 April 1788

Der Krautschneider (Spl, 4, Schikaneder), Regensburg, ?3 May 1788 [? same as Kaspar der Krautschneider, Vienna, Leopoldstadt, 21 April 1785]

Der dumme Gärtner aus dem Gebirge, oder Die zween Anton (Spl, 2, Schikaneder), Vienna, Wieden, 12 July 1789, *A-Wn*, vs (Vienna, 1789), collab. F. X. Gerl; also known as Die beyden Anton [1st 'Anton' Spl]

Jakob und Nannerl, oder Der angenehme Traum (3, Schikaneder), Vienna, Wieden, 25 July 1789; also attrib. Gerl, F. X. Pecháček

Die verdeckten Sachen (Spl, 2, Schikaneder), Vienna, Wieden, 26 Sept 1789, *Wgm*, *I-Fc*, collab. Gerl and J. G. Lickl [2nd 'Anton' Spl]

Was macht der Anton im Winter? (Spl, 2, Schikaneder), Vienna, Wieden, 6 Jan 1790, *A-Wgm*, *I-Fc*, collab. Gerl and others [3rd 'Anton' Spl]

Der Fall ist noch weit seltner, oder Die geplagten Ehemänner (Spl, 2, Schikaneder), Vienna, Wieden, 10 May 1790, *D-Mbs*; sequel to Martín y Soler: Lilla, oder Schönheit und Tugend [Una cosa rara]

Der Frühling, oder Der Anton ist noch nicht tot (Spl, 2, Schikaneder), Vienna, Wieden, 18 June 1790, *A-Wgm* collab. Gerl and others [4th 'Anton' Spl]

Der Stein der Weisen, oder Die Zauberinsel (heroisch-komische Oper, 2, Schikaneder), Vienna, Wieden, 11 Sept 1790, *D-B*, *I-Fc*, vs (Frankfurt, 1796), collab. Gerl ?and Mozart

Die Wiener Zeitung (Spl, 3, K. L. Gieseke), Vienna, Wieden, 12 Jan 1791, collab. Gerl

Anton bei Hofe, oder Das Namensfest (Spl, 2, Schikaneder), 4 June 1791, collab. Gerl and others [5th 'Anton' Spl]

Das Schlaraffenland (Spl, 2, Gieseke), Vienna, Wieden, 23 June 1792, collab. Gerl

Der Renegat, oder Anton in der Türkei (Spl, 2, Schikaneder), Vienna, Wieden, 15 Sept 1792, collab. Gerl and others [6th 'Anton' Spl]

Die Antwort auf die Frage: was begehrt alles Frauenzimmer, arm und reich, jung und alt ohne Ausnahme am heftigsten? (komische Oper, 3), Vienna, Landstrasse, ?16 Dec 1792; also known as Frage und Antwort, oder Ein altes Haus kann auch was Gutes stiften

Der eifersüchtige Bauer, oder Der Schulmeister im Ofenloch (2, G. Korndorfer), Vienna, Landstrasse, 28 Jan 1793; also known as Der [*sic*] beiden Lieschen

Der wohltätige Derwisch, oder Die Schellenkappe (Spl, 3, Schikaneder), Vienna, Wieden, 10 or 11 Sept 1793, collab. Gerl, Henneberg ?and others; also known as Die Zaubertrommel, *D-MH*

Die beiden Nannerln, oder Das chinesische Feuerwerk zu Ehren der Nannerln (Spl, 2), 26 July 1794

Der Zauberbrief (romantisch-komische Oper, 3), Vienna, Josefstadt, 1 Jan 1795

Das Häuschen im Walde, oder Antons Reise nach seinem Geburtsort (Spl, 2, Schikaneder), ?6 Jan 1795, collab. others [7th 'Anton' Spl]

*

F. J. Lipowsky: *Baierisches Musik-Lexikon* (Munich, 1811), 297

AMZ, xxix (1827), 519

E. Komorzynski: *Emanuel Schikaneder* (Berlin, 1901, 2/1951)

R. Haas: Preface to Ignaz Umlauf: *Die Bergknappen*, DTÖ, xxxvi, Jg.xviii/1 (1911)

E. K. Blümml and G. Gugitz: *Alt-Wiener Thespiskarren* (Vienna, 1925)

F. Hadamowsky: *Das Theater in der Wiener Leopoldstadt, 1780–1860* (Vienna, 1934)

O. E. Deutsch: *Das Freihaustheater auf der Wieden 1787–1801* (Vienna, 2/1937)

H. Endrös: 'Emanuel Schikaneder und das Augsburger Theater', *Zeitschrift des Historischen Vereins für Schwaben*, lv–lvi (Augsburg, 1942–3), 203–98

E. Komorzynski: *Der Vater der Zauberflöte: Emanuel Schikaneders Leben* (Vienna, 1948)

A. Bauer: *Das Theater in der Josephstadt zu Wien* (Vienna, 1957)

K. M. Pisarowitz: 'Ein Weib ist das herrlichste Ding auf der Welt', *Mitteilungen der Internationalen Stiftung Mozarteum*, vii/1–2 (1958), 5–7

LINDA TYLER

Schafer, R(aymond) Murray (*b* Sarnia, Ont., 18 July 1933). Canadian composer and author. One of Canada's most innovatory and successful composers, he studied composition with John Weinzweig at the Royal Conservatory in Toronto, but his rebellious nature led to quick expulsion in 1954. Thereafter, apart from brief study with Peter Racine Fricker, Schafer was self-taught. Except for ten years' teaching at Simon Fraser University (1965–75) and short residencies elsewhere, Schafer has supported himself by his compositions and writings, which include contributions in many areas. Offended by the routine of much school music, he wrote several influential pamphlets urging the cultivation of creativity in children; these have been collected and widely translated. He has written a book on E. T. A. Hoffmann and edited the musical writings of Ezra Pound, whose opera *The Testament of François Villon* he directed for the BBC (1962). Most notable is Schafer's unprecedented study of the sonic environment, or 'soundscape', most fully articulated in his book *The Tuning of the World*(New York, 1977). These ideas are inseparable from his development as a composer.

Schafer's first works were neo-classical in style, but in the 1960s he rapidly assimilated a range of avant-garde techniques, encompassing serialism, spatial deployment, electronic sound and graphic notations. These were all brought together in his first opera, *Loving* (1966). This is both the summation of his early development and the first step towards his 'theatre of confluence', a contemporary variant of the Wagnerian *Gesamtkunstwerk*, fusing many artistic media. Critical of 19th-century operatic conventions, Schafer has blended several dramaturgical influences (Brecht, Piscator, Meyerhold) with his own special concerns. He has made use of ritualistic theatre, notably in the dramatic choral work *Apocalypsis* (composed 1976–7), and has devised ingenious forms of audience participation. Most daringly, he has explored unorthodox performance sites, beginning with *Music for Wilderness Lake* (1979), written for 12 trombones dispersed around a small lake in the wilderness, in two parts, performed at dawn and dusk. In this and subsequent larger works, the soundscape emerges as the centre of Schafer's musical thought.

After *Loving*, Schafer began a series of multi-media theatre pieces under the collective title *Patria*. Planned as a trilogy, *Patria* has grown to 12 full-length dramatic works, of which seven are now completed. These are intended to be performed separately, but the whole cycle, interconnected by musical and narrative themes, is certainly the most ambitious and imposing theatrical project ever conceived in Canada. Performances in Canada and Europe have received both public and critical acclaim. Schafer's output includes many solo vocal and choral works. A prolific composer, he has also been successful in orchestral and chamber music (including a remarkable series of string quartets), but even his concert music often has a theatrical flavour. His many honours include the Fromm Foundation Award, a Guggenheim Fellowship, the Prix Honegger from France, an honorary LlD from Carleton University and the first Glenn Gould Prize.

See also LOVING and PATRIA.

music-theatre works unless otherwise stated; all texts by the composer

Loving [Toi; Loving/Toi] (op, 1), Montreal, CBC TV French Network, 3 Feb 1966
Patria (cycle):
- Patria 2: Requiems for the Party Girl, Stratford (Ont.) Festival, 23 Aug 1972
- Patria 1: Wolfman (formerly The Characteristics Man), 1974, Toronto, The Shaw Festival, 21 Nov 1987
- Patria Prologue: The Princess of the Stars, Heart Lake, Ont., 26 Sept 1981
- Patria 6: RA, Toronto, Science Center, Comus Music Theatre, 4 May 1983
- Patria 3: The Greatest Show, Peterborough (Ont.) Festival of the Arts, 6 Aug 1987
- Patria 4: The Black Theatre of Hermes Trismegistos, Liège Festival, 9 March 1989
- Patria 5: The Crown of Ariadne, concert perf., Toronto, Jane Mallet, 2 March 1992

Apocalypsis, 1976–7, London, Ont., Centennial Hall, 28 Nov 1980

WRITINGS

'Opera and Reform', OC, v (1964), 10
Patria and The Theatre of Confluence (Indian River, Ont., 1991); repr. in *Descant*, xxii/2 (1991) [whole issue]

*

B. Mather: 'Notes sur "Requiems for the Party Girl"', *Canada Music Book* (1970), 91–7
S. Adams: *R. Murray Schafer* (Toronto, 1983)
K. Garebian: 'The Dusk to Dawn Journey of "Ra"', *Performing Arts* (1986), 12
S. Adams: 'Murray Schafer's *Patria*: The Greatest Show on Earth?', *Journal of Canadian Studies*, xxiii/1–2 (1988), 199–207
P. Dutton: 'The Broken Thread: Ariadne in the Work of R. Murray Schafer', *Descant*, xix (1988), 47
K. MacKenzie: *A Twentieth-Century Musical/Theatrical Cycle: R. Murray Schafer's 'Patria' (1966–)* (diss., U. of Cincinnati, 1991)

STEPHEN J. ADAMS

Schäferspiel. *See* PASTORAL.

Schäffer, Bogusław (*b* Lwów, 6 June 1929). Polish composer. He studied at the Kraków Conservatory, where he was professor of composition (from 1963); he then worked extensively for Polish radio in Warsaw, notably at the Experimental Studio (from 1965). He has consistently pursued an iconoclastic path through Polish culture, not only as an avant-garde composer, but also, since the mid-1970s, as a writer, painter and, most recently, a playwright and theatre director. These activities have often arisen from his reaching a compositional impasse or from his frustration with prevailing musical attitudes. His compositions are highly gestural and conceptual, frequently employing graphic notation and electronic means. They include over 20 pieces of music theatre often described as 'happenings', whose duration might be anything from less than a minute to eight hours. The early *Non-stop* for piano (1960) was followed by two major compositions of 1963, *TIS MW2* and *TIS GK. TIS MW2* (performed 1964, Kraków), is built around excerpts from K. Irzykowski's novel *Pałuba* (1903), and explores the state of humanity through a dream-based sequence of aleatory combinations of sections and performers, who include an actor, mime artist and ballerina in addition to a soprano and four instrumentalists. The score is typical of Schäffer's ingenuity in inventing notational methods to suit experimental compositional needs.

Actors feature largely in his music-theatre works, sometimes alone, as in *Scenario for a Non-Existent but Possible Instrumental Actor* (1963), in groups, as in *PR-I V* (1964), or in combination with instrumental forces, as in his setting of fragments from Alan Ginsberg's *Howl* (1966), *Hommage à Czyżewski* (1972), *Autogenic Composition* for soprano, flute, cello, piano and four actors (1980) and *Teatrino fantastico* for actor, piano, violin, tape and multimedia (1983). Perhaps his most theatrical and amusing work – Schäffer is a noted wit – is the *Quartet* for four actors (1966), in which he explores the world of the members of a string quartet, deprived of their instruments. Schäffer's one radio opera, *Monodrama* (1968), uses texts by George Seferis and Yannis Ritsos in an instrumental and electronic environment not far removed from Varèse's *Poème électronique*, and is strongly characterized by the female protagonist reliving her past passions and disappointments.

*

B. Schäffer: 'Composer's Workshop', *Polish Music* (1969) no.1, 16–23
J. Olkuśnik: 'Polish Radio Operas', *Polish Music* (1971) no.2, 15–21

ADRIAN THOMAS

Schalk, Franz (*b* Vienna, 27 May 1863; *d* Edlach, 2 Sept 1931). Austrian conductor. A pupil of Bruckner at the Vienna Conservatory, he became first conductor at the Vienna Hofoper in 1900, under Mahler's directorship. In 1918 he became director there himself, jointly with Richard Strauss, whose *Die Frau ohne Schatten* he conducted at its first performance in 1919; and on Strauss's resignation in 1924, he was in sole control until 1929. He conducted the first uncut *Ring* in the USA at the Metropolitan Opera during the 1898–9 season, and conducted at Covent Garden in 1898, 1907 and, finally, in 1911, when his performances of the *Ring* cycle were much admired. DERYCK COOKE

Scharley, Denise (*b* ?1918). French contralto. She studied in Paris and made her début in 1942 at the

Opéra-Comique as Geneviève (*Pelléas et Mélisande*), then sang Carmen, Dulcinée (*Don Quichotte*), Mignon, Taven (*Mireille*) and Charlotte. She sang at La Monnaie (1947–8) and made her début at the Opéra in 1951 as Maddalena (*Rigoletto*); her other roles there included Delilah, Amneris, Bellone (*Les Indes galantes*), the Nurse (*Boris Godunov*), Mary (*Der fliegende Holländer*), Puck (*Oberon*), Erda, Fricka, Emilia (*Otello*), Ulrica, Young David/Bathsheba (Honegger's *Le roi David*) and Madame de Croissy in the Paris première of *Dialogues des Carmélites* (1957), a role she also recorded. She appeared at Rome, Barcelona, Geneva, Lyons and Marseilles, where she sang the Countess in *The Queen of Spades* (1961) and Madame Flora in *The Medium* (1962). A powerful actress with a vibrant voice, especially strong in the lower register, she made a convincing Carmen and Delilah and a magnificent Madame de Croissy. ELIZABETH FORBES

Schat, Peter (*b* Utrecht, 5 June 1935). Dutch composer. He studied composition with Van Baaren at the Utrecht Conservatory (1952–8), took lessons with Seiber for a year in London, and was a pupil of Boulez in Basle (1960–62). From 1974 to 1983 he taught composition at the Royal Conservatory of The Hague, and since then he has been a full-time composer.

Schat's musical language has developed through different stages: after using 12-note serialism he combined expanded serial techniques with aleatory form; he later abandoned academic compositional procedures and included elements of pop music. In the early 1980s he created a 'Tone Clock' system, based on the 12 notes of the octave and containing 12 'tonalities' or modes; the resulting music is neither strictly tonal nor atonal.

Schat has written four operas, and also collaborated on the 'morality' *Reconstructie*. *Labyrinth* (1966), 'a kind of opera', as the composer calls it, is a complex production that combines music, acting, dance and film projection. Each musical and theatrical aspect moves independently, resulting in a multi-layered structure: the 'singing layer' contains a mythological story about a woman called Noéma (contralto); the choir, situated among the audience, represents her people; the 'acting story' is about a female called Beauty Kitt; the sense of confusion is enhanced by the autonomous role of the film and the dancers.

The circus opera *Houdini* was inspired by the life of the escape artist, Ehrich Weiss (1874–1926), alias Harry Houdini. The plot derives its dramatic tension from the fact that Houdini (tenor), who strongly rejects spiritualism and occultism – symbolized by the character of Sir Arthur Conan Doyle (bass) – is, at the same time, longing to have contact with his deceased mother. The Holland Festival première of the cartoon opera *Aap verslaat de Knekelgeest* ('Monkey Subdues the White-bone Demon', 1980) took place in a tent in Amsterdam. Schat wrote the text, using an episode from the adventures of the Monkey character in the 16th-century Chinese book *The Pilgrimage to the West*. The powerful and magical Monkey (tenor) assists his teacher, Hsuan-Tsang, a Buddhist monk (countertenor), in his search for the 'Holy Writings'. During their pilgrimage Monkey has to protect Hsuan-Tsang from the White-bone Demon (soprano), who wants to eat the meat of this 'holy man' so that he can become immortal.

The libretto of *Symposion* combines recent research about the death of Tchaikovsky (baritone) with the dialogue about Love from Plato's *Symposium*. Each character is represented by one of the chromatic tonalities from the 'Tone Clock'.

See also RECONSTRUCTIE.

Labyrinth op.15 (3, L. de Boer, after L. P. Boon: *De paradiisvogel*), Amsterdam, Carré, 23 June 1966
Reconstructie (morality, 2 pts, H. Mulisch and H. Claus), Amsterdam, Carré, 29 June 1969, collab. L. Andriessen, R. de Leeuw, M. Mengelberg and J. van Vlijmen
Houdini op.25 (circus op, 3, A. Mitchell), Amsterdam, Carré, 29 Sept 1977
Aap verslaat de Knekelgeest op.28 [Monkey Subdues the White-bone Demon] (cartoon op, 2, P. Schat, after *The Pilgrimage to the West*), Amsterdam, 7 June 1980
Symposion op.33, 1982–9 (3, G. Komrij, after Plato)

*

P. Schat: 'Labyrinth: a Kind of Opera', *Opera* 66, ed. C. Osborne (London, 1966), 250
R. Koopmans: 'On Music and Politics – Activism of Five Dutch Composers', *Key Notes*, no.4 (1976), 19–35
H. Koegler: 'Houdini, a Circus Opera', *Key Notes*, no.6 (1977), 33–40
P. Schat: 'Monkey Subdues the White-bone Demon: the Development of Characters Composed', *Key Notes*, no.12 (1980), 17
'Peter Schat: Aap verslaat de Knekelgeest', *MR*, xlv (1984), 317–18
P. Schat: *De toonklok: essays en gesprekken over muziek* (Amsterdam, 1984)
L. Samama: *Zeventig jaar nederlandse muziek* (Amsterdam, 1986), 281
P. Schat: *De wereld chromatisch: een muzikaal reisverslag* (Amsterdam, 1988)
L. Samama: 'Peter Schat: een profeet in eigen land', *Schat in Groningen*, ed. P. van Reijen (Groningen, 1989), 43–57

MICHAEL VAN EEKEREN

Schatzgräber, Der ('The Treasure-Seeker'). Opera in a prologue, four acts and an epilogue by FRANZ SCHREKER to his own libretto; Frankfurt, 21 January 1920.

Schreker's most popular opera relocated his preoccupations with art and sexuality in the fairy-tale German 'middle ages'. He added the motif of worldly 'treasure', whose hidden presence is mysteriously divined by the lute of Elis, the scholar-minstrel (tenor). The treasure in question is the stolen jewellery of the Queen, who believes her youth and beauty are ensured by it. It is collected from mysterious sources by Els (soprano), the self-willed daughter of a forest innkeeper, through suitors whom she has subsequently murdered. She falls in love with Elis, who is falsely accused of, and almost hanged for, the murder of her most recent suitor, but who is then enlisted by the King's Fool (tenor) in the search for the treasure. In the celebrated love scene in Act 3, opening with her delicate lullaby ('Klein war ich noch'), Els appears to Elis wearing little but the royal jewels, which she subsequently gives to him, permitting no question. But the crime is discovered and Els is saved only by the King's Fool, who claims her as his prize for securing the jewels. In an epilogue (a year later), Elis is summoned to Els's deathbed in the mountain retreat where the Fool has chastely protected her. Elis sings of the fairy-tale palace of dreams where, together, they will find the greatest of treasures. PETER FRANKLIN

Schauspieldirektor, Der ('The Impresario'). Singspiel in one act, K486, by WOLFGANG AMADEUS MOZART to a libretto by GOTTLIEB STEPHANIE the younger; Schönbrunn, Orangery, 7 February 1786.

Der Schauspieldirektor was performed on 7 February 1786 at Schönbrunn Palace as part of an Imperial entertainment for the Governor-General of the Netherlands. It was played (at the opposite end of the room) before Salieri's *Prima la musica*; three public performances followed.

Frank (spoken role, originally Stephanie), the impresario, and Puf (bass, though no singer; Josef Weidmann) are assembling a company of actors and singers, who squabble over pre-eminence and pay. There are five other spoken roles, including a banker. Besides Mozart's music, extracts from three plays were used for the 'auditions'.

The overture is a sonata allegro with full development. Frank auditions actors, then Mme Herz (soprano, Aloysia Lange): the pathetic style ('Da schlägt des Abschieds Stunde'), yields to a brilliant conclusion. There follows Mlle Silberklang (soprano, Catarina Cavalieri) with an elegant rondò ('Bester Jüngling'). Unfortunately they cannot both be prima donna, and they argue in a hilarious trio ('Ich bin die erste Sängerin'), with Vogelsang, the company's tenor (Johann Valentin Adamberger), keeping the peace (Mme Herz displays her f''' and illustrates the words 'adagio' and 'allegro'). Both ladies are promised large salaries and star billing; quarrels are ended for the sake of art. In the finale, Puf joins in.

Stephanie's *Gelegenheitsstück* ('pièce d'occasion': Mozart called it 'comedy with music', the singers being minor characters) makes a crude contrast with the short opera by Salieri. Nevertheless this silly farce provided the opportunity, which Mozart seized, to write serious arias which could adorn a real opera or concert programme, while the overture is of scintillating ingenuity and charm. JULIAN RUSHTON

Schech, Marianne (*b* Geitau, 18 Jan 1914). German soprano. She studied at the Munich Conservatory, made her début in 1937 at Koblenz as Marta (*Tiefland*), and joined the Münster Stadttheater. During the 1940s she sang with the Munich, Düsseldorf and Dresden companies; she rejoined the Staatsoper in Munich after the war. She built an international reputation in the 1950s, with débuts in 1956 at Covent Garden as Venus and at the Metropolitan; in 1959 she sang in the American première of *Die Frau ohne Schatten*, at San Francisco. Other engagements took her to the Vienna Staatsoper and major German centres, and to Brazil, Portugal and Spain. She recorded several Wagner and Strauss roles, including Elsa under Kempe (1952), Senta and Venus under Konwitschny (1960) and Chrysothemis and the Marschallin under Böhm (1960). Her singing was distinguished more for strong character than for technique. NOËL GOODWIN

Schechner-Waagen [née Schechner], **Nanette** [Anna] (*b* Munich, 1806; *d* ?Munich, 29 April 1860). German soprano. Under the patronage of the Queen of Bavaria she was sent to study in Italy from 1822; she reappeared in Munich as a principal, at first in Italian opera (including the role of Countess Almaviva), and then moved to Vienna, where she made her début as Emmeline in Weigl's *Die Schweizerfamilie* on 22 May 1826. Schubert wrote that she 'pleased exceedingly' (letter of May 1826). She turned exclusively to German opera in 1827 on accepting an engagement at Berlin. From 1829 to 1835 she sang at the Theater an der Wien; her career was interrupted by a chest disease (of nervous origin, according to Fétis) which led to a serious decline, commented on by Mendelssohn in a letter of 6 June 1830, and forced her to retire. Schechner was described as possessing in her prime an exceptionally rich and full-toned voice, and a natural, unpretentious dramatic talent. Her most successful roles were Leonore, Donna Anna, Euryanthe, Reiza, the *Tauris* Iphigenia and Spontini's Giulia.

*

FétisB

L. Eisenberg: *Grosses biographisches Lexicon der deutschen Bühne im XIX. Jahrhundert* (Leipzig, 1903) JOHN WARRACK

Scheff, Fritzi (*b* Vienna, 30 Aug 1879; *d* New York, 8 April 1954). Austrian soprano. She studied with her mother, the soprano Anna Jäger, and then in Munich and Frankfurt, where she made her début in 1896 as Gounod's Juliet. After singing Martha at Nuremberg she was engaged at the Hofoper in Munich, making her début in 1897 as Marie (*La fille du régiment*). In 1900 she first appeared at Covent Garden as Nedda and at the Metropolitan as Marzelline. Her repertory included Cherubino, Zerlina, Marguerite, Elsa and Asa, which she sang in the American première of Paderewski's *Manru* (1902, New York). She created the title roles of two Victor Herbert operettas, *Babette* (1903) and *Mlle Modiste* (1905). Having scored an enormous success in these works, both written specially for her, she abandoned the opera house for Broadway.

*

'Tales of an Enfant Terrible: Chapters from the Unpublished Memoirs of Fritzi Scheff', *ON* viii/12 (1943–4), 4–9; viii/13 (1943–4), 8–14 HAROLD ROSENTHAL/R

Scheidemantel, Karl (*b* Weimar, 21 Jan 1859; *d* Weimar, 26 June 1923). German baritone. He studied with Julius Stockhausen, making his début in 1878 as Wolfram at Weimar, where he was engaged until 1886. He then sang at Dresden until 1911. After a guest appearance in Munich (1882) as Wolfram, he made his London début at Covent Garden in the same role (1884), and also sang Pizarro, Telramund, Kurwenal, and Rucello in Stanford's *Savonarola*; he returned in 1899 to sing Hans Sachs. He appeared at every Bayreuth Festival from 1886 to 1892, alternating as Klingsor and Amfortas in *Parsifal*, and singing Kurwenal, Hans Sachs and Wolfram, a part he also sang in Vienna (1890) and at La Scala (1892). A stylish singer with a fine, well-placed voice, he was as successful in Italian as in German roles; at Dresden, he sang Alfio in *Cavalleria rusticana* (1891), David in *L'amico Fritz* (1892) and Scarpia in *Tosca* (1902), all first local performances. He created Kunrad in *Feuersnot* (1901) and Faninal in *Der Rosenkavalier* (1911).

For illustration *see* DRESDEN, fig.8.

*

H. Rosenthal: *Two Centuries of Opera at Covent Garden* (London, 1958)

K. Neupert, ed.: *Die Besetzung der Bayreuther Festspiele* (Bayreuth, 1961)

N. Del Mar: *Richard Strauss* (London, 1962–72)

G. Skelton: *Wagner at Bayreuth* (London, 1965, enlarged 2/1976)

ELIZABETH FORBES

Scheidl, Theodor (*b* Vienna, 3 Aug 1880; *d* Tübingen, 22 May 1959). German baritone. As a young man he was an Olympic swimmer and began his operatic studies at the age of 26. He made his début as the Herald in *Lohengrin* at the Vienna Volksoper in 1910 and then sang successively at Olmütz (Olomouc), Augsburg and Stuttgart, where he remained from 1913 to 1921. From then until 1932 he was at the Berlin Staatsoper, singing a wide repertory but most closely associated with the Wagnerian roles. At Bayreuth he was heard first in 1914 as Klingsor and Donner; from 1924 to 1930 his roles were Amfortas and Kurwenal. He also made guest appearances throughout Europe and sang for a year at the Deutsches Theater in Prague (1932). He sang Scarpia at Stuttgart in 1955 to celebrate his 75th birthday. Recordings made around 1930 show an authoritative style and a powerful, resonant voice with a particularly strong upper register. J. B. STEANE

Scheidt, Robert vom (*b* Bremen, 16 April 1879; *d* Frankfurt, 10 April 1964). German baritone. He studied in Cologne and made his début there in 1897. In 1903 he was engaged at Hamburg. The next year he sang Biterolf (*Tannhäuser*), Donner and Klingsor at Bayreuth. In 1912 he moved to Frankfurt, where he remained until his retirement in 1940. He created Tamare in Schreker's *Die Gezeichneten* (1918) and Vogt in Schreker's *Der Schatzgräber* (1920), and took part in the first performance of Egk's *Die Zaubergeige* (1935). His large repertory included Wotan, Hans Sachs, Telramund, Kurwenal and the Dutchman, as well as Verdi's Falstaff, Borromeo (*Palestrina*) and Boris, which he sang in the first Frankfurt performance of Musorgsky's opera (1921). ELIZABETH FORBES

Schelb, Josef (*b* Bad Krozingen, nr Freiburg, 14 March 1894; *d* Freiburg, 8 Feb 1977). German composer. After studying with Hans Huber and others, he made concert tours as accompanist to the violinist Juan Manén. From 1924 he taught at the Karlsruhe Conservatory (later Musikhochschule), eventually becoming professor (1932–59). His music was strongly influenced by Reger and by French impressionism, although he also used 12-note techniques. The opera *Charlotte Corday*, composed between 1940 and 1943 to a libretto by F. Baser, is set in the French Revolution, with a prologue in the temple, three acts in Normandy and Paris and an epilogue; it could not be performed during the Nazi era, but a copy of the score survived. His other opera *Die Falken*, 1967 (A. Bergengruen), was also never performed. FRIEDRICH BASER

Schenck [Schenk], **Johannes** [Johann, Joan, Jan] (*b* Amsterdam, bap. 3 June 1660; *d* after 1716). Netherlands composer. He was first active as a viola da gamba player and composer in Amsterdam before he entered the service of Johann Wilhelm, Elector Palatine in Düsseldorf, in about 1696. It is not known what became of him after the Düsseldorf musical establishment was disbanded with the elector's death in 1716. In his Amsterdam period, Schenck composed music for one of the earliest *zangspelen* (light theatre plays on Dutch texts with a mixture of sung and spoken words), namely *Opera op de zinspreuk 'Zonder spys en wyn, kan geen liefde zyn'* (pubd 1686) by Goverd Bidloo, which was staged at the Amsterdam Stadsschouwburg. The airs from this *zangspel* were published separately as *Eenige gezangen uit de opera van Bacchus, Ceres en Venus* (Amsterdam, 1687).

*

K. H. Pauls: 'Der kurpfälzische Kammermusikus Johannes Schenck', *Mf*, xv (1962), 157–71; xix (1966), 288–9 RUDOLF A. RASCH

Schenk, Johann Baptist (*b* Wiener Neustadt, 30 Nov 1753; *d* Vienna, 29 Dec 1836). Austrian composer. (According to his autobiographical sketch he was born on 30 November 1761.) He studied with Anton Stoll, choirmaster at Baden and later a friend of Mozart's, and while still a boy composed songs and other pieces, becoming a proficient violinist and keyboard and wind player. In 1773 he went to Vienna, where he was Wagenseil's pupil for counterpoint and composition. In 1780 he began to compose for the theatre. Although his incidental music to Blumauer's tragedy *Erwine von Steinheim* (1780) was successful, he did not press for performance of five early Singspiels; even the pronounced success of the two works he wrote anonymously for Marinelli's Theater in der Leopoldstadt (*Die Weinlese*, 1785; *Die Weihnacht auf dem Lande*, 1786) did not diminish his diffidence. These two Singspiels, with their important roles for the comic character Kasperl (played by La Roche), were followed by works written for the Kärntnertortheater and Schikaneder's Theater auf der Wieden. In the late 1780s Schenk also met with success as an instrumental composer; he remarked in his autobiography on Haydn's complimentary and encouraging comments about his symphonies.

It was the mid-1790s before Schenk established himself at the court theatres. His Singspiel *Achmet und Almanzine* had five performances in 1795, and brought him in an honorarium of 225 gulden. Some commentaries confuse it with *Achmet und Zenide*, a play by Iffland performed four times in 1796–7. A more widespread and serious confusion surrounds an operetta *Der Bettelstudent, oder Das Donnerwetter*, held to have been performed at the Kärntnertortheater on 9 February 1796 with music by Schenk and text by Paul Weidmann. But there is good reason to think that this represents a confusion with Weidmann's comedy of this name; as there is no record of Schenk's receiving payment for a *Bettelstudent*, and no trace of a score, it must be considered highly doubtful if Schenk did write this work.

With *Der Dorfbarbier* (autumn 1796), Schenk's masterpiece, the ground is firmer. In 1799 a new Schenk Singspiel, *Die Jagd*, was given with limited success. His last, *Der Fassbinder* (1802), is sometimes attributed to Ignaz Umlauf (who had died six and a half years earlier), or held to be a ballet, or assumed to be identical with the original Audinot–Gossec *Le tonnelier*, which as *Der Fassbinder* had often been heard in Vienna since 1776. But there is no doubt that the score for the 1802 production is a new and original work by Schenk, and that the (anonymous) libretto is different from the earlier text. Schenk's *Der Fassbinder* had 43 performances in the court theatres until 1810, and was also staged at Eisenstadt in 1805 and in the Theater in der Leopoldstadt in 1812. It is a charming piece, not markedly below *Der Dorfbarbier* in musical (or dramatic) quality. Schenk stated in his autobiographical sketch that he also began to write a grand opera at the turn of the century, but was obliged to abandon it owing to lack of progress and ill-health.

For the rest of his long life Schenk lived in the shadow of *Der Dorfbarbier*, an undisputed if minor masterpiece, and after 1802 he wrote no further works for the stage (though at the time of his death he was revising *Die Jagd* with the help of his friend, the dramatist and poet Eduard von Bauernfeld). His later years were spent mainly in teaching. He referred in his interesting but factually unreliable autobiographical sketch to his preference for 'a peaceful and withdrawn private life'. He is frequently mentioned in Beethoven literature as having aided Beethoven in 1793 with counterpoint and composition exercises. He was a friend of Mozart's and Schubert's; his pupils included the daughter of Joseph Weigl; to Weigl himself Schenk bequeathed his music (now in *A-Wgm*).

See also DORFBARBIER, DER.

all Singspiels and first performed in Vienna unless otherwise stated

WK – *Kärntnertortheater* WL – *Theater in der Leopoldstadt*
WWD – *Freihaus-Theater auf der Wieden*

Der Schatzgräber (op), 1780, unperf., *A-Wgm**
Die Weinlese (3, Wiest), WL, 12 Oct 1785, frags. *Wgm*
Die Weihnacht auf dem Lande (3, Wiest), WL, 14 Dec 1786, *Wgm**
Im Finstern ist nicht gut tappen (2, L. Hiesberger), WK, 12 Oct 1787, *Wgm**, *Wn*
Das unvermutete [unterbrochene] Seefest (3), WWD, 9 Dec 1789, *Wgm**
Das Singspiel ohne Titel (Operette, 3, Hiesberger), WWD, ?4 Nov 1790, *Wgm**, *Wn**
Der Erntekranz [Ärndtekranz], oder Das Schnitterfest (2, ? K. Mayer, after C. F. Weisse), WWD, ?9 July 1791, frags. *Wgm*
Achmet und Almanzine (2, after Lesage and D'Orneval), WK, 17 July 1795, *Wgm**, *Wn*
Der Dorfbarbier (1, P. and J. Weidmann), WK, 30 Oct 1796, or Burg, 6 or 7 Nov 1796, *Wgm**, many MS copies, ed. R. Haas, DTÖ, lxvi, Jg. xxxiv (1927)
Pantomime and Singspiel for Empress Maria Theresia's name-day, Laxenburg, 15 Oct 1798, *Wgm**
Die Jagd (2, after Weisse), WK, 7 May 1799, *Wgm**; inc. rev., 1836
Der Fassbinder (1, after Audinot), WK, 18 or 17 Dec 1802, *Wgm**, *Wn*

Lost: 4 Singspiels, 1780–85, unperf.; 2 Singspiels, perf. privately at Prince Karl von Auersperg's estate, sum. and aut. 1794

Arias in *Gk*, *Wgm*, *Wn*

Doubtful: Der Bettelstudent, oder Das Donnerwetter (Operette, 2, P. Weidmann), WK, ? 9 Feb 1796

*

Obituary, *AMZ*, xxxix (1837), 165
E. Bauernfeld: 'Johann Schenk, eine biographische Skizze', *Wiener Zeitschrift für Kunst, Literatur, Theater und Mode* (Vienna, 1837), nos.5–7
C. von Wurzbach: *Biographisches Lexicon des Kaiserthums Oesterreich*, xxix (Vienna, 1875), 198ff
E. Hanslick: 'Der Dorfbarbier von Schenk', *Aus dem Tagebuch eines Musikers* (Berlin, 1892), 122ff
F. Staub: *J. B. Schenk, eine Skizze seines Lebens* (Wiener Neustadt, 1900)
E. Mandyczewski: *Zusatzband zur Geschichte der kais. kgl. Gesellschaft der Musikfreunde in Wien* (Vienna, 1912), 114–15 [incl. list of Schenk autographs]
E. Rosenfeld[-Roemer]: *Johann Baptist Schenk als Opernkomponist* (diss., U. of Vienna, 1921)
F. Hadamowsky: *Das Theater in der Wiener Leopoldstadt* (Vienna, 1934)
F. K. Rieger: *Johann Schenk, ein Altmeister des deutschen Singspiels* (St Pölten, 1944)
A. Bauer: *Opern und Operetten in Wien* (Graz and Cologne, 1955)
K. Adel: 'Paul Weidmann', *Jb der Gesellschaft für Wiener Theaterforschung*, xv–xvi (1966), 127–78
F. Hadamowsky: *Die Wiener Hoftheater (Staatstheater), 1776–1966*, i: *1776–1810* (Vienna, 1966)

PETER BRANSCOMBE

Schenk, Manfred (*b* Stuttgart, 23 Jan 1930). German bass. He studied in Stuttgart and sang in the radio chorus there for three years. In 1967 he was engaged at Frankfurt, where he remained for over 20 years. He sang Sarastro at Glyndebourne (1973), Hunding at the Metropolitan (1977), Daland at Orange (1980) and King Henry at Covent Garden (1981). At Bayreuth (1981–91) he sang Pogner, King Henry, Fasolt and Gurnemanz; he has also appeared in Vienna, Munich, Rome, Bologna and Salzburg. His repertory ranges from Neptune (*Il ritorno d'Ulisse*), the Commendatore and Rocco to Hans Sachs, Wotan, King Mark, Padre Guardiano, Kecal and Pimen. He has a fine, sonorous voice and an imposing presence. ELIZABETH FORBES

Schenk, Otto (*b* Vienna, 12 June 1930). Austrian actor and director. He studied acting at the Max Reinhardt Seminar and theatre at Vienna University and began his theatrical career as an actor. In 1957 he began a successful career as an opera director with *Die Zauberflöte* at the Salzburg Landestheater. He directed the same work at the Salzburg Festival in 1963, by which time he had already directed successful productions of von Einem's *Dantons Tod* and Berg's *Lulu* at the Vienna Festival. In 1965 he was appointed resident director at the Vienna Staatsoper, where most of his acclaimed productions have been staged: *Der Rosenkavalier* (with Leonard Bernstein) in 1969, *Der Freischütz* (with Karl Böhm) in 1972 and *L'elisir d'amore* (at the Theater an der Wien) in 1973. During the 1970s he became one of the most sought-after opera directors on the international circuit, making his début at the Metropolitan Opera with *Tosca* (1968; *Fidelio* followed in 1970), at La Scala with *Le nozze di Figaro* (1974) and at Covent Garden with *Un ballo in maschera* (1975).

These productions – often in collaboration with the designer Jürgen Rose – were notable for their attention to stylish period detail. In the 1980s and 90s he has remained an arch-traditionalist, turning his back on the fashionable modernism of his German contemporaries. His romantic production of *Der Ring des Nibelungen* at the Metropolitan Opera (1986–9) can be seen as a reaction against the political interpretations of Götz Friedrich, Patrice Chéreau and Harry Kupfer. Schenk is at his most assured in comedy, and his productions of Viennese operetta, above all of *Die Fledermaus*, which he has directed all over the world, have a charm and taste which few can rival. His interpretation of the spoken role of the gaoler Frosch in *Die Fledermaus* is justly famous. HUGH CANNING

Scherchen, Hermann (*b* Berlin, 21 June 1891; *d* Florence, 12 June 1966). German conductor. Mainly self-taught as a musician, in 1912 he worked with Schoenberg in preparing *Pierrot lunaire* for performance, and made his début as a conductor during the German tour that followed the work's Berlin première, showing the support for new musical trends that characterized most of his later work. After World War I he returned to Berlin (1918) where he founded the Neue Musikgesellschaft and, in 1919, the militant musical journal *Melos*. He also conducted frequently at the ISCM festivals from 1923. In 1924 he conducted the première of the Three Fragments from *Wozzeck* at Frankfurt (the year before the opera was first staged under Kleiber), and Hába's *Matka* at Munich in 1931.

After settling in Switzerland in 1933 he brought fresh vigour to the propagation of new music through his founding of the Ars Viva edition in Zürich in 1950 and by conducting the premières of works such as Dallapiccola's *Il prigioniero* (1950, Florence), Dessau's *Das Verhör des Lukullus* (1951, Berlin) and the original version of Henze's *König Hirsch* (1956, Berlin). His Darmstadt performance in 1951 of the 'Dance round the Golden Calf' from *Moses und Aron* was the first music to be heard from Schoenberg's opera. He edited the score for the opera's Hamburg radio première under Rosbaud in 1954 and conducted the 1959 production at the Berlin Städtische Oper that was regarded as decisive for the work's wider success.

One of the 20th century's outstanding musical pioneers, Scherchen dedicated his career to the better understanding of contemporary music. His conducting, which usually disdained the use of a baton, was functional, clear and scholarly, but it combined knowledge of detail with vitality of spirit. He continued to work until four days before his death, when he had a heart attack during a performance of Malipiero's *L'Orfeide* at Florence. GERHARD BRUNNER

Scheveningen. *See* HAGUE, THE.

Schiassi, Gaetano Maria (*b* Bologna, 10 March 1698; *d* Lisbon, 1754). Italian composer. He was a member of the Accademia Filarmonica in Bologna as a *suonatore*, and a violinist among the virtuosos at the ducal court of Alderano Cybo Malaspina. From about 1727 he was employed by the Landgrave of Darmstadt. During this period several of his operas and oratorios were performed on Italian stages; Barilli noted that his setting of *Didone abbandonata* was extremely successful ('incontrò a meraviglia'). Of special interest is his comedy *La Zanina finta contessa*, partly written in Bolognese dialect in the manner of G. M. Buini.

From at least the end of 1734 he lived in Lisbon, where he served in the royal chapel and was active as a composer, teacher and singer. His letters to Padre Martini from 3 January 1735 to 30 September 1753 (now in *I-Bc*) provide insights into performing practice and taste in 18th-century Lisbon, where the king refused to allow women to take roles in operas and prohibited all kinds of entertainment during his illness except oratorios and church festivals.

Schiassi's vocal music is often in a pastoral style similar to that of G. A. Perti and other Bolognese composers of the first half of the 18th century. His output also includes several collections of instrumental music.

La Rosinda, Cento, Vicini, Sept 1726
La Zanina finta contessa, Modena, Molza, carn. 1728
L'amor fra' nemici (P. A. Bernardoni), Bologna, Marsigli-Rossi, carn. 1732
La fede ne'tradimenti (G. Gigli), Bologna, Marsigli-Rossi, carn. 1732
Stratonica (A. Salvi), Ravenna, Teatro di Ravenna, spr. 1732
Il Demetrio (P. Metastasio), Milan, Ducale, 28 Aug 1732, aria *I-Rsc*
Alessandro nelle Indie (Metastasio), Bologna, Formagliari, carn. 1734, 1 aria *D-Dlb*
Il Demofoonte (Metastasio), Venice, Grimani, carn. 1735, *B-Bc*
Didone abbandonata (Metastasio), Bologna, Formagliari, spr. 1735
Le vicende amorose, o L'enigma disciolto (Metastasio), Bologna, Angelelli, 4 Feb 1736
Anagilda (dramma), Lisbon, Academia da Trindade, 1737
Artaserse (Metastasio), Lisbon, 1737

Arias in *D-Dlb*

*

A. Barilli: *Zibaldone* (MS, *I-Bu*)
C. Ricci: *I teatri di Bologna nei secoli XVII e XVIII* (Bologna, 1888)
R. Haas: *Die estensischen Musikalien: thematisches Verzeichnis mit Einleitung*, i (Regensburg, 1925) ANNE SCHNOEBELEN

Schiava liberata, La ('The Slave Freed'). *Opera seria-comica* in three acts by NICCOLÒ JOMMELLI to a libretto by GAETANO MARTINELLI; Ludwigsburg, Schlosstheater, 18 December 1768.

Selim (soprano castrato), son of Solimano (tenor), returns home triumphantly with three European captives: the noblewoman Dorimene (soprano) and her betrothed servants, Giulietta (soprano) and Pallottino (tenor). Selim falls in love with his beautiful captive, spurning Elmira (soprano), daughter of Albumazar (bass). After Solimano orders him to remain faithful to Elmira, Selim engages Pallottino to disguise himself as a rug merchant and purchase Dorimene for him. But Pallottino is distracted when he realizes that Albumazar has designs on Giulietta. During the Act 1 finale, the two men are discovered in the harem dressed in female attire.

At the beginning of Act 2, Don Garzia (alto castrato) attempts unsuccessfully to ransom Dorimene. Dorimene intercepts the dagger Elmira has intended for the sleeping Selim, and he wakes to find her clutching it. Despite her apparent treachery, he again engages Pallottino to secure Dorimene, this time by posing as a French consul. Albumazar learns of the plot, and in the finale of Act 2 he appears in a similar disguise, spouting fractured French. The impostors are soon exposed. Elmira recognizes the advantages of removing her rival from the scene and persuades Solimano to free the captives. In the finale of Act 3, the Europeans take their leave, and Selim reluctantly returns to Elmira.

La schiava liberata represents a blending of comic and serious elements only possible outside Italy. Martinelli built this harem-rescue story around the conflict between love and filial duty, a typical theme of *opera seria*. He also borrowed ideas from the stage settings of *opera seria*. In the first act finale, as in some finales in *opera seria*, the number of singers on stage diminishes until only the humiliated Albumazar remains – a striking departure from the usual additive finales of comic operas. On the other hand, Martinelli relies on stock characterizations of *opera buffa*. The comic characters amuse themselves with bluff and bluster: flirtatious repartee, extravagant boasting, ineffectual disguises, broken French and 'catalogue' arias. The *buffo* bass, Albumazar, is difficult to categorize; although he has a comic role, he is also a member of the nobility and must command a certain amount of respect.

Jommelli's music matches the contrasts of the libretto. The part of Selim was sung by the primo uomo, Giuseppe Aprile, whose music attests to his vocal prowess. Jommelli wrote arias of stunning virtuosity ('Se il mio valor'), ravishing beauty ('Dolce sonno, amor pietoso') and stark contrasts ('So che pietosa sei'). His arias take the form of the shortened rondò, often found in comic opera after the mid-18th century. Selim becomes involved in the comic intrigue and joins the other noble characters in establishing a serious tone in the finales. Jommelli proves to be equally adept at composing charming, lighthearted arias for Giulietta, and *buffo* patter and parody arias for Pallottino and Albumazar. He comes closest to Mozart in his finales, where he foregoes the usual succession of closed forms in favour of more fluid and dramatic structures in which closure is continually avoided. Sections are delineated by textural climax and abrupt changes of tempo, tonality and mode. As in Mozart's operas, Jommelli's opera shows evidence of careful tonal planning, both within the finales and spanning the opera as a whole.

Indirectly, Martinelli's libretto served as a model for Mozart's *Die Entführung aus dem Serail*. Joseph Schuster composed music to Martinelli's libretto for Dresden (1777). Bretzner's reworking, entitled *Belmont und Constanze*, was performed in Leipzig in 1781 with music by André. This work in turn was the model for Stephanie's libretto for Mozart's *Die Entführung*. Mozart's Selim is a composite of Jommelli's Solimano and Selim. Jommelli's Giulietta and Pallottino became

Mozart's Blonde and Pedrillo, Dorimene and Don Garzia became Belmonte and Konstanza, and Albumazar became Osmin. MARITA P. McCLYMONDS

Schiavo, Lo [*O escravo*] ('The Slave'). *Opera seria* in four acts by CARLOS GOMES to a libretto by Rodolfo Paravicini after a drama by the Viscount of Taunay; Rio de Janeiro, Teatro Lírico, 27 Sept 1889.

The story is set in Brazil in the 16th century, and deals with the impossible love between Américo (tenor), son of Count Rodrigo (baritone), and Ilara (soprano), their Indian maid. To prevent their marriage, Rodrigo sends his son to join the Portuguese armada against a revolt of the Tamoio Indians. Before his departure, Américo releases the slave Iberê (baritone) who had been shackled for an insignificant reason. Soon after Américo's departure, Iberê and Ilara are seized and forced to be married. Although Iberê hopes that Ilara will accommodate herself to their life together, she cannot forget Américo and declares that she would prefer death.

An alliance of Indian tribes led by Iberê plans to fight the Portuguese and to attack Rodrigo's property. Iberê is tormented by the thought that Américo will come to take Ilara from him. After a long scene involving the three, Américo understands Iberê's noble gesture of having respected Ilara, out of gratitude to Américo. Iberê hands Ilara over to Américo, and the couple run away. As the Indians enter demanding Américo as their prisoner, Iberê stabs himself and dies.

Gomes received the suggestion for the subject of this opera from his friend the Viscount of Taunay during a sojourn in Brazil in 1880. At that time the movement towards the abolition of slavery was gathering force in Brazil, and the main characters of Taunay's drama were to be black slaves. But the librettist decided on fundamental changes in order to submit to the standard 'scenic necessities' of Italian opera. Black slaves were replaced by Indians, and the action was transposed from the 18th century to the 16th.

Lo schiavo is considered in Brazil to be the best of Gomes's operas, as it reflects a national subject which required and was given a new treatment. Although he did not draw on indigenous materials, he used certain rhythmic traits associated with dance music of the late 19th century. For example, the well-known 'Dance of the Tamoios' is based on a melodic motif (ex. 1*a*) whose

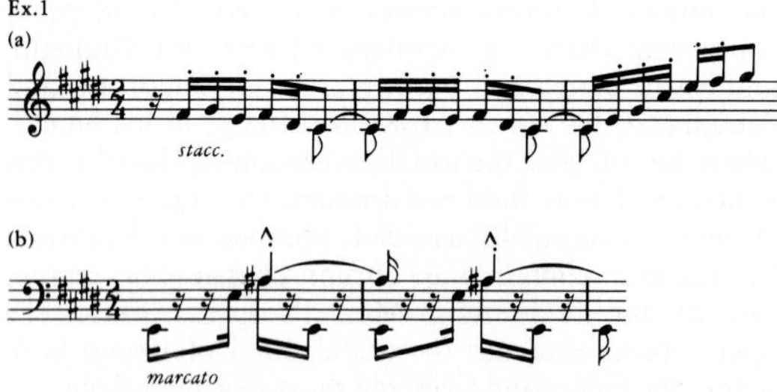

rhythmic figuration has a clear popular flavour and whose accompaniment recalls the habanera syncopation (ex. 1*b*). The melodic line in several arias is reminiscent of the expressive Luso-Brazilian *modinha* (sentimental song type), and adds to the intense lyricism of the work. Marcello Conati found the melodic invention of *Lo schiavo* sober and elegant, with a 'refined and penetrating expression'. The first part of the fourth act includes an intermezzo known as *Alvorada* ('Dawn'), intended to describe daybreak in a Brazilian forest. This passage is considered Gomes's best realization in orchestral writing and may have been a model for Mascagni's 'Inno al sole' in *Iris*. GERARD BÉHAGUE

Schiavo di sua moglie, Lo ('The Slave of his Wife'). *Melodramma* in three acts by FRANCESCO PROVENZALE to a libretto by Francesco Antonio Paolella; Naples, Palazzo Reale, 1672.

Of Provenzale's six operas only this and *La Stellidaura vendicata* (1674) survive in a form that more or less corresponds with their first stage productions. The plot, in an elaborate and faintly mocking manner characteristic of many late 17th-century Italian librettos, dramatizes the power of love to enslave men of valour and apparent good sense. Three Greek warriors, Teseo (tenor), Ercole (bass) and Timante (tenor), collectively engaged in a war against the Amazons, fall under the spell of the Amazon queen, Ippolita, and her sister Melanippa (both sopranos). By the start of Act 2 Timante and Ercole both love Melanippe, Melanippe is enamoured of Teseo, and Teseo of Ippolita. Further thoughts of war evaporate as each tries to pursue his or her own aims amid a welter of mutual recriminations and misunderstandings. The position is complicated by the fact that Timante is really Leucippe, husband of Melanippe, in disguise (she believes Leucippe to be dead, and is much struck by Timante's resemblance to him). At the beginning of Act 3, redisguised as a Turkish slave, he manages to get himself engaged by Melanippe as her servant (hence the opera's title) to observe her actions more closely. In an emotive scene he appears to her in his true guise just at the moment she awakens from a deep sleep. Not knowing whether, at the sight of Leucippe, she is awake or dreaming, she flees. In despair he attempts suicide but is prevented by his friend Areste (alto). At the end of the opera Ercole renounces his claim on Melanippe, and husband and wife are reunited. Ippolita becomes engaged to Teseo.

The generally farcical nature of the opera is underlined by the appearance of three comic characters, an old nurse called Melinta (alto), Lucillo (soprano), a page, and Sciarra (tenor), a 'foolish gardener' who uses Neapolitan dialect. Besides acting as companions or messengers for their employers, they have scenes of their own in which they pursue their own amorous game and make caustic comments.

The music contains a mixture, characteristic for that period, of recitatives, ariosos, and short arias and ensembles in various set forms. The arias in quadruple and triple time are about equal in number, many of those in triple time being in a simple, dance-like style which imparts a youthful quality to the characters singing them (the male ones especially). MICHAEL F. ROBINSON

Schibler, Armin (*b* Kreuzlingen, Lake Constance, 20 Nov 1920; *d* Zürich, 7 Sept 1986). Swiss composer. He studied in Zürich with Burkhard and others and in England with Tippett in 1946. His work was also influenced by the Darmstadt summer courses (1949–53) given by Fortner, Leibowitz, Krenek and Adorno. As a young man he was one of Switzerland's best-known composers, writing in a style ranging from neo-baroque to late romantic and impressionist, reminiscent of Burkhard. For a number of years from about 1950 he used 12-note techniques; the opera *Die späte Sühne* (1954) is the main work from this rather expressionistic period. His subsequent works were influenced by dance and jazz rhythms. Made aware by Theodor Adorno of the sociological implications of music, he adopted melodramatic techniques to draw reciprocal relationships between words and music. His disenchantment with traditional music theatre led him, in the 1970s, to write multi-media works which he called 'Hörwerke'. These combine text and music without recourse to the stage; however, some are suitable for the theatre, for example *Enkidus Tod* (1974), based on the Gilgamesh legend. His final stage works, including two parts of a Thornton Wilder trilogy, remain unperformed.

Der spanische Rosenstock op.20, 1947–50 (lyrische Oper, 3, M. Allenspach, after W. Bergengruen), Berne, 1950
Der Teufel im Winterpalais op.27, 1950–52 (Spieloper, 3, G. Specht and J. Kapp, after Bergengruen), unperf.
Die späte Sühne [Die Füsse im Feuer] op.42 (Kammeroper, 1, Schibler, after C. F. Meyer), Zürich, 1954
Urs und Flurina op.58, 1955–6 (Jugendoper, 3, Schibler, after S. Könz and A. Carigiet), unperf.
Orpheus – Die Unwiederbringlichkeit des Verlorenen (Hörwerk, A. Goldmann), Lausanne, 1970
The Point of Return (Hörwerk, Schibler), Basle, 1972
Enkidus Tod (episch-dramatisches Vokalwerk, A. Goldmann), Basle, 1974
La folie de Tristan (musikalisches Mysterium, M. de France, J. Bédier and Schibler), Montreux, 1980
Antoine und die Trompete (Kammermusical, Schibler), Zürich, 1983
Amadeus und der graue Bote (Kammeroper, 1, T. Wilder), Berne, 1986 [pt 1 of trilogy]
Königinnen von Frankreich, 1986 (musikalisches Kammer-Lustspiel, 1, Wilder), unperf. [pt 2 of trilogy]
Schlafwagen Pegasus, 1986 (Kammeroper, 1, Wilder), unperf. [pt 3 of trilogy]
Sansibar oder die Rettung, 1984–6 (musikdramatische Szenenfolge, 2, Schibler, after A. Andersch), unperf.

*

A. Schibler: 'Selbstporträt', *Musik der Zeit* (1953), no.10
K. H. Wörner: *Armin Schibler* (Amriswil, 1953)
P. Mieg: 'Armin Schibler', *40 Schweizer Komponisten der Gegenwart* (Amriswil, 1956)
A. Schibler: *Zur Oper der Gegenwart* (Amriswil, 1956)
——: *Das Werk 1986* (Adliswil, 1986)

FRITZ MUGGLER, ANDREW CLARK

Schick [née Hamel], **Margarete (Luise)** (*b* Mainz, 26 April 1773; *d* Berlin, 29 April 1809). German singer. She studied singing in Würzburg with Dominicus Steffani and in Mainz with Righini, and sang under Mozart at Frankfurt in 1790; her stage début was in 1791. After a guest appearance at Hamburg in 1793 she became chamber and theatre singer at the Berlin court and from 1794 she sang at the Nationaltheater. She was renowned for her expressive performances of Mozart and of Gluck, in whose *Iphigénie en Tauride* she sang her most famous role, Iphigenia. Both her daughter Julie and granddaughter Pauline von Schätzel were opera singers.

*

ADB (H. Wetti)
K. von Levezow: *Leben und Kunst der Frau Margarete Luise Schick, gebornen Hamel* (Berlin, 1809)

GAYNOR G. JONES

Schickele, Peter (*b* Ames, IA, 17 July 1935). American composer and humorist. He studied music at Swarthmore College, then went to the Juilliard School, where he continued his composition studies with Persichetti and Bergsma. In 1959 he studied with Milhaud at the Aspen Music School. He was composer-in-residence to the Los Angeles public schools, then taught at Swarthmore for a year before returning to teach at Juilliard.

In 1959, as a student at the Juilliard School, Schickele co-founded the Composers Circle, which presented concerts of works by members of the group. His serious compositions show a diversity of influences, including jazz, rock and nontonal styles. Childhood interests in theatre, pop and rock songs, and the slapstick burlesque of a style reminiscent of songs by Spike Jones began to find their place in Schickele's output when he invented P. D. Q. Bach, a persona through whom he lampooned Baroque and Classical music and musicology. Pieces by P. D. Q. Bach include orchestral, chamber and vocal parodies as well as three operas; they are full of surprising violations of familiar styles, musical forms and phrase structures, harmonic conventions and orchestration. Schickele has also written music for television and films, and songs for musicals including *Oh! Calcutta!*

As P. D. Q. Bach

The Stoned Guest ('half-act opera'), New York, Carnegie Hall, Dec 1967
Hansel & Gretel & Ted & Alice (1), Houston or Dallas, March 1972
A Little Nightmare Music (spoof, 1), New York, Carnegie Hall, 27 Dec 1982
The Abduction of Figaro (comic parody, 3, P. Schickele), Minneapolis, Orpheum, 24 April 1984
The Magic Bassoon (1), Denver, Oct 1986
Oedipus Tex (spoof, 1), Minneapolis, 15 March 1988
Prelude to Einstein on the Fritz ('undiscovered opera'), New York, Carnegie Hall, 1989

DEANE L. ROOT

Schidlowsky, Leon (*b* Santiago, 21 July 1931). Israeli composer of Chilean birth. He attended Santiago Conservatory (1940–47) and read philosophy and psychology at the University of Chile (1948–52) while continuing to study harmony, counterpoint and composition privately. After further studies at Detmold and in Barsbüttel he returned to Chile in 1955 and held a number of important teaching and administrative posts. In 1969 he settled in Tel-Aviv and began teaching at the Rubin Academy of the university.

Schidlowsky has progressed from free atonality through 12-note serialism, total serialism and aleatory writing to graphic composition, on which he concentrated from 1969. Whatever the style or means, however, he has always been powerfully influenced by contemporary events, particularly the Holocaust of World War II. His output has been divided evenly between orchestral and choral works, chamber and instrumental music, and graphically notated compositions (some intended for staged performance); he has also written a number of staged vocal works.

Schidlowsky's one completed opera, *Die Menschen*, composed in 1969, is based on a play by Walter which strongly anticipates the 'theatre of the absurd' of Beckett and Ionesco. It is an intensely expressionistic, multi-media theatre piece demanding large forces (25 characters, mixed choir, children's choir, symphony orchestra) and various scenic effects. Four of the five acts have five scenes, and the stage is divided so that five different scenes can take place simultaneously. There is no definite plot, since the work depicts the gamut of (sometimes violent) events that may occur in a man's lifetime. In 1980 Schidlowsky began a projected three-act opera, *The Dybbuk*, based on Ansky's play dealing with the life and suffering of the Jewish people. After abandoning it for some years, he resumed work on it in 1990.

WILLIAM Y. ELIAS

Schiebeler, Daniel (*b* Hamburg, 25 March 1741; *d* Hamburg, 19 Aug 1771). German librettist. The son of a businessman, he studied law at Göttingen and Leipzig. After taking his doctorate in 1768 he returned to Hamburg, where he died of tuberculosis when only 30. As a student at Leipzig he collaborated with J. A. Hiller on two German operas, and at Hamburg provided C. P. E. Bach with the text of his oratorio *Die Israeliten in der Wüste* (1769). He adored Metastasio, memorized entire scenes from his works, and sought to imitate him in *Die Grossmuth des Scipio* (1768). As a poet he also made significant contributions to the Romanze.

Basilio und Quitera, oder Don Quiscotte der Löwenritter (dramatische Singgedicht), Telemann, 1761; *Lisuart und Dariolette, oder Die Frage und die Antwort* (Operette), Hiller, 1766; *Die Muse* (Comödie), Hiller, 1767; *Die Grossmuth des Scipio* (dramatische Singgedicht), J. Schuback, 1768

THOMAS BAUMAN

Schieferdecker [Schiefferdecker], **Johann Christian** (*b* Teuchern, nr Weissenfels, 10 Nov 1679; *d* Lübeck, 5 April 1732). German composer. The son of a Kantor and organist, he came of a long line of ministers and church musicians. He attended the Thomasschule, Leipzig, 1692–7; later, when he was a university student in Leipzig, two of his operas were staged. In 1702 he became accompanist to the Hamburg Opera, where three of his operas were first performed or revived. On 23 January 1707 Schieferdecker succeeded Buxtehude as organist and parish clerk of the Marienkirche, Lübeck, marrying his predecessor's daughter in 1707. Thereafter he focussed his attention on the church.

Der von dem Ackerpflug zu den Thron erhobene Kaiser Justinus (3), Leipzig, 1700
Medea, Leipzig, 1700
Der königliche Printz Regnerus (3), Weissenfels, 1701
Der siegende König der Gothen Alarikus (3, Nothnagel), Hamburg, 1702
Viktor Hertzog der Normannen [Act 1] (3, H. Hinsch), Hamburg, 1702 [Act 2 by Mattheson, Act 3 by Bronner]

*

H. C. Wolff: *Die Barockoper in Hamburg, 1678–1738* (Wolfenbüttel, 1957)

G. B. SHARP/R

Schierbeck, Poul (Julius Ouscher) (*b* Copenhagen, 8 June 1888; *d* Copenhagen, 9 Feb 1949). Danish composer. In 1906, while engaged in law studies, he began composition lessons with Nielsen and with the church musician Thomas Laub; he also studied the piano, the organ and conducting. He served as an artillery lieutenant during World War I, but continued to pursue his musical interests. From 1916 until his death he held a post as church organist and from 1931 was on the staff of the Copenhagen Conservatory, where he became an influential teacher of composition and instrumentation. Among the honours he received was membership of the Royal Swedish Academy of Music (1947).

Schierbeck made a most important contribution to the literature of Danish song, and also composed valuable material for Danish children's songbooks. From 1923 to 1930 he worked on the opera *Fête galante* op.25 (M. Lobedanz; Copenhagen, Kongelige, 1 Sept 1931); the first performance was directed by Victor Schiøler, with Sylvia Larsen, the composer's wife, as Suzon. Although the piece was well applauded, the critics all commented on its excessive length, and it was taken off after six performances. Schierbeck undertook revisions in the expectation of further stagings, but it was not until after his death that a shortened version was broadcast by Danish radio (1949), and there was no complete performance again until the opera returned to the Kongelige Teater in 1960; that production met with success, but the work failed to gain a place in the repertory. Disappointed by the problems surrounding his opera, Schierbeck found an outlet for his inclination towards dramatic composition in editing and arranging *Tiggerens opera* op.36 (after Gay and Pepusch: *The Beggar's Opera*; Danish radio, November 1936) and in collaborating with the Danish film maker Carl Theodor Dreyer.

*

G. Fjelrad: 'Poul Schierbeck in memoriam', *Sanger bladet* (1949), no.3
J. Maegaard: 'En glemt opera?', *Nordisk musikkultur* iv/4 (1955), 113–15 [on *Fête galante*]
O. Mathison: *Bogen om Poul Schierbeck* (Copenhagen, 1988)

WILLIAM H. REYNOLDS

Schiff, David (*b* Bronx, NY, 30 Aug 1945). American composer. He became interested in the new-music movement at Columbia and Cambridge universities in the 1960s, and attended the Juilliard School. His teachers included Roger Smalley, John Corigliano, Ursula Mamlok and Elliott Carter. Perhaps his most successful work has been the opera *Gimpel the Fool*, with a Yiddish libretto by Isaac Bashevis Singer. The work was composed in 1976 as an hour-long vaudeville with piano accompaniment but was later expanded for a small orchestra suggestive of a klezmer band. It was first performed in New York on 20 May 1979. Originally sung in Yiddish with English narration, the opera was given entirely in English for a 1985 production. *Gimpel* is eclectic and written with a shrewd grasp of language and theatre; it also draws upon the kaleidoscopic variety of the Jewish musical heritage. CAROL J. OJA

Schikaneder [Schickaneder], **Emanuel (Johann Joseph** [Baptist]**)** (*b* Straubing, 1 Sept 1751; *d* Vienna, 21 Sept 1812). Austrian dramatist, theatre director, actor, singer and composer of German origin. Educated at the Jesuit Gymnasium at Regensburg, where he was a cathedral chorister, Schikaneder may briefly have been a town musician before he became an actor with F. J. Moser's troupe in 1773 or 1774. In 1774 he danced in a court ballet at Innsbruck, where his Singspiel *Die Lyranten* (of which he wrote both words and music) was performed in 1775 or 1776. The Innsbruck company, then under Andreas Schopf and Theresia Schimann, moved in 1776 to Augsburg, where on 9 February 1777 he married Maria Magdalena (known as Eleonore) Arth (*b* Hermannstadt, 1751; *d* Vienna, 22 June 1821), an actress in the company. In 1777–8 they were in Nuremberg with Moser's company, and in December 1777 Schikaneder made a famous guest appearance as Hamlet at the Munich court theatre, where he was obliged to repeat the final scene as an encore. From January 1778 he was director of the troupe, appearing at Ulm, Stuttgart, Augsburg, Nuremberg, Rothenburg and elsewhere. In 1780 they went to Laibach (now Ljubljana), Klagenfurt and Linz before beginning a lengthy season at Salzburg in September, during which Schikaneder became friendly with the Mozarts. Further travels through Austria included summer seasons at Graz in 1781 and 1782, the winter of 1782–3 in Pressburg (now Bratislava), and a guest appearance in summer 1783 at the Kärntnertortheater, Vienna.

After further visits to Pest and Pressburg, where Joseph II saw him perform in October 1874, Schikaneder was invited to play in Vienna. He and Hubert Kumpf began a three-month season of operas and Singspiels at the Kärntnertor on 5 November. Thereafter, Schikaneder was a member of the Nationaltheater, performing in plays and operas, from 1 March 1785 until 28 February 1786. During this time his own troupe was run by his wife and Johann Friedel and touring in southern Austria until it moved into the Freihaus-Theater auf der Wieden, Vienna, in November 1788. Schikaneder himself, in February 1786, had been granted an imperial licence for the building of a suburban theatre but did not make use of it for 15 years, forming instead a new company specializing in Singspiels and operas, which he took to Salzburg, Augsburg and Memmingen. In February 1787 he took over the Prince of Thurn and Taxis's court theatre at Regensburg. When Johann Friedel died at the end of March 1789 Schikaneder and his wife took over the Freihaus-Theater, bringing from Regensburg the singer-composers Schack and Gerl. Schikaneder's reign at the Freihaus began on 12 July 1789 with the first performance of his 'Anton' opera *Der dumme Gärtner*, and from this time dates the beginning of his steady series of plays, opera and Singspiel librettos which were the backbone of the repertory of his theatre (but which were also performed in other theatres, sometimes with new musical scores).

Schikaneder's years of travel had seen the production of more straight plays than operas; in Vienna he placed the emphasis firmly on opera, and commissioned settings of his own texts from Mozart (*Die Zauberflöte*), Süssmayr (*Der Spiegel von Arkadien*), Wölfl (*Der Höllenberg*), Mederitsch and Winter (one act each of *Babylons Pyramiden*; Winter also set *Das Labyrinth*, a sequel to *Die Zauberflöte*). He also received scores from his theatre Kapellmeister, Henneberg (*Die Waldmänner*), Haibel (*Der Tiroler Wastel*) and Seyfried (*Der Löwenbrunnen* and *Der Wundermann am Rheinfall*). As the 1790s advanced, Schikaneder began to suffer from increasing financial difficulties as he strove to surpass the achievements of his rivals and of his own greatest successes. In 1799 he handed over the management of the theatre to Bartholomäus Zitterbarth while continuing his artistic direction. Of the 12 greatest successes at the Freihaus, which closed on 12 June 1801, eight – including the first five – were written by Schikaneder himself.

On 13 June 1801 Schikaneder opened the new Theater an der Wien, using the licence he had previously been granted; it was the most lavishly equipped and one of the largest theatres of its age, and has continued in almost unbroken use. It opened with Teyber's setting of Schikaneder's libretto *Alexander*, but a change in public taste and a decline in Schikaneder's standards and powers of judgment were influential in the decision to sell the licence to Zitterbarth after less than a year. Schikaneder continued to supply plays and librettos, and to act, but despite two further periods as artistic director his fortunes were waning. After the sale of the theatre in 1806 Schikaneder left Vienna and took over the Brno Theatre. At Easter 1809 he was back in Vienna, but financial ruin and failing mental health darkened his last years. On his way to Budapest to take up an appointment as director of a new German theatre company in 1812 he became mad, returned to Vienna, and died in penury shortly after; a performance of his

Emanuel Schikaneder as Papageno in Mozart's 'Die Zauberflöte'; engraving (1791) by Ignaz Alberti

play *Die Schweden vor Brünn* was given for his benefit at the Theater in der Leopoldstadt on 18 July 1812 – an uncommon tribute from a rival theatre, albeit one that had successfully staged his plays since the early 1780s and would continue to do so until the 1850s.

Schikaneder was one of the most talented and influential theatre men of his age. Although it is fashionable to decry his plays (of which there are nearly 50) and librettos, they more than satisfied the demands of their day. Goethe praised his skill at creating strong dramatic situations, and though the verse is often trite the libretto of *Die Zauberflöte* (Gieseke's claims to the authorship of which were proved false by Komorzynski and more scientifically by Rommel) is by no means unworthy of Mozart's music. Some of Schikaneder's comedies (the 'Anton' plays, *Der Tiroler Wastel*, *Das abgebrannte Haus*, *Der Fleischhauer von Ödenburg*, *Die Fiaker in Wien*) continued to be much performed for many years and strongly influenced the later development of the Viennese *Lokalstück* ('local play'). Early in his career Schikaneder composed two, and perhaps several more, theatre scores: it has long been known that the music as well as the text of *Die Lyranten* was his work; and for the production of his Singspiel *Das Urianische Schloss* (1786, Salzburg) at the Theater in der Leopoldstadt in November 1787 a score by him is specifically mentioned by Wenzel Müller in his diary ('Opera by Em: Schikaneder, music, and book').

Schikaneder's brother, Urban (1746–1818), was an actor and singer; he sang First Priest in the première of *Die Zauberflöte* in 1791 and took a part in the administration of his brother's travelling company. Urban's daughter Anna (or Nanny or Nanette; 1767–1862) sang First Boy in the *Zauberflöte* première and was later a member of the Theater in der Leopoldstadt company, singing the Queen of Night when that company first gave *Die Zauberflöte* in 1811. Her brother KARL SCHIKANEDER was also a man of the theatre.

Der Müllertomerl, oder Das Bergmädchen [Kaspar der Müllertomerl] (ländliche Oper), 1785; *Der Luftballon* (Operette), Schack, ?1786; *Die drei Ringe, oder [Kaspar] der Lächerliche Mundkoch* (Spl), Schack, ?1786; *Lorenz und Suschen* (Spl), Schack, 1788; *Der Krautschneider* (komische Spl), Schack, 1788; *Der dumme Gärtner aus dem Gebirge, oder Die zween Anton* (komische Oper), Schack and Gerl, 1789 [1st 'Anton' Spl]; *Jakob und Nannerl, oder Der angenehme Traum* (komische Oper), Schack and/or Gerl, 1789

Die verdeckten Sachen (komische Oper), Schack, Gerl and Lickl, 1789 [2nd 'Anton' Spl]; *Was macht der Anton im Winter?* (komische Oper), Schack, Gerl and others, 1790 [3rd 'Anton' Spl]; *Die schöne Isländerin, oder Der Mufti von Samarkanda* (Zauberkomödie mit Gesang), 1790; *Der Fall ist noch weit seltner, oder Die geplagten Ehemänner* (Oper), Schack, 1790; *Der Frühling, oder Der Anton ist noch nicht tot* (komische Oper), Schack, Gerl ?and others, 1790 [4th 'Anton' Spl]

Der Stein der Weisen, oder Die Zauberinsel (heroisch-komische Oper), Schack, Gerl ?and Mozart, 1790; *Anton bei Hofe, oder Das Namensfest* (komische Oper), Schack, Gerl ?and others, 1791 [5th 'Anton' Spl]; *Die Zauberflöte* (grosse Oper), Mozart, 1791; *Der redliche Landmann* (ländliches Familiengemälde mit Musik), 1792; *Johanna von Weimar* (Ritterschauspiel mit Gesang), Henneberg, 1792; *Der Renegat, oder Anton in der Türkei* (komische Oper), Schack, Gerl ?and others, 1792 [6th 'Anton' Spl]

Die Kriegsgesetze, oder Die deutsche Griechin (militärische Szenen mit Gesang), 1792; *Die Eisen-Königin* (Zauberspiel), Henneberg, 1793; *Der Zauberpfeil, oder Das Kabinett der Wahrheit* (grosse Oper), Lickl, 1793; *Der wohltätige Derwisch, oder Die Schellenkappe* [Die Zaubertrommel] (Lust- und Zauberspiel), Schack, Gerl, Henneberg ?and others, 1793; *Die Wäldmänner* (komische Oper), Henneberg, 1793; *Die Hirten am Rhein* (magisch-komische Oper), 1794

Der Spiegel von Arkadien (grosse heroisch-komische Oper), Süssmayr, 1794; *Das Häuschen im Walde, oder Antons Reise nach seinem Geburtsort* (komische Oper), ? Schack and others, 1795 [7th 'Anton' Spl]; *Der Scherenschleifer* (Faschings Oper), Henneberg, 1795; *Der Königssohn aus Ithaka* (grosse heroisch-komische Oper), Hoffmeister, 1795; *Der Höllenberg, oder Prüfung und Lohn* (heroisch-komische Oper), Wölfl, 1795; *Der Tiroler Wastel* (Oper), Haibel, 1796

Östreichs treue Brüder, oder Die Scharfschützen in Tirol [Der Landsturm] (patriotisches Spl), Haibel, 1796 [pt 2 of Der Tiroler Wastel]; *Das medizinische Konsilium* (komische Oper), Haibel, 1797; *Der Löwenbrunn* [Der Löwenbrunnen] (heroisch-komische Oper), Seyfried, 1797; *Babylons Pyramiden* (grosse heroisch-komische Oper), Mederitsch and Winter, 1797; *Das Labyrinth, oder Der Kampf mit den Elementen* (grosse heroisch-komische Oper), Winter, 1798 [sequel to Die Zauberflöte]

Die Ostindier vom Spittelberg [Die Rückkehr aus Ostindien] (komisches Spl), Seyfried, Stegmayer and others, 1799; *Konrad Langbart von Friedburg, oder Der Berggeist* (Ritterschauspiel mit Gesang), Henneberg, 1799; *Mina* [Minna] *und Peru, oder die Königspflicht* (heroisch-komisches Spl), Henneberg and Seyfried, 1799; *Der Papagei und die Gans, oder Die zisalpinischen Perücken* (ländlich-komisches Familiengemälde mit Gesang), Haibel, 1799

Der Wundermann am Rheinfall (grosse komische Oper), Seyfried, 1799; *Die Spinnerin am Gatterhölzl, oder Der Stock-am-Eisen-Platz* (österreichische Volkssage mit Gesang), 1800; *Amors Schiffchen in der Brigittenaue* (komische Oper), Seyfried and others, 1800; *Proteus und Arabiens Söhne* (Zaubersingspiel), Seyfried and Stegmayer, 1801; *Alexander* (grosse heroische Oper), F. Teyber, 1801; *Tsching! Tsching! Tsching!* (Spl), Haibel, 1802

Die Entlarvten (Oper), A. Fischer, 1803 [sequel to Die Waldmänner]; *Pfändung und Personal-Arrest* (komisches Spl), Teyber, 1803; *Swetards Zaubertal* (grosse Oper), Fischer, 1805; *Vestas Feuer* (grosse heroische Oper), J. Weigl, 1805 [also frag. setting by Beethoven]; *Die Kurgäste am Sauerbrunn* (Original Spl), Diabelli, 1806; *Das Zaubermädchen im Schreywald* (Oper), *Das Fest der Götter* (Karikatur-Oper), libs. passed by Brno censor before Nov 1809

Librettos and music: Die Lyranten, oder Das lustige Elend (Operette, 3), Innsbruck, 1775/6; Das Urianische Schloss (Spl), Salzburg, 1786

*

ADB (A. Sauer); *LoewenbergA*; *WurzbachL*

Theater-Kalender (Gotha, 1775–98)

J. K. Schikaneder: 'Emanuel Schikaneder', *Der Gesellschafter*, xviii (Berlin, 1834), nos.71–4

E. von Komorzynski: *Emanuel Schikaneder: ein Beitrag zur Geschichte des deutschen Theaters* (Berlin, 1901, 2/1951)

L. Eisenberg: 'Schikaneder', *Grosses biographisches Lexikon der deutschen Bühne im 19. Jahrhundert* (Leipzig, 1903), 881ff

E. K. Blümml: *Aus Mozarts Freundes- und Familienkreis* (Vienna, 1923)

F. Hadamowsky: *Das Theater in der Wiener Leopoldstadt* (Vienna, 1934)

O. E. Deutsch: *Das Freihaus-Theater auf der Wieden* (Vienna, 1937)

H. Endrös: 'E. Schikaneder und das Augsburger Theater', *Zeitschrift des Historischen Vereins für Schwaben*, lv–lvi (1942–3), 203–98

E. von Komorzynski: *Der Vater der Zauberflöte: Emanuel Schikaneders Leben* (Vienna, 1948)

K. Goedeke: *Grundriss zur Geschichte der deutschen Dichtung*, xi/1 (Düsseldorf, 2/1951), 132; xi/2 (Düsseldorf, 2/1953), 376ff, 381ff

A. Bauer: *150 Jahre Theater an der Wien* (Vienna, 1952)

H. Pigge: *Geschichte und Entwicklung des Regensburger Theaters 1786–1859* (diss., U. of Munich, 1953)

A. Bauer: *Opern und Operetten in Wien* (Graz and Cologne, 1955)

W. Senn: 'Schikaneders Weg zum Theater', *Acta mozartiana*, ix (1962), 39–46

P. Branscombe: '*Die Zauberflöte*: some Textual and Interpretative Problems', *PRMA*, xcii (1965–6), 45–63

F. J. Fischer: 'Emanuel Schikaneder und Salzburg', *Jb der Gesellschaft für Wiener Theaterforschung*, xv–xvi (1966), 179–216

E. M. Batley: *A Preface to The Magic Flute* (London, 1969)

D. Koenigsberger: 'A New Metaphor for Mozart's *Magic Flute*', *European Studies Review*, v (1975), 229–75

K. Honolka: *Papageno* (Salzburg and Vienna, 1984)

PETER BRANSCOMBE

Schikaneder, Karl (*b* Freising, 1770; *d* Prague, 25 March 1845). German composer, dramatist, actor, singer and director, son of Urban Schikaneder. After a period with the Freihaus-Theater company of his uncle, Emanuel Schikaneder, he became a director (Regisseur) at the Theater in der Josefstadt in 1803. He moved to Steyr, Karlsbad and Brno (where he was a member of the company his uncle directed in 1807). In 1811, and again from 1816 to 1819, he was a member of the Theater in der Leopoldstadt, being employed as dramatist, singer and actor. He moved to Prague in 1819, where he was appointed opera director, retiring in 1834. He was the author of a once-popular series of plays and composed a number of musical scores, including at least six to his own texts (others of which were set by Wenzel Müller, Franz Teyber and Franz Volkert).

WL – *Vienna, Theater in der Leopoldstadt*

Die Frau Everl vom Altserbach (Posse, 3, K. Schikaneder), WL, 13 Oct 1810

Die schwarze Burg, oder Der Höllenhammer (komische Zauberoper, 3, Schikaneder), WL, 20 June 1810

Die Ausforderung (Operette, 1, Schikaneder), WL, 4 May 1811

Der Vetter Michel aus dem Ratzenstadel, oder Die Braut Harifax aus England (Posse mit Gesang, 3), WL 13 June 1812

Kasperl der lustige Flickschneider (komische Oper, 1, M. Fenzl), WL, 25 July 1812

Božena, oder Der Kampf mit dem Lindwurm (Schauspiel mit Gesängen, 4, F. J. Korntheuer), Brno, 1814

Die bezauberten Hortensien, oder Der Feen-Streit (komisches Zauberspiel mit Gesang, 3), Prague, 9 Feb 1828

Der Wettlauf zu Kronäuglstadt, oder Das Wahrzeichen (parodistische Posse, Schikaneder), Prague, 12 Jan 1832
Die steinerne Braut mit Fleisch und Bein, oder Hans Kröpfelbergers Genie-Streiche (parodierende Posse, after *Zampa*), Prague, 30 Jan 1834

Librettos for other composers: *Der Schiffmeister von Straubing* (Lustspiel mit Gesängen), F. Teyber, 1807; *Die Zauberhöhle, oder Die steinernen Brüder* (Zauberspiel), K. Nanke, 1810; *Der Talisman im Magnetgebirge* (Zauberoper), Nanke, 1811; *Theophrastus Paracelsus, oder Die Basilisken-Kluft* (Zaubermärchen mit Gesang), Volkert, 1811; *Der Ball beim Schwarzen Hasen, oder Die Ehemänner auf Reisen* (Lustspiel), Volkert, 1814; *Die Prellerei in der Narrengasse* (Posse), W. Müller, 1816; *Die unvermutete Hochzeit* (Spl), Müller, Vienna, 1816; *Der Kampf mit der Riesenschlange, oder Der Leuchtturm auf der Rubineninsel* (Zauberspiel), Volkert, 1817; *Die englischen Waren* (Spl), Vienna, 1819; *Die Brillantnadel und das Zauberkäppchen* (Zauberspiel), 1827; *Nachtschatten* (Zauberoper, 3), F. J. Škroup, Prague, 1829; *Die Erdgeister und der Brillenhändler* (Zauberspiel), Müller, 1833; *Der unverhoffte Schatz* (Posse mit Gesang), 1839; *Der Glasfabrikant* (Posse mit Gesang), 1840

PETER BRANSCOMBE

Schiller, (Johann Christoph) Friedrich von (*b* Marbach, 10 Nov 1759; *d* Weimar, 9 May 1805). German dramatist, poet, aesthetician and historian. The son of an army officer, he had an unsettled childhood and youth. During his years as a student (of law, then medicine) at the Karlsschule in Stuttgart (1773–80) he wrote his first play, *Die Räuber*. Shortly after its première, in Mannheim in 1782, he was obliged to flee from Stuttgart and settled in Mannheim, where he wrote *Fiesco* and *Kabale und Liebe*. In 1785, encouraged by C. G. Körner, he moved to Leipzig and Dresden where, between 1785 and 1787, he completed *Don Carlos* and considered writing a libretto for Naumann. In 1787 he went to Weimar, where he was to settle in 1799; in 1789 he became professor of history at Jena. He married Charlotte von Lengefeld, a keen amateur pianist, in 1790, and at about this time he became acquainted with Rochlitz and Reichardt. From 1794 Schiller was on very friendly terms with Goethe, developing with him the most famous artistic collaboration in the history of German letters. Apart from their joint ventures Schiller's Weimar years saw the completion and production of the *Wallenstein* trilogy (1798–9), *Maria Stuart* (1800), *Die Jungfrau von Orleans* (1801), *Die Braut von Messina* (1803), *Wilhelm Tell* (1804) and the unfinished *Demetrius*. The theme of these dramas is to a more or less marked extent the search for moral freedom, though political freedom is as much the subject of *Wilhelm Tell* as it had been of the early revolutionary plays.

Schiller was no musician, and indeed there is little evidence that he understood or appreciated music to any great extent. His tastes were conservative; Gluck alone among his great contemporaries found a ready appreciation from him. However, he stated that 'a certain musical state of mind [*Gemütsstimmung*]' was for him the precursor of poetic inspiration. Much of Schiller's verse has a kind of musicality, as well as rhythmic élan – qualities found in his lyrics and ballads as well as in the great dramatic dialogues and monologues. Incidental music plays a modest part in most of Schiller's plays; in one, *Die Braut von Messina*, he strove to recreate the mood and conditions of Greek classical tragedy, with an important role for the chorus.

Around 1800 Goethe and Schiller were concerned to effect a closer alliance between music and drama. Schiller justified his use of the chorus in *Die Braut von Messina* in the essay 'Über den Gebrauch des Chors in der Tragödie', with which he prefaced the play, stating that the chorus acted not only as a commentator but also as a 'living wall', distancing the spectators from the action and pointing up the idealistic and universal nature of art. His intention to accompany the choric interludes instrumentally was dropped on the advice of Körner. Schiller's views on music are scattered among his letters and aesthetic essays. In 'Über das Pathetische' (1793) he argued that the primary concern of tragic art is the depiction of suffering and moral resistance to it. His deep mistrust of the emotional, even sensual effect of music is clear, music for Schiller even at its most intellectual having 'a closer affinity to the senses *by nature of its material* than true aesthetic freedom allows'. A summary of his views on the relationship between music and the other arts may be found in Letter 22 of his 'Über die ästhetische Erziehung des Menschen' (1795):

> Music in its highest perfection must become form [*Gestalt*] and make its effect on us with the calm power of the antique world; fine art in its highest perfection must become music and touch us through its direct sensuous presence; poetry in its most perfect form must, like music, seize us powerfully, but at the same time, like the plastic arts, surround us with calm clarity.

Apart from the operas that Rossini and Verdi based on Schiller plays there are numerous other, largely forgotten settings. Mercadante as well as Verdi set *Die Räuber*; Lalo wrote an (unperformed) *Fiesque* (1866–8); Verdi's *Luisa Miller* was preceded by a once popular Viennese musical parody of Schiller's *Kabale und Liebe*, by Bäuerle and Drechsler; Michael Costa wrote a *Don Carlos* (1844). Not surprisingly, Schiller's grandest achievement, the *Wallenstein* trilogy, has tempted numerous composers to try their hand with incidental music and tone poems, but there have also been several operatic settings. *Maria Stuart* gave birth to several operas, but even more numerous are the settings based on *Die Jungfrau von Orleans*, from a very varied list of composers besides Tchaikovsky and Verdi. Many composers have based operas on Schiller's adaptation of Gozzi's *Turandot*; an Italian translation of Schiller's *Turandot*, itself a reworked translation of Gozzi, was the starting-point for Puccini's opera. *Die Braut von Messina* has inspired one particularly distinguished setting, Fibich's *Nevěsta messinská*. Schiller's last completed drama, *Wilhelm Tell*, ineradicably associated with Rossini's final opera, also spawned Henry Bishop's adaptation *Hofer, the Tell of the Tyrol* (1830).

Die Räuber (1782): Mercadante (I briganti), 1836; Verdi (I masnadieri), 1847; Zajc (Amelia), 1860; Klebe, 1957
Die Verschwörung des Fiesco zu Genua (1783): G. Hellmesberger, comp. 1848–9; Lalo, comp. 1866–8 (Fiesque)
Kabale und Liebe (1784): Bäuerle and Drechsler, 1827; Verdi (Luisa Miller), 1849; von Einem, 1976
Don Carlos (1787): Deshayes, 1800; Nordal, 1843; M. Costa, 1844; Bona, 1847; Ferrari, 1854; Moscuzza, 1862; Ferrara, 1863; Verdi, 1867
Der Taucher (ballad, 1798): Reichardt, 1811
Die Bürgschaft (ballad, 1798): Schubert, 1816, inc.; F. P. Lachner, 1828; G. Hellmesberger, 1851
Wallenstein (trilogy, 1799): Seyfried, 1813; Adelburg, *c*1860; Verdi (La forza del destino, 1 scene), 1862; Musone, 1873; Denza, 1876; Ruiz, 1877; Weinberger, 1937; Shabelsky, 1950; Zafred, 1965
Das Lied von der Glocke (poem, 1799): Knecht, 1807 (melodrama); D'Indy (Le chant de la cloche), 1912
Maria Stuart (1800): P. Casella, 1813; Mercadante, 1821; Coccia, 1827; Donizetti, 1834 (initially as Buondelmonte); Niedermeyer, 1844; Palumbo, 1874; Lavello, 1895
Die Jungfrau von Orleans (1801): Carafa (Jeanne d'Arc à Orléans), 1821; Vaccai (Giovanna d'Arco), 1827; Pacini (Giovanna d'Arco), 1830; Balfe (Joan of Arc), 1837; Vesque von Püttlingen

(Johanna d'Arc), 1840; Verdi (Giovanna d'Arco), 1845; Langert (1861); Tchaikovsky (The Maid of Orléans), 1881; Rezniček, 1887; Klebe (Das Mädchen aus Dorémy), 1976
Die Braut von Messina (1803): Kastner (Beatrice), comp. 1839; Vaccai, 1839; Oertzen, 1840; Bonawitz, 1874; Fibich (Nevěsta messinská), 1884; Mai, 1904
Wilhelm Tell (1804): Rossini, 1829; Van Overeen, 1906
Der Gang nach dem Eisenhammer (ballad, 1804): B. A. Weber, 1810; Schoenfeld, 1832; C. Kreutzer (Fridolin), 1837; Terry, 1861
Turandot (adaptation of Gozzi, 1804): Blumenröder, 1809; Danzi, 1816; Reissiger, 1835; Vesque von Püttlingen, 1838; Lowenskjold, 1854; Konradin, 1866; Busoni, 1917; Puccini, 1926
Demetrius (1805, unfinished): Joncières, 1876; Dvořák, 1882

*

A. Schaefer: *Historisches und systematisches Verzeichnis sämtlicher Tonwerke zu den Dramen Schillers ...* (Leipzig, 1886)
A. Kohut: *Schiller in seinen Beziehungen zur Musik* (Stuttgart, 1905)
E. Bienenfeld: 'Verdi and Schiller', *MQ*, xvii (1931), 204–8
G. Baruch: *Verdi und Schiller: Quellenkundliche Studien zum Librettoproblem* (diss., U. of Prague, 1935)
P. Weigand: 'Schiller's Dramas as Opera Texts', *Monatshefte*, xlvi (1954), 249–59
A. C. Keys: 'Schiller and Italian Opera', *ML*, xli (1960), 223–37
L. K. Gerhartz: 'Verdi und Schiller', *Verdi: Bollettino dell'Istituto di studi verdiani*, ii/6 (1966), 1589–1610, 2063–95
R. M. Longyear: *Schiller and Music* (Chapel Hill, 1966)
P. J. Branscombe: 'Schiller and Music', *Forum for Modern Language Studies*, iv (1968), 396–403
Congresso internazionale di studi verdiani: Verona, Parma, Busseto 1969 [articles on Schiller and Verdi, esp. *Don Carlos*]
E. Inasaridse: *Schiller und die italienische Oper: das Schillerdrama als Libretto des Belcanto* (Frankfurt am Main, 1989)
L. Sharpe: *Friedrich Schiller: Drama, Thought and Politics* (Cambridge, 1991)
PETER BRANSCOMBE

Schillings, Max von (*b* Düren, 19 April 1868; *d* Berlin, 24 July 1933). German composer, conductor and opera administrator. He learnt the violin, piano and theory in Bonn, before attending the University of Munich, where he studied law, philosophy, literature and art history. There he began a lifelong friendship with Richard Strauss who encouraged him to devote his energies towards a musical career. In 1892 he was appointed assistant stage conductor at Bayreuth, becoming chorus master there ten years later. Gradually he came to be recognized as one of the leading musical figures in Munich, working as composer, conductor and teacher. His reputation was sealed in 1903 when he was appointed Königlicher Professor at Munich, where his pupils included Furtwängler and Heger. In 1908 he became assistant to the Intendant of the Royal Opera House in Stuttgart, remaining there for the next ten years. His tenure was marked by several notable performances, including the première of the first version of Strauss's *Ariadne auf Naxos* (1912) with the composer conducting and Schillings's own adaptation of Berlioz's *Les Troyens* (1913). He also arranged recitatives for Mozart's *Die Entführung aus dem Serail* (1910).

Schillings's operatic output began with *Ingwelde*, a music drama based on a poem by Count Ferdinand von Sporck, which recounts the Scandinavian *Svarfdälasaga* in Zedlitz's *Altnordische Bilder*. First performed in Karlsruhe in 1894 under Felix Mottl, initially it was greeted with critical approval and received further performances under Richard Strauss in Munich in 1897. But like countless other operas of the period, including Strauss's *Guntram*, d'Albert's *Gernot* and Weingartner's *Sakuntala*, *Ingwelde* suffered from a poor text and an all-too-obvious imitation of Wagner's style, particularly that of the *Ring*. Not only was the plot closely related to Nibelungen sagas, but the characterization of the heroine bore a strong resemblance to Brünnhilde.

In *Der Pfeifertag*, first produced at Schwerin in 1899, Schillings moved away from the sombre tragedy of his first opera and attempted to write a comedy in the manner of Wagner's *Die Meistersinger*. The poem, again by Sporck, is set in medieval times and tells of the noble patron of a piper who has been outwitted by his son and daughter and eventually agrees to a wedding which was not in accordance with his rank. Unlike Wagner, however, Schillings betrays little feeling for dramatic action and the leitmotifs are less distinctive and less well developed. The best sections of the opera are lyrical and include an effective symphonic intermezzo entitled 'Von Spielmanns Leid und Lust'.

Schillings's third opera, *Moloch*, constituted yet another response to Wagnerian music drama and is closely modelled on *Parsifal*. Here Gerhäuser's scenario, based on a dramatic fragment by Hebbel, concerns the Moloch priest Hiram who inflames the Northern Land of Thule with a new faith that threatens the country's stability. The old king remains loyal to the old beliefs of his people, while his son becomes dependent upon these new idols. Eventually the son pays for such treachery with his life. In many respects *Moloch*, first performed in Dresden under Ernst von Schuch in 1906, reflects the composer's attitude towards contemporary musical developments in his own country. The new gods, in effect, are representative of Schillings's fear that foreign elements were affecting the purity of German music – a fear that grew with the passing of time.

Such evident conservatism was masked by Schillings's activities in Stuttgart where he conducted such operas as Strauss's *Salome* in 1908 and *Elektra* in 1910. Indeed, these compositions, as well as the increasing popularity in Germany of Italian *verismo*, exercised a considerable impact upon the composer's final and most successful opera *Mona Lisa*. Completed in four and a half weeks during 1915, this work exemplified a deliberate attempt on the part of the composer to exploit sensationalism in the theatre. The story centres around the enigmatic smile of Mona Lisa which arouses the suspicions of her husband Francesco del Giaconda, a pearl dealer by trade. He lures her lover into his gem cupboard, thereby suffocating him, but Mona Lisa takes her revenge by inducing Francesco to enter the cupboard and locking him in to share her lover's fate. As the story is somewhat insubstantial, the action is framed by a prologue and epilogue in which the three characters are identified with a modern honeymoon couple and their lay-brother tourist guide. Of all Schillings's operas, *Mona Lisa* enjoyed the greatest longevity on the stage and became a notable vehicle for the talents of his second wife Barbara Kemp, as well as Maria Jeritza. The score is a typical late-Romantic effusion which perhaps lacks thematic distinction, but demonstrates considerable expertise in theatrical effects.

Schillings's final years at Stuttgart were increasingly marked by personal difficulties with his first wife and disputes with his employer. In 1918 he resigned his position and in the following year was appointed Intendant at the Berlin Staatsoper, a post he retained until 1925. Becoming extremely disillusioned with the artistic climate of the Weimar Republic, he virtually gave up composition. Nonetheless, as an administrator he made strenuous efforts to conceal his nationalist sympathies by presenting a balanced repertory at the Staatsoper. The most important works produced during his tenure included Pfitzner's *Palestrina*, Schreker's *Die Gezeichneten*, Strauss's *Die Frau ohne Schatten*, Busoni's *Turandot* and *Arlecchino*, and Braunfels's *Die Vögel*. In 1925 he publicly clashed with Carl Becker, the Prussian Minister of Culture, over artistic policy and was summarily dismissed from his post. This action provoked a scandal which united even those who were temperamentally and politically opposed to Schillings's attitudes.

Freed from administrative burdens, Schillings spent the next few years touring Europe and America as conductor of a travelling German opera ensemble. He also served as conductor at the Zoppoter Waldoper (until 1932) and became General Music Director in Riga. In 1929 he returned to the Berlin Staatsoper to conduct Strauss and Wagner and even contemplated writing another opera entitled *Karl V*, a subject subsequently set by Krenek. Yet his influence upon German musical life was essentially marginal until the Nazis gained more prominence. In 1931 *Der Pfeifertag* enjoyed a revival and in the following year Schillings was appointed to several prestigious positions including that of President of the Prussian Academy of Arts. He proved a willing instrument in purging this institution of 'alien' influences and in March 1933 was rewarded by the new regime with the position of Intendant at the Berlin Städtische Oper in succession to the dismissed Carl Ebert. Although Schillings's premature death in July 1933 prevented him from playing a crucial role in the development of artistic policy during the Third Reich, his early operas were rehabilitated during the next few years with *Ingwelde* produced at the Berlin Staatsoper in 1938. Inevitably a reaction against his music set in after World War II, but *Mona Lisa* enjoyed a successful revival in Karlsruhe in 1984.

See also MONA LISA.

Ingwelde (3, F. von Sporck), Karlsruhe, Hof, 13 Nov 1894 (Leipzig, 1894)
Der Pfeifertag (3, Sporck), Schwerin, Hof, 26 Nov 1899 (Berlin, 1900); rev. 1931
Moloch (musical tragedy, 3, E. Gerhäuser, after fragment by F. Hebbel), Dresden, Sächsisches Staats, 8 Dec 1906 (Berlin, 1907)
Mona Lisa (prol., 2, epilogue, B. Dovsky), Stuttgart, Kleines, 26 Sept 1915 (Munich, 1915)

*

R. Louis: *Max von Schillings* (Leipzig, 1909)
J. Korngold: 'Max Schillings "Mona Lisa" ', *Deutsches Opernschaffen der Gegenwart* (Vienna, 1922), 356–66
A. Richard: *Max Schillings* (Berlin, 1922)
P. Ehlers: 'Max von Schillings', *Zfm*, c (1933), 914–16
W. Raupp: *Max von Schillings: der Kampf eines deutschen Künstlers* (Hamburg, 1935)
P. Schwers: 'Schillings "Ingwelde" wieder in der Berliner Staatsoper', *AMZ*, new ser., lx (1938), 392–3
F. von Lepel: *Max von Schillings und seine Oper 'Mona Lisa'* (Berlin, 1954)
D. Satzky: 'Schillings, Max von', *Rheinische Musiker*, iv, ed. K. G. Fellerer (Cologne, 1966), 141–7
J. Guenich and K. Strahn, eds.: *Gedenkschrift Max von Schillings* (Düren, 1968)
C. M. Gruber: 'Max von Schillings: an almost forgotten Composer', *Opera*, xxxiv (1983), 963–8
R. Schlötterer: *Richard Strauss-Max von Schillings: ein Briefwechsel* (Pfaffenhofen, 1987) ERIK LEVI

Schimon, Adolf (*b* Vienna, 29 Feb 1820; *d* Leipzig, 21 June 1887). Austrian composer. The son of a painter well known for his portraits of Beethoven, Weber and Spohr, he entered the Paris Conservatoire at the age of 16, studying the piano, composition (with Berton and Halévy) and singing (with Bordogni and Banderali). In the 1840s he travelled to Italy for further study in singing and in 1846 his opera *Alessandro Stradella* (L. Cemini) was produced in Florence. From 1850 to 1853 he was *maestro al cembalo* at Her Majesty's Theatre, London, and he also toured with Balfe, Sims Reeves and Clara Novello. While *maestro al cembalo* at the Théâtre Italien, Paris (1854–9), his comedy *List und List* (C. Nurrey and H. Lemonnier) was produced in Schwerin in 1858 under Flotow and became popular in several theatres in north Germany. He was especially well known as a singing teacher in Leipzig and Munich.

Schimon's wife, Anna Regan (1841–1902), was a singer of some distinction. She made her début in Siena and went on to sing at the court theatre in Hanover. She toured widely until her marriage in 1872.

*

MGG (E. Badura-Skoda)
'Nachrichten', *AMZ*, xxxix (1837), 182; xlviii (1846), 342

Schindelmeisser, Louis (Alexander Balthasar) (*b* Königsberg, 8 Dec 1811; *d* Darmstadt, 30 March 1864). German conductor and composer. He studied in Berlin and then in Leipzig with his stepbrother Heinrich Dorn (1831), later Hofkapellmeister in Berlin and an opponent of Wagner. He became a friend of Wagner in Leipzig, and in 1832 was named Kapellmeister of the theatre in Salzburg. He then occupied similar posts in Innsbruck, Graz and the Königstadt, Berlin (1837). In 1838 he went to the German theatre in Pest, and from 1847 worked successively in Hamburg, Frankfurt and Wiesbaden. From 1853 he was Hofkapellmeister in Darmstadt.

Schindelmeisser was one of the early admirers and enthusiastic partisans of Wagner. It was probably on his recommendation that Wagner was appointed musical director in Riga in 1837. In 1852–3 he arranged for the first performances in Wiesbaden and Darmstadt of *Tannhäuser*, *Rienzi* and *Lohengrin*. In spite of this, there is hardly a trace of Wagner's influence in Schindelmeisser's compositions, not even in his last opera *Melusine* (1861). They are, rather, in the style of the older Romantic operatic tradition of Weber and Spohr, though frequently their artless conglomeration of naive dramatic effects and routine orchestration testifies to the decaying state of that tradition.

Mathilde (grosse heroische Oper, 3, K. Pichler), Innsbruck, 19 Oct 1834
Die zehn glücklichen Tage (romantische Oper, 4, J. Schuller), Graz, Nov 1835
Die Giftmischerin, oder Die Marquise von Brinvilliers (3, F. Genée), Pest, Deutsches, Sept 1838
Peter von Szapáry (3), Pest, Deutsches, 8 Aug 1839
Malwina (romantische Oper, 4, Uffer), Pest, Deutsches, 20 Dec 1841
Der Rächer (heroische romantische Oper, 3, O. Prechtler, after P. Corneille: *Le Cid*), Pest, Deutsches, 4 April 1846
Melusine (romantische Oper, 4, E. Pasqué), Darmstadt, Grossherzogliches Hof, 29 Dec 1861 (Berlin, n.d.)

*

StiegerO
Obituary, *Niederrheinische Musikzeitung*, xii (1864), 127
H. Dorn: *Ergebnisse aus Erlebnissen* (Berlin, 1877)
W. Weissheimer: *Erlebnisse mit Richard Wagner, Franz Liszt und vielen anderen Zeitgenossen nebst deren Briefen* (Stuttgart, 1898)
O. Dorn: 'Das Wiesbadener Theaterorchester und seine Dirigenten', *Die Musik*, ii/4 (1902–3), 179–85 KLAUS RÖNNAU

Schindler, Povl Christian (*b* Copenhagen, 1648; *d* Copenhagen, 1740). Danish composer. After training at

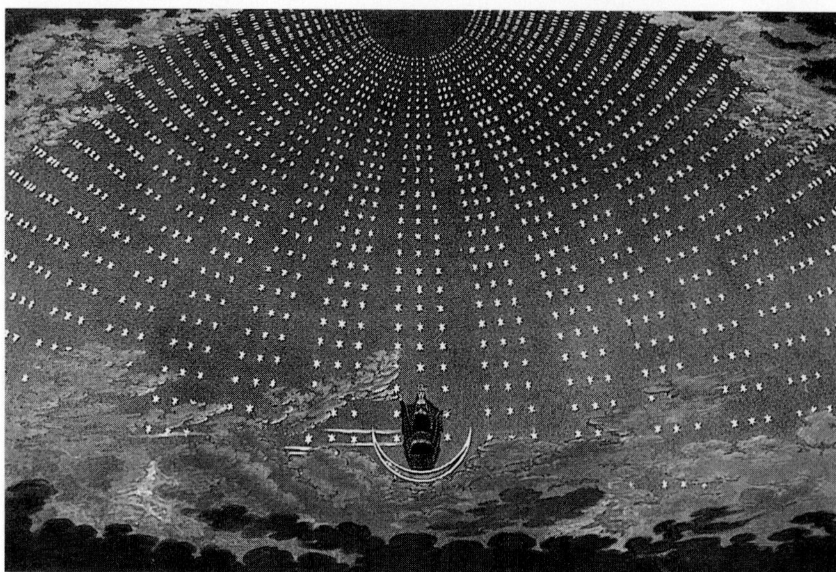

Design by Karl Friedrich Schinkel for the Queen of Night scene in Act 1 of Mozart's 'Die Zauberflöte' in the production by the Berlin Royal Opera, 1816

the court of Gottorf and in Dresden, he returned to Denmark and became a court musician to Christian V in 1674. Though appointed a viola da gamba player, he was increasingly called upon to compose and thus had responsibility for the musical celebration of Christian V's birthday on 15 April 1689. For this occasion he wrote what is regarded as the first Danish opera (though to a German text), *Der vereinigte Götterstreit*; it was performed in an opera house erected for the occasion as an extension of the queen mother's residence, Sofie Amalienborg Palace.

The music is lost, but from the libretto it seems that *Der vereinigte Götterstreit* was conceived in emulation of the operas produced with such success since 1678 at Hamburg. The text was written by a student at the university, Peter Anton Burchard (*d* 1714), who later became a pastor. It consists of a prologue, in which the homage of the occasion is presented and the dispute on Olympus is revealed in a little pastorale, and four short acts; a comic intermezzo, involving the shepherd and shepherdess Corydon and Phillis, occurs between Acts 2 and 3. The gods violently disagree as to whether the four gods of war (Act 1) or the four of peace (Act 2) shall be the protectors of Christian V. The confrontation (Act 3) continues (Act 4) until Mercury brings Jupiter's judgment that all shall have a share in the Danish king.

So great was the opera's success that it was decided to perform it a second time for a broader public on 19 April. The theatre was festively decorated and soon after the performance had begun, some branches caught fire, spreading the flames rapidly throughout the house. It is reported that within 15 minutes the wooden building had burnt to the ground, killing some 200 people including Schindler's wife and daughter. The fire spread quickly to the palace, which was also destroyed. Such a tragedy understandably discouraged the cause of opera in Denmark for a time, but in 1703 a new opera house of brick and stone was opened as a public theatre and in 1710 a court theatre was built in Copenhagen Castle. The taste was now for Italian opera, however, and Schindler was bypassed as director of music in favour of Bartolomeo Bernardi.

*

C. Thrane: *Fra hofviolonernes tid* (Copenhagen, 1908)

A. Hammerich: *Dansk musikhistorie indtil ca.1700* (Copenhagen, 1921)

N. Schiørring: *Musikkens historie i Danmark*, i (Copenhagen, 1977)

JOHN BERGSAGEL

Schinkel, Karl Friedrich (*b* Neuruppin, 13 March 1781; *d* Berlin, 9 Oct 1841). German architect, stage designer and painter. He moved to Berlin in 1794 and studied architecture under David and Friedrich Gilly, completing his studies in Italy and France (1803–5), where he developed his interest in painting. On returning to Berlin he started to work as a painter of panoramas and dioramas (mainly for the Gropius brothers' establishment), exhibiting monumental views with musical accompaniments, lighting and transparency effects and movable staffage. Count Brühl, Intendant of the royal theatre in Berlin, made Schinkel chief designer (1815–28). As architect and assessor to the Prussian Ministry of Public Buildings from 1810, he also had a definitive influence on theatre construction.

Inspired by philosophical idealism and the pathos of the Wars of Liberation against Napoleon, Schinkel aimed at creating a kind of theatre which would educate and purify the public. This didactic end required that the same degree of participation should be experienced by each member of an audience, and that the stage should be visible from all points of the auditorium, which was not possible with the traditional proscenium arch and wings. He envisaged sets consisting of nothing more than a monumental view on a backcloth, like a panorama or diorama, thus reduced to the 'symbolic background' of the action which would take place in the neutral proscenium area. The orchestra pit should be sunk for optical and acoustic reasons. As the architect of the Berlin Schauspielhaus (1817–21), a royal theatre, Schinkel was unable to realize this 'democratic' ideal, but as a designer for the stage, he put it into practice, partly at least, in the historically accurate, formally perfect panoramic sets for *Die Zauberflöte* (1816) and more than 40 other operas, ballets and plays. His stage designs, first published in 1819, had an extraordinary influence on the style of operatic production that followed in Germany. His ideas for the reform of theatrical construction influenced Gottfried Semper and Wagner.

For further illustration *see* BERLIN, fig.4; STAGE DESIGN, fig.12 and *UNDINE* (i).

*

ES (G. Schöne)
Decorationen auf den beiden königlichen Theatern in Berlin (Berlin, 1819–24, rev. 4/1874)
F. Kugler: 'Die Dekorationsmalerei der Bühne und Schinkels Entwürfe', *Deutsches Kunstblatt*, vi (1855), 101–05; also in *Zeitschrift für Bauwesen*, xv (1855), 396–406
A. von Wolzogen: *Aus Schinkels Nachlass* (Berlin, 1862–4)
P. Mahlberg: *Schinkels Theaterdekorationen* (diss., U. of Greifswald, 1916)
L. Nusser: *Schinkel und Brückner in ihrer Bedeutung für die Bühnenmalerei im 19. Jahrhundert* (diss., U. of Würzburg, 1922)
F. B. Biermann: *Die Pläne für die Reform des Theaterbaues bei K. F. Schinkel und G. Semper* (Berlin, 1928)
P. O. Rave: *Karl Friedrich Schinkel* (Berlin, 1935) [bibliography]
——: *Schinkel: Berlin*, i: *Bauten für die Kunst, Kirchen, Denkmalpflege* (Berlin, 1941), 79ff
G. Schöne: 'Trois mises en scène de "La flûte enchantée" de Mozart: Berlin 1816, Weimar 1817 et Munich 1818', *Anatomy of an Illusion: 4th International Congress on Theatre Research: Amsterdam 1965*, 45–9
M. Boetzkes: 'K. F. Schinkel', *The Age of Neo-Classicism* (London, 1972), 623–4, 946–9 [exhibition catalogue]
H. G. Pundt: *Schinkel's Berlin* (Cambridge, MA, 1972)
T. Eggeling: 'Bühnendekorationen nach 1815: die kunstgeschichtliche Stellung der Bühnendekorationen Schinkels', *Karl Friedrich Schinkel: Architektur, Malerei, Kunstgewerbe* (Berlin, 1981), 269–89
C. Blechen: 'Der Bühnenbildner' *Du*, xl (1981), 46–51
F. Chaslin: 'Schinkel, architecte d'opéra', *Feuilles*, ix (1984), 77–81

MANFRED BOETZKES

Schiøtz, Aksel (Hauch) (*b* Roskilde, 1 Sept 1906; *d* Copenhagen, 19 April 1975). Danish tenor. He studied in Copenhagen and with John Forsell. He made his début in 1939 at the Royal Opera, Copenhagen, as Mozart's Ferrando; the next year he sang the title role of *Faust* and Sverkel in Hartmann's *Liden Kirsten*. In 1946 he shared the role of Male Chorus with Peter Pears in the first performances of *The Rape of Lucretia* at Glyndebourne. After retiring he taught in Minnesota, Toronto, Colorado and Copenhagen. A fine Mozart singer, he had a voice of silvery quality, which he used with elegance and feeling. He wrote a book on singing, *The Singer and his Art* (New York, 1969), and made many recordings.

*

H. Rosenberg: 'Aksel Schiøtz', *Nationale diskotek katalog* (Copenhagen, 1966), no.6 [discography]

ALAN BLYTH

Tito Schipa as Des Grieux in Massenet's 'Manon'

Schipa, Tito [Raffaele Attilio Amadeo] (*b* Lecce, 2 Jan 1888; *d* New York, 16 Dec 1965). Italian tenor, the outstanding *tenore di grazia* of his generation. He made his début in 1910 in *La traviata* at Vercelli, and by the 1915–16 season had reached La Scala in *Prince Igor* and *Manon*. He soon began to specialize in the lighter and more lyrical roles, and in 1917 became the first Ruggero in Puccini's *La rondine* at Monte Carlo. His beautiful, flexible voice was at its peak during his years in America: in Chicago from 1919 until 1932, and for the three following seasons (and during one later one, in 1941) at the Metropolitan. During the 1930s he sang regularly at La Scala, and in later years frequently in Rome, concentrating increasingly on a central repertory consisting of the lighter and more graceful Italian roles and on a smaller French group including the romantic heroes of *Lakmé*, *Mignon*, *Manon* and *Werther*. His attractive voice, so well produced as to carry with ease in large theatres, was employed with exquisite skill and taste. His refined musical phrasing and clear enunciation are well displayed in his numerous recordings, which include a complete performance of Donizetti's *Don Pasquale*. He wrote an operetta, *La Principessa Liana* (3, A. Santoro and E. Neri; Rome, Adriano, 2 June 1929), and several songs.

*

GV (R. Celletti; R. Vegeto)
T. Hutchinson and S. Winstanley: 'Tito Schipa', *Record Collector*, xiii (1960–61), 77–109 [with discography]
T. Schipa: *Si confessa* (Genoa, 1961) [with discography]

DESMOND SHAWE-TAYLOR

Schipper, Emil (Zacharias) (*b* Vienna, 19 Aug 1882; *d* Vienna, 20 July 1957). Austrian baritone. He studied in Milan, then made his début in 1904 at the Neues Deutsches Theater, Prague, as Telramund. After engagements at Linz, the Vienna Volksoper and the Vienna Hofoper, in 1916 he joined the Munich Hofoper, where he remained until 1922; he then returned to the Vienna Staatsoper until 1938 and was made an Austrian *Kammersänger*. In Munich he sang Meister Florian in the 1920 revised version of *Das Spielwerk und die Prinzessin* and Barak in the first performance there of *Die Frau ohne Schatten*. He appeared regularly at Covent Garden (1924–8) as the Dutchman, Kurwenal, Hans Sachs, Wotan, Telramund, John the Baptist and Amonasro, in Chicago (1928–9) and at the Teatro Colón. Schipper sang Agamemnon in *Iphigénie en Aulide* at the 1930 Salzburg Festival and returned there in 1935–6 as Kurwenal. He also made guest appearances in France, the Netherlands, Spain and Belgium. His voice was powerful and dramatic, but he did not always use it with subtlety. He married the mezzo-contralto Maria Olczewska.

*

Obituary, *Record News* [Toronto], ii (1957–8), 33–5 [with discography]

HAROLD ROSENTHAL/R

Schippers, Thomas (*b* Kalamazoo, MI, 9 March 1930; *d* New York, 16 Dec 1977). American conductor. After studying at the Curtis Institute, Philadelphia, and privately with Olga Samaroff, he made his professional conducting début in 1948 with the Lemonade Opera Company in New York. In 1950 he became conductor of Menotti's *The Consul* shortly after its première, beginning an association with the composer that continued with Schippers's appointment as music director of Menotti's Festival of Two Worlds at Spoleto, where his impassioned but natural, fluent performances became increasingly admired. He joined the staff of the New York City Opera in 1951, and in 1955 made débuts at the Metropolitan and at La Scala. In 1963 he conducted the new production of *Die Meistersinger* at Bayreuth. Having established himself as a young American opera conductor of international stature, he was a natural choice to conduct the première of Barber's *Antony and Cleopatra* when the Metropolitan opened its new house at Lincoln Center in September 1966. A vigorous interpreter, Schippers was probably best known for his work in the Romantic repertory.

BERNARD JACOBSON

Schira, Francesco (*b* Malta, 21 Aug 1809; *d* London, 15 Oct 1883). Italian composer, conductor and singing teacher. He studied under Basili at the Milan Conservatory. At 23 he was commissioned by La Scala to write an opera, *Elena e Malvina* (1832), which was well received. He held appointments at the S Carlos Theatre and the conservatory in Lisbon and became director of music at the newly opened Princess's Theatre, London, in 1842. From 1843 to 1848 he conducted seasons under Alfred Bunn's management at Covent Garden and Drury Lane. His opera *Kenilworth* (1848), after Scott, was rehearsed but not produced; *Mina* (1849) and *Thérèse, or The Orphan of Geneva* (1850), produced at the Princess's Theatre, were well received.

Schira conducted Bunn's 1852 season at Drury Lane, but thereafter taught singing (his most famous pupil was Louisa Pyne), while continuing to compose. His opera *Niccolò de' Lapi* was given at Her Majesty's Theatre in 1863; in 1875 he achieved his greatest success with *Selvaggia* at Venice, but after *Lia* the following year he composed no more. He was totally opposed to any style other than the Italian, which led the *Musical Times* to declare, on his death, that 'his music suffered mainly from the disadvantage of being out of fashion'. He was awarded the title Commendatore by Humbert I. Despite his narrow musical tastes, Schira was, after Verdi, one of the outstanding Italian opera composers of his generation. Arditi, who conducted the première of *Niccolò de' Lapi*, justly described the work as 'a patriotic opera ... written in the genuine Italian style ... fervid, melodious, and free from pretence or assumption'. *Selvaggia*, his masterpiece, is even more powerful: its through-composed texture sustains a consistent dramatic tension which clearly foreshadows the methods of Puccini, and the climax of the second act is a *coup de théâtre* of such brilliance that it, alone, justifies the opera's revival.

Elena e Malvina (melodramma, 3, F. Romani), Milan, Scala, 17 Nov 1832
Il fanatico per la musica (ob, 2, G. Rossi), Lisbon, S Carlos, sum. 1835
Os cavalleiros de Valenca [I cavalieri di Valenza, ossia Isabella di Lara] (melodramma tragico, 2, Rossi), Lisbon, S Carlos, 22 Sept 1836
Kenilworth (os, Schira, after W. Scott), 1848, unperf.
Mina (romantic op, 2, W. Morris and G. Linley), London, Princess's, 8 Dec 1849
Thérèse, or The Orphan of Geneva (romantic op, 3, C. Jefferys), London, Princess's, 26 April 1850, vs (London, 1851)
Niccolò de' Lapi, ossia L'assedio di Firenze (dramma lirico, 4, S.M. Maggioni), London, Her Majesty's, 7 May 1863, vs (London, 1864)
Alina (2), London, St George's Hall, 7 April 1871
The Ear-Ring (operetta, 1, D. L. Ryan), London, St George's Hall, 21 May 1872, vs (London, 1873)
Selvaggia (dramma lirico, prol., 3, G. T. Cimino), Venice, Fenice, 20 Feb 1875, vs (Milan, 1875)
Lia (dramma lirico, 3, M. M. Marcello), Venice, Fenice, 25 March 1876

*

LoewenbergA; *StiegerO*
C. L. Kenney: *Memoir of Michael William Balfe* (London, 1875), 178
W. A. Barrett: *Balfe: his Life and Work* (London, 1882), 189
Obituary, *MT*, xxiv (1883), 612
L. Arditi: *My Reminiscences* (London, 1896), 123–4
J. W. Davison: *From Mendelssohn to Wagner* (London, 1912), 440
H. Rosenthal: *Two Centuries of Opera at Covent Garden* (London, 1958), 61, 80, 142

NIGEL BURTON, KEITH HORNER

Schiuma, Alfredo Luis (*b* Spinazzola, 21 June 1885; *d* Buenos Aires, 23 July 1963). Argentine composer and conductor. Born in Italy, he was taken as a child to Argentina, where he received his musical training and developed his professional career. Many other members of his family were active in music in Buenos Aires. He wrote a number of italianate operas which were first performed in the city: *Biancafiore* (1915), *Amy Robsart* (1920) and *La sirocchia* (1922, produced later in Spanish as *Litigio de amor*). In 1925 his most successful opera, *Tabaré*, based on the poem of the same name by José Zorrilla de San Martín, received its première at the Colón. Set during the period of the Spanish conquest, it contains reminiscences of Argentine folk music. In 1939 his other work in Spanish, *Las vírgines del sol*, was performed at the Colón. (Its libretto was also set to music at the same time by another Argentine, E. M. Casella). *El manto mágico*, a comic opera in three acts, was not performed.

Schiuma was also active as a conductor: he founded the Teatro Lírico Argentino (*c*1930) to promote operas by native composers, many of which received their first performances there (for example Casella's *Latapera*, 1934).

all premières in Buenos Aires

Biancafiore (2, A. Magno), Politeama Argentino, 8 Jan 1915
Amy Robsart (4, after W. Scott), Coliseo, 24 April 1920
La sirocchia (comedia lírica, 1, Magno), Odeón, 23 April 1922; as Litigio de amor, Colón, 15 Sept 1932
Tabaré (3, J. Servetti Reeves, after J. Zorrilla de San Martín), Colón, 6 Aug 1925
Las vírgenes del sol (3, A. Herrera), Colón, 9 June 1939
El manto mágico, *c*1949 (ópera cómica, 3), unperf.

*

M. García Acevedo: *La música argentina contemporánea* (Buenos Aires, 1963)

JUAN MARÍA VENIARD

Schjelderup, Gerhard (Rosenkrone) (*b* Kristiansand, 17 Nov 1859; *d* Benediktbeuren, 29 July 1933). Norwegian composer. In 1878 he went to Paris, where he studied composition with Massenet. Thereafter he was active principally in Germany, serving as a professor in Dresden and Munich. The most decisive influence on him was a performance of the *Ring* at Karlsruhe in 1887. From that time he saw music drama as his life's work, although his stated objectives were different from those of Wagner: 'I am constantly seeking something nearer to us, something more intimate than Wagner's gods and heroes ... I will try not only to give the outward appearance of reality ... but, so to speak, to open humanity's heart and reveal the riches which often hide behind the simplest exterior'. He had neither Wagner's feeling for drama nor his sense of line; the strength of his operas lies rather in their detailed characterization and fine lyrical atmosphere. Most of them were composed to his own texts and their principal theme is the victory of ideal love. His harmony is complex and mainly local in its effects; thorough working of motivic material can sometimes make the forms a little obscure; and the instrumentation, while it has many good details, tends to be too full. His writings include *Richard Wagner: hans liv og verker* (Copenhagen, 1907, 2/1913).

Østenfor sol og vestenfor måne [East of the Sun and West of the Moon], Act 1, Munich, 1890
Sampo Lappelill, begun 1890, unperf.
Sonntagsmorgen, Munich, 1893
Norwegische Hochzeit [Bruderovet (The Abduction)], 1894, Prague, 1900
En hellig aften [A Holy Evening], 1895, Oslo, 1915
Et folk i nød [A People in Need], unperf.
Vaarnat [Spring Night], Dresden, 1908; rev. as Stjernenaetter [Starry Nights]
Opal, Dresden, 1915
Die scharlachrote Blume (after Baroness Orczy: *The Scarlet Pimpernel*), unperf.
Sturmvögel, Schwerin, 1926

*

W. Altmann: 'Gerhard Schjelderup im heutigen Musikbetrieb', *ZfM*, Jg.100 (1933), 317–27
I. E. Kindem: *Den norske operas historie* (Oslo, 1941)
O. M. Sandvik: 'Gerhard Schjelderup (1859–1933)', *SMz*, lxxxviii (1948), 383–6
G. Schjelderup: *Gerhard Schjelderup: en norsk operakomponists liv og virke* (Oslo, 1976) KARI MICHELSEN

Schlemm, Anny (*b* Neu-Isenburg, 22 Feb 1929). German soprano, later mezzo-soprano. She studied in Berlin and made her début in 1946 at Halle; in 1949 she was engaged at the Berlin Staatsoper. She also appeared in Cologne, Frankfurt, Munich, Hamburg, Stuttgart, Düsseldorf, and at Glyndebourne, where she sang Zerlina in 1954. During this period her repertory included Susanna, Donna Elvira, Desdemona, Mařenka, Berlioz's Marguerite, Giorgetta, Manon Lescaut, Octavian, the Marschallin, Arabella and Boulotte, which she sang in Felsenstein's production of *Barbe-Bleue* at the Komische Oper (1963). Later, as her voice darkened, she became a famous exponent of Clytemnestra, Herodias, the Innkeeper (*Boris Godunov*), the Kostelnička and Kabanicha. At Bayreuth (1978–86) she sang Mary (*Der fliegende Holländer*). A superb singing-actress, she was equally effective as Métella (*La vie parisienne*), Mrs Peachum or Madelon (*Andrea Chénier*), which she sang at Covent Garden (1984). ELIZABETH FORBES

Schlesinger, John (Richard) (*b* London, 16 Feb 1926). English director. Educated at Oxford, he began his career as a film actor. He then turned to directing, making several documentaries for television and some celebrated feature films. As associate director at the National Theatre, London, he produced Shaw's *Heartbreak House* (1975). His first opera production was of *Les contes d'Hoffmann* (1980), followed by *Der Rosenkavalier* (1984), both at Covent Garden. His *Ballo* at Salzburg in 1989, given in the original Stockholm setting, was criticized for putting more faith in spectacle and extravagant display than in the work's dramaturgy. BARRY MILLINGTON

Schlosser, Max [Karl] (*b* Amberg, Bavaria, 17 Oct 1835; *d* Utting am Ammersee, 2 Sept 1916). German tenor. After singing in Zürich, St Gallen and Augsburg, in 1868 he was engaged at the Hofoper, Munich, where he remained until 1904. He sang David in the first performance of *Die Meistersinger* (1868) and Mime in the first performance of *Das Rheingold* (1869). He also sang Mime in *Siegfried* at Bayreuth in the first complete *Ring* cycle (1876). In 1882 he accompanied Angelo Neumann's Wagner tour of Europe, singing Mime in the first London performance of the *Ring*, at Her Majesty's Theatre. His repertory included Almaviva (*Barbiere*), Tonio (*La fille du régiment*), Lyonel (*Martha*) and Max (*Der Freischütz*). Towards the end of his career he sang baritone roles, including Beckmesser and the Nightwatchman (*Die Meistersinger*), which he sang at his farewell performance in Munich, in his 70th year.
ELIZABETH FORBES

Schlusnus, Heinrich (*b* Braubach, 6 Aug 1888; *d* Frankfurt am Main, 18 June 1952). German baritone. He trained as a postal official but also studied singing in Frankfurt and made a successful début at Hamburg in 1915 as the Herald in *Lohengrin*. He sang at the Nuremberg Staadttheater (1915–17), then at the Berlin Staatsoper (1917–45), becoming their leading Verdi baritone. In 1932 he sang Guy de Montfort at the Berlin première of *Les vêpres siciliennes*. He toured extensively, to Amsterdam (1919), Barcelona (1922), Chicago (Wolfram, 1927) and Bayreuth (Amfortas, 1933). His voice, particularly easy in the high register, was steady and smooth, his style economical. Besides excelling in opera he was an outstanding lieder singer. His recordings are extensive.

*

E. von Naso and A. Schlusnus: *Heinrich Schlusnus, Mensch und Sänger* (Hamburg, 1957)
E. Csan and A. G. Ross: 'A Schlusnus Discography', *Record News* [Toronto], iii (1958–9), 164–81, 196–206, 319–24, 402–5; iv (1959–60), 136–40
S. Smolian: 'Heinrich Schlusnus: a Discography', *British Institute of Recorded Sound Bulletin* (1959), no.14, pp.5–24; (1960), no.15–16, pp.16–26
J. B. Steane: *The Grand Tradition* (London, 1974), 213–14
CARL L. BRUUN/R

Schlüter, Erna (*b* Oldenburg, 5 Feb 1904; *d* Hamburg, 1 Dec 1969). German soprano. She sang as a contralto at Mannheim and Düsseldorf between 1925 and 1939; her roles included Lady Macbeth, Fricka, Azucena and Ortrud. She sang Brünnhilde at Frankfurt in 1936 and by 1940 had graduated to the dramatic soprano repertory. At Hamburg, where she sang from 1944 to 1956, she was Ellen Orford in the first German performance of *Peter Grimes*. Performances at the Wagner festival at Zoppot (1939–42) were followed by Leonore (*Fidelio*) at the 1948 Salzburg Festival. She took part in the Strauss Festival organized by Beecham in London in 1947 and sang Electra under Erich Kleiber at Covent Garden in the same year. Her only Metropolitan appearances were as Isolde and the Marschallin in the 1947–8 season. DAVID CUMMINGS

Schmedes, Erik (*b* Gentofte, nr Copenhagen, 27 Aug 1866; *d* Vienna, 23 March 1931). Danish tenor. He studied in Berlin and Paris and made a brilliant baritone début as the Herald in *Lohengrin* at Wiesbaden in 1891. From 1894 to 1897 he was engaged at Dresden. In 1898 he made his tenor début in Vienna as Siegfried; he remained there until 1924 and was the first Viennese Pedro (*Tiefland*), Parsifal, Palestrina (Pfitzner) and Herod. In 1899 he sang Siegfried and Parsifal at Bayreuth, returning there for several years until 1906. He appeared at the Metropolitan for the 1908–9 season, making his début as Siegmund and also singing Siegfried, Pedro, Tristan and Parsifal. His voice was of pleasing quality, rather declamatory in style, and he was an excellent actor.

*

GV [with discography by R. Vegeto] CARL L. BRUUN/R

Schmid, Adolf. *See* MÜLLER, ADOLF.

Schmidt, Franz (*b* Pressburg [now Bratislava], 22 Dec 1874; *d* Perchtoldsdorf, nr Vienna, 11 Feb 1939). Austrian composer. Mainly self-taught as a pianist and composer, he studied briefly with Bruckner, Robert Fuchs and Ferdinand Hellmesberger at the Vienna conservatory. While working as a cellist in the Vienna Hofoper orchestra (1896–1911) he taught the cello at the conservatory of the Gesellschaft der Musikfreunde (1901–9). In 1914 he was appointed professor of piano at the Vienna Staatsakademie, serving as its director from 1925 until 1927 when he succeeded Joseph Marx as a director of the Musikhochschule; he retired in 1937, owing to failing health.

His compositions, which include four symphonies, chamber and organ music and the oratorio *Das Buch mit sieben Siegeln* (composed 1935–7 and first staged at the 1987 Salzburg Festival), show sensitive melodic invention and reveal the influence of Bruckner, Mahler, Reger, Schoenberg and Debussy. Romanticism, expressionism and atonality can all be found in his music. In his first opera, *Notre Dame* (1902–4; 2, L. Wilk and F. Schmidt, after V. Hugo; Vienna, Staatsoper, 1 April 1914), the stylized gypsy theme of the main character Esmeralda (soprano) typifies his predilection for a full orchestral sound. The work brought Schmidt international fame although its *verismo* style is not characteristic of his output. An immensely better opera, with distinctive counterpoint is *Fredigundis* (1916–21; B. Hardt-Warden and I. M. Welleminsky, after F. Dahn; Berlin, Preussische Staatsoper, 19 Dec 1922), an enthralling historic story of old France concerning the wicked Merovingian queen Fredigundis (soprano). The work was not so well received, however. Richard Strauss noted scornfully: 'It is indeed not necessary for a composer to make his job so difficult', continuing that he could have written four operas with the thematic inventions of *Fredigundis*. In the last few years Schmidt's works have seen a renaissance in concert performances and recordings.

*

J. Korngold: *Deutsches Opernschaffen der Gegenwart* (Vienna and Leipzig, 1922)
C. Nemuth: *Franz Schmidt: ein Meister nach Brahms und Bruckner* (Vienna, 1957)
N. Tschulik: *Franz Schmidt* (Vienna, 1972)
H. Herrmann: 'Franz Schmidts Harmonik', *ÖMz*, xxix (1974), 534–40 PETER P. PACHL

Schmidt, Giovanni (Federico) (*b* Livorno, *c*1775; *d* Naples, after 1840). Italian librettist. Schmidt settled early in Naples, remaining there for the rest of his life. Between 1800 and 1840 he wrote some 45 librettos, nearly all of them for the S Carlo, where he was employed as a poet. With Tottola, he dominated the writing of librettos in Naples in the first quarter of the 19th century, for which he has received a deservedly bad press; his librettos were prolix, pedestrian and cliché-ridden. He is best remembered for his four librettos for Rossini (two of which had previously been set by Pavesi), and as a translator, notably of Spontini's *La vestale*. Pacini described him as 'a man of some talent', adding that 'misery was his constant companion, so that his personality, distressing beyond description, inspired melancholy just on seeing him'.

dgm – *dramma giocoso per musica* dm – *dramma per musica*
dssm – *dramma semiserio per musica*

Idante (dm), Portogallo, 1800; *Gli americani* (dm), Tritto, 1802 (Pacini, 1825, as Amazilia); *Piramo e Tisbe* (dm), Andreozzi, 1803; *Leonora* (dssm), Paer, 1804; *Cesare in Egitto* (dm), Tritto, 1805; *Sofonisba* (dramma serio per musica), Paer, 1805; *Andromeda* (dramma mitologico), Trento, 1805; *Elisabetta regina d'Inghilterra*, Pavesi, 1809 (Rossini, 1815); *Odoardo e Cristina* (dm), Pavesi, 1810 (Rossini, 1819, as Eduardo e Cristina); *Il salto di Leucade* (melodramma tragico), L. Mosca, 1812; *Ecuba* (tragedia per musica), N. A. Manfroce, 1812

Marco Curzio (melodramma tragico), Capotorti, 1813; *La lavandara* (dramma giocoso), Raimondi, 1813; *L'affricano generoso* (dssm), Valentino Fioravanti, 1814; *Manfredi*, Manfroce, 1816; *Armida* (dm), Rossini, 1817; *Adelaide di Borgogna* (dm), Rossini, 1817; *Trajano*, D. Tritto, 1818; *L'apoteosi d'Ercole* (dm), Mercadante, 1819; *Anacreonte in Samo* (dm), Mercadante, 1820; *Lo sposo di provincia* (commedia per musica), Cordella, 1821; *La sposa indiana* (dm), Generali, 1822; *Anco Marzio* (dm), Pavesi, 1822; *Argene ed Alsindo* (dm), Generali, 1822

I cavalieri del nodo (dm), Pavesi, 1823; *L'amante virtuoso* (dgm), G. Balducci, 1823; *Argia* (componimento drammatico), Raimondi, 1823; *Rodrigo* (dm), A. Sapienza, 1823; *Le nozze de' Sanniti* (dm), Raimondi, 1824; *Alessandro nelle Indie* (dm), Pacini, 1824; *Pompeo in Siria* (dm), F. Sampieri, 1825; *Elvida* (dm), Donizetti, 1826; *Meleagro* (dramma tragico per musica), D. Pagliani-Gagliardi, 1826; *Dev'esser uno e sono quattro* (dgm), G. Festa, 1827; *Osmano pascià d'Egitto* (dssm), G. Magagnini, 1828

Malvina (dm), M. Costa, 1829; *Leonilda* (dramma serio per musica), M. Salvioni, 1830; *Ernesto e Zelinda* (dssm), Pagliani-Gagliardi, 1832; *Il tutore e il diavolo* (dgm), P. Bona, 1832; *La tragedia buffa* (dgm), G. A. Speranza, 1833; *La fedeltà alla prova* (dgm), P. Mandanici, 1835; *Alfonso d'Aragona* (azione melodrammatica), various, 1835; *Il dono a Partenope* (azione melodrammatica), various, 1840; *Le nozze campestri* (dm), various, 1841; *Il dono a Pallade* (azione melodrammatica), various, 1852

*

G. Pacini: *Le mie memorie artistiche* (Florence, 1865)

JOHN BLACK

Schmidt, Gustav (*b* Weimar, 1 Sept 1816; *d* Darmstadt, 11 Feb 1882). German conductor and composer. He studied in Weimar under Hummel, Eberwein and Lobe, and in Leipzig with Mendelssohn. He conducted at the theatre in Brünn (now Brno; 1841–4), then in Würzburg (1845), Frankfurt (1846), Wiesbaden (1849), Frankfurt (1851–61), Leipzig (1864–76) and Mainz. He finally became court Kapellmeister in Darmstadt in 1876. His operas (for some of which he wrote his own texts) include the successful *Prinz Eugen* (1847) and *Die Weiber von Weinsberg* (1858). Much admired as a conductor, he was an early champion of Wagner and introduced *Tannhäuser* and *Lohengrin* to Frankfurt; he also sought to make Berlioz's music better known in Germany. Liszt, who conducted *Die Weiber von Weinsberg* in Weimar, took an interest in his plan for a conference of Kapellmeisters to increase both their artistic standing in music and their musical standards. Schmidt also wrote popular songs and choruses.

Prinz Eugen, der Edle Ritter (3, Schmidt and A. Rost), Frankfurt, 27 July 1847
Loreley die Rheinnixe (romantische komische Oper), Mainz, 8 Dec 1851
Die Weiber von Weinsberg, oder Weibertreue (komisch-romantische Oper, 3, Schmidt), Frankfurt, 16 Feb 1858 (Frankfurt, ?1860)
La Réole (3, C. Birch-Pfeiffer), Breslau, 24 Jan 1863, vs (Berlin and Posen, ?1865)
Alibi, oder Die Fahrt ins Philisterium (komische Operette, 3), Darmstadt, Hof, 1 Feb 1880, vs (Hamburg, 1880)

*

StiegerO JOHN WARRACK

Schmidt, Heinrich (*b* Lübeck, 1809; *d* Leipzig, 1854). German tenor. He studied in Vienna, making his début in 1830 as Don Ottavio at Brunswick. After singing at Kassel and Breslau (now Wrocław) he was engaged at Leipzig (1838–54) until an accident cut short his career. There he created Görg in Lortzing's *Hans Sachs* (1840) and Baron Kronthal in *Der Wildschütz* (1842). He also sang Rossini's Otello, Auber's Fra Diavolo, Chapelou in *Le postillon de Lonjumeau* and Eléazar in *La Juive*, roles which displayed the brilliant top register of his powerful voice. ELIZABETH FORBES

Schmidt, Johann Christoph. *See* SMITH, JOHN CHRISTOPHER.

Schmidt, Johann Philipp Samuel (*b* Königsberg, 8 Sept 1779; *d* Berlin, 9 May 1853). German composer. He made some early appearances as a pianist, including in his own works, before studying law in Königsberg. He then travelled extensively in Germany, settling briefly in Berlin as a pupil of J. G. Naumann, and eventually returning there to work in a government post. At the same time he wrote songs for the *Liedertafel*founded there by Zelter and soon resumed his musical career, performing in public and writing essays on music as well as composing operas and other works.

Schmidt's operas and Singspiels are of a popular nature, in what has been described as a light and melodically attractive post-Mozartian style displaying Biedermeier sensibilities (Härtwig). One of the most popular was *Das Fischermädchen*, which Weber, in an essay written before he conducted the Dresden première in 1818, praised for its musical characterization, among other things. *Das verborgene Fenster* was described by Zelter in a letter to the composer as pleasant and cheerful though somewhat lacking in depth and permanence.

Das Dankopfer, oder Die gestiftete Eintracht (Prolog, C. Steinberg), Königsberg, 1796
Der Schlaftrunk (komische Oper, C. Bretzner), Königsberg, Interims, 1797
Das ländliche Fest (Prolog, L. von Baczko), Königsberg, 1798
Der Onkel (operetta, K. Herklots), Königsberg, Interims, 1804
Eulenspiegel (Posse, 1, A. von Kotzebue), Berlin, Königstädtliches, 19 Sept 1806
Der blinde Gärtner, oder Die blühende Aloë (Liederspiel, 1, Kotzebue), Danzig, 1810
Feodore (Spl, 1, Kotzebue), Berlin, Königliche, 12 June 1812
Die Alpenhütte (Spl, 1, Kotzebue), Berlin, Königliche, 28 Aug 1816
Der Kyffhäuserberg (Volksmärchen mit Gesang, 1, Kotzebue), Berlin, Königliche, 18 June 1817
Das Fischermädchen, oder Hass und Liebe (lyrisches Drama, 1, T. Körner), Leipzig, 5 Aug 1818
Das verborgene Fenster, oder Ein Abend in Madrid (Spl, 3, L. Tenelli), Berlin, Königliche, 4 Feb 1824
Alfred der Grosse, König von England (2, Körner), Berlin, Königliche, 28 Nov 1830
Die Doppelflucht (Spl, 3), Berlin, 1836

*

MGG (D. Härtwig); *StiegerO*
G. Kaiser, ed.: *Sämtliche Schriften von Carl Maria von Weber* (Berlin and Leipzig, 1908), 305, 396
S. Goslich: *Die deutsche romantische Oper* (Tutzing, 1975)
JOHN WARRACK

Schmidt, Trudeliese (*b* Saarbrücken, 7 Nov 1934). German mezzo-soprano. She began a commercial career before taking up singing studies with Hans Richrath in Saarbrücken, and later in Rome, and made her stage début at the Saarbrücken Landestheater in 1965. In 1967 she joined the Deutsche Oper am Rhein, Düsseldorf, where she specialized in trouser roles (Cherubino, Octavian, Siébel, Orlofsky) and played Dorabella and Suzuki, making her British début with that company at the 1972 Edinburgh Festival. The next year she toured with the Bavarian Staatsoper in Japan. She made débuts in 1974 at the Vienna Staatsoper as Octavian and Covent Garden as Cherubino, in 1975 at Bayreuth in the *Ring*, and in 1976 at Glyndebourne as Dorabella. Other engagements took her to the Salzburg and Holland Festivals, Moscow and Leningrad. A singing actress of grace and spirit, she has made numerous recordings, adding to some of the roles already mentioned others in *Dido and Aeneas*, *Mathis der Maler*, *Der Barbier von Bagdad* and Janáček's *Cunning Little Vixen*. NOËL GOODWIN

Schmidt-Isserstedt, Hans (*b* Berlin, 5 May 1900; *d* Holm-Holstein, nr Hamburg, 28 May 1973). German conductor and composer. He studied in Berlin at the Musikhochschule and at the university where he wrote a dissertation on the Italian influences on instrumentation in Mozart's early operas. After engagements at various German theatres, he was appointed principal Kapellmeister at the Hamburg Staatsoper in 1935, and in 1943 opera director at the Deutsche Oper in Berlin, where he became general music director in 1944. As a guest conductor he gave memorable performances of *Le nozze di Figaro* at Glyndebourne (1958) and of *Tristan und Isolde* at Covent Garden (1962).

Schmidt-Isserstedt aimed at a transparent orchestral texture and strict rhythmic precision, rejecting all superfluous gestures and mannerisms. After World War II he became the advocate of Bartók, Stravinsky and Hindemith, whose music had long been outlawed in Germany, but his chief love was Mozart, whose works he conducted in a remarkably relaxed and delicate way. This is shown particularly by his recordings of *Idomeneo* and *La finta giardiniera*. His own compositions include the opera *Hassan gewinnt*, first performed in Rostock in 1928. HANS CHRISTOPH WORBS

Schmiedt, Siegfried (*b* Suhl, Thuringia, *c*1756; *d* Suhl, 1799). German composer. He was a proofreader for Breitkopf & Härtel in Leipzig, notably of operas by Mozart and Dittersdorf, and briefly ran a music shop there. A charming, unassuming figure among the Rococo song and keyboard composers in Leipzig, he left works that show the influence of both the Berlin lied school and J. A. Hiller's philanthropic, folklike lieder. His two stage works were a historical-allegorical melodrama, *Die Feier des 18. Jahrhunderts* (1, C. F. Schlenkert), one of his best works, and an opera, *Melida*; both works were first performed and published in vocal score at Leipzig, in 1794 and 1797 respectively.
DIETER HÄRTWIG

Schmied von Gent, Der ('The Blacksmith of Ghent'). *Grosse Zauberoper* in three acts by FRANZ SCHREKER to his own libretto after Charles de Coster's 'Smetse Smee' from *Vlämischen Mären*; Berlin, Städtische Oper, 29 October 1932.

Schreker's last opera developed the new style of his *Der singende Teufel* (1928) and reflected ideals set out in his 1932 foreword to *Christophorus*, where he described 'folk-like tunes' effecting 'redemption through absolute music', and envisaged the renewal of opera as traditional theatrical entertainment. The skilful libretto, not without contemporary political overtones, traces the adventures of Smee (baritone), a merry Flemish smith. Reduced to poverty by the slander of his neighbour Slimboek, he seals a pact with the devil for seven years of work and good living. He then loses his wealth, but outwits the messengers of Hell. In Act 3 he dies and journeys to heaven, to be denied entry until St Joseph, finding that Smee's concern for freedom of conscience outweighs his bad deeds, invites him into paradise.

PETER FRANKLIN

Schmittbaur [Schmittbauer], **Joseph Aloys** (*b* Bamberg, 8 Nov 1718; *d* Karlsruhe, 24 Oct 1809). German composer. He received his musical education from the organ builder J. P. Seuffert in Würzburg and was a musician at the Rastatt court from about 1753 until its dissolution in 1771. There he was Konzertmeister in 1762 (leading the orchestra from the harpsichord) and Kapellmeister from 1765. In 1772 he became Konzertmeister at the Karlsruhe court, but in 1775 he went to Cologne as Kapellmeister at the cathedral and director of public concerts. Although his stay was brief, he had a lasting influence on Cologne's musical life through his sacred compositions and through his introduction of modern orchestral methods in the style of the Mannheim school. In 1777 he returned to Karlsruhe as Kapellmeister, where he was also a teacher and maker of glass harmonicas.

Schmittbaur's compositions were highly esteemed in the 1780s, but his pre-Classical style was soon outdated. His earliest dramatic work, the serenata *L'isola disabitata*, shows the influence of Jommelli, who was in Stuttgart after 1753; his *Endymion*, for the wedding of the Crown Prince Karl Ludwig in 1774, reflects the opera reforms of Gluck, whom he knew personally.

L'isola disabitata (serenata, 1, P. Metastasio), Rastatt, 1762
Herkules auf dem Oeta (Vorspiel mit Gesang, 1, J. B. Michaelis), Hanover, Schloss, 4 June 1771 [also attrib. Schlager or Schweitzer]
Lindor und Ismene (Spl, F. J. Soden von Sassanfort), Karlsruhe, 1771, *D-DS*; rev. as Ein Grab in Arkadien, 1779, song in Bibliothek der Grazien, i (Speyer, 1789)
Endymion (Operette/serenata, Metastasio), Karlsruhe, 1774
Schuss von Gänsewitz, oder Betrug aus Liebe (H. F. Möller), Karlsruhe, 3 Jan 1787

*

C. L. Junker: *Zwanzig Komponisten* (Berne, 1776)
L. Schiedermair: 'Die Oper an den badischen Höfen des 17. und 18. Jahrhunderts', *SIMG*, xiv (1912–13), 200, 510–50
K. W. Niemöller: 'Joseph Aloys Schmittbaurs Werke und ihre Würdigung im 18. Jahrhundert', *Festschrift Karl Gustav Fellerer* (Regensburg, 1962), 377–90
——: 'Schmittbaur, Joseph Aloys', *Rheinische Musiker*, ii, ed. K. G. Fellerer (Cologne, 1962), 88–95

KLAUS WOLFGANG NIEMÖLLER

Schmitt-Walter, Karl (*b* Germersheim, 23 Dec 1900; *d* Kreuth, 14 Jan 1985). German baritone. He studied in Munich and Nuremberg, where he made his début in 1921. In the following years he appeared at Oberhausen, Saarbrücken and Dortmund, then from 1929 to 1935 at Wiesbaden. His Berlin début in *Il trovatore* led to a long career with the Staatsoper where he sang in a comprehensive repertory of lyrical roles. He sang Papageno at Salzburg in 1949 and a highly acclaimed Beckmesser at Bayreuth from 1956 to 1961. Guest appearances took him to Vienna, Paris and London, where he appeared as the Count in the first performances in England of *Capriccio*, given by the Bayerische Staatsoper in 1953. He retired from opera in 1964 but continued to give concerts and was for many years a valued teacher. His many recordings show him as a highly accomplished artist in both opera and song. In later years his voice lost some of its steadiness, but before the war he was one of the best lyrical baritones then singing.

J. B. STEANE

Schmuck der Madonna, Der. Opera by Ermanno Wolf-Ferrari; *see* GIOIELLI DELLA MADONNA, I.

Schnaut, Gabriele (*b* Mannheim, 1953). German mezzo-soprano, later soprano. She studied in Frankfurt and Berlin, making her début in 1976 at Stuttgart as a mezzo-soprano. She sang Waltraute (*Die Walküre*) and Second Norn at Bayreuth (1977) and was engaged at Darmstadt (1978) and Mannheim (1980). Her roles during that period included Octavian, Dorabella, Brangäne, Fricka, Carmen and the Nurse (*Die Frau ohne Schatten*). She became a dramatic soprano in 1985 and sang Isolde at Dortmund, Venus and Third Norn at Bayreuth, adding Sieglinde in 1986. She created Ophelia in Rihm's *Die Hamletmaschine* (1987, Mannheim), then made her Covent Garden début in 1988 as Ortrud. She has also sung at Hamburg, Düsseldorf, Cologne (where she sang Brünnhilde in 1990) and Geneva. She made her American début in 1991 at San Francisco as Isolde. Her repertory includes Lady Macbeth, Marie (*Wozzeck*) and Els (Schreker's *Der Schatzgräber*). Although not always under perfect control, her large, penetrating and lustrous voice ensures that her performances are noteworthy.

ELIZABETH FORBES

Schnebel, Dieter (*b* Lahr, 14 March 1930). German composer. He studied music from the age of 12 and attended the Freiburg Musikhochschule, 1949–52. At the University of Tübingen (1952–5) he studied music, philosophy and theology; he was ordained in 1955 and has taught theology. From 1949 he attended the Darmstadt Ferienkurse, where he encountered the music of the post-Webern avant garde. His first published scores, grouped together under the title of *Versuche*, date from his university years; his early music was heavily influenced by Stockhausen (on whose early works he wrote a theoretical study) and, from 1959, by Cage.

Much of Schnebel's subsequent output has been concerned with the relationship between speech and music, and with the production of vocal sounds themselves; explorations began in *Glossolalie* (1959–61) for speaker and instruments and continued through *:!(Madrasha 2)* for three choral groups (1958–68) and the pieces belonging to the *Produktionprozesse* series (1968–75). In these works and in *dt 316* for 12 vocal groups (1956–8), Schnebel incorporated theatrical and gestural elements, and in the series of graphic and verbal scores (such as *ki-no*) that he composed in the 1960s and to which he gave the generic title of 'Meta-musik', he sought to create a kind of scenario that translated musical experience into purely visual terms. From 1978

Scene from Wagner's 'Das Rheingold' at the Metropolitan Opera House, New York, 1988, with sets designed by Günther Schneider-Siemssen

onwards he worked with the experimental theatre group Die Maulwerker, and collaborated with the director and designer Achim Freyer on versions of his *Maulwerke* (1968–74) and *Cage-up*, evening-long presentations of Cage's works. In the 1980s Schnebel continued his experiments in the synthesis of vocal and physical gestures (in *Laut-Gesten-Laute* and *Zeichen-Sprache*); his *Chili*, for three narrators, four singers and instruments (1989–91), bears the subtitle 'Music and pictures on Kleist'. ANDREW CLEMENTS

Schneider, Hortense (**Catherine** [Caroline]-**Jeanne**) (*b* Bordeaux, 30 April 1833; *d* Paris, 6 May 1920). French soprano. She made her début in 1853 at Agen, as Inès in *La favorite*, and first appeared in Paris at the Bouffes-Parisiens in 1855 in a double bill including Offenbach's *Le violoneux*. The following year she sang in Offenbach's *Tromb-al-Cazar* and *La rose de St-Flour* and Adam's *Les pantins de Violette*. She appeared at the Variétés for two seasons and from 1858 to 1864 at the Palais-Royal. She had decided to leave the stage when Offenbach persuaded her to return to the Variétés for *La belle Hélène* (1864); her triumphant success as Helen was equalled by her Boulotte in *Barbe-bleue* (1866) and surpassed in *La Grande-duchesse de Gérolstein* (1867; *see* OPERETTA, fig.2). A visit to London was followed by *La Périchole* (1868) and *La diva* (1869), but the Franco-Prussian War brought to an end the Second Empire and the moral climate in which the great Offenbach operettas had flourished. Schneider sang in St Petersburg (1872) and in Paris for a few more years and then retired. Her voice was small though well projected; she had superb enunciation and was a talented actress.

For further illustration *see* BELLE HÉLÈNE, LA.

*

L. Schneider: *Offenbach* (Paris, 1923)

M. Rouff and T. Casevitz: *Hortense Schneider: la vie de fête sous le Second Empire* (Paris, 1931)

S. Kracauer: *Jacques Offenbach und die Paris seiner Zeit* (Paris, 1937)

E. Forbes: 'Hortense Schneider', *Opera*, xxxii (1981), 1236–42

ELIZABETH FORBES

Schneider, Peter (*b* Vienna, 26 March 1939). Austrian conductor. After singing with the Vienna Boys Choir he studied at the Vienna Akademie für Musik (conducting with Swarowsky). His operatic début was at the Salzburg Landestheater in 1959 (Handel's *Giulio Cesare*). He worked at Heidelberg from 1961 and was first conductor at the Deutsche Oper am Rhein from 1968, directing operas by Wagner, Mozart, Verdi, Berg and Dallapiccola and a complete Janáček cycle. He has appeared regularly at Bayreuth, conducting *Der fliegende Holländer* (1981), then *Lohengrin* (1984) and a *Ring* cycle (1987). He was music director at Mannheim (1985–7), and has conducted opera in London (*Die Zauberflöte*, 1986), Madrid, Berlin, Hamburg and Tokyo (*Der Rosenkavalier* with the company of the Vienna Staatsoper, 1986). He was appointed music director of the Bayerische Staatsoper, Munich, from 1993. DAVID CUMMINGS

Schneider-Siemssen, Günther (*b* Augsburg, 7 June 1926). Austrian scene designer of German birth. He was guided to study scene design by Clemens Krauss, through whom he gained early experience in scene painting at the Staatsoper in Munich, where he studied with Sievert, Preetorius and Rudolf Hartmann. From 1947 to 1954 he designed for theatres and films in Berlin, Munich and Salzburg. In 1952 he began his 20-year association with the Salzburg marionette theatre, eventually revolutionizing the design of the puppet stage and creating several new productions of Mozart operas. In 1954 he was named chief of design at the Bremen Staatstheater, where he designed his first *Ring*. After collaborating with Karajan on *Pelléas et Mélisande* at the Vienna Staatsoper in 1960 he became Karajan's personal adviser on production, moving in 1962 to Vienna where he was appointed chief designer for the Staatsoper, the Burgtheater and the Volksoper. He made his Covent Garden début in 1962 designing Peter Ustinov's production of Schoenberg's *Erwartung*, and then designed the *Ring* directed by Hotter and conducted by Solti (1962–4). With Karajan he worked on numerous productions for the Salzburg festivals including *Boris Godunov* (1965), *Don Giovanni* (1967),

Otello (1969), the *Ring* (1967–70, later given in modified form in New York), *Fidelio* (1971) and *Tristan und Isolde* (1972). He also designed *Le nozze di Figaro* at La Scala in 1973 and *Jenůfa* at the Metropolitan Opera in 1974.

His designs, particularly for Wagner, are outstanding for the epic, cosmic world they create on stage. Light and projection in sweeping, swirling patterns evoke with powerful symbolism a universe that coincides perfectly with the visions of the directors with whom he has most often worked, Karajan, August Everding and Otto Schenk. In 1988 Schneider-Siemssen's second Metropolitan *Ring* was completed. Harking back to the Bayreuth 1897 production, though criticized by some for being over-pretty and reactionary, it created a sensational effect, contrasting with the modern interpretative trend among directors and designers. Schenk's romantic fairy-tale conception was produced using all the stage machinery and lighting equipment available to the modern theatre. The following year Schneider-Siemssen and Everding created an entirely different, modern-dress *Ring* for the Wielki Theatre in Warsaw, the first time the complete cycle had been given in Poland. Among many other notable productions Schneider-Siemssen designed are Dvŏrák's *Armida* (1961), *Palestrina* (1964, Vienna), *La fanciulla del West* (1982, Berlin), *Les contes d'Hoffmann* (1982, Metropolitan) and *Un re in ascolto* (1984, Salzburg).

See also STAGE DESIGN, §7. For further illustration *see* LIGHTING, fig.13.

*

C. Abbate and others: *The Ring at the Metropolitan* (New York, 1988)

PAUL SHEREN

Schnittke, Alfred. *See* SHNITKE, AL'FRED.

Schnitzer, Ignaz (*b* Pest, 20 Dec 1839; *d* Vienna, 18 June 1921). Austrian librettist. In Budapest he founded and edited the *Neues Pesther Journal* from 1869. He settled in Vienna in 1880, making a name for himself as a translator and adapter of Hungarian literature. The major success of his career as a librettist came when he collaborated with Johann Strauss on a substantially adapted version of a story by the Hungarian writer Mór Jókai: *Der Zigeunerbaron* (1885). More serious than Strauss's previous operettas, the work was a success, and led to a projected further collaboration with Strauss on an adaptation of Heine's *Schelm von Bergen*. This foundered, ostensibly because its leading character was an executioner, an idea that had been a feature of Sullivan's *The Mikado*. Schnitzer later adapted this libretto for *Bruder Straubinger*, set by Edmund Eysler (1903), with whom he also enjoyed some success with *Pufferl* (1905). However, Schnitzer never repeated the success of *Der Zigeunerbaron*. In 1920 he published a two-volume set of reminiscences of his collaboration with Strauss, *Meister Johann*.

Operetten unless otherwise stated

Muzzedin (romantische komische Oper), S. Bachrich, 1883; *Rafaela* (with A. Schirmer), M. Wolf, 1884; *Der Goldmensch* (Schauspiel), A. Müller jr, 1885; *Der Zigeunerbaron* (after M. Jókai), J. Strauss, 1885; *Die Königsbraut* (romantische komische Oper), R. Fuchs, 1889; *Das Orakel*, J. Hellmesberger, 1889; *Hand in Hand* (Volksstück, with Friesch), F. Roth, 1891; *Husarenblut*, H. Felix, 1894; *Bruder Straubinger* (with M. West, after H. Heine: *Schelm von Bergen*), E. Eysler, 1903; *Pufferl* (with S. Schlesinger), Eysler, 1905; *Der Hexenspiegel*, Eysler, 1905; *Der Elektriker* (with Schlesinger), C. J. Fromm, 1906; *Tip-Top* (with Schlesinger), Stritzko, 1907; *Kreolenblut* (with E. von Gatti), H. Berté, 1910; *Anno 1814* (Zeitbild, with H. Regel), P. Eisler, 1914

ANDREW LAMB

Schnorr von Carolsfeld, Ludwig (*b* Munich, 2 July 1836; *d* Dresden, 21 July 1865). German tenor. While still a student at the Leipzig Conservatory he was engaged by Eduard Devrient for the Karlsruhe Hofoper, making his first solo appearances in 1854–5 in *Norma* and *Der Freischütz*. He became principal tenor of the company in 1858 and two years later moved to Dresden, where he quickly made a reputation in lieder, oratorio and opera, especially as Tannhäuser and Lohengrin. He began studying Tristan, but his fears about the demands of the role led him to abandon it. Then in 1862 at Biebrich he and his wife, the soprano Malvina Garrigues, sang Tristan and Isolde to Wagner, who was much moved by Schnorr's singing and praised his artistic sympathy and quickness of understanding. The couple were, with Bülow, primarily responsible for the success of the première on 10 June 1865. It was largely the strain of the experience that caused Schnorr to develop a feverish chill. His last public appearance was in Munich as Erik in *Der fliegende Holländer* (9 July 1865), though he sang excerpts from the *Ring* and *Die Meistersinger* before Ludwig II on 12 July. Returning to Dresden, he rehearsed *Don Giovanni* on the 15th, but on the 16th developed what he termed a 'rampant gout' that began in his knee and led to delirium. He burst into song on his deathbed, calling repeatedly on Wagner's name.

A powerfully built man, with baritone colour in his tenor voice, Schnorr was praised for his smoothness of line, his portamento, and his 'elegiac, somewhat veiled' tone (Prölss). Wagner regarded him as inferior vocally to Tichatschek but greatly superior in dramatic power and intelligence; his death affected Wagner profoundly, on both personal and artistic grounds.

Schnorr's wife, Malvina Garrigues (*b* Copenhagen, 7 Dec 1825; *d* Karlsruhe, 8 Feb 1904), studied in Paris with the younger Manuel García and sang in Breslau (1841–9), making her début in *Robert le diable*, then in Coburg, Gotha, Hamburg and (from 1854) in Karlsruhe. She was praised for her powerful, ringing soprano and her fluent technique. After her husband's death she was unable to continue her career.

*

R. Wagner: 'Meine Erinnerungen an Ludwig Schnorr von Carolsfeld', *Gesammelte Schriften und Dichtungen*, viii (Leipzig, 1873, 5/1911), 221; Eng. trans., W. Ashton Ellis, iv (London, 1895)

R. Prölss: *Geschichte des Hoftheaters zu Dresden* (Dresden, 1878)

E. Schuré: *Souvenirs sur Richard Wagner: la première de 'Tristan et Iseult'* (Paris, 1900)

C. H. N. Garrigues: *Ein ideales Sängerpaar* (Copenhagen, 1937)

E. Newman: *The Life of Richard Wagner*, iii–iv (London, 1945–7)

E. Zuckerman: *The First Hundred Years of Wagner's Tristan* (New York, 1964)

O. Schneider: 'Vor 100 Jahren starb: Ludwig Schnorr von Carolsfeld', *ÖMz*, xx (1965), 378–9

JOHN WARRACK

Schoberlechner, Franz (*b* Vienna, 21 July 1797; *d* Berlin, 7 Jan 1843). Austrian composer. He studied the piano with Hummel and E. A. Förster and in 1814 made a concert tour to Italy. While in Florence he wrote a requiem and the opera *I virtuosi teatrali* (1817). After visits to Rome and Naples he was engaged as Kapellmeister by the Duchess Marie Louise of Lucca, for whom he composed *Gli arabi nelle gallie* (1819). He returned soon afterwards to Vienna and in due course, armed with letters of introduction, set off for Russia. In

Ludwig Schnorr von Carolsfeld and his wife Malvina in the title roles of Wagner's 'Tristan und Isolde' which they created in Munich, 1865

St Petersburg in 1824 he married the singer Sophie Dall'Occa (1807–64). After travelling in Russia, Germany and Italy, the couple returned to St Petersburg, where Sophie sang with great success at the Italian Opera for three years (1827–30), including appearances with Malibran; her husband wrote *Il barone di Dolzheim* for her. In 1831 they bought an estate near Florence, but continued to make further concert tours. Schoberlechner's operas had some success in their day.

I virtuosi teatrali (ob), Florence, 1817
Gli arabi nelle gallie, Lucca, 1819
Der junge Onkel (operetta, 1, H. Blangini), Vienna, Kärntnertor, 14 Jan 1823, *A-Wn*
Il barone di Dolzheim (F. Romani), St Petersburg, Imperial, 1828
Il desertore per l'amore [Lyubovnoye zel'yo], St Petersburg, Kammeniy ostrov, sum. 1830
Rossane (G. Rossi, after V. Hugo: *Marie Tudor*), Milan, 9 Feb 1839, *I-Mr*

*

FétisBS; *ME* [incl. Dall'Occa family]; *StiegerO*
A. Vol'f: *Khronika petersburgskikh teatrov*, i (St Petersburg, 1877)
Yu. Keldïsh and others: *Istoriya russkoy muzïki*, v (Moscow, 1988), 471

JOHN WARRACK

Schock, Rudolf (Johann) (*b* Duisburg, 4 Sept 1915; *d* Gürzenich, 13 Nov 1986). German tenor. He studied in Cologne and with Laurenz Hofer in Hanover, and joined the Duisburg opera chorus at the age of 18, later studying with Robert von der Linde in Berlin. He began singing major roles at Brunswick in 1937; after wartime service he resumed his career, singing in Hanover, Berlin and as a member of the Hamburg Staatsoper (1947–56). His Covent Garden début was in 1949 as Rodolfo (with Schwarzkopf as Mimì), followed by Alfredo, Pinkerton and Tamino in the same season. During the 1950s he was admired at the Vienna Staatsoper and at the Salzburg Festival, where he played Idomeneus and sang in the 1954 première of Liebermann's *Penelope*, and in 1959 appeared as Walther at Bayreuth. He recorded this role under Kempe in 1956, as he did Bacchus with Karajan in 1954 and Max under Keilberth in 1959. Later he became popular in operetta, musical films and television, and was acclaimed as a successor to Tauber. Schock was a lyric tenor with a strong top register, which allowed him to play such heroic roles as Florestan and Lohengrin; his voice was warmer and more flexible than his acting, which benefited from strong direction.

NOËL GOODWIN

Schodel, Róza [Rozália] (*b* Kolozsvár [now Cluj-Napoca], 29 Nov 1811; *d* Nyáregyháza, nr Budapest, 19 Aug 1854). Romanian soprano. She studied first at the singing school in Kolozsvár and then privately with János Schodel, who married her and later conducted some of the performances in which she took part. She sang her first roles in Pozsony and achieved critical notice as Agathe in *Der Freischütz*. Further study in Vienna led to a three-year contract at the Kärntnertortheater (1833–6). During a three-week tour of Berlin in 1834 she was offered a lifetime contract there, but Vienna would not release her. In 1837 she had great success at the Hungarian Theatre in Pest and after appearing as Norma at the newly-founded National Theatre, she was engaged by the company at a salary three times that of the other performers. Despite her wilful and capricious nature she was given nearly complete artistic control. She sang Lucia, Linda (*Linda di Chamounix*), Lucretia, Norma, Lady Macbeth (H.-A. Chélard's *Macbeth*) and Leonore (*Fidelio*); her greatest creation was Erzsébet Szilágyi in Erkel's *Hunyadi László*. She left in 1840 after an onion wreath was thrown at her feet during an ovation. In 1841 and 1842 she toured widely, appearing in Hanover, Mainz, London and Cologne. She returned to Pest in 1843 and retired in 1849. Her voice was even, vibrant, yet capable of an engaging softness.

*

K. Benyovszky: *Schodel Rozália* (Bratislava, 1927)

Schoeck, Othmar (*b* Brunnen, 1 Sept 1886; *d* Zürich, 8 March 1957). Swiss composer. The son of a landscape painter, he studied at the Zürich Conservatory and with

Max Reger in Leipzig (1907–8). On returning to Switzerland he held various choral conducting posts in Zürich and from 1917 to 1944 was director of the town concerts at St Gall. He seems to have been content to lead a useful but unambitious public life, though much of his music suggests that his inner life was not tranquil. As a composer, Schoeck is principally known for his more than 400 songs, which include some notable cycles and extended over the whole of his creative life. He also wrote instrumental and choral music.

Schoeck had a preference for German Romantic poetry and for the work of the Swiss writer Gottfried Keller. Among contemporary authors he favoured Hermann Hesse, a personal friend. His discrimination extended to the literary origins of his stage works. He wrote incidental music for Goethe's Singspiel *Erwin und Elmire* (1916, Zürich) and *Das Wandbild*, a 'scene and pantomime' to a scenario by Ferruccio Busoni (1921, Halle). Kleist and Balzac were the sources for *Penthesilea* and *Massimilla Doni*, Grimm for *Vom Fischer un syner Fru* and Holberg for *Don Ranudo*; *Venus* was based on the story *La Vénus d'Ille* by Prosper Mérimée; his last opera, *Das Schloss Dürande*, on the story of the same name by Joseph von Eichendorff. Although four of them were first produced in major German opera houses, these accomplished and unusual operas have so far found no regular place in the repertory even in the composer's native country. *Venus*, concerned with the irruption into French provincial society of pagan influences, was described by Schoeck's biographer Corrodi as a *Bekenntnisswerk*, an artistic credo, in which the whole man is revealed. An antique bronze statue of Venus, newly excavated (represented by a mime or dancer), comes to life and infatuates and kills a young man about to marry a local girl. The considerable demands of the tenor role may explain why *Venus* has been infrequently performed. *Massimilla Doni* is a Venetian comedy and conversation piece; the connoisseurs' discussion of their singer-protégés anticipates the aesthetic debates of Strauss's *Capriccio*. *Das Schloss Dürande* is set in Provence and Paris during the Revolution. Renald Vomholz, gamekeeper to Count Dürande, discovers that his sister Gabrielle is in love with his employer's son, Armand. He assumes (wrongly) that she has been seduced by Armand, kills her (by accident) and Armand (intentionally), then blows up the castle and himself. The first performance took place in 1943 during the Allied bombing of Berlin. The public found the final explosion too close to reality for comfort. Goering sent a furious telegram of protest to the Staatsoper about the libretto but the performances continued.

Schoeck had an instinct for matching style to content. Under a diverse, often highly chromatic surface that may be classed as late-Romantic he made use of closed forms – in solos, duets and ensembles and in the variation structure of *Vom Fischer un syner Fru*. His practical experience as a musician and song composer shows in the grateful vocal writing, in inventive orchestration and in the ability to present sensational, even melodramatic, events with a formal grasp and concentration that sharpen the intensity and immediacy of feeling.

See also MASSIMILLA DONI; PENTHESILEA; and VOM FISCHER UN SYNER FRU.

Don Ranudo op.27 (comic op, 4, A. Rüeger, after L. Holberg), Zürich, 16 April 1919, vs (Leipzig, 1919); rev. version, Dresden, Staatsoper, 3 Oct 1930

Venus op.32 (3, Rüeger, after P. Mérimée: *La Vénus d'Ille*), Zürich, 10 May 1922, vs (Leipzig, 1925); rev. version, Zürich, 26 Nov 1933

Penthesilea op.39 (1, Schoeck, after H. von Kleist), Dresden, Staatsoper, 8 Jan 1927 (Zürich, 1927)

Vom Fischer un syner Fru op.43 (dramatic cantata, 1, Schoeck, after P. O. Runge and J. L. and W. C. Grimm), Dresden, Staatsoper, 3 Oct 1930, vs (Leipzig, 1930)

Massimilla Doni op.50 (4, Rüeger, after H. de Balzac), Dresden, Staatsoper, 2 March 1937, vs (Vienna, 1936)

Das Schloss Dürande op.53, 1938–9 (4, H. Burte, after J. F. von Eichendorff), Berlin, Staatsoper, 1 April 1943, vs (Vienna and Leipzig, 1942)

*

H. Corrodi: *Othmar Schoeck: eine Monographie* (Frauenfeld and Leipzig, 1931, enlarged 2/1936, 3/1956)

W. Vogel: *Thematisches Verzeichnis der Werke von Othmar Schoeck* (Zürich, 1956) [incl. bibliography]

——: *Othmar Schoeck: Leben und Schaffen im Spiegel der Selbstzeugnissen und Zeitgenossenberichten* (Zürich, 1976)

RONALD CRICHTON

Schoemaker, Maurice (*b* Anderlecht, Brussels, 27 Dec 1890; *d* Brussels, 24 Aug 1964). Belgian composer. He studied with Ysaÿe and Paul Gilson, and was associated with the 'Synthétistes' group. His opera *Swane* (E. de Bom, after S. Streuvels; Antwerp, 1933), which embraces the jocular and the tragic, shows a brilliance of colour typical of his music; his second opera was *Arc-en-Ciel*, written in 1937 (M. de Ghelderode; Antwerp, 1951), and his third, *De toverviool*, composed in 1954 ('The Magic Violin'; ob, 4, A. van de Velde; Radio Brussels, 1960). He also wrote much incidental music as well as orchestral, other instrumental and vocal works.

CORNEEL MERTENS/R

Schoenberg [Schönberg], **Arnold** (**Franz Walter**) (*b* Vienna, 13 Sept 1874; *d* Los Angeles, 13 July 1951). Austro-Hungarian, later American composer. He was born into a Jewish family of rather modest means. His father died when he was 16, and he was obliged to leave school and take a job. He therefore received no formal musical education, though his near-contemporary Alexander von Zemlinsky gave him lessons in counterpoint and composition. He very quickly made up for his late start. The string sextet *Verklärte Nacht* (1899) initiated a series of works in which he expanded the boundaries of tonality so far that by 1909 he became the first composer to overstep them. Each new piece was greeted by a greater outcry than the last. While he could earn almost nothing from his music, his name, at least, gradually became known internationally.

His first operas, *Erwartung* (1909) and *Die glückliche Hand* (1910–13), belong to what may be called his expressionist period, after his break with tonality, and are highly idiosyncratic works. Yet opera had never been far from his mind. He was a constant opera-goer and knew the standard repertory well. He arranged the vocal score of Zemlinsky's first opera *Sarema* (1897), and scored many operettas to increase his meagre income from teaching. In 1901 he married Zemlinsky's sister Mathilde, and he not only followed his friend's increasing operatic output with admiration but looked for subjects to tackle himself. Three unfinished librettos from about this time survive: *Die Schildbürger* (1901), *Aberglaube* and *Odoaker*. Unaware of Debussy's setting he considered an opera on *Pelléas et Mélisande* before composing the symphonic poem of 1902–3, and in 1906–7 he sketched a prelude and the opening recitatives for an operatic version of Gerhart Hauptmann's new play *Und Pippa tanzt*. It took time for him to realize that he would be able to commit himself fully only to a conception of his own.

Although Marie Pappenheim supplied the subject as well as the libretto for *Erwartung* she clearly knew the kind of psychological situation that Schoenberg wished to explore at that time; its companion piece, *Die glückliche Hand*, is entirely his own work, symbolizing the spiritual crisis through which he was passing. For the next few years he was deeply absorbed in a quest for religious faith. It gave rise to several large-scale plans for an opera, oratorio or symphony which remained unrealized partly because his ideas moved on too quickly for his interest to be sustained. In 1912 he contemplated a vast three-evening operatic version of *Séraphita*, Balzac's novel based on the theosophy of Swedenborg, and later composed the opening bars of an oratorio on its final scene. The following year his imagination was caught by *Merlins Geburt*, a new play by Eduard Stucken, whom he knew. He recommended it as an operatic subject to Zemlinsky. While tempted to set it himself he admitted that Zemlinsky was better equipped to solve its dramatic problems than he was and returned to the *Séraphita* project, with which Pappenheim was now helping him. Eventually, however, Balzac's conception provided the framework for his oratorio *Die Jakobsleiter* (1917).

The years after World War I brought many changes in Schoenberg's life. He had moved to Berlin in 1911 to escape difficulties in Vienna for which anti-Semitism was partly responsible, and his music began at last to make some headway with the public. The war brought material hardship and, after his return to Vienna in 1915, spells of military service which damaged his health, but by the early 1920s his fortunes began to improve again. It was at this time that he devised his very influential 12-note serial method. His religious beliefs began to move decisively towards Judaism, which he had abandoned early in life (he had even been a baptized member of the Lutheran Church for a brief period from 1898). In 1923 his wife died, and the next year he married Gertrud Kolisch. Then, early in 1926, he moved back to Berlin to take charge of the masterclass in composition at the Prussian Academy of Arts, where he enjoyed a better position and more leisure to compose than he had ever known or was to find again.

Although Schoenberg's chamber and orchestral music of this period seemed to some even harder to grasp than his expressionistic works, he saw it as upholding traditional values. Thus his opera *Von heute auf morgen* (1928), though humorous and in externals more traditional than its predecessors, is no less personal, for it defends enduring values in life, as in art, against the threat posed by the superficial and the modish. Opera too was the form that he chose for his great profession of faith, *Moses und Aron* (1930–32), though he never composed the music for the third act. He did not write for the stage again. In 1933 he was dismissed from his post on racial grounds. He went briefly to Paris, where he formally re-embraced the Jewish faith, and thence to a teaching position in Boston. The following year he moved to Los Angeles, where he remained for the rest of his life.

See also ERWARTUNG; GLÜCKLICHE HAND, DIE; MOSES UND ARON; and VON HEUTE AUF MORGEN.

Erwartung op.17, 1909 (Monodram, 1, M. Pappenheim), Prague, Neues Deutsches, 6 June 1924 (Vienna, 1916)

Die glückliche Hand op.18, 1910–13 (Drama mit Musik, 1, Schoenberg), Vienna, Volksoper, 14 Oct 1924 (Vienna, 1916)

Von heute auf morgen op.32, 1928–9 (1, M. Blonda [G. Schoenberg]), Frankfurt, Opernhaus, 1 Feb 1930 (Berlin, 1929)

Moses und Aron, 1930–32 (3, Schoenberg), Act 3 not composed; Der Tanz um das goldene Kalb perf. in concert, Darmstadt, 2 July 1951; Acts 1–2 perf. in concert, Hamburg, Nordwestdeutscher Rundfunk, 12 March 1954; Acts 1–2 staged, Zürich, Stadt, 6 June 1957 (Mainz, 1958)

WRITINGS

Briefe, selected and ed. E. Stein (Mainz, 1958; Eng. trans., enlarged, 1964)

Style and Idea, ed. L. Stein (London, 1975)

Gesammelte Schriften, i, ed. I. Vojtěch (Frankfurt, 1976)

*

H. Keller: 'Schoenberg's "Moses and Aron"', *The Score*, no.21 (1957), 30–45

——: 'Schoenberg's Comic Opera', *The Score*, no.23 (1958), 27–36

J. Rufer: *Das Werk Arnold Schönbergs* (Kassel, 1959, 2/1975; Eng. trans., 1962)

K. H. Wörner: *Gotteswort und Magie* (Heidelberg, 1959; Eng. trans., 1963, as *Schoenberg's 'Moses and Aron'*)

T. Wiesengrund-Adorno: 'Sakrales Fragment', *Quasi una fantasia* (Frankfurt, 1963), 306–38

K. H. Wörner: '"Die glückliche Hand", Arnold Schönbergs Drama mit Musik', *SMz*, cciv (1964), 274–83

H. Buchanan: 'A Key to Schoenberg's "Erwartung"', *JAMS*, xx (1967), 434–49

D. Lewin: 'Moses und Aron: some General Remarks and Analytical Notes for Act I, Scene I', *PNM*, vi/1 (1967), 1–17

K. H. Wörner: 'Schönberg's "Erwartung" und das Ariadne-Thema', *Die Musik in der Geistesgeschichte* (Bonn, 1970), 91–117

J. Crawford: 'Die glückliche Hand: Schoenberg's Gesamtkunstwerk', *MQ*, lx (1974), 583–601

C. Dahlhaus: 'Ausdrucksprinzip und Orchesterpolyphonie in Schönbergs "Erwartung"', *Kongress der Internationalen Schönberg-Gesellschaft: Vienna 1974*, 34–8

H. Stuckenschmidt: *Schönberg: Leben, Umwelt, Werk* (Zürich, 1974; Eng. trans., 1977)

H. Boventer, ed.: *'Moses und Aron': zur Oper Arnold Schönbergs* (Bensberg, 1979)

E. Budde: 'Arnold Schönbergs Monodrama "Erwartung": Versuch einer Analyse der ersten Szene', *AMw*, xxxvi (1979), 1–20

J. Crawford: '"Die glückliche Hand": Further Notes', *Journal of the Arnold Schoenberg Institute*, iv (1980), 68–76

S. Mauser: 'Forschungsbericht zu Schönbergs "Erwartung"', *ÖMz*, xxxv (1980), 215–19

A. L. Ringer: 'Schoenberg, Weill and Epic Theater', *Journal of the Arnold Schoenberg Institute*, iv (1980), 77–98

A. Serravezza: 'Critica e ideologia nel "Moses und Aron"', *RIM*, xv (1980), 204–29

E. Steiner: 'The "Happy" Hand: Genesis and Interpretation of Schoenberg's Monumentalkunstwerk', *MR*, xli (1980), 207–22

J. Laborda: *Studien zu Schönbergs Monodram 'Erwartung' Op.17* (Laaber, 1981)

O. Steck: *Moses und Aron: die Oper Arnold Schönbergs und ihr biblischer Stoff* (Munich, 1981)

R. Weaver: 'The Conflict of Religion and Aesthetics in Schoenberg's "Moses and Aaron"', *Essays on the Music of J. S. Bach and other divers Subjects: a Tribute to Gerhard Herz* (Louisville, 1981), 291–303

S. Mauser: *Das expressionistische Musiktheater der Wiener Schule: stilistische und entwicklungsgeschichtliche Untersuchen zu Arnold Schönbergs 'Erwartung', op.17, 'Die glückliche Hand', op.18, und Alban Bergs 'Wozzeck', op.7* (Regensburg, 1982)

P. White: 'The Genesis of "Moses und Aron"', *Journal of the Arnold Schoenberg Institute*, vi (1982), 8–55

O. Neighbour: 'Veraltete Sentimentalität: Arnold Schoenberg in Defence of Richard Strauss', *Festschrift Albi Rosenthal* (Tutzing, 1984), 253–7 [on *Von heute auf morgen*]

J. Stengel: 'Die Apokalypse einer Liebe: Arnold Schönbergs Monodram "Erwartung"', *Kongress der Internationalen Schönberg-Gesellschaft: Vienna 1984*, 64–72

E. Weissweiler: '"Schreiben Sie mir doch einen Operntext, Fräulein!" Marie Pappenheims Text zu Arnold Schönbergs "Erwartung"', *NZM*, cxlv/6 (1984), 4–8

P. White: *Schoenberg and the God-Idea: the Opera "Moses und Aron"* (Ann Arbor, 1985)

H. Mäckelmann: ' "Die glückliche Hand": eine Studie zu Musik und Inhalt von Arnold Schoenbergs "Drama mit Musik" ', *HJbMW*, x (1988), 7–36

J. Auner: 'Schoenberg's Aesthetic Transformations and the Evolution of Form in "Die glückliche Hand" ', *Journal of the Arnold Schoenberg Institute*, xii (1989), 103–28 O. W. NEIGHBOUR

Schoening, Alwina. *See* VALLERIA, ALWINA.

Schöffler, Paul (*b* Dresden, 15 Sept 1897; *d* Amersham, 21 Nov 1977). Austrian bass-baritone of German birth. After studying music at the Dresden Conservatory he concentrated on singing, his teachers including Staegemann at Dresden, Grenzebach at Berlin and Sammarco at Milan. He was a member of the Dresden Staatsoper from 1925 to 1937, when he joined the Vienna Staatsoper. He was first heard at Covent Garden in 1934 (Donner, Švanda); later London heard him as Gunther, Scarpia, Kurwenal, Figaro, Don Giovanni, John the Baptist and Wotan (*Rheingold*). At Bayreuth he sang Hans Sachs (1943–4) and the Dutchman (1956). His Metropolitan début was in 1950 (as John the Baptist), and he sang 14 roles there, up to 1964; at Salzburg in 1952 he created Jupiter at the first public performance of *Die Liebe der Danae*. He was a notable Cardillac and Mathis (*Mathis der Maler*), and created von Einem's Danton (1947, Salzburg). He sang character parts such as the Music-Master (*Ariadne auf Naxos*) and Antonio (*Figaro*) when well over 70.

Schöffler's careful musicianship and fine stage presence were supported by a warm, expressive voice which made him a fine Wagner interpreter as well as a master of the Mozart repertory. He was also a successful concert singer.

*

GV (R. Celletti; R. Vegeto)

H. Christian: *Paul Schöffler: Versuch einer Würdigung* (Vienna, 1967) [with discography] PETER BRANSCOMBE

Scholz, Bernhard (*b* Mainz, 30 March 1835; *d* Munich, 26 Dec 1916). German composer. Among his teachers were Heinrich Esser and S. W. Dehn. He taught theory at the Königliche Musikschule in Munich from 1856, then conducted the opera in Zürich and Nuremberg before becoming assistant court Kapellmeister to Marschner in Hanover, 1859–65. Subsequently he conducted the concerts of the Società Cherubini in Florence (1865–6) and, in Berlin, the Philharmonic Concerts and the Cecilia Choir. From 1871 he directed the concerts of the Breslau Orchestral Society. He succeeded Raff as director of Hoch's Conservatory in Frankfurt in 1883, a position he retained until his retirement in 1908.

Scholz belonged to the circle of Brahms, Joachim and Clara Schumann, and was among those who signed the famous manifesto of March 1860 against the New German School. He worked assiduously to promote the works of Brahms, whose influence is most evident in his compositions.

Carlo Rosa (komische Oper, 3, Scholz), Nuremberg, Staat, 16 Dec 1858

Ziethen'sche Husaren (komische Oper, 3, T. Rehbaum), Breslau, 26 Nov 1869

Morgiane (romantische Oper, 3, Rehbaum), Munich, Hof, 18 Sept 1870

Der Nachtwächter (1, Rehbaum), 1871

Golo (romantische Oper, 4, Scholz), Nuremberg, 4 April 1875

Der Trompeter von Säckingen (komische Oper, 4, Rehbaum), Wiesbaden, 20 Jan 1877

Die vornehmen Wirte (komische Oper, 3, P. Schumacher), Leipzig, 10 March 1883

Gustav Wasa, Kassel, 1886

Ingo (4, Scholz), Frankfurt, 27 Feb 1898

Anno 1757 (3, R. Scholz), Berlin, Kgl, 18 Jan 1903

Mirandolina (3, Rehbaum), Darmstadt, Hof, 1 March 1907

*

StiegerO

W. Nagel: Obituary, *Neue Musik-Zeitung*, xxxviii (1917), 123 GAYNOR G. JONES

Schönbach, Dieter (*b* Stolp, Pomerania, 18 Feb 1931). German composer. After studies in Detmold and Freiburg with Bialas and Fortner, he was music director at the Bochum Schauspielhaus (1959–73); he also worked in theatres in Münster (Westphalia) and Basle. In 1972 he was joint winner of the Stamitz Prize of Stuttgart with Wolfgang Steffen and Hans Otte.

Schönbach is, with Riedl, one of the foremost German exponents of mixed-media composition. He has engaged in collaborative ventures with visual artists, choreographers and film directors, and even in his 'pure' works he makes use of Kandinsky's theory of elements in pictorial form, disposing his materials as 'surfaces', 'points', 'silences' and 'curves'. Many of his pieces require graphic projections, sometimes prepared by other artists.

Die Geschichte von einem Feuer (mixed-media op, after E. Borchers), Kiel, June 1968, collab. E. Kieselbach, O. Piene, B. Völkle and G. Weseler

Canzona da sonar 6 (mixed-media show with puppets), 1970, collab. Weseler

Bedrohung und Überleben (multi-media opera), Cologne, 11 May 1971, collab. Kieselbach and Piene

Hysteria – Paradies schwarz (mixed-media op), Cologne, 9 Oct 1971, collab. D. Wellershoff, Kieselbach, K. Geldmacher, K. Göhling, P. Brühning and Weseler

Der Sturm (mixed-media show, after W. Shakespeare: *The Tempest*), Wiesbaden, 1971, collab. Kieselbach

Hymnus II – Morgen nach dem Feuer (mixed-media show), Munich, 1972

Come S Francesco, 1975–6 (chamber op) [after A. Scarlatti], Münster, Sept 1979

*

D. Gojowy: 'Multimedia und graphische Komposition', *Musik und Bildung*, ii (1970), 273–8

D. Schönbach: 'Neue Aspekte für das totale Theater', *Musik und Bildung*, iii (1971), 525–30 DETLEF GOJOWY

Schönbrunn. Palace in the south-western suburbs of Vienna; a court theatre was built there in 1747 and used for imperial entertainments, including opera. The theatre is now used for chamber opera. *See* VIENNA, §§2 and 5.

Schöne, Lotte (*b* Vienna, 15 Dec 1891; *d* Paris, 23 Dec 1977). Austrian soprano, later naturalized French. She studied in Vienna, made her début at the Volksoper in 1915, and sang at the Staatsoper from 1917 to 1926 and at the Salzburg festivals from 1922 to 1935. Hearing her there, Bruno Walter engaged her for the Berlin Städtische Oper, where she remained from 1926 to 1933. In Vienna and Berlin she was especially famous in all the lighter Mozart roles, as Adele in *Die Fledermaus* and Norina in *Don Pasquale*, as Verdi's Gilda and Oscar, and as Strauss's Sophie and Zerbinetta. Among several Puccini roles she excelled as Liù, which she sang with great success at Covent Garden in 1927. The latter part of her artistic life was sadly disrupted by the coming to power of the Nazis in 1933. Thereafter she made her home in Paris, where her Mélisande was much admired, but she was obliged to go into hiding in southern France during the war. A beautiful woman, she had a charming stage presence, of which her light and well-schooled soprano seemed the natural counterpart. The best of her many recordings are those made in Berlin between 1927 and 1931.

A. Tubeuf: 'Lotte Schoene', *Record Collector*, xx (1971–2), 77–89 [with discography] DESMOND SHAWE-TAYLOR

Schöne, Wolfgang (*b* Bad Gandersheim, 9 Feb 1940). German baritone. After studying in Hanover and Hamburg, he became a concert singer. He was engaged at Stuttgart in 1973, and has sung at Vienna, Hamburg, Geneva, Berlin and Basle; in 1983 he created Tom in Henze's *The English Cat* at Schwetzingen. His repertory includes Guglielmo, Don Giovanni, Wolfram, Gunther, Amfortas, Germont, Renato, Ford, Yevgeny Onegin, Golaud, Father Grandier (*The Devils of Loudun*), Barak and Mandryka. He sang the Count (*Capriccio*) at Salzburg (1985) and Florence (1987), and Dr Schön at the Théâtre du Châtelet, Paris (1991). He has a warm-toned, lyrical voice, used with great expressiveness, and is also a talented actor.

For illustration *see* ENGLISH CAT, THE. ELIZABETH FORBES

Schöne Galathee, Die ('Beautiful Galathea'). *Operette* in one act by FRANZ SUPPÉ to a libretto by 'Poly Henrion' (L. Kohl von Kohlenegg); Berlin, Meysel's, 30 June 1865.

The sculptor Pygmalion (tenor) has produced a statue of a beautiful woman, Galathea, which the wealthy art collector Mydas (*buffo* baritone) wishes to buy; but Pygmalion will not part with it. He wishes that the beautiful creature could be alive and prays to Venus to this end. Galathea does come to life (soprano), but causes havoc with her flirtations with Pygmalion's servant Ganymede (mezzo-soprano), her extraction of jewels from Mydas, her taste for wine and her tantrums. Pygmalion's prayer that Galathea be returned to stone is answered, but Mydas's jewels are turned to stone too. Pygmalion is now only too happy to let Mydas buy the statue.

A Viennese response to Offenbach, Suppé's richly melodic score includes Mydas's 'Meinem Vater Gordios', Galathea's awakening ('Sie regt sich, sie erwacht'), her drinking song 'Hell im Glas', Ganymede's 'Wir Griechen', the treasure trio 'Seht den Schmuck' and Ganymede's kissing duet with Galathea 'Ach, mich zieht's zu dir'. At the first production Anna Grobecker of the Carltheater, Vienna, made a guest appearance as Ganymede. ANDREW LAMB

Schöne Schusterinn, Die [*Die schöne Schusterinn, oder Die pücefarbenen Schuhe* ('The Beautiful Shoemaker's Wife, or The Puce-Coloured Shoes')]. Singspiel in two acts by IGNAZ UMLAUF to a libretto by GOTTLIEB STEPHANIE after the Marquis de Ferrière's *Les souliers mors-dorés* (1776); Vienna, Burgtheater, 22 June 1779.

The shoemaker's wife Lehne (alto), lured into the quarters of the high-spirited but good-hearted Baron von Pikourt (tenor), is whisked behind a curtain on the unexpected arrival of her husband Sock (baritone). Told she is the baron's mistress, he measures her protruding feet for a new pair of shoes. Her loutish stepson Hanns (tenor) arrives and tells Sock that it is Lehne in the Baron's room, but Pikourt explains the prank and vouches for her honour.

Umlauf's cheerful and undemanding score was his greatest popular success in Vienna. The part of Lehne was written for the rich alto voice of Marianne Weiss, who made her début in the role (in later productions at Vienna and elsewhere the role was usually transposed). Stephanie's musical texts were largely plagiarized from the earlier translation by the composer Johann André. THOMAS BAUMAN

Schöne und getreue Ariadne, Die ('The Beautiful and Faithful Ariadne'). Opera in three acts by JOHANN GEORG CONRADI to a libretto by CHRISTIAN HEINRICH POSTEL; Hamburg, Theater am Gänsemarkt, 1691.

The opera is freely based on the classical myth of Ariadne (soprano), daughter of Minos, King of Crete (baritone), who falls in love with Theseus, Prince of Athens (tenor). Theseus has come to Crete to try to stop the terrible practice of offering up young Athenian men and women as sacrifices to the Minotaur, a monster with the head of a bull and the body of a man. It was confined by Minos in a labyrinth built by Daedalus, and fed annually seven youths and seven maidens. In the version presented by this opera Theseus loves Phaedra (soprano), Ariadne's sister. After he learns from Ariadne the secret of escape from the labyrinth, he abandons her on an island and flees with Phaedra. Bacchus (tenor), who appears earlier in the opera disguised as Evantes, arrives and immediately falls in love with Ariadne. They are met by Venus and her Graces, and in the finale are raised to the heavens, where Ariadne is transformed into the constellation Corona Ariadne (i.e. Corona Borealis).

Ariadne is important as the earliest surviving score from the repertory of the Hamburg opera and is thus a significant document in the history of German opera. The music consists of a mixture of Venetian, German, and French musical styles, but French musical taste dominates everything except the recitatives, including the arias, ensembles, and orchestral passages. The recitatives, the earliest extant examples written for Hamburg, are in a highly dramatic, emotion-laden style that originated in the works of Venetian opera composers. GEORGE J. BUELOW

School for Fathers **(i).** Opera by Charles Dibdin; *see* LIONEL AND CLARISSA.

School for Fathers (ii). Opera by Ermanno Wolf-Ferrari; *see* QUATRO RUSTEGHI, I.

Schorr, Friedrich (*b* Nagyvarád, 2 Sept 1888; *d* Farmington, CT, 14 Aug 1953). Hungarian bass-baritone, later naturalized American. He studied with Adolf Robinson, sang some small roles in Chicago in early 1912, and made his true début in Graz on 20 June 1912 as Wotan in *Die Walküre*. After brief engagements in Graz, Prague and Cologne, he came to wider prominence when engaged by the Berlin Staatsoper in 1923. During his seven Berlin years and thereafter, he was to tackle roles from a surprisingly wide repertory; but it was above all in the great Wagnerian bass-baritone parts that he excelled, not only in Berlin, but at Bayreuth (1925–31), at Covent Garden (1925–33), and especially at the Metropolitan (every season from 1924 to 1943). His Wotan and Hans Sachs long dominated the international operatic scene; he was beyond question the outstanding exponent of these and of numerous other Wagnerian roles, especially the Dutchman. His voice had majesty and unfailing beauty; he never fell into the notorious 'Bayreuth bark', but maintained a steady legato flow of tone even in declamatory passages. The most important part of his recorded legacy consists of the extensive Wagnerian excerpts made in his prime, in which his impeccable enunciation plays an important part in the impression of authority that he conveys. One can believe in the grandeur of a Wotan whose utterances are so commandingly distinct, and in the poetic sensibility of a Hans Sachs to whom words are of such evident importance.

*

GV (L. Riemens; R. Celletti; R. Vegeto)
A. Frankenstein, E. Arnosi and B. Semeonoff: 'Friedrich Schorr', *Record Collector*, xix (1970–71), 245–84 [with discography by J. Dennis]
DESMOND SHAWE-TAYLOR

Schott, Anton (*b* Schloss Staufeneck, Swabia, 24 June 1846; *d* Stuttgart, 6 Jan 1913). German tenor. He studied in Munich and made his début in 1870 at Frankfurt as Max (*Der Freischütz*). After engagements at Munich, Berlin and Schwerin, in 1877 he went to Hanover, where he sang Benvenuto Cellini and created Azim in Stanford's *The Veiled Prophet* (1881). Meanwhile he appeared at Her Majesty's Theatre, London, as Rienzi and Lohengrin (1880) and returned for Tannhäuser (1882). After touring with Angelo Neumann's company in the *Ring* throughout Europe, in 1884–5 he toured the USA with the Damrosch Opera Company and sang Tannhäuser and Siegmund at the Metropolitan, returning in 1894 as Siegfried (*Götterdämmerung*). In 1889 he accompanied Neumann's company to Russia.
ELIZABETH FORBES

Schreier, Peter (*b* Meissen, 29 July 1935). German tenor. He studied privately with Polster and then with Winkler, 1956–9. In 1959 he joined the Dresden Staatsoper school and in 1961 made his début as the First Prisoner in *Fidelio*, then went as leading lyric tenor to the Berlin Staatsoper. He sang at Salzburg, the Metropolitan (début as Tamino, 1967), La Scala and the Teatro Colón (1968), and then in most European centres, appearing regularly in Vienna, Salzburg and Munich. By the mid-1960s he was acclaimed as a lively, elegant and accomplished Mozart tenor. His best roles are perhaps Belmonte, Don Ottavio, Tamino and Ferrando, but he has also sung Fenton, Alfred (*Die Fledermaus*), Rossini's Almaviva, Des Grieux, the Holy Fool (*Boris Godunov*), Strauss's Leukippos and Dancing-Master, Loge, David, Lensky and the Physicist (Dessau's *Einstein*). He sings with seamless legato, a distinctive, slightly nasal colouring to his tone and fastidious phrasing, yet never loses the simplicity and sense of proportion that make his art so appealing and distinguished. He embarked on a conducting career in 1970 which has included a well-received *Idomeneo* in Berlin (1981).

*

G. Schmiedel: *Peter Schreier: für Sie porträtiert* (Leipzig, 1976)

Schreker, Franz (*b* Monaco, 23 March 1878; *d* Berlin, 21 March 1934). Austrian composer. The eldest child of an early-widowed mother, he managed to complete musical studies at the Vienna Conservatory while contributing to the family income. He then adopted a somewhat dissolute lifestyle, composing and gathering experiences that were to bear fruit in the conception of *Der ferne Klang*. As director of the Philharmonic Choir from 1907, however, he began to play a prominent role in Vienna's musical life as a significant champion of modern music (he conducted the first performance of Schoenberg's *Gurrelieder* in 1913). His reputation as one of the 'Neutöner' was further strengthened by the

Friedrich Schorr as Hans Sachs in Wagner's 'Die Meistersinger von Nürnberg'

success of his ballet pantomime *Der Geburtstag der Infantin* (to Oscar Wilde's story) at the 1908 modernist *Kunstschau.*

Schreker's first, one-act opera, *Flammen*, had been given a concert performance, with the composer at the piano, in 1902, but it was not until 1912 that the long gestation period of *Der ferne Klang* concluded with its remarkably successful performance in Frankfurt under Ludwig Rottenberg. Schreker's almost instantaneous reputation as a leading composer of new opera led to the double première in the following year of *Das Spielwerk und die Prinzessin* in Frankfurt (again under Rottenberg) and Vienna (under Hugo Reichenberger). It confused even his admirers with its dense symbolism, eroticism, innovative staging and a musical language that incorporated all that was currently new as well as older Wagnerian mannerisms. In Vienna, Julius Korngold accused Schreker of formless eclecticism in the music and poetic ineptitude in the libretto. In Frankfurt, however, Paul Bekker suggested that Schreker had to be understood not as someone who simply composed operas to texts, but as the creator of 'stage works for music out of a musical-dramatic inspiration'. This notion he was to elaborate on in a short study (1919) of Schreker, whom he hailed as the most significant musical-dramatist after Wagner. Bekker's continuing support of Schreker, in the *Frankfurter Zeitung* and elsewhere, played an important part in the subsequent success of the composer's most popular operas: *Die Gezeichneten* (1918) and *Der Schatzgräber* – the latter first performed in 1920, the year in which Schreker's celebrity as both a composer and a teacher of composition (at the Academy of Music) led to his being offered the prestigious post of Director of the Hochschule für Musik in Berlin. His pupils there and in Vienna included Ernst Krenek, Alois Hába, Jascha Horenstein and Max Brand.

The early years in Berlin, where Schreker presided over an impressive teaching staff (to which he added composers with different creative inclinations from his own, such as Hindemith) coincided with the height of his fame. The appearance of *Irrelohe* in 1924, however, occasioned influentially negative reviews. Although public interest in Schreker's works persisted for some years, the composer was sufficiently hurt to reconsider his artistic values. He consulted Schoenberg over drafts of *Christophorus* (he worked on it simultaneously with *Der singende Teufel*, 1928), in which the language was already turning towards closed neo-Baroque forms and Hindemithian counterpoint.

Plans for staging *Christophorus* were effectively blocked by the Nazis, pressure from whom led to Schreker's 'resignation' from the Hochschule in 1931. He had already been seeking a position in the USA, but this came to nothing. After his last opera, *Der Schmied von Gent*, had been staged in Berlin in 1932 (occasioning anti-semitic demonstrations), Schreker's enforced retirement from the Prussian Academy of Arts in December 1933 seems to have precipitated the stroke which led to his death in 1934. Sketches of a projected opera, *Memnon*, remain, although only the overture was completed (*Vorspiel zu einer grossen Oper*, 1933, unpublished).

Schreker was celebrated in the 1920s for a rich musical language that linked the aesthetic worlds of symbolism, expressionism and Viennese *Jugendstil*. In terms of operatic technique, he was particularly successful in writing flexible arioso lines, adopting the rhythm of spoken language, against recherché textures of almost tactile harmonic and orchestral subtlety. Surviving recordings confirm the delicate lyricism of his wife Maria Schreker in roles such as Els in *Der Schatzgräber*, in which she began her career as an operatic soprano in 1923. Schreker was equally at home, however, with effects of Straussian magnificence (if tending always towards quasi-expressionistic fragmentation) and the manipulation of graphic leitmotifs which seemed, to some, disarmingly appropriate to the manner of his librettos. These were condemned for their 'penny-dreadful' characteristics and linked by German critics with the baleful influence of Puccini, although their reflection of such literary figures as Wedekind, Hauptmann, Ibsen and Nietzsche is of considerable interest. Much of the debate about Schreker reflected annoyance at his demonstration of a practical alternative to both classical propriety and élitist avant-garde idealism. Theodor Adorno was to go further in a 1959 radio talk, where he characterized Schreker's 'shamelessness' as 'voicing doubt in culture itself'. This observation offers itself tantalizingly to more recent debate about early 20th-century modernism, and argues persuasively for the re-examination of Schreker's once famous 'sound', which even Adorno described as attaining 'smouldering subliminality and, in its highest moments, that sweetness which thrives where weeping could be as little repressed as happiness'.

See also CHRISTOPHORUS; FERNE KLANG, DER; GEZEICHNETEN, DIE; IRRELOHE; SCHATZGRÄBER, DER; SCHMIED VON GENT, DER; SINGENDE TEUFEL, DER; and SPIELWERK, DAS.

Flammen op.10, 1901 (1, D. Leen), concert perf., Vienna, Bösendorfersaal, 24 April 1902, *GB-Lbl**

Der ferne Klang, *c*1901–10 (3, Schreker), Frankfurt, 18 Aug 1912 (Vienna and Leipzig, 1912)

Das Spielwerk und die Prinzessin, 1909–12 (prol., 2, Schreker), Frankfurt and Vienna, Hofoper, 15 March 1913, vs (Vienna and Leipzig, 1912); rev. as Das Spielwerk, 1915–19 (Mysterium, 1, Schreker), Munich, National, 30 Oct 1920, vs (Vienna and Leipzig, 1919)

Die Gezeichneten, 1913–15 (3, Schreker), Frankfurt, 25 April 1918, vs (Vienna and Leipzig, 1916)

Der Schatzgräber, 1915–18 (prol., 4, epilogue, Schreker), Frankfurt, 21 Jan 1920 (Vienna, 1919)

Irrelohe, 1919–23 (3, Schreker), Cologne, 27 March 1924 (Vienna and New York, 1923)

Der singende Teufel, 1924–8 (4, Schreker), Berlin, Staatsoper, 10 Dec 1928 (Vienna and Leipzig, 1928)

Christophorus, oder Die Vision einer Oper, 1925–9 (prol., 2, epilogue, Schreker), Freiburg, 1 Oct 1978, vs (Berlin, 1931)

Der Schmied von Gent, 1929–32 (Grosse Zauberoper, 3, Schreker, after C. de Coster: *Smetse Smee*, from the Flemish folktale), Berlin, Städtische Oper, 29 Oct 1932 (Vienna and Leipzig, 1932)

*

P. Bekker: *Franz Schreker: Studie zur Kritik der modernen Oper* (Berlin, 1919)
Musikblätter des Anbruch, ii/1–2 (1920) [special issue]
F. Schreker: *Dichtungen für Musik* (Vienna and Leipzig, 1920–21)
J. Kapp: *Franz Schreker: der Mann und sein werk* (Munich, 1921)
F. Schreker: 'Memnon, Oper in zwei Aufzügen (vier Blätter)', *Blätter der Staatsoper* (Berlin), i/3 (1921)
P. Bekker: *Klang und Eros* (Stuttgart and Berlin, 1922)
Musikblätter des Anbruch, vi/2 (1924) [special issue]
F. Schreker: *Die tönenden Sphären, Operndichtung in zwei Aufzügen (drei Bildern) und einem Epilog* (Vienna, 1924)
G. Neuwirth: *Franz Schreker* (Vienna, 1959)
T. Adorno: 'Schreker', *Quasi una fantasia*, Musikalische Schriften, ii (Frankfurt, 1963); repr. in T. Adorno: *Musikalische Schriften I–III, Gesammelte Schriften*, vi (Frankfurt, 1984), 272–5
H. Schreker-Bures: *El Caso Schreker* (Buenos Aires, 1969); Ger. trans., rev., with contributions by H. H. Stuckenschmidt and W. Oehlmann, as *Franz Schreker* (Vienna, 1970)
——: *Horen, denken, fühlen – Eine kleine Studie über Schrekers Operntexte* (Buenos Aires, 1970)
P. Granzow: *Franz Schrekers Kompositionstil in seiner Oper 'Die Gezeichneten'* (diss., U. of Innsbruck, 1972)
G. Neuwirth: *Die Harmonik in der Oper 'Der ferne Klang' von Franz Schreker* (Regensburg, 1972)
S. Döhring: 'Franz Schreker und die grosse musiktheatralische Szene', *Mf*, xxvii (1974), 175–86
R. Blackburn: 'Franz Schreker, 1878–1934', *MT*, cxix (1978), 224–8
C. Hailey: 'Franz Schreker in seiner Schriften', *ÖMz*, xxxiii/3 (1978), 119–27
O. Kolleritsch, ed.: *Franz Schreker am Beginn der neuen Musik*, Studien zur Wertungsforschung, xi (Graz, 1978)
R. Zondergeld: 'Traum und Klang zum Phantastischen in der Operndichtungen Franz Schrekers', *Phaicon 3. Almanach der phantastischen Literatur* (Frankfurt, 1978), 131–43
E. Budd and R. Stephan, eds.: *Franz-Schreker-Symposion*, Schriftenreihe der Hochschule der Künste Berlin (Berlin, 1980)
S. Döhring: 'Das Trivialitäts-Missverständnis: Schrekers *Gezeichneten* in Frankfurt', *Werk und Wiedergabe: Musiktheater exemplärisch interpretiert*, ed. S. Wiesmann (Bayreuth, 1980), 336–47
H. Schreker-Bures: *Spaziergang durch ein Leben* (Buenos Aires, 1981)
C. Hailey: 'Der Schmied von Gent', *Opera Journal*, xv/1 (1982), 3–13
P. Franklin: 'Style, Structure and Taste: Three Aspects of the Problem of Franz Schreker', *PRMA*, cix (1982–3), 134–46
R. Erman, ed.: *Franz Schreker (1978–1934) zum 50. Todestag* (Aachen, 1984)
P. Franklin: 'Schreker's Decline', *The Idea of Music, Schoenberg and Others* (London, 1985), 139–60
M. Brzoska: *Franz Schrekers Oper 'Der Schatzgräber'*, suppl. xxvii to *AMw* (Stuttgart, 1988)
P. Franklin: 'Distant Sounds – Fallen Music: *Der ferne Klang* as "Women's Opera"', *COJ*, iii (1991), 159–72
C. Hailey: *Franz Schreker* (Cambridge, 1992)

PETER FRANKLIN

Schröder-Devrient [née Schröder], **Wilhelmine** (*b* Hamburg, 6 Dec 1804; *d* Coburg, 26 Jan 1860). German soprano. Her father, Friedrich Schröder (1744–1816), was the first German Don Giovanni. She made her début at the Kärntnertortheater as Pamina (20 January 1821), when the freshness and confidence of her singing made a great impression. She followed this with Emmeline (Weigl's *Die Schweizerfamilie*) and Marie (Grétry's *Raoul Barbe Bleu*, in German); she also sang Agathe on 7 March 1822 with Weber conducting. Her greatest triumph, and the performance that laid the foundations of her international fame, was as Leonore on 3 November 1822. She first sang in Dresden that year, and in 1823 was given a two-year contract at the Hoftheater; she remained associated with Dresden until 1847.

Schröder-Devrient impressed audiences everywhere with the dramatic power of her performances, especially as Donna Anna, Euryanthe, Reiza, Norma, Romeo, Valentine and Rossini's Desdemona. She had an outstanding success in Berlin in 1828, though she offended Spontini by refusing to sing the title role of *La vestale* (she sang it a year later in Dresden). In Paris in May 1830 she made triumphant appearances as Agathe and Leonore. She returned to sing Italian opera in 1831–2, appearing with Malibran in *Don Giovanni* and *Otello*. From May to July 1832 she also appeared at the King's Theatre in London 30 times, in *Fidelio*, *Don Giovanni* and Chelard's *Macbeth*. In the following season she was heard in *Der Freischütz*, *Die Zauberflöte*, *Euryanthe* and *Otello*, less successfully owing to the rival attractions of Taglioni and Fanny Elssler. After Malibran's death she was encouraged to return to London in 1837, and sing in *Fidelio*, *La sonnambula* and *Norma*. From that time a decline in her vocal powers was noticeable. She seemed tired of the stage and inclined to drag the tempo and to declaim rather than sing; but she continued to have successes in Germany, creating Adriano (*Rienzi*, 1842), Venus and Senta (both 1845) in Dresden, and also singing Gluck's Iphigenia (*Aulide*). Her last appearance was at Riga on 17 December 1847.

In an age when few singers matched their vocal prowess with equal dramatic skill, Schröder-Devrient impressed audiences especially with her interpretation of Leonore; many reports give details of its dramatic effect. Weber thought her the best of all Agathes, and to have disclosed more in the part than he had believed was there; however, on hearing her sing Leonore in 1822 he discerned the deficiencies that later (1842) disturbed Berlioz, who deplored her exaggerated acting, her vehement declamation and her failures of style. According to Chorley, 'Her voice was a strong soprano ... with an inherent expressiveness of tone ... Her tones were delivered without any care, save to give them due force'. However, he praised her acting, despite her increasingly exaggerated characterization. It was her Leonore that roused the 16-year-old Wagner to his sense of vocation as a dramatic composer; in *Über Schauspieler und Sänger*, dedicated to her memory, he gave a moving and detailed critical evaluation of her art. Her vocal deficiencies were partly due to shortcomings in her training; as a singer who brought new dramatic powers to the art of opera she was influential on the course of German Romantic opera.

For further illustration *see* EURYANTHE.

Wilhelmine Schröder-Devrient as Leonore in Beethoven's 'Fidelio': lithograph by W. Santer

*

L. Rellstab: 'Wilhelmine Schröder-Devrient', *Gesammelte Schriften*, ix (Leipzig, 1844)
H. Chorley: *Modern German Music* (London, 1854)
——: *Thirty Years' Musical Recollections* (London, 1862, 2/1926)
C. von Glümer: *Erinnerungen an Wilhelmine Schröder-Devrient* (Leipzig, 1862, 3/1905)
E. Genast: *Aus dem Tagebuch eines alten Schauspielers* (Leipzig, 1862–6)
A. von Wolzogen: *Wilhelmine Schröder-Devrient* (Leipzig, 1863)
H. Berlioz: *Mémoires* (Paris, 1870; Eng. trans., 1969)
R. Wagner: 'Über Schauspieler und Sänger', *Gesammelte Schriften*, ix (Leipzig, 1873; Eng. trans., v, 1896), 157–230
G. Bonacci: 'Guglielmina Schröder-Devrient e Gasparo Spontini', *Nuova antologia*, no.106 (1903), 306–19
C. Hagemann: *Wilhelmine Schröder-Devrient* (Berlin, 1904, 2/1947)
J. Bab: *Die Devrients* (Berlin, 1932)

JOHN WARRACK

Schröder-Feinen, Ursula (*b* Gelsenkirchen, 21 July 1936). German soprano. She studied in Gelsenkirchen with Maria Helm and joined the opera chorus there in 1958. In 1961 she sang Aida. Her repertory at Gelsenkirchen included Handel's Cleopatra, Leonore, Oscar, Chrysothemis, Salome, Turandot and Gershwin's Bess. From 1968 to 1972 she was engaged at the Deutsche Oper am Rhein, Düsseldorf, adding Electra, Kundry and Brünnhilde (*Die Walküre*) to her repertory. She sang at the Metropolitan (1970–78), at Bayreuth (as Senta, Ortrud, Kundry and Brünnhilde) from 1971, and at Salzburg (as the Dyer's Wife and Ortrud) from 1975, the year of her British début as Salome at the Edinburgh Festival. She made her Paris Opéra début as Brünnhilde in 1976. Her repertory included Jenůfa and Isolde. Schröder-Feinen was a singer in the great German *hochdramatisch* tradition, but sang many roles that were too heavy for her gleaming, warm-toned voice. She retired in 1979. HAROLD ROSENTHAL/R

Schroeder, Jeanne Charlotte. *See* SAINT-AUBIN, JEANNE CHARLOTTE.

Schubaur, Johann Lukas (*b* Lechfeld, bap. 23 Dec 1749; *d* Munich, 15 Nov 1815). German composer. He attended the theological seminary in Neuburg an der Donau, where he also acquired a comprehensive musical education. He gave up the monastic life because of illness, and studied medicine in Vienna, making a living by giving piano lessons and writing short occasional compositions. From 1775 he practised in Neuburg an der Donau; soon afterwards he settled in Munich and held several important medical posts.

Schubaur's activities as a dilettante composer were linked with the efforts of the Palatine court in Munich to develop an independent German Singspiel alongside Italian and French comic opera. His first attempt, *Melide, oder Der Schiffer*, translated freely by Schubaur himself from a French model and performed in 1782 in Munich, failed utterly and aroused discussion only after the success of his next Singspiel, *Die Dorfdeputierten*. For this work Schubaur chose a lighter text which had already been set by E. W. Wolf and later appeared in a well-known setting by Dieter and Teyber. It was his greatest artistic and commercial success (largely because of the vocal score, which he published himself) and is said to have received over a hundred performances in Munich alone, as well as frequent stagings throughout Germany as late as 1813. After the resounding failure of *Das Lustlager* (1784) and the only moderate success of *Die treuen Köhler* (1786) Schubaur gave up writing for the theatre. Among his works only *Die Dorfdeputierten* and *Die treuen Köhler* are extant; additional works, mentioned by Eitner and Lipowsky, cannot be authenticated as Schubaur's.

first performed at Munich, Nationaltheater

Melide, oder Der Schiffer (Spl, Schubaur, after F. de Falbaire), 24 Sept 1782

Die Dorfdeputierten (Spl, 3, G. E. Heermann, after C. Goldini: *Il feudatorio*), 8 May 1783, vs (Mannheim and Munich, *c*1783)

Das Lustlager (Spl, 2, F. M. Babo), 4 Aug 1784

Die treuen Köhler (Spl, 2, Heermann), 29 Sept 1786, vs (Munich, 1786)

*

EitnerQ

F. J. Lipowsky: *Baierisches Musik-Lexikon* (Munich, 1811)

E. Reipschläger: *Schubaur, Danzi und Poissl als Opernkomponisten* (diss., U. of Rostock, 1911; biographical extracts, Berlin-Mariendorf, 1911)

GERHARD ALLROGGEN

Schubert, Franz (Peter) (*b* Vienna, 31 Jan 1797; *d* Vienna, 19 Nov 1828). Austrian composer. He completed 11 works of various kinds for the theatre and left sketches or unfinished manuscripts of seven others. Thus his operas formed a major part of his total output.

1. Life. Schubert was born into a respectable lower-professional class home in a suburb of Vienna of first-generation Viennese parents (his father was Moravian, his mother Silesian). In his early years, living conditions in the capital were grim as the Napoleonic Wars gradually reduced Austria to bankruptcy (in 1811). His father, a dedicated primary school teacher and headmaster, acquired a reputation which resulted in his receiving honorary Viennese citizenship in 1826. He recognized the talents of some of his children, not least Franz's exceptional musical gifts. At the age of 11 Schubert was accepted as a choirboy in the Imperial Hofkapelle. Apart from the musical experience this offered him, there was the added advantage of an excellent general education at the Akademisches Gymnasium and residence in the Stadtkonvikt nearby where musical activities were further encouraged.

When in July 1812 Schubert's voice broke and he could no longer sing in the chapel choir he was allowed to continue at the Gymnasium, but in autumn 1813 he decided to leave and concentrate on music. He was probably persuaded by his father to acquire a professional qualification (after one year's training) as a primary school teacher, and he enrolled at the Normalhauptschule in Vienna. He was to teach in his father's school intermittently from 1815 probably until 1818.

While still at the Stadtkonvikt Schubert was caught up in the Viennese enthusiasm for opera, which reached a peak in 1814–15, during and immediately after the Congress of Vienna. He attended performances at the Kärntnertortheater (the court theatre) and the Theater an der Wien. His first recorded theatre visits were to see Joseph Weigl's popular Singspiels *Das Waisenhaus* and *Die Schweizerfamilie* in 1810–11. It was probably in December 1811, shortly before his 15th birthday, that Schubert began composing his first opera, the three-act Singspiel *Der Spiegelritter*, to a text by the prolific and popular German playwright August von Kotzebue. But the task proved too much for him and he finally put it aside early in 1813, before he had completed the first act. In about 1812 he saw several of the operas from Paris that were now favourites (in German versions) in Vienna, such as Cherubini's *Médée* and Spontini's *La vestale*, as well as *Die Zauberflöte*.

Schubert began lessons in composition with Antonio Salieri in June 1812. Salieri had been a pupil of Gluck and was one of several established composers, among them Beethoven and Weigl, who deplored the frivolous tastes of Viennese audiences. Under his tutelage a great change took place in Schubert's compositions as the relatively free writings of his childhood gave way to more profound music created by a young man with a professional technique and grasp. Schubert devoted intensive study to the operas of Gluck, Mozart and Salieri himself. In October 1813, just before he left the Stadtkonvikt, Schubert began work on his second three-act Singspiel, *Des Teufels Lustschloss*; evidence of Salieri's criticism is found in Schubert's autograph manuscripts of the opera, in two versions, most of which have survived. Meanwhile, in May 1814, Schubert attended a performance of Beethoven's *Fidelio*, an experience which was to have considerable influence on his own theatre music.

About this time Schubert's music began to be heard not only in the circle of family and friends but also publicly. The steady flow of songs in 1814 grew into a veritable torrent in 1815. In that year, despite his work as an unwilling school teacher, he composed two symphonies (nos.2 and 3), two masses, instrumental pieces, 150 songs and four Singspiels. Of these last, the first was the comic one-act piece *Der vierjährige Posten*, which he wrote in 12 days during May. In this opera a young soldier, who absented himself to marry, is saved from execution for desertion by resuming after four years his former position as a sentry. As Schubert left much of the dialogue to be spoken and set only one example of each musical form – aria, duet, trio etc. – it is likely that he composed the music as an exercise rather than with performance in view. For the one-act, serious Singspiel *Fernando*, which followed in June and July, Schubert's school friend Albert Stadler created a poor play which combined themes from Beethoven's *Fidelio* and an earlier Kotzebue drama. The music, also written in Beethoven's shadow, is again experimental. Of his next theatre work, Goethe's Liederspiel *Claudine von Villa Bella*, the last two acts were destroyed during the 1848 revolution. The text, a minor early work of Goethe's, was far superior to Stadler's amateur and immature effort, and the play accompanied by Schubert's completed score might have been worthy of performance. The final Singspiel of this remarkable year was the promising two-act comic piece *Die Freunde von Salamanka* to a text by Schubert's poet friend Johann Mayrhofer (the dialogue is now lost). The plot, which reveals a debt to *Twelfth Night*, is not without virtues, and presented Schubert with a variety of scenes, characters and set pieces and the opportunity for some promising large ensembles. The writing of this Singspiel, probably begun in November at about the same time as his Mass in B♭, occupied Schubert into the early part of 1816.

Schubert may have looked at another Singspiel text, based on a tale of medieval Minnesingers, before he turned in May 1816 to his first opera on a classical theme, *Die Bürgschaft*. The autograph manuscript of *Die Bürgschaft* shows that it was another student work written under Salieri's critical eye. After completing two acts and the entr'acte before Act 3, Schubert gave up, in the middle of an ensemble. The librettist is unknown and the connecting dialogue is lost: but the poverty of the text suggests that this was another amateurish effort by one of Schubert's friends.

Early in 1816 Schubert made the first of several unsuccessful applications for a salaried appointment, on this occasion as music teacher at a teachers' training college in Laibach (now Ljubljana), a post no doubt more to his taste than one involving the teaching of small children. Soon after this he left home and schoolmastering to move into lodgings in Vienna where, with no steady income, the pattern of his life changed radically. Regular lessons with Salieri ceased, and for some two years he rested from operatic composition. He was now more concerned with receiving paid commissions and having his music performed and published than with writing time-consuming pieces for the theatre which stood little chance of performance. His professional life continued to develop during 1817; he met Johann Michael Vogl, the operatic high baritone who was to introduce his songs to a wide public; and to two more symphonies written in 1816 (nos.4 and 5) he added no.6, besides composing songs and solo piano music.

Schubert spent the summer of 1818 as music tutor to the family of Count Johann Esterházy at Zseliz in Hungary. Soon after his return to Vienna in the early autumn he was invited by the management of the Kärntnertortheater to compose music for the one-act farce *Die Zwillingsbrüder*, in which Vogl was to play the double role of the twin brothers. The text, based on a French model, by Georg von Hofmann, later resident librettist at this theatre, was of a trivial kind for which Schubert felt little affinity; but this commission, procured through Vogl's good offices, gave him his first opportunity in the professional theatre. He completed the music early in 1819; it was performed in June 1820. The shallow tale of mistaken identities was of a kind briefly popular in Vienna (the censorship laws were severely restrictive of serious theatre). Such plays were generally set to music of at best ephemeral charm by second-rate composers, and this was not Schubert's metier. Late in 1819 he set to work on his next opera, *Adrast*, again on a classical subject and to another Mayrhofer text. This was a serious work, potentially of some importance in his development as a composer; but he laid it aside unfinished, probably in February 1820, to concentrate on the remarkable dramatic oratorio for Easter, *Lazarus* (which he also left unfinished).

A commission followed, this time from the Theater an der Wien, for another Hofmann play, the three-act melodrama *Die Zauberharfe*. He composed long passages of descriptive music to accompany the spoken word, as well as choruses and a tenor solo. The first of eight performances took place in August 1820. Before the final performance of his melodrama Schubert embarked on a new work for the theatre, a three-act opera *Sacontala*, a classical Sanskrit tale of a kind common in early German Romantic opera. Romantic love and high ideals are put to the test, while magic and scenic transformations add spice to the dramatic and musical possibilities. But *Sacontala* too was fated to be left in fragmentary form. From this time dates another Singspiel fragment, usually referred to as *Sophie* after the name of the heroine.

In January 1821 Schubert applied for a position on the music staff of the Kärntnertortheater and worked there briefly as a répétiteur. He received another small commission to write a comic duet and an aria to be inserted into a German version of Hérold's *La clochette* (*Das Zauberglöckchen*), based on the Aladdin story; these were favourably received at the first performance, in June.

In September 1821, on the brink of a promising start in the theatre, Schubert began work on a three-act 'grand Romantic opera', *Alfonso und Estrella*. The librettist was his close friend Franz von Schober; the plot was similar in many respects to Shakespeare's *As you Like it*. Work was well under way by 3 November when the two young men attended the first Viennese performance of Weber's *Der Freischütz*. Here was an event of considerable importance to supporters of German Romantic opera in Vienna, providing a short respite in the losing battle against the flood of enthusiasm for the operas of Rossini. Schubert was familiar with several of these Italian operas; he praised the best of them but was critical of others. Sadly, from 1821 his own fate as an opera composer must be linked with Rossini's success and the concomitant rejection of German operas. On its completion, *Alfonso und Estrella* was turned down by all the theatres that were approached. Both the Kärntnertortheater and the Theater an der Wien were in financial difficulties when, in December 1821, they fell under the management of the Italian impresario Domenico Barbaia. As his principal aim was to keep the theatre doors open, Italian operas, which drew in the largest audiences, predominated in the repertory. Barbaia tried to encourage German composers, however, by commissioning new operas, including one from Weber (*Euryanthe*) and, after the rejection of *Alfonso*, another from Schubert (*Fierrabras*).

There was a break of some months before Schubert received the libretto for *Fierrabras* and, still hoping for further success in the theatre, he composed between November 1822 and April 1823 music for the one-act comic Singspiel *Die Verschworenen*, to a text by the popular local poet and dramatist Ignaz Castelli. It was based on Aristophanes' *Lysistrata* and *Ekklesiazusae*, transferred to a medieval crusader background (under pressure from the censors, the title was changed to *Der häusliche Krieg*). Although rejected by theatres when it was composed, *Die Verschworenen* was to become immensely popular later in the century. In May Schubert made some fragmentary sketches for a serious Romantic opera, *Rüdiger*, similar in background to *Fierrabras*, possibly to words by his patron and adviser Ignaz von Mosel. This he discarded when he received the libretto for the grand, three-act heroic-romantic opera *Fierrabras* from Josef Kupelwieser, then secretary (general manager) at the Kärntnertortheater and older brother of Schubert's close friend, the artist Leopold

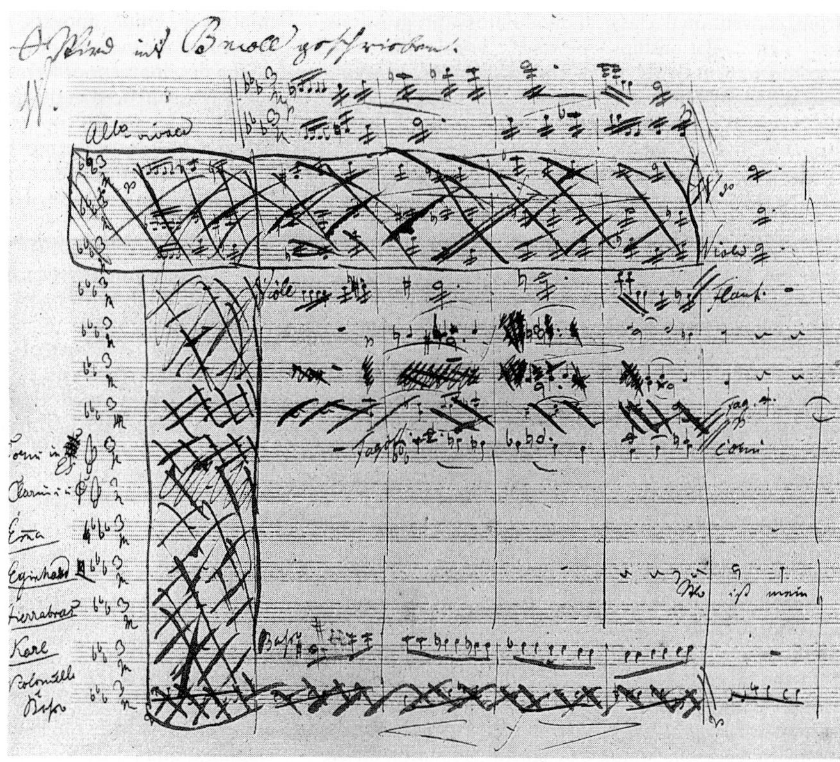

Autograph score of 'Fierrabras' (composed 25 May–2 October 1823) showing alterations Schubert made to the Act 3 quartet; these were necessary after the withdrawal of a preceding trio section, and include the direction that the Allegro vivace should be transposed from C minor to B♭ minor

Kupelwieser. *Fierrabras* is a love story told against the background of the reign of Charlemagne and his battles against the Moorish infidels. Such themes were becoming increasingly popular in the German theatre; on 25 October, only three weeks after Schubert finished his composition, Weber's *Euryanthe* of a similar type, to a text by Helmina von Chezy, had its première at the court theatre. The failure of Weber's opera was perhaps the final blow for German Romantic opera in Vienna, and certainly helped to destroy any chances that Schubert's *Fierrabras* might have had of performance, when the management turned its back on the possibility of a further expensive medieval catastrophe.

The two performances of Chezy's disastrously unsuccessful play *Rosamunde* in December – only Schubert's incidental music was well received – saw the end of his dreams of success in the theatre. All attempts thereafter to get *Alfonso und Estrella*, *Die Verschworenen* and *Fierrabras* into production failed. In Vienna the craze for Italian opera only briefly restrained a decline in the popularity of the genre which was to continue until long after Schubert's death. The theatres were frequently closed for extended periods and there was virtually no interest in German works. Schubert's scores sank into oblivion. From the period of these three operas come Schubert's Mass in A♭, the *Wanderer* Fantasy, the Unfinished Symphony (in 1822) and *Die schöne Müllerin* (1823). These years also saw the onset of his tragic syphilitic illness and a period of several weeks in hospital.

At the beginning of 1824, ill and depressed, and with the failure of his theatre works weighing on his mind, Schubert abandoned the writing of operas; he concentrated over the next three years on songs and instrumental music – including first quartets, then his long-planned Symphony in C major (1825–6). During 1825 he travelled in Austria to mountains and lakes. By this time many of his songs and much piano music (especially dances) had been published, and he was far from unknown in Vienna. But his reputation was no help to him when ne vainly applied for the position of Hoforganist or, in the following year, that of vice-Kapellmeister at the Hofkapelle.

Some time in 1825–6 Schubert persuaded his new friend, the dramatist Eduard von Bauernfeld, to write an opera libretto for him on the subject of *Der Graf von Gleichen*. Set at the time of the Crusades in the Orient and the Occident, the story tells of the bigamous marriage of the Count of Gleichen to a young Egyptian princess who had helped him escape from imprisonment. Unaccountably, Schubert was determined to set the play despite the censors' rejection of the text. He did not start work on it until June 1827, after he had completed the first part of *Winterreise*. He put the two-act opera manuscript aside in March 1828, fully sketched except for the last two numbers, in order to prepare for an important public concert of his music in the Philharmonic Society Hall at the end of that month. Other thoughts and compositions absorbed his attention for his remaining eight months. He may have been contemplating another ecclesiastical appointment when, during the summer, he wrote six sacred works. Finally, in a burst of phenomenal inspiration, came the String Quintet, the last three piano sonatas and the *Schwanengesang* songs.

2. Operas. Just as Schubert developed his techniques, structures, power and range of expression in his songs and instrumental music, from his early student efforts to the great works of his mature years, so too did his operatic style evolve. The music grew richer, increasingly colourful and dramatically more powerful. Throughout his dramatic music there is evidence of his concern for orchestral colour, for expressive digressions

from conventional classical modulatory progressions, for new relationships between vocal line and accompaniment in set pieces and in dialogue, in recitative and in melodrama, and for the expansion, using all the means at his disposal, of the Singspiel into a longer, Romantic operatic whole.

The most important changes in Schubert's composing for the stage took place in 1820–21, as he approached maturity as a composer. These years covered his composition of *Adrast*, the dramatic oratorio *Lazarus* and the melodrama *Die Zauberharfe*. In *Adrast* he experimented with new orchestral timbres, especially in the combination of lower string tones, and in the use of trombones (four of them in the chorus, no.3), particularly in soft passages. He had used trombones already with some daring in his earliest operas, but did not use them in his comic Singspiels, except in the last, *Die Verschworenen*. He continued to experiment with instrumental colours in *Lazarus*, producing some ravishing new orchestral sounds. Schubert made advances here, too, in the setting of recitatives, with some telling and varied orchestral accompaniments, blending instrumental ideas with passages of lyrical declamation which flow easily into arias and ensembles in this unusual and remarkable through-composed work.

In the magical play *Die Zauberharfe* recitative gave way to melodrama, in which speech is accompanied or punctuated by music. Apart from solo passages for the tenor, Palmerin, including a delightful Romance, all the vocal music is choral; the instrumental music within the work is entirely in melodrama. Schubert developed these movements from thematic and rhythmic ideas and figurations rather than from his until then more usual melodic material. Some such ideas recur throughout the play as reminiscence motifs, often in skilfully varied forms; he was to use such motifs again in his two grand Romantic operas.

Schubert's penchant for unexpected or startling changes of key is much in evidence in his theatre music. In *Die Zauberharfe*, during the angry dialogue between Arnulf and Melinde in the melodrama no.6, for example, the music modulates rapidly and into apparently unrelated tonalities, frequently in a stepwise progression (as from D minor to E♭ or F minor to G♭). Schubert used key changes of this kind only in moments of particular intensity in his operas. Thus in *Alfonso und Estrella* such modulations are used to emphasize the threat of Adolfo and his followers in the conspirators' ensemble and the despair of Mauregato in his last-act aria; in *Fierrabras*, they colour Roland's impressive description in Act 1 of Fierrabras's valour in battle and Florinda's fiery aria in Act 2. As in *Die Zauberharfe*, the moments of greatest tension in the melodramas of *Fierrabras* are similarly marked. Schubert's harmonic excursions into tonalities linked by the interval of a 3rd (major or minor) are a familiar fingerprint of his music, and occur most meaningfully in his later operas in moments of tender expression. The attraction of the exquisite, gentle duet for Florinda and Maragond in Act 2 of *Fierrabras* lies both in the beautiful interweaving of the vocal lines and in the easy flow back and forth from the home key of A♭ to A♭ minor and C♭. This flow continues even into the final six bars of the piece, the music only coming to rest in the home key of A♭ major in the penultimate bar. Another magical transformation in the music of the same opera occurs in the first-act 'balcony scene' as, after Eginhard's opening serenade in the minor key, Emma appears, reassuring her beloved with a repeat of the melody, now in the relative major.

The development of lyrical declamation in Schubert's songs was mirrored in the development of recitative and arioso style in his operas. From the declamatory passages of *Lazarus* he moved easily to the recitatives of *Alfonso*, also, and rather surprisingly for the time, in through-composed form. These recitatives are dramatically and musically impressive, as is illustrated by the tense dialogue in recitative between Adolfo, Mauregato and Estrella near the start of the first-act finale. But in *Fierrabras*, except for some fine descriptive passages of dialogue in recitative in the first act, Schubert almost dispensed with this form of word-setting, perhaps rejecting it for reason of its close association with Italian opera. He now seemed to prefer either the spoken word or, for dramatic high points, melodrama, the latter often structured on an almost symphonic scale. However, Schubert returned to the inclusion of recitatives in his final theatre work, the unfinished *Der Graf von Gleichen*.

As early as 1815–16, when Schubert composed the Singspiels *Fernando* and *Die Freunde von Salamanka*, he showed signs of seeking a broader operatic scenario than could be contained in the Singspiel. In his two grand operas of 1821–2 and 1823 he found what he was looking for. Whereas *Alfonso* is marked by some imposing scenes and its increasing level of action, *Fierrabras* is notable for its wide range of ensembles of all kinds, including a quintet of somewhat Mozartian character. In addition, the large chorus, subdivided into several groupings, in the new style of Romantic operas, plays a vital part in the development of the drama. In both these operas, Schubert called for a large orchestra.

Schubert's music for the theatre has long been dismissed as dramatically unsatisfactory. As the music has become more accessible this view has progressively been modified. Schubert was without doubt involved with the development of German opera, aware of its inadequacies but deeply conscious of its potential; and he experimented with its vocal, instrumental and structural possibilities. Had he seen either of his grand operas on the stage or even in rehearsal he would surely have made revisions, as have so many composers before and since. He was a mere 26 years old when he completed his last opera (the age at which Mozart wrote *Die Entführung aus dem Serail*). Had the state of Vienna's theatres been more favourable towards German operas, Schubert might well have been inspired to greater heights after 1823. However, it is clear from the music he did write for the theatre that, although he was sensitive to the feelings and situations of his characters, as his music reflects, they tend to remain the means of describing a story rather than representing lively and distinctive personalities which develop during the course of the work. In addition, Schubert did not acquire sufficient sense of dramatic timing. He might, with more experience, have come to understand better the need to build up tension and release it before interest begins to sag, to introduce more elements of surprise, and to bring his characters on and to see them off the stage at an acceptable pace. His delightfully decorative treatment in sound of the scenes of nature described in the texts could intensify atmosphere but in no way enhance dramatic effect.

Despite any such criticisms, Schubert's works for the theatre include music of outstanding beauty and interest which well merits occasional hearing. He failed during his short lifetime to win success in the field of serious opera (none of his operas was published during his lifetime), and he had no influence upon its development, except possibly through his settings of German texts to music in his songs. This failure, however, was matched by every other Viennese composer during the remainder of the 19th century; it was in operetta that the Viennese were to excel.

See also ALFONSO UND ESTRELLA; FIERRABRAS; VERSCHWORENEN, DIE; and ZWILLINGSBRÜDER, DIE.

Editions: *F. Schuberts Werke: kritisch durchgesehene Gesamtausgabe*, ed. E. Mandyczewski, J. Brahms and others (Leipzig, 1884–97) [SW, ser./vol., p.]
F. Schubert: Neue Ausgabe sämtlicher Werke, ed. W. Dürr, A. Feil, C. Landon and others (Kassel, 1964–) [NSA, ser./vol.]
Texts: *Franz Schubert: Bühnenwerke: Kritische Gesamtausgabe der Texte*, ed. C. Pollack (Tutzing, 1988) [P, p.nos.]

Items are ordered by D number as enumerated in W. Dürr, A. Fiel, C. Landon and others: *Franz Schubert: thematisches Verzeichnis seiner Werke in chronologischer Folge von Otto Erich Deutsch*, Neue Ausgabe sämtlicher Werke, viii/4 (Kassel, 1978)

first performed in Vienna unless otherwise stated

D	*title*	*genre, acts*	*librettist*	*composition*	*first performance*	*SW; NSA*	*P*
11, 966	Der Spiegelritter	Spl, 3; only ov. and most of Act 1 complete	A. von Kotzebue	Dec 1811–late 1812 or early 1813	Swiss Radio, 11 Dec 1949	xxi/1, 1, xv/7, 107; ii/11	357–415
84	Des Teufels Lustschloss [1st version]	Zauberoper, 3	Kotzebue	30 Oct 1813–15 May 1814	Musikvereinsaal, 12 Dec 1879 (as pubd in 1888)	xv/1; ii/1*a*	15–74
	[2nd version]			completed 22 Oct 1814		–; ii/1*b*	
137	Adrast	Oper, 2 or 3; unfinished	J. Mayrhofer	?late 1819–early 1820	Redoutensaal, 13 Dec 1868	xv/7, 315; ii/11	417–32
190	Der vierjährige Posten	Spl, 1	T. Körner	8–19 May 1815	Dresden, 23 Sept 1896	xv/2, 1; ii/2	75–91
220	Fernando	Spl, 1	A. Stadler	June–9 July 1815	13 April 1907	xv/2, 109; ii/2	93–116
239	Claudine von Villa Bella	Spl, 3; only ov. and Act 1 survive	J. W. von Goethe	begun 26 July 1815	Gemeindehaus Wieden, 26 April 1913	xv/7, 1; ii/12	433–92
326	Die Freunde von Salamanka	komisches Spl, 2	Mayrhofer	18 Nov–31 Dec 1815 (?early 1816)	Halle, 6 May 1928	xv/2, 169; ii/3	117–45
435	Die Bürgschaft	Oper, 3; Acts 1 and 2 only		2 May 1816–?late sum.	7 March 1908	xv/7, 201; ii/12	493–508
644	Die Zauberharfe	Zauberspiel mit Musik (melodrama), 3	G. von Hofmann	?May–Aug 1820	An der Wien, 19 Aug 1820	xv/4, 1; ii/4, 3	147–64
647	Die Zwillingsbrüder	Posse, 1	Hofmann, after *Les deux Valentins*	?Dec 1818–Jan 1819	Kärntnertor, 14 June 1820	xv/3, 1; ii/5	165–96
701	Sacontala	Oper, 3, sketches for Acts 1 and 2 only	J. P. Neumann, after Kalidasa	Oct 1820–early 1821	12 June 1971	–; ii/13	531–54
732	Alfonso und Estrella	Oper, 3	F. von Schober	20 Sept 1821–27 Feb 1822	Weimar, Hof, 24 June 1854	ov. xv/4; xv/5, 1; ii/6	197–244
787	Die Verschworenen (Der häusliche Krieg)	Spl, 1	I. F. Castelli, after Aristophanes: *Lysistrata* and *Ecclesiazusae*	?late 1822–April 1823	Frankfurt, 29 Aug 1861 (concert perf., Vienna, Musikvereinsaal, 1 March 1861)	xv/3, 113; ii/7	245–283
791	Rüdiger	Oper, sketches for nos. 1–2 only	?I. von Mosel	begun May 1823	Redoutensaal, 5 Jan 1868	–; ii/14	555–9
796	Fierrabras	heroisch-romantische Oper, 3	J. Kupelwieser, after J. G. G. Büsching and F. H. von der Hagen's story in *Buch der Liebe* (1809), and F. de la Motte Fouqué: *Eginhard und Emma* (1811)	25 May–2 Oct 1823	Karlsruhe, Grossherzögliches Hof, 9 Feb 1897	xv/6, 1; ii/8	285–346
918	Der Graf von Gleichen	romantische Oper, 2, sketches only	E. von Bauernfeld	19 June 1827–1828		–; ii/14 (facs., 1988)	561–615

D	title	genre, acts	librettist	composition	first performance	SW; NSA	P
981	Der Minnesänger	Oper, unfinished, lost					
982	[Sophie]	Oper, sketches, 3 nos. only		?spr. 1821		–; ii/14	617–22

Duet and aria (D723) in Hérold: Das Zauberglöckchen [La clochette], Kärntnertor, 20 June 1821

F. Liszt: 'Alfonso und Estrella', *NZM*, xli (1854), 101–5
H. Kreissle von Hellborn: *Franz Schubert* (Vienna, 1865; Eng. trans., 1869)
R. Krott: *Die Singspiele Schuberts* (diss., U. of Vienna, 1921)
O. E. Deutsch: *Schubert: a Documentary Biography* (London, 1946)
H. Graeser: 'Schuberts musikdramatisches Werk', *ZfM*, cxiv (1953), 653–7
O. E. Deutsch: *Schubert: Memoirs by his Friends* (London, 1958)
M. J. E. Brown: 'Schubert's Two Major Operas', *MR*, xx (1959), 104–18
E. N. McKay: 'Schubert's Incidental Music to "Rosamunde" ', *MR*, xxi (1960), 8–15
——: 'Publisher's Errors in Schubert's Overture to "Die Zauberharfe" ', *MR*, xxiii (1962), 128–31
——: *The Stage-Works of Schubert, Considered in the Framework of Austrian Biedermeier Society* (diss., U. of Oxford, 1962)
F. Racek: 'Franz Schuberts Singspiel "Der häusliche Krieg" und seine jetzt aufgefundene Ouvertüre', *Biblos*, xii (1963), 136–43
E. N. McKay: 'Schubert's Music for the Theatre', *PRMA*, xciii (1966–7), 51–66
M. J. E. Brown: 'Schubert's "Fierrabras" ', *MT*, cxii (1971), 338–9
M. J. Citron: *Schubert's Seven Complete Operas: a Musico-Dramatic Study* (diss., U. of North Carolina, 1971)
W. Szmolyan: 'Schubert als Opernkomponist', *ÖMz*, xxvi (1971), 282–9
G. R. Cunningham: *Franz Schubert als Theaterkomponist* (diss., U. of Freiburg, 1974)
R. Van Hoorickx: 'A Schubert Manuscript Identified', *MT*, cxv (1974), 127
——: 'Les opéras de Schubert', *RBM*, xxviii–xxx (1974–6), 238–59
P. J. Branscombe: 'Schubert and his Librettists, I: Settings of Existing Librettos', *MT*, cxix (1978), 943–7
O. E. Deutsch: *Schubert: Thematisches Verzeichnis seiner Werke* (Kassel, 1978)
——: 'Schubert's "Rosamunde" im Theater an der Wien', *ÖMz*, xxxiii (1978), 179–84
E. Forbes: 'Schubert's "Claudine" ', *Opera*, xxix (1978), 1168–71
E. Hilmar: *Verzeichnis der Schubert-Handschriften in der Musiksammlung der Wiener Stadt- und Landesbibliothek* (Kassel, 1978)
E. Badura-Skoda and P. J. Branscombe, eds.: *Schubert Studies: Problems of Style and Chronology* (Cambridge, 1982) [incl. P. J. Branscombe: 'Schubert and the Melodrama', 105–41; E. N. McKay: 'Schubert as a Composer of Opera', 85–104]
M. A. Wischusen: *The Stage Works of Franz Schubert: Background and Stylistic Influences* (diss., U. of New Jersey, 1983)
E. Hilmar: *Franz Schubert in seiner Zeit* (Vienna, 1985)
——: 'Kann Schuberts "Fierrabras" eine lebensfähige Oper sein?', *ÖMz*, v (1988), 241–4
E. N. McKay: 'Schuberts "Fierrabras" – eine Wiener Oper', *ÖMz*, v (1988), 234–40
T. Denny: 'Wo haben Kupelwieser und Schober ihre Sujets für Schubert gefunden', *Mitteilungen des Internationales Franz Schubert Instituts*, v (1990), 32–7
T. G. Waidelich: 'Einige Korrekturen zu "Alfonso und Estrella" ', ibid, 31–2
E. N. McKay: *Franz Schubert's Music for the Theatre* (Tutzing, 1991)
T. G. Waidelich: *Franz Schuberts 'Alfonso und Estrella': Problemfall einer frühen durchkomponierten Oper* (Tutzing, 1991)

ELIZABETH NORMAN McKAY

Schubert, Johann Friedrich (*b* Rudolstadt, 17 Dec 1770; *d* Mülheim an der Ruhr, Oct 1811). German composer. After studying in Sondershausen his skill on the violin and bassoon impressed E. L. Gerber, who drew him into the court concerts there. In 1791 he joined the orchestra of the Döbbelin Troupe in Berlin as second violinist and moved with it to Stettin (now Szczecin), where he was appointed director of music after the successful première of his two-act opera *Die nächtliche Erscheinung* (1798). He was director of music at the theatre at Glogau (now Głogów) from 1801 and held a similar post with a theatrical society in Ballenstedt from 1804. Soon after, he became a leader of concerts in Mülheim.

Schubert was the author of a treatise on singing, *Neue Singe-Schule, oder Gründliche und vollständige Anweisung zur Singkunst* (Leipzig, 1804), a valuable guide to contemporary practice in such matters as ornamentation and portamento. DIETER HÄRTWIG

Schubert, Richard (*b* Dessau, 15 Dec 1885; *d* Oberstaufen, 12 Oct 1959). German tenor. He studied with Rudolf von Milde and made his début as a baritone in 1909 at Strasbourg. After further study in Milan and Dresden, he returned in 1911 as a tenor, singing first at Nuremberg and then at Wiesbaden (1913–17), where he concentrated on the Wagnerian repertory. His career was then divided largely between Hamburg and Vienna. He sang in the première of Korngold's *Die tote Stadt* (1920, Hamburg), and was also closely associated with Strauss in early performances of *Ariadne auf Naxos*, *Die Frau ohne Schatten* and *Die ägyptische Helena*. Abroad he sang in Paris, Buenos Aires and Chicago. He had a wide repertory of lyric and dramatic roles in Italian and French opera, including Rodolfo, Faust, Radames and Otello. His last appearance in Vienna was as Eisenstein in *Die Fledermaus* in 1937, after which he sang and directed the opera at Osnabrück and then retired to teach. His recordings show a vividly expressive and unusually lyrical style in the Wagnerian repertory; in association with his attractive stage presence these qualities understandably gave him a leading position among the German tenors of his time. J. B. STEANE

Schuch, Ernst, Edler von (*b* Graz, 23 Nov 1846; *d* Kötzschenbroda, nr Dresden, 10 May 1914). Austrian conductor. He studied at Graz with Eduard Stolz and at Vienna with Otto Dessoff before becoming music director of Lobe's theatre in Breslau in 1867. After periods at Würzburg (1868–70), Graz (1870–71) and Basle (1871) he was engaged by Pollini at Dresden in 1872. From sharing conducting duties with Julius Rietz and then Franz Wüllner, he rose to assume sole direction of the Hofoper in 1882 and in 1889 became general music director. During his tenure the company came to rank among the greatest in the world, witnessing 51 world premières as well as the addition of 117 other works to the repertory. Schuch conducted the premières of Strauss's *Feuersnot* (1901), *Salome* (1905), *Elektra* (1909) and *Der Rosenkavalier* (1911), brought Wagner's *Ring*, *Tristan und Isolde* and *Die Meistersinger von Nürnberg* to the Dresden stage, and introduced Puccini's operas and Mascagni's *Cavalleria rusticana* to German audiences; he also gave the first local performances of works by Bungert, Paderewski, Dohnányi and Wolf-Ferrari. Because he cultivated a close working relationship with his orchestra and singers, it was with reluctance that he moved the rostrum back to the rail from the middle of the orchestra nearer the footlights, a position that had been used in Dresden for many years, during the regimes of Weber, Wagner and others.

In 1884 Schuch conducted the opera orchestra in excerpts from *Parsifal* and later indicated his support of contemporary music in his concert programmes. He also appeared as a guest conductor in Europe, Russia and the USA. A man of wide culture and great intelligence, he was a conductor of exceptionally fine technique, taste and inspiration, whose regime of more than a quarter-century was one of the most brilliant periods in the musical history of Dresden. He was ennobled in 1898. Schuch was married to the singer Clementine Schuch-Proska. Their daughter, Liesel von Schuch, was a coloratura soprano of the Dresden opera.

*

P. Sakolowsky: *Ernst von Schuch* (Leipzig, 1901)
P. Adolph: *Vom Hof- zum Staatstheater* (Dresden, 1932)
F. von Schuch: *Richard Strauss, Ernst von Schuch und Dresdens Oper* (Dresden, 1952, 2/1953)
G. M. Henneberg and U. Püschel: 'Virtuosentum und Ensemblegedanke', *300 Jahre Dresdner Staatstheater*, ed. W. Höntsch and U. Püschel (Berlin, 1967)

Schuch-Proska [née Procházka], **Clementine** (*b* Sopron, 12 Feb 1850; *d* Kötzschenbroda, nr Dresden, 8 June 1932). Hungarian soprano. She studied at the Vienna Academy with Mathilde Marchesi, and from 1873 to 1904 was engaged at the Hofoper, Dresden, as leading coloratura soprano. She first sang in Vienna in 1879, and made her Covent Garden début in 1884 as Eva (*Die Meistersinger*). She also appeared as Aennchen (*Der Freischütz*). In 1886 she made a guest appearance in Munich, singing Rosina and Susanna. At Dresden in 1894 she took part in Haydn's *Lo speziale* (sung in German as *Der Apotheker*), which was also performed in Vienna the following year. Her repertory included Amina, Blonde, Zerlina and Violetta; these, along with Eva, were her principal roles. Her voice was light, brilliant and flexible, and she had the impeccable technique of a Marchesi pupil. She was married to the conductor Ernst von Schuch.

*

A. Ehrlich: *Berühmte Sängerinnen der Vergangenheit und Gegenwart* (Leipzig, 1895)

ELIZABETH FORBES

Schüchter, Wilhelm (*b* Bonn, 15 Dec 1911; *d* Dortmund, 27 May 1974). German conductor. He studied at the Cologne Hochschule für Musik with Hermann Abendroth and Philipp Jarnach and made his début in Coburg in 1937 conducting *Cavalleria rusticana* and *Pagliacci*. He held conducting appointments in opera houses in Würzburg (1937–40), Aachen (1940–42), where he worked closely with Karajan, and Berlin (Städtische Oper, 1942–3). After working in Hamburg and Tokyo, he became Generalmusikdirektor at Dortmund, 1962–5, his radical improvement of standards gaining him the position of artistic director and general manager of the Dortmund Städtische Oper, which opened its new house in 1966. Schüchter remained at Dortmund until his death. His tenure was not without controversy, but he was generally considered the principal architect of Dortmund's musical advance in the late 1960s. His recordings, remarkable for their opulent and spacious orchestral sound, are sometimes considered heavily Wagnerian; his performances of Wagner's music dramas at Dortmund won well-deserved acclaim.

LESLIE EAST

Schuh, Oscar Fritz (*b* Munich, 15 Jan 1904; *d* Salzburg, 22 Oct 1984). German director and administrator. He studied philosophy at Munich University and began his theatrical career in Munich, directing Gerhart Hauptmann's *Hanneles Himmelfahrt* (1923). He proceeded by way of Oldenburg, Osnabrück, Darmstadt, Gera and Prague (German Theatre) to become resident producer at the Vienna Opera before joining the Freie Volksbühne in West Berlin as Intendant. From 1959 to 1962 he was Intendant of the Städtische Bühnen, Cologne, and from 1962 to 1968 of the Deutsches Schauspielhaus, Hamburg. At Salzburg, he directed the premières of Egk's *Irische Legende*, von Einem's *Dantons Tod* and *Der Prozess*, Liebermann's *Penelope* and Orff's *Antigonae*. He staged *Le nozze di Figaro* at Covent Garden in 1962 and was noted for his productions of Mozart and Strauss operas in Munich, Salzburg and Vienna.

*

ES (I. A. Chivsano)
O. F. Schuh: *Salzburger Dramaturgie* (Vienna, 1951)

HUGH CANNING

Schuh, Willi (*b* Basle, 12 Nov 1900; *d* Zürich, 4 Oct 1986). Swiss music critic and musicologist. He studied in Aarau, Berne and Munich, where he was a pupil of Anton Beer-Walbrunn. He then studied musicology in Munich with Sandberger (1922–4) and in Berne with Kurth (1924–7). He took the doctorate at Berne in 1927 and in 1928 became music critic of the *Neue Zürcher Zeitung*, of which he was subsequently also music editor (1944–65). He taught at the Winterthur Music School, the St Gall Handelshochschule and Zürich Conservatory (1930–44), and was co-editor of the *Mitteilungen der Schweizerischen musikforschenden Gesellschaft* (1934–6) and editor-in-chief of the *Schweizerische Musikzeitung* (1941–68).

Schuh's work as a music critic for the *Neue Zürcher Zeitung* was of great importance to Swiss musical life. His carefully prepared reviews are of permanent value for their emphasis on thorough analysis and evaluation. Many of his reviews have been republished in the four volumes of *Kritiken und Essays* (1947–8, 1955) and in *Umgang mit Musik* (1970). Schuh's research centred on the works of Richard Strauss, who chose him as his biographer; they were in continual contact from 1936 to the composer's death, and their correspondence was published in 1969.

ed.: *Die Briefe Richard Wagners an Judith Gautier* (Zürich, 1936)
ed.: *Ferruccio Busoni: Briefe an seine Frau* (Zürich, 1936)
Othmar Schoeck: Verzeichnis sämtlicher Werke, Bearbeitungen und Ausgaben (Leipzig, 1936)
ed.: *Othmar Schoeck: Festgabe der Freunde zum 50. Geburtstag* (Erlenbach, 1936)
Kritiken und Essays, i: *Über Opern von Richard Strauss* (Zürich, 1947)
In memoriam Richard Strauss (Zürich, 1949)
ed.: *Richard Strauss: Betrachtungen und Erinnerungen* (Zürich, 1949, 3/1981)
ed.: *Richard Strauss und Hugo von Hofmannsthal: Briefwechsel: Gesamtausgabe* (Zürich, 1952, 4/1964)
'Goethe-Vertonungen', *Goethe-Gedenkausgabe*, ii (Zürich, 1953), 665–739

'Der Rosenkavalier: die ursprüngliche Fassung des II. Aktes', *Neue Rundschau*, lxiv (1953), 357–91
ed.: *R. Strauss: Briefe an die Eltern* (Zürich, 1954)
ed.: R. Strauss and H. von Bülow: 'Briefwechsel', *Richard Strauss Jb 1954*, 7–88; Eng. trans. (1955)
ed.: *Igor Strawinsky: Leben und Werk, von ihm selbst* (Zürich and Mainz, 1957)
ed.: *Richard Strauss und Stefan Zweig: Briefwechsel* (Frankfurt, 1957)
Renoir und Wagner (Zürich, 1959)
ed., with G. K. Kende: *Richard Strauss und Clemens Krauss: Briefwechsel* (Munich, 1963)
Hugo von Hofmannsthal und Richard Strauss: Legende und Wirklichkeit (Munich, 1964)
Ein paar Erinnerungen an Richard Strauss (Zürich, 1964)
with E. Roth: *Richard Strauss: Gesamtverzeichnis* (London, 1964)
Der Rosenkavalier: vier Studien (Olten, 1968)
ed.: *Richard Strauss und Willi Schuh: Briefwechsel* (Zürich, 1969)
Umgang mit Musik: über Komponisten, Libretti und Bilder (Zürich, 1970)
Richard Strauss: Jugend und frühe Meisterjahre, Lebenschronik 1864–1898 (Zürich, 1976; Eng. trans., 1982)
Straussiana aus vier Jahrzehnten (Tutzing, 1981)

*

SML [with list of writings to 1964]
A. Briner: 'Fünfundzwanzig Jahre Schriftleitung Dr Willi Schuh', *SMz*, cvi (1966), 196–7
A. Briner: 'In Beziehung zu Strauss: "Richard Strauss – Briefwechsel mit Willi Schuh"', *Neue Zürcher Zeitung* (1969), no.169
J. Stenzl, ed.: *Art Nouveau, Jugendstil und Musik* (Zürich, 1980)

JÜRG STENZL

Schuhu und die fliegende Prinzessin, Der ('The Bird-Man and the Flying Princess'). Opera by UDO ZIMMERMANN to a libretto by Eberhard Schmidt and the composer after Peter Hacks's fairy-tale; Dresden, Staatsoper, 30 December 1976.

Zimmermann's fourth opera, written in 1976, was commissioned by the Dresden Staatsoper, and first performed by them under Max Pommer with Harry Kupfer as director. The 'Schuhu' is a bird-man who can 'see by night, solve all riddles and give advice'. His actions 'are like those of a man who accepts things as he finds them but does not seem to be quite of this world'. The fable, which was taken as criticism of the utopian ideas of social realism, runs thus: a Tailor (tenor) and his Wife (soprano) produce an egg as their tenth child. With great difficulty, a Smith breaks it open and a Schuhu (baritone) is born. He has magic powers and tries to use them for his parents' good, but those around him are suspicious and cast him out. He travels widely, hoping to put his great gifts to the service of a strong lord, as did St Christopher, but finds himself always distrusted and rejected. At last he obtains a humble position as a nightwatchman in the imperial gardens at Ctesiphon. Here the Princess of Tripolis (soprano), who can also fly, notices him when he plays his horn and falls in love with him; consequently, she refuses offers of marriage from her powerful suitors. Although previously at odds with each other, the suitors now form an alliance to catch, roast and eat the Schuhu. However, he succeeds in destroying their fleets in the manner of cunning Odysseus. Now husband of the Princess, he seems to have all he could desire, but she falls in love with a nobleman from Holland (bass-baritone) and leaves the Schuhu. In the end they are reunited in resignation, to fly away to a promised land far off in the Caucasus.

Der Schuhu is scored for groups of solo instruments and includes music for hurdy-gurdy, musical saw and tape. The way in which Zimmermann constructs 'mountains of sound' is reminiscent of the blocks of textures employed by the Polish School; the 'new simplicity' of his tonal language makes the music accessible to the public. *Der Schuhu* has been staged in many German cities and in Amsterdam, Brussels, Budapest, Prague, Vienna, Warsaw and Zagreb. DETLEF GOJOWY

Schuldrama (Ger.: 'School drama'). From the early 16th century, in Catholic schools and universities and later in Protestant ones as well, the performance of Latin plays formed an important part of the educational programme, cultivating in their youthful executants a mastery of Latin and the social bearing needed for the positions in society they were to assume. At first comedies by Terence and other Roman playwrights were used, but at many schools members of the faculty wrote new Latin plays in imitation of classical models but without their erotic allusions. Important contributors after the mid-century include the Augsburg Mastersinger Sebastian Wild.

Typically, the plays used no decorations and only amateur actors. They were performed either in the school's auditorium or in public; in some towns the student stage functioned as a civic theatre. The plays show little if any literary finesse, with the main action normally drawn from the Bible but freely embellished in order to provide a forceful sense of realism. There was a pronounced tendency to incorporate elements that would fix the attention of an audience often little acquainted with Latin – spectacle, dances, live animals and scenes of physical violence as well as of excessive eating and drinking. Music's role was ordinarily confined to choruses, *intermedi* of various sorts and occasional hymns and songs.

Under the music-loving Prince-Archbishop von Schrattenbach, students at the University of Salzburg performed five-act Latin tragedies interspersed with musical pantomimes and comic intermezzos at Shrovetide, for important visitors and at the end of each term. Michael Haydn contributed both pantomimes and German Singspiels for these occasions between 1767 and 1771, as did the young Mozart with his three-act Latin intermezzo *Apollo et Hyacinthus* (13 May 1767).

*

J. B. Trenkle: *Über süddeutsche geistliche Schulkomödien* (Freiburg, 1866)
E. Riedel: *Schuldrama und Theater* (Hamburg, 1885)
P. E. Schmidt: *Die Bühnenverhältnisse des deutschen Schuldramas und seiner volkstümlichen Ableger im 16. Jahrhundert* (Berlin, 1903)
H. Levinger: *Augsburger Schultheater*, Theater und Drama, ii (Berlin, 1931)
G. Skopnik: *Das Strassburger Schultheater: sein Spielplan und seine Bühne* (Frankfurt, 1935)

THOMAS BAUMAN

Schuller, Gunther (Alexander) (*b* New York, 22 Nov 1925). American composer. The son of a violinist, he began his career as a horn player; he was principal horn at the Metropolitan Opera from 1945 to 1959. As a composer he is entirely self-taught. His interests range widely over both popular and classical traditions, and he has amalgamated diverse elements into syntheses that have a distinctive viability, vividness and communicative power. His earliest published work, the Suite for wind quintet (1944), reveals his lifelong quest for assimilating disparate elements into variegated, though coherent, forms. After this piece his development was marked by a protean absorbing of styles and genres (especially of jazz), an unerring instinct for orchestration, a decreasing dependence on accompanied melody and a movement away from selfconscious rhetoric towards a fuller integration of powerful gestures into the deeper structure. He has drawn on techniques developed by 20th-century composers: on Stravinsky's rhythm, Schoenberg's serialism, Webern's orchestration, Varèse's manipulation of planes and volumes and on Babbitt's principles of 'combinatoriality'. His Symphony (1965) revives symphonic procedures that had been regarded as inappropriate to serial music.

Though Schuller's output as a composer is prodigious, he has written only two operas. In his three-act opera *The Visitation* (Hamburg, 12 October 1966), which is based on Kafka's novel *Der Prozess*, he typically amalgamates jazz and art music in the manner he himself termed 'third stream music'. *The Fisherman and his Wife*, a chamber opera for children (libretto by J. Updike, based on a Grimm fairy-tale) was first performed in Boston on 7 May 1970. His book *Musings: The Musical Worlds of Gunther Schuller* (New York, 1986) includes an article, 'The Future of Opera', written in 1967.

See also VISITATION, THE.

*

R. L. Larsen: *A Study and Comparison of Samuel Barber's 'Vanessa', Robert Ward's 'The Crucible', and Gunther Schuller's 'The Visitation'* (diss., U. of Indiana, 1971)
C. J. Stuessy: *The Confluence of Jazz and Classical Music from 1950 to 1970* (diss., Eastman School of Music, 1977)

AUSTIN CLARKSON

Schuloper (Ger.: 'school opera'). A German opera written for didactic use in schools; its suitability for performance by children is a secondary consideration. Early examples, which belong more strictly to the category of 'school drama' (*see* SCHULDRAMA), derived from 15th-century humanism and concentrated on religious training and the teaching of Latin; music was confined to choruses and short interludes. Although Singspiels were written for children during the 18th and 19th centuries, the *Schuloper* belongs to the 20th century. Interest in the idea was reawakened in the late 1920s through the influential musical Jugendbewegung and through the concern for amateur music shown by leading contemporary composers. The pedagogic content concentrated on the teaching of music, drama and a community spirit. The most important examples are Weill's *Der Jasager* (1930), which also encouraged political thinking, and Hindemith's *Wir bauen eine Stadt* (1930), the latter well suited to performance by children in junior and middle schools.

*

MGG ('Schuldrama'; K.-G. Hartmann and J. Bužga); *RiemannL 12*

IAN KEMP

Schultz, Johann Abraham Peter. *See* SCHULZ, JOHANN ABRAHAM PETER.

Schultz, Svend S(imon) (*b* Nykøbing Falster, 30 Dec 1913). Danish composer. He studied the piano and composition at the Royal Danish Conservatory with Schierbeck and others (1933–8). He worked as a teacher and as a music critic (1942–9), and was appointed choir conductor and instructor for Danish Radio in 1949. As a pianist and conductor he toured Scandinavia, Italy and Switzerland with his own works. In his compositions he has concentrated on chamber and vocal music, although his output includes symphonies and concertos. Through a series of short, melodic, often *buffo*-like operas for small ensembles he has continued with public success the Danish tradition of Børresen and Schierbeck. His dramatic works also include a ballet, a pantomime and the church drama *Eva* (1968; M. Balslev).

Bag Kulisserne [Behind the Scenes], 1946 (1, Schultz), Copenhagen, Kongelige, 24 May 1949
Solbadet [The Sunbath], 1947 (Schultz), Århus, 26 Nov 1949
Høst [Harvest] (E. Falk-Rønne), Århus, 1950
Bryllupsrejse [The Honeymoon] (ob, 1, H. Boland), Copenhagen, Odd Fellows, 4 Sept 1951
Hosekræmmeren [The Stocking Peddler], 1955 (M. Balslev, after S. S. Blicher); rev. 1975; rev. 1985, Århus, 4 May 1990
Tordenvejret eller Da Søren blev Mand [The Thunderstorm] (Falk-Rønne), Copenhagen, Kongelige, 11 April 1956
Dommer Lynch [Judge Lynch], 1959, inc.
Marionetterne (marionette op for television, Falk-Rønne), 1959
Konen i muddergrøften [The Woman in the Muddy Ditch] (television op, Boland), 18 April 1965
Støv, 1969 (television op, Schultz), unperf.
Svinedrengen (school op, I. H. Jacobsen, after H. C. Andersen), 1970
Lykken og forstanden (children's op, Jacobsen), 1972

*

V. Jensen: '"Bag kulisserne", Omkring Sv. S. Schultz' forste opera', *Dansk Musiktidsskrift*, xxiv (1949), 227–30
V. Jensen: 'Kendt komponist sigtet: "Høst" og "Bryllupsrejse" af Svend S. Schultz', *Dansk Musiktidsskrift*, xxvi (1951), 185–8

NIELS MARTIN JENSEN

Schulz [Schultz], **Johann Abraham Peter** (*b* Lüneburg, 31 March 1747; *d* Schwedt an der Oder, 10 June 1800). German composer. He studied music with the local organist of Lüneburg, J. S. Schmügel, and at 15 travelled to Berlin, where he sought out C. P. E. Bach and Joseph Kirnberger for help in furthering his career. They persuaded him, however, to return to Lüneburg to complete his education. When he was 18 he returned to Berlin; Kirnberger accepted him as a pupil, and in 1768 recommended him for the position of accompanist and music teacher to Princess Sapieha Woiwodin von Smolensk of Poland. Schulz travelled with the princess throughout Europe for three years, during which time his musical horizons were greatly expanded. He was particularly impressed with Gluck's music, which was to have a major influence on his operatic composition. He also met Grétry during this period. Schulz returned to Berlin in 1773 and Kirnberger enlisted his help in writing the music articles for J. G. Sulzer's *Allgemeine Theorie der schönen Künste*. Schulz wrote all the music articles from S to Z, and assisted with several others. About this time he wrote his first work for the musical stage, a prologue, *Das Opfer der Nymphen*, for the birthday of Frederick the Great in 1774. He wrote his first full stage work in the following year, a three-act operetta *Clarissa, oder Das unbekannte Dienstmädchen*, to a libretto by J. C. Bock. Eight songs from the work were later to appear in Schulz's chief song collection, *Lieder im Volkston* (Berlin, 1782–90), implying that he considered them folklike in character.

In 1776, on J. F. Reichardt's recommendation, Schulz was appointed music director of the newly built French Theatre in Berlin. Two years later, he was given a similar position at the private theatre of the Prussian crown princess, Friederike Luise. He wrote several stage works in this period. The first, composed in 1779, was a one-act *comédie mêlée d'ariettes* entitled simply *Musique de l'impromptu en vers*. The second, *La fée Urgèle, ou Ce qui plait aux dames*, to a text by C.-S. Favart, was written during the 1780–81 season. It was revised and translated into German in 1789 and presented at the Nationaltheater in Berlin; it would later be translated into Danish by Theodor Thaarup and presented in Copenhagen in 1792. Schulz's third French work was *La vérité*, written in 1784 for the court at Rheinsberg where he had been appointed court composer to the Prussian king's younger brother, Prince Heinrich, in spring 1780. The melodramatic *divertissement Panomphée* dates from about 1785. His next work, a five-act opera based on the Racine tragedy *Athalie* and written for Rheinsberg, was one of Schulz's most successful stage compositions. His final stage work written in Prussia was the three-act French opera *Aline, reine de Golconde*, to a libretto by Michel-Jean Sedaine. It was composed in Rheinsberg during summer 1787 for the private French opera house of Prince Heinrich.

During his tenure as director of the French Theatre, the private theatre of the crown princess and court theatre of Prince Heinrich in Rheinsberg, Schulz championed new music, producing, in addition to his own works, French operettas and new works by Gluck, Piccinni and Sacchini. This advocacy brought him into disfavour with the royal family, however, and the fury with which Princess Amalie reacted to his dedication to her of *Athalie* (a queen who massacred her entire family save for one grandson) was the final blow that led to his resignation in 1787. Schulz was shortly appointed to an even more important position, that of Hofkapellmeister and director of the Kongelige Teater at the Danish court in Copenhagen, on the recommendation of C. F. Cramer and Count Stolberg. He took with him the opera *Aline*. It was translated into German by Cramer, and into Danish by Theodor Thaarup as *Aline, dronning af Golconda*, presented in Copenhagen in 1789. In Copenhagen Schulz reorganized the royal chapel, staged works that reflected Denmark's concern for problems such as land reform, founded a benefit fund for musicians' widows and wrote a major treatise on music education. Because of his varied activities, Copenhagen soon became one of the leading musical centres of Europe. Schulz also wrote three Danish Singspiels, *Indtoget* ('Entry'), *Høstgildet* ('Harvest Home') and *Peters bryllup* ('Peter's Wedding'). All deal with the political subject of land reform and freedom for the peasants – *Peter's Wedding* being a sequel both textually and musically to *Harvest Home* – and all remained in the Copenhagen repertory for several decades.

Schulz was extremely influential in Denmark and has been called the pioneer of that country's national music, even though he was not Danish. His stage works written there were important as embodiments of current political ideas. The composer was pensioned in 1795, aged 48, having contracted tuberculosis. He sailed for Portugal that autumn, but his ship was forced ashore by bad weather at Arendal, on the southern coast of Norway, where he stayed the winter at great detriment to his health. The following spring he visited his birthplace in Lüneburg, then returned to Prussia. For the remainder of his life he divided his time between Berlin and Rheinsberg, with frequent visits to Schwedt for medical reasons. He died in Schwedt at 53.

See also ATHALIE.

Das Opfer der Nymphen (prol., C. W. Ramler), Berlin, Koch's, 24 Jan 1774, lost

Clarissa, oder Das unbekannte Dienstmädchen (Operette, 3, J. C. Bock), Berlin, Döbbelin's, 26 May 1775, 8 songs in Lieder im Volkston (Berlin, 1782–90)

Musique de l'impromptu en vers, 1779 (cmda, 1), *B-Bc*

La fée Urgèle, ou Ce qui plait aux dames (comédie avec ariettes, 4, C.-S. Favart), ?Rheinsberg, 1782; rev. as Was den Damen gefällt, Berlin, National, 1789, vs *D-Bds*

La vérité (épilogue, G. de Morveau), Rheinsberg, 1784, lost

Panomphée, *c*1785 (divertissement), lost

Athalie (5, Schulz and F. C. Cramer, after J. Racine), Rheinsberg, French Theatre, 1785; rev. version, Berlin, Corsicascher Konzertsaal, 1786, choruses, songs in Polyhymnia, vs (Hamburg and Kiel, 1786)

Minona, oder Die Angelsachsen (tragisches Melodram, 4, H. Gerstenberg), Hamburg, 1786, lost

Aline, reine de Golconde (4, M.-J. Sedaine), Rheinsberg, sum. 1787; as Aline, dronning af Golconda, Copenhagen, Kongelige, 1789, vs (Copenhagen, 1790)

Indtoget, 1789–90 (Singspiel, 2, P. A. Heiberg), Copenhagen, 26 Feb 1793, vs (Copenhagen, 1793)

Høstgildet (Singspiel, 1, T. Thaarup), Copenhagen, Kongelige, 16 Sept 1790, vs (Copenhagen, 1790)

Peters bryllup (Singspiel, 2, Thaarup), Copenhagen, 12 Dec 1793, vs (Copenhagen, *c*1791)

Contribs. to Die Hochzeit des Figaro, Le barbier de Seville (1786) and Goetz von Berlichingen (1787)

*

M. Seiffert: 'J. A. P. Schulz' "dänische" Oper', *AMw*, i (1918–19), 422–31

H. Gottwaldt, ed.: 'Drei Fragmente einer eigenen Lebensbeschreibung,' *Lüneburger Blätter*, vi (1955); xi–xii (1961)

G. Hahne, ed.: *Briefwechsel zwischen J. A. P. Schulz und J. H. Voss* (Kassel and Basle, 1960) RAYMOND A. BARR

Schulzová, Anežka (*b* Prague, 24 March 1868; *d* Prague, 4 Nov 1905). Czech librettist. The well-educated daughter of the literary critic and historian Ferdinand Schulz, she wrote theatre reviews from the age of 20 and made translations from French, Danish and English. She also studied the piano (from 1886) and later composition (1892) with Fibich. The close friendship that developed between the two was recorded in Fibich's *Nálady, dojmy a upomínky* ('Moods, Impressions and Reminiscences'), his 'erotic diary' for piano, and led, in 1897, to Fibich's leaving his wife for her. Schulzová wrote the librettos for Fibich's last three operas – *Hedy* (after Byron's *Don Juan*; 1896), *Šárka* (1897) and *Pád Arkuna* ('The Fall of Arkona', 1900) – all employing operatic conventions notably different from those of his earlier works. Later she published a biography and a more personal memoir.

Zdenko Fibich: eine musikalische Silhouette (Prague, 1900) [under pseud. C. L. Richter]

'Zdenko Fibich: hrstka upomínek a intimních rysů' [Zdenko Fibich: a Handful of Reminiscences and Intimate Traits], *Květy*, xxiv (1902), bk 68, no.6, pp.768–83, bk 69, no.1, pp.67–84; ed. L. Boháček (Prague, 1950); also in *Zdeněk Fibich: sborník dokumentů*, ed. A. Rektorys, ii (Prague, 1952), 141–99

*

Obituary, *Dalibor*, xxvii (1905), 357

Z. Nejedlý: *Zdeňka Fibicha milostný deník: Nálady, dojmy a upomínky* [Zdeněk Fibich's Erotic Diary: Moods, Impressions and Reminiscences] (Prague, 1925, 2/1948; Eng. summary in G. Abraham: 'An Erotic Diary for Piano', *Slavonic and Romantic Music* (London, 1968), 70–82

V. Hudec: *Zdeněk Fibich* (Prague, 1971)

J. Tyrrell: *Czech Opera* (Cambridge, 1988)

For further bibliography *see* FIBICH, ZDENĚK. JOHN TYRRELL

Schuman, William (Howard) (*b* New York, 4 Aug 1910; *d* New York, 15 Feb 1992). American composer. An early interest in popular music led him to take up formal musical studies in 1930. He began composing concert music while at Columbia University Teachers College, and subsequently studied with Roy Harris. In 1938 his Second Symphony won a nationwide contest, and in 1943 he was awarded the first Pulitzer Prize in music, for *A Free Song*. He was later also prominent as a teacher and administrator, serving as president of the

Juilliard School (1945–62) and Lincoln Center for the Performing Arts (1962–69).

The Mighty Casey, the first of Schuman's two one-act operas, had its première on 4 May 1953 at the Burns School auditorium in Hartford, Connecticut. It was inspired by Ernest L. Thayer's poem, long enshrined in baseball folklore, about a legendary batsman who strikes out in his team's hour of need. The opera is traditional in format and eclectic in style; Harold Schonberg observed that the music accompanying Casey's strike-out 'carries suggestions of Prokofiev's "Scythian Suite", Beethoven's Ninth Symphony, Times Square on a Saturday evening, and the Queen Mary coming into dock'. Schuman's suggestion that performers 'should evoke the softened feeling of recollection' rather than the excitement of the game provides a clue to his intentions in making Casey a mute protagonist and emphasizing the reactive role of the spectators' chorus. The composer's imprint is evident in the athletic rhythms, leaping vocal lines, major-minor chords and use of ostinatos and semitonal clashes to produce tension. He later recast the work as a cantata, making minor adjustments to the score, enlarging the orchestra and eliminating the spoken dialogue. *Casey at the Bat* was first heard in this form on 6 April 1976 in Washington, DC.

Schuman's second opera, *A Question of Taste*, was commissioned by Glimmerglass Opera, which gave the first performance on 24 June 1989 at its theatre near Cooperstown, New York. J. D. McClatchy's libretto is based on a story by Roald Dahl in which a wealthy businessman stakes his daughter's hand in marriage on a blind wine-tasting test. As in *Casey*, Schuman's music is richly coloured and expansive, despite the prevalence of terse rhythmic motifs. Both works draw obliquely on popular idioms: *Casey* on jazz and parlour songs, *A Question of Taste* on waltzes which evoke the hedonism of turn-of-the-century New York and propel the masterful build-up of suspense in the final scene.

*

H. Schonberg: 'Casey Bats Again with Same Result', *New York Times* (5 May 1953)

A. H. and C. B.: 'William Schuman's Opera The Mighty Casey Given First Performance', *MusAm*, lxxiii/8 (1953), 7

W. Spiegelman: 'Schuman at Glimmerglass', *Wall Street Journal* (7 July 1989), A7

R. H. Kornick: *Recent American Opera: a Production Guide* (New York, 1991), 277–9

HARRY HASKELL

Schumann, Elisabeth (*b* Merseburg an der Saale, 13 June 1888; *d* New York, 23 April 1952). German soprano, later naturalized American. She studied with Natalie Hänisch, Marie Dietrich and Alma Schadow, and made her début at the Hamburg Stadttheater, as the Shepherd in *Tannhäuser*, in 1909, remaining a member of that company until 1919, when Richard Strauss persuaded her to join the Vienna Staatsoper. She became a firm favourite in Vienna and remained there until 1938, when the Nazi annexation of Austria decided her to leave the country. Having sung several roles with the Metropolitan Opera in 1914–15, she was first heard at Covent Garden in 1924, when she had a great success as Sophie in *Der Rosenkavalier*, and thereafter in many Mozart roles. Her pure and beautifully controlled high soprano, together with a charming stage presence, made her a delightful Susanna, Blonde, Zerlina and Despina; Strauss's Sophie has also remained inseparably linked with her name, especially for her delivery of those long, soaring phrases with which the girl acknowledges the gift of the rose in Act 2. In the concert hall her popularity became even greater, and Strauss was so charmed by her singing of his songs that he toured the USA as her accompanist in 1921. She excelled also in the more lyrical, playful and purely decorative songs of Schubert. From 1938 she lived in New York, and after the war made many further recital appearances in Britain. Her many recordings, especially the famous abridged version of *Der Rosenkavalier* and a long series of lieder, particularly of Schubert, are among the happiest of their kind ever made. The second of her three husbands was the German conductor Carl Alwin (1891–1945).

Elisabeth Schumann as Sophie in Richard Strauss's 'Der Rosenkavalier', Hamburg, 1911

*

E. Schumann: *German Song* (London, 1948)

F. Juynboll and J. Seddon: 'Elisabeth Schumann Discography', *Record Collector*, xxxiii (1988), 55–116

DESMOND SHAWE-TAYLOR

Schumann, Robert (Alexander) (*b* Zwickau, Saxony, 8 June 1810; *d* Endenich, nr Bonn, 29 July 1856). German composer, one of the leaders of the Romantic movement. He is in many ways the quintessential Romantic composer, with his emphasis on self-expression and keen concern with extra-musical (especially literary) associations. His piano music and songs are particularly notable.

1. LIFE. Schumann's father was a bookseller and publisher. By the age of 11 Robert was a good pianist and spent much time playing the music in his father's shop; at the house of a wealthy neighbour he was also becoming familiar with the best Classical chamber music. From the age of 14 he developed a passion for Romantic literature, and again there was a wealth of books at his

disposal in the shop. There was an element of mental imbalance in the family; his sister Emilie was mentally afflicted, and when she committed suicide in 1826 at the age of 19, the shock resulted in the death of the father, who was also in poor health. Schumann's mother now insisted he prepare for a secure career, and he was sent to Leipzig University to study law. Here, however, he devoted most of his time to music, enrolling as a piano student with Friedrich Wieck. Damage to his right hand in 1832 meant that he had to abandon his planned career as a virtuoso, and he concentrated on composition. From 1828 to 1839 he published a large amount of piano music, wonderfully free and original in construction, melody and harmony. Many of his works during this period, as well as critical articles he wrote for the magazine he founded, the *Neue Zeitschrift für Musik*, are signed 'Florestan', representing the impetuous side of his personality, or 'Eusebius', representing the quiet, reflective side.

In 1837 he became engaged to Wieck's virtuoso pianist daughter Clara, against the implacable hostility of her father, who was able to delay the marriage until 1840, when she was 21. In 1840 Schumann composed more than a hundred published songs and developed the art of the song cycle in such works as *Dichterliebe* and *Frauenliebe und -leben*. Now settled into his blissfully happy marriage and artistic partnership with Clara, Schumann began to explore other compositional genres. In 1841 he turned his attention to the orchestra, writing among other works the 'Spring' Symphony and the first version of the D minor Symphony. Chamber music dominated 1842, with the three string quartets, the Piano Quintet and the Piano Quartet, and in 1843 the oratorio *Das Paradies und die Peri* was composed and performed.

In 1844, after his first serious mental breakdown, Schumann resigned the teaching appointment he held at the Leipzig Conservatory, as well as the editorship of the *Neue Zeitschrift für Musik*, and settled at Dresden, where for the next six years he lived quietly, devoting his time almost exclusively to composition. It was in these years that he produced three masterpieces which could be described as dramatic: the incidental music to Byron's *Manfred* (1848–9), which was staged by Liszt at Weimar in 1852; the *Szenen aus Goethes Faust* (1844–53), also performed by Liszt at Weimar; and his only completed opera, *Genoveva*. In 1850 he was appointed director of music and conductor of the orchestra at Düsseldorf: despite his onerous duties, orchestral and choral works in particular continued to flow from his pen. The Düsseldorf post was, however, completely unsuited to a dreamy artist like Schumann, and the strain induced by administrative matters and difficult rehearsals led to his complete mental breakdown. He attempted suicide in the Rhine in 1854 and was removed to a mental hospital, where he died two years later.

2. Works. During his lifetime most of the musical public found Schumann's music puzzlingly 'modern' and 'difficult'. Only gradually during the three decades after his death was he accepted in Germany, France and Russia as a composer of the front rank. Recognition came later still in England, where mid-19th-century reviews of his music were usually cold and hostile. But there can be no doubt that he was one of the greatest and most original composers of piano music and songs, and he made a distinctive contribution in the fields of orchestral, chamber and choral music. Nor is his stage music without merit.

Schumann took a persistent interest in opera and made several attempts at opera composition. 'Every morning and evening my prayer is for German opera', he wrote in 1842, and he searched long for a suitable subject. Early subjects he considered included E. T. A. Hoffmann's *Doge und Dogaressa* and *Die Bergwerke zu Falun*, Till Eulenspiegel, *Hamlet*, *The Tempest*, Abélard and Héloïse, Mary Stuart, Tristan and Isolde, King Arthur and the *Odyssey*, but all were discarded. In 1844 he commissioned Owsald Marbach to write a libretto based on Byron's *The Corsair*, but composition extended only to a chorus based on 'O'er the glad waters' and a fragment of an aria for the pirate Conrad. Then early in 1847 he decided that the story of his own opera was to be based on the medieval legend of St Genevieve of Brabant (which, incidentally, has also been the basis of librettos for operas by, among others, Fabbrini, 1685; Haydn, written for the marionette theatre at Eszterháza, 1777; Offenbach, 1859; and Satie, for a marionette theatre, 1899).

The legend had also been the source of many German literary works from the 17th century to the 19th. Unfortunately for the unity of the libretto the two sides of Schumann's character were attracted to two totally incompatible versions of the legend. It seems that at first he settled on Ludwig Tieck's play *Leben und Tod der heiligen Genoveva* (1799). The central character here was Genoveva, the pure devoted wife, left alone when her husband goes to the wars, faithful amid the passionate advances and all-pervading power of Golo, the young knight commanded by her husband to look after her. This play, in praise of married fidelity, appealed to the 'Eusebius' side of Schumann, who early in 1847 commissioned the poet Robert Reinick to set to work on a libretto based on it. Reinick had completed more than half the libretto when by chance Schumann lighted on Friedrich Hebbel's *Genoveva* (1842). This was written as a counterblast to Tieck's play; it revolves around Golo and is a deep psychological study of his passionate love for Genoveva and with it the almost impossible position he finds himself in. This play appealed to Schumann's 'Florestan' side, which sympathized with the highly charged emotional character of Golo; Schumann provided music to match the ardent young man we meet in Act 1, as well as that showing understanding of his degeneration into treachery and crime.

Schumann now asked Reinick to fuse these two plays but was dissatisfied with both the draft librettos he received. In July 1847 he invited Hebbel to his house with a view to his helping with the libretto, but the meeting was unfruitful. At this point he decided that he himself would write the text, based on Reinick's second draft. Reinick, not liking this, refused to acknowledge any hand in the finished libretto, and the opera was published as being 'after L. Tieck and F. Hebbel – by Robert Schumann'. (A more accurate title might have been 'Two Perspectives on the Legend of Genoveva of Brabant by Florestan and Eusebius'.)

Schumann's diary for 1 April 1847 notes that he was reading Hebbel's *Genoveva*. Then for 5 April he records, 'First sketch of *Genoveva* overture completed. Joy.' However, the delays over the libretto, and his preoccupation with composing his piano trios in D minor and F major, meant that work on the opera proper could not start before December. But then it proceeded rapidly, and the full score is carefully annotated with the completion date of each act: 23 January, 30 March, 13 June and 4 August 1848. Schumann at once approached Julius Rietz, director of the Leipzig Opera, who accepted *Genoveva* for performance. Rietz, on a closer acquaintance with the score, seems to have had doubts about it, however, and delay followed delay. It was eventually given on 25 June 1850. Schumann conducted the first two performances and then sat in the audience for the third and final one. From the first the work was controversial. It was, however, praised by Spohr and also by Liszt, who resolved to stage the work at Weimar, which he did in 1855.

Schumann envisaged two more opera projects, but neither went beyond their orchestral preludes, which were published separately as concert overtures. The first (1850–51) was to Schiller's play *Die Braut von Messina*, a story of feuding twin brothers and their mother who desperately tries to preserve peace between them. The second (1851) was to Goethe's *Hermann und Dorothea*, a charming love story with a happy ending set in the Rhenish countryside at the time of the French Revolution.

See also GENOVEVA.

W. von Wasielewski: *Robert Schumann: eine Biographie* (Dresden, 1858, Eng. trans., 1886; enlarged 4/1906)
H. Abert: 'Robert Schumann's "Genoveva"', *ZIMG*, xi (1909–10), 277–89
R. H. Schauffler: *Florestan: the Life and Work of Robert Schumann* (New York, 1945)
J. Chissell: *Schumann* (London, 1948, 5/1989)
G. Abraham: 'The Dramatic Music', *Schumann: a Symposium* (London, 1952), 260–82
F. Cooper: 'Operatic and Dramatic Music', *Robert Schumann: the Man and his Music*, ed. A. Walker (London, 1972, 2/1976), 324–49
B. Schlotel: 'The Orchestral Music', ibid, 277–323
L'avant-scène opéra, no.71 (1985) [*Genoveva* issue]

BRIAN SCHLOTEL

Schumann-Heink [née Rössler; Heink], **Ernestine** [Tini] (*b* Lieben, nr Prague, 15 June 1861; *d* Hollywood, 17 Nov 1936). Austrian contralto and mezzo-soprano, later naturalized American. Among her teachers was G. B. Lamperti (the younger). She made her opera début at Dresden as Azucena on 15 October 1878, and remained there for four seasons. After marriage to Ernst Heink, she obtained an engagement at Hamburg under Pollini, and remained there until 1897, taking part in the company's London season under the young Mahler in 1892, when she was much applauded as Erda, Fricka, Waltraute and Brangäne. In 1893, having divorced her first husband, she married the actor Paul Schumann, assuming the familiar hyphenated form of her surname. A long and fruitful relationship with Bayreuth lasted from 1896 to 1914. During that period she took part in four consecutive Covent Garden seasons (1897–1901), and became a regular member of the Metropolitan company for a similar period (1898–1903), returning subsequently for single seasons only. By then she had begun the series of popular and profitable cross-country American concert tours that occupied much of the rest of her long career and made her into a national legend. In 1909 she returned to Dresden to sing the part of Clytemnestra in the première of *Elektra*. Although she could sing (and very well) virtually anything, her English and American stage career centred on Wagner; and it was as Erda that she bade farewell to the Metropolitan in 1932, still captivating the audience, as the American critic Olin Downes wrote, with 'knowledge and imagination embodied in the tone and in every syllable of the text she delivered so memorably'. These words well describe the effect vividly conveyed by her Erda and Waltraute recordings made less than three years before.

Ernestine Schumann-Heink as Waltraute in Wagner's 'Ring'

For further illustration *see* ELEKTRA.

M. Lawton: *Schumann-Heink: the Last of the Titans* (New York, 1928; repr. 1977 with discography by W. R. Moran)
J. McPherson: 'Ernestine Schumann-Heink', *Record Collector*, xvii (1967–8), 99–144 [with discography by W. R. Moran], 154–9; xx (1971–2), 165; xxv (1979–80), 75–7

DESMOND SHAWE-TAYLOR

Schunk, Robert (*b* Neu-Isenburg, 5 Jan 1948). German tenor. After studying at Frankfurt, he made his début in 1973 at Karlsruhe as Jack (*The Midsummer Marriage*), then sang in Bonn and Dortmund. At Bayreuth (1977–86) he has sung Siegmund, Melot, Erik and Walther (*Tannhäuser*). He has also sung at Hamburg, Munich, Vienna, Cologne, Berlin, Geneva, Chicago and San Francisco. He made his Metropolitan début (1986) as Florestan and his Covent Garden début (1987) as the Emperor (*Die Frau ohne Schatten*). He sang Siegmund in the 1987 Munich production of the *Ring* and in 1991 sang in *Das Liebesverbot* in Palermo. His repertory includes Parsifal, Walther (*Die Meistersinger*), Don Carlos, Max, Dmitry, Hoffmann and the Officer (*Cardillac*). He has an expressive, supple voice with ringing top notes and excellent diction.

ELIZABETH FORBES

Schürer, Johann Georg (*b* ?Raudnitz [now Roudnice], Bohemia, *c*1720; *d* Dresden, 16 Feb 1786). German composer. He was working in about 1746 as resident composer and music director of an opera troupe that appeared in Dresden with the Mingotti company at the Zwinger; the Dresden repertory had been dominated by Hasse since 1734. On 29 October 1746 they performed Schürer's opera *Astrea placata* (which had been given in Warsaw on 7 October in honour of the king's birthday); it was repeated several times. On 8 November of the same year his *Galatea* was given at Dresden, and repeated with new settings in the presence of the court a week later and again on 28 June 1747, the day before Gluck's festival opera *Le nozze d'Ercole e d'Ebe* was given at Pillnitz. During the 1747 court festivities Schürer's opera *L'Ercole sul Termodonte* and his German Singspiel *Doris* were performed. His last opera was *Calandro*, a comedy, performed in 1748 in the little Zwinger theatre; thereafter he confined himself to composing sacred music, becoming *Kirchencompositeur* in royal service.

Schürer was thus one of a notable succession of musicians, headed by Hasse, who worked at the Dresden court of August II. His principal occupation was composing, which he did with enormous industry, though his output seems to have ceased in his last years in office. He retired in 1780.

Although Schürer, according to Reichardt, was a 'very skilful composer', master of his craft and of counterpoint, his music met with only limited appreciation in Dresden because he did not bow to the prevalent neo-Neapolitan taste. His operas exemplify the changing style of his time, combining use of the traditional figured bass with delicate Rococo sentiment. Stylistically his music places him between the mature Telemann and the 12-year-old Mozart; but his melodic ideas are limited and eventually become tedious. The pastorale *Galatea* and the German Spingspiel *Doris* have *galant*, Rococo features also found in Mozart's *Bastien und Bastienne*.

Astrea placata, ovvero La felicità della terra (dramma per musica, 1, B. Campagnari, after P. Metastasio), Warsaw, 7 Oct 1746, lib. *D-B*

La Galatea (componimento drammatico, 2, Metastasio), Dresden, 8 Nov 1746, *Dlb*; also 4 arias in Ger.

L'Ercole sul Termodonte (dramma per musica, 3, C. F. Bussani), Dresden, 9 Jan 1747, *Dlb*

Doris (Spl, 2), Dresden, 13 Feb 1747, *Dlb*

Calandro (commedia per musica, 3, S. Pallavicino), Dresden, 20 Jan 1748, *Dlb*

Several other operas, presumed lost

*

MGG (D. Härtwig)

J. F. Reichardt: *Briefe eines aufmerksamen Reisenden*, ii (Frankfurt and Breslau, 1776), 176

G. J. Dlabacž: *Allgemeines historisches Künstler-Lexikon* (Prague, 1815)

M. Fürstenau: *Zur Geschichte der Musik und des Theaters am Hofe zu Dresden*, i (Dresden, 1861)

R. Haas: *J. G. Schürer (1720–1786): ein Beitrag zur Geschichte der Musik in Dresden* (Dresden, 1915) [with complete list of works]

O. Schmid: *Musik im alten Dresden*, i (Dresden, 1921)

L. Schiedermair: *Die deutsche Oper* (Leipzig, 1930, 2/1940)

G. Pietzsch: *Sachsen als Musikland* (Dresden, 1938)

H. Schnoor: *Dresden: 400 Jahre deutsche Musikkultur* (Dresden, 1948)

DIETER HÄRTWIG

Schürmann [Schurmann, Scheuermann], **Georg Caspar** (*b* Idensen, nr Hanover, 1672–3; *d* Wolfenbüttel, 25 Feb 1751). German composer. He began his career at the age of 20 in Hamburg where he found engagements as a male alto both at the opera and in various churches. During the next six years he performed in an ideal musical milieu for a young musician, especially at the opera where Conradi, Kusser and Keiser were involved with productions of their works, and the music of Steffani (among other outstanding composers) was often heard. In 1697 he travelled with the Hamburg opera company for a series of guest appearances at the Brunswick court of Duke Anton Ulrich of Brunswick-Lüneburg. Soon after, Duke Anton Ulrich appointed Schürmann as solo alto to the court and also, according to Walther, as a conductor for the opera and court church.

Except for two periods of absence, Schürmann remained at the Brunswick-Wolfenbüttel court until his death 54 years later. He quickly established himself as a gifted composer, and in 1700 his first dramatic work, the Italian pastorale *Endimione*, was performed at the court theatres at Salzthal and Wolfenbüttel. The following year he wrote and produced two sacred operas, *Salomon* and *Daniel*. In late 1701 Duke Anton Ulrich sent him to Venice, no doubt to complete his education in the Italian operatic style. Walther said that he made the acquaintance of the most famous composers and musicians while in Venice, and one can speculate that these would have included Antonio and Carlo Francesco Pollarolo, Tomaso Albinoni, Francesco Gasparini and Francesco Pistocchi. Nothing specific is known of Schürmann's Italian period, and apparently he returned to Germany after only one year to become, on loan from the Duke of Brunswick, Kapellmeister and composer at the court of Meiningen. He remained there until at least 1706 and wrote several operas and ballets and many church cantatas. In 1706 Schürmann went to produce an opera at Naumburg, where each year an important opera festival was maintained at court during the Petri-Pauli fair (beginning on 29 June and lasting eight days).

Walther stated that Schürmann returned permanently to Brunswick-Wolfenbüttel in 1707. Over more than 30 years his productivity was enormous. After 1739 he is not known to have composed operas, but he remained immersed in court musical life as a conductor, producer of operas, and translator and arranger of the Italian operas which had become the mainstay of the theatre. Schürmann rearranged many of his own works, inserting arias by other composers and creating numerous pasticcios. In his final years he continued to compose occasional pieces for special court festivals.

Schürmann, together with Conradi, Kusser, Keiser and Telemann, was an outstanding contributor to German Baroque opera. It is regrettable that of the more than 25 operas he is known to have written only three seem to survive in their entirety and excerpts from another nine remain in manuscripts; none of the three principal manuscripts has been published in a complete modern edition. An outstanding study of Schürmann's operas was written by G. F. Schmidt, who examined the music in great detail.

Schürmann's operas demonstrate a successful blending of the operatic style developed in north Germany, especially in Hamburg in the music of Keiser, with the Italian practices he observed in Venice. His operas are aria-orientated, and each aria, in characteristic Baroque fashion, is planned to express a single affection or emotional idealization. Most of the arias have fairly extensive da capo structures, but Schürmann filled these stereotyped forms with richly inventive melodic ideas, strong textural variety (including frequent contrapuntal interplay between the voice and instrumental parts) and colourful solo instrumental writing. The recitatives are in the north German tradition of affective, rhetorical declamation, in which vocal line, harmonic colour (in the continuo part as well as the melody) and dramatic accent add strength and theatrical effectiveness. This is not the recitative of contemporary Italian opera, with its rapid parlando patter, and frequent 'dry' punctuations of cadential harmonic formulae in the accompanying harpsichord continuo realization. For Schürmann, as for the Hamburg opera composers, the recitative was still an important component of the musical drama.

Schürmann's melodic gift, undoubtedly in part the result of his own lengthy career as an operatic singer, makes his works impressively lyrical. The voice parts are never overshadowed by the orchestra, and the instrumental parts generally take on the melodic characteristics of the vocal style – not the reverse procedure, as one finds, for example, in Keiser's operas. Schürmann continued the Hamburg opera composers' proclivity for folklike melodies and for arias based on dance rhythms (especially the siciliano, barcarolle and minuet). The dance is in fact a major part of each work, although for the most part other composers (frequently French ones) supplied the music for such ballet insertions. Although Schürmann gave his soloists ample opportunity to excel in written-out coloratura ornamentation, this kind of vocal virtuosity never dominated his arias, as it did for example in much of Keiser's music.

However, Schürmann's operas move clearly beyond his Hamburg heritage and in many ways remind one of the later works of Handel. While the textures are frequently contrapuntal, the use of counterpoint occurs as an element of variation, not as a basic compositional procedure. Harmonic rhythm, especially in his last surviving opera, *Ludovicus Pius*, is markedly slow, at times static, and often similar to that of the early Classical style in Germany. Bass lines, then, are not generally melodic, and indeed often seem to be in the early Classical mould with their tendency to serve a purely harmonic function. Schürmann's music, in fact, points strongly in the direction of the Classical style and suggests that this composer, who worked with both C. H. Graun and Hasse at Wolfenbüttel, may have played a significant part in the style's development in Germany during the first half of the 18th century.

performed in Brunswick and music lost unless otherwise stated

Endimione (favola per musica, 3, F. de Lemene), Salzthal, 1700

Salomon (Spl, 3, Duke Anton Ulrich of Brunswick and/or J. C. Knorr von Rosenroth), wint. 1701, *D-SWl*

Daniel (Spl, 3, Knorr von Rosenroth), sum. 1701

Leonilde, oder Die siegende Beständigkeit (Spl, 3, G. Fiedler), 1704 or 1705, 4 arias *Bds*

Das verstöhrte Troja (Spl, 5, ? J. C. Frauendorf), wint. 1706, arias and duets *B*

Telemaque (4, ?Frauendorf), Naumburg, sum. 1706; rev. as Telemachus und Calypso (3), Aug 1717

Giasone, overo Il conquisto del vello d'oro (dramma per musica, 3, F. Parisetti, Ger. trans. Schürmann), 1707, pasticcio incl. music by various It. composers, *Bds*

Die schöne Psyche (Spl, 3, C. Postel), 1708 [?adaptation or partial recomposition of R. Keiser: Die wunderschöne Psyche]

Issé, oder Die vergnügende Liebe (pastorale, 3, A. H. de Lamotte), Wolfenbüttel, 3 Oct 1710 [?adaptation or partial recomposition of opera by A. Destouches]

Procris und Cephalus (Spl, 3, F. C. Bressand), wint. 1714, pasticcio incl. music by Keiser, A. Lotti and others

Regnero (dramma per musica, prol., 3, P. Pariati), wint. 1715 [?only prol. by Schürmann]

Heinrich der Löwe (3, O. Mauro, Ger. trans. Fiedler), wint. 1716, pasticcio with music largely by A. Steffani

L'amor insanguinato, oder Holofernes (Spl, 5, J. Beccau), 1716, pasticcio

Die Plejades, oder Das Siebengestirn (Spl, 3, Bressand), 1716

Atis, oder Der stumme Verliebte (3, L. von Bostel), wint. 1717

Claudio ed Agrippina (dramma per musica, prol., 3), wint. 1717 [?only prol. by Schürmann]

Heinrich der Vogler, pt 1 (Spl, 3, J. U. König), 1 Aug 1718

Porsenna [Clelia] (Spl, 5, Bressand), 1718, excerpts *B*

Tiridate, ovvero L'amor tirannico (dramma per musica, 3, D. Lalli), 1718

Die getreue Alceste (3, König, after P. Quinault), Feb 1719, *B* (1719, Hamburg)

Heinrich der Vogler, pt 2 (Spl, König), 11 Jan 1721

Das eroberte Jerusalem, oder Armida und Rinaldo (Spl, 3, J. S. Müller, after G. C. Corradi), wint. 1722

Ixion (3, Fiedler), wint. 1722, excerpts *B*

Orlando furioso (dramma per musica, 3, G. Braccioli, arr. and Ger. trans. Schürmann, after A. Ariosti), wint. 1722, pasticcio

Rudolphus Habspurgicus (3, 2 'Anreden', Müller), 4 Feb 1723

Ludovicus Pius, oder Ludewig der Fromme (3, C. E. Simonetti), Feb 1726, incl. some arias by C. H. Graun, ballet music partly from operas by Destouches and A. Campra, *Bsommer*; partial edn in PÄMw, xvii (1890)

Hannibal in Capua (3, N. Beregan, arr. Schürmann), wint. 1726

Orpheus (3, Bressand, ?arr. Schürmann), wint. 1727 [?music by Schürmann and Keiser]

Der von Londinen zugleich geliebte und ungeliebte Pharasmanes, König von Iberien (Spl, 3, J. F. von Uffenbach), ?1729

Magnus Torquatus (3, Müller), wint. 1730

Single arias from operas in *Bds, SWl, W*

Doubtful: Mario (3, S. Stampiglia), Leipzig, 1709 [?collab. J. D. Heinichen with some music by G. B. Bononcini]; Herodes (Spl, 4, Müller), Wolfenbüttel or Salzthal, 28 May 1718; Doppia festa d'Himeneo (favola pastorale, 25 scenes, Mauro), Salzthal, 1718 [? music partly or entirely by Steffani]; Cadmus (3, König), 1720; Justinus (3, Simonetti, after Beregan), sum. 1725; Ninus and Semiramis (3), sum. 1730

*

WaltherML

F. Chrysander: 'Geschichte der Braunschweig-Wolfenbüttelschen Capelle und Oper vom 16.–18. Jahrhundert', *Jb für musikalische Wissenschaft*, i (1863), 147–286

H. Sommer: 'Die Oper Ludwig der Fromme von Georg Caspar Schürmann', *MMg*, xiv (1882), 48-51, 53-5

G. F. Schmidt: *Die frühdeutsche Oper und die musikdramatische Kunst Georg Caspar Schürmanns* (Regensburg, 1933–4)

R. Brockpähler: *Handbuch zur Geschichte der Barockoper in Deutschland* (Emsdetten, 1964)

GEORGE J. BUELOW

Schuster, Ignaz (*b* Vienna, 20 July 1779; *d* Vienna, 6 Nov 1835). Austrian actor, singer and composer. He was a treble, and later a bass, chorister at the Schottenstift in Vienna; Eybler and Franz Volkert were among his teachers. At about the same time he was offered posts as a bass in the Esterházy musical household and at the Theater in der Leopoldstadt in Vienna. He chose the latter, and despite his rather small, misshapen figure he quickly established himself as a comic actor and singer after a successful début in December 1801. From 1804 he began to figure as a composer too (*Baron Baarfuss*), supplying some 30 or 40 scores for farces, parodies and pantomimes, some of them enjoying a long and distinguished life. He showed a particularly happy touch in his music for parodies and satires, making witty points without lapsing into maliciousness. In 1806 he was appointed a solo singer at the Hofkapelle – such was the urbanity of Vienna's cultural life that nothing untoward was felt about the city's leading comic actor (which Schuster had by then become) being also employed as singer in the imperial and royal chapel, and in St Stephen's Cathedral.

A notable date in his career was 22 October 1813, when he created the role of Staberl in Bäuerle's *Die Bürger von Wien* and thereby inaugurated the last of the comic *personae* that from Hanswurst via Kasperl formed the principal sources of public delight in the old Viennese popular theatre. He earned special admiration for his brilliant imitation of Madame Borgondio in the Bäuerle-Müller parody of Rossini's *Tancredi* in 1817. The following year he appeared in the title role of *Die falsche Primadonna in Krähwinkel* (the censor had forbidden its original title of *Die falsche Catalani*), for which he also composed the music. This work, the finest of the long line of Krähwinkel plays that followed Kotzebue's *Die deutschen Kleinstädter*, was frequently imitated but never equalled until eclipsed in 1848 by Nestroy's *Freiheit in Krähwinkel*; *Die falsche Primadonna* was given throughout the German-speaking lands, and in the Leopoldstadt alone it was performed 161 times in 40 years. Despite the rising popularity of the dramatist and actor Ferdinand Raimund, which provoked jealousy from the older Schuster, he continued to enjoy triumphs as actor, singer and composer. His manuscripts and some printed works are preserved in the major Vienna libraries.

selective list; all first performed in Vienna, Theater in der Leopoldstadt

Baron Baarfuss, oder Der Wechselthaler (Zauberoper, 3, J. Perinet), 16 Aug 1804
Es ist Friede, oder Die Zurückkunft des Fürsten (vaterländisches Gemälde, 3, J. A. Gleich), 18 Jan 1806, collab. F. Kauer and W. Müller
Othello, der Mohr in Wien (Posse, 1, J. F. Kringsteiner), 28 May 1806
Werthers Leiden (Posse, 1, Kringsteiner), 17 Nov 1806
Der Tanzmeister (Posse, 3, Kringsteiner), 6 Feb 1807, collab. F. Kauer and W. Müller
Hamlet (Karikatur, Perinet), 5 Nov 1807
Romeo und Julie (Quodlibet von Charakteren, 2, Kringsteiner), 18 March 1808
Der Zauberspiegel (Burleske, 3, I. Schuster), 16 Feb 1811
Kora die Sonnenjungfrau (Karikatur-Oper, 3, Perinet), 17 Oct 1812
Der Baum der Diana (travestierte Oper, 3, Perinet), 19 Dec 1812
Der Herr Johannes vom Parisergartel (Posse, 1, H. Herzenskron), 23 Jan 1813
Der travestierte Fridolin (Karikatur-Oper, 3, Perinet), 24 April 1813
Die Schwabenwanderung (Posse, 3, K. Meisl), 22 Nov 1817
Die falsche Primadonna in Krähwinkel (Posse, 2, A. Bäuerle), 18 Dec 1818
Die Abenteuer eines echten Shawls in Wien (Lokal-Gemälde, 3, Meisl), 11 Jan 1820
Die natürliche Zauberei (Posse, 3, Bäuerle), 18 May 1821
Der Mädchenraub (Schwank, 2, Gleich), 27 Sept 1822
Jupiter in Wien (Zauberposse, 2, F. X. Told), 15 April 1825
Die Benefizvorstellung (Posse, 2, Meisl), 7 April 1827, collab. J. Drechsler and W. Müller

*

StiegerO; *WurzbachL*
Biographical sketch, MS, *A-Wgm* [with inc. list of works]
L. Eisenberg: *Grosses biographisches Lexikon der deutschen Bühne im XIX. Jahrhundert* (Leipzig, 1903), 942
E. von Bauernfeld: *Erinnerungen aus Alt-Wien* (Vienna, 1923)
F. Hadamowsky: *Das Theater in der Wiener Leopoldstadt 1781–1860* (Vienna, 1934)

PETER BRANSCOMBE

Schuster, Joseph (*b* Dresden, 11 Aug 1748; *d* Dresden, 24 July 1812). German composer. The son of a court musician in Dresden, he studied first with his father and with J. G. Schürer. With a scholarship from the elector, and accompanied by Franz Seydelmann, he spent the years 1765–8 with J. G. Naumann in Italy, studying counterpoint. In 1772 both he and Seydelmann were appointed church composers in Dresden. From 1774 to 1777 Schuster again visited Italy, where he studied with Padre Martini in Bologna, composed operas for Naples and Venice and received the honorary title of *maestro di cappella* to the King of Naples. His first *opera seria*, *Didone abbandonata* (1776, Naples), to a text by Metastasio, established his popularity with the Italian public. Contracts for new operas brought about his last journey to Italy, 1778–81, when he established closer relations with J. A. Hasse and had further stage successes in Naples and Venice. By this time he was also admired in Germany as a composer of *opera buffa* and Singspiel: his *Der Alchymist, oder Der Liebesteufel* (1778), one of the most charming and successful examples of the genre, remained popular in Germany into the 19th century. From 1781 he conducted in the Dresden court church and theatre (in turn with Naumann, Schürer and Seydelmann), and in 1787 he was appointed Kapellmeister to the elector, again at the same time as Seydelmann.

Schuster had an easy social manner, was attracted by everything fashionable and was a very productive composer, writing much sacred and instrumental music. Apart from his work as a conductor, his most important duties at court included managing the elector's chamber music and court concerts, giving music instruction, acquiring new music (primarily from Vienna, including works by Haydn, Mozart and Pleyel) and handling new appointments. He also participated enthusiastically in Dresden's concert life; his role in it during the last two decades of the 18th century was significant, and during the 1780s he was at the height of his creativity and international success, particularly in opera. By 1792 he was recognized throughout Germany as 'one of our most popular composers' (Gerber).

See also ALCHYMIST, DER and WÜSTE INSEL, DIE (i).

DKT – *Dresden, Kleines Kurfürstliches Theater*
NC – *Naples, Teatro S Carlo* VM – *Venice, Teatro S Moisè*

La fedeltà in amore (ob, 2), DKT, 1773, *D-Dlb*
L'idolo cinese (ob, 3, G. Lorenzi), DKT, 1776, *Dlb*
L'amore artigiano (ob, 3, C. Goldoni), VM, 1776, *B-Bc*
La Didone abbandonata (os, 3, P. Metastasio), NC, 1776, *D-Dlb*, *I-Nc*, 1 song [also attrib. G. Gazzaniga] (London, *c*1790)
Demofoonte (os, 3, Metastasio), Forlì, Nuovo, 1776, *D-Dlb*, *F-Pc*
La schiava liberata (op seria-comica, 3, G. Martinelli), DKT, 2 Oct 1777, *D-Dlb*
Der Alchymist, oder Der Liebesteufel (comische Oper, 1, A. G. Meissner, after M. A. Le Grand: *L'amour diable*), DKT, March 1778, *A-Wn*, *D-Bds*, *Dlb*, *DS*, *Rp*; vs, ed. G. Sartorius, *Mbs* (*R*1985: GOB, v); ed. R. Engländer (Kassel, 1958)
Bradamante [Ruggiero e Bradamante] (dramma per musica, C. Mazzolà), Padua, Nuovo, June 1779
Creso in Media (os, 3, G. Pagliuca), NC, 1779, *Dlb*, *I-Nc*
Die wüste Insel (Spl, 1, Meissner, after Metastasio: *L'isola disabitata*), Leipzig, Ranstädter Tor, 1779, *A-Wn*, *D-B*
Amor e Psyche (os, 2, after M. Coltellini), NC, 1780, *Dlb*, *I-Nc*
Il bon ton (ob, 2), VM, 1780, ?lost
Il marito indolente (ob, 2, C. Mazzolà), DKT, 1782, *D-Dlb*; Ger. trans. as Der gleichgültige Ehemann, *Bds*
Il pazzo per forza (ob, 2, Mazzolà), DKT, 1784, *Dlb*
Lo spirito di contradizione (ob, 2, Mazzolà), DKT, 1785, *Dlb*; Ger. trans. as Dr Murner, *DS*
Gli avari in troppola (ob, 2, Mazzolà), DKT, 1787, *Dlb*
Rübezahl, ossia Il vero amore (ob 2, Mazzolà), DKT, 14 Feb 1789, *Dlb*, vs *A-Wgm*
Il servo padrone, ossia L'amore perfetto (ob, 2, Mazzolà), DKT, 1793, *D-Dlb*
Osmano dey d'Algeri (ob, 2, ? G. Cinti), DKT, 1800, *Dlb*
L'amor prigionero (Metastasio), DKT, 1801
Il giorno natalizio (ob, 2, Cinti), pasticcio, DKT, 24 Feb 1802, *Dlb*
Der Schauspieldirector (Spl), *DS* [doubtful; cited in *EitnerQ*]

*

GerberL; *StiegerO*
M. Fürstenau: *Beiträge zur Geschichte der königlich sächsischen musikalischen Kapelle* (Dresden, 1849)
R. Engländer: 'Die Opern Joseph Schusters (1748–1812), *ZMw*, x (1927–8), 257–91

DIETER HÄRTWIG

Schütz, Françoise Jeanne. *See* LITVINNE, FÉLIA.

Schütz, Hans (*b* Vienna, 16 Dec 1862; *d* Wiesbaden, 12 Jan 1917). Austrian baritone. He studied in Vienna and made his début in 1891 at Linz. In 1893 he moved to Zürich and in 1896 to Düsseldorf. He was engaged in Leipzig from 1898 to 1908, then in Wiesbaden until his death. Known chiefly as a Wagner singer, at Bayreuth he sang Amfortas (1899), Donner and Klingsor (1901–2). He sang at Covent Garden in 1904, as Telramund, Kurwenal, Wolfram and Beckmesser.

ELIZABETH FORBES

Schütz, Heinrich [Henrich] [Sagittarius, Henricus] (*b* Köstritz [now Bad Köstritz], 14 Oct 1585; *d* Dresden, 6 Nov 1672). German composer. He received his early musical training as a choirboy at the court of Landgrave Moritz of Hessen-Kassel (1599–1608), then matriculated as a law student at Marburg, but Moritz provided funds for him to study in Venice with Gabrieli (1609–12). He returned to his duties in Kassel before moving to the Dresden court of the Elector of Saxony, Johann Georg I, in 1615. There he became Kapellmeister, retaining the post until 1657, although he left Dresden during certain periods, including a second visit to Venice (1628–30) and two visits to Copenhagen (1633–5 and 1642–4).

Schütz's most important musical dramas date from after his second trip to Italy, during which he studied with Monteverdi. In a letter of 6 February 1633 to the Saxon agent in Hamburg, Friedrich Lebzelter, Schütz stated:

> during my recent journey to Italy I engaged myself in a singular manner of composition, namely how a comedy of diverse voices can be translated into declamatory style and be brought to the stage and enacted in song – things that to the best of my knowledge ... are still completely unknown in Germany.

But the patronage, in his early years, of the Landgrave Moritz, at whose court lavish festivals were held, also contributed to his development as a composer of musical-dramatic works; and festivities at the Dresden court provided him with occasions for composing dramatic music. His opera *Dafne* (libretto by Martin Opitz) was performed on 13/23 April 1627 in Torgau after the wedding of Johann Georg's eldest daughter. Subsequent marriages of the elector's children, his youngest daughter on 5/15 October 1634 to the Danish Prince-Elect in Copenhagen and his heir Johann Georg on 13/23 November 1638 in Dresden, gave rise to the composition of more musical dramas: two four-act plays by Johann Lauremberg, *Wie Aquilo der Regent mitternächtigen Länder die edle Princessin Orithyjam heimführet* and *Wie die Harpyiæ von zweyen septentrionalischen Helden verjaget; und König Phineus entlediget wird* (texts published as *Zwo Comoedien*, Copenhagen, 1635), a ballet (1634) initiated by Duke Frederik (later Frederik III of Denmark) and an operatic ballet *Orpheo und Euridice* (1638, libretto by August Buchner).

Although *Dafne* is heralded as the first extant German opera, not until Lauremberg's *Musicalisch Schawspiel* (1655, Copenhagen) does German-language opera have madrigal verse and alternating recitative and aria. *Dafne, Zwo Comoedian* and *Orpheo und Euridice* are spoken plays with vocal inserts, usually in the form of strophic lieder, an early form of opera which persisted in German-speaking lands. None of Schütz's dramatic music is extant, although music does survive for a strophic song, 'Gesang der Venus-Kinder' SWV278, performed as part of a masqued tournament invention for the Copenhagen wedding in 1634 and published there that year. Other occasional works with extant dramatic texts for which Schütz provided music include *Wunderliche Translocation des weitberümbten und fürtrefflichen Berges Parnassi* (Dresden, 25 July 1617, for the visit of the Emperor Matthias), *Glückwündschung des Apollinis und der neun Musen* (Dresden, 5 March 1621, for the birthday of Johann Georg I) and *Theatralische neue Vorstellung von der Maria Magdalena* (Wolfenbüttel, December 1644; text by J. G. Schottelius).

*

M. Fürstenau: *Zur Geschichte der Musik und des Theaters am Hofe zu Dresden* (Dresden, 1861–2)

A. Hammerich: *Musiken ved Christian den Fjerdes Hof* (Copenhagen, 1892)

C. Elling: 'Die Musik am Hofe Christian's IV. von Dänemark: nach Angul Hammerich', *VMw*, ix (1893), 62–98; rev. S. A. E. Hagen, as 'Angul Hammerich: *Musiken ved Christian den Fjerdes Hof* (Copenhagen, 1892)', *Historisk tidsskrift*, 6th ser., iv (1892–4), 420–44 [review of Hammerich 1892]

E. H. Müller von Asow, ed: *Heinrich Schütz: Gesammelte Briefe und Schriften* (Regensburg, 1931)

I. Becker-Glauch: *Die Bedeutung der Musik für die Dresdener Hoffeste bis in die Zeit August des Starken* (Kassel, 1951)

W. Osthoff: 'Monteverdis *Combattimento* in deutscher Sprache und Heinrich Schütz', *Festschrift Helmuth Osthoff* (Tutzing, 1961), 195–227

J. P. Larsen: 'Schütz und Dänemark', *Sagittarius*, ii (1969), 9–16; repr. in *BMw*, xiv (1972), 215–220

S. Köhler: 'Dafne und die Folgen: Anmerkungen zum Opernschaffen des Heinrich Schütz', *Der Komponist und sein Adressat: musikästhetische Beiträge zur Autor-Adressat-Relation* (Halle, 1977), 40–45

K. Gudewill: 'Der "Gesang der Venuskinder" von Heinrich Schütz (1634)', (Kiel, 1978); repr. in *Schütz Jb*, vi (1984), 72–92

M. Rank and H. Seeger: 'Leitmotive der Dresdener Operngeschichte', *Oper heute*, ii (1979), 7–28

J. J. Berns: '"Theatralische neue Vorstellung von der Maria Magdalena": ein Zeugnis für die Zusammenarbeit von Justus Georg Schottelius und Heinrich Schütz', *Schütz Jb*, ii (1980), 120–29

W. Breig: 'Höfische Festmusik im Werk von Heinrich Schütz', *Daphnis*, x (1981), 711–33; repr. in *Heinrich Schütz in seiner Zeit*, ed. W. Blankenburg (Darmstadt, 1985), 375–404

W. Braun: 'Zur Gattungsproblematik des Singballets', *Gattung und Werk in der Musik-Geschichte Norddeutschlands und Skandinaviens,* Kieler Schrifter zur Musikwissenschaft, xxvi, ed. F. Krummacher and H. W. Schwab. (Kassel, 1982), 41–50

Dresdener Hefte, iv (1985) [whole issue]

D. Arnold: 'The Second Venetian Visit of Heinrich Schütz', *MQ*, lxxi (1985), 359–74

E. Möller: 'Heinrich Schütz und das Jahr 1617', *Heinrich Schütz im Spannungsfeld seines und unseres Jahrhunderts: Dresden 1985*, 69–80

M. Radice: 'Heinrich Schütz and the Foundations of the *Stile recitativo* in Germany', *Bach*, xvi/4 (1985), 9–23

G. Stephan and H. John, eds.: *Dresdener Operntraditionen*, i: *Die Dresdener Oper von Heinrich Schütz bis Johann Adolf Hasse* (Dresden, 1986)

J. Aikin: 'Creating a Language for German Opera: the Struggle to Adapt Versification in Seventeenth-Century Germany', *Deutsche Vierteljahresschrift*, lxii (1988), 266–89

J.-U. Fechner: 'Zur literargeschichtlichen Situation in Dresden 1627: Überlegungen im Hinblick auf die "Dafne"-Oper von Schütz und Opitz', *Schütz Jb*, x (1988), 5–29

A. Ørbæk and O. Kongsted, eds.: *Heinrich Schütz und die Musik in Dänemark zur Zeit Christians IV*. (Copenhagen, 1989)

M. R. Wade: 'Heinrich Schütz and "det store Bilager" in Copenhagen (1634)', *Schütz Jb*, xi (1989), 32–52

W. Steude: *Dresdener Hefte*, xxi (1990)

M. R. Wade: 'Zwei unbekannte Seitenstücke zu Opitz' *Dafne*', *Wolfenbütteler Barock-Nachrichten*, xix (1992)

MARA R. WADE

Schützendorf, Gustav (*b* Cologne, 1883; *d* Berlin, 27 April 1937). German baritone. He studied in Cologne and Milan, and made his début in Krefeld in 1905 as Don Giovanni. From 1914 to 1920 he sang with the Munich Hofoper. After two seasons at the Berlin Staatsoper (1920–22) he was engaged by the Metropolitan; he made his début as Faninal in 1922 and remained with the company until 1935, taking a wide range of roles including Beckmesser, Alberich and Klingsor. He sang the Foreman of the Mill in Janáček's *Jenůfa* (1924), the Chamberlain in Stravinsky's *The Nightingale* (1926) and the Devil in Weinberger's *Švanda the Bagpiper* (1931), all American premières. His younger brother Leo Schützendorf and his elder brothers Guido (1880–1967), bass, and Alfons (1882–1946), bass-baritone, were opera singers of international stature; Alfons sang Klingsor at Bayreuth (1910–12) and Wotan at Covent Garden (1910). A famous performance of *Die Meistersinger* at Bremen in 1916 featured Guido as Kothner, Alfons as Hans Sachs, Gustav as Pogner and Leo as Beckmesser, the only time all four brothers appeared in the same performance.

HAROLD ROSENTHAL/R

Schützendorf, Leo (*b* Cologne, 7 May 1886; *d* Berlin, 18 Dec 1931). German bass-baritone, brother of Gustav Schützendorf. He studied with D'Arnals in Cologne and made his début at Düsseldorf in 1908. After engagements in Krefeld, Darmstadt, Wiesbaden and Vienna, he joined the Berlin Staatsoper in 1920. In nine years he made 445 appearances in a repertory of 47 roles, including Ochs, Boris, Beckmesser, Faninal, Méphistophélès and Wozzeck, which he created in 1925. In 1929 he sang in *Der Bettelstudent* at the Metropoltheater, Berlin, but as he had not obtained leave from the Staatsoper he was dismissed, an event that contributed to his final breakdown and early death. He was a versatile actor, as much at home in tragic roles as in comic ones.

*

J. Dennis: 'Leo Schützendorf', *Record Collector*, xvi (1964–66), 229–37 [with discography]

HAROLD ROSENTHAL/R

Schütz-Oldosi, Amalia (*b* *c*1800; *d* after 1839). Austrian soprano and mezzo-soprano. After singing in the chorus of the Vienna Hofoper, she was engaged at the Théâtre de l'Odéon in Paris, where she also sang Ellen (*La donna del lago*) at the Théâtre Italien (she repeated the role at the King's Theatre, London, in 1828). Having made her début at La Scala in 1830 as Bellini's Giulietta (*I Capuleti e i Montecchi*), she sang Rosina there in 1831. Under contract to the impresario Lanari, in 1833 she sang Norma at Lucca and Florence where, according to Duprez, she 'made a sensation'. She created Serafina in *Il campanello di notte* at the Teatro Nuovo, Naples, in 1836 and took the title role of *Beatrice di Tenda* at Bologna in 1837. The same year she sang Norma at the Teatro Apollo, Rome (on this occasion *Norma* was given as *La foresta d'Irminsul* with Delia as the main character). She returned to La Scala in 1839 in the title role of *Anna Bolena*. Brilliant and flexible, her voice was in the mezzo range; after hearing her in *I Capuleti*, Bellini wrote: 'the opera made half the effect that one felt at Venice … in all the ensemble pieces the voices of the two donnas cannot be effective, as they are both mezzos'.

*

G. L. Duprez: *Souvenirs d'un chanteur* (Paris, 1880)
C. Gatti: *Il Teatro alla Scala nella storia e nell'arte (1778–1958)* (Milan, 1963)
S. Corti: *Edizione critica delle lettere del tenore G. L. Duprez nell'archivio dell'impresario teatrale Alessandro Lanari presso la Biblioteca nazionale di Firenze* (diss., U. of Pisa, 1991)

SANDRO CORTI, ELIZABETH FORBES

Schwan, Christian Friedrich (*b* Prenzlau, 1733; *d* Heidelberg, 29 June 1815). German librettist and publisher. In 1765 Schwan opened a bookshop in Mannheim. His German translations of French comic operas were frequently used for performances by local troupes. *Der Kaufmann von Smyrna* (1770), a translation of Chamfort's comedy, was especially popular and was set by G. J. Vogler (1771), C. D. Stegmann (1773), O. F. Holý (1773) and F. Seydelmann (1778). Together with the poet Anton Klein, Schwan helped establish the Deutsche Gesellschaft at Mannheim in 1775. His *Rheinische Beiträge zur Gelehrsamkeit*, begun in 1777, served as its polemical voice and contributed to the establishment of the Mannheim Nationaltheater. Schwan's original Singspiel *Azakia*, intended for C. Cannabich, was set by J. André (1778) and, with minor revisions, by F. Danzi (1780). In 1790 he reissued *Der Kaufmann von Smyrna* in an expanded two-act version entitled *Die Sklavenhändler*; it was set by P. Ritter for the Mannheim Nationaltheater.

*

F. Walter: *Geschichte des Theaters und der Musik am kurpfälzischen Hofe* (Leipzig, 1898)
T. Bauman: *North German Opera in the Age of Goethe* (Cambridge, 1985)

PAUL CORNEILSON

Schwanda the Bagpiper. Opera by Jaromír Weinberger; *see* ŠVANDA THE BAGPIPER.

Schwanenberger [Schwanberg, Schwanberger], **Johann Gottfried** (*b* probably at Wolfenbüttel, *c*1740; *d* Brunswick, 29 March 1804). German composer. The birthdate 28 December 1737 (or 1740) given by Gerber is not confirmed by church records. He studied in Wolfenbüttel with G. C. Schürmann and Ignazio Fiorillo, and from 1756 to 1761 (on a court stipend) in Venice with Hasse, Gaetano Latilla and Giuseppe Saratelli. From 1762 to 1802 he was Kapellmeister at the court of the Duke of Brunswick. During this period he made a number of competent settings of Italian *opere serie* for the court, which though unimportant to the development of the genre reflect the court's prevailing taste for Italian melody. He later declined an invitation from Frederick the Great to succeed Agricola as court composer in Berlin. His operas and keyboard works were highly praised by Burney (and by Burney's translator Ebeling, who regretted that so few reached print); he was also known as an excellent keyboard player.

all performed in Brunswick; some MSS in D-W, Wa

Adriano in Siria (os, 3, P. Metastasio), Aug 1762
Il Temistocle (os, 3, Metastasio), Aug 1762
Solimano (os, 3, G. A. Migliavacca), 4 Nov 1762
La Galatea (favola pastorale, Metastasio), Feb 1763
Ezio (os, 3, Metastasio), 1763
La buona figliuola maritata (dg, 3, ? C. Goldoni), Feb 1764
Talestri regina delle amazoni, 1764
La Didone abbandonata (os, 3, Metastasio), Aug 1765
Zenobia (Metastasio), 1765
L'Issipile (os, Metastasio), 1766; rev. 10 Feb 1767 with 3 new ballets
Antigono (os, 3, Metastasio), 2 Feb 1768
Romeo e Giulia (os, 2, J. R. Sanseverino), 1776
Le isole fortunate (festa teatrale), 1778

L'Olimpiade (os, 3, Metastasio), 1782
Il trionfo della Costanze (2, D. Poggi), 13 March 1790
Recits in Il Creso, 1760

*

GerberL; *GerberNL*; *Burney GN* HEINRICH SIEVERS

Schwartz, Arthur (*b* Brooklyn, New York, 25 Nov 1900; *d* Kintersville, PA, 3 Sept 1984). American composer. He learnt to play the piano almost secretly, having to circumvent the opposition of his father, a lawyer. He eventually acquiesced in his father's insistence that he become a lawyer, too, but also turned to playing the piano for money and to composing. He wrote the songs for 17 New York shows, four London musicals and numerous films. Most of his American songs were written for the lyricist Howard Dietz. One tremendous irony encompasses all of Schwartz's writing for Broadway. The revues he composed for were almost all major successes, but none of his musical comedies was commercially successful. His best score is often said to be that for *The Band Wagon* (1931), widely considered the best revue ever given in New York. One of Broadway's most underrated composers, Schwartz was instrumental in popularizing the smoky harmonies so characteristic of the 1930s. He ranged skilfully from moody ballads to sprightly rhythm numbers.

all musicals; performance details are for New York premières

Revenge with Music (H. Dietz), New Amsterdam, 28 Nov 1934; Virginia (L. Stallings and O. Davis; lyrics A. Stillman), Center, 2 Sept 1937; Between the Devil (Dietz), Imperial, 22 Dec 1937; Stars in your Eyes (J. P. McEvoy; lyrics D. Fields), Majestic, 9 Feb 1939; Park Avenue (N. Johnson and G. S. Kaufman; lyrics I. Gershwin), Shubert, 4 Nov 1946; A Tree Grows in Brooklyn (B. Smith and G. Abbott; lyrics D. Fields), Alvin, 19 April 1951; By the Beautiful Sea (H. Fields and D. Fields; lyrics D. Fields), Majestic, 8 April 1954; The Gay Life (F. Kanin and M. Kanin, after A. Schintzler: *The Affairs of Anatol*; lyrics Dietz), Shubert, 18 Nov 1961; Jennie (A. Schulman; lyrics Dietz), Majestic, 17 Oct 1963

*

S. Green: *The World of Musical Comedy* (New York, 1960, 4/1980)
G. Bordman: *American Musical Theatre: a Chronicle* (New York, 1978, 2/1986) GERALD BORDMAN

Schwarz, Hanna (*b* Hamburg, 15 Aug 1943). German mezzo-soprano. She studied at Essen and Hanover, where she made her début as Maddalena in *Rigoletto* in 1970. In Hamburg her roles included Cherubino and Dorabella; at Bayreuth in 1975 she graduated to Rhinemaiden and Valkyrie, appearing as Erda the following year. Her American début (San Francisco, 1977) as Fricka was praised in *Opera* as 'radiant-toned', and at Covent Garden in 1980 her Waltraute was 'stunningly sung'. Thought to be miscast as Carmen in San Francisco and as Charlotte in Amsterdam, she scored a particular success as Dido in *Les Troyens* at Hamburg in 1983. She has sung parts as diverse as the Princess in *Adriana Lecouvreur* and Prince Orlofsky in *Die Fledermaus*, but has continued to appear regularly at Bayreuth, and her Waltraute was widely considered to be vocally the greatest asset of Covent Garden's *Götterdämmerung* in 1990. Her rich, steady voice has taken well to recording, though the voice alone hardly suggests the attractiveness and animation of her stage appearance. J. B. STEANE

Schwarz, Joseph (*b* Riga, 10 Oct 1880; *d* Berlin, 10 Nov 1926). German tenor. He studied in Berlin and Vienna, making his début in 1900 as Amonasro at Linz. After appearances in Riga, Graz and St Petersburg, he was engaged at the Vienna Volksoper and then at the Hofoper, where he made his début in 1909 as Luna. In 1915 he became a member of the Berlin Hofoper (later the Staatsoper). He made his American début in 1921 at Chicago as Rigoletto, returning as Iago and Germont; he sang Rigoletto again at the Paris Opéra (1923) and at Covent Garden (1925). He had a lyrical voice of considerable beauty of tone but, although an excellent actor, he had an unimpressive stage presence.

LEO RIEMENS/ELIZABETH FORBES

Schwarz, Paul (*b* Vienna, 30 June 1887; *d* Hamburg, 24 Dec 1980). German tenor. After seasons at Bielitz (now Biała) and the Vienna Volksoper he joined the Hamburg Stadttheater (later Staatsoper) in 1912. Until he was obliged to leave in 1933 he sang more than four thousand performances of 145 roles: he was best known as David, Pedrillo and Jaquino and in other *buffo* parts, but was also heard as Manrico, Turiddu, Mime, Alfredo and Rodolfo. He sang as a guest in Berlin, Vienna, Paris and Amsterdam. Although he left Europe for America, he returned to sing Monostatos at the 1936 Glyndebourne Festival. His last role was Don Basilio in *Figaro* (1949, Hamburg). DAVID CUMMINGS

Schwarz, Vera (*b* Agram, 10 July 1888; *d* Vienna, 4 Dec 1964). Yugoslav soprano. She studied in Vienna and made her début in operetta at the Theater an der Wien in 1908. Her clear voice and good looks quickly brought her leading roles such as Rosalinde (*Die Fledermaus*). She graduated to opera, first at Hamburg, then with the Berlin Staatsoper, and in 1921 at Vienna, where she had a great success as Tosca. Known as 'the poor man's Jeritza', she sang in a repertory ranging from Countess Almaviva to Aida, Ariadne, Marietta (*Die tote Stadt*) and even Carmen. In 1927 she sang in the Viennese première of *Jonny spielt auf* and in the Berlin première of Lehár's *Der Zarewitsch*. This marked the beginning of a noted partnership with Richard Tauber in Lehár operettas. In 1938 at short notice she appeared at Glyndebourne as Lady Macbeth, where her acting was found 'outstandingly impressive' though her voice sounded tired. She spent the next ten years in the USA, singing and later teaching, and returned to Europe in 1948 to give classes at Salzburg and Vienna. Her versatility, as well as a less than perfect technical control over a fine but hard-worked voice, is well illustrated on records. J. B. STEANE

Schwarze Maske, Die ('The Black Mask'). Opera in three acts by KRZYSZTOF PENDERECKI to a libretto by HARRY KUPFER and the composer after Gerhart Hauptmann's play; Salzburg Festival, 15 August 1986.

The composition of *Die schwarze Maske*, Penderecki's third opera (1984–6), followed that of the operatic *rappresentazione Paradise Lost* (1975–8). The two works share many musical characteristics (including an evident economy of musical means), although the more grotesque and lurid aspects of the plot of *Die schwarze Maske* lend themselves more readily to Penderecki's brand of chromaticism than do the purer elements of *Paradise Lost*.

Gerhart Hauptmann lived and worked in central Silesia until his death in 1946. This area of what is now Poland is just to the north-west of Penderecki's own birthplace, and no doubt this is one link binding their two imaginations. The other is the fascination with the surreal and inquisitorial that had already surfaced in Penderecki's first opera, *THE DEVILS OF LOUDUN*. The setting of *Die schwarze Maske* (whose three short acts run without a break) is the home in the Silesian town of Bolkenhain of the mayor Silvanus Schuller (tenor) and his wife Benigna (soprano) in 1662. Against a backdrop of plague and a carnival, a banquet takes place for a very odd assortment of characters, ranging from the Jansenist Jadidja Potter (*buffo* tenor, who bursts regularly into chorales) through a Huguenot gardener, various members of the aristocracy, an organist and local worthies, to the black intruder Johnson (speaking role). Although Johnson says only a few lines, his appearance at the start of Act 2 is catalytic. He is a symbol of mortality, avenging past misdeeds by leading the assembled company in a dance of death.

Penderecki treats this crazed, irrational drama with a frantic whirlwind of musical gestures, mostly based on lines of semitones and tritones. Certain figures, such as the first chordal theme, recur at significant points, as also do some of the 'imported' musical ideas. Baroque chorales, chants, and period dances on recorders, alongside quotations from Penderecki's own *Te Deum* and *Polish Requiem*, lend the opera a quixotic character that will be recognized by anyone familiar with his *St Luke Passion* (1963–6) or the Second Symphony (1980). The persistence of 'horror movie' chromatic writing might prove over-indulgent were it not for Penderecki's surefooted dramatic control, the rare oases of quiet, eerie orchestration or the towering power of Benigna's repudiations of Johnson and their hidden past together – one of her guests is the young mulatto Arabella (soprano leggiero). Benigna dominates the second half of the opera from the middle of Act 2, her music broadening to include 3rds and perfect 4ths in an extended scena of high lyrical expressivity which puts much of the rest of the opera in the shade. ADRIAN THOMAS

'Die schwarze Maske' (Penderecki): scene from the original production at the Salzburg Festival, 15 August 1986, with Charleston Marquis as Johnson (wearing the black mask) and Josephine Barstow as Benigna

Schwarzendorf. *See* MARTINI, JEAN-PAUL-EGIDE.

Schwarzkopf, (Olga Maria) Elisabeth (Friederike) (*b* Jarotschin, Posen province, 9 Dec 1915). German soprano. The outstanding lieder singer of the postwar decades and pre-eminent among women as was Fischer-Dieskau among men, she was an operatic artist in whom personal beauty, beauty of tone and line, and rare musical intelligence were combined. She entered the Berlin Hochschule für Musik in 1934, studying voice with Lula Mysz-Gmeiner (but for a year only; the celebrated lieder singer wished to make a contralto of her). In 1938 she joined the Berlin Städtische Oper, making her début as a flowermaiden and soon graduating from second-soprano roles to Adele, Musetta, Zerbinetta etc. Recordings from this period show a rather dark middle voice and a brilliant coloratura top. She became a pupil of Maria Ivogün, whom she regards as her real teacher. Karl Böhm invited her to join the Vienna Staatsoper, and after the war it was as a leading member of this troupe that she made her Covent Garden début (Donna Elvira, and Marzelline in *Fidelio*) in 1947. Invited to join the newly founded Covent Garden company, she remained with it for five seasons, singing not only in the German repertory (Pamina, Susanna, Eva, Sophie) but also Violetta, Gilda, Mimì, Butterfly and Massenet's Manon – all in English. The voice became a lustrous, powerful lyric soprano, full-toned, warm and flexible, and her international reputation grew. At the Salzburg Festival (début in 1947, Mozart's Susanna) she appeared most years until 1964; at La Scala (début in the 1948–9 season, Countess Almaviva) most years until 1963; with the San Francisco Opera (début in 1955, Marschallin) most years until 1964. Internationally she was sought as, above all, a peerless Fiordiligi, Countess Almaviva, Donna Elvira and Marschallin (Metropolitan début as the last, 1964; Donna Elvira, 1964), but her repertory ranged from Mélisande, Marguerite and Iole in Handel's *Hercules*, all at La Scala, to Mařenka in an English *Bartered Bride* in San Francisco.

In 1951 Schwarzkopf created the role of Anne Trulove in Stravinsky's *The Rake's Progress* in Venice. Although Italian opera played a relatively small part in her career after she left Covent Garden, one notable exception was her inimitably merry, dexterous Alice Ford in Verdi's *Falstaff* (Milan, Salzburg, Vienna) – happily captured on gramophone records, as was her Bayreuth Eva of 1951. Schwarzkopf's fame was furthered by many excellent recordings; in 1953 she married Walter Legge, artistic director of EMI records, and the two perfectionists combined to record a great deal of her theatre repertory and also some Johann Strauss (ii) and Lehár operetta heroines. Richard Strauss's Ariadne, Arabella (in excerpt) and Countess (*Capriccio*) are among her best recorded performances. All Schwarzkopf's interpretation and execution was marked by great care for detail; the care was often apparent, and she did not escape charges of overinflection and artfulness, particularly in later years when the voice had lost its earlier freedom. She retired from the stage after singing *Rosenkavalier* in Brussels in 1972; she was made a DBE in 1992.

*

W. Mann: 'Elisabeth Schwarzkopf', *Gramophone Record Review*

Elisabeth Schwarzkopf as the Marschallin in Richard Strauss's 'Der Rosenkavalier'

(1958), no.56, p.659 [with discography by F. F. Clough and G. J. Cuming]
G. Moore: *Am I Too Loud?* (London, 1962), 162ff
A. Porter: *A Musical Season* (New York, 1974), 93ff
J. B. Steane: *The Grand Tradition* (London, 1974), 348ff
W. Legge: 'Her Master's Voice', *ON*, xxxix/22 (1974–5), 9; also in *Opera*, xxvii (1976), 316–24
E. Greenfield: 'Elisabeth Schwarzkopf', *Gramophone*, liv (1976), 555, 751
L'avant-scène opéra (1983) [whole issue] ANDREW PORTER

Schweigsame Frau, Die ('The Silent Woman'). *Komische Oper* in three acts by RICHARD STRAUSS to a libretto by STEFAN ZWEIG after BEN JONSON's play *Epicoene*; Dresden, Staatsoper, 24 June 1935.

Sir Morosus	*a retired admiral*	bass
Widow Zimmerlein	*his housekeeper*	contralto
Schneidebart	*a barber*	high baritone
Henry Morosus	*nephew of the admiral*	high tenor
Aminta	*his wife*	coloratura soprano
Isotta	*members of an operatic troupe*	coloratura soprano
Carlotta		mezzo-soprano
Morbio		baritone
Vanuzzi		deep bass
Farfallo		deep bass
The Parrot		

Other players, neighbours

Setting The drawing-room of Sir Morosus's house in London, cluttered with mementoes of his naval career; about 1780

With the unexpected death in 1929 of Hofmannsthal, his junior by a decade, the 65-year-old Strauss was bereft – midway through their *Arabella* – of the librettist he had counted upon as a lifelong collaborator. Friends proposed new candidates in vain, while he strove to pull the *Arabella* sketches together and then tinkered with their earlier semi-failure *Die ägyptische Helena*. At length he was put in touch with Stefan Zweig, a distinguished younger writer, politicized intellectual and occasional dramatist, who was flattered to the point of obsequiousness. In 1931 Zweig proposed two ideas: a grandiose, humanitarian, multi-media pantomime – which Strauss rejected gently but firmly (just as Zweig later declined to write the *Semiramis* libretto Strauss had so long wanted) – and a domestic-scale comedy based on Ben Jonson's *Epicoene, or The Silent Woman* (1609). That the composer approved, and when the *Schweigsame Frau* libretto was finished in January 1933 he greeted it as the best comic-opera text since Da Ponte's *Figaro*.

Zweig's attraction to the English playwright had begun several years earlier, when upon reading a summary of Jonson's *Volpone* he wrote forthwith a successful version of his own. For *Die schweigsame Frau* he consulted translations of the *Epicoene* play, which was widely known. (Not only had Salieri drawn an opera from it, and the forgotten Mark Lothar too for Dresden in 1930, but at second or third hand it inspired Donizetti's *Don Pasquale*.)

Jonson's 'epicene' creature was a mere pageboy, got up as a woman to fool old Morose into a ruinous marriage; Zweig preferred to make him a real woman, as in *Don Pasquale* – indeed the gentle wife of the real schemer, Morosus's nephew. Yet again Strauss promised to write a swift 'operetta'-style piece, and it was agreed that there should be plenty of spoken repartee. In the event most of that went to the conniving barber Schneidebart, an obvious Figaro cousin. By November 1934 the score was complete but for its potpourri overture.

Despite a notable cast (Karl Böhm conducted Cebotari's Aminta, the 61-year-old Plaschke's Morosus, Martin Kremer's Henry and Matthieu Ahlersmeyer's Barber), the opera had a fraught première. Even in 1935, Strauss had to battle with Nazi officialdom to get his Jewish librettist acknowledged on the Dresden Opera handbills, whereupon Hitler and Goebbels decided not to attend. Its postwar resuscitation has been fitful, long drawn out and uncertain. For what amounts merely to 'grand operetta', the demands upon all the principal singers – and long-sitting audiences – are formidable, and the piece cannot work without a Morosus of crustily disarming, larger-than-life personality (Kurt Böhme was one such). Though Strauss composed the role *con amore*, his music remains a little bland without some extra-musical spicing – as might be said of the rest of the score.

ACT 1 There is a prefatory 'potpourri' in A – little more than four minutes long, but Strauss's first proper overture since his first opera *Guntram*. The label is mock-deprecatory: though based upon tunes from the opera, this bright curtain-raiser is polyphonic and shapely as well as sprightly.

Arriving for his daily appointment with Sir Morosus, the Barber is delayed by his garrulous Housekeeper. She bewails the rich old Admiral's lonely condition, exacerbated by his absolute intolerance of noise, and imagines the comfort a modest, quiet wife would bring him: a mature lady, of course, not a young one. When the Barber becomes impatient, their loud mutual abuse provokes the furious entry of Morosus and the widow's speedy exit. Morosus delivers a long diatribe against rackety modern London – its noisy entertainments (the orchestra cites several guilty operas), even its church bells. Shaving and soothing him, Schneidebart conjures up a vision of a silent, devoted young bride. (In the matching scene of Rossini's *Barbiere* Figaro is already practising a deception upon Don Bartolo, but here a notion for one is just taking form.) Lulled by the Barber's innocent *canzone*, Morosus begins to warm to the idea.

A commotion heralds the return of a prodigal, his scapegrace nephew Henry. The old man is touchingly overjoyed; now he has a companionable heir again, and any wife would be redundant. When Henry confesses that he has brought his 'Truppe' with him, the proud uncle expects a squad of soldiers. In fact Henry has become an operatic tenor, and the troupe that enters (to a 'Kleiner humoristischer Marsch') is a gaggle of Italian singers who hope to play the Haymarket; worse still, he has married the leading soprano. Scandalized, Morosus disowns his nephew, orders the Barber to find him a silent bride and stamps out, after an F minor ensemble of protests.

With his offended colleagues, Henry is nonplussed: he was hoping for some money. Schneidebart assures him that there is £60 000 or £70 000 in the cellar (a new ensemble, in E, impressed and excited), explains the Admiral's irascibility to the others – a naval explosion disordered his hearing – and urges them not to despair. Henry refuses to give up his beloved Aminta, as she suggests (their duet, in A, becomes a septet with chorus); his colleagues Isotta and Carlotta, in their own ariettas, reject the Barber's idea that one of them might marry Morosus (Aminta joins them for a ladies' trio, in B). He offers another plan: trick Uncle into a mock wedding with a meek 'bride', who will then prove an ear-splitting termagant; that should make him value the lot of a peaceful gentleman-bachelor with a deserving heir. Though gentle Aminta has a pang of sympathy for the old man, everybody embraces the prospect in a very long, strenuously bright octet-finale in G, with chorus.

ACT 2 After a preludial minuet, the unhappy Housekeeper helps Morosus prepare to interview three prospective fiancées, whom Schneidebart has found and now ushers in with another fluent *canzone*. Signor Vanuzzi's troupe plays the charade to the hilt: Carlotta is a hopelessly thick peasant girl, Isotta flashy and loquacious, Aminta – at considerable length – virginally mild as 'Timidia'. Morosus makes the obvious choice, and Vanuzzi and Morbio, masquerading as priest and notary, set up the 'wedding' (to music Strauss adapted from the Fitzwilliam Virginal Book, by way of period effect). The old man addresses himself to his 'bride' with a simple candour and sweetness that touch her heart. But the charade must go on: once the ceremony is completed (with a heartfelt sextet, in A♭), and Farfallo – claiming to have served under the Admiral – has crashed in with a large, boisterous 'wedding party' and crashed out again, and after a brief, tender idyll (in D♭) alone with her 'husband', Aminta's cue now is to scream on high C. At the top of her lungs she emits a torrent of outrageous demands and threats, meanwhile assaulting the marine mementoes. Horrified but impotent, Morosus collapses. Henry comes providentially to the rescue; he quells 'Timidia', promises his uncle to arrange an immediate divorce and packs him off to bed, overcome with gratitude and exhaustion. Now Henry and Aminta enjoy their own clandestine idyll (also in D♭), though she has twinges of self-reproach. From his distant bedroom, Morosus calls out his sleepy thanks again.

ACT 3 The orchestral introduction starts with a fugato – like the third act of *Der Rosenkavalier*, but here in a brisk, practical C major quite different from those *sotto voce* Mendelssohnian scurryings – and reaches a polythematic climax. The curtain rises upon a domestic upheaval: 'Timidia' has hired workmen to change everything in the house, with maximal hullabaloo. Her raucous parrot installed and the Housekeeper's faint protests brushed aside, she begins a coloratura lesson with her 'music master' – Henry in disguise of course, as in Rossini's *Barbiere*, with Farfallo at the harpsichord. (For their songs, Strauss raided Monteverdi and Legrenzi.) The Admiral staggers in with his ears stopped, adding his voice to an anxious ensemble with the Housekeeper and the parrot. Now the Barber announces (in D minor) the imminent divorce hearing, and does some preliminary dickering with 'Timidia' and Morosus. While the latter goes off to dress in his official best, Vanuzzi and the company arrive, to more music from the Fitzwilliam Virginal Book (a John Bull 'In Nomine'), as the 'Lord Chief Justice' with cohorts. Finding themselves briefly alone, all the conspirators gloat in a D major *prestissimo*.

Morosus returns in full fig, and the proceedings begin – duologues, solo outbursts and ensembles, running from B♭ major to minor. First there are legal questions about whether 'Timidia', who protests her devotion, is the wife he meant to marry. Then Isotta and Carlotta testify that she has 'known' another man. Henry claims to be that man (in a passionate D♭ love song and a new disguise), and Aminta swears that she has been strictly faithful to her husband – all of which is indeed true. When the verdict seems to be going in the Admiral's favour, Farfallo reverses it by a fresh quibble: the contract never required 'Timidia' to be *virgo intacta*. Amid a cruel chorus of suggestions that he might still appeal, the old man crumples in despair.

Abruptly, Henry and Aminta expose the whole charade, with heartfelt apologies. The uncle is astounded, then furious, and finally – over a huge orchestral explosion of relief – amused and forgiving. The naughty performers, who will get what they wanted, retire with a paean of praise. 'How beautiful music is', Morosus muses, 'especially when it's over.' With a glass of wine, his pipe, and his dear nephew and wife at hand he drowses off, in simple E♭ and blissful content.

* * *

There is more 'light music' in *Die schweigsame Frau*, fluent but two-dimensional, than in any other Strauss opera – the comedians' music in *Ariadne* has more sap, and the *Intermezzo* intermezzos more satirical point. The chromatic excursions are second-hand; the house-overturning music instantly recalls the *Rosenkavalier* ructions, and the Morosus-Barber banter *Ariadne*. The protracted ensembles invite comparison with Rossini, and lose by it; where Rossini's ensembles dramatize confusion and conflict, too many of the Strauss-Zweig ones are unanimous declarations, operatically redundant. Only a brilliant cast can cover over the dramatic faults:

the unprepared change of heart for Morosus at the crux, long character numbers for marginal figures in the drama, a central ruse in which the sympathetic main couple are inexplicably cruel – including a shy, tender heroine who switches to relentless sadism and back again. Yet a vein of kindly, Indian-summer warmth runs through the score, and in a sensitive performance it makes an impression that outlasts the foolery.

DAVID MURRAY

Schweinitz, Wolfgang von (*b* Hamburg, 7 Feb 1953). German composer. He studied composition in Washington, DC, then in Hamburg, eventually with Ligeti, and spent a year in Stanford at the Center for Computer Research in Music and Acoustics. Serialism guided his earlier pieces, but after the song cycle *Papiersterne* (1981) he began to explore both tonal and serial possibilities in his compositions of the 1980s, chiefly a dramatic Mass and his long opera *Patmos*. A musical action in an introit and seven acts, *Patmos* had its première at the Munich Biennale on 28 April 1990. It sets the entire text of the *Revelation* in Martin Luther's version (in German and English), arranged by David Sattler. The narrative role of St John is divided between two singers, tenor and baritone; besides several other solo voices, there are women's and children's choruses and a forceful chamber orchestra; a substantial dance element is presupposed. Responsibility for the visual realization is left to the director. Part of the Munich audience took angry offence at Ruth Berghaus's production, which illustrated the Apocalypse with oblique references to the Holocaust. Schweinitz's elaborately organized score is notable for its lucid, original harmonic idiom and for the strong lyrical impulse in the vocal writing.

DAVID MURRAY

Schweitzer, Anton (*b* Coburg, bap. 6 June 1735; *d* Gotha, 23 Nov 1787). German composer. As a young man he served the Duke of Hildburghausen as chamber musician. To groom him in composition, the duke sent him to Bayreuth (1758) and later Italy (1764–6), after which he promoted him to Kapellmeister. When financial pressures forced the duke to dissolve his opera company in 1769, Schweitzer found employment as music director of the itinerant theatrical company of Abel Seyler, which was just beginning to add German operas to its spoken offerings.

Schweitzer's first work for the Seyler company, the one-act occasional piece *Elysium* (1770), gained considerable popularity as a musical afterpiece and was published in vocal score in 1774. He composed other celebratory pieces on mythological themes, but also comic operas. His re-setting of the popular musical farce *Der lustige Schuster* is lost, but surviving arias from *Walmir und Gertraud* show the italianate clarity and verve of Schweitzer's comic style. Seyler sent his music director on an expedition to recruit new singers in order to expand and elevate his musical productions in directions towards which Schweitzer's music clearly pointed. By a stroke of good fortune, the music-loving Duchess Anna Amalia of Saxe-Weimar engaged Seyler's company at this time (1771), and Schweitzer's ambitions were at last given full rein.

A heated rivalry with the duchess's leading musician (later Kapellmeister), Ernst Wilhelm Wolf, flared up immediately. Through a series of bold new works composed in collaboration with major writers, Schweitzer quickly established himself as the superior figure. While Wolf continued composing the Hillerian comic operas in which the duchess delighted, Schweitzer turned to the witty, more urbane tone of F. W. Gotter's farce *Die Dorfgala* (1772). On a more elevated plane, he composed not only celebratory dramas but also several dramatic ballets for the birthdays of the duchess and her sons, Karl Eugen and Konstantin.

Two other experiments at Weimar opened new vistas for the German theatre. In May 1772 the Seyler company gave the première of the first German melodrama, Schweitzer's setting of a translation of Rousseau's *Pygmalion*. A year later it was able to mount a serious five-act opera in German, Christoph Martin Wieland's *Alceste*, the achievement for which Schweitzer is chiefly remembered. Theatrical collaboration between Schweitzer and Wieland had begun in mid-1772 with the dramatic ballet *Idris und Zenide* and continued that year with two dramatic prologues of Metastasian stamp, *Aurora* and *Die Wahl des Herkules*. When Wieland proposed the *Alceste* project to the duchess, he insisted that Schweitzer and not Wolf compose it.

A brilliant success at Weimar, *Alceste* made its way quickly to many other German stages, establishing at a stroke *seria*-style opera in German as a musical reality. Out of practical necessity, the singing roles had been limited to just four, but the virtuoso part of Parthenia (Alcestis' sister and confidante), written for the brilliant voice of Josepha Hellmuth, yields to no other opera of the day in difficulty. Elsewhere, the moderation of tone that Wieland thought proper to dramatic music predominates in the arias and extensive obbligato recitatives of Alcestis, Admetus and even the champion of virtue Heracles. Musically, the score is northern – expressively rich but monochromatic and formally conservative, without so much as a trace of Gluck's inspiration. Its high points are poignant, reflective moments in the obbligato recitatives of Alcestis and Admetus.

After *Alceste* Schweitzer began work on a new melodrama, *Ariadne auf Naxos*, adapted from a cantata text by H. W. von Gerstenberg by a member of the Seyler company, Johann Christian Brandes, in order to display the talents of his wife Charlotte. The work was only partly complete when a fire destroyed the Hoftheater at Weimar in May 1774. The Seyler troupe, by now one of the most respected in Germany, was immediately engaged by Duke Ernst II at the nearby court of Gotha. There Schweitzer found a far more formidable rival than Wolf in the court Kapellmeister Georg Benda. Benda supplanted Schweitzer almost immediately as the chief purveyor of important new dramatic compositions. The first of these, tellingly, was Brandes's melodrama *Ariadne auf Naxos* (27 January 1775); it eclipsed the rather tame, if lyrical, specimen in the same genre that Schweitzer produced that April, *Polyxena*, to a text by the Weimar courtier F. J. Bertuch.

As Benda scored one triumph after another, creative inertia seemed to overcome Schweitzer. His artistic ties remained firmly with the Weimar court, the scene of his greatest triumphs. In 1775 he set Goethe's early German libretto, *Erwin und Elmire*, but the opera was not performed at Gotha. When the Seyler company left Gotha, he elected not to travel with it, but remained as music director of the Gotha Hoftheater, which Duke Ernst II founded to replace the departed troupe in 1776. That March Schweitzer's incidental music to Goethe's tragedy *Clavigo* made a deep impression. Other than that he composed nothing for the new enterprise except for the brief occasional piece with which it was inaugurated, *Das Fest der Thalia*.

Schweitzer's main compositional challenge during these years came from elsewhere. The success of *Alceste* in 1775 at Schwetzingen and Mannheim prompted the Palatine court to commission another serious opera from Wieland and Schweitzer in 1777. Possibly the example of Holzbauer's *Günther von Schwarzburg* induced Wieland to contemplate a more full-blooded drama. Against his own inclinations, he worked hard to make his *Rosamunde* 'everything that a true Mannheim opera should be'. Schweitzer composed it with enthusiasm, and travelled to Mannheim in December 1777 to conduct rehearsals. The death of the Bavarian Elector Maximilian III Joseph on 30 December forestalled the performance, however, and the opera was not produced until two years later, at the Mannheim Nationaltheater, without success.

After *Rosamunde* Schweitzer wrote nothing more for the stage. He remained in Gotha as Benda's successor after the latter resigned as the duke's Kapellmeister in 1778. The Hoftheater was disbanded in September of the following year. Early in 1780 Benda remarked acidly in a letter to the composer F. W. Rust: 'For the labours one now demands of a Kapellmeister here my successor Schweitzer is quite good, for he has nothing to do and does just that.'

Although *Die Dorfgala* showed how well Schweitzer could acquit himself in 'the valley of the farce' (in the words of its librettist, Gotter), his fame was made by devoting himself to serious opera, both in the occasional pieces he was required to compose during his first years with Seyler, and in his two through-composed operas, *Alceste* and *Rosamunde*. It was *Alceste* alone, however, that sustained his reputation to the end of the century, and that inspired other composers to establish opera of a more or less Metastasian character on the German stage. Both the libretto and the music evoked censure as well as praise. The young Goethe was revolted that Wieland could claim Euripides as his model for such 'meaningless pap'. Mozart found Schweitzer hopeless as a composer for the voice and the tone of the opera dreary. Gerber summed up the opera's fortunes in 1792: 'Many and diverse things have the critics found to fault in it, and indeed not without cause. In spite of this, it has now held up on our German stage for 16 years, always with the same enthusiastic praise and applause.'

See also ALCESTE (iv); DORFGALA, DIE; and ROSAMUNDE.

Walmir und Gertraud, *c*1769 (Operette, 3, J. B. Michaelis), 2 arias pubd in *Gothaer Theater-Kalender* (Gotha, 1776)

Elysium (Vorspiel mit Gesang, 1, J. G. Jacobi), Hanover, Schloss, 18 Jan 1770, *D-Dlb, LEm, GB-Lcm* (vs), vs (Königsberg, 1774)

Der lustige Schuster (komische Oper, 3, C. F. Weisse, after C. Coffey: *The Merry Cobler*), Celle, 21 May 1770

Apollo unter den Hirten (Vorspiel mit Gesang, 1, Jacobi), Halberstadt, 4 June 1770, *RU-KAu**

Pygmalion (Melodram, 1, J.-J. Rousseau, trans. J. C. F. Schmidt), Weimar, Hof, 13 May 1772

Die Dorfgala (komische Operette, 3, F. W. Gotter), Weimar, Hof, 18 May 1772; rev. version (2), Hamburg, Gänsemarkt, 21 Jan 1779, *D-Bds, Dlb, F, US-Wc*, vs (Leipzig, 1777)

Aurora (Vorspiel, 1, C. M. Wieland), Weimar, Hof, 24 Oct 1772, *D-LEm**

Ariadne auf Naxos, 1772–3 (Duodrama, 1, J. C. Brandes, after H. W. von Gerstenberg), inc.

Alceste (Spl, 5, Wieland, after Euripides: *Alkestis*), Weimar, Hof, 28 May 1773, *A-Wn, Wgm, D-B, Dlb, Ds, LEm, F-Pc, US-Wc*, vs/short score (Leipzig, 1774)

Die Wahl des Herkules (lyrisches Drama, 1, Wieland, after Xenophon: *Memoirs*), Weimar, Hof, 4 Sept 1773, *D-Bds*

Polyxena (lyrisches Monodram, 1, F. J. Bertuch), Gotha, Schloss Friedenstein, 7 April 1775, *F**; (Weimar, 1793)

Erwin und Elmire, 1775 (Schauspiel mit Gesang, 2, J. W. von Goethe, after O. Goldsmith: *The Vicar of Wakefield*), unperf., aria pubd in *Gothaer Theater-Kalender* (Gotha, 1777)

Rosamunde, 1777 (Spl, 3, Wieland, after J. Addison), Mannheim, National, 20 Jan 1780, *B, US-Wc*

*

GerberL; *GerberNL*

C. M. Wieland: 'Briefe an einen Freund [F. H. Jacobi] über das deutsche Singspiel, *Alceste*', *Der deutsche Merkur*, i (1773), no.1, pp.34–72; no.3, pp.223–43

E. C. Dressler: *Gedanken, die Vorstellung der Alceste, ein deutsches ernsthaftes Singspiel betreffend* (Frankfurt and Leipzig, 1774)

[G. J. Vogler]: 'Ueber die Musik der Oper *Rosamunde*', *Rheinische Beiträge zur Gelehrsamkeit*, no.6 (Mannheim, 1780); repr. in Klein (1781)

A. Klein: *Ueber Wielands 'Rosamund', Schweizers Musik und die Vorstellung dieses Singspiels in Mannheim* (Frankfurt and Leipzig, 1781)

E. Istel: *Die Entstehung des deutschen Melodramas* (Berlin, 1906)

J. Maurer: *Anton Schweitzer als dramatischer Komponist* (Leipzig, 1912)

A. A. Abert: 'Der Geschmackswandel auf der Opernbühne, am Alkestis-Stoff dargestellt', *Mf*, vi (1953), 214–35

J. van der Veen: *Le mélodrame musical de Rousseau au Romantisme* (The Hague, 1955)

T. Bauman: 'Wieland's *Aufklärungsoper*', *IMSCR*, xii *Berkeley 1977*, 245–9

——: *North German Opera in the Age of Goethe* (Cambridge, 1985)

THOMAS BAUMAN

Schweizerfamilie, Die ('The Swiss Family'). *Lyrische Oper* in three acts by JOSEPH WEIGL to a libretto by I. F. Castelli after C. G. d'Aucour de Saint Just; Vienna, Kärntnertortheater, 14 March 1809.

The plot is not, as has sometimes been claimed, drawn from J. D. Wyss's *The Swiss Family Robinson*, which was not published until 1841. A Swiss family in exile is living in an unspecified alpine country. Unknown to her parents Gertrude (mezzo-soprano) and Richard Boll (baritone), young Emmeline (soprano) is betrothed to a Swiss boy, Jakob Friburg (tenor). Her parents are worried about her failing health and her sanity as she, believing she will never see Jakob again and to allay their fears, attempts to hide her unhappiness behind a show of cheerfulness. A local Count (bass), whose life Richard saved, tries to help the family, while a local youth Paul (tenor) falls in love with Emmeline and believes she returns his love. His older companion Durmann (tenor) attempts to restrain him. Jakob, after long searching for Emmeline, arrives on the scene (playing his flute) and is eventually reunited with her amidst general rejoicing.

Die Schweizerfamilie was Weigl's most successful opera – a gentle, pastoral, romantic love story with little action but considerable musical variety and charm. It was immensely popular in the early 19th century, and was performed throughout Europe in many languages. Apart from two overtures, which incorporate music from the opera, there are 19 well-ordered numbers including one each of aria, lied, *romance* and *cavatine*, five duets, three trios, a quartet, a quintet and choral ensembles. A section of melodrama occurs shortly before Emmeline is reunited with Jakob. The numbers are formally concise in classical Singspiel tradition, whereas Weigl's orchestral colouring, use of themes with 'Swiss' character, reminiscence motifs and moments of sentimental expression are typical of German Romantic opera.

ELIZABETH NORMAN McKAY

Schwerin. City in north Germany, capital of Mecklenburg-Vorpommern. Performances of drama and opera were forbidden by the pietist Duke Friedrich between 1756 and 1785, on the grounds that they were 'dissolute' – a prohibition which put an end to the promising inception of a German national theatre begun by the duke's father Christian Ludwig II after 1751, with the hiring of the Schönemann theatrical company and the founding in 1753 of the first drama academy in Germany. Graun's *Montezuma* and Hasse's *Didone abbandonata* were among the productions that had been staged. In 1785 the actor and musician I. C. C. Fischer of Güstrow put forward a plan for a national theatre in Mecklenburg, and in 1790 he became director of the Ballhaus am Alten Garten, recently converted into a theatre. Three performances of *Don Giovanni* were given in 1790, among other works.

The Ballhaus burnt down in 1831, and a new theatre was opened on 17 January 1836, producing French and Italian operas as well as works of Mozart, Beethoven, Weber and Lortzing. Jenny Lind had many triumphs here in operas by Bellini, as did the fine local singer Luise Schlegel in *Les Huguenots* and *Fidelio*. The initiative of Wagner's niece Franziska and the choirmaster Julius Stock brought a production of *Tannhäuser* as early as 26 January 1852. Flotow was director of the opera, 1855–63; his engagement of the Hofkapellmeister Georg Aloys Schmitt (1856–92), who immediately reorganized the orchestra and the company, brought Schwerin's operatic stage up to modern standards of quality. Under Schmitt's direction the Schwerin Hoftheater was the first German theatre after Bayreuth to produce *Die Walküre* and *Siegfried*, both in 1878. Schmitt's deputy, Richard, gave the first performance of his own comic opera *Der Musikfeind* in 1862.

The theatre burnt down on 16 April 1882, and Karl von Ledebur (director, 1883–1913) opened the new Hoftheater of the Grand Duchy of Mecklenburg-Schwerin (730 seats) on 3 October 1886 with Gluck's *Iphigénie en Aulide*. The Kapellmeisters Karl Gille (1892–7) and in particular Herman Zumpe (1897–1901) further extended the strength and reputation of the company. In 1899 it toured with Zumpe, performing Schillings's *Ingwelde* eight times in Berlin, and in the same year his *Pfeifertag* was first performed in Schwerin; Zumpe's *Sâwitri* also had its première here. Further first performances include those of operas by the local composer Robert Alfred Kirchner (1889–1946) – *Der Tod des Musikers* (1925), *Sündflut* (1926), *Marionetten* (1929) and *Abenteuer des Don Quichotte* (1941) – and of Schjelderup's *Sturmvögel* (1926). After the 1918 revolution an operetta company was added, and the court theatre was renamed the Mecklenburg Landestheater, becoming the Staatstheater in 1926. Paul Graener's *Friedemann Bach* was first performed here in 1931, and Mark Lothar's revision of Haydn's *Il mondo della luna*, as *Die Welt auf dem Monde*, in the following year. In 1936 Pfitzner brought his *Der arme Heinrich* to the Schwerin theatre, which suffered no damage in World War II and resumed performances in May 1945. The repertory laid emphasis on operas by Slav composers as well as classical and contemporary works. Recent Kapellmeisters include Rudolf Neuhaus, Karl Schubert, Kurt Masur, Klaus Tennstedt, Hartmut Haenchen, Johannes Winkler, and since 1990 Ruslan Raichew.

*

H. W. Bärensprung: *Versuch einer Geschichte des Theaters in Mecklenburg-Schwerin* (Schwerin, 1837)

F. Chrysander: 'Musik und Theater in Mecklenburg', *Archiv für Landeskunde in den Grossherzogthümern Mecklenburg* (1854), 105

F. Wedemeier: 'Beiträge zur Geschichte des Grossherzoglichen Hoftheaters in Schwerin', *Archiv für Landeskunde in den Grossherzogthümern Mecklenburg*, x (1860), 705

K. von Ledebur: *Aus meinem Tagebuch: ein Beitrag zur Geschichte des Schweriner Hoftheaters* (Schwerin, 1897)

C. Meyer: *Die Geschichte der Mecklenburg-Schweriner Hofkapelle* (Schwerin, 1913)

H. Tank-Mirow: 'Geschichte des Schweriner Hoftheaters, 1836–1855 und 1855–1882', *Jb des Vereins für mecklenburgische Geschichte und Altertumskunde*, lxxxvii (1923), 72; lxxxviii (1924), 59

W. Golther: 'Die Wagner-Überlieferung an den mecklenburgischen Theatern Schwerin und Rostock', *Mecklenburgische Monatshefte*, xii (1935), 599

D. Härtwig: 'Zur Geschichte des Musiktheaters in Schwerin 1836–1945', *Festschrift 125 Jahre Mecklenburgisches Staatstheater Schwerin* (Schwerin, 1961) DIETER HÄRTWIG

Schwertsik, Kurt (*b* Vienna, 25 June 1935). Austrian composer. After studying at the Vienna Academy of Music (1949–57), where his composition teachers were Joseph Marx and Karl Schiske, he combined a career as an orchestral horn player with further study in Cologne and Darmstadt with Stockhausen. In 1958 he founded the Viennese new music ensemble Die Reihe with Cerha. Though Schwertsik had involved himself in the postwar avant garde and absorbed its techniques, his own music moved rapidly in a very different direction, embracing a richly allusive tonal idiom, the purpose of which was to entertain and suprise as much as it was to extend his expressive range. The first performance of *Liebesträume* for seven instruments caused an uproar at Darmstadt in 1962; four years later Schwertsik founded the Vienna Salonkonzerte with Otto Zykan, with a plea for 'more amusement, more tolerance and fewer ethical ambitions', publishing a manifesto in which he made clear his dissatisfaction with the preoccupations of the avant garde.

His first opera, *Der lange Weg zur grossen Mauer* op.24, in two acts to an original libretto by Richard Bletschacher based on a Chinese folktale, received its first performances in 1975 on consecutive days in Ulm (13 May) and Lucerne (Stadttheater, 14 May) in two different productions. The chamber opera for children *Das Märchen von Fanferlieschen Schönefüsschen* op.42 was commissioned by the Württemberg Staatstheater for the Kammertheater, Stuttgart: it was first performed on 24 November 1983. The libretto, by Karin and Thomas Körner, based on one of Brentano's fairy-tales, reduces a complex narrative to a sequence of ten scenes interspersed with orchestral interludes and replaces Brentano's highflown prose with vivid doggerel. Schwertsik's music also contains many vernacular associations, but the idiom remains personal, its highly coloured mix of stylistic references lyrical and surreal by turns.

*

K. Schwertsik: 'Looking into the Mirror: Fragments from Diaries, Reports and Manifestos', *Tempo*, new ser., nos.161–2 (1987), 52–67 ANDREW CLEMENTS

Schwestern von Prag, Die ('The Sisters from Prague'). Singspiel in two acts by WENZEL MÜLLER to a libretto by JOACHIM PERINET after PHILIPP HAFNER's burlesque *Der von dreyen Schwiegersöhnen geplagte Odoardo, oder Hannswurst und Crispin, die lächerlichen Schwestern*

von Prag (*c*1762); Vienna, Theater in der Leopoldstadt, 11 March 1794.

Herr von Brummer's daughter Wilhelmine (soprano) is desired in marriage by three suitors: a feeble poetaster, Herr von Sperlingshausen (tenor), a French fop, Chevalier Chemise (tenor) and Herr von Gerstenfeld (tenor), a good, honest gentleman. Brummer (bass) will not agree to his daughter's engagement without the approval of his sister, who is expected from Prague. Krispin (tenor) and Johann (bass), the servants of the poet and of the favoured suitor, Gerstenfeld, independently pretend to be the sister; both are unmasked, but not before Brummer has agreed to let Gerstenfeld marry Wilhelmine. Her maid Lorchen (soprano), who has been wooed by the three valets, gives her hand to Johann, and all ends happily.

The witty, tuneful score is one of Müller's best. 12 of the 21 numbers are arias (for the serious characters), or neatly contrasted songs; there are also four duets, a trio, a quartet, an ensemble including chorus and two extensive finales. The most familiar piece, thanks to Beethoven's Variations op.121a, is Krispin's 'Ich bin der Schneider Kakadu'. But the most ambitious and interesting is the Act 1 finale, in which the heroine and her maid are serenaded at their window by a succession of suitors, who accompany themselves on a variety of instruments, until Brummer comes out to complain about the din. A general mêlée is briefly stilled by the offstage cry of the nightwatchman, but the neighbours join in the racket and it takes the arrival of the watchman and lamplighters to restore order. Despite the simultaneous involvement of ten solo voices, and later of chorus too, the vocal writing only briefly extends to five parts. But the foreshadowing of the conclusion of Act 2 of Wagner's *Die Meistersinger von Nürnberg* is unmistakable.

PETER BRANSCOMBE

Schwetzingen. Town in south-west Germany, near Mannheim and Heidelberg. In the 18th century the palace served as the summer residence of the court of the Elector Palatine. Its Rococo Schlosstheater (now with 466 seats for opera performances) was designed by Nicolas de Pigage and inaugurated in 1752; it survives as the only German theatre of its kind faithful to its original form (later extensions of the stage house and amenities were kept in strict historical style). Early opera performances included Holzbauer's *Il figlio delle selve*, *L'isola disabitata* and *Don Chisciotte*, and Gluck's *La Cythère assiégée*. Since 1952 the park, palace and theatre have been the setting for the annual Schwetzingen Festspiele, held from late April to early June under the patronage of Süddeutscher Rundfunk, Stuttgart, whose symphony orchestra plays for the two or three opera productions for which individual opera companies are invited. As an ideal showcase for Baroque and Classical operas, the festival has pursued a policy of reviving neglected chamber operas; side by side with these are contemporary works, many of which are specially commissioned. These include Werner Egk's *Der Revisor* (1957), Hans Werner Henze's *Elegy for Young Lovers* (1961), Wolfgang Fortner's *In seinem Garten liebt Don Perlimplin Belisa* (1962), Giselher Klebe's *Das Märchen von der schönen Lilie* (1969), Aribert Reimann's *Melusine* (1971), Günter Bialas's *Der gestiefelte Kater* (1975), Udo Zimmermann's *Die wundersame Schustersfrau* (1982), Rudolf Kelterborn's *Ophelia* (1984), Hans-Jürgen von Bose's *Die Leiden des jungen Werthers* (1986), Georg Katzer's *Gastmahl, oder Über die Liebe* (1988) and Manfred Trojahn's *Enrico* (1991).

*

K. Martin: *Die Kunstdenkmäler des Amtsbezirks Mannheim: Stadt Schwetzingen* (Karlsruhe, 1933), 96–109 [designs for the Schwetzingen theatre]

L. Fehrle-Burger: *Die Welt der Oper in den Schlossgärten von Heidelberg und Schwetzingen* (Karlsruhe, 1977)

HORST KOEGLER

Sciammarella, Valdo (*b* Buenos Aires, 20 Jan 1924). Argentine composer. He studied composition under Célica Schiuma de Diana and Julián Bautista in Buenos Aires, and for many years was a chorus master at the Teatro Colón. In 1956 and 1957 he wrote *Marianita limeña*, a one-act lyrical comedy, which was given a successful first performance on 11 November 1957 at the Teatro Presidente Alvear in Buenos Aires by the Teatro de Cámara de Buenos Aires; Enrique Sivieri conducted. The following year it was put on at the Brussels World Festival, then at the Teatro Argentino in La Plata (1961) and at the Colón (1962, 1966 and 1970). In 1960 it was recorded for television. To a libretto by Francisco Javier, the opera is based on a story from Ricardo Palma's *Tradiciones peruanas*, set in Lima in 1750. Marianita is a young girl married to an old count, to whom she has granted a year to make her fall in love with him and consummate the marriage. At the end of the year she runs away. There are three scenes, each containing a moralizing madrigal. An important role is played by the disorderly crowd, who provide pointed comments in popular songs and exclamations taken from Palma's story which add local colour to the work. Tonality is freely treated, and Sciammarella uses harmonies and rhythms that evoke a Spanish or Latin American atmosphere, but without using traditional or folkloric material.

JUAN MARÍA VENIARD

Sciarrino, Salvatore (*b* Palermo, 4 April 1947). Italian composer. A precocious autodidact, Sciarrino began painting at the age of four, progressed to abstract, informal canvases, and thence, during his teens, to music. From his early 20s he based himself in Rome, where his distinctive scores (soon widely imitated) quickly earned him attention. In 1977 he was appointed artistic director of the Teatro Comunale in Bologna, where he worked for three years. He has taught extensively, principally in Milan, Florence and Città di Castello. His choice of musical materials is fastidious and idiosyncratic. Obsessive gestures are built up from marginal sounds (string and wind harmonics, ancillary performance noises and the more unexpected reaches of the human voice). An analogous sensibility is at work in his wry, surreal theatre works, which scrutinize familiar myths – whether ancient or modern – from unfamiliar perspectives. In his first opera, *Amore e Psiche* (1972), myth is dissolved into a series of symbolical images, a process essentially repeated in *Aspern* (1977–8), where Henry James's story *The Aspern Papers* freezes into images of 'a lifeless existence'. But with *Cailles en sarcophage* (1979) and *Vanitas* (1981) even the allusion to a narrative frame is abandoned in favour of surrealist montage. The myths in question are now those of this century (in *Cailles* Greta Garbo, Marlene Dietrich, etc.), and Sciarrino accordingly draws upon his encyclopaedic knowledge of classic American songs from the 1930s and 40s, fragments from which rotate obsessively.

With his two operas drawn from Laforgue Sciarrino embarks with relish upon the subversion of familiar stories. Both *Lohengrin* and *Perseo e Andromeda* demonstrate the same basic thesis: that long-awaited airborne heroes may prove a disappointment in practice. In both instances the protagonists' attempts at relationships regress into a hopeless (but sometimes hilarious) solipsism. However, Sciarrino treats the two stories quite differently. *Lohengrin* is a virtuoso vehicle for a single female vocalist, using every aspect of the voice to impersonate her two protagonists but breaking into song only at the end. *Perseo e Andromeda*, on the other hand, employs four singers (including a male duet for Perseus) and elaborates a mannered lyricism against a backdrop of live electronics.

See also LOHENGRIN (ii).

Amore e Psiche (1, A. Pes), Milan, Piccola Scala, 2 March 1973
Aspern (Spl, 2, G. Marini and S. Sciarrino, after H. James: *The Aspern Papers*, with fragments from L. da Ponte), Florence, Pergola, 8 June 1978
Cailles en sarcophage (atti per un museo delle ossessioni, 3 pts, G. Marini), Venice, Malibran, 26 Sept 1979; rev., Venice, Fenice, 17 Oct 1980
Vanitas (natura morta, 1, text assembled by Sciarrino from anonymous sources, Sempronius, G. B. Marino, R. Blair, J. de Sponde, M. Opitz, J. C. Günther and C. von Grimmelhausen), Milan, Piccola Scala, 11 Dec 1981
Lohengrin (azione invisibile, Sciarrino, after J. Laforgue: *Lohengrin fils de Parsifal* from *Moralités légendaires*), Milan, Piccola Scala, 15 Jan 1983
Perseo e Andromeda (1, Sciarrino, after Laforgue: *Moralités légendaires*), Stuttgart, Staats, 27 Jan 1991

*

M. Bortolotto: 'Intervista con Salvatore Sciarrino', *Spettatore musicale*, vii/6 (1972), 9
A. Pes: 'Amore e Psiche: introduzione–vicenda–argomento', *Spettatore musicale*, vii/6 (1972), 12
M. Mazzolini: 'Dell'interrogare: incontro con Salvatore Sciarrino', *Sonus*, ii/3 (1990), 45 [on *Vanitas*, *Lohengrin* and *Perseo e Andromeda*]

DAVID OSMOND-SMITH

Scimone, Claudio (*b* Padua, 23 Dec 1934). Italian conductor and musicologist. He studied with Ferrara, Mitropoulos and Zecchi, and in 1959 founded the chamber ensemble I Solisti Veneti. At first specializing in 18th-century Italian instrumental music and contemporary works, the ensemble subsequently also became involved in opera as a result of Scimone's musicological research. In the 1970s Scimone became closely associated with the Rossini revival originating at Pesaro, conducting theatre or concert performances of such works as *Mosè in Egitto* and *Maometto II* at Pesaro in the 1980s, *Ermione* at Padua in 1986, *Armida* at Amsterdam and *Zelmira* at Venice in 1988. At Venice in 1984 he conducted his own reconstruction from the Vienna autograph of Albinoni's *Il nascimento dell'aurora* (*c*1710). Outside Italy his operatic work has included *L'elisir d'amore* at Covent Garden in 1981, and *Il barbiere di Siviglia* at Melbourne in 1989. His recordings include *L'italiana in Algeri* (1980) with Horne, *Maometto II* (1985), *L'elisir d'amore* (1986), *Zelmira* (1989) and such rarities as Vivaldi's *Catone in Utica*.

CLAUDIO CASINI, NOËL GOODWIN

Scio, Etienne (*b* Bordeaux, 1766; *d* Paris, 21 Feb 1796). French composer. He made his début as a composer at the Grand Théâtre, Marseilles, where he was engaged as first violinist in 1788. The impresario Boursault-Malherbe brought him and his colleague Joseph Arquier to Paris in June 1791, when he opened the Théâtre Molière and acted as its first conductor. He left it in 1792 to play second violin in the orchestra of the Théâtre Feydeau, where his wife (née Julie-Angélique Legrand) sang the principal female roles. Scio's two main operas were performed there. *Lisidore et Monrose* (1792) was criticized for plagiarizing Grétry's *Richard Coeur-de-lion* and Dalayrac's *Raoul sire de Créqui*; nevertheless it was a success. *Lisia* (1793), on an exotic subject derived from Dalayrac's *Azémia*, is notable for the important part played by the chorus and for its constant search for novel sonorities within the French operatic tradition.

all first performed in Paris; printed works published in Paris

Le réveil de Kamailliaka, ou Le mariage de la folie (2, Monnet), Molière, 4 July 1791
Le sopha (opéra féerie mêlé de vaudevilles et d'ariettes, 2), Molière, 26 Aug 1791, *F-Mc*
La France régénérée (comédie mêlée de vaudevilles et d'airs nouveaux, 1, Chaussard), Molière, 14 Sept 1791
Lisidore et Monrose (drame héroï-lyrique, 3, Monnet, after F.-T.-M. de Bacular d'Arnaud: *Le sire de Créqui*), Feydeau, 26 April 1792, excerpts (n.d.)
Lisia (cmda, 2, Monnet), Feydeau, 8 July 1793, *F-Pc**, excerpts (n.d.)
Le tambourin de Provence, ou L'heureuse incertitude (comédie mêlée de chant et de danses, 1, Monnet), Palais-Variétés, 13 Sept 1793

*

StiegerO

MICHEL NOIRAY

Scio [Le Grand], **Julie-**[Claudine-]**Angélique** (*b* Lille, 1768; *d* Paris, 14 July 1807). French soprano. She made her début in 1786 under the name of Mlle Grécy. After engagements at Montpellier, Avignon and Marseilles, she made her Paris début in 1792 at the Opéra-Comique, later singing at the Opéra. At the Théâtre Feydeau she created the title role of Cherubini's *Médée* (1797) and Constance in *Les deux journées* (1800). She also took part in the premières of works by H.-M. Berton, Le Sueur and Dalayrac. Married to the violinist Etienne Scio, she was reputed to have been a highly dramatic singing actress. She died of tuberculosis at the height of her career.

ELIZABETH FORBES

Scipione ('Scipio'). Opera in three acts by GEORGE FRIDERIC HANDEL to a libretto by PAOLO ANTONIO ROLLI based on ANTONIO SALVI's *Publio Cornelio Scipione* (1704, Livorno), after Livy, *Historiarum ab urbe condita*, xxvi, 50; London, King's Theatre, 12 March 1726.

Scipione was Handel's eighth full-length opera for the Royal Academy of Music. There were 13 performances in the first run, with a cast consisting of the castratos Senesino and Antonio Baldi (Luceio [Luceius] and Scipio), the sopranos Francesca Cuzzoni and Livia Costantini (Berenice and Armira), the tenor Luigi Antinori (Lelio [Laelius]) and the bass Giuseppe Boschi (Ernando). The opera was written in unusual haste; Handel completed the score only ten days before the first performance, having taken – according to the librettist, Rolli – just three weeks to compose the music; signs of hurry are occasionally apparent both in the music (the overture borrows from two of Handel's recorder sonatas) and the libretto (the last recitative repeats the words of an earlier aria). Handel's original intention had been to produce *Alessandro* as his first new opera of the season, with both Cuzzoni and her newly engaged rival Faustina Bordoni in the leading roles, but the late arrival of Faustina caused him to interrupt composition of *Alessandro* and to write *Scipione* for the existing company, presumably to meet pressing demands for a new opera. There was a further complication: the opera was first written for a cast of seven singers, but the contralto Anna Vincenza Dotti (intended for the role of Rosalba, Berenice's mother) dropped out, forcing Handel to remove her part and make other changes which compounded the mismanaged continuity of Rolli's libretto.

That Handel was conscious of defects in his 1726 score is suggested by the extensive revisions made for his single revival at the King's Theatre on 3 November 1730. Only Senesino retained his part: Scipio became a tenor (Annibale Pio Fabri), Laelius and Armira female altos (Francesca Bertolli and Antonia Merighi); Anna Maria Strada del Pò sang Berenice. The new version was almost a pasticcio, with 14 numbers included from earlier Handel operas, but the title role is strengthened with the passionate 'Dimmi crudele' from *Muzio Scevola* and two new arias. Chrysander's score in the Händel-Gesellschaft edition gives a confused and incomplete treatment of all versions of the opera, though the 1726 and 1730 performing versions can be reconstructed (with the exception of some passages of 1730 recitative) from sources which were available to him. The first modern revival of the opera was given at Göttingen on 27 June 1937 and the first in Britain by the Handel Opera Society under Charles Farncombe at the Queen Elizabeth Hall, London, on 9 October 1967 (revived at Sadler's Wells Theatre in 1970 and 1979). The first revival of Handel's 1726 performing score (with some cuts) was at the Guildhall School of Music and Drama, London, on 15 November 1989, conducted by Clive Timms.

The historical context of the action is the capture of the Spanish port of New Carthage (Cartagena) by Publius Cornelius Scipio (237–183 BC) in 209 BC. Livy's account of how the young general refrained from exercising the rights of a conqueror over a beautiful female captive, a story known as 'The Continence of Scipio', was noted as a moral precept in the Renaissance and was popular with 17th- and 18th-century painters as well as being the subject of opera librettos by Salvi, Zeno and Piovene. Handel's opera opens with the triumphant entry of Scipio (alto) into New Carthage, accompanied by Laelius (tenor), one of his captains, and the captives Berenice (soprano) and Armira (soprano); Berenice is the daughter of Ernando, King of the Balearic Islands. Scipio admits he is attracted by Berenice, while Laelius prefers Armira. Berenice mentions the name of her fiancé Luceius, a Celtiberian prince whom Laelius knows and respects. Luceius (alto) learns of Berenice's capture and decides to disguise himself as a Roman soldier in order to rescue her. Laelius makes polite overtures to Armira and tries to comfort Berenice. As Berenice wonders where her lover is, the voice of Luceius himself answers as he approaches her. He assures her of his love, but she is anxious for his safety and tells him to hide when Scipio arrives.

As Scipio's compliments to Berenice become warm, Luceius intervenes. Berenice pretends to Scipio that Luceius is mad and dismisses him with a show of anger. Laelius tells Scipio that 'Erennius' (Luceius's assumed Roman name) is a soldier who served Scipio's father and partly lost his senses because of harsh enemy treatment. This satisfies Scipio, but Luceius is not sure that Berenice's dismissal of him was pretence. Ernando (bass), arriving to ransom Berenice, is welcomed by Laelius. Scipio declares his love to Berenice but she explains who she is and declares her fidelity to Luceius. After Scipio leaves, Laelius arrives with Luceius, but Berenice again sends Luceius away, making him jealous and angry. Armira rejects Laelius's advances but keeps him in hope in order to gain time until news of her capture reaches her father Indibilis. Luceius returns in search of Berenice. His conversation with Armira is partly overheard and misunderstood by Berenice. Armira is offended and leaves.

As Berenice and Luceius quarrel Scipio appears: Luceius reveals his identity and attempts to challenge Scipio, but is disarmed and led away. Scipio urges Berenice to love a Roman, but she declares herself faithful to Luceius. Ernando gains an audience with Scipio, who asks him for his daughter's hand. Ernando refuses: he too has given his word to Luceius. Scipio tells Laelius that Luceius is to be taken to Rome as a prisoner. Berenice asks Scipio to return Luceius to her or send her with him. Scipio, moved, assures her that she will be happy. In a throne room Scipio receives Ernando's ransom tribute and releases Berenice to him. Laelius discovers that Armira is the daughter of Indibilis, a Roman ally, and offers her freedom, prompting her to admit that she loves Laelius. In the final scene Scipio yields Luceius to Berenice and presents him with Ernando's ransom as dowry; all praise his magnanimity.

* * *

The character of Scipio, written as the secondary male role, is established confidently in the fine opening scene (beginning with the famous march) but is later enfeebled by dainty arias in minuet style; his most striking music, an accompanied recitative in which he considers his moral dilemma, seems never to have been performed by Handel. Luceius and Berenice have their best moments at the end of Act 2, as Luceius defies Scipio in the heroic aria 'Cedo a Roma' and Berenice declares her constancy in the soaring vocal line of 'Scoglio d'immota fronte'; their other arias tend to be musically exquisite rather than dramatically compelling. The amorous bantering of Laelius and Armira contrasts nicely with the high-minded sentiments of the other characters, and their arias are appropriately lighter in style. ANTHONY HICKS

Scipione affricano ('Scipio Africanus'). *Drama per musica* in a prologue and three acts by FRANCESCO CAVALLI to a libretto by NICOLÒ MINATO; Venice, Teatro SS Giovanni e Paolo, 9 February 1664.

During the celebration of Scipio's victory over the army of Asdrubale [Hasdrubal] (tenor), the captured Carthaginian princess Ericlea (soprano) is brought in chains before Scipio (soprano). He is immediately smitten with her beauty and spirit, but she is faithful to Prince Luceio [Luceius] (soprano), to whom she has been betrothed. Luceius and his brother Polinio [Polinius] (soprano) soon arrive in Carthage, not to attempt to rescue Ericlea but to test the virtue of the fiancée whom Luceius has never met. He and Ericlea fall in love immediately.

Meanwhile, the hapless Siface [Syphax] (alto), king of the defeated Masaesyles, has been imprisoned in a tower on a lonely beach by Scipio's ally Massanissa [Masinissa] (bass), who has also secretly abducted Syphax's wife Sofonisba [Sophonisba] (soprano). Determined to save her, Syphax fashions a parachute from his sheet and floats to freedom. Before he flees, he places in a corpse's hand a false suicide note telling of Sophonisba's imprisonment. Scipio finds the note and learns about Masinissa's treachery. In Masinissa's apartment Sophonisba sings a touching lament about her predicament, 'Di misera regina strano destin'.

Ericlea intercepts a letter to Sophonisba from Masinissa: 'Either bind yourself with these chains or drink your death with this poison'. She thinks the letter is from Scipio and wonders how someone who professes to love her could be so cruel. She begins to drink the poison, whereupon Masinissa admits his crime to Scipio. However, instead of returning Sophonisba, Masinissa forces her to hide in a deserted ship. When Scipio orders the ship to be set on fire, Masinissa again spirits Sophonisba away. Syphax swims to save his wife. Not finding her, he demands that Masinissa bring her forward. Masinissa finally reunites the couple, who surrender themselves to Scipio. Scipio realizes that he has no hope of winning Ericlea and presents her to Luceius. All sing in praise of love.

Syphax was one of the most famous characters in 17th-century Venetian opera. His engaging personality demonstrates great wit and courage, especially in his daring escape from the tower. The castrato Giovanni Francesco Grossi achieved such acclaim when he sang the role in the Rome revival of 1671 that he adopted Siface as his stage name. MARTHA NOVAK CLINKSCALE

Sciroli [Schiroli, Scivoli, Siroli], **Gregorio** (*b* Naples, 5 Oct 1722; *d* after 1781). Italian composer. He was a pupil of Fago and Leo and followed an operatic career characteristic of the time: from 1747, for some ten years, he composed intermezzos, farsettas and full-length comic works for the smaller theatres of Naples, Rome and Palermo. Having then gained some reputation, he appears to have spent the next decade mostly in north Italy writing more important (and better-paid) serious operas for Pisa, Venice, Milan and Bologna.

In his early years he began to teach singing, notably to the soprano Giuseppe Aprile who made his Neapolitan début at the Teatro di S Carlo in December 1753, and who derived his nickname 'il Scirolino' from his teacher. In 1752 Sciroli was *maestro di cappella* to the Prince of Bisignano, and he also directed the Palermo Conservatory (1753–7). Meanwhile the S Carlo engaged him for the season of 1753–4 as second harpsichordist, even though, as the appointment reads, he might find himself obliged to go to Palermo for production of his comic works (in fact, none is known to have been performed in Sicily then). His contract in 1756 with the Teatro dei Fiorentini is illustrative of production practices of the time. Sciroli was to write the season's first and third comic operas, to rehearse and conduct the performances and 'to alter arias, recitatives, duets, quartets, finales and even whole acts, in case of need'. The first of these works was perhaps *La Zita correvata*; P. Mililotti, who adapted the libretto of the other, *La marina di Chiaia*, complained that the production had been beset with constant difficulties, not least of which was Sciroli's need to be in Rome to oversee performances there, and that hence the whole undertaking had had to be put together in greatest haste.

Sciroli may later have held a church post, judging from the amount of his surviving sacred music. His serious opera *Merope*, for Carnival 1761 in Milan, achieved some *réclame*, and in November that year, when he was in Genoa, the S Carlo impresario urged the king in Naples to recall him to work at home. Sciroli then received commissions to compose the prologue for the theatre's Carnival opening (perhaps Cafaro's *Ipermestra* or the revival of J. C. Bach's *Alessandro nell'Indie*) and the spring opera, *Sesostri*. But the latter, which may have been a revival of music written for Pisa in 1759, was a failure, and he seems then to have left Naples permanently; he may have settled in Venice about 1766. In 1777 he was in Milan, whence he recommended to the S Carlo management the tenor Gaetano Scovelli (he was eventually engaged for the 1779–80 season).

Sciroli's surviving operas are professionally competent but unimaginative. *Merope*, written when many new forces were making themselves felt in *opera seria*, is a conservative work containing arias mechanically following the full da capo form, with the middle section almost invariably in the subdominant. Towards the end of each part of the first section the vocalise had become so stereotyped a feature that it could occur on any word containing the right vowel, regardless of meaning. He had little gift for affective lyricism and constructed his melodies almost obsessively out of triadic members and half-octave scale passages; the number of arias opening with such patterns must make the opera as a whole monotonous. His harmonic vocabulary was limited and the arias contain frequent long activated tonic or dominant pedals. Although he regularly used a fuller orchestra than some composers of the period, with oboes and horns either in C or G, the accompaniments contain little contrapuntal interest. Perhaps the most attractive aria in the opera is 'Misero core amante', marked 'Alla veneziana', a piece in 6/8 metre with some flavour of a popular song, and a frequently repeated rhythmic motif to open phrases. His uninspired melodic style may be more effective in comic arias, where it is mitigated by livelier rhythmic effects, achieved especially through use of rests that interrupt regularity of phrasing.

Capitan Giancocozza (farsa, D. A. Di Fiore), Naples, Fiorentini, carn. 1747

La Smorfiosa (int), Rome, Valle, carn. 1748

Madama Prudenza (farsetta), Rome, Valle, carn. 1749

Ulisse errante (dramma per musica, G. Badoaro), Palermo, S Cecilia, carn. 1749

Lo Corrivo (ob, P. Trinchera), Naples, Pace, carn. 1751–2

Lo Barone deluso (int, G. Petrosellini), Rome, Capranica, carn. 1752

Li nnamorate correvate (ob, Trinchera), Naples, Nuovo, aut.–wint. 1752

Il finto pastorello (ob, A. Palomba), Naples, Nuovo, sum. 1755

La caffettiera astuta (farsetta), Rome, Capranica, carn. 1756 [or Florence, Cocomero, carn. 1757], *I-Gl*

La Zita correvata (ob, P. Mililotti, after G. A. Federico), Naples, Fiorentini, 1756

La marina di Chiaia (ob, B. Saddumene), Naples, Fiorentini, carn. 1757

Il Conte Gian Pascozio in villeggiatura (farsetta), Rome, Capranica, Jan 1757, *Gl*

La sposa alla moda (int), Rome, Pace, carn. 1758

La contadina scaltra (int), Lucca, Pubblico, carn. 1759

Sesostri re d'Egitto (dramma per musica, after P. Pariati), Pisa, Pubblico, spr. 1759, *P-La* [a perf. with this title in Naples, S Carlo, 30 May 1762 may have had new music]

Bellerofonte (dramma per musica), Genoa, Falcone, spr. 1760

Olimpiade (dramma per musica, P. Metastasio), Venice, S Benedetto, aut. 1760, *La*

Merope (dramma per musica, Zeno), Milan, Regio Ducal, Jan 1761, *I-Nc*, *P-La*

Lo Saglemmanco [Act 1] (ob), Naples, ?Nuovo, 1762

Prologo, Naples, S Carlo, carn. 1762

Alessandro nelle Indie (dramma per musica, Metastasio), Bologna, Pubblico, 31 May 1764, *La*

Solimano (dramma per musica, G. A. Migliavacca), Venice, S Cassiano, 22 Nov 1766, *La*

Le nozze in campagna (dg, ?C. Goldoni), Venice, S Moisè, aut. 1768

Il vagabondo fortunato (ob, A. Papi), Brescia, Erranti, Aug 1769

La finta ammalata (int), *I-Gl* [incl. aria by G. Cocchi and trio by R. da Capua]

La villanella innocente (ob), *Gl* (Act 3 missing)

Duets and arias in P. Guglielmi: Antigono, Cremona, carn. 1776–7

Doubtful: Achille in Sciro (dramma per musica, Metastasio), Naples, 1751; Artaserse (Metastasio), 1752, aria *Gl*; Li negromanti (ob), Naples, Nuovo, 1752; La commediante (ob, after Palomba), Naples, ?before 1754; Zemira e Azor, Nice, 1777

Arias in *Fc*, *Gl*, *MAav*

*

M. Scherillo: *L'opera buffa napoletana durante il settecento: storia letteraria* (Naples, 1883, 2/1917), 259–60, 281
G. Sorge: *I teatri di Palermo* (Palermo, 1926), 399
E. Santaro: *Il teatro di Cremona* (Cremona, 1969), i, 141, 273

JAMES L. JACKMAN

Sciutti, Graziella (*b* Turin, 17 April 1927). Italian soprano. She studied in Rome and made her début as Lucy in *The Telephone* at the 1951 Aix-en-Provence Festival. There she also sang Susanna, Despina and Zerlina and in 1954 created the title role of Sauguet's *Les caprices de Marianne*. That year she made her British début as Rosina at Glyndebourne and sang the Duchess in Paisiello's *Don Chisciotte* to reopen the restored Teatrino di Corte in Naples. In 1955 she sang Carolina (*Il matrimonio segreto*) to inaugurate the Piccola Scala. She appeared many times in both the smaller and the larger auditoriums; her parts included the title role in *La Cecchina*, Adèle (*Le comte Ory*), Norina and Paisiello's Nina.

Sciutti made her Covent Garden début as Oscar in 1956 and returned to sing Nannetta, Susanna and Despina. She made her American début at San Francisco in 1961 as Susanna. She sang regularly at Salzburg and in Vienna and also appeared in Paris in Sacha Guitry and Reynaldo Hahn's *Mozart* and as Polly (*Die Dreigroschenoper*). In 1970 she returned to Glyndebourne as Fiorilla and in 1977 she sang in her own production of *La voix humaine* there. Her vivacity, pointed phrasing and crystal-clear diction made her an outstanding soubrette singer. In the 1980s she worked as a director in New York and Chicago.

*

GV (R. Celletti, incl. discography)
H. Rosenthal: *Great Singers of Today* (London, 1966)

HAROLD ROSENTHAL/R

Scolari, Giuseppe (*b* Vicenza, ?1720; *d* ?Lisbon, after 1774). Italian composer. He appears to have led the life of a travelling opera composer, with no fixed appointment. For many years he was in Venice, but from 1750 to 1752 or 1753 he was evidently at Barcelona. He may have been married to the Bolognese singer Barbara Narici (who is called Narici Scolari in one of the Barcelona librettos). Perhaps as early as 1766, certainly by 1768, he was in Lisbon; the presence of a fairly extensive collection of his scores (including one dated 1774) in the library of the Palácio Nacional da Ajuda suggests that he died in Lisbon some years later.

Scolari was among the first north Italian composers to take up the new style of comic opera that emanated from Naples and Rome in the early 1740s and dominated the European stage in the second half of the century. Though overshadowed by Galuppi and others, he appears to have enjoyed considerable success, notably with *La cascina*, written for him by Goldoni, which spread far and wide (in Spain it eventually joined the nascent zarzuela repertory, as *Las queseras*); and since the libretto has very little merit, the credit for the opera's success must be imputed to Scolari, who displayed a gift for ingratiating melody in some of its best numbers.

See also CASCINA, LA.

dg – *dramma giocoso* dm – *dramma per musica*

Il Pandolfo (commedia per musica, 3), Venice, S Samuele, aut. 1745
La fata maravigliosa (dg, 3), Venice, S Cassiano, carn. 1745–6
L'olimpiade (dg, 3, P. Metastasio), Venice, S Moisè, carn. 1746–7
Il vello d'oro (dm, 3, G. Palazzi), Venice, S Cassiano, carn. 1748–9
Alessandro nell'Indie (dm, 3, Metastasio), Vicenza, Piazza, carn. 1749, arias *I-Gl*
Il chimico (dg, A. Palomba), Barcelona, Santa Cruz, 23 Sept 1750
Didone abbandonata (dm, 3, Metastasio), Barcelona, Santa Cruz, 30 May 1752; rev., Ferrara, carn. 1763
Chi tutto abbraccia nulla stringe (dg, 3, B. Vitturi), Venice, S Moisè, aut. 1753, *D-Dlb* according to Eitner; as L'avaro schernito, Lugo, 1754; as L'avaro burlato, Copenhagen, aut. 1762
Adriano in Siria (dm, 3, Metastasio), Venice, S Samuele, carn. 1753–4
Cajo Fabricio (dm, 3, A. Zeno), Rome, Capranica, 2 Jan 1755, *P-La*
La cascina (dm, 3, C. Goldoni), Venice, S Samuele, 26 Dec 1755, *F-Pn*, *I-Fc*, *P-La*; as La Campagna, Bassano, 1763; also as Las queseras
Statira (dm, 3, Goldoni), Venice, S Samuele, Ascension 1756, duet *I-MOe*
L'Andromaca (dm, G. M. Viganò), Lodi, Sociale, 20 Jan 1757
Artaserse (dm, 3, Metastasio), Pavia, Homodei, carn. 1757, aria *Nc*, aria *CMbc*
Rosbale (dg, 3, F. Silvani), Padua, Nuovo, June 1757, *P-La*
La conversazione (dg, 3, Goldoni), Venice, S Samuele, carn. 1758, *A-Wn*, *I-Fc*
Il ciarlatano (dg, 3), Venice, S Moisè, aut. 1759; as Il finto cavaliero, Modena, 1760
La buona figliuola maritata (dg, 3, Goldoni), Murano, 24 April 1762
Il viaggiatore ridicolo (dg, 3, Goldoni), Milan, Ducale, sum. 1762 [with some music from Mazzoni setting of 1757], *F-Pc*
La famiglia in scompiglio (dg, 3), Parma, Ducale, 26 Oct 1762, *D-Dlb* according to Eitner
Il Tamerlano (dm, 3, A. Piovene), Milan, Ducale, 26 Dec 1763, *I-Nc*, *P-La*
Cajo Mario (dm, 3, G. Roccaforte), Milan, Ducale, Jan 1765, *I-Nc*, *P-La*
Il ciarlone (int, Palomba), Rome, Valle, carn. 1765
La schiava riconosciuta (dg, 3, 'Alcindo Isaurense, P.A.'), Bologna, Formagliari, sum. 1765, collab. Piccinni; rev., Venice, 1766, ?entirely by Scolari
La donna stravagante (dg, 3, 'Alcindo Isaurense, P.A.'), Venice, S Samuele, carn. 1765–6, *La*
Antigono (dm, 3, Metastasio), Naples, S Carlo, 30 May 1766, *La*; *S-Skma* according to Eitner
L'Arcifanfano (dg, 2, Goldoni), Lisbon, rua dos Condes, Sept 1768
Il viaggiatore ridicolo (dg, Goldoni), Lisbon, 1770 [? unrelated to 1762 setting]
Il Bejglierbej di Caramania (dg, G. Tonioli), Lisbon, Bairro Alto, sum. 1771
Eponina (dm, 3, G. F. Fattiboni), Cádiz, 20 Jan 1772
Alle dame (burletta), ?Lisbon, 1774, *P-La*
Giulia Mammea, *F-Pn*

Substitute arias in G. M. Rutini's I matrimoni in maschera, as Il tuttore burlato (dg, 3), Rovigo, aut. 1764

*

EitnerQ; *GerberL*
G. Ortolani and others, eds.: *Carlo Goldoni: opere complete* (Venice, 1907–71)
E. Cotarelo y Mori: *Origines y establicimiento de la ópera en España hasta 1800* (Madrid, 1917)
——: *Historia de la zarzuela* (Madrid, 1934)

PIERO WEISS

Scontrino, Antonio (*b* Trapani, Sicily, 17 May 1850; *d* Florence, 7 Jan 1922). Italian double bass player and composer. His father, a carpenter, was an ardent music lover and amateur instrument maker. Antonio joined the family orchestra at the age of seven, playing a cello adapted to serve as a double bass. From 1861 to 1870 he studied at the Palermo Conservatory, where his teachers included Platania. He then toured as a virtuoso on the double bass in southern Italy. He studied German music in Munich (1871) and in 1874 was a member of Mapleson's orchestra in England. He then taught in

Milan and later at Palermo and Florence.

In 1871 he obtained a libretto from Leopoldo Marenco, but the opera, *Matelda*, was not produced until 1879. Four more operas were staged before the end of the century, some in important theatres; but inspired as they were by Italian *melodramma*, they did not persist in the face of the emerging popularity of *verismo*. Scontrino's output also included chamber, orchestral and choral works, songs and incidental music.

Matelda (4, L. Marenco), Milan, Verme, 19 June 1879 (Milan, 1879)
Il progettista (farse, 1, U. Barbieri), Rome, Argentina, 18 Feb 1882 (Milan, 1882)
Il sortilegio (3, G. de Nobili), Turin, Alfieri, 21 June 1882 (Milan, 1882)
Gringoire (1, Cordelia, after T. de Banville), private perf., Milan, 24 or 27 May 1890 (Milan, 1890)
Cortigiana (4, G. F. Cimino), Milan, Verme, 30 Jan or 5 Feb 1896 (Milan, 1896)

Scopabirba, Gasparo. *See* ANELLI, ANGELO.

Scotland. For discussion of opera in Scotland *see* EDINBURGH and GLASGOW.

Scott, Mrs. English mezzo-soprano; *see* YOUNG family, (4).

Scott, Cyril (Meir) (*b* Oxton, Cheshire, 27 Sept 1879; *d* Eastbourne, 31 Dec 1970). English composer. He studied with Humperdinck at the Hoch Conservatory, Frankfurt, and then continued his studies in Liverpool; in 1895 he returned to Frankfurt, where his teacher was Iwan Knorr. He returned to Liverpool to teach in 1898.

A long series of impressionist piano pieces and songs, together with frequent recitals and his own strikingly romantic appearance, established Scott's reputation as a 'modernist' composer. His study of Indian philosophy led to his becoming a Vedantist and finally a follower of the Higher Occultism. Between the wars his music was much performed on the Continent, and a high point in his career came in 1925 when his one-act opera *The Alchemist* (1917), for which he had written his own libretto, was produced at Essen on 28 May with Felix Wolfe conducting. In 1918 he completed a second one-act opera, also to his own libretto, *The Shrine* (originally entitled *The Saint of the Mountain*); it has not been performed. In the 1930s large-scale works by Scott were heard at the Norwich and Leeds festivals, but thereafter his reputation as a composer declined.

By 1944 Scott had decided to abandon composition, but according to his own account, a significant occult sign led him to continue. The fruits of this renewed activity included the three-act opera *Maureen O'Mara* (1946), again to his own libretto and as yet unperformed, an oratorio and a considerable quantity of orchestral and chamber music. None of his more extended works has remained in the repertory. As his only staged opera, and as an expression of his philosophy of the superiority of spiritual over material desires, *The Alchemist* must be regarded as Scott's most important contribution, even though *Maureen O'Mara* is more ambitious in scope. Though sumptuous, his impressionist, bitonal harmonies, largely presented as a stream of parallel chords, create a somewhat enervating effect that is not entirely relieved by exclusively parlando vocal lines. MICHAEL HURD

Scott, Sir **Walter** (*b* Edinburgh, 15 Aug 1771; *d* Abbotsford, 21 Sept 1832). Scottish poet and novelist. The image of Scotland was a major influence on the Romantic movement in Europe. In about 1770 Goethe was swept off his feet by J. G. Herder's translations of *Border Ballads* (from Thomas Percy's *Reliques of Ancient English Poetry*, 1765); at the same time the epics attributed to the Celtic harpist Ossian were being translated into German and other languages, and compared, not to their disadvantage, with the *Odyssey*. Scotland, the source of these strange poems, had the further fascination of being a little-known land on the very edge of Europe, and so the first Scotsman who wrote in attractive detail of his country's customs and history was welcomed with enthusiasm. By the 1820s Scott was being read in translation all over Europe.

Scott was over 40 when he became dispirited with his long narrative poems and turned to novels, and of these the earlier ones about the Lowlands of Scotland are now thought to be the best. *Ivanhoe* was the first that he based on English history, and its success led him to write as many novels set in England as in Scotland. The novels proved to be excellent for stage adaptations. Their characters were heroic yet realistic, and they were set sufficiently far in the past to make operatic treatment acceptable. *Ivanhoe* and *Kenilworth* were especially popular as models for librettos (Beethoven once contemplated an opera on *Kenilworth*). Scott was in Paris in 1826 and saw *Ivanhoé*, a pastiche concocted from Rossini's music without the composer's permission. He wrote: 'It was superbly got up ... but it was an opera, and, of course, the story sadly mangled, and the dialogue, in part, nonsense'. Scott's view was predictable: a libretto can hardly hope to preserve his vivid dialogue at all social levels, the historical detail, the geographical reality, and the narrative flow. If the plot sinks as well, then there can be nothing of the original left. In the *Ivanhoe* opera that Scott saw, Rowena and Richard Coeur de Lion do not appear, and Ivanhoe marries Rebecca. The libretto of Bizet's *La jolie fille de Perth* never mentions the two main events of the story, and makes Scott's level-headed heroine go mad at the end. Much of the powerful plot survives in Donizetti's *Lucia di Lammermoor*, the best of the Scott operas; true, Cammarano's libretto leaves out Scott's most memorable villainess, Lucia's mother, but at the climax the opera fashions the novel's realistically crazy heroine into a powerful, mythic figure by melding her image with that of Ophelia.

The British operas that were staged in London very soon after the publication of the earlier novels did do some justice to the plots, but their spoken dialogue was written in stage fustian; the blank verse dialogue in the first of these operas, Bishop's *The Knight of Snowdoun* (taken from *The Lady of the Lake*), was especially deplorable. Although Scott had no knowledge of music, he enjoyed national songs, especially when he knew something of their historical background, and his novels are full of them. The operas often included some fine old Scots songs, and the eventual popularity of *Auld lang syne* owed much to its being sung in John Davy's *Rob Roy Macgregor*. Scott himself was unexpectedly sympathetic towards these adaptations; he even wrote some new lyrics for the operatic *Guy Mannering*, perhaps in fear of others writing something worse.

LITERARY WORKS ON WHICH OPERAS HAVE BEEN BASED

novels unless otherwise stated

The Eve of St John (lyric, 1800): Mackenzie, 1924
The Lady of the Lake (poem, 1810): Bishop, 1811, as The Knight of

Snowdoun; Rossini, 1819; Vesque von Püttlingen, 1830; pastiche from operas of Rossini, 1846
Rokeby (poem, 1813): Reeve, 1813, as Rokeby Castle; sketch by Glinka, 1824
The Lord of the Isles (poem, 1814): Rodwell, 1834
Waverley (1814): Rodwell, 1824; pastiche from operas of Rossini, 1825; Dulcken, 1865, as MacIvor; Holstein, 1872, as Der Erbe von Morley
Guy Mannering (1815): Bishop, 1816; Bertin, 1825; Boieldieu, 1825, as La dame blanche [title role from *The Monastery*]
The Antiquary (1816): Bishop, 1820
Old Mortality (1816): Bishop, 1820, as The Battle of Bothwell Brigg; Peellaert, 1827, as L'exilé
The Black Dwarf (1817): Horn, 1817, as The Wizard
Rob Roy (1818): Davy, 1818; A. Curmi, 1832; Flotow, 1836; De Koven, 1894
The Heart of Midlothian (1818): Bishop, 1819; Carafa, 1833, as La prison d'Edimbourg; F. Ricci, 1838, as La prigione di Edimburgo; MacCunn, 1894, as Jeanie Deans
The Bride of Lammermoor (1819): Carafa, 1829; L. Rieschi, 1831; Damse, 1832; I. Bredal, 1832; Mazzucato, 1834; Donizetti, 1835, as Lucia di Lammermoor
The Legend of Montrose (1820): Bishop, 1822, as Montrose, or The Children of the Mist
Ivanhoe (1820): J. Parry, 1820; pastiche from operas of Rossini, 1826; Marschner, 1829, as Der Templer und die Jüdin; G. Pacini, 1832; O. Nicolai, 1840, as Il templario; Sullivan, 1891
Kenilworth (1821): Auber, 1823, as Leicester; Donizetti, 1829, as Elisabetta al castello di Kenilworth; Damse, 1832; Weyse, 1832, as Festen paa Kenilworth; Loewe, comp. 1842, as Emmy; Schira, comp. 1848; Macfarren, 1880; De Lara, 1893, as Amy Robsart; B. O. Klein, 1895
The Fortunes of Nigel (1822): Bishop, 1823, as Nigel
Peveril of the Peak (1822): Horn, 1826
Quentin Durward (1823): H. Laurent, 1848; Gevaert, 1858; Maclean, 1920
Redgauntlet (1824): Gomis y Colomer, 1833
The Talisman (1825): Bishop, 1826, as The Knights of the Cross; Riotte, 1827, as König Richard in Palästina; Loewe, comp. 1832, as Malek-Adhel; Balfe, inc., as The Knight of the Leopard, arr. M. Costa, 1874, as Il talismano
The Fair Maid of Perth (1828): Bizet, 1867

*

E. Forbes: 'Sir Walter Scott and Opera', *Opera*, xix (1968), 872–8
A. Benedetti: *Le traduzioni italiane da Walter Scott e i loro anglicismi* (Florence, 1974)
J. Mitchell: *The Walter Scott Operas: an Analysis of Operas Based on the Works of Walter Scott* (Birmingham, AL, 1977)

ROGER FISKE

Scotti, Antonio (*b* Naples, 25 Jan 1866; *d* Naples, 26 Feb 1936). Italian baritone. He made his début at the Circolo Filarmonico, Naples, in March 1889 as Cinna in *La vestale*, then sang in Malta, Madrid, Buenos Aires, Moscow and the principal Italian cities before making his La Scala début (1898–9). He was noted for smooth delivery, variety of colour, a fine legato, facility in the upper register and elegance in his acting, his repertory including the typically 'noble' baritone roles in *Don Giovanni*, *Les Huguenots*, *I puritani*, *La favorite*, *Ernani* and *Don Carlos*, as well as Falstaff and Tonio. After his début as Don Giovanni both at Covent Garden (8 June 1899) and the Metropolitan (23 November 1899), his appearances were confined mainly to England and the USA (in London until 1910, and in 1913–14; in New York until 1933) and coincided with the ascent of the actor over the singer and of 'character' over 'noble' baritone roles – Iago, Marcel, Scarpia, Sharpless; his voice soon lost its beauty, becoming thick and inflexible, but his already remarkable abilities as singer and actor were further refined. In 1919 he formed the Scotti Grand Opera Company, which for four seasons brought Italian opera and Italian singers – many of them from the Metropolitan company – on tour to cities throughout North America.

Antonio Scotti as Scarpia in Puccini's 'Tosca'

GV (R. Celletti; J. P. Kenyon)
G. Gatti-Casazza: *Memories of Opera* (New York, 1941)
G. Lauri-Volpi: *Voci parallele* (Milan, 1955), 166f
G. Davidson: *Opera Biographies* (London, 1955), 274ff
P. G. Hurst: *The Golden Age Recorded* (Lingfield, 1963), 129ff
W. Ashbrook: *The Operas of Puccini* (New York, 1968)
D. Reutlinger: 'Antonio Scotti', *The Maestro*, i (1969), nos.1–2, pp.35–8; nos.3–4, p.31 [with discography]
M. F. Bott: 'On Tour with Scotti – 1921', *Opera*, xxvii (1976), 1101–7

RODOLFO CELLETTI

Scottish Opera. Opera company founded in GLASGOW in 1962.

Scotto, Renata (*b* Savona, 24 Feb 1934). Italian soprano. After studying in Milan, she made her début in 1952 at Savona as Violetta, repeating the role at Milan (Teatro Nuovo) in 1953. She first sang at La Scala in 1954 as Walter (*La Wally*), then appeared in Rome and Venice. In 1957 she made her London début (Stoll Theatre) as Mimì, then sang Adina, Violetta and Donna Elvira. She replaced Callas as Amina in one performance of *La sonnambula* at Edinburgh for La Scala, with whom she later sang Elvira (*I puritani*), Antonida (*A Life for the Tsar*), Marguerite, Nannetta and Bellini's Giulietta. She made her American début (1960) in Chicago as Mimì and her Covent Garden début (1962) as Butterfly; later roles included Gilda, Manon, Amina and Lady Macbeth. At the Metropolitan (1965–87) she took on heavier roles from 1974, singing Leonora (*Il trovatore*), Luisa Miller, Amelia (*Ballo*), Hélène (*Les vêpres siciliennes*), Desdemona, Elisabeth de Valois, Manon Lescaut, Musetta, Giorgetta, Angelica, Lauretta, Berthe (*Le prophète*), Adriana Lecouvreur, La Gioconda, Francesca da Rimini and Norma. Her repertory included *Lucia di Lammermoor*, *Maria di*

Rohan, *Anna Bolena* and *La straniera*. Her singing offered a rare combination of vocal agility, pathos and dramatic power.

*

E. Gara: 'Renata Scotto', *Opera*, xxii (1971), 199–206
R. Scotto and O. Roca: *Scotto: More than a Diva* (New York, 1984)

ALAN BLYTH

Scovelli, Gaetano (*fl* 1767–92). Italian tenor. He sang in *opera seria* at Modena in Carnival 1767 but did not begin a sustained career until 1771. In 1771–3 he was at Cádiz, resuming Italian engagements in 1777 at leading theatres, with later absences in 1782–4 (London) and 1788–90 (Spain). He retired from the stage in 1792. Unattractive physically, he was noted for his bravura singing. DENNIS LIBBY

Scovotti, Jeanette (*b* New York, 5 Dec 1936). American soprano. In 1960 she sang Despina (*Così fan tutte*) with the New England Opera Theater in Boston, then appeared at Santa Fe, as Gianetta (*The Gondoliers*), Clorinda (*La Cenerentola*) and Lauretta (*Gianni Schicchi*). She made her San Francisco début in 1962 as Blonde, returning in 1967 for the Queen of Night and Miss Hampton in Schuller's *The Visitation*. In 1966 she began a longstanding association with the Hamburg Staatsoper, where her roles included Rosina, Zerlina, Despina, Donizetti's Norina and Lucia, Gilda, Glinka's Lyudmila, Carolina (*Il matrimonio segreto*), Aminta (*Die schweigsame Frau*) and the Italian Singer (*Capriccio*); she also sang the title role in the first performance of Krenek's *Sardakai* (1970). Scovotti appeared with the Bavarian Staatsoper at Covent Garden as Zerbinetta (1972) and sang the Queen of Shemakha (*The Golden Cockerel*) at Dallas (1973) and Offenbach's Olympia at Turin (1974); she has also sung in Buenos Aires, Vienna and Bonn. Her limpid tone and the extreme flexibility of her voice were well displayed as Costanza in a concert performance of Vivaldi's *Griselda* in London (1978). ELIZABETH FORBES

Scribe, (Augustin) Eugène (*b* Paris, 24 Dec 1791; *d* Paris, 20 Feb 1861). French dramatist and librettist. After the early death of his father, a Parisian shopkeeper, he was brought up in straitened circumstances by his mother, but a scholarship enabled him to attend the Collège Sainte-Barbe. His mother sent him to study for the legal profession with Louis-Ferdinand Bonnet (1760–1839), one of the greatest advocates of his day. Scribe was, however, irresistibly attracted to the theatre which, profiting from newly won freedoms from strict regulation, was then astonishingly lively and varied in Paris, even if there was little new drama of genuinely high quality. His own first efforts achieved scant success with audiences that were tempestuous at the best of times and noisily scathing when displeased. He persisted, however, learning his trade with dogged thoroughness, and even in a period when there was an insatiable appetite for new plays, whose runs were often very short, he was astonishingly prolific. Though academic critics rarely approved wholeheartedly of his work, Scribe was elected to the Académie Française in 1836. The distinction made no difference to his attitude to his vocation; he simply went on writing theatrical works of various sorts, happily collaborating with other authors all his life and, despite the occasional protest, providing opera composers with just the sort of librettos they needed. Scribe did not, it seems, see drama as a medium of self-expression; instead, he found satisfaction in the craft of writing and in varying his style in accordance with changing tastes.

Scribe first made his mark with *comédies-vaudevilles* – conventional and ephemeral little plays, often spiced with topicality, if not satire, and interspersed with songs, some of which would be sung to the popular tunes of the day. A frequent collaborator at the time was Delavigne, with whom he had become friendly at the Collège Sainte-Barbe. Nowadays Scribe is remembered more for his 'well-made' plays, such as *Le verre d'eau* of 1840. With no great interest, apparently, in contemporary social or political issues, Scribe concentrated above all in his dramas on the deft management of the plot. The characters' fortunes are reversed again and again in a series of contrasting scenes as the action moves inexorably and with increasing rapidity towards a final confrontation – the *scène à faire* ('obligatory scene') often referred to by 19th-century theatre critics. Though the characters themselves are only dimly aware of the forces that bring the action to this culmination, which is artfully delayed until the latest possible moment, the audience is allowed a comfortable sense of superior knowledge and can foresee the outcome, observe the characters with detachment and appreciate the dextrous manipulation of the dramatic action. Whether in contemporary settings or the historical situations that were in fashion, Scribe used language which, though plain and rather colourless, has the great virtues of clarity and simplicity, which makes the frequent 19th-century criticisms of its lack of literary grace appear pedantic and mistaken. These plays, even if no longer performed, may still be seen as an influence in realistic theatre and its various descendants.

Turning from the *comédies-vaudevilles* of his youth towards the 'well-made' plays did not in any way reduce Scribe's involvement in drama with music. As well as preparing ballet scenarios, including such important early Romantic works for the choreographer Jean Aumer as *La somnambule* (1827, music by Hérold), *La belle au bois dormant* (1829, Hérold) and *Manon Lescaut* (1830, Halévy), Scribe became one of the most significant and influential librettists of the 19th century, making a particular contribution to the development of French grand opera. To his librettos Scribe brought the same indefatigable industry that distinguished him as a dramatist, the same readiness (perhaps forced on him by the necessity of producing texts quickly) to work with collaborators, both literary and musical, and the same devotion to craftsmanship. His contemporaries admired him, and many composers sought to recruit his skills. Yet, though the list of his librettos is long and contains a number of works that will always figure in the history of opera, his contribution was not really original; he was content to follow fashion, even exaggerating it to some degree, in order to satisfy the public of the day. Even towards the end of his career, when he might well have been able to pick and choose, he was not very particular. His concern was, it seems, more for the moment than for posterity.

Scribe's first librettos were unremarkable, and even as late as 1828 he was content with conventional hackwork, collaborating with Delestre-Poirson on the amalgamation of two one-act playlets to provide Rossini with *Le comte Ory*. By then, however, he had already given Boieldieu the libretto of *La dame blanche*, and what was to prove a long association with Auber resulted in *La muette de Portici*. After that Scribe

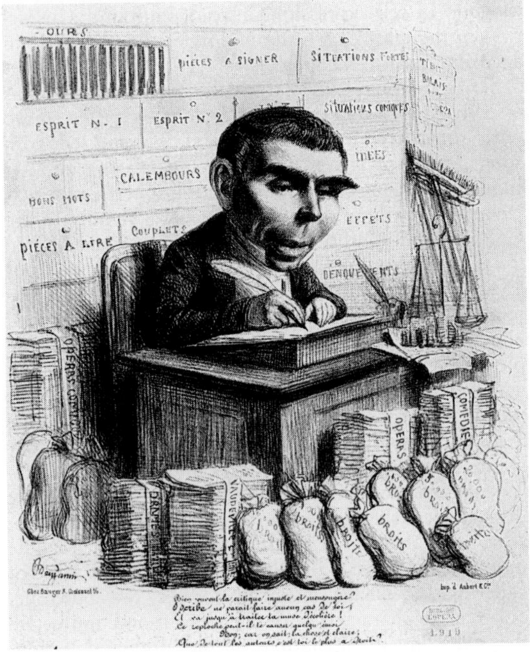

Eugène Scribe: caricature by Benjamin from the series 'Panthéon charivarique' from the journal 'Le Charivari' (1841)

worked with most of the leading composers of the age, including Bellini, Donizetti, Gounod, Halévy, Verdi and, most notably and characteristically, Meyerbeer.

Part of Scribe's success as a librettist comes from his application of the principles of construction used in his plays. The changing fortunes of his characters allow for effectively contrasted musical treatment, while confrontations naturally provide excellent opportunities for ensembles. Although he could make do in other circumstances with simple staging, for opera Scribe did not hesitate to indulge the taste for grandiose spectacle that swept Paris in the age of Ciceri. He took up the effects that Hugo and Dumas *père* had borrowed from the melodramas of the Boulevard and from the Gothic novel: emotion runs riot, love is always passionate and usually tragic, and stirring conflicts take place between races, religions and classes in period settings, often the Middle Ages or the Renaissance. There is abundant scope for spectacle, including ballet, even if for the most part the local and historical colour is superficial. Crowd scenes create enthralling situations for chorus participation, and the personal drama is often played out against a background of popular revolt or of public rejoicing at some festivity. Above all, Scribe's sequences of striking scenes leading inevitably towards confrontation were a natural preparation for grand finales at the ends of acts and, of course, of the opera itself.

Scribe's grand opera librettos do not make impressive or even very pleasant reading; in general the language is hackneyed, pedestrian and full of theatrical clichés. Time and again moments of towering emotion seem to be brought down to a level that is either prosaic or, worse still, reminiscent of the facile style of Offenbachian *opéra bouffe*. Such criticisms, however, miss their mark. In French grand opera there is little need for subtle distinctions in verbal expression, for the concern is not with psychological nuance so much as with broad theatrical emotions within situations that allow of their fullest expression in music and spectacle. Local and historical colour is not supplied to a large extent by the librettist's choice of vocabulary, but more by the settings, which were often imaginatively lit, and by the costumes. Where language, whether for the principals or the chorus, does matter is in exposition and at the climaxes. If the key words are to be heard as the singers rise above the orchestra, clarity is needed – not great poetic eloquence or unusual formulations – and here, as in all Scribe's work for the theatre, his professional readiness to bow to the practical demands of the stage paid dividends.

Edition: *E. Scribe: Oeuvres complètes* (Paris, 1874–85)

La chambre à coucher (oc), Guénée, 1813
La perruque et la rédingote (oc), R. Kreutzer and Kreubé, 1815
La comtesse de Troun (oc), Guénée, 1816
L'ours et le pacha (folie-vaudeville, with J. X. B. Saintine, 1820), Audran, 1862 (Bazin, 1870)
La meunière (oc, with Mélesville [A.-H.-J. Duveyrier]), García, 1821
Michel et Christine (comédie-vaudeville, with H. Dupin), Aimon, 1821
Le paradis de Mahomet (oc, with Mélesville), Kreutzer and Kreubé, 1822
Le petite lampe merveilleuse (opéra-féerique, with Mélesville), L. A. Piccinni, 1822
Leicester (oc, with Mélesville), Auber, 1823
Le valet de chambre (oc, with Mélesville), Carafa, 1823
La neige (oc, with Delavigne), Auber, 1823
Les trois genres (prol d'ouverture), Auber and Boieldieu, 1824
Concert à la cour (oc, with Mélesville), Auber, 1824
Léocadie (opéra, with Mélesville), Auber, 1824
Robin des Bois (opéra-fantastique, with Castil-Blaze), music arr. from Weber's Der Freischütz, 1824
Le maçon (oc, with Delavigne), Auber, 1825 (Eng., Rodwell, 1828)
La dame blanche (oc), Boieldieu, 1825 (Eng., T. S. Cooke, 1826)
La vieille (oc, with Delavigne), Fétis, 1826
Le timide (oc, with Saintine), Auber, 1826
Fiorella (oc), Auber, 1826
Le loup-garou (oc, with E. Mazères), Bertin, 1827
La lettre posthume (oc, with Mélesville), Kreubé, 1827
La somnambule (ballet-pantomime, with Aumer) [after La somnambule, vaudeville, 1816], Hérold, 1827 (It., Bellini, 1831)
Le mal du pays (with Mélesville), Adam, 1827
La muette de Portici (with Delavigne), Auber, 1828 (Eng., T. S. Cooke, 1829, as Masaniello)
Yelva (vaudeville, with Devilleneuve and Desvergers, 1828), Eng., Bishop, 1829, as The Orphan of Russia
Le comte Ory (with Delestre-Poirson) [after Le comte Ory, vaudeville, 1816], Rossini, 1828
La fiancée (oc), Auber, 1829
La belle au bois dormant (ballet-pantomime, with Aumer), Hérold, 1829
Le deux nuits (oc, with Bouilly), Boieldieu, 1829
Alcibiade, Hanssens, 1829
Fra Diavolo (oc), Auber, 1830
L'amazone (with Mélesville, Delestre-Poirson and L. J. A. de Beauplan, 1830)
Manon Lescaut (ballet-pantomime, with Aumer), Halévy, 1830 (Auber, 1856)
Le dieu et la bayadère (opéra-ballet), Auber, 1830
L'enlèvement (oc, with Saint-Victor), P.-J.-G. Zimmermann, 1830
Le philtre, Auber, 1831 (It., Donizetti, 1832, as L'elisir d'amore; Eng., Macfarren, 1863, as Jessy Lea)
L'orgie (ballet-pantomime, with Coralli), Carafa, 1831
La marquise de Brinvilliers (drame-lyrique, with Castil-Blaze), Auber, Batton, Berton, Blangini, Boieldieu, Carafa, Cherubini, Hérold and Paer, 1831
Robert le diable (with Delavigne), Meyerbeer, 1831 (Kastner, 1845, as Les nonnes de Robert-le-diable, unperf.)
Le serment (with Mazères), Auber, 1832
La médecine sans médecin (oc, with Bayard), Hérold, 1832
Gustave III (opéra-historique), Auber, 1833 (It., Verdi, 1859, as Un ballo in maschera)
La prison d'Edimbourg (oc, with de Planard), Carafa, 1833
Ali-Baba (opéra, with Mélesville), Cherubini, 1833
Lestocq (oc), Auber, 1834
Le fils du prince (oc), de Feltre, 1834

Le chalet (oc, with Mélesville), Adam, 1834 (It., Donizetti, 1836, as Betly; Moniuszko, 1852, as Betly)
La Juive, Halévy, 1835
Le cheval de bronze (opéra-féerique), Auber, 1835
Le portefaix (oc), Gomis y Colomer, 1835
Actéon (oc), Auber, 1836
Les Huguenots (with E. Deschamps), Meyerbeer, 1836
Les chaperons blancs (oc), Auber, 1836
Le mauvais oeil (oc, with Lemoine), L. Puget, 1836
L'ambassadrice (oc, with J.-H. Vernoy de Saint-Georges), Auber, 1836
Le remplaçant (oc, with Bayard), Batton, 1837
Le domino noir (oc), Auber, 1837 (It., L. Rossi, 1849)
Le fidèle berger (oc, with Saint-Georges), Adam, 1838
Guido e Ginevra, Halévy, 1838
La volière (ballet-pantomime, with T. Elssler), C. Gide, 1838
Marguerite (oc, with de Planard), L. Boieldieu, 1838
La figurante (oc, with Dupin), Clapisson, 1838
L'Africaine, 1838, Meyerbeer, 1865
Régine (oc), Adam, 1839
Le lac des fées (opéra, with Mélesville), Auber, 1839
Les treize (oc, with P. Duport), Halévy, 1839
Polichinelle (oc, with Duveyrier), Montfort, 1839
La tarentule (ballet-pantomime, with Coralli), Gide, 1839
Le shérif (oc), Halévy, 1839
La reine d'un jour (oc, with Saint-Georges), Adam, 1839
La xacarilla, Marliani, 1839
Le duc d'Albe (with Duveyrier) [after *Les vêpres siciliennes*, parodie-vaudeville, 1819], Donizetti, 1839 (inc.) (It., rev. Scribe and Duveyrier, for Verdi, 1855, as Les vêpres siciliennes)
Le drapier, Halévy, 1840
Les martyrs (after P. Corneille: *Polyeucte*), Donizetti, 1840
Zanetta (oc, with Saint-Georges), Auber, 1840
L'opéra à la cour (oc, with Saint-Georges), arr. Grisar and L. Boieldieu, 1840
Le guitarrero (oc), Halévy, 1841
Les diamants de la couronne (oc, with Saint-Georges), Auber, 1841
Carmagnola, Thomas, 1841
Le main de fer (oc, with de Leuven), Adam, 1841
Le diable à l'école (oc), Boulanger, 1842 (Swed., Söderman, 1856, as Hin Ondes första lärospån)
Le duc d'Olonne (oc, with Saintine), Auber, 1842
Le code noir (oc), Clapisson, 1842
Le kiosque (oc, with Duport), J. F. Mazas, 1842
Le part du diable (oc), Auber, 1843
Le puits d'amour (oc, with de Leuven), Balfe, 1843
Lambert Simnel (oc, with Mélesville), Monpou, completed by Adam, 1843
Dom Sébastien, roi de Portugal (after P. H. Foucher), Donizetti, 1843
Cagliostro (oc, with Saint-Georges), Adam, 1844
Oreste et Pylade (oc, with Dupin), A. Thys, 1844
La sirène (oc), Auber, 1844
La barcarolle (oc), Auber, 1845
Le ménétrier (oc), Labarre, 1845
La charbonnière (oc, with Mélesville), A. Montfort, 1845
Ne touchez pas à la reine! (oc, with Vaëz), D. F. X. Boisselot, 1847
Le sultan Saladin (oc, with Dupin), L. Bordèse, 1847
Une femme qui se jette par la fenêtre (vaudeville, with Lemoine, 1847), Cz., Kovařovic, 1886, as Cesta oknem (It., Zandonai, 1919, as La via della finestra)
Haydée (oc), Auber, 1847
La nuit de Noël (oc), Reber, 1848
Jeanne la folle, Clapisson, 1848
Adrienne Lecouvreur (drame, with Legouvé, 1849), It., Cilea, 1902 (Setaccioli, inc., 1904–7)
Le prophète, Meyerbeer, 1849
La fée aux roses (opéra-féerique, with Saint-Georges), Halévy, 1849
La statue équestre (oc), Clapisson, 1850
La tempestà (trans. Giannone, after W. Shakespeare), It., Halévy, 1850
Giralda (oc), Adam, 1850
La chanteuse voilée (oc, with de Leuven), Massé, 1850
L'enfant prodigue, Auber, 1850 (It., Ponchielli, 1880)
La dame de pique (oc), Halévy, 1850
Zerline, Auber, 1851
Florinda (trans. Giannone), It., Thalberg, 1851
Mosquita la sorcière (oc, with Vaëz), Boisselot, 1851
Le juif errant (with Saint-Georges), Halévy, 1852
Le vieux château (oc), Van der Doës, 1852
Les mystères d'Udolphe (oc, with Delavigne), Clapisson, 1852
Marco Spada (oc, with J. Mazelier), Auber, 1852
La lettre au bon Dieu (oc, with C. de Courcy), Duprez, 1853
Le nabab (oc, with Saint-Georges), Halévy, 1853
L'étoile du nord (oc), Meyerbeer, 1854
La fiancée du diable (oc, with H. Romand), Massé, 1854
La nonne sanglante (with Delavigne), Gounod, 1854
Jenny Bell (oc), Auber, 1855
Jacqueline (oc, with Battu), Comte d'Osmond and J. Costé, 1855
Les vêpres siciliennes, 1855: see *Le duc d'Albe*, 1839
La chatte métamorphosée en femme (oc, with Mélesville) [after folie-vaudeville, 1827], Offenbach, 1858
Broskovano (oc, with Boisseaux), L. Deffès, 1858
Les trois Nicolas (oc, with B. de Lopez and G. de Lurien), Clapisson, 1858
Les petits violons du roi (oc, with H. Boisseaux), Deffès, 1859
Yvonne (drame-lyrique, after d'Herbanges), Limnander de Niewehove [A. M. Guillain], 1859
Le nouveau Pourceaugnac (oc, with Delestre-Poirson) [after folie-vaudeville, 1817], A. J. L. Hignard, 1860
Barkouf (oc, with Boisseaux), Offenbach, 1860
La circassienne (oc), Auber, 1861
Madame Grégoire (oc, with Boisseaux), Clapisson, 1861
La beauté du diable (oc, with de Najac), G. E. A. Alary, 1861
La fiancée du roi de Garbe (oc, with Saint-Georges), Auber, 1864

Addns to: *La favorite* (Royer and Vaëz), Donizetti, 1840

*

N. C. Arvin: *Eugène Scribe* (New York, 1924)
A. L. Crosten: *French Grand Opera* (New York, 1948)
A. Scherle: 'Eugène Scribe und die Oper des 19. Jahrhunderts', *Maske und Kothurne*, iii (1957), 141–58
P. Smith: *The Tenth Muse* (New York, 1970)
K. Pendle: 'Eugène Scribe and French Opera of the 19th Century', *MQ*, lvii (1971), 535–61
——: *Eugène Scribe and French Opera of the 19th Century* (Ann Arbor, 1979)
A. Gerhard: *Der Verstädterung der Oper* (Stuttgart, 1992)

CHRISTOPHER SMITH

Sculthorpe, Peter (Joshua) (*b* Launceston, Tasmania, 29 April 1929). Australian composer. He studied music at the University of Melbourne and at Wadham College, Oxford. While in the USA, 1966–7, he was composer-in-residence at Yale University, and he was visiting professor at the University of Sussex, 1972–3. In 1974 he was awarded a three-year Fellowship by the Australia Council, which allowed him to take leave from the University of Sydney music department (where he was appointed reader in 1968) and compose full-time.

Aware of the handicap distance imposed on Australian composers competing for attention with European and American composers, the young Sculthorpe rejected serialism and atonality; he believed that they stemmed from the European psyche, formed in a particular physical and historical context which was not valid for a people who had a different historical perception of its origins. He sought personal modes of expression outside the accepted norms, finding models in Copland, whose individualism and non-European perception of the USA he admired, and in Bloch, whose aural vistas of a Jewish wilderness of the soul heightened his own consciousness of the vast Australian deserts and of national aspirations, at a time when Australian identity was under close examination. Sculthorpe's early nationalism, however, bears little resemblance to what is usually conveyed by that term. Like most of his generation he was aware of the dangers inherent in the new freedom from European ties. He was also conscious of the symbolism of the Australian landscape and the problems arising from cohabitation with the indigenous peoples. Attracted to quick, ritualistic, non-melodic and non-harmonic textures and slow, harmonically static melodies, he rejected musical development as a

European trait. This has led him to rely 'on repetitive variational patterns and taut miniature forms' (Hannan 1982) and to explore the music of Australia's neighbours in the region – in particular Bali and Japan – in pursuit of the Australian context.

Sculthorpe did not come to opera until 1972. His previous stage work, a five-part ballet in his *Sun Music* series, had great success, but neither that nor his early incidental music for the theatre prepared him for a commission for the first full-length Australian opera to be performed by Australian Opera in the new Sydney Opera House, and he was overconscious of the responsibility. The merits of *Rites of Passage*, first performed on 27 September 1974, have been hotly debated. The deliberately monotonous vocal lines coupled with evocative and emotional instrumental writing, allied to the composer's own near-plotless libretto, which uses symbolic language, proved confusing. Sculthorpe responded by rewriting the work for the concert hall, in keeping with the mood of the time: because of the expense involved in operatic staging and consequent difficulty in achieving staged performances, Australian composers tended to favour works of music theatre, which could be performed in the concert hall with minimal action. So far only the chorales of this version of the work have been performed, at Sydney Opera House on 6 May 1989.

Sculthorpe's next opera, *Quiros*, was written for television in 1982 and was broadcast on 1 July of that year by ABC; it remains television-bound, since it would need extensive rewriting before it could be staged. The libretto, by Brian Bell, concerns the fruitless search of a 17th-century Portuguese sea-captain for the promised land, Terra Australis, which is paralleled by a philosophical voyage into the mind. The music is, in a broad sense, tonal, with much use of leitmotifs and semi-spoken material. An easily accessible, lyrical work, *Quiros* includes elements of folksong and liturgical chant within a tightly controlled framework.

See also RITES OF PASSAGE.

*

E. Wood: *Australian Opera, 1842–1970* (diss., U. of Adelaide, 1979), i, 195–7

M. Hannan: 'Peter Sculthorpe', *Australian Composition in the Twentieth Century*, ed. F. Callaway and D. Tunley (Melbourne, 1978), 136–45

——: *Peter Sculthorpe: his Music and Ideas 1929–1979* (Brisbane, 1982)

Peter Sculthorpe, Australian Composers Series, v (Sydney, 1988)

THÉRÈSE RADIC

Scuola de' gelosi, La ('The School of Jealousy'). *Dramma giocoso* in two acts by ANTONIO SALIERI to a libretto by CATERINO MAZZOLÀ; Venice, Teatro S Moisè, 27 December 1778.

Typical of the late 18th-century *opera buffa* in the spirit of Goldoni, *La scuola de' gelosi* presents characters from three distinct social classes. The nobility are represented by Count Bandiera (tenor) and his Countess (soprano), the bourgeoisie by the grain-dealer Blasio (bass) and his wife Ernestina (soprano), and the working class by Blasio's servant Lumaca (bass), who loves the chambermaid Carlotta (soprano). The link between the classes and the chief instigator of the plot is the Lieutenant (tenor), cousin of Blasio and friend of the Count. The Count finds Ernestina attractive. His attempts to seduce her inflame the jealousy of both the Countess and Blasio, who is so angry he locks up his wife. The Lieutenant advises Blasio and the Countess to make their spouses jealous. (The Lieutenant, the teacher of the 'school', has an analogous role to that of Don Alfonso in *Così fan tutte, ossia La scuola degli amanti.*) Following the Lieutenant's advice, Blasio leaves a woman's portrait for Ernestina to find; the Lieutenant writes the Countess a love letter for the Count to discover. The tricks work; the jealousy that is aroused restores the equilibrium, and the opera ends happily.

This was one of Salieri's most successful comic operas, and one of the few that became popular in Italy as well as Germany. During the 1780s it was performed in no fewer than ten Italian cities, and its fame spread to Eszterháza, Vienna, Dresden, Brunswick, London, Warsaw and St Petersburg. In 1783 it was chosen to inaugurate Joseph II's new comic opera troupe in Vienna, where Francesco Benucci, who later created the roles of Figaro and Guglielmo, sang Blasio and Nancy Storace, the original Susanna, sang the Countess. Audiences throughout Europe seem to have agreed with the *Morning Post and Daily Advertiser*, which announced when *La scuola de' gelosi* was performed in London in 1786: 'The whole together is a masterly composition, and does great honour to Salieri, whose reputation as a composer must rise infinitely in the musical world, from this very pleasing specimen of his abilities'. JOHN A. RICE

Scutta, Andreas (*b* Vienna, 1806; *d* Prague, 24 Feb 1863). Austrian composer, actor and singer. The experience of taking part in a performance of Rossini's *Mosè in Egitto* (given as *Moses*) at the Theater an der Wien determined him to take up music as a career. He studied singing at Count Palffy's conservatory, and in 1824 went to Graz (and later to Linz and Zagreb) to gain experience. Illness cost him his fine and expressive singing voice in 1829 and he began to take comic parts in plays. After two years in the provinces he was engaged at the Theater in der Leopoldstadt following a successful guest appearance in 1831, soon making a name for himself not only as a skilful comic actor but also as the composer of music for a series of farces and parodies. After some years of successful appearances as a guest in various theatres he went to Prague in 1852 and performed in the German theatre there for ten years.

Among Scutta's 30 scores, written mainly for the Theater in der Leopoldstadt but including also some for the Theater an der Wien and Theater in der Josefstadt, the following were the most successful: *Der Zauberdrache*, *Robert der Wau Wau*(a parody of Meyerbeer's *Robert le diable*), *Der errungene Preis*, *Der Wasserfall im Feenhain* and *Eisenbahnheiraten* (with nearly 60 performances, his most often-heard score).

all first performed in Vienna

WJ – *Theater in der Josefstadt*
WL – *Theater in der Leopoldstadt*
WW – *Theater an der Wien*

Der Zauberdrache (pantomime, 2, J. Fenzl), WL, 16 Nov 1831, incl. music by other composers

Amintha und Odiosa, oder Der Kampf der Zwietracht mit der Liebe (Feenmärchen mit Gesang, 2, J. Schickh), WL, 2 June 1832

Die elegante Bräumeisterin (Posse, 2, Schickh, after J. F. Kringsteiner), WL, 28 July 1832

Der Zauberkranz, oder Die Zeit bringt Rosen (romantisch-komisches Märchen, 2, J. E. Gulden), WL, 29 Nov 1832

Robert der Wau Wau (Parodie, 2, Schickh), WL, 18 July 1833

Er verdirbt Alles, oder Lauter Malheur (Posse, 2, F. Tomaselli), WL, 11 Jan 1834

48 Stunden in Ichsl [Baden], oder Die Schicksale der Familie Schwalbenschweif (Posse, 3, F. X. Told), WL, 18 March 1834

Das Turnier zu Kronstein, oder Die drei Wahrzeichen (Spektakel-Lustspiel, 5, F. von Holbein), WL, 7 June 1834
Adelaïde oder Zehn Jahre aus dem Leben einer Sängerin (Gemälde neuerer Zeit, 4, Schickh), WL, 4 Sept 1834
Das Zauber-Ridikül, oder Liebe stärker als Zaubermacht (Parodie, 2, Schickh), WL, 27 Nov 1834
Der errungene Preis, oder Pierrot als Wasserträger (komische Pantomime, 2, Fenzl), WL, 20 May 1835
Der Wasserfall im Feenhain, oder Der unsichtbare Freier (Zauberposse, 2, D. F. Reiberstorffer), WL, 12 Sept 1835
Die Quellennymphe, oder Ehestandsleiden (Posse, 2, W. Brabbée), WL, 7 Nov 1835
Der goldgelockte Maxl, oder Hochmut kommt vor den Fall (Posse, 3, ? A. Platzer), WJ, 30 Jan 1836
Amanda, oder Liebe ohne Geld und Geld ohne Liebe (lokales Märchen, 2, E. Weil), WL, 9 April 1836
Der elegante Hafnermeister (Posse, 2, Schickh), WL, 21 Jan 1837
Kleon, oder Die Grotte der Wahrheit (Zauberspiel, 3, Schickh), WL, 4 Jan 1838
Der Phantast, oder Lustig ohne Geld und traurig ohne Grund (Zauberspiel, 2, Gulden), WL, 10 Feb 1838
Stanzerl und Siegwart, oder Jetzt und Rococo (Posse, 3, Gulden), WL, 17 Nov 1838
Die Lokalsängerin und ihr Vater, oder Das Theater im Theater (Fresco-Gemälde, 2, Schickh), WJ, 19 Oct 1839
Der Hut als Heiratsstifter, oder Die Komödie beim Harfenisten (Posse, 2, J. B. Hilar), WL, 17 March 1840
Der Ehefeind (Posse, 3, Brabbée), WL, 23 Oct 1840
Philadelphia, oder Der unterbrochene Darstellung aus dem Gebiete der scheinbaren Zauberei (Posse, 2, Schickh), WJ, 12 Dec 1840
Die Braut des Waldes, oder Die Lebenszweige (Schwank, 2, E. L. Hofzinser), WL, 23 Oct 1841
Das Glück verlässt die Seinen nicht (komische Skizze, 3, ?C. Juin), WL, 18 Jan 1842
Das Haus der Tratschereien, oder Die zwei Putzgreteln (Familiengemälde, 2, Schickh), WW, 24 Sept 1842
Der Fiaker (Posse, 2, Juin), WL, 23 Nov 1842
Eisenbahnheiraten, oder Wien, Neustadt und Brünn (Posse, 3, J. N. Nestroy), WW, 3 Jan 1844
D. B. W. G., oder Die Jägermädchen (Posse, 2, F. Hopp), WL, 11 Jan 1845
Rebus an allen Ecken (Posse, 2, Lödl), WL, 14 March 1845

*

StiegerO
L. Eisenberg: *Grosses biographisches Lexikon der deutschen Bühne im XIX. Jahrhundert* (Leipzig, 1902), 950
F. Hadamowsky: *Das Theater in der Wiener Leopoldstadt 1781–1860* (Vienna, 1934)
A. Bauer: *150 Jahre Theater an der Wien* (Zürich, 1952)
——: *Das Theater in der Josefstadt zu Wien* (Vienna, 1957)

PETER BRANSCOMBE

Scylla. *Tragédie en musique* in a prologue and five acts by THEOBALDO DI GATTI to a libretto by JOSEPH-FRANÇOIS DUCHÉ DE VANCY after OVID; Paris, Opéra, 16 September 1701.

The plot is particularly gory. It concerns the obstacles to the love between Scylla (soprano), daughter of the King of Megara, and Minos (bass), King of Crete: Scylla is promised to Dardanus (*haute-contre*), Crete and Megara are at war, and the jealous Capis (soprano) has enlisted sorcery to prolong the war. In desperation Scylla cuts her father's hair, supposedly the source of his country's strength. When he is killed in battle, Scylla, overcome with remorse, takes her own life in the presence of the victorious Minos, the only one of the principal characters surviving to the end of the opera. *Scylla*'s most remarkable musical feature is a full-blown *air italien avec la symphonie*, 'Per vincer pugnando', one of the earliest overt manifestations of the italianate vocal writing that began to infiltrate French opera in the early 18th century. CAROLINE WOOD

Scylla et Glaucus ('Scylla and Glaucus'). *Tragédie en musique* in a prologue and five acts by JEAN-MARIE LECLAIR to a libretto by D'Albaret after OVID'S *Metamorphoses* (books 10, 13 and 14); Paris, Opéra, 4 October 1746.

PROLOGUE

The Chief of the [Amanthon] people	baritone
First Propoetida	soprano
Second Propoetida	haute-contre
Vénus [Venus]	soprano
L'Amour [Cupid]	soprano

TRAGÉDIE

Scylla *a nymph*	soprano
Témire [Temire] *her confidante*	soprano
Glaucus *a marine god*	haute-contre
Licas *his confidant*	baritone
Circé [Circe] *a sorceress*	soprano
Dorine *her confidante*	soprano

DIVERTISSEMENT

A Shepherd } *in love with Scylla*	tenor
A Sylvan } *in love with Scylla*	baritone
A Shepherdess	soprano
A Dryad	soprano
Hécate [Hecate]	haute-contre
A Sicilian Girl	soprano

People of Amanthus, Propoetides, shepherds, sylvans, Circe's attendants, sea divinities, gods of the underworld, Sicilians

Setting Sicily

Despite a star cast including the singers Marie Fel and Pierre de Jélyotte and the dancers Marie-Anne Cupis de Camargo and Louis Dupré, *Scylla* was only a qualified success; it was given 18 times, a respectable but not outstanding total. From the eighth performance, the work was followed by a new ballet pantomime, *Une jardinière et un jardinier*, danced by Mlle Dallemand and Pietro Sodi and using the overture to Rameau's *Hippolyte et Aricie*. Beffara's statement (*Dictionnaire*) that performances of *Scylla* were followed by the Italian *intermède La soubrette maîtresse* (Pergolesi's *La serva padrona*) is mistaken: although that work, later to be so controversial, had its French première on the same day as Leclair's, it was given not at the Opéra but at the Comédie-Italienne. In December *Scylla* seems to have been privately performed at the home of the composer's patron, the Comtesse de La Mark, to whom the engraved score is dedicated. The work was never revived in Paris, though several numbers found their way into revivals of Lully's *Thésée* and Marais' *Alcyone* and individual items were published separately (notably the overture as part of Leclair's Trio op.13 no.3). In 1747, and possibly again in the 1750s, *Scylla* was given in Lyons in an abridged concert version prepared by the composer's brother Jean-Marie Leclair *le cadet* (1703–77); the work was divided to form two *concerts*, the second preceded by 'une seconde ouverture de la composition de Mr Leclair l'aîné' (possibly that published by his widow as part of the Trio op.14).

PROLOGUE *The temple of Venus* The Propoetides, a cult of young women from Amanthus, interrupt the worship in the temple and impiously deny the divinity of Venus. For this, the goddess turns them to stone (thus foreshadowing the ending of the *tragédie* proper). The ensuing celebration, and particularly the ensemble 'Que digne fils du plus grand des vainqueurs', is a glorification

– unusual at the Opéra by 1746 – of Louis XV and the Dauphin.

ACT 1 *A forest opposite a vast landscape* In a soliloquy 'Non, je ne cesserai jamais de fuir tes dangereuses chaînes', Scylla confesses her fear of love. During a *divertissement* in her honour, a shepherd and a sylvan try to woo her (their musette-chorus 'Loin de nos retraites' is especially seductive), but she declares that her heart will always remain indifferent. Glaucus, arriving after the shepherds have gone, is surprised when his own wooing arouses Scylla's anger. He resolves to enlist the help of the sorceress Circe in softening his beloved's heart.

ACT 2 *Circe's palace, where various animals have been metamorphosed by the sorceress* Circe is apprehensive. Having learnt by her magic art that 'a rebuffed lover' approaches, she feels emotionally vulnerable. When Glaucus appears, Circe is immediately infatuated. Outwardly she agrees to use her art on his behalf, and summons her ministers to that end. But during a long choral *passacaille* ('Amours dont le prix') the magicians bewitch Glaucus, who finds himself inflamed with love for Circe. However, the charm's effects are short-lived. Glaucus's confidant comes to tell him that Scylla now laments his absence: at the name 'Scylla' the spell is broken. Glaucus leaves the palace precipitately, to Circe's consternation and mounting fury. She and her ministers swear vengeance.

ACT 3 *The seashore* Scylla is now smitten with love for Glaucus. In an *air* 'Serments trompeurs, tendre langage' she interprets Glaucus's absence as a sign of fickleness. When he reappears, she accuses him of succumbing to Circe's charms. Glaucus affirms his constancy, and Scylla, embarrassed at her *volte face*, admits her love for him. They sing a brief love duet, 'Que le tendre amour nous engage'. Glaucus summons the sea divinities to celebrate his victory. During the chorus 'Dieu charmant, répondez à notre impatience' a cloud descends. In their euphoria, everyone expects it to contain Cupid. To their dismay the cloud opens to reveal Circe. The lovers and sea divinities flee. Circe, torn between love and revenge, resolves once more to gain Glaucus's heart, but threatens a terrible punishment for him if she fails.

ACT 4.i *Mount Etna in the distance; the surrounding countryside parched and covered with ashes* Glaucus politely parries Circe's attempts to win his love, most eloquently expressed in her *air* 'Reviens, ingrat mais cher amant' (accompanied by flute, violin and harpsichord). But when she threatens to kill Scylla, Glaucus becomes alarmed. Promising to renounce his love as long as Scylla remains unharmed, he consents to leave with Circe. Before he can do so, Scylla arrives. During the passionate exchanges that follow, Circe pretends to be taken in by Glaucus's tears. In a short but moving *air* ('Allez, couple fidèle', built over a ground bass) she even appears to give them her blessing. As soon as the lovers have departed, however, Circe plans her revenge.

4.ii *Mount Etna emitting flames* As the moon rises, Circe summons the gods of the underworld. Together, in a series of forceful solos and choruses interspersed with three vigorous *airs de démons*, they invoke Hecate, goddess of spells and incantations. The moon, Hecate's emblem, is seen to grow pale, then suddenly fall to earth. As the earth opens, Hecate appears. To a tremolando accompaniment she presents Circe with a herb culled from the banks of the river Phlegeton in Hades, with which to poison Scylla.

ACT 5.i *A place near a fountain, prepared for a celebration* Although Scylla is now convinced of Glaucus's fidelity, she remains apprehensive. Glaucus tries unsuccessfully to persuade her that Circe is no longer a threat. A group of Sicilians arrive to commemorate the day on which their country was delivered from the Cyclops' tyranny. During their celebration Glaucus gives thanks to Cupid in a bravura *ariette*, 'Chantez l'Amour, chantez ses douces flammes'. He shows Scylla the fountain in which he had first seen her reflection. As she looks into the fountain, the waters, poisoned by Circe, drive her insane and she eventually faints. Glaucus and the onlookers mourn, thinking her dead; but when they shout her name she revives and, still deranged, rushes out. Before Glaucus can follow, a triumphant Circe appears in mid-air, mounted on a dragon, and reveals that Scylla has drowned. During a powerful *symphonie* characterized by violent inverted dotted rhythms and rushing scales, she causes the scene to change to reveal Scylla's fate.

5.ii *The Straits of Sicily: on the Italian side the promontory of Reggio with the whirlpool of Charybdis, on the Sicilian side a massive siren-shaped rock surrounded by monsters who appear to be baying* As Glaucus laments, Circe warns that the petrification of Scylla must be a memorial to her rage. The violent *symphonie* is repeated. GRAHAM SADLER

Seal-Woman, The. Celtic folk opera in two acts by GRANVILLE BANTOCK to a libretto by Marjory Kennedy-Fraser after her collection *Songs of the Hebrides*; Birmingham, Repertory Theatre, 27 September 1924.

The seal-women are bewitched daughters of the King of Lochlann who revert to human form three times a year. An Isleman (tenor) has seen one of them bathing on such an occasion and has fallen in love with her. He takes away her sea-robe, thus preventing her from returning to the sea; they marry and have a child, but after seven happy years the Seal-Woman (mezzo-soprano) regains her robe and leaves them to return to the sea, no longer able to resist its call.

Bantock, always susceptible to things Celtic, had admired Marjory Kennedy-Fraser's collected folksongs and from 1913 he arranged several of them as partsongs and used others in two symphonies. The opera sets and links 20 songs, in both Bantock's and Kennedy-Fraser's arrangements, evocatively scored for a small orchestra. Kennedy-Fraser herself took the part of the Cailleach, the old crone (contralto), in the original production.

STEPHEN BANFIELD

Searelle, (William) Luscombe (*b* Devon, 1853; *d* 1907). New Zealand composer. He emigrated to New Zealand in about 1862 and completed his education at Christ's College, Christchurch. Originally intending to study law, he succumbed to an early fascination for the performing arts, having shown creative flair as a playwright and as a composer. His stage works were produced in Australia, New Zealand and in Britain. Those performed included the comic operas *Estrella* (Sydney, 27 September 1884), *Bobadill* (Sydney, 22 November 1884) and *Isadora*, re-titled *The Black Rover* (Melbourne, 7 July 1885). All three operas follow the techniques of light opera in which spoken dialogue is interspersed with solo, ensemble and chorus settings, entr'actes and incidental music, often culminating in ensemble finales. A contemporary review of *Estrella* speaks of 'well varied and brightly arranged music, with considerable originality, many cheerful melodies and a straightforward unaffected style recalling Donizetti, and an overture in a modern style introducing themes to be subsequently heard in the opera'.

*

F. C. Brewer: *The Drama of New South Wales* (Sydney, 1892), 84–5
E. Wood: *Australian Opera 1842–1970: History of Australian Opera with Descriptive Catalogues* (diss., Adelaide U., 1979)
E. Irvin: *Dictionary of the Australian Theatre 1788–1914* (Sydney, 1985)

ANDREW D. McCREDIE

Searle, Humphrey (*b* Oxford, 26 Aug 1915; *d* London, 12 May 1982). English composer. He studied at the RCM (1937) and at the New Vienna Conservatory (1937–8). While in Vienna he had private lessons with Webern. From 1946 onwards he made systematic and regular use of 12-note techniques in all his principal works. He was for many years a leading figure in contemporary music circles and had a special interest in the music of Liszt, whose methods of thematic transformation influenced his own work.

His Romantic leanings and his concern with extreme forms of human behaviour are reflected both in his major choral trilogy (*Gold Coast Customs*, *The Riverrun* and *The Shadow of Cain*) and in his operas: these are for the most part through-composed, without set numbers or formal divisions. In *The Diary of a Madman* and *The Photo of the Colonel* he found congenial themes which allowed him to exploit a vein of surrealist humour already foreshadowed in settings of Edward Lear. In *Hamlet* he adopted a leitmotif technique, deriving themes for the principal characters from a single note-row, itself introduced at the soliloquy 'To be, or not to be'. There is direct parody of Romantic music in the Player's speech and in the play scene, while Ophelia and the gravediggers are given 'untonal folksongs'. The opera was given its première at Hamburg in 1968 and its British première on 18 April 1969 (owing to the illness of the principal baritone and of his understudy, only the first of the London performances was given complete). *Hamlet* was better received in Germany than in England, where Andrew Porter summed up the general opinion: '*Hamlet* ... has its striking and enjoyable moments, but the idiom is inadequate to the play'.

The Diary of a Madman op.35 (1, Searle, after N. Gogol), Berlin, Staatsoper, 1959 [Ger. version]; London, Sadler's Wells, 26 April 1964
The Photo of the Colonel op.41 (1, Searle, after E. Ionesco), BBC radio, 8 March 1964; stage, Frankfurt, Staatsoper, 3 June 1964
Hamlet op.48 (3, Searle, after W. Shakespeare), Hamburg, Staatsoper, 4 March 1968 [Ger. version]; Toronto, Royal Conservatory of Music, 12 Feb 1969

*

M. Kingsbury: 'Humphrey Searle's Hamlet', *MT*, cx (1969), 369–71

HUGO COLE

Season. A period, more or less fixed, during which opera is given each year. The idea of regular seasons came in with public performances before a paying audience. Such performances were timed to catch the maximum number of residents and visitors, to take advantage of favourable weather, and to avoid closures imposed during public holidays. As opera developed, a system of regular seasons enabled artists to plan their professional and audiences their social lives. The system, however, largely disintegrated towards the end of the 19th century with the coming of repertory opera and of railways, which allowed familiar works to be put on and taken off within days.

The earliest operas, given in the households of rulers or of great nobles by artists most of them permanently employed, celebrated important events – dynastic marriages, birthdays, name-days or military victories. The performance was timed for whatever date suited the great persons in command. When, however, public performances began in Venice in 1637, they exploited the recognized period of winter merrymaking which was also the height of the local tourist season. This, lasting from 26 (or 27) December to Shrove Tuesday (a shifting date in February or early March), was best observed in Catholic Europe, where it was known as carnival (the season beginning on 26 December 1750 would be 'Carnival 1751'); besides Venice, towns noted for their carnival celebrations were Rome, Vienna and Munich. Down to about 1860 a carnival season offered the chance not only of attracting a wealthy audience but also of profiting from the masked balls and banquets that were held in the opera house (with the stalls emptied of seats or covered over); these were the high spot of the social year, and as many as ten or twelve might be held in the last hectic days before Lent.

The other main occasion for opera in the mid-17th century was the trade fair which a number of Italian and German towns put on for anything from two to six weeks at some time between April and October (for a *fiera* season); as early as 1645 Landi's *Sant'Alessio* (first given privately in Rome in 1631 or 1632) was performed during the fair at Reggio Emilia, which for the next two centuries or more went on ranking as an important season. Other towns with notable fair seasons – none of them the seat of a court – were Padua (with two), Bergamo and, in the early 19th century, Senigallia; in Germany, Augsburg, Leipzig and Frankfurt. Regular fairs lost much of their importance for opera with the coming of railways and the vogue for occasional international exhibitions.

The seasonal system developed in Italy because there opera was at once more rapidly commercialized and more widely dispersed than in other countries: in Paris from 1669 and in Hamburg from 1678 – each in its way unique as a musical and theatrical centre – opera seems to have been understood as taking place through much of the year (at the slow rate of two or three performances a week); as late as 1831 the management contract for the Paris Opéra specified a minimum of three performances a week but not the number of weeks during which the theatre should be open. In Italy by the end of the 17th century carnival seasons were firmly established in a number of towns besides Venice. A letter of 13 January 1690 from the musician Antonio Alamanni (*I-MOs* Archivio per Materie, Musici b. 2) describes a Livorno season, with two operas on historical subjects – the model for a fashionable Italian carnival season over the next century and a half. Rome in the carnival of 1696 had, besides the operas at the two main public theatres, 45 dramatic productions, spoken or sung, between public and private theatres, not counting embassies ('Avvisi di Roma', 14 January–3 March, *I-Rvat* Cod. Ottob. Lat. 3361 ff. 4–16).

As opera performances multiplied in the 18th century, new seasons were exploited, chiefly spring (*primavera*: April to end June) and autumn (*autunno*: late August or September to end November). There were occasionally Ascension seasons (*ascensione*: May to June). Short

November seasons beginning before Advent were occasionally held, known as *avvento* or (principally if not exclusively in Rome) *autunnino*. Summer (*estate*: June to August) was on the whole a time to avoid: the landed classes, the part of the audience no management could do without, tended to leave town for their country estates so as at once to escape the heat – intense in most continental cities – and oversee the harvest, as well as shoot, an activity at its height once the harvest had cleared the fields of crops. There were, however, opera performances at the summer residences of rulers (Laxenburg near Vienna, Pratolino near Florence, Posillipo near Naples etc.); so far as is known, these were generally of operas that were also given in public theatres under the rulers' influence. The Prague opera troupe run by Pasquale Bondini in the 1780s spent the summers in Leipzig, where a merchant-dominated audience could still be found. In the 19th century the concentration of gambling as a pastime of the European rich in a single holiday resort (first Lucca with its neighbouring baths, then Baden-Baden, finally Monte Carlo) made for fashionable late summer opera seasons in the first two towns: Berlioz's *Béatrice et Bénédict* (1862, Baden-Baden) was one of the very few notable operas to have its first performance in August.

With the vogue for comic opera in the latter half of the 18th century there developed in Italy cheap summer seasons, often in very small towns. These stood at the bottom of a hierarchy of seasons. Carnival was generally the most fashionable, particularly in theatres that were privileged to put on *opera seria*, the most exalted and expensive genre; the grandest theatres, such as the Regio, Turin, and La Fenice, Venice, for many years were open at this season alone. There were exceptions. Naples ran a 'theatrical year' (starting on 30 May) rather than a seasonal system; its main winter session (sometimes called the *inverno* season rather than *carnevale*) might begin on St Charles's Day, 4 November, rather than 26 December. At Bologna the fashionable season was, to begin with, spring (then, in the 19th century, autumn); the point may have been to capitalize on Bologna's role as the hub of the Italian musical profession by employing the best singers at a time when they were not in demand in the best-funded royal opera houses, and would take more modest fees. Singers' fees in autumn especially (when attendance was often slack as members of the élite lingered on in the country) could be half of what they earned in carnival.

The final step in the making of an operatic seasonal calendar was the annexation of religious holidays, particularly Lent. Before the 1780s, most governments forbade performances in Lent, not always successfully: a ruling prince of Parma, on holiday in Venice, upset many senators by putting on a 'private' opera in his own house (G. M. Giannini to Duke of Modena, 27 March 1683, *I-MOs* Archivio per Materie, Musici b. 1/B). In Vienna and Prague the Empress Maria Theresa's regulations banned performances on a further 50 days, including Advent (15–25 December), Easter Week and two or three days around each of the main Christian, including Marian, festivals (Epiphany, Ascension, Pentecost, Trinity, Corpus Christi, Assumption, Immaculate Conception, All Saints, All Souls) as well as around the birthdays and name-days of her parents and the date of her father's death. In Naples the calendar was much the same, with further closures during the novena and octave of the local patron saint, St Januarius (17 days in April–May, 16 days in mid-September), which went on into the 19th century even after the rest had been given up. France with its Gallican tradition seems always to have been more lax, with only a three-week Easter closure.

Lent, however, was – in Catholic countries especially – a time for oratorios and religious processions and sermons, which could be seen as affording dramatic entertainment. The cooling of religious faith among the educated in the late 18th century, as much as the increasing demand for opera, may explain why governments came to allow staged performances of 'sacred dramas' (operas on biblical subjects) in Lent. Such permission was given in Munich as early as 1734. Prague followed suit in 1749, but Maria Theresa tried to hold the line; she allowed some relaxation from 1772, and after her death her sons Joseph II and Leopold II opened up Lent, all but Holy Week (Austrian lands, 1788; Tuscany, 1791); so did Naples in 1787. The real problem in contemporary eyes was whether to allow ballet, potentially the most scandalous genre because it exploited sexual attraction. The French Revolution for a time abolished the entire Christian calendar, as well as bringing about an explosion of opera and other theatre in Paris throughout the critical years 1793–5; the Napoleonic conquests in Italy and Germany made Lent into an ordinary opera (and ballet) season tacked on to carnival. Despite attempts by the restored monarchical governments after 1814 (in France as well as in Italy) to go back to former closure periods or to restrict Lent to 'sacred drama', the Napoleonic arrangements were back in place by 1830. The only 'sacred drama' still current in our own day (apart from Handel's dramatic oratorios) is Rossini's *Mosè in Egitto* (1818, Naples). Lent seasons were sometimes called *Quaresima*, from the late 18th century; in Venice and Florence *Quadragesima* (the first Sunday in Lent) was the term favoured for a Lent season.

Outside Italy, 18th-century opera houses tended to engage singers and musicians by the year, in part because of old habits of court employment, in part because of the difficulties of long-distance travel. The season, as in London in Handel's day, was often theoretically meant to last from September to June. This was to be the 19th- and 20th-century practice in many places, not only in capital cities but, from the 1840s, in a French provincial town such as Béziers. Meanwhile each town had its own habits which shaped the opera calendar. Munich seems to have concentrated it into carnival and (on the pretext of various name-days etc.) autumn. Vienna did much the same in the late 17th century but, by the late 1740s, was running a cosmopolitan mixture of serious and comic opera (Italian, French, German), plays, and (especially from about 1770) ballet; there was some tendency for serious opera to be concentrated into spring and autumn seasons, and in the period of Italian management, 1823–48, a fashionable Vienna spring season fitted in neatly with carnival seasons in Italy. In general, the more popular the audience for a particular theatre (in Vienna as elsewhere) the more it seems to have played all the year round, in a mixture of genres and with a fast changing repertory: artisans, shopkeepers and clerical workers did not go away on holiday until well into our own century. In Naples in 1832–8, out of an average of some 700 opera performances a year, 427 were given in the popular Nuovo and La Fenice against 188 in the royal S Carlo and Fondo.

In 18th-century London the fashionable opera season

in practice ran (with hiccoughs due to various crises) from November to June, but from the early 19th century down to 1939 it coincided with the 'London season' when Parliament sat and landed and other wealthy persons were in town. It generally ran from late March or April till some time in the summer – as late as 1862 till late August, then till late July, then, between the two world wars, till somewhere about late June. The season shrank at times of economic crisis – in the agriculturally depressed 1880s, and again between the wars, when it seldom lasted more than six or seven weeks. There were, however, fairly frequent autumn or winter seasons, less fashionable and often in English.

Since 1947 both London opera houses have run continuous seasons of nine or ten months. This is generally the aim of leading modern opera houses; in countries with reliably hot summers, most of the USA included, there are also open-air seasons in or near some large cities. In South America the fashionable season (a good deal shrunk from its heyday in 1860–1940) is the southern winter (June–September). Almost everywhere the old cheap off-season performances have vanished.

*

O. Teuber: *Geschichte des Prager Theaters* (Prague, 1883–8), i, 203–4, 281–2; ii, 146–7

C. L. Curiel: *Il Teatro San Pietro di Trieste* (Milan, 1937), 158, 272

H. Rosenthal: *Two Centuries of Opera at Covent Garden* (London, 1958)

H. Bolongaro-Crevenna: *L'arpa festante: Die Münchner Oper 1651–1825* (Munich, 1963)

F. Hadamowsky: *Die Wiener Hoftheater (Staatstheater) 1776–1966* (Vienna, 1966–75), i, chronological appx

G. Zechmeister: *Die Wiener Theater nächst der Burg und nächst dem Kärntnerthor von 1747 bis 1776* (Vienna, 1971)

R. M. Isherwood: *Music in the Service of the King: France in the Seventeenth Century* (Ithaca, NY, 1973)

J. N. Black: *Donizetti's Operas in Naples 1822–48* (London, 1982), 9–10

——: *The Italian Romantic Libretto* (Edinburgh, 1984), 6

J. Gourret: *Ces hommes qui ont fait l'Opéra* (Paris, 1984), 263–7

J. Rosselli: *The Opera Industry in Italy from Cimarosa to Verdi: the Role of the Impresario* (Cambridge, 1984)

J. Bèges and A. Bèges: *Mémoire d'un théâtre* (Béziers, 1987), 109–10, 115

W. Dean and J. M. Knapp: *Handel's Operas 1704–1726* (Oxford, 1987), 151–2

P. Fabbri and R. Verti: *Due secoli di teatro per musica a Reggio Emilia* (Reggio Emilia, 1987)

J. Rosselli: 'Artisti e impresari', *Il Teatro di San Carlo* (Naples, 1987), i, 25–60, esp. 47–8

JOHN ROSSELLI (with RICHARD MACNUTT)

Seating. The space theatregoers occupy while witnessing a performance, whether they are sitting or not, and, if they are sitting, whether they are sitting on an actual seat or not (they may be on the floor); the seating capacity of a theatre often includes an estimate of how many standing spectators ('standees') can be accommodated.

The ancient Greeks divided their seating area into pie-shaped sectors and distributed tablets to show which space spectators (or the state, for them) had purchased. Some seats were considered more desirable, distance from the stage being the simplest way of 'scaling' the house. Seats for dignitaries were closest, in a semicircle on the rim of the orchestra performing area. These were not necessarily the best places for witnessing a performance; since the auditoria were on steep hillsides, people further back and higher up had a better view and just as good hearing. Even in modern houses, where all seats are supposedly good, people willingly pay higher prices for those thought to be especially favourable – closer to the stage or in a place best noticed by others.

Court playhouses of the Renaissance and Baroque periods were patterned after ancient theatres but with some important differences: they were usually indoors and within rectangular spaces, often banquet halls. The semicircular seating plan of classical times was reshaped into a U to make the best use of the oblong area. Chief dignitaries were on a 'state' or platform facing the stage at the back of the U; other spectators would not presume to sit in front of the state, so that space became a kind of forestage and was used by dancers, who could perform more easily there than on the raked and uneven stage floor in any case (see fig.1; *see also* INTERMEDIO and SOCIOLOGY OF OPERA, fig.1). The rest of the seating at court theatres was usually open: bench-like structures along the sides and back of the hall, sometimes on one level, sometimes on two or occasionally more. Segregation into boxes was unnecessary, since the audience was socially of a piece, but those of lesser rank took places along the sides nearest the stage, where the view of the painted perspective scenery was not ideal. That probably did not matter, since the performance was as much a social as a theatrical event.

Most opera houses today are based not so much on the court theatres of old as on indoor public theatres, both those used for plays and those for the new aristocratic toy, opera. These theatres had to accommodate enough people to pay expenses (and in the case of operas the cost was, and still is, enormous) as well as people from different social and economic classes. It was during the 17th century that theatres began to take the form that most opera houses now follow. Remarkably, the general layout, both in the auditorium and backstage, was and still is much the same from country to country (see figs.2–11), one of the reasons being that operas and performers travelled all over Europe and theatre plans and practices tended to become standardized. With a few exceptions, opera houses everywhere were differentiated from legitimate theatres chiefly by being larger and grander and with acoustics suitable for music.

All seats in a theatre should face the stage, but if that ideal is sought, capacity may have to be curtailed to keep the last row reasonably close (approximately 22 metres away if possible). There are two solutions: add levels of seating over the rear of the auditorium and/or put seats along the sides. Most opera houses since the early 17th century have done both, and some have that rare combination of large capacity in a small cubic space, reasonable sightlines for most spectators and acceptable acoustics.

The seating areas thus created have many names, the terms used – pit, boxes, galleries etc. – being usually a matter of national or local preference (see Table 1). The auditorium floor seating is called variously the stalls, orchestra, pit, parterre or parquet. In the 17th and 18th centuries the seats there were benches (at first backless; *see* THEATRE ARCHITECTURE, fig.6) with hinged flaps which formed aisles when lifted and extra seating when lowered. This arrangement evolved into continental seating (as at the Bayreuth Festspielhaus; see fig.10; *see also* BAYREUTH, fig.3) that provides more leg room in each row and no aisles except at the sides. At the back of this seating area is normally a place for standees. In the 17th and 18th centuries in France, however, the forward portion of the floor, the parterre, was left open for standees, and behind them and just below the first tier of

1. *Theatre in the Palazzo Reale, Naples, during a performance (6 November 1747) of Giuseppe de Majo's serenata 'Il sogno d'Olimpia': engraving by G. Vasi after Vincenzo Re from 'Narrazione delle solenni reali feste fatte per celebrare in Napoli ... la nascita di ... Filippo Principe delle Due Sicilie' (Naples, 1748)*

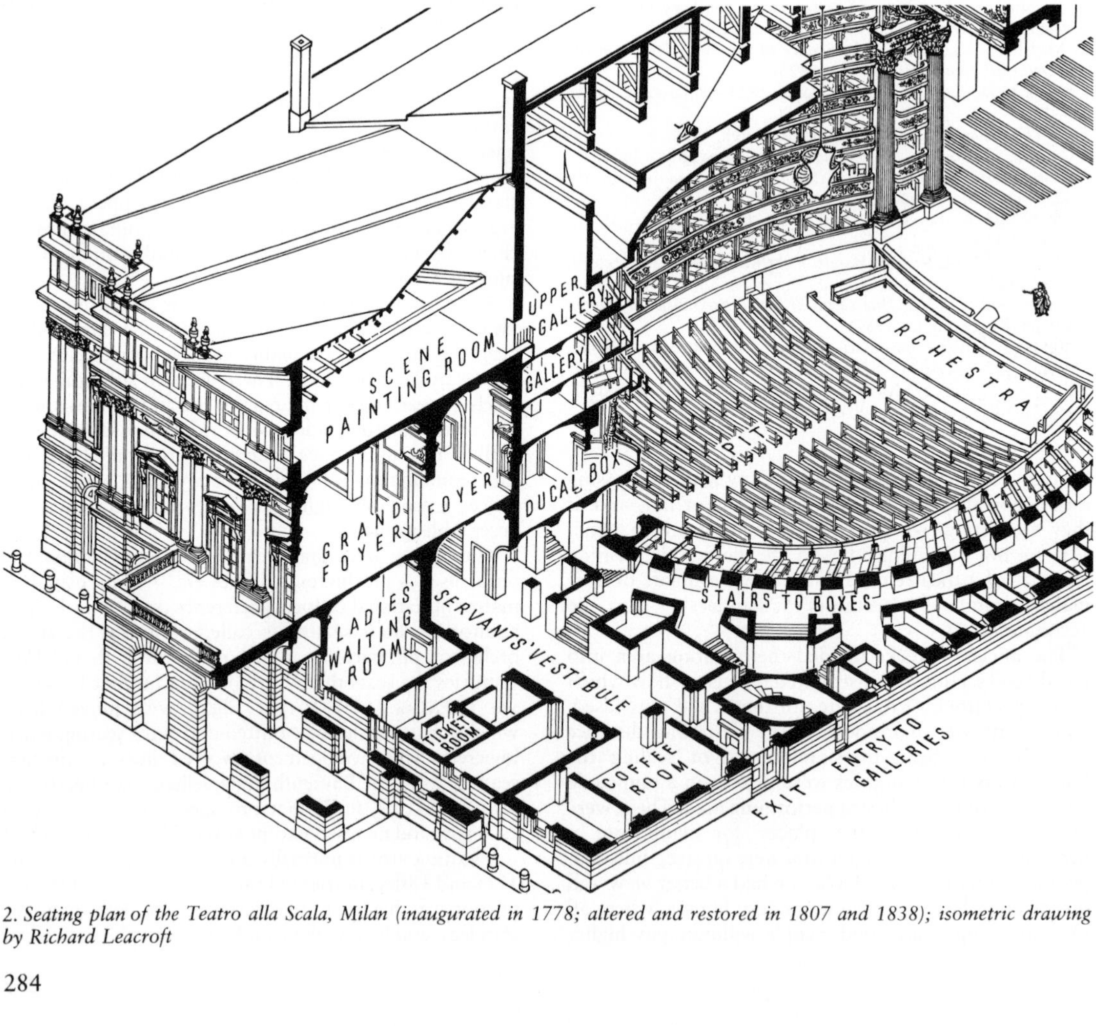

2. *Seating plan of the Teatro alla Scala, Milan (inaugurated in 1778; altered and restored in 1807 and 1838); isometric drawing by Richard Leacroft*

The Crown Gallery
PIT
PIT DOOR
PIT DOOR
PRINCE's SIDE
Stage
KING's SIDE

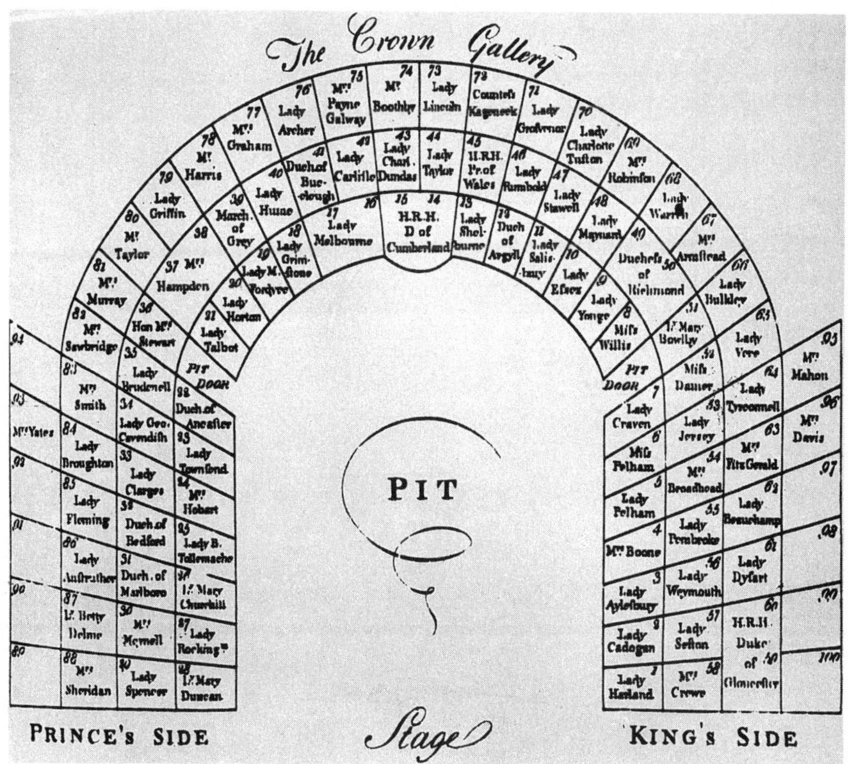

3. Box seating plan, from the box bookkeeper's book, King's Theatre, Haymarket, London, 1783; above the third tier of front boxes (facing the stage) was the five-shilling or crown gallery and, above that, the three-shilling gallery

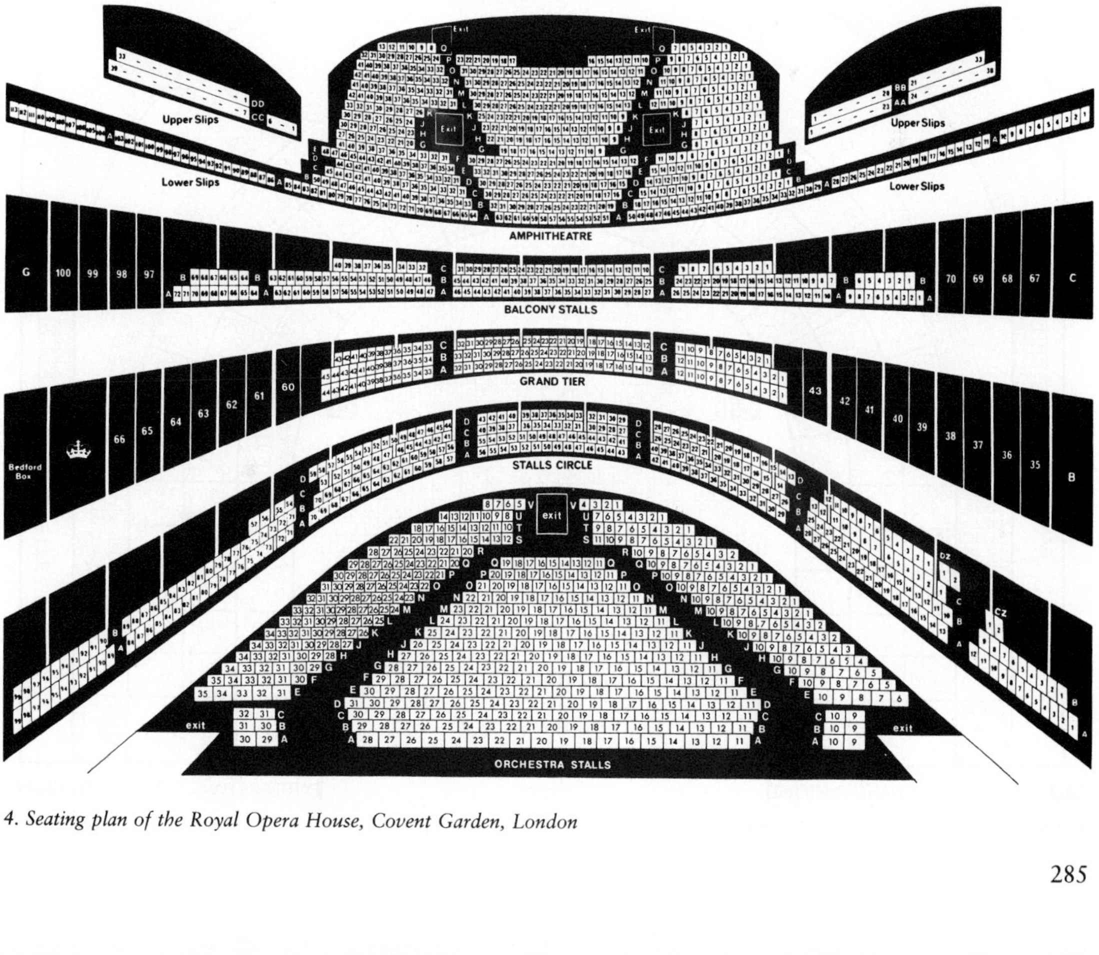

Upper Slips
Upper Slips
Lower Slips
Lower Slips
AMPHITHEATRE
BALCONY STALLS
GRAND TIER
STALLS CIRCLE
Bedford Box
ORCHESTRA STALLS
exit
exit

4. Seating plan of the Royal Opera House, Covent Garden, London

2. Rang
1. Rang
Hochparkett
HP-Loge Mitte rechts
HP-Loge Mitte links
1. Rang Loge A
1. Rang Loge B
1. Rang Loge C
1. Rang Loge D
2. Rang Loge A
HP Loge A
HP Loge B
HP Loge C
rechts
Parkett
links

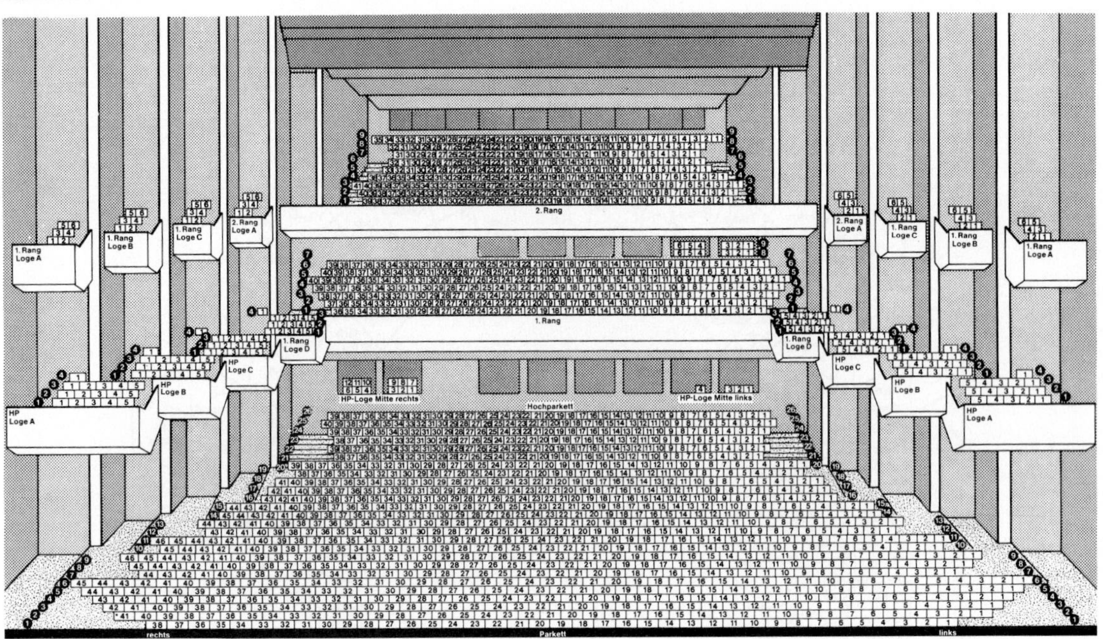

5. Seating plan of the Deutsche Oper, Berlin

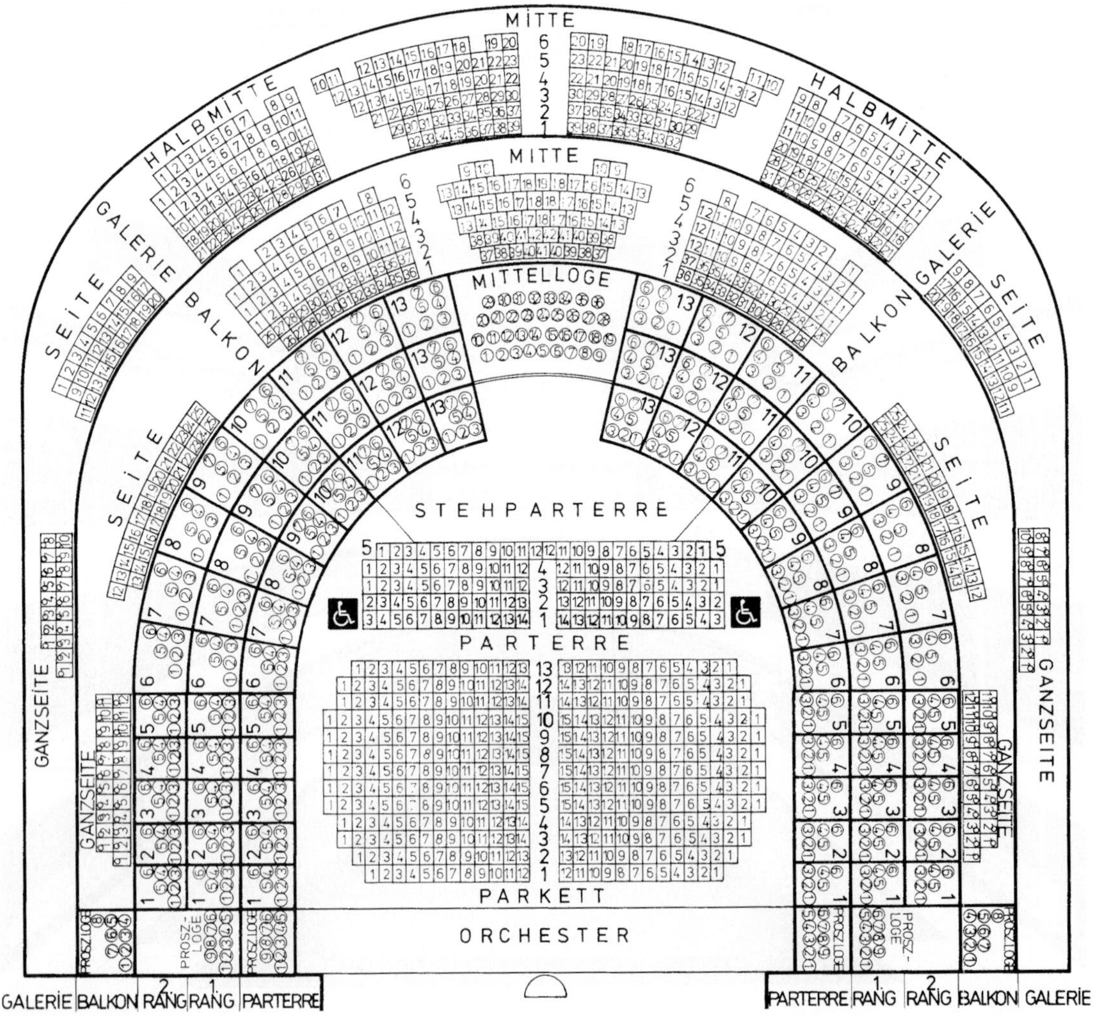

MITTE
HALBMITTE
GALERIE
SEITE
MITTE
BALKON
MITTELLOGE
STEHPARTERRE
PARTERRE
GANZSEITE
PARKETT
ORCHESTER
PROSZ.-LOGE
GALERIE BALKON 2. RANG 1. RANG PARTERRE
PARTERRE 1. RANG 2. RANG BALKON GALERIE

6. Seating plan of the Staatsoper, Vienna

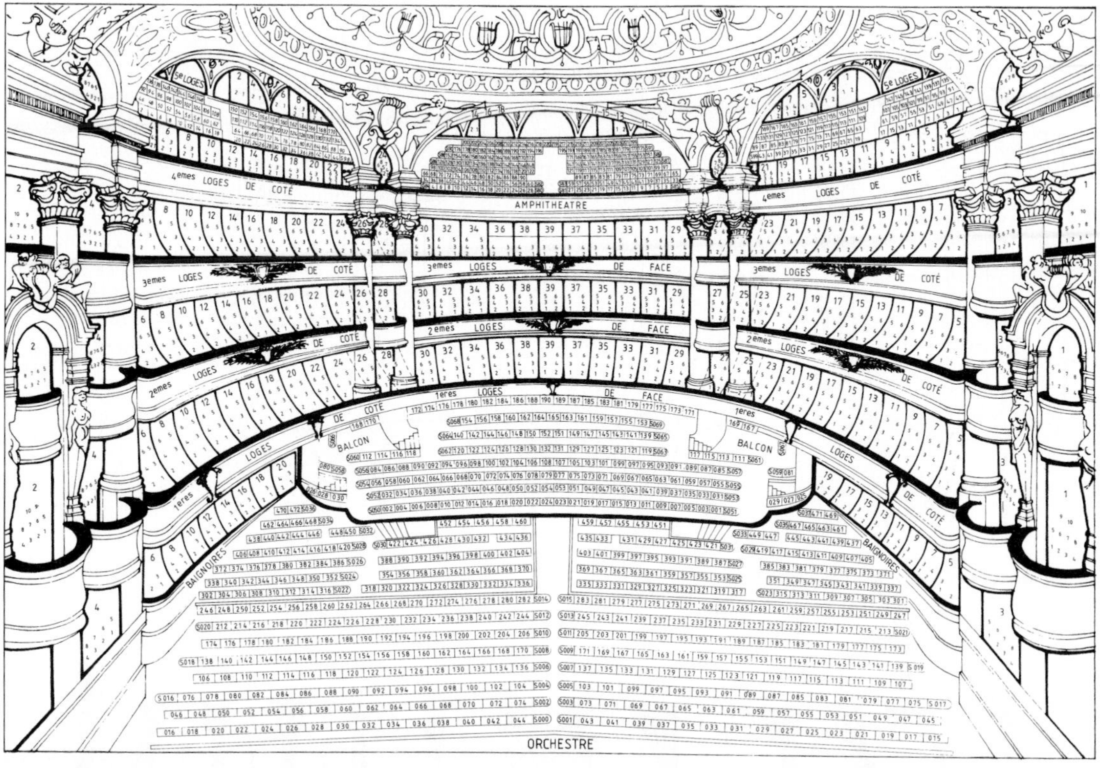

7. *Seating plan of the Palais Garnier ('Opéra'), Paris*

8. *Auditorium of the Metropolitan Opera House, New York*

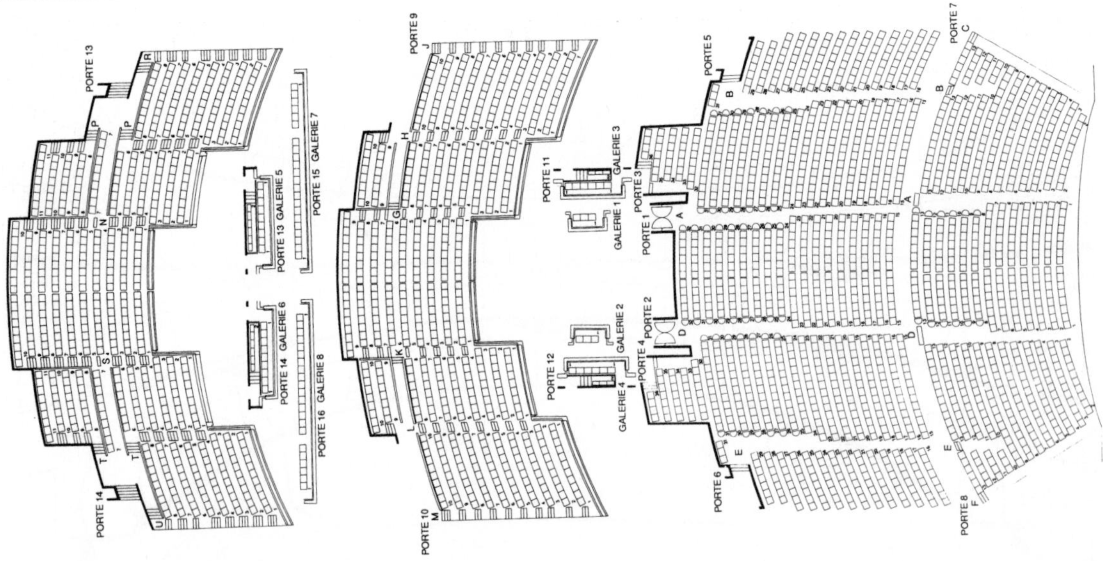

9. *Seating plan of the Opéra Bastille, Paris*

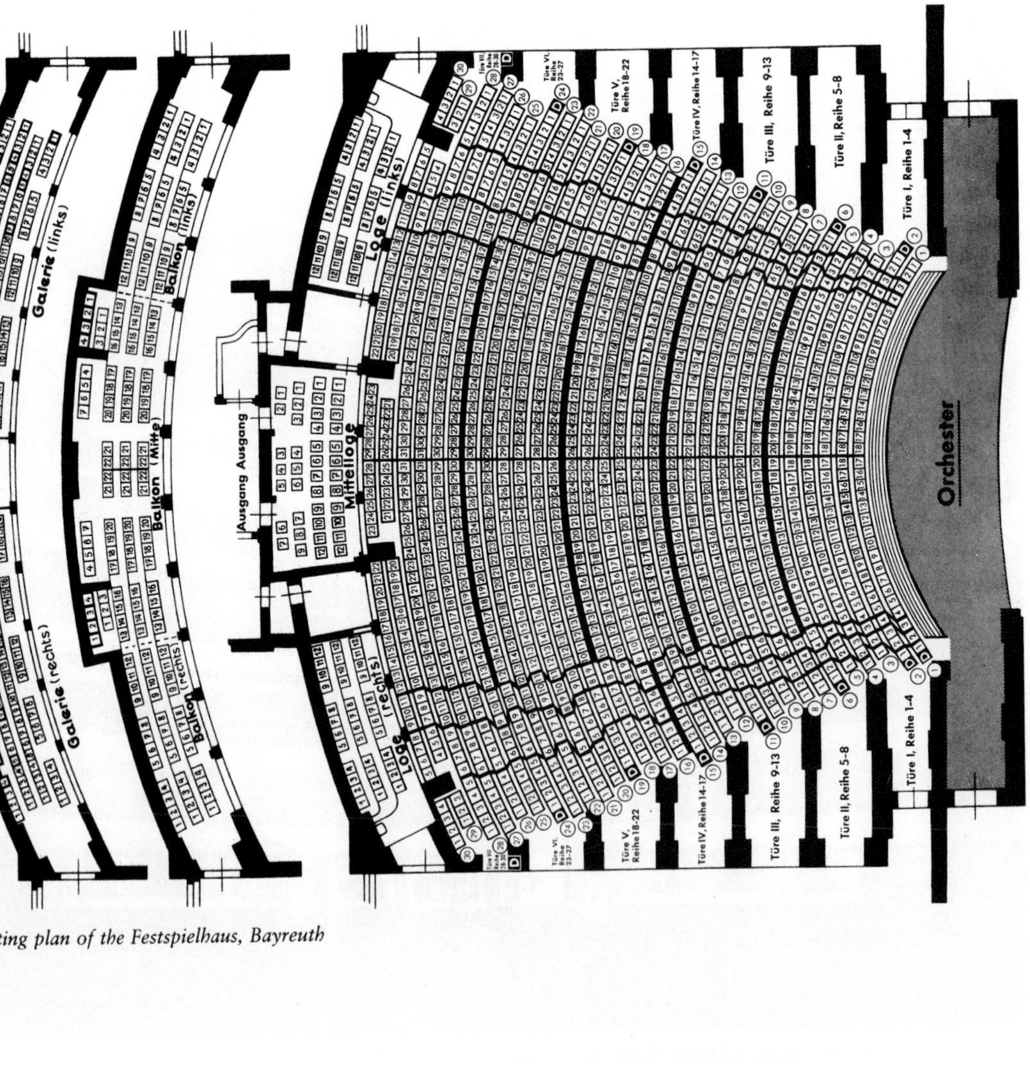

10. *Seating plan of the Festspielhaus, Bayreuth*

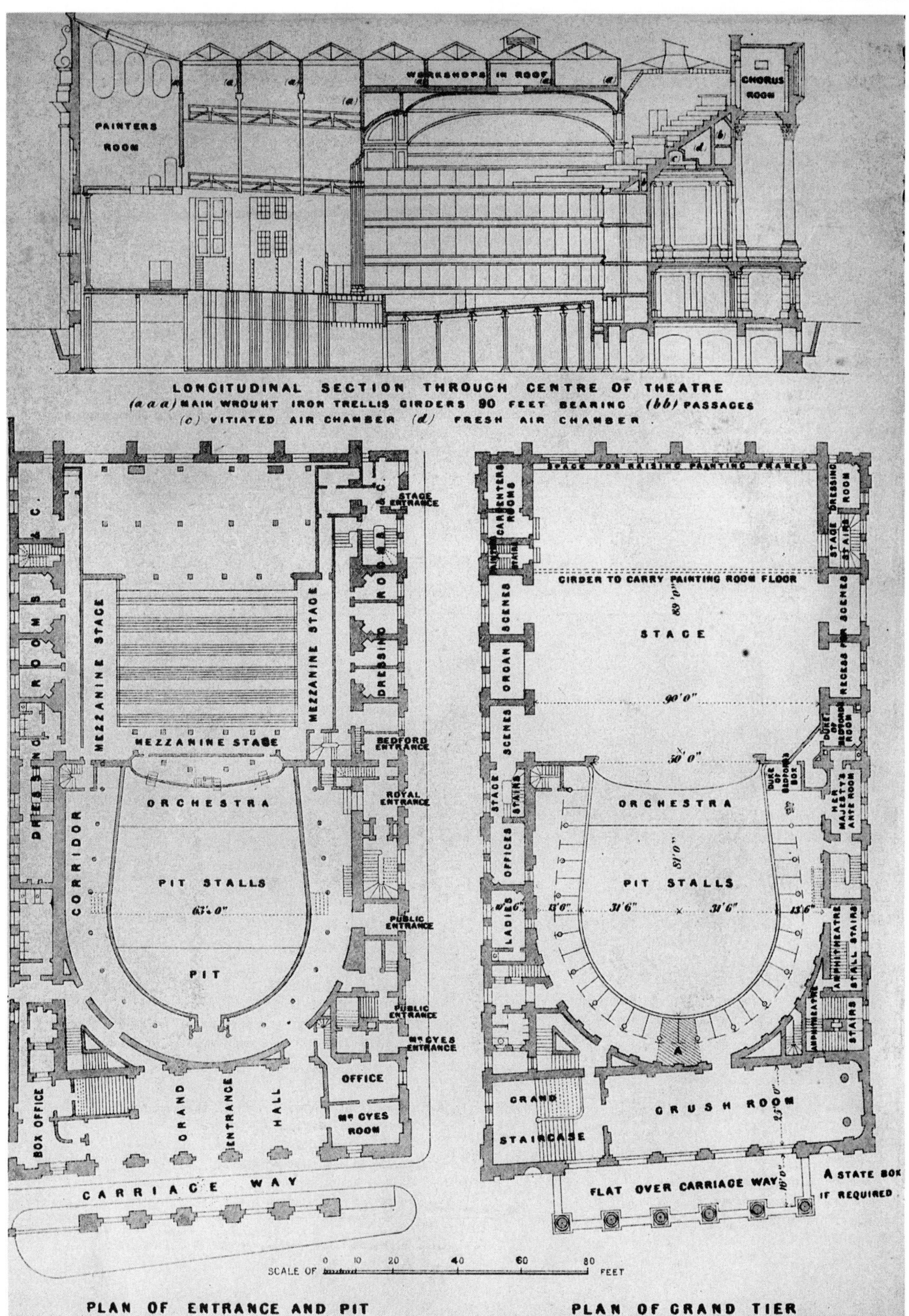

11. The Royal (Italian) Opera House, Covent Garden (1856–8) designed by E. M. Barry: longitudinal section above, and plans of the entrance and pit (below left), and grand tier: from 'Transactions of the Royal Institute of British Architects', 1st ser., x (1859–60)

TABLE 1: Seating terms*

English	*French*	*German*	*Italian*
auditorium/hall	salle	Zuschauerraum	sala
balcony	balcon	Balkon	balconata
circle		Rang	
box	loge	Loge	palco
dress circle/first balcony	premier balcon/balcon	erster Rang/Balkon	prima balconata
gallery/second balcony	paradis	Galerie/Rang	galleria/balconata
mezzanine	mezzanine	Zwischenrang/Hochparterre	mezzanino
orchestra seats [stalls and pit]	fauteuils d'orchestre	Parterrevordersitze/Parkett	poltrone
parquet [main floor]			
parquet circle [main floor beneath galleries]			
pit [rear orchestra seats]		Sitzparterre/Parterre	platea
seating plan	plan des locations	Sitzplan	pianta dei posti
stalls [front orchestra seats]	fauteuils d'orchestre	Parterrevordersitze/Parkett/erstes Parterre	poltrone/platea
tier	gradin	Galerie/Rang	fila
upper circle	deuxième galerie	zweiter Rang	seconda balconata
upper gallery/ 'gods'	paradis	Galerie	

*Developed from K. Rae and R. Southern: *An International Vocabulary of Technical Theatre Terms* (New York, 1960)

TABLE 2: The configuration of seating areas in some modern opera houses

(arranged by levels; configurations may change)

Bayreuth, Festspielhaus (cap. *c*1900)

1 Parkett
2 Loge
3 Balkon
4 Galerie
} no side seats

Berlin, Deutsche Oper (cap. *c*1900)

1 Parkett (front); Hochparkett (rear); Hochparkett Loge (rear)
2 Rang 1 (rear); Hochparkett and Rang 1 Loge (sides)
3 Rang 2 (rear); Rang 1 and Rang 2 Loge (sides)

London, Royal Opera House, Covent Gardent (cap. 2186)

1 orchestra stalls
2 stalls circle (rear and sides)
3 grand tier (rear); grand tier boxes (sides)
4 balcony stalls (rear and sides); balcony boxes (sides)
5 amphitheatre (rear); upper and lower slips (sides)

Milan, Teatro alla Scala (cap. 3000)

1 poltrona (front); poltroncina (rear)
2 palchi 1 (rear and sides)
3 palchi 2 (rear and sides)
4 palchi 3 (rear and sides)
5 galleria 1 (rear and sides)
6 galleria 2 (rear and sides)

New York, Metropolitan Opera House (cap. 3788)

1 orchestra (front); standing room (rear)
2 parterre boxes (rear and sides)
3 grand tier (rear); grand tier boxes (sides)
4 dress circle (rear); dress circle boxes (sides)
5 balcony (rear); balcony boxes (sides)
6 family circle (rear); family circle boxes (sides)

Paris, Opéra Bastille (Grand Salle, cap. 2700)

1 parterre
2 1er balcon (rear); galeries (lower, sides)
3 2ème balcon (rear); galeries (upper, sides)

Paris, Palais Garnier ('Opéra') (cap. *c*2100)

1 orchestre
2 balcon (rear); baignoires (sides)
3 1ères loges (rear and sides)
4 2ème loges (rear and sides)
5 3ème loges (rear and sides)
6 amphithéâtre (rear); 4ème loges (sides)
7 5ème loges (rear and sides); stalles (sides)

Vienna, Staatsoper (cap. *c*2200)

1 Parkett (front); Parterre (rear); Stehparterre (rear)
2 Parterre Loge (rear and sides)
3 Mittelloge (rear); Rang 1 Loge (rear and sides)
4 Rang 2 Loge (rear and sides)
5 Balkon (rear and sides)
6 Galerie (rear and sides)

boxes, were bench-type seats forming the *amphithéâtre* (see fig.12). Remnants of the latter can still be seen at the Paris Opéra (see fig.7 above), though by the 1760s in France standees were placed behind rather than forward of the pit seating area.

Until fire regulations were imposed, many houses did not have proper aisles and sufficient exits; indeed, in England in the 18th century houses were sometimes quite literally packed, and the entrances to the pit area screwed closed (*Morning Chronicle*, 6 February 1790). In some English theatres in the 19th century seating on the auditorium floor was divided into fairly uncomfortable benches nearer the stage (the stalls) and very uncomfortable benches behind them (the pit).

The seating on the auditorium floor could be altered. On special occasions, such as the première of a new work, the pit, as they sometimes advertised in England, would be 'laid into boxes' – sectioned off to add prestige and justify raised prices. (For such occasions as banquets or masquerades, the entire pit might be floored over, level with the stage.)

Along the flanks and back of the auditorium of a typical opera house today are usually two or more levels of divided boxes (loges). These seating coves are descendants of the special seating for dignitaries in classical times, but in public indoor Renaissance theatres they may have been born of engineering necessity as much as social gratification. Levels of seating one above the other required pillars, and these not only supported the tier above but, in effect, divided the seating into segments; walls between segments were added, and thus boxes were created. The partitions in

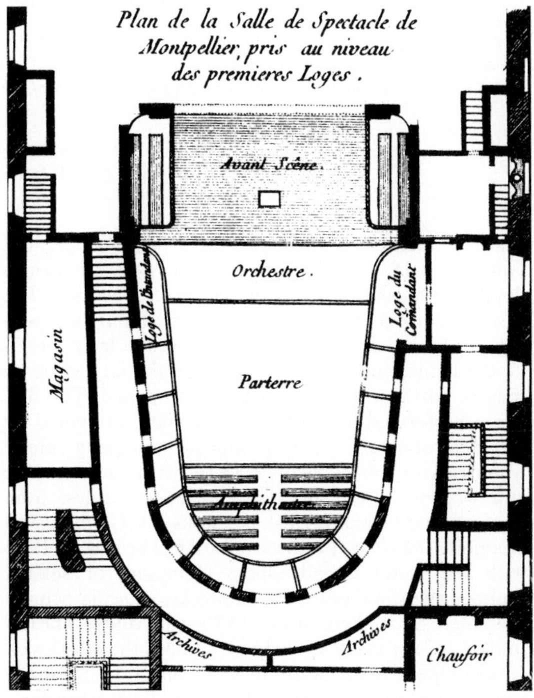

12. Plan of the forestage (avant scène; the railed-off benches on each side were for spectators), orchestra, ground-floor standing (parterre) and seating (amphithéâtre), and first tier of boxes (loges) at the first public theatre in Montpellier (1755); the splayed-U design and the standing area in front of the seating were features of a number of French theatres: from G. Dumont, 'Parallèle de plans des plus belles salles de spectacles d'Italie et de France' (Paris, c1764)

13. A box at the Paris Opéra, 1789: engraving by Patas after J. M. Moreau the younger (note the draw curtain to allow some occupants to watch the performance while others dallied behind, and the roller curtain that could provide total privacy)

some theatres separated the boxes completely. Curtains were installed, as illustrations show, so that patrons could close themselves off from the entertainment and from the eyes of the rest of the audience (see fig.13; *see also* LIGHTING, fig.2 and THEATRE ARCHITECTURE, fig.10).

Floor-to-ceiling walls made for miserable sightlines towards the stage in the side boxes, and eventually in many theatres these dividers, if they were not weight-bearing, were cut down to seat level. By the late 18th century seating tiers were cantilevered, and supporting columns could be moved to behind box spectators (at first some theatregoers were fearful that their floor was unsupported). Low partitions remained in the 19th century to give wealthy patrons the feeling that they were special, but in effect the levels of boxes evolved into democratic, semi-open seating except for a few fully segregated boxes (*see* OPERETTA, fig.1).

At the centre rear of the first level of boxes in many old houses, facing the stage, is the most favoured (often royal or ducal) box (*see* MUNICH, fig.1 and THEATRE ARCHITECTURE, fig.5), though by the late 18th century many such special places were not at the back of the auditorium but on each side of the stage, near the proscenium arch (*see* THEATRE ARCHITECTURE, fig.6). The capacity of boxes varies, six to eight being typical, and the seats are sometimes individual chairs (a hazard in case of panic). The best boxes had (some still have) anterooms for the convenience of patrons, containing whatever amenities they might wish. In some court theatres, as at Versailles and Drottningholm, there are private boxes with lattice façades allowing one to see the show without being seen (see fig.14).

Rear seats in boxes, especially those along the sides near the proscenium, have poor sightlines, but recently architects have designed tiers of side arms reaching into the auditorium, as at the Berlin Deutsche Oper (1961, fig.5 above), with all seats orientated towards the stage.

14. Auditorium of the Drottningholm court theatre (1766) showing the boxes (one with latticed front for incognito members of the audience), bench seating, and centrally-placed seats for royalty

A degree of box-like segregation is achieved by a stepped-down design that also improves the sightlines for those sitting further back.

The names of the levels of boxes vary from country to country and even theatre to theatre. The simplest and most descriptive in English are first tier, second tier, or first circle, second circle, and so on. Designations such as dress and family circle are attempts by managers to indicate acceptable fashions. Access to the box levels is sometimes by way of an entrance through which patrons going to other seating areas also pass, but in most older theatres different seating areas are reached by separate ways.

Boxes could on occasion be created on the stage; in Baroque France the practice of permitting spectators on stage was so common (until they were banned by Voltaire in 1759) that plans of theatres show relatively permanent, railed-in, bench seating along the sides of the acting area (see fig.12; *see also* ORCHESTRA, fig.6), quite ruining any effect the scenery might have had. The practice was also common in London until David Garrick banished stage spectators in 1762.

Above the tiers of boxes, along the sides and back of an opera auditorium, are open balconies or galleries with each higher level raked more steeply to improve sightlines (fig.11; *see also* SOCIOLOGY OF OPERA, fig.3). The highest and least expensive seats (in the top balcony, gallery, amphitheatre – however designated) sometimes have a fair view of the stage floor but no view of the setting; hence the 'peanut gallery', 'gods', '*paradis*'. Along the sides on the uppermost level are sometimes desks with lamps for people following scores. The cheaper the seats the more difficult and dingy the access to them, the plainer the bar and lounge (if any), the harder the seats once you get to them, and the poorer the sightlines. The sound, however, is not always as bad in the worst seats as one would expect and is often far better than in the most expensive seats near the stage.

LS

E. O. Sachs and E. A. E. Woodrow: *Modern Opera Houses and Theatres* (London, 1896–8)

S. T. Worsthorne: *Venetian Opera in the Seventeenth Century* (Oxford, 1954, enlarged 2/1968)

T. E. Lawrenson: *The French Stage and Playhouse in the XVIIth Century* (Manchester, 1957, 2/1986)

M. Baur-Heinhold: *The Baroque Theatre: a Cultural History of the 17th and 18th Centuries* (New York, 1967)

B. Gascoigne: *World Theatre* (Boston, 1968)

R. Leacroft and H. Leacroft: *Theatre and Playhouse* (London, 1984)

EDWARD A. LANGHANS

Seattle. American city, in the state of Washington. Founded in 1851 and incorporated in 1869, it began to develop as an artistic centre in the late 19th century. The first recognized theatre in Seattle was Squire's Opera House, established in 1879. Five years later Frye's Opera House (cap. 1300), said to be the largest opera theatre north of San Francisco, was opened. The first opera performed in Seattle was *Carmen*, presented by the Metropolitan Opera's touring company under Maurice Grau in November 1899, with Emma Calvé and Giuseppe Campanari in the leading roles. John Spargur conducted English versions of *Carmen* and Gounod's *Faust* at the Metropolitan Theatre in 1914 with the Stand Grand Opera Company of Seattle, founded the same year. The impresario Cecilia Schultz presented *La traviata* at the 1650-seat Moore Theater (built 1907) in 1940; she helped establish the Northwest Grand Opera Association, in 1951 and brought many great artists to Seattle over 30 years. Two other forerunners of the Seattle Opera were the Festival Opera Company, established by Stanley Chapple, and the Wester Opera Company. The Seattle Opera Association, founded in the early 1960s by Glynn Ross, its first general director, presented the world premières of Floyd's *Of Mice and Men* in 1970 and Pasatieri's *Black Widow* in 1972. In 1975 he initiated the Pacific Northwest Wagner Festival, held each summer, at which productions of Wagner's entire *Ring* cycle have been given both in German and in English. Speight Jenkins, who succeeded Ross in 1983, initiated a new production of the cycle (in German, with English surtitles) in 1985 with *Die Walküre* (the full cycle was given in 1986). In 1989 *Die Meistersinger* was the focus of the festival, supported by a conference on the opera, and the following year *War and Peace* was given. The festival returned to the *Ring* in 1991. In its regular season in 1988, the Seattle Opera presented the first production in the USA of Gluck's *Orphée et Euridice* (the 1774 version), and the first West Coast production of Glass's *Satyagraha*. In 1989 the company presented Massenet's *Werther* in his own revision for baritone, recently discovered in Rome.

*

J. Burks: 'Opera is Alive and Well in Seattle', *ON*, xxxiii/13 (1968–9), 14–16

M. Salem: *Organizational Survival in the Performing Arts: the Making of the Seattle Opera* (New York, 1976)

R. Downey: 'Seattle: Towards the *Ring*', *Opera* (1985), festival issue, 119–22

MAXINE CUSHING GRAY

Sébastian [Sebestyen], **Georges** (*b* Budapest, 17 Aug 1903; *d* nr Paris, 12 April 1989). French conductor of Hungarian birth. He studied at the Budapest Academy and with Walter in Munich, joining the staff of the Munich Opera in 1922 (then under Walter) and of the Metropolitan Opera in 1923. After holding posts at Hamburg and Leipzig between 1924 and 1927 he became principal conductor at the Berlin Städtische Oper (1927–31), during which time he gave the first Berlin performances of Bartók's *Bluebeard's Castle* and Krenek's *Jonny spielt auf*. After working as music director of Moscow Radio he moved to the USA, appearing at the San Francisco Opera; he also conducted in Argentina and Brazil. After World War II he returned to Europe; he made his début at the Paris Opéra in 1947 with *Rigoletto*, settled in Paris and took French nationality. He became principal conductor at the Opéra, giving several important Wagner performances with Flagstad and presiding over the début there of Callas in 1958 in a concert which also included a staged account of *Tosca* Act 2 (with Gobbi). He conducted at the Opéra-Comique and at various festivals including Aix-en-Provence (*Ariadne auf Naxos* in 1966 with Crespin and Troyanos). His commercial recordings are few; they include *Mignon* and *Thaïs* (both 1952), excerpts from *Lucia di Lammermoor* with Mesplé (1960) and *Iphigénie en Tauride* with Crespin from a live performance in 1964 at the Teatro Colón, Buenos Aires.

CHRISTIANE SPIETH-WEISSENBACHER, NOËL GOODWIN

Sebenico, Giovanni [Šibenčanin, Ivan] (*b* ?Šibenik, Croatia, *c*1640; *d* Cividale del Friuli or Corbola, Veneto, Nov 1705). Composer of Croatian origin. Probably a pupil of Legrenzi, he worked as vice-*maestro di cappella* at Cividale del Friuli, 1660–63, and as a tenor at St Mark's, Venice, 1663–6. He was next at Charles II's court in London, in 1668 as 'Master of Italian Music', returning to Italy in 1673 to become *maestro di cappella* at the court of Savoy in Turin, a position he held until 1690. He was then most probably in Venice for two years before returning to Cividale del Friuli in 1692 as *maestro di cappella*.

In his own day Sebenico was best known as a performer and as a composer of operas. The two operas he is known to have written were performed in Turin – *L'Atalanta* (Bianca; Teatrino della Venaria Reale, 6 Dec 1673) and *Leonida in Sparta* (1689). *Leonida in Sparta* was given a new libretto (although the music was unchanged) and was performed in Venice at SS Giovanni e Paolo in 1692, as *L'oppresso sollevato*. The music to both operas is believed to be lost, but the librettos of *Leonida in Sparta* and *L'oppresso sollevato* have survived.

*

M. M. Velimirović: 'Giovanni Sebenico (prispevek k biografiji)', *MZ*, i (1965), 49–58

LOVRO ŽUPANOVIĆ

Šebor, Karel Richard (*b* Brandýs-nad-Laben, 13 Aug 1843; *d* Prague, 17 May 1903). Czech composer and conductor. He studied the violin and composition (with J. B. Kittl) at the Prague Conservatory, 1854–60. He began his theatrical career as a conductor in Erfurt, then worked in 1865 as second conductor and chorus master at the Czech opera (at the Provisional Theatre) in Prague and in 1866–70 as third conductor. After disagreements with the management he decided to leave Czech musical life. He worked in many places abroad, and became conductor of the opera orchestra in Lemberg (now L'viv, Ukraine), 1870–71, then for a short time was conductor of the Carltheater in Vienna. In 1900 he returned to Czech musical life and became a member of a committee which drew up the repertory of the National Theatre in Prague.

Šebor's impact as a composer was considerable. His historical romantic opera *Templáři na Moravě* ('The Templars in Moravia', 1865) received its première when he was 22; the first Czech opera to an original Czech text to be produced after František Škroup's *Dráteník* ('The Tinker'), it was given at the first permanent Czech stage in Prague, the Provisional Theatre. The musical public hailed it as a promise of the long-expected Czech national opera, and at the time Šebor was considered a rival of Smetana. In the opera Šebor followed the concept of French *grand opéra* and succeeded in mastering both its dramatic and its theatrical qualities (the concert performances in Plzeň and Litomyšl in 1981 confirmed this, revealing music of remarkable dramatic power). The successful run was interrupted by the composer himself owing to financial disagreements; there were only eight performances up to 1867.

The Templars was followed in close succession by two further Czech operas, and Šebor seemed to be devoting his efforts exclusively to national opera. The 'grand romantic opera' *Drahomíra* (1867) was also a success, receiving 19 performances. Its subject matter is more strictly historical, and concerns the Czech legend of Wenceslas and the dramatic power of the female protagonist, a Czech counterpart to Lady Macbeth. This work as a whole conforms more to the contemporary trends in Italian opera. Šebor's greatest success, however, was the 'grand romantic opera' *Nevěsta husitská* ('The Hussite Bride'), which had 43 performances in Prague between 1868 and 1894 and was among the representative Czech works prepared for the International Exhibition of Music and Theatre in Vienna in 1892 (in the end this production was not realized). The opera was originally written to a German text and subsequently translated into Czech; in the 1870s, when trying to have it staged in Vienna, Šebor revised it using a new German text. The libretto, based on a conflict of love and duty in 15th-century Bohemia, makes full use of the types of dramatic situation characteristic of

French *grand opéra*. This influence is obvious also in the use of quotation, in this case of the Hussite chorale *Ktož jsú boží bojovníci* ('Ye who are God's warriors'); Šebor thus initiated the symbolic use of this chorale in Czech music by Smetana, Dvořák, Bendl, Suk and others. The opera has long integrated sections, with a through-composed orchestral part playing an important role. Šebor's 'fantastic romantic opera' *Blanka* (1870) was surprisingly withdrawn from the repertory after four performances. The reasons for the disagreements about this work and for Šebor's departure from Prague are not yet clear. It too was written to a German text and later translated into Czech, but the libretto, which deals with the interaction between the fairy world and that of medieval knights and monks, is not so clearcut and did not allow the public to identify with the characters. Conforming with Šebor's compositional development as a whole, the opera tends to use large structural units and vast dramatic scenes, and in some ways integrates the influences of contemporary Italian and German opera.

After leaving Prague Šebor seemed to have abandoned Czech opera. In fact he was working on a new version of *The Hussite Bride*, and it is now clear that he also orchestrated the operas *Svatojanské proudy* ('The St John's Rapids') and *Záviš z Falkenštejna* ('Záviš of Falkenstein') for his friend J. R. Rozkošný. In an attempt to reserve Šebor's talent for Czech opera, he was offered a comic libretto, *Zmařená svatba* ('The Frustrated Wedding'). He was obviously not at ease with the folklike character of this text, which suggested a comic number opera with spoken dialogue. His setting uses intentionally simple structures, and the music is rather primitive, especially in the solo songs. Again a successful series of performances (ten in 1879–80) was interrupted, because of Šebor's financial demands. The composer lost interest in the work; he did not replace the spoken dialogue with recitatives as he had intended, and he failed even to realize his further operatic plans. With the exception of some incidental music he wrote only one more work for the stage, the ballet *Memoiren aus dem Zauberreich*, which was turned down by the National Theatre in Prague in 1890 because of its high production expenses and unrealistic technical demands. Šebor's works demonstrate the high standard of Czech operatic composition that surrounded the masterpieces of Smetana and Dvořák. They remain to be fully assessed from the standpoint of musicology as well as that of theatrical practice.

all first performed in Prague

Templáři na Moravě [the Templars in Moravia] (historical romantic op, 3, K. Sabina), Provisional, 19 Oct 1865, *CS-Bm**, excerpts, vs (Prague, n.d.; Hamburg, n.d.)

Drahomíra (grand romantic op, 4, J. Böhm, after F. Šír), Provisional, 20 Sept 1867, *Bm**

Nevěsta husitská [The Hussite Bride] (grand romantic op, 5, E. Rüffer, trans.), New Town, 27 Sept 1868, *Bm**, love duet, Act 3, vs (Prague, n.d.); rev. (Ger. lib. rev. T. Fallerau, trans.), *Pnd*, extract in Burghauser

Blanka (fantastic romantic op, 4, Rüffer, trans.), Provisional, 8 March 1870, *Bm**

Zmařená svatba [The Frustrated Wedding] (national op, 3, M. Červinková-Riegrová, after Fr. vaudeville Le petit Pierre), Provisional, 25 Oct 1879, *Bm**, excerpts, vs (Prague, n.d.; Hamburg, n.d.)

*

E. Chvála: *Ein Vierteljahrhundert böhmischer Musik* (Prague, 1887)

V. A. J. Hornové [V. Horn, A. Horn and J. Horn]: *Česká zpěvohra* [Czech Opera] (Prague, 1903)

L. Bráfová: *Rieger, Smetana, Dvořák* (Prague, 1913)

J. Bartoš: *Prozatímní divadlo a jeho opera* [The Provisional Theatre and its Opera] (Prague, 1938)

J. Plavec: 'Karel Šebor', *České umění dramatické*, ii: *Zpěvohra* [Czech Dramatic Art, ii: Opera], ed. J. Hutter and Z. Chalabala (Prague, 1941), 174–7

V. Svobodová: 'Opery Karla Šebora v Prozatímním divadle' [The Operas of Karel Šebor at the Provisional Theatre], *Časopis Moravského musea v Brně, vědy společenské*, xxxviii (1953), 150–62

J. Němeček: *Opera Národního divadla v období Karla Kovařovice 1900–1920* [The Opera of the National Theatre during the Kovařovic Era 1900–20] (Prague, 1968–9)

M. Pospíšil: 'Balada v české opeře 19. století' [The Ballad in Czech 19th-Century Opera], *HV*, xvi (1979), 3–25

M. Ottlová and M. Pospíšil: 'K problematice české historické opery 19. století' [The Problems of Czech Historical Operas of the 19th century], *HRo*, xxxiv (1981), 169–72; Ger. trans. in *The Musical Theatre: Brno XV 1980*, 267–81

——: 'Karel Šebor', *Mladá Smetanova Litomyšl 1981* (Prague, n.d.), 20–24 [programme]

J. Burghauser, ed.: *Národnímu divadlu: vklad zakladatelské generace* [Towards a National Theatre: the Investment by the Founding Generation] (Prague, 1983)

M. Ottlová: 'Die französische grand opéra in der Entwicklung der tschechischen Nationaloper', *2. Romantikkonferenz: Dresden 1982*, 82–90; Eng. summary in *Muzyka*, xxix (1984), 50–51

O. Hostinský: *Z hudebních bojů let sedmdesátých a osmdesátých: výbor z operních a koncertních kritik* [From the Musical Battles of the 1870s and 80s: a Selection of Opera and Concert Reviews], ed. E. Vítová (Prague, 1986)

J. Tyrrell: *Czech Opera* (Cambridge, 1988)

MARTA OTTLOVÁ, MILAN POSPÍŠIL

Secco (It.: 'dry'). Short for *recitativo secco*. A 19th-century term for RECITATIVE accompanied (normally) by a harpsichord or other keyboard instrument (in some contexts with a cello and/or a double bass) rather than by the orchestra.

Sechter, Simon (*b* Friedberg, Bohemia, 11 Oct 1788; *d* Vienna, 10 Sept 1867). Austrian composer. Though known to posterity as a music theorist and teacher (among his pupils were Schubert, briefly, and Bruckner), he was also an extremely prolific composer. He moved to Vienna in 1804. In 1824 he was appointed assistant Hoforganist, and succeeded Voříšek as principal Hoforganist the following year. From 1851 until 1863 he was professor of thoroughbass and counterpoint at the Vienna Academy. He seems not to have begun writing operas until he was in his 50s, and all five of his known stage works were probably composed within a ten-year period (no firm date is known for *Des Müllers Ring*). *Ali Hitsch-Hatsch*, his only performed opera, was also one of his few published works. A commentator observed of this opera: 'if one took no notice of the text one believed one was listening to veritable church music' (*AMZ*, 1871). The libretto of *Melusine*, by Sechter's pupil Grillparzer, was originally intended for Beethoven and had been set by Conradin Kreutzer in 1833.

Das Testament des Magiers, 1842 (Posse, 3)

Ezzeline, die unglückliche Gefangene aus Delikatesse, 1843 (komische Oper), unperf.

Ali Hitsch-Hatsch (3, Ernst Heiter ['Serious Merry', pseud. of a pupil of Sechter]), Vienna, Josefstadt, 12 Nov 1844, vs (Vienna, *c*1845)

Melusine, 1851 (romantische Oper, 3, F. Grillparzer), unperf.

Des Müllers Ring (Localunsinn, 3), unperf.

*

S. Sechter: 'Einiges über mich selbst', *Wiener allgemeine Musikzeitung*, nos.153–4 (1845), 619–20

'Vermischte literarische Mitteilungen', *AMZ*, new ser., vi (1871), 606

C. F. Pohl: *Simon Sechter* (Vienna, 1888)

MAURICE J. E. BROWN/CLIVE BROWN

Seckendorff, Karl Siegmund, Freiherr **von** (*b* Erlangen, 26 Nov 1744; *d* Ansbach, 26 April 1785). German amateur composer and courtier. In addition to his studies in law and literature at Erlangen, he may have studied music briefly at Bayreuth. After a decade of military service to Austria he joined the court of Duchess Anna Amalia at Weimar in late 1775. The Hofkapelle was placed under his supervision, and he took an active role in general artistic and literary activities at court. He translated *Werther* into French and composed music for several of Goethe's stage works, not always as the poet's first choice; Goethe maintained a rocky relationship with him and thought little of his music. Seckendorff also orchestrated compositions by the duchess, including her setting of Goethe's *Erwin und Elmire* (first version), and provided the libretto for E. W. Wolf's *Superba* and his own *Der Blumenraub* (both 1784). His stage music favours a simple idiom, tinged at times with folklike elements of the lied, to which he also contributed during his Weimar years. Disillusioned, he left the court in 1784 and moved as a Prussian diplomat to Ansbach, where he died soon after.

See also PROSERPINA.

all first performed at Weimar, Neues Theater

Lila (Spl, 4, J. W. von Goethe), 1777, *D-WRtl* [first version of text, now lost]

Proserpina (monodrama, 1, Goethe), 30 Jan 1778, *DS* [included in *Der Triumph der Empfindsamkeit* (1778)]

Jery und Bätely (Spl, 1, Goethe), 12 July 1780

Der Blumenraub (operette, 2, Seckendorff), 1784

*

W. Bode: *Die Tonkunst in Goethes Leben* (Berlin, 1912)

V. Knab: 'Karl Siegmund von Seckendorff (1744–1785): ein Beitrag zur Geschichte des deutschen volkstümlichen Liedes und der Musik am weimarischen Hof im 18. Jahrhundert', *Jahresbericht des Historischen Vereins für Mittelfranken*, lx (1914), 17–184

F. A. Hohenstein: *Weimar und Goethe* (Weimar, 1958)

THOMAS BAUMAN

Seconda donna. In 18th-century *opera seria* the seconda donna sang (as a rule) one of two female parts, less prominent than the PRIMA DONNA but still substantial; examples are Celia in Mozart's *Lucio Silla* and Servilia in his *La clemenza di Tito*. With the late 18th-century inflation of titles denoting status she came to be known by the euphemism *altra* ['other'] prima donna; perhaps because the Rome courts in 1835 chose to interpret this term literally, at the impresario's expense, a secondary but substantial woman's part (such as Fenena in Verdi's *Nabucco*, 1842) was later known as comprimaria. The term seconda donna was now applied to small parts, typically those of confidantes or nurses. A Genoa court confirmed in 1866 that seconda parts were inferior in status to comprimarie.

*

G. Valle: *Cenni teorico-pratici sulle aziende teatrali* (Milan, 1823), 35–45

P. Ascoli: *Della giurisprudenza teatrale* (Florence, 1871), 101–2

E. Rosmini: *La legislazione e la giurisprudenza dei teatri* (Milan, 1872), 158–62

JOHN ROSSELLI

Secondary title. *See* ALTERNATIVE TITLE.

Secret, The [*Tajemství*]. Comic opera in three acts by BEDŘICH SMETANA to a libretto by ELIŠKA KRÁSNOHORSKÁ; Prague, New Czech Theatre, 18 September 1878.

Malina *a town councillor*	bass
Miss Róza *his sister*	contralto
Blaženka *his daughter*	soprano
Kalina *a town councillor*	baritone
Vít *his son (a hunter)*	tenor
Bonifác *a retired soldier*	baritone
Skřivánek *a ballad-singer*	tenor
Master Mason	baritone
Landlady	soprano
Jirka *a bell-ringer*	tenor
Spirit of Friar Barnabáš	baritone
Bagpiper	silent

Town councillors, neighbours, young lads and lasses, threshers, bricklayers, ghosts and apparitions in Kalina's dream

Setting Bezděz and its environs at the end of the 18th century

After the success of *The Kiss* in early November 1876 Smetana was anxious to keep the same librettist, Eliška Krásnohorská, for his next opera. She at once (22 November 1876) hinted at a new libretto (the setting, she suggested, could be around the mountain of Bezděz – familiar summer holiday territory for Smetana) but it was not until 17 July 1877 that Smetana received the first instalment (Act 1). Six days later he began his pencil sketch and on 30 September, contrary to his practice, began orchestrating this single act, which he completed on 6 December. He received the remaining two acts on 19 October 1877 and by 31 January 1878 had completed the pencil sketch of Act 2 and 419 bars of the orchestration (completing that on 4 April). Act 3 was complete in full score on 31 May 1878, the overture on 15 July. With few exceptions Smetana set every word that was given him, his only requests were to enlarge parts for favoured singers: an independent song for Bonifác (Karel Čech) and an extension of Kalina's aria (for Josef Lev). Bonifác's song was added after Smetana had completed his piano sketch of Act 2; Kalina's aria – an extension of 115 bars – was introduced at the 11th performance (28 February 1879).

Smetana composed all the main parts for singers he knew from the Provisional Theatre company. As with *The Kiss*, the première was conducted by Adolf Čech and produced by Edmund Chvalovský. The public did not take to *The Secret* as enthusiastically as to *The Kiss*: by the time of Smetana's death in 1884 it had been performed only 24 times, and it has never been one of Smetana's more popular operas.

Like *Dalibor*, *The Secret* is virtually a monothematic opera. The motto theme (ex.1) announced in the Largo

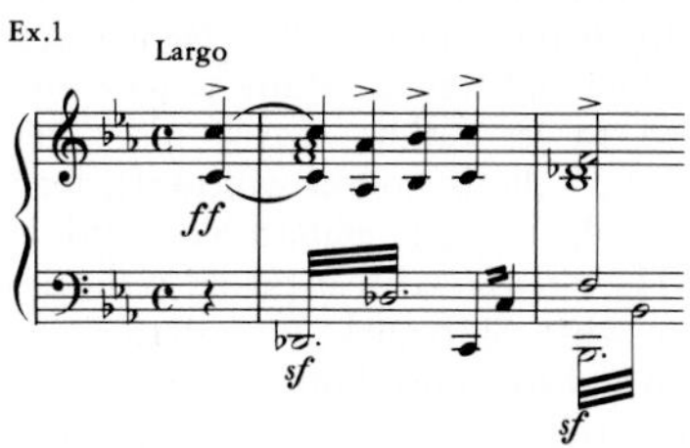

opening of the independent overture soon gives way to an Allegro vivo variant on which the greater part of the

'The Secret' (Smetana): scenes from the original production at the New Czech Theatre, Prague, 18 September 1878; engraving after a drawing by Ant. Gareise

overture is built, concluding with a four-part fugato and accelerating to a brilliant finish.

ACT 1 *The square of a small town below Bezděz, Malina's house on the right, Kalina's new house on the left* *The Secret* is one of only four Smetana operas to begin with a chorus, here threshers, the sound of whose flails is heard as the curtain rises. The solo characters introduced in quick succession include the retired soldier Bonifác, Miss Róza (on whom Bonifác has designs), her brother Malina and Kalina. Many years earlier Malina had refused to let Kalina marry his sister. Kalina married another (he is now a widower), leaving Miss Róza resentful, himself embittered, and the town polarized. These tensions are exposed in the next scenes, for instance when Skřivánek the ballad-singer arrives. He is instructed to praise both parties in his strophic song, but his attempts end in a row – a spirited ensemble for chorus and seven soloists followed by bitter recriminations between Kalina and Róza. She maintains that their adviser, the late Friar Barnabáš, promised that he would show Kalina a secret that could unite them (ex.1 is heard in the orchestra), but Kalina denies he knows any such secret. As the sun sets the arrival of a bagpiper adds another diversion which again becomes a pretext for factional violence. This time it is their children, Blaženka and Vít, who appeal to their fathers to stop. Blaženka goes off with her aunt, leaving Vít, as darkness falls, to express his love for her in a brief Andante amoroso.

Bonifác, meanwhile, has picked up an old document that has surfaced in the building of Kalina's house and gives it to Kalina – it is in Friar Barnabáš's hand. Kalina pockets it and extracts a promise from Vít and Bonifác not to tell anyone about it. Kalina goes off with Vít. Left alone with the Master Mason, Bonifác immediately tells him the secret, naturally first demanding his silence. In the same way the secret is passed on to the Landlady and a couple of women neighbours, and then to Jirka. In a final scene Blaženka and Vít agree to meet on Bezděz. They celebrate the 'secret' of their love in a brief duet while Jirka, now in his bell-tower, calls down to

Skřivánek with Kalina's rather different secret.

ACT 2 *On Bezděz, an overgrown, rocky landscape with ruins of a monastery and a castle in the distance* Kalina is introduced by a short prelude. In a long *scena* he declares that he is deeply in debt – the building of the house is just bravado – and expresses his divided emotions about Miss Róza and his desire for riches. He falls asleep and in his dreams he hears Friar Barnabáš calling up earth spirits guarding a treasure. This small ensemble soon mingles with a more pious chorus, a hymn sung by a procession of young girls led by Skřivánek. Kalina is abashed and leaves. Blaženka and Vít meet and sing an exultant duet, but the unpleasant reality of their situation intrudes and, in a long solo, Blaženka has to reassure Vít of her undying love. Vít responds defiantly: let the whole world know their secret. It soon does, in the shape of all the townspeople who have come on the pilgrimage up the mountain. The concertato ensemble that this discovery provokes reverses Italian tradition: a *presto* stretta, then, after the children's vain appeal to their fathers, a touching Largo, 'O klamné domnění' ('Oh vain delusion'). In a solo Miss Róza regrets that Kalina had not similarly defied her brother. This encourages Bonifác to try his luck, singing a song of his military prowess to impress her. However, his most powerful argument is that by marrying him she would be punishing the 'treacherous Kalina'. He is about to disclose the 'secret' (Miss Róza duly swears) when a resolute Kalina appears with a lamp and a shovel. Friar Barnabáš's instructions have led him to Bezděz – the entrance to his treasure is here. Kalina descends into the tunnel and cannot be restrained even by the pleas of Miss Róza.

ACT 3 *A room in Malina's house at midnight* The act opens with a chorus framing a strophic 'folksong' sung by Blaženka. The townsfolk gathered here include Miss Róza and the Master Mason, who in a trio plead with Malina to allow Blaženka to marry Vít. He agrees, providing Kalina comes to ask in person. Strange bangings frighten the company; to keep up their spirits Skřivánek is told to sing. He does so (a three-verse song with Bonifác then the chorus joining in the refrain). But when the bangings resume everyone except Miss Róza runs away. A hole opens up and Kalina appears – the secret passage from the mountain has led to Malina's house. The couple are at last united when both realize Friar Barnabáš's intention: Miss Róza was to be Kalina's 'treasure' and the company returns to find them embracing. Kalina asks Malina for Blaženka for his son and Róza for himself. To the joy of the company both requests are granted.

* * *

Although containing many of the same ingredients as its predecessor *The Kiss*, *The Secret* has never had the same appeal for Czech audiences. It shares the same gentle lyricism and message of reconciliation, but the humour is forced, and with its more complicated story and larger cast there is less room for the psychological development of its characters. JOHN TYRRELL

Secunde, Nadine (*b* Independence, OH, 21 Dec 1953). American soprano. She studied at Oberlin, at Indiana University with Margaret Harshaw and in Stuttgart. In 1980 she was engaged at Wiesbaden. In 1985 she moved to Cologne, making her début as Kát'a. She has sung in Karlsruhe, Munich, Hamburg, Vienna, Zürich, and at Bayreuth, where she sang Elsa and Sieglinde. In 1988 she made her Covent Garden début as Elsa and sang Elisabeth (*Tannhäuser*) in Chicago. Her repertory includes Elvire (*La muette de Portici*), Eva, Freia, Mařenka, Jenůfa, Arabella and Ariadne. In 1991 she sang Cassandra (*Les Troyens*) at Los Angeles and Chrysothemis (*Elektra*) at San Francisco. She has a vibrant, flexible voice of great tonal beauty and is a powerful actress. ELIZABETH FORBES

Sedaine, Michel-Jean (*b* Paris, 2 June 1719; *d* Paris, 17 May 1797). French librettist and playwright. He was the most successful and most important librettist of *opéra comique* in the later 18th century, taking a major role in the transformation of that genre from its mid-century identity (dominated by Favart) to its operatic maturity at the outset of the Revolution. He collaborated with the leading exponents of *opéra comique*: Philidor, Monsigny and Grétry.

Sedaine began his career as a stone-mason and apprentice architect. By his 30s he was writing poetry while still engaged on building projects. In 1752 his *Pièces fugitives de M. S+++* appeared, and in 1756 *Le vaudeville*, a 'poème didactique'. He collected his works in a *Recueil de poésies de M. Sedaine* (1760, 2/1780). In 1754, attracted by his verse, Jean Monnet (manager of the Opéra-Comique) tried to persuade him to write for the company. He did not succeed until 1756, when Sedaine adapted *Le diable à quatre* from Coffey's *The Devil to Pay* (*see* PARIS, fig.8). Its good reception did not deflect Sedaine from 'making houses' (Sedaine 1841–3). In 1759 Monnet's successor persuaded Sedaine to write again: he produced *Blaise le savetier* because of 'the pleasure in attempting a whole scene in music, one composed of several participants acting at the same time' (ibid). The result was an important quintet, 246 bars long, and other ensembles.

From then on he was naturally in demand, and could lay down the conditions that interested him. He continually expanded the scope of his field, always developing the constituent role of music. *Le roi et le fermier* (set by Monsigny, 1762) was one pivotal work, both for its theme of royal recognition of common justice and for its three-act length. The other pivotal collaboration with Monsigny was *Le déserteur* (1769), which had universal success. Its daring 'English' mixture of comedy and near-tragedy was as significant as its variety of musical ensembles and the through-composed final scenes.

In 1765 the Comédie-Française produced Sedaine's best play, *Le philosophe sans le savoir*, and in 1766 *Aline, reine de Golconde* succeeded at the Opéra: Sedaine thus had major works running simultaneously on the three leading stages of France. In the 1770s Sedaine developed his interest in subjects from the Middle Ages; the outstanding results, set by Grétry, were *Aucassin et Nicolette* (1779) and *Richard Coeur-de-lion* (1784).

By this time Sedaine's technique involved the total dramatic integration of music and disguising the moral fable that gave rise to his subject. He never lost the ability, shown in his early works, to create 'living' characters, if necessary using unconventional theatrical diction.

His mentor was Diderot, and he was greatly inspired by Shakespeare. The prefaces to his librettos discuss his precepts: that acting should not stop during the musical portions of a work; that acting directions must be specified; that complex ensembles are good and achieve effects unknown to the spoken theatre; and that drama must educate. His chosen subjects mark him as a *philosophe*, as do lines like 'Tous les hommes sont bons', sung in *Le déserteur*. Doubtless, he saw *opéra comique* as a vehicle for popularizing ideas. The extraordinary aspect of his work was his continual recognition that the librettist's job was to exploit the contribution of music; though, as Grétry put it, 'He was not at all a musician, sacrificing nothing to music, that is why his pieces have unity'.

Sedaine was elected to the Académie Française in 1786. In his acceptance speech he discussed the twin needs of dramatic language and music, and articulated the wish for 'a man gifted with the sublime talents of poetry and of music, carried to the same degree'.

LIBRETTOS

Anacréon (pastorale-héroïque en vaudevilles), 1754; *Le diable à quatre, ou La double métamorphose* (oc, partly 'en vaudevilles'), Baurans, F.-A. D. Philidor and J.-L. Laruette, 1756 (Gluck and others, 1759; B. Porta, 1790; J.-P. Solié, 1809); *Blaise le savetier* (oc), Philidor, 1759; *L'huître et les plaideurs, ou Le tribunal de la chicane* (oc), Philidor, 1759; *Les troqueurs dupés* (cmda), C. Sodi, 1760; *On ne s'avise jamais de tout* (oc), P.-A. Monsigny, 1761; *Le bon compères, ou Les bons amis* (oc), J.-B. de La Borde, 1761, as Les bons amis; *Le jardinier et son seigneur* (oc), Philidor, 1761

Le roi et le fermier (comédie mêlée de morceaux de musique), Monsigny, 1762; *L'anneau perdu et retrouvé* (oc), La Borde, 1764 (L.-C.-A. Chardiny, 1788); *Rose et Colas* (comédie en prose et musique), Monsigny, 1764; *Aline, reine de Golconde* (ballet-héroïque), Monsigny, 1766; *Philémon et Baucis* (opéra), Monsigny, 1766; *Les sabots* (oc, after J. Cazotte), E. Duni, 1768; *Le déserteur* (drame mêlé de musique), Monsigny, 1769; *Thémire* (pastorale mêlée d'ariettes), Duni, 1770; *Le mort marié* (oc), F. Bianchi, 1771; *Le faucon* (oc), Monsigny, 1771

Le magnifique (comédie mise en musique, after J. de La Fontaine), A.-E.-M. Grétry, 1773; *Ernelinde* (tragédie-lyrique, after A. A. H. Poinsinet), Philidor, 1773; *Les femmes vengées* (oc), Philidor, 1775; *Félix, ou L'enfant trouvé* (comédie mise en musique), Monsigny, 1777; *Aucassin et Nicolette, ou Les moeurs du bon vieux temps* (comédie), Grétry, 1779; *Pagamin de Monègue* (opéra lyrico-comique), Monsigny, comp. 1782 (Porta, 1792, as Pagamin, ou Le calendrier des vieillards); *Thalie au nouveau théâtre* (prol.), Grétry, 1783; *Richard Coeur-de-lion* (comédie mise en musique), Grétry, 1784

Alcine (opéra, with N. E. Framery), Lacépède, 1785; *Amphitryon* (opéra, after Molière), Grétry, 1786; *Le comte d'Albert* (drame, after La Fontaine), Grétry, 1786; *La Suite du Comte d'Albert* (oc), Grétry, 1786; *Raoul Barbe-bleue* (cmda, after C. Perrault), Grétry, 1789; *Guillaume Tell* (drame, after A.-M. Lemierre), Grétry, 1791; *Basile, ou A trompeur, trompeur et demi* (after M. de Cervantes), Grétry, 1792; *La blanche haquenée* (oc), Porta, 1793; *Robin et Marion*, Monsigny, lib. dated 1795, unperf.; *Protogène* (opéra), unperf.; *L'amoureux goutteux* (oc), S. Champein, n.d., rev. 1807 [cited in Brenner 1947]

*

M.-J. Sedaine: *Discours de réception* [1786, on his election to the Académie Française], repr. in *Choix de discours de réception à l'Académie française*, ii (Paris, 1808), 339ff

A. D'Origny: *Annales du Théâtre italien depuis son origine jusqu'à ce jour* (Paris, 1788)

A.-E.-M. Grétry: *Mémoires, ou Essais sur la musique* (Paris, 2/1797)

Obituary, *Almanach des spectacles de Paris ... pour l'an VIII* (Paris, 1799), 300–04

[M.-J. Sedaine]: 'Quelques réflexions inédites de Sedaine sur l'opéra comique', in *Théâtre choisi de G. Pixérécourt*, iv (Paris, Nancy, 1841–3), 501–16

M. Gisi: *Sedaine: sein Leben und sein Werk* (Berlin, 1883)

L. Günther: *L'oeuvre dramatique de Sedaine* (Paris, 1908)

A.-E.-M. Grétry: *Réflexions d'un solitaire*, ed. L. Solvay and E. Closson (Brussels and Paris, 1919–24), iii, 97

C. D. Brenner: *A Bibliographical List of Plays in the French Language 1700–1789* (Berkeley, 1947, 2/1979)

M. A. Rayner: *The Social and Literary Aspects of Sedaine's Dramatic Work* (diss., U. of London, 1960)

D. Charlton: *Grétry and the Growth of Opéra-Comique* (Cambridge, 1986)

E. A. Cook: *The Operatic Ensemble in France, 1673–1775* (diss., U. of East Anglia, 1989)

M. Noiray: 'Les créations d'opéra à Paris de 1790 à 1794', *Orphée phrygien: les musiques de la Révolution*, ed. J. R. Julien and J. C. Klein (Paris, 1989), 193–204

DAVID CHARLTON

Sedgwick, Thomas (*d* Somers Town, London, 9 Oct 1803). English bass. Originally an ironmonger, he was taught to sing by the glee composer Richard Stevens and performed for clubs such as the Anacreontic Society. This led to a stage appearance as Artabanes in *Artaxerxes* in October 1787 and then a regular career at Drury Lane from 1788. He had limited acting abilities, but Storace wrote good songs for him in most of his English operas. In Attwood's pasticcios *The Prisoner* (1792) and *The Mariners* (1793) he performed adaptations of Figaro's and Sarastro's most famous arias.

*

BDA; *LS*

[F. G. Waldron]: *Candid and Impartial Strictures on the Performers* (London, 1795)

J. Roach: *Authentic Memoirs of the Green Room* (London, 1796)

OLIVE BALDWIN, THELMA WILSON

Sedlmair, Sophie (*b* Hanover, 25 Jan 1857; *d* Hanover, 14 Oct 1939). German soprano. She appeared first in operetta at Leipzig, then was engaged at Mainz, and at Dresden (1880–85). After a season in Amsterdam, appearances at the Thalia Theatre in New York (1887) and a spell in Berlin, she went to Vienna to renew her studies. In 1893 her career as a dramatic soprano began with what amounted to a second début, in *Fidelio* at Danzig. Guest performances at Budapest in 1896 were followed by a ten-year engagement at the Vienna Staatsoper. Her roles included both lyric and dramatic parts: in *Die Walküre*, for instance, she would sing either Brünnhilde or Sieglinde – the latter was said to have been a portrayal of 'magical tenderness'. In her single Covent Garden season (1897) she sang Isolde and the *Siegfried* Brünnhilde in performances with Jean de Reszke; *The Times* recognized her intelligence but thought the voice not quite powerful enough for the house. Her recordings show both the grandeur of the dramatic soprano and the spirited lightness of a singer experienced in operetta, but are marred by her excessive use of portamento.

J. B. STEANE

Seedo [Sidow], Mr (*b c*1700; *d* ?Prussia, *c*1754). German composer. His father may have come to London from Prussia as early as 1700, perhaps with Pepusch. By the mid-1720s Seedo was working at the Little Theatre in the Haymarket. In 1727 he married the singer Maria Manina. After Pepusch had helped to make *The Beggar's Opera* a success at Lincoln's Inn Fields, Seedo worked on imitations for Drury Lane from 1731 to 1734.

The Devil to Pay failed in its full-length version (42 airs), but as an afterpiece (16 airs) it was by far the most popular ballad opera of the century, apart from *The Beggar's Opera*; it was given regular London performances until well into the 19th century. In a translation by von Borcke it became popular in Germany as well, and was a major influence on the development of Singspiel. Like most ballad operas, it was originally published with only the melodies of the airs; for provincial productions someone on the spot must have provided the accompaniments. Thus it is that two early sets of MS parts survive for *The Devil to Pay* with completely different basses, and sometimes with instrumental preludes and postludes of a different length (*GB-Lbl* R.M. 21.c.43 and *Lcm* 2232). On 20 October 1740 the engraver George Bickham advertised in the *London Daily Post* a new edition 'with the Scene engrav'd in Picture Work on the top of each Song, as represented at the Old Playhouse', and 'a new Bass to the Whole'.

Bickham's basses cannot be by Seedo, and it may well be that the ones in the MS sets are not by him either. But Seedo arrangements (without preludes and postludes) were published anonymously for the 21 songs in *The Devil of a Duke*; an advertisement in other ballad opera librettos, for instance Robert Drury's *The Fancy'd Queen*, says they were 'Sett by Mr Seedo for the Spinnet, Harpsichord, German Flute, Violin and Hautboy, and a thorough bass to each Tune'. Seedo directed the band for all these ballad operas, and in the Drury Lane revival of Fielding's *The Author's Farce* he even spoke:

LUCKLESS: Mr Seedo, have you not provided a new overture for the occasion?
SEEDO [*in the orchestra pit*]: I have provided one.

This does not survive, and nor does the music for three more of Seedo's stage works: an all-sung masque, *Venus, Cupid and Hymen* (Drury Lane, 21 May 1733); the overture and incidental music for James Miller's comedy *The Mother-in-law* (Haymarket, 20 Feb 1734); and the music of *Harlequin in the City* (Goodman's Fields, 25 Sept 1734). About 1736, deep in debt, he went to Potsdam to work with the Royal Band.

Contribs. to ballad operas (all first performed at Drury Lane): The Devil to Pay [1 song] (C. Coffey), afterpiece version, 16 Aug 1731; The Lottery [10 songs] (H. Fielding), 1 Jan 1732; The Mock Doctor [3 songs] (Fielding, after Molière), 23 June 1732; The Devil of a Duke [1 song] (R. Drury), 17 Aug 1732; The Boarding School, or The Sham Captain [3 songs] (Coffey), 29 Jan 1733; The Author's Farce [1 song] (Fielding), revival, 15 Jan 1734

*

W. H. Rubsamen: 'Mr Seedo, Ballad Opera, and the *Singspiel*', *Miscelanea en homenaje a Monseñor Higini Anglès* (Barcelona, 1958–61), ii, 775–809
E. V. Roberts: 'Mr Seedo's London Career and his Work with Henry Fielding', *Philological Quarterly*, xlv/Jan (1966), 179–90
R. Fiske: *English Theatre Music in the Eighteenth Century* (London, 1973, 2/1986) ROGER FISKE/IRENA CHOLIJ

Seefehlner, Egon (*b* Vienna, 3 June 1912). Austrian administrator. After studying at Vienna University he pursued a business and literary career until he became, in 1946, secretary general of the Vienna Konzerthausgesellschaft, a post he held until 1951. He was deputy director of the Vienna Staatsoper (1954–61), during difficult years as assistant to Böhm, and later Karajan, and was appointed deputy general manager of the Deutsche Oper in West Berlin when it was established in 1961, becoming director general in 1972. In 1976 he became general administrator at the Vienna Staatsoper, leaving in 1986 when Claudio Abbado became musical director. DAVID CUMMINGS

Seefried, Irmgard (*b* Köngetried, Swabia, 9 Oct 1919; *d* Vienna, 24 Nov 1988). Austrian soprano of German birth. She studied with her father and at the age of 11 sang Gretel in Humperdinck's opera. After further study at the Augsburg conservatory she was engaged by Karajan for the Aachen Opera in 1939. In 1943 she made her début at the Vienna Staatsoper as Eva in *Die Meistersinger* under Karl Böhm, and remained a member of the company. She sang the Composer in the performance of *Ariadne auf Naxos* at Vienna in honour of Strauss's 80th birthday (1944). She became known for Mozart and Strauss roles, and after the war made a series of guest appearances in Europe and the USA. She first sang at Covent Garden with the Vienna Staatsoper in September 1947 (as Fiordiligi and Susanna), and soon became a regular soloist at such festivals as Salzburg, Edinburgh and Lucerne, as well as singing in some 20th-century works and developing a parallel career in lieder and recitals. Seefried's beautiful lyric soprano voice, charm and pleasing stage deportment soon made her a favourite, although she occasionally overplayed the soubrette aspects of some of her favourite Mozart and Strauss roles. Her last stage appearance was in the title role of *Kát'a Kabanová* in Vienna in 1976.

*

F. Fassbind: *Wolfgang Schneiderhan, Irmgard Seefried* (Berne, 1960)
E. Werba: 'Irmgard Seefried', *Opera*, xvii (1966), 611
J. Schumann: 'Irmgard Seefried Discography', *Fono-forum*, ix (1974), 812, 1226
A. Blyth: 'Irmgard Seefried: an Appreciation', *Opera*, xl (1989), 35–6 PETER BRANSCOMBE

Seelewig [*Das geistliche Waldgedicht oder Freudenspiel genant Seelewig* ('The Sacred Forest Poem or Play of Rejoicing called Seelewig')]. Singspiel in a sung prologue

'Seelewig' (S. T. Staden), Act 3 scene i: woodcut from G. P. Harsdörffer's 'Frawenzimmer Gesprächspiele', iv (Nuremberg, 1644)

and epilogue and three acts by SIGMUND THEOPHIL STADEN to a libretto by GEORG PHILIPP HARSDÖRFFER; Nuremberg, 1644.

Seelewig is the earliest Singspiel for which the music survives. It falls within the tradition of early sacred dramatic works (e.g. Cavalieri's *Rappresentazione*, 1600) in presenting, in pastoral guise, the struggle between the body and the soul. The cast of Seelewig (soprano), her antagonist Trügewalt (bass), three shepherdesses and three shepherds is supported by an instrumental ensemble of three violins, three flutes, three shawms and a horn. Staden's music is through-composed and, in the early German *Liedoper* tradition, adapts an italianate madrigal style to German strophic song.

Harsdörffer based his text on that of a Counter-Reformation school play, *Ein gar schön geistliches Waldgetichte genannt Die glückseelige Seele* (1637), which was a translation of Nicolò Negri's *L'Anima felice favola boschareccia* (Rome, 1606). The text and music were published in Harsdörffer's *Frawenzimmer Gesprächspiele* (vol. iv, Nuremberg, 1644), an eight-volume collection of conversational narratives; the commentary of the six participants in the narrative presents Harsdörffer's ideas about performing the work, with references to the sets, costumes and music.

Seelewig was to influence the development of German-language opera, notably through the works of the Nuremberg poet Sigmund von Birken (1626–81) and of Anton Ulrich, Duke of Brunswick-Wolfenbüttel. Sophie Elisabeth, Duchess of Brunswick-Wolfenbüttel, had a performance mounted at Wolfenbüttel in 1654, and it was revived at Augsburg in 1698. After a long period of neglect it was staged in the 1970s and 80s in Germany, the Netherlands and Oberlin, Ohio.

MARA R. WADE

Segalini, Sergio (*b* Castell'Arquato, 1 Dec 1944). French critic of Italian birth. He studied at the Sorbonne and soon became established as an authority on singing and opera and a broadcaster on the subject for Radio France. He was appointed editor of the journal *Opéra international* in 1979; he serves on singing and record juries and teaches at the Accademia Rossiniana, Pesaro. In 1991 he became artistic director of the Accademia di Osimo. His books include studies of several singers, including Callas, Schwarzkopf and Berganza, volumes on Meyerbeer and La Scala, and *Divas, parcours d'un mythe.*

CHARLES PITT

Segerstam, Leif (Selim) (*b* Vasa, 2 March 1944). Finnish conductor. He studied at the Sibelius Academy, Helsinki (1952–63), and then at the Juilliard School (1963–5). He was a conductor of the Finnish National Opera (1965–8) and the Royal Opera of Stockholm (1968–72, becoming chief conductor in 1971); he became chief conductor of the Deutsche Oper, Berlin (1971–3), and director of the Finnish National Opera (1973–4). In 1973 he conducted at Covent Garden (*Tosca*) and at the Metropolitan (*La bohème* and *Manon Lescaut*). A regular conductor at the Savonlinna Festival, he has conducted operas including *Boris Godunov* (1976), *Don Carlos* (1979–85), *Aida* and *Der fliegende Holländer* (both 1988). Also a prolific composer, he has eschewed the restraints of any system and has preserved an intuitive and colourful idiom at the expense of formal stringency.

ERIK WAHLSTRÖM

Segreto di Susanna, Il [*Susannens Geheimnis*] ('Susanna's Secret'). 'Intermezzo' in one act by ERMANNO WOLF-FERRARI to a libretto by ENRICO GOLISCIANI; Munich, Hoftheater, 4 December 1909.

This most frequently performed of Wolf-Ferrari's operas owes its success partly to its disarming simplicity. Lasting barely 45 minutes, with only two singing characters, it is conveniently cheap to produce; and the slender but distinctive idea of the libretto, combined with the elegant if rather miscellaneous charm of the music, has an obvious appeal which even subsequent cancer research has not seriously undermined.

The plot centres on a simple misunderstanding which is resolved only after repeated delays. Count Gil (baritone) smells tobacco smoke around his house, and jumps to the conclusion that his young wife Susanna (mezzo-soprano) must have a secret lover. This seems confirmed by the fact that he has once caught sight of her out in the street without his permission. But he eventually finds that she herself is the smoker, and that the destination of her secret outing was the tobacconist's shop. Gil celebrates their reconciliation by taking up smoking too.

The justly famous little overture establishes a zestfully comic atmosphere by almost literally imitating the manner and spirit of 18th-century *opera buffa*. The subsequent music also touches on a variety of more recent styles – with recognizable allusions to the opening of Debussy's *Prélude à l'après-midi d'un faune* to represent cigarette smoke. There is little attempt to disguise this extreme eclecticism, and Wolf-Ferrari's distinctive personal voice is only intermittently audible. Although this hardly matters in so unassuming a work, the result gives little idea of the composer's true stature, as seen in his best operas such as *I quatro rusteghi* and *Il campiello*.

JOHN C. G. WATERHOUSE

Seguin [née Childe], **Anne** [Ann] (*b* London, ?1809–14; *d* New York, Aug 1888). English soprano. After training at the RAM, she married the bass Arthur Seguin about 1831 and was engaged at the King's and Drury Lane theatres; in 1837 she sang Donna Anna in an English version of *Don Giovanni.* She appeared with success in the USA, particularly as Arline in *The Bohemian Girl.* On stage she was handsome, graceful and vivacious, and an accomplished actress.

*

'Seguin, Ann', *Appleton's Encyclopedia of American Biography* (New York, 1888)

NICHOLAS E. TAWA

Seguin, Arthur (Edward Shelden) (*b* London, 7 April 1809; *d* New York, 9 Dec 1852). English bass. He studied at the RAM, where he appeared in student performances of Italian operas. His professional début was as Polyphemus in Handel's *Acis and Galatea* in London in 1831; he also sang at Covent Garden (1833–4), the King's Theatre (Count Robinson in *Il matrimonio segreto*) and Drury Lane (1835–8). In 1838 he went to New York, making his début at the National Theatre in Rooke's *Amilie* on 13 October; he formed an opera company which toured in the USA and Canada. His voice was a deep bass, rich and even in quality; he was noted as a superlative actor. He was married to the soprano Anne Seguin (née Childe).

*

W. T. Parke: *Musical Memoirs*, ii (London, 1830), 266ff

Obituaries: *New York Daily Times* (14 Dec 1852); *Dwight's Journal of Music* (18 Dec 1852); *The Athenaeum* (22 Jan 1853)

Seguin Opera Company. English travelling company formed by Anne and Arthur Seguin, active in the USA from the early 1840s to 1852; the company dominated the performance of English-language opera in the USA during the 1840s, and it mounted the American première of Balfe's *The Bohemian Girl* in 1845. *See* TRAVELLING TROUPES, §5(i).

Segurola, Andrés de (*b* Valencia, 27 March 1874; *d* Barcelona, 22 Jan 1953). Spanish bass. He studied in Barcelona where he made his début in 1895. He made early appearances in France and at La Scala. From 1902 he sang at the Metropolitan Opera, notably as Alvise (*La Gioconda*), Colline, Varlaam and Geronte (*Manon Lescaut*). He created Jake in *La fanciulla del West* (1910) and Didier in Victor Herbert's *Madeleine* (1914), in addition to singing in the first Metropolitan performances of Rabaud's *Mârouf* (1917) and Mascagni's *Lodoletta* (1918). His stagecraft was particularly admired in the role of Leporello (1910, Salzburg). After his retirement in 1931 he taught in Hollywood and appeared in films (e.g. *One Night of Love*, with Grace Moore). DAVID CUMMINGS

Sehlbach, (Oswald) Erich (*b* Barmen, 18 Nov 1898; *d* Essen, 31 Oct 1985). German composer. He studied at the Leipzig Conservatory; later he became lecturer in composition and counterpoint and finally professor at the Essen Folkwangschule, where he was also director of opera classes. Writing in a style somewhere between Schoeck and Hindemith but entirely his own, he produced works in every genre. Except for *Baal* op.96 (composed in 1932, but revised in 1959), his operas date from before World War II, all of them to his own librettos. The manuscript scores of most of them were destroyed during the war, but printed vocal scores have survived.

Die Stadt op.17 (Sehlbach), Krefeld, 1935
Galilei op.19 (Sehlbach), Essen, 1937
Signor Caraffa op.21 (Sehlbach), Duisburg, 1938
Hadlaub op.42, 1940 (Sehlbach)
Baal op.96, 1932, rev. 1959 (Sehlbach) KLAUS L. NEUMANN

Seidel, Friedrich Ludwig (*b* Treuenbrietzen, 1 June 1765; *d* Berlin, 5 May 1831). German composer. He was a pupil of Georg Benda in Berlin, although Reichardt, who took him into his house, must have taught him a good deal. He lived in Berlin all his life. In 1792 he was organist at the Marienkirche, in 1801 assistant conductor at the Nationaltheater (at the instigation of B. A. Weber, who had heard his Singspiel *Claudine von Villa Bella*), in 1808 musical director of the royal chapel, and in 1822 court Kapellmeister. He was pensioned in 1830.

Besides *Claudine*, the score of which is now lost, Seidel wrote a number of operas and theatrical pieces, including *Der Dorfbarbier Zweiter Theil, oder Die Schmids-Wittwe* (one-act farce, a sequel to Schenk's opera; Berlin, 14 Dec 1807) and *Die Postkutsche zu Bocksdorf* (Lustspiel, 5, C. Reinhold, after Picard; Berlin, 15 Sept 1808). He also wrote three ballets and incidental music to plays by Goethe, Schiller and Shakespeare. Much of the vocal music was published, separately and in anthologies, between 1795 and 1815; most of the surviving MSS are in the Staatsbibliothek Preussischer Kulturbesitz, Berlin.

Seider, August (*b* Leverkusen, 11 Feb 1901; *d* Gräfelfing, 18 Nov 1989). German tenor. He made his début at Cologne in 1926 as Paolino in *Il matrimonio segreto*. After appearing at Halle, he was engaged at Leipzig (1930–45) and with the Bayerische Staatsoper, Munich (1946–61). He sang Walther at Salzburg in 1938 and made his Covent Garden début in 1947 as Tristan opposite Flagstad; in 1950 he sang Tristan at Rome opposite Callas. His roles included Max, Tannhäuser, Siegmund, the Drum Major (*Wozzeck*) and King Pollux, which he sang in the British première of *Die Liebe der Danae* during the visit of the Bayerische Staatsoper to Covent Garden in 1953. Though he did not have a voice of truly heroic quality or proportion, he was an intelligent singer and an excellent character actor. ELIZABETH FORBES

Seidl, Anton (*b* Pest, 7 May 1850; *d* New York, 28 March 1898). Austro-Hungarian conductor. Following studies with Hans Richter, he became a protégé of Wagner, in whose house he lived from 1872, and for whom he helped prepare the first complete performance of the *Ring* in 1876. Ever after Seidl's mission was to propagate the Wagner canon, and as an interpreter he consciously embodied the ideals set forth in Wagner's essay 'On Conducting'. He became chief conductor for Angelo Neumann's Leipzig Opera in 1879, and then for Neumann's Richard Wagner Opera Company in 1882–3, introducing the *Ring* throughout central Europe and in England. He subsequently conducted for Neumann's Bremen Opera (1883–5), and appeared with great success both at Covent Garden and Bayreuth in 1897. After 1885, however, Seidl's career was based in the USA. He became an American citizen and made New York his permanent home. He succeeded Leopold Damrosch as principal conductor at the Metropolitan Opera during the German seasons of 1885 to 1891, and led the New York Philharmonic Society from 1891 to 1898.

At the Metropolitan, assisted by a devoted ensemble including Lilli Lehmann and Albert Niemann, Seidl conducted the American premières of *Die Meistersinger* (1886), *Tristan und Isolde* (1886), *Siegfried* (1887), *Götterdämmerung* (1888) and *Das Rheingold* (1889). He also conducted abridged concert performances of *Parsifal* in Brooklyn (1890–91). Even in his orchestral programmes – in New York, in Brooklyn (including Brighton Beach, where he conducted 14 times a week during the summer) and on tour – Wagner's music was performed more than any other. Seidl became the central figure in an American Wagner cult. Arthur Farwell, in a typical encomium, wrote in 1944: 'For all those in any degree sensitive to the spirit of music and romance, the presence of Anton Seidl ... tinged the atmosphere and the consciousness of [New York City] with a peculiarly individual and glowing quality of feeling such as it has not known before or since'. In the USA, no other operatic conductor has ever exerted such influence. The discriminating response by New York to the interpretations of Wagner by Mahler and Toscanini at the Metropolitan before World War I bears eloquent testimony to Seidl's legacy.

H. T. Finck, ed.: *Anton Seidl: a Memorial by his Friends* (New York, 1899)
H. Krehbiel: *Chapters of Opera* (New York, 1909)
A. Farwell: 'America's Gain from a Bayreuth Romance: the Mystery of Anton Seidl', *MQ*, xxxv (1944), 448–57
J. Horowitz: 'Anton Seidl and America's Wagner Cult', *Wagner in Performance*, ed. B. Millington and S. Spencer (New Haven and London, 1992) JOSEPH HOROWITZ

Seidl-Kraus [née Kraus], **Auguste** (*b* Vienna, 28 Aug 1853; *d* Kingston, NY, 17 July 1939). Austrian soprano. She studied with Mathilde Marchesi in Vienna, making her début at the Hofoper in 1877 singing minor roles. In 1879 she sang Wellgunde and the Woodbird in the first Vienna performance of the *Ring*. In 1881 she was engaged at Leipzig, where she met the conductor Anton Seidl, whom she later married. She took part in Angelo Neumann's Wagner tour of Europe in 1882, visiting London (Her Majesty's Theatre), Paris, Switzerland and Italy. In 1883 she was engaged at Bremen and the following year sang at the Metropolitan, making her début as Elisabeth (*Tannhäuser*). Between 1885 and 1888 she sang Sieglinde, the Woodbird and Gutrune in the first New York *Ring* cycle, and also Elsa, Eva and Maria (Nessler's *Der Trompeter von Säkkingen*). She retired in 1898. ELIZABETH FORBES

Seinemeyer, Meta (*b* Berlin, 5 Sept 1895; *d* Dresden, 19 Aug 1929). German soprano. She studied in Berlin, making her début there in 1918 at the Deutsches Opernhaus in *Orphée aux enfers*. She remained there until 1925, singing such roles as Elsa, Elisabeth, Agathe and Countess Almaviva. In 1923–4 she toured the USA with Hurok's German Opera Company, singing Elisabeth and Eva in New York. After a guest appearance as Marguerite at the Dresden Staatsoper, she was engaged there from 1925 until her death; she created the Duchess of Parma in Busoni's *Doktor Faust* (1925), sang Maddalena in the German première of *Andrea Chénier* (1926), and also Manon Lescaut and Leonora in *La forza del destino*. She appeared at the Colón, Buenos Aires (1926), the Vienna Staatsoper (1927) and Covent Garden (1929), where she sang Sieglinde, Eva and Elsa a few months before her death from leukaemia. As her recordings demonstrate, she had a highly individual voice, dark-toned and moving, while her singing displayed the spontaneity often attributed to Lotte Lehmann.

*

J. Dennis: 'Meta Seinemeyer', *Record Collector*, xiv (1961–2), 158–68 [with discography by J. W. C. Hesser]

LEO RIEMENS/ELIZABETH FORBES

Sekar-Rozhansky [Rozhansky], **Anton Vladislavovich** (*b* 6/18 May 1863; *d* 28 Jan 1952). Russian tenor. He graduated from the St Petersburg conservatory in 1891 and for the next five years sang at opera houses in Rostov, Kharkiv and Tbilisi. He made a successful début at the Mariinsky Theatre in 1896, but after only two months left St Petersburg for Moscow, joining Zimin's Private Opera company, where he was principal tenor until 1914. He had a big voice, strongest in the middle register and baritonal in quality: it was said that when he sang in duet with Battistini it was hard to tell which was the baritone. He was criticized for poor diction and intonation, faults offset by his imposing stage presence and brilliant acting. The title role in Rimsky-Korsakov's *Sadko* was written for him, as was an interpolated aria for Guidon in *The Tale of Tsar Saltan*; he also created the part of Likov in *The Tsar's Bride* (1899, Moscow). After retiring from the stage he taught at the conservatories in Moscow and Warsaw. BORIS SEMEONOFF

Sekles, Bernhard (*b* Frankfurt, 20 March 1872; *d* Frankfurt, 8 Dec 1934). German composer. He studied with Knorr at the Hoch Conservatory in Frankfurt, and was later a pupil of Humperdinck. In 1893–4 he was Kapellmeister at the Heidelberg Opera and in 1895–6 at the Mainz Opera. He returned to teach at the Hoch Conservatory, which he directed from 1923 to 1933; his pupils included Hindemith. Among his stage works are the three-act opera *Scheherazade* op.26 (1917) and the comic opera *Die zehn Küsse* (1926). His style incorporates elements of jazz and Slavonic and oriental music; though essentially conservative, it is one of great variety and individuality in its approach to form, rhythm and harmony.

Scheherazade op. 26 (3, G. von Bassewitz), Mannheim, Hof, 2 Nov 1917
Die blaue Marie (Märchenspiel, F. Jungnickel), Frankfurt, Neues, 16 April 1918
Bettelchristel (Märchenspiel, Jungnickel), Frankfurt, Neues, 16 April 1918
Die Hochzeit des Faun (Traumspiel, 2, R. Moor), Wiesbaden, Landes, 1 Dec 1921
Die zehn Küsse (heitere Oper, after H. C. Andersen: *The Swineherd*), Frankfurt, 1926

*

StiegerO GEORGE W. LOOMIS

Seleuco, re di Siria ('Seleucus, King of Syria'). *Opera seria* in three acts by FRANCESCO BIANCHI to a libretto by MATTIA BOTTURINI after APOSTOLO ZENO and PIETRO PARIATI's *Antioco*; Venice, Teatro S Benedetto, 26 December 1791.

Antioco [Antiochus] (soprano castrato), son of Seleucus (tenor), is enamoured of his father's betrothed, Stratonica (soprano), who returns his affections. The plot centres on the terrible conflict between love and loyalty that the couple face, and on Seleucus's attempts to ease his son's despair. At last he learns the truth and unites the lovers in a two-scene finale, which also celebrates a triumphant sea battle. The work is significant for its several ensembles (one incorporating chorus and dance), its choruses (sometimes functioning as a 'character' in the drama), and its multi-sectional, action-ensemble finale. MARITA P. McCLYMONDS

Sellars, James (Edward) (*b* Fort Smith, AR, 8 Oct 1943). American composer. He studied at the Manhattan School with Vittorio Giannini, Nicolas Flagello and David Diamond, and also attended Southern Methodist University and North Texas State University, Denton. In 1976 he became associate professor at the Hartt School of Music, Hartford. At his best in chamber music and songs, Sellars has evolved stylistically from the neo-romanticism of his teachers through serialism and dada to an eclectic post-modernism containing some popular elements. His stage works are generally on a small scale: *Chanson dada*, first staged by Sellars himself, is a monodrama in three sections for soprano and small orchestra; *Beulah in Chicago*, using poems by Frank O'Hara, is in the style of a nightclub floor show, and comprises five movements, including a 12-note habanera; *The World is Round*, scheduled for performance in 1993, is based on Gertrude Stein's book of that name. Sellars's most ambitious stage work, *The Turing Opera*, begun in 1984, is still incomplete; the libretto is based on documents from the life of the mathematician Alan Turing, and the music quotes from the period in a score reflecting the complexity of the subject.

The Family, 1960 (television op, 1, W. Giorda), Tulsa, Oklahoma Educational TV, 1963 [withdrawn]
Chanson dada (monodrama, 3 pts, T. Tzara), Jaffrey, NH, 29 Aug 1980 (Hartford, CT, 1990)

Beulah in Chicago (1, after F. O'Hara: *Suite for Military Band*), Albany, NY, Albany Institute of Art, 28 March 1982 (Hartford, 1989)
The Turing Opera, 1984– (3, T. Meyer), vs (Hartford, 1992) [Act 1]
The World is Round, 1992 (1, J. Rockwell, after G. Stein)

YVAR MIKHASHOFF

Sellars, Peter (*b* Pittsburgh, 27 Sept 1957). American theatre and opera director. He studied at Harvard University and formed his own group, the Explosives B Cabaret, which put on several plays. In 1980 he staged Gogol's *The Inspector General* for the American Repertory Theater, Cambridge, Massachusetts, in a modernist, anti-realist style. For the same theatre he directed in 1981–2 a production of Handel's *Orlando* in which the central character was an astronaut stationed at Cape Canaveral, and for the Chicago Lyric Opera a version of *The Mikado* located in present-day Japan. Sellars became the director of the Boston Shakespeare Company in 1983, and embarked on an adventurous repertory that included the American première of Maxwell Davies's *The Lighthouse*. In 1984 he was appointed director of the American National Theater Company at the Kennedy Center, Washington, DC.

A series of Mozart productions has included a widely acclaimed *Così fan tutte* (1986, Purchase, New York; based on the 1984 production at Castle Hill, Boston), set in a neon-lit diner, with an invented relationship between Despina and Don Alfonso. *Don Giovanni* (1987, Purchase), set among drug dealers, was felt to have weakened the tensions and balance of the plot to some extent; *Le nozze di Figaro* (1988, Purchase), however, was entertainingly set in a new apartment block in New York. His production for Glyndebourne in 1990 of *Die Zauberflöte*, interestingly updated to the West Coast of the 1950s, provoked adverse criticism for its cutting of all the spoken dialogue (some restored in the 1991 revival), with detrimental effects on the coherence of the work. Sellars's first production in the UK was an oblique one of the equally enigmatic *The Electrification of the Soviet Union* (Glyndebourne Touring Opera, 1987), a collaboration between Sellars, Craig Raine (text) and Nigel Osborne (music). Other notable productions have included a richly comic *Giulio Cesare* (1985, Purchase) and the première of John Adams's *Nixon in China* (1987, Houston). In this, as in his production of Adams's *The Death of Klinghoffer* (1991, Brussels, La Monnaie), he has worked closely with composer, librettist and choreographer. The static, oratorio-like style of *Klinghoffer* and the amplification of the voices, within the striking steel girder set, distanced the subject of the work and emphasized the minimalism of the music.

Sellars's iconoclastically untraditional approach, with its strong visual element, is influenced both by the European avant garde and, in its emphasis on gesture and symbol, by oriental stagecraft. He shows an unusual sensitivity to the theatrical workings of music in opera and musical comedy, but his inventiveness has sometimes led to productions in which the overlay of symbols and performance styles has seemed diffuse and complicated.

*

R. Dyer: 'Is Peter Sellars for Real?', *Boston Globe Magazine* (7 Feb 1982)
J. Allen: 'The Many Directions of Peter Sellars', *Esquire*, cii/6 (1984), 146–56
T. Eckert, jr: 'Taking Issue', *ON*, l/1 (1985–6), 10–14
G. Kay: 'Watching the Tanks Roll In', *Classical Music* (26 Sept 1987), 13–15

STEVEN LEDBETTER

Sellin [Selle], Mlle (*b c*1700; *d* after 1726). German soprano. She was probably related to the Hamburg Kantor Thomas Selle. She sang at the Gänsemarkt Opera, appearing in 1722 as Melite in Telemann's *Sieg der Schönheit* and as a Singende Gratie in Keiser's *Ariadne*. In 1724 she sang Juno in the prologue and Doris in the main part of Destouches' *Omphale*, adapted by Telemann, appearing the following year in Keiser's *Bretislaus* (as a nymph) and *Die Hamburger Schlachtzeit* (Lisette) and as Zaida in Handel's *Tamerlano*. Her last role there seems to have been Pallas in Keiser's *Mistevojus* in 1726.

*

K. Zelm: 'Die Sänger der Hamburger Gänsemarkt-Oper', *HJbMw*, iii (1978), 70

HANS JOACHIM MARX

Sellitto [Sellitti], **Giuseppe** (*b* Naples, 22 March 1700; *d* Naples, 23 Aug 1777). Italian composer. He began his career as dramatic composer with *Amor d'un ombra e gelosia d'un aura*, performed in spring 1725 at the Teatro Nuovo, Naples. For that theatre in autumn 1731 he and Pietro Pulli made some amendments and additions to Leonardo Vinci's *La mogliere fedele*. Most of his subsequent life was spent in Naples, but he is known to have visited Venice, where he wrote two operas in 1733, and Rome, where he had a hand in the composition of three operas, in 1742 and 1746. The exact number of works by Sellitto has yet to be determined. In two petitions dated November and December 1771 written to the King of Naples, Sellitto claimed that he had written 46 operas in all, 32 for Naples and 14 for Rome, Venice, Bologna and Florence, as well as oratorios and other vocal works. The list of his known operas is well short of the 46 total, and it is not yet established when he might have been in Florence or Bologna – though presumably he passed through those cities on his way to and from Venice in 1732–3. In 1760 he was appointed organist of the church of S Giacomo degli Spagnuoli, Naples, a post he held until his death. In his later years he also taught singing. His other extant music includes a wedding cantata and a few arias and duets.

Amor d'un ombra e gelosia d'un aura (ob, C. de Palma, after C. S. Capece), Naples, Nuovo, spr. 1725
L'Oronte, ovvero Il custode di se stesso (ob, B. Saddumene), Naples, Fiorentini, 1730, *I-Rn*
Nitocri (os, A. Zeno), Venice, S Giovanni Grisostomo, carn. 1733, *D-Bds*, *Dlb*
Ginevra (os, A. Salvi, after L. Ariosto), Venice, S Samuele, Ascension 1733
Siface (os, P. Metastasio), Naples, S Bartolomeo, 4 Dec 1734, collab. others; perf. with La franchezza delle donne (int, T. Mariani), *I-Nc*
Drusilla e Strabone (int); perf. with F. Mancini's Demofoonte (dramma per musica, 3, Metastasio), Naples, S Bartolomeo, 20 Jan 1735, *Nc*, collab. Leo and Sarro
La vedova ingegnosa (int, Mariani); perf. with Leo's Emira, Naples, S Bartolomeo, 12 July 1735, *D-Hs*
Il finto pazzo per amore (ob, Mariani), Naples, Fiorentini, wint. 1735
I due baroni (ob, G. A. Federico), Naples, Fiorentini, sum. 1736
Sesostri re d'Egitto (os, P. Pariati), Rome, Capranica, 2 Jan 1742, *A-KR*
Farnace [Act 3] (os, A. M. Lucchini), Rome, Capranica, Jan 1742 [Acts 1 and 2 by G. Arena]
Le innocenti gelosie (ob, A. Villani), Naples, Nuovo, aut. 1744
Orazio Curiazio (os), Rome, Dame, carn. 1746, *I-Vnm*
Gl'inganni fortunati (ob), Naples, Fiorentini, wint. 1747
L'amor comico (ob, A. Palomba), Naples, Fiorentini, carn. 1750
Donna Laura Pellecchia (ob), Naples, Fiorentini, aut. 1750
Il cinese rimpatriato (divertimento scenico), Paris, Opéra, 1753; Fr. parody as Les Chinois (C.-S. Favart, Naigeon), Paris, Comédie-

Italienne, 18 March 1756, *F-Pn*, *Po* (Paris, 1763–72), collab. others
L'amore alla moda (ob, Palomba and P. Mililotti), Naples, Fiorentini, wint. 1755

*

U. Prota-Giurleo: 'Giuseppe Sellitto', *Gazzetta musicale di Napoli*, iv (1958), 53
G. Hardie: 'Neapolitan Comic Opera, 1707–1750: Some Addenda and Corrigenda for *The New Grove*', *JAMS*, xxxvi (1983), 125, 127
MICHAEL F. ROBINSON

Šelma sedlák. Opera by Antonín Dvořák; *see* CUNNING PEASANT, THE.

Selva, Antonio (*b* Padua, 1824; *d* Padua, Sept 1889). Italian bass. He sang in the chorus of La Fenice and in 1844 was chosen by Verdi to sing the part of Silva in the first performance of *Ernani*. At S Carlo he sang Balthazar in *La favorite* (1848) and created Count Walter in *Luisa Miller* (1849). He sang in Rome and Milan and at the Théâtre Italien, Paris, specializing in Verdi roles such as Zaccaria (*Nabucco*). From 1864 to 1874 he was engaged at the Teatro Real, Madrid.
ELIZABETH FORBES

Selva sin amor, La ('The Forest without Love'). *Egloga pastoral* in seven scenes by Filippo Piccinini and Bernardo Monanni (music lost) to a text by FÉLIX LOPE DE VEGA; Madrid, *salón grande* of the Alcázar, 18 December 1627.

That this was the first opera performed in Spain is stressed both in the Florentine diplomatic correspondence (Whitaker, 1984) and in Lope de Vega's dedication to his text as printed in his *Ellaurel de Apolo, con otras rimas* (Madrid, 1630). It was, however, composed and produced by Italians. Shortly after his arrival at the Madrid court of Philip IV in 1626, the stage designer Cosimo Lotti had begun to plan a short play with machines (*comedietta di macchine*) in the hope of impressing the king, an endeavour in which he was supported by the secretary Bernardo Monanni and other members of the Tuscan embassy staff. Lope de Vega, the most prolific and highly regarded dramatist of the day, was asked to provide the Spanish text. The Bolognese lutenist Piccinini, at the court since 1613 and one of the king's favourite musicians, composed the music with the aid of Monanni.

While the score is lost, the text (only 672 lines including the prologue) has long been accepted as a libretto. Unlike other stage works by Lope, it is in one act divided into seven scenes, composed entirely in Italian poetic metres with lines of 7 and 11 syllables (hence the designation *égloga pastoral*), except for the duet of Filis and Flora that opens the fourth scene. The work unfolds in an imaginary forest consecrated to Daphne in Madrid. In the prologue, designed for Lotti's invention of a flowing river complete with leaping fish, Venus chides Amor [Cupid] for his negligence and encourages him to intervene in the affairs of the loveless shepherds. Amor uses his famous arrows to influence Silvio, Jacinto, Filis and Flora and to transform the 'forest without love' (*selva sin amor*) into the 'forest of loves' (*selva de amores*). The work was set mainly in recitative, a genre completely new to the Spanish court. Although Philip IV was delighted by the new musical style and the italianate staging, no further operas were produced in Spain until about 1660, and recitative was reintroduced only after about 1650 in works by Calderón de la Barca (music probably by Juan Hidalgo).

M. Menéndez Pelayo, ed.: *Obras de Lope de Vega*, v (Madrid, 1895); repr. as vol. xi, Biblioteca de Autores Españoles, clxxxvi (Madrid, 1965), 58–63; vol.xiii, ibid, clxxxviii (Madrid, 1965), 187–98
F. Pedrell: 'L'eglogue La forêt sans amour de Lope de Vega, et la musique et les musiciens du théâtre de Calderón', *SIMG*, xi (1909), 55–104
E. Cotarelo y Mori: *Orígenes y establecimiento de la ópera en España hasta 1800* (Madrid, 1917), 7–24
J. Subirá: *La participación musical en el antiguo teatro español* (Barcelona, 1930), 19–28
E. Cotarelo y Mori: *Historia de la zarzuela, ó sea el drama lírico en España, desde su origen a fines del siglo XIX* (Madrid, 1934), 5–42
C. V. Aubrun: 'Les débuts du drame lyrique en Espagne', *Le lieu théâtral à la Renaissance: CNRS Royaumont 1963*, 423–44
J. Subirá: 'La ópera castellana en los siglos XVII y XVIII', *Segismundo*, i (1965), 23–42
S. B. Whitaker: 'Florentine Opera comes to Spain: Lope de Vega's *La selva sin amor*', *Journal of Hispanic Philology*, ix (1984), 43–61
L. K. Stein: *Music in the Seventeenth-Century Spanish Secular Theater, 1598–1690* (diss., U. of Chicago, 1987), 159–77
——: 'Opera and the Spanish Political Agenda', *AcM*, lxiii (1991), 125–66
——: *Songs of Mortals, Dialogues of the Gods: Music and Theatre in Seventeenth-Century Spain* (Oxford, 1992)
LOUISE K. STEIN

Sembach [Semfke], **Johannes** (*b* Berlin, 9 March 1881; *d* Bremerhaven, 20 June 1944). German tenor. He studied in Vienna and later with Jean de Reszke in Paris. In 1900 he made his début at the Vienna Staatsoper, and from 1905 to 1913 was principal dramatic tenor at Dresden, where he created Aegisthus in *Elektra* (1909). In 1910 he was admired at Covent Garden as an excellent Loge and Siegmund, adding Parsifal, Lohengrin and Walther in 1914. His *mezza voce* was the subject of special praise and the lyric beauty of his voice was again noticed when he sang the title role of Méhul's *Joseph* in its London première. At the Metropolitan he enjoyed a notable success, first as Parsifal (1914), then as Tamino, Florestan and Adolar (Weber's *Euryanthe*). He showed further versatility in the following seasons, turning from Siegfried to Pylades (*Iphigénie en Tauride*) and in 1920 learning the Wagnerian repertory in English as required in the immediate postwar years. Sembach returned to New York at the Mecca Temple (later the City Center) in 1931 and also made successful appearances in South America. On stage he presented a more credible hero than most Wagnerian tenors and on records his voice is heard as a strong, incisive instrument, often attractively used.
J. B. STEANE

Sembrich, Marcella [Kochańska, Prakseda Marcelina] (*b* Wiśniewczyk, Galicia, 15 Feb 1858; *d* New York, 11 Jan 1935). Polish soprano, naturalized American. She studied in Milan and made her début in Athens on 3 June 1877 as Elvira in *I puritani*. In 1878, after studying the German repertory, she made a successful début as Lucia in Dresden, where she remained for two years. On 12 June 1880, again as Lucia, she made her first appearance at Covent Garden, returning for five consecutive seasons and establishing herself as a worthy colleague of Patti and Albani in the florid repertory; she reappeared there in 1895, as Susanna and Violetta. By then she was in demand in Russia, France, Spain and the USA. Her first appearance at the Metropolitan Opera was on 24 October 1883, once more as Lucia. On the last night of that season she displayed her musicianship and versatility at a benefit concert, playing Chopin on the piano and two movements from Bériot's Violin Concerto no.7 as well as singing Rosina in Act 2 of *Il barbiere di Siviglia*. She reappeared at the Metropolitan in 1898, and returned for every season but one until her farewell on 6 February 1909. Besides all the expected florid parts, her roles had included Elsa, Eva, Mimì, and Elvira in *Ernani*. After her retirement she taught in Philadelphia and New York, numbering among her pupils Alma Gluck, Maria Jeritza and Dusolina Giannini.

Sembrich's voice, singularly perfect in quality, with a compass from *c′* to *f‴*, had considerable volume and was capable of true expressiveness. She was among the finest coloratura singers in the world, while as a singer of songs she displayed beautiful tone combined with musical intelligence. Her records, nearly all made late in her career, do not do her full justice, but they reveal the purity of tone and elegance of style that made her so great a favourite.

*

G. Arnim: *Marcella Sembrich und Herr Prof. Julius Hey* (Leipzig, 1898)

H. G. Owen: *A Recollection of Marcella Sembrich* (New York, 1950)

——: 'A Recollection of Marcella Sembrich', *Record Collector*, xviii (1968–9), 101–38 [with discography by W. R. Moran]; xx (1971–2), 165

***Semele* (i).** Serious opera in three acts by JOHN ECCLES to a libretto by WILLIAM CONGREVE after OVID'S *Metamorphoses*, composed about 1706 but not performed; London, St John's, Smith Square, 22 April 1972.

Congreve wrote the libretto of *Semele* in 1705–6, near the end of his association with John Vanbrugh, architect and first manager of the Queen's Theatre in the Haymarket. The opera was perhaps intended to open the new building, but that plan was spoilt by Christopher Rich, manager of the Theatre Royal, Drury Lane, who introduced the first Italian operas on the London stage in 1705 before the Haymarket opened. Eccles, a close friend of Congreve, probably finished the score of *Semele* in November or December 1706, but by that time the Lord Chamberlain, in a clumsy attempt to placate the actors over the high salaries being paid to singers, had given Rich and Drury Lane a monopoly on opera. Encouraged by their patron the Earl of Halifax, Congreve and Eccles swallowed their pride and agreed with Rich that *Semele* should be produced at Drury Lane during the 1706–7 season. But Rich, notoriously duplicitous, shelved Eccles's opera and instead mounted *Thomyris*, an italianate pasticcio arranged by J. C. Pepusch. Though *Semele* was never performed, Congreve published the libretto in 1710, and Eccles's autograph full score survives (*GB-Lcm*); Handel is most unlikely to have seen the score when, in 1743, he transformed the opera into 'a musical drama' (that is, a secular oratorio). It should be emphasized that Eccles's setting is a true English opera, intended for the stage, which Handel's (with the addition of choruses) is not.

Rich's refusal to produce Eccles's opera is understandable in the light of the failure of Clayton's setting of Addison's *Rosamond* (March 1707) – like *Semele*, a through-composed opera in English. The tide had turned decisively towards imported *opera seria*. Yet *Semele* is in every way superior to the other operas, English and italianate, performed in London between the death of Purcell and Handel's *Rinaldo* (1711). Its main strengths are the dramatic libretto (an archetypal story of consuming ambition), in which arias and ariettas frequently advance the action; the liberal use of instrumental music to set the scene and underscore important events; the invention of a style of rapid text declamation, less formulaic and more expressive than *secco* recitative; and a remarkable variety of aria types – from simple binary songs to full-blown da capos (the first, to emphasize his status, is Jupiter's initial utterance), with motto openings and imaginative orchestration, including pizzicato effects far in advance of their time. Outstanding items are the strophic aria for the jealous Juno (soprano) on hearing that Jupiter (bass) has taken a mortal mistress; Somnus's (bass) opening lines, 'Leave me, loathsome light', Handelian in manner though hardly anticipating Handel's immortal setting; and Jupiter's grave response to Semele's (soprano) request that he appear to her in his full omnipotence ('Ah! take heed what you press'), set over a throbbing, descending bass, which is followed by a monologue in recitative with a measured refrain (' 'Tis past, 'tis past recall, / She must a victim fall') – a rondo-like scene clearly owing something to *tragédie lyrique*. Admittedly, Eccles's tunes are rarely memorable and his imitation of Purcell is sometimes embarrassing; but *Semele* would be eminently worthy of revival had not modern directors found Handel's far greater setting so easy to turn into an opera.

The non-performance of *Semele* in 1707 confirmed the demise of the short-lived English opera tradition, which had begun with Blow's *Venus and Adonis* (*c*1683) and includes Purcell's *Dido and Aeneas* (*c*1685–9), Eccles and Finger's *The Loves of Mars and Venus* (1696), the four settings of *The Judgment of Paris* (1701) and Clayton's *Arsinoe* (1705) and *Rosamond* (1707). Congreve's libretto is dramatically much more sophisticated than that of any contemporaneous *opera seria*, and Eccles met the considerable challenge posed by English recitative. For the rest of the ingredients (except the da capo arias), he was heavily indebted to Purcell, though he lacked Purcell's genius for melody and was following fashion in eschewing counterpoint.

CURTIS PRICE

***Semele* (ii).** Opera in three acts by GEORGE FRIDERIC HANDEL to a libretto by WILLIAM CONGREVE after OVID'S *Metamorphoses*; London, Covent Garden, 10 February 1744 (concert performance).

Cadmus *King of Thebes*	bass
Semele *his daughter*	soprano
Ino *her sister*	contralto
Athamas *Prince of Boeotia*	countertenor
Jupiter	tenor
Juno	contralto
Iris *Juno's attendant messenger*	soprano
Somnus *god of sleep*	bass
Apollo	tenor

Thebans, priests, augurs, loves, zephyrs, nymphs, swains, attendants

Setting Thebes, in mythological times

In the early 1740s the performance of oratorios at Covent Garden represented Handel's chief concert activity in London. His biblical oratorios had some relationship to Greek tragedy and it is perhaps not surprising that he decided to venture into the world of classical drama. It may have been Thomas Arne's recent setting of Congreve's *Judgment of Paris* text that suggested to him *Semele*, of which the original setting (*see* SEMELE (i)) had never been performed. He composed the music in June and July 1743. The considerable adjustment that the text required may have been undertaken by Newburgh Hamilton, who had performed a similar service in respect of *Samson*; this involved the provision or adaptation of words for the choruses, new material for the end of Act 2 (where Congreve had prescribed a 'dumb shew' and 'rural sports', presumably a French-style *divertissement*) and changes in the balance and positioning of recitatives and lyrical numbers. The additional words are largely drawn from Congreve's own verse and from Pope's (including the best-known number, 'Where'er you walk'). The work has been interpreted as a parable about social advancement through sexual favours, and specific targets, in Congreve's time and in Handel's, have been proposed.

Although Congreve, and its original composer Eccles, had intended *Semele* to be given on the stage, Handel designed and performed it 'in the Manner of an *Oratorio*': that is, in concert form. It had only modest success; its amorous topic – it is essentially a creation of the late Restoration period – seems not to have pleased those who attended the Lenten seasons for a different kind of uplift, and it irritated the supporters of true (Italian) opera. There were four performances in February, then two more at the King's Theatre in December, with changes and additions, including arias in Italian, and with some of the sexually more explicit lines removed; it had no further revivals in Handel's lifetime and was perhaps unsurely matched to the spirit of the time. The original cast included Elisabeth Duparc ('La Francesina') in the title role, John Beard as Jupiter, Esther Young as Ino and Juno and Henry Reinhold in the bass parts (though in fact Handel seems to have interchanged some of the music between singers).

Semele had its first modern stage revival in Cambridge in 1925 and its London stage première in 1954; it had four productions by the Handel Opera Society under Charles Farncombe (1959, 1961, 1964 and 1975) and entered the repertories of the English National Opera (then Sadler's Wells Opera) in 1970 and Covent Garden in 1982, conducted on both occasions by Charles Mackerras. Its stage première in the USA was at Evanston in 1959 and it was given at Washington, DC, in 1980.

ACT 1 Cadmus, his family and priests have foregathered in the temple of Juno for the solemnization of the marriage of Semele to Athamas. The omens seem propitious, but Semele invents reasons for delay and, aside, pleads to Jupiter for help. Ino, herself in love with Athamas, is also distressed (quartet, 'Why dost thou thus untimely grieve?'). Thunder is heard, and the flame on Juno's altar grows feeble. All flee save Ino and Athamas; but he takes her words to him as merely an expression of sympathy. Cadmus returns and tells of the events he has just witnessed: Semele, with 'azure flames' around her head, was snatched heavenward by 'an eagle of mighty size, on purple wings descending', leaving a diffusion of 'celestial odour and ambrosial dew'. But the priests and augurs celebrate rather than mourn her translation, and from a distance her voice is heard in a joyous gavotte ('Endless pleasure, endless love, Semele enjoys above'; Congreve had assigned it to a Second Augur), taken up by all present.

ACT 2 In a 'pleasant country', Iris tells Juno of the newly erected palace that her errant husband has built for Semele on Mount Cithaeron. The incensed Juno swears vengeance on Semele and her line, and resolves to call on Somnus, god of sleep, to help her gain access to the heavily guarded palace.

Semele, in the palace, attended by Loves and Zephyrs, calls on sleep to return ('O sleep, why dost thou leave me?') and restore her erotic 'visionary joys'. Jupiter enters, in human form, and reassures her; she responds amorously. The chorus sing of the pains and joys of love. But Jupiter, detecting her discontent and her aspirations to immortality ('I must with speed amuse her'), thinks it wise to send for Ino as a companion. Then he turns the scene to Arcadia and celebrates rural delights ('Where'er you walk'). Ino arrives and describes her remarkable journey, conveyed by Zephyrs, and the sweet music she has heard; the sisters and the chorus sing of the joys of music ('Bless the glad earth with heav'nly lays').

ACT 3 Juno comes to Somnus's cave to awaken the unwilling god ('Leave me, loathsome light'). When she promises him his favourite nymph, Pasithea, he agrees to do her bidding: he is to put Ino and the palace sentinels to sleep, and to provide Jupiter with an erotic dream that leaves him prey to any demand that Semele might make of him (duet, 'Obey my will').

Semele is alone and discontent ('My racking thoughts') when Juno, disguised as Ino, enters. She has a magic mirror that deceives Semele into thinking herself more beautiful than ever ('Myself I shall adore': the air's reflecting musical figures suggest the mirror). 'Ino' advises her to refuse Jupiter her bed until he promises to grant any wish to her, and then to require that he come not in mortal guise but 'like himself, the Mighty Thunderer', as only then (she says) will Semele become immortal. Semele thanks her; Juno retires, elated.

Jupiter enters, inflamed ('Come to my arms'), but Semele keeps him at a distance ('I ever am granting'). He swears an irrevocable oath, calling Olympus itself as witness (distant rumblings are heard), to grant any demand. She asks as Juno bade her: 'Ah, take heed what you press', Jupiter responds, but she stands firm, supposing him unwilling to accord her immortality ('No, no, I'll take no less'). Jupiter bitterly regrets his hasty oath: if he comes to her in his own guise 'she must a victim fall', for all his 'softest lightning' and 'mildest melting bolt'. Juno, observing, gloats over her triumph. Semele sees Jupiter descending, as a fiery cloud, and realizes too late the consequence of her vanity; consumed by his flames, she dies.

Ino, returned to Thebes, joins Cadmus and the priests, who have witnessed the death of Semele as a storm. Ino relates Semele's fate and Jupiter's command that she and Athamas wed. Apollo appears and prophesies that, phoenix-like, Bacchus, god of wine, will rise from Semele's ashes; the chorus celebrates this fortunate outcome ('Happy shall we be').

* * *

As in Handel's other works written for concert performance, the many and sometimes extended choruses pose serious problems in production; there exists no conventional framework within the aesthetic of Baroque performance for their staging. The tradition to which they belong, in style, form and function, is that of Handel's English oratorios. Yet, as its history in the 20th century demonstrates, *Semele* invites realization on the stage because of the eminently theatrical quality of much of its music. That Handel thought of it as akin to his Italian operas is attested by the modifications he required in the libretto, and in particular the adjustments that allowed the inclusion of arias in the operatic da capo form (14 of the 25) where none had existed before. But the work also draws on that spirited, wilful vein of melody, distinctively English, familiar from his earlier *Acis and Galatea* and going back at least to Purcell, which so happily catches the vein of humour that pervades the work. Another striking feature of *Semele* is its abundance of accompanied recitatives, which are more numerous than in any other of his extended English works or indeed his Italian operas, and which are also important in intensifying the drama and the characterization.

Of the characters, it is the women who are the more sharply and perceptively drawn; Jupiter himself appears as little more than an eloquent and ardent lover. Juno's cunning and jealousy, and her natural authority, are speedily established from the moment of her peremptory summons to Somnus in an accompanied recitative at the beginning of Act 3, and consistently maintained up to the jubilant da capo aria to which she departs, her quest for vengeance satisfied. But the music for the hedonistic Semele herself, often deeply sensuous, but not without hints of coquetry and vanity when her ambitions are aroused, represents a tour de force of female character drawing; and the principal scene in Act 2, from her 'Sleep Song' to the final celebration of love and music, stands as one of the great musical paeans to the joys of humankind. STANLEY SADIE

Semi-opera [dramatic opera; English opera; ambigue]. A play with four or more separate episodes or masques which include singing, dancing, instrumental music and spectacular scenic effects such as transformations and flyings. The form, which flourished in England between 1673 and 1710, is further characterized by a clear demarcation between the main characters, who only speak, and minor characters – spirits, fairies, shepherds, gods and the like – who only sing or dance. Most semi-operas are tragicomedies adapted from earlier plays. The finest examples are those with music by Henry Purcell: *Dioclesian*, *King Arthur* and *The Fairy-Queen*.

Although its roots lie in the Jacobean masque and early Restoration play with music, semi-opera was invented in 1673 at the Duke's Company, Dorset Garden, London. The actor-manager THOMAS BETTERTON, who had probably seen Lully's *comédies-ballets* and early *tragédies lyriques* in Paris, was determined to produce an English equivalent. He and his collaborators, the playwright Thomas Shadwell and the composer MATTHEW LOCKE, recognized that all-sung opera of the Italian type would not suit 'rational' English taste, which was deeply rooted in the spoken play tradition. Their solution was to increase the already plentiful amount of music and dance in the early Restoration adaptations of Shakespeare and to exploit the scenic potential of the new Dorset Garden Theatre, which had been equipped as an opera house. Their first great success was a scenically enhanced version of *The Tempest* (1674), with music by Locke, James Hart, Pietro Reggio, Pelham Humfrey and John Banister. While closely following Davenant and Dryden's 1667 adaptation of the play, they expanded the Ariel scenes as well as the Masque of Devils in Act 2 and the Masque of Neptune in Act 5. Though the resulting work is far removed from the original play of the same name, the music grows naturally from the plot and contributes to it, an integration generally characteristic of the early semi-operas even though music and speech are clearly separated. This barrier was substantially removed in the next major musical work, *Psyche* (1675), by Shadwell and Locke. The composer disavowed much continental influence, claiming in fact to have created 'an English opera' distinct from French and Italian models, although *Psyche* was based on the *tragédie-ballet* of the same name. Locke's elaborately orchestrated music promises more than it delivers, but in the character of Venus, who both speaks and sings, semi-opera was brought close to the continental mainstream.

After the lavish though musically inferior *Circe* (1677), text by Charles Davenant, there were no more new semi-opera productions for many years, a consequence partly of financial hard times in the theatres but also of the death in that year of Locke, the only English composer of his generation (besides Blow) to show much gift for the theatre. In 1684 Dryden wrote what he described as a play in 'blank Verse, adorn'd with Scenes, Machines, Songs and Dances' (the classic definition of a semi-opera), but this work, which he later called *King Arthur*, was not produced at the time. Semi-opera was resurrected in 1690 by Betterton, who adapted Philip Massinger and John Fletcher's tragicomedy *The Prophetess* (or *Dioclesian*) for Purcell. This was a notable success and helped establish a pattern of production which lasted for many years. Because semi-opera involved all the theatre's resources – full acting and singing casts, dancers, orchestra, scene painters and machinists – it was very expensive. Only one new work was possible each year; rehearsals began after Christmas for a première in May or June. *The Tempest*, *Psyche* and all Purcell's semi-operas were revived from time to time, often updated with new music.

Purcell's semi-operas differed in conception from earlier works of their kind, in that the music is mostly concentrated into self-contained masques which do not advance the plot. Little attempt was made to integrate music and spoken drama, except at a metaphorical level; for example, in *The Fairy-Queen* the Masque of Seasons in Act 3 symbolizes the renewal of Oberon and Titania's marriage vows. Purcell also preferred to write for professional singers, rather than the actor-singers who could not do justice to his more difficult music, and this tended to distance even further the spoken parts from the musical ones. Such compartmentalization seemed to retard rather than hasten the development of all-sung opera in England.

After Purcell's death in 1695, the Theatre Royal continued to mount new semi-operas. The most notable, *The Island Princess* (1699), enjoyed more performances than any English opera until *The Beggar's Opera* (1728). Adapted by Peter Anthony Motteux from earlier plays of John Fletcher and Nahum Tate, it had music by Richard Leveridge, Daniel Purcell and Jeremiah Clarke. Earlier in the same season had appeared John Dennis and John Eccles's *Rinaldo and Armida* (1698); unusually for semi-opera, it was a tragedy, and it gave rise to three other works of the same genre, *The Grove* by John Oldmixon and Daniel Purcell (1700), *The Rival Queens* (1701), adapted from Nathaniel Lee's play with music by Daniel Purcell and Godfrey Finger, and Elkanah Settle's *The Virgin Prophetess* (1701), music by Finger.

Contrary to general supposition, the semi-opera did not die out because there was no composer of Purcell's genius available to sustain this curious hybrid of music drama; rather, it was killed off by theatre politics. With the introduction of Italian opera in 1705–6, the London stage, which had survived several years of vicious competition between the two houses Drury Lane and Lincoln's Inn Fields (later the Queen's Theatre in the Haymarket), reeled under the strain of the high salaries demanded by foreign singers. Drury Lane tried to accommodate both musical plays and Italian opera by squeezing the actors' wages. After several crises, the Lord Chamberlain stepped in and ordered a separation of genres between the two theatres: Drury Lane was permitted to put on plays, but without music, while the Haymarket could produce any kind of opera. The Order of Separation (December 1707), which also restricted actors to Drury Lane, effectively sank semi-opera, which required both actors and singers. George Granville's *The British Enchanters* and D'Urfey's weird comic semi-opera *Wonders in the Sun* (1706), the first of which at least had been enjoying considerable success, were accordingly stripped of music and abandoned. Semi-opera returned to the London stage a few years later when the genre restriction was eased, but no new works were written.

In Spain, several of the complex three-act mythological court plays by Pedro Calderón de la Barca were performed as semi-operas, with music by Juan Hidalgo. In these *comedias* with integrated operatic scenes, the gods sing their dialogues as recitative and address the mortals with persuasive airs or *tonadas* (mostly in strophic form, some with refrains). The mortal characters sing only common songs, largely drawn from a pre-existing repertory of well-known or popular songs. The prototypes for the genre in Spain seem to have been Calderón's *La fiera, el rayo, y la piedra* (1652; music lost) and *Fortunas de Andrómeda y Perseo* (1653; music in *US-CA*). These plays were produced at court with elaborate italianate staging by Baccio del Bianco. Later semi-operas by Calderón and Hidalgo include *Fieras afemina amor* (1670 or 1672), and *La estatua de Prometeo* (*c*1670–75). In Spain, where only three operas were produced in the 17th century, hybrid genres such as the semi-opera and the zarzuela dominated the repertory at court in the latter half of the century. No other dramatists cultivated the semi-opera (the lighter, pastoral zarzuelas without sung dialogue were easier to produce), but the Calderón-Hidalgo works were revived at court up to the end of the century.

*

E. J. Dent: *Foundations of English Opera* (London, 1928)
D. Arundell: *The Critic at the Opera* (London, 1957)
R. Luckett: 'Exotick but Rational Entertainments: the English Dramatick Operas', *English Drama: Forms and Development*, ed. M. Axton and R. Williams (Cambridge, 1977), 123–41
E. W. White: *A History of English Opera* (London, 1983)
C. A. Price: *Henry Purcell and the London Stage* (Cambridge, 1984)

CURTIS PRICE (with LOUISE K. STEIN)

Semiramide ('Semiramis'). *Melodramma tragico* in two acts by GIOACHINO ROSSINI to a libretto by GAETANO ROSSI after VOLTAIRE's *Sémiramis*; Venice, Teatro La Fenice, 3 February 1823.

Idreno *an Indian king*	tenor
Oroe *high priest of the Magi*	bass
Assur *prince, descended from Baal*	bass
Semiramide *Queen of Babylon, widow of King Nino*	soprano
Arsace *commander of Semiramide's forces*	contralto
Azema *princess, descended from Baal*	soprano
Mitrane *captain of the royal guard*	tenor
Nino's ghost	bass

Satraps, Magi, Babylonians, princesses, cithara players, foreign women, royal guards, temple priests, Indians, Scythians, Egyptians, slaves

Setting Babylon, in the 8th century BC

Semiramide was the last opera Rossini wrote in Italy. He worked on it at Castenaso, his country house outside Bologna, in the late summer and autumn of 1822 immediately following his spectacularly successful visit to Vienna. In many respects, the opera is an extended, formally stabilized and dramatically more powerful version of the musical and dramatic archetypes first essayed in *Tancredi* (1813), a work similarly based on a drama by Voltaire adapted by the librettist Gaetano Rossi. On this occasion, though, there is evidence of close and thorough collaboration between Rossini and his librettist: Rossi was obliged to live at Castenaso during the principal period of composition. (His comments on this can be found in his correspondence at the time with the young Giacomo Meyerbeer.) At the first performance, the title role was sung by Isabella Colbran, the last of many roles created for her by Rossini, whom she had married on 16 March 1822. The other roles at the *prima* in Venice were taken by Rosa Mariani (Arsace), Filippo Galli (Assur), John Sinclair (Idreno), Matilde Spagna (Azema) and Luciano Mariani (Oroe).

The opera quickly reached Milan (see illustration), Naples and Vienna. Rossini himself supervised the first British performances at the King's Theatre, Haymarket, in the spring of 1824, with Giuditta Pasta in the title role, as well as the Paris première in December 1825 with Joséphine Fodor-Mainvielle. Maria Malibran made her Paris début in the title role in 1828. In autumn 1829 a production, with which Rossini may have been connected, was mounted in Bologna. The opera was first staged in New York, in abridged form, in 1835 and in full in 1845. In 1847 there was an important revival by the Royal Italian Opera at Covent Garden with Giulia Grisi, Marietta Alboni and Antonio Tamburini, conducted by Rossini's friend and advocate, Michael Costa (for illustration *see* GRISI, GIULIA). In 1860 Rossini ceded the French rights to Michele Carafa whose lavish new staging, with additional ballet music, was seen at the Paris Opéra on 9 July. The production starred the sisters Carlotta and Barbara Marchisio as Semiramide and Arsace; Rossini wrote of them at the time 'they are possessors of that song which is sensed in the soul'. In 1894 Melba sang the title role at the Metropolitan Opera. In 1922 Gustav Kobbé announced '*Semiramide* seems to have had its day', but it was spectacularly revived at La Scala, Milan, in 1962 with Joan Sutherland, Giulietta Simionato, Gianni Raimondi and Wladimiro Ganzarolli, conducted by Gabriele Santini. The outstanding Arsace of recent times, however, has been Marilyn Horne. She recorded the role in December 1965 with Joan Sutherland, conducted by Richard Bonynge. One of the classic Rossini recordings, it has remained unchallenged for over a quarter of a century. Horne also sang in a distinguished revival of the opera at the Metropolitan in December 1990 directed by John Copley and conducted by James Conlon, with Samuel Ramey as Assur and June Anderson and Lella Cuberli alternating in the title role.

'Semiramide' (Rossini), Act 2 scene v (within the monument of King Nino): design by Alessandro Sanquirico for the first Milan production at La Scala, 9 October 1824

The autograph manuscript of the opera, in the archive of the Teatro La Fenice, Venice, is entirely in the composer's hand; changes, mainly cuts, were made by Rossini for the London and Paris performances in 1824–5. For Paris he redrafted the opera's denouement, mitigating the rapidity of Arsace's change from grieving matricide to triumphantly proclaimed king.

ACT 1.i *Within the precincts of the temple of Baal* Semiramide and Prince Assur have murdered her husband, King Nino, and attempted to murder her son, Arsace. But Arsace has survived and now, 15 years later and no longer known to his mother or would-be stepfather, has become a brilliant young commander on one of the kingdom's furthest frontiers.

The opera is prefaced by one of Rossini's finest overtures, a powerfully worked version of the familiar Rossini archetype, containing, unusually for him, thematic material that recurs in the opera. At the start of the long opening scene sombre orchestral colours determine the mood of gloom and unease as the high priest, Oroe, stands before the altar of Baal. A huge crowd has gathered outside the temple, impatient for the nomination of a male successor to the throne that Semiramide has occupied since the death of Nino. Prince Assur has pretensions to the throne but fears that Oroe has secret information about him. Idreno, an Indian king, appears at the sanctuary to ask the gods' blessing on his love for the princess Azema. But it is Semiramide's arrival that provides the culmination of Rossini's huge 700-bar exposition: as she approaches the altar there is a blinding flash and the sacred flame is extinguished. The people flee but Oroe returns; at the sanctuary he is confronted by Arsace, back in the city by royal summons. He, too, has an interest in the princess Azema, whom he once rescued from bandits; he also carries a casket containing a sword and scrolls, the property of his late father, which Oroe appears to recognize. When Assur meets Arsace, he remonstrates with him for leaving his border post. But it soon becomes clear that Arsace distrusts Assur; if Assur succeeds in his claim to the throne, Arsace will never recognize him as king.

1.ii *The Hanging Gardens of Babylon* Semiramide is overjoyed that Arsace, the young commander, has returned. Her cavatina 'Bel raggio lusinghier', a famous soprano showpiece, is the score's most dazzling number, a love song that irradiates the queen's entire personality. An ambiguously worded pronouncement arrives from the oracle at Memphis. Believing the gods at last appeased, Semiramide summons Arsace. In a duet of mutual misunderstanding 'Serbami ognor sì fido', she talks of Assur's treachery but mistakes Arsace's love for Azema as love for herself; this is one of Rossini's most eloquent duets, an E♭ andantino in 6/8 time. The use of the crescendo subject from the overture as a transition with the cabaletta proves abortive, but the coda is gloriously shaped with augmented rhythms in the voice part and seething figurations beneath.

1.iii *The throne room of the palace* The Act 1 finale is a 900-bar six-movement structure. Semiramide announces that Arsace is to be both king and her consort. Arsace is appalled, Assur furious. Meanwhile, Azema will be given in marriage to Idreno. As the high priest is about to unite them in marriage, the ghost of King Nino rises up. Arsace will be king, he announces, but there are crimes to be expiated and Arsace must descend into the vault and offer up a sacrifice to Nino's ashes. The first episode of the finale, a slow section in E♭ where allegiance is sworn to Semiramide, treats the overture's solemn horn subject in unaccompanied choral form. Later in the finale there are two especially impressive episodes in the minor key. 'Quel mesto gemito', Semiramide's stunned response to the rumblings from Nino's tomb, deploys a sombre ostinato similar to that which Verdi was to use in the 'Miserere' in *Il trovatore*. The later episode in which the ghost of Nino addresses Arsace is equally powerful, in a restless F minor. Henry Chorley noted that the terror is created here as much by the rhythm as by the declamation.

ACT 2.i *A room in the palace* Semiramide reminds Assur of their past crimes and threatens to expose him. In a magnificent duet of mutual recrimination, 'Quella, ricordati', they quarrel, like the Macbeths, over events that are beginning to overshadow them. In the andantino Assur reminds Semiramide of 'the night of death' in phrases which are both suave and terrifying.

2.ii *The palace sanctuary* Oroe and the Magi assemble to lead Arsace to Nino's tomb. Oroe now reveals to Arsace that he is Nino, son of the late king, and that the king was murdered by his mother and Assur. Killing Assur is easily contemplated, but Arsace prays that his father's spirit will show leniency to Semiramide.

2.iii *The queen's apartments* Arsace reveals to his mother that he knows all. In a scene distantly reminiscent of the closet scene in *Hamlet*, Nino is also tacitly present; Rossini even accords him a brief theme of his own. The truth revealed, Semiramide offers her life to her son ('Ebben ... a te, ferisci'), but Arsace's response is generous. However hateful Semiramide is in the sight of the gods, she is his mother. The music is now lyric and serene as she perceives her son's sincerity through his tears.

2.iv *The palace, by the tomb of King Nino* Assur is determined to kill Arsace but is told that Oroe has revealed his crimes to the people; he is now on the verge of madness. Colours implicit in the opera's first scene are broodingly remixed as Assur becomes subject to terrible visions. The scene, written for the great bass Filippo Galli, is full of fractured declamation and fraught rhythms. Even the transition to the cabaletta brings its rich cargo of effects as Rossini charts Assur's hazy return to consciousness before the stirring *marziale* conveys to us the resolve of the newly restored man. This remarkable scene is a possible inspiration for the great Banquet Scene in Verdi's *Macbeth*.

2.v *Within the monument of King Nino* Arsace enters the monument as do Assur and Semiramide, who fears for her son's life. Her prayer, 'Al mio pregar t'arrendi', is followed by a trio, the characters circling one another in the gloom. When Arsace strikes, he strikes his mother in error. Her death throes, extended by Rossini in his Paris revision, make Arsace's accession to the throne less abrupt, though no less harrowing, as the people acclaim their new and rightful king.

* * *

With *Semiramide*, Rossini brought his Italian career to a spectacular close. After a series of operas in which the primary areas of interest were either vocal or architectural, Rossini once again drew vocal, dramatic, and architectural elements into harmony with one another. The strategic planning is formidable, with an opening movement of over 700 bars and an Act 1 finale of over 900 bars; the work points directly forward to the huge structural spans of *Guillaume Tell* (1829). The *Semiramide* story, popular with composers of the period, is to some extent locked into an 18th-century Metastasian aesthetic, and Rossini has yet to rid himself of the *travesti* contralto hero. But his treatment of key scenes has great musico-dramatic impact, far removed from the kind of musical tinsel served up by Marcos António Portugal in his *La morte di Semiramide* (1801) where vocal display obscures the thrust of those archetypal relationships and situations which Rossini's music powerfully engages.

See also VENDETTA DI NINO, LA. RICHARD OSBORNE

Semiramide riconosciuta ('Semiramis Recognized') [Semiramide]. Libretto by PIETRO METASTASIO, first set by Leonardo Vinci (1729, Rome).

*'Semiramide riconosciuta', final scene of Act 3 (*SIBARI: *'My people, to you I reveal a deception: open your eyes, a fragile woman encumbers your empire'): engraving from the 'Opere' of Pietro Metastasio (Paris: Hérissant, 1780–82)*

Scitalce, an Indian prince, masquerading under the name of Idreno, won the love of the Egyptian princess, Semiramide, with whom he eloped. He made an attempt on her life, however, when Sibari, also in love with her, suggested that she was unfaithful. Surviving the ordeal, Semiramide made her way to Assyria where she became the wife of Nino, the king; upon his death, she disguised herself as their son and heir, also named Nino, and now rules Assyria.

ACT 1 Sibari has arrived in Babylon to witness Tamiri, princess of Bactria, select a consort from among three contenders: Ircano, a Scythian prince; Scitalce, the Indian prince; and Mirteo, a prince from Egypt, raised in Bactria, and brother of Semiramide (whom he believes dead). Although Semiramide and Scitalce recognize each other, both remain silent; but when Tamiri shows a clear preference for Scitalce, the disguised queen is quick to postpone an official announcement. Meanwhile, Sibari learns that, although his position as a rival for Semiramide remains unknown to Scitalce, the letter he wrote accusing her of infidelity is still in Scitalce's possession. When Semiramide urges Mirteo and Ircano to plead their cases more strongly with Tamiri, the latter resolves instead to murder Scitalce.

ACT 2 The chosen suitor will demonstrate his acceptance of Tamiri in proposing a toast. Sibari informs Ircano that he plans to kill Scitalce by poisoning the cup. Scitalce, however, unable to accept Tamiri, sets the cup aside. When Tamiri then turns to Ircano, he is unwilling to take up the poisoned cup; indignant,

Tamiri condemns Scitalce to death. Semiramide insists, however, that Sibari take him prisoner. While Sibari then assists Ircano in planning the abduction of Tamiri, Semiramide reveals herself to Scitalce, who rejects her.

ACT 3 When the abduction attempt fails, Ircano challenges Sibari to a duel. Mirteo comes to his aid, taking Ircano prisoner, and learns from Sibari that Scitalce is his sister's murderer. Semiramide, learning that Mirteo wants revenge, frees and warns Scitalce, then pleads her own cause, again without success. Ircano exposes the treachery of Sibari over the poisoned cup and Scitalce, anxious to explain his past actions to Mirteo, produces Sibari's letter. Sibari, thwarted, reveals the true identity of the disguised Semiramide. Acclaimed by her people, she is reunited with Scitalce and pardons Sibari. Tamiri turns to Mirteo.

* * *

Ctesias, in his *Persica* (book 1), related a series of fables surrounding Queen Semiramis that were retold 300 years later by Diodorus Siculus in the *Bibliotheca* (book 2). These legends place Semiramis at the beginning of the third millennium BC and, together with such sources as the Strabo *Geographica* (books 2 and 16) and Justin's epitome of the Trogus *Historiae* (book 1), provide the substance for most plots that bring Semiramis on to the stage. In book 1 of his *Historiae*, however, Herodotus referred to Semiramis as having lived five generations before Nitocris, another famous queen from around the period 600 BC. This dovetails more closely with what recent scholars have outlined as the period of the Assyrian empire and with their identification of Semiramis as the historical figure Sammuramat, wife of the Assyrian king Shamshi-Adad V, who reigned from 824 to 810 BC. Their son, Adad-nirari III, then ruled across the period 810–782 BC, but since he came to the throne as a minor, his mother assumed political control during the first years of his reign. Metastasio's locations and the names of most of his characters can be traced to Diodorus, although he confessed, in his *argomento*, to the substitution of Egypt for Syria as a place of origin for Semiramis. That Semiramis ruled Assyria disguised as her son, Ninias, is one of Justin's claims that was to resurface in several treatments of the legend, such as the Spanish plays of Cristóbal de Virués (*La gran Semíramis*, published 1609) and Calderón de la Barca (*La hija del aire*, *c*1653). In France *Sémiramis* dramas were written by Gabriel Gilbert (1646), Nicolas Desfontaines (1647), Madeleine Gomez (1716), Crébillon (1717) and Voltaire (1748). Of all these only Gomez refrained from making Semiramis responsible for the death of her husband Ninus, and Virués, Desfontaines, Crébillon and Voltaire dispatched their title character either by her own hand or by that of her son. In Pierre Roy's libretto (1718) this task is accomplished by the gods. The Italians took a different approach. In his pastoral piece *Semiramis boscareccia* (1593) Muzio Manfredi suppressed the violence, as did the librettists Giovanni Moniglia (*La Semiramide*, 1667), Francesco Silvani (*Semiramide*, 1713), Apostolo Zeno (*Semiramide in Ascalona*, 1725) and Metastasio, all with different but equally complex plots. Metastasio's *Semiramide*, with fewer than 40 settings, fell short in popularity of such other early librettos as *Artaserse* and *Alessandro nell'Indie*. This may be partly explained by the rivalry of Silvani's text and others that were to draw on Voltaire's drama, such as Giovannini's LA VENDETTA DI NINO, Sografi's *La morte di Semiramide* and, ultimately, Rossi's *Semiramide* for Rossini. Gluck made his operatic début in Vienna with the first mounting of an opera on the subject in that city, staged to celebrate the reopening of the renovated Burgtheater on Maria Theresa's birthday in 1748. Metastasio revised the text for Carlo Broschi (Farinelli), then theatre director in Madrid, in 1752, and in 1764 Sacchini's setting was particularly well received in Rome.

For a list of settings *see* METASTASIO, PIETRO. DON NEVILLE

Semiramide riconosciuta ('Semiramis Recognized'). *Dramma per musica* in three acts by NICOLA PORPORA to a libretto by PIETRO METASTASIO (*see* SEMIRAMIDE RICONOSCIUTA above) with minor alterations, perhaps by DOMENICO LALLI; Venice, Teatro S Giovanni Grisostomo, Carnival 1729.

The first two settings of this text, by Leonardo Vinci and by Porpora, received their premières in Rome and Venice respectively during the same carnival season of 1729. The Porpora setting was designed for a formidable cast that included Farinelli (in the part of Mirteo), Nicola Grimaldi (Idreno), Lucia Facchinelli (Semiramide), and Domenico Gizzi (Sibari). The score reflects the strong casting; the six characters all have da capo arias of rather similar length and difficulty. Porpora's elaborate and expressive vocal lines require superlative singing to make them effective.

MICHAEL F. ROBINSON

Semkow, Jerzy [Georg] (*b* Radomsko, 12 Oct 1928). Polish conductor. He studied at Kraków and at the Leningrad Conservatory, becoming assistant to Mravinsky with the Leningrad PO until 1956. He had further studies with Erich Kleiber in Prague and with Walter, and was conductor at the Bol'shoy, 1956–8. After working with Serafin in Italy, Semkow returned to Poland as artistic director and principal conductor of the Warsaw National Opera (1959–62). He was principal conductor of the Danish Royal Opera, 1966–76, and first appeared at Covent Garden in 1970, conducting *Don Giovanni*. He has held orchestral appointments in the USA in Cleveland, St Louis and Rochester, as well as Rome (RAI). His recordings include *Prince Igor* and the first to use the original version of *Boris Godunov* (with Talvela and Polish forces).

MIECZYSŁAWA HANUSZEWSKA

Semper Oper. The familiar name for the Königliches Sächsisches Hoftheater (Royal Saxon Opera House) built in DRESDEN in 1841 by the architect Gottfried Semper. It was destroyed by fire in 1869, rebuilt in 1878, renovated in 1912 and destroyed by bombs in 1945. The third opera house on the site, built to a design essentially faithful to Semper's original, was opened as the 'Semper Oper' in 1985.

Semplice (It.: 'simple'). Term used since the 18th century in the context *recitativo semplice* ('simple recitative'), to signify recitative accompanied only by continuo; it is more commonly (if less historically) called *recitativo secco*. *See* RECITATIVE.

Sem'ya Tarasa ('The Taras Family'). Opera in four acts, op.47, by DMITRY BORISOVICH KABALEVSKY to a libretto by Sergey Alexandrovich Tsenin after Boris Gorbatov's short novel *Nepokorenniye* ('The Unvanquished'); Moscow, Stanislavsky–Nemirovich-

Danchenko Music Theatre, 2 November 1947; second version, Leningrad, Kirov Theatre of Opera and Ballet, 7 November 1950; third version, Moscow, Stanislavsky–Nemirovich-Danchenko Music Theatre, 17 November 1967.

The Taras Family was one of many works to be inspired by the patriotic fervour of World War II. Kabalevsky had already written numerous choral and instrumental works on war topics, and this was his second opera on the same theme. He salvaged the best music from the unsuccessful *V ogne* ('Into the Fire', 1943) for the new opera, which eventually proved one of the most successful of its type. The clearcut dramatic conflict between the heroic Soviet people and the invading fascist enemy is accentuated by sharp musical contrasts, and there is some use of leitmotif techniques. Kabalevsky was awarded the State Prize, Second Grade, for *The Taras Family* in 1950.

The action takes place in central Russia. An old factory foreman, Taras (bass), bids farewell to his sons Stepan (baritone) and Andrey (tenor) as they go off to war. His young daughter, Nastya (soprano), laments her lost childhood and separation from her schoolfriend, Pavlik (tenor). Taras's wife Yefrosin'ya (mezzo-soprano) and Andrey's wife Antonina (soprano) pray for the safety of their loved ones, and the factory workers resolve to destroy the factory before letting it fall into the hands of the approaching Germans. Taras and his family cower behind locked doors. Wailing is heard, and through the window they watch a procession of Russian women being led into slavery by the Nazis. Taras vows never to submit to the fascists. Stepan directs the partisans behind enemy lines and puts Pavlik in charge of bombing the German headquarters located in their former school. Taras arrives, and father and son are joyously reunited. Taras listens proudly as his son describes the latest Red Army offensive and then returns to the settlement. Andrey unexpectedly returns home after his escape from a German prison camp, but his father is ashamed of his cowardice. Andrey leaves, promising that they will hear from him again.

At German headquarters – the school – a ball is in progress. Village youths gather at the fence; Pavlik goes with others to set the bomb while Nastya stands guard. Meanwhile, a German officer wants the workers to repair the factory to make tanks. When Taras refuses, the German wounds him. As the workers threaten the officer, the sound of aeroplanes and bombs is heard. The Russians have broken through the front. The youths plot at Taras's house and, led by Stepan, they leave to blow up the bridge that is the Germans' sole route of escape. When they have gone, Pavlik returns en route to join the Red Army. He and Nastya declare their love and, once he has left, she reflects on their future happiness. But the Germans arrive unexpectedly to seize Nastya; they know she participated in the school bombing and press her to betray the other conspirators. She resists them defiantly and, despite the pleas of her mother, she is taken away to be shot. When Russian troops arrive triumphantly the next morning, Andrey, who has redeemed his honour, is among them.

LAUREL E. FAY

Semyon Kotko. Opera in five acts, op.81, by SERGEY PROKOFIEV to a libretto by the composer and Valentin Katayev after Katayev's novella *Ya–sïn trudovogo naroda* ('I am a Son of the Labouring Masses'); Moscow, Stanislavsky Opera Theatre, 23 June 1940.

Katayev's novella was a typical product of its high-Stalinist time: a sort of *Bildungsroman* in which a simple soldier (Semyon Kotko), returning home from World War I after the Russian withdrawal, receives his political education at the hands of heroic Bolsheviks defending the populace against black-hearted counter-revolutionaries and German interventionists as the post-revolutionary Civil War is played out on Ukrainian soil. The peg on which the plot turns is the Romeo-and-Juliet-like love of Semyon (tenor) and Sof'ya (soprano), the daughter of the Bolsheviks' chief antagonist Tkachenko (bass-baritone), who almost succeeds in having Semyon executed and his daughter married off to the village landowner's heir, but is thwarted at the last minute and executed himself. The opera was written in March–June 1939 and conducted at its première by Mikhail Zhukov.

The narrative's dramaturgical strategy, as can already be seen, consists in its crude deployment of 'contrasting elements: there is the love of the young people versus the hatred of the representatives of the old world, heroic struggle and tearful loss versus the merry pranks that are so endemic to Ukrainian humour'. The quoted words are Prokofiev's. The composer, eager to achieve a major stage success in the period immediately following his return to his homeland (and the fiasco of *The Fiery Angel*), turned, on the advice of the novelist Alexey Tolstoy, to Katayev's work as a mine of time-honoured, surefire devices of contrast dramaturgy such as those on which the 'classical' traditions of Russian opera had rested. (In the aftermath of Shostakovich's disgrace over *Lady Macbeth of the Mtsensk District* those traditions were being asserted as a veritably official requirement for Soviet opera.) It was surely the Nazi-Soviet pact, in force by the time he wrote about his opera in 1940, that caused Prokofiev to omit from his list the contrast that emerged most clearly of all in his music: that between the twisted, dissonant, marching tunes of the German invaders and the open-hearted diatonicism of the positive characters, full of melodic turns appropriated from Russian and Ukrainian folk music. (One character – Semyon's young sister Frosya, a soprano with mezzo extension – sings an authentic Ukrainian folk melody that had previously served Tchaikovsky in *Vakula the Smith*; she avoids violating Prokofiev's literalistic standards of operatic realism by actually singing it as a song in the course of the action, rather than expressing her own feelings to the melody the way Tchaikovsky allowed his Vakula to do.) Such a contrast had lain behind the musical dramaturgy of *A Life for the Tsar*, the very fountainhead of the classical Russian repertory. That Prokofiev was thinking consciously of Glinka's opera is suggested by the scene in *Semyon Kotko* (fashioned by conflating two separate scenes in the novella) in which the Germans intrude upon the hero and heroine's betrothal ceremony, exactly as the Poles interrupt a similar scene of Glinka's.

But if such devices were old hat in Russian opera, they were new to Prokofiev. Never before had he paid the slightest attention to genre music or national character, and his strongly held dramaturgical convictions had hitherto rejected contrast in favour of a 'steady dramatic crescendo' (as he had called *The Gambler*) – i.e. a sustained, cumulative sweep. He still insisted on prose for the libretto (for which reason Katayev thought him pedantic), but was more ready than ever to cast the prose – according to the 'melodic mould' technique (*see* PROKOFIEV, SERGEY, §1) – in rounded periods at 'sung'

'Semyon Kotko' (Prokofiev): costume design for the title role (left) and set design for Act 1 by A. G. Tyshler for the original production at the Stanislavsky Opera Theatre, Moscow, 23 June 1940

tempos, not even eschewing occasional expressive melismata. In addition, he seized upon every pretext (such as recurrent phrases of recitative, the repetitions of which he sometimes considerably augmented) for constructing conspicuous leitmotifs on which to base the thematic structure of the music. As a result of all these efforts – at 'lyricalizing', at exploiting dramatic contrast, at incorporating folk material, at deploying leitmotifs – *Semyon Kotko* represented Prokofiev's sincerely motivated attempt to deradicalize his operatic style and make his work accessible to the musically untutored, as a Soviet composer was expected to do.

Modernist prejudices notwithstanding, such an attempt did not automatically imply debasement. Indeed, the climactic finale of Act 3 was arguably Prokofiev's finest operatic achievement to date. A mad scene for a partisan martyr's bereaved fiancée against a background of mass destruction, it effectively distilled into one concentrated and compelling dose the obsessive atmosphere and ostinato-driven idiom the composer had so overdone in *The Fiery Angel*.

Despite everything, *Semyon Kotko* was not a success. The adaptation of novella into opera was somewhat clumsy, chiefly because of Soviet censorship conditions and the requirement that revolutionary themes be given heroic treatment. Remenyuk (bass), the head of the village Soviet and the chief representative in the novella of Soviet power, could not be martyred in the opera as he was in the book (for the same reason that Verdi could not show a king's assassination on stage in *Un ballo in maschera*), but survives and functions to the end as a crude *deus ex machina*. The martyrs that remained – Tsaryov (a sailor, baritone) and Ivasenko (bass, Remenyuk's stand-in) – are 'secretly' buried in a bombastic ceremonial scene (Act 3.iii) built around a sonorous (and therefore unbelievable) chorus on 'Testament', the most famous poem by Taras Shevchenko, the Ukrainian national poet. (In Katayev's novella, a pair of lines from Shevchenko had served as an epigraph to one of the chapters.) The original production was further hampered by the Hitler-Stalin pact. With the Germans now 'sworn friends' (in a famous catch-phrase of the day), they could not be portrayed on the Soviet stage as enemies; they were spuriously replaced by Austrians. Yet another pall was cast by the arrest of the director, the great Vsevolod Meyerhold, in the final stages of production, and his replacement by the greenish Serafima Birman.

The main reason for the failure of Prokofiev's opera, however, was that despite his best efforts he could not bring it down to the level the Stalinist cultural establishment now required. That signal achievement was the young Tikhon Khrennikov's. His 'song-opera' *V buryu* ('Into the Storm') had its première the same season as *Semyon Kotko* and in the same theatre. The mandatory invidious comparison was of great moment in the history of the Russian musical stage. It set the tone for Soviet opera – one to which Prokofiev was doomed never to succeed in reconciling himself despite repeated agonizing attempts – for the rest of the Stalin period, which coincided exactly with the rest of the composer's life. After its initial season *Semyon Kotko* went unplayed until 1957 and unstaged until 1960.

RICHARD TARUSKIN

Sénéchal, Michel (*b* Tavery, 11 Feb 1927). French tenor. He studied in Paris, making his début in 1950 at La Monnaie, where he sang for three seasons. Established at the Paris Opéra and Opéra-Comique, as well as other French theatres, he sang lyric roles such as Ferrando, Don Ottavio, Tamino, Almaviva, Count Ory, Paolino (*Il matrimonio segreto*), Hylas (*Les Troyens*), Georges Brown (*La dame blanche*) and also many character roles. In 1956 he sang Rameau's Platée at Aix-en-Provence, scoring a triumph in the travesty role of an elderly nymph, which he repeated at Amsterdam, Brussels and the Opéra-Comique (1977). Other roles in this category included Erice (*L'Ormindo*), Monsieur

Senesino (left), Francesca Cuzzoni and Gaetano Berenstadt in a scene from an Italian opera, probably by Handel (possibly 'Flavio'): engraving by J. Vanderbank

Triquet, Scaramuccio (*Ariadne auf Naxos*), Trabuco, Valzacchi, Rodriguez (*Don Quichotte*) and Teapot/ Arithmetic (*L'enfant et les sortilèges*). He sang Gonzalve (*L'heure espagnole*) at Glyndebourne (1966); the Brahmin (*Padmâvatî*) at Florence (1971); Don Basilio and Le Dancaïre (*Carmen*) at Salzburg (1972–88), and Don Jerome in the French première of *Betrothal in a Monastery* at Strasbourg (1973). Having made his Metropolitan début in 1982 as the four *Contes d'Hoffmann* tenor comics, he returned as Don Basilio and Guillot (*Manon*). In 1985 he created Fabien in Landowski's *Montségur* at Toulouse and Pope Leo X in Boehmer's *Docteur Faustus* at the Opéra. His high, smooth, agile voice and unrivalled ability as a character actor were evident still in 1990 when he sang the *Hoffmann* comics at Geneva.

ANDRÉ TUBEUF/ELIZABETH FORBES

Sénéchal de Kerkado, Mlle **Le.** *See* KERKADO, LE SÉNÉCHAL DE.

Senesino [Bernardi, Francesco] (*b* Siena; *d* ?Siena, by 27 Jan 1759). Italian alto castrato. He sang at Venice in five operas in 1707–8; in the first two, by G. M. Ruggeri and G. Boniventi, he played Rinaldo. In 1709 he appeared in Caldara's *L'inimico generoso* at Bologna; in the same year (and again in 1712 and 1720) at Genoa; in 1711 in Rome (Ottoboni's private theatre); in 1713–14 in Lotti's *Irene Augusta* and two operas by C. F. Pollarolo at Venice, and also in Reggio and Brescia; in 1715–16 in six operas at Naples, including A. Scarlatti's *Carlo re d'Alemagna* and *La virtù trionfante*. He was engaged for Dresden from 1 September 1717 at a huge salary and sang in Lotti's *Giove in Argo* (1717), *Ascanio* (1718) and *Teofane* (1719). He was dismissed early in 1720 when, at rehearsals of Heinichen's *Flavio Crispo*, he refused to sing an aria and tore up Berselli's part. Handel engaged him for London in 1720; he accepted the Royal Academy's offer of 3000 guineas and joined the company in September 1720. He made his début on 19 November in G. Bononcini's *Astarto* and remained a member of the company until June 1728, singing in all 32 operas produced during that period, among them 13 by Handel, eight by Bononcini and seven by Ariosti. His success was spectacular and he was constantly eulogized in newspapers and private letters in such terms as 'beyond all criticism' (of his performance in Handel's *Giulio Cesare*), though his arrogant temper clashed with Handel's.

After the break-up of the Academy in 1728 Senesino sang in Paris in 1728 and Venice in 1729. He apparently gave Handel a cold reception when they met in Italy, but in 1730 he was re-engaged for the second Academy, and in the next three years sang in four new Handel operas and many revivals as well as in oratorios. His popularity remained great, but with his increasing antipathy to Handel he was among those who worked to set up a rival company, the so-called Opera of the Nobility, which occupied Lincoln's Inn Fields (1733–4) and then the King's Theatre, with Porpora as chief composer and Senesino, Farinelli and later Cuzzoni as the leading singers. In three seasons (1733–6) Senesino sang in five operas by Porpora and others by Bononcini, Hasse, Handel (*Ottone*), Sandoni and Veracini. When he left, a song called *The Lady's Lamentation for the Loss of Senesino* haunted the theatre bills for several years. He sang in operas at Florence in 1737–9, and was engaged in 1739–40 for Naples, but the public there found his style old-fashioned. His last known performances were in Porpora's *Il trionfo di Camilla* at the S Carlo in 1740.

Senesino's quality as an artist may be estimated from the superb parts Handel composed for him. Of his 20 roles in Handel's operas, 17 were original: Mucius Scaevola, Floridante, Ottone, Guido in *Flavio*, Julius Caesar, Andronicus in *Tamerlano*, Bertarido in *Rodelinda*, Luceius in *Scipione* and the title roles in *Alessandro*, *Admeto*, *Riccardo Primo*, *Siroe*, *Tolomeo*, *Poro*, *Ezio*, *Sosarme* and *Orlando*. His compass in Handel was narrow (*g* to *e''* at its widest), yet he was equally renowned for brilliant and taxing coloratura in heroic arias and expressive *mezza voce* in slow pieces. Hawkins said that 'in the pronunciation of recitative [he] had not his fellow in Europe', and Burney quoted opinions that he was unsurpassed in the accompanied recitatives of *Giulio Cesare* and *Admeto*. According to the same writer his best style was 'pathetic, or majestic', but his 'articulate and voluminous voice' could bring off the most difficult divisions. Quantz wrote:

He had a powerful, clear, equal and sweet contralto voice, with a perfect intonation and an excellent shake. His manner of singing was masterly and his elocution unrivalled. Though he never loaded Adagios with too many ornaments, yet he delivered the original and essential notes with the utmost refinement. He sang Allegros with great fire, and marked rapid divisions, from the chest, in an articulate and pleasing manner. His countenance was well adapted to the stage, and his action was natural and noble. To these qualities he joined a majestic figure.

His private character, by all accounts, was marred by touchiness, insolence and an excess of professional vanity.

'Herrn Johann Joachim Quantzens Lebenslauf von ihm selbst entworfen', in F. W. Marpurg: *Historisch-kritische Beyträge zur Aufnahme der Musik*, i (1754), 197–250; repr. in W. Kahl: *Selbstbiographien deutscher Musiker des XVIII. Jahrhunderts* (Cologne, 1948), 104–57; Eng. trans. in P. Nettl: *Forgotten Musicians* (New York, 1951), 280–319

L. Cellesi: 'Un poeta romano e un sopranista senese', *Bollettino senese di storia patria*, new ser., i (1930), 320–23

A. Mazzeo: *I tre 'Senesini': musici ed altri cantanti evirati senesi* (Siena, 1979)

WINTON DEAN

Senger-Bettaque, Katherine (*b* Berlin, 2 Aug 1862; *d* ?Berlin, after 1909). German soprano. She studied with Heinrich Dorn in Berlin and made her début there in 1879, in *Feramors* by Anton Rubinstein. After appearances in Leipzig, Bremen and Hamburg she joined the Munich Hofoper in 1893, remaining until 1906. She sang Ortrud and Brünnhilde but was more successful as Eva, which she sang at the first Bayreuth performance of *Die Meistersinger*, in 1888. At Covent Garden in 1892 she appeared as Freia, Sieglinde and Gutrune in the *Ring* performances conducted by Mahler. At the Metropolitan (1888–9 and 1904–5) she was heard as Marguerite, Sélika (*L'Africaine*), Elsa, and Elisabeth in *Tannhäuser*. Other roles included Venus, Leonore and Maria in *Der Trompeter von Säkkingen* by Viktor Nessler (British première, Drury Lane, 1892).

DAVID CUMMINGS

Sens, Ginetta [Genoveffa]. *See* CIGNA, GINA.

Sentenza, La ('The Sentence'). Opera in one act by GIACOMO MANZONI to a libretto by Emilio Jona; Bergamo, Teatro Donizetti, 13 October 1960.

In the Chinese village of Vutan, Sun-Te (soprano), wife of a labourer, Li-Scen (baritone), saves the life of a fugitive partisan, Sen-Ko (tenor), by claiming that he is her husband. Li-Scen is dragged in, and identifies his house and his wife; Sun-Te says she does not know him. Li-Scen is shot. After the partisans' victory a judge and jury deliberate on the events of the first scene: the verdict is 'neither condemnation nor absolution', but Sun-Te protests that she wants justice and peace in her heart. The chorus reply 'If you want a sentence, it must come from you'. Manzoni wrote throughout in a stark, gestural dodecaphony, but included demanding choral sections.

DAVID OSMOND-SMITH

Sepolcro (It.: 'sepulchre'). A 17th-century genre of sacred dramatic music in Italian related to the oratorio and performed on Maundy Thursday and Good Friday at the Habsburg court chapels in Vienna. Other terms used for the genre were AZIONE SACRA and RAPPRESENTAZIONE SACRA. The libretto of a *sepolcro* is invariably based on the Passion or an Old Testament story interpreted as prefiguring the Passion. The earliest examples date from the 1660s, the latest from about 1705. A *sepolcro* tends to be shorter than an oratorio and in one structural part rather than the two common for the Italian oratorio. Bearing a close relationship to opera, the *sepolcro* was characteristically performed with scenery, costumes and action. References to the scenery and action are commonly found in both the printed librettos and music manuscripts of the numerous *sepolcri* set by Antonio Draghi to librettos by Nicolò Minato. These sources invariably begin with a comment on the replica of the Most Holy Sepulchre of Christ, the main element of the scenery, before which the personages in the drama play their parts. In addition to the Sepulchre, a large painted backdrop often depicted a scene appropriate to the drama. In the Draghi-Minato *Il sagrificio non impedito* (1692), for instance, the Sepulchre was in the foreground, while the painted scene represented the summit of a mountain on which Abraham's sacrifice of Isaac was in progress. Among the leading composers of *sepolcri* are, besides Draghi, Antonio Bertali, P. A. Ziani, Antonio Cesti, G. B. Pederzuoli, and the emperor Leopold I.

R. Schnitzler: *The Sacred Dramatic Music of Antonio Draghi* (diss., U. of North Carolina, 1971)

H. E. Smither: *A History of the Oratorio*, i (Chapel Hill, 1977)

HOWARD E. SMITHER

Septet (Fr. *septuor*; Ger. *Septett*; It. *settimino*). An ensemble for seven voices. Septets are rare as separate numbers outside the context of an act finale. In one early example, Alessandro Scarlatti's *Eraclea* (1700), the seven voices never sing together but rather sing a short melody in turn. The earliest septet in *opéra comique* appears in Monsigny's *Le roi et le fermier* (1762), which preceded another, in Philidor's *Le bûcheron*, by three months. In Monsigny's the voices are rapidly combined, while Philidor introduces them more gradually; both develop into music of some contrapuntal complexity. There are no septets as such in Mozart's operas, though occasionally (as in *Le nozze di Figaro*, Act 2) seven characters sing together in a finale; there is a finale septet, unaccompanied, in Rossini's *Matilde di Shabran* (1821), and one in the *introduzione* to Verdi's *Stiffelio* (1850). There is a true septet (sometimes called the Duel Septet) in Meyerbeer's *Les Huguenots* (1836) and one of outstanding beauty in Berlioz's *Les Troyens* (1863), 'Tout n'est que paix et charme' (drawing on Shakespeare's 'On such a night as this', from *The Merchant of Venice*).

See also FINALE.

JULIAN BUDDEN

Sequi, Sandro (*b* Rome, 10 Nov 1933). Italian director. After graduating from Rome University, where he studied literature and philosophy, he became a dance critic and embarked on a directorial career with *La sonnambula* at La Fenice in 1961. His predisposition towards realistic *mises-en-scène* with a touch of opulence was evident in such productions as *I puritani* (1971, Florence; 1976, Metropolitan), *Guillaume Tell* (1972, Florence) and *Les contes d'Hoffmann* (1975, Dallas).

BARRY MILLINGTON

Serafin, Tullio (*b* Rottanova di Cavarzere, Venice, 1 Sept 1878; *d* Rome, 2 Feb 1968). Italian conductor. He studied at the Milan Conservatory and made his conducting début at Ferrara in 1898. After experience in various Italian cities, and making his Covent Garden début in 1907, he became principal conductor at La Scala, 1909–14, returning in 1917–18. There he conducted the first Italian productions of *Der Rosenkavalier* and *Feuersnot*, *Oberon*, operas by Dukas, Humperdinck and Rimsky-Korsakov, and the premières of Montemezzi's *L'amore dei tre re* (1913) and *La nave* (1918). At the Metropolitan Opera (1924–34) he conducted the first American productions of *Simon Boccanegra*, *Turandot* and operas by Falla, Giordano, and Musorgsky, and gave the premières of Deems Taylor's *The King's Henchman* (1927) and *Peter Ibbetson* (1931), Louis Gruenberg's *The Emperor Jones* (1933) and Howard Hanson's *Merry Mount* (1934). At New York he did much to develop the careers of several singers, especially Rosa Ponselle, who appeared with him at Covent Garden in 1931 in the first production there of *La forza del destino*, and in *Fedra*, by her teacher, Romano Romani.

Returning to Europe in 1934, Serafin was appointed artistic director of the Rome Teatro Reale. He remained there until 1943, conducting new operas by Alfano, Pizzetti and others, the *Ring* in Italian and the Italian première of *Wozzeck* with Gobbi in the title role. He conducted at the Florence Maggio Musicale, and returned to La Scala for the first postwar season, which included the first Italian production of *Peter Grimes*. During the 1950s, when he had a spell at the Chicago Opera (1956–8), he became closely associated with the career of Maria Callas, both in the opera house and on many noteworthy recordings. In 1959 he coached and conducted Joan Sutherland in her first appearance in *Lucia di Lammermoor* at Covent Garden. Three generations of singers owed much to his skill and encouragement, and it has been said that without him the postwar revival of interest in Italian ottocento opera and the bel canto style would have been impossible. In Gobbi's opinion he was 'an infallible judge of voice and character and an invaluable guide to young singers'. He remained active as a conductor into his 80s, being appointed artistic adviser to the Rome Opera in 1962 and conducting Verdi's *Otello* there that year. With Alceo Toni he wrote *Stile, tradizioni e convenzioni del melodramma italiano del settecento e dell'ottocento* (Milan, 1958). Serafin was modest and retiring in personality, quietly incisive in rehearsal and ruthless only in eradicating carelessness; he often achieved an unparalleled balance of musical line and emotional expression in performance, to which many of his gramophone records testify.

*

W. Weaver and others: 'Tullio Serafin (1878–1968)', *Opera*, xix (1968), 273–7

Obituary, *Opera*, xix (1968), 330

J. B. STEANE, NOËL GOODWIN

Seraglio, The. Opera by W. A. Mozart; *see* ENTFÜHRUNG AUS DEM SERAIL, DIE. (The title has also been used for Mozart's unfinished, untitled opera ZAIDE, which is a setting of a libretto originally entitled *Das Serail*.)

Serail, Das. Opera by W. A. Mozart; *see* ZAIDE.

Serban, Andrei (*b* Bucharest, 21 June 1943). Romanian director. He studied at the Theatre Institute, Bucharest, and directed several plays before going to New York, where his productions for the experimental theatre group La Mama included Greek tragedies (in the original language) and *The Cherry Orchard*. Receiving much acclaim, *The Cherry Orchard* set the tone for his first opera productions, in which stylized but traditional settings framed an acting style of emotional intensity, often illuminated by dreams and fantasies. His first production, *Yevgeny Onegin* (WNO, 1980), began in a setting of wide open cornfields, but showed Onegin and Tatyana progressively enclosed by restricting doors and windows. His staging of *I puritani* (WNO, 1982; also seen at the Netherlands Opera and the Opéra-Comique, Paris) was an intense psychological study of Elvira's mental breakdown. With *Turandot*, which had its première in Los Angeles in 1984 and was also his first production for Covent Garden, Serban and his designer Sally Jacobs successfully integrated the techniques of kabuki and Chinese theatre with those of grand opera. Further London productions have included a controversial *Fidelio*, much influenced by the designs of Beethoven's contemporary William Blake, and a lavish *Prince Igor* in collaboration with the Royal Ballet. In the late 1980s Serban directed the première of Philip Glass's *The Juniper Tree* in Boston, productions of *Alcina* and *Norma* in New York and a violent and experimental version of Prokofiev's *The Fiery Angel* in Los Angeles. He also directed a classically restrained *Elektra* in Geneva. In 1990, after the revolution in Romania, he was made Artistic Director of the National Theatre in Bucharest. MIKE ASHMAN

Serbia. Serbia freed itself from Ottoman rule in the first half of the 19th century; organized musical life in the country dates from the second half of the century. At first the prevailing taste was for a type of Singspiel containing folk and oriental elements which was introduced in the 1840s by Josef Schlesinger, the first director of music at the court of the Prince of Serbia. Davorin Jenko (1835–1914), a Slovene by birth, was particularly successful in this genre. In the first national operas, Stanislav Binički's *Na uranku* ('At Dawn', 1903) and Isidor Bajić's *Knez Ivo od Semberije* ('Prince Ivo of Semberija', 1911), oriental elements were a means of underlining the dramatic contrast between the cultures of the Slavonic population and the occupying Ottomans. Orientalism became a mannerism difficult to shake off and as late as 1927 proved a limitation in Petar Krstić's *Zulumćar* ('The Ruffian'). On the other hand, Milenko Paunović tried in his *Čengić-Aga* (after 1918) to use a more advanced idiom of the music drama.

Belgrade Opera gained a high reputation in the 1920s, when the city became the capital of the newly formed Yugoslavia, but in spite of this few Serbian composers wrote operas. In the 1920s and 30s distinguished works came from Petar Konjović, whose individual language was based on Musorgsky and Janáček: his *Koštana* (1931) is considered the greatest Serbian opera. In *Suton* ('In the Dusk', 1925) Stevan Hristić combined impressionist orchestration with the intimate atmosphere of a chamber opera.

After World War II only Stanojlo Rajičić, Mihovil Logar and Nikola Hercigonja showed a sustained interest in the genre. Rajičić's *Simonida* (1957) is a notable work by a one-time member of the avant garde who turned to a more conventional language. Logar tried in his *Četrdesetprva* ('1941'), completed in 1961, to write a modern yet accessible opera on a theme from World War II. Hercigonja avoided fully staged or sung operas: his *Gorski vijenac* ('The Mountain Wreath', 1957) is an opera-oratorio, and *Stav'te pamet na komediju* ('Let's Do a Comedy', 1964), an opera-ballet. In the early 1960s successful contributions to the genre of comic opera came from Dušan Radić and Dušan Kostić. Since the 1970s several Belgrade composers have turned their attention to operas for television. There are permanent opera companies in Belgrade and Novi Sad.

For further information on operatic life in the country's principal centres *see* BELGRADE and NOVI SAD.

*

S. Djurić-Klajn: *Serbian Music through the Ages* (Belgrade, 1972)
D. Cvetko: *Musikgeschichte der Südslawen* (Kassel and Maribor, 1975)
J. Sivec: *Opera skozi stoletja* ['Opera through the Centuries'] (Ljubljana, 1976)
K. Kovačević, ed.: *Leksikon jugoslavenske muzike* (Zagreb, 1984)

BOJAN BUJIĆ

Serenade (Fr. *sérénade*; Ger. *Serenade*, *Ständchen*; It. *serenata*). An Italian serenade convention, in the modern sense of a song addressed by a lover to his (occasionally her) beloved, existed from the 18th century. Such *serenate*, following a Venetian tradition, are almost always 11-syllable verse with music in 6/8 time and an accompaniment that mimics the thrumming of a guitar. Examples (not all of them so entitled) include 'Chi s'impaccia di moglie cittadina' (*L'infedeltà delusa*, Haydn, 1773), 'Deh vieni, non tardar' (*Le nozze di Figaro*, Mozart, 1786), 'Deh vieni alla finestra' (*Don Giovanni*, Mozart, 1787) with mandolin accompaniment, 'Com'è gentil' (*Don Pasquale*, Donizetti, 1843), 'O Lola ch'hai di latti la cammisa' (*Cavalleria rusticana*, Mascagni, 1890; in Sicilian dialect) and 'O Colombina, il tenero Arlecchin' (*Pagliacci*, Leoncavallo, 1892). 'La gaia canzon fa l'eco languir' (*La Gioconda*, Ponchielli, 1876) is an unaccompanied choral serenade sung behind the scenes as background to an attempted poisoning.

JULIAN BUDDEN

Serenata (It.). A dramatic cantata, normally celebratory or eulogistic in intent, for two or more singers with orchestral accompaniment. The name is derived from Italian 'sereno', meaning 'a clear sky at night', and alludes to the fact that such cantatas were often performed by artificial light in the open air at night time. Through semantic contamination 'serenata' has become associated with 'sera' (evening), possibly by analogy with 'mattinata' (i.e. music for the 'mattina', or morning). However incorrect this etymology may be, it has certainly influenced the interpretation of the word from early times. The term is cognate with English 'serenade' and has been used to denote not only the genre under consideration here but also a lover's serenade in folk or art music or a purely instrumental composition (e.g. Mozart's *Serenata notturna* K239).

The first serenatas appear to have been written in Italy and in Vienna (at the time an Italian literary colony) shortly after the emergence of the solo cantata as a distinct genre. Two early examples are Antonio Bertali's *Gli amori d'Apollo con Clizia* (1661, Vienna) and Antonio (or possibly Remigio) Cesti's *Io son la primavera* (1662, Florence). The genre petered out in the early 19th century, its social and aesthetic basis having been lost through the *embourgeoisement* of aristocratic culture and the universal reaction against Classicism and Arcadianism. The choral cantata is partly its linear descendant, partly its substitute.

Poets and audiences of the 17th and 18th centuries viewed the serenata as a dramatic genre in the Aristotelian sense: the singers represent characters who speak (sing) in their own voice without external narration. However, it was not necessarily dramatic in the more modern senses of being acted on stage or having an identifiable plot. This apparently contradictory nature has given rise in our own day to differing opinions about the nature of the genre, which has been seen by some as a species of overblown cantata and by others as a type of miniature opera. In reality, the serenata is a quite distinct genre, although its literary texts, like those of opera, go by a bewildering number of alternative descriptions that suggest greater diversity than actually exists.

'Serenata' is best understood as a catch-all term like 'opera' or 'oratorio'. It is very often the actual description applied by the poet to his text and by the composer to his setting. Even when it is not, it is the term that one is most likely to encounter in contemporary references to the work (in diaries, letters etc.). The term 'cantata' was also used in the same sense from early times and in the late 18th century was in fact generally preferred, the risk of confusion with the chamber cantata having receded after the decline of that genre, while the rise of the instrumental serenade made the continued use of the description 'serenata' potentially misleading. Poets liked to substitute terms that conveyed something of the special essence of their work. An 'applauso per musica', for example, is explicitly a congratulatory piece, an 'epitalamio musicale' a work written for a wedding; a 'festa teatrale' is a celebratory piece to be performed in an actual or improvised theatre, an 'azione teatrale' a work for theatrical performance that contains some form of action (*azione*). Certain poets used a particular description simply as a kind of trademark: Minato writes 'composizioni per musica', Pasquini 'feste di camera', Bernardoni 'poemetti musicali', and Cassani 'intrecci scenico-musicali'. These are not subgenres lying within the general ambit of the serenata but merely grandiloquent titles.

The serenata shares important features with three genres: the chamber cantata, oratorio and opera. Like the cantata, it was usually a courtly entertainment performed privately before an invited audience. There were exceptions: learned societies (academies) and colleges also promoted serenatas, and in Venice the custom arose of performing a serenata instead of a full-length opera in public theatres on the last night of Carnival in order to leave more time afterwards for banqueting and visiting the gaming-house. Since serenatas were so often given in open spaces, they could also on occasion attract an outer circle of uninvited listeners and so become *de facto* public events. Serenatas usually formed part of a larger celebration, or *festa*, with whose programme they were closely integrated. Sometimes, when a celebration spread over several days, whole cycles of serenatas came into being, such as the five performed at the Contarini palace at Piazzola sul Brenta on 7 and 8 August 1685 (see fig.1). As in chamber cantatas, the singers in serenatas normally read from their parts and remained more or less stationary during the performance. This meant that, relieved of the burden of memorizing, they could if the composer wished tackle more complex music than would be feasible in an opera. Similarly, the poet had the opportunity

1. The dramatic cantata 'Il ritratto della Gloria donato all'Eternità', by Domenico Freschi, performed in the hall of the Villa Contarini, Piazzola sul Brento, on 7 August 1685 (the instrumentalists are girls from the conservatory established by Marco Contarini in Piazzola): engraving from 'L'orologia del piacere' (1685) by the librettist Francesco Maria Piccioli

to introduce greater literary artifice than the operatic stage would tolerate. However, in order to enhance the visual impact and sense of occasion, singers of serenatas were frequently costumed in operatic style and profiled against scenic backgrounds; in 17th-century serenatas, elaborate stage machinery was also often used.

In dramaturgical respects the serenata most closely resembles the Baroque oratorio. Many serenatas, exactly like oratorios, contain allegorical characters personifying abstract concepts such as duty and honour, and their texts usually contain a strong moralizing strain. Another similarity is the frequent division of the composition into two approximately equal parts (but whereas an oratorio was normally broken to accommodate a sermon, the interval of a serenata was commonly used for the serving of refreshments).

It is in its musical style and resources that a serenata comes closest to true opera. The rise of the genre coincided exactly with that of the orchestra in the modern sense (having strings in four or five doubled parts), and its instrumental accompaniment was orchestral almost from the very beginning. Wealthy patrons sometimes recruited mammoth orchestras for serenatas in a spirit of frank ostentation: Cardinal Melchior de Polignac, for instance, needed 130 players in 1729 for the celebration of the dauphin's birth in *La contesa de' numi* (text by Metastasio, music by Vinci; *see* ROME, fig.3). Like operas, serenatas sometimes include choruses, although movements described as 'coro' often turn out merely to be ensembles for the full cast of principals.

The length of a serenata is highly variable. Cassani's *Il nome glorioso in terra, santificato in cielo* (1724, set by Albinoni) represents something close to the average, with five closed numbers in its first part, six in its second; this is equivalent to slightly more than one act of a three-act *dramma per musica.* Extreme brevity is represented by Metastasio's *La rispettosa tenerezza* (1750, set by Reutter), which contains only one closed number, extreme length by *Il nascimento dell'Aurora* (*c*1710, set by Albinoni), which contains 25 closed numbers (one repeated) and amazingly eschews the customary division into two parts.

One special feature of serenatas that distinguishes them from most operas is that the importance of the roles is usually kept very equal, even when these number as many as six or seven. Arias are often organized in 'rounds' containing one aria for each singer (to prevent excessive uniformity, successive rounds usually vary the order of singing). In many cases the division into rounds coincides with a structural division of the text.

Since the settings in which serenatas were performed varied so much – only a minority were heard in purpose-built theatres – one cannot easily generalize about the manner of their production. Enormous ingenuity was expended by architects, carpenters and scenery painters in the creation of 'theatres for a day'. One favourite motif was the opposition between land and water. The *Serenata fatta sull'Elba* (1719, music by Heinichen) had the performers on a boat moored in the Elbe and the Saxon court watching from the bank (see fig.2). Conversely, *Le gare delle lodi di Sua Eccellenza conte di Melgara*, with which Marco Contarini regaled a visitor to Piazzola in 1686, placed the audience on a boat and left the performers on dry land.

The poets and musicians commissioned to write serenatas were nearly always local talents. This can be explained by the extreme pressure of time under which both often had to work (amusingly satirized in Metastasio's *Il Parnaso confuso*, 1765; *see* VIENNA, fig.4) and the need for close liaison with the commissioning patron. Although most of the authors and composers of the serenatas are also known from their operatic activity, quite a few minor figures and *dilettanti* to whom operatic commissions were never offered made a contribution to the genre. The only author of serenatas who can truly be said to have operated at an international level, receiving commissions from afar, was Metastasio, many of whose librettos achieved the status of 'classic' texts that were set and reset by one composer after another in exactly the same way as his opera librettos. In addition, the serenata offered high-born amateur singers (such as members of the Habsburg dynasty) a socially acceptable means of appearing publicly in dramatic music, free from the taint of the professional theatre.

The occasions that called forth serenatas can be divided into those that could usually be predicted and prepared for well in advance (e.g. birthdays, name-days, weddings, annually recurring ceremonies and official visits), and those which could not be predicted with the same degree of certainty and had to be celebrated as soon as possible after the event (e.g. births, military victories and peace treaties). Nearly all serenatas contain as a matter of course a clear allusion to the event celebrated. The re-use or adaptation of a complete text for a later festive occasion occurred relatively rarely, perhaps because this was thought disrespectful to both the old and the new recipient of homage; however, the borrowing of short portions of text or music from earlier works was not precluded, although it was done less blatantly than in opera. Once again, the great exception is Metastasio, whose most important serenata texts seem to have reduced topical reference to the minimum in order to make them more re-usable; a good example is his *L'isola disabitata*, which in 1753 received its première in Madrid in a setting by Bonno and during the next 30 years was set successively by Holzbauer, Uttini, Sales, Jommelli, Perez, Traetta, Calegari, J. G. Naumann, Astarita, Haydn and Gatti.

Most serenatas lack a plot in the ordinary sense, although a few include a small amount of dramatic action (a good example is Handel's *Aci, Galatea e Polifemo*); indeed, Metastasio's *azioni teatrali* owe their description as such to the presence of a plot. The *dramatis personae* of serenatas, when not allegorical figures as described above, can be deities, semi-deities or denizens of Arcadia; only rarely do actual historical figures appear, as in Metastasio's *Il sogno di Scipione*, 1743. The absence of a plot poses a problem for the poet, who has to work towards the climax (which can often be equated with the final revelation of the person and/or event celebrated) at a very leisurely pace. Two favourite models of construction are employed. The first can be termed the 'debate' or 'contest' model, and is frequently indicated by the words *gara* or *contesa* (or their opposites, *unione* and *concordia*) in the title. Jacques Joly refers to this type very appositely as the 'joute oratoire', or oratorical tourney. As in the debates of academies, the characters put forward different points of view which finally become reconciled or synthesized. The second common model is that of the 'quest', in which the characters discover in stages the object of their celebration.

Topical references are customarily veiled in Arcadian language. For example, an Austrian emperor may be alluded to merely by use of the adjective 'augusto', while Venice often appears as 'L'Adria' (the Adriatic). Sometimes the allusions are very oblique indeed. Vivaldi's *Serenata a tre* RV690 apparently commemorates the imprisonment of a Jansenist propagandist, Amable de Tourreil; the refusal of the shepherd Alcindo, standing for Tourreil himself, to pay more than lip-service to erotic love symbolizes the refusal of his sect to submit

2. Festival of Diana on the Elbe, a serenata, with music by Heinichen, given as part of the festivities in honour of the marriage of Crown Prince Friedrich August II to Maria Josepha (daughter of Joseph I of Austria) in Dresden in August 1719: pen and ink drawing with wash (artist unknown)

wholeheartedly to papal authority. Flights of fancy that would have been regarded as risky deviations in opera find an occasional place in the serenata. For instance, a fifth of *Il nascimento dell'Aurora* (mentioned above) is given over to a dramatically irrelevant word-game played by the five characters, which gives rise to banter of astonishing liveliness.

Essentially an Italian conception, the serenata soon spread beyond the Alps to centres of Italian culture in northern Europe. In Lutheran states vernacular versions appeared. The works by J. S. Bach that we commonly know today as 'secular cantatas' could accurately be described as German serenatas; two (BWV66*a* and 173*a*) are actually titled 'serenata'. In England the venerable court ode normally took the form of a serenata by the start of the 18th century; good examples of the type are the birthday odes for the sovereign composed by Kusser in Dublin, which run in a continuous series from 1709 to 1727, or the birthday and New Year odes of William Boyce, from 1751 to 1779. Only France resisted the serenata, rather strangely in view of its successful naturalization of both opera and the cantata.

The extinction of the serenata began when aristocratic culture, classicizing language and Arcadian imagery came into conflict with democratic sentiments, Romanticism and the pursuit of realism. An extraordinary mismatch of style and content is already apparent in *Mantova assediata* (text by G. Artusi, music by V. Trento), performed at the Venetian theatre of S Salvatore in 1799 in homage to Emperor Francis II, victor over the French. Alongside the traditional allegorical characters Manto, symbolizing Mantua, and Liberty (later revealed as Falsehood), symbolizing French revolutionary philosophy, we find such realistic figures as a French officer, a German adjutant and an unwillingly conscripted French soldier, formerly an innkeeper. The loss of Italian musical hegemony north of the Alps hastened the serenata's demise there; it lingered on in Italy until the end of the Rossinian epoch.

Most music-lovers and probably most musicologists do not yet appreciate in either qualitative or quantitative terms how significant the serenata genre was in its time. From a modern point of view, it sits rather uncomfortably between the stage and the concert hall, and has suffered as a result. Fortunately, the growth in recent years of music theatre as distinct from traditional opera has encouraged the development of an aesthetic that is more tolerant of forms of presentation intermediate between a full staging and a concert performance, opening the door to an imaginative revival of the best works in the serenata tradition in a style that respects its essential nature.

For further illustration *see* SEATING, fig.1.

*

AllacciD

F. M. Piccioli: *L'orologio del piacere* (Piazzola, 1685)

Catalogo delle compositioni musicali continente oratori sacri, componimenti da camera, serenate et opere composte e rappresentate sotto il gloriosissimo governo … di Carlo VI (MS, *A-Wn*)

J. Mattheson: *Der vollkommene Capellmeister* (Hamburg, 1739)

F. S. Quadrio: *Della storia e della ragione d'ogni poesia*, iii/2 (Milan, 1744), 333

B. Valmarana: *Drammaturgia compilata in seguito a quella pubblicata dell'Allacci* (MS, 1842, *I-Vnm*)

P. Camerini: *Piazzola* (Milan, 1925)

I. Becker-Glauch: *Die Bedeutung der Musik für die Dresdener Hoffeste bis in die Zeit Augusts des Starken* (Kassel and Basle, 1951)

F. Hadamowsky: 'Barocktheater am Wiener Kaiserhof, mit einem Spielplan (1625–1740)', *Jb der Gesellschaft für Wiener Theaterforschung 1951–52* (Vienna, 1955), 7–117

O. Jander: *Alessandro Stradella and his Minor Dramatic Works* (diss., Harvard U., 1962)

R. Monelle: 'Gluck and the *festa teatrale*', *MQ*, liv (1973), 308–25

T. J. Walsh: *Opera in Dublin 1705–1797: the Social Scene* (Dublin, 1973)

T. Griffin: *Alessandro Scarlatti's Serenata Erminia, Tancredi, Polidoro e Pastore* (diss., UCLA, 1975)

U. Hofmann: *Die Serenata am Hofe Kaiser Leopold I. 1658–1705* (diss., U. of Vienna, 1975)

S. Dahms: 'Mozart's festa teatrale "Ascanio in Alba" ', *ÖMz*, xxxi (1976), 15–24

J. Joly: *Les fêtes théâtrales de Métastase à la cour de Vienne (1731–1767)* (Clermont-Ferrand, 1978)

L. Kantner: 'Le opere di Francesco Gasparini a Vienna', *Francesco Gasparini (1661–1727): Camaiore 1978*, 59–65

H. Seifert: 'Die Aufführungen der Opern und Serenate mit Musik von Johann Joseph Fux', *SMw*, xxix (1978), 9–27

H. E. Samuel: 'John Sigismond Cousser in London and Dublin', *ML*, lxi (1980), 158–71

M. Talbot: 'Vivaldi's Serenatas: Long Cantatas or Short Operas?', *Antonio Vivaldi: teatro musicale, teatro e società: Venice 1981*, 67–96

M. Gemin: 'L'Adria Festosa per Federico Cristiano: la lunga visita', *L'invenzione del gusto: Corelli e Vivaldi: mutazioni culturali, a Roma e Venezia, nel periodo post-barocco* (Milan, 1982), 191–212

M. Talbot: 'The Serenata in Eighteenth-Century Venice', *RMARC*, no.18 (1982), 1–50

T. Griffin: *The Late Baroque Serenata in Rome and Naples: a Documentary Study with Emphasis on Alessandro Scarlatti (Italy)* (diss., UCLA, 1983)

L. Zoppelli: 'Il pensiero conservato dagli affetti: psicologia retorica e linguaggi interni della rappresentazione festiva leopoldina (Vienna, 1690)', *Il tranquillo seren del secol d'oro: musica e spettacolo musicale a Venezia e a Vienna fra seicento e settecento* (Milan, 1984), 9–39

A. Cetrangolo and G. De Padova: *La serenata vocale tra viceregno e metropoli: Giacomo Facco dalla Sicilia a Madrid* (Padua, 1990)

M. Talbot: *Tomaso Albinoni: the Venetian Composer and his World* (Oxford, 1990)

MICHAEL TALBOT

Sereni, Mario (*b* Perugia, 25 March 1928). Italian baritone. He studied at the Accademia Chigiana in Siena and the Accademia di S Cecilia in Rome and privately with Basiola. His début was in 1953 at the Florence Maggio Musicale in Lualdi's *Il diavolo nel campanile*, and he went on to sing in Buenos Aires, Chicago, Mexico City, Milan, Naples, Palermo, Rome, Verona and Vienna. After his Metropolitan Opera début in 1957, as Carlo Gérard in *Andrea Chénier*, he became a mainstay of the company, singing over 380 performances of 26 roles. His robust but flexible voice has allowed him to span the baritone repertory from the lyric to the dramatic, from lighter roles such as Belcore, Rossini's Figaro and Malatesta to Verdi's Iago, Macbeth and Nabucco, and the *verismo* Scarpia and Tonio.

CORI ELLISON

Serio, Luigi (*b* Vico Equendo, 1744; *d* 13 June 1799). Italian poet. He was named *poeta di corte* for Naples in 1778 as part of a reform of the theatrical administration and held the post until 1795. His duties included writing prologue and cantata texts for special occasions and vetting and adapting librettos for operas produced in all Neapolitan theatres. His *Ifigenia in Aulide*, set by Vicente Martín y Soler for Naples in 1779, was reset by Alessio Prati for Florence in 1784. Serio's version of this often reworked *opera seria* plot can be identified by the absence of Clytemnestra and the presence of Elisena, the 'other' Iphigenia, who dies instead of the heroine. This calls into question attributions to Serio of settings by

Lorenzo Rossi (1784) and Giuseppe Giordani (1786) and suggests that the London production, with music by Bertoni, was based on Serio's libretto and not Cigna-Santi's. Serio's *Oreste*, set by Cimarosa for Naples in 1783, represents a unique treatment of the circumstances surrounding Orestes' exile to Argos and a rare example of an *opera seria* with an unhappy ending. Also forward-looking are the sizable finales and the vestigial third act with only two scenes. MARITA P. McCLYMONDS

Sernicola, Carlo (*fl* 1787–95). Italian poet. He was a member of the Arcadian Academy active in Naples. His first known libretto was for an oratorio set for Naples by Giuseppe Giordani in 1787. The following year he produced an oratorio for Guglielmi; the comic opera *I matrimoni per fanatismo*, set by Anfossi in the same year, may also be by him. His two tragedies of the 1790s both have happy endings, unlike their counterparts in the north. Sernicola was one of the first to treat the bloody story of the Orazi and the Curiazi in operatic form. In his version Orazia is reconciled with her brother, whereas she dies at his hands in Sografi's version for Cimarosa a year later (1796, Milan). In *Sofronia ed Olindo*, the villain dies in the extended action finale. Both Sernicola's comic and his serious operas contain a number of ensembles in addition to introductory ensembles and finales. *Gli Orazi* makes extensive use of chorus.

Debora e Sisara [secularized as *Arsineo e Breno*] (azione sacra), P. A. Guglielmi, 1788; *Sofronia ed Olindo* [*Amelia ed Ottiero*] (azione tragica), Andreozzi, 1793; *Gli Orazi* (azione tragica), Zingarelli, 1795, as Gli Orazi e i Curiazi

*

M. McClymonds: 'The Venetian Role in the Transformation of Italian Opera Seria during the 1790s', *I vicini di Mozart: Venice 1987*, 221–40 MARITA P. McCLYMONDS

Serov, Alexander Nikolayevich (*b* St Petersburg, 11/23 Jan 1820; *d* St Petersburg, 20 Jan/1 Feb 1871). Russian composer and critic. Although he never occupied any official position, never taught, and belonged to no organized group or faction, Serov was the most significant and, except for Anton Rubinstein, the most influential Russian musician of the 1860s. His critical writings, modelled on Wagner's and closely resembling them in their idealism, are unrivalled in his country's literature for breadth and weight. Many of his essays have gone through numerous reprints and have continued to exert a strong authority during the Soviet period. (A new collected edition, inaugurated in 1984, had reached five out of seven volumes by 1990.) His operas, also modelled on Wagner's but much less closely resembling them, were the outstanding contributions to the Russian musical stage between Dargomïzhsky's *Rusalka* and the early works of Tchaikovsky and The Five. They have not survived in the repertory.

1. Background, influences. 2. The operas: style and reception.

1. BACKGROUND, INFLUENCES. Serov's development as a composer may have been the most retarded in the history of music; it could have happened only in Russia. He was born into the family of a well-placed civil servant, and educated for a similar career. It was at the Imperial School of Jurisprudence, an institution that trained gifted youths for civil service sinecures, that his musical inclinations flourished, partly as a result of a powerful friendship with Vladimir Stasov, his schoolmate and later his chief critical antagonist. Another major influence on his decision to devote himself to music was Glinka, with whom he became acquainted in 1842. At that time there were no institutions in Russia for professional training in musical composition, a calling that had no social standing there. Since Serov's family, though highly cultured, was neither aristocratic nor independently wealthy, he had no leisure to pursue music as a full-time avocation, as Glinka and Dargomïzhsky had done. While on his first civil service posting, in the Crimean resort town of Simferopol', Serov had a few counterpoint lessons by correspondence with Osip Hunke, a Czech pedagogue on the staff of the court choir school in St Petersburg; these were the sum total of his formal training as a composer. For the rest he learnt by painful trial and error. Early operatic projects (1843–54), documented chiefly in a huge correspondence with Stasov, include *Basurman* ('The Infidel'), after a historical novel about Tsar Ivan III by Ivan Lazhechnikov (1838); *Vindzorskiye prokaznitzï* ('The Merry Wives of Windsor'); *Mel'nichikha v Marli*, after Duveyrier's popular vaudeville *La meunière de Marly* (1840); and Gogol's Ukrainian tale *Mayskaya noch', ili Utoplennitsa* ('May Night, or The Drowned Maiden', 1831), later set by Rimsky-Korsakov. The last was completed, according to Serov's autobiographical sketch, but destroyed owing to an insufficiency of national character, brusquely pointed out by Stasov. Fragments from it (and from *Mel'nichikha*) survive and have seen scattered publication. The first two projects never got beyond the planning stage.

Serov's career as critic began during a brief period (1851–2) in which, having impulsively resigned his civil service commission to devote himself to composition, he found himself in a state of near-starvation. From then until 1865, when a crown stipend at last assured his livelihood, he maintained a frenzied literary productivity that made him an extraordinary reputation but virtually eclipsed his true musical vocation. His critical voice was from the first that of a frustrated operatic composer: all of his most important essays were prolix, high-minded and compulsively polemical tracts on the aesthetics (which for him amounted to the ethics) of dramatic music.

The first of these programmatic pieces was *Spontini i yego muzïka* ('Spontini and his Music', 1852), in which he gave first Russian voice to the well-worn reformist position (there attributed to Gluck) that the criteria of musical drama 'are the same as those of spoken drama, that music drama must be, in fact, and above all, *drama*'. For this blessed union to come about, he asserted, it would be necessary to reconcile the demands of musical beauty with those of 'truth of expression', which implied the rapprochement of the Italian and German schools. Disillusioned with Meyerbeer, he looked forward to the advent of 'a new operatic genius, inclined towards the tragic genre', who would 'loose the Gordian knot'.

Within months of writing these words, Serov discovered *Oper und Drama*, and this began his long involvement – personal, professional and propagandistic – with Wagner, in whom he instantly recognized a kindred spirit. He met Wagner in Weimar in 1858, immediately after being bowled over by *Tannhäuser*. In 1863 he heralded Wagner's Russian tour and proclaimed himself a disciple. His incautious advocacy of a composer from whom other Russian musicians tended to hold aloof did his reputation more immediate harm than good, and has also affected posterity's view of him, placing him in an unfortunate double bind. His aesthetic position is often described as wholly derivative from Wagner's, though the Spontini article shows it to have been basically in place by the time of his 'conversion'. More seriously, the fact that his subsequent creative work does not so obviously derive from Wagner has been taken as evidence not merely of a lesser gift, but of inconstancy and opportunism as well.

This unfair assessment is due to Stasov, with whom Serov fell out over a divergent view of Glinka's legacy (and over Stasov's brief amorous entanglement with Serov's sister). As a partisan of the Balakirev circle, Stasov upheld *Ruslan and Lyudmila* as a model of Russian national music despite its dramaturgical shortcomings. Serov, true to his puritanical idealism, rejected *Ruslan* in favour of the dramatically stronger *A Life for the Tsar*. Their estrangement erupted into a bitter and protracted press war after Glinka's death, in which Serov was portrayed as a blind 'Zukunftist' hostile to the 'New Russian School', despite his uniformly warm critical reception of Balakirev, Cui, Musorgsky and Rimsky-Korsakov on their respective débuts. (His later hostility to Balakirev and Cui was a response to overt provocation.) Stasov, who outlived Serov by more than 30 years, continued to besmirch his memory in a torrent of abusive writings, including the great synoptical articles that formed the basis for Western reception of Russian music in the early 20th century.

Whatever disadvantages may have accrued to Serov from his Wagnerian leanings, they were amply outweighed by the simple fact that it was Wagner's example – the proof, as it were, that the ideal was attainable – that reawakened Serov's dormant appetite for musico-dramatic creation. In 1857 he turned to another Russian Wagnerite – Konstantin Zvantsov, an official of the Imperial Theatres who later translated *Tannhäuser* and *Lohengrin* for their Russian premières – with a proposal that they become a team. Serov proposed an opera on Pushkin's *Poltava* (later the basis for Tchaikovsky's *Mazepa*). Zvantsov countered with F. H. C. de la Motte Fouqué's *Undine* (already the basis of a Russian opera by Alexey L'vov). For three years they got nowhere; but on the night of 20 December 1860/1 January 1861, the two of them were sitting together in a box at the Mariinsky Theatre when the touring Italian tragedienne Adelaida Ristori, speaking her own language, scored a sensation as the title character in *Giuditta* by Paolo Giacometti. This was it at last: two and a half years later, at the same theatre, the 43-year-old Serov finally made his operatic début with *Yudif'* ('Judith').

2. THE OPERAS: STYLE AND RECEPTION. *Judith* was a thing of paradoxes. To begin with, Russia's most unrelentingly anti-Italian critic had conceived it as an Italian opera and offered it as a vehicle to Emmy Lagrua, the reigning diva at the St Petersburg Italian Opera from 1859 to 1862. A quixotic bid for prestige on the part of an understandably impatient composer, the scheme foundered when Lagrua refused the work (statutorily unperformable by the Italian troupe in any case since it was by a Russian composer). The libretto, commissioned by Serov through Zvantsov from a local Italian teacher and *improvisatore* named Giustiniani, had to be translated into Russian. This Zvantsov did, together with a younger writer, Dmitry Lobanov; towards the end Apollon Maykov, a major poet of the period whom Serov knew through the civil service (where they both worked as censors of the foreign press), contributed some aria verses. Although his opera's libretto was thus the work of a committee, Serov maintained, and believed, that he was – according to the Wagnerian prescription – author of the text as well as the music; that is because he had planned the scenario. According to a theory he had asserted as early as his pre-Wagnerian Spontini essay, the actual words of the libretto were not a fully fledged constituent of the musical drama, which consisted of 'musico-theatrical frescoes' in which the only significant impressions were those carried to the eyes by the movements of the *dramatis personae*, and to the ears by the music. In keeping with this precept, Serov composed the music of his opera before he received the verbal texts. This was by no means an unheard-of procedure, especially in Russia, where a precedent had been established by Glinka himself. Serov, however, may be the only operatic composer to have worked in this way out of principled conviction.

The music of *Judith* is raw, blatant and stylistically anonymous. It also exhibits what César Cui, no friend of its composer, had to recognize as 'a nose for theatre' coupled with a respectably 'conscious attempt to embody a truly contemporary view of art'. Wagnerian affinities are not to be sought in the musical details but in the flexible formal design, in which full closes are avoided for exceedingly long stretches. The opera enjoyed far more than the predicted *succès d'estime*. In the words of the theatrical chronicler Alexander Vol'f, 'the public listened attentively, but with comparative reserve, to the uncommonly serious music; but the more the drama unfolded, the more the opera appealed; applause rang out more and more frequently and at the end the composer was unanimously cheered several times'. The mounting success was surely due in part to a canny scenario that followed a pair of severe acts depicting the besieged Hebrews with a pair of gaudy ones set in the Assyrian camp. *Judith* played 20 times to full houses during its first season, an extraordinary success for a Russian opera.

The critical reception was also unusually friendly, with an especially lengthy and appreciative review from the poet Apollon Grigor'yev, through whom Serov was introduced to a literary circle known as *pochvenniki* ('men of the soil'), clustered round Dostoyevsky's journals *Vremya* ('Time') and *Epokha*. It was in this conservatively nationalistic milieu that Serov's second opera, a patriotic historical hodgepodge known as *Rogneda*, gradually took shape. Set in 10th-century Kiev at the time of the christianization of Russia, it celebrated the union of the Russian church and state. True to his critical principles (or so he imagined), Serov copied the dramaturgical shape of *A Life for the Tsar*, opposing 'pagan' and 'Christian' music (as Glinka had opposed Russian and Polish) in an accelerating rhythm of confrontation, meanwhile planting a melody for multifarious symbolic reprise and eventual blazing culmination, 'thematic' in a dual sense (ex.1). Carried away with aesthetic-cum-ethical zeal, Serov composed a pompous preface to the opera's libretto, in which he again claimed authorship of 'both the canvas and the music', although the actual words were written (again to waiting music) by Dmitry Averkiyev, a poetaster who later collaborated (more normally) with Anton Rubinstein. 'My ideal is dramatic truth in tone', Serov asseverated, boasting that for the sake of his ideal he 'had to sacrifice "conventional" beauty, the "jewelled" elegance of musical form', and warning that any criticism of this sacrifice 'will expose, in my eyes, only the immaturity' of the critic.

['Submit to the cross, enlighten thy people, affirming the true faith to all the land. And formidable to its foes, and in eternal glory, the Holy Russian land shall live.']

(b) Historical song *Pro tatarskiy polon* ('On the Tatar captivity'), no. 2 of *Sobraniye russkikh narodnïkh pesen*, ed. M. A. Stakhovich, iv (1854)

['There is no noise, no thunder rumbles']

The ease with which Serov's antagonists (chiefly Stasov and Cui) were able to hoist the poor composer with his own petard, even as the old-guard press was extolling his 'civic deed', has made the critical reception of *Rogneda* a famous tragicomedy. The action, pieced together from miscellaneous factual and fictional sources, could hardly have been less coherent; the opera's historical gaffes could scarcely have been more glaring; nor, despite the composer's claims, was it at all short on conventional operatic trappings or formal numbers, many – especially the folklike ones – of a triviality it was only too easy to expose.

The opera was also the most sensational success in the history of the Russian musical stage. Vol'f, a detached and therefore credible witness to the incredible, describes the unprecedented visit of the tsar (Alexander II) and tsarina to the normally despised Russian Opera in order to witness the phenomenal triumph (12/24 November 1865). Serov, summoned to their box, was awarded a lifetime pension on the spot, thus becoming Russia's unofficial composer laureate. The Grand Duchess Yelena Pavlovna, patroness supreme of Russian art music, commissioned a libretto for Serov from the court poet Yakov Polonsky, based on Gogol's *Christmas Eve*, a story that itself celebrates imperial largesse. Needless to say, the composer of *Rogneda* was accused of pandering – 'Why shouldn't Serov's operas succeed?', sniffed Dargomïzhsky, 'there are camels in the first and dogs in the second' – but the only evidence of that was his success. The undeniable triteness of his score was not cynical; the way the truculent autodidact cleaved to his exalted models even as he fell so laughably short of them is, at a century's remove, oddly touching.

Serov did not live to write *Christmas Eve* (a posthumous piano suite was published by his widow Valentina Serova, herself a composer, who claimed to have worked from sketches that have not survived). By the time he received that commission he had already set his heart on another operatic venture, to be his last. Although he spent more than five years on the project (twice as long as he had worked on his other operas), it was still unfinished at his untimely death from a heart attack. The reason was the huge, paralysing rift that developed between the cantankerous composer and his librettist, the famous playwright Alexander Ostrovsky. It was a great pity, for *Vrazh'ya sila* ('The Power of the Fiend') was on its improbable way to becoming a genuine masterpiece, as far removed in concept as one could imagine from the gaudy monumental spectacles on which Serov had made his reputation. Even in its ersatz redactions (first by the composer's widow in collaboration with Nikolay Solov'yov, later by the Soviet scholar Boris Asaf'yev), the work represents the highwater-mark of 'genre realism' (the realism of simple everyday life) in Russian opera, and the most thoroughgoing integration of Russian folk idioms into art music ever attempted.

Genre realism implies an unpretentious, even casual formal design, and Serov, with fine theatrical instinct, cast the work in an unashamed numbers format not far removed from the lowly status of the vaudeville, a genre still current on the St Petersburg stage, where an active French theatre (both spoken and modestly musical) remained popular throughout the 19th century. In place of spoken dialogue, however, Serov concocted an idiosyncratic sort of recitative that was no less imbued than the lyric numbers with the 'intonations' of urban folksong. And, having decided to end the opera with a bloody denouement to replace Ostrovsky's happy ending (the source of their falling-out), Serov composed music that for studied ugliness had no precedent in the music of his time. In the best scenes (the Act 3 finale, the Shrovetide panorama in Act 4) the combination really jelled; the opera has an originality of style and an integrity of tone at which nothing in Serov's earlier output had so much as hinted.

What *The Power of the Fiend* hints at is a tremendous aesthetic kinship between Serov and that other militant realist of the Russian operatic stage, Musorgsky – a kinship lamentably obscured by the artistic politics of their day and the conventional historiography of ours. When this is realized – in the 19th century only Hermann Laroche perceived it – concrete parallels between all three of Serov's operas and the work of his younger contemporary suddenly loom up. They include some of Musorgsky's most memorable conceptions: Boris Godunov's hallucination (compare Holofernes' in *Judith*, Act 4); the famous tritone tintinnabulations in Tsar Boris's coronation scene (anticipated in the Royal Hunt from *Rogneda*, Act 3); the folksong recitatives in *The Fair at Sorochintsï* (compare *The Power of the Fiend*, passim). Rimsky-Korsakov also paraphrased Serov from time to time – and not altogether unconsciously, as he admitted in his marvellously candid autobiography. The Assyrians in the middle acts of *Judith* lurk behind Borodin's Polovtsï in the middle acts of *Prince Igor*. Not even Tchaikovsky was immune to Serovian reminiscence: there is more than a passing whiff of the *Judith* title role in that of *The Maid of Orléans*, and as late as 1892, only a year before his death, Tchaikovsky told an interviewer that, next to *A Life for the Tsar*, Serov's first opera was the Russian opera he loved best. Much as Stasov may have hated the idea, his much-maligned antagonist was a vital and necessary link between the Russian opera of the early 19th century and the late-19th-century works that dominate the repertory.

See also ROGNEDA; VRAZH'YA SILA; and YUDIF'.

Basurman [The Infidel] (after I. Lazhechnikov), scenario described in letter to V. Stasov, 18/30 Aug 1843, ed. in Gozenpud and Obram, i (1961)

Vindzorskiye prokaznitzï [The Merry Wives of Windsor], 1844 (V. R. Zotov, after W. Shakespeare), project described in correspondence with Stasov, ed. in Gozenpud and Obram, i (1961), and Zotov (1896)

Mel'nichikha v Marli [The Miller-Girl from Marly], 1844 (after C. Duveyrier), several nos., excerpt in Findeyzen, facs. in Gozenpud and Obram, i (1961); complete opera attempted 1845–7 (D'yachenko), autograph facs. of 1 aria in Gozenpud and Obram, ii (1966)

Mayskaya noch' [May Night], 1850–54 (2 or 3, P. Bakunina, after N. V. Gogol), 10 nos., ?destroyed; frag. in *RMG*, iii (1896)

Poltava (K. Zvantsov, after A. S. Pushkin), projected *c*1857

Undine (Zvantsov, after F. H. C. de la Motte Fouqué), projected, ?sketched *c*1858–60

Yudif' [Judith], 1861–3 (5, Serov, with I. A. Giustiniani, Zvantsov, D. Lobanov and A. Maykov, after the Apocrypha, P. Giacometti and F. Hebbel), St Petersburg, Mariinsky, 16/28 May 1863, vs (Moscow, 1885)

Rogneda (5, Serov, with D. V. Averkiyev, after M. N. Zagoskin, K. Rïleyev and historical chronicles), St Petersburg, Mariinsky, 27 Oct/8 Nov 1865, vs (St Petersburg, 1866)

Noch' pod rozhdestvo [Christmas Eve], 1866 (3, Ya. Polonsky, after Gogol), sketches only

Vrazh'ya sila [The Power of the Fiend; Hostile Power], 1867–71 (5, A. N. Ostrovsky, P. Kalashnikov and A. Zhokhov, after Ostrovsky: *Ne tak zhivi, kak khochetsya* [Live Not the Way You'd Like]), inc.; completed and ed. V. S. Serova and N. F. Solov'yov, St Petersburg, Mariinsky, 19 April/1 May 1871, vs (Moscow, 1885); completed and ed. B. Asaf'yev, Moscow, Bol'shoy, 30 May 1947

Gusitï [Hussites] (trilogy), projected; described by Serov in Khubov, i (1950), 77

WRITINGS

ed. N. Stoyanovsky, V. Stasov and others: *Kriticheskiye stat'i* [Critical Essays] (St Petersburg, 1892–5)

ed. G. Khubov: *Izbrannïye stat'i* [Selected Essays] (Moscow, 1950 and Leningrad, 1957)

ed. A. Gozenpud and V. Obram: 'A. N. Serov: Pis'ma k V. V. i D. V. Stasovïm' [Letters to V. V. and D. V. Stasov], *Muzïkal'noye nasledstvo* [Musical Heritage], i (Moscow, 1961), 65–312; ii/1 (Moscow, 1966), 44–267; iii (Moscow, 1970), 27–207

ed. V. Protopopov and others: *Stat'i o muzïke* [Essays on Music] (Moscow, 1984–)

*

F. M. Tolstoy [Rostislav]: 'A. N. Serov: vospominaniya' [Reminiscences of Serov], *Russkaya starina* (1874), no.2

A. Vol'f: *Khronika Peterburgskikh teatrov s kontsa 1855 do nachala 1881 goda* [A Chronicle of Petersburg Theatres from the End of 1855 to the Beginning of 1881] (St Petersburg, 1884)

D. Lobanov: *Serov i ego sovremenniki* [Serov and his Contemporaries] (St Petersburg, 1886)

A. Molchanov: *Bibliograficheskiy ukazatel' literaturï o A. N. Serove i ego proizvedeniyakh* [A Bibliographical Directory of the Literature on Serov and his Works] (St Petersburg, 1888)

K. Zvantsov: *Aleksandr Nikolayevich Serov v 1857–1871 gg.: vospominaniya o nyom i ego pis'ma* [Reminiscences about Serov and his Letters] (St Petersburg, 1888)

V. Baskin: *A. N. Serov: biograficheskiy ocherk* [A Biographical Study] (Moscow, 1890)

V. Zotov: 'Aleksandr Nikolayevich Serov i pervaya zadumannaya im opera' [Serov and his First Projected Opera], *Nablyudatel'* (1896), no.1

N. Findeyzen: *Aleksandr Nikolayevich Serov: ego zhizn' i muzïkal'naya deyatel'nost'* [Serov's Life and Musical Activities] (Moscow, 1900, 2/1904)

V. Serova: *Serovï, Aleksandr Nikolayevich i Valentin Aleksandrovich: vospominaniya* [Reminiscences of A. N. and V. A. Serov] (St Petersburg, 1914)

O. von Riesemann: 'Alexander Seroff and his Relations to Wagner and Liszt', *MQ*, ix (1923), 450–68

M. D. Calvocoressi and G. Abraham: *Masters of Russian Music* (London, 1936) [incl. G. Abraham: 'Serof', 76–96]

G. Khubov: *Zhizn' A. Serova* [Life of Serov] (Moscow and Leningrad, 1950)

G. Abraham: 'The Operas of Serov', *Essays Presented to Egon Wellesz* (Oxford, 1966), 171–83; repr. in *Essays on Russian and East European Music* (Oxford, 1985), 40–55

T. Livanova: *Opernaya kritika v Rossii* [Opera Criticism in Russia], ii/3 (Moscow, 1969)

A. Gozenpud: 'Opernoye tvorchestvo A. N. Serova' [Serov's Operatic Works], *SovM* (1971), no.7, pp.91–102

R. Ridenour: *Nationalism, Modernism, and Personal Rivalry in 19th-Century Russian Music* (Ann Arbor, 1981)

A. Stupel: *Aleksandr Nikolayevich Serov (1820–1871)* (Leningrad, 1981)

R. Taruskin: *Opera and Drama in Russia* (Ann Arbor, 1981)

M. Cherkashina: *Aleksandr Nikolayevich Serov* (Moscow, 1985)

R. Taruskin: 'Serov and Musorgsky', *Slavonic and Western Music: Essays for Gerald Abraham* (Ann Arbor and Oxford, 1985), 139–62

Yu. Keldïsh: 'Opernoye tvorchestvo A. N. Serova' [Serov's Operatic Works], *Istoriya russkoy muzïki*, vi (Moscow, 1989), 134–67

Judith

A. Grigor'yev: '*Yudif'*, opera v pyati aktakh A. N. Serova' [*Judith*: an Opera in Five Acts by A. N. Serov], *Yakor'* (1863), no.12

M. Musorgsky: Letter to M. Balakirev (10/22 June 1863), *Pis'ma* [Letters], ed. E. Gordeyeva (Moscow, 1984), 44–51; trans. in J. Leyda and S. Bertensson: *The Musorgsky Reader* (New York, 1947), 48–55

A. Serov: Preface to *Yudif'* (St Petersburg, 1863) [libretto]

F. M. Tolstoy [Rostislav]: *Razbor operï A. N. Serova 'Yudif''* [A Critique of Serov's Opera *Judith*] (St Petersburg, 1863)

V. Odoyevsky: '18-e predstavleniye Yudifi – operï A. N. Serova' [The 18th Performance of Serov's Opera *Judith*]; 'Uslïshim li mï operu Yudif' v Moskve?' [Shall we Hear the Opera *Judith* in Moscow?; both orig. pubd 1864], in V. F. Odoyevsky: *Muzïkal'no-literaturnoye naslediye* [Musical-Literary Legacy], ed. G. Bernandt (Moscow, 1956), 286–91

D. Lobanov: 'A. N. Serov i ego opera "Yudif'": iz vospominaniy' [Serov and his Opera *Judith*: from Reminiscences], *Vestnik Yevropï* (1871), no.6

A. Gozenpud: *Russkiy opernïy teatr XIX veka* [Russian Operatic Theatre of the 19th Century], iii (Leningrad, 1971), 62–84

R. Taruskin: 'Opera and Drama in Russia: the Case of Serov's *Judith*', *JAMS*, xxxiii (1980), 501–43

Rogneda

A. Serov: Preface to *Rogneda* (St Petersburg, 1865) [libretto]; repr. in *Izbrannïye stat'i* [Selected Essays], ed. G. Khubov, ii (Leningrad, 1957), 63–5

C. Cui: '"Rogneda", opera v pyati deystviyakh A. N. Serova, stikhi D. V. Averkiyeva (po programme kompozitora)' [*Rogneda*: An Opera in Five Acts by Serov, Libretto by Averkiyev], *Sankt-peterburgskiye vedomosti* (6/18 Nov 1865)

H. Laroche [G. Larosh]: '"Rogneda", novaya russkaya opera' [*Rogneda*: a New Russian Opera], *Russkaya stsena* (1865), no.9 [signed 'Uchenik konservatorii', 'A Conservatory Student']

——: 'Yeshchyo o "Rognede"' [More on *Rogneda*], *Russkaya stsena* (1865), no.13 [signed 'Uchenik konservatorii', 'A Conservatory Student']

C. Cui: 'Zhurnal'nïye tolki o "Rognede" g. Serova' [Magazine Gossip about Serov's *Rogneda*], *Sankt-peterburgskiye vedomosti* (14/26 Jan 1866)

V. Stasov: 'Arkheologicheskaya zametka k postanovke "Rognedï"' [An Archaeological Note on the Production of *Rogneda*], *Vestnik Yevropï* (1866), no.3 [with note by N. Kostomarov]; repr. in *Sobraniye sochineniy*, iii (St Petersburg, 1894), 187–91

——: 'Verit' li?' [Can You Believe it?], *Sankt-peterburgskiye vedomosti* (16/28 March 1866); repr. in *Izbrannïye sochineniya* [Selected Works], ed. E. D. Stasova and others (Moscow, 1952), i, 141–51

C. Cui: 'Vtoroye izdaniye "Rognedï", dopolnennoye i ispravlennoye' [The Second Edition of *Rogneda*, Supplemented and Corrected], *Sankt-peterburgskiye vedomosti* (8/20 Dec 1866)

V. Odoyevsky: 'Rogneda i drugaya novaya opera Serova v ego kontserte 10 marta, v voskresen'ye, v Bol'shom teatre' [*Rogneda* and Another New Opera by Serov at his Concert on Sunday, 10 March, at the Bol'shoy], *Sovremennïye izvestiya* (9/21 March 1868); repr. in V. F. Odoyevsky: *Muzïkal'no-literaturnoye naslediye* [Musical-Literary Legacy], ed. G. Bernandt (Moscow, 1956), 340–43

F. M. Tolstoy [Rostislav]: *Muzïkal'nïy razbor 'Rognedi'* [A Musical Critique of *Rogneda*] (St Petersburg, 1870)

P. I. Tchaikovsky: 'Vozobnovlyonnaya "Rogneda", opera Serova' [The Revival of Serov's Opera *Rogneda*; orig. pubd 1872], *Muzïkal'no-kriticheskiye stat'i* [Critical Essays on Music] (Leningrad, 4/1986), 43–7

A. Gozenpud: *Russkiy operniy teatr XIX veka* [Russian Operatic Theatre in the 19th Century], iii (Leningrad, 1971), 108–23
G. Abramovsky: '"Rogneda" A. N. Serova', *SovM* (1976), no.12, pp.92–101
R. Taruskin: *'Pochvennichestvo* on the Russian Operatic Stage', *Opera and Drama in Russia* (Ann Arbor, 1981), 79–140
——: 'Christian Themes in Russian Opera: a Millennial Essay', *COJ*, ii (1990), 83–91

The Power of the Fiend

A. Grigor'yev: 'Russkiy teatr v Peterburge' [The Russian Theatre in Petersburg], *Epokha* (1864), no.3, pp.220–44
C. Cui: 'Muzïkal'nïye zametki': "Vrazh'ya sila", opera A. N. Serova' [Musical Notes: Serov's Opera *The Power of the Fiend*] *Sankt-peterburgskiye vedomosti* (24 April/6 May 1871)
F. M. Tolstoy [Rostislav]: *Novaya opera A. N. Serova 'Vrazh'ya sila'* [Serov's New Opera *The Power of the Fiend*] (St Petersburg, 1871)
H. Laroche [G. Larosh]: '"Vrazh'ya sila", posmertnaya opera g. Serova' [Serov's Posthumous Opera *The Power of the Fiend*], *Golos* (6/18 July 1872)
V. Maslikh: 'A. N. Ostrovsky i A. N. Serov', *A. N. Ostrovsky i russkiye kompozitorï* [Ostrovsky and Russian Composers], ed. E. Kolosova and V. Filippov (Moscow, 1937), 90–140
A. Gozenpud: *Russkiy operniy teatr XIX veka* [Russian Operatic Theatre in the 19th Century], iii (Leningrad, 1971), 240–76
R. Taruskin: 'Drama Revealed through Song: an Opera after Ostrovsky', *Opera and Drama in Russia* (Ann Arbor, 1981), 141–248
RICHARD TARUSKIN

Serova [née Bergman], **Valentina Semyonovna** (*b* Moscow, 1846; *d* Moscow, 24 June 1924). Russian composer and writer on music, wife of Alexander Serov. She entered the St Petersburg Conservatory in 1862 to study the piano with Anton Rubinstein, but left to study composition privately with Serov, whom she married in 1863. Together they published *Muzïka i teatr* (1867–8). When his *Vrazh'ya sila* ('The Power of the Fiend') was in production, in January 1871, Serov died, leaving Act 5 incomplete. Valentina, aided by Nikolay Solov'yov, finished it in time for the première (19 April/1 May 1871). The intense emotional experience revived her interest in composition and resulted in her composing four original operas; *Marie d'Orval* is set in the French Revolution, *Il'ya Muromets* (given by the Mamontov Private Opera) is based on a Russian heroic tale, and the last relates to the political unrest of 1904–5. She also wrote music criticism in the leading Russian musical, literary and educational journals between 1865 and 1915 and vigorously promoted music education among ordinary people.

Uriel Acosta (5, Serova and P. Blaramberg, after C. von Gutschow's novel), Moscow, Bol'shoy, 15/27 April 1885, vs (Moscow, 1892)
Marie d'Orval, 1880s (5, Serova), lost
Il'ya Muromets (4, Serova), Moscow, Solodovnikov, 22 Feb/6 March 1899
Vstrepenulis' [They Roused Themselves Up], 1904–5 (5, Serova), lost

*

ME (Yu. V. Keldïsh)
V. Serova: *Serovï, Aleksandr Nikolayevich i Valentin Aleksandrovich: vospominaniya* [Reminiscences of A. N. and V. A. Serov] (St Petersburg, 1914)
N. Yefimova-Simonovich: 'Pamyati muzïkanta-obshchestvennika V. S. Serovoy' [Memoirs of the Musician and Social Figure V. S. Serova], *SovM* (1947), no.4, pp.56–60
G. B. Bernandt: 'Uriel Acosta', 'Il'ya Muromets', *Slovar' oper* [A Dictionary of Operas] (Moscow, 1962)
G. B. Bernandt and I. M. Yampol'sky: 'Serova (urozh. Bergman)', *Kto pisal o muzïke* [Writers on Music] (Moscow, 1974–89)
MALCOLM HAMRICK BROWN

Serpilla e Bacocco [*Bajocco*]. Intermezzo by G. M. Orlandini; *see* *MARITO GIOCATORE E LA MOGLIE BACCHETTONA, IL.*

Serra, Luciana (*b* Genoa, 4 Nov 1946). Italian soprano. She studied at the Genoa Conservatory and with Michele Casato, and made her début at Budapest in 1966 as Eleonora in Cimarosa's *Il convito* with the Italian Opera Giacosa company. She sang in Teheran, 1969–76, acquiring a repertory of coloratura and other roles including Susanna, Zerlina and the Queen of Night, as well as Adina, Lucia, Norina, Gilda and Violetta. Engagements following her return to Italy included Covent Garden (1980) as Olympia, and La Scala as Lucia; she was also especially admired as Amina. Her American début at Charleston as Violetta was followed by Lakmé with the Chicago Lyric Opera, and she has appeared in South America and South Africa. Her recordings include *I Capuleti e i Montecchi*, *Aureliano in Palmira* and *Fra Diavolo*, as well as the Queen of Night under Colin Davis (1985) and Norina under Campanella (1989). Her light, flexible voice serves well in lyric-coloratura music, and is accompanied by a spirited stage personality.

*

H. Canning: 'Luciana Serra, Covent Garden's Sleepwalker', *Classical Music* (3 July 1982), 11 [interview]
NOËL GOODWIN

Serrana. *Ópera cómica* in three acts by ALFREDO KEIL to a libretto by Henrique Lopes de Mendonça, after Camilo Castelo Branco's novel *Como ela amava*; Lisbon, Teatro S Carlos, 13 March 1899.

The action takes place in a village in the Serra da Estrela around 1820 and concerns the rivalry between two neighbouring villages, personified in the three main characters: the mountain girl Zabel (soprano) and her two suitors, Pedro (tenor) and Marcelo (baritone). Structurally, the opera is in the Italian Romantic tradition, with choruses to open each act, and such characteristic episodes as a storm and the death of the heroine in Act 3. Nationalist traits may be seen in the use of the Portuguese *desafio* (a challenge or duel song) in Act 1, and the folksong-like melodies of the choruses, but the most obvious influence on the opera's style is Italian *verismo*.

Considered the first Portuguese nationalist opera, because the first to be written to a Portuguese libretto, it was however first performed in Italian. A considerable success, it was often revived. LUISA CYMBRON

Serrano (y Ruiz), Emilio (*b* Vitoria, 13 March 1850; *d* Madrid, 9 April 1939). Spanish composer. He studied at the Royal Conservatory in Madrid with Eslava and Arrieta, and later taught successively solfège, piano and composition there until 1920. He succeeded Arrieta as professor of composition, and his pupils included José Subirá, Conrado del Campo and others of the so-called *generación de maestros* ('master generation'). He was a strong partisan of Spanish opera and succeeded in securing premières of four works at the Teatro Real, Madrid, where he was artistic director. Although his roots were in the Italian tradition, he practised a simple type of nationalism, using folk themes, and his operatic work showed Wagnerian influence. His last work, *La maja de rumbo*, commissioned for the unsuccessful Teatro Lírico, was given its first performance in Buenos Aires; it is typical of his best work, perhaps because it follows more faithfully a Spanish line. He composed music in a variety of genres and was court musician to the infanta Isabel. His speech of acceptance to the Royal Academy of S Fernando, entitled 'Estado actual de la música en el teatro', dealt with the zarzuela and opera in Spain.

Mitrídates (lyric drama, 3, M. Capdepón), Madrid, Real, 14 Jan 1882 [perf. in It.]
Doña Juana la Loca (4, Serrano, after Tamayo and Baus), Madrid, Real, 2 March 1890
Irene de Otranto (3, J. Echegaray), Madrid, Real, 17 Feb 1891
Gonzalo de Córdoba (prol., 3, Serrano), Madrid, Real, 6 Dec 1898
La maja de rumbo (musical comedy, 3, C. Fernández Shaw), Buenos Aires, Colón, 24 Sept 1910
La bejarana (zar, 2, L. Fernández Ardavín), Madrid, Apolo, 31 May 1924, collab. F. Alonso

*

J. Subirá: *Historia y anecdotario del Teatro Real* (Madrid, 1949)
——: *Historia de la música española e hispanoamericana* (Barcelona, 1953)
C. Gómez Amat: *Historia de la música española: el siglo XIX* (Madrid, 1984, 2/1988)
A. Iglesias: *Escritos de Julio Gómez* (Madrid, 1986)

CARLOS GÓMEZ AMAT

Serrano (Simeón), José (*b* Sueca, Valencia, 14 Oct 1873; *d* Madrid, 8 March 1941). Spanish composer. He came from a musical family and studied first with his father, conductor of the town band, and then with Salvador Giner at the Valencia Conservatory. He composed a mass, fugues and songs in Valencia, but his interest lay in the theatre. He therefore moved to Madrid, but made little progress until becoming assistant to Manuel Fernández Caballero during the latter's period of blindness. Caballero gave him opportunities to compose, and in 1900 the success of *El motete* finally launched Serrano on a career as a theatre composer. He ranked with Vives as the most successful young zarzuela composer of the first decade of the century, but unlike Vives he continued to specialize in one-act works. These included several of the big successes of the period. He was a fluent composer of richly melodic, vibrant and sensuous music, as much at home in intensely Spanish creations as in evoking Venice in *El carro del sol* (1911) and the Bay of Naples in *La canción del olvidó* (1916). The death of a son inspired a larger-scale, more serious work, *La dolorosa* (1930), after which he largely retreated from the public scene.

zarzuelas, unless otherwise stated; most published in vocal score in Madrid

La casta de Pepe (Carbonel), Seville, Feb 1900; El motete (1, S. Alvarez Quintero and J. Alvarez Quintero), Madrid, Apolo, 24 April 1900; Las zarzuelistas (Péon), San Fernando, 10 June 1900; El corneta de Ordenes, Madrid, Apolo, June 1900; La venta de los gatos (opera, 3, S. Alvarez Quintero and J. Alvarez Quintero), Madrid, Circo, 1901; El olivar (A. Melantuche and G. García Artista), Madrid, Jan 1902, collab. T. Barrera; Don Miguel de Mañara (F. Pérez Capo), 1902
La maja de rumbo (C. Fernández Shaw), Madrid, 1902; La mazorca roja (F. Tristán Larios), 1902; El vals de las olas (A. Paso), Madrid, Cómico, 23 Oct 1903; La reina mora (1, S. Alvarez Quintero and J. Alvarez Quintero), Madrid, Apolo, 11 Dec 1903; El pelotón de los torpes (Paso and R. Asensio Mas), 1903; El solo de trompa (Paso and D. Jiménez Prieto), 1903; El trébol (Paso and J. Abati), Madrid, 19 Feb 1904, collab. Q. Valverde; Las estrellas (C. Arniches), Madrid, 31 Dec 1904, collab. Q. Valverde
El mal de amores (1, S. Alvarez Quintero and J. Alvarez Quintero), Madrid, Apolo, 28 Jan 1905; La casita blanca (M. Thous and E. Cerdá), Madrid, Eldorado, Feb 1905; Moros y cristianos (1, Thous and Cerda), Madrid, Zarzuela, 27 April 1905; El perro chico (Arniches and E. García Alvarez), Madrid, Apolo, 5 May 1905, collab. Q. Valverde; La reja de la Dolores (Arniches), Madrid, Apolo, 26 Sept 1905, collab. Q. Valverde; La infanta de los bucles de oro (Mento and S. Delgado), Madrid, Zarzuela, 6 Jan 1906
La mala sombra (S. Alvarez Quintero and J. Alvarez Quintero), Madrid, 25 Sept 1906; La noche de Reyes (Arniches), Madrid, Zarzuela, 15 Dec 1906; El pollo Tejada (1, Arniches and García Álvarez), 1906, collab. Q. Valverde; La suerta loca, Madrid, Apolo, June 1907; Alma de Dios (1, Arniches and Garcí Álvarez), Madrid, Comico, 17 Dec 1907; La banda Nueva (Thous and Cerdá), 1907, collab. E. Brú; La alegría del batallón (1, Arniches and F. Quintana), Madrid, Apolo, 11 March 1909
El trust de los tenorios (Arniches and García Alvarez), Madrid, Oct 1910; El palacio de los duendes (1, Delgado), Madrid, Apolo, 28 Dec 1910, collab. Vives; Barbarroja (1, Delgado), Madrid, Apolo, 1911; El carro del sol (1, Thous), 1911; La gentuza (Arniches), 1913; Si yo fuera rey (A. López Monís), Madrid, Apolo, 1913/14; El amigo Melquíades, ó Por la boca muere el pez (1, Arniches), 1914, collab. Q. Valverde; La canción del olvidó (1, F. Romero and G. Fernández Shaw), Valencia, Lirico, 17 Nov 1916
La sonata de Greig (1, Romero and Fernández Shaw), 1916; La canción del soldado (Delgado), 1917; La venta de los ojos (intermedio, 1, J. Fernández del Villar), Madrid, Zarzuela, 31 Oct 1919; Los leones de Castilla (1, J. Moyrón), Madrid, 19 Dec 1919; El príncipe carnaval (opereta-revista, 2, J. J. Cadenas and Asensio Mas), Madrid, Reina Victoria, 17 Dec 1920, collab. Q. Valverde; El príncipe se casa (revue), Madrid, Reina Victoria, April 1922; Danza de apaches (L. Germán), 1924; La maga de Oreinte (Delgado), 1924, collab. E. Rosillo
Magda la tirana (R. Millán Astray), 1926; Los de Aragón (1, J. J. Lorente), Madrid, Centro, 16 April 1927; Las hilanderas (1, F. Oliver), Barcelona, Eldorado, 3 Dec 1927; Los claveles (1, L. Fernández de Sevilla, A. C. Carreño), Madrid, Fontalba, 6 April 1929; La dolorosa (2, Lorente), Valencia, Apolo, 23 May 1930; El fallero (Thous), Valencia, Apolo, 1931; Golondrina de Madrid (Fernández de Sévilla), S Sebastián, 1944, completed J. M. Izquierdo

Other works: Las sotanas (Carlos Leines); El saloncilla (revue); El cornetila; Copias y canas

*

'Serrano Siméon (José)': *Enciclopedia universal ilustrada europeo-americana* (Barcelona, 1907–), lv, 601; appx ix, 1248; suppl. 1940–41 (Madrid, 1948), 367
E. Cotarelo y Mori: *Historia de la zarzuela, o sea el drama lírico* (Madrid, 1934)
A. Sagardía: *El compositor José Serrano (Vida y obra)* (Madrid, 1972)
A. Fernández-Cid: *Cien años de teatro musical en España (1875–1975)* (Madrid, 1975)
J. Arnau and C. M. Gomez: *Historia de la zarzuela* (Madrid, 1979)
R. Alier and others: *El libro de la zarzuela* (Barcelona, 1982, rev. 1986 as *Diccionario la zarzuela)*

ANDREW LAMB

Serrao, Paolo (*b* Filadelfia, Catanzaro, 1830; *d* Naples, 17 March 1907). Italian composer. Most of his professional life was spent at the Naples Conservatory, first as a student (composition with Carlo Conti), and from 1863 as composition professor. He was considered one of the best teachers in Naples and was a friend of Rossini and Verdi. Among his pupils were Cilea, Leoncavallo, Giordano, Martucci and Mugnone. His compositions include liturgical works, chamber music and five operas, of which three were performed. The most successful, *La duchessa di Guisa* (1865), has a traditional plot concerning an unfaithful wife whose life ends tragically as her husband's honour is avenged; it is an old-fashioned number opera, filled with romanzas and *giuramento* scenes. Although antiquated in its excessive use of recitative (e.g. to begin the opera) and Donizettian aria forms (andante – cabaletta), it is more advanced in imitations of Verdi's *La traviata* (in the Valzer e Duetto an onstage orchestra playing a waltz is used as background to the principals singing in parlando style; unlike Verdi's scene, however, the voices double the orchestral line a great deal). The opera is also filled with reminiscence themes and has a prayer for the soprano and a ballata for the page, all typical features of a mid-19th-century Italian opera.

L'imperatore, 1850, unperf.
Leonora dei Bardi (L. Badiali), 1853, unperf.
Pergolesi (3, F. Quercia), Naples, Fondo, 19 July 1857
La duchessa di Guisa (4, F. A. Piave), Naples, S Carlo, 8 Dec 1865
Il figliuol prodigo (4, A. de Lauzières), Naples, S Carlo, 23 April 1868

MARVIN TARTAK

Serse ('Xerxes'). Opera in three acts by GEORGE FRIDERIC HANDEL to an anonymous revision of SILVIO STAMPIGLIA's libretto *Il Xerse* (Rome, 1694) based on Nicolo Minato's *Il Xerse* (Venice, 1654); London, King's Theatre, 15 April 1738.

Serse [Xerxes] *King of Persia*	mezzo-soprano
Arsamene *his brother, in love with Romilda*	mezzo-soprano
Amastre *heiress to the kingdom of Tagor, betrothed to Xerxes*	alto
Ariodate *a prince, vassal to Xerxes*	bass
Romilda *his daughter, in love with Arsamene*	soprano
Atalanta *her sister, secretly in love with Arsamene*	soprano
Elviro *servant of Arsamene*	bass

Setting Abydos, Persia, in ancient times

Handel composed *Serse* between 26 December 1737 and 14 February 1738. It was to be his last opera for the King's Theatre, which he shared with Pescetti for the 1737–8 season. He based it not only on the version of the libretto prepared by Stampiglia for Bononcini's setting of 1694 but to some extent on Bononcini's score, from which he had been borrowing musical material since 1734. In *Serse* itself he tended to follow Bononcini in matters of tonality and style rather than use direct thematic quotation; indeed, the considerable degree of rewriting in the score attests to a determination to produce a thoroughly original work on Bononcini's model. The libretto is largely fictional, but has a historical background derived from Herodotus's account of the Graeco-Persian wars (*Histories*, vii). The title role represents the Persian king Xerxes I (reigned 485–65 BC), and the action supposedly takes place at the time of his expedition against Greece, about 470 BC. Reference is made to Xerxes' attempt to bridge the Hellespont with boats and (in the famous opening number of the opera) to his reverence for a plane tree. For the most part, however, the action is a court intrigue involving the rivalry between Xerxes and his brother Arsamene for the love of Romilda, and the rivalry of Romilda and her mischievous sister Atalanta for the love of Arsamene. Amastre (a character derived from Xerxes' historical wife), betrothed to Xerxes but abandoned by him, performs a key role in resolving the complications.

The original cast included the celebrated castrato Gaetano Majorano, known as Caffarelli, as Xerxes, Maria Antonia Marchesini ('La Lucchesina') as Arsamene, Elisabeth du Parc ('La Francesina') as Romilda, Antonia Merighi as Amastre, Margherita Chimenti ('La Droghierina') as Atalanta, and Antonio Montagnana as Ariodate. *Serse* was little appreciated by its original audiences and after only five performances was replaced by repeats of the heroic operas given earlier in the season. It was not heard again until the production of Oskar Hagen's arrangement at Göttingen on 5 July 1924, but soon became one of the most frequently performed of Handel's operas; there were three productions in the USA between 1928 and 1935. The first British revival was at the Pollards Opera Festival, Loughton, Essex, on 15 June 1935. One of the most successful recent productions was that by Nicholas Hytner for the ENO, first given at the London Coliseum on the tercentenary of Handel's birth (23 February 1985), which vindicated the use of the uncut score.

The place of the action (unspecified in Handel's libretto) is presumably Abydos.

ACT 1 In a garden, with a summer house on one side, Xerxes addresses affectionate praise to the shade of a plane tree ('Ombra mai fù'). Arsamene and his clownish servant Elviro watch as sweet music is heard and Romilda, in the summer house, sings in gentle mockery of Xerxes: he loves a tree, but it responds only with the rustle of its leaves. Arsamene (who, unknown to Xerxes, is Romilda's lover) tells his brother he does not know who the singer is. As Romilda's singing grows livelier Xerxes becomes captivated by her: he loves her, wants her as his wife. He orders the dumbfounded Arsamene to tell Romilda of his wishes, but Arsamene pleads shyness and Xerxes determines to do his own wooing. Arsamene warns Romilda of what is about to happen, so giving hope to Romilda's sister Atalanta that Romilda will yield to Xerxes and leave Arsamene for her. Xerxes bans Arsamene from the court and declares his love to Romilda, but she remains unmoved. Amastre appears, disguised as a man; she is betrothed to Xerxes but, abandoned by him, seeks revenge. Romilda's father Ariodate announces a Persian victory and presents enemy insignia and prisoners to Xerxes; in reward the king promises Ariodate a royal husband, 'equal to Xerxes', for Romilda. Arsamene gives Elviro a letter for Romilda, grieving at his separation from her. Atalanta tells Romilda that Arsamene has found a new lover, but Romilda sees through her lie and says her love will remain true.

ACT 2 In a public square, Amastre encounters Elviro, disguised as a flower seller and speaking in dialect. She questions him and is grief-stricken and angry to learn that Xerxes is to marry Romilda (disapproved of by Elviro as a vassal's daughter). Atalanta appears and Elviro makes himself known to her; she says she will deliver Arsamene's letter, telling Elviro that Romilda has abandoned Arsamene and now loves Xerxes. Elviro curses Romilda and leaves as the king approaches. Xerxes finds Atalanta reading the letter, and asks to see it. It is a declaration of love which Xerxes recognizes to be in Arsamene's hand. Atalanta claims that the letter is hers and it is she whom Arsamene truly loves. Xerxes is delighted, and takes the letter; Atalanta reminds him that Arsamene will deny he loves her. He now confronts Romilda with the letter: she insists she will always love Arsamene. Xerxes is furious but cannot bring himself to reject her. Elviro prevents Amastre from killing herself. He tells Arsamene what Atalanta said about Romilda and Xerxes; Arsamene is heartbroken.

By Xerxes' new bridge joining the shores of the Hellespont, a chorus of mariners congratulates him on the achievement. Xerxes tells Ariodate that he will shortly advance into Europe. He meets the despondent Arsamene and tells him he is no longer angry: he gladly gives Arsamene permission to marry the woman he really loves, Atalanta. Arsamene declares he loves only Romilda and remains determined to win her. Xerxes advises Atalanta to forget Arsamene but she says she cannot. Elviro remarks on the gathering storm, which threatens to wreck the bridge, and seeks solace in drink. Xerxes meets Amastre, who claims to have been wounded while serving Xerxes in the wars. Their strained conversation is interrupted by Romilda. The king again asks her to marry him but Amastre intervenes, calls Xerxes a traitor and draws her sword. She is arrested by the royal guards, but released on the orders of Romilda, who delivers a ringing tribute to those faithful in love.

ACT 3 Arsamene and Romilda are quarrelling, but are swiftly reconciled when Atalanta admits her deception and resigns herself to finding another lover. Xerxes again presses Romilda to marry him. She tells Xerxes to seek her father's permission; she will obey her father's orders. Reproached by Arsamene, she says it is death, not marriage, that awaits her. Xerxes again asks Ariodate if he is happy for Romilda to marry 'a person equal to us, and of our blood', and Ariodate, assuming that Arsamene is the person in question, gladly agrees. Romilda now resolves to reject Xerxes, telling him that Arsamene is her lover and that they have kissed. Xerxes says this is a ruse to thwart him but orders Arsamene's execution. Amastre offers to help Romilda by giving her a letter to take to Xerxes, and reflects on the grief she has brought on herself by loving one who has betrayed her. Arsamene blames Romilda for his death sentence.

The final scene takes place in the temple of the sun. Romilda and Arsamene enter, still quarrelling, but when Ariodate joins their hands and tells them they are married with Xerxes' consent they are joyfully reconciled. Now Xerxes appears, to marry Romilda, and is furious when Ariodate explains what he has done. His anger is intensified when a page brings a letter from Romilda, upbraiding him for his betrayal in love, and is not assuaged when the letter is revealed to be from Amastre. He draws his sword and orders Arsamene to kill Romilda with it. But Amastre intervenes, asking Xerxes if he truly wishes treachery to be avenged: he agrees, and Amastre, revealing who she is, turns the sword on him. Xerxes begs her pardon, and receives it; his love for her will be renewed. He blesses the marriage of Romilda and Arsamene. All celebrate the union of love and honour.

* * *

Serse is not Handel's only comic opera, as it has sometimes been described, but it is the finest of his operas with comical or satirical elements and shows the greatest deviation from the standard forms of *opera seria*. Most of the arias are short, and about half are through-composed, without da capo. In many scenes the music is precisely moulded to the action in a manner which seems prophetically modern (notably at the start of Act 1, with its delightful mix of sinfonias, recitative and short arias), though it in fact derives from the early Venetian origins of the libretto. Only Elviro is a wholly comic role: all the other characters exhibit some degree of seriousness and are sharply and sympathetically drawn. Xerxes is a rather absurd figure but never wholly foolish: the threat of his arbitrary power gives an underlying tension to the drama, and his music, with its big set-piece arias, emphasizes his importance. The heart of Act 2 is his exchange with Romilda: in a duet as simple as it is moving he fails to persuade her to relinquish her love for Arsamene, then reacts with the aria 'Se bramate d'amar chi vi sdegna', a stunning outburst of fury and anguish expressed by alternating fast and slow tempos, and harmonic surprise. His amorous address to the plane tree in the opening scene, 'Ombra mai fù', is presumably satirical, but its perfectly shaped melody and grave beauty have made it the most famous of Handel's opera songs (often entitled 'Handel's Largo', though the tempo is actually Larghetto). The deepest emotions are found in the minor-key songs for Romilda, Arsamene and Amastre, and Handel nicely contrasts the music for Atalanta with that for her sister, epitomizing their characters in the closing arias of the first two acts. Atalanta's 'Un cenno leggiadretto', ending Act 1, is charmingly teasing; Romilda's 'Chi cede al furore', at the end of Act 2, has a noble, seamless melodic line aptly expressing her constancy. The occasional choruses, two with solo trumpet and one with a pair of horns, give additional variety to the score. Though other Handel operas may contain greater music, *Serse* is one of the composer's most consistently satisfying scores, moving surefootedly between farce and tragedy and always responding with insight to the emotions of its very human characters. ANTHONY HICKS

Sertor, Gaetano (*b* ?Venice, *c*1760; *d* 1805). Italian librettist. In the libretto to *Protesilao* he is identified as 'abate Sertor di Venezia'. He was among the first to incorporate into his librettos elements that Verazi had introduced in his controversial librettos for the opening of La Scala, Milan, during the 1778–9 season. He apparently collaborated with Giovannini in writing *Epponina*, later revised by Giovannini for Sarti as *Giulio Sabino*; Sertor also revised the text for Anfossi as *Tito nelle Gallie*. In 1780 Sertor began working with Bianchi; their association spanned 11 years and resulted in six works. Their operas of the early 1780s – *Arbace*, *Zemira*, *Piramo e Tisbe* and *Aspardi* – depart from the traditional pattern of recitatives and arias. Ensembles of increasing or diminishing numbers of personnel, and arias and duets with interjections by other characters or the chorus, occur sparingly. Sertor follows Verazi's lead in borrowing from comic opera the *introduzione* and the finale incorporating some action. In Bianchi's *Piramo e Tisbe*, a reworking of Coltellini's serenata for Hasse, Sertor planned to conclude the work with three suicides but in the performance he replaced the original ending with a happy one in which none of the characters dies. The original tragic ending was used in Borghi's setting for Florence later the same year – a significant move towards the restoration of staged death in *opera seria*.

In *Osmane*, written for Venice in 1784, Sertor's interest in blending lyrical and declamatory elements into more fluid and dramatic constructions becomes more evident. In a solo scene near the end of Act 2, Zadira's aria grows out of the obbligato recitative. In the midst of a second section in a quicker tempo, the vocal line moves back into recitative at the sounds of battle. The singer remains on stage to participate in a fast-moving, emotionally charged trio finale, which also grows out of the obbligato recitative. *Enea e Lavinia* and *Armida abbandonata* incorporate some French-inspired spectacle. *Enea e Lavinia*, which Guglielmi composed for Naples, contains two terrifying appearances of Dido's ghost, scenes from Verazi's *Enea nel Lazio*. In Act 1 Dido interrupts the sacrifice scene: during a programmatic trio, lightning and thunder announce the ghost's arrival. In Act 2 the ghost of Dido interrupts Lavinia's 'sleep' aria to warn her of Aeneas's faithlessness. Like Mozart's *Idomeneo* (1781), also written for Munich, *Armida* contains lavish spectacle, choruses, ballets, pantomimes and a quartet; with the exception of several cavatinas and arias without exit, however, the work adheres formally to the Italian tradition.

Sertor's libretto *La morte di Cesare*, after Shakespeare's *Julius Caesar*, proved to be his most influential work, ushering in a series of 'morte' operas in the 1790s. Murders had been staged in Florence and Milan during the preceding three years, but in Sertor's libretto for Venice the assassination of Caesar took place behind closed doors. The tragic ending was still a break with tradition, and audiences would have been shocked to view the corpse of Caesar lying on stage during the final scenes. The chorus assumes a prominent role in the drama, participating in the ensembles and the act finale. They offer interjections in Caesar's solo aria in Act 2. A ballet is incorporated into the coronation scene, and a pantomime is used to portray Calpurnia's dreadful premonition. The opera also contains a duet for two men and an oath scene (*giuramento*), which closes the opera.

In his librettos of the early 1790s, Sertor continued to reduce the number of exit arias by replacing them with aria-length cavatinas and by increasing the number of ensembles. Staged deaths, ballets and choruses appear frequently in Venetian theatres after 1791. For *Idomeneo* he provided a violent ending with several deaths as well as an alternative ending in which none of the characters dies. By 1792, introductions, ballets, action ensembles and multiple choruses (alone and in combination with ensembles and solos) were becoming commonplace. *Tarara* contains two scene complexes – combining cavatina, chorus, instrumental music and dance bound together with obbligato recitative – one serving as the finale to Act 1, the other occurring within Act 2. Such scene complexes eventually replaced ensemble finales in Venetian opera. Sertor's reworkings of *Le danaidi* and *Tarara* (based on librettos of Salieri's operas for Paris) close with French-inspired spectacle. In *Tarara*, Virtù and Felicità appear in the clouds to celebrate the death of the tyrant. In *Le danaidi*, the wicked Danaus is dragged down to Hades, where the murdered Danaidi and the Furies ensure his eternal torment. Late in his career Sertor also wrote a comic piece, *Il divorzio senza matrimonio*.

drammi per musica unless otherwise stated

Epponina (with P. Giovannini), G. Giordani, 1779 (P. Anfossi, 1780, as Tito nelle Gallie); *Arbace*, Bianchi, 1781 (Andreozzi, 1781; F. Alessandri, 1781; G. B. Borghi, 1782; rev. Andreozzi, 1785); *Zemira*, Bianchi, 1781 (P. Morandi, 1782; Anfossi, 1782); *Piramo e Tisbe*, Bianchi, 1783 (Borghi, 1783); *Aspardi, principe di Battriano*, Bianchi, 1784; *Osmane*, Giordani, 1784; *Armida abbandonata*, A. Prati, 1785; *Enea e Lavinia*, P. A. Guglielmi, 1785; *La morte di Cesare*, Bianchi, 1788 (F. Robuschi, 1789; Andreozzi, 1790; N. Zingarelli, 1790); *Protesilao*, J. F. Reichardt (Act 1), J. G. Naumann (Act 2), 1789; *Zenobia in Palmira*, Anfossi, 1789; *Aspasia*, Giordani, 1790; *Idomeneo*, G. Gazzaniga, 1790 (F. Paer, 1794); *Angelica e Medoro*, F. G. Bertoni, 1791 (Andreozzi, 1792); *Le danaidi*, G. Isola, 1792 (A. Tarchi, 1794); *Tarara, o sia La virtù premiata* (dramma), Bianchi, 1792; *Sarabes*, G. Scolari, 1793; *Il divorzio senza matrimonio, ossia La donna che non parla* (dg), Gazzaniga, 1794; *Griselda*, Guglielmi, 1796

*

M. McClymonds: '"La morte di Semiramide ossia La vendetta di Nino" and the Restoration of Death and Tragedy to the Italian Operatic Stage in the 1780s and 90s', *IMSCR* xiv: *Bologna 1987*, 285–92

——: 'The Venetian Role in the Transformation of Italian Opera Seria during the 1790s', *I vicini di Mozart: Venice 1987*, 221–40

MARITA P. McCLYMONDS

Servandoni, Giovanni Niccolò [Servandony, Jean-Nicolas] (*b* Florence or Lyons, 2 May 1695; *d* Paris, 19 Jan 1766). Italian or French stage designer. It is not known whether he was a Florentine who took French citizenship or a Frenchman who followed fashion and italianized his name. He was a pupil of the *capriccio* painter Giovanni Panini and later studied architecture in Rome. He settled in Paris in 1724, and in 1726 the Académie Royale de Musique asked him to design a set showing the Palace of Ninus for the première of Rebel and Francoeur's first opera, *Pyrame et Thisbé*. In 1728 he was appointed chief scene painter at the Opéra. There are only a couple of sketches definitely attributed to him, but the *Mercure de France* gives detailed accounts of his *veduta* work for opera, including Lully's *Proserpine*, with a waterfall of silver gauze (1727), Lacoste's *Orion*, a Nile landscape with pyramids (1728), Lully's *Thésée*, mixing real and painted perspective (1729), Rameau's *opéra-ballet Les Indes galantes* (1735) and Rebel and Francoeur's opera *Scanderberg*, the peak of his achievement, an enchanted palace in the shape of an exotic mosque (1735).

In 1738 he opened a *spectacle d'optique* in the Salle des Machines in the Tuileries, the largest stage in Paris (43 metres deep), on which he mounted pantomime plays to music, illustrated with motifs from mythology and the epics, that mixed mechanical and mobile figures with live actors. Lighting was an essential and expensive element. These *son et lumière* spectacles, in a darkened auditorium (a practice not generally followed before 1800), were immensely popular; they used lighting and staging techniques that were copied in Italy and Germany and further developed by Daguerre and others.

Servandoni worked in Lisbon (1742) and Bordeaux (1745) and was employed by John Rich at Covent Garden from 1747. In London he designed a set-piece for the fireworks display in St James's Park to celebrate the treaty of Aix-la-Chapelle (1748) and scenery for Handel's *Alceste* (1749), though the latter project was abandoned. In Dresden (1755–6) he was responsible for the lighting of large operas at court, including *Ezio*, which had as its climax a 25-minute triumphal procession into nocturnal Rome. He also worked in Vienna (1760) and Württemberg (1763).

Servandoni's careful studies of perspective helped him to modify stage space to increase verisimilitude and the impression of spaciousness. He broke with the principle of symmetrical, regular perspective, introducing oblique perspective (*per angolo*) to the Opéra. He alternated transverse space with space seen in depth, but above all, and it was in this that he showed his greatest originality, he made use of the entire height of the stage. He suggested vast proportions by showing fragments of architecture in the foreground, their height increasing as the eye approached the back of the stage, and by representing only the lower part of a column or tree. As the upper part was unseen, the spectator could supply and extend it as his own imagination suggested. Diderot described Servandoni as a 'grand machiniste, grand architecte, bon peintre et sublime décorateur'. He was the most influential neo-classical artist of his time, leading the reaction against Baroque style in the theatre. His innovations affected stage decor until the end of the 19th century. Some of his designs and plans are preserved in Vienna (Albertina), New York and Stockholm (the Tessin collection), but our knowledge of his work comes chiefly from descriptions in the *Mercure de France* from 1726 to 1758.

*

ES (E. Povoledo)

P. Bjurström: 'Servandoni décorateur de théâtre', *Revue de la Société d'histoire du théâtre*, iii (1959)

C. Heybrock: *Jean-Nicolas Servandoni: eine Untersuchung seiner Pariser Bühnenwerke* (Cologne, 1970)
D. Oenslager: *Stage Design* (London, 1975)
G. M. Bergmann: *Lighting in the Theatre* (Stockholm, 1977)

DAVID J. HOUGH, NICOLE WILD

Serva padrona, La ('The Maid as Mistress'). Intermezzo in two parts by GIOVANNI BATTISTA PERGOLESI to a libretto by GENNARO ANTONIO FEDERICO after Jacopo Angello Nelli's play; Naples, Teatro S Bartolomeo, 5 September 1733.

Uberto *an elderly gentleman*	bass
Serpina *his servant*	soprano
Vespone *another servant*	silent role

Setting A room in Uberto's house

La serva padrona was first performed between the acts of Pergolesi's *opera seria Il prigioniero superbo*, commissioned for the birthday celebrations of the Empress Elisabeth Christina, consort of Charles VI. It became one of the most popular examples of intermezzo in the 18th century. Federico based his text on a spoken play of the same title written by Nelli (1673–1767), an erudite member of the Accademia dei Rozzi in Siena. Published in 1731, the play contains the essence of Federico's plot, which uses familiar stock characters of the *commedia dell'arte*.

For two decades after its creation *La serva padrona* survived in the repertory almost intact, with minimal changes; this was most unusual for the genre. During that period it was performed in more than 60 theatres in Italy and throughout Europe, from Malta and Spain in the south to St Petersburg in the north. The only change to the music over those two decades occurred in Act 2, where the original duet, 'Contento tu sarai', was sometimes supplanted by 'Per te ho io nel core' from Pergolesi's *Flaminio* (1735).

When first performed in Paris on 4 October 1746 the intermezzo passed almost unnoticed. But during its second Paris presentation, in August 1752, when it was coupled with Lully's *Acis et Galatée*, it became the centre of a controversy that was to affect the future development of opera in Paris and the creation of *opéra comique*. *La serva padrona* was one of the 14 Italian works given in Paris between 1752 and 1754 by a group of Italian *buffo* singers led by Eustachio Bambini. The comic Italian style projected in these works was new to the French public, which split into two camps and voiced their opinions in numerous pamphlets and newspaper articles (the QUERELLE DES BOUFFONS). The Philosophes and Encyclopedists, such as Rousseau, Grimm and Diderot, were supporters of the Italian comic style and were active participants. Pergolesi, called 'divine' by his supporters, was the chief representative of this new musical style, and six of the 14 compositions given by Bambini's company contained his music. They included Latilla's *La finta cameriera* (with Pergolesi's duet 'Per te ho io nel core'), Orlandini's *Il giocatore* (with Pergolesi's duet 'Contento tu sarai'), *Il maestro di musica*, which though attributed to Pergolesi was a pasticcio incorporating only some of his music, and *Tracollo, medico ignorante*, a reworking of Pergolesi's intermezzo *Livietta e Tracollo* (1734).

Through Pergolesi's music the French gradually came to terms with the Italian comic idiom, especially after Rousseau used *La serva padrona* as a model for his own French intermezzo, *Le devin du village* (1752). Two years later Pierre Baurans translated and revised Pergolesi's intermezzo as *La servante maîtresse*; new names were given to the characters, new numbers were added and the recitative replaced by spoken French dialogue.

Pergolesi's intermezzo continued to be performed in Paris and London throughout the second half of the 18th century. In London it was translated into English and enjoyed a great success in outdoor performances, especially at Marylebone Gardens in 1759 in a version by Stephen Storace senior (*c*1725–81) and James Oswald, with an additional act and a new character. It was also performed at the King's Theatre, Drury Lane, Ranelagh Gardens and Covent Garden, and over the years inspired several English versions, including *The Maid the Mistress* (1770) with a text by Bickerstaff and entirely new music by Dibdin, which was later revised as *He Wou'd if he Could* (1771). Paisiello made a new setting of Federico's libretto in 1781 during his sojourn in Russia.

INTERMEZZO 1 Uberto angrily emerges from his bedroom and launches directly into an aria, 'Aspettare e non venire'. Serpina, who refuses to take orders from him, has been delinquent in bringing him his chocolate; Uberto's dissatisfaction with her is depicted in the opening line, which includes a descending octave jump, and the phrase is repeated three times at successively higher pitches. The ensuing patter is accompanied by repeated figures in the orchestra. Uberto is all the more frustrated with Serpina since, as her guardian, he has cared for her throughout her adolescent years, and now she is behaving in an ungrateful and insolent manner. In his first full-length da capo aria, 'Sempre in contrasti', patter phrases such as 'e qua e la', 'e su e giù' and 'e si e no' break the continuity of the phrases into short melodic and rhythmic motifs, depicting his relationship with Serpina in a constant battle of words. Uberto decides to improve the domestic atmosphere by marrying; he orders Vespone to go out and find him a wife. Serpina insists that he marry her instead, and in her aria 'Stizzoso, mio stizzoso' she promises to lock the doors to prevent him from seeking a wife. A duet of conflicting opinions, 'Lo conosco a quegl'occhieti', closes the first part of the intermezzo.

INTERMEZZO 2 Serpina enlists the aid of Vespone, whom she has frequently mistreated in the past, to help her to marry Uberto. In return she promises him continued employment and a secure future in her household when she becomes its mistress. To arouse Uberto's jealousy she has Vespone disguise himself as a soldier and announces her intention to marry him. In 'A Serpina penserete', a cleverly constructed sentimental aria, Serpina manipulates Uberto's emotions by convincing him that he will miss her when she leaves. The aria is in several sections of contrasting metres and tempos, portraying changes in mood. Throughout the piece Serpina comments in asides on the effect her words are having on Uberto. In his aria 'Son imbrogliato io gia' he begins to weaken as he considers marriage. The final duet of reconciliation, 'Contento tu sarai', was later supplanted by 'Per te ho io nel core' from Pergolesi's comic opera *Flaminio* (1735).

* * *

La serva padrona calls for a chamber orchestra of strings and continuo. The unison playing of the first and second violins, and the doubling of the bass line by the violas, produces a thin, two-part texture. The work is

'La serva padrona': scene from part 2 of an early Paris production of Pergolesi's intermezzo: engraving (18th century)

remarkable for the suppleness of its melodic phrases and for the vivacity of its arias. Syllabic patter songs, octave jumps and frequent repetition of cadential material were not only components of the new comic idiom, developed in the early decades of the century by Pergolesi, Leo, Sarro, Hasse, Orlandini and others, but also constituted the basis of the pre-classical style.

GORDANA LAZAREVICH

Serve rivali, Le [*Le due serve rivali* ('The Two Rival Servants')]. *Burletta* in three acts by TOMMASO TRAETTA to a libretto by PIETRO CHIARI; Venice, Teatro S Moisè, autumn 1766.

The lovers Giacinta (mezzo-soprano) and Giannino (tenor) are caught in a typically Italian web of amorous intrigue. Letanzio (tenor) is pursuing Giacinta and Palmetta (soprano) has designs on Giannino. Carlina (soprano) wishes to marry Don Grillo (tenor) but is betrothed to someone else. Three acts full of plotting and masquerading finally resolve happily.

A fine example of Traetta's mature manner, the music both charms and amuses, with an array of contrasting moods, tempos and styles, ranging from unembellished syllabic *buffo* bluster to lyric and tastefully florid cantabiles. There is a playful duet for the comic lovers incorporating action and divided into several sections, and an aria and storm scene for Giannino in which Traetta displays his skill in programmatic orchestral effects as well as his melodic gifts. The work also includes stock comic ingredients, such as dialogue in fractured French, a love song with guitar accompaniment and a *buffo* aria that builds up through great crescendos and accelerates to rapid, repetitive parlando. The finales of Acts 1 and 2, in several sections of contrasting tempos and metres, never stray beyond closely related keys. The Act 3 finale is a joyful sextet for the entire cast.

Traetta's most often performed work, the opera enjoyed modest success and international attention with 20 or more productions over a 15-year period. It was heard in most of the major theatres in Italy, as well as in Vienna, Dresden, London, Bonn and Brunswick.

MARITA P. McCLYMONDS

Servières, Jules. Pseudonym of LUDOVIC HALÉVY.

Servilia [*Serviliya*]. Opera in five acts by NIKOLAY ANDREYEVICH RIMSKY-KORSAKOV to his own libretto, after the drama by Lev Alexandrovich Mey; St Petersburg, Mariinsky Theatre, 1/14 October 1902.

At once Rimsky-Korsakov's grandest opera and his least significant, *Servilia* was given seven times in St Petersburg in the autumn of 1902, six times in Moscow in the autumn of 1904, and thereafter disappeared unregretted into Lethe. The action, set in Neronian Rome (AD 67), concerns the fate of a senator's daughter (the title character, soprano) who, converted to Christianity by the example of a secret Christian (Nevoleya, soprano) who saves her life, in turn converts, by dying innocently, a whole stageful of Romans in time for the final curtain, which falls on a choral Credo à la Palestrina (originally composed as an 'Amen' to end the 1877 revision of Rimsky's *Maid of Pskov*). The opera is dedicated to the memory of Mey; the première was conducted by Felix Blumenfeld, with Ivan Yershov as Valery, Andrey Labinsky as Afer and Vladimir Kastorsky as the old man.

Rimsky's lengthy account in his autobiography of the opera's gestation emphasizes the freedom he felt the antique setting would give him to invent music as he wished, rather than having to conform to an existing idiom as Russian national subjects demanded. Still, he concluded, even ancient Roman music must have had a national style; so he invented one out of a combination of traditional Russian 'orientalism' and the Greek-Byzantine modal idiom he thought he could discern in contemporary Orthodox church music. In the end, the best word Rimsky-Korsakov could find to characterize the style of his new opera was 'pale'. Its one big detachable number, Servilia's Act 3 aria 'Tsvetï moi' ('My flowers!'), is cast in a declamatory style perhaps most reminiscent of 'Suicidio!' from *La Gioconda*. It makes its dramatic point by a series of appoggiaturas to diminished 7th and dominant 9th chords, reflected at the climax by a direct (if at once resolved) leap of a diminished octave, mildly wild for the date.

RICHARD TARUSKIN

Sesostri, re di Egitto ('Sesostris, King of Egypt'). Libretto by PIETRO PARIATI, first set by Francesco Gasparini (1710, Venice). It was long but mistakenly supposed to be a joint work of Pariati and Apostolo Zeno.

Aprio, king of Egypt, has been murdered by Amasi, who has usurped the throne. Each had a son, brought up secretly. Many years later, Aprio's son Sesostris kills Amasi's son Osiride, whom he then impersonates. Under this disguise, 'Osiride' presents himself to Amasi, who commands him to explain to Nitocri (widow of Aprio) how he killed her son (Sesostris). She vows revenge and attempts to involve Artenice, betrothed to Sesostris in childhood. Meanwhile, Artenice has fallen in love with 'Osiride', a situation further complicated by Amasi's decision to wed her. Nitocri is imprisoned when she is discovered attempting to kill 'Osiride'. Then Sesostris is arrested when Osiride's tutor, Canopo, testifies that Osiride is dead by the hand of Sesostris. Amasi offers the unsuspecting Nitocri the opportunity to kill Sesostris, but Sesostris narrowly escapes when Artenice tells Nitocri she is about to kill her own son. Amasi is condemned and Sesostris is hailed as the new king of Egypt, with Artenice as his bride.

Gasparini's setting was revived in Rome (1713, 1718), Florence (1714) and Bologna (1719). Other early settings (Bononcini, 1716; Conti, 1717) remain faithful to the original text, but Fiorè's (1717) adds the role of Nirene, confidante to Nitocri. The first significant revision, an expansion of Nitocri's first murder attempt, occurred in Terradellas's opera (1751) and set a pattern for later versions. Many of these omit the role of Canopo (Cocchi, 1752; Galuppi, 1757; Monza, 1760; Sciroli, 1759, rev. 1762; Guglielmi, 1766, rev. 1768). The libretto for the London performance (1768) of Guglielmi's 1766 setting was revised by G. G. Bottarelli, who predictably cut large sections of recitative and whole scenes. A radical revision of the libretto by A. Carasale was set by Hasse in 1726, as *Il Sesostrate*; the only original characters are Amasi and Sesostri. The libretto *Le feste d'Iside* by Gaetano Rossi shares an Egyptian setting with Pariati's *Sesostri*, but is otherwise unrelated to it.

For a list of settings *see* PARIATI, PIETRO. REBECCA GREEN

Sessi, Marianna (*b* Rome, 1776; *d* Vienna, 10 March 1847). Italian soprano. She made her début, at 16, in the performance of Paisiello's *I giuochi d'Agrigento* which opened the Teatro La Fenice, Venice. She sang with much success in Vienna from 1793 but left the stage between 1795 and 1804, following her marriage to Franz-Wilhelm Natorp. On resuming her career she appeared in Stockholm, London, Dresden, Berlin, Naples and Copenhagen. Her agile coloratura was particularly admired in the operas of Mozart, Zingarelli and Mayr. Her sisters Imperatrice Sessi (1784–1808) and Anna Maria Sessi (1790–1864) sang in Italy and Vienna. DAVID CUMMINGS

Sessions, Roger (Huntington) (*b* Brooklyn, NY, 28 Dec 1896; *d* Princeton, NJ, 16 March 1985). American composer and teacher. He initiated work on a number of operas, two of which he completed. Although rarely performed, the second, *Montezuma*, has often been cited as a masterpiece of the genre.

After graduating from Harvard University at the age of 18, he studied composition with Horatio Parker at Yale and with Ernest Bloch in New York. He then taught at Smith College and the Cleveland Institute (1917–25) where he was Bloch's assistant. From 1926 to 1933 he lived principally in Europe, residing mainly in Florence and Rome. Sessions later commented that his experience of the rise of European fascism during these years contributed crucially to his interest in the story of Montezuma, with its exploration of the themes of conquest, political suppression and colonization. Moving to Berlin briefly during the early 1930s at Klemperer's suggestion, he became especially engrossed in the city's vital opera scene, attending numerous performances of repertory works as well as recent Strauss operas.

He settled in the USA in 1933 and taught at several institutions, for the most part in New York and Boston, before joining the Princeton faculty in 1935. He remained there until 1944, taught at the University of California at Berkeley from 1944 to 1953 and returned to Princeton in 1953, remaining there until his retirement in 1965. He continued teaching at the Juilliard School during the 1970s and he also held distinguished professorships at Berkeley and Harvard. Sessions was a key figure in the development of American music and an exemplary citizen of the musical community. He was arguably the most important American composition teacher of his era, counting Milton Babbitt, Leon Kirchner, Earl Kim, Andrew Imbrie, Peter Maxwell Davies, Donald Martino, John Harbison and Fred Lerdahl among his pupils. As pedagogue, theorist, critic and cultural commentator, Sessions produced numerous essays and several books, including *The Musical Experience* (1945), *Questions about Music* (1971) and *Harmonic Practice* (1951).

Ineluctably an American composer while deeply committed to the techniques and aspirations of the European high art tradition, Sessions composed music notable for its consistent structural depth, broad scope, sweeping line and noble ambition. His early works were considered Stravinskian but by the time of the Violin Concerto (1935) his music embodied a highly evolved technique and an utterly original voice. From the end of the 1930s, with the *Pages from a Diary* (1939), he began to explore more freely chromatic, dissonant voice-leading procedures, an investigation that culminated in his adoption of 12-note techniques. During this period he wrote his first opera, the one-act *The Trial of Lucullus*, and began his second, *Montezuma*, his longest composition. As his operatic impulses came to fruition, Sessions's music generally became more receptive to dramatic contrasts and bolder juxtapositions. In both the operatic and non-dramatic works, this impulse towards more mercurial and contrasted materials was tempered by his ongoing predilection for classical forms and formal balance. Sessions was especially productive in the 1960s and 70s, his work retaining its characteristic vigour, lucidity and sophistication.

The Trial of Lucullus, based on a radio play by Brecht, was written in 13 scenes, for the Drama Department at Berkeley. Sessions conducted the première there on 18 April 1947, only three months after he began its composition. *Lucullus* shares with *Montezuma* a preoccupation with military authority and the ethical and judicial issues of armed conflict. It is one of Sessions's most accessible and pictorially vivid works. The three-act *Montezuma* is equally immediate in its dramatic effects and gestural mimicry, but it unfolds a much more complex structure, texturally and colouristically dense yet with sweeping continuity. The opera calls for a dozen principal and secondary roles with as many minor roles, two choruses, a large orchestra (including six percussionists) and about 15 instrumentalists on stage. In its concerns with cultural assimilation and conflict and the ambiguous relations between colonizers and colonized, *Montezuma* seems to reflect Sessions's own predicament as an American composer coming to terms with European musical culture. The composition of *Montezuma* occupied Sessions intermittently for 15 years. It was first performed in Berlin in 1964 and Sarah Caldwell conducted the American première with the Boston Opera Company in 1976.

See also MONTEZUMA (ii).

*

B. Boretz: 'Current Chronicle', *MQ*, xlvii (1961), 393–6
E. Laufer: 'Roger Sessions: *Montezuma*', *PNM*, iv/i (1965), 95–108
D. Drew: 'Out of Limbo', *New Statesman* (24 June 1966)
M. Steinberg: 'Enter Montezuma', *ON*, xi/19 (1975–6), 10–16
J. Harbison: 'Roger Sessions and Montezuma', *Tempo* (1977), no.121, pp.2–5
R. Sessions: *Roger Sessions on Music: Collected Essays*, ed. E. T. Cone (Princeton, 1979)
C. N. Mason: *A Comprehensive Analysis of Roger Sessions's Opera 'Montezuma'* (diss., U. of Illinois, Urbana-Champaign, 1982)
A. Porter: 'A Magnificent Epic', *New Yorker* (8 March 1982)
A. Olmstead: 'The Plum'd Serpent: Antonio Borgese and Roger Sessions's *Montezuma*', *Tempo* (1985), no.152, pp.13–22
——: *Roger Sessions and His Music* (Ann Arbor, 1985)

MARTIN BRODY

Sestetto (It.). SEXTET.

Sestini, Giovanna (*fl* 1772–91). Italian soprano. She came to London from Lisbon in 1774 and was a popular performer in Italian comic operas at the King's Theatre for many seasons and at the Smock Alley Theatre, Dublin, in 1777–8. Mount Edgcumbe remembered her as 'handsome, sprightly and a good actress' but considered that she was 'nothing of a singer, except for lively comic airs'. She also performed in English operas at Covent Garden (1782–4), in Dublin (1784–5) and in five summer seasons at the Haymarket. O'Keeffe, who designed the part of Lorenza in *The Castle of Andalusia* for her, called her 'Lovely, charming, tuneful, clever' and made an English adaptation of *La serva padrona* for her. She was particularly successful in travesty fop roles such as Jessamy in Dibdin's *Lionel and Clarissa*. Her husband came with her as 'last man' in the King's company, but by 1783 she was the sole support of eight children. She disappeared from the stage after 1791, but apparently remained in England and died in poverty.

*

BDA; *BurneyH*; *LS*
R. Mount Edgcumbe: *Musical Reminiscences* (London, 1824, 4/1834)
M. Kelly: *Reminiscences* (London, 1826, 2/1826); ed. R. Fiske (London, 1975)
J. O'Keeffe: *Recollections* (London, 1826)
T. J. Walsh: *Opera in Dublin 1705–1797* (Dublin, 1973)
M. C. de Brito:*Opera in Portugal in the Eighteenth Century* (Cambridge, 1989)

OLIVE BALDWIN, THELMA WILSON

Setaccioli, Giacomo (*b* Tarquinia, 8 Dec 1868; *d* Siena, 5 Dec 1925). Italian composer. He studied with C. De Sanctis in Rome at the S Cecilia conservatory, where he later taught. In 1925 he was invited to succeed Pizzetti as director of the Florence Conservatory. His pupils included Vittorio Gui and Renzo Rossellini.

Setaccioli's music typifies the prevailing taste in Rome at the turn of the century. The opera *Il mantellaccio*, given on Italian Radio in 1954, contains noble music, closer to Zandonai and Cilea than to more obviously *verismo* works. The loss of his other three operas, and of most of his other music, militates against any analysis of his style, but a string quartet reveals a solid grounding in counterpoint and an individual approach to harmony. According to Loewenberg, *La sorella di Mark* was written for the soprano Gemma Bellincioni. Setaccioli was also active as an orchestral conductor and wrote some theoretical works including *Il contenuto musicale di 'Gianni Schicchi' di G. Puccini* (Rome, 1920).

L'ultimo degli Abenceragi (E. Palermi, after F. R. Chateaubriand), Rome, 1893
La sorella di Mark (3, E. Golisciani), Rome, Costanzi, 7 May 1896
Adriana Lecouvreur, 1904, unperf.
Il mantellaccio, 1913 (S. Benelli), RAI, 1954

*

DEUMM (R. Cognazzo); *LoewenbergA*

Setaro, Nicolà (*b* Somma, *c*1730; *d* Bilbao, *c*1774). Italian impresario and bass. Active in the Iberian peninsula, he directed a Neapolitan opera company taken to Barcelona by the Marqués de Mina. Its first performance, Auletta's pasticcio *Il maestro di cappella*, was in the Captain General's palace in 1750. The company staged Pergolesi's *La serva padrona* at the Teatro de la Santa Cruz (with Setaro singing) and gave premières of three works by the company's *maestro di cappella*, Giuseppe Scolari. Leaving part of the company in Barcelona under Giuseppe Ambrosini, Setaro took the others to Jerez de la Frontera (1753) and Puerto de Santa Maria (1753–4), but because of legal difficulties his singers returned to Barcelona.

In 1761 a Setaro company, including many of Nicolà's family and colleagues, performed in Cádiz and Seville. Nicolà was active as impresario at the Teatro do Corpo da Guarda, Oporto, from 1762, when he and his daughter Anna sang in Ciampi's *Il trascurato*. In August 1768 he staged *Il maestro di cappella* at Santiago de Compostela with a company made up largely of his family. In December that year he established himself in La Coruña, where he built a theatre and obtained the patronage of important merchants. He performed there until Carnival 1769, but the theatre had to be demolished (partly because of urban development) and he went on to Ferrol, where he opened a theatre in 1769 (it burnt down in 1807). Later he opened the Teatro de la Franja in La Coruña, where he performed in 1771–2; it was then taken over by the city authorities, and survived until 1842. With a new *maestro di cappella*, Girolamo Sertori, Setaro moved from Pamplona to Bilbao. In 1773 he was denounced for nefarious conduct and condemned to death; he was later acquitted, but died in prison. The theatre continued under the direction of his son-in-law, Alfonso Niccolini. Setaro remains a figure unique in the diffusion of Italian opera in Spain and Portugal for his attempts at setting up theatres with paid admission.

*

X. M. Carreira: 'La tasa y regulación del Coliseo de Operas y Comedias fabricado por Setaro (Coruña, 1772)', *RdMc*, x (1987), 601–21
M. C. de Brito: *Opera in Portugal in the Eighteenth Century (1708–1793)* (Cambridge, 1989)
X. M. Carreira: 'El teatro de opera en la peninsula ibérica ca. 1750–1775: Nicolà Setaro', *De música hispánica et aliis: miscelánea en honor al Prof. Dr. José López-Calo*, ii (Santiago, 1990), 27–117

XOÁN M. CARREIRA

Set piece [closed number]. Any piece of music within an opera that forms a self-sufficient unit, marked off from its surroundings by a recognizable beginning and end. From about 1680 operas consisted, generally speaking, entirely of numbers linked by passages of recitative or, in *opéra comique*, Singspiel and other vernacular genres, spoken dialogue. In *tragédie lyrique* the boundaries were generally more fluid. During most of the 18th and 19th centuries set pieces (each followed by applause for performers and composer, except where composers specifically avoided it for dramatic reasons), formed the staple of operatic construction, first losing their identity in the music dramas of Wagner, extracts from which, when given in the concert hall, have to be furnished with special endings. Elsewhere the rule of set pieces within a continuous texture remained in force, although they decreased in number as operas increasingly came to be organized in whole acts. By the 20th century they are exceptional outside operetta, being confined mostly to the occasional aria, for example 'Un bel dì vedremo' (*Madama Butterfly*, 1904), 'Depuis le jour' (*Louise*, Charpentier, 1900), the recitative and aria 'Grossmächtige Prinzessin' (*Ariadne auf Naxos*, Strauss, rev. 1916), or instrumental interlude, for example the Dance of the Seven Veils from *Salome* (Strauss, 1905), the intermezzo from *I gioielli della Madonna* (Wolf-Ferrari, 1911) or the Four Sea Interludes from *Peter Grimes* (Britten, 1945). JULIAN BUDDEN

Sette canzoni. Opera by G. F. Malipiero, part 2 of the triptych ORFEIDE, L'.

Settimino (It.). SEPTET.

Séverac, (Marie-Joseph-Alexandre) Déodat de (*b* St Félix de Caraman en Lauragais, Haute Garonne, 20 July 1872; *d* Céret, Pyrénées-Orientales, 24 March 1921). French composer. He was born into a provincial aristocratic family. Except for the period during which he studied at the Schola Cantorum in Paris (1896–1907), he spent most of his life in southern France, convinced that a composer should draw his musical resources from his native land. Although the Schola orientated its students towards chamber and symphonic music, Séverac wrote several theatrical works, including one important opera and two *tragédies lyriques*. These reflect his lifelong interest in folk music and past traditions. *Le coeur du moulin*, begun in 1902 and first performed in 1909, sets a lyrical play in two acts by Maurice Magre. Séverac originally called it *Le retour*, for it tells of a young man who returns to his birthplace only to find his sweetheart married to someone else. For these simple characters and the nostalgic evocation of Nature, he composed sober lines, set in a Debussy-like orchestration. Critics praised the work for its melodic invention and spontaneity of feeling, but objected to the incomprehensible offstage voices singing of past memories.

Héliogabale, first performed in 1910 at the Béziers arena to an audience of 15 000, centres on the decadence of classical Rome, the tyranny of its illegitimate ruler Heliogabalus and the mysticism of the early Christians. Its form recalls that of the *tragédies lyriques* of Rameau. Séverac uses large forces and juxtaposes the Christians' hymns and Gregorian chant with the Roman courtesans' melodies, using Hindu and Phrygian modes. Four *cobla* (Basque folk instruments) are used to accompany the final masquerade. Séverac composed another *tragédie lyrique*, *La fille de la terre* (1913), an *opéra bouffe Le roi pinard* (1919) and *Les antibels*, an opera based on a novel by Emile Pouvillon, as well as incidental theatre music.

Le coeur du moulin (2, M. Magre), Paris, OC (Favart), 8 Dec 1909
Héliogabale (tragédie lyrique, 3, E. Sicard), Béziers, Arènes, 21 Aug 1910 [with prol. Les deux triomphes, C. Guéret, and epilogue ballet-mime La résurrection d'Adonis, G. Boissy]
La fille de la terre (tragédie lyrique, 3, Sicard), Coursan, July 1913
Le roi pinard (opéra bouffe, Séverac and A. Bausil, after L. Lointier: *Les princesses d'Hokifari*), 1919
Les antibels, lost

*

Grove6 (E. Brody)
P. Lalo: 'La Musique' [review of *Le coeur du moulin*], *Le Temps* (14 Dec 1909)
V. Debay: 'Le coeur du moulin', *Courrier Musical* (15 Dec 1909)
R. Davray: 'Héliogabale', *Courrier Musical* (1–15 Sept 1910)
J. Pillois: 'Héliogabale', *Courrier Musical* (15 March 1911)
B. Selva: *Déodat de Séverac* (Paris, 1930)
Centenaire Déodat de Séverac (Céret, 1972) [Musée d'Art Moderne pamphlet]
JANN PASLER

Severini, Carlo (*b* Bologna, 1793; *d* Paris, 15 Jan 1828). Italian director. After a period of military service in his native Bologna, he moved to Paris in 1817. He soon gained employment at the Théâtre Italien as a stage manager's assistant. Through sheer industry he worked his way up the theatre hierarchy and in 1825 became co-director with Edouard Robert. Their tenure was one of the high points in the history of the Théâtre Italien, a period that featured the Parisian premières of works such as *Anna Bolena* and *La sonnambula*, the world première of *I puritani* and regular appearances by such great singers as Grisi, Rubini, Tamburini and Lablache. In 1828 Severini met a premature death in a fire at the theatre, apparently in an attempt to save administrative papers. STEVEN HUEBNER

Sevil'. Opera in four acts by FIKRET AMIROV to a libretto by Talet Eyubov after Jafar Jabarli's play; Baku, Azerbaijani Theatre of Opera and Ballet, 25 December 1953.

Described as a 'national lyrical-psychological opera', *Sevil'* depicts the liberation of Azerbaijani women from Islamic repression in 1918–19, and the fourth act, set in 1929, paints a rosy picture of their improved situation under Soviet Socialist rule. The heroine Sevil' (soprano) stands for the suffering Azerbaijani woman, oppressed by stereotypical religious and capitalist elements. By concerted action with her similarly oppressed sisters she brings about revolutionary change, the climax of the revolt taking place in the second act, which incorporates the melodies of the *varsovienne*, the revolutionary song *Smelo tovarishchi* ('Bravely Comrade') and the Internationale. Despite this use of non-indigenous material, *Sevil'* was much praised on its first appearance for its strongly national style and for this reason it holds an important position in the history of Azerbaijani national music. Critics also praised the dramatic conflicts and the musical characterization, particularly of Sevil' herself.

Amirov's experiences in writing his first two symphonic *mugam* (1948), based on the Azerbaijani song-dance form of that name, gave him valuable experience in marrying folk styles with Western, and particularly Russian, symphonic elements. *Sevil'* also makes use of simple leitmotif techniques, with particularly important themes for the heroine and 'the people'. In addition there is a kind of 'leit-instrumentation', with leading characters allotted specific instrumental sounds, often in imitation of native folk instruments. *Sevil'* was revised twice: important choral parts were introduced in the 1955 version, and in 1959 some of the allegedly too complex orchestral polyphony was removed. STEPHEN JOHNSON

Seville (Sp. Sevilla; It. Siviglia). Spanish city, the capital of Andalusia. Although its colourful and exotic image has made it a favourite setting for operas, the city has itself had only a sporadic history of operatic performance. Strict government censorship in the 17th century and the intransigent attitude of local bishops in the 18th meant that few theatrical performances could be given. For a brief period in 1729–33 when the Spanish king and court were in residence, operas and serenatas were given in the Alcázar by the company of the Teatro de los Caños del Peral from Madrid. Later, in 1761–5, a series of plays and operas including Piccinni's *La buona figliuola* and the pasticcio *Il maestro di cappella* (with music by Auletta) was given in a public theatre by a visiting Italian company; there is some evidence to suggest cooperation between this theatre and others in Cádiz and Lisbon. Then, from 1767 to 1778 at the Teatro de S Eloy, the impresario José Chacón staged operas such as *Demofoonte* and *Ezio* in Spanish translations by Ramón de la Cruz (composers unknown) and *opere buffe* including *La frascatana*. Finally, in 1795 permission was granted for the opening of the Teatro Cómico, giving chiefly drama but also Italian opera and ballet and, between 1804 and 1808, French opera; among the works presented were Fioravanti's *Le cantatrici villane* and Cimarosa's *Il matrimonio segreto* (both in 1805) and Boieldieu's *Le calife de Bagdad* (1807). Though disrupted in the 1820s by the effects of the Peninsular War, the Cómico reopened and remained active until 1858. Meanwhile, the Anfiteatro had opened on 19 September 1846 (with Verdi's *Ernani*) and the luxurious Teatro de S Fernando (cap. 3000, designed by French architects) with *I Lombardi* on 21 December 1847. For more than a century the S Fernando mounted plays, operas and zarzuelas.

On 2 May 1991 the Teatro de la Maestranza (cap. 1774) opened with a gala performance. Designed by Luís Marín de Terán and Aurelio del Pozo, it incorporates the façade of the old Maestranza barracks. It was the scene of an extended Expo 92 season from April to October 1992, partly given by companies from the leading European opera houses and the Metropolitan, New York. Opera is occasionally given at Santiponce, 11 km from Seville, at the Roman amphitheatre of Itálica (cap. 1014) and the experimental Teatro Central (cap. up to 990).

Seville, however, remains most famous in the world of opera as a setting, notably for *Le nozze di Figaro*, *Don Giovanni*, *Fidelio*, *Il barbiere di Siviglia* and *Carmen*. In this context it has frequently been used for filming cinema and television productions and as a venue for opera conferences.

*

F. Aguilar Piñal: *Sevilla y el teatro en el siglo XVIII* (Oviedo, 1974)

XOÁN M. CARREIRA

Sextet (Fr. *sextuor*; Ger. *Sextett*; It. *sestetto*). An ensemble for six voices. Sextets are rare as separate numbers outside the context of an act finale. Early examples appear in Hasse's *Antigono* and Graun's *Artasese* (both 1743); these are settings of items added to the original Metastasio librettos. Sextets are popular in *opéra comique*, being especially favoured by the librettists Anseaume and Sedaine; the earliest is in E. Duni's *L'isle des foux* (1760; the libretto was written by Anseaume in conjunction with Marcouville who, two years before, had written the first known text for a quintet). The sextet is not uncommon in *opera buffa* and *semiseria*. Outstanding examples include Mozart's 'Riconosci, in questo amplesso' in *Le nozze di Figaro* (1786), Act 3, and his 'Solo in bujo loco' in *Don Giovanni*, Act 2 (1787; the latter may have been planned as an act finale); both are action ensembles, unlike the contemplative sextet 'Quest' è un nodo avviluppato', from Rossini's *La Cenerentola* (1817), which offers a brilliant display of florid part-writing. The most famous operatic sextet is 'Chi mi frena in tal momento', from Donizetti's *Lucia di Lammermoor* (1835), which is in fact the *pezzo concertato* with chorus in the Act 2 finale.

See also FINALE. JULIAN BUDDEN, STANLEY SADIE

Seydelmann [Seidelmann], **Franz** (*b* Dresden, 8 Oct 1748; *d* Dresden, 23 Oct 1806). German composer. He studied with J. C. Weber and the composers J. G. Schürer and (from 1764) J. G. Naumann. He and his fellow pupil Joseph Schuster accompanied Naumann on a study tour of Italy from 1765 to 1768. He completed his education in Naples, Palermo, Bologna and Padua. In 1772 he was appointed a church composer to the court in Dresden and in 1787 Kapellmeister, in both cases simultaneously with Schuster. Among his duties were the care of sacred music in the Catholic court church and the 'Accompagnement der opera buffa'; occasionally the direction of the operas lay entirely in his hands because both Naumann and Schuster frequently took extended leave of absence. In 1773 Seydelmann's earliest known stage work, *La serva scaltra*, was performed at the Kleines Kurfürstliches Theater in Dresden, followed by several other operas in succeeding years. His 'Chinese' spectacle *Il mostro, ossia Da gratitudine amore* (1786) was particularly successful, as was his best Italian opera, *Il turco in Italia* (1788), which Constanze Mozart described after a performance in Vienna in 1789. Although his operatic output virtually ceased in 1790 with *Amore per oro*, he wrote sacred music until the end of his life.

Seydelmann wrote fewer operas than his Dresden colleagues, but their quality, at least in the most successful, met the exacting standards of the city. His works make use of thematic recall in the manner of Naumann, contain many grandiloquent through-composed sections and rich orchestration, and occasionally reach a tone of deep conviction; on the other hand, the arias and melodic structure show many conservative, even conventional, traits. Seydelmann also contributed to the cultivation of German Singspiel at Dresden. In the fairy-tale Singspiel *Arsene* (1779) traces of Georg Benda's monodrama can be seen, while the German comic opera *Der lahme Husar* (1780) has the naturalness of Singspiel.

DKT – *Dresden, Kleines Kurfürstliches Theater*

La serva scaltra (ob, 3), DKT, 1773, *D-Dlb*

Der Kaufmann von Smyrna, DKT, 1778, lost, recit and aria in J. A. Hiller, ed.: Sammlung der vorzüglichsten, noch ungedruckten Arien und Duetten des deutschen Theaters, v (Leipzig, 1780)

Arsene [Die schöne Arsene] (Spl, 4, A. G. Meissner, after C.-S. Favart), DKT, 3 March 1779, *Dlb*, vs (Leipzig, 1779)

Das tartarische Gesetz (F. W. Gotter), *c*1779, lost

Der lahme Husar (komische Oper, 2, F. C. Koch), Leipzig, Ranstädter Tor, 17 July 1780, *Dlb*, 2 songs in J. A. Hiller, ed.: Sammlung der vorzüglichsten, noch ungedruckten Arien und Duetten des deutschen Theaters, vi (Leipzig, 1780)
Il capriccio corretto (ob, 2, C. Mazzolà), DKT, 1783, *Dlb*, *B-Bc*, vs, *D-Dlb*, terzetto in Auswahl der neuesten italiänischen, frantzösischen und deutschen Singestücken (Dresden, *c*1793)
Der Soldat (komische Oper), Gotha, 1784
La villanella di Misnia (ob, 2, Mazzolà), DKT, 5 March 1786; Ger. trans. as Das sächsische Bauernmädchen, Frankfurt, 1791, *Dlb*
Il mostro, ossia Da gratitudine amore (ob, 2, Mazzolà), DKT, 5 March 1786, *Dlb*
Il turco in Italia (ob, 2, Mazzolà), DKT, 1788, *Dkh*, *Dlb*, song in Bibliothek der Grazien, ii (Speyer, 1790)
Amore per oro (ob, 2, ?Mazzolà), Dresden, Hof, 7 April 1790, *Dlb*
Le fils reconnaissant (Spl, 1), Oels, 25 April 1795, lost [possibly identical to Der Soldat]

*

StiegerO
M. Fürstenau: *Beiträge zur Geschichte der königlich sächsischen musikalischen Kapelle* (Dresden, 1849)
R. Cahn-Speyer: *Franz Seydelmann als dramatischer Komponist* (diss., U. of Munich, 1908; Leipzig, 1909) [incl. chronological index of works]
DIETER HÄRTWIG

Seyfried, Ignaz (Xaver), Ritter **von** (*b* Vienna, 15 Aug 1776; *d* Vienna, 27 Aug 1841). Austrian composer and conductor. His brother Joseph (1780–1849) was a prolific dramatist, librettist and writer. Ignaz von Seyfried is said to have studied keyboard with Mozart and Kozeluch, and composition with Albrechtsberger and Winter. He studied philosophy in Prague in 1792–3, intending to take up law, but eventually devoted himself to music. From 1797 he was a conductor in Schikaneder's Freihaus-Theater, furnishing it and later the Theater an der Wien with innumerable scores; in 1826 he resigned as Kapellmeister, though he continued to supply occasional works and arrangements for other theatres. It has been estimated that his music was heard on 1700 evenings in the Theater an der Wien alone. He was on friendly terms with Beethoven, whose *Fidelio* he conducted at its première in 1805, and his versatility won him a unique place in Vienna's musical life; however, almost none of his music is marked by real originality or distinction.

Four of Seyfried's scores (including his setting of Schikaneder's *Der Wundermann am Rheinfall*, 1799, about which Haydn wrote him a complimentary letter) were among the 12 most often performed works in the Freihaus-Theater; many of his operas and Singspiels, as well as pantomimes, for the Theater an der Wien also enjoyed frequent performance. He was highly regarded not least for his biblical music dramas, which include *Saul* (1810), *Abraham* (1817), *Die Makabäer* (1818) and *Noah* (1819). Among his many arrangements were *Ahasverus, der nie Ruhende* (1823) and *Der hölzerne Säbel* (1830), both based on melodies by Mozart, and *Rochus Pumpernickel* (1809), a pasticcio by Stegmayer for which the music was arranged by Seyfried and Jakob Haibel. He also reorchestrated or composed numbers for many earlier works, including *La clemenza di Tito* and *Zémire et Azor.* Plays for which he wrote incidental music include Schiller's *Die Räuber* (1808) and *Die Jungfrau von Orleans* (1811) and Grillparzer's *Die Ahnfrau* (première, 1817). Himself the author of music for several parodies, his opera *Idas und Marpissa* (1807, text by Stegmayer) was parodied by Perinet and Tuczek under the same title in 1808, both works proving highly popular. A large number of Seyfried's works were published in Vienna, and some in Germany; his MSS may be found in the important libraries in Vienna.

all first performed in Vienna

WF – *Freihaus-Theater auf der Wieden*
WJ – *Theater in der Josefstadt*
WK – *Kärntnertortheater* WW – *Theater an der Wien*

Der Friede, oder Die Prüfung der Herzen (Spl, 2, P. Weidmann), WF, 11 May 1797, collab.; Der Löwenbrunn (heroisch-komische Oper, 2, E. Schikaneder), WF, 15 July 1797; Die travestierte Agnes Bernauerin (Lustspiel, 3, K. L. Gieseke), WF, 11 Nov 1797; Orion, oder der Fürst und sein Hofnarr (Hofgemälde, 4, J. Perinet), WF, 8 Jan 1798; Der Feenkönig (Zauber-Spl, 3, M. Stegmayer), WF, 10 Feb 1798; Eins und drei, oder Ein Gesicht und drei Menschen (Spl, 3, Perinet), WF, 18 Feb 1798, collab. Stegmayer
Die Schneiderhochzeit (Spl, 2 parts, each of 2 acts, Perinet), part 1, WF, 19 May 1798, part 2, Martinls Freisprechung, WF, 25 July 1798, collab. Stegmayer; Das Jägermädchen (Spl, 3, Stegmayer), WF, 25 Sept 1798, collab. Henneberg and Haibel; Drei Väter und zwei Kinder (komische Oper, 1, Stegmayer), WF, 18 Dec 1798, collab. Hoffmeister; Die Ostindier vom Spittelberg (Spl, 2, Schikaneder), WF, 2 Feb 1799, collab. Stegmayer; Die Pfaueninsel (Zauber-Oper, 2, C. L. Gieseke), WF, 26 March 1799, collab. Stegmayer; Minna und Peru, oder Die Königspflicht (Spl, 2, Schikaneder), WF, 30 April 1799, collab. Henneberg
Der rote Geist im Donnergebirge (heroische Oper, 2, Stegmayer), WF, 5 June 1799, collab. Triebensee; Amor's Flügel (heroisch-komisches Märchen, 3, J. Hutt, Seyfried and others), WF, 13 July 1799; Der travestierte Aeneas (farce, 3, Gieseke), WF, 13 Aug 1799, collab. Stegmayer; Der Wundermann am Rheinfall (heroische Oper, 2, Schikaneder), WF, 26 Oct 1799; Holga, die Göttin des Kristallengebirges (Spl, 3), WF, 1 Feb 1800, collab. Henneberg and Stegmayer; Amors Schiffchen in der Brigittenaue (komische Oper, 1, Schikaneder), WF, 27 Feb 1800
Die Jungbrunn-Nymphe bei Klosterneuburg (österreichische Volkssage, 3, J. F. Kringsteiner), WF, 14 April 1800 collab. Stegmayer; Hilda, oder Die Alte in den Ruinen von Fronstein (Zaubermärchen, M. Voll), WF, 24 May 1800, collab.; Das Urteil des Paris (Travestie, 1, J. Richter), WF, 9 Aug 1800, collab. Stegmayer; Alceste (Travestie, 2, Richter), WF, 2 Dec 1800, collab. Stegmayer; Proteus und Arabiens Söhne (Zauber-Spl, 3, Schikaneder), WF, 31 Jan 1801, collab. Stegmayer; Der Schuh ohne Fuss (Operette, 1), WF, 21 Feb 1801; Die Sonnenjungfrau (Travestie, 5), WF, 6 April 1801, collab. Stegmayer
Die Druiden (grosse Oper, 3), WW, 1 Aug 1801; Die Mühle am Arpennerfelsen (Melodram, 3, I. F. Castelli, after G. Pixérécourt), WW, 14 Oct 1802; Cyrus in Persien (grosse heroisch Oper, 3, J. von Seyfried), WW, 22 Nov 1803; Die Ehemänner nach der Mode (komisches Spl, 1, Seyfried), WW, 25 June 1804; Montezuma, oder Tippo Saib (Melodram, 3, Seyfried), WW, 19 Dec 1804; Untreue aus Liebe (Zauberoper, 2, Stegmayer), WW, 16 Feb 1805; Zum goldenen Löwen (1, J. Sonnleithner), WW, 12 Nov 1806, perf. WK, 1807
Alamar, der Maure (3, Castelli, after Cuvier), WW, 1 Jan 1807; Mitternacht (Spl, 1), WW, 22 April 1807; Roderich und Kunigunde, oder Der Eremit auf dem Berge Prazzo (Parodie, 4, Castelli), WW, 1 Aug 1807; Idas und Marpissa (romantische Oper, 3, Stegmayer), WW, 10 Oct 1807; Der politische Schuster (Posse, 5, J. Seyfried, after L. Holberg), WW, 1 Feb 1808; Der Ehedoktor (Posse, 3, Castelli), WW, 27 Feb 1808; Der Briefbote (Operette, 1, after B.-J. Marsollier), WW, 14 Oct 1808; Rochus Pumpernickel (Quodlibet, 3, Stegmayer), WW, 28 Jan 1809, collab. Haibel
Bertha von Werdenberg (historische Oper, 2, Stegmayer), WW, 21 Sept 1809; Die Familie Pumpernickel (Quodlibet, 3, Stegmayer), WW, 13 Feb 1810; Saul, König in Israel (Melodram, 3, Seyfried), WW, 7 April 1810; Die rote und die weisse Rose (historische Oper, 3, Castelli), WW, 19 Oct 1810; Pumpernickels Hochzeitstag (Quodlibet, 3, Stegmayer), WW, 14 Feb 1811; Feodora (Operette, A. Kotzebue), WW, 9 Sept 1811; Das lebendige Weinfass (Posse, 3, Stegmayer), WW, 25 Jan 1812; Die kluge Frau im Walde, oder Der stumme Ritter (Zauberspiel, 5, Kotzebue), WW, 25 Feb 1813
Moses (Melodram, 5, A. Klingemann), WW, 24 April 1813; Der Teufelssteg am Rigiberge (Melodram), WW, 30 April 1814; Er hält wahrhaftig Wort (komisches Spl, 2, F. X. Gewey), WW, 17 June 1815; Der Hund des Aubri de Mont Didier (heroisch-romantisches Drama, 3, Pixérécourt, trans. Castelli), WW, 26 Sept 1815; Der süsse Brei (Zauberspiel, 3, K. F. Grüner), WW, 3 Feb 1816; Drei Treppen hoch (Posse, 1, Castelli, after M.-A.-M. Desaugiers), WW, 28 Oct 1816; Der Rosenhügel am Blocksberg (Zauberspiel, 3, after Kotzebue), WW, 28 Dec 1816

Die Waise und der Mörder (Melodram, 3, after Frédéric), WW, 12 Feb 1817; Montag, Dienstag, Mittwoch (komisches Spl, 3), WW, 16 May 1817, collab. J. Kinsky and Gyrowetz; Undine, die Braut aus dem Wasserreiche (Zauberspiel, after F. Fouqué), WW, 16 Aug 1817; Abraham (Melodrama, 4), WW, 28 Nov 1817; Salmonea und ihre Söhne (Die Makabäer) (biblisches Drama, 4, Castelli), 21 Nov 1818; Noah (biblisches Drama, 3, A. Eckschläger), WW, 19 Oct 1819; Die Waise aus Genf (Melodram, 3, Castelli, after Victor), WW, 28 June 1821; Ugolino, oder Der Hungerturm (Melodram, 4, F. von Biedenfeld), WW, 26 Sept 1821; Mangadola, oder Die Wunderperle (Märchen, 4), WW, 17 Jan 1822

Timur, der Tartar Chan (Melodram, 3, Seyfried, after M. G. Lewis), WW, 14 Sept 1822; Der unsichtbare Prinz (Zauberspiel, 4, Castelli), WW, 9 Sept 1823; Sintram (nordische Rittersage, 3, A. Schumacher, after W. Scott), WW, 9 Oct 1823; Der kurze Mantel [Act 3] (Feenspiel, 3, J. G. Seidl), WW, 6 Nov 1824 [Act 1 by Riotte, Act 2 by Blumenthal]

Additions to and arrs. of numerous stage scores

*

StiegerO; *WurzbachL*
A. Schmidt: *Denksteine: Biographien von Ignaz Ritter von Seyfried ...* (Vienna, 1848), 1–39
E. Komorzynski: *Emanuel Schikaneder: ein Beitrag zur Geschichte des deutschen Theaters* (Berlin, 1901, 2/1951)
T. Frimmel: *Beethoven-Handbuch*, ii (Leipzig, 1926)
O. E. Deutsch: *Das Freihaus-Theater auf der Wieden* (Vienna, 1937)
A. Bauer: *150 Jahre Theater an der Wien* (Zürich, Leipzig and Vienna, 1952)
——: *Opern und Operetten in Wien* (Graz, 1955)

PETER BRANSCOMBE

Seyler, Abel (*b* Liestal, nr Basle, 23 Aug 1730; *d* Rellingen, nr Hamburg, 25 April 1800). Swiss impresario and actor, active in Germany. He was one of the founders of the German Nationaltheater in Hamburg in 1767. After the death of his first wife, or perhaps his divorce from her, his infatuation with the actress Sophie Hensel, whom he later married, led to his wholehearted espousal of the theatre. He gained a controlling interest in the Hamburg theatre but in 1769 financial difficulties forced him to accept a post as director of George III's theatre at Hanover; there he formed an excellent company which settled in Weimar (1772), then Gotha (1774), before Seyler obtained a licence to perform in Saxony (1775). From 1777 he performed in Frankfurt, Mainz, Cologne and Mannheim, where for two seasons from 1779 he was artistic director of the Elector Carl Theodor's Nationaltheater; he left after an unfortunate incident provoked by his wife's jealousy, and for most of the next 11 years he served as director of the Schleswig court theatre. In 1792 he returned briefly to Hamburg before retiring.

Seyler was in advance of his time in appointing a resident theatre poet and a musical director; from 1769 the latter post was held by the experienced Anton Schweitzer. By that time the musical side of the company had been strengthened by the arrival of two very good singers. Schweitzer wrote several Singspiels for the company, including a setting of Weisse's *Der lustige Schuster* 'in Piccinis Manier'. During the period that the company spent in Weimar and Gotha, librettos by Gotter, Wieland and Brandes were available, and they gave the first performances of works by E. W. Wolf, Georg Benda and Schweitzer; these included Benda's *Ariadne auf Naxos*, *Medea* and *Der Jahrmarkt*, and Schweitzer's *Alceste*, to a text by Wieland. Seyler's company also played an important part in the popularization of Shakespeare in Germany.

*

ES (A. M. Nagler)
C. H. Schmid: *Chronologie des deutschen Theaters* (Leipzig, 1775); ed. P. Legband (Berlin, 1902)
R. Schlösser: *Vom Hamburger Nationaltheater zur Gothaer Hofbühne* (Hamburg and Leipzig, 1895)
E. Pies: *Prinzipale: zur Genealogie des deutschsprachigen Berufstheaters vom 17. bis 19. Jahrhundert* (Ratingen, Kastellaun and Düsseldorf, 1973), 308
T. Bauman: *North German Opera in the Age of Goethe* (Cambridge, 1985)

PETER BRANSCOMBE

Seyler [née Sparmann; Hensel], **(Friederike) Sophie** (*b* Dresden, 1738; *d* Schleswig, 22 Nov 1789). German actress and writer. At the end of an unhappy childhood she took to the stage. In 1754 she married the actor Hensel, but they separated three years later. She worked with various troupes and appeared several times in Vienna. After the collapse of the Hamburg Nationaltheater, she took up with the impresario Abel Seyler in 1769, and married him three years later, by which time she was recognized as Germany's foremost tragedienne. Lessing praised her passionate and majestic acting at Hamburg, and Benda and F. W. Gotter wrote their chilling melodrama *Medea* to set off her skills in 1775. At the end of her career she wrote a five-act libretto *Hüon und Amande*, based on Wieland's epic poem *Oberon* and set by the Schleswig music director Karl Hanke in 1789. The text was adapted for Paul Wranitzky shortly thereafter by Gieseke as *Oberon, König der Elfen*, one of the first and most popular of Viennese magic operas. THOMAS BAUMAN

Seymour, John Laurence (*b* Los Angeles, 18 Jan 1893; *d* San Francisco, 1 Feb 1986). American composer. Between 1923 and 1928 he studied composition with Ildebrando Pizzetti and Felice Boghen in Italy and with d'Indy in France. Subsequently he devoted himself primarily to teaching: from 1928 to 1936 he served as lecturer in opera and drama at the University of California, Berkeley, and for many years he was chairman of the theatre department of Sacramento Junior College. He was a librarian at Southern Utah College, Cedar City, 1969–85.

Seymour's opera *In the Pasha's Garden*, based on a tale by H. G. Dwight, received the David Bispham Memorial Award and was performed at the Metropolitan Opera, with Lawrence Tibbett in the title role, on 24 January 1935, with two repeat performances. In 1940 he received the PhD in English literature from Berkeley; his dissertation, *Drama and Libretto*, consisted of four adaptations of two Shakespeare plays. In 1977 his opera in Spanish, *Ollanta, el Jefe Kolla*, won prizes in the cultural division of the Bolivarian Games in La Paz. Fluent in several languages, Seymour made translations from French and Russian drama and was the author of several plays. His operas have been praised for their italianate lyricism and complex orchestral textures.

Antigone (heroic op, 3, after Sophocles), 1920
The Protégé of the Mistress (4)
Les précieuses ridicules (oc, after Molière), 1920
The Bachelor Belles (operetta, R. Seymour), 1922
The Devil and Tom Walker, 1926 (operetta, 3, H. C. Tracy, after W. Irving), 1942
In the Pasha's Garden (1, Tracy, after H. G. Dwight), New York, Met, 24 Jan 1935
Golden Days (operetta, J. L. Seymour), 1936
Hollywood Madness (operetta, J. L. Seymour), 1936
Two Gentlemen of Verona op.38 (operetta, 2, J. L. Seymour and Tracy, after W. Shakespeare), 1937
The Three Brothers (operetta, after E. Bulwer-Lytton), 1942
Ming Toy (musical), 1949
The Lure and the Promise (musical), 1960

Ramona (Tracy), Provo, UT, Brigham Young U., 11 Nov 1970
Measure for Measure op.69 (musical, J. L. Seymour), 1973
Ollanta, el Jefe Kolla (F. Diaz de Medina), La Paz, 1977

YVAR MIKHASHOFF

Sforza-Cesarini, Duke **Francesco** (*b* *c*1772; *d* Rome, , 16 Feb 1816). Italian impresario. He inherited the Teatro Argentina, one of the three leading opera houses in Rome, built by his family in 1732; he acted as its impresario, as a rule with a humbler dependant as front man. During periods of French domination (1798–9 and 1809–14) he supported first the republican and then the Napoleonic regime, without afterwards incurring penalties from the restored papal government; in 1809–14 he held various official posts, among them that of supervisor of theatres, and suffered heavy losses by keeping not only the Argentina but the Teatro Valle going in adverse economic circumstances. In Carnival 1816, denied an official subsidy for the usual *opera seria* season at the Argentina, he fell back on comic opera; he contracted Rossini, assembled a company at the last moment and with great difficulty, but died suddenly four days before the première of *Il barbiere di Siviglia.*

*

Correspondence: Prefect and Mayor of Rome, 1810 (Paris, Archives Nationales Série F[1] 139)
L. Madelin: *La Rome de Napoléon* (Paris, 1906), 262–3, 659
M. Rinaldi: *Due secoli di musica al Teatro Argentina* (Florence, 1978)

JOHN ROSSELLI

Shacklock, Constance (*b* Sherwood, Nottingham, 16 April 1913). English mezzo-soprano. She studied in London at the Royal Academy of Music. In 1946 she joined the newly formed Covent Garden Opera Company, singing in Purcell's masque *The Fairy-Queen*. She remained with the company for a decade, starting with small roles such as Mercedes (*Carmen*) and graduating to leading parts: Carmen, Marina (*Boris Godunov*), Magdalene (*Die Meistersinger*), Mrs Sedley (*Peter Grimes*), Brangäne, Azucena, Amneris, Octavian, Fricka, Herodias, Ortrud and Erda (*Siegfried*). In 1953 she shared the title role of Britten's *Gloriana* with Joan Cross. A dramatic singer, she was a valued member of the company.

ELIZABETH FORBES

Shade, Ellen (*b* New York, 17 Feb 1944). American soprano. She studied in New York and made her début in 1972 at Frankfurt as Liù. She made her Metropolitan début in 1976 as Eva, returning as Sieglinde. At Chicago (1976–82) she sang Emma (*Khovanshchina*), Amelia (*Simon Boccanegra*) and Luisa Miller. She sang Donna Elvira at San Francisco (1978) and for her New York City Opera début (1981) and Donna Anna at Aix-en-Provence (1981). At Santa Fe (1982–6) she has sung Countess Almaviva, Arabella, Handel's Delilah and Kát'a; at La Monnaie (1982–5) she sang Luisa, Amelia, Kát'a and Rosalinde; at Cincinnati (1984–5) she sang Elisabeth de Valois and Aida. Her repertory includes Elsa, Agathe, Alice Ford, Giulietta, Salud (*La vida breve*), the title roles of *Ariane et Barbe-bleue* (1990, Geneva), *Iphigénie en Tauride* (1991) and *Die Frau ohne Schatten* (1992), both at Amsterdam. Her rich, warm-toned voice has developed in power without losing its lyricism as she has taken on heavier Verdi and Strauss roles.

CHARLES JAHANT/ELIZABETH FORBES

Shade, Nancy (*b* Rockford, IL, 31 May 1949). American soprano. After studying at Indiana University at Bloomington she made her début with the Kentucky Opera in 1968 as Leonora in *Il trovatore*. Her Musetta at the New York City Opera in 1971 was followed by Manon Lescaut at Spoleto (1973) and Giorgetta in *Il tabarro* at Covent Garden (1974). Further guest appearances have taken her to Munich, Milan, Geneva and Salzburg in a repertory including Konstanze, Donna Anna, the Queen of Night and Gilda. Among her modern roles are Berg's Lulu and Marie, Strauss's Zerbinetta, Marie in Zimmermann's *Die Soldaten* (1983, Lyons; 1988, Stuttgart; 1990, Vienna) and the Young Woman in Henze's *We Come to the River* (American première, 1984, Santa Fe). She sang Kát'a at Chicago in 1987.

DAVID CUMMINGS

Shakespeare, William (*b* Stratford-on-Avon, bap. 26 April 1564; *d* Stratford-on-Avon, 23 April 1616). English playwright.

1. General. 2. Settings of plays: (i) *Romeo and Juliet* (ii) *Hamlet* (iii) *Antony and Cleopatra* (iv) *The Tempest* (v) *The Winter's Tale* (vi) *The Taming of the Shrew* (vii) *A Midsummer Night's Dream.* 3. Verdi's Shakespeare operas. 4. Uncompleted projects.

1. General. Of about 270 operas (among over 380 vocal theatre works) based for the most part obliquely on the plays of Shakespeare only a handful have any musical or dramatic worth, and fewer have achieved a place in the repertory of professional companies. Nowadays only Verdi's three masterpieces, *Macbeth*, *Falstaff* and *Otello*, Britten's *A Midsummer Night's Dream* and, on the Continent, Nicolai's *Die lustigen Weiber von Windsor* and Thomas' *Hamlet* continue to receive performances; and the survival of the many new works that have had performances in recent years is far from assured. It is remarkable how few Shakespeare operas have been successful in over 300 years, given that Shakespeare has proved the single most popular source of inspiration for opera, ahead of such fashionable but perhaps dated playwrights as Goldoni, Goethe, Schiller, Hugo and Racine.

A Shakespearean opera is one whose plot, though possibly shaped by other sources just as the original plays were, contains uniquely Shakespearean elements. Many operas share short titles with Shakespeare plays but otherwise have little or no connection with them. Walton's *Troilus and Cressida*, for example, is based on Chaucer, and many late 18th- and 19th-century *Hamlets* and *Tempests* derive from sources other than Shakespeare. Few 'Caesar' or 'Coriolanus' operas are dependent on Shakespeare. Other operas contain Shakespearean characters but are arguably non-Shakespearean. The most striking example of these is Bellini's *I Capuleti e i Montecchi* (1830). Long regarded as the best of a group of early 19th-century Italian operas based on *Romeo and Juliet*, it turns out on closer examination to be something else: Romani's libretto is derived from the one he wrote in 1825 for Vaccai, after Foppa's *Giulietta e Romeo* (1795) and Luigi Scevola's play of the same name (1818).

Musical cues and references to music abound in Shakespeare's plays. Music itself appears at differing levels of dramatic sophistication, ranging from straightforward entertainment and diversion to integrated theatrical function, especially in the later plays. Themes of love, an essential ingredient in opera, predominate in both the tragedies and the comedies. Despite the significance of music and song, most of the plays in their original form are not well suited to operatic treatment.

Much of Shakespeare's theatrical art depends on lightning verbal wit and word-play not easily integrated with music. Even when incorporated into the action of a play, as in *The Tempest*, music remains incidental to the medium of artistic expression, namely the poetic language. In opera that medium is the music in which the emotions of the characters are expressed. Only one full-length opera wholly based on Shakespeare's text (albeit considerably cut) can be said to be successful, namely Britten's *A Midsummer Night's Dream* (1960). Barkworth's *Romeo and Juliet* (1916), using Shakespeare's text with a minimum of alteration, demonstrates the unhappy transference of medium from play to opera. Other successful operas are adaptations of Shakespeare texts, often far removed from the original.

Opera is in itself a clearly identifiable, though multi-faceted, art form; a play, however, needs extensive modification to shape it into a libretto. The quality and verbal intricacy of Shakespeare's plays and, not least, audience familiarity with them, demand that the opera be not simply a musical version of the play but a valid artistic endeavour on its own terms. Some of the plays – *Romeo*, *Merchant*, *Shrew*, *Winter's Tale*, *Antony*, *Lear*, *Othello*, *Macbeth*, *Tempest*, *Midsummer Night's Dream* and *Merry Wives* – are more obviously suited to operatic setting than others. (The rest have nonetheless been set in considerable number.)

2. SETTINGS OF PLAYS.

(i) 'Romeo and Juliet'. Of the tragedies, *Romeo and Juliet* lends itself most readily to operatic treatment, as its popularity with composers attests. Its theme, of young love set against a background of family disapproval and quarrelling, is a stereotype of opera. It has beautiful *ingénu* roles in the two lovers, a large character role in the old nurse and impressive chorus possibilities in the opening riot and the ballroom scene. The great structural scenes – the balcony, the orchard and the finale in the graveyard and tomb – are also immediately opera types. Moreover, the rich and lyrical text is already close to Romantic libretto language. The earliest libretto, by J. R. Sanseverino (1773; set by Schwanenberger, 1776), departs significantly from Shakespeare. There are only three characters and the lovers both survive and happily marry in the finale. This Italian version with its Classical rationality contrasts with F. W. Gotter's impassioned Singspiel adaptation of 1776, again far removed from Shakespeare and likewise eschewing a tragic ending. Daniel Steibelt's *opéra comique* (1793), to a libretto by Alexandre de Ségur, is arguably the finest 18th-century setting; it has a typical Revolution format, opening with domestic comedy, progressing to more serious stuff and culminating in a dramatic climax and a happy ending.

During the second half of the 19th century librettists attempted increasingly to respect the original text, in keeping with a general trend in both opera and drama. Marchetti was at pains to point this out in the preface to his *Romeo & Giulietta* (1865). Such conventions as climactic ensemble finales, as well as certain idiosyncrasies, however, continued to intrude: Gounod, for example (*Roméo et Juliette*, 1867), could not resist introducing a wedding and, in the 1888 Paris Opéra revival, a ballet. The opera has rather more Gounod in it than Shakespeare, notably in Juliet's delightful dance arias, but it does use Shakespeare's Prologue and Mercutio's Queen Mab soliloquy for the first time.

20th-century attempts have little to commend them from either a Shakespearean or an operatic point of view. Ranging from Sutermeister's cluttered and histrionic version (1940) to Blacher's terse radio representation (1947), all lack the musical clarity and dramatic consistency of Schwanenberger or Steibelt. Perhaps the most successful adaptation has been Bernstein's *West Side Story* (1957), in which Capulets and Montagues are replaced by rival New York street gangs.

(ii) 'Hamlet'. Among Shakespeare's plays *Hamlet* poses the greatest number of difficulties for the opera composer because its plot is diffuse, its verse introspective and muted, and its forms dominated by the figure of Hamlet, with no compelling relationships allowing scope for duets and ensembles. Only the Ghost and Ophelia have real potential as opera roles. None of these difficulties has been overcome in the numerous adaptations.

Of special interest (but variable musical worth) is Faccio's *Amleto* (1865) for its use of Boito's first libretto, already well fashioned and superbly adapted while preserving the integrity and mood of the play. Little is altered or omitted, operatic conventions notwithstanding, except that Boito has Ophelia die on stage, and Gertrude is not referred to by the Ghost. A mixture of good and bad is to be found in Thomas' still popular *Hamlet* (1868). To a contracted plot with significantly altered detail Thomas variously applied Gounod's sentimental, Rossini's exuberant and Verdi's grandiose styles, sometimes to good effect, as in the Ghost's two scenes (the first on the battlements, the second interpolated at Ophelia's funeral), but at other times less successfully, for example in Ophelia's uninspired love music, the Danish March and the ballet. Scandinavian themes occur primarily because Thomas devised the role of Ophelia for the Swedish soprano Christine Nilsson, and not because of Hamlet's regal connections with Denmark. As if confirmation were needed of the work's doubtful artistic integrity, Julius Hopp's operetta (1874) is a biting comic parody of it. In the 20th century only Searle's large-scale but stylistically uncertain version (1968) has attracted significant critical acclaim. It has not, however, remained in the repertory.

(iii) 'Antony and Cleopatra'. Scope for extensive characterization is present in abundance in *Antony and Cleopatra*, notably of Cleopatra in her many changing moods and in her closing scene as she sings of her 'immortal longings' in all her imperial glory. All versions, mainly 20th-century, amply reflect the grandeur and extravagance of the play's Roman-Egyptian setting, though Malipiero confines his *mise en scène* to Egypt. The scale of Barber's setting, commissioned for the opening of the Metropolitan Opera House in 1966, is matched only by the extent of its initial failure. Zeffirelli's film-like adaptation of the original Shakespeare was altered mainly by Menotti for the 1975 revision, which relies almost exclusively on Shakespeare's text, though with some cuts and rearrangement.

(iv) 'The Tempest'. Of all the plays, *The Tempest* has generated the most operas, particularly in Germany. The original play has more music in it than any other, serving specific dramatic functions ranging from accompanying Ariel's magic to conveying atmospheric nuances. It has a delicate Romanticism in the discovery of young love in Ferdinand and Miranda, and in the

pitting of the fallen human world, with its jealousies and intrigues, against the purity of the supernatural, with its powers of magical intervention; it also has a storm and shipwreck, adventure and discovery – all embraced by the simple but powerful allegory of good and evil. Moreover the action observes the unities of time and place, resulting in a coherent plot and uncomplicated setting with comparatively few scene changes. All the more surprising, therefore, that no composer has written an altogether successful 'Tempest' opera.

In 1667 a much altered contemporary version of *The Tempest* made by Davenant and Dryden was produced at the Duke's Theatre. In 1674 that adaptation was further 'improved' by Thomas Shadwell and 'made into an opera'. A slightly revised version of this text was the basis of an opera long thought to be by Henry Purcell, but now, following Laurie (1963–4), accepted as by John Weldon, and probably first produced in 1712. Only two of Ariel's songs, 'Come unto these yellow sands' and 'Full fathom five' preserve the original Shakespeare, while a dialogue for devils is inserted into Act 2 and various new airs (including the delicate 'Dear pretty youth', probably by Purcell) are introduced. Baroque symmetries in both music (exact sequences) and plot (Miranda/Hippolito, Caliban/Sycorax), italianate da capo arias, recurring ritornellos, ornamentation (roulades) of purely musical significance and other devices common in contemporary italianate opera are present. Singing and speaking characters are for the most part clearly differentiated.

The first important German version of *The Tempest* was *Die Geisterinsel*, written by F. H. von Einsiedel in 1778 and reworked by Gotter in 1790–91. It was highly esteemed, especially by its authors, and offered to various famous composers. Mozart accepted the libretto only a few months before he died (Einstein, 1958). It was next submitted to Dittersdorf (in 1792) but withdrawn after he had demanded substantial textual revisions. Agreement was finally reached with Fleischmann in 1796, and his opera *Die Geisterinsel* received its first performance in 1798. Other settings followed in the same year by Reichardt and Zumsteeg and in 1799 by Haack. That Mozart saw opera potential in this adaptation, distant from Shakespeare in tone, dramatic emphasis and verbal movement, affirms its Singspiel nature, with its mixture of spectacle, farce, serious moralizing, magic, love and discovery. Reichardt's setting is clearly in the *Zauberflöte* mould, particularly in the musical characterization, but without any of its subtlety, accomplishment or memorability, while Zumsteeg's version is an altogether more serious work, notably in ensembles; its characterization, however, is less effective. Ritter's *Der Sturm* (1799), to J. W. Döring's libretto *Der Sturm, oder Die bezauberte Insel*, is closely related to the Singspiel, as shown in J. D. Hensel's *Die Geisterinsel* (1799, after Gotter's *Die Geisterinsel* and Döring's libretto), which claims to be more expressive and direct than Mozart and his followers. Wenzel Müller's *Der Sturm*, to a libretto by K. F. Hensel (1798), and presumably Hoffmeister's *Der Schiffbruch* (1792) suggest that he was following the then fashionable Viennese practice of mixing the heroic with the comic in a banal but spectacular manner, accompanied by appropriate music.

More faithful to Shakespeare, according to its author, was a libretto by Scribe, rejected in 1846 by Mendelssohn (who had already turned down one by Karl Immermann in 1832) but accepted shortly afterwards by Halévy; it was translated into Italian for its London première in 1850. Both libretto and music, in their insipid mannerisms and conventionality, have little to commend them except historical interest. All the 19th-century 'Tempest' operas depend less on Shakespeare than on the ideals and techniques of German Romanticism. Even Fibich's *Bouře* (1895) is a heavy-handed exercise in Teutonic moralizing and Wagnerian leitmotifs. There is little Czech in it. 20th-century approaches to *The Tempest* range between the extremes of Sutermeister's extravagant *Die Zauberinsel* (1942), with its diatonic tunes in unnecessarily irregular metres, and Frank Martin's austere and literal *Der Sturm* (1956), whose libretto follows Schlegel's translation with one or two cuts. Somewhere in the middle come the inconsequential English lyric romantic settings by Hale (1912) and Gatty (1920).

(v) 'The Winter's Tale'. The other play to appeal to the fervent sentimentality of the German Romantics was *The Winter's Tale*. Comic elements are taken out, Autolycus and the Clown disappear, and the librettos assume such 19th-century melodramatic stereotypes as child-snatching, women fainting, earthquakes, storms, weird visions (*Traumbilder*), shipwrecks, sailors' choruses and cradle songs in their main plots. The most extreme setting is Goldmark's *Ein Wintermärchen* (1908), which ranges in style from Weber to Richard Strauss, and indulges in rich chromatic harmony at the expense of musical invention.

(vi) 'The Taming of the Shrew'. Except for Goetz, the German Romantics ignored *The Taming of the Shrew*. Its comic situation, much rushing in and out, fervent quarrelling, grand finale, implied scenes (for example, the marriage in Act 3 scene ii), ensemble of characters deftly portrayed in gentle verse, lusty rather than weighty heroic roles for Katharine and Petruchio, render the play unsuited to plot development. Goetz's *Der widerspänstigen Zähmung* (1874) is unsatisfactory mainly because its comedy, occasionally effective as in the Act 1 serenade, is overlaid with sentimentality. In Giannini's version (1953) naive pastiche (of Schumann, Puccini, Bizet and others) and neo-Romantic heaviness detract from any attempted wit. By contrast, the Russian composer Shebalin (1955) is more successful in his obvious humour couched in a traditional Tchaikovskian musical style. Both Goetz and Shebalin follow Shakespeare's play closely. Such lightness of touch was eventually realized in Cole Porter's memorable musical, *Kiss me, Kate* (1948).

(vii) 'A Midsummer Night's Dream'. The earliest use of *A Midsummer Night's Dream* for opera was in Purcell's *The Fairy-Queen* (1692). The manuscript for the first production has not survived, but the revised version mounted in February 1693 'with Alterations, several Additions, and several new Songs' has. Although only about 750 lines come from Shakespeare's original 2100, and another 400 are clearly derivative, the ethos of *The Fairy-Queen* is that of Shakespeare's *A Midsummer Night's Dream*. Unlike other Restoration 'improvements' for opera (notably *The Tempest*) the unnamed author(s) did not falsify but rather simplified the plot, cutting over 900 lines and adding 200 spoken and 250 sung lines as extraneous episodes. Both Purcell and the librettist(s) (variously identified as Thomas Betterton, John Dryden and Elkanah Settle) modernized *A Midsummer Night's Dream*, making 'creative use of current

local traditions and conventions' (Savage, 1973). None of the surviving songs has a Shakespeare text, though the air 'The woosel-cock so black of hue' (Act 3 scene i) may have been the only genuine Shakespeare text in *The Fairy-Queen* and in all Purcell's songs. This semi-opera has a special character in that the music does not advance the drama but instead creates a mood.

There is a significant link between the first opera based on *A Midsummer Night's Dream* and a much later one, certainly the best setting since. In 1967 Britten, helped by Imogen Holst, produced an edited concert version of Purcell's work only a few years after the completion of his own opera, first performed in 1960 at Aldeburgh. Like Purcell's, Britten's music is superbly atmospheric and evocative. The emphasis is on the make-believe world of the fairies, couched in the bewitching context of night and dreaming, a theme that fascinated Britten as early as 1937 in his *On This Island*, based on Auden's *Nocturne*. The theme recurs later in the opposition of the natural and the supernatural in the menacing *Turn of the Screw* (1954) and in his own *Nocturne* (1958). Each of the three acts opens in the woods with fairies, and closes with the fairies in command. In Shakespeare the mortal world is portrayed before the magical. In Britten and Pears's libretto the original play is appropriately shortened for opera; only one line is invented; some scenes are repositioned (notably the entry of Theseus and Hippolyta with their court, which opens the play but is transferred to the last section of the opera); and several lines are transposed, especially Puck's, many of whose lines are given to the chorus of fairies. Only Shakespeare's Egeus and Philostrate disappear. All the adaptations are plausible and ingeniously managed. That the opera matches the play in spirit and artistry is arguably everywhere apparent. Britten accomplished in his music the wonderful and effective transformations, paralleling Shakespeare, from simple humour to sophisticated love, and from ordinariness to enchantment.

3. VERDI'S SHAKESPEARE OPERAS. The three other operas that have assured Shakespeare a continued place in the opera house are Verdi's *Macbeth*, *Otello* and *Falstaff*. They have done so mainly because of their quintessentially Verdian qualities, but the Shakespearean element has also aroused considerable interest. Verdi's lifelong interest in Shakespeare is confirmed in his defensive and now famous letter of 28 April 1865 to Léon Escudier: 'He is a favourite poet of mine, whom I have had in my hands from earliest youth and whom I read and reread constantly.' When *Macbeth*, his first Shakespearean opera, had its première in Florence in 1847, Verdi manifested an affinity with Shakespeare extraordinary in Italy at the time and unique among composers. Although Verdi's was not the first Italian Shakespearean opera (Rossini's *Otello* was a famous precedent), it was the first attempt to represent Shakespeare in opera with any integrity. Unlike Rossini, whose setting is Shakespearean only in Act 3, Verdi aimed to set the original.

The Shakespeare that Verdi had to hand for his *Macbeth* was principally Carlo Rusconi's deplorable prose version (1838). The dull heaviness of Rusconi's translation adversely affects the spirit and movement of the libretto. Moreover, in keeping with widespread theatrical tradition, the work's many changes to the original (reordering, sectionalized extending or contracting, glossing and embellishing) produce a spectator 'operatic' *Macbeth* out of the original audience drama, affording pre-eminence to what is seen rather than to what is heard. The result is an emphasis on the supernatural, 'promoting Hecate and the Witches to the rank of main characters', and elevating Lady Macbeth to a dominant position. The sleepwalking scene in Act 4 becomes a climactic point in the opera, transforming it from Shakespeare's scene of recollection into a moment of grand operatic assertion.

Similar romanticizing occurs in both *Otello* and *Falstaff*. In *Otello* the most obvious difference between the source and the opera is the omission of virtually all of Act 1. One reason for this may have been a lingering neo-classical longing for unity of place, but it also reflects the librettist's reinterpretation of basic themes and characterization, and his thoroughgoing transformation of a complex, often mysterious play into an opera of broader, simple values and characters. If Shakespeare's play presents the confused and often contradictory, sometimes inexplicable aspects of human nature, with subtle and disturbing uncertainties, the opera shows, in Dryden's words, 'nature, but nature wrought up to a higher pitch': it is heroic, demonic or innocently pure.

Shakespeare's Act 1 presents an Othello calm, dignified and reasonable, whose set speech to the senate, 'Most potent, grave, and reverend signiors', is self-deprecating, low-key and manly. The opera retains only fragments of this act, transformed significantly into the intensely romantic and passionate love duet which closes Act 1. This, in short, is what the libretto as a whole does to the character of Othello. It dispenses with his quieter, thoughtful, restrained elements and his own doubts about himself and his marriage; it straightens out his wavering, doubting and agonized path to jealousy, and creates a simplified two-sided hero of heightened and rhetorically magnified nobility, coupled with an equally exaggerated savagery. It is not surprising that this approach finds no room for the self-questioning, terrible reluctance and beauty of the great soliloquy over the sleeping Desdemona, 'It is the cause, it is the cause my soul'.

The character of Desdemona is also simplified: in the opera she embodies an uncomplicated image of purity, innocence and utterly devoted love, surrounded by imagery and music of religious and saintly connotation; but Shakespeare's Desdemona is a more complex human creature – stronger, braver and sometimes wilful, the Desdemona who dared to enter into a secret and unorthodox marriage after encouraging Othello's early approaches, who can jest (almost improperly with Iago) and coax and inveigle to get her way. Her lively humanity is necessary for Shakespeare's tragedy, to be contrasted with Othello's false image of her perfect beauty and faultless purity, a semi-divine image which Iago finds easy to smash, thus bringing about chaos. But the opera needs this simpler character in order to present an angelic image; the Ave Maria inserted in Act 4 completes the holy image of Desdemona, on to whose deathbed Emilia could not be allowed to drag her dying body.

The same movement to a less ambiguous, bolder characterization can be seen in the handling of Iago, in the opera a demonic figure forming a striking trio with Othello's heroism and Desdemona's purity. The Iago of Shakespeare's Act 1 is an apparently jolly comrade, a joker, a bustling plotter of mischief, moved by a simple hatred arising from frustrated ambition. He is a pragmatist, taking the opportunity which presents itself, with no hint of a devilish strategy with a distant but known end. Ultimately Shakespeare's Iago is unexplained, his various confessed motives hardly believable. But the opera adds the completely un-Shakespearean Credo of Act 2 – 'Credo in un Dio crudel che m'ha creato', emphatically and simply establishing Iago's diabolic motivation, and from that moment the third huge figure for the heroic triptych is ready to go forward without further complex analysis. Such simplification of outline, plot and character is a necessary move from play to opera. It is for the music to add the depths and suggestiveness of emotion and characterization. It is here, particularly in the opening dramatic storm and the powerfully evocative 'Willow Song', that Verdi is so masterly.

In *Falstaff*, the adaptation of the source follows the simplification of structure and character found in *Otello*. The purpose of this is to produce a leaner plot with no unnecessary characters cluttering the action. The main two-episode Falstaff plot is combined with a romantic subplot developed charmingly behind a screen in the laundry-basket episode, and consummated with intrigue and disguise in the forest scenes. A number of characters are dispensed with, including Justice Shallow and his stupid nephew, Sir Hugh Evans, Nym and even Mr Page, which leaves Mrs Page as a freelance intriguer, while Nannetta becomes one of the Ford family. The plot is thus moved forward by a tighter and clearer band of characters.

A subtler and less mechanical transformation occurs between the two plays, in the general tone and the final view of life they leave with, us. Shakespeare's play is above all a 'gulling' comedy involving a series of humiliations, and for all its farcical episodes it has a thread of malice and cruelty. The opera offers a more rumbustious, affirmative and happy world, where the gulling is enjoyed for the sheer fun of intriguing and plotting, where no one takes Falstaff's offence very seriously, except as an excuse for engineering a theatre of ludicrous situations. It is also a world of romance where the Fenton-Nannetta plot brings in the truly operatic world of sonnets and love duets and even a screen episode in Act 2 scene ii, beloved of librettists, though without a contrived discovery. In this world of good-humoured romp and romance Falstaff is not the dejected gull, but a positive, even a creative power. He is the root cause of all this fun and frolic, someone we laugh with as well as at, as he leads the symbolic fugue of acceptance, forgiveness and tolerance, blended into glorious harmony in his final apotheosis.

4. Uncompleted projects. If Shakespeare has turned out to be the single most popular source for opera librettos, the list of established composers who have failed to realize their ambition of completing a Shakespeare opera indicates that he has also been one of the most intractable. More established composers have foundered in their attempts to write an opera on *Hamlet* than on any other play. Bizet wrote to his mother in 1859 that he was considering *Hamlet* as the basis of an opera – 'J'ai la tête pleine de Shakespeare: Hamlet! Macbeth! Mais un poète?' – but the idea remained unrealized. In 1842–3 Glinka worked on a 'Hamlet' opera, but it was never finished. Respighi, too, started one some time before 1937 but gave up. Prokofiev planned a 'Hamlet' opera, but, although he succeeded in supplying incidental music, nothing came of it. There is also a brief outline of a 'Hamlet' opera by Mendelssohn (*GB-Ob*, Deneke collection). In a letter to his mother dated 12 December 1830, Schumann affirmed: 'Next, you are right about the big opera: I am all on fire, and revel all day long in sweet fairy-like sounds. The opera is called *Hamlet*: the thought of glory and immortality gives me strength and imagination'. This heroic dream never materialized. Verdi wrote to the librettist Giulio Carcano on 17 June 1850 about the difficulties of setting *Hamlet*.

After *Hamlet*, the source of the greatest number of documented abortive attempts has been *King Lear*. Verdi's lifelong ambition to write *Re Lear* was never fulfilled, even though he came close to attempting it in the 1850s and Boito pressed him hard after the success of *Falstaff*. Difficulties with musical characterization and a lack of 'parola evidente e scenica' caused by the intricacy within the bold extremity of Shakespeare's text most obviously deterred him, as it did most other composers. (Reimann, however, using Eschenburg's 1775 translation for his *Lear* (1978), found that this complexity offered his music scope to develop. A huge score and a skilful libretto by H. Henneberg which faithfully condenses Shakespeare's original without reducing it at least fulfils its musical and dramatic aims.) Britten was frightened off *Lear* in the early 1960s after what he felt was undue publicity. Similarly, Bloch abandoned his *Lear* project (with the librettist Edmond Fleg) in 1910 after the adverse criticism of his *Macbeth*. Mascagni abandoned *Re Lear* after Verdi's example. According to Mosco Carner (*Puccini: a Critical Biography*, 1974), Puccini seriously considered a Lear opera.

The most frequently set play, *The Tempest*, has created some difficulties. Mendelssohn twice considered 'Tempest' librettos, but did not attempt to set them. In 1890 Hugo Wolf wrote about his projected *Tempest* in letters to Schur and Grohe. Ligeti expressed ideas for a 'Tempest' opera in 1984. Mozart's flirtation with *Die Geisterinsel* is well known (Deutsch 1966). As for other plays, Beethoven became disaffected with *Macbeth* after the death in 1811 of the librettist H. J. von Collin, who had managed to complete only Act 1 and half of Act 2. In the mid-1950s Chausson gave up his *Macbeth*, a 'drame lyrique en trois actes, d'après Shakespeare'. Tchaikovsky's *Othello*, following a scenario by Stasov, came to nothing. Berlioz contemplated but did not compose an opera based on *Antony* (*c*1859), and even Debussy's long involvement (1886–1917) with *As you Like it* did not bear fruit (see Lockspeiser 1965). It is known that between 1902 and 1904 he was working on an operatic version with the librettist P.-J. Toulet, and at other times he was involved in projects to write incidental music. Another early comedy, *Love's Labour's Lost*, attracted both Henze and Stravinsky. In an interview in April 1965 Henze said that he wanted to set *Love's Labour's Lost* and had asked Ingeborg Bachmann to adapt the text. Far from doing so, Bachmann produced instead *Der junge Lord* in the same year. The libretto by Auden and Kallman used by Nabokov in 1972 stirred Stravinsky to remark that he would have liked to compose the music for *Love's Labour's Lost*, especially as he had already set 'When daisies pied' in 1953. Finally, one of the few plays for which no operatic setting survives was not totally ignored. In a letter of 28 July 1898 to Modest Tchaikovsky, Rakhmaninov requested the libretto for *Richard II* which they had discussed a few months earlier, but nothing came of the project. About 1917,

Havergal Brian also considered adapting *Richard II*, but his plans, too, failed to materialize.

It may not seem surprising, then, that so many attempts to set Shakespeare by many eminent composers came to nought. The characteristics of individual plays notwithstanding. Shakespeare's theatrical art depends more on verbal wit, the quickness of words, eloquent speech, and characterization than on plot. Opera is a more diverse art involving words as only part of its effect – a small part if Richard Strauss is to be believed in stating (to Hofmannsthal) that the composer will find it difficult to make his words audible, no matter how hard he tries. That there are close parallels, even a synonymy (according to Schmidgall 1990), between Shakespeare and opera such as prosodic alternation (including prose and verse), textual contrast (soliloquy – aria and crowd-scene – ensemble), rhetoric (simple and impassioned utterance) and much more is not especially significant: these relationships can be found between many dramas and operas. They are, however, more noticeable in late 18th- and 19th-century Romanticism, which may explain why most successful Shakespearean operas come from this period. It is above all the quality of the music interacting with and bringing out aspects of Shakespeare's portrayal of character that distinguishes a fine transformation of a Shakespeare play into opera.

See also CLEOPATRA.

All's Well that Ends Well

K. A. von Lichtenstein, *Ende gut, alles gut* (1, F. X. Huber), Dessau, 1800
M. R. Lacy, *All's Well that Ends Well, or Love's Labour Won* (F. Reynolds), London, 1832
E. Hamel, *Malvina* (3, A. Steppes), Hamburg, 1855 (private perf.); Stadttheater, 1857
F. David, *Le saphir* (3, A. de Leuven, M. Carré and T. Hadot), Paris, 1865
M. Castelnuovo-Tedesco, *All's Well that Ends Well/Tutto è bene quello che finisce bene*, 1955–8 (3,Castelnuovo-Tedesco)
N. Bicât, *All's Well that Ends Well* (Bicât), Oxford, 1978
S. Anderson, *All's Well that Ends Well*, Los Angeles, 1979
D. Winkler, *All's Well that Ends Well* (Winkler), New York, 1987

Antony and Cleopatra

J. Mattheson, *Die unglückselige Cleopatra, Königin von Egypten* (3, F. C. Feustking), Hamburg, 1704
V. Sacchi, *Cleopatra* (3, P. Rabitti, after Shakespeare and Plutarch), Milan, 1877
F. E. Wittgenstein, *Antonius und Kleopatra* (4, H. S. Mosenthal), Graz, 1883
S. V. Yuferov, *Antony i Kleopatra*, 1900 (Yuferov)
L. Ardin, *Antony and Cleopatra*, 1919 (Ardin)
M. Logar, *Četiri scene iz Šekspira* [Four Scenes from Shakespeare], comp. 1927–36, broadcast Belgrade, 1988
G. F. Malipiero, *Antonio e Cleopatra* (3, Malipiero), Florence, 1938
L. Gruenberg, *Antony and Cleopatra*, 1951–61 (3, Gruenberg)
J. van Durme, *Antonius und Kleopatra*, 1957–9 (3)
S. Barber, *Antony and Cleopatra* (3, F. Zeffirelli), New York, 1966, rev. 1975
E. Bondeville, *Antoine et Cléopâtre* (3, Bondeville), Rouen, 1974
F. P. Glonti, *Kleopatra* (R. Tabukashvili), Tbilisi, 1976 (concert perf.); staged Tbilisi, 1981
V. Soukup, *Cleopatra*, 1976 (R. Rouček)
K. Nürnberg, *Alpha et Omega*, 1979–85 (Nürnberg)

As you Like it

F. M. Veracini, *Rosalinda* (P. Rolli), London, 1744
M. Elliston, *Six Musical Episodes from Shakespeare with Original Setting for Children* (Elliston, after 7 plays), Southampton, 1894
F. Wickham, *Rosalind* (Wickham), Dresden, 1938
J. Balamos, *As you Like it* (D. Seitz and T. Seitz), Westport, CT, 1964
G. Meyer, *As you Like it*, 1965 (Meyer)
N. C. Engleberg, *As you Like it*, 1969 (rock musical, Engleberg)
M. Gibbons, *As you Like it (Shakespeare Transmogrified)*, 1972 (F. L. Bluth)
R. E. Winters, *As you Like it*, 1974 (L. Shane and J. P. Watkins)
P. Hasquenoph, *Comme il vous plaira* (F. Didelot), Strasbourg, 1982
W. Bromley and others, *Arden* (Bromley, R. Augustine, D. Bromley and J. Mustacchi)

The Comedy of Errors

S. Storace, *Gli equivoci* (2, L. da Ponte), Vienna, 1786
R. Rodgers, *The Boys from Syracuse* (G. Abbott; L. Hart), New Haven, CT, 1938
A. Lorenz, *Irrungen*, 1887 (Lorenz), Stettin, 1939
F. Wödl, *Komödie der Irrungen* (R. Gugg), Beuthen, 1941
I. Krejčí, *Pozdvižení v Efesu* [Scandal in Ephesus] (2, J. Bachtík), Prague, 1945
J. Slade, *Comedy of Errors* (L. Harris and R. McNab), BBC TV, 1954; London, 1956
F. Koch, *Comedy of Errors* (Koch and M. F. Bill), Cleveland, 1974
A. Kagan, *Comedy of Errors* (P. James), Tel-Aviv, 1975
G. Woolfenden, *Comedy of Errors* (T. Nunn), Stratford-on-Avon, 1976
R. Leslee, *Comedy of Errors* (Leslee and S. Elkin), Buffalo, NY, 1979
A. Wilson-Dickson, *Comedy of Errors* (Wilson-Dickson), London, 1980
I. Madarász, *Tévedések vígjátéka* (D. Sztevanovity), Békéscaba, 1981
M. Valenti, *Oh, Brother!* (D. Driver), Washington DC, 1981

Coriolanus

T. S. Cooke, *Coriolanus* (R. W. Elliston), London, 1820
A. Baeyens, *Coriolanus* (1, L. A. J. Burgersdijk), Antwerp, 1941
S. Šulek, *Koriolan* (3, Šulek), Zagreb, 1958
J. Cikker, *Coriolanus* (3, Cikker), Prague, 1974

Cymbeline

R. Kreutzer, *Imogène, ou La gageure indiscrète* (3, J. E. B. Dejaure), Paris, 1796
J. F. E. Sobolewski, *Imogen* (3, Sobolewski), Königsberg, 1832
N. van Westerhout, *Cimbelino* (E. Golisciani), Naples, 1887 (private perf.); Rome, 1892
M. Elliston, *Six Musical Episodes from Shakespeare with Original Setting for Children* (Elliston, after 7 plays), Southampton, 1894
E. J. L. Missa, *Dinah* (4, M. Carré and P. de Choudens), Paris, 1894
A. Eggen, *Cymbeline* (Eggen, after trans. by H. Rytter; incl. material from *The Winter's Tale*), Oslo, 1951
C. Arrieu, *Cymbeline*, 1958–63 (2, J. Tournier and M. Jacquemont), ORTF, 31 March 1974

Hamlet

F. Gasparini, *Ambleto* (3, A. Zeno and P. Pariati), Venice, 1706
D. Scarlatti, *Ambleto* (Zeno and Pariati), Rome, 1715
G. Carcani, *Ambleto* (Zeno and Pariati), Venice, 1742
G. Andreozzi, *Amleto* (2, G. Foppa), Padua, 1792
M. Maraczek, *Hamlet* (3, Maraczek), Brno, 1840
W. Thau, *Hamlet* (J. Sigma), Vienna, 1841
A. Zanardini, *Amleto* (Zanardini), Venice, 1854
A. Stadtfeld, *Hamlet* (5, J. Guillaume), Darmstadt, 1857
F. Faccio, *Amleto* (4, A. Boito), Genoa, 1865
J. L. A. Hignard, *Hamlet*, 1868 (5, P. de Garal), Nantes, 1888
A. Thomas, *Hamlet* (5, J. Barbier and M. Carré), Paris, 1868
M. Cooney, *Hamlet* (?Cooney), New York, 1870
J. Hopp, *Hamlet* (2, Hopp), Vienna, 1874
M. Elliston, *Six Musical Episodes from Shakespeare with Original Setting for Children* (Elliston, after 7 plays), Southampton, 1894
J. Kalniņš, *Hamlets* (3, Kalniņš, after trans. by A. P. Chekhov), Riga, 1936
E. S. Lindsey, *Hamlet*, *c*1946 (Lindsey), Chattanooga, TN, 1952
E. Roters, *Hamlet*, *c*1957 (T. Robinsohn and Roters)
M. Zafred, *Amleto* (3, L. Zafred and M. Zafred), Rome, 1961
S. Kagen, *Hamlet* (Kagen), Baltimore, 1962
A. Machavariani, *Gamlet* (Machavariani, after trans. by I. Machabeli), Tbilisi, 1965
H. Searle, *Hamlet* (3, Searle), Hamburg, 1968
S. Szokolay, *Hamlet* (3, Szokolay, after trans. by J. Arany), Budapest, 1968
H. U. Engelmann, *Ophelia* (M. Goldschmidt), Hanover, 1969
K. Horký, *Jed z Elsinoru* [Poison from Elsinore] (V. Renč, after M. Rejnuš), Brno, 1970
P. Bentoiu, *Hamlet* (2, Bentoiu), Bucharest, 1971 (concert perf.); staged Marseilles, 1974
J. K. Forest, *Die Hamlet-Saga* (Forest, after Saxo Grammaticus, F. de Belleforest and trans. by A. W. von Schlegel), Berlin, 1973
C. Jones, *Kronborg: 1582* (rock musical, Jones), Charlottetown, Prince Edward Island, 1975

H. Reutter, *Hamlet* (2, Reutter, after trans. by Schlegel), Stuttgart, 1980
K. Munakata, *Noh Hamlet* (Munakata), Tokyo, 1983
R. Kelterborn, *Ophelia* (H. Meier), Schwetzingen, 1984
S. M. Slonimsky, *Gamlet*, 1990 (3, Ya. Gordin)
E. Morgeson and M. E. Wise, *Hamlet, the Musical* (rock musical, R. A. Briggs)

Henry IV (pts 1 and 2)

G. Pacini, *La gioventù di Enrico V* (2, G. Tarducci or J. Ferretti), Rome, 1820
S. Mercadante, *La gioventù di Enrico V* (4, F. Romani), Milan, 1834
G. Verdi, see *Merry Wives of Windsor, The*
G. Holst, *At the Boar's Head* (1, Holst), Manchester, 1925
J. P. Webber, *Falstaff* (B. Hooker), New York, 1928
R. A. Barbie, *Good King Hal* (Barbie), Bismarck, ND, 1979
G. Getty, *Plump Jack* (4 scenes, Getty), San Francisco, 1987

Henry V

R. Boughton, *Agincourt*, 1918 (1 scene), Glastonbury, 1924
E. Misterly, *Henry V* (C. R. Bulla), Los Angeles, 1969, inc.

Julius Caesar

J. C. F. Bach, *Brutus* (J. G. Herder), Bückeburg, 1774
J. García Robles, *Julio César* (3, N. Guille), Barcelona, 1880
M. Carl, *Julius Cäsar*, comp. *c*1880
A. Consorti, *Giulio Cesare* (A. Lega), 1923
G. F. Malipiero, *Giulio Cesare* (3, Malipiero), Genoa, 1936
G. Klebe, *Die Ermordung Cäsars* (1, Klebe), Essen, 1959
A. Schmitz, *Julius Caesar* (Schmitz), New Brunswick, NJ, 1978
G. D. Rasmussen, *Julius Caesar* (Rasmussen), excerpts Fort Lauderdale, FL, 1983

King Lear

V. Séméladis, *Cordelia* (E. Deschamps and E. Pacini), Versailles, 1854
A. Cagnoni, *Il re Lear*, 1883 (4, A. Ghislanzoni)
A. Raynaud, *Le roi Lear* (4, H. Lapierre), Toulouse, 1888
H. Litolff, *Le roi Lear*, 1890 (3, J. Adenis and E. Adenis)
G. Cottrau, *Cordelia* (2, Cottrau), Padua, 1913
V. Frazzi, *Re Lear*, 1922–8 (3, G. Papini), Florence, 1939
M. Logar, *Četiri scene iz Šekspira* [Four Scenes from Shakespeare], comp. 1927–36, broadcast Belgrade, 1988
A. Ghislanzoni, *Re Lear* (3, Alberto Ghislanzoni), Rome, 1937
J. van Durme, *König Lear*, 1955–7 (2)
F. C. Gerhard, *König Lear* (Gerhard), Wuppertal, 1956
D. Schaaf, *The Witness and Revelation of the New Tragedy of King Lear*, 1970 (Schaaf)
D. Carnochan, D. O'Neal and R. Rosenberg, *Lear*, 1972 (rock musical, J. Manlove)
A. Reimann, *Lear* (2 pts, C. H. Henneberg), Munich, 1978
P. Dambis, *Karālis Līrs*, 1983 (3)
D. Božič, *Kralj Lear* (Božič), Maribor, 1986

Love's Labour's Lost

A. Beecham, *Peines d'amour perdues*, 1934 (2, ?Beecham, trans. J. Chantavoine)
C. F. Swier, *Love's Labour's Lost* (B. Bruestle), Tulsa, 1969
F. Darvas, *Mannerschwüre, oder Verlorene Liebesmüh'*, 1973 (D. Mesziely, Ger. trans. K. Eidam)
N. Nabokov, *Love's Labour's Lost* (W. H. Auden and C. Kallman), Brussels, 1973
B. Williams, *Love's Labour's Lost* (D. Vando), Washington DC, 1974
S. Quesnel and T. Dunn, *Love's Investments Lost*, 1976 (Quesnel and Dunn)
R. Leslee, *Love's Labour's Lost* (Leslee and K. Welsh), Buffalo, NY, 1986
G. Bush, *Love's Labour's Lost*, 1988 (2)

Macbeth

R. Leveridge, *Macbeth* (musical scenes, Davenant), London, 1702
H.-A.-B. Chelard, *Macbeth* (3, C. J. Rouget de Lisle), Paris, 1827; (5), Weimar, 1861
L. A. Piccinni, *Macbeth* (prol., 5, V. Ducange and A. Bourgeois), Paris, 1829
G. Verdi, *Macbeth* (4, F. M. Piave and A. Maffei), Florence, 1847
W. Taubert, *Macbeth* (5, F. H. Eggers), Berlin, 1857
Lauro Rossi, *Biorn* (5, F. Marshall), London, 1877
E. Bloch, *Macbeth*, 1904–6 (prol., 3, E. Fleg), Paris, 1910
L. Collingwood, *Macbeth* (Collingwood), London, 1934
N. Gatty, *Macbeth*, before 1947 (4, Gatty)
A. F. Gedike, *Makbet* (5), excerpts, 1947 (concert perf.)
A. Calabrese and R. Calabrese, *Murdering Macbeth* (Calabrese and Calabrese, after W. S. Gilbert), New York, 1960
H. Fries, *Eine schottische Tragödie*, *c*1965 (Fries, after trans. by D. Tieck)
S. Halpern, *Macbeth* (?Halpern), New York, 1965
H. Koppel, *Macbeth* (A. Koppel and H. Koppel, after trans. by V. Østerberg), Copenhagen, 1970
B. Koblenz, *Hexenskat, oder Der Streik der Hexen* (Koblenz, after H.-C. von Dadelsen), Saarbrücken, 1984
T. Ward, *Nightshriek* (rock musical), London, 1986

Measure for Measure

R. Wagner, *Das Liebesverbot, oder Die Novize von Palermo* (2, Wagner), Magdeburg, 1836
J. L. Seymour, *Measure for Measure*, 1973 (Seymour)

The Merchant of Venice

C. Pinsuti, *Il mercante di Venezia* (4, G. T. Cimino), Bologna, 1873
L. P. Deffès, *Jessica* (5, J. Adenis and H. Boisseaux), Toulouse, 1898
J. B. Foerster, *Jessika* (3, J. Vrchlický, after Ger. trans. by R. Batka), Prague, 1905
H. de Saussine, *Le marchand de Venise* (4, Saussine), Paris, 1907
F. Alpaerts, *Shylock* (3, H. Melis), Antwerp, 1913
O. Taubmann, *Porzia* (3, R. Wilde), Frankfurt, 1916
A. Beecham, *The Merchant of Venice* (?Beecham), Brighton, 1922
W. La Violette, *Shylock* (?La Violette), excerpts Chicago, 1930
M. Logar, *Četiri scene iz Šekspira* [Four Scenes from Shakespeare], comp. 1927–36, broadcast Belgrade, 1988
F. Brumagne, *Le marchand de Venise* (5, P. Spaak), Brussels, 1933
R. Hahn, *Le marchand de Venise* (3, M. Zamacoïs), Paris, 1935
T. Chatburn, *The Gay Venetians* (Chatburn), Derby, 1955
M. Castelnuovo-Tedesco, *The Merchant of Venice/Il mercante di Venezia* (3, Castelnuovo-Tedesco), Florence, 1961
K. Nürnberg, *Il mercante di Venezia*, 1973 (Nürnberg)
R. Haines, *Shylock* (2, P. Bentley), Edinburgh, 1974
A. Tchaikowsky, *Merchant of Venice*, 1974–82 (J. O'Brien)
J. Smith, *A Musical Merchant of Venice* (T. Tanner), New York, 1975
E. Hildebrand, *Der Kaufmann von Venedig* (Hildebrand), comp. 1980
J. Glover and M. Glover, *The Merchant of Venice*, 1981 (J. Seay)
I. Heywood, *Shylock* (?Heywood), Chester, 1981

The Merry Wives of Windsor

Papavoine, *Le vieux coquet, ou Les deux amies* (3, A. Bret), Paris, 1761
P. Ritter, *Die lustigen Weiber von Windsor* (3, G. C. Römer), Mannheim, 1794
C. Ditters von Dittersdorf, *Die lustigen Weiber von Windsor* (2, Römer), Oels, 1796
A. Salieri, *Falstaff, ossia Le tre burle* (2, C. P. Defranceschi), Vienna, 1799
C. E. Horn, J. Parry, S. Webbe and others, *The Merry Wives of Windsor*, London, 1824
M. Balfe, *Falstaff* (2, S. M. Maggioni), London, 1838
O. Nicolai, *Die lustigen Weiber von Windsor* (3, S. H. Mosenthal), Berlin, 1849
A. Adam, *Falstaff* (1, J.-H. Vernoy de Saint-Georges and A. de Leuven), Paris, 1856
G. Verdi, *Falstaff* (3, A. Boito), Milan, 1893
M. Elliston, *Six Musical Episodes from Shakespeare with Original Setting for Children* (Elliston, after 7 plays), Southampton, 1894
J. P. Webber, *Falstaff* (B. Hooker; incl. material from *Henry IV* pts 1 and 2), New York, 1928
R. Vaughan Williams, *Sir John in Love* (4, Vaughan Williams), London, 1929
C. F. Swier, *When the Cat's Away* (B. Bruestle), Philadelphia, 1941
J. Gilbert, *Good Time Johnny* (J. More; Gilbert and More), Birmingham, 1971
F. Gilbert and E. W. Rogers, *The Genuine Music Hall Version of The Merry Wives of Windsor* (Gilbert and Rogers), New York, 1977
N. Alifantis, *Nevestele vesele din Windsor* (Alifantis), Piatra-Neamt, 1978
A. Rea, *Falstaff In and Out of Love* (1, W. Monson), Fresno, CA, 1982

A Midsummer Night's Dream

H. Purcell, *The Fairy-Queen* (prol., 5), London, 1692
R. Leveridge, *Pyramus and Thisbe* (1, Leveridge), London, 1716
J. F. Lampe, *Pyramus and Thisbe* (1, ?Lampe), London, 1745

J. C. Smith, *The Fairies* (3, D. Garrick or Smith; song texts from other plays and by others), London, 1755
E. W. Wolf, *Die Zauberirrungen, oder Die Irrtürmer der Zauberei* (F. H. von Einsiedel), Weimar, 1785
G. C. Grosheim, *Titania, oder Liebe durch Zauberei* (2, Oberst von Weber), Kassel, 1792
H. R. Bishop, *A Midsummer Night's Dream* arr., after Burney, Handel, J. C. Smith, R. J. S. Stevens and others (3, F. Reynolds, after D. Garrick and G. Colman (i), 1763), London, 1816
A. A. Alyab'yev, *Volshebnaya noch'* [The Enchanted Night] (3, A. F. Veltman), rehearsed Moscow, 1938
F. von Suppé, *Ein Sommernachtstraum* (3, E. Straube), Vienna, 1844
M. Elliston, *Six Musical Episodes from Shakespeare with Original Setting for Children* (Elliston, after 7 plays), Southampton, 1894
R. Leoncavallo, *Songe d'une nuit d'été* (?Leoncavallo), Paris, 1899 (private perf.)
U. Roti, *Il sogno d'una notte d'estate* (M. Olmi), Turin, 1899
J. Lloret, *Nochecita de San Juan* (J. R. Martín and E. F. Revenga), Madrid, 1919
V. Vreuls, *Un songe d'une nuit d'été* (3, P. Spaak), Brussels, 1925
L. Mancinelli, *Sogno di una notte d'estate* (3, F. Salvatori), excerpts Rome, 1922
D. Arundell, comp. 1930
M. Logar, *Četiri scene iz Šekspira* [Four Scenes from Shakespeare], comp. 1927–36, broadcast Belgrade, 1988
J. Van Heusen, *Swingin' the Dream* (G. Seldes and E. Charell; E. de Lange), New York, 1939
F. Ghisi, *Piramo e Tisbe*, 1941–3 (1), Plauen, 1955
M. Delannoy, *Puck*, 1943–5 (3, A. Boll), Strasbourg, 1949
J. Doubrava, *Sen noci svatojanské*, 1945–9 (Doubrava and R. Vonásek), Opava, 1969
B. Britten, *A Midsummer Night's Dream* (3, Britten and P. Pears), Aldeburgh, 1960
R. Besoyan, *Babes in the Wood* (Besoyan), New York, 1964
N. Bruce, *Pyramus and Thisbe* (1 scene), Tuscaloosa, 1965
R. Tallman, *Midsummer Night's Dream* (Tallman and S. Mackenroth), Dallas, 1973/4
M. Alaszewski, *Ein Sommernachtstraum* (K. Pankiewicz), E. Berlin, 1975
E. Siegmeister, *Night of the Moonspell* (3, E. Mabley), Shreveport, LA, 1976
R. Leslee, *A Hollywood Midsummer Night's Dream* (Leslee, S. Elkin), Buffalo, NY, 1980
S. Margoshes, *Midsummer Night's Dream* (J. Vaccaro), New York, 1980
M. Pagani, *Sogno di una notte d'estate*, Milan, 1981
R. Convery, *Pyramus and Thisbe* (2 scenes, Convery), Waterford, CT, 1982
L. Mosca, *Il sogno di Titania* (P. Garcia), Milan, 1982
J. Martin, *Midsummer Night's Dream*, Sterling Forest, Tuxedo, NC, 1983
G. Cummings-Knight, *Midsummer Night's Dream* (C. Cowling), Hurstpierpoint, Sussex, 1984
R. Gerber, *Le songe d'une nuit d'été* (2, Gerber), Biel, 1984
J. Kurtz, *Bottom's Dream* (J. Mazzonelli; incl. material from *The Tempest*), New York, 1984
L. J. Werle, *En midsommarnattsdröm* (L. Söderström), Malmö, 1985
D. F. Urrows, *Midsummer Night's Dream* (Urrows, after J. C. Smith, The Fairies), excerpts Cambridge, MA, 1986
C. Fox, *Midsummer Night's Dream* (K. Friedman; N. Gimbel)

Much Ado about Nothing

H. Berlioz, *Béatrice et Bénédict* (2, Berlioz, after trans. by B. Laroche), Baden-Baden, 1862
A. Doppler, *Viel Lärm um Nichts* (3, A. Harlcher), Leipzig, 1896
P. Puget, *Beaucoup de bruit pour rien* (4, E. Blau), Paris, 1899
C. V. Stanford, *Much Ado about Nothing* (*The Marriage of Hero*) (4, J. Sturgis), London, 1901
R. Hahn, *Beaucoup de bruit pour rien* (4, J. Sarment), Paris, 1936
H. Henrich, *Viel Lärm um Nichts* (Henrich), Frankfurt/Oder, 1956
T. N. Khrennikov, *Mnogo shuma ... iz-za serdets* [Much Ado about Hearts] (2, B. Pokrovsky), Moscow, 1972
H. Conrad, *Ta-Dah!*, 1978 (Conrad), New York, 1981
J. G. Chēn [Chin. version], Anhui, 1986

Othello

G. Rossini, *Otello, ossia Il moro di Venezia* (3, F. Berio di Salsa), Naples, 1816
G. Verdi, *Otello* (4, A. Boito), Milan, 1887
D. Božič, *Jago*, 1968 (Božič, after Shakespeare and W. Heinrich)
T. J. White, *Catch my Soul* (rock musical, J. Good), Los Angeles, 1968

Pericles

G. Cottrau, *Pericle re di Tiro*, c1915 (prol., 4, ?Cottrau)
A. Hovhaness, *Pericles* (Hovhaness), excerpts Shippensburg, PA, 1979
R. Leslee, *Americles* (Leslee and S. Elkin), Buffalo, NY, 1983

The Rape of Lucrece

O. Respighi, *Lucrezia* (1, C. Guastalla, after Shakespeare and Livy), Milan, 1937
B. Britten, *The Rape of Lucretia* (2, R. Duncan, after A. Obey), Glyndebourne, 1946

Richard III

G. Salvayre, *Riccardo III* (4, E. R. Blavet), St Petersburg, 1883
J. van Durme, *König Richard der Dritte*, 1960–61 (3)
P. Turok, *Richard III*, 1975 (Turok), Philadelphia, 1980 (concert perf.)
I. Kuljerić, *Rikard III*, 1984 (2, N. Turkalj), Zagreb, 1987
F. Testi, *Riccardo III* (Testi), Milan, 1987

Romeo and Juliet

G. Benda, *Romeo und Julie* (3, F. W. Gotter), Gotha, 1776
J. G. Schwanenberger, *Romeo e Giulia* (2, J. R. Sanseverino), Brunswick, 1776
S. von Rumling, *Roméo et Juliette* (?Rumling), Stuttgart, 1784
N.-M. Dalayrac, *Tout pour l'amour, ou Roméo et Juliette* (4, J.-M. Boutet de Monvel), Paris, 1792
D. Steibelt, *Roméo et Juliette* (3, A. de Ségur), Paris, 1793
P. C. Guglielmi, *Romeo e Giulietta* (S. Buonaiuti), London, 1810
L. Damrosch, *Romeo und Julia* (Damrosch), Breslau, 1862
F. Marchetti, *Romeo e Giulietta* (4, M. Marcello), Trieste, 1865
C. Gounod, *Roméo et Juliette* (5, J. Barbier and M. Carré), Paris, 1867
P. X. D. d'Ivry, *Les amants de Vérone* (4, Ivry), Paris, 1867; (5), Paris, 1878
A. Mercadal y Pons, *Romeo e Giulietta* (?Mercadal y Pons), Mahon, Minorca, 1873
H. R. Shelley, *Romeo and Juliet* (3, ?Shelley), New York, 1901
G. W. L. Marshall-Hall, *Romeo and Juliet* (4, Marshall-Hall), excerpts Melbourne, 1912
C. del Campo, *Los amantes de Verona* (4, F. de Iracheta), Madrid, 1916
J. Barkworth, *Romeo and Juliet* (4, Barkworth), Middlesbrough, 1916
R. Zandonai, *Giulietta e Romeo* (3, A. Rossato, after L. da Porto and Shakespeare), Rome, 1922
H. Sutermeister, *Romeo und Julia* (2, Sutermeister), Dresden, 1940
B. Blacher, *Romeo und Julia* (3, Blacher), Berlin-Zehlendorf Radio, 1947; staged Salzburg, 1950
G. F. Malipiero, *Romeo e Giulietta* [Act 2 of *Mondi celesti e infernali*] (Malipiero), RAI, 1950; staged Venice, 1961
K. Fribec, *Romeo i Julija* (Fribec, after trans. by M. Bogdanovich), Zagreb, 1955
L. Bernstein, *West Side Story* (2, A. Laurents; S. Sondheim), Washington DC, 1957
R. Gerber, *Roméo et Juliette*, 1957–61 (Gerber, after trans. by A. Koszul and P. le Tourneur)
W. Harper, *Sensations* (rock musical, P. Zakrzewski), New York, 1970
B. Matuszczak, *Julia i Romeo* (5 scenes, Matuszczak and J. Iwaszkiewicz), Warsaw, 1970
W. E. Black, *Romeo & Juliet: New Wave* (Black), New York, 1984

The Taming of the Shrew

F. Bertoni, *Il duca d'Atene* (C. F. Bedini), London, 1780
T. S. Cooke, J. Braham and others, *The Taming of the Shrew* (F. Reynolds, after D. Garrick: *Catherine and Petruccio*, 1756, and other Shakespeare plays), London, 1828
H. Goetz, *Der Widerspänstigen Zähmung* (4, J. V. Widmann), Mannheim, 1874
F. Le Rey, *La mégère apprivoisée* (3, E. Deshays), Rouen, 1895
S. Samaras, *La furia domata* (3, E. A. Butti and G. Macchi), Milan, 1895
R. Chapí, *Las bravías* (1, C. Fernández Shaw and J. López Silva), Madrid, 1896
C. Silver, *La mégère apprivoisée* (4, H. Cain and E. Adenis, after adaptation by P. Delair), Paris, 1922
R. Bossi, *Volpino il calderaio* (1, L. Orsini), Milan, 1925

E. Wolf-Ferrari, *Sly, ovvero La leggenda del dormiente risvegliato* (3, G. Forzano), Milan, 1927
P. Bottagisio, *La bisbetica domata* (M. Spiritini), Verona, 1928
M. Persico, *La bisbetica domata* (A. Rossato), Rome, 1931
H. Biggs, *Shrew* (J. Staton and H. Moore), Seattle, 1939
P. G. Clapp, *The Taming of the Shrew*, 1945–8 (Clapp)
C. Porter, *Kiss me, Kate* (S. Spewack and B. Spewack; Porter), Philadelphia, 1948
H. Groth, *Petruchio* (?Groth), Conway, AK, 1954
V. Giannini, *The Taming of the Shrew* (3), Cincinnati, 1953 (concert perf.); NBC TV, 1954; stage, New York, 1958
V. I. Shebalin, *Ukroshcheniye stroptivoy* (4, A. A. Gozenpud), Moscow, 1955 (concert perf.); stage, Kuybïshev, 1957
T. Eastwood, *Christopher Sly* (R. Duncan), London, 1960
D. Argento, *Christopher Sly* (2, J. Manlove), Minneapolis, 1963
R. A. Barbie, *Shrew!* (Barbie), Bismarck, ND, 1977
R. Leslee (Leslee and S. Elkin), Buffalo, NY, 1982

The Tempest

J. Bannister, P. Humfrey, M. Locke and others, *The Tempest, or The Enchanted Islands* (T. Shadwell, after W. Davenant and J. Dryden), London, 1674
J. Weldon, *The Tempest* (Shadwell, after Davenant and Dryden), London, ?1712
J. C. Smith, *The Tempest* (D. Garrick; song texts by Dryden and others), London, 1756
J. H. Rolle, *Der Sturm, oder Die bezauberte Insel* (1, J. S. Patzke), Magdeburg, 1782 (concert perf.); staged Berlin, 1782
F. A. Hoffmeister, *Der Schiffbruch* (Korndorfer), Vienna, 1792
L. Caruso, *La tempesta* (2), Naples, 1799
F. Fleischmann, *Die Geisterinsel* (3, F. W. Gotter and F. H. von Einsiedel), Weimar, 1798
W. Müller, *Der Sturm, oder Die Zauberinsel* (2, K. F. Hensler), Vienna, 1798
J. F. Reichardt, *Die Geisterinsel* (3, Gotter), Berlin, 1798
P. Winter, *Der Sturm* (2, F. X. Kaspar), Munich, 1798
J. R. Zumsteeg, *Die Geisterinsel* (3, Gotter), Stuttgart, 1798
J. D. Hensel, *Die Geisterinsel* (Hensel, after Gotter and J. W. Döring), Hirschberg, 1799
P. Ritter, *Der Sturm, oder Die bezauberte Insel* (2, Döring), Mannheim, 1799
F. W. Haack, *Die Geisterinsel* (Gotter), ? Stettin, 1799
K. F. L. Schäffer, *Der Orkan*, 1805 (Schäffer)
A. J. Emmert, *Der Sturm*, Salzburg, 1806
P. J. Riotte, *Der Sturm, oder Prosperos Geisterinsel* (3, J. G. Seidl), Brno, 1833
A. A. Alyab'yev, *Burya*, ?1830s (3, ? A. A. Shakhovskoy, ? N. M. Satin and ? M. A. Gamazov)
F. Halévy, *La tempestà* (3, P. Giannone and E. Scribe), London, 1850
E. Frank, *Der Sturm* (3, J. V. Widmann), Hanover, 1887
A. Urspruch, *Der Sturm* (3, E. Pirazzi), Frankfurt, 1888
M. Elliston, *Six Musical Episodes from Shakespeare with Original Setting for Children* (Elliston, after 7 plays), Southampton, 1894
Z. Fibich, *Bouře* (3, J. Vrchlický), Prague, 1895
R. del Frate, *La tempesta* (3, U. Fleres), Livorno, 1900
N. I. Kazanli, *Miranda: poslednyaya bor'ba* [Miranda: the Last Struggle] (Kazanli), St Petersburg, 1910
A. M. Hale, *The Tempest* (3, Hale), excerpts London, 1912
A. Farwell, pt arr., *Caliban: the Shakespeare Tercentenary Masque* (P. MacKaye), New York, 1916
P. Canonica, *Miranda*, 1917 (3, C. Bernardi and Canonica), Sanremo, 1937
N. Gatty, *The Tempest* (3, R. Gatty), London, 1920
F. Lattuada, *La tempesta* (prol., 3, A. Rossato), Milan, 1922
H. Brearley, *The Duke of Milan* (?Brearley), Blackburn, Lancs., 1929
H. Sutermeister, *Die Zauberinsel* (2, Sutermeister), Dresden, 1942
K. Atterberg, *Stormen* (7 scenes, Atterberg), Stockholm, 1948
F. Martin, *Der Sturm* (3, Martin, after trans. by A. W. von Schlegel), Vienna, 1956
K. Honolka, arr., *Die Wunderinsel*, after Schubert, Alfonso und Estrella (Honolka), Stuttgart, 1958
P. Kont, *Der Sturm*, Vienna, 1968
S. Šulek, *Oluja* (3, Šulek), Zagreb, 1969
D. Post, *The Tempest* (Post), San Antonio, TX, 1979
L. Berio, *Un re in ascolto* (2 pts, Berio, after I. Calvino, W. H. Auden and Gotter), Salzburg, 1984
J. Petosa, *Shakespeare's The Tempest* (Petosa), Washington DC, 1984
P. Westergaard, *Tempest*, 1972–90 (3, Westergaard), Lawrenceville, NJ, 1992
J. C. Eaton, *The Tempest* (3, A. Porter), Santa Fe, 1985
J. Kenny, *Tempest Now* (P. Stebbings), Huddersfield, 1985
L. Hoiby, *The Tempest* (3, M. Shulgasser), Indianola, IA, 1986
M. Nyman, *La princesse de Milan*, Avignon, 1991
M. Malamet, *Dreamstuff: the Musical Tempest* (H. Ashman; D. Green)

Timon of Athens

J. Tunick, *Timon of Athens* (?Tunick), New York, 1971
K. Nürnberg, *Timon*, 1985 (Nürnberg)
S. Oliver, *Timon of Athens* (2, Oliver), London, 1991

Troilus and Cressida

W. Zillig, *Troilus und Cressida* (3, Zillig), Düsseldorf, 1951
G. Macdermot, *Troilus and Cressida*, 1969–70 (rock op, J. Papp)

Twelfth Night

E. Steinkühler, *Cesario, oder die Verwechslung* (3, K. Gollmick), Düsseldorf, 1848
M. Anger, *Viola*, 1872 (J. Böhm)
W. Rintel, *Was ihr wollt*, Berlin, 1872
W. Taubert, *Cesario, oder Was ihr wollt* (3, E. Taubert), Berlin, 1874
B. Smetana, *Viola*, 1874–84, inc. (E. Krásnohorská), Prague, 1900 (concert perf.); staged Prague, 1924
K. Weis, *Viola* (3, B. Adler, R. Schubert and V. Novohradský), Prague, 1892
A. Kirchner, *Viola* (3, Kirchner), Hermannstadt, 1904
F. Hart, *Malvolio* (3, Hart), Melbourne, 1918 (Act 1 only)
G. Farina, *La dodicesima notte, o Quel che volete* (E. Possenti), Milan, 1929
A. Kusterer, *Was ihr wollt* (Kusterer, after trans. by A. W. von Schlegel), Dresden, 1932
H. Holenia, *Viola* (3, O. Widowitz), Graz, 1934
K. Brüggeman, *Illyrisches Abenteuer*, 1937–9 (Brüggeman)
A. de Filippi, *Malvolio*, 1937 (Filippi)
A. A. Shenshin, *Bliznetsï* [The Twins] (V. G. Shershenevich), Moscow, 1939
L. Hess, *Was ihr wollt* (Hess), Stettin, 1941
C. A. Gibbs, *Twelfth Night*, 1946–7 (3, M. Currie)
C. F. Swier, *Twelfth Night* (B. Bruestle), Tulsa, 1957
I. Jirko, *Večer tříkrálový* (Jirko), Liberec, 1967
D. Amram, *Twelfth Night* (2, J. Papp), Glens Falls, NY, 1968
P. Blatný, *Aprílová komedie* [Capricious Comedy] (V. Renč), Brno, 1968
S. J. Gelber, *Love and Let Love* (J. Lollos; Lollos and D. Christopher), New York, 1968
H. Hester, *Your Own Thing* (D. Driver; Hester and D. Apolinar, after their *The London Look*), New York, 1968
J. Wilson, *Twelfth Night* (3, H. Moulton), Wexford, 1969
B. I. Zeydman, *Dvenadtsataya noch'* (Zeydman), Tashkent, 1969
D. Vulchev, *Dvanaiseta nosht* (P. Spasov), Sofia, 1970
R. Adler, *Music Is* (G. Abbott; W. Holt), New York, 1976
Shen Li Qun and others, *Di shi er yi* (Zhong Shui He), Shanghai, 1986
J. Klusák, *Viola* (Klusák), Olomouc, 1987

The Two Gentlemen of Verona

J. L. Seymour, *The Two Gentlemen of Verona*, 1937 (2, Seymour and H. C. Tracy)
F. Emmert, *Veronští šlechtici*, Brno, 1964
G. Macdermot, *Two Gentlemen of Verona* (rock musical, J. Guare and M. Shapiro; Guare), New York, 1971
A. Linstaedt, *Drei Herren aus Verona* (rock musical, H. Artmann and N. Brieger), Nuremberg, 1972
F. Fonseca, *The Two Gentlemen of Verona* (Fonseca), Miami, 1985
C. Frezza, *The Two Gentlemen of Verona* (Frezza), Pittsburgh, 1987
P. Taylor, *The Two Gentlemen of Verona* (Taylor), Edinburgh, 1987

The Winter's Tale

C. E. Barbieri, *Perdita, oder Ein Wintermärchen* (4, K. Gross), Leipzig, 1865
M. Bruch, *Hermione* (4, E. Hopffer), Berlin, 1872
J. Nešvera, *Perdita* (3, J. Kvapil), Prague, 1897
M. Elliston, *Six Musical Episodes from Shakespeare with Original Setting for Children* (Elliston, after 7 plays), Southampton, 1894
H. Bereny, *Das Wintermärchen*, 1898 (A. Prasch)
B. Zimmermann, *Ein Wintermärchen* (3, Zimmermann, after trans. by K. Simrock), Erfurt, 1900

L. Pillaut, *Perdita*, ?1904 (L. Gallet)
K. Goldmark, *Ein Wintermärchen* (3, A. M. Willner), Vienna, 1908
K. Nürnberg, *Leontes*, 1966 (Nürnberg)
H. Burrell, *Ostragobolus* (D. Cowan), Edinburgh, 1973
J. Harbison, *The Winter's Tale*, 1974 (2, Harbison), San Francisco, 1979
D. Douglas, *The Winter's Tale* (D. Axelrod; K. James), Burbank, CA, 1984

Venus and Adonis

H. Weisgall, *The Gardens of Adonis*, 1959, rev. 1977–81 (3 scenes, J. Olon-Scrymgeour, after A. Obey and Shakespeare)

Works inspired by Shakespeare

A. Thomas, *Le songe d'une nuit d'été* (3, J. B. Rosier and A. de Leuven), Paris, 1850
T. Benvenuti, *Guglielmo Shakespeare* (F. M. Piave), Parma, 1861
D. Božič, *Telemah*, 1989 (after R. Bolt: *A Man for all Seasons* and Shakespeare)

*

E. Istel: 'Richard Wagners Oper Das Liebesverbot auf Grund der handschriftlichen Originalpartitur dargestellt', *Die Musik*, viii (1908–9), 3–47
F. Dubitzky: 'Shakespeares Dramen als Opern', *Bühne und Welt*, xv (1913), 318
A. Luzio and G. Cesari: *I copialettere di Giuseppe Verdi* (Milan, 1913)
L. Collison-Morley: *Shakespeare in Italy* (Stratford-on-Avon, 1916), 98–150
E. J. Dent: 'The Musical Interpretation of Shakespeare on the Modern Stage', *MQ*, ii (1916), 523–37
C. Wilson: *Shakespeare and Music* (London, 1922)
F. Erckmann: 'Sir John Falstaff in Opera', *Chesterian*, 2nd ser., v/ Sept (1923)
W. Deetjen: '*Der Sturm* als Operntext bearbeitet von Einsiedel und Gotter', *Shakespeare-Jb*, lxiv (1928), 77–89
A. C. Keys: *Les adaptations musicales de Shakespeare en France* (Paris, 1933)
E. W. McMullen: *The Earliest Operatic Adaptations of Shakespeare* (diss., Columbia U., 1939)
C. E. Ward: 'The Tempest: a Restoration Opera Problem', *Journal of English Literary History*, xiii/June (1946), 119–30
P. van Tieghem: *Le Préromantisme: études d'histoire littéraire européenne*, iii: *La découverte de Shakespeare sur le continent* (Paris, 1947)
O. F. Babler: 'Shakespeare's *Tempest* as an Opera', *Notes and Queries*, cxcvi (1951), 30–31 [incl. extract from letter of Wolf]
J. Kerman: 'Verdi's *Otello*, or Shakespeare Explained', *Hudson Review*, vi (1953–4), 266–77
——: 'Verdi's *Otello*: Traditional Opera and the Image of Shakespeare', *Opera as Drama* (New York, 1956), 129–67; (2/1988), 109–39
A. Einstein: 'Mozart and Shakespeare's *The Tempest*', *Essays on Music* (London, 1958), 200–06
K. H. Ruppel: 'Shakespeare und die Oper', *Shakespeare-Jb*, xcv (1959), 178–92
M. Laurie: 'Did Purcell set "The Tempest"?', *PRMA*, xc (1963–4), 43–57
W. Dean: 'Shakespeare and Opera', *Shakespeare in Music*, ed. P. Hartnoll (London, 1964), 89–175
——: 'Shakespeare and Italian Opera – Without the Prince', *Opera*, xv (1964), 224–32
J. W. Klein: 'Verdi's "Otello" and Rossini's, *ML*, xlv (1964), 130–40
C. A. Niemeyer: 'Shakespeare and Opera', *Union College Symposium* (sum. 1964), 17–23
H. Sutermeister: 'Gedanken zu Shakespeares Bedeutung für die Geschichte des Musiktheaters', *Shakespeare-Jb*, c (1964), 109–16
W. Dean: 'Shakespeare in the Opera House', *Shakespeare Survey*, xviii (1965), 75–93
E. Lockspeiser: 'Projects for *As you Like it*', *Debussy: his Life and Mind*, ii (London, 1965), 246–53
O. E. Deutsch: 'Mozart und Shakespeares *Sturm*', *ÖMz*, xxi (1966), 3–5
W. Dean: 'Verdi's "Otello": a Shakespearian Masterpiece', *Shakespeare Survey*, xxi (1968), 87–96
G. J. Buelow: 'An Evaluation of Johann Mattheson's Opera, *Cleopatra* (Hamburg 1704)', *Studies in Eighteenth-Century Music: a Tribute to Karl Geiringer* (London, 1970), 92–107
R. E. Aycock: 'Shakespeare, Boito, and Verdi', *MQ*, lviii (1972), 588–604
R. Hapgood: '*West Side Story* and the Modern Appeal of *Romeo and Juliet*', *Deutsche Shakespeare-Gesellschaft West Jb* (1972), 99–112
R. Savage: 'The Shakespeare-Purcell *Fairy Queen*: a Defence and Recommendation', *EMc*, i (1973), 201–21
H. Gatti: 'Arrigo Boito discepolo di Shakespeare', *Studi inglesi* [Bari], no.1 (1974), 317–65
D. Kimbell: 'The Young Verdi and Shakespeare', *PRMA*, ci (1974–5), 59–73
J. R. Elliott jr: 'The Shakespeare Berlioz Saw', *ML*, lvii (1976), 292–308
P. Conrad: *Romantic Opera and Literary Form* (Berkeley and Los Angeles, 1977)
R. Craft: 'Verdi, Shakespeare and *Falstaff*', *Current Convictions: Views and Reviews* (New York, 1977), 114–24
W. Osthoff: 'Il sonetto nel *Falstaff* di Verdi', *Il melodramma italiano dell'ottocento: studi e ricerche per Massimo Mila* (Turin, 1977), 157–83
G. Schmidgall: *Literature as Opera* (New York, 1977)
G. J. Williams: 'Madame Vestris' *A Midsummer Night's Dream* and the Web of Victorian Tradition', *Theatre Survey*, xviii/Nov (1977), 1–22
T. Bauman: 'Opera versus Drama: *Romeo and Juliet* in 18th-Century Germany', *Eighteenth-Century Studies*, xi/wint. (1977–8), 186–203
D. Linthicum: 'Verdi's *Falstaff* and Classical Sonata Form', *MR*, xxxix (1978), 39–53
F. Noske: '*Otello*: Drama through Structure', *Essays on Music for Charles Warren Fox* (Rochester, NY, 1979), 14–47
J. A. Hepokoski: 'Verdi, Giuseppina Pasqua, and the Composition of *Falstaff*', *19th Century Music*, iii (1979–80), 239–50
A. Porter: 'Translating Shakespeare's Operas', *Opera*, xxxi (1980), 527–34, 639–44, 753–9
H. Heinsheimer: 'In Search of *Lear*', *ON*, xlv/June (1980–81), 13–14, 16 [on Reimann's setting]
F. Noske: 'Verbal to Musical Drama: Adaptation or Creation?, *Themes in Drama*, iii: *Drama, Dance and Music*, ed. J. Redmond (Cambridge, 1981), 143–52
W. Weaver: 'Verdi, Shakespeare and the Italian Audience', *Otello*, ed. N. John (London, 1981), 23–6 [ENO Opera Guide]
D. Cooke: 'Shakespeare into Music', *Vindications: Essays on Romantic Music* (Cambridge, 1982), 175–80
P. Weiss: 'Verdi and the Fusion of Genres', *JAMS*, xxxv (1982), 138–56
J. Hepokoski: *Giuseppe Verdi: Falstaff* (Cambridge, 1983)
H. Lindenberger: *Opera: the Extravagant Art* (Ithaca, NY, 1984)
W. Oehlmann: *Oper in vier Jahrhunderten* (Stuttgart, 1984)
W. Weaver: 'The Shakespeare Verdi Knew', *Verdi's Macbeth: a Sourcebook*, ed. D Rosen and A. Porter (New York, 1984), 144–8
G. Schmidgall: 'Verdi's *King Lear* Project', *19th Century Music*, ix (1985–6), 83–101
H.-J. Genzel: 'Die Oper und Shakespeare: Bemerkungen und Beispiele zur Adaptation', *Shakespeare Jb*, cxxii (1986), 159–76
J. Hepokoski: *Giuseppe Verdi: Otello* (Cambridge, 1987)
——: 'Boito and F.-V. Hugo's "Magnificent Translation": a Study of the Genesis of the *Otello* Libretto', *Reading Opera*, ed. A. Groos and R. Parker (Princeton, 1988), 34–59
E. R. Hotaling: *Shakespeare and the Musical Stage: a Guide to Sources, Studies, and First Performances* (Boston, 1990)
G. Schmidgall: *Shakespeare and Opera* (Oxford, 1990)
B. N. S. Gooch and D. Thatcher, eds.: *A Shakespeare Music Catalogue* (Oxford, 1991)

CHRISTOPHER R. WILSON

Shakh-Senem. Opera in three acts by REYNGOL'D MORITSEVICH GLIER after an Azerbaijani legend; Baku, 17 March 1927 (revised version, Baku, 1934).

The opera tells of the wandering 'Ashug' musician Kerib (tenor), who takes part in a singing competition for the hand of the Shah's beautiful daughter, Shakh-Senem (soprano). He wins, but the Shah (baritone) is angered by his poverty and his championship of the oppressed people. He banishes Kerib, but the people, who have sided with the young Ashug, mutiny, and Shakh-Senem defies her father, vowing to be faithful to Kerib. Her patience is rewarded in Act 3, when her lover returns in triumph to claim her hand and liberate the people from the Shah's tyranny.

Glier wrote *Shakh-Senem* (including possibly all or part of the libretto) shortly after his invitation to Azerbaijan to assist in the development of Soviet-style musical life. This was his first large-scale attempt to fuse the republic's indigenous folk styles with his own conservative Russian style, and it found immediate official favour. The ethnomusicologist Uzeir Gajibekov described *Shakh-Senem* as 'the basis of the strong beginning of new Azerbaijani operatic culture', though certain stylistic impurities, in particular a strong Persian colouring, had to be removed in the revision. *Shakh-Senem* contains some fine music, and the work has made a stronger impact than any of Glier's four later operas.

STEPHEN JOHNSON

Fyodor Shalyapin in the title role of Boito's 'Mefistofele'

Shalyapin [Chaliapin], **Fyodor (Ivanovich)** (*b* nr Kazan', 1/13 Feb 1873; *d* Paris, 12 April 1938). Russian bass. Widely considered the greatest singing actor of his day, he was largely self-taught and sang with small provincial companies before having any formal training. After study (1892–3) in Tbilisi he successfully sang a wide variety of roles there and in St Petersburg, where he belonged to the Imperial Opera (at the Mariinsky Theatre), 1894–6, leaving to join Mamontov's private opera in Moscow. There he became renowned for his carefully thought-out performances of such roles as Boris and Varlaam, Dosifey (*Khovanshchina*), Ivan the Terrible (*The Maid of Pskov*), the Viking Guest (*Sadko*), the Miller (Dargomïzhsky's *Rusalka*) and Holofernes (Serov's *Judith*), as well as creating Rimsky-Korsakov's Salieri in 1898. He was a member of the Bol'shoy Opera in Moscow, 1899–1914, and made frequent guest appearances at the Mariinsky and in the provinces. His international career began in 1901 at La Scala, as Boito's Mefistofele. He made his Metropolitan Opera début on 20 November 1907 in the same role and during the 1907–8 season sang Don Basilio (*Il barbiere*), Leporello and Faust. He took part in the Dyagilev seasons in Paris (1908, 1909, 1910 and 1913), sang in London (1913–14) and rejoined the Mariinsky Theatre as soloist and artistic director (1918). In 1921 he left Russia and, on 9 December, sang Boris at the Metropolitan. He continued to sing throughout the world until his final illness. He made two films and some 200 recordings.

Shalyapin's voice was sufficiently flexible to allow him to sing baritone roles like Yevgeny Onegin, Valentin (*Faust*) and Rubinstein's Demon, as well as such bass roles as Oroveso (*Norma*) and Philip II (*Don Carlos*). In *Prince Igor* he sang Galitsky, Konchak and Igor. He was a perfectionist as far as his own make-up, costuming, and musical and dramatic preparation were concerned, and untiringly attentive to the staging of the operas he appeared in. Those who worked with him or who knew him off stage testify to his almost superhuman vital force, warmth, and fierce intolerance of artistic mediocrity.

For further illustration *see* DON QUICHOTTE.

WRITINGS

Stranitsï iz moyey zhizni: avtobiografiya (Leningrad, 1926; Eng. trans. as *Pages from my Life*, 1927)

Maska i dusha: moi sorok let na teatrakh (Paris, 1932; Eng. trans. as *Man and Mask*, 1932)

Chaliapin: an Autobiography as Told to Maxim Gorky (London, 1968) [incl. different trans. of parts of the two above]

*

GV (R. Celletti; R. Vegeto)

H. T. Finck: 'Chaliapine, the Russian "Mephistopheles"', *The Century*, new ser., lxxxi (1910–11), 230–37

R. Newmarch: *The Russian Opera* (London, 1914)

B. Semeonoff: 'Feodor Chaliapine', *Record Collector*, v (1950), 124–41 [with discography]

E. Grosheva, ed.: *Fyodor Ivanovich Shalyapin: literaturnoye nasledstvo* [Literary Legacy] (Moscow, 1960) [incl. lists of roles, concert repertory, discography]

B. Semeonoff: 'Chaliapin's Repertoire and Recordings', *Record Collector*, xx (1971–2), 173–230 [with discography by A. Kelly]

D. Ewen: *Musicians since 1900: Performers in Concert and Opera* (New York, 1978)

HAROLD BARNES

Shamus O'Brien. Romantic comic opera in two acts, op.61, by CHARLES VILLIERS STANFORD to a libretto by George H. Jessop after a poem by Joseph Sheridan Le Fanu; London, Opera Comique, 2 March 1896.

The opera is set immediately after the 1798 rebellion in the mountains and bogs of Cork, whither the outlaw Shamus O'Brien (baritone) leads the British army a dance in Act 1 while his wife Nora (mezzo-soprano) confides to the priest Father O'Flynn (bass) that she has heard the Banshee's wail and fears for Shamus's life. Her sister Kitty (soprano) provides the subplot by flirting with the English Captain Trevor (tenor). Mike Murphy (tenor) betrays Shamus to the British and then tries to buy Nora's love in return for the promise of his release, but Shamus effects a last-minute escape from the gallows with the help of Father O'Flynn. Mike, pursuing him, is shot by the soldiers. Shamus escapes; the Banshee was crying for Mike.

The music, redolent of Irish song and dance and full of chorus material, is interspersed with spoken dialogue. The original principals were partly drawn from the RCM and included Kirkby Lunn, as Nora, at the beginning of her career. All in all, it is easy to see why the work became a West End success and transferred to the provinces and Broadway.

STEPHEN BANFIELD

Shane, Rita (Frances) (*b* New York, 15 Aug 1940). American soprano. She attended Barnard College, New York, and studied privately with Beverly Peck Johnson and on the Santa Fe Opera Apprentice Program (1962–3), making her début as Olympia in *Les contes d'Hoffmann* in Chattanooga in 1964. Her New York City Opera début was in 1965, as Donna Elvira; she subsequently sang with most American companies and in Amsterdam, Chicago, Geneva, Milan, Munich and Salzburg. She is best known for her portrayal of the Queen of Night, her début role at the Metropolitan in 1973. In 1979 she created the title role in Argento's *Miss Havisham's Fire* at New York City Opera. Her penetrating voice, combined with an impressive top extension and coloratura facility, have established her in roles including Konstanze, Lucia, Lulu, Violetta and Zerbinetta. CORI ELLISON

Shanewis [*The Robin Woman: Shanewis*]. Opera in one act by CHARLES WAKEFIELD CADMAN to a libretto by Nelle Richmond Eberhart; New York, Metropolitan Opera, 23 March 1918.

The plot is partly based on the life of the Creek Indian Tsianina Redfeather, Shanewis being a phonetic approximation of her name. She herself assisted Cadman in the lectures he gave on Indian music throughout the USA.

Mrs Asher Everton (contralto) gives a party for her protégée Shanewis (mezzo-soprano), who is a singer, and her daughter Amy (soprano), engaged to Lionel Rhodes (tenor). Lionel, who is attracted to Shanewis, follows her when she returns to her people in Oklahoma. When she learns of his unfaithfulness to Amy, she repulses him, and in revenge Shanewis's foster brother Harjo (baritone) kills Lionel as Amy watches. The opera is in two scenes separated by an intermezzo.

Shanewis was the first opera with a contemporary American setting (including an onstage jazz band) to be produced by the Metropolitan Opera, and it was one of Cadman's last works to use American Indian themes, one of the songs in the opera, 'The Spring Song of the Robin Woman', being originally sung to him by Tsianina Redfeather. Percussion accompanies the Indian scenes, contrasting with chromatically embellished tertiary harmonies for the music of the whites.

See also BLACKSTONE, TSIANINA REDFEATHER.

THOMAS WARBURTON

Shanghai. Chinese city; for an account of operatic activity there *see* CHINA.

Shanks, Donald (*b* Brisbane, 5 July 1940). Australian bass. He began his stage career in Gilbert and Sullivan, then in 1965 sang Baron Douphol (*La traviata*) on tour with the Sutherland-Williamson Company. With the Elizabethan Trust Opera, later Australian Opera, he has sung an enormous range of both comic and dramatic roles since 1964; the former category includes Rossini's Don Basilio, Osmin, Don Pasquale, Dulcamara, Rocco, Pistol, Kecal, Colline and Don Magnifico; among the latter are Sarastro, the Commendatore, Oroveso, Giorgio (*I puritani*), Ramfis, Ferrando (*Il trovatore*), Zaccaria, Padre Guardiano, Philip II and the Grand Inquisitor, Fiesco, Banquo, Timur, Pimen and Boris. His repertory includes many Wagner roles: Daland, the Landgrave, King Henry, Pogner, King Mark, Hunding and Fafner, which he also sang at Covent Garden (1974) and the Opéra (1976). He sang Gounod's Méphistophélès in Brisbane (1991). His imposing stage presence and his rich, dark-coloured voice are best employed, despite a great talent for comedy, in serious dramatic roles. ANN CARR-BOYD/ELIZABETH FORBES

Shaporin, Yury Alexandrovich (*b* Glukhovo, 27 Oct/8 Nov 1887; *d* Moscow, 9 Dec 1966). Russian composer. Despite showing early talent for composition, he initially studied philology at Kiev University (1906). He then read law in St Petersburg and in 1913 entered the conservatory, where his teachers were Sokolov, Shteynberg and Tcherepnin. His style was formed in the nationalist tradition, particularly as represented by Rimsky-Korsakov. On graduating, however, he allied himself with revolutionary movements in drama and stage production, founding the Grand Drama Theatre with Gorky, Lunacharsky and Blok in 1919; he was music director there until 1928, after which he was associated with the Academic Drama Theatre (now the Pushkin Theatre) until 1934. During that period he wrote a great deal of theatre music, some of it showing experimental tendencies. With Asaf'yev he was a founder-member of the progressive Association for Contemporary Music (1926), which encouraged closer ties with new Western music. At about that time he planned an opera based on Gorky's *Mat'* ('The Mother'), though this was abandoned after the writer's death.

In the 1930s, Shaporin's career took a new direction. His rate of composition slowed and the scale of his works increased. Of these later works the best known is his only opera *Dekabristï* ('The Decembrists'), based on an idea by Alexey Tolstoy. Shaporin had begun work on it as early as 1920, and in 1925 a first, incomplete version, consisting of two scenes and entitled *Polina Gyobel'*, was performed in Leningrad. After 1930 he worked on it with new determination, a commission from the Moscow Bol'shoy in 1935 providing added incentive; he moved to Moscow in 1936, and from 1939 taught at the conservatory. Another version of the opera was completed in 1938, but Shaporin was dissatisfied and revised it drastically. The last period of intensive effort came in 1953, when Shaporin began close collaboration with his final librettist, Vsevolod Rozhdestvensky. *The Decembrists* was completed and had its première that year on 23 June, at the Bol'shoy Theatre, Moscow. It remained in the Soviet repertory, but was not performed elsewhere.

See also DECEMBRISTS, THE.

*

G. Abraham: *Eight Soviet Composers* (London, 1943), 89–98
V. Vasina-Grossman: *Yu. A. Shaporin* (Moscow, 1946)
E. Groshyova: *Yury Alexandrovich Shaporin* (Moscow, 1957)
S. Katonova: *Shaporin Yu.: Dekabristï opera* (Leningrad, 1959)
I. Martïnov: *Yury Shaporin* (Moscow, 1966)
B. Schwarz: *Music and Musical Life in Soviet Russia 1917–1970* (London, 1972, 2/1983) RITA McALLISTER

Shaposhnikov, Adrian Grigor'yevich (*b* St Petersburg, 29 May/10 June 1887; *d* Moscow, 22 June 1967). Russian composer. He studied at the St Petersburg Technical Institute (1905–9) while taking music lessons with Kalafati, and in 1913 graduated from the St Petersburg Conservatory. After working in Moscow as an engineer-economist and freelance composer (1920–35), he lived in Ashkhabad (1937–48), directing the Composers' Union of the Turkmen SSR. He returned to

Moscow in 1949. His opera *Zokhre i Takhir* (1941) was among the first Turkmenian examples of the genre.

Otravlenniy sad [The Poisoned Garden] (opera-poem, F. Sologub), 1913
Zokhre i Takhir (B. Amanov), Ashkhabad, 6 Nov 1941; rev. (A. Karliyev), Ashkhabad, 6 April 1953; collab. V. Mukhatov
Gyul' i bil'bil' [Rose and Nightingale] (K. Burunov), Ashkhabad, 6 March 1943
Shasenem i Garib (Burunov), 1944; rev., Ashkhabad, 25 Oct 1955; collab. D. Ovezov
Kemine i kazï [Kemine and the Goat], 1945–6 (comic op, Burunov and I. Keller), Ashkhabad, 26 Nov 1947, collab. L. Mukhatov
Ayna, 1957, collab. S. Ovezov DETLEF GOJOWY

Sharp, Frederick (Charles) (*b* Mansfield Woodhouse, Notts., 19 Oct 1911; *d* Tadworth, Surrey, 20 April 1988). English baritone. He studied in London at the RCM. He made his début in 1946 as Junius in *The Rape of Lucretia* at Glyndebourne, where the following year he created Sid in *Albert Herring* for the English Opera Group. He then joined Sadler's Wells Opera, where he remained until 1960, singing a large variety of roles that included Don Giovanni, Germont, Rigoletto, Scarpia, Paolo (*Simon Boccanegra*) and Yevgeny Onegin, his finest and most successful interpretation. Though his voice was not large, it was strongly projected, and he was an actor of fierce intensity.

For illustration *see* ALBERT HERRING. ELIZABETH FORBES

Shaw, (George) Bernard (*b* Dublin, 26 July 1856; *d* Ayot St Lawrence, Herts., 2 Nov 1950). Irish dramatist, music critic and polymath. Born into a musical family, Shaw was early introduced to Italian opera and to Mozart. He moved to London in 1876, writing his first music criticism that year, reviewing Wagner as genius composer and neurotic conductor at the Albert Hall the following year. *Love among the Artists*, the third of his novels (1881), has for hero a composer-pianist, and in 1887 he wrote the short story *Don Giovanni Explains*; but it was in his criticism for *The Star* (from 1888) that he first revealed his passionate commitment to the highest standards in music and a loathing for those who traduced them. His seriousness of purpose was disguised with rapier wit and the jester's ability to stand ideas on their head. His major musical essay, on the *Ring*, was published in 1898 as *The Perfect Wagnerite*.

A friendship with Elgar, ripening from 1921, suggested the possibility of a libretto. But Shaw demurred, claiming that his plays set themselves to a music of their own; moreover, opera writing was mere piffle to such as Elgar, who had shown in *Falstaff* the true way to set drama to music. Among Shaw's plays *Arms and the Man* provided the basis in 1908 for Oscar Straus's musical comedy *Der tapfere Soldat*, and in 1956 *Pygmalion* inspired Loewe's musical *My Fair Lady*.

*

P. M. Young, ed.: *Letters of Edward Elgar* (London, 1956)
D. H. Laurence, ed.: *Shaw's Music* (London, 1981) [collected writings on music] ROBERT ANDERSON

Shaw, Carlos Fernández. *See* FERNÁNDEZ SHAW, CARLOS.

Shaw (y Iturralde), Guillermo Fernández. *See* FERNÁNDEZ SHAW, GUILLERMO.

Shaw, John (*b* Newcastle, NSW, 12 Oct 1924). Australian baritone. He was engaged for leading roles by the J. C. Williamson touring Italian company of 1955 and was a principal in the first two seasons (1956–7) of the Elizabethan Trust (now Australian) Opera. He was recommended to Covent Garden by Elsie Morison and Joan Hammond, who had appeared with him in *Tosca* and *Otello*, and engaged for the title role in *Rigoletto* in 1959 (with Sutherland as Gilda) and for many other parts subsequently. He made guest appearances with eminent companies in Europe and the USA. A resident member of the Australian Opera from 1974 to 1989, he was associated particularly with such roles as Jack Rance, Amonasro and, above all, Scarpia. Virile in manner, he has a strong voice which is sometimes blurred in focus; though his acting is broadly generalized, he is also capable of vividly detailed performances, an outstanding late example of which was his appearance as Gianni Schicchi. ROGER COVELL

Shaw, Martin (Fallas) (*b* London, 9 March 1875; *d* Southwold, 24 Oct 1958). English composer. He studied at the RCM, where he was a pupil of Stanford and then worked with Gordon Craig and Isadora Duncan in connection with the stage both in England and abroad. He founded the Purcell Operatic Society, which produced *Dido and Aeneas* in 1900. He worked as a church organist (1908–24) and was appointed OBE in 1955.

Shaw's first stage success was his ballad opera *Mr Pepys*. This was modelled on *The Beggar's Opera* and contains many short songs that make use of folklike rhythms. The musical content of two later ballad operas, *Waterloo Leave* and *Faithful Jenny Dove*, is developed considerably; the first act of *Faithful Jenny Dove* concludes with an ambitious ensemble. Shaw's most adventurous work is his opera *The Thorn of Avalon*. Based on a religious theme, it is sung throughout and includes several large choruses. His autobiography *Up to Now* (London, 1929) contains many reminiscences of his diverse theatrical career.

all first performed and published in London

Brer Rabbit and Mr Fox (musical frolic, 5 scenes, M. Dearmer), vs (1914)
Mr Pepys (ballad op, 3, C. Bax), Hampstead, Everyman, 11 Feb 1926, vs (1926)
The Thorn of Avalon (3, B. Baron), Crystal Palace, 6 June 1931, vs (1931)
Philomel (operetta, E. Farjeon and Bax), Ambassador's, 1932, 1 song (1932)
Waterloo Leave (ballad op, Bax), ?unperf.
Faithful Jenny Dove (ballad op, Farjeon), ?unperf.

ELISABETH COOK

Shaw [née Postans], **Mary** (*b* Lea, Kent, 1814; *d* Hadleigh Hall, Suffolk, 9 Sept 1876). English contralto. She studied at the RAM and afterwards with Sir George Smart. After five years as a concert singer, in 1839 she made her operatic début at Novara as Arsace, then sang Malcolm (*La donna del lago*). At La Scala she sang Cuniza in the première of Verdi's first opera, *Oberto*. She returned to England in 1842 and sang at Covent Garden, also scoring great successes in *Il matrimonio segreto* and *La donna del lago* at Drury Lane, where in 1844 she appeared in the first performance of Benedict's *The Brides of Venice*. Later that year her husband went insane, and the shock affected her voice so that she had to retire from the stage while at the height of her career.

HAROLD ROSENTHAL/R

Shawān, Aziz. *See* EL-SHAWĀN, AZIZ.

Shawe-Taylor, Desmond (Christopher) (*b* Dublin, 29 May 1907). Anglo-Irish music critic. Before World War II his field was mainly literary criticism. In 1945 he was appointed music critic of the *New Statesman*, and was gramophone critic of *The Observer* (1950–58), then chief music critic of the *Sunday Times* (1958–82). From 1951 to 1973 he contributed a quarterly article to the *Gramophone* surveying recordings of vocal music. His particular interests are opera (especially 19th-century Italian and Czech), vocal technique and interpretation, and recorded music. His judgments are based on a wide knowledge and keen discernment, particularly as regards the human voice.

Covent Garden (London, 1948)
with E. Sackville-West: *The Record Guide* (London, 1951, 2/1955, with A. Porter and W. Mann; suppl., 1956)
with E. Sackville-West and A. Porter: *The Record Year* (London, 1952); *The Record Year 2* (London, 1953)

Shchedrin, Rodion Konstantinovich (*b* Moscow, 16 Dec 1932). Russian composer and pianist. The son of a composer and theorist, Shchedrin attended the Moscow Choral School (1945–50). He then studied at the Moscow Conservatory, graduating in 1955 from the piano class of Yakov Fliyer and in 1959 from the post-graduate composition class of Yury Shaporin. Regarded in his own country as one of the leading postwar composers, Shchedrin has long been a prominent figure in Soviet musical life. From 1965 to 1969 he taught at the Moscow Conservatory. In 1962 he joined the governing board of the Union of Soviet Composers, and in 1973 he succeeded Shostakovich as chairman of the Union of Composers of the RSFSR, a post he held until 1990. He has been the recipient of numerous prizes and honours including the Order of the Red Banner (1971), a State Prize (1971), the Order of Lenin (1982) and the Lenin Prize (1984). In 1981 he was named People's Artist of the USSR.

Shchedrin's compositional promise, especially evident in his attraction to the infectious melodic style and rhythms of the urban folk *chastushka* and his flair for vivid and effective orchestration, was identified early and nurtured carefully. Over the years his palette expanded to include atonality and he flirted with many of the trends and modern styles of the late 20th century, though his aesthetic has remained firmly rooted in the lyrical and accessible. His first work for the theatre, the fairy-tale ballet *Konyok-gorbunok* ('The Little Humpbacked Horse'), was a success at its première in 1960 and its popularity has endured.

Shchedrin's first opera, *Ne tol'ko lyubov'* ('Not for Love Alone'; 3, V. A. Katanyan, after S. Antonov), with its setting on a somewhat idealized contemporary collective farm, also capitalized on the appeal of the *chastushka*. In his more ambitious second three-act opera, *Myortvïye dushi* ('Dead Souls'), Shchedrin turned to the literary classic by Nikolay Gogol. In his approach to the literary original and his careful attention to the nuances of characterization and text-setting, he placed himself in the best Russian traditions of Musorgsky and Shostakovich. Shchedrin's interpretation sets itself apart, however, by the juxtaposition and resultant symbolism of two contrasting planes of dramatic action. Both of his operas, and all his ballets, have been given their premières by the Bol'shoy Theatre, *Not for Love Alone* on 25 December 1961 and *Dead Souls* on 7 June 1977; *Not for Love Alone* was first performed in a revised version on 20 January 1972 at the Chamber Opera in Moscow. Shchedrin has also composed works for orchestra – including four piano concertos and two symphonies – as well as choral and chamber music.

See also Myortvïye dushi and Ne tol'ko lyubov'.

*

L. Genina: 'Novo, talantlivo' [New and Talented], *SovM* (1961), no.7, pp.23–39
L. Dobrïnina: ' "Ne tol'ko lyubov' " ...', *SovM* (1962), no.9, pp.42–7
'Materialï obsuzhdeniya operï R. Shchedrina "Ne tol'ko lyubov' ", sostoyavshegosya 13 yanv. 1962 g. v SK SSSR' [Material from the Discussion of the Opera *Not for Love Alone* which Took Place on 13 January 1962 in the USSR Composers' Union], *SovM* (1962), no.3, pp.82–6
I. Likhachyova: *Muzïkal'niy teatr Rodiona Shchedrina* (Moscow, 1977)
M. Tarakanov: 'Poema Gogolya na opernoy stsene' [A Poem of Gogol on the Opera Stage], *SovM* (1977), no.10, pp.85–97 [on *Dead Souls*]
V. Komissinsky: *O dramaturgischeskikh printsipakh tvorchestva R. Shchedrina* [On the Dramaturgical Principles of the Work of Shchedrin] (Moscow, 1978)
M. Cherkashina: ' "Myortvïye dushi" – v partiture i na stsene' [*Dead Souls* in the Score and on the Stage], *Muzïka Rossii*, ed. A. Grigor'yeva, iii (Moscow, 1980), 69ff
R. Kosachyova: 'Zametki o novatorstve i traditsiyakh opernogo zhanra (opera R. Shchedrina "Myortvïye dushi")' [Remarks on Novelty and Tradition in the Operatic Genre (Shchedrin's Opera *Dead Souls*)], *Sovetskaya muzïkal'naya kul'tura: istoriya, traditsii, sovremennost'* [Soviet Musical Culture: History, Traditions and the Present], ed. D. Daragan (Moscow, 1980), 83–106
M. Tarakanov: *Tvorchestvo Rodiona Shchedrina* [The Work of Rodion Shchedrin] (Moscow, 1980)
I. Likhachyova: *Opera 'Myortvïye dushi' R. Shchedrina: putevoditel'* [Shchedrin's Opera *Dead Souls*: a Guide] (Moscow, 1981)
H. Gerlach: *Zum Schaffen von Rodion Schtschedrin* (Berlin, 1982)
I. Balázs: 'Rodion Schtschedrin: *Die toten Seelen*: Opernszenen nach Gogol in 3 Aufzügen, 19 Bildern, Aspekte zum Problem der Operndramaturgie', *Melos*, l/1 (1988), 55–105
I. Prokhorova: *Rodion Shchedrin: nachalo puti* [Shchedrin: the Beginning of his Path] (Moscow, 1989)

LAUREL E. FAY

Shebalin, Vissarion Yakovlevich (*b* Omsk, 29 May/11 June 1902; *d* Moscow, 28 May 1963). Russian composer. He was admitted to the Moscow Conservatory in 1923 on the recommendation of Myaskovsky, who influenced him for some years, counterbalancing his interest in Skryabin and the French musical impressionists. On graduating with the highest honours in 1928, Shebalin joined the conservatory staff, becoming a professor (1935) and head of composition (1941). His many honours include the title People's Artist of the RSFSR (1947) and two Stalin prizes. His dismissal from the conservatory during the 1948 purges came as a shock, although he had spoken out with great courage during the public discussions earlier that year. He was reinstated in 1951 and, despite a stroke that left him partly paralysed on the right side, he continued to compose. His four-act comic opera *Ukroshcheniye stroptivoy* ('The Taming of the Shrew') op.46, to a libretto by A. A. Gozenpud, after Shakespeare, was given its concert première at the Central House of Art Workers, Moscow, on 1 October 1955. The stage première, at Kuybïshev (now Samara) on 25 May 1957, was an outstanding success. It was followed on 9 June 1958 at Moscow by the first performance of *Solntse nad step'yu* ('Sun over the Steppe') op.27, in three acts, on which Shebalin had been working since 1939. In both its style and its typically Soviet theme (revolutionary heroes and White Guard villains) it is a more conventional work than its predecessor. Shebalin has also provided a widely admired version of Musorgsky's fragmentary opera *The Fair at Sorochintsï* (1931–2).

See also UKROSHCHENIYE STROPTIVOY.

*

G. Abraham: *Eight Soviet Composers* (London, 1943)
I. Bel'za: *Vissarion Shebalin* (Moscow, 1945)
M. Sabinina: 'Ukroschcheniye stroptivoy', *SovM* (1957), no.10, p.94
V. Shebalin: 'O proydennom puti' [My Journey through Life], *SovM* (1959), no.2, p.74; *SovM* (1962), no.6 [incl. 60th-birthday tributes]
I. Bel'za and V. Protopopov, eds.: *V. Ya. Shebalin: stat'i, vospominaniya, materialï* [Shebalin: Articles, Reminiscences, Materials] (Moscow, 1970)
B. Schwarz: *Music and Musical Life in Soviet Russia 1917–1970* (London, 1972, 2/1983)
D. Gojowy: *Neue sowjetische Musik der 20er Jahre* (Laaber, 1980)
N. Listova: *V. Ya. Shebalin* (Moscow, 1982)
E. Bonch-Osmaolovskaya: *V. Ya. Shebalin: monografiya* (Leningrad, 1983) BORIS SCHWARZ/STEPHEN JOHNSON

Shekhter, Boris Semyonovich (*b* Odessa, 8/20 Jan 1900; *d* Moscow, 16 Dec 1961). Russian composer. He completed his studies with Maliszewski at the Odessa Conservatory in 1922 and with Vasilenko and Myaskovsky at the Moscow Conservatory in 1929. In 1925 he was a co-founder of Prokoll, the 'production collective' of composition students at the Moscow Conservatory, where he taught from 1929. Together with Alexander Davidenko he represented and defended a popular art which was anti-modernist and free from Western influence. As well as operas he composed many popular songs and choruses.

1905 god [The year 1905] (3, S. Mstislavsky), Moscow Radio, 1935; rev. 1955; collab, A. A. Davidenko
Yusup i Akhmet (A. Kurbanov, K. Burunov and A. Minnikh), Ashkhabad, 12 June 1942, collab. A. Kuliyev
Sejide, 1942–3 (K. Burunov), collab. S. Ovesov
Pushkin v Mikhaylovskom [Pushkin in Mikhaylovskoye], 1954–5 (I. A. Novikov and M. N. Novikova), Moscow, University, 1958 as Pushkin v izgnanii [Pushkin in Exile]

*

E. Dobrïnina: 'Pushkin-geroy operï' [Pushkin – an Opera Hero], *SovM* (1959), no.6, pp.46–51
B. Shekhter: 'Iz vospominaniy ob A. Davidenko' [From Memories of Davidenko], *SovM* (1959), no.6, pp.52–7 DETLEF GOJOWY

Shelley, Harry Rowe (*b* New Haven, CT, 2 June 1858; *d* Short Beach, CT, 12 Sept 1947). American composer. He studied with Stoeckel at Yale University and later in New York with Dudley Buck and Dvořák. A professional organist from the age of 20, he taught harmony and counterpoint in New York and composed extensively for the organ. In larger forms he was less prolific – a handful of orchestral works and two operas. The earlier and larger opera was an ambitious three-act version of *Romeo and Juliet*, in which Shelley adapted the libretto from Shakespeare, preserving much of the original text and retaining the most famous scenes. Though the scenario is well shaped, the libretto, heavy with iambic pentameter, is verbose. Shelley's setting, often little more than highly rhythmicized recitative with many repeated notes, lacks the kind of melodic élan that might give life to the drama. The publication of the score (1901) with text in English and German suggests that Shelley hoped for European productions, but the work seems never to have been performed.

Old Black Joe, a one-act opera on a libretto by Clay M. Green, was produced privately at a New York theatrical club, 'The Lambs', on 26 February 1911; the four principal parts, including one female role, were performed by men, suggesting that the work was a club event never intended for public performance. The dated plot, in stereotyped minstrel-show dialect and full of unlikely situations, takes place on a southern plantation near the end of the American Civil War. Stephen Foster's familiar song *Old Black Joe* is quoted (the text adjusted somewhat at its entrance), and the opera ends with an apotheosis of General Grant.

STEVEN LEDBETTER

Shepherd's Lottery, The. Musical entertainment in two parts by WILLIAM BOYCE to a libretto by Moses Mendez; London, Drury Lane, 19 November 1751.

Conceiving the work as a sequel to *THE CHAPLET* (1749), Mendez and Boyce must have calculated that *The Shepherd's Lottery*, with its similar pastoral plot and sublimated ballad style, would match the success of its predecessor. The libretto hinges on the implausible Arcadian convention that on May Day the shepherds draw lots for their future wives. The young lovers Phillis (soprano) and Thyrsis (treble) fear that the draw may not sanction their union. The cynical Daphne (soprano) affects not to care whom she gets and makes an assignation with Dorylas (tenor) with no intention of fulfilling it. The carefree Colin (tenor) is interested only in the nymphs who yield and refuses to participate in the draw at all – much to Daphne's displeasure. Having appealed to Venus for a happy outcome, Phillis has her dearest wish granted her.

The Shepherd's Lottery received 20 performances during its first season at Drury Lane, but only seven more before it was dropped in 1754. The reasons for its relative failure are not clear since the music, with its deftly contrasted airs, compares favourably with that of *The Chaplet*. However, with even less dramatic motivation and little distinctive character of its own, *The Shepherd's Lottery* suffered from having to compete in the repertory with *The Chaplet* itself. Phillis's intensely lyrical song to Venus, 'Goddess of the dimpling smile', with oboe obbligato, offers a high point similar to Laura's lament in *The Chaplet*, while in Colin's first air, 'The drum is unbrac'd', the pastoral scene is colourfully evoked by sopranino recorder and horns. *The Shepherd's Lottery* was the first English opera to have a vaudeville finale. The irrepressible overture in F, embracing the most memorable of gavotte finales, was included in Boyce's *Eight Symphonys* (London, 1760).

IAN BARTLETT

Shere, Charles (*b* Berkeley, CA, 20 Aug 1935). American composer. He studied composition with Berio and Robert Erickson and from 1973 to 1984 he taught at Mills College, Oakland. He was art and music critic for the Oakland *Tribune* (1972–88) and he edited and published *Ear* (1973–8), a magazine concentrating on avant-garde music. The first public performance of his music was of incidental music for Tennessee Williams's play *Camino Real*, given at the University of California, Berkeley, in 1958. Other stage works include a full-length opera, *The Bride Stripped Bare by her Bachelors, Even*, based on Marcel Duchamp's painting *La mariée mise à nu par ses célibataires, même*, and a cycle of three chamber operas, setting plays by Gertrude Stein: *Ladies Voices*, *I Like it to Be a Play* and *What Happened*. The trilogy can be staged as a single work of about 40 minutes' duration, or any of the three operas can be given separately.

The Bride sets the many notes and memoranda kept by Duchamp while he was elaborating his curious painting, now in the collection of the Philadelphia Museum. The painting itself serves as Shere's scenario. The music forms an analogue of Duchamp's pictorial and aesthetic procedures and recapitulates most of the compositional procedures current during the time of the opera's composition (1963–84): graphic notation, random procedures, serial and 12-note writing, extended techniques, etc. Its abstraction and pictorial nature draw on the precedent of Virgil Thomson's *Four Saints in Three Acts* (*The Bride* is dedicated to Thomson), but elements of its structure recall those of Berg's *Wozzeck*: a piano concerto and a violin concerto, for example, intertwine in the accompaniment in the centre of the second act. The general direction of *The Bride* moves from the experimental, open-form, small-ensemble writing at the opening, especially in Act 1 scene i, through the obsessive rhythms of Act 2, to the parodies and 'found music' of Act 3.

The Bride Stripped Bare by her Bachelors, Even, 1963–86 (3, Shere, after M. Duchamp); Act 1 scene i as The Box of 1914, San Francisco, Conservatory, 30 Jan 1981; Act 1 complete and Act 2 scenes i–iii, Oakland, CA, Mills College, 1 Dec 1984

Ladies Voices (chamber op, prol., 4, G. Stein), Berkeley, Berkeley Art Center, 30 Oct 1987 [pt 1 of trilogy]

I Like it to Be a Play (chamber op, 1, Stein), San Francisco, Hatley Martin Gallery, 6 Feb 1989 [pt 2 of trilogy]

What Happened, 1991 (chamber op, 5, Stein) [pt 3 of trilogy]

*

R. H. Kornick: *Recent American Opera: a Production Guide* (New York, 1991), 279–80

ROBERT HUGHES

Sheridan, Margaret (*b* Castlebar, Co. Mayo, 15 Oct 1889; *d* Dublin, 16 April 1958). Irish soprano. She studied with William Shakespeare at the RAM (1909–11), then in Italy with Alfredo Martino. Her début was in *La bohème* (1918, Rome). She appeared at Covent Garden in 1919 (as Mimì, and in the first London performance of Mascagni's *Iris*) and returned there in 1925–6 and 1928–30, but sang mostly in leading Italian theatres, including La Scala (1922–4). Her voice was pure and colourful, naturally suited to the gentle and sentimental, but at times also passionate, music of Puccini. A fine actress, she was outstanding as Manon, Mimì, Butterfly and as Maddalena (*Andrea Chénier*) and Wally (which she sang under Toscanini in 1922).

*

GV (L. Riemens; J. B. Richards)

RODOLFO CELLETTI

Sheridan, Richard Brinsley (*b* Dublin, 30 Oct 1751; *d* London, 7 July 1816). Irish playwright, politician, theatre owner-manager and opera impresario active in London. A major figure in the House of Commons for over 30 years, much of the time effectively as leader of the opposition, Sheridan is chiefly remembered as a playwright, author of *The Rivals* (1775) and *The School for Scandal* (1777). He was also successful in English opera: *THE DUENNA* (1775), with music composed and arranged by his father-in-law THOMAS LINLEY (i), was so popular that Sheridan delayed its publication for nearly 20 years to prevent pirating. With his permission, however, *The Duenna* was translated into an Italian opera, *La governante* (1779), by Carlo Francesco Badini and set by Francesco Bertoni. Later settings of the play include those by Roberto Gerhard (1949) and T. N. Khrennikov (1983).

Sheridan's lifelong ambition, which was unfulfilled, was to control the London patent theatres. As a first step he bought Garrick's interest in Drury Lane in 1776. But the most coveted prize was the King's Theatre in the Haymarket, the Italian opera house. In January 1778 he agreed with Thomas Harris (principal owner and manager of Covent Garden, the other patent theatre) to purchase a majority interest in the Haymarket. They completed the transaction on borrowed money, saddling the theatre with mounting debts from which it never recovered. Unfamiliar with the world of Italian opera and illiterate in the Italian language, Sheridan appointed Antoine Le Texier to run the artistic side of the company. In 1781 he brought the later notorious WILLIAM TAYLOR into the company as comptroller, which only exacerbated its financial problems. By then, however, Sheridan was deeply involved in the day-to-day running of the theatre and was even taking artistic decisions. In 1781 the tenor Giovanni Ansani refused to sing in Sacchini's *Mitridate* with his rival and enemy Francesco Roncaglia, a castrato; Sheridan's suggestion for a new scene for Ansani pleased no one. At the end of the season, he handed over his interest in the opera house to Taylor, whose even less competent management soon led to the theatre's bankruptcy with even the principal performers' salaries unpaid – an inevitable result of Sheridan's unsecured purchase of the house. The playwright had no further involvement with Italian opera until 1791–2 when, as co-proprietor of Drury Lane and a man of considerable political and social influence, he helped arrange the so-called Opera Settlement: Italian opera was re-established at the new Haymarket theatre after the Pantheon opera house fire of January 1792. Sheridan's actual connection with opera was brief, but the ruinous debts with which he saddled the King's Theatre, Haymarket, were to have a disastrous effect on opera in London for fully 60 years.

*

F. H. W. Sheppard, ed.: *Survey of London*, xxix, xxx (London, 1960)

C. Price, ed.: *The Letters of Richard Brinsley Sheridan* (Oxford, 1966)

——: *The Dramatic Works of Richard Brinsley Sheridan* (London, 1973)

CURTIS PRICE

Shicoff, Neil (*b* New York, 2 June 1949). American tenor. He studied at the Juilliard School, where he sang in Thomson's *Lord Byron* (1972). In 1975, after making his professional début in Washington as Narraboth, he sang Ernani at Cincinnati and Paco (*La vida breve*) at Santa Fe. He made his Metropolitan début in 1976 as Rinuccio, later singing the Duke, Lensky, Massenet's Des Grieux, Werther, Hoffmann, Don Carlos, Faust and Cavaradossi (1991). Since making his Covent Garden début in 1978 as Pinkerton, he has sung Rodolfo, Macduff, Alfredo, the Duke and Hoffmann, one of his finest roles, which he has also sung in Florence, Hamburg and Barcelona and at the Opéra Bastille (1992). He sang Werther, another favourite role, at Houston, Zürich, Vienna and Aix-en-Provence and made his début at Chicago (1979) as Rodolfo, at San Francisco (1981) as Edgardo (*Lucia*) and at the Paris Opéra (1981) as Romeo. His voice, at first essentially lyrical, has developed and darkened so that he can take on heavier roles such as Don José, which he first sang at Seattle (1987) and repeated at Macerata and Nîmes; and Rodolfo (*Luisa Miller*), which he sang at Amsterdam (1991).

*

G. D. Lipton: 'Playing to Win', *ON*, xlviii/9 (1983–4), 8

RICHARD LeSUEUR/ELIZABETH FORBES

Shield, William (*b* Swalwell, nr Newcastle upon Tyne, 5 March 1748; *d* London, 25 Jan 1829). English composer. As the son of a music teacher, he learnt the rudiments of music early, but he was apprenticed to a boat builder, Edward Davison of South Shields, after the death of his father in 1757. He eventually resumed musical studies with Charles Avison of Newcastle, playing the violin in local concerts. After finishing his apprenticeship he became leader of the theatre band and conductor of the concerts first at Scarborough and then at Durham. During this time he made the acquaintance of the radical Thomas Holcroft, an actor and author who was later to provide him with the chance to compose a comic opera for London. In 1771 Shield moved to London to play second violin at the King's Theatre, transferring to principal viola the following season. He held that position for 18 years, even after replacing Michael Arne as house composer to Covent Garden in autumn 1784. The position at Covent Garden paid him £7 a week, and he remained in it until summer 1797 (except for the 1791–2 season, when, after an altercation with the manager, he left to travel in Europe).

Shield's first comic opera, *The Crisis* (1778), was a collaboration with his old friend Holcroft and did not see print. Like all comic operas in England, it had spoken dialogue instead of recitative. The next project, however, brought Shield to public notice. *The Flitch of Bacon* stole the 1778 summer season at the Haymarket and became one of the theatre's most profitable and often performed pieces. This pasticcio typifies much of Shield's theatrical writing: of the afterpiece's 14 musical numbers, nine are by Shield, the rest being borrowed from an assortment of sources, including Italian opera, Tudor songbooks and British folksong. Shield emphasized the military slant of the libretto with appropriate rhythms that contrast nicely with the numerous pastoral and romantic pieces in 6/8, and the older borrowings reflect the traditional roots of the Dunmow flitch tradition.

Rosina (1782), Shield's most often performed work, follows the same blend of charming original and borrowed music, with perhaps more Irish and Scots traditional songs than were usually heard at the theatres royal. The overture contains a folktune, to be played while bassoons imitate the bagpipe, which was revised and attached to the poem 'Auld Lang Syne' after Robert Burns's death. As *Rosina* shows, Shield already excelled in harmonizing traditional music without destroying its character. He could also write more complex, italianate arias like 'When William at eve' and 'Light as Thistledown'. Unlike some earlier comic opera composers, Shield did not fall into the habit of assigning traditional ballads to rustics and italianate arias to the gentry: in *Rosina*, all the principal characters sing both types of music, and the blend seemed to please audiences. *Rosina* and its successor, *The Poor Soldier*, were the afterpieces most often performed in the London theatres (over 200 performances each in less than 20 years). According to the Covent Garden accounts, Shield received £100 for the music (not £40, as Parke claimed in his memoirs) six months after the opera opened.

The Poor Soldier (1783) relied on an Irish slant in the music to reflect its setting, and O'Keeffe claimed to have sung to Shield tunes that he remembered from his youth in Ireland so that they could be used in the opera (Fiske, 1973, traced the sources of many). Also, the presence of John Johnstone, a successful tenor in the Covent Garden company, no doubt encouraged Shield to write Irish parts for him. Shield was greatly interested in preserving musical heritages, both in his theatrical work and in his collaborations with the antiquarian Joseph Ritson. Together they edited *Select Collection of English Songs* (London, 1783) and *Scotish Songs* (London, 1794). He incorporated in his comic operas much native folk music, which Isaac Bickerstaff, the creator of comic opera in the 1760s, had regarded as a tasteless abomination. Shield's work with O'Keeffe included many works with Celtic settings that allowed for appropriate music: *Love in a Camp* (1786), *The Highland Reel* (1788), *The Lad of the Hills* (1796). Shield could also mimic the folk idiom. For example, 'Sweet Transports' from *Rosina* makes generous use of the Scotch snap. The song in *The Farmer* (1787) about a ploughboy with social and political aspirations was arranged by Benjamin Britten in a collection of folksongs. Other musical cultures also interested Shield: in *The Czar* (1790), a comic opera about Peter the Great's shipbuilding days in Deptford, he incorporated Russian folksongs, some obtained from Muzio Clementi.

Covent Garden needed to keep abreast of fashions to compete with Drury Lane, which had developed increasingly spectacular musical works, and as house composer, Shield provided music for the latest tastes in his comic operas and pantomimes. In the 1780s he wrote comic operas with rural settings and romantic plots about characters of obscure birth: the successful *Rosina* (1782) and the unsuccessful *The Noble Peasant* (1784). The pastoral operas displayed his talents best. When the Romantic movement began taking root, he wrote operas with medieval settings. *Robin Hood* (1784) stands as an early example, Shield no doubt having been influenced by Ritson's research into the ballads about Robin Hood. Some of his later gothic operas also had evocative music: *The Mysteries of the Castle* (1795) accented its Sicilian setting with the newly published tune 'Sicilian Mariners'.

Other operas made use of recent events. *The Highland Reel* (1788) followed soon upon the publication of Boswell's *Journal of a Tour to the Hebrides* (1786). *The Crusade* (1790) featured 'Turkish' rhythms that capitalized on the fact that Turkey had sent its first ambassador to London that year. *The Woodman* (1791) exploited the season's rage for female archery. This work borrows some devices from the rival theatre by adding spectacular onstage rainstorms and archery contests. The music contains the usual mix of borrowed operatic arias and folksongs interspersed with original glees and arias, but critics noted that music now had the primary, not the secondary, role, as was the case in works at Drury Lane. Shield's acquaintance Haydn saw a performance on 10 December 1791 with Elizabeth Billington in the role of Emily, and he complained about the sleepiness of the orchestra and the impertinence of the audience in the galleries. *The Italian Villagers* (1797) focusses on the newly fashionable Swiss Alps and contains patter songs and ensembles in the increasingly popular Mozartian style.

Although Shield experimented widely with orchestration and exotic flavours in his music, the operas that contained large doses of middlebrow glees, strophic songs and vaudeville finales succeeded best with Covent Garden audiences and established his fame. During the 1790s Drury Lane composers such as Stephen Storace set a more spectacular style that Shield could not, or would not, adopt, and after 1797, Shield retired as house composer to Covent Garden. He turned his talents to theoretical matters, publishing two anthology-textbooks of music: *An Introduction to Harmony* (London, 1800) and *The Rudiments of Thoroughbass* (London, 1815), which discuss such matters as how to harmonize folksongs. In 1817 Shield became Master of the King's Music, and in 1818 he wrote the last court ode. On his death he left his viola to George IV and his library to his wife, Ann Stokes Shield. He was buried in the south cloister of Westminster Abbey.

See also FLITCH OF BACON, THE and ROSINA.

mostly pasticcios with spoken dialogue; first performed in London unless otherwise stated; vocal scores published in London soon after performance

LCG – *Covent Garden* LDL – *Drury Lane*

aft – *afterpiece* mf – *musical farce*

The Shamrock, or The Anniversary of St Patrick (comic op aft, 2, J. O'Keeffe), Dublin, Crow Street, 15 April 1777, and LCG, 7 April 1783; as The Poor Soldier, LCG, 4 Nov 1783, vs/*R*1981 in Link; ed. W. Brasmer and W. Osborne (1978); music selected by librettist
The Crisis, or Love and Fear (comic op aft, 2, T. Holcroft), LDL, 1 May 1778
The Flitch of Bacon (comic op aft, 2, H. Bate, later Sir H. Bate Dudley), Haymarket, 17 Aug 1778, vs
The Cobler of Castlebury (mf, 2, C. Stuart), LCG, 27 April 1779, some music by Gehot
The Siege of Gibraltar (mf, 2, F. Pilon), LCG, 25 April 1780, vs
Rosina (comic op aft, 2, F. M. Brooke, after C.-S. Favart: *Les moissonneurs*), LCG, 31 Dec 1782, vs; ed. J. L. Hatton and J. Oxenford in English Ballad Operas (1874); MS orch parts *GB-Lbl*
The Campaign, or Love in the East Indies (comic op, 3, R. Jephson and N. Barry), Dublin, Smock Alley, 30 Jan 1784, and LCG, 12 May 1785, partly compiled by Tenducci, ov. by Haydn, 1 duet pubd; reduced as Love and War (aft, 2), LCG, 12 March 1787
Robin Hood, or Sherwood Forest (comic op, 3, L. MacNally and E. Lysaght, after popular ballads and O. Goldsmith: *The Vicar of Wakefield*), LCG, 17 April 1784, vs; ov. from Baumgarten: William and Nanny (1779); reduced (aft, 2), 28 Nov 1789
The Noble Peasant (comic op, 3, Holcroft), Haymarket, 2 Aug 1784, vs
Fontainbleau, or Our Way in France (comic op, 3, O'Keeffe), LCG, 16 Nov 1784, vs
The Nunnery (comic op aft, 2, W. Pearce), LCG, 12 April 1785, vs
The Choleric Fathers (comic op, 3, Holcroft), LCG, 10 Nov 1785, vs
Love in a Camp, or Patrick in Prussia (mf, 2, O'Keeffe), LCG, 17 Feb 1786; sequel to The Poor Soldier
Richard Coeur de Lion (comic op, 3, MacNally, after M.-J. Sedaine), LCG, 16 Oct 1786, vs; reduced (aft), 24 Oct 1786; free rev. of Grétry: Richard Coeur-de-lion
Nina (op aft, 1, B. J. Marsollier des Vivetières, trans. J. Wolcot), LCG, 24 April 1787, vs; after Dalayrac: Nina, ou La folle par amour, arr. with W. Parke
The Farmer (mf, 2, O'Keeffe), LCG, 31 Oct 1787, vs/*R*1981 in Link; ov. by T. Giordani
Marian (comic op aft, 2, Brooke), LCG, 22 May 1788, vs
The Highland Reel (comic op, 3, O'Keeffe), LCG, 6 Nov 1788, vs; reduced (aft, 3), 8 Dec 1788
The Prophet (comic op, 3, R. Bentley), LCG, 13 Dec 1788, vs; reduced (aft, 2), 4 Feb 1789; ov. by Salieri
The Czar (comic op, 3, O'Keeffe), LCG, 8 March 1790, 1 song pubd; reduced as The Fugitive (aft, 2), 4 Nov 1790; lib. printed as The Czar Peter
The Crusade (musical drama, 3, F. Reynolds), LCG, 6 May 1790, vs, part in full score
The Woodman (comic op, 3, H. Bate Dudley), LCG, 26 Feb 1791, vs
Hartford Bridge, or The Skirts of a Camp (mf, 2, Pearce), LCG, 3 Nov 1792, vs
The Midnight Wanderers (comic op aft, 2, Pearce), LCG, 25 Feb 1793, vs; ov. from J. G. Naumann: Amphion
To Arms, or The British Recruit (musical interlude, 1, T. Hurlstone), LCG, 3 May 1793; incl. music by T. Giordani and Dr Stevenson of Dublin; as The British Recruit, or Who's Afraid?, 16 March 1795
Sprigs of Laurel (comic op aft, 2, O'Keeffe), LCG, 11 May 1793, vs; reduced as The Rival Soldiers (musical entertainment, 1), 17 May 1797
The Travellers in Switzerland (comic op, 3, Bate Dudley), LCG, 22 Feb 1794, vs
Netley Abbey (mf, 2, Pearce), LCG, 10 April 1794, vs; ov. and 1 song by Parke, finale by W. Howard
Arrived at Portsmouth (mf, 2, Pearce), LCG, 30 Oct 1794; reduced (1), 13 Jan 1796
The Mysteries of the Castle (musical drama, 3, M. P. Andrews and Reynolds), LCG, 31 Jan 1795, vs
The Irish Mimic, or Blunders at Brighton (mf, 2, O'Keeffe), LCG, 23 April 1795
Lock and Key (mf, 2, P. Hoare), LCG, 2 Feb 1796, vs; ov. by Parke
The Lad of the Hills, or The Wicklow Gold Mine (comic op, 3, O'Keeffe), LCG, 9 April 1796, vs; reduced as The Wicklow Mountains (aft, 2), 7 Oct 1796; Act 2 finale by Parke
Abroad and at Home (comic op, 3, J. G. Holman), LCG, 19 Nov 1796, vs
The Italian Villagers (comic op, 3, Hoare), LCG, 25 April 1797
The Village Fete (occasional interlude, 1, R. Cumberland), LCG, 18 May 1797, to commemorate the marriage of the Princess Royal
Two Faces under a Hood (comic op, 3, T. Dibdin), LCG, 17 Nov 1807, vs

*

BDA; *DNB* (R. Legge); *ES* (R. Brindle); *LS*; *NicollH*
J. O'Keeffe: *Recollections of the Life of John O'Keeffe* (London, 1826)
W. T. Parke: *Musical Memoirs* (London, 1830)
C. Pohl: *Mozart und Haydn in London* (Vienna, 1867)
J. Robinson: *Life of William Shield* (Newcastle upon Tyne, 1891)
M. Winesanker: *The Record of English Musical Drama, 1750–1800* (diss., Cornell U., 1944)
——: 'Musico-Dramatic Criticism of English Comic Opera, 1750–1800', *JAMS*, ii (1949), 87–96
G. Hauger: 'William Shield', *ML*, xxxi (1950), 337–42
R. Fiske: *English Theatre Music in the Eighteenth Century* (London, 1973, 2/1986)
H. C. R. Landon: *Haydn: Chronicle and Works*, iii: *Haydn in England, 1791–95* (London, 1975)
S. Hall: *English Dialogue Opera, 1762–96* (diss., U. of Toronto, 1980)
F. Link, ed.: *The Plays of John O'Keeffe* (New York, 1981)
L. Troost: *The Rise of English Comic Opera, 1762–1800* (diss., U. of Pennsylvania, 1985) LINDA V. TROOST

Shilling, Eric (*b* London, 12 Oct 1920). English bass-baritone. He studied at the GSM with Walter Hyde and at the RCM with Dorothea Webb and Clive Carey, later with Frank Titterton. While still a student he made his début with Sadler's Wells Opera in 1945 as Marullo (*Rigoletto*) as part of six months' practical work. For several seasons he toured Britain and abroad with Intimate Opera as principal baritone and producer, performing in small-scale piano-accompanied repertory including specially composed works such as *Three's Company* by Antony Hopkins. From 1959 he was a regular principal with Sadler's Wells (later the ENO) for 30 years, with outstanding success in comedy roles including Don Pasquale, Gianni Schicchi, Frank (*Die Fledermaus*) and Jupiter (*Orphée aux enfers*), but embracing a large repertory from Leporello to Alberich and Daland. He sang Count Rostov in the first British performance of *War and Peace* in 1972 and created roles in *Our Man in Havana* and *The Violins of St Jacques* by Malcolm Williamson, Richard Rodney Bennett's *A Penny for a Song*, Gordon Crosse's *The Story of Vasco* and Holloway's *Clarissa* (Screwtape; 1990). He has toured in America and Australia, made numerous television appearances and recordings of character roles, and given more than 500 lecture-recitals with his wife, the soprano Erica Johns. His musical perception and clarity of diction are complemented by complete mastery of stagecraft. NOËL GOODWIN

Shilovsky, Konstantin Stepanovich [Loshivsky] (*b* 1849; *d* 1893). Russian amateur poet and actor. He was a close friend of Tchaikovsky. After trying strenuously to interest the composer in a grand-opera libretto he had concocted on a pseudo-biblical subject – *Ephraim*, after a scenario called *Tsaritsa ponevole* ('Empress against her Will') – Shilovsky won his meed of immortality by helping to adapt Pushkin's *Yevgeny Onegin* (1877), among other things writing Triquet's couplets for the first scene of Act 2 in Tchaikovsky's opera. His younger brother Vladimir (1852–93), a gifted musical amateur, took lessons in composition from Tchaikovsky, who complimented his pupil by incorporating a brief orchestral piece by Shilovsky as the entr'acte to Act 2 of *Oprichnik* (1874).

*

N. Kashkin: *Vospominaniya o P. I. Chaykovskom* [Reminiscences of Tchaikovsky] (Moscow, 1896)
P. Chaykovsky: Polnoye sobraniye sochineniy: literaturnïye proizvedeniya i perepiska [Complete Collection of Writings: Literary Works and Correspondence], v (Moscow, 1959)

RICHARD TARUSKIN

Shimell, William (*b* Brentwood, Essex, 23 Sept 1952). English baritone. After studying in London he made his début in 1980 with Kent Opera as an Usher (*Rigoletto*). He sang Young Scrooge in Musgrave's *Christmas Carol* (Sadler's Wells, 1981) and Count Almaviva at Glyndebourne (1984). He has sung with Opera North, Scottish Opera, the WNO and the ENO, in Paris and Amsterdam, and at La Scala, where he sang Baron Dourlinski (Cherubini's *Lodoïska*) in 1991, and Covent Garden, where he made his début in 1985 as Schaunard, returning as Guglielmo, Albert (*Werther*) and the Count in *Capriccio*, which he also sang in San Francisco (1990). His repertory includes Mozart's Figaro, Papageno, Dandini, Malatesta, Mercutio, Tomsky, Marcello, Sharpless and Nick Shadow. His incisive, flexible voice and handsome stage presence make him an ideal Don Giovanni. ELIZABETH FORBES

Shimizu, Osamu (*b* Osaka, 4 Nov 1911; *d* Tokyo, 29 Oct 1986). Japanese composer. The son of a gagaku player, he became familiar with traditional Japanese music early on and studied European music at the Tokyo Music School (1936–9). In 1939 he won a prize at the Mainichi Music Competition with an orchestral work, but he soon established himself primarily as a composer of vocal music. Indeed, his choral pieces are among the most frequently performed Japanese works, a position they owe to their memorable melodies, smooth harmony, familiar subjects (legendary or Romantic) and generally popular character; among the most successful is *Yama ni inoru* ('The Prayer to the Mountains') for reciter, male chorus and orchestra (1960).

After World War II Shimizu became more interested in dramatic music, composing more than a dozen operas and operettas. His first opera, *Shuzenji monogatari* ('The Tale of Shuzenji'), won the National Art Festival Prize in 1954 and has been one of the more successful in postwar Japan. He then composed a series of shorter operettas and chamber operas, based on folklore or fairy-tale, all written for a small number of singers with a small instrumental ensemble. Some of these works have become popular because of their adaptability to a simpler presentation and for their intimate and easy musical style, for example *Sumiyaki-hime* ('Princess Sumiyaki', 1956) and *Sero-hiki no Gōshu* ('Gōshu the Cellist', 1957), which uses Japanese instruments (koto and percussion) within a European orchestra. *Shunkan* (1965), after a kabuki play with a tragic historical figure as the title role, was successful primarily because of its dramatic role for baritone.

In 1968, at the invitation of the University of California, Shimizu composed a comic opera, *Muko erabi* ('The Marriage Contest'); it was performed by young Japanese singers with the Los Angeles SO at five theatres in California. In 1970 he wrote *Daibutsu kaigan* ('The Great Image of Buddha') for the government-sponsored Art Festival. Dealing with an 8th-century story about the building of the great Buddha in Nara it was the most ambitious of his works, though it was not successful. The works on a more modest scale which followed were better received, including *Yokobue* (1973), a mono-opera for soprano, and *Kicchomu shōten* ('The Assumption of Kicchomu', 1973), commissioned by a company in Ōita and based on an Ōitan folktale.

See also SHUZENJI MONOGATARI.

performed in Tokyo unless otherwise stated; most autograph MSS in Tokyo, Nihon Kindai Ongakukan Documentation Centre of Modern Japanese Music

Shuzenji monogatari [The Tale of Shuzenji] (1, Kidō Okamoto), Osaka, Asahi Hall, 4 Nov 1954, vs (Tokyo, 1962)
Sumiyaki-hime [Princess Sumiyaki] (operetta, 1, N. Uno), NHK, 1 Nov 1956; stage, Nihon Seinenkan Hall, 11 Oct 1957, vs (Tokyo, 1956)
Aozora o utsu otoko [The Man who Shoots the Blue Sky] (radio op, 1, S. Tanigawa), ABC, 26 Nov 1956; stage, Nihon Seinenkan, 24 April 1959
Sero-hiki no Gōshu [Gōshu the Cellist] (1, K. Miyazawa), Nihon Seinenkan, 11 Oct 1957
Sunekotanpako [The Little Demon of a Child] (radio op, 1, I. Wakabayashi), NHK, 10 Nov 1961
Utai gaikotsu [The Singing Skeleton] (chamber op, 1, Kazuhiko Okamoto), NHK, 26 Nov 1961; stage, Metropolitan Festival Hall, 15 March 1962 [pt 3 of Mittsuno mukashiko (Three Old Tales); pt 1 by Moroī; pt 2 by Irino]
Shunkan [Shunkan, the exile] (1, Shimizu and Kazuhiko Okamoto, after a kabuki), Metropolitan Festival Hall, 9 March 1965
Yûfuku shijin [Merciful Poet] (radio operetta, 1, Kazuhiko Okamoto, after R. Kōda), NHK Nagoya, Dec 1965
Muko erabi [The Marriage Contest] (1, Kazuhiko Okamoto), Riverside, CA, University, 3 Oct 1968
Daibutsu kaigan [The Great Image of Buddha] (3, H. Nagata), Nissei, 2 Oct 1970
Ikutagawa [The Ikuta River] (chamber op, 1, Kazuhiko Okamoto, after O. Mori), Metropolitan Festival Hall, Small Hall, 10 Nov 1971
Yokobue (mono-op, 1, Kazuhiko Okamoto, after C. Takayama), Yûbin Chokin Hall, 15 June 1973
Kicchomu shōten [The Assumption of Kicchomu] (2, H. Sakata), Ōita, Kenmin Opera, 1 Oct 1973
Shishi-odori no hajimari [The Origin of the Deer Dance] (1, H. Terasaki, after K. Miyazawa), Yûbin Chokin Hall, 4 Oct 1978
Yama ni inoru [The Prayer to the Mountains], 1979 (chamber op, 1, Shimizu, after his choral suite), unperf.
Kaguyahime [Princess Kaguya], 1980 (chamber op, 1, H. Terasaki), unperf. MASAKATA KANAZAWA

Shirinsky, Vasily Petrovich (*b* Ekaterinodar [now Krasnodar], 17 Jan 1901; *d* Mamontovka, nr Moscow, 16 Aug 1965). Russian composer. He studied at the Moscow Conservatory until 1928, and from 1923 was second violinist in the Conservatory Quartet, later named the Beethoven Quartet. He taught at the Conservatory from 1939 and led the Soviet RSO (1932–6), working at the Stanislavsky Opera Theatre at the same time. Other appointments took him to the music department of the Red Army Central Theatre (1939–41) and the Komsomol Theatre (1943–4). He wrote two operas (neither performed), for which he also provided the librettos: *P'yer i Lyus* ('Pierre and Louise', 1943–6; after R. Rolland) and *Ivan Grozniy* ('Ivan the Terrible', 1951–4; after A. Tolstoy). DETLEF GOJOWY

Shirley, George (Irving) (*b* Indianapolis, IN, 18 April 1934). American tenor. He studied in Washington and New York, making his début in 1959 as Eisenstein at Woodstock, New York. In 1960 he sang Rodolfo at the Teatro Nuovo, Milan, and in 1961 made his New York City Opera and San Francisco débuts in the same role. At Spoleto he sang Herod (1961) and Don José (1962). In 1961 he also sang in Verdi's *Aroldo* (New York) and made his Metropolitan début as Ferrando; later roles there included Don Ottavio, Alfredo, Pinkerton, Romeo and Almaviva. At Santa Fe he sang Alwa in *Lulu* (1963), then Apollo in *Daphne* (1964) and Leandro in Henze's *König Hirsch* (1965), all American premières. He made his British début at Glyndebourne in 1966 as Tamino, then sang Idomeneus and Percy (*Anna Bolena*) there. Having made his Covent Garden début in 1967 as Don Ottavio, he returned for David (*Die Meistersinger*), Pelléas and Loge, which he repeated in Berlin (1984). He created Romilayu in Kirchner's *Lily* (New York City Opera, 1977). He had a bright-toned voice of considerable dramatic power and acted intelligently.

ALAN BLYTH

Shirley, James (*b* London, bap. 7 Sept 1596; *d* London, bur. 29 Oct 1666). English dramatist. After spending two years as a schoolmaster at St Albans he settled in London in 1625 and started to write plays, 34 of which are extant. In 1634 he provided the text for an elaborate masque, *The Triumph of Peace* (set by William Lawes and Simon Ives), which was staged by the Inns of Court, as a demonstration of their loyalty to the crown, at Whitehall on 3 February 1634 and in the Merchants' Hall a few days later (ed. M. Lefkowitz, *Trois masques à la cour de Charles Ier d'Angleterre*, Paris, 1970). It consisted of a series of unrelated spectacular scenes and marks a decline in the masque form. Many details of the performance are preserved in the papers of Bulstrode Whitelocke (see Lefkowitz 1965).

Because of the Civil War, Shirley reverted to schoolteaching in 1644, and his last dramatic works were designed for school performance. These included two masques: *The Triumph of Beautie*, with music partly by William Lawes (published in 1646) and *Cupid and Death* (with music by Christopher Gibbons). The latter was given privately on 26 March 1653 and revived, with additional music by Matthew Locke, in 1659. Both these masques were less elaborate and more dramatic than the later court masques had been. In *Cupid and Death* especially, speech and music, masque and antimasque are integrated into a consistent dramatic plot to form the most important English work of its kind at that period (ed. in MB, ii, 1951, 2/1965).

*

BurneyH
A. H. Nason: *James Shirley, Dramatist: a Biographical and Critical Study* (New York, 1915)
E. J. Dent: *Foundations of English Opera* (Cambridge, 1928)
M. Lefkowitz: *William Lawes* (London, 1960)
——: 'The Longleat Papers of Bulstrode Whitelocke: New Light on Shirley's *Triumph of Peace*', *JAMS*, xviii (1965), 42–60
A. J. Sabol: 'New Documents on Shirley's Masque "The Triumph of Peace"', *ML*, xlvii (1966), 10–26
L. Potter: 'The Triumph of Peace and The Cruel War: Masque and Parody', *Notes and Queries*, ccxxv (1980), 345–8

MARGARET LAURIE

Shirley-Quirk, John (*b* Liverpool, 28 Aug 1931). English bass-baritone. He studied with Roy Henderson and made his début in 1962 at Glyndebourne as the Doctor (*Pelléas et Mélisande*). For the English Opera Group he created the Ferryman (*Curlew River*, 1964), Shadrach (*The Burning Fiery Furnace*, 1966), the Father (*The Prodigal Son*, 1968) and seven baritone roles in *Death in Venice* (1973), which he also sang at the Metropolitan (1974). He created Spencer Coyle in *Owen Wingrave* (BBC Television, 1971), repeating the role at Covent Garden (1973), where he created Lev in *The Ice Break* (1977) and sang the High Priest (*Alceste*) and Rangoni (*Boris Godunov*). For Scottish Opera he sang Count Almaviva, Don Alfonso (also for the Glyndebourne touring company), Mittenhofer (*Elegy for Young Lovers*), Golaud and Yevgeny Onegin. He was appointed CBE in 1975. He had a mellow voice, refined phrasing and intensity of expression. In 1982 he became an associate artistic director of the Aldeburgh Festival. ALAN BLYTH

Shirreff [Shireff], **Jane** (*b* 1811; *d* London, 23 Dec 1883). Scottish soprano. Her operatic début was at Covent Garden as Mandane in Arne's *Artaxerxes* (1831). Until 1838 she sang at Covent Garden or Drury Lane Theatre as well as at the Philharmonic Concert and the Concert of Ancient Music. Her American début (1838) was in the title role of W. M. Rooke's *Amilie* which was the operatic and theatrical hit of the season. Shirreff subsequently spent 20 highly successful months touring with John Wilson (who assumed the role of her protector), appearing in English opera and concerts in New York, Boston, Providence, RI, Washington, DC, Baltimore, Philadelphia, Charleston, SC, and elsewhere. An attractive and skilful actress, she had perfect intonation and a voice that was full-toned and powerful; her upper notes were described as 'clear and bell-like'. According to Ireland she was the 'most admired English prima donna between the days of Mrs Wood and those of Louisa Pyne'. She returned to England in May 1840, married and retired from the stage.

*

J. N. Ireland: *Records of the New York Stage from 1750 to 1860* (New York, 1866–7)
J. D. Brown and S. S. Stratton: *British Musical Biography: A Dictionary of Musical Artists, Authors, and Composers* (London, 1897)
K. K. Preston: *Travelling Opera Troupes in the United States, 1825–1860* (diss., City U. of New York, 1989)

KATHERINE K. PRESTON

Shnitke, Al'fred [Schnittke, Alfred] (*b* Engel's, 24 Nov 1934). Russian composer. His musical education began in 1946 in Vienna, where his German-born father worked for two years as a journalist; among his strongest impressions from that time was a performance of *Die Entführung aus dem Serail* conducted by Knappertsbusch. He then studied choral conducting in Moscow and from 1953 attended the Moscow Conservatory (instrumentation with Nikolay Rakov, counterpoint and composition with Yevgeny Golubev, with whom he remained for postgraduate studies, 1958–61). He also met Filipp Herschkowitz, the Romanian-born Webern pupil who gave many Russian composers their first encounter with the music of the Second Viennese School. From 1962 until 1972 Shnitke taught composition and theoretical subjects at the conservatory; he also wrote several articles on Russian and Western contemporary music.

His own music is intensely dramatic and has a direct emotional appeal. At first blending modernist techniques with more traditional rhythmic and gestural invention, his style underwent a change in the late 1960s, incorporating quotations, pastiche and juxtaposed historical references in a manner summed up by the composer as 'polystylistic'. This principle has exerted an enormous influence in Shnitke's homeland, and he came to enjoy the highest international reputation of any Russian composer since Shostakovich. In 1985 he suffered the first of several strokes, which have slowed but by no means halted his prolific output. In 1989 he moved to Hamburg where he took charge of a composition class at the conservatory.

Though known mainly for his orchestral and chamber works, including five symphonies and numerous concertos, Shnitke has also composed a small number of ballet and theatre scores and two operas. His first opera was completed in 1962 in piano score but was neither orchestrated nor staged. Entitled *Odinnadtsataya zapoved'* ('The 11th Commandment') and to a libretto by Marina Churova, Georgy Anisimov and the composer, it is concerned with the conscience of a pilot who has dropped an atom bomb. *Zhizn' s idiotom* ('Life with an Idiot') is based on a 1980 novella by Viktor Yerofeyev, who also provided the libretto. For an unspecified offence a university lecturer ('I') and his wife are forced to share their flat with an asylum patient (Vova) who then wrecks their marriage, sleeps with both in turn, murders the wife and leaves 'I' insane. In the first production, by Netherlands Opera conducted by Mstislav Rostropovich (Amsterdam, Muziektheater, 13 April 1992), the director Boris Pokrovsky underlined the element of political satire by presenting Vova as a caricature of Lenin. Shnitke's episodic and parodistic setting suggests the continuing influence of Shostakovich's Gogol opera *The Nose*. A longstanding project for an opera on the Faust legend remains unrealized.

*

'... und möchte nicht darüber sprechen', *Musik für die Oper? Mit Komponisten im Gespräch*, ed. G. Belkius and U. Liedtke (Berlin, 1990), 243 [interview on Shnitke's projected Faust opera]

V. Kholopova and Ye. Chigaryova: *Al'fred Shnitke: ocherk zhizni i tvorchestva* [Al'fred Shnitke: a Sketch of his Life and Work] (Moscow, 1990)

DAVID FANNING

Shostakovich, Dmitry (**Dmitriyevich**) (*b* St Petersburg, 12/25 Sept 1906; *d* Moscow, 9 August 1975). Russian composer. His central importance as a composer of symphonic and chamber music is not matched by his contribution to opera, which was greatly affected by his brush with political authority in the 1930s.

1. Early works. 2. Later projects.

1. Early works. A precocious musical talent, Shostakovich enrolled in 1919 at the Petrograd Conservatory, where he studied the piano with Leonid Nikolayev and composition with Maximilian Shteynberg; he graduated as a pianist in 1923. His diploma work for the composition course, the Symphony no.1 (1925), was first performed successfully in Leningrad in 1926, conducted by Nikolay Mal'ko, and helped launch his international career, a career both spectacular and unique in the spotlight it cast, and continues to cast, on the conflict between the aesthetic prerogatives of the creative artist and his indenture to the social and political demands of the state. Chiefly acclaimed as one of the finest symphonists of the 20th century, with his cycle of 15 symphonies spanning more than 40 years from 1925 to 1971, as well as the composer of an equally impressive cycle of 15 string quartets, composed between 1938 and 1974, and much other symphonic and chamber music, Shostakovich began his career as one of the most promising operatic composers of the century.

He was attracted to the theatre early. Among surviving juvenilia – composed before commencing studies at the conservatory – is an undistinguished setting of three numbers for *Tsïgane* ('The Gypsies'; *c*1918–19), a projected opera based on the poem by Alexander Pushkin. As a student and young professional in the 1920s, a period noted for innovatory experiments in the Soviet dramatic theatre, Shostakovich followed the latest developments avidly. His first completed opera, a setting of Nikolay Gogol's comic story *Nos* ('The Nose') op.15, was a deliberate experiment designed to inject modernistic freshness and vitality into Soviet opera. Composed in 1927–8 to a libretto by the composer, Yevgeny Zamyatin, Georgy Ionin and Alexander Preys, the absurd tale of a petty bureaucrat who wakes one morning to find his nose missing and the scandalous adventures of his personified proboscis on the streets of 19th-century St Petersburg was an unlikely subject for an opera. Clearly influenced by the theatrical principles of Vsevolod Meyerhold, at whose Moscow theatre he was employed as a pianist in the winter of 1928 while still working on his opera, Shostakovich spoke of *The Nose* as a 'theatre symphony', a work in which music and text were evenly balanced. The musical language – showing the influences of Stravinsky and Berg as well as that of popular idioms – was astringent and angular, grotesque in its emphasis on musical parody and the clash of tone-colour extremes. Also evident was the composer's sure grasp of fast-paced, 'cinematic' timing, a skill he may have absorbed as a student during long hours accompanying silent films to support his impoverished family.

By the time *The Nose* was staged, after elaborate preparations, at the Malïy Theatre, Leningrad, in January 1930, tolerance of modernistic experiments in the Soviet arts had succumbed to the strident polemics of the self-appointed proletarian cultural watchdogs. *The Nose*, an opera with a subtle and sophisticated musical language that made no pretence at immediate mass accessibility and with no obvious relevance to the socialist agenda, was an obvious target for these critics. Despite enthusiastic support among the artistic intelligentsia, *The Nose* did not provide a foundation for the development of Soviet opera nor did it establish itself in the repertory; it ran for 16 performances before it was withdrawn by early 1931. It was performed in numerous Western cities in the 1960s and was successfully rehabilitated in the Soviet Union in 1974 in a production prepared with the participation of the composer and conducted by Gennady Rozhdestvensky at the Moscow Chamber Opera Theatre.

Though disappointed by the failure of his first opera – his request to the Malïy's administration for the withdrawal of *The Nose* from the repertory as early as April 1930 went unheeded – Shostakovich immediately applied the valuable lessons he had learnt to his next operatic project, an adaptation of Nikolay Leskov's *Ledi Makbet Mtsenskogo uyezda* ('Lady Macbeth of the Mtsensk District') which he began in late 1930. While he turned again to 19th-century Russian literature for his topic, claiming that a search for worthy librettos on contemporary subjects had proved fruitless, his approach to the literary source differed significantly from that of *The Nose*. There Shostakovich strove for fidelity to the letter and spirit of Gogol's original. In *Lady Macbeth*, he deliberately reinterpreted Leskov's story of the passion and murderous brutality of Katerina Izmaylova, the wife of a provincial merchant. Whereas Leskov's Katerina is vile and her actions indefensible, Shostakovich sought to transform the heroine, who murders husband and father-in-law to sustain the liaison with her serf lover, into the victim of her social environment in 19th-century Russia, misguided in her quest for love but deserving of the spectators' sympathy. Collaborating again with Alexander Preys on the libretto, the composer made small but significant changes to the plot.

It was the music, however, that was intended to humanize the heroine by distinguishing her from those around her. Labelling his opera a 'tragedy-satire', Shostakovich reserved music of poignancy and lyrical feeling for his heroine, painting her family, lover, workers, police and clergy, by contrast, as grotesque caricatures with his most acerbic music. While it retained the momentum and cinematic pacing of *The Nose* as well as other stylistic similarities, *Lady Macbeth* – with a realistic, action-packed plot plus generous doses of sex and violence, all set in a more accessible tonal framework – was intended to appeal to a wider audience than its predecessor.

Shostakovich worked on the opera for two years, completing it in December 1932. He contemplated it initially as the first of a trilogy (later expanded to a tetralogy) of operas examining the lot of women at different periods of Russian history, to culminate with an opera about the new Soviet woman. *Lady Macbeth* was produced simultaneously in two cities. In Leningrad, Smolich, Dmitriyev and Samosud, the same collaborators who had mounted the composer's first opera, teamed up again to present the première of the opera at the Malïy Theatre on 22 January 1934. This was followed two days later by the première of the production alternatively entitled 'Katerina Izmaylova' at the Stanislavsky–Nemirovich-Danchenko Music Theatre, Moscow. Despite significant differences in approach, both productions enjoyed enormous success. In the two-year period after its première the opera received approximately 200 performances in Moscow and Leningrad; it was performed in Europe, Scandinavia, North and South America, and was widely hailed as the first major Soviet opera. Shostakovich, still under the age of 30, was an international celebrity.

On 26 December 1935 a second Moscow production was staged at the filial of the Bol'shoy Theatre, under the direction of Smolich. During January 1936, when the Malïy brought its production on tour to Moscow, three different versions were available to Moscow audiences. On 26 January 1936, Stalin, accompanied by an entourage of the government élite, attended a performance of the new, Bol'shoy production. Shostakovich was in attendance, but he did not have the opportunity to speak with the dignitaries, who left without explanation before the final act. His feeling of ominous foreboding was warranted; on 28 January 1936 the central government newspaper *Pravda* published a scathing attack, unsigned, on his opera, entitled 'Sumbur vmesto muzïki' ('Muddle instead of Music') that was to change the course not only of his own career but of Soviet cultural history. In an unprecedented stream of invective, the article savaged both the music and drama of Shostakovich's opera, its pretensions as social satire and as art worthy of the Soviet people. The broader political agenda implicit in its insinuated threats took effect immediately. During the early months of 1936, artists of all disciplines were required to study the 'historic document', to recant their own errors and condemn those of others. *Lady Macbeth* became the most prominent sacrificial victim in an official campaign to subjugate Soviet artists to the absolute creative control of the Communist Party and state, the symbolic catchword for artistic 'formalism', the unhealthy antithesis of the aesthetic principles of socialist realism demanded of all Soviet artists.

2. Later projects. Until the political imbroglio instigated by the condemnation of *Lady Macbeth* in 1936, the development of Shostakovich's compositional career had been closely linked to the theatre. In addition to his two operas, he had composed three ballet scores – the third of which, *Svetlïy ruchey* ('The Limpid Stream'), also became a conspicuous target in the 1936 cultural crackdown – incidental music for a range of dramatic productions, including a collaboration with Meyerhold and Vladimir Mayakovsky in 1929 on the staging of the latter's *Klop* ('The Bedbug'), and a half-dozen film scores. He had already been intrigued by the notion of creating a hybrid 'film-opera', not simply a film record of a staged operatic production, but a uniquely conceived fusion of the genres. He had demonstrated a penchant for comic and satiric subjects; among projects eventually abandoned was the comic opera *Bol'shaya molniya* ('The Big Lightning'), commissioned in 1932 by the Malïy Theatre on a libretto by N. Aseyev. The surviving fragments, discovered and first performed in concert by Rozhdestvensky in 1981, are closer in style to the music for dramatic theatre than to his operas, foreshadowing the tuneful style of his operetta *Moskva, Cheryomushki*, composed in 1958.

The most obvious result of the attack on *Lady Macbeth*, after the inevitable removal of the work from the repertory, was that Shostakovich – one of the most original and talented dramatic composers of his generation – abandoned his idea of an operatic cycle about Russian women and never completed another opera, an incalculable loss for operatic posterity. He did not recant publicly or denounce *Lady Macbeth*. His Fifth Symphony, first performed on 21 October 1937, became the vehicle for a triumphant public rehabilitation. It marked a broad shift – along with the Fourth Symphony, completed in 1936 but withdrawn from rehearsal and first performed only in 1961 – in the composer's emphasis from theatrical to instrumental genres; his natural dramatic instincts were henceforth sublimated in his symphonies and chamber music. It also signalled the shift from the whimsical humour of much of his youthful music to the tragic intensity of that of his mature years.

After its suppression, *Lady Macbeth* remained unperformed in the Soviet Union until after Stalin's death. In late 1954, immediately after the death of his first wife, to whom he had dedicated *Lady Macbeth*, Shostakovich dusted off his opera and began to make revisions. He polished passages of awkward vocal scoring, purged some of the more offensive naturalistic text, and composed two new entr'actes. Various schemes to stage the revised version in the mid-1950s proved premature; the political climate had not yet thawed sufficiently to allow the opera's rehabilitation. The revised opera, which uses a distinctive title and opus number, *Katerina Izmaylova* op.114, finally received its official première in January 1963 at the Stanislavsky–Nemirovich-Danchenko Music Theatre, Moscow, directed by L. Mikhaylov and conducted by Gennady Provatorov. In the West the composer's designation of the revised opera as the definitive one has been discounted and in recent years the original version has found greater favour.

Shostakovich's determination to avoid the operatic genre after 1936 was not unyielding. There was rarely a time in his career when he was not at least contemplating an operatic project. Among the subjects to which he devoted more than passing attention were *Volochayevskiye dni* ('Volochayev Days'), an opera contracted by the Kirov Theatre in 1937 concurrent with his work on the film of the same name; *Katyusha Maslova*, undertaken in 1940, to a libretto by Anatoly Mariengof about the heroine of Lev Tolstoy's novel 'Resurrection'; *Tikhiy Don* ('Quiet Flows the Don'), a 1964 project on a libretto by Yu. Lukin and A. Medvedev featuring different episodes taken from the same Sholokhov novel as Dzerzhinsky's opera of the same name; and *Chyornïy monakh* ('The Black Monk'), a story by Anton Chekhov, one of Shostakovich's favourite authors. He was attracted by the musical and structural properties of this story as early as the 1940s, but definite plans for an opera apparently took shape only in 1972, and proceeded as far as the arrangement of the Serenade by Gaetano Braga, central to Chekhov's story.

One project progressed well beyond the planning stages. Immediately after completing work on his Seventh Symphony (the 'Leningrad') in evacuation in Kuybïshev (now Samara) in December 1941, Shostakovich turned again to Gogol and commenced an operatic setting of his play about the cheating of a credulous card-sharper, *Igroki* ('The Gamblers'). Following in the traditions of Dargomïzhsky's setting of *The Stone Guest* and Musorgsky's musical 'realism', Shostakovich decided to set the play without adaptation or cuts. The musical style, tart and witty, harked back to that of *The Nose*. He continued work on the opera steadily through most of 1942, informing only his closest friends of its progress. In late 1942 Shostakovich abandoned work as abruptly as he had begun; having composed 50 minutes of music, setting less than a third of Gogol's text, he concluded that the dimensions of the completed opera would be too unwieldy. He subsequently incorporated themes from the unfinished setting in his last work, the Sonata for viola and piano (1975). The completed portion of *The Gamblers* was given its concert première in 1978; it was staged at the Moscow Chamber Theatre on 24 January 1990. A completion of Shostakovich's opera, making cuts in Gogol's play, was undertaken by the Polish composer Krzysztof Meyer in 1980–81 and was first performed at the Wuppertal Opernhaus in 1983.

Besides his own operas, Shostakovich became actively involved with the operas of others. His professional expertise and activity were instrumental in salvaging Dzerzhinsky's *Quiet Flows the Don* from humble beginnings and seeing it to the stage in 1935, all the more ironic as *Quiet Flows the Don* was the work that became the role model for Soviet opera after the condemnation of *Lady Macbeth*. After the death of his student Veniamin Fleyshman, defending Leningrad in the early days of World War II, Shostakovich rescued and completed Fleyshman's major work, *Rothschild's Violin*, a one-act opera on the story by Chekhov. His most extensive involvement, however, and the most telling in its influence on his own music, was with the operas of Modest Musorgsky, one of his favourite composers. On a commission from the Bol'shoy Theatre, in late 1939 Shostakovich respectfully undertook a new orchestration of Musorgsky's masterpiece *Boris Godunov* with the aim of fleshing out the original, minus Rimsky-Korsakov's accretions, into more contemporary, theatrically viable dimensions. Completed in 1940, Shostakovich's orchestration did not receive its first performance until 4 November 1959 at the Kirov Theatre, Leningrad. In the meantime, in 1958, he began an orchestration of *Khovanshchina* for a film version of the opera. He restored the cuts made by Rimsky-Korsakov, and re-composed the sections left incomplete by the composer, in the hope that the opera might find its way into the operatic repertory. The film was released in 1959 and Shostakovich's version of *Khovanshchina* was first staged at the Kirov on 25 November 1960. While *Boris* is performed most frequently now in Musorgsky's own orchestration, Shostakovich's version of *Khovanshchina* can indeed be credited with facilitating this opera's acceptance into the repertory.

See also GAMBLERS, THE; *KATERINA IZMAYLOVA*; *LADY MACBETH OF THE MTSENSK DISTRICT*; and *NOSE, THE*.

Nos [The Nose] op.15, 1927–8 (3, Shostakovich, Y. Zamyatin, G. Ionin and A. Preys, after N. V. Gogol), Leningrad, Malïy, 18 Jan 1930

Ledi Makbet Mtsenskogo uyezda [Lady Macbeth of the Mtsensk District] op.29, 1930–32 (4, Shostakovich and A. Preys, after N. Leskov), Leningrad, Malïy, 22 Jan 1934; rev. as Katerina Izmaylova op.114, 1955–63, Moscow, Stanislavsky–Nemirovich-Danchenko Music Theatre, 8 Jan 1963

Bol'shaya molniya [The Big Lightning], ?1931–2 (comic op, N. Aseyev), inc., concert performance of frags., Leningrad, Philharmonic Bol'shoy Hall, 11 Feb 1981

Igroki [The Gamblers], 1941–2 (after Gogol), inc., concert perf, Leningrad, Philharmonic Bol'shoy Hall, 18 Sept 1978 (concert perf.), Moscow, Chamber Music Theatre, 24 Jan 1990; completed by K. Meyer (3), Wuppertal, Opernhaus, 12 June 1983

Moskva, Cheryomushki, 1958 (operetta, V. Mass and M. Chervinsky), Moscow, Operetta, 24 Jan 1959

*

S. Gres: 'Ruchnaya bomba anarkhista' [The Hand Bomb of an Anarchist], *Rabochiy i teatr* (1930), no.10, p.6 [on *The Nose*]

D. Shostakovich and N. Mal'kov: *Nos: opera v 3 deystviyakh, 10 kartinakh po N. V. Gogolyu, muzïka D. Shostakovicha* (Leningrad, 1930) [incl. lib.]

D. Shostakovich, I. Sollertinsky and V. Dmitriyev: *'Nos': opera v 3-kh aktakh po N. V. Gogolyu, 15-ye sochineniye D. Shostakovicha* (Leningrad, 1930)

I. Sollertinsky: '"Nos" – orudiye dal'noboynoye' [*The Nose* – a Long-Range Gun], *Rabochiy i teatr* (1930), no.7, pp.6–7

D. Zhitomirsky: '"Nos" – opera D. Shostakovicha', *Proletarskiy muzïkant* (1930), nos.7–8, pp.33–9

M. Sokol'sky: 'Opera i kompozitor', *Sovetskoye iskusstvo* (16 Oct 1932); repr. in *Musorgsky, Shostakovich: stat'i, retsenzii* (Moscow, 1983), 85–8

A. Ostretsov: '"Ledi Makbet Mtsenskogo uyezda", opera Dmitriya Shostakovicha', *SovM* (1933), no.6, pp.9–32

B. Asaf'yev: 'O tvorchestve D. Shostakovicha i ego opere "Ledi Makbet Mtsenskogo uyezda"' [On Shostakovich's Composition and his Opera *Lady Macbeth*], *Ledi Makbet Mtsenskogo uyezda*, ed. S. N. Gisin (Leningrad, 1934), 27–31; repr. in *D. Shostakovich: stat'i i materialï*, ed. G. Shneerson (Moscow, 1976), 150–59

L. Kaltat, ed.: *Katerina Izmaylova* (Moscow, 1934) [incl. articles by Shostakovich, V. Nemirovich-Danchenko and A. Ostretsov]

D. Shostakovich and others: *Ledi Makbet Mtsenskogo uyezda* (Leningrad, 1934)
I. Sollertinsky: '"Ledi Makbet Mtsenskogo uyezda"', *Rabochiy i teatr* (1934), no.4, pp.2–3; repr. in idem: *Kriticheskiye stat'i*, ed. M. S. Druskin (Leningrad, 1963), 73–6
B. Asaf'yev: 'Volnuyushchiye voprosï' [Stirring Questions], *SovM* (1936), no.5, pp.24–7
'Sumbur vmesto muzïki ob opere "Ledi Makbet Mtsenskogo uyezda" D. Shostakovicha' [Muddle instead of Music: on Shostakovich's Opera *Lady Macbeth of the Mtsensk District*], *Pravda* (28 Jan 1936); *SovM* (1936), no.2, pp.4–5
V. Bogdanov-Berezovsky: 'Operï D. Shostakovicha', *Sovetskaya opera* (Leningrad and Moscow, 1940), 111–43
A. Veprik: 'Tri orkestrovïye redaktsii pervoy kartinï prologa operï Musorgskogo "Boris Godunov"' [Three Orchestral Editions of the First Scene of the Prologue of Musorgsky's Opera *Boris Godunov*], *Ocherki po voprosam orkestrovïkh stiley* [Essays on the Problems of Orchestral Styles] (Moscow, 1961, 2/1978), 75–125
K. Sakva: 'Novaya vstrecha s *Katerinoy Izmaylovoy*' [A New Encounter with *Katerina Izmaylova*], *SovM* (1963), no.3, pp.57–62; Ger trans. in *Musik und Gesellschaft*, xiii (1963), 428–32
G. Grigor'yeva: 'Pervaya opera Shostakovicha "Nos"' [Shostakovich's First Opera, *The Nose*], *Muzïka i sovremennost'* [Moscow], iii (1965), 68–103
N. Shumskaya: 'Traditsiya i novatorstvo v opere Shostakovicha "Katerina Izmaylova"' [Tradition and Innovation in *Katerina Izmaylova*], ibid, 104–21
G. Ordzhonikidze: 'Vesna tvorcheskoy zrelosti' [The Spring of Creative Maturity], *SovM* (1966), no.9, pp.38–48
M. Sabinina: 'Zametki ob opere "Katerina Izmaylova"' [Notes on *Katerina Izmaylova*], *Dmitry Shostakovich*, ed. L. Danilevich (Moscow, 1967), 132–66
V. Gurevich: 'Shostakovich v rabote nad "Khovanshchinoy"' [Shostakovich at Work on *Khovanshchina*], *Voprosï teorii i estetiki muzïki* [Leningrad], xi (1972), 84–108
L. Bubennikova: 'Meyyerkhol'd i Shostakovich: iz istorii sozdaniya operï "Nos"' [Meyerhold and Shostakovich: from the History of the Creation of the Opera *The Nose*], *SovM* (1973), no.3, pp.43–8
A. Bretanitskaya: 'O muzïkal'noy dramaturgii operï "Nos"' [On the Musical Dramaturgy of the Opera *The Nose*], *SovM* (1974), no.9, pp.47–53
L. Bubennikova: 'K probleme khudozhestvennogo vzaimodeystviya muzïkal'nogo i dramaticheskogo teatrov' [On the Problem of the Artistic Interaction of Musical and Dramatic Theatres], *Problemï muzïkal'noy nauki*, [Moscow], iii (1975), 38–63 [on Meyerhold and *The Nose*]
A. Bretanitskaya: 'Vtoroye rozhdeniye "Nosa"' [The Second Birth of *The Nose*], *Muzïka Rossii: muzïkal'noye tvorchestvo i muzïkal'naya zhizn' respublik Rossiyskoy Federatsii, 1973–74* [The Music of Russia: Musical Creations and Life in the Russian Republic], i (Moscow, 1976), 310–23
G. Fedorov: 'Vokrug i posle "Nosa"' [Around and After *The Nose*], *SovM* (1976), no.9, pp.41–50
L. Rotbaum: 'V poiskakh stsenicheskogo resheniya 'Katerinï Izmaylovoy' [In Search of Scenic Solutions for *Katerina Izmaylova*], *Muzïka Rossii*, i (Moscow, 1978), 337–51
A. Bogdanova: *Operï i baletï Shostakovicha* (Moscow, 1979)
——: 'Shostakovich: znakomïy i neznakomïy' [Shostakovich: Familiar and Unfamiliar], *Muzïkal'naya zhizn'* (1979), no.11, pp.8–9 [on *The Gamblers*]
G. Norris: 'Shostakovich's *The Nose*', *MT*, cxx (1979), 393–7
L. E. Fay: 'Musorgsky and Shostakovich', *Musorgsky: In Memoriam, 1881–1981*, ed. M. H. Brown (Ann Arbor, 1982), 215–26
E. Fischer: 'Engagement und ironische Distanz: Schostakowitsch: "Ledi Makbet Mzenskowo ujesda"', *Zur Problematik der Opernstruktur: das kunstlerische System und seine Krisis im 20. Jahrhundert* (Wiesbaden, 1982), 119–57
G. Norris: 'An Opera Restored: Rimsky-Korsakov, Shostakovich and the Khovansky Business', *MT*, cxxiii (1982), 672–5
——: 'The Operas', *Shostakovich: the Man and his Music*, ed. C. Norris (London, 1982), 105–24
A. Bretanitskaya: *'Nos' D. D. Shostakovicha* (Moscow, 1983)
A. Bogdanova: 'O nekotorïkh osobennostyakh stilya operï D. D. Shostakovicha "Igroki"' [On some Peculiarities of the Style of *The Gamblers*], *Muzïkal'nïy sovremennik* [Moscow], v (1984), 75–89; Ger trans. in *Sowjetische Musik: Betrachtungen und Analysen*, ed. H. Gerlach (Berlin, 1984), 162–9
R. S. Brown: 'The Three Faces of Lady Macbeth', *Russian and Soviet Music: Essays for Boris Schwarz* (Ann Arbor, 1984), 245–52
L. E. Fay: 'The Punch in Shostakovich's *Nose*', ibid, 229–45
G. Ordschonikidze: 'Das Operntheater Dmitri Schostakowitschs', *Dmitri Schostakowitsch 1984/5: wissenschaftliche Beiträge, Dokumente, Interpretationen, Programme* (Duisburg, 1984), 157–63
E. Kröplin: *Frühe sowjetische Oper: Prokofjew, Schostakowitsch* (Berlin, 1985)
L. D. Mikhaylov: '"Katerina Izmailova" D. D. Shostakovicha', *Sem' glav o teatre* [Seven Chapters on Theatre] (Moscow, 1985), 66–90
C. Emerson: 'Back to the Future: Shostakovich's Revision of Leskov's "Lady Macbeth of Mtsensk District"', *COJ*, i (1989), 59–78
I. D. Glikman: 'Kazn' "Ledi Makbet"' [The Execution of 'Lady Macbeth'], *Sovetskaya kul'tura* (23 Sept 1989)
I. Kharkhuta: 'K voprosu tonal'nosti v opere D. Shostakovicha "Nos"' *Problemï muzïkal'noy nauki*, vii (1989), 158–73
R. Taruskin: 'The Opera and the Dictator: the Peculiar Martyrdom of Dmitri Shostakovich', *New Republic* (20 March 1989)

LAUREL E. FAY

Shostakovich, Maxim (Dmitryevich) (*b* Leningrad [now St Petersburg], 10 May 1938). Russian conductor and pianist, son of Dmitry Shostakovich. He studied at the Moscow Conservatory, and conducting with Nikolay Rabinovich and Alexander Gauk, later with Rozhdestvensky and Igor Markevich. He began orchestral conducting in 1963, becoming principal conductor of the State Radio SO and touring widely in the West. His work has been mostly in the concert repertory; his first opera in the theatre was his father's *The Nose* for the New Opera Company in association with the ENO at the London Coliseum in 1979. His American opera début was in *Lady Macbeth of the Mtsensk District* at the Juilliard American Opera Center, New York, in 1984; *Yevgeny Onegin* at Washington the next year was less favourably reviewed. He has been more warmly approved in his father's works, as again with *Lady Macbeth* at the Hamburg Staatsoper in 1990 when his own son, Dmitry, also participated as the onstage pianist in the police-station scene.

NOËL GOODWIN

Shtokolov, Boris Timofeyevich (*b* Kuznetsk, 19 March 1930). Russian bass. He joined the Sverdlovsk (now Yekaterinburg) opera company in 1951 while still a student at the Ural Conservatory in that city. He completed his studies there in 1954 and sang as a soloist until 1959, when he transferred to the Kirov Opera. His voice is a *basso cantante*, characterized by an expressive, seldom obtrusive vibrato. He can be heard in his favourite roles of Boris (original version) and Ruslan in the Kirov recordings of 1962 and 1979 respectively. His other recordings include excerpts from Dzerzhinsky's opera *Sud'ba cheloveka* ('The Fate of a Man'), in which he created the role of Andrey Sokolov. The breadth of his interests is reflected in his identification with contemporary opera and the care he devoted to his interpretation of the role of Boris, which he sang in the Rimsky-Korsakov and Shostakovich versions as well as in the composer's rarely performed original. He was awarded the title of People's Artist of the USSR in 1966 and the Glinka prize in 1976.

BORIS SEMEONOFF

Shuard, Amy (*b* London, 19 July 1924; *d* London, 18 April 1975). English soprano. She studied at Trinity College of Music, London, and later with Eva Turner. After singing Aida, Venus and Giulietta (*Les contes* *d'Hoffmann*) in Johannesburg, in 1949 she joined the Sadler's Wells Opera, remaining there until 1955, and singing the title role of *Kát'a Kabanová* in the British première in 1951. Her repertory also included Magda Sorel (*The Consul*), Carmen, Eboli, Tatyana and Tosca. In 1954 she joined Covent Garden Opera, where she distinguished herself first in the Italian repertory as Aida, Turandot and Lady Macbeth in the first production there of Verdi's *Macbeth*, then in the German repertory as Sieglinde, Brünnhilde, Kundry and Electra. She sang the title role in *Jenůfa* in the opera's first stage production in Britain in 1956, and the Kostelnička in its 1972 and 1974 revivals. She sang Isolde in Geneva in 1972, and also appeared in Bayreuth, Vienna, Buenos Aires, San Francisco and Milan.

*

H. Rosenthal: 'Amy Shuard', *Opera*, xi (1960), 257–62

HAROLD ROSENTHAL/R

Shuter, Edward [Ned] (*b* London, ?1728; *d* London, 1 Nov 1776). English actor and singer. Creator of the roles of Mr Hardcastle in *She Stoops to Conquer* and Sir Anthony Absolute in *The Rivals*, he was described by Garrick as the greatest comic genius he had ever seen. He sang well enough to be given roles in several English operas. Dibdin wrote that 'nothing upon earth could have been superior to his Midas' (in the burletta of that name) and he was the first Justice Woodcock in *Love in a Village* (1762), Sir Harry Sycamore in *The Maid of the Mill* (1765) and Squire Western in *Tom Jones* (1769).

For illustration *see* LOVE IN A VILLAGE.

*

BDA; *DNB* (J. Kennedy); *LS*

Theatrical Biography, ii (London, 1772)

C. Dibdin: *A Complete History of the English Stage*, v (London, 1800)

OLIVE BALDWIN, THELMA WILSON

Shuzenji monogatari ('The Tale of Shuzenji'). Opera in one act by OSAMU SHIMIZU after Kidō Okamoto's drama; Osaka, Asahi Hall, 4 November 1954.

The deposed shogun Yoriie (tenor) is confined in the village of Shuzenji, where Yashaō (baritone), a master of mask-making, lives with his daughters, Katsura and Kaede (both soprano), and Kaede's husband, Haruhiko (tenor) a disciple of Yashaō. Yoriie asks the master to carve a mask in his image, but it takes a long time to finish. Irritated by this, Yoriie finally visits Yashaō's house and finds a beautifully carved mask in his own likeness. The master, however, is not satisfied, as the mask has no spirit and is dead. Yoriie, who is satisfied with it, insists on taking it with him, and also Katsura who has attracted him. Later that evening, Yoriie is with Haruhiko at a rendezvous with Katsura, when an assassin (bass) approaches him. Gorō (tenor), Yoriie's servant, fights while Haruhiko runs to alert Yashaō. Back in Yashaō's workshop, Haruhiko arrives with news of the ambush and is followed by a fatally wounded samurai, who turns out to be Katsura dressed like Yoriie and wearing his mask. Learning from a priest of Shuzenji temple (bass) that Yoriie is also dead, the master realizes that he predicted the death of the deposed shogun by carving his mask without spirit. The music is tonal and lyrical, and the composer successfully sets Japanese text within European idioms. The opera won both the government-sponsored Art Festival Prize and the Mainichi Music Prize. MASAKATA KANAZAWA

Shvanda the Bagpiper. Opera by Jaromír Weinberger; *see* ŠVANDA THE BAGPIPER.

Sibelius, Jean [Johan] (**Julius Christian**) (*b* Hämeenlinna, 8 Dec 1865; *d* Järvenpää, 20 Sept 1957). Finnish composer. He studied in Helsinki, 1886–9, and later in Berlin and Vienna. His only opera is *Jungfrun i tornet* ('The Maiden in the Tower'; 1, R. Herzberg, Helsinki, 1896). The libretto, in Swedish, is based on a folk ballad about a young woman captured by a scheming bailiff and eventually rescued by a gallant knight. The weakness of the libretto is the opera's principal fault: the story is banal and undramatic, and the music is on the whole uninteresting. The work does not approach Sibelius's achievements as a symphonist and song composer. He considered as an opera subject *Veenen luominen* ('The Creation of the Boat'), based on legends from the *Kalevala*, but completed only the prelude, which became known as *Tuonelan joutsen* ('The Swan of Tuonela'); another of the 'Lemminkäinen' legends, *Lemminkäinen Tuonelassa* ('Lemminkäinen in Tuonela'), would seem to owe some of its thematic substance to operatic origins. Sibelius also toyed with Aïno Ackté's libretto *Juha*, only to reject it (it was later set by Aarre Merikanto and Leevi Madetoja). ERKKI ARNI

Siberia. Opera in three acts by UMBERTO GIORDANO to a libretto by LUIGI ILLICA; Milan, Teatro alla Scala, 19 December 1903.

The action takes place in Russia and Siberia during the 1850s. Act 1 opens in a palace in St Petersburg where the demi-mondaine Stefana (soprano) has been installed by her latest protector, Prince Alexis (tenor). Stefana is awaited by her anxious housekeeper Nikona (mezzo-soprano). When Alexis arrives with two friends, Nikona tells them that her mistress is still asleep, whereupon they sing her a *mattinata* ('O bella mia') and retire. Stefana returns from a secret assignation with her lover, Vassili (tenor), a young infantry officer who, she tells Nikona, knows nothing of her circumstances ('Nel suo amore rianimata'). Her manager, Gleby (baritone), ridicules this new passion. It turns out, however, that Nikona is Vassili's old nurse; and when he comes to bid her farewell before setting out for the Crimean War he and Stefana recognize one another. Their duet is interrupted by Alexis, who draws his sword on the intruder. In the ensuing fight Alexis is wounded. Vassili is arrested and led away to prison.

In Act 2, set at a frontier post on the Siberian border thronged by peasants and pedlars, a party of convicts arrive on their way to a prison camp. Among them is Vassili, condemned to hard labour. He is joined by Stefana, who has come to share his fate. Act 3 begins amid the rigours of a Siberian winter with the lovers longing for freedom. Stefana is startled by the unexpected presence of Gleby among the camp's inmates. He too has fallen into disgrace and been sentenced to deportation, but he tells her of a hidden escape route through a dried-up well and begs her to join him there. When she refuses he proclaims to all the secret of her past life. She retorts by denouncing him as her first lover, who sold her into prostitution. A fracas is prevented by the appearance of the Prison Governor (bass), who delivers the Easter message. During the evening's celebration Stefana and Vassili attempt to escape through the well; but the alarm is raised, shots are fired and Stefana, mortally wounded, dies in her lover's arms.

Siberia was Giordano's own favourite among his operas. The prestigious première, which it owed to the postponement of Puccini's *Madama Butterfly*, featured Rosina Storchio (Stefana), Giovanni Zenatello (Vassili) and Giuseppe De Luca (Gleby); the conductor was Cleofonte Campanini. At the opera's performance in Paris in 1905 Fauré pronounced it the best product of the GIOVANE SCUOLA. In 1911 *Siberia* achieved the rare distinction of a performance in French at the Paris Opéra, the first to be accorded to a work by a living Italian composer since Verdi's *Otello* (1894). Giordano later revised the opera into its definitive form, first presented at the Teatro alla Scala in Milan in 1927.

Especially notable are the ensembles, from the *mattinata* of Act 1 for four voices with chorus to the entire second act, which is conceived as a massive genre canvas. No other Italian opera makes such extensive use of authentic Russian melody. The first act opens with an offstage chorus of harmonized orthodox plainchant and closes with the tsarist anthem played by the stage band. Act 2 contains the hymn 'Slava', familiar from Beethoven, Musorgsky and Rimsky-Korsakov, and the folktune 'Oy, ne khodi, Gritsyu', also quoted by Donizetti and Glinka and, most strikingly of all, 'The Song of the Volga Boatmen' which forms the basis of the prisoners' chorus. The Easter scene of Act 3 includes a balalaika band which plays a number of traditional tunes including 'U vorot', recognizable from Tchaikovsky's *1812* overture. The opera's only recurring motif is a sinuous theme connoting Siberia that is first heard in the prelude to Act 2 and later forms the opening strain of Vassili's solo 'Orride steppe'.

JULIAN BUDDEN

Sibilla [Gronamann, Sybilla; Mrs Pinto] (*d* before 1766). ?German soprano. A pupil of Arne, she made her début in his *Comus* at the Aungier Street Theatre, Dublin, and took the title role in his *Rosamond* (1743). Her first London appearance was in Arne's *The Temple of Dullness* (1745) at Drury Lane, where she sang for three seasons, mostly in theatre pieces by Arne but also in Lampe's *Dragon of Wantley* and Leveridge's *Macbeth* music. In 1747 she joined the King's Theatre company, appearing in the Handel pasticcio *Lucio Vero* and Hasse's *Didone* and *Semiramide riconosciuta*. She sang in Handel's oratorio seasons of 1748 and 1749. The tessitura and compass (c' to a'', the latter note once only) of his parts for her suggest a limited voice with a mezzo timbre. Her daughter Julia Pinto sang leading parts at Dublin in Arne's *Artaxerxes* and operas by Michael Arne, Gazzaniga and Piccinni between 1774 and 1777.

WINTON DEAN

Sibiryakov, Lev (**Mikhailovich**) (*b* St Petersburg, 1869; *d* Antwerp, Oct 1942). Russian bass. He studied in Milan and made some guest appearances in Italy before returning to Russia, where he made his début in 1895. Singing first in the provinces, he established himself as a leading bass at the Mariinsky Theatre in St Petersburg and then developed an international career in Europe and the USA. He sang Don Basilio in *Barbiere* (in Russian) with the Boston Opera Company in 1910 and Marcel in *Les Huguenots* at Covent Garden in 1911. Back in Russia, he continued for some years, leaving for Western Europe after the Revolution. In 1932 he sang in *Aida* and *La favorita* at Monte Carlo and made a final appearance in the title role of *Boris Godunov* at Brussels in 1938. 6′ 6″ tall and with a voice of proportionate volume, he was often compared with Shalyapin. Recordings show a deep-toned voice with an extensive upper range and remarkable control throughout, though for power of vocal characterization he can hardly approach his great contemporary.

J. B. STEANE

Siboni, Erik Anthon Valdemar (*b* Copenhagen, 26 Aug 1828; *d* Frederiksberg, 11 Feb 1892). Danish composer, son of Giuseppe Siboni. After early training in Copenhagen he went to the Leipzig Musikhochschule in 1847 to study the piano with Moscheles and theory with Hauptmann. After serving in the Danish army during the Three Years War, he went to Vienna in 1851 to study with Sechter. Returning to Copenhagen in 1853, he established himself as a composer and as a teacher of, among others, the princesses Alexandra and Dagmar, later Queen of England and Empress of Russia, respectively. He succeeded Peter Heise as organist and singing teacher at Sorø Academy in 1865, and retired for reasons of health in 1883.

Most of Siboni's published music consists of songs and piano pieces, but he also wrote orchestral and choral music. Though his father occupied a leading position in the operatic life of Copenhagen, he died when Siboni was only 10 years old, and this was perhaps why the operatic tradition did not come to play a larger part in Siboni's career. Apart from a one-act opera, *Loreley*, with which he is credited in early work-lists (Riemann, Squire) but which is not otherwise known, he composed *Carl den Andens flugt* ('The Flight of Charles II'), an opera in three acts with a libretto by Thomas Overskou, now best known for his history of the Kongelige Teater in Copenhagen, where it was performed in 1861. Although it was said to be a success, it received only six performances. The title character of the opera is Charles II of England.

*

Grove1 (W. B. Squire); *RiemannL*

T. Overskou: *Den danske skueplads* [The Danish Theatre], i–vii (Copenhagen, 1854–76)

E. Gigas: 'Siboni, Erik Anthon Valdemar', *DBL* (Copenhagen, 1887–1905)

H. V. Schytte: *Nordisk musik-lexicon*, i–iii (Copenhagen, 1888–1906)

S. Lunn: 'Siboni, Erik Anthon Valdemar', *DBL* (Copenhagen, 3/ 1979–84)

JOHN BERGSAGEL

Siboni, Giuseppe (**Vincenzo Antonio**) (*b* Forlì, 27 Jan 1780; *d* Copenhagen, 28 March 1839). Italian tenor. He made his début at Rimini in 1797 and then sang in Florence. He sang in Bologna (1798), in Genoa (1800) and at La Scala (1805). He made his first appearance in London at the King's Theatre (1806), in *Il principe di Taranto* by Paer, who later wrote many roles for him. During that season he also sang in Portugal's *Il ritorno di Serse* and *La morte di Mitridate*, in Paisiello's *Il barbiere di Siviglia* and in Nasolini's *La morte di Cleopatra*. He sang again in London three years later, in operas by Pucitta, Farinelli and Paisiello. During his career he also appeared in Paris, Vienna, Prague and St Petersburg and throughout Italy. In 1819 he became director of singing at the Royal Theatre in Copenhagen.

*

P. Ingerslev-Jensen: 'Giuseppe Siboni: Selvbiografiske notater 1780–1818', *Det Kongelige Danske Musikkonservatorium: Aarsberetning for 1961* (Copenhagen, 1962), 21–53

G. Schepelern: *Giuseppe Siboni* (Copenhagen, 1989)

ELIZABETH FORBES

Siciliani, Francesco (*b* Perugia, 3 March 1911). Italian music administrator and composer. He took a diploma in composition at the Florence Conservatory with Frazzi and Pizzetti (1935) as well as receiving university degrees in law and in political science. Though successful in the 1930s as a composer, he decided on a career in administration which he pursued in the most important opera houses in Italy: he was artistic director successively of S Carlo, Naples (1940–48), of the Teatro Comunale and the Maggio Musicale, Florence (1948–57), and of La Scala, Milan (1957–66 and 1980–83). He founded and directed the Sagra Musicale Umbra of Perugia (1947), an international festival. From 1983 to 1990 he was president of the S Cecilia Conservatory in Rome, and he has been president of the Panatenee Pompeiane since 1985. In 1988 he was awarded the Venetian prize 'Una vita per la musica'.

CAROLYN GIANTURCO

Sieben Todsünden, Die ('The Seven Deadly Sins'). *Ballet chanté* in eight parts by KURT WEILL to texts by BERTOLT BRECHT; Paris, Théâtre des Champs-Elysées, 7 June 1933.

Anna I (soprano) and her sister, Anna II (dancer), set out from Louisiana. In seven years they hope to earn enough in the big cities to return and build a house for their Family (two tenors, a baritone and a bass – the last is 'Mother'). Anna II is pretty, Anna I is practical. With just one savings book between them, they are really two sides of the same person.

Sloth The family lives in the hope of Anna II becoming industrious. Its prayers are punctuated by the proverb: 'The devil makes work for idle hands'. Meanwhile, Anna II falls asleep during the exploit she and her sister have devised: Anna II makes a scene by accosting strange men in the park; Anna I then offers to remove her for a fee.

Pride In Memphis Anna II learns that 'pride is something for the rich'. She thinks of her dancing as art, but the cabaret audiences demand striptease for their money.

Anger In Los Angeles the sisters work as film extras. When Anna II protests at the ill-treatment of a horse, she is sacked. Her sister teaches her to curb her anger in the interests of getting on. Complaining of the paltry sums coming in, the Family prays that 'our children may know the way that leads to prosperity'.

Gluttony In Philadelphia Anna II is engaged as a solo dancer. She must watch her weight (two servants with revolvers assist her) or break her contract.

Lust In Boston the sisters find a man called Edward who has money. But Anna II loves Fernando, who has none. She is forced against her will to remain faithful to Edward.

Avarice Anna II spells financial ruin for Edward, who shoots himself. Others follow suit. Now in Baltimore, she achieves fame. But eventually her naked displays of greed turn her fame into notoriety.

Envy In San Francisco Anna II is envious of all those who commit sins with impunity. She is rebuked by her sister and repents.

Epilogue After seven years away, the two Annas return to live in their little house in Louisiana.

The above synopsis is culled from the ballet's sung texts, written by Brecht, and the scenario. The latter was not by Brecht, as later assumed, but by the impresario Edward James and the artistic director BORIS YEVGEN'YEVICH KOCHNO. James had agreed to fund the first season of Kochno's and Balanchine's Parisian company 'Les Ballets 1933', provided they commissioned a new work from Weill. That work, *Die sieben Todsünden*, turned out to be the collaboration of mutually estranged exiles. Weill, recently arrived from Germany, initially wanted to work with Cocteau. James however insisted on Brecht, from whom Weill had become alienated during the Berlin production of *Aufstieg und Fall der Stadt Mahagonny*. The text and vocal score were written in April 1933, the full score during the following month. Lotte Lenya, with whom Weill was going through divorce proceedings (they later remarried), was also summoned. She sang the part of Anna I (her current lover, Otto von Pasetti, who came from Vienna with her, was given a tenor part in the Family). The dancer, for whose appeasement James had devised the ballet, was his wife, Tilly Losch, who divorced him the following year. Caspar Neher (with whose wife Weill was having an affair) was persuaded to serve as stage designer.

Each 'sin' is conceived as a separate musical number. The Family, all-male quartet, sings in all but the outer movements, providing a kind of linking refrain, now with quasi-religious intonations, now in the style of a German *Singverein*, now like a barbershop quartet, at all times in parodistic vein. There is also a musical link with the transformation of the recurring opening motif. The score represents a remarkable fusion of popular and classical styles with an almost symphonic coherence.

Despite the personal complications of the original production, it proved a huge critical success. When the troupe transferred to the Savoy Theatre in London on 28 June (the title having been changed to *Anna-Anna* after intervention by the Lord Chamberlain) the critical reception was lukewarm. Lenya's revival of the work in the 1950s gave birth to a new version, with Anna I's numbers transposed down a perfect 4th. She thereby inaugurated a frequently-copied style of performance at odds with her husband's original intentions.

STEPHEN HINTON

Sieber, Ferdinand (*b* Vienna, 5 Dec 1822; *d* Berlin, 19 Feb 1895). Austrian singer and teacher. The son of a bass singer, Kaspar Sieber (1796–1827), who appeared in theatres in Vienna, Berlin and elsewhere, he was a pupil of J. A. Miksch in Dresden and had some career as a singer in Detmold and other German cities before studying in Italy under Ronconi and Farini. He appeared in Spain, Russia and in Germany before settling in 1854 as a teacher and critic in Berlin, where he had great influence through his numerous publications. He composed songs and other works, especially solfeggi (of which he wrote 696). His didactic works include *Völlständiges Lehrbuck der Gesangskunst* (Magdeburg, 1858, 2/1878), *Die Aussprache des italienischen in Gesang* (1860), *Katechismus der Gesangskunst* (1862, 6/1903), a series of volumes *Kurze Anleitung zum gründlichen Studium der Gesangskunst* opp.30–35 and 42–9 (Leipzig, 1865 etc.; opp.42–3 form a *Schule der Geläufigkeit*), *Die Kunst des Gesänges* opp.110–11 (Offenbach, 1877; Eng. trans. 1972) and *Il bel canto* (Berlin, 1886), as well as many sets of exercises and similar works.

Siège de Corinthe, Le [*L'assedio di Corinto* ('The Siege of Corinth')]. *Tragédie lyrique* in three acts by GIOACHINO ROSSINI to a libretto by Luigi Balocchi and

'Le siège de Corinthe' (Rossini): design by Auguste Caron for the final scene in Act 3 in the original production at the Paris Opéra, 9 October 1826

Alexandre Soumet after Cesare della Valle's libretto for Rossini's *Maometto II*; Paris, Opéra, 9 October 1826.

Though the setting is now Corinth, with a renamed cast of characters, the action of the opera is similar to that of Rossini's *MAOMETTO II*, of which this is a carefully edited, theatrically effective revision. Cléomène (tenor), Governor of Corinth, is advising surrender to the Turks and their leader Mahomet II (bass). But Néocles (tenor), a young Greek officer, urges a fresh attack. Impressed by the valour of Néocles, Cléomène offers him the hand of his daughter Pamyre (soprano). But she has fallen in love with a stranger – in reality Mahomet, who had earlier spied for his father in Corinth – a fact which incenses her father. In the fresh assault, the Greeks are driven back and Cléomène is taken prisoner. Rushing to intervene, Pamyre is recognized by Mahomet who offers to make peace with the Greeks if she will marry him. Cléomène insists that she marry Néocles, but she refuses and is abandoned to Mahomet by the Greek leaders. In Act 2 Mahomet prepares to marry Pamyre, whose loyalties are still divided, but the wedding preparations are interrupted by Néocles demanding Pamyre's return. She defends him, pretending that he is her brother, and they flee leaving Mahomet vowing to kill every Greek by sunset. In Act 3 Néocles goes to the city's catacombs where the Greeks are gathering for their final defence. Greek women are heard in prayer in the distance and Cléomène laments Pamyre's private disloyalty. After the failure of further peace overtures, Mahomet determines to rout the Greeks and win Pamyre by military means. Pamyre goes to the catacomb where Néocles reconciles her with her father before the raising and blessing of the banners as the Greeks recall famous victories at Marathon and Thermopylae. The Turks are victorious in the ensuing battle, but when Mahomet comes to claim his bride he finds that she and her women have killed themselves.

By scaling down the huge musical structures of *Maometto II*, Rossini simplified the piece but made it more stageworthy. Unduly florid vocal lines are calmed and the *travesti* role of Calbo becomes the theatrically more credible role of the tenor, Néocles. There is little new music in the revision; the only newly composed longer structure is the Act 2 finale incorporating the chaste but sensuous *hymne* 'Divin prophète'. The third act, however, is substantially changed: it is no longer, like Act 2 of *Maometto II*, the glorification of a single woman's sacrifice. Pamyre's suicide is placed firmly within a context of national fervour and national suffering occasioned by the trauma of war. The opening scene, prayer and air, and its scene and trio, are taken from Act 2 of *Maometto II* but the blessing of the Greek banners, 'Quel nuage sanglant', is new. Pamyre's F♯ minor prayer, 'Juste ciel, ah! ta clémence', is from Act 1 of *Maometto II*, but Rossini's depiction of the sack of Corinth is a skilful reworking of fragments gathered from the original finale, with the orchestra alone drawing the drama to a close. RICHARD OSBORNE

Siege of Belgrade, The. Mainpiece dialogue opera in three acts by STEPHEN STORACE to a libretto by JAMES COBB partly after LORENZO DA PONTE's libretto *Una cosa rara*; London, Drury Lane, 1 January 1791.

The Siege of Belgrade, a 'comic' opera with spoken dialogue, was one of Storace's two most popular operas. After 47 performances in its first half-season, it remained a regular part of the Drury Lane repertory well into the 19th century, though with an increasing number of musical additions and substitutions. The actor John Philip Kemble, who was manager at Drury Lane at the time of its première, wrote in his diary that day that 'New Year's Day requires the strongest Pieces that can be acted', so demonstrating well-founded confidence in the opera from the start. Cobb and Storace borrowed part of the plot and music from *Una cosa rara* (1786, Vienna), which had a libretto by Lorenzo Da Ponte and music by Vicente Martín y Soler. Cobb changed the location from Spain to Turkey and transformed the Spanish prince into the Seraskier. He added a second, more serious, strand to the plot, based on the unsuccessful siege of Belgrade by the Turks under Mehmet II in 1456. This event provided an excuse for a spectacular onstage battle. The two plots alternate but remain separate for Acts 1 and 2; in Act 3 they become interwoven. Cobb added a few twists of his own to the characters of the magistrate, Lilla's lover and the Seraskier.

The plot encompasses several captures and escapes, disguises and mistaken identities, while highlighting differences between Christian and Muslim values. The Seraskier (tenor) intends to add Lilla (soprano), a village girl, to his seraglio; he has already captured Catherine (soprano), the wife of an Austrian colonel. The Seraskier permits Lilla to marry her lover, Leopold (baritone) – by which means she stops the unwelcome suit of the corrupt local magistrate – but continues his pursuit and finally captures her. The colonel (spoken role), caught trying to infiltrate the Seraskier's camp, is condemned to death. Lilla escapes, and discovers where the magistrate has hidden his ill-gotten wealth; she returns it to its rightful owners. After battles between the Austrians and the Turks in which the colonel is rescued and the Seraskier is captured, the colonel spares the Seraskier's life.

Storace used single-movement overtures for his first three English operas, but the overture here is in three movements, perhaps to conform to the taste of his English contemporaries. The curtain rises on the last movement, which becomes the opening chorus with Turkish peasant dances. Storace borrowed its themes from Mozart's 'Rondo alla turca' in the Piano Sonata K331/300*i*. The musical relationship with *Una cosa rara* is in some respects close. Storace borrowed from nine vocal numbers by Martín y Soler, each (except for one which became the second movement of the overture) associated with the part of Cobb's plot borrowed from the parallel situation in Da Ponte's libretto. Storace and Cobb therefore retained the dramatic contexts of these numbers. Storace abbreviated most of the borrowings and added substantial portions of new music to some. Cobb's new strand of plot is set almost entirely with newly composed music. Both Nancy Storace and Michael Kelly had sung in *Una cosa rara* in Vienna, Nancy in the same role of Lilla and Kelly as Corrado, the prince's confidant. Lilla's borrowed music in *The Siege of Belgrade* was therefore sung again by Nancy Storace, but only because of consistency of dramatic context, not any direct relationship between singers and borrowings.

The music varies from elaborate numbers for the main singers to simple strophic songs, especially those for subsidiary characters. The few action ensembles do not include the finales, which are reflective. *The Siege of Belgrade* takes a middle place in Storace's development of the full-length English opera with integrated music and drama, with greater involvement than *The Haunted Tower* but less than his next collaboration with Cobb, *The Pirates*. The style of Storace's music is Mozartian, not least because of direct borrowings in the overture and opening chorus.

For illustration *see* LONDON, fig.6 and PLAYBILL, fig.2.

JANE GIRDHAM

Siege of Rhodes, The. Heroic opera in five acts by Henry Cooke, Henry Lawes, MATTHEW LOCKE, Charles Coleman (*see* COLEMAN family, (1)) and George Hudson to a libretto by WILLIAM DAVENANT; London, Rutland House, September 1656.

The first all-sung English opera, it had no immediate successors yet was highly influential; the music is now lost. The librettist, Sir William Davenant, was poet laureate at the time of the execution of Charles I and was briefly in exile in France. He returned to England in 1650 and, after two years in the Tower of London, persuaded the Council of State to allow him to establish a theatre dedicated to the moral and political education of the common people. Having built a small theatre at the back of his house in Charterhouse Yard, Davenant devised a 'Morall Representation' of various historical subjects with scenery and illustrative incidental music: *The First Dayes Entertainment at Rutland-House, by Declamations and Musick* was given on 23 May 1656. Encouraged by the silent approval of the Puritan authorities, Davenant was emboldened to undertake a more ambitious work a few months later; this was *The Siege of Rhodes*, which was designed to be acted 'with an Italian Musick', that is, all-sung with recitative.

Having collaborated with Inigo Jones on *The Temple of Love* (1635), a lavish court masque, Davenant was no stranger to music drama. Charles I had granted him a patent in 1639 to build a theatre for plays and 'musical presentments', a project that foundered at the outbreak of civil war. Davenant's promotion of opera in the mid-1650s was tacitly approved by the Puritan authorities and does not therefore seem to have been motivated by a need to avoid the ban on plays. *The Siege of Rhodes* is a plausible libretto, given the author's inexperience in the genre. It is to some extent indebted to Richard Flecknoe's unperformed libretto *Ariadne Deserted by Theseus* (1654). In his preface Flecknoe traces the development of Italian opera, particularly the recitative, and suggests how English dramatic poetry could be adapted as *dramma per musica* by writing short lines with emphasis on open vowels and avoiding diphthongs and feminine endings, advice that Davenant heeded. Yet *The Siege of Rhodes* resembles no contemporary Venetian libretto. Its domination by recitative dialogue suggests that Davenant may have conceived it as a play. There are very few aria texts; any lyrical reflection is provided by the chorus (which had all but disappeared from Italian opera by this time). Its stilted and formulaic appearance at the end of each scene tediously disrupts the otherwise excellent plot.

The Siege of Rhodes was based on an historical event (which also distinguishes it from most 17th-century French and Italian operas): the Ottoman defeat of the Knights of St John at Rhodes in 1522. Besieged by the sultan Solyman and the Turks, Duke Alphonso of Sicily permits his wife Ianthe to embark in search of reinforcements. She is captured by the Turks but released by Solyman, who admires her courage. The themes of valour and conjugal love were to become the principal preoccupation of the later heroic plays. In spite of the tiny dimensions of the Rutland House stage (11 feet high, 15 feet deep), the opera was enhanced by elaborate scenes painted by John Webb, a pupil of Inigo Jones: Rhodes at peace (see illustration); Rhodes under siege; Solyman's pavilion with a throne; his castle on Mount Philermus; the general assault.

The music was composed by 'the most transcendent of *England* in that Art'. In overall charge was Captain Henry Cooke, who composed the second and third entries or acts. (He was also to re-establish the Chapel Royal choir after the Restoration.) The other composers

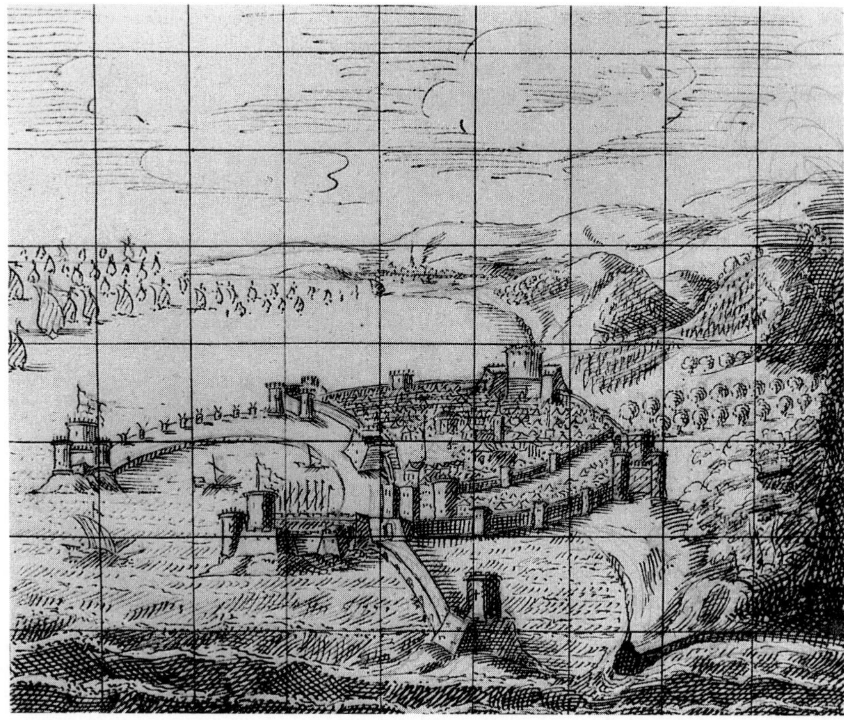

'The Siege of Rhodes' (Davenant): design by John Webb for the first scene (Rhodes at peace) of the original production at Rutland House, London, September 1656; pen and ink drawing

were Henry Lawes, master of the declamatory air (first and fifth entries), and Matthew Locke, the most important English stage composer of the 1660s and 1670s (fourth entry). Charles Coleman and George Hudson provided the instrumental music. The *dramatis personae* included Cooke and Locke themselves as Solyman and the Admiral of Rhodes respectively, Henry Purcell (the composer's uncle) as Mustapha and, as Ianthe, Mrs Edward Coleman, one of the first women to appear on the public stage in England.

The degree of success of the original production is unknown, though it was transferred to the Cockpit, Drury Lane, in 1658. After the Restoration *The Siege of Rhodes* was revived, but in what form is unclear. John Dryden, writing 10 years after the event, recalled that Davenant 'review'd' the opera and then had it 'acted as a just Drama', that is, spoken instead of sung; but Dryden may have confused this revival with *The Second Part of the Siege of Rhodes*, a new play by Davenant for the opening of his theatre in Lincoln's Inn Fields on 28 June 1661. Adding to the confusion, the diarist John Evelyn wrote that *The Second Part* was acted 'in *Recitativa Musique*', which is surely a mistake. None of the music of the original *Siege of Rhodes* survives, though on 31 October 1665 Pepys heard Mrs Coleman sing one of Lawes's songs from the opera. While it led to no other all-sung opera, *The Siege of Rhodes* influenced the development of heroic drama and, indirectly, SEMI-OPERA.

CURTIS PRICE

Siege of Rochelle, The. Grand opera in two acts by MICHAEL WILLIAM BALFE to a libretto by EDWARD FITZBALL, after Stéphanie Félicité Brulart de Sillery, Comtesse de Genlis's novel *Le siège de La Rochelle*; London, Drury Lane, 29 October 1835.

Clara (soprano), the daughter of Count Rosenberg (bass), has been given in infancy into the care of the villainous Montalban (bass), and believes that she is his child. Montalban, seeing that Clara intends to marry the widowed Marquis de Valmour (tenor), and wishing to obtain his inheritance, kills Valmour's young son. He is detected by Clara, who is falsely accused of the murder but cannot bring herself to betray her own father. During the siege of La Rochelle she learns that Rosenberg is her true father and denounces Montalban. The French are victorious, and Valmour claims her as his bride.

The Siege of Rochelle was Balfe's first English opera, and ran for 73 performances during its opening season. The music is youthful, extravagant and exhilarating. Edward Fitzball has left a vivid account of the opera's production in his *Thirty-Five Years of a Dramatic Author's Life* (London, 1859).

NIGEL BURTON

Siegfried. Second day of *DER RING DES NIBELUNGEN* in three acts by Richard Wagner (*see* WAGNER family, (1)) to his own libretto; Bayreuth, Festspielhaus, 16 August 1876.

Siegfried	tenor
Mime	tenor
The Wanderer	bass-baritone
Alberich	bass-baritone
Fafner	bass
Erda	contralto
Brünnhilde	soprano
Woodbird	soprano†

† originally 'boy's voice'

The first sketches for *Jung-Siegfried* (the opera's original title, subsequently changed to *Der junge Siegfried*) date probably from 3–24 May 1851. The prose draft followed between 24 May and 1 June, and two days later Wagner began the versification, ending at midday on 24 June. Following the writing of the poems for *Die Walküre* and *Das Rheingold*, Wagner subjected his texts for *Der junge Siegfried* and *Siegfrieds Tod* (later

Götterdämmerung) to revision (Nov–Dec 1852). The final poem was incorporated into the private printing of the entire *Ring* text in February 1853. *Der junge Siegfried* and *Siegfrieds Tod* were definitively named *Siegfried* and *Götterdämmerung* in 1856.

Some preliminary musical sketches were made for *Der junge Siegfried* in 1851, but the composition proper was begun in 1856 (probably early September) with the first complete draft. To avoid the problems he had experienced with *Die Walküre*, Wagner took each act through from first draft to score before embarking on the next. He also worked in tandem between the first complete draft (in pencil) and the second (in ink, on at least three staves – two instrumental and one vocal – elaborating details of the orchestral texture). In June 1857 he broke off work on the drafts, with Siegfried resting under the linden tree (Act 2), partly because the *Ring* was becoming a drain on his financial resources, partly because he wished to try out his increasingly chromatic style on the subject of Tristan. Nevertheless, he briefly took up again the composition of Act 2 shortly after, finishing the first complete draft on 30 July 1857 and the second on 9 August. Not until 27 September 1864 was the task of making a fair copy of the score of Act 1 resumed and between 22 December of that year and 2 December 1865 the scoring of Act 2 was undertaken. Work on Act 3 began on 1 March 1869, after the fair copy of the Act 1 and 2 scores had been finished. The scoring of the whole work was completed on 5 February 1871.

ACT 1 *A cave in the rocks in the forest* Opening with a subdued drum roll and a pair of brooding bassoons, the prelude sets the scene in the dark forest, where the dragon Fafner has his lair, at the same time alluding to the crafty scheming of the dwarf Mime. The contrabass tuba joins in with a motif associated (in *Das Rheingold*) with the hoard and then the dotted Nibelungs' motif is introduced as an ostinato accompaniment to it. The tempo becomes more animated and the motifs of the Ring and Sword are heard, the latter on the bass trumpet in its familiar key of C major, though without disturbing the Nibelungs' tonality of B♭ minor in which the prelude as a whole is set. The curtain rises on Mime hammering away at an anvil (to the rhythm of the Nibelungs' motif), cursing his wearisome labour and his hopeless attempts to forge a sword that the boy Siegfried cannot break in two. The giant Fafner has transformed himself into a fierce dragon, Mime tells us (a Dragon motif growls low on tubas), the better to guard the Nibelung treasure. If only he, Mime, could forge together the fragments of Nothung, the sword of Siegfried's father, Siegmund, the boy might kill the dragon with it and the ring would come to Mime.

Siegfried enters to the exuberant strains of his motif (ex.1). He is leading in a huge bear and he laughs all the

Ex.1

way to a top C as it chases Mime round the cave. He demands to see Mime's work but on testing it (to the strains of another motif to be associated with his heroism, ex.2), he scornfully smashes it on the anvil; he

Ex.2

berates Mime to yet another motif (ex.3). His

Ex.3

annoyance with the prattling dwarf is hardly diminished when Mime tells him (to a modified form of the Nibelungs' motif, ex.4) that he should show more

Ex.4

gratitude to his guardian. He knocks the proffered meat and soup out of Mime's hands, whereupon the latter embarks upon what Siegfried later calls his 'starling song', 'Als zullendes Kind', telling Siegfried how Mime has nurtured him: one of the several self- contained song forms incorporated into the structure of this act. Siegfried's response, a litany of loathing (exx.3 and 4), inspires only a further attempt at ingratiation, the lyrically tender ex.5. If Mime is his father, Siegfried asks, where

Ex.5

is his mother? He forcefully extracts the whole story from Mime, to reminiscences of the themes of the Volsungs and their love. Hearing about the fragments of Nothung, Siegfried excitedly instructs Mime to reforge the sword and rushes off into the forest, leaving Mime sitting dejectedly at the anvil.

The Wanderer (Wotan in disguise) appears and asks for hospitality (scene ii): 'Heil dir, weiser Schmied!'. The textural and motivic contrast between his music, with its noble tread, and Mime's enables the Riddle Scene, as it is sometimes called, to be analysed as a Baroque ritornello structure (see Newcomb 1989). The Wanderer stakes his head on answering correctly three questions. Mime asks the name of the races that live in the earth, on the face of the earth and in the cloudy heights. The Nibelungs, the giants and the gods ruled by Wotan, come the answers, duly illustrated with the appropriate motifs, often in their original tonality. To Mime's horror, the Wanderer then demands the same in exchange. His first question concerns the tribe treated harshly by Wotan though dearest to him. The Volsungs, replies Mime confidently. As to the name of the sword to be wielded by the hero Siegfried, he correctly replies Nothung. But when asked who will forge the sword, Mime jumps up in alarm: he has no idea. The answer, the Wanderer tells him against the growls of the Dragon motif, is 'one who has never known fear'. He leaves Mime's head forfeit to the fearless one and departs.

The orchestra paints a dazzling picture of flickering lights and roaring flames as the terrified Mime imagines the dragon looming in the forest (scene iii). Siegfried returns and Mime determines to teach him fear (tremolo strings), but Siegfried's curiosity is only whetted. Mime looks on aghast as Siegfried begins to forge the fragments of the sword himself, to the accompaniment of a transformation of ex.1, its vigour enhanced by

'Siegfried' (Wagner): design by Joseph Hoffmann for Act 1 (Mime's cave in the rocks in the forest) for the original production at the Festspielhaus, Bayreuth, 16 August 1876

augmented triad colouring. On being told the name of the sword, Nothung, Siegfried launches his Forging Song with it: 'Nothung! Nothung! Neidliches Schwert!' This song, also coloured by augmented chords, begins as a strophic structure (the second and third stanzas slightly varied), but after interruptions by Mime, the form dissolves under the pressure of the dramatic momentum. Mime plots how he will offer Siegfried a drugged drink after his battle with the dragon, and then kill him with his own sword. At last the forging is done, and Siegfried crashes the sword down on the anvil, splitting it in two.

ACT 2 *Deep in the forest* Two motifs are dominant in the prelude to Act 2: the growling of the dragon, outside whose cave the scene is set, and the Curse. Alberich is keeping watch over the cave and is surprised by the appearance of the Wanderer. Bitterly recalling how, as Wotan, he stole the ring from him, Alberich taunts him (to frequent repetitions of the Spear motif) with his ambitions for world supremacy. Wotan remains quietly philosophical and even warns Alberich of the approach of Siegfried and Mime. He surprises Alberich further by arousing Fafner on his behalf and asking him to yield up the ring. The dragon, extending the giants' falling perfect 4th to an augmented one, is unmoved.

Mime arrives with Siegfried (scene ii) and describes to him the fearsome dragon; Siegfried is concerned only to know where is the dragon's heart, so that he can plunge in his sword. Mime leaves Siegfried alone and to the mellifluous strains of the Forest Murmurs (shimmering muted strings supporting woodwind solos), the boy expresses his relief that the ugly dwarf is not his father after all. (The rippling movement of the Forest Murmurs is anticipated more than once in the preceding pages of the score, effectively integrating it into the scene as a whole.) Hearing the song of the Woodbird, Siegfried tries to imitate it with a pipe made from a reed, but after several abortive attempts (comically rendered on the english horn) he gives up. He blows his horn instead (exx.1 and 2) and a somnolent Fafner drags himself out of his cave. After an exchange of banter and a battle depicted by the conflict of their motifs, Siegfried stabs Fafner in the heart with Nothung. Fafner, in his last gasp, tells Siegfried his history. Putting his burning hand involuntarily to his mouth, Siegfried tastes the dragon's blood. At last he understands the song of the Woodbird: it tells him to take the ring and Tarnhelm from the cave.

As Siegfried disappears into the cave, Mime and Alberich appear from opposite sides (scene iii). To a shambling, syncopated accompaniment they argue angrily about the rightful ownership of the treasure. Mime offers to relinquish the ring, provided he be allowed the Tarnhelm. Their argument is halted by the reappearance of Siegfried with both items; a chorus of horns, wafting the Rhinemaidens' motif, reminds us of the origin of the gold. The Woodbird tells Siegfried to beware Mime, who now approaches and hails him unctuously. As Mime cajoles Siegfried and offers him his drugged drink, his actual words keep betraying his intention to make an end of him (a comic device which Wagner apparently borrowed from a 19th- century farce on the Faust legend). Finally, Siegfried, in an access of revulsion, kills Mime with a blow of the sword.

He tosses Mime's body into the cave and drags Fafner's over its mouth. Lying down under the linden tree, he listens again to the song of the Woodbird and asks its advice. The bird tells him of the bride that awaits him on a mountain top surrounded by fire. Siegfried jumps up and follows the bird as it leads the way.

ACT 3.i–ii *The foot of a rocky mountain* The prelude is a symphonic development of a number of major motifs, notably the dotted rhythm pervading the prelude, associated with Wotan, the Valkyries and their riding; the Erda motif and its inversion the Twilight of the Gods; the flattened mediant harmonies of the Wanderer; the falling semitone associated in *Rheingold* with Alberich and the baleful power of his ring; and the Magic Sleep. The Wanderer appears and, summoning

Erda (the earth goddess) from her slumber, demands to know more of the earth's secrets: 'Wache, Wala!'. First she refers him to the Norns as they weave the rope of destiny, and then to the daughter she bore him, Brünnhilde. When he tells her that Brünnhilde is being punished for her disobedience, she expresses surprise that the one who taught defiance is now punishing it. The technical advance represented by this scene, written after the long break during which Wagner composed *Tristan* and *Die Meistersinger*, is immediately evident. Powerfully conceived vocal lines completely abandoning recitative in favour of heightened arioso are supported by an orchestral texture of unprecedented richness and motivic density. The scene takes the form of a dialogue between the Wanderer and Erda, in which the characteristic material of each is subjected to variation. The form threatens to disintegrate as the emotional temperature rises, until a climax is reached with the Wanderer's announcement that he now looks forward to the end of the gods. The gravity of the moment is signalled with a noble new motif (ex.6); leitmotifs of

Ex.6

such expansiveness and autonomy are henceforth to play a major role in the *Ring*. The Wanderer bequeaths his inheritance to the Volsung hero, Siegfried. Erda sinks back into the earth.

As the Wanderer waits by the cave, Siegfried comes into view, led by the Woodbird. In answer to the old stranger's questions, Siegfried tells, to the accompaniment of the appropriate motifs, how he killed the dragon, about the deceit of Mime, and how he himself forged the sword. Siegfried, irritated by the stranger, treats him with contempt. The Wanderer is finally moved to try to block Siegfried's path, but his spear is shattered by a stroke of Siegfried's sword; the motif of the Spear, and hence of Wotan's authority, is symbolically fragmented. The Wanderer vanishes and Siegfried plunges into the flames.

3.iii *On the peak of Brünnhilde's rock* During an orchestral interlude constructed from motifs associated with Siegfried and the fire, the scene changes to the rocky summit of the end of *Die Walküre*. The first violins, unaccompanied, scale the heights as Siegfried climbs to the top of the rock. He mistakes the form of the sleeping Brünnhilde for that of a man, even after removing her helmet (his doubts and irresolution prompting a brief return to the quasi-recitative style). His eventual realization, on removing the breastplate, that it is a woman causes a frenzy of fear and excitement (depicted in a series of flourishes characteristic of the post-*Tristan* Wagner). Now for the first time he has been taught fear, yet he longs to waken her. In desperation he kisses her on the lips, at which she opens her eyes and raises herself to a sitting position. With a flurry of harps, and in a bright C major, Brünnhilde greets the daylight: 'Heil dir, Sonne!'. She tells him that she has always loved him, even before he was conceived. Siegfried wonders if the woman is in fact his mother, but she tells him how she was confined on the rock for shielding him. This first part of their extended duet introduces a pair of new thematic ideas (exx.7 and 8), which will return to dominate the close of the act.

The confusion engendered by Siegfried's mixed emo-

tions soon gives way to impetuous desire, the excitability of the vocal line being matched by tumescence in the orchestra. These effusions alternate with slower passages of a darker colour as Brünnhilde becomes increasingly conscious of her vulnerability, stripped as she is of her godhead. When Siegfried tries to embrace her, she pushes him away in terror. Now it is she who is prey to conflicting emotions, and motifs associated with Wotan's agony in Act 2 of *Die Walküre* and even the Curse well up from the depths of the orchestra. She begs him not to destroy the purity of their love, embarking on a monologue almost self-contained in its thematic content (the music is familiar from the *Siegfried Idyll*, composed the following year): 'Ewig war ich'. Gradually she is won over by the intensity of Siegfried's passion and is able to accept her new mortal status. To a riotous profusion of themes, including exx.6, 7 and 8, as well as a new one, ex.9, which combines the boyish

Ex.9

vigour and falling 4ths of ex.3 with a suggestion of the cycle's principal Love motif (*see* RHEINGOLD, DAS, ex.4), they embrace in ecstasy. Brünnhilde bids farewell to the world of the gods, and, transformed by each other's love, they invoke 'laughing death'.

* * *

The long span of 15 years over which the composition of *Siegfried* took place accounts for much of the stylistic inconsistency identifiable in the work. Acts 1 and 2 continue the style of *Rheingold* and *Walküre*, but with some interesting experiments in formal structure, while Act 3, written after the composition of *Tristan* and *Die Meistersinger*, demonstrates a new-found flexibility and maturity. The role of Siegfried, in which the singer is required to dominate the stage for the best part of four hours, culminating in a strenuous final scene with the newly awakened Brünnhilde, is one of the most testing in the tenor repertory. BARRY MILLINGTON

Sieglitz, Georg (*b* Mainz, 26 April 1851; *d* Munich, 3 Nov 1917). German bass. He studied in Berlin, making his début in 1880 at Hamburg as Masetto. Successively engaged at Poznán, Düsseldorf, Nuremberg, the Kroll Opera, Berlin, and the German Theatre, Prague, in 1898 he became a member of the Munich Hofoper. There he sang in the first performances of Siegfried Wagner's *Der Bärenhäuter* (1899) and of Wolf-Ferrari's *Le donne curiose* (1903) and *I quatro rusteghi* (1906). His repertory included Leporello, Bartolo (*Le nozze di Figaro*), the title role of Cornelius's *Der Barbier von Bagdad* and Beckmesser as well as Caspar (*Der Freischütz*), Bertram (*Robert le diable*), Marcel (*Les Huguenots*), King Henry (*Lohengrin*), Daland and Pogner. ELIZABETH FORBES

Siegmeister, Elie (*b* New York, 15 Jan 1909; *d* Manhasset, NY, 10 March 1991). American composer. He studied theory and composition with Seth Bingham at Columbia College and counterpoint with Wallingford Riegger. From 1927 to 1931 he studied with Boulanger in Paris and from 1935 to 1938 conducting with Albert Stoessel at the Juilliard School. He held teaching positions at Brooklyn College (1934), the New School for Social Research (1937–8), the University of Minnesota (1948) and Hofstra University (1949–76), and helped found the American Composers Alliance (1937) and the American Ballad Singers (1939). He was vice-president of the American Music Center (1960–65) and from 1977 served on the board of directors of ASCAP. He was a recipient of numerous awards and commissions from the Ford Foundation (1971), the NEA (1974, 1980), the American Academy and Institute of Arts and Letters (1978) and the Library of Congress (1983).

Like other American composers of the 1930s and early 1940s, Siegmeister composed music for the 'common folk'. As other composers' interest in this type of utilitarian approach to music waned in the early 1950s, Siegmeister's commitment continued, and his significant accomplishments in the genre of musical theatre and opera show the skilful development of his music's ability to speak to the masses.

Early efforts in the genre are the play with music *Doodle Dandy of the USA* (1942) and the musical *Sing Out, Sweet Land* (1944). The first work tells the story of Doodle Dandy who helps the people of a small town rid themselves of a would-be dictator. He alerts the townspeople to the dangers of dictatorship and arouses them to action. Ultimately he outwits the dictator through a series of pranks, and gets his message to the people. *Sing Out, Sweet Land*, a Broadway musical, makes extensive use of American popular music. Both works exhibit uncomplicated musical styles that emphasize the message, rather than a sophisticated compositional language. The vocal writing shows a similar approach: melodies moving mainly in stepwise motion, with little use of chromaticism, and limited in range.

If Siegmeister's early works are blatantly American to the core, his middle works show a composer just as committed to providing a message, but using a subtler approach. His next three operas concern the lives of everyday Americans, exemplifying how they share the same problems and moral dilemmas. *Darling Corie* (1952) focusses on the lives of mountain folk, its story possibly derived from a folk ballad of the same title. The musical style follows logically from his earlier works, cast in a contemporary Broadway idiom, but uses some modal, folklike tunes for contrast. The age-old struggle between overprotective father and worldly, yet naive, daughter provides the subject matter for *Miranda and the Dark Young Man* (composed 1955). Influenced by jazz, Siegmeister displays here a penchant for off-the-beat vocal entrances and jazz-inspired use of chromaticism. The vocal writing continues to use limited ranges, marking this work as a successful vehicle for the opera workshop environment. The work's only obvious flaw is an alternating line rhyme scheme giving the text a choppy and stilted effect, and making the libretto seem more trite than it actually is. In his final opera of this middle period Siegmeister turned to a more fantastical subject, while still conveying a universal message. *The Mermaid in Lock no.7* (1958) tells the story of a sailor who is rescued by, and falls in love with, a mermaid. On returning home the sailor is smitten with a nightclub singer who warns that the mermaid is 'different' and will lure him to his death, which she does.

The first of Siegmeister's mature operatic works, *The Plough and the Stars* (1969; originally *Dublin Song*, 1963), based on O'Casey's play, depicts dramatic situations that develop between individuals during the Irish Rebellion of 1915–16, contrasting revolutionary rhetoric with the everyday lives of the Dubliners. For *Night of the Moonspell* (1976), Shakespeare's *A Midsummer Night's Dream* is updated to the turn of the century and set in the bayou and forest country of Louisiana. The musical style of these works draws heavily on the composer's experience in American musical theatre, exhibiting a mixture of Broadway, opera, folk music and jazz. *Night of the Moonspell* experiments with giving a separate musical identity to each group of characters. Both works possess music of vivid orchestral colouring and vocal writing that is immensely rich and varied.

The final operatic works, *Angel Levine* and *The Lady of the Lake* (both composed 1984–5), find Siegmeister exploring his Jewish identity in subject matter and musical style, the former employing Hebrew chants and intonations. Although off-the-beat entrances in the voice and orchestra and an extensive use of syncopation relate *Angel Levine* to an earlier style, the vocal lines possess a wider range, show an adventurous use of chromaticism and are more rhythmically interesting than in earlier works. *The Lady of the Lake* exhibits much the same style, but is more lyrically expansive in manner than previously found.

Doodle Dandy of the USA (play with music, S. Lancourt), New York, 26 Dec 1942, vs (New York, 1942)
Sing Out, Sweet Land (musical, W. Kerr), Hartford, CT, 10 Nov 1944
Darling Corie, 1952 (1, L. Allan), Hempstead, NY, Hofstra College, 18 Feb 1954, vs (New York, 1954)
Miranda and the Dark Young Man (1, E. Eager), Hartford, CT, Hartt School, 9 May 1956, vs (New Rochelle, NY, 1957)
The Mermaid in Lock no.7 (1, E. Mabley), Pittsburgh, Point State Park, 20 July 1958, vs (New York, 1958)
Dublin Song (3, Mabley, after S. O'Casey), St Louis, Washington U., 15 May 1963; rev. as The Plough and the Stars, Baton Rouge, Louisiana State U., 16 March 1969
Night of the Moonspell (3, Mabley, after W. Shakespeare: *A Midsummer Night's Dream*), Shreveport, LA, 14 Nov 1976
The Marquesa of O (3, N. Rosten, after H. von Kleist), 1982
Angel Levine (1, Mabley, after B. Malamud), New York, Kaufmann Auditorium (92nd Street Young Men's-Young Women's Hebrew Association), 5 Oct 1985, vs (New York, 1985)
The Lady of the Lake (1, Mabley, after Malamud), New York, Kaufmann Auditorium, 5 Oct 1985

*

E. Siegmeister: 'A Long, Long Road', *ON*, xxxiv/20 (1969–70), 27–9 [*The Plough and the Stars*]
D. K. Allen: *Drama and Characterization in Opera Settings of A Midsummer Night's Dream by Britten and Siegmeister* (thesis, North Texas State U., 1982)
C. J. Oja: 'Composer with a Conscience: Elie Siegmeister in Profile', *American Music*, vi/2 (1988), 158–80
R. H. Kornick: *Recent American Opera: a Production Guide* (New York, 1991), 280–82

JAMES P. CASSARO

Siehr, Gustav (*b* Arnsberg, Westphalia, 17 Sept 1837; *d* Munich, 18 May 1896). German bass. He studied in Berlin, making his début in 1863 at Neustrelitz as Oroveso. After singing in Göteborg, Prague and Wiesbaden, in 1881 he was engaged at the Munich Hofoper, where he remained until his death. At Bayreuth he sang Hagen in the first *Ring* cycle (1876), Gurnemanz in *Parsifal* (1882–9) and King Mark (1886). His wide repertory included Sarastro, the

Commendatore, Caspar (*Der Freischütz*), Bertram (*Robert le diable*), Daland and Pogner.

ELIZABETH FORBES

Siemonn, Mabel. *See* GARRISON, MABEL.

Siems, Margarethe (*b* Breslau [now Wrocław], 30 Dec 1879; *d* Dresden, 13 April 1952). German soprano. She studied with Orgeni, a pupil of Viardot and Marchesi. She was engaged for the Prague May Festival in 1902, when she sang Marguerite de Valois, and that autumn joined the Prague Opera. In 1908 she became principal dramatic coloratura soprano at Dresden, where she sang until 1920, creating Chrysothemis (1909) and the Marschallin (1911); she also created Zerbinetta (1912, Stuttgart). In 1913 she made her Covent Garden début as the Marschallin in the first London performance of *Der Rosenkavalier*. Siems was an extraordinarily versatile singer and actress. Her repertory included the coloratura soprano roles of Bellini, Donizetti and Meyerbeer, as well as the Queen of Night; she successfully undertook the heavier Verdi parts (Leonora, Amelia and Aida) and Wagnerian roles such as Venus and Elisabeth (she often sang both on the same evening), and even Isolde. Strauss considered her the ideal Marschallin.

For illustration *see* *ARIADNE AUF NAXOS* (ii), fig.1.

*

P. Wilhelm: 'Margarethe Siems', *Record News* [Toronto], ii (1957–8), 421–7 [with discography] HAROLD ROSENTHAL/R

Siena. Italian city in Tuscany. The Teatro dei Rinnovati in the Palazzo Pubblico was long associated with the Accademia dei Rinnovati and was used for *commedie* from 1560; in 1670 the academy mounted the first opera performed at the theatre, Cesti's *Argia*. At this time the theatre was renamed the Teatro Grande; it burnt down in 1742 and 1751, and was rebuilt the second time by Antonio Galli-Bibiena, opening in 1753. It fell into disrepair during the 19th century but was restored in 1950, and since then has been in regular use as the Teatro dei Rinnovati. The Congrega dei Rozzi, founded in 1531, also produced *commedie* and pastoral plays with musical *intermedi*; Grand Duke Cosimo III granted them a theatre in 1690, and they became the Accademia dei Rozzi in the following year. The Teatro dei Rozzi, rebuilt in 1836, still stands.

During the 18th and 19th centuries Siena's musical life declined to a provincial level. But in the 20th century the tradition of the Sienese academies was revived by Count Guido Chigi Saracini, who in 1932 founded the Accademia Musicale Chigiana. Opera received a particular stimulus when in 1939 Saracini devised with Alfredo Casella the festival Settimana Musicale Senese. Inaugurated with a revival of Vivaldi's *Olimpiade* – which led to something of a Vivaldi renaissance – the festival has gained international renown for its successful presentation of little-known Italian works. Outstanding productions have included Alessandro Scarlatti's *Il trionfo dell'onore*, Pergolesi's *Il Flaminio*, Galuppi's *L'amante di tutte*, Cimarosa's *I tre amanti* and *I due baroni di Rocca Azzurra*, Traetta's *Le serve rivali*, Cesti's *Orontea*, Cherubini's *Pimmalione*, Rossini's *L'inganno felice* and *Adina*, Salieri's *Falstaff* and Donizetti's *Parisina*, many of these works receiving their first modern performances in specially commissioned revisions. The festival takes place in the summer.

R. Morrocchi: *La musica in Siena* (Siena, 1886)
L. Pinzauti: *L'Accademia musicale chigiana da Boito a Boulez* (Milan, 1982) GUIDO BURCHI

Siepi, Cesare (*b* Milan, 10 Feb 1923). Italian bass. After private vocal studies, he made his début as Sparafucile at Schio near Vicenza in 1941. In 1946 he sang Zaccaria (*Nabucco*) at La Scala, appearing at Covent Garden during the Scala company's visit in 1950. That autumn he opened Rudolf Bing's first Metropolitan season as Philip II; a member of the Metropolitan for 24 years, he performed the major *basso cantante* roles of the Italian repertory as well as Méphistophélès in *Faust*, Boris, and Gurnemanz in *Parsifal*. He has been especially admired for his Mozart roles, particularly Figaro and Don Giovanni which he sang in Salzburg in 1953 under Furtwängler. Like his predecessor, Ezio Pinza, he also attempted a Broadway musical comedy (*Bravo, Giovanni!*, 1962), but with little success. With a pleasantly warm, pliant, evenly schooled voice, he could always be relied on for intelligent, consistent, professional performances rather than interpretations of arresting artistic individuality.

*

GV (G. Gualerzi; R. Vegeto) PETER G. DAVIS

Sierra, Roberto (*b* Vega Baja, Puerto Rico, 9 Oct 1953). Puerto Rican composer. He studied in Puerto Rico, then in London and Utrecht and at the Hochschule für Musik in Hamburg (1979–82), where he was a pupil of Ligeti. He returned to Puerto Rico in 1982 and subsequently his works won many international prizes and gained more performances than those of any other Puerto Rican composer. In September 1989 he began a three-year appointment as composer-in-residence with the Milwaukee Symphony Orchestra.

Sierra's musical style is marked by the vigorous movement of melodic lines within a context of dissonant harmony, yet retains a traditional foundation. His two-act opera *El mensajero de plata*, to a libretto by Myrna Casas, was first performed at the Interamerican Festival, San Juan, on 9 October 1986. It represents a successful synthesis of many elements and tendencies previously evident in his instrumental and vocal music, including the stylization of Caribbean rhythms and melodic contours, while placing a Puerto Rican folk subject within the context of art music. *El mensajero de plata* is the first opera to have been composed and produced in Puerto Rico in the 20th century.

*

F. Cordero: 'Estreno de opera', *El mundo* [San Juan] (11 Oct 1986)
S. Cherson: 'Estreno plateado de "El mensajero de plata"', *El nuevo día* [San Juan] (12 Oct 1986)
D. Thompson: 'A Fine Puerto Rican Opera', *San Juan Star* (13 Oct 1986)
S. Lamoutte: 'Un "Mensajero" maravilloso', *El nuevo día* [San Juan] (13 April 1988) DONALD THOMPSON

Sievert, Ludwig (*b* Hanover, 17 May 1887; *d* Munich, 11 Dec 1966). German stage designer. After studying scene painting at the Stadttheater and at the school of applied arts in Aachen, he worked in various, chiefly Rhenish, scenic studios as a painter, 1904–9. He then became artistic director of the Werkstätte für Bühnenkunst in Munich (1910) and of the important Studio Lüttkemeyer in Coburg (1911), before going to the Städtische Bühnen in Freiburg (1912–14) as artistic director. There followed engagements as director of design at Mannheim (1914–18), Frankfurt (1918–37)

Design by Ludwig Sievert for the poet Goldhaar's garret in the original production of Krenek's 'Der Sprung über den Schatten' at the Opernhaus, Frankfurt, 9 June 1924: gouache and watercolour

and Munich (1937–43), as well as invitations to work at other European and American opera houses.

Sievert's work was at first influenced by neo-romanticism and the reforms of *Jugendstil*. He played a part in the development of the anti-historicist and anti-naturalist *Stilbühne*, to which he gave a craftsmanlike, ornamental stamp which asserted itself later, especially in his Mozart productions. The radicalization of the *Stilbühne* concept under the influence of expressionism, which he had undertaken with the director F. L. Hoerth in his Freiburg Wagner productions, was continued in Mannheim and Frankfurt. He developed an art of expression tending towards abstraction, rich in symbols, which in influential productions (e.g. *Sancta Susanna*, 1922, Frankfurt and Krenek's *Der Sprung über den Schatten*, 1924, Frankfurt; see illustration) sought to make visual the idealized, almost irrational emotional appeal of expressionist music drama through cubist forms, expressive colours and suggestive lighting effects. Elements of expressionism could still be traced in his sketches (especially for Wagner productions) until the 1950s, but after 1925 his work tended towards the concrete objectivity of the 'new realism'. This style, at first working with modernism (e.g. in the première of *Von heute auf morgen*, 1930, Frankfurt), then increasingly moving towards three-dimensional genre-painting and historicism, resulted in creditable artistic achievements even under the constraints imposed by fascism – which however enforced a flight into a conservatism based on craftsmanlike solidity, to which he remained committed even after World War II.

For further illustration *see* FRIEDENSTAG and STAGE DESIGN, fig.19.

'Das Bühnenbild', *Frankfurter Theater-Almanach*, iv (1920–21), 43
'Das Bühnenbild der Oper', *Hellweg*, iii (1923), 867–8; *Blätter der Städtischen Bühnen Frankfurt am Main*, ii (1925), 93
'So ist es ...!?', *Die Szene*, xviii (1928), 13–14
Bühnenbilder: 96 mehrfärbige und einfarbige Wiedergaben aus dem vergriffenen Werk 'Lebendiges Theater' (Munich, 1944)
with E. L. Stahl: *Lebendiges Theater: Drei Jahrzehnte deutscher Theaterkunst* (Munich, 1944)

ES (H. Grosse and E. Povoledo) [incl. list of works]
L. Wagner: *Der Szeniker Ludwig Sievert* (Berlin, 1926)
G. Frette: 'Gli scenografi dell'espressionismo', *Sipario*, xiii (1958), no.141, p.9
C. Niessen: *Der Szeniker Ludwig Sievert* (Cologne, 1959)
H. Grosse: 'Ludwig Sievert', *Bühnentechnische Rundschau*, liv/5 (1960), 16
A. R. Mohr: *Die Frankfurter Oper 1924–1944* (Frankfurt, 1971)

MANFRED BOETZKES

Siface. *See* GROSSI, GIOVANNI FRANCESCO.

Siface re di Numidia ('Syphax, King of Numidia') [*Siface*; *Viriate*]. Libretto by PIETRO METASTASIO, first set by Francesco Feo (1723, Naples).

ACT 1 Siface, King of Numidia, has sought peace with the King of Lusitania by offering marriage to his daughter, Viriate, even though he loves Ismene, daughter of Orcano, a Numidian nobleman. Ismene ignites Siface's animosity towards Viriate when she threatens to reject him if she cannot have the throne. Viriate, however, gains the support of Erminio, general of the Numidian armies, who, in love with Ismene, is distressed by her conduct, as is Orcano. Viriate also gains the respect of Libanio, Siface's confidant, when she repels his advances. Orcano threatens Ismene with his sword, then offers his own life to Viriate in reparation for his daughter's conduct. Viriate blames herself for his distress and urges Ismene to leave the palace; this she refuses to do.

ACT 2 Viriate is imprisoned; when Orcano protests, Siface charges her with infidelity. Erminio attempts to rescue her, fails, and is also imprisoned. Siface then reads a spurious letter to Orcano, supposedly written by Viriate to Erminio, in which the king's assassination is planned. Both Viriate and Erminio deny such duplicity in spite of rewards offered by Siface for confessions.

ACT 3 Libanio brings Viriate a cup of poison and a dagger and bids her choose her means of death. She asks permission to write a letter to her father, which Siface, suspecting treachery, snatches from her – only to discover a request for his pardon. Although moved, he still insists upon Viriate's death, in response to which she requests his sword. This, however, she uses to defend him when Orcano and Erminio rush in to rescue her. Overwhelmed, Siface yields. Orcano and Erminio are pardoned, and Ismene and Erminio are reunited.

* * *

Although Metastasio regarded *Didone abbandonata* as his first serious drama, *Siface*, an adaptation of Domenico David's *La forza della virtù*, preceded it by one year. David had based his plot on the Spanish historical figure, Pedro the Cruel (1334–69), King of Castile from 1350. In love with María de Padilla, Pedro was forced into marriage with Blanche, daughter of the Duke of Bourbon, to secure a Franco-Castilian alliance against England; he abandoned Blanche immediately after the marriage (1353) and María remained his mistress until her death in 1361. David did not use the historical names for his characters, and Metastasio changed them yet again, reducing their number, and moving the location from Spain to Numidia. His rewriting resulted in a more tightly organized text with the actions better motivated. Emotional expression, however, is more restrained, particularly in the case of Ismene and the heroine, Viriate, with whom there is a greater focus on moral duty than is the case with David's counterpart. Siface [Syphax] was a Numidian prince, erroneously called King of Numidia in some classical sources. By substituting Siface for Pedro, Metastasio associated his text with the popular Sophonisba dramas of his time (one was set by Traetta, as *SOFONISBA*), and with such names as Gian Giorgio Trissino, Jean Mairet and Pierre Corneille. Variously based on classical accounts, these dramas also involved a second love interest for a married partner and the offering of poison to the central female figure. There, however, the similarities end. In France, Pedro's story was dramatized by Charles Regnault as *Blanche de Bourbon reyne d'Espagne* (1641), and subsequently by Pierre de Belloy as *Pierre le Cruel* (1772) and Voltaire as *Don Pèdre*, published in 1774 but never performed. Although Metastasio generally suppressed *Siface*, it was set at least 13 times; Feo's version (1723, Naples) is regarded as one of his best works.

For a list of settings *see* METASTASIO, PIETRO. DON NEVILLE

Sigismondo. *Dramma* in two acts by GIOACHINO ROSSINI to a libretto by GIUSEPPE MARIA FOPPA; Venice, Teatro La Fenice, 26 December 1814.

A failure with the public at the time, and arguably Rossini's most unrevivable serious opera, *Sigismondo* concerns the destructive advice given by a minister Ladislao (tenor) to Sigismondo, King of Poland (contralto), regarding his wife, Aldimira (soprano), daughter of the King of Hungary. Chance encounters, military defeat and private remorse all help bring Sigismondo to his senses; and his queen is eventually restored to her rightful throne. Rossini later used music from *Sigismondo* in his considerably more succesful *Elisabetta, regina d'Inghilterra* (1815, Naples) and fragments even appear in the *introduzione* and 'Calumny' aria of *Il barbiere di Siviglia* (1816, Rome).

RICHARD OSBORNE

Sigismondo, Giuseppe (*b* Naples, 13 Sept 1739; *d* Naples, 10 May 1826). Italian historian and composer. He studied both music (with Porpora) and law, and devoted much of his time to acting 'all'improvviso' in an amateur theatrical company for which he wrote many comedies, some of which were published. He was also active as a singing teacher and amateur composer, and the music of three stage works survives in autograph. Of more interest, he provided Saverio Mattei with material for his important book (1784) on Jommelli, of whom he had been a close friend (some say pupil). Mattei later had Sigismondo appointed archivist-librarian at the Pietà dei Turchini Conservatory (1794). Although Sigismondo gathered materials for a history of music in Naples, he never published them. His four-volume manuscript (1820) became instead the fully-acknowledged basis of the Marchese di Villarosa's *Memorie dei compositori di musica del regno di Napoli* (Naples, 1840).

Endimione, ?1764/5 (P. Metastasio), ?unperf., *I-Nc**
L'isola disabitata (op teatrale, 1, Metastasio), Naples, S Bartolomeo, 1766, *Nc**
La prosuntuosa delusa (int), Arienzo, 1783, *Nc**
Demetrio, 1 aria *Nc* DENNIS LIBBY

Signor Bruschino, Il [*Il Signor Bruschino, ossia Il figlio per azzardo* ('Mr Bruschino, or Son by Accident')]. *Farsa giocosa* in one act by GIOACHINO ROSSINI to a libretto by GIUSEPPE MARIA FOPPA after the play *Le fils par hasard, ou Ruse et folie* by Alissan de Chazet and E.-T. Maurice Ourry; Venice, Teatro S Moisè, 27 January 1813.

The setting is the country house of Gaudenzio Strappapuppole (bass), the guardian of Sofia (soprano). She is in love with Florville (tenor) but there is no hope of their marrying because Gaudenzio has long been a sworn enemy of Florville's father. However, the sudden death of old Florville encourages his son to restake his claim. Unfortunately, Gaudenzio has promised Sofia to the son of his old friend Signor Bruschino. At a local inn young Bruschino has run up a huge bill, much to the consternation of the innkeeper Filiberto (bass). When Florville hears of this, he offers to pay the bill, provided young Bruschino is detained at the inn for a suitable time; meanwhile, he resolves to present himself to Gaudenzio as Bruschino's son. This he does; but the unexpected arrival of old Bruschino (bass), in a thoroughly bad mood because of the heat, upsets everything. Bruschino is surprised to hear of his son's escapades and even more surprised to be presented with a young man who is palpably not his son. After a central ensemble of confusion, Sofia attempts to intercede with old Bruschino in her aria, 'Ah! donate il caro sposo', but to no avail. In a series of misunderstandings over names and handwriting, everyone, including the Police Officer (bass), concludes that Florville is Bruschino's son: Bruschino, they believe, is simply trying to wriggle out of his contract with Gaudenzio. With the drama now verging on comedy of menace, old Bruschino is brought to the edge of breakdown as he is baited like a bear at the stake. But the innkeeper has not been paid and when old Bruschino offers to settle on the spot Filiberto tells all. Bruschino now has the upper hand, and when he learns that Florville is the son of Gaudenzio's old enemy he determines to exact revenge by recognizing Florville as his son and urging his immediate marriage with Sofia. Despite the arrival of the real young Bruschino (tenor), stuttering out his one line of apology to a bedraggled minor-key march, old Bruschino, like Falstaff in Windsor Forest, has the last laugh while Florville and Sofia are happily married.

Il Signor Bruschino is the last of the *farse* written for the S Moisè in Venice and more or less perfects the kind of sustained 80-minute musical structure that was shortly to serve Rossini so well in the first acts of such works as *L'italiana in Algeri*. At the same time, it introduces into his style new elements of acerbity and comic realism. RICHARD OSBORNE

Signor dottore, Il ('The Doctor'). *Dramma giocoso per musica* in three acts by DOMENICO FISCHIETTI to a libretto by CARLO GOLDONI; Venice, Teatro S Moisè, autumn 1758.

The tailor Beltrame (bass) has invested considerable money in the education of his son, Bernardino (tenor). When Bernardino returns from university with a doctorate in law, Beltrame sees this as an opportunity to marry off both his son and his daughter, Pasquina (soprano), to rich parties from a higher social rank. For his son he chooses the widowed countess Clarice (soprano), who enjoys using her suitors for her own amusement – as has been the case with Don Alberto (soprano castrato). She pretends willingness to marry Bernardino in order to play a joke on both father and son. The town apothecary Fabrizio (tenor) is in love with Pasquina, while his own sister Rosina (contralto) is in love with Bernardino, who is now ignoring her as she is no longer good enough for him. But Rosina brings Bernardino to his senses when the countess and Don Alberto reveal that he has never attended university and has usurped his father's money. Since Pasquina can no longer aspire to marry someone rich, she settles for Fabrizio. Beltrame reconciles himself to life as an impecunious tailor.

The libretto satirizes the artificiality of social rank and social climbers. Along with *Il mercato di Malmantile*, *Il signor dottore* was regarded as Fischietti's most successful opera. It had a lifespan on European stages of at least two decades, with a revival in Pavia as late as 1787. Rosina's Act 2 aria 'No che non son più quella' ('I am not the one') became a particularly popular number.

GORDANA LAZAREVICH

Signorini, Francesca Caccini. *See* CACCINI family, (2).

Sigurd. *Opéra* in four acts and nine tableaux by ERNEST REYER to a libretto by CAMILLE DU LOCLE and Alfred Blau; Brussels, Théâtre de la Monnaie, 7 January 1884.

Blau's libretto, versified by Du Locle, was based on a French translation of the *Nibelungenlied*. When Reyer embarked on the opera, probably between 1862 and 1866 (although this remains uncertain), Reyer knew no Wagner later than *Lohengrin* and was certainly unaware that he was engaged on a vast opera on the same subject. The fact that *Sigurd* was not performed until 1884, when French Wagnerism was rapidly gaining ground, caused unfortunate comparisons to be made. It is to the opera's credit that in spite of such overwhelming competition it was remarkably successful. Its Brussels première was followed swiftly by productions in Lyons and Paris, where it remained in the repertory for half a century.

The characters Gunther (baritone), Hagen (bass-baritone), Brunehild (soprano), Sigurd (tenor) and the three Norns (silent roles) are shared with *Götterdämmerung*. Gunther's sister is named Hilda (soprano). Longing for a hero she has seen in her dreams, she refuses the hand of Attila the Hun. Sigurd arrives and challenges Gunther in rivalry for the rescue of Brunehild, who has been confined in an impregnable castle by Odin. But Gunther is conciliatory, since Sigurd once rescued Hilda from captivity, and they swear an oath of brotherhood instead. After drinking a magic potion Sigurd is struck by Hilda's beauty.

Concealing his face with a visor, Sigurd rescues Brunehild on Gunther's behalf, and then claims Hilda as his reward. All is well until Brunehild confesses her true passion for Sigurd and learns from Hilda that it was Sigurd, not Gunther, who rescued her. Gunther is full of remorse until Hagen tells him he has seen Sigurd and Brunehild meeting secretly at night. Sigurd falls to Gunther's sword; Brunehild joins him on his funeral pyre.

The libretto is wordy and old-fashioned in tone, and the score, for all its strong invention, is long and spacious. Reyer bitterly resisted cuts, however. It has a prominent group of motifs, well characterized, but the style recalls not Wagner but more often Weber, Meyerbeer, Gounod and Berlioz (the old nurse full of foreboding may be compared with Berlioz's Cassandra in *Les Troyens*). It is a full-blooded score that yields very little to the French taste for the purely decorative.

HUGH MACDONALD

Si j'étais roi ('If I were King'). *Opéra comique* in three acts by ADOLPHE ADAM to a libretto by Adolphe Philippe d'Ennery and Jules Brésil; Paris, Théâtre Lyrique, 4 September 1852.

Zéphoris (tenor), a young fisherman in 16th-century Goa, rescues an unknown girl from drowning ('J'ignore son nom, sa naissance'). When he discovers that she is Princess Nemea (soprano), he dreams of becoming a king so that he may be worthy enough to marry her. His wish is granted by the real King (baritone), a benevolent monarch, for just a single day, during which Zéphoris manages to win his royal bride, despite the machinations of the wicked Prince Kadoor (baritone), who wants to marry her himself. The gentle fantasy of the text is perfectly matched by the imagination of the music, written in the composer's most delightful style. Though as melodious as ever, a feeling of elegiac tenderness has become apparent, while the delicacy of the orchestration is even more noticeable than in earlier works. Less popular than either *Le chalet* in France or *Le postillon de Lonjumeau* abroad, *Si j'étais roi* can lay claim to be Adam's finest and most enduring opera.

ELIZABETH FORBES

Silbersee, Der [*Der Silbersee: ein Wintermärchen* ('The Silverlake: a Winter's Fairy-Tale')]. Play with music in three acts by KURT WEILL to a libretto by Georg Kaiser; simultaneous premières at Leipzig, Altes Theater; Erfurt, Stadttheater; and Magdeburg, Stadttheater, 18 February 1933.

After raiding a grocery store, Severin (tenor) and his comrades are fired upon by the country policeman Olim (singing actor; baritone). Severin, who has stolen only a pineapple, is wounded and arrested. Olim feels such remorse that he alters his report to feign Severin's innocence, and retires from duty. He then wins the lottery and buys a castle. There he devotes himself to serving as Severin's generous but guilty benefactor. Severin, confined to a wheelchair and seething with revenge, is initially ignorant of his host's identity.

Frau von Laub (mezzo-soprano), Olim's housekeeper, is intrigued by the relationship between the two men. In order to discover more she enlists her charming and guileless niece Fennimore (soprano). Through

'Der Silbersee' (Weill): Act 1 scene ii (the grocery store) from the original production at the Stadttheater, Magdeburg, 18 February 1933, designed by Ernst Rufer

Fennimore, Severin discovers Olim's secret. Severin's doctor prescribes music, which Fennimore provides, accompanying herself on the harp in the 'Ballad of Caesar's Death'. But the song only fuels the patient's wrath, as does Fennimore's dance performed by two bananas on the ends of forks (as in Chaplin's film *The Gold Rush*): Severin's attention is drawn to the fruit bowl and hence to the original booty from the raid, a pineapple. Hiding in the attic from the vengeful Severin, Olim is duped by Frau von Laub into signing away his property to her.

Frau von Laub enlists Olim's former colleague, the portly country policeman (spoken) to reveal Olim's identity. But Fennimore encourages a reconciliation after Severin has systematically overcome his anger: 'Whoever must continue', she had advised, 'will be supported by the silver lake'. Instead of drowning, as they intended, Olim and Severin escape across the frozen 'silver' lake. A gust of wind blows away the snow and reveals the green countryside, and with bright sunshine sparkling on the ice, winter is transformed into spring.

For his last work written in Germany, Weill turned again to Georg Kaiser, the expressionist playwright with whom he had collaborated on *Der Protagonist* and *Der Zar lässt sich photographieren.* The description 'play with music' belies the composer's substantial contribution and also the considerable demands of the score. The closest model is the Singspiel, except that *Der Silbersee* was written for theatre companies, not opera houses, from which Weill could have expected little support in 1933. Yet the work is less the product of expediency than of Weill's abiding concern with generic reform for which he was keen to enlist leading playwrights. Given the complex score, with its 16 numbers, including solo songs, duets, choruses and melodramas, and an orchestra comprising at least 30 musicians, the cast will tend to be singers who can act rather than vice versa. The full title *Der Silbersee: ein Wintermärchen* alludes to three works: *Der Schatz im Silbersee*, a popular late 19th-century Wild West story by Karl May; Shakespeare's *The Winter's Tale*; and Heine's *Deutschland: ein Wintermärchen*, a sardonic commentary on Germany from Parisian exile. That Weill and Kaiser had similarly sardonic intentions is beyond question. A central theme of *Der Silbersee*, also found in much of Kaiser's more overtly expressionist work, is the renewal of man. In the economic and political turmoil of 1932–3 prospects of renewal must have seemed to require nothing short of a mystical transfiguration. As a constitutive part of the drama, the music often transports the action into the realm of the fantastic. Some of the songs, which have become detached from the work as pieces in their own right, also provide scarcely veiled commentary on current affairs, racial origin ('Ich bin eine arme Verwandte'), capitalism ('Was zahlen Sie für einen Rat') and demagogy ('Cäsars Tod'). The triple première met with considerable critical acclaim. Universal Edition published both a vocal score and a volume containing six of the songs. But by March civil liberties had been suspended, following the Reichstag fire, and all further performances were banned. Weill wisely left for France. For a production in West Berlin in 1955 Boris Blacher and others arranged a somewhat shortened version of the score for five musicians. David Drew has made both a concert version (1971) and a concert suite (1975). In 1980 the New York City Opera staged a freely adapted version, entitled *Silverlake*, with book and lyrics by Hugh Wheeler and a musically continuous score by Lys Symonette incorporating material from other Weill compositions. While Wheeler objected to the original's 'pissy-assed socialism', Drew has described the New York version as 'wellnigh indefensible'.

STEPHEN HINTON

Silja, Anja (*b* Berlin, 17 April 1935). German soprano. She studied with her grandfather, Egon van Rijn, making her début in 1955 as Rosina at Brunswick, where her roles included Micaëla, Zerbinetta and Leonora (*Il trovatore*). In 1959 she sang the Queen of Night at the Aix-en-Provence Festival. In 1960 Wieland Wagner engaged her for Bayreuth as Senta; during the next seven years (as Elsa, Elisabeth, Eva, Freia and Venus) she became the most controversial singing actress at post-war Bayreuth. Her close association with Wieland Wagner continued at Brussels, Cologne, Stuttgart and Frankfurt, where she sang Isolde, Brünnhilde, Leonore, Lulu, Marie (*Wozzeck*), Renata (*The Fiery Angel*), Kát'a, Desdemona, Salome and Electra. She made her London début at Sadler's Wells (1963) with the Frankfurt Opera in *Fidelio*, which she also sang at her Covent Garden début in 1967; other Covent Garden roles included Cassandra (*Les Troyens*) and Marie. She made her American début as Senta in Chicago (1968). At the Metropolitan (1972) she sang Leonore and Salome. Engaged at the Hamburg Staatsoper from 1974 to 1984, she created Luise (*Kabale und Liebe*) in Vienna (1976). She sang Regan (Reimann's *Lear*) at San Francisco (1985), Emilia Marty (*The Makropulos Affair*) at Boston (1986), Lady Macbeth (1987) and Grete (*Der ferne Klang*) at Brussels (1988). At the 1989 Glyndebourne festival she sang the Kostelnička in *Jenůfa*. Silja is a performer of great magnetism. Her early assumption of heavy dramatic roles put pressure on her bright, strong lyric soprano, but her wholehearted stage portrayals command admiration. She married the conductor Christoph von Dohnányi.

For illustration *see* WINDGASSEN, WOLFGANG.

*

W. Schwinger: 'Anja Silja', *Opera*, xx (1969), 193–8

HAROLD ROSENTHAL/R

Silkkirumpu ('The Damask Drum'). Opera in one act by PAAVO HEININEN to a libretto by Eeva-Liisa Manner and the composer after Motokiyo Zeami's noh play; Helsinki, Aleksanterinteattri, 5 April 1984.

The Damask Drum is set in the gardens of a palace. An old and lonely Gardener (baritone) falls in love with a Princess (soprano). He is encouraged to beat a drum hanging from a laurel tree by the lake, believing that if the sound carries to the palace, he may see his adored Princess again. However, no sound emerges from the drum. The Gardener beats it increasingly desperately, until he realizes that he has been mocked. In fury he throws himself in the lake and is turned into a demon. He takes possession of the Princess's mind and causes her in turn to beat the drum, but she cannot escape the Gardener's revenge, for she too has become a demon.

The work, defined by the composer as a 'concerto', is constructed as a succession of scenes connected by orchestral interludes and comments from the chorus. The music is uncompromisingly avant-garde, but also intensely colourful. The opera was well received and quickly established in the Finnish National Opera repertory.

ERKKI ARNI

Silla ('Sulla'). Opera in three acts by GEORGE FRIDERIC HANDEL to a libretto by GIACOMO ROSSI; possibly performed privately at the Queen's Theatre, London, 2 June 1713.

The circumstances of the composition and performance of *Silla* are obscure. One copy of a printed wordbook survives, in Italian only and entitled 'L. C. Silla'; it bears a dedication by Rossi to the Duc d'Aumont, the recently appointed French Ambassador, dated 2 June 1713. A performance on that date is therefore likely, but the venue is not mentioned, no cast is given and no specific record of a performance has been found. If the opera was staged, it was surely in the Queen's Theatre, presumably privately hired for the occasion: the complex scenic effects often echo those in previous operas at the Queen's and could have been realized by the same machines.

Rossi's libretto is based on Plutarch's account of the life of Lucius Cornelius Sulla (138–78 BC). The action takes place in and near Rome. Sulla (alto) returns to the city after military victories and, to the dismay of his wife Metella (soprano) and his friend the tribune Lepido [Lepidus] (soprano), becomes its tyrant. Lepidus's wife Flavia (soprano) has a vision of Rome being burned by a monster. Sulla is opposed by the Roman knight Claudio [Claudius] (alto) who is in love with Celia (soprano), the daughter of one of Sulla's lieutenants; she conceals her love for him because he is Sulla's enemy. A god (bass) – or Hecate, according to the wordbook – appears to Sulla in a dream and inspires him to order the slaughter of refugees in the temple of Berecynthia. Sulla's viciousness is further emphasized by his lascivious advances to both Flavia and Celia. When Claudius and Lepidus try to defend the honour of their women, Sulla orders his favourite Scabro [Scabrus] (silent role) to have Lepidus stabbed and Claudius thrown to the lions; but Metella arranges with Scabrus to get them released. Sulla decides to leave Rome, but first torments Celia with a report of Claudius's death. When she proves resolute, he tries a similar trick on Flavia with equal lack of success. Both women are reunited with their true lovers. Sulla embarks on a sea journey, is shipwrecked, and is rescued by Metella. On the steps of the Capitol, Lepidus and Claudius proclaim the end of tyranny; the god Mars (silent role) appears in glory. Sulla begs pardon for his sins and renounces his titles, to general acclamation.

Handel's score survives nominally complete in five manuscript copies, which broadly conform to the extant fragments of the autograph but do not include music for some of the lines in the wordbook and have no instrumental music to cover the scene transformations. Perhaps a more complete version of the score was made in a source that has not come down to us, or perhaps the opera was cancelled at the last minute and was never finished for performance. The score in its surviving form thus often seems perfunctory, and the characters are not sharply drawn. Yet there are several arias and arioso passages of high quality, especially in the parts of the sorely tried Flavia and Celia, and the scene in which the god appears to Sulla has real dramatic power. The fact that a significant amount of musical material was re-used in Handel's next opera, *Amadigi*, suggests that the composer never regarded *Silla* as more than a *pièce d'occasion.*

ANTHONY HICKS

Sills, Beverly [Silverman, Belle] (*b* Brooklyn, NY, 25 May 1929). American soprano and opera director. When she was seven she began vocal studies with Estelle Liebling; she made her operatic début as Frasquita with the Philadelphia Civic Opera in 1947, and sang with the San Francisco Opera. In 1955 she joined the New York City Opera and became the company's diva. She gained great recognition for her Cleopatra in Handel's *Giulio Cesare* (1966), continuing in bel canto roles, including Donizetti's trio of Tudor queens, Mary Stuart, Anne Boleyn and Elizabeth in *Roberto Devereux*. Appearances in major European opera houses quickly followed, including the Queen of Night in Vienna (1967), Rossini's *Le siège de Corinthe* at La Scala (1969) and *Lucia di Lammermoor* at Covent Garden (1970). Her formal début at the Metropolitan was in 1975, as Pamyre in *Le siège de Corinthe*. Sills was general director of the New York City Opera, 1979–89. Although a singer of secure and often brilliant technical accomplishment, she lacked the dramatic weight of Callas and the sheer tonal beauty of Caballé or Sutherland. As a consequence the lighter, less dramatically commanding roles such as Lucia and Elvira (*I puritani*) seemed more suited to her voice and temperament. An excellent actress with a warm ingratiating stage personality, she perhaps found her most congenial part in Massenet's Manon. In 1980 she received the Presidential Medal of Freedom, and in 1985 a Kennedy Center Honor.

*

W. Sargent: 'Beverly Sills', *Divas* (New York, 1973), 77–103
J. B. Steane: *The Grand Tradition* (New York, 1974), 401ff
R. Jacobson: 'At Long Last!: on the Occasion of her Met Debut Beverly Sills talks with Robert Jacobson', *ON*, xxxix/21 (1974–5), 54
B. Sills: *Bubbles: a Self-Portrait* (New York, 1976, 2/1981 as *Bubbles: an Encore*)
J. Hines: 'Beverly Sills', *Great Singers on Great Singing* (Garden City, NY, 1982), 302–12
B. Sills: *Beverly: an Autobiography* (New York, 1987)

PETER G. DAVIS

Silva, João Cordeiro da (*fl* 1756–1808). Portuguese composer. He may have studied in Naples but on 21 November 1756 he was admitted to the Irmandade de S Cecília, the musicians' benevolent association of Lisbon. In 1763 he was already organist and composer of the Real Capela de Ajuda, and the following year he started to receive a yearly salary of 240 000 réis from the royal theatres. He was praised in a letter from the director of the royal theatres to Jommelli dating from 1767, which also indicates that by then he was responsible for all operatic productions at the Lisbon court, including the adaptation of Jommelli's own operas for local conditions. In his own compositions he attempted to follow Jommelli's style as closely as possible. He may have replaced João de Sousa Carvalho after his retirement as music master to the princes. In 1808 he was earning 170 000 réis as first *mestre* to the future King João VI but was considered too old to follow the royal family to Brazil. None of his dramatic works, which were all written for the Lisbon court, has received a modern revival.

all first performed in Lisbon

dm – *dramma per musica*

Untitled 'componimento drammatico', Ajuda, 6 June 1764
Il natal di Giove (serenata, P. Metastasio), Queluz Palace, 21 Aug 1778, *P-La*
Edalide e Cambise (dm, 1), Ajuda, 17 Dec 1780, *La*
Il ratto di Proserpina (dm da cantarsi, 1, G. Martinelli), Queluz Palace, 25 July 1784, ov. *Em*
Archelao (dm da cantarsi, 1, Martinelli), Queluz Palace, 21 Aug 1785, *La*
Telemaco nell'isola di Calipso (dm, 1), Ajuda, 21 Aug 1787, *Em*, inc.
Megara tebana (dm, 1, Martinelli), Ribeira Palace, 25 July 1788, *La*, ov. *Em*
Bauce e Palemone (dm, 1, Martinelli), Ajuda, 25 April 1789, *La*, ov. *Em*
Lindane e Dalmiro (dramma serio-comico, 2, Martinelli), Ajuda, 17 Dec 1789, *La*

Doubtful: L'Arcadia in Brenta (dramma giocoso, 3, C. Goldoni), Salvaterra, carn. 1764, *La*

*

F. Mazza: *Dicionário biográfico de músicos portugueses* (MS, *P-EVp*, Cx IV 1–26); ed. J. A. Alegria, *Ocidente*, xxiii-vi (1944–5); pubd separately (Lisbon, 1945), 82
F. M. de Sousa Viterbo: 'Os musicos e mais pessoal dos theatros regios no tempo do Principe regente (depois D. João VI)', *Arte musical*, xii (1910), 106
M. P. McClymonds: *Niccolo Jommelli: the Last Years, 1769–1774* (Ann Arbor, 1981)
M. C. de Brito: *Opera in Portugal in the Eighteenth Century* (Cambridge, 1989)

MANUEL CARLOS DE BRITO

Silvana. Romantische Oper in three acts, J87, by CARL MARIA VON WEBER to a libretto by Franz Carl Hiemer after a text by Carl von Steinsberg; Frankfurt, 16 September 1810.

Silvana was the first of Weber's operas to win some success. It was composed between July 1808 and February 1810, partly from material used in his earlier *Das Waldmädchen* (1800), for which Steinsberg had written the libretto. The original intention of producing it in Stuttgart was frustrated by Weber's banishment over a financial scandal. Its première in Frankfurt was not particularly successful, but at its production in Berlin two years later it was enthusiastically received. For this production Weber completely rewrote nos.4 and 10. It was among the first operas that Weber produced in Dresden after taking up his post there in 1817.

The plot, like many of the period, is complex and packed with incident; it concerns the trials and tribulations of a pair of lovers. Count Rudolf (tenor) falls in love with Silvana, the mute heroine, after finding her living wild in the forest. He, however, is betrothed to Mechtilde (soprano), whom he does not love. He is not aware that she does not wish to marry him since she is actually in love with Albert (tenor). The problem is that Albert is the son of Hanns von Cleeburg, the old enemy of Mechtilde's father, Adelhart (bass). Years earlier Hanns had kidnapped Adelhart's other daughter, Ottilie. Eventually it transpires that Silvana is the lost Ottilie; she recovers her voice, and the opera ends with the usual universal rejoicing. There are also several squires and servants who provide additional complications to the plot and a certain amount of comic relief.

Though the music of *Silvana* is obviously that of an immature composer, it contains many elements which hint at Weber's later mastery and a number of passages which are impressive in themselves. Weber's music is particularly effective when it is inspired by nature; the forest scene at the beginning of the first act and the orchestral introduction to Act 3, which represents a storm in the forest, are especially fine. Weber also shows flashes of his later skill in characterization; Adelhart is a more rounded figure than many of his type in the operas of the period and Rudolf, too, is shown to be more than the conventional heroic tenor. At many points in the opera Weber displays his feelings for sensitive and colourful orchestration. CLIVE BROWN

Silvani, Francesco [Valsini, Frencasco] (*b* Venice *c*1660; *d* 1728–44). Italian librettist. He was an abbot; little else is known about his life. He issued his first two works, which are discussed in the *Mercure galant* of March 1683, under the anagram 'Frencasco Valsini'. Between 1691 and 1716 he produced librettos under his own name for various Venetian theatres almost every year. The title-pages of his librettos document that he served Ferdinando Carlo, Duke of Mantua, from 1699 to 1705. The duke granted Silvani his patent after Silvani wrote *L'oracolo in sogno* for a production in Mantua in June 1699, but it is not known how much time Silvani spent there. He was usually on hand for the Venetian productions of his works. He reached the height of his career in the years 1708–14 when he wrote for the Teatro S Giovanni Grisostomo, the most important theatre in Venice.

Silvani's identification with reform librettists, such as Zeno, Pariati and Frigimelica Roberti, stems from his clearly motivated plots, elevated diction, and extensive passages of recitative. He occasionally borrowed from earlier literary works. *Armida abbandonata* and *Armida al campo* are based on Tasso's *Gerusalemme liberata*, and *La pace generosa* is indebted to Seneca's *Troades* ('The Trojan Women'). Two works are based on French neo-classical dramas: *I veri amici* on Pierre Corneille's *Héraclius empereur d'Orient*, and *La costanza combattuta in amore* on Nicolas Pradon's *Statira*. For autumn productions he often wrote pastorals, suited to the nobles' return from *villeggiatura*. His carnival works, which are heroic, usually have historical characters, although the plots are not always historically founded. He reacted strongly to charges of plagiarism. In the preface to *L'innocenza giustificata*, he declared it to be his policy to place his name on the title-pages of only those works that were entirely his own in invention, disposition and elocution. He pointed to *Il principe selvaggio* as a work that he wrote with the advice and assistance of others; hence it does not bear his name on the title-page.

Silvani was fond of long, abstract titles; later productions often shortened the original title to a character's name. The high literary esteem Silvani's work enjoyed is clear from the publication after his death of 24 librettos in a collected edition, *Opere drammatiche del signor Abate Francesco Silvani* (Venice, 1744).

Ottone il grande, Biego, 1682; *Marzio Coriolano*, Perti, 1683; *L'inganno scoperto per vendetta*, Perti, 1691 (Ariosti, 1725, as Dario); *La virtù trionfante dell'amore e dell'odio*, M. A. Ziani, 1691 (Vivaldi, Micheli and N. Romaldi, 1724, as La virtù trionfante dell'amore, e dell'odio, overo Il Tigrane; Hasse, 1729, as Tigrane; Arena, 1741, as Tigrane); *La moglie nemica*, Ziani, 1694 (L. Tavelli, 1726, as Ottone amante and Amore e sdegno); *Il principe selvaggio*, M. A. Gasparini, 1695

La costanza in trionfo, Ziani, 1696 (Schürmann, 1704, as Leonilde, oder Die siegende Beständigkeit; Handel, 1721, as Floridante); *L'ingratitudine gastigata*, Albinoni, 1698 (Caldara, ?1698; comp. unknown, 1701, as Alarico re de' vandali; F. Gasparini, Albinoni and others, 1705, as Alarico, ovvero L'ingratitudine gastigata); *L'innocenza giustificata*, Vinaccesi, 1698 (comp. unknown, 1699, as Carlo re d'Alemagna; Chelleri, 1711; Orlandini, 1713, as Carlo re d'Alemagna; Ger., J. G. Hamann, Chelleri, Telemann and Handel, 1732, as Judith, Gemahlin Kayser Ludewigs des Frommen, oder Die siegende Unschuld; Vivaldi, 1739, as Feraspe)

La fortezza al [in] cimento, Aldrovandini, 1699 (Albinoni, 1707; A. Guerra and Vivaldi, 1726, as La tirannia gastigata; G. Bencini, 1727, as Nerone; *L'oracolo in sogno*, Caldara, Quintavalle and C. F. Pollarolo, 1699 (various comps., 1700; A. M. Bononcini, 1721, as Rosiclea in Dania); *Il duello d'amore e di vendetta*, Ziani, 1700 (Handel, 1707, as Vincer se stesso è la maggior vittoria [Rodrigo]; G. M. Buini, 1725, as Gli sdegni cangiati in amore; B. Galuppi, 1729, as L'odio placato)

La pace generosa, Ziani, 1700; *L'inganno innocente*, Albinoni, 1701 (Albinoni and Stuck, 1702, as Rodrigo in Algeri; Gluck, Maccari, Lampugnani and Vinci, 1744, as La finta schiava); *L'arte in gara con l'arte*, Albinoni, 1702; *Gl'imenei stabiliti dal caso*, Gasparini, 1702 (various comps., 1720, as La sorte nell'amore); *Il più fedel fra i vassalli*, Gasparini, 1703 (Aldrovandini, 1705; Perti and others, 1710; comp. unknown, 1714, as Il più fedel fra i vassalli ossia L'innocenza trionfante; Ger., Gasparini, 1716, as Die unverfälschte Landestreu, das ist Antiochus der Getreueste unter den Untertanen im Lande)

Il miglior d'ogni amore per il peggior d'ogni odio, Gasparini, 1703 (Graun, 1727, as Sancio und Sinilde; Telemann, 1727, as Sancio, oder Die siegende Grossmuth); *La fede tradita e vendicata*, Gasparini, 1704 (Orlandini, 1709; Gasparini, Orlandini and others, 1712; Vivaldi, 1726; Vinci, 1726, as Ernelinda; various comps., 1726, as Rodoaldo re di Norvegia; Bioni, 1729; Galuppi, 1744, as Ricimero); *La maschera levata al vizio*, Gasparini, 1704 (Buini, 1730, and 1735, as Il filosofo ippocrita); *Fredegonda*, Gasparini, 1705

Il principato custodito dalla frode, Gasparini, 1705; *La fede tra gl'inganni*, Albinoni, 1707; *Armida abbandonata*, Ruggieri, 1707 (Buini, 1716; Bioni, 1725); *Armida al campo*, Boniventi, 1708 (Bioni, 1726); *Arrenione*, Ruggieri, 1708 (?Vignati, 1720, as Aquilio in Siracusa; Ariosti, 1724, as Aquilio consolo); *Sofonisba*, Caldara, 1708; *Il tradimento tradito*, Albinoni, 1709; *La ninfa riconosciuta* (melodramma pastorale), Pollarolo, 1709 (Buini, 1724); *Ama più chi men si crede* (melodramma pastorale), Lotti, 1709; *Il comando non inteso et ubbidito*, Lotti, 1710 (Gasparini, 1713)

Il tradimento traditor di se stesso, Lotti, 1711 (Lotti and F. Mancini, 1713, as Artaserse re di Persia; various comps., 1721, as Artaserse; Porpora, 1742, as Statira); *La forza del sangue*, Lotti, 1711 (L. A. Predieri, 1736, as Zoe); *L'infedeltà punita*, Lotti and Pollarolo, 1712; *I veri amici* (with Lalli), A. Paulati, 1712 (Vivaldi, 1720, as Candace, o siano Li veri amici; Albinoni, 1722; Fiorè and Giai, 1728; Lampugnani, 1740, as Candace; Leo, 1731, as Evergete); *La verità nell'inganno*, Gasparini, 1713 (Caldara, 1717, as Tiridate, overo La verità nell'inganno, and 1727, as La verità nell'inganno, ossia Arsinoe; Capelli, 1726, as I fratelli riconosciuti; Porpora, 1726; Hasse, 1728, as Attalo, re di Bitinia; Chinzer, 1743, as Atalo)

Irene augusta, Lotti, 1713; *Semiramide*, Pollarolo, 1714 (Vivaldi, 1732); *La costanza combattuta in amore*, Giovanni Porta, 1716 (A. Galeazzi, 1731, as Il trionfo della costanza in Statira vedova d'Alessandro; Paganelli, 1742, as Barsina); *Amor in gara col fasto*, Pollarolo, 1718; *La sorte nemica*, Porta, 1725, as Amor e fortuna

*

Chassebras de Cramailles: Reviews of 'Ottone il grande' and 'Marzio Coriolano', *Mercure galant* (March 1683)

V. Coronelli: *Guida de' forestieri* (Venice, 1700)

R. Strohm: 'Händel in Italia: nuovi contributi', *RIM*, ix (1974), 152–74

——: 'Händel und seine italienischen Operntexte', *HJb 1975–6*, 101–59; rev. and trans. in *Essays on Handel and Italian Opera* (Cambridge, 1985), 34–79

——: *Italienische Opernarien des frühen Settecento (1720–1730)*, *AnMc*, no.16 (1976)

W. Dean and J. M. Knapp: *Handel's Operas (1704–1726)* (Oxford, 1987)

L. Bianconi and G. La Face Bianconi, eds.: *I libretti italiani di Georg Friedrich Händel e le loro fonti* (Florence, 1992–)

HARRIS S. SAUNDERS

Silver, Charles (*b* Paris, 16 April 1868; *d* Paris, 10 Oct 1949). French composer. A student of Dubois and Massenet, Silver won the Prix de Rome in 1891. He subsequently entered the army and composed highly esteemed military music. His first opera, *La belle au bois dormant*, though based on leitmotifs, is nonetheless clearly French in its transparent and highly coloured orchestration. His first work to be staged in Paris was *Le clos*. Set in Normandy, it is the story of a girl who marries a wealthy landowner in order not to lose the family smallholding. Implored by her former lover to leave, she remains faithful to her husband and their love is renewed. *Neigilde*, although accepted for performance at the Opéra-Comique, was finally created in Monte Carlo owing to its extreme choreographic demands. *La mégère apprivoisée*, an adaptation of *The Taming of the Shrew*, was widely performed in France and abroad. *Quatre-vingt-treize* was revived at the Opéra-Comique after its première in Nice.

all vocal scores printed in Paris

La belle au bois dormant (féerie lyrique, 4, M. Carré and P. Collin), Marseille, Jan 1902, vs (1901)

Le clos (oc, 4, Carré, after A. Achard), Paris, OC (Favart), 6 June 1906, vs (1906)

Neigilde (ballet-opéra, prol., 2, epilogue, J. Lorraine, after H. C. Andersen), Monte Carlo, Grand, 10 April 1909, vs (1908)

Myriane (drame lyrique, 3, P. Ferrier and P. de Choudens), Nice, Opéra, 12 Feb 1913, vs (1912)

La mégère apprivoisée (comédie lyrique, 4, H. Cain and E. Adenis, after P. Delair's adaptation of W. Shakespeare: *The Taming of the Shrew*), Paris, Opéra, 30 Jan 1922, vs (1921)
Pepita, ou le diplomate amoureux, 1924 (3, G. Duval and E. Adenis, after E. Scribe and G. Delavigne), ?unperf., *F-Pn**
La grand-mère (comédie lyrique, 2, P. Milliet, after V. Hugo), Paris, OC (Favart), 7 Oct 1930, vs (1930)
Quatre-vingt-treize (épopée lyrique, 4, Cain, after Hugo), Nice, Opéra, March 1935
Fantasio (comédie lyrique, 4), ?unperf.

*

P. Locard: 'Jean Nouguès, Ch. Silver, André Bloch, Francis Bousquet', *Le théâtre lyrique en France* (Paris, 1937–9) [pubn of Poste National/Radio Paris], iii, 245–8

RICHARD LANGHAM SMITH

Silveri, Paolo (*b* Ofena, nr Aquila, 28 Dec 1913). Italian baritone. He studied in Florence and Rome, where he made his début as a bass in 1939 as Hans Schwarz (*Meistersinger*). He retrained as a baritone, and in 1944 sang Germont in Rome. He made his London début at Covent Garden with the S Carlo company in 1946 as Marcello, and then appeared with the Covent Garden Opera, 1947–9, as Rigoletto, Escamillo and Boris (in English), returning in 1950 to sing Ford and Iago with the Scala company. In 1948 he appeared at the Edinburgh Festival as Don Giovanni, returning the following year as Renato (*Ballo*); from 1950 to 1953 he sang at the Metropolitan Opera. In 1959 he sang the title role in Verdi's *Otello* (a tenor part) in Dublin, but in 1960 reverted to baritone roles. He retired in 1967. He was gifted with a fine stage presence, and his virile, resonant voice was especially impressive in Verdi. In his later years he tended to sacrifice delicacy and precision to mere volume. HAROLD ROSENTHAL/R

Silverlake. Opera by Kurt Weill; *see* SILBERSEE, DER.

Silverman, Stanley J(oel) (*b* New York, 5 July 1938). American composer. He attended Mills College, where his teachers were Leon Kirchner and Milhaud, and also studied at Columbia University with Henry Cowell and Vladimir Ussachevsky (1958–9) and at the Berkshire Music Center with Roberto Gerhard (1961). He has acted as music director or consultant for several theatres and theatrical festivals, and received grants from the National Opera Institute (1976) and other bodies, as well as awards for *Elephant Steps* (1968) and *Dr. Selavy's Magic Theatre* (1972).

Silverman's career has centred around the musical theatre in both the USA and Canada, where he has written incidental music for more than 20 plays, and some 11 operas. The stage works are marked by a sensitivity to dramatic action, which is enhanced rather than overpowered by the music. Silverman often adjusts his style to the period of the drama, writing for example in a 16th-century idiom for a Renaissance play and using 20th-century techniques such as the 12-tone method for contemporary dramas. Typically, orchestrations are clear and economical, achieving the fullest effect with the least number of instruments.

Elephant Steps (2, R. Foreman), Tanglewood, MA, 7 Aug 1968
Dr. Selavy's Magic Theatre (T. Hendry and Foreman), Stockbridge MA, Lenox Arts Center, 12 Aug 1972
Hotel for Criminals (2, Foreman), Stockbridge, Lenox Arts Center, 14 Aug 1974
Madame Adare (1, Foreman), New York, City Opera, 9 Oct 1980
The Columbine String Quartet Tonight! (2, T. Howe), Stockbridge, Lenox Arts Center, 2 July 1981
Up from Paradise (musical play, 2, A. Miller, after his *The Creation of the World and Other Business*), New York, Jewish Repertory, 1983
The Golem, 1984 (musical play, H. Leivick)
Africanus Instructus (musical play, 2, Foreman), New York, 14 Jan 1986
A Good Life (1, J. Moss), Washington, Kennedy Center, April 1986
Black Sea Follies [Shostakovich] (2, P. Schmidt), Stockbridge, Lenox Arts Center, 6 Aug 1986
Love and Science, 1990 (Foreman)

*

R. H. Kornick: *Recent American Opera: a Production Guide* (New York, 1991), 283–6

JAMES G. ROY

Simándy, József (*b* Budapest, 18 Sept 1916). Hungarian tenor. He studied with Emilia Posszert, joining the Budapest Opera House chorus in 1940. He made his début at the Szeged National Theatre in 1946 as Don José. The following year he returned to the Budapest Opera, and was its leading heroic tenor until 1984. Between 1956 and 1960 he was a regular performer in Munich. Although he undertook a wide range of lyric and spinto tenor roles, Simándy was, in dramatic and vocal character, best suited to heroic roles, notably Radames, Otello and Lohengrin. His recordings include the title roles in Erkel's *Bánk bán* and *Hunyadi László*.

*

L. Dalos: *Bánk bán elmondja* [Bánk bán Tells it] (Budapest, 1983)

PÉTER P. VÁRNAI

Simeonov, Konstantin Arsen'yevich (*b* Kaznakovo, Tverskaya province, 7/20 June 1910; *d* Kiev, 3 Jan 1987). Russian conductor. He studied conducting at the Leningrad Conservatory with Alexander Gauk and Il'ya Musin. After being active as a symphonic conductor (1930–60), he was chief conductor of the Kiev Opera and Ballet Theatre from 1961 until 1967, when he moved to the Leningrad Opera and Ballet Theatre; in 1974 he returned to the Kiev post. He won the 1964 All-Union Conductors' Competition in Moscow, and the same year was one of the conductors with the Bol'shoy company at La Scala. He conducted *The Queen of Spades* during this visit and was highly praised for the balance of voices and orchestra, and for his evocation of dramatic atmosphere. His opera performances in the USSR were distinguished by emotional power and dramatic tension, excelling in choral scenes such as those of Musorgsky's *Khovanshchina* and Shostakovich's *Katerina Izmaylova*. He was also admired for his performances of operas by Dzerzhinsky, Lysenko, Mayboroda and Paliashvili, among others. He was made a People's Artist of the USSR in 1962.

I. M. YAMPOL'SKY

Simile aria [metaphor aria]. An aria in which the text makes a comparison between the singer's situation or thoughts and some natural phenomenon or activity in the world at large; the music provides appropriate illustration. Its literary origins are found in the elaborate metaphorical style of Giambattista Marino (1569–1625), whose influence on 17th-century Italian literature extended to the opera libretto; aria texts using conceits broadly similar to those favoured by Metastasio are common in the 17th century. Arias of this kind offered composers an opportunity to introduce a wide variety of imagery. An example from Handel is Caesar's aria 'Va tacito e nascosto' in *Giulio Cesare* (1724), where a solo horn alludes to the hunter who must go cautiously in pursuit of his prey and the text makes a comparison with the intriguer who conceals his real intentions. Favourite topics for simile arias were ships at sea in a storm, gently flowing streams and birds, all of which provided opportunity for attractive illustrative writing. In Gay's *The Beggar's Opera* (1728) the beggar claims to have 'introduc'd the similes that are in all your celebrated *Operas*' and the texts include several parodies of the type, e.g. 'I'm like a skiff on the Ocean tost'. The convention was increasingly criticized during the 18th century and had nearly died out by the end of it. A late example is 'Come scoglio' in Mozart's *Così fan tutte* (1790), which parodies the convention, in that Fiordiligi compares her resolution – which the audience knows will prove weak – to a rock unaffected by the battering it receives from a stormy sea. JACK WESTRUP

Simionato, Giulietta (*b* Forlì, 12 May or 15 Dec 1910). Italian mezzo-soprano. She studied at Rovigo with Locatello and Palumbo. She made her début in 1935 in the première of Pizzetti's *Orsèolo* at Florence and first sang at La Scala in 1939 as Beppe (*L'amico Fritz*). During the next few years she sang Cherubino, Rosina, Hänsel, Dorabella and Mignon. From 1946 she appeared regularly at La Scala, where her repertory included Charlotte (*Werther*), Jane Seymour (*Anna Bolena*), Cenerentola, Isabella (*L'italiana in Algeri*), Carmen, Asteria (*Nerone*) and Léonor. She made her British début as Cherubino at the 1947 Edinburgh Festival; she first sang at Covent Garden in 1953 as Adalgisa, Amneris and Azucena. In 1954 she sang Romeo (*I Capuleti e i Montecchi*) in Palermo and made her American début at Chicago. She sang at Salzburg (1957–63) as Mistress Quickly, Eboli, Orpheus and Azucena and at the Metropolitan from 1959 to 1963. In 1962 she sang Valentine at La Scala. She retired in 1966, making her farewell as Servilia at the Piccola Scala. Simionato's agile coloratura mezzo had a personal and seductive timbre in its lower register. She had a charming stage presence, vivacious in comedy, dignified and moving in tragedy.

*

GV (R. Celletti; R. Vegeto)

I. Kolodin: 'Great Artists of our Time: Giulietta Simionato', *HiFi*, xi (1959), 37

A. Natan: 'Simionato, Giulietta', *Prima donna* (Basle, 1962) [with discography]

G. Gualerzi: 'Giulietta Simionato', *Opera*, xv (1964), 87–92

G. Lauri-Volpi: 'Il riposo di Carmen', *Musica e dischi* (1969), no.274, p.61 HAROLD ROSENTHAL/R

Simon, Anton Yulyevich (*b* Paris, 5 August 1850; *d* Moscow, 19 Jan/1 Feb 1916). Russian composer and conductor of French birth. He studied at the Paris Conservatoire with Antoine Marmontel (piano) and Jules Duprato (composition). In 1871 he went to Moscow on the staff of the newly organized Théâtre Bouffe, where for several years he conducted French casts in the latest hits by Offenbach and Lecocq. Afterwards he remained in Moscow, became a Russian subject, and taught piano both privately and at the training school of the Moscow Philharmonic Society. In 1897, with the help of a friend, the conductor Ippolit Altani, he was appointed to the bureaucracy of the Imperial Theatres (as 'inspector of orchestras'), and began conducting at the Moscow Bol'shoy Theatre, where his own operas and ballets were chiefly produced.

Simon's most ambitious opera was his first, the five-act *Rolla* op.40 to a libretto by A. M. Nevsky. Set in 16th-century Genoa and Florence, it melodramatically portrays the fate of a sculptor who in a moment of frenzied doubt destroys a statue of his beloved and thereafter imagines that he has killed her. It was first performed at the Bol'shoy on 17/29 April 1892 under Altani, to whom it is dedicated. *Pesn' torzhestvuyushchey lyubvi* ('The Song of Love Triumphant') op.46, in three acts, was adapted by the librettist N. N. Vilde from Turgenev's eponymous novella, a bathetic tale of death and resurrection smacking, in one critic's biting phrase, of 'the second-rate atmosphere of the medium's consulting room'. Its Bol'shoy première, also under Altani, took place on 2/14 December 1897. The veristic *Rïbaki* ('The Fishermen') op.51, to a libretto by Vilde in one act after Hugo's poem *Les pauvres gens*, was Simon's most successful work for the stage, making effective use of stylized *chansonettes* and Breton folk tunes. It was first performed at the Bol'shoy on 23 February/7 March 1899, under the composer's baton.

In his choice of subject matter, his reliance on routine forms, his small-boned lyric gift (suitable to the extent that the desired result was piquant or intimate) and his predilection for decorative harmony laced with syncopes and suspensions, Simon has often been compared as an operatic composer with his contemporary César Cui, another Russian with strong ancestral and cultural ties to France.

RICHARD TARUSKIN

Simon Boccanegra. Opera in a prologue and three acts by GIUSEPPE VERDI to a libretto by FRANCESCO MARIA PIAVE (with additions by Giuseppe Montanelli) after ANTONIO GARCÍA GUTIÉRREZ's play *Simón Bocanegra*; Venice, Teatro La Fenice, 12 March 1857 (revised version, with additions and alterations by ARRIGO BOITO, Milan, Teatro alla Scala, 24 March 1881).

PROLOGUE

Simon Boccanegra *a corsair in the service of the Genoese Republic*	baritone
Jacopo Fiesco *a Genoese nobleman*	bass
Paolo Albiani *a Genoese goldsmith*	bass
Pietro *a Genoese popular leader*	baritone

Sailors, populace, Fiesco's servants etc.

DRAMMA

Simon Boccanegra *the first Doge of Genoa*	baritone
Maria Boccanegra *his daughter, under the name Amelia Grimaldi*	soprano
Jacopo Fiesco *under the name Andrea*	bass
Gabriele Adorno *a Genoese gentleman*	tenor
Paolo Albiani *the Doge's favourite courtier*	bass
Pietro *another courtier*	baritone
A Captain of the Crossbowmen	tenor
Amelia's Maidservant	mezzo-soprano

Soldiers, sailors, populace, senators, the Doge's court, African prisoners of both sexes

Setting In and around Genoa, about the middle of the 14th century; between the Prologue and Act 1, 25 years pass

Verdi was approached to write a new opera for the Teatro La Fenice in Venice (his last première there had been of *La traviata* in 1853) at the instigation of the librettist Francesco Maria Piave in the spring of 1856. By May of that year a contract had been agreed with the theatre, the subject to be Gutiérrez's *Simón Bocanegra*, and Piave set to work according to precise instructions from the composer. In fact, Verdi himself supplied a complete prose sketch of the action, one so detailed that he insisted that his sketch rather than a draft of the libretto be submitted to the censors for approval. From August 1856 Verdi was in Paris, and in part because communication was difficult with the Italian-based Piave, he took on a local collaborator, the exiled revolutionary Giuseppe Montanelli, who drafted several scenes. Verdi began composing in the autumn of 1856 and, as the date of the première approached, showed his usual close concern with the staging and choice of performers. The première, whose cast included Leone Giraldoni (Boccanegra), Giuseppe Echeverria (Fiesco), Luigia Bendazzi (Amelia) and Carlo Negrini (Gabriele), was only a moderate success; the libretto in particular received some harsh criticism. Subsequent revivals in the late 1850s were occasionally successful, although the 1859 La Scala première was a complete fiasco.

Doubtless in reaction to this lack of public acclaim, Verdi considered revising the score during the 1860s; but it was not until 1879 that he finally decided to make substantial alterations, in part to test the possibility of working with Arrigo Boito as librettist on the larger project of *Otello*. Looking over the score, Verdi pronounced it 'too sad' and decided that, although the prologue and final two acts could remain more or less unchanged, the first act needed a thorough overhaul, in particular by the injection of contrast and variety. This idea eventually gave rise to the famous Council Chamber scene; but in the end Verdi (somewhat reluctantly) found it necessary to make large adjustments to several other portions of the score (details are given below). The revised version had a resoundingly successful première at La Scala, directed by Franco Faccio and with a cast including Victor Maurel (Boccanegra), Edouard de Reszke (Fiesco), Anna D'Angeri (Amelia) and Francesco Tamagno (Gabriele).

PROLOGUE *A square in Genoa* The 1857 version begins with a prelude in which various themes from the opera are briefly juxtaposed; the opening scene is the barest of declamatory recitatives. In 1881 Verdi underpinned the opening conversation between Paolo and Pietro with an undulating string theme, rich in harmonic inflections and clearly meant to introduce the maritime *tinta* of the score. The two men discuss who is to be the next Doge, Pietro persuading Paolo to support the corsair Boccanegra. As Pietro departs to rally the plebeian vote, Boccanegra himself appears. He is at first indifferent to assuming high office, but is persuaded to seek it by Paolo's reminder that his position will help win him his beloved Maria, imprisoned in her father Fiesco's home. From here to the end of the prologue the two versions largely correspond, although Verdi made numerous small revisions for 1881. First comes a chorus during which Paolo and Pietro convince the workers that they should vote for Boccanegra. The scene, remarkable for its restraint, centres on 'L'atra magion vedete?', in which Paolo describes the Fieschi's gloomy palace, which holds Maria prisoner.

As the crowd disperses, Fiesco emerges from his home, stricken with grief at the death of his daughter. After a stern recitative he sings the famous 'Il lacerato spirito', a minor–major *romanza* notable for its extreme melodic simplicity but powerful emotional effect. Fiesco is then joined by Boccanegra for the first grand duet of the opera. The first movement shows the usual violent alternation of moods: Fiesco accuses, Boccanegra tries to placate him, the old man agrees to pardon Boccanegra if he will give up the daughter Maria has borne him. But in a second movement, 'Del mar sul lido', again dominated by maritime figures in the orchestra, Boccanegra narrates how his daughter has mysteriously disappeared from her remote hiding place. Fiesco, who contributes little to this movement, turns his back on Boccanegra, pretending to leave, but hides nearby. In a third movement, full of passionately anxious string figures, Boccanegra enters the palace in search of Maria. His cries of anguish at discovering her body are immediately countered by offstage cheers. To a jarring festive theme – a kind of cabaletta substitute – the people enter to hail Boccanegra their new leader.

ACT 1.i *The gardens of the Grimaldi palace outside Genoa* 25 years have passed. An evocative orchestral prelude depicting the rising dawn introduces Amelia, whose French-style ternary aria, 'Come in quest'ora bruna', is notable for its delicately varied accompaniment and its injection of narrative mystery in the middle section. Gabriele's offstage voice is now heard in two stanzas of a *Trovatore*-like serenade, 'Cielo di stelle orbato'. In the 1857 version this leads to a cabaletta for Amelia, 'Il palpito deh frena', which in 1881 was replaced by a few bars of recitative. In the first movement of the lovers' ensuing duet, Gabriele tries to calm Amelia's fears for the future; in the second, the gentle Andantino 'Vieni a mirar la cerula', they pause to admire the sea around Genoa, although thinking too of enemies within the city walls. At the close of the Andantino the pair are joined by Pietro, who asks permission for the Doge to visit later that day. Amelia, sure that he is planning for her to marry Paolo, sends Gabriele away to prepare for their own wedding. In a final cabaletta, 'Sì, sì, dell'ara il giubilo', much reduced in 1881, they swear to defy the whole world.

Amelia hurries into the palace, but Gabriele is detained by Fiesco (who is posing under the name Andrea, and has long been watching over Amelia). Fiesco, informed of Amelia's and Gabriele's marriage plans, warns Gabriele that his intended bride is not of noble birth but an orphan who replaced the real Amelia Grimaldi, long since dead. In 1857 the episode was rounded off by a duet cursing Boccanegra, thought responsible for the death; in 1881 there is a *religioso* duet in which Fiesco gives a father's blessing to Gabriele.

Offstage trumpets herald Boccanegra. In a brief scena the Doge gives Amelia a paper showing that he has pardoned her presumed brothers (the Grimaldi). In the first movement of the ensuing duet, 'Dinne, perchè in quest'eremo', which is underpinned by a sinuous orchestral melody, Amelia admits her love for Gabriele and, feeling gratitude to Boccanegra, decides to tell him of her lowly birth. This she does in a second movement, the *racconto* 'Orfanella il tetto umile', in the last section of which Boccanegra joins her with a gathering sense of her true identity. The third movement, in which Boccanegra confirms that she is his long-lost daughter, quickly gives way to a cabaletta of mutual joy, 'Figlia! a tal nome io palpito', subtly varied in the 1881 version to increase the sense that both individuals have distinct musical personalities. Amelia leaves, and Boccanegra roughly tells Paolo to abandon hope of marrying her. When Boccanegra himself departs, Paolo tells Pietro of his plan to abduct Amelia.

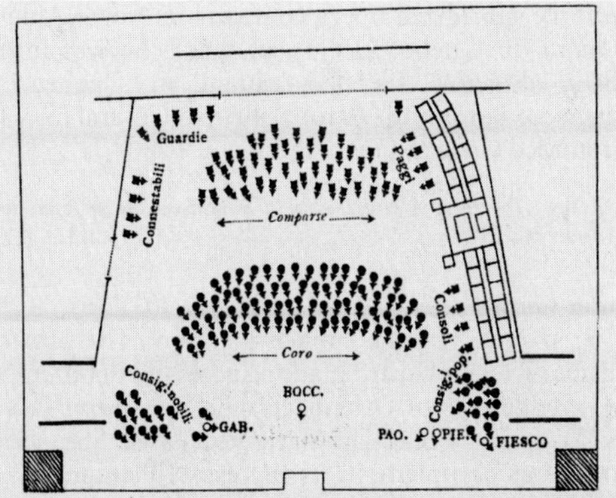

Le parole: *Vendetta!* devono essere rivolte dal **Coro** al **Doge, con** molta fierezza agitando in alto le scuri, le donne stendendo il braccio destro: l'agitazione fra il popolo dev'essere continua: **Boccanegra rimarrà** calmo ed impassibile, poi si avanzerà di due passi e dirà **ironicamente**: *Questa è dunque del popol la voce?* poi volgendosi a destra dirà a **Gabriele**: *Adorno perchè impugni l'acciar?* mentre ad un di lui cenno i due popolani che tenevano afferrato per le braccia **Gabrielè,** lo lasceranno libero ritraendosi di un passo. Il popolo, sempre eccitato, interromperà con ira le parole di **Gabriele**: il **Doge** indignato, esclamando: *Ribaldo,* si ritrarrà con disgusto da **Gabriele,** in modo che rimanga uno spazio libero fra loro due. In questo frattempo **Amelia** entrerà dal fondo e si collocherà nel centro, in mezzo ai Cori, in modo che non sia scorta dal pubblico (1).

Alla parola: *Muori,* **Gabriele** alza la spada e fa per slanciarsi per ferire il **Doge**: ma viene subito afferrato dai due popolani, mentre **Amelia** sortendo improvvisamente dal mezzo del popolo s'interpone fra il **Doge** e **Gabriele,** dicendo a questi: *Ferisci!*

(1) Si prega l'artista che rappresenta AMELIA a non farsi far largo dai Coristi, quasi ad avvertire il pubblico che sta per arrivare la prima donna: è AMELIA stessa che deve farsi largo fra il popolo ed apparire improvvisamente.

Page from the disposizione scenica (production book) compiled by Giulio Ricordi after the original production of Verdi's 'Simon Boccanegra' at La Scala, Milan, 24 March 1881: the Council Chamber of the Doge's Palace (Act 1 scene ii). The strictly scenic preparation for Amelia's climactic entrance is meticulous, and the footnote, which instructs that the chorus should avoid warning the audience of her appearance by allowing space for her entrance, suggests an increasing desire for 'realistic' stage effect.

1.ii *The Council Chamber of the Doge's Palace* This scene was almost entirely recomposed for the 1881 version. The 1857 finale is set in a large square in Genoa, and is a conventional four-movement concertato finale, a grand ceremonial scene in which the Doge appears amid festivities and is interrupted by Fiesco and Gabriele who accuse him of abducting Amelia. As the scene reaches its climax Amelia herself appears, protesting the Doge's innocence and thus precipitating the central Andantino. Amelia then narrates her abduction and escape, but she refuses to reveal publicly who was responsible, and all join in a stretta calling for the guilty one to be brought to justice.

In 1881 Verdi altered this traditional plan, vastly expanding the first movement, eliminating the last, and fashioning new music almost throughout. The scene begins with a stormy orchestral introduction, after which the Doge urges the Council to preserve peace between Genoa and Venice. A riot is heard outside as the plebeians demand death for the patricians and the Doge. Boccanegra orders the crowd to be brought in, and a mass of people appears with Fiesco and Gabriele as captives, accused of killing Lorenzino, a leader of the plebeians. Gabriele in turn accuses the Doge of having Amelia abducted and is about to stab him when Amelia enters and interposes herself between them. She narrates her abduction and escape in 'Nell'ora soave', but refuses to reveal publicly who was responsible. A new argument develops between the opposing factions, this time violently quelled by the Doge, who launches the central Andante mosso, 'Plebe! Patrizi!', a magnificent ensemble movement in which the Doge's and Amelia's pleas for peace calm the crowd. The Andante over, the Doge pronounces a solemn curse on Amelia's abductor, forcing Paolo to repeat the words. As the chorus reiterate the curse, Paolo falls down in horror.

Act 2 *The Doge's room in the Ducal Palace at Genoa* In 1881 Verdi expanded Paolo's brief 1857 scena into a powerful recitative during which he meditates on the curse that has fallen on him and then puts poison in Boccanegra's drink. Fiesco and Gabriele are led in and, in spite of his hatred for Boccanegra, Fiesco refuses to be involved in Paolo's plot against the Doge. Fiesco leaves and Paolo informs Gabriele that the Doge wishes Amelia for himself. Left alone, Gabriele breaks into a fit of jealous anger that culminates in the two-movement aria 'Sento avvampar nell'anima', the first movement driven by a furious orchestral figure, the second a lyrical Largo enhanced by delicate chromatic details in the vocal line.

There follows a highly condensed four-movement duet for Amelia and Gabriele. During the opening movement Gabriele accuses Amelia of betrayal; she denies this but will elaborate no further. In the second-movement Andante, 'Parla, in tuo cor virgineo', Gabriele begs her to explain herself while she continues to protest her innocence. A tiny connecting movement starts as Amelia hears the Doge approaching. Gabriele refuses to leave, but in a short cabaletta she succeeds in making him hide on the balcony. The Doge enters and in a stormy recitative learns that she loves Gabriele, whom he now knows to be conspiring against him. Left alone, he drinks from the poisoned cup and lapses into sleep. Gabriele reappears and after some deliberation decides to murder the Doge; but he is stopped by the sudden appearance of Amelia. Boccanegra awakes and eventually reveals that Amelia is his daughter, the three principals cementing their newfound connection in the lyrical Andante 'Perdon, perdon, Amelia'. But a warlike chorus is heard in the distance: the people are rebelling against the Doge. Gabriele offers to sue for peace, and vows to fight at Boccanegra's side.

Act 3 *Inside the Doge's Palace* An orchestral introduction and choral cries in praise of the Doge precede the appearance of Fiesco and Paolo. In an impassioned recitative, Paolo reveals that it was he who abducted Amelia and poisoned the Doge. He is led off to execution. A Captain orders that all the lights in the city be extinguished in honour of the dead. The Doge himself appears, a sluggish, chromatic string theme depicting the moving of the poison through his body. In a shimmering arioso, he delights in his beloved Genoese sea, 'Oh refrigerio! ... la marina brezza!', before being joined by Fiesco. In the first movement of their duet, 'Delle faci festanti al barlume', which contains the usual series of sharply contrasting episodes, Fiesco challenges the Doge and then admits his true identity. As the lights are gradually extinguished, Boccanegra reveals that 'Amelia' is really Fiesco's granddaughter. At this Fiesco breaks into tears, and the lyrical second movement, the Largo 'Piango, perchè mi parla', sees bass and baritone gradually reconciled. But ominous rhythmic figures in the orchestra warn us that Boccanegra is nearing death, and Fiesco tells him he has been poisoned. Amelia and Gabriele appear and Boccanegra blesses them in a final concertato, 'Gran Dio, li benedici'. With his dying breath he nominates Gabriele as his successor.

* * *

Simon Boccanegra is the mature Verdian opera most thoroughly revised by the composer, and the fact that these revisions were effected more than 20 years after the original version leaves the opera with some startling stylistic disjunctions. The 1857 drama was remarkably forward-looking for its time, particularly from the point of view of conventional operatic characterization: there are no secondary female characters, but a preponderance of low male voices; and though a baritone protagonist was no longer exceptional, Boccanegra has very few opportunities to show vocal brilliance and is assigned no conventional arias. However, this excitingly unusual vocal constellation is connected with, and in part causes, an important problem, one of which Verdi himself was well aware: the opera was, he felt, too consistently dark in colour, too gloomy.

The 1881 revisions do much to improve this aspect of the work. Though the distribution of voices remains the same, in retouching various scenes the mature Verdi invariably added new levels of harmonic and instrumental colour to the opera. And, perhaps most importantly, by adding the new Act 1 finale (the famous Council Chamber scene), he injected into the heart of the work an episode of enormous vividness and power, enriching the character of Boccanegra in such a way that his subsequent death scene gains considerably in impressiveness.

It has been argued, however, that the revisions – especially the addition of the new Act 1 finale – create a further general problem, one of what we might call dramatic balance. The sheer weight of Boccanegra's new presence tends to overpower the other principals, Gabriele in particular, making their concerns seem unimportant or at least under-articulated. But perhaps critics tend to exaggerate the extent to which these essentially 'narrative' matters are crucial to the success of an opera. In recent years, audiences have been in no doubt that *Simon Boccanegra* contains some of the mature Verdi's greatest dramatic music, and there seems little doubt that the opera will retain its new status as one of the composer's most compelling creations.

ROGER PARKER

Simoneau, Léopold (*b* Saint-Flavien, Quebec, 3 May 1916). Canadian tenor. He studied in Montreal with Salvator Issaurel, and made his début there in 1941 as Hadji in *Lakmé* with the Variétés Lyriques. After successful appearances in *Così fan tutte* and *Die Zauberflöte*, he studied in New York with Paul Althouse. He made his Opéra-Comique début in 1949, in *Mireille*, and remained in Paris for five seasons. His reputation as a Mozart specialist, elegantly lyrical in style, was first established at the Aix-en-Provence and (from 1951) Glyndebourne festivals, where he sang Idamantes and Don Ottavio. He sang in Mozart operas at La Scala (1953), in London with the Vienna Staatsoper (1954), at the Teatro Colón, at the Salzburg Festival (1956) and with the Metropolitan (début 1963, as Don Ottavio). He was Tom in the French première of *The Rake's Progress*, at the Opéra-Comique in 1953. Other roles included Bizet's Nadir. In 1946 he married the soprano Pierrette Alarie with whom he has often appeared. He played a leading part in forming the first statutory subsidized opera company in North America, L'Opéra du Québec (1971), of which he was initially artistic director. He has taught in Quebec, San Francisco, Banff and Victoria, British Columbia, where he founded Canada Opera Piccola in 1986.

*

R. Maheu: *Pierrette Alarie, Léopold Simoneau, deux voix, un art* (Montreal, 1988)

GILLES POTVIN

Simon-Girard [née Girard], **Juliette** (*b* Paris, 8 May 1859; *d* Nice, 1954). French soprano. The attractive and characterful Girard made a successful début at 18 in the juvenile role of Offenbach's *La foire Saint-Laurent* (1877) at the Folies-Dramatiques, Paris. She shot to stardom as Serpolette in its successor, Planquette's *Les cloches de Corneville* and, having wed her co-star Simon-Max, called herself thereafter Mme Simon-Girard. At 19 she created the title role in Offenbach's *Madame Favart* (1878) and the next year his *La fille du tambour-major*, establishing herself among Paris's most popular performers. She remained so for some 30 years, creating many further roles (in Varney's *Fanfan la tulipe*, Lecocq's *La princesse des Canaries*, Messager's *La fauvette du temple*), playing the classic repertory and reappearing in her own great roles, including a Serpolette as late as 1908.

KURT GÄNZL

Simoni, Renato (*b* Verona, 5 Sept 1875; *d* Milan, 5 July 1952). Italian critic, playwright and librettist. His main career was in journalism; in 1894 he became drama critic of the *Adige* (Verona), moving in the same capacity to *Tempo* (Milan) in 1899. In 1903 he assumed the editorship of the *Corriere della sera*, acting as its drama critic from 1913 until his death. From 1906 until 1924 he was editor of the review *La lettura* in succession to Giuseppe Giacosa – a fact which probably recommended him to Puccini as a suitable partner for Giuseppe Adami on the libretto of *Turandot* (1926). In the meantime he had written five comedies, one of them in Venetian dialect, and furnished Giordano with the text of *Madame Sans-Gêne* (1915). His only other libretto of note was *Il Dibuk* (1934), written for Ludovico Rocca. He translated a number of operettas, including Ivan Caryll's *The Duchess of Danzig* (on the same subject as *Madame Sans-Gêne*). He was well known for many years as a writer of elegant children's verses under the pseudonym 'Turno'.

JULIAN BUDDEN

Simonov, Yury Ivanovich (*b* Saratov, 4 March 1941). Russian conductor. The son of opera singers, he showed a talent for conducting when aged 12, studied at the Leningrad Conservatory with Nikolay Rabinovich, and in 1963 conducted the first of several opera productions there, Dargomïzhsky's *Rusalka*. He won the Accademia di Santa Cecilia conductors' competition at Rome in 1968, made his début at the Bol'shoy Theatre with *Aida* the next year, and was principal conductor there, 1970–85, covering a wide repertory of Western as well as Russian opera. He appeared with the Bol'shoy Opera at the Metropolitan, New York, in 1975 with Prokofiev's *War and Peace*, and has toured with the company to other cities in the USA, Europe and Japan, as well as taking guest engagements. His Covent Garden début was in 1982 with *Yevgeny Onegin*, and he returned in 1986 for *La traviata*. He has worked with the opera company in Budapest, conducting *Tristan und Isolde* (1988) and *Tannhäuser* (1990). In 1990 he also performed *The Queen of Spades* at the Los Angeles

Music Center. His performances achieve a balance between the letter and spirit of the score in freely expressive interpretation. His recordings include Glinka's *Ruslan and Lyudmila* (1983). A professor at the Moscow Conservatory since 1975, he has been a regular jury member for the Vittorio Gui conductors' competition, Florence. He was named People's Artist of the RSFSR and the USSR.

I. M. YAMPOL'SKY/NOËL GOODWIN

Simonsen, Martin (*b* 30 Jan 1830; *d* Melbourne, 29 Nov 1899). Australian impresario. A violinist of German-Jewish descent, he went to Australia in 1865 as a touring concert artist with his French wife Fannie (née Dehaes, 1835–96), a soprano. In 1866 the couple joined W. S. Lyster's opera company, in which Fannie had great success as Sélika in *L'Africaine* and Martin a less shining stint as conductor. In 1876, after alternating for some years between Australia and Europe, the couple formed a touring *opéra bouffe* company whose chief production was Maillart's *Les dragons de Villars*. When, after Lyster's death in 1880, his successor George Musgrove withdrew from the promotion of grand opera, Simonsen seized the opportunity to recruit a large Italian company, which toured with great success in 1886–7. A second Simonsen Italian company (1888) was of lesser calibre. Depressed by encroaching deafness and blindness, he died by his own hand. Three of his daughters by Fannie became professional singers, the best known being Frances Saville (1865–1935), a leading soprano at the Metropolitan and at the pre-1914 Vienna Hofoper. The Metropolitan prima donna Frances Alda was their granddaughter and received her early training from Fannie.

*

F. Alda: *Men, Women and Tenors* (Boston, 1937)
B. Mackenzie and F. Mackenzie: *Singers of Australia* (Melbourne, 1967)
H. Love: *The Golden Age of Australian Opera* (Sydney, 1981)
A. Simpson: 'On Tour with the Simonsens', *Opera in New Zealand: Aspects of History and Performance* (Wellington, 1990), 19–32
——: 'The Simonsen Opera Company's 1876 Tour of New Zealand', *The Turnbull Library Record*, xxiii (1990)

HAROLD LOVE

Simplicius Simplicissimus [*Simplicius Simplicissimus: drei Szenen aus seiner Jugend* ('Simplicius Simplicissimus: Three Scenes from his Youth')]. Chamber opera in three scenes by KARL AMADEUS HARTMANN to a libretto by HERMANN SCHERCHEN, Wolfgang Petzet and the composer after Johann Jakob Christoffel von Grimmelshausen's novel *Der abenteuerliche Simplicissimus* (1669); first version as *Des Simplicius Simplicissimus Jugend*, broadcast, Munich, Bavarian Radio, 2 April 1948; stage, Cologne, Theater der Stadt, Kammerspiele, 20 Oct 1949; second version, Mannheim, Nationaltheater, 9 July 1957.

The action takes place in Germany during the Thirty Years War. In the introduction a Narrator underlines the political and social background to the war, drawing attention to the figure of Simplicius Simplicissimus. Scene i shows Simplicius (soprano), a simple and unworldly peasant boy, tending his parents' sheep. He falls asleep and dreams about a tree whose branches are so overladen with people that its roots experience pain. On waking up he is confronted by a Mercenary (baritone) who demands to know the way to his parents' farm. The Mercenary pushes him aside, causing both Simplicius and his parents to flee. In scene ii Simplicius, the only member of his family to survive, seeks refuge in a forest, where he encounters a Hermit (tenor). The Hermit, who becomes fully aware of the boy's innocence, tries to educate him in the ways of the world but dies leaving Simplicius once again alone. Simplicius is subsequently captured by mercenaries who transport him to the Governor's banqueting hall, where (scene iii) he assumes the role of court jester. However, when the Governor (tenor) asks him to make a speech, Simplicius recalls his dream. In suddenly understanding that the tree's painful roots symbolize the oppressed members of society, Simplicius makes common cause with the peasants who force their way into the hall and kill everyone apart from him. The Narrator reappears and recapitulates the material stated in the introduction.

Apart from the early *Wachsfigurenkabinett* (1929–30), *Simplicius Simplicissimus* remains Hartmann's only stage work. The composer wrote the opera as a protest against war and, in particular, against the social and political repressions of the Nazi era. In its first version the work contained extended sections of spoken dialogue. These were eliminated in the second version, which was conceived for larger instrumental forces and included three substantial symphonic interludes that strengthen the opera's overall structure. Although in dramatic terms *Simplicius Simplicissimus* is modelled on the epic theatre, its musical idiom, which does not reject tonality, is strongly influenced by the Second Viennese School.

ERIK LEVI

Sinclair, John (*b* nr Edinburgh, 9 Dec 1791; *d* Margate, 23 Sept 1857). Scottish tenor. His first, anonymous, stage appearance was as Captain Cheerly in Shield's *Lock and Key* at the Haymarket Theatre, 7 September 1810. He was then engaged at Covent Garden, where he appeared on 20 September 1811 as Don Carlos in *The Duenna*. He remained for several seasons, creating the tenor roles in Bishop's *Guy Mannering* and *The Slave* (1816). He later studied in Paris with Pellegrini and in Milan with Banderali and also had instruction from Rossini in Naples in 1821. In 1822 he sang Rossini operas throughout Italy. In 1823 he was engaged for Venice and created Idreno (*Semiramide*), written for him. That year he reappeared at Covent Garden as Prince Orlando in Dibdin's *The Cabinet*. In 1828–9 he sang at the Adelphi, in 1829–30 at Drury Lane. He also visited the USA in 1830. In Italy his technique was said to be remarkable, especially in runs.

Sinclair, Monica (*b* Evercreech, Somerset, 23 March 1925). English contralto. She studied at the Royal Academy and Royal College of Music in London and joined the Carl Rosa Company in 1948, making her début as Suzuki in *Madama Butterfly*. This was also her first role at Covent Garden, where from 1949 to 1967 she was heard in a wide variety of roles including Azucena, Cherubino and Pauline (*The Queen of Spades*). In 1952 she sang Margret in the English première of *Wozzeck*, and in 1954 created Evadne in Walton's *Troilus and Cressida*. From 1954 to 1960 she was a favourite at Glyndebourne, especially as Ragonde in *Le comte Ory* and Marcellina in *Le nozze di Figaro*. She was an asset in comic operas and crowned the latter part of her career with appearances at the Metropolitan as the Marquise in *La fille du régiment*. This was with Joan Sutherland and Richard Bonynge, in whose revivals of Baroque and early 19th-century opera she played a prominent part. She developed exceptional fluency over a wide range, which in combination with her powerful and penetrating tone proved valuable in the productions of *Alcina* at Covent Garden and Venice, in which she sang Bradamante. She also appeared regularly with the Handel Opera Society in London. In 1955 she sang the title role of Lully's *Armide* in Bordeaux, and in the 1960s toured Australia with a company headed by Sutherland. Her recordings include *Alcina* and *La fille du régiment* and some very effective performances as the gorgon-contralto in Gilbert and Sullivan. J. B. STEANE

Sinfonia (It.). A term – from the Latin 'symphonia', which in turn derives from the Greek 'syn-phōnē', 'sounding together' – which has been in use since the late 16th century to designate several types of piece for or with instrumental ensemble, most notably the concert symphony. In Italian opera, 'sinfonia' was used from the beginning to refer to any sort of instrumental number or section other than functional dance or march music (in France and England, 'symphonies' was similarly used). The term has thus been applied not only to the overture (the 'sinfonia avanti l'opera') and to preludes to individual acts but also to scene-setting or scene-changing music and to short pieces introducing, punctuating or concluding a vocal number that might sometimes equally be considered ritornellos (sometimes called 'sinfonie da ritornello'). Over the first two centuries of operatic history the different types of sinfonia became increasingly specialized, the overture growing in size and substance while the sinfonias within acts lost their separate identity and became components of larger complexes. After 1800 the term 'sinfonia' normally means 'overture' when applied to opera. In modern writing about older opera 'sinfonia' is sometimes used exclusively to mean ITALIAN OVERTURE, the type of operatic sinfonia that most closely approaches the concert symphony, but this restriction of the meaning is ahistorical.

See also OVERTURE. STEPHEN C. FISHER

Sinfonia avanti l'opera (It.: 'symphony before the opera'). An early term for a SINFONIA used to begin an opera, that is, as an OVERTURE, as opposed to one serving to begin a later section of the work or as an instrumental number within an act. STEPHEN C. FISHER

Singende Teufel, Der ('The Singing Devil'). Opera in four acts by FRANZ SCHREKER to his own libretto; Berlin, Staatsoper, 10 December 1928.

Schreker linked an often spare and more contrapuntally linear style to one of his most remarkable librettos. Set in Germany in the early Middle Ages, it juxtaposes the worlds of an enclosed monastic community and a nature-worshipping pagan people. They confront each other through the love of Lilian (soprano) for the monk Amandus (tenor), who is trying to complete a great organ, partly constructed by his father. Like the 'Spielwerk' of Schreker's earlier opera *Das Spielwerk und die Prinzessin* the organ is misused to terrify the local people as a 'singing devil'. Seeking to release Amandus from his chaste obsession, Lilian burns down the monastery. She dies beside the organ, whose white-hot pipes finally emit angelic sounds. PETER FRANKLIN

Singer, George (*b* Prague, 6 Aug 1908; *d* Tel-Aviv, 1 Oct 1980). Israeli conductor of Czech birth. After studying with Zemlinsky at the Prague Music Academy (1924–6), he made his début as an opera conductor in 1926 at the Neues Deutsches Theater, Prague, with Kinzl's *Evangele Mann*. He conducted there until 1930, when he went to Hamburg to conduct the Staatsoper. In 1934 he returned to Prague, where he gave the first radio performance of the concert version of Dvořák's first opera *Alfred*. In 1939 he settled in Palestine and on the establishment of the Israel National Opera in 1947 he became its permanent guest conductor. He also toured widely in Europe and the USSR and made his American début in 1968 with the New York City Opera in *La bohème*. He conducted the premières of Avidom's *Alexandra the Hasmonean* (Israel National Opera, 1959), Karel Salmon's *Vows* and Yehuda Wohl's *The Fence*. WILLIAM Y. ELIAS

Singgedicht. *See* APPLAUSUS MUSICUS.

Singher, Martial (Jean-Paul) (*b* Oloron Ste Marie, Pyrénées-Atlantiques, 14 Aug 1904; *d* Santa Barbara, CA, 9 March 1990). American baritone of French birth. He studied at the Ecole Normale Supérieure de St Cloud (1925–7) and with Gresse at the Paris Conservatoire (1927–30), where he won *premiers prix* in both opera and *opéra-comique* singing. He continued his studies with Juliette Fourestier and in November 1930 made his début in Amsterdam as Orestes in *Iphigénie en Tauride* under Monteux. He first sang at the Opéra a month later, as Athanaël in *Thaïs*, and remained a principal baritone of that company as well as singing at the Opéra-Comique. At Paris his roles included Wagner's Dutchman, Telramund and Gunther, much Verdi, Thomas' Hamlet and Rossini's Figaro.

Singher settled in the USA and made his Metropolitan début in 1943 as Dapertutto in *Les contes d'Hoffmann*. He continued as a member of the Metropolitan until 1959, singing Pelléas, Count Almaviva and Figaro in *Figaro*, all four baritone roles in *Hoffmann*, Lescaut in *Manon* and Mercutio in *Roméo et Juliette*, Wolfram and Amfortas. The lean, clearly focussed, rather dry timbre of his voice was not one of great natural beauty, but he was a fastidious musician and an elegant interpreter, particularly of French music. After he retired from the stage he became a singing teacher; among his pupils were James King, Gramm, Reardon, Louis Quilico, Valente, Blegen and Altmeyer.

GV (L. Riemens; R. Vegeto)

PETER G. DAVIS, DENNIS K. McINTIRE

Singing: a bibliography.

The list that follows contains a variety of materials on singing technique, voice production, ornamentation, registers, national and historical styles, interpretation, diction and pronunciation. The great majority of the items listed are concerned with the kind of singing associated with opera, but a number of more general works have been included for their relevance to vocal art; among these are several texts from the first half of the 17th century and a few works on accompaniment and the interpretation of song. Excluded for the purposes of this bibliography are vocalise, solfeggio, sight-singing and ear-training manuals, as well as publications relating primarily to choral and sacred music and music in schools. Dates of first and last editions are given where known, and important title changes are noted. Facsimiles, reprints and modern editions are given for early works, and the translations cited are all to English unless otherwise stated. Journals relating specifically to opera are listed in PERIODICALS; some of these, such as the *NATS Bulletin*, published since 1944 by the National Association of Teachers of Singing, contain numerous articles on technique. Further information about singing can be found in the entries on individual singers elsewhere in this dictionary.

For further bibliography *see* CASTRATO, COUNTERTENOR, ORNAMENTATION, SOPRANO and TENOR.

*

16TH AND 17TH CENTURIES

A. Ornithoparchus: *Musicae activae micrologus* (Leipzig, 1517, 5/1535 as *De arte cantandi micrologus*), bk 4; trans. J. Dowland as *Andreas Ornithoparcus, his Micrologus* (London, 1609); both works *R*1973

N. Vicentino: *L'antica musica ridotta alla moderna prattica* (Rome, 1555, 2/1557; *R*1959 [1555]: Documenta musicologica, 1st ser., xvii)

G. C. Maffei: *Delle lettere del S.or Gio. Camillo Maffei ... dove ... v'è un discorso della voce e del modo d'apparare di cantar di garganta*, bk 2 (Naples, 1562); 1 letter repr. in *RdM*, xxxviii (1956), 3–34

G. de' Bardi: *Discorso mandato ... a Giulio Caccini detto Romano sopra la musica antica e il cantar bene* (MS, *c*1578, *I-Rvat*); pubd in Doni (1763)

G. della Casa: *Il vero modo di diminuire con tutte le sorti di stromenti di fiato et corda et di voce humana* (Venice, 1584/*R*1970: BMB, 2nd ser., xxiii)

G. Bassano: *Ricercate, passaggi et cadentie* (Venice, 1585); repr. in Italienische Diminutionslehre, i (Zürich, 1976)

R. Rognoni: *Passaggi per potersi essercitare nel diminuire* (Venice, 1592) [lost; MS copy by F. Chrysander, *US-SFsc*]

L. Zacconi: *Prattica di musica utile et necessaria si al compositore ... si anco al cantore per assicurarsi in tutte le cose cantabili* (Venice, 1592–1622/*R*1967: BMB, 2nd ser., i–ii)

G. L. Conforto: *Breve e facile maniera d'essercitarsi ... a far passaggi ... per cantare* (Rome, 1593/*R*1922: VMPH, ii)

G. B. Bovicelli: *Regole, passaggi di musica, madrigali e motetti passeggiate* (Venice, 1594/*R*1957: Documenta muscicologica, 1st ser., xii)

E. de' Cavalieri: 'A lettori', *Rappresentatione di Anima, et di Corpo* (Rome, 1600/*R*1967); ed. in Solerti (1903), 5–12

J. Peri: 'A lettori', *Euridice* (Florence, 1600/*R*1981: RRMBE, xxxvi–xxxvii, with trans.)

A. Banchieri: *Cartella, overo Regole ... imparare il canto figurato* (Venice, 1601, 3/1614 as *Cartella musicale*, 5/1623 as *La Banchierina*; *R*1968 [3/1614]: Documenta musicologica, 2nd ser., xxvi)

G. Caccini: 'Ai lettori', *Le nuove musiche* (Florence, 1601/2; trans., RRMBE, ix, 1970)

O. Durante: Preface to *Arie devote, le quali contengono in se la maniera di cantar' con gratia l'imitation' delle parole, et il modo di scriver passaggi, et altri affetti* (Rome, 1608)

G. Caccini: 'A discreti lettori', *Nuove musiche e nuova maniera di scriverle* (Florence, 1614/*R*1978: RRMBE, xxviii, with trans.)

D. Friderici: *Musica figuralis, oder Newe klärliche richtige und vorstentliche Unterweisung der Singe-Kunst* (Rostock, 1618, 6/1677); ed. E. Lanlelütje (Berlin, 1901)

M. Praetorius: 'Instructio ... zum singen tragen, vff jetzige italianische Manier zu informiren', *Syntagmatis musici*, bk 3, chap.9 (Wolfenbüttel, 1618, 2/1619); ed. E. Bernouilli (Leipzig, 1916)

F. Rognoni Taegio: *Selva di varii passaggi secondo l'uso moderno, per cantare e suonare* (Milan, 1620/*R*1983: BMB, 2nd ser., cliii)

V. Giustiniani: *Discorso sopra la musica* (Rome, 1628); repr. in Solerti (1903), 98–128; trans., MSD, ix (1962)

G. B. Doni: *Trattato della musica scenica* (MS, 1633–5); pubd in Doni (1763); extracts in Solerti (1903), 195–228

M. Mersenne: *Harmonie universelle*, bk 1, ii: 'Traitez de la voix et des chants' (Paris, 1636/*R*1963); trans. E. Le Roy: *Marin Mersenne's 'Harmonie universelle'* (diss., Juilliard School, 1978)

L. Ribovius: *Enchiridion musicum, oder Kurzer Begriff der Singkunst* (Königsberg, 1638)

G. B. Doni: 'Discorso sesto sopra il recitare in scena con l'accompagnamento', *Annotazioni sopra il Compendio de' generi e de' modi della musica* [1635] (Rome, 1640); extracts ed. C. Gallico, *RIM*, iii (1968), 286–302

P. della Valle: *Della musica dell'età nostra* (MS, 16 Jan 1640); pubd in Doni (1763); repr. in Solerti (1903), 148–85

J. A. Herbst: *Musica practica sive instructio pro symphoniacis, das ist Eine kurtze Anleitung zum Singen, wie die Knaben und andere ... auff itzig italienische Manier ... können informiret und unterrichtet werden* (Nuremberg, 1642, 2/1653 as *Musica moderna prattica, overo Maniera del buon canto*)

J. Playford: *A Breefe Introduction to the Skill of Musick for Song and Violl* [later titles vary] (London, 1654, 7/1674/*R*1966, 19/1730)

C. Bernhard: *Von der Singe-Kunst, oder Maniera* (MS, *c*1657); trans. W. Hilse, *Music Forum*, iii (1973), 1–196

J. Crüger: *Musicae practicae praecepta brevia et exercitia pro tyronibus varia/Der rechte Weg zur Singekunst* (Berlin, 1660)

C. Simpson: *The Principles of Practical Musick ... Instruction ... in Singing or Playing* (London, 1665, enlarged 2/1667 as *A Compendium of Practical Musick*, 9/?1775); ed. P. J. Lord (Oxford, 1970)

J. Millet: *La belle méthode, ou L'art de bien chanter* (Besançon, 1666)

B. de Bacilly: *Remarques curieuses sur l'art de bien chanter* (Paris, 1668, enlarged 2/1679 as *L'art de bien chanter*, 4/1681); trans. of 1668 edn by A. B. Caswell as *A Commentary upon the Art of Proper Singing* (Brooklyn, NY, 1969)

J. R. Ahle: *Brevis et perspicua introductio in artem musicam, das ist Eine kurze Anleitung zu der lieblichen Singekunst* (Mühlhausen, 1673; ed. J. G. Ahle as *Kurze doch deutliche Anleitung zu der lieblich-löblichen Singekunst*, 1690, enlarged 2/1704)

B. Bismantova: *Compendio musicale* (MS, 1677, *I-REm*: *R*1979)

W. C. Printz: *Musica modulationis vocalis, oder Manierliche und zierliche Singkunst* (Schweidnitz, 1678)

J. Rousseau: *Méthode claire, certaine et facile pour apprendre à chanter la musique* (Paris, 1678, 6/1707); trans. R. A. Green in *Annotated Translation and Commentary of the Works of Jean Rousseau* (diss., Indiana U., 1979)

A. B. Philo-Mus.: *Synopsis of Vocal Musick, containing the Rudiments of Singing Rightly any Harmonical Song* (London, 1680)

G. Falk [Falck]: *Idea boni cantoris, das ist Getreu und gründliche Anleitung* (Nuremberg, 1688)

W. C. Printz: *Compendium musicae signatoriae et modulatoriae vocalis, das ist Kurtzer Begriff aller derjenigen Sachen, so einem, der die Vocal-Music lernen will zu wissen von nöthen seyn* (Dresden, 1689, 2/1714)

P. Berthet: *Leçons de musique, ou Exposition des traits le plus necessaires pour apprendre à chanter sa partie à livre ouvert* (Paris, 1691, 2/1695)

1700–50

S. de Brossard: *Dictionaire des termes grecs, latins et italiens* (Paris, 1701, enlarged 2/1703/*R*1965 as *Dictionaire de musique*; trans. [of 2/1703], 1982)

J. B. Peyer [Beyer]: *Primae lineae musicae vocalis* (Freiburg, 1703/*R*1977, abridged 2/1730)

M. H. Fuhrmann: *Musicalischer-Trichter, dadurch ein geschickter Informator seiner Informandis die edle Singe-Kunst nach heutiger Manier ... einbringen kan* (Frankfurt an der Spree, 1706, 2/1715 as *Musica vocalis in nuce*)

Z. Tevo: *Il musico testore* (Venice, 1706)

D. Robinson: *An Essay upon Vocal Musick* (Nottingham, 1715)

B. Marcello: *Il teatro alla moda, o sia Metodo sicuro e facile per il ben comporre ed eseguire l'opere italiane in musica all'uso moderno* (Venice, 1720); trans., *MQ*, xxxiv (1948), 371–403; xxxv (1949), 85–105

P. F. Tosi: *Opinioni de' cantori antichi e moderni, o sieno Osservazioni sopra il canto figurato* (Bologna, 1723); ed. in Leonesi (1904), in Della Corte (1933) and in R. M. Mori: *I maestri del bel canto* (Rome, 1953); trans. J. E. Galliard as *Observations on the Florid Song*, 1742, 2/1743/*R*1978) [see also Agricola (1757)]

P. Prelleur: 'An Introduction to Singing', *The Modern Musick-Master, or The Universal Musician* (London, 1731, ?1785; *R*1965 [1731]: Documenta musicologica, 1st ser., xxvii)

M. P. de Montéclair: *Principes de musique* (Paris, 1736), esp. pt iii

F. David: *Méthode nouvelle ou principes généraux pour apprendre facilement la musique et l'art de chanter* (Paris, 1737)

J. Mattheson: *Der vollkommene Capellmeister* (Hamburg, 1739/*R*1954; trans., 1981), pt i, chap.6; pt ii, chaps.1, 3, 11

F. Chigi Zondadari: *Riflessioni fatte da Euchero Pastore Arcade sopra alla maggior facilità che trovasi nell'apprendere il canto con l'uso di un solfeggio di dodici monosillabi* (Venice, 1746)
C. Denis: *Nouveau système de musique pratique* (Paris, 1747, *c*1760 as *Nouvelle méthode pour apprendre ... la musique et l'art de chanter*)

1750–1800

C. Buterne: *Méthode pour apprendre la musique vocale et instrumentale* (Rouen, 1752)
G. De Cattaneo: *La libertà nel cantare* (Lucca, 1752)
J. J. Quantz: 'Herrn Johann Joachim Quantzens Lebenslauf von ihm selbst entworfen', in F. W. Marpurg: *Historisch-kritische Beyträge zur Aufnahme der Musik*, i (Berlin, 1754/*R*1970); trans. in P. Nettl: *Forgotten Musicians* (New York, 1951)
J.-A. Bérard: *L'art du chant* (Paris, 1755/*R*1972; trans. 1969)
J. F. Agricola, ed.: *Anleitung zur Singekunst* (Berlin, 1757) [heavily annotated Ger. trans. of Tosi (1723)]
J.-J. Rousseau: 'Goût du chant', in D. Diderot and J. le R. D'Alembert, eds.: *Encyclopédie* (Paris, 1757); repr. in J.-J. Rousseau: *Dictionnaire de musique* (Paris, 1768/*R*1969), 283
M. Corrette: *Le parfait maître à chanter: méthode pour apprendre facilement la musique vocale et instrumentale* (Paris, 1758, enlarged 2/1782)
G. B. Doni: *Lyra Barberina amphichordos*, ed. A. F. Gori and G. B. Passeri (Florence, 1763/*R*1974)
I. F. X. Kürzinger: *Getreuer Unterricht zum Singen mit Manieren* (Augsburg, 1763, 5/1821)
F. W. Marpurg: *Anleitung zur Musik überhaupt und zur Singkunst besonders* (Berlin, 1763)
F. J. Chastellux: *Essai sur l'union de la poésie et de la musique* (The Hague and Paris, 1765)
J. Lacassagne: *Traité général des élémens du chant* (Paris, 1766/*R*1972) [see also P. Boyer: *Lettre à M. Diderot* (Paris, 1767) and Lacassagne: *L'uni-cléfier musical pour servir de supplement au Traité* (Paris, 1768)]
L'Ecuyer: *Principes de l'art du chant* (Paris, 1769/*R*1972)
B. Marcello: *Il teatro alla moda, o sia Metodo sicuro e facile per il ben comporre ed eseguire l'opere italiane in musica all'uso moderno* (Venice, 1770)
A. Bayly: *A Practical Treatise on Singing and Playing with Just Expression and Real Elegance* (London, 1771)
——: *The Sacred Singer, containing an Essay on Grammar, the Requisites of Singing* (London, 1771)
Raparlier: *Principes de musique, les agréments du chant, et un essai sur la prononciation, l'articulation et la prosodie de la langue françoise* (Lille, 1772/*R*1972)
J. A. Hiller: *Anweisung zur Singekunst in der deutschen und italienischen Sprache* (Frankfurt and Leipzig, 1773)
——: *Anweisung zum musikalisch-richtigen Gesange* (Leipzig, 1774, enlarged 2/1798) [incl. pt 2: *Exempelbuch*; see also Martini (1792)]
G. B. Mancini: *Pensieri e riflessioni pratiche sopra il canto figurato* (Vienna, 1774, enlarged 3/1777 as *Riflessioni pratiche*); extract, 1807 as *Metodo per ben insegnare ed apprendere l'arte del cantare*; 3/1777 edn partly repr. in Della Corte (1933); trans. as *Practical Reflections* (1967)
P. Duval: *Méthode agréable et utile pour apprendre facilement à chanter juste avec goût et précision* (Paris, 1775/*R*1972)
J. Hawkins: *A General History of the Science and Practice of Music* (London, 1776, 3/1875)
G. J. Vogler: *Stimmbildungskunst* (Mannheim, 1776)
S. Bertezen: *Principi di musica teorico-prattica* (Rome, 1780, abridged 2/1780 as *Principi della musica*, 3/1782 as *Extract of the Work Entitled 'Principles of Music'*)
J. A. Hiller: *Anweisung zum musikalisch-zierlichen Gesange* (Leipzig, 1780); trans. S. J. Beicken (diss., Stanford U., 1980)
S. Marchesi: *Lodi caratteristiche del celebre cantore Signor Luigi Marchesi* (Siena, 1781)
E. de Arteaga: *Le rivoluzioni del teatro musicale italiano dalla sua origine fino al presente* (Bologna, 1783–8, enlarged 2/1785; *R*1969: BMB, 3rd ser., vi) [vol.iii contains extracts of Manfredini's review of vol.i]
G. F. Tenducci: *Instruction of Mr. Tenducci to his Scholars* (London, ?1785)
D. van der Hooch: *De zangkunst gemaklijk gemaakt, of Musykaal handboek* (Amsterdam, 1788)
V. Manfredini: *Difesa della musica moderna e de' suoi esecutori* (Bologna, 1788) [commentary on vol.iii of Arteaga (1783–8)]
G. Aprile: *The Modern Italian Method of Singing* (London, 1791, *c*1810)
J. P. Martini: *Mélopée moderne, ou L'arte du chant* (Paris, ?1792, 2/*c*1800) [draws heavily on Hiller (1774)]
F. Trisobio: *La scuola del canto, or A New ... Method of Acquiring Perfection in Singing according to the Most Modern Italian Stile* (London, 1795)
W. Heinse: *Hildegard von Hohenthal* (Berlin, 1795–6) [novel with references to 18th-century operatic repertory and technique]
V. Manfredini: *Regole armoniche, o sieno Precetti ragionati* (Venice, enlarged 2/1797) [first edn is not relevant to singing]
J. B. Lasser: *Vollständige Anleitung zur Singkunst* (Munich, 1798, 2/1811)
J. Corfe: *A Treatise on Singing* (London and Bath, 1799)
M. López Remacha: *Arte de cantar, o Compendio de documentos músicos respectivos al canto* (Madrid, 1799)
F. Tomeoni: *Théorie de la musique vocale, ou des dix règles qu'il faut connoitre et observer pour bien chanter ... avec des remarques pour la prononciation des langues françoise et italienne* (Paris, 1799)

1800–25

C. H. Wilson: *The Myrtle and Vine, or Complete Vocal Library ... with an Essay on Singing and Song-Writing* (London, *c*1800, 3/*c*1802)
N. d'Aubigny von Engelbrunner: *Briefe an Natalie über den Gesang* (Leipzig, 1803, enlarged 2/1824)
B. Mengozzi: *Méthode de chant du Conservatoire de musique*, ed. H. F. M. Langlé (Paris, 1804, *c*1815)
J. F. Schubert: *Neue Singe-Schule, oder Gründliche und vollständige Anweisung zur Singkunst* (Leipzig, 1804)
Metodo per ben insegnare ed apprendere l'arte del cantare (Florence, 1807)
G. Baini: *Difesa del solfeggiamento regolato dalla variazione de' tuoni* (MS, 1808); described in A. de La Fage: *Essais de dipthérographie musicale* (Paris, 1864), 257ff
A. Calegari: *Modi e maniere onde adornare le spoglie cantilene* (MS, 1809, *I-Pl*; pubd posth., Milan, 1836, as *Modi generali del canto ... onde adornare o rifiorire le nude o semplici melodie e cantilene giusta il metodo di Gaspare Pacchiarotti*)
A. de Garaudé: *Méthode de chant* op.25 (Paris, 1809, 3/1854) [other Garaudé methods incl. opp.40, 53, 55 and 62]
G. Lanza: *The Elements of Singing* (London, 1809, 1843)
D. Corri: *The Singer's Preceptor, or Corri's Treatise on Vocal Music* (London, 1810)
G. Crescentini: Preface to *Raccolta di esercizi per il canto all'uso del vocalizzo, con un discorso preliminare* (Milan, *c*1810; trans., 1825) [other Crescentini collections pubd to 1835]
A. M. Pellegrini Celoni: *Grammatica o siano regole di ben cantare* op.6 (Rome, 1810, 2/1817)
M. Perrino: *Osservazioni sul canto* (Naples, 1810)
A. F. G. Pacini: *Ecole moderne de chant* (Paris, *c*1810–15)
E. Imbimbo: *Observations sur l'enseignement mutuel appliqué à la musique ... précédées d'une notice sur les conservatoires de Naples* (Paris, 1811)
A. Benelli: *Regole per il canto figurato, o siano Precetti ragionati ... per imparare a cantare/Regeln für den figurirten Gesang* (Dresden, 1814, 2/1819)
K. F. S. Liskovius [Liscovius]: *Theorie der Stimme* (Leipzig, 1814)
C. J. Smyth: *Six Letters on Singing from a Father to his Son* (Norwich, 1817)
G. G. Ferrari: *Breve trattato di canto italiano* (London, 1818; trans. W. Shield as *A Concise Treatise on Italian Singing*, 1818)
H.-P. Gérard: *Considérations sur la musique en général et particulièrement sur tout ce qui a rapport à la vocale* (Paris, 1819)
A. Clifton: *New Vocal Instructer* (Baltimore, 1820, 3/1846)
W. Kitchiner: *Observations on Vocal Music* (London, 1821)
J. B. Roucourt: *Essai sur la théorie du chant* (Brussels, 1821)
G. L. B. Wilhem: *Guide de la méthode élémentaire et analytique de musique et de chant* (Paris, 1821–4, 6/1845 as *Guide complet*)
I. Nathan: *An Essay on the History and Theory of Music and on the Qualities, Capabilities and Management of the Human Voice* (London, 1823, 2/1836 as *Musurgia vocalis*)
A. M. Pellegrini Celoni: *Metodo breve e facile per conoscere il piantato della musica e sue diramazioni* (Rome, 1823)
R. M. Bacon: *Elements of Vocal Science, being a Philosophical Enquiry into some Principles of Singing* (London, 1824)
A. Costa: *Considerations on the Art of Singing* (London, 1824)
P. von Winter: *Vollständige Singschule* (Mainz, 1824, 2/1874; abridged by L. Benda, n.d.)

1825–50

A. B. Marx: *Die Kunst des Gesanges, theoretisch und praktisch* (Berlin, 1826)
G. Brivi: *Brevi notizie intorno ad alcuni più celebri compositori di musica: cenni sullo stato presente del canto italiano* (Rovereto, 1827)
S. Dyer: *Dyer's Vocal Preceptor, containing a Concise Introduction to the Art of Singing* (New York, 1828)
H.-N. Gilles: *The Complete Vocal Instructor* (Baltimore, 1828)
T. Goodbau: *A New and Complete Introduction to Singing* (London, *c*1829)
E. J. B. Pastou: *Méthode de musique vocale* op.15 (Paris, 6/?1830)
A. Bagioli: *Bagioli's New Method of Singing* (New York, *c*1833)
N. Tacchinardi: *Dell'opera in musica sul teatro italiano e de' suoi difetti* (Florence, 2/1833)
J. Turner: *A Manual of Instruction in Vocal Music* (London, 1833/*R*1983: Classical Texts, vii)
N. Vaccai: *Metodo pratico di canto italiano per camera diviso in 15 lezioni, ossiano Solfeggi progressivi elementari sopra parole di Metastasio* (n.p., *c*1833; London, 1834, enlarged 2/1840, ed., with commentary, E. Battaglia, 1990) [numerous Vaccai methods, 1865 onwards]
G. Malagoli: *Metodo breve, facile e sicuro per apprendere bene il canto* (Bologna, 1834)
H. F. Mannstein: *Das System der grossen Gesangsschule des Bernacchi von Bologna dargestellt* (Leipzig, 1834, 2/1848)
T. Williams: *A Treatise on Singing* (London, 1834)
J. Addison: *Singing, Practically Treated in a Series of Instructions* (London, 1836)
H. Wainewright: *Critical Remarks on the Art of Singing* (London, 1836)
G. L. B. Wilhem: *Manuel musical à l'usage des collèges, des institutions et des cours de chant* (Paris, 1836, 7/1849); trans. J. A. Hamilton as *Singing for the Million* (1843) [see also Hullah (1841)]
M. Anfossi: *Trattato teorico-pratico sull'arte del canto/A Theoretical and Practical Treatise on the Art of Singing* (London, 1837, 2/*c*1840)
A. Costa: *Analytical Considerations on the Art of Singing* (London, 1838)
F. Ermagora: *Teorica del canto* (Venice, 1838, 2/1863)
H. F. Mannstein: *Geschichte, Geist und Ausübung des Gesanges von Gregor dem Grossen bis auf unsere Zeit* (Dresden, 1839)
——: *Die sogenannte Praktik des klassischen Gesange* (Dresden and Leipzig, 1839)
A. Panseron: *Méthode de vocalisation* (Paris, 1839) [numerous Panseron vocalization methods, 1839 onwards]
G. M. Bordogni: *Méthode de chant* (Paris, 1840) [other Bordogni vocalization methods, 1837 onwards]
G. Concone: *Introduzione all'arte per ben cantare, ossia Metodo elementare di canto* op.8 (Turin, *c*1840) [numerous Concone singing and vocalization methods, 1846 onwards]
E. Devrient: *Reisebriefe aus Paris* (Berlin, 1840)
P.-Y. Escudier and L. Escudier: *Etudes biographiques sur les chanteurs contemporains, précédées d'une esquisse sur l'art du chant* (Paris, 1840)
F. Florimo: *Breve metodo di canto* (Naples, *c*1840, enlarged 3/1865)
M. P. R. Garcia: *Traité complet de l'art du chant* (Paris, 1840, 2/1847/*R*1985, 3/1851 as *Ecole de Garcia*, 11/1901); trans. D. V. Paschke as *A Complete Treatise on the Art of Singing* (1972); Eng. edn as *Hints on Singing*, trans. B. Garcia (London, 1894, 2/1911)
L. Lablache: *Méthode de chant* (Paris, *c*1840 2/1851, enlarged 1894; trans., 1840)
A. Belgioioso: *Sull'arte del canto: breve osservazioni* (Milan, 1841; trans., *c*1860)
D. F. Crivelli: *L'arte del canto, ossia Corso completo d'insegnamento sulla coltivazione della voce* (London, 1841; trans., ?1843, 2/1844)
F. Despiney: *Physiologie de la voix et du chant* (Bourg, 1841)
M. P. R. Garcia: *Mémoire sur la voix humaine* (Paris, 1841)
J. Hullah: *Wilhem's Method of Teaching Singing, adapted to English Use* (London, 1841, 1842/*R*1983: Classical Texts, vi) [see also Wilhem (1836)]
C. G. Nehrlich: *Die Gesangkunst, oder die Geheimnisse der grossen italienischen und deutschen Gesangmeister alter und neuer Zeit vom physiologischen, psychologischen, ästhetischen und pädagogischen Standpunkt aus betrachtet* (Leipzig, 1841, enlarged 2/1853, 1860)
J. Barnett: *Systems and Singing Masters: an Analytical Comment upon the Wilhem System … and Critical Remarks upon Mr John Hullah's Manual* (London, 1842) [see also Wilhem (1836) and Hullah (1841)]
J. Barnett: *School for the Voice, or The Principles of Singing* (London, 1844)
E. Chevé: *Méthode élémentaire de musique vocale* (Paris, 1844, ?2/1863)
F. Avventi: *Mentore teatrale: repertorio di leggi, massime, norme e discipline per gli artisti melodrammatici* (Ferrara, 1845)
G.-L. Duprez: *L'art du chant* (Paris, 1845, ?1860; trans., 1847)
W. Harker: *Elements of Vocal Music, or A Collection of the Established Principles and Best Usages of Composition* (London, 1845)
A. Martineau: *Nouvelle grammaire de la langue musicale … ou principes de musique et de chant* (Paris, 1845)
G. W. Fink: *Der musikalische Hauslehrer, oder Theoretisch-praktische Anleitung für Alle* (Leipzig, 1846)
G. A. Perotti: *Guida per lo studio del canto figurato* (Milan, 1846)
R. Platt: *A New, Easy and Correct System of Vocal Music* (London, 1847)
F. Casella: *Compendio dell'opera e delle teorie per l'arte del canto* (Rome, 1848)
H. H. Curtis: *Voice Building and Tone Placing* (New York, 1848, 3/1909)
J. Gothard: *Thoughts on Singing, with Hints on the Elements of Effect and the Cultivation of Taste* (Chesterfield, 1848)
H. F. Mannstein: *Die grosse italienische Gesang-schule nebst praktischen Übungstücken* (Dresden and Leipzig, enlarged 2/1848)
L. A. Segond: *Hygiène du chanteur … causes principales de l'affaiblissement de la voix* (Paris, 1848)
M. H. Callcott: *The Singer's Alphabet, or Hints on the English Vowels* (London, 1849)
L. Cinti-Damoreau: *Méthode de chant composée pour ses classes du Conservatoire* (Paris, 1849)
B. Fontana: *The Musical Manual, containing both the Theory and Practice of Instrumental and Vocal Music* (London, 1849)
A. Mueller: *Der dramatische Sänger* (Darmstadt, 1849)

1850–75

A. Mueller: *Nouvelle méthode de chant/Neue vollständige Gesangschule* (Vienna, ?1850)
P. Pargetti: *Treatise on Singing* (London, 1850)
G. Vitelli: *A Treatise on the Formation, Cultivation and Development of the Voice, with General Directions for Singing … as adopted by Mdlle Jenny Lind* (London, *c*1850)
B. F. Baker and L. H. Southard: *A Complete Method for the Formation and Cultivation of the Voice* (Boston, 1852)
S. de la Madelaine: *Théories complètes du chant* (Paris, 1852, 3/1868)
L. Plet: *Sopra la vocale lettura della musica e sopra l'arte del canto* (Venice, 1852)
J. A. Hamilton: *Hamilton's Modern Instructions for Singing* (London, 1853)
H. Panofka: *L'art de chanter: théorie et pratique* op.81 (Paris, 1854) [incl. 'Vade-mecum du chanteur, contenant des exercises'; other Panofka methods, 1849 onwards]
F. Schmitt: *Grosse Gesangschule für Deutschland* (Munich, 1854, 2/1864)
C. Bloxsome: *Fundamental Principles for the Vocal Student* (London, 1855)
M. P. R. Garcia: *Nouveau traité sommaire de l'art du chant* (Paris, 1856; trans. as *Garcia's New Treatise on the Art of Singing*, 1857, also subsequent edns)
M. W. Balfe: *A New Universal Method of Singing without the Use of Solfeggi* (London, 1857)
C. Bassini: *Bassini's Art of Singing: an Analytical, Physiological and Practical System for the Cultivation of the Voice*, ed. R. S. Willis (Boston, 1857, 1869 as *Bassini's New Method*)
C. Bloxsome: *Elementary Practice for the Vocal Student* (London, 1857)
J. Fodor-Mainvielle: *Réflexions et conseils sur l'art du chant* (Paris, 1857)
J. Wass: *Complete Singing Method* (London, 1857)
A. Cordero y Fernández: *Escuela completa de canto en todos sus géneros y principalmente en el dramatico espanol y italiano* (Madrid, 1858)
F. Sieber: *Vollständiges Lehrbuch der Gesangskunst* (Magdeburg,

1858, 2/1878; trans. as *The Art of Singing*, 1872) [numerous Sieber vocalization methods, 1872 onwards]
W. Williams: *The Singer's Manual* (Boston, 1858)
W. Schwarz: *System der Gesangskunst nach physiologischen Gesetzen* (Hanover, 1859)
F. de Courcy: *The Art of Singing, its Theory and Practise* (London, 1860)
O. Guttmann: *Die Gymnastik der Stimme* (Leipzig, 1860, 7/1908; trans., 1882, 6/1893)
W. Matthias: *Praktische Singschule ... Text und Melodienbuch* (Berlin, 1860)
L. Meignen: *The Art of Singing* (Philadelphia, 1860)
F. Sieber: *Die Aussprache des Italienischen im Gesang* (1860, 2/1880)
W. W. Cazalet: *The Voice, or The Art of Singing* (London, 1861)
C. Everest: *Vocal Instructor* (Philadelphia, 1861)
E. Seiler: *Altes und neues über die Ausbildung des Gesangorganes* (Leipzig, 1861; trans. as *The Voice in Singing*, 1868, enlarged 1909)
M. H. Schmidt: *Gesang und Oper: kritisch-didaktische Abhandlungen in zwanglosen Heften* (Magdeburg, 1861–4)
C. Bassini: 'Exercises for the Training of the Singer', *The New Olive Branch*, ed. T. J. Cook and T. E. Perkins (New York, 1862)
H. Berlioz: *A travers chants* (Paris, 1862); ed. L. Guichard (Paris, 1971) [incl. 'Sur l'état actuel de l'art du chant', 89–103; 'Les mauvais chanteurs, les bons chanteurs, le public, les claqueurs', 104–7]
F. Sieber: *Katechismus der Gesangskunst* (1862, Leipzig, 6/1903)
C.-A. Battaille: *Nouvelles recherches sur la phonation*, ii: *De l'enseignement du chant* (Paris, 1863)
F. N. Erith: *The Voice and the Principles of Singing: a Lecture* (London, 1864)
L. Giraldoni: *Guida teorico-pratica ad uso dell'artista cantante* (Bologna, 1864)
F. Lamperti: *Guida teorico-practico-elementare per lo studio del canto* (Milan, 1864; trans. as *The Singer's Guide*, 1868)
H. F. Mannstein: *Katechismus des Gesanges im Lichte der Naturwissenschaft, Sprache und Logik* (Leipzig, 1864)
K. J. Formes: *Karl Formes' Method of Singing* (San Francisco, 1865, 2/1885)
B. Gamucci: 'Del costume di rifiorire le melodie vocali italiane', *Atti dell'Accademia del reale istituto musicale di Firenze* (Florence, 1865)
F. Sieber: *Kurze Anleitung zum gründlichen Studium der Gesangeskunst* opp.30–35, 42–9 (Leipzig, 1865) [incl. 'Schule der Geläufigkeit' opp.42–3]
F. Chiaromonte: *L'art de phraser et de cadencer* (Paris, 1866)
F. B. Faure: *La voix et le chant: traité pratique* (Paris, 1866)
F. Hauser: *Gesangslehre für Lehrende und Lernende* (Leipzig, 1866)
G. Toscano: *Sullo stato dell'arte del canto* (Naples, 1866)
L. Celentano: *Intorno all'arte del cantare in Italia nel secolo decimonono* (Naples, 1867)
Lucius: *American and Italian Cantatrici, or A Year at the Singing Schools of Milan* (London, 1867)
H. Zopff: *Practical Advice for Singers and Singing Teachers ... for Voices that are Poor or Spoiled* (Leipzig, 1867)
G. Carulli: *Méthode de chant* (Paris, 1868)
G. Lovati: *Guida per gli esordienti nell'arte melodrammatica* (Milan, 1868)
S. de la Madelaine: *Etudes pratiques de style vocale* (Paris, 1868)
G. Weiss: *Allgemeine Stimmbildungslehre für Gesang und Rede mit anatomisch-physiologischer Begründung dargestellt* (Brunswick, 1868)
J. Ella: *Musical Sketches* (London, 1869, 3/1878)
F.-J. Fétis: *Méthode des méthodes de chant, basée sur les principes des écoles les plus célèbres de l'Italie et de la France* (Paris, 1870)
G. Carlberg: *Die Kunst Sänger zu werden* (Vienna, *c*1870)
——: *Über Gesangskunst und Kunstgesang* (Vienna, 1870)
C. Delprat: *L'art du chant* (Paris, 1870)
G. Durant: *Hygiene of the Voice: its Physiology and Anatomy* (New York, 1870)
F. Lamperti: *L'arte del canto: norme tecniche e consigli agli allievi ed agli artisti* (Milan, *c*1870; trans. 1884)
H. Panofka: *Voix et chanteurs* (Paris, *c*1870)
Singing Made Easy, explaining the Pure Italian Method of Producing and Cultivating the Voice, the Management of the Breath (London, 1870)
F. W. Abt: *Praktische Gesangschule* op.474 (Brunswick, 1871; trans., 1893) [Eng. edn incl. M. Spicker: 'A Short Practical Treatise on the Art of Singing', ii–iv]
B. Carelli: *Cronaca d'un respiro* (Naples, 1871, 2/1875)
W. Ludden: *School for the Voice, being an Analytical, Theoretical and Practical Treatise upon the Proper Use and Development of the Vocal Organs* (Boston, 1871)
H. R. Streeter: *Voice Building: a New and Correct Theory for the Mechanical Formation of the Human Voice* (Boston, 1871)
G. J. Webb and C. G. Allen: *Voice Culture: a Complete Method of Theory and Practice for the Cultivation and Development of the Voice* (New York, 1871, 2/1884)
J. Eastes: *The Vocalists' Vade Mecum, or Pocket Companion: Practical Hints on Singing* (London, 1872) [other Eastes singing exercise books with instructions under name variants, from *c*1865]
G. Nava: *Method of Instruction*, ed. C. Santley (London, 1872) [other Nava vocalization methods pubd contemporaneously]
G. Weldon: *Hints for Pronunciation in Singing* (London, 1872, 3/1882)
G. Roberti: *Corso elementare di musica vocale* (Florence, 1872–4)
B. Carelli: *L'arte del canto* (Naples, 1873)
W. H. Daniell: *The Voice and How to Use it* (Boston, 1873; also as *How to Sing*)
G. Fantoni: *Storia universale del canto* (Milan, 1873)
F. W. Root: *F. W. Root's School of Singing* (Cincinnati, 1873) [other Root methods, from 1901]
W. Barnes: *How to Improve the Voice* (London, 1874)
W. Cooper: *The Voice, the Music of Language and the Soul of Song: a Short Essay on the Art of Singing* (London, 1874)
E. Delle Sedie: *L'art lyrique* (Paris, 1874)
A. Laget: *Le chant et les chanteurs* (Paris, 1874)
T. Lemaire: 'L'art du chant en Italie', *Chronique musicale*, iii (1874), 61–6
G. L. Osgood: *Guide in the Art of Singing, based on the Reliable Traditions of the Italian School of Vocalization and Practical Developments of Modern Science* (Boston, 1874)

1875–1900

C. Lunn: *The Philosophy of Voice* (London, 1875, enlarged 3/1880, as *Vox populi* 10/1906)
S. de la Madelaine: *Oeuvres complètes sur le chant: théorie et pratique* (Paris, 1875)
J. Audubert: *L'art du chant, suivi d'un traité de maintien théatral avec figures explicatives* (Paris, 1876)
L. Browne: *Medical Hints on the Production and Management of the Singing Voice* (London, 1876)
E. Delle Sedie: *Arte e fisiologia del canto* (Milan, 1876; trans. in *Vocal Art*, 1886; abridged in *A Complete Method of Singing*, 1894)
A. Lacombe: *La science du méchanisme vocal et l'art du chant* (Paris, 1876)
A. Orsini: *Considerazioni generali sull'arte del canto* (Rome, 1876)
E. G. J. Grégoir: *Panthéon musical populaire* (Brussels, 1876–7) [incl. 'Méthode de chant' and exercises]
S. A. Ciccolini: *De diepe ademhaling, hare verhouding tot de gezondheid en de zangkunst* (1877; trans. as *Deep Breathing as a Means of Promoting the Art of Song and Curing Weaknesses ... of the Throat and Lungs*, 1883)
A. J. Ellis: *Pronunciation for Singers* (London, 1877, 10/*c*1910)
E. Franceschi: *L'arte della parola nel discorso, nella drammatica e nel canto* (Milan, 1877)
E. Polko: *Vom Gesange: musikalische Winke und Lebensbilder* (n.p., 1877)
F. Sieber: *Die Kunst des Gesangs* opp.110–11 (Offenbach, 1877; trans. as *The Art of Singing*, 1972)
V. Cirillo: *Vocal Method* (Boston, 1878)
A. J. Ellis: *Speech in Song* (London, 1878)
C. Lunn: *Vocal Expression, Empirical or Scientific* (London, 1878)
A. A. Pattou: *The Voice as an Instrument* (New York, 1878)
F. Penna: *Singing: an Essay* (London, 1878)
A. Filippi: *Del tremulo della voce nel canto: mezzi per prevenirlo o curalo* (Florence, 1879)
E. Behnke: *Mechanism of the Human Voice* (London, 1880, 18/*c*1900)
G. Bozzelli: *Brevi considerazioni sull'arte del canto* (Menaggio, 1880)
F. Coletti: *La scuola di canto in Italia* (Rome, 1880)
G. H. Federlein: *Common Sense in Singing: an Essay on the 'Practical School of Vocal Culture'* (New York, 1880)
——: *Gottlieb Federlein's Practical School of Voice Culture* (New York, 1880)

G. Galvani: *Osservazioni pratiche sull'organo della voce dell'artista di canto* (Venice, 1880)
G. Holmes: *The Science of Voice Production and Voice Preservation: for Use of Speakers and Singers* (London, 1880)
B. Lutgen: *To Students of Singing and Declamation: How to Sound the Letter 'R'* (London, 1880)
C. E. Pinsuti: *Hints to Teachers on Singing* (London, 1880)
E. Delle Sedie: *Riflessioni sulle cause della decadenza della scuola di canto in Italia* (Paris, 1881)
H. Hiles: *First Lessons in Singing* (Manchester, 1881)
T. Lemaire and H.-M.-F. Lavoix: *Le chant, ses principes et son histoire* (Paris, 1881)
R. Matteini: *Riflessioni sull'arte del canto* (Rome, 1881)
W. H. Walshe: *Dramatic Singing Physiologically Estimated* (London, 1881)
W. Ward: *The Throat in its Relation to Singing: a Series of Popular Papers* (London, 1881)
C. Camillo: *Über Erziehung und Erhaltung der Stimme* (Vienna, 1882)
A. A. Pattou: *The Art of Voice-Production with Special Reference to the Methods of Correct Breathing* (New York, 1882)
A. B. Bach: *On Musical Education and Vocal Culture* (Edinburgh, 1883, 5/1898)
L. Browne and E. Behnke: *Voice, Song and Speech* (London, 1883, 23/*c*1920)
S. H. Dow: *Artistic Singing* (Boston, 1883)
L. Kofler: *The Old Italian School of Singing* (Albany, NY, 1883)
E. J. Myer: *Truths of Importance to Vocalists* (New York, 1883)
L. Browne: *Science and Singing* (Albany, NY, 1884)
C. Lunn: *Artistic Voice in Speech and Song* (London, 1884)
J. Stockhausen: *Julius Stockhausens Gesangs-Methode* (Leipzig, 1884; trans. as *A Method of Singing*, 1884)
J. Williams: *The Elocution of Singing* (London, 1884)
A. B. Bach: *The Principles of Singing* (Edinburgh, 1885, 2/1894); partly repr. as *The Art of Singing* (Edinburgh, 1886)
J. F. Botume: *Modern Singing Methods, their Use and Abuse* (Boston, 1885, 4/1896)
F. Campanella: *Sulla decadenza del canto in Italia* (Naples, 1885)
E. Delle Sedie: *L'estetica del canto e dell'arte melodrammatica* (Livorno, 1885 [in Eng., It. and Fr.]; trans. in *Vocal Art*, 1886; abridged in *A Complete Method of Singing*, 1894)
F. Penna: *The Art of Singing* (London, *c*1885)
A. Guagni-Benvenuti: *L'odierna scuola di canto in Italia* (Rome, 1886)
G. C. Guidi: *La ginnastica della voce giusta, i principii della fisiologia, dell'arte e dell'igiene* (Bergamo, 1886)
J. Hey: *Deutsche Gesangs-Unterricht: Lehrbuch des sprachlichen und gesanglichen Vortrags* (Mainz, 1886; ed. F. Volbach and H. E. Hey, 1913)
J. Howard: *The Physiology of Artistic Singing* (Boston, 1886)
M. Mackenzie: *The Hygiene of the Vocal Organs: a Practical Handbook for Singers and Speakers* (London, 1886, 9/1928)
M. Marchesi: *Ecole Marchesi: méthode de chant théorique et pratique* op.31 (Paris, 1886; trans. as *Bel Canto*, n.d., and as *The Marchesi School*, 1896) [numerous Marchesi methods, 1863 onwards, some as *L'art du chant*]
E. J. Myer: *The Voice from a Practical Stand-Point, with Exercises* (New York, 1886)
J. Rand: *Practical Method of Singing, based upon Natural and Artistic Principles* (Boston, 1886)
J. Stockhausen: *Julius Stockhausen's Gesangstechnik und Stimmbildung* (Leipzig, 1886)
W. Bartoschek: *Gesangstechnik im Lichte neuerer Erkenntnisse* (Berlin, *c*1887)
C. Saint Germaine: *The Growth and Cultivation of the Voice in Singing* (London, 1887)
H. Tilla: *Why We Sing and Where the Voice is Formed and Placed* (New York, 1887)
R. Dannenberg: *Kathechismus der Gesangskunst: Max Hesses illustrierte Katechismen* (Leipzig, 1888, 5/1920 as *Handbuch der Gesangskunst*)
A. Labanchi: *Dell'arte del canto in Italia: studi e riforme* (Naples, 1888)
G. Oiram: *Cenni sulla soluzione del problema vocale* (Milan, 1888)
F. Quatremayne: *Correct Voice Production: a Concise Gymnastic for the Singing Voice* (London, 1888)
C. Ristori: *Manuale pratico di declamazione ad uso degli studiosi d'arte rappresentativa applicata pure al canto* (Turin, 1888)
T. W. Barth: *The Cheapest Singing Lesson in the World: the Only Secrets of the Italian Method … for Singing and Speaking* (London, 1889)
M. A. C. Carr: *Illustrated Manual of the Vowel Sounds in Voice Production and Singing* (London, 1889)
A. Galli: *Il canto da sala e da teatro* (Milan, 1889)
L. Giraldoni: *Metodo analitico, filosofico e filologico per la educazione della voce* (Milan, 1889)
L. Kofler: *The Art of Breathing as the Basis of Tone-Production* (New York, 1889, 7/1897)
L. Mastrigli: *L'azione drammatica dell'artista lirico: consigli e precetti* (Rome, 1889)
——: *Igiene del cantante* (Rome, 1889)
G. Nuvoli: *Sull'uso delle vocali nell'insegnamento del canto* (Turin, 1889)
L. Vivarelli: *Ancora della decadenza dell'arte del canto* (Milan, 1889)
T. Chater: *Scientific Voice, Artistic Singing and Effective Speaking* (London, 1890)
L. O. Emerson: *Emerson's Vocal Method* (Boston, 1890)
H. Goldschmidt: *Die italienische Gesangsmethode des XVII. Jahrhunderts und ihre Bedeutung für die Gegenwart nach Quellen jener Zeit* (Berlin, 1890)
B. Müller-Brunow: *Tonbildung oder Gesangsunterricht?* (Leipzig, 1890, 6/1912)
A. Kohut: *Die grössten und beruhmtesten deutschen Soubtretten des neunzehnten Jahrhunderts* (Dusseldorf, 1890)
L. Mastrigli: *Manuale del cantante* (Milan, 1890)
F. Arlberg: *Försök till en naturlig och fornuftig grandlaggning af tonbildningsläran* [An Attempt at a Natural and Sensible Basis for Tone Production] (Stockholm, 1891)
B. Carelli: *Torniamo a cantare: maestri e cantanti* (Naples, 1891)
F. Chrysander: 'Ludovico Zacconi als Lehrer des Kunstgesanges', *VMw*, vii (1891), 337–40
E. J. Meyer: *Vocal Reinforcement* (New York, 1891)
E. Palermi: *Sunto di nozioni fisiologiche sugli organi vocali e brevi cenni sull'insegnamento del canto* (Rome, 1891)
A. Raggi: *Regole e precetti del canto* (Cesena, 1891)
J. W. Bernhardt: *Vox humana: Voice Production and Development and the Art of Singing* (London, 1892)
S. Dunn: *The Art of Singing* (London, 1892)
H. Goldschmidt: *Der Vokalismus des neuhochdeutschen Kunstgesanges und der Buhnensprache: eine sprach- und gesangsphysiologische Studie* (Leipzig, 1892)
W. H. Griffiths: *Human Voice, its Cultivation and Preservation* (London, 1892)
C. R. Hennig: *Die Unterscheidung des Gesangregister auf physiologischer Grundlage, mit besonderer Berücksichtigung der Voix mixte* (Leipzig, 1892)
G. Henschel: *Progressive Studies for the Voice* op.49 (London, 1892)
A. G. Labanchi: *Gli eunuchi e le scuole del canto del secolo XVIII* (Florence, 1892, 2/1893)
R. Miles: *Chart of the Whole Art of Singing* (Deptford, 1892)
P. A. Roche: *Avviamento allo studio del canto con nozioni speciali per la voce di baritono* (Naples, 1892)
V. Boccabadati: *Oservazioni pratiche per lo studio del canto* (Pesaro, 1893)
M. H. B. Hart: *Practical Hints on Singing and Pianoforte Playing* (London, 1893)
J. Joal: *De la respiration dans le chant* (Paris, 1893; trans., 1895)
F. Maccabe: *Frederic Maccabe on Voice Production, the Arts of Speaking, Singing, Acting and Ventriloquism* (Wolverhampton, 1893)
A. Randegger: *Singing* (London, 1893)
C. K. Rogers: *The Philosophy of Singing* (London, 1893)
F. C. M. De Rialp: *The Legitimate School of Singing* (New York, 1894)
L. Leonesi: *La decadenza dell'arte del canto: causa e rimedio* (Bologna, 1894)
W. S. Rockstro: *Jenny Lind, a Record and Analysis of the 'Method' of the Late Madame Jenny Lind-Goldschmidt* (London and New York, 1894)
O. Sefferi: *Neue Rationelle* (Leizig, 1894)
F. H. Tubbs: *Science and Art of Breathing* (New York, 1894)
J. W. Bernhardt: *A Singing Lesson, from Shorthand Notes of a Lecture on Vocal Method* (London, 1895)
A. Iffert: *Allgemeine Gesangsschule* (Leipzig, 1895, 4/1903)
J. Mayan: *Il canto e la voce: studio completo dell'arte lirica* (Trieste, 1895) [orig. in Fr.]
A. Piltan: *The Human Voice, its Mechanism: a New and Original*

Book on Singing (London, 1895)
F. Walker: *Letters of a Baryton* (London, 1895)
H. H. Curtis: *Voice Building and Tone Placing* (New York, 1896)
A. Ehrlich: *Berühmte Sängerinnen* (Leipzig, 1896)
P. Garnault: *Cours théorique et pratique de physiologie, d'hygiène et de thérapeutique de la voix parlée et chantée* (Paris, 1896)
L. Lehmann-Kalisch: *Was ich über die moderne Gesangskunst denke* (Berlin, 1896)
C. Pierre: *L'école de chant de l'Opéra (1672–1807) d'après des documents inédits* (Paris, 1896)
F. W. Root: *The Polychrome Lessons in Voice Culture* (Cincinnati, 1896)
G. E. Thorp: *20 Lessons on the Development of the Voice* (London, 1896, 5/1930)
G. E. Thorp and W. Nicholl: *Textbook on the Natural Use of the Voice* (London, 1896)
H. J. Wood: *To my Pupils: Brief Notes [on Singing] to be Kept in Memory* (London, 1896)
G. Fante: *Alcune osservazioni intorno lo studio dell'arte del canto* (Pesaro, 1897)
A. Guillemin: *Sur la génération de la voix et du timbre* (Paris, 1897)
L. W. Mason, K. L. Beidler and K. Unglaub: *Handbuch für Lehrer zu der neuen Gesangschule* (Leipzig, 1897)
L. Mastrigli: *La decadenza del canto in Italia: cause e rimedi* (Rome, 1897)
E. J. Myer: *Position and Acting in Singing* (New York, 1897)
J. S. Brown: 'The Literature of Voice Production and the Art of Singing: a Bibliography', *Musician* [Philadelphia], iii (1898), 45, 73, 101, 133
B. Carelli: *L'arte del canto: metodo* (Naples, 1898)
J. Deggau: *Eine neue Methode der Stimmbildung: eine Einführung in die Kuypers'sche 'Anleitung zur Stimmbildung und zum flüssigen Sprechen'* (Giessen, 1898)
E. Holland: *Voice Production* (London, 1898)
A. Kuijpers: *Anleitung zur Stimmbildung* (Leipzig, *c*1898, 3/1902, 1910)
K. I. Mikhaylov-Stoyan: *Genezis, analiz i metod estestvennago pieniya: rukovodstvo k bistromu dostizheniyu pravilnago i khoroshago pieniya* [The Origins, Analysis and Method of Natural Singing: Instruction for the Quick Attainment of Correct and Good Singing] (Moscow, 1898)
C. E. Rowley: *The Voice, or The Physiologist versus the Singing Master* (London, 1898)
W. Shakespeare: *The Art of Singing* (London, 1898–9, 2/1921)
A. M. de Gordon y de Acosta: *Consideraciones sobre la voz humana* (Havana, 1899)
L. Janácek: *Návod pro vyučování zpěvu* [Instructions for Singing Lessons] (Brno, 1899; ed. M. Duchoňová and L. Faltus, 1980)
L. Mastrigli: *La respirazione nel canto* (Rome, 1899)
T. P. Sykes: *Notes on Singing* (London, 1899)

1900–25

W. A. Aikin: *The Voice: its Physiology and Cultivation* (London, 1900; ed. H. St John Rumsey, 3/1951)
B. Campana: 'L'arte del canto', *Cronaca musicale*, v (1900), 182–92
S. Reeves: *Sims Reeves on the Art of Singing* (London, 1900)
C. Santley: *The Singing Master* (London, 1900)
B. Baylis: *The Often Mis-Used Voice* (London, 1901)
T. Beretta: *Practical Notes on Singing and the Production of the Voice* (London, 2/1901)
W. H. Lawton: *The Singing Voice and its Practical Cultivation* (New York, 1901)
M. Marchesi: *Ten Singing Lessons* (New York, 1901)
G. Vogel: *Italienische und deutsche Gesangskunst* (1901)
T. Coli: *Il canto* (Milan, 1902)
L. Crépaux: *Palatal Tone-Placing: Articulation in Singing* (San Francisco, 1902)
A. Giovannini: *Manualetto di nozioni utili per chi vuol dedicarsi al magistero del canto* (Milan, 1902)
A. Göttmann: 'Gesangstudium und Gesangmethode', *Die Musik*, ii (1902), 188–92
M. Kuhn: *Die Verzierungskunst in der Gesangs Musik des XVI. und XVII. Jahrhunderts* (Leipzig, 1902)
L. Lehmann: *Meine Gesangskunst* (Berlin, 1902, 11/1980; trans. as *How to Sing*, 1902, enlarged 3/1924)
S. Marchesi: *A Vademecum for Singing-Teachers and Pupils* (New York, 1902)
E. J. Myer: *The Renaissance of the Vocal Art: a Practical Study … through Flexible, Elastic Bodily Movements* (Boston, 1902)
J. M. B. Ranske: *Health, Speech and Song: a Practical Guide to Voice-Production* (London and New York, 1902)
G. Armin: *Gesammelte Aufsätze über Stimmbildung, Gesangskritik, moderne Sänger und Schauspeiler* (Berlin, 1903)
J. Clarkson: *Practical Guide to Articulation for Singing or Speaking* (Manchester, 1903)
G. Ferreri: *La voce nel linguaggio e nel canto* (Rome, 1903)
H. H. Hulbert: *Breathing for Voice Production* (New York, 1903)
M. I. James: *Scientific Tone Production: a Manual for Teachers and Students of Singing and Speaking* (Boston, 1903)
W. H. Neidlinger: *A Primer on Voice and Singing* (Chicago, 1903)
A. Solerti, ed.: *Le origini del melodramma: testimonianze dei contemporanei* (Bologna, 1903) [incl. Cavalieri (1600), Peri (1600), Caccini (1601/2), Giustiniani (1628), Doni (1633–5), Della Vale (1640)]
G. E. Stubbs: *The Adult Male Alto or Counter-Tenor Voice* (London, 1903, 2/1908)
J. H. Wagenmann: *Neue Aera der Stimmbildung für Singen und Sprechen* (Berlin, 1903)
C. van Zanten and E. C. Poser: *Leitfaden zum Kunstgesang* (Leipzig, 1903)
W. A. Armstrong: 'Madame Marchesi: Some of her Teaching Principles', *Etude*, xxii (1904), 139–40
W. H. Breare: *Vocalism: its Structure and Culture from an English Standpoint* (New York and London, 1904)
J. Howard: *Expression in Singing, including Thirty-One Exercises for Voice Culture*, ed. T. Drury (London and New York, 1904)
R. Imhofer: *Die Krankheiten der Singstimme für Ärzte* (Berlin, 1904) [incl. M. Wallerstein: 'Gesangstechnik']
L. Leonesi: *La scuola di canto dell'epoca d'oro (sec. XVII)* (Naples, 1904)
C. Lunn: *The Voice: its Downfall, its Training and its Use* (London, 1904)
G. Armin: *Das Stauprinzip, oder Die Lehre von dem Dualismus der menschlichen Stimme* (Leipzig, 1905, ?2/1912)
D. T. Ffrangcon-Davies: *The Singing of the Future* (London and New York, 1905, 6/1920); abridged in *David Ffrangcon-Davies, his Life and Book*, ed. M. Ffrangcon-Davies (London, 1938), 67–185
G. B. Lampert and M. Heidrich: *The Technics of Bel Canto* (New York, 1905) [orig. in Ger.]
G. Magrini: *Arte e tecnica del canto* (Milan, 1905)
L. A. Russell: *English Diction for Singers and Speakers* (Boston, 1905)
O. Rutz: *Die Rutz'schen Tonstudien und die Reform des Kunstgesanges* (Munich, 1905)
'A Singer': *Singing, or Method of Song and Speech* (London, 1905)
G. Somigli: *G. Stockhausen e la scuola del canto artistico* (Chicago, 1905)
B. Ziller: 'Das Geheimnis des "Bel canto" (Schöngesang): einige aufklärende Worte für Gesangfreunde, Gesangstudierende und Gesanglehrer', *AMz*, xxxii (1905), 534–5
P. Bruns-Molar: *Neue Gesangs-Methode nach erweiterten Grundlehren von primären Ton* (Berlin, 1906)
G. Clerici: *Perfection in Singing, being Criticisms, Essays, Remarks and Useful Hints* (London, 1906)
H. A. K. Gutzmann: *Stimmbildung und Stimmpflege* (Wiesbaden, 1906, 3/1920)
W. J. Henderson: *The Art of Singing* (New York, 1906, enlarged 2/1938)
——: *The Art of the Singer: Practical Hints about Vocal Technics and Style* (New York, 1906)
A. Kohut: *Die Gesangsköniginnen in den letzen drei Jahrhunderten* (Berlin, 1906)
W. Mills: *Voice Production in Singing and Speaking, based on Scientific Principles* (Philadelphia and London, 1906, 5/*c*1915)
C. W. Palmer: *Voice Simplified: a Condensed and Practical Treatise on Singing* (London, 1906)
J. Pownall: *The Singing Voice and its Development* (London, 1906)
W. Reinecke: *Die Kunst der idealen Tonbildung* (Leipzig, 1906, enlarged 2/1910)
I. San Carolo and P. Daniel: *The Common-Sense of Voice Development* (New York, 1906)
C. E. Seashore: *The Tonoscope and its Use in the Training of the Voice* (Iowa City, IA, 1906)
W. H. Breare: *Vocal Faults and their Remedies* (New York and London, 1907)
E. Drummond: *Useful Hints for Those Who Wish to Sing but Who Cannot Get Tuition* (London, 1907)
H. Goldschmidt: *Die Lehre von der vokalen Ornamentik* (Berlin, 1907)

H. H. Hulbert: *Voice Training in Speech and Song* (London, *c*1907, 4/1912)
M. Jpes-Speet: *Wie ich über Sprechen und Singen denke* (Berlin, 1907)
L. A. Russell: *The Commonplaces of Vocal Art: a Plain Statement Singing* (Boston, 1907)
J. Smith: *Voice and Song: a Practical Method for the Study of Singing* (New York, 1907)
J. A. van Broekhoven: *The True Method of Voice Production* (New York, 1908)
E. Byron: *Fallacies in the Art of Singing* (Leicester, 1908)
L. Cappiani: *Practical Hints and Helps for Perfection in Singing* (New York, 1908)
W. H. Griffiths: *The Voxaphone System of Singing: a Method of Teaching Singing by Means of Gramophone Records* (London, 1908)
M. Heidrich: 'Zum Verfall der Gesangskunst', *Signale für die musikalische Welt*, lxvi/6 (1908), 105–8
B. Lütgen: *Die Kunst der Kehlfertigkeit/Studies in Velocity* (New York, 1908)
A. L. Manchester: *Twelve Lessons in the Fundamentals of Voice Production* (Boston, 1908)
O. Rutz: *Neue Entdeckungen von der menschlichen Stimme* (Munich, 1908)
C. Santley: *The Art of Singing and Vocal Declamation* (London and New York, 1908)
K. Scheidemantel: *Stimmbildung* (Leipzig, 1908, enlarged 7/1920)
A. Spanuth: 'Wagner-Gesang und Bel Canto', *Signale für die musikalische Welt*, lxvi/6 (1908), 169–74
D. C. Taylor: *The Psychology of Singing* (New York, 1908)
B. Ulrich: 'Die älteste Anleitung zum Kunstgesang', *Die Stimme*, iii (1908–9), 10–19 [about Maffei (1562)]
M. Cléricy Blanc du Collet: *Méthode naturelle, scientifique, physiologique de pose de la voix* (Paris, 1909)
H. Klein: *The Hermann Klein Phono-Vocal Method, based upon the Famous School of Manuel Garcia* (New York, 1909)
E. Kreuz: *Dramatic Singing and Opera in English* (London, 1909)
C. F. H. Mills: *Voice and Vocalism, including … Treating of the Subtile Influence of Singing* (Mt Vernon, IA, 1909)
L. Tetrazzini and E. Caruso: *The Art of Singing* (New York, 1909, 1975 as *Caruso and Tetrazzini on the Art of Singing*)
E. G. White: *Science and Singing: a Consideration of the Capabilities of the Vocal Cords and their Work in the Art of Tone Production* (London, 1909, enlarged 1918 as *The Voice Beautiful in Speech and Song*, 3/1922)
F. Fechter: 'Italienische Stimmbildung und deutsches Musikdrama', *AMz*, xxxvii (1910), 235–8, 263–6
M. Heinrich: *Correct Principles of Classical Singing, containing Essays on Choosing a Teacher, the Art of Singing* (Boston, 1910)
M. S. Mackinlay: *The Singing Voice and its Training* (London and New York, 1910)
E. Michotte: *Souvenirs: une soirée chez Rossini à Beau-Séjour (Passy) 1858* (Brussels, *c*1910; trans., 1968)
F. E. Miller: *The Voice: its Production, Care and Preservation* (New York, 2/1910)
G. Monaldi: *Cantanti celebri del secolo XIX* (Rome, *c*1910)
G. E. Moure and A. Bouyer: *The Abuse of the Singing and Speaking Voice: Causes, Effects and Treatment* (London, 1910) [orig. *Du malménage de la voix chantée et parlée*]
C. K. Rogers: *My Voice and I, or The Relation of the Singer to the Song* (Chicago, 1910)
G. Armin: *Automatische Stimmbildung* (Leipzig, 1911)
C. Biaggi: 'I segreti dell'arte del canto', *Lettura* (1911)
T. Fillebrown: *Resonance in Singing and Speaking* (Boston, 1911, 3/1911)
S. Garsó: *Schule der speziellen Stimmbildung auf der Basis des losen Tones* (Berlin, 1911)
C. Gib: *Vocal Science and Art* (London, 1911)
J. Griset: *Prononciation et expression musicales* (Paris, 1911)
W. E. Haslam: *Style in Singing* (New York, 1911)
J. Isnardon: *Le chant théatral* (Paris, 1911)
J. Kennedy: *Common Sense and Singing* (London, 1911)
B. Kwartin: *Prinzipien für Stimmbildung und Gesang* (Leipzig, 1911); Eng. edn as *Fundamentals of Vocal Instruction* (New York, 1941)
L. Parisotti: *A Treatise on Speaking and Singing according to the Principles of the Old Italian School* (London and New York, 1911)
O. Rutz: *Sprache, Gesang und Körperhaltung* (Munich, 1911, 2/1922)
S. Sonky: *Théorie de la musique vocale* (Paris, 1911)
C. Tree: *How to Acquire Ease of Voice Production: the Preservation of the Voice* (London, 1911)
J. H. Wagenmann: *Enrico Caruso und das Problem der Stimmbildung* (Altenburg, 1911, 3/1924)
A. R. Broad: *How to Attain the Singing Voice* (London, 1912)
T. Gerold: *Zur Geschichte der französischen Gesangskunst im 17. Jhdt.* (diss., U. of Strasbourg, 1912; pubd as *L'art du chant*, Strasbourg, 1921)
R. L. Herman: *An Open Door for Singers: Hints and Vocalists* (New York, 1912)
H. Lavielle: *De l'enrouement chez les chanteurs: étude physiopathologique de la voix chantée* (Bordeaux, 1912)
L. Mantler: *Die Bildung des Belcanto* (Vienna and Leipzig, 1912)
A. Minoja: *Lettera sopra il canto* (Milan, 1912)
O. Noë and H. J. Moser: *Technik der deutschen Gesangskunst* (Leipzig, 1912, 3/1955)
W. Reinecke: *Vom Sprechton zu Sington: von der Mischstimme zur Vollstimme (Schwellton)*, pt ii: *Die natürlich Entwicklung der Singstimme* (Leipzig, 1912)
C. K. Rogers: *English Diction in Song and Speech* (n.p., 1912)
O. Schwartz: *Das Opernstudium: Repertoire der verschiedenen Stimmfächer* (Berlin, 1912, 2/1914)
B. Ulrich: *Die Grandsätze der Stimmbildung … 1474–1640* (Leipzig, 1912; trans., 1973)
E. Caruso: *How to Sing* (New York, 1913)
H. J. Frossard: *La science et l'art de la voix* (Paris, 1913, 2/1927)
C. Gib: *The Art of Vocal Expression* (London, 1913)
D. D. Jones: *Lyric Diction for Singers, Actors and Public Speakers* (New York and London, 1913)
M. Marchesi and B. Marchesi: *Truths for Singing Teachers and Students* (Philadelphia, 1913)
E. J. Myer: *The Vocal Instructor* (Philadelphia, 1913)
K. Scheidemantel: *Gesangsbildung* (Leipzig, 1913, 2/1921)
G. Silva: *Il canto ed il suo insegnamento razionale* (Turin, 1913)
C. Thurwanger: *French Musical Diction: an Orthologic Method for Acquiring a Perfect Pronunciation … Especially in the Singing of the French Language* (New York and London, 1913)
A. E. White: *Practical Lessons in Singing and Voice Production for Beginners* (London, 1913)
W. H. Breare: *Vocal Technique* (London, 1914)
M. A. C. Carr: *Keep Breathing: How to Do It, and Why … for Speech, Singing* (London, 1914)
C. A. Eitz: *Der Gesangunterricht als Grundlage der musikalischen Bildung* (Leipzig, 1914)
H. Frossard: *La science et l'art du chant* (Paris, 1914, 2/1927)
G. Garcia: *A Guide to Solo Singing, containing Full Instructions on Singing with a Detailed Analysis of some Well-Known Works and Songs* (London, 1914)
W. Graziani: *Il canto: la chiave del piazzamento della voice: guida d'insegnamento al mio metodo di canto* (Turin, 1914)
H. V. Hemery: *The Artistic Singing of Songs* (London, 1914)
F. Martienssen: *Johannes Messchaert: ein Beitrag zum Verständnis echter Gesangskunst* (Berlin, 1914, 2/1920 as *Die echte Gesangskunst)*
T. Paul: *Systematische Gehör-, Treff- und Rhythmus-Übung und allgemeine Musikkunde* (Breslau, 1914)
W. W. Shaw: *The Lost Vocal Art and its Restortion, with Practical Exercises* (Philadelphia, 1914)
D. C. Taylor: *Self Help for Singers … based on the Old Italian Method* (New York, 1914)
G. Binetti: *Per la carriera lirica* (Milan, 1915)
C. W. Emerson: *Psycho Vox, or The Emerson System of Vocal Culture* (Millis, MA, 1915)
F. S. Muckey: *The Natural Method of Voice Production in Speech and Song* (New York, 1915)
J. M. B. Ranske: *Voice and Nerve Control* (New York, 1915)
V. Ricci: *La crisi del bel canto* (Florence, 1915)
C. C. Rossiter: *Singing Without a Master* (London, 1915)
D. C. Taylor: 'Voice Culture Past and Present: a General View of a Perplexing Subject', *MQ*, i (1915), 453–71
C. Cooke: *Practical Singing* (London, 1916, 2/1927)
J. F. Cooke: *Great Singers on the Art of Singing* (London, 1916, 2/1921)
M. M. van Gelder: *The Foundations of Artistic Singing* (Atlanta, GA, 1916)
H. S. Kirkland: *Expression in Singing* (Boston, 1916)
J. J. M. Levien: *The Singing-Master's Decalogue* (London, 1916)
O. Saenger: *The Oscar Saenger Course in Vocal Training* (Camden, NJ, 1916)

D. C. Taylor: 'L'antico sistema italiano di coltivazione vocale', *RMI*, xxiii (1916), 140–47

——: *New Light on the Old Italian Method: an Outline of the Historical System of Voice Culture, with a Plea for its Revival* (New York, 1916)

E. S. Thomas: *Scientific Singing: a Study of the Voice from a Logical Common-Sense Basis* (San Francisco, 1916)

D. A. Clippinger: *The Head Voice and Other Problems* (Boston, 1917)

G. Heller: *The Voice in Song and Speech* (London, 1917, 2/*c*1920)

M. Moestue: *Sangkunstens historie indtil midten av 19 aarhundrede* (Kristiana [Oslo], 1917)

E. J. Myer: *A Revelation to the Vocal World ... the Physical, Mental and Emotional Production, Reinforcement and Control of the Singing Voice* (Philadelphia, 1917)

C. W. Palmer: *Voice and Singing Practically Explained* (London, 1917)

W. H. Zay: *Practical Psychology of Voice and Life* (New York, 1917)

L. Graveure: *'Super-Diction': Twelve Studies in the Art of Song* (New York, 1918)

H. Hackmann: *Die Wiedergeburt der Tanz- und Gesangskunst aus dem Geiste der Natur* (Jena, 1918)

S. D. Duff: *Simple Truths Used by Great Singers* (Boston, 1919)

A. Weissmann: *Die Primadonna* (Berlin, 1919)

H. M. Brower: *Vocal Mastery: Talks with Master Singers and Teachers* (New York, 1920)

G. Cunelli: *Sui modi per rovinare la voce, il cantante e l'artista* (Rome, 1920)

H. W. Greene: *The Singer's Ladder, revealing the Necessity of a Serious Approach to the Most Attractive and Most Difficult Study in the World of Art* (New York, 1920)

R. Hahn: *Du chant* (Paris, 1920; trans. as *On Singers and Singing*, 1990)

E. McLellan: *Voice Education* (New York and London, 1920)

V. Ricci: *La tecnica del canto in rapporto con la pratica antica e la teoria moderna* (Livorno, 1920)

K. Rutz and O. Rutz: *Typenstimmbildung, zugleich die neue Ausdruckskunst für Bühne und Konzert* (Leipzig, 1920)

G. Armin: *Von der Urkraft der Stimme* (Leipzig, 1921)

J. Forchhammer: *Theorie und Technik des Singens und Sprechens in gemeinverständlicher Darstellung* (Leipzig, 1921)

W. J. Henderson: *Early History of Singing* (New York, 1921)

G. Silva: 'L'arte del canto', *La vita musicale dell'Italia d'oggi: Turin 1921*, 211–16

F. H. Haywood: *Universal Song: a Voice-Culture Course* (New York, 1921–33)

P. Bruns: *Carusos Technik in deutscher Erklärung* (Berlin, 1922)

S. Fucito and B. J. Beyer: *Caruso and the Art of Singing, including Caruso's Vocal Exercises and his Practical Advice* (New York, 1922)

C. Gib: *Vocal Success* (London, 1922)

F. C. Maghee: *Rhythmic Phonetic Training for Voice and Speech* (Boston, 1922)

P. M. Marafioti: *Caruso's Method of Voice Production* (New York, 1922, ?3/1958)

F. Martienssen-Lohmann: *Das bewusste Singen: Grundlegung des Gesangstudiums* (Leipzig, 1922, 2/1926)

F. E. Miller: *Vocal Art-Science and its Application* (New York, 2/1922)

H. Schmid-Kayser: *Der Kunstgesange* (Berlin, 1922)

G. Silva: 'The Beginnings of the Art of "Bel Canto": Remarks on the Critical History of Singing', *MQ*, viii (1922), 53–68

R. Temple: *Young Singers: What They Should Know* (Boston, 2/1922)

R. Denbigh: *Singing as a Career* (London, 1923)

J. Forchhammer: *Stimmbildung auf stimm- und sprachphysiologischer Grundlage* (Munich, 1923, 2/1937–8)

F. Haböck: *Die Gesangskunst der Kastraten*, i (Vienna, 1923; also as *Die Kastraten und ihre Gesangskunst*, Stuttgart, 1927)

H. Klein: *The Bel Canto, with Particular Reference to the Singing of Mozart* (London, 1923)

F. H. Martens: *The Art of the Prima Donna and Concert Singer* (New York, 1923)

E. Newman: *Solo Singing* (Glasgow, 1923)

L. Nordica: *Lillian Nordica's Hints to Singers*, ed. W. Armstrong (New York, 1923)

F. Proschowski: *The Way to Sing: a Guide to Vocalism, with Thirty Practical Exercises* (Boston, 1923)

V. Ricci: *Il bel canto* (Milano, 1923)

L. Tetrazzini: *How to Sing* (New York, 1923)

I. W. Voorhees: *Hygiene of the Voice* (New York, 1923)

J. H. Williams: *Voice Production and Breathing for Speakers and Fundamental Studies for Singers* (London, 1923)

J. Arger: *Initiation à l'art du chant* (Paris, 1924)

W. H. Breare: *Vocal Analyses: Sensitising Breath – Emotional Revolution* (London, 1924)

G. Desargues: *De l'art de bien chanter* (Washington DC, 1924)

N. Douty: *What the Vocal Student Should Know: an Introduction to the Art of Singing* (Philadelphia, 1924)

W. S. Drew: *Voice Training* (London, 1924)

R. Haas: 'Josse de Villeneuves Brief über den Mechanismus der italienischen Oper von 1756', *ZMw*, vii (1924–5), 129–63

C. Lagourgue: *The Secret: Vocal Feelings and Reactions* (Chicago, 1924, 2/1945)

W. Shakespeare: *Plain Words on Singing* (London and New York, 1924, 3/1929)

A. Thausing: *Die Sängerstimme: ihre Beschaffenheit und Entstehung, ihre Bildung und ihr Verlust* (Stuttgart and Berlin, 1924, 3/1957)

V. Vannini: *Della voce umana, ma principalmente delle voce del soprano* (Florence, 1924)

H. Wohlmuth: *Die Grundsätze deutscher Gesangs-Kultur 1750–90* (diss., U. of Vienna, 1924)

1925–50

A. Buzzi-Peccia: *How to Succeed in Singing* (Philadelphia, 1925)

G. Cauda: *Cantanti d'altri tempi* (Milan, 1925)

G. R. Dodds and J. D. Lickey: *The Control of the Breath* (London, 1925, 2/1935)

R. Duhamel: 'Le chant moderne: sa matière, sa nature, sa forme et ses moyens', *RMI*, xxxii (1925), 80–97, 219–38, 599–620

M. Gautier: *Principes et technique du chant* (Paris, 1925)

H. G. Hast: *The Singer's Art: Letters from a Singing Master* (London, 1925)

W. Lyle: *How to Become a Vocalist: Singing Made Easy* (London, 1925)

J. McKerrow: *The Vocal Movements and Some Others* (London and New York, 1925)

P. M. Marafioti: *The New Vocal Art* (New York, 1925)

L. Melchissédec: *Le chant: la déclamation lyrique, le mécanisme et l'émission de la voix* (Paris, 1925)

W. Reinecke: *Praktische Übungen zur Gewinnung der Gesangsmeisterschaft* (Leipzig, *c*1925)

C. K. Rogers: *Your Voice and You ... a Practical Application of Psychology to Singing* (Boston, 1925)

H. Witherspoon: *Singing: a Treatise for Teachers and Students* (New York, 1925)

W. Zimmerman: *Passives Singen: die psychologische Basis des Belkanto* (Leipzig, *c*1925)

K. E. Behnke: *Singer's Difficulties: How to Overcome Them* (London, 1926)

R. Duhamel: 'La question de la vocalise dans le chant français', *RMI*, xxxiii (1926), 363

H. P. Greene: *Three Short Talks on Singing* (London, 1926)

G. Henschel: *Articulation in Singing ... with Practical Examples and Exercises* (London, 1926)

M. Laird-Brown: *Singers' French* (New York, 1926)

G. Magrini: *Il canto, arte e tecnica* (Milan, 3/1926; ed. F. Gagliati, 1938)

N. Melba: *Melba Method* (Melbourne, 1926)

B. Pierpont: *A Short Practical Text Book on the Singing Voice* (London, 1926)

G. R. Dodds: *Practical Hints for Singers* (London, 1927)

W. B. Downing: *Vocal Pedagogy for Student, Singer and Teacher* (Boston, 1927)

A. T. Grechaninov: *Ecole du chant* (London, 1927)

F. Proschowski: *The Singing School of Frantz Proschowski* (Philadelphia, 1927)

E. W. Scripture: *Anwendung der graphischen Methode auf Sprache und Gesang* (Leipzig, 1927)

T. Van Borre: *Le chant humain* (Paris, 1927)

E. G. White: *Light on the Voice Beautiful* (London, 1927–8)

H. J. Wood: *The Gentle Art of Singing* (London, 1927–8, abridged 2/1930)

W. Bitterling: *Im Anfang war der Vokal* (Leipzig, 1928, 2/1929)

H. Brown: *The Principles of Expression in Song* (London, 1928)

M. Clark and R. D. C. Leland: *Secrets of Correct Singing* (Boston, 1928)

E. T. Evetts and R. A. Worthington: *The Mechanics of Singing* (London, 1928)
C. Novello-Davies: *You Can Sing* (London, 1928)
E. Ross: *Deutsche und italienische Gesangsmethode* (Kassel, 1928)
G. Silva and G. Gradenigo: *Il maestro di canto: saggi di pedagogia del canto, preceduti da elementi di acustica e di fonetica* (Turin, 1928)
C. Armin: *Enrico Caruso: eine Untersuchung der Stimme Carusos* (Berlin, 1929)
H. Biehle: *Staue dich Gesund! Stimmheilung durch Stimmkrise* (Leipzig, 1929)
D. A. Clippinger: *Fundamentals of Voice Training* (Boston and New York, 1929)
A. Guercia: *L'arte del canto italiano* (Milan, 1929)
H. Killer: *Die Tenorpartien in Mozarts Opern: ein Beitrag zu Geschichte und Stil des Bühnengesanges* (Kassel, 1929)
G. A. Murphy: *The Voice and Singing* (Grand Rapids, MI, 1929)
W. Reinecke: *Das Sänger-A-B-C: Bausteine zur Bildungs, Pflege und Erhaltung der Singstimme, für Opern- u. Konzertsänger* (Leipzig, 1929)
R. Rosner: *Benjamino Gigli und die Kunst des Belcanto* (Vienna, 1929)
D. Stanley: *The Science of Voice: a Book on the Singing and Speaking Voice* (New York, 1929, enlarged 5/1958)
H. Biehle: 'Die ästhetischen Grundlagen der französischen Gesangs-Kunst im 17. und 18. Jahrhundert', *ZMw*, xii (1929–30), 161–7
E. Cameron [Brownsmith]: *Natural Singing and Speaking* (London, 1930)
E. Carducci: 'The Tenor Voice in Europe', *ML*, xi (1930), 318–23
D. Freer: *The Student of Singing and the Gramophone* (London, 1930)
A. Gescheidt: *Make Singing a Joy: Normal Natural Voice Development* (New York, 1930)
E. Maitland: *The Science of Voice Training as an Introduction to the Art of Singing* (Portsmouth, c1930)
F. Proschowski: *Tone Thinking* (Kansas City, MO, 1930)
T. G. Samuels: *Singing and its Mastery* (London, 1930)
W. W. Shaw: *Authentic Voice Production* (Philadelphia and London, 1930)
H. W. Witherspoon: *Thirty-Six Lessons in Singing for Teacher and Student* (Chicago, 1930)
A. Allerup: *Die 'Musica Pratica' des Johann Andreas Herbst und ihre Entwicklungsgeschichte Bedeutung* (Kassel, 1931)
R. Benedito: *Cómo se enseña el canto y la música* (Madrid, 2/1931)
W. E. Brown: *Vocal Wisdom: Maxims of Giovanni Batista Lamperti* (New York, 1931, ?2/1957)
A. Crabbé: *Conversation et conseils sur l'art du chant* (Brussels, 1931)
P. Judd: *Singing Technique* (London, 1931)
H. Klein: *Great Women Singers of My Time* (London, 1931)
F. Pandolfini and L. Labbaraque: *Education de la voix chantée* (Paris, 1931)
W. Reinecke: *Der freie Gesangston und seine Gestaltung* (Leipzig, 1931)
M. Signorelli: 'Il tramonto del bel canto', *Musica d'oggi*, xiii (1931), 354–8
C. Somigli: 'La technica del canto artistico, inartistico', *RMI* (1931–2)
H. N. Spohr: *Art and Practice of Singing* (Riverside, CA, 1931)
J. H. Wagenmann: *Der sechzigjährige deutsche Meistersänger Heinrich Knote in seiner Stimmbildung Bedeutung und im Vergleich mit anderer Sängern* (Munich, 1931)
A. Wicart: *Le chanteur* (Paris, 1931, 4/1944)
J. Woodside: *Style in Singing and Song Interpretation* (New York, 1931)
H. Biehle: *Die Stimmkunst* (Leipzig, 1931–2)
A. C. Beltrán: *Arte de canto: recopilación de los principales y más importantes preceptos y teorías desde el siglo XVII hasta nuestros días* (Mexico City, 1932)
B. Marchesi: *The Singer's Catechism and Creed* (London, 1932)
L. Matha and G. de Parrel: *Education et rééducation de la voix chantée* (Paris, 1932)
H. G. Mowe: *Fundamentals of Voice Use in Song and Speech* (New York, 1932)
K. Schubert: *Spontinis italienischen Schule* (Strasbourg, 1932)
H. G. Seashore: *An Objective Analysis of Artistic Singing* (Iowa City, IA, 1932)
H. Arlberg: *Belcanto: der lückenlose Weg zur altitalienischen Gesangstechnik* (Leipzig, 1933)
S. T. Barrows: *The Voice: How to Use It* (Boston, 1933)
Z. Bhotiva: *La magie dans l'art du chant* (Paris, 1933)
D. A. Clippinger: *The Clippinger Class-Method of Voice Culture* (Boston, 1933)
A. Della Corte: *Canto e bel canto* (Turin, 1933) [incl. Tosi (1723); Mancini (1774, 3rd edn); Della Corte: 'Vicende degli stili del canto dal tempo di Gluck al '900', 231–72]
A. M. Henderson: *Speech and Song (a Direct Approach to Singing)* (London, 1933)
K. Kephren: *De l'interprétation dans le chant* (Paris, 1933)
E. R. G. Passe: *The Singing Voice: a Description of the Relationship of the Structure to the Functions of the Voice-Producing Organs* (London, 1933)
C. K. Scott: *Word and Tone: an English Method of Vocal Technique* (London, 1933)
D. Stanley and J. P. Maxfield: *The Voice, its Production and Reproduction* (London, 1933)
B. Ulrich: *Die altitalienische Gesangsmethode: die Schule des Belcanto, auf Grund der Originalschriften zum ersten Male dargestellt* (Leipzig, 1933)
D. Arbenin: *Postanovka golosa: theoriya i analiz vokal'nïkh printsipov* [Voice Training] (Riga, 1934)
G. Armin: *Altitalienische Gesangsmethoden auf dem Papier: eine Abrechnung* (Berlin, 1934)
P. Bekker: *Wandlungen der Oper* (Zürich and Leipzig, 1934)
L. Bocci-Brunacci: *Del bel canto: fisiologia e arte, patologia e decadenza* (Rome, 1934)
H. Brown: *The Complete Singing Teacher* (London, 1934)
P. Claudel: 'La voix humaine', *ReM*, xv (1934), 337–9
T. Vironi: *Theorie der Stimmbildung der Jetztzeit: Hygiene und Technik* (Tallinn, 1934)
J. H. Allen: *The Technique of Modern Singing* (London, 1935)
E. Bruschini: *La tecnica del bel canto* (Florence, 1935)
H. Feller: *Die Gesangskoloratur in Rossinis Opern und ihre Ausführung* (Berlin, 1935)
H. Francillo-Kauffmann: *Von Caruso zu Dir: Gesangstechnisches aus der Praxis und für die Praxis* (Vienna, 1935)
J. Müller-Blattau, ed.: *Hohe Schule der Musik*, iii (Potsdam, 1935) [incl. E. Ross: 'Gesang und Gesangsmethoden', 1–75; F. Martienssen-Lohmann: 'Die Ausbildung der menschlichen Stimme', 76–143]
J. C. Wilcox: *The Living Voice: a Study Guide for Song and Speech* (New York, 1935, 2/1945)
S. Auteri: *Il canto nella sua essenza artistica e scientifica* (Bologna, 1936)
J. Berntsen: *Ein Meister der Stimmbildungskunst* (Leipzig, 1936)
G. A. Brouillet: *Voice Manual* (Brookline, MA, 1936)
M. Conklin: *Fundamental Vocal Technique* (Philadelphia, 1936)
E. F. Herbert-Caesari: *The Science and Sensations of Vocal Tone* (London, 1936)
G. Krasnoff: *How to Improve your Voice* (New York, 1936)
E. H. Melling: *Voice Production for Elocution and Singing* (London, 1936)
C. M. Pitts: *Pitts Voice Class Method for Class and Studio* (Chicago, 1936)
K. N. Westerman: *Modern Phonetization Applied to Singing* (Adrian, MI, 1936, 2/1938)
G. Baruetto: *Metodo di canto* (Chieri, 1937)
W. S. Drew: *Singing: the Art and the Craft* (London, 1937)
P. Lopes Moreira: *Compendio di technica vocal* (Rio de Janeiro, 1937)
P. Séveilhac and J. René-Celles: *L'étude et la pratique du chant* (Bordeaux, 1937)
C. H. Wood: *Vocal Vigor in Speech and Song* (Worcester, MA, 1937)
M. Barbereux-Parry: *Barbereux System of Constructive Voice Production* (Los Angeles, 1938)
W. W. Combs: *Voice in Singing, its Care and Development* (Dallas, 1938)
M. Gerar: *A la recherche du chant perdu* (Paris, 1938)
Internationale Kongress Singen und Sprechen: Frankfurt am Main 1938 [incl. H. Osthoff: 'Der Gesangstil der frühdeutschen Oper', 11–16; A. Cairati: 'Gibt es einen geschmaklichen, technischen oder methodischen Unterschied dem italienischen und dem deutschen Gesang, oder beruht der Unterschied nur auf dem verschiedenen Aufbau der beiden Sprachen?', 161–5; Kreichgauer: 'Akustische Probleme der Opern- und Sprechbühne', 319–31]
L. Labarraque: 'La science phonétique, base essentielle de l'éducation de la voix chantée', *Third International Congress of Phonetic Sciences: Ghent 1938*, 207

J. F. Lissfelt: *Basic Principles of Artistic Singing* (Boston, 1938)
A. Martino and C. G. Rex: *Today's Singing* (New York, 1938, 2/ c1953)
J. L. Orton: *Voice Culture Made Easy* (London, 1938)
L. Siotto-Pintor: *I segreti del bel canto* (Milan, 1938)
E. G. White: *Sinus Tone Production* (London, 1938)
E. Wilcke: *German Diction in Singing*, ed. B. Crist (New York, c1938)
E. F. Herbert-Caesari: 'The Decline of Singing', *MO*, lxii (1938–9), 501–12, 698–9
H. Brown: *Success in Amateur Opera: Instructions on Auditions … Training Soloists, Diction, Conducting* (London, 1939)
L. Cocchi: *Il canto artistico e il suo insegnamento* (Milan, 1939)
H. V. Hemery: *The Physiological Basis of the Art of Singing* (London, 1939)
J. Lewis: *Singing without Tears: a Handbook for Beginners of All Ages* (London, 1939)
L. Medicus: *Die Koloratur in der italienischen Oper des 19. Jahrhunderts* (Zürich, 1939)
D. Silvestrini: *L'insegnamento del canto fisiologico* (Bologna, 1939)
V. van Hemel: *De zangkunst … methodes* (Antwerp, c1940, 2/ 1958)
J. J. M. Levien: *Some Notes for Singers* (London, c1940)
I. H. Nicoll and C. M. Dennis: *Simplified Vocal Training* (New York, 1940)
W. Ruth: *Über die Kunst des Gesanges: ihr Gesetz und ihre Erlernung* (Berlin, 1940)
J. Schmidt: *Die männlichen Stimmcharaktere in den Opern Verdis* (diss., U. of Erlangen, 1940)
M. Barbereux-Parry: *Vocal Resonance, its Source and Command* (Boston, 1941) [pt i, MS, 1927; pt ii, pubd 1938 as *Vocalized Speech*]
A. J. Boruttau: *Über Grundlagen, Ausbau und Grenzen der Stimmkunst* (Munich, 1941)
H. C. Divver: *Teaching Notes and Treatise on Singing* (Newton, MA, 1941)
I. Hibbs: 'Rameau's Thoughts on Voice Culture', *Etude Music Magazine*, lix (1941), 699ff
E. Johnson: 'Styles in Singing', *Be your own Music Critic*, ed. R. E. Simon (Garden City, NY, 1941), 41–59
J. J. M. Levien: *Letters on Singing (Reprinted from the 'Musical Times')* (London, 1941)
——: *Letters to the Editor of 'Musical Opinion' on the Decline of Singing* (London, 1941)
R. L. Weer: *My Views on Voice Production* (Boston, 1941)
V. Andréossy: *L'esprit du chant: essai sur la philosophie de l'art du chant* (Geneva, 1942, 2/1979)
F. L. Dunkley: *The Buoyant Voice, acquired by Correct Pitch-Control* (Boston, 1942)
J. S. Gould: *Successful Singing, based on the Italian Method of Singing* (East Greenwich, RI, 1942)
A. Lancelotti: *Le voci d'oro* (Rome, 1942)
P. Lohmann: 'Das Legato des deutschen Sängers', *Von deutscher Tonkunst: Festschrift Peter Raabe* (Leipzig, 1942), 182–6
L. S. Samoiloff: *The Singer's Handbook* (Philadelphia, 1942)
K. N. Westerman: *The Vibrato* (Columbus, OH, 1942)
E. Liebling: *The Estelle Liebling Coloratura Digest* (New York, 1943)
F. Martienssen-Lohmann: *Berufung und Bewährung des Opernsängers* (Mainz, 1943, 1970 as *Der Opernsänger*)
M. Sands: 'The Teaching of Singing in Eighteenth-Century England', *PRMA*, lxx (1943–4), 11–31
L. Bachner: *Dynamic Singing: a New Approach to Free Voice Production* (New York, 1944)
F. D. Lawson: *The Human Voice: a Concise Manual on Training the Speaking and Singing Voice* (New York, 1944)
K. Nygren-Kloster: *Rösten i tål och sang* [Voice in Speech and Song] (Stockholm, 1944)
C. R. Dengler: *Read This and Sing: for Voice Students, Chorus and Choir Singers* (Philadelphia, 1944–5)
E. C. Bairstow and H. P. Greene: *Singing Learned from Speech* (London, 1945)
N. Bazzetta de Vemenia: *Cantanti italiane dell'ottocento* (Novarra, 1945)
K. E. Behnke: *The Technique of Singing* (London, 1945, 3/1947)
E. Kuester: *This Voice Question* (New York, 1945)
J. J. M. Levien: *The Singing of John Braham* (London, 1945) [incl. C. G. Cathcart: 'A Scientific Justification of the Historic Method of Voice Production', 22–82]
T. Longo: *Fundamentals of Singing and Speaking* (New York, 1945)
C. Panzéra: *L'art de chanter* (Paris, 1945)
D. Stanley: *Your Voice: Applied Science of Vocal Art, Singing and Speaking* (New York and Chicago, 1945, 2/1950)
B. Storey and E. Barnard: *A Key to Speech and Song* (London, 1945)
U. Tegani: *Cantanti di una volta* (Milan, 1945)
R. M. Brown: *The Singing Voice* (New York, 1946)
A. Crabbé: *L'art d'Orphée: la physiologie du chant* (Brussels, 1946)
F. Freemantel: *High Tones and How to Sing Them* (New York, 1946)
M. Marshall: *The Singer's Manual of English Diction* (New York and London, 1946)
F. Schweinsberg: *Stimmliche Ausdrucksgestaltung im Dienste der Kirche* (Heidelberg, 1946)
J. Tarneud: *Le chant, sa construction, sa destruction* (Paris, 1946)
K. Vikrot: *Rösten, dess skolning och vård* [The Voice, its Training and Care] (Lund, 1946)
G. Baker: *This Singing Business* (London, 1947)
M. Elwin: *The Maurice Elwin Postal Method of Voice-Production and Singing* (London, 1947)
V. A. Fields: *Training the Singing Voice* (New York, 1947)
A. Jeri: *Belle gole* (Milan, 1947)
H. Lázaro: *Mi método de canto* (Barcelona, 1947)
G. Loiseau: *Notes sur le chant* (Neuilly, 1947)
M. L. Mansion: *L'étude du chant: technique de la voix parlée et chantée* (Buenos Aires, 1947; trans. as *How to Sing*, 1952)
I. Warren: *The Grammar of Singing by Way of Questions and Answers* (London, 1947)
S. P. Yudin: *Pevets i golos* [The Singer and the Voice] (Moscow, 1947)
F. Farga: *Die goldene Kehle: Meistergesang aus drei Jahrhunderten* (Vienna, 1948)
J. A. Fracht: *Sing Well, Speak Well* (New York, 1948)
R. Lodron: *Kleiner Katechismus für Sänger: 7 Fragen und Antworten* (Vienna, 1948)
A. Machabey: *Le 'bel canto'* (Paris, 1948)
A. Arnholtz: 'Det sangbares problem', *Dansk musiktidsskrift*, xxiv (1949), 151–61
G. Baum: 'Vom Singen', *Musica* [Kassel] (April 1949), 137–9
W. Bitterling: *Der Kunstgesang* (Veytaux, nr Montreux, 1949)
F. Martienssen-Lohmann: *Ausbildung der Gesangsstimme* (Potsdam, 1949)
W. Vennard: *Singing: the Mechanism and the Technic* (New York, 1949, enlarged 5/1968)

1950–75

ES ('Canto'; F. d'Amico)
G. Baum: 'Gesangstechnik Kompositionstechnik', *Musikleben*, iii (1950), 12–15
A. Bergman: *Creating and Developing a Singing Voice* (New York, 1950)
W. Ehmann: *Erbe und Auftrag musikalischer Erneuerung* (Kassel, 1950)
F. C. Field-Hyde: *The Art and Science of Vocal Training* (London, 1950)
J. Forchhammer: 'Sangkunst', *Dansk musiktidsskfrift*, xxv (1950), 76–9
C. N. Granville: *The Granville Vocal Study Plan* (New York, 1950)
S. Kagen: *On Studying Singing* (New York, 1950)
F. Kelsey: *The Foundations of Singing* (London, 1950)
J. Laurens: *Bel canto et émission italienne: le problème de la décadence de l'art lyrique française* (Paris, 1950)
M. Montell: *Montell Vocal Technique* (Miami, 1950)
C. L. Reid: *Bel Canto: Principles and Practices* (New York, 1950)
R. Boas: 'La Scala and the Art of Singing', *MO*, lxxiv (1950–51), 143–5
P. A. Duey: *Bel Canto in its Golden Age: a Study of its Teaching Concepts* (New York, 1951)
E. F. Herbert-Caesari: *The Voice of the Mind* (London, 1951, 2/ 1963)
M. Högg: *Die Gesangskunst der Faustina Hasse und das Sängerinnenwesen ihrer Zeit in Deutschland* (diss., U. of Berlin, 1951)
P. Judd: *Vocal Technique* (London, 1951)
B. Marcello: *The Voice of the Mind* (London, 1951)
M. Accortini: *Elementi di tecnica del canto* (Milan, 2/1952)
D. L. Aspelund: *Razvitye pevtsa i yego golosa* (Moscow and Leningrad, 1952); Ger. edn, as *Die Entwicklung des Sängers und seiner Stimme* (Dresden, 1954)
H. B. Bowman: *A Study of the Castrati Singers and their Music* (diss., Indiana U., 1952)
O. Hensel: *Die geistigen Grundlagen des Gesanges* (Kassel, 1952)

N. A. Punt: *The Singer's and Actor's Throat* (Melbourne, 1952, 3/1979)
M. Sands: 'The Decline and Revival of the Counter-Tenor', *MMR*, lxxxii (1952), 115–20
H. Egenolf: *Die menschliche Stimme … eine Praktikum* (Stuttgart, 1953)
E. Gerhardt: *Recital* (London, 1953)
G. Moore: *Singer and Accompanist* (London, 1953)
V. Nevina: *Voice Production in Singing* (London, 1953)
G. M. Young: *What Happens in Singing: a Short Manual of Vocal Mechanics and Technique* (London, 1953)
H. Abraham: *Un art de l'interpretation* (Paris, 1954; trans. as *Claire Croiza: the Singer as Interpreter*, 1989)
R. M. Graves: *Singing for Amateurs* (London, 1954)
N. Fortune: 'Italian 17th-century Singing', *ML*, xxxv (1954), 206–19
L. Riemens: *Uren der zangkunst* (Amsterdam, 1954)
C. K. Scott: *The Fundamentals of Singing: an Inquiry into the Mechanical and Expressive Aspects of the Art* (London, 1954)
C. R. Thorpe: *Teach Yourself to Sing* (London, 1954, 1968 as *A Short Course in Singing*)
G. W. Beckman: *Tools for Speaking and Singing* (New York, 1955)
H. Biehle: *Stimmkunde für Beruf, Kunst und Heilzwecke* (Berlin, 1955, 2/1970 as *Stimmkunde für Redner, Schauspieler, Sänger und Stimmkranke*)
R. Foster: *Competitive Singing and Public Performance* (London, 1955)
G. Lauri-Volpi: *Voci parallele* (Milan, 1955, 2/1960)
J. T. Lawson: *Full-Throated Ease: a Concise Guide to Easy Singing* (Toronto, 1955)
P. W. Peterson: *Natural Singing and Expressive Conducting* (Winston-Salem, NC, 1955, 2/1966)
L. Roma: *The Science and Art of Singing* (New York, 1955)
G. Rossi della Riva: *Aclaraciones sobre la escuela italiana del 'bel canto'* (Buenos Aires, 1955)
K. N. Westerman: *Emergent Voice* (Ann Arbor, MI, 2/1955)
N. Bridgman: 'Giovanni Camillo Maffei et sa lettre sur la chant', *ReM*, xxxviii (1956), 3–34
E. Downes: 'Bel canto in 1956', *Opera Annual*, iii (1956), 48–51
A. Heriot: *The Castrati in Opera* (London, 1956)
E. Liebling: *The Estelle Liebling Vocal Course* (New York, 1956) [separate books for men and women singers]
F. Martienssen-Lohmann: *Der wissende Sänger: Gesangslexikon in Skizzen* (Zürich, 1956, 3/1981)
H. Pleasants: 'Bel Canto through the Microphone: Has our Singing been Afflicted by Gigantism?', *HiFi*, v (1956), 34–45, 106–7
F. Puritz: *The Teaching of Elisabeth Schumann* (London, 1956)
F. Reusch: *Der kleine Hey: die Kunst des Sprechens* (Mainz, 1956, 2/1975)
A. Stampa: *Atem, Sprache und Gesang* (Kassel, 1956)
A. Berg: 'La voix dans l'opéra', *Ecrits*, ed. and trans., H. Pousseur (Monaco, 1957)
A. Cranmer: *The Art of Singing* (London, 1957)
L. Fugère and R. Duhamel: *Nouvelle méthode pratique de chant français par l'articulation* (Paris, 1957)
E. Gara: 'I cantanti d'oggi oltre il muro del rimpianto', *RaM*, xxvii (1957), 103–12
E. Heller: 'Zur Technik und Ästhetik des Belkanto', *OM*, xii/2 (1957), 59–62
H. Kopf: *Kleines Sängerbrevier (Sänger und Arzt)* (Munich, 1957)
A. Raymond: *Précis moderne de technique vocale* (Arthabaska, Quebec, 1957)
L. Strongin, ed.: *Vocal Technique* (New York, 1957)
R. De Young: *The Singer's Art: an Analysis of Vocal Principles* (Chicago, 1958)
E. F. Herbert-Caesari: *Tradition and Gigli, 1600–1955* (London, 1958, 2/1973)
H. Höltzen: *Die methodisch-pädagogischen Grundsätze deutschen Gesangskultur im 19. Jahrhundert* (diss. U. of Münster, 1958)
R. M. Taylor: *Acoustics for the Singer* (Emporia, KS, 1958)
T. Serafin and A. Toni: *Stile, tradizioni e convenzioni del melodramma italiano del settecento e dell'ottocento* (Milan, 1958)
G. Cornut: *La mécanique respiratoire dans la parole et le chant* (Paris, 1959)
A. Cuartero: *Voz libre* (Barcelona, 1959)
I. Franca: *Manual of Bel Canto* (New York, 1959)
N. Mari: *Canto e voce: difetti causati da un errato studio del canto* (Milan, 1959, 2/1970)
W. E. Ross: *Secrets of Singing* (Bloomington, IN, 1959)
L. Rousselot: *Le chant acte réflexe: éléments rationnels d'une pédagogie vocale moderne* (Paris, c1959)
G. Sciortino: *La tecnica del bel canto descritta in ordine al metodo d'insegnamento dell'antica scuola italiana* (Palermo, 1959)
H. C. Wolff: 'Vom Wesen des alten Belcanto', *Händel: Halle 1959*, 95–9
R. Husson: *La voix chantée* (Paris, 1960)
L. V. Mayer: *Notebook for Voice and Diction* (Dubuque, IA, 1960)
I. Trusler and W. Ehret: *Functional Lessons in Singing* (Englewood Cliffs, NJ, 1960, 3/1987)
A. Berkman: *Singing Takes More than a Voice* (Los Angeles, 1961)
V. A. Christy: *Expressive Singing* (Dubuque, IA, 1961, 3/1974)
F. Herzfeld: *Magie der Stimme: die Welt des Singens, der Oper und der grossen Sänger* (Berlin, 1961)
O. Merlin: *Le bel canto* (Paris, 1961)
C. Wyss: *Ce que chanter veut dire* (Paris, 1961)
J. Garbarino: *Phonologie, la voix chantée, ses secrets, ses énigmes* (Marseille, 1962)
K. J. Kutsch and L. Riemens: *Unvergängliche Stimmen: kleines Sängerlexikon* (Berne, 1962; trans., 1969)
J. Litante: *A Natural Approach to Singing* (London, 1962)
A. Rose: *The Singer and the Voice* (London, 1962, 2/1971)
A. Armhold: *Singing Based on Irrefragible Laws* (Cape Town, 1963)
G. Baker: *The Common Sense of Singing* (Oxford and New York, 1963)
V. Fuchs: *The Art of Singing and Voice Technique* (London and Dublin, 1963)
E. J. Kay: *Bel Canto and the Sixth Sense … Italian Physical Style of Singing Examined by Means of the Facilities of Modern Science* (London, 1963)
E. Mannheit: *Vom Gesang und dessen Grundlegenden Problemen* (Vienna, 1963)
F. Müller-Heuser: *Vox humana: ein Beitrag zur Untersuchung der Stimmästhetik des Mittelalters* (Regensburg, 1963)
W. Ruth: 'Die Kastraten und ihre Gesangskunst', *Bühnengenossenschaft*, xv (1963), 259–62
F. Viñas: *El arte del canto: datos históricos, consejos y ejercicios musicales para la educación de la voz* (Barcelona, 2/1963)
A. B. Caswell: *The Development of Seventeenth-Century French Vocal Ornamentation and its Influence upon Late Baroque Ornamentation Practice* (diss., U. of Minnesota, 1964)
R. Celletti: *Le grandi voci: dizionario critico-biografico dei cantanti* (Rome, 1964)
B. Coffin: *Phonetic Readings of Songs and Arias* (Boulder, CO, 1964, 2/1982)
E. Fischer-Junghann: *Gesangsbildungslehre: der Gesang am Scheidewege* (Heidelberg, 1964)
E. Gara: 'Cantanti mascagnani tra preguidizio e verità', *Pietro Mascagni*, ed. M. Morini (Milan, 1964), i, 201–49
K. H. Adler: *The Art of Accompanying and Coaching* (Minneapolis, 1965)
V. A. Christy: *Foundations in Singing: a Basic Textbook in the Fundamentals of Technic and Song Interpretation* (Dubuque, IA, 1965, 5/1990)
N. Flack: *Singing can be Ecstasy* (New York, 1965)
G. Griffith: *Artistry in Singing* (New York, 1965)
E. F. Herbert-Caesari: *The Alchemy of the Voice* (London, 1965)
F. Husler and Y. Rodd-Marling: *Singing, the Physical Nature of the Vocal Organ: a Guide to the Unlocking of the Singing Voice* (London, 1965, 2/1976)
R. M. Mason: *A Study of the Physiological Mechanisms of Vocal Vibrato* (diss., U. of Illinois, 1965)
C. L. Reid: *The Free Voice: a Guide to Natural Singing* (New York, 1965)
E. Rossi: *Neue Grundlagen für den Sprech- und Gesangsunterricht* (Munich and Basle, 1965)
F. Aranda: *Direct, Complete and Basic New Scientific Method of How to Educate Perfect Free Voice for Singing and Speaking* (Rio de Janeiro, 1966)
C. Berberian: 'La nuova vocalità nell'opera contemporanea', *Discoteca* (1966) no.62, pp.34–5
R. Celletti: 'L'interpretazione di Verdi nel secolo XIX', *I° congresso internazionale di studi verdiani: Venice 1966*, 308–13
W. Dürr and U. Siegele: 'Cantar d'affetto: zum Vortrag monodischer Musik', *GfMKB: Leipzig 1966*, 208–15
E. Gara: 'Come ha da essere un cantante verdiano? ', *I° congresso internazionale di studi verdiani: Venice 1966*, 314–18
P. Kaelin: *Pour mieux chanter* (Paris, 3/1966)
M. Lewitas: *Darkhe shemirah, ripui u-pituah ha-kol le-dovrim ule-*

mezamrim [Development of the Voice for Lecturers and Singers] (Tel-Aviv, *c*1966)
H. Pleasants: *The Great Singers* (New York, 1966)
K. Wichmann: *Der Ziergesang und die Ausführung der Appoggiatura* (Leipzig, 1966)
R. Winsel: *The Anatomy of Voice: an Illustrated Manual of Vocal Training* (New York, 1966)
B. Coffin: *Word by Word Translations of Songs and Arias* (New York, 1966–72)
K. H. Adler: *Phonetics and Diction in Singing* (Minneapolis, 1967)
D. R. Appelmann: *The Science of Vocal Pedagogy: Theory and Application* (Bloomington, IN, 1967)
M. Breazu: 'Noţiuni noi în teoria emisiei vocale' [New Ideas in the Theory of Vocal Production], *LM*, iii (1967), 209–14
R. Celletti: 'La vocalità al tempo del Tosi', *NRMI*, i (1967), 676–84
L. Kettelkamp: *Song, Speech and Ventriloquism* (New York, 1967)
J. J. Klein and O. A. Schjeide: *Singing Technique: How to Avoid Vocal Trouble* (Princeton, NJ, 1967)
W. Whitlock: *Facets of the Singer's Art* (Champaign, IL, *c*1967)
——: *Master Lessons on Fifty Opera Arias* (Champaign, IL, 1967)
R. Schollum: 'Gedanken zur Ganzlichkeit des Gesangsunterrichtes', *Musikerziehung*, xxi (1967–8), 72–80
Yu. Barsov: *Vokal'no-ispolnitel'skiye i pedagogicheskiye printsipï M. Glinki* [The Vocal Performance and Teaching Principles of Glinka] (Leningrad, 1968)
P. M. Capponi: 'L'educazione di una virtuosa nel secolo XVII', *Spettatore musicale*, iii (1968), May, 12–15
R. Celletti: 'L'insegnamento del canto nell'ottocento', *Educazione musicale*, v/3 (1968), 71–7
——: 'Origini e sviluppi della coloratura rossiniana', *NRMI*, ii (1968), 872–919
——: 'Il vocalismo italiano da Rossini a Donizetti', *AnMc*, no.5 (1968), 267–94; no.7 (1969), 214–47
J. Pahn: *Stimmübungen für Sprechen und Singen* (Berlin, 1968)
E. Radò: 'Gesangstechnik als Basis des künstlerischen Gestaltens', *ÖMz*, xxiii (1968), 677–81
W. Rosenberg: *Die Krise der Gesangskunst* (Karlsruhe, 1968)
E. Sittner: 'Stimmbildungsprobleme der Gegenwart', *ÖMz*, xxiii (1968), 673–7
——: *Wege zum Kunstgesang* (Vienna, 1968)
——: 'Zur historischen Entwicklung der Gesangskunst', *ÖMz*, xxiii (1968), 668–73
F. Thomas: *Die Lehre des Kunstgesanges nach der altitalienischen Schule* (Berlin, 1968)
H. Trenner: *Zur Stilgeschichte der Koloratur von Monteverdi bis Verdi* (diss., Innsbruck U., 1968)
O. Watrin: *Worauf es beim Singen ankommt: grundlegende Anweisungen zur Erlernung des Belcanto Gesanges unter besonderer Berücksichtigung von Atemtechnik, Tonstützungen, Stimmbandfunktion* (Cologne, 1968)
W. Whitlock: *Bel Canto for the Twentieth Century* (Champaign, IL, 1968)
R. Zimmerman: *Sing Out Like Never Before: a Handbook on Voice Production* (Tucson, AZ, 1968)
J. C. Collins: 'Singing: a Comparative Analysis', *NATS Bulletin*, xxv/3 (1968–9), 32–5; xxv/4 (1968–9), 12–19
E. Foreman: 'Bel Canto: a New Definition', *NATS Bulletin*, xxv/3 (1968–9), 49
E. Sittner: 'Atemschulung als Hauptfaktor elementarer Stimmbildung', *Musikerziehung*, xxii (1968–9), 161–4
V. L. Chaplina, ed.: *Voprosï vokal'noy pedagogiki* [Problems in Vocal Pedagogy] (Moscow, 1969)
R. Celletti: 'A colloquio con Magda Olivero', *NRMI*, iii (1969), 1096–1104
——: 'Il virtuosismo vocale nel melodramma di Händel', *RIM*, iv (1969), 77–101
E. Fischer: *Handbuch der Stimmbildung* (Tutzing, 1969)
E. V. Foreman: *A Comparison of Selected Italian Vocal Tutors of the Period circa 1550 to 1800* (diss., U. of Illinois, 1969)
D. Galliver: '"Favolare in armonia": a Speculation into Aspects of 17th Century Singing', *MMA*, iv (1969), 129–46
E. F. Herbert-Caesari: *Vocal Truth* (London, 1969)
B. Kaczyński: 'Ada Sari – pédagogue', *Ruch muzyczny*, xiii/14 (1969), 16–17
E. Leipp and M. Castellengo: 'L'intelligibilité de la parole dans le chant', *Festival international du son I: Paris 1969*, 15–34
R. Mancini: *L'art du chant* (Paris, 1969)
O. Merlin: *Le chant des sirènes: le bel canto* (Paris, 1969)
A. Schiøtz: *The Singer and his Art* (New York, 1969)
Vocal Registers in Singing: San Diego and Cleveland 1969 [pubn of the Acoustical Society of America]
V. Werbeck-Svärdström: *Die Schule der Stimmenthüllung: ein Weg zur Katharsis in der Kunst des Singens* (Dornach, 2/1969)
J. Wildgruber: 'Zur Entwicklung der Sopranfächer in der deutschen Oper des 19. Jahrhunderts', *Beiträge zur Geschichte der Oper*, ed. H. Becker (Regensburg, 1969), 147–64
C. Brambarow: 'The Training and Career of the Opera Singer', *International Music Educator*, ii/1 (1969–70), 10–13, 22–30, 32–7, 47–51
A. Gerstl-Duschak: 'Musical Style as a Stimulant to Vocal Technique', *NATS Bulletin*, xxvi/2 (1969–70), 30–33
O. D. Simmons: 'A Conceptual Approach to Singing', *NATS Bulletin*, xxvi/1 (1969–70), 15–18
M. Aspinall: 'Il cantante nelle interpretazioni delle opere rossiniane', *Bolletino del Centro rossiniano di studi*, new ser., iv (1970)
E. Colorni: *Singers' Italian: a Manual of Diction and Phonetics* (New York, 1970)
R. G. Cox: *The Singer's Manual of German and French Diction* (New York and London, 1970)
T. Culley: *Jesuits and Music*, i (Rome and St. Louis, MO, 1970)
A. D. Hewlett: *Think Afresh about the Voice: a Reappraisal of the Teaching of Ernest George White* (Deal, 1970, 3/1981)
H. W. Hitchcock: 'Vocal Ornamentation in Caccini's "Nuove musiche"', *MQ*, xlv (1970), 389–404
W. Lopez Temperan: *Las tecnicas vocales: analisis acustico y psicofisiologico de la voz humana y de la pedagogia vocal* (Montevideo, 1970)
R. M. Mori: *Coscienza della voce nella scuola italiana di canto* (Milan, 1970)
C. L. Reid: 'Functional Vocal Training', *Journal of Orgnonomy*, iv (1970), 231–49; v (1971), 36–64
L. F. Sunderman: *Artistic Singing: its Tone Production and Basic Understandings* (Metuchen, NJ, 1970)
K. Mitchells: 'Operatic Characters and Voice Type', *PRMA*, xcvii (1970–71), 47–58
C. W. Chapman: *Survey of Elementary Concepts of Voice Production Reflected in American Monographs on Vocal Pedagogy from 1875 to 1920* (diss., U. of Texas, 1971)
Collegium Medicorum Theatri: Buenos Aires 1971, 130–79 [In Fr. and Eng.; papers on numerous aspects of singing]
L. Hăngănut: 'Aspecte ale activităţii şi pedagogiei vocal- interpretative a lui George Stephănescu' [Aspects of Stephănescu's Vocal and Interpretative Teaching Methods], *LM*, vii (1971), 45–59 [with summaries in various languages]
M. V. Mykysha: *Praktychy osnovy vokal'nogo mystetstva* [The Practical Foundations of the Vocal Art] (Kiev, 1971)
K. A. Pahlen: *Grosse Sänger unserer Zeit* (Vienna, 1971)
H. Pleasants: 'A Shorter Vocabulary of Vocalism', *Stereo Review*, xxvi/5 (1971), 69–72
R. Rushmore: *The Singing Voice* (New York, 1971, 2/1984)
M. Sauter-Falbriard: *Die physiologischen Gesetze des Belcanto* (Berne, 1971)
R. Smolover: *The Vocal Essence: a Practical Handbook for Singers ... Voice Teachers, Vocal Coaches* (Scarsdale, NY, 1971)
R. Stanton: *Steps to Singing for Voice Classes* (Belmont, CA, 1971, 3/1983)
J. A. Stark: 'Giulio Caccini and the "Noble Manner of Singing"', *Canadian Association of University Schools of Music Journal*, i/2 (1971), 39–53
D. Uris: *To Sing in English: a Guide to Improved Diction* (New York and London, 1971)
H. Baer: 'Establishing a Correct Basic Technique for Singing', *NATS Bulletin*, xxviii/4 (1971–2), 12–14, 27
L. Lampe: 'The Impact of Effective Singing', *NATS Bulletin*, xxviii/3 (1971–2), 10–12
G. Newton: 'Random Notes for a Study of Interpretation', *NATS Bulletin*, xxviii/4 (1971–2), 22–7
E. Battaglia: 'Voci verdiane: equivoco di scuola?', *NRMI*, vi (1972), 526–44
K. Borg: *Suomalainen laulajan aapinen* [A Finnish Singer's Alphabet] (Helsinki, 1972)
E. Brand-Seltei: *Belcanto: eine Kulturgeschichte der Gesangskunst* (Wilhelmshaven, 1972)
J. Carone: *Master Vocal Study* (Hollywood, 1972)
R. Celletti: 'Caratteri della vocalità di Verdi', *3o congresso internazionale di studi verdiani: Milan 1972*, 81–8
——: 'Lo stile vocale di Verdi e di Wagner', *AnMc*, no.11 (1972), 28–41
G. Friedrich: 'Moderne Ausbildung von Sängern für die Musikbühne', *Theater der Zeit*, xxvii/1 (1972), 44–5

D. Galliver: 'Vocal Colour in Singing in 17th Century Italy: the Contribution of Caccini', *IMSCR*, xi *Copenhagen 1972*, 385–7
B. Lupo: 'La scuola della voce', *NRMI*, v (1972), 207–17
A. Riesch: *Lebendige Stimme: Stimmbildung für Sprache und Gesang* (Mainz, 1972)
H. J. Scholz: *Das Registerproblem in der deutschen Gesangspädagogik von Johann Friedrich Agricola bis Friedrich Schmitt* (diss., U. of Cologne, 1972)
H. Ainsaar: *Laulufysiologian perusteet viron-, saksan- ja suomen kielissä* [The Fundamentals of Singing Physiology in Estonian, German and Finnish] (Helsinki, 1973)
J. C. Burgin: *Teaching Singing* (Metuchen, NJ, 1973)
R. Celletti: 'La vocalità rossiniana e "La gazza ladra"', *Bollettino del Centro rossiniano di studi* (1973), no.2, pp.5–21
G. Cunelli: *Voice No Mystery: Half a Century of Recollections in the Arts of Singing and Speaking* (London and New York, 1973)
J. Delaquerrière: *Savoir chanter* (Montreal, 1973)
D. Galliver: 'Cantare con la gorga – the Coloratura Technique of the Renaissance Singer', *SMA*, vii (1973), 10–18
B. Goldovsky and A. Schoep: *Bringing Soprano Arias to Life* (New York, 1973)
J. Gourret: *La technique du chant en France depuis le XVIIe siècle* (Paris, 1973, 2/1976)
J. Moriarty: *An Outline of Italian, French and German Diction* (Boston, 1973)
D. Rexroth: 'Die Grundlagen des Wagnerschen Gesangstils', *Hifi-stéreophonie*, xii (1973), 1255–62
J. A. Stark: *The Rise of Virtuoso Singing* (diss., U. of Toronto, 1973)
E. Surian: 'Metastasio, i nuovi cantanti, il nuovo stile: verso il classicismo', *Venezia e il melodramma nel settecento: Venice 1973*, i, 341–62
G. A. Beouillet: *Voice Manual* (Boston, 1974)
S. Bergol'ts: 'O razvitii muzïkal'nosti pevtsa' [On the Development of the Singer's Musical Ear], *Istoriya i teoriya muzïki* (Baku, 1974), 18–28
W. Bregy: *Elementy techniki wokalnej* [Elements of Vocal Technique] (Kraków, 1974)
L. Dmitriev: *V klasse professora M. Ė. Donec-Tessejr* (Moscow, 1974)
D. Galliver: 'Cantare con affetto – Keynote of the Bel Canto', *SMA*, viii (1974), 1–7
A. E. Grotzinger: *Die Behebung der Krise der Gesangs- und Sprechkunst* (Uelzen, 1974)
R. Husson: *Pevcheskiy golos: issledovaniye osnovnïkh fiziologicheskikh i akusticheskikh yavleniy pevcheskogo golosa* [The Singers's Voice: a Study of the Main Physiological and Acoustical Phenomena of a Singer's Voice] (Moscow, 1974)
L. Manén: *The Art of Singing* (London, 1974, 3/1987 as *Belcanto: the Teaching of the Classical Italian Song-Schools, its Decline and Restoration*)
J. Patterson and M. Patterson: *Who Wants to Sing? What it's All About* (Belfast, 1974, 2/1978)
P. Petrobelli: 'Un cantante fischiato e le appoggiature di mezza battuta: cronaca teatrale e prassi esecutive alla metà del '700', *Studies in Renaissance and Baroque Music in Honor of Arthur Mendel* (Kassel and Hackensack, NJ, 1974), 363–76
H. Piper-Ziethen: 'Alto naturale oder: von der Kunst des Falsettierens Countertenor Paul Esswood', *Fono Forum*, xi (1974), 607–9
S. Reiner: 'La vag'Angioletta (and others)', *AnMc*, no.14 (1974), 26–8
J. B. Steane: *The Grand Tradition: Seventy Years of Singing on Record* (London, 1974)
R. M. Resch: 'George Bernard Shaw's Criticism of Singers and Singing', *NATS Bulletin*, xxxi/2 (1974–5), 2–10
M. Zaczkowska: 'Ergebnisse einer Arbeitstagung über Probleme der Stimmerziehung', *Musikerziehung*, xxviii (1974–5), 118–23

SINCE 1975

E. Battaglia: 'Il cantante italiano e l'antica vocalità', *Convegno di studi palestriniani: Palestrina 1975*, 33–48
G. Boerdner: *Die natürliche Gesangslinie/The Natural Song Method* (Brunswick, 1975)
H. M. Brown: *Embellishing Sixteenth-Century Music* (London, 1975)
A. Caswell: 'Mme Cinti-Damoreau and the Embellishment of Italian Opera in Paris: 1820–1845', *JAMS*, xxviii (1975), 459–92
E. S. Daniels: *Performing for Others* (New York, 1975)
A. Greene: *The New Voice: How to Sing and Speak Properly* (New York, 1975)
R. S. Hines: *Singer's Manual of Latin Diction and Phonetics* (New York, 1975)
J. Moriarty: *Diction: Italian, Latin, French, German: the Sounds and 81 Exercises for Singing Them* (Boston, 1975)
G. Nielsen: *A New Guide to Good Singing: Practical Hints* (Ontario, 1975)
A. Schoch: *Opernschule: Lehrbuch der szenischen Darstellung für Sänger* (Wiesbaden, 1975)
R. F. Sheil: *A Manual of Foreign Language Dictions for Singers* (New York, 1975)
C. R. Watson: *Teaching the Mechanical Art of Song* (Minneapolis, 1975)
B. Coffin: 'Articulation for Opera, Oratorio and Recital', *NATS Bulletin*, xxxii/3 (1975–6), 26–41
F. Frank and others: 'Stimmgattungen in der modernen Vokalliteratur ab 1900 bis heute', *Musikerziehung*, xxix (1975–6), 157–62, 205–8
I. Atanelov: *Ispolnitel'skaya deyatel'nost' i vokal'no-pedagogicheskiye principï D. Ja. Andguladze i ego uchenikov* [The Performance and Vocal Pedagogical Principles of Andguladze] (diss., Leningrad Conservatory, 1976)
B. Coffin: *Sounds of Singing: Principles and Applications of Vocal Techniques* (Boulder, CO, 1976, 2/1987)
K. Linklater: *Freeing the Natural Voice* (New York, 1976)
K. Rüs and F. Bonde-Peterson: 'The Function of the Body during Singing', *Musik und forskning*, ii (1976), 66–82
P. Tronina: *Iz opïta pedagoga-vokalista* [From the Experience of the Singing Teacher] (Moscow, 1976)
M. Uberti and O. Schindler: 'Contribution à la recherche d'un art vocal monteverdien: la couleur', *L'avant-scène opéra*, no.5 (1976), 78–89 [*Orfeo* issue]
H. W. Balk: *The Complete Singer-Actor: Training for Music Theater* (Minneapolis, 1977)
A. Berkman: *The Psychology of Singing* (Los Angeles, 1977)
G. J. Buelow: 'A Lesson in Operatic Performance Practice by Madame Faustina Bordoni', *A Musical Offering: Essays in Honor of Martin Bernstein* (New York, 1977), 19–96
R. Celletti: 'La vocalità', *Storia dell'opera*, ed. G. Barblan and A. Basso, iii/1 (Turin, 1977), 3–317
M. Cyr: 'On Performing 18th-Century *Haute-Contre* Roles', *MT*, cxviii (1977), 291–5
F. A. Fields: *Foundations of the Singer's Art* (New York, 1977)
G. Marchesi: 'I cantanti', *Storia dell'opera*, ed. G. Barblan and A. Basso, iii/1 (Turin, 1977), 321–435
T. Mellos: *About Singing and Singers* (1977)
R. Miller: *English, French, German and Italian Techniques of Singing: a Study in National Tonal Preferences and How They Relate to Functional Efficiency* (Metuchen, NJ, 1977)
E. Sąsiadek: 'O technice wokalnej i realizacji ozdobników w utworach Monteverdiego' [On Vocal Technique and the Execution of Mordents in Monteverdi's Works], *Ruch muzyczny*, xxi/14 (1977), 6–7
M. K. Warren: *Theories on Vocal Registers* (diss., U. of Maryland, 1977)
L. Wierenga: *French Diction for the Singer* (New York, 1977)
A. L. Barresi: 'The Singing Voice as an Aid to the Instrumental Conductor and Performer', *Dialogue in Instrumental Music Education*, ii (1978), 38–44
D. Bourlet: *Le vlac! approche napolitaine du chant lyrique* (Paris, 1978)
S. Butenschon: *Stemme og sang: en studie av anatomiske, fysiologiske og fonetiske aspekter ved stemme- og sangfunksjønen* (Oslo, 1978; trans., 1982)
D. Craig: *Singing Onstage* (New York, 1978, 2/1990)
R. D. Fee: *Basic Ideas about Singing: the Teaching of Theodore Harrison, an American Vocal Maestro* (Washington DC, 1978)
H. Fischer-Klotz: *Zu einigen gesangswissenschaftlichen Grundsätzen und methodisch- pädagogischen Empfehlungen für die Gesangsausbildung: ein Betrag zur Klärung Gesangsterminologischer Probleme* (diss., Martin Luther King U., Halle, 1978)
C. Grindea, ed.: *Tensions in the Performance of Music: a Symposium* (London, 1978) [incl. W. Gruner: 'Voice Production and Body Coordination', 56–73; L. Howard: 'Freeing the Voice for Actors and Opera Singers', 74–83]
R. A. Hammar: *Singing – an Extension of Speech* (Metuchen, NJ, 1978)
G. Hewitt: *How to Sing* (London, 1978)
B. J. Monahan: *The Art of Singing: a Compendium of Thoughts on*

Singing Published between 1777 and 1927 (Metuchen, NJ, 1978)
H. G. Nägeli: *Die Individual-Bildung: sieben Aufsätze über Solo-Gesangbildung* (Zurich, 1978)
A. Ransome: 'Towards an Authentic Vocal Style and Technique in Late Baroque Performance', *EMc*, vi (1978), 417–19
G. Rienäcker: 'Zu einigen Aspekten der Struktur und Funktion des Singens im Musiktheatei', *Material zum Theater* (Berlin, 1978), 3–38
W. Seidner: *Die Sängerstimme: phoniatrische Grundlagen für die Gesangsausbildung* (Berlin, 1978)
R. S. Slaughter: *Notes on the Science of Singing* (West Babylon, NY, 1978)
J. Stanislav: *Hudba, zpěv, řeč* [Music Song, Speech] (Bratislava, 1978)
J. Wall and R. Weatherspoon: *Anyone Can Sing* (Garden City, NY, 1978)
V. Andréossy: *L'esprit du chant: essai sur la philosophie de l'art du chant* (Plan-de-la-Tour, 1979)
E. Bishop: *The Urge to Sing and How it Grows* (Babylon, NY, 1979)
E. de Lys: *Jean de Reszke Teaches Singing to Edith de Lys: a True Copy of the Lesson Notebooks of Edith de Lys* (San Francisco, 1979)
C. N. Gattey: *Queens of Song* (London, 1979)
P. Gerritz: *Zenger ken uw stem* [Singer, Know your Voice] (Naarden, 1979)
H. B. Grossman: *Song Literature: a Singer's Guide* (West Babylon, NY, 1979)
T. Grubb: *Singing in French: a Manual of French Diction and French Vocal Repertoire* (New York, 1979)
C. Henius: 'Zur Problematik des Sängerkarriere', *Revue musicale suisse*, cxix (1979), 27–30
V. Kamaryt: 'Gesangspraktische Aspekte des Musicals', *Musica*, xxxiii (1979), 468–9
L. Manén: 'Vocal Timbres, the Essence of the Classical School of Singing', *SMA*, xiii (1979), 34–43
D. L. B. Mitchell: *Luisa Tetrazzini's Explanation of Bel Canto Vocal Technique: a Physiological and Acoustical Analysis* (diss. Brigham Young U., 1979)
S. A. Sanford: *A Guide to Singing the French Language according to the Principles in Seventeenth- and Eighteenth-Century Treatises* (Stanford, CA, 1979)
——: *Seventeenth- and Eighteenth-Century Vocal Style and Technique* (diss., Stanford U., 1979)
E. Sąsiadek: 'O specyfice głosu kontratenorowego' [Concerning the Countertenor Voice], *Ruch muzyczny*, xxiii/17 (1979), 10–12
W. Simmons: *The Human Voice* (Pleasantville, NY, 1979) [incl. filmstrip and recordings]
J. Sundberg: *Chest Vibrations in Singers* (Paris, 1979)
E. Stone: 'Francesco and Giovanni Lamperti: a Comparative Study of their Vocal Pedagogy', *NATS Bulletin*, xxxvi/4 (1979–80), 20–25, 30
R. Celletti: 'Stendhal e l'arte del canto', *Martinella di Milano*, xxxiv/2–3 (1980), 13–20
B. Coffin: *Coffin's Overtones of Bel Canto: Phonetic Basis of Artistic Singing, with 100 Chromatic Vowel-Chart Exercises* (Metuchen, NJ, 1980)
M. Cyr: 'Eighteenth-Century French and Italian Singing: Rameau's Writing for the Voice', *ML*, lxi (1980), 318–37
W. Goldhan: *Kennzeichen der Sängerstimme* (Leipzig, 1980)
J. Hanson: *Me and My Red Shadow* (London, 1980)
J. Krassowski, ed.: *Oddychanie w śpiewie i w grze na instrumentach dętych* [Breathing for Singing and for Playing Wind Instruments] (Gdańsk, 1980) [summary in Eng.]
C. J. Large, ed.: *Contributions of Voice Research to Singing* (Houston, 1980)
P. P. Lewis: *The Alexander Technique: its Relevance for Singers and Teachers of Singing* (diss., Carnegie-Mellor U., 1980)
J. Sundberg: *Röstlara: fakta om rosten i tal och sang* (Stockholm, 1980; trans. as *The Science of the Singing Voice*, 1987)
T. Wishart: 'Extended Vocal Technique', *MT*, cxxi (1980), 313–4
C. Barr: *The Claudio Barr Method of Voice Production* (London, 1981)
A. Blackwood: *The Performing World of the Singer* (London, 1981)
C. Frazes-Hoffman: 'Hebrew for Singers', *Choral Journal*, xxii/3 (1981), 19
R. Jacobs: 'Le chant baroque italien', *Goûts réunis* (1981), Oct, 2–9
Care of the Professional Voice: New York 1981 [incl. papers on singing]
W. Odom: *German for Singers: a Textbook of Diction and Phonetics* (New York and London, 1981)
J. Ott and B. Ott: *La pédagogie de la voix et les techniques européennes du chant* (Issy-les-Moulineaux, 1981) [incl. tape recordings]
F. Piperno: 'Francesco Gasparini: le sue abitazioni romane, i suoi allievi|coabitanti (1717–1727)', *Esercizi: arte musica|spettacolo*, iv (1981), 104–15
Autoperception, Computer Synthesis, Emotion, Health, Voice Source, ed. Royal Swedish Academy of Music: Committee for the Acoustics of Music (Stockholm, 1981)
M. I. Soet: *De stem: handleiding voor het goede gebruik* [The Voice: Method for its Proper Use] (Amsterdam, 1981)
L. Spitzer, ed.: *Probleme der Sängerausbildung* (Vienna, 1981)
M. Tellier: 'La respiration', *Goûts réunis* (1981), Oct, 29–45
P. S. Wormhoudt: *Building the Voice as an Instrument* (Oskaloosa, IA, 1981)
A. Yakovleva: 'K voprosu e dostizhenii rovnosti golosa metstso-soprano' [Concerning the Attainment of a Consistent Mezzo-Soprano Voice], *Problemï muzïkal'noy pedagogiki* (Moscow, 1981)
J. Baker: *Full Circle* (London, 1982)
Dynamics of the Singing Voice (Vienna, 1982)
R. Celletti: 'I cantanti a Roma nel XVIII secolo', *Le muse galanti: La musica a Roma nel settecento: Rome 1982*, 101–7
Y. Dagdelen: 'Muttersprache Stimmklang Stimmbildung', *Musikerziehung*, xxxvi (1982), 3–113
J. B. van Deinse: *The Technique of Singing: a Comparative Study* (The Hague, 1982)
S. Durante: 'Alcune considerazioni sui cantanti di teatro del primo settecento e la loro formazione', *Antonio Vivaldi*, ed. L. Bianconi and G. Morelli (Florence, 1982), 533–46
P. Giles: *The Counter Tenor* (London, 1982)
G. W. Gruber: 'Kastratensänger und Countertenors', *ÖMz*, xxxvii (1982), 390–94
G. Heldt and B. Heldt: *Ein Leben für di Oper: Jean Cox* (Laaber, 1982) [incl. W. Wagner: 'Was verlangt man von einem Sänger'; A. Varnay: 'Singen und Darstellen'; G. Heldt: 'Ein "deutscher Bel Canto" ?' and 'Zum Wesen des Wagner-Gesangs']
J. Hines: *Great Singers on Great Singing* (Garden City, NY, 1982)
F. J. Huie-Armbrister: *The Lyric Soprano Voice: Pedagogy and Repertoire from 1600–1980* (diss., Columbia U., 1982)
H. N. Jacobi: *Building your Best Voice* (Englewood Cliffs, NJ, 1982)
M. Langdon: *Notes from a Low Singer* (London, 1982)
V. L. Lawrence, ed.: *Care of the Professional Voice* (New York 1982) [transcripts of 40 papers on singing technique and voice]
J. C. McKinney: *The Diagnosis and Correction of Vocal Faults* (Nashville, 1982)
D. Mason: *The Singing Voice* (London, 1982)
C. Menotti: *Secrets of Voice Production* (New York, 1982)
P. Mioli: 'La voce umana cantante come strumento irrecuperabile: verifica nel settecento', *Restauro, conservazione e recupero di antichi strumenti musicali: Modena 1982*, 129–42
L. Rasponi: *The Last Prima Donnas* (New York, 1982)
G. K. Rhyming: 'Quelques remarques sur l'art vocal français de la seconde moitié du 17e siècle', *Revue musicale suisse*, cxxii/1 (1982), 1–7
J. L. Santos: 'Los castrati', *A tempo*, ii (1982), 9–12
E. Sittner: *Grossen Sängern abgelauscht: Anweisung und Übungen zur Erlangung von Stimmkraft, Piano, Geläufigkeit* (Vienna, 1982)
G. Troup: 'The Physics of the Singing Voice', *Journal of Research in Singing*, vi (1982), 1–26 [orig. pubd in *Physics Reports*, 1981]
J. R. Joiner: 'The Garcia Legacy: Charles Aimable Battaille', *NATS Bulletin*, xxxix/5 (1982–3), 7–12
S. Zucker: 'Seismic Shocker: the High C from the Chest ... was Popularized by the Frenchman Gilbert-Louis Deprez', *ON*, lxvii/8 (1982–3), 12–14, 44
M. Alió: *Reflexiones sobre la voz* (Barcelona, 1983)
P. Brunger: 'Zwischenbericht zu einer Untersuchung über Geschmack für Singstimmen', *Musikalische pädagogische Forschung*, iv (1983), 242–63
R. Celletti: *Storia del belcanto* (Florence, 1983, 2/1986; trans., 1991)
K. Faulkner: *Voice* (London, 1983)
E. Häfliger: *Die Singstimme* (Berne and Stuttgart, 1983)
H. Krones and R. Schollum: *Vokale und allgemeine Aufführungspraxis* (Vienna and Cologne, 1983)
K. E. Miller: *Principles of Singing* (Englewood Cliffs, NJ, 1983)
J. Pierlot: *Le chant: le libre geste vocal* (Paris, 1983)
C. L. Reid: *A Dictionary of Vocal Terminology: an Analysis* (New York, 1983)

G. K. Rhyming: *Den franska sångkonsten och Benigne de Bacilly, färgstark personlighet i 1600-talets Paris* (Stockholm, 1983)

D. Rossell: *Voice: a Dramatic New Concept for Singing and Speaking* (Seattle, 1983)

R. Russell: 'The Best Voice for Mozart', *Choral Journal*, xxiii/5 (1983), 5–8

O. Tajetti and A. Colzani: *Aspetti della vocalità secentesca* (Como, 1983)

J. Vermeil: 'Les nouveaux castrats: un autre regard sur la voix', *Diapason*, no.285 (1983), July–Aug, 32–5

W. Crutchfield: 'Vocal Ornamentation in Verdi: the Phonographic Evidence', *19th Century Music*, vii (1983–4), 3–54

A. Arnaud: *Les hasards de la voix* (Paris, 1984)

E. Careri: 'Le tecniche vocali del canto italiano d'arte tra il XVI e il XVII secolo', *NRMI*, xviii/3 (1984), 359–75

R. Christiansen: *Prima Donna: a History* (London, 1984)

M. Collins and E. K. Kirk, ed.: *Opera and Vivaldi* (Austin, 1984) [incl. H. M. Brown: 'Embellishing Eighteenth-Century Arias: on Cadenzas', 258–76; R. Covell: 'Voice Register as an Index of Age and Status in Opera Seria', 193–210]

T. Gobbi: *Tito Gobbi on his World of Italian Opera* (London, 1984)

J. Gourret and J. Labayle: *L'art du chant et la médicine vocale* (Paris, 1984)

R. W. Harpster: *Technique in Singing* (New York and London, 1984)

R. Lee: *Learn to Sing Step by Step* (New York, 1984)

G. Newton: *Sonority in Singing: a Historical Essay* (New York, 1984)

P.-L. Otonkoski: *Fonetiikkaa laulajille* [Phonetics for Singers] (Helsinki, 1984)

J. Schmidinger: *Biodynamische Stimmbildung: ein praktischer Lehrgang bis zum deutschen Belcanto* (Vienna, 1984)

J. Schmidt: *Basics of Singing* (New York, 1984, 2/1989)

V. Thordal: *Sangteknik p stemmens praemisser* [The Technique of Singing on Vocal Premises] (Copenhagen, 1984)

D. E. Winters: *Vocal Pedagogy: a Guide to Singing Skills* (Hattiesburg, MI, 1984)

R. H. Cowden: *Concert and Opera Singers: a Bibliography of Biographical Materials* (Westport, CT, 1985)

D. Fischer-Dieskau: *Töne sprechen, Worte klingen: zur Geschichte und Interpretations des Gesangs* (Munich and Stuttgart, 1985)

B. Harlow: *You, the Singer* (Chapel Hill, 1985)

I. von Heijne and others: *Barockboken* (Stockholm, 1985) [incl. essays on vocal articulation and technique]

E. Hehr: 'How the French Viewed the Differences between French and Italian Singing Styles of the 18th Century', *IRMAS*, xvi/1 (1985), 73–85

S. Lachowicz: *Włodzimierz Kaczmar: artysta, piewak i padagog* (Kraków, 1985)

C. E. Lindsley: *Fundamentals of Singing* (Belmont, CA, 1985)

S. Mamy: 'Tradizione pedagogica del canto a Napoli: Giuseppe Aprile', *Musicisti nati in Puglia: Lecce 1985*, 281–98

J. Proubasta: 'El misteri de la timbrica vocal', *Revista musical catalana*, viii (1985), 25–9

Profession chanteur: 1st International Colloquium on the Training of Singers: Rennes 1985

D. Rees-Rohrbacher: *A Spanish Diction Manual for Singers* (diss., Indiana U., 1985)

S. Riggs: *Singing for the Stars: a Complete Program for Training your Voice* (Sherman Oaks, CA, 1985)

S. E. Stedman: *Singing and Self: the Psychology of Performing* (diss., Northwestern U., 1985)

R. Blanchard and R. de Candé: *Dieux et divas de l'opéra: des origines au Romantisme* (Paris, 1986)

H. John: 'Die Kastraten und ihre Gesangskunst in Dresden', *Dresdner Operatraditionen: Dresden 1986*, 197–207

A. Juvarra: 'Il trattamento del settore acuto della voce cantata: aspetti foneticoacustici e metodologici', *NRMI*, xx (1986) 416–26

J. Kesting: *Die grossen Sänger* (Düsseldorf, 1986)

H. Matheopoulos: *Bravo: Today's Great Tenors, Baritones and Basses Discuss their Roles* (London, 1986)

R. Miller: *The Structure of Singing: System and Art in Vocal Technique* (New York and London, 1986)

O. Schindler and N. Mari: *Il canto come tecnica, la foniatria come arte* (Padua, 1986)

K.-H. Viertel: 'Überlegungen zur Gesangsausbildung während Webers Kapellmeisterzeit', *Carl Maria von Weber und der Gedanke der Nationaloper: Dresden 1986*, 327–35

S. Durante: 'Theorie und Praxis der Gesangsschulen zur Zeit Händels: Bemerkungen zu Tosis *Opinioni de' cantori antichi e moderni*', *Händel auf dem Theater: Karlsruhe 1986–7*, 59–77

XIV congresso della Società internazionale di musicologia: Bologna 1987, ii [incl. S. Durante: 'Condizioni materiali e trasmissione del sapere nelle scuole di canto a Bologna a metà settecento', 175–89; P. Lescat: 'L'enseignement du chant italien en France de la fin de l'Ancien Régime à la Restauration: transmission ou transformation?', 190–97 and E. Rosand: '"Senza necessità del canto dell'autore": Printed Singing Lessons in Seventeenth-Century Italy', 214–25]

S. D. Boardman: *Voice Training for the Musical Theater Singer* (diss., U. of Cincinnati, 1987)

J. Bourgeois: 'Vers une renaissance de l'école française de chant', *L'avant-scène opéra*, no.100 (1987), 134–6 [*La Juive* issue]

M. Callas: *Callas at Juilliard: the Master Classes*, ed. J. Ardoin (New York, 1987)

M.-F. Castarède: *La voix et ses sortilèges* (Paris, 1987)

D. Colas: 'Les chanteurs lyriques français: formation et débouchés', *Le théâtre lyrique française, 1945–1985: Paris 1987*, 139–46

D. Craig: *On Performing: a Handbook for Actors, Dancers, Singers on the Musical Stage* (New York, 1987)

S. Durante: 'Il cantante', *SOI*, iv (1987), 347–415

P. J. Jarvis: *The Mature Female Voice in Transition* (diss., Arizona State U., 1987)

J. Kenney: *Becoming a Singing Performer* (Dubuque, IA, 1987)

I. Mayerhoffer: '*... und der Kehlkopf bewegt sich doch!' oder was das Singen wirklich ist: die Urfunktion des richtigen Singens!* (Vienna, 1987)

L. F. Wiens: *A Practical and Historical Guide to the Understanding of the Counter Tenor Voice* (diss., Indiana U., 1987)

K. J. Kutsch and L. Riemens: *Grosses Sängerlexikon* (Basle, 1987–91)

B. M. Doscher: *The Functional Unity of the Singing Voice* (Metuchen, NJ, 1988)

B. Göpfert: *Handbuch der Gesangskunst* (Wilhelmshaven, 1988)

A. Legge: *The Art of Auditioning: a Handbook for Singers, Accompanists and Coaches*, ed. T. Ford (London, 1988)

G. Moens-Haensen: *Das Vibrato in der Musik des Barock: ein Handbuch zur Aufführungspraxis für Vokalisten und Instrumentalisten* (Graz, 1988)

S. Mamy: L'importation des solfèges italiens en France à la fin du XVIIIe siècle', *L'opera tra Venezia e Parigi*, ed. M. T. Muraro (Florence, 1988), 67–89

E. Vecchiarelli: *Il canto rossiniano e la critica* (Pesaro, 1988)

C. Ware: *Voice Adventures: a Process of Exploring, Discovering and Developing Vocal Potential* (St Paul, MN, 1988)

P. Barbier: *Histoire des castrats* (Paris, 1989)

C. Caballero: *Cómo educar la voz hablada y cantada* (Mexico City, 4/1989; also as *Manual para educar la voz hablada y cantada*)

R. Celletti: *Il canto* (n.p., 1989)

B. Coffin: *Historical Vocal Pedagogy Classics* (Metuchen, NJ, 1989)

G. Di Stefano: *L'arte del canto* (Milan, 1989)

E. W. Jones: *Sound, Self and Song: Essays on the Teaching of Singing* (Metuchen, NJ, 1989)

E. Klusen: *Singen: Materialien zu einer Theorie* (Regensburg, 1989)

A.-P. Noyer: *Dictionnaire des chanteur francophones de 1900 à nos jours* (Paris, 1989)

E. Salaman: *Unlocking your Voice: Freedom to Sing* (London, 1989)

B. White: *Singing Techniques and Vocal Pedagogy* (New York, 1989)

J. Steane: 'An Assortment of Voices', *Opera Now* (April 1989 to Dec 1990) [monthly articles on voice types]

L. Bloch-Morhange: *Vies de divas* (Paris, 1990)

B. Bruckboeg: *Literatur der Gesangskunst Bibliographie* (Mainz, 1990)

L. Magiera: *Luciano Pavarotti: metodo e mito* (Milan, 1990)

——: *Mirella Freni: Metodo e mito* (Milan, 1990)

H. W. Balk: *The Radiant Performer: the Spiral Path to Performing Power* (Minneapolis, 1991)

S. C.-T. Cheng: *The Tao of Voice: a New East-West Approach to Transforming the Singing and Speaking Voice* (Rochester, VT, 1991)

R. Cross: *La voix dévoilée* (Paris, 1991)

H. Deighton: *Singing and the Etheric Tone: Gracia Ricardo's Approach to Singing, based on her Work with Rudolf Steiner* (Hudson, NY, 1991)

J. Rosselli: *Singers of Italian Operas* (Cambridge, 1992)

Z. M. Szweykowski: *Między kunsztem a ekspresją/From Virtuosity to Expression* (Kraków, 1992) [with summaries in Eng.]

Singspiel (Ger.: 'sung play'). A term generally understood to signify a light German opera of the 18th century.

1. Terminology. 2. History.

1. TERMINOLOGY. 'Singspiel' as a designation for a German opera with spoken dialogue and a comic or sentimental plot is a modern application of the term, one that became stabilized throughout German-speaking lands only in the 19th century. The word itself can be traced back to at least the end of the 16th century, at which time 'singets Spil' or 'singents Spil' was the common genre label for the crude farces in verse acted and sung to popular tunes by English comedians performing in Germany and by their German imitators. The Nuremberg poet and dramatist Jakob Ayrer (*c*1543–1605) published ten such works in his *Opus theatricum* (1624), for example *Eulenspiegel mit dem Kauffman und Pfeiffenmacher, ein schöns neus singents Spil mit sechs Personen.*

With the cultivation of Italian opera and the beginnings of an indigenous operatic tradition at German courts in the 17th century, 'Singspiel' came to serve as the German equivalent of the Italian 'dramma per musica'; that is how the term is defined in the dictionaries of Kaspar Stieler (1691) and Matthias Kramer (1702). It could also carry broader implications than 'opera', since it was frequently applied to sacred as well as secular representations in verse. For most of the 17th century, poets showed a decided preference for the pastoral and morally didactic in both categories. Further, a characteristically German emphasis on the text's primacy over the music occurs in early theoretical discussions. As one of the interlocutors in the 'Vorspiel' to Georg Philipp Harsdörffer's libretto *Seelewig* (1644) explains, the final element in a compound noun like 'Singspiel' expresses the genre's essential attribute: 'The last word carries the basic meaning, the preceding word the nuance. If the play is a song or exists within the singing, then formally it may be called a "Spielgesang"; if, however, the singing exists within the play, then it must be called a "Singspiel"'.

As a synonym for 'opera', 'Singspiel' could refer to Italian or German works – the Hamburg Opera during the age of Keiser favoured the term 'Singe-Spiel' for a wide variety of comic and tragic representations including those that mixed both languages. Until the mid-18th century the term tended to be restricted to operas that were sung throughout rather than to musical plays with spoken dialogue (which were in the main confined to the popular stages plied by travelling companies). The *Breslauer Anleitung* (1725) notes that 'an opera ... is also called a Singspiel, since everything is sung'. Under 'Singspiel' J. C. Gottsched's *Handlexikon* of 1760 says simply 'see Opera', a practice followed by H. C. Koch's *Musikalisches Lexikon* (1802) and Gustav Schilling's *Encyclopädie* (1838). Christoph Martin Wieland restricted the term to serious German opera more or less directly modelled on Metastasian opera in the critical and historical essays he published in connection with his own five-act verse libretto *Alceste, ein Singspiel in fünf Aufzügen* between 1773 and 1775.

The first works to fit the modern definition of 'Singspiel' are the comic operas of J. A. Hiller and his imitators which sprang up in profusion in Saxony, Thuringia and Prussia beginning in 1766. Yet contemporaneous printed librettos, scores and criticism very seldom make use of the word 'Singspiel' as a generic term for these works. Hiller himself and his chief librettist, C. F. Weisse, labelled every one of their collaborations a 'komische Oper' (most probably a translation of the French 'opéra comique'). The related terms 'Operette' and 'komische Operette' also saw much use into the 1780s and beyond for many German operas with spoken dialogue.

Goethe introduced 'Schauspiel mit Gesang' for works of broader emotional compass with his first librettos, *Erwin und Elmire* (1775) and *Claudine von Villa Bella* (1775), but when he redrafted both works in the 1780s as recitative operas in the Italian manner he relabelled each of them 'Singspiel'. The change, directly counter to Harsdörffer's semantic analysis of the term, may be taken as symbolic of the primacy that music came to assume at that time in North Germany with the increased cultivation of an Austro-Italian repertory. Similarly, the use by other librettists and composers of 'mit Gesang' in various generic designations, implying as it does music's subordination to the play's spoken text, waned considerably in the 1790s.

In Austria, 'Singspiel' continued to be used as the German equivalent of 'opera' in its most general sense. The company of singers established by Joseph II in 1778 to perform German opera at the Vienna Burgtheater was named the National-Singspiel. On the organization's playbills 'Singspiel' betokened any opera in the repertory, even translations of French or Italian works, and the German-language playbills for the Italian company that succeeded the National-Singspiel continued to use the term for their fare (the one announcing the première of *Così fan tutte* called it 'ein komisches Singspiel'). In his printed libretto Stephanie the younger called *Die Entführung aus dem Serail* (1782) as well as his other German opera texts 'Singspiel', whereas Mozart used 'Oper' whenever he mentioned either *Die Entführung* or *Die Zauberflöte* (1791). Dittersdorf designated nearly all his comic operas of the 1780s and 1790s 'komische Singspiele'. In 1779 the fashionable Leipzig librettist C. F. Bretzner entitled a collection of his German opera texts *Operetten*; a second set, issued in 1796 and wholly in the Italian manner (including one called *Opera buffa*), carried the title *Singspiele.*

In the early 19th century, however, the modern terminological distinction began to crystallize. In both Austria and Germany the term 'Oper' came to be restricted to full-scale works, often with an accompanying adjective such as 'romantisch', a combination used by C. M. von Weber for *Silvana* (1810), *Der Freischütz* (1821) and *Oberon* (1826). 'Singspiel' was most often reserved for one- or two-act works of a lighter and more cheerful nature, such as Weber's *Abu Hassan* (1811). Franz Schubert, too, distinguished consistently between the three-act 'Oper' and the lighter 'Singspiel' in one or two acts. The adjective 'grand' tended to indicate a serious, through-composed work, for example Weber's *Euryanthe* ('grosse heroisch-romantische Oper', 1823).

Hermann Mendel's *Musikalisches Conversations-Lexikon* of 1878, in adopting a historical perspective on the issue, cast the distinction between 'Singspiel' and 'Oper' once more in terms of the balance struck between the text and music, rather than the presence or absence of spoken dialogue:

> Previously, one tended to seek the distinguishing feature in the spoken dialogue and to call those dramatic works in which it was introduced 'Singspiele', and to call those in which recitative was deployed 'Oper'. Yet the whole historical course of both forms in-

dicates that it is only the role that the music plays in the dramatic portrayal that determines the distinguishing mark.

In sum, at various times the term could mean a through-composed German opera or one with spoken dialogue, one in which the text was the chief ingredient or one in which musical considerations predominated, a synonym for 'opera' or a distinctive category. The historical overview that follows adopts the modern definition of 'Singspiel' offered by Peter Branscombe:

In a precise and limited sense, the term normally covers those dramatic works that have a liberal infusion of song and occasionally of more ambitious musical forms and that, following the success of the English ballad opera, from the time of Standfuss in the 1750s and Hiller in the 1760s, offered a popular and vernacular alternative to the operas (of the court and permanent public opera houses) that were sung throughout.

2. History. In the restricted sense of the term given above, the German Singspiel coalesced as a distinctive genre not from a prior operatic tradition but within that of the German spoken theatre during its popular renaissance in the second half of the 18th century. Before that time, music had played a role that was clearly subordinate and ornamental in the spoken offerings of itinerant theatrical companies on civic stages in Germany. Scattered arias, incidental music and ballet seasoned many works – farcical, comic and serious – in their repertories.

In 1743, in Berlin, the Schönemann theatrical company performed *Der Teufel ist los*, a German translation of Charles Coffey's ballad opera *The Devil to Pay* (1731), but this early adaptation remained an isolated phenomenon. Another impresario, Heinrich Gottfried Koch, asked the poet C. F. Weisse to retranslate the same play and solicited a new setting from his music director Johann Standfuss to replace the original English tunes Schönemann had used. The success of this version at Leipzig in 1752 led to a bitter pamphlet war, initiated by Gottsched, further kindling public interest in the new genre.

After the Seven Years War Koch persuaded Weisse to revise his text, now renamed *Die verwandelten Weiber*, and enlisted J. A. Hiller to recompose much of it. The instant and overwhelming popularity of the new version led to further collaborations. The sequel to Coffey's ballad opera was first (*Der lustige Schuster*, 1766), but then with *Lottchen am Hofe* (1767) and *Die Liebe auf dem Lande* (1768) Weisse turned to the rustic-sentimental *opéra comique* as a more refined model, one he himself had experienced first-hand at Paris during the war years. His collaboration with Hiller and Koch reached its zenith with *Die Jagd* (1770), very popular well into the 19th century and still occasionally revived in Germany.

Essentially, these early Singspiels were spoken comedies, with large casts and extensive dialogue, to which modest musical numbers had been added in order to strengthen the drama's ambience and to help delineate its characters. When drawing on models from *opéra comique*, Weisse and others tended to choose early works that made few dramatic demands on the music. Hiller kept his music tuneful and deliberately simple, owing partly to the idealized *Volkston* of the operas but more especially to the indifferent musical skills of the actor-singers in Koch's troupe, only one of whom (Caroline Steinbrecher) had a trained voice. This enforced simplicity not only made a virtue of necessity but also made it attractive for nearly every theatrical company across northern and southern Germany, no matter how modest its resources, to take up the new genre.

In northern and central Germany the Hiller-Weisse prototype found many imitators, including especially E. W. Wolf, Anton Schweitzer and Hiller's pupils C. G. Neefe and J. F. Reichardt, both of whom returned at least in part to the farcical spirit Weisse and Hiller had subordinated to French-derived rustic sensibility. Schweitzer marked a high point in this vein with *Die Dorfgala* (1772), as did the Gotha Kapellmeister Georg Benda with *Der Jahrmarkt* (1775). Both composers became involved with more serious and musically ambitious works that moved outside the circumscribed aesthetic of the Singspiel – Schweitzer's German *opera seria Alceste* (1773), and Benda's domestic drama *Romeo und Julie* (1776, with *seria*-style numbers and a *lieto fine* but spoken dialogue). Benda significantly broadened the expressive world and musical dimensions of the rustic-sentimental sort of Singspiel with his 'ernsthafte Operette' *Walder* (1776). Few North Germans followed his lead. During a brief flirtation with German opera, Dresden produced several important new works by the Italian-trained Joseph Schuster (*Der Alchymist*, 1778, and *Die wüste Insel*, 1779) and Franz Seydelmann (*Arsene*, 1779).

The pioneering works of Schweitzer and Benda, which include their German melodramas, were all written for theatres supported by the small and enlightened courts at Weimar and Gotha. In both the North and South, the Singspiel was able to move with ease from the civic stages that had nurtured the genre to private court theatres. Duchess Anna Amalia of Weimar, to whom *Die Jagd* is dedicated, showed great fondness for German opera and herself composed several of Goethe's librettos after his arrival at Weimar in 1775. As the cases of Schweitzer and Benda illustrate, the more stable theatres under court subvention allowed companies to take advantage of superior vocal and instrumental resources and to pursue new stylistic paths.

With the general awakening of the German theatre as an important cultural institution during the 1770s, civic stages also grew more stable and enterprising. The Singspiel saw further development as a public art form at Berlin, especially after the arrival of Johann André as music director of the Döbbelin company in 1777. André's style, without forsaking Hiller's tuneful simplicity, strove for greater variety, seen also in his choice of librettos. He was the first to set his friend Goethe's *Erwin und Elmire* (1775), and later collaborated with the most popular new librettist of the era, C. F. Bretzner, who sought out new sources of inspiration in the exotic (*Belmont und Constanze, oder Die Entführung aus dem Serail*) and the supernatural (*Das wütende Heer, Der Irrwisch*). In contrast to Weisse's librettos, Bretzner's were taken up eagerly by Viennese composers, and in exchange, by the early 1780s, companies like Döbbelin's were beginning to perform new Austrian and Italian operas as their musical resources improved.

In southern Germany composers of Singspiel at first took their lead from the North. The new genre was eagerly embraced by travelling companies that had hitherto relied mostly on French comic operas in translation. At the Stuttgart court, Christian Ludwig Dieter set several North German librettos that won abiding popularity there, including Bretzner's *Belmont und Constanze* (1784). At Munich the amateur composer Johann Lukas Schubaur recomposed several

'Die Bergknappen' (Umlauf), scene xii from the original production at the Burgtheater, Vienna, 17 February 1778: engraving by Carl Schütz

librettos that the Weimar courtier G. E. Heermann had written for E. W. Wolf. Schubaur was the most significant contributor of new Singspiels to the Munich court's efforts in the 1780s to establish a creditable German opera company alongside its French and Italian establishments.

The most serious exertions in this direction came from Joseph II at Vienna, who established the National-Singspiel in 1778 as an adjunct to the distinguished National Theater he had created in 1776 to promote German drama. Between its founding and its demise in 1783 the National-Singspiel by and large disappointed hopes for a significant outpouring of new German operas. Mozart's *Entführung* (1782) was an isolated triumph, if a spectacular one. Salieri's deputy, Ignaz Umlauf, fared best among local composers. The one-act inaugural opera he wrote for the enterprise, *Die Bergknappen* (1778; see illustration), shows the richness and variety of styles the Viennese expected, and among his later operas *Die schöne Schusterinn* (1779) and *Der Irrwisch* (1782) enjoyed considerable popularity and were revived at later dates. Salieri himself contributed a very italianate German opera to the National-Singspiel in 1781, *Der Rauchfangkehrer*, which proved to be the season's greatest attraction. Stephanie the younger, the poetic mainstay of the undertaking, furnished many of its new German texts; he also translated and adapted copiously from the Italians and French when the National-Singspiel turned to music from abroad to flesh out its repertory. Vienna, its sympathies clearly in the Italian camp, showed no interest in importing anything more than the texts of North or South German operas.

Austria had a rich popular theatrical tradition of improvised comedy with music, a local variant of the *commedia dell'arte* that by the 1780s was firmly entrenched in Vienna's suburban theatres, all of them under private management. Music had been an ingredient in the Viennese popular theatre since the beginning of the century, and after the middle of the century impresarios like Josef Kurz began to seek out new music for works in this repertory, including Haydn's *Der neue krumme Teufel* (possibly composed in 1751, now lost). This tradition, indigenous and quite independent of German operatic developments elsewhere, contributed vitally to the character of the magic operas that dominated Vienna's suburban theatres in the last decade of the century (*see* ZAUBEROPER).

After the collapse of the National-Singspiel, a second effort was made by the Viennese court to foster German opera, this time at the Kärntnertortheater. During its brief lifetime, from 1785 to 1788, Dittersdorf scored a series of unprecedented popular successes on this stage with *Der Apotheker und der Doktor*, *Der Betrug durch Aberglauben* (both 1786), *Die Liebe im Narrenhause* (1787), *Das rote Käppchen* and *Hieronymus Knicker* (1789). Their happy blend of the *opera buffa* style dear to Viennese hearts and the folklike tunefulness by now associated everywhere with the Singspiel kept these works high in public affection for decades and provided a paradigm for German comic opera outside the tradition of magic opera, in which Dittersdorf showed no interest. Especially popular examples by later Viennese composers include Wenzel Müller's *Die Schwestern von Prag* (1794), Johann Schenk's *Der Dorfbarbier* (1796) and Joseph Weigl's *Die Schweizerfamilie* (1809).

In North Germany the 1780s were arid years for indigenous operatic production as repertories came ever more under the sway of Viennese and Italian opera. By the 1790s, most successful composers and librettists in the North were writing in imitation of *opera buffa* and Viennese magic opera. F. W. Gotter's *Die Geisterinsel* (1796), originally intended for Mozart, artfully combined Northern and Southern traditions, blending careful craftsmanship and literary polish with spectacle, the supernatural and a mixing of high and low comic elements. It received four settings before the end of the decade, the most important being those of Reichardt (1798, Berlin) and Johann Rudolf Zumsteeg (1798, Stuttgart).

During the 19th century the Singspiel, if we restrict the term to the definition given earlier, continued as a secondary byway, subordinated to the more serious artistic pretensions of German Romantic opera. Major monuments like Beethoven's *Fidelio* and Weber's *Der Freischütz*, whose lighter elements illustrate Romantic opera's indebtedness to the 18th-century Singspiel, belong nonetheless to a newer tradition that one cannot comfortably subsume under the old. Already in 1796 Peter von Winter's *Das unterbrochene Opferfest* had taken up the heightened dramatic and expressive innovations of French revolutionary opera and along with them a new consciousness of opera as a vehicle of socio-political discourse.

*

J. C. Gottsched: *Versuch einer critischen Dichtkunst* (Leipzig, 1730, enlarged 4/1751), 731–55
J. Mattheson: *Die neueste Untersuchung der Singspiele* (Hamburg, 1744)
J. F. Reichardt: *Ueber die deutsche comische Oper* (Hamburg, 1774)
C. H. Schmid: *Chronologie des deutschen Theaters* (1755); repr. in *Schriften der Gesellschaft für Theatergeschichte*, i (1902)
J. G. Stephanie der Jüngere: 'Vorrede', *Sämmtliche Singspiele* (Liegnitz, 1792)
H. M. Schletterer: *Das deutsche Singspiel von seinen Anfängen bis auf die neueste Zeit* (Augsburg, 1863)
J. Minor: *Christian Felix Weisse und seine Beziehungen zur deutschen Literatur des achtzehnten Jahrhunderts* (Innsbruck, 1880)
W. Martinsen: *Goethes Singspiele im Verhältnis zu den Weissischen Operetten* (Dresden, 1887)
R. Eitner: 'Die deutsche komische Oper', *MMg*, xxiv (1892), 37–92
J. Bolte: *Die Singspiele der englischen Komödianten und ihrer Nachfolger in Deutschland, Holland und Skandinavien*, Theatergeschichtliche Forschungen, vii (Hamburg and Leipzig, 1893)
K. M. Klob: *Beiträge zur Geschichte der deutschen komischen Oper* (Berlin, 1903)
F. Brückner: 'Georg Benda und das deutsche Singspiel', *SIMG*, v (1903–4), 571–621
G. Calmus: *Die ersten deutschen Singspiele von Standfuss und Hiller* (Leipzig, 1908)
L. Riedinger: 'Karl von Dittersdorf als Opernkomponist: eine stilkritische Untersuchung', *SMw*, i (1914), 212–349
L. Schiedermair: *Die deutsche Oper: Grundzüge ihres Werdens und Wesens* (Leipzig, 1930, 3/1943)
W. Stauder: 'Johann André: ein Beitrag zur Geschichte des deutschen Singspiels', *AMw*, i (1936), 318–60
F. Brüggemann: *Bänkelgesang und Singspiel vor Goethe* (Leipzig, 1937)
K. Wesseler: *Untersuchungen zur Darstellung des Singspiels auf der deutschen Bühne des 18. Jahrhunderts* (diss., U. of Cologne, 1955)
W. Rubsamen: 'Mr. Seedo, Ballad Opera, and the Singspiel', *Miscellánea en homenaje a Mons. Higinio Anglés* (Barcelona, 1958–61), 775–809
H. Kindermann: *Theatergeschichte Europas*, iii–v (Salzburg, 1959–62)
A. R. Neumann: 'The Changing Concept of the *Singspiel* in the Eighteenth Century', *Studies in German Literature*, ed. C. Hammer (Baton Rouge, 1963), 63–71
R. Pröpper: *Die Bühnenwerke Johann Friedrich Reichardts: ein Beitrag zur Geschichte der Oper in der Zeit des Stilwandels zwischen Klassik und Romantik* (Bonn, 1965)
E. M. Batley: 'The Inception of Singspiel in Eighteenth-Century Southern Germany', *German Life and Letters*, xix (1965–6), 167–77
——: *A Preface to The Magic Flute* (London, 1969)
K. Kawada: *Studien zu den Singspielen von Johann Adam Hiller (1728–1804)* (Marburg and Lahn, 1969)
O. Michtner: *Das alte Burgtheater als Opernbühne: von der Einführung des deutschen Singspiels (1778) bis zum Tod Kaiser Leopolds II. (1792)* (Vienna, 1970)
P. Branscombe: 'The Singspiel in the Late 18th Century', *MT*, cxii (1971), 226–8
——: 'Music in the Viennese Popular Theatre of the Eighteenth and Nineteenth Centuries', *PRMA*, xcviii (1971–2), 101–12
H.-A. Koch: *Das deutsche Singspiel* (Stuttgart, 1974)
G. Flaherty: *Opera in the Development of German Critical Thought* (Princeton, 1978)
R. Schusky, ed.: *Das deutsche Singspiel im 18. Jahrhundert: Quellen und Zeugnisse zu Ästhetik und Rezeption* (Bonn, 1980)
R. Gruenter, ed.: *Das deutsche Singspiel im 18. Jahrhundert* (Heidelberg, 1981)
T. Bauman: *North German Opera in the Age of Goethe* (Cambridge, 1985)
B. van Boer: 'Coffey's *The Devil to Pay*, the Comic War, and the Emergence of the German *Singspiel*', *Journal of Musicological Research*, viii (1988), 119–39
M. R. Wade: *The German Baroque Pastoral 'Singspiel'* (Berne, 1990)

THOMAS BAUMAN

Sinimberghi, Gino (*b* Rome, 26 Aug 1913). Italian tenor. He studied in Rome and was engaged at the Berlin Staatsoper from 1937 to 1944, then returned to Italy, where he continued to appear until 1968. He sang Ismaele (*Nabucco*) at S Carlo in 1949 with Callas; in Rome he sang Grits'ko (*The Fair at Sorochintsi*), Sobinin (*A Life for the Tsar*) and Don Ramiro (*La Cenerentola*), also taking part in the Italian première of Hindemith's *The Long Christmas Dinner* (1962). His other roles included Števa (*Jenůfa*), Herod and Aegisthus. When his originally light, lyrical voice darkened, he became a character tenor of some distinction.

ELIZABETH FORBES

Sïn mandarina ('The Mandarin's Son'). *Opéra comique* in one act by CÉSAR ANTONOVICH CUI to a libretto by VIKTOR ALEXANDROVICH KRÏLOV; St Petersburg, Artists' Club, 7/19 December 1879.

A primitive yet stylistically orthodox (i.e. French-sounding) little vaudeville of mistaken identity – Muri the scullion (tenor) turns out to be the Mandarin's son and heir, so he can marry the Innkeeper's daughter Iedi (soprano), despite her father's contract with Zaï-Zang (*basso buffo*) – it originated in domestic circumstances (a birthday present for the composer's wife). It was performed at the very first 'private spectacle' the members of the as-yet-unchristened 'mighty kuchka' organized for their own amusement (22 February/6 March 1859): Malvina Cui sang Iedi, her husband accompanied (Balakirev joined him for the overture) and Musorgsky sang Kau-Tsing, the Mandarin (bass). The first performance with orchestra was still semi-private. Not until the early 1890s did the piece reach the public stage, when Rimsky-Korsakov heard it and was not amused.

Indeed, one might have expected Russia's severest critic of opera to be embarrassed or annoyed at the late public airing of this *péché de jeunesse*; yet Cui never stood in its way, because (as he wrote to a friend in 1911) alone of his operas it enjoyed some popular success. Bernandt (*Slovar' oper*, Moscow, 1962) lists 11 productions by the time of the Revolution, to which a 12th (1913, Ryazan') may be added.

RICHARD TARUSKIN

Sinopoli, Giuseppe (*b* Venice, 2 Nov 1946). Italian conductor and composer. He combined medical studies at Padua with composition at the Venice Conservatory, where he became professor of contemporary and electronic music in 1972. Further studies with Bruno Maderna and Franco Donatoni were combined with conducting under Hans Swarowsky in Vienna; after making his conducting début at the Royan Festival (1975) he taught conducting at the Paris Conservatoire in 1977. His opera début was with *Aida* at Venice the following year.

While pursuing further operatic engagements he wrote his own two-act opera, *Lou Salomé*, to a libretto by Karl Dietrich Gräwe; it was first performed at the Munich Staatsoper on 10 May 1981. Its action mixes biographical and symbolical elements, drawing images from Lou Salomé's relationships with Rainer Maria Rilke, Friedrich Nietzsche and the atheist thinker Paul Rée. The whole is framed by two choruses on the theme of freedom. Each scene is given its specific musical character by the use of carefully delimited harmonic resources – often fixed pitch fields of only six or seven components. The retrospective subject matter is complemented by the presence of tonal references, though they are not allowed to take on any larger structural functions.

Sinopoli's operatic and concert careers both developed rapidly in the early 1980s. He conducted mainly Puccini and Verdi at Berlin, Hamburg and Vienna, and made his Covent Garden début with *Manon Lescaut* in 1983 and his American début with *Tosca* at the Metropolitan in 1985. That year he first appeared at Bayreuth (*Tannhäuser*), and returned there in 1990 for a new production of *Der fliegende Holländer*. Having conducted the Vienna Staatsoper production of *Manon Lescaut* in Japan in 1986, he inaugurated the Suntory Hall, Tokyo, the next year with concert performances of *Madama Butterfly* with the Philharmonia from London, of which he became music director in 1987 after three years as its principal conductor.

Sinopoli was appointed general music director at the Deutsche Oper, Berlin, in 1990, beginning with a production of *Salome*; however, because of controversy over his terms of contract (signed a decade earlier), he did not take up the post. He was appointed principal conductor of the Dresden Staatskapelle for the 1991–2 season. His conducting style has been no less controversial, adversely criticized for corpulent tempos, muddled textures and rhythmic indulgence. He has defined his intentions as 'making singers and players perform above their ability' and his performances have been admired for his continuing search for the music's interior logic, as well as for a wealth of instrumental detail and shading to complement the voices. He has recorded several Verdi, Puccini and Wagner operas, some in video versions.

*

J. H. Sutcliffe: 'Support for Sinopoli', *Opera*, xli (1990), 1470–71

NOËL GOODWIN, DAVID OSMOND-SMITH

Sior Todero brontolon. Opera by G. F. Malipiero; *see* *TRE COMMEDIE GOLDONIANE.*

Siqueira, José (de Lima) (*b* Conceição Paraíba, 24 June 1907; *d* Rio de Janeiro, 22 April 1985). Brazilian composer. A bandmaster's son, he entered the Instituto Nacional de Música in Rio de Janeiro in 1926, where he studied composition with Francisco Braga. In 1935 he was appointed to teach harmony at the institute and, after successfully competing for the position, he became a regular member of the faculty in 1938. His intensive activity as an orchestral conductor began in the late 1930s and in 1940 he founded the Brazilian SO, which he directed for eight years. He was responsible for the foundation of the Sociedade Artística Internacional (1946), the short-lived Rio de Janeiro SO (1949) and the Clube do Disco (1951) for promoting recordings.

Siqueira began to compose in about 1933, following a neo-classical style, but in 1943 he turned to musical nationalism and established himself as one of the foremost Brazilian proponents of that trend of his generation. He carried out field research in north-east Brazil, particularly of the Afro-Brazilian and *caboclo* musics of the region. His output shows a predilection for programmatic orchestral music, although he also wrote choral works based on Afro-Brazilian ritual music. His three-act comic opera *A Compadecida*, produced in 1961, uses folksong themes to characterize the main roles. He also wrote the *drama lírico Gimba* (1960), in two acts and a prologue, on verses by the poet Gianfrancesco Guarnieri, which remains unperformed.

See also COMPADECIDA, A.

*

E. Nogueira Franca: 'Festival José Siqueira', *Revista brasileira de música*, ii (1963)

J. Ribeiro: *Maestro José Siqueira: artista e o líder* (Rio de Janeiro, 1963)

G. Béhague: 'Rasgos afrobrasileños en obras nacionalistas escogidas de compositores brasileños del siglo XX', *Revista musical chilena*, no.158 (1982), 53–9

GERARD BÉHAGUE

Širca, Friderik. *See* SAVIN, RISTO.

Sir John in Love. Opera in four acts by RALPH VAUGHAN WILLIAMS to his own libretto after WILLIAM SHAKESPEARE's play *The Merry Wives of Windsor*, with interpolations from other Shakespeare plays and other authors; London, Royal College of Music, 21 March 1929.

Vaughan Williams here sets the same plot as Verdi's *Falstaff* but stays closer to Shakespeare. For extra arias and choruses he went to other Shakespeare plays (e.g. 'Sigh no more, ladies', from *Much Ado about Nothing*) and to other poets, particularly Ben Jonson, whose 'See the chariot at hand' forms the melodic climax of the last scene. Ten folksongs are incorporated into the score, the best-known being 'Greensleeves', which Mrs Ford (mezzo-soprano) sings at the beginning of Act 3; the orchestral introduction to this act was later issued separately as the *Fantasia on Greensleeves*. Two English folkdances are also used. However, the folktunes represent only a fraction of the score; Vaughan Williams's original melodies, particularly that for 'See the chariot', are in his most lyrical vein. Falstaff's Act 2 love song, 'O that joy so soon should waste', is especially effective.

For a production in Bristol in 1933, Vaughan Williams added a Prologue (later withdrawn) and two short scenes. Five of the choruses – the third of them considerably expanded – were published in 1931 as the cantata *In Windsor Forest*.

MICHAEL KENNEDY

Sirmay, Albert. *See* SZIRMAI, ALBERT.

Siroe (i) [Siroe re di Persia ('Siroes, King of Persia')]. Opera in three acts by GEORGE FRIDERIC HANDEL to a libretto adapted by NICOLA FRANCESCO HAYM from PIETRO METASTASIO's *Siroe* as revised for Naples (1727); London, King's Theatre, 17 February 1728.

Siroe was Handel's twelfth full-length opera for the Royal Academy of Music and the fourth of the group of five operas in which the leading female roles were designed for the rival sopranos Francesca Cuzzoni and Faustina Bordoni; they sang Laodice and Emira. The other singers were the alto castratos Senesino as Siroe and Antonio Baldi as Medarse, with the basses Giuseppe Maria Boschi as Cosroe and Giovanni Battista Palmerini as Arasse (this part has no arias). Some of the music was originally composed for a version of Beregan's libretto *Genserico* (1669, Venice), which Handel abandoned before completing the first act. The new libretto was the first of the three by Metastasio used by Handel, and had been first set, by Vinci, two years earlier in Venice. (For details of the plot, *see* SIROE RE DI PERSIA, below.)

Handel completed the score on 5 February 1728. Its production 12 days later at the King's Theatre had a good run of 18 performances, but Handel never revived the work. There were productions in Brunswick in August 1730 and February 1735. The first modern revival was at Gera in December 1925, arranged by R. Meyer.

The choice of a recent Metastasio libretto suggests a desire (perhaps on the part of the Academy directors rather than Handel) to keep up with the latest Italian fashion. Unfortunately Metastasio's excessively contrived plotting robs the characters of credibility, with the consequence that the many excellent arias (there are no duets or other vocal ensembles) seem abstracted from the drama; exceptions are Laodice's 'Mi lagnerò tacendo' (of which the theme derives from the Israelites' lament in *Esther*), Cosroe's 'Gelido in ogni vena' (a slow minor-key aria with chromatic inflections, not at all typical of a Boschi role) and Siroe's fine prison *scena*, 'Son stanco ... Deggio morire, o stelle'.

ANTHONY HICKS

Siroe **(ii)** [Siroe re di Persia ('Siroes, King of Persia')]. *Opera seria* in three acts by JOHANN ADOLF HASSE to a libretto by PIETRO METASTASIO; Bologna, Teatro Malvezzi, 2 May 1733 (second setting, Dresden, Hoftheater, and Warsaw, Imperial Theatre, Carnival 1763).

The castrato Farinelli sang the title role in the original version of this opera in Bologna; on 4 November 1747 it was revived at the S Carlo, Naples. 30 years after the initial production, Hasse made a second setting for the Elector of Saxony (who as King of Poland also resided in Warsaw during the Seven Years War); this new version was the last opera written and performed at the Saxon court. While the second *Siroe* shows a greater regard for Metastasian dramatic conventions and a deeper, more mature command of musical form in the construction of its da capo arias, with longer phrases, stronger rhythmic drive and more contrapuntal orchestral accompaniments, the earlier setting is nevertheless a fine example of the heights Hasse's creative powers had reached only a few years after he went to Dresden. The aria 'Spresso tra vaghe rose' (once attributed to Pergolesi and other composers) was extracted from *Siroe* and used in comic operas and intermezzos, for example in the famous pasticcio *Il maestro di musica* performed in Paris in the 1750s. (For details of the plot, *see* SIROE RE DI PERSIA, below.)

HOWARD MAYER BROWN

Siroe re di Persia ('Siroes, King of Persia') [Siroe]. Libretto by PIETRO METASTASIO, first set by Leonardo Vinci (1726, Venice).

ACT 1 Cosroe, King of Persia, has slain Asbite, King of Cambaya, in combat. Emira, Asbite's daughter, seeks revenge, and enters the court of Cosroe in male attire under the assumed name of Idaspe; only Siroe, elder son of Cosroe and in love with Emira, knows her identity. Meanwhile, Medarse, younger son of Cosroe, has methodically ingratiated himself with his father in order to displace Siroe as heir. Affronted that Cosroe should consider choosing between his sons, Siroe incurs his father's anger while Medarse gains the promise of the throne. When Siroe refuses to aid Emira's cause, she

Design by Giambattista Crosato for Giuseppe Scarlatti's setting of Metastasio's 'Siroe re di Persia' (Teatro Regio, Turin, 1750): tempera

spurns his love and spitefully suggests to Laodice, in love with Siroe and loved by Cosroe, that her affections are reciprocated. Outraged when Siroe corrects this fabrication, Laodice informs Cosroe that Siroe is his rival and has attempted to seduce her. This Siroe overhears while concealed in Cosroe's chambers, where he has left an anonymous note warning the king that his life is in danger; he also overhears Medarse name him as traitor. Siroe reveals his presence, an act that only compounds the accusations against him.

ACT 2 Laodice, remorseful, gains Siroe's pardon for her slander but is unable to suppress her love for him as he requests. Emira, still disguised as Idaspe, repeats her demand for the death of Cosroe, in response to which Siroe, torn between the roles of son and lover, draws his sword to kill himself. Cosroe, entering unexpectedly, construes this gesture as an attempt upon Idaspe. Siroe, longing for death, pleads guilty, and his imprisonment affords Emira the opportunity to embark upon the immediate assassination of Cosroe. Interrupted, however, she presents her drawn sword to the king as an act of loyalty, a deception that is then matched by the dissembling Medarse who informs his father of his willingness to yield the succession to his brother. Cosroe fruitlessly offers Siroe full pardon if, not guilty of treason, he will name the traitor. Laodice, meanwhile, begs Emira (as Idaspe) to plead her cause with Siroe, to which 'Idaspe' replies that 'his' own love for Laodice renders such action impossible.

ACT 3 Cosroe orders Arasse, general of the Persian armies, to execute Siroe. Laodice, alarmed by a mob that champions Siroe and now surrounds the palace, appeals to Cosroe who informs her of his order. In response, she confesses her falsehood and pleads Siroe's innocence. 'Idaspe', also distressed by the rebellion and horrified to learn of the sentence upon Siroe, persuades the king to revoke his order. When Arasse announces that this decision comes too late, Emira rails against Cosroe and reveals her identity. Arasse, on the pretence of taking Emira into custody, informs her that Siroe still lives, and she enters the dungeons in time to prevent Medarse from murdering him. Siroe and Emira, followed by Arasse and other supporters, make a timely arrival at the scene where Medarse's coronation was to have taken place and save Cosroe from the rebels. At Siroe's bidding, Laodice and Medarse are pardoned and Emira renounces her quest for revenge. Cosroe proclaims Siroe king.

* * *

Khosrau II Parvez (Chosroes II) ruled Persia across the years AD591–628 and was deposed by his son, Kavadh II Shiruya (Siroes), who thus prevented the throne passing to his brother, Merdaza (Medarses). Accounts of this story are to be found in the Zonaras *Epitomae* (bk 14); the Elmacinus *Historia saracenica* (bk 1); and the Baronio *Annalium* (vol. xi), drawn from the Theophanes, *Chronographia* (*A.M.* 6118). For Metastasio, Jean de Rotrou's *Cosroès* (1649) and Zeno's *Ormisda* (1721) could have provided contemporary models, the latter dealing with the same dynasty and a similar plot placed one generation earlier. Success was assured for the *Siroe* première with Marianna Benti-Bulgarelli ('La Romanina') and Nicolini, the two leading singers from *Didone abbandonata* (1724), heading the cast. Although *Siroe* achieved over 35 settings, however, it was never to gain the popularity of the earlier opera. Handel, in 1728, introduced London audiences to their first Metastasian opera with a *Siroe* setting, and in 1740 Majorano Caffarelli and Giovanni Manzuoli sang in a setting that established Perez in Naples as an opera composer. For Conforto, *Siroe* (1752) was one of the operas that secured him a position as opera composer at the court in Madrid, and in Munich, Venanzio Rauzzini, newly appointed to the court of Maximilian Joseph II, made his début in Traetta's *Siroe* in 1767.

For a list of settings *see* METASTASIO, PIETRO. DON NEVILLE

Širola, Božidar (*b* Žakanj, 20 Dec 1889; *d* Zagreb, 10 April 1956). Croatian composer. In 1921 he took a doctorate in musicology at the University of Vienna, with a dissertation on Istrian folksong. He taught mathematics and physics in Zagreb for nearly 30 years; from 1935 to 1941 he was administrative director of the secondary school of music within the Zagreb Academy of Music, and he was also important as an ethnomusicologist, organologist, lecturer and critic, becoming curator and then director of the Ethnographic Museum in the city. A prolific composer, Širola was often inspired by elements of the folk music of various Croatian regions; he is remembered particularly for three operas and an oratorio commemorating SS Cyril and Methodius (1927). In his comic opera *Citara i bubanj* ('The Cithara and the Drum') he succeeded in depicting the typical atmosphere of a small Croatian seaside town, using elements of folk music and flexible declamation. His other works include ballets, melodramas and incidental music.

Stanac (musical grotesque, 1, after M. Držić), Zagreb, 29 Oct 1915; rev., Zagreb, 3 Oct 1936
Citara i bubanj ili neobični svatori [The Cithara and the Drum, or an Unusual Wedding] (comic op, 3, V. Dezelić the younger, after V. Novak), Zagreb, 22 Nov 1930
Z Griča na Trešnjevku [From Grič to Trešnjevka], 1931 (operetta, 3)
Mecena [Maecenas], 1934 (grotesque satire, 1, A. Kostelić)
Grabancijaš [The Student of Black Arts] (comic op, 1, Deželić, after T. Brezovački), Zagreb, 3 Oct 1936
Mladi gospodin [The Young Gentleman], 1940 (3, Deželić, after A. Šenoa), unperf.
Kameni svatovi [The Stone Wedding Guests], 1954 (folk op, 3, M. Širola, after A. Šenoa), unperf.
Godišnji odmor [The Holiday], 1955 (operetta, 3, Širola)

*

K. Kovačević: *Hrvatski kompozitori i njihova djela* [Croatian Composers and their Works] (Zagreb, 1960), 447–64
J. Andreis: *Music in Croatia* (Zagreb, 1974)
Arti musices, xvi/1–2 (1985) [Širola issue] KORALJKA KOS

Sismano nel Mogol ('Sismano among the Moguls'). *Opera seria* in three acts by GIOVANNI PAISIELLO to a libretto by GIOVANNI DE GAMERRA; Milan, Regio Ducal Teatro, Carnival 1773.

Sismano (tenor), King of Persia, arrives to celebrate the marriage of his daughter Zeira (soprano) to Siface (soprano castrato), the Grand Mogul. The treacherous Sismano plans to kill Siface and give Zeira to Idreno (soprano castrato), who in turn is loved by Arsinda (soprano), Zeira's friend. In private Sismano tells Zeira that he is not her father but her protector, and that he intends to marry her. Dismayed, Zeira recognizes Siface's danger and persuades him to flee. Sismano drags Zeira to the temple for the marriage; Idreno confronts him and joins with the Moguls to rout the Persians. Sismano threatens to kill Zeira in revenge. All arrive to rescue her, and Sismano is captured, but the reunited couple pardon him.

The opera is noteworthy for the early example of an action ensemble finale, to Act 2. This begins with a pantomime of Idreno's defection and continues through Sismano's capture, moving from duo (Sismano and Zeira) to quintet as her three rescuers enter. The last scene of the opera has an unusually extensive chorus, pantomime and duo as Sismano enters in chains to witness the uniting of Siface and Zeira. The opera was revived for Cremona in 1785. MARITA P. McCLYMONDS

Sitsky, Larry (*b* Tientsin, China, 10 Sept 1934). Australian composer of Russian descent. He migrated to Australia with his parents in 1951, graduating from the New South Wales State Conservatorium in 1956 after studies with the pianist Winifred Burston and the composer Raymond Hanson. From 1959 to 1961 he studied at the San Francisco Conservatory of Music with Egon Petri. He taught at the Queensland State Conservatorium of Music, 1961–5, and in 1966 was appointed to the staff of the Canberra School of Music. Sitsky is a prolific composer and has written seven operas, all in collaboration with the poet Gwen Harwood.

Until 1965 Sitsky was known as a composer of highly intellectualized instrumental music. Though an underlying Romanticism is discernible in much of his work, the overwhelming technical virtuosity can hinder the music's accessibility. While *The Fall of the House of Usher* (1965), his first opera, is vocally stilted, the work is powerfully dramatic in its instrumental writing. By the time Sitsky and Harwood began *Lenz*, their second collaboration, in 1970, the librettist's sense of staging had developed; the work is better constructed dramatically, prompting the composer to more dynamic writing than had been apparent in *The Fall*. Nevertheless, there is an air of claustrophobia about these early operas, because of the concentration on internal argument and logic rather than on dramatic development and resolution. They are, however, the works on which Sitsky's reputation as an opera composer is based. His next work, *Fiery Tales* (1976), derived from two stories by Chaucer and Boccaccio, is in a lighter dramatic vein and, musically, an occasional piece; it was first performed with George Dreyfus's *King Charles* at the 1976 Adelaide Festival. *Voices in Limbo* (composed 1977), an ABC/FM commission, uses voices altered by computer and electronic devices. *The Golem* was completed in 1980 as a commission from the Australian Opera. Sitsky's next operatic endeavour was *De profundis* (1982), a short monodrama for baritone, percussion and two string quartets. In 1989 he composed *Three Scenes from Aboriginal Life*, described as three short music-theatre pieces, which can be performed separately and which employ children's voices.

See also FALL OF THE HOUSE OF USHER, THE (ii) and LENZ.

The Fall of the House of Usher, 1965 (1, G. Harwood, after E. A. Poe), Hobart, Royal, 18 Aug 1965, vs (Sydney, 1974)
Lenz, 1970 (1, Harwood, after G. Büchner), Sydney, Opera House, 14 March 1974
Fiery Tales (1, Harwood, after G. Chaucer and G. Boccaccio), Adelaide, Scott, 23 March 1976
Voices in Limbo, 1977 (radio op, Harwood), ABC, 1977
The Golem, 1980 (3, Harwood)
De profundis (monodrama, Harwood, after O. Wilde), concert perf., Canberra, School of Music, 31 Oct 1982; stage, Sydney, U. of NSW, 8 April 1987
Three Scenes from Aboriginal Life, 1989 (children's op, Harwood), Canberra, School of Music, Oct 1991

R. Covell: *Australia's Music: Themes of a New Society* (Melbourne, 1967)
L. Sitsky: 'Sitsky on Sitsky', *Music Now* (April 1971), 5–12
J. Murdoch: *Australia's Contemporary Composers* (Melbourne and Sydney, 1972)
D. Thornton: 'Larry Sitsky', *Australian Composition in the Twentieth Century*, ed. F. Callaway and D. Tunley (Melbourne, 1978)
E. Wood: *Australian Opera, 1842–1970* (diss., U. of Adelaide, 1979)
Larry Sitsky, Australian Composer Series, vi (Sydney, 1988)
THÉRÈSE RADIC

Sitzprobe (Ger.: 'seat-rehearsal'). Term used in opera houses, in virtually all countries, for what is normally the first rehearsal of an opera with orchestra, during which the singers remain seated on the stage; this, undertaken when the singers have learnt their parts, is intended to show them how their own music fits into the total musical texture as supplied by the orchestra and the other singers without the distraction of acting. *See* REHEARSAL, §2(i).

Šivic, Pavel (*b* Radovljica, 2 Feb 1908). Slovene composer. He studied composition with Osterc at the Ljubljana Conservatory (until 1931) and with Suk, Hába and Kurz in the Prague Conservatory masterclasses (1933). He taught at the Ljubljana Conservatory (1934–9) and at the academy of music, where he was made professor in 1961. Throughout his career he has been an enthusiastic follower of new compositional trends. Šivic's *Cortesova vrnitev* ('Cortés's Return'; 1974) is written in an atonal style and is considered to be one of the finest achievements in the field of Slovene opera. *Svitanje* ('The Daybreak'; 1979) is a selection of scenes drawn from the cultural life of fighting partisans, and although it is based mainly on abstract elements, there are a few authentic folk melodies and words interwoven into the texture. His later works became more melodic, particularly the children's opera *Kaznovana radovednost* ('Curiosity Punished'; 1988). He has also been active as a pianist and as a writer on music.

Oj, ta prešmentana ljubezen [Oh, that Cursed Love] (operetta, 3, M. Simončič), 29 April 1931
Cortesova vrnitev [Cortés's Return], 1971 (3, Šivic, after A. Hieng), 20 March 1974
Svitanje [The Daybreak] (1, Šivic, after B. Šömen), 10 May 1979
Samorog [The Unicorn], 1981 (3, Šivic, after G. Strniša)
Kaznovana radovednost [Curiosity Punished] (children's op, 1, Šivic and V. Rudolf), 9 Feb 1988 ANDREJ RIJAVEC

Skazaniye o nevidimom grade Kitezhe i deve Fevronii. Opera by N. A. Rimsky-Korsakov; *see* LEGEND OF THE INVISIBLE CITY OF KITEZH AND THE MAIDEN FEVRONIYA, THE.

Skazka o Tsare Saltane. Opera by N. A. Rimsky-Korsakov; *see* TALE OF TSAR SALTAN, THE.

Skilondz, Adelaide von [Andrejewa de] (*b* St Petersburg, 15/27 Jan 1882; *d* Stockholm, 5 April 1969). Russian soprano. She studied in St Petersburg and sang there from 1904, notably as the Queen of Shemakha in the local première of *The Golden Cockerel* (1909). She sang at the Berlin Hofoper until the outbreak of World War I, when she moved to Stockholm. Until 1920 she was successful there in such coloratura roles as the Queen of Night, Lucia and Gilda. She sang in concert performances until 1930 and later taught singing in Stockholm: Kerstin Meyer, Kim Borg and Elisabeth Söderström were among her pupils. DAVID CUMMINGS

Skilton, Charles Sanford (*b* Northampton, MA, 16 Aug 1868; *d* Lawrence, KS, 12 March 1941). American composer. After graduating from Yale, he studied from 1891 to 1893 at the Berlin Hochschule für Musik, where his teachers included Woldemar Bargiel. He taught at Salem and in New Jersey before becoming professor at the University of Kansas in 1903. Skilton belonged to a group of American composers of the first quarter of the 20th century who saw American Indian music as a vital new source, and who incorporated tribal melodies and folklore into their major works, albeit in a conventionally romantic style. His three-act opera *Kalopin* (composed 1927), to a libretto by V. N. Palmer, is based on the Indian legendary explanation of the events causing the New Madrid earthquake of 1811. Although unperformed, the opera received the David Bispham Memorial Medal of the American Opera Association of Chicago (1930). Skilton's *The Sun Bride* (L. W. Spencer) is also based on an Indian tale, of Pueblo sun-worship. A one-act radio opera incorporating music from the composer's *Suite Primeval*, it was first broadcast by NBC on 17 April 1930. A third stage work, *The Day of Gayomair* (prol., 2 scenes, A. Crafton, after F. Gerstacker), was composed in 1936 but remains unperformed. DAVID E. CAMPBELL

Sklavos, Georgios (*b* Braila, Romania, 20 Aug 1888; *d* Athens, 19 March 1976). Greek composer. He studied at the Athens Conservatory, graduating in 1913, and may have been a pupil of Lavrangas. Sklavos taught at both the Athens and Piraeus conservatories, and translated many French, Italian and Russian operas into Greek, but his translations are naive. During the civil war of 1946–9 he was appointed director general of the Greek National Opera, and from 1964 he was a member of its administrative board. In his operas he favoured folk or historical subjects, drawing accordingly on either folk melodies or Byzantine music (as in *Kassiani*). His orchestration is colourful and his romantic harmonies tend increasingly towards chromaticism and density of texture.

first performed in Athens unless otherwise stated

Niove (comic op, 3, I. Efthymiou, after H. Paulton), Scherzo (Act 1) and Ballet (Act 3) perf. 27 Jan 1920
Lestenitsa, 1923 (1, T. Daralexis), National Opera, 14 March 1947
Kassiani, 1929–36 (4, S. Sperantzas), National Opera, 30 Oct 1959
To krino st' akroyali [Lily on the Seashore], 1937–41 (3, Sperantzas), National Opera, 26 Feb 1966
Amphitryon, 1955–60 (lyrical comedy, 3, Sperantzas), unperf.
St' Ai Yoryou to paniyiri [At St George's Fair], 1961–2 (1, Sperantzas), unperf.

*

Megali elliniki engyklopaedia [Great Greek Encyclopedia] (Athens, 1934)
A. S. Theodoropoulou: 'Synchronoi ellines moussikoi: 2. Georgios Sklavos' [Contemporary Greek Musicians], *Anglohelleniki epitheorissi*, iii/2 (1947), 56–7
M. Doumias: 'G. Sklavos: Kassiani', *Kathimerini* (5 Nov 1959) [review]; repr. in *Moussikokritika* (Athens, 1963), 261–3
GEORGE LEOTSAKOS

Skopje. City in the Macedonian region of the former Yugoslavia. The establishment after World War II of opera and ballet companies at the Makedonski Naroden Teatar (Macedonian People's Theatre) encouraged Macedonian composers to write for the stage. At first, however, the opera company relied on repertory classics to attract and help build up an audience; the first performance was of *Cavalleria rusticana* on 9 May 1947. The greatest contribution to the company's rapid development was made between 1948 and 1952 by Lovro von Matačić, who also launched the careers of many young artists. The Macedonian Opera has performed successfully both at home and abroad, giving the premières of all operas (most with a strong folk element) by the Macedonian composers Trajko Prokopiev (1909–79), Kiril Makedonski (1925–84), Toma Proshev (*b* 1931), Sotir Golabovski (*b* 1937), Risto Avramovski (*b* 1943), Blagoj Trajkov (*b* 1944) and Dimitrie Buzharovski (*b* 1952). DRAGOSLAV ORTAKOV

Skram, Knut (*b* Hjörundfjord, 18 Dec 1937). Norwegian baritone. He obtained an architect's diploma from Montana University in the USA, but while there began singing studies with George Buckbee, and on his return to Europe continued with Paul Lohmann in Wiesbaden and Luigi Ricci in Rome. His début was in 1964 at Oslo as Amonasro. After winning the 1967 Munich international competition he became principal baritone at the Norwegian Royal Opera, where he has sung over 50 roles, ranging from Don Giovanni and Yevgeny Onegin to Scarpia and Kurwenal. His British début was in 1969 at Glyndebourne as Guglielmo, and he returned in eight further seasons, notably as Figaro in Peter Hall's 1973 production. In 1988 he first sang at the Moscow Bol'shoy, playing Scarpia, and at the Colón, Buenos Aires, as Pizarro. His American début was in 1979 with the Kentucky Opera as Papageno. A versatile baritone of musical perceptiveness and flexible technique, he is also admired as a lieder singer.
NOËL GOODWIN

Skripka Rotshil'da ('Rothschild's Violin'). Opera in one act by VENIAMIN IOSIFOVICH FLEYSHMAN, 1939–41 (completed by Dmitry Shostakovich, 1944), to a libretto by the composer after a story by ANTON PAVLOVICH CHEKHOV; Leningrad, Experimental Chamber Opera Studio of the Leningrad Conservatory, 24 April 1968 (previous concert performance, Moscow, Central House of Composers, 20 June 1960).

When it became apparent that his gifted young student, Fleyshman, had perished in the early days of World War II, Shostakovich resolved that the major work composed under his supervision, the one-act opera *Rothschild's Violin*, should not be lost to posterity. From his evacuation in Kuybïshev (now Samara), Shostakovich made concerted efforts to track down the score. Late in 1943 the manuscript was finally delivered to him, and he took the necessary steps to complete the score and make a fair copy, dated 5 February 1944. Not wanting to undermine the integrity of Fleyshman's work, Shostakovich was extremely modest in delineating his own contribution and claimed only to have completed the unfinished orchestration. It appears, however, that he was also responsible for realizing some incomplete vocal lines and polishing other details of the score.

Yakov Matveyevich Ivanov, nicknamed Bronza (bass), is a coffin maker and amateur fiddler in a provincial Russian town, a man of cupidity and spleen. His world revolves around his losses, real and imaginary. What might he have earned if circumstances had been different? The only bright spot in his existence is his violin, which he occasionally plays in a local Jewish band. Even here, though, all is not well. He vents his anger and scorn at the poor flautist Rothschild (tenor), who is periodically sent to fetch him. Largely through philosophical reflection, by the end of the opera Yakov comes to a new understanding of the meaning of life and death. This is mirrored musically in the gradual shift from a declamatory style reminiscent of Musorgsky and writing which is sometimes deliberately trite and grotesque to a warmer, more lyrical style. The death of Yakov's wife Marfa (mezzo-soprano), whom he has ignored for the 50 years of their marriage, is the turning-point. Modal writing and other characteristic traits also lend a somewhat Jewish flavour to the work. Though Yakov reflects that his whole life consists of losses and that death alone can bring unconditional gain, he realizes that he cannot take his violin to the grave nor orphan it. Instead, he bequeaths it to the unsuspecting Rothschild. The final tender melody on Yakov's violin is elevated into an orchestral apotheosis.

LAUREL E. FAY

Škroup [Schkroup, Skraup], **František Jan** (*b* Osice, 3 June 1801; *d* Rotterdam, 7 Feb 1862). Czech composer and conductor. He was a descendant of several generations of teachers, which in 18th-century Bohemia almost automatically meant good musicians. His father, Dominik Škroup (1766–1830), a teacher and composer, introduced František to music. At the age of 11, already a good flautist, he went to Prague to finish primary school, and supported himself as a choirboy. He continued his schooling at one of the most important Czech national revival movement centres, Hradec Králové, where he was a choirboy at the cathedral and studied with the local choirmaster and composer Franz Volkert (1767–1831); then he returned to Prague to attend university. From 1822 he studied law but also pursued acting, music teaching and performing. He was particularly involved in Czech amateur charity opera productions, which started on 28 December 1823 when the Prague Estates Theatre first gave a Czech version of Weigel's *Die Schweizerfamilie*. This was followed by works by Cherubini, Weber, Méhul, Rossini and Mozart.

The aim of the young Czech national revival movement – to express the intellectual power of the Czech nation and its language in opera as one of the highest achievements of art – soon led from translations to more ambitious ventures, and inspired Škroup to compose his first opera, *Dráteník* ('The Tinker', 1826), a two-act Singspiel in 14 numbers to a libretto by J. K. Chmelenský (1800–39), a lawyer, poet, literary and music critic and publisher of the first Czech music magazine. The plot is of the Viennese Singspiel type, a lyrical comedy of love and disguise, where the tinker's cloak and hat and also his homesickness play an important role. The libretto uses both Czech and Slovak (the main character is a wandering Slovak tinker). *The Tinker*, for small orchestra, eight characters and no chorus, uses spoken dialogues and recitatives; the music is in a fairly simple, agreeable musical style owing less to Mozart than to early Romantic Italian and French opera and German Singspiel. As required by the national revival feelings, Škroup tried to imitate Czech national song. *The Tinker* used to be regarded as the first Czech opera; in fact, since most of Škroup's principal predecessors and contemporaries wrote to German or Italian texts, he was a pioneer in this field only for his period and his circle, for there are many Czech 'folk' operas of the 18th century.

After the success of *The Tinker*, in which Škroup sang the title role, he devoted himself entirely to music, theatre music especially. In 1827 he became second Kapellmeister at the Estates Theatre, in 1837 first Kapellmeister. He directed the company successfully up to 1857 when he was dismissed because of a disagreement with the director, J. A. Stöger. He then conducted various concert groups and opened a singing school; in 1860 he became Kapellmeister at Rotterdam opera, where again he achieved great success.

The opera and Singspiel repertory given by Škroup in Prague consisted mostly of the works required by public taste: historical dramas, genre-scenes, fairy-tales and thrillers. But he did introduce to Prague many valuable works by Marschner, Spohr, Halévy, Meyerbeer, Lortzing and others, among them Gluck's *Iphigénie en Tauride* and Verdi's *Nabucco, Rigoletto* and *Il trovatore*. He also gave the first Prague Wagner productions, *Tannhäuser* in 1854 and *Lohengrin* and *Der fliegende Holländer* in 1856 (when he organized a special Wagner week). He also gave Beethoven's *Fidelio* and works by Mozart, and he wrote insertions for *La Juive*, Cherubini's *Médée* and Bellini's *Beatrice di Tenda*. In his role as Kapellmeister he wrote much incidental music, especially for plays by J. K. Tyl, of which the most famous is *Fidlovačka* ('Shoemakers' Feast', 1834), a farce describing Prague society on the background of the Easter fair and guild feast. The music consists of 21 numbers – overture, interludes, dances, songs and choruses, some of them quoting popular folk melodies. One song, 'Kde domov můj' ('Where is my home') soon became a national hymn, and shortly after the foundation of Czechoslovakia in 1918 a part of the national anthem.

After *The Tinker*, Škroup wrote other, but less successful, Czech and German operas and Singspiels. To meet the taste of the wider Prague public he composed four fairy-tales, of which only *Der Nachtschatten* (1830) survives; the score shows the influence of Weber. His first attempt at a historical drama in music was *Oldřich a Božena* ('Oldřich and Božena', 1828). Chmelenský's libretto dealt here with the half-mythical story of love and marriage of a Czech 11th-century prince. In 1833 Škroup's opera also appeared in a German version (*Udalrich und Božena*). Also based on Czech legendary history was his and Chmelenský's last Czech opera, *Libušin sňatek* ('Libussa's Wedding'), composed and performed in 1835, rewritten in 1849 and given again in 1850. The libretto deals with the origins of Bohemia and the foundation of the first Czech princely dynasty, the Přemyslids (a popular subject that gave rise to numerous plays and operas, including works by Albinoni, Kreutzer, Grillparzer and, perhaps most important, Smetana). Škroup's *Drahomíra*, written to a German text by a philologist, student of aesthetics and gymnasium professor Václav Alois Svoboda-Navarovský (1848), was to picture the life and death of St Wenceslas and his mother, Princess Drahomíra, against the background of the struggle between pagans and Christians in 10th-century Bohemia (again a popular subject in music and drama, widely used, notably by Dvořák in his oratorio *St Ludmila*). Affected by the revolutionary movements of 1848, Škroup turned in 1851 to the history of the Netherlands. *Der Meergeuse* (to a libretto by the Prague writer and newspaper editor J. C. Hickel, who worked as theatre repertory adviser in Prague and Vienna), describes an episode of the Dutch revolt against Spanish rule in the 16th century; it was the most successful opera première of the year in Prague and brought Škroup one of his greatest triumphs in Rotterdam in 1861. His most important musical work, *Columbus*, based again on a libretto by Hickel and composed in 1855, was never performed during his lifetime.

Škroup's enterprise in his choice of the repertory for the Estates Theatre is only modestly reflected in his own work. The strongest points of his compositions are the fresh *buffo* scenes, the moving lyrical songs and the use of well-balanced and colourful orchestration. He based *The Tinker* on the late Classical opera idiom, coloured by national elements. But the fresh, *buffo* naivety so successful there did not suit his other operas. The sophisticated poetic structure of Chmelenský's later librettos for *Oldřich and Božena* and *Libussa's Wedding*, with their historical plots which required such careful handling, led to works that are dramatically lifeless. The best of each work is found in the individual songs that became popular. *Der Meergeuse*, with a plot concerning a different part of Europe and a libretto full of theatrical effects (Hickel had served in the army and drew on his experience in his dramatic works) offered a freer field to explore. The work is influenced by contemporary German and Italian opera – in places it even shows a neo-romantic feeling – and is dramatically well built. The same applies to *Columbus*, which was influenced by French grand opera. Škroup's style might be called eclectic, based on his work as a Kapellmeister; his work is chiefly of value as a successful experiment in the composition not simply of Czech but European music. This was not easy in the Bohemia of his time; the barriers erected by the nationalist revival movement, which wanted to make the music serve their artistic objectives through the use of folksong, were to be fully overcome only in the work of Smetana and Dvořák.

all first performed in Prague

Dráteník [The Tinker] op.1 (Spl, J. K. Chmelenský), Estates, 2 Feb 1826 (Prague, 1913)
Oldřich a Božena op.19 (3, Chmelenský), 14 Dec 1828; as Udalrich und Božena, 12 Feb 1833; 2 songs in F. J. Škroup and J. K. Chmelenský, eds.: Věnec ze zpěvů vlastenských [Garland of Patriotic Songs], i (Prague, 1835), iii (Prague, 1837)
Der Nachtschatten, 1827 (3, K. Schikaneder), Jan 1830
Der Prinz und die Schlange (Spl, 3, F. V. Ernst), 1829; Cz. version 1835; lost
Libušin sňatek [Libussa's Wedding] op.20 (3, Chmelenský), 6 Nov 1835; rev. version, 11 April 1850; excerpts in Věnec zpěvů vlastenských, i (Prague, 1835), iv (Prague, 1838)
Die Drachenhöhle bei Röthelstein, oder Der Hammer um Mitternacht (Spl, I. Kollmann), 28 May 1832, lost
Die Geisterbraut (Ernst, after W. Irwing), 17 Nov 1836, lost
Drahomíra (3, V. A. Svoboda-Navarovský), 20 Nov 1848
Der Meergeuse op.34 (3, J. C. Hickel), 29 Oct 1851
Columbus op.38, 1855 (3, Hickel), 1942

*

J. B. Pešek: *František Škroup* (Prague, 1901)
J. Plavec: *František Škroup* (Prague, 1941)
M. Kopecká: *Vztah slova a hudby v lyrických částech jevištních děl a kupletech Františka Škroupa* [The Relationship of Words and Music in the Lyrical Sections of the Dramatic Works and Couplets of František Škroup] (diss., Charles U., Prague, 1973)
J. Tyrrell: *Czech Opera* (Cambridge, 1988)

MICHAELA FREEMANOVÁ

Škroup [Skraup], **Jan Nepomuk** (*b* Osice, 15 Sept 1811; *d* Prague, 5 May 1892). Bohemian composer and conductor, brother of František Jan Škroup. He became a vice-Kapellmeister of the Prague Estates Theatre in 1836. From 1838 he was choirmaster, and in 1840 he became second Kapellmeister. In 1843 he conducted the Czech opera performances in the Prague Růžová Street theatre, for whose opening in 1842 he had written the *Slavná overtura* ('Festival Overture'). He left the theatre to become a director of the Sophien-Akademie (1844–9) and Kapellmeister of Prague Cathedral (from 1845). In 1874 he returned to the Estates Theatre as second Kapellmeister and choirmaster.

For the theatre Škroup wrote incidental music, overtures and other pieces. His first opera, *Elfriede*, may have been intended for children. In 1845 he wrote *Švédové v Praze* ('The Swedes in Prague'), but only the first act was performed, at a benefit concert, and with no great success. It was not given complete until 1867, with its libretto reworked. Nothing is known of *La fiancée du gnome*, mentioned by Wurzbach and Teuber. As far as can be judged from *Švédové v Praze*, Škroup's style was based more on national music than on the Italian, French and German operatic idioms he must have met during his years spent in the theatre.

Elfriede (? children's op, 3, J. Siegl), Prague, before 1828
La fiancée du gnome, ?1836 or ?1850 [according to Wurzbach and Teuber]
Švédové v Praze [The Swedes in Prague], 1845 (3, J. Pečírka); lib. rev. by E. Züngel, Prague, Provisional, 22 April 1867
Der Liebesring (comic op, 3, H. T. Schmid), Prague, 18 Dec 1861
Vineta, 1864 (3, Schmid), Prague, 11 June 1870

*

WurzbachL; *ČSHS*
O. Teuber: *Geschichte des Prager Theaters von den Anfängen des Schauspielwesens bis auf die neueste Zeit*, iii (Prague, 1888)
J. Plavec: *František Škroup* (Prague, 1941)
E. Léblova-Crhová: *Jan Nepomuk Škroup a jeho opera 'Švédové v Praze'* (thesis, Charles U., Prague, 1953)
J. Tyrrell: *Czech Opera* (Cambridge, 1988)

MICHAELA FREEMANOVÁ

Skuherský, František Zdeněk (Xavier Alois) (*b* Opočno, 31 July 1830; *d* Budweis [now České Budějovice], 19 Aug 1892). Bohemian composer. He attended the Prague Organ School, 1846–7, and in 1850 studied composition with Kittl. In 1854 he left for Innsbruck as a theatre conductor. However, having had no grounding in theatre work he soon became director of the music society and choirmaster at the university church. In 1866 he was appointed director of the Prague Organ School, where his pupils included Janáček, and from 1879 he taught at Prague University. Organ and sacred works form the nucleus of his output; his secular compositions lack individuality. The strongest aspect of Skuherský's talent was his melodic invention, which explains the popularity of individual scenes from his none-too-successful operas.

The opera subjects chosen by Skuherský reflect his love of history, a characteristic of Czech culture after 1850. The plot of the unfinished *Samo* is set in the 7th century in Samo's empire on Czech territory. *Der Apostat* describes the struggle between Christians and pagans in 9th-century Bulgaria; modified, in Czech, as *Vladimír, bohů zvolenec* ('Vladimir, the Gods' Chosen One'), it stayed in the repertory of the Provisional Theatre for several years. *Der Liebesring*, Skuherský's only opera to be staged in the original German version, is a fairy story about a magic ring. The plot of his comic opera *Der Rekrut* is set in Prague in 1547 and concerns a military episode in the life of a student of theology. An unusual feature is the sermon in the second act.

Samo (J. B. Staněk), inc., excerpts, Prague, 16 March 1854, lost
Der Apostat, before 1860 (historical op, 4, J. V. Frič), unperf.; in Cz. as Vladimír, bohů zvolenec [Vladimir, the Gods' Chosen One] (H. Mostecký [pseud. of Frič]), Prague, Provisional, 27 Sept 1863, *Cs-Pnm**
Der Liebesring, before 1860 (romantische Oper, 3, H. T. Schmid), Innsbruck, 26 Feb 1861; in Cz. as Lóra (2, K. Krása), Prague, Provisional, 13 April 1868, *Pnm**
Der Rekrut, before 1860 (comic op, 3, E. Züngel, after Raupach: *Vor hundert Jahren*); in Cz. as Rektor a generál [Rector and General], Prague, Provisional, 28 March 1873, *Pnm**, excerpts arr. pf (Prague, 1873)
Smrt krále Václava [King Wenceslas's Death], 1868 (J. Wenzig), inc., lost
Jaroslav ze Šternberka [Jaroslav Sternberg], 1873 (E. Krásnohorská, after Dvůr Králové MS), inc., lost

*

J. Bartoš: *Prozatímní divadlo a jeho opera* [The Provisional Theatre and its Opera] (Prague, 1938), 90–92, 253
J. Tyrrell: *Czech Opera* (Cambridge, 1988) JITKA LUDVOVÁ

Skulte, Ādolfs (*b* Kiev, 15/28 Oct 1909). Latvian composer. He graduated from the Latvian State Conservatory in 1934 and continued his studies in the practical composition class, 1934–6. He taught there from 1936 holding the chair in composition from 1948 to 1972 (professor from 1952).

Skulte is a versatile composer, one of the most remarkable in Latvia, who has shown a particular liking for large symphonic forms and music for the stage. A master of brilliant orchestral colour and displaying a penchant for picturesque programme music, he has an individual style which often leans on the melodic and metrical characteristics of Latvian folk music. In 1950 he was awarded the USSR State Prize for the music to the film *Rainis* (1949). His fairy-tale opera *Princese Gundega* ('Princess Gundega'; 4, after A. Brigadere) was first performed in Riga in 1971. This moral philosophical fairy-tale becomes a large-scale, romantic psychological music drama, wherein the orchestra is the most important means of expression and is treated in a neo-impressionistic manner; vocal parts are masterly and are melodically developed. The children's fairy-tale opera *Eža kazociņš* ('The Hedgehog's Coat', 1979; 3, after V. Plūdonis) has a picturesque colour and musical witticisms.

*

V. Briede-Bulavinova: *Opernoye tvorchestvo latyshkih kompozitorov* [Operas of Latvian Composers] (Leningrad, 1979)
I. Lukašinska: *Ādolfs Skulte* (Riga, 1987)
JĒKABS VĪTOLIŅŠ, ARNOLDS KLOTIŅŠ

Skupoy. Opera by V. A. Pashkevich; *see MISER, THE.*

Skupoy rïtsar'. Opera by S. V. Rakhmaninov; *see MISERLY KNIGHT, THE.*

Skylight Opera. American company, founded in 1960 in MILWAUKEE.

Slater, Montagu (*b* Millom, Cumberland, 23 Sept 1902; *d* London, 19 Dec 1956). English librettist. Benjamin Britten, after writing incidental music for three of Slater's plays and puppet-plays (1936–8), chose him as the librettist of *Peter Grimes*. The subject, derived from George Crabbe's poem, had already been shaped by Britten and Peter Pears, but Slater worked on the libretto in 1942–3 and composition took place in 1944–5. Its first performance was on 7 June 1945 at the postwar reopening of Sadler's Wells Theatre. That *Peter Grimes* won international acceptance and has remained the most performed of Britten's operas owes much to the character of the passionate hero (or anti-hero) created by Slater, and no less to the robust diversity of the surrounding personages, though the language itself is occasionally strained or improbable. Britten's *Ballad of Heroes* (1939) was dedicated to Slater and his wife Enid. Known chiefly as a poet and dramatist, Slater also wrote the libretto for Denis ApIvor's opera *Yerma* (broadcast 1961). ARTHUR JACOBS

Slatinaru, Maria (*b* Iaşi, 25 May 1938). Romanian soprano. She studied in Bucharest, where she made her début in 1969 as Elisabeth de Valois. She has sung in Germany, France and Switzerland. Though her roles include Wagner's Elisabeth, Senta, Sieglinde and Elsa, as well as Leonore, Abigaille (*Nabucco*) and Amelia (*Simon Boccanegra*), her rich voice with its powerful middle register is especially well suited to the veristic repertory: Santuzza, Maddalena (*Andrea Chénier*), Puccini's Manon Lescaut, Minnie, Giorgetta, which she sang in Paris (1982) and Florence (1983), and above all Tosca, which she sang in San Francisco (1985), Dallas (1988) and at many other theatres. ELIZABETH FORBES

Slavina, Mariya (*b* St Petersburg, 24 May/5 June 1858; *d* Paris, 1951). Russian mezzo-soprano. She studied at the St Petersburg Conservatory with Natalia Iretzkaya and Camillo Everardi. In 1879 she made her début as Amneris at the Mariinsky Theatre, St Petersburg, where she later created the roles of Hanna in Rimsky-Korsakov's *May Night* (1880), Konchakovna in *Prince Igor* (1890), the Countess in *The Queen of Spades* (1890) and Clytemnestra in Taneyev's *Oresteia* (1895). Her best role was Carmen, which she introduced to Russian audiences, and she was a notable Olga (*Yevgeny Onegin*), Fidès (*Le prophète*), Ortrud, Fricka and Waltraute. She left Russia at the time of the Revolution and taught singing in Paris. DAVID CUMMINGS

Slezak, Leo (*b* Schönberg [now Šumperk], Moravia, 18 Aug 1873; *d* Egern am Tegernsee, Austria, 1 June 1946). Austrian-Czech tenor. Discovered and trained by the well-known baritone and teacher Adolf Robinson, he first appeared at Brno on 17 March 1896, as Lohengrin. His early career was somewhat chequered; and his Covent Garden début, again as Lohengrin, on 18 May 1900, was ruined by the pandemonium aroused by the news of the relief of Mafeking. By contrast, his career in Vienna, whither he was called by Mahler in 1901, was brilliant and prolonged; he remained one of the leading tenors of the house until the mid-1920s, and made occasional guest appearances as late as 1933. His international fame grew after a period of study with Jean de Reszke in 1907. A marked improvement was noted on his reappearance as Otello at Covent Garden in 1909; this remained one of his most successful parts, and served for his New York début on 17 November of the same year. He remained with the Metropolitan company for four consecutive seasons, singing his main Wagner roles (Tannhäuser, Lohengrin, Siegfried, Walther), Verdi's Manrico and Radames, and Tchaikovsky's Hermann (see illustration overleaf). His autobiographical books show his irrepressible sense of fun; and a similar volume by his son, the actor Walter Slezak, called *What Time's the Next Swan?* (New York, 1962), alludes to the tenor's celebrated stage whisper on an occasion when the *Lohengrin* swan began to move off before he had stepped aboard.

Leo Slezak as Siegfried in Wagner's 'Ring'

L. Slezak: *Song of Motley* (London, 1938)
J. Dennis: 'Leo Slezak', *Record Collector*, xv (1964), 197–235 [with discography by T. G. Kaufman] DESMOND SHAWE-TAYLOR

Šlezinger, Josif (*b* Sombor, 1794; *d* Belgrade, 1870). Serbian composer and conductor of Jewish origin. He taught music in Šabac and held a conducting post in Novi Sad. Invited in 1831 to the court of Prince Miloš Obrenović, he founded and directed the prince's Serbian Orchestra, which played in his Serbian Theatre in Kragujevac and Belgrade. In 1840 he moved with the court to Belgrade, where he was active until 1864. He was the outstanding figure of early Serbian stage life and composed and arranged music for several plays, containing overtures and vocal and instrumental numbers: many of the songs were influenced by Serbian or oriental folktunes and achieved wide popularity. Owing to its musical richness *Ženidba cara Dušana* ('The Marriage of Tsar Dušan'; 1840, Kragujevac) is regarded as an opera, although Šlezinger conceived the music to accompany Atanasije Nikolić's play.

*

S. Đurić-Klajn: 'Razvoj muzičke umetnosti u Srbiji' [The Development of the Art of Music in Serbia], in J. Andreis, D. Cvetko and S. Đurić-Klajn: *Historijski razvoj muzičke kulture u Jugoslaviji* (Zagreb, 1962), 531–709
B. Stojković: *Istorija srpskog pozorišta od srednjeg veka do modernog doba* [The History of Serbian Theatre from the Medieval to the Modern Period] (Belgrade, 1977)

ROKSANDA PEJOVIĆ

Slippers, The. Opera by P. I. Tchaikovsky; *see* CHEREVICHKI.

Slobodskaya, Oda (*b* Vilna [now Vilnius], 10 Dec 1888; *d* London, 29 July 1970). Russian soprano. She studied at the St Petersburg Conservatory and made her début, as Lisa (*Queen of Spades*), at the Mariinsky Theatre in 1919. During the following years she sang there many of the principal soprano parts of the Russian and international repertories. In 1922 she sang Parasha at the first performance, in Paris, of Stravinsky's *Mavra*; she also sang, in Italian, the heroine of Rimsky-Korsakov's *Invisible City of Kitezh* at La Scala in 1933. A greater career might well have been hers but for the vicissitudes of exile from Russia during a time of war and international confusion. Nevertheless, she appeared in London with Shalyapin in Dargomïzhsky's *Rusalka* (Lyceum, 1931), as Venus in *Tannhäuser* (Covent Garden, 1932), and as Palmyra in the British première, under Beecham, of Delius's *Koanga* (Covent Garden, 1935). In England, where she eventually made her home, she became famous for her live and broadcast recitals of Russian song, of which she made many brilliant recordings to a surprisingly advanced age.

*

O. Slobodskaya (as told to G. Eves): 'Reminiscences', *Recorded Sound*, xxxv (1969), 495–511 [with discography by H. Barnes and S. Junge]
M. Leonard: *Slobodskaya: a Biography of Oda Slobodskaya* (London, 1979) [with discography]

DESMOND SHAWE-TAYLOR

Slonimsky, Sergey Mikhaylovich (*b* Leningrad [now St Petersburg], 12 Aug 1932). Russian composer. He studied at the Leningrad Conservatory, graduating from O. Yevlakhov's composition class in 1955 and from V. Nilsen's piano class in 1956. In 1959 he was appointed to teach theory at the Leningrad Conservatory; he joined the composition faculty there in 1967. He was awarded the State Prize of the RSFSR in 1983 and was named People's Artist of the RSFSR in 1987. One of the post-Stalin generation of Soviet composers, Slonimsky gained a reputation from the 1960s for stretching the limits of the permissible in Soviet music. He was among the first Soviet composers to experiment with 12-note and aleatory techniques, graphic notation and extended instrumental resources, as well as with the fusion of popular and serious genres. Extensive participation in folklore expeditions also left a perceptible mark on the composer's style, in a predilection for modal and microtonal melodic inflections and asymmetrical rhythmic patterns.

A large proportion of Slonimsky's output has consisted of vocal and choral music. His innate lyrical gift was underlined by a powerful flair for the dramatic in his first opera, *Virineya* (1967), based on a tale of the confusion and conflicting passions in post-revolutionary Russia. His second opera, *Master i Margarita*, based on Bulgakov's masterpiece, attracted attention for other reasons. Completed in 1972, it fell victim to the Soviet cultural bureaucracy; for 17 years, until its concert première in Moscow in 1989, the opera was regarded as a conspicuous symbol of artistic repression in Soviet society. His third opera, *Mariya Styuart*, was less controversial in its treatment of the familiar historical subject and in its highly accessible musical idiom. Since the staging of the opera in 1981, the composer has turned his attention to the composition of instrumental music.

See also MARIYA STYUART; MASTER I MARGARITA; and VIRINEYA.

Virineya (3, S. Tsenin, after L. Seyfullina), Leningrad, Malïy, 30 Sept 1967; rev. version, Leningrad, Malïy, Feb 1976

Master i Margarita [The Master and Margarita], 1970–72 (chamber op, 3, Yu. Dimitrin and V. Fialkovsky, after M. Bulgakov), concert perf., Moscow, Bol'shoy Hall of the Conservatory, 20 May 1989; stage, Moscow, Mossovet, 11 Feb 1991
Mariya Styuart [Mary Stuart] (opera-ballade, 3, Ya. A. Gordin, after S. Zweig), Kuybïshev, Opera and Ballet Theatre, 31 Jan 1981; Leningrad, Maliy, 18 April 1981
Gamlet, 1990 (dramma per musica, 3, Ya. Gordin, after W. Shakespeare: *Hamlet*)

*

'Na obsuzhdenii "Virinei" S. Slonimskogo' [Discussing Slonimsky's 'Virineya'], *SovM* (1968), no.4, pp.31–46
S. Slonimsky: 'O "Virinee" v Moskve' [On 'Virineya' in Moscow], *SovM* (1969), no.2, pp.22
V. Smirnov: ' "Virineya" S. Slonimskogo', *Voprosï teorii i estetiki muzïki* [Problems of Theory and Aesthetics in Music], ed. L. Raaben, xi (Leningrad, 1972), 50–67
A. Milka: *Sergey Slonimsky: monograficheskiy ocherk* (Leningrad, 1976)
G. Belov: 'Novaya redaktsiya "Virinei" ' [A New Approach to 'Virineya'], *SovM* (1977), no.1, pp.79–84
A. Kenigsberg: 'Mary Stuart: Sergey Slonimsky's New Opera', *Music in the USSR* (1982), no.2, p.48
A. Milka: 'Yarkaya partitura, interesnoye voploshcheniye' [A Vivid Score, an Interesting Composition], *SovM* (1982), no.2, pp.26–31 [on *Mary Stuart*]
A. Klimovitsky: 'Opernoye tvorchestvo Sergeya Slonimskogo' [The Operas of Sergey Slonimsky], *Sovremennay Sovetstaya opera* [Contemporary Soviet Opera] (Leningrad, 1985), 24–59
'Passions Raging on the Stage: a Leipzig Production of Sergey Slonimsky's Mary Stuart', *Music in the USSR* (1985), April–June, 12–13
V. Kholopova: '"Filosofskaya kamerata" Sergeya Slonimskogo', *SovM* (1989), no.10, pp.22–5 [on *Master and Margarita*]
A. Klimovitsky: 'Procrastination Still at Work', *Music in the USSR* (1989), July–Sept, 14–17 [on *Master and Margarita*]
M. Rïtsareva: *Kompozitor Sergey Slonimsky: monografiya* (Leningrad, 1991) LAUREL E. FAY

Slorach, Marie (*b* Glasgow, 8 May 1951). Scottish soprano. She studied at the Royal Scottish Academy of Music and in 1974 joined Scottish Opera, with whom her roles have included Marzelline, Gretel, Zerlina, Mimì, Musetta, Adina, Tatyana, Leïla, Eva, Liù, Mařenka, the Governess (*The Turn of the Screw*), Jenifer (*The Midsummer Marriage*) and Fiordiligi. At Wexford she sang Maliella (*I gioielli della Madonna*) and Vendulka (*The Kiss*). With the ENO she has sung Lisa (*The Queen of Spades*) and Donna Elvira; with Glyndebourne Touring Opera, Donna Anna, Electra (*Idomeneo*) and Amelia (*Simon Boccanegra*); with Opera North, Micaëla, Kát'a and Ellen (*Peter Grimes*). A strongly dramatic singer, she excels in portraying passionate characters such as Lisa or Mozart's Electra.

ELIZABETH FORBES

Slovakia. The republic of Slovakia differs from Bohemia and Moravia (the other parts of Czechoslovakia) in several crucial respects, and the history of Slovak opera is quite unlike that of Czech opera. While the Czechs had maintained an independent kingdom until 1620, the Slovaks had been part of Hungary since 1018 and were brought together with Bohemia and Moravia in 1526 under Habsburg rule. Despite the similar tongue (until the 1840s Slovak was generally treated as a dialect of Czech), the adjacent areas were never integrated. An administrative boundary divided the Czech lands – part of the Austrian (Cisleithan) region – from Slovakia – part of the Hungarian (Transleithan) region; the division was made even more rigid in the dual monarchy of 1867. In the 1860s, when the Czechs were taking advantage of the Habsburgs' faltering grip by creating their own cultural institutions, the Hungarians were promoting a policy of aggressive magyarization at the expense of the minorities (including the Slovaks) who happened to fall in their orbit. Thus while the Czechs were able to establish a continuous tradition of Czech-language opera from the 1860s, Slovak culture was being fast eroded. Bratislava, through its proximity to Vienna and its years as the coronation capital of Hungary during the Turkish occupation, had become an important cultural centre in the 18th century, but as a German and increasingly a Hungarian city.

Opera composers of Slovak origin existed, but, like 18th-century Czech composers, they made their contribution in other languages, and to other cultures. Maciej Kamieński (Kamenický) wrote the first Polish opera in 1778, Jozef Chudý wrote the first Hungarian opera in 1793, and József Ruzitska (Jozef Ružička) wrote the oldest surviving Hungarian opera in 1822. Even a century later, a figure as substantial as Ján Levoslav Bella, the 'father of Slovak music', wrote his only completed opera in German. When independence came to the country in the form of political union with Bohemia and Moravia in 1918, there was not a single Slovak opera that the newly established Slovak national opera (1920) could perform.

Slovak operas were written in the 1920s by Viliam Figuš-Bystrý, František Dostalík and Jozef Grešák. Czech opera inevitably provided a model, both through the training of Slovak composers (many of whom studied under Vítězslav Novák) and in the pattern of development, with an emphasis on regional folksong (Figuš-Bystrý's *Detvan*, 1928) and on subjects derived from history or folklore. None of these operas forms part of a national repertory today, but some of those by composers who came into prominence in the 1930s, Jozef Rosinský, Alexander Moyzes and Ladislav Holoubek, have proved more durable.

The turning-point in Slovak opera came after World War II with the première of Eugen Suchoň's *Krútňava* ('The Whirlpool', 1949), a work that soon came to be regarded as the quintessential Slovak opera despite its evident stylistic debts to Janáček, Strauss, Busoni and Berg. A decade later Suchoň followed this tragic opera based on folklore with a historical opera, *Svätopluk*, based on the Great Moravian Empire. With the completion in the 1950s of the first operas of Ján Cikker it soon became clear that Slovakia had two opera composers of a calibre unmatched in postwar Czech opera. Cikker wrote operas at a much faster rate than Suchoň and soon discarded Slovak-conscious material. From his third and fourth operas (based respectively on Dickens and Tolstoy) he began to adopt a style that was more aware of international developments, and its influence can be detected in the operas of the next generation of Slovak composers, including Juraj Beneš, Tadeáš Salva and Juraj Hatrík.

For further information on operatic life in the country's principal centres *see* BANSKÁ BYSTRICA; BRATISLAVA; and KOŠICE.

*

Š. Hoza: *Opera na Slovensku* [Opera in Slovakia] (Martin, 1953–4)
P. Eckstein: *Czechoslovak Opera: a Brief Outline* (Prague, 1964)
——: *Die tschechoslowakische zeitgenössischer Oper/The Czechoslovak Contemporary Opera* (Prague and Bratislava, 1967)
Z. Nováček: *Hudba v Bratislave* [Music in Bratislava] (Bratislava, 1978) [text in Slovak, Ger., Eng. and Russ.]
L. Polyakova: *Cheshkaya i slovatskaya opera XX. veka* [Czech and Slovak Opera of the 20th Century], i (Moscow, 1983)
I. Vajda: *Slovenská opera* [Slovak Opera] (Bratislava, 1988)

JOHN TYRRELL

Slovenia. The sub-Alpine region between the gulf of Trieste and the river Drava, though populated by Slavs, was divided between several Austrian duchies in the Middle Ages and remained within Austria-Hungary until its incorporation in 1918 into the state of Yugoslavia; in 1992 it became an independent republic. Dramatic performances with music were a strong feature in the Ljubljana Jesuit theatre in the 17th century, but a lack of sustained patronage meant that until the second half of the 18th century operatic activity was sporadic. Seasons of German and Italian opera became a regular feature after 1770. In the 1770s and 80s Zollner's and Schikaneder's troupes paid regular visits to Ljubljana and provided a stimulus for the first Singspiel in Slovenian, J. B. Novak's *Figaro* (1790). In spite of a rich musical tradition in the region, Slovenian Romantic opera was slow to develop since the domination of the German and Italian repertory was ensured by the German Ständisches Theater in Ljubljana (later the Landestheater, where Mahler conducted during the season 1881–2). The first crop came late in the century with the works of Anton Foerster, Benjamin Ipavec and Viktor Parma. Risto Savin quickly moved away from a simple Romantic idiom using elements of Wagner's and Strauss's language. In the 1920s Slovenian composers came much closer to the central European mainstream than their contemporaries in the rest of the newly-formed state of Yugoslavia: Marij Kogoj, Slavko Osterc and Matija Bravničar wrote in advanced harmonic as well as atonal idioms. Kogoj's *Črne maske* ('Black Masks', 1929) is a powerful, if uneven, expressionist work; Osterc moved from his early historical *Krst pri Savici* ('Baptism at the Savica Waterfall', composed 1921) towards expressionist operas and 'opéras minutes' written between 1919 and 1931.

A particularly fruitful period came after World War II with the operas by Danilo Švara and Marijan Kozina, although stylistically the composers at first retracted from the advanced idiom of the pre-war period. From the 1960s several Slovenian composers have succeeded in giving an individual mark to works reflecting current tendencies in opera and music theatre in Western Europe; among them Pavel Šivic's *Cortesova vrnitev* ('Cortés's Return', composed 1971) stands out. Darijan Božič combines sung and spoken word and uses a wide range of vocal sonorities in works that unite elements of opera, play and musical in a post-modernist manner: *Ares-Eros* (1971) was followed by *Lizistrata '75* (1980) and *Kralj Lear* (1986). An interesting example of bilingualism is to be found in Pavle Merkù's *La libellula* (1976): the music fits both Italian and Slovenian versions of the libretto without any need for adjustments. There are permanent opera companies in Ljubljana and Maribor.

For further information on operatic life in the country's principal centres *see* LJUBLJANA and MARIBOR.

*

J. Škerlj: *Italijanske predstave od XVII do XIX stoletja v Ljubljani* [Italian Performances in Ljubljana from the 17th to the 19th Centuries] (Ljubljana, 1936)

J. Sivec: *Opera v Stanovskem gledališču v Ljubljani od leta 1790–1861* [Opera in the Estates Theatre in Ljubljana from 1790 to 1861] (Ljubljana, 1971)

D. Cvetko: *Musikgeschichte der Südslawen* (Kassel and Maribor, 1975)

J. Sivec: *Opera skozi stoletja* [Opera through the Centuries] (Ljubljana, 1976)

Slovenska opera v evropskem okviru: ob njeni 200-letnici: Ljubljana 1982 [Slovene Opera Within the European Framework: on the Occasion of its Bicentenary]

BOJAN BUJIĆ

Sly [*Sly, ovvero La leggenda del dormiente risvegliato* ('Sly, or The Legend of the Sleeper Awoken')]. Opera in three acts by ERMANNO WOLF-FERRARI to a libretto by GIOVACCHINO FORZANO after the 'Induction' to WILLIAM SHAKESPEARE's *The Taming of the Shrew*; Milan, Teatro alla Scala, 29 December 1927.

Only the earlier part of this strange work (to a libretto that had been turned down by Puccini) bears any relationship at all to Shakespeare's comedy. As the opera unfolds, the action becomes increasingly tragic, until the protagonist – driven to despair by the treacherous twists and turns of his experience – takes his own life. Although very remote from the lightheartedly satirical subjects that usually brought out the best in Wolf-Ferrari, this disturbing story clearly struck a special chord with him in the aftermath of the personal crisis through which he had passed during World War I. The result, though much less widely known than *I gioielli della Madonna*, is surely the most deeply felt of his few serious operas.

As at the beginning of *The Taming of the Shrew*, Christopher Sly (tenor) collapses into a drunken stupor in an alehouse. Also present is a lord – identified here as the 'Conte di Westmoreland' (baritone) – who, like his anonymous Shakespearean prototype, decides to play an elaborate practical joke at Sly's expense: he tells his servants to convey the besotted drunkard (who in the opera is an impoverished poet rather than a tinker) to his castle. Still unconscious when he arrives there, Sly awakes to find himself dressed in splendid clothes and decked in jewellery. Bewildered, he is made to believe that he is a wealthy aristocrat who for ten years has been suffering from loss of memory. Westmoreland's mistress Dolly (soprano) plays a crucial part in the deception, by impersonating the wife whom Sly is led to believe he has forgotten. But it gradually dawns on her that she really loves him, and she feels moved to assure him of this after the cruel hoax has been revealed for what it is and Sly has been locked away in the castle cellar. In the last act Dolly secretly visits him in his confinement; but she finds him bleeding to death, having slashed his wrists with a broken bottle.

Viewed objectively, this plot may seem rather tortuous and implausible; and the music, too, may on paper seem dangerously eclectic. Verdi, Wagner and even Dvořák have all contributed something to the mixture; and more modern elements include unexpected suggestions of Weill at a few points in the alehouse scene. It is perhaps understandable that *Sly*, being so remote from most people's image of a typical Wolf-Ferrari opera, was for so many years neglected. Yet recent revivals in Germany, including an impressive recording, have shown that a good performance can have a surprisingly powerful impact, culminating in Sly's remarkable tragic monologue that dominates Act 3.

JOHN C. G. WATERHOUSE

Smallens, Alexander (*b* St Petersburg, 20 Dec 1888/1 Jan 1889; *d* Tucson, AZ, 24 Nov 1972). American conductor of Russian birth. He studied at the New York Institute of Musical Art and, from 1909, at the Paris Conservatoire, returning to the USA as assistant conductor of the Boston Opera, 1911–14. After two years as conductor of Pavlova's touring company, including a South American tour, he returned to become conductor of the Chicago Opera, 1919–23. He took American citizenship in 1919. His Chicago association began when he replaced Hasselmans as conductor for the première of Reginald De Koven's *Rip van Winkle* in 1920. He was musical director of the Philadelphia Civic Opera (1924–31), where he gave the American premières of Strauss's *Feuersnot* (1927) and *Ariadne auf Naxos* (1928). Later he moved towards a lighter repertory, conducting the première of Gershwin's *Porgy and Bess* at Boston in 1935 and taking a production of it on a European tour in 1952 that included its British stage première at the Stoll Theatre, London. From 1947 to 1950 he was music director of Radio City Music Hall, New York. BERNARD JACOBSON

Smareglia, Antonio (*b* Pola, Istria, 5 May 1854; *d* Grado, 15 April 1929). Italian composer. He found his vocation listening to the music of Mozart, Beethoven and Wagner in Vienna and Graz where he was studying mathematics. In 1871 he moved to Milan to study composition with Franco Faccio, first privately then at the conservatory from 1872 to 1877. The 1873 Milan première of *Lohengrin* found Smareglia among the work's staunchest supporters, and Wagnerian opera later exercised a major influence on his own works.

His formative years in Milan were influenced by the *Scapigliatura*, the late Romantic, progressive trend led by Faccio, Boito and Praga. The choice of subjects and the stylistic references of Smareglia's early works reflected the *scapigliati*'s tastes and attitudes and were to become similarly decadent. Boito became Smareglia's closest friend and mentor, sharing his enthusiasm for German Romanticism and German music. Within the *Scapigliatura* circle, Smareglia's apprenticeship and experiences were very similar to those of Alfredo Catalani, who attended the Milan Conservatory during the same period. His one-act 'Oriental eclogue' *La falce* and Smareglia's dramatic sketch *Caccia lontana* were performed in the Conservatory theatre in the summer of 1875 within weeks of each other and established their composers as the most promising young musicians in Milan. They also earned the support of the progressive publisher Giovanna Lucca, who printed Smareglia's first two operas and nearly all those of Catalani.

Smareglia's *Preziosa* (1879) and *Bianca da Cervia* (1882) seem disappointingly conventional, based as they are on the uninspired imitation of Verdi's middle-period style and *grand opéra*. Sequences of unremarkable vocal numbers strung together by dull recitatives characterize these early works which Smareglia later disowned as 'contemptible nonsense', though they were well received by Milanese audiences and critics. A third opera, *Re Nala*, was written in Milan and had its première in Venice in 1887. This was the only failure in Smareglia's career and was subsequently destroyed by the composer. It also brought to an end his Milanese period.

In the next few years, Smareglia moved away from Italian models and assimilated Wagnerian compositional techniques, in pursuit of a more congenial form of music theatre that favoured symphonic treatment at the expense of vocal supremacy. *Il vassallo di Szigeth* (1889), *Cornill Schut* (1893) and *Nozze istriane* (1895) marked innovative stages in Smareglia's artistic evolution, and the librettist, Luigi Illica, mediated between contemporary trends and the composer's sensibility. *Il vassallo* followed the fashion for funereal and demonic subjects that flourished in the 1880s. As a belated product of the *Scapigliatura*, *Il vassallo* has a weird and muddled story, set in 13th-century Hungary, and featuring Andor, master of Szigeth, his brother Milos (both in love with Naja) and their satanic vassal Rolf, who causes the woman's death by poison and Andor's killing at the hands of Milos. The opera was first performed with great success in Vienna under Hans Richter and praised by Brahms. *Cornill Schut* (dealing with 17th-century Flemish painters) was also successfully performed in Dresden and Prague, and then in Vienna under Richter. Reviewing *Il vassallo* Hanslick noted how Smareglia had mastered 'all the new skills of orchestration'.

In 1894 Smareglia returned to Istria and stayed for a few months in Dignano where he was joined by Illica who was to work with him on the adaptation of Flaubert's *Tentation de Saint Antoine*. Illica, however, suggested that, after the furore caused by *Cavalleria rusticana*, a veristic subject might prove a better choice. The village life of Dignano was ready at hand to be portrayed by the librettist, and the composer was obviously familiar with the customs and folklore of his own land. *Nozze istriane* was written in the summer of 1894 and had its première in Trieste with the first interpreters of *Cavalleria*, Gemma Bellincioni and Roberto Stagno, in the leading roles. In 1908 the opera reached the Volksoper in Vienna. The critic of the *Neue Musik-Zeitung*, Max Dietz, praised the work as an original synthesis of the German, Italian and Slav musical traditions. *Nozze istriane* had little in common with the *verismo* of the 1890s: the vocal parts are delicately combined with a minute and transparent instrumental embroidery; there are no violent outbursts or naturalistic shouts; the action allows for humorous scenes of Rossinian subtlety (for example, the duets between the old miser Menico and the marriage-broker Biagio). Similarities could more easily be found with Smetana's *The Bartered Bride* than with contemporary veristic operas.

A crucial turning-point in Smareglia's production came with *La falena* (1897) and *Oceàna* (1903), the best examples of his allusive, purely musical theatre. Wagner's *Tristan* and *Das Rheingold* had a clear influence on the last phase of the composer's evolution, but the music bears the imprint of a strong personality and the aesthetic conception has a different, original character. *La falena* and *Oceàna* are undramatic, oneiric fantasies consisting of vast, symphonic movements which convey a psychological mood (anguish, erotic frenzy) or suggest an ambience (harvest time, a seascape, night and dawn), but blur contrasts and dampen action. The texts were arranged by the young writer Silvio Benco (1874–1949), who artfully combined decadent and symbolist elements: the lustful Falena is Baudelaire's 'Sorcière au flanc d'ébène, enfants des noirs minuits' seen through D'Annunzian eyes; the evanescent sea creatures of *Oceàna*, as Benco himself wrote, are akin to the fairies of *A Midsummer Night's Dream*, and to the tritons and nereids painted by Arnold Böcklin.

Benco also wrote the libretto of Smareglia's last opera, *Abisso* (1914), an overtly D'Annunzian imitation. Like *Oceàna*, it was performed at La Scala only thanks to the wholehearted support of Boito and Toscanini. The hostility of Italy's major publisher, Ricordi, as well as Smareglia's awkward character (worsened by the total blindness that struck him in 1900), have been blamed for the undeserved oblivion into which his operas fell. In the years that saw the creation of *Pelléas et Mélisande* and *Salome*, Smareglia remained a late 19th-century Romantic composer, a fine lyricist and an excellent orchestrator. As Benco put it in his *Ricordi*:

He did not belong to this world intellectually and psychologically saturated with refined drugs: he was an unsophisticated and sound man who would not conceive of leading music through the sense of sin or the fluctuations of the uncertainty of existence.

See also FALENA, LA; NOZZE ISTRIANE; and OCEÀNA.

Caccia lontana (scena melodrammatica), Milan, Conservatory, 10 Aug 1875
Preziosa (dramma lirico, 3, after H. W. Longfellow: *The Spanish Student*), Milan, Dal Verme, 20 Nov 1879, *I-Mr**, vs (Milan, 1880)
Bianca da Cervia (dramma lirico, 4, F. Fulgonio [F. Pozza]), Milan, Scala, 7 Feb 1882, *Mr**, vs (Milan, 1882)
Re Nala (melodramma, 4, V. Valle, after A. De Gubernatis: *Il ritorno*), Venice, Fenice, 9 Feb 1887 [destroyed by composer]
Il vassallo di Szigeth (os, 3, L. Illica and F. Pozza), as Der Vasall von Szigeth, Vienna, Hofoper, 18 June [or ?4 Oct] 1889, vs (Leipzig, n.d.); in orig. It., Pola, Ciscutti, 4 Oct 1930
Cornill Schut (dramma lirico, 3, Illica), as Cornelius Schut, Dresden, Hofoper, 6 June 1893 [according to A. Loewenberg: *Annals of Opera* and others, 1st perf. Prague, 20 May 1893]; in orig. It., Trieste, Comunale, 17 Feb 1900, vs (Leipzig, n.d.); rev. as Pittori fiamminghi, Trieste, Verdi, 21 Jan 1928, vs (Milan, 1927)
Nozze istriane (dramma lirico, 3, Illica), Trieste, Comunale, 28 March 1895, vs (Trieste, n.d.)
La falena (leggenda, 3, S. Benco), Venice, Rossini, 6 Sept 1897, vs (Leipzig, ?1908)
Oceàna (commedia fantastica, 3, Benco), Milan, Scala, 22 Jan 1903, vs (Milan, 1902)
Abisso (dramma lirico, 3, Benco), Milan, Scala, 10 Feb 1914, vs (Vienna, ?1913)

*

E. Hanslick: 'Der Vasall von Szigeth', *Die moderne Oper*, vi: *Aus dem Tagebuche eines Musikers* (Berlin, 1892), 147–54
——: 'Cornelius Schut', *Die moderne Oper*, vii: *Fünf Jahre Musik (1891–1895)* (Berlin, 1896), 124–31
I. Valetta: 'Antonio Smareglia e *La Falena*', *Nuova Antologia*, xxxii (1897), 535–42
M. Kalbeck: 'Cornelius Schut', *Opernabende* (Berlin, 1898), 54
——: 'Der Vasall von Szigeth', ibid, 46
L. Torchi: 'Oceàna', *RMI*, x (1903), 309–66
R. Specht: *Oceàna-Ouverture* (Vienna, *c*1907)
——: *Oceàna-Suite* (Vienna, *c*1907)
M. Dietz: 'Istrianische Hochzeit', *Neue Musik-Zeitung*, xxix/10–11 (1908), 221–3
J. Korngold: 'Istrianische Hochzeit', *Die romantische Oper der Gegenwart* (Vienna, 1908), 216ff
R. Wallascheck: 'Istrianische Hochzeit', *Die Zeit* (Vienna, 1908)
L'illustrazione istriana, i (1923), no.4 [complete issue on Smareglia]
G. Zuccoli: *Antonio Smareglia* (Trieste, 1923)
'*Abisso* di Antonio Smareglia a Trieste', *Cronache musicali*, ii/4 (1926), 2
V. Levi: 'Un grande operista italiano: Antonio Smareglia', *RMI*, xxxvi (1929), 600–15
A. Smareglia: *Vita ed arte di Antonio Smareglia: un capitolo di storia del teatro lirico italiano* (Lugano, 1932, 2/1936)
M. Smareglia: *Antonio Smareglia nella storia del melodramma italiano: raccolta di critiche musicali e di altri documenti* (Pola, 1934)
V. Levi: *Oceàna di Antonio Smareglia: guida attraverso l'opera* (Trieste, 1949)
B. Bidussi: 'Antonio Smareglia e la critica italiana', *Pagine istriane* (1950), 315–18
V. Levi: *Nozze istriane: nel centenario della nascita di Antonio Smareglia* (Trieste, 1954)
H. Tomicich: *Der grosse Einsame* (Berlin, 1954)
V. Levi, G. Botteri and I. Bremini: *Il Comunale di Trieste* (Udine, 1961)
G. Viozzi: 'Civica onoranza ad Antonio Smareglia', *Umana*, xiii/7–9 (1964), 13–16
S. Benco: *Ricordi di Antonio Smareglia* (Duino, 1968)
G. Botteri: *Trieste 1868–1918* (Trieste, 1968)
V. Levi: *La vita musicale a Trieste: cronache di un cinquantennio (1918–68)* (Milan, 1968)
S. Benco: *Scritti musicali* (Milan and Naples, 1974)
R. Tedeschi: *Addio fiorito asil: Il melodramma italiano da Boito al verismo* (Milan, 1978)
E. Perpich: *Il teatro musicale di Antonio Smareglia* (Trieste and Rovigno, 1990)

MATTEO SANSONE

Smetana, Bedřich (*b* Litomyšl, 2 March 1824; *d* Prague, 12 May 1884). Czech composer. Smetana was the most important of the new generation of Czech opera composers writing from the 1860s. His eight operas established a canon of Czech operas to serve as models for Czech nationalist opera and have remained in the Czech repertory ever since. His comic opera *Prodaná nevěsta* ('The Bartered Bride') was by far the most popular of these and from the 1890s was the only Czech opera before Janáček's to be regularly performed abroad.

1. Life. 2. Operatic genres. 3. Smetana and Czech nationalist opera. 4. Operatic conventions and voice types. 5. Smetana and his librettists. 6. Smetana and the 'Czech' style.

1. LIFE. Smetana came from the small town of Litomyšl, where his father was a master brewer, and attended school there and in other provincial towns. After studying for a year in Prague (1839–40) he completed his schooling in Plzeň (1840–43). He played the violin and the piano from an early age and composed by the age of eight. The range of music he came across was haphazard: Beethoven, Mendelssohn, Chopin and Liszt (from his Prague concerts in 1840), but also light virtuoso piano music, military band music and popular dance music. He showed an early passion for the polka, and wrote many for the piano.

In 1843 he settled in Prague with a view to becoming a professional musician. He had theory lessons from Josef Proksch (1843–7) and earned his living as a private music tutor to the family of Count Leopold Thun (1844–7). At Proksch's musical institute, where he took part in concerts, his education proceeded more systematically with a grounding in music from Bach to Berlioz (whose Prague visit took place during this period). His own compositions became more varied. In addition to virtuoso piano pieces he wrote his first orchestral and first vocal compositions (to German and Latin texts). His first published work was the *Six morceaux caractéristiques* for piano which he sent to Liszt in an attempt to win his support for a musical institute he founded in 1848. Though Liszt did not help him financially, he found a publisher for the pieces and became an influential model. In 1849 Smetana married Kateřina Kolářová (1827–59), who bore him four daughters. Smetana continued to write piano pieces, but also more substantial works such as the Triumphal Symphony (1854) and a fine Piano Trio in G minor (1855) in memory of his eldest daughter (of the four only one grew to adulthood).

In the autumn of 1856 he took up an offer (via the pianist Alexander Dreyschock) to teach the piano in the Swedish town of Göteborg. Smetana opened an institute there and conducted the local choral society. A year later his wife and surviving daughter joined him. He did not complete a third season in Sweden: in April 1859 his wife became ill and died in Dresden on the way back to Bohemia. Smetana taught in Göteborg for two more seasons, in the second accompanied by his new wife, Bettina Ferdinandová (1840–1908), whom he married in July 1860 (there were two daughters from this union). Of the compositions from the Swedish period, the most important were three Lisztian tone poems, and a piece left in a rough piano score, *Macbeth a čarodějnice* ('Macbeth and the Witches').

In the spring of 1861 the Smetanas settled in Prague. By this time political conditions were much improved, allowing Czech cultural organizations to flourish, in particular the opening of a permanent Czech opera house, the Provisional Theatre, in 1862. Smetana had hoped to become chief conductor there or (in 1865) to succeed Kittl as director of the Prague Conservatory. In the event he had to make do with a mixture of private pupils and reviewing, working as chorus master at the Prague Hlahol (a choral society; 1863–5) and teaching at a musical institute he ran with Ferdinand Heller (1863–6). In response to the competition organized by Count Harrach for a Czech opera, he wrote *Braniboři v Čechách* ('The Brandenburgers in Bohemia', composed 1862–3). The work was performed in January 1866 and a few months later it took first prize in the Harrach competition. His next two operas, *The Bartered Bride* (1863–6) and *Dalibor* (1865–7), followed in quick succession.

With the political readjustments that took place after the Austro-Prussian war of 1866, the administration changed at the Provisional Theatre and Smetana replaced Jan Nepomuk Maýr as chief conductor. He held this post for eight years, during which period he did his best to promote his vision of Czech opera. Of his own works only *Dalibor* and *Dvě vdovy* ('The Two Widows', 1873–4) were given during this time; *Libuše*, which he wrote in between (1869–72), he kept in reserve for the opening of the National Theatre. His time at the theatre was not easy. He was a finer musician than his predecessor, but a slacker disciplinarian. He had vision, but lacked administrative skills. He drew criticism from within the company and without, and most notably from the influential singing teacher František Pivoda. Attempts to unseat him failed, however, until in October 1874 he became almost completely deaf (a symptom of his syphilitic condition) and had to give up his post as conductor. Maýr replaced him, and Smetana devoted himself entirely to composition (receiving a salary from the theatre in return for the performance rights to his operas). All attempts to find a cure for his condition were unsuccessful, and Smetana wrote the rest of his works in total deafness. These included five of the magnificent cycle of six symphonic poems *Má vlast* ('My Fatherland') and two string quartets, and his three last operas, *Hubička* ('The Kiss', 1875–6), *Tajemství* ('The Secret', 1877–8) and *Čertova stěna* ('The Devil's Wall', 1879–82), all to librettos by Eliška Krásnohorská – the librettist of *Viola*, which Smetana had worked on briefly in 1874. Smetana returned to *Viola* in 1883 but was now extremely ill and did little other than orchestrate the few scenes he had completed. On 20 April 1884 his mental condition had so deteriorated that he was committed to the Prague Lunatic Asylum, where he died a few weeks later.

2. Operatic genres. Smetana's eight operas fall into three groups: three serious operas based on Czech history and myths (*The Brandenburgers in Bohemia*, *Dalibor* and *Libuše*), two comic operas conceived as *opéras comiques* (*The Bartered Bride* and *The Two Widows*) – the spoken dialogue was later adapted to recitative – and the three final operas all to librettos by Krásnohorská. *Libuše*, with its static monumentality, is best described as a sort of musical *tableau vivant* (a popular genre in Prague at that time). Paradoxically the other two overtly nationalist operas are the nearest to common European patterns: *The Brandenburgers in Bohemia* a rather clumsy French grand opera, and *Dalibor* a straightforward tragedy with the death of hero and heroine at the end.

The five other operas share a common thread. All are comedies, the later ones increasingly serious, and all concern the healing of a central relationship. This relationship has been soured either by a failure of communication (Jeník and Mařenka in *The Bartered Bride*), or by the passing of years – Smetana's later central couples are distinctly middle-aged, one of them usually a widow or a widower, or long unmarried. In *The Two Widows* healing is achieved by shock treatment, but in the Krásnohorská operas it is internal, and suggested by physical metaphor: in the deep forest (*The Kiss*), the dark tunnel (*The Secret*) or by a perilous crossing of the swollen waters of the Vltava (*The Devil's Wall*). Such plots have little to do with contemporary operatic models and much more to do with Shakespeare's comedies and romances or Mozart's *Die Zauberflöte* – the Viennese musical, magical 'quest' plays transplanted easily to the Prague stage and their Czech successors were a dominant strain in Czech theatre of the generation before Smetana and Krásnohorská.

3. Smetana and Czech nationalist opera. Smetana is regarded as the 'father of Czech opera' (and indeed of Czech 'modern' music) not because he was the first composer to write operas in Czech, but because his operas were the first to stay in the Czech repertory and thus form the basis for a continuous tradition which has lasted to this day. Professional composers such as František Škroup wrote operas in Czech from the 1820s onwards (Škroup himself was preceded by half a century of semi-amateur attempts), but apart from Škroup's *Dráteník* ('The Tinker') none was given more than a couple of times.

The opening of the Provisional Theatre provided the greatest incentive towards the establishment of a permanent Czech operatic tradition. The first opera given there was Cherubini's *Les deux journées* – there was no suitable Czech piece – but 19 years later when the National Theatre was finally opened, it was with Smetana's *Libuše* (1881). In between these dates all but one of Smetana's completed operas were performed at the theatre or its summer alternatives. Smetana was not alone in taking advantage of the new possibilities. Even before his first opera, *The Brandenburgers*, had been staged in 1866 a German opera by his older contemporary Skuherský had been translated into Czech and given at the Provisional Theatre, and *Templáři na Moravě* ('The Templars in Moravia') by Smetana's younger contemporary Šebor had narrowly anticipated Smetana's première. As well as Šebor, other Czech composers of the new generation such as Bendl, Rozkošný and Blodek were all enthusiastically composing operas – their premières mingled with those of Smetana – but of their operas only a single one, Blodek's unassuming one-act *V studni* ('In the Well'), has maintained a place in the Czech repertory. It is the canon of Smetana's eight completed operas which dominate the early history of Czech opera and consciously provided models for his contemporaries and successors.

4. Operatic conventions and voice types. Smetana's mission did not prevent his drawing on existing traditions of European opera. His attitude towards these can

be inferred from the reviews that he wrote in *Národní listy* (1864–5) and from the repertory he maintained and introduced at the Provisional Theatre during his time there as chief conductor. Most of the objections in his reviews were to the Italian repertory, which he found faded and dramatically inept. German opera – in the language of the oppressor – was understandably unpopular (and was anyway available in Prague at the German opera house), so Smetana sought to move towards the inclusion of more Slavonic repertory and, despite the cramped resources, with tiny chorus and orchestra, towards the French repertory.

There is some echo of French grand opera particularly in his early works. *The Brandenburgers in Bohemia*, for instance, is based on the Scribe-Meyerbeerian canvas of large-scale historical events against which the characters enact their own dramas. The build-up of atmosphere in Act 1 scene ii, with its genre choruses, ballet, and 'revolutionary chorus', has similarities with Auber's *La muette de Portici* rather than with later Meyerbeer works – there is for instance no exploitation of double-chorus confrontations which the plot would suggest (in fact apart from a single soldier, there is no musical depiction of any Brandenburger). Most of these 'French' traits in *The Brandenburgers*, however, can be traced back more to the librettist than to the composer.

Where Smetana made compositional choices he seems to have taken Italian rather than French models. There are several cantabile-cabaletta arias and duets in *The Brandenburgers*, and the outer acts both make use of the concertato-stretta formula. Indeed such traits are sometimes present in Smetana's later operas: Act 1 of his most advanced opera, *Dalibor*, concludes with a cabaletta duet, and there are elements of the concertato reactive ensembles in all his later operas. Even when, in the later operas, the repetitions characterizing a cabaletta structure disappear, the slow–fast cantabile–cabaletta design underlies many of the solo arias and some of the duets. Such survivals are puzzling in view of Smetana's stated aversions, but can be partly explained by the conditions in which he worked. Most of the singers at the Provisional Theatre were trained in the Italian school and felt more comfortable with its traditions. Smetana, furthermore, regularly complied with their requests for extra arias. Thus Act 3 of *The Brandenburgers*, dramatically far from clear, is further confused by two specifically requested insert arias. The first, for the baritone Josef Lev (as Jan Tausendmark), shows off his cantabile legato so well that there is danger of this villain appearing too sympathetic.

Such habits cannot be dismissed merely as the composer's lack of assertiveness at the beginning of his operatic career: in the Hamburg revisions to *The Two Widows* (1882) he added a cabaletta ending for Anežka's aria as requested; by the time of *The Secret* (1877–8) he was still adding music for Josef Lev, for instance the 115-bar expansion to his Act 2 aria inserted after the première. Smetana's admiration for Lev's especial gifts (wholly lyrical and undramatic) and his tailoring of leading baritone parts to them, meant that after *The Brandenburgers* baritone villains virtually disappeared from his operas. Similarly, the fact that the Provisional Theatre lacked dramatic sopranos and Heldentenors as permanent members of the ensemble, meant that Smetana generally avoided writing for these heavier voices in his operas: he learnt his lesson in *Dalibor*. And for all his reservations about italianate traits he included coloratura when appropriate to the singer. The leading Czech prima donna Eleonora z Ehrenbergů did not hide her contempt for a part she was allocated in *The Bartered Bride* (Mařenka) with no scope for her talents. Thereafter Smetana made sure to give something to please her (such as Jitka's melismatic flourishes over the Act 2 soldiers' chorus in *Dalibor* or the trill-laden part of the First Reaper in *Libuše*). This also accounts for the presence in *The Kiss* of Barče's 'lark song', written expressly for the coloratura soubrette talents of Marie Laušmannová. The small and fairly stable group of singers assembled at the Provisional Theatre during Smetana's time there had a lasting effect on his future voice types – even in his final opera, *The Devil's Wall*, he was writing with their specific voices in mind. In general Smetana confined himself to light, lyrical voices; and after the unsatisfiable demands of *The Brandenburgers* (three tenors, including a Heldentenor) and *Dalibor*, he and his last librettist, Krásnohorská, were careful to write for what was on hand.

5. Smetana and his librettists. The role of Krásnohorská as Smetana's last librettist was a particularly dominant one. She chose the subjects of his last three completed operas (two of them her invention) and determined the voice types and the conventions. She believed in ensembles (as she wrote forcefully to Fibich when negotiating the libretto of *Blaník* with him), and consequently included many in her librettos. She determined where there was duet writing and where there were formal solos. Smetana took what was given him (he mentioned that he had left out only four lines of Act 1 in *The Secret*) and, apart from obliging favoured singers, made no specific requests other than for more 'comedy' in the final opera.

Most of their work together was done when Smetana was at his most vulnerable – deaf, and with rapidly deteriorating health – so it is not surprising that he was so passive. However, the scanty evidence available suggests that Smetana was no more assertive in his relationships with earlier librettists. The texts for *Dalibor* and *Libuše* were written ahead of any commission; similarly it would seem Smetana had no great say in the subject matter of the two texts he received from Karel Sabina, *The Brandenburgers* and *The Bartered Bride*, apart from specifying a comic opera for the latter and, for the former, a serious historical opera that would comply with the conditions for the Harrach competition. Conventions of ensemble and simultaneous singing tended to vary with the librettists. Sabina, lacking the time, patience and skills for the equal-length lines needed, provided little usable material for ensembles. Thus *The Bartered Bride* has few ensembles (compared, for instance, to *The Two Widows*, which benefited from Emanuel Züngel's much greater experience as an opera translator and versifier), and those in *The Brandenburgers* had to be eked out from scanty and unpromising material. *Dalibor* has so few ensembles that one suspects that its librettist, Josef Wenzig, conceived it originally as a play – only in the monumental *Libuše* did Wenzig attempt to provide material for ensembles.

6. Smetana and the 'Czech' style. Smetana wrote opera in a medium that was politicized almost the moment he began. In his preamble for his Czech opera competition, Count Harrach had suggested that use should be made of Czech folksong and 'old chorales' to establish a Czech identity. This was a position which

became associated with the conservative faction of Czech politics (the *staročeši*), whereas Smetana belonged to the progressive wing (the *mladočeši*) and was against the quotation of Czech folksong. Accordingly there are almost no direct quotations in his operas and the few that he employs (for instance the pastorella lullaby in *The Kiss*) are there for specific reasons. There are, however, pseudo-folksongs and/or choruses in all of Smetana's operas. The suggestion of folksong was usually made by the use of strophic structures, repetitive tunes and variable metres or tempos (a slow, ruminative beginning accelerating into a more regular and faster continuation, e.g. Ludiše's 'folksong' in *The Brandenburgers*).

Smetana may well have decided that his 'progressive', Lisztian orientation (which resulted for instance in the near monothematic construction of *Dalibor*) was not compatible with the quotation of folk music. But a crucial factor was that he was not particularly well acquainted with it in the first place: the music that he imbibed in his youth was popular dance music from the town rather than genuine Czech folk music from the country. It is dance rhythms rather than folktunes that provide the closest link between Smetana and vernacular music. A number of dances are specifically named, for instance the *skočná* and the *furiant* in *The Bartered Bride*. He also made frequent use of the *sousedská* (a Ländler-type waltz), but the most common dance of all in his operas was the polka. Thus fast 2/4 pieces with well stressed beats and polka-like rhythmic figures underlie many of Smetana's operas from *The Bartered Bride* onwards. Lukáš's ironic serenade to Vendulka in *The Kiss* is 'à la polka'. When the country folk celebrate at the end of *The Two Widows*, it is with a named polka, but many unnamed polkas (specifically allowed for in the predominantly trochaic libretto), can be heard throughout the opera, most noticeably in the Act 2 Prelude and the associated duet for the two widows.

Other sources of 'Czechness' reside in the setting of the Czech language itself but, at least in Smetana's early operas, this is compromised by his poor word-setting (only by his fourth opera, *Libuše*, did he manage to avoid mis-stressings), and by the fact that in two operas, *Dalibor* and *Libuše*, the Czech text follows the rhythms and metres of the German originals. Although in the later operas the word-setting is fully idiomatic, Krásnohorská's penchant for high-style iambics (alien to the Czech language's distinctive first-syllable stress) led to less natural-sounding word-setting than Smetana achieved with the trochees in *The Two Widows*. If Czech audiences perceived Smetana's operas musically as particularly 'Czech' it may well be that familiarity with *The Bartered Bride* rather than the use of dance rhythms or idiomatic setting of the Czech language led to Smetana's personal voice being taken as the clearest expression of 'Czechness' in music.

See also BARTERED BRIDE, THE; BRANDENBURGERS IN BOHEMIA, THE; DALIBOR; DEVIL'S WALL, THE; KISS, THE; LIBUŠE; SECRET, THE; and TWO WIDOWS, THE.

Editions: *Souborná díla Bedřicha Smetany* [Smetana's Collected Works], ii–iv, ed. O. Ostrčil (Prague, 1932–6) [SD]
Studijní vydání děl Bedřicha Smetany [Study Scores of Smetana's Works], ed. F. Bartoš, J. Plavec and others (Prague, 1940–) [SV]

all first produced in Prague; MSS in CS-Pnm; printed works published in Prague unless otherwise stated

title	*genre, acts*	*libretto*	*composed*	*first performance*	*publication*	*edition*
Braniboři v Čechách [The Brandenburgers in Bohemia]	op, 3	K. Sabina	1862–3	Provisional, 5 Jan 1866	vs (1899)	SV ix
Prodana nevěsta [The Bartered Bride]	comic op	Sabina				
1st version	2		1863–6	Provisional, 30 May 1866		
2nd version	2		1869	Provisional, 29 Jan 1869		
3rd version	3		1869	Provisional, 1 June 1869		
4th (definitive) version	3		1869–70	Provisional, 25 Sept 1870	vs (1872); full score (Berlin, 1893)	SD ii-iv, SV i
Dalibor	op, 3	J. Wenzig [Ger.], Cz. trans. E. Špindler	1865–7, rev. 1870	New Town, 16 May 1868	vs (1884)	SV v
Libuše	festival op, 3	Wenzig [Ger.], Cz. trans. Špindler	1869–72	National, 11 June 1881	vs (1881)	SV vi
Dvě vdovy [The Two Widows]	comic op, 2	E. Züngel, after P. J. F. Mallefille: *Les deux veuves*				
1st version			1873–4	Provisional, 27 March 1874		
2nd (definitive) version			1877	Provisional, 15 March 1878		SV vii
addns for 1st publication			1882		unauthorized version (Berlin, 1893)	

title	genre, acts	libretto	composed	first performance	publication	edition
Viola, frag.	romantic op	Krásnohorská, after W. Shakespeare: *Twelfth Night*	1874, 1883–4	concert perf., 15 March 1900; stage, National, 11 May 1924	vs (1902)	
Hubička [The Kiss]	folk op, 2	E. Krásnohorská, after K. Světlá	1875–6	Provisional, 7 Nov 1876	vs (1880)	SV iii
Tajemství [The Secret]	comic op, 3	Krásnohorská	1877–8	New Czech, 18 Sept 1878	vs (1892)	SV x
Čertova stěna [The Devil's Wall]	comic-romantic op, 3	Krásnohorská	1879–82	New Czech, 29 Oct 1882	vs (1902)	SV xii

CATALOGUES

K. Teige: *Příspěvky k životopisu a umělecké činnosti mistra Bedřicha Smetany*, i: *Skladby Smetanovy: kommentovaný katalog všech skladeb mistrových v chronologickém postupu* [Contributions to the Biography and Artistic Activities of Maestro Bedřich Smetana, i: Smetana's Compositions: Annotated Catalogue of All the Maestro's Works in Chronological Order] (Prague, 1893)

M. Očadlík: 'Soupis dopisů Bedřicha Smetany' [List of Smetana's Letters], *MMC*, xv (1960), 5–134; see also F. Bartoš: 'Příspěvky k soupisu dopisů Bedřicha Smetany' [Contributions to the List of Smetana's Letters], *HV*, i (1964), 645–82

R. Budiš and V. Kafková: *Bedřich Smetana: vyběrová bibliografie* [Selective Bibliography] (Prague, 1963)

J. R. Bennett: *Smetana on 3000 Records* (Tarrant Hinton, nr Blandford, 1974)

O. Čechová and J. Fojtíková: *Bedřich Smetana (inventář fondu)* (Prague, 1984)

J. Berkovec: *Tematický katalog díla Bedřicha Smetany* [Thematic Catalogue of the Works of Bedřich Smetana] (in preparation)

SOURCE MATERIAL

critical edition of librettos

Operní libretу Bedřicha Smetany [Bedřich Smetana's Opera Librettos]: i: *K. Sabina: Braniboři v Čechách* [The Brandenburgers in Bohemia], ed. Z. Nejedlý (Prague, 1918); ii: *K. Sabina: Prodaná nevěsta* [The Bartered Bride], ed. Z. Nejedlý (Prague, 1930); iii: *E. Krásnohorská: Hubička* [The Kiss], ed. M. Očadlík (Prague, 1942); iv: *E. Krásnohorská: Čertova stěna* [The Devil's Wall], ed. M. Očadlík (Prague, 1946); v: *J. Wenzig and E. Špindler: Dalibor*, ed. J. Bartoš (Prague, 1944); vi: *J. Wenzig and E. Špindler: Libuše*, ed. J. Bartoš (Prague, 1951); vii: *E. Züngel: Dvě vdovy* [The Two Widows], ed. M. Očadlík (Prague, 1962)

correspondence

O. Hostinský, ed.: 'Smetanovy dopisy' [Smetana's Letters], *Dalibor*, vii–ix (1885–7), passim

K. Teige: *Příspěvky k životopisu a umělecké činnosti mistra Bedřicha Smetany*, ii: *Dopisy Smetanovy: kommentovaný výbor šedesáti čtyř mistrových dopisů* [Contributions to the Biography and Artistic Activities of Maestro Bedřich Smetana, ii: Smetana's Letters: a Selection with Commentary of 64 of the Maestro's Letters] (Prague, 1896)

L. Zelenka-Lerando: *B. Smetana a E. Züngel* (Nymburk, 1903)

A. Kraus: 'Bedřich Smetana v Göteborgu', *Věstník České akademie císaře Františka Josefa pro vědy, slovesnost a umění*, xv (1906), 1–8, 81–7, 283–9, 356–64, 401–13 [Smetana's letters to his Swedish friends in the orig. Ger.]

J. Löwenbach, ed.: *Bedřich Smetana a dr. Ludevít Procházka: vzájemná korespondence* [Mutual Correspondence] (Prague, 1914)

V. Balthasar: *Bedřich Smetana* (Prague, 1924) [incl. letters from Smetana to Srb-Debrnov and to his publishers; also transcripts of Smetana's conversations with Velebín Urbánek]

F. Bartoš, ed.: *Smetana ve vzpomínkách a dopisech* [Smetana in Letters and Reminiscences] (Prague, 1939, enlarged 9/1954; Ger. trans., 1954; Eng. trans., 1955) [Ger. trans. gives orig. text of Ger. documents]

M. Očadlík, ed.: *Eliška Krásnohorská – Bedřich Smetana: vzájemná korespondence* [Mutual Correspondence] (Prague, 1940)

J. Jiránek: *Smetanův žák vzpomíná* [Smetana's Pupil Remembers] (Prague, 1941, 2/1957 as *Vzpomínky a korespondence s Bedřichem Smetanou* [Reminiscences and Correspondence with Bedřich Smetana])

F. Bartoš and Z. Němec: *Z dopisů Bedřicha Smetany* [From Bedřich Smetana's Letters] (Prague, 1947)

other

Z. Nejedlý: 'Opera Tajemství ve Smetanových dennících' [*The Secret* in Smetana's Diaries], *HR*, i (1908), 377–9

M. Očadlík, ed.: *Bedřich Smetana: To, co my komponisté jako v mlhách tušíme* (Prague, 1940) [Smetana's statements on creating a national style]

——, ed.: 'Smetanovy skizzy' [Smetana's Sketches], *Volné směry*, xxxvi (1941), no.7 [incl. transcr. of omitted passage from *Dalibor*]

——, ed.: *Bedřich Smetana: Zápisník motivů* [Bedřich Smetana: Notebook of Motifs] (Prague, 1942) [facs.]

——, ed.: *Prodaná nevěsta: první náčrtek Bedřicha Smetany* (*The Bartered Bride*: Smetana's First Sketch] (Prague, 1944) [facs.]

V. H. Jarka, ed.: *Kritické dílo Bedřicha Smetany* [Bedřich Smetana's Critical Works] (Prague, 1948)

M. Očadlík: *Rok Bedřicha Smetany v datech, obrazech, zápisech a poznámkách* [Bedřich Smetana's Year in Dates, Pictures, Reports and Notes] (Prague, 1950)

T. Volek and S. Jareš: *Dějiny české hudby v obrazech* [The History of Czech Music in Pictures] (Prague, 1977)

J. Clapham: 'Smetana's Sketches for "Dalibor" and "The Secret"', *ML*, xli (1980), 136–46

J. Smolka: 'Nově nalezené skici Bedřicha Smetany k Mé vlasti, Viole a Snění' [Newly-Found Sketches by Bedřich Smetana for *My Fatherland*, *Viola* and *Dreams*], *Sborník Národního muzea v Praze*, ser. A, xl (1986), 171–202

MEMOIRS AND BIOGRAPHICAL STUDIES

E. Krásnohorská: *Bedřich Smetana: nástin života i působení jeho uměleckého* [Bedřich Smetana: an Outline of his Life and Artistic Activity] (Prague, 1885); repr. in *Výbor z díla* [Selected Works], ed. Z. Pešat and J. Křesálková, ii (Prague, 1956), 363–90

V. V. Zelený: *O Bedřichu Smetanovi* (Prague, 1894)

O. Hostinský: *Bedřich Smetana a jeho boj o moderní českou hudbu* [Bedřich Smetana and his Battle for Modern Czech Music] (Prague, 1901, 2/1941 ed. B. Hostinsky)

E. Špindler: 'Několik vzpomínek na mistra B. Smetanu' [Some Reminiscences of Bedřich Smetana], *HR*, ii (1909), 248–53

B. Kalenský: 'Maýr a Smetana: jejich správa vykonné zpěvohry české' [Maýr and Smetana: Their Administration of the Performance of Czech Opera], *Dalibor*, xxxv (1912–13), 2–3, 25–7, 45–7, 105–6

L. Bráfová: *Rieger, Smetana, Dvořák* (Prague, 1913)

E. Krásnohorská: 'Ze vzpomínek na Bedřicha Smetana' [From my Reminiscences of Bedřich Smetana], *Ruch* (1913–14); addns in *Ženské listy* (1915); repr. in *Co přinesla léta* [What the Years Brought], ed. F. Strejček, ii (Prague, 1928), 5–46

E. Chvalovský: 'Premiera Smetanových "Dvou vdov"' [The Première of Smetana's *The Two Widows*], in J. Schwarz and others: *Vzpomínky na Bedřicha Smetanu* [Reminiscences of Bedřich Smetana] (Prague, 1917), 47–61

A. Heller: 'Vzpomínky Ferdinanda Hellera' [Ferdinand Heller's Reminiscences], ibid, 9–35

Z. Nejedlý, ed.: Ladislav Dolanský: *Hudební paměti* [Musical Memoirs] (Prague, 1918, 2/1949)

K. Šípek: *Vzpomínky na Prozatímní* [Reminiscences of the Provisional Theatre] (Prague 1918)

Almanach na památku tisícího provedení Prodané nevěsty [Almanach to Commemorate the 1000th Performance of *The Bartered Bride*] (Prague, 1927) [incl. memoirs]

A. Hnilička: *Studie k etapám vývoje epochy Bedřicha Smetany* [Studies in the Stage of the Evolutionary Epochs of Bedřich Smetana] (Prague, 1937)

J. Clapham: 'The Smetana-Pivoda Controversy', *ML*, iii (1971), 353–64

P. Daněk and J. Vyšohlídová: 'Dokumenty k operní soutěži o cenu hraběte Harracha' [Documents Concerning Count Harrach's Operatic Prize Competition], *MMC*, xxx (1983), 147–75

O. Bořík, R. Khel and J. Boříková: 'Ušní onemocnění Bedřicha Smetany' [Bedřich Smetana's Ear Disease], *OM*, xvi (1984), 294–304; see also ibid, 308–10

R. Útrata: 'Feminní element v životě Bedřicha Smetany' [The Feminine Element in the Life of Bedřich Smetana], *OM*, xvi (1984), 305–7

R. Khel: 'Bedřich Smetana – čtenář' [Bedřich Smetana – Reader], *OM*, xviii (1986), 104–118

LIBRETTOS AND LIBRETTISTS

J. Štolba: 'Libretto pro Bedřicha Smetanu' [A Libretto for Bedřich Smetana], *Z mých pamětí* [From my Memoirs] (Prague, 1906–7), i, 243–59

F. Šelepa: 'K otázce libretta Smetanova "Dalibora"' [On the Question of the Libretto to Smetana's *Dalibor*], *HR*, ii (1909), 471–3

A. Šilhan: 'Smetanův "Dalibor": příspěvek k historii jeho vzniku' [Smetana's *Dalibor*: a Contribution to the History of its Origins], *HR*, ii (1909), 209–17

O. Zich: 'Smetanova "Čertova stěna"' [Smetana's *The Devil's Wall*], *HR*, ii (1909), 222–8

O. Fischer: 'K Smetanovým librettům: 1. K Daliboru'; '——: 2. K Libuši', [On Smetana's Librettos: 1, *Dalibor*; 2, *Libuše*], *HR*, viii (1915), 153–62; 205–15

Z. Nejedlý: 'Eliška Krásnohorská a Bedřich Smetana', *Smetana*, xii (1922), 129–34; repr. in *Zdeněk Nejedlý o Bedřichu Smetanovi*, ed. J. Jiránek (Prague, 1980), 116–24

M. Očadlík: 'Mezi Shakespearem a Smetanou' [Between Shakespeare and Smetana], *Eliška Krásnohorská*, ed. P. Antošová (Brno, 1947), 93–114

——: *Smetanovi libretisté* [Smetana's Librettists] (Prague, 1948)

Z. Vokurka: 'Ještě k vavřínům Smetanovy Hubičky' [Once More to the Laurels of Smetana's *The Kiss*], *OM*, ii (1970), 198–203

M. Suchá and M. Ulčová: 'Plzeňské počátky libretistické spolupráce Elišky Krásnohorské s Bedřichem Smetanou' [The Plzeň Beginnings of Eliška Krásnohorská's Collaboration with Bedřich Smetana], *Bedřich Smetana: Plzeň 1840–1843* (Plzeň, 1974), 97–117

J. Jiránek: 'Sabinovo libreto ke Smetanově první opeře' [Sabina's Libretto to Smetana's First Opera], *Česká literatura*, xxvii (1979), 206–18

see also 'Source Material: critical edition of librettos'; 'Memoirs and Biographical Studies'

SPECIAL TOPICS

J. B. Theurer: 'Fragment opery Violy od B. Smetany' [The Fragment of the Opera *Viola* by Bedřich Smetana], *Dalibor*, xxi (1899), 9–14

O. Zich: 'Bezprostřední styky skladeb Smetanových s lidovou písní' [The Immediate Contacts of Smetana's Works with Folksong], *Český lid*, xviii (1909), 353–6

J. A. Theurer: 'Smetana a české pěvectvo' [Smetana and Czech Singing], *Věstník pěvecký a hudební*, xxviii (1924), 13–22

J. Racek: *Idea vlasti, národa a slávy v díle Bedřicha Smetany* [The Idea of Fatherland, Nation and Glory in the Work of Bedřich Smetana] (Brno, 1933, enlarged 2/1947)

M. Očadlík: *Libuše: vznik Smetanovy zpěvohry* [*Libuše*: the Origin of Smetana's Opera] (Prague, 1939)

——: *Zavišův zpěv z náčrtu k Čertově stěně* [Záviš's (Omitted) Song from the Sketch for *The Devil's Wall*] (Prague, 1944) [incl. transcr.]

G. Abraham: 'The Genesis of "The Bartered Bride"', *ML*, xxviii (1947), 36–49; repr. in G. Abraham: *Slavonic and Romantic Music* (London, 1968), 28–39

F. Bartoš: 'Ke genesi Smetanovy Prodané nevěsty' [On the Genesis of *The Bartered Bride*], *Musikologie*, iv (1955), 7–31

J. Zich: *Instrumentace Smetanova Dalibora* (Prague, 1957)

J. Jiránek: 'Vztah hudby a slova ve Smetanově Prodané nevěstě' [The Relationship of Music and Words in Smetana's *The Bartered Bride*], *HV*, viii (1971), 19–40 [Ger. summary, 123–4]

L. Jehne: 'K problematice smetanovských hlasových oborů a pěveckých typů' [Problems in Smetana's Voice Types and Types of Singers], *HV*, xi (1974), 125–34 [Ger. summary, 135]

J. Jiránek: 'Problém hudebně dramatické reprezentace Krasavy ve Smetanové Libuši' [The Problem of the Musico-dramatic Representation of Krasava in Smetana's *Libuše*], *HV*, xi (1974), 250–73 [Ger. summary, 274–7]

——: 'Krystalizace významového pole Smetanovy Libuše' [Crystallization of the Range of Meaning in Smetana's *Libuše*], *HV*, xiii (1976), 27–54 [Ger. summary, 55–8]

——: *Vztah hudby a slova v tvorbě Bedřicha Smetany* [The Relation of Music and Word in the Works of Bedřich Smetana] (Prague, 1976) [incl. Ger. summary, 173–7]; for abridged Ger. version see 'Das Problem der Beziehung von Musik und Wort im Schaffen Bedřich Smetanas', *Music and Word: Brno IV 1969*, 107–37

M. Pospíšil: 'Balada v české opeře 19. století' [The Ballad in Czech 19th-Century Opera], *HV*, xvi (1979), 3–25

J. Jiránek, ed.: Zdeněk Nejedlý: *O Bedřichu Smetanovi* [On Bedřich Smetana] (Prague, 1980)

M. Ottlová and M. Pospíšil: 'Český historismus a opera 19. století (Smetanova Libuše)' [Czech Historicism and 19th-Century Opera: Smetana's *Libuše*], *Uměnovědné studie*, iii (1981), 83–99

——: 'K problematice české historické opery 19. století' [The Problem of 19th-Century Czech Historical Opera], *HRo*, xxxiv (1981), 169–72; Ger. version in *The Musical Theatre: Brno Colloquia XV 1980*, 267–81 [on *The Brandenburgers in Bohemia*]

P. Vít: 'Libuše – proměny mýtu ve společnosti a v umění' [*Libuše*: the Transformations of Myth in Society and in Art], *HV*, xix (1982), 269–73; Ger. trans. in *The Musical Theatre: Brno Colloquia XV 1980*, 282–91

A. Houtchens: 'Libuše and Vanda, Legendary and Operatic Sisters', *The Smetana Centennial: San Diego 1984* (unpubd; some material in *A Critical Study of Antonín Dvořák's 'Vanda'*, diss., U. of California at Santa Barbara, 1987)

B. Srba: 'Bedřich Smetana a soudobá divadelní konvence' [Bedřich Smetana and Theatrical Conventions of his Time], *OM*, xvii (1985), 71–81, 97–107

J. Tyrrell: *Czech Opera* (Cambridge, 1988)

M. Ottlová and M. Pospíšil: 'Francouzská veselohra v kontextu české opery Smetanovy Dvě vdovy' [French Comedy in the Context of the Czech Opera, Smetana's *The Two Widows*], *Proudy české umělecké tvorby 19. století: smích v umění: Plzeň 1989*, 156–67

see also historical introductions by F. Bartoš to the opera volumes in the critical edition (*Studijní vydání děl Bedřicha Smetany*)

PERFORMANCE AND RECEPTION STUDIES

F. A. Šubert: *České Národní divadlo na první mezinárodní divadelní výstavě ve Vídni r. 1892* [The Czech National Theatre at the First International Theatre Exhibition in Vienna 1892] (Prague, 1892) [incl. reviews of *The Bartered Bride* and *Dalibor*]

J. Machač: *Bedřich Smetana a cizina* [Bedřich Smetana and Abroad] (Hradec Králové, 1910)

F. Pujmann: *Poznámky o dramaturgii Smetanových oper* [Remarks on the Dramaturgy of Smetana's Operas] (Prague, 1919) [from *Dalibor* to *The Devil's Wall*]

O. Zítek: *O novou zpěvohru: k dramaturgii a režii hudebního dramatu* [On the New Opera: Dramaturgy and Direction of Music Drama] (Prague, 1920) [incl. chaps. on *Libuše*, *The Two Widows* and *The Devil's Wall*]

——: *Smetanova Čertova stěna s hlediska dramaturgického* [Smetana's *The Devil's Wall* from the Dramaturgical Point of View] (Prague, 1922)

Almanach na památku tisícího provedení Prodané nevěsty [Almanach to Commemorate the 1000th performance of *The Bartered Bride*] (Prague, 1927) [incl. statistics of performances and interpreters]

Památník: 200 představení Tajemství [Memorial Volume: 200 Performances of *The Secret*] (Prague, 1927) [incl. statistics]

J. Bartoš, ed.: J. B. Foerster: *O Bedřichu Smetanovi: referáty v Národních listech 1884–1893* [On Bedřich Smetana: Reviews in the *Národní listy* 1884–93] (Prague, 1929)

Z. Nejedlý: *Opera Národního divadla do roku 1900* [Opera at the National Theatre until 1900] (Prague, 1935); *Opera Národního divadla od roku 1900 do převratu* [Opera at the National Theatre from 1900 until the Coup d'état] (Prague, 1936); both vols., 2/1949 as *Dějiny opery Národního divadla* [The History of Opera at the National Theatre]

L. Firkušný: *Prodaná nevěsta a její historie na brněnském jevišti* [*The Bartered Bride* and its History on the Brno Stage] (Brno, 1936) [incl. statistics, photographs and stage designs]

J. Bartoš: *Prozatímní divadlo a jeho opera* [The Provisional Theatre and its Opera] (Prague, 1938)

H. Thein: *Mé režijní poznámky k Prodané nevěstě* [My Production Notes on *The Bartered Bride*] (Unhošť', 1940)
M. Rutte, O. Šourek and others: *Smetanův operní epilog: k novým dramaturgickým úpravám Čertovy stěny* [Smetana's Operatic Epilogue: on the New Dramaturgical Adaptation of *The Devil's Wall*] (Prague, 1942)
L. Novák: *Stará garda Národního divadla* [The Old Guard at the National Theatre] (Prague, 1944)
M. Očadlík: *Poslední dramaturgická úprava Smetanovy Čertovy stěny* [The Last Dramaturgical Adaptation of Smetana's *The Devil's Wall*] (Prague, 1946)
Památník třistého provedení slavnostní zpěvohry Bedřicha Smetany 'Libuše' [Memorial Volume for the 300th Performance of Bedřich Smetana's Festival Opera *Libuše*] (Prague, 1946) [incl. statistics]
P. Pražák: *Smetanovy zpěvohry* [Smetana's Operas] (Prague, 1948)
M. Nedbal, ed.: Ludevít Procházka: *Slavná doba české hudby: výbor z kritik a článků* [A Glorious Era of Czech Music: a Selection from Reviews and Articles] (Prague, 1958)
P. Pražák: *Smetanova Prodaná nevěsta: vznik a osudy díla* [Smetana's *The Bartered Bride*: Origin and Further History of the Work] (Prague, 1962)
Opera Národního divadla v období Otakara Ostrčila [The Opera of the National Theatre during the Ostrčil Era]: F. Pala, i–iv (Prague, 1962–70); V. Pospíšil, v–vi (Prague, 1983–9)
J. Němeček: *Opera Národního divadla v období Karla Kovařovice 1900–1920* [The Opera of the National Theatre in the Kovařovic Era] (Prague, 1968–9)
S. Jareš: 'Obrazová dokumentace nejstarších inscenací Prodané nevěsty' [Pictorial Documentation of the Earliest Productions of *The Bartered Bride*], *HV*, xi (1974), 195–8
B. Srba: 'Jevištní výprava představení Smetanovy Libuše v Národním divadle z let 1881 a 1883' [Stage Sets for the Performances of Smetana's *Libuše* at the National Theatre in 1881 and 1883], *Divadlo v české kultuře 19. století: Plzeň 1983*, 167–87
M. Dosoudilová: 'Pujmanova režijní koncepce Smetanova Dalibora' [Pujman's Production Conception of Smetana's *Dalibor*], *HRo*, xxxviii (1985), 178–84, 221–4, 284–7
M. Kuna, ed.: *Sto let odkazu Bedřicha Smetany: Praha 1984* (Prague, 1985) [incl. articles on reception and performance problems of Smetana's operas]
M. Hůrka: 'Prodaná nevěsta a film' [*The Bartered Bride* and Film], *HRo*, xxxix (1986), 186–92
M. Dosoudilová: 'Geneze Pujmanova pojetí Prodané nevěsty' [The Genesis of Pujman's Conception of *The Bartered Bride*], *HV*, xxviii (1991), 125–33

CRITICAL COMMENTARIES AND GUIDES

V. J. Novotný: *Uvedení do Smetanovy slavnostní zpěvohry Libuše* [Introduction to Smetana's Festival Opera *Libuše*] (Prague, 1882)
O. Hostinský: 'O zpěvohrách Smetanových' [Smetana's Operas], *Bedřich Smetana a jeho boj o moderní českou hudbu* (Prague, 1901, 2/1941 ed. B. Hostinský), 377–439 [2nd edn]
V. A. J. Hornové [V. Horn, A. Horn and J. Horn]: 'Bedřich Smetana', *Česká zpěvohra* [Czech Opera] (Prague, 1903), 250–76
W. Ritter: 'Les huit opéras', *Smetana* (Paris, 1907), 70–196
Z. Nejedlý: *Zpěvohry Smetanovy* [Smetana's Operas] (Prague, 1908, 3/1954)
O. Zich: *Smetanova Hubička: hudebně estetické rozbor* [Smetana's *The Kiss*: a Musico-aesthetical Analysis] (Prague, 1911)
M. Očadlík: *Čertova stěna: výklad opery* [*The Devil's Wall*: an Account of the Opera] (Prague and Brno, 1938)
——: *Smetana – Dalibor: výklad opery* [Smetana's *Dalibor*: an Account of the Opera] (Prague and Brno, 1938)
——: *Smetana – Tajemství* [Smetana: *The Secret*] (Prague and Brno, 1938)
H. Doležil: 'Bedřich Smetana', *České umění dramatické*, ii: *Zpěvohra* [Czech Dramatic Art: Opera], ed. J. Hutter and Z. Chalabala (Prague, 1941), 49–97
M. Očadlík: *Smetanova Prodaná nevěsta* [Smetana's *The Bartered Bride*] (Prague, 1951)
F. Pala: *Smetanův Dalibor* [Smetana's *Dalibor*] (Prague, 1952)
M. Očadlík: *Smetanovi Braniboři v Čechách* [Smetana's *The Brandenburgers in Bohemia*] (Prague, 1953)
B. Large: *Smetana* (London, 1970)
J. Clapham: *Smetana* (London, 1972), 90–115
J. Smolka: *Smetanova vokální tvorba: písně, sbory, kantáta* [Smetana's Vocal Works: Songs, Choruses, Cantatas] (Prague, 1980) [incl. commentaries on choruses in the operas]
L. Šíp: 'Bedřich Smetana', *Česká opera a její tvůrci: průvodce* [Czech Opera and its Creators: Guide] (Prague, 1983), 19–69
J. Jiránek: *Smetanova operní tvorba* [Smetana's Operatic Works] (Prague, 1984–9)
J. Smaczny: 'Smetana's Romantic Comedy' [*The Devil's Wall*], *Opera*, xxxviii (1987), 134–9
JOHN TYRRELL

Smirnov, Dmitry (Alexeyevich) (*b* Moscow, 7/19 Nov 1882; *d* Riga, 27 April 1944). Russian tenor. He studied with Emiliya Pavlovskaya and apparently in Milan. He made his début as Gigi in the first performance of Esposito's *Camorra* at the Hermitage Theatre, Moscow, in 1903. After a trial début as Sinodal in Rubinstein's *The Demon* he sang at the Bol'shoy (1904–10). From 1910 until 1917 he was a member of the Imperial Opera, St Petersburg. He often sang in western Europe (Paris, in the Dyagilev seasons, Monte Carlo, Brussels, Madrid, Barcelona), and appeared at the Metropolitan, 1910–12 (début as the Duke in *Rigoletto*). In 1911 he sang in *Lakmé* with the Boston Opera and toured Latin America. He took part in Beecham's Drury Lane Russian opera productions in summer 1914. After 1919 he sang widely in Paris, Brussels and London. Besides his large French and Italian repertory, he sang many Russian roles, including Lensky, Grigory (*Boris*) and Levko (*May Night*), as well as Lohengrin. He made approximately 90 recordings between 1909 and the late 1920s.

*

J. Stratton: 'Dmitri Smirnoff', *Record Collector*, xiv (1961–2), 245–77 [with discography]
HAROLD BARNES

Smirnov, Dmitry Nikolayevich (*b* Minsk, 2 Nov 1948). Russian composer. He was born into a family of opera singers and from 1967 to 1972 studied at the Moscow Conservatory with Nikolay Sidel'nikov, Edison Denisov and others. He worked as an editor at the publishing house *Sovetskiy kompozitor* until 1980, and thereafter has devoted himself to composition full-time. He is married to the composer Yelena Firsova. Smirnov has composed works in a wide variety of genres. He has discovered a particular affinity with the works of William Blake and has written a number of compositions inspired by them, including two operas, both written on his own parallel English and Russian librettos: the three-act *Tiriel* (*Tiriel'*) op.41, a lush score with echoes of Wagner and Strauss, was written between 1983 and 1985 and given its première in Freiburg at the Freiburger Theater Grosses Haus on 28 January 1989. The more intimate one-act chamber opera, *The Lamentations of Thel* (*Zhalobï Teli*) op.45, was completed in 1986 and first performed by the Théâtre de Complicité at the Almeida Theatre, London, on 9 June 1989.

*

G. McBurney: 'Smirnov's "Tiriel"', *Tempo*, no.169 (June 1989), 61–2
T. Slyusarenko: 'I v mig odin uvidet' vechnost'' [And Perceive Eternity in a Single Moment], *SovM* (1990), no.12, pp.11–15
LAUREL E. FAY

Smit, Leo (*b* Philadelphia, 12 Jan 1921). American composer. He received his first instruction in piano and theory from his father, a professional violinist. From 1930 to 1932 he studied the piano with Isabelle Vengerova and at the Curtis Institute, then received private instruction from José Iturbi (piano) and Nicholas Nabokov (composition). As a pianist with Balanchine's American Ballet company (1936–7) he associated closely with Stravinsky, whose influence can be detected in Smit's neo-classical style of the 1950s. His earlier works were strongly American in flavour but since about 1960 he has arrived at a synthesis of styles, with occasional atonality surfacing. He has taught at Sarah Lawrence College (1947–9), the University of California at Los Angeles (1957–63) and the State University of New York at Buffalo (1962–84).

An interest in vocal music has been present throughout Smit's career. His three-act opera *The Alchemy of Love* (composed 1969), to a libretto by the astronomer and science-fiction writer Fred Hoyle, has a futuristic scenario about attempts of a thought-control official from an alien planet to wrest a secret formula for producing gold from an innocent young alchemist by seduction and less subtle means. A production was prepared in 1973 by the Manhattan School of Music, directed by George Schick, but was cancelled at the last minute. On 29 and 30 October 1979 Smit conducted performances of his one-act opera, *Magic Water*, staged by the University of Buffalo Opera Workshop, at Buffalo Seminary. The libretto, written by the composer, is based on Nathaniel Hawthorne's short story *Dr. Heidegger's Experiment*, in which an ageing femme fatale and a group of roués are offered water from the fountain of youth and suddenly become young, only to begin repeating the same follies all over again. A review in the *Buffalo Evening News* (30 October 1979) called Smit's opera a 'light, musical morality play, ... clear and uncluttered with very singable lines against old-time dissonances ... [and] witty musical quotations'.

HERMAN TROTTER

Smith, Donald (*b* Bundaberg, Queensland, 1922). Australian tenor. After singing in light opera, he studied in London and Italy, then sang in Brisbane (1955) and Sydney as Tamino, Almaviva and Pinkerton. In 1961 he joined Sadler's Wells Opera, making his début as Don José and later singing the Duke, Jeník, Dick Johnson, Foresto (*Attila*), Riccardo (*Ballo*), Ernani and Don Alvaro. He sang Calaf at Covent Garden (1965) and Corrado (*Il corsaro*) at the Camden Festival (1966). Returning to Sydney in 1968, he sang Manrico, Cavaradossi, Canio, Luigi (*Il tabarro*), Radames, Florestan and Carlo (*I masnadieri*). In 1978 he sang his only Wagnerian role, Erik, at Melbourne, with his son Robin Donald (*b* 1942) as Steersman. He retired in 1982. He had a vibrant, italianate voice with ringing top notes, and was an immensely exciting performer, especially in his many Verdi roles. ELIZABETH FORBES

Smith, Harry B(ache) (*b* Buffalo, NY, 28 Dec 1860; *d* Atlantic City, NJ, 2 Jan 1936). American lyricist and librettist. The most prolific of all American stage writers, he is said to have written over 300 librettos and more than 6000 lyrics. Best remembered among his stage works, which were produced between 1887 and 1932, are *Robin Hood* (1891) and *The Fortune Teller* (1898). Among his few lyrics still heard today are those for 'Gypsy Love Song' and 'Play, Gypsies – Dance, Gypsies'. His brother, Robert (*b* Chicago, 4 June 1875; *d* New York, 6 Nov 1951), wrote the lyrics and books for nearly 30 shows between 1902 and his early retirement in 1920. His most famous lyrics were those for Victor Herbert's operetta *Sweethearts* (1913).

*

H. B. Smith: *First Nights and First Editions* (Boston, 1931)

GERALD BORDMAN

Smith, Jennifer (Mary) (*b* Lisbon, 13 July 1945). British soprano. She studied in Lisbon and made her début there as the Voice from Heaven in *Don Carlos* in 1968. In 1971 she moved to London where she had further tuition from Winifred Radford and Pierre Bernac. Her roles include Mozart's Countess Almaviva (1979, WNO) and Amyntas (1987, Lisbon), and Rameau's Alphise in the stage première of *Les Boréades* (1982, Aix-en-Provence); she made her American début as Cybele in Lully's *Atys* in New York in 1988. Other parts include Gluck's Eurydice and Rameau's Folly (*Platée*). She has also appeared with Scottish Opera and Kent Opera, and in 1991 sang the Queen of Night in Toronto and Reine Berthe/La Vieille (Duni's *La fée Urgèle*) at the Opéra-Comique. Smith is a versatile artist able on the one hand to bring grandeur and pathos to her interpretations and on the other to sustain light-hearted, comic and mischievous roles as she has demonstrated in *Platée*. Though her concert repertory is wide she has recorded mainly the Baroque repertory for which she is best known: Purcell's *Fairy-Queen* and *King Arthur*, Marais's *Alcyone* and Rameau's *Castor et Pollux*, *Naïs*, *Les Indes galantes*, *Platée* and *Les Boréades*.

NICHOLAS ANDERSON

Smith, John Christopher [Schmidt, Johann Christoph] (*b* Ansbach, 1712; *d* Bath, 3 Oct 1795). British composer of German parentage. He was the son of Johann Christoph Schmidt (1683–1763), who was brought to London by Handel in 1716 as his treasurer and principal copyist. The younger Schmidt arrived in 1720 and both adopted the anglicized form of their name. Smith appears to have had some lessons from Handel around 1725, but also learnt from Pepusch and Thomas Roseingrave, with whom he lodged in Wigmore Street. In the 1730s he was taken up by Arbuthnot, one of the librettists of Handel's *Acis and Galatea*, and through him met many literary figures, including Alexander Pope and Jonathan Swift. In 1736 he married the sister of Thomas Pakenham (later Lord Longford), but their children did not survive infancy and she died in 1742. During the mid-1740s, Smith was abroad in charge of an invalid youth. He also met Robert Price and Benjamin Stillingfleet, who were later to provide him with librettos and, according to Burney, gave him 'a taste for, and procured him admission into, good company; so that he formed his character on models of a higher class than that of a mere musician'. On his return from the Continent, Smith resumed his connection with Handel when the older composer required assistance to offset his oncoming blindness, though Smith's role went beyond that of an amanuensis. On the death of his father in 1763, Smith inherited Handel's manuscripts, which he in turn bequeathed to George III. Smith's second wife, formerly Mrs Coxe, whom he had married after her husband's death in 1760, died in 1785, upon which he retired to Bath to live with his stepdaughter.

In the early 1730s Smith was drawn into the elder Thomas Arne's project to provide a repertory of italianate, all-sung operas with English words. *Teraminta* (1732), for which only one air survives, is set in Cuba and takes the theme of a lost child of aristocratic parents being identified and returned to his natural sphere. The existing *Teraminta* score, previously thought to have been Smith's, is now attributed to John Stanley (*see* TERAMINTA) and considered to date from the early 1750s. The three performances that the box office sustained were few enough, but they reflected greater interest than the single benefit staging of *Ulysses* in 1733. The uneven though occasionally brilliant score, with its many da capo arias, was not assisted by Samuel Humphreys's lifeless libretto, which is devoid of incident. The next decade opened promisingly with his one-act 'musical drama' *Rosalinda*, to a libretto by John Lockman, first performed by the Apollo Society in Hickford's Rooms, Brewer Street, in 1740. Smith's Metastasian operas, however, which all date from the 1740s, appear never to have been staged, and those that are not lost are either unfinished or survive incomplete. It is likely that *Artaserse* at least was written during Smith's travels to Geneva and Aix-en-Provence.

In the 1750s Smith was introduced to David Garrick and agreed to collaborate with him on *The Fairies*, based on Shakespeare's *A Midsummer Night's Dream*. This was yet another feeble attempt to establish English as a rival operatic language to Italian and, like the efforts of Colley Cibber, Arne and Lockman, it was ineffectual. *The Fairies* had performances in the 1755–6 and 1756–7 seasons, and in New York in 1786. An adaptation of *The Tempest* followed, borrowing material haphazardly from previous versions of the play and introducing song texts from other sources. Smith's infelicitous setting and the preponderance of da capo arias must have made both works seem old-fashioned, although there is evidence that by this time he was trying to use a lighter style, shortening the numbers and including such features as a hornpipe and the fashionable Scotch snap.

Smith's last collaboration with Garrick was on the afterpiece *The Enchanter* (1760), with a text wholly attributed to Garrick. As with most operatic afterpieces, it had simple airs and was fairly successful, demonstrating that English audiences were not necessarily against singing or recitatives but opposed the total exclusion of spoken drama from an evening's entertainment. *The Enchanter* takes its cue from Thomas Arne's earlier 'eastern' masque *The Sultan* (1756): both feature harems and a heroine called Zaida. His final opera, *Medea*, was not completed because, if Coxe is to be believed, it 'was deemed equally improper for public exhibition, from the horror and catastrophe, and therefore after finishing the first two acts, Mr. Smith relinquished the task of setting the remainder of the music'. After that, Lenten oratorios occupied Smith as a composer until the 1770s; the rest of his output consists of occasional works, harpsichord lessons and a few songs.

See also FAIRIES, THE and ULYSSES (ii).

performed in London unless otherwise stated; all printed works published in London

Teraminta (3, H. Carey), Lincoln's Inn Fields, 20 Nov 1732, 1 air in British Musical Miscellany, iv (1735)

Ulysses (3, S. Humphreys, after Homer: *Odyssey*, bks 16–24), Lincoln's Inn Fields, 16 April 1733, *D-Hs*; incl. 2 choruses from Smith's funeral ode The Mourning Muse of Alexis, 1729

Rosalinda (musical drama, 1, J. Lockman), Hickford's Rooms, 4 Jan 1740

The Seasons, 1740 (serenade op, 2, Lockman), unperf., *Hs**

Issipile, 1743 (3, P. Metastasio), unperf., *GB-Lbl** (without recits.)

Il Ciro riconosciuto, 1745 (3, Metastasio), unperf., *D-Hs** (without recits.); ov. used in The Tempest

Dario, 1746 (3), unperf.

Artaserse, ?1748 (3, Metastasio), inc.; 'Dando impero al gusto al Prode' in Coxe (1799) possibly for this opera

The Fairies (comic op, 3, D. Garrick or Smith, after W. Shakespeare: *A Midsummer Night's Dream*), Drury Lane, 3 Feb 1755, excerpts (1755), ov. in Six Favourite Overtures (1760), prol. in *The Gentleman's Magazine*, xxv (1755), 86; ov. from pastoral cantata Daphne, 1744; incl. song texts by Hammond, Lansdowne, J. Milton, Shakespeare and E. Waller

The Tempest (3, Garrick, after Shakespeare), Drury Lane, 11 Feb 1756, excerpts (1756), ov. in Six Favourite Overtures (1760); ov. from Il Ciro riconosciuto; incl. song texts by J. Dryden and others

The Enchanter, or Love and Magic (musical drama afterpiece, 2, Garrick), Drury Lane, 13 Dec 1760, excerpts (1760), ov. in Six Favourite Overtures (1760)

Medea, 1760–61 (3, B. Stillingfleet), inc., *Hs**, 1 air in Coxe (1799)

*

[W. Coxe]: *Anecdotes of George Frederick Handel and John Christopher Smith* (London, 1799)

W. Coxe: *Literary Life and Select Works of Benjamin Stillingfleet* (London, 1811)

G. W. Stone jr: '*A Midsummer Night's Dream* in the Hands of Garrick and Colman', *Publications of the Modern Language Association of America*, liv (1939), 467–82

A. Loewenberg: 'Midsummer Night's Dream Music in 1763', *Theatre Notebook*, i (1945), 23–6

M. Sands: 'The Problem of "Teraminta"', *ML*, xxxiii (1952), 217–22

W. C. Smith: 'More Handeliana', *ML*, xxxiv (1953), 11–24

J. S. Hall: 'John Christopher Smith, Handel's Friend and Secretary', *MT*, xcvi (1955), 132–4; Ger. trans. in *HJb 1957*, 126–32

G. W. Stone jr: 'Shakespeare's *Tempest* at Drury Lane during Garrick's Management', *Shakespeare Quarterly*, vii (1956), 1–7

J. S. Hall: 'John Christopher Smith [sr]: his Residence in London', *HJb 1957*, 133–7

J. P. Larsen: *Handel's 'Messiah': Origins, Sources, Composition* (Copenhagen, 1957), 260ff

K. Sasse: 'Neue Daten zu Johann Christoph Schmidt', *HJb 1957*, 115–25

A. D. McCredie: 'John Christopher Smith as a Dramatic Composer', *ML*, xlv (1964), 22–38

J. S. Hall: 'John Christopher Smith (1712–1795)', *HJb 1964–5*, 59–69

R. Fiske: *English Theatre Music in the Eighteenth Century* (London, 1973, 2/1986)

A. G. Williams: 'Stanley, Smith and "Teraminta"', *ML*, lx (1979), 312–15

J. M. Knapp: 'English Theatrical Music in Garrick's Time: *The Enchanter* (1760) and *May Day* (1775)', *The Stage and the Page*, ed. G. W. Stone jr (Berkeley, 1981), 123–35

N. Gillespie: 'The Text of Stanley's "Teraminta"', *ML*, lxiv (1983), 218–24

A. C. Hicks: 'The Late Additions to Handel's Oratorios and the Role of the Younger Smith', *Music in Eighteenth-Century England: Essays in Memory of Charles Cudworth* (Cambridge, 1983), 147–69

A. Mann: 'Handel's Successor: Notes on John Christopher Smith the Younger', ibid, 135–45 MICHAEL BURDEN

Smith [Vielehr], **Julia (Frances)** (*b* Denton, TX, 25 Jan 1911; *d* New York, 27 April 1989). American composer. She studied composition with Frederick Jacobi, Bernard Wagenaar and Rubin Goldmark at the Juilliard Graduate School (1932–9), and at the same time was pianist for the Orchestrette Classique of New York. Between 1941 and 1946 she taught at Hartt College, where she founded the department of music education. Her music, which includes orchestral and chamber music with an appealing directness, is tonal, often dissonant and incorporates elements of jazz, folk and 20th-century French harmony. All six of her operas have been performed. *Cynthia Parker*, her first but also her most recently revised opera, was composed for the Texas Centennial but not completed in time. A complete performance took place in Austin for the Texas Sesquicentennial on 5 December 1985. The opera concerns the tragic conflicts between white and native American cultures in the 19th century. The music recalls folk music of both cultures in a conservative tonal idiom. Of the last four operas, which are for children, *Cockcrow* employs Anglo-American folk music with some reference to popular music of the period, and is lyrical, harmonically conservative and easily accessible.

Daisy, based on the life of Juliette Gordon Low, the founder of the Girl Scouts of America, was first performed by the Opera Guild of Greater Miami on 3 November 1973, and has since received more than 30 performances.

Cynthia Parker (3, J. Fortune), partial perf., Denton, North Texas State U., 16 Feb 1939; rev. 1977; first complete perf., Austin, 5 Dec 1985
The Stranger of Manzano, 1943 (1, J. W. Rogers), Denton, North Texas State U., 1 May 1946
The Gooseherd and the Goblin (1, J. F. Royle), New York, Municipal Broadcasting Station, 22 Feb 1947
Cockcrow (fairy-tale op, 1, C. D. Mackay), Austin, 22 April 1954
The Shepherdess and the Chimneysweep (Christmas op, 1, Mackay, after H. C. Andersen), Fort Worth, 28 Dec 1966
Daisy (2, B. Harding), Miami, 3 Nov 1973

*

C. Ammer: *Unsung: a History of Women in American Music* (Westport, CT, 1980)
J. W. LePage: *Women Composers, Conductors, and Musicians of the Twentieth Century*, ii (Metuchen, NJ, 1983), 274–304
R. H. Kornick: *Recent American Opera: a Production Guide* (New York, 1991), 286–8 ADRIENNE FRIED BLOCK

Smith, Patrick J(ohn) (*b* New York, 11 Dec 1932). American writer. He studied at Princeton and worked as an independent writer on music, founding in 1970 an adventurous periodical *The Musical Newsletter* that produced many worthwhile articles during its seven years' life. Smith served as president of the Music Critics' Association, 1977–81, and in 1985 became director of the Opera-Musical Theater Program of the National Endowment of the Arts; he relinquished that position in 1989 to become editor of *Opera News*. A well-informed writer with a marked interest in the literary aspects of opera, Smith produced the first English-language historical book on the opera libretto, *The Tenth Muse* (New York, 1970), and has also written *A Year at the Met* (New York, 1983).

Smith, Robert B(ache). American lyricist and librettist, brother of HARRY B. SMITH.

Smock Alley. Theatre in DUBLIN, built in 1662 and closed in 1787.

Smutný, Jiří (*b* Prague, 1 April 1932). Czech composer. In 1951 he completed his studies at the Prague Conservatory and enrolled at the academy, where his composition teachers were Karel Janeček, and Bořkovec. He became accompanist at the singing department of the academy in 1955, moving in 1956 to a similar appointment with the opera company at the National Theatre in Prague. His music draws on Janáček and Prokofiev in particular, and its dramatic vividness has led him to specialize in works for the stage. Smutný's extensive theatrical output, covering a wide range of subjects, genres and compositional techniques, has rendered his music more notable for its solid workmanship than for individuality. *Noční rozhovor* ('Night Conversation', 1967) and *Dvojník* ('The Double', 1974), both based on works by Dürrenmatt, reveal a deep concern for humanity, an opposition to violence and to the suppression of free thought.

Když dva dělají totéž, aneb Ženská ctnost [When Two do the Same, or Women's Virtue] (op-scherzo, 1, I. Havlů, after G. Boccaccio), Ústí nad Labem, 31 Dec 1960
Věštkyně [The Fortune-Teller], 1961 (1, J. M. Průša, after K. Čapek), Prague, Czechoslovak TV, 29 March 1964
Dalskabáty, hříšná ves [The Sinful Village of Dalskabaty] (comic op, after J. Drda), Prague, Czechoslovak TV, 14 Oct 1962
Budapešťský rychlík [The Budapest Express], 1962 (1, Průša, after E. E. Kische), unperf.
Ženska historie [A Woman's Story] (op-scherzo, 2, Průša, after E. Bass), Prague, Academy of Fine Arts, Opera Studio, 9 Nov 1965
Noční rozhovor [Night Conversation] (1, Smutný and B. Černik, after F. Dürrenmatt), Prague, Czechoslovak Radio, 11 Sept 1967
Klementina (radio op, 2, Smutný, after Vercors), Prague, Czechoslovak Radio, 5 Nov 1969; rev. for stage, 1969
Cesta za hvězdou [Journey to a Star], 1969 (radio op, J. Melč, after Vercors), Prague, Czechoslovak Radio, 17 Oct 1971
K smrti odsouzeni [The Death Sentence], 1970–74 (op-oratorio, K. Pietschmann), unperf.
Dvojník [The Double] (chamber op, 1, Smutný and Černik, after Dürrenmatt), Gelsenkirchen, 10 June 1974

OLDŘICH PUKL, HELENA HAVLÍKOVÁ

Smyth, Dame Ethel (Mary) (*b* Marylebone, 22 April 1858; *d* Woking, 8 May 1944). English composer. Born into a military family, she showed strong will and determination from the start and pursued music despite parental opposition. In 1877 she entered the Leipzig Conservatory and studied for a time with Reinecke and Jadassohn, but, dissatisfied, she turned for private tuition to Heinrich von Herzogenberg. At Leipzig her early essays in chamber music met with approval, derivative though they were, and she was further encouraged by meetings with Brahms, Grieg, Tchaikovsky, Dvořák, Clara Schumann and Joachim – all of whom accepted her as a promising and serious composer. She first appeared before English audiences in April 1890 with a Serenade for orchestra, and in October of the same year with an overture *Antony and Cleopatra*. The full implications of her ambition and achievement were recognized at the Albert Hall in January 1893 when her Mass in D was performed. The striking power of this work (quite unprecedented in a woman's composition) made a deep impression.

Her most considerable successes were yet to come, and in a field in which English musical conditions offered little opportunity: opera. *Fantasio*, highly commended in an international opera competition in 1895, was successfully produced under Stavenhagen in Weimar and revived by Mottl in Karlsruhe in 1901. A comedy of errors, it was constructed along conventional operatic lines and later regarded by its composer as journeyman work. She came to feel that its handling as a *Bildungsroman* fantasy was overdone and in 1916 she burnt most of the scores. *Der Wald*, whose première under Muck in Berlin in 1902 was followed by productions at Covent Garden and the Metropolitan, is a one-act tragedy of great concentration showing Smyth's German Romanticism at its height but lacking lyrical sublimity. This last could also be said of her greatest opera, *The Wreckers*, but here the vehement characterization of the harsh and oppressed Cornish village community and the more restless, electric musical style are ample compensation. It was written to her own French text, because at the time a French production seemed more likely; but in the event *The Wreckers* (*Les naufrageurs*) was first produced in Leipzig in 1906 (under the title *Standrecht*). The opera was then given in Prague and was espoused by Beecham, going on to enjoy professional revivals in England until 1939 and forming an important if unacknowledged link between Romantic music drama and the realism of *Peter Grimes*. Her later, less than full-length operas were not produced on the Continent; *The Boatswain's Mate* marks a turning towards indigenous traditions, being based symphonically on folksongs and her own *March of the Women* (one of her many contributions to the suffragette movement), and including spoken dialogue. Given under Beecham in 1916, it later passed into the repertory of the Old Vic where it met with considerable success. Its humorous vein was tapped less successfully in *Entente cordiale* (1925), an occasional piece about the war. *Fête galante* (1923), a miniature essay in idiosyncratic neo-classicism, stands apart from this development and is probably the least flawed of Smyth's operas. She wrote an autobiography (*Impressions that Remained*, 1919) and eight further witty books of memoirs.

See also BOATSWAIN'S MATE, THE and WRECKERS, THE.

Fantasio, 1892–4 (phantastische Komödie, 2, H. Brewster and Smyth, after A. de Musset), Weimar, Hof, 24 May 1898, *GB-Lbl**, vs (Leipzig, 1899)
Der Wald, 1899–1901 (Musik-Drama, 1, Brewster and Smyth), Berlin, Kgl, 9 April 1902; as The Forest, London, Covent Garden, 18 July 1902, *Lbl**; (London, 1902)
Les naufrageurs [The Wreckers], 1902–4 (lyrical drama, 3, Brewster and Smyth); trans. H. Decker and J. Bernhoff as Strandrecht, Leipzig, Neues, 11 Nov 1906; trans. A. Strettell and Smyth, London, His Majesty's, 22 June 1909; *Lbl**, vs (Leipzig, 1906)
The Boatswain's Mate [Der gute Freund], 1913–14 (comedy, 1, Smyth, after W. W. Jacobs), London, Shaftesbury, 28 Jan 1916, *Lbl**, vs (Vienna, 1915)
Fête galante (dance-dream, 1, E. Shanks and Smyth, after M. Baring), Birmingham, Repertory, 4 June 1923, *Lue*, vs (Vienna, 1923); arr. as ballet (Vienna, 1933)
Entente cordiale (postwar comedy, 1, Smyth), London, RCM, 22 July 1925; Bristol, Royal, 20 Oct 1926, *Lfm*, vs (London, 1925)

*

Kobbé10
C. Forsyth: *Music and Nationalism: a Study of English Opera* (London, 1911)
H. Foss: 'Fête galante', *MT*, lxiv (1923), 468–70
T. Beecham: *A Mingled Chime* (London, 1944), 84–6
C. St John: *Ethel Smyth: a Biography* (London, 1959)
F. Howes: *The English Musical Renaissance* (London, 1966), 65–7
N. Burton: 'Opera: 1865–1914', *The Romantic Age: 1800–1914*, ed. N. Temperley (London, 1981), 355–7
E. W. White: *A History of English Opera* (London, 1983), 354–64
D. Hyde: 'Ethel Smyth (1858–1944): a Reappraisal', *New-Found Voices: Women in Nineteenth-Century English Music* (Liskeard, 1984), 138–65
S. Banfield: 'British Opera in Retrospect', *MT*, cxxvii (1986), 205–7
——: 'The Early Renaissance: Mackenzie, Stanford and Smyth', *British Opera in Retrospect* (n.p., 1986) [pubn of the British Music Society], 63–8
J. Bernstein: '"Shout, Shout, up with your Song!": Dame Ethel Smyth and the Changing Role of the British Woman Composer', *Women Making Music: the Western Art Tradition, 1150–1950*, ed. J. Bowers and J. Tick (London, 1986), 304–24
R. Crichton, ed.: *The Memoirs of Ethel Smyth* (Harmondsworth, 1987) [incl. list of works]
E. Wood: 'Gender and Genre in Ethel Smyth's Operas', *The Musical Woman: an International Perspective*, ii, ed. J. L. Zaimont (New York, 1987), 493–507 STEPHEN BANFIELD, MICHAEL HURD

Smythe, Russell (*b* Dublin, 19 Dec 1949). British baritone. He studied at the Guildhall School of Music and the London Opera Centre. In 1976 he created Stephen Oliver's *Tom Jones* for English Music Theatre. With the WNO he sang Rossini's Figaro (1977), Yeletsky, Billy Budd, Almaviva, Papageno and Yevgeny Onegin, and for the ENO he has sung Rossini's Figaro (1981), Pelléas, Tarquinius and Andrey (*War and Peace*). He made his Covent Garden début in 1984 as Ned Keene, returning as Malatesta, Falke and Guglielmo. He has sung at Hamburg, Paris, Lyons, Vancouver and Vienna, and his repertory includes Harlequin (*Ariadne*), Sherasmin (*Oberon*), Lord Cockburn (*Fra Diavolo*) and the title role of Donizetti's *Torquato Tasso*, which he sang at Buxton (1988). A stylish singer, he has a light, flexible and incisive voice. ELIZABETH FORBES

Snape. Village in Suffolk, England, near ALDEBURGH; its former malt-house, converted into a concert hall (The Maltings) in 1967, is used for opera performances connected with the Aldeburgh Festival and houses the Britten-Pears School of Advanced Musical Studies.

Snegurochka. Opera by N. A. Rimsky-Korsakov; *see* SNOW MAIDEN, THE.

Snow Maiden, The [*Snegurochka*]. Springtime tale (*vesennyaya skazka*) in a prologue and four acts by NIKOLAY ANDREYEVICH RIMSKY-KORSAKOV to his own libretto after the 'springtime fairy-tale' by ALEXANDER NIKOLAYEVICH OSTROVSKY (1873); St Petersburg, Mariinsky Theatre, 29 January/10 February 1882.

PROLOGUE

Vesna-Krasna [The Bonny Spring]	mezzo-soprano
Ded Moroz [Grandfather Frost]	bass
Devushka-Snegurochka [Snow Maiden] *their daughter*	soprano
Leshiy [Forest Sprite]	tenor
The Shrovetide Straw-Dummy	bass
Bobïl'-Bakula ('Poor Peasant Bakula')	tenor
Bobïlikha *his wife*	mezzo-soprano

Berendeyans of both sexes and all ages; Spring's retinue, birds: cranes, geese, ducks, rooks, magpies, starlings, skylarks etc.

OPERA

Snow Maiden	soprano
Lel' *a shepherd*	alto
Kupava *a young maiden, daughter of a wealthy villager*	soprano
Mizgir' *visiting trader from the Berendey settlement*	baritone
Tsar Berendey	tenor
Bobïl'-Bakula	tenor
Bobïlikha	mezzo-soprano
The Bonny Spring	mezzo-soprano
Bermyata *boyar in attendance*	bass
First Crier	tenor
Second Crier	bass
Royal Page	mezzo-soprano
Forest Sprite	tenor

Boyars, their wives, and the tsar's retinue of psalterists, blind bards, minstrels, fiddlers, pipers; shepherds, lads and lasses, Berendeyans, forest sprites, flowers (Spring's retinue)

Setting The land of the Berendeyans in prehistoric times

Although it is seldom remarked, Rimsky-Korsakov's romantic tale of nature made animate is every bit as entitled as Dargomïzhsky's *Stone Guest* or Musorgsky's *Marriage* – those pillars of 'realism' – to be classified as a 'sung play'. Its libretto is simply the text of its literary source, unaltered but for considerable condensation: whole parts, including the major role of Kupava's father, were dropped from the cast of characters. Perhaps condensation should have gone further: even its greatest admirers – including the composer, who supplanted the original score of 1881 in about 1895 with an abridgment containing recommendations for further cutting – have acknowledged that the opera is overlong because of its fastidious retention of texts not meant to be slowed by music.

Yet in every other way Ostrovsky's play was already a virtual libretto. Composed in verse, it contained so many interpolated songs and dances (sometimes to folk texts that had well-known attendant melodies) that performance without music was virtually unthinkable. For the gala first production (at the Maliy Theatre, Moscow, in 1873), an elaborate incidental score had been commissioned from Tchaikovsky (op.12, 19 numbers), which contains many of the same songs and choruses as Rimsky's opera, sometimes set to the same folk melodies, as specified.

The première of the opera was conducted by Eduard Nápravník; Fyodor Stravinsky sang Grandfather Frost.

PROLOGUE *Midnight, the end of winter: a snow-covered landscape at the Red Hill (a river running at its foot and the Berendeyan capital visible on its opposite bank)* The Forest Sprite announces the change of season; the Bonny Spring enters with her entourage of birds. The birds remind her with their shivering that the season is yet chill because the Snow Maiden, the love-child she has borne of Grandfather Frost, has angered the sun god Yarilo. She bids the birds dance to warm themselves (chorus, on two folksongs transcribed by the composer). Frost arrives and sings of his pleasure in spreading cold. Spring asks after the Snow Maiden; Frost calls her out of the forest. The Snow Maiden asks to be allowed to live among humans for the sake of their songs and games; she admits she listens to Lel''s warm songs particularly, which are so beautiful 'you listen and melt'. At 'melt' Frost takes fright and warns the Snow Maiden to avoid Lel', but he grants her request and asks the Forest Sprite to watch over his daughter; Spring promises to help the Snow Maiden if the need arises. Villagers approach with a Shrovetide effigy, who sings of the changing season (the score incorporates three choral songs from Rimsky-Korsakov's own anthology of 1877). Bobïl' and Bobïlikha spy the Snow Maiden, who begs them to adopt her; when they agree, she calls farewell to the forest. The villagers disperse in fright when the forest answers her cry.

ACT 1 *Bobïl's hut; evening* The orchestral introduction contains horn calls associated with Lel', based on shepherds' pipe tunes the composer recalled from childhood. Bobïl' welcomes Lel' (his identifying tune is based on a shepherd call Lyadov gave Rimsky) and invites him to sing for the Snow Maiden; unable to understand why he wants something as paltry as a kiss as payment, she offers a flower instead. Lel' sings two songs, the first melancholy, the second gay. Some girls call to Lel'; willingly he runs off to them, tossing the Snow Maiden's flower aside. She is left lamenting the cold heart she has inherited from her father. Kupava enters and comforts the Snow Maiden; she tells of her betrothal to Mizgir'. Mizgir' enters and enacts the wedding ritual of purchasing Kupava from her friends (this scene incorporates three songs from Rimsky-Korsakov's collection). Mizgir' is about to leave with Kupava when he sees the Snow Maiden and falls in love with her (the background chorus is based on a *khorovod* ('The Linden Tree') from Rimsky-Korsakov's anthology); Kupava leaves, distraught. Bobïl' and Bobïlikha tell the Snow Maiden to get rid of Lel' and pursue her rich admirer. The villagers return from the field and question Mizgir' on his fickleness. He insults Kupava and declares his love for the Snow Maiden. Kupava curses Mizgir'. All resolve to take the matter to the tsar.

ACT 2 *Tsar Berendey's court* A chorus of blind psalterists sing the tsar's praises. Bermyata complains of the unseasonable cold; the tsar resolves to celebrate a mass wedding ceremony on Yarilo's day (i.e. Kupala) to placate the god. Kupava enters and tells her story to the tsar. The criers call for all to assemble and hear the tsar's decree; the court assembles to an orchestral march. The Berendeyans, led by Kupava and Lel', sing a hymn to their vatic ruler (chorus *a cappella*). Mizgir', confronted with his crime, confesses and is banished. The Snow Maiden arrives; her beauty dazzles the tsar (Berendey's cavatina, 'Polna, polna chudes': 'How full of wonders'). On learning that the Snow Maiden, for all her beauty, has never loved, he offers a reward to any who may make the Snow Maiden fall in love. Lel' is the favoured candidate, but Mizgir' asks to be released so that he too may try. Berendey, knowing that the Snow Maiden's love will end his kingdom's deep freeze, assents. All sing a hymn to the tsar.

ACT 3 *A forest clearing* The villagers sing and dance while their tsar looks on in approval (choral fantasy on 'The Linden Tree', already heard in Act 1). Bobïl' dances in imitation of a beaver (based on a *khorovod* from Rimsky-Korsakov's anthology). The tsar thanks everyone for their contribution, asks his minstrels for a final dance ('Dance of the Skomorokhi', popularly known as the 'Dance of the Buffoons', on a folktune in Stakhovich's collection) and commands Lel' to sing a final song. As reward, Lel' is allowed to claim a kiss from the maiden of his choice; he picks Kupava, to the Snow Maiden's torment. After everyone leaves, Mizgir' returns and protests his love to the Snow Maiden; she flees, assisted by the Forest Sprite, who bars Mizgir''s path with suddenly appearing foliage and misleads him with hallucinations of the Snow Maiden. Lel' and Kupava return and declare their love; the Snow Maiden reappears and reproaches Kupava for stealing Lel', but Lel' rebuffs her, reminding her that her heart is still cold. The Snow Maiden resolves to learn to love.

ACT 4 *The sacred valley of the sun, with a lake, surmounted by Yarilo's sacred hill; dawn* The Snow Maiden calls to her mother, who rises from the lake. At her entreaties, Spring grants her the gift of love. Suddenly nature explodes into life; the flowers sing to the Snow Maiden; Spring leaves with her retinue. Mizgir' overtakes the Snow Maiden who, to his amazement, now returns his passion. Remembering her father's warning, she begs Mizgir' to protect her from the sun. The tsar and villagers arrive to celebrate the Kupala and the ordained wedding ceremony (chorus, based on two *khorovod* tunes in Balakirev's collection, also used for the opening chorus in *May Night*). Mizgir' presents the Snow Maiden as his bride. As she confesses her love, the first rays of the sun strike her and she melts away; Mizgir' throws himself in the lake in despair. The tsar interprets these events to his people: they signify their release from the sun's wrath. He orders a hymn in praise of Yarilo (concluding chorus in a famous 11/4 metre).

* * *

The composer, who thought *The Snow Maiden* his finest work, intended to write a book on the opera, analysing it from standpoints both technical and poetic. He only managed, in the summer of 1905, to jot down an outline and a preliminary classification of themes. He divided the characters into four categories: (a) wholly mythological, representative of animated nature (Frost,

Spring, Forest Sprite); (b) mixed types ('half-mythological, half-real'), who inhabit the human world as links with the world of nature (the Snow Maiden, Lel', the vatic Tsar Berendey); (c) humans (Kupava, Mizgir'); and (d) the chorus, supplier of the impersonal folk background. Their respective musical idioms differ symbolically. The unalloyed avatars of nature (especially the Forest Sprite) are characterized by tritones and 'artificial' harmonies (chiefly whole-tone), the humans by the conventional idiom of Romantic opera, the chorus by 'modal' folksongs (often in unusual, asymmetrical metres, or simple units grouped into asymmetrical hypermetres). The mixed characters are of course the most varied and *sui generis*, their style responding to the exigencies of the action.

Rimsky classified the musical materials of the opera into three grades, as it were. The first consists of complexes of leitmotifs (Rimsky listed 12) associated with the various characters; unlike Wagnerian leitmotifs, they are not woven into complex symphonic textures to any great extent (although they are very extensively developed and transformed). The second class includes complete and rounded melodies out of which the lyrical and decorative set pieces are constructed. The third comprises themes or motifs that appear transiently, 'serving as temporary characterization of individual moments' rather than as identifying or recalling themes; sometimes they are used as a foundation (in the orchestra) on which a musical structure is erected – thus 'they serve symphonic, not operatic, ends'. (No examples are given, but the sumptuous music accompanying the betrothal kiss in Act 3 must be a prime one.) Rimsky-Korsakov's fragmentary analysis of *The Snow Maiden* is of interest as a rare quasi-theoretical profession of the pragmatic, semi-systematic method of operatic composition for which he has since been revered and reviled in equal measure.

RICHARD TARUSKIN

Sobinov, Leonid Vital'yevich (*b* Yaroslavl, 26 May/7 June 1872; *d* Riga, 14 Oct 1934). Russian tenor. After embarking on a law career he studied singing in Moscow, where he made his operatic début in small roles with a visiting Italian troupe (1893–4). He sang at the Bol'shoy from 1897, then with private opera companies and at the Moscow and St Petersburg imperial theatres, at La Scala (1903, 1905, 1911), Monte Carlo and Berlin (1905) and Madrid (1908). He made numerous appearances throughout Russia. Among his best roles were Lensky, Sinodal (Rubinstein's *Demon*, his Bol'shoy début role), Dubrovsky (in Nápravník's opera), Vladimir (*Prince Igor*), Berendey (*Snow Maiden*), Levko (*May Night*), Werther, Faust, Romeo, Des Grieux, Ernesto (*Don Pasquale*), the Duke, Alfredo, Lohengrin and Orpheus (Gluck). Even after he left the stage (1924) he was active at the Bol'shoy in various capacities. He had a profoundly poetic approach to his roles and studied every aspect of them in detail. His attractive stage presence and his even, expressive voice endeared him to a vast public. He made 66 recordings between 1901 and 1910. Two volumes of his letters, articles, speeches and reminiscences were published, with a discography, in Moscow in 1970.

*

GV (R. Celletti; J. Stratton and R. Vegeto)

HAROLD BARNES

Sobolewski, (Johann Friedrich) Eduard [Edward] (*b* Königsberg [now Kaliningrad], 1 Oct 1804; *d* St Louis, 17 May 1872). American conductor and composer of Polish birth. He studied composition with Zelter in Berlin and Weber in Dresden (1821–4). In 1830 he became director of music at the theatre in Königsberg, where he presented his operas *Imogen* (1832), *Velleda* (1835), *Salvator Rosa* (1848) and *Der Prophet von Khorassan* (1850); the last, his greatest success, received widespread publicity. He also worked as a critic and writer, notably for the *Neue Zeitschrift für Musik*, and published his judgment of Wagner's essays and works in his *Reaktionäre Briefe aus dem Feuilleton der Ostpreuss. Zeitung* (Königsberg, 1854; Eng. trans. in *The Musical World*, xxxiii, 1855), which in turn became part of the controversy surrounding the Berlioz-Wagner season in London (1855). In 1854 he moved to Bremen as music director of the theatre; at that time he was developing his own style of motivic construction and continuous music which he used in *Komala* and explained in *Oper, nicht Drama* (Bremen, 1857; *D-BMs*). After its 1857 première, *Komala* was produced by Liszt at Weimar in 1858, the first of Sobolewski's operas to be performed outside his Kapellmeister posts. Richard Pohl, in a lengthy review (1859), placed it within the camp of the moderns, thereby bringing it into an already raging debate.

Sobolewski left Bremen for the USA and settled in Milwaukee in July 1859. There his opera *Mohega, die Blume des Waldes*, based on the Pulaski episode in the Revolutionary War, was performed with the help of the Musical Society on 11 October and 1 November 1859; the first opera on a native American Indian theme to be composed in the USA, it followed many of the same principles as *Komala* and caused a major controversy in Milwaukee. His melodrama *An die Freude* was given in a Schiller festival there the same year. After founding and conducting briefly the Milwaukee Philharmonic Society Orchestra, in June 1860 he moved to St Louis, where he became conductor of the Philharmonic Society. He resigned in 1866 to devote himself to teaching and composition. Although most of his compositions are lost, detailed reviews with musical examples are extant. A gifted composer who produced striking ideas, Sobolewski seldom spent time in revision and reflection to perfect his works. They nonetheless form part of the history of exoticism in opera.

Imogen (3, Sobolewski), Königsberg, Stadt, 6 Dec 1832

Velleda, die Seherin des Brockens, Königsberg, Stadt, 1835

Salvator Rosa, Königsberg, Stadt, 22 Feb 1848

Der Prophet [Der Seher] von Khorassan (3, Sobolewski, after T. Moore: *Lalla Rookh*), Königsberg, Stadt, early 1850, lib. *D-LÜh*

Ziska vom Kelch (after A. Meissner), Königsberg, Stadt, 14 Feb 1851

Ein Lied als Verräther (comic op, H. Hartung), Königsberg, Stadt, 1852

Komala [Comala], die Königstochter von Inisthore (3, Sobolewski, after J. Macpherson: *Fingal*), Bremen, Stadt, early 1857

Mohega, die Blume des Waldes (amerikanische Nationaloper, 3, Sobolewski), Milwaukee, 11 October 1859, lib. *US-SLug*

*

'Der Prophet von Khorassan', *Illustrierte Zeitung*, xiv (11 May 1850) [review]

'Der Seher von Khorassan', *NZM*, xxxii (1850), 128–31 [review]

L. Köhler: 'Sobolewski's Oper: Ziska vom Kelch', *NZM*, xxxiv (1851), 100–01, 109–11

Hoplit [R. Pohl]: 'Comala', *NZM*, l (1859), 6–7, 16–18, 33–4, 39–42, 57–8, 68–9, 82–3, 92–3, 111–12, 124–6

O. Burckhardt: *Der Musikverein von Milwaukee* (Milwaukee, 1900)

R. T. Laudon: 'Eduard Sobolewski, Frontier Kapellmeister: from Königsberg to St Louis', *MQ*, lxxiii (1989), 94–118

JAMES M. BURK, ROBERT T. LAUDON

Sociology of opera. Two lines of inquiry have developed in recent years which might be described as 'sociology of opera', though neither has as yet run to much of the quantitative study characteristic of sociology as a modern academic discipline.

1. Opera as a social statement. 2. Opera in society: (i) Introduction (ii) Early opera (iii) The impresario (iv) 18th-century developments (v) From patronage to the market (vi) The 20th century.

1. OPERA AS A SOCIAL STATEMENT. The first is concerned with the inner workings of opera as a genre and of particular operas. It asks what these tell us about social relations in the cultures from which opera (or particular operas) sprang: opera, it assumes, is a revealing witness because, in the elaboration of the artistic means brought to bear on it, the genre lends itself to embodying projections of the fears, desires and conflicts at work within society. Inquiries of this kind have so far been few. Wagner's *Der Ring des Nibelungen* has called up several, the best-known being the still controversial essays by Bernard Shaw, Thomas Mann and Theodor Adorno: this is hardly surprising, since the *Ring* itself originated in a conception in part sociological.

More recent studies include one or two by musicologists (Carl Dahlhaus and Francesco Degrada) but also those of Catherine Clément (from a feminist perspective) and Peter Conrad, as well as a few essays by Luigi Baldacci and by one or two of the American scholars edited by Arthur Groos and Roger Parker. The latter group – literary critics with an interest in opera – are concerned far more with the libretto than with the music of the works they deal with. A study of the libretto is in itself legitimate and useful. The recent invention of surtitles, besides, makes the words of operas far more present to audiences' minds than they ever were in the past, even when they were sung in the audience's own language; it may end by tilting the balance towards the literary and away from the musical component. It does however seem rash to put forward far-ranging sociological analyses of operas while taking only scant notice of the music. In practice, and until further notice, opera remains an art led by music.

2. OPERA IN SOCIETY. The second line of inquiry, also recent, concerns itself with – to borrow a title from a seminal article by Lorenzo Bianconi and Thomas Walker – the 'production, consumption and political function' of opera, in different countries and at different times. It studies how opera has been financed and managed, and how it has been influenced by (or has influenced) its patrons and audiences. It is historically based, as sociological inquiry can be but (in practice) seldom is, and may be thought of as an interdisciplinary pursuit on the borders of musicology, sociology and economic and social history.

(i) Introduction. That opera is, among the arts, unusually revealing of pressures within the society that creates it is not a new idea. Early in the 20th century, Edward J. Dent was aware of it as well as knowledgeable about the pressures themselves, but he did not care to deal with the question systematically. What has brought about a new approach is the rapid spread, from the mid-1970s, of an interest in social science and in the social or collective dimension of history, partly under the influence of the group of French historians (Marc Bloch, Fernand Braudel, Emmanuel Le Roy-Ladurie etc.) associated with the journal *Annales*. The change may be seen at work in the short period that elapsed between the appearance of two Italian multi-volume histories, the *Storia dell'opera* edited by Guglielmo Barblan and Alberto Basso (1977), which was organized by countries, genres, schools and periods, and the *Storia dell'opera italiana* edited by Bianconi and Giorgio Pestelli, the first volume of which to appear (in 1987) bore the subtitle 'The System of Production and its Responsibilities'.

Opera has been from its inception a public art drawing on many and diverse resources and is correspondingly expensive. Requiring as it does singers, musicians, sometimes dancers, scenery and costumes, stagehands, front-of-house personnel, as well as both a literary and a musical creator, it could never be performed in private in the sense that chamber music was for a long time by definition private, if only because the many people involved in its production themselves made up a kind of audience; when, most unusually, a private performance of opera took place (as when Ludwig II of Bavaria arranged to be the only spectator at performances of some of Wagner's operas) it was seen as a contradiction in terms and a sign of the king's eccentricity.

(ii) Early opera. The new art grew out of diverse kinds of entertainments current in Italy about the turn of the 16th and 17th centuries, all of them patronized by courts or by nobles whose establishments were in effect miniature courts; the cardinals of the Roman Catholic Church, the chief patrons in Rome, were both noble and, some of them, nephews to the pope, that is, members of the ruling family in the Papal States. Even COMMEDIA DELL'ARTE, one of the contributory streams, was at that time patronized by the great, and should not be thought of as an affair of ragged strolling players.

The seeming contrast between opera as given in rulers' courts and public opera as it developed in Venice from 1637 should not be taken too far. True, the differences are obvious. At court, an opera was given a few performances at most, before the ruler, his courtiers and invited guests; it was performed by musicians already in the ruler's regular employ or specially borrowed from fellow-rulers or nobles; it was managed by the ruler's officials, with possibly a good deal of direct interest from the ruler himself; it was lavishly financed from the ruler's purse, with no thought of recouping any of the expenditure; its purpose was to display the ruler's 'magnificence', to enhance his prestige and confirm his supremacy within the court, and to carry the message beyond the confines of the household or the state as well. The opera libretto itself might be designed to glorify the ruler, both explicitly (e.g. by proclaiming the triumph of Austrian arms over the Turks in an opera written for the Vienna court) and implicitly (by an astounding display of monumental scenery and elaborate flying machines). This description applies to the operas composed by Monteverdi for the Mantuan court (*Orfeo*, 1607, and others now lost), to those put on in Rome by cardinals of the Barberini family in the middle decades of the 17th century, and to those commissioned by the courts of Leopold I in Vienna and of Louis XIV in France.

Venetian opera was public in the sense that most of the audience paid to get in, either at the doors or by buying or renting boxes. It was put on for a run of performances (at first only during the carnival season, lasting a couple of months or so, later during the shorter

Ascension fair season as well). The opera house belonged not to a ruler but to a noble family, and, by the mid-17th century, a number of competing theatres – generally six or seven – were putting on opera at the same time. The management of the season was as a rule entrusted to an individual or a group of persons known as the IMPRESARIO, who ostensibly bore the financial risk. The company were hired on contract for the season, and were not in the regular employ of either the theatre owners or the impresario, though a few members might be in the employ of a ruler away from Venice who allowed them to take up a lucrative opportunity. The operas themselves might allude to public events involving Venice, but on the whole were aimed at entertaining the audience: hence, in the 17th century, a strong emphasis on erotic appeal mixed with scenes of low comedy. Though spectacular scenery was not absent, singers were the great draw; the instrumental forces used were, until 1675 or thereabouts, much smaller than in court operas, as for instance in Monteverdi's *Il ritorno d'Ulisse in patria* (1640), in contrast with his *Orfeo*.

Although this was the 'Venetian model', it was rapidly exported about mid-century to other parts of Italy, in particular to Naples, by AF01the short-lived but influential troupes called Febiarmonici. This in turn made possible the growth of what has been identified (by Bianconi and Walker) as a third mode of production, whereby opera was put on under municipal patronage on the occasion of a trade fair, with an impresario or impresarios managing the season but with the ruler (or possibly a group of nobles) meeting the deficit. Here the occasion, as in Venice, was the entertainment of visitors, but the purpose was to enhance the standing as well as the tourist attractions of the city and the state.

Real though the differences are between these various sets of arrangements, they do not mark off straightforward 'court' and 'commercial' modes of production. How far the Venetian nobles who built opera houses pursued profit is unclear. That they had some notion of at least recouping their expenditure follows from the practice of selling or letting boxes, and of entrusting the season to an impresario who (until the late 18th century) was charged rent; payment for admission made the whole thing, in contemporary eyes, a 'mercenary' enterprise. The steward of a family allied to the theatre-owner Grimani rejoiced in 1694 that the Grimani would not, as had been feared, have to stand a loss on the current carnival season. On the other hand it is also clear that ownership of a theatre conferred prestige. Those involved were leading families who provided doges and high officials; when Cardinal Vincenzo Grimani was Viceroy of Naples in the Austrian interest during the War of the Spanish Succession he used singers and scene designers as counters, both in diplomacy and in forwarding the combined interests of his own Naples opera and of the Grimani theatres in Venice. There were fierce struggles for dominance among Venetian theatre-owning families; in these the primary motive was not commercial. It is thus possible to assert that in 17th-century Italy 'opera theatre [was] first and foremost an instrument of political authority' (Bianconi and Walker). If this was true in the leading commercial city in Italy, in Hamburg, another great commercial city, Johann Mattheson could write as late as 1728: 'Opera is more for kings and princes than for merchants or shopkeepers'.

(iii) The impresario. The impresario, too, when examined closely turns out to have been less than a risk-taking capitalist. This figure was to remain central to opera production in Italy until the late 19th century, as public opera spread (from the turn of the 17th and 18th centuries) to more towns and seasons; impresarios, often Italian, also came to operate in the German-speaking lands, the British Isles, the Iberian peninsula and Eastern Europe (in Britain, 18th-century German and Italian impresarios were succeeded by British managers who worked in much the same way). The one important European country that resisted the system, as it resisted Italian opera itself, was France, where serious opera remained for long an entertainment under royal control, and theatres up to recent times were run by permanent managers (*directeurs*); it was the incursion of Italian troupes that helped to bring about the growth of (rapidly Frenchified and less directly controlled) *opéra comique*.

Rather than a venture capitalist, an opera impresario was an intermediary who stood to the controllers of an opera house in a relation somewhere between that of a partner and that of a dependant. The management, if held by a nobleman or a group of nobles (as often happened in the 18th century), was in practice a kind of executive acting on behalf of the ruler (in a royal theatre) or of the noble family or association who owned the theatre or the boxes. A plebeian manager, on the other hand – generally a member of the musical or dancing professions, or a tradesman with theatrical connections, e.g. a costume hirer or printer – depended on the controllers of the opera house for a subsidy, and was sometimes little less than a retainer of theirs in everyday life; as late as the 1810–40 period one of the leading Rome impresarios was a tenant of the Capranica theatre-owning family, whom he supplied with chocolate and candles. The subsidy was not (until the early 19th century) necessarily regular or laid down in advance, nor was it always paid in cash; it might consist in a number of boxes which the impresario could dispose of (as he could not dispose of boxes in general), or in the sometimes highly profitable gambling concession attached to 18th-century theatres, or in a cash subvention either agreed beforehand by the theatre owner(s) or the boxholders, or granted by them or by the ruler to make up a deficit. This did not mean that the impresario took no risks: some of the various forms of subsidy were uncertain and might prove inadequate, leading to the impresario's failure, signalled by his fleeing the town and leaving the company unpaid; on the other hand, until well into the 19th century, authority could at times be successfully appealed to for further help.

(iv) 18th-century developments. In Italy, the movement during the 18th century was towards the formation of a market for opera management and especially for the engagement of opera personnel: cash rewards and short-term contracts gradually superseded relations of patronage and dependence. During the 17th century, opera engagements had been too few to provide a regular living; most musicians and singers (themselves, in the first half of the century, not clearly differentiated from instrumental musicians) were employed in church music and sometimes in chamber music as well, which might well mean permanent attachment to a great personage or to an institution. An incidental reason for the growth of a market was the almost uninterrupted series of wars on both Italian and German soil between

1689 and 1714, which drew some rulers' attention elsewhere and often precluded them from paying musicians. More fundamental in accounting for the change was the notable multiplication of theatres and seasons. Already in the period of the wars a kind of circuit had grown up among the courts of Mantua, Modena, Parma and Tuscany, with some allied town theatres, along which musicians circulated. By the 1750s the opera habit was firmly implanted among the upper classes of many north and central Italian towns; many theatres had been built, if only, as yet, semi-permanent wooden ones; and spring and autumn seasons had come to be regularly given as well as the traditional ones held during carnival and summer fairs. This made a dense network where opera personnel could find employment all year round at a wide variety of levels of imputed quality and financial reward. The network also enabled them to concentrate on opera, some of them to the exclusion of all other work.

In the many German-speaking states, opera became divided between court theatres (sometimes maintained by a great nobleman who was a virtual petty sovereign, like Haydn's employer Prince Esterházy), some ambitious municipal theatres as in the free city of Hamburg, and humbler town theatres used by itinerant troupes who got a princely or municipal subsidy. Save for a few important capitals such as Vienna, Munich and Dresden, the coming of opera was delayed by the ill effects of the Thirty Years War until late in the 17th century, and it remained subject to sudden financial constraints or to the accession of a new sovereign with little interest in music, who might close it down. Arrangements which in Italy were becoming archaic still went on in Germany down to the Napoleonic Wars, such as the engagement of musicians and singers for a term of years (sometimes lifelong) to perform in church and chamber as well as in the opera house. In large cities such as Vienna, Prague and Dresden, however, public opera houses could be run by Italian impresarios and with a mixture of Italian and German musicians. Expensive wars, again, between 1740 and 1763 drew opera away from court and towards a town opera house under less direct imperial or royal supervision; it was for this latter kind of theatre that Mozart's late Italian comic operas were written.

In London it used to be held that distinctly commercial arrangements prevailed, with opera run by committees of the aristocracy and the upper merchant class on (at least in intention) business lines; but recent studies have suggested that the system by which Handel's operas were put on was not markedly unlike the Italian, since it included an impresario working on behalf of a boxholders' committee, and a subsidy (though a relatively modest one) from the king. True, opera artists in London were never dependants of the ruler or of any individual noble; their engagements were seasonal and contractual and payment was strictly in cash, whereas on the Continent part payment in kind (easier to come by and held to be more honorific) went on, gradually diminishing through the rest of the century. Again, in this matter German courts and noble households remained archaic, so that until 1790 Haydn and the company at Eszterháza were paid partly in beef, cabbages and firewood.

(v) From patronage to the market. As the production and organization of opera moved from patronage to the market, so the make-up and the visible array of the audience changed over time.

In 17th-century court opera the audience focussed on the ruler or other great person whose bounty had made the performance possible (*see* MUNICH, fig.1); in Venice and occasionally elsewhere the paying audience was more heterogeneous and the glory shed on the noble family or group ultimately responsible for the performance more diffused. Between about 1700 and 1850 the single great man or family gradually came to play a less active and more decorative role, if indeed such a single focus remained. Instead, the most visible part of the audience – the boxholders – collectively put themselves on display, still with a nicely graduated hierarchy signalled by the architecture of the opera house itself (see fig.2). In this display the aristocracy generally bore a large part, together with the upper stratum of the professional and official classes; at widely varying times, a more clearly defined middleclass element became conspicuous, but where it prevailed it tended ultimately to impose a modified architecture and a new, less obviously hierarchical array.

The earliest Renaissance theatres went back to antiquity for a model and seated most of the audience on stepped stands (for illustration *see* INTERMEDIO; *see also* VICENZA). The earliest opera houses, as they were first worked out in Italy and then copied all over Europe, instead took up much of the outer skin of the auditorium with vertically arranged tiers of boxes, set out in horseshoe, bell or rectangular shape; the tiers numbered anything from two to six. There were technical reasons for this: voices had less far to travel, even in a very large six-tier house such as the S Carlo, Naples (1737; *see* NAPLES, fig.2), than in a stepped theatre laid out in depth. But the main reason was the enhanced possibility of displaying an audience of boxholders, in the first place to each other, and of arraying them in hierarchical order (*see* SEATING and THEATRE ARCHITECTURE).

The horseshoe or similar shape ensured that the occupants of every box were visible from every other box. It also made possible the provision, across a corridor running behind the boxes, of a dressing-room corresponding to each box: here servants could prepare meals and drinks; the family occupying the box enjoyed a home from home. The vertical arrangement made possible a clear, graduated hierarchy, taken over from the vertical hierarchy of an Italian palazzo (and not very different from that of a noble palace in Vienna or Prague). The second tier invariably ranked highest; this was where the ruler (if there was one resident in the town) had his or her box, and save in exceptional circumstances the other boxes were occupied almost wholly by the aristocracy, at any rate in the main opera season (exceptions were certain commercial towns with little resident nobility, such as Trieste). The first and third tiers ranked somewhat lower than the second, and any tiers above the third somewhat lower still; the sixth tier in a very large theatre might still harbour the odd impoverished noble, but was generally given over to a shopkeeping, artisan or soldier audience as well as to some of the vast number of servants of the aristocracy attending the opera (who in some places had free entry). Boxes at the side of each tier ranked a little lower, and cost a little less, than those in the centre, but their inconvenience was less marked than it is now, because the stage and the singers were thrust farther forward into the auditorium. The downstairs area, in Britain called the stalls, in America the orchestra, and in a number of

1. Performance of an opera in the private theatre of the Turin royal palace as part of the celebrations marking the arrival of the Princess of Piedmont in 1722: engraving by A. Aveline after Filippo Juvarra

continental countries the parterre, in the 18th century might also be filled with servants, but upper ones: at La Scala, between the opening of the theatre in 1778 and the coming of the revolutionary French army in 1796, the stalls gave admission at a preferential rate to the 'black cloaks' – the majordomos, secretaries and stewards of the nobles occupying the boxes, who were thus enabled to call on their services whenever they chose. But the stalls were also the place for officers, government officials, passing travellers and, in university towns, students.

The coming of an audience more middle-class in composition and tone was not sudden or uniform. It happened first in economically advanced places where a growing middle class was willing or eager to take an interest in opera. France in the last years of the *ancien régime* – a good deal more economically advanced, in relative terms, than popular cliché has it – was such a place: as soon as the shackles of official monopoly were removed from opera at the Revolution there occurred an explosion both of new works and of opera performances, not only in Paris but along a dense network of provincial towns; between October 1793 and August 1795 there were 1643 performances of operas by Dalayrac in 36 provincial towns and, in nine months of 1795–6, 1552 performances of operas by Grétry. This was one among many changes that could be only partly reversed, whether by Napoleon or by the restored monarchy: at Lille, a middle-sized town, the theatre in 1815–16 gave more than 250 performances of all genres, of which 134 were of opera and ballet. In the period immediately after Waterloo an attempt was made to put the Paris Opéra back under royal and aristocratic control, but the 1830 revolution brought in a selfconsciously bourgeois regime both in the state and in the opera house. Provincial opera houses continued to provide a largely bourgeois audience with abundant fare; as France was also unusual at this time in having an effective system of copyright for both the text and the music of French-language operas, Italian composers such as Donizetti and Verdi were keen to see French versions of their works going round this circuit, quite apart from the works they wrote specifically for Paris.

A similar change took place under French influence in

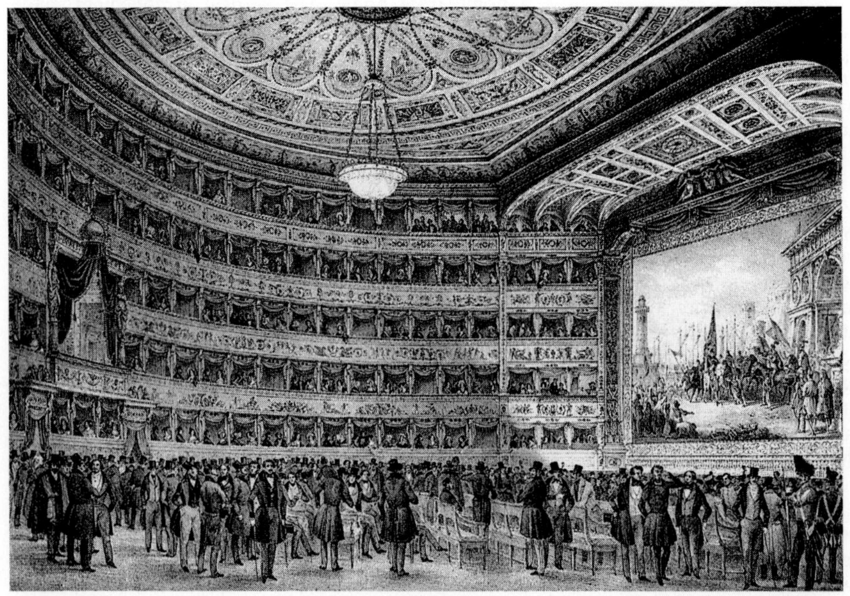

2. Interior of La Fenice, Venice, soon after it was rebuilt in 1837: lithograph (dedicated to the contralto Karoline Unger)

parts of Italy and Germany, but piecemeal and more slowly. Milan, chosen by Napoleon as his Italian capital, developed a considerable middle class which by the 1820s was occupying much of the space formerly taken up by 'black cloaks'; it was also the first place in Italy to get rid of hierarchical pricing by class and genre (i.e. higher prices for nobles, lowest for servants; higher for serious opera, lower for comic). Whether and how fast such changes came about depended on the general social and economic make-up of the town and the pattern of control over particular theatres. The main opera house in the capital of a small German or Italian State was likely still to be dominated by the court; in Venice, the leading theatre, the aristocratically controlled La Fenice, resisted making the top tier into an undivided gallery (seen as relatively 'popular') until 1878, but other Venice theatres were less fussy.

A special case was Britain, economically the most advanced country in the first two-thirds of the 19th century, but with a middle class of whom many avoided opera, some through religious scruples about all theatre-going, others out of a longstanding preference for native mixed genres (ballad opera, pantomime etc.). George Eliot, representative of the Victorian middle class at its finest, associated opera with the appurtenances of 'good society' – 'claret', 'velvet carpets', 'dinner engagements six weeks deep', 'faery ballrooms' – an association it has never wholly shaken off. True, there was, alongside the taste for opera as an imported luxury, a middle-class following for the modest line of native operas (by Balfe, Wallace etc.) and for the Pyne-Harrison company which gave opera in English. In the USA opera remained an exotic import (first Italian or French, then German). Religious objections had some force with the overwhelmingly middle-class audience here as well, though they did not prevent a stream of young women singers from going to Europe for training and a début; Emma Abbott (1850–91) did interpolate 'Nearer, my God, to Thee' in a performance of *La sonnambula* in Milan (it was hissed) and later declined to sing *La traviata* on moral grounds, though she relented in her American touring days (she stressed the sentiment and the Worth gowns).

The Latin-American countries shared the North American propensity to consume opera as a luxury import from Italy or France, along with zarzuela from Spain; German opera did not arrive in strength until the 20th century. The audience here was heavily dominated by the Iberian-descended 'oligarchy'; from the 1860s it provided rich pickings for European troupes that took advantage of the South American winter, corresponding to the slack season in the northern hemisphere, and were prepared to face the attendant risks of yellow fever and coups d'état. In the last third of the 19th century, large Italian immigrant populations built up in Argentina, Uruguay and Chile: these supported an Italian popular opera, based on a few of the most familiar repertory works.

By that time, repertory opera had become the norm in Italy itself, as well as in France, Germany, Austria and Bohemia – the homelands of opera. Much the same group of works (headed by *Il barbiere di Siviglia*, *Lucia di Lammermoor*, *Lohengrin*, *Rigoletto*, *Il trovatore*, *La traviata*, *Faust*, *Mignon*, *Roméo et Juliette*, *Aida*, *Carmen*) were diffused year after year through many theatres of varying prestige, some of them frankly appealing to a middle- and lower-middle-class public. These theatres were often recently built; by 1880, when an ambitious new opera house (the Teatro Costanzi, now the Teatro dell'Opera) opened in Rome, it had only three tiers of boxes but two large undivided upper balconies, an arrangement which to begin with struck some people as insufficiently hierarchical, though it was soon accepted (see fig.3). From then on, boxes were on the retreat and balconies increasingly the norm. The many opera houses of the second or third rank were no longer dominated either by an aristocratic audience or by a demand for a steady diet of new works; opera and the new, highly popular genre of operetta often alternated, though the two (outside the German-speaking countries) remained distinct in their personnel and their management structures, operetta being more often put on by touring companies headed by a singer-manager. In these countries, the period between about 1860 and 1914 probably saw more and larger audiences for opera than at any time before or since, but far fewer new crea-

3. Auditorium of the Teatro Costanzi, Rome (designed by Achille Sfondrini; inaugurated 1880): engraving (c1884) after D. Paolocci; note the undivided upper balconies above the three tiers of boxes

4. A live relay from the Royal Opera House, London, of Rossini's 'Il viaggio a Reims', shown on a giant screen in the Covent Garden piazza, 4 July 1992

tions than in the 18th century or the early 19th. It was also a period of some economic strain, particularly for the more traditional aristocratic opera houses. The so-called 'great depression' of 1873–96, really a period of falling prices and lower profits (but on the whole of rising incomes for much of the urban population), damaged some aristocratic fortunes, and the coming of even limited suffrage and representative government brought subsidies for opera under attack. In Italy from 1860 (but in Germany not till 1918) the old state capitals lost their courts and with them much of the money and patronage that had made for notable opera seasons. Formerly important opera houses – at Naples, Venice, Florence, Parma, Modena – lost much of their quality though not (as Verdi grumbled apropos of Naples) their complacency.

(vi) The 20th century. Strains of this kind were exacerbated in the 20th century by the coming of new technology in popular entertainment with which opera could not compete, and by a long-term rise in labour costs which an expensive art such as opera could not absorb.

The cinema from the 1910s, radio from the 1930s and television from the 1950s have diverted the great public from the opera house, though all three in their different ways (followed now by video) have made opera available to a wide audience in conditions radically unlike those experienced in the theatre. (In Britain, this outcome is masked by the growth since World War II of regional opera companies and of long, regular London opera seasons; the devastating effects of the new media on the opera-going habit can best be perceived in France and Italy, where the habit was most rooted, though there has been some recovery since the 1960s.) Gramophone records, already important in the 1900s, have had a complex effect on both the production and the consumption of opera. In the early part of the century, they reinforced the cult of the aria and the solo voice, hence the cult of singers such as Caruso. More recently, long-playing records have made part of the audience familiar with entire works and with more works than ever before, but at the cost of further distancing it from what actually goes on in the opera house; on occasion, too, a new opera production is in effect a tryout of a recording. For singers and conductors, opera engagements may become incidents in a career focussed on the recording industry.

The rise in costs is essentially the result of paying decent wages to the rank and file of an opera company (chorus, orchestra etc.) in a country with a steadily rising standard of living. It has debarred impresarios from any longer attempting to manage opera. Even in the USA, the last impresario to run a popular opera company giving regular seasons, FORTUNE T. GALLO, gave up soon after World War II. Opera in the USA nevertheless can still be run on a mixture of private and civic patronage, with corporate patronage playing an important role, as for example in the Metropolitan Opera broadcasts, sponsored by Texaco. The British government has wished opera companies in Britain to move in the same direction, but so far American levels of private patronage have been unattainable; opera in postwar Britain (as in continental countries since the

1920s at least) has depended on state subsidy and been run by non-profit-making institutions responsible to an intermediary body, the Arts Council (on the Continent, to an appropriate ministry). In Britain the perennial drawback of this system is inadequate funding and the threat of insidiously falling standards; on the Continent it is more often political interference, as in Italy, where the superintendence of an opera house is 'allotted' to a nominee of this or that political party. But that may confirm that where opera is thought important it remains, as a public art, inextricably bound up with political power.

*

OPERA AS A SOCIAL STATEMENT

L. Baldacci: *Libretti d'opera* (Florence, 1974)
P. Conrad: *Romantic Opera and Literary Form* (Berkeley, 1977)
C. Clément: *L'opéra ou la défaite des femmes* (Paris, 1979; Eng. trans. as *Opera, or the Undoing of Women*, 1988)
F. Degrada: *Il palazzo incantato* (Fiesole, 1979)
C. Dahlhaus: *Musikalischer Realismus: zur Musikgeschichte des 19. Jahrhunderts* (Munich, 1982; Eng. trans. as *Realism in Nineteenth-Century Music*, 1985)
P. Conrad: *A Song of Love and Death* (London, 1987)
A. Groos and R. Parker, eds.: *Reading Opera* (Princeton, 1988)

OPERA IN SOCIETY

ES ('Impresario'; R. Celletti)
W. L. Crosten: *French Grand Opera: an Art and a Business* (New York, 1948)
W. J. Baumol and W. G. Bowen: *Performing Arts: the Economic Dilemma* (New York, 1966)
M. F. Robinson: *Naples and Neapolitan Opera* (Oxford, 1972)
R. M. Isherwood: *Music in the Service of the King* (Ithaca, 1973)
N. Mangini: *I teatri di Venezia* (Milan, 1974)
M. Blaug, ed.: *The Economics of the Performing Arts* (London, 1976)
B. Brévan: *Les changements de la vie musicale parisienne (1774–1799)* (Paris, 1980)
H. C. R. Landon: *Haydn: Chronicle and Works*: iv, *Haydn at Eszterháza* (London, 1980)
R. Strohm: 'Aspetti sociali dell'opera italiana del primo settecento', *Musica/Realtà*, ii (1981), 117–41
M. De Angelis: *Le carte dell'impresario* (Florence, 1982)
J. Milhous and R. D. Hume: *Vice-Chamberlain Coke's Theatrical Papers 1706–15* (Carbondale, IL, 1982)
——: 'New Light on Handel at the Royal Academy of Music in 1720', *Theatre Journal*, xxxv (1983), 149–67
L. Trezzini and A. Curtolo: *Oltre le quinte: idee, cultura e organizzazione del teatro musicale in Italia* (Venice, 1983)
L. Bianconi and T. Walker: 'Production, Consumption and Political Function of Seventeenth-Century Opera', *Early Music History*, iv (1984), 209–96
J. Milhous: 'Opera Finances in London 1674–1738', *JAMS*, xxxvii (1984), 567–92
J. Rosselli: *The Opera Industry in Italy from Cimarosa to Verdi: the Role of the Impresario* (Cambridge, 1984)
C. Ehrlich: *The Music Profession in Britain since the Eighteenth Century* (Oxford, 1985)
J. Mongrédien: *La musique en France des Lumières au Romantisme (1789–1830)* (Paris, 1986)
F. Piperno, J. Rosselli and F. Nicolodi: 'Il sistema produttivo', *SOI*, iv (Turin, 1987), 1–229
J. Fulcher: *French Grand Opera as Politics* (London, 1988)
J. Rosselli: 'From Princely Service to the Open Market: Singers of Italian Opera and their Patrons, 1600–1850', *COJ*, i (1989), 1–32

JOHN ROSSELLI

Socor, Matei (*b* Iaşi, 15 Sept 1908; *d* Bucharest, 30 May 1980). Romanian composer and conductor. He studied at the Bucharest Conservatory (1927–9) with Alfonso Castaldi (harmony and counterpoint) and Constantin Brăiloiu (folklore, music history), and then at the Leipzig Conservatory (1930–33) with Sigfrid Karg-Elert and Hermann Grabner (composition). He became a researcher at the Institute of Folklore in Bucharest, chairman of Romanian Broadcasting (1945–52) and then president of the Union of Composers (1949–54). His only opera, *Conu Leonida faţă cu reacţiunea* ('Mr Leonida Face to Face with Reaction'), is a musical farce in one act to a libretto by I. L. Caragiale, first performed on 28 December 1978 at the Romanian Opera House, Bucharest. A veritable swansong, it represents a synthesis of his ironic style, permeated by traces of popular song. A parlando-rubato style for the arias alternates with arioso declamation, intended to complement Caragiale's inspired text.

*

G. Constantinescu: *Matei Socor* (Bucharest, 1983)

VIOREL COSMA

Sodeika, Antanas (*b* Jurbarkas, 23 Jan 1890; *d* Vilnius, 12 Sept 1979). Lithuanian baritone. He studied music privately in his native town. From 1907 to 1920 he lived in America, taking part in various musical activities organized by Lithuanian emigrés. After graduating from M. Petrauskas's music school in Boston in 1920 he returned to Lithuania, where he became one of the founders of the Kaunas Opera; he sang Germont in *La traviata*, its first local production. During two periods of study in Italy he added Rigoletto to his repertory. He sang at the Kaunas and, later, at the Vilnius Operas until 1950, his roles including Boris, Prince Igor, Yevgeny Onegin, Rubinstein's Demon, Escamillo, Amonasro and Scarpia. He made several recordings, and published his memoirs in Vilnius in 1958. Sodeika's brothers Stasys (1897–1980) and Stepas (1903–64) were also opera singers.

ADEODATAS TAURAGIS

Söderström(-Olow), (Anna) Elisabeth (*b* Stockholm, 7 May 1927). Swedish soprano. Trained at the Royal Academy of Music and Opera School in Stockholm, she made her début as Mozart's Bastienne in the Drottningholm Court Theatre in May 1947. She joined, and has remained a member of, the Swedish Royal Opera; she has also pursued an international career in a wide variety of roles ranging from Nero in Monteverdi's *Poppea*, through Mozart's Countess Almaviva and Susanna, Tchaikovsky's Tatyana, Strauss's Octavian, Christine and Marschallin, Debussy's Mélisande, Britten's Ellen Orford and Governess, to Janáček's Jenůfa and Emilia Marty. She made her Glyndebourne début in 1957, as the Composer in Strauss's *Ariadne auf Naxos*, and remained a favourite there (singing Strauss, Mozart, Beethoven and Tchaikovsky). Her Metropolitan début was as Susanna (1959) and she first appeared at Covent Garden with the Royal Swedish Opera as Daisy Dodd in Blomdahl's *Aniara* (1960); her Australian début was as Emilia Marty (1982, Adelaide). She combines a quick musical intelligence and a vivid and engaging stage personality with a protean voice not especially powerful but well able to express both soubrette mirth and tragic passion. Among her many contemporary roles have been Elisabeth Zimmer in Henze's *Elegy for Young Lovers* (1961) and Juliana Bordereau in the première of Argento's *The Aspern Papers* at Dallas in 1988 (for illustration *see* VON STADE, FREDERICA). She has published *I min tonart* (Stockholm, 1978; Eng. trans. as *In my own Key*, 1979).

ANDREW PORTER

Sodi [Sody], **Charles** [Carlo] (*b* Rome, *c*1715; *d* Paris, Sept 1788). Italian composer active in France. After joining his younger brother Pietro, a dancer and choreographer, in Paris around 1749, he obtained a position as violinist in the orchestra of the Comédie-Italienne and also became music master to Mme Favart. He provided the music for a number of ballets choreographed by his brother and staged mainly at the Comédie-Italienne during the early 1750s, but enjoyed greater success with his parodies of Italian intermezzos. He was granted a pension by the Comédie in 1765, and retired to teach the mandolin.

Baïocco et Serpilla (1753) was one of the first in a series of works by various librettists and composers parodying the popular repertory of the Bouffon troupe, which performed in Paris between 1752 and 1754. Parody techniques – the borrowing of text or music, or both – were important in preparing the ground for a more sophisticated type of *opéra comique* in which original librettos were set to original music. The text of *Baïocco* was adapted by C.-S. Favart from *Il giocatore* (performed by the Bouffons in August 1752), and the new French verses, interspersed with spoken dialogue, were set by Sodi as italianate *ariettes* and dialogue duets. Further parodies followed: *Le charlatan* (1756), based on the Bouffons' *Tracollo medico ignorante*, and *La femme orgueilleuse* (1759), based on *La donna superba*. The latter, whose music A.-J.-B.-A. Origny found 'extrêmement agréable' (*Annales du théâtre italien*, Paris, 1788), enjoyed a modest success at the Comédie-Italienne and remained in the repertory for over three years. By the end of the 1750s parody techniques had been superseded by original composition as the basis for *opéra comique*. Sodi subsequently set a new libretto by Sedaine, *Les troqueurs dupés*, in 1760, but this was a failure.

Baïocco et Serpilla (intermède, 3, C.-S. Favart, after the Bouffons: *Il giocatore*), Paris, Comédie-Italienne (Bourgogne), 6 March 1753 (Paris, *c*1765)

Le charlatan (cmda, 2, J. Lacombe, after the Bouffons: *Tracollo medico ignorante*), Paris, Comédie-Italienne (Bourgogne), 17 Nov 1756, excerpts in J. Dubreuil: *Dictionnaire lyrique portatif* (Paris, 1764)

La femme orgueilleuse (parodie, 2, A.-F. Quétant, after the Bouffons: *La donna superba*), Paris, Comédie-Italienne (Bourgogne), 8 Oct 1759, excerpts in Dubreuil

Les troqueurs dupés (cmda, 1, M.-J. Sedaine), Paris, OC (Foire St-Germain), 6 March 1760

ELISABETH COOK

Soffel, Doris (*b* Hechingen, 15 May 1948). German mezzo-soprano. She studied the violin first, and then singing with Marianne Schech in Munich, making her début at the Bayreuth Youth Festival in 1972 in Wagner's *Das Liebesverbot*. After winning the Berlin national competition that year she was engaged at the Stuttgart Opera, 1973–82, singing a wide repertory including Rosina, Carmen, Eboli and Octavian. At Bayreuth she sang Waltraute (1976) and Fricka (1983). She created Ma Ubu in Penderecki's *Ubu Rex* at Munich (1991). Her voice is noted for its tonal richness, particularly in the lower register. She sings regularly in leading opera houses and in concerts, and her recordings include Nancy in Flotow's *Martha* and roles in *Die Zauberflöte*, *Parsifal* and Wolf's *Der Corregidor* under Albrecht (1987).

NOËL GOODWIN

Sofia. Capital of Bulgaria. Situated on the main route from Istanbul to central Europe, it is Bulgaria's cultural centre. Liberation from the Turks in 1878 brought about dynamic changes and in 1891 the Dramatichesko-operna Trupa (Dramatic Opera Company), which consisted of Bulgarian and Czech singers, began to stage excerpts from operas. However, early problems of organization within the company and conflicts over repertory resulted in the formation later that year of Salza i Smyah (Tears and Laughter), an independent drama group, and Stolichna Operna Trupa (Sofia Opera Company). Encouraged by better material conditions and with assistance provided by the School of Music and the Bulgarian Music Union, together with the help of actors from Russia, Konstantin Mikhaylov-Stoyan, Ivan Vulpe and others founded the Bulgarska Operna Druzhba (Bulgarian Opera Society). The company first played in 1908 at the Naroden Teater (National Theatre), later performing at Slavyanska Beseda. World War I restricted its activities but some excellent Bulgarian singers joined. In 1922 Operna Druzhba became the Sofiyska Narodna Opera (Sofia National Opera). The National Theatre burned down on 10 February 1923 and the company performed in the Svoboden Teater (Free Theatre) and Renesans Teater (Renaissance Theatre) before returning to the new National in 1929. More Bulgarian operas were added to the standard European repertory and the National Opera achieved a high artistic standard. Besides Mikhaylov-Stoyan its soloists included Peter Raichev and Todor Mazarov.

The theatre was destroyed in 1944 and after the war opera was given first in the Balkan Theatre and then in the rebuilt National Theatre. Many Bulgarian operas were performed, including Pipkov's *Momchil* (24 April 1948). In 1953–4 the company moved to a new building (seating 1400) on Zabunov Street. After 1944, its new music directors organized training courses and a fresh generation of singers (e.g. Nicolai Ghiaurov and Dmitar Uzunov) went on to establish international careers. During the 1950s and 60s a nucleus of strong lead singers was built up and the conductors Assen Naidenov and Athanas Margaritov developed the sense of ensemble performance for which the theatre is renowned; notable productions have included Mikhail Hadjimishev's *Die Zauberflöte*, Dragan Kardjiev's *I quatro rusteghi* and Boris Pokrovskiy's *War and Peace*. In addition to the standard repertory, the company has staged many Russian operas and taken productions of *Boris Godunov* and *Khovanschchina* on international tours. The Sofia Opera contines to be the source of soloists (e.g. Stefka Evstatieva and Nikola Gyuzelev) for stages throughout the world; its conductors have included Ruslan Raichev, Mikhail Angelov, Boris Hinchev and Dimitar Manolov. The company's name became simply Sofiyska Opera in 1991.

The Darzhaven Musikalen Teater 'Stefan Makedonski', opened in 1947, specializes in operetta and musical comedy.

*

V. Krastev, ed.: *Entsiklopediya na bulgarskata muzikalna kultura* (Sofia, 1967)

R. Biks: *Bulgarski operen teatar* (Sofia, 1976)

MAGDALENA MANOLOVA

Sofonisba ('Sophonisba'). *Opera seria* in three acts by TOMMASO TRAETTA to a libretto by MATTIA VERAZI after ANTONIO MARIA ZANETTI and Girolamo Zanetti; Mannheim, Hoftheater, 4 November 1762.

Sophonisba (soprano) and Siface [Syphax] (tenor), King of Numidia, are married and have a child. When Syphax fails to return from battle against the

Romans, Massinissa [Masinissa] (soprano castrato), Sophonisba's former suitor, renews his advances. Syphax appears among the captives and rejoins his wife; they fail in their attempt to escape from their Roman captors. Afraid that she will be marched in chains through the streets of Rome, Sophonisba poisons herself and is dying when the news arrives that all has been resolved.

The libretto closely follows that of Jommelli's opera for Venice (1746), which Allacci attributed to the Zanettis. Jommelli's is unusual for the married status of the principal couple, whose child acquires a singing role in Verazi's libretto; even more remarkable is Sophonisba's staged suicide and death, a radical departure from Italian dramaturgical conventions, which proscribed staged deaths and required a happy ending. The tragic ending of Jommelli's opera presents a sharp contrast to earlier ones that treat the same subject – Minato's *Scipione affricano* for Cavalli (1664) and Silvani's *Sofonisba* for Caldara (1708) – both of which end happily. Verazi's version is acceptable because the dying Sophonisba, like Cato in Metastasio's revised version of *Catone in Utica*, is still alive when she exits, leaving the horrified company to sing the final chorus. Librettos entitled *Scipione nelle Spagne* by Zeno and Piovene and *Scipione in Cartagena* by Giunti are related but treat the historical material differently. A few years before, in Parma, Traetta had set Frugoni's French-inspired librettos, which incorporated spectacular elements that had been banished from Italian opera early in the century; these might have inspired Verazi, though the innovations in *Sofonisba* go far beyond those in the operas for Parma. Together Verazi and Traetta achieved an operatic spectacle with a dramatic power and intensity of expression entirely new to *opera seria*.

Sofonisba opens with a programmatic sinfonia accompanying the successful battle and breaching of the city wall. Later, a triumphant procession leads to a pantomime ballet and chorus depicting gladiatorial games. Verazi infused his aria texts with action and exclamatory language, which allowed Traetta to move seamlessly from recitative with orchestral accompaniment to fragmented, declamatory arias in multiple tempos punctuated with recitative. In several arias Traetta abandoned the predominant dal segno form for a variety of through-composed forms, including the shortened rondo (*ABA′B′*) common in *opera buffa*. For the trio finale of Act 2 Sophonisba and Syphax exit, leaving Masinissa alone on stage to express his frustration and rage. In the quintet at the end of the opera Traetta used material from the second movement of the sinfonia; he set Sophonisba's last words in an intensely dramatic recitative. MARITA P. McCLYMONDS

Sogner, Pasquale (*b* Naples, 1793; *d* Naples, 28 Dec 1842). Italian composer of Spanish descent. He studied with his father, a composer and teacher in Livorno. By the age of 16 he had already written and had performed a comic opera, *La vedova bizzarra*. When he left home he probably went first to Venice and then to Naples, to write music for the comic theatre (usually providing his own librettos) and, according to Fétis, for the ballet. His librettos show that he lived in Naples long enough to learn the Neapolitan dialect. Despite their melodic distinction, his operas appear to have been only moderately successful, and for a time he supported himself by teaching. The success of his opera *La figlia cameriera del padre* in Venice in 1834 recalled him to the notice of Neapolitan impresarios, giving him hopes (later substantiated) of a commission for the coming year: *Margehereta di Fiandra* was produced in Naples in 1835.

librettos by the composer and music lost unless otherwise stated

La vedova bizzarra (ob, 2, G. Checcherini), Livorno, Accademia dei Floridi, spr. 1809
Le avventure di Gilotto (dg, 2), Florence, Pergola, carn. 1814 [?unperf. according to *SchmidI*], *I-Fc*, arias *Nc*
Maria Stuarda, ossia I carbonari di Scozia (melodramma eroicomico), Venice, S Moisè, carn. 1815
Amore per finzione (opera comica, 2), Naples, Nuovo, ?spr. 1822
Generosità e vendetta (melodramma, 2), Naples, Fondo, 9 March 1824
Quattro prigionieri ed un ciarlatano (ob, 1), Naples, Nuovo, sum. 1832
La cena alle montagne russe (commedia, 2), Naples, Fondo, 1832
La figlia cameriera del padre, Venice, Fenice, ?spr. 1834
Margehereta di Fiandra (2), Naples, 1835

*

FétisB; *FlorimoN*; *SchmidlDS*
C. Gervasoni: *Nuova teoria di musica* (Parma, 1812), 275–6
U. Prota-Giurleo: *La grande orchestra del R. Teatro San Carlo nel settecento* (Naples, 1927), 61
A. Bonaventura: *Musicisti livornesi* (Livorno, 1930), 47
JAMES L. JACKMAN

Sogno di Scipione, Il ('The Dream of Scipio'). *Azione teatrale* in one act, K126, by WOLFGANG AMADEUS MOZART to a libretto by PIETRO METASTASIO; possibly Salzburg, Archbishop's Palace, May 1772.

It seems likely that *Il sogno di Scipione*, Mozart's first full-length Metastasio setting, was planned for the 50th anniversary of Archbishop Schrattenbach's ordination, and accordingly was composed before *Ascanio in Alba*. Schrattenbach however died in December 1771, and it may have been performed as a serenata in the Salzburg palace the next year during the installation ceremonies for Archbishop Colloredo.

Il sogno di Scipione belongs to the Viennese court tradition of moral theatre pieces. In his dream Scipio (tenor) is claimed by Fortuna [Fortune] (soprano), promising earthly rewards, and Costanza [Constancy] (soprano), representing unselfish virtue. In Elysium he meets his adopted father Publio [Publius] (tenor) and his real father Emilio [Emilius] (tenor), but they will not dictate his choice. Fortune impatiently demands an answer; Constancy is more persuasive and despite the threats of Fortune (the only obbligato recitative) Scipio elects to follow her. There follows a *licenza* in praise of the Archbishop.

The solos are arranged symmetrically round the aria for Emilius, the other singers each having two. The series of abbreviated da capo forms is mitigated by variation of tempo and metre, the short second aria for Publius and two choruses. The overture, lacking a third movement, is linked to the first scene; Mozart later added a finale to make a separate symphony, K141*a*. The final recitative is harmonically and instrumentally adventurous; otherwise, as befits its function, *Scipione* is elegant rather than dramatic. JULIAN RUSHTON

Sografi, Simeone Antonio [Antonio Simeone] (*b* Padua, 29 July 1759; *d* Padua, 4 Jan 1818). Italian librettist. Although he belonged to a family of famous surgeons, Sografi received a degree in law from the University of Padua. He moved to Venice where, after practising law for a time, he devoted himself completely to literary endeavours. Sografi made his début as a librettist with *Giovanna d'Arco*, an *opera seria* for the Teatro Eretenio in Vicenza during summer 1789. His first Venetian opera, *Gli Argonauti in Colco*, was produced at the S Samuele during the carnival season of 1790. He became a prolific dramatist, writing comedies, farces and dramas, both serious and semi-serious, as well as librettos for many of the foremost opera composers of his time. After the fall of the Venetian Republic he returned to Padua, where he built a theatre in the garden of his home and served as writer, director and impresario for its amateur troupe.

On the merit of Sografi's work in general, scholars of Italian literature have been less than enthusiastic. They have recognized his technical ability and facility of invention, but have faulted him for producing works that catered to the changing tastes of the public. Much of this research is outdated, as it focusses narrowly on Sografi's reputation as an author of spoken farce and, more specifically, on his *Le convenienze teatrali* (1794) and its sequel *Le inconvenienze teatrali* (1800). These two farces satirize the pretensions and foibles of opera singers, impresarios, librettists and others engaged in the production of opera and belong to a long tradition of operatic parody which includes Marcello's *Teatro alla moda* and Calzabigi's *Opera seria*. However, the exaggerated attention given to them belies Sografi's real contribution to opera: with regard to his operatic librettos, those of the comic genre make up a very small part of his total output.

Unlike his contemporaries, Sografi called his comic operas *commedie*, instead of the usual *drammi giocosi*. Such a choice indicated Sografi's preference for Goldonian-style comedies of character and his rejection of the visual gags and slapstick that had been the legacy of the *commedia dell'arte*. Sografi's target for satire was the bourgeoisie, and, like Goldoni's, his characters demonstrated a refinement in comedic manners, often expressing their feelings in language and in verse forms that resemble those from serious opera. Nevertheless, Sografi did not hesitate to round out his casts with such traditional types as the buffoon doctor, the wily maid and foreigners who speak with distinctive accents. In *I bagni d'Abano* (based on a Goldoni play), Sografi lampooned both the medical profession and the opera world. He gave the character Geltrude, a 'prima donna dall'Opera Seria di Padova', a Metastasian-style simile aria. In the same opera, Sografi spoofed the ghost scene, which was quickly becoming a convention in serious opera. (The most famous such scene was from his own *La morte di Semiramide*.)

The majority of Sografi's operatic comedies are in two acts. Many of the arias have four or more stanzas and use two different metres (i.e. four stanzas of *settenari*, followed by two stanzas of *quinari*). Ensembles are integral to the development of the plot, the most complex appearing at the ends of the two acts. Sografi generates comic verve in his finales by juxtaposing, in rapid succession, stanzas of various lengths and metres.

Sografi's serious librettos far outweigh his comic ones in importance. For subject matter he drew not only on the traditional sources of mythology and ancient history but also from more recent historical material (e.g. Peter the Great and Joan of Arc) and from French enlightenment authors (e.g. Rousseau and Voltaire). The serious librettos range in length from one act (*Pimmalione*) to four (*Giovanna d'Arco*), although all his late serious operas are in two acts.

In Sografi's serious librettos the Italian operatic theatre took on many of the characteristics of the French *tragédie lyrique*. Many begin with lengthy scene complexes that integrate soloists with chorus, and they occasionally include ballet. His finales exhibit a free dramatic interplay between solos, small and large ensembles, and chorus. In fact, in Sografi's hands the chorus becomes a fully participating character. This flexible dramatic approach, combined with Sografi's keen sense of the spectacular, brought a new level of theatricality to the operatic stage, and the serious works are rarely without some type of spectacle, be it a sacrificial scene (*Gli Argonauti in Colco*), a divination scene (*Saffo*) or a wedding scene (*Alceste*).

Although exit arias remain a prominent feature, arias also appear at the beginning and in the middle of scenes. Arias of two four-line stanzas of *settenari* or *ottonari* are commonplace, but increasingly in his later operas Sografi wrote arias that use *senari* and *quinari*, as well as arias of three and four strophes. Stanzas of *decasillabi* appear infrequently, and then usually for the chorus. Duets, trios, quartets and large ensembles often have a mixture of metres, grouped into strophes of two, four or six lines, although five-line stanzas occasionally appear. Act 2 scene ii of *Alceste* effectively demonstrates Sografi's style: an opening chorus sets the tone of sorrow with two strophes of *ottonari*. During Alceste's ensuing recitative the chorus comments on her agitated state. Alceste begs the gods to spare the life of her husband in an aria made up of one strophe of *settenari*. At the prompting of the high priests Alceste determines to die in her husband's stead. Sografi indicates a change in mood by writing an aria of two five-line stanzas of *quinari*. The scene ends with Alceste and the chorus sharing a closing stanza of *settenari*. This scene not only demonstrates the flexible use of solo and chorus, but also the basic formula of the cantabile/cabaletta scena that would become standard in Italian opera of the early 19th century.

As a member of the Venetian Società Filodrammatica, Sografi associated with Alessandro Pepoli and other advocates of operatic tragedy. His *Gli Orazi e i Curiazi* (Cimarosa, 1796) was the most influential *tragedia per musica* of that era, and it remains his most famous libretto. The story is based on Roman history and like most neo-classical operas deals with the conflict between duty and love. However, this conflict is resolved with a level of dramatic tension unprecedented in operas of that period. The protagonist Orazio, fulfilling his duty to Rome, has had to kill the husband of his sister, Orazia. To the strains of a triumphal chorus he rides at the head of a military parade. In a series of solos and duets Orazia confronts her brother, taunting him and finally cursing both him and the Roman republic. Orazio then stabs her and violently throws her down a flight of stairs. The curtain falls on two conflicting choruses, one singing the praises of Orazio and the fatherland, the other horrified at Orazia's brutal slaying. With *Gli Orazi*'s flexible dramatic structures, its spectacle, its high-pitched confrontation and sombre ending, Sografi began to move away from neo-classicism into the realm of Romanticism.

Giovanna d'Arco, ossia La pulcella d'Orléans (dm), Andreozzi, 1789; *Gli Argonauti in Colco* (dm), Gazzaniga, 1789; *Pimmalione* (scena drammatica), Cimador, 1790 (Giuseppe Rossi, 1793); *La morte di Semiramide* (tragedia, after Giovannini), Nasolini, 1790 (Borghi, 1791); *Ercole al Termodonte, ossia Ippolita regina delle Amazzoni* (dm), Nasolini, 1791; *La morte di Cleopatra* (tragedia), Nasolini, 1791; *Telemaco in Sicilia* (dm), A. Calegari, 1792; *Pietro il Grande ossia Il trionfo dell'innocenza* (dramma eroico), Rossi, 1793; *Apelle* (dm), Zingarelli, 1793

I bagni d'Abano ossia La forza delle prime impressioni (commedia), Capuzzi, 1793; *Saffo ossia I riti d'Apollo Leucadio* (dm), Mayr, 1794; *Il primo navigatore* (pastorale), Himmel, 1794; *La principessa filosofa ossia Il contraveleno* (commedia after A. Moreto: *Donna Diana*), Andreozzi, 1794 (reworked as *Il disprezzo vinto dal disprezzo* (commedia), Andreozzi, 1795); *Gli Orazi e Curiazi* (tragedia), Cimarosa, 1796 (Portugal, 1798); *L'amante servitore* (commedia), Paer, 1796; *La morte di Mitridate* (tragedia), Nasolini, 1796 (Zingarelli, 1797; Portugal, 1806)

Telemaco nell'isola di Calipso (dm), Mayr, 1797; *Timoleone* (dm), Nasolini, 1798; *Alceste* (tragedia), Portugal, 1798; *Il trionfo di Clelia* (dm), Nasolini, 1798; *L'uomo di quarant' anni* (f), Trento, 1799; *Annibale in Capua* (dm), Salieri, 1801; *I Manli* (mel), G. Nicolini, 1801; *Il Cid della Spagna* (dm), G. Farinelli, 1802; *Edipo a Colone* (tragedia), Zingarelli, 1802; *La caduta della nuova Cartagine* (dm), Farinelli, 1803; *La vergine del sole* (dm), Farinelli, 1804; *Il Corradino* (dm), Morlacchi, 1808; *Le Danaide romane* (dm), Pavesi, 1816

*

ES (N. Mangini)
G. Vedova: *Biografia degli scrittori padovani* (Padua, 1836)
G. Bonfio: *Cenni biografici di Antonio Sografi* (Padua, 1854)
L. Lamberto: 'Simeone Antonio Sografi, commediografo padovano del secolo XVIII', *Nuovo archivio veneto*, vii (1894), 107–47
L. Miragoli: *Il melodramma italiano nell'ottocento* (Rome, 1924)
I. Sanesi: *La commedia*, ii (Milan, 1935)
B. Brunelli: 'Un commediografo dimenticato: Antonio Sografi', *Rivista italiana del dramma*, i (1937), 171–88
A. Della Corte: *Satire e grotteschi di musiche e di musicisti d'ogni tempo* (Turin, 1946)
R. Angermüller: 'Grundzüge des nachmetastasianischen Librettos', *AnMc*, no.21 (1982), 192–235
D. Goldin: 'Aspetti della librettistica italiana fra 1770 e 1830', *AnMc*, no.21 (1982), 128–91; repr. in *La vera fenice: librettisti e libretti fra sette e ottocento* (Turin, 1985), 3–72
G. Morelli and E. Surian: Introduction to D. Cimarosa: *Gli Orazi e i Curiazi* (Milan, 1985)
M. McClymonds: 'The Venetian Role in the Transformation of Italian Opera Seria during the 1790s', *I vicini di Mozart: Venice 1987*, 221–40
——: '*La morte di Semiramide ossia La vendetta di Nino* and the Restoration of Death and Tragedy to the Italian Operatic Stage in the 1780s and 90s', *IMSCR*, xiv *Bologna 1987*, 285–92
C. Questa: *Semiramide redenta* (Urbino, 1989)

RONALD SHAHEEN

Sokal's'ky, Petro Petrovych (*b* Kharkiv, 14/26 Sept 1832; *d* Odessa, 30 March/11 April 1887). Ukrainian composer, critic and folksong collector. His father was a professor of economic science and his grandfather a conductor. He studied natural sciences at Kharkiv University, leaving in 1855, and was a schoolteacher before going to New York in 1857 as secretary to the Russian consulate. Returning to Russia in 1859 he turned to journalism, writing on science and economics; he also wrote often outspoken but perceptive reviews of concerts and new music. In 1859 he refounded the Odessa Philharmonic Society, and in 1864 he formed a choir. He wrote three operas, *Mazeppa* (composed 1858–9), *Mays'ka nich* ('May Night', 1876) and *Osada Dubno* ('The Siege of Dubno', 1878), as well as a cantata, orchestral pieces, piano music and songs. Many of his works, particularly the operas, contain folksongs: some critics hailed *The Siege of Dubno* as an excellent example of nationalist opera, though Serov considered that *May Night* was almost totally devoid of local colour. Sokal's'ky was also a pioneer collector and analyst of Russian and Ukrainian folk music; a volume that he edited was published in 1903.

Mazepa, 1858–9 (after A. S. Pushkin: *Poltava*), inc.
Mays'ka nich [May Night] (after N. Gogol), Odessa, 1876
Osada Dubno [The Siege of Dubno] (after Gogol: *Taras Bulba*), Odessa, 1878, extracts (St Petersburg, 1884)

T. Karïsheva: 'Iz istorii ukraniskoy muzïkal'noy kul'turï: P. P. Sokal'sky', *SovM* (1950), no.4, pp.83–8
——: *P. P. Sokal'sky* (Kiev, 1950)

JENNIFER SPENCER

Sokolovsky, Mikhail Matveyevich (*b c*1750; *d* ? late 18th century). Russian composer. A staff violinist and (probably) conductor at Michael Maddox's theatre (later the Petrovsky Theatre) in Moscow, he also gave singing lessons at Moscow University. He composed and arranged the music (much of it derived from folk and popular tunes) for Alexander Ablesimov's enormously popular comic opera *Mel'nik – koldun, obmanshchik i svat* ('The Miller who was a Wizard, a Cheat and a Matchmaker'), which had its première at Maddox's theatre on 20/31 January 1779 (ed. I. Sosnovtseva, Moscow, 1984; excerpts in Ginzburg 1968). Sokolovsky's wife and sister were also on the payroll of the theatre and took part in the production: the former sang the role of the Mother (soprano), the latter sang in the chorus and danced. Although the *Dramaticheskiy slovar'*, a dictionary of drama published in Moscow in 1787, informed its readers that the score of *The Miller* 'was arranged from old-Russian [*russkiye*] songs by the contemporary Russian [*Rossiyskiy*] musician of the Moscow theatre Mr Sokolovsky', his name did not appear either in the original printed libretto (Moscow, 1782) or in any surviving performance material (in *RU-SPtob*); the music, on account of its quality, was attributed to Yevstigney Fomin, the most accomplished dramatic composer of the period, and first published under his name (vocal score, Moscow, 1884). The matter was cleared up in 1927 by Fomin's biographer, Alexey Finagin, but the correct attribution was initially met with scepticism and the false one has proved hardy.

See also MILLER, THE.

*

A. Finagin: 'Yevstigney Fomin: zhizn' i tvorchestvo' [Life and Work], *Muzïka i muzïkal'nïy bït staroy Rossii: materialï i issledovaniya* [The Music and Musical Life of Old Russia: Documents and Research Essays] (Leningrad, 1927), 94–5
N. F. Findeyzen: *Ocherki po istorii muzïki v Rossii s drevneyshikh vremyon do kontsa XVIII veka* [Studies in the History of Music in Russia from Ancient Times to the End of the 18th Century], ii (Moscow and Leningrad, 1929), 217–18
A. S. Rabinovich: *Russkaya opera do Glinki* [Russian Opera Before Glinka] (Moscow, 1948)
T. N. Livanova: *Russkaya muzïkal'naya kul'tura XVIII veka v eyo svyazyakh s literaturoy, teatrom i bïtom* [Russian Musical Culture of the 18th Century and its Connections with Literature, the Theatre and Everyday Life], ii (Moscow, 1953), 129–30
D. Lehmann: *Russlands Oper und Singspiel in der zweiten Hälfte des 18. Jahrhunderts* (Leipzig, 1958)
Yu. Keldïsh: *Russkaya muzïka XVIII veka* (Moscow, 1965), chap.6
S. L. Ginzburg, ed.: *Istoriya russkoy muzïki v notnïkh obraztsakh* [History of Russian Music in Examples], i (Moscow, 2/1968), 113–38, 487–8
S. Oreshnikov: 'U istokov …' [At the Origins …], *SovM* (1976), no.3, pp.49–57
I. Sosnovtseva: Commentary to *Mel'nik – koldun, obmanshchik i svat*, Pamyatniki russkogo muzïkal'nogo iskusstva [Monuments of Russian Art Music], x (Moscow, 1984), 227–63
S. Karlinsky: *Russian Drama from its Beginnings to the Age of Pushkin* (Berkeley and Los Angeles, 1985), chap.5
O. Levasheva: 'Nachalo russkoy operï' [The Beginning of Russian Opera], in Yu. Keldïsh and others: *Istoriya russkoy muzïki v desyati tomakh* [History of Russian Music in Ten Volumes], iii (Moscow, 1985), 5–45
L. Hughes, ed. and trans.: 'A. Ablesimov: *The Miller who was Wizard, Cheat and Matchmaker*', *Russian Literature Triquarterly*, xx (1987), 21–49

RICHARD TARUSKIN

Soldaten, Die ('The Soldiers'). Opera in four acts by BERND ALOIS ZIMMERMANN, to a libretto by the composer after JAKOB MICHAEL REINHOLD LENZ's play; Cologne, Opernhaus, 15 February 1965.

Wesener *a fancy-goods merchant in Lille*	bass
Marie } *his daughters*	dramatic soprano
Charlotte } *his daughters*	mezzo-soprano
Wesener's old mother	contralto
Stolzius *a draper in Armentières*	high baritone
Stolzius's mother	contralto
Obrist *Count of Spannheim*	bass
Desportes *a young French nobleman*	very high tenor
A Young Huntsman *in the service of Desportes*	spoken
Pirzel *a captain*	high tenor
Eisenhardt *an army chaplain*	baritone
Major Haudy	baritone
Major Mary	baritone
Three Young Officers	high tenors
Countess de la Roche	mezzo-soprano
The Young Count *her son*	high lyric tenor
An Andalusian Waitress	dancer
Three Cadets	dancers
Mme Roux *hostess of the coffee house*	silent
The Countess's Servant	spoken
The Young Cadet	spoken
A Drunken Officer	spoken

18 officers and cadets, ballet, doubles of the actors and dancers

Setting French-speaking Flanders, yesterday, today and tomorrow

Zimmermann began work on his only opera in 1957; the following year it was formally commissioned by Cologne Opera. The first version was rejected by the opera house as technically impossible, and in 1963–4 Zimmermann prepared a simplified version, scaling down the forces and narrowing the dramatic scope. Although the published score (1966) still prescribes multiple acting levels and three projection screens to preserve the simultaneities of the action, Zimmermann's original concept had involved up to 12 acting areas each with its own instrumental ensemble. The première in Cologne was conducted by Michael Gielen and directed by Hans Neugebauer; the production was later the basis of a commercial recording. Following the success of the première, when *Die Soldaten* was proclaimed the most significant German opera since Berg's *Lulu*, it received a succession of stagings that varied considerably in their fidelity to Zimmermann's staging instructions: Gerd Albrecht conducted the Kassel production in 1968; Gielen was the conductor for Vaclav Kaclik's staging at Munich in 1969; the 1971 Düsseldorf production, conducted by Günter Wich, was brought to the Edinburgh Festival in 1972. In 1981 at Frankfurt Gielen conducted a production by Alfred Kirchner that stimulated yet more interest in the score; a staging at Stuttgart in 1988, conducted by Bernhard Kontarsky, was the basis of a second commercial recording. The American première in Boston in 1982 was conducted by Sarah Caldwell, and in 1991 the work was staged to much acclaim by the New York City Opera, conducted by Christopher Keene and produced by Rhoda Levine.

ACT 1.i *In Lille, Wesener's house* After a long, complex and turbulent introduction (Preludio) which unfolds over an insistent rhythmic motif, the first scene shows Marie writing a letter to Madame Stolzius in Armentières. While staying there she has fallen in love with Stolzius, though she will not reveal her feelings to her sister Charlotte.

1.ii (Ciacona I) *In Armentières, Stolzius's house* The melancholy Stolzius too has fallen for Marie, and when his mother eventually shows him the letter she has received his mood brightens; Madame Stolzius, however, disapproves of the liaison.

1.iii (Ricercari I) *Lille* After an interlude of sustained 'colour chords' (Tratto I) Desportes visits Marie; his courtesies are couched in elaborate coloratura, but she rejects his advances, telling him that her father has warned her against men's deceptions. Wesener himself enters, and Desportes uses the opportunity to ask if he can take Marie to the theatre; the father refuses and, when Marie betrays her disappointment, justifies his strictness by pointing out that she is his only delight.

1.iv (Toccata I) *Armentières, a public place* The army officers – Obrist, Haudy, Mary and Pirzel, with the chaplain Eisenhardt – discuss moral issues with their colleagues. They compare the theatre with the pulpit, and their discussion leads inevitably to the subject of women: does the theatre encourage army officers to seduce respectable girls? Haudy maintains that a whore will always be a whore.

1.v (Nocturne I) *Lille, Marie's room* To a background of stage percussion Wesener asks Marie whether Desportes can be trusted. She shows her father a love poem the nobleman has sent her, and the prospective match begins to appeal to him. Yet he advises Marie not to sever her connections with Stolzius until Desportes has proposed. Left alone, Marie reveals her continuing love for Stolzius in an increasingly passionate and wide-ranging aria, to which the orchestra provides a violent postlude.

ACT 2.i (Toccata II) *Armentières, a café* The officers assemble to drink and play cards; during the scene the score specifies rhythms that they tap out with their cups and spoons. Their banter gives way to a dance full of jazz inflections and led by Madame Roux and her Andalusian waitress. As it subsides Stolzius enters and is immediately teased about Marie; she has been seen around Lille with Desportes. He denies all knowledge of her behaviour or of his rival suitor and leaves.

2.ii (Capriccio, Chorale and Ciacona II) *Lille, Wesener's house* After an interlude (Intermezzo) dominated by organ and onstage percussion, Marie is seen in despair. She has received a reproachful letter from Stolzius, which she shows to Desportes. He pretends anger and dictates Marie's reply, using the opportunity to begin to seduce her. The scene becomes the dramatic and musical pivot of the opera: as the couple's love-making continues the scene simultaneously depicts Stolzius in Armentières, grief-stricken over the letter he has received from Marie and vowing vengeance upon Desportes, and Wesener's mother, watching her granddaughter's downfall and foreshadowing her fate. The grandmother's cynical commentary is set to a folktune, quoted from Lenz, while the orchestra borrows the chorale 'Ich bin's, ich sollte büssen' from Bach's *St Matthew Passion*.

ACT 3.i (Rondino) *Armentières* After a short Preludio Eisenhardt and Pirzel are found in the throes of

'Die Soldaten' (Zimmermann): set design by Max Bignens for the original production at the Opernhaus, Cologne, 15 February 1965, showing the multiple stages and the three projection screens

another arcane philosophical debate on the meaning of military life.

3.ii (Rappresentazione) *Lille, Mary's room* Dressed as a soldier, the highly wrought Stolzius successfully applies to be batman to Major Mary.

3.iii (Ricercari II) *Lille, Wesener's house* Charlotte upbraids Marie for transferring her attentions to Mary in Desportes' absence; she refuses to accept her sister's excuses. Mary enters and is greeted with elaborate courtesy by Marie; as the trio prepare to leave, the sisters notice the major's batman and his likeness to Stolzius. The following interlude is an elaborate and extended Romanza which steadily thins down its textures until only a solo guitar remains.

3.iv (Nocturne II) *Lille, the house of the Countess de la Roche* The Countess awaits the return of her son late at night, reflecting in her aria on the pain that sons cause their mothers throughout their lives; her elaborate and wide-ranging set piece develops into a duet with the arrival of her son, as the Countess declares that Marie is an unsuitable partner for him. She herself will oversee the girl's future.

3.v (Tropi) *Lille, Wesener's house* Mary appears to have abandoned Marie, though she disputes this with Charlotte. Their argument is interrupted by the arrival of the Countess, who patronizingly declares herself to be Marie's best ally and advises her to ignore the gossip about the town. She offers Marie a place in her own household, and as the Countess urges her to consider the offer carefully the act ends in an extended trio for the three women, which takes the final scene of *Der Rosenkavalier* as its reference point.

ACT 4.i (Toccata III) *Armentières, the café* The final act opens, after another orchestral Preludio, with the most ambitious and extensive of Zimmermann's explorations of simultaneity. The scene charts Marie's final downfall and degradation in a nightmarish sequence of tableaux, portrayed on film and by singers, dancers and doubles, in which past, present and future are telescoped. Mary finds Marie at the Countess's house, and after a meeting in a garden is interrupted by the Countess, Marie runs away and cannot be found. Desportes instructs his huntsman to pick up Marie; he does so and rapes her. She becomes a prostitute. Stolzius hears of what has happened, and buys rat poison to exact his revenge. The scene, which begins with a huge, sustained, wordless chord for all the main characters, ends with a densely interwoven chorus on the words 'Must those who suffer injustice tremble, and can only those who do wrong be happy!'.

4.ii (Ciacona II) *Armentières, Mary's room* After an interlude (Tratto II) for organ and percussion, Desportes is seen dining with Mary; they are waited on by Stolzius, who overhears their conversation. Desportes is dismissive of Marie's fate: she was only a whore in the first place, and he tells his friend how he had arranged for his huntsman to intercept her before she could find him again. Though Mary protests that he would have married her himself, Desportes is adamant that she got no worse than she deserved. Stolzius poisons Desportes' soup, and as he dies in agony screams Marie's name into his face; Stolzius himself then takes poison.

4.iii (Nocturno III) *A road on the banks of the River Lys* Wesener's final meeting with his daughter is embedded in an aural and visual collage of pre-recorded tape, film footage and musical cross-reference. Offstage voices provide a background of sustained chords and isolated syllables; the officers continue to visit Madame Bischof's café; Eisenhardt is heard proclaiming the Lord's Prayer; the screens show soldiers of many nationalities endlessly marching. A beggar woman accosts Wesener and asks for money; he at first refuses, but then relents, remembering the fate of his own daughter. He has not recognized Marie, who falls to the ground weeping. The sounds of marching become ever louder until everything else is overwhelmed.

* * *

Though the forces involved in *Die Soldaten* are so massive – in his score Zimmermann provides the option of siting the percussion in another performing space and conveying its sounds to the stage electronically – they are used with great discrimination and selectivity; chamber sonorities frequently accompany the voices. The vocal lines develop the techniques of Berg's operas – the exceptionally demanding role for Marie, with its high-lying coloratura and expressionist extremes, echoes both her namesake in *Wozzeck* and Lulu; elsewhere the parts move freely between speech, parlando, Sprechgesang and unfettered arioso.

As the indications in the summary of the plot suggest, the plan of each scene is based upon a well-defined formal structure, derived again from Berg, within which Zimmermann contains his strictly organized serial material and extensive stylistic borrowings. His use of collage and quotation is more effective dramatically here than in any of his non-operatic works and was arguably the most influential aspect of the opera when it was first performed. Zimmermann's attempt to convey separate and simultaneous dramatic strands by the use of multiple stages and ensembles appears to have influenced Henze's similar techniques in *We Come to the River* (1976). ANDREW CLEMENTS

Soldatenliebschaft, Die ('The Soldier's Love Affair'). Singspiel in one act by FELIX MENDELSSOHN to a libretto by Johann Ludwig Casper, probably after a French source; private performance, Berlin, possibly 1820 (first public performance, Wittenberg, 28 April 1962).

Die Soldatenliebschaft, Mendelssohn's second operatic attempt, shows how rapidly the 11-year-old boy's abilities were developing, for it is considerably more ambitious and assured than the brief domestic scene, *Ich J. Mendelssohn*, composed earlier in the same year.

The action, set during the Napoleonic occupation of Spain, concerns the clandestine love affairs of a French colonel, Felix (tenor), with Elvire (soprano), a widowed Spanish countess, and the colonel's sergeant Victor (tenor) with Zerbine (soprano), the countess's maid. The countess's steward, Tonio (baritone), is also enamoured of Zerbine. Puzzled and concerned by the mysterious appearance of flowers on his mistress's balcony, Tonio constructs a system of alarm bells; Victor, climbing to the balcony, sets them off, and confusion ensues. From his vantage point Victor sees the colonel and the countess together and uses this information to exact permission for his marriage to Zerbine. The opera ends with the union of both couples.

The characterization is primitive and the debt to stock characters of the German Singspiel tradition obvious. Elvire and Felix are a pair of romantic lovers, Zerbine a soubrette and the insouciant Victor her typical tenor counterpart, while Tonio belongs in the tradition of the German *buffo* bass. The music is unpretentious but charming and skilfully constructed; the orchestration in particular shows the young Mendelssohn's feeling for instrumental colour. CLIVE BROWN

Soler, José (*b* Barcelona, 22 Feb 1904). Uruguayan tenor. He studied in Montevideo under Frasca Mónaco and made his operatic début as Manrico in 1945, singing the same role at the Teatro Colón under Panizza in 1946. After that came foreign invitations, including his Italian début at San Remo. In 1947 he sang in *La traviata* at La Scala with Carosio and Tagliabue under Serafin. Soler partnered Callas, Tebaldi, Caniglia and Simionato, among others. His repertory was Italian: Verdi, Puccini, Donizetti and Mascagni; he sang Ernani at the centenary performance at the Teatro Solís, Montevideo. He was noted for his strong and expressive voice. His recordings include *Andrea Chénier* with Tebaldi. SUSANA SALGADO

Soler, Vicente Martín y. *See* MARTÍN Y SOLER, VICENTE.

Solera, Temistocle (*b* Ferrara, 25 Dec 1815; *d* Milan, 21 April 1878). Italian librettist and composer. Everything about him was larger than life: his Herculean physique, his torrents of words and invective and, above all, his career of almost unbelievable contrasts. While his father languished in the dreaded Spielberg prison, he was educated in Vienna, ran away to join a circus, completed his studies in Milan and Pavia and, in his early twenties, published books of verse. His first operatic task was to rework a text by Piazza for Verdi (*Oberto conte di San Bonifacio*, 1839). Four more librettos followed quickly, two of which he set to music himself, before Verdi's setting of *Nabucodonosor* (*Nabucco*) brought him fame. *I Lombardi alla prima crociata*, *Giovanna d'Arco* and *Attila* continued the collaboration with Verdi but before the last was finished he followed his wife, the soprano Teresa Rosmina, to Spain, where he became director of productions in Madrid (and, reputedly, the favourite of Queen Isabella). *Attila* was completed by Piave, in the face of Solera's bitter recriminations. He was soon back in Italy and after 25 years of extraordinary, picaresque adventures, he died in abject poverty.

He never worked with Verdi after *Attila*, though he pressed several librettos on him. Verdi refused to have further dealings with him, but in 1861 he contributed anonymously to a fund to help him. Solera always spoke of Verdi with the warmest praise, taking credit for his success. Verdi however held that Solera had only himself to blame; had he applied himself to his career, he could have been the foremost librettist of the day. Solera's successful librettos show an eye for a theatrical situation, an unquenchable flow of colourful language, an ability to express emotional and patriotic sentiments in phrases which evoked a strong response from Verdi, and a style of versification which propelled his lines forward. Nothing he wrote later matches the force of his Verdi librettos; if their dramatic structure creaks at times, the words carry all before them.

dl – *dramma lirico*

Oberto conte di S Bonifacio (dramma, rev. of A. Piazza), Verdi, 1839 (Graffigna, 1842, as I Bonifazi ed i Salinguerra); *Ildegonda* (dramma), Solera, 1840 (Arrieta, 1845; Morales, 1865); *Gildippe ed Odoardo* (melodramma), O. Nicolai, 1840; *Il contadino d'Agliate* (melodramma), Solera, 1841; *Galeotto Manfredi* (tragedia lirica), C. Herman, 1842; *Nabucodonosor* (dl), Verdi, 1842; *I Lombardi alla prima crociata* (dl), Verdi, 1843

Genio e sventura (dl), Solera, 1843; *Giovanna d'Arco* (dl), Verdi, 1845; *Attila* (dl, Act 3 completed by Piave), Verdi, 1846; *La conquista de Granada* (dl), Arrieta, 1850; *La hermana de Pelayo* (dl), Solera, 1853; *La fanciulla delle Asturie* (tragedia lirica), B. Secchi, 1856; *Sordello*, A. Buzzi, 1856; *Pergolesi*, S. Ronchetti-Monteviti, 1857; *Vasconcello*, Villanis, 1858; *Una notte di festa*, Villanis, 1859; *L'espiazione*, A. Peri, 1861; *Zilia* (dl), Villate, 1877

E. Checchi: 'Librettisti e libretti di Giuseppe Verdi', *Nuova antologia*, no.167 (1913), 529–40

A. Luzio, ed.: 'La tragicommedia di Temistocle Solera', *Carteggi verdiani*, iv (Rome, 1947), 244–9

J. Subirá: *El teatro del Real palacio* (Madrid, 1950)

A. C. Ramelli: *Libretti e librettisti* (Milan, 1973)

M. Mila: 'Lettura dell' Attila di Verdi', *NRMI*, xvii (1983), 247–76

JOHN BLACK

Soler Sardà, Josep (*b* Vilafranca del Penedès, nr Barcelona, 25 March 1935). Spanish composer. He studied first in Spain, and at the beginning of the 1960s went to Paris; there he received advice from René Leibowitz, but his principal teacher, from 1960 to 1964, was Cristòfor Taltabull. He was a professor at the Barcelona Conservatory, then became director of the Badalona Conservatory. Soler has written chamber, piano and organ music, as well as orchestral and sacred works, and he has published numerous essays, especially on the process of musical creation. His music is firmly rooted in the tradition of the Second Viennese School, especially Alban Berg, and he has developed an original musical language blending the 12-note concept with a re-interpretation of 'Tristan' harmony. Soler's interest in opera has proved more persistent than that of his contemporaries: by 1990 he had composed eight operas, although only *Edipo y Yocasta*, his best-known work, has been performed. *Edipo* explores the theme of predestination and is musically well organized. The original tone row is used in both the orchestra and chorus; Jocasta has a tone row of her own, the inversion of which serves as that for Oedipus; two other rows, similar to the original one, are used for other characters.

Less conventional is *Macbeth* (1990), in which the main characters speak in low voices against an orchestra playing mainly pianissimo. The difficulty of achieving the desired atmosphere in an opera house led the composer to think of *Macbeth* as an opera not to be staged but to be recorded on compact disc, in order to eliminate extraneous noise and to provide a truly effective means of conveying the whispered, frightening atmosphere to the listener.

Agamemnon, 1960, rev. 1973 (1, after Seneca)

La tentation de St Antoine, 1964 (2, after G. Flaubert)

Edipo y Yocasta, 1972 (2, after Seneca and Sophocles), concert perf., 30 Oct 1974; stage, Barcelona, Liceo, 1986

Jesús de Nazaret, 1974–85 (2 pts, after the Gospels)

La Belle et la Bête, 1982 (Leprince de Beaumont)

Nerón, 1985 (2, J. Soler)

Murillo, 1989 (after R. M. Rilke)

Macbeth, 1990 (2, after W. Shakespeare)

R. Leibowitz: '"Josep Soler" apéndice', *14 compositores españoles de hoy* (Oviedo, 1982)

J. Soler: 'Notas sobre la opera *Edipo y Yocasta*', *Recerca musicològica*, ii (1982), 55–80

ANGEL MEDINA

Solerti, Angelo (*b* Savona, 20 Sept 1865; *d* Massa Carrara, 10 Feb 1907). Italian philologist and musicologist. After attending the Istituto di Studi Superiori in Florence, he graduated in arts from the University of Turin in 1887 and spent his career mainly in education. Through his philological studies he made important contributions to the documentation of the origins of opera. *Le origini del melodramma: testimonianze dei contemporanei* (Turin, 1903) is largely an edition of prefaces and other accounts of early opera, including a list of operas performed before 1640. *Gli albori del melodramma* (Milan, 1904–5), a history of the opera in the first half of the 17th century, contains critical editions of many early librettos and the complete works for music of Rinuccini and Chiabrera. *Musica, ballo e drammatica alla corte medicea dal 1600 al 1637: notizie tratte d'un diario ... con appendice di testi inediti e rari* (Florence, 1905) is one of the earliest full-scale archival studies of an aspect of Italian musical life. Solerti contributed many articles to the *Rivista musicale italiana* and other periodicals.

V. Cian: 'Prefazio: Angelo Solerti', *Rime disperse di Francesco Petrarca o a lui attribuite*, ed. A. Solerti (Florence, 1909), pp.v ff [incl. complete list of writings, pp.xv ff]

LEONARDO PINZAUTI

Solfeggio (It.; Fr. *solfège*). Term originally referring to the singing of scales, intervals and melodic exercises to solmization syllables. P. F. Tosi's *Opinioni de' cantori antichi e moderni* (1723) emphasizes the young musician's need to 'solfeggiar la scaletta'. There have been numerous approaches to *solfeggio*, fashioned to meet the theoretical and practical needs of the time. In the 17th century the meaning of the term was extended to include textless exercises composed by Italian singing masters to assist in the development of vocal agility and the art of ornamentation (i.e. 'florid song'). These rarely came into print, since one of the hallmarks of the competent singing teacher was his ability to compose such exercises himself. Tosi (Eng. trans., 2/1742) recommended that

> If the Master does not understand Composition, let him provide himself with good Examples of *Sol-Fa*-ing [i.e. *solfeggio*] in divers Stiles, which insensibly lead from the most easy to the more difficult, according as he finds the Scholar improves; with this Caution, that however difficult, they may be always natural and agreeable, to induce the Scholar to study with Pleasure.

Solfeggi of this kind were too elaborate to be sung to solmization syllables, and single vowel sounds were used. G. B. Mancini (*Pensieri, e riflessioni pratiche sopra il canto figurato*, 1774) advocated the use of the vowels 'a' and 'e' only.

Italian pedagogical methods were widely disseminated and emulated in the 18th century, and with the founding of the Paris Conservatoire in 1795 training in *solfeggio* was a basis of the curriculum. *Solfège* developed there during the 19th century into an elaborately systematic regimen in basic musicianship. French interest in Italian methods of instruction is coeval with the first publications of *solfeggi*, all of them in Paris. The first important collection was *Solfèges d'Italie avec la basse chiffrée* (containing examples by Leo, Durante, Scarlatti, Hasse, Porpora and others), which first appeared in 1772. Others were Girolamo Crescentini's *Raccolta di esercizi per il canto ... solfeggi ed esercizi vari* (*c*1810) and Rossini's *Gorgheggi e solfeggi per soprano* (1827). The most important later method was *Solfèges des solfèges* by Danhauser, Lemoine and Lavignac (1910–11), an elaborate course extending to three volumes. The French tradition has served as a point of departure for numerous methods of teaching basic musical skills developed in other countries. OWEN JANDER

Solié [Solier, Sollié, Soulié, Soulier], **Jean-Pierre** (*b* Nîmes, 1755; *d* Paris, 6 Aug 1812). French composer and singer. The son of a cellist in the theatre at Nîmes, he became a choirboy in the local cathedral. For a long time he gave singing and guitar lessons in towns in the south of France and played the cello in theatre orchestras. In 1778 he was in Avignon where Grétry's *La rosière de Salency* was being produced; he replaced a sick actor, and had such success that he was immediately engaged as a tenor. After performing in the provinces he was summoned to the Comédie-Italienne, making his début on 31 August 1782 in Monsigny's *Félix* and Grétry's *L'amant jaloux* with moderate success. He then went to Nancy and to Lyons, where he worked for three years. Recalled to Paris in 1787, he played secondary parts for two years until he was asked to stand in for Jean-Baptiste Clairval in Propiac's *La fausse paysanne* on 26 March 1789. This time he was a great success and established a reputation. His voice, which had taken on a baritone quality (then novel at the Comédie-Italienne), inspired Méhul to write parts for him in *Euphrosine* (Alibour), *Stratonice* (the Doctor) and *Joseph* (Jakob). In 1790 he embarked on a career as a dramatic composer by introducing some airs from Gluck's *La rencontre imprévue* into *Les fous de Médine*. He produced *Jean et Geneviève* at the Théâtre Favart in 1792; the piece was revived 28 years later.

Although pleasant and facile, Solié's compositional style was not assertive enough to achieve lasting success. He is, however, remembered for *Le secret* and *Le jockey* (works which owe much to the librettist Hoffman) and for occasional pieces such as *L'opéra au village* (1807), written for the emperor's return and the signing of the peace. His last work, *Les ménestrels* (1811), was a failure.

Solié's second son, Emile Solié (*b* 1801; *d* after 1867), was a writer on music whose works include *Histoire du Théâtre royal de l'Opéra-Comique* (Paris, 1847) and a *Notice sur l'Opéra national* (Paris, 1847). Emile's son, Charles Solié (*d* after 1912), was a conductor and director at the Nantes Grand-Théâtre in the 1860s and later conductor at the Nice Théâtre-Français. He composed a successful *opéra comique*, *Scheinn Baba, ou L'intrigue au harem* (Nice, 5 April 1879), and light orchestral music.

opéras comiques, first performed in Paris, unless otherwise stated; printed works published in Paris

Le séducteur (comédie, 5, G.-F. de Bièvre), Fontainebleau, 4 Nov 1783
Les fous de Médine, ou La rencontre imprévue (3, L. Dancourt), OC (Favart), 1 May 1790, with H.-M. Berton and others
Le franc Breton, ou Le négociant de Nantes (opéra, 1, J.-C. Dejaure), OC (Favart), 3 Nov 1792 (n.d.), collab. R. Kreutzer
Jean et Geneviève (1, G.-F. de Favières), OC (Favart), 3 Dec 1792 (*c*1798)
L'école de village (1, C.-A. Sewrin), OC (Favart), 10 May 1793
La moisson (2, Sewrin), OC (Favart), 5 Sept 1793
Le plaisir et la gloire (1, Sewrin), OC (Favart), 19 Jan 1794
Le congrès des rois (cmda, 3, Desmaillot [A. F. Eve]), OC (Favart), 26 Feb 1794, collab. Dalayrac, Grétry, Méhul and 8 others
La soubrette, ou L'étui de harpe (1, F.-B. Hoffman), OC (Favart), 3 Dec 1794
L'entreprise folle (1), OC (Favart), 1795
Le jockey (1, Hoffman), OC (Favart), 6 Jan 1796 (*c*1796)
Le secret (1, Hoffman), OC (Favart), 20 April 1796 (*c*1796)
Azelina (3, Hoffman), OC (Feydeau), 5 Dec 1796, air (1798)
La femme de quarante-cinq ans (1, Hoffman), OC (Favart), 19 Nov 1798
Le chapitre second (1, E. M. Dupaty), OC (Favart), 17 June 1799 (*c*1799)
Une matinée de Voltaire, ou La famille Calas à Paris (1, J.-B. Pujoulx), OC (Favart), 22 May 1800
Une nuit d'été, ou Un peu d'aide fait grand bien (1, N. Gersin), OC (Favart), 7 June 1800
Oui, ou Le double rendez-vous (opéra, 1, J.-F.-T. Goulard), OC (Favart), 29 Aug 1800
La rivale d'elle-même (1, P.-J.-R. Bins de Saint-Victor), OC (Favart), 3 Oct 1800
La pluie et le beau temps, ou L'été de l'an VIII (vaudeville, 1, Dupaty), OC (Favart), 17 Nov 1800
Le petit Jacquot (1, Alexandre), Jeunes Artistes, 27 April 1801
Quatre maris pour un (1, R. C. G. de Pixérécourt), Jeunes Artistes, 27 April 1801
Plutarque (1, F.-P.-A. Leger and Alissan de Chazet), OC (Feydeau), 20 Jan 1802
Le séducteur amoureux (comédie, 3, C. de Longchamp), Français, 25 Jan 1803 (1803)
Henriette et Verseuil (1, Guillet and E. Hus), OC (Feydeau), 30 July 1803
L'incertitude maternelle, ou Le choix impossible (1, Dejaure), OC (Feydeau), 6 Aug 1803 (n.d.)
L'oncle et le neveu (1, A.-J. Grétry), Montansier, 26 Nov 1803
Louise, ou La malade par amour (1, Hoffman), OC (Feydeau), 16 April 1804 (n.d.)
L'époux généreux, ou Le pouvoir des procédés (1, Dejaure), Italien, 1804 (n.d.)
Les deux oncles (opéra, 1, Grétry and N. J. Forgeot), OC (Favart), 3 Jan 1805
Chacun son tour (1, J. Gensoul), OC (Feydeau), 26 Oct 1805 (n.d.)
L'opéra au village (divertissement, 1, Sewrin), OC (Feydeau), 30 July 1807
L'amante sans le savoir (opéra, 1, C. A. Creuzé de Lesser), OC (Feydeau), 1807
Anna, ou Les deux chaumières (opéra, 1, Sewrin), OC (Feydeau), 20 Feb 1808 (n.d.)
Mademoiselle de Guise (3, Dupaty), OC (Feydeau), 17 March 1808 (n.d.)
Le hussard noir (opéra, 1, Dupaty), OC (Feydeau), 10 Dec 1808
Le diable à quatre, ou La femme acariâtre (3, Creuzé de Lesser, after M.-J. Sedaine), OC (Feydeau), 30 Nov 1809 (n.d.)
La victime des arts (2, L.-M. d'Estourmel), OC (Feydeau), 27 Feb 1811, collab. Isouard and H.-M. Berton
Les ménestrels (3, J. M. de Reveroni Saint-Cyr), OC (Feydeau), 27 April 1811

Unperf.: Les trois tantes, 1797 (Pixérécourt); Victor, 1797 (drame lyrique, Pixérécourt) [accepted by Théâtre Feydeau, but never perf.]

E. Campardon: *Les comédiens du roi de la troupe italienne* (Paris, 1880)
A. Pougin: *L'Opéra-comique pendant la Révolution* (Paris, 1891)
C. Pierre: *Musique des fêtes et cérémonies de la Révolution française* (Paris, 1899) PAULETTE LETAILLEUR

Soliman den andra [*Soliman den andra, eller De tre sultaninnorna* ('Soliman II, or The Three Sultanas')]. Drama with music in three acts and a *divertissement* by JOSEPH MARTIN KRAUS to a libretto by Johan Gabriel Oxenstierna after CHARLES-SIMON FAVART's *Soliman II, ou Les trois sultanes*; Stockholm, Royal Dramatic Theatre, 22 September 1789.

Soliman (speaking role) agonizes over which of three women – an outspoken French slave, Roxelane (soprano), a conniving Spanish aristocrat, Elmire (a dancer), or a shy Circassian songstress, Delia (soprano) – will be his sultana. Aided by his vizier, Osmin (speaking role), and Roxelane, he is able to judge the superficiality of both Delia's and Elmire's love. But Roxelane insults him publicly, and he condemns her to exile. Only a declaration of her hidden love prevents this, and the opera ends with a *divertissement*, 'Roxelane's kröning' ('Roxelane's Coronation'), in which the people of both Turkey and France hail the new sultana. First performed privately before the Swedish court in 1788 in a version for actors, *Soliman* remained in the repertory in Stockholm until 1817, and saved the Royal Opera from the financial ruin caused by Carl Stenborg's competing comic theatre; it was revived at Drottningholm in May 1989. One of the few Swedish examples of the 18th-century Turkish opera, it is strictly a hybrid work consisting of one-third ballet, one-third music and one-third spoken dialogue. Kraus's musical style is light, tuneful and rhythmically complex; the orchestration makes extensive use of exotic percussion instruments such as the Turkish crescent. BERTIL H. VAN BOER

Solimano ('Suleyman'). Libretto by GIOVANNI AMBROGIO MIGLIAVACCA, first set by J. A. Hasse (1753, Dresden).

Suleyman, the Turkish emperor, has sent his two sons to wage war against Persia. The mother of Osmino [Osmin] wants him to inherit the throne rather than his half-brother Selimo [Selim], the legitimate heir. She and Rusteno intrigue against Selim, until Suleyman, suspicious, confronts Selim in Persia. Meanwhile, the brothers have fallen in love with their prisoners, Narsea and Emira, daughters of Tacmante, the Persian king; they want to end the war and get married. Selim confesses his love for Narsea to his father, who tries to separate the pair. Rusteno produces a letter in which Selim asks Tacmante for Narsea's hand in return for a military alliance against Suleyman; angered, Suleyman orders Selim's death. Osmin refuses to believe that Selim was a traitor and discovers that Rusteno wrote the letter himself. Acomate appears with Selim, announcing that a slave died in Selim's place. Suleyman promises peace and blesses the lovers' alliances.

This text, with slight modifications, was set eight times between 1753 and 1762, notably by Traetta (1759). A second version, with a Turkish love interest for Osmino and without the character of Rusteno, retained the basic plot and much of the dialogue. It was set by Perez (1757), B. Galuppi (1760), Sciroli (1766) and J. G. Naumann (1773). A third version, with music by G. M. Curcio (1782, rev. ? J. Durandi), uses much of Migliavacca's original text with a new sequence of scenes. There were at least three pasticcios (1758 and 1765, London; 1778, Florence).

For a list of settings *see* MIGLIAVACCA, GIOVANNI AMBROGIO.

JENNIFER GRIESBACH

Solimano ('Suleyman'). *Dramma per musica* in three acts by DAVID PEREZ to a libretto by GIOVANNI AMBROGIO MIGLIAVACCA (*see* SOLIMANO above); Lisbon, Ajuda, Carnival 1757.

The opera was revived with alterations in 1768 for Lisbon, and the synopsis that follows relates to that version. The Turkish emperor Suleyman (tenor) has sent his oldest sons and half-brothers Selimo [Selim] (alto castrato) and Zanghire [Cihangir] (soprano castrato) to war against Tammase [Tahmasp], Shah of Persia. Selim has negotiated a peace in which he is to marry Tahmasp's daughter Persane (soprano) and receive Persia as her dowry. Cihangir's mother, Roselane [Roxelana], wishing to be rid of Selim so that her son may inherit the throne, has joined with the Grand Vizier Rustamo [Rustem] in persuading Suleyman that Selim is plotting against him. Suleyman comes to Babylon with Osmino [Osmin] (tenor), captain of the guard, and his sister Barsina (soprano), who is betrothed to Cihangir. Cihangir, loyal to his brother, exposes the conspiracy against Selim and kills Rustem. Suleyman and Selim are reconciled, and the two pairs of lovers are allowed to marry.

Solimano is Perez's acknowledged masterpiece. It contains 14 dal segno arias, one cavatina and six accompanied recitatives of exceptional scope. Its formal flexibility, dramatic contrasts and musical vitality are largely due to a juxtaposition of *buffa* and *seria* idioms and to an interchange of style between aria and accompanied recitative. The integration of numbers into large-scale complexes of scenes with continuous orchestral accompaniment shows that Perez, though composing outside the main operatic centres, was a major participant in the operatic reforms of the 1750s.

STEPHEN C. FISHER, PAUL J. JACKSON

Soliva, Carlo Evasio (*b* Casale Monferrato, Piedmont, 1792; *d* Paris, 20 Dec 1851). Italian composer, teacher and conductor. He studied with Asioli and Federici at the Milan Conservatory and in 1815 was engaged as a conductor at La Scala, where four of his five operas were produced. In 1821 he moved to Warsaw, where he became one of the foremost figures in musical life, as teacher at the conservatory, director of the School of Singing and Declamation (from 1827) and as conductor of operas and concerts. In 1832 he moved to St Petersburg, where he was director of the opera from 1834. In 1841, after a visit to Italy, he settled in Paris. His other works include sacred, instrumental, chamber and piano music. He also wrote a textbook on singing.

La testa di bronzo ossia La campana solitaria (opera comica, 2, F. Romani), Milan, Scala, 3 Sept 1816
Berenice d'Armenia (os, 3, J. Ferretti), Turin, Regio, Jan 1817
La zingara delle Asturie (opera semiseria, 2, Romani), Milan, Scala, 5 Aug 1817
Giulia e Sesto Pompeo (os, 2, B. Perotti), Milan, Scala, 24 Feb 1818
Elena e Malvina (opera semiseria, 2, Romani), Milan, Scala, 22 May 1824 ZOFIA CHECHLIŃSKA

Solovey. Opera by Igor Stravinsky; *see* NIGHTINGALE, THE.

Solov'yov, Nikolay Feopemptovich (*b* Petrozavodsk, 27 April/9 May 1846; *d* Petrograd, 14/27 Dec 1916). Russian composer, critic and educator. He studied composition at the St Petersburg Conservatory under Nikolay Zaremba (a pupil of A. B. Marx), graduating in 1872. From 1874 until 1909 he taught theory and composition there himself. While still a student Solov'yov was entrusted with the orchestration of sections of Alexander Serov's posthumous opera *Vrazh'ya sila* (1871), completed by the composer's widow. In 1874 he competed unsuccessfully against Tchaikovsky for the prize awarded by the Russian Musical Society in memory of Serov for the best setting of Polonsky's libretto after Gogol, *Kuznets Vakula* ('Vakula the Smith'); Solov'yov's setting, titled *Vakula kuznets* to distinguish it from Tchaikovsky's, was performed on 29 April/11 May 1880 by an amateur opera club in St Petersburg as a benefit for Bulgarian war orphans. Excerpts from an unfinished opera on Pushkin's comic poem *Domik v Kolomne* ('The Little House in Kolomna') were published in a St Petersburg music magazine in 1899; Stravinsky's *Mavra* is based on the same literary source. Solov'yov's magnum opus was the Gounodesque *Kordeliya* ('Cordelia'), based on

Victorien Sardou's play *La haine* (libretto by Pavel Konstantinovich Bronnikov). It was first performed, under the title *Mest'* ('Revenge'), at the Bol'shoy Theatre, St Petersburg, on 12/24 November 1885 (Eduard Nápravník conducting); a revised version followed in 1898 (St Petersburg, Mariinsky Theatre, Nápravník conducting). Its best number is a reconditely harmonized choral *Ave Maria*. RICHARD TARUSKIN

Solov'yov-Sedoy, Vasily Pavlovich (*b* St Petersburg, 12/25 April 1907; *d* Leningrad [now St Petersburg], 2 Dec 1979). Russian composer. At the age of eight he taught himself to play the balalaika, and by the age of 13 he was taking part in a young people's theatre group, accompanying its productions with piano improvisations. He studied at the Musorgsky Music School (1929–31) and at the Leningrad Conservatory (1931–6), where his interest in folk music was encouraged. His opera *Mat'* ('Mother'), based on a text by Maxim Gorky, was performed in Moscow in 1941. Several operettas followed, including *Vernïy drug* ('A Loyal Friend', 1945) and *Samoye zavetnoye* ('Most Cherished Possession', 1952). His last operetta, *Zhil-bïl Shel'menko* ('Once Upon a Time Shel'menko Lived'), was produced in Tarnopol' in 1978. Solov'yov-Sedoy was best known for his many songs, but his work was largely for the theatre. He received the Order of Lenin in 1957 and the Lenin Prize in 1959.

operettas unless otherwise stated

Mat' [Mother] (opera, after M. Gorky), Moscow, 1941

Vernïy drug [A Loyal Friend] (V. Mikhaylov), Kuybïshev [now Samara], Opera, Operetta and Musical Comedy Theatre, 6 Oct 1945

Samoye zavetnoye [Most Cherished Possession], 1945 (V. Mass and M. Cervinki); rev. 1951, Moscow, Operetta Theatre, 2 Oct 1952

Olimpiyskiye zvyozdï [Olympic Stars], Leningrad, Musical Comedy Theatre, 1962

Vosemnadtsat' let [18 years], Leningrad, Musical Comedy Theatre, 1967

U rodnogo prichala [In Home Port], Odessa, Musical Comedy Theatre, 1970

Vendetta, 1970

Neravnïy brak [The Unequal Marriage], 1971

Zhil-bïl Shel'menko [Once Upon a Time Shel'menko Lived], Tarnopol', Musical Comedy Theatre, 1978

*

M. Grinberg: '"Samoye zavetnoye"', *SovM* (1952), no.12, pp.77–80

A. Sokhor: *V. P. Solov'yov-Sedoy* (Leningrad and Moscow, 1952, 2/1967)

Yu. Kremlyov: *V. P. Solov'yov-Sedoy: ocherk zhizni i tvorchestva* [Solov'yov-Sedoy: Outline of his Life and Work] (Leningrad, 1960) M. ARANOVSKY (with MARINA NEST'YEVA)

Solti, Sir **Georg** [György] (*b* Budapest, 21 Oct 1912). British conductor of Hungarian birth. After studies with Dohnányi, Bartók and Kodály at the Liszt Academy, Budapest, he began his career as a pianist and joined the Budapest Opera as répétiteur. He was music assistant to Toscanini at Salzburg (1936–7), and made his conducting début with *Le nozze di Figaro* at Budapest in 1938. Finding that Jews were barred from contract appointments there, he sought refuge in Switzerland, returned to the piano and some voice coaching, and won the Geneva International Piano Competition in 1942. A chance invitation to conduct *Fidelio* at Munich in 1946 led to his appointment as music director of the Bayerische Staatsoper (1946–52), where he laid the foundation of its postwar reputation and obtained advice from Richard Strauss on the conducting of his operas.

Solti was Generalmusikdirektor at Frankfurt, 1952–61, touring with the opera company to Paris, Florence and Salzburg, where he conducted Mozart at the festival, notably *Idomeneo* and *Die Zauberflöte.* The latter he again conducted for his British début at the 1952 Edinburgh Festival with the Hamburg Staatsoper. His American début was with *Elektra* at San Francisco in 1953; he conducted *Don Giovanni* at Glyndebourne in 1954, and first appeared at the Metropolitan in 1960 with *Tannhäuser.* At his Covent Garden début in 1959 he conducted *Der Rosenkavalier.* Its success led to his appointment as music director of the Royal Opera (1961–71) where he went a long way towards fulfilling his declared intention of making Covent Garden 'the best opera house in the world'. He conducted new productions of more than 20 operas during this time, including the British première of Schoenberg's *Moses und Aron*, the first Covent Garden production of *Die Frau ohne Schatten* and memorable performances of the *Ring* and Britten's *Billy Budd* and *A Midsummer Night's Dream.* His work was recognized by the award of an honorary CBE in 1968, which was advanced to KBE in 1971, and he took British nationality the next year.

He has been a frequent conductor at the Vienna Staatsoper, and was music adviser to the Paris Opéra (1971–3) while serving as music director of L'Orchestre de Paris; he became a Commandeur of the Légion d'honneur in 1974. He had influential orchestral posts with the Chicago SO (1969–90) and the LPO (1977–83), conducted the *Ring* at Bayreuth in a controversial production by Sir Peter Hall (1983) and continued to conduct widely into the 1990s, being named artistic director for the Salzburg Easter Festival from 1992. He celebrated his 80th birthday by conducting a series of *Otello* performances at Covent Garden. During earlier years he galvanized performances to a pitch of sustained intensity that could make them sound hard-driven; later he became mellower and more relaxed, but never less than supremely communicative.

Solti made the first complete *Ring* recording between 1958 and 1966. From 1967, beginning with *Salome* (with Birgit Nilsson), he made pioneering use of stereo recording technique for Decca, and his many recordings include major works of Strauss, Wagner and Mozart, Verdi's *Aida*, *Simon Boccanegra*, *Otello* and *Falstaff*, and several video-cassettes including *Arabella*, *Hänsel und Gretel* and *Falstaff.*

*

P. Robinson: *Solti* (London, 1979)

W. Mann: 'Solti, Champion of Strauss', *Opera*, xxxv (1984), 1298–1308, 1394 ARTHUR JACOBS, NOËL GOODWIN

Sołtys, Mieczysław (*b* Lwów, 7 Feb 1863; *d* Lwów, 11 Nov 1929). Polish composer. He studied in Lwów and in Paris, where he was a composition pupil of Saint-Saëns. On his return to Lwów he became editor of an arts periodical and from 1899 until his death he was director of the conservatory and the musical society, for which he conducted a great number of orchestral concerts. He was also active as a journalist and administrator. His works include five operas, composed during the period 1894 to about 1925. Until 1910 his music, in its early Romantic style influenced by Moniuszko, seemed academic and outdated. Later his technique developed, his harmony becoming more venturesome and his melody richer in a Wagnerian manner, but his music was never strikingly original. The composer considered *Nieboska komedia* ('Undivine Comedy') to be his best and most mature work.

Panie Kochanku, 1890 (3, H. Kopija, after J. I. Kraszewski), Lwów, 3 May 1924
Rzeczpospolita Babińska [Republic of Babin], 1894 (3, A. Kiczman and A. J. Popławski), Lwów, 27 April 1905
Jezioro-dusza [Lake-Soul], 1907 (12 scenes, K. Brzozowski) (Lwów, 1921), unperf.
Opowieść ukraińska [A Ukraine Story] op.22 (1, Sołtys, after A. Malczewski), Lwów, 16 Feb 1909 (Lwów, 1910)
Nieboska komedia [Undivine Comedy], *c*1925 (after Z. Krasiński), unperf.

*

W. Poźniak: 'Opera po Moniuszce' [Opera after Moniuszko], Z *dziejów polskiej kultury muzycznej*, ii (Krakow, 1966), 306–28
TERESA CHYLIŃSKA

Somers, Harry (Stuart) (*b* Toronto, 11 Sept 1925). Canadian composer. He was a composition pupil of John Weinzweig at the Toronto Conservatory (1942–3 and 1945–9) and although he showed exceptional promise as a pianist, in 1948 he turned decisively to composition. The following year he was awarded a Canadian Amateur Hockey Association Scholarship to study for a year in Paris with Milhaud. Somers has never held a teaching position or sought permanent employment. In the 1950s he earned a living in a variety of odd jobs, briefly driving a taxi, working as a part-time music copyist and playing the guitar professionally. From 1960 he supported himself through commissions from major institutions and orchestras. He also became involved in broadcasting, serving as a writer, commentator and host on a variety of CBC radio and television music programmes. In 1972 he was made a Companion of the Order of Canada, the country's highest award.

Somers might be considered an eclectic in that he has, throughout his career, absorbed many influences, among them the music of Weinzweig, Bartók and Ives, Baroque counterpoint, serial technique and Gregorian chant. However, he has always selected those elements most compatible with his own strong creative personality. From the beginning he developed a musical language of great originality. One important characteristic of his style has always been the extended, lyrical melodic line, used to achieve intensity and continuity. His preoccupation with serial pitch organization and with the juxtaposition of different styles within one work occurred in the 1950s. Both can be seen in his one-act chamber opera *The Fool* (1953). Much of the opera is written in Somers's own style using a 12-note series, but in two places this is abandoned in favour of an archaic tonal idiom, intruding upon the work's mildly dissonant musical language. *The Fool* was given its first stage performance in Toronto on 15 November 1956. In 1955 Somers composed a second dramatic work in collaboration with the librettist Michael Fram, the television operetta *The Homeless Ones*.

Serialism and a counterpoint of styles are present above all in the three-act opera *Louis Riel*, Somers's most important achievement. It focusses sympathetically on the character and aspirations of the Métis spokesman who led unsuccessful uprisings in Manitoba in 1869–70 and 1884–5. Commissioned by the Floyd S. Chalmers Foundation for the Canadian Centennial in 1967, the work received international acclaim. It was performed eight times during 1967–8 and was broadcast in 1969 by CBC television. The libretto, in English and French with some Cree and Latin, was provided by Mavor Moore (Jacques Languirand collaborated on the French sections). The music is in four distinct styles: lean, atonal orchestral writing (used for dramatic intensity and to evoke the Canadian northwest); popular songs of the Riel period (e.g. 'Orangemen Unite', used for a political gathering); folksong (notably Marguerite's beautiful aria 'Kuyas'); and electronic sounds (used to create maximum tension, as in the battle scene in Act 1). Although he has worked extensively in the studios of Toronto University, this opera contains Somers's only use of electronic sounds. Among the most intense parts of the work are two virtually unaccompanied arias, one for Louis, the other for Marguerite, his wife. These arias may be seen as a further stage in the development of Somers's masterful and individual extended melody.

Mario and the Magician, Somers's next opera, to a libretto by Rod Anderson, is based on the novella by Thomas Mann and concerns the rise of fascism in Italy; its première took place in Toronto in 1992.

See also LOUIS RIEL.

The Fool, 1953 (1, chamber op, M. Fram), Toronto, 15 Nov 1956
The Homeless Ones (television operetta, Fram), CBC TV, 31 Dec 1955
Louis Riel (3, M. Moore and J. Languirand), Toronto, O'Keefe Centre, 23 Sept 1967
Improvisation (music-theatre piece), Montreal, 5 July 1968
Death of Enkidu: Part I (chamber op, M. Kinch, after the epic of Gilgamesh), Toronto, 7 Dec 1977
Mario and the Magician (3, R. Anderson, after T. Mann), Toronto, Elgin, 19 May 1992

*

EMC ('The Fool', F. Hayes; 'Louis Riel', K. Winters)
H. Rosenthal: Review of 'Louis Riel', *Opera*, xviii (1967), 865–7
J. Graham: 'Louis Riel', *CBC Times*, xxii (1969), no.18, p.2
R. M. Schafer: 'Louis Riel: a Case Study', *The Public of the Music Theatre*, Universal Edition Report, i (Vienna, 1972)
B. Cherney: *Harry Somers* (Toronto, 1975)
P. Dyson: 'A New Mann Opera', *Opera*, xliii (1992), 928–30 [review of *Mario and the Magician*]
BRIAN CHERNEY

Somigli, Domenico (*b* Florence, Aug 1756; *d* after 1798). Italian librettist and dramatist. He decided to be a poet and actor, but became blind and was forced to dedicate himself to singing and writing poetry. His earliest known dramas were spoken tragedies. His prose comedy *Il conte villano* of 1787 was later adapted for music by Foppa under the title *Un pazzo ne fa cento* and was set by Mayr (1796) and Paer (1812). Beginning with the intermezzo *L'autunno* (1788), he subsequently wrote stage works exclusively for Florence which were set to music mainly by Tuscan composers. They embrace comic operas, intermezzos and farces and were mostly small-scale dramas designed for the minor theatres – the Cocomero, Piazza Vecchia and Borgo Ognissanti. In 1797 he wrote *Il medico burlato* and *Il padre fanatico* for the more august Intrepidi theatre. More than any other librettist working in Florence in this period, he typified the clever, humane and sentimental comedy of the Tuscan school. He may have retired in the face of the upheavals of the first French invasion of Tuscany of 1799.

L'autunno (int), Neri Bondi, 1788; *La baronessa giardiniera* (farsa), F. Rutini, 1791; *Le nozze all'inferno* (farsa), Moneta, 1791; *Il finto astronomo, o sia Il mondo della luna* (farsa), Neri Bondi, 1791; *La cameriera raggiratrice, o sia La guerra aperta* (int), Neri Bondi, 1793; *I tre desideri, o sia Il taglialegne* (farsa), Rutini, 1794; *La semplice* (dg), Rutini, 1795; *Il finto medico per amore* (int), Rutini, 1795; *Amor vince tutti* (int), A. Riccomini, 1796; *Le nozze fra i boschi, o siano I finti turchi* (int), Riccomini, 1797
L'unghero giardiniere (int), 1797; *Gli sponsali in villa, o siano Gli scherzi della villeggiatura* (dg), G. Aloisi, 1797; *Chi è minchio suo danno, o sia Pasquino e Marforio* (dg), Rutini, 1797; *Il medico burlato* (dg), F. Giuliani, 1797; *Il padre fanatico, o sia L'amante*

volubile (dg), Rutini, 1798; *Adelina, o sia L'incostanza vinta* (dg), Rutini, *c*1798; *Le donne s'attaccano sempre al peggio, o sia Il ganzatore burlato* (dg), Rutini, 1798

*

D. Somigli: *Rime* (Florence, 1782) [incl. important preface by publisher, A. Argivo]
L. Rasi: *I comici italiani* (Florence, 1905)
Enciclopedia biografica e bibliografica italiana, 9th ser., i–ii (Milan, 1936)
M. de Gnechis: *Melodramma spettacolo e musica nella Firenze dei Lorena* (Florence, 1991)
R. L. Weaver and N. Weaver: *A Chronology of Music in the Florentine Theater 1751–1800* (Warren, MI, 1992)

ROBERT LAMAR WEAVER

Somigli, Franca [Clark, Marion Bruce] (*b* Chicago, 17 March 1901; *d* Trieste, 14 May 1974). American soprano. Her vocal studies were in Milan with Storchio and Votto. She made her début as Mimì in Rovigo in 1927 and went on to sing dramatic roles such as Sieglinde, Kundry, Minnie, Salome and Giordano's Fedora in major Italian theatres. Her Chicago début was in 1934 as Maddalena in *Andrea Chénier*, and in 1936 she sang Alice in *Falstaff* under Toscanini at Salzburg. In 1935 Somigli created Contarina in Pizzetti's *Orséolo* in Florence, and made her Metropolitan début in 1937 in *Madama Butterfly*. CORI ELLISON

Somma, Antonio (*b* Udine, 28 Aug 1809; *d* Venice, 8 Aug 1864). Italian librettist. Following studies at Padua, he settled in Trieste as a poet and playwright. His successful tragedy *Parisina*, written while he was still a student, brought him the superintendency of the Teatro Comunale there. He later practised law in Venice. There he met Verdi, who entrusted him with the libretto of *Il re Lear* on Cammarano's death; when this project collapsed, he prepared the *melodramma Un ballo in maschera* instead. Verdi admired his poetic gifts and patriotic sentiments, but found him ignorant of the requirements of musical setting. Somma wrote several plays, but no other librettos, though he is often credited as one of the authors (with Dall'Ongaro and Gazoletti) of the *melodramma Un duello sotto Richelieu* (set by Federico Ricci, 1839); the extent of his participation is uncertain.

*

A. Pascolato, ed.: *Opere scelte di Antonio Somma* (Venice, 1865)
A. Pascolato: *Re Lear e Ballo in maschera: lettere di Giuseppe Verdi ed Antonio Somma* (Città di Castello, 1902)
A. C. Ramelli: *Libretti e librettisti* (Milan, 1973)
G. Schmidgall: 'Verdi's King Lear Project', *19th Century Music*, ix (1985–6), 83–101

JOHN BLACK

Sommeil (Fr.: 'sleep'). A scene-type in late 17th- and 18th-century French opera. The sleep is usually a magical event, brought about at the instigation of a god or sorcerer as an expression of power: as the main character sleeps, dreams reveal future events. Musically, some or all of the following characteristics are present: stepwise movement in slurred pairs of notes; the presence of *flûtes* (recorders), often in alternation with strings; and some use of pedal notes. The definitive *sommeil* occurs in Lully's *Atys* (1676): it is one of the most highly organized scenes in all Lully's operas. Subsequent examples are not necessarily so extended, but echoes of the style are to be found not only in operas such as Desmarets' *Circé* (1694) and Montéclair's *Jephté* (1732) but in other genres, such as the cantata.

*

C. Wood: 'Orchestra and Spectacle in the *Tragédie en musique*, 1673–1715: Oracle, *Sommeil* and *Tempête*', *PRMA*, cviii (1981–2), 25–46

CAROLINE WOOD

Sommer, Hans [Zincke, Hans Friedrich August] (*b* Brunswick, 20 July 1837; *d* Brunswick, 26 April 1922). German composer. He studied mathematics at Göttingen, where he later became a professor of physics. From 1859 to 1884 he taught at the Technische Hochschule in Brunswick, becoming director in 1875 and founding a Verein für Konzertmusik there. In 1883 he gave up science to devote himself to music, and in the following year visited Liszt in Weimar. He moved to Berlin in 1885, to Weimar (where he befriended Richard Strauss) in 1888, and returned to Brunswick in 1898; in that year he joined with Strauss, Schillings and Rösch in founding the protective Genossenschaft Deutscher Komponisten (from 1903 Genossenschaft Deutscher Tonsetzer).

Sommer was most successful as a composer for the theatre, especially for his later works in imaginative forms. He placed great importance on the literary quality of his librettos and corresponded with numerous librettists and composers. In addition to his operas he wrote incidental music to Hans von Wolzogen's *Das Schloss der Herzen* (1891), which was first performed in 1897 in Berlin, in concert form.

Der Nachtwächter (1), Brunswick, ? 22 Nov 1865, vs (Brunswick, 1865)
Der Vetter aus Bremen, unperf., vs (Brunswick, 1865)
Lorelei (3, G. Gurski), Brunswick, ? 12 April 1891, vs (Leipzig, 1890)
Saint Foix (1, H. von Wolzogen), Munich, 31 Oct 1894, vs (Leipzig, 1892)
Der Meermann (1, Wolzogen), Weimar, 19 April 1896, vs (Leipzig, 1895)
Münchhausen (Schelmenstück, 3, Wolzogen and F. Sporck), ? Brunswick, 1904, vs (Leipzig, 1897)
Augustin (Wolzogen), unperf., vs (Leipzig, 1898)
Rübezahl und der Sackpfeifer von Neisse (4, E. König), Brunswick, 15 May 1904, vs (Leipzig, 1902–3)
Riquet mit dem Schopf (Märchenoper, 3, König), Brunswick, 14 April 1907, vs (Leipzig, 1905–6)
Der Waldschratt (3, König), Brunswick, 31 March 1912, vs (Leipzig, 1908–11)

*

MGG (E. Valentin); *StiegerO*
E. Valentin: *Hans Sommer* (Brunswick, 1939)

Son and Stranger. Opera by Felix Mendelssohn; *see* HEIMKEHR AUS DER FREMDE, DIE.

Sondheim, Stephen (Joshua) (*b* New York, 22 March 1930). American composer and lyricist. Inescapable if contentious doyen of the American musical, he assimilated its stylistic traditions early and has subsequently developed its potential for innovatory and serious theatrical expression, notably in partnership with the directors Harold Prince and more recently James Lapine, the orchestrator Jonathan Tunick, the musical director Paul Gemignani and writers including Hugh Wheeler, John Weidman and James Goldman. Some of Sondheim's professional work has been as lyricist for the music of others, particularly at the start of his career, but it is as a theatre songwriter who moulds his own music and lyrics in order to convey dramatic character that he is recognized as unsurpassed. With ten Broadway shows to his credit he seems to have outstripped all other postwar composers in quantity, though he challenges audiences too much to be as popular as his Broadway predecessors. Several of his works contain much continuous music, with complex thematic cross-references and motivic developments, yet he has eschewed the influence of rock opera, with its all-sung dialogue, and continues to favour the older naturalistic mode of speech and sung lyrics. Despite his frequently ambitious musical demands (notably in ensembles), his approach to wit, verbal clarity, pacing and teamwork remains that of Broadway with its singing actors and the need for long commercial runs based on immediate critical approval. Nevertheless, *Sweeney Todd* has been produced successfully by the New York City Opera (1984) and other companies, *Pacific Overtures* somewhat less so by the ENO (1987).

Four of his early musicals were written as part of an intensive course of private study (1946–52) in writing for the musical theatre with Oscar Hammerstein II, a family friend. Later the award of the Hutchinson Prize for music at Williams College enabled him to study analysis privately with Milton Babbitt. His first professional assignments included co-writing television scripts for the *Topper* series, but it was as lyricist for Bernstein's *West Side Story* (1957) and Jule Styne's *Gypsy* (1959) that he made his name. As a composer recognition came more slowly, since the music for *A Funny Thing Happened on the Way to the Forum* (1962) was seen as a utilitarian part of the show's success, and *Anyone Can Whistle* (1964) failed after nine performances. *Company* (1970) and *Follies* (1971), marking the start of Sondheim's collaboration with Prince, established his pre-eminence in the musical theatre, the former (with its songs of incisive criticism of contemporary *mores*) a landmark in the development of the plotless 'concept musical', the latter a masterpiece of pastiche with deep layers of irony. *A Little Night Music* (1973), containing Sondheim's most popular song, 'Send in the clowns', explored the genre of European operetta, while *Pacific Overtures* (1976) broke new ground with its use of Japanese kabuki theatre techniques. *Sweeney Todd, the Demon Barber of Fleet Street* (1979) is his biggest work, and over three quarters of the drama is set to music. Highly characterized numbers, including intricate duets, ensembles, parlour pastiches and comedy songs (prime among them the Act 1 waltz finale, 'A little priest'), are interwoven with much 'symphonic' material in the form of transformational motifs which gives clues to the story. The whole is bounded by the rondo theme of 'The ballad of Sweeney Todd', which is based melodically on the *Dies irae*.

Sondheim's structuralist propensity not to dissociate form and content attracted him to melodrama in *Sweeney Todd* as it had to farce in *A Funny Thing Happened on the Way to the Forum*. A similar emphasis on musical 'plotting' informs the score of *Merrily we Roll Along* (1981), whose chronology and musical development operate in reverse. *Sunday in the Park with George* (1984), inspired by the painting *Dimanche, après-midi à l'île de la Grande Jatte* (1884–6) by the artist Georges Seurat, found Sondheim conveying his images of the pointillist style through passages of musical minimalism, an idiom with which he had first shown clear affinities in *Pacific Overtures*. But this technique has receded in *Into the Woods* (1987), in whose fairy-tale enactments, complex enough as a theatrical plot, a new simplicity of musical material is attained in accordance with the show's powerful contemporary message of universality and rebirth. Different again is *Assassins* (1991), in which his critique of disaffection in American history is also a critique, often harsh, of vernacular American music, including Sousa marches, gospel, folk and pop music. Sondheim has composed music for plays and films, and the first of several revues of his songs, *Side by Side by Sondheim*, entered the repertory in 1977.

His musical language, in which melody and harmony are closely argued, retains strong affinities with Ravel and Copland, while making sophisticated use of jazz and dance idioms. It is intensely personal, often bittersweet, in its expression. Sondheim is a member of the Dramatists Guild and served as its President from 1973 to 1981; he was elected to the American Academy and Institute of Arts and Letters in 1983. In 1990 he became the first Visiting Professor of Contemporary Theatre at Oxford University. Most of his scores have won Tony and New York Drama Critics' Circle Awards, and *Sunday in the Park with George* was awarded the 1985 Pulitzer Prize for Drama.

musicals unless otherwise stated, all to lyrics by Sondheim; dates are of first New York productions (not including workshop performances) unless otherwise stated; all published in New York

By George (2), Bucks County, PA, George School, 25 May 1946, collab. M. Dubin and J. Lincoln, *US-MAhs*

Phinney's Rainbow (2, J. Horton), Williamstown, MA, Williams College, 30 April 1948, 3 songs (1948)

All That Glitters (2, Sondheim, after G. S. Kaufman and M. Connelly: *Beggar on Horseback*), Williamstown, MA, Williams College, 18 March 1949, *MAhs*, 5 songs (1949)

High Tor, 1949 (Sondheim, after M. Anderson), inc., *MAhs*

Mary Poppins, 1950 (Sondheim, after P. L. Travers), inc., *MAhs*

Climb High, 1950–52 (2, Sondheim), unperf., *MAhs*

Saturday Night, 1954 (2, J. Epstein and P. Epstein), unperf., *MAhs*

The Lady or the Tiger, 1954 (television musical, 2, after F. Stockton), collab. M. Rodgers, inc., *MAhs*

Mizners (after A. Johnston: *The Legendary Mizners*), inc., *MAhs*

The Last Resorts, 1956 (J. Kerr), inc., *MAhs*

I Believe in You (television musical, 2, E. Carrington), inc., *MAhs*

The Jet Propelled Couch, 1958 (S. Roberts), unperf., *MAhs*

Happily Ever After, 1959 (television musical, 2, J. Stein), unperf.

Passionella (minimusical), Huntingdon, NJ, 1962, *MAhs*, 1 song (1990)

A Funny Thing Happened on the Way to the Forum (2, B. Shevelove and L. Gelbart, after Plautus), Alvin, 8 May 1962, *MAhs*, vs (1964)

Anyone Can Whistle (3, A. Laurents), Majestic, 4 April 1964, *MAhs*, vs (1968)

Evening Primrose (television musical, 2, J. Goldman, after J. Collier), ABC, 16 Nov 1966, 2 songs (1980, 1987)

Company (2, G. Furth), Alvin, 26 April 1970, vs (1970)

Follies (1, Goldman), Winter Garden, 4 April 1971, vs (1971); rev. version (2), London, Shaftesbury, 21 July 1987, selections (London, 1987)

A Little Night Music (2, H. Wheeler, after I. Bergman: *Smiles of a Summer Night*), Shubert, 25 Feb 1973, vs (1974)

The Frogs (play with music, 1, Shevelove, after Aristophanes), New Haven, Yale U. Paine Whitney Gymnasium swimming-pool, 20 May 1974, 2 songs (1987)

Pacific Overtures (2, J. Weidman, with Wheeler), Winter Garden, 11 Jan 1976, vs (1977)

Sweeney Todd, the Demon Barber of Fleet Street (musical thriller, 2, Wheeler, after C. Bond), Uris, 1 March 1979, vs (1981)

Merrily we Roll Along (2, Furth, after Kaufman and M. Hart), Alvin, 16 Nov 1981, vs (1984)

Sunday in the Park with George (2, J. Lapine), Booth, 2 May 1984, vs (1987)

Into the Woods (2, Lapine), Martin Beck, 5 Nov 1987, vs (1989)

Assassins (1, Weidman), Playwrights Horizon, 27 Jan 1991

Lyrics: West Side Story, Bernstein, 1957; Gypsy, J. Styne, 1959; 1 song for Hot Spot, M. Rodgers, 1963; Do I Hear a Waltz?, R. Rodgers, 1965; 1 song for The Mad Show, M. Rodgers, 1966; A Pray by Blecht, Bernstein, comp. 1968, inc.; addl material for Candide (rev. version), Bernstein, 1973

*

AG (S. S. Brylawski)

S. Sondheim: 'Theatre Lyrics', *Dramatists Guild Quarterly*, viii/3 (1971), 6–36; repr. in *Playwrights, Lyricists, Composers on Theater*, ed. O. L. Guernsey jr (New York, 1974), 61–97

P. Sheren and T. Sutcliffe: 'Stephen Sondheim and the American Musical', *Theatre '74*, ed. S. Morley (London, 1974), 187–215
C. Zadan: *Sondheim & Co.* (New York, 1974, 3/1990)
S. Sondheim: 'The Musical Theater', *Dramatists Guild Quarterly*, xv/3 (1978), 6–29
T. P. Adler: 'The Musical Dramas of Stephen Sondheim: some Critical Approaches', *Journal of Popular Culture*, xii (1978–9), 513–25
J. Lahr: 'Sondheim's Little Deaths: the Ironic Mode and its Discontents', *Harper's*, cclviii/April (1979), 71–8; rev. as 'Stephen Sondheim', *Automatic Vaudeville: Essays on Star Turns* (New York, 1984), 5–21
H. Prince and S. Sondheim, with G. Cryer: 'On Collaboration between Authors and Directors', *Dramatists Guild Quarterly*, xvi/3 (1979), 14–34
M. C. Adams: *The Lyrics of Stephen Sondheim: Form and Function* (diss., Northwestern U., 1980)
S. Sondheim: 'Larger than Life: Reflections on Melodrama and Sweeney Todd', *Melodrama*, ed. D. Gerould (New York, 1980), 3–14
D. J. Cartmell: *Stephen Sondheim and the Concept Musical* (diss., U. of California, Santa Barbara, 1983)
J. Rockwell: 'Urban Popular Song, the Broadway Musical, the Cabaret Revival & the Birth Pangs of American Opera: Stephen Sondheim', *All American Music: Composition in the Late Twentieth Century* (New York, 1983), 209–20
C. Blyton: 'Sondheim's "Sweeney Todd" – the Case for the Defence', *Tempo*, no.149 (1984), 19–26
S. G. Freedman: 'The Creative Mind: the Words and Music of Stephen Sondheim', *New York Times Magazine* (1 April 1984)
M. Katutani: 'How Two Artists Shaped an Innovative Musical', *New York Times* (10 June 1984)
E. K. Bristow and J. K. Butler: '*Company*, about Face! The Show that Revolutionized the American Musical', *American Music*, v (1987), 241–54
D. van Leer: 'Putting it Together: Sondheim and the Broadway Musical', *Raritan*, vii (1987), 113–28
T. Sutcliffe: 'Sondheim and the Musical', *MT*, cxxviii (1987), 487–90
N. Mankin, ed.: 'The *PAJ* Casebook 2: *Into the Woods*', *Performing Arts Journal*, xi/1 (1988), 46–66
L. F. Orchard: *Stephen Sondheim and the Disintegration of the American Dream: a Study of the Work of Stephen Sondheim from 'Company' to 'Sunday in the Park with George'* (diss., U. of Oregon, 1988)
D. Savran, ed.: 'Stephen Sondheim', *In Their Own Words: Interviews with American Playwrights* (New York and London, 1988); repr. in *Sunday in the Park with George* (Royal National Theatre programme booklet, 1990)
F. Hirsch: *Harold Prince and the American Musical Theatre* (Cambridge, 1989)
C. Ilson: *Harold Prince: from 'Pajama Game' to 'Phantom of the Opera'* (Ann Arbor, 1989)
'Sondheim's Technique: Stephen Sondheim Interviewed by Trevor Herbert', *Contemporary Music Review*, v (1989), 199–214
J. Gordon: *Art Isn't Easy: the Achievement of Stephen Sondheim* (Carbondale, IL, 1990)
M. Ratcliffe: 'Putting it Together', *Sunday in the Park with George* (Royal National Theatre programme booklet, 1990)
J. P. Swain: *The Broadway Musical: a Critical and Musical Survey* (New York, 1990)
C. Bond: Introduction to *Sweeney Todd* (New York, 1991)
R. H. Kornick: *Recent American Opera: a Production Guide* (New York, 1991), 288–96
J. Tunick: Introduction to *A Little Night Music* (New York, 1991)

STEPHEN BANFIELD

Sonnambula, La ('The Sleepwalker'). *Melodramma* in two acts by VINCENZO BELLINI to a libretto by FELICE ROMANI after EUGÈNE SCRIBE and J.-P. Aumer's ballet-pantomime *La somnambule, ou L'arrivée d'un nouveau seigneur*; Milan, Teatro Carcano, 6 March 1831.

Bellini wrote his sixth professional opera for a remarkable season at the Teatro Carcano which opened with Donizetti's *Anna Bolena*, using the same principals, Giuditta Pasta (Amina) and Giovanni Battista Rubini (Elvino). It was the only occasion on which Bellini was able to write for both together:

Lisa *an inn hostess, in love with Elvino*	soprano
Alessio *a villager, in love with Lisa*	bass
Amina *an orphan raised by Teresa, betrothed to Elvino*	soprano
Teresa *a mill-owner*	mezzo-soprano
A Notary	tenor
Elvino *a wealthy landowner in the village*	tenor
Count Rodolfo *lord of the village*	bass

Country villagers

Setting A village in Switzerland in the early 19th century

Luciano Mariani sang Count Rodolfo and Lisa was sung by Elisa Taccani. Until a late stage Bellini planned to set *Ernani*, from Hugo's play; he did not start on *La sonnambula* until 2 January, and wrote the second act in two weeks, from about 9 February.

The theme of somnambulism was common; the present libretto has a different plot from those of Foppa's *La sonnambula* (1800) for Paer, Scribe's *La somnambule* (1819) and Romani's *Il sonnambulo* (1824) for Carafa. Also independent are Romani's *Amina* (1824) for Rastrelli and Ferretti's *Amina, ossia L'orfanella di Ginevra* (1829) for Luigi Ricci.

Much of the opera is pitched very high. Rubini's part (Elvino) was originally higher than it appears in Ricordi's printed scores (see Boosey's vocal score, 1849), ascending to *d''* in the duets and Act 2 aria and rarely falling below *a*. Bellini may not have intended the original pitches for anyone other than Rubini, who used a mellifluous head voice; transpositions are justifiable, but the current scores produce abrupt key changes. The part of Amina, for Giuditta Pasta, ascends to *d'''* in the second duet and to *e♭'''* (not in the autograph) in the final 'Ah! non giunge uman pensiero'.

The opera was very successful (as Glinka recorded in his *Memoirs*) and was presented with Pasta and Rubini in London (28 July 1831) and Paris (24 October) before being seen again in Italy (1832, Florence). The role of Amina was quickly taken up by Maria Malibran, first in an English adaptation by Bishop (vocal score, London, 1833); it was also a favourite role of Giuseppina Strepponi. Famous exponents in England were Jenny Lind (1847) and Adelina Patti, who made her Covent Garden début as Amina (1861). Some of Lind's embellishments were written down and published by Rockstro (London, 1894); closer to Bellini's own time are those by Laure Cinti-Damoreau (see Caswell 1975). In the 20th century, famous interpreters of Amina included Luisa Tetrazzini, Amelita Galli-Curci and Toti dal Monte, who sang the role at La Scala in 1935, the centenary of Bellini's death. Maria Callas also sang Amina at La Scala and then at the Edinburgh Festival in 1957. On the latter occasion the final performances were sung by Renata Scotto, who was later to make a speciality of the role.

ACT 1.i *The village square with an inn, a mill and hills in the background* There is no overture, but an orchestral introduction supported by offstage band leads to the offstage chorus of villagers, 'Viva Amina'. In a cavatina, 'Tutto è gioia, tutto è festa', Lisa laments that, amid the general rejoicing, she alone is sad, at the prospect of losing Elvino. Alessio rushes in and embraces the unenthusiastic Lisa. As the villagers arrive,

1. Giuditta Pasta as Amina and Giovanni Battista Rubini as Elvino in Act 1 scene i of the original production of Bellini's 'La sonnambula' at the Teatro Carcano, Milan, 6 March 1831, with (below) the opening of their duet 'Prendi, l'anel ti dono': lithograph by A. Lanzani

he organizes them around Amina's dwelling at the mill and joins in their praises of the girl. Amina comes out of the mill with Teresa and thanks her fellow villagers. She expresses her joy in the cavatina 'Come per me sereno' and the cabaletta 'Sovra il sen la man mi posa', a brilliant show piece of a length unprecedented in Bellini's works; this was his first opportunity to write for the great contemporary diva, Giuditta Pasta. Amina naively wishes Alessio and Lisa well, and Lisa's sour reaction is noted by Teresa.

A notary enters, announcing the arrival of Elvino, who greets Amina and explains that he has been singing her praises in front of his mother's tomb. Before the notary he pledges her everything he possesses; she replies that she has only her heart to offer him in return. In the duet, 'Prendi, l'anel ti dono', Elvino gives Amina a ring that belonged to his mother and a bunch of wild flowers. The couple are now betrothed and in 'Ah! vorrei trovar parola' Amina wishes she could find words to express her love. The sound of coach wheels is heard, and Count Rodolfo enters; he is on his way to the castle, but accepts Lisa's invitation to stay the night at her inn. Though unrecognized by the villagers, he remembers the mill and the countryside that he left years before, and evokes the memories in a cavatina, 'Vi ravviso, o luoghi ameni'. He is much taken with Amina, whom he compares with a love of his youth (a relic of Romani's complication, specifically rejected by Bellini, whereby Amina is the fruit of an earlier indiscretion).

It is now dusk and Teresa tells everyone to leave promptly, warning Rodolfo of a phantom swathed in white that haunts the area at night. The villagers support Teresa's fears and in the chorus 'A fosco cielo, a notte bruna' describe the ghostly noctambulist to the incredulous Rodolfo. He takes a gallant farewell of Amina, much to Elvino's indignation. Left alone, the lovers quarrel and then make it up again in a duet, 'Son geloso del zeffiro errante', which contains some of Bellini's most delicate exchanges of vocal fioriture.

1.ii *A room at Lisa's inn* Rodolfo is flirting with Lisa, who informs him that he has been recognized as the new lord of the castle. They are disturbed by a noise and Lisa hurriedly departs, dropping her kerchief. Amina, all in white, comes in by the window; she is walking in her sleep, and Rodolfo realizes that she must be the villagers' 'phantom'. In disjointed phrases Amina speaks of her forthcoming marriage, of Elvino's jealousy and their quarrel. Rodolfo refrains from taking advantage of 'this pure and innocent flower', and goes out by the window, leaving Amina asleep on his sofa. The villagers, arriving to welcome their new lord, are amused to discover a girl in his room; they are about to leave discreetly when Lisa ushers in Elvino and Teresa, triumphantly pointing to the sleeping girl. Everyone exclaims in shocked surprise as they recognize Amina. Woken by the noise, she is confused and completely ignorant of what has happened. She is denounced by all; only Teresa, who picks up Lisa's kerchief (mistaking it for Amina's) and puts it round Amina's neck, believes the girl's protestation of innocence, 'D'un pensiero e d'un accento', with which Amina launches the superb final ensemble. Elvino calls off the wedding and the villagers condemn Amina.

ACT 2.i *A shadowy valley between the village and the castle* The villagers rest on their way to the castle to put Amina's case to Count Rodolfo ('Qui la selva è più folta ed ombrosa'). Amina tells Teresa that she is her only support in her grief and is comforted by her foster-mother. (Bellini cut a long cantilena, mainly for two trumpets, from the orchestral prelude to this scene; it is printed, however, in the Boosey vocal score edited by Pittman and Arthur Sullivan, and is restored on a recording made by Sutherland in 1980.) Elvino soliloquizes on his misery in 'Tutto è sciolto'. Seeing Amina, he reproaches her in 'Pasci il guardo, e appaga l'alma'. When the villagers return, announcing that the Count has exonerated Amina, Elvino furiously snatches his ring from Amina and in 'Ah! perchè non posso odiarti' regrets that he can neither hate her, nor entirely banish her from his heart.

2.ii *The village square* Brushing off Alessio, Lisa sings of her joy at marrying Elvino ('De' lieti auguri a voi son grata') who kisses her hand and leads her towards the church. Rodolfo, arriving with the villagers, proclaims Amina's innocence. In the quartet with chorus, 'Signor Conte agli occhi miei', the Count tries to explain to a disbelieving Elvino that Amina was sleep-walking. Teresa begs the villagers to make less noise as Amina has fallen asleep; she is shocked to see Elvino about to marry Lisa, who points out that she was not found in another man's room. When Teresa produces the kerchief dropped by Lisa, Elvino realizes that Lisa is a liar.

Amina appears sleep-walking on the eaves of the mill-house roof (it was reputedly Jenny Lind who introduced the bridge across the mill-wheel; for illustration *see* LIND, JENNY). The villagers kneel and pray silently for her safety; they sigh with relief in a soothing

2. 'La sonnambula' (Bellini): lithograph after Alessandro Sanquirico's design for the sleep-walking scene in Act 2 in the original production at the Teatro Carcano, Milan, 6 March 1831

cadence ('È salva!') as she descends to the ground and, in a typically Romantic 'mad scene' accompanied by reminiscent themes in the orchestra, Amina imagines that she is reunited with Elvino. In the cantabile 'Ah! non credea mirarti' she addresses the flowers, now dead, that he had given her. Elvino awakens her by replacing his ring on her finger. Her happiness restored, Amina gives way to feelings of joy in the brilliant cabaletta 'Ah! non giunge uman pensiero'.

* * *

Throughout the 19th century *La sonnambula* was regarded in Italy along with Donizetti's *Linda di Chamounix* as a *locus classicus* of the pastoral genre, which persisted well into the age of Italian grand opera, as may be seen from Autori-Manzocchi's *Dolores* (1875) and Ponchielli's *Lina* (1877). It was a particular favourite with Victorian audiences. Two of Sullivan's wittiest operatic parodies, the sextet 'A nice dilemma' (*Trial by Jury*, 1875) and 'Carefully on tiptoe stealing' (*H.M.S. Pinafore*, 1878), are modelled on, respectively, the concertato 'D'un pensiero e d'un accento' and the chorus 'Tutto tace: e dorme certo', both from the finale of Act 1. In George Eliot's novel *The Mill on the Floss* Maggie Tulliver's rejected suitor Philip Wakem reproaches her with Elvino's cabaletta 'Ah! perchè non posso odiarti'.

In *La sonnambula* Bellini's mature style appears finally crystallized, a synthesis of heartfelt melody, expressive declamation and coloratura from which all Rossinian hedonism has been banished. The rustic setting together with the subject of an innocent village maiden traduced and finally vindicated would seem to place it in the category of 'opera semiseria', were it not for the absence of the statutory *basso buffo* (and spoken dialogue). The opera is therefore subheaded 'melodramma' *tout court*. The forms are mostly shorter and more flexible than in Bellini's previous works; and there is a plentiful use of orchestral 'parlanti'. The recitatives often take on the quality of arias in low relief, merging into the formal numbers with the smoothest of transitions. Likewise a considerable dramatic advance is achieved, as in *I Capuleti e i Montecchi* (1830), by the interventions of other singers into solo arias. Among the latter 'Ah! non credea mirarti' stands out as an example of the composer's 'long, long, long melodies' (Verdi's phrase), extending over 36 bars of slow tempo with no element of reprise. At the same time the chorus that opens Act 2, with its strangely Gluckian overtones, bears witness to Bellini's roots in an older, classical tradition.

JULIAN BUDDEN, ELIZABETH FORBES, SIMON MAGUIRE

Son na Volge ('A Volga Dream'). Opera in four acts, op.16, by ANTON STEPANOVICH ARENSKY, in part to a libretto by ALEXANDER NIKOLAYEVICH OSTROVSKY originally prepared for Tchaikovsky's first (later withdrawn) opera, *Voyevoda*; Moscow, Bol'shoy Theatre, 21 December 1890/2 January 1891.

The plot concerns a love triangle involving Nechay Shalïgin (baritone), the old military governor (voyevoda) of a Volga province, Mar'ya Dyuzhaya (soprano), the younger daughter of a landowner to whose elder daughter the voyevoda was previously engaged, and Stepan Bastryukov (tenor), scion of a boyar family to whom the voyevoda has sworn enmity. Of course, the young lovers triumph in the end, the old voyevoda being driven nearly mad by nightmares (whence the title) and unseated by order of the tsar.

Arensky began work on *Son na Volge* in Rimsky-Korsakov's composition class in 1882 and completed it as his op.16 in 1888. It is throughout an epigonous study in 'kuchkist' style, full of national colour and extended dramatic recitative, for which the nightmare scene (Act 4 scene i) was a natural outlet. It filled Rimsky-Korsakov with nostalgia. 'Nowadays no one writes like this any more,' he told his Boswell, Vasily Yastrebtsev, shortly after the opera's St Petersburg première in 1903, 'it smacks of something irretrievable.'

RICHARD TARUSKIN

Sonneck, Oscar G(eorge) T(heodore) (*b* Lafayette [now in Jersey City], NJ, 6 Oct 1873; *d* New York, 30 Oct 1928). American musicologist, librarian and editor. He went to Germany to study the piano in 1883, later developing interests in philosophy, musicology and composition. He returned to the USA in 1899. He then travelled for three years collecting references to American musical life before 1800, and in 1902 was made head of the new music division of the Library of Congress, where he organized and developed what was to become one of the most comprehensive collections in the world of printed music, manuscripts and books on music. He established its unrivalled archive of opera scores and librettos, and in 1908 acquired the Albert Schatz collection of about 12 500 opera librettos and additional documentation. In 1917 he resigned and became director and then vice-president (1921) of G. Schirmer, whose *Musical Quarterly* he had edited since its first issue in 1915. Sonneck's work for American music scholarship was much undervalued during his life. His scheme of music classification (1904, the basis of the organization of music collections in the Library of Congress) and his work on opera librettos before 1800 remain the outstanding reference works of their kind.

Dramatic Music: Catalogue of Full Scores in the Collection of the Library of Congress (Washington DC, 1908, 2/1917)
Catalogue of Opera Scores (MS, 1912, *US-Wc*)
Catalogue of 19th Century Librettos (MS, 1914, *US-Wc*)
Catalogue of Opera Librettos Printed before 1800 (Washington DC, 1914)
Early Opera in America (New York, 1915)

JON NEWSOM

Sonnenfest der Braminen, Das ('The Sun Festival of the Brahmins'). *Heroisch-komisches Original-Singspiel* in two acts by WENZEL MÜLLER to a libretto by KARL FRIEDRICH HENSLER; Vienna, Theater in der Leopoldstadt, 9 September 1790.

One of the most successful and influential of a new type of Singspiel in the Viennese theatre, it combines elements of the 'mercy opera' (in the tradition of Gluck's *La rencontre imprévue* and Mozart's *Die Entführung*) with religious and humanitarian concerns. Eduard (tenor), a young Englishman, and his English servant, Barzalo (bass), arrive on an Indian island in the hope of releasing Eduard's betrothed, Laura (soprano), from captivity. The confrontation between the outwardly harsh tenets of Brahminism and the familiar idealized Enlightenment attitudes of the Europeans provides much of the dramatic interest, though the choral utterances of the Brahmins proclaiming the blessings of wisdom and nature, duty and love, already point towards the eventual happy outcome. Apart from the choruses, the songs for Barzalo and the gardener, Pirokko (tenor), were admired by contemporaries; *Das Sonnenfest*, Müller's first major achievement as a composer, was mounted in numerous theatres in Austria and Germany at the end of the 18th century and in the early decades of the 19th. It was also given in Poland, the Netherlands and in Paris, and in the Leopoldstadt it achieved nearly 100 performances in 15 years. Although the story is clearly derived from Kotzebue's *Die Sonnenjungfrau*, Hensler constructed a lively, colourful libretto to which Müller responded with a witty and tuneful, and at times impressively sombre, score.

PETER BRANSCOMBE

Sonnleithner [Sonnleitner], **Joseph von** (*b* Vienna, 3 March 1766; *d* Vienna, 26 Dec 1835). Austrian librettist. He was born into a prominent Viennese musical family. A lover of the fine arts, he edited the Viennese *Theater-Almanach*, 1794–6, and helped found the Gesellschaft der Musikfreunde in 1812 along with, in 1817, the conservatory associated with it. He was secretary of the court theatres until 1814 and of the Gesellschaft until his death. A multi-volume history of music, planned with Johann Forkel, never saw the light of day. Sonnleithner wrote and translated opera librettos for Cherubini, Seyfried, Weigl and Gyrowetz, but his best-known contribution remains the translation and adaptation of Bouilly's libretto *Léonore* for Beethoven. Although basically a translation, it attempts to increase the opportunities for musical drama by the addition of several numbers. Sonnleithner's additions created opportunities for some of Beethoven's finest music in the first version of the opera, but many critics have blamed the initial failure of *FIDELIO* on his libretto. The expansion – which creates two acts from Bouilly's Act 1 – involves the least dramatic part of the story, thus slowing the action; however, the limitations of Beethoven's setting have also been noted. The libretto for Cherubini's *Faniska* (1806) has received even harsher criticism (a 'disastrous hotch-potch'), although both Haydn and Beethoven admired the work. A staunch musical patron until his death, Sonnleithner greatly enriched the archival holdings of the Gesellschaft and the conservatory with his bequest of instruments, material concerning opera librettos and his extensive personal library.

Fidelio (after J. N. Bouilly), Beethoven, 1805; *Faniska*, Cherubini, 1806; *Zum goldenen Löwen*, Seyfried, 1806; *Agnes Sorel* (after Bouilly), Gyrowetz, 1806; *Kaiser Hadrian* (after P. Metastasio), Weigl, 1807; *Emericke* [Die Zurechtweisung] (komische Oper), Gyrowetz, 1807; *Die Pagen des Herzogs von Vendôme* (Singspiel, after J. M. A. M. Dieulafoy), Gyrowetz, 1808

*

A. Sandberger: 'Léonore von Bouilly und ihre Bearbeitung für Beethoven durch Joseph Sonnleithner', *Ausgewählte Aufsätze zur Musikgeschichte*, ii (Munich, 1924), 141–53, 283–365
W. Hess: *Beethovens Oper Fidelio und ihre drei Fassungen* (Zürich, 1953, enlarged as *Das Fidelio-Buch*, 1986)
A. Bauer: *Oper und Operetta in Wien* (Zürich, 1955)
M. Ruhnke: 'Die Librettisten des Fidelio', *Opernstudien: Anna Amalie Abert zum 65. Geburtstag* (Tutzing, 1975), 121–40

KRISTIN M. KNITTEL

Sontag [Sonntag], **Henriette (Gertrud Walpurgis)** (*b* Koblenz, 3 Jan 1806; *d* Mexico City, 17 June 1854). German soprano. Her first appearance in opera was as Salome in Kauer's *Das Donauweibchen* (probably in Darmstadt in 1811). After her father's death she moved with her mother to Prague, entering the conservatory in 1815. She made her mature début in 1821 as the Princess in Boieldieu's *Jean de Paris*. She moved to Vienna where in 1823 Weber heard her in Rossini's *La donna del lago* and offered her the title role in *Euryanthe*, in which she triumphed. After a brief but highly successful season in Leipzig (1825), when she sang in *Der Freischütz* and *Euryanthe*, she was engaged for the Berlin Königstädtisches Theater, making her début on 3 August 1825 as Isabella (*L'italiana in Algeri*).

Sontag's international career dates from her brilliant Paris début at the Théâtre Italien in 12 roles, initially as Rosina on 15 May 1826 (for illustration *see BARBIERE DI SIVIGLIA, IL* (ii)). After further German appearances, she returned in January 1828, including Donna Anna and Semiramide in her repertory. Her English début was also in 1828, as Rosina at the King's Theatre on 19 April. After marrying a Sardinian diplomat she was obliged to renounce the stage in 1830, and for some years made only select private and concert appearances in cities to which her husband was posted. She returned to the stage when financial difficulties intervened and

Henriette Sontag as Ellen in Rossini's 'La donna del lago' at the King's Theatre, London, 16 May 1828

when the King of Sardinia's abdication ended her husband's career in 1849. Lumley offered her a six-month contract at Her Majesty's, where she sang Rossini, Donizetti and Mozart. After an English tour she went to Paris, returning to create Miranda in Halévy's *La tempesta* (1850, Her Majesty's), and again singing in Paris and London in 1851. She reappeared in Germany, and in 1852 went to America. In 1854 she toured Mexico with an Italian company. Her last appearance was as Lucrezia Borgia on 11 June; the following day she was taken ill with cholera.

In spite of the long interruption to her career, Sontag was one of the most consistently successful and popular German sopranos of her time. On her return to the stage her vocal powers appear to have been undiminished, her artistry more mature. Of great beauty and charm of presence, she possessed a lively and attractive voice which she used with great skill: her range was from *a* to *e‴* and technically she was said to be the equal or superior of any singer of her day, including Catalani and her bitter rival Malibran. But she was essentially a singer of light and brilliant parts which demanded little dramatic feeling. J. E. Cox gave a description of her 1828 London appearances: '[Her voice's] greatest merit consists in its wonderful flexibility ... Execution is with her everything, expression as nothing ... that coolness of temperament which her acting seems to denote has most likely exercised a joint influence in determining the character of her singing'. But Berlioz, in an eloquent obituary tribute, described her as possessing 'all the gifts of art and nature: voice, musical feeling, dramatic instinct, style, exquisite taste, passion, reflectiveness, grace, everything and still something more'.

T. Gautier: *L'ambassadrice: biographie de la Comtesse Rossi* (Paris, 1850)

J. E. Cox: *Musical Recollections of the Last Half-Century* (London, 1872)

A. Ehrlich: *Berühmte Sängerinnen der Vergangenheit und Gegenwart* (Leipzig, 1895)

H. Stümcke: *Henriette Sontag* (Berlin, 1913)

E. Pirchan: *Henriette Sontag: die Sängerin des Biedermeier* (Vienna, 1946) [incl. extensive bibliography]

JOHN WARRACK

Sonzogno. Italian firm of publishers. It was founded in Milan at the end of the 18th century by G. B. Sonzogno, whose grandson Edoardo (*b* Milan, 21 April 1836; *d* Milan, 14 March 1920) began in 1874 to specialize in music. His first music publication was an arrangement for piano of *Il barbiere di Siviglia*. Among the firm's notable achievements were obtaining the Italian rights for *Carmen* in 1897 and, later, those for Thomas' *Mignon* and *Hamlet*; the Sonzogno Competition was instituted in 1883 (also held in 1889, 1892 and 1903 – the young Mascagni won that of 1889, with his *Cavalleria rusticana*). The firm promoted the *verismo* school associated with Mascagni, Giordano, Filiasi, Leoncavallo and Cilea, as well as some foreign composers, and operettas by Hervé, Lecocq and Offenbach. Its greatest successes were *Pagliacci*, *Andrea Chénier*, *Fedora*, *L'amico Fritz* and *La Gioconda*. In 1875 Edoardo Sonzogno took over the management of the Teatro S Redegonda in Milan; the experiment was repeated with lasting success in 1894, when on 22 September he opened a theatre of his own, the Lirico Internazionale (founded on the site of the Canobbiana), with *La martire*, based on a theatre piece by Luigi Illica, with music by Spyridon Samaras. Sonzogno also published the periodical *Il teatro illustrato* (1881–92).

On Edoardo's retirement in 1909 the publishing house came under the direction of his son Riccardo (*d* 1915), who was succeeded by his cousin Renzo (1877–1920). Renzo had been introduced to music and publishing by his uncle and had worked with the separate firm Lorenzo Sonzogno, founded in 1910 to promote Italian and foreign operettas, and comic and serious operas, among which were Mascagni's *Parisina* and Pizzetti's *Fedra*. The firms amalgamated in 1915; the Società per Azioni Sonzogno remains active.

Catalogo delle pubblicazioni musicali dell'editore E. Sonzogno (Milan, 1911)

Catalogo generale 1916–1917 della casa musicale Sonzogno (Milan, 1917)

C. Sartori: *Dizionario degli editori musicali italiani* (Florence, 1958)

Soomer, Walter (*b* Liegnitz [now Legnica], 12 March 1878; *d* Leipzig, Aug 1955). German bass-baritone. He studied in Berlin, made his début in 1902 at Colmar and was engaged by the Halle Opera for the next four years. With his powerful voice and imposing physique it was natural that he would specialize in the Wagnerian roles and he quickly came to notice in Bayreuth, where he sang first in 1906 and for the last time in 1925, shortly after which he retired to teach. Throughout his career he was a member of the Leipzig company, though he also appeared abroad, notably at Covent Garden in the 1905 season, when he sang Hans Sachs, and at the Metropolitan (1908–11). In later years he relinquished the bass-baritone repertory in favour of deeper roles such as Hagen and Hunding. Records show a fine, evenly produced voice of impressive range and resonance.

J. B. STEANE

Soot, Fritz [Friedrich] (**Wilhelm**) (*b* Wellesweiler-Neunkirchen, Saar, 20 Aug 1878; *d* Berlin, 9 June 1965). German tenor. He studied with Scheidemantel in Dresden and made his début there in 1908 as Tonio (*La fille du régiment*). While at Dresden he created the Italian Tenor in *Der Rosenkavalier* (1911). He was a member of the Stuttgart Opera (1918–22), then moved to the Berlin Staatsoper, where his creations included the Drum Major in *Wozzeck* (1925). He was also the first Berlin Laca in *Jenůfa* (1924), Mephistopheles in *Doktor Faust* (1927) and Babinski in *Švanda dudák* (1929). But it was as a Wagner tenor that he was best known and in 1924 and 1925 he sang Siegmund, Siegfried, Tristan, Erik and Walther at Covent Garden; his repertory also included Parsifal, Palestrina and Otello. He returned to the Berlin Staatsoper after World War II and continued to sing character roles there until 1952, taking part in the première of Dessau's *Die Verurteilung des Lukullus* (1951). HAROLD ROSENTHAL/R

Sooter, Edward (*b* Salina, KA, 8 Dec 1934). American tenor. He studied at Kansas University and in Hamburg with Helmut Melchert. After singing Florestan at Bremerhaven in 1966, he appeared widely in Germany in the Heldentenor repertory and as Manrico, Canio and Don José. Appearances at the Metropolitan (from 1980) have included Otello, Tannhäuser, Aeneas (*Les Troyens*), Lohengrin and Tristan. He has been praised for the intelligence of his interpretations but in such roles as Siegfried (1984, Seattle) has been found wanting in vocal weight. DAVID CUMMINGS

Sophie [Sophia] **Elisabeth,** Duchess of Brunswick-Lüneburg (*b* Güstrow, 20 Aug 1613; *d* Lüchow, 12 July 1676). German composer and poet. She received musical training at the court of her father, Duke Johann Albrecht of Mecklenburg-Güstrow. In 1629 she was obliged to flee from the Thirty Years War and for some years lived at the Kassel court, a lively centre of music. In July 1635 she married Duke August the Younger of Brunswick-Lüneburg. She played a leading role in the court music at Brunswick and Wolfenbüttel; her musical adviser and composition teacher was Heinrich Schütz, whom she appointed senior Kapellmeister in 1655. Most of her compositions are sacred songs, but she also contributed music and texts to numerous secular celebrations and theatrical performances. Allegorical celebratory plays, ballets and masquerades were performed annually, most of them in honour of Duke August's birthday (10 April) and with the participation of the ducal family. Sophie Elisabeth played an essential part in establishing this tradition and apparently composed the music for most of the productions up to 1656. In 1654 she presented Harsdörffer and Staden's *Seelewig*. Her librettos include *Der Natur Banquet* (1654), *Ballet der Zeit* (1655), *Der Minervae Banquet* (1655) and *Glückwünschende Wahrsagung und Ankunft der Königin Nicaulae* (1656). The music of only two of her dramatic works has survived. In *Friedens Sieg* (1642, Brunswick), to a text by J. G. Schottelius, the spoken voice, solo and choral singing, instrumental music and dance are combined within an operetta-like action. *Glückwünschende Freudensdarstellung* (published Lüneburg, 1652) is conceived in the manner of a scenic festival cantata; it includes two instrumental pieces, five lieder and a *Schlusschor*.

M. Schneider: 'Ein Braunschweiger Freudenspiel aus dem Jahre 1648', *Musik und Bild: Festschrift Max Seiffert* (Kassel, 1938), 87–94 [incl. musical excerpts]

H. Sievers: 'Aus den Anfängen zum Nationaltheater', *250 Jahre Braunschweigisches Staatstheater 1690–1940* (Brunswick, 1941), 26

H.-G. Roloff, ed.: *Sophie Elisabeth, Herzogin zu Braunschweig und Lüneburg: Dichtungen*, i: *Spiele* (Frankfurt, 1980)

HORST WALTER

Sophocles [Sophokles] (*b* Colonus, nr Athens, *c*496 BC; *d* Athens, 406 BC). Greek dramatist. He is said to have studied under Aeschylus and to have written some 123 plays. His public career included distinguished military service against the Samians and service on embassies to foreign states. Seven tragedies survive and about 400 lines of a satyr play, the *Ichneutae* ('The Investigators'). He is credited with the introduction of a third actor in his plays, allowing more complex plots than in Aeschylus, more interaction between characters and heightened drama. Aristophanes could easily parody Aeschylus and Euripides in *The Frogs*; he made no assault on the classic poise and measured dignity of Sophocles. In Sophocles the trilogy had less unity than in Aeschylus, so that the three 'Theban' plays of Sophocles, *Oedipus tyrannus*, *Oedipus at Colonus* and the *Antigone*, were presented at separate festivals. The compelling power of *Oedipus tyrannus*, with its close-wrought plot, and such notable tragic heroines as Antigone and Electra, have appealed greatly to opera librettists and composers: Stravinsky's *Oedipus rex* (1928), most of Enescu's *Oedipe* (1936) and Harry Partch's *Oedipus* (1952) are based on the story of *Oedipus tyrannus*; Sacchini's *Oedipe à Colone* (1786) and Act 4 of Enescu's *Oedipe* use material from *Oedipus at Colonus*; Antigone has been the subject of about 30 operas from Orlandini (1718) to Orff (1949), including works by Zingarelli (1790) and Honegger (1927); and Electra has been treated by Strauss (1909) and Haeffner (1787). The satyric *Ichneutae* was championed by Roussel (*La naissance de la lyre*, 1925).

See also ANTIGONE. ROBERT ANDERSON

Sopot. Resort near GDAŃSK.

Soprano (It.; Fr. *dessus*, *soprano*; Ger. *Sopran*). The highest female voice, normally written for in the range *c'* to *a''*, which may be extended at either end. In the 17th and 18th centuries the term was more regularly applied to the higher range of castrato voice, and it is also sometimes used for a boy treble (that is why it takes a masculine term: *il soprano*, not *la soprano*, is correct). The word is built on the root 'sopra' or 'sovra', ultimately from the Latin *superius*, the most common term for the uppermost voice in 15th-century polyphony.

1. Italian opera up to 1750. 2. French dessus singers. 3. 1750–1800. 4. After 1800: voice types. 5. Singers and roles: 19th century: (i) French and Italian opera (ii) German opera. 6. 20th century.

1. ITALIAN OPERA UP TO 1750. The female soprano was the latest of the voices to achieve a place in art music; until the late 15th century most female musicians were courtesans and only at the time of the rise of the madrigal in the early 16th century did female singing become a socially accepted pursuit. The cult of the female voice was developed late in the 16th century, with the famous *concerto delle donne* (a consort of high voices) at the Ferrara court and the admiration universally accorded to Vittoria Archilei, who sang in the Florentine *intermedi* of 1589 and may have created the title role in Peri's *Euridice*. It was with the expressive power of Caterina Martinelli in mind that Monteverdi composed the lament for *Arianna*; although she died and could not sing it, reports after the performance say that among the audience 'there was not a woman who did not shed tears'. It was normal throughout the 17th century for virtually all female roles in opera to be written for sopranos, except for the occasional character

part (older women, nurses and the like were sometimes written for contraltos); the term 'soprano' was however more often applied to the high castrato singer. Women's parts were most usually written in the range *c′ to g″*, sometimes (for example in the role of Penelope in Monteverdi's *Il ritorno d'Ulisse*, 1640) with a voice in mind closer to what would now be regarded as a mezzo-soprano tessitura than a soprano one.

It is difficult to glean information about specific singers in this period. Most of the female singers – who were admired and enjoyed for their beauty and other capacities as much as for their singing (see Rosselli 1989) – had only brief careers, and then as much in the private *cappella* of a noble patron as in the opera house. Inevitably, they were in some degree dependent on their protectors. Sopranos of the period included Anna Renzi, active mainly in Venice, the first Octavia in Monteverdi's *Poppea*; Giulia Masotti, active in Rome in the 1660s and later in Vienna; Anna Venturi, who was noted for her ill-tuned singing in Verona and Venice; Maria Maddalena Musi, from Bologna, who sang at the S Luca theatre managed by the Vendramin family in Venice early in the 18th century; Ottavia Monteneri, who was active in Modena in 1689; and Diamante Scarabelli, who sang mainly at the Venetian and Bolognese theatres.

Female sopranos were sometimes cast as men. There are several examples in Handel's operas; one of his earliest sopranos, Margherita Durastanti, specialized in men's roles and created the title role in *Radamisto* (1720) and the part of Sextus in *Giulio Cesare* (1724) as well as Agrippina (1709) and Gismonda in *Ottone* (1723). That was the opera in which his most famous soprano, Francesca Cuzzoni, made her début; among the other roles she created for Handel between 1723 and 1728 were Cleopatra and Asteria in *Tamerlano* (both 1724), Rodelinda (1725), Berenice in *Scipione* and Lisaura in *Alessandro* (both 1726) and Antigona in *Admeto* (1727). She also sang in several Bononcini operas, and in 1734 joined the rival 'Nobility Opera'; it is clear from the praise lavished upon her that she was a superlative artist with a unique 'warble' to her voice, adept in rapid divisions, 'complete mistress' of embellishment and rubato, and capable of pathos and charm, and dependable for perfect intonation and beauty of tone. In her last performances with Handel she had to share the stage with a rival, Faustina Bordoni, whose voice was pitched about a tone lower and is properly reckoned a mezzo-soprano. The chief soprano in Handel's operas from 1729 (*Lotario*) until 1737 (*Berenice*) was Anna Maria Strada del Pò, a singer of great brilliance and wide emotional range, to judge by contemporary critics and the music Handel wrote for her, which includes such roles as Cleofis (*Poro*), Elmira (*Sosarme*), Angelica (*Orlando*) and above all Ginevra (*Ariodante*) and Alcina.

2. FRENCH DESSUS SINGERS. In France, the term 'soprano' was applied only to Italian singers well into the 18th century, and DESSUS was preferred as late as the time (1829) of the first edition of Rossini's *Guillaume Tell*. The most famous soprano (or *dessus*) during Lully's era was Marie Le Rochois, who, succeeding Saint-Christophle (creator of the title role in *Alceste*, 1674), was noted for her powerful acting and fine declamation; she joined the Académie Royale de Musique in 1678 and sang there for 20 years, creating six Lully roles (she was specially admired in the title role of *Armide*, 1686, and Charpentier's *Medea*, 1693). Desmatins, active there from 1682 for more than a quarter of a century, sometimes alternated with Le Rochois, notably in Destouches' *Issé*; she also created the title role of Marais' *Alcyone*. During this period Marie Aubry was also a leading soprano, creating five Lully roles in the years 1675–82. Among their contemporaries were the Moreau sisters, of whom Fanchon sang in 27 operas in the 20 years from 1683, creating three Lully roles, and the spectacular Maupin, active between 1690 and 1705, singer of Clorinde in Campra's *Tancrède* and possessor of a slightly lower voice. The next generation of French sopranos includes Marie Antier, who joined the Académie in 1711 and sang there for 30 years, taking principal roles as early as 1712 (Campra's *Idomenée*) and singing Phaedra in Rameau's *Hippolyte et Aricie* (1733); she was admired for the nobility of her tone and the flexibility of her singing. The main soprano role, Telaira, in *Castor et Pollux* (1737) and Iphise in *Dardanus* were sung by Marie Pélissier, active at the Opéra in the period 1726–41; her declamatory power and eloquent acting were her strongest assets. Her principal rival, who supplanted her in several Rameau roles (and created Iphise in Montéclair's *Jephté*, 1732), was Catherine-Nicole Lemaure, who had a stormy career at the Académie between 1721 and 1744, with several breaks. But the most famous of Rameau sopranos was Marie Fel, noted for her 'light and brilliant voice, its tone ringing like silver, as pure as gold from the furnace' (Grimm, *Le petit prophète de Boehmischbroda*, 1753) and the intelligence of her singing; she sang at the Académie between 1734 and 1757 in over 100 roles, creating nine for Rameau including Hebe (1739), Amélite in *Zoroastre* and Naïs (both 1749). Fel's successor was her pupil Sophie Arnould, a leading singer at the Académie from 1757 to 1778, a striking actress with a sweet and expressive voice, who sang principal roles in many revivals of operas by Rameau and Lully; her most famous new role was Iphigenia in Gluck's first Paris opera, *Iphigénie en Aulide*, and she also sang Eurydice in the première of his *Orphée* (both 1774), but the more powerful Rosalie Levasseur was preferred for the title role in *Alceste* (1776) and to create those in *Armide* (1777) and *Iphigénie en Tauride* (1779).

3. 1750–1800. A number of sopranos, mostly from Italy or of Italian descent, achieved European reputations during the second half of the 18th century. One of the most admired was Caterina Gabrielli, from Rome, probably a Porpora pupil, who sang at Vienna in the late 1750s (Metastasio himself was her protector), creating roles by Gluck, and singing at Parma in important reformist works by Traetta in 1759–60. This 'most intelligent and best-bred virtuosa' (Burney), noted for her charm and skill, also appeared in St Petersburg and London as well as widely in Italy; Leopold Mozart however called her a 'conceited fool' and Wolfgang said that her strength lay in brilliant and eccentric coloratura but that she lacked a technique for sustained singing. The Mozarts had a much higher opinion of Lucrezia Aguiari (known as 'La Bastardella'), whose career, apart from a brief visit to Paris and longer ones (1775–7) to London, was confined to Italy, where she held a post at Parma; her range was phenomenal, from *g* ('a good deep alto', wrote Leopold Mozart) to *c″″* ('as beautifully as an octave stop in an organ'). Burney wrote of her majestic style, her precise execution and her full, rounded tone, and her taste and expression were also much praised.

Another singer of wide range and exceptional agility was Anna Lucia de Amicis, who began as a comic singer in Naples and elsewhere in Italy and graduated to serious opera in J. C. Bach's *Orione* in London (1763); she later appeared regularly in Italy, singing in Jommelli operas in Naples in 1769–72 and in Venice during the same period, and creating Junia in Mozart's *Lucio Silla* in Milan in 1772. The Mozarts much admired her technical skill in difficult passage-work and her musical singing, and Metastasio praised her fire, boldness and expressiveness. She sang the title role in the Italian première of Gluck's *Alceste* in 1778. Mozart's other prima donna in Italy, the German Antonia Bernasconi (Aspasia in *Mitridate*, 1770), had created Alcestis at the première in Vienna in 1767, where she had earlier sung in *opera buffa*; she sang in London, 1778–80, but her career was principally in Italy. She was in Vienna in the early 1780s, singing (according to Mozart) very sharp ('a good comma higher than anyone else – a great achievement, for she always stays in tune'), still a fine tragic singer but 'a total failure' in comic roles. Another famous German soprano was Gertrud Elisabeth Mara, who sang in the Berlin opera in the 1770s, in London in the period between 1784 and 1802 and occasionally in Italy, but she was an indifferent actress and much of her career was outside the theatre.

Of the singers for whom Mozart wrote in his mature operas, probably the most notable were Nancy Storace, the English soprano who created Susanna (1786) and many other roles in Viennese *opere buffe* of the time (works by Salieri and Martín y Soler, for example) as well as English operas in the 1790s, and was admired more for her charm and her lively manner than her slightly harsh voice; and Caterina Cavalieri, Konstanze in *Die Entführung* (1782) and Donna Elvira in the Viennese première of *Don Giovanni* (1788), an Austrian who sang primarily in German opera and had a strong, agile voice. Among her rivals was Mozart's sister-in-law Aloysia Lange, noted for her high and brilliant singing; Mozart wrote only one operatic role for her, in *Der Schauspieldirektor* (1786), where she sang (in the role of her stage rival) alongside Cavalieri, as she did as Donna Anna in *Don Giovanni.* Her eldest sister, Josepha Hofer, created the Queen of Night in *Die Zauberflöte* (1791), but her modest career was confined to the German theatres of Vienna; so was that of Anna Gottlieb, the first Barbarina and Pamina, whose career was longer. Of the sopranos who created roles in his Da Ponte operas the most distinguished were Luisa Laschi, the first Countess Almaviva and Zerlina in the 1788 *Don Giovanni*, who came from Florence, and Adriana Ferrarese, who went to Vienna after some career in Italy and London, sang Susanna in the 1789 revival of *Figaro* and the first Fiordiligi (*Così fan tutte*, 1790); she was noted for her strong lower register and was most successful in serious roles. The fact that the same singer can have played Susanna and Fiordiligi, or the Countess Almaviva and Zerlina, shows how flexible singers were expected to be and how little casting was based on voice type at this date.

4. After 1800: voice types. That situation began to change early in the 19th century. In the 18th, an age when composers wrote for the occasion rather than for posterity, it had generally been the practice for a composer to write each role to suit the particular capacities of its first interpreter, for the first interpreter was often the last: operas were rarely revived, and when they were the music would customarily be altered to suit the new singer or replaced (indeed Mozart composed two new arias for Susanna when Ferrarese assumed the role). But in the 19th, a consolidated international repertory began to develop and singers were increasingly called upon to sing music that had not been written for them, although in Italy especially the preference for composing for a particular singer, and maximizing the likelihood of an opera's initial success, persisted well into the second half of the century. But the nature of the international operatic world, and the new diversity of styles in which singers were required to perform – Beethoven's final version of *Fidelio* had its première within weeks of that of Rossini's *Il turco in Italia* – increasingly predicated the categorization of sopranos (and indeed the other voices too) into types: among them are the coloratura soprano (or in France the 'soprano à roulades'), the lyric soprano, the two characteristic French voices, the 'Falcon' and the 'Dugazon' (named after particular singers), the Italian and more dramatic *spinto* and *lirico spinto*, and the dramatic or heroic soprano, primarily a German type of voice.

In the Italian early 19th-century repertory the lyric coloratura type was central, in the roles of Rossini and Bellini: most famous among them were such singers as Giuditta Pasta, Jenny Lind and later Adelina Patti. Developments in opera composition however did not favour their delicacy of voice or their preoccupation with technical virtuosity suitable for operas that soon came to be dismissed as old-fashioned. The growth of naturalism in drama suggested that progress seemed to lie in the abandonment of formal rules such as the provision of a set-piece aria exhibiting the singer's skill in legato to be followed by a cabaletta that calls upon accomplishment in florid work, scales, passages, trills and so forth. Further, the larger opera houses and heavier orchestration of the mid-19th century demanded voices of more power. The later operas of Verdi and Wagner were prime influences in effecting a change of direction for the soprano as for others. By the early years of the 20th century the traditional skills in florid singing had fallen in the esteem of many musical people, so that the so-called coloratura sopranos had become specialists who still retained a certain popular following (witness the acclaim of singers such as Luisa Tetrazzini and Amelita Galli-Curci), though it was one from which 'serious' musicians generally dissociated themselves.

Their preferred type was the lyric-dramatic, who had been in evidence since the early years of the 19th century in such roles as Beethoven's Leonore, sung by Anna Milder in all three premières and later, apparently making an indelible impression in the opera's 1822 revival in Vienna, Wilhelmine Schröder-Devrient, noted too for her Agathe (*Der Freischütz*). This type is represented in the early 20th century by Emmy Destinn and then by Lotte Lehmann and Elisabeth Rethberg; these, it was felt, had more humanity in their voices and a richer musical background than the coloratura soprano whose traditions were basically Italian. The other type that gained in importance over these years was the heroic soprano, whose ultimate charge was to cater for the Wagnerian repertory. A first-generation Bayreuth soprano who became a leading exponent of the heroic roles was Lilli Lehmann, exceptional in her ability to combine activity in this sphere with a mastery of parts such as Norma and Violetta. Later singers of Isolde and

Brünnhilde were confined much more rigidly, so that once Kirsten Flagstad in the 1930s had been internationally recognized as the great heroic soprano of the age, audiences rarely had a chance to hear her in operas other than Wagner's. Her successor Birgit Nilsson maintained a more broadly based repertory, and in the later years of the 20th century there has been a tendency for sopranos to move with relative freedom from one category to another. It might also be observed that in the same period sopranos able to fulfil the requirements of the Wagner roles seem to have become rarer than ever.

By contrast, these same years have been well provided in probably the least expected area, that of the coloratura soprano, now no longer limited to a few arias and bird-songs with flute obbligato, but playing a prominent part in the revival of interest in Baroque music, particularly in the operas of Handel, and in the comparable opening-up of the bel canto repertory, with its consequent reappraisal of Rossini and Donizetti. The great personal success of Maria Callas in the 1950s has sometimes been credited with having set all of this in motion, and certainly it was a powerful influence. One immediate effect was to strengthen the hand of those who foresaw an artistic triumph if Joan Sutherland were to sing *Lucia di Lammermoor*, which she did for the first time in 1959. Over the next two decades she and her husband Richard Bonynge did much to encourage singers to equip themselves for work in this field. A generally beneficial outcome has been the recognition that a thorough training in some of the older traditions is now necessary for sopranos of every type, from the soubrette or light soprano who will be involved in Rossini productions, to the heroic soprano who may, like Lilli Lehmann, be called upon for *Norma*.

Another development in the 20th century, accelerating in the second half, has been the reduction of national differences in singing. Early recordings illustrate national schools clearly. The Italian preference for brilliance of tone contrasts with the German taste for mellowness. A characteristic of French sopranos has been a brightness of tone with less richness of the chest register than is favoured by the Italian school. This has been shared to some degree by the Russians while the English soprano was known for a purity that in turn appealed more in German than in Latin cultures. There also seem to have been different levels of tolerance and liking in matters of vibrato, tremolo or 'wobble'. Earlier in the century Italy and Spain produced many sopranos whose quick reiterative vibrato was welcomed in their home countries as adding to the excitements of performance, while the 'straighter' teutonic and Anglo-Saxon soprano voice seemed somewhat cold and lacking in temperament. Germans seemed to find it easier to accept the slower kind of vibrato – the 'beat' or 'wobble' – and in Slavonic opera houses it has sometimes appeared to be a *sine qua non*.

Though the wobble still thrives, the quick vibrato was effectively banished in the late 20th century. One reason may be that it does not record well; recording tends to exaggerate it to an extent not approved by a large part of the record-buying public. Recording must also have played a part in the reduction of national differences, another influence in which has been the emergence of American singers as world leaders. These are usually the products of mixed schools and ethnic backgrounds, so that it would be difficult to identify any particular national characteristic in the voice and method of recent and modern sopranos such as Grace Bumbry, Jessye Norman, Cheryl Studer, Carol Vaness or Barbara Bonney.

5. SINGERS AND ROLES: 19TH CENTURY.

(i) French and Italian opera. The advent of Rossini in the second decade of the 19th century, offering a new kind of opera, led to a need for new types of singer in all the voice categories. One type of soprano was personified by Isabella Colbran, the Spanish singer for whom Rossini wrote roles in ten of his serious operas between 1815 and 1823, including *Elisabetta, regina d'Inghilterra*, *Otello*, *Mosè in Egitto*, *La donna del lago*, *Maometto II* and *Semiramide*. Colbran was a striking singing actress with a fine coloratura technique; her powerful if harsh voice was extremely flexible and Rossini provided her with music that was both dramatic in character and highly decorated in style. The soprano roles in Rossini's operas written or adapted for Paris (1826–9), *Le siège de Corinthe*, *Moïse et Pharaon*, *Le comte Ory* and *Guillaume Tell*, were intended for Laure Cinti-Damoreau, the leading soprano at the Opéra, whose voice was lighter and less dramatic but even wider in range and more dazzling in coloratura technique. Elvire in Auber's *La muette de Portici* and Isabelle in *Robert le diable* (1831), both extremely florid roles, were also written for Cinti-Damoreau. Alice, the real heroine of Meyerbeer's first French opera, was created by Julie Dorus-Gras, who succeeded Cinti-Damoreau at the Opéra; she also had a high, flexible voice and became a noted Isabelle, a role that probably suited her better.

The part of Alice was later sung, at her début, by Cornélie Falcon. Though Falcon's career lasted only a few years, after which she lost her voice, she left an indelible mark on French opera, lending her name to the type of lyrico-dramatic soprano personified by Alice, and by Rachel (*La Juive*, 1835) and Valentine (*Les Huguenots*, 1836), two roles written expressly for her; Falcon's nobility of voice and classical style of singing were perhaps best displayed in the role of Julia in Spontini's *La vestale*. The lighter, higher coloratura parts of Marguerite de Valois in *Les Huguenots* and Eudoxie in *La Juive* were intended for and first sung by Dorus-Gras.

In Italy, Bellini inaugurated another new style of vocalism, one that still required great agility from the singer, the soprano in particular, but above all demanded the ability to draw long, flowing, seamless melodic lines. This style, hinted at in his early operas, *Bianca e Gernando*, *Zaira*, *Il pirata* and *La straniera*, all of whose heroines were created in the years 1826–9 by Henriette Méric-Lalande, a French soprano with the necessary vocal flexibility as well as the legato line, came to full maturity in *La sonnambula* (1831), whose title role (Amina) was composed for Giuditta Pasta. Pasta's magnificently vibrant voice, ranging from *a* to *e‴*, and her powerful gifts as an actress, exerted a great influence on Bellini, who also wrote the more dramatic roles of *Norma* (1831) and *Beatrice di Tenda* (1833) for her. At the première of *Norma*, the role of Adalgisa, now usually sung by a mezzo-soprano, was created by Giulia Grisi, then a high-voiced lyric soprano, later a majestic Norma herself; it was for Grisi that Bellini composed the part of Elvira in his last opera, *I puritani* (1835), first performed at the Théâtre Italien in Paris where she was prima donna; although less dramatic in character than the roles for Pasta, Elvira nonetheless embodies the stylistic elements of a typical Bellini soprano heroine, combining vocal agility with the long-breathed melodic phrases.

Another opera composed round Pasta's talents was Donizetti's *Anna Bolena* (1830), the first of his operas to gain a wide international acceptance, quickly reaching London and Paris with Pasta in the title role. In the first-night audience for *Anna Bolena* was Mikhail Glinka, who was greatly impressed by Pasta's voice and talent; the vocal lines of *A Life for the Tsar*, especially those for Antonida, the soprano, betray a strong Italian influence. Mariya Stepanova, who first sang that role (1836), and that of Lyudmila in his second opera *Ruslan and Lyudmila* (1842), had a lyric-dramatic voice not unlike Pasta's in weight and flexibility. Yuliya Platonova, who made her début as Antonida, sang Marina (usually a mezzo role) in *Boris Godunov* (1874); she also created Donna Anna in Dargomïzhsky's *The Stone Guest* (1872) and Olga in Rimsky-Korsakov's *The Maid of Pskov* (1873); her voice appears to have been a type of 'Falcon' – her roles included Valentine (*Les Huguenots*), which Falcon had created.

The most famous of Donizetti's soprano roles, 'poor mad Lucy' in *Lucia di Lammermoor* (1835), typified the tragic heroine of the Romantic movement; there had been mad scenes for sopranos before, notably those in Paisiello's *Nina* and Bellini's *La sonnambula* and *I puritani*, but that in *Lucia* was in a class by itself. Fanny Tacchinardi-Persiani, by whom it was first sung, had a brilliant voice of exceptionally wide compass; her amazing coloratura technique was fully exploited by Donizetti, who wrote equally florid roles for her in *Rosmonda d'Inghilterra* (1834) and *Pia de' Tolomei* (1837). He wrote five roles, including Queen Elizabeth I in both *Maria Stuarda* (1835) and *Roberto Devereux* (1837), for Giuseppina Ronzi de Begnis, a soprano with rather less flexibility of voice than Tacchinardi-Persiani but one who used a great deal more force and dramatic expression. The four archetypal Donizetti soprano roles written for Karoline Unger, an Austrian contralto with a phenomenally wide compass and, according to Rossini, 'brazen lungs, a silver voice and golden talent', included Parisina (1833) and Antonina in *Belisario* (1836). Donizetti also wrote roles for sopranos previously better known as interpreters of Bellini's operas: one was Méric-Lalande, whose fiery personality and declamatory style were generously used in *Lucrezia Borgia* (1833), and another was Giulia Grisi, who brought a tragic intensity to Elena in *Marino Faliero* (1835) and intoxicating high spirits and good humour to Norina in *Don Pasquale* (1843).

In Verdi's first major success, *Nabucco* (1842), Abigaille, the villainous female protagonist, has the hallmarks of the typical early Verdi soprano, including a wide compass and great violence of emotion, expressed through torrents of coloratura. The role was created by Giuseppina Strepponi, although not specially written for her. Verdi, like any other Italian composer of the period, usually tailored the role to the singer: Sophie Loewe, the first Elvira (*Ernani*, 1844) and Odabella (*Attila*, 1846); Erminia Frezzolini, the first Giselda (*I Lombardi*, 1843) and Joan of Arc (1845); and Marianna Barbieri-Nini, the first Lucrezia Contarini (1844), Lady Macbeth (1847) and Gulnara (*Il corsaro*, 1848), were all sopranos with voices powerful enough, particularly in the middle register, to penetrate Verdi's orchestration (found extremely noisy by contemporary critics) and yet flexible enough to cope with the considerable florid sections of their music. On the other hand, Amalia in *I masnadieri* (1847) was perfectly suited to Jenny Lind, whose voice was lighter, higher-placed, more brilliant in tone and more flexible.

With Hélène in *Les vêpres siciliennes* (1855), his first original work for the Paris Opéra, Verdi returned to the forceful and vengeful heroines of his early operas. Sophie Cruvelli, the German soprano for whom the part was written, had an opulent voice with a range of nearly three octaves and sang with a ferocity perfectly suited to the part and to such roles as Abigaille or Odabella. Elisabeth de Valois, in Verdi's next French opera, *Don Carlos* (1867), combines a beautiful lyricism with powerful dramatic expression; the part was first sung by Marie Sasse, the Belgian soprano who had created Sélika in Meyerbeer's *L'Africaine* (1865), and had also sung Elisabeth in *Tannhäuser* at the disastrous Paris première of Wagner's opera (1861).

Gounod's *Faust* received its première in 1859 at the Théâtre Lyrique, Paris; there the reigning soprano was Caroline Carvalho, whose smooth, light, lyric voice and excellent coloratura were displayed to great advantage by the role of Marguerite. Carvalho also created Gounod's Baucis, Mireille and Juliet (1860–67), heroines perfectly adapted to her vocal talents. The first London Juliet, Adelina Patti, was also a fine Marguerite and a superb Dinorah. The title role of *La jolie fille de Perth* (1867), also produced at the Théâtre Lyrique, was written for the ultra-flexible and brilliant-toned voice of the Swedish soprano Christine Nilsson, who was however too busy scoring a triumph at the Opéra in *Hamlet* (1868) as Ophelia, a part Thomas had modelled for her voice and talents; she never sang Bizet's Catharine. Aline in Berwald's *Drottningen av Golconda* was another role composed expressly for Nilsson that she never sang.

Verdi wrote lyric soprano roles, such as Gilda, Violetta and Amelia in *Simon Boccanegra*, but increasingly he preferred more dramatic heroines, such as Amelia in *Un ballo in maschera* and Leonora in *La forza del destino*, even when there was no ideal interpreter for them. At the first performance of the revised version of *La forza* (1869), Leonora was sung by Teresa Stolz, the Bohemian soprano who was also the first Italian Elisabeth de Valois (1867) and later the first Italian Aida (1872). In Stolz, whose voice was described as 'vigorous, flexible, dramatic, limpid, brilliant', Verdi found an ideal interpreter of such roles. The younger composers to emerge from Verdi's shadow included Ponchielli, whose *La Gioconda* (1876) offered a magnificent role for his wife, the dramatic soprano Teresa Brambilla-Ponchiello, while the title role of *Marion Delorme* (1885) was written for Romilda Pantaleoni, whose magnetic personality and voice inspired Verdi's Desdemona (1887) and Tigrana in Puccini's *Edgar* (1889).

The rise of *verismo* and its overwhelming success heralded a new generation of sopranos with the generous voices required to surmount the luxuriant orchestration favoured by Mascagni, Leoncavallo, Giordano and Puccini, and also with the dramatic conviction that these composers demanded. While Adelina Stehle, the creator of Nedda in *Pagliacci* (1892) and also Nannetta in *Falstaff* (1893), was a lyric soprano in traditional mould, Gemma Bellincioni, the first Santuzza (1890) and Fedora (1898), and also the first Italian Salome, had an altogether more opulent voice. Hariclea Darclée, creator of Wally (1892), Iris (1898) and Tosca (1900); Cesira Ferrani, the first Manon Lescaut (1893) and Mimì (1896), and Emma Calvé, the French soprano who created Suzel in *L'amico Fritz* (1891), were also dramatic singers with powerful voices. Anita in *La Navarraise* (1894) and Fanny Legrand in *Sapho* (1897), both strong, independent characters, were written for Calvé by Massenet, who was always eager to please his singers; susceptible to more than beautiful voices, Massenet composed *Esclarmonde* (1889) and *Thaïs* (1894) for Sybil Sanderson, the handsome American soprano whose lyrical, high-lying, silver-toned voice he greatly admired.

(ii) German opera. Anna Milder, the Austrian soprano who first sang Leonore in all three versions of *Fidelio*, was only 19 when she took part in the première in 1805 of Beethoven's opera at the Theater an der Wien, Vienna; a role now considered the province of the dramatic soprano could easily be sung by a young girl in that small theatre, with the orchestral instruments of the period. Something of her progress from lyric to dramatic soprano may be inferred from the changes to Leonore's vocal line between the first and last versions (1814) of the score. Cherubini composed the title role of *Faniska* for her (1806), and she was also the first Viennese Medea. In Berlin Milder-Hauptmann, as she had become, created two roles in operas by Spontini, Namouna in *Nurmahal* (1822) and Irmengard in *Agnes von Hohenstaufen* (1829). Particularly admired for her classical style as Gluck's Alcestis, Armida and both Iphigenias, she had perfect intonation and was noted for her intense, penetrating vocal power.

The first London Leonore was Wilhelmine Schröder-Devrient, who had studied the role with Beethoven; Chorley described her voice as: 'a strong soprano – not perfect in quality ... but with an inherent expressiveness of tone, which made it more attractive on the stage than a more faultless organ'. She created Spohr's Jessonda (1823) and was considered by Weber as one of the finest interpreters of Agathe. Schröder-Devrient was also admired by Wagner, whose Adriano (*Rienzi*), Senta and Venus she created in the years 1842–5. Johanna Wagner (the composer's niece by adoption) sang Elisabeth at the première of *Tannhäuser*; she claimed that Brünnhilde was written for her, but when the first complete *Ring* cycle was given at Bayreuth she sang only a Valkyrie and a Norn.

As Wagner began to dominate German-speaking opera houses, singers had to be found with voices powerful enough to cope with the heavy orchestration of his operas. The Danish soprano Malvina Schnorr von Carolsfeld, the first Isolde (1865), Sophie Stehle, the first Fricka (*Das Rheingold*, 1869) and the first Brünnhilde (*Die Walküre*, 1870) and a conspicuously successful Senta, and Therese Vogl, creator of Sieglinde (1870) and a famous Isolde and the first London Brünnhilde, were among the first generation. Amalie Materna, who sang Brünnhilde in the first *Ring* cycle at Bayreuth (1876), Kundry at the première of *Parsifal* (1882) and became the first Metropolitan Brünnhilde, also created the title role of Goldmark's *Die Königin von Saba* (1875), while Lilli Lehmann, who had begun her career in such florid roles as Philine (*Mignon*), Violetta and Sulamith (*Die Königin von Saba*), became a magnificent Isolde and Brünnhilde, while continuing to sing Donna Anna and Norma.

When Richard Strauss conducted *Tannhäuser* at Bayreuth in 1894, Elisabeth was sung by Pauline de Ahna, who earlier that year had created Freihild in *Guntram* (1894), his first opera; though her career was relatively short, she had an incalculable influence on Strauss, whom she subsequently married, as a composer for the soprano voice. De Ahna, who was to have sung Hänsel at the première of Humperdinck's opera (1893) but was indisposed, had an even, silver-toned lyric soprano voice whose echo is heard in many of her husband's operas.

6. 20TH CENTURY. On 10 April 1900 a young, unknown Scottish soprano, Mary Garden, who had not yet made her official début at the Opéra-Comique, caused a sensation when she took over the title role of Charpentier's *Louise* in the middle of a performance. Two years later she became the first Mélisande, on Debussy's insistence (Maeterlinck would have preferred Georgette Leblanc). Massenet, who admired Garden as Manon, wrote the title role of *Chérubin* for her (1905); she also sang Thaïs, Fanny Legrand (*Sapho*), Cleopatra and Jean (*Le jongleur de Notre-Dame*), a tenor part. Lucienne Bréval, the soprano for whom Massenet composed roles in *Grisélidis* (1901), *Ariane* (1906) and *Bacchus* (1909), had a larger, more dramatic voice than Garden's silvery tones. Bréval sang roles such as Brunehild in Reyer's *Sigurd* as well as Wagner's Venus, Kundry and Brünnhilde. She also created the title role in Fauré's *Pénélope* (1913). Nellie Melba, who had made her reputation singing high, florid roles such as Lucia and Juliet with impeccable taste and technique, created Saint-Saëns' Hélène at Monte Carlo (1904), but the role was taken by Garden in Paris. Melba, beloved at Covent Garden and the Metropolitan, went on to a wider range of roles but was especially admired as Mimì.

The Czech soprano Emmy Destinn, the first Tatyana in *Yevgeny Onegin* at Covent Garden, had a magnificent, even-toned voice, larger and quite unlike that of the creator of the role in Moscow, the 22-year-old student Mariya Klimentova, who continued to sing Tatyana throughout her career and also took part in another Tchaikovsky première, as Oxana in *Cherevichki* (1887). Destinn, also Covent Garden's first Butterfly, sang Minnie at the première of *La fanciulla del West* (1910) at the Metropolitan; she was the first Berlin and Paris Salome, a role in which she excelled. Other sopranos who specialized in Strauss included Annie Krull, the first Diemut (*Feuersnot*, 1901) and Electra (1909), who appears to have sung the latter role rather more lyrically than later interpreters; Margarethe Siems, who created Chrysothemis, the Marschallin (Strauss considered her ideal) and Zerbinetta (1912), also sang the coloratura heroines of Bellini and Donizetti with dazzling ease. The ideal Sophie of this era was Elisabeth Schumann, noted for the purity of her tone and style, which also fitted her ideally for the lighter Mozart roles (Susanna, Zerlina, Despina). Maria Jeritza, the glamorous Czech soprano who first sang the title role of *Ariadne auf Naxos* (both versions, 1912 and 1916) and the Empress in *Die Frau ohne Schatten* (1919), introduced Minnie to Vienna and Janáček's Jenůfa to New York. Lotte Lehmann, who created the Composer, the Dyer's Wife and Christine in *Intermezzo* (1924), was also a renowned Marschallin, while Elisabeth Rethberg, the first Egyptian Helen (1928), excelled in Italian roles, particularly Aida and Desdemona. Viorica Ursuleac, who created Arabella (1933), Maria (*Friedenstag*, 1938), Countess Madeleine (*Capriccio*, 1942) and Danae (at the public dress rehearsal in 1944), was the last of the sopranos for whom Strauss wrote such wonderful roles. Other

Strauss singers to have made the familiar journey from Sophie or Octavian to the Marschallin during the course of their careers include Sena Jurinac and Lisa della Casa, the one admired for her purity and evenness of tone, the other for her warm, creamy singing; both were also distinguished Mozart singers. Perhaps the supreme interpreter of Strauss in middle and late 20th century however was Elisabeth Schwarzkopf, whose command of tone and line and their coupling with a high level of musical perception won her almost unalloyed praise.

Geraldine Farrar, the American soprano who created the Goose Girl in *Königskinder* (1910) and was the Metropolitan's first Butterfly, sang Suor Angelica at the première of Puccini's *Trittico* (1918). Giorgetta in *Il tabarro* was created by Claudia Muzio; a much loved Mimì, Manon Lescaut and Tosca, she also sang Turandot, the role created in 1926 by Rosa Raisa, the Polish soprano whose thrilling voice and commanding personality also made her a fine Norma. Another successful Turandot, the English soprano Eva Turner, was also an excellent Brünnhilde.

From the turn of the century a succession of powerful interpreters of Wagner's dramatic soprano roles had presented themselves: Anna Bahr-Mildenburg, who sang Kundry and Ortrud at Bayreuth (1897–1914), was also an outstanding Isolde; Olive Fremstad, the Swedish-American soprano whose superbly sung Sieglinde, Brünnhilde and Isolde dominated the Metropolitan in the years 1903–14, had a wide enough range to sing mezzo roles; Frida Leider, her successor in the Wagnerian dramatic repertory, had great tonal brilliance enhanced by the clarity of her diction; and her successor in turn, Kirsten Flagstad, the Norwegian soprano whose golden-toned, seamless voice was of unsurpassable richness and unprecedented volume. Other distinguished Wagner sopranos of the period were Martha Mödl and Astrid Varnay.

Between the wars, while Verdi's operas kept their popularity and even gained in reputation, those of Bellini and Donizetti came to be considered old-fashioned. *Norma* survived as long as a dramatic soprano such as Rosa Ponselle was available for the title role, but *Lucia di Lammermoor* became the property of coloratura sopranos with light voices such as Toti dal Monte and Lily Pons. Not until 1949, when Maria Callas – beyond question the outstanding dramatic as well as coloratura soprano of her era – sang Elvira (*I puritani*) between two series of performances of Brünnhilde (*Die Walküre*) and alternated Norma with Turandot, did Bellini regain credibility as a serious composer. After Joan Sutherland, who had sung Agathe, Desdemona and Eva and created Jenifer in *The Midsummer Marriage* (1955), earned a spectacular success in *Lucia di Lammermoor*, Donizetti's rehabilitation was also on the way, a process to which Callas and Montserrat Caballé, a singer of great refinement whose early repertory included Elsa, Elisabeth, Eva and Salome, also contributed. These three sopranos, all with voices of dramatic weight as well as great flexibility, exhumed many other long-neglected bel canto operas. Renata Tebaldi, whose magnificent voice and classic style were heard to best advantage in Verdi, in particular as Desdemona and Leonora (*La forza del destino*), was also a splendid Mimì, Tosca, Butterfly, Manon Lescaut and Minnie; her own favourite role was Adriana Lecouvreur, in which her declamation of the monologue from Racine's *Phèdre* was spine-chilling. Another superb Adriana, Magda Olivero, who was Cilea's preferred interpreter, sang the role at Edinburgh in 1963.

Puccini and Strauss may have written the last truly popular operas, but composers continued to provide roles for specific singers. Britten wrote Ellen Orford (*Peter Grimes*, 1945), the Female Chorus in *The Rape of Lucretia* (1946), Lady Billows (*Albert Herring*, 1947) and Queen Elizabeth I (*Gloriana*, 1953) for Joan Cross, a lyric soprano then approaching the end of her career; Francis Poulenc wrote Thérèse in *Les mamelles de Tirésias* (1947), Blanche in *Dialogues des Carmélites* (1957) and Elle in *La voix humaine* (1959) for Denise Duval, who had begun her career singing at the Folies-Bergères; she also made an ideally waif-like Mélisande. Heather Harper, an even-toned lyric soprano who sang Elsa at Bayreuth, created Mrs Coyle in Britten's television opera *Owen Wingrave* (1971) and Nadia at the première of Tippett's *The Ice Break* (1977); Josephine Barstow, whose voice defies categorization, but is specially effective in 20th-century music, created Denise in *The Knot Garden* (1970) and became an ideal exponent of Shostakovich's Katerina Izmaylova. A fine Russian interpreter of Katerina, Galina Vishnevskaya, who had a richer and more vibrant voice, also sang Tatyana, Lisa in *The Queen of Spades*, Aida and Tosca with great success.

Evelyn Lear created several roles written specially for her, including Lavinia in Levy's *Mourning Becomes Electra* (1967), Arkadina in Pasatieri's *The Seagull* (1974) and Ranyevskaya in Kelterborn's *Kirschgarten* (1984); her repertory ranged from Monteverdi's Poppaea and Handel's Cleopatra to Marie (*Wozzeck*) and Lulu. Another famous Marie, Christel Goltz, a dramatic soprano with a compass of three octaves, sang Orff's *Antigonae* (1949) and Liebermann's *Penelope* (1954). Lulu in the three-act version was first sung by Teresa Stratas and later by Karan Armstrong, both lyric sopranos, and then by Patricia Wise, a coloratura soprano.

Birgit Nilsson was the most powerful dramatic soprano since Flagstad; her penetrating, secure and brilliant-toned voice was suitable for Donna Anna, Tosca, Salome, Electra and Turandot as well as for Isolde, Brünnhilde and other Wagner roles. Another noted exponent of these emotionally demanding roles was Ljuba Welitsch. A superb Sieglinde and Elsa whose voice opened out with exciting strength at the top, Leonie Rysanek was also a magnificent Empress in *Die Frau ohne Schatten*; in *Elektra* she sang first Chrysothemis, then Electra and, after more than 40 years, Clytemnestra. Anja Silja, admired as Leonore, Eva, Senta, Elisabeth and Elsa, also sang Cassandra in *Les Troyens* and later became a spectacular Ortrud. Gwyneth Jones, long a vocally and dramatically convincing Brünnhilde, also made a powerful Electra and Turandot. Sopranos who began their careers in Mozart and have moved on to heavier roles include Kiri te Kanawa, a creamy-voiced Countess Almaviva and Donna Elvira, who also sings Desdemona, Amelia (*Simon Boccanegra*) and Arabella; Carol Vaness, a stylish Vitellia and Donna Anna, who has become a noted Violetta, Amelia (*Un ballo in maschera*) and Anna Bolena; and Felicity Lott, who progressed from the Countess Almaviva and Donna Elvira to Strauss's Arabella, the Marschallin, the Countess Madeleine and Christine in *Intermezzo*, roles for which her pure, silvery-toned voice is well suited. Jessye Norman, whose repertory ranges from Rameau's Phaedra (*Hippolyte et Aricie*) and Gluck's Alcestis to Wagner's

Elisabeth and Strauss's Ariadne, combines a powerful voice with a magnificent stage presence.

*

M. and L. Escudier: *Vie et aventures des cantatrices célèbres* (Paris, 1856)
A. Kohut: *Tragische Primadonnenehen* (Leipzig, 1887)
H. Sutherland Edwards: *The Prima Donna: her History and Surroundings from the Seventeenth to the Nineteenth Century* (London, 1888)
A. Ehrlich: *Berühmte Sängerinnen der Vergangenheit und Gegenwart* (Leipzig, 1895)
L. C. Strang: *Famous Prima Donnas* (Boston, 1900)
A. Kohut: *Die Gesangs-Königinnen in den letzten drei Jahrhunderten* (Berlin, 1906)
A. Weissmann: *Die Primadonna* (Berlin, 1920)
H. Klein: *Great Women Singers of my Time* (London, 1931)
H. Rosenthal: *Sopranos of Today* (London, 1956)
K. Honolka: *Die grossen Primadonnen* (Stuttgart, 1960)
J. Wildgruber: 'Zur Entwicklung der Sopranfächer in der deutschen Oper des 19. Jahrhunderts', *Beiträge zur Geschichte der Oper*, ed. H. Becker (Regensburg, 1969), 147
F. J. Huie-Armbrister: *The Lyric Soprano Voice: Pedagogy and Repertoire from 1600 to 1980* (diss., Columbia U., 1982)
R. Blanchard and R. de Candé: *Dieux et divas de l'opéra* (Paris, 1986)
J. Rosselli: 'From Princely Service to the Open Market: Singers of Italian Opera and their Patrons, 1600–1850', *COJ*, i (1989), 1–32

For further bibliography *see* SINGING: A BIBLIOGRAPHY.

OWEN JANDER, STANLEY SADIE, J. B. STEANE, ELIZABETH FORBES

Sor [Sors], **(Joseph) Fernando** [Ferrán] (**Macari**) (*b* Barcelona, 13 Feb 1778; *d* Paris, 10 July 1839). Catalan composer. He was a virtuoso guitarist and composed a wide range of works, including a highly successful opera, *Telemaco nell'isola di Calipso*, first performed at the Teatro de Santa Cruz in Barcelona in 1796 and then at least another 15 times in the same theatre over the next two years. He began a second opera, *Don Trastulio*, while in the service of the Duchess of Alba in Madrid (*c*1801–2) but abandoned it on her death in 1802. He also wrote a 'melodrama' while in the service of the Duke and Duchess of Medinaceli, probably in 1802.

*

B. Jeffery: *Fernando Sor: Composer and Guitarist* (London, 1977)
A. Martín Moreno: *Historia de la música española*, iv: *Siglo XVIII* (Madrid, 1985), 337–8

JACK SAGE

Sorcerer, The. Operetta in two acts by ARTHUR SULLIVAN to a libretto by W. S. GILBERT; London, Opera Comique, 17 November 1877.

The story, a burlesque of Donizetti's *L'elisir d'amore*, relates how two lovers, Alexis (tenor) and Aline (soprano), use a magic potion supplied by the family sorcerer, John Wellington Wells (baritone), to induce amorous relationships among the villagers, with unforeseen consequences for their parents, Sir Marmaduke Pointdextre (baritone) and Lady Sangazure (contralto), and the vicar, Dr Daly (baritone). Songs that gained popularity include 'It is not love' and the patter number 'My name is John Wellington Wells'. For a revival in 1884 the work was revised and a new overture arranged by Hamilton Clarke. DAVID RUSSELL HULME

Sorceress, The. Opera by P. I. Tchaikovsky; *see* *ENCHANTRESS, THE.*

Soriano Fuertes (**y Piqueras**), **Mariano** (*b* Murcia, 28 March 1817; *d* Madrid, 26 March 1880). Spanish composer. He received early training from his father, Indalecio Soriano Fuertes, the music director of the royal chapel in Madrid. Abandoning a career in the military, in 1842 Mariano founded, with Joaquín Espín y Guillén, the periodical *La Iberia musical*, in which he promoted a national school of musical theatre. He also contributed to the revival of the zarzuela through his stage works. His first success was *Jeroma la Castañera*, first performed in Madrid in 1842 and later enthusiastically received in the provinces and Latin America. Initially mislabelled a *tonadilla*, it was in fact a zarzuela, consisting of one act and 11 musical numbers; it was followed in 1843 by two more zarzuelas, *El ventorillo de Alfarache* and *La feria de Santiponce*, performed by the amateur society La Union in Madrid. In 1844 Soriano Fuertes assumed the directorship of the Liceo Artístico y Literario in Córdoba, where he composed religious as well as theatrical works, including the Christmas zarzuela *A Belén van los zagales* (1844). In 1849 he moved to Seville to become director of the Liceo there. During a brief stay in Cádiz, he composed *El tío Caniyitas, ó El mundo nuevo de Cádiz*. In this his most popular work, the lively, simple music is based on native folksong and reflects the unsophisticated view of the people of Andalusia presented in Pérez's drama. It won enormous favour with the public (both in Spain and Latin America) but earned the scorn of the musical intelligentsia, which accused him of writing for the people and not for art. He became director of the Teatro de San Fernando in Seville, then returned to Cádiz in 1850 to take up a similar post at the Teatro Principal and La Comedia. In 1852 he moved to Barcelona as director of music at the Liceo. His final stage work, *Buen viaje señor don Simón*, was successfully produced there in 1853. Thereafter he devoted himself more to scholarship, and wrote his celebrated *Historia de la música española desde la venida de los fenicios hasta el año 1850* (Madrid and Barcelona, 1855–9), which contains valuable autobiographical information.

zarzuelas unless otherwise stated

La pastora de Manzanares, Madrid, Instituto, 1842, collab. J. Sobejano and F. La Hoz
Jeroma [Geroma] la Castañera (1, M. Fernández), Madrid, Príncipe, 3 April 1842, vs and pts *E-Msa*
El ventorillo de Alfarache (F. de Montemar), Madrid, 1843
La feria de Santiponce (Montemar), Madrid, 1843
A Belén van los zagales (2), Córdoba, 1844
La venta del puerto, ?Cádiz, 1847, collab. C. Ourid
El tío Caniyitas, ó El mundo nuevo de Cádiz (ópera cómica, 2, J. Sans Pérez), Seville, S Fernando, Nov 1849, vs and pts *Msa*
La fábrica de tabacos de Sevilla (ópera cómica, S. Albarrán), Seville, S Fernando, 1850
Lola la Gaditana, Cádiz, Principal, 1850, duet *Msa*
Buen viaje señor don Simón, Barcelona, Liceo, 1853, collab. C. Puig, N. Manent and T. Solera

*

J. Parada y Barreto: *Diccionario técnico, histórico y biográfico de la música* (Madrid, 1868), 357–8
B. Saldoni: *Diccionario biográfico-bibliográfico de efemérides de músicos españoles* (Barcelona, 1868–81), ii, 170–74; iv, 160–62
A. Peña y Goñi: *Historia de la zarzuela* (Madrid, 1881), 475–80
E. Cotarelo y Mori: *Historia de la zarzuela* (Madrid, 1934), 299–304
J. Subirá: *Historia de la música española e hispano-americana* (Barcelona, 1953)
J. A. Garcia Seco: 'Mariano Soriano-Fuertes y Piqueras: músico murciano del siglo XIX', *Primera semana de estudios murcianos*, vi (2–8 May 1961), 85–93

WALTER AARON CLARK

Sorochinskaya yarmarka ('Sorochintsy Fair'). Opera by M. P. Musorgsky; *see* *FAIR AT SOROCHINTSÏ, THE.*

Sorosina, Benedetta (*fl* 1722–32). Italian soprano. A Venetian in the service of the Elector Palatine, she sang in operas at Venice in 1722–3 (C. F. Pollarolo's *Arminio* and two others) and 1727–8 (four, three of them by Vivaldi), Naples in 1723 (three, including Vinci's *Silla dittatore*), Genoa in 1727, Florence in 1728 (Porpora's *Arianna e Teseo*), and was engaged for Milan, 1731–2. In 1725 she sang in London, in Handel's *Giulio Cesare* (as Nerina, a female part expanded from Nirenus), Ariosti's *Dario* and the Vinci-Orlandini *Elpidia*. Handel's two arias for her have a compass of *d′* to *g″* and a mezzo-soprano tessitura. WINTON DEAN

Sorozábal (Mariezcurrena), Pablo (*b* San Sebastián, 18 Sept 1897; *d* Madrid, 26 Dec 1988). Spanish composer and conductor. He studied first in his native city and later under Alfredo de Larrocha (violin) and Beltrán Pagola (harmony and composition). He became a member of the Orfeón Donostiarra and later the orchestra of the Casino, playing under his violin teacher and Enrique Fernández Arbós. In 1918 he moved to Madrid as a member of the Philharmonic Orchestra and in 1920 he went to Leipzig. There he studied with Hans Sitt (violin) and Stephan Krehl (composition), supporting himself by playing in symphony orchestras and as a café musician, and made his conducting début in 1922. In 1931 he returned to Spain for the first performance of *Katiuska*, which remained one of the greatest of many successes in its genre. With Federico Moreno Torroba he was one of the last major exponents of the zarzuela, bringing to it technical refinement and a distinctive grasp of regional styles. He also composed chamber, choral and orchestral music, and was conductor of the Madrid Municipal Band, the Madrid PO and of many zarzuela recordings.

Katiuska (opereta, 2, E. González del Castillo and M. Martí Alonso), Barcelona, Victoria, 27 Jan 1931; La guitarra de Figaro (comedia musical, 1, E. Enderiz and J. Roa, after P. Baroja), Bilbao, Arriaga, 1931; La isla de las perlas (opereta, 2, González del Castillo and Martí Alonso), Madrid, Coliseum, 1933; Adiós a la bohemia (op chica, 1, Sorozábal, after Baroja), Madrid, Calderón, Dec 1933; El alguacil rebolledo (tonadilla, A. Cuyás de la Vega), Madrid, Calderón, 1934; Sol en la cumbre (zar, 2, A. Carreño), Madrid, Rialto, 1934; La del manojo de rosas (sainete madrileño, 2, Carreño and R. de Castro), Madrid, Fuencarral, 13 Nov 1934

No me olvides (opereta, prol., 2, F. Romero and G. Fernández Shaw), Madrid, Zarzuela, 1935; La tabernera del puerto (romance marinero, 3, Romero and Fernández Shaw), Barcelona, Tivoli, 1936; La Rosario (sainete catallán, 1, Romero and Fernández Shaw), Valencia, Apolo, 1941; Cuidado con la pintura (sainete madrileño, 1, Romero and Fernández Shaw), Valencia, Apolo, 1941; Black, el payaso (opereta, prol., 3, F. Serran Anguita), Barcelona, Coliseum, 21 April 1942; Don Manolito (sainete madrileño, 1, Carreño and L. Fernández Sevilla), Madrid, Reina Victoria, 1943; La eterna canción (sainete madrileño, 2, Fernández Sevilla), Barcelona, Principal Palace, 1945

Los burladores (zar, 3, S. Alvarez Quintero and J. Alvarez Quintero), Madrid, Calderón, 10 Dec 1948; Entre Sevilla y Triana (sainete andaluz, 2, Fernández Sevilla and L. Tejedor), Madrid, Price, 1950; La ópera del mogollón (zar bufa, R. Peña), Madrid, Fuencarral, 1954; Brindis (revista, 2, Fernández Sevilla and Tejedor), Madrid, Lope de Vega, 1955; Las de Caín (comedia musical, 3, S. Alvarez Quintero and J. Alvarez Quintero), Madrid, Zarzuela, 1958, collab. P. Sorozábal jr; Juan José (drama lírico popular, 3, J. Dicenta), unperf.

Arrs. (all perf. Madrid): H. Berté: Die Dreimäderlhaus (after Schubert), Zarzuela, 1935; Albéniz: San Antonio de la Florida, Fuencarral, 1954; F. A. Barbieri: Pan y toros, Retiro, 1960; Albéniz: Pepita Jiménez, Zarzuela, 1964

*

A. Fernández-Cid: *Cien años de teatro musical en España (1875–1975)* (Madrid, 1975)

R. Alier and others: *El libro de la zarzuela* (Barcelona, 1982, 2/1986 as *Diccionario de la zarzuela*)

P. Sorozábal: *Mi vida y mi obra* (Madrid, 1986) ANDREW LAMB

Sors, Fernando. *See* SOR, FERNANDO.

Sortita (It.: 'coming out'). A term denoting a principal singer's first entrance, especially when marked by an important piece of music. A CAVATINA in the mid-19th century sense is sometimes described as an 'aria di sortita'. Bellini refers to the great quartet in *I puritani* (1835) as the 'sortita di Rubini', since that is the number in which the tenor makes his first appearance.

JULIAN BUDDEN

Sosarme [*Sosarme, re di Media* ('Sosarmes, King of Media')]. Opera in three acts by GEORGE FRIDERIC HANDEL to a libretto anonymously adapted from ANTONIO SALVI's *Dionisio re di Portogallo* (1707, Pratolino); London, King's Theatre, 15 February 1732.

Handel completed the score of *Sosarme* on 4 February 1732. His original title was *Fernando re di Castiglia*, and most of the first two acts were composed with the Portuguese setting (in Coimbra) and the characters of Salvi's original libretto, among them the Portuguese king Dionysius (reigned 1279–1325), his son Alfonso IV and King Ferdinand IV of Castile (reigned 1295–1312). Presumably to avoid offence to the royal family of Portugal, Britain's oldest ally, the setting was changed to Sardis in Lydia and the characters acquired new, fictional names: Dionysius became Haliate of Lydia, Alfonso became Argone and Ferdinand became Sosarme of Media. The other characters are Haliate's queen, Erenice; their daughter Elmira (Argone's sister), betrothed to Sosarme; Melo, Haliate's illegitimate son; and Altomaro, the treacherous counsellor of Haliate. In the original run of 11 performances the cast consisted of the castratos Senesino and Campioli (Sosarme and Argone), Anna Maria Strada del Pò (Elmira), Anna Bagnolesi (Erenice), Francesca Bertolli (Melo), Giovanni Pinacci (Haliate) and Antonio Montagnana (Altomaro). The opera was very well received. Viscount Percival thought it 'one of the best I ever heard', and the compiler of the so-called 'Colman Opera Register' observed that it 'took much' and 'was much crowded to some peoples admiration'. Handel revived it on 27 April 1734 for three performances in a much altered version incorporating arias from *Riccardo Primo* and with adjustments to accommodate the higher voices of the castratos Carestini and Scalzi as Sosarme and Argone; the soprano Margherita Durastanti took over the tenor role of Haliate. *Sosarme* was not heard again until the broadcast of Act 2 by the BBC Third Programme in 1948 and of the complete work in January 1955, both conducted by Anthony Lewis, whose pioneer L'Oiseau-Lyre recording also appeared in 1955. The first staged revival was by Unicorn Opera at Abingdon on 8 September 1970.

The action begins in the great square of Sardis. The city is under siege from Haliate (tenor) because it holds the rebel forces of his son Argone (alto). Argone orders an attack on the besieging army to obtain supplies. Outside the city, Erenice (mezzo-soprano) tells her daughter Elmira (soprano) of a dream which warned her that the feud will end only 'with the royal blood shed by a son'; she believes that her husband or her son must die, and she resolves to stop Argone from attacking his father.

The royal counsellor Altomaro (bass) tells his grandson Melo (alto), Haliate's illegitimate son by Altomaro's daughter, that he has been declared Haliate's successor in place of Argone; Melo is loath to gain advancement by such means. Sosarme (alto), betrothed to Elmira, tells Melo that he intends to make peace. He begins by warning Haliate: if the king treats Elmira as he has Argone, Sosarme will oppose him. As Argone is about to begin the sortie he is held back by Elmira and by Erenice, who warns him that she will die if he attacks his father, but soldiers' cries stiffen his resolve. The women reflect on their conflicting loyalties.

At the start of Act 2, Elmira tells Erenice that Sosarme has entered the battle against Argone, who appears with 'royal blood' on his sword: the women assume he has killed his father, but he says the blood is Sosarme's, and Elmira faints. Melo reports to Haliate that the Medians are deserting him with demands for Sosarme's freedom. Altomaro accuses Melo of starting the mutiny; Haliate denounces Melo and tells Altomaro to seek reconciliation with Argone. Melo refuses to be turned against Haliate by Altomaro. In a small room, Sosarme, merely wounded, is being nursed by Elmira; their suffering has intensified their love. Erenice announces messengers of peace from Haliate; Argone agrees to peace if he receives his rights as Haliate's son. But the prospect of reconciliation is shattered by Altomaro, who reports (falsely) that Haliate has demanded single combat with Argone. Argone angrily accepts, but Erenice resolves to plead with Haliate and asks Sosarme to pacify Argone. He and Elmira look forward to their marriage.

In Act 3, Altomaro tells Haliate that Argone, encouraged by Erenice, challenges him to single combat. Haliate orders Erenice's arrest and puts her under Melo's care. Her comments lead Melo to realize Altomaro's treachery, and he resolves to intervene. Sosarme and Elmira try to pacify Argone. On the duelling field, Altomaro appears as Haliate's second. Swords are presented to Haliate and Argone, but as they fight Erenice and Melo intervene and both are wounded, Erenice by Argone and Melo by Haliate. The combatants are filled with remorse and Altomaro flees. After explanations, Sosarme brings news of Altomaro's suicide. All are reconciled.

* * *

The music of *Sosarme* is of high quality throughout, but its beauties are not always placed in the service of the drama. Partly this is the result of the original casting, which caused the most powerful dramatic element (the family conflict) to be played out between the less important singers, one of whom (Campioli as Argone) was not good enough even to be given an aria. Erenice and Haliate are nevertheless memorably portrayed, Erenice vigorous and tender by turns, and Haliate covering a wide emotional range in arias of anger, clemency and bitterness, the second ('Se discordia ne disciolse') being especially fine. Altomaro's three arias have a major-key geniality at odds with his villainous nature. Melo is treated with special sympathy, his first two arias deepened by minor-key melancholy. The greatest riches of the score, however, are found in the several exquisite arias for Sosarme and Elmira, and above all in their two duets, the first of which ('Per le porte del tormento' in Act 2) transcends its dramatic context with music of sublime and piercing radiance. Though not the best exemplar of Handel's skills as a musical dramatist, *Sosarme* consistently illustrates his greatness as a composer. ANTHONY HICKS

Sotin, Hans (*b* Dortmund, 10 Sept 1939). German bass. He studied privately with F. W. Hezel and Dieter Jacob. His début was in Essen in 1962, as the Police Inspector in *Der Rosenkavalier*; in 1964 he joined the Hamburg Staatsoper, taking small roles, but soon graduated to virtually all the leading bass roles in the Hamburg repertory, as well as singing Wotan in *Das Rheingold* and *Die Walküre*. He made his Glyndebourne début as Sarastro in 1970, subsequently appearing at the Chicago Lyric Opera (début as the Grand Inquisitor, 1971), the Metropolitan (Sarastro, 1972), Bayreuth (the Landgrave, 1972), the Vienna Staatsoper (King Mark, 1973), Covent Garden (Hunding, 1974) and La Scala (Ochs, 1976). He has also sung Pogner, Don Alfonso and van Bett (*Zar und Zimmermann*). His rolling, voluminous tones, his sympathetic stage presence and interpretative independence make him one of the most valuable German basses of his generation. MARTIN BERNHEIMER

Soubrette (Fr.: 'servant girl'). A stock character of 18th-century French theatre, the clever but impertinent servant girl who comments wryly on the behaviour of the ladies and gentlemen of the household, and who often becomes an agent of intrigue. The word, said to be of Old Provençal origin, an adjective meaning 'coy' or 'shrewd, cunning', has been adopted in English and German for operatic soubrettes, examples of whom include Serpina in Pergolesi's *La serva padrona*, Despina in Mozart's *Così fan tutte* and Adele in Johann Strauss's *Die Fledermaus*; the type goes back to the servant girls of early Venetian operas such as *L'incoronazione di Poppea*. The soubrette is typically a rather lightweight secondary character, but in the cases of Susanna (*Le nozze di Figaro*) and Zerlina (*Don Giovanni*) Mozart created personalities of unusual breadth. The term 'soubrette' is sometimes extended to refer to operatic roles calling for a light, agile soprano voice, for example Papagena and Marzelline (*Fidelio*), and also to a range of operetta roles including those by Sullivan.

See SOPRANO. OWEN JANDER, J. B. STEANE

Souez [née Rains], **Ina** (*b* Windsor, CO, 3 June 1908). American soprano. She trained at Denver and then in Milan. Her début as Mimì at Ivrea in 1928 led to engagements in Palermo and London, where she sang Liù to Eva Turner's Turandot in 1929. Her repertory also included *Trovatore*, *Faust*, *Mefistofele* and *Madama Butterfly*, but it was in Mozart at Glyndebourne that the most enduring part of her reputation was made. She sang Fiordiligi in the opening season of 1934, added Donna Anna in 1936, and appeared regularly in both roles until 1939. She also sang at the Stockholm Opera but, in 1941, retired from the operatic stage. Her voice, light for Covent Garden, developed a hardness that sometimes limited enjoyment of her work at Glyndebourne, yet hers was probably the greatest personal success there in the early seasons, and her singing of Micaëla in the Covent Garden *Carmen* of 1935 was described as a 'joy to hear'. She recorded both Mozart operas with Fritz Busch. J. B. STEANE

Souffleur (Fr., Ger.). PROMPTER.

Soulacroix, Gabriel (*b* Villeneuve-sur-Lot, 11 Dec 1853; *d* Paris, 16 Aug 1905). French baritone. He studied at Toulouse and Paris, making his début in 1878 at La Monnaie as Beckmesser in the theatre's first production of *Die Meistersinger*. In 1885 he joined the Opéra-Comique, singing the leading role in the première of Messager's *La basoche* in 1890. He was also Ford in the first French performance of *Falstaff* and at the Gaîté-Lyrique appeared in the French première of *La bohème*. At Covent Garden his high baritone enabled him to take the tenor role of Pedrillo in *Die Entführung aus dem Serail*. His other roles there, from 1881 to 1884, included Escamillo and Rossini's Figaro; in 1889 he returned to sing such varied roles as Alfio, Mercutio and Beckmesser, a part he also sang at La Scala. Some of his best work was done at Monte Carlo, where he appeared regularly from 1889 until 1904: the title role in Hérold's *Zampa* and Iago to Tamagno's Otello were among his more notable undertakings. About 30 rare recordings preserve his finely produced voice, showing an elegance and fluency remarkable even for their period.

J. B. STEANE

Soulié [Soulier], **Jean-Pierre.** *See* SOLIÉ, JEAN-PIERRE.

Souliotis, Elena (*b* Athens, 25 May 1943). Greek soprano. Her family emigrated to Buenos Aires; she studied there and in Milan. Her début was in 1964 as Santuzza in Naples, and her American début was at Chicago in 1966 as Helen of Troy in Boito's *Mefistofele*. The same year she made her first appearance at La Scala, as Abigaille (*Nabucco*), and in 1968 caused a sensation in the same part at a concert performance in London. Her first appearances at Covent Garden and the Metropolitan were both in 1969 as Lady Macbeth; at Covent Garden, Abigaille and Santuzza followed in 1972 and 1973. Her career proved short-lived, largely because she lacked the discipline to husband her appreciable resources. On stage she was a vivid though controversial performer.

ALAN BLYTH

Sourdéac, Marquis de [Rieux, Alexandre de] (*fl c*1659–71; *d* ?Paris, 7 May 1695). French machinist and opera manager. He was the son of Guy de Rieux, *premier écuyer* to Marie de' Medici, and showed an affinity for machines at an early age. In the late 1650s he collaborated with Pierre Corneille on the machine tragedy *La toison d'or*, providing an array of spectacular effects; the play was first performed in 1660 in a specially constructed theatre in Sourdéac's castle in Neubourg, Normandy, and was staged in the Théâtre du Marais, Paris, in 1661. In December 1669, six months after PIERRE PERRIN had obtained royal consent to establish the 'Académies d'Opéra', Sourdéac became one of Perrin and Cambert's business managers. He was also appointed machinist and designed the adventurous and much-admired machine effects for the inaugural production, *Pomone*, in 1671; rehearsals were held during 1670 in Normandy. Financial greed, however, led him and his business partner Champeron to swindle the company out of the substantial profits; this left Perrin insolvent and facing imprisonment. Nonetheless, Sourdéac designed the machines for *Les peines et les plaisirs de l'amour* (staged early in 1672), and was planning the spectacle for a third opera (probably Perrin's revised *Ariane*) when the Académies were forced to close.

Sourdéac's machinery allowed fantastic and exciting effects. *Pomone* included thunder, lightning, a burning cloud, flying bottles and a wine fountain, while in *Les peines et les plaisirs* chariots and a throne descended from the heavens. According to the *Mercure galant* (1673), the machines for the third opera were 'so beautiful, novel and surprising that people would have come from the four corners of the globe to see them'. Sourdéac made a considerable artistic contribution to the establishment of French opera; it was possibly his awareness of this that led him to exploit his position for personal financial gain.

*

C. Nuitter and E. Thoinan: *Les origines de l'opéra français* (Paris, 1875)

A. Adam, ed.: *Tallement des Réaux: Historiettes* (Paris, 1960–61)

A. Niederst, ed.: *Pierre Corneille: théâtre complet*, iii/1 (Rouen, 1986), 93–7

C. Bashford: 'Perrin and Cambert's "Ariane, ou Le mariage de Bacchus" Re-examined', *ML*, lxxii (1991), 1–26, esp. 20–21

CHRISTINA BASHFORD

Sousa Carvalho, João de. *See* CARVALHO, JOÃO DE SOUSA.

South Africa. Operatic performances took place fairly regularly at the Cape from the beginning of the 19th century. The first theatre in Cape Town, the so-called African Theatre, opened in 1800. The earliest performances were of *opéras comiques* and English comic operas; some were later given in Dutch translations. A number of spoken plays also included music from the works of several composers. Performances were frequently given by French musicians who stayed at the Cape on their way to Mauritius. Operas included Méhul's *Une folie* and Rousseau's *Pygmalion*; among the English works were *The Devil to Pay* (libretto by Charles Coffey) and *The Poor Soldier* (libretto by John O'Keeffe).

The first serious opera production took place in 1831, when an amateur company performed *Der Freischütz* in English. In the latter part of the 19th century a number of touring companies performed in Cape Town and Durban, and later also in Johannesburg. They generally concentrated on the Italian repertory but also included Wagner operas, such as *Die Meistersinger* and *Die Walküre*. Opera was provided by visiting companies well into the 20th century.

The University of Cape Town Opera Company presented regular seasons from 1929 onwards; it flourished under the direction of Erik Chisholm (1951–65) and Gregorio Fiasconaro (1952–80). Productions included numerous South African premières as well as first performances of a number of Chisholm's operas and John Joubert's *Silas Marner* (1961). The company toured widely in southern Africa. The Eoan Group, an amateur company, performed several operas between 1956 and 1969, under the direction of Joseph Manca. Gordon Jephtas and Fiasconaro were also associated with the group. The University of the Witwatersrand in Johannesburg presented opera on a more modest basis, the most interesting production being Weber's *Abu Hassan* in 1951. The provincial arts councils were formed in 1963 and assumed responsibility for performances of drama, ballet and opera. With their establishment the influence of smaller companies, such as the University of Cape Town Opera Company, waned. An arts council was formed for each province, even for Namibia.

Since most first-class South African singers pursued careers in Europe, many overseas singers were engaged for local productions. In the early 1990s – partly because of the cultural boycott of South Africa – this trend was reversed and more local singers were employed. There is now a well-established local operatic tradition, but South African composers have largely ignored the medium, though the Department of National Education offers encouragement through opera competitions. Operas of note written for performance in South Africa have mainly been by British composers – such as W. H. Bell and Chisholm – who were resident there.

For further information on operatic life in the country's principal centres *see* CAPE TOWN; DURBAN; and JOHANNESBURG.

*

J. Bouws: *Musiek in Suid-Afrika* (Bruges, 1946)
——: *Die musieklewe van Kaapstad: 1800–1850* (Cape Town, 1966)
P. R. Kirby: *Wits End* (Cape Town, 1967)
G. S. Jackson: *Music in Durban: 1850–1900* (Johannesburg, 1970)
D. Talbot: *For the Love of Singing: 50 Years of Opera at UCT* (Cape Town, 1978)
JAMES MAY

Soutullo (Otero), Reveriano (*b* Puenteáreas, Pontevedra, 11 July 1884; *d* Madrid, 29 Oct 1932). Spanish composer. He received his initial musical education from his father, director of the municipal band in Puenteáreas, and then became a military bandsman in Murcia. In 1902 he matriculated from the Madrid conservatory with a first prize in composition which permitted further study in Germany, Italy and France. On his return he worked mostly on zarzuelas, ultimately composing well over one hundred. It was in collaboration with Juan Vert that he achieved lasting renown, especially through *La leyenda del beso* (1924), *La del Soto del Parral* (1927) and *El último romántico* (1928), works that combined Latin passion with fluent lyricism and rich melody. He also composed orchestral music and one opera, *La devoción de la Cruz* (after P. Calderón), which appears not to have been performed.

selective list of zarzuelas, all first performed in Madrid

La paloma del barrio (G. Cantó and E. Calonge), Novedades, 1911; El capricho de una reina (2, A. Paso *hijo* and J. Vidal), Apolo, 13 May 1919, collab. J. Vert; Justicias y ladrones (S. Delgado), Apolo, 1919–20, collab. Vert; Guitarras y bandurrias (Paso and F. García Pacheco), Centro, 1920, collab. Vert; La esnigotina (2, Paso and García Pacheco), Apolo, 30 Dec 1921, collab. Vert; La leyenda del beso (2, E. Reoyo, Paso and S. Aramburu), Apolo, 18 Jan 1924, collab. Vert; Encarna, la misterio (2, Luque and Calonge), Apolo, 8 May 1925, collab. Vert; La del Soto del Parral (2, A. Carreño and L. Fernández Ardavín), Latina, 26 Oct 1927, collab. Vert; El último romántico (2, J. Tellaeche), Apolo, 9 March 1928, collab. Vert; Luces de verbena (S. Anguita and Tellaeche), Calderón, 1935, completed by G. Baudor and F. Moreno Torroba

*

A. Fernández-Cid: *Cien años de teatro musical en España (1875–1975)* (Madrid, 1975)
J. Arnau and C. M. Gomez: *Historía de la zarzuela* (Madrid, 1979)
R. Alier and others: *El libro de la zarzuela* (Barcelona, 1982, 2/1986 as *Diccionario de la zarzuela*)
ANDREW LAMB

Souzay [Tisserand], **Gérard (Marcel)** (*b* Angers, 8 Dec 1920). French baritone. He studied with Pierre Bernac and at the Paris Conservatoire. After 15 years as a concert singer, he sang Purcell's Aeneas at Aix-en-Provence (1960) and then the title role of Monteverdi's *Orfeo* with the New York City Opera. His operatic appearances included Golaud at Rome (1962), the Opéra-Comique, Paris (1963), Florence (1966) and Wiesbaden (1976); Don Giovanni at the Paris Opéra (1963), Munich (1965) and Lausanne (1967); and Count Almaviva at the Metropolitan and Glyndebourne (1965), where he had to withdraw through illness after one performance. He sang in the British première (concert performance) of Roussel's *Padmâvatî*. His recordings of Rameau's Pollux, Berlioz's Méphistophélès, Albert (*Werther*), both Lescaut and the Chevalier des Grieux in *Manon*, Alaouddin (*Padmâvatî*) and in particular Golaud, his finest role, perfectly illustrate his warm-toned voice, firm but flexible, and his superb diction.
MARTIN COOPER/ELIZABETH FORBES

Soviero, Diana (*b* Jersey City, NJ, 19 March 1946). American soprano. After singing Lauretta and Massenet's Manon at St Paul (1974), Violetta at Norfolk, Virginia, and Anne Trulove at Lake George (1975), she joined the New York City Opera in 1976, then sang at Chicago, Miami, San Francisco and the Metropolitan, where she made her début in 1986 as Juliet. She has also sung at Hamburg, Cologne, Paris, Vienna, Zürich, Rome, Florence and La Scala. Her repertory includes Norina, Micaëla, Leïla, Mimì, Butterfly, Tosca, Manon Lescaut and Angelica. In 1988 she sang Gounod's Marguerite at San Diego, Boito's Margherita at Philadelphia and Busoni's Gretchen at Geneva. A stylish singer, she excels in roles such as Nedda, in which she made her Covent Garden début in 1989.
ELIZABETH FORBES

Soviet Union. UNION OF SOVIET SOCIALIST REPUBLICS.

Soyer, Roger (Julien Jacques) (*b* Paris, 1 Sept 1939). French bass. He studied at the Paris Conservatoire and made his début in small roles at the Paris Opéra in 1963; that year he also sang in *Les mamelles de Tirésias* at the Piccola Scala. In 1965 he sang Pluto in Monteverdi's *Orfeo* at Aix-en-Provence; he returned on many occasions, singing Don Giovanni, Don Basilio and Arkel among other roles. In 1968 he sang Ralph (*La jolie fille de Perth*) at the Wexford Festival and made his American début in Miami as Friar Laurence (*Roméo et Juliette*). At the 1973 Edinburgh Festival he sang Don Giovanni, the role of his Metropolitan début the previous year and one which he played in many theatres including the Paris Opéra, where he also sang Ferrando (*Il trovatore*), Procida (*Les vêpres siciliennes*), Colline, Méphistophélès, Rangoni (*Boris Godunov*) and Mr Broderick (Stanton Coe's *Sud*), which he created in 1972. He sang Rodolfo (*La sonnambula*) at Geneva (1982) and Sulpice (*La fille du régiment*) at Dallas (1983). A genuine *basse chantante*, Soyer sang with great elegance.
HAROLD ROSENTHAL/R

Spadavecchia, Antonio Emmanuilovich (*b* Odessa, 21 May/3 June 1907; *d* Moscow, 7 Feb 1988). Ukrainian composer of Italian descent. He graduated from Shebalin's composition class at the Moscow Conservatory in 1937 and had lessons from Prokofiev in 1944. In 1963 he received the title Honoured Artist of the RSFSR. His biggest success was with the opera *Ovod* ('The Gadfly'), which received its first performance in 1957.

Ak-buzat Volshebnïy kon' [Ak-buzat the Magic Horse] (S. Miftakhov), Ufa, 7 Nov 1942; rev. 1952; collab. Kh. Zaimov
Nezhdannaya svad'ba [The Unforeseen Wedding] (musical comedy), Ufa, 1944
Khozyayka gostinitsï [The Hostess], 1947 (S. Tsenin, after C. Goldoni), Moscow, Stanislavsky–Nemirovich-Danchenko Music Theatre, 24 April 1949
Khozhdeniye po mukam [The Way of Sorrow] (I. Keller, after A. Tolstoy), Perm', 29 Dec 1953; rev. as Ognennïye godï [The Fiery Years], Perm', 1966
Ovod [The Gadfly] (4, Keller, after E. Voynich), Perm', 8 Nov 1957, vs (Moscow, 1961)

Serdtse skripki [The Violin's Heart] (musical comedy), Orenburg, 1959
Braviy soldat Shveyk [The Good Soldier Švejk] (after J. Hašek), Sverdlovsk, 1963
K zvyozdam [To the Stars] (triptych, Tsiolko sky), Elektrostal', 1967
Vïstrel v temnote [The Shot in the Dark] (musical comedy), Orenburg, 1969
Yukki/Prazdnik fonarey [Holiday of the Lanterns] (3, Keller, after H. Pfeiffer), Sverdlovsk, 1969, vs (Moscow, 1974)
Pis'mo neznakomki [The Letter of an Unknown Woman] (mono-op, after S. Zweig: *Brief einer Unbekannten*), Kislovodsk, 1975
Kapitanskaya dochka [The Captain's Daughter], 1977
Zolushka (children's op), Engels, 1977
Volshebnaya lampa Aladina [Aladdin's Magic Lamp] (musical comedy), Orenburg, 1978 DETLEF GOJOWY

Spagna, Arcangelo (*b* Viterbo, *c*1632; *d* Rome, 3 May 1726). Italian librettist. He was an abbot and canon, and served various Roman cardinals including Francesco Barberini, Carlo Ciceri and Pietro Ottoboni. He seems to have spent most of his life in Rome, where he published 30 oratorios in two collections (1706 and 1720), seven *melodrammi scenici* (1709 and 1713), and about 12 *commedie in prosa* (1711–17). First performances of his oratorios ranged from 1656 to 1716. A chronology of his secular works has not been established because many were written for household productions and the texts were not published at the time of the performance. The only exception is *La gelosa di se stessa*, which was produced at the Palazzo Barberini on 17 February 1689 and printed four months later. In the preface to his collection of six *melodrammi scenici*, all comedies for a few rustic characters, he declares that they were 'written mainly in my juvenile years'. They seem to be ordered by number of singers: *Lo sdegno con lo sdegno si vince* (*a* 3), *Il pastor finto*, *Chi può s'ingegni* and *La gelosa di se stessa* (all *a* 4), *La fortuna tra le disgratie* (*a* 6) and *Amor, donna et ingegno* (*a* 8). The seventh, *Non si scherzi con amore* (*a* 3), was printed separately in 1713. It is not known who first set Spagna's opera librettos. An anonymous score for *La gelosa* (*I-Rvat* Barb.lat.4213–15) and fragments (*IBborromeo*) survive; the latter have not been examined, but the former contains an early 18th-century revision of the text with, presumably, a completely new musical setting.

*

A. Schering: 'Neue Beiträge zur Geschichte des italienischen Oratoriums im 17. Jahrhundert', *SIMG*, viii (1906–7), 43–70
H. E. Smither: *A History of the Oratorio*, i: *The Oratorio in the Baroque Era: Italy, Vienna, Paris* (Chapel Hill, NC, 1977)
S. Franchi: *Drammaturgia romana: repertorio bibliografico cronologico dei testi drammatici pubblicati a Roma e nel Lazio, secolo XVII* (Rome, 1988)

LOWELL LINDGREN

Spagnoletto. *See* CATRUFO, GIOSEFFO.

Spagnoletto, Lo. *See* GARCÍA FAJER, FRANCISCO JAVIER.

Spagnoli, Clementina (*b* Rome, *c*1735; *d* after 1778). Italian soprano. She sang in *opera buffa* at Venice in 1752–3 but rose to prima donna in *opera seria* at Florence in Carnival 1754 and was then engaged in leading Italian theatres up to Carnival 1772, reappearing at Faenza in Carnival 1778. The intricacy of some of her music suggests a highly skilled musician (range approximately *d'* to *d'''*), but she was criticized for performances completely worked out beforehand, with no element of spontaneity, a major failing in the aesthetic of the genre. DENNIS LIBBY

Spain.

1. The 17th century. 2. The 18th century: (i) The court theatres (ii) Public theatres. 3. The 19th century and early 20th. 4. Since 1936.

1. THE 17TH CENTURY. Opera began in Spain probably in the first third of the century, but the word itself was not used until 1698: on 27 January two companies in Madrid united to give a 'fiesta de ópera', and in February the same companies performed an 'ópera cantada'. Critical writers as well as the great dramatists of Spain's Golden Age – Cervantes, Lope de Vega, Tirso de Molina, Luis Vélez de Guevara and above all Calderón – attached great importance to music. *Comedias*, *autos sacramentales*, zarzuelas and the organization of players imply substantial use of music in drama, and Spain thus possessed an artistic tradition that naturally led to opera. Guitar music, popular songs, dances accompanied by singing and instrumental music were all integrated into the drama, with simple music serving the text and providing various effects as required by the text. Opera in Spain emerged from this tradition, dating back to Juan del Encina and reaching its peak with Calderón, enhanced by awareness of what was happening in this field in Italy, with which there were strong cultural ties. Both the Florentine stage designer Cosimo Lotti and the Tuscan Giulio Rospigliosi, papal nuncio and author of librettos for Stefano Landi, worked in Spain in this period.

It seems certain that the first opera performed in Spain was Lope de Vega's *La selva sin amor*, given at the Coliseo del Buen Retiro, the theatre in the royal palace, Madrid, on 18 December 1627, with stage machinery by Lotti. Lope's famous prologue includes some significant phrases: 'acted in singing ... something new to Spain ... my verses were the least important element', but he does not name the composer, and the music is lost. Other works were performed in the succeeding years, such as Bocángel y Unceta's *El nuevo Olimpo* in 1648; their descriptive titles do not confirm but suggest their nature: 'representación real y festiva máscara', 'fiesta', 'representación musical'.

The next significant works, both given probably in 1660 at the royal palace in Madrid, had librettos by Calderón. *La púrpura de la rosa* was performed on 17 January; the music, again, is lost, nor is the name of the composer known for certain, but it may have been Juan Hidalgo, who certainly wrote the next opera, *Celos aun del aire matan* (? 5 December). That the former was a true opera seems confirmed by Calderón in the prologue, in which one of the characters says: 'Do you not see what a risk it is, to expect Spanish impatience to tolerate a play that is sung?' Other important evidence indicates that it was sung in recitative style, with pieces for solo singers alone and in ensembles, and instrumental passages.

Celos aun del aire matan, a 'fiesta grande cantada', is the earliest surviving Spanish opera. The subject is a mythological one from Ovid's *Metamorphoses*. Hidalgo's music is a succession of dialogue recitatives, expressive and dramatic, and arias in triple time; at moments of particular dramatic importance there are short homophonic choruses, a common feature of Spanish music for the theatre. Not until Sebastián Durón's *La guerra de los gigantes*, probably composed between 1700 and 1707, do we encounter another extant fully fledged Spanish opera.

2. THE 18TH CENTURY.

(i) The court theatres. The establishment of the Bourbon

dynasty in Spain in 1700 had significant consequences for public entertainment, the most important of which was undoubtedly Italian opera. Philip V celebrated the birthday of his first queen, Maria Luisa of Savoy, on 25 August 1703 with a performance in the Coliseo del Buen Retiro of Act 3 of *Il pomo d'oro* (music perhaps by Cesti). Because in this opera Mercury transforms himself into Truffaldino, the company which introduced Italian opera into Spain became known as the Trufaldines, and they settled in the Calle de Alcalá, Madrid. As court employees they did not observe the normal practice of contributing a proportion of their earnings to the city's hospitals, and this led to serious conflicts with Spanish companies working at the Teatro del Príncipe and Teatro de la Cruz, and also with the municipality. Political crises obliged them to leave their premises in 1707 and return to the Buen Retiro, before moving the following year to the Teatro de los Caños del Peral, where they continued to function until 1714.

In 1716, under the Duke of Alberoni, a new Italian company was set up under exceptionally favourable conditions, again at the Caños del Peral theatre. When Alberoni fell in 1719 he was succeeded by Annibale Scotti, the favourite of the new queen, Isabella Farnese, and the Italians kept all their privileges. There are few extant records of their activities, but one opera they are known to have performed, in 1722, was Gioacchino Landi's *L'interesse schernito dal proprio inganno*.

The Italian company accompanied the court when it moved to Seville in 1728. In 1733 they left Seville and followed the court to Aranjuez and La Granja. Meanwhile the Spanish companies regained their standing in Madrid, and as a result the Italians left the Caños del Peral theatre soon after their return. In 1735 the new season at the theatre opened with a company formed from the best singers from the Cruz and Príncipe theatres to sing in Spanish Italian operas by Corselli, Corradini (the leading figure in the 1730s and early 40s) and Mele, who all lived in Madrid.

A new opera house on the Caños del Peral site opened, under Scotti, on 16 February 1738 with Hasse's *Demetrio*. The enormous running costs and the limited repertory, as well as Scotti's fall from power, soon led to the closing of the theatre, but it was open again between 1743 and 1746 for further productions of operas in Italian or in translation by Spanish companies; the composers included Corradini and Nebra.

The Coliseo del Buen Retiro, meanwhile, was gaining new importance through Farinelli. He was engaged on very favourable terms to alleviate Philip V's bouts of depression, and he acquired great power at court, which he used exclusively to the benefit of Italian opera. When performances were suspended at the Caños del Peral theatre the best voices in the company remained in the king's service as chamber singers, and Farinelli used them to reopen the Buen Retiro on 9 May 1738 with Corselli's *Alessandro nell'Indie*. The success of the opera led to the rebuilding of the theatre, which was transformed into one of the leading opera houses in Europe. From 1740 the company performed at the Buen Retiro and at Aranjuez many operas, intermezzos and serenatas by such composers as Bonno, Galuppi, Hasse, Jommelli and Pergolesi, and many well-known singers appeared, including Anton Raaff.

After the death of Philip V in 1746, his son Ferdinand VI made Farinelli even more powerful: he put him in charge of court festivities, which became ever more sumptuous. But on the accession of Charles III in 1759 Farinelli returned to Italy, and the rest of the company failed to maintain their success, largely owing to the influence of the Archbishop of Toledo, who thought that 'such pernicious spectacles should not be allowed'.

In 1766 the Count of Aranda, a distinguished soldier, was appointed prime minister, and he gave the theatre an important place in his political programme. He created the Compañía de los Reales Sitios, which was intended to accompany the court on its various moves; and it performed operas, as well as ballets and plays. The company was disbanded in 1777, and the history of court theatres came to an end. During this period opera performances in emulation of the court had also been given in noble houses in other cities, including Mondoñedo, Palma de Mallorca, Saragossa (Joaquín Martínez de la Roca's *Los desagravios de Troya*, 29 July 1712, published in Madrid in the same year), Seville and Valencia.

(ii) Public theatres. In the legal system of the *ancien régime*, responsibility for public entertainment rested with the local authorities and it was customary for the takings of theatres to go to charity hospitals. The enlightened Spanish system saw theatrical performance as a powerful instrument of popular education. The agents of the central power were the captains-general and the military governors, who became the protectors of Italian opera. Their confrontations with municipalities and the Church were a constant feature of the second half of the 18th century.

Opera was most successful in those cities that were particularly flourishing or undergoing a renaissance during this period as a result of maritime commerce (Cádiz, La Coruña) or ship-building (Ferrol, El Puerto de Santa María) and where there was an important foreign colony and local power was divided or insignificant. In traditional cities, however, the establishment of opera could be achieved only through the direct intervention of the captain-general (Jerez de la Frontera, Santiago de Compostela) or the political representative of the government (Seville), directly from Madrid (Pamplona, Valladolid) or through pressure exerted by enlightened local nobility (Córdoba, Granada, Palma de Mallorca). In some populous cities (Valencia, Saragossa) it was the hospital which fostered entertainment that brought them rich benefits, and the municipality which resisted its introduction. Occasional operatic performances were given by companies who had time to spare and obtained permission to perform for a few weeks in cities not on their usual circuit (Ávila, Burgos, Estella, Logroño, Palencia, Salamanca, Zamora). Some cities, too, had single public performances provided by noblemen or ecclesiastics.

The rivalry between Italian opera companies and Spanish dramatic companies was highly significant, as was the unfairness of the Italians, whose political and economic privileges enabled them to disregard the obligations to pay municipal taxes and the customary dues to the hospitals, while the Spaniards not only had to pay the taxes but also saw their takings dwindle. The Spanish companies reacted by trying to produce Spanish musical entertainments, first based on the great dramas of their repertory produced with magic and elaborate stage machinery, and trying to rescue the old Baroque zarzuela, and then by giving the *entremeses* (intermezzos) of the classical theatre a musical form which became an independent genre, the *tonadilla escénica*.

Occasionally impresarios such as José Lladó and Carlos Vallés founded opera companies with varying numbers of Spanish singers, which sometimes performed in Spanish and even, with the composer Rodríguez de Hita and the librettist Ramón de la Cruz, created a new popular genre something like comic opera, also known as zarzuela. During the latter half of the century there was continual friction between actors and opera singers, and the situation was only resolved when the Italians were driven out.

There are at least three distinct periods in the spread of Italian opera as a public spectacle in Spain. The first, 1750–55, was marked by the arrival of Nicolà Setaro's company in Barcelona, brought from Parma by the captain-general the Marquis de Mina. In 1753 Setaro left part of his company in Barcelona and took the rest to Jerez de la Frontera, where he founded the Teatro de Puerto de Santa María. Immediately after the Lisbon earthquake of 1755, Ferdinand VI suspended dramatic performances throughout Spain. Only the Marquis de Mina got round the ban, and performances in Barcelona continued for several months. The deaths of the queen in 1758 and of the king in 1759 kept the theatres closed.

The second period, 1760–78, coincided with the final stages of the Teatro de los Reales Sitios, when the political leader was Count de Aranda. The most important companies were those of Setaro and Ribaltoni. Cádiz and Seville in Andalusia and La Coruña and Ferrol in Galicia were the most important cities. In Valencia, to mention another city, there were companies led by Petronio Setti (1763–4), Luigi Marescalchi and Francisco Creus (1768–70), Francesco Formentari and Teresa Taveggia (1774–6) and Giuseppe Croce (1777–8) – significant operatic activity rivalling that in Barcelona or Saragossa. There were also several lesser companies performing on a regional basis. Important lawsuits included the inquisitorial trial of Setaro in Bilbao in 1773, as a result of which he was condemned to death, and that against Ribaltoni and Setti's itinerant company in 1769 over the upkeep of the Córdoba opera house. A fire at the Saragossa theatre on 12 November 1778, which caused many deaths, was the signal for the effective disappearance of the Italians from Spain except in La Coruña, Ferrol and perhaps occasional performances in Cádiz.

The final period, 1787–1800, coincided with the reopening of the Teatro de los Caños del Peral in Madrid and the spread from there of a new type of entertainment, the *ballet d'action*, prompted by the presence of some of the leading dancers and choreographers of the time. But many operas were staged in Madrid during this period, the composers including Anfossi, Cimarosa, Gazzaniga, Grétry, Martín y Soler, Paër, Paisiello, Salieri and Sarti.

The second most important public opera house was that at Cádiz, directed by the choreographer C.-A. Favier. Those at La Coruña and Ferrol operated, as they had earlier, in conjunction with the house at Oporto. Operatic activity at Barcelona depended largely on Madrid, and singers were engaged on their way to or from Italy and France; and besides Italian operas, works by Spanish composers were performed. The Valencia opera house presented the company of Francesco Curioni from 1790. Many other cities had flourishing houses too, whether permanent as at Seville or temporary as at Salamanca, performing a variety of operas and ballets.

Early in the century leading opera composers included Durón, Literes and Nebra. Later in the century the principal composers were Terradellas, Martín y Soler and García Fajer. All three of these, however, developed their careers outside Spain, and Martín y Soler was the only one whose operas and ballets were frequently performed in his own country.

3. The 19th century and early 20th. The history of opera in the 19th century is one of the most dramatic and controversial chapters in Spanish music. From the outset opera was the genre most cultivated by composers, providing the bulk of published music and inspiring the construction of most Spanish theatres. It is also a difficult subject to treat since little research has been done on 19th- and early 20th-century opera in Spain.

The creation of a specifically Spanish opera to compete with French, German and Italian opera was a long-lived problem which both theorists and composers sought to solve throughout the 19th century, and some thought to be impossible. Peña y Goñi claimed that 'Spanish opera does not exist, Spanish opera has never existed'.

Ever since the influx of Italian musicians in the 18th century, the chronicle of reciprocal influences, of attempts by composers to free themselves from Italian models, and of the idolization of the Italian style continued until nationalism and the influence of Wagner produced some change. Opera in the 19th century was largely a continuation of that of the 18th; in 1792 Moratín described Spanish opera thus: 'Music for the theatre is like the rest, backward and debased ... as far as the music is concerned it is a collection of unconnected imitations, lacking unity, character, novelty, elegance, taste.'

The first decade and a half of the new century saw the first attempts to hispanize opera: a proclamation dated 28 December 1799 prohibited 'the acting, singing or dancing of pieces which are not in the Spanish language or performed by Spanish actors and actresses'. This prohibition meant that operas had to be sung in Spanish (except in Catalonia, which had its own laws), but this did not alter the situation, since the composers performed continued to be Italian, except for Manuel García, who left Spain in 1807.

A second phase, marked by passionate enthusiasm for Rossini, began in Barcelona in 1815 with the first Spanish performance of *L'italiana in Algeri* and in Madrid in 1816 with the opera's arrival there. Although the revolution of 1820 interrupted this fervour, in 1821 the prohibition against singing in Italian was repealed and especially after 1826 Italian opera and singers were again dominant, at first almost entirely with works by Rossini, to which were added a little later works by Donizetti and Bellini and then Pacini and Mercadante, as well as Meyerbeer. In Barcelona in the 1830s the amateur Sociedad Dramática was founded, the origin of the Liceu theatre, later the Liceo Filarmónico-Dramático de Doña Isabel II. One outcome of the Italian monopoly was Bretón de los Herreros's satire *El furor filarmónico*, another a passion for bel canto. In 1838 a very successful opera received its first performance in Barcelona and was considered to be a portent of the resurrection of Catalan music, *La Fattucchiera* by Cuyas y Borés; but it was in Italian, and its chief claim to glory in the eyes of critics and public alike was its similarity to Italian models.

Operas composed in Spain used librettos in Italian: Carnicer, who became a fierce partisan of Italian opera, composed operas in the Italian style and language during the 1820s and 30s, as did composers such as Genovés y Lapetra, Saldoni and Eslava. But most of these works were staged to fill gaps between Italian operas or at the end of a season, sung by little-known artists and then forgotten; very few works in Castilian were given.

The question of language was becoming a central one. It was much treated in writings both literary and theoretical from the 1820s on, and was a frequent topic of discussion from the 1850s to the 70s, when Spanish was usually defended as a suitable language for opera. The first practical attempt to change the situation was the founding in 1842 of the first journal to express and defend Spanish music, *La Iberia musical* (soon to be *Iberia musical y literaria*). Its promotion of Spanish opera was echoed by many journals and associations which arose as the century progressed. Yet they continued to compare and discuss Italian opera and idolize the early Romantic Italian composers and, after a cool welcome, Verdi. The result was further controversy.

During the 1840s several operas were written in Spanish by composers such as Arrieta and, above all, Joaquín Espín y Guillén (founder of *La Iberia musical*), whose *Asedio de Medina* was well received. A decisive solution was achieved through the development of a new and successful type of 'grand' zarzuela in four acts, which finally put an end to the possibility of a Spanish national type of opera, once F. A. Barbieri and other composers, as well as Peña y Goñi, could envisage Spanish opera as deriving only from it. The success of works such as Hernando's *Colegiales y soldados* and *El duende* (both 1849) and, above all, Barbieri's *Gloria y peluca* (1850), *Jugar con fuego* (1851) and *Pan y toros* (1864) established a new and definitive type of zarzuela, and their example was followed by some of the best composers, such as Gaztambide, Arrieta and Oudrid. The 1850s and 1860s were the great years of the zarzuela, and the abundance of significant pieces in the genre left opera in second place. Statistics of productions in the two most important theatres, the Liceu, Barcelona, and the Teatro Real, Madrid, show that almost 90 cer cent of works given their premières were foreign, usually Italian.

Controversy died away during the 1870s and better results were achieved as the new ideologies of nationalism and Wagnerism began to have an effect. In 1869 the publishers Bonifacio Eslava and Antonio Romero, with the composer Arrieta, made a final effort in Madrid to encourage Spanish opera by arranging a competition, won by Enrique Barrera Gómez with *Atahualpa*. In fact the best 19th-century Spanish operas were written in the last three decades to librettos by leading Spanish dramatists; they included Arrieta's *Marina*, Tomás Bretón's *Guzmán el bueno*, *Los amantes de Teruel*, *Garín* and *La Dolores*, Chapí's *Las naves de Cortés*, *Roger de Flor* and *Margarita la tornera* and Emilio Serrano's *Doña Juana la Loca* and *Gonzalo de Córdoba*.

To the late 1870s belong the operas of Marcial del Adalid and Guillermo Morphy, composed for the Théâtre Italien, Paris. Both composers were different from the others mentioned here in not being professional musicians and in being well aware of contemporary European music and unaffected by the demands of the Spanish public.

As for nationalism, the 1880s brought the first signs of musical consciousness to Catalonia, with the beginning of a cultural renaissance in the essentially expressive genre of opera, and with an outstanding personality in Pedrell, whose influence was to be felt throughout Spain. This led to other nationalisms, Basque, Galician, Valencian and so on, and thus to the question of language: naturally opera had to take account of local languages, a subject treated by Pedrell in his manifesto *Por nuestra música* (Barcelona, 1891). What was happening here, and elsewhere in Europe, was to a great extent an intellectual neo-historicist movement, affected also by the most 'modern' music of the day: Wagner, the Russian school and late Verdi. Pedrell spoke of the need to create a national school based on popular song; but this popular song was made up of a wide spectrum which included the classical past, especially the Spanish Golden Age.

The results can be heard in the operas of Pedrell himself – *Els Pireneus*, *La Celestina* and *El Comte Arnau* – and a number of important composers linked with him: Nicolau with *La tempestad*, Vives with *Euda d'Uriac* and Morera with *Emporium*, as well as the early works of Albéniz and Granados. Above all there was the following generation, in the early 20th century, including such important composers of opera as Jaime Pahissa, with his *Gala Placidia*, *La morisca* and *La princesa Margarida*, and Juan Manén, with *Nerón i Acté*. Basque opera composers included Buenaventura Zapirain, Usandizaga and Guridi. Galician nationalism, after Adalid, was expressed in the operas of Baudot-Puente and Rodríguez-Losada Rebellón.

Well-known composers such as Falla and Joaquín Turina also wrote operas, but by the 1930s the so-called Generation of '27 had deserted opera and wrote in other dramatic forms such as ballet; and the closing of the Teatro Real, Madrid, in 1925 was a symbolic act.

4. SINCE 1936. The horrors of the Civil War and the persistence of the Franco regime for 40 years blighted the achievements and promise of the preceding years. The only surviving opera house was the privately owned Liceu, Barcelona, which in addition to the classical repertory has staged several first performances of works by Spanish and Spanish-born composers, such as Montsalvatge's *Una voz en off* (1962), Matilde Salvador's *Vinatea* (1974), José Soler's *Edipo y Yocasta* (1986) and Leonardo Balada's *Cristóbal Colón* (1989).

The celebration in 1964 of '25 Years of Peace' (to commemorate the Civil War victory) had important consequences for the musical world. The touring Festivales de España made performances possible in towns whose normal financial resources were inadequate, but these also prevented the existence of local initiatives of which the political system disapproved. In Madrid the news that the Teatro Real was to be converted into a concert hall was tempered by the creation in 1964 of the so-called Madrid Opera Festival at the small Teatro de la Zarzuela with a revival of Albéniz's *Pepita Jiménez*. Operas receiving their premières there included Tomás Marco's *Selene* and Oscar Esplá's *El pirata cautivo* (both in 1974). The return of democracy in 1976 had little effect on the criteria of the festival, which was financed entirely from the public treasury. The fact that it was not possible to put on the first performance of Pablo Sorozábal's *Juan José* produced an outcry since, given the composer's radical stance, the staging of this opera had been considered a touchstone of the festival's democratization. The socialist administration decided to back operatic activity to the extent of providing the Teatro de la Zarzuela, now officially the Teatro Lírico Nacional La Zarzuela, with a management and a permanent orchestra, so that it could put on its own productions, for example the premières of two operas by Luís de Pablo (who had been coordinator of the musical activities of the '25 Years of Peace'): *Kiú* (1983) and *El viajero indiscreto* (1990).

From 1986 the Teatro Lírico Nacional commissioned chamber operas from young composers without stage experience for performance in the very inadequate Sala Olimpia (which had specialized in contemporary theatre and has no pit). Each of these operas was required to have a plot taken from one of the works in the Zarzuela's programme. The total lack of clarity in these commissions has understandably led to significant protests. The restoration of the Teatro Real started in 1988, in order to provide a home for the Teatro Lírico Nacional, and heavy public investment in operatic production is likely to be maintained.

In other Spanish cities, given the impossibility of private management of opera seasons, the initiative is taken by the Asociaciones de Amigos de la Opera (La Coruña, Bilbao and Oviedo were the pioneers), which from the 1950s organized short opera festivals centred on the 19th-century repertory. An unusual event was the première at Castellón in 1943 of Salvador's *La filla del rei Barbut*. During the recent democratic years the initiatives of the autonomous regional governments and of some municipalities, combined with the restoration of 19th-century theatres, have led to the putting on of opera seasons in some of the larger cities and to the organization of performances in many others, as well as the revival of early operas and the staging of new works such as J. L. Turina's *Ligazón* (Cuenca, 1982). In 1991 the Teatro de la Maestranza was inaugurated in Seville, with a programme selected by Plácido Domingo. In 1992, on the occasion of the Barcelona Olympics, Joan Guinjoan's opera *Laudí* was staged.

For further information on operatic life in the country's principal centres *see* BARCELONA; BILBAO; CÁDIZ; LA CORUÑA; MADRID; SEVILLE; TOLEDO; and VALENCIA. *See also* LAS PALMAS; MAHÓN; PALMA DE MALLORCA; and SANTA CRUZ DE TENERIFE.

*

J. Rius: *Opera española* (Barcelona, 1841)
F. A. Barbieri: *La ópera española* (Madrid, 1880)
A. Peña y Goñi: *La ópera española y la música dramática en España en el siglo XIX* (Madrid, 1881, 2/1967 as *España desde la ópera a la zarzuela*)
F. Pedrell: *Teatro lírico español anterior al siglo xix* (La Coruña, 1897–8)
E. Cotarelo y Mori: *Origenes y establecimiento de la ópera en España hasta 1800* (Madrid, 1917)
——: *Historia de la zarzuela, ó sea el drama lírico* (Madrid, 1934) [also in *Boletín de la Real academia española*, xix–xxiii (1932–6)]
G. Chase: 'Origins of the Lyric Theater in Spain', *MQ*, xxv (1939), 292–312
J. Subirá: *Historia de la música teatral en España* (Barcelona, 1945)
N. D. Shergold: *A History of the Spanish Stage from Medieval Times until the End of the Seventeenth Century* (Oxford, 1967)
J. Sage: 'Nouvelles lumières sur la genèse de l'opéra et la zarzuela en Espagne', *Journées internationales d'étude du baroque: Montauban 1970*, 107–114
A. Fernandez-Cid: *Cien años de teatro musical en España* (Madrid, 1975)
J. Gomez: *Problemas de la ópera española* (Madrid, 1975)
J. López-Calo and J. Subirá: 'L'opera in Spagna', *Storia dell'opera*, ed. G. Barblan and A. Basso, ii/1 (Turin, 1977), 489–536
J. Sage: 'Seventeenth-Century Spanish Music Drama and Theatre', *IMSCR*, xii *Berkeley 1977*, 701–5
J. López-Calo: 'El italianismo operístico en España en el siglo XIX', *La ópera in España: Oviedo 1984*
X. M. Carreira: 'Centralismo y periferia en el teatro musical español del siglo XIX', *España en la musica de Occidente: Salamanca 1985*
D. Becker: 'Lo hispánico y lo italiano en el teatro lírico español del siglo XVII', *RdMc*, x (1986)
T. Marco: 'El teatro musical en España hoy', *La música para teatro in España: Cuenca 1986*, 701–8
M. Querol Gavaldá: 'Debate sobre el teatro lírico español del Barroco y las influencias musicales italianas', *La música para teatro in España: Cuenca 1986*, 559–62
C. M. Fernandez-Fernandez: 'Espectáculos, ópera y hospitales en España', *RdMc*, xiii (1989), 569–89
X. M. Carreira: 'El teatro de ópera en la Península Ibérica *ca.* 1750–1775: Nicolà Setaro', *De musica hispánica et aliis: miscelánea en honor al Prof. Dr. José López-Calo* (Santiago, 1990), ii, 27–117
L. K. Stein: 'Opera and the Spanish Political Agenda', *AcM*, lxiii (1991), 125–66
M. C. de Brito: 'La penisola iberica', *SOI*, ii (forthcoming)

EMILIO CASARES (1, 3), XOÁN M. CARREIRA (2, 4)

Spalato (It.). SPLIT.

Spangler, (Maria) Maddalena [Magdalena] **(Rosalie)** (*b* Vienna, 4 Sept 1750; *d* Vienna, 29 Aug 1794). Austrian soprano. The daughter of Johann Michael Spangler, who befriended Haydn in Vienna before his appointment at Eisenstadt, she was appointed at Eszterháza in September 1768, and left with her husband Karl Friberth in September 1776. Haydn wrote a number of roles for her, in which she usually played against her husband; her most elaborate was that of the minx Vespina in *L'infedeltà delusa*. An anonymous writer in the *Historisch-kritische Theaterkronik* noted her 'pleasant' voice and pretty figure, and remarked on her timidity on stage.

*

D. Bartha and L. Somfai: *Haydn als Opernkapellmeister* (Budapest, 1960)
H. C. R. Landon: *Haydn: Chronicle and Works*, ii: *Haydn at Eszterháza 1766–1790* (Bloomington, IN, 1978)

MARY HUNTER

Spani, Hina [Tuñón, Higinia] (*b* Puán, Buenos Aires, 15 Feb 1896; *d* Buenos Aires, 11 July 1969). Argentine soprano. She studied in Buenos Aires and in Italy, where in 1915 she made her début at La Scala as Anna in Catalani's *Loreley*. Returning to Argentina, she performed at the Teatro Colón, notably as Nedda (*Pagliacci*) with Caruso and Ruffo. After World War I she gained prominence among the lyric sopranos in Italy, while adding to her repertory Wagner's Elsa, Elisabeth and Sieglinde and such dramatic roles in Verdi as Aida and Amelia (*Ballo*). She reappeared at La Scala as Margherita in *Mefistofele* (1924), sang in France and Spain and toured Australia with Melba and the J. C. Williamson company (1928). In the 1930s she performed in Monteverdi's *L'incoronazione di Poppea* and *Orfeo*, Rameau's *Castor et Pollux* and (at the Colón) Verdi's *Oberto*. Her voice had a finely concentrated dramatic power with an exquisite pianissimo, and she was among the most stylish singers of her time.

*

W. Moran and R. Turró: 'Hina Spani', *Record Collector*, ix (1954), 81–99 [incl. discography]

J. B. STEANE

Spanish Lady, The. Unfinished opera in two acts by EDWARD ELGAR to a libretto by Barry Jackson based on BEN JONSON's play *The Devil is an Ass*; London, St John's, Smith Square, 15 May 1986.

The cast-list includes Fitzdottrel (bass), 'a middle-aged fool; vain and stupidly cunning'; Meercraft (baritone), 'a plausible rogue'; Wittipol (tenor), 'a sprightly young man'; Manly (tenor), 'a more solid young man'; Frances (soprano), 'a young lady of great estate and ward to Fitzdottrel who would wed her'; Lady Tailbush (mezzo-soprano), 'a lady of fashion desirous of freedom and fortune'; and Lady Eitherside (coloratura soprano), 'a much withered echo of Lady Tailbush and of vinegar spirit'. The plot, a savage indictment of the times in Ben Jonson's original, was made more respectable by Jackson. It concerns Meercraft's plans to cheat Fitzdottrel with fantastic schemes and make him duke of Drowndland. Wittipol is determined it is he who shall marry Frances and not Fitzdottrel; this he achieves by disguising himself as the Spanish lady of the title. Elgar aimed high: 'It is going to be very grand, and it is going to out-Meistersinger the Meistersinger'. He himself did much work on the libretto, tapping a range of sources, in Jonson and outside. For the music he used ideas sketched over a period of more than 50 years. The longest connected passage is a duet using material from a projected Simon of Gitta scene in *The Kingdom* (1906). Plans for the opera spanned the years 1929–33; it was abandoned because of the BBC commission for a Symphony no.3, also unfinished. ROBERT ANDERSON

Spartaco ('Spartacus'). *Dramma per musica* in three acts by GIUSEPPE PORSILE to a libretto by GIOVANNI CLAUDIO PASQUINI; Vienna, Kleines Hoftheater, 21 February 1726.

The former Roman slave and gladiator Spartacus (tenor), now ruler of Capua, is in love with his captive, Vetturia (soprano), a Roman woman of high birth. However, she loves Licinio (alto castrato), a Roman nobleman who has secretly entered Capua in advance of the Roman army. Disguised as Vetturia's brother, Licinio wins Spartacus's favour. Spartacus attempts to persuade his daughter Gianisbe (mezzo-soprano) to marry Licinio, but she prefers Popilio (alto castrato), a Capuan gentleman. As the Roman army enters Capua, Spartacus is driven mad; the pairs of lovers, however, are happily united.

The cast for Vienna included four internationally acclaimed singers: the mezzo-soprano Faustina Bordoni, the tenor Francesco Borosini, the soprano Regina Schoonjans and the alto castrato Gaetano Orsini. Porsile exploited their full vocal potential, requiring of Schoonjans high tessituras, of Borosini dramatic melodic leaps, and of all four singers extremely florid patterns and long-breathed phrases. The initial success of *Spartaco*, according to Zeno (*Lettere*, iv, 98), rested chiefly upon the beauty of Porsile's music and the brilliance of Faustina's singing. Giuseppe Galli-Bibiena was the scenic designer; there were ballets by Alessandro Philebois and Simone Pietro Levassori della Motta to music by Nicola Matteis.

Probably because of the Habsburgs' conservative taste and Fux's influence, Porsile's music seems comparatively old-fashioned, but in most respects *Spartaco* is representative of the period. In virtually all the arias and ensembles the orchestra plays in not only the ritornellos but also the vocal sections, often in the quasi-contrapuntal style favoured at the court. Although most of the arias are cast in the type of da capo form that was preferred in the 1720s, not all conform slavishly to that stereotype. For dramatic purposes Porsile frequently modified the number and length of ritornellos. His tendency towards greater structural freedom is most apparent in the Rodope-Trasone duet, 'Così oppresa'/'S'egli morto' (Act 3 scene x), and in the climactic aria of Spartacus's mad scene (Act 3 scene xi); here he abandoned the traditional da capo design and showed an adventurous approach to key relationships.

LAWRENCE E. BENNETT

Spasov, Bozhidar [Bojidar] (*b* Sofia, 13 Aug 1949). Bulgarian composer. In 1975 he graduated in composition from the Moscow Conservatory, then became a research associate at the Musicology Institute of the Bulgarian Academy of Sciences. Spasov is familiar with contemporary developments, including those of Stockhausen and Berio, and is representative of the generation of young Bulgarian composers of the 1970s and 80s in that he distances himself from his material to achieve musical clarity. His orientation is to the deeper levels of consciousness, specifically to medieval texts, whose complex semanticism he has sought to codify with a variety of effects and contrasts in instrumental and vocal music. In *Glagolicheskiyat kontsert* ('Glagolitic Concerto'), based on 13th-century sources, the solo female voice is intertwined in the multi-layered texture as an additional timbre, using the text as musical sound-material. The chamber opera-ballet *Omagyosaniyat* ('The Bewitched') is a parable about love, jealousy and unfaithfulness, and freedom and its denial. Dramatically it is close to Stravinsky, and the work may be seen as a mosaic of various compositional styles.

Omagyosaniyat [The Bewitched] (chamber opera-ballet, 1, Spasov, after *Malleus maleficarum*, *Carmina burana*, *Des Knaben Wunderhorn* and S. Brant: *Das Narren Schyff*), Moscow Conservatory, June 1975 (in Russ.); Dresden, Staatsoper, 1979 (in Ger.); Blagoevgrad, 30 Sept 1985 (in Bulg.); also television version

Printsesata i svinaryat, 1980 [The Princess and the Swineherd] (chamber opera-ballet, Spasov, after H. C. Andersen), unperf.

*

E. Schmidt: 'Vielfalt der Formen und Sujets', *Oper heute*, iv (1981), 141–78

MAGDALENA MANOLOVA

Spech, János (*b* Pozsony [now Bratislava], 18 Dec 1767; *d* Oberlimbach, 24 Nov 1836). Hungarian composer. He studied first in Pozsony, a lively centre of music, where operas were staged at a theatre which opened in 1776; weekly performances were given by Count Erdődy's company from 1787 – including works by Haydn, Mozart and Paisiello. These surroundings must have encouraged Spech's musical development, although in 1792 he became a clerk in Buda. He continued his music studies, however, completing them with Haydn in Vienna in 1800. After leaving Vienna (1804) he was a piano teacher in Buda and from 1809 a composer to Baron Podmaniczky. He was conductor at the German Town Theatre of Pest from 1812 to 1815 and during that period his first opera, *Ines és Pedro* (2, after S. Kisfaludy: *Tátika*; MS score in *A-Wgm*), was performed there as *Ines und Pedro, oder Die Johannisnacht* (30 March 1814). From 1816 to 1818 he lived in Paris, and his style must have been influenced by the French and Italian music there. He returned to Pest, where his light opera *Der Vogel des Bruder Philipp* was performed in the Town Theatre (11 June 1821). His other works for the theatre were the 'romantic fairy-tale' *Felizie* and an overture to Schink's *Der verlorene Sohn*. From 1824 he lived in Vienna.

Spech's music is basically Germanic, incorporating stylistic elements from late Mozart to Schubert, though not untouched by French and Hungarian influences.

*

J. Spech: 'A muzsikának mai állapotjáról s abbeli izléséről Párizsban' [On the Present State of Music and Taste in Paris], *Tudományos gyűjtemény* (Pest, 1822), no.4, pp.50–64 [Ger. version in *Allgemeine musikalische Zeitung mit besonderer Rücksicht auf den österreichischen Kaiserstadt*, vi (1822), 169–72, 177–9, 185–8, 193–5]
I. Bartalus: *Magyar Orpheus* (Pest, 1869) DEZSŐ LEGÁNY

Spech-Salvi [née Spech], **Adelina** (*b* Milan, 18 Aug 1811; *d* Bologna, Aug 1886). Italian soprano. She studied with her father, the tenor Giuseppe Spech. In the 1830s she sang at the S Carlo and at the Teatro Valle, Rome, where she created Eleonora d'Este in Donizetti's *Torquato Tasso* (1833). Her repertory included Norma and Amina (*La sonnambula*). She was married to the tenor Lorenzo Salvi. ELIZABETH FORBES

Special effects. *See* MACHINERY, §6.

Spelman, Timothy (Mather) (*b* Brooklyn, New York, 21 Jan 1891; *d* Florence, 21 Aug 1970). American composer. He studied with Harry Rowe Shelley in New York (1908), with Albert Spalding and Edward Burlingame Hill at Harvard (1909–13), and with Walter Courvoisier at the Munich Conservatory (1913–15). Several early stage works were produced during these years, including the melodrama *How Fair, How Fresh were the Roses*, the pantomime *Snowdrop* and the 'wordless fantasy' *The Romance of the Rose*. Spelman coached American military bands during World War I and in 1918 moved to Florence; he remained there for the rest of his life, except for the period 1935–47, when he lived in New York. In 1920 he wrote his first opera, *La magnifica* (vocal score, 1924), to a libretto by his wife, the poet Leolyn Louise Everett. A tale of political and amorous intrigue set in colonial South America, this one-act opera blends elements of Italian *verismo* and French impressionism in a style characteristic of Spelman's mature work. The Spelmans collaborated on many songs and at least two other dramatic works: *The Sea-Rovers* (1924), a three-act opera strikingly reminiscent of the Boito-Verdi *Otello*, and *Babakan* (1933), a one-act lyric comedy with an Arabian setting. Spelman himself wrote the librettos for *Lizzie Hexam* (4 acts, 1927–9), *The Sunken City* (3 acts, 1930) and *The Courtship of Miles Standish* (3 acts, after H. W. Longfellow, 1941). The Peabody Institute in Baltimore holds manuscript scores and sketches of several of his stage works. HARRY HASKELL

Spendiaryan [Spendiarov], **Alexander (Step'anos Afanas)** (*b* Kakhovka, Crimea, 20 Oct/1 Nov 1871; *d* Erevan, 7 May 1928). Armenian composer. With Komitas he is considered one of the founders of the 20th-century Armenian national school, though like his teacher Rimsky-Korsakov he explored east European folk styles as well as those of the Near East. On finishing his musical studies in 1900 he returned from St Petersburg to the Crimea, where he played an important part in the creation of musical and music-educational institutions. He also worked as a conductor. In 1916 Spendiaryan met the poet Hovhannes T'umanyan, on whose poem *T'mkaberdi arumê* ('The Capture of T'mkaberd'), in an adaptation by himself and S. Parnok, he was to base his opera *Almast*, which occupied him from about 1918 to the end of his life; it was completed by T. Akhumyan and performed in Moscow in 1930. In 1925 he was made a People's Artist of the Armenian SSR. Though some of his orchestral works were praised in their time for their imaginative post-Rimskian orientalism, it is for *Almast* that Spendiaryan is now chiefly remembered.

See also ALMAST.

*

E. Abasova: *Opera 'Almast' A. Spendiarova* (Baku, 1958)
STEPHEN JOHNSON

Speransky, Nikolay Ivanovich (*b* 18/30 July 1877; *d* Moscow, 5 March 1952). Russian bass-baritone and opera director. After early musical education in Saratov, he went to study law in Moscow, where he had lessons in singing from Camillo Everardi and Battistini and in piano from Rakhmaninov. He made his début in 1901 at the Moscow Private Opera, spent two years at the Tbilisi Opera, and returned to Moscow in 1905 as leading soloist with Zimin's opera company, where he created the roles of Dodon (*The Golden Cockerel*, 1909) and Suleyman in Ippolitov-Ivanov's *Izmena* ('The Betrayal', 1910). His repertory spanned almost the entire range of bass and baritone parts, from the Miller (*Rusalka*) and Kochubey (*Mazepa*) to Escamillo and Amonasro; in *Boris Godunov* he sang Varlaam and Rangoni, as well as the title role. He gave up singing in 1916 and devoted his time to organizing opera and teaching in provincial cities. From 1939 he taught at the Moscow Conservatory. BORIS SEMEONOFF

Speranza, Giovanni Antonio (*b* Mantua, 1811; *d* Milan, 1850). Italian composer. He studied at the Naples Conservatory under Zingarelli, and his first operas were produced there. Speranza composed with considerable regularity but, with the exception of the widely produced *I due Figaro* (1839), success eluded him. He belongs to a large group of his generation who retained the conventions of Rossini's time without succeeding in revitalizing them. He led a rather disorderly life and died insane.

La tragedia buffa (dg, 1, G. F. Schmidt), Naples, Nuovo, aut. 1833
Gianni di Parigi (dg, 2, F. Romani), Naples, Nuovo, spr. 1836
I due Figaro, ossia Il soggetto d'una commedia (melodramma giocoso, 2, Romani), Turin, Carignano, 30 Oct 1839
L'Aretino (melodramma giocoso, 2, G. Giachetti), Turin, Carignano, 17 Oct 1840
Il postiglione di Longjumeau (melodramma, 3, A. P.), Lucca, Pantera, 26 Dec 1841
Saul (tragedia lirica biblica, 2, Romani), Florence, Pergola, 8 April 1844
Il mantello, ovvero Lo sposo statua (ob, 2, F. Rubino), Turin, Sutera, carn. 1845
Scherzo melodrammatico (ob), Florence, Feb 1847
Yava [Java] (commedia, 2, G. di Giurdignano), Naples, Fondo, 2 April 1847
La figlia di Domenico, ossia Quattro prove per una recita (farsa, 1), Florence, Pergola, carn. 1848; rev. as Il padre dell'esordiente, Livorno, Rossini, Jan 1848
L'alloggio militare (ob, Torrignini), unperf.

WILLIAM ASHBROOK

Spetrino, Francesco (*b* Palermo, 2 July 1857; *d* Rome, 27 July 1948). Italian conductor and composer. He studied with Pietro Platania at the Palermo Conservatory. Most of his life was spent conducting theatre orchestras throughout Europe and in North America. From 1876 to 1892 he conducted in the major Italian theatres to great acclaim; he conducted at the Wielki

Theatre, Warsaw, for five years and at the Hofoper, Vienna (1903–8). In 1901 in Lemberg he conducted Paderewski's opera *Manrù* with great success. With Toscanini, he conducted at the Metropolitan Opera in the 1908–9 season. Spetrino composed two operas: *Filippo II*, which was performed in Palermo in 1876, and *Celeste*, to a libretto by A. Ghislanzoni, which was first staged in Bucharest in 1891. He also translated *Parsifal* into Italian for the publisher Sonzogno.

MARVIN TARTAK

Spezia-Aldighieri, Maria. *See* ALDIGHIERI, MARIA SPEZIA-.

Speziale, Lo **(i)** ('The Apothecary'). *Dramma giocoso per musica* in three acts by VINCENZO PALLAVICINI (Act 1) and DOMENICO FISCHIETTI (Acts 2 and 3) to a libretto by CARLO GOLDONI; Venice, Teatro Grimani di S Samuele, 26 December 1754.

The plot concerns an apothecary, Sempronio (bass), who is outwitted in his love for his ward Grilletta (soprano) by his assistant Mengone (tenor); a series of subplots involves Sempronio's daughter Albina (soprano) and her lover Lucindo (soprano), and alternative lovers, Volpino (tenor) and Cecchina (soprano), for the central couple. (For a fuller account of the story *see* SPEZIALE, LO (ii).)

This collaborative work was the first setting of Goldoni's highly successful libretto, which was commissioned in 1752 by the *buffo* singers Francesco Baglioni (*see* BAGLIONI family, (1)) and Francesco Carattoli (Sempronio and Mengone respectively), who then took the opera to a number of other Italian theatres where they continued to sing the lead roles. Lucindo was originally sung by a woman. Although the libretto gives Carnival 1755 as the date of the première, the original Venetian edition of Goldoni's complete works gives 1753, the date that the libretto was apparently printed. The opera was presented at the Haymarket in London in 1769 and in Treviso in 1779 as *Il bottanico novellista*.

GORDANA LAZAREVICH

Speziale, Lo **(ii)** [*Der Apotheker* ('The Apothecary')]. *Dramma giocoso* in three acts by JOSEPH HAYDN to a libretto by CARLO GOLDONI, possibly revised by CARL FRIBERTH; Eszterháza, autumn 1768.

Goldoni's libretto of 1752, first set by Fischietti and Pallavicini (Carnival 1755, Venice), was considerably altered and shortened for Haydn; the revisions were probably the work of the tenor, producer and librettist Carl Friberth, who sang Sempronio, the apothecary. The serious characters were removed, leaving just four singers. Apart from Sempronio (tenor), the plot includes Mengone, the apothecary's assistant (tenor, originally sung by Leopold Dichtler), Sempronio's foster daughter Grilletta (soprano, sung by Maddalena Spangler), and Volpino, a man-about-town and the ultimately disappointed lover (soprano; shortage of singers made this a trouser role, taken by Barbara Dichtler).

Mengone, a typical love-sick apprentice, is pounding powders as he sings; he has a low opinion of the industry and skill of his master, whose sole interests are reading the papers in search of exotic news and his ward, whom he intends to marry. His aria 'Questa e un'altro novità' includes an obvious pictorial device of a held note followed by a rising scale to *c''* to represent the expanse of the arena at Verona over the height of the tower at Cremona, conveyed by a drop of two octaves followed by a leap of an octave and a 6th. Volpino, under the pretence of having prescriptions made up, comes to see Grilletta, but Mengone keeps him at bay. In the best-known aria of the opera the latter sings the praises of a good laxative: 'Per quel che ha mal di stomaco' (Haydn wrote 'NB' at the appropriate point in his autograph score). When Grilletta enters, Volpino makes no headway, and she mocks him in a gently playful aria (there are two versions, the first with alternating Moderato assai and Presto sections, the other, written for the 1770 revival, marked Adagio, is gentler in spirit). Volpino's anger at being outwitted by Grilletta and Mengone is expressed in a fiery G minor aria. After his departure Grilletta and Mengone timidly admit their mutual attraction, but at Sempronio's sudden entry they are lucky to escape detection. In the trio finale they are caught hand in hand when the apothecary returns from fetching something. The finale is an agreeable three-section number, increasing in tempo.

In Act 2 Volpino draws an affronted refusal when he asks Sempronio for Grilletta's hand, but tries to worm his way back into favour by telling a choice anecdote from France, in an elegant 6/8 Allegretto in E major; here, for the first time, a flute joins the oboes and horns in the orchestral texture. Sempronio responds to Volpino's tale by singing an aria in which he claims to be wise to girls' tricks: a stick brings them back to their senses. Grilletta calls Mengone's bluff and bids him leave her in an aria through which tenderness gleams. She says that Mengone must be taught a lesson, but she goes further than she intends when she accepts Sempronio's proposal of marriage. The notary who has been summoned turns out to be Volpino in disguise. Mengone also appears as a notary, to Volpino's annoyance. The quartet finale opens with the apothecary dictating his marriage contract, each notary making a copy. The double deception is recognized, and the act ends in confusion.

Only two numbers survive from Act 3, though the libretto is complete. Lost are, apart from some recitatives, an aria for Sempronio and a duet for Grilletta and Mengone. The aria that does survive is a mock-Turkish one for a disguised Volpino, a delightful and impressively short number in which a bassoon makes its first and only specified appearance. Sempronio agrees that Grilletta should be given in marriage to a Turk – it turns out to be Mengone, of course. Volpino and Sempronio can only agree, in the brief finale, that they have been outwitted by the happy young couple.

Although *Lo speziale* survives in an incomplete form, it has probably been given more times than the rest of the Haydn operatic canon together, thanks to the German edition of Robert Hirschfeld as *Der Apotheker* (1895), which was taken up by Mahler, Weingartner and others, and has lived on after 1945 in performances by the Vienna Boys' Choir. First performed to inaugurate the new opera house, the only later performances known from Haydn's lifetime were two given by the Esterházy musicians at Baron Sumerau's Vienna residence on 21 and 22 March 1770. *Lo speziale* was recorded by Hungaroton under György Lehel in 1978 and has been revived in Batignano and Vienna (1980), Cheltenham (by the Warsaw Chamber Opera, 1982) and London (Musica nel Chiostro, 1984); it was staged at Stoke by Nayland in 1991 by Opera Restor'd.

PETER BRANSCOMBE

Spiegel von Arkadien, Der ('The Mirror from Arcadia'). *Heroisch-komische Oper* in two acts by

FRANZ XAVER SÜSSMAYR to a libretto by EMANUEL SCHIKANEDER; Vienna, Freihaus-Theater auf der Wieden, 14 November 1794 (text revised by CHRISTIAN AUGUST VULPIUS as *Die neuen Arkadier*, Weimar, Hoftheater, 2 February 1796).

Enjoying over a hundred performances by 1804, this work was one of the most successful of the many operas produced in the wake of *Die Zauberflöte* at the Freihaus-Theater in the 1790s. The story focusses on two couples: a noble pair, Ballamo (tenor) and Philanie (soprano), and a comic duo, the viper-catchers Metallio (bass) and Giganie (soprano). Jupiter (bass), Juno (soprano) and two genii (sopranos) descend to assist these Arcadians against the evil Tarkeleon (bass). In the opera's central intrigue Tarkeleon provides Metallio with a magic mirror that gives him, when he speaks to a woman, the outward appearance of the man she loves. This device incites jealousy in Ballamo – he hears Philanie expressing her love to Metallio, whom, because of the mirror, she sees as Ballamo. When Ballamo shuns her, the distraught Philanie chooses to pursue the island's 'Path to Evil' and ends up imprisoned in Tarkeleon's palace. Although Ballamo attempts to rescue her, the gods must intervene to punish Tarkeleon and reunite the couple. Süssmayr's music follows the precedent set by Mozart in *Die Zauberflöte*, drawing especially on the German folk and Italian lyrical styles.

LINDA TYLER

Spieloper (Ger.). Term used for a 19th-century comic opera with spoken dialogue between set musical numbers; there is no clear distinction between *Spieloper* and SINGSPIEL. Examples include Kreutzer's *Das Nachtlager in Granada* (1834), Lortzing's *Zar und Zimmermann* (1839) and *Der Wildschütz* (1842), Flotow's *Martha* (1847), Nicolai's *Die lustigen Weiber von Windsor* (1849) and Cornelius's *Der Barbier von Bagdad* (1858). It has also been used for non-German works such as Berlioz's *Béatrice et Bénédict* (1862) and Smetana's *The Bartered Bride* (1866).

The term has alternatively been applied in the sense of an all-sung opera as opposed to one with spoken dialogue (a *Sprechoper*).

Spiel von Liebe und Tod, Ein. Opera by Ján Cikker; *see* HRA O LÁSKE A SMRTI.

Spielwerk, Das. 'Mysterium' in one act by FRANZ SCHREKER to his own libretto; Munich, National, 30 October 1920 (revised version of *Das Spielwerk und die Prinzessin*, in two acts with sung Prelude, Vienna and Frankfurt, 15 March 1913).

An internal dream-interlude from the first version became the overture to this complex symbolic fantasy, in which the power of music is presented both as the intoxicant of the nihilistic, erotomane Princess (soprano) – particularly when emanating from Meister Florian's strange mechanical music-box – and the gift of a young wayfarer (tenor), who redeems her with his innocently simple flute-playing. A schematized succession of scenes leads to a transfiguring round-dance of life and love, set against the moving lullaby of Old Liese (contralto), comforting the soul of her recently dead son, whose apparition had halted a mob intent upon burning the ambivalent 'Spielwerk'.

PETER FRANKLIN

Spiess, Ludovic (*b* Cluj, 13 May 1938). Romanian tenor. He was trained in Braşov and Bucharest, then studied further (1965–6) in Milan with Antonio Narducci. He made his stage début at the Musical Theatre of Braşov in 1962 and sang with the Bucharest Operetta Theatre (1962–4), notably in *Der Zigeunerbaron* and Dendrino's *Let me Sing*; he joined the Bucharest Opera in 1964. Karajan chose him to sing Grigory in *Boris Godunov* at the 1967 Salzburg Festival, and he has sung Radames at the Vienna Staatsoper, the Metropolitan and Covent Garden (début, 1973). A dramatic tenor with a naturally forceful voice and a clear upper register, he also sings Cavaradossi, Rodolfo, Calaf, Lohengrin and Florestan.

VIOREL COSMA

Spinalba [*La Spinalba, ovvero Il vecchio matto* ('Spinalba, or The Old Madman')]. *Dramma comico* in three acts by FRANCISCO ANTÓNIO DE ALMEIDA to a libretto by an unknown author; Lisbon, Palácio da Ribeira, Carnival 1739.

The action takes place in Rome. Spinalba (soprano) disguises herself as a man in order to enter the service of her unfaithful Roman lover, Ippolito (tenor). Her father, the Florentine merchant Arsenio (bass), does not know where she is, and as a result becomes mad with grief. Other characters involved in the plot include Spinalba's mother, Dianora (mezzo-soprano), her cousin Elisa (soprano), Elisa's lover Leandro (tenor), and the servants Vespina (soprano) and Togno (bass).

One of the first Italian operas performed in Portugal, at King João V's court, *La Spinalba* is the only opera by Almeida that has survived complete. Written six years after Pergolesi's *La serva padrona*, it is close in style to that intermezzo and reflects the Italian patterns of the time, with abundant use of *secco* recitative and a predominance of da capo arias. But there are also strophic and bipartite arias, for Togno (Act 1 scene viii) and Vespina (Act 1 scene vi) respectively, and each act ends with an ensemble. The pronounced lyricism of the work is apparent from the start in Spinalba's first aria. Since the rediscovery of the score in the 1960s *La Spinalba* has been widely revived in Europe.

LUISA CYMBRON

Spinazzari, Alessandro (*fl* 1672–4). Italian composer. The published librettos of three operas by him survive: *L'Alcatrasso geloso* (C. A. Marchesini; 1672, Vicenza, *US-Wc*); *Agripina minore* (Marchesini; 15 Oct 1673, Verona, *I-Mb*); and *La più giusta vendetta contro i più crudi tiranni* (P. A. Bettanini; Dec 1674, Vicenza, *Mb*). He contributed music to a setting of Nicolò Minato's libretto *Iphide Greca* which also had music by Freschi, Partenio and Gasparo Sartorio and was performed in Verona on 22 October 1675. According to the Minato libretto he was *maestro di cappella* at Vicenza in 1674.

Spindler, (Franz) Stanislaus (*b* Steingaden, 4 May 1763; *d* Strasbourg, 8 Sept 1819). German composer. From 1782 he worked as a singer or opera director at various theatres, including those in Augsburg, Regensburg, Innsbruck and Brno, where he continued his studies with Dittersdorf. From 1793 to 1797 he worked at Breslau, where he sang, among other roles, Tamino, and then, after a stage accident and a period as an invalid, 'from which he arose a bass' (Obituary, *AMZ*, xxi, 1819, col.698), Don Giovanni and Count Almaviva. After various interim engagements, he went via Vienna to Strasbourg, where in 1808 he became Kapellmeister at the cathedral.

Spindler's compositions, which are known only by title, include 16 stage works (mainly Singspiels), songs and church music. Spohr and several other contemporaries praised the Singspiel *Das Waisenhaus*, which was successfully produced at Strasbourg in 1807; Spindler then sent it to the Vienna Hoftheater, where it was rejected. However, its text (by Franz Moll), as the above-mentioned obituary and Spohr credibly state, was secretly copied in Vienna and reset by Weigl in 1808 (see Loewenberg).

Die Reue vor der Tat (Spl, 1, G. F. W. Grossmann, after M. Monvel), Frankfurt, 1783
Pyramus und Thisbe (melodrama), Innsbruck, National, 1785
Balders Tod, Augsburg, 1786
Kain und Abel (melodrama), Innsbruck, National, 1786
Die Liebe in der Ukraine (Spl, 4, H. C. Pleissner), Innsbruck, National, 1786
Der Wundermann (Spl, Spindler), Graz, Landständisches, April 1789
Freitags Reisen (Spl), Brno, 1790
Amor und graue Haare (komisches Spl, 2), Brno, Oct 1791
Der Liebhaber im Schlafrock (komische Oper, 2), Brno, 1791
Die vier Vormünder (komisches Spl, 2), Brno, 1792
Achmet und Zenaide, Breslau, 1796
Don Quixote (2), Breslau, 1797
Der Alte überall und nirgends (Zauberoper, 3, W. Vogel), Mannheim, 1807
Das Waisenhaus (2, F. Moll), Strasbourg, 1807
Der Triumph mütterlicher Liebe (Spl), Karlsruhe, 1 Oct 1808
Das Loch in der Mauer (2), Strasbourg, Deutsches, 1810

*

LoewenbergA; *MGG* (A. Würz); *StiegerO*
F. J. Lipowsky: *Baierisches Musik-Lexikon* (Munich, 1811)
L. Spohr: *Selbstbiographie*, i (Kassel, 1869), 243–4

KLAUS RÖNNAU

Spinelli, Nicola (*b* Turin, 29 July 1865; *d* Rome, 17 Oct 1909). Italian composer. On his mother's side he was related to the composers Bonifazio Asioli and Isidoro Rossi. His teachers included Ernesto Becucci and Luigi Mancinelli in Florence and Trouvé-Castellani and Giovanni Sgambati in Rome; he completed his studies with Costantino Palumbo and Paolo Serrao in Naples. His graduation piece, the comedy *I guanti gialli*, was performed at the conservatory in 1881. His first publicly performed work was *Labilia*. This was placed second to Mascagni's *Cavalleria rusticana* in a competition for one-act operas organized by the publisher Edoardo Sonzogno in 1888. It was performed on 7 May 1890 at the Teatro Costanzi in Rome, its success owing much to the conductor Leopoldo Mugnone and the singers Gemma Bellincioni (Labilia) and Roberto Stagno (Volello), the same artists who appeared in *Cavalleria* ten days later. In his review in *L'opinione* (11 May 1890) D'Arcais remarked that Spinelli, although as yet lacking a musical personality of his own, had achieved the rapidity of movement required by 'modern melodrama', and possessed the ability to link scenes together and to distribute tone colour.

Between 1889 and 1894 Spinelli made several successful tours as a pianist and conductor. He returned to the theatre with *A basso porto*, a *verismo* low-life tragedy, which received international acclaim, although critics drew attention to the difficulty, implicit in the libretto, of reconciling the squalor of the ambience and characters and their rough speech with their expression in verse. Spinelli started work on setting Luigi Illica's *La trilogia di Dorina*, but a serious illness impaired his mind and led to his early death.

See also A BASSO PORTO.

I guanti gialli (3, E. Golisciani), Naples, Conservatory, March 1881
Labilia (1, V. Valle, after a Corsican tale), Rome, Costanzi, 7 May 1890
A basso porto (3, E. Checchi, after G. Cognetti: *Scene napoletane*), in Ger. trans., Cologne, Stadt, 18 April 1894, vs (Leipzig, 1894); in It., Rome, Costanzi, 11 March 1895
La trilogia di Dorina (L. Illica), inc.

*

R. Celletti: 'Gli ultimi cent'anni', *Storia dell'opera*, ed. G. Barblan and A. Basso (Turin, 1977), iii/1, 282–98
V. Frajese: *Dal Costanzi all'Opera*, i: *Cronache, recensioni e documenti* (Rome, 1978), 111, 135–6

FRANCESCO BUSSI

Spinto (It.: 'pushed'). Term applied to voices with a capacity for power and incisiveness at dramatic climaxes. It is most often applied to a TENOR, and occasionally to a SOPRANO; it is not, as might be supposed, pejorative. Of the tenor, it indicates a type of voice which, though lacking the weight of a full heroic tenor, nevertheless has a quality that is more dramatically exciting than that of the pure lyric type. Roles for the 'spinto' (or 'lirico spinto') include Ernani, Don Alvaro in *La forza del destino*, Chénier, and Dick Johnson in *La fanciulla del West*; soprano roles include Leonora (*La forza del destino*) and Mimì. Among Italian tenors of the 20th century, Giovanni Martinelli (1885–1969) and Franco Corelli (*b* 1921) come under the heading.

J. B. STEANE

Spirito di contradizione, Lo ('The Spirit of Contradiction'). *Opera buffa* in three acts by Pietro Alessandro Guglielmi (*see* GUGLIELMI family, (1)) to a libretto by GAETANO MARTINELLI; Venice, Teatro S Moisè, Carnival 1766.

In 1763 Guglielmi had supplied the overture, three finales and one aria for Anfossi's *Lo sposo di tre e marito di nessuna*, to a libretto in Neapolitan dialect by Antonio Palomba. He used the same plot and the same finales and introductory ensembles for this Venetian version three years later. The plot revolves around a charlatan, Don Cesarino (tenor), who convinces three rich women, Lisetta, Cecchina (sopranos) and the Countess Flaminia (mezzo-soprano), that he is going to marry each one of them. His plan, to pocket all three dowries and to leave quickly, is achieved close to the end of the second act. The Act 2 finale consists of his capture and chastisement. Fortunately there are other men waiting for the deceived women: Orazio Capocchio (tenor), who loves Lisetta, the notary Agabito (tenor) who loves Cecchina but gets Nanetta (soprano), and Nanetta's brother, the governor Asdrubale (tenor), who gets Cecchina. Don Cesarino is banished 'a denti asciutti' (i.e. with no wife), and the Countess, having rejected the ignorant Asdrubale, also remains single. As befits the libretto, Guglielmi does not make strong contrasts between characters and the music never reaches extremes of either heroism or sentimentality. Although in Act 1 Orazio's aria and the Countess's cavatina tend respectively towards these two modes of expression even this variety seems motivated more by the need for musical diversity than by dramatic necessity. The arias are in a variety of binary-like and through-composed forms, with Guglielmi's characteristically concise melodies and lively accompaniments which punctuate the text with gestural motifs, or enliven the rhythmic background of the vocal line.

MARY HUNTER

Split (It. Spalato). City in Croatia. A theatrical tradition has existed in Split since medieval times. Since the middle of the 19th century Italian opera troupes have visited annually to perform contemporary repertory. Two theatres were built during the 19th century; at the time they were the largest in the Balkans. The Teatro Bajamonti was built in 1859 and burnt down in 1881; the Općinsko Kazalište (Municipal Theatre), built in 1893 in the neo-Renaissance style, was damaged by fire in 1970 and restored in 1979. Initially, the operas performed in the civic theatre were staged by companies from Italy, Zagreb, Osijek and Bohemia. In 1911 Split saw its first operatic première by a native composer, Josip Hatze's *Povratak*, performed by the Zagreb Opera. Before 1945, opera was given only intermittently because of financial problems. Only since 1945 has the Split Opera been a permanent company, building an extensive repertory of Italian, Slavonic and native opera. Since 1954 its performances have formed the nucleus of the Splitsko Ljeto (Split Summer) festival, held during July and August in the ancient and imposing courtyard of the palace of the Roman Emperor Diocletian, built in AD 305. As a stage this courtyard is spatially and acoustically unique; such operas as *Aida*, *Otello* and *Nabucco*, Boito's *Nerone* and Monteverdi's *L'incoronazione di Poppea* have been extremely effective.

*

Narodno kazalište Split 1893–1953 [The National Theatre in Split, 1893–1953] (Split, 1953)

B. Buljan: 'Splitska opera i njen 15-godišnji kontinuirani rad u periodu poslije Oslobodenja' [The Split Opera and its 15 Years of Continuous Activity in the Period after the Liberation], *Splitska scena*, viii (1961), 1–2

J. Andreis: *Music in Croatia* (Zagreb, 1974) KORALJKA KOS

Spohr, Louis [Ludewig, Ludwig] (*b* Brunswick, 5 April 1784; *d* Kassel, 22 Oct 1859). German composer. His parents were accomplished amateur musicians who fostered the development of his musical talent and encouraged his early efforts at composition. Among these was an abortive attempt to write a Singspiel after the pattern of J. A. Hiller's *Die Jagd* and *Lottchen am Hofe*, of which his mother possessed vocal scores. Shortly after Spohr's 13th birthday his father, a country doctor, sent him to Brunswick to be educated. Because he was already a good violinist he was soon allowed to play in the Brunswick theatre orchestra, and this became a regular part of his duties when he was appointed *Kammermusicus* at the Brunswick court in 1799. This experience led to a particular admiration for the operas of Mozart and Cherubini, composers who were to influence him significantly during the first phase of his development as an opera composer.

After a period of study with the Mannheim violinist Franz Eck, Spohr rapidly gained recognition as an outstanding violinist. During a concert tour to Leipzig and Berlin his playing and compositions were highly praised in the pages of the influential *Allgemeine musikalische Zeitung* and at the age of 21 he was appointed Konzertmeister to the ducal court in Gotha. This position offered him security (increased by his marriage to the talented harpist Dorothea [Dorette] Scheidler in 1806) and an enlarged scope for his compositional activities. Hitherto his compositions had been almost exclusively for the violin, but during his first few years in Gotha he broadened his range to include orchestral and vocal music. In furtherance of his suit for Dorette's hand he wrote a scena, *Oskar*, for her mother, a court singer, in 1805. Despite the fact that Gotha possessed no theatre, he composed a one-act operetta, *Die Prüfung*, in autumn 1806. It was performed at a court concert, but by then he was dissatisfied with it, and except for the overture, published as op.15, and a tenor aria (no.4), which he performed at a few subsequent concerts, he suppressed the piece.

Spohr's operatic aspirations soon reasserted themselves, however, and his next attempt was much more ambitious. *Alruna, die Eulenkönigin*, a 'grand Romantic opera' in three acts, was composed during summer and autumn 1808. Emboldened by the success of concert performances of sections of the work in Gotha, Spohr offered it for production at the theatre in nearby Weimar, where Goethe was Intendant. It was put into rehearsal, but Goethe's objections to the iambic verse of the libretto and Spohr's own growing dissatisfaction with the opera caused him to withdraw it. Only the overture was published, but other material was used in later works. Two more years elapsed before Spohr returned to operatic composition. By 1810 his reputation as a composer had grown considerably and during a concert tour to Hamburg early in 1810 he was commissioned to compose one of four operas for the opening of F. L. Schröder's new theatre company in 1811. After a number of alterations had been made to the not altogether satisfactory libretto, Spohr wrote the music of *Der Zweikampf mit der Geliebten* during winter 1810–11. The production, delayed until 15 November 1811, was well received, but Spohr himself was by no means satisfied, realizing too late how the work could have been improved. However, a vocal score was published in 1813 and, although the opera did not find a place in the repertory, a number of selections and arrangements were subsequently published.

Spohr's next opera, *Faust*, was composed in 1813 in Vienna, where he had been appointed to direct the orchestra of the Theater an der Wien the previous year. It marks a decisive stage in his development as an opera composer; for the first time he felt he had truly found his own operatic style and a satisfactory solution to the problems of theatrical composition. *Faust* received its première under Weber at Prague in 1816 while Spohr was on a concert tour in Italy. Having spent the years 1815–17 travelling and giving concerts, Spohr settled down again in 1818 as director of the Frankfurt opera. After his production there of *Faust* in 1818, for which he composed a new aria, 'Liebe ist die zarte Blüthe', the work began to gain wider appreciation and gradually achieved the status of a repertory piece. Spohr's appointment in Frankfurt encouraged him to look for another opera text. He began work on a libretto based on Apel's story *Der schwarze Jäger*, but when he heard that Weber was writing an opera (*Der Freischütz*) on the same subject he abandoned it. Instead he accepted a libretto by the Frankfurt theatre director J. J. Ihlée, based on Marmontel's *Zémire et Azor*, which had been set by Grétry in 1771. He completed *Zemire und Azor* in February 1819 and it was staged two months later. Spohr's skilful musical treatment of the story and its wealth of fine melodic writing won it a modest place in the German repertory until late in the century.

Spohr resigned his Frankfurt post shortly after the première of *Zemire und Azor* and was without a fixed position for the next three years. While visiting Paris in 1821 he came across Lemièrre's play *La veuve de Malabar*; he recognized its potential as an opera plot and when he moved to Dresden in October 1821 he asked a local literary amateur, Eduard Gehe, to turn it into a libretto. Work on it was briefly delayed by Spohr's appointment as Kapellmeister in Kassel in January 1822 (a post which he was to retain for the rest of his life) and the new opera, *Jessonda*, took shape more slowly than was usual with Spohr. As he recalled in his memoirs, he felt so convinced of the importance of this opera that he worked on it only when he felt really inspired; nevertheless, it was completed by the end of the year. Unlike his earlier operas, *Jessonda* was a grand opera, without spoken dialogue. German grand opera was rare at that time; among Spohr's contemporaries only Poissl and Mosel had made significant contributions to the genre, but neither of these composers was able to invest it with the necessary Romantic spirit and musical interest to achieve a lasting success. Schubert's flawed masterpiece *Alfonso und Estrella*, completed some ten months before *Jessonda*, was not produced in his lifetime. Weber's *Euryanthe*, completed a few months after *Jessonda*, contained much exceptionally fine music but was weighed down by an impossible libretto. Thus Spohr's *Jessonda*, which came to be regarded as his operatic masterpiece, stood alone during the 1820s and 30s as the one really successful German grand opera and is now acknowledged to be a significant forerunner of Wagner's music drama. It became a particular favourite of Brahms, was admired by Richard Strauss and remained in the German repertory until after World War I.

Shortly after returning from the triumphant Leipzig production of *Jessonda* in February 1824, Spohr received a request from the Elector of Hesse to compose a new opera for the celebration of his daughter's wedding in March 1825. The resulting work, *Der Berggeist*, continued musically in the direction Spohr had taken with *Jessonda*. At Spohr's request the librettist, Georg Döring, eschewed rhyming verse. The subject, however, was stale and the libretto uninspired, and, despite its initially enthusiastic reception, the opera failed to achieve the success of *Jessonda*. For his next two operas, *Pietro von Abano* (1827) and *Der Alchymist* (1830), Spohr reverted to the use of spoken dialogue, though it played a much smaller role than in his earlier works. Neither opera achieved the success he expected, but they both contain some excellent music and are by no means unstageworthy. In the case of *Pietro von Abano*, moral and religious objections to aspects of the text limited its circulation. The reasons for the failure of *Der Alchymist* are more difficult to discern; a reviewer of the vocal score firmly laid the blame for the opera's neglect on unimaginative theatre managements and an uncultured public. He observed that they preferred 'even very trivial foreign rubbish' while 'German works by really first-rate men are allowed to sleep peacefully for years' (*AMZ*, xxxiv, 1832, col. 689).

Discouraged by the unpropitious climate for German opera, which was exacerbated by the political upheavals of 1830, Spohr did not seriously consider writing for the stage again for almost 14 years. It seems likely that his last opera, *Die Kreuzfahrer*, in which he reverted to the grand-opera format, resulted partly from the stimulus of the young Richard Wagner, of whose *Der fliegende Holländer* Spohr had mounted a highly successful production in Kassel in June 1843. Together with his second wife, Marianne, Spohr himself adapted the libretto for *Die Kreuzfahrer* from Kotzebue's play of 1803. The opera was respectfully received and quietly forgotten. With his roots in an earlier aesthetic tradition (he found Wagner's avoidance of regular cadences distressing), Spohr had nothing more to contribute to the development of German opera. His final operatic effort was a new version of his *Faust*, which he was induced to make in 1852. At the request of Frederick Gye of the Royal Italian Opera in London, he replaced the spoken dialogue with musical sections and remodelled the opera in a number of ways, while retaining all the original music. Peters immediately published a vocal score and in its new form *Faust* was performed in other German theatres.

During the first quarter of the 19th century Spohr was in the forefront of developments in German Romantic opera. He drew his initial inspiration from German Singspiel, from Mozart and from French opera, particularly Cherubini, and in his first three operas he formed his own distinctive style and approach. His mature musical language, which was highly chromatic but firmly wedded to Classical principles, was capable of great expressiveness; it became an alluring model for younger composers and pointed the way for Wagner's more radical development of chromaticism. Structurally, Spohr strove for continuity and dramatic cohesiveness; he moved away from the concept of opera as a string of individual, self-contained numbers. His concern for scene-building is evident as early as *Alruna*, and in his subsequent works he moved increasingly towards the idea of opera as a connected series of open-ended units. This led logically to his championship of grand opera and his crucial role in the creation of a model for German Romantic grand opera with *Jessonda*. Another important product of Spohr's concern for continuity and coherence was his exploration of the idea of musical motif as a form of unification. The highly sophisticated scheme of motifs that he developed in *Faust* seems to have no obvious precedent in earlier opera; it went far beyond the use of musical reminiscence employed in late 18th-century French opera. But the originality of Spohr's procedure in *Faust*, and its importance for the later development of leitmotif, have not been widely appreciated. Weber, who recognized its significance in 1816, adopted a similar approach in *Der Freischütz* and especially in *Euryanthe*, but it was left to Wagner to exploit it more fully in his mature operas.

Although they contain much fine music and are by no means unstageworthy, Spohr's operas have not stood the test of time. Some of them are fine examples of early Romantic opera (notably *Faust*, *Zemire und Azor* and *Jessonda*) and are arguably worthy of revival. But Spohr lacked Weber's flair for theatrical effect; he often painted his musical canvas in too great detail where a bolder, perhaps even cruder, stroke would have been more telling.

See also FAUST (i); JESSONDA; PIETRO VON ABANO; and ZEMIRE UND AZOR.

Edition: *Selected Works of Louis Spohr (1784–1859)*, ed. C. Brown and others (New York, 1988–90) [SB]

Die Prüfung (Operette, 1, E. Henke), Gotha, 1806, *D-Ksp**, ov. pubd as op.15 (Bonn, 1809)

Alruna, die Eulenkönigin, 1808 (grosse romantische Oper, 3), unperf., *US-Bp**, ov. pubd as op.21 (Offenbach, 1812)

Der Zweikampf mit der Geliebten (3, J. F. Schink), Hamburg, 15 Nov 1811, autograph (private collection), *D-B*, vs (Hamburg, n.d.)

Faust, 1813 (romantische Oper, 2, J. C. Bernard), Prague, Estates Theatre, 1 Sept 1816, vs (Leipzig, 1822), ov. pubd as op.60 (Leipzig, 1857); rev. 1852 as 3-act grosse Oper, CG, 15 July 1852, vs (Leipzig, 1853); SB i

Zemire und Azor (romantische Oper, 2, J. J. Ihlée, after J. F. Marmontel: *Zémire et Azor*), Frankfurt, 4 April 1819, *Mbs*, vs (Hamburg, n.d.)

Jessonda (grosse Oper, 3, E. Gehe, after A.-M. Lemièrre: *La veuve de Malabar*), Kassel, Hof, 28 July 1823, vs (Leipzig, 1824), full score (Leipzig, 1881/*R*1988: SB ii)

Der Berggeist (romantische Oper, 3, G. Döring), Kassel, Hof, 24 March 1825, *Mbs*, vs (Leipzig, 1827)
Pietro von Abano (romantische Oper, 2, C. Pfeiffer, after L. Tieck), Kassel, Hof, 13 Oct 1827, *F-Pn**/R1989: SB iii, vs (Berlin, 1831)
Der Alchymist (romantische Oper, 3, F. G. Schmidt [pseud. of Pfeiffer], after W. Irving: *The Student of Salamanca*), Kassel, Hof, 28 July 1830, *D-B*, vs (Berlin, 1831)
Die Kreuzfahrer (grosse Oper, 3, L. Spohr and M. Spohr, after A. von Kotzebue), Kassel, Hof, 1 Jan 1845, *B*, vs (Hamburg, 1845)

*

I. J. Ebers: *Spohr und Halévy* (Breslau, 1837)
W. H. Riehl: 'Zwanzig Jahre aus der Geschichte der romantischen Oper, III: Spohr, Weber und Meyerbeer', *Musikalische Charakterköpfe*, i (Stuttgart, 1853, 8/1899), 332–400
L. Spohr: *Selbstbiographie*, i–ii (Kassel and Göttingen, 1860–61; Eng. trans., 1865, 2/1878); ed. E. Schmitz (1954–5) [abridged adaptation of *Lebenserinnerungen*, autograph MS, lost]
——: 'Briefe L. Spohrs an das Haus Peters in Leipzig', *AMZ*, new ser., ii (1867), 290–91
A. Schöne, ed.: *Briefe von Moritz Hauptmann an Franz Hauser*, i-ii (Leipzig, 1871)
F. Hiller, ed.: *Briefe von Moritz Hauptmann an Louis Spohr und andere* (Leipzig, 1876)
La Mara [pseud. of M. Lipsius]: 'Aus Spohrs Leben', *Classisches und Romantisches aus der Tonkunst* (Leipzig, 1892)
P. Spitta: 'Jessonda', *Zur Musik* (Berlin, 1892), 235–66
W. Altmann: 'Spohrs Beziehungen zur Generalintendantur der Königl. Schauspiele zu Berlin', *NZM*, lxxi (1904), 199–202
R. Wassermann: *Louis Spohr als Opernkomponist* (diss., U. of Rostock, 1909)
E. Istel: 'Fünf Briefe Spohrs an Marschner', *Festschrift ... Rochus Freiherrn von Liliencron* (Leipzig, 1910), 110–15
E. Schmitz: 'Louis Spohrs Jugendoper Alruna', *ZIMG*, xiii (1911–12), 293–9
E. Speyer: *Wilhelm Speyer der Liederkomponist* (Munich, 1925)
S. Goslich: *Beiträge zur Geschichte der deutschen romantischen Oper, zwischen Spohrs 'Faust' und Wagners 'Lohengrin'* (Leipzig, 1937)
E. Schmitz: 'Louis Spohrs erster Opernversuch', *AMf*, vii (1942), 84–9
F. Uhlendorff: 'Kasseler Kapelle, Kapellmeister und Konzertmeister im Zeitraum 1814–1852', *Festschrift 450 Jahre heissischer Staatskapelle* (Kassel, 1952)
——: 'Chronik des Kasseler Musiktheaters 1814–1944', *Theater in Kassel* (Kassel, 1959)
F. Göthel, ed.: *Louis Spohr: Briefwechsel mit seiner Frau Dorette* (Kassel, 1957)
D. Greiner: *Louis Spohrs Beiträge zur deutschen romantischen Oper* (diss., U. of Kiel, 1960)
R. Lebe: *Ein deutsches Hoftheater in Romantik und Biedermeier* (Kassel, 1964)
A. A. Abert: 'Webers "Euryanthe" und Spohrs "Jessonda" als grosse Opern', *Festschrift für Walter Wiora* (Kassel, 1967), 435–40
F. Göthel, ed.: *L. Spohr: Lebenserinnerungen* (Tutzing, 1968)
C. Brown: 'Spohr's "Jessonda"', *MT*, cxxi (1980), 94–7
F. Göthel: *Thematisch-bibliographisches Verzeichnis der Werke von Louis Spohr* (Tutzing, 1982)
C. Brown: *Louis Spohr: a Critical Biography* (Cambridge, 1984)
——: 'Spohr, Faust and Leitmotif', *MT*, cxxv (1984), 25–7

CLIVE BROWN

Spoleto. Italian city in the province of Perugia, Umbria. There is evidence for musical and theatrical performances given in the palaces of the nobility from the end of the 16th century under the aegis of the Accademia degli Ottusi. In 1639, having been banished to Spoleto, Loreto Vittori composed his opera *La Galatea* there. The Accademia was also responsible for the construction of the Teatro de' Nobili in the Piazza del Duomo, built over the remains of the Palazzo della Signoria which had been left unfinished in the 14th century. Authorization for its construction was granted on 8 March 1657; for Carnival 1661 Francesco Vannarelli's *La Fedra* was performed there. The rectangular wooden hall was altered to a horseshoe shape in 1667 and equipped with 60 boxes in four tiers. In 1737 the theatre staged Pergolesi's intermezzo *La serva padrona*. Between 1749 and 1751 the number of boxes was increased from 15 to 18 per tier, and the theatre was re-inaugurated in autumn 1751 with Niccolò Jommelli's *Ipermestra*, composed for the occasion. Subsequent productions included Gioacchino Cocchi's *Farsetta in musica* and, for Carnival 1783, Cimarosa's *Il pittor parigino*. The theatre was again restored and reopened in 1802 with *I tre Orfei* by Marcello Bernardini. In the 19th century operas by Donizetti, Verdi, Bellini and Rossini were performed there. 1880 saw the completion of a reconstruction in masonry of the old wooden theatre, which had gradually become unusable; it was renamed the Teatro Cajo Melisso.

The Teatro Nuovo, designed by Ireneo Aleandri, was built in 1854–64 on the site of the church of the monastery of Sant'Andrea, itself built on Roman foundations. On a horseshoe plan, it has four tiers of boxes and about 1200 seats. The theatre was inaugurated on 3 August 1864 with a season of opera and ballet consisting of Errico Petrella's *Ione*, Verdi's *Il trovatore*, and *Giusemberga da Spoleto*, composed for the occasion by Filippo Sangiorgi. Every year performances are given there by the Teatro Lirico Sperimentale, a group founded in 1947 to provide opportunities for young singers.

It was as a result of this enterprise that Gian Carlo Menotti chose Spoleto as the seat of the Festival dei Due Mondi (Festival of Two Worlds), which was inaugurated in 1958 and takes place in June and July each year. The festival, experimental in character, revolves around music drama with the addition of chamber and symphony concerts, as well as ballet, plays, films and exhibitions. An important catalyst of the festival was Thomas Schippers, artistic director until 1965 and musical director until 1975. The artistic direction, after being in the hands of Menotti in 1966 and 1967, passed to Massimo Bogianckino (1968–71), Romolo Valli (1972–8), Rafaello de Banfield (1979) and Menotti (1984). The musical director from 1978 was Christian Badea, who was succeeded in 1987 by Spiros Argiris.

The collaboration of Luchino Visconti as director was also very important. He staged *Macbeth* for the inaugural festival (1958), followed by *Il duca d'Alba* (1959), *Salome* (1961), *La traviata* (1963) and *Manon Lescaut* (1973). Other memorable productions at the Festival were *Don Giovanni* with scenery by Henry Moore (1961), *Carmen* with Shirley Verrett (1962) and revivals of forgotten or little-known operas such as Donizetti's *Il furioso all'isola di San Domingo* (1967), Mercadante's *Il giuramento* (1970), Bizet's *Le Docteur Miracle* (1975), Cavalli's *L'Erismena* (1980) and *L'Ormindo* (1984), Gluck's *L'ivrogne corrigé* (1981), Gounod's *La colombe* (1982), Rameau's *Platée* (1986) and Graun's *Montezuma* (1987). Contemporary works, particularly those of Menotti, have also been well-attended. The custom has arisen of identifying each year of the festival by the name of the most important opera performed. The old Teatro Cajo Melisso, having declined into use as a cinema, was restored by Roberto De Luca in time for the first festival. The horseshoe-shaped auditorium is in late 19th-century style and the foyer communicates by means of a staircase with the floor below, the Sala dei Armigeri of the old Palazzo della Signoria. Productions are also staged in churches and the Roman theatre, the castle and gardens of the city, making the festival a unique attraction in the panorama of summer festivals in Italy. In May 1977 the festival was expanded to Charleston, South Carolina (representing the other of the two worlds); productions from Spoleto are performed there each year during May and June.

*

ES

O. Sansi: *Il teatro nuovo di Spoleto: notizie cronistoriche dal 1840 al 1864* (Spoleto, 1914)

——: *Il Nobile Teatro di Spoleto* (Spoleto, 1922)

L. Fausti: 'Memorie storiche dell' Accademia Spoletina', *Atti dell'Accademia Spoletina (1923–26)* (Spoleto, 1926)

O. Sansi: 'Notizie cronistoriche aggiunte al Nobile Teatro di Spoleto', ibid

M. Rinaldi: 'Storia di un teatro', *La Scala* (1953), no.44, pp.15–18

C. Jolly: 'The Festival of Two Worlds', *Opera*, ix (1958), 551–7

W. Weaver: '25 anni di musica', *Spoleto Festival 1982* (Spoleto, 1982), 65–83

M. Natale, ed.: *Spoleto trent'anni di Festival: gli spettacoli, gli autori, i partecipanti, gli artisti 1958–1987* (Spoleto, 1987)

GALLIANO CILIBERTI, PAOLO GALLARATI

Spoleto Festival. American branch of Menotti's Festival of Two Worlds, situated in CHARLESTON, South Carolina, since 1977.

Spontini, Gaspare (Luigi Pacifico) (*b* Maiolati, near Iesi, 14 Nov 1774; *d* Maiolati, 24 Jan 1851). Italian composer. He dominated serious grand opera of the early 19th century in Paris and later in Berlin.

1. 1774–1802: Italy. 2. 1803–20: Paris. 3. 1820–42: Berlin. 4. 1842–51: Return to Italy. 5. Works.

1. 1774–1802: ITALY. The son of an artisan and smallholder, Spontini was destined for the church, but when his musical talent came to be recognized, in 1793, he entered the Conservatorio della Pietà dei Turchini in Naples. Here he composed various *opere buffe*, the first of which was performed in Rome in 1796. The Bourbon court moved temporarily from Naples to Palermo in 1798, and there is evidence that Spontini was there too in 1800, before he moved to Paris at the end of 1802. At least 12 of his operas had their first performances in Italy, and it seems that he must have visited Rome, Florence and perhaps Venice between 1796 and 1802 – although little research has been done into the details of his early career or the dates of performance of several of his works (many of the scores are not preserved). Nor is much known for certain about his teachers. He must have been taught by Nicola Sala and Giacomo Tritto at the conservatory; his later claim that he was a pupil of Cimarosa cannot be substantiated. In any event, he won no more than occasional recognition in the first six years of his career, and in no way stood out among the many minor operatic composers who were his contemporaries.

2. 1803–20: PARIS. Spontini began his career in Napoleonic Paris by giving singing lessons. His first success came in 1804, at the Théâtre Italien, with a revised version of *La finta filosofa*. But his first French-language work, *La petite maison*, ran into widespread anti-Italian feeling at its troubled first performance, on 12 May 1804, and had only three performances in all (though the fiasco at least made Spontini better known). *Milton*, described as a *fait historique*, was first performed at the Opéra-Comique in the same year. Its librettist, Etienne de Jouy, further offered Spontini a libretto he had already written for *La vestale*. After writing his last work in the Italian *opera buffa* style in 1805 (*Julie, ou Le pot de fleurs*), Spontini devoted himself to work on *La vestale*, his first *tragédie lyrique*, which was completed in draft in 1805, the year in which he was first described as *compositeur particulier de la chambre* to the Empress Josephine. Josephine's patronage, to which Spontini responded with such occasional works as the cantata *L'eccelsa gara* and the vaudeville *Tout le monde a tort* (both 1806), proved a decisive influence on his career; only Josephine's persistent intervention brought about the long-delayed first performance of *La vestale* on 15 December 1807. The work's triumphant success meant that Spontini was now seen as one of the leading composers in Paris, and he was commissioned to provide propaganda for Napoleon's Spanish campaign in the form of an opera about Hernán Cortés and his conquest of Mexico. Napoleon himself, with the kings of Saxony and Westphalia, attended the première of *Fernand Cortez* on 28 November 1809.

Although *Fernand Cortez* was taken out of the repertory in 1810, that year proved to be the peak of Spontini's career. In February he was appointed *directeur de la musique de l'opéra buffa* at the Théâtre de l'Impératrice and was able to put his ideas for repertory – concentrating on performances of Cimarosa and Mozart – into practice at the Théâtre Italien. In July he was awarded a newly created prize for the best opera of the decade, for *La vestale*, and in the same month he married Marie-Cathérine-Céleste Erard, daughter of the pianoforte maker and publisher Jean-Baptiste Erard. After Napoleon's fall from power Spontini withdrew from the public eye for some time, but he greeted the return of the Bourbon kings in August 1814 with *Pélage* and he was restored for a time to the position at the Théâtre Italien which he had given up in 1812. After collaborating on the opera *Les dieux rivaux* (1816), written for the wedding of the heir to the throne, and achieving success with a new version of *Fernand Cortez* and an adaptation of Salieri's *Les Danaïdes* (both 1817), he obtained French naturalization in November 1817 and in May 1818 was granted a pension by the king.

As early as 1814, the King of Prussia had invited Spontini to Berlin. For some time he delayed making a decision, but he accepted the appointment in 1819, when his tacit hopes for a prominent position in the musical life of Paris were becoming increasingly nebulous and the production of *Olimpie* had run into various difficulties; it was eventually performed on 22 December 1819, when it was attacked by liberal reviewers. Spontini took up his position in Berlin on 1 February 1820.

3. 1820–42: BERLIN. As the leading court musician, with the title of Generalmusikdirektor, Spontini was warmly welcomed by King Friedrich Wilhelm III and by many of the city's intellectuals such as E. T. A. Hoffmann. But he also came under attack, even more vigorously than he had during his last years in Paris. Leading critics expressed resentment at the status accorded to a foreigner, whom they despised as an interloper, drawing a contrast with the circumstances of Weber and the emerging German Romantic opera. In the musical running of the Hofoper, conflicts with the administrator Brühl (who had been opposed to Spontini's appointment) were inevitable, since their spheres of jurisdiction were never clearly delineated. Nevertheless, Spontini's three main Parisian works, *La vestale*, *Fernand Cortez* and *Olimpie*, were frequently performed, and he also won recognition as a conductor of the operas of other composers. His own creative rhythm, however, was slowing down. Of the operas he wrote in Berlin, all first

performed on the occasion of royal weddings, neither *Nurmahal* (1822) nor *Alcidor* (1825) was popular with the general public, nor was *Agnes von Hohenstaufen*, although after the première of its first act on 28 May 1827 Spontini repeatedly revised it, as perseveringly as he had previously revised *Fernand Cortez* and *Olimpie*.

When Brühl left the Hofoper in 1828, Spontini, who had no aptitude for intrigue, became even more entangled in conflicts with his successor, Redern, and was the target of increasingly virulent attacks led by the critic Rellstab. Worse was to come after the king's death in June 1840. Some phrases in a statement Spontini had made (he was not proficient in German) led to his being accused of *lèse majesté*, and on 2 April 1841 the audience drove him out of the opera house after the overture to a performance of *Don Giovanni*. In July he was sentenced to nine months' imprisonment and dismissed from his post. However, in May 1842 Friedrich Wilhelm IV lifted the sentence, which had been confirmed by the court of appeal. He had already, in August 1841, guaranteed the continued payment of Spontini's salary despite his dismissal.

4. 1842–51: RETURN TO ITALY. In 1842, as none of his previous hopes for a triumphant return to Paris had materialized, the embittered Spontini had to acknowledge that his day in France was long since over. In disregard of the facts, however, he ascribed the general lack of interest in his work entirely to intrigue, for which he held Meyerbeer chiefly responsible, and he took refuge in an exaggerated sense of self-esteem (satirized in Wagner's reminiscences of his visit to Dresden in November 1844). Notable among the many distinctions Spontini received in these years was his appointment by the pope to the title of Count of San Andrea on 21 January 1845. After some years spent alternately in Paris and travelling, he returned to his birthplace in the Papal States (to which he had already sent generous donations) in September 1850. In 1939, in recognition of the improvements Spontini had made possible, the town was renamed Maiolati Spontini.

5. WORKS. In Italy Spontini, like any other professional opera composer, had met the demand for new operas with scores that only occasionally add individual touches to the established style of Neapolitan opera around 1800. A gulf seems to separate this early phase from his later works. Although some of the early works already contain expressive accompanied recitatives, *sforzati* on unstressed beats and large-scale instrumental combinations, they hardly foreshadow the great qualitative stride the composer was to take in Paris.

In Paris, he began by writing works related to his *opere buffe*, such as *La petite maison* and *Julie*; but in *Milton*, an opera which, well before Berlioz's *Benvenuto Cellini* and Wagner's *Tannhäuser*, treats the issue of the artist's role in society, he revealed a high-minded attitude for which there is no precedent in his only serious opera before that date, *Teseo riconosciuto*. However, Spontini did not excite much attention until *La vestale*. In this work he succeeded in reviving the spirit of the *tragédie lyrique* of the Gluck era, retaining the pathetic declamatory style of that genre yet at the same time incorporating the characteristic pomp of many post-Revolutionary French operas, with their solemn hymns. He succeeded in combining rhetorical grandeur with a fundamentally Italian melodic style in which 'singability' is paramount. Yet his melodies are very restricted in their scope, and his harmony has been described, not without some justification, as crude (as is his sometimes mannered use of dotted rhythms and syncopated *sforzati*); yet his calculated use of relatively simple methods is always direct and effective. The salient characteristics of Spontini's style are no more adequately described by such details of compositional technique than they are explained as betraying the influence of (at isolated moments) Paisiello, Cimarosa, Cherubini, Méhul and, above all, Mozart (whom Spontini venerated all his life). The qualities that made him the most successful opera composer in the Paris of his day, besides involving him in stylistic contradictions that could never be fully resolved, must rather be described as entirely original.

Spontini's fondness for marches, for example, found as early as *La vestale*, has more than picturesque significance: the forward-thrusting character of the march rather pervades the dramaturgical aspect of his operas (with its carefully judged ebb and flow of tension), which regularly culminate in grandiose final tableaux. Like Gluck, Spontini preferred short and well-defined arias to solo numbers in several parts and used simple but gesturally clear instrumental motifs to achieve sharp characterization. These arias, however, like the rather casually handled recitatives in *La vestale*, are always subordinate to the formal dynamics which bring each act together as a unity. An important factor here was the *récitatif obligé*, which could become arioso; Spontini used it again and again to differentiate between heroic pathos and musico-dramatic vitality, while disregarding traditional forms. Another was the stretta finale as the musical culmination of an entire act, a feature previously unusual in French opera and originating in *opera buffa*.

This dramatization of musical form, so successfully executed in the second act of *La vestale*, and the feeling for sharp contrasts through many *lontano* effects and in the use of opposed choruses – contrasts which dominated Spontini's work after *Fernand Cortez* – made him the first composer after Beethoven to find convincing expression for the perceptions of an age overtaken by the extraordinary dynamics of historical and military events. Despite this reinvigoration of the course of music drama Spontini, himself a political reactionary, clung to some of the neo-classical aesthetic of the 18th century, when only affairs of state were considered worthy of dramatic representation, and he was apt to allow the most complicated intrigue peter out in the static *divertissement* of a *lieto fine*.

But although Spontini also amassed all available musical means, even in ballet and festal scenes extraneous to the plot, the hybrid idea of the *Gesamtkunstwerk* can already be discerned behind the monumental result. Even the much-derided appearance of 17 live horses in *Fernand Cortez* and three elephants in the 1821 *Olimpia* shows not just the uncritical use of spectacular developments taken over from other theatrical arts but also Spontini's unswerving determination to win for opera the kind of artistic status Beethoven had just procured for the symphony. Not least in his readiness to spend several years composing an opera – very unusual at the time – he showed a progressive outlook on opera as an ideal art form, one that was not fully accepted until Wagner's time, with claims to an absolute artistic value: an approach to his art that is not easy to reconcile with the office of court composer. With the contradictions of his *Fernand Cortez*, first devised in honour of Napoleon and repeatedly revised, Spontini was already paying the price for his anachronistic ingratiation with artistically reactionary courts. The dramatization of events from more recent history would have been in line with the new interest in the historical novel, but Spontini was not ready to exploit the melodramatic effects of spectacular staging in the depiction of romantically flawed characters and the gradual unfolding of a complex plot. While the radical changes in the various versions of *Fernand Cortez* show that it was possible for him to shift individual arias, in *Olimpie* he turned his innovative energies entirely to the expression of delicate shades of feeling by the idealized characters. *Olimpie*, with its classical splendour, more in tune with the spirit of the Empire, was bound to appear old-fashioned to a public keen on the novels of Sir Walter Scott; and it was Spontini's misfortune that in Berlin he again came into open conflict with the sometimes provincial currents of German Romanticism, which rejected him as a royal favourite.

The move to exotically coloured magical themes in *Nurmahal* and *Alcidor* seemed, perhaps, to offer a way out. But, with his preference for aristocratic characters, his emphasis on the static qualities of his dramatic art in numerous *tableaux vivants*, and his recourse to italianate coloratura arias and aesthetic models from the *opéra-féerie* genre, Spontini increasingly distanced himself from an epoch which preferred to see the unreconciled co-existence of marked contrasts in all the arts. In the face of the emerging German national opera, these works were as little able to stake their claim as was *Agnes von Hohenstaufen*, which Spontini believed to be his greatest work but which like them was never performed beyond Berlin in the 19th century. In the finale of the second act of this, his last completed opera – still impressive for its monumental conception – he pursued the tendency, foreshadowed in *Olimpie*, to elevate spectacular *coups de théâtre* and finely chiselled contrasts into grand ensembles where opposing musical structures were piled one upon another, raising the art of ensemble to a peak never again reached in the 19th century.

Such techniques had been prefigured as early as his first Paris operas, although there they were confined to the orchestration. In contrast with most opera composers before Wagner, Spontini also cultivated a complex blend of sounds by the most extravagant means; his music was accordingly sometimes criticized as noisy. In *Agnes von Hohenstaufen*, for instance, he took particular pains over an invisible orchestra imitating the sound of the organ, whereas other composers made the organ itself a stage instrument. Even the use of anvils in a chorus in *Alcidor* (though taken from *Pélage*), which was denounced as the height of absurdity by hostile Berlin critics, makes them part of a complex sound combination.

Although Spontini's 20 years in Berlin represent a mere episode in the development of German opera, he was very important in the development of modern conducting. He was sternly fanatical in his insistence on rehearsals; he was one of the first conductors to use a baton; and his achievements in the production of a powerful orchestral sound are beyond dispute. Of his operas, however, only the French works had any immediate effects on operatic history. While the influence of his bold 'tableau' style can be seen most clearly in the grand opera of the 1830s, his further influence on the operatic composers of the following generation, from Rossini through Schubert, Weber and Meyerbeer to Wagner, can hardly be overestimated, although only Berlioz, who greatly admired Spontini, was ready to admit as much.

See also AGNES VON HOHENSTAUFEN; FERNAND CORTEZ, OU LA CONQUÊTE DU MEXIQUE; NURMAHAL, ODER DAS ROSENFEST VON KASCHMIR; OLIMPIE; and VESTALE, LA (i).

title	*genre, acts*	*libretto*	*first performance*	*sources, remarks*
Li puntigli delle donne	farsetta per musica, 2		Rome, Pallacorda di Firenze, carn. 1796	*I-Nc**
Il finto pittore			? Rome, 1797/8; Palermo, S Cecilia, 1800	lost
Adelina Senese, o sia L'amore secreto	dramma giocoso, 2	G. Bertati: *La principessa d'Amalfi*	Venice, S Samuele, 10 Oct 1797	*US-NYbroude** (Act 1)
L'eroismo ridicolo	farsa per musica, 1	D. Piccinni	Naples, Nuovo, carn. 1798	*I-Nc*
Teseo riconosciuto	dramma per musica, 2	C. Giotti	Florence, Intrepidi, 22 May 1798	*Fc*
La finta filosofa	commedia per musica, 2	?Piccinni	Naples, Nuovo, sum. 1799	3 arias *Nc*, lib. *Bc*; expanded from L'eroismo ridicolo
2nd version	dramma giocoso per musica, 3		Paris, Théâtre Italien (Favart), 11 Feb 1804	*D-Dlb*, *US-Bp*, excerpts (Paris, ?1804 and 1807)
La fuga in maschera	commedia per musica, 2	G. Palomba	Naples, Nuovo, carn. 1800	
Gli Elisi delusi	melodramma buffo, 2	M. Monti	Palermo, S Cecilia, 28 Aug 1800	*I-PLcon* (ov. and Act 1), lib. *PLcom*
I quadri parlanti	melodramma buffo		Palermo, S Cecilia, 1800	lost
Gli amanti in cimento, o sia Il geloso audace	dramma giocoso, 2	?Bertati: *Il geloso in cimento*	Rome, Valle, 3 Nov 1801	lost
Le metamorfosi di Pasquale, o sia Tutto è illusione nel mondo	farsa giocosa per musica, 1	G. Foppa	Venice, S Samuele, carn. 1802	lost
La petite maison	opéra comique, 3	A. M. Dieulafoy and N. Gersin	Paris, OC (Feydeau), 12 May 1804	*A-Wn*, *GB-Lbl*, excerpts (Paris, 1805)
Milton	fait historique, 1	E. de Jouy and Dieulafoy	Paris, OC (Favart), 27 Nov 1804	(Paris, ?1805)

title	genre, acts	libretto	first performance	sources, remarks
Julie, ou Le pot de fleurs	comédie en prose, mêlée de chants, 1	A. G. Jars	Paris, OC (Favart), 12 March 1805	(Paris, ?1806); collab. E. Fay
Tout le monde a tort	vaudeville		Malmaison, 17 March 1806	*F-Pn*
La vestale	tragédie lyrique, 3	Jouy	Paris, Opéra, 15 Dec 1807	*Po**; (Paris, ?1808/*R* 1979: ERO, xlii)
Fernand Cortez, ou La conquête du Mexique	opéra, 3	Jouy and J. A. d'Esmenard, after A. Piron	Paris, Opéra, 28 Nov 1809	*Po**; (Paris, ?1809)
2nd version	3	rev. Jouy	Paris, Opéra, 28 May 1817	*US-Eu* *; (Paris, ?1817/*R* 1980: ERO, xliii)
3rd version (as Ferdinand Cortez, oder Die Eroberung von Mexiko)	Oper, 3	rev. M. Théaulon de Lambert, trans. J. C. May	Berlin, Kgl Opernhaus, 6 April 1824	*F-Po**, vs (Leipzig, ?1825)
4th version		rev. K. von Lichtenstein	Berlin, Kgl Opernhaus, 26 Feb 1832	music lost, lib. *D-B*
Pélage, ou Le roi et la paix	opéra, 2	Jouy	Paris, Opéra, 23 Aug 1814	*F-Po*, vs [single nos.] (Paris, ?1814)
Les dieux rivaux ou Les fêtes de Cythère	opéra-ballet, 1	Dieulafoy and C. Brifaut	Paris, Opéra, 21 June 1816	*Po*, excerpts (Berlin, n.d.); collab. Kreutzer, Persuis and H.-M. Berton
Olimpie	tragédie lyrique, 3	Dieulafoy and Brifaut, after Voltaire	Paris, Opéra, 22 Dec 1819	*US-STu*, vs (Paris, 1820)
2nd version (as Olimpia)	grosse Oper, 3	rev., trans. E. T. A. Hoffmann	Berlin, Kgl Opernhaus, 14 May 1821	vs (Berlin, ?1825)
3rd version (as Olimpie)	tragédie lyrique, 3		Paris, Opéra, 28 Feb 1826	*F-Po**; (Paris, 1827/*R* 1980: ERO, xliv)
Lalla Rûkh	Festspiel	S. H. Spiker, after T. Moore: *Lalla Rookh*	Berlin, Kgl Schloss, 27 Jan 1821	vs (Berlin, ?1822)
Nurmahal, oder Das Rosenfest von Kaschmir	lyrisches Drama mit Ballet, 2	C. A. Herklots, after Moore: *Lalla Rookh*	Berlin, Kgl Opernhaus, 27 May 1822	*D-Bds*, *F-Po**, vs (Berlin, 1824) ; reuses Grand Bacchanale (*B-Lc*, written for the revival of Salieri's Les Danaïdes, Paris, Opéra, 22 Oct 1817), parts of Lalla Rûkh and Les dieux rivaux
Alcidor	Zauber-Oper mit Ballet, 3	Théaulon de Lambert, after Rochon de Chabannes; Ger. trans. Herklots	Berlin, Opera, 23 May 1825	*D-Bds*, *F-Po**
Agnes von Hohenstaufen	lyrisches Drama, 2	E. Raupach	Berlin, Kgl Opernhaus, 28 May 1827 [Act 1 only]	*US-Wc** (frag.)
2nd version	grosse historisch-romantische Oper, 3	Raupach	Berlin, Kgl Opernhaus, 12 June 1829	*Wc** (inc.)
3rd version	grosse historisch-romantische Oper, 3	rev. Lichtenstein	Berlin, Kgl Opernhaus, 6 Dec 1837	*D-B*, *Bds*, *F-Po**

Doubtful: Chi più guarda meno vede, ? Florence, 1798, ? Venice, 1802 [existence uncertain]

LETTERS AND DOCUMENTS

Des dramatischen Leib-Compositeurs, kgl.-preuss. General-Musikdirectors ... Herrn Ritters Gasparo Spontini Klagen über den Verfall der dramatischen Musik (Leipzig, 1837) [anonymous pamphlet]

H. Berton, M. Carafa and G. Spontini: *Reconstruction de la Salle Favart: observations à MM. les membres de la Chambre des députés* (Paris, ?1839)

[G. K. F.] Kunowski: *Vertheidigungsschrift zweiter Instanz in Sachen wider ... Herrn Ritter Spontini* (Berlin, 1841)

J.-B. Weckerlin: *Musiciana* (Paris, 1877), 309–11

La Mara, ed.: *Musikerbriefe aus fünf Jahrhunderten*, ii (Leipzig, 1886), 23–35

G. Radiciotti: *Lettere inedite di celebri musicisti, annotate e precedute dalle biografie di Pietro, Giovanni e Rosa Morandi a cui sono dirette* (Milan, ?1892), 119–26

A. de Eisner-Eisenhof, ed.: *Lettere inedite di Gaetano Donizetti* (Bergamo, 1897), 88

L. Geiger: 'Archivalische Notizen über Spontini und Paganini', *SIMG*, i (1899–1900), 686–7

J. S. Shedlock: 'Letters from Weber to the Abbé Vogler and to Spontini', in R. Grey, ed.: *Studies in Music by Various Authors* (London, 1901), 233–51

E. Rychnovsky: 'Ein Brief Spontinis an Napoleon', *ZIMG*, iv (1902–3), 6–8

J.-G. Prod'homme: 'Une lettre inédite de Spontini à Lesueur', *ZIMG*, v (1903–4), 54–6

——: 'Spontini et Ch. Gounod', *ZIMG*, xi (1909–10), 325–8

J. Tiersot: 'Lettres de musiciens écrites en français du XVe au XXe siècle', *RMI*, xxi (1914), 52–85; pubd separately (Turin, 1924), 363–98

E. Pfeiffer: 'Lettere inedite di G. Spontini', *Musica d'oggi*, xi (1929), 199–203

J. Heugel: 'Une lettre inédite de Spontini', *Le ménestrel*, xcii (1930), 344

A. Gentili: 'Spontini: a Hitherto Unpublished Letter', *MMR*, lxii (1932), 199–202

G. Radiciotti and E. Pfeiffer: 'Lettere inedite di G. Spontini', *NA*, ix (1932), 23–40

R. Sassi: 'Lettere inedite di Gaspare Spontini', *NA*, xii (1935), 165–83
M. Pincherle: *Musiciens peints par eux-mêmes: lettres de compositeurs écrites en français (1771–1910)* (Paris, 1939), 64–72
C. Daubray: *Victor Hugo et ses correspondants* (Paris, 1947), 258–9
A. Belardinelli: *Documenti spontiniani inediti* (Florence, 1955)
F. Schlitzer: *Frammenti biografici di Gaspare Spontini con lettere inedite*, Quaderni dell'Accademia Chigiana, xxxiii (Siena, 1955)
——: *Circonstanze della vita di Gaspare Spontini con lettere inedite*, Quaderni dell'Accademia Chigiana, xxxvii (Siena, 1958)
Pis'ma zarchyeezhn'ikh muz'ikantov ne russkukh arkhuvov [Letters by Musicians from Abroad in the Russian Archives] (Leningrad, 1967), 238–9
G. Gaetti, ed.: *Epistolario familiare e documenti vari dal 1774 al 1851 di Gaspare Spontini* (Maiolati Spontini, 1974)
H. Becker and G. Becker, eds.: *G. Meyerbeer: Briefwechsel und Tagebücher*, iii (Berlin, 1975), 696
P. Citron, ed.: H. Berlioz: *Correspondance générale*, iii (Paris, 1978), 134, 138–9, 355–7, 385–6
G. Gaetti, ed.: *Céleste Erard, dolce sposa di Gaspare Spontini: epistolario* (Maiolati Spontini, 1978)

MEMOIRS

W. Każyński: *Notatki z podróży muzykalnej po Niemczech odbytej w roku 1844* [Notes from a Musical Journey through Germany in 1844] (St Petersburg, 1845); ed. W. Rudziński (Kraków, 1957), 197–216
A. Gathy: 'Berlioz über Spontini', *Neue Berliner Musikzeitung*, v (1851), 88–90, 97–8
H. Heine: *Lutetia* (Hamburg, 1854), letter 12
A. B. Marx: *Erinnerungen: aus meinem Leben* (Berlin, 1865), i, 218–58; ii, 1–17
H. Dorn: 'Ritter Gasparo Spontini', *Aus meinem Leben: musikalische Skizzen* (Berlin, 1870–86), iii, 1–34
R. Wagner: 'Erinnerungen an Spontini', *Gesammelte Schriften*, v (Leipzig, 1872), 109–32
——: *Mein Leben* (Munich, 1911), 331–47

CRITICISM

FétisB
J.-M.-B. Bins de Saint-Victor: *Réflexions d'un amateur sur l'opéra 'La vestale'* (Rouen, 1809)
E. T. A. Hoffmann: 'G. Spontini: *Lalla Rükh*', *Zeitung für Theater und Musik* (24 Feb 1821); 'Nachträgliche Bemerkungen über Spontinis Oper *Olympia*', ibid (9, 16, 23 and 30 June, 14, 21 and 28 July, 4, 18 and 25 Aug, 1, 8 and 22 Sept 1821); repr. in *Schriften zur Musik*, ed. F. Schnapp (Munich, 1981), 338–95
L. Rellstab: *Über mein Verhältnis als Kritiker zu Herrn Spontini als Komponisten und Generalmusikdirektor in Berlin* (Leipzig, 1827)
A. B. Marx: 'Eine Betrachtung über den heutigen Zustand der deutschen Oper, angeknüpft an *Nurmahal* von Spontini und *Oberon* von Weber', *Caecilia*, vii (1828), 135–82
[? H. S. von Bittkow]: *Spontini in Deutschland, oder Unpartheiische Würdigung seiner Leistungen* (Leipzig, 1830)
C. F. Müller: *Spontini und Rellstab: einige Worte zur Beherzigung der Parteien* (Berlin, 1833)
E. M. Oettinger: *Spontini* (Leipzig, 1843)
[L. de Loménie]: 'Spontini', *Galérie des contemporains illustres par un homme de rien*, x (Paris, ?1847)
G. I. Montanari: *Elogio del cavaliere Gaspare Spontini, conte di S Andrea, letto nel 20 febbrajo 1851, nella chiesa plebale di Majolati* (Ancona, 1851)
H. Berlioz: 'Spontini: esquisse biographique', *Soirées de l'orchestre* (Paris, 1852; Eng. trans., 1965) [12th and 13th soirée]
D. Raoul-Rochette: 'Notice historique sur la vie et les ouvrages de M. Spontini', *Institut national de France: Académie des beaux-arts, séance publique annuelle du … 2 octobre 1852* (Paris, 1852)
W. H. Riehl: 'Der musikalische Dramatiker des französischen Kaiserthums: Gasparo Spontini', *Musikalische Charakterköpfe: ein kunstgeschichtliches Studienbuch*, i (Stuttgart, 1853), 181–204
[W. Neumann]: *Gaspare Spontini: eine Biographie* (Kassel, 1855)
F. Poland: *Die Musik eine Sprache, am Beispiel von Spontini's Vestalin erläutert* (Dresden, 1870)
A. Jullien: 'Les Commencements de Spontini (1774–1807)', *Chronique musicale*, x (1875), 31–43, 59–71
A. Moretti: *Vita di Gaspare Spontini* (Imola, 1875)
T. de Lajarte: 'Spontini: *La vestale* et *Fernand Cortez*: histoire de ces deux ouvrages', *Curiosités de l'Opéra* (Paris, 1883), 133–83
C. Robert: *Gasparo Luigi Pacifico Spontini: eine biographische Skizze* (Berlin, 1883)
P. Spitta: 'Spontini in Berlin', *Zur Musik* (Berlin, 1892), 291–353
W. Altmann: 'Spontini an der Berliner Oper: eine archivalische Studie', *SIMG*, iv (1902–3), 242–92
A. Pougin: 'Les dernières années de Spontini', *RMI*, xxix (1922), 54–80, 236–63
A. Maecklenburg: 'Der Fall Spontini-Weber: ein Beitrag zur Vorgeschichte der Berliner Erstaufführung der *Euryanthe*', *ZMw*, vi (1923–4), 449–65
C. Bouvet: *Spontini* (Paris, 1930)
K. Schubert: *Spontinis italienische Schule* (Strasbourg, 1932)
W. Wahle: '*Ferdinand Cortez* von Spontini als Vorbild zu Wagners *Rienzi*', *AMz*, lxvi (1939), 3–4
G. Abraham: 'The Best of Spontini', *ML*, xxiii (1942), 163–71
A. Ghislanzoni: *Gaspare Spontini: studio storico-critico* (Rome, 1951)
L. Ronga: 'Gasparo Spontini (1774–1851)', *RaM*, xxi (1951), 1–14
Studi spontiniani: Iesi, Maiolati, Fabriano, Ancona 1951
Studi spontiniani: Firenze 1954
P. Fragapane: *Spontini* (Bologna, 1954, 2/1983)
L. Ronga: 'L'*Agnese di Hohenstaufen* di Spontini e l'*Euryanthe* di Weber', *RMI*, lvi (1954), 247–57
H. Engel: 'Wagner und Spontini', *AMw*, xii (1955), 167–77
H. Mueller von Asow: 'Gasparo Spontinis Briefwechsel mit Wolfgang von Goethe', *Chronik des Wiener Goethe-Vereins*, lxi (1957), 42–58
F. Schlitzer: *La finta filosofa di Gaspare Spontini* (Naples, 1957)
F. Schnapp: 'E. T. A. Hoffmanns Textbearbeitung der Oper *Olimpia* von Spontini', *Jb des Wiener Goethe-Vereins*, lxvi (1962), 126–43
P. Fragapane: 'Spontini e la sua *Julie* (1805)', *Chigiana*, new ser., v (1968), 253–63
D. A. Libby: *Gaspare Spontini and his French and German Operas* (diss., Princeton U., 1969)
D. Charlton: *Orchestration and Orchestral Practice in Paris, 1789–1810* (diss., U. of Cambridge, 1973)
A. Vander Linden: 'Notes de Madame Gaspare Spontini sur la vie et l'oeuvre de son mari', *RBM*, xxviii–xxx (1974–6), 222–37
G. Carli Ballola: '*Milton*: opera prima', *Chigiana*, new ser., xi (1976), 343–6
E. J. Dent: *The Rise of Romantic Opera* (Cambridge, 1976), 95–109
D. Libby: 'Spontini's Early French Operas', *MT*, cxvii (1976), 23–4
S. Döhring: 'Spontinis Berliner Opern', in C. Dahlhaus, ed.: *Studien zur Musikgeschichte Berlins im frühen 19. Jahrhundert* (Regensburg, 1980), 469–89
N. Miller: 'Der musikalische Freiheitskrieg gegen Gaspare Spontini', *Preussen: dein Spree-Athen*, ed. H. Kühn (Reinbek bei Hamburg, 1981), 200–27
J. Joly: 'Les ambiguités de la guerre napoléonienne dans *Fernand Cortez* de Spontini', *La bataille, l'armée et la gloire: Clermont-Ferrand 1983*, 239–54
Studi spontiniani: Maiolati Spontini, Iesi 1983
J. Mongrédien: *La musique en France des lumières au Romantisme* (Paris, 1986)
R. S. Ridgway: 'Voltairian bel canto: Operatic Adaptations of Voltaire's Tragedies', *Studies on Voltaire and the Eighteenth Century*, no.241 (1986), 125–54
M. Walter: 'Hoffmann und Spontini: zum Problem der romantischen Oper', *E. T. A. Hoffmann et la musique*, ed. A. Montandon (Berne, 1987), 85–119
G. Buschmeier: *Die Entwicklung von Arie und Szene in der französischen Oper von Gluck bis Spontini* (Tutzing, 1991)
A. Zecca Laterza, ed.: *Catalogo tematico delle opere di Spontini* (Maiolati Spontini, forthcoming)

ANSELM GERHARD

Spoorenberg, Erna (*b* Jogyakarta, Java, 11 April 1926). Dutch soprano. She studied in Hilversum and Amsterdam, making her début in 1949 at the Vienna Staatsoper, as well as embarking on a concert career. With Netherlands Opera (1958–62) she sang Marie (*Zar und Zimmermann*), Fiordiligi, Eurydice, Constanze, Nicolai's Mrs Ford, Pamina and Violetta, and took part in the première of Badings's *Martin Korda DP* in 1960. She appeared with the Deutsche Oper am Rhein and at the Hamburg Staatsoper, where in 1961 she sang Mélisande, one of her finest roles, which she recorded for Ansermet and for which her charming appearance and clear, limpid vocal timbre were well suited. In 1963 she created Julie in Frank Martin's *Monsieur de Pourceaugnac* at Geneva.

*

E. Spoorenberg: *Daar lig je dan* (The Hague, 1962)

TRUUS DE LEUR/ELIZABETH FORBES

Sportonio, Marc'Antonio ['Il Bolognese'] (*b* ?Bologna, *c*1631; *d* ?Palermo, after 1696). Italian soprano castrato and composer. A pupil of Carissimi, nominally in the service of the Duke of Modena from 1645, he went to Paris in 1646 to take part in Luigi Rossi's *Orfeo* (1647), remaining there in the service of the French queen-regent. From 1653 he was at Palermo, where he sang in an 'attione tragica', *Costantino* (stage music by G. B. Fasolo). In 1655, with other Palermo singers, the 'Musici accademici sconcertati', he organized the first opera performance there, Cavalli's *Giasone*, in which he sang Delfa. The leading figure in public theatre life at Palermo, he appeared as the composer of *Elena* (Carnival 1661, text by Minato). *La Flavia imperatrice* (text by F. Beverini, 1669) was described as his fourth opera; in 1675 he signed the libretto of *Caligola* and in 1678 he composed one of the few operas of local origin, *La Fiordispina* (text by Antonio Salamone, a writer active in Palermo; it was repeated at court in 1680 and at the Teatro S Bartolomeo, Naples, in Carnival 1683). Sportonio used his international theatrical experience at the court of the viceroy: in February 1659 he sang, in a flying carriage, the introduction to a dancing festivity. From at least 1655 to 1696 he was a member of the Cappella Palatina in Palermo.

*

H. Prunières: *L'opéra italien en France avant Lulli* (Paris, 1913), 91, 101, 136, 377
R. Pagano: 'La vita musicale a Palermo e nella Sicilia del seicento', *NRMI*, iii (1969), 448, 455
L. Bianconi: 'Funktionen des Operntheaters in Neapel bis 1700 und die Rolle Alessandro Scarlattis', *Colloquium Alessandro Scarlatti: Wurzburg 1975*, 20, 26–7, 76
L. Bianconi and T. Walker: 'Dalla *Finta pazza* alla *Veremonda*: storie di Febiarmonici', *RIM*, x (1975), 393, 404
R. Pagano: 'Giasone in Oreto: considerazioni sull'introduzione del melodramma a Palermo', *I quaderni del Conservatorio*, i (Palermo, 1988), 11–18
A. Tedesco: *Il Teatro Santa Cecilia e il seicento musicale palermitano* (Palermo, 1992)

LORENZO BIANCONI

Sposa fedele, La ('The Faithful Bride'). *Opera buffa* in three acts by Pietro Alessandro Guglielmi (*see* GUGLIELMI family, (1)) to a libretto by PIETRO CHIARI; Venice, Teatro S Moisè, Carnival 1767.

Rosinella (soprano) and Pasqualino (tenor) have eloped but have been separated in a shipwreck. They land close to the estate of the Marchese del Vento Ponente (tenor), but do not discover each other's presence. Rosinella's arrival (she introduces herself as Donna Aurora del Campo) diverts the Marchese and Conte Lelio from their previous amorous situations; both fall in love with her. Rosinella reciprocates the Marchese's tenderness until she realizes that Pasqualino has landed safely and has been employed as her servant. The couple do not divulge their true identities, and Act 2 ends with a series of confused meetings in the dark. Act 3 ends with the Marchese permitting the lovers to marry, once he knows that Pasqualino is of an appropriate social class for the 'Donna Aurora del Campo'. A main characteristic of this piece is the enlarged middle ground between comic and serious characters. Pasqualino and Rosinella both have significant elements of comedy and pathos; this is evident in the text and in their music, which includes simple melodies, similar to folktunes, highflown noble pieces and sentimental arias.

This was perhaps Guglielmi's most successful (and according to some modern critics, his best) *opera buffa*; it may have been performed first in Cremona in 1765. In addition to Italian productions throughout Europe (as *La Rosinella, ossia La sposa fedele*; *La fedeltà in amore*; *La sposa costante* and *La costanza di Rosinella*), it was given in German as *Robert und Kalliste, oder der Triumph der Treue*; an abridged German vocal score was published in Berlin and Leipzig in 1777.

MARY HUNTER

Sposi malcontenti, Gli ('The Discontented Newly-Weds'). *Opera buffa* in two acts by STEPHEN STORACE to a libretto by Gaetano Brunati; Vienna, Burgtheater, 1 June 1785.

In spring 1783 the Austrian emperor Joseph II had disbanded his German opera ensemble and established an Italian opera group. Nancy Storace was engaged from Italy as *prima buffa*, and became a great favourite of the Emperor. It was probably due to her influence that her brother, a young man of 23 with no previous experience of writing for the stage, was commissioned to write an opera. In addition to Nancy Storace as Eginia (soprano), the singers at the first performance included Michael Kelly as Valente (tenor), Vincenzo Calvesi as Casimiro (tenor), Stefano Mandini as Artidoro (baritone), Francesco Benucci as Rosmondo (bass), Catarina Cavalieri as Enrichetta (soprano) and Therese Teyber as Bettina (soprano).

The scene is 18th-century Genoa. Eginia has married Casimiro at her father's wish, but feels unable to love him. Valente, a middle-aged scholar, is angered at being rejected by Casimiro's sister Enrichetta, who loves Artidoro, a previous suitor of Eginia, and he plans to revenge himself by spreading the rumour that Artidoro and Eginia are having an affair. Since Artidoro is in fact trying to elope with Enrichetta, he easily raises the suspicions of Casimiro and his domineering father, Rosmondo. The maidservant, Bettina, pretends to help Valente, but actually tells his plans to Artidoro, who arranges for Casimiro and Rosmondo to be in the garden that night so that Valente can be unmasked. It then becomes clear who has been causing all the trouble. Eginia's innocence and honour are vindicated, Artidoro can marry Enrichetta and even Valente is forgiven. Although anticipations of *Figaro* can be found in the plot – Artidoro hiding behind and on the sofa, and the disguisings and mistaken identities in the dark garden – these were probably borrowed from Beaumarchais' comedy *Le mariage de Figaro*, which was still banned. The libretto is well constructed, and Storace manages to infuse the farcical misunderstandings with touching humanity. The music has a Mozartian flavour, combined with an English quality sometimes tending towards the ballad air.

Despite a first-night catastrophe when Nancy Storace lost her voice in the middle of Act 1 (her place was taken by Celestine Coltellini), the opera was a surprising success. It went into the repertory of the Burgtheater, and was performed there regularly. Performances were given the following year at Prague and Leipzig, and in 1789 at Dresden. It was translated into German, and in 1790 a French version was given in Paris. There is even a contemporary arrangement of some of the arias for wind band by Johann Went, a sign that the tunes were in popular circulation. Storace re-used two of the songs in *The Pirates* (1792) and the overture in *The Cherokee* (1794), and more of the music found its way into *Mahmoud* (1796). An English version (translation by Brian Trowell) had its première on 28 March 1985 at the New Theatre, King's College, London.

RICHARD PLATT

Sposo deluso, Lo ('The Deluded Bridegroom'). *Opera buffa*, K430/424*a*, by WOLFGANG AMADEUS MOZART to a libretto after *Le donne rivali*; unfinished.

Lo sposo deluso was composed in 1783–4. Its libretto, surviving complete with Mozart's intended casting for the Italian company resident in Vienna, was formerly attributed, without evidence, to Lorenzo da Ponte. Campana (1990) has shown that the libretto is based on a Roman intermezzo, possibly written by Giuseppe Petrosellini.

The first three numbers were drafted and a trio completed. The overture's Allegro begins with a sprightly fanfare; following an Andante, the reprise opens with a quartet, the first number. Pulcherio (tenor, or high baritone, Francesco Bussani) laughs at Bocconio, the title role (bass, Francesco Benucci) for aspiring to a young bride, Eugenia. Bettina (soprano, Catarina Cavalieri), his niece, and Don Asdrubale (tenor, Stefano Mandini) deride the old man's pretensions. Eugenia (soprano, Nancy Storace) arrives; the sketched aria (the second number) reveals a lady of spirit. Pulcherio's aria (the third) is addressed to the ill-matched couple. Eugenia and Asdrubale, former lovers tragically separated, contrast in the trio with the bafflement of Bocconio, expressed in a phrase used again in Bartolo's aria in Act 1 of *Le nozze di Figaro*.

Only the trio suggests the style of the future Da Ponte operas. Some lively invention notwithstanding, the rest, in line with the conventional libretto, represents surprisingly little advance on *La finta giardiniera*.

JULIAN RUSHTON

Sprechgesang [Sprechstimme] (Ger.: 'speech-song' ['speech-voice']). A type of vocal enunciation intermediate between speech and song. Sprechgesang, using the notation in ex.1*a*, was introduced by Humperdinck

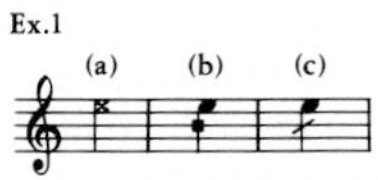

in *Königskinder* (1897), though in the edition of 1910 he replaced it by conventional singing. It could well have been an attempt to prescribe a kind of articulation already being used by singers of both lieder and popular song, and certainly its most celebrated embodiment is in Schoenberg's *Pierrot lunaire* (1912, notation as in ex.1*b*), where the soloist hinges between those worlds. However, Schoenberg also used Sprechgesang in quite different contexts: chorally in *Die glückliche Hand* (1924) and for the role of Moses in *Moses und Aron* (composed 1930–32). It was used too by Berg in *Wozzeck* (1925) and *Lulu* (1937), the latter work introducing a new shade, 'half sung' (notated as in ex.1*c*), between Sprechgesang and song. In a prefatory note to *Wozzeck* Berg insisted that passages in Sprechstimme (his term) 'are not to be sung' but must be delivered as 'a spoken melody' (*Sprechmelodie*): 'in singing the performer stays on the note without change; in speaking he strikes the note but leaves it immediately by rising or falling in pitch'.

However, the realization of Sprechgesang remains problematic, partly because the pitch range of speaking voices is narrow, partly because there is no clear middle point between speech and song but rather a haze of alternatives. The operas of many composers since the 1950s, including Berio and Kagel, have worked within that haze, while classic Sprechgesang has tended, if only because of the prestige of *Pierrot lunaire* and *Wozzeck*, to imply some kinship to German expressionism. It has been used, though, by composers from Britten (*Death in Venice*, 1973) to Rihm.

PAUL GRIFFITHS

Sprechstimme (Ger.: 'Speech-voice'). Term used interchangeably, in general, with SPRECHGESANG. Berg used the term in *Wozzeck*, specifying pitched speech rather than singing.

Staatsoper (Ger.: 'state opera', 'national opera'). The term given to the national opera companies in the German-speaking lands that succeeded the court opera companies, mostly at the time of World War I. The best-known companies bearing the name are those of Vienna (Wiener Staatsoper), Berlin, Munich (Bayerische Staatsoper) and Dresden (Dresdner Staatsoper).

Mariano Stabile in the title role of Verdi's 'Falstaff'

Stabile, Mariano (*b* Palermo, 12 May 1888; *d* Milan, 11 Jan 1968). Italian baritone. He studied in Rome under Cotogni and made his début in his native Palermo in 1911, as Marcello in *La bohème*. His selection by Toscanini to sing the title role in Verdi's *Falstaff* for the opening of the 1921–2 season at La Scala, with thorough coaching by both Toscanini and De Luca, proved to be the turning-point of his career: he scored an enormous success and sang the part nearly 1200 times in the course of 40 years. During his first Covent Garden season, in 1926, he appeared as Falstaff, Iago and Don Giovanni, and later became a notable Gianni Schicchi and Scarpia. He was greatly admired at Glyndebourne as Figaro and as Dr Malatesta in *Don Pasquale*; also as Don Alfonso in the Glyndebourne production of *Così fan tutte* at the 1948 Edinburgh Festival. He repeated some of these parts between 1946 and 1949, during the long postwar seasons of Italian opera mounted by the Russian-born impresario Jay Pomeroy at the Cambridge and Stoll Theatres. Stabile's vocal powers were not exceptional, and his great attainments were the result of a spontaneous dramatic exuberance tempered by a fine sense of style. His enunciation was unusually clear, and his mastery of dramatic inflection and gesture complete. These qualities found full scope in *Don Pasquale* and *Così fan tutte*, and in both these operas his relish of the approaching discomfiture of his victims always delighted the audience. Malatesta's 'Bella siccome un angelo' has been more smoothly vocalized by other singers, but there was something irresistibly comical in the gusto with which Stabile would arouse Don Pasquale's desires by his account of Norina's charms while at the same time holding him at arm's length with imperious gestures of restraint.

*

G. Gualerzi: 'Stabile – a Centenary Tribute', *Opera*, xxxix (1988), 1190–94

DESMOND SHAWE-TAYLOR

Stabinger [Stabingher, Staubinger], **Mathias** [Mattia] (*b* probably in Germany, *c*1750; *d* Venice, 1815). Composer and conductor. His theatrical career took him first to France, thence to Italy, where he had his first big success, with *Le astuzie di Bettina* (1780); this work was rapidly taken up in other countries, particularly Germany. He then made his way to St Petersburg by way of Warsaw, where he played the harpsichord in the opera orchestra. Arriving in the Russian capital in 1782, he moved straight away to Moscow, where he conducted a season of Italian opera, including his own *Il finto pazzo per amore*, at Michael Maddox's theatre on Petrovka Street. He left Russia with the troupe to which he was attached and spent the next two years in Italy, composing operas and ballets for Venice and Bologna.

After returning to Moscow in his own right in 1785, Stabinger made that city his base for the rest of his creative life, directing the orchestra at Maddox's theatre (which was by then called the Petrovsky Theatre) from the year of his return until 1799. The works he wrote for the Moscow operatic stage during this period were all comic operas with dialogue set to Russian librettos. Two of the latter, both on fantastic subjects, were by Prince Dmitry Gorchakov, a member of Moscow's leading literary family. *Baba-Yaga* is based on folklore, except that the title character (played, as the Witch often is in *Hänsel und Gretel*, in travesty) is a benign sorceress rather than the traditional Russian witch. *Schastlivaya Tonya* ('Lucky Tonya'), drawn from *The Thousand and One Nights*, remained a staple of the Moscow repertory until the end of the century.

Calipso abbandonata, Milan, Scala, *c*1777

Le astuzie di Bettina (ob, 2), Genoa, S Agostino, 1780, *F-Pn*

Il finto pazzo per amore (ob, 2, ? T. Mariani), Moscow, Maddox's, 25 Oct/5 Nov 1782

La morte d'Arrigo VI, Bologna, 1784

Schastlivaya Tonya [Schastliviy nevod] (Lucky Tonya [The Lucky Net]) (comic op, 4, D. Gorchakov), Moscow, Petrovsky, 14/25 Jan 1786

Baba-Yaga (comic op, 3, Gorchakov), Moscow, Petrovsky, 2/13 Dec 1786

Pigmalion, ili Sila lyubvï [Pygmalion, or The Power of Love] (drama with music, 1, V. Maykov, after J.-J. Rousseau), Moscow, Petrovsky, 20/31 Dec 1787

Neudachnaya zhenit'ba [The Unhappy Marriage] (trans. from It.), Moscow, Petrovsky, 16/27 Feb 1788

*

N. F. Findeyzen: *Ocherki po istorii muziki v Rossii s drevneyshikh vremyon do kontsa XVIII veka* [Studies in the History of Music in Russia from Ancient Times to the End of the 18th Century], ii (Moscow and Leningrad, 1929)

R.-A. Mooser: *Annales de la musique et des musiciens en Russie au XVIIIme siècle*, ii (Geneva, 1951)

T. Livanova: *Russkaya muzïkal'naya kul'tura XVIII veka v eyo svyazyakh s literaturoy, teatrom i bïtom* [Russian Musical Culture of the 18th Century and its Connection with Literature, the Theatre and Everyday Life], ii (Moscow, 1953)

A. A. Gozenpud: *Muzïkal'nïy teatr v Rossii ot istokov do Glinki: ocherk* [The Music Theatre in Russia from its Origins up to Glinka: a Study] (Leningrad, 1959)

Yu. Keldïsh and others: *Istoriya russkoy muzïki v desyati tomakh* [History of Russian Music in Ten Volumes], iii (Moscow, 1985)

RICHARD TARUSKIN

Stabreim (Ger.: 'stave-rhyme', 'alliterative verse'). Alliteration is found in all the oldest surviving forms of Germanic verse, from the Old English *Beowulf* to the Old High German *Hildebrandslied* and the Old Norse Poetic Edda. Each line of verse is made up of two half-lines, each of which consists of two – sometimes three – semantically important, stressed syllables (*Hebungen* or 'lifts'), with a variable number of weakly stressed syllables (*Senkungen* or 'dips') dividing them. The lines are linked together alliteratively: the main stress or 'stave' is located on the first lift of each second half-line, while the two lifts in the preceding half-line are treated as supporting staves, one or both of which must alliterate with the main stave.

Initial rhyme was replaced by end-rhyme in the 9th century in German, somewhat later in Old English and Old Norse. It was revived in the 19th century by Friedrich de la Motte Fouqué in *Der Held des Nordens*, from where it was taken over by Wagner into *Der Ring des Nibelungen*. Drawing on Romantic theories of language, Wagner believed that primitive communities had expressed themselves instinctively in alliterative verse: the libretto of the *Ring* was based, therefore, on the premise that the more insistent the *Stabreim* and the more archaic the language, the more 'authentic' the text would be as an expression of 'purely human' emotions. By mistaking the conscious and highly elaborate artistry of his Eddic sources for a spontaneous outpouring of the popular spirit, Wagner has counterfeited a style which proves more of a hindrance than a help in our understanding of the text. His experiment found few imitators.

*

R. Wagner: *Oper und Drama*, Gesammelte Schriften (Leipzig, 1871–83, 5/1911), iii–iv; Eng. trans. (1892–9), ii

E. Sievers: *Altgermanische Metrik* (Halle, 1893)

H. Wiessner: *Der Stabreimvers in R. Wagners Ring des Nibelungen* (Berlin, 1924)

D. Borchmeyer: *Das Theater Richard Wagners* (Stuttgart, 1982; Eng. trans., 1991)

STEWART SPENCER

Stade, Frederica von. *See* VON STADE, FREDERICA.

Staden, Sigmund Theophil (*b* Kulmbach, bap. 6 Nov 1607; *d* Nuremberg, bur. 30 July 1655). German composer. He is historically important as the composer of *Seelewig* (1644), the earliest extant score for a German Singspiel. He studied with his father, with Jakob

Paumann in Augsburg and with Walter Rowe in Berlin. From 1627 he was paid by the city of Nuremberg as an instrumentalist and from 1634 also as organist at St Lorenz. In 1643, together with the Nuremberg pastor Johan Michael Dilherr, he organized and performed in a 'Historisches Konzert' in which he attempted to trace the development of music from its beginnings up to his own day; in addition to his own compositions, he included in it works by Lassus, Hassler, Giovanni Gabrieli and his own father.

Following that concert Staden began to collaborate with two members of the Pegnesischer Blumenorden (a German language society, also known as the Pegnitzschäfer), George Philipp Harsdörffer and Johann Klaj. Harsdörffer wrote the text and Staden the music for *Das geistliche Waldgedicht oder Freudenspiel genant Seelewig*, a three-act pastoral Singspiel for a small cast and instrumental ensemble (libretto and score in Harsdörffer's *Frawenzimmer Gesprächspiele*, iv, Nuremberg, 1641–57; ed. R. Eitner, *MMg*, xiii, 1881, pp.65–147; the collection also contains strophic songs by Staden). A through-composed *Liedoper* in the 'Italian manner', *Seelewig* requires an ensemble of three violins, three flutes, three shawms and a horn, as well as three sopranos, two altos, two tenors and a bass; in the text Harsdörffer suggested possible alternatives for performance. The arias are strophic songs, a form that remained popular in German-language opera until the turn of the century; the recitatives are the only ones Staden wrote. *Seelewig* and the three *Friedens-Gesänge* (1651) are the only longer compositions by Staden that are still extant.

Staden composed music for sacred works, so-called *Redeoratorien* (1644–50, lost) with texts by Klaj, which are also important in the development of dramatic music in Nuremberg; Staden's music (solo, choral and instrumental) served to accompany Klaj's declaimed texts. He also composed incidental music for Klaj's *Der leidende Christus* (1645) and probably for Klaj's six other *Redeoratorien* as well.

See also SEELEWIG.

*

F. van Ingen: 'Bericht über die *Seelewig*-Aufführung in Utrecht', *Inszenierung und Regie barocker Dramen: Wolfenbütteler Arbeiten zur Barockforschung* (Hamburg, 1976), 69–73

P. Keller: *Die Oper 'Seelewig' von Sigmund Theophil Staden und George Philipp Harsdörffer* (Berne and Stuttgart, 1977)

J. Leighton: 'Die Wolfenbütteler Aufführung von Harsdörffers und Stadens *Seelewig* im Jahre 1654', *Wolfenbütteler Beiträge 1978*, 115–28

M. R. Wade: '*Seelewig*: the Earliest Extant German Opera and its Antecedent', *Daphnis*, xiv (1985), 559–78

S. R. Huff: 'The Early German Libretto: some Reconsiderations Based on Harsdörffer's "Seelewig"', *ML*, lxix (1988), 345–55

M. R. Wade: 'Music in the Works of the Early Pegnitzschäfer', *Daphnis*, xvii (1988), 633–46

——: *The German Baroque Pastoral 'Singspiel'* (Berne, 1990)

J. P. Aikin: 'Narcissus and Echo: a Mythological Subtext in Harsdörffer's Operatic Allegory "Seelewig"', *ML*, lxxii (1991), 359–71

MARA R. WADE

Stading, Sofia Francisca (*b* Berlin, 1763; *d* Dresden, 1837). German soprano active in Sweden. Arriving in Stockholm at the age of 10, she was accepted as a student in the Royal Opera school, making her début as Myris in Favart's *opéra comique Arsène* in 1780. She achieved success as Iphigenia in Gluck's operas in 1781, and in 1782 sang Cora in Naumann's *Cora och Alonzo* at the dedication of the new theatre for the Royal Opera. Her voice was considered light and versatile, and she won considerable applause for her beauty and poise on stage. She was pensioned in 1806 and returned to Germany.

*

F. Dahlgren: *Anteckningar om Stockholms teatrar* [Notes on Stockholm's Theatres] (Stockholm, 1866)

BERTIL H. VAN BOER

Stadler, Abbé **Maximilian** [Johann Karl Dominik] (*b* Melk, 4 Aug 1748; *d* Vienna, 8 Nov 1833). Austrian composer. After studying at the Jesuit College in Vienna, in 1766 he entered the Benedictine abbey of Melk and in 1772 was ordained; he was elected prior in 1784. Appointed abbot of Lilienfeld two years later, he then held the same post at Kremsmünster (1789) where his administration was marked by his support of secular music, including performances of operas by Paisiello, Salieri and Umlauf. He moved to Linz in 1791 as consistorial adviser to the bishop, and in 1796 settled in Vienna, where he became musical adviser to Mozart's widow. After his secularization in 1803 he worked as a parish priest until 1815.

Stadler wrote mainly vocal music and experimented early with lied and melodrama. Both forms are found in the Viennese-influenced Singspiel, *Das Studenten-Valete* (U. Petrack; Melk, 6 Sept 1781; *A-M*), his single operatic endeavour. He also composed incidental music, sacred works and keyboard pieces, and made string sextet arrangements of other composers' operas, an activity undoubtedly arising out of his close friendship with Ignaz von Mosel, director of the Imperial court theatres, 1820–29. A prominent figure in Viennese musical life, in his day he was admired as a keyboard player; his history of music in Austria, written between about 1816 and 1826, is believed to be the earliest of its kind.

*

I. F. von Mosel: 'Nekrolog: Abbé Maximilian Stadler', *Wiener Zeitschrift für Kunst, Literatur, Theater und Mode* (1833), nos.149–50, cols.1213, 1221

H. Sabel: *Maximilian Stadlers weltliche Werke und seine Beziehungen zur Wiener Klassik* (diss., U. of Cologne, 1941)

A. Kellner: *Musikgeschichte des Stiftes Kremsmünster* (Kassel, 1956)

K. Wagner: *Abbé Maximilian Stadler* (Kassel, 1974)

R. N. Freeman: *The Practice of Music at Melk Abbey* (Vienna, 1989)

ROBERT N. FREEMAN

Stadsschouwburg. Municipal theatre in AMSTERDAM, opened in 1774 and rebuilt in 1894.

Städtische Oper (Ger.: 'city opera', 'municipal opera'). The term given to court opera houses in German-speaking lands that were taken over by city or town authorities, mostly about the time of World War I. The Vienna Volksoper company has officially been called the Städtische Volksoper since being taken over by the municipality of Vienna in 1938.

Staempfli, Edward (*b* Berne, 1 Feb 1908). Swiss composer. After studying medicine for two years, he studied music in Cologne, then with Dukas in Paris, where the circle of Mihalovici, Martinů, Harsányi and Conrad Beck had some influence on him. In 1935 he attended Scherchen's conducting course in Brussels, where he was awarded the Henri Le Boeuf Prize. After the outbreak of World War II he returned to Switzerland, remaining there until 1951. In 1954 he settled in Berlin. His first opera, *Ein Traumspiel*, was completed in 1943 and is partly atonal. In 1949 Staempfli adopted a 12-note technique, and this is the dominant characteristic of his second opera, *Medea*, completed in

1954. The one-act opera *Der Zöllner Matthäus*, which followed 20 years later, takes account of Staempfli's development of serial procedures. His fourth opera, *Caligula*, dating from 1981, is in four acts and has a French libretto based on the play by Camus. His later music is free of dogmatic adherence to serialism and shows an increasing interest in tone colour. None of his operas has been performed.

all librettos by the composer; all unperformed

Ein Traumspiel, 1943 (3, after A. Strindberg)
Medea, 1954 (3, after F. Grillparzer)
Der Zöllner Matthäus, 1974 (1, after M.-L. Kaschnitz)
Caligula, 1981 (4, after A. Camus) ANDREW CLARK

Stafford, Thomas (*fl* from 1653). English singer and composer active in Italy. Little is known about his life. At the beginning of 1653 he was in Rome, where he probably studied with Luigi Rossi. He was a member of the Italian company which on 14 April 1654 performed Carlo Caproli's *opéra-ballet Le nozze di Peleo e di Teti* in the great hall of the Petit Bourbon in Paris. Stafford took the role of Prometheus and also sang in the chorus of the Nereids. Some of his own compositions are in the Playford collections, *Choice Ayres, Songs and Dialogues* (London, 1675) and *New Ayres and Dialogues* (London, 1678).

*

H. Prunières: *L'opéra italien en France avant Lulli* (Paris, 1913)
G. Barblan and A. Basso, eds.: *Storia dell'opera*, ii (Turin, 1977), 11
PAOLA BESUTTI

Stage band (It. *banda*). A group of instruments that perform on stage level, either behind the scenes or in view of the audience. It may include the string ensembles in the ballroom scenes of Mozart's *Don Giovanni* (1787) and Verdi's *Rigoletto* (1851) and *Un ballo in maschera* (1859), the Militär- and Wirtshausmusik in Berg's *Wozzeck* (1926) and the assortment of archaic instruments featured in the court scenes of Britten's *Gloriana* (1953). Mostly, however, it designates the miscellaneous wind band which originated with Paisiello's *Pirro* (1787) and became a fairly constant feature of Italian opera of the 19th century, beginning with Rossini's *Ricciardo e Zoraide* (1818). As the 'banda' was under separate direction and its composition varied from theatre to theatre, the bandmaster scored in detail what the composer wrote out on two staves, as for a piano reduction. Clarinets predominated in the upper register, brass in the middle and lower, including such instruments as the 'flicorno' (flugelhorn) and the 'bombardone'. At the Paris Opéra the 'fanfare téâtrale' consisted entirely of brass instruments, among which the presence of Adolphe Sax as director during the mid-century ensured a family of saxhorns of various pitches. The rise of the professional operatic conductor put an end to the stage band as an independent unit. The 'banda' music in Mascagni's *L'amico Fritz* (1891) and Puccini's *La bohème* (1896) is fully scored by the composer. JULIAN BUDDEN

Stage design [scene design; scenography] (Fr. *décor*; Ger. *Bühnenbild*; It. *scenografia*). Stage design represents the sum of the visual elements of theatrical production combining all forms of scenery, lighting, makeup and costumes (and sometimes the actual space in which the production is presented) to create an illusion of a place, space and time. Stage design is an ephemeral theatrical art, capable of realizing its full potential only in the context of a performance. Not only is stage design governed, to a certain extent, by the requirements of both the libretto and the music, but also by the political, economic and social demands of current modes of tastes of the society in which opera is performed. This was particularly true during the era of the French *grand opéra*.

For the purposes of this article, the discussion of stage design will be limited to the more commonly accepted concept of 'scene design'; that is, the scenic elements of operatic production in which the visual attention of the public is focussed on to a predetermined acting space (or area) during the performance. For other information falling within the broader concept of stage design, *see also* COSTUME, LIGHTING, PRODUCTION, MACHINERY and THEATRE ARCHITECTURE, as well as entries on individual designers.

1. Sources. 2. Before 1600. 3. The 17th century: (i) The Italian transformation stage (ii) North of the Alps. 4. The 18th century. 5. The 19th century. 6. 1900–45. 7. After World War II. 8. The late 20th century.

1. SOURCES. A vast quantity of original source materials and theoretical publications pertinent to the study of stage design exists. Original designs can be studied in basically two forms. There are, first, engravings published in librettos or 'festival' books, which depicted the stagings of royal festivals such as marriages, births and triumphal entries into a city; most such books date from the 16th and 17th centuries. Secondly, there are hand-drawn and coloured drawings. Most of the surviving original materials relating to opera can be found in major libraries and museums, especially those with an emphasis on the performing arts. In Europe, the outstanding collections are those in the Österreichisches Theatermuseum, Vienna (formerly the Theatersammlung, Österreichische Nationalbibliothek); the Bibliothèque de l'Opéra, the Collections Rondel and Arts et Spectacle in the Bibliothèque de l'Arsenal, Paris; the Museo Teatrale alla Scala, Milan; the Biblioteca e Raccolta Teatrale del Burcardo, Rome; and the Sammlung Niessen and the holdings of the Institut für Theater- Film- und Fernsehwissenschaft at the University of Cologne, Germany. Notable local collections in Italy include the Museo Correr and Fondazione Giorgio Cini, Venice; the Biblioteca Reale and Museo Civico, Turin; and the Museo San Martino, Naples. In Germany, other notable collections are in the Theatermuseum, Munich, and the Institut für Theaterforschung, Hamburg. The major theatrical collection in Britain is the Enthoven Collection, now housed in the Theatre Museum, Covent Garden, with other materials in the holdings of the Victoria and Albert Museum, both in London. In the USA there are several outstanding major collections, encompassing the entire history of scene design: the Oenslager Collection (for both designs and historical treatises), now in the Pierpont Morgan Library, New York, the Robert Tobin Collection of the McNay Museum, San Antonio, Texas, the Harvard Theater Collection at Harvard University and the Cooper-Hewitt Collection in New York City. Other important collections include the New York Public Library for the Performing Arts at Lincoln Center, and the Center for the Humanities of the University of Texas in Austin, Texas.

2. BEFORE 1600. The basis for operatic stage design began with the theatrical art created by ancient Greeks and Romans for the performances of spoken dramas

and comedies in amphitheatres. Together with the use of the space between the *skene* (i.e. the stage house to the rear of the acting area) and the orchestra with the use of movable stage machinery, such as the *periaktoi*, the viewing audience was able to partake in the illusion created for the duration of the theatrical performance. Vitruvius (*De Architectura*) documented the uses of interchangeable units of painted scenery mounted on the *periaktoi*, a revolving three-sided, prism-like device. He further noted that in this era three types of representative scenes were possible: the tragic scene, with a design of a royal palace; the comic scene, with a depiction of ordinary houses; and the satyric stage, representing a wooded landscape. Other architectural features, such as the *proskenion* (proscenium), were developed and later became an integral part of both scene design and theatre architecture.

Although some elements of spectacle were used in ancient times, such as splendid decorations and large choruses, the morality and religious plays of the 13th century made greater use of spectacle in the naturalistic style of production. Biblical representations occasionally spanned a number of stages, but often a single stage was built in the main centre of a community. The craftsmen from the local guilds supplied materials to create, sometimes metaphorically and sometimes with great detail, what were thought to be realistic scenes such as the entrances to, and scenes in, heaven and hell. The elements of spectacle continued to evolve; the stage settings became more and more elaborate. New theatrical machinery was invented to create even greater effects. Spectacle and machinery became an integral part of stage design; all the elements of theatrical production were used to reflect the power and glory of the ruling families of the major population centres of Europe, especially in the city-states of northern Italy.

During the 15th and 16th centuries communities evolved from a feudal society and, particularly in northern Italy, they grew greater in culture, material wealth and political power. In this way the ruling leaders with their families embraced the growth of humanism through the acceptance and study of learning, science and the arts. Humanism, in opening up science and art related to reality, made an essential contribution to the growth of the secular theatre alongside the sacred. The favourite medium of entertainment of the ruling families was the court festivities; these included *intermedi*, ballets, concerts, weddings, triumphal entries and great events in the grand streets and piazzas. These events did not yet require a formal stage setting, but there emerged an event aesthetically distinct from other activities which necessitated a scenic setting as a separate unit of decor. Four factors were decisive in this: the influence of the staging of religious plays; the study of the ancient theatre through the publications of works such as that of Vitruvius; the discovery and practice of central perspective in the early to mid-15th century; and the theory and practice of contemporary drama.

Central perspective had a decisive effect on scene design by providing a scientific method of reproducing the illusion of physical reality. It was distinguished from the perspective representation of antiquity and the Middle Ages by its central vanishing-point and the mathematical regularity of its 'visual pyramid'. Filippo Brunelleschi is considered its inaugurator; its laws were formulated and published in L. B. Alberti's treatise, *Della pittura* (1436). From the art of illusionist painting, the technique of large-scale perspective painting developed and this facilitated the growth in the early 16th century of the painted backcloth (or backdrop), which could both depict a segment of reality and provide an image of an absolute courtly social order. Through this, the full effect of the central perspective was revealed only to those occupying the royal seats in the centre of the seating area; the focal point of the performance centred on royal personages.

The development of the perspective stage was influenced by the growth of an Italian dramatic art which, though dependent on the Latin classics, had also evolved an aesthetic seeking to combine rational humanism with the realities of court life through a system of poetic rules. The conception of the perspective stage was favoured by the concept of 'plausibility', which linked the theatre with aesthetic and social norms. The rule concerning unity of place presupposed the existence of the perspective stage which, significantly, came into use in comedies conforming to the new aesthetic. Pellegrino da Udine painted perspective views of towns for plays by Ariosto performed early in the 16th century at the court of Ferrara; similar town scenes were created by other artists.

Under Horace's influence, late Renaissance drama was grouped into three theoretical genres, each corresponding with a particular social stratum: tragedy (ruling classes), comedy (middle classes) and the pastoral, which developed from the satyr play (peasant classes). This related to Vitruvius's three types of decor; thus theatrical decor too was affected by a class hierarchy. Illustrations from about 1540 represent scenes for tragedy and comedy as architectural backcloths showing aristocratic and middle-class buildings respectively and that for the pastoral as a landscape.

3. The 17th century.

(i) The Italian transformation stage. Attempts were made early in the 16th century to expand the background of painted perspective into an illusionistic area containing the action. By the 1530s, perspective painting was extended from the backcloth to four angular wings at the rear of the stage, marking the diagonal axes of the perspective. A next step was the use of rotating triangular prisms (*periaktoi*), painted on all sides, with a larger prism at the rear; by rotation, three different painted scenes could be presented, emphasizing the depth of the stage (for illustration *see* Machinery, fig.13). This was subsequently improved by the invention of machines for transformation effects, with the use of horizontally movable sliding flats instead of prisms (*see* Machinery, figs.1 and 2).

The advances in illusionist techniques also influenced the structure of court theatre halls. While perspective backcloths required merely a wooden scaffold at a suitable distance from the prince and the rest of the audience (generally in rising tiers), the more complicated transformation stages necessitated a proscenium frame that screened the theatrical machinery from the spectators and partly hid the lighting apparatus (candles, oil lamps). With the erection of a proscenium arch, as early as the 1560s, the spatial separation of the audience area from the stage was achieved, underlined by the curtain. Early 17th-century theatre architects made a space for the orchestra in front of the stage (Florence in 1622; Parma in 1627–8) and, following the example of the Renaissance courts enclosed by multi-storey galleries and tournament theatres, conceived the audience area as a construction of rows of boxes built vertically to each

1. *Design by Bernardo Buontalenti for the fifth intermedio for Bargagli's comedy 'La pellegrina', performed in Florence, 2 May 1589, for the marriage celebrations of Ferdinando I de' Medici and Christine of Lorraine: etching by Epifanio d'Alfiano*

other, on a groundplan at first right-angled and later horseshoe- or bell-shaped. This emphasized the privileged position of the princes, seated on the central axis of the perspective, and the 'parterre noble' around them. Stage design and theatre construction were discussed in numerous 16th- and 17th-century books that elucidated and refined the laws of perspective and their application.

In the evolution of theatrical machinery, Italian scenography attempted to do justice to a dramatic art which in the late 16th century increasingly suppressed plausibility in favour of the 'marvellous'. To display a 'marvel' – something contrary to nature but also credible and even, with divine intervention, plausible – was seen from the mid-16th century as the essence of drama. It was only logical that writers should thereafter ascribe the introduction of the catharsis in drama primarily to the stage marvels produced by the designers and machine technicians. The prestige of the 'marvellous' in late 16th-century theatre was based on its appropriateness to absolutist courts, where mythological and allegorical subjects mirrored the social structure. The main vehicle for the 'marvellous' was the musical *intermedio*, which accompanied dramatic presentations at court and became a spectacular genre which impressively communicated the rulers' power; this is exemplified in Bernardo Buontalenti's decor, machines and costumes for the Florentine *intermedi* of 1586 and 1589. Corresponding with the Platonist texts by Bardi and the music by members of the Camerata, Buontalenti drew on mythology to pay homage to the Medici, creating a sequence of symbolic stage sets (temple, garden, forest, sea coast (see fig.1), underworld, Mount Olympus) metaphorically linking court life with the life of the gods. Often, the princely ruler was depicted in the role of a god entering the stage through scenic devices of the *deus ex machina*.

Opera was staged according to the same principles. The performance of Giulio Caccini's *Il rapimento di Cefalo* in the Teatro Uffizi (1600; decor by Buontalenti) showed that the *stile rappresentativo* could easily be combined with the ostentatious style of the *intermedio*. Offering a conjunction of all the arts cultivated at court festivities, opera took over the representative function of the *intermedio* at many Italian courts during the early 17th century. It brought on to the stage pastoral and romantic subjects, even themes from the lives of the saints; and an extension of the principles of scenography was introduced, using new motifs of architecture and landscape. These motifs were visible in the stage sets of Ludovico Cigoli (Peri's *Euridice*, 1600, Florence), A. M. Viani (Monteverdi's *Orfeo* and *Arianna*, 1607 and 1608, Mantua), Giulio Parigi (Marco da Gagliano's *La regina Sant'Orsola*, 1624, Florence; for illustration *see* PRODUCTION, fig.3), Alfonso Parigi (Gagliano and Peri's *La Flora*, 1628, Florence (engravings; *see* FLORENCE, fig.1); Coppola's *Le nozze degli dei*, 1637, Florence), Francesco Guitti (Monteverdi's *Mercurio e Marte*, 1628, Parma), Alfonso Rivarola (Sances's *Ermiona*, 1636, Padua), Pietro da Cortona (Landi's *Sant'Alessio*, 1632, Rome) and G. F. Grimaldi (Cecchini's *La Sincerità trionfante* and Marazzoli's *La Vita humana*, 1638 and 1656, Rome; for illustration *see* CASTELLI, OTTAVIANO; MARAZZOLI, MARCO; and ROME, fig.1). Despite the concern for greater variety, operatic stage design in the early 17th century clung to the concept of unity between court auditorium and stage: its 'marvels' remained firmly tied to the world of the court and to iconographical tradition.

With the opening of the first public theatre, in 1637 (S Cassiano, Venice), scene design and the production of opera entered a new phase. It became a commercial enterprise dependent on the interest and patronage of the upper and prosperous middle classes; composers such as Monteverdi, Sacrati, Cavalli, Cesti and Legrenzi created a form of drama that endeavoured to cater to the new public with new subjects, mostly taken from history, and sometimes mythology as well. The spectacular success of Venetian opera was based also on the contributions of stage designers and machine technicians such as Alfonso Rivarola (named 'Chenda'), Giuseppe Alabardi, Giovanni Burnacini and, above all, Giacomo Torelli (see fig.2). Most of these artists had worked at court and adapted its methods to the new conditions of theatrical production, which differed in the diminution of the role of machines and the 'marvellous' to a merely

2. Design by Giacomo Torelli for a square in the city of Nasso in Act 2 of Sacrati's 'Venere gelosa', first performed at the Teatro Novissimo, Venice, in 1643: engraving

entertaining function. Venetian stage design brilliantly varied the traditional formal principles and exploited the artistic possibilities of central perspective focussing at infinity. At the same time its importance for European stagecraft lay in its ingenious innovations, above all the technique developed by Torelli of simultaneous *a vista* changes of settings, in view of the audience, with extensive use of wing flats as an important part of the theatrical experience.

This style of scene design, already used by Torelli and Burnacini, became an important and very refined form of theatrical production which increased in significance as mythology and elaborate effects produced by stage machinery largely lost their meaning for the younger generation of designers such as Francesco Santurini, Ippolito Mazzarini and the Mauro brothers. The elaborate settings modelled after contemporary court interiors such as atriums, large halls, cabinets and bedrooms reflected not so much the qualities of the ruling families, but were intended more to glorify *Serenissima*, Venice herself. Some of the constraints of scene design were dictated by the economic conditions of commercial opera production; the paying public not only made possible a more realistic theatrical representation but also enforced in the settings, the music and the libretto a reduction of expressive means to the 'typical'. The opera impresario, in contrast to the subsidized court theatre, had to maintain a good supply of generic and, at the same time elaborate, changeable stage settings and costumes as a fundamental business requisite in order to

3. Design by Jean Berain for Campra's 'Hésione', first performed at the Paris Opéra (Académie Royale de Musique), 21 December 1700

offer entertainment, spectacle and splendour at an acceptable price.

In Italy, stage designers, notably Ferdinando Tacca, Gaspare Vigarani, Giacomo Cipriotti and Girolamo Fontana, took up the ideas suggested by Venetian practice and developed them in the context of court theatres. As a feature of absolutist courtly culture the Italian perspective stage spread throughout Europe in the late 16th and 17th centuries. By 1650 the perspective art was well known, even outside princely residences, as evinced by numerous popular graphic publications, such as the illustrations in the *Orbis sensualium pictus* (Nuremberg, 1659) of J. A. Komenský (Comenius).

(ii) North of the Alps. In France from about 1610 the perspective stage was successfully adapted for the *ballet de cour* by the Florentines Tommaso and Alessandro Francini and further developed by Georges and Denis Buffequin. It was given decisive new impetus by Torelli, who went to Paris in 1645 with Mazarin's opera troupe. It was Torelli's successor Gaspare Vigarani (in Paris from 1659) who with his son Carlo (the co-beneficiary of Lully's operatic privilege from 1672 to 1680) inaugurated the characteristic stage design of Louis XIV's Académie Royale de Musique. Opposed to Venetian opera's gestures towards realism, it sought to preserve the domination of the 'marvellous' with formalized architectural and landscape backcloths and with accomplished mechanical artistry. This conservative conception of the theatre also influenced Vigarani's successor Jean Berain (see fig.3), who designed over 80 productions from Lully's *Cadmus et Hermione* (1673) to Campra's *Les fêtes vénitiennes* (1710).

The princely residences of the German-speaking countries may have been familiar with the Italian perspective stage by the late 16th century. It began to flourish with the cultivation of Italian opera in the 17th century. Often German artists who had worked in Italy introduced new ideas: J. W. Baur, who in 1627 presented the most recent Italian stage techniques at the Viennese court; Joseph Furttenbach of Ulm, a pupil of Parigi; and the writer G. P. Harsdörffer, whose *Frawenzimmer Gesprächspiele* (Nuremberg, 1641–57) contributed to the popularization of the new type of stage among the middle classes. In 1651 Giovanni Burnacini, one of the most important Venetian designers, went to Vienna. His son Ludovico, active at the imperial court for over 50 years, inaugurated a style of spectacular stage presentation using a Baroque multiplicity of forms and stupendous machines; among his most notable designs were those for Cesti's *Il pomo d'oro* (1668; see fig.4, and for further illustration *see* POMO D'ORO, IL) and Draghi's *La monarchia latina trionfante* (1678).

4. Design by Ludovico Burnacini for Act 2 scenes vi–ix (the mouth of hell) of Cesti's 'Il pomo d'oro', performed at the Hoftheater auf der Cortina, Vienna, 12 July 1668: engraving by Matthäus Küsel

As a result of the willingness of Venetian stage designers in Germany such as Francesco Santurini, the Mauro brothers and Tommaso Giusti, and German designers such as Kaspar Amort, J. A. Gumpp, Elias Gedeler and Martin Kletzel, to meet the representational requirements of the courts, this style became obligatory for italianate musical theatre at German princely residences in the late 17th century. Only in the northern and central German opera houses with strong middle-class influence (Hamburg, Brunswick, Wolfenbüttel, Hanover, Leipzig etc.), towards the end of the century, could a realistic type of design be developed for both Italian and German opera. Its most important representative was Johann Oswald Harms (see fig.5), who designed sets, mostly in Brunswick, for numerous operas by Kusser, Steffani, Krieger, Reinhard Keiser (notably *Störtebecker und Jödge Michaels*, 1701, Hamburg), the young Handel and others.

While on the Continent the perspective stage was used in public theatres, in Jacobite and Stuart England it remained a court preserve. In 1605, for a performance

5. Designs for wing flats by Johann Oswald Harms: pen and ink drawing with colour wash (late 17th century)

in Oxford of a pseudo-antique sequence of dramas (*Masque of Blackness*) for a visit by James I, Inigo Jones designed the first stage decor in England painted in perspective. He adopted the perspective stage designs in his later court masques where, especially after his journey to Italy (1613–15), he conceived the stage as an illusionistic space on the Italian model, constructed with stage machinery that he developed to suit the genre. The puritanical spirit of the Commonwealth was manifested in the pared-down, topographically precise stage designs of his pupil John Webb for the operatic ventures of Davenant (*The Siege of Rhodes*, 1656; for illustration *see* SIEGE OF RHODES, THE). Stage design in the Restoration period, of which the chief representatives were Isaac Fuller, Robert Streeter and Thomas Stephenson, developed both at court and in most public theatres a largely French-influenced theatre of machines which, judged by visitors from abroad, came up to current European standards.

4. THE 18TH CENTURY. Despite the 17th-century trends towards realism, the domination of theatre machinery did not end until the early 18th century, when the Arcadian reform of such poets as Stampiglia and Zeno sought to blend the ideology of court absolutism with bourgeois rationalism and to banish not only the comic elements of later Venetian librettos but also all 'marvellous' subjects. With *opera seria*, the fruit of this compromise, conditions of theatrical production were altered. More commercial companies were founded, and there was a substantial growth of middle-class audiences which were catered for by the adoption of elements characteristic of the Enlightenment (notably by Metastasio), but *opera seria* essentially remained a work of art for the princely court. Its rationalist structure in text, music and affects, formalized in a courtly manner, was matched by a scenic framework that translated feudal ideology, not by traditional theatrical machinery, but with the calculated and refined effects of optical illusion through architectural perspective painting. The scenic art thus inclined to the expression of the monumental and making refined use of *trompe l'oeil*. Its basic techniques – angular perspective (*scena per angolo*), diagonal viewpoint which provided a view of several areas, and worm's- and bird's-eye views – derived from quadrature painting, especially from the Bolognese school of Dentone, Mitelli and Colonna.

The first to use this procedure systematically in the theatre was Ferdinando Galli-Bibiena, in his designs for Sabadini's *Dido Giuliano* (1687, Piacenza). Bibiena later published the mathematical requirements for creating a scene to be viewed at an angular perspective and other quadraturist techniques in a seminal treatise, *L'architettura civile* (Parma, 1711; see fig.6). The primary feature is the ability to move the vanishing point of the perspective view from the centre of the scene to different places within that view. The eye of the audience was no longer restricted to one single locus, but was able to wander to different points of view within the scene. This theory, and others, spread a new art of perspective throughout Europe, and considerably enlarged the theatre's imaginative potential. Besides the Galli-Bibiena family, other important representatives of this style were Pietro Righini, G. D. Barbieri, G. B. Medici and the brothers Giuseppe and Domenico Valeriani. Such technically brilliant scene painting was effectively complemented by elegant costumes, delineating the standardized characters who wore them and essentially adhering to the courtly dress and the typology of the 17th century.

With the development of bourgeois culture, courtly *opera seria* declined. In bourgeois drama (exemplified in plays by George Lillo, Denis Diderot and G. E. Lessing) and the new types of musical theatre (*opera buffa*, *opéra comique*, *ballet d'action*, ballad opera, Singspiel) along with the 'reform operas' of Gluck and others, the central concern of bourgeois art was evident: the replacement of courtly formalism by an approach to individual and social existence through the natural and the universally human. Plausibility no longer consisted in the endorsement of traditional aesthetic and social norms but rather in its concordance with empirical nature – which however was reproduced not in its plain appearance but in a typical, idealizing selection that raised theatrical art above 'common reality'.

A vital aspect of the new aesthetic was the coordination of the theatrical arts: stage designer and costume designer were both expected to produce a truthfulness of representation corresponding to the work being performed. The adoption of this concept by the musical theatre (J.-G. Noverre: *Lettres sur la danse*, 1760) meant the end of the formalistic brilliance of Galli-Bibiena's school. Although the operatic theorists of the second half of the century – notably Algarotti (*Saggio sopra l'opera in musica*, 1755), Planelli (*Dell'opera in musica*, 1772) and Arteaga (*Le rivoluzioni del teatro musicale italiano*, 1783–8) – acknowledged the significance of Ferdinando Galli-Bibiena's innovations in the art of perspective (with the exception of Planelli), they cited the lack of plausibility in attacking the bizarre architectural fantasies of his followers. They supported the idea of a pictorially composed stage, communicating moods and local colour; such an art had already emerged in the first half of the century in the work of Filippo Juvarra (for example in his sets for Alessandro Scarlatti's *Ciro*, 1712; for illustration *see* SCARLATTI). This tendency is also evident in sets designed by Antonio Jolli and Luigi Vanvitelli in Rome and Marco Ricci and Bernardo Bellotto in Venice; with the Piedmontese brothers Fabrizio and Bernardino Galliari it began to characterize Italian stage design as a whole (see fig.7).

In spite of compromises with court traditions, these designers reflected the current processes of change in musical theatre. Genre scenes from the comic theatre constituted much of the artistic output and furthered interest in appropriate representation. Enthusiasm for nature (even in *opera seria*) and the new feeling for the aesthetic qualities of landscape led to the displacement of the architectural scenes which had dominated the stage; the tendency of designers to provide visual counterparts of the intentions of the text and the music was reinforced. The generation of the Galliari brothers largely shared the ideal enlightened artist whose 'imagination was guided by erudition' (Algarotti, *Saggio*, 2/1763, p.57). With the adoption, if superficially, of historical and exotic stylistic features propagated by Algarotti, Noverre and F. Milizia (*Trattato completo formale e materiale del teatro*, 1771) to characterize the scene of action, it embodied – at least in principle – the requirement for historically correct stage representation.

Such artists as L.-R. Boquet, Noverre's collaborator, and Leonardo Marini, the Galliaris' partner in Turin, applied these principles to their costumes. Though they often retained the courtly style, by using elements of contemporary and historical popular and national dress, they created costumes of a variety and expressiveness hitherto unknown. This appearance of more realistic decor and costumes reflected middle-class cultural needs, though despite the universality sought in the theatre the art of classical antiquity remained the central point of reference, the republican traditions of the Greeks and Romans increasingly forming an ideal contrast with the contemporary weakening of feudal and absolutist monarchies. This romantic version of classicism was influential not only in musical theatre but had a significant influence on important scenic designers in Italy, notably Pietro Gonzaga, Francesco Fontanesi and Carlo Caccianiga.

The German and Austrian princely residences, where *opera seria* had become an essential element of courtly self-representation, was the centre of the Galli-Bibienas' activities in the first half of the 18th century. In the few

6. Courtyard seen from an angle, illustrating 'operazione 67a: Per disegnare le scene vedute per angolo', in Ferdinando Galli-Bibiena's 'L'architettura civile' (Parma, 1711): engraving by an unknown artist

7. Design by Fabrizio Galliari for a scene from Holzbauer's 'Nitteti', performed at the Teatro Regio, Turin, in 1758

centres of German opera, designers such as Tobias Querfurt in Brunswick asserted an attitude of greater realism, and in the mid-18th century the scenographers of Italian opera troupes came round to a similar position. During the second half of the century G. P. Gaspari, Jacopo Fabris, Innocente Colomba, Giovanni Maria Quaglio the elder, Bartolomeo Verona and Lorenzo Sacchetti (see fig.8) arrived at scenic ideas similar to those of the Galliaris, but the dominant role of architectural scenery long remained a feature of German theatre. In the designs of Lorenzo and Giulio Quaglio, J. H. Zimmermann and Joseph Platzer, the genre-type themes of the Singspiel came to the fore along with classical subjects.

In France, Jean Berain the younger, as scenic director of the Académie Royale de Musique, continued his father's tradition, which had meanwhile fossilized into convention. An important artist such as Claude Gillot (the elder Berain's assistant from about 1697) could threaten this monopolistic situation but not break it down. Only after Berain's death (1726) did French stage design renew its links with international developments in the perspective art of G. N. Servandoni, who, as the Académie's leading stage designer (1726–44) and the organizer of *spectacles de décoration* in the Tuileries (Salle des Machines, 1738–58), combined the tradition of the French theatre of machines with the Italian innovations in perspective. His successor as scenic director to the Académie (1744–8) was François Boucher, the principal master of the Rococo in France, who had been responsible for opera designs from about 1737. His picturesque landscapes and genre scenes translated the world of *fêtes galantes* on to the stage, although they were not always well adapted to the requirements of contemporary musical theatre. The criticism levelled by the Encyclopedists (J. F. Blondel in particular) at the

8. Design (1781) for the royal palace of Apollo by Lorenzo Sacchetti: model of a stage set for an unknown opera

theatrical dilettantism of 'peintres de chevalet' was doubtless aimed at Boucher, yet his influence on French stage design was great, extending (despite the classical tendencies of the Slodtz brothers and C. M.-A. Challe) far into the second half of the century. Boucher influenced the production style of Jean Monnet's Opéra-Comique, and during the 1760s he produced many design sketches for the Académie. Only with Gluck's reform operas did the dominance of the Rococo style cease in French stage design; the classicism that appeared in the designs of J.-M. Moreau, F.-J. Belanger and P.-A. Pâris (see fig.9) was to spread far beyond France, above all in its romantic interpretation by Louis-Jean Desprez in Rome and Stockholm. Desprez' atmospheric landscapes and effective tableaux, as exemplified in his sets for J. G. Naumann's *Gustaf Wasa* (1786; for illustration *see* GUSTAF WASA), foreshadowed principles that were to be developed in Romantic opera design.

In late 17th-century England a form of stage design evolved in the public theatres which, while unpretentious compared with continental practice, was characterized by an element of bourgeois realism; this affected the style of Italian opera design in London, as early as the simple sketches of James Thornhill for Clayton's italianate *Arsinoe* (1705; for illustration *see* ARSINOE). Subsequently Italian designers brought to England the perspective art of the Galli-Bibienas, particularly scenes viewed at an angle, but the most important designers working for the King's Theatre, such as Marco Ricci (1708–16), Servandoni (1720–21), Antonio Jolli (1746–8), Innocente Colomba (1774–80) and Michael Novosielski (1781–95), did not follow the formalism associated with court theatres. A more important part was played in the development of a realistic type of stage design, however, by the popular genres of musical theatre such as English-language opera, burlesque and pantomime. Their parodies of courtly opera and mythology found in the pseudo-Baroque stage designs of John Devoto (*fl* 1708–52) a form of visual expression – picturesque genre scenes, topographical views and fairy-tale or exotic sets – that was apt to their themes of everyday life, current political events or romantic incidents. With the striking depictions of Nature by P. J. de Loutherbourg and Robert Carver the scenic realism of the 18th century, though primarily throwing romantic subjects into relief, reached its apex.

The evolution of a more realistic style later necessitated a modification of the 17th-century stage structure, with its symmetrical wings, borders and backcloth. The adoption of quadraturist techniques by Galli-Bibiena had made the backcloth the main medium of illusion, laying the foundations for a primarily 'painterly' art of stage design, though at the same time the development of the 'cut cloth' (or 'cut drop') had created the possibility of plastic effects (Ferdinando Galli-Bibiena, *Direzioni delle prospettive teoriche*, Bologna, 1732, operazione 69). The favourite theatrical aesthetic formula of the Enlightenment, in which the stage is described as a 'living painting' (Cahusac, Noverre), signifies not the restriction of the scene to two dimensions but a realistic art corresponding to contemporary landscape and genre painting. Even more thoroughly than Galli-Bibiena, Juvarra attempted to achieve this by wings often placed asymmetrically and by a backcloth broken up into juxtaposed (and in part perforated) smaller units of decor, thus giving an effect of greater depth and plasticity. In the second half of the century the concept of a 'natural' stage area was further developed, above all by the Galliari brothers at La Scala in Milan, who staggered the acting surfaces with draped trestles, stairs, platforms and other props while retaining the basics of the wing, border and backcloth system. It was perfected, at least in landscape scenes, by Loutherbourg with his naturalistically shaped cut cloths, movable scenery and floor-pieces (see fig.10). On the other hand, the application of 'naturalness' to the construction of interiors barely passed the experimental stage; difficulties of lighting precluded widespread dissemination of the 'box set' introduced in Hamburg in the early 1790s by F. L. Schröder.

9. Design by Pierre-Adrien Pâris for the prison of Orestes and Pylades in a production of Gluck's 'Iphigénie en Tauride' at the Paris Opéra (Académie Royale de Musique) between 1779 and 1792

10. Stage set by P. J. de Loutherbourg for an unknown production: (a) the component pieces, including movable scenery and floor pieces (b) the constructed set in place on the stage (the large central back piece is missing)

5. THE 19TH CENTURY. The 19th-century theatre not only reflected the progress and social change of the Industrial Revolution but also based its organization and production on the governing principles of the industrial age. Encouraged by the suppression or relaxation of the previous conventions, musical theatre in most of Europe was freed of its court associations. The more trivial genre of musical drama that now flourished in the cities catered for the expanding middle-class society as, increasingly, did opera and ballet productions.

The theatre's vital role in this society was in part expressed by its outward appearance, its characteristic architecture marking it out as a centre of bourgeois culture. The new class system (as the old had been) was manifested in most 19th-century theatres by hierarchical tiers of boxes. This kind of theatre, typified by Garnier's Paris Opéra (1875), prevailed partly because the amphitheatre-type conception favoured by progressive architects could not be satisfactorily combined with the illusionist perspective stage. Richard Wagner's Bayreuth

Festspielhaus (1876) was a notable exception, for it had few direct successors. Its example led late 19th-century theatre architects to strive for a combination of the tiered and amphitheatre style such as became obligatory in the 20th century, especially after World War II.

The facilities offered by the 18th-century stage system were increased through refinements offered by new industrial techniques. Decisive factors in this process, besides the building of more spacious stage areas allowing greater mechanization, were gas and electric lighting. Coal gas lighting was first used in London (Drury Lane and Lyceum, 1817) and was soon taken up by all the larger European theatres; it provided a relatively strong, controllable and safe light which not only made possible the introduction of the closed-in 'box set' (important in the evolution of realism) but also considerably enhanced the illusionist techniques of the Romantic musical theatre such as the panorama (1785), the diorama (*c*1820) and the moving panorama (*c*1820). The installation of gas lighting in the Paris Opéra in 1820 gave an important impetus to scene design. Particularly intense lighting effects could be produced by limelight, invented in 1825 but not generally used in theatres until the 1840s. The theatrical use of electricity began with the carbon arc (used for the sun in the première of Meyerbeer's *Le prophète* at the Opéra in 1849), installed during the second half of the 19th century primarily as a spotlight and projection lamp; the general electrification of the stage came about only after the invention of the dynamo (1866) and the incandescent lamp (1879). After the experimental electric illumination of the auditorium and foyer of the Opéra, in 1881, the large theatres of Europe all came to be fitted with electric stage lighting, beginning in the same year with the Savoy, London. Munich followed in 1883, and the Vienna Hofoper in 1887.

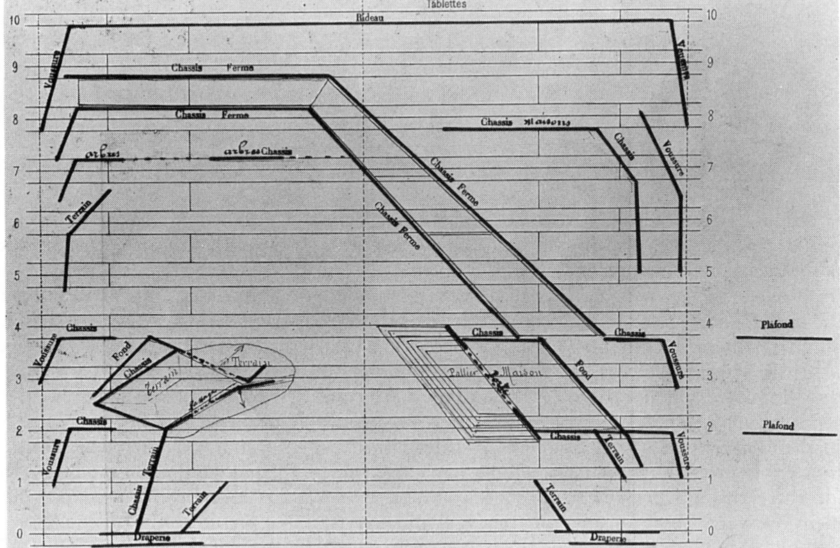

11. Stage set designed by J. B. Lavastre for a courtyard in the palace of the King of Granada (Act 4) in Massenet's 'Le Cid', first performed at the Paris Opéra, 30 November 1885: ground plan (above) and model (below)

12. *Design by Karl Friedrich Schinkel for a performance of Spontini's 'Fernand Cortez' at the Schauspielhaus, Berlin (1818)*

The integration of these new technologies into artistic production was possible only through the development of the art of stage management, which sprang both from the ideals of the Enlightenment as to the coordination of the production as a self-contained work of art and from an interest in local colour, styles and milieux. The idea of artistic stage production had already been apparent in the 18th-century *ballet d'action*, but in opera the concept was applied, first in France, only as a consequence of the rationalization that resulted from the introduction of commercial principles in opera management. However, this practice was based on a 'common agreement between the egoisms' of the individual arts, dependent, in Wagner's view, on the public taste, which resulted in only a 'pseudo-unification'; it was only in a *Gesamtkunstwerk*, akin to a Utopian model of society, that each art could be deployed to its fullest extent (*Das Kunstwerk der Zukunft*, 1849).

Theatrical production in the 19th century is marked by its attempts to standardize the theatrical work and so make it reproducible for other theatres, primarily in the provinces. By the late 18th century, commercial theatrical agencies in Paris were successfully publishing production books; this procedure, which became standard, gave Parisian box-office successes the status of model productions, particularly after 1820 with the publication of the production book detailing the settings and staging of *La muette de Portici* at the Opéra, and was to be copied by provincial and foreign theatres. The reproduction of sets, properties and costumes was taken over by scenic studios – workshops run as private enterprises by the designers of large theatres; the first of these was founded in 1822 by P.-L.-C. Ciceri, scenic director of the Opéra, whose historical sets for Meyerbeer's *Robert le diable* were remarkably detailed and accurate (*see* GRAND OPERA, fig.4). Within a few decades the production of sets was predominantly in the hands of workshops similar to Ciceri's in most of Europe and North America. Such technical and organizational innovations increased the stage's visual potential to a new degree and gave rise to a relatively uniform international style of staging, even if with specific national characteristics.

Aided by the survival of forms of *opera seria*, and influenced by the international success of grand opera, many stage designers of the early 19th century clung first of all to the enlightened early bourgeois concept, as propagated by F. C. Beuther in *Dekorationen für die Schaubühne* (1824), of an art raised above 'common reality', and hence to the idealism of neo-classicism, even if such men as Karl Friedrich Schinkel (see fig.12), chief designer at the Berlin Königliche Schauspiele from 1815 to 1828, used new illusionist techniques. Other representatives of this movement were Ignazio Degotti and J.-B. Isabey (Paris), Paolo Landriani (Milan), Giuseppe Borsato (Venice), Giacomo Pregliasco (Milan), Giuseppe Quaglio and his son Angelo the elder (Munich) and Gaetano Marinari (London).

However, with the continuing decline of the distinct traditional genres and the emergence of Romantic opera, subjective tendencies began to dominate scene design, in reaction against early industrial society. For the designers of early Romantic opera, among them Giorgio Fuentes (Frankfurt), Alessandro Sanquirico (Milan), Anton de Pian (Vienna), Angelo Quaglio (Munich) and William Capon (London), the formal rules of classicism, such as those systematized in Lorenzo Sacchetti's *Quanto sia facile l'inventare decorazioni teatrali* (1830), were relevant. With the increasingly predominant medieval ('Gothick'), exotic and supernatural themes, however, they were appropriated in a stock of motifs within a historic-idyllic style coloured by personal sentiment and characterized by atmospheric architecture, picturesque landscapes and genre scenes.

This subjective conception predominated until after the mid-century, though it was increasingly mixed with realistic tendencies. Triggered by social conflicts during the French Restoration, and stimulated by the rediscovery of national historical and cultural traditions, there was a revival of interest in primarily realistic art for historical subjects (*couleur locale*). From the late

1820s Ciceri, his collaborators and his students exploited the most modern stage and lighting techniques and used highly coordinated production methods along with the help of costume designers to create effective scenic settings. These scenes depicted precisely the relevant historical milieu for the grand operas of Auber, Halévy and Meyerbeer. Although some historical depiction was achieved, it was supplemented not only through meticulous scenic reconstruction but also through familiar social elements such as the revolutionary gesture (highly effective in *La muette di Portici*, which touched off a political revolution in Brussels, 1830), massive crowd scenes (as in Act 4 of *Le prophète*) and special technical scenic effects (the eruption of Vesuvius in *La muette de Portici*; *see* MUETTE DE PORTICI, LA, fig.2).

The elements of spectacle achieved greater status in French grand opera, for the genre itself became an instrument of state. Up to the latter part of the 19th century, the Opéra was granted by the government a large budget to create and achieve grand scenic effects particularly for the operas of Meyerbeer and Halévy. The results, with their subsequent popularity, served to propagate the glory and stability of the French state.

The production style of French grand opera achieved international dissemination; its influence on stage design was to be found above all where opera was a vehicle for political ideas: in pre-1848 Germany (Wagner's *Rienzi*), Italy of the Risorgimento (especially with Verdi's *Ernani*, *La battaglia di Legnano* and *Attila*) and in other countries striving for independence such as Belgium, Poland, Hungary and the Czech lands. However, the work of many scene designers, such as Giuseppe and Pietro Bertoia, Domenico Ferri, C. W. Gropius (see fig.13), Hermann Neefe, Joseph Mühldorfer, Antonio Sacchetti and Andreas Roller, though formally dependent on the Paris school of grand opera, remained in many respects within the bounds of idyllic early Romanticism.

In England early 19th-century stage designers such as John Henderson Grieve and his sons Thomas and William, as well as Robert C. Andrews, David Roberts and, above all, Clarkson Stanfield, linking up with the tradition of English landscape painting, were able with the aid of an accomplished stage technique to outdo anything on the Continent. However, their technique was inseparable from genres such as pantomime, extravaganza, burletta etc., in which realism had increasingly been sacrificed to colour, ostentation and triviality, and in which a tendency to exploit effect for its own sake had developed. European stage design during the second half of the century, particularly French grand opera, was dominated by such tendencies, manifesting in a preoccupation with detail, a bourgeois historicism and a flight into myths and exotic dream worlds.

With the evolution of grand opera, the visual aspect of production acquired a still greater importance, but the integrated visual impact was lost in favour of academic virtuosity which, above all else, demanded a stage and costume designer with an encyclopedic knowledge, best described by Théophile Gautier (*Portraits contemporains*, Paris, 1874):

> [The designer (*décorateur*)] must have an intimate knowledge of every country, every historical epoch, all styles; he must have a thorough knowledge of geology, the flora and the architecture of the five continents of the world. And even that is not enough. Lost civilizations, splendours of the antediluvian world, the azure pastures of Paradise, the red blazes of Hell, the coral grottos of the ocean, Babel, Enochia, Nineveh, Tyre, Memphis and the entire dominion of the fairies, all that exists and all that does not exist.

The most impressive contributions to this universal panorama reduced to the perspective of the middle classes were provided by numerous stage designers associated with various scenic studios, among them Joseph Thierry in France, Carlo Ferrario (Verdi's favourite designer) in Italy (see fig.14), and in Germany and Austria the court scene-painters Angelo Quaglio the younger (see fig.15), Heinrich Döll and in Vienna, Carlo and Anton Brioschi.

In addition to this theatrical art, screening off or ignoring social realities of the time, there evolved other genres of musical theatre which approached reality either satirically, as did Offenbach and his followers, or in a critically descriptive way, as with *verismo* at the end of the century. While parodistic operettas caricatured conventional sets and costumes (as in the stage designs by Jules Draner and costumes by Alfred Grévin for the

13. Design by C. W. Gropius for the Act 3 finale from the original production of Weber's 'Der Freischütz' at the Schauspielhaus, Berlin, 18 June 1821

14. Design by Carlo Ferrario for the first performance of Verdi's 'Don Carlos' in four acts at La Scala, Milan, 10 January 1884

15. Model of the set designed by Angelo Quaglio (ii) for Tristan's castle in Brittany (Act 3) for the original production of Wagner's 'Tristan und Isolde' at the Königliches Hof- und Nationaltheater, Munich, 10 June 1865

Théâtre des Variétés in Paris), *verismo* introduced objective, functional design placed wholly at the service of the drama. However, apart from the stagings by Georg von Meiningen and the Naturalist school, there was little unifying principle behind *verismo* stage designs. In the designs of Marcel Jambon, Bailly, Lucien Jusseaume, the former *féerie* specialist Amable, Adolf Hohenstein and Georg Hacker for the operas of Charpentier, Bizet, Mascagni, Leoncavallo, Puccini and others, there was an eclectic mixture of historical, naturalistic, impressionistic and neo-romantic elements. The novelty of the style lay in its preference for realistic, flexible pieces of decor to complement the illusionistic painting.

Descriptive realism made an even more important appearance in Russian opera during the late 19th century, although it was basically restricted to the private opera productions for the magnate Vlassa Ivanovich Mamontov in Abramtsevo and Moscow (1885–7). Apart from some naturalistic designs by Ivan Petrovich Andreyev for the Imperial Court Theatre in St Petersburg, it was otherwise dominated by the Romantic tradition of stage design associated with Andreas Roller. The painters in Mamontov's circle at Abramtsevo worked as his stage designers, and their work was inspired by the realism of Russian folk art; among those who were outstanding were the designers Viktor Andreyevich Simov and Viktor Mikhailovich Vasnetzov.

6. 1900–45. In the early 20th century, during the period of political and economic expansion, the artist's traditional identification with the society around him was shattered. The naturalists might have been able to make their social criticism artistically productive; but the subsequent generation of designers, raising its own lack of solutions into a principle, rejected confrontation with the inhuman and threatening outside world of an industrial society. Instead, they explored an 'inner world'

of the soul, dreams and the 'unsullied' world of exoticism. Unlike Freud's attempts to form a theory of the unconscious mind, the artistic concepts of the symbolists and of their successors, the neo-romantics, were characterized by escapism, anti-realism and irrational, élitist mystical impulses. The resultant autonomous art of the theatre would have remained without decisive influence on 20th-century stage design had it not contained vital progressive elements in its opposition to 'bourgeois' decor and its demands that a style of staging older and contemporary dramatic works be suitable to the works themselves. During the course of the century, the theatre as a tool for education, both subtly and overtly, and as a means of propaganda grew in importance and relevance.

Until then, works from the cultural heritage were performed in a way that attempted to bring the respected 'original conception' into a harmonious relationship with the new emancipating goals of the middle classes, theatrical conventions and censorship. The scenic interpretations of the neo-romantics were achieved in ways that derived from the inherent characteristics of the works themselves, often leading to an exaggerated attitude of 'art for art's sake'. Under the influence of the 'vital philosophy' of Bergson, Nietzsche and Dilthey, and in particular through a trivialized application of hermeneutic method, the 'inner vision that a work awakens in its later re-creators' (R. Specht, *Gustav Mahler*, Berlin, 1913) came to be a decisive criterion in performance. This concept inevitably led to a break with traditional theatrical production. Staging no longer meant an effective coordination of the stage activities, but rather the realization of an intuitively grasped interpretation, to be applied to all aspects of the production.

This concept also embraced the latest refinements and newest inventions in modern theatre technology. Although it was designed primarily to improve the naturalistic and historical styles of scenic illusion, new technology provided essential elements in the evolution of the scenic art. These included the refinement and widespread use of the circular horizon (otherwise known as the cyclorama) which, combined with an effective lighting system, assisted in creating stage spaces freed from cumbersome wings, legdrops and borders previously required to mask offstage areas from the view of the audience. Technological improvements in lightbulbs (stronger filament bulbs replacing arc lights) allowed refinements in lighting the stage with spotlights and projection lamps as well as greater control in manipulating levels of light intensity. Motorized revolving stages were introduced in Munich (1896) and Vienna (1900). Large portions of the stage floor as well as smaller traps were mechanized through electricity or hydraulics, and mechanically operated flies became standard resources of the modern opera house.

A major contribution to the break in the traditional forms of theatrical production were the theories of the Swiss designer and reformer, Adolphe Appia. He opposed the domination of the stage by elaborate scenic painting, be it conventional or avant-garde. The singing actor should be the central intermediary between the author and public, the music and the stage. In his pioneering publication *Die Musik und die Inszenierung* (1899), Appia firmly believed that the music should govern the staging; he appealed for absolute visual simplicity and, more significantly, in what was to lead towards a fundamental shift in the scenic art, a new and different method of stage lighting. Borderlights and footlights were de-emphasized and stress was placed on individual and combined spotlights to shape and form through lighting (distinct from simply illuminating the stage) in order to achieve the full plasticity and depth of the scene. Less emphasis was placed on scenic painting, whose role as the medium of colour was transferred to lighting. The plasticity of the design also involved the performer in a three-dimensional stage setting which should manifest the dramatic 'vision issuing from the womb of the music' corresponding to the action on the stage itself (see fig.16).

In some essentials Appia's abstract designs were close to the work of Edward Gordon Craig (*The Art of the Theatre*, 1905), who constructed his poetic productions for the London Purcell Operatic Society (1900–03) largely with the use of coloured curtains and atmospheric lighting. After 1905, however, Craig strove towards an architectonic scenic form whose functional problems were solved around 1907 in a highly original

16. Set design (1892) by Adolphe Appia for Act 3 of Wagner's 'Die Walküre', depicting Wotan on the rock of the Valkyries after having sent Brünnhilde to sleep: drawing

way with the development of kinetic 'screens' (*The Mask*, vii, 1914–15, p.139).

During the first decade of the 20th century the influence of Appia and, later, Craig spread throughout central Europe. With the development and refinement of stage devices such as the cyclorama, and significant technical and artistic improvements in stage lighting, some theatres offered the practical conditions in which the concepts of Appia and Craig could be applied. But most of the established theatrical institutions were conservative and refused to entertain their radical ideas, even though a few experimental productions proved their practicability and attracted attention among artists and patrons of the *belle époque*.

Combined with the introduction of new stage technologies and refinements in lighting, many producers and stage directors began to make more use of artists rather than stage designers. It was avant-garde painters who were approached to revitalize stage design. In Vienna, during Gustav Mahler's directorship at the Hofoper (1897–1907), Mahler's concepts of stagecraft combined with the ideals of the *Gesamtkunstwerk* – despite its neo-romantic individualism – were influenced through his contact with the reformative functionalism of *art nouveau*, as reflected in the Austrian *Sezession* and the German *Jugendstil*, which strove towards a synthesis of the arts. Alfred Roller, a key member of the *Sezession*, was engaged by Mahler as chief designer (1903–09). Roller used architectural simplicity and clarity as well as clear, intense colour and lighting. He cleared the stage of excessive scenic and decorative clutter and through the unity of the arts an atmosphere was created in which the attention of the audience was focussed on the drama on the stage. Roller was among the first to put into reality basic ideas of the *Gesamtkunstwerk* similar to those espoused by Richard Wagner, Appia and Craig. His productions (notably *Tristan und Isolde*, 1903; see VIENNA, fig.8, and *Don Giovanni*, 1905; see fig.17) influenced the work of numerous designers, including Karl Walser and Bernhard Pankok. In Berlin, the director Max Reinhardt engaged such painters as Lovis Corinth, Emil Orlik, Edvard Munch and Ernst Stern. In the same spirit of revitalized stagecraft, Josef Wenig was active in Bohemia and Karol Frysz in Poland.

The Russians used many avant-garde painters as well. *Jugendstil* and French symbolism were great influences on stage designers at the influential Mamontov Opera in Moscow (1896–9) which included folk realists of the Abramtsevo circle, members of Princess Tenisheva's circle of artists, and a group associated with the journal *Mir iskusstvo* ('World of Art', founded by Serge Dyagilev in 1898). Under the influence of Dyagilev and Alexandre Benois, S. M. Volkonsky, director of the Imperial Theatre from 1899, and his successor V. A. Telyakovsky followed Mamontov's lead and entrusted members of the *Mir iskusstvo* circle with the designs for numerous productions in St Petersburg and Moscow. These included Benois, Konstantin Korovin, Alexander Golovin, Leon Bakst and Nikolay and Valentin Serov. The opera impresario S. I. Zimin also followed the Mamontov tradition, engaging painters such as Fedor Fedorovsky and Ivan Bilibin, both closely linked with Russian folk art.

From about 1905, Russian stage directors associated with symbolism – Vsevolod Meyerhold, Nikolay Yevreynov, Fyodor Komisaryevsky and Konstantin Stanislavsky – also sought to collaborate with the artistic circle associated with *Mir iskusstvo*, many of whom later became influential designers in opera and ballet. Golovin in particular collaborated with Meyerhold at the Mariinsky Theatre in St Petersburg in Gluck's *Orfeo ed Euridice* in 1911. In the productions of Dyagilev's Ballets Russes, founded in Paris in 1909 with members (including Benois) of the imperial theatres in St Petersburg and Moscow, the design and staging principles previously developed in Russia were followed and carried even further. Dyagilev and Benois claimed to have realized the idea of the *Gesamtkunstwerk*, but it was the stage designs and costumes of the *Mir iskusstvo* painters that dominated these imaginative 'spectacles de rêve' of the *belle époque*. Their international success assured artistic scene-painting a prominent place in music theatre outside Russia, and associated it more firmly with contemporary trends in the fine arts, an association strengthened by Dyagilev's collaboration with avant-garde painters such as Natalia Goncharova and Mikhail Laryonov (see fig.18). In Paris Jacques Rouché followed this example and, in operatic and balletic experiments at the Théâtre des Arts (1910–13) and in productions at the Opéra, he collaborated with Maxime Dethomas, René Piot, Jacques Drésa and Maurice Denis.

17. Design by Alfred Roller for the graveyard scene (Act 2) of Mahler's production of Mozart's 'Don Giovanni' at the Vienna Hofoper, 21 December 1905

18. Design by Mikhail Laryonov for the original production of Stravinsky's 'Renard' performed by Dyagilev's Ballets Russes at the Paris Opéra, 18 May 1922

The neo-romantic dream of an aesthetic existence apart from reality was shattered first by increasingly acute social and economic conflicts and eventually by the experience of World War I. Among progressive artists, the idealistic protest movement took on an activist guise, with expressionism, futurism and constructivism combating and destroying previous formal traditions. The passionate activism of expressionism did not conflict with its basis in the irrational: it dealt not with 'facts' but with 'human hearts', which the artist 'with a soul' renewed with the 'pathos of the unequivocal' and the 'melody of the grand gesture' (P. Kornfeld: 'Der beseelte und der psychologische Mensch', *Das junge Deutschland*, i, 1918, p.12). On the stage, taking the concepts of Appia and Craig to radical extremes, this occurred through a pathos-orientated arrangement of geometric basic forms and expressive colours, with a 'soul' instilled by effective lighting. From 1912 onwards, in the symbolically designed, near-abstract spatial compositions of the most important representative of this tendency, Ludwig Sievert (see fig.19), there appeared a peculiarly suggestive visual manifestation of the intuitively conceived, subjective, emotional world of the expressionist drama and also of the freshly reappraised classical music drama. Essential contributions to the development of expressionist design were made in Germany by Emil Pirchan, Hans Strohbach, Hein Heckroth (Handel festivals in Göttingen and Münster, from 1924), Panos Aravantinos and others; in Czechoslovakia by Vlastislav Hofmann, Bedřich Feuerstein and František Muzika; in Poland by Wincenty Drabik; in France by Andrée Parr and Gaston Baty; in Sweden by Isaac Grünewald; and in England by Paul Shelving and Laurence Bradshaw.

From about 1910 onwards the Italian futurists, primarily by means of burlesque, demonstrated in

19. Design by Ludwig Sievert for the 1921 production of Korngold's 'Die tote Stadt' at the Vereinigtes Stadttheater, Frankfurt

numerous 'theatrical syntheses' their rejection of traditional forms, their irrational innovations and their desire for dynamism and activism at any price (including that of the war). Their aim of 'hurling the spectator through the labyrinth of sensory perceptions' (F. T. Marinetti and others: *Manifesto del teatro futurista*, 1915) appeared in the abstract, dynamic archi tectures of colours, light and space by Giacomo Balla (Stravinsky's *Fireworks*, Ballets Russes, 1917, Rome), Fortunato Depero (*Balli plastici* by Alfredo Casella, Malipiero and others, 1918, Rome) and Enrico Prampolini.

While the futurists were celebrating the machine as a sort of blind nemesis, the fascination with the technique of Russian cubist futurism and of the constructivist movement from which it grew was more orientated to reality and marked by the desire to liberate man, with the aid of the machine, from his dependence on nature and traditional social structures. Kasimir Malevich's stage designs for the first manifestation of cubist futurism in the musical theatre – M. V. Matyushin's 'suprematist' Singspiel *Pobeda nad solnzem* ('The Victory over the Sun'; 1913, St Petersburg; see fig.20) – sought to treat this demand as its theme, though it was still chiefly a painterly conception. The growing interest of progressive stage directors such as A. J. Tairov, Meyerhold and Nemirovich-Danchenko in the work of the constructivists played its part, after the October Revolution, in the emergence of a conception of a dynamic and technique-orientated spatial stage. Partly strictly formal and partly frivolous, its functionalism exercised a lasting influence on the scenography of Soviet musical theatre. Constructivism was introduced to French musical theatre in the 1920s and had considerable influence in eastern Europe.

20. Design by Kasimir Malevich for the original production of M. V. Matyushin's 'The Victory over the Sun' at the Luna Park theatre, St Petersburg, 1913: from the cover of the libretto (St Petersburg, 1913)

Similar social Utopianism was represented by the Bauhaus in Weimar, Dessau and Berlin (1919–33). After an early expressionist phase under Lothar Schreyer, stage design at the Bauhaus was under Oskar Schlemmer (from 1923); he took special interest in the relationship between man and space, similar to the Dutch *de stijl* movement (Piet Mondrian, Theo van Doesburg) and the Berlin G-Gruppe (Ludwig Mies van der Rohe, Friedrich Kiesler), and successfully tackled the clarification of form and basic construction. Bauhaus stage design sought to realize Walter Gropius's aim of 'a new unity of art with technique' by mechanizing not only the constructivist spatial articulation of the stage but all theatrical and musical means of expression. Some of its experiments influenced the progressive professional musical theatre, particularly the productions of the Berlin Kroll Opera under Klemperer (1927–31). This applied less to the purist abstract constructions of Schlemmer (Hindemith's *Das triadische Ballet*, 1922, Stuttgart) and Vasily Kandinsky (Musorgsky's *Pictures at an Exhibition*, 1928, Dessau) than the creation of a functional constructional representation of reality exemplified by László Moholy-Nagy (Offenbach's *Les contes d'Hoffmann*, 1929, Berlin) and Roman Clemens (Hindemith's *Neues vom Tage*, 1930, Dessau). The cubist scenic space of Klemperer's favoured designer Ewald Dülberg (*Fidelio*, 1927) also bore the imprint of Bauhaus ideas.

The circumstances in Russia (1917) and Germany (1918) caused many progressive artists to break with the idealism and romanticism of the expressionists and constructivists and to face social and economic reality. From the revolutionary socialist Berlin dadaists there grew a group of *verismo* artists among whom George Grosz and John Heartfield saw the theatre, especially in the productions of Erwin Piscator, as an effective instrument of aggressive and sometimes cynical social criticism. This type of realism influenced the early productions of Brecht, mostly realized in collaboration with the producer Erich Engel and the stage designer Caspar Neher (see fig.22). It was the basis of a critical realistic 'epic' drama exhibiting the economic driving forces of its action partly through the reduction of its human terms and partly through commentary provided by a blending of banners, projections and film. Neher in particular realized this concept not only in the works of Brecht and Weill but also in repertory operas

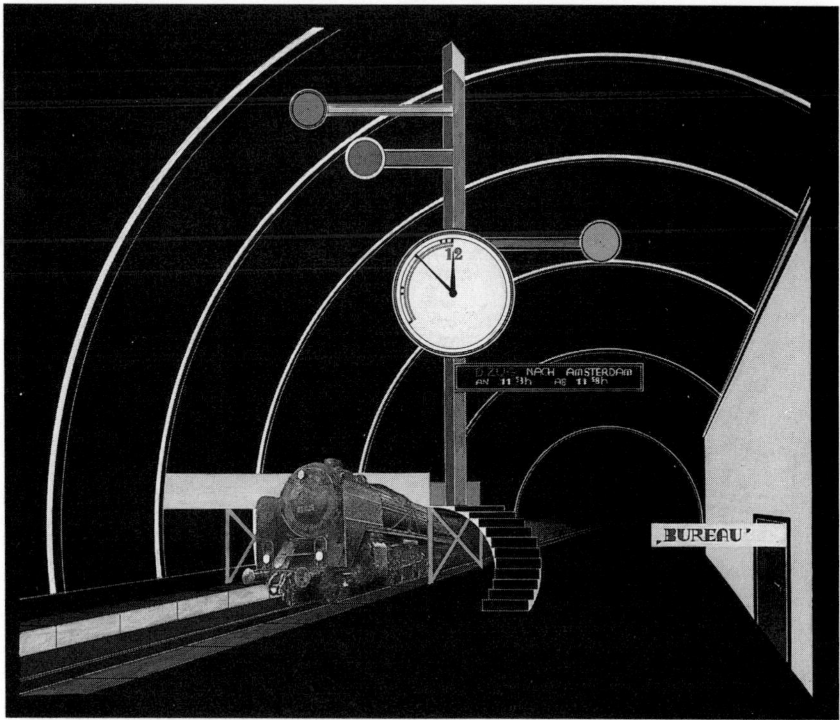

21. Design by Roman Clemens for the 1928 Dessau production of Krenek's 'Jonny spielt auf'

such as *Carmen* at the Berlin Kroll Opera in 1928.

During the mid-1920s a further trend emerged in Germany alongside this socially committed art (later suppressed by the Nazis) which, though similarly orientated towards objectivity, renounced the critical attitude. It embraced a variety of formal trends linked by their aspiration towards objectivity. This is exemplified by the 'New Functionalism' in the works of Wilhelm Reinking, Lothar Schenk von Trapp and Gerd Richter; these were significant through their updated stagings of the classics. They renounced the Utopianism but not the techniques or the technological rationalism of constructivism and the Bauhaus. New Functionalism shared this tendency towards the affirmative with the 'magical realism' of Cesar Klein and the surrealism of Heckroth, and also with the work of anti-modernists such as the Wagner specialist Emil Preetorius, who expressed a preference for classical monumentality, or Leo Pasetti and Josef Fenneker, who imprinted it with lyrical romantic features. Except for Heckroth, these 'objective', monumental, romantic or surrealistic designers, together with former expressionists such as Sievert and Schröder, became after 1933 the most important German stage designers under Nazism. Benno von Arent, who progressed from a revue painter to 'stage designer by order of the Reich', introduced a

22. Design by Caspar Neher for Act 3 scene iv of Weill's 'Aufstieg und Fall der Stadt Mahagonny' for the original production at the Neues Theater, Leipzig, 9 March 1930

23. Model of the set designed by Oliver Messel for the 1956 Glyndebourne production of Mozart's 'Die Entführung aus dem Serail'

form of neo-historicism; his preference for a monumental neo-Baroque and neo-classical formal language typifies the ostentatiousness of the period (*Die Meistersinger*, 1936, Berlin).

In Italy, the experiments of the futurists continued, and the *pittura metafisica* occasionally influenced musical theatre in the 1920s; but they were unable to break the domination of 19th-century historicist painting exemplified by the works of Carlo Ferrario. The studio of Luigi Sapelli, who designed under the pseudonym of Caramba, set the style well into the 1930s not only at La Scala, Milan, but also in the provincial Italian and foreign opera houses, including the Metropolitan Opera, New York. At La Scala, Appia (*Tristan und Isolde*, 1923) and Nicola Benois (from 1926) introduced fresh, if sometimes dated, stimuli but the rise of fascism in 1923 resulted in a general architectonic monumentality of style evinced in the designs of Ettore Fagiuolo, Guido Marussig, Effisio Oppo and Pietro Aschieri. Only in 1933 with the Maggio Musicale Fiorentino was an Italian forum created for modern design; by that time, however, formal radicalism had been abandoned. The designs of the former futurist Gino Severini for Florence, like those of the representatives of the *pittura metafisica*, were distinguished by clear, classicistic formal language. At the same time, a picturesque neo-historicism developed with the designs of Gino Sensani, Aldo Calvo, Giorgio de Chirico, Mario Sironi and Felice Casorati.

In France, collaborations between producers and painters at the Ecole de Paris, after the examples of Dyagilev and Rouché, affirmed the painterly conception and remained largely uninfluenced by isolated experiments along expressionist or constructivist lines. Furthermore the partly symbolist, partly romantic *belle époque* style, exemplified by the work of Maurice Denis, Jacques Drésa, René Piot, Emile Berlin and Alexandre Benois, long remained a vital force at the Opéra, extending into the 1930s and to some extent the 1940s. In the 1920s, under the influence of cubists such as Picasso, Léger and Braque and former fauvists such as Matisse, Rouault and Dufy, and above all in the productions of Dyagilev's Ballets Russes and R. de Maré's Ballet Suédois, there evolved an aesthetically independent and 'distant' decor accompanying the production in an analytical or illustrative way and containing an element of the naive as seen in the work of André Derain and Hélène Perdriat. Prepared through the efforts of Chirico (Jean Börlin's *La Jarre*, 1924, Paris), Max Ernst and Juan Mirò (Constant Lambert's *Romeo and Juliet*, 1926, Monte Carlo), surrealism became the dominant style in French scenic design in the early 1930s; vital contributions to its development in musical theatre were made by André Masson, Christian Bérard, Jean Cocteau and others.

In England, neo-romantic scene painting survived into the 1920s, as in the scenic work of George Sherringham and Adrian Allinson. The nostalgic historicism of Cecil Beaton, Rex Whistler, Oliver Messel (see fig.23) and the Motley studio, along with the personal 'impressions' of Sophie Fedorovich, still showed strong elements of neo-romanticism during the 1930s and 40s. During that period, however, surrealism also exerted a significant influence, stimulated by the visits of the Ballets Russes and their successors. Designers such as the Fedoroviches, Gwendolin Raverat, William Chappell, Leslie Hurry and Roger Furse were influenced, at least for a time, by an art that evoked the 'surreal' or the 'magical' objectivity of the *pittura metafisica*, though for the most part in the 1940s they were already turning to a concrete representation of reality, even if without striving towards the authenticity of Tanya Moiseiwitsch's realistic stage constructions.

Under the influence of social drama and social comedy, a realistic form of stage design evolved in the USA during the 1920s, further developing the formal heritage of the neo-romanticists, expressionists and constructivists. The theories of Appia and Craig influenced many American designers, leading them away from the extreme naturalistic styles popularized by David Belasco, particularly with simplified settings and the use of lighting as an expressive device. During the Depression designers such as Cleon Throckmorton and especially Mordechai Gorelik were capable of strong social criticism, but with economic stability stage design followed objective, if not affirmative, trends. This realistic style came to exert a vital and lasting influence on the genres of American musical theatre, primarily with musical comedy but also opera and ballet. In an eclectic yet effective way, stage designers of the expressionist generation, chiefly Robert Edmond Jones, Norman Bel Geddes (see fig.24), Lee Simonson, Donald Oenslager, Joseph Urban and Boris Aronson, staged their varied musical-dramatic subjects through a rich diversity of forms, from naturalism through a selective form of realism to an ironic, romanticizing or historicizing manner. During the 1930s and 40s surrealism found its way into American stage design through Pavel Tchelichew, Eugene Berman and Serge Soudeikin. The scenic and costume designs for Soudeikin's most successful work, Gershwin's *Porgy and Bess* (1935, New York), revealed an often naive, characteristically American realism (for illustration *see* PORGY AND BESS).

In Russia, the era of the consolidation of the Revolution provided a secure foundation for realistic stage design. Bearing the imprint of a socialist image of man, there developed during the late 1920s and 1930s a scenic art of socialist realism, whose diverse influences include the tradition of neo-romantic painting, the constructivists' social-revolutionary functionalism, psychological realism (further developed by Stanislavsky's opera studio and its stage designers V. A. Simov and B. A. Matrunin), the *verismo* stage production associated with the Jewish theatre in Moscow (whose grotesque comedy was introduced at the Bol'shoy Theatre in 1927 by Rabinovich in Prokofiev's *The Love for Three Oranges*) and, not least, folk art, already applied by the *Mir iskusstvo* circle. This polymorphic realism (not only folk art) was further developed by such artists as M. J. Kurilko (Glier's *Red Poppy*, 1927, Moscow) and P. V. Williams (Prokofiev's *Romeo and Juliet*, 1946, Moscow).

7. AFTER WORLD WAR II. In many countries, political restoration after World War II was accompanied by conservative tendencies in the theatre. Many stage designers of the period renounced the objectivity of the previous decades in favour of approaching the content of a work through subjectivity and immanence and its form through eclecticism (of a kind long practised in the USA). The scenic interpreter, arguing in favour of a visual presentation appropriate to each specific work, on a pragmatic basis according to his emotional response, rather than following any preconceived series of ideals, felt himself free to draw on the abundant stock of available forms – he 'assumes many styles, working in one production as a realist or a surrealist, in another as an expressionist' (*Donald Oenslager: Stage Designer and Teacher*, Detroit, 1956, p.10). In this way, such artists as John Piper, Georges Wakhevich, Teo Otto, Ita Maximowna, Rouben Ter-Arutunian, Nicholas Georgiadis, Jürgen Rose and Jörg Zimmermann were

24. Design by Norman Bel Geddes for the first American production of Gluck's 'Iphigénie en Aulide' at the Academy of Music, Philadelphia, 1935: sanguine drawing

able to bring out their artistic individuality and to contribute significantly through their fertile imaginations to opera and ballet stage design. Since their eclecticism frequently involved not only the 'style' but also the constructional and material properties of the stage itself, and could draw on a constantly advancing technology, the conflict between painted and constructed decor was now largely a dramaturgical matter.

Eclecticism was spurned, however, by artists who had established a personal style outside the theatre, such as the painters Maurice Utrillo, Bernard Buffet and Oscar Kokoschka or the sculptors Alexander Calder, Barbara Hepworth and Fritz Wotruba (and more recently Giacomo Manzù, Victor Vasarely, Bernhard Schultze, David Hockney and Maurice Sendak). Another ostensible renunciation of the eclecticism was represented by the search for an operatic stage reduced to abstract, plastic formal components, a quest begun in the late 1940s in Kiel and Essen by Gustav Rudolf Sellner with the stage designers Franz Mertz and Paul Haferung and continued in Darmstadt by Michael Raffaeli.

Similar endeavours sustained the productions of Wieland and Wolfgang Wagner at Bayreuth; from 1951 onwards they attempted to overcome the festival's traditional historicism, and by borrowing from Appia's formal language of symbolism and expressionism they worked out a form of Wagnerian stage that used lighting 'as an aid to dramaturgical expression, and deployed stylistic elements of contemporary art – visionary "symbols", geometric abstractions, symbolic colours and forms – in the articulation of the stage area' (Wieland Wagner, 'Denkmalsschutz für Wagner?', *Richard Wagner und das neue Bayreuth*, Munich, 1962, p.235). Wieland Wagner worked as his own producer and designer (see fig.25), paving the way for an increasing number of scene designers who became their own producers, among them Franco Zeffirelli, Jean-Pierre Ponnelle and Pier Luigi Pizzi.

Bayreuth's modernistic symbolism, de-historicizing the work of Wagner and other composers with a considerable display of technique and, by stylization, rendering it into 'timeless', 'archetypal musical theatre' (Wieland Wagner), was represented outside Bayreuth by Wieland Wagner himself in Stuttgart and other German opera houses as well as by Heinrich Wendel, Alfred Siercke, Günther Schneider-Siemssen and (in most of his productions) Josef Svoboda, who, reactivating the tradition of constructivism, brought formal modernism and technological performance (including shadowless laser lighting) to a new peak. He was followed by Jan Brazda, Sean Kenny, Timothy O'Brien, John Bury and notably Ralph Koltai.

This emphatically subjective attitude of de-historicizing stands in opposition to the attempts of many designers to produce objective scenic re-creation, exemplified by the neo-historical movement, which started in Italy and which aimed at scenic authenticity in re-creating the style of decor of the period in which the libretto is set or prevalent at the time of the work's composition. This movement, through the work of designers such as Zeffirelli, Lila de Nobili, Filippo Sanjust, Salvatore Fiume, Fabrizio Clerici, Pier Luigi Samaritani, Desmond Heeley, Beni Montresor, Julia Trevelyan Oman and Terence Emery found a home in many of the world's leading opera houses.

In contrast with this decorative historicism, which embodied some element of subjective nostalgia and spectacle for its own sake, Walter Felsenstein began working in 1947 at the Komische Oper in East Berlin with such designers as Heinz Pfeiffenberger, Rudolf Heinrich and Reinhart Zimmermann to develop a musical theatre of the 'literal', a form of scenic art that did not 'accompany' but rather 'contained' the work being performed (W. Felsenstein, 'Der Weg zum Werk', *Musiktheater*, 1961, pp.50, 54). The work's visual presence could stretch over three interacting dimensions: the period of the action, the period of the music and the period of the interpretation. This framework, it was claimed, could 'release the historical proceedings from their context so that they could speak with a present-day voice' and thus 'actualize' them, presenting them 'in their historical clothing for comparison with present-day problems and proceedings', but also 'leave them in their historicity, in the alien world of the historical', and

25. Wieland Wagner's 1956 Bayreuth production of 'Die Meistersinger von Nürnberg' (Act 2)

26. Götz Friedrich's production of 'Die Walküre' (Act 2) at Covent Garden, London, 1974, designed by Josef Svoboda

by portraying this exactly 'present it to view as if at a distance' (R. Zimmermann, 'Bühnenbild im Musiktheater', *Bühnenbildarbeit in der Deutschen Demokratischen Republik*, 1971, p.41).

Felsenstein's dialectical realism, founded partly on Brecht's theories of epic theatre and alienation, admitted philosophical and political ideas into the opera house and demanded dynamic collaborations between theatrical directors with a committed vision and their designers. This is particularly evident in the operatic work of Giorgio Strehler and his stage designers, including Luciano Damiani and Ezio Frigerio. Other notable collaborations between director and designer in this Brechtian style have been between Felsenstein and N. Zolotaryov (*Carmen*, 1969, Moscow), Joachim Herz and Heinrich (*Ring*, 1973–6, Leipzig), Götz Friedrich and Svoboda (*Ring*, Covent Garden, 1974–6), Ponnelle (Mozart cycles, Cologne, Salzburg etc.) and August Everding and Ming Cho Lee (*Boris Godunov*, 1974, New York).

Selected *Ring* cycles since the 1950s exemplify the prevalent style of postwar scene design for opera. Wieland Wagner's 1951 and 1965 Bayreuth productions were scenic abstractions painted with light. Schneider-Siemssen's, for Herbert von Karajan (1967–70, Salzburg), continued in that vein. Constructivist settings relying on stage technology and space age materials distinguished Svoboda's cycle at Covent Garden (1974–6; see fig.26) as well as Koltai's for the Sadler's Wells Opera (1970–73). Patrice Chéreau's iconoclastic Bayreuth production (1976) depended upon Richard Peduzzi's anti-romantic settings with their strong anachronistic elements (for illustration *see* PRODUCTION, fig.24), offset by the subsequent Bayreuth offering in 1983 in which William Dudley created eclectic picturesque decor. John Conklin returned to neo-romanticism for the San Francisco *Ring* (1985), while Ruth Berghaus's much acclaimed Frankfurt cycle (1985–7) was definitive poetic theatre, its powerful abstractions supported by the superb technical facilities of the Frankfurt opera house.

8. THE LATE 20TH CENTURY. The profile of operatic design in the late 20th century is essentially defined by the peculiar nature of an operatic repertory that has consolidated into a corpus of work almost entirely dating from before 1945. A feature of the period is that the divisions of responsibility for staging are often blurred between director, designer, lighting designer and choreographer. Relative to previous generations, fewer opportunities are offered for designers to collaborate on the creation of new operas; but often such new works, when they arise, challenge accepted notions of opera, and the designer is vital to the creation of a theatrical style that accommodates them: a notable example is the collaboration of Jocelyn Herbert in the long genesis of Harrison Birtwistle's *The Mask of Orpheus* (1986, London; for illustration *see MASK OF ORPHEUS, THE*). The divergence of public taste away from modern music is, however, countered by a trend in favour of earlier operas that often have no performance tradition at all. As a result, designers face the challenge of effectively 'creating' a work written centuries ago by finding a style which mediates between three periods – that of the composition, that of the action and that of the performance.

Because the passion for authenticity in performance is an aspect of a general crisis of confidence in the way we assimilate our past, this search for a style is infinitely complex. It calls into question the whole acting style of a production, and hence a feature of much operatic design is the resurgence of interest in ballet, or choreographed movement. The monumental designs for Philip Glass's *Akhnaten* by Achim Freyer (1984, Stuttgart; see fig.27) were conceived to preclude all but the most stylized gesture, and John Conklin's Kabuki chic costumes for Robert Wilson's *Die Zauberflöte* (1991, Paris, Bastille) were designed as sculptural shapes. The issue is very evident in the multiplicity of approaches to the Baroque repertory. Carlo Tommasi and Patrice Cauchetier designed the production by Jean-Marie Villégier of Lully's *Atys* (1987, Paris, Opéra-Comique): the single set of a magnificent black marble hall made no attempt

27. Scene from Achim Freyer's production of Philip Glass's 'Akhnaten' at the Staatstheater, Stuttgart, 1984

to recreate the 17th-century spectacle of machines, but the period costumes and wigs allowed the performers to move in both choreographed and naturalistic styles. The designer-director Pier Luigi Pizzi has pursued a more stylized approach in his Baroque productions, often denying any free movement to the singers in favour of extravagant costumes and moving plinths on which they are trundled about by actors. By contrast the work in Zürich and London of Opera Factory director David Freeman (Monteverdi's *Orfeo*, 1981 and *Il ritorno d'Ulisse in patria*, 1989) proposes a very raw physical style, in designs by David Rodger which strip away 17th-century conventions in favour of 'timeless' peasant costumes and abstract sets.

Theatre designers' versatility in working within many different conventions is tested to its extreme by opera because some of the most frequently performed works are based on dramatic genres that no longer hold the spoken stage. The stimulus is increased by the amount of opera now given new productions, as more opera houses move over to a *stagione* system in which they can be properly prepared for a season of performances, and by the variety of venues where they are given, from intimate auditoriums to sports arenas. Perhaps most importantly, because audiences are as unfamiliar with late 20th-century art as they are with its music, there is no shared visual vocabulary on which designers can rely.

The peculiar level of funding in postwar Berlin, both East and West, made it a breeding ground for an opera of ideas. Felsenstein's Komische Oper trained an ensemble spirit of perfection, encompassing design, which has been perpetuated by the directors Joachim Herz, Götz Friedrich and Harry Kupfer in their international careers; their belief in the ultimate seriousness and (in the broadest sense) the political significance of the operatic enterprise is harnessed to a boundless appetite for rehearsal and preparation to ensure an ideal spontaneity in performance. Apart from the important productions mentioned in the previous section, perhaps the most controversial designs have been those for Kupfer's Bayreuth *Ring* by Peter Sykora and Reinhard Heinrich (1988), in which the full extent of the Festspielhaus stage area and indeed beyond was opened up for a laser light tunnel and enormous metal constructions that accentuated the physical prowess of the performers who were literally running and climbing around them. Ruth Berghaus, doyenne of the Berlin Staatsoper until the demise of East Germany, was associated in the 1980s at the Frankfurt Opera with the vibrant abstract designs of the painter Axel Manthey. Sharing the Berlin heritage of intellectual engagement, she has to some extent pioneered the use of stylized movement as an addition to design to encourage detachment from, as well as involvement in, performance. The controversial effect often alienates audiences unfamiliar with the style: a well-received example was Dukas' *Ariane et Barbe-Bleue* (1991, Paris, Châtelet), with surrealist sets by Hans Dieter Schaal and costumes by Marie Luise Strandt.

In Berlin the Schaubühne in the Lehninerplatz, co-founded in 1970 by Peter Stein, gradually acquired an almost legendary status for the rehearsal of spoken drama in rejection of the conventions of theatrical illusion. His designer Karl-Ernst Herrmann established an aesthetic of design dependent on the highest quality of craftsmanship allied to a brilliant theatrical imagination. The refinement of his designs, with attention to exquisite detail and genuine period materials, combined to make the stage itself a work of art, a precious machine in which the artists could express themselves with the maximum truth. Herrmann applied this style to opera as a director in his own right with a series of Mozart productions in Brussels, beginning with *La clemenza di Tito* (1981) and including a memorable *La finta giardiniera* (1986). The conspicuous sumptuousness of *La traviata* (1987) was followed by Gluck's *Orfeo ed Euridice* (1988; see fig.28) in a disused warehouse, where the audience gazed down at the characters as they performed on a constructed world of earth and water, a labyrinth of Hades and staircase to Elysium. The contrast with Kupfer's 1989 production of the same opera (designed by Hans Schavernoch and Eleonore Kleiber), conceived as a psychological drama, and set in a modern city with video monitors for the vision of Eurydice, could hardly be greater. Stein's own productions of *Otello* (1986) and *Falstaff* (1988) for Welsh National Opera were designed by Lucio Fanti (sets) and Moidele Bickel (costumes), and their period images – drawn from paintings of the Italian Renaissance or Elizabethan England – were conceived through the lens of the 19th-century theatre. Herrmann and Bickel worked with Stein on *Pelléas et Mélisande* (WNO, 1992) in similar vein, interestingly closing off large sections of the stage for some scenes, isolating the performer in a vertical or horizontal shaft of light. The seductive beauty of these effects was a revelation for audiences accustomed to the uncompromising statements of East Berlin design.

None of this is to deny the decorative naturalism of much opera design on the stages of major houses. Managements are cautious of the response of singers and audiences to controversial production and design – the Vienna Staatsoper cancelled Kupfer's *Ring* cycle as too daring, but then cancelled Filippo Sanjust's as too traditional. Nor is it to underestimate the impact of the architectural and atmospheric vision of designers such as Ezio Frigerio (working with the costume designer Franca Squarciapino), or Gaia Aulenti, or the designers for Patrice Chéreau, Richard Peduzzi and Patrice Schmidt.

British design retains an idiosyncratic flavour, fed by the vitality of London as a theatrical centre. The enormous budgets (unthinkable in the subsidized theatres) of commercial musicals have enabled some designers to achieve international renown for breathtaking feats of engineering and spectacle. Maria Björnson (*Phantom of the Opera*, 1986; *Aspects of Love*, 1989), John Napier and Andreane Neofitou (*Les misérables*, 1985; *Miss Saigon*, 1989) and David Fielding (Pet Shop Boys' World Tour, 1991) have put their operatic experience towards popular music events and in so doing have explored technical possibilities that were otherwise inaccessible. Showmanship with a high degree of intellectual and erotic charge is the hallmark of Stefanos Lazaridis, whose fruitful if conventional partnership with John Copley in the 1970s led to a series of designs for the director David Pountney, at the English National Opera, for example in Dvořák's *Rusalka* (1983; for illustration *see* LAZARIDIS, STEFANOS), set in an Edwardian nursery, *Lady Macbeth of the Mtsensk District* (1987), with the visual metaphor of an abattoir, and an expressionist *Wozzeck* (1990), while their sensational *Der fliegende Holländer* was seen on the floating stage at the Bregenz Festival (1989). Equally theatrical, but more painterly and less mechanical in approach, the designs of David Fielding, Tom Cairns, Anthony Macdonald and Hildegard Bechtler explore the emotional world of an opera in symbolic designs. A very different talent is that of the director Jonathan Miller, whose grasp of the cultural context of opera is matched by an art-historian's approach to design: paintings by Chardin, Baudoin and Lavreince inform his vision of *Le nozze di Figaro* (1978, ENO, designed by Patrick Robertson and Rosemary Vercoe; 1991, Vienna, Theater an der Wien, Richard Hudson); he also acknowledges the influence of film and his updating of *Rigoletto* (1982, ENO, Robertson and Vercoe) to Little Italy in New York showed the impact of the *Godfather* films (as well as Edward Hopper), or *Tosca* (1986, Florence, Maggio Musicale, designed by Lazaridis) to Fascist Rome, inspired by Luchino Visconti's *Roma Aperta*. He has written (*Subsequent Performances*, 1986, pp.183–5):

> I feel the same reluctance to shift the period of Mozart's operas as I do with much of Shakespeare ... most 19th-century composers ... dealt rather carelessly with the past as they transposed opera into almost any period ... This stands in strong contrast to earlier composers like Mozart, for example, who are either working right in their own period ... or in remote antiquity.

Such an argument has not deterred the young American director Peter Sellars, who works with the designers Adrianne Lobel and Duná Ramicová, from updating Mozart to modern New York, with Don Giovanni peddling heroin, Count Almaviva in the Trump Tower and Despina managing 'Despina's Diner' (1987–9, PepsiCo Festival, New York), or from setting *Die Zauberflöte* as a West Coast fantasy on a freeway (1990, Glyndebourne). The rewards and dangers of such a literal conversion of the poetry of opera to modern vernacular are obvious.

28. Scene from Karl-Ernst Herrmann's production of Gluck's 'Orfeo ed Euridice' at La Monnaie, Brussels, 1988

The following designers (or directors with strong influence on design) have entries in this dictionary: AMICONI, JACOPO; ANISFELD, BORIS IZRAYELEVICH; APPIA, ADOLPHE; BARBIERI, GIOVAN DOMENICO; BARDON, HENRY; BEL GEDDES, NORMAN; BELLAVITE, INNOCENTE; BENOIS, ALEXANDRE; BENOIS, NICOLA; BERAIN, JEAN; BÉRARD, CHRISTIAN; BERGHAUS, RUTH; BERMAN, EUGENE; BERTHÉLÉMY, JEAN-SIMON; BERTOLI, ANTONIO DANIELE; BEUTHER, FRIEDRICH CHRISTIAN; BIGARI, FRANCESCO; BOQUET, LOUIS-RENÉ; BRIOSCHI; BROOK, PETER; BUONTALENTI, BERNARDO; BURNACINI, GIOVANNI; BURNACINI, LUDOVICO OTTAVIO; BURY, JOHN; CAMBON, CHARLES-ANTOINE; CAPOBIANCO, TITO; CICERI, PIERRE-LUC-CHARLES; CIGOLI; CLERICI, ROBERTO; COLOMBA, INNOCENTE; COLONELLO, ATTILIO; CONKLIN, JOHN; COSTA, GIOVANNI FRANCESCO; CRAIG, EDWARD GORDON; CROSATO, GIAMBATTISTA; DAGUERRE, LOUIS-JACQUES-MANDE; DE NOBILI, LILA; DESPREZ, LOUIS-JEAN; DEVOTO, JOHN; FABRIS, JACOPO; FAGGIONI, PIERO; FELSENSTEIN, WALTER; FERRARIO, CARLO; FONTAINE, PIERRE-FRANÇOIS-LÉONARD; FONTANA, GIROLAMO; FONTANESI, FRANCESCO; FRIGERIO, EZIO; FUENTES, GIORGIO; GALLIARI; GALLI-BIBIENA; GASPARI, GIOVANNI PAOLO; GEORGIADIS, NICHOLAS;

Gérard, rolf; Ghiglia, lorenzo; Gillot, claude; Gonzaga, pietro; Goupy, joseph; Greenwood, thomas; Grimaldi, giovanni francesco; Guitti, francesco; Halmen, pet; Harms, johann oswald; Heinrich, rudolf; Hockney, david; Hurry, leslie; Jolli, antonio; Jones, inigo; Jones, robert edmond; Juvarra, filippo; Kenny, sean; Kletzel, martin; Koltai, ralph; Lazaridis, stefanos; Leuven, adolphe de; Lingwood, tom; Loutherbourg, philip james de; Majewski, andrej; Marinari, gaetano; Marini, leonardo; Martin, jean baptiste; Mauro; Maximowna, ita; Ménageot, françois-guillaume; Messel, oliver; Ming cho lee; Montresor, beni; Neher, caspar; Neumann-spallart, gottfried; Novosielski, michael; Oenslager, donald; Oman, julia trevelyan; Otto, teo; Parigi, giulio; Pâris, pierre-adrien; Peduzzi, richard; Pirchan, emil; Pizzi, pier luigi; Platzer, joseph; Ponnelle, jean-pierre; Preetorius, emil; Quaglio; Re, vincenzo; Ricci, marco; Richards, john inigo; Righini, pietro; Rivarola, alfonso; Roller, alfred; Rooker, michael angelo; Rose, jürgen; Sacchetti, lorenzo; Sanjust, filippo; Sanquirico, alessandro; Santurini, francesco (i); Schinkel, karl friedrich; Schneider-siemssen, günther; Servandoni, giovanni niccolò; Sievert, ludwig; Sourdéac; Strehler, giorgio; Svoboda, josef; Tacca, ferdinando; Thomson, brian; Thornhill, james; Torelli, giacomo; Urban, josef; Valeriani, giuseppe; Vanvitelli, luigi; Varona, josé luciano; Verona, bartolomeo; Vigarani, carlo; Vigarani, gaspare; Visconti, luchino; Vlachopoulos, michalis; Wakhévitch, georges; Walker, david; Wallmann, margarita; Webb, john; Wilson, robert; Zambello, francesca; Zeffirelli, franco; and Zimmermann, johann heinrich f.

*

GENERAL

ES ('Scenografia'; E. Povoledo)

A. Pougin: *Dictionnaire historique et pittoresque du théâtre et des arts qui s'y rattachent* (Paris, 1885)

G. Bapst: *Essai sur l'histoire du théâtre: la mise en scène, le décor, le costume, l'architecture, l'éclairage, l'hygiène* (Paris, 1893)

G. Ferrari: *La scenografia: cenni storici dall'evo classico ai nostri giorni* (Milan, 1902)

M. Hammitzsch: *Der moderne Theaterbau* (Berlin, 1906)

J. Gregor: *Wiener szenische Kunst*, i: *Die Theaterdekoration der letzten drei Jahrhunderte nach Stilprinzipien dargestellt* (Vienna, 1924)

Denkmäler des Theaters (Munich, 1926–30; with addl Eng. text as *Monumenta scenica*, 1926–30; new ser., 1954–)

C. Niessen: *Das Bühnenbild: ein kulturgeschichtlicher Atlas* (Bonn, 1924)

A. Nicoll: *The Development of the Theatre* (London, 1927, 5/1966)

F. Kranich: *Bühnentechnik der Gegenwart* (Munich, 1929–33)

J. Gregor and F. Hadamowsky, eds.: *Kataloge der Theatersammlung der Nationalbibliothek in Wien*, ii: *Die Handzeichnungen der Theatersammlung* (Vienna, 1930)

V. Mariani: *Storia della scenografia italiana* (Florence, 1930)

C. Ricci: *La scenografia italiana* (Milan, 1930)

A. de Angelis: *Scenografi italiani di ieri e di oggi: dizionario degli architetti teatrali, scenografi, scenotechnici, figurinisti, ecc.* (Rome, 1938)

C. W. Beaumont: *Ballet Design Past and Present* (London, 1946)

L. Simonson: *The Art of Scenic Design* (New York, 1950)

J. Laver: *Drama, its Costume and Décor* (London, 1951)

R. Southern: *Changeable Scenery* (London, 1952)

G. Altman and others: *Theater Pictorial* (Berkeley, 1953)

N. Décugis and S. Raymond: *Le décor de théâtre en France du moyen âge à 1925* (Paris, 1953)

A. H. Mayor, M. Viale, A. Della Corte and A. G. Bragaglia: *Tempi e aspetti della scenografia* (Turin, 1954)

F. Kindermann: *Theatergeschichte Europas*, iv–v (Salzburg, 1961–2)

M. N. Pozharskaya: 'Dekoratsionnoye iskusstvo', *Teatral'naya entsiklopediya*, ii (Moscow, 1963), 353

F. Mancini: *Scenografia italiana dal Rinascimento all'età romantica* (Milan, 1966)

E. Povoledo: 'Scenography: Western Europe', *Encyclopaedia of World Art*, xii (New York, 1966), 753–93

H. C. Wolff: *Oper: Szene und Darstellung von 1600 bis 1900* (Leipzig, 1968, 2/1979)

F. Mancini: 'L'allestimento scenico nell'opera dei trattatisti', *Scritti in onore di Roberto Pane* (Naples, 1972), 289

M. Fagioli dell'Arco: *La scenografia dalle sacre rappresentazioni al futurismo* (Florence, 1973)

S. Rosenfeld: *A Short History of Scene Design in Great Britain* (Oxford, 1973)

M. Monteverdi: 'Scenografia e costumi', *Musei e gallerie di Milano*, iii: Museo teatrale alla Scala (Milan, 1975)

D. Oenslager: *Stage Design: Four Centuries of Scenic Invention* (New York, 1975)

S. Leopold: 'Bibliographie der italienischen Literatur zur Szenographie des Musiktheaters', *AnMc*, no.17 (1976), 296–309

G. M. Bergman: *Lighting in the Theatre* (Stockholm, 1977)

R. Hartmann: *Oper: Regie und Bühnenbild heute* (Stuttgart, 1977; Eng. trans., 1977)

G. Ricci: *Duecento anni di teatro alla Scala: la scenografia* (Bergamo, 1977)

R. Stoddard: *Stage Scenery, Machinery, and Lighting: a Guide to Information Sources* (Detroit, 1977)

E. Berckenhagen and G. Wagner: *Bretter die die Welt bedeuten* (Berlin, 1978)

H. R. Cohen and M.-O. Gigou: 'La conservation de la tradition scénique sur la scène lyrique en France au XIXe siècle: les livrets de mise en scène et la Bibliothèque de l'Association de la régie théâtrale', *RdM*, lxv (1978), 253–67

C. F. Baumann: *Bühnentechnik im Festspielhaus Bayreuth* (Munich, 1980)

O. K. Larson: 'New Evidence on the Origins of the Box Set', *Theatre Survey*, xxi/2 (1980), 79–92

M. Viale Ferrero: *Storia del Teatro regio di Torino*, iii: la scenografia dalle origini al 1936 (Turin, 1980)

A. Blumenthal: *Theater Designs in the Collection of the Cooper-Hewitt Museum* (New York, 1986)

W. Greisenegger: 'Das Bühnenbild', *Die Wiener Oper*, ed. A. Seebohm (Fribourg, 1986; Eng. trans., 1987)

F. Mancini: *Il Teatro San Carlo 1737–1987*, iii: *le scene, i costumi* (Naples, 1987)

C. F. Baumann: *Licht im Theater: von der Argand-Lampe bis zum Glühlampen-Scheinwerfer* (Stuttgart, 1988)

O. Pausch: *Vom Bild zum Raum: Bühnen Modelle 1781–1987* (Vienna, 1988)

R. T. Lacy: *A Biographical Dictionary of Scenographers: 500 B.C. to 1900 A.D.* (Westport, CT, 1990)

PERIODICALS

Bühnentechnische Rundschau (Zürich, 1907–)

Tabs: Stage Lighting International (London, 1937–)

Szenográfia (Budapest, 1960–)

Theater Design and Technology (Charlottesville, 1965–)

Theater Crafts (New York, 1967–)

Interscena (Prague, 1971–)

BEFORE 1600

E. K. Chambers: *The Medieval Stage* (Oxford, 1903)

M. Bieber: *The History of Greek and Roman Theater* (Princeton, 1939, 2/1961)

G. R. Kernodle: *From Art to Theater: Form and Convention in the Renaissance* (Chicago, 1944)

H. Leclerc: *Les origines italiennes de l'architecture théâtrale moderne* (Paris, 1946)

L. Magagnato: *Teatri italiani del cinquecento* (Venice, 1954)

T. B. L. Webster: *Greek Theatre Production* (London, 1956)

G. Wickham: *Early English Stages 1300 to 1660* (London, 1959–72)

E. Battisti: *Rinascimento e barocco* (Turin, 1960), 96ff

L. Schrade: *La représentation d'Edipo tiranno au Teatro olimpico (Vicenza, 1585)* (Paris, 1960)

C. Molinari: *Spettacoli fiorentini del quattrocento* (Venice, 1961)

W. F. Michael: *Frühformen der deutschen Bühne* (Berlin, 1963)

A. Parronchi: *Studi su la dolce prospettiva* (Milan, 1964)

I. Lavin: 'The Campidoglio and Sixteenth-Century Stage Design', *Essays in Honor of Walter Friedlaender* (New York, 1965), 114–18

A. M. G. Little: *Roman Perspective Painting and the Ancient Stage* (Wheaton, 1971)

M. Angiolillo: *Leonardo, feste e teatri* (Naples, 1979)

G. Spadolini: *Filippo Brunelleschi: la sua opera e il suo tempo* (Florence, 1980)

Il teatro italiano del Rinascimento (Milan, 1980)

M. Doglio and G. Tintori: *Leonardo e gli spettacoli del suo tempo* (Milan, 1983)

J. Orrell: *The Human Stage: English Theatre Design, 1567–1640* (Cambridge, 1988)
R. Savage and M. Sansone: '"Il corago" and the Staging of Early Opera: Four Chapters from an Anonymous Treatise circa 1630', *EMc*, xvii (1989), 495–511

17TH CENTURY

Il corago, o vero Alcune osservazioni per metter bene in scena le composizioni drammatiche (MS, *c*1630, *I-MOe*); ed. P. Fabbri and A. Pompilio (Florence, 1983)
P. Zucker: *Die Theaterdekoration des Barock* (Berlin, 1925)
A. Tessier: 'La décoration théâtrale à Venise à la fin du XVIIe siècle', *Revue de l'art ancien et moderne*, liv (1928), 181–90, 217–34
F. Biach-Schiffmann: *Giovanni und Ludovico Burnacini: Theater und Feste am Wiener Hofe* (Vienna, 1931)
G. Freedly, ed.: *Theatrical Designs from the Baroque through Neoclassicism* (New York, 1940)
J. Eisenschmidt: *Die szenische Darstellung der Opern Händels auf der Londoner Bühne seiner Zeit* (Wolfenbüttel, 1940–41)
G. Guerrieri and E. Povoledo: *Il secolo dell'invenzione teatrale* (Venice, 1951)
A. M. Nagler, ed.: *Sources of Theatrical History* (New York, 1952; as *A Source Book in Theatrical History*, 1959)
T. E. Lawrenson: *The French Stage in the 17th Century: a Study in the Advent of the Italian Order* (Manchester, 1957, 2/1985)
A. S. Jackson: 'Restoration Scenery 1586–1680', *Restoration and 18th Century Theatre Research*, iii/2 (1964), 25–38
A. M. Nagler: *Theatre Festivals of the Medici 1539–1637* (New Haven, 1964)
A. Parronchi: *Studi su la dolce prospettiva* (Milan, 1964)
M. Baur-Heinhold: *Theater des Barock* (Munich, 1966; Eng. trans., 1967)
R. Strong: *Festival Designs by Inigo Jones: an Exhibition of Drawings for Scenery and Costumes for the Court Masques of James I and Charles I* (Washington DC, 1967)
N. Pirrotta: *Li due Orfei: da Poliziano a Monteverdi* (Turin, 1969; Eng. trans. as *Music and Theatre from Poliziano to Monteverdi*, 1975, 2/1982 [incl. E. Povoledo: 'Origins and Aspects of Italian Scenography', 281–383])
M. Viale Ferrero: *Filippo Juvarra: scenografo e architetto teatrale* (New York, 1970)
A. Cavicchi: 'Scenotecnica e macchinistica teatrale in un tratto inedito di Fabrizio Carini Motta (Mantova, 1688)', *Venezia e il melodramma nel seicento: Venice 1972*, 359–77
F. Marotti: 'Lo spazio scenico del melodramma, esaminato sulla base della trattatistica teatrale italiana', *Venezia e il melodramma nel seicento: Venice 1972*, 349–57
G. Kernodle: 'Perspective Scenery: Science and Symbol', *Theatre Studies*, xxii (1975), 5–15
A. Blumenthal: *Theater Art of the Medici* (Hanover, NH, 1980)
M. Weil: *Baroque Theatre and Stage Design* (St Louis, MO, 1983)
J. Milhous: 'The Multimedia Spectacular on the Restoration Stage', *British Theatre and the Other Arts, 1660–1800*, ed. S. S. Kenny (Washington DC, 1984), 41–61
N. Pirotta: 'Theater, Sets, and Music in Monteverdi's Operas', *Music and Culture in Italy from the Middle Ages to the Baroque* (Cambridge, MA, 1984), 254
R. A. Foakes: *Illustrations of the English Stage 1580–1642* (Stanford, CA, 1985)
E. Povoledo: 'Incontri romani: Francesco Bibiena e Giovanni Paolo Pannini (1719–1721)', *RIM*, xx (1985), 296–327
A. Blumenthal: *Giulio Parigi's Stage Designs: Florence and the Early Baroque Spectacle* (New York, 1986)
O. Larson, ed. and trans.: *F. Carini Motta: The Theatrical Writings: Trattato sopra la struttura de' Teatri e scene, 1676; and Costruzione de' teatri e machine teatrali, 1688* (Carbondale, IL, 1987)
L. Lindgren: 'The Staging of Handel's Operas in London', *Handel Tercentenary Collection*, ed. S. Sadie and A. Hicks (London, 1987), 93–119
C. Durand: 'The Apogee of Perspective in the Theatre: Ferdinando Bibiena's "Scena per angolo"', *Theatre Research International*, xiii (1988), 21–9

18TH CENTURY

F. Galli-Bibiena: *L'architettura civile* (Parma, 1711)
B. Marcello: *Il teatro alla moda, o sia Metodo sicuro e facile per il ben comporre ed eseguire l'opere italiane in musica all'uso moderno* (Venice, *c*1720; Eng. trans., *MQ*, xxxix (1948), 222–33, 371–403 and xxxv (1949), 85–105; abridged, in *Source Readings in Music History*, ed. O. Strunk, New York, 1950)
F. Algarotti: *Saggio sopra l'opera in musica* (Bologna, 1755, 2/1763; Eng. trans., 1767); extract repr. in *Source Readings in Music History*, ed. O. Strunk (New York, 1950), 657–72
Boullet: *Essai sur l'art de construire les théâtres, leurs machines et leurs mouvemens* (Paris, 1801; Eng. trans., 1986)
E. Cotarelo y Mori: *Estudios sobre la historia del arte escénico en España* (Madrid, 1896–1902)
P. Zucker: *Die Theaterdekoration des Klassizismus* (Berlin, 1925)
F. Hadamowsky: *Die Familie Galli-Bibiena in Wien: Leben und Werk für das Theater* (Vienna, 1962)
M. Viale Ferrero: *La scenografia del '700 e i fratelli Galliari* (Turin, 1963)
F. Mancini: *Scenografia napoletana dell'età barocca* (Naples, 1964)
E. Nölle: *Die Theatermaler Gaspari* (Munich, 1966)
M. T. Muraro: *Scenografie di Pietro Gonzaga* (Venice, 1967)
M. T. Muraro and E. Povoledo: *Disegni teatrali dei Bibiena* (Vicenza, 1970)
S. Hansell: 'Stage Deportment and Scenographic Design in the Italian *Opera Seria* of the *Settecento*', *IMSCR*, xi *Copenhagen 1972*, i, 415–24
A. M. Nagler: 'J. N. Servandonis und F. Bouchers Wirken an der Pariser Oper', *Bühnenformen–Bühnenräume–Bühnendekorationen … : Herbert A. Frenzel zum 65. Geburtstag* (Berlin, 1974), 64
F. Mancini, M. T. Muraro and E. Povoledo: *Illusione e pratica teatrale: proposte per una lettura dello spazio scenico dagli intermedi fiorentini all'opera comica veneziana* (Vicenza, 1975)
S. Rosenfeld: *Georgian Scene Painters and Scene Painting* (Cambridge, 1981)
J. de la Gorce: 'Décors et machines à l'Opéra de Paris au temps de Rameau', *RMFC*, xxi (1983), 145
S. Angrisani: *I Galliari primi scenografici della Scala* (Florence, 1984)
A. F. Ivaldi: 'Giovanni Battista Olivieri scenografo nel teatro romano di Tordinona (1737)', *NRMI*, xvii (1984), 376–405
C. Ault, ed.: *Scenes and Machines from the Eighteenth Century: the Stagecraft of Jacopo Fabris and Citoyen Boullet* (New York, 1986)
J. Hilmera, T. Volek and V. Ptáčková: *Mozart's "Don Giovanni" in Prague* (Prague, 1987)
C. Ault: 'The "Scena per Angolo" at the Teatro della Fortuna', *Theatre History Studies*, viii (1988), 206–210
W. Greisenegger: 'Der Szenenraum des Don Giovanni – Zur Wiener Szenenraumgestaltung', *Weg zu Mozart "Don Giovanni"* (Vienna, 1988), 67–78
M. Viale Ferrero: *Scenografi scaligeri tra settecento e ottocento* (Milan, 1988)
M. Beaumont: *Eighteenth-Century Scenic and Architectural Design: Drawings by the Galli-Bibiena Family: from the Collections in Portugal* (Alexandria, VA, 1990)

19TH CENTURY

G. Ferarrio: *500 bozetti scenografici* (Turin, 1919)
G. M. Ciampelli: *Le opere verdiane al Teatro alla Scala (1839–1929)* (Milan, 1929)
G. Adami: *Un secolo di scenografia alla Scala (1845–1945)* (Milan, 1945)
A. Appia: 'Notes de mise en scène pour l'Anneau de Nibelungen (1891–1892)', *Revue d'histoire du théâtre*, vi (1954), 46–59
J. G. Kernodle: 'Wagner, Appia and the Idea of Musical Design', *Education Theatre Journal*, vi (1954), 223
V. Hepner: *Scénická výprava na jevišti Národního divadla: v letech 1883–1900* [Set Designs on the Stage of the National Theatre in the Years 1883–1900] (Prague, 1955)
B. Król: 'Antoni Sacchetti – dekorator romantyczny: działalnośc w latach 1829–1845', *Pamiętnik teatralny*, viii (1959), 219–60
G. Damerini: *Scenografi veneziani dell'ottocento: Francesco Bagnara – Giuseppe e Pietro Bertoja* (Venice, 1962)
M. T. Muraro: 'Le scenografie delle cinque "Prime Assolute" di Verdi alla Fenice di Venezia', *1° congresso internazionale di studi verdiani: Venice 1966*, 328–34
I. Hanl: *Der Bühnenbildner Alessandro Sanquirico: Leben und Werk* (diss., U. of Vienna, 1970)
D. Petzet and M. Petzet: *Die Richard Wagner-Bühne Ludwigs II* (Munich, 1970)
E. Ibscher: *Theaterateliers des Deutschen Sprachraums im 19. und 20. Jahrhundert* (diss., U. of Cologne, 1972)
N. Wild: 'Un demi-siècle de décors à l'Opéra de Paris, Salle le Peletier (1822–1873)', *Regards sur l'Opéra* (Paris, 1976), 11–22
H. R. Cohen: 'On the Reconstruction of the Visual Elements of French Grand Opera: Unexplored Sources in Parisian Collections', *IMSCR*, xii *Berkeley 1977*, 463–80

N. Wild: 'La recherche de la précision historique chez les décorateurs de l'Opéra de Paris au XIXe siècle', ibid, 453–63
H. R. Cohen and M.-O. Gigou: 'La conservation de la tradition scénique sur la scène lyrique en France au XIXe siècle: les livrets de mise en scène et la Bibliothèque de l'Association de la régie théâtrale', *RdM*, lxiv (1978), 253–67
D. Coe: 'The Original Production Book for *Otello*: an Introduction', *19th Century Music*, ii (1978–9), 148–58
C. Baumann: *Bühnentechnik im Festspielhaus Bayreuth* (Munich, 1980)
H. J. Gund: *Die Wagner-Bühnenbilder der Pariser Oper von 1891 bis 1914* (diss., U. of Freiburg, 1980)
F. Mancini: *Scenografia napoletana dell'ottocento: Antonio Niccolini e il neoclassico* (Naples, 1980)
M. Ambrose: 'Walter Scott, Italian Opera and Romantic Stage Setting', *Italian Studies*, xxxvi (1981), 58–78
M. Conati: 'Aspetti della messinscena del "Macbeth" di Verdi', *NRMI*, xv (1981), 374–404
B. Daniels: 'Cicéri and Daguerre: Set Designers for the Paris Opéra, 1820–1822', *Theater Survey*, xxii (1981), 69–90
A. Tubeuf: *Bayreuth et Wagner: cent ans d'images, 1876–1976* (Paris, 1981)
H. R. Cohen: *Les gravures musicales dans l'Illustration 1843–1899* (Stuyvestant, NY, 1982)
E. Nölle: *Richard Wagner 1813–1883: Ur- und Erstaufführungen seiner Werke in München* (Munich, 1983)
M. Viale Ferrero: *La scenografia della Scala nell'età neoclassica* (Milan, 1983)
M. Bucci: *Drawings for the Stage – Italian Set Designs from 1790–1860* (New York, 1984)
M. Viale Ferrero: 'La scenografia italiana ai tempi di Ponchielli e gli allestimenti delle sue opere', *Amilcare Ponchielli 1834–1886 saggi e ricerchi nel 150. anniversario della nascita* (Soresina, 1984)
——: *Liverani e Verdi* (Modena, 1984)
H. R. Cohen: 'A Survey of French Sources for the Staging of Verdi's Operas: "Livrets de mise en scène", Annotated Scores and Annotated Libretti in Two Parisian Collections', *Studi verdiani*, iii (1985), 11–44
E. Greisenegger-Georgila: *Naturmotiv in Angebot eines Theaterdekorationsateliers des 19. Jahrhunderts: das Atelier Brioschi und seine Tradition in der K.u.K. Hofoper in Wien* (diss., U. of Vienna, 1985)
N. Grilli: *Filippo Peroni – scenografo alla Scala, 1849–1867* (Milan, 1985)
M. Ottlova and M. Popíšil: 'Oper und Spektakel im 19. Jahrhundert', *Mf*, xxxviii (1985), 1–8
P. Trarieux: *L'Opéra-Comique de Paris et son décor* (diss., U. of Paris-Sorbonne, 1985)
H. R. Cohen and M.-O. Gigou: *Cent ans de mise en scène lyrique en France (env. 1830–1930)* (Stuyvestant, NY, 1986)
J. Fulcher: *French Grand Opera as Politics and Politicized Art* (Cambridge, 1987)
N. Wild: *Décors et costumes du XIXe siècle, i: Opéra de Paris: catalogues de la bibliothèque de l'Opéra* (Paris, 1987)
G. Guccini: 'Direzione scenica e regia', *SOI*, v (1988), 123–56
C. Join-Diéterle: *Les décors de scène de l'Opéra de Paris à l'époque Romantique* (Paris, 1988)
M. Viale Ferrero: 'La spettacolarità – Luogo teatrale e spazio scenico', *SOI*, v (1988), 1–122
N. Wild: *Dictionnaire des théâtres parisiens au XIXe siècle* (Paris, 1989)

20TH CENTURY

A. Appia: *La mise en scène du drame wagnérien* (Paris, 1895; Eng. trans., 1982)
——: *Die Musik und die Inszenierung* (Munich, 1899; Eng. trans., 1962; Fr. orig., 1963)
E. Gordon Craig: *The Art of the Theatre* (Edinburgh, 1905)
K. MacGowan and R. E. Jones: *Continental Stagecraft* (New York, 1922)
M. Gorelick: *New Theatres for Old* (New York, 1940)
W. Felsenstein and S. Melchinger: *Musiktheater* (Bremen, 1961)
D. Bablet: *Esthétique générale du décor de théâtre de 1870 à 1914* (Paris, 1965)
G. von Einem and S. Melchinger: *Caspar Neher* (Hanover, 1966)
W. R. Volbach: *Adolphe Appia: Prophet of the Modern Theatre* (Middletown, CT, 1968)
H. Curjel: *Experiment Krolloper 1927–1931* (Munich, 1975)
G. Lise: 'Le scene di Lodovico Pogliaghi per il "Nerone" di Boito', *Rassegna di studi e notizie – Castello Sforzesco*, ii/3 (1975), 243–84
D. Mack: *Der Bayreuther Inszenierungsstil (1876–1976)* (Munich, 1976)
A. M. Nagler: *Malaise in der Oper: Opernregie in unseren Jahrhundert* (Rheinfelden, 1980; Eng. trans. as *Misdirection: Opera Production in the Twentieth Century*, 1981)
S. Angrisani: *I giovani ottant'anni di Nicola Benois* (Milan, 1981)
V. Cavicchioni: *Piero Simonini: 25 anni di scenografia* (Reggio Emilia, 1981)
R. Hartmann: *Richard Strauss: the Staging of his Operas and Ballets* (New York, 1981)
S. Sinisi and F. C. Villari: *Artisti scenografi italiani 1915–1930* (Rome, 1981)
D. Bablet: *Adolphe Appia, 1862–1928: Actor – Space – Light* (London, 1982)
O. Bauer: *Richard Wagner: die Bühnenwerke von der Uraufführung bis heute* (Fribourg, 1982; Eng. trans., 1982)
V. Ptáčková: *Česká scénografie XX. století* (Prague, 1982)
M. L. Bablet-Halin, ed.: *A. Appia: oeuvres complètes*, i–iv (Berne, 1983)
M. Friedman: *Hockney Paints the Stage* (New York, 1983)
C. Innes: *Edward Gordon Craig* (Cambridge, 1983)
J. M. Walton, ed.: *Craig on Theatre* (London, 1983)
A. Aronson: *American Stage Design* (New York, 1985)
M. C. Ewans: 'Two Centenary Productions of *The Ring* at Bayreuth. I: the Bayreuth Centenary *Ring* by Patrice Chéreau and Pierre Boulez', *MMA*, xiv (1985), 167–74
J. Gaulme: *Architectures scénographiques et décors de théâtre* (Paris, 1985)
W. Greisenegger: 'Szenenbilder – Szenenbildner in der ersten Hälfte des 20. Jahrhunderts', *Ladislav Hoffmann* (Vienna, 1985)
R. M. Jacobson: *Magnificence: Onstage at the Met – Twenty Great Opera Productions* (London, 1985)
C. Castle: *Oliver Messel* (New York, 1986)
G. Isgrò: *Fortuny e il teatro* (Palermo, 1986)
F. Peixoto: *Opera e encenacão* (Rio de Janeiro, 1986)
J. Willett: *Caspar Neher: Brecht's Designer* (London and New York, 1986)
D. Harris: 'Full Cycle: how the *Ring* has been Staged since Wagner's Day', *ON*, li/12 (1986–7), 12–14, 45
J. M. Gillette: *Theatrical Design and Production: an Introduction to Scene Design and Construction, Lighting, Sound, Costume and Make-up* (Palo Alto, CA, 1987)
B. Millington: '*The Ring* according to Berghaus', *MT*, cxxviii (1987), 491–2
F. Rich: *The Theatre Art of Boris Aronson* (New York, 1987)
R. C. Beacham, ed.: *Adolf Appia: Essays, Scenarios, and Designs* (Ann Arbor, 1989)
W. Greisenegger: 'Alfred Roller: Neubedeutung des szenischen Raumes', *SM*, xxxi (1989), 271–81
O. Larson: *American Stage Design, 1915–1990* (Fayetteville, AR, 1989)
W. Willaschek: *Jean-Pierre Ponnelle: Arbeiten für Salzburg 1968–1988* (Salzburg, 1989)
L. Damiani: *Luciano Damiani al Teatro alla Scala* (Milan, 1990)
A. Aronson: 'Postmodernist Stage Design', *Theater Journal*, xliii (1991), 1–13
N. van Norman Baer: *Theatre in Revolution: Russian Avant-Garde Stage Design 1913–1935* (New York, 1991)
D. Rothschild: *Picasso's Parade: from Street to Parade* (New York, 1991)
W. Greisenegger: *Alfred Roller* (Vienna, 1992)
E. Baker: *Alfred Roller's Production of Mozart's "Don Giovanni": a Break in the Scenic Traditions of the Vienna Court Opera* (diss., New York U., 1993)

MANFRED BOETZKES, EVAN BAKER (1–7), NICHOLAS JOHN (8)

Stagione (It.). (1) SEASON.

(2) The term is used in the English-speaking world and in Germany for a particular system of repertory management in which each opera performed has a short 'season' of performances. This method, favoured by most houses in Great Britain and the USA, many large international houses elsewhere and smaller houses in Italy, has the advantage that a cast can be assembled for a period of, say, three weeks in which an opera can be rehearsed and a series of performances given. In smaller houses, only one opera may be seen during a period of two or three weeks; in larger ones, the seasons of the

different operas tend to overlap, so that two or three operas may be seen within a few days. This system is naturally favoured where casts have to be assembled rather than drawn from a resident company; where there is a resident company, the REPERTORY system is normally preferred.

Stagno, Roberto [Andrioli, Vincenzo] (*b* Palermo, 11 Oct 1840; *d* Genoa, 26 April 1897). Italian tenor. He studied in Milan with Lamperti, then made his début in 1862 at Lisbon as Rodrigo in Rossini's *Otello*. He appeared at Madrid, Venice, Rome, Naples, Florence and the Metropolitan, where he sang Enzo in the first New York performance of *La Gioconda* (1883). His repertory included Don Ottavio, Elvino, Pollione, Gennaro (*Lucrezia Borgia*), Poliuto, Raoul, Robert le diable, Manrico, Radames, Romeo, Faust and Lohengrin. He also sang Verdi's Otello in Buenos Aires (1888). He created Turiddu in *Cavalleria rusticana* at the Teatro Costanzi, Rome (1890), and sang in the first performance of Giordano's *Mala vita* at the Teatro Argentina, Rome (1892). His powerful, flexible voice could encompass a great variety of roles. He was married to the soprano Gemma Bellincioni; their daughter Bianca Stagno-Bellincioni (1888–1980), also a soprano, sang in Naples, Barcelona, Rome and Lisbon, and appeared at Covent Garden (*Bohème* and *Manon Lescaut*) in 1914. ELIZABETH FORBES

Stahlman, Sylvia (*b* Nashville, TN, 5 March 1929). American soprano. She attended the Juilliard School and began her career singing in Broadway musicals. From 1951 to 1954 she sang under the name Giulia Bardi at the Théâtre de la Monnaie, Brussels, making her début as Elvira in *I puritani*. She was a member of the Frankfurt Opera (1958–60) and also sang in Amsterdam, Brussels, Frankfurt and Vienna. She appeared at the New York City Opera as Blonde in 1956, in San Francisco in *Médée* in 1958, and in Chicago in 1960. In 1959 she sang Ilia at Glyndebourne and in 1964 took part in the American première of *Daphne* in Santa Fe. Excelling in coloratura and soubrette roles, she appears on recordings as Lisa in *La sonnambula* and Oscar in *Un ballo in maschera*. CORI ELLISON

Stahmer-Andriessen, Pelagie. *See* GREEFF-ANDRIESSEN, PELAGIE.

Stalinabad. DUSHANBE.

Stamford. American city, in Connecticut. It is the base of Connecticut Grand Opera/Stamford State Opera, a professional company formed in 1986 by the merger of the two formerly independent institutions. Connecticut Grand Opera had been established in Bridgeport in 1978, Stamford State Opera in 1968. Since the merger, the company has mounted three or four productions a season, with one performance each in Stamford (Palace Theatre of the Arts, capacity 1584) and in Bridgeport (Klein Memorial Auditorium, capacity 1500). In 1988 it presented the American stage première of Busoni's *Turandot*. Laurence Gilgore was appointed artistic director in 1990. STEVEN P. METCALF

Stamm, Harald (*b* Frankfurt, 29 April 1938). German bass. After studying in Frankfurt, he was engaged at Gelsenkirchen (1968), Kassel, Cologne and Frankfurt (1973). In 1975 he took part in the première of Bialas's *Der gestiefelte Kater* (Hamburg Staatsoper at Schwetzingen). He has sung in Berlin, Vienna, Düsseldorf, Munich, Rome, Venice and at the Metropolitan. He sang Antinous in Henze's version of *Il ritorno d'Ulisse* at Salzburg (1985) and made his Covent Garden début as Raimondo (*Lucia*) in 1987. In 1990 he sang Wagner's King Henry in Brussels and Lisbon. His repertory includes Sarastro, Mozart's Bartolo, Rocco, Daland, King Mark, Hunding, Philip II, the Grand Inquisitor, Procida, Fiesco, Don Quichotte and Madruscht (*Palestrina*). A fine actor, he has a resonant voice which is very strong in the lowest register. ELIZABETH FORBES

Stampiglia, Silvio (*b* Civita Lavinia [now Lanuvio], nr Rome, 14 March 1664; *d* Naples, 26 Jan 1725). Italian librettist. In 1690 he was a founder-member of the Accademia dell'Arcadia, using the name Palemone Licurio. Until 1696 he served two fellow Arcadians in Rome, Gran Contestabile Filippo Colonna and his brother-in-law, Luigi della Cerda, Duke of Medinaceli. His first dramatic works were oratorios, serenatas and reworkings of opera librettos by other writers for production at the Teatro di Tordinona between 1692 and 1695 (*Xerse*, *Tullo Ostilio*, *Muzio Scevola* and possibly as many as five others). *Xerse* is the first of these revisions on which his name appears. He completely reworked the internal structure of Minato's libretto, shifting the focus to exit arias, but preserved the characters and the story. The lighthearted elements that he retained, for example King Xerxes' befuddled behaviour throughout the work, are well known from performances of Handel's 1738 setting.

Stampiglia's first five original librettos were written for Naples, where he again served the Duke of Medinaceli, who had become Viceroy and who did much to increase the splendour of the Teatro S Bartolomeo. In these works he continued to mingle comic and serious scenes, and his noble characters were often made even more ridiculous than their servants. The farcical delights of *Camilla* and *Partenope* may well explain why these two were the most successful among Stampiglia's librettos. *Camilla* had 38 productions in 70 years, of which the three in London totalled 111 performances between 1706 and 1728. *Partenope* was produced 36 times in the first half of the 18th century; the setting by Manuel Zumaya for the theatre of the Viceroy of Mexico in 1711 made it the first Italian opera known to have been produced in the New World.

Driven from Naples by the War of the Spanish Succession (1701–14), Stampiglia moved to Rome, where his most notable commissions were from Prince Ferdinando de' Medici. His work during the war years was apparently largely piecemeal and is therefore difficult to trace. By the end of 1706, he had moved to Vienna, where thanks to the influence of Giovanni Bononcini he had been named imperial poet to Joseph I, succeeding Donato Cupeda. Stampiglia began at the splendid salary of 3000 florins annually (600 more than the other imperial poet, P. A. Bernardoni), which was then raised to 4000. Between 1707 and 1711 five of his operas, eight serenatas and one oratorio were given. He seems to have remained in Vienna until about November 1718, when Apostolo Zeno replaced him as imperial poet. Stampiglia continued to receive imperial commissions from Vienna for serenatas and oratorios when he was in Rome (1718–22) and Naples (1722–5). His last known work, the serenata *Imeneo* set by Porpora (1723), features a highly amusing mad scene at its climax. It enjoyed continued success as an opera, *Imeneo in Atene* (1726, Venice), and even as an 'operetta' in a new setting by Handel (1740, London, and 1742, Dublin).

In 1725 Apostolo Zeno declared that Stampiglia was 'more ingenious than wise' ('più ingegnoso che dotto') and that his dramas manifested 'più di spirito che di studio'. Indeed, their zestful spirit is quite foreign to the studious *opere serie* that Zeno and other 'reformers' were writing from the 1690s onwards. Anna Mondolfi (*ES*) has observed that even Stampiglia's magnanimous heroes (e.g. Caius Graccus) make crude parodistic remarks, so that his works seem to counter the purgative movement of his day. As might be expected, his outdated comic scenes and other irregularities were usually excised by the expurgatorial editors of revivals, who thus removed much of the spirited wit found in the first editions. Even so, the works clearly remained viable, for they were frequently restaged during the early 18th century.

drammi per musica

Xerse (after N. Minato), G. Bononcini, 1694 (Handel, 1738, as Serse); *Tullo Ostilio* (after A. Morselli), Bononcini, 1694; *Muzio Scevola* (after Minato), Bononcini, 1695 (rev., Bononcini, 1710; Handel, 1721); *Il trionfo di Camilla, regina de' Volsci*, Bononcini, 1696 (rev. as La rinovata Camilla, 1698; Fiore, 1713; Vinci, 1725; Leo, 1726; Porpora, 1740; V. Ciampi, 1750; Scolari, 1767); *La caduta de' Decemviri*, A. Scarlatti, 1697 (Ballarotti, 1699; Porta, 1723; Vinci, 1727)

Partenope, Mancia, 1699 (Caldara, 1708 [? or 1701]; Predieri, 1710; Zumaya, 1711; Quintavalle, 1713; Sarro, 1724; Vinci, 1725, as La Rosmira fedele; Handel, 1730; Vivaldi, 1738, as Rosmira; G. Scarlatti, 1749; Cocchi, 1753, as La Rosmira fedele); *L'Eraclea*, A. Scarlatti, 1700 (Vinci, 1724); *Tito Sempronio Gracco*, A. Scarlatti, 1702 (Sarro, 1725); *Turno Aricino*, 1702 (A. Scarlatti, 1704; Bononcini, 1707; Leo, Vinci and others, 1724)

L'incoronazione di Dario (after Morselli), Aldrovandini, 1705 (rev. as Li tre rivali al soglio, 1711); *Lucio Manlio l'imperioso*, Scarlatti, 1705; *L'Etearco*, Bononcini, 1707; *Mario fuggitivo*, Bononcini, 1708 (F. Mancini, 1710); *L'Abdolomino*, Bononcini, 1709 (with addns by Mancini, 1711); *Caio Gracco*, Bononcini, 1710 (Leo, 1720)

Doubtful: *Cirene*, P. Pellegrini, 1742

*

ES (A. Mondolfi)

A. Ricchi: *Teatro degli uomini illustri nelle armi, lettere e dignità, che fiorirno nel regno antichissimo de' Volsci* (Rome, 1721), 149–50

P. Zeno: 'Elogio di Silvio Stampiglia romano', *Giornale de' letterati d'Italia*, xxxviii/2 (1733), 117–33

A. Zeno: *Lettere* (Venice, 2/1785), i, 317, 341, 412; ii, 341–2; iv, 21

A. von Weilen: 'Zur Wiener Theatergeschichte: die von Jahre 1629 bis zum Jahre 1740 am Wiener Hofe zur Aufführung gelangten Werke theatralischen Charakters und Oratorien', *Mittheilungen des Österreichischen Vereins für Bibliothekswesen*, ii (1898), suppl.

A. Koczirz: 'Exzerpte aus den Hofmusikanten des Wiener Hofkammerarchivs', *SMw*, i (1913), 286

M. Fabbri: *Alessandro Scarlatti e il Principe Ferdinando de' Medici* (Florence, 1961)

H. Powers: 'Il Serse trasformato', *MQ*, xlvii (1961), 481–92; xlviii (1962), 73–92

R. Freeman: 'The Travels of *Partenope*', *Studies in Music History: Essays for Oliver Strunk* (Princeton, 1968), 356–85

H. Powers: 'Il *Mutio* tramutato, i: Sources and Libretto', *Venezia e il melodramma nel seicento: Venice 1972*, 227–58

A. Ford: 'Music and Drama in the Operas of Giovanni Bononcini', *PRMA*, ci (1974–5), 107–20

L. Lindgren: 'I trionfi di *Camilla*', *Studi musicali*, vi (1977), 89–160

——: '*Camilla* and *The Beggar's Opera*', *Philological Quarterly*, lix (1980), 44–61

E. Kanduth: 'Silvio Stampiglia, poeta cesareo', *L'opera italiana a Vienna prima di Metastasio: Venice 1984*, 43–63

C. Hill: *Handel's 'Imeneo': a Pre-Edition Study* (Armidale, NSW, 1987) [incl. facs. of libs. for Naples, 1723; London, 1740; and Dublin, 1742]

S. Franchi: *Drammaturgia romana: repertorio bibliografico cronologico dei testi drammatici pubblicati a Roma e nel Lazio, secolo XVII* (Rome, 1988)

C. Lampe: 'L'arcade Silvio Stampiglia da Civita Lavinia (1664–1725)', *Eruditi e letterati del Lazio: Lunario Romano 1989*, ed. R. Lefevre (Rome, 1988), 107–20

L. Bianconi: *I libretti italiani di Georg Friedrich Händel e le loro fonti*, i: *Da 'Vincer se stesso è la maggior vittoria' (1707) a 'L'Elpidia' (1725)* (Florence, 1992)

LOWELL LINDGREN

Stamps. The postage stamp was conceived by Sir Rowland Hill and the first example, the 'Penny Black' showing a portrait of Queen Victoria, was issued by Great Britain on 6 May 1840. Other countries soon took up this convenient method of prepaying postage, adorning their stamps with portrayals of their own head of state or with appropriate symbols. The hobby of stamp collecting started at almost the same time. It was not until the early 20th century that the design of stamps developed beyond portraits and symbols and pictorial subjects, generally in commemoration of people, events and places, began to appear. The first music stamps were issued as early as 1889, when the Hamburg suburb of Altona issued three small stamps portraying Beethoven, Mozart and Wagner. Among themes represented on stamps, music is the tenth most popular; more than 10 000 stamps with musical connotations have been issued. These can be subdivided under such headings as Instruments, Composers, Dance, Jazz, Festivals and Paintings, as well as Opera.

1. Chronological survey. 2. Particular topics: (i) Musical notation (ii) Operatic scenes (iii) Singers (iv) Opera houses (v) Miscellaneous (vi) Auxiliaries.

1. CHRONOLOGICAL SURVEY. Few specific opera stamps were issued until the 1950s. Noteworthy early sets came from Germany, Italy, Austria, Czechoslovakia and the USSR. The first important set was issued by Germany in 1933 to commemorate the 50th anniversary of Wagner's death. Nine of his operas are depicted in exquisitely engraved detail: *Der fliegende Holländer*, *Lohengrin*, *Das Rheingold*, *Die Walküre*, *Siegfried*, *Die Meistersinger von Nürnberg*, *Tristan und Isolde* and *Parsifal* (interestingly, *Götterdämmerung* was not included); the stamps carried a surcharge for charity and, as a political gesture, a watermark of swastikas. The stamps were sold to raise money for Nazi Party funds. Also from Germany before World War II were commemorative portraits of Bach, Handel and Schütz in 1935; a portrait of Mozart for the 150th anniversary of his death followed in 1941.

Italy issued a fine set of 11 stamps to commemorate the centenary of Bellini's death in 1935, including portraits and allegories, his house, his piano and a scene from *La sonnambula*. In 1942 the 150th anniversary of Rossini's birth was celebrated with a set of four stamps, his portrait and a reproduction of the monument in front of the Rossini Conservatory in Pesaro. Spontini, Pergolesi, Donizetti, Cimarosa, Bellini, Leopardi, Verdi and Catalani portraits were also issued between 1937 and 1954. Another Italian commemorative was the set of three stamps issued in 1951 on the 50th anniversary of Verdi's death: the 10 lire stamp shows a photograph of the composer, the Teatro Reale and the Cathedral in Parma; 25 lire shows Verdi's head from the monument by Secchi, Roncole Church and its organ; and 60 lire shows the bust of Verdi by Gemito, La Scala and Milan Cathedral.

Postage stamp issued in Monaco (1987) for the bicentenary of the première of Mozart's 'Don Giovanni', with a portrait of the composer and several scenes from the opera

Austria produced a series of elegantly engraved composers' portraits in 1922: Beethoven, Mozart, Haydn, Schubert, Bruckner, the younger Johann Strauss and Wolf. In 1926 a set of 'Nibelung Legends' was issued, and in 1931 a portrait of J. M. Nestroy. The Linz Landestheater was illustrated in 1953.

Czechoslovakia issued portraits of Smetana and Dvořák in 1934, the Smetana stamp showing music from his opera *Libuše*; further portraits of each composer followed in 1951. The 150th anniversary of Mozart's death was commemorated by Bohemia in 1941 with four stamps, with attached labels: two showed the Tyl Theatre in Prague, with labels carrying notation from *Don Giovanni*, the others the Posch relief of Mozart with labels showing Mozart's piano.

French issues between 1936 and 1952 include noteworthy portraits of Berlioz, Debussy, Massenet, Gounod, d'Indy, Saint-Saëns and Chabrier (the last referring to *Gwendoline*). A USSR issue of three portrait stamps for Tchaikovsky, in 1940, includes one with music from *Yevgeny Onegin*; in a Rimsky-Korsakov issue of 1944 two of four stamps show the score of *Mlada*. The first of many depictions of the Moscow Bol'shoy Theatre appeared in 1946, followed by the opera houses in Baku, Riga, Tallinn and Alma-Ata in 1950 and Tbilisi in 1951; 1951 also saw a multi-portrait stamp showing Glinka, Tchaikovsky, Musorgsky, Borodin and Rimsky-Korsakov with the Bol'shoy Theatre.

These early stamps form the foundation of a collection of opera stamps and represent a rational approach to the issuing of stamps. In the mid-1950s governments came to realize the potential financial gains of issuing stamps. In Europe this was kept within reasonable bounds, but countries not directly concerned with the composers were less discriminating. The period 1967–73 saw the appearance of gaudy 'wallpaper'-type stamps from small Middle East kingdoms such as Ajman (*Norma*, *Carmen*, *Die Zauberflöte*), Ras Al Khaima (Boldoni's magnificent portrait of Verdi, *Otello*, *Faust*, *Aida*, *Madama Butterfly*, *Lohengrin*, *Die Entführung*) and Sharjah (Mozart and *Die Zauberflöte*).

In 1985, named as European Music Year because of the anniversaries of Handel, Bach, Schütz, Domenico Scarlatti and others, the European Postal Authority required each member country to issue music stamps. Of the some 350 that appeared in the year a number are concerned with opera.

2. PARTICULAR TOPICS.

(i) Musical notation. Musical excerpts, generally from the overture or from an aria, are often shown on stamps. The overture to Mozart's *Die Zauberflöte* appears on a miniature sheet of 1981 from the German Democratic Republic. Music from *Andrea Chénier* forms the background to Giordano's portrait on an Italian stamp of 1967. Smetana's *The Bartered Bride* is seen on a Czech miniature sheet of 1966. Great Britain used part of the score of Tippett's *The Midsummer Marriage* on a stamp issued to celebrate the 50th anniversary of the British Council in 1984. Gluck's *Armide* is shown on a German stamp of 1987. There are many further examples.

(ii) Operatic scenes. Scenes from operas, often lavishly reproduced, can be seen on many stamps. While individual stamps are generally issued to commemorate an anniversary, many scenes are issued in sets independent of a particular occasion. Sometimes sets are confined to a single composer, but often they represent the works of several.

Among single Italian stamps can be mentioned Puccini's *La bohème* (1958), Leoncavallo's *Pagliacci* (1958), Boito's *Mefistofele* (with portrait, 1968) and Ponchielli's *La Giaconda* (with portrait, 1986). Puccini's *Madama Butterfly* is beautifully illustrated, together with a portrait, on a Monaco issue of 1983. Of particular interest is a Monaco 1987 issue on the bicentenary of the première of *Don Giovanni*; alongside a portrait of Mozart is a composite picture showing the opening scene, in which Giovanni kills the Commendatore, and the final scene, in which he is consumed by the flames of hell while the Commendatore's ghost-statue looks on: a masterpiece of stamp design (see illustration).

Hungary issued an opera set in 1967 showing *Prince Igor*, *Der Freischütz*, *Die Zauberflöte*, *Bluebeard's Castle*, *Carmen*, *Don Carlos*, *Tannhäuser* and *Hunyadi László*. There was also a set of seven composers in 1953, which included scenes from five Hungarian operas alongside portraits of their composers: *Verbunkos* (J.

Bihari), *Bánk bán* (Erkel), *Szép Ilonka* (Mosonyi), *Die Königin von Saba* (Goldmark) and *Háry János* (Kodály). Monaco has issued several tasteful operatic scenes, among them four from *Carmen* in 1975 celebrating the centenary of the première. A set including five opera scenes appeared in 1979 on the centenary of the Salle Garnier opera house in Monte Carlo; the operas, all of which had their premières there, were Massenet's *Le jongleur de Notre Dame* and *Don Quichotte*, Ganne's *Hans, le joueur de flûte*, Ibert and Honegger's *L'aiglon* and Ravel's *L'enfant et les sortilèges*. A Swedish issue of 1983 shows a scene from Blomdahl's *Aniara*.

(iii) Singers. A Romanian issue of 1964 shows portraits of singers costumed for a role: George Folescu (in *Boris Godunov*), Elena Teodorini (*Carmen*), Hariclea Darclée (*Tosca*), Ion Bajenaru (*Petru Rares*), Jean Athanasiu (*Rigoletto*), N. Leonard (*Les contes d' Hoffmann*), Doru Popovici (Alberich in the *Ring*) and Trian Grosavescu (*Rigoletto*); the set is completed with a portrait of George Stephănescu, a founder of Romanian opera. Among other singers portrayed on stamps are Melba (Australia 1961), Shalyapin as painted by Serov (USSR 1965) and by Korovin (USSR 1973), Caruso (Italy, 1973), Slezak (Austria 1973), Lind (Sweden 1975), Aïno Akté (Finland, 1976), Albani (Canada 1980), Callas (Greece 1980), Ghiaurov (Bulgaria 1980), Birgit Nilsson (Sweden, 1981) and Margaret Sheridan (Ireland 1989).

In 1975 Nicaragua issued an interesting set of opera stamps, 'Grandes cantantes de opera', with 15 stamps showing singers in costume alongside an operatic excerpt. The choice was made in a poll of critics and personalities of the opera world. The singers are Jussi Björling (*La bohème*), Callas (*Tosca*), Caruso (*La Juive*), Giuseppe de Luca (*Rigoletto*), Flagstad (*Tristan und Isolde*), Gobbi (*Simon Boccanegra*), Lotte Lehmann (*Der Rosenkavalier*), Melba (*La traviata*), Giovanni Martinelli (*Otello*), Melchior (*Parsifal*), Nilsson (*Turandot*), Pinza (*Don Giovanni*), Ponselle (*Norma*) and Sutherland (*La fille du régiment*).

Another interesting item is the miniature sheet issued by Austria on the centenary of the Vienna Staatsoper in 1969. The sheet of nine stamps includes seven operas, a ballet and a central vignette of the opera house. Each opera has some special significance for the house in terms of anniversaries and premières. The designer disclaims that he depicted recognizable artists but all the scenes are based on photographs; the operas and singers on these beautifully detailed stamps are Eberhard Waechter (*Don Giovanni*), Walter Berry (*Die Zauberflöte*), Anton Dermota (*Fidelio*), Wolfgang Windgassen and Elisabeth Grümmer (*Lohengrin*), Sena Jurinac and Paul Schöffler (*Don Carlos*), Rudolf Schock and Jean Madeira (*Carmen*) and Christa Ludwig and Anneliese Rothenberger (*Der Rosenkavalier*).

(iv) Opera houses. Among the opera houses shown on stamps are La Scala, Milan (1951 and others), the Staatsoper, Vienna (1955), the Paris Opéra (1964), Sydney Opera House (1973), the Festspielhaus, Bayreuth (1976), the Royal Opera House, Covent Garden, in a painting by Sir Hugh Casson (1980), the Metropolitan, New York (1983; for illustration *see* NEW YORK, fig.8) and the S Carlo, Naples (1987). Architects of opera houses have also been depicted, including E. von der Null and A. von Siccardsburg (Vienna Staatsoper, 1934) and G. W. von Knobelsdorf (Berlin Staatsoper, 1953).

(v) Miscellaneous. Mozart anniversaries have been duly celebrated. The 1941 wartime commemoration was modest, but 1956 saw issues from Austria, Belgium, Bulgaria, Czechoslovakia, Germany, Romania and the USSR. The charming Czechoslovak set of six gives portraits of Mozart's friends in Prague and reference to *Don Giovanni* with the theatre in which it was first performed. Monaco noted the 225th anniversary of Mozart's birth in 1981 with a triptych. 1991 saw issues from more than a dozen countries, the Austrian offering of a triptych souvenir sheet being of particular interest. It shows the Papageno fountain in the Mozart Platz, Vienna, depicting Tamino and Pamina from *Die Zauberflöte*, while the Czechoslovak stamp shows music from *La clemenza di Tito*.

Composers shown conducting include Richard Strauss (West Berlin 1949 and Austria 1989) and Carl Maria von Weber (in triptych, in the engraving by J. Hayter, conducting *Der Freischütz*, Germany 1986). Other well-known conductors depicted include Mahler (Austria, 1960), Toscanini (Italy 1967 and others), Beecham (Great Britain 1980), Klemperer (Germany 1985), and Mitropoulos (Greece 1985).

Librettists depicted include Maeterlinck (Belgium 1952), C. F. Ramuz (Switzerland 1972) and Hofmannsthal (Austria 1974).

Opera posters reproduced on stamps include one for Gounod's *Faust* by Jan Lenica (Poland 1968) and one for the première of *Der Freischütz* (German Democratic Republic 1986). Chopin's piano arrangement of 'La ci darem' from *Don Giovanni* is on a Polish stamp of 1960. Wagner's patron King Ludwig II of Bavaria is on a German stamp of 1960. Among opera critics, George Bernard Shaw appears and Vladimir Stasov is on a Russian stamp of 1973. Among music festivals celebrated on stamps are Salzburg (1970) and Bregenz (1979), and from Ireland the Wexford Festival as one of a set of three (1987).

(vi) Auxiliaries. Stamps are not the only way in which postage may be prepaid. Postal stationery, which consists of cards and envelopes already printed with a stamp, is widely used. Germany issued such a card for the Bayreuth Festival in 1933; in Italy cards have been produced (for example of Zandonai in 1983) in lieu of stamps. Many were issued in the USSR.

An important adjunct to a stamp is the cancellation. When new stamps are issued, the 'first day cancel' may portray a composer, musical notation or an appropriate scene from an opera. Many such have also been produced in Italy on anniversaries of musicians or librettists never shown on a stamp (Augusto Massari, Lorenzo da Ponte, Placido Domingo). Metermarks, which replace stamps, should also be mentioned: Texaco advertises the Metropolitan Opera of New York, which they sponsor. Among 'Cinderellas' – stamp-like labels (also called 'vignettes' or 'seals'), generally issued for charity or for advertising purposes – is a French set, 'Aide aux Musiciens' (1944), including scenes from Massenet's *Manon*, Lalo's *Le roi d'Ys* and Chabrier's *Gwendoline*; the bicentenary of La Scala was liberally celebrated in 1978 with the issue of 14 sheets, each of 12 to 25 vignettes showing composers and their works and famous singers associated with La Scala.

*

J. Watson: *Stamps and Music* (London, 1962)
J. S. Papa: *Opera Checklist* (1966; suppl., 1969)

The Baton: Magazine of the Philatelic Music Circle (1969–) [incl. many articles on opera stamps]
M. J. Whitehead: *Checklist of Opera on Stamps* (1989)

IRENE LAWFORD

Standfuss, J(?ohann) C. (*d* ? after 1759). German composer. He was a violinist and répétiteur with G. H. Koch's theatre company about 1750, wrote what is often regarded as the earliest German Singspiel and, despite Gerber's report that he died in a Hamburg hospital in 1756, was presumably still alive in 1759, in which year two further Singspiels by him were first performed. Although the term 'Singspiel' had long been used in Germany for both comic and serious works, and by this period a flourishing Viennese tradition had been established, Standfuss's setting of C. F. Weisse's first version of Charles Coffey's *The Devil to Pay, or The Wives Metamorphos'd* (London, 1731) opened an era in the German musical theatre. Under the title *Der Teufel ist los, oder Die verwandelten Weiber* it was performed for the first time on 6 October 1752 in Leipzig by Koch's company. Coffey's original, in a translation by the former Prussian ambassador to London, C. W. von Borck, had been given in Berlin nine years earlier, probably with the original English tunes; works on the subject were frequent in the 18th century. As Koch had some good singers in his company it is reasonable to assume that *Der Teufel ist los* was well performed. Not the least significant aspect of its success was the battle of pamphlets to which it gave rise, Gottsched and his adherents objecting in vain to the demise of good taste evinced by the comic Singspiel. A sequel, *Der lustige Schuster, oder Der zweyte Theil vom Teufel ist los*, based on Coffey's *The Merry Cobbler* (London, 1735), appeared seven years later. Both parts of *Der Teufel ist los* were revised by C. F. Weisse and J. A. Hiller at Leipzig in 1766 and were published in vocal score there in 1770 and 1771 respectively.

Standfuss's scores have not survived, but Hiller took over many of Standfuss's numbers into his own versions; in his preface to *Der lustige Schuster* Hiller spoke appreciatively of 'a certain gaiety, a not infelicitous expressiveness in the low comic vein, and now and again a witty touch' in Standfuss's music, the historical importance of which he clearly realized. The last of Standfuss's known works, the (lost) Singspiel *Jochem Tröbs, oder Der vergnügte Bauernstand*, to a libretto by an actor in Koch's company, was given in Hamburg on 17 September 1759.

Der Teufel ist los, oder Die verwandelten Weiber (Spl, C. F. Weisse), Leipzig, 6 Oct 1752
Der lustige Schuster, oder Der zweyte Theil vom Teufel ist los (Spl, Weisse), Lübeck, 18 Jan 1759
Jochem Tröbs, oder Der vergnügte Bauernstand [Der stolze Bauer Jochem Tröbs] (Spl, J. C. Ast), Hamburg, 17 Sept 1759, music and text lost

*

GerberNL
C. F. Weisse: *Selbstbiographie*, ed. C. E. Weisse and S. G. Frisch (Leipzig, 1806)
C. H. Schmid: *Chronologie des deutschen Theaters*, ed. P. Legband, Schriften der Gesellschaft für Theatergeschichte, i (Berlin, 1902), 102, 128, 157, 175
G. Calmus: 'Die ersten deutschen Singspiele von Standfuss und Hiller', *Publikationen der Internationalen Musikgesellschaft, Beihefte*, 2nd ser., vi (Leipzig, 1908), 1–15

PETER BRANSCOMBE

Stanford, Sir **Charles Villiers** (*b* Dublin, 30 Sept 1852; *d* London, 29 March 1924). Irish composer. He was brought up in the cultured Protestant professional circle in Dublin. His undergraduate career at Queens' College, Cambridge, was a brilliant one, and by 1873 he had become organist of Trinity College and conductor of the Cambridge University Musical Society, which he built into a major choral and orchestral body (later he was also conductor of the London Bach Choir and the Leeds Festival). Trinity permitted him to study further in Berlin and Leipzig and he travelled widely on the continent at this time. He was appointed professor of composition and orchestral playing at the RCM from its opening in 1883 and professor of music at Cambridge in 1887, holding both posts until his death, though his relations with Cambridge became strained in later years and he lived in London.

Stanford's great influence on several generations of British composers as composition teacher at the RCM never found effective manifestation in vernacular opera, for, unlike Ethel Smyth, he mustered neither singlemindedness nor diplomacy to influence its painfully slow headway in English society. Yet his list of works and his articles show what a central concern it was. His initial problem was how to transplant early continental successes to English opera houses, his later one how to forge a national idiom.

His first opera, *The Veiled Prophet of Khorassan* (composed 1877–9), was championed by Ernst Frank and given a fine production in Hanover in 1881 (as *Der verschleierte Prophet*), which was followed by others in Germany. Cosmopolitan and pre-Wagnerian in its ethos (the influence of Meyerbeer has been suggested), it must have seemed old-fashioned by the time it appeared at Covent Garden in 1893. *Savonarola* (1883) shows more individuality, though Stanford's aesthetic is essentially a contained one and hence no real match for its heroic scenario; again success attended its première in Germany but not at Covent Garden later in the same year (9 July 1884), apparently owing to indispositions. It is less easy to account for the neglect of *The Canterbury Pilgrims* (1883), following its excellent first production by Carl Rosa (though Stanford would not risk taking it further after the failure of *Savonarola* less than three months later), and for the demise of *Much Ado about Nothing* (1900), after two London performances in 1901, though it was well received in Leipzig the following year. In these two operas Stanford developed a refulgent approach to high comedy which, although too reminiscent of *Die Meistersinger* in *The Canterbury Pilgrims* to withstand comparison with it and not quite able to handle the wit and wealth of Shakespeare's subplots in *Much Ado*, marked a notable step forward in English opera, equal to (and doubtless modelled on) the achievements of Goetz and Nicolai in Germany. The ensembles, love music and orchestration in *Much Ado* are particularly fine.

Shamus O'Brien (1895), a light opera with spoken dialogue, was Stanford's one measurable success. Although it would probably not have withstood the more searching climate of the Irish renaissance a decade or so later, it was at the time a refreshing alternative to satirical or titillating operettas. Its modest yet surefooted musical handling of a bittersweet Irish plot involved the use of folksongs and was well paced, with the pert and the sentimental thoroughly integrated. It ran consecutively for a good while in London and then toured the provinces and reached Broadway in 1897.

Stanford's best operatic music was still to come, however, in *The Critic* (1915) and *The Travelling Companion* (1916). *The Critic* is a clever attempt to present Sheridan's backstage comedy in operatic terms. Only a professional production will determine whether it works as a *jeu d'esprit*, with its many musical jokes and quotations; there is plenty of lyrical warmth besides, in an overtly English frame of reference. Simple yet potentially profound lyricism, now in the context of a dramatic allegory which is a close and worthy companion to Humperdinck's fairy-tale operas, is also the legacy of *The Travelling Companion*. Here, in his last completed opera, Stanford found the English dramatic context, that of the spiritual wayfarer (or Everyman), which suited him best. Still Brahmsian in style, it came too late for it to pave the way for others (in fact the music is based on a piano piece which Stanford composed as early as 1875), though it is worth noting that Tippett produced it at the Barn Theatre, Oxted, as a young man.

Since the 1920s Stanford's operas have received only occasional productions, largely amateur. While their musical resources are conservative and circumscribed, they are nonetheless the work of an experienced professional with a distinctively warm style and a realizable personal vision, and only with professional productions will it be possible to reach an assessment of their contribution to the renaissance of British music.

See also CRITIC, THE; *SHAMUS O'BRIEN*; and *TRAVELLING COMPANION, THE*.

The Veiled Prophet of Khorassan, 1877–9 (grand op, 3, W. B. Squire, after T. Moore: *Lalla Rookh*); as Der verschleierte Prophet, Hanover, Hof, 5 Feb 1881, *GB-Lbl**, *Lcm**, vs (Berlin, 1881), rev. vs (London, 1893)
Savonarola (grand op, prol., 3, G. A. A'Beckett); in Ger., Hamburg, Stadt, 18 April 1884; in Eng., London, CG, 9 July 1884; *Lcm**, vs (Leipzig, 1884)
The Canterbury Pilgrims (3, A'Beckett), London, Drury Lane, 28 April 1884, *Lcm**, vs (London, 1884)
The Miner of Falun, 1888 (3, Squire and H. F. Wilson, after E. T. A. Hoffmann), unperf., Act 1 *Lcm**, unpubd
Lorenza op.55, 1894 (dramma lirico, prol., 2, A. Ghislanzoni and F. Fontana), unperf., MS, Newcastle, University Library, unpubd
Shamus O'Brien op.61 (romantic comic op, 2, G. H. Jessop, after J. S. Le Fanu), London, Opera Comique, 2 March 1896, *Lbl**, vs (London, 1896)
Christopher Patch [The Barber of Bath] op.69, 1897 (comedy op, 2, B. C. Stephenson and Jessop), *Lbl** (inc.), *Lcm**, unperf., unpubd
Much Ado about Nothing [The Marriage of Hero] op.76a, 1900 (4, J. Sturgis, after W. Shakespeare), London, CG, 30 May 1901, *Lcm**, vs (London, 1901)
The Critic, or An Opera Rehearsed op.144 (2, L. C. James, after R. B. Sheridan), London, Shaftesbury, 14 Jan 1916, vs *Lcm**, vs (London, 1915)
The Travelling Companion op.146, 1916 (4, H. Newbolt, after H. C. Andersen), Liverpool, David Lewis, 30 April 1925, *Lcm**, vs (London, 1919)

*

GänzlBMT
'The Veiled Prophet', *New Quarterly Musical Review*, no.2 (1893), 63–76
Pitt: 'Shamus O'Brien', *Magazine of Music*, xiii (1896), 249–50
C. V. Stanford: 'The Case for National Opera', *Studies and Memories* (London, 1908), 3–23
C. Forsyth: *Music and Nationalism: a Study of English Opera* (London, 1911)
C. V. Stanford: *Pages from an Unwritten Diary* (London, 1914)
J. F. Porte: *Sir Charles V. Stanford* (London, 1921)
J. A. Fuller Maitland: 'Stanford's Seven Operas', *The Music of Parry and Stanford* (Cambridge, 1934), 79–93
H. Plunket Greene: *Charles Villiers Stanford* (London, 1935), 183–201
F. Howes: *The English Musical Renaissance* (London, 1966), 156–7
G. Norris: *Stanford, the Cambridge Jubilee and Tchaikovsky* (Newton Abbot, 1980)
N. Burton: 'Opera: 1865–1914', *Music in Britain: the Romantic Age, 1800–1914*, ed. N. Temperley (London, 1981), 330–57
E. W. White: *A History of English Opera* (London, 1983), 346–7
G. Hauger: 'Stanford's Early Operas', *Opera*, xxxv (1984), 724–9
S. Banfield: 'British Opera in Retrospect', *MT*, cxxvii (1986), 205–7
——: 'The Early Renaissance: Mackenzie, Stanford and Smyth', *British Opera in Retrospect* (n.p., 1986) [pubn of the British Music Society], 63–8
L. Foreman: *From Parry to Britten: British Music in Letters 1900–1945* (London, 1987), 12–13

STEPHEN BANFIELD

Stanislavsky [Alexeyev], **Konstantin Sergeyevich** (*b* Moscow, 5/17 Jan 1863; *d* Moscow, 7 Aug 1938). Russian theatre and opera producer and theorist. He directed and performed in operettas in his family's private theatre and prepared for an opera career with the tenor Fyodor Komissarzhevsky, turning to drama only because his voice proved unsuitable for opera. In 1898 he and VLADIMIR IVANOVICH NEMIROVICH-DANCHENKO founded the Moscow Art Theatre, where they encouraged new playwrights such as Chekhov and Gorky and experimented with naturalistic staging. Out of this distinguished ensemble developed the Stanislavsky system, the theatre's most widespread approach to acting and directing. According to the system actors prepare their roles from within instead of concentrating on external presentation; they determine their character's psychological and social background, even extending beyond the specific dramatic situation. Combined with the actor's self-awareness and 'emotion memory', this leads to complete identification with the character, in turn resulting in an intensely realistic performance. Stanislavsky approached setting, costume, movement, light and sound with similarly studied concern for detail and accuracy. His early musical training and Shalyapin's influence made him especially sensitive to tempo and rhythm, and he proposed classes in music for his actors. He was among the first producers to 'orchestrate' serious dramatic scenes with music and sound effects to support underlying moods and ideas. He believed that dramatic art was moving towards 'the synthesis of music and drama, of words and sound'.

Stanislavsky's last 20 years were devoted more to opera than to theatre. In 1918 he organized the Bol'shoy Theatre Opera Studio whose aims were to set up a laboratory for research in the art of lyric drama; to renovate archaic traditions of opera production; to apply the system to opera acting; and to fuse in performance music, singing, words and movement. He maintained that the score, not the libretto, must be the point of departure in producing opera, and he depended upon the music to supply his motivation and truth, as well as tempo and rhythm. Immediately successful and ultimately influential, his studio productions were noted for narrative clarity and consistency, convincing acting and unmannered singing. By 1926 the studio, detached from the Bol'shoy, was renamed the Stanislavsky Opera Theatre Studio. Illness prevented Stanislavsky from taking sole responsibility for productions after 1928, but he continued planning and supervising opera until his death. His studio productions included: *Yevgeny Onegin*, 1919 (Act 1), 1922 (complete); *Werther*, 1921; *Il matrimonio segreto*, 1925; *The Tsar's Bride*, 1926; *La bohème*, 1927; *May Night*, 1928; *Boris Godunov*, 1929; *The Queen of Spades*, 1930; *The Golden Cockerel*, 1932; *Il barbiere di Siviglia*, 1933; *Carmen*, 1935; *Don Pasquale*, 1936; *Madama Butterfly*, 1938; and, posthumously produced, *Rigoletto*, 1939.

My Life in Art (London, 1923; Russ. orig., *Moya zhizn' v iskusstve*, 1926)

An Actor Prepares (London, 1936; Russ. orig., *Rabota aktyora nad soboy*, i, 1938)
Rabota aktyora nad soboy, ii (Moscow, 1948; Eng. trans. as *Building a Character*, 1949)
Creating a Role (London, 1949; Russ. orig., *Rabota aktyora nad rol'yu*, 1957)
ed. D. Magarshack: *Stanislavsky on the Art of Stage* (London, 1950)
ed. M. N. Kedrov: *K. S. Stanislavsky: sobraniye sochineniy* [Collected Works] (Moscow, 1954–61)

*

K. E. Antarova, ed.: *Besedï K. S. Stanislavskogo v Studii Bol'shogo v 1918–22 gg.* [Conversations with Stanislavsky at the Bol'shoy Studio during the Years 1918–22] (Moscow, 1939, 3/1952)
P. I. Rumyantsev: 'Rabota Stanislavskogo nad *Borisom Godunovïm*' [Stanislavsky's Work on *Boris Godunov*], *Teatral'nïy al'manakh* (1946), no.1, p.120
——: 'Sistema Stanislavskogo v opernom teatre' [Stanislavsky's System in the Opera Theatre], *Yezhegodnik Moskovskogo khudozhestvennogo teatra* (1947), 375–523
V. O. Toporkov: *K. S. Stanislavsky na repetitsii: vospominaniya* (Moscow, 1950; Eng. trans. as *Stanislavski in Rehearsal: the Final Years*, 1979)
G. V. Kristi: *Rabota Stanislavskogo v opernom teatre* [Stanislavsky's Work in the Opera Theatre] (Moscow, 1952)
P. I. Rumyantsev: *Rabota Stanislavskogo nad operoy Rigoletto* [Stanislavsky's Work on *Rigoletto*] (Moscow, 1955)
I. N. Vinogradskaya, ed.: *Zhizn' i tvorchestvo K. S. Stanislavskogo: letopis'* [The Life and Work of Stanislavsky: a Chronicle], iii (Moscow, 1973)
E. R. Hapgood, ed.: *Stanislavsky on Opera* (New York, 1975) [incl. recollections by P. I. Rumyantsev of Stanislavsky's productions]
J. Benedetti: *Stanislavski: an Introduction* (London, 1982)
L. Strasberg: *A Dream of Passion: the Development of the Method* (London, 1988)

PAUL SHEREN

Stankovych, Yevhen [Stankovich, Yevgeny] (*b* Svalyava, Transcarpathia, 19 Sept 1942). Ukrainian composer. In 1970 he graduated from the Kiev Conservatory, where he had been a pupil of Borys Lyatoshyns'ky and Miroslav Skorik. A connoisseur of Ukrainian folklore, he was strongly attracted to symphonic forms of expression. Among his works are symphonies for large and small orchestra, chamber and choral works and ballet music. Stankovich designated his single opera *Tsvit paporoti* ('The Fern's Bloom', 1979) as a folk opera; the libretto is by Alexander Stel'mashenko on subjects from Gogol. Aspects of human life – birth, work, love, conflict with the enemy, leisure, death – are transformed into ceremonial folkloristic forms. The three acts consist of three epic canvases: the everyday life of the Zaporozhian Sech' (the self-governing Cossack community); a cycle of traditional religious festivities related to St John's Eve (24 June in the Orthodox Calendar); and aspects of the heroic life of the people. The work is notable for the interaction of two different musical and stylistic layers. The first is vocal and related to dance (in the style of a *duma* or Ukrainian folk ballad), and to historical song, lament and *kazachok* (a Cossack dance), all either genuinely traditional or created by the composer in appropriate style, and all intended for performance by a folk choir. The second is the highly developed instrumental writing for symphony orchestra. In the song and dance material Stankovich's style embraces polyphony, antiphonal singing by choral groups, differently elaborated choral layers and other types of choral writing. The orchestral language is more complex and piquant than the vocal, with polytonal stratification, aleatory effects and tone clusters. The sophisticated instrumental commentary allows the song or folktune material to be developed into large-scale, fresco-like scenes. The opera remains unperformed: having been accepted for performance in Kiev the production was cancelled after only two rehearsals, a victim of the campaign against nationalism.

MARINA NEST'YEVA

Stanley, John (*b* London, 17 Jan 1712; *d* London, 19 May 1786). English composer. He was blinded by a domestic accident at the age of two. When he was seven he began organ lessons, and soon after he transferred to Maurice Greene. Progress with Greene was so rapid that in 1723 he was appointed organist of All Hallows, Bread Street. He later obtained posts at St Andrew's, Holborn (1726) and the Temple Church (1734), both of which he held until his death. After Handel died in 1759 he joined J. C. Smith as co-director of the Lenten oratorios at Covent Garden (and later Drury Lane) and in 1779 succeeded William Boyce as Master of the King's Music. Stanley married Sarah Arlond in 1738, but had no children.

Stanley's stage works included incidental music to T. Southerne's *Oroonoko* (adapted by J. Hawkesworth; 1759) and music for R. Lloyd's and A. Murphy's masque *The Tears and Triumphs of Parnassus* (London, Drury Lane, 17 Nov 1760), both of which are now lost. Two works which have survived are the one-act pastoral *Arcadia, or The Shepherd's Wedding* (Lloyd; Drury Lane, 26 Oct 1761; broadcast, BBC, 1986; *GB-Lcm*), written in celebration of George III's marriage to Queen Charlotte, and the three-act opera *Teraminta* (H. Carey; *GB-Lcm*), which seems to have remained unperformed until a BBC radio broadcast in the 1950s. Like most English composers of the early Georgian period Stanley drew heavily on the Corelli-Handel tradition for his musical style. Later in life, however, he was influenced by the *galant* style of J. C. Bach, traces of which are clearly audible in his last works.

See also TERAMINTA.

*

BurneyH; *LS*
H. Carey: *Dramatick Works* (London, 1743)
D. E. Baker: *The Companion to the Play-House* (London, 1764)
[W. Coxe]: *Anecdotes of George Frederick Handel and John Christopher Smith* (London, 1799)
G. Finzi: 'John Stanley (1713–1786)', *PRMA*, lxxvii (1950–51), 63–75
M. Sands: 'The Problem of *Teraminta*', *ML*, xxxiii (1952), 217–22
G. Finzi: 'John Stanley', *Tempo*, new ser., no.27 (1953), 21–7
E. Bell: 'New Light on John Stanley', *New Beacon*, xli (1957), 193–5
W. Dean: *Handel's Dramatic Oratorios and Masques* (London, 1959)
R. Fiske: *English Theatre Music in the Eighteenth Century* (London, 1973, 2/1986)
G. Williams, H. D. Johnstone and M. Boyd: 'New Light on Stanley', *MT*, cxvii (1976), 810–15
A. G. Williams: *The Life and Works of John Stanley (1712–86)* (diss., U. of Reading, 1977)
——: 'Stanley, Smith and "Teraminta"', *ML*, lx (1979), 312–15

A. GLYN WILLIAMS

Stanzani, Tommaso (*b* Bologna, *c*1647; *d* 27 April 1717). Italian librettist. He spent most of his life in Bologna apart from an exile in Venice, 1682–7, and was a member of various academies including, in 1712, the Arcadian where he took the name Atresio Geonuntino. At first he wrote mainly melodramas which were presented regularly at the Teatro Formagliari, and in Venice he wrote and staged two more; after his return to Bologna, however, he diversified into comedy (*Zelida*), rustic drama (*La Bernarda*, adapted from a prose text in dialect) and works treating the conflict between heroism and love (*Attilio Regolo*) and heroic virtue (*Griselda*).

Stanzani's melodramas are mostly historical and retain the typical 17th-century narrative and formal structure. Among his works *Arsinoe* is notable for its intense dramatic style in the handling of the 'throne versus love' subject.

L'Oronte di Menfi (dramma musicale), P. Franceschini, 1676; *L'Arsinoe* (dramma musicale), Franceschini, 1676 (Clayton, 1705, as Arsinoe, Queen of Cyprus); *Apollo in Tessaglia* (dramma musicale), Franceschini, 1679; *Atide* (dramma musicale), G. F. Tosi, Degli Antoni and Perti, 1679; *Erismonda* (dramma), Tosi, 1681; *L'anarchia dell'impero* (dramma musicale), Legrenzi, 1683; *Rodoaldo re d'Italia* (dramma), D. Gabrielli, 1685 (B. Soliani, 1688)

Il riposo d'Italia (trattenimento musicale), G. M. Righi, 1689; *La Bernarda* (dramma rusticale), Righi, 1694; *Zelida, ovvero La scuola delle mogli* (dramma musicale), comp. unknown, 1696; *Attilio Regolo in Africa* (dramma musicale), P. P. Laurenti, 1701; *Esone ringiovenito* (trattenimento musicale), Laurenti, 1706; *La virtù in trionfo o sia La Griselda* (after A. Zeno), L. A. Predieri, 1711

A. A. Sacco: *Notizie istoriche degli Arcadi morti* (Rome, 1720–21), iii

G. Fantuzzi: *Notizie degli scrittori bolognesi* (Bologna, 1781–94)

M. G. Bergamini: *La Colonia Renia: profilo documentario e critico dell'Arcadia bolognese*, ed. M. Saccenti, i: *Documenti bio-bibliografici* (Modena, 1988)

MARIA GRAZIA ACCORSI

Stapp, Olivia (*b* New York, 31 March 1940). American soprano. She studied in New York and Italy, singing Beppe (*L'amico Fritz*) at Milan in 1960. Engaged at the Vienna Volksoper and Wuppertal, she made her New York City Opera début in 1972 as Carmen. At first a mezzo-soprano, in 1980 she became a soprano, and made her Metropolitan début in 1982 as Lady Macbeth. She has sung in Rome, Vienna, San Francisco, Chicago, Geneva, Hamburg and at La Scala. Her repertory includes Norma, Anne Boleyn, Mary Stuart, Elvira (*Ernani*), Hélène (*Les vêpres siciliennes*), Aida, Abigaille, Strauss's Electra, Santuzza, Tosca and Minnie. Her strong and flexible voice, dark-coloured in timbre, is ideal for Lady Macbeth, which she has sung in Berlin, Washington, DC, Zürich and at the Paris Opéra.

ELIZABETH FORBES

Stara Zagora. Bulgarian city. Situated on the crossroads from Western Europe, the East and Russia, the city was at first visited by foreign companies. In 1897 the Kaval music society was founded, which staged its first full-scale performance, Georgi Atanasov's *Gergana*, in 1925. The Southern Bulgarian Regional Opera was formed in 1931. In 1933–4 the opera house came under the administration of the city; it became state run in 1946, opening as the Narodna Opera Stara Zagora (Stara Zagora National Opera) on 19 June with *Il barbiere di Siviglia*. Leading figures have included the music director Romeo Raichev, Zlatan Stanchev and the conductors Dobri Christov, Yosif Yossifov and Dimitar Dimitrov. Since the early 1970s Stara Zagora has hosted the only festival especially for opera and ballet in Bulgaria. The first purpose-built opera house in Bulgaria (seating 700) opened with Lyubomir Pipkov's *Momchil* in 1972. During the 1980s the repertory was orientated towards large-scale operas such as *Boris Godunov*, *Der fliegende Holländer*, *Norma* and Marin Goleminov's *Trakiyski idoli* ('Thracian Idols'). Until the theatre burnt down in 1991, there were each year 150 performances including five premières, one of which was an operetta or musical; opera and drama was performed on alternate days.

Entsiklopediya na bulgarskata muzikalna kultura (Sofia, 1967)

R. Biks: *Bulgarski operenteatar* (Sofia, 1985), ii

MAGDALENA MANOLOVA

Starer, Robert (*b* Vienna, 8 Jan 1924). American composer of Austrian birth. His musical training began in Vienna and continued at the Juilliard School where he taught from 1949 to 1974 and at Brooklyn College from 1963. He has composed two full-length and two chamber operas. *The Intruder* (1956), a one-act chamber opera, is set in the kitchen of an isolated New England farmhouse occupied by a widow and two daughters. Starer brings irony and humour to the Intruder's disruption of the family.

Starer's largest opera, *Pantagleize* (composed in 1967), in three acts, has a cast of 14 singers, chorus and dancers. The action takes place in a European city on the morrow of one war and the eve of another. After the première Andrew Porter wrote: 'Starer has done more than set a good and unusual play to music ... Ghelderode's *Pantagleize* now seems to have been reshaped by Starer in musical form' (*New Yorker*, 21 April 1973). The opera has been compared to *Wozzeck*, for the similarity of musical setting and the anti-hero protagonist.

The Last Lover (1975), a one-act chamber opera, was described by the librettist, Gail Godwin, as a 'musical morality play'. Its three singers play five parts between them and are accompanied by a woodwind quintet which also takes part in the action. The story is based on the legend of St Pelagia, who lived in Antioch during the 4th century: a woman of easy virtue is so impressed by a holy man that she not only gives up her way of life but also her gender and becomes 'Brother Pelagius'. *Apollonia*, in two acts, has a cast of nine singers, and a mime as the young Apollonia. The adult Apollonia (soprano) has the power to help people transform themselves into whatever they would like to be. Whenever she uses her magic powers, Starer employs an electric keyboard for the 'magic' music, in addition to the conventional orchestra.

The Intruder (1, M. A. Pryor), New York, Cherry Lane, 4 Dec 1956

Pantagleize, 1967 (3, Starer, after M. de Ghelderode), New York, Brooklyn College Opera Theater, 8 April 1973

The Last Lover (1, G. Godwin), Katonah, NY, Caramoor Festival, 2 Aug 1975

Apollonia [The Ideal Self] (2, Godwin), St Paul, MN, 22 May 1979

A. Porter: 'May Day', *Musical Season: a Critic from Abroad in America* (New York, 1974), 233

R. Starer: *Continuo, a Life in Music* (New York, 1987)

A. Porter: *Musical Events: a Chronicle, 1983–1986* (New York, 1989), 289

R. Starer: 'Writing an Opera is a Composer's Ultimate Challenge', *New York Times* (29 April 1990)

R. H. Kornick: *Recent American Opera: a Production Guide* (New York, 1991), 296–8

DOROTHY LEWIS-GRIFFITH

Starzer, Joseph (*b* 1726–7; *d* Vienna, 22 April 1787). Austrian composer. In collaboration with the choreographer Franz Hilverding he helped to lay the foundations for the Viennese reform of ballet by Gluck and Gasparo Angiolini (Hilverding's pupil), and thereby also for the Gluckian reform of opera. From 1752 he was a violinist in the orchestra of the Vienna Burgtheater (directed by Gluck after *c*1755), and composer of music for pantomime ballets performed there and at the German (Kärntnertor) theatre, and for ballets given with *opéras comiques* and Italian operas. With his highly gestural, pictorial music, Starzer ably seconded Hilverding's efforts at integrating pantomime and dance. Though in his early works he relied heavily on binary dances, he ensured continuity through returns of movements and tonal concatenation of numbers – techniques exploited by Gluck in both *Don Juan* and *Orfeo ed Euridice*. Starzer followed Hilverding to the Russian court early in 1759; while there he wrote dances for Raupach's *opéra-ballet Pribezhishche dobrodeteli* ('The Refuge of Virtue'), among other works. Hilverding returned to Vienna in 1765 and Starzer in 1768, in which year Hilverding died. During the 1770s he created several large-scale pantomime ballets with Jean-Georges Noverre, accommodating Noverre's preference for free-flowing, through-composed music.

He was also an early contributor to Viennese operatic reform, providing dance music for Wagenseil's *Le cacciatrici amanti* (1755), which La Borde termed a true *opéra-ballet* in the French manner, and probably also for Gluck's *L'innocenza giustificata*. Besides developing techniques useful to opera, Starzer also borrowed from the genre, using instrumental recitative as early as 1757 in his ballet *La guirlande enchantée*. His music shows a strong folk element, and a varied and imaginative instrumental palette, for example chalumeaux depicting sirens' voices in the ballet *Circé et Ulisse* (1756–7), and janissary music in *Le turc généreux* (1758). His works were highly appreciated in Italy, beginning in the 1750s, but especially in later restagings of Noverre's ballets. Late in his career Starzer composed a passion oratorio which was much admired, and arranged Handel oratorios for concerts given by Baron Gottfried van Swieten, a responsibility assumed by Mozart on Starzer's death. One of the founders of Vienna's Tonkünstlersozietät, Starzer was well represented as a symphonist on its concert programmes. Burney, a guest at a quartet party in 1772, praised the 'uncommon feeling and expression' of his playing on the violin.

all dates are of ballet first performances

Ballets in operas: Adolfati: La clemenza di Tito, 1753; Gluck: La danza, 1755; Les amours de Bastien et Bastienne [M.-J.-B. Favart parody of J.-J. Rousseau: Le devin du village], 1755; Wagenseil: Le cacciatrici amanti, 1755; La vengeance inutile [C.-S. Favart parody of Mondonville: Titon et l'Aurore], 1755, *CS-K*; Tircis et Doristée [C.-S. Favart parody of Lully: Acis et Galatée], 1756; G. Reutter: L'amor prigionero, 1756; Le Chinois poli en France [L. Anseaume parody of Sellitto: Il cinese rimpatriato], 1756, *I-Tn*; A. Bret: Le déguisement pastoral, 1756; Gluck: Il re pastore, 1756; Gluck: La fausse esclave, 1758; Gluck: L'île de Merlin, ou Le monde renversé, 1758; Raupach: Pribezhishche dobrodeteli [The Refuge of Virtue; L'asile de la vertu], 1759; Raupach: Siroe, re di Persia, 1760; Manfredini: Carlo Magno, 1763

Doubtful works: Die Wildschützen (Lustspiel mit Gesängen, 3, G. Stephanie the Younger), Vienna, Burg, 1777, *A-Wn*; Die drei Pächter (Spl, 2), Vienna, 1778; ballet in Gluck: L'innocenza giustificata (1755)

*

BurneyGN
Journal encyclopédique, Jan 1756–Dec 1759 passim
J. von Stählin: *Nachrichten von der Musik in Russland*, in J. J. Haigold [A. L. von Schlözer]: *Beylagen zum neuveränderten Russland* (Riga and Leipzig, 1769–70)
C. F. D. Schubart: *Ideen zu einer Ästhetik der Tonkunst* (Vienna, 1806)
R. Haas: *Gluck und Durazzo im Burgtheater* (Vienna, 1925)
L. Braun: 'Die Ballettkompositionen von Joseph Starzer', *SMw*, xiii (1926–7), 38–56
R. Haas: 'Die Wiener Bühnentanz von 1740 bis 1767', *JbMP 1937*, 77–93
R.-A. Mooser: *Opéras, intermezzos, ballets, cantates, oratorios joués en Russie durant le XVIIIe siècle* (Geneva, 1945, 3/1964)
——: *Annales de la musique et des musiciens en Russie au XVIIIme siècle* (Geneva, 1948–51)
K. Hansell: 'Il ballo teatrale e l'opera italiana', *SOI*, v (1988), 175–306
B. A. Brown: *Gluck and the French Theatre in Vienna* (Oxford, 1991)

BRUCE ALAN BROWN

Stasov, Vladimir Vasil'yevich (*b* St Petersburg, 2/14 Jan 1824; *d* St Petersburg, 10/23 Oct 1906). Russian arts publicist. Born into the family of a famous architect, Stasov was sent to the élite School of Jurisprudence in St Petersburg. There he studied piano with Adolf Henselt and made friends with A. N. Serov, with whom he carried on a voluminous correspondence in the 1840s and the early 1850s that has served scholars as a mirror of the Russian artistic and intellectual atmosphere at the time. (By the time Serov embarked on his career as a composer he and Stasov had fallen out, partly because of a furious debate over the dramatic merits of Glinka's operas.) After a 30-month stay abroad (1851–4), during which he catalogued Fortunato Santini's music library, Stasov returned to St Petersburg and joined the staff of the Imperial Public Library, where he remained for the rest of his long life, from 1872 as the head of the Department of Fine Arts.

The grounds for Stasov's claim to immortality was his service as friend, confidant, factotum, browbeater, inspirer and indefatigable tribune to generations of Russian painters and composers, particularly those of maverick persuasion. In art, he attached himself to the realist painters known as 'Peredvizhniki' ('The Wanderers'); in music, he was virtually the sixth member of 'The Five', whose Russian sobriquet *moguchaya kuchka* ('Mighty Little Heap') Stasov inadvertently coined in an article of 1867 (*Sankt-peterburgskiye vedomosti*, 13 May). He collaborated extensively with all his artist and musician friends, and in this informal capacity he had a hand in making history as well as reporting it. A list of his 'Suggestions to artists' that he included shortly before his death in a letter to his niece and biographer includes the following operas: *Mel'nichikha v Marli* and *Rogneda* (Serov); *Andzhelo* (Cui); *Prince Igor* (Borodin); and *The Tale of Tsar Saltan*, as well as 'significant portions' of *Sadko* and *The Maid of Pskov* (Rimsky-Korsakov). Stasov also took full credit for the idea behind Musorgsky's *Khovanshchina* ('the consequence of my reading, while still a boy, Konstantin Masalsky's novel *The Streltsy*'), but this is doubtful. Yet even if he did not directly inspire it, that opera (like *Prince Igor*) was one in which Stasov's actual creative input was particularly strong. He also supplied Musorgsky with incidental texts for *Boris Godunov* (Varlaam's song, the hostess's and children's songs, the Jesuits' Latin hymn).

As a self-confessed follower of the literary critic Vissarion Belinsky (1811–48), Stasov sought to foster and defend an art that would engage with serious social and historical issues. He vigilantly opposed aestheticism on the one hand, and the levelling propensity of institutions on the other (hence he resisted the founding of a Russian conservatory in 1862). His gradual migration from a liberal 'realist' position, as understood in the 1860s, to one of conservative jingoism was typical of his generation. By the late 1880s he was allied, in music, with the academic and provincial Belyayev school, which took its name from its patron, the timber-merchant Mitrofan Petrovich Belyayev. His late writings, mainly fulminations at 'decadent' art, are far less valuable than his vigorous youthful propaganda on behalf of his chosen ones when their work was new. His entire oeuvre was canonized during the Stalinist period and turned into Soviet scripture; regularly used as a weapon of state against 'formalist' tendencies (especially by Zhdanov in 1948), Stasov's legacy has become equivocal.

Stasov's natural medium was the polemical *feuilleton*, of which he wrote hundreds. He also produced a number of biographical and obituary essays – on Glinka (1857), Dargomïzhsky (1875), Musorgsky (1881), Borodin (1889), Rimsky-Korsakov (1890), Cui (1894) – that have established themselves as important primary sources on their subjects. More extended, synoptical efforts followed, of which the most substantial, *Dvadtsat' pyat' let russkogo iskusstva* (1882), contains summaries of Russian creative achievement over 25 years in painting, sculpture, architecture and music (the last is translated in Jonas 1968). A curious companion-piece, *Tormozï novogo russkogo iskusstva* (1885), is an exhaustive chronicle of negative criticism directed against the artists and composers Stasov upheld. To Stasov also belongs the distinction of writing the earliest general survey of the arts in the 19th century (*Iskusstvo XIX veka*, 1901). All of these works are of great interest and utility to historians, provided they allow for Stasov's egregious partisanship and can endure his annoyingly hectoring tone, itself evidence of the atmosphere in which 19th-century artists worked. Yet perhaps Stasov's most precious bequest is his fantastically voluminous correspondence. Besides that with Serov (of which only Serov's side has been published), there have been superb annotated editions of his correspondence with Rimsky-Korsakov, Balakirev (ed. A. S. Lyapunova, 1970) and Musorgsky. A comprehensive edition of his letters to various cultural figures has also appeared. Most extensive of all, and especially informative, is Stasov's collected family correspondence.

Editions: *V. V. Stasov: Sobraniye sochineniy 1847–1906* [Collected Works 1847–1906] (St Petersburg, 1894–1906) [writings on music in vols.iii, iv]

V. V. Stasov: Izbrannïye sochineniya [Selected Works], ed. E. D. Stasova and others (Moscow, 1952) [IS]

V. V. Stasov: Izbrannïye stat'i o M. P. Musorgskom [Selected Articles on Musorgsky], ed. A. Ossovsky and A. Dmitriyev (Moscow, 1952)

V. V. Stasov: Stat'i o Rimskom-Korsakove [Articles on Rimsky-Korsakov], ed. V. Kiselyov (Moscow, 1953)

V. V. Stasov: Pis'ma k rodnïm [Family Correspondence] (Moscow, 1953–62)

V. V. Stasov: Izbrannïye stat'i o M. I. Glinke [Selected Articles on Glinka], ed. T. Livanova and V. Protopopov (Moscow, 1955) [G]

V. V. Stasov: Pis'ma k deyatelyam russkoy kul'turï [Letters to Russian Cultural Figures], ed. N. Chernikov (Moscow, 1962–7)

Vladimir Stasov: Selected Essays on Music, trans. F. Jonas (London and New York, 1968) [J]

V. V. Stasov: Stat'i o muzïke [Articles on Music], ed. V. Protopopov (Moscow, 1974–80)

'Mikhail Ivanovich Glinka', *Russkiy vestnik* (Oct–Dec 1857); pubd separately (Moscow, 1953) [IS: i, 379–524]

'Muchenitsa nashego vremeni' [A Martyr of our Time], *Russkiy vestnik*, xx/1 (1959) [on *Ruslan and Lyudmila*; orig. pubd as 'Mnogostradal'naya opera'; G: 50–67]

'Chekhi i russkaya opera', *Sankt-peterburgskiye vedomosti* (10 March 1867) [IS: i, 161–70]

'Pis'ma iz-za granitsï' [Letters from Abroad], *Sankt-peterburgskiye vedomosti* (1869), nos.262–3 [on Wagner and Liszt; J: 38–51]

'Pervonachal'nïy plan operï "Ruslan i Lyudmila"' [The Original Plan of Ruslan and Lyudmila], *Russkaya starina* (March 1871) [G: 122–32]

'Dvadtsat' pyat' let russkogo iskusstva: nasha muzïka' [25 Years of Russian Art: our Music], *Vestnik Yevropï* (1882), no.10 [J: 66–116]

'Tormozï novogo russkogo iskusstva' [The Brakes on New Russian Art], *Vestnik Yevropï* (1885), nos.2–5 [IS: ii, 569–689]

'Po povodu "Knyazya Igorya" Borodina na Mariinskoy stsene' [On the Occasion of Borodin's *Prince Igor* at the Mariinsky], *Severnïy vestnik* (1890), no.12

'Po povodu 50-letiya "Ruslana i Lyudmilï"' [The 50th Anniversary of *Ruslan and Lyudmila*], *Istoricheskiy vestnik* (Nov 1892) [G: 214–42]

'Radost' bezmernaya' [Boundless Joy], *Novosti* (1898), no.55 [on Shalyapin; IS: iii, 229–31]

'17 pisem V. V. Stasova k A. M. Kerzinu', *MS* (1916), no.2

*

Nezabvennomu V. V. Stasovu [Collection of Reminiscences] (St Petersburg, 1908)

V. Karenin [pseud. of V. Komarova-Stasova]: *Vladimir Stasov: ocherk yego zhizni i deyatel'nosti* [Essay on his Life and Work] (Leningrad, 1927)

A. N. Rimsky-Korsakov: 'Stasov i muzïka', *Vladimir Vasil'yevich Stasov 1824–1906: k 125-letiyu so dnya rozhdeniya*, ed. E. D. Stasov (Moscow and Leningrad, 1949)

Yu. Kremlyov: *Russkaya mïsl' o muzïke* [Russian Thought on Music], i (Leningrad, 1954)

T. Livanova: *Stasov i russkaya klassicheskaya opera* (Moscow, 1956)

E. Viner and others, eds.: *Vladimir Vasil'yevich Stasov: materialï k biografii, opisaniye rukopisey* [Materials for a Biography, List of Manuscripts] (Moscow, 1956) [incl. comprehensive list of writings]

T. Livanova: 'Polemika V. V. Stasova i A. N. Serova ob operakh Glinki', *Pamyati Glinki: issledovaniya i materialï* (Moscow, 1958), 333–61

M. Curran: *Vladimir Stasov and the Development of Russian National Art: 1850–1906* (diss., U. of Wisconsin, 1965)

A. Lebedev and A. Solodovnikov: *V. V. Stasov: zhizn' i tvorchestvo* [Life and Works] (Moscow, 1966, 2/1976)

G. Abraham: 'V. V. Stasov: Man and Critic', in F. Jonas, trans.: *Vladimir Stasov: Selected Essays on Music* (London and New York, 1968), 1–13

T. Livanova: *Opernaya kritika v Rossii*, ii/3–4 (Moscow, 1969–73)

A. Markevich: 'K izucheniyu naslediya V. V. Stasova' [On Stasov's Legacy], *SovM* (1974), no.7, pp.91–5

A. Gozenpud: 'Velikiy pobornik realizma' [A Great Champion of Realism], *Kritika i muzïkoznaniye* (Leningrad, 1975)

R. Taruskin: 'Glinka's Ambiguous Legacy and the Birth Pangs of Russian Opera', *19th Century Music*, i (1977–8), 142–62

Y. Olkhovsky: *Vladimir Stasov and Russian National Culture* (Ann Arbor, 1983)

RICHARD TARUSKIN

State Opera of South Australia. Australian company based in ADELAIDE; founded in 1957 as Intimate Opera, it became the New Opera in 1973 and the State Opera of South Australia in 1976.

Statira **(i)** [*La Statira*]. *Dramma per musica* in three acts by Alessandro Scarlatti (*see* SCARLATTI family, (1)) to a libretto by Cardinal PIETRO OTTOBONI; Rome, Teatro Tordinona, 5 January 1690.

The action takes place in Persia in 333 BC. The Persians are defeated by the army of Alessandro il Magno [Alexander the Great] (soprano castrato); the Persian king, Darius III, is killed and his daughter Statira (alto castrato) taken prisoner. Alexander becomes enamoured of Statira, who is betrothed to the Persian prince Oronte (tenor), and what follows revolves around the attempts of Oronte to reclaim Statira and of Campaspe (soprano castrato), who is in love with Alexander, to have her put to death. To this end Campaspe enlists the help of the Macedonian general Demetrio (bass), who loves her, but in the end she is united with the court painter Apelle (tenor), who also has loved her all along. Alexander, impressed by the love Oronte and Statira show to each other, is ready not only to reunite them but also to bestow his throne and his empire on them, but Oronte's honour will not allow him to accept such a sacrifice and he withdraws in Alexander's favour. The goddess Diana (soprano castrato) appears on a cloud to bless the marriage of the two pairs of lovers.

La Statira inaugurated the reopening of the Tordinona theatre, which had been closed during the pontificate of Innocent XI. It was performed at least three more times that season and was also heard (though perhaps not seen) at Ottoboni's palace, the Cancelleria, in April. Critical reaction was mixed, and the opera seems not to have been seen again during Scarlatti's lifetime, but it was probably his music that accompanied a revival of two acts in a concert version at the Cancelleria on 10 February 1706.

Scarlatti's music shows a keen feeling for characterization, although the arias and duets (mostly in da capo form) are too numerous and too brief for many of them to make a strong impression without a second strophe, which occurs in 11 cases out of 54. In this context 'Casta dea, fo voto e giuro', an aria accompanied by full strings in which Demetrio vows to abjure love, makes an effect out of proportion to its means. MALCOLM BOYD

Statira (ii). *Dramma per musica* in three acts by TOMASO GIOVANNI ALBINONI to a libretto by APOSTOLO ZENO and PIETRO PARIATI; Rome, Teatro Capranica, Carnival 1726.

The princesses Statira and Barsina (sopranos) both claim the Persian throne. Profiting from their dissension and angry that Statira refuses to wed him, the Scythian king Oronte (tenor) defeats the Persians and takes the princesses captive. Statira continues to reject his marriage proposal, since he killed her father in battle and she is betrothed to Arsace (soprano), a Persian prince; Barsina, however, schemes to win Oronte's heart. Prince Idaspe (contralto), pursuing a private vendetta, fails to assassinate Oronte and implicates Arsace to protect himself. Oronte seeks Arsace's death, but is stopped by Barsina, who secretly loves the prince; meanwhile Barsina seeks Statira's death, but is impeded by Oronte's continued hope of winning her. Eventually the deadlock is broken by Idaspe's voluntary confession of guilt. Oronte generously agrees that Statira become Queen of Persia, while Barsina is granted a neighbouring kingdom.

Albinoni identified *Statira*, probably with some exaggeration, as his 70th opera. Lightly touched by the *galant* style introduced during the 1720s by Neapolitan composers, it reveals his gift for melody and sound craftsmanship. While its recitatives convey the ebb and flow of dramatic tension very effectively, its arias, for all their lyrical charm, are perhaps too abstractly conceived to delineate the characters clearly. MICHAEL TALBOT

Statkowski, Roman (*b* Szczypiórno, nr Kalisz, 24 Dec 1859; *d* Warsaw, 12 Nov 1925). Polish composer. After law studies at Warsaw University he studied with Żeleński at the Warsaw Music Institute and with Nikolay Solov'yov and Rubinstein at the St Petersburg Conservatory, where he graduated in 1890. For some time he taught in Kiev. In 1903 he won first prize in the London International Opera Competition with his opera *Filenis*, which he had composed in 1897 (2, Statkowski, after H. Erler; Warsaw, 14 September 1904); a vocal score was later published in Berlin (*c*1910). In 1903–4 Statkowski wrote another opera, *Maria*, also on his own libretto (3, after A. Malczewski; Warsaw, 1 March 1906; overture published Kraków, 1951). From 1904 he was professor at the conservatory in Warsaw and in 1911 was a founder-editor of the *Kwartalnik muzyczny*.

Statkowski was influenced by Russian music, particularly that of Musorgsky, and by contemporary German music, especially Strauss's symphonic poems and Pfitzner's operas. Lyrical and richly melodic, his work represents a link between the post-Moniuszko composers and the generation of Szymanowski. The plots of both his operas are strongly constructed and the fluent, expressive melodies are supported by clear and colourful orchestration. *Filenis* contains no traditional arias or ensembles and uses leitmotif techniques, but is closer in style to the oratorios of Mendelssohn and Schumann than to Wagner. *Maria* is imbued with elements of Polish and Ukrainian folk music; its freshness and sincerity make it one of the best Polish operas. It was revived in Warsaw (1919 and 1924), Poznań (1936), Kraków (1951) and Wrocław (1965).

*

W. Poźniak: 'Opera po Moniuszke' [Opera after Moniuszko], *Z dziejów polskiej kultury muzycznej* (Kraków, 1966), 306–28

TERESA CHYLIŃSKA

Staubinger, Mathias. *See* STABINGER, MATHIAS.

Staudigl [née Koppmayer], **Gisela** (*b* Branau, 4 Sept 1864; *d* Karlsruhe, 22 Feb 1929). Austrian mezzo-soprano. She studied with Mathilde Marchesi and made her stage début in Hamburg as Amneris (1882). She joined the Karlsruhe Hoftheater in 1884 and married Josef Staudigl the following year. In 1886 she was the first Bayreuth Brangäne and toured with the Metropolitan as Adriano (*Rienzi*) and as Goldmark's Queen of Sheba: she visited Milwaukee, Boston and Cincinnati with the Damrosch Opera Company in the season 1897–8. At the court opera houses of Vienna, Munich and Berlin she was successful as Orpheus, Fricka, Azucena, Amneris, Waltraute and Venus.

DAVID CUMMINGS

Staudigl, Joseph (*b* Vienna, 18 March 1850; *d* Karlsruhe, 21 April 1916). Austrian baritone, son of the bass Joseph Staudigl (1807–61). He studied with Rokitansky at the Vienna Conservatory. During 1874–83 he sang at the Karlsruhe Hoftheater and also at court. From 1884 to 1886 he was principal baritone at the Metropolitan Opera, where he appeared as Pogner in the American première of *Die Meistersinger* (4 January 1886) as well as the Dutchman, Wolfram, Wotan, Pizarro and Escamillo. In 1886 he also sang Don Giovanni at Salzburg, thereafter appearing in many operas in Germany (including Bayreuth), the Netherlands and Switzerland. Staudigl was also in demand as a concert singer. DAVID CHARLTON

Steane, J(ohn) B(arry) (*b* Coventry, 12 April 1928). English critic. He studied English at Cambridge, and was a teacher, 1952–88; he joined the staff of *Gramophone* in 1972, primarily as a reviewer of recordings (including historical ones) of opera and other vocal music. His commanding knowledge and refined judgment of singing in the first half of the 20th century are seen in his *The Grand Tradition: Seventy Years of Singing on Record* (London, 1974), his many reviews and his article series in *Opera* (1981–3) and *Opera Now* (1989–91), and his broader view of singing and its reception in *Voices, Singers and Critics* (London, 1992).

Stearns, Theodore Pease (*b* Berea, OH, 10 June 1880; *d* Los Angeles, 1 Nov 1935). American composer. He studied the violin at the Oberlin Conservatory before travelling to Germany in 1896 to attend the Würzburg Conservatory. After returning to America he earned a living conducting theatre pieces and operetta. From 1922 to 1926 he was a music critic for the *New York Morning Telegraph* and *The Chicago Herald Examiner*, and in 1932 he became chairman of the music department at UCLA. Stearns completed three stage works. *Snowbird* (1923) concerns a prince who hides as a hermit after he has stolen an amulet from his father, and a young girl whom he has rescued from a storm and wrapped in a white robe calling her his 'Snowbird'. Tragically, she is killed when she is discovered with the missing amulet. Stearns won the Bispham Medal in 1925 for *Snowbird* and received a Guggenheim Fellowship (1927–8) to study in Germany. *Atlantis* recounts the legend of the lost island from the perspective of two present-day lovers who remember their former lives as the last king and queen of Atlantis.

Endymion (Stearns), 1895
Snowbird (lyric episode, 1, Stearns), Chicago Civic Opera, 13 Jan 1923
Atlantis (lyric drama, 2, Stearns), Dresden, Staatsoper, 1926
Hiawatha, inc.

*

E. E. Hipsher: *American Opera and its Composers* (Philadelphia, 1927)
BRADLEY H. SHORT

Steber, Eleanor (*b* Wheeling, WV, 17 July 1916; *d* Langhorne, PA, 3 Oct 1990). American soprano. After studying privately with Paul Althouse and William Whitney, and appearing in Boston in 1936, she won the 1940 Metropolitan Auditions of the Air. This led to her début on 7 December as Sophie, and she remained a leading soprano with the Metropolitan until 1963. As her voice matured, its silvery sheen gave way to greater warmth and breadth, and she began to undertake heavier roles such as the Marschallin, Elsa, Desdemona, Tosca and Donna Anna. She was particularly noted for the suavity and poise of her Mozart heroines – the Countess Almaviva, Fiordiligi, Pamina, Donna Elvira and Konstanze, which she sang at the Metropolitan première of *Die Entführung* in 1946. She also created the title role in Barber's *Vanessa* (1958), sang the title role in the American première of *Arabella* (Metropolitan, 1955), and Marie in the first Metropolitan *Wozzeck* (1959). She appeared at the Edinburgh Festival, Bayreuth, Vienna and Florence as well as with numerous American companies; she sang Miss Wingrave in the American première of Britten's opera (1973, Santa Fe). In later years she appeared in musical comedy.
MARTIN BERNHEIMER

Štědroň, Miloš (*b* Brno, 9 Feb 1942). Czech composer. He studied musicology and Czech at Brno University (1959–64; doctorate 1967), and composition and music theory at the Brno Academy (1965–70). From 1963 to 1972 he worked at the Moravian Museum in Brno, researching into Janáček's music and organizing concerts, and from 1972 he taught music theory at Brno University. His theoretical work has been concerned with Janáček's relationship with the western European avant garde, the use of computers in musical practice and analysis, and the problems of employing new musical ideas and of using modality in contemporary music. His own music makes use of modality together with collage forms. Štědroň's compositional interests have included music for tape, collaboration with jazz bands and pop groups, collective composition and work for the theatre, television and cinema. His theatrical works include three operas and the musical *Mann ist Mann* (after Brecht). *Aparát* ('Machinery'; six scenes and six interludes) combines the sonorities of a contemporary music ensemble, including electronic sounds, with those of children's 'Schulwerk' instruments. In this work, Štědroň uses collage techniques (with passages echoing Renaissance, rock and Romantic music), as well as aleatory and dance music. In this overall vision of evil, only the children's spontaneity and naivety stand out as a glimmer of hope against the calculating world of the adults. *Kuchyňské starosti* ('Culinary Cares') was inspired by Beethoven's conversation books through which he communicated his everyday needs. The subtle humour of the opera lies in the contrast between great genius and everyday life – the latter evoked through the inclusion of servants' songs. *Chameleon, aneb Joseph Fouché* ('The Chameleon, or Joseph Fouché') is a piece of synthetic music theatre originally created for the Brno drama workshop, Divadlo na Provázku (Theatre on a String). It is a drastically satirical portrayal of a careerist in the French Revolution, using collage techniques.

Štědroň has also been involved with the authentic realization of Baroque and Classical works.

Aparát [Machinery] (chamber op, 1, Štědroň, after F. Kafka), concert perf. Brno, Dům Umění, 3 April 1970
Kuchyňské starosti ['Culinary Cares'] (opera-int, 1, Štědroň), Brno, Reduta, 25 April 1979
Chameleon aneb Joseph Fouché [The Chameleon, or Joseph Fouché] ('new op', prol., 2 pts, epilogue, Štědroň and L. Kundera), Brno, 16 May 1984
JIŘÍ FUKAČ, HELENA HAVLÍKOVÁ

Stefani, Jan (*b* Prague, 1746; *d* Warsaw, 24 Feb 1829). Polish composer. He studied music in Italy and about 1765 became a violinist in the court orchestras of Count G. Kinsky and Joseph II in Vienna. In 1779 he moved to Warsaw, becoming violinist and conductor of the orchestra of King Stanisław August Poniatowski. He occasionally conducted opera performances at the National Theatre in Warsaw in the mid-1790s, and from 1799 to 1818 was first violinist there. His own operas date from the period of his contact with the theatre, and for the most part are like Singspiels, simple in texture, with arias replaced by songs and with choruses that are mainly homophonic. Stefani also wrote cantatas, masses, songs, chamber works and about a hundred orchestral polonaises, but he is principally remembered as the composer of *Cud mniemany* ('The Supposed Miracle'), the best Polish opera of the 18th century, and the only one by him to have survived intact. It became the most popular opera in Poland in the first half of the 19th century; indeed, at the time it was regarded as the most nationalistic, its libretto describing Polish folk customs and hinting at the contemporary political situation, and its music using both national dance and folk rhythms. *The Supposed Miracle* is also the first Polish opera in which both music and text draw on dialect (though not actually from the region in which it is set). It was staged throughout Poland and is still in the repertory.

Several of Stefani's children were musicians, including Karolina (1784–1803) and Eleonora (1802–31), both opera singers, and Józef Stefani.

See also CUD MNIEMANY.

all first performed at the National Theatre, Warsaw

Król w kraju rozkoszy [The King of Cockaigne] (3, F. Zabłocki, after M.-A. Legrand: *Le roi de Cocaigne*), 3 Feb 1787
Cud mniemany, czyli Krakowiacy i górale [The Supposed Miracle, or Kracovians and Highlanders] (4, W. Bogusławski, after A.-A.-H. Poinsinet: *Le sorcier*), 1 March 1794, *PL-Wtm** (Kraków, 1856)
Drzewo zaczarowane [The Magic Tree] (Spl, Zabłocki, after P. L. Moline), 17 April 1796
Wdzięczni poddani panu, czyli Wiejskie wesele [Thankful Serfs, or The Country Wedding] (Spl, 3, T. Drozdowski), 28 April 1796
Frozyna, czyli Siedem razy jedna [Frozine, or Seven Times Dressed Up] (Spl, 1, J. Adamczewski, after J. B. Radet), 21 Feb 1806
Rotmistrz Górecki, czyli Oswobodzenie [Captain Górecki, or The Liberation] (3, W. Pękalski, after J. Lipiński), 3 April 1807
Polka, czyli Oblężenie Trembowli [The Polish Woman, or The Siege of Trembowla] (3, J. Wybicki), 22 May 1807
Stary myśliwy [The Old Huntsman] (3, Pękalski, after Francis and Tournay), 31 Jan 1808
Papirus (Papirius), czyli Ciekawość dawnych kobiet [Papyrus, or The Curiosity of Women in Ancient Times] (oc, 1, Adamczewski, after N. Gersin and P. A. Vieillard), 15 May 1808

*

Z. M. Szweykowski and others, eds.: *Z dziejów polskiej kultury muzycznej* [History of Polish Musical Culture], ii (Kraków, 1966), 33–5

ZOFIA CHECHLIŃSKA

Stefani, Józef (*b* Warsaw, 16 April 1800; *d* Warsaw, 19 March 1876). Polish composer, son of Jan Stefani. He studied music with his father, then with Elsner. At the age of 13 he began to sing in the chorus of the National (later Wielki) Theatre in Warsaw, and later played in its orchestra. Between 1827 and 1858 he conducted ballet performances as well as teaching singing there. Operas, ballets and choral works form the main part of his output. As many of the operas do not survive, and the scant information about them derives from contemporary journals, it is not always possible to say whether they were indeed operas, or merely consisted of incidental music to spoken plays. From those that do survive it would appear that for Stefani there was no essential difference, in form or character, between operetta and the Singspiel. His works are simple and designed to have a wide appeal. Solos, which predominate, are modelled on popular song and are devoid of virtuosity, while the rare choruses tend to be homophonic; Polish folkdance rhythms, especially those of the mazurka and polonaise, are widely used. Some of the operas enjoyed considerable success in their day, but are now of only historical interest.

all first performed in Warsaw

Dawne czasy [Old Times] (K. Godebski), National, 26 April 1826, collab. J. Damse, 1 aria *PL-Wtm*
Lekcja botaniki [The Botany Lesson] (operetta, 2, F. Szymanowski), National, 15 March 1829, excerpts, vs (Warsaw, 1829)
Figle panien [A Young Girl's Frolics] (Spl, 1, F. Skarbek), Rozmaitości, 6 Aug 1832
Jest temu lat szesnaście [16 Years Ago] (3, W. Olechowski, after V. H. J. Ducange), Poznań, 26 July 1838; opera of this name first perf. Wielki, 17 March 1833, composer not named
Talizman [Talisman] (Spl, 5, B. Gwozdecki, after J. Nestroy), Rozmaitości, 7 Dec 1849
Żyd, wieczny tułacz [The Wandering Jew] (5, J. T. S. Jasiński, after E. Sue), Wielki, 1 Jan 1850
Piorun [Thunderbolt] (Spl, B. Halpert, after Clairville), Rozmaitości, 21 May 1856, frags. *Wtm**
Trwoga wieczorna [Evening Fear] (operetta, 1), Letni, 25 July 1872, *Wtm**

Unperf.: Nowy dziedzic [A New Squire] (1, J. N. Kamiński), *Kj**; Oj, żoneczka [Oh, Wife!] (Spl), *Wtm**; Trzy grzechy [Three Sins] (Spl, 1), *Wtm**

ZOFIA CHECHLIŃSKA

Stefano, Giuseppe di. *See* DI STEFANO, GIUSEPPE.

Steffani [Stefani, Stephani], **Agostino** (*b* Castelfranco, nr Venice, 25 July 1654; *d* Frankfurt, 12 Feb 1728). Italian composer. His works represent an attractive blend of late 17th-century Italian and French styles and exerted a considerable influence on the rise of opera in Germany.

At the age of 13 Steffani was taken to Munich, where he stayed for 21 years. He may have sung in November 1667 in *Le pretensioni del sole* by the Kapellmeister, Johann Caspar Kerll, who later gave him organ lessons (1668–71). In October 1672 he went to Rome to study composition with Ercole Bernabei, *maestro di cappella* at St Peter's; there he wrote sacred music and probably composed the first of his celebrated chamber duets – the cornerstone of his output.

After returning to Munich in 1674 Steffani was appointed court organist in 1675 and director of chamber music on 1 January 1681. His first opera, *Marco Aurelio* (libretto by his brother, Ventura Terzago, *b* 1648), was first performed later that month and revived in October. He composed four further operas between 1685 and 1688 – to two more librettos by Terzago and two by Luigi Orlandi. *Servio Tullio* was written for the wedding of the young Elector Maximilian II Emanuel and Maria Antonia, Archduchess of Austria, in 1686, and was produced on an extravagant scale (*see* MUNICH, fig.2). His other Munich works include a serenata 'alla maniera d'Italia', the music for a tournament, a set of motets and further duets and cantatas.

In summer 1688 Steffani was appointed Kapellmeister to Duke Ernst August of Hanover. His arrival coincided with the establishment of the first permanent opera company there and the construction of a magnificent new theatre – part of the duke's successful campaign to secure an electorate. Of the ten works performed there between 1689 and 1697 Steffani probably composed the first eight, all to librettos by Ortensio Mauro. *Henrico Leone*, in which Francesco Borosini sang, inaugurated the opera house and marked the 500th anniversary of the battle of Bardowick (1189). *I trionfi del fato* and *Baccanali* were repeated in November 1695 to celebrate the marriage of Princess Charlotte Felicitas to Rinaldo d'Este of Modena. But the heyday of opera at Hanover was ended by the death of Ernst August in 1698.

The last 30 years of Steffani's life were largely devoted to matters of church and state. He had been a priest since 1680 and acquired considerable diplomatic experience at Munich and Hanover. In March 1703 he moved to Düsseldorf, where his formal responsibilities were entirely political and ecclesiastical. In 1707 he was made Bishop of Spiga and in 1709 Apostolic Vicar of northern Germany. He moved back to Hanover in November 1709 and, apart from a brief spell in Italy (1722–5), was based there for the rest of his life.

From 1707, at least, his music circulated under the name of Gregorio Piva. His three 'Düsseldorf' operas can be boiled down to one. *Arminio* is a pasticcio, assembled from some of his earlier operas, in which he may have had no hand, and *Amor vien dal destino*, though first performed in Düsseldorf, seems to have been written for Hanover in 1694. Only *Il Tassilone*, in which Pellegrini appeared, is certainly a new composition; there were plans to revive this in London under Bononcini, in 1720–21, but they came to naught.

Steffani's operas, which impress by their quality rather than their quantity, are based on the late 17th-century Venetian style. His Munich works involve numerous characters (some of them comic), elaborate scenes and machines and large numbers of arias (60 to 70 per opera). Most of the arias are in da capo form, and many are based on ostinatos. About half are accompanied by instruments, the remainder by continuo only. The orchestra comprises four- or five-part strings, flutes, bassoon and continuo, often with trumpets and drums. *Alarico* also requires two piffari, and *Niobe* four viols. The latter is particularly remarkable for its richness of musical language and detailed instrumental and expressive indications.

His operas also reflect the influence of the French style. Most of his Munich works included ballets choreographed by François Rodier and composed by Melchior d'Ardespin, but they also contain dances, and arias in dance styles, by Steffani himself. Features of the French style are even more evident in his Hanover operas, the *ouvertures* of which are in the Lullian mould and incorporate trios for oboes and bassoon. These works take full advantage of the stage effects available in the new theatre at Hanover, but the number of characters is somewhat reduced, as is the number of arias (40 to 50 per opera). Vocal lines are sometimes virtuoso, and ostinatos almost disappear. Orchestral accompaniment is more common and is better integrated with the vocal line, and the da capo form is more fully developed. As well as ensembles of three to six characters, the Hanover operas include an exceptionally large number of duets in a contrapuntal style which, as Mattheson observed (1739), was unusual in dramatic works.

The six full-length Hanover operas were translated into German by Gottlieb Fiedler and staged in Hamburg during the period 1695–9. Fiedler tried not to change a note of Steffani's music, which he described as 'incomparable'. The Hamburg productions were quickly followed by others elsewhere. Arias from *Orlando generoso* were printed at Lübeck (1699) and Amsterdam (*c*1704–5), and instrumental music from the operas was published by Roger as *Sonate da camera* (*c*1705). By such means Steffani's music had a powerful influence on opera in Germany and on such composers as Keiser, Wilderer, Schürmann, Telemann and Handel (who borrowed extensively from *La lotta d'Hercole con Acheloo*, especially in *Theodora*). It seems fitting that four of Steffani's operas (*Alarico*, *Henrico Leone*, *Arminio* and *Tassilone*) are based not on standard classical or mythological subjects but on episodes from German history.

Edition: *A. Steffani: Ausgewählte Werke*, iii, ed. H. Riemann, DTB, xxiii, Jg.xii/2 (1912) [R]

Marco Aurelio (drama per musica, 3, V. Terzago, after Aelius Spartianus and Julius Capitolinus in *Scriptores historiae Augustae*), Munich, Court, Jan 1681, *GB-Lbl**, excerpts in R

Solone (drama per musica, 3, Terzago, after M. C. H. Desjardins: *Les amours des grands hommes*), Munich, Court, carn. 1685

Audacia e rispetto (torneo, Terzago), Munich, Court, carn. 1685

Servio Tullio (drama per musica, prol., 3, Terzago, after Livy: *Ab urbe condita libri*), Munich, Court, Jan 1686, *A-Wn*, excerpts in R; ?rev., Weimar, 1697

Alarico il Baltha, cioè L'audace re de' gothi (drama per musica, 3, L. Orlandi, after P. Orosius, Paul the Deacon, Jornandes, St Augustine, Procopius and E. Tesauro), Munich, Court, 18 Jan 1687, *Wn*, *D-SWl*, in DTB, xxi, Jg.xi/2 (1911)

Niobe, regina di Tebe (drama per musica, 3, Orlandi, after Ovid: *Metamorphoses*), Munich, Court, carn. 1688, *A-Wn**, *D-SWl*, excerpts in R

Henrico Leone (dramma, 3, O. Mauro, after H. Göding and H. Meibom), Hanover, Schloss, 30 Jan 1689, *B*, *Bds*, *SWl*, *GB-Lbl**, excerpts in R; Ger. trans., Hamburg, 1696; as Mechtilde, Stuttgart, 1701; rev. G. C. Schürmann, Brunswick, 2 Feb 1716, *D-SWl*, ed. in Musikalische Denkwürdigkeiten, i (Hanover, 1926)

La lotta d'Hercole con Acheloo (divertimento drammatico, 1, Mauro, after Ovid: *Metamorphoses*), Hanover, Schloss, sum. 1689, *B*, *Bds*, *Mbs*, *SWl*, *GB-Lbl*, *US-NYp*; facs. in HS, ix (1986), excerpts in R

La superbia d'Alessandro (drama, prol., 3, Mauro), Hanover, Schloss, Feb 1690; rev. as Il zelo di Leonato, Hanover, Feb 1691, *D-B*, *Bds*, *SWl*, *GB-Lbl**, excerpts in R; Ger. trans., Hamburg, 1695

Orlando generoso (drama, 3, Mauro, after L. Ariosto: *Orlando furioso*), Hanover, Schloss, Feb 1691, *A-Wn*, *D-B*, *Bds*, *HVs*, *SWl*, *GB-Lbl**; arias (Lübeck, 1699; Amsterdam, *c*1704–5), excerpts in R; Ger. trans., Hamburg, 1696

Le rivali concordi (drama, 3, Mauro), Hanover, Schloss, Feb 1692, *A-Wn*, *D-B*, *Bds*, *SWl*, *GB-Lbl**, *Lbl*, *I-MOe*, *US-NYp*; facs. in IOB, xiv (1978), excerpts in R; Ger. trans. as Die vereinigten Mit-Buhler, oder Die siegende Atalanta, Hamburg, 1698

La libertà contenta (drama, 3, Mauro, ? after Plutarch), Hanover, Schloss, 3 Feb 1693, *D-B*, *Bds*, *Dl*, *SWl*, *GB-Lbl**, excerpts in R; Ger. trans. as Der in seiner Freyheit vergnügte Alcibiades, Hamburg, 1697

Il Turno, 1693–7 (dramma, 3, Mauro, after Virgil: *Aeneid*), Düsseldorf, Jan 1709 as Enea o Amor vien dal destino, *D-HVl*, *GB-Lbl**, excerpts in R

I trionfi del fato (drama, 3, Mauro, after Virgil: *Aeneid* and Livy: *Ab urbe condita libri*), Hanover, Schloss, Feb 1695; rev. as I trionfi del fato, o Le glorie d'Enea; *D-B*, *Bds*, *Dl*, *Hs*, *SWl*, *GB-Lbl**, excerpts in R; Ger. trans., Hamburg, 25 Nov 1699; rev. Schürmann as Enea in Italia, Brunswick, 1716

Baccanali ([divertimento], 1, Mauro), Hanover, Picciolo Elettorale, Feb 1695, *Lbl*; rev. Schürmann as Doppia festa d'Himeneo, Salzthal (Brunswick), 12 Sept 1718; as La festa di Minerva, Wolfenbüttel, 15 May 1719

Arminio (tragedia per musica, 5, S. B. Pallavicino, ? after Tacitus), Düsseldorf, carn. 1707, *D-WD*, *GB-Lbl* [pasticcio]

Il Tassilone (tragedia per musica, 5, Pallavicino), Düsseldorf, 17 Jan 1709, *D-B*, *E-Mn*, *GB-Lbl*; ed. in Denkmäler rheinischer Musik, viii (Düsseldorf, 1958), excerpts in R

*

J. Mattheson: *Der vollkommene Capellmeister* (Hamburg, 1739)

F. Chrysander: *G. F. Händel* (Leipzig, 1858–67), i, 309–27

A. Neisser: *Servio Tullio: eine Oper aus dem Jahre 1685 von Agostino Steffani* (Leipzig, 1902)

G. Fischer: *Musik in Hannover* (Hanover, 1903), 12–19

H. Riemann: 'Bibliographie der in Handschriften und Drucken nachweisbaren 18 Bühnenwerke von Agostino Steffani', DTB, xxi, Jg.xi/2 (1911), pp.vii–xvi

——: 'Agostino Steffani als Opernkomponist', DTB, xxiii, Jg.xii/2 (1912), pp.vii–xxiii

T. W. Werner: 'Agostino Steffanis Operntheater in Hannover', *AMf*, iii (1938), 65–79

G. Croll: Preface to A. Steffani: *Tassilone*, Denkmäler rheinischer Musik, viii (Düsseldorf, 1958) [review by P. H. Lang, *MQ*, xlv (1959), 412–17]

——: *Agostino Steffani (1654–1728): Studien zur Biographie, Bibliographie der Opern und Turnierspiele* (diss., U. of Münster, 1960)

——: 'Zur Chronologie der "Düsseldorfer" Opern Agostino Steffanis', *Festschrift K. G. Fellerer zum 60. Geburtstag* (Regensburg, 1962), 82–7

A. Della Corte: 'Qualche lettera e qualche melodramma di Agostino Steffani', *RaM*, xxxii (1962), 25–38

P. Keppler: 'Agostino Steffani's Hannover Operas and a Rediscovered Catalogue', *Studies in Music History: Essays for Oliver Strunk* (Princeton, 1968), 341–54

R. E. Wallbrecht: *Das Theater des Barockzeitalters an den welfischen Höfen Hannover und Celle* (Hildesheim, 1974)

C. Timms: 'Gregorio Piva and Steffani's Principal Copyist', *Source Materials and the Interpretation of Music: a Memorial Volume to Thurston Dart* (London, 1981), 169–90 COLIN TIMMS

Steffek, Hanny (*b* Biala, Poland, 12 Dec 1927). Austrian soprano. She studied in Vienna and Salzburg, making her début in 1951 at Wiesbaden. At Salzburg (1951–3) her roles included Blonde and Papagena. She sang in Graz and Frankfurt, then in 1958 joined the Staatsoper in Munich, also appearing frequently at the Vienna Volksoper. She made her Covent Garden début in 1959 as Sophie (*Der Rosenkavalier*) and in 1960 sang Susanna at Aix-en-Provence. Her roles included Monteverdi's Proserpina, Gluck's Eurydice, Despina, Zerlina, Marzelline, Marguerite (*Faust*), Nannetta, the title role of Orff's *Die Kluge* and Christine, which she sang in the British première of *Intermezzo* (1965) at Edinburgh. She sang Vespina (Haydn's *L'infedeltà delusa*) at Bregenz (1970). A most attractive artist, she had a sweet-toned voice of some strength, ideal for Mozart's soubrette roles. ELIZABETH FORBES

Steffens, Walter (*b* Aachen, 31 Oct 1934). German composer. He studied with Jarnach in Hamburg and taught there before moving to the Nordwestdeutsche Musikakademie (now the Musikhochschule) in Detmold, where he became professor of composition and music theory in 1971. His operas are consciously based on the tradition of grand opera rather than the experimental forms of late 20th-century German music theatre. His music has also been influenced by the works of painters, from Leonardo da Vinci to Picasso. His first opera, *Eli*, was the first to be commissioned by the new Grosses Haus in Dortmund. Dealing with the death of a Jewish boy in World War II, the music is atonal in the style of Webern; *Grabbes Leben*, written for the 150th anniversary of the death of the playwright C. D. Grabbe, and *Der Philosoph*, in the style of Goldoni, both show the development of an individual harmonic language, a synthesis between tonal and atonal expression.

Eli (3, after N. Sachs: *Mystery of the Sorrow of Israel*), Dortmund, Grosses, 5 March 1967
Unter dem Milchwald (3, after D. Thomas), Hamburg, Staatsoper, 5 Oct 1973
Grabbes Leben (3, P. Schütze), Detmold, Landes, 12 Sept 1986
Der Philosoph (1, Schütze), Detmold, Landes, 11 April 1990
Die Judenbuche, 1992 (musikalisches Volksdrama, 10 scenes, Schütze, after A. von Droste-Hülshoff)

HANSPETER KRELLMANN/ANDREW CLARK

Stegmann, Carl David (*b* Staucha, nr Meissen, 1751; *d* Bonn, 27 May 1826). German tenor and composer. He began his career as a singer, actor and harpsichordist in Breslau in 1772 (with the Wäser theatre company), working in Königsberg (now Kaliningrad) in 1773, Heilsberg in 1774 (as court harpsichordist to the Bishop of Ermeland), Danzig (now Gdańsk) in 1775, Königsberg again in 1776 (with the Schuch company) and later in Gotha (at the court theatre). From 1778 to 1783 he made the first of two extended visits to Hamburg, winning particular renown as a harpsichordist. By that time five of his operas and Singspiels, first produced earlier in Königsberg and Danzig, were attracting performances elsewhere in northern Germany. In 1783 he left Hamburg to join the Grossmann company in Bonn. He then became attached to the court theatre at Mainz, in association with which he made highly acclaimed guest appearances in Frankfurt. He sang in the first German-language *Don Giovanni* (Mainz, 13 March 1789), produced or conducted other operas by Mozart, Salieri, Gluck and Gassmann, composed incidental music (e.g. to Bürger's version of *Macbeth*, 30 August 1785) and acted in dramas by Lessing and Schiller.

The summit of Stegmann's activities in Frankfurt was the production of his allegorical coronation opera *Heinrich der Löwe* (15 July 1792) to celebrate the coronation of Emperor Franz II. By the time of his return to Hamburg in November 1792, he was esteemed as a leading operatic producer and adapter, which compensated for the declining vocal prowess that forced him to restrict his appearances to comic roles. In 1798 he joined the directorate of the Hamburg theatre, remaining there until 1811.

As a composer for the theatre (including ballet and incidental music), Stegmann has attracted attention for his harmonic and tonal organization and for using antecedent forms of the leitmotif, showing an early interest in dramatic and psychological continuity.

Clarisse, oder Das unbekannte Dienstmädchen (komische Operette, 3, J. C. Bock), Hamburg, Gänsemarkt, Nov 1778
Der Kaufmann von Smyrna (komische Oper, 1, C. F. Schwan, after N.-S. de Chamfort), Königsberg, 1773, *B-Bc*, vs (Leipzig and Königsberg, 1773)
Die Rekruten auf dem Lande (komische Oper, 3), Danzig and Königsberg, 1775, *D-Dlb**
Das redende Gemählde (komische Oper, 2, J. Anseaume), Königsberg, 1775, vs (Mitau and Hasenboth, 1775)
Erwin und Elmire (Schauspiel mit Gesang, 2, J. W. von Goethe), Königsberg, Kreutzenplatz, 1776, vs (Königsberg and Leipzig, 1776)
Philemon und Baucis (Spl, Echof), Gotha, 1777
Montgolfier (opera-ballet), Bonn, 1788
Sultan Wampum, oder Die Wünsche (3, after A. von Kotzebue), Mainz, National, 7 March 1791
Heinrich der Löwe (coronation op, 2, H. G. Schmieder), Frankfurt, National, 15 July 1792, ov. (Vienna, 1792)
Der Triumph der Liebe, oder Das kühne Abentheuer (4, O. Jester), Hamburg, Gänsemarkt, 27 Feb 1796, *B*, vs arr. Stegmann (Königsberg, 1796); rev. as Die Roseninsel (3, K. L. Costenoble), Hamburg, 24 Nov 1806, *Dlb*

*

A. Peiba: *Gallerie von teutschen Schauspielern und Schauspielerinnen* (Vienna, 1783); repr. in *Schriften der Gesellschaft für Theatergeschichte*, xiii (Berlin, 1910)
J. F. Schütze: *Hamburgische Theatergeschichte* (Hamburg, 1794)
E. Metzel: 'Karl David Stegmann: aus dem Leben eines Bühnenkünstlers des 18. Jahrhunderts', *Archiv für Theatergeschichte*, i (Berlin, 1904), 129
A. Gottron: *Mainzer Musikgeschichte von 1500 bis 1800* (Mainz, 1959)

ANDREW D. McCREDIE

Stegmayer, Matthäus (*b* Vienna, 29 April 1771; *d* Vienna, 10 May 1820). Austrian composer, dramatist and singer. A powerful treble choirboy in Vienna, he toured the provinces with itinerant theatre troupes after completing his secondary education. In 1792–3 he joined the Theater in der Josefstadt, where he took leading parts and composed Singspiels and occasional music. In 1796 he moved to Schikaneder's Freihaus-Theater auf der Wieden, first appearing as composer there with a score for Gieseke's *Die zwölf schlafenden Jungfrauen*. During the next 25 years he wrote many plays and much theatre music, frequently sharing the task with Seyfried, Henneberg and other composers (as with his own *Holga die Göttin des Kristallengebirges*, 1800). He gradually gave up composition but continued to write plays. Although he left Schikaneder for the court theatre (probably in 1800) he continued to supply works for the former. After a period as chorus director and producer at the court theatre he joined the Theater an der Wien in 1804 as actor and chorus master, while continuing to supply librettos, including the popular *Idas und Marpissa* (1807), with music by Seyfried; his greatest success was the quodlibet *Rochus Pumpernickel* (after Molière's *Monsieur de Pourceaugnac*, with music by Haibel and Seyfried).

Stegmayer's son Ferdinand (*b* Vienna, 25 Aug 1803; *d* Vienna, 6 May 1863) was music director at the Königstädtisches Theater, Berlin, from 1823; after serving as

Kapellmeister in Prague and Leipzig he returned to Vienna in 1852, where he founded the Singakademie (1858).

*

WurzbachL
M. Stegmayer: Autobiographical sketch (*A-Wgm*)
F. Blitzenetz: *Matthäus Stegmayer* (diss., U. of Vienna, 1929)
O. E. Deutsch: *Das Freihaus-Theater auf der Wieden* (Vienna, 1937)
A. Bauer: *150 Jahre Theater an der Wien* (Zürich, Leipzig and Vienna, 1952)
——: *Opern und Operetten in Wien* (Graz and Cologne, 1955)

PETER BRANSCOMBE

Stehle, Adelina (*b* Graz, 30 June 1860; *d* Milan, 24 Dec 1945). Austrian, later Italian, soprano. She studied in Milan and made her début as Amina at Broni in 1881. In the following years she sang in many of the leading Italian houses before going to La Scala in 1890, where she appeared in several world premières, most notably those of *La Wally* and *Falstaff*, both in 1892; in the latter, she sang Nannetta to the Fenton of her husband, Edoardo Garbin. In 1892 at the Teatro Dal Verme she was the first Nedda in *Pagliacci*, and in 1895 at La Scala she took the leading soprano roles in two Mascagni premières, *Guglielmo Ratcliff* and *Silvano*. With Garbin at Palermo in 1896 she sang in the performances of *La bohème* that first established the opera's popularity. In 1902 she toured South America and in 1905 was a member of the distinguished Sonzogno company at the Théâtre Sarah Bernhardt in Paris; she also sang in St Petersburg, Berlin and Vienna. Her voice, originally that of a light lyric and coloratura soprano (with Ophelia and Gilda among her roles), developed into a more dramatic instrument, and she was admired as a leading exponent of *verismo* roles such as Adriana Lecouvreur and Giordano's Fedora. On retirement she became a teacher, her best-known pupil being Giannina Arangi-Lombardi. Her only two recordings, a duet and quartet, reveal little about her voice and art. J. B. STEANE

Stehle, Sophie (*b* Sigmaringen, 15 May 1838; *d* Schloss Harterode, Hanover, 4 Oct 1921). German soprano. She studied in Augsburg and Munich, where she made her début at the Hofoper in 1860 as Emmeline in Weigl's *Die Schweizerfamilie*. During the next 14 years she sang a wide variety of roles, including Marguerite, Agathe, Rachel (*La Juive*), Pamina, Amazili (Spontini's *Fernand Cortez*), Sélika (*L'Africaine*), Anna (Marschner's *Hans Heiling*), Senta, Elisabeth and Elsa. She sang Fricka in the first performance, in Munich, of *Das Rheingold* (1869) and Brünnhilde in *Die Walküre* (1870). She made her farewell in 1874 as Gretchen in Lortzing's *Der Wildschütz*. ELIZABETH FORBES

Steibelt, Daniel (Gottlieb) (*b* Berlin, 22 Oct 1765; *d* St Petersburg, 20 Sept/2 Oct 1823). French composer of German birth. He entered the Prussian army in his late teens, but deserted in 1784 and travelled for six years, appearing as a pianist throughout Saxony and Hanover, visiting Paris and probably Vienna, and finally settling in Paris by the beginning of 1790. By 1793 he had completed his first opera, *Roméo et Juliette*, to a libretto by his patron Vicomte Alexandre de Ségur, and submitted it to the Académie Royale de Musique. Lacking the financial resources to stage new works, however, they rejected it. Steibelt then replaced the sung recitative with spoken dialogue and it was finally performed as an *opéra comique* at the Théâtre Feydeau on 9 October 1793. Its success brought Steibelt much acclaim. For the next 15 years he divided his time between Paris and London, performing extensively in those cities and on tour in most of the major European capitals. He wrote many instrumental works as well as ballets and a pasticcio opera, *Albert and Adelaide* (1798, London). In 1806 his 'festival intermezzo' *La fête de Mars*, composed in honour of Napoleon's victory at Austerlitz, was staged at the Opéra.

Steibelt was one of many European musicians lured to Russia by generous offers from the government of Alexander I in the first decade of the 19th century. In 1808 his second full-scale opera, *La princesse de Babylon*, was given its première in St Petersburg. The following year he brought out his ballet *La fête de l'empereur* and possibly another opera, *Paul et Virginie*, while beginning work on *Cendrillon*, first staged on 14/26 October 1810. He was named director of the imperial French theatre there before the end of that year, succeeding Boieldieu, and soon after his appointment completed another three-act opera, *Sargines*, and a pasticcio, *Les folies amoureuses*. In 1817 he revised *Roméo et Juliette*, restoring the sung recitative; another opera, *Phèdre*, is reported to have received its première in 1818 in St Petersburg. His final opera, *Le jugement de Midas*, was begun some time after 1820 but never completed, as he had by then developed a protracted illness to which he finally succumbed in 1823.

Steibelt was principally a composer of vocal music, and his greatest works were undoubtedly his operas. His reputation in this field, though based solely on *Roméo et Juliette* (his only real opera known outside Russia), was not inconsiderable. Berlioz cited *Roméo* as the best of the five settings of the Shakespeare play in existence and was obviously influenced by Steibelt's innovatory orchestration, his harmonies and individual writing for chorus, which included unison passages in a choral-recitative style and the use of the chorus as another 'instrument' in the orchestra. In Steibelt's operas dramatic requirements always take precedence over purely musical considerations. *Roméo et Juliette* held the stage for at least 30 years after its première and was translated into four languages and performed in opera houses from New Orleans to Moscow. His only other published opera, *Cendrillon*, also an *opéra comique*, has never been heard outside Russia. It too has a striking and bold dramatic style coupled with characteristic instrumentation and form.

See also ROMÉO ET JULIETTE (i).

Roméo et Juliette (oc, 3, A.-J.-P. de Ségur, after W. Shakespeare), Paris, Feydeau, 9 Oct 1793 (Paris, 1793); restored (orig.) version, St Petersburg, 1817, *D-B*
Albert and Adelaide, or The Victim of Constancy (grand heroic romance, 3, S. Birch, after B. J. Marsollier des Vivetières and J. M. Boutet de Monvel), London, CG, 11 Dec 1798, pf score of ov. pubd, collab. Attwood, ? incl. music by Cherubini
La fête de Mars (int, J. A. d'Esménard), Paris, Opéra, 4 March 1806, *F-Po*
La princesse de Babylon (3), St Petersburg, 1808
La fête du 4 fevrier, Paris, 1809
Paul et Virginie, St Petersburg, 1809
Cendrillon (3, C. G. Etienne), St Petersburg, 14/26 Oct 1810, ed. in Hagberg (1976)
Les folies amoureuses, St Petersburg, *c*1810, pubd [pasticcio]
Sargines (3), St Petersburg, 1811
Phèdre, St Petersburg, 1818
Le jugement de Midas, *c*1823, inc., ? St Petersburg

*

M. Dietz: *Geschichte des musikalischen Dramas in Frankreich während der Revolution* (Vienna, 1885, 2/1893), 301ff, 449ff

V. Stasov: *Russikiia i inostrannyia opery ispolniavshiiasia na Imperatorskikh teatrakh v Rossii v xviii i xix stoltiiakh* [Russian and Foreign Operas Performed at the Imperial Theatres in Russia in the 18th and 19th Centuries] (St Petersburg, 1898)

E. Prout: 'Some Forgotten Operas, iii: Steibelt's *Roméo et Juliette*', *MMR*, xxxiv/9–11 (1904)

A. A. Gozenpud: *Muzïkal'nïy teatr v Rossii ot istokov do Glinki* [Musical Theatre in Russia from its Origins up to Glinka] (Leningrad, 1959)

G. B. Bernandt, ed.: *Slovar' oper … 1736–1959* [Dictionary of Opera] (Moscow, 1962)

W. Dean: 'Shakespeare and Opera', *Shakespeare and Music*, ed. P. Hartnoll (London, 1964), 89–175

K. A. Hagberg: *Daniel Steibelt's Cendrillon: a Critical Edition with Notes on Steibelt's Life and Works* (diss., U. of Rochester, 1976)

KAREN A. HAGBERG

Stein, Gertrude (*b* Allegheny, PA, 3 Feb 1874; *d* Paris, 27 July 1946). American writer. She was at the centre of the philosophical and artistic revolutions of the early 20th century and became a natural emblem for modernism, both through her own writing and through her influence as a catalyst of the avant garde. Her well-known associations with writers like Sherwood Anderson and Hemingway and painters like Picasso and Matisse have to some extent eclipsed her involvement with music; but as a student at Radcliffe College (1893–7) she had been attracted to opera (particularly Wagner), and after settling in Paris in 1903 she became acquainted with Satie. Although her approach to music was as idiosyncratic as her writing, several composers were drawn to her work, including Bernstein, Paul Bowles, Petre Kotik, Meyer Kupferman and, most notably, VIRGIL THOMSON, whose collaboration with Stein in the operas *Four Saints in Three Acts* and *The Mother of Us All* brought composer and librettist great success. Both works, which present an unconventional view of the development of modern America, were abstract and required Maurice Grosser to create a scenario for context after the words and music were completed. Lord Berners commissioned a libretto on the Faust story, *Doctor Faustus Lights the Lights*, but did not write the music. While the metaphors most often employed to explain Stein's writing come from the visual arts (cubism and the cinema), her experiments with prose rhythms and her repetitive interweaving of themes also invite comparison with the rise, fall and repetition of musical themes, an aspect of her work explored by Sutherland (1951).

Four Saints in Three Acts (op to be sung, 1927): V. Thomson, 1934

Doctor Faustus Lights the Lights (1938): Kupferman, 1953; Ahlstrom, 1982

The Mother of Us All (play, 1946): Thomson, 1947

Three Sisters who are not Sisters (1946): Ahlstrom, 1953; Rorem, 1971

In a Garden: Kupferman, 1948

A Cabaret Opera (chamber op, with W. H. Auden, E. E. Cummings, E. Pound and others): Russo, 1970

Photograph 1920 (comedy): Kalmanoff, 1972

Ladies Voices (play): Shere, 1987 [pt 1 of trilogy]

I Like it to Be a Play (play): Shere, 1989 [pt 2 of trilogy]

What Happened (play): Shere, 1991 [pt 3 of trilogy]

*

C. van Vechten: Introduction to Gertrude Stein: *Last Operas and Plays* (New York, 1949), pp.vii–xix

D. Sutherland: *Gertrude Stein: a Biography of her Work* (New Haven, CT, 1951)

R. Jackson: *The Operas of Gertrude Stein and Virgil Thomson* (diss., Tulane U., 1962)

J. McCaffrey: '"Any of mine without music to help them": the Operas and Plays of Gertrude Stein', *Yale/Theatre*, iv (1973), 27–39

G. L. Jeffers: *Non-narrative Music Dramas: Settings by Virgil Thomson, Ned Rorem and Earl Kim of Plays by Gertrude Stein and Samuel Beckett* (diss., UCLA, 1981)

E. Burns, ed.: *The Letters of Gertrude Stein and Carl van Vechten, 1913–1946* (New York, 1986)

T. Page and V. W. Page, eds.: *Selected Letters of Virgil Thomson* (New York, 1988)

BROOKS LANDON

Stein, Horst (*b* Elberfeld, 2 May 1928). German conductor. After studying music in Cologne and a first engagement at the Städtische Bühnen, Wuppertal, he was appointed Kapellmeister at the Hamburg Staatsoper in 1951. He was Kapellmeister at the Berlin Staatsoper, 1955–61, and Generalmusikdirektor in Mannheim, 1963–70; in 1970 he was appointed principal conductor at the Vienna Staatsoper, and from 1972 to 1979 he was Generalmusikdirektor at the Hamburg Staatsoper. A conductor of wide experience, always intent on achieving a satisfactory balance between singer and orchestra, he has been most successful with Wagner's works. He has conducted the *Ring* at Bayreuth, *Parsifal* at the Paris Opéra and *Tristan und Isolde* at the Teatro Colón, Buenos Aires. He also conducts Mozart frequently and was regularly engaged at the Salzburg Festival and elsewhere into the 1990s. His recordings include *Carmen* in German (1961), with Christa Ludwig, and Verdi's *Don Carlos* (1970).

HANS CHRISTOPH WORBS, NOËL GOODWIN

Stein [Rosenstein], **Leo** (*b* Lemberg [now L'viv], 25 March 1861; *d* Vienna, 28 July 1920 or 1921). Austrian librettist. He studied law and began writing song lyrics while supporting himself with an office job with the Südbahngesellschaft. In due course he was able to devote himself full-time to writing. He collaborated most notably with Victor Léon on the Strauss-Müller *Wiener Blut* (1899) and Lehár's *Die lustige Witwe* (1905), and with Béla Jenbach on Kálmán's *Die Csárdásfürstin* (1915); he wrote Nedbal's *Polenblut* (1913) independently. Stein was much sought after as one of the most inventive and conscientious writers of operetta librettos, and as one who paid ample attention to the sound construction of a libretto.

operettas unless otherwise stated

Lachende Erben (with J. Horst), C. Weinberger, 1892; *Münchner Kindl* (with A. Landesberg), Weinberger, 1893; *Die Königin von Gamara* (burleske Operette, with R. Genée), Alexander Neumann, 1894; *Lady Charlatan* (with P. von Schönthan), A. Müller jr, 1895; *Die Lachtaube* (with Landesberg), Weinberger, 1895; *Der Löwenjäger* (with Schönthan), G. Verő, 1896; *Der Pumpmajor* (with Horst), Neumann, 1896; *Der Wunderknabe* (with Landesberg), E. von Taund, 1896

Der Pfiffikus (Spl, with Horst), Müller, 1896; *Die Blumenmary* (with Landesberg), Weinberger, 1897; *Der Dreibund* (with Landesberg), Taund, 1898; *Frau Reklame* (with Horst), L. Roth, 1898; *Der Blondin von Namur* (with Horst), Müller, 1898; *Gräfin Kuni* [Der Minnesänger] (with Schönthan), F. Baumgartner, 1899; *Die wahre Liebe ist das nicht* (with Horst), F. Skallitzky, 1899; *Wiener Blut* (with V. Léon), Müller, after J. Strauss, 1899

Der griechische Sklave [trans. of O. Hall: *A Greek Slave*], S. Jones, 1899; *Der Sechsuhrzug* (with Léon), Heuberger, 1900; *Das süsse Mädel* (with Landesberg), H. Reinhardt, 1901; *Das gewisse Etwas* (Vaudeville-Operette, with Léon), Weinberger, 1902; *Clo-Clo* (Vaudeville-Operette, with Landesberg), F. Pagin, 1902; *Der liebe Schatz* (with Landesberg), Reinhardt, 1902; *Der Göttergatte* (with Léon), Lehár, 1904

Der Generalkonsul (with Landesberg), Reinhardt, 1904; *Das Garnisonmädel* (with Landesberg), R. Mader, 1904; *Der Schnurrbart* (with C. Lindau), Verő, 1905; *Die Schützenliesl* (with Lindau), E. Eysler, 1905; *Die lustige Witwe* (with Léon), Lehár, 1905; *Künstlerblut* (with Lindau), Eysler, 1906; *Der selige Vincenz* (with Landesberg), Mader, 1907; *Tausendundeine Nacht* (komische Oper, Lindau), E. Reiterer, after J. Strauss, 1907; *Vera*

Violetta (Vaudeville-Operette), Eysler, 1907; *Das Glücksschweinchen* (with Lindau), Eysler, 1908

Johann der Zweite (with Lindau), Eysler, 1908; *Lumpus und Pumpus*, Eysler, 1910; *Das Puppenmädel* (with A. M. Willner), Fall, 1910; *Die Sirene* (with Willner), Fall, 1911; *Die kleine Freundin* (with Willner), Straus, 1911; *Der Natursänger* (with B. Jenbach), Eysler, 1911; *Der Frauenfresser* (with Lindau), Eysler, 1911; *Die Premiere* (musikalische Schwank, with Jenbach), J. G. Hart, 1912; *Der fliegende Rittmeister* (with Jenbach), H. Dostal, 1912; *Polenblut*, Nedbal, 1913

Der Nachtschnellzug (with Léon), Fall, 1913; *Ein Tag im Paradies* (musikalische Posse, with Jenbach), Eysler, 1913; *Die Csárdásfürstin* (with Jenbach), E. Kálmán, 1915; *Die – oder keine* (with Jenbach), Eysler, 1915; *Die Winzerbraut* (with J. Wilhelm), Nedbal, 1916; *Bloch und Co* (Spl, R. Wengraf), Stolz, 1918; *Das Hollandweibchen* (with Jenbach), Kálmán, 1920; *Die blaue Mazur* (with Jenbach), Lehár, 1920; *Die Scheidungsreise* [Wer wird denn weinen ...!] (Vaudeville-Operette), H. Hirsch, 1922; *Mädi* (with A. Grünwald), Stolz, 1923 ANDREW LAMB

Stein, Peter (*b* Berlin, 1 Oct 1937). German director. He joined the Munich Kammerspiele in 1964, where his first assignment as a director was Edward Bond's *Saved* (1967). He also directed Brecht and Weiss in Munich, as well as Goethe and Schiller in Bremen, before co-founding the Schaubühne Company in Berlin (1970), for which he directed many classics both at home and on international tours; he relinquished his artistic directorship in 1985. His first venture into opera was a controversial production of *Rheingold* in Paris (1976). His *Otello* (1986) and *Falstaff* (1988) for the WNO marked a return to more traditional values with their assiduous concern for harmony of action and music.

*

M. Patterson: *Peter Stein: Germany's Leading Theatre Director* (Cambridge, 1981) BARRY MILLINGTON

Steinberg, William [Wilhelm] **(Hans)** (*b* Cologne, 1 Aug 1899; *d* New York, 16 May 1978). American conductor of German birth. He studied conducting with Hermann Abendroth at the Cologne Conservatory. After appointments at the Cologne Opera (as Klemperer's assistant, then first conductor from 1924) and Prague (1925) he moved in 1929 to Frankfurt as musical director; while there he conducted the premières of Schoenberg's *Von heute auf morgen* and Antheil's *Transatlantic* and an early performance of Weill's *Mahagonny*. He also conducted regularly at the Berlin Staatsoper, but after Hitler came to power his activities were restricted. Following an invitation from Toscanini to become associate conductor of the NBC SO in 1938 he emigrated to America. Thereafter his energies were devoted mostly to orchestral conducting, though he appeared as a guest conductor with the San Francisco Opera.

A cultivated man and an exceedingly private personality, Steinberg embodied the probity and selflessness of Toscanini and Klemperer, the two conductors so influential in his career. Though in his 70s his economical gestures became minimal, in his best years his stick technique was unsurpassed in cleanness and clarity. MICHAEL STEINBERG

Stein der Weisen, Der [*Der Stein der Weisen, oder Die Zauberinsel* ('The Philosophers' Stone, or The Enchanted Island')]. *Heroisch-komische Oper* in two acts by BENEDIKT SCHACK and FRANZ XAVER GERL to a libretto by EMANUEL SCHIKANEDER; Vienna, Freihaus-Theater auf der Wieden, 11 September 1790.

This work, frequently mentioned as a forerunner to *Die Zauberflöte*, and the first of Schikaneder's magic operas, was long thought to be lost. However, a vocal score was discovered by Alfred Einstein in Florence, there is a printed libretto from a Frankfurt production of 1796 in the Library of Congress, and engravings of scenes from the original production survive in Schikaneder's *Almanach für Theaterfreunde auf das Jahr 1791*. The story, loosely derived from the tale of the same name in the first volume of Wieland's collection *Dschinnistan*, involves a young couple who are exposed to various trials, and a comic couple with their own problems. The one comparatively familiar number from the work is a duet ('Nun, liebes Weibchen') for the comic pair, Lubano and Lubanara, in which she can only mew like a cat; this number was orchestrated, and perhaps partly composed, by Mozart (K625/592*a*; for evidence about Mozart's contributions to the operas of Schack, see Constanze Nissen's letter to him of 16 February 1826). PETER BRANSCOMBE

Steiner, Elisabeth (*b* Berlin, 17 March 1933). German mezzo-soprano. She studied in Berlin, making her début there at the Städtische Oper in 1961 as Wanda (Blacher's *Rosamunde Floris*). Engaged at the Hamburg Staatsoper, she sang there for nearly 30 years, taking part in the premières of many contemporary operas, including *The Devils of Loudun* (1969). She sang Artemis (*Iphigénie en Aulide*) at Salzburg (1962) and created Mary in Einem's *Jesu Hochzeit* in Vienna (1980). She sang many trouser roles, including Cherubino, Annius (*La clemenza di Tito*), Hänsel, Adriano (*Rienzi*), Ascanio (*Benvenuto Cellini*), Fyodor, Nicklausse (*Les contes d'Hoffmann*), Orlofsky and the High-School Boy (*Lulu*), as well as Dulcinée (*Don Quichotte*), Mignon, Concepción (*L'heure espagnole*), Nancy (*Albert Herring*) and Bianca in the British première of Zemlinsky's *Eine florentinische Tragödie* at Edinburgh (1983). A fine musician with an attractive stage presence, she had a rich-toned voice of considerable volume. ELIZABETH FORBES

Steingruber, Ilona (*b* Vienna, 8 Feb 1912; *d* Vienna, 12 Dec 1962). Austrian soprano. After study at the Vienna Akademie für Musik she sang regularly for Vienna Radio (1939–42). After the war she was heard widely in Europe as a concert singer, notably in contemporary music, and sang roles in the coloratura repertory at the Vienna Staatsoper (1948–51 and 1959–62). She appeared in the *Ring* cycles conducted by Furtwängler at La Scala in 1950 and was a regular visitor to Palermo between 1951 and 1957. Among her recordings are *Bluebeard's Castle*, Schubert's *Die Verschworenen* (*Der häusliche Krieg*) and *Lulu*, conducted by Mitropoulos. DAVID CUMMINGS

Stella, Antonietta (*b* Perugia, 15 March 1929). Italian soprano. She studied in Perugia and Rome, making her début in 1950 at Spoleto as Leonora (*Il trovatore*). In 1951 she sang Leonora (*La forza del destino*) at the Rome Opera and in 1954 appeared at La Scala as Desdemona. In 1955 she made her Covent Garden début as Aida and in 1956 first sang at the Metropolitan, in the same role. She appeared at all the leading European theatres, singing Butterfly, Tosca, Santuzza, Elisabeth de Valois, Violetta and Amelia (*Un ballo in maschera*). She also sang Wagner's Senta, Elisabeth, Elsa and Sieglinde. In 1974 she created the title role of De Bellis's *Maria Stuarda* at Naples. Her beautiful voice was used with great style. ELIZABETH FORBES

Stella [Lotti], **Santa** ['La Santini'] (*fl* 1703–41; *d* 18 Sept 1759). Italian soprano. Originally from Venice or Bologna, she was one of the most famous singers of her generation. From 1706 to 1714 her name appears in librettos as a *virtuosa* of the Duke of Mantua, but she is not listed among those who received salaries from Duke Ferdinando Carlo, who died in 1708. She married the composer Antonio Lotti and travelled with him around Europe. She performed at Casale Monferrato (1703 and, in 1704, in the title role of *Il gran Pompeo*), in Genoa (1704, 1705), and in Pavia (1705). She sang in many productions in Venice at the S Cassiano and S Giovanni Grisostomo theatres, 1706–8, and may also have appeared in London as prima donna in 1709. From 1710 she was again in Venice, and from 1711 to 1714 she sang only in the principal theatre in leading roles. After appearances in Parma in 1714 her career appears to have culminated with the grand productions in Dresden of 1718 and 1719, the year in which she took the title role in her husband's *Teofane*. She sang at Munich in 1737 in Francesco Peli's *La costanza in trionfo* and perhaps at Turin in 1739 in *Ciro riconosciuto* (though this last reference to an appearance by her may be due to a confusion of names).

*

P. F. Tosi: *Opinioni de' cantori antichi e moderni* (Bologna, 1723; Eng. trans. by J. E. Galliard, 1742, 2/1743, as *Observations on the Florid Song*)

E. Selfridge-Field: *Pallade veneta: Writings on Music in Venetian Society, 1650–1750* (Venice, 1985)

L. Lindgren: 'Venice, Vivaldi, Vico and Opera in London, 1705–17: Venetian Ingredients in English Pasticci', *Nuovi studi vivaldiani*, ed. A. Fanna and G. Morelli (Florence, 1988), 633–66

SERGIO DURANTE

Stenborg, Carl (*b* Stockholm, 25 Sept 1752; *d* Stockholm, 1 Aug 1813). Swedish singer, composer, translator and impresario. The son of the impresario and actor Petter Stenborg, he grew up in the household of Count Adam Horn, who underwrote his education at Uppsala University and supported his appointment to a government post in 1767. At the age of 14 he made his début in the public concerts of Stockholm and began to study composition under Ferdinand Zellbell. His début as an opera singer was as Thetis in Uttini's *Thetis och Pelée* on 18 January 1773, and during the following decade he achieved considerable success as the leading singer in Stockholm, in such works as Handel's *Acis and Galatea*, Gluck's *Orfeo* (a scene of which was painted by the artist Per Hilleström), Uttini's *Birger Jarl och Mechtilde* and Naumann's *Gustaf Wasa*. In 1782 he was appointed court secretary, and in 1783 he was elected to the Royal Swedish Academy of Music.

In 1780 Stenborg took over the management of his father's theatre in Eriksberg, receiving from Gustavus III permission to stage comic operas both there (and later at the Munkbro Theatre) and at the Bollhus Theatre. He engaged successively J. C. F. Haeffner and J. D. Zander as his musical directors and, with the librettist Carl Envallsson, offered Swedish translations of *opéras comiques* by Grétry, Dalayrac, Duni, Monsigny and others. He also performed Swedish works by C. I. Hallman, O. Kéxel and D. G. Björn (his leading comic actor), including the parodies *Caspar och Dorothea* (1775), *Skeppar Rolf* (1778) and *Petis och Thelée* (1779), for all three of which he composed music. His theatre often rivalled the Royal Opera in popularity during 1788–9, and he maintained his standing in both theatres as impresario and principal singer until 1796. After the theatre closed in 1799 Stenborg toured the Swedish provinces with a troupe until his retirement from the Royal Opera in 1806. He married the daughter of Elisabeth Olin, his leading lady, in 1793.

Stenborg's voice was known for its dexterity, soft expressivity and dark tone colour, and was nearer to a baritone than to a tenor. His ability to bring considerable emotion to his roles made him a particular favourite at the Royal Opera; his portrayal of Gustavus Vasa, the first king of Sweden, for example, won him fame for its realistic patriotic fervour. As a composer, he was well trained in technique, according to contemporary sources, and his music is characterized by lyrical melodic lines coupled with a solid sense of form and harmony. He composed music for nine stage works, mostly parodies and Singspiels.

all first performed in Stockholm

Caspar och Dorothea (oc, 3, C. I. Hallman), 31 Aug 1775, *S-St* [parody of Handel: Acis and Galatea]

Konung Gustaf Adolfs jagt (comedy with song, 3, A. F. Ristell, after C. Collé and R. Dodsley), 25 June 1777, *Skma*

Kärlek utan strumpor [Love without Stockings] (tragédie lyrique burlesque, 5, J. H. Wessel and Stenborg), 17 Oct 1777, *Skma*

Skeppar Rolf och Gunnild (comedy with song, 3, Hallman), 6 July 1778, *St* [parody of Uttini: Birger Jarl och Mechtilde]

Petis och Thelée (comedy with song, 3, Hallman), 27 Sept 1779, *St* [parody of Uttini: Thetis och Pelée]

Don Micco och Lesbina (oc, 1, Biancolelli, after J. A. Romagnesi), 11 Aug 1780

Så blefvo alla nögda [Thus are all Happy] (comic op, 1, C. Envallsson), 18 Aug 1782, *St*

Donnerpamp (comedy with song, 1, Hallman), 21 June 1783, collab. J. D. Zander [parody of Piccinni: Roland]

Gustaf Ericsson i Dalarne (drama with song, 3, Envallsson), Munkbro, 29 Oct 1784, *Skma*

*

F. Dahlgren: *Anteckningar om Stockholms teatrar* (Stockholm, 1866)

J. Flodmark: *Stenborgska skådebanorne* [Stenborg's Theatres] (Stockholm, 1893)

——: *Elisabeth Olin och Carl Stenborg* (Stockholm, 1903)

N. Personne: *Svenska teatern under Gustavianska tidehvarfvet* (Stockholm, 1913)

S. Lindström: 'Vårt första nationella sångspel', *STMf*, xxiv (1942), 68–83

BERTIL H. VAN BOER

Stendhal [Beyle, Henri] (*b* Grenoble, 23 Jan 1783; *d* Paris, 22 March 1842). French writer. His musical education was limited to a few lessons. He attached himself to Angelina Bereyter, seconda diva of the Odéon, of whose performances in *Il matrimonio segreto* he claimed to have attended 60 to 100 between 1811 and 1813. His passionate love of Italy and the Italians derived from his fascination with Italian opera. He regretted that he had not devoted his life to music and, when in Milan, certain that he was a born composer, would study the libretto of the opera he was to attend and instinctively add his own music. Cimarosa was the composer he most admired, followed by Mozart and Rossini, and, as distant emulators, Paisiello, Pergolesi and Simon Mayr. In later years he found Cimarosa trifling and Rossini flighty. Stendhal's *Vie de Rossini* is witty and urbane, erroneous in detail, yet stimulating as a work of art. He claimed to have met Rossini and bragged he had long been in his intimacy, but Rossini later declined to be introduced to him and never read the book. His remarks on Haydn were all plagiarized from Giuseppe Carpani's *Le Haydine, ovvero Lettere sulla vita e le opere del celebre maestro Giuseppe Haydn* (1812); he even appropriated Carpani's private reminiscences of Haydn and Vienna, in *Lettres ... sur le célèbre compositeur Haydn* published under the pseudonym of César Bombet (1814).

Lettres ... sur le célèbre compositeur Haydn, suivies d'une vie de Mozart et de considérations sur Métastase ... (Paris, 1814, 2/1817 as *Vies de Haydn, de Mozart et de Métastase*; Eng. trans., 1818 and 1972)

Vie de Rossini (Paris, 1824, rev. H. Prunières, 2/1922; Eng. trans., 1956, 2/1970)

*

R. Rolland: 'Stendhal et la musique', *Revue de Paris*, cv (1913), 462–82

J. W. Klein: 'Stendhal as Music Critic', *MQ*, xxix (1943), 18–31

V. del Litto: Preface to *Vie de Rossini*, Les oeuvres de Stendhal, ed. V. del Litto and E. Abravanel, iii (Lausanne, 1960), 9

R. Celletti: 'Stendhal et l'arte del canto', *Martinella di Milano*, xxxiv/2–3 (1980), 13–20

O. Matteini: *Stendhal e la musica* (Turin, 1981)

A. RICHARD OLIVER

Stenhammar, (Karl) Wilhelm (Eugen) (*b* Stockholm, 7 Feb 1871; *d* Göteborg, 20 Nov 1927). Swedish composer. Largely self-taught in composition, he was first influenced by Beethoven and Wagner, and later by Sibelius and Nielsen. His early three-act opera, *Gildet på Solhaug* ('The Feast at Solhaug'; autograph in *S-Skma*), a setting of Ibsen's play (in the original Norwegian) composed in 1892–3, shows the influence not only of Scandinavian composers such as Södermann, Grieg, Svendsen and Hallström, but also of Wagner, especially in *Parsifal*. The two styles are woven together to create a personal, expressive language, all the more remarkable as the composer had had little experience of theatre music. The language of the opera may also be traced in the contrasting styles of his 1891 ballads, *Florez och Blanzeflor* and *Snöfrid*, together with folktunes and dance rhythms. The orchestration is particularly impressive, given the composer's youth, and is at all times linked closely to the drama. *Gildet* received its première at the Stuttgart Hoftheater on 12 April 1899 but was not performed in Stockholm until 1902. Although well received by the public, it suffered at the hands of the influential critic Wilhelm Peterson-Berger, an ardent Wagnerian and a composer himself.

Peterson-Berger was equally disenchanted with Stenhammar's second opera, a setting of Anna Broberg's *Tirfing* (autograph in *St*, autograph vocal score in *Smf*). The two-act 'mystical saga poem' with prologue and epilogue was composed in 1897 and first performed at the Stockholm Royal Opera on 9 December 1898. In *Tirfing* Stenhammar questioned the aesthetics of Romanticism, including Wagner; his musical language had developed considerably, though his orchestral language was still influenced by Wagner. Stenhammar's use of leitmotif was never understood by Peterson-Berger, who was probably equally bemused by the opera's intense atmosphere and poetry, especially in the four solo scenes for the principal role of Hervor (mezzo-soprano). It is regrettable that Stenhammar abandoned opera (though he later wrote excellent incidental music and also left sketches for an opera based on Shakespeare's *Twelfth Night*), as he had a dramatic gift which, in its power and consistency, no other Swedish composer has equalled.

*

B. Wallner: *Wilhelm Stenhammar och hans tid* (Stockholm, 1991)

ANDERS WIKLUND

Stepanova, Mariya Matveyevna (*b* 1811 or 1815; *d* 1903). Russian soprano. Engaged at the Bol'shoy Theatre, St Petersburg (1834–46), she created Antonida in *A Life for the Tsar* (1836) and Lyudmila in *Ruslan and Lyudmila* (1842). She also sang at the Bol'shoy Theatre, Moscow (1846–55), returning to St Petersburg in 1850 (when she was heard as Antonida by the ten-year-old Tchaikovsky) and in 1852, when she created Kseniya in Rubinstein's first opera *Dmitry Donskoy* (*Kulikovskaya bitva*, 'The Battle of Kulikovo').

ELIZABETH FORBES

Stepanova, Yelena Andreyevna (*b* Moscow, 5/17 May 1891; *d* Moscow, 26 May 1978). Russian soprano. She studied singing with M. Polli. From 1908 she sang in the Bol'shoy chorus until, after a successful début as Antonida (*A Life for the Tsar*), she became a soloist in 1912. Stanislavsky, who had great influence on her, prepared her for the roles of Gilda (1919) and Tatyana (1921); she was also influenced by the conductors Václav Suk, Cooper and Golovanov and the director Lossky, as well as by Shalyapin, Sobinov and Nezhdanova. Her singing was distinguished by rare clarity, crystalline coloratura and artistic sensitivity. Her Rimsky-Korsakov portrayals were fascinating: Marfa (*The Tsar's Bride*), the Snow Maiden, Pannochka-Rusalka (*May Night*) and the Queen of Shemakha (*Golden Cockerel*), among others. Her repertory also included Glinka's Lyudmila, Violetta, Elsa, Meyerbeer's Marguerite de Valois and Lakmé. She left the opera stage in 1944.

*

E. A. Stepanova (Moscow, 1953)

K. Konstantinov: 'E. A. Stepanova: k 70-letiyu so dnya rozhdeniya' [Stepanova: for her 70th Birthday], *Muzïkal'naya zhizn'* (1961), no.10, pp.11–12

I. M.YAMPOL'SKY

Step'anyan, Haro Levon (*b* Elizavetpol [now Gyandzha], Azerbaijan, 13/25 April 1897; *d* Erevan, 9 Jan 1966). Armenian composer. He studied at the Moscow music college (1923–7) and at the Leningrad Conservatory (1926–30), then settled in Erevan, teaching at the conservatory and holding the presidency of the Armenian Composers' Union (1938–48). His operatic, orchestral and chamber music played an important part in the development of Armenian music in the 1930s and 40s; though he followed the Armenian tradition, and in particular the work of Komitas, he drew into it certain features from Prokofiev and Shostakovich. Folk music remained an essential source of thematic material. Step'anyan's operas cover a wide range, from the improbable, satiric *K'adj Nazar* ('Brave Nazar') to the epic *Sasuntsi Davit'*, from the revolutionary *Lusabatsin* ('At Dawn') to the historical, romantic *Nune*. The use of the chorus shows great ingenuity, whether in the dynamic material of *Lusabatsin* or the static, oratorical writing of *Sasuntsi Davit'*, in which the archaic setting is evoked through the use of *sharakan* melodies, hymns, heavy rhythms and strict polyphony.

K'adj Nazar [Brave Nazar] (4, D. Demirdjyan), Erevan, 1935

Sasuntsi Davit' [David of Sasun] (4, Demirdjyan, after traditional epic), 1936

Lusabatsin [At Dawn] (5, T. Hakhumyan), Erevan, 1938

Nune (4, A. Adamyan and V. Vagharshyan), 1947

Herosuhi [The Heroine] (4, Adamyan), Erevan, 1950

*

G. Tigranov: *Armyanskiy muzïkal'nïy teatr*, ii (Erevan, 1960), 71–125

M. Katsakhyan: *Haro Step'anyan* (Erevan, 1962)

G. Tigranov: *Aro Stepanyan: 1897–1966* (Moscow, 1967)

SVETLANA SARKISYAN

Stephan, Rudi (*b* Worms, 29 July 1887; *d* nr Tarnopol, Galicia, 29 Sept 1915). German composer. He studied in Frankfurt with Sekles and then in Munich, where he also studied philosophy. In addition to instrumental pieces, which attracted attention for their avoidance of established forms and of programmes, in 1914 he composed the opera *Die ersten Menschen*, to a libretto by O. Borngräber, a work looking back to Beethoven and Gluck; it was first performed in Frankfurt in 1920.

*

A. D. McCredie: 'The Munich School and Rudi Stephan (1887–1915): some Forgotten Sources and Byways of Musical Jugendstil and Expressionism', *MR*, xxix (1968), 197–222

Stephănescu, George (*b* Bucharest, 13 Dec 1843; *d* Bucharest, 25 April 1925). Romanian composer, conductor and teacher. He studied at the Bucharest Academy (1864–7), and at the Paris Conservatoire (1867–71) with Auber and Thomas (composition), Marmontel (piano) and Enrico delle Sedie (singing). At the Bucharest Academy he taught singing (1872–1904), his pupils including Darclée, Theodorini, Nuovina, D. Popvici-Bayreuth and Giovanni Dimitrescu. He was conductor of the Romanian Opera in 1879, and founded and conducted the ensemble Opera Româna (1885–6). A fervent supporter of opera in the vernacular, he translated many foreign works. Besides chamber, orchestral and choral works, his compositions include incidental music for stage plays and several operas and operettas. His music is characterized by broad melodic lines, solid architecture and orchestration which reflects folk influences, as in the shepherd's pipe song in the fairy-tale *Sînziana şi Pepelea*.

Peste Dunăre [Across the Danube] (operetta, G. Ventura), Bucharest, National, 1880
Sînziana şi Pepelea [Sînziana and Pepelea] (musical fairy-tale, V. Alecsandri), Bucharest, National, 29 March 1881
Scaiul bărbaţilor [Sticking to a Man like a Leech], 1884 (operetta, G. Bengescu-Dabija), Bucharest, Edison, 29 March 1910
Mama soacră [The Mother-in-law], 1894 (comic op, 3, T. Speranţia), Bucharest, Edison, 1902
Cometa (operetta, T. Sperania), 1900
Petra, 1902 (lyrical drama, 1, E. Aslan), inc.

VIOREL COSMA

Stephanie, Gottlieb (*b* Breslau, 19 Feb 1741; *d* Vienna, 23 Jan 1800). German actor, playwright and librettist active in Vienna. Called Stephanie der Jüngere (the younger) to distinguish him from his elder brother, the actor Christian Gottlob, Stephanie was prevented from studying law by his conscription into the army of Frederick the Great. He was captured at Landshut and later joined the Austrian forces; after serving as a recruiter, he began a career in 1769 as an actor in Vienna but soon turned to writing plays (40 in all, 29 of them written before 1780). He involved himself actively in theatrical affairs, ingratiated himself at court, and was named one of the five inspectors of the Nationaltheater, established by Joseph II in 1776. He also participated in the National-Singspiel, created in 1778, as a translator and adapter of French and Italian comic operas. In 1781 its direction was placed in his hands.

Stephanie earned a dark reputation as an inveterate intriguer, but he remained a warm supporter and friend of Mozart's, facilitating the commissioning of *Die Entführung aus dem Serail* in 1781 as well as choosing and adapting the text. After the demise of the National-Singspiel in 1783, he continued to provide texts for the German companies at the Kärntnertortheater, including several of Dittersdorf's most successful operas.

As a playwright Stephanie enjoyed sustained popularity in Vienna but scant critical acclaim. His librettos vary considerably in tone, plot and characterization, depending on the stage for which they were intended. Those for the National-Singspiel are more refined than his later texts for the Kärntnertor. As a translator of foreign operas for the National-Singspiel, he showed uncommon skill in placing new German texts beneath the original music. In his own operas his verses gained little esteem and he often resorted to pilfering from or adapting other poets for this purpose. He frequently adapted German texts for new settings by local composers, although the extent of his revisions of C. F. Bretzner's *Belmont und Constanze* for Mozart is unusual. Bretzner publicly ridiculed the new musical numbers Stephanie wrote for *Die Entführung*. In 1792 Stephanie published his original librettos and included an informative preface on many of the conventions that governed German comic opera at Vienna during the 1780s.

Da ist nicht gut zu rathen (comische Oper), J. Bartha, 1778; *Die schöne Schusterinn, oder Die puecefarbnen Schuhe* (komisches Spl), I. Umlauf, 1779; *Das Irrlicht* [adaptation of C. F. Bretzner: *Der Irrwisch*] (Spl), Umlauf, 1782; *Die Entführung aus dem Serail* [adaptation of Bretzner: *Belmont und Constanze*] (Spl), Mozart, 1782; *Rose, oder Pflicht und Liebe im Streit* (komisches Spl), Mederitsch, 1783; *Der Apotheker und der Doktor* [*Doktor und Apotheker*] (komisches Spl), Dittersdorf, 1786; *Der Schauspieldirektor* (Gelegenheitsstück), Mozart, 1786; *Die glücklichen Jäger* (Spl), Umlauf, 1786; *Die Liebe im Narrenhause* (komische Oper), Dittersdorf, 1787; *Hieronymus Knicker* [*Lucius Knicker*; *Chrisostomus Knicker*] (komische Operette), Dittersdorf, 1789; *List und Ungefähr* (Spl), E. Lange, 1793; *Die Freiwilligen* (Spl), Süssmayr, 1796

*

H. Bussmann: *Die Schauspielkunst Gottlieb Stephanies d.J.* (diss., U. of Jena, 1923)
S. Hochstöger: 'Gottlieb Stephanie der Jüngere', *Jb der Gesellschaft für Wiener Theaterforschung*, xii (1960), 3–82

THOMAS BAUMAN

Stephens, Catherine (*b* London, 18 Sept 1794; *d* London, 22 Feb 1882). English soprano and actress. From 1807 she studied singing with Gesualdo Lanza and in 1812 sang small parts with an Italian company at the Pantheon in London. On 23 September 1813 she made her début at Covent Garden as Mandane in Arne's *Artaxerxes*, later appearing as Polly (*The Beggar's Opera*), Rosetta (*Love in a Village*) and Clara (*The Duenna*). She remained there until 1822, when she went to Drury Lane, returning in 1828. It was as an exponent of 'English style on Italian rudiments' that she became one of the most popular artists of the day. She appeared in ballad operas, in operas and entertainments by Bishop and others, and in arrangements of operas from abroad which, by 20th-century standards, are extraordinary. She sang Susanna in the first performance in English of *Le nozze di Figaro* (1819, Covent Garden), having previously sung Zerlina in *The Libertine*, an afterpiece based on Shadwell's play, with Mozart's music, which is counted as the first performance in English of *Don Giovanni* (1817, Covent Garden). Stephens was one of three sopranos who sang Agnes (Agathe) in Hawes's English adaptation of *Der Freischütz* (1824, English Opera House). She retired in 1835 and married the Earl of Essex in 1838. Contemporary writers agreed on the sweetness of her voice, which was rich if not outstandingly brilliant. William Hazlitt compared her 'simple, artless manner'

favourably with Braham's elaborate artifice, and Leigh Hunt praised her 'exquisite vein of gentle pathos'.
RONALD CRICHTON

Sterbini, Cesare (*b* Rome, 1784; *d* Rome, 19 Jan 1831). Italian librettist. An official of the Vatican treasury and a poet, he was fluent in Greek, Latin, French and German. His first libretto *Paolo e Virginia* (set by Vincenzo Migliorucci, 1812) was written for the benefit night of the Mombelli sisters, and although described as a cantata it was evidently staged. He replaced Jacopo Ferretti as librettist for Rossini's *Torvaldo e Dorliska* (1815), producing a badly written and ill-organized libretto which failed to stimulate the composer. By contrast, *Almaviva*, also for Rossini (*Il barbiere di Siviglia*, 1816), was a sparkling and flawless text, and it is not to decry Sterbini's achievement to point out that Beaumarchais' comedy – on which it was based – itself had all the necessary elements for a comic opera. The rest of Sterbini's short career as librettist was undistinguished. Although his choice of subjects and handling of forms were sometimes forward-looking his texts tended to retain elements of Metastasian style; however, it is hard not to see the influence of Ferretti in this.

Paolo e Virginia (cantata), V. Migliorucci, 1812; *Torvaldo e Dorliska* (dramma semiserio), Rossini, 1815; *Almaviva* [set as Il barbiere di Siviglia] (commedia), Rossini, 1816 (Dall'Argine, 1868; Graffigna, 1879; A. Torazza, 1924); *Il credulo deluso* (dg), Tadolini, 1817; *Il contraccambio* (dg), Cordella, 1818 (as La rappresaglia: Stuntz, 1819; Poissl, 1820; F. Cianciarelli, 1822); *Il gabbamondo* (dg), Generali, 1819; *Isaura e Ricciardo* (dramma per musica), F. Basili, 1820

*

A. Cametti, ed.: *Una conferenza ineditat di Jacopo Ferretti sulla storia della poesia melodrammatica romana* (Pesaro, 1896)
G. Radiciotti: *Gioacchino Rossini* (Tivoli, 1927)
M. Rinaldi: *Due secoli di musica al Teatro Argentina* (Florence, 1978)
D. Goldin: 'Il *Barbiere di Siviglia* da Beaumarchais all'opera buffa', *La vera fenice* (1985), 164–89
JOHN BLACK

Sternberg, Erich Walter (*b* Berlin, 31 May 1891; *d* Tel-Aviv, 15 Dec 1974). Israeli composer. He graduated in law from the University of Kiel but in 1918 decided to make music his career, studying composition with Hugo Leichtentritt and the piano with H. Praetorius. In 1932 he settled in Palestine, which he had been visiting regularly since 1925. He taught at the Tel-Aviv conservatory and formed the Palestine SO (later the Israel PO) with Bronislaw Huberman. His opera-oratorio *Dr Doolittle* (1937; Sternberg, after H. Lofting) was never completed because Sternberg omitted to obtain the author's consent to set the story to music; however, a performance of the completed parts did take place in Israel (1939) and, in 1941, Sternberg composed an orchestral suite, based on the opera, which has been performed several times. Later he collaborated with his niece, the American librettist and writer Renate Alsberg Hunter, to create a new opera using the musical material from *Dr Doolittle*. The result was *Pacifica* (1974), a three-act children's opera first performed at the Eastman Theatre, Rochester, New York (1 June 1979).
WILLIAM Y. ELIAS

Sternefeld, Daniel (*b* Antwerp, 27 Nov 1905; *d* Uccle, Brussels, 2 June 1986). Belgian composer and conductor. He studied at the Antwerp conservatory (1918–24), then privately, and in 1931–2 pursued conducting studies with Clemens Krauss and Karajan in Salzburg. He joined the orchestra of the Royal Flemish Opera, Antwerp, as a flautist (1929), becoming second conductor in 1938 and principal conductor in 1944; later he was conductor of the Belgian RSO. *Mathis der Maler* and *Peter Grimes* are among the many works whose Belgian premières he directed. The pressure of his conducting career forced him to give second place to composition, but he nevertheless wrote several dramatic works: the opera *Mater dolorosa* (1934; W. Gijssels, after H. C. Andersen; Antwerp, 21 Dec 1935), three ballets and incidental music.
CORNEEL MERTENS

Sternfeld, F(rederick) W(illiam) (*b* Vienna, 25 Sept 1914). British musicologist of Austrian birth. He studied with Lach and Wellesz at the University of Vienna from 1933 and with Dent at Cambridge, then emigrated to the USA (1938), where he completed the doctorate under Schrade at Yale University (1943). From 1940 to 1956 he taught at Wesleyan University, Middletown, then at Dartmouth College. He moved to England in 1956 as lecturer at Oxford University and subsequently became reader in the history of music (1972).

Sternfeld's work ranges from antiquity to the 20th century; he has been especially concerned with the relation of music to the other arts and to cultural and intellectual history in general. A long series of Shakespeare studies is headed by the classic *Music in Shakespearean Tragedy* (London, 1963, 2/1967), and his interest in English drama has produced work on the 17th-century masque. He has also worked extensively on the *intermedio* and the early development of opera, on Gluck and on the symbolic role of the Orpheus figure in the pre-history, rise and later development of opera.

*

J. Caldwell, ed.: *'The Well Enchanting Skill: Music, Poetry and Drama in the Culture of the Renaissance' – Essays in Honour of F. W. Sternfeld* (Oxford, 1990) [incl. list of writings]

Stettin (Ger.). SZCZECIN.

Stevens [Steenberg], **Risë** (*b* New York, 11 June 1913). American mezzo-soprano. She sang with the New York Opera-Comique company before becoming a pupil of Anna Schoen-René. Approached by the Metropolitan, she turned a deaf ear and sailed for Europe to study with Marie Gutheil-Schoder. She then made her formal operatic début in Prague in 1936 as Thomas' Mignon; she also sang with the Vienna Staatsoper and in Buenos Aires. Returning to the USA, she made her début with the Metropolitan on tour in Philadelphia in 1938 as Octavian, appearing a month later in New York as Mignon. She remained with the company until 1961 but also sang with other companies (among them Glyndebourne in 1939 and, as Cherubino, 1955). Her repertory included Carmen, Delilah and Gluck's Orpheus. She had a warm lyric mezzo of specialized repertory, unsuited to Wagner and the heavy Verdi roles.

*

K. Crichton: *Subway to the Met: Risë Stevens' Story* (Garden City, NY, 1959)
J. Hines: 'Risë Stevens', *Great Singers on Great Singing* (Garden City, NY, 1982), 313–22
MAX DE SCHAUENSEE/R

Stevenson, Sir **John (Andrew)** (*b* Dublin, Nov 1761; *d* Kells, Co. Meath, 14 Sept 1833). Irish composer. A chorister and vicar-choral in Dublin at Christ Church and St Patrick's cathedrals, he obtained an honorary MusD at Dublin in 1791 and his knighthood in 1803. In

1814 he was appointed the first organist and musical director at the Castle Chapel. He composed music for several theatrical productions in Dublin and London and contributed songs to a few more, but he is best known for his perhaps over-elaborate 'symphonies and accompaniments' to Thomas Moore's collection of Irish melodies, in which he showed himself a follower of Haydn.

first performed in Dublin unless otherwise stated

The Contract (comic op, R. Houlton), Smock Alley, 14 May 1782; rev. as The Double Stratagem, Capel Street, 20 May 1784; collab. P. Cogan

Love in a Blaze (comic op, 3, J. Atkinson, after J. de Lafont: *Le naufrage*), Crow Street, 29 May 1799

The Bedouins, or The Arabs of the Desert (comic op, 3, E. Irwin), Crow Street, 1 May 1801, vs (London, *c*1811)

The Patriot, or The Hermit of Saxellen (melodrama, H. B. Code), Hibernian, 1811, vs (London, *c*1811)

The Spanish Patriots, or A Thousand Years Ago (dramatic romance, Code), London, Lyceum, 22 Sept 1812, vs (London, *c*1812)

Edwin and Angelina (after O. Goldsmith), 1815, collab. J. Clifton

The Cavern, or The Outlaws (comic op, S. Isdell), Hawkins Street, 22 April 1825

*

DNB (J. C. Haddon)

J. S. Bumpus: *Sir John Stevenson: a Biographical Sketch* (London, 1893)

I. Hogan: *Anglo-Irish Music* (Cork, 1966)

T. J. Walsh: *Opera in Dublin, 1705–1797* (Dublin, 1973)

BRUCE CARR

Stewart, Nellie (*b* Sydney, 20 Nov 1858; *d* Sydney, 22 June 1931). Australian soprano and actress. The daughter of Theodosia Yates-Stirling, former chorus mistress at Drury Lane, London, and a singer-actress of great versatility, she made her first stage appearance at the age of five, and followed her mother's example by excelling in both sung and spoken theatre. She sang the leading role in Offenbach's *La fille du tambour-major* in April 1881 for George Musgrove's management and played Yum-Yum in the Australian première of *The Mikado* in 1885. A descendant of one of David Garrick's leading ladies, she was the most popular operetta and musical comedy performer in Australia before Gladys Moncrieff. ROGER COVELL

Stewart, Thomas (James) (*b* San Saba, TX, 29 Aug 1926). American baritone. He studied at the Juilliard School, New York, where he made his début in 1954 as La Roche in the American première of *Capriccio*. He also sang at the New York City Opera and in Chicago. In 1958 he was engaged by the Berlin Deutsche Oper, making his début as Escamillo; he sang the role at Covent Garden in 1960, returning as Gunther, Don Giovanni and the Dutchman. In 1960 he sang Donner, Gunther and Amfortas at Bayreuth, where he appeared regularly until 1975, adding Wotan and Wolfram to his repertory; he also sang Wotan in the Salzburg Easter Festival. He made his Metropolitan début in 1966 as Ford and returned there regularly until 1980, singing Iago, Golaud, John the Baptist, the Hoffmann villains and Hans Sachs, which he had first sung at Nuremberg (1971). He sang the title roles in the American premières of *Cardillac* (1967) at Santa Fe and *Lear* (1981) at San Francisco, where he had sung since 1962 as Valentin, Golaud, Yevgeny Onegin and Wotan. He married the soprano Evelyn Lear. His voice, more lyrical than dramatic, was nevertheless incisive and of sufficient volume to encompass the heroic Wagner roles.

HAROLD ROSENTHAL/R

Stich-Randall, Teresa (*b* West Hartford, CT, 24 Dec 1927). American soprano. She studied at the Hartford School of Music and Columbia University, New York, where she created Gertrude Stein in *The Mother of Us All* (1947) and the title role of Luening's *Evangeline* (1948). In 1949 she sang the High Priestess in Toscanini's broadcast and recording of *Aida* and in 1950 Nannetta in his *Falstaff*. She made her European début at Florence in 1951 as the Mermaid in *Oberon*. After a season at Basle she was engaged by the Vienna Staatsoper, where her first role was Violetta. From 1953 to 1971 she appeared at the Aix-en-Provence Festival as Fiordiligi, Countess Almaviva, Konstanze, Donna Anna and Pamina. She sang Gilda at Chicago in 1955 and made her Metropolitan début as Fiordiligi in 1961. She took part in the première of Martin's *Le mystère de la Nativité* (1960, Salzburg) and sang throughout Italy, as Strauss's Ariadne and in the Mozart repertory. She sang Norma at Trier in 1971, the year of her retirement from the stage. Her pure, sweet voice was sometimes used in an excessively mannered way, but at its best her cultivated style won wide praise.

*

GV (G. Gualerzi; R. Celletti)

H. Rosenthal: *Great Singers of Today* (London, 1966), 173–4

HAROLD ROSENTHAL/R

Stiedry, Fritz (*b* Vienna, 11 Oct 1883; *d* Zürich, 8 Aug 1968). American conductor of Austrian birth. After studying at the Vienna Academy of Music, he was engaged on Mahler's recommendation as assistant to Ernst von Schuch at Dresden, 1907–8. He held appointments at Teplice, Poznań, Prague, Nuremberg and Kassel, and in 1914 became principal conductor at the Berlin Staatsoper, where he remained until 1923; he then succeeded Weingartner as director of the Vienna Volksoper (1924–5), conducting the première of Schoenberg's *Die glückliche Hand* in 1924. From 1928 to 1933 he was again in Berlin, as principal conductor at the Städtische Oper where he collaborated with Carl Ebert on productions of *Macbeth* and *Simon Boccanegra*, operas then seldom performed, and conducted the first performance of Weill's *Die Bürgschaft* (1932). Forced to leave his post by the Nazi regime in 1933, he conducted in Russia before settling in the USA in 1937. He conducted at the Chicago Civic Opera, 1945–6, and regularly at the Metropolitan, 1946–58, specializing in Verdi and Wagner. In 1947 he conducted Gluck's *Orfeo ed Euridice* at Glyndebourne, in a renewed collaboration with Ebert; Kathleen Ferrier sang Orpheus and the performance was recorded. He first appeared at Covent Garden in 1953–4 to conduct a new production of the *Ring* and a revival of *Fidelio*. His performances then were criticized as musically unpolished, but in general he was a direct, unfussy conductor in the best tradition of Austrian-trained musicians. ALAN BLYTH

***Stiffelio*.** Opera in three acts by GIUSEPPE VERDI to a libretto by FRANCESCO MARIA PIAVE after Emile Souvestre's and Eugène Bourgeois' play *Le pasteur, ou L'évangile et le foyer*; Trieste, Teatro Grande, 16 November 1850.

As was becoming the pattern, Verdi's April 1850 contract for the work that would become *Stiffelio* was signed not with a theatre but with a publisher, in this as in most other cases Ricordi. The librettist was again to be Piave, who himself suggested an adaptation of *Le*

Stiffelio *an Ahasuerian preacher* tenor
Lina *his wife* soprano
Stankar *an old colonel, count of the Empire and Lina's father* baritone
Raffaele von Leuthold *a nobleman* tenor
Jorg *an old preacher* bass
Federico di Frengel } *Lina's cousins* tenor
Dorotea } *Lina's cousins* mezzo-soprano

The Count's friends, Stiffelio's disciples, Ahasuerians

Setting Austria, in and around Stankar's castle by the river Salzbach, at the beginning of the 19th century

pasteur, a French play that had received its première only the previous year but was already available in Italian translation. It was a bold choice, a far cry from the melodramatic plots of Byron and Hugo: modern, 'realistic' subjects were unusual in Italian opera, and the religious subject matter seemed bound to cause problems with the censor.

Ricordi decided to have the première staged at Trieste – the theatre that had recently given such a lukewarm reception to *Il corsaro* – and, true to expectation, the local censorship insisted on a number of important changes, in particular muting the action of the final scene so as (in the composer's view) to make it ridiculous. The première cast included Gaetano Fraschini (Stiffelio), Marietta Gazzaniga Malaspina (Lina) and Filippo Colini (Stankar), and its reception was not much better than that accorded *Il corsaro*. *Stiffelio* had occasional revivals in subsequent years, but was continually dogged by censorship difficulties, and in the mid-1850s Verdi decided to 'rescue' his music by revising it to fit a different, less sensitive plot, *Aroldo*. The original *Stiffelio* disappeared from the repertory and won its first modern revival only in the 1960s. Since then it has received a fair number of performances, and is ranked by many as Verdi's most unjustly neglected opera.

The overture is of the potpourri type: a sequence of contrasting melodies, some of which return in the subsequent action. Its predominantly martial atmosphere (even the main cantabile melody is scored for solo trumpet) seems, curiously, better suited to *Aroldo* than to the original subject.

Act 1.i *A hall on the ground floor of Stankar's castle* The opera immediately pronounces its unusual formal exterior by beginning without the customary introductory chorus. Instead, Jorg offers up an intense, chromatic prayer on behalf of Stiffelio, who has just returned from a mission. Stiffelio appears, surrounded by his family and friends, and in the ensuing *racconto*, 'Di qua varcando sul primo albore', narrates that a boatman reported to him how at first light he saw a young man and a woman at an upstairs window, clearly up to no good, and how the man threw himself from the window into the river, letting fall some papers as he did so. Stifled outbursts from Lina and Raffaele suggest their guilty consciences, but Stiffelio puts their fears to rest by magnanimously casting the documents into the fire. All join in a septet, 'Colla cenere disperso', after which Stiffelio's friends sing a welcoming chorus, 'A te Stiffelio un canto', based on a theme heard in the overture.

The crowd disperses, leaving Stiffelio alone with his wife. The first part of his ensuing double aria is a complex, articulated structure, responding as it does to Lina's reactions. First comes 'Vidi dovunque gemere', in which he describes the moral collapse he has seen everywhere on his journey; then he has a reassuring word for his wife in 'Ah no, il perdono è facile'; and finally come the loving words of 'Allor dunque sorridimi' as he takes her hand and asks for a smile such as she gave him on their wedding day. But his melody suddenly breaks off as he sees that her ring is missing. She can give no answer to his inquiries about it and his suspicions burst out in the cabaletta 'Ah! v'appare in fronte scritto'. The final bars are interrupted by Stankar, who asks Stiffelio to join his friends; with a reminder that he will soon return, the pastor hurries away.

Lina offers a prayer, 'A te ascenda, o Dio clemente', delicately scored and with those elaborate cadential harmonies so characteristic of the later Verdi. She decides to write her husband a letter of confession but is interrupted by Stankar, who reads the first line and is confirmed in his suspicions of her infidelity. Their ensuing duet follows the conventional four-movement pattern. The first movement is dominated by an accusing Stankar, while the second, 'Ed io pure in faccia agl'uomini', is of the 'dissimilar' type, Lina answering his impassioned declamation with obsessively repeated 'sobbing' figures. Stankar forbids Lina to reveal the truth; she reluctantly agrees and they seal the bargain with the cabaletta 'Or meco venite', sung *sotto voce* almost throughout.

In a brief *scena*, Raffaele conceals a letter to Lina inside a book, Klopstock's *Messias*. Federico enters to take the book away and, observed by Jorg, he and Raffaele depart.

1.ii *A reception hall in the castle* The jubilant opening chorus, 'Plaudiam! Di Stiffelio s'allegri', fashioned on a waltz-time variant of one of the overture's main themes, is interspersed with fragments of conversation as Jorg tells Stiffelio of the hidden letter and his (mistaken) suspicions about Federico. Stiffelio is called upon to describe his forthcoming sermon, and with bitter declamation says it will concern the evils of betrayal. As if to illustrate his point, he asks Federico for the *Messias*. But the book is locked, and Stiffelio's demand for Lina's key leads to the Adagio of the concertato finale, 'Oh qual m'invade ed agita', a magnificently imposing movement that builds to a climax of rare power. Stiffelio forces the lock; the letter falls out, but Stankar seizes it and, in spite of the preacher's protests, tears it up. Stiffelio's anger bursts on Stankar in the stretta 'Chi ti salva o sciagurato', Lina pleading for her father's protection while Stankar arranges a duel with Raffaele.

Act 2 *An ancient graveyard* The sombre orchestral prelude is one of Verdi's most evocative to date. Lina, drawn by an 'unknown force', finds the tomb of her mother and in the Largo 'Ah! dagli scanni eterei' – whose luminous scoring makes a striking contrast to the prelude – begs for divine support. Raffaele appears, refusing to renounce his love for Lina even when she directs at him the imploring cabaletta 'Perder dunque voi volete'. But they are interrupted by Stankar, who provokes Raffaele to a duel by insulting his lineage. They defy each other in 3rds and 6ths and begin to clash swords as Stiffelio appears, calling on them to stop in the name of God. The intervention is too much for

Stankar, who blurts out that Raffaele is Lina's seducer. This precipitates a magnificent concertato quartet movement, 'Ah no, è impossibile!', one which prefigures the famous quartet in *Rigoletto* in its welding together of strongly contrasting musical material. It is dominated by Stiffelio, who develops an imposing musical presence through his powerful declamatory style. Stiffelio continues to control the next movement, in which he takes upon himself Stankar's challenge to Raffaele. At the height of the action a chorus within the church is heard singing of divine forgiveness. In spite of the others' pleading, Stiffelio cannot renounce his thirst for vengeance, and eventually falls down in a faint at the sight of a nearby cross.

ACT 3.i *An antechamber with doors leading to various rooms* First comes a double aria for Stankar in which his sense of dishonour leads him to thoughts of suicide. After an unusually complex recitative, the Andante 'Lina, pensai che un angelo' shows Verdi already along the road to the baritone cantabile movements of his later works, while the cabaletta 'O gioia inesprimibile', performed almost entirely *sotto voce*, approaches the level of suppressed energy so pervasive in *Il trovatore*. As Stankar leaves, Stiffelio appears with Jorg, whom he immediately sends off to warn the congregation of his arrival. He meets Raffaele and, questioning him about Lina's future, leads him to a side room where, Stiffelio says, he will 'hear all'. Lina herself now appears before Stiffelio. This is the key confrontation in the opera: a duet difficult to understand in terms of the standard four-movement pattern, so closely are its various stages fashioned around the rapidly changing reactions of the main characters. First comes Stiffelio's 'Opposto è il calle', in which, to a deceptively simple melody charged with harmonic tension, he demands divorce. Lina's violent response is countered by a yet more restricted period from Stiffelio, but then Lina takes over and in 'Non allo sposo' begs him to listen as a priest if not as a husband. Her final plea, 'Egli un patto proponeva', accompanied by solo english horn, is the most touching of all: she declares that her love for Stiffelio has never wavered. Stiffelio, understanding that Raffaele is to blame, goes to the side room to confront him. But Stankar appears, bloody sword in hand, to announce that honour is now satisfied. The closing cabaletta, 'Ah sì, voliamo al tempio', is (as befits the moment) of the 'dissimilar' type, and concludes as Stiffelio is dragged by Jorg towards the church.

3.ii *The interior of a Gothic church* This very brief final scene is remarkable in being based almost entirely on stage effect: there are hardly any sustained melodies, merely declamation and atmospheric choral interpolations. The congregation, Lina included, is at prayer as Stiffelio and Jorg appear. Stiffelio opens the Bible, determined to take inspiration from whatever passage he finds. He reads the episode of the woman taken in adultery and, as he reaches the phrase 'and she rose up, forgiven', the congregation repeats his words in a stirring choral close.

* * *

Much has been made of *Stiffelio* in recent times, some even claiming that it deserves an equal place beside the operas it immediately precedes, *Rigoletto*, *Il trovatore* and *La traviata*. Its 'modern' plot and subject matter are certainly in tune with contemporary sensibilities, and the tendency of its most powerful moments to avoid or radically manipulate traditional structures has been much praised. There are, though, a few drawbacks, not least the manner in which the progress of the action is occasionally unclear. And even the 'forward-looking' dramaturgical structures seem at times to lack necessary durational weight, almost as though the composer were working out new formal balances as he progressed. It is, for instance, significant that many of the alterations made for *Aroldo* are not governed by the new plot but are inserted because Verdi felt he could improve the dramatic articulation. However, *Stiffelio* undoubtedly deserves a better fate than its present neglect, and has in its protagonist one of Verdi's finest tenor roles.

ROGER PARKER

Stignani, Ebe (*b* Naples, 10 July 1903; *d* Imola, 5 Oct 1974). Italian mezzo-soprano. She studied at the Naples Conservatory and made her début at the S Carlo in 1925 as Amneris. In 1926 Toscanini engaged her for La Scala, where she first appeared as Eboli in *Don Carlos*. In successive seasons at La Scala she added to her repertory all the leading mezzo-soprano parts in Italian opera and a large number of other roles including Delilah, Ortrud, Brangäne and Gluck's Orpheus. But it was in the tragic characters of Verdi, above all Azucena in *Il trovatore*, that she found the greatest scope and won her greatest successes. At Covent Garden she sang Amneris (1937, 1939 and 1955), and Azucena (1939 and 1952), and Adalgisa to the Norma of Maria Callas (1952 and 1957). She had a voice of rich quality and ample range, extending from *f* to *c'''*. Judged by older standards, neither her vocalization nor her phrasing was impeccable, yet her singing was always grandiose and authoritative and she brought to the fierce mezzo parts of Verdi – as to the mezzo part in his Requiem – an intensity and dramatic fire that made her for many years the leading exponent of this music.

*

GV (R. Celletti; R. Vegeto)
H. Rosenthal: 'Ebe Stignani', *Opera*, vi (1952), 334–40
E. Davidson: 'All about Ebe', *ON*, xxxv/21 (1970–71), 28–9

DESMOND SHAWE-TAYLOR

Stile concitato (It.: 'agitated style'). Term used by Monteverdi to denote a particular style of composition. Following Greek philosophers, he believed that music should express three main emotional states, 'anger, moderation, and humility or supplication'. Music must therefore have three equivalent styles or manners: 'agitated' (*concitato*), 'soft' (*molle*) and 'moderate' (*temperato*). He equated the first with Plato's description of music which would imitate the utterances and accents of a man engaged in warfare. The Greeks describe the pyrrhic measure as useful for warlike dances; Monteverdi's equivalent was to divide a single semibreve into 16 semiquavers for the 'agitated' style. These are repeated on a single note, thus resembling superficially the modern tremolo, but they must be strictly measured.

Monteverdi worked out the concept in some detail in *Combattimento di Tancredi e Clorinda* (1624) and in works published in his *Madrigali guerrieri et amorosi* (1638); there are also frequent passages in his late operas where suitable words are set in the *concitato* manner. Later composers to use the technique include Francesco Cavalli.

DENIS ARNOLD

Stile rappresentativo (It.: 'theatrical style'). One of several terms applied in the early 17th century to the affective styles of the 'new music'. According to Pietro de' Bardi (1634), 'il canto in istile rappresentativo' was developed by Vincenzo Galilei in Giovanni de' Bardi's CAMERATA, and the term first appeared in print on the title-page of Giulio Caccini's *Euridice* (1600: 'composta in stile rappresentativo'). Other composers linking the term with the theatre include Girolamo Giacobbi, whose *Aurora ingannata* (1608) includes 'canti rappresentativi', and Monteverdi, in his *Madrigali guerrieri et amorosi* (1638).

Like the closely related 'stile recitativo', the term was not restricted to stage music. 'Stile rappresentativo', 'musica rappresentativa', 'genere rappresentativo' etc. are used for *seconda prattica* madrigals (Aquilino Coppini describing Monteverdi's Fifth Book in 1608), solo songs or duets – in the preface to Caccini's *Le nuove musiche* (1602), the 'lettera amorosa' and 'partenza amorosa' in Monteverdi's *Concerto* (1619), Francesco Rasi's *Dialoghi rappresentativi* (1620) and Monteverdi's *Lamento della ninfa* of 1638 – and even sacred *concerti* (Bernardino Borlasca in 1609). Thus the term can denote music for the theatre, music in a recitative style, or music that adopts a particularly dramatic or emotional approach to representing its text.

The theorist Giovanni Battista Doni attempted to clarify the terminology. In the *Trattato della musica scenica* (1633–5), he distinguished between the 'stile recitativo', 'espressivo' and 'rappresentativo' (the last used on the stage). But the differences remain obscure: the 'stile espressivo' is more a heightened recitative than a separate style, and the 'stile rappresentativo' is 'almost the same as today's recitative', although 'some things should be added, and others taken away, to bring it to perfection'. More fruitful was Doni's subsequent notion of three sub-species of the 'stile detto recitativo' (or 'stile monodico') in his *Annotazioni sopra il Compendio de' generi e de' modi della musica* (1640): 'narrativo' (e.g. Daphne's report of Eurydice's death in Peri's *Euridice*, 1600), 'recitativo' or 'recitativo speciale' (e.g. the prologue to *Euridice*, with its more formal strophic organization) and 'espressivo' (e.g. Monteverdi's *Lamento d'Arianna*, 1608). The confusion reflects the difficulties faced by composers of the 'new music' in giving a rational account of their essentially intuitive endeavours. Nevertheless, the term 'stile rappresentativo' is as good as any to suggest the vivid, emotional and dramatic qualities now sought in music.

*

A. Solerti: *Le origini del melodramma* (Turin, 1903)

P. Fabbri: 'Lessico monteverdiano: intorno al "genere rappresentativo"', *La musica nel veneto dal XVI al XVIII secolo*, ed. F. Passadore (Adria, 1984), 89–97

TIM CARTER

Still, William Grant (*b* Woodville, MS, 11 May 1895; *d* Los Angeles, 3 Dec 1978). American composer. Both his parents were musical, and after his father died Still's mother married a man who had a particular interest in opera. A legacy from his father enabled Still to study at the Oberlin Conservatory, and scholarships made study possible with both Chadwick and Varèse. In New York he worked as recording director for the Black Swan Phonograph Company and as an arranger for Paul Whiteman. His *Afro-American Symphony*, composed in 1930, reveals his assimilation of blues melodies. Howard Hanson, who championed the work, dubbed him the 'dean of America's negro composers'. In the early 1930s Still moved to Los Angeles, where he began to compose operas in collaboration with the librettist Verna Arvey, whom he married in 1939. He lived to see three of his operas performed. The first performance of *Troubled Island*, in Spring 1949, was the first world première given by the City Center Opera Company (later New York City Opera); the work was the first opera by a black composer to be performed by a company of standing. *Highway No. 1, U. S. A.*, begun with the title *A Southern Interlude*, was first performed in 1963, and Opera South's 1974 production of *A Bayou Legend* was later presented on television (PBS) in 1981.

Most of Still's operas have North American settings. *Troubled Island*, concerning the overthrow of Dessalines, is set in Haiti, and Haitian dancers appeared in its first performance. *Highway No. 1, U. S. A.*, *A Bayou Legend*, *Blue Steel* and *Minette Fontaine* are all set in the deep South or the South-east; voodoo provides the mainspring for the plots of the last two. Both *Mota* and *The Pillar* deal with Indian subjects set in the Southwest, while *Costaso* (performed 1992) has a Spanish-American setting. *Blue Steel*, *Troubled Island*, *Costaso*, *Mota* and *The Pillar* centre on struggles for power between two main characters. A love triangle dominates the operas *A Bayou Legend*, *Highway No. 1, U. S. A.*, *Minette Fontaine*, *Troubled Island*, *Costaso* and *Mota*. All the operas reveal Still's gift for melody couched in a tonal, mildly dissonant harmonic idiom, but they avoid direct quotation of folk material.

Blue Steel, 1934 (3, B. Forsythe, after C. Moss), unperf.
Troubled Island, 1937–49 (3, L. Hughes and V. Arvey), New York, City Center Opera, 31 March 1949
A Bayou Legend, 1941 (3, Arvey), Jackson, MS, 15 Nov 1974
Highway No. 1, U. S. A., 1942–63 (2, Arvey), Coral Gables, FL, High School (U. of Miami), 11 May 1963
Costaso, 1949 (3, Arvey), Pasadena, John Muir High School, 23 May 1992
Mota, 1951 (3, Arvey), unperf.
The Pillar, 1955 (3, Arvey), unperf.
Minette Fontaine, 1958 (3, Arvey), Baton Rouge, LA, 24 Oct 1985

*

R. H. Kornick: *Recent American Opera: a Production Guide* (New York, 1991), 299–305

THOMAS WARBURTON

Stiller, Andrew [Drew] (*b* Washington DC, 6 Dec 1946). American composer and writer. He received the PhD in composition in 1976 from the State University of New York at Buffalo, where he studied with Lejaren Hiller and Morton Feldman. He plays the clarinet, bassoon and recorder in ensembles and has held faculty positions at Empire State College, Buffalo (1974–86), and SUNY, Buffalo (1979–86). He has been a critic and writer for *Musical America/Opus Magazine* and the *Philadelphia Inquirer*, and has written *Buffalo Philharmonic Orchestra: a History* (published privately, 1985) and an exhaustive *Handbook of Instrumentation* (Berkeley, 1985). His output includes a number of instrumental works. Stiller's chamber opera *Lavender* was staged by Opera Antica e Moderna, a predominantly student group, in the Baird Hall of SUNY, Buffalo on 25 and 26 May 1978. It is an almost literal transference to the stage of a brief, underground comic strip of the same name by Trina Robbins. Scored for three voices, four strings, four bassoons and harpsichord, the opera is a mythological fantasy about the sorceress Lavender and the attempt by her former husband to steal a magic book; he is foiled by the ministrations of her lady-in-waiting, amidst oaths of feminine solidarity and a wistful tear over the lost lover. A review in the *Buffalo Evening News* described the music as 'closer to declamatory than lyrical but quite attractive, its open textured scoring partly archaic and partly contemporary, with whimsical Wagnerian quotations'. HERMAN TROTTER

Stilwell, Richard (*b* St Louis, MO, 6 May 1942). American baritone. After studying with Frank St Leger and later with Daniel Ferro in New York, he began his career as a soloist with the US Army Chorus. He made his operatic début in April 1970 with the New York City Opera as Pelléas; his evenly modulated light baritone, dramatic intensity and youthful ardour made him a virtually ideal interpreter of this role, which was to bring him worldwide prominence. At the Kennedy Center, Washington, DC, in January 1974 he sang the title role in the American stage première of Monteverdi's *Il ritorno d'Ulisse in patria*, which he had sung at Glyndebourne the year before. He created roles in two operas by Pasatieri: Konstantine in *The Seagull* (1974, Houston Opera) and the leading male role in *Inez de Castro* (1976, Baltimore). Stilwell's elegantly delineated performances have also been admired at La Scala, the Metropolitan (début as Guglielmo, 1975), Chicago, San Francisco, Covent Garden and many other leading European and American houses and festivals. His roles include Don Pasquale, Billy Budd, Don Giovanni, Count Almaviva, Papageno, Yevgeny Onegin, Dandini (*La Cenerentola*), Otho (*L'incoronazione di Poppea*) and Olivier (*Capriccio*).

For illustration *see* VON STADE, FREDERICA.

MARTIN BERNHEIMER

Stockhausen, Karlheinz (*b* Burg Mödrath, nr Cologne, 22 Aug 1928). German composer. As the leading figure in the post-1945 German avant garde, closely associated with serialism, electronic music and indeterminacy, Stockhausen was converted to opera late in life, at the age of 49. Several reasons may be advanced for this: the highly abstract, constructivist style of his earlier music; an innate aversion to all traditional musical genres; and a religious-mystical preoccupation which may, as with his teacher Messiaen, have made the generally secular medium of opera unattractive. However, certain theatrical elements are evident in works from the 1960s such as *Originale* and *Momente*, and a number of 'music theatre' projects were sketched during the late 1960s (including one called simply 'Opera'), though none were actually realized. In the early 1970s came many examples of what Stockhausen calls 'scenic music' – instrumental and/or vocal works in which staging, lighting and movement are exactly specified (e.g. *Trans* for orchestra, *Sirius* for singers, instrumentalists and electronic music, and the chorus opera *Atmen gibt das Leben*).

In 1977, a few years after espousing a tightly organized yet more overtly melodic style ('formula composition'), Stockhausen suddenly decided to devote the next 25 years to the composition of a cycle of seven operas, with the collective title *Licht* ('Light'); each opera is named after a day of the week. The aspirations of these innately sacred works are basically post-Parsifalian. In addition to a latter-day leitmotif system, they extend the Wagnerian idea of the *Gesamtkunstwerk* in that the composer has sought to define and interrelate music, text, movement and staging. Up to 1990 three operas had been completed.

See also DONNERSTAG AUS LICHT; LICHT; MONTAG AUS LICHT; and SAMSTAG AUS LICHT.

Atmen gibt das Leben, 1974 [for chorus]; rev. 1977 (chorus op), Cologne, 10 Feb 1979

Donnerstag aus Licht, 1978–81 (greeting, 3, farewell, Stockhausen), Milan, Scala, 15 March 1981 (inc.); complete, 3 April 1981

Samstag aus Licht, 1981–3 (greeting, 4, Stockhausen), Milan, Palazzo dello Sport, 25 May 1984

Montag aus Licht, 1984–8 (greeting, 3, farewell, Stockhausen), Milan, Scala, 7 May 1988

*

R. Frisius: 'Komposition als Versuch der strukturellen und sematischen Synthese – Karlheinz Stockhausen und sein Werk-Projekt "Licht"', *Neuland*, ii (Bergisch-Gladbach, 1982), 160–78

J. Kohl: 'The Evolution of Macro- and Micro-time Relations in Stockhausen's Recent Music', *PNM*, xxii (1983–4), 147–85

——: 'Stockhausen at La Scala', ibid, 483–501

K. Stockhausen: 'Elektronische Musik zu "Kathinkas Gesang als Luzifers Requiem"', *Neuland*, v (Bergisch-Gladbach, 1985), 31–49

P. Britton: 'Stockhausen's Path to Opera', *MT*, cxxvi (1985), 515–21

G. Canella and L. Ferrari: 'Interview with Stockhausen', *NZM*, Jg.146, no.1 (1985), 2 [*Samstag*]

A. Clements: 'Thursday's Child', *Opera*, xxxvi (1985), 988–93

R. Frisius: 'Reihen – Schichten – Bedeutung: zu Karlheinz Stockhausens Werk-Projekt "Licht"', *Melos*, xlviii/3 (1986), 82–129

M. Tannenbaum: *Converations with Stockhausen* (Oxford, 1987)

M. Kurtz: *Stockhausen – eine Biografie* (Kassel, 1988)

H. Conen and J. Hennlich: 'Before and after *Samstag aus Licht*', *Contemporary Music Review*, v (1989), 267–97

R. Maconie and K. Stockhausen: *Stockhausen on Music* (London, 1989)

J. Kohl: 'Into the Middleground: Formula Syntax in Stockhausen's "Licht"', *PNM*, xxviii/2 (1990), 262–91

R. Maconie: *The Works of Karlheinz Stockhausen* (Oxford, 2/1990)

RICHARD TOOP

Stockholm. Capital of Sweden. It was founded in 1255 as a small island fortress between Lake Mälaren and the Baltic. Although art music in general and opera in particular were to be dominated for centuries by the music and musicians of continental Europe, a modest indigenous output of vernacular plays with incidental music was created during the 16th and 17th centuries, starting with *Tobie comedie* (probably written in 1550 by the Swedish Lutheran reformer Olaus Petri); these were performed mainly by students from the cathedral schools. The period 1611–1718 was one of cultural as well as political and economic expansion. In 1620 the Swedish *hovkapell* was enlarged and greatly improved by an ensemble of 20 German musicians. During the reign of Queen Christina (1632–54) the court ballet was highly esteemed: a French ballet-master and a troupe of six French violinists were engaged and several ballets created. In 1652 an Italian opera company under the direction of Vincenzo Albrici arrived; among the singers were some prominent castratos. It is not known, however, whether the company performed complete operas before they left Sweden on Christina's abdication in 1654. At the turn of the century a French theatre company, the Rosidor troupe, visited Stockholm (1699–1706) and gave performances at court and at the Bollhuset (the Tennis Court Theatre). Their repertory consisted mainly of French classical drama (Corneille, Racine), comedies and ballets (Lully). After Charles XII's fatal war with Russia and the departure of the Rosidor company, opera was performed only sporadically by a few visiting troupes.

Operatic activity was organized on a more regular basis by Queen Lovisa Ulrika in the middle of the 18th century. The sister of Frederick the Great, she took a lively interest in music, theatre and literature. At her initiative a French theatre company was engaged by the Swedish court in 1753. The troupe remained in Sweden for almost 20 years, during which time it presented a substantial repertory of French vaudevilles and *opéras comiques*. Meanwhile in 1755 an Italian opera company arrived. It dispersed after a few years, but its director, the composer F. A. B. Uttini, settled in Stockholm. He wrote several Italian and, later, Swedish operas for the court and in 1767 was appointed *hovkapellmästare*. It was Lovisa Ulrika who was responsible for the building of the theatres at the palaces of Ulriksdal (the Confidence, inaugurated in 1753) and DROTTNINGHOLM (1754), near Stockholm. The first theatre at Drottningholm burnt down in 1762 but was replaced by a larger building in 1766, now one of the best-preserved Baroque theatres in Europe. After the assassination of Gustavus III in 1792 the theatres at Ulriksdal and Drottningholm fell into disuse. The Drottningholm theatre was 'rediscovered' and restored in the 1920s; performances of operas and ballets, mainly from the 17th and 18th centuries, are given there every summer. The Confidence at Ulriksdal was restored and reopened in the 1980s, and also gives regular performances in the summer season.

Culturally the reign of Gustavus III (1771–92) was one of the most glorious in Swedish history. The king himself, keenly interested in theatre and opera and a talented playwright, aimed to create a national culture. He founded the Royal Swedish Academy of Music in 1771 and the Royal Swedish Opera in 1773, the first company in northern Europe to give regular performances in the vernacular, not merely of Singspiels and vaudevilles but also of great heroic operas. The first opera in Swedish, Uttini's *Thetis och Pelée*, was performed in 1773. In the following years a broad repertory of French and Italian works in Swedish translation was presented. Most important were the productions of Gluck's reform operas, which became the stylistic ideal for the new, Gustavian works. The king himself wrote the plots for several operas on national topics, though for the music he was dependent on foreign, mainly German, composers. The most spectacular were *Gustaf Wasa* (1786), with music by J. G. Naumann, and *Gustav Adolph och Ebba Brahe* (1788) by G. J. Vogler, both with sets by Desprez. Gustavian classicism culminated in the opera *Aeneas i Cartago* (1799) by J. M. Kraus.

In 1782 an opera house in central Stockholm (designed by Adelcrantz) opened with a performance of *Cora och Alonzo* by Naumann. The building was also used for concerts and masked balls, the most famous of which was the one in March 1792, when Gustavus III was shot (the subject of operas by Auber, Verdi and Werle). From the late 18th century several private companies appeared in smaller theatres, notably the Nya Svenska Teatern (New Swedish Theatre), directed by Carl Stenborg (1784–1801), with a large repertory of *opéras comiques* and Swedish Singspiels, and the Mindre Teatern (Little Theatre; 1846–63), directed by Edvard Stjernström with August Söderman as chief conductor and composer of music for national Singspiels. After a period of decline the Royal Opera was revived from about 1810 under the direction of skilful *kapellmästare* such as Edouard Du Puy, J. F. Berwald, Jacopo Foroni and Ludwig Norman. More operas in Swedish, mainly based on Swedish subjects, were written by native composers, and a national musical style based on folk music began to develop. Light Singspiels on rural topics with inserted folktune arrangements became very popular, such as *En majdag i Värend* ('A May Day in Värend', 1843) with music arranged by J. F. Berwald and, most successful of all, *Värmlänningarna* ('The Värmländers', 1846), with music by Andreas Randel. In 1835 Jenny Lind made her début in A. F. Lindblad's opera *Frondörerna* ('The Fronde Rebels'); she created many leading parts at the Stockholm opera before leaving the country in 1844. The first stage performance of an opera by Franz Berwald, *Estrella de Soria*, took place in 1862. Later several operas based on Nordic history and mythology were created, among them *Den bergtagna* ('The Bride of the Mountain King', 1874) and *Vikingarna* ('The Vikings', 1877) by Ivar Hallström, *Harald Viking* (1881) by Andreas Hallén and *Arnljot* (1910) by Wilhelm Peterson-Berger.

In 1891 the old Gustavian opera house was demolished, to be replaced in 1898 by a new building designed by Axel Anderberg. Here Jussi Björling, Set Svanholm, Birgit Nilsson, Nicolai Gedda, Elisabeth Söderström and other famous singers made their first appearances. The postwar period, under the direction of Svanholm, Gentele and others, has been a progressive one, with productions of *Wozzeck* (1957), *The Rake's Progress* (1961, directed by Ingmar Bergman) and the world première of Ligeti's *Le Grand Macabre* (1978). In addition, many Swedish operas have been given, including *Marionetter* by Hilding Rosenberg (1939, one of the few Swedish comic operas), *Tranfjädrarna* ('The Crane Feathers') by S.-E. Bäck (1958), *Aniara* by K.-B. Blomdahl (1959), *Drömmen om Thérèse* ('Dream about Thérèse') by L. J. Werle (1964) and *Bachanterna* ('The Bacchants') by Daniel Börtz (1991). A private theatre, the Oscarsteatern (opened 1906), has specialized in operetta and musical comedy, while several new companies, such as Folkoperan (1976) and the Stockholms Musikdramatiska Ensemble (1978), have been established in the city and its suburbs. Higher operatic training is given at the Operahögskolan (formerly Statens Musikdramatiska Skola, founded in 1968) and at the Musikhögskolan (formerly the conservatory of the Royal Swedish Academy of Music).

*

F. Dahlgren: *Anteckningar om Stockholm's teatrar* [Notes on Stockholm's Theatres] (Stockholm, 1866)
R. Engländer: *Johann Gottlieb Naumann als Opernkomponist (1741–1801), mit neuen Beiträgen zur Musikgeschichte Dresdens und Stockholms* (Leipzig, 1922)
M. Tegen: *Musiklivet i Stockholm 1890–1910* (Stockholm, 1955)
R. Engländer: 'Die Gustavianische Oper', *AMw*, xvi (1959), 314–27
K. Ralf, ed.: *Operan 200 år: jubelboken* (Stockholm, 1973)
——, ed.: *Kungliga Teatern i Stockholm, repertoar 1773–1973* (Stockholm, 1974)
L. Roth, ed.: *Musical Life in Sweden* (Stockholm, 1987)
A. Johnson: 'Stockholm in the Gustavian Era', *The Classical Era*, ed. N. Zaslaw (London, 1989), 327–49
I. Mattsson, ed.: *Gustavian Opera: an Interdisciplinary Reader in Swedish Opera, Dance and Theatre 1771–1809* (Stockholm, 1991)

ANNA JOHNSON

Stöckl-Heinefetter, Clara. German soprano, sister of SABINE HEINEFETTER.

Stockman, David (*b* Göteborg, 30 Nov 1879; *d* Stockholm, 2 Dec 1951). Swedish tenor. He studied in Breslau, making his début in 1906 as Wilhelm Meister (*Mignon*) at the Royal Opera, Stockholm, where he was engaged until 1942. He was the first Swedish Chénier, Mârouf, Hermann (*The Queen of Spades*) and Gennaro (*I gioielli della Madonna*); he also sang Romeo, Raoul (*Les Huguenots*) and Hoffmann as well as Lohengrin,

Tristan and Parsifal. A very stylish singer, he had a smooth, well-managed voice. ELIZABETH FORBES

Stojanović, Petar (*b* Budapest, 7 Sept 1877; *d* Belgrade, 11 Sept 1957). Serbian composer. He studied in Budapest (with Jenő Hubay) and Vienna. A professional violinist, he inclined towards instrumental composition, but also wrote operas, operettas and ballets. His comic opera *Der Tiger* (to a German libretto) is a joyful and serene work, which shows an awareness of the problems of dramatic composition; specific motifs are used to represent the individual characters. The music drama *Blaženkina zakletva* ('Blaženka's Oath'), which concerns the tragic events on the Croatian coast in the 15th century, is in Wagnerian style, with emotional arioso vocal parts, rich harmony and sonorous orchestral writing; the orchestral texture carries leitmotifs referring to love, hate, youth and death. Events follow quickly one after another and the main characters are faithfully portrayed, especially those in love with Blaženka.

Der Tiger (musikalisches Lustspiel, 1, R. von Perger, after B. Michel and M. Michel), Budapest, 14 Nov 1905
Liebchen am Dach (operetta, V. Léon), Vienna, 1917
Der Herzog von Reichstadt (operetta, Léon and H. Reichert), 1921
Blaženkina zakletva [Blaženka's Oath], 1934 (music drama, 3, M. Jelušić), unperf.

*

V. Peričić: *Muzički stvaraoci u Srbiji* [Musical Creators in Serbia] (Belgrade, 1969) ROKSANDA PEJOVIĆ

Stoker, Richard (*b* Castleford, Yorks., 8 Nov 1938). English composer. He studied composition with Winifred Smith and Harold Truscott at the Huddersfield Music School, with Lennox Berkeley at the RAM and, as a Mendelssohn scholar, with Boulanger in Paris. He was professor of composition at the RAM, 1963–87, and edited *Composer*, 1969–80. Stoker's music, though it often has serial leanings, is freely organized and, without overt dissonance, is quite easily accessible to the listener. He published his autobiography, *Open Window – Open Door*, in 1985.

The Birthday of the Infanta op.19 (children's op, 1, S. Vincent, after O. Wilde), London, St Pancras Town Hall, 12 July 1963
Johnson Preserv'd op.30 (3, J. Watt), London, St Pancras Town Hall, 4 July 1967
Make Me a Willow Cabin op.44 (operatic scena, Stoker, after W. Shakespeare), London, Purcell Room, 14 Feb 1973
Thérèse Raquin op.50, 1975 (2, T. Hawkes, after E. Zola)
Chinese Canticle op.68 (3 scenes, Stoker, after S. Chien: *Records of the Historian*), London, Purcell Room, 24 Oct 1991

*

E. Brophy: 'Richard Stoker's Dr Johnson Opera', *Opera*, xviii (1967), 543–6
C. Norris: 'Richard Stoker', *Music and Musicians*, xxiii/6 (1974–5), 16–22 RICHARD TOWNEND

Stokes, Eric (Norman) (*b* Haddon Heights, NJ, 14 July 1930). American composer. He studied music at Lawrence College, the New England Conservatory, and the University of Minnesota (PhD 1964), where his teachers included Dominick Argento and Paul Fetler. Between 1961 and 1988 he taught at the University of Minnesota, where he founded the university's electronic music programme (1970) and the new music ensemble programme, including the performing group the First Minnesota Moving & Storage Warehouse Band (1971). Stokes's music exhibits a variety of styles including an early tonal period (1955–62), the use of collage, theatre and mixed-media elements in conjunction with the spatial deployment of forces (from 1963) and the incorporation of found sounds (from 1980). His interest in American subjects is a vital element in his work and dates from the early 1960s.

Stokes has written seven operas. *Horspfal* (1969), commissioned by the Center Opera Company (now the Minnesota Opera Company), is a satirical and panoramic vision of American history, focussing on the tragic impact on the American Indian and the devastating effect on the land of many forms of white exploitation from the revolutionary era to the present. It is a collage work combining vocal and instrumental forces with film; the orchestra of 17 instruments requires up to five conductors. *HAPP, or Orpheus in Clover* (1977) is a micro-opera in one scene, with lyrics slowly spelling out 'Happy Birthday'. *The Jealous Cellist and Other Acts of Misconduct* (1979) was written with the aid of grants from the NEA and the Jerome Foundation. It is a comic love story, told in the form of a science fiction parable, about two groups of people who are abruptly switched in place and time. *Itaru the Stonecutter* (1982), written for children, is based on a classic Japanese folktale. *Apollonia's Circus* (1985) places the Orpheus myth in a contemporary circus setting. *We're Not Robots, you Know* (1986), written for stage or television, revolves around a suburban family of marionettes who acquire two all-purpose robots programmed to perform various household tasks. It received its television première at the Minneapolis Institute of Art in autumn 1986. In *The Further Voyages of the Santa Maria* (1990), the ghost of Columbus accompanies astronauts on future voyages of space ships sailing under the name of Santa Maria.

all published in Minneapolis

Horspfal (2, A. Greenberg), Minneapolis, Guthrie, 15 Feb 1969 (1969)
HAPP, or Orpheus in Clover (micro-opera, 1, Stokes), Minneapolis, 11 Oct 1977 (1977)
The Jealous Cellist and Other Acts of Misconduct (2, Greenberg), Minneapolis, 2 Feb 1979 (1979)
Itaru the Stonecutter (op for children, 1, Stokes, after Jap. folktale), Roseville, MN, Brimhall School, 25 March 1982 (1982)
Apollonia's Circus, 1985 (3, Greenberg) (1985)
We're Not Robots, you Know (puppet op for stage/TV, 1, K. Gunderson), broadcast, Synergenesis Corporation, aut. 1986; stage, Chicago, 15 May 1988 (1986)
The Further Voyages of the Santa Maria, 1990 (3, Greenberg) (1990)

*

A. Holbert: 'Horspfal: Fable without Moral', *Minneapolis Tribune* (9 Feb 1969)
H. Schonberg: 'Minneapolis Opera Makes an Original Try', *New York Times* (17 Feb 1969)
T. Willis: 'Most American Opera Yet', *Chicago Tribune* (18 Feb 1969)
'Hell's Bells', *Newsweek* (10 May 1976)
M. Anthony: 'Sound for the Joy of Sound', *Minneapolis Tribune* (28 Jan 1979)
M. Lynch: 'We're Not Robots, you Know', *Opera for Youth News*, xii/1 (1989), 4–5 WILLIAM DUCKWORTH

Stolle, Philipp (*b* Radeburg, Saxony, 1614; *d* Halle, 4 Oct 1675). German composer. In the 1630s he served at the Dresden court as a singer and string player. In 1650 he moved to the court chapel in Halle, where four years later he became director. Duke August had made Halle a centre of opera, to which Stolle was immediately drawn. He wrote a number of operas, all but one now apparently lost; in 1660 he gave up his position as Kapellmeister to devote himself entirely to opera but remained, next to the new director David Pohle, the highest-paid musician at court.

Stolle's importance lies in his contributions to early German Singspiel and in his songs. The one surviving Singspiel definitely attributable to him is the five-act *Charimunda oder Beneideter Liebes-Sieg*, which is in the German pastoral tradition with a large cast; in the preface to the published libretto (Halle, 1658) Stolle refers to a recent performance. There is one solo song accompanied by lute in Act 1, and each of the first four acts ends with a chorus. These five numbers survive at the end of the printed text, scored for soprano and figured bass. They are simple, syllabic, strophic songs requiring only modestly gifted singers. Their charm lies in the unusual variety of harmony, which in Charimunda's aria in Act 1 even includes an augmented 6th chord. The anonymous Singspiel *Die Hochzeit der Thetis*, which opened the court opera in Halle in 1654, and other anonymous operas produced in Halle to 1680 have been attributed to Stolle because of their similarity to *Charimunda* and because he was the leading composer there at that time. JOHN H. BARON

Stoll Theatre. London theatre built in 1911 and known as the London Opera House until 1916; *see* LONDON, §II, 2.

Stoltz, Rosine [Noël, Victoire] (*b* Paris, 13 Feb 1815; *d* Paris, 28 July 1903). French mezzo-soprano. She made her début in 1832 at the Théâtre de la Monnaie, Brussels, singing small parts and in the chorus. She then sang at Spa, Antwerp, Amsterdam and Lille, before returning to Brussels, where she sang Alice in *Robert le diable* (1835) and Rachel in *La Juive* (1836). She made her Paris Opéra début in 1837 as Rachel. During the ten years that she was engaged at the Opéra she sang in the first performances of Halévy's *Guido et Ginevra* (1838), *La reine de Chypre* (1841), *Charles VI* (1843) and *Le lazzarone* (1844). She created Ascanio in Berlioz's *Benvenuto Cellini* (1838), Marguerite in Auber's *Le lac des fées* (1839), Léonor in *La favorite* (1840) and Zayda in *Dom Sébastien* (1843). Her other roles included Donna Anna, Valentine (*Les Huguenots*), Desdemona (Rossini's *Otello*) and Isolier (*Le comte Ory*). In 1847 she was forced to resign and did not return to the Opéra until 1854. She made her last appearance at Lyons in 1860. Despite a flamboyant private life, Stoltz was a serious and genuinely talented interpretative artist, with a fine voice and a magnificent stage presence.

For illustration *see* FAVORITE, LA.

*

H. Berlioz: *Mémoires* (Paris, 1870; Eng. trans., 1969)
G. Bord: *Rosina Stoltz de l'Académie royale de musique* (Paris, 1909)
J.-G. Prod'homme: *L'Opéra (1669–1925)* (Paris, 1925)
H. Weinstock: *Donizetti and the World of Opera in Italy, Paris and Vienna in the First Half of the 19th Century* (New York, 1963)
ELIZABETH FORBES

Stolz, Robert (Elisabeth) (*b* Graz, 25 Aug 1880; *d* Berlin, 27 June 1975). Austrian composer and conductor. He received his initial musical training from his parents, Jacob Stolz, a conductor and music teacher, and Ida Bondy, a concert pianist. Later he studied under Robert Fuchs at the Vienna Conservatory and with Humperdinck in Berlin. Between 1897 and 1907 he worked as a répétiteur and conductor in Graz, Marburg an der Drau, Salzburg and Brno, marrying the soprano Grete Holm in 1904. In 1907 he took over as conductor of *Die lustige Witwe* from about its 420th performance at the Theater an der Wien and conducted various other major Viennese operettas in their initial runs. His music for a Singspiel, *Studentenulke*, was followed by various operettas, but his first major success as composer was achieved by a popular song, *Servus Du* (1911). This was followed by several other successful Viennese songs before he gained international popularity with the song 'Hallo, du süsse Klingelfee' (1919) and with the operetta *Der Tanz ins Glück* (1921), produced in England as *Whirled into Happiness* and in the USA as *Sky High*. In 1924 Stolz took a job in cabaret in Berlin, and his period of greatest success began with songs for early German film musicals and with the operetta *Wenn die kleinen Veilchen blühen* (1932). In 1940 he went to the USA, where he composed music for Hollywood films and conducted concerts of Viennese music. He returned to Vienna in 1946, becoming celebrated as the last major survivor of Viennese operetta from before World War I. He conducted recordings of classical operettas for Ariola-Eurodisc in the 1960s, which remain important documents, and was also commissioned to provide new operettas, though these often turned out to be revisions of earlier works. Besides his stage works he composed several hundred individual songs and dances, and received honours and decorations from many countries.

selective list

Studentenulke op.15 (Spl, F. Haller), Marburg, Stadt, 21 March 1901
Schön Lorchen op.17 (Operette, A. Moisson), Salzburg, Stadt, 3 March 1903
Manöverliebe op.26a (Operette, K. Waldeck and G. Bondi), Brno, Stadt, 15 April 1906
Die lustigen Weiber von Wien op.59 (Operette, 1, J. Brammer and A. Grünwald), Vienna, Colosseum, 6 Nov 1908
Die Commandeuse (Operette, 1), Vienna, Colosseum, 1 Sept 1909
Der grosse Name op.67 (Schauspiel mit Musik, V. Léon and L. Feld), Berlin, Deutsches Volks, 2 Oct 1909
Das Glücksmädel op.72 (Operette, 3, R. Bodanzky and F. R. Thelen), Vienna, Raimund, 28 Oct 1910
Der Minenkönig (Operette, 1, E. Marischka and G. Beer), Vienna, Apollo, 1 Nov 1911
Die eiserne Jungfrau op.90 (Operette, 3, Léon), Vienna, Raimund, 11 Nov 1911
Du liebes Wien op.143 (Operette, O. Hein and K. Robitschek), Vienna, Intimes, 24 Jan 1913
Das Lumperl op.219 (Operette, Léon), Stuttgart, Hof, 31 July 1915
Die Varietédiva (Spl, 1, Robitschek and Hein), Vienna, Ronacher, 1 Dec 1915
Die schöne Katharin (Operette, 1, L. Hirschfeld and Hein), Vienna, Ronacher, 11 Jan 1916
Der Favorit op.221 (Operette, 2, F. Grünbaum and W. Sterk), Berlin, Komische Oper, 7 April 1916
Mädel, küsse mich op.245 (Revue-Operette, 5, B. Hardt-Warden and E. Schwarz), Vienna, Lustspiel, 29 April 1916
Das Mäderlhaus (Operette, 3, W. Sterk), Vienna, Kabarett Fledermaus, 26 Aug 1916
Die Bauernprinzessin op.260 (Spl, A. Aldermann and F. Lunzer), Munich, Volks, 1916
Die anständige Frau (Spl, 1, Hein), Vienna, Budapester Orpheum, 19 Jan 1917
Eine einzige Nacht op.274 (Spl, Hein and B. Wengraf), Vienna, Budapester Orpheum, 15 March 1917; rev., op.501 (R. Oesterreicher and L. Jacobson), Vienna, Carl, 23 Dec 1927
Lang, lang ist's her op.275 (Operette, 2, Hardt-Warden), Vienna, Lustspiel, 28 March 1917
Die Familie Rosenstein (Spl, 1, Hein and Wengraf), Vienna, Budapester Orpheum, 12 Oct 1917
Die Hose des Tenors (Spl, 1, W. Berg and Hein), Vienna, Budapester Orpheum, 1 Jan 1918
Muschi (Spl, 1, F. Löhner-Beda), Vienna, Gartenbau, 1 Jan 1918
Brautersatz (Operette, 1, Gutbach), Vienna, Gartenbau, 1 March 1918
Bloch und Co (Spl, 1, Wengraf and L. Stein), Vienna, Budapester Orpheum, 5 April 1918

Leute von heute (Operette, Lunzer and Rebner), Vienna, Bundes, 22 June 1918, collab. E. Eysler and A. M. Werau
Das Busserlschloss op.307 (Operette, Grünbaum), Vienna, Ronacher, 1 Aug 1918
Muzikam (Operette, 1, Hein and Wengraf), Vienna, Budapester Orpheum, 2 Sept 1918
Dagobert, wo warst du? (Operette, 1), Vienna, Budapester Orpheum, 8 Aug 1919
Funserls Entdeckung (Spl, 1), Vienna, Budapester Orpheum, 1 Nov 1919
Ein toller Tag (Operette, 1), Vienna, Budapester Orpheum, 1 Jan 1920
Die Rosen der Madonna (op, 1, Hardt-Warden and O. Tumlirz), Vienna, 1 March 1920
Das Sperrsechserl [Wiener Gemütlichkeit] op.360 (Operette, 2, R. Blum and Grünwald), Vienna, Komödienhaus, 1 April 1920
Das Haus des Schreckens (Operette, 1, Hein and Wengraf), Vienna, Künstlerspiele Pan, 1 May 1920
Der Tanz ins Glück op.372 (Operette, 3, Bodanzky and Hardt-Warden), Vienna, Raimund, 28 Oct 1920; rev. as Hallo, das ist die Liebe, op.1310, Vienna, Raimund, 1958
Kirikiri (Operette, 1), Vienna, Budapester Orpheum, 1 Jan 1921
Die Tanzgräfin op.375 (Operette, 3, Bodanzky and L. Jacobson), Berlin, Wallner, 1921
Eine fesche Landpartie (Operette, 1), Vienna, Budapester Orpheum, 1 March 1921
Eine Sommernacht op.400 (Operette, 3, Bodanzky and Hardt-Warden), Vienna, Johan Strauss, 23 Dec 1921
Die Liebe geht um op.425 (Operette, 3, Hardt-Warden), Vienna, Raimund, 22 June 1922
Mädi op.450 (Operette, 3, Grünwald and Stein), Berlin, Berliner, 2 April 1923
Der Hampelmann op.451 (Vaudeville-Operette, Beer and Lunzer), Vienna, Komödienhaus, 9 Nov 1923
Ein Ballroman [Der Kavalier von zehn bis vier] op.452 (Operette, 3, Oesterreicher, A. M. Willner and F. Rotter), Vienna, Apollo, 29 Feb 1924
Ein Rivieratraum [Das Fräulein aus 1001 Nacht] op.453 (Vaudeville-Operette, Hardt-Warden, K. Farkas and Rotter), Vienna, Robert-Stolz-Bühne, 8 Oct 1924
Due Baci (Operette, G. Forzano and R. Simoni), Milan, 1925
Märchen im Schnee op.467 (Operette, 1, Robitschek and P. Morgan), Berlin, Kabarett der Komiker, 1 Dec 1925
Der Mitternachtswalzer op.470 (Operette, Willner and Oesterreicher), Vienna, Bürger, 28 Oct 1926
Prinzessin Ti-Ti-Pa op.480 (Operette, 3, Beer and Lunzer), Vienna, Carl, 15 May 1928
Gloria und der Clown op.520 (Operette, J. Horst and R. Gilbert), 1929
Peppina op.530 (Operette, Oesterreicher), Berlin, Komische Oper, 22 Dec 1930
Wenn die kleinen Veilchen blühen op.590 (Operette, 2, Hardt-Warden, after A. Kehm and M. Frehsee: *Als ich noch im Flügelkleide*), The Hague, Princess, 1 April 1932
Venus in Seide op.600 (Operette, 3, Grünwald and L. Herzer), Zürich, Stadt, 10 Dec 1932
Der verlorene Walzer [Zwei Herzen im Dreivierteltakt] (Operette, 3, P. Knepler, J. M. Welleminsky and Gilbert, after W. Reisch and F. Schulz), Zürich, Stadt, 30 Sept 1933
Grüezi! [Himmelblaue Träume/Servus! Servus!] op.633 (Operette, G. Burckhard and Gilbert), Zürich, Stadt, 3 Nov 1934; rev. as Hochzeit am Bodensee (Gilbert, Burckhard and H. Wiener), Bregenz, Lake Stage, 22 July 1969
Ein Mädel hat sich verlaufen op.638 (musikalisches Lustspiel, Hardt-Warden and Gilbert), Berlin, Berliner, 1934
Zum goldenen Halbmond [Zum goldenen Kipferl] op.646 (Operette, F. Koselka), Osnabrück, Deutsches National, 1935; rev. as Wiener Café (Gilbert, Koselka and W. Göttig), Graz, Opera House, 1965
Rise and Shine (musical play, H. Graham and D. Carter, after F. Arnold and Bertram [Gilbert]), London, Drury Lane, 7 May 1936
Der süsseste Schwindel der Welt op.696 (musikalisches Lustspiel, 3, R. Weys and Gilbert), Vienna, Scala, 21 Dec 1937
Die Reise um die Erde in 80 Minuten op.699 (Revue-Operette, H. Gilbert, R. Gilbert and Wiener), Vienna, Volksoper, 22 Dec 1937
La Montagne Bleu (A. Willemetz), Paris, Chatelet, 1 Sept 1939
Night of Love (musical, R. Leigh, after *Tonight or Never*), New York, Hudson, 7 Jan 1941
Mr Strauss Goes to Boston op.750 (musical, Grünwald, F. Brentano, L. L. Levinson and R. Sour), Boston, Shubert, 13 Aug 1945
Schicksal mit Musik op.790 (musical, Farkas), Vienna, Apollo, 24 Nov 1946
Drei von der Donau op.820 (musical, Oesterreicher and R. Gilbert, after J. N. Nestroy: *Lumpazivagabundus*), Vienna, Stadt, 24 Sept 1947
Fest in Casablanca op.855 (Operette, G. Schwenn and W. Frank), Nuremburg, Opera House, 19 March 1948
Ein Lied aus der Vorstadt (musikalisches Lustspiel, D. M. Brandt and G. Fraser), Vienna, Deutsches Volks, 19 April 1948
Frühling im Prater op.850 (Operette, 2, Marischka), Vienna, Stadt, 22 Dec 1949
Das Glücksrezept op.890 (musikalisches Lustspiel, R. Martiné and Wiener), Vienna, Bürger, 1 May 1951
Rainbow Square op.901 (musical, G. Bolton and H. Purcell), London, Stoll, 21 Sept 1951
Ballade vom lieben Augustin op.916 (Spl, U. Becher and P. Preses), Vienna, Arkadenhof, 1 June 1953
Signorina op.967 (musical, P. Schwenzen and R. Gilbert), Nuremberg, Opera House, 26 April 1955; rev. as Trauminsel [Weit her von Yucatan], Bregenz, Lake Stage, 21 July 1962
Behalt mich lieb, Chérie op.970 (Funkoperette, A. Morenau), Vienna, Rundfunk, Oct 1955
Kleiner Schwindel in Paris op.977 (musical, Weys and R. Gilbert), Vienna, Josefstadt, 31 Dec 1956
Kitty und die Weltkonferenz op.1312 (musical, K. Nachmann and Preses), Vienna, Josefstadt, 4 Feb 1959; rev. as Die kleine und die grosse Welt (G. Neumann), Berlin, 1963
Joie de Vivre (musical play, T. Rattigan and P. Dehn, after Rattigan: *French Without Tears*), Oxford, New, 3 May 1960
Ein schöner Herbst (musikalisches Lustspiel, H. Weigel, after B. Schuppler: *Junger Herr von vierzig Jahren*), Vienna, Josefstadt, 5 June 1963
Frühjahrsparade (Operette, 2, Wiener, after Marischka), Vienna, Volksoper, 25 March 1964 [based on film music]

*

G. Holm: *Im Dreivierteltakt durch die Welt* (Linz, 1948)
W.-D. Brümmel and F. van Booth: *Robert Stolz: Melodie eines Lebens* (Stuttgart, 1967)
O. Herbrich: *Robert Stolz: König der Melodie* (Vienna and Munich, 1975)
R. Stolz and E. Stolz: *Servus Du: Robert Stolz und sein Jahrhundert* (Munich, 1980)

ANDREW LAMB

Stolz [Stolzová], **Teresa** [Teresina, Terezie] (*b* Elbekosteletz [now Kostelec nad Labem], 2 or 5 June 1834; *d* Milan, 23 Aug 1902). Bohemian soprano. She was trained at the Prague Conservatory; in 1856, in Trieste, she had lessons from the composer Luigi Ricci and in 1857 made her operatic début in Tbilisi. For some five years she sang in Odessa, Constantinople, and often Tbilisi. Her earliest Italian appearances to have been traced were in Turin, autumn 1863. Her successes in Nice (*Il trovatore*, December 1863) and Granada (*Ernani*, April 1864) led to a *Trovatore* in Spoleto (September 1864), and then *Ernani* and *Guillaume Tell* in Bologna. In 1867 she was chosen for the Italian première of *Don Carlos*, in Bologna, and two years later for the revised *La forza del destino*, at La Scala, where, in 1872, she was the first Italian Aida. In 1874 she sang in the first performances of Verdi's *Requiem*. Verdi's operas had from the start been prominent in her repertory and, both in Italy and abroad, she became a leading and frequent interpreter of his later heroines, from Amelia in *Un ballo in maschera* to Aida. After 1872, her only non-Verdian roles were Alice in *Robert le diable* and Rachel in *La Juive*. Her last operatic engagement was in St Petersburg (1876–7). Stolz was the Verdian dramatic soprano par excellence, powerful, passionate in utterance but dignified and disciplined in manner, with a voice that extended securely from *g* to *c*♯‴.

*

G. Cenzato: 'Verdi e la Stolz', *Corriere della sera* (30 Oct 1932); repr. in *Itinerari verdiani* (Parma, 1949), 148–61; (Milan, 2/1955), 127–36

A. Luzio, ed.: 'Il carteggio di Verdi con la Stolz e la Waldmann', *Carteggi verdiani*, ii (Rome, 1935), 222–91; other Stolz letters, *Carteggi verdiani*, iv (Rome, 1947), 189–97
F. Walker: *The Man Verdi* (London, 1962), 283–446

ANDREW PORTER

Stolze, Gerhard (*b* Dessau, 1 Oct 1926; *d* Garmisch-Partenkirchen, 11 March 1979). German tenor. He studied in Dresden and Berlin, then in 1949 was engaged by the Dresden Staatsoper, where he made his début as Augustin Moser (*Die Meistersinger*). From 1953 to 1961 he was a member of the Berlin Staatsoper. At Bayreuth he took minor roles in 1951, then in 1956 sang David and in 1957 Mime, a role he continued to sing there until 1969 and in which he made his Covent Garden début in 1960. He created roles in Egk's *Der Revisor* (1957, Schwetzingen), Erbse's *Julietta* (1959, Salzburg), Orff's *Oedipus der Tyrann* (1959, Stuttgart), the stage première of Martin's *Le mystère de la Nativité* (1960, Salzburg) and Klebe's *Jacobowsky und der Oberst* (1965, Hamburg). In 1968 he sang Loge at the Metropolitan. His musical intelligence and dramatic gifts specially suited him to such character roles as Herod, the Captain in *Wozzeck*, and Oberon in Britten's *A Midsummer Night's Dream*. HAROLD ROSENTHAL/R

Stölzel [Stöltzel, Stölzl], **Gottfried Heinrich** (*b* Grünstädtel, nr Schwarzenberg, Erzgebirge, 13 Jan 1690; *d* Gotha, 27 Nov 1749). German composer. In 1707 he went to Leipzig University, but felt himself drawn more towards the opera, recently reopened there, and to the collegium musicum (founded by Telemann and at that time directed by Melchior Hofmann). He proved to be a helpful copyist to Hofmann, who soon recognized his gifts as a composer. Stölzel's first works were performed under his teacher's name (Emanuel Kegel); they appeared only later under his own. In 1710 he went to Breslau, where he taught singing and keyboard in aristocratic circles. He also composed for the collegium musicum and produced his first dramatic work, *Narcissus*. He went next to Halle, wrote a pastorale for the court at Gera, and received a commission from the Zeitz court for which he composed three operas for the fair at Naumburg. Afterwards he received from both Gera and Zeitz offers of the post of court Kapellmeister, which he refused.

At the end of 1713 Stölzel went to Italy, meeting Gasparini, Alessandro Marcello, C. F. Pollarolo and Vivaldi in Venice, and Antonio Bononcini and Domenico Scarlatti in Rome. In 1715 he went to Prague, where he remained for three years; he took a lively part in the musical activities there, and composed dramatic works, oratorios, masses and instrumental music.

By the beginning of 1718 Stölzel was Kapellmeister at the court at Gera, and on 24 February 1720 he was appointed to the same post at the court at Saxe-Gotha. For 30 years he held this appointment, which obliged him to compose for the church, the opera and other court festivities. He also executed commissions for the courts at Sondershausen and Gera. About this time he allowed some of his works to be copied, notably church cantatas, and his reputation grew. From the evidence of various applications to his patrons, it seems that Stölzel wrote the texts of his own vocal works. He acquired authority as a teacher and theorist, and in 1739 was elected a member of Lorenz Christoph Mizler's Societät der Musikalischen Wissenschaften.

The extent of Stölzel's reputation is reflected in the fact that Mizler placed him above J. S. Bach in his list of leading German composers. Bach himself valued Stölzel's music, but it was increasingly forgotten during the later 18th century and an extensive collection of his MSS in Gotha was lost during the time of his successor, Georg Benda.

Stölzel's *Abhandlung vom Recitativ* (MS, *A-Wgm*, ed. in Steger), the first major specialized treatise on recitative, reflects his unrivalled superiority in this field, and was acknowledged by his contemporaries. Stölzel had a special preference for recitative with a number of voices which both alternated and combined. The traditional da capo aria, which he favoured, serves to provide development, imagery and contrast. Because Stölzel was so prolific over a short period there are inevitably superficialities in his work; but his best music shows skill in composition and richness of idea.

unattributed librettos may be by Stölzel

Narcissus (musikalisches Dramat or Drama, Stölzel), Breslau, 1711 or 1712; ?rev. version, Gotha, 1734–5
Valeria (Stölzel), Naumburg, 1712
Rosen und Dornen der Liebe (Pastorale), Gera, 1713
Artemisia (opera or Spl, Stölzel), Naumburg, 1713
Orion (Stölzel), Naumburg, 1713
Venus and Adonis [Adonis] (musikalisches Dramat, Stölzel), Prague, 1715–17; rev. version, Altenburg, 1728–30
Acis und Galathea [Die triumphirende Liebe] (musikalisches Dramat, Stölzel), Prague, 1715–17, lib. *D-Bds*; ?rev. version, Gotha, 1729
Das durch Liebe besiegte Glück (Stölzel), Prague, 1715–17
Diomedes, Bayreuth, 1718
Der Musenberg (Drama, Stölzel), Gotha, 1723
Die beglückte Tugend (Pastorale), Gotha, 1723
Hercules Prodicius, oder Die triumphirende Tugend (Dramat, Stölzel), Gotha, 1725, lib. *Bds*, *ALa*
Die Ernde der Freuden [Die Freuden-Ernde] (Pastorale), Gotha, 1727, lib. *Ju*; ?rev. version, Altenburg, 1727
Thersander und Demonassa, oder Die glückliche Liebe (Pastorale), Gotha, 1733
L'amore vince l'inganno (drama pastorale), Gotha, 1736, lib. *US-Wc*
Endymion (musikalisches Schäfer-Spiel), Gotha, 1740, lib. *D-Gs*
Die gekrönte Weisheit (Singe-Spiel), Gotha, 1742
Die mit Leben und Vergnügen belohnte Tugend (musikalisches Singe-Spiel), Gotha, 1744, lib. *HAu*

*

J. Mattheson: *Grundlage einer Ehren-Pforte* (Hamburg, 1740); ed. M. Schneider (Berlin, 1910)
L. C. Mizler: *Neu eröffnete Musikalische Bibliothek*, iv (Leipzig, 1754)
F. W. Marpurg: *Historisch-kritische Beyträge zur Aufnahme der Musik*, i (Berlin, 1754–5)
J. A. Hiller: *Lebensbeschreibungen berühmter Musikgelehrten und Tonkünstler*, i (Leipzig, 1784)
G. Lutze: *Aus Sondershausens Vergangenheit*, ii (Sondershausen, 1909)
E. W. Böhme: 'Gottfried Heinrich Stölzel in Gera', *ZMw*, xiii (1930–31), 333–4
——: *Die frühdeutsche Oper in Thüringen* (Eisenberg and Stadtroda, 1931)
A. Fett: *Musikgeschichte der Stadt Gotha* (diss., U. of Freiburg, 1952)
F. H. Neumann: *Die Theorie des Rezitativs im 17. und 18. Jahrhundert* (diss., U. of Göttingen, 1955)
W. Steger: *Gottfried Heinrich Stölzels 'Abhandlung vom Recitativ'* (diss., U. of Heidelberg, 1962)

FRITZ HENNENBERG

Stolzing, W. di. *See* MONLEONE, DOMENICO.

Stone Guest, The [*Kamenniy gost'*]. Opera in three acts by ALEXANDER SERGEYEVICH DARGOMÏZHSKY set directly to the verse tragedy of ALEXANDER SERGEYEVICH PUSHKIN; St Petersburg, Mariinsky Theatre, 16/28

February 1872 (revised version, Moscow, Bol'shoy Theatre, 19 December 1906/1 January 1907).

Don Juan	tenor
Leporello *his servant*	bass
Donna Anna	soprano
Don Carlos	baritone
Laura	mezzo-soprano
A Monk	bass
First Guest	tenor
Second Guest	bass
Statue of the Commander	bass

Setting Spain; time unspecified

The opera, unfinished at the time of Dargomïzhsky's death in 1869, was completed by César Cui and orchestrated by Nikolay Rimsky-Korsakov; the première was conducted by Eduard Nápravník, with Fyodor Komissarzhevsky as Don Juan, Osip Petrov as Leporello, Julia Platonova as Donna Anna and Ivan Mel'nikov as Don Carlos. Rimsky-Korsakov reorchestrated it in 1898–1902, and also retouched the score, in the process rewriting the duel music in Act 2 and Don Juan's arioso 'Kogda b ya bïl bezumets' ('If I were a madman') in Act 3. The prelude, based on a number of themes and leitmotifs from the opera, was added in 1903. This second version, now regarded as the standard one, was conducted at its première by Václav Suk.

Pushkin's 'little tragedy' of 1830 was inspired in part by the first Russian-language production of Mozart's *Don Giovanni*, which had taken place in St Petersburg two years earlier (with the title role transposed for Vasily Samoylov, a popular tenor). Although Pushkin adopted a certain amount from Da Ponte's libretto, including the character Leporello, his treatment of the Don Juan legend differs strikingly from the established tradition of Don Juan plays – a tradition Pushkin must have known, since he revived Tirso de Molina's original subtitle (*El convidado de piedra*; it seems unlikely that the Russian poet would have known the similarly titled operas by Vincenzo Righini or Giuseppe Gazzaniga). Where all previous Don Juan plays had been essentially farcical up to the last scene, Pushkin's is high romantic tragedy, diluted only by the *buffo* role he had taken over from Da Ponte. Everything points inexorably to the horrific expiation. The plot – which is also that of Dargomïzhsky's opera in every detail – is simplicity itself.

ACT 1.i *Before the fence of a monastery, at the gates of Madrid; evening* Don Juan has secretly returned from exile, where he had been sent in punishment for having killed the Commander, Don Alvaro. In the north he had 'all but died of boredom'. With the help of his manservant Leporello he has decided to steal into Madrid, where a rendezvous with the actress Laura awaits him. The familiar sights of the city bring back memories of Inez, an old, dead love. From a chance conversation with a monk, Don Juan learns that Donna Anna, the widow of the slain Commander, comes to the monastery every evening to visit her husband's grave, and that she is beautiful. Don Juan is inflamed with desire to meet her. Catching sight of the woman on her arrival, her face mysteriously hidden behind a black widow's veil, Don Juan is even more strongly drawn to her. Night falls, and while the moon is as yet unrisen Don Juan and Leporello set out under cover of night into the city.

1.ii *Laura's room* Laura is dining, surrounded by her admirers. At their request she sings two songs. One of the guests – the volatile Don Carlos, the Commander's brother – has appealed to her; he reminds Laura of her old love, Don Juan, whom she has not been able to forget. A knock at the door is heard; it is Don Juan. Don Carlos, who has long hated his brother's killer, now challenges him to a duel. They fight, and Don Carlos is mortally wounded.

ACT 2 *In the cemetery, before the Commander's statue* Calling himself 'Don Diego del Calvado', Don Juan, disguised as a monk, has gained entry into the monastery. He meets Donna Anna and with impassioned avowals and artful speeches succeeds in enticing her. She consents to receive him at home the next evening. Drunk with success, Don Juan gives Leporello an impudent order: to invite the Statue of the Commander to stand sentry at Donna Anna's door while he is there. To their horror, Don Juan and Leporello see the Statue nod in assent.

ACT 3 *Donna Anna's room* Don Juan reveals his secret to Donna Anna; the widow realizes that before her stands her husband's murderer. And yet she has not the strength to resist him. They agree to meet again the next day and as a sign of forgiveness Donna Anna bestows a kiss upon Don Juan. Suddenly there is a loud knocking at the door; the Statue has come as invited. The stone guest seizes Don Juan's hand and drags him down to hell.

* * *

The most obvious difference from the familiar libretto – that Donna Anna is the Commander's widow, not his daughter – makes Don Juan's crimes seem that much more odious and the drama's denouement that much more ethically justified. Yet Pushkin's Don Juan, compared with Mozart's, is curiously passive, stalked everywhere by death and attracted to it (he loved Inez for 'her voice so soft and weak, like an invalid's'; he confesses his love to Donna Anna in a cemetery; both his trysts end in death, first Don Carlos's, then his own). His only bold or wilful act is the invitation to the statue, and there, obviously, he does not expect results. Nor does he seek the duel with Don Carlos; when it is over he expresses not triumph but resignation. His meeting with Donna Anna is fortuitous, and he woos her without bravado. Once he sees her he is in the grip of forces beyond his control. One can only explain his revealing his identity to Donna Anna by the fact that (as he says) for the first time Don Juan is truly in love. And no sooner is he touched by true love than he, like all his victims, must perish. He is killed, as it were, by his own sword, wielded by Donna Anna, her husband's inadvertent avenger.

Except for the duel, there is little action in Pushkin's play, and it is generally taken for granted that the poet never meant it for the stage. It is in effect not a tiny play but an extended lyric meditation on love and death. Its merits are precisely those normally shunned by librettists as inimical to music; its beauties are of nuance and detail.

So it was the natural, inevitable choice to serve as basis for the most demonstratively 'reformist' opera ever written. To set a pre-existing play to music as it stands, with no mediating libretto at all, was to reject not only 'numbers' but the whole concept of *dramma per musica*, and to imply that the criteria of opera and those of spoken drama were ideally identical. To ignore the demand that an operatic text make suitable provision for the unfolding of musical structure – whatever the particular structure or the means of its unfolding – was manifestly to devalue musical 'form' and to uphold the idea that (as Nikolay Chernïshevsky put it) 'emotion and form are opposites'. Dargomïzhsky's letters are full of slogans just as categorical ('I want sound directly to express the word; I want truth' – to which Tchaikovsky, in his diary, made rejoinder in kind: 'If there is anything more hateful and *false* than this unsuccessful attempt to introduce *truth* into a branch of art where everything is based on *pseudo* ... I do not know it').

It is a tricky matter to decide to what extent such a posture was born of commitment to the realist ferment that took hold in Russian art and literature in the 1850s and 60s, and to what extent it was the reaction of an embittered Russian autodidact whose operatic ambitions had been systematically thwarted by the inimical conditions in which he had to work. That the latter fed the former there can be no doubt. But that Dargomïzhsky had professed an early commitment 'to develop the dramatic side of our national character' is no less true; and it is reflected in the remarkable accompanied recitatives that gave his earlier opera *Rusalka* its chief claim to the attentions of the younger generation of Russian composers, whose support comforted, and decisively influenced, Dargomïzhsky in his last decade. In his encyclopedic review of the original production, Alexander Serov singled out for special praise the confrontation of the Miller and the Prince in Act 3 of *Rusalka*, a scene cast entirely in accompanied recitative and set to Pushkin's original verses, or, in other words, composed to the formula that was to characterize the whole of *The Stone Guest*. Dargomïzhsky thanked him by letter for his 'uncommonly deep penetration of my innermost and even unconscious thoughts'. As soon as he had begun 'amusing myself with Pushkin's *Don Juan*', he became a cult object – an honorary member of the Balakirev circle and the focus of a frantic journalistic crusade on the part of Vladimir Stasov and César Cui. Long before the opera was finished it had achieved the quasi-legendary status it has never lost, however infrequent its performances.

It is the infrequency of performances that accounts for the inaccuracy of the legend. For despite its billing, *The Stone Guest* is emphatically not a recitative opera. It is, rather, almost unabatedly lyric in its fundamental impulse – far more so, in fact, than are the recitative scenes in *Rusalka*. The true sources of its style are to be found in the through-composed romances of Dargomïzhsky's late years (see ex.1, in which song and opera excerpt have whole bars in common).

Ex.1

(a) Dargomïzhsky: Romance, *Mne vsyo ravno* ('I don't care'), words by F. Miller

['Let them deride me, let them laugh, I don't care!']

(b) *The Stone Guest*, scene i

p
A go-los u ney bïl tikh i
dim.
pp

['And her voice was soft and weak, like an invalid's . . . ']

Cui coined the term 'melodic recitative' to describe the romance-like style of Dargomïzhsky's last opera, in which the accompaniments are full of continuous figuration and regular harmonic rhythm, and in which the melodic phrases consist of what Mikhail Druskin termed 'rounded intonational periods', that is, a series of (mostly) quavers surrounded by a pair of crotchets. This is anything but naturalistic reproduction of Russian speech.

Laroche, reviewing the première, rightly characterized the idiom of *The Stone Guest* as 'recitative-in-song, much closer to cantilena than to the Italian recitative'. The opera is in effect one gargantuan through-composed romance, the perfect counterpart to Pushkin's text as characterized above. The special 'realist' quality comes from the virtual absence of repetition (hence, absence of 'form'). When the text contains repetitions, the music follows suit, so that minuscule 'arias' do emerge at a couple of points: one for Don Carlos in Act 2; the other, in Act 3, built around a threefold rhetorical repetition by Don Juan: 'Kogda b ya bïl bezumets' ('If I were a madman'). Still, the only detachable numbers in the opera are Laura's two Spanish romances in Act 2, where Pushkin had merely specified 'she sings'. Both were songs already in Dargomïzhsky's portfolio. The first of them, 'Odelas' tumanom Grenada' ('Granada is shrouded in mist'; 1856), has as its ritornello a Spanish tune familiar from Glinka's *Jota Aragonesa*. The second, 'Ya zdes', Inezil'ya' ('Inezilia, I'm here'), is a setting of a Pushkin lyric (after Barry Cornwall). Its ritornello furnished the curtain music for Act 2. (Laroche made the droll prediction that in the new age of realism one of the 'chief tasks [of librettos] will be creating situations and inventing characters to ask one another to sing'.)

Another aspect of Dargomïzhskian realism lay in the studied ugliness of much of the music. Some of this, especially in the gory duel scene, was removed by Rimsky-Korsakov; but the statue music, on which the opera's climax is constructed, consists of novel explorations of whole-tone harmony, striking for the date.

RICHARD TARUSKIN

Stoppelaer, Michael (*d* London, 1777, will proved 4 July). Irish tenor and actor. From 1731 Stoppelaer sang leading roles on the London stage in numerous ballad opera afterpieces such as *The Devil to Pay* and Fielding's *The Lottery* and *The Intriguing Chambermaid*. He had a small part in Handel's *Ariodante* (1735). In 1737 John Beard took over his roles and for the rest of his long career Stoppelaer was primarily a comic actor singing occasional songs.

BDA; *LS*
R. Ryan: *Dramatic Table Talk*, ii (London, 1825)

OLIVE BALDWIN, THELMA WILSON

Nancy Storace as Euphrosyne in the masque 'Comus', with music by Thomas Arne: engraving (1791) by Condé after De Wilde

Storace, Nancy [Ann Selina; Anna] (*b* London, 27 Oct 1765; *d* Dulwich, 24 Aug 1817). English soprano, the daughter of Stefano Storace, an Italian double bass player, translator of Italian opera into English and adapter, and sister of STEPHEN STORACE. A vocal prodigy, she appeared in Southampton in 1773 as 'a Child not eight Years old'; her first London concert was at the Haymarket Theatre in April the following year. On 29 February 1776 she appeared with the celebrated Caterina Gabrielli in the première of Venanzio Rauzzini's *Le ali d'amore*. Her teachers in London were Rauzzini and Sacchini. In 1778 she followed her brother to Italy where she began her career in *opera seria*, singing seconda donna roles, Phoebe and Ebe, in Bianchi's *Castore e Polluce* (1779, Florence); this was followed by appearances in revivals of comic opera (1780–81) in which she took both *prima seria* and *prima buffa* roles. In 1782 she sang in Milan, Turin, Parma, Rome and Venice. The first opera composed for her specifically was one of the most acclaimed of its time, Sarti's *Fra i due litiganti il terzo gode* (1782, Milan); Kelly, who sang with her in Venice at the Teatro S Samuele in 1783 recalled that she 'drew overflowing houses' and was 'quite the rage' and when 'she announced a benefit, the first ever given to any performer at Venice ... the kind-hearted and liberal Venetians not only paid the usual entrance money, but left all kinds of trinkets, watch chains, rings, &c., to be given her'.

This celebrity caused the Viennese ambassador to Venice, Count Giacomo Durazzo, to engage her for the newly-organized Italian opera in Vienna the same year. For her début she sang the role created for her at the S Samuele, the Countess in Salieri's *La scuola dei gelosi*. During her first season at the Burgtheater, Storace sang in half of the 14 productions; her contract provided for a salary achieved by only the most sought-after singers of the day. In late 1783 she married the composer J. A. Fisher, but he apparently treated her cruelly and they soon parted; in 1786–7 she had a close relationship with Lord Barrard. Her years in Vienna (1783–7) are important for the roles that major composers (Paisiello, Martín y Soler, Mozart) created for her. Her early vocal training and her experience in serious opera in Italy had helped her acquire vocal and dramatic resources that she could integrate into her comic performances; composers responded with roles of stylistic richness and variety. Her vocal qualities can be inferred from her music in the greatest operas written for her, Mozart's *Le nozze di Figaro* and Martín y Soler's *Una cosa rara* (this latter the greatest popular triumph of Viennese music theatre). Both Susanna and Lilla exploit her formidable dramatic talents, her precise declamation and her preference for melodies within a limited vocal range and in *nota e parola* style. Mozart's sensitivity to Storace's low tessitura caused him to begin composing the role of Susanna below that of the Countess (subsequently reversed). Although Storace's music on occasion contained bravura elements, it is rarely ambitious in range or difficulty. Similar vocal writing is found in Mozart's other compositions for Storace, which include a single aria from the aborted *Lo sposo deluso* and the concert aria 'Chi'io mi scordi di te ... Non temer amato bene' (for her farewell concert in Vienna).

In February 1787 Storace, her mother, the composer Thomas Attwood and Michael Kelly left for London where on 24 April she appeared in Paisiello's *Gli schiavi per amore* at the King's Theatre, Haymarket, for which she was provided additional arias by her brother, Corri and Mazzinghi. Stephen wrote that his sister 'has had great opposition from the Italians – who consider it as an infringement on their rights – that any person should be able to sing that was not born in Italy'. In 1789 she moved to Drury Lane to join her brother for the 1789–90 season, and on 24 November 1789 she made her début as Adelia in her brother's *The Haunted Tower*, for which she received top billing (unusual for a woman on London playbills); its great success was in large measure due to its prima donna and her large-scale italianate piece, 'Be mine tender passion'. Other leading roles in operas by her brother included Margaretta in *No Song, no Supper*, Lilla in *The Siege of Belgrade* and Fabulina in *The Pirates*. There is reason to think she had a close relationship with the Prince of Wales in the early 1790s, when he, the Duke of Bedford and the Marquis of Salisbury attempted to hire her for their secret court theatre at the Pantheon concert hall in Oxford Street (see Price, 66ff). She sang at the King's Theatre for a season in 1793. After her brother's death in 1796 she left Drury Lane and in 1797 she and her lover, the tenor JOHN BRAHAM, left for a tour of the Continent. Her farewell performance, and that of her friend Kelly, was at Drury Lane in *No Song, no Supper* in 1808.

After her death in 1817 Storace was underpraised by English writers. Burney called her 'a lively and intelligent actress' but said her voice had 'a certain crack and roughness' and 'a deficiency of natural sweetness'. Lord Mount Edgcumbe wrote that she was unfitted for serious opera and was undoubtedly most successful in comic parts: 'In her own particular line ... she was unrivalled, being an excellent actress, as well as a masterly singer'. These evaluations suggest that it could not have been her virtuosity or purity of tone that made her voice so compelling to composers but rather that her intelligence, wit and charm inspired some of the most vocally and dramatically incisive music of its time.

*

BurneyH
The Thespian Dictionary (London, 1802, rev. 1805)
W. Bingley: *Musical Biography* (London, 1814, rev. 1834)
Earl of Mount Edgcumbe: *Musical Reminiscences* (London, 1824, 4/1834)
M. Kelly: *Reminiscences* (London, 1826, 2/1826); ed. R. Fiske (London, 1975)
B. Matthews: 'The Childhood of Nancy Storace', *MT*, cx (1969), 733–5
R. Fiske: *English Theatre Music in the Eighteenth Century* (London, 1973, 2/1986)
F. C. Petty: *Italian Opera in London 1760–1800* (Ann Arbor, 1980)
K. Geiringer and I. Geiringer: 'Stephen and Nancy Storace in Vienna', *Essays on the Music of J. S. Bach and Other Divers Subjects: a Tribute to Gerhard Herz* (Louisville, 1981), 235–44
B. Matthews: 'Nancy Storace and the Royal Society of Musicians', *MT*, cxxviii (1987), 325–7
J. C. Girdham: *Stephen Storace and the English Opera Tradition of the Late Eighteenth Century* (diss., U. of Pennsylvania, 1988)
——: 'The Last of the Storaces', *MT*, cxxix (1988), 17–18
C. Price: 'Italian Opera and Arson in late Eighteenth-Century London', *JAMS*, xlii (1989), 55–107
H. C. R. Landon: *Mozart: the Golden Years* (London, 1989), 187
P. Lewy Gidwitz: *Vocal Profiles of Four Mozart Sopranos* (diss., U. of California, Berkeley, 1991)

PATRICIA LEWY GIDWITZ, BETTY MATTHEWS

Storace, Stephen (John Seymour) (*b* London, 4 April 1762; *d* London, 15 or 16 March 1796). English composer. His father, Stephano (later Stephen) Storace was an Italian double bass player, who was working in Dublin in 1750, and in London by 1758. His mother (née Elizabeth Trusler) was the daughter of the owner of Marylebone Gardens. After learning the violin as a youth, he was sent to the S Onofrio Conservatory in Naples to study composition. Thomas Jones, a painter who took him on sketching expeditions around Naples in the late 1770s, indicated that Storace treated his studies lightheartedly. His parents and his younger sister, Nancy, visited him in late 1778, and then the whole family travelled in Italy. By autumn 1779 he and his sister were performing in Florence, she singing, he playing second harpsichord at the opera house. In Livorno they met the Irish tenor Michael Kelly, who became their friend and colleague and whose memoirs include many anecdotes about the Storace family. Storace's earliest known composition, *Orfeo negli elisi*, a cantata for two voices (now lost), was from this time.

In the early 1780s Storace returned to England, where he tried to settle in both London and Bath. His earliest published works were songs and chamber music from this period, but his later output was to be mainly operatic. He made several trips to Vienna, where his sister was employed as a singer. His two *opere buffe*, *Gli sposi malcontenti* (1785, Vienna) and *Gli equivoci* (1786, Vienna), were probably commissioned through Nancy's influence on Emperor Joseph II. Storace was in Vienna for the premières of these two operas, in both of which his sister and Michael Kelly sang. The Storaces became friends of Mozart and invited him to London, but this plan never came to fruition. Although Storace was clearly influenced by Mozart, there is no evidence that he was Mozart's pupil, as is sometimes claimed.

Back in London, both Stephen and Nancy Storace joined the Italian opera company at the King's Theatre. In 1787 they made their London operatic débuts in Paisiello's *Gli schiavi per amore*, he as director. Storace's Italian opera for London, *La cameriera astuta*, received only a few performances, all in 1788. In the same year he sued the publishers Longman & Broderip for printing his substitute aria 'Care donne che bramate' without permission, and eventually won his case.

By the beginning of the 1788–9 season, Storace had moved to Drury Lane, where Thomas Linley (i), the house composer and a family friend, seems to have happily delegated his responsibilities. (Storace never officially became composer to the theatre because Linley, a part-owner, retained his title until his death only shortly before Storace's.) For his first project, Storace worked with James Cobb, Linley's librettist, in using Dittersdorf's *Doktor und Apotheker* as the basis for an afterpiece. In the following season they followed that success with a full-length opera, *The Haunted Tower*.

For the rest of his career Storace composed almost entirely for the Drury Lane company, usually collaborating with Cobb for mainpieces and with Prince Hoare for afterpieces. Storace and Hoare first worked together on *No Song, No Supper* (1790). All of their afterpieces were first staged as benefits for Storace's principal singers – Nancy Storace and Michael Kelly, and their less distinguished partners, John Bannister and Anna Maria Crouch – and subsequently adopted into the repertory of the theatre. Storace derived his own income from sharing benefit nights with his librettists and by selling the copyright of his music to publishers – normally his operas were published in vocal score as soon as they were established as successes on stage.

Several of Storace's works were composed for specific occasions. *Poor Old Drury*, a prelude with songs by Storace, was produced when the Drury Lane company moved to the King's Theatre in 1791. (They were without their own theatre for almost three years while it was rebuilt.) In the 1792–3 and 1793–4 seasons Storace again directed Italian operas at the King's Theatre, along with Michael Kelly. He wrote his own serious English opera *Dido, Queen of Carthage* (1792) for performance by the Drury Lane company there, but it was a failure. Another occasional work was the afterpiece *The Glorious First of June*, staged in July 1794 to raise money for the dependents of sailors killed in Lord Howe's victorious battle against the French on 1 June.

Storace's two early Viennese operas are typical *opere buffe*, and he thought well enough of parts of them to incorporate sections into his English works. In his earliest works for the Drury Lane company, he quite blatantly set out to please the English audience, modelling his operas on those of Thomas Linley (i), Shield and Arnold. He then gradually modified the model – a series of dramatically inessential musical numbers alternating with spoken dialogue – towards a greater integration of drama and music, especially in ensembles. This trend reached its height in *The Pirates* (1792) and *The Cherokee* (1794), his last two completed mainpiece operas. With these he became the sole proponent of action finales on the English stage. His operatic songs run the gamut from simple folklike strophic songs to bravura numbers in complex forms. In most of his operas he followed the English tradition of using borrowed numbers side by side with those he had composed himself. Most of his overtures are in one movement, following the continental European model rather than the old three-movement overture retained by other English composers.

Storace was taken ill in March 1796 during rehearsals for *The Iron Chest* and died a few days after its première; his death has been attributed to gout. He was buried in Marylebone Church on 21 March, an event recorded in John Philip Kemble's diary (*GB-Lbl*). Nancy Storace and possibly Michael Kelly made his unfinished opera *Mahmoud* stageworthy by adding music from other sources. Prince Hoare wrote a prologue in Storace's memory for its première on 30 April, and on 11 May it was performed as part of a benefit night for Storace's widow and child. In 1797 Joseph Dale, who had been Storace's main publisher, brought out the *The Iron Chest* and *Mahmoud* together for their benefit.

When Storace died at the age of 34, his career in the English theatre had lasted less than eight years. His innovations had little influence on his contemporaries and successors, who continued to segregate drama and music. Although some of his operas remained popular for several decades, his contribution to the history of English opera was small: while audiences accepted his tactfully introduced innovations, other English composers rejected them in favour of the status quo.

For illustration *see* GREENWOOD, THOMAS (*Lodoiska*); LONDON, fig.6; and PLAYBILL, fig.2 (both *The Siege of Belgrade*).

See also DIDO, QUEEN OF CARTHAGE; EQUIVOCI, GLI; HAUNTED TOWER, THE; IRON CHEST, THE; LODOISKA (i); NO SONG, NO SUPPER; PIRATES, THE; SIEGE OF BELGRADE, THE; and SPOSI MALCONTENTI, GLI.

afterpieces and mainpieces are dialogue operas unless otherwise stated; librettos published unless otherwise stated

LDL – *London, Theatre Royal, Drury Lane*
LKH – *London, King's Theatre in the Haymarket*
LLH – *London, Little Theatre in the Haymarket*

aft – *afterpiece*   a-s – *all-sung*

Gli sposi malcontenti (ob, a-s, 2, G. Brunati), Vienna, Burg, 1 June 1785, *A-Wn*, *D-Dlb* (2 copies), ov. pubd pf 4 hands

Gli equivoci (ob, a-s, 2, L. da Ponte, after W. Shakespeare: *The Comedy of Errors*), Vienna, Burg, 27 Dec 1786, *A-Wn*, *D-Dlb* (2 copies), *US-Wc*, lib. unpubd; ed. R. Platt as The Comedy of Errors, MB (forthcoming)

La cameriera astuta (ob, a-s, 2), LKH, 4 March 1788, ov. pubd in kbd arr., 2 arias and qt pubd in full score (all London, 1788)

The Doctor and the Apothecary (aft, 2, J. Cobb, after G. Stephanie the younger), LDL, 25 Oct 1788, vs (London, 1788); incl. music from Dittersdorf: Doktor und Apotheker

The Haunted Tower (mainpiece, 3, Cobb), LDL, 24 Nov 1789, vs (London, 1789)

No Song, No Supper (aft, 2, P. Hoare), LDL, 16 April 1790, *GB-Lcm*, vs (London, 1790); ed. R. Fiske, MB, xvi (1959)

The Siege of Belgrade (mainpiece, 3, Cobb, partly after Da Ponte: *Una cosa rara*), LDL, 1 Jan 1791, vs (London, 1791); incl. music from V. Martín y Soler: Una cosa rara

The Cave of Trophonius (aft, 2, Hoare), LDL, 3 May 1791, lib. unpubd

Poor Old Drury (prelude with music, 1, Cobb), LKH, 22 Sept 1791, text unpubd

Dido, Queen of Carthage (mainpiece, a-s, 3, Hoare, after P. Metastasio: *Didone abbandonata*), LKH, 23 May 1792

The Pirates (mainpiece, 3, Cobb), LKH, 21 Nov 1792, vs (London, 1792), lib. unpubd; rev. with new text, as Isidore de Merida, London, LDL, 29 Nov 1827

The Prize (aft, 2, Hoare), LLH, 11 March 1793, vs (London, 1793)

My Grandmother (aft, 2, Hoare), LLH, 16 Dec 1793, vs (London, 1794)

Lodoiska (aft, 3, J. P. Kemble, after J. E. B. Dejaure), LDL, 9 June 1794, vs (London, 1794); incl. music from R. Kreutzer: Lodoiska and L. Cherubini: Lodoïska

The Glorious First of June (aft, 1, Cobb and others), LDL, 2 July 1794, vs (London, 1794), lib. unpubd

The Cherokee (mainpiece, 3, Cobb), LDL, 20 Dec 1794, vs (London, 1795)

The Three and the Deuce (aft, 3, Hoare), LLH, 2 Sept 1795, vs (London, 1795)

The Iron Chest (mainpiece play with music, 3, G. Colman (ii), after W. Godwin: *Caleb Williams*), LDL, 12 March 1796, vs (London, 1797)

Mahmoud (mainpiece, 3, Hoare), LDL, 30 April 1796, vs (London, 1797), lib. unpubd; music probably completed by N. Storace and M. Kelly

*

LS
Obituaries, *The Oracle* (17 and 18 March 1796)
The Thespian Dictionary (London, 1802, rev. 1805)
W. Bingley: *Musical Biography* (London, 1814, rev. 1834)
M. Kelly: *Reminiscences* (London, 1826, 2/1826); ed. R. Fiske (London, 1975)
'Memoir of Stephen Storace', *The Harmonicon*, vi (1828), 1–3
W. T. Parke: *Musical Memoirs* (London, 1830)
'Musical Biography No. X. Stephen Storace', *Musical World*, xli, new ser., vii (1840), 212–15
T. Jones: *Memoirs of Thomas Jones* (London, 1951)
R. Graves: 'The Comic Operas of Stephen Storace', *MT*, xcv (1954), 530–32
R. Fiske: 'The Operas of Stephen Storace', *PRMA*, lxxxvi (1959–60), 29–44
J. A. Anderson: *The Viennese Operas of Stephen Storace* (diss., Catholic U. of America, 1971)
R. Fiske: *English Theatre Music in the Eighteenth Century* (London, 1973, 2/1986)
F. C. Petty: *Italian Opera in London 1760–1800* (Ann Arbor, 1980)
K. Geiringer and I. Geiringer: 'Stephen and Nancy Storace in Vienna', *Essays on the Music of J. S. Bach and Other Divers Subjects: a Tribute to Gerhard Herz* (Louisville, 1981), 235–44
M. Velimirović: 'Beograd kot tema glasbenih Kompozicij [Belgrade as Subject of Musical Compositions]', *Muzikološki Zbornik/ Musicological Annual*, xvii/1 (1981), 147–64
J. Platoff: *Music and Drama in the 'opera buffa' Finale: Mozart and his Contemporaries in Vienna, 1781–1790* (diss., U. of Pennsylvania, 1984)
D. Hunter: 'Music Copyright in Britain to 1800', *ML*, lxvii (1986), 269–82
J. C. Girdham: *Stephen Storace and the English Opera Tradition of the Late Eighteenth Century* (diss., U. of Pennsylvania, 1988)

JANE GIRDHAM

Storchio, Rosina (*b* Venice, 19 May 1872; *d* Milan, 24 July 1945). Italian soprano. A pupil at the Milan Conservatory, she made her début there in 1892 at the Teatro Dal Verme as Micaëla. She sang in the provinces, then at La Scala in 1895 as Sophie in *Werther*; at Venice in 1897 she took part in the first performance of Leoncavallo's *La bohème*, as Musetta. The best years of her career began when she sang the title role in the première of his *Zazà* (Milan, Teatro Lirico, 1900), and continued with La Scala successes as Donizetti's Linda

(1902), Stefana in the first performance of Giordano's *Siberia* (1903), Norina (1905) and Violetta (1906). She also created Butterfly (1904) at La Scala and returned there occasionally until 1918. She sang frequently in Barcelona, 1898–1923, and in Buenos Aires, 1904–14. In 1921 she appeared at the Manhattan Opera House, New York, and in Chicago. Among her notable parts were Mimì, Massenet's Manon, and the title role in Mascagni's *Lodoletta*, which she sang at the first performance (1917, Rome). Her voice was not large, but flexible, pure and sweet; at the height of the popularity for *verismo* she personified the lyrical, refined, gentle and sensitive school of singing. Her plaintive, fragile Butterfly was typical of this approach, but in roles such as Violetta or Manon her acute sensitivity led to characterizations of passionate and touching impulsiveness.

For illustration *see* MADAMA BUTTERFLY, fig.2.

*

R. Celletti: 'Rosina Storchio', *Musica e dischi*, no.91 (1954), 4

T. Hutchinson: 'Rosina Storchio', *Record Collector*, xii (1958–60), 53–60 [with discography]

R. Celletti and K. Hardwick: 'Rosina Storchio', *Record News* [Toronto], iv (1959–60), 429–36 RODOLFO CELLETTI

Story of a Real Man, The [*Povest' o nastoyashchem cheloveke*]. Opera in four acts, op.117, by SERGEY PROKOFIEV to a libretto by the composer and MIRA ALEXANDROVNA MENDELSON (Prokof'yeva) after Boris Polevoy's novella (1946); Leningrad, Kirov Theatre, 3 December 1948 (closed run-through without sets or costumes); first public performance, Moscow, Bol'shoy Theatre, 8 October 1960.

Serving as a wartime correspondent (in which role he makes an 'appearance' in the last scene of Prokofiev's opera), Boris Polevoy became acquainted at the Kursk battlefront with Alexey Meres'yov, a flyer who had lost both his legs in a crash, yet managed to return to active duty with the help of a double prosthesis. Later, at the Nuremberg Trials, Polevoy heard Hermann Göring testify that the Germans lost the war because they did not know the Russians, 'who have always been and remain a riddle for the West'. The author came to conceive of Alexey Meres'yov's story – so he later wrote – as a sort of answer to the riddle; this was the inspiration for one of the great Soviet bestsellers of the immediate postwar period.

The story's turning-point is a scene in which an old Commissar, convalescing in the same sanitorium ward as Alexey, finds a way of rousing the wounded flyer from his gloom and mobilizing his will to succeed. He hands Alexey a magazine story about a Russian flyer in World War I who had lost a leg but continued to fly.

> 'Have you read it?' slyly asked the Commissar.
> (Alexey was silent, but his eyes went on scanning the lines.) 'Well, what do you say?'
> 'He only lost one leg.'
> 'But you, you're a Soviet man.'
> 'He flew a "Farman". You call that an airplane? It's a glider. Who couldn't fly it? You don't need speed, you don't need reflexes to control it.'
> 'But you're a Soviet man!', the Commissar insisted.
> 'A Soviet man', Alexey mechanically repeated, still without taking his eyes off the article; then his pale face began to glow with some kind of inner ruddiness, and he looked round at everyone with uncanny joy.

Prokofiev and Mendelson saw operatic possibilities here, and opportunities of another kind. The second part of their opera *War and Peace* having been suppressed in July of 1947 for unstated ideological reasons, the composer was desperate to win back a measure of official favour. On 30 October the newspaper *Vechernyaya Moskva* carried an interview in which Prokofiev announced that he was basing an opera on this most patently conforming of all Soviet war stories and 'dedicating [it] to Soviet Man and his limitless courage'. Before he completed it he was officially censured at the 'hearings' leading up to the Communist Party's 'Resolution on Music' of February 1948. In his compulsory 'self-critique', Prokofiev again cited *The Story of a Real Man* as the work in which he would make amends:

> I am highly gratified that the Resolution has pointed out the desirability of polyphony, particularly in choral and ensemble singing ... In my [new] opera, I intend to introduce trios, duets and contrapuntally developed choruses, for which I will make use of some interesting northern Russian folksongs. Lucid melody, and as far as possible, a simple harmonic language, are elements which I intend to use in my opera.

Prokofiev's handling of the exchange between Meres'yov (baritone) and the Commissar (bass), which went into the opera practically verbatim, exemplifies these points; it shows, too, how the composer maintained some continuity with his earlier operatic habits despite all the concessions he was forced to make to totalitarian demands. One of the 'folksongs' in the opera – first sung by a group of villagers hiding from the Nazis in a wood, who find Alexey and nurse him back to (relative) health – is in fact *Pesnya o rodine* ('The Song of the Fatherland', op.79 no.1), a propagandistic 'mass song' Prokofiev had composed in 1939. The melody runs through the opera as a motto. In the scene with the Commissar, Alexey sings his protests in typically scrupulous recitative, the kind of proudly prosy speech-song that had been a Prokofiev hallmark ever since *The Gambler*. The Commissar, however, sings his part throughout to the tune of *The Song of the Fatherland*, each repetition of the phrase 'But you're a Soviet man!' transposed a semitone higher than the last. Finally, the Commissar is wheeled out. Alexey, left alone to reflect, takes up the refrain, and pushes it up yet another pair of semitones. The motto theme represents a 'higher' reality than speech-song, much as Socialist Realism was supposed to reveal a higher truth than what Soviet critics call naturalism.

The Song of the Fatherland was only one of nine Prokofiev compositions of the 1930s and 40s that went into his last opera as representatives of 'contemporary Soviet reality' (they include additional mass songs, a couple of interpolated folksong arrangements, a waltz and even a rumba). In the end, it seems to have been precisely this wealth of genre detail at the expense of heroic rhetoric that doomed *The Story of a Real Man*. Vasily Kukharsky, the head of the all-powerful Committee on Artistic Affairs that had suppressed the work after its Leningrad trial performance, attacked it savagely in the government press as 'a striking example of the artist's detachment from real life'. This was a typical Stalinist inversion; but, alas, its lesson was one Prokofiev might have gleaned from the fate of his earlier Soviet opera, *Semyon Kotko*.

Perhaps the most interesting feature of the opera is its application of cinematic techniques such as flashback and montage to motivate the ensembles Prokofiev promised in response to the Resolution. The fifth scene, for example, shows Alexey in the hospital, delirious after his double amputation. The operation itself, his consultations with the surgeons, his mother (mezzo-soprano), his sweetheart Ol'ga [Olga] (soprano) and his best friend Andrey Degtyarenko (bass), all appear to him, and the characters sing in various combinations.

The 1960 production, which has been recorded, redistributed the scenes into three acts, omitted several numbers, introduced a multitude of cuts, and otherwise departed from the author's text; this version is available in vocal score (Moscow, 1962). RICHARD TARUSKIN

Story of Vasco, The. Opera in three acts, op.29, by GORDON CROSSE to a libretto by Ted Hughes after Georges Schehadé's play *L'histoire de Vasco*; London, Coliseum, 13 March 1974.

Set in the midst of war, vaguely in the 19th century and somewhere in Europe perhaps, the subject is war and its absurdity and poignancy. Vasco (lyric tenor), a timid village barber who is the unwitting centre of the military action and ultimately its hero, is actually no more in evidence than Caesar (high tenor), a crazy self-styled scholar and father of Marguerite (lyric soprano), who dreams she is engaged to Vasco and who follows him as far as she can on his mission. Her ecstatically amorous visions inspire an elaborate vocal line and the most lyrical music of a score which, while reflecting the influence of Britten and Messiaen in particular among the composer's contemporaries, is entertainingly resourceful in meeting the harsh realism, broad comedy, and surreal poetry of an extravagantly imaginative text.
GERALD LARNER

Stoska, Polyna [Stošku, Apoltéonija] (*b* Worcester, MA, 1911). American soprano of Lithuanian parentage. She studied at the Juilliard School with Sembrich and in Berlin with Charlotte Gadski-Busch. Her début was in 1939 in the title role of *Euryanthe* at the Deutsche Oper, Berlin, where she remained until 1941, when she returned to the USA. At the New York City Opera (1944–6) she sang roles including the Composer, Mařenka and Senta, and also took part in operettas and Broadway shows. In 1947 she created Ann Maurrant in the première of Weill's *Street Scene* on Broadway; the same year she made her Metropolitan Opera début as Donna Elvira, singing there for six seasons. In 1953 she visited Barcelona, Berlin and Vienna. On retiring from the opera stage she taught at the University of Indiana, Bloomington, and later at Boston University. Her warm but powerful voice was specially effective in the heavier Mozart and lighter Wagner roles. CORI ELLISON

Stoyanov, Veselin (*b* Shumen, 20 April 1902; *d* Sofia, 29 June 1969). Bulgarian composer. He received his first music lessons from his father and his brother. In 1922 he enrolled at the State Musical Academy in Sofia, completing his studies at the Vienna Hochschule (1926–30), where Franz Schmidt was his composition teacher. On returning to Bulgaria, Stoyanov worked as a concert pianist, conducted at the operetta and taught at the State Musical Academy, where he was later Rector (1956–62). For one season (1953–4) he was also director of the National Opera in Sofia. Classically balanced forms, an optimistic outlook and a keen awareness of contemporary trends are the prevalent features of his music, resulting from his Viennese studies. The late Romantic style as exemplified in Musorgsky, Wagner, Debussy and Strauss, which he absorbed into his own writing, was a new departure in Bulgarian opera which in the early part of the 20th century had been heavily Italian-influenced. In *Zhensko tsarstvo* ('The Kingdom of Women', 1935), the first modern Bulgarian comic opera, the prose libretto makes extensive use of recitative, strongly influenced by patterns of speech. Stoyanov's next work, *Salammbo* (1940), was an important contribution to the development of national opera in Bulgaria; the declamatory style and the dramatic as well as musical use of the orchestra were combined with the spectacle and lavishness of late Romantic style. His later comic opera *Hitar Petar* ('Cunning Peter', 1958) uses the melodic and rhythmic structures of Bulgarian folksong.

all first performed at the National Opera, Sofia

Zhensko tsarstvo [The Kingdom of Women] (comic op, S. Kostov, after Kostov), 5 April 1935

Salammbo (musical drama, B. Borozonov, after G. Flaubert), 22 May 1940

Hitar Petar [Cunning Peter] (comic op, V. Stoyanov and M. Moskov), 23 March 1958 MAGDALENA MANOLOVA

Stracciari, Riccardo (*b* Casalecchio di Reno, 26 June 1875; *d* Rome, 10 Oct 1955). Italian baritone. After singing in the chorus in operetta (1894), he studied with Ulisse Masetti at Bologna. In 1901 he appeared at Lisbon, then at La Scala (1904–5), Covent Garden (1905), the Metropolitan (1906–7, début as Germont), the Paris Opéra (1909), the Real, Madrid (1909–10), and other leading theatres. He then sang mostly in Italy, Spain and Argentina, though from 1917 to 1919 he was a member of the Chicago Opera. His vocal decline can be dated from 1928, but though he devoted himself to teaching, first in Naples (1926), then in Rome, he did not leave the stage until 1942 and in 1944 appeared again in *La traviata* at the Teatro Lirico, Milan. His mellow, velvety voice, resonant over its whole range, with an extended and penetrating upper register, made him between 1905 and 1915 the rival of Ruffo and Amato. He sang all the great baritone roles; among the dramatic ones he preferred those in *Il trovatore*, *Rigoletto* and *Aida*. But, thanks to a technique characteristic of the best 19th-century traditions, he excelled in works which allowed him to display his courtly enunciation, smooth singing, elegant phrasing and musical delicacy: *La favorite*, *Ernani* and above all *La traviata*, in which he played Germont with exceptional, gripping effect. He was also a noted Figaro in *Il barbiere di Siviglia* – a role, along with Rigoletto, that he recorded in 1929. Christoff and Silveri were among his pupils.

M. de Schauensee: 'Fourteen Hundred Times Figaro: a Visit with Riccardo Stracciari', *ON*, xix/7 (1954–5), 8–9

R. Celletti: 'Per lungo tempo Stracciari è stato il "Figaro" più ammirato', *Musica e dischi*, no.106 (1955), 18 [with discography by R. Vegeto]

R. Celletti and K. Hardwick: 'Riccardo Stracciari', *Record News* [Toronto], iii (1958), 75–82 [with discography by F. A. Armstrong] RODOLFO CELLETTI

Strada del Pò, Anna Maria (*b* Bergamo; *fl*1719–40). Italian soprano. She sang in four operas in Venice in 1720–21, the first of them Vivaldi's *La verità in cimento*, then in Milan in 1721 and Lucca in 1724. She appeared at the S Bartolomeo, Naples (1724–6), in Vinci's *Eraclea* and *Astianatte*, Porpora's *Semiramide*, Leo's *Zenobia in Palmira* and two operas by Porta, and married Aurelio del Pò, for a time manager of the theatre. In 1729 Handel engaged her for London, where she made her début as Adelaida in *Lotario* and was the leading soprano in all his operas and oratorios until 1737. She sang more major Handel parts than any other singer, appearing in at least 24 operas, the opera-ballet *Terpsicore* and many other works, and was the only member of his company who did not go over to the Opera of the Nobility in 1733. Handel composed many roles for her: Adelaida in *Lotario* (1729), Parthenope (1730), Cleofis in *Poro* (1731), Fulvia in *Ezio* and Elmira in *Sosarme* (1732), Angelica in *Orlando*(1733), Arianna and Erato in *Terpsicore* (1734), Ginevra in *Ariodante* and Alcina (1735), Atalanta (1736) and Thusnelda in *Arminio*, Ariadne in *Giustino* and Berenice (1737). She sang in 11 Handel revivals, taking eight roles composed for Cuzzoni and one for Faustina; nearly all were modified or included new or adapted arias. She also appeared in a number of pasticcios under Handel and in his revival of Ariosti's *Coriolano* (1732). She refused to sing for Bononcini in 1732. In 1738 she left London for Breda; she sang in Naples in 1739–40 and then retired to Bergamo.

Burney attributed Strada's success largely to Handel, calling her:

> a singer formed by himself, and modelled on his own melodies. She came hither a coarse and aukward singer with improvable talents, and he at last polished her into reputation and favour ... Strada's personal charms did not assist her much in conciliating parties, or disposing the eye to augment the pleasures of the ear; for she had so little of a Venus in her appearance, that she was usually called the *Pig*. However, by degrees she subdued all their prejudices, and sung herself into favour.

These prejudices are attested by Rolli and Mrs Pendarves ('her person *very bad* and she makes *frightful mouths*'), though she was clearly no negligible artist. Rolli called her 'a copy of Faustina with a better voice and better intonation, but without her charm and brio', and quoted Handel as saying that

> she sings better than the two who have left us, because one of them [Faustina] never pleased him at all and he would like to forget the other [Cuzzoni]. The truth is that she has a penetrating thread of a soprano voice which delights the ear, but oh how far removed from Cuzzona!

She was famous for her shake, and seems to have combined something of Faustina's dramatic flair with the seductive warbling for which Cuzzoni was renowned. Her parts point to a wide range in emotional and expressive power as well as in compass (*c′* to *c‴*, later (1737) *d′* to *b♭″*). WINTON DEAN

Stradella, Alessandro (*b* Nepi, 3 April 1639; *d* Genoa, 25 Feb 1682). Italian composer. Though originally from Fivizzano (Tuscany), the aristocratic Stradella family moved to Nepi (near Viterbo) in 1575. Alessandro's father Marcantonio was a member of the Cavalieri di S Stefano, the order of knights that the Medici founded in Pisa. From 1653 to 1660 Alessandro was a page to the Lante family in Rome; in 1659, and again in 1664, he was said to be 'from Bologna'. The first notice of him as a musician dates from 1667. He began his operatic career in 1668 by writing the prologue 'O di Cocito oscure deità' for Jacopo Melani's comedy *Il Girello*, first given in the Palazzo Colonna, Rome, and then performed successfully throughout Italy. For Rome's first public opera theatre, the Tordinona, Stradella composed prologues, intermezzos and arias for the Venetian imports of 1671–2. He also wrote sacred and secular works in all vocal and instrumental genres for the Roman aristocracy, such as his considerable incidental music, reminiscent of *commedia dell'arte* practices, for the prose play *Il Biante* (probably 1670–71, to celebrate the wedding of Cleria Cesarini and Filippo Colonna). In 1675, the year of his oratorio *S Giovanni Battista*, he had an honorary position as *cameriere extra* at the papal court.

Although well-connected and a nobleman, Stradella was apparently without funds. He and the castrato Giovan Battista Vulpio received a large sum of money from an 'old and ugly' woman to arrange a marriage between her and Cardinal Cibo's nephew. To evade the anger of the Cibo family, Stradella fled to Venice, where his patron Polo Michiel welcomed him. While there, he may have composed an opera on a libretto by Gianfrancesco Saliti, but it was not performed. After a few months he fled again, this time to Turin, and later to Genoa, where he arrived in December 1677. Through the good offices of Anna Pamphili (whom he knew from Rome) and her husband Duke Giovanni Andrea Doria, he was immediately employed by the Teatro Falcone to coach the singers and play continuo in the orchestra, but by the next season he was impresario. For the Falcone he composed *La forza dell'amor paterno* (15 performances from 10 November 1678), *Le gare dell'amor eroico* (from 1 January 1679) and *Il Trespolo tutore* (from 30 or 31 January 1679). In May 1681 he completed *Moro per amore* on a libretto by a Roman patron and collaborator, Flavio Orsini, Duke of Bracciano, but it does not seem to have been performed publicly.

Stradella enjoyed great success in Genoa. After *La forza* the audience tossed laudatory sonnets to him, and some admirers gave him a gold tray which he said was worth more than his income for the entire season. Moreover, several noblemen were so pleased with him that they agreed to pay him 100 Spanish doubloons a year and to give him a house, a servant and food simply to have him stay in the city. Stradella continued to compose music in all genres for local patrons, as well as for those in other cities. His good fortune was not to continue, however: for reasons which are not clear, he was fatally stabbed in the back by an unidentified assassin. His decorous burial in one of Genoa's most fashionable churches, the Chiesa delle Vigne, was proof of the respect in which he was held.

Stradella's largest contribution was to the cantata, both sacred and secular for small and larger forces. However, his extant theatre works – four operas (plus one unfinished), 11 prologues, nine intermezzos, several arias and a duet for other composers' operas and incidental music for a play – prove his competence in this area too. The operas are scored for an orchestra of two violin parts and continuo and require professional voices capable of sustaining occasionally florid lines. *La forza dell'amor paterno* and *Le gare dell'amor eroico* are reworkings of librettos written by Minato for Venice: *Seleuco* and *Mutio Scevola* respectively. *Moro per amore* offers similar fare, being an *opera regia* (one in which the main characters are royal). But *Il Trespolo tutore* is a true comedy. Based on a prose play by Giovanni Battista Ricciardi, adapted by Giovanni Cosimo Villifranchi, it belongs to the tradition of Tuscan comic plays and operas so popular in the mid-17th century; the two mad scenes here, like those in *La forza*, however, follow a Venetian preference. Arias in the operas are accompanied variously by continuo alone and by the orchestra; there are two-strophe arias, as well as *AA′*, *AB* and *ABA* forms, and instrumental ritornellos offering brief imitative treatments of aria themes. Frequently an 11-syllable line of recitative just before an aria is treated more lyrically (i.e. as arioso). Examples of accompanied recitative are to be found in *Il Corispero, La forza* and *Le gare*, as well as throughout Stradella's non-operatic music; *Moro per amore* has an echo scene. Most of Stradella's prologues and intermezzos are in comic style, an idiom in which he excelled, and much of the music for *Il Biante* (a prologue, sinfonia, balletto, 20 arias, two duets and two trios) is also comic. The importance of comedy in Rome, as evidenced through Stradella's works, has yet to be fully researched.

Stradella's style typically features fluent melodic lines which pay careful attention to textual form and underlay; it is also characterized by a frequent and delightful use of counterpoint, and of basses which are either strictly or freely ostinato. The language is tonal, but unusual progressions may occasionally surprise the listener. His music constitutes an important link in the period between Cesti and Handel.

O di Cocito oscure deità (prol., G. F. Apolloni), Rome, Palazzo Colonna, 4 Feb 1668, perf. as prol. to J. Melani: Il Girello, *GB-Lbl, I-MOe, Nc, Rvat, Tn**

Che nuove? Oh, ragionevoli (prol.), probably Rome, May–June 1668, *Tn**

Con meste luci (prol., F. M. Sereni), probably Rome, May–June 1668, *MOe, Tn**

Reggetemi, non posso più (prol., F. Orsini), ?Rome, 5 Dec 1668, *MOe, Tn**

Soccorso, aita, ohimè (int, ?Apolloni), ?Rome, 1668, intended for Melani: Il Girello, *MOe, Tn**

Fermate, omai, fermate (prol., Apolloni), Rome, Tordinona, 8 Jan 1671, with F. Cavalli: Scipione Affricano, *MOe, Rvat, Tn**

Amanti, che credete? (int, ?Apolloni), Rome, Tordinona, 8 Jan 1671, between Acts 2 and 3 of Cavalli: Scipione Affricano, *MOe, Rvat* (inc.), *Tn**

Su, su, si stampino (int, ?Apolloni), Rome, Tordinona, 8 Jan 1671, between Acts 1 and 2 of Cavalli: Scipione Affricano, *MOe, Rvat* (partly another version), *Tn**

Questo è il giorno prefisso (prol., Apolloni), Rome, Tordinona, 24 Jan 1671, with Cavalli: Il novello Giasone, *MOe, Tn* (partial autograph)

Dormi, Titone, addio (prol., Apolloni), Rome, Tordinona, 31 Dec 1671, with A. Cesti: La Dori, *B-Bc, I-MOe, Tn**

Che fai, Dorilla mia? (int), ?Rome, Tordinona, 1671, with Cesti: La Dori, *MOe, Tn** (inc.)

Chi mi conoscerà (int, ?Apolloni), ?Rome, 1671, intended for Cavalli: Scipione Affricano but not used, *MOe, Tn**

Aita, numi, aita (prol., F. Acciaiuoli), Rome, Tordinona, 12 Feb 1672, with Cesti: Il Tito, *MOe, Tn**

Oh, ve' che figuracce! (int, Acciaiuoli), Rome, Tordinona, 12 Feb 1672, between Acts 2 and 3 of Cesti: Il Tito, *MOe, Tn**

La forza dell'amor paterno (3, after N. Minato: *Seleuco*), Genoa, Falcone, 10 Nov 1678, *MOe, Tn**

Le gare dell'amor eroico (3, after Minato: *Mutio Scevola*), Genoa, Falcone, 1 Jan 1679, *GB-Lbl* (inc., entitled Porsenna), *I-MOe* (entitled L'Oratio)

Il Trespolo tutore (3, G. C. Villifranchi, after G. B. Ricciardi: *Amore è veleno e medicina degl'intelletti, o vero Trespolo tutore*), Genoa, Falcone, 30 or 31 Jan 1679, *MOe*

E dovrò dunque in solitaria stanza (prol.), ?intended for Rome, 1679, *MOe, Tn* (2 autograph copies)

La ruina del mondo (int), ?Genoa, Falcone, 1679, with Le gare dell'amor eroico, *Tn** (inc.)

Moro per amore, 1681 (3, Orsini), unperf., *A-Wn* (*R*1979: IOB, x), *D-Mbs* (inc.), *F-Pn* (entitled Il Rodrigo), *I-MOe* (entitled Il Floridoro), *Tn* (partial autograph)

Chi me l'avesse detto (int), *Tn**

Dal luminoso impero (prol.), *MOe, Tn**

Il Corispero, *MOe* (inc.)

?La Doriclea, lost

Lasciai di Cipro il soglio (prol.), *Tn**

Su, miei fiati canori (int), *Tn* (text inc.)

Letters to P. Michiel, *I-Vmc*, PD. C. 1065, nn.218, 348 and 1066, n.577; to F. Orsini, *Rasc*, 1.279, n.487

H. Hess: *Die Opern Alessandro Stradella's* (Leipzig, 1906)

A. Gentili: 'Un'opera di Alessandro Stradella ritrovata recentemente', *Il pianoforte*, viii (1927), 210–13

A. della Corte: '*La forza d'amor paterno* di Alessandro Stradella', *Musica d'oggi*, xiii (1931), 389–96

A. Cametti: *Il Teatro Tordinona, poi di Apollo* (Tivoli, 1938)

M. Tiberti: 'Un importante rinvenimento musicale, *La Doriclea*, opera di Alessandro Stradella', *Musica d'oggi*, xx (1938), 85–8

J. A. Westrup: 'Stradella's *Forza d'amor paterno*', *MMR*, lxxi (1941), 52–9

G. Roncaglia: '*Il Trespolo tutore* di Alessandro Stradella: la prima opera buffa', *RMI*, lvi (1954), 326–32

O. Jander: 'The Prologues and Intermezzos of Alessandro Stradella', *AnMc*, no.7 (1969), 87–111

C. Gianturco: *The Operas of Alessandro Stradella (1644–1682)* (diss., U. of Oxford, 1970)

——: 'Caratteri stilistici delle opere teatrali di Stradella', *RIM*, vi (1971), 211–45

——: 'Sources for Stradella's *Moro per amore*', *Quadrivium*, xii/2 (1971), 129–40

——: 'The Revisions of Alessandro Stradella's *Forza dell'amor paterno*', *JAMS*, xxv (1972), 407–27

——: 'A Possible Date for Stradella's *Il Trespolo tutore*', *ML*, liv (1973), 25–37

——: '*Il Trespolo tutore* di Stradella e Pasquini: due diverse concezioni dell'opera comica', *Venezia e il melodramma nel settecento: Venice 1973*, 185–98

——: 'Evidence for a Late Roman School of Opera', *ML*, lvi (1975), 4–17

C. Gianturco and G. Rostirolla, eds.: *Alessandro Stradella e il suo tempo: Siena 1982*

C. Gianturco, ed.: *Alessandro Stradella e Modena* (Modena, 1985)

C. Gianturco and E. McCrickard: *Alessandro Stradella (1639–1682): a Thematic Catalogue of his Compositions* (Stuyvesant, NY, 1991)

CAROLYN GIANTURCO

Straesser, Joep (*b* Amsterdam, 11 March 1934). Dutch composer. He studied musicology at Amsterdam University (1952–5) and organ, music theory and composition (with Ton de Leeuw) at the Amsterdam Conservatory. He was a lecturer at Utrecht Conservatory (1962–89).

As a composer, Straesser has risen to the challenge of the serial and post-serial techniques in the music of Schoenberg and Webern and their followers. His one opera, *Über Erich M.: ein komi-tragisches Singspiel*, was first given, in concert performance, on 6 November 1987 in the Royal Conservatory in The Hague; the libretto is by Stanny Straesser-Verster and the composer, after the German writer Erich Mühsam (1878–1934). *Über Erich M.* is a cantata-opera containing two stories: the satirical opera, in two acts, derives from a story in Mühsam's *Die Psychologie der Erbtante*; a prologue, interlude and epilogue alternate with the two acts of the opera to form a cantata, its text based on Mühsam's war poems, *Brennende Erde*. The opera received the 1988 Matthijs Vermeulen prize. MICHAEL VAN EEKEREN

Strakosch, Maurice (*b* Gross-Seelowitz [now Židlochovice], ?15 Jan 1825; *d* Paris, 9 Oct 1887). American impresario of Czech birth. He was a pianist and composer, and trained as a singer and coach. He arrived in New York in 1848, where he became associated with Salvatore Patti; that winter he began a two-year American tour with a small company including Patti's daughter Amalia, whom he later married. He managed and coached Amalia's eight-year-old sister, Adelina, after her concert début (1851), and he, Amalia, Adelina and the violinist Ole Bull toured the USA (1852–4). In February 1855 Strakosch, Bull and Max Maretzek presented opera at the Academy of Music in

New York, but the partnership collapsed within weeks. Strakosch managed his own company from 1856 to 1857, merging with Bernard Ullman's troupe in February 1857. The Ullman-Strakosch Opera Company presented opera at the Academy of Music and toured the East Coast until 1860; its final season was a near-disaster, rescued only by Adelina Patti's operatic début.

Strakosch managed Adelina Patti from 1860 to 1868; in 1861 he and the Pattis moved to Europe, where he also recruited performers for his brother Max Strakosch (*b* Gross-Seelowitz, 27 Sept 1835; *d* New York, 17 March 1892). Max had assisted Maurice (1857–61), and then managed Louis Moreau Gottschalk. From 1865 until the mid-1870s he managed singers and presented opera, frequently as his brother's partner; essentially a businessman, he relied on Maurice's artistic judgment. The brothers presented Christine Nilsson (1870–74) and also managed Clara Kellogg, Emma Thursby and Minnie Hauk. From 1877 to 1880 Max directed the Max Strakosch English Opera Company and Maurice toured with Bull. Thereafter Maurice worked primarily in Europe, often with his son Robert or his brother Ferdinand. He was an efficient manager; on his American tours he concentrated on small towns rather than urban centres, a pattern followed by his brother Max. His nephew Karl Strakosch (*b* c1859; *d* Hartford, CT, 23 Oct 1916) was also an impresario. He married Clara Kellogg (1887), and managed her career from the mid-1880s.

*

M. Strakosch: *Souvenirs d'un imprésario* (Paris, 1887)

L. M. Lerner: *The Rise of the Impresario: Bernard Ullman and the Transformation of Musical Culture in Nineteenth Century America* (diss., U. of Wisconsin, 1970), 38, 122

WILLIAM BROOKS

Stralia [Fischer], **Elsa** (*b* Adelaide, 1881; *d* Melbourne, 5 Aug 1945). Australian soprano. She studied with her father, the baritone Hugo Fischer, and at the Melbourne Conservatory, before pursuing further training in London and Italy. In 1912 she made her début at Genoa, and on returning to England she took over from Melba at an Albert Hall concert, which led to her engagement at Covent Garden. Her Donna Elvira was well received and in the following season 'a vast improvement' was noted. She soon became a leading figure in British opera, appearing with Beecham at Drury Lane during World War I and in postwar seasons at Covent Garden, where her roles included Elisabeth in *Tannhäuser*, Yaroslavna in *Prince Igor* and Aida, a performance in which several good judges considered her the equal of Emmy Destinn. In 1922 and again in 1929 she toured the USA and sang in New York under Walter Damrosch who was greatly impressed by her power, beauty of tone, and ability to turn from dramatic music to the coloratura repertory. She also toured South Africa and Australia, where she retired in 1933. Her recordings probably dull the effect of her full-bodied voice but the quality remains impressive. J. B. STEANE

Strandrecht. Opera by Ethel Smyth; *see* WRECKERS, THE.

Straniera, La ('The Stranger'). *Melodramma* in two acts by VINCENZO BELLINI to a libretto by FELICE ROMANI after Victor-Charles Prévôt's novel *L'étrangère*; Milan, Teatro alla Scala, 14 February 1829.

After the great success of *Il pirata*, Bellini delayed before accepting this commission, trying to get the tenor Rubini freed from a contract in Naples. He eventually preferred the singers at Milan to those offered by Turin, then insisted on a libretto to be written by Romani, who was left to decide on the actual subject matter. Bellini began work some time around 10 September 1828; the première was planned for 26 December but Romani's illness delayed it. The first cast included Henriette Méric-Lalande as Alaide, the 'stranger' of the title, Caroline Unger as Isoletta, Domenico Reina as Arturo and Antonio Tamburini as Valdeburgo. When the opera was revived at La Scala in 1830, Rubini sang Arturo and Bellini raised the tessitura of the part. The opera quickly became popular in Italy and there were productions in Palermo, Naples, Trieste, Venice, Rome and other cities during the next few years. *La straniera* reached the king's Theatre, London, and the Théâtre Italien, Paris, in 1832, when Alaide was sung by Giuditta Grisi. More recently the opera was staged at Palermo in 1968, when Renata Scotto sang Alaide; at Catania in 1980 with Olivia Stapp; and at the 1987 Wexford Festival.

The setting is Brittany, in and around the castle of Montolino, in about 1300. Arturo, Count of Ravenstal (tenor), has become infatuated with 'la straniera', Alaide (soprano), despite his betrothal to Isoletta (soprano). The peasants have asked Arturo to find out if Alaide is a witch. He does not know that she is really Agnese, the sister of Baron Valdeburgo (bass) and once married to the King of France. Forced to return to Isemberga, his discarded wife, the king has banished Agnese to Brittany. She now roams the countryside heavily veiled.

There is no overture. At the castle Isoletta's forthcoming wedding is being celebrated but she reveals to Valdeburgo that Arturo is in love with the mysterious stranger. Arturo, trying to discover the stranger's identity, comes to her hut. Alaide's voice, accompanied by a lute, is heard in the distance singing a *romanza*, 'Sventurato il cor che fida', which is punctuated by interjections from Arturo. Gradually drawing nearer she enters the hut. In a duet, 'Serba, serba i tuoi segreti', Alaide admits that she returns Arturo's love, but tells him he must not see her again.

In the forest a chorus of huntsmen sings of the pleasures of the chase. Arturo tells Valdeburgo, who has been searching for him, that he no longer loves Isoletta. When Alaide appears Valdeburgo recognizes her and runs to greet her, causing Arturo to suspect that Valdeburgo is her lover. In the trio 'No: non ti son rivale', Valdeburgo tries to reassure him.

At a remote place by the lake near Alaide's hut, Arturo is sunk in reflection, his dark thoughts matched by an impending thunderstorm. Unseen, he watches Valdeburgo take affectionate leave of Alaide in a trio 'Ah! non partir ... gia stende oscura notte il velo'. Alaide goes inside the hut and Arturo attacks Valdeburgo, wounding him. Valdeburgo falls into the lake and Alaide, disturbed by the noise, emerges again. When she tells Arturo that Valdeburgo was her brother, Arturo jumps into the lake to try and rescue his victim. Alaide calls for help and armed men rush in. Finding her covered in blood with Arturo's sword in her hand they accuse her of murder. The storm reaches its climax, Alaide becomes hysterical and in an aria 'Un grido io sento' accuses herself of causing her lover's death. She is arrested and taken away.

Act 2 opens with Alaide's trial before the tribunal of the Knights Hospitallers. She denies having killed

Valdeburgo but refuses to unveil or tell the Prior (bass) her true identity. Arturo enters and confesses his guilt. The court is about to sentence them both, when Valdeburgo appears, to the amazement of everyone. He exonerates both Alaide and Arturo and, in 'Meco tu vieni, o misera', invites the former to leave with him. Alaide reveals her face to the Prior, who recognizes her, and she is allowed to leave with Valdeburgo. Back in the forest outside Alaide's hut Arturo longs to see her again and ask her forgiveness for his suspicions. Valdeburgo comes out of the hut and, in the duet 'Sì ... Sulla salma del fratello', dissuades Arturo from going in as Alaide is still deeply upset. However, he will allow Arturo to see his sister once more in return for Arturo's promise to marry Isoletta. In her room at the castle, Isoletta expresses her unhappiness in 'Ah! se non m'ami più'. When her ladies inform her that Arturo will marry her after all, her grief turns to joy.

At the porch of the chapel of the Hospitallers, a chorus praises the betrothed couple. Arturo lingers on the threshold as the Prior and his Knights enter the chapel. Alaide arrives unobserved and hides behind a tomb. In the quartet 'Che far vuoi tu? ... Qual sarà dolor che uccide' (which derives partly from a student work, *Tantum ergo*), Valdeburgo urges the reluctant Arturo to fulfil his promise. Isoletta renounces her marriage, while Arturo, recognizing Alaide, declares his love for her. Alaide leads Isoletta and Arturo back into the chapel followed by Valdeburgo. Shortly afterwards Alaide comes out by herself and, in 'Ciel pietosa, in si crudo momento', an expressive aria that anticipates Bellini's mature style, prays for forgiveness for her unhappiness at the marriage. As the chorus celebrates the union, Arturo rushes from the chapel, followed by the Knights and the Prior, who recognizes Alaide as Agnese and announces that, as Isemberga has died, she is now Queen of France. Arturo kills himself with his sword and Alaide, after a short cabaletta 'Or sei pago, o ciel tremendo', in which she prays for death, falls unconscious on the ground.

Stylistically more unified than *Il pirata*, *La straniera* depicts another impetuous Romantic tenor hero, described by the composer as 'un disperato'. The opera represents the extreme point of Bellini's abnegation of Rossinian melodic decoration, with little opportunity for vocal display. At the same time, there is a substantial gain in dramatic tension, particularly in the trial scene at the beginning of the second act, where the potentially risible situation of a woman who believes she is responsible for the deaths of her lover and her brother, both of whom then turn up alive and well, becomes dramatically effective because of its musical content and structure. SIMON MAGUIRE, ELIZABETH FORBES

Strasbourg (Ger. Strassburg). French city on the Rhine in Alsace. It was a free imperial city from the 13th century until 1681, when it was incorporated into France. From 1871 to 1919 it was part of the German Empire. Opera was probably first given at the local fairs and at the Zimmerhof Theatre (built 1603). The first opera house was opened in the Place Broglie in a converted granary in 1701. This theatre burnt down in 1800 and opera was provisionally transferred to the Petit Théâtre, built in 1733 by the drapers' corporation, then to the converted church of St Etienne. A new opera house in the Place Broglie, the Théâtre Municipal, with a capacity of 1500 in stalls and four galleries, was built by the architect Casimir Robin and inaugurated in 1821 with Grétry's *La fausse magie*. It flourished until its destruction, apart from the exterior walls, during the German bombardment in 1870. The city's new administration quickly had the theatre rebuilt in identical style (by the architect J. G. Conrath). It reopened in 1873, the circular back façade being added in 1888. During the German occupation, the opera had a succession of famous musical directors: Otto Lohse (1897–1904), Robert Heger (1907), Pfitzner (1910–19) and Furtwängler (1910–11), with Klemperer (1914–17) and Szell (1917–19) as first conductors.

When the city was returned to France in 1919, the house was run with Paul Bastide as musical director (1919–38); another German occupation brought Hans Rosbaud to the company as musical director. Bastide returned in 1945 and strengthened the ensemble and the repertory. During his first administration Strauss's *Die ägyptische Helena* was given its first performance in France (1932) with the composer conducting. Bastide's second administration saw the first French staging of *Béatrice et Bénédict* (1945), the first French performance of Wolf-Ferrari's *Le donne curiose* (1946) and the world première of Henri Rabaud's *Martine* (1947). Roger Lalande, director from 1948 to 1953, presented the premières of Delannoy's *Puck* and Arrieu's *Noé* (1950) and the first French productions of *Peter Grimes* (1949), *Mathis der Maler* (1951) and *The Rake's Progress* (1952). His successor, Pierre Deloges, gave the first French productions of *Bluebeard's Castle* (1954) and *The Love for Three Oranges* (1955).

The remarkable French conductor Frédéric Adam was director from 1955 to 1972 (for the first five years with the conductor Ernest Bour as co-director). His regime saw the *Ring* in 1956 with the French début of Birgit Nilsson, and the French premières of Bizet's *Don Procopio* (1958), Dallapiccola's *Il prigioniero* (1961), Stravinsky's *Oedipus rex* (1961), *Jenůfa* (1962), *Die Frau ohne Schatten* (1965), Henze's *Der junge Lord* (1967) and Smetana's *Dalibor* (1968). In 1960 Adam opened his season with the then rarely heard *Les Troyens*.

In 1972 Strasbourg joined with Mulhouse and Colmar to form the Opéra du Rhin, first with Alain Lombard as director and, since 1980, René Terrasson. In a season running from October to May, seven or eight productions are each given six to eight performances in Strasbourg before being shown in Mulhouse and Colmar; often they are co-productions with the Badische Staatstheater in Karlsruhe. Large-scale productions are mounted by the Opéra du Rhin in the recently built Palais de la Musique et des Congrès (2500 seats). The Strasbourg Music Festival, the oldest in France, founded in 1932, includes opera productions by visiting companies as well as by the Opéra du Rhin. Britten's *A Midsummer Night's Dream* (sung in French) received its first performance in France at the festival, in 1965; *Die Soldaten* was given by the Stuttgart Opera in 1988.

*

L. J. Brote: 'L'Opéra du Rhin: l'art lyrique régionalise', *Le théâtre lyrique français 1945–1985* (Paris, 1987), 383–94

CHARLES PITT

Strassburg (Ger.). STRASBOURG.

Straszny dwór. Opera by Stanisław Moniuszko; *see HAUNTED MANOR, THE.*

Stratas, Teresa [Strataki, Anastasia] (*b* Toronto, 26 May 1938). Canadian soprano of Greek descent. She studied with Irene Jessner and made her début in Toronto with Canadian Opera in 1958 as Mimì (also the role of her 1961 Covent Garden début). Having won the 1959 Metropolitan Opera Auditions of the Air, she made her début at the Metropolitan that October as Poussette (*Manon*). Her regular appearances in New York have included those as Sardula (Menotti's *Le dernier sauvage*), Lisa (*The Queen of Spades*), Liù, Nedda, Micaëla, Zerlina, Cherubino, Despina and Hänsel. In 1961 she created the title role in Peggy Glanville-Hicks's *Nausicaa* at the Athens Festival. She has appeared regularly as a guest in Munich, Hamburg and Paris, and has also performed at Salzburg and the Bol'shoy. Her repertory includes Verdi's Joan of Arc, Violetta, Tatyana, Mélisande and Lulu, which she sang at the opera's first complete performance (1979, Paris). She sang Violetta to Domingo's Alfredo in Zeffirelli's film (1983), appeared on Broadway in *Rags* in 1986, and took the role of Marie Antoinette in the 1991 première at the Metropolitan of Corigliano's *The Ghosts of Versailles*. Stratas has a lyric-dramatic voice of individuality and a keen sense of the stage. Deep involvement in her roles distinguishes all her appearances.

Straus, Oscar (*b* Vienna, 6 March 1870; *d* Bad Ischl, 11 Jan 1954). Austrian composer and conductor. On the recommendation of Brahms he studied with Hermann Grädener and in 1891 went to Berlin as a pupil of Bruch. Advised by the younger Johann Strauss to gain practical experience in the provinces, he conducted between 1893 and 1899 in Pressburg (now Bratislava), Brno, Teplitz (now Teplice), Mainz and Hamburg, composing stage works and a good deal of salon music during the same period. He was conducting in Berlin when, in 1900, he was engaged as pianist and composer in the newly founded Überbrettl cabaret, and he enjoyed his first popular successes with songs such as *Die Musik kommt* and *Der lustige Ehemann*. Having returned to Vienna he began a series of operettas, of which *Ein Walzertraum* in particular rivalled *Die lustige Witwe* in its popularity and first brought Straus international success. Its successor, *Der tapfere Soldat* (1908), an adaptation of Shaw's *Arms and the Man*, gained particular success in the USA as *The Chocolate Soldier*. Subsequent operettas added little to those successes until *Der letzte Walzer* (1920), featuring Fritzi Massary, around whom several of Straus's works were written. These included *Eine Frau, die weiss, was sie will* (1932), produced in London as *Mother of Pearl*. Of later works, *Drei Walzer* (1935), which used the music of Johann Strauss I and II in the first two acts and that of Straus himself in the third, achieved its greatest success with Yvonne Printemps in Paris. In 1939 Straus left Vienna and lived in France (where he was awarded membership of the Légion d'honneur), New York and Hollywood, finally returning to settle in Bad Ischl in 1948. He continued to conduct his music on concert tours and recordings and enjoyed a remarkable success with his theme tune for the film *La ronde* (1950). Besides his works for the theatre, he composed chamber music, two ballets, several hundred songs, piano pieces and music for many films. Straus composed much cheerful, lilting music in the Viennese operetta style, eminently piquant and charming without ever matching Lehár's passion and sensuousness. His son Erwin (1910–66) was a pianist and composed several stage works including *Denk an mich* (1930) and *Der tanzende Shylock*.

See also TAPFERE SOLDAT, DER and WALZERTRAUM, EIN.

most published in vocal score in Vienna or Berlin

Der Weise von Cordoba (komische Oper, 1, M. Singer), Bratislava, 1 Dec 1894; Die Schwedin vor Brünn (Festspiel, 3), Brno, Stadt, 10 Aug 1895; Der schwarze Mann (komische Oper, 1, R. Schanzer, after T. von Trotha and G. von Moser), Berlin, Secessions, 23 Dec 1901; Lolotte (Monodram, 4 scenes, L. Heller), Prague, 5 Aug 1903; Colombine (1, A. Pserhofer, after E. Korn), Berlin, Westens, 13 Feb 1904; Die lustigen Nibelungen (burleske Operette, 3, Rideamus [F. Oliven]), Vienna, Carl, 12 Nov 1904; Zur indischen Witwe (Operette, 3, I. Schnitzer and S. Schlesinger), Berlin, Zentral, 30 Sept 1905; Hugdietrichs Brautfahrt (komische Märchen-Operette, 3, Rideamus), Vienna, Carl, 10 March 1906; Mam'zell Courage (Bild: Szene aus dem Dreissigjährige Krieg, Korn), Vienna, Lustspiel, 16 March 1906; Ein Walzertraum (Operette, 3, F. Dörmann and L. Jacobson, after H. Müller: *Das Buch der Abenteuer*), Vienna, Carl, 2 March 1907; Der Frauenmörder (melodramatische Szene, 1, V. Léon), Vienna, Orpheum, 8 Nov 1907

Der tapfere Soldat [Der Praliné-Soldat] (Operette, 3, R. Bernauer and Jacobson, after G. B. Shaw: *Arms and the Man*), Vienna, An der Wien, 14 Nov 1908; Didi (Operette, 2, Léon), Vienna, Carl, 23 Oct 1909; Der tapfere Kassian (Spl, 1, A. Schnitzler), Leipzig, Stadt, 30 Oct 1909; Venus im Grünen (musikalisches Scherzspiel, 1, R. Lothar), Leipzig, Stadt, 30 Oct 1909; Das Tal der Liebe (musikalische Komödie, 3, Lothar, after M. Dreyer), Vienna, Volksoper and Berlin, Komische Oper, 23 Dec 1909, rev. as Die galante Markgräfin (3, F. Dörmann), Vienna, Volksoper, 24 Jan 1919; Mein junger Herr (Operette, 3, F. Stollberg), Vienna, Raimund, 23 Dec 1910; Die anderen Herren sind nicht so (melodramatische Szene, 1, Léon), Vienna, Hölle, 1 Feb 1911; Die kleine Freundin (Operette, prelude, 2, L. Stein and A. M. Willner), Vienna, Carl, 20 Oct 1911

The Dancing Viennese [Eine vom Ballett] (Operette, 2, J. Brammer and A. Grünwald), London, Coliseum, 3 June 1912; Love and Laughter (komische Oper, 3, F. Fenn and A. Wimperis), London, Lyric, 3 Sept 1913; Die himmelblaue Zeit (Spl, 3, P. Wertheimer and R. Batka), Vienna, Volksoper, 21 Feb 1914; Rund um die Liebe (Operette, 3, R. Bodanzky and F. Thelen), Vienna, Johann Strauss, 9 Nov 1914; Die schöne Unbekannte (Operette, 2, postlude, Jacobson and Stein), Vienna, Carl, 15 Jan 1915; Man steigt nach (Posse, 3, Léon and H. Reichert), Vienna, Carl, 2 May 1915; Liebeszauber (Operette, 4, Léon), Vienna, Bürger, 28 Feb 1916; Nachtfalter (Spl, 3, Jacobson and Bodanzky), Vienna, Ronacher, 12/13 March 1917; A maranymeny asszony (Operette, 3, E. Haltai), Budapest, Lustspiel, 19 April 1917, as Niobe (Operette, 3, O. Blumenthal), Berlin, Lessing, 1 June 1917; Eine Ballnacht (Operette, 1, Jacobson and Bodanzky), Vienna, Johann Strauss, 11 Oct 1918; Dorfmusikanten (Operette, 3, Jacobson and Bodanzky), Vienna, An der Wien, 26 Nov 1919

Der letzte Walzer (Operette, 3, Brammer and Grünwald), Berlin, Berliner, 12 Feb 1920; Nixchen (Operette, 3, Willner and R. Oesterreicher), Berlin, Wallner, 10 Sept 1921; Die törichte Jungfrau (Operette, 3, Florido [H. Saltenburg]), Berlin, Grosses Schauspielhaus, aut. 1922; Die Perlen der Cleopatra (Operette, 2, Brammer and Grünwald), Vienna, An der Wien, 17 Nov 1923; Der Tanz um die Liebe (Operette, 3, Jacobson and Saltenburg), Berlin, Deutsches Künstler, 25 Sept 1924; Riquette (Operette, 3, R. Schanzer and E. Welisch), Berlin, Deutsches Künstler, 17 Jan 1925; Die Teresina (Operette, 3, Schanzer and Welisch), Berlin, Deutsches Künstler, 11 Sept 1925; Die Königin (Operette, 3, E. Marischka and B. Granichstaedten), Berlin, Deutsches Künstler, 4 Nov 1926; Mariette, ou Comment on écrit l'histoire (musikalische Komödie, 3, S. Guitry), Paris, Edouard VII, 1 Oct 1928, as Marietta (trans. Grünwald), Vienna, An der Wien, 25 Oct 1929; Hochzeit in Hollywood (Operette, 4, Jacobson and B. Hardt-Warden), Vienna, Johann Strauss, 21 Dec 1928

Die erste Beste (Operette, 3, Schanzer and Welisch), Prague, Deutsches, 19 Oct 1929; Der Bauerngeneral (Operette, 3, Brammer and G. Beer), Vienna, An der Wien, 28 March 1931; Eine Frau, die weiss, was sie will (Operette, 3, Grünwald, after L. Verneuil), Berlin, Metropol, 1 Sept 1932, rev. as Manon, Munich, Kammerspiele, Oct 1952; Zwei lachende Augen (Operette, 3, L. Hirschfeld and Oesterreicher), Vienna, An der Wien, 22 Dec 1933; Das Walzerparadies (Operette, 3, Grünwald, after Verneuil), Vienna, Scala, 15 Feb 1935; Drei Walzer (Operette, 3, P. Knepler and A. Robinson), Zürich, Stadt, 5 Oct 1935, as Trois valses (F. L. de Marchand and A. Willemetz), Paris, Bouffes-Parisiens, 22 April 1937; Mes amours (Operette, 2, de Marchand and Willemetz, after E. Childs-Carpenter: *Bachelor Father*), Paris, Marigny, 2 May 1940; Die Musik kommt (musikalische Komödie, 3, Knepler, Robinson and R. Gilbert), Zürich, Stadt, 1948, rev. as Ihr erster Walzer, Munich, Gärtnerplatz, 31 March 1950; Božena (3, Brammer and Grünwald), Munich, Gärtnerplatz, 16 May 1952

*

B. Grun: *Prince of Vienna: the Life, Times and Melodies of Oscar Straus* (London, 1955)

R. Traubner: *Operetta: a Theatrical History* (New York, 1983)

F. Mailer: *Weltbürger der Musik: eine Oscar-Straus-Biographie* (Vienna, 1985)

ANDREW LAMB

Strauss, Johann (Baptist) (*b* Vienna, 25 Oct 1825; *d* Vienna, 3 June 1899). Austrian composer. He was the most celebrated member of a distinguished Viennese family of musicians who made their names directing and composing for their own dance orchestras. His father, the elder Johann Strauss (1804–49), had begun the family tradition, gaining acclaim during the second quarter of the 19th century not only in Vienna but also on extensive tours that included Britain in Queen Victoria's coronation season. Since the father opposed his sons following in his footsteps, the younger Johann was at first intended for a banking career. However, with his mother's encouragement, he took violin lessons from a member of his father's orchestra and subsequently studied theory with Joseph Drechsler (1782–1852). In October 1844 he made his début with his own small orchestra at a *soirée dansante* and soon began to establish himself as his father's most serious rival – a rivalry heightened when the two supported opposing factions in the revolution of 1848.

After the father's death the younger Johann continued to extend the family reputation both in Vienna and further afield. He eventually inherited from his father the popular accolade of 'Waltz King', and in 1863 he was appointed to the official position of *Hofballmusikdirektor* ('music director of the court balls'). With the demand for his services increasing, he was fortunate to be able to enlist the services of his brothers Josef (1827–70) and Eduard (1835–1916), permitting the orchestra to be split. Johann himself conducted summer concerts at Pavlovsk in Russia annually from 1856 to 1865 and in several subsequent summers, and visited Paris and London in 1867 and Boston and New York in 1872.

The 1860s were the years of major Strauss waltzes such as *Morgenblätter* (1864), *An der schönen blauen Donau* and *Künstlerleben* (1867), *Geschichten aus dem Wienerwald* (1868) and *Wein, Weib und Gesang* (1869). By 1870, however, Strauss was increasingly recoiling from the stress of constant concert-giving and incessant public adulation. At roughly the same time Viennese theatrical impresarios, alarmed at the dominance of the Viennese musical theatre by the imported works of Offenbach, had seen in Strauss the one popular composer of the stature to mount a local challenge. Encouraged also by his first wife, the singer Jetty Treffz (1818–78), he took it up. He resigned his position as 'k.k. Hofballmusikdirektor' and, with Josef now dead, left the direction of the family orchestra to Eduard. For the rest of his life he concentrated almost entirely on composition for the stage, while contriving to provide new material for the ballroom by adapting themes from his operettas.

When his first completed operetta, *Indigo und die vierzig Räuber*, reached the stage in 1871, Strauss was already 45. The work was an undoubted success, but already the strengths and limitations of Strauss's theatrical writing were evidenced by the even wider success of the waltz *Tausend und eine Nacht* on themes from the operetta. By contrast, the weaknesses were demonstrated by fact that the operetta was repeatedly revised, with a new libretto, *La reine Indigo*, being substituted in Paris in 1875 which was then translated into German for a production in Vienna in 1877. His second operetta, *Carneval in Rom* (1873), fared somewhat similarly, but with his third, *Die Fledermaus* (1874), he achieved what was to remain the greatest success of 19th-century Viennese operetta.

Its successors were inevitably relative disappointments. *Cagliostro in Wien* (1875), about the exploits of an Italian adventurer, was the first that had a role created by Alexander Girardi, who was to become Strauss's leading interpreter. It was followed by a satirical Offenbachian piece *Prinz Methusalem* (1877) that scarcely suited Strauss's talents and by an undisguised failure, *Blindekuh* (1878). Greater success returned with *Das Spitzentuch der Königin* (1880), a work featuring Cervantes as a character. It was a particular success in the USA and was the source of the waltz *Rosen aus dem Süden*. Then came *Der lustige Krieg* (1881), which in Strauss's lifetime remained perhaps the most successful of his operettas after *Die Fledermaus* and *Der Zigeunerbaron*. After his death, though, that position was assumed by his next work, *Eine Nacht in Venedig* (1883), which has survived perpetual attempts to improve its libretto to be recognized as, perhaps, the most purely beautiful of all his operettas.

His disenchantment over the problems of the book of *Eine Nacht in Venedig* ended his association with Vienna's leading librettists Zell and Genée, the latter having acted not merely as lyricist but also as something of a musical amanuensis to the theatrically uneasy Strauss. *Der Zigeunerbaron* followed in 1885, on the eve of Strauss's 60th birthday, and its more serious mien and closer integration of text and music represented a step towards Strauss's ambition, under the influence of his young third wife Adele, to compose a genuine opera. He next attempted a work based on Heine's *Der Schelm von Bergen*, but the project foundered on a combination of circumstances which included one remarkable coincidence. The leading comic role intended for Alexander Girardi was an executioner who could not stand the sight of blood. Just at that time Sullivan's *The Mikado* was going the rounds of German stages, and the similarity of the character Ko-Ko meant that the work could not go ahead.

In its place Strauss set to work with the young Victor Léon on *Simplicius*, set in the Thirty Years War. It turned out to be another disappointment, though Strauss thought enough of it to have the book revised subsequently. His next work was the genuine opera after which he had striven. He worked on *Ritter Pázmán* for three years, and it was received politely enough at the Vienna Hofoper in January 1892 and subsequently in Prague and Berlin, but it failed to hold the stage. He immediately settled back into the potentially more commercial field of operetta, setting *Fürstin Ninetta* without even seeing the complete libretto. Now nearing 70, he composed only three more operettas – *Jabuka* (1894) for the celebration of his artistic golden jubilee, *Waldmeister* (1895) and *Die Göttin der Vernunft* (1897). This last represented the nadir of his always uneasy relations with his librettists. He was persuaded to complete the music only by the threat of legal action. He did not attend the première, and after his death music and text were formally divorced. The music was re-used with a completely new text for *Reiche Mädchen* (1909), while the libretto was reworked for Lehár's *Der Graf von Luxemburg*. Strauss's very last stage work was a ballet, *Aschenbrödel*.

If incompatibility of text and music have proved a bar to lasting currency of most of Strauss's stage works in their original form, the appeal of their music has ensured the survival of the greatest – albeit (in the case of *Eine Nacht in Venedig* especially) with frequent revision of both book and music. Likewise Strauss's music has remained a happy hunting ground for arrangers. He himself gave approval to the trend by permitting the younger Adolf Müller to adapt some of his published dance compositions for the operetta *Wiener Blut*, and later examples have included *Tausend und eine Nacht* (1906), *Casanova* (1928), *Walzer aus Wien* (1930) and *Die Tänzerin Fanny Elssler* (1934).

Strauss's strong point as an operetta composer remained the same as for his dance music, namely his irresistible melodic grace and vitality. To these he was able to add an ability, demonstrated in his waltz introductions, to set atmosphere and mood, most notably in *Eine Nacht in Venedig*. But wit and portrayal of character were never his strong points, and only in the sparkle of *Die Fledermaus* did all his undeniable genius for popular music combine irresistibly with a book of sufficient quality to produce a work incontrovertibly a classic.

See also FLEDERMAUS, DIE; NACHT IN VENEDIG, EINE; WALZER AUS WIEN; WIENER BLUT; and ZIGEUNERBARON, DER.

WW – *Vienna, Theater an der Wien*

Die lustigen Weiber von Wien, *c*1868 (burleske Operette, 3, J. Braun), inc., lib. *A-Wst*

Romulus, *c*1871, inc., frags. *Wst*

Indigo und die vierzig Räuber (komische Operette, 3, M. Steiner), WW, 10 Feb 1871, inc. autograph *Wst*, vs (Vienna, 1871)

Carneval in Rom (komische Operette, 3, Braun and C. Lindau, after V. Sardou: *Piccolino*), WW, 1 March 1873, inc. autograph *Wst*, vs (Vienna, 1873)

Die Fledermaus (komische Operette, 3, C. Haffner and R. Genée, after H. Meilhac and L. Halévy: *Le réveillon*), WW, 5 April 1874, *Wst**, vs (Vienna, 1874), full score (Zürich, 1968)

Cagliostro in Wien (komische Operette, 3, F. Zell and Genée), WW, 27 Feb 1875, autograph frags. *Wst*, vs (Vienna, 1875)

Prinz Methusalem (komische Oper, 3, C. Treumann, after Delacour and Wilder), Vienna, Carl, 3 Jan 1877, autograph frags. *Wst*, vs (Vienna, 1877)

Blindekuh (Operette, 3, R. Kneisel), WW, 18 Dec 1878, vs (Hamburg, 1879)

Das Spitzentuch der Königin (Operette, 3, H. Bohrmann-Riegen and Genée, after M. de Cervantes), WW, 1 Oct 1880, autograph frags. *Wst*, vs (Hamburg, 1880)

Der lustige Krieg (Operette, 3, Zell and Genée), WW, 25 Nov 1881, autograph frags. *Wst*, vs (Hamburg, 1881)

Eine Nacht in Venedig (komische Oper, 3, Zell and Genée, after E. Cormon and M. Carré: *Château Trompette*), Berlin, Friedrich Wilhelmstädtisches, 3 Oct 1883; WW, 9 Oct 1883, *US-STu**, vs (Hamburg, 1883), full score (Vienna, 1970)

Der Zigeunerbaron (Operette, 3, I. Schnitzer, after M. Jókai), WW, 24 Oct 1885, *A-Wst**, vs (Hamburg, 1886)

Der Schelm von Bergen, 1886 (Schnitzer, after H. Heine), inc., autograph sketches *Wst*

Simplicius (Operette, prelude, 2, V. Léon, after J. J. C. von Grimmelhausen: *Der abenteuerliche Simplicissimus*), WW, 17 Dec 1887, vs (Hamburg, 1888); rev. version, Vienna, WW, 19 Sept 1894, *Wst**

Ritter Pázmán (komische Oper, 3, L. Dóczi, after J. Arany), Vienna, Hofoper, 1 Jan 1892, *Wst**, vs (Berlin, 1892)

Fürstin Ninetta (3, H. Wittmann and J. Bauer), WW, 10 Jan 1893, autograph frags. *Wst*, vs (Hamburg, 1893)

Jabuka (3, M. Kalbeck and G. Davis), WW, 12 Oct 1894, autograph frags. *Wst*, vs (Vienna, 1894)

Waldmeister (Operette, 3, Davis), WW, 4 Dec 1895, vs (Berlin, 1896)

Die Göttin der Vernunft (Operette, 3, A. M. Willner and B. Buchbinder), WW, 13 March 1897, inc. autograph *Wst*, vs (Vienna, 1897)

ARRANGEMENTS BY OTHERS

selective list

Le reine Indigo (opérette, 3, A. Jaime and V. Wilder), Paris, Renaissance, 27 April 1875, vs (Paris, 1875); Ger., WW, 10 Oct 1877 [arr. from Indigo and other Strauss music]

La tzigane (opérette, 3, Wilder and A. Delacour), Paris, Renaissance, 30 Oct 1877, vs (Paris, 1877); Ger., Graz, Stadt, 16 Nov 1985 [arr. from Die Fledermaus, Cagliostro in Wien]

Wiener Blut (Operette, 3, Léon and L. Stein), Vienna, Carl, 25 Oct 1899, vs (Hamburg, 1899) [arr. A. Müller from pubd dances]

Gräfin Pepi (Operette, 3, Léon), Vienna, Venedig in Wien, 5 July 1902, vs (Leipzig, 1902) [arr. E. Reiterer from Simplicius, Blindekuh]

Tausend und eine Nacht (Operette, prelude, 2, Stein and C. Lindau), Vienna, Venedig in Wien, June 1906, vs (Leipzig, 1906) [arr. Reiterer from Indigo]

Reiche Mädchen (Operette, 3, F. Stollberg), Vienna, Raimund, 30 Dec 1909, vs (Vienna, 1909) [arr. from Die Göttin der Vernunft]

Der blaue Held (Operette, 3, Stollberg), WW, 18 Sept 1912 [arr. from Carneval in Rom]

Faschingshochzeit (Operette, O. Friedmann and F. Lunzer), Vienna, Carl, 25 May 1921 [arr. J. Klein]

Casanova (Operette, 7 scenes, R. Schanzer and E. Welisch), Berlin, Grosses Schauspielhaus, 1 Sept 1928, vs (Leipzig, 1928) [arr. R. Benatzky]

Walzer aus Wien [Waltzes from Vienna, The Great Waltz] (Spl, 3, Willner, H. Reichert and E. Marischka), Vienna, Stadt, 30 Oct 1930, vs (Vienna, 1930) [arr. J. Bittner, E. W. Korngold, after J. Strauss and J. Strauss (the elder)]

Die Tänzerin Fanny Elssler (Operette, 3, H. Adler), Berlin, Deutsches, 22 Dec 1934, vs (Leipzig, 1935) [arr. O. Stalla]

Die Straussbuben (Spl, 2, H. Marischka and R. Weis), Vienna, Raimund, 20 Oct 1946 [arr. Stalla from Johann and Josef Strauss]

*

L. Eisenberg: *Johann Strauss: ein Lebensbild* (Vienna, 1894)

E. Hanslick: 'Johann Strauss als Operncomponist', *Die moderne Oper*, ix (Berlin, 1900), 305–6

R. von Procházka: *Johann Strauss* (Berlin, 1900, 2/1903)

R. Heuberger: *Im Foyer* (Leipzig, 1901)

R. Specht: *Johann Strauss* (Berlin, 1909, 2/1922)

E. W. Engel: *Johann Strauss und seine Zeit* (Vienna, 1911) [calendar]

F. Lange: *Johann Strauss* (Leipzig, 1912)

P. Lindau: *Nur Erinnerungen*, ii (Stuttgart and Berlin, 1917)

E. Neumann: *Die Operetten von Johann Strauss: ihre Formen und das Verhältnis von Text und Musik* (diss., U. of Vienna, 1919)

I. Schnitzer: *Meister Johann: bunte Geschichten aus der Johann Strauss-Zeit* (Vienna, 1920)

E. Decsey: *Johann Strauss* (Stuttgart, 1922, 2/1948)

S. Loewy: *Johann Strauss: der Spielmann von der blauen Donau* (Vienna, 1924)

K. Kobald: *Johann Strauss* (Vienna, 1925)

A. Strauss, ed.: *Johann Strauss schreibt Briefe* (Berlin, 1926)

H. E. Jacob: *Johann Strauss und das neunzehnte Jahrhundert: die Geschichte einer musikalischen Weltherrschaft* (Amsterdam, 1937, 3/1962)

W. Jaspert: *Johann Strauss: sein Leben, sein Werk, seine Zeit* (Vienna, 1939, 2/1949)

E. Schenk: *Johann Strauss* (Potsdam, 1940)

J. Pastene: *Three-quarter Time: the Life and Music of the Strauss Family of Vienna* (New York, 1951)

M. Schönherr: 'Beiträge zu einer Bibliographie der Dynastie Strauss', *ÖMz*, xix (1964), 33–4

F. Racek: Preface to J. Strauss: *Eine Nacht in Venedig* (Vienna, 1970) [full score]

O. Schneidereit: *Johann Strauss und die Stadt an der schönen blauen Donau* (Berlin, 1972)

D. Stoverock: *Die Fledermaus* (Lichterfelde, 1973)

J. Wechsberg: *The Waltz Emperors* (London, 1973)

F. Racek: Preface to J. Strauss: *Die Fledermaus* (Vienna, 1974) [full score]
F. Mailer: *Das kleine Johann Strauss-Buch* (Salzburg, 1975)
——: '"Man tut mir zuviel Ehre an": Gedenken zum Persönlichkeitsbild von Johann Strauss', *ÖMz*, xxx (1975), 257–63
M. Prawy: *Johann Strauss: Weltgeschichte in Walzertakt* (Vienna, 1975)
F. Racek: *Johann Strauss zum 150. Geburtstag: Ausstellung der Wiener Stadtbibliothek 22. Mai bis 31. Oktober 1975* (Vienna, 1975)
——: 'Zur Entstehung und Aufführungsgeschichte der "Fledermaus"', *ÖMz*, xxx (1975), 264–72
A. Weinmann: 'Die Johann Strauss-Literatur: Versuch einer Zusammenfassung', *ÖMz*, xxx (1975), 298–302
A. Lamb: 'Johann Strauss and Operetta', *Opera*, xxvii (1976), 21–5, 122–5
——: 'Nights in Venice', *MT*, cxvii (1976), 989–92
——: 'Die Fledermaus: from Vaudeville Theatre to Opera House', *About the House*, v/4 (1977), 4–9
A. Blyth: 'Opera on the Gramophone: *Die Fledermaus*', *Opera*, xxix (1978), 22–34
N. Linke: *Johann Strauss (Sohn) in Selbstzeugnissen und Bilddokumenten* (Hamburg, 1982)
L'avant-scène opéra, no.49 (1983) [*Fledermaus* issue]
F. Mailer: *Johann Strauss (Sohn): Leben und Werk in Dokumenten* (Tutzing, 1983–)
A. Lamb: '*A Night in Venice* and *The Gipsy Baron*', *Opera on Record 3*, ed. A. Blyth (London, 1984), 248–63
P. Kemp: *The Strauss Family: Portrait of a Musical Dynasty* (Tunbridge Wells, 1985, 2/1989)
A. Lamb: '*Die Fledermaus* and Tradition', *Opera*, xlii (1991), 1405–09

ANDREW LAMB

Strauss, Richard (Georg) (*b* Munich, 11 June 1864; *d* Garmisch-Partenkirchen, 8 Sept 1949). German composer, the leading figure in German opera in the first half of the 20th century.

1. Before 1900. 2. After 1900. 3. Operas after 1900.

1. BEFORE 1900. Despite his operatic penchant for waltzes, Richard Strauss was no kin to the old Viennese waltz firm of Josef and the two Johanns. In fact he owed his surname to a decent gesture by his Bavarian grandfather Urban Strauss, who had permitted his illegitimate children – Richard's father Franz and a sister – to bear his name, but chose a different wife. Franz proved to be a fine natural musician, like his maternal uncles and younger stepbrothers, and he rose to become one of Germany's leading horn players: 42 years in the Munich court orchestra, and regularly summoned by Wagner to play first horn at Bayreuth (though Franz disapproved of both the man and his music). At 31 he had lost his first wife and family to the cholera epidemic of 1853, but he made a fortunate second marriage to a daughter of the renowned Bavarian brewers Pschorr. 'Pschorrbräu' – and 'Hackerbräu', brewed by a family who soon merged with the Pschorrs – are still honoured labels; and at the Pschorrbräu-Haus in Munich, Neuhauserstrasse 11–13, the menu-cards declare proudly that this was the *Geburtshaus* of Richard Strauss.

Financially secure, Franz could raise his new son and his daughter Johanna in comfort, and Richard was educated well. He had piano lessons from the age of four, and violin lessons from seven; in between he began regular, assiduous composing, a habit that was to last for some 80 years. At ten he was enrolled at the Ludwigsgymnasium for his secondary schooling, but from 11 he also learnt standard music theory, harmony and instrumentation from the conductor Friedrich Wilhelm Meyer – another of Franz's Munich court orchestra colleagues, like his earlier teachers. For longer than that, he had enjoyed free access to their orchestral rehearsals: a priceless advantage for a budding composer. At 13 he became a back-desk violinist in Franz's own semi-professional orchestra, and moved steadily forward. Many of his early piano pieces and songs survive (none, however, so precociously effective as to have entered the repertory). While still at the Ludwigsgymnasium, which instilled in him a lifelong reverence for classical culture, he composed a chorus from Sophocles' *Electra*. Before he turned 17, his String Quartet in A, a D minor Symphony and a *Festmarsch* (his published op.1) were all performed in Munich.

Though his father sought to protect him from Wagner's music as long as possible, Richard had heard *Tannhäuser* at 10, and then *Siegfried* and *Lohengrin*. He thought himself unimpressed; but at 17 he succumbed to *Tristan* (68 years later, he wrote of having 'positively wolfed the score of *Tristan*, as if in a trance') and soon also to the *Ring*. Around the time of the *Tristan* revelation, Strauss was composing the first of his pieces that would travel beyond his native city, the Cello Sonata in F, and – dedicated to the virtuoso Oscar Franz, but surely inspired by his own father Franz – the E♭ Horn Concerto no.1 (no.2 came 60 years later), and in the same key a Serenade for 13 wind instruments, which Hans von Bülow and his Meiningen court orchestra introduced to Berlin in 1883. In none of that music are there more 'Wagnerian' traces to be detected than in the work of many of his young contemporaries; it takes its place in the sturdily diatonic post-Weber tradition, with passing nods towards Schumann and Brahms.

Though Strauss's musical education had been thoroughly pragmatic, innocent of anything like radical theory or advanced speculation, it would have seemed redundant to send him on to a music academy. Once he matriculated at the Gymnasium (in 1882, the year of Wagner's *Parsifal* première) his formal studies ran no further than two terms at Munich University, where he read philosophy, aesthetics and art history. Then he made his first visit to Bayreuth. The experience of Wagner would reverberate in his music for most of his life – certainly as far as his penultimate opera *Die Liebe der Danae*: perhaps only in his final *Capriccio* (which he preferred modestly to call 'a conversation-piece') did he at last refine everything he had taken from Wagner into pure Strauss. Nonetheless, the young man whose imagination was seized by the Master was already a composer of individual character, with the basis of a professionally confident style. In due course he did produce one all-too-Wagnerian work, his first opera *Guntram* – but only ten years later; in the interim, he had established himself as the leading spirit of new German music.

After Strauss's 1883 Bayreuth trip his father paid his way to Leipzig and to Dresden, where the court orchestra under Franz Wüllner played his op.7 wind serenade, and then to Berlin for a much longer stay. That winter, Bülow not only performed the Serenade but commissioned a Suite from him for a similar band ('op.4': these early opus numbers are chronologically all awry). By luck the American conductor Theodore Thomas visited old Franz when the ink was just dry on Richard's new F minor Symphony, and the New York Philharmonic gave its première in December 1884; soon after, Wüllner conducted the first German performance, in Cologne. In retrospect, however, what looms largest in that period is Strauss's prolific output of lieder, of which perhaps a dozen have earned the status of evergreens – all with Straussian fingerprints (certain cadences at turning-points, teasing feints in the vocal lines, specially rapt treatment of some Romantic words) which would remain constant in his mature music.

In the summer of 1885 Bülow made him his assistant conductor at Meiningen. Soon Strauss played Mozart's C minor Piano Concerto with the orchestra, and then conducted his own F minor Symphony. When Brahms came to Meiningen to prepare the October première of his Fourth Symphony, he lent an interested ear (somewhat critical) to the young composer's work. In November, quite suddenly Bülow resigned and moved to Hamburg. The Duke of Saxe-Meiningen was happy to leave Strauss in charge of the orchestra – but with the senior conductor gone, the duke also set about reducing it to a mere 39 players. In April 1886 Strauss chose prudently, on Bülow's advice, to give up Meiningen in favour of a three-year contract with the Munich Hofoper. Before returning to Munich, however, he made his first visit to Italy (as recommended by Brahms); and the impression it left inspired an expansive 'symphonic fantasy' in four movements. In March 1887, under his own baton, the première of *Aus Italien* had a mixed but lively reception at the Munich Odeon. That fantasy, like the *Burleske* for piano and orchestra which he had drafted in Meiningen, still maintains a toehold in the repertory. He harboured doubts about the *Burleske*, which had to wait another three years for its first performance (along with that of his much newer *Tod und Verklärung*): again conducted by himself, but in Eisenach, with his friend Eugen d'Albert as soloist.

In both of the earlier works Strauss displayed a new concern with Brahmsian orchestral counterpoint, to the point of over-stuffing – leavened in the *Burleske* by pawky humour, in *Aus Italien* by picturesque colour and breezy tunes; but at Meiningen he had already begun *Macbeth*, the first of the 'tone poems' which would secure his lasting fame. It marked the fateful influence of another friend, his senior by some 30 years: Alexander Ritter, a first violin at Meiningen, impressively well-read and full of ideas about the true future of music. Where Bülow, once a firm Wagnerian (his wife Cosima, Liszt's daughter, had left him for the Master), had transferred his allegiance to the Brahms camp, Ritter – still married to a Wagner niece – was passionately devoted to the symphonic-dramatic ideals of Berlioz and Liszt as well as Wagner's. With a proselyte's fervour he expounded their scores to the 21-year-old Strauss, to whom much of that music was quite new. More, he electrified him with Wagnerian notions about the potential of music to represent and enact the deepest spiritual issues.

Nothing in Strauss's already extensive output had betrayed ambitions of that order. At most he aimed either to produce competent, original pieces in the established instrumental forms, or to illustrate poetry, as in his songs and his 1884 *Wandrers Sturmlied* chorus after Goethe. Even the puckish variety of the *Burleske* is contained under the umbrella of a Rondo; and though the finale of *Aus Italien* reviews earlier themes – neither more nor less arbitrarily than his French contemporaries liked to do, on César Franck's 'cyclical' plan – the whole remains a suite of contrasted movements. *Macbeth* announced a new model, the fruit of his intensive colloquies with Ritter, and ultimately of those Wagnerian preludes and interludes where fraught motifs are set in contrapuntal contention. He strove to capture the dynamic gist of a tragedy in one long, self-supporting, through-composed movement, stern and febrile by turns, with explicit story episodes but more genuinely symphonic than the Liszt exemplars. (In his orchestral works Liszt, like Berlioz, 'recalled' his tag-themes more often for dramatic effect than to find them fresh musical employment; his grand piano sonatas were more cogently 'symphonic' than most of his 'symphonic poems'.) But *Macbeth* hung fire for a long time, while Strauss made fretful revisions – an important one prompted by Bülow's comment that whereas an *Egmont* overture might close with the triumphal Egmont, no *Macbeth* one should culminate in the triumph of Macduff – which delayed its première until 1890 (in Weimar). Revised again for its second performance, it was warmly received in Berlin in 1892. Long before that Strauss had completed his *Don Juan*, much more swiftly and fluently, and in November 1889 conducted its acclaimed Weimar première only a month after taking up his new contract there.

Don Juan was written in Munich, and immediately after it most of *Tod und Verklärung* too, but Strauss was happy to depart for the Weimar Hofkapelle as full partner to the conductor Edward Lassen. In the larger city he had been frustrated as a mere third conductor, learning the current repertory – often with disdain – but rarely entrusted with the principal works. (An exception was Mozart's *Così fan tutte*, then gravely underrated, which he loved more than any opera but *Tristan*; a decade later he performed it with his own accompaniments to the *secco* recitatives, imaginative and much admired, and in 1910 he was still praising its 'superior ironies'.) Between ending his Munich term in July 1889 and going to Weimar, he agreed to work as a mere répétiteur at Bayreuth, where he would return five years later as conductor, with his wife as heroine.

She was the soprano PAULINE DE AHNA, the intelligent, wilful, prickly daughter of a General who was himself a doughty amateur baritone. Strauss met her in summer 1887 while visiting a Pschorr aunt in Feldafing, and was entranced. She had trained at the Munich Conservatory, without any professional outcome; in the spirit of Rossini's *Barbiere*, Strauss volunteered to give her advanced singing lessons. Her talent was genuine, and their relationship warmed rapidly. (He had had earlier affairs, but *Don Juan*, composed during the year after they met, was his first musical essay in erotic passion.) Once he was installed at Weimar, he managed to bring Pauline into the company. She sang Mozart's Pamina and Elvira, Wagner's Elisabeth, Elsa and Eva, and Hänsel in Humperdinck's opera – though not in its first-ever performance, which had fallen by luck to Weimar and Strauss when the intended Munich première was delayed: Pauline was disabled by a hurt foot, and took up her role later in the run. In May 1894 she created Freihild in Strauss's own *Guntram*, and he announced their engagement. In July, en route to Munich once more to become Hermann Levi's associate at the Opera, Strauss made his first Bayreuth appearance conducting *Tannhäuser*, with Pauline as Elisabeth; in September they were married. As a wedding gift, he wrote her the four famous songs of op.27.

The Weimar contract had been a mixed pleasure: satisfaction in his greater musical responsibilities and his own successful premières, disappointment with the modest numbers and resources of the Weimar company. Twice he fell seriously ill there, with a long convalescent break in Greece, Italy and Egypt during the winter of

1. Richard Strauss with his wife, the soprano Pauline De Ahna, and their son Franz

1892. Apart from completing *Tod und Verklärung*, what Strauss chiefly composed at Weimar was *Guntram*. The idea for the opera had come in 1887 from Ritter, who challenged him to meet Wagner's standard by writing his own libretto. All too earnestly, Strauss complied. For two years in Munich he laboured over the text, with a sedulously Wagnerian setting and situations – knights and Minnesingers, lofty conflict between *Bruderbund* duty and heartfelt impulse, even the names: Guntram, Freihild, Friedhold. (His dramaturgy drew some astute criticism from father Franz.) Then in Weimar he set it to music, for forces greatly exceeding the Weimar norm; and meanwhile he conducted a pair of one-act comedies by Ritter himself, for whom he preserved a lifelong admiration. In some of Strauss's next operas, his requirements would stretch the resources of any opera house.

Guntram enjoyed some *succès d'estime* at Weimar, and Mahler – whose acquaintance he had made in Munich earlier – praised the score at first glance. Strauss therefore had high expectations for the opera in his own city. He was shaken and wounded by the reception it got in November 1895, so loftily dismissive that the first performance became the last (though Pauline again had a personal success as Freihild). The drama was judged inept, incredible and interminable, despite the cuts he had made to his hero's strenuous role. On closer study of the music Mahler had already withdrawn his first opinion, and to the Wagnerian loyalists Guntram's ultimate choice – a Straussian departure from Ritter's original idea – signified a betrayal of the true faith. Unlike his obvious role models, Tannhäuser and Parsifal, Guntram renounces the *Bruderbund* at last and wills his own fate: the Wagnerites scented a Nietzschean apostasy. (Young Nietzsche's philosophical raptures over *Tristan* had made him welcome in Wagner's circle, but later he found *Parsifal* so repellently drenched in Schopenhauer's pessimism and quietism that he renounced Wagner in favour of the hypocrisy-free, 'Mediterranean' vitality of *Carmen*.) Indeed, Strauss was already at work on his Nietzschean tone poem *Also sprach Zarathustra*.

Its predecessor *Till Eulenspiegels lustige Streiche* was acclaimed at Cologne in the very month when *Guntram* foundered at Munich. Strauss's first plan for the folktale scamp Till had been to make an opera of him, but after lengthy, unconfident work on a libretto he decided instead to build a tone poem around his scapegrace history. In later years Strauss always claimed that the *Guntram* disaster had nearly wrecked his operatic ambitions; at the time, however, he must also have reflected that his notional *Till* opera had found a better realization as an orchestral piece, more boldly inventive than any of his *Guntram* music. In Frankfurt, *Zarathustra* made a great impression under his own baton in 1896. It was soon followed by *Don Quixote*, on a subject with obvious operatic potential – which he rendered instead as a cello concerto, in the form of 'fantastical variations on a theme of knightly character'. Though he composed it in Munich, the 1898 première went to Cologne. In the same year he was summoned to Berlin, to take Felix Weingartner's place as Royal Kapellmeister of the Hofoper; he completed *Ein Heldenleben* there, and conducted its triumphant Frankfurt première in 1899.

2. AFTER 1900. The above chronology should underline a remarkable fact about Strauss's long career: that by the end of the 19th century he had composed all the tone poems that ensured his lasting fame, but no successful opera, whereupon he devoted his half of the 20th century to opera above all. *Ein Heldenleben* had described a valedictory curve, with the concluding 'Hero's Works of Peace' illustrated by citations from Strauss's own past works – though he was only 34. He was to write just two more big orchestral pieces (not counting his ballets, the *Josephs-Legende* op.63 and *Schlagobers* op.70, nor his fine postwar string elegy, the 1945 *Metamorphosen*). The *Symphonia domestica* was completed in 1902–3, just before his decisive operatic breakthrough with *Salome*, and *Eine Alpensinfonie* (1911–15) came between the first and second versions of *Ariadne auf Naxos*. Though both 'symphonies' trace

scenarios as explicit as *Don Juan* or *Till* with a wealth of Straussian invention, they lack any cogent impetus, dramatic or symphonic. The earlier piece goes fluently through the motions of the late-Romantic German symphony, with no guiding purpose beyond evoking the random joys of domestic life (that of the *Familie* Strauss); the 'Alpine Symphony' is a scenic trip up and down an Alp, crying out for a movie to accompany it. Both pieces came from his time at the Berlin Hofoper, where after ten years he was promoted to Generalmusikdirektor and stayed ten years more; neither of them has entered the central Strauss canon.

In short, once Strauss was recognized as a significant operatic composer, his interest in other musical forms dwindled fast – except in lieder, which he continued to write as long as he lived (less frequently after Pauline's retirement from the concert platform, where he had been her regular accompanist). He admitted later that he always needed a text to get him started. But his priorities were the reverse of his close contemporary Hugo Wolf's: where Wolf had aimed at unimprovable refinement in his lieder, whilst vaguely imagining operas he might generate from them, Strauss's 20th-century songs were mostly wayside flowers along his determined operatic path. When accompanying them, he treated the published piano parts as mere raw material, and his singers had to brace themselves for spur-of-the-moment variations. There is complementary evidence from Alfred Orel, who turned Strauss's pages during an early 1920s recital with Elisabeth Schumann, to show how seriously he regarded his operas. Between songs, Orel reported, the composer

> fingered the keys apparently at random. Great was my amazement when I realized that it was always passages from his operas with which he made the transition to the new song, and specifically passages which were musically closely related to the song in question, but revealed that close relationship only now in the way he played them. Thus before 'Du meines Herzens Krönelein' he played very softly – apparently entirely for himself – the famous closing duet from *Der Rosenkavalier*.

After two decades at the Hofoper, Strauss spent one more year in Berlin as director of the new Staatsoper, and then moved to Vienna to take up a five-year contract (1919–24) as director – jointly with Franz Schalk – of the Staatsoper there. Even his librettist Hofmannsthal advised him against that; having to make invidious decisions about staging his own and/or other composers' operas, he was bound to incur criticism. So he did, in the event, but in hindsight his Vienna record looks honourable: under his directorship his contemporaries Korngold, Franz Schmidt, Schreker, Bittner, Zemlinsky and Weingartner all enjoyed Staatsoper productions of their work. His contract expired after his 60th birthday, upon which both Vienna and Munich had honoured him with the freedom of the city. Vienna also gave him a plot of land in the Belvedere, and he had a sumptuous villa built upon it, though the family's Garmisch villa remained his real home. Strauss never held another permanent post, for he no longer needed one; his international royalties and his appearances as guest conductor provided sufficient income.

When his Vienna term ended, he devised two substantial orchestral works with left-hand solo piano (unjustly forgotten now) to commissions from the one-armed pianist Paul Wittgenstein, brother of the philosopher Ludwig. Even those sprang from scenarios: the op.73 concerto 'Parergon' to the *Symphonia domestica* (1924) dramatized a Strauss family crisis, when their son Franz had been gravely ill and then recovered, and the elaborate musical frieze of the op.74 *Panathenäenzug*, 'Symphonic Studies in the form of a Passacaglia' (1927), depicted the grandest festival-procession of ancient Athens. Otherwise Strauss devoted himself to continuing his operatic collaboration – lifelong, as he supposed – with Hofmannsthal. In 1929 the untimely death of his junior partner left him grievously bereft, at the age of 65. Eventually he was persuaded to take on a new librettist, Stefan Zweig, and later Zweig's friend Joseph Gregor; meanwhile Hitler rose to power, and as the apolitical Strauss reached his eighth decade he found himself embroiled in ugly problems for which he had no stomach. As Germany's most famous living composer, he could mount crusty short-term defences for Jewish colleagues like Zweig; on the other hand, he dared not refuse his appointment by Goebbels to the presidency of the Reichsmusikkammer in 1933, and when in the same year Toscanini withdrew from a Bayreuth *Parsifal* on anti-Fascist grounds Strauss agreed to take his place. He was much criticized abroad. Still, an artist like Thomas Mann could exile himself by way of moral protest, and go on writing novels; for old Strauss, a professional composer of German operas for German companies and German audiences, there was nowhere else to go. Of his last five operas, *Die schweigsame Frau* (to Zweig's libretto) and the pacifist *Friedenstag* (Zweig/Gregor) met official disfavour, and *Die Liebe der Danae* was denied its Salzburg Festival première in 1944 when the war went badly for Germany.

Only in his last years did Strauss return to 'pure' music-making – sonatinas for wind band, the Oboe Concerto, the Duet-Concertino, and arguably his final opera *Capriccio* too – modestly disclaiming any intention beyond civilized, craftsmanly entertainment. While Germany surrendered to the Allies, however, he composed the grave, disconsolate *Metamorphosen* for strings. Then he retreated with Pauline to Switzerland, making visits abroad to conduct his own music and re-reading Goethe, until his official 'denazification' in 1948. They went home to Garmisch, where he wrote the Four Last Songs (a fifth, *Malven*, was published long after them) and died in peace. Dying, he declared, turned out to be 'just as I composed it in my *Death and Transfiguration*'.

3. Operas after 1900. After his luckless *Guntram*, Strauss wrote 14 more successful operas. *Feuersnot*, the earliest of them (1900–01), counts as a light comic intermezzo between *Guntram* and the third-time-lucky *Salome*. It was a rude squib, a bawdy old tale re-told by Strauss's friend Wolzogen as a parable about the narrow-minded Müncheners who had scorned *Guntram* and its Wagnerian inheritance. *Guntram* had been unremittingly sober and high-minded; for *Till Eulenspiegel* Strauss had already found a robust new vein of comedy, but it took *Feuersnot* to make operatic room for it (and probably some material from the abandoned *Till* opera, too). Though *Feuersnot* is an engaging piece, it was too much of its time – and particularly of its Bavarian place – to travel safely. It was quickly taken up nevertheless, first in Germany and Austria and then further afield, propelled by its enticing whiff of indelicacy and scandal.

That was a scent Strauss relished, as several more of his operas would testify. It was always more of an asset than a liability, despite prompting occasional disputes with local censors (in Berlin, the outraged Kaiser himself

sagt. Ah! ich will ihn jetzt küssen . . . Aber warum siehst du mich nicht an, Jochanaan? Deine Augen, die so schrecklich waren, so voller Wuth und Verachtung, sind jetzt geschlossen. Warum sind sie geschlossen? Öffne doch deine Augen! Erhebe deine Lider, Jochanaan! Warum siehst du mich nicht an? Hast du Angst vor mir, Jochanaan, dass du mich nicht ansehen willst? . . . Und deine Zunge, ~~die wie eine rothe, giftsprühende Schlange war, sie bewegt sich nicht mehr~~, sie spricht kein Wort, Jochanaan, diese Scharlachnatter, die ihren Geifer auf mich spie. Es ist seltsam, nicht? Wie kommt es, dass die rothe Natter sich nicht mehr rührt? . . . ~~Du wolltest mich nicht haben, Jochanaan! Du wiesest mich von dir.~~ Du sprachst böse Worte gegen mich, ~~Du benahmst dich gegen mich wie gegen eine Hure, wie gegen ein geiles Weib~~, gegen mich, Salome, die Tochter der Herodias, Prinzessin von Judäa! Nun wohl, ich lebe noch, aber du bist tot, und dein Kopf gehört mir. Ich kann mit ihm thun, was ich will. Ich kann ihn den Hunden vorwerfen und den Vögeln der Luft. Was die Hunde übrig lassen, sollen die Vögel der Luft verzehren . . . Ah! Jochanaan, Jochanaan, ~~du warst der Mann, den ich allein von allen Männern liebte! Alle anderen Männer waren mir verhasst.~~ Doch du warst schön! Dein Leib war eine Elfenbeinsäule auf silbernen Füssen.

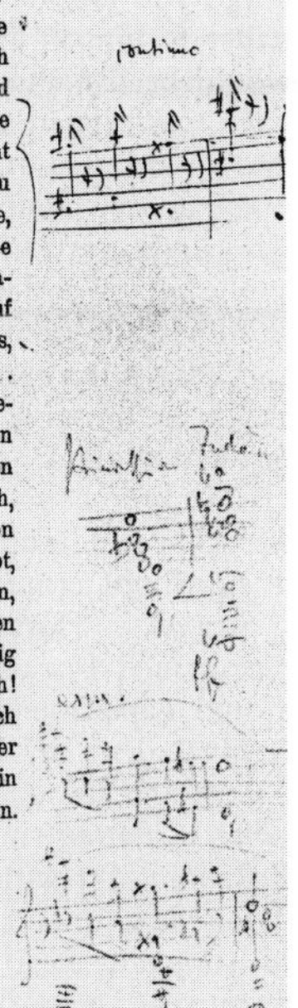

2. Opening from Strauss's working copy of Oscar Wilde's 'Salome' (1896), translated by H. Lachmann, with illustrations by Aubrey Beardsley

had the run of *Feuersnot* broken off); and generally it arose from something too central to the plot or situation to be either overlooked or hygienically expunged – Baron Ochs's gloating indecency in *Rosenkavalier*, the incestuous undercurrents of *Elektra*, the crucial bedtime deception in *Arabella*, the indelicately candid sketch of Strauss's own Pauline in *Intermezzo*. One should remember that his early battles with censors had to do with *operatic* propriety, with the limits thought proper to opera as refined spectacle. By contrast, stage plays written for Berlin and Vienna – by Wedekind, Kraus, Horvath, Hofmannsthal himself – revelled from the turn of the century until the rise of the Nazis in 'Freudian' subjects unknown to opera houses (though such stuff would have been suppressed in London, and New York would have recoiled). Strauss demanded no more than an equal licence for opera. His 1905 triumph with *Salome* emboldened other composers: Franz Schreker, for example, had let his own opera about sexual degradation, *Der ferne Klang*, hang fire until Strauss chanced his arm and won.

Salome, the start of his real career as an opera composer, was guaranteed scandalous, as in England the Lord Chamberlain had already judged Oscar Wilde's original play to be. The opera culminates in Salome's love-making to the severed head of John the Baptist – and Strauss's music, strictly faithful to the action, supplies an erotic charge far beyond the verbal fancies of Wilde's arch, bejewelled text. (A supposed photograph of the author, chastely robed to play his own heroine in a private performance, shows how different his imagined Salome was from the opera's nymphet Isolde.) What makes the opera work, however, and not merely titillate, is its superbly achieved musico-dramatic form. We may note that both *Salome*, which Wilde himself judged to have a 'musical' form, and Strauss's next opera *Elektra* resulted from his having seen the original plays staged by a master producer, Max Reinhardt. Instead of coping with untried librettos on paper, as with *Guntram* and *Feuersnot*, Strauss was devising musical expansions for texts he had already seen brilliantly played in real stage time. He never did that again; but at this point in his career, the luxury of writing music for known, well-paced theatrical successes must have been invaluable.

Both of those one-act plays offered him blueprints for realising the ideal mentioned earlier: a single 'symphonic' movement, through-composed but with room for pictorial episodes, which would capture the gist of a tragic drama. By now Strauss's symphonic technique had matured enormously through his tone poems. Where his earlier operatic attempts, with leitmotifs sedulously attached to characters and specific emotions in devout Wagnerian style, were still 'number-operas' in effect, *Salome* and *Elektra* generated whole symphonic spans. Each has a prologue for minor characters, at once an 'exposition' of principal themes – not, of course, an orderly Classical exposition – and of the dramatic situation. The advent of the heroine, who thereafter never leaves the stage, marks the start of the symphonic 'development' but brings a new theme or two as well. All that is developed purposefully towards a Romantic apotheosis, rather than a mere Classical recapitulation. The ultimate deserts of any Strauss heroine are not fated but passionately self-willed, and the Classical sense of an inevitable return would be out of place. Strauss was too thoroughly steeped in the Austro-German symphonic tradition, however, to feel as free as an Italian composer to introduce brand new tunes for finales; in all his operas he preferred to engineer some kind of recapitulation – usually illuminating, sometimes flat routine.

Elektra (1909) was Strauss's first opera to a text by Hugo von Hofmannsthal (who had vainly proposed a ballet to him in 1900, *Der Triumph der Zeit*). There would be five more, but to purpose-written librettos. Each was argued out by the collaborators, in structure and in detail – mostly through letters, because they made uneasy companions. The younger Hofmannsthal, who knew very little about music, was hyper-literary, sophisticated and keenly 'psychological'; partly in reaction, Strauss soon assumed the role of plain, down-to-earth Bavarian and practical musical showman. They chose to preserve an unlimited mutual respect at a prudent distance (something which Hofmannsthal was glad to keep between himself and the daunting Pauline, too). The resultant correspondence offers a uniquely full document of a rare operatic partnership.

Strauss's Hofmannsthal operas are sometimes represented as tracing a downward curve from the bold atonal experiments of *Elektra*, through a bourgeois retrenchment in *Der Rosenkavalier* and *Ariadne auf Naxos* and the quasi-Wagnerian exercises of *Die Frau ohne Schatten* and *Die ägyptische Helena*, to a *Rosenkavalier*-with-water reprise in *Arabella*. That is a dated view, one in which atonality was destined rather to supplant tonal music than merely to extend its resources. The great atonalist Schoenberg himself never thought that: he allowed that there was plenty of good music still to be written in C major. (It is worth remarking that Schoenberg composed his soprano monodrama *Erwartung* four years after *Salome*, at about the time of the *Elektra* première – and that he began his wryly 'modern', domestic comedy *Von heute auf morgen*, to a libretto by his wife, four years after the première of *Intermezzo*, Strauss's bourgeois comedy about himself and Pauline.) As a dramatic composer Strauss was primarily concerned with *Affekt*, and no less anxious than Verdi to find a 'tinta', a special musical colour, for each new opera. Skittish tonal dislocations had been apt for *Salome*; when he played the score to his father, who died six months before the première, old Franz exclaimed that it was 'just like having mayflies in one's pants'. For *Elektra*, the composer was anxious to disguise the close resemblance of its ground-plan to that of *Salome* with a palpably different sound-palette; furthermore the desperate tensions of *Elektra* needed to be more profoundly disorienting, and so it brandishes much longer passages of lurid, tonally rootless music. But Strauss, unlike Schoenberg, never saw atonality as a brave new musical realm to be systematically conquered; in *Elektra* it is only a theatrical recourse, sensationally orchestrated and effective, but not musically systematic at all – and the vital emotional moments, just as in *Salome*, are rooted in full-blooded tonality.

There are 'advanced' passages in most of his later operas – even in *Rosenkavalier* – which slip their tonal moorings by subtler, more musicianly steps. Had Strauss ever got hold of another blood-boltered tragedy, like the notional *Semiramis* that he proposed vainly to each new librettist, he might have explored that vein more deeply. After *Elektra*, however, he wanted first to make a contrasting hit with something operetta-ish, light, comic and sentimentally appealing – something very like *Die Fledermaus*, in fact. *Der Rosenkavalier* (1911) was meant to be that, but Strauss could not help responding to Hofmannsthal's rich text in depth, breadth and orchestral weight. Then their *Ariadne*, conceived as a miniature number opera, outgrew its limits; and later the light touch they intended for *Die ägyptische Helena* and *Arabella* was compromised by the playwright's penchant for deep psychology and Strauss's concern to do it full justice. Yet the composer never gave up his ambition to produce at least one cheerful piece with a bright, simple surface: without Hofmannsthal, he undertook four other operas in that hopeful spirit, with varying results. For none of them would he have dreamt of using anything but sunny major keys as their bases. As an operatic professional he knew his audiences very well, and respected the musical limits upon what they could perceive as the right *Affekt*.

Besides, Strauss himself associated particular keys with specific *Affekte*, instinctively and tenaciously. As music in the 20th century became chromatically volatile, most musicians came to regard such key associations as old-fashioned myths or at best inherited conventions, scientifically groundless. Not Strauss: for him D♭ major is always the tonality for serenely elevated rapture (whereas C♯, its enharmonic twin, comes with an uncanny shimmer), plain C is honest and upstanding, E♭ warmly expansive, C minor and D minor threatening and tragic in distinct ways, and so on for virtually all the other keys. If such verbal formulae are tendentious, Strauss's operatic practice leaves no doubt about his precise tonal convictions – normal enough by Romantic standards, but abnormally particularized. A careful comparison of what he chose to set in A major rather than in D or E, or between his uses of F and B♭, would discover fine distinctions beyond anything sanctified in tradition. Very often, if one can guess the expressive character Strauss would discern in a certain passage of a scenario, one can also predict the key in which he will compose it. To the ear – especially to ears that do not discern absolute pitch – Strauss's consistency about that is obscured by all his 'mayfly' modulations; in his printed scores, however, the key signatures change more slowly, displaying what he took to be the basic key of this or that number even where there are continual chromatic twists.

On the other hand, after his one-movement *Salome* and *Elektra* Strauss attached little importance to overall key structure in his operas. Every Mozart opera, like every Classical symphony, has a fundamental tonality which is significantly regained by the end; if a Mahler symphony concludes in a new key ('progressive tonality' is the usual label), that too makes a point. With Strauss, the fact that *Der Rosenkavalier* begins in E and ends in G seems arbitrary, like the tritone gap between the start and the finish of *Die schweigsame Frau*, or *Daphne*'s slide from G to F♯. To that extent he jettisoned a defining feature of 'symphonic' music. He may have judged that in highly chromatic modern writing like his own, few listeners would detect long-range tonal plans; or perhaps he just let his keys be dictated by the dramatic situations, scene by scene.

In Strauss as in mature Wagner, almost every detectible theme is pressed into service as a theatrical leitmotif too, and when woven together they can – with the help of programme notes, or the thematic catalogues that all Wagnerians know – 'tell a story'. Yet there is a marked difference between Wagner's use of the method, especially in the *Ring* and *Die Meistersinger*, and Strauss's as he developed it. Wagner's leitmotifs acquire their 'meanings' in many and various ways: by accompanying the entry of a certain character, or an onstage deed, or a mere verbal mention of something, or by being sung to crucial words. Sometimes they arrive even before the audience can learn their meanings (very rare in Strauss), but thereafter they are meant to evoke the things they stand for, not necessarily the dramatic situations in which they were first heard. They are strongly characterized and contrasted by rhythm and diction, by memorable harmonies or turns of phrase or instrumental colour, so that in contrapuntal conjunction they still stand out separately. The ones that really are signature tunes – for Siegfried, say, or Parsifal – can be treated as musical stand-ins for those characters, acquiring more sonorous traits as the characters mature.

Strauss's instinctive practice went another way. As his string of operas grew longer, he was less and less inclined to deploy leitmotifs like name tags (and programme notes become less confident about identifying their 'meanings'). Instead they recall moments of the drama already seen and heard, to fix the sense of the current scene. Even in *Salome*, what a programme note might call 'the Jokanaan themes' serve less to evoke the Prophet himself than the original force of his exalted scorn; in *Rosenkavalier*, the 'Heut' oder morgen' theme 'means' neither the Marschallin nor Fated Romantic Loss, but recalls her attempt in Act 1 to make Octavian understand that their affair will have a natural end. These are back-references, strictly internal to the music drama – there is no pretence that the characters or their ideals have some independent fictional existence beyond the stage action, as in Wagner's myths. There was a beautiful inevitability about Strauss's choice of a truly 'deconstructionist' piece as his operatic swansong, the 1942 *Capriccio*: the whole operatic action, as eventually we learn, is merely an opera written about the events of that day by the participants – whom we have not after all met, for we have been watching and hearing only their own representations of themselves. No opera could be more urbanely self-contained.

Furthermore Strauss's leitmotifs, unlike Wagner's, fall into increasingly distinct categories. Those that *are* primarily labels or mottos (in his 1919 *Frau ohne Schatten*, for example, the Falcon's cry and the warning that the Emperor will turn to stone) are gnomically memorable, too quirky to be digested in a running symphonic treatment. Contrariwise, the far more pervasive themes that carry emotional *Affekt* – the real threads of the musical drama – remain within the limits of Strauss's favoured lyrical idiom: poignant enough, but much narrower than the heroic range of Wagner's material. Though they answer perfectly to Hofmannsthal's delicately introspective studies, nothing in Strauss's operas after *Elektra* is comparable to Wagner's great orchestral episodes; the themes have too little muscular variety to generate a thrust of that order. When called upon to deliver 'epic' stuff for *Die Frau ohne Schatten*, Strauss fell back upon memories of *Lohengrin* and *Die Meistersinger*. Yet his resourceful fluency in lyrical, informal counterpoint is potently expressive on its own scale, and apt for capturing the private (bourgeois) crises of feeling that were Hofmannsthal's chief concern. It was a mode that required a tonal focus; from *Der Rosenkavalier* onwards Strauss confined his extra-tonal experiments to spooky scenes, momentary violence and local colour, and carried the main drama upon mellifluous harmony, freshly wrought in a wistful, backward-looking spirit.

After Hofmannsthal's abrupt demise, Strauss completed their *Arabella* slowly and painfully, and then brought himself to consider other librettists. He chose an intellectual Jewish writer, Stefan Zweig, who wrote him an astringent period-comedy – *Die schweigsame Frau* (1935) – which pleased him so much that he over-upholstered it with music. When the Nazi regime cut their collaboration short, Strauss took on Zweig's donnish friend Joseph Gregor in his stead, without enthusiasm. He accepted Gregor's completion of Zweig's *1648* (as *Friedenstag*), but fretted over Gregor's own *Daphne* text to the point where he threw Gregor's ending away and adopted a Clemens Krauss alternative. He allowed Gregor to draft a *Liebe der Danae* only when he remembered that Hofmannsthal himself had envisaged an opera on the Danae story; then he let Gregor try his hand at a 'words-versus-music' comedy that Zweig had originally suggested (after the Abbé Casti), but soon lost patience with him and wrote his own text for *Capriccio* with Krauss.

About those five post-Hofmannsthal operas no general remarks can be made with confidence, because three of them are still almost unknown and unexplored in the theatre. Even *Arabella* took some 30 years to enter the repertory, which the earlier *Ägyptische Helena* has never yet managed to do. Then *Capriccio* and *Daphne* – in that order – gained footholds, initially on the strength of the ravishing soprano soliloquies which end them (in quite different ways); but *Die schweigsame Frau* has rarely enjoyed a production with the large, expert cast that it needs, *Friedenstag* is all but forgotten (its dour single act is unseductive and awkward to programme), and the opulent *Danae* – for which Strauss wrung everything possible out of Gregor's torpid imagination, expecting it to be his last operatic testament – is forbiddingly expensive to cast and produce to the elegant standard required. Until we know them better, generalizations about 'late Strauss operas' are hazardous. The composer took a long, relaxed view of such problems: for the midpoint of 'Beim Schlafengehen', now the best-loved of his Four Last Songs, he lifted the rapt violin solo straight from Act 1 of the failed *Guntram* he had composed 56 years earlier.

See also ÄGYPTISCHE HELENA, DIE; ARABELLA; ARIADNE AUF NAXOS (ii); CAPRICCIO; DAPHNE; ELEKTRA; FEUERSNOT; FRAU OHNE SCHATTEN, DIE; FRIEDENSTAG; GUNTRAM; INTERMEZZO; LIEBE DER DANAE, DIE; ROSENKAVALIER, DER; SALOME; and SCHWEIGSAME FRAU, DIE.

op.	*title*	*genre, acts*	*libretto*	*first performance*	*remarks*
25	Guntram	3	R. Strauss	Weimar, Grossherzogliches Hof, 10 May 1894	comp. 1892–3; rev. 1934–9, Weimar, Deutsches, 29 Oct 1940
50	Feuersnot	Singgedicht, 1	E. von Wolzogen	Dresden, Hof, 21 Nov 1901	comp. 1900–01
54	Salome	Musikdrama, 1	O. Wilde, trans. H. Lachmann	Dresden, Hof, 9 Dec 1905	comp. 1903–5
58	Elektra	Tragödie, 1	H. von Hofmannsthal, after Sophocles: *Electra*	Dresden, Hof, 25 Jan 1909	comp. 1906–8
59	Der Rosenkavalier	Komödie für Musik, 3	Hofmannsthal	Dresden, Königliches, 26 Jan 1911	comp. 1909–10

op.	title	genre, acts	libretto	first performance	remarks
60	Ariadne auf Naxos		Hofmannsthal		
	1st version	Oper, 1		Stuttgart, Hof, 25 Oct 1912	comp. 1911–12; to be played after Molière: *Le bourgeois gentilhomme*
	2nd version	prol., 1		Vienna, Hof, 4 Oct 1916	
65	Die Frau ohne Schatten	Oper, 3	Hofmannsthal	Vienna, Staatsoper, 10 Oct 1919	comp. 1914–17
72	Intermezzo	bürgerliche Komödie mit sinfonischen Zwischenspielen, 2	Strauss	Dresden, Staatsoper, 4 Nov 1924	comp. 1918–23
75	Die ägyptische Helena	Oper, 2	Hofmannsthal	Dresden, Staatsoper, 6 June 1928	comp. 1923–7; rev. version Salzburg, Festspielhaus, 14 Aug 1933
79	Arabella	lyrische Komödie, 3	Hofmannsthal	Dresden, Staatsoper, 1 July 1933	comp. 1929–32
80	Die schweigsame Frau	komische Oper, 3	S. Zweig, after B. Jonson: *Epicoene*	Dresden, Staatsoper, 24 June 1935	comp. 1933–4
81	Friedenstag	Oper, 1	J. Gregor	Munich, Staatsoper, 24 July 1938	comp. 1935–6
82	Daphne	bukolische Tragödie, 1	Gregor	Dresden, Staatsoper, 15 Oct 1938	comp. 1936–7
83	Die Liebe der Danae	heitere Mythologie, 3	Gregor	dress rehearsal for cancelled première, Salzburg, Festspielhaus, 16 Aug 1944; première, Salzburg, Festspielhaus, 14 Aug 1952	comp. 1938–40
85	Capriccio	Konversationsstück für Musik, 1	Strauss and C. Krauss	Munich, Staatsoper, 28 Oct 1942	comp. 1940–41

OTHER STAGE WORKS

op.	title	genre, acts	libretto	first performance	remarks
	Iphigénie auf Tauris [C. W. von Gluck]			Weimar, Hof, 1890	new version
	Die Ruinen von Athen [L. van Beethoven]			Vienna, Staatsoper, 20 Sept 1924	new version, with Hofmannsthal, with borrowings from Beethoven's *Prometheus*
	Idomeneo [W. A. Mozart]			Vienna, Staatsoper, 16 April 1931	new version, with Wallerstein
	Des Esels Schatten	Komödie in sechs Bildern [school op]	Gregor and H. Adler	Ettal, Gymnasium, 7 June 1964	comp. 1947–8, inc., completed K. Haussner

CORRESPONDENCE

F. Strauss, ed.: *Richard Strauss: Briefwechsel mit Hugo von Hofmannsthal* (Berlin, 1925; Eng. trans., 1928)

Richard Strauss et Romain Rolland: correspondance, fragments de journal (Paris, 1951; Eng. trans., 1968)

F. von Schuch: *Richard Strauss, Ernst von Schuch und Dresdens Oper* (Leipzig, 1952, 2/1953)

W. Schuh, ed.: *Richard Strauss und Hugo von Hofmannsthal: Briefwechsel: Gesamtausgabe* (Zürich, 1952, enlarged 2/1955; Eng. trans., 1961)

R. Tenschert, ed.: *Richard Strauss und Joseph Gregor: Briefwechsel 1934–1949* (Salzburg, 1955)

W. Schuh, ed.: *Richard Strauss, Stefan Zweig: Briefwechsel* (Frankfurt am Main, 1957; Eng. trans., 1977)

E. Müller von Asow: 'Richard Strauss und Giuseppe Verdi', *ÖMz*, xvi (1961), 348–53

H. Fähnrich: 'Richard Strauss über das Verhältnis von Dichtung und Musik (Wort und Ton) in seinem Opernschaffen', *Mf*, xiv (1961), 22–35

G. K. Kende and W. Schuh, eds.: *Richard Strauss, Clemens Krauss: Briefwechsel* (Munich, 1963, 2/1964)

G. K. Kende: 'Aus dem Briefwechsel Richard Strauss/Clemens Krauss: 12 unveröffentlichte Briefe', *SMz*, cvi (1966), 2–10

W. Schuh, ed.: *Richard Strauss: Briefwechsel mit Willi Schuh* (Zürich, 1969)

K. W. Birkin: 'Strauss, Zweig and Gregor: Unpublished Letters', *ML*, lvi (1975), 180–95

F. Trenner, ed.: *Cosima Wagner–Richard Strauss: ein Briefwechsel* (Tutzing, 1978)

H. E. Mutzenbecher: 'In memoriam Joseph Gregor', *Richard-Strauss-Blätter*, new ser., no.4 (1980), 5–17

CATALOGUES, DOCUMENTARY MATERIAL, MEMOIRS, ICONOGRAPHY

S. Zweig: *Die Welt von gestern: Erinnerungen eines Europäers* [1942] (Stockholm, 1944; Eng. trans., 1943)

E. Roth, ed.: *Richard Strauss: Bühnenwerke* (London, 1954) [text in Ger., Eng., Fr.]

W. Schuh: *Das Bühnenwerk von Richard Strauss in den unter Mitwirkung des Komponisten geschaffenen letzten Münchner Inszenierungen* (Zürich, 1954)

F. Trenner: *Richard Strauss: Dokumente seines Lebens und Schaffens* (Munich, 1954)

A. Jefferson: *The Operas of Richard Strauss in Britain 1910–1963* (London, 1963)

L. Kusche: *Richard Strauss im Kulturkarussell der Zeit 1864–1964* (Munich, 1964)

O. Ortner, ed.: *Richard-Strauss-Bibliographie, Teil 1: 1882–1944* (Vienna, 1964)

W. Schuh and E. Roth, eds.: *Richard Strauss: Complete Catalogue* (London, 1964)

W. Deppisch: *Richard Strauss in Selbstzeugnissen und Bilddokumenten* (Reinbek, nr Hamburg, 1968)

G. Brosche, ed.: *Richard-Strauss-Bibliographie, Teil 2: 1944–1964* (Vienna, 1973)

A. Jefferson: *Richard Strauss* (London, 1975)
G. Jaaks and A. W. Jahnke, eds.: *Richard Strauss 1864–1949: Musik des Lichts in dunkler Zeit, vom Bürgerschreck zum Rosenkavalier* (Mainz, 1980)

SPECIAL PERIODICAL ISSUES

Die Musik, iv/8 (1905)
Tempo, no.12 (1949)
Mitteilungen der Internationalen Richard-Strauss-Gesellschaft, i–lxiii (Berlin, 1952–69)
W. Schuh, ed.: *Richard Strauss Jb 1954*
——: *Richard Strauss Jb 1959–60*
Tempo, no.69 (1964) [centenary number]
Richard-Strauss-Blätter, nos.1–12 (Vienna, 1971–8)
Richard-Strauss-Blätter, new ser. (Tutzing, 1979–)

LIFE, WORKS

E. Urban: *Richard Strauss* (Berlin, 1901)
——: *Strauss contra Wagner* (Berlin, 1902)
P. Marsop: 'Italien und der "Fall Salome", nebst Glossen zur Kritik und Ästhetik', *Die Musik*, vi/2 (1906–7), 139–57
E. Newman: *Richard Strauss* (London, 1908)
W. Reich: 'Bemerkungen zum Strauss'schen Opernschaffen, anlässlich des 70. Geburtstages', *Der Auftakt*, xiv (1934), 101–5
J. Kapp: *Richard Strauss und die Berliner Oper* (Berlin, 1934–9)
E. Krause: *Richard Strauss: Gestalt und Werk* (Leipzig, 1955, 6/1980; Eng. trans., 1964)
H. Friess: 'Richard Strauss and the Bavarian State Opera', *Tempo*, no.43 (1957), 26–9
R. Tenschert: 'Richard Strauss: Gedenken der Rheinoper', *ÖMz*, xiv (1959), 421–2
S. von Scanzoni: *Richard Strauss und seine Sänger: eine Plauderei über das Musiktheater in den Wind gesprochen* (Munich, 1961)
N. Del Mar: *Richard Strauss: a Critical Commentary on his Life and Works* (London, 1962–72/*R* with corrections 1978)
F. Trenner: 'Richard Strauss and Munich', *Tempo*, no.49 (1964), 5–14
L. Wurmser: 'Richard Strauss as an Opera Conductor', *ML*, xlv (1964), 4–15
G. R. Marek: *Richard Strauss: the Life of a Non-Hero* (New York, 1967)
F. Grasberger: *Richard Strauss und die Wiener Oper* (Tutzing, 1969)
A. Jefferson: *The Life of Richard Strauss* (Newton Abbot, 1973)
M. Kennedy: *Richard Strauss* (London, 1976)
W. Schuh: *Richard Strauss: Jugend und Meisterjahre: Lebenschronik 1864–98* (Zürich, 1976; Eng. trans., 1982)
K. Wilhelm: *Richard Strauss: an Intimate Portrait* (London, 1989)

OPERAS

General

E. Schmitz: *Richard Strauss als Musikdramatiker: eine aesthetischkritische Studie* (Munich, 1907)
P. Bekker: *Das Musikdrama der Gegenwart* (Stuttgart, 1909)
G. Gräner: *Richard Strauss: Musikdramen* (Berlin, 1909)
O. R. Hübner: *Richard Strauss und das Musikdrama: Betrachtungen über den Wert oder Unwert gewisser Opernmusiken* (Leipzig, 1910)
M. Steinitzer: *Richard Strauss in seiner Zeit, mit einem Abdruck der auf der Strausswoche zu Stuttgart im Kgl. Hoftheater gehaltenen Rede und einem Bildnis* (Leipzig, 1914)
A. Rosenzweig: *Zur Entwicklungsgeschichte des Strauss'schen Musikdramas* (diss., U. of Vienna, 1923)
R. Specht: 'Von *Guntram* zur *Frau ohne Schatten*', *Almanach der deutschen Musikbücherei*, ed. G. Bosse (Regensburg, 1923), 150–63
K. Westphal: 'Das musikdramatische Prinzip bei Richard Strauss', *Die Musik*, xix (1926–7), 859–64
K. H. Ruppel: 'Richard Strauss und das Theater', *Melos*, xiii (1934), 175–9
K.-J. Krüger: *Hugo von Hofmannsthal und Richard Strauss: Versuch einer Deutung des künstlerischen Weges Hugo von Hofmannsthals, mit einem Anhang: erstmalige Veröffentlichung der bisher ungedruckten einzigen Vertonung eines Hofmannsthalschen Gedichtes durch Richard Strauss* (Berlin, 1935)
J. Gregor: *Richard Strauss: der Meister der Oper* (Munich, 1939, 2/1942)
R. Tenschert: 'Hosenrollen in den Bühenwerken von Richard Strauss', *ZfM*, Jg.106 (1939), 586–90
A. Mathis: 'Stefan Zweig as Librettist and Richard Strauss', *ML*, xxv (1944), 163–76, 226–45
O. Gatscha: *Librettist und Komponist: dargestellt an den Opern Richard Strauss'* (diss., U. of Vienna, 1947)
W. Schuh: *Über Opern von Richard Strauss* (Zürich, 1947)
O. Erhardt: 'The Later Operatic Works of Richard Strauss', *Tempo*, no.12 (1949), 23–31
F. Trenner: *Die Zusammenarbeit von Hugo von Hofmannsthal und Richard Strauss* (diss., U. of Munich, 1949)
R. Schopenhauer: *Die antiken Frauengestalten bei Richard Strauss* (diss., U. of Vienna, 1952)
W. Schuh, ed.: *Richard Strauss und Hugo von Hofmannsthal: Briefwechsel: Gesamtausgabe* (Zürich, 1952, enlarged 2/1955; Eng. trans., 1961)
E. Wellesz: 'Hofmannsthal and Strauss', *ML*, xxxiii (1952), 239–42
G. Hausswald: *Richard Strauss: ein Beitrag zur Dresdener Operngeschichte seit 1945* (Dresden, 1953)
W. Wendhausen: *Das stilistische Verhältnis von Dichtung und Musik in der Entwicklung der musikdramatischen Werke Richard Strauss'* (diss., U. of Hamburg, 1954)
R. Tenschert: 'Composer and Librettist', *Tempo*, no.41 (1956), 24–8
G. Baum: *'Hab' mir's gelobt, ihn lieb zu haben …': Richard Strauss und Hugo von Hofmannsthal nach ihrem Briefwechsel dargestellt* (Berlin, 1962)
A. A. Abert: 'Stefan Zweigs Bedeutung für das Alterswerk von Richard Strauss', *Festschrift Friedrich Blume zum 70. Geburtstag* (Kassel, 1963), 7–15
A. Natan: *Richard Strauss: die Opern* (Basle, 1963)
L. Lehmann: *Five Operas and Richard Strauss* (New York, 1964; as *Singing with Richard Strauss*, London, 1964)
W. Mann: *Richard Strauss: a Critical Study of the Operas* (London, 1964)
W. Schuh: *Hugo von Hofmannsthal und Richard Strauss: Legende und Wirklichkeit* (Munich, 1964)
R. Tenschert: 'Richard Strauss und Stefan Zweig', *ÖMz*, xxiii (1968), 75–9
H. Becker: 'Richard Strauss als Dramatiker', *Beiträge zur Geschichte der Oper* (Regensburg, 1969), 165–81
P. Burwik: *Die Bühnenbilder zu den Wiener Aufführungen von Richard Strauss-Opern, 1902–1964* (diss., U. of Vienna, 1970)
W. Schuh: 'Richard Strauss und seine Libretti', *GfMKB, Bonn 1970*, 169–73
A. A. Abert: *Richard Strauss: die Opern: Einführung und Analyse* (Hanover, 1972)
J. Knaus: 'Leoš Janáček und Richard Strauss', *NZM*, Jg.133 (1972), 128–30
A. A. Abert: 'Richard Strauss' Anteil an seinen Operntexten', *Musicae scientiae collectanea: Festschrift Karl Gustav Fellerer* (Cologne, 1973), 1–11
O. Hafner: 'Richard Strauss und die Grazer Oper', *ÖMz*, xxxiv (1979), 498–503
A. Giubertoni: 'L'ombra tra Hofmannsthal e Strauss', *NRMI*, xiv (1980), 205–15
R. Hartmann: *Die Bühnenwerke von der Uraufführung bis heute* (Fribourg, 1980; Eng. trans., 1981)
M. Prawy: '"Hab' mir's gelobt …": die Aria Richard Strauss', *Oper heute: ein Almanach der Musikbühne*, ed. H. Seeger and M. Rank, iii (Berlin, 1980), 137–49
N. Del Mar: *The Anatomy of the Orchestra* (London, 1981)
B. Gilliam: 'Stefan Zweig's Contribution to Strauss Opera after *Die schweigsame Frau*', *Richard-Strauss-Blätter*, new ser., no.5 (1981), 48–57
K. W. Birkin: 'Collaboration out of Crisis (Strauss-Zweig-Gregor)', *Richard-Strauss-Blätter*, new ser., no.9 (1983), 50–76
C. Osborne: *Complete Operas of Richard Strauss* (London, 1988)
D. B. Greene: *Listening to Strauss' Operas: the Audience's Multiple Standpoint* (New York, 1991)

Die ägyptische Helena

H. von Hofmannsthal: *Die ägyptische Helena*, *Insel-Almanach* (1929); also in *H. von Hofmannsthal: Selected Writings*, ed. M. Hottinger, T. Stern and J. Stern, iii: *Selected Plays and Libretti* (London and New York, 1963), 756–70

Arabella

W. Schuh: 'Eine nicht komponierte Szene zur *Arabella*', *SMz*, lxxxiv (1944), 231–5
——: '*Arabella*: die ursprüngliche Fassung des I. Aktes', *Die neue Rundschau*, lxiv (1953), 357–91

R. Tenschert: '*Arabella*: die letzte Gemeinschaft von Hugo von Hofmannsthal und Richard Strauss', *ÖMz*, xiii (1958), 323–7
N. John, ed.: *Arabella* (London, 1985) [ENO Opera Guide]
K. Birkin: *Richard Strauss: Arabella* (Cambridge, 1989)

Ariadne auf Naxos

F. Torrefranca: 'La nuova opera di Riccardo Strauss', *RMI*, xix (1912), 986–1031
B. Diebold: 'Die ironische *Ariadne* und der *Bürger als Edelmann*', *Deutsche Bühne*, i (1918), 219–44
P. Nicolai: *Der Ariadne-Stoff in der Entwicklungsgeschichte der deutschen Oper* (Viersen, 1919)
K. K. Eberlein: 'Problem im Barock', *Das National-Theater*, iv (Berlin, 1933), 12–19
E. Lismann: 'Ariadne auf Naxos', *Tempo*, no.28 (1953), 25–8
D. G. Daviau and G. J. Buelow: *The 'Ariadne auf Naxos' of Hugo von Hofmannsthal and Richard Strauss* (Chapel Hill, 1975)
W. Schuh: 'Hofmannsthals Randnotizen für Richard Strauss im *Ariadne* Libretto', *Für Rudolf Hirsch: zum siebzigsten Geburtstag* (Frankfurt, 1975), 224–35
——: 'Metamorphosen einer Ariette von Richard Strauss', *Opernstudien: Anna Amalie Abert zum 65. Geburtstag* (Tutzing, 1975), 197–208
G. Brosche: 'Der Schluss der Oper *Ariadne auf Naxos*: neue Aspekte zur Entstehung des Werkes', *ÖMz*, xxxiv (1979), 329–34
C. Erwin: 'Richard Strauss's Presketch Planning for *Ariadne auf Naxos*', *MQ*, lxvii (1981), 348–65
K. Forsyth: *'Ariadne auf Naxos' by Hugo von Hofmannsthal and Richard Strauss: its Genesis and Meaning* (London and Oxford, 1982)
L'avant-scène opéra, no.77 (1985) [*Ariadne auf Naxos* issue]

Capriccio

R. Hartmann: *Capriccio: ein Konversationsstück für Musik in 1 Aufzug von Clemens Krauss und Richard Strauss, op.85: Regieangaben nach Erfahrungen der Uraufführung, Staatsoper München, 28. Oktober 1942* (Berlin, 1943)
G. Becker: *Das Problem der Oper an Hand von Richard Strauss' Capriccio* (diss., U. of Jena, 1944)
R. Tenschert: 'The Sonnet in Richard Strauss's Opera "Capriccio"', *Tempo*, no.47 (1958), 7–11
H. F. Redlich: '"Prima la musica ...?": a Ruminative Comment on Richard Strauss' Final Opera', *MR*, xxiv (1963), 185–9
R. H. McConnaughey: *Richard Strauss's 'Capriccio': a Conversation Piece in One Act* (diss., Boston U., 1986)
D. H. Saunders: *Capriccio, by Richard Strauss and Clemens Krauss: Theoretical Discussion as Theatrical Presentation, together with Three Recitals of Selected Works of Strauss, Wagner, Verdi, Mozart, Britten and Prokofiev* (diss., North Texas State U., 1986)

Daphne

J. Gregor: 'Zur Entstehung von Richard Strauss' *Daphne*', *Almanach zum 35. Jahr des Verlags R. Piper & Co., München* (Munich, 1939), 104
B. R. Gilliam: *Richard Strauss's Daphne: Opera and Symphonic Continuity* (diss., Harvard U., 1984)
K. Birkin: *Friedenstag and Daphne: an Interpretative Study of the Literary and Dramatic Sources of Two Operas by Richard Strauss* (New York and London, 1989)

Elektra

P. Bekker: '*Elektra*: Studie', *Neue Musik-Zeitung*, xxx (1909), 293–8, 333–7, 387–91
E. Fischer-Plasser: *Einführung in die Musik von Richard Strauss und Elektra* (Leipzig, 1909)
C. Mennicke: 'Über Richard Strauss' *Elektra*', *Riemann-Festschrift* (Leipzig, 1909), 503–24
F. Torrefranca: 'Riccardo Strauss e l'*Elektra*', *RMI*, xvi (1909), 335–84
E. Hutcheson: *Elektra by Richard Strauss: a Guide to the Opera with Musical Examples from the Score* (New York, 1910)
W. Klein: 'Die Harmonisation in *Elektra* von Richard Strauss: ein Beitrag zur modernen Harmonisationslehre', *Der Merker*, ii (1911), 512–14, 540–43, 590–92
R. Wittelsbach: 'Betrachtungen zu *Salome* und *Elektra*', *Festschrift 1817–1967: Akademie für Musik und darstellende Kunst in Wien* (Vienna, 1967), 93–9
K. Overhoff: *Die Elektra-Partitur von Richard Strauss* (Salzburg, 1978)
M. Enix: 'A Reassessment of *Elektra* by Strauss', *Indiana Theory Review*, ii/3 (1979), 31–8
S. E. Bales: *Elektra: from Hofmannsthal to Strauss* (diss., Stanford U., 1984)
R. A. Kaplan: *The Musical Language of 'Elektra': a Study in Chromatic Harmony* (diss., U. of Michigan, 1985)
L'avant-scène opéra, no.92 (1986) [*Elektra* issue]
B. R. Gilliam: 'Strauss Preliminary Opera Sketches, Thematic Fragments and Symphonic Continuity', *19th Century Music*, ix (1986), 176–88
N. John, ed.: *Salome/Elektra* (London, 1988) [ENO Opera Guide]
N. R. Adams: *'Elektra' as Opera and Drama* (diss., U. of Pennsylvania, 1989)
D. Puffett, ed.: *Richard Strauss: Elektra* (Cambridge, 1990)

Die Frau ohne Schatten

R. Specht: 'Vom *Guntram* zur *Frau ohne Schatten*', *Almanach der Deutschen Musikbücherei*, ed. G. Bosse (Regensburg, 1923), 150–63
J. Gregor: 'Die west-östlich Gedankenwelt von Hofmannsthals "Die Frau ohne Schatten"', *Programmheft des Operntheaters Wien*, viii (1931), 2–20
H. Röttger: *Das Formproblem bei Richard Strauss, gezeigt an der Oper 'Die Frau ohne Schatten', mit Einschluss von 'Guntram' und 'Intermezzo'* (diss., U. of Munich, 1935; abridged, Berlin, 1937)
O. Erhardt: 'Richard Strauss's *Die Frau ohne Schatten*', *Tempo*, no.17 (1950), 24–8
S. Beinl: 'A Producer's Viewpoint: Notes on *Die Frau ohne Schatten*', *Tempo*, no.24 (1952), 29–31
J. Knaus: *Hugo von Hofmannsthal und sein Weg zur Oper Die Frau ohne Schatten* (Berlin, 1971)
G. I. Ascher: *Die Zauberflöte und Die Frau ohne Schatten: ein Vergleich zwischen zwei Operndichtungen der Humanität* (Berne, 1972)
S. Pantle: *'Die Frau ohne Schatten' by Hugo von Hofmannsthal and Richard Strauss: an Analysis of Text, Music and their Relationship* (Berne, 1978)

Friedenstag

P. M. Potter: 'Strauss's *Friedenstag*: a Pacifist Attempt at Political Resistance', *MQ*, lxix (1983), 408–24
C. Dahlhaus: 'Was it an Aesthetic of Resistance? The Case of Richard Strauss' *Friedenstag*', *BMw*, xxviii (1986), 18–22

Guntram

H. Röttger: *Das Formproblem bei Richard Strauss, gezeigt an der Oper 'Die Frau ohne Schatten', mit Einschluss von 'Guntram' und 'Intermezzo'* (diss., U. of Munich, 1935; abridged, Berlin, 1937)

Intermezzo

W. Virneisel: 'Richard Strauss' *Intermezzo*', *ZfM*, Jg.96 (1929), 131–5, 201–4
H. Röttger: *Das Formproblem bei Richard Strauss, gezeigt an der Oper 'Die Frau ohne Schatten', mit Einschluss von 'Guntram' und 'Intermezzo'* (diss., U. of Munich, 1935; abridged, Berlin, 1937)
E. Graf: 'Die Bedeutung von Richard Strauss' *Intermezzo*', *ÖMz*, xviii (1963), 241–9

Die Liebe der Danae

D. Lindner: *Richard Strauss/Joseph Gregor: Die Liebe der Danae: Herkunft, Inhalt und Gestaltung eines Opernwerkes* (Vienna, 1952)
W. Schuh, ed.: *Hugo von Hofmannsthal: Danae oder die Vernunftheirat: Szenarium und Notizen* (Frankfurt, 1952)
R. Tenschert: 'A "Gay Myth": the Story of *Die Liebe der Danae*', *Tempo*, no.24 (1952), 5–11
W. Keller: '*Die Liebe der Danae*: ein Wagner-Oper von Richard Strauss? Ein Beitrag zur ästhetischen Manipulation', *NZM*, Jg. 134 (1973), 628–33
K. Birkin: 'The Last Meeting: "Die Liebe der Danae" Reconsidered', *Tempo*, no.153 (1985), 13–19

Der Rosenkavalier

F. Torrefranca: 'Il Rosenkavalier di Riccardo Strauss', *RMI*, xviii (1911), 147–79
E. Blom: *The Rose Cavalier* (London, 1930)
G. Röttger: *Die Harmonik in Richard Strauss' Der Rosenkavalier: ein Beitrag zur Entwicklung der romantischen Harmonik nach Richard Wagner* (diss., U. of Munich, 1931)
A. Pryce-Jones: *Richard Strauss: Der Rosenkavalier* (London, 1947)
F. Staiger: 'Betrachtungen zum *Rosenkavalier*', *Musik und Dichtung* (Zürich, 1947), 86–98; also in *Universitas*, v (1950), 919–25

W. Schuh: 'Die Entstehung des *Rosenkavalier*', *Trivium* [Zürich], ix/2 (1951), 65–91
——: '*Der Rosenkavalier*: die ursprüngliche Fassung des II. Aktes', *Die neue Rundschau*, lxiv (1953), 357–91
K. Pörnbacher: *Hugo von Hofmannsthal/Richard Strauss: Der Rosenkavalier* (Munich, 1964)
R. Gerlach: *Don Juan und Rosenkavalier* (Berne, 1966)
H. Schnoor: *Die Stunde des Rosenkavalier: 300 Jahre Dresdner Oper* (Munich, 1968)
W. Schuh: *Der Rosenkavalier: 4 Studien* (Olten, 1968)
O. Schneider: '*Der Rosenkavalier* in Salzburg', *ÖMz*, xxiv (1969), 451–3
A. Wasdruszka: 'Das *Rosenkavalier* Libretto', *ÖMz*, xxiv (1969), 440–45
W. Schuh, ed.: *Hugo von Hofmannsthal, Richard Strauss: Der Rosenkavalier: Fassungen, Filmszenarium, Briefe* (Frankfurt, 1971)
R. Gerlach: 'Die ästhetische Sprache als Problem im Rosenkavalier', *Melos/NZM*, i (1975), 95–101, 278–86
D. Zimmerschied: 'Integration in Liebe oder brutale Vertreibung? Versuche zur Deutung der Sängerepisode im "Rosenkavalier"', *Mf*, xxxii (1979), 291–7
N. John, ed.: *Der Rosenkavalier* (London, 1981) [ENO Opera Guide; incl. articles by D. Puffett, M. Kennedy, P. Branscombe, libs. in Ger. and Eng.]
R. Sussman Stewart, ed.: *Der Rosenkavalier* (London, 1983) [Met Opera Classics; incl. articles by G. R. Marek, A. Burgess, libs. in Ger. and Eng.]
L'avant-scène opéra, nos.69–70 (1984) [*Rosenkavalier* issue]
W. Mann: '*Der Rosenkavalier* or the Country-Cousin', *About the House*, vii/1 (1984), 4–7
B. R. Gilliam: 'Strauss Preliminary Opera Sketches, Thematic Fragments and Symphonic Continuity', *19th Century Music*, ix (1986), 176–88
A. Jefferson, ed.: *Richard Strauss: Der Rosenkavalier* (Cambridge, 1986)

Salome

L. Gilman: *Strauss' Salome: a Guide to the Opera* (New York, 1906)
L. Torchi: '*Salome* di Richard Strauss', *RMI*, xiv (1907), 113–56
H. Daffner: *Salome: ihre Gestalt in Geschichte und Kunst, Dichtung, bildender Kunst, Musik* (Munich, 1912)
W. Schuh: 'Zur harmonischen Deutung des *Salome*-Schlusses', *SMz*, lxxxvi (1946), 452–8
H. Grabner: 'Eine denkwürdige Erstauf-Erstaufführung', *40 Jahre steierischer Tonkünstlerbund* (Graz, 1967), 49–51
R. Wittelsbach: 'Betrachtungen zu *Salome* und *Elektra*', *Festschrift 1817–1967: Akademie für Musik und darstellende Kunst in Wien* (Vienna, 1967), 93–9
C. Höslinger: '*Salome* und ihr österreichisches Schicksal, 1905–1919', *ÖMz*, xxxii (1977), 300–09
M. Hurlimann: 'Wie-schön-ist-die-Prinzessin-Salome-heut-nacht', *Du-Kunstzeitschrift* (1981), no.8, pp.20–23
L'avant-scène opéra, nos.47–8 (1983) [*Salome* issue]
D. Puffett, ed.: *Richard Strauss: Salome* (Cambridge, 1989)

DAVID MURRAY

Stravinsky, Fyodor Ignat'yevich (*b* Rechitskiy, Minsk province, 8/20 June 1843; *d* St Petersburg, 21 Nov/4 Dec 1902). Russian bass of Polish descent, father of Igor Stravinsky. He studied in St Petersburg, and sang Don Basilio in a student production of *Il barbiere* in 1873. Engaged at Kiev the same year he made his début as Rodolfo (*La sonnambula*). In 1876 he was appointed a principal bass at the Mariinsky Theatre, St Petersburg, where he continued to sing until 1902, making 1235 appearances in 64 roles, both serious and comic. He sang in three Tchaikovsky premières, creating His Highness in *Vakula the Smith* (1876); Dunois in *The Maid of Orléans* (1881) and Mamïrov in *The Enchantress* (1887); he also created Grandfather Frost in *The Snow Maiden* (1882). Other roles in Russian opera included Holofernes (Serov's *Yudif'*); the Miller (Dargomïzhsky's *Rusalka*); Rangoni and Varlaam (a role he sang at the request of Rimsky-Korsakov); Panas (*Christmas Eve*), the Village Head (*May Night*) and Nápravník's Dubrovsky. As Farlaf (*Ruslan and Lyudmila*) he was considered by Serov as 'the worthy successor to Osip Petrov'. His non-Russian roles included Mephistopheles (Gounod and Boito), Marcel and Gessler. An intelligent performer who made a thorough psychological study of each character he portrayed, he was also an authority on make-up and costume design. His powerful voice, though not intrinsically beautiful, was over two octaves in range, and he used it with equal success for musical and dramatic purposes.

For illustration *see* MAY NIGHT.

*

E. A. Stark: 'Fyodor Ignat'yevich Stravinsky', *EIT 1903–4*, suppl. to xiv, 116–79
I. Stravinsky: *Chronique de ma vie* (Paris, 1935–6, 2/1962; Eng. trans., 1936 as *An Autobiography*)
E. Stark: *Peterburgskaya opera i eyo mastera, 1890–1910* (Leningrad, 1940)
V. Bogdanov-Berezovsky: *Fyodor Stravinsky* (Moscow and Leningrad, 1951)
M. Montagu-Nathan: 'Shaliapin's Precursors', *ML*, xxxiii (1952), 232–8
E. D. Stasova and others, eds.: *V. V. Stasov: Izbrannïye sochineniya* [Selected Works], iii (Moscow, 1952)
A. Gozenpud, ed.: *F. Stravinsky: stat'i, pis'ma, vospominaniya* [Articles, Letters, Reminiscences] (Leningrad, 1972)

JENNIFER SPENCER/ELIZABETH FORBES

Stravinsky, Igor (Fyodorovich) (*b* Oranienbaum [now Lomonosov], 5/17 June 1882; *d* New York, 6 April 1971). Russian composer, son of the bass FYODOR IGNAT'YEVICH STRAVINSKY, expatriate from 1910, later of French (1934) and American (1945) nationality.

1. Life. 2. Attitude to opera and first attempt. 3. *Renard* and *Mavra*. 4. Later works.

1. LIFE. Stravinsky studied the piano from the age of nine, and later took harmony lessons. He spent eight terms (1901–5) studying liberal arts at St Petersburg University. In 1902 he first consulted Rimsky-Korsakov, whose protégé and pupil he became. In 1909 the impresario Sergey Dyagilev, impressed by his *Scherzo fantastique*, invited Stravinsky first to arrange and compose for him; then *The Firebird* was given in Paris in 1910 by the company that the next year became the Ballets Russes. *Petrushka* and *The Rite of Spring* followed over the next three years; Stravinsky's first opera, *Solovey* ('The Nightingale'), was finished soon after and also performed by Dyagilev. During the war years Stravinsky and his family were in Switzerland; *Renard* belongs to this period, as do *The Soldier's Tale* and *The Wedding*. In 1920 he settled in Paris, where he lived until 1939, though he travelled widely (including three visits to the USA); *Mavra* dates from these years, as does the opera-oratorio *Oedipus rex*. He moved to the USA in 1939; *The Rake's Progress*, his last opera, was completed in 1951. He lived in Los Angeles until 1969 and then New York, where he died; he was buried in Venice.

2. ATTITUDE TO OPERA AND FIRST ATTEMPT. Opera occupies a relatively small place in Stravinsky's output. This is in one sense ironic, given the composer's family background and schooling. Besides his father Fyodor, his brother Gury (1884–1917) was an operatic bass whose promising career was cut short by conscription and death on the Romanian front during World War I. Rimsky-Korsakov, but for elementary training Stravinsky's only teacher, was almost exclusively an opera composer during the time Stravinsky knew him. It seemed inevitable to critics in Russia during the period

of Stravinsky's first fame that he would carry on the tradition, and *The Firebird*, that most operatic of ballets, only confirmed the impression. As one Moscow paper put it, 'Russian opera, so pitifully muted since the death of Rimsky-Korsakov, must now pin its hopes on Stravinsky' (*Utro Rossii*, 24 August 1912).

In another sense, given the notorious 'anti-Papa politics' that runs like a cantus firmus through Stravinsky's autobiography and memoirs, his turn away from opera seems in hindsight equally inevitable. Yet it required a catalyst. The last project Stravinsky embarked on before his teacher's death was *Solovey* ('The Nightingale'), an opera after Andersen's fairy-tale retelling of the Orpheus myth, that would have been in many ways derivative of Rimsky's operatic manner. The choice of fantastic subject matter, and the specific theme of the magical bird, both recall *The Golden Cockerel*, Rimsky's last opera, as yet unperformed at the time of its composer's death. The scenario for *The Nightingale* was drafted by Stravinsky and Stepan Mitusov, his friend and librettist, at the home of Vladimir Bel'sky, the librettist of *The Golden Cockerel*, and with his active participation. Very likely Bel'sky's was the idea of using Andersen's Fisherman as a scene-framing 'Greek chorus' (like the Astrologer in Rimsky's opera).

The music for the first act of *The Nightingale* is typical of that produced by the youngest generation of Rimsky-Korsakov pupils. There is an aestheticist (then called 'decadent') striving after recondite harmonies and timbres, and some awareness of advanced contemporary music in Germany (Strauss) and France (Debussy – especially pronounced at the beginning of *The Nightingale* with its near-quotation of *Nuages*); but all novelty is traceable by small logical steps to the Rimskian fount. Indeed, marginalia in the draft scenario testifies to Stravinsky's reverence for his teacher's example: one of the stranger chords is marked 'Leitharmonie', the term Rimsky had coined for the whole-tone sonority associated with the Forest Sprite in his opera *The Snow Maiden*. The expansion of the Wagnerian system of recollection motifs to incorporate individual harmonies and timbres was considered by Rimsky-Korsakov's disciples to be his essential operatic contribution. This network of associations was to be subordinated – contra *Salome* and contra *Pelléas* – to a traditional voice-dominated numbers format, and Stravinsky's lushly accompanied but formally simple Fisherman's song is evidence that he meant to honour Rimsky's operatic priorities.

It was after one act of *The Nightingale* was complete and fully scored that Stravinsky received the call from Dyagilev to compose *The Firebird*, his first ballet and the launching-pad from which his phenomenal international career took off. Here was the anti-operatic catalyst. Dyagilev had become a ballet impresario by default, his operatic projects having failed at the box office. To justify the switch Dyagilev had begun noisily denigrating opera as outmoded and aesthetically impure, adopting a position long advanced within his circle by the painter and designer Alexandre Benois, a staunch balletomane, who saw in dance an essential aesthetic clarity the operatic mixture of media had bemired. Once he had joined their circle Stravinsky was subjected to heavy indoctrination along these lines; and, bolstered by the gratification of enormous success and lionization as a ballet composer, he propagated the Dyagilev line, becoming its loudest and most influential spokesman. Interviews with Stravinsky, which after 1910 began filling the columns of newspapers both in Russia and abroad, were never complete without arch pronouncements like these:

> Opera does not attract me at all ... Opera is falsehood pretending to be truth, while I need falsehood that pretends to falsehood. Opera is a competition with nature (*Birzheviye vedomosti* [St Petersburg], 25 September 1912).

> I dislike opera. Music can be married to gesture or to words – not to both without bigamy. That is why the artistic basis of opera is wrong and why Wagner sounds at his best in the concert-room. In any case, opera is a backwater. What operas have been written since 'Parsifal'? (*Daily Mail* [London], 13 February 1913).

Stravinsky made a conscious decision never to finish *The Nightingale*, but rather to publish the first act as a sort of Arcadian tone poem with voices. What made him change his mind was a very lucrative offer from Alexander Sanin (*né* Schoenberg, 1869–1956), Dyagilev's former opera stage director and now co-founder of the Moscow Free Theatre, to furnish a full-length opera for the new theatre's first season (1913–14). There was no question, now that Stravinsky had completed three sensationally 'maximalist' scores for Dyagilev, of going back to the 'modest, rationalized impressionism' (as Asaf'yev called it) of his Rimskian incubator. The composer tried to explain away the immense stylistic disparity between the part of *The Nightingale* that had been composed before *The Firebird* and the part composed after *The Rite of Spring*, on the basis of the change in setting between Acts 1 and 2: poetic nature versus brilliant palace pomp. But there were other disparities. Where the first scene had been conventionally operatic in its balance of words and music, Stravinsky, having lost faith in words as music's ally, now demanded a radically stripped libretto that would keep words to an absolute minimum, leaving most of the dramatic presentation to movement and mime supported by orchestral music. The correspondence between Stravinsky and Mitusov during the summer of 1913 is a veritable education in the difference between true opera and 'opera-pageant ballet', as the septuagenarian Stravinsky somewhat shamefacedly characterized the later acts of *The Nightingale* in his memoirs. While these acts surely have a brilliance the composer could never have achieved had he composed the work straight through in 1908–9, just as surely they are burdened with a 'period' flavour stemming from the composer's transient aesthetic dogmas. At Dyagilev's suggestion, Stravinsky put them out of their misery, as it were, by turning them into ballet plain (*Chant du rossignol*, 1917).

The other pre-war operatic project in which Stravinsky participated was the reconstruction of Musorgsky's *Khovanshchina*, which Dyagilev mounted as a vehicle for Shalyapin in 1913. Stravinsky's job was to replace Rimsky-Korsakov's final chorus with one composed on the themes Musorgsky designated for that number, minus the reprise of Peter the Great's triumphal march with which the earlier arranger had trumped the Old Believers' suicide psalm. More than a musical alteration, it fundamentally changed the opera's historiographical outlook, restoring some of its still-controversial mystical pessimism. Stravinsky's audacity in revising his teacher's work, much remarked at home, estranged him from the Rimsky-Korsakov family forever.

3. 'Renard' and 'Mavra'. During the period 1915–20 Stravinsky wrote a great deal of stage music, much of it

vocal, but none of it in any ordinary sense operatic. The work that comes closest is *Renard* [Reynard] (or *Bayka pro Lisu, Petukha, Kota da Barana*, 'Fable of the Vixen, the Cock, the Cat and the Ram', 1915–16), after some Russian barnyard fables collected by the 19th-century folklorist Afanas'yev. This 'merry performance with singing and [instrumental] music' is operatic to the extent that its story unfolds through continuous singing. The singers are placed within the orchestra, however, while the four roles of the title are played by clowns, ballet dancers or acrobats (standing in for archaic Russian folk entertainers) on a trestle stage.

The idea for such a division of labour between singers and mimes derived from Dyagilev's epochal 1914 production (conceived by Benois) of *The Golden Cockerel*. *The Nightingale*, which shared a double bill with that production, was similarly affected by it, and it told as well on the greatest stage work with voices from Stravinsky's 'Russian' period – the singularly abstract, wholly unclassifiable *The Wedding*. Yet that work is in no conceivable sense operatic. Its action is wholly expressed by dance; the text is a non-narrative collage of folksong and ritual in a bizarrely telescoped non-progressive 'present tense' akin to what literary historians now call spatial form. The singers do not assume specific roles; any voice of either gender can fleetingly portray any character. The spectacle's closest affinities are not to other stage genres but to liturgical ones.

With his postwar conversion to 'neo-classicism' (proclaimed by his future collaborator Cocteau as the 'call to order'), Stravinsky made a peace of sorts with opera by radically distinguishing it from 'music drama', its putative antithesis. A sort of vulgar Wagnerism stood on its head, the new dogma received its most polished 'theoretical' formulation in *La poétique musicale*, the set of six lectures (ghostwritten by Alexis Roland-Manuel) which Stravinsky delivered in French at Harvard during the academic year 1939–40 while holding the Charles Eliot Norton chair of poetry. 'The vogue of the music drama had a pathological origin', he declared. It smacked of disorder and, what was worse, improvisation. A return to the formalities of opera properly so-called would be a renewal of 'pure music'. Stravinsky undertook to revive 'the freshness of the Russo-Italian tradition ... a tradition that continued to live apart from the main stream of the present, and in which circulated a salubrious air, well adapted to delivering us from the miasmic vapours of the music drama'.

The pivotal work was *Mavra*, a little 'opéra bouffe' after a comic poem by Pushkin, which Stravinsky put together in 1921–2 with the help of Boris Kochno, Dyagilev's teenage secretary. Hardly more than a skit, it seems to have been intended originally for a Russo-Parisian cabaret, Nikita Baliyev's Théâtre de la Chauve-Souris à Moscou (known on its British and American tours as 'The Bat Theatre of Moscow'). The resounding failure that greeted this fragile kickshaw on its incongruous Paris Opéra première made it a *cause célèbre* with the composer, the subject of an exorbitant apology in his autobiography (*Chroniques de ma vie*), in *La poétique musicale*, and in his son Théodore's polemical pamphlet, *Le message d'Igor Strawinsky*. While the work was arguably a landmark in Stravinsky's development and a beacon to such younger Parisian composers as Poulenc and Milhaud (both of whom joined in its public defence), its status owes relatively little to its specifically operatic qualities. Rather, it was the site of Stravinsky's rediscovery of tonal harmony (i.e. harmony that relies on the dominant function) and of what he called the 'cadenced phrase' – aspects of elementary musical etiquette that had been 'reviled and drowned out by the clang and clatter of the music drama'. Both re-findings are delightfully displayed in the opening 'chanson russe', which the composer later extracted both as an independent concert number and as an instrumental encore. The essential *Mavra*, however, is to be found in its ensembles (two duets and a quartet), where vocal lines redolent of Glinka and Dargomïzhsky are jostled by an instrumental accompaniment exuberating with ragtime rhythms.

4. Later works. Slight as it is and unimportant as it seems, *Mavra* did set the Stravinskian agenda where the lyric stage was concerned. A flaunted commitment to mannered and conventionalized formal procedures would henceforth be a *sine qua non*. Prospective librettists would always be warned that (as Stravinsky wrote to Auden) 'I will compose *not* a musical drama, but just an opera with definitely separated numbers'. Yet however rigorously conventionalized, the remaining sung dramatic works of the interwar years were anything but conventional. Their loftily, even haughtily depersonalized tone was quite alien to what was then taken for a normal operatic manner: in the unfolding of a drama, no less than in the composing of 'pure music', Stravinsky had a horror of anything that smacked of spontaneity. Writing in 1982 of the neo-classical myth-plays of the period, Paul Griffiths neatly observed that 'In *Oedipus rex* (1926–27) opera had been frozen into oratorio and in *Perséphone* (1933–34) it had been dissolved into cantata and, once again, ballet'.

Cocteau, who adapted the libretto of *Oedipus rex* from Sophocles' tragedy, had to rewrite it three times before the composer was satisfied that it was sufficiently ceremonious and stiff to merit the designation 'opera-oratorio'. The main characters are directed to behave like statues or figures in a frieze. The lines Cocteau wrote for them were translated (by Jean Daniélou) into Latin, a language Stravinsky thought 'not dead but turned to stone', before being set to suitably lapidary music. No work better exemplifies that thirst for monumentality which seized so many artists in the confusing decade that followed World War I.

In its renunciation of every vestige of 'illusionist' theatre, and in its use of a narrator-interpreter (designated 'Le Speaker' in the cast-list) who provides 'the vulgar' with preliminary, coyly simplified summaries of its action, *Oedipus rex* has been variously compared with Brechtian epic theatre and with medieval liturgical drama. As the composer came to see it, he was simply protecting his prerogatives: 'I wished to leave the play, as play, behind', he wrote in *Dialogues and a Diary*; 'I thought to distil the dramatic essence by this, and to free myself for a greater degree of focus on a purely musical dramatisation'. Thanks to a vivid use of tonality-symbolism, a powerful thematic recapitulation at the climax, and a masterly transmutation of the title character's fatal progress into a stylistic metamorphosis (florid melisma into stony syllabic simplicity), the immobilized opera manages against all ostensible odds to achieve stunning catharsis.

In contrast to *Oedipus*, of which he was the indubitable mastermind, Stravinsky had little hand in planning *Perséphone*. The terms of the commission from Ida

Rubinstein, a famous mime, stipulated the text (an early verse drama by André Gide, adapted for the occasion by the author) as well as the casting of the title role for a speaking voice (her own). Subtitled 'melodrama in three scenes', the work presents its action through recitation, dance and choral song; the only solo singer is Eumolpus, a priest, whose role is closer to that of the speaker-narrator in *Oedipus rex* than to a true dramatic participant. Eumolpus was Stravinsky's own idea, and that must be the slender reason why the composer chose to classify *Perséphone* among his operas at all. Otherwise the work has no more claim to that designation than the Stravinsky-Ramuz *Soldier's Tale* (1918), a narrated Faust-play-with-music in which one character (the Devil) briefly recites his part to notated rhythms co-ordinated with the instrumental accompaniment. But it is fitting withal to invoke the myth of Persephone in a discussion of Stravinsky's operas, since it – or rather its close relative, the myth of Venus and Adonis – is a vital part of the background to Stravinsky's last contribution to the genre, *The Rake's Progress* (1947–51).

Given his eccentric track record, one would scarcely have predicted a fully fledged full-length opera as Stravinsky's valedictory to the genre; yet *The Rake's Progress*, inspired by and loosely following the implied plot of William Hogarth's famous series of paintings, was just that. It is the composer's longest work by far, all his other operas and quasi-operas taking well under an hour to perform; and it staked Stravinsky's unexpected claim to consideration as one of the major opera composers of his time.

Many have been unwilling to grant it. The opera's aura of pastiche and its welter of in-jokes and allusions (some of them deemed at first 'unwholesome') have made it a critical battleground. But it has won an unshakable place in the repertory, with perhaps more productions worldwide than any other opera composed since World War II, its only possible rivals being *War and Peace*, *Peter Grimes*, *Dialogues des Carmélites* and (in America) Thomson's *The Mother of Us All.*

The reason for such lasting success cannot be merely the composer's colossal name, nor even the superb technical refinement for which both the music and the text, by W. H. Auden and Chester Kallman, are justly if still somehow grudgingly celebrated. The fact is, alongside (not to say despite) all its artifice and conscious virtuosity, the opera is fundamentally and unambiguously humane – and, what is less expected (from Stravinsky, anyway), human. This pastoral allegory of errancy and redemption, to quote Kerman's unsurpassed early appreciation, 'has all necessary urgency, timeliness, universality and pathos', and at the same time its musical manner is comfortingly relaxed. There is little left of the 'dehumanized', disjunct style on which Stravinsky had set such store in the forbidding neoclassical works of the 1920s and 30s. What is more, the composer was evidently so far reconciled to the 'music drama' that he could allow the shape of several crucial scenes – and particularly the graveyard denouement – to play far more naturally and spontaneously than, in his more tightly corseted days, he could have countenanced. Was it the American environment (in which he had been living since 1939, as a citizen since 1945) that loosed the corset and in a double sense naturalized his muse? Hearing the brothel and Baba scenes with their chastened but unmistakable hints of Broadway, and reflecting on the generally lessened intransigence that characterized other aspects of the new American's outlook (his political views, for instance), one has to allow it. Having let his guard down and been rebuked for it by a new generation of musical intransigents, Stravinsky would beat a quick retreat into serialism; but his operatic career ends here, at what was surely one of the happiest, most optimistic junctures of his life. *The Rake's Progress* is its precious memento.

See also MAVRA; NIGHTINGALE, THE; OEDIPUS REX; PERSÉPHONE; RAKE'S PROGRESS, THE; and RENARD.

Solovey [The Nightingale], Act 1, 1908–9, Acts 2 and 3, 1913–14 (lyric tale, 3, S. Mitusov, after H. C. Andersen); as Le rossignol, Paris, Opéra, 26 May 1914, cond. Monteux, vs (Berlin, 1914); rev. version, full score (London, 1962)

Bayka pro Lisu, Petukha, Kota da Barana [Fable of the Vixen, the Cock, the Cat and the Ram], 1915–16 ('merry performance with singing and [instrumental] music', Stravinsky, after A. Afanas'yev); as Renard [Reynard], Paris, Opéra, 18 May 1922, cond. Ansermet, vs (Geneva, 1917), full score (London, 1930)

Mavra (opéra bouffe, 1, B. Kochno, after A. Pushkin: *Domik v Kolomne* [The Little House at Kolomna]), Paris, Hôtel Continental, 27 May 1922; stage, Paris, Opéra, 3 June 1922, cond. Fitelberg, vs (Berlin, 1922), full score (London, 1969).

Oedipus rex, 1926–7 (opera-oratorio, 2, J. Cocteau, after Sophocles), Paris, Sarah Bernhardt, 30 May 1927; stage, Vienna, Staatsoper, 23 Feb 1928, cond. Wallerstein, vs (Berlin, 1927); rev. 1948, full score (London, 1949)

Perséphone [Persephone], 1933–4 (melodrama, 3 scenes, A. Gide), Paris, Opéra, 30 April 1934, cond. Stravinsky, vs (Berlin, 1934); rev. 1949, full score (London, 1950)

The Rake's Progress, 1947–51 (3, epilogue, W. H. Auden and C. Kallman), Venice, Fenice, 11 Sept 1951, cond. Stravinsky (London, 1951)

WRITINGS

with W. Nouvel: *Chroniques de ma vie* (Paris, 1935–6, 2/1962; Eng. trans., 1936 as *An Autobiography*; Sp. trans., 1936–7; Ger. trans., 1937; Russ. trans., 1963; Bulg. trans., 1966; Hung. trans., 1969)

La poétique musicale (Cambridge, MA, 1942; Eng. trans., 1947; Ger. trans., 1949, 3/1966; It. trans., 1954; Dan. trans., 1961; Rom. trans., 1967; Eng.-Fr. edn, 1970)

Leben und Werk (Zürich and Mainz, 1957) [reprints of Ger. trans. of *Chroniques de ma vie* and *La poétique musicale* with 'Answers to 35 Questions', incl. one question omitted in *Conversations*]

with R. Craft: *Conversations with Igor Stravinsky* (London and New York, 1959; Russ. trans., 1971)

——: *Memories and Commentaries* (London and New York, 1960; Russ. trans., 1971)

——: *Expositions and Developments* (London and New York, 1962; Russ. trans., 1971)

——: *Stravinsky in Conversation with Robert Craft* (Harmondsworth, 1962; Ger. trans., 1961) [= *Conversations* and *Memories*]

——: *Dialogues and a Diary* (New York, 1963, enlarged London, 1968; Russ. trans., 1971)

——: *Themes and Episodes* (New York, 1966, 2/1967)

——: *Retrospectives and Conclusions* (New York, 1969)

Themes and Conclusions (London, 1972; Ger. trans., 1972) [items by Stravinsky only from *Themes and Episodes* and *Retrospectives and Conclusions*]

L. S. D'yachkova, ed.: *Stat'i materialï* [Articles and Materials] (Moscow, 1973) [incl. 60 letters]

R. Craft, ed.: *Stravinsky: Selected Correspondence* (New York, 1982–5)

*

T. Strawinsky: *Le message d'Igor Strawinsky* (Lausanne, 1948; Ger. trans., 1952; Eng. trans., 1953)

M. Lederman, ed.: *Stravinsky in the Theatre* (London and New York, 1949) [articles repr. from *MM*, 1924–46]

E. W. White: *Stravinsky: the Composer and his Works* (London, 1966, enlarged 2/1979)

L. Klein: 'Stravinsky and Opera: Parable as Ethic', *Les cahiers canadiens de musique*, no.4 (1972), 65 [special issue: *Dossier Stravinsky: Canada 1937–67*]

V. Thomson: 'Stravinsky's Operas', *Musical Newsletter*, iv/4 (1974), 3–7

V. Stravinsky and R. Craft: *Stravinsky in Pictures and Documents* (London and New York, 1978)

A. Schouvaloff and V. Borovsky: *Stravinsky on Stage* (London, 1982)

L. Andriessen and E. Schönberger: *Het Apollinisch uurwek: over Stravinsky* (Amsterdam, 1983; Eng. trans., 1989)

P. van den Toorn: *The Music of Igor Stravinsky* (New Haven and London, 1983)

S. Walsh: *The Music of Stravinsky* (London, 1988)

D. Albright: *Stravinsky: the Music Box and the Nightingale* (New York, 1989)

R. Taruskin: *Stravinsky and the Russian Traditions: a Biography of the Works through Mavra* (Berkeley and Los Angeles, forthcoming)

STUDIES OF INDIVIDUAL WORKS

The Nightingale

M. Calvocoressi: 'Igor Stravinsky's Opera: "The Nightingale"', *MT*, lv (1914), 372–4

V. V. Smirnov: *Tvorcheskoye formirovaniye I(gorya) F(yodorovicha) Stravinskogo* [The Creative Development of Stravinsky] (Leningrad, 1970)

N. Kinkul'kina: 'Pis'ma I. F. Stravinskogo i F. I. Shalyapina k A. A. Saninu' [Stravinsky's and Shalyapin's Letters to Sanin], *SovM* (1978), no.6, pp.92–6

R. Craft, ed.: *Selected Correspondence*, ii (New York, 1984), 197–218, 432–47

A. Bayeva: 'Tendentsiya k zhivopisno-kartinnoy organizatsii materiala v opere "Solovey"' [The Tendency towards a Painterly-Picturesque Organization of Material in *The Nightingale*], *Igor' Stravinsky: Stat'i i vospominaniya* [Articles and Memoirs], ed. G. Alfeyevskaya and I. Vershinina (Moscow, 1985), 176–95

D. Albright: *Stravinsky: the Music Box and the Nightingale* (New York, 1989), chap.4

L. Kazanskaya: 'Stepan Mitusov', *SovM* (1990), no.12, pp.82–8

Khovanshchina

R. Threlfall: 'The Stravinsky Version of *Khovanshchina* in Collaboration with Ravel', *SMA*, no.15 (1981), 106–15

I. Vershinina: 'Musorgsky i Stravinsky (o Dyagilevskoy postanovke "Khovanshchinï")' [Musorgsky and Stravinsky (on Dyagilev's Production of *Khovanshchina*)], *M. P. Musorgsky i muzïka XX veka* [Musorgsky and 20th-Century Music], ed. G. L. Golovinsky (Moscow, 1990), 192–217

Mavra

D. Milhaud: 'Strawinskijs neue Bühnenwerke', *Musikblätter des Anbruch*, iv (1922), 260–62; Eng. synopsis, *MT*, lxiv (1923), 40

F. Poulenc: 'La musique: à propos de "Mavra" de Igor Strawinsky', *Feuilles libres*, no.27 (1922), 222–4

A. Lur'ye [Lourié]: 'Dve operï Stravinskogo' [Two Operas of Stravinsky], *Vyorstï*, iii (1928), 109–26; partial Fr. trans., *ReM*, viii (1926–7), 240–53; partial Ger. trans., *Blätter der Staatsoper*, viii/19 (1928), 9–13

J. Cocteau: 'Critics and the Comic Spirit', *Igor Stravinsky*, ed. E. Corle (New York, 1949), 21–4 [orig. written 1922]

S. Campbell: 'The "Mavras" of Pushkin, Kochno and Stravinsky', *ML*, lviii (1977), 304–17

L. Dan'ko: '*Mavra* I. Stravinskogo i *Nos* D. Shostakovicha', *Muzïkal'nïy sovremennik*, ii (1977), 73–84

Oedipus rex

A. Lur'ye [Lourié]: 'Dve operï Stravinskogo' [Two Operas of Stravinsky], *Vyorstï*, iii (1928), 109–26; partial Fr. trans., *ReM*, viii (1926–7), 240–53; partial Ger. trans., *Blätter der Staatsoper*, viii/19 (1928), 9–13

J. Cocteau: 'La collaboration Oedipus rex', *ReM*, no.212 (1952), 51 [special issue]

J. Kerman: 'Armchair Opera', *Hudson Review*, vii (1954–5), 436–44

W. Mellers: 'Stravinsky's Oedipus as 20th-Century Hero', *MQ*, xlviii (1962), 300–12; repr. in *Stravinsky: a New Appraisal of his Work*, ed. P. H. Lang (New York, 1963), 34–46

I. Stravinsky: 'On *Oedipus rex*', *Encounter*, xviii (1962), 30–39; repr. in I. Stravinsky and R. Craft: *Dialogues and a Diary* (New York, 1963), 3–16

R. Zinar: *Greek Tragedy in Theatre Pieces of Stravinsky and Milhaud* (diss., New York U., 1968)

T. Sorokina: '*Tsar' Edip* kak primer neoklassicheskoy manerï Stravinskogo' [*Oedipus rex* as an Example of Stravinsky's Neo-Classical Manner], *Nauchno-metodicheskiye zapiski* (Novosibirsk, 1970)

P. H. Lang: 'Stravinsky', *The Experience of Opera* (New York, 1971), 269–73

A. Schoenberg: 'Stravinsky's *Oedipus*', *Style and Idea*, ed. L. Stein (London, 1975), 482–3 [orig. written 1928]

L. Bernstein: *The Unanswered Question* (Cambridge, MA, 1976), 391–418

G. Alfeyevskaya: '*Tsar' Edip* Stravinskogo: k probleme neoklassitsizma' [Stravinsky's *Oedipus rex*: on the Problem of Neo-Classicism], *Teoreticheskiye problemï muzïki XX veka*, ii (Moscow, 1978), 126–68

M. Hansen: 'Igor Strawinskys "Oedipus rex"', *Musik und Gesellschaft*, xxviii (1978), 329–34

R. Zinar: 'Stravinsky and his Latin Texts', *College Music Symposium*, xviii (1978), 186

D. Möller: *Jean Cocteau und Igor Strawinsky: Untersuchungen zur Ästhetik und zu Oedipus rex* (Hamburg, 1981)

R. Craft, ed.: *Stravinsky: Selected Correspondence*, i (New York, 1982), 71–106 [with Cocteau]

G. Vinay: 'Da "Oidipous" a "Oedipus rex" e ritorno: un itinerario metrico', *RIM*, xvii (1982), 333–45

J. Engelhardt: *Gestus und Verfremdung: Studien zum Musiktheater bei Strawinsky und Brecht/Weill* (Munich, 1984)

D. Albright: *Stravinsky: the Music Box and the Nightingale* (New York, 1989), chap.6

N. John, ed.: *Oedipus rex/The Rake's Progress* (London, 1991) [ENO Opera Guide]

Perséphone

I. Stravinsky and R. Craft: *Memories and Commentaries* (London and New York, 1960), 135–43

R. Craft, ed.: *Stravinsky: Selected Correspondence*, iii (New York, 1985) [appx B, '*Perséphone*: the Evolution of the Libretto', 475–507]

The Rake's Progress

Lord Harewood: 'Strawinsky and *The Rake's Progress*', *Opera*, ii (1951), 610–18

C. Mason: 'Stravinsky's Opera', *ML*, xxxiii (1952), 1–9

J. Kerman: 'Opera à la mode', *Hudson Review*, vi (1953–4), 560–77; repr. in *Opera*, v (1954), 411–15, 491–5; answered by G. McFadden in *Hudson Review*, viii (1955–6), 105–12, with surrebuttal on p.319

R. Craft: 'Reflections on *The Rake's Progress*', *The Score*, no.9 (1954), 24–30

I. Stravinsky: '*The Rake's Progress*', *Memories and Commentaries*, with R. Craft (London and New York, 1960), 144–67 [incl. correspondence and draft scenario]

D. Cooke: '*The Rake* and the 18th Century', *MT*, ciii (1962), 20–23

W. H. Auden: *The Dyer's Hand* (London, 1963)

V. Stravinsky: '*The Rake's Progress*: "La prima assoluta"', in I. Stravinsky and R. Craft: *Themes and Episodes* (New York, 1966, 2/1967) 51–4

A. A. Abert: 'Strawinsky's *The Rake's Progress*: strukturell betrachtet', *Musica*, xxv (1971), 243–7

W. H. Auden: *Forewords and Afterwords* (New York, 1973)

R. Craft: 'The Poet and the Rake', *W. H. Auden: a Tribute*, ed. S. Spender (London, 1975)

G. Josipovici: '*The Rake's Progress*: Some Thoughts on the Libretto', *Tempo*, no.113 (1975), 2–10

V. Stravinsky and R. Craft: *Stravinsky in Pictures and Documents* (New York, 1978)

G. Ordzhonikidze: 'Nravstvennïye uroki nasmeshlivoy pritchi' [Moral Lessons of a Mocking Parable], *SovM* (1979), no.1, pp.56–61

R. Craft, ed.: *Stravinsky: Selected Correspondence*, i (New York, 1982), 299–324 [with W. H. Auden]; iii (New York, 1985) [appx C, '*The Rake's Progress*: the Evolution of the Libretto and the Sketches', 508–12]

P. Griffiths, ed.: *Igor Stravinsky: The Rake's Progress* (Cambridge, 1982)

J. Jacquot: 'The Rake's Progress et la carrière de Stravinsky', *RdM*, lxviii (1982), 110–27

R. Kirkpatrick: 'Recollections of Two Composers: Hindemith and Stravinsky', *Yale Review*, lxxi (1982), 627–40

D. Hamilton: '*The Rake's Progress*: a Novel Work Vividly Aware of its Past', *Opus*, i (1985), 24–6

D. Albright: *Stravinsky: the Music Box and the Nightingale* (New York, 1989), chaps.7, 10

J.-M. Vaccaro, ed.: '*The Rake's Progress: un opéra de W. Hogarth, W. H. Auden, C. Kallman et I. Stravinsky, une réalisation de J. Cox et D. Hockney* (Paris, 1990)

M. Hunter: 'Igor and Tom: History and Destiny in *The Rake's Progress*', *OQ*, vii (1990–91), 38–52

N. John, ed.: *Oedipus rex/The Rake's Progress* (London, 1991) [ENO Opera Guide]

RICHARD TARUSKIN

Strecker, Ludwig. *See* ANDERSEN, LUDWIG.

Street Scene. American opera in two acts by KURT WEILL to a libretto by Elmer Rice after his own play, with lyrics by Langston Hughes and Rice; Philadelphia, Shubert Theatre, 16 December 1946; New York, Adelphi Theatre, 9 January 1947.

Ann Maurrant	soprano
Frank Maurrant *her husband*	bass-baritone
Rose Maurrant *their daughter*	soprano
Sam Kaplan *poet, in love with Rose*	tenor
Abraham Kaplan	tenor
Greta Fiorentino	high soprano
Carl Olsen	bass
Emma Jones	mezzo-soprano
Olga Olsen	contralto
Henry Davis *janitor*	high baritone
Daniel Buchanan	tenor
George Jones	baritone
Lippo Fiorentino	tenor
Jennie Hildebrand	soprano
Two Graduates	soprano, mezzo-soprano
Mrs Hildebrand	mezzo-soprano
Harry Easter	high baritone
Mae Jones	singer-dancer
Dick McGann	singer-dancer
Willie Maurrant	boy soprano
First Nursemaid	soprano
Second Nursemaid	mezzo-soprano
Shirley Kaplan Steve Sankey Vincent Jones Dr Wilson Officer Murphy City Marshal Fred Cullen	spoken

Policemen

Setting A sidewalk in front of house no.346 in New York City in June

Weill saw a production of Elmer Rice's *Street Scene* in Berlin before emigrating to the USA (the play was first performed on Broadway in 1929). During rehearsals for *Johnny Johnson* in 1936, he met Rice and suggested a musical version of his drama, which had meanwhile been awarded a Pulitzer Prize. Rice rejected the idea as premature, but finally consented when the two men met ten years later. Much of the spoken dialogue was retained in abridged form, and the black poet Langston Hughes was engaged to write the lyrics. Weill himself described the changes:

> The political element in the original play will be considerably toned down. The love story between Sam and Rose will be made more passionate; Sam, instead of being always the beaten Jew, will be the young poet trying to adjust to the world and to the hateful surroundings he is living in ... His aria, 'Lonely House', is almost a theme song for the show: the house as a prison for the human spirit.

The New York première was a critical success. The cast featured Polyna Stoska and Norman Cordon as Ann and Frank Maurrant, with Anne Jeffreys as Rose and Brian Sullivan as Sam. Maurice Abravanel conducted. High running costs forced it to close after 148 performances – 'a mediocre run for a "dramatic musical"', as Kim Kowalke remarked, 'but an impressive string of consecutive performances for an American opera'. Recent revivals include those by New York City Opera, Scottish Opera and English National Opera.

The orchestral prelude introduces two recurring motifs: the swooping, yearning melody of Sam Kaplan's 'Lonely House' (no.10) and the bustling syncopations that depict (among other things) New York. The meteorological frame for the ensuing drama, which adheres to the classical unities, is provided by the ensemble which opens and closes the work: it is a sweltering hot evening and day in New York City. While the principals enact the double plot – the murder of Ann Maurrant by her jealous and bibulous husband Frank, and the ultimately unrequited love of a romantic intellectual, Sam Kaplan, for the Maurrants' daughter Rose – the minor characters gossip about their neighbours and provide much local colour with set pieces (nos.2, 7, 9, 11, 13 and 15). The more or less self-contained numbers are linked by spoken dialogue. Some dialogue is accompanied, with leitmotifs, by the orchestra as in melodrama.

ACT 1 *Evening* The women who live in the house are sitting on the steps, complaining about the heat (no.1, introduction and ensemble, 'Ain't it awful the heat!'). They talk to the janitor, Henry Davis, who comes up from the cellar singing his blues song (no.2, 'I got a marble and a star'), and they gossip about Mrs Maurrant's love life (no.3, scene and trio, 'Come in, come in wherever you are'). They also make fun of Daniel Buchanan, whose wife is having a baby, and sing with him 'When a woman has a baby' (no.4, arietta). Mrs Maurrant expresses her troubled mind and her secret desires in the aria 'Somehow I never could believe' (no.5). This is followed by a scene and quartet, 'Get a load of that!' (no.6) and the Ice-Cream Sextet (no.7, 'First time I come to da America'). Maurrant wishes to 'Let things be like they always was' (no.8, aria). The young girls come home from their graduation exercises (no.9, scene and ensemble, 'Hail to the school', 'Wrapped in a ribbon and tied in a bow') and Sam Kaplan sings of adolescent melancholy (no.10, arioso). Rose Maurrant's 'boss', Mr Easter, is trying to lure her into a different sort of life (no.11, scene and song, 'Wouldn't you like to be on Broadway'), but Rose decides to go her own way (no.12, cavatina and scene, 'What good would the moon be'). Dick and Mae sing and dance, 'Moon-faced, starry-eyed' (no.13). The act ends with a love duet and 'Finaletto', in which Rose and Sam dream of lilac bushes and happiness (no.14, 'Remember that I care').

ACT 2.i *The following morning* The scene opens with the morning music, the awakening of the house and the Children's Game (no.15, 'Fat, Fat the Water Rat'). After a scene and trio for Maurrant, Mrs Maurrant and Rose (no.16, 'There'll be trouble'), Mrs Maurrant sings touchingly of her little son (no.17, 'A boy like you'). In a passionate duet, Sam and Rose tell of their decision to take life into their own hands (no.18, 'We'll go away together'). This is followed by an interlude (an orchestral reprise of no.17).

2.ii *Afternoon, the same day* The two Nursemaids are trying to sing the babies to sleep with a lullaby (no.20, 'Sleep, baby dear') while gossiping about their

'Street Scene' (Weill): scene from the original production at the Adelphi Theatre, New York, 9 January 1947

parents. The Finale (no.22) begins as Rose sees her father for the last time: he has killed his wife (but sings 'I loved her too') and is being taken away by the police. Rose and Sam reminisce ('Do you remember'), but Rose realizes that she has to say goodbye to Sam too ('Don't forget the lilac bush'). The opera ends with a reprise of the opening ensemble.

* * *

Weill considered *Street Scene* his chef d'oeuvre. In a note for the cast recording (1947), he described it as 'two dreams come true'. The first dream was for a form of musical theatre 'that would completely integrate drama and music, spoken word, song and movement'. All his previous works thus became 'stepping stones in this direction'. The second was that of an 'American opera' – something he had first glimpsed with the 1935 première of Gershwin's *Porgy and Bess*. There can be little doubt that the first dream came true, in a number of his American works. Whether the same goes for the second is debatable, not unrelated to the first dream. In other words, is the generic description 'American opera' a contradiction in terms? It has proved a stumbling-block, not least for Weill, who changed it twice. Cautious about invoking the concept of opera, he initially billed the work as a 'dramatic musical', but re-christened it later as a 'Broadway opera'. Finally, for the vocal score, he decided on 'American opera'. Critics have used this apparent uncertainty to suggest an inherent separateness between the work's traditionally 'operatic' parts and its more popular 'Broadway musical' elements. For example, Larry Stempel: 'If the two musical worlds thus demand equal attention, the problem is that they are made simply to coexist without one shedding much light on the other' ('*Street Scene* and the Enigma of Broadway Opera', *A New Orpheus*, ed. K. Kowalke, New Haven, 1986, p.333). This criticism ignores the complexities of style and idiom in Weill's later dramatic work, where to search for stylistic consistency and absolute musical coherence is basically misguided. Style and idiom are at all times subservient to the drama, never ends in themselves. In *Street Scene* Weill frequently switches idioms, since as he observed:

> the play lent itself to a great variety of music, just as the streets of New York themselves embrace the music of many lands and many people. I had the opportunity to use different forms of musical expression, from popular songs to operatic ensembles, music of mood and dramatic music, music of young love, music of passion and death – and, overall, the music of a hot summer night in New York.

Moreover, irony is never far from the surface. 'Hail to the school' at the beginning of the graduation ceremony (no.9), for instance, quotes an original school song of the Julia Richman School in New York. And although 'Wrapped in a ribbon and tied in a bow', which follows it, is Weill's own composition, its style is no less appropriate to the event. It is also one of the numbers (along with no.13) where Weill resorted to traditional Broadway practice and left the orchestration to another hand (Ted Royal). In defence of no.9, one might say that neither its musical style nor its orchestration is a mere concession, whether to box office or to exigencies of production. Weill's musical concern was less with originality than with authenticity. The cloying sentimentality is a function of the drama. It also demonstrates how Weill adjusted his musical voice as the drama demanded. *Street Scene* contains European elements, including allusions to Puccini, even to Wagner. The drama demanded them, too. The description 'American opera' nonetheless applies: it is an opera *for* America – that is, for a Broadway public; and it is an opera *about* America, both musically and in terms of plot. STEPHEN HINTON

Strehler, Giorgio (*b* Barcola, Trieste, 14 Aug 1921). Italian director. He studied at the Accademia di Filodrammatici, Milan, and began his career as an actor in 1940. Three years later he directed his first theatre production and in 1947 was a co-founder of the Piccolo Teatro in Milan, which soon became the leading Italian art theatre. Strehler's radical productions and rehearsal methods were major influences on contemporary European staging. His style was one of heightened realism, marrying extreme visual beauty of setting to an often intensely physical acting style. Most of his work in opera and music theatre has been at La Scala and the Piccola Scala, the experimental studio he helped found in 1955. He began with *La traviata* in 1947, going on to direct the Italian premières of *The Love for Three Oranges*, *Lulu*, *Aufstieg und Fall der Stadt Mahagonny* and Mario Peragallo's *La collina*, as well as the première of J. J. Castro's *Proserpina y el extranjero* (1952). In 1956 Strehler restored much of the original power of *Die Dreigroschenoper* by setting it in the 'Little Italy' district of New York at the turn of the century. It was extravagantly praised by Brecht himself, who had important discussions with the director (later published).

Strehler's international opera career began with *Die Entführung aus dem Serail* (1965, Salzburg Festival), a work to which he frequently returned. The production was noted for its *commedia dell'arte* influences and use of silhouettes. His production of *Simon Boccanegra* (1971, La Scala and elsewhere) placed great emphasis on class and political struggles and was compactly designed to play with just one interval. His *Macbeth* (1975, La Scala) steered Verdi's work closely along the lines of Shakespeare's tragedy; memorable use of cloths and costumes provided haunting appearances for the witches and for Lady Macbeth in the sleepwalking scene. Also noteworthy were two further Mozart productions, a dark, serious *Die Zauberflöte* (1974, Salzburg) and a *Figaro* (1973, Versailles and elsewhere) in which the scenery extended unseen into the wings to build atmosphere for the cast. In the 1980s Strehler became increasingly occupied with the specially created Théâtre de l'Europe at the Odéon, Paris, though he has been active elsewhere; his production of *Don Giovanni* at La Scala in 1988 revealed a profound serio-comic relationship between Giovanni and Leporello and contained an eerily virtuoso treatment of Giovanni's descent to hell. Strehler's reflections on his work, in a series of conversations with the drama critic Ugo Ronfani, were published as *Io, Strehler* (Milan, 1986).

*

G. Guazotti: *L'opera da tre soldi di Bertolt Brecht e Kurt Weill* (Bologna, 1961)

F. Battistini: *Giorgio Strehler* (Rome, 1980)

MIKE ASHMAN

Streich, Rita (*b* Barnaul, 18 Dec 1920; *d* Vienna, 20 March 1987). German soprano. She studied with Domgraf-Fassbänder, Ivogün and Berger, making her début at Aussig (now Ústí nad Labem) in 1943 as Zerbinetta. From 1946 to 1951 she sang at the Berlin Staatsoper in such roles as Zerlina, Blonde, Gilda, Sophie and Olympia. In 1951 she joined the Berlin Städtische Oper, extending her repertory to include the Queen of Night and Konstanze. She was engaged at the Vienna Staatsoper in 1953 and made her London début with that company at the Festival Hall in 1954 as Zerlina and Susanna. She made her American début at San Francisco in 1957 as Sophie and sang Zerbinetta in the first performance there of *Ariadne auf Naxos* and at her Glyndebourne début in 1958. She also appeared at Salzburg, where she created the title role of Erbse's *Julietta* (1959), Aix-en-Provence and Bayreuth, where she sang the Woodbird (1952). She was at her best in medium-sized auditoriums, for her exquisite art and voice were lost in larger theatres.

HAROLD ROSENTHAL/R

Strepponi, Giuseppina [Clelia Maria Josepha] (*b* Lodi, 8 Sept 1815; *d* Sant'Agata, nr Busseto, 14 Nov 1897). Italian soprano, second wife of Verdi. She was the eldest daughter of Feliciano Strepponi (1797–1832), organist of Monza Cathedral and composer of several operas, of which *Ullà di Bassora* enjoyed some success at La Scala in 1831. She studied the piano and singing at the Milan Conservatory, winning the first prize for bel canto in her final year. She made her début at Adria in Luigi Ricci's *Chiara di Rosembergh* in December 1834; her first triumph was in Rossini's *Matilde di Shabran* in Trieste in spring 1835. In the same year she appeared in Vienna as Adalgisa in *Norma* and as the heroine of *La sonnambula*, which became one of her most famous roles. She often appeared with the tenor Napoleone Moriani and the baritone Giorgio Ronconi. She was now the breadwinner of her family: her unremitting activity, combined with liaisons which resulted in three illegitimate children, considerably shortened her career. During the late 1830s, however, she aroused fanatical enthusiasm; Donizetti wrote his *Adelia* (1841, Rome) for her.

Strepponi made her début at La Scala in 1839. In 1842 she created the role of Abigaille (*Nabucco*), but by then her powers were in decline. Apart from a disastrous season in Palermo in 1845, she thereafter appeared only sporadically (mostly in operas by Verdi) until her retirement in February 1846. In October that year she moved to Paris, where Verdi joined her the following summer; from then on her history is that of his life-partner, though they were not legally married until 1859. Strepponi was described as having a 'limpid, penetrating, smooth voice, seemly action, a lovely figure; and to Nature's liberal endowments she adds an excellent technique'; her 'deep inner feeling' was also praised. She interpreted Donizetti's Lucia, Bianca in Mercadante's *Il giuramento* and most of Bellini's heroines especially well. She was equally at home in comedy, as Adina in *L'elisir d'amore* and Sandrina in Luigi Ricci's *Un'avventura di Scaramuccia*. Yet the most famous of all the roles she created, Verdi's Abigaille, was probably the one least suited to her vocal means. Although she was highly talented, she never sang outside Italy after 1835.

*

E. De Amicis: 'Giuseppina Verdi-Strepponi', *Nuovi ritratti letterari ed artistici* (Milan, 1902); repr. in *Verdi: bollettino dell'Istituto di studi verdiani*, i/2 (1960), 779–84

A. Luzio: 'La "Traviata" e il dramma intimo di Verdi', *Nuova antologia*, no.390 (1937), 270–92; repr. in *Carteggi verdiani*, iv (Rome, 1947), 250–76

M. Mundula: *La moglie di Verdi: Giuseppina Strepponi* (Milan, 1938)

E. Gara: 'La misteriosa giovinezza di Giuseppina Strepponi', *Corriere della sera* (27 Jan 1951)

M. Medici: '"Quel prete" che sposò Verdi', *Verdi: bollettino dell' Istituto di studi verdiani*, i/2 (1960), 657–61

F. Walker: *The Man Verdi* (London, 1962)

'Ebbe una figlia a Trieste la moglie di Giuseppe Verdi', *Corriere della sera* (6 March 1965)

C. Sartori: 'La Strepponi e Verdi a Parigi nella morsa quarantottesca', *NRMI*, viii (1974), 239–53

M. De Angelis: *Le carte dell'impresario: melodramma e costume teatrale nell'ottocento* (Florence, 1982)

JULIAN BUDDEN

Stretta [stretto] (It.: 'grip', 'tightening'; Fr. *strette*). In opera, the rapid, concluding movement of an ensemble. It probably originates in the fast concluding sections to the 'ensemble of confusion' that traditionally ends the intermediate act finales in 18th-century *opere buffe*, such as that in the Act 2 finale of *Le nozze di Figaro* (the 'Più allegro' at bar 783, to the words 'Son confuso, son stordito'). During the first half of the 19th century, from Rossini's time onwards, the stretta forms a regular constituent of a central finale, balancing the PEZZO CONCERTATO as the 'cabaletta' balances the 'cantabile' of an aria or duet. Usually, by this period, led by one voice, it can be particularly effective in comedy, as for example the uproarious 'Va sossopra il mio cervello' (*L'italiana in Algeri*, Rossini, 1813), 'Mi par d'esser con la testa' (*Il barbiere di Siviglia*, 1816) and 'Son tradito, son tradito' (*Don Pasquale*, Donizetti, 1843). In tragic opera its mood of generic excitement can often prove trivializing; hence a growing tendency at the mid-century to abandon it. For examples of 'strette dell'introduzione', see 'Trema il tempio, infausto evento' (*Semiramide*, Rossini, 1823) and 'Sull'orlo dei tetti' (*Il trovatore*, Verdi, 1853). In duets the term is sometimes loosely used as an alternative to 'cabaletta'; it can more legitimately be applied to any short concluding duet movement that avoids cabaletta form, for example 'In arcion! in arcion!' (*Ernani*, Verdi, 1844).

JULIAN BUDDEN

Stricker, Augustin Reinhard (*d* after 1720). German composer. He joined the royal orchestra in Berlin as a tenor and violinist in 1702. From 1714 to 1717 he was Kapellmeister at Cöthen, where he was J. S. Bach's predecessor. In autumn 1717 he went to Neuburg an der Donau in the service of the Elector Palatine Carl Philipp. He probably died before 1723. Stricker wrote two German operas for the Berlin court, *Der Sieg der Schönheit über die Helden* (J. von Besser; December 1706; collab. J. B. Volumier and G. Finger) and *Alexanders und Roxanens Heirat* (Besser; 28 November 1708). For the Neuburg court he set parts of two Italian operas, in 1717 *Crudeltà consuma amore* (G. M. Rapparini; overture by Finger, Acts 1 and 3 by J. Greber, Act 2 by Stricker) and in March 1718 *L'amicizia in terzo, overo Il Dionigio* (G. M. Rapparini; overture and ballet music by Finger, Act 1 by an amateur, 'Cavaliere Messa', Act 2 by Stricker, Act 3 by J. D. Heinichen). None of his operatic music survives.

Striegler, Kurt (*b* Dresden, 7 Jan 1886; *d* Wildthurn, nr Landau, 4 Aug 1958). German conductor and composer. He attended the choir school of the Catholic Hofkirche in Dresden from 1896 to 1900, and from 1900 to 1905 studied composition with Draeseke and conducting with Kutzschbach at the Dresden Conservatory. In 1905 Schuch appointed him solo répétiteur to the Dresden Opera. This was the beginning of a valuable 50 years of involvement with the institution of which he was made Kapellmeister in 1913. Subsequently he became deputy director of the Opera and Kapellmeister of the state of Saxony. He also taught at the conservatory (1905–45), was its artistic director (1933–6) and was artistic director of the opera school (1936–45). From 1914 to 1920 he directed the Dresden Volkssingakademie, and at a later date other amateur choirs. In 1950 Striegler moved to Munich, but he remained permanent guest conductor of the Dresden State Opera and was made an honorary member in 1955. He worked as a freelance for Bavarian radio in Munich, and was engaged by the Bayreuth Festival in 1951.

Besides a number of orchestral and chamber works, songs, choral and organ compositions, he wrote five operas. His works embody a good deal of Dresden musical history, arising from the tradition of Weber, Wagner and Reissiger, though stylistically they are closer to the music of Richard Strauss and Hans Pfitzner. His compositions are practical, in the best sense of the word, rather than rarefied academic music.

Der Thomaskantor op.37 (3, F. A. Geissler), concert perf., Bautzen, Stadt, 1928

Hand und Herz op.43 (2, L. Anzengruber), Dresden, Staatsoper, 1923

Dagmar op.67 (3, R. Bosshart, after T. Storm), Dresden, Staatsoper, 1927

Die Schmiede op.70 (3, W. Staegemann), Hanover, Städtische Bühnen, 1933

Der Spielmann op.85 (Märchenoper, 3, P. Neuhaus), Coburg, 1949

E. Schmitz: 'Der 50jährige K. Striegler und sein Schaffen', *Dresdner Nachrichten* (10 Jan 1936)

H. Schnoor: *Dresden – 400 Jahre deutsche Musikkultur* (Dresden, 1948)

E. Sprink: *Ein halbes Jahrhundert im Dienste der Dresdner Staatstheater: zur Ehrung K. Strieglers am 9. Januar 1955* (Dresden, 1955)

——: 'K. Striegler', *Blätter der Staatskapelle Dresden* (1955–6), no.3

H. Böhm: 'Kurt Striegler', *Musica*, xii (1958), 624–5

DIETER HÄRTWIG

Strienz, Wilhelm (*b* Stuttgart, 2 Sept 1900; *d* Frankfurt, 10 May 1987). German bass. His teachers included Oskay Schroeter, Theodor Scheidl, Luise Reuss-Belce and Louis Bächner. In 1922 he made his début in Berlin as the Hermit in *Der Freischütz* and in 1924 he joined the Wiesbaden Opera. He gained popularity in operatic productions on German radio (1926–32), where his roles included Osmin, Leporello, Rocco, Hagen and King Mark. His short stature limited his stage career, which was further curtailed by the establishment of the Nazi party with which he was out of sympathy and favour. His reappearance in opera in the 1938 season at Covent Garden came about as a result of his recording of Sarastro in *Die Zauberflöte* under Beecham the previous year. On stage his Sarastro was found 'nervous', and according to Cardus he sang the part 'without the note of wisdom in his voice'. His other role, that of King Henry in *Lohengrin*, was scarcely more successful. A prolific recording artist, he can be heard as a communicative singer able to draw on a wide repertory in opera, lieder and popular song.

J.-U. Völmecke: 'Wilhelm Strienz', *Record Collector*, xxxv (1990), 52–82

J. B. STEANE

Striggio, Alessandro [Alessandrino] (*b* Mantua, ?1573; *d* Venice, ?15 June 1630). Italian librettist. He was the son of the madrigal composer Alessandro Striggio (*d* 1592). He appears as a viol player in the list of musicians who took part in the Florentine *intermedi* of 1589. Having studied law at Mantua in preparation for a diplomatic career, he became secretary to Duke Vincenzo I Gonzaga in June 1611, and for some years served as ambassador to Milan. First a count, then a marquis, he was also elevated to the rank of chancellor in January 1628. During the war over the succession to Vincenzo II he attempted to obtain military and political aid for Mantua in Madrid and then in Venice, where he died of the plague.

Striggio's most important link with the musical world was through his collaboration with Monteverdi, for whom he wrote the libretto of *Orfeo* (1607, Mantua), probably the ballet *Tirsi e Clori* (1616) and the lost dramatic cantata *Apollo*. After Monteverdi moved to Venice in 1613 Striggio's position as his patron and closest ally at the Mantuan court is eloquently documented by their correspondence, for the majority of Monteverdi's extant letters are addressed to him.

Orfeo was modelled on *Euridice* (1600) by Ottavio Rinuccini, who had altered the received version of the myth to effect a happy ending. Although Striggio's libretto adheres to the original tragic outcome (Orpheus loses his bride for ever and is dismembered by the Bacchantes), in Monteverdi's published score (1609) Orpheus is rescued by a *deus ex machina*. This discrepancy may have resulted from the circumstances of the 1607 performances, which did not allow for the use of machinery; but it is also likely that aesthetic considerations prompted Monteverdi to resort to the *lieto fine*.

Orfeo is in five acts, each having a different formal design centred around its own climax. Although Striggio's verse contains many echoes of Rinuccini's libretto, it is structurally more varied. There are passages in blank verse inviting the flexibility of recitative, others in traditional lyrical forms such as *terza rima* demanding strophic repetition, as well as sections that move between these extremes in novel ways. Interesting as the large-scale formal act-schemes are, however, Striggio's versification is less subtle rhetorically than that of Rinuccini, with whom Monteverdi subsequently collaborated.

Striggio also wrote texts for *Il trionfo d'onore* and *Il balletto d'Ifigenia*, both set by Marco da Gagliano and performed in Mantua in June 1608. He was a member, known as 'il Ritenuto' ('the reserved one'), of the Accademia degli Invaghiti, which promoted the first production of *Orfeo*.

*

A. Solerti: *Gli albori del melodramma*, iii (Milan, 1904)
K. Ringger: 'Monteverdis Libretti und die Anfänge der italienischen Tragödie', *Arcadia*, iii/2 (1978), 146–60
B. R. Hanning: *Of Poetry and Music's Power: Humanism and the Creation of Opera* (Ann Arbor, 1980)
R. Donington: *The Rise of Opera* (New York, 1981)
N. Pirrotta: 'Monteverdi and the Problems of Opera' and 'Theater, Sets, and Music in Monteverdi's Operas', *Music and Culture in Italy from the Middle Ages to the Baroque: a Collection of Essays* (Cambridge, MA, and London, 1984), 235–53, 254–70
F. W. Sternfeld: 'The Orpheus Myth and the Libretto of *Orfeo*', *Claudio Monteverdi: 'Orfeo'*, ed. J. Whenham (Cambridge, 1986), 20–33

BARBARA R. HANNING

Strinasacchi, Teresa (*b* Ostiglia, nr Mantua, 1768; *d* after 1830). Italian soprano. One of the leading female *buffa* singers of her time, she studied in Prague, according to Teuber, making her début in 1787 at Verona or Mantua in Paisiello's *Le due contesse*. She subsequently appeared in many Italian cities, including Chioggia and Treviso (1791) and Volterra (1792–3). She was a member of Guardasoni's company in Prague, 1793–7, singing in Czech in Singspiels by Czech composers from 1795. Schmidl says she was in Vienna in 1797, but between then and 1801 she sang in 17 operas at Venice.

From May 1801 to winter 1804–5 Strinasacchi was in Paris, where she enjoyed enormous success as Carolina in Cimarosa's *Il matrimonio segreto*. Stendhal (*Vie de Métastase*) referred to her finesse, fire and grace in this part, which she later performed at La Scala (1806), the Théâtre Italien, Paris (1816), London (1823) and Padua (1830). She also sang in Venice (1806–7), Padua (1810) and Florence (1814–15).

Strinasacchi was married to the *buffo* singer Giuseppe Ambrogetti. A Marianna Strinasacchi and a Teresa Strinasacchi Avogadro, probably her daughters or nieces, were active as opera singers in northern Italy in the 1830s and 40s. Her sister Anna was also a singer, and Regina Strinasacchi (1759–1839) was a well-known violinist.

*

DEUMM; *ES* (R. Celletti); *SchmidlD*
O. Teuber: *Geschichte des Prager Theaters* (Prague, 1883–7)

COLIN TIMMS

Strindberg, (Johan) August (*b* Stockholm, 22 Jan 1849; *d* Stockholm, 14 May 1912). Swedish writer and dramatist. He grew up in a musical household in which his parents and siblings all played instruments. Though he did not play himself, he frequented musical circles and enjoyed the friendship of such musicians as Tor Aulin. He favoured Beethoven, Bach and Chopin, and his experience of their music plays an important part in many of his works; but it was after the 'inferno crisis' (1894–6) that his perceptions of music as an art deepened, and that music assumed for him a moral, even religious function. He also studied harmony and developed his own theories about tonality and rhythm. In 1907 he published in the magazine *Idun* a thesis about music theory and notation, in which he advocated free tonality and a greater degree of chance and subjectiveness in music (theories which bear a striking resemblance to those of the Second Viennese School).

Strindberg gave careful instructions as to the nature and placing of music in his plays. For *Kronbruden* ('The Crown Bride') he also composed (or arranged) the 'Song of the Neck' and for *Samum* he wrote a bizarre, non-tonal melody. The only opera project Strindberg participated in was *Kronbruden*; the young Ture Rangström approached him for discussions about his setting, and Strindberg sanctioned the omission of the last two acts. His plays, notably *Ett drömspel* ('A Dream Play'), continue to attract the attention of opera composers.

Den fredlöse [The Outlawed] (play, 1872): I. Wikström, 1985
Lycko-Pers resa [Lucky-Peter's Travels] (play, 1882): Williamson, 1969
Fadren [The Father] (play, 1887): W. Runnström, 1980
Fröken Julie [Miss Julie] (play, 1888): Rorem, 1965; Bibalo, 1975; W. Amlyns, 1976; Hallin, 1989
Den starkare [The Stronger] (play, 1888–9): Weisgall, 1952; Hallin, 1990
Samum [Simoon] (play, 1889): J. Röntgen, 1926; Meyerowitz, 1948; Chisholm, 1953
Dödsdansen [Dance of Death] (play, 1900): Reimann, 1983
Kaspers fettisdag [Kasper's Shrove Tuesday] (play, 1900): Rosenberg, 1954
Ett drömspel [A Dream Play] (play, 1901): Weismann, 1922–4; Staempfli, 1944; E. Blomberg, 1964–5; Reimann, 1965; Williamson, 1968; T. Sullivan, 1988; I. Lidholm, 1991
Kronbruden [The Crown Bride] (play, 1901): Rangström, 1918
Svanevit [Swan White] (play, 1901): Weismann, 1919–20
Holländarn [The Dutchman] (play, 1902): I. Lidholm, 1967
Ett halvt ark papper [Half a Sheet of Paper] (play, 1903): F. Glans, 1966
Stora grusharpan [The Great Gravel-Harp] (play, 1903): M. Maros, 1982
Spöksonaten [The Ghost Sonata] (play, 1907): Weismann, 1929–30; Reimann, 1984

*

L. Sundman: *Strindberg och musiken* (diss., U. of Uppsala, 1971)
G. Ollén: *Strindbergs dramatik* (Stockholm, 1982)

ANDERS WIKLUND

Strobel, Otto (*b* Munich, 20 Aug 1895; *d* Bayreuth, 23 Feb 1953). German musicologist. He studied musicology at Munich University, where he took the doctorate in 1924 with a dissertation on Wagner. During the rise of Nazism and the concomitant enthusiasm for Wagner, he sifted and evaluated the Wagner family's autograph manuscripts and was archivist of the Wahnfried Archives, Bayreuth (from 1932), and director of the short-lived Richard Wagner Forschungsstätte (from 1938). He wrote extensively on Wagner's sketches and working methods, mostly in short articles for the *Bayreuther Festspielführer* and local periodicals, and edited some important documents, including the manuscript texts of the *Ring*. Although his exclusive and largely uncritical devotion to Wagner limited the intellectual perspective of his writing, his work is regarded as a foundation-stone of Wagner scholarship.

Richard Wagner über sein Schaffen: ein Beitrag zur 'Künstlerästhetik' (Munich, 1924)
Richard Wagner: Skizzen und Entwürfe zur Ring-Dichtung (Munich, 1930)
Genie am Werk: Richard Wagners Schaffen und Wirken im Spiegel eigenhandschriftlicher Urkunden: Führer durch die einmalige Ausstellung einer umfassenden Auswahl von Schätzen aus dem Archiv des Hauses Wahnfried (Bayreuth, 1933, 2/1934)
König Ludwig II und Richard Wagner: Briefwechsel (Karlsruhe, 1936)
Richard Wagner: Leben und Schaffen: eine Zeittafel (Bayreuth, 1952) JOHN DEATHRIDGE

Stroe, Aurel (*b* Bucharest, 5 May 1932). Romanian composer. He studied the piano with Manya Botez and Maria Fotino and then attended the Bucharest Conservatory (1951–6), studying with Marţian Negrea (harmony), Mihail Andricu (composition) and Theodor Rogalski (orchestration); from 1966 to 1969 he attended the Darmstadt summer school. He was professor of composition at the Bucharest Conservatory from 1962 to 1985 and at the University of Mainz from 1988. In addition to dramatic works, his output includes orchestral, vocal and chamber works. His highly original music explores unusual sonorities, mixing basic instruments (metal and wooden plates, gongs and cattle bells), to evoke the ancient world, with electronic equipment (magnetic tape, organ). He draws on microtonal harmonies and explores vocal techniques ranging from Sprechstimme and spoken recitative to shouting; vocal soloists are required to play instruments and instrumentalists to act on stage.

De Ptolemaco, 1970 (mini-opera), tape
Nu va primi premiul Nobel [Ça n'aura pas le Prix Nobel] (3 pts, P. Sterian), Kassel, Staats, 12 Nov 1971 (Mainz, 1969)
La paix (anti-opera, 3, Stroe, after Aristophanes) (Paris, 1973)
Les Choéphores [Orestia II] (music-theatre piece, 3, Stroe, after Aeschylus), Bucharest, radio broadcast, 13 Nov 1978
Agamemnon [Orestia I] (music-theatre piece, 3, Stroe, after Aeschylus), Bucharest, radio broadcast, 1 March 1983
Eumenides [Orestia III] (3, Stroe, after Sophocles), Timişoara, radio broadcast, 1986 VIOREL COSMA

Strohm, Reinhard (*b* Munich, 4 Aug 1942). German musicologist. He studied musicology at the University of Munich with Thrasybulos Georgiades and Wolfgang Osthoff, as well as Latin and Italian literature, then at the Technische Universität, Berlin, with Carl Dahlhaus. During this time he spent several periods of study in Italy. From 1964 to 1970 he collaborated with the Deutsche Arbeitsgruppe of *RISM*, and since 1970 he has been an editor of the Richard-Wagner-Gesamtausgabe. In 1975 he was appointed lecturer in music at King's College, London. He was awarded the Dent medal of the Royal Musical Association in 1977. Strohm's field of research ranges from early polyphony to 19th-century opera. He has made fundamental contributions to the documentation of the life and works of Handel and to the editing of Wagner's operas.

'Händels Pasticci', *AnMc*, no.14 (1974), 208–69
'Hasse, Scarlatti, Rolli', *AnMc*, no.15 (1975), 220–57
'Händel und seine italienischen Operntexte', *HJb 1975–6*, 99–157
Italienische Opernarien des frühen Settecento (1720–1730), AnMc, no.16 (1976) [whole vol.]
Essays on Handel and Italian Opera (Cambridge, 1985)

Stromentato (It., now *strumentato*: 'scored for instruments'). A term used, in the context recitativo stromentato, for recitative in which the orchestra enhances the sense of the words with expressive or dramatic writing; the terms 'recitativo obbligato' and 'orchestral recitative' are usually preferred. *See* RECITATIVE.

Strong, Susan (*b* Brooklyn, NY, 3 Aug 1870; *d* London, 11 March 1946). American soprano. She went to London at an early age and studied at the RCM. She made her operatic début as Sieglinde in 1893, and two years later sang the role at Covent Garden, as well as that of Elsa in *Lohengrin*. In 1897 she returned in the Grand Season with a 'powerfully sung' Brünnhilde in *Siegfried*. She also sang Aida, adding Venus, Donna Anna and Freia in *Rheingold* to her repertory during the 1900 season. She appeared at Vienna and Naples, and for a few years had some success in New York, singing with Mapleson's company in 1896 and then at the Metropolitan, where W. J. Henderson later remembered her as an underrated singer. She continued in concert work, mostly in London, and then ran a laundry in Baker Street. Her few recordings, mostly of songs, show an imaginative artist with a voice probably not meant by nature for the heavy roles she undertook. J. B. STEANE

Stronger, The. Opera in one act by HUGO WEISGALL to a libretto by Richard Hart after AUGUST STRINDBERG's play *Den starkare*; Westport, CT, White Barn Theatre, 9 August 1952 (with piano); revised version, New York, Columbia University, January 1955 (with orchestra).

Within the short duration of this dramatic monologue, three lives are brought sharply into focus, those of Estelle (soprano), her husband Harold, and Lisa (silent). Harold never appears in the opera but figures significantly in the action. Set in a bar on Christmas Eve afternoon, the work portrays Estelle's bitterness towards Lisa's friendship with Harold. As Estelle downs one cocktail after another, she becomes openly hostile to Lisa's silence and failure to respond to her jealous accusations. At the height of drunkenness, Estelle, in a rage and full of self-pity, accuses Lisa of trying to take Harold from her, as so many others have tried, as well as dominating every aspect of Estelle's domestic life. In an effort to determine who is 'the stronger' of the two, Estelle expresses her hysterical suspicions, portraying Lisa as a monster of hatred and guile. Having unburdened herself of thoughts that have afflicted her for some time, Estelle, convinced she is 'the stronger', regains composure and bids Lisa a 'Merry Christmas' as she exits.

Weisgall's musical setting is appropriate to the text's inherent drama. His music is atonal, consistently dissonant, tense and nervous. There are some uses of jazz, providing a kind of 'piano-bar' mood that re-establishes the reality of setting when the dramatic action warrants it. Although the musical tension may seem relentless, the music does have movement, reaching climaxes through linear motion in the vocal and orchestral parts. The harmonic scheme is complex, the orchestral colour vivid. A tour de force for solo soprano, Weisgall's vocal writing is inspired. Though the setting of the text is mostly syllabic, there are instances of melismatic writing. These sections are devised in a way that skilfully portrays the heroine's insinuations and biting accusations. The effective libretto rearranges and updates some events of the original play, but remains true to Strindberg's dramatic intentions. JAMES P. CASSARO

Strophic. A term applied to a song or aria in which all stanzas of the text are sung to the same music. In early Italian opera, arias often took the form of strophic variations, in which the bass usually remained the same from verse to verse while the melodic line was elaborated: 'Possente spirto', from Monteverdi's *Orfeo* (1607), is the outstanding example of strophic variations in opera. Strophic songs have in general not been greatly used by opera composers, because of their essentially undramatic character. They are generally reserved for situations in which their use conveys some particular dramatic point, for instance the bucolic simplicity of Papageno in *Die Zauberflöte* or the static and repetitive occupation of spinning as practised by Senta or Marguerite.

Strouse, Charles (Louis) (*b* New York, 7 June 1928). American composer. He began to write songs at the age of 12 and studied under Bernard Rogers at the Eastman School of Music. He was later a pupil of Copland at the Berkshire Music Center and in 1951 spent several months in Paris with Nadia Boulanger. On his return to the USA he continued his studies under Arthur Berger, Israel Citkowitz and David Diamond. At the same time he worked on Broadway as a rehearsal pianist, played in dance bands and, in collaboration with the lyricist Lee Adams (*b* 1924), wrote songs for summer-camp shows and off-Broadway revues. In 1960 they wrote their first complete score, *Bye-Bye Birdie*, which won a Tony award for the best musical of the year, as did their later success, *Applause* (1970). Strouse has since worked with other lyricists on shows for Broadway, but only *Annie* (1977) has achieved a similar popularity. He has also written film scores, and orchestral and instrumental music. Strouse's musical style, inventive if traditional in his early shows, has become more venturesome and free-ranging in his later ones.

musicals in two acts; dates are of first New York performances (librettist; lyricist)

Bye-Bye Birdie (M. Stewart; L. Adams), Martin Beck, 14 April 1960; All American (M. Brooks; Adams), Winter Garden, 19 March 1962; Golden Boy (C. Odets and W. Gibson; Adams), Majestic, 20 Oct 1964; It's a Bird, it's a Plane, it's Superman! (B. Comden and A. Green; Adams), Alvin, 29 March 1966; Applause (Comden and Green; Adams), Palace, 30 March 1970; Six (Strouse; Strouse), Cricket, 12 April 1971; I and Albert (J. Allen; Adams), London, Piccadilly, 6 Nov 1972; The Member of the Wedding, 1975; Annie (T. Meehan; M. Charnin), Alvin, 21 April 1977; A Broadway Musical (W. F. Brown; Adams), 21 Dec 1978

Flowers for Algernon (D. Rogers after D. Keye; Rogers), London, Queen's, 1979 (rev. as Charlie and Algernon, New York, Helen Hayes, 14 Sept 1980); Bring Back Birdie (Stewart; Adams), Martin Beck, 5 March 1981; Nightingale (children's op, Strouse, after H. C. Andersen: *The Nightingale*; Strouse), Buxton, Opera House, July 1982 (London, Hammersmith, Lyric, Dec 1982); Dance a Little Closer (A. J. Lerner, after R. E. Sherwood: *Idiot's Delight*; Lerner), Minskoff, 11 May 1983; Mayor (W. Leight, after E. Koch; Strouse), Top of the Gate, 13 May 1985; Rags (J. Stein; S. Schwartz), Hellinger, 21 Aug 1986

*

S. Green: *The World of Musical Comedy* (New York, 1960, 4/1980)
G. Bordman: *American Musical Theatre* (New York, 1978, 2/1986)

GERALD BORDMAN, ANDREW LAMB

Strozzi, Giulio [Zorzisto, Luigi] (*b* Venice, 1583; *d* Venice, 31 March 1652). Italian librettist, poet and dramatist. The singer-composer Barbara Strozzi was his adopted (probably illegitimate) daughter. He was himself the illegitimate (later legitimized) son of Roberto Strozzi, a Venetian banker and member of a prominent Florentine family. He was educated in Venice and at the University of Pisa, where he graduated in law. He then moved to Rome, where he attained the rank of apostolic prothonotary and was instrumental in founding, in about 1608, the Accademia degli Ordinati. This literary circle, which met at the house of Cardinal Giovanni Battista Deti, was formed in opposition to the influential Accademia degli Umoristi. Strozzi later resigned from the position of prothonotary and left Rome, where he seems to have become a controversial figure. He worked for a time at Padua, where he wrote the tragedy *Erotilla* (Venice, 1615), and at Urbino, where he served the duke as 'prefect of the bedchamber'. He finally returned to Venice, probably in the early 1620s, and spent most of the rest of his life there.

Strozzi was active in Venice in both literary and musical circles. In company with several of the early librettists of Venetian opera he was a member of the Accademia degli Incogniti and shared the academy's libertine philosophy. He himself founded two other academies at Venice. The first of these met at the house of the Marquis Martinenghi Malpaga. The second – the Accademia degli Unisoni, founded in 1637 – met at Strozzi's home and was devoted not only to the reading of academic discourses but also to musical performances in which Barbara Strozzi played a major role; the published papers of the academy (*Veglie de' Signori Unisoni*, Venice, 1638) are dedicated to her. Strozzi and his academy seem to have achieved some notoriety: both were attacked in an anonymous and strongly worded series of satires dating probably from late 1637 or early 1638.

Strozzi's literary output includes orations, plays, poetry and descriptions of Venetian ceremonial, several of which contain useful information on Venetian musical life; and his *Le glorie della Signora Anna Renzi romana* (Venice, 1644) contains biographical information about, and a critical appreciation of, the famous operatic soprano. He is best known, however, for the dramatic texts that he wrote for musical setting from the mid-1620s onwards. The five-act comic opera *La finta pazza Licori*, developed from an existing dramatic dialogue in 1627 and intended for performance at Mantua, is known only from Monteverdi's letters. Monteverdi wrote with enthusiasm about Strozzi's text and about the problems of a musical depiction of madness. According to Tomlinson (1983), however, he probably set no more than part of Act 1 before the project was abandoned.

From about the same period dates the earliest of Strozzi's small-scale dramatic texts to survive in its musical setting. This is the pastoral dialogue *La Gelosia placata* (Licoris, Tityrus, chorus), of which Giovanni Rovetta, assistant choirmaster at St Mark's, included a setting in his first book of madrigals (1629). The text, adapted from Act 3 scene i of Strozzi's comedy *Il natal di Amore, anacronismo* (Venice, rev. 4/1629), is cleverly constructed and is distinguished by its unusually energetic language; the musical setting foreshadows stylistic features of early Venetian opera and employs the Monteverdian *stile concitato* (texts and music in Whenham 1982). Strozzi's second collaboration with Monteverdi, *Proserpina rapita*, commissioned by the Venetian patrician Girolamo Mocenigo for the wedding of his daughter, was first performed on 16 April 1630 in a room above Mocenigo's apartments in the Palazzo Dandolo (now the Danieli Royal Hotel), Venice. The libretto survives, as does a brief description of the wedding banquet and performance (see Zoppelli 1986–7; another, and slightly varied, copy of the description cited by Zoppelli survives in *A-Wn*, Cod. 6263, ff.111*v*–112*r*). A setting for three voices and continuo of a section of the text, 'Come dolce hoggi l'auretta', was published in a posthumous collection of Monteverdi's *Madrigali e canzonette* (1651). (*Proserpina rapita* was not, as has previously been asserted, reset by Francesco Sacrati in 1644.)

Strozzi was one of the most original, important and influential of the small group of librettists involved in the creation of Venetian opera. Badoaro and Busenello were his friends. The latter contributed a laudatory ode for the publication of Strozzi's *La Venetia edificata* (Venice, 1624) and also dedicated several poems to Strozzi. Another librettist, Paolo Vendramin, was a member of the Accademia degli Unisoni. Several of Strozzi's librettos (all extant) were set for performance at the new public opera houses. *La Delia, o sia La Sera sposa del Sole*, written in 1630–31, was set by Francesco Manelli (music lost) and performed for the opening of the Teatro SS Giovanni e Paolo in 1639. Osthoff (1964) described it, rather than the work of Benedetto Ferrari, as 'the prototype of Venetian opera'. Even more important was *La finta pazza* (reprinted in Della Corte 1958; not to be identified with *La finta pazza Licori*); it was first performed with music by Sacrati for the opening of the Teatro Novissimo, Venice, on 14 January 1641 and subsequently presented in several other Italian cities. A score of the opera used by a touring company – the Febiarmonici – and dating from no earlier than 1644 has recently been rediscovered. The most notable revival of the opera took place in Paris in 1645, with stage designs by Giacomo Torelli and choreography by G. B. Balbi; for this, one of the earliest performances of Italian opera in Paris, some of the recitatives were replaced by spoken dialogue. Of the music for *La finta savia* (1643, Venice, SS Giovanni e Paolo; music by several composers), only the arias contributed by Filiberto Laurenzi survive. The setting of *Il Romolo e 'l Remo* (1645, Venice, SS Giovanni e Paolo), attributed on uncertain grounds to Cavalli, is lost, but Cavalli's score for Strozzi's last libretto, *Veremonda, l'amazzone d'Aragona* (1652, Naples, and probably 1653, Venice), survives. On the title-page of the libretto, which was a reworking of G. A. Cicognini's *Celio* (1646, Florence), Strozzi's name appeared anagrammatically as Luigi Zorzisto.

La finta pazza Licori, Monteverdi, inc., 1627; *Proserpina rapita*, Monteverdi, 1630; *La Delia, o sia La Sera sposa del Sole* (poema dramatico), Manelli, 1639; *La finta pazza* (drama), Sacrati, 1641; *La finta savia* (drama), F. Laurenzi, T. Merula, C. Crivelli, B. Ferrari, possibly later addns by A. Leardini and V. Tozzi, 1643; *Il Romolo e 'l Remo* (drama), ?Cavalli, 1645; *Veremonda, l'amazzone d'Aragona* (drama), Cavalli, 1652

*

Grove6 (J. Whenham)
Il cannochiale per La finta pazza (Venice, 1641)
Feste theatrali per La finta pazza, dramma del Sig.r Giulio Strozzi ... e da Giacomo Torelli da Fano inventore (Paris, 1645)
G. B. Balbi: *Balletti d'invenzione nella Finta pazza* (n.p., n.d.)
G. Spini: *Ricerca dei libertini* (Rome, 1950)
A. Della Corte: *Drammi per musica dal Rinuccini allo Zeno* (Turin, 1958), i, 333–430
W. Osthoff: *Das dramatische Spätwerk Claudio Monteverdis* (Tutzing, 1960)
D. Arnold: *Monteverdi* (London, 1963, rev. 3/1990)
W. Osthoff: 'Maske und Musik', *Castrum Peregrini*, lxv (1964); It. trans., *NRMI*, i (1967), 16–44
C. Sartori: 'Un fantomatico compositore per un'opera che forse non era un'opera', *NRMI*, v (1971), 788–98
T. Walker: 'Gli errori di "Minerva al tavolino": osservazioni sulla cronologia delle prime opere veneziane', *Venezia e il melodramma nel seicento: Venice 1972*, 7–20
G. Morelli and T. Walker: 'Tre controversie intorno al San Cassiano', ibid, 97–120, esp. 114
W. Osthoff: 'Filiberto Laurenzis Musik zu "La finta savia" in Zusammenhang der frühvenezianischen Oper', ibid, 173–97
D. de' Paoli, ed.: *C. Monteverdi: Lettere, dediche e prefazioni: edizione critica* (Rome, 1973)
L. Bianconi and T. Walker: 'Dalla Finta pazza alla Veremonda: storie di Febiarmonici', *RIM*, x (1975), 379–425
B. Brancaforte and C. L. Brancaforte: *La primera traducción del 'Lazarillo de Tormes' por Giulio Strozzi* (Ravenna, 1977)
E. Rosand: 'Barbara Strozzi, virtuosissima cantatrice: the Composer's Voice', *JAMS*, xxxi (1978), 241–81
D. Stevens, ed. and trans.: *C. Monteverdi: Letters* (London, 1980)
J. Whenham: *Duet and Dialogue in the Age of Monteverdi* (Ann Arbor, 1982)
G. Tomlinson: 'Twice Bitten, Thrice Shy: Monteverdi's "finta" *Finta pazza*', *JAMS*, xxxvi (1983), 303–11
L. Zoppelli: 'Il rapto perfettissimo: un'inedita testimonianza sulla "Proserpina" di Monteverdi', *Rassegna veneta di studi musicali*, ii-iii (1986–7), 343–5
P. Fabbri: *Il secolo cantante: per una storia del libretto d'opera nel seicento* (Bologna, 1990)
E. Rosand: *Opera in Seventeenth-Century Venice: the Creation of a Genre* (Berkeley and Los Angeles, 1990)
L. Bianconi and T. Walker, eds.: *F. Sacrati: La finta pazza*, DMV, i (1991)

JOHN WHENHAM

Strungk, Nicolaus Adam (bap. Brunswick, 15 Nov 1640; *d* Dresden, 23 Sept 1700). German composer. He received his musical education in Brunswick and Lübeck, and held posts from 1660 as first violinist and Konzertmeister of the Hofkapellen of Wolfenbüttel, Celle and Hanover. His first close contact with opera came in 1662 on a visit to Vienna, where he performed before the emperor. Working in Hanover, where opera began to flourish after 1672, he encountered Cesti's *Orontea* and P. A. Ziani's *L'Antigona delusa da Alceste*, and he must certainly have known operas by Antonio Sartorio, who was then directing the Italian Kapelle there. He also met the theatre architect Girolamo Sartorio. In 1679 he became director of both city and cathedral music in Hamburg; he made his mark during the early days of the Hamburg Opera with his first operas, *Doris*, *Esther* and *Alceste*. In June 1682 he returned to Hanover as court composer. By now French had superseded Italian opera at the court. While living in Hanover Strungk continued to compose for Hamburg, where his operas *Theseus* and *Floretto* were produced in 1683. In 1685 and 1686 he stayed in Venice with Duke Ernst August, but returned to Germany without his permission and was dismissed from his post. However, his visits to Italy may have led to his appointment in 1688 as vice-Kapellmeister and chamber organist at the Dresden court, since Elector Johann Georg III and Carlo Pallavicino, director of the Dresden Opera, visited Venice during this period. He completed Pallavicino's opera *Antiope* for the elector after the composer's death (Telemann was its conductor briefly from 1701), and in 1692 he became Kapellmeister.

On 13 June 1692 the Elector Johann Georg IV granted Strungk permission to present 'a German Singspiel at his own and his associates' expense' with 'foreign musicians' in Leipzig during the fair. Not least of the reasons behind this enterprise was Strungk's desire to improve his financial situation. Assisted by special licences granted by the elector, he succeeded in establishing an opera house on the Brühl; among his associates was Girolamo Sartorio, who built the theatre and then remained as director and as designer of scenery and stage effects. The theatre was opened on 8 May 1693 at the Easter Fair with Strungk's *Alceste*, performed in the presence of the elector. Strungk remained the principal composer of operas; *Nero* (1693) and *Syrinx* (1694) were particularly well received. His daughters, who appeared with the company as singers, continued running it with their mother Christine after his death (Telemann was its conductor briefly from 1701), and it remained in existence until 1720. Singers from outside were also engaged, particularly students and even choristers from the Thomaskirche, giving rise to a complaint from the Kantor, Kuhnau. In 1697 Strungk lost his position in Dresden. His financial situation improved slightly in 1699, when he was appointed principal director of the *Landmusik*, but he left a heavy burden of debt to his family on his death.

Together with Johann Theile, J. W. Franck and J. P. Förtsch, Strungk was one of the first Germans to apply himself to the development of a national German opera, and he was particularly important for the founding and direction of his opera company in Leipzig. His dramatic works were performed on many German stages in his day. Nothing survives of their music except arias from the sacred opera *Esther*, the authorship of which was proved by H. C. Wolff (1957). Schering ascribed several other operas to him; his authorship of further works attributed by Berend and Schiedermair cannot be proved, as no music is extant. The arias from *Esther*, which have been preserved almost complete, were published without attribution (Hamburg, 1684) together with arias from *Semiramis*, an opera once also believed to be by Strungk but ascribed by Wolff (1957) on stylistic grounds to Franck. Strungk initially employed the Italian style in his Hamburg operas, at the same time adapting foreign forms. According to Wolff (1957), textual repetition and extended coloratura passages were first used for affective purposes at the Hamburg Opera in *Esther*, achieving an expressive power comparable to that of Schütz. Strungk used ostinato bass in the Venetian manner to link coloraturas and provide overall shape, and his symmetrical motivic patterns suggest the influence of Cavalli and Cesti. His arias represent an advance on those of Theile. Following the style of cantatas such as Buxtehude's, he attempted to develop German strophic song and compose different music for each stanza. In employing the variation principle and unexpected harmonic changes, he distanced himself from Italian models and gave his music personal and indeed national features. He also put counterpoint to the service of textual interpretation. The many ritornellos emphasize the concertante element, while the choruses (in two parts with continuo) are self-contained pieces. The libretto of *Esther* is not, as with most Hamburg operas of the period, a translation from Italian but an original German text. In completing Pallavicino's *Antiope*, Strungk adapted his style almost seamlessly to the Venetian composer's; most of Act 3 seems to be his. His Leipzig operas were based on Italian librettos. Pleasing melodic writing, with echoes of the convivial student songs of the time, may have been characteristic of his Leipzig opera *Alceste* (1693).

Die liebreiche, durch Tugend und Schönheit erhöhete Esther (Spl, J. M. Köler), Hamburg, 1680, 36 arias in Ein Hundert auserlesene Arien zweyer Hamburgischen Operen mit beygefügten Ritornellen (Hamburg, 1684)
Doris, oder Der königliche Sclave (Spl, trans. J. P. Förtsch), Hamburg, 1680
Alceste (Spl, P. Quinault, trans. Förtsch), Hamburg, 1680
Theseus (Quinault, trans. L. von Bostel), Hamburg, 1683
Floretto (after C. Weise: Die triumphirende Keuschheit), Hamburg, 1683
Antiope (dramma per musica, S. B. Pallavicino), Dresden, Feb 1689, *D-Dlb* [by C. Pallavicino, completed by Strungk]
Alceste (P. Thymich, after A. Aureli: L'Antigona delusa da Alceste), Leipzig, 8 May 1693
Nero (3, Thymich, after G. C. Corradi), Leipzig, 1693
Syrinx, Leipzig, 1694

Attrib. by Schering (all libs. by C. L. Boxberg): Phocas, Leipzig, 1696; Ixion (after Perisetti: L'Isione), Leipzig, 1697; Scipio und Hannibal, Leipzig, 1698; Agrippina, Leipzig, 1699; Erechtheus, Leipzig, 1700

M. Fürstenau: *Zur Geschichte der Musik und des Theaters am Hofe der Kurfürsten von Sachsen* (Dresden, 1861)
J. O. Opel: 'Die ersten Jahrzehnte der Oper in Leipzig', *Neues Archiv für sächsische Geschichte und Altertumskunde*, v (Dresden, 1884), 116–41
J. Sittard: *Geschichte des Musik- und Concertwesens in Hamburg* (Altona, 1890)
F. Zelle: 'Drei Beiträge zur Geschichte der ältesten deutschen Oper, II', *Programm des Humboldt-Gymnasiums* (Berlin, 1891)
H. Kretzschmar: 'Das erste Jahrhundert der deutschen Oper', *SIMG*, iii (1901–2), 270–93
F. Berend: *Nicolaus Adam Strungk, 1640–1700: sein Leben und seine Werke, mit Beiträgen zur Geschichte der Musik und des Theaters in Celle, Hannover und Leipzig* (Freiburg, 1915)
G. F. Schmidt: 'Die älteste deutsche Oper in Leipzig am Ende des 17. und Anfang des 18. Jahrhunderts', *Festschrift zum 50. Geburtstag Adolf Sandberger* (Munich, 1918), 209–57
——: 'Zur Geschichte, Dramaturgie und Statistik der frühdeutschen Oper (1627–1750)', *ZMw*, v (1922–3), 582–97, 642–65; vi (1923–4), 129–57, 496–530
F. Reuter: *Geschichte der deutschen Oper in Leipzig, 1693–1720* (diss., U. of Leipzig, 1922)
A. Schering: *Musikgeschichte Leipzigs*, ii (Leipzig, 1926)
L. Schiedermair: *Die deutsche Oper* (Leipzig, 1930)
I. Schreiber: *Dichtung und Musik der deutschen Opernarien, 1680–1700* (diss., U. of Berlin, 1934)
H. C. Wolff: *Die Venezianische Oper in der 2. Hälfte des 17. Jahrhunderts* (Berlin, 1937)
W. Schulze: *Die Quellen der Hamburger Oper – 1678–1738* (Hamburg and Oldenburg, 1938)
H. Schnoor: *Dresden – 400 Jahre deutsche Musikkultur* (Dresden, 1948)
H. C. Wolff: *Die Barockoper in Hamburg (1687–1738)* (Wolfenbüttel, 1957)

DIETER HÄRTWIG

Stubborn Lovers, The [*Tvrdé palice*]. Comic opera in one act by ANTONÍN DVOŘÁK to a libretto by Josef Štolba; Prague, New Czech Theatre, 2 October 1881.

In a small country town, the widower Vávra (baritone) and widow Říhová (contralto) agree that their respective children, Toník (tenor) and Lenka (soprano), will marry. Knowing the stubborn nature of the two young people, the godfather Řeřicha (bass) warns that they probably will not agree to their parents' wishes. The opera is taken up with the implementation of Řeřicha's plan in which Toník and Lenka are duped into thinking that each one is going to marry the other's parent. During the course of the opera the two stubborn lovers admit to Řeřicha that they do love one another, but it is only in the penultimate scene that they tell each other. With Řeřicha's design exposed, the young ones are free to marry and the final scene commemorates the happy outcome with rejoicing.

Although *The Stubborn Lovers* had its première in 1881, it was written in 1874 – completed shortly after Dvořák had finished the second version of *King and Charcoal Burner*. Despite Štolba's awkward libretto, *The Stubborn Lovers* marks a considerable advance on Dvořák's first comic opera and on the Provisional Theatre's most popular one-act opera, Blodek's *V studni* ('In the well'). Despite a number of set pieces, the opera is through-composed with the continuity ensured by a single theme associated with Řeřicha and his ruse.

Melodically, the work is much richer than *King and Charcoal Burner*, at times anticipating Dvořák's 'Czech national style' as exemplified by the first set of Slavonic Dances (1878). Dvořák's treatment of the comedy and characterization is also surprisingly developed, foreshadowing similar village types in *The Jacobin* and *The Devil and Kate*. JAN SMACZNY

Stuck [Stück], **Jean-Baptiste** [Batistin, Baptistin] (*b* 1680; *d* Paris, 8 Dec 1755). Italian composer of German descent. He began his career in Italy (in Florence, Livorno and Naples), and went to France about 1705. In his four books of cantatas (Paris, 1706–14) he is described as 'ordinaire de la musique de ... Monseigneur le Duc d'Orléans'. A virtuoso cellist, he played in Paris under the patronage of the Prince of Carignan. He apparently left France about 1714 and spent some time in the service of the Elector of Bavaria before travelling to Italy, where he wrote an opera, *Il Cid*, for Livorno at Carnival 1715. In France again, he was given a pension in 1718 as *ordinaire de la musique du Roy*. According to La Gorce (1986), he married Bonne-Françoise, daughter of Jean Bérain, Louis XIV's artistic designer, in 1727. Famous as a composer of cantatas, Stuck had one of his motets played at the Concert Spirituel in 1738.

Stuck composed three operas for the Académie Royale de Musique: *Méléagre* in 1709, *Manto la fée* in 1711 (a spectacular fairy drama) and *Polidore* in 1720 (according to Girdlestone, on a libretto by Pellegrin writing under the pseudonym of La Serre). Only *Polidore*, which had the best libretto, was ever revived (in 1739). These works were not very successful, as they were not in line with the established aesthetic. Rochemont associates them with 'musical beauties of a new taste and a genre more elevated than our ordinary routine' (*Réflexions d'un patriote sur l'opéra français*, Paris, 1754).

Musically *Méléagre* is the most interesting because of its freshness; here Stuck often seems closer in style to the young Handel (e.g. Althée's aria and the chorus 'Hâtez notre bonheur' in Act 1 scene v) than to his French contemporaries, except perhaps for the Duke of Orléans. Composed less than five years after Stuck's arrival in France, *Méléagre* adopts the French style in the tradition of Lully, particularly in its recitatives (despite the occasional clumsiness of the verse). But there are also many italianate touches, notably in the treatment of the orchestra and the thematic development. Stuck introduced a genuine Neapolitan aria in the prologue, 'Su la bella Navicella', and he was to do the same in *Manto* with a 'Lieto brilla il cor' (5.v). The prologue to *Méléagre*, as *L'union de la musique italienne et française*, was performed several times at the Concert François in 1728–9. In Stuck's later works the Italian element gradually disappears; *Polidore* shows almost no trace of it.

Méléagre (tragédie lyrique, prol., 5, F. A. Jolly, after Ovid: *Metamorphoses*), Paris, Opéra, 24 May 1709, reduced score (Paris, 1709)

Manto la fée (opéra, 5, Mennesson), Paris, Opéra, 29 Jan 1711, reduced score (Paris, 1711)

Il [gran] Cid (G. G. Alborghetti), Livorno, S Sebastiano, carn. 1715 (Massa, 1715)

Polidore (opéra, 5, La Serre [S.-J. Pellegrin]), Paris, Opéra, 15 Feb 1720 (Paris, 1720, 2/1739)

Orion, 1725 (J. de La Font), inc., 1 air pubd in *Mercure de France* (Feb 1725)

Airs in: Rodrigo in Algeri (1702); Thétis et Pélée (1708)

S. Milliot: 'Jean-Baptiste Stück', *RMFC*, ix (1969), 91–8

C. Girdlestone: *La tragédie en musique (1673–1750) considérée comme genre littéraire* (Paris, 1972)

J. R. Anthony: *French Baroque Music from Beaujoyeulx to Rameau* (London, 1973, 2/1978)

E. Lemaître: *L'orchestre dans le théâtre lyrique français chez les continuateurs de Lully, 1687–1715* (diss., Paris Conservatoire, 1977)

J. de La Gorce: *L'opéra sous le règne de Louis XIV: le merveilleux ou les puissances surnaturelles (1671–1675)* (diss., U. of Paris, 1978)

——: *Bérain dessinateur du roi* (Paris, 1986)

JEAN DURON

Stückgold [née Schneidt], **Grete** (*b* London, 6 June 1895; *d* Falls Village, CT, 13 Sept 1977). German soprano, later naturalized American. She studied in Munich and made her début in 1917 at Nuremberg. In 1922 she was engaged at the Berlin Staatsoper, where in 1929 she created Laura in Hindemith's *Neues vom Tage* at the Kroll Theater. In 1927 she sang Aida at Covent Garden and made her début as Eva at the Metropolitan, where she continued to sing until 1939; her repertory included Wagner's Elisabeth, Elsa and Sieglinde as well as Agathe, Octavian and the Marschallin. She also appeared at Chicago, San Francisco and Philadelphia. Her warm and generous voice is preserved on recordings made in the 1920s. RICHARD LeSUEUR, ELIZABETH FORBES

Studer, Cheryl (*b* Midland, MI, 24 Oct 1955). American soprano. After studying at Interlochen and in Vienna with Hans Hotter, in 1980 she joined the Bayerische Staatsoper in Munich, where she has sung Mařenka, Irene (*Rienzi*), Euryanthe, Sieglinde, the Empress (*Die Frau ohne Schatten*) and Daphne. In 1984 she made her American début at Chicago as Micaëla, and sang Elisabeth at Bayreuth, Eva at San Francisco and Freia at the Deutsche Oper, Berlin. She returned to Bayreuth (1987) for Elsa, the role of her Covent Garden début (1988). At La Scala she sang Mathilde (*Guillaume Tell*) in 1988, Hélène (*Les vêpres siciliennes*) in 1989 and Odabella in 1991. She made her Vienna Staatsoper début as Chrysothemis, which she also sang at Salzburg. At the Metropolitan she has sung Donna Anna (1990) and Mozart's Electra (1991). Her repertory includes Countess Almaviva, Pamina, Lucia and Violetta. An eloquent singer, she has sometimes taken on parts too heavy for her beautiful, flexible voice.

ELIZABETH FORBES

Stümer, Heinrich [Carl] (*b* Frödenwald, Prussia, 1789; *d* Berlin, 27 Sept 1856). German tenor. He studied in Berlin, making his debut there in 1811 as Belmonte at the Hofoper, where he was engaged for 20 years. His repertory included Florestan and Max (*Der Freischütz*), which he created at the Berlin Schauspielhaus in 1821; he was particularly renowned for his singing of Gluck's Pylades, Achilles, Admetus, Renaud and Orpheus.

ELIZABETH FORBES

Stuntz, Joseph Hartmann (*b* Arlesheim, nr Basle, ? 23 July 1793; *d* Munich, 18 June 1859). Swiss composer of German origin. He studied with Peter von Winter in Munich (1808–12) and with Salieri in Vienna (1813–16) and then became conductor of the Italian Opera in Munich. His first opera, *La rappressaglia*, written during his first stay in Italy (1818–20), was well received on both sides of the Alps; it was produced successively in Munich, Vienna, Stuttgart and Berlin in a German translation as *Das Schloss Lowinsky*. This success, however, was not matched by his next operas, and Stuntz decided to settle in Munich, where in 1825 he was appointed Winter's successor as first conductor of the Hofoper. Because of his conducting methods (he tended to slow tempos, and preferred the new way of leading the orchestra from the piano rather than as first violinist) he was replaced by Franz Lachner, but continued as conductor of the court orchestra until his death.

While his Italian operas are written in a neo-Neapolitan style, his two German dramatic works written for Munich, the Singspiel *Heinrich IV. zu Ivry* and the tragic opera *Maria Rosa*, fail as attempts at 'deutsche Oper'. *Garibaldi der Agilolfinger* (1824), arranged for King Maximilian's 25th jubilee, is a rather odd adaptation of Mozart's *La clemenza di Tito*; only the introduction and the second finale are original. Stuntz also wrote a large number of ballets, cantatas, masses and other works for official occasions. He was the founder of the male-choir tradition in Munich, and his songs and choruses became popular in southern Germany.

La rappressaglia, ossia Il contracambio (komische Oper, 2, C. Sterbini), Milan, Scala, 2 Oct 1819; Ger. trans. as Das Schloss Lowinsky

Constantino (P. A. Tindorio Dalmiro), Venice, Fenice, 12 Feb 1820

Heinrich IV. zu Ivry (Spl, 3, J. J. Sendtner, after Voltaire), Munich, Hof, 8 Sept 1820

Argene e Dalmiro (2, A. Peracchi), Turin, Regio, 26 Dec 1820

Elvira e Lucindo (2, L. Romanelli), Milan, Scala, 9 June 1821

Garibaldi der Agilolfinger (C. M. Heigel, after P. Metastasio), Munich, Hof, 16 Feb 1824, music adapted from Mozart's La clemenza di Tito

König Stanislaus (2, J. von Seyfried), Berlin, Königstadt, 3 Aug 1827

Maria Rosa (romantische Oper, 3, Lessner), Munich, Hof, 23 Feb 1845

*

StiegerO

K. Gross: *Joseph Hartmann Stuntz als Opernkomponist* (diss., U. of Munich, 1934; part pubd, Würzburg, 1936)

C. Gruber: *Opern Uraufführungen*, ii (Vienna, 1987)

F. R. BOSONNET

Stünzner, Elise (*b* Altenburg, 10 Jan 1886; *d* Dresden, 19 Sept 1975). German soprano. She studied at Leipzig and then Dresden, making her début there in 1909 while still a student as the Shepherd Boy in *Tannhäuser*. Engaged at the Hofoper (later Staatsoper) until her retirement in 1935, she sang the Milliner at the first performance of *Der Rosenkavalier* (1911) and her repertory included many Strauss roles: Octavian, Diemut (*Feuersnot*), the Composer (*Ariadne auf Naxos*), the Dyer's Wife and Salome, which she sang in the 25th-anniversary performance of the opera (1930). She created the Mother in d'Albert's posthumously performed *Mister Wu* (1932). ELIZABETH FORBES

Stuttgart. City in Germany, capital of Baden-Württemberg.

1. To 1800. 2. After 1800.

1. To 1800. From 1609 the ducal court at Stuttgart mounted French-style ballets and other spectacles involving singing and dancing to mark special festive occasions. *Wirtschaften*, or court masquerades, were added in 1676. In 1674 the 'musicalischer Freudenspil' *In der Frembde erworbene Lavinia* (text by Michael Schuster, composer unknown) was mounted in the new Komödienhaus that replaced the old Lusthaus.

Opera at Stuttgart flowered under Duke Eberhard Ludwig (reigned 1677–1733) with the arrival of J. S. Kusser from Paris, where he had studied with Lully. Appointed Kapellmeister in 1700, he produced operas by himself and others in German until his departure in 1704. Reinhard Keiser resided at Stuttgart from 1719 to 1722 but was unable to secure an appointment in the increasingly Italian atmosphere. In 1733 the duchy passed to the Winnenthal line and Duke Carl Alexander. On his sudden death in 1737 he left an expanded Kapelle and considerable debts for the regents who ruled until the accession of the 16-year-old Duke Carl Eugen in 1744, when there began a brilliant and ruinously extravagant period of opera, theatre and ballet at court. In 1750 the duke had the old Lusthaus converted into an opera house at a cost of 300 000 gulden; it opened on 30 August with C. H. Graun's *Artaserse*, which Carl Eugen had heard at Berlin in 1743.

Ignaz Holzbauer served as court Kapellmeister from 1751 to 1753, but the duke's fondest wish was to secure Niccolò Jommelli, whose *Ezio* was produced on the duke's birthday, 11 February 1751. Carl Eugen met the composer at Rome in 1753 and appointed him Kapellmeister that October. Between then and his departure in 1769 Jommelli wrote 14 serious operas, as well as serenatas and comic operas for Stuttgart. The duke gave him complete charge of operatic activities, although he chose the two librettos for the new carnival operas. These were almost invariably by either Metastasio (adjusted by Jommelli himself) or the court poet Matteo Verazi. The winter season began on the duke's name-day, 4 November, and carnival began with a new opera immediately after New Year's Day; the second and most sumptuous production took place on Carl Eugen's birthday, 11 February. The chief singers during the Jommelli years included Maria Masi-Giura and Giuseppe Aprile. Burney reported that in 1772 the orchestra included 18 violins, 6 violas, 3 cellos, 4 basses, 4 oboes, 2 flutes, 3 horns and 2 bassoons. A ballet, established in 1758, achieved widespread fame under J.-G. Noverre from 1760 to 1767.

In 1764 animosity between the townspeople and the duke had prompted Carl Eugen to move his court to Ludwigsburg, about 10km north of Stuttgart. Occasional productions of Italian opera had been mounted at the Schlosstheater there since 1728; upon Carl Eugen's installation in 1764 he immediately turned every resource to the swift completion of an immense new opera house, the scene of his final extravagances. But in 1767 relentless pressure from the Estates and the influence of his new mistress, Franziska von Leutrum, forced Carl Eugen to reverse his ways. Noverre and half the ballet were dismissed, along with the entire French acting company; further reductions followed over the next six years. In 1775 the palace and opera house at Ludwigsburg were closed and the court moved back to Stuttgart.

While still at Ludwigsburg the duke had established a theatrical school in 1770 as part of the military conservatory (after 1775 the Carlsschule) and in 1773 added an Ecole des Demoiselles. As a further economizing measure these institutions supplied singers and musicians for subsequent operatic productions at court. In 1777 the court began charging admission to theatrical events, and travelling companies performing Italian and German plays and operas began visiting Stuttgart, including Schikaneder's troupe in 1778. A smaller theatre, the Kleines Schauspielhaus auf der Planie, was built in 1779. Here German, Italian and later French operas were

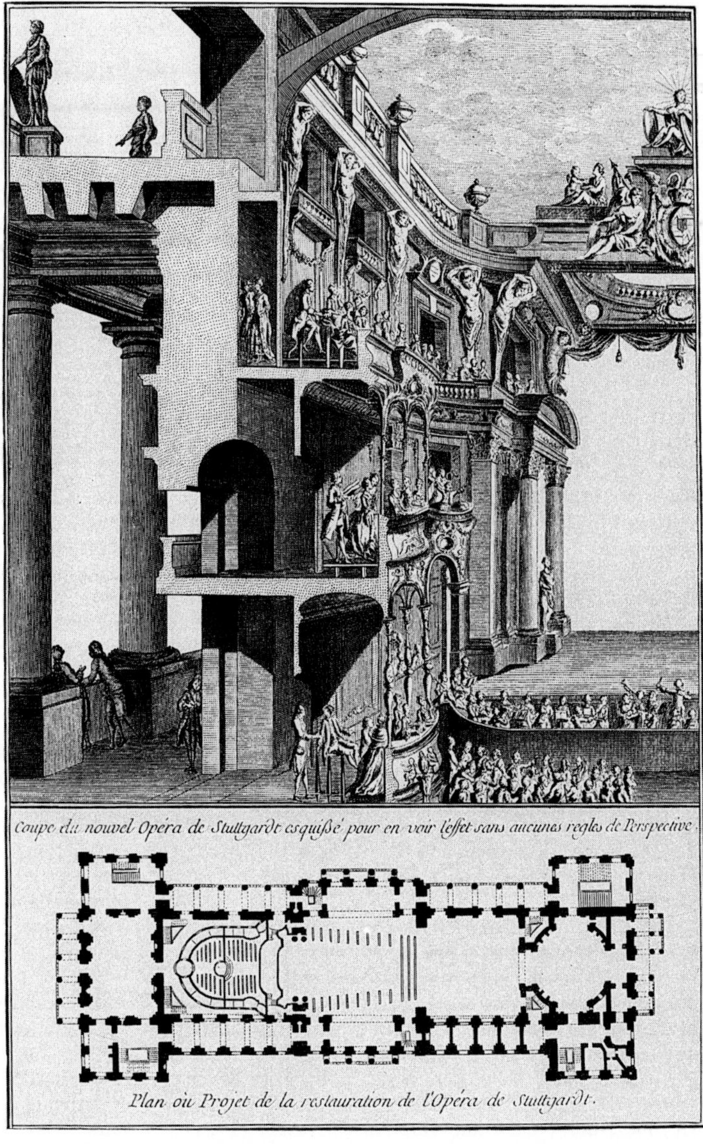

1. *Plan and cross-section of the Stuttgart opera house rebuilt (1758–9) to a design by Philippe de le Guêpièrre: engraving from Diderot and D'Alembert, 'Encyclopédie', x (planches) (1772)*

given until the house burnt down on 17 April 1802.

The court's German theatre, under C. F. D. Schubart from 1787 to his death in 1791, began to rival in importance the Italian company, under Kapellmeister Agostino Poli from 1782 to 1792. J. R. Zumsteeg, like Schubart a graduate of the Carlsschule, replaced his teacher Poli as Kapellmeister from 1793 (the year of Carl Eugen's death) to 1802; he was the first German to hold the post since Holzbauer. Zumsteeg, a firm champion of Mozart's works, crowned his own career as an operatic composer with his setting of Gotter's *Die Geisterinsel*, given at the big opera house on 7 November 1798.

2. Ater 1800. After the death of Duke Carl Eugen the court theatre underwent some drastic economic measures with dire results, commented on by Goethe when he visited Stuttgart in 1797. Weber worked as secretary to Duke Ludwig in Stuttgart, 1807–10, and there composed *Silvana* and incidental music for Schiller's reworking of Gozzi's *Turandot*; Conradin Kreutzer was Hofkapellmeister, 1812–16, to be followed by Hummel, 1816–18, but they all ran into difficulties with the administration and soon left. The former Lusthaus was renovated in 1812 and again in 1845, and continued to serve as a court theatre (seating about 1250) until it burnt down in 1902.

Standards improved under Peter von Lindpaintner, who was Hofkapellmeister from 1819 to 1856, with Ignaz Lachner as his deputy. He improved the quality of the orchestra, which was praised by both Mendelssohn and Berlioz, and introduced many new works to the repertory, including some of his own. Mozart was a great favourite, with *Die Entführung*, *Figaro*, *Don Giovanni*, *Die Zauberflöte* and *La clemenza di Tito* as stalwarts, while *Così*, in spite of several stagings, never succeeded. Weber's *Freischütz* had its Stuttgart première in 1822. With two opera performances a week, the 1824 season offered 32 different works by 17 composers.

The 1830s saw the advance of Meyerbeer, with *Robert le diable* in 1834 and *Les Huguenots* in 1838; Meyerbeer himself conducted his *Etoile du nord* in 1854 and *Dinorah* in 1859 with great success. Stuttgart's first Verdi production was *Nabucco* in 1844, while Wagner

2. Poster for a Richard Strauss festival in Stuttgart (1912), showing Max Littmann's Grosses Haus (right), and the Kleines Haus (left) which was inaugurated with the première of 'Ariadne auf Naxos' on 25 October 1912

made his local bow in 1859 with *Tannhäuser*, to be followed by *Holländer* (1865), *Lohengrin* (1869) and guest performances of the *Ring* by Angelo Neumann's troupe in 1883; the first locally produced *Ring* followed in 1890. Under Johann Joseph Abert, Hofkapellmeister 1867–88, and his assistant Karl Doppler, Stuttgart's reputation received fresh impetus. Verdi and Wagner were the audience's favourites during these decades. By the end of the century about 120 performances of between 40 and 60 operas were given each year. When the house burnt down early in 1902 a temporary theatre (1140 seats) was erected immediately; this opened in October that year with *Tannhäuser* and served the Stuttgart audience until a new Hoftheater complex, designed by Max Littman and consisting of the Grosses Haus and the Kleines Haus, was inaugurated in 1912 (see fig.2).

The Kleines Haus opened on 25 October 1912 with the première of Strauss's *Ariadne auf Naxos*, produced by Max Reinhardt. With Max von Schillings as musical director, 1908–18, new works became a regular feature of the repertory, among them his own *Mona Lisa* (1915) and Zemlinsky's *Eine florentinische Tragödie* (1917). He was followed from 1918 to 1922 by Fritz Busch, whose premières included those of Hindemith's *Mörder, Hoffnung der Frauen* and *Das Nusch-Nuschi* (1921). During the period when Carl Leonhard was Stuttgart's musical director (1922–37) long-term planning resulted in a complete Weber cycle in his anniversary year, 1926, and performances of all Wagner's operas in 1933. Special emphasis was placed on works by Gluck, but Handel, too, was favoured, and among contemporaries Schreker, Hindemith, Busoni, Krenek and Weill, as well as Strauss, figured prominently.

After 1933 a different brand of contemporary composer was preferred: Paul von Klenau, Paul Höffer, Hugo Herrmann and Marc André-Souchay, as well as operetta composers such as Franz Grothe and Nico Dostal. Cautious modern reforms of opera production were introduced under such directors as Franz Ludwig Hörth and Otto Erhardt. With Gustav Deharde as Generalintendant (1937–44; his musical director was Herbert Albert) the house inevitably yielded increasingly to Nazi doctrines, although this was more strongly evident in the drama than in the opera repertory.

The Kleines Haus was bombed in 1944, but the Grosses Haus was one of the few German theatres to survive World War II undamaged. After being used for a time by French and American forces as a club, it was restored to its legitimate function as an opera house, while the drama company of what became the Württembergische Staatstheater had to perform in makeshift halls until the Kleines Haus was rebuilt in 1962. With Walter Erich Schäfer as its enlightened Generalintendant (1949–72) and Ferdinand Leitner as musical director (1950–69), the Stuttgart Staatsoper joined the front rank of German opera companies. Carl Orff headed the list of contemporary composers; his *Comoedia de Christi resurrectione* (1957), *Oedipus der Tyrann* (1959) and *Ludus de nato infante mirificus* (1960) all received their premières in Stuttgart, and his other works became regular repertory staple. With *Fidelio* in 1954 Wieland Wagner started his series of productions which earned Stuttgart the reputation of 'the winter Bayreuth'; these were complemented by those of Günther Rennert between 1955 and 1975.

Performances abroad, a strong emphasis on model productions of contemporary operas (by Stravinsky, Wolfgang Fortner, Hermann Reutter, Giselher Klebe and Penderecki) and the high standard of the Stuttgart Ballet under the direction (1961–73) of John Cranko further contributed to Stuttgart's international reputation. Hans Peter Doll, who succeeded Schäfer as Generalintendant from 1972 to 1985, continued on the same lines, with Silvio Varviso as musical director (1972–80), followed by Dennis Russell Davies (1980–87). Under Doll, and with Wolfram Schwinger as opera director, contemporary composers whose works were especially cultivated included Kagel (première of *Die Erschöpfung der Welt*, 1980), Henze (*The English Cat* at the Schwetzingen Festival in 1983) and Philip Glass (*Satyagraha*, 1981; première of *Akhnaten*, 1984; *Einstein on the Beach*, 1988) – all in productions by Achim Freyer. In 1985 Wolfgang Gönnenwein was appointed Generalintendant, with García Navarro as musical director. When Navarro left in 1991 Gabriele Ferro was appointed to succeed him. While Henze and Glass continued to spearhead the contemporary repertory, close links were established with the Ludwigsburg Festival, of which Gönnenwein is the artistic director.

*

J. Sittard: *Zur Geschichte der Musik und des Theaters am Württembergischen Hofe* (Stuttgart, 1890–91)

H. Abert: 'Die dramatische Musik', *Herzog Karl Eugen von Württemberg und seine Zeit* (Esslingen, 1905)

R. Krauss: *Das Stuttgarter Hoftheater* (Stuttgart, 1908)

H. Abert: 'Zur Geschichte der Oper in Württemberg', *IMusSCR*, iii *Vienna 1909*, 186–92

J. Völckers: *Johann Rudolph Zumsteeg als Opernkomponist* (Erfurt, 1944)
A. Yorke-Long: 'Charles Eugene of Württemberg', *Music at Court: Four Eighteenth Century Studies* (London, 1954), 41–70
U. Becker, ed.: *Die Oper in Stuttgart: 75 Jahre Littman-Bau* (Stuttgart, 1987) THOMAS BAUMAN (1), HORST KOEGLER (2)

Styne, Jule [Stein, Julius Kerwin] (*b* London, 31 Dec 1905; *d* New York, 6 Oct 1989). American composer. He was taken to the USA as a child and studied at the Chicago College of Music. He worked as a concert pianist and dance-band leader before turning to composition. In the 1940s he was one of the most prolific and successful writers of songs for films. His first Broadway success was *High Button Shoes* (1947) and during the next two decades he went on to become the most prolific and one of the most successful Broadway composers. His scores include those for *Gentleman Prefer Blondes* (1949), *Peter Pan* (1954) and *Bells are Ringing* (1956); but his best-remembered, most revived works are *Gypsy* (1959) and *Funny Girl* (1964). Styne, exceptional in his field for orchestrating some of his material, wrote what are fundamentally traditional theatre songs but had a gift for catchy melodies and a penchant for surprising yet ultimately logical turns of musical phrase that justified his popularity and durability.

all musicals; names of librettists and lyricists are given in that order; dates are of first New York performance

High Button Shoes (S. Longstreet; S. Cahn), Century, 9 Oct 1947; Gentlemen Prefer Blondes (J. Fields and A. Loos; L. Robin), Ziegfeld, 8 Dec 1949, rev. as Lorelei (K. Solms and G. Parent; B. Comden and A. Green), 1974; Peter Pan (after J. M. Barrie; Comden and Green), Winter Garden, 20 Oct 1954, collab.; Bells are Ringing (Comden and Green), Shubert, 29 Nov 1956; Gypsy (A. Laurents; S. Sondheim), Broadway, 21 May 1959

Do Re Mi (G. Kanin; Comden and Green), St James, 26 Dec 1960; Subways are for Sleeping (lib. and lyrics by Comden and Green), St James, 27 Dec 1961; Funny Girl (1, Lennart; B. Merrill), Winter Garden, 26 March 1964; Fade Out – Fade In (lib. and lyrics by Comden and Green), Hellinger, 26 May 1964; Hallelujah, Baby! (Laurents; Comden and Green), Beck, 26 April 1967; Sugar (P. Stone; Merrill), Majestic, 9 April 1972

*

T. Taylor: *Jule* (New York, 1979) GERALD BORDMAN

Subirá (Puig), José (*b* Barcelona, 20 Aug 1882; *d* Madrid, 5 Jan 1980). Spanish musicologist. He studied the piano and composition at the Madrid Conservatory, but when he failed to win the 1905 Prix de Rome he dedicated himself to writing about music. His immense output is particularly remarkable since he never held any remunerative musical post, living with rigorous economy as an employee of Madrid City Council and similar organizations. In 1952 he was elected a member of the Real Academia de Bellas Artes de San Fernando in Madrid, and from 1950 until his retirement was head of the Madrid section of the Instituto Español de Musicología. Along with Anglès, Subirá was the finest 20th-century Spanish musicologist. His work is distinguished by its remarkable diversity and originality. His chief interest was theatrical music in Spain, especially Madrid. As well as original studies, such as *La tonadilla escénica* and his books on Iriarte and the Teatro Real, Subirá translated and adapted German and Italian books and wrote more general histories; he also prepared editions of many *tonadillas*.

La tonadilla escénica (Madrid, 1928–30)
Tonadillas teatrales inéditas: libretos y partituras (Madrid, 1932)
'Celos aun del aire matan': opera del siglo XVII, texto de Calderón y música de Juan Hidalgo (Barcelona, 1933) [incl edn of Act 1]
La tonadilla escénica: sus obras y sus autores (Barcelona, 1933)
Historia de la música teatral en España (Barcelona, 1945)
La ópera en los teatros de Barcelona (Barcelona, 1946)
Historia y anecdotario del Teatro Real (Madrid, 1949)
El compositor Iriarte (1750–1791) y el cultivo español del melólogo (melodrama) (Barcelona, 1949–50)
El teatro del Real palacio (1849–1851), con un bosquejo preliminar sobre la música palatina desde Felipe V hasta Isabel II (Madrid, 1950)
Cien óperas: autores, personajes, argumentos (Madrid, 1967)

*

'Homenaje a la tonadilla escénica y al Académico D. José Subirá', *Academia: anales y boletín de la Real academia de bellas artes de San Fernando*, xxx (1970), 29–70 [with list of publications to 1970]
F. J. León Tello: 'D. José Subirá cumple 90 años', *Revista de ideas estéticas*, xxxi (1973), 47–54
L. Romero Tobar: 'Conversación con Subirá', *Anales del Instituto de estudios madrileños*, ix (1973), 631–40
J. M. Llorens: 'Excmo. Sr. Don José Subirá Puig', *AnM*, xxxiii–xxxv (1978–80), 1–3

Sucher [née Hasselbeck], **Rosa** (*b* Velburg, Bavaria, 23 Feb 1849; *d* Eschweiler, nr Aachen, 16 April 1927). German soprano. In 1871 she was engaged at the Hofoper, Munich, for small roles. In 1875 she appeared as Agathe (*Der Freischütz*) at the Kroll Opera, Berlin. She sang Sieglinde in the first Leipzig *Ring* cycle (1878), and was then engaged at Hamburg. She made her London début in 1882 as Elsa at Drury Lane, and later sang Senta, Elisabeth, Eva in the first London *Meistersinger* and Isolde in the first London *Tristan*. She also sang Isolde at Hamburg (1882), Bayreuth (1886) and Munich (1893). Her other roles at Bayreuth were Kundry (1886), Eva (1888), Venus (1891) and Sieglinde (1896). Her Wagner performances were marked by great warmth and intensity, while she was also a compelling actress. In Vienna, she sang in *Der Freischütz*, *Euryanthe* and *Oberon* during 1886, the Weber centenary year. From 1888 to 1898 she was engaged at the Hofoper, Berlin, where she sang Leonore (*Fidelio*) and Brünnhilde in *Götterdämmerung* (1888). In 1892 she appeared at Covent Garden, singing Brünnhilde (*Siegfried*) and Isolde. She made her New York début as Isolde with the Damrosch Opera Company at the Metropolitan in 1895. She retired in 1903 after a final performance of Sieglinde in Berlin.

*

A. Ehrlich: *Berühmte Sängerinnen der Vergangenheit und Gegenwart* (Leipzig, 1895)
H. Klein: *Thirty Years of Musical Life in London* (London, 1903)
R. Sucher: *Aus meinem Leben* (Leipzig, 1914)
J. Kapp: *Geschichte der Staatsoper Berlin* (Berlin, 1937)
H. Fetting: *Die Geschichte der Deutschen Staatsoper* (Berlin, 1955)
H. Rosenthal: *Two Centuries of Opera at Covent Garden* (London, 1958) ELIZABETH FORBES

Suchoň, Eugen (*b* Pezinok, 26 Sept 1908). Slovak composer. He studied the piano and composition at the Bratislava Academy from 1927 and attended Vítězslav Novák's masterclasses at the Prague Conservatory (1931–3). He was professor of theory at the Bratislava Academy from 1933 before becoming professor of music theory at Bratislava University (1959–74), after which he retired as professor emeritus. He played an important role in a number of Slovak musical organizations: he was permanent president of the Slovak performing rights society, president of the Slovak Composers' Union (from 1972) and the Czechoslovak Composers' Organization (from 1973). He has also received a number of state and civic awards. The best known and most original Slovak composer, Suchoň has written a large number of choral and other vocal works, most of which provide a vehicle for his strong dramatic instinct, a quality that is evident from his earliest mature compositions, the Violin sonata in A♭ (1929–30) and the String Quartet of 1930–31. The majestic oratorio-cantata *Žalm zeme podkarpatskej* ('Psalm of the Sub-Carpathian Land', 1937–8) stands as an independent operatic study, its musical language anticipating that of Suchoň's first opera, *Krútňava* ('The Whirlpool'; Bratislava, Slovak National Opera, 10 Dec 1949).

Suchoň is neither the first Slovak opera composer, nor the most prolific. His second opera, *Svätopluk* (Suchoň, I. Stodola and J. Krcmery-Vrtel'ova; Bratislava, Slovak National Opera, 10 March 1960) achieved only a *succès d'estime*; a third, comic opera, *Hannibal on Television*, begun in the 1970s, has remained unfinished. But the production of his first opera *The Whirlpool* in 1949 is a turning point in Slovak opera and in Slovak music in general. This single work, which was immediately popular at its first production, has seen over 40 productions in Czechoslovakia and abroad and gave Slovak opera the confidence to challenge the much better established operatic traditions of its Czech sister nation.

The Whirlpool (to a libretto by Suchoň and Š. Hoza, after M. Urban) is in some ways a continuation of the Czech tradition of village opera, seen in its serious mode in Janáček's *Jenůfa*. The parallels with *Jenůfa* are striking, particularly in colourful folk scenes which set into relief a powerful personal drama resolved only when truths are faced and acknowledged. While seemingly concerned with the establishment of the paternity of Katrena's child, the opera is actually about personal development; this is the obvious link between *The Whirlpool*, *Jenůfa* and Smetana's late 'comedies'. But Suchoň's strong musical and dramatic personality ensured that the opera establishes its own world. Its musical style is akin to that of Janáček only in a few regards (for instance the extensive use of ostinatos), and for all its modal inflections was clearly abreast of developments in European music. Although the language is far removed from that of Berg, Suchoň uses principles of large-scale organization similar to those that lie behind *Wozzeck*. *The Whirlpool* is conceived as a sonata form, and its successor *Svätopluk* as a double fugue which breaks down into smaller forms by act (a palindrome in Act 1, a rondo in Act 2). This could not be further from the episodic, improvisatory structures in Janáček. Similarly rigorous is the motivic generation of *The Whirlpool* from a single melodic cell (a rising perfect 4th with a descending minor 3rd) and a single harmonic idea (two tritones a major 2nd apart).

The Whirlpool can be characterized by its concision, its dramatic thrust (the story-line is that of a thriller) and its psychological penetration. *Svätopluk*, on the other hand, is altogether grander and more monumental, a conscious reflection of the epic-history tradition of nationalist opera such as *Boris Godunov* or *Libuše*. The latter celebrates the legendary foundress of Prague; *Svätopluk*, based on a tragedy by Ivan Stodola, is on safer historical grounds, celebrating King Svätopluk, the founder of the Great Moravian Empire which briefly united all the lands of Czechoslovakia and beyond. That the opera's appeal is narrower than that of *The Whirlpool* is both explained by and compensated by its richer musical language, a more developed approach to leitmotivic characterization, and a musical palette that ranges from unaccompanied vocal writing to a sumptuous orgy of orchestral sound.

See also SVÄTOPLUK and WHIRLPOOL, THE.

*

V. Donovalová: 'Charakteristika postáv v Suchoňovej opere Krútňava' [Characteristic Forms in Suchoň's Opera *The Whirlpool*], *Hudobnovedné štúdie*, v (1961), 5–91

——: 'K hudobnej dramaturgii Suchoňovho Svätopluka' [Towards a Musical Dramaturgy of Suchoň's *Svätopluk*], *Hudobnovedné štúdie*, vi (1963), 5–55

J. Kresánek and I. Vajda: *Národný umelec Eugen Suchoň* [National Artist Suchoň] (Bratislava, 1978), 68–80

L. Polyakova: *Cheshskaya i slovatskaya opera XX. veka* [Czech and Slovak Opera of the 20th Century], ii (Moscow, 1983), 114–82

V. Yegorova: *Yevgen Suchoň: zhizn' i tvorchestvo* [Eugen Suchoň: Life and Work] (Moscow, 1987), 96–155, 178–238

I. Vajda: *Slovenská opera* (Bratislava, 1988), 37–60, 234–6

IGOR VAJDA (with JOHN TYRRELL)

Suda, Stanislav (*b* Starý Plzenec, 30 April 1865; *d* Plzeň, 1 Sept 1931). Czech composer. Blind from early childhood, he was educated in Prague and was taught to play the violin, the flute and later the piano. In 1880–81 he was an external student of the Organ School, where he studied composition under F. Z. Skuherský. After the National Theatre burnt down he gave concerts to raise money for its rebuilding and made a concert tour of Germany in 1884–5. He settled in Plzeň in 1887 as a teacher and piano tuner.

Between 1893 and 1927 Suda wrote five operas. The first, *U božích muk* ('At a Wayside Cross', 1897; first performed as *Boží muka*), is a Czech Singspiel, influenced by Smetana; the protagonist of *Il divino boemo* (1927) is the 18th-century composer Mysliveček. *Lešetínský kovář* ('The Smith of Lešetín', 1903), based on the famous poem by Svatopluk Čech, brought him the greatest success of all his operas. The poem had long been banned by Austrian censorship for its anti-German content (Karel Weis composed an opera on the same theme 20 years later). In this work Suda found his way from a purely arioso concept of operatic writing to a more expressive and dramatic declamatory style.

U božích muk [At a Wayside Cross] (1, K. Želenský), as Boží muka, Plzeň, Old, 13 March 1897

Lešetínský kovář [The Smith of Lešetín] (3, int, P. Nebeský and E. Šimek, after S. Čech), Plzeň, New Town, 4 April 1903

Bar Kochba (3, K. Jonáš, after J. Vrchlický), Plzeň, New Town, 8 April 1905

Il divino boemo, 1909–12 (3, Jonáš), Plzeň, New Town, 30 Dec 1927

Mše svatováclavská [St Wenceslas Mass], 1917 (Jonáš, after J. Neruda), unperf.

*

J. Fábera: 'Stanislav Suda', *Za hudebním vzděláním*, iii (1927–8), 85

B. Vomáčka: *Stanislav Suda* (Prague, 1933)

M. Mrázek: 'Operní dílo Stanislava Sudy' [The Operatic Works of Stanislav Suda], *Sborník vědeckých prací Pedagogické fakulty v Plzni* (Plzeň, 1968), 87–101

EVA HERRMANNOVÁ

Sud'ba cheloveka ('The Fate of a Man'). Opera in three acts by IVAN IVANOVICH DZERZHINSKY, orchestrated by others, to his own libretto after Mikhail Alexandrovich Sholokhov's story; Moscow, Bol'shoy Theatre, and simultaneously Leningrad (now St Petersburg), Kirov Theatre, 17 October 1961.

Long attracted to the works of Sholokhov, Dzerzhinsky was predictably interested when his war story *Sud'ba cheloveka* was published in 1956–7. He fashioned his own libretto, making slight changes and incorporating verses by a number of poets. When the piano score of the opera – which had spoken dialogue – was completed in 1959, opera companies in Moscow, Leningrad and Kiev accepted it for production, intending to present it in conjunction with the opening of the

22nd Congress of the Communist Party. Each theatre commissioned its own orchestration: for the Bol'shoy production the opera was orchestrated by A. S. Melik-Pashayev, for the Kirov by V. Sayko and for Kiev by B. Yarovinsky. For the production in Leningrad, recitatives composed by I. Chelishchev were substituted for the spoken dialogue.

The action takes place during World War II and is presented as a casual reminiscence by the central character, Andrey Sokolov (bass). Parting from his wife Irina (mezzo-soprano) and his children, Andrey is mobilized at the beginning of the war and captured by the Germans. In a church in occupied territory, he is interned with other Russian prisoners in inhuman conditions where he witnesses the shooting of an old prisoner. Andrey's dreams of his family are interrupted again by overhearing the treachery of another prisoner; he kills him. As dawn breaks the Commandant (baritone) separates the prisoners into work parties.

Andrey voices his complaints about the working conditions and is taken for punishment to the Commandant's office, where German officers are drinking and taunting Zinka (mezzo-soprano), a female prisoner; to help characterize the Germans, Dzerzhinsky employs a distorted quote from Kurt Weill's *Dreigroschenoper*. Andrey is sentenced to death, but Zinka agrees to sing for the soldiers in order to distract their attention. The song, about her Russian homeland, brings new resolve to Andrey, who drinks proudly to his own death. Impressed by his courage, the Commandant commutes his sentence and makes Andrey his chauffeur. Andrey manages to drive the sleeping German through the front lines to deliver him to Soviet forces. In the meantime, however, his son has gone to the front, his wife and daughters have died and his home has been destroyed. During the celebrations in liberated Berlin, the final blow falls: Andrey hears of the death of his son. He returns to his home and examines its smouldering remains. Discovering an orphan, Vanya, playing in the dirt, he adopts him as his own; finally he takes him by the hand and departs.

The Fate of a Man does not escape stereotype and excessive sentimentality either in subject or in musical treatment. Andrey is a monochrome heroic figure who dominates the musical fabric as well as the dramatic. The musical style is lyrical, with emphasis on simple, folklike tunes and their unsophisticated development.

LAUREL E. FAY

Suett, Richard (*b* Chelsea, London, 1755; *d* London, 6 July 1805). English actor and singer. As a boy he sang at St Paul's and in the London pleasure gardens. He worked for several years in the north of England in Wilkinson's company before making his Drury Lane début as Ralph in *The Maid of the Mill* (1780). Tall and thin with a lugubrious face, he became a popular comic actor; Lamb wrote that 'Shakespeare foresaw him, when he framed his fools and jesters'. Although his adult voice was not of fine quality his musical ability and comic genius led Storace and Kelly to create many roles for him. His greatest success was the barber-factotum Dicky Gossip in Storace's *My Grandmother* (1793). His published compositions include a set of sonatas, six glees and a number of songs, mainly sentimental ballads.

BDA; *DNB* (J. Kennedy); *LS*
T. Wilkinson: *The Wandering Patentee*, i–ii (London, 1795)
The Thespian Dictionary (London, 1802, 2/1805)
T. Gilliland: *The Dramatic Mirror*, ii (London, 1808)
Elia [C. Lamb]: 'On Some of the Old Actors', *Essays* (London, 1823)
W. Oxberry: 'Memoir of Richard Suett', *Dramatic Biography*, iii (1825), 217–27

OLIVE BALDWIN, THELMA WILSON

Sugar Reapers, The. Opera in two acts by ALAN BUSH to a libretto by Nancy Bush; Leipzig, Opernhaus, 11 December 1966 (as *Guyana Johnny*).

The action takes place in 1953, shortly before Guyana gained independence. Johnny (bass), a workers' leader, and the wealthy Indian, Maraj (baritone), are both in love with Sumuntra (soprano). Her father, Panasar (baritone), favours Maraj but Sumuntra loves Johnny, so Panasar gives his blessing to their union. Act 1 ends joyfully with celebrations of the engagement and the news that the popular party (in which Indians and Africans are united) have won a decisive victory in the elections. In Act 2 the government has overriden the popular verdict and is arresting the people's leaders. Maraj blackmails Johnny's brother, Joseph (tenor), into giving false evidence against him, and he is arrested on a trumped-up charge in the middle of the wedding celebrations. Sumuntra and the repentant Joseph resign themselves to wait in patience for Johnny's release.

The Sugar Reapers is the most lighthearted and colourful of Bush's four principal operas. Love interest and political message are convincingly integrated. He combines a syllabic treatment of dialogue, which moves the action forward, with more sensuous, melismatic music for the Indian wedding, while the introduction of Caribbean rhythms adds further to the opera's interest and variety.

HUGO COLE

Suggeritore (It.). PROMPTER.

Suitcase aria. Term used for arias that singers carried around with them, to insert in any or every performance in which they sang, during the period in the 18th century when such practices were accepted. *See* PASTICCIO.

Suitner, Otmar (*b* Innsbruck, 16 May 1922). Austrian conductor. He studied at the Innsbruck Conservatory, and from 1940 to 1942 at the Salzburg Mozarteum with Clemens Krauss. After making his début as an operatic Kapellmeister at the Innsbruck Landestheater in 1942, he was appointed civic music director of Remscheid (1952–7), and then music director of the Ludwigshafen Palatinate Orchestra (1957–60). He was principal conductor of the Dresden Staatsoper, 1960–64, and conducted the gala performance there of *Der Rosenkavalier* in 1961 on the 50th anniversary of its first performance. As music director of the Berlin Staatsoper, 1964–71 and 1975–90, he conducted the first performances of Dessau's operas *Puntila* (1966), *Einstein* (1973) and *Leonce und Lena* (1979). Suitner has appeared as guest conductor in most European countries, in North and South America and in Japan. He has also appeared at the Bayreuth Festival, where he worked with Wieland Wagner (1964–6) on *Der fliegende Holländer*, *Tannhäuser* and the *Ring*. His recordings include *Die Entführung*, *Figaro*, *Così*, *Il barbiere*, *Hänsel und Gretel* and *Salome*.

Suitner is the ideal theatrical Kapellmeister, finding a particular affinity with Mozart, Wagner and Strauss.

His organized and methodical approach strives for clarity and differentiation of style. Elegance and lightness characterize his interpretations of Mozart, and in Wagner he avoids pathos and broad tempos. In Strauss he lightens the colour and depth of the orchestral element to bring out the words; by agreement with the composer, he adapted *Der Rosenkavalier* for performance with a small orchestra.

*

W. Neumeister and G. Hausswald: *Dirigenten in Schrift und Bild* (Berlin, 1965)
H. Schaefer: 'Otmar Suitner', *Theater der Zeit*, xxi (1965), 33
E. Krause: 'Begegnung mit Otmar Suitner', *Sonntag* (9 Nov 1969)

DIETER HÄRTWIG

Suk, Václav [Váša, Vyacheslav Ivanovich] (*b* Kladno, 16 Nov 1861; *d* Moscow, 12 Jan 1933). Russian conductor and composer of Czech birth. After studying at the Prague Conservatory and privately with Fibich he became leader of an opera orchestra in Kiev, 1880–82, and then from 1882 to 1887 was a violinist in the orchestra of the Bol'shoy Theatre. From 1885 he became known as a conductor in various Russian cities and from 1906 to 1933 he was a conductor at the Bol'shoy (chief conductor 1928–33). Beginning in 1927 he was also principal conductor of the Stanislavsky Opera Theatre in Moscow. He was much esteemed for his thoroughness in operatic preparation, and A. A. Gozenpud called him one of the best interpreters of Rimsky-Korsakov's works. Suk's opera *Lesův pán* ('Lord of the Forests'), to a Czech libretto by J. V. Frič based on K. H. Mácha's verse classic, *Maj* ('May'), was first produced in Russian translation at Kharkiv in 1900, and in Czech at Prague in 1903. ARTHUR JACOBS

Sukis, Lilian (*b* Kaunas, Lithuania, 29 June 1939). Canadian soprano. She arrived in Canada as a wartime refugee and studied at the Royal Conservatory of Music, Toronto, with Irene Jessner among others. At the Metropolitan she sang Pamina and various minor roles (1967–8). From 1969 she sang in the lyric repertory at the Munich Opera as Violetta, Countess Almaviva, Fiordiligi and Micaëla; she was particularly admired as Strauss's Daphne. In 1972 she created the title role in *Sim Tjong* by Isang Yun. Mozart's *Ascanio in Alba* and *La finta giardiniera* are among her recordings.

DAVID CUMMINGS

Šulek, Stjepan (*b* Zagreb, 5 Aug 1914; *d* Zagreb, 16 Jan 1986). Croatian composer. He studied the violin and then taught it, first at the Zagreb Conservatory and later at the Zagreb Academy of Music, where he was also a composition professor (1947–75). He was active as a conductor. As a composer he developed an individual style, blending Baroque polyphony with Classical form and Romantic expressiveness. He wrote two three-act operas, both to his own librettos, based on Shakespeare. The musical drama *Koriolan* (Zagreb Opera, 12 Oct 1958) is a symphonic work both in structure and in its treatment of the orchestra: each act, in which leitmotifs play an important part, is in a different mood from the one preceding it. The interlude between Acts 1 and 2 comprises a triple fugue depicting the confusion of war. The nature of the text of *Koriolan* dictates the use of recitative rather than bel canto singing. *Oluja* ('The Tempest'; Zagreb Opera, 28 Nov 1969) is quite a different work due to the fantastical nature of its plot. The scenes involving the ethereal Ariel (mezzo-soprano), strongly contrasted with the other characters, are particularly effective.

*

K. Šipuš: *Stjepan Šulek* (Zagreb, 1961)
I. Supičić: 'Estetika Stjepana Šuleka: Sintetični pregled osnovnih koncepcij' [Stjepan Šulek's Aesthetics: a Synthetic View of the Basic Concepts], *MZ*, v (1969), 101–10
J. Andreis: *Music in Croatia* (Zagreb, 1974)
Stjepan Šulek 1914–1986, Spomenica [Memorial] (Zagreb, 1987) [pubn of the Yugoslav Academy of Arts and Sciences; incl. study by K. Kovačević and list of works]

KORALJKA KOS, KREŠIMIR KOVAČEVIĆ

Sullivan, Sir **Arthur** (**Seymour**) (*b* Lambeth, London, 13 May 1842; *d* London, 22 Nov 1900). English composer and conductor. His place in operatic history is assured chiefly through his series of operettas (the 'Savoy Operas') written in collaboration with the librettist W. S. GILBERT.

1. LIFE. Sullivan's mother was of Italian descent and his father an Irishman whose career in military music culminated in a professorship at the Royal Military School of Music, Kneller Hall. Showing early promise, Arthur Sullivan entered the Chapel Royal as a chorister in 1854 and two years later became the first holder of the Mendelssohn Scholarship at the RAM, studying composition with William Sterndale Bennett and John Goss. An extension of the scholarship enabled him to enter the Leipzig Conservatory (1858–61), where his composition teachers included Moritz Hauptmann, Julius Reitz and Carl Reinecke. Among Sullivan's works performed at Leipzig was incidental music to *The Tempest* (1861), which brought him immediate recognition when heard at the Crystal Palace in 1862. A succession of choral settings and orchestral works produced during the 1860s and early 70s established his position among the foremost British composers, while his wider popularity was assured by songs and other music for the drawing-room.

Of an opera begun about 1862, *The Sapphire Necklace* (libretto by the critic Henry Chorley), only excerpts were ever performed and little of the music is extant, though apparently the score was completed. *Cox and Box* (1866), Sullivan's earliest surviving operatic work, was conceived as entertainment for a sociable musical group. F. C. Burnand of *Punch* adapted a popular farce by J. Maddison Morton, and, with the composer improvising a piano accompaniment, the operetta received its private première. After seeing *Cox and Box* at a later charity performance, Thomas German Reed commissioned a new work from Sullivan and Burnand for St George's Hall. *The Contrabandista* (1867) was reasonably successful, but Reed, unable to sustain the expenditure, returned to small-scale entertainments at the Royal Gallery of Illustration. There, in 1869, *Cox and Box* received its first professional production. It was during this run that the composer Frederic Clay introduced Sullivan to the comic writer and dramatist William Schwenck Gilbert. Two years later they were to collaborate on *Thespis* for John Hollingshead's Gaiety Theatre. Although moderately successful, the piece was never revived and most of the music is lost.

During the 1870s Sullivan's conducting commitments increased. He also became principal of the newly established National Training School (forerunner of the RCM) from 1876 to 1881. With less time for composition, his serious output diminished as his success in operetta grew. It was the suggestion by Richard D'Oyly

Carte that Sullivan and Gilbert might write a short work for the Royalty Theatre which led to the composition of *Trial by Jury* (1875). Capitalizing on its popularity, Sullivan soon composed another one-act piece, *The Zoo* (1875), to a libretto by B. C. Stephenson. That this was less successful – the music remained unpublished until 1969 – may have persuaded Sullivan to throw in his lot with Gilbert and to support Carte in establishing a company to perform their joint work, along with other British pieces, at the Opera Comique Theatre. The first fruit of the venture was *The Sorcerer* (1877), but it was the production of *HMS Pinafore* in the following year that firmly established the collaborators at the forefront of British operetta.

The popularity of *HMS Pinafore* spread to the USA, where unauthorized productions proliferated. To combat this financial and artistic affront, Carte took the authoritative production to New York, where a new work, *The Pirates of Penzance* (1879), was also unveiled. Such was the success of the Gilbert and Sullivan partnership – the librettist's name took priority at an early stage – that Carte built the Savoy Theatre to house their works. It was during the run of *Patience* (1881) that the company moved to the new theatre, whose name was to provide the generic title for the entire Gilbert and Sullivan canon. The first Savoy première was that of *Iolanthe* (1882), one of their finest collaborations. This was followed, in 1884, by *Princess Ida*, a reworking of a blank verse play by Gilbert (who often drew on his earlier material). It was rather less successful. Withdrawal caught the partners without a successor, so *The Sorcerer* was revised and presented in a double bill with *Trial by Jury*. Thus began a distinguished series of revivals, produced under the direction of author and composer, which kept their works before the Savoy audiences.

Although Sullivan approached the composition of operetta with integrity, his attitude to it remained ambivalent, for it had undoubtedly distracted him from more serious composition. What he regarded as his subservient role in the collaborations with Gilbert also rankled. Frustrated, he decided to write no more for the Savoy. Gilbert's idea (which he had previously rejected) for a new work, in which characters were transformed on eating a magic lozenge, only hardened this resolve. What Sullivan called the 'lozenge plot' epitomized, for him, Gilbert's commitment to the fantastic, whereas he preferred 'to set a play of human interest and probability' in which the music could have greater prominence. Eventually differences were settled, and out of the tumult arose *The Mikado* (1885). Generally considered their greatest work, it has sustained an enormous popularity and is the only Sullivan operetta to have gained a foothold outside the English-speaking world.

Sullivan's conductorship of the Leeds Triennial Festival (1880–98) led to the composition in 1886 of one of his most substantial serious works, the cantata *The Golden Legend*. The broader technical scope, both harmonic and orchestral, of this work is also evident in *Ruddigore* (1887) and *The Yeomen of the Guard* (1888). *Ruddigore* was not entirely successful at its première, but after revision it settled down to achieve a respectable run. With *The Yeomen of the Guard* Gilbert experimented in writing a Savoy libretto which was essentially romantic rather than comic or fantastic. Sullivan responded with a more serious and operatic score which stands apart from his other Gilbert collaborations. The public response did not, however, encourage Gilbert to continue in this vein. Unwilling to return to the earlier style, Sullivan again refused to collaborate. He might have continued to do so had he not been commissioned to write a grand opera to open Carte's Royal English Opera House. This prospect resolved some of Sullivan's artistic conflicts, and in a particularly happy spirit of mutual understanding he and Gilbert produced *The Gondoliers*, their final masterpiece, in 1889. The goodwill was soon destroyed, however, by the so-called 'carpet quarrel' over expenses at the Savoy, which eventually led to conflict in open court. Sullivan did work with Gilbert again, but neither *Utopia Limited* (1893) nor *The Grand Duke* (1896) achieved any great success.

When Queen Victoria knighted Sullivan in 1883 she urged him to write a grand opera. Carte's commission provided the opportunity and the outcome was *Ivanhoe* (1891), an adaptation by Julian Sturgis of Scott's novel. (Gilbert declined to provide a libretto.) Lavishly staged, the work achieved an impressive run of 161 performances, but thereafter failed to retain a place in the repertory. Although containing much fine music, the opera as a whole lacks dramatic impetus and in time came to represent a considerable disappointment to its composer.

After the 'carpet quarrel' Sullivan turned to a new collaborator. Sydney Grundy's libretto for *Haddon Hall* (1892), though undistinguished, satisfied Sullivan's desire for a romantic story of human interest, and the work was moderately well received. For *The Chieftain* (1894) Sullivan was persuaded by Burnand to expand their earlier collaboration, *The Contrabandista*, but their efforts produced no particular success. The nadir of Sullivan's fortunes at the Savoy box office was reached, however, in 1898 with the production of *The Beauty Stone*. Described as a 'romantic musical drama', the setting of a libretto by Pinero and Comyns Carr was a further attempt by Sullivan to bring a more serious class of work to the Savoy. At a time when public taste was being won over to the frivolities of musical comedy he had miscalculated: it ran for less than two months.

The 1890s had been a decade of disappointment. Sullivan's already erratic health declined markedly and this was paralleled by a falling off in the quality of musical inspiration. Illness and probably a conviction that greatness as a composer had eluded him – he wrote no serious work of consequence after *Ivanhoe* – seemed to devitalize his creative faculties. The turn of the century, however, brought renewed fortunes. In *The Rose of Persia* (1899) Sullivan regained some of his old form (perhaps because Basil Hood's libretto aped Gilbert's style) and the work's enthusiastic reception encouraged further collaboration with its author. On Sullivan's death in November 1900, however, *The Emerald Isle* was only partly set. It was completed by Edward German.

2. WORKS. Sullivan clearly had Offenbach in mind when he wrote *Cox and Box*, particularly in the stylistic burlesque of grander musical forms. Such humour is a mainstay of the earlier Sullivan operettas, but reliance on it diminishes after *The Pirates of Penzance*. As operetta became the main focus of his creative energies, Sullivan understandably sought expression through his own musical style – one which combined originality and eclecticism, drawing on both English and continental traditions and incorporating elements of Victorian

church music, drawing-room ballad and opera. His synthesis of Victorian musical predilections was undoubtedly a factor in the enormous contemporary popularity his music enjoyed in Britain.

Sullivan's operettas are notable for a surefooted technical mastery which places them in a class apart. The ingenuity of tonal sequences in 'Three little maids' (*The Mikado*) and 'When the night wind howls' (*Ruddigore*), for example, testifies to his characteristically unassuming resourcefulness. Sullivan's facility is particularly evident in his orchestration. He scored at great speed, yet the result is rarely perfunctory. Infinitely varied, and particularly sensitive in its use of woodwind, it impresses by subtlety rather than brilliance.

Rhythm was generally the starting-point for Sullivan's vocal settings. His comic numbers may keep the verbal wit to the fore by simple syllabic treatment but elsewhere he experimented with alternative rhythms, achieving naturalness yet avoiding the obvious. Undoubtedly Gilbert's metrical ingenuity was often a spur to invention, although instances of an undistinguished lyric being raised to distinction by the composer's imaginative setting (especially in non-Gilbert works) are numerous. 'The sun whose rays' (*The Mikado*) and 'Now, Marco dear' (*The Gondoliers*), for example, reveal a subtle handling of the English language which is an important part of Sullivan's contribution to the renaissance of British music.

Sullivan's music avoids emotional extremes. There are few moments of real pathos, and melancholy is usually tinged with wistfulness. Gaiety, wit and good humour abound, but abandoned frivolity hardly ever occurs. Although Sullivan's principal characters rarely reveal musical individuality, he shows a remarkable gift for capturing a sense of locale and for group characterization. The tang of the brine pervades the music of *HMS Pinafore* as surely as the spirit of the grim old Tower of London hangs over every bar of *The Yeomen of the Guard*; whether it is for the yokels of *The Sorcerer*, the aesthetic maidens of *Patience* or the ghosts of *Ruddigore*, the music reflects their identities as surely as the costumes they wear. Indeed, by combining contrasting melodies, first presented separately by different character groups, Sullivan creates one of his most characteristic effects, the double chorus.

Although Sullivan's serious works and non-Gilbert operettas are beginning to emerge from the neglect which befell them following the composer's death, it is his collaborations with Gilbert which sustain his wider reputation. Their partnership is unique in theatrical history. Sullivan, a respected composer of symphonic and choral music, channelled his gifts into a field generally the province of more limited musicians. Gilbert, by an innovatory approach to stage direction as well as by the quality and originality of the texts themselves, brought a new sophistication to light musical theatre. Together they raised the artistic and social status of British operetta far above any it had hitherto enjoyed.

The very originality and success of the Savoy operettas have, ironically, had a somewhat restrictive influence on the growth of the continuing tradition which they might have been expected to encourage. For many, British operetta and Gilbert and Sullivan are synonymous and their ideal realizations those of the D'Oyly Carte Opera Company. Until the expiry of copyright in 1961, this company held a monopoly on professional performances and imprinted its generally traditional approach on countless amateur and school productions. Such presentations continue to draw an enthusiastic following and, freed from copyright restrictions, the works have been taken up with considerable success by leading professional companies. Their popularity outside English-speaking countries, however, remains limited – the difficulty of translating Gilbert's librettos and the peculiarly British elements in his humour do not wholly explain such neglect – yet Sullivan's operettas reveal an inventiveness, artistic sensibility, technical resource and, above all, variety which place him among the greatest composers for the genre, and the Savoy operettas at the pinnacle of its achievements.

See also COX AND BOX; GONDOLIERS, THE; HMS PINAFORE; IOLANTHE; MIKADO, THE; PATIENCE; PIRATES OF PENZANCE, THE; PRINCESS IDA; RUDDIGORE; SORCERER, THE; TRIAL BY JURY; and YEOMEN OF THE GUARD, THE.

Edition: *The Gilbert and Sullivan Operas: a Critical Edition*, ed. P. Young and G. Hendrie (New York, in preparation)

first performed and (where printed) published in London unless otherwise stated

LST – *Savoy Theatre*

title	*genre, acts*	*libretto*	*first performance*	*sources; remarks*
The Sapphire Necklace [The False Heiress]	opera, 4	H. F. Chorley	Crystal Palace, 13 April 1867 (excerpts)	madrigal *US-NYpm**, autograph otherwise lost; 1 song, ov. arr. military band, madrigal (1885–98); most music lost; composed beginning *c*1862
Cox and Box; or, The Long-Lost Brothers	operetta, 1	F. C. Burnand, after J. M. Morton: *Box and Cox*	private perf. (pf acc.), ? 26 May 1866; Adelphi, 13 May 1867 (orch version)	vs (1869), full score ov. (1966), *NYpm**
The Contrabandista; or, The Law of the Ladrones	operetta, 2	Burnand	St George's Hall, 18 Dec 1867	(1868), *GB-MYrees**; rev. 1894 as The Chieftain
Thespis; or, The Gods Grown Old	operetta, 2	W. S. Gilbert	Gaiety, 26 Dec 1871	1 song (1872), autograph lost; ? some ballet music survives; most music lost; 1 chorus reused in The Pirates of Penzance
Trial by Jury	operetta, 1	Gilbert	Royalty, 25 March 1875	vs (1875), full score (New York, n.d.), *US-NYpm**

title	genre, acts	libretto	first performance	sources; remarks
The Zoo	operetta, 1	B. Rowe [pseud. of B. C. Stephenson]	St James's, 5 June 1875	vs (1969), *GB-MYrees**
The Sorcerer	operetta, 2	Gilbert	Opera Comique, 17 Nov 1877	vs (1877), rev. LST, 11 Oct 1884, vs (1884), *US-NYwolfson**
HMS Pinafore; or, The Lass that Loved a Sailor	operetta, 2	Gilbert	Opera Comique, 25 May 1878	vs (1878); Ger. adaptation, as Amor an Bord (Brunswick, 1882); (New York, n.d.), *NYpm**
The Pirates of Penzance; or, The Slave of Duty	operetta, 2	Gilbert	Paignton, Royal Bijou, 30 Dec 1879; New York, Fifth Avenue, 31 Dec 1879	vs (1880), full score (New York, n.d.); *NYpm**
Patience; or, Bunthorne's Bride	operetta, 2	Gilbert	Opera Comique, 23 April 1881	vs (1881), full score (New York, n.d.), *GB-Lbl**
Iolanthe; or, The Peer and the Peri	operetta, 2	Gilbert	LST, 25 Nov 1882	vs (1883), full score (New York, n.d.), London, D'Oyly Carte Opera Trust*
Princess Ida; or, Castle Adamant	operetta, 3	Gilbert, after Tennyson: *The Princess*	LST, 5 Jan 1884	vs (1884), *Ob**
The Mikado; or, The Town of Titipu	operetta, 2	Gilbert	LST, 14 March 1885	vs (1885), full score (Leipzig, n.d.), *Lam**
Ruddigore; or, The Witch's Curse	operetta, 2	Gilbert	LST, 22 Jan 1887	vs (1887), full score (New York, 1987), *Lst**
The Yeomen of the Guard; or, The Merryman and his Maid	operetta, 2	Gilbert	LST, 3 Oct 1888	vs (1888), full score (New York, n.d.), ov. (1979), *Lcm**
The Gondoliers; or, The King of Barataria	operetta, 2	Gilbert	LST, 7 Dec 1889	vs (1890), full score (New York, n.d.) (1984), *Lbl**
Ivanhoe	opera, 3	J. Sturgis, after W. Scott	Royal English Opera House, 31 Jan 1891	(1891), *US-NYwolfson**; rev., Liverpool, Court, 14 Feb 1895
Haddon Hall	operetta, 2	S. Grundy	LST, 24 Sep 1892	vs (1892), *GB-MYrees**
Utopia Limited; or, The Flowers of Progress	operetta, 2	Gilbert	LST, 7 Oct 1893	vs (1893), autograph lost
The Chieftain	operetta, 2	Burnand	LST, 12 Dec 1894	vs (1895), *MYrees**; rev. of The Contrabandista, 1867
The Grand Duke; or, The Statutory Duel	operetta, 2	Gilbert	LST, 7 March 1896	vs (1896), *US-NYwolfson**
The Beauty Stone	romantic musical drama, 2	A. W. Pinero, J. Comyns Carr	LST, 28 May 1898	vs (1898), autograph privately owned
The Rose of Persia; or, The Story-Teller and the Slave	operetta, 2	B. Hood	LST, 29 Nov 1899	vs (1900), ? full score (Leipzig, ?1901), autograph privately owned
The Emerald Isle; or, The Caves of Carrig-Cleena	operetta, 2	Hood	LST, 27 April 1901	vs (1901), completed by E. German, *GB-MYrees**

BIOGRAPHY

Grove6 (A. Lamb)

A. H. Lawrence: *Sir Arthur Sullivan: Life Story, Letters and Reminiscences* (London, 1899)

W. J. Wells: *Souvenir of Sir Arthur Sullivan, Mus. Doc., M.V.O.* (London, 1901)

H. S. Wyndham: *Arthur Sullivan* (London, 1903) [incl. E. Ford: 'Sullivan as a composer', 53–61]

B. W. Findon: *Sir Arthur Sullivan: his Life and Music* (London, 1904, 2/1908 as *Sir Arthur Sullivan and his Operas*)

H. S. Wyndham: *Arthur Seymour Sullivan* (London, 1926)

H. Sullivan and N. Flower: *Sir Arthur Sullivan: his Life, Letters and Diaries* (London, 1927, 2/1950)

H. Pearson: *Gilbert and Sullivan* (London, 1935)

L. Baily: *The Gilbert and Sullivan Book* (London, 1952, 3/1966)

——: *Gilbert & Sullivan and their World* (London, 1973)

R. Allen and G. R. D'Luhy: *Sir Arthur Sullivan: Composer and Personage* (New York, 1975)

C. Brahms: *Gilbert and Sullivan: Lost Chords and Discords* (London, 1975)

A. Jacobs: *Arthur Sullivan: a Victorian Musician* (Oxford, 1984, 3/1992)

J. Wolfson: *Sullivan and the Scott Russells* (Chichester, 1984)

PERSONAL REMINISCENCES AND PERIOD STUDIES

G. Grossmith: *A Society Clown: Reminiscences* (Bristol, 1888)

G. Thorne: *Jots* (Bristol, 1897)

R. Barrington: *Rutland Barrington – by Himself* (London, 1908)

——: *More Rutland Barrington – by Himself* (London, 1911)

H. A. Lytton: *The Secrets of a Savoyard* (London, 1922)

J. Bond: *The Life and Reminiscences of Jessie Bond the Old Savoyard* (London, 1930)

ANALYTICAL AND HISTORICAL

GänzlBMT

P. H. Fitzgerald: *The Savoy Operas and the Savoyards* (London, 1894, 2/1899)

A. C. Mackenzie: 'The Life-work of Arthur Sullivan', *SIMG*, iii (1901–2), 539–64

C. Maclean: 'Sullivan as National Style-builder', *PMA*, xxviii (1901–2), 89–104

E. Ford: *A Short History of Music in England* (London, 1912)

F. Cellier and C. Bridgeman: *Gilbert, Sullivan and D'Oyly Carte* (London, 1914, 2/1927)

H. M. Walbrook: *Gilbert and Sullivan Opera* (London, 1922)

S. J. A. Fitz-Gerald: *The Story of the Savoy Opera* (London, 1924)

A. H. Godwin: *Gilbert and Sullivan* (London, 1926)

S. Mackinlay: *Origin and Development of Light Opera* (London, 1927)

T. F. Dunhill: *Sullivan's Comic Operas: a Critical Appreciation* (London, 1928)

I. Goldberg: *The Story of Gilbert and Sullivan* (London, 1929)

I. Parrott: 'Arthur Sullivan (1842–1900)', *ML*, xxiii (1942), 202–10
W. A. Darlington: *The World of Gilbert and Sullivan* (New York, 1950)
A. Jacobs: *Gilbert and Sullivan* (London, 1951)
E. W. White: *The Rise of English Opera* (London, 1951)
A. Williamson: *Gilbert and Sullivan Opera: a New Assessment* (New York, 1953, 2/1982)
W. Cox-Ife: *Training the Gilbert and Sullivan Chorus* (London, 1955)
——: *How to Sing both Gilbert and Sullivan* (London, 1959)
G. Hughes: *The Music of Arthur Sullivan* (London, 1960)
——: *Composers of Operetta* (London, 1962)
R. Mander and J. Mitchenson: *A Picture History of Gilbert and Sullivan* (London, 1962)
F. L. Moore: *The Handbook of Gilbert and Sullivan* (London, 1962)
C. Rollins and R. J. Witts: *The D'Oyly Carte Opera Company in Gilbert and Sullivan* (London, 1962)
T. Rees: *Thespis: a Gilbert and Sullivan Enigma* (London, 1964)
M. Cooper: 'The Fickle Philistine', *ON*, xxxii/25 (1967–8), 8–12
A. Lamb: 'G & S and the Gaiety', *MT*, cxii (1971), 1162–4
P. M. Young: *Sir Arthur Sullivan* (London, 1971)
L. Ayre: *The Gilbert & Sullivan Companion* (London, 1972)
A. Lamb: 'Ivanhoe and the Royal English Opera', *MT*, cxiv (1973), 475–8
S. Meares: *Performing Sullivan's Ivanhoe* (Chesham Bois, 1975) [private circulation]
C. Hibbert: *Gilbert and Sullivan and their Victorian World* (London, 1976)
J. Wolfson: *Final Curtain: the Last Gilbert and Sullivan Operas* (London, 1976)
A. Hyman: *Sullivan and his Satellites* (London, 1978)
S. Ledbetter: 'Managed by a Job?', *MT*, cxx (1979), 642–4
G. Emmerson: *Arthur Darling* (London, Ont., 1980)
N. Burton: 'Opera: 1865–1914', *Music in Britain: the Romantic Age, 1800–1914*, ed. N. Temperley (London, 1981), 348–65
I. Bradley: *The Annotated Gilbert and Sullivan* (Harmondsworth, 1982–4)
G. Smith: *The Savoy Operas* (London, 1983)
E. W. White: *A History of English Opera* (London, 1983)
J. Wolfson: *Sullivan and the Scott Russells* (Chichester, 1984)
D. R. Hulme: 'Princess Ida: some Notes on the Autograph Full Score', *Princess Ida*, ed. D. Eden (Saffron Walden, 1984), 45–54
——: 'Trial by Jury: towards a First Night Text', *Trial by Jury and The Sorcerer*, ed. D. Eden (Saffron Walden, 1984), 15–17
A. Jefferson: *The Complete Gilbert and Sullivan Opera Guide* (Exeter, 1984)
R. Traubner: *Operetta: a Theatrical History* (London, 1984)
R. Wilson and F. Lloyd: *Gilbert and Sullivan: the D'Oyly Carte Years* (London, 1984)
D. Eden: *Gilbert and Sullivan: the Creative Conflict* (London, 1986)
D. R. Hulme: *The Operettas of Sir Arthur Sullivan: a Study of Available Autograph Full Scores* (diss., U. of Wales, Aberystwyth, 1986)
A. Jacobs: 'The Mask of "The Mikado"', *Opera*, xxxvii (1986), 882–6
D. Lisle: 'Arthur Sullivan', *British Opera in Retrospect* (n.p., 1986) [pubn of the British Music Society], 57–62
C. Hayter: *Gilbert and Sullivan* (London, 1987)
D. R. Hulme: 'Ruddigore: an Investigation of Musical Sources', *Ruddygore*, ed. D. Eden (Saffron Walden, 1987), 48–56
N. Burton: '"The Yeomen of the Guard": Apogee of a Style', *MT*, cxxix (1988), 656–9
M. Yates: 'Musical Unity in the "Yeomen" Score', *The Yeomen of the Guard*, ed. D. Eden (Saffron Walden, 1988), 22–3

DAVID RUSSELL HULME

Sullivan, Daniel (*d* Dublin, 13 Oct 1764). Irish countertenor. He appeared at Chester with the Lampes in 1741 and made his London début at Drury Lane in 1743 as Moore in *The Dragon of Wantley*, singing in several other stage pieces by Lampe at Drury Lane and the New Haymarket (1743–5). Handel engaged him for his 1744 oratorio season, when he created the part of Athamas in *Semele*. According to Mrs Delany he was '*a block* with a very fine voice', which put Handel 'mightily out of humour'. He was a low alto, with a compass of *g* or *a* to *c″*. He returned to Dublin (1745–6), rejoined the Drury Lane company (1746–8) and was engaged for Dublin (Smock Alley) in 1748. Most of his later career was spent there and at Bath. In Dublin he appeared in stage works by Purcell, Boyce, Arne and Carey, and as Macheath in *The Beggar's Opera*. WINTON DEAN

Sullivan, Timothy (*b* Ottawa, 16 Dec 1954). Canadian composer. He studied music at Harper College, Palatine, Illinois (1972–4), and composition at the Toronto Conservatory (1974–8). In 1977 he entered Toronto University, where he studied with John Beckwith and Walter Buczynski. He began teaching theory and composition at the Conservatory in 1979, became head of the composition department (1985–9), and also taught composition at the University of Victoria (1989–90). In 1987–8 he was one of the first composers-in-residence for the Canadian Opera Company.

His first opera, *Tomorrow and Tomorrow* (1986), for soprano solo and instrumental ensemble, combines a variety of vocal styles, including declamation, parlando and set arias. This very contemporary work has classical characteristics; it consists of one scene and one character, and the music was created to serve the text. The opera's theme is broken love and contemporary loneliness perceived through the suicide of a woman, the symbolic world of her unconscious and flashbacks of her life. It was first performed in New York on 28 March 1987. Sullivan describes his second opera, *Dream Play* (1988), as '… designed in form and style to be imitative of a dream. A journey of confusion, pain and exalted beauty merge in this poetic canvas of life'.

Tomorrow and Tomorrow (monodrama, 1 scene, Sullivan), New York, DeJur Playhouse, 28 March 1987
Dream Play (1, Sullivan, after A. Strindberg), Toronto, Texaco Opera, 19 May 1988
The Imaginary Couple, 1990 (Sullivan, after Molière: *Sganarelle, ou Le cocu imaginaire*)
Florence, 1990 (A. McPherson)

*

'The Loneliness of Love', *Macleans* (13 April 1987), 51
'Towards Tomorrow's Opera', *Music Magazine*, xi/5 (1988), 28–9

RUTH PINCOE

Sully, Mariette (*b* ?Brussels, Dec 1874; *d* Paris, ? 1940). Belgian soprano. She made her début as the Page in Lecocq's *La petite mariée* at the Casino, Nice, in 1892. After appearing in Monte Carlo and Bucharest (as Irma in Audran's *Le grand mogol*), she joined the company at the Bouffes-Parisiens, where she appeared in Varnay's *Les forains*. Afterwards, at the Gaîté, she created Alesia in Audran's *La poupée*, Caterina in Planquette's *Panurge* and Thérèsette in his *Mam'zelle Quat'sous*; she later created the title role in Messager's *Véronique* (1898, with Jean Périer) and many other roles. In 1925 a gala benefit was given in her honour at the Théâtre Sarah Bernhardt. Called 'Mademoiselle Vif-Argent', her style was described as 'ornée d'un charme tout particulier, qui fit, jadis, si delicieuse la poupée qu'elle créa'. PATRICK O'CONNOR

Summer and Smoke. Opera in two acts, op. 27, by LEE HOIBY to a libretto by Lanford Wilson after Tennessee Williams's play of the same title; St Paul, Minnesota, O'Shaughnessy Auditorium, 19 June 1971.

Summer and Smoke is the first opera to be based on a Williams play. It tells the story of Alma Winemiller (soprano), the inhibited daughter of a Southern minister and an unbalanced mother. Alma, in the words of Williams, 'suffocated in smoke from something on fire inside her', for she could not release her love for the young doctor John Buchanan (baritone) until it was too late. The dramatic changes that take place in the attitudes of the potential lovers are tragically reflected in Alma's line at the close of the opera: 'I came here to say you need not be a gentleman, but you're telling me I've got to remain a lady'. In anguish and desperation, she gives herself casually to a man she meets in the town park where, as a young girl, she first met John.

The work was commissioned by the St Paul Opera Association. Mary Beth Peil and John Reardon took the chief roles at its first performance, which was conducted by Igor Buketoff and directed by Frank Corsaro. On 12 March 1972 it was produced by the New York City Opera, conducted by Julius Rudel. It continues to be performed with substantial success, and its 1980 production by the Chicago Opera Theater was broadcast in June 1982 by PBS-TV (WTTW), Chicago, and seen nationally. For its production during the Lee Hoiby Festival at California State University, Long Beach in 1989 (31 March–9 April), Hoiby added a new scene in Act 1 drawn from his *Three Women: Scenes for Soprano, Saxophone and Piano* (1988).

Summer and Smoke is a skilful interweaving of offstage music and spoken passages. It is a lyrical, poetic and compelling work that critics praised as America's most successful opera to date. Paul Hume (writing in the *Washington Post*) considered it an 'opera of immense emotional power flooded with music of great beauty'. Its lush orchestral score and insistent theme associated with the main character have been compared with Samuel Barber's *Vanessa. Summer and Smoke* shows the composer's individuality: his creative sensitivity to the inner conflict of the characters is notable in the final passages of the Anatomy Lesson scene with the poignant line, 'Eternity and Alma have such cool hands'. This scene has been recorded by New World Records (NW 305). The vocal score was published in New York (1972). ELISE K. KIRK

Summers, Jonathan (*b* Melbourne, 2 Oct 1946). Australian baritone. He studied in Melbourne and with Otakar Kraus in London, making his début in 1975 as Rigoletto with Kent Opera. In 1976 he sang Falstaff for Glyndebourne Touring Opera and in 1977 made his Covent Garden début as Kilian (*Der Freischütz*); he has since sung Sonora (*La fanciulla del West*), the Herald (*Lohengrin*), Balstrode, Sharpless, Malatesta, Figaro (Rossini and Mozart), Albert (*Werther*), Marcello, Demetrius, Papageno, Paolo (*Simon Boccanegra*), Faninal, Animal Tamer (*Lulu*) and Ford there. For the ENO he has sung Tonio, Posa, Rigoletto, Yevgeny Onegin, Boccanegra, Renato (*Ballo*), Macbeth (1990) and Rodrigo (1992). He has sung with Opera North and Scottish Opera, in Paris, Geneva, Brussels, Sydney, San Diego, Florence and at the Metropolitan, where he made his début in 1988 as Marcello. His repertory includes Gluck's Orestes and Hercules, Luna, Germont, Nabucco, Gérard, the four villains (*Les contes d'Hoffmann*) and the traveller (*Death in Venice*). A powerful actor, he has an expressive, keenly focussed voice well suited to Verdi. ELIZABETH FORBES

Sundine, Stephanie (*b* Illinois, 1954). American soprano. At the New York City Opera (1981–4), her roles included Boito's Margherita/Helen of Troy, Ariadne and Santuzza. She sang the title role in Prokofiev's *Maddalena* at St Louis (1982); The Nice Caroline in Sallinen's *The King Goes Forth to France* (1986) and the title role in Matthus's *Judith* (1990) at Santa Fe, all American premières. Her repertory includes Tosca, La Gioconda, Wally, Elsa, Isolde, Emilia Marty, Chrysothemis and Salome, which she has sung at Toronto, Cologne, Brisbane, with the WNO and for her Covent Garden (1988) début. Engaged to sing Fusako in the première of Henze's *Das verratene Meer* at the Deutsche Oper, Berlin, in 1990, she was unwell on the first night and had to mime the role (which was sung by Beverly Morgan) but sang in later performances. A powerful actress of handsome appearance, she has a full, bright-toned and vibrant voice. ELIZABETH FORBES

Suor Angelica ('Sister Angelica'). Opera in one act by GIACOMO PUCCINI to a libretto by GIOVACCHINO FORZANO; New York, Metropolitan Opera, 14 December 1918 (as no.2 of *Il trittico*).

Sister Angelica	soprano
The Princess *her aunt*	contralto
The Abbess	mezzo-soprano
The Monitress	mezzo-soprano
The Mistress of the novices	mezzo-soprano
Sister Genovieffa	soprano
Sister Osmina	soprano
Sister Dolcina	soprano
The nursing sister	mezzo-soprano
The alms sisters	sopranos
The novices	sopranos
The lay sisters	soprano/mezzo soprano

Offstage chorus of women, children and men

Setting A convent, towards the end of the 17th century

Forzano's drama about a nun who takes her own life on hearing of the death of her child had originally been planned as a spoken play. In the winter of 1916–17 he offered it to Puccini for his projected 'triptych' (*Il trittico*). The composer accepted without hesitation, despite its close resemblance to Giordano's *Mese Mariano* of 1910. Composition proceeded swiftly through the spring and summer of 1917. For local colour Puccini turned to his sister Igenia, Mother Superior at the covent at Vicepelago, and was permitted to visit her establishment and play the score to the assembled nuns, all of whom were moved to tears. Another valuable source of information was Puccini's lifelong friend, the priest Father Pietro Panichelli, who supplied the text for what the composer flippantly referred to as the 'Marcia reale della Madonna' of the final scene.

The work was completed on 25 July, Puccini's name-day, and was first given along with its two companion-pieces, *Il tabarro* and *Gianni Schicchi*, the following year in America. Geraldine Farrar was Sister Angelica, Flora Perini the Princess; the conductor was Roberto Moranzoni. For the Italian première (11 January 1919), at the Teatro Costanzi, Rome under Gino Marinuzzi with Gilda dalla Rizza as Angelica and Matilde Blanco Sadun as her antagonist, Puccini was persuaded to extend Angelica's 'Senza mamma, bimbo, tu sei morto' ('Without your mother, child, you died') over a reprise of the long orchestra-based melody that occurs when the Princess's carriage is first seen arriving at the convent. In subsequent performances Gilda dalla Rizza regularly cut a short aria sung by Angelica as she gathers the flowers from which she distils the poison for her suicide, 'Amici fiori, voi mi compensate' – a remarkably modern piece with polyonal implications, which some scholars have compared to Malipiero. Puccini eventually replaced it with a 16-bar extension of the preceding intermezzo, over which the soprano sings an altered text containing an ironical reference to the 'wasp' episode that he had originally marked as an optional cut. The aria can still be heard, though dimly, on a recording made by Lotte Lehmann in 1920. The only printed score to carry it is the first edition (1918) of the entire *Trittico*.

The garden of the cloister It is a fine spring evening and the air is full of birdsong. From the chapel come the strains of an *Ave Maria*, in which Angelica's voice can be distinguished. As the nuns emerge into the garden the Monitress assigns condign punishment to two late-comers, to one Sister Lucilla for causing laughter during the service and to Sister Osmina for concealing red roses within her habit. The nuns proceed to disport themselves. Sister Genovieffa notices that the fountain is about to be turned to gold by the rays of the setting sun – a sign of divine grace, says the Monitress, that occurs only on three evenings during May. An air of melancholy descends as they remember the Sister who died a year ago. Surely, Genovieffa exclaims, her spirit would desire a libation from the gilded fountain. In a brief cantabile ('I desideri sono i fiori dei vivi') Angelica declares that desires flower only for the living; those of the dead are fulfilled before they can utter them. The Monitress maintains that to nuns all desires are forbidden; but Sister Genovieffa disagrees. Brought up as a shepherdess she yearns to fondle a pet lamb ('Soave Signor mio'). Sister Dolcina too has a wish – the sisters reply, laughing, that her wish is for some tasty morsel. And Sister Angelica? She denies wishing for anything. The sisters murmur, shocked, that that is untrue. They know that she is consumed by longing for news of the noble family that has mysteriously forced her to take the veil.

The Nursing Sister hurries in much distressed. One of the sisters has been stung by a wasp and is in agony. Angelica swiftly prepares a floral remedy and the Nursing Sister retires, praising Angelica's skill. Two Alms Sisters enter with donkey and cart and distribute provisions. The harmonic movement comes to a virtual standstill for 20 bars, until they mention having seen a magnificent coach arrive at the convent; whereupon the orchestra launches the principal melody of the opera, a long, sustained cantilena over which the voices chatter at first casually, then with growing excitement, Angelica showing particular agitation. They go into the cloister as the Abbess comes to summon Angelica to meet an important visitor. The Princess enters, a formidable personage dressed in black and leaning on an ebony stick. Her frigid demeanour is conveyed in the music by a bleak unison figure that winds upward and comes to rest on an unrelated chord. She has come to ask Angelica to sign away her share of her parents' heritage to a younger sister, who is about to be married – to a man who can overlook the dishonour that Angelica has brought upon their family. Angelica protests that her aunt is inexorable. Deeply offended, the Princess tells of frequent visits to her own sister's grave, where their spirits commune ('Nel silenzio di quei raccoglimenti'). But always her thoughts return to her niece's sin and the need for its expiation.

'Suor Angelica' (Puccini): final scene of the original production (designed by Pietro Stroppa) at the Metropolitan Opera, New York, 14 December 1918, with Geraldine Farrar as Sister Angelica

Angelica, duly humble, insists nonetheless that she will never forget her beloved child, only to learn that he has died of a fever. She collapses sobbing, but recovers sufficiently to sign the parchment and when her aunt has left pours out her grief in the aria 'Senza mamma, bimbo, tu sei morto'. Singing of divine grace ('La grazia è discesa dal cielo') the nuns proceed to their cells followed by Angelica, who presently reappears carrying a jar into which she pours a lethal draught distilled from flowers. Bidding the sisters a tender farewell she drinks the poison and is immediately overcome by guilt at having committed mortal sin. She prays frantically for salvation; the doors of the chapel open revealing a host of angels. In their midst is the Virgin Mary leading Angelica's child by the hand towards the dying mother, as the 'Royal March of the Madonna' swells to a climax.

* * *

In the dismemberment of the *Trittico* which followed the early performances, *Suor Angelica* was the first to be discarded (much to the annoyance of Puccini, who claimed it as his favourite among the three). Managements were put off by the problems of an all-female cast. Protestant audiences were alienated by the subject. Even in Italy the prevailing sweetness of the idiom held little appeal for a generation familiar with the explorations of Pizzetti and Malipiero into the austere ecclesiastical traditions of the past. Finally it may be questioned whether Puccini rose adequately to the challenge of the culminating miracle, which ideally calls for the kind of transfiguration that lay outside his range.

JULIAN BUDDEN

Supertitles. *See* SURTITLES.

Supervia [Supervía], **Conchita** (*b* Barcelona, 9 Dec 1895; *d* London, 30 March 1936). Spanish mezzo-soprano. She can have had little musical training when at the age of 14 she made her operatic début in minor roles with a touring Spanish company at the Teatro Colón, Buenos Aires. In November 1911, not yet 16, she was chosen as the Octavian of the Rome première of *Der Rosenkavalier*; in the 1915–16 season she appeared in Chicago as Charlotte, Mignon and Carmen, and during the 1920s sang widely in Spain, and at La Scala (Octavian, Cherubino, Humperdinck's Hänsel and Ravel's Concepcion) and elsewhere in Italy. Her international fame began with her assumption of the brilliant Rossini mezzo parts in *L'italiana in Algeri*, *La Cenerentola* and *Il barbiere*; these roles, together with that of Carmen, formed the centre of her stage repertory during the last decade of her life, and brought her to Covent Garden in 1934 and 1935. By then she had married an Englishman, Ben Rubenstein, and settled in London, becoming very popular also on the concert platform. She died after childbirth when her career was at its height. Supervia possessed exceptional gifts of musicianship and temperament. Her rich and vibrant mezzo attained a high degree of flexibility. Few singers conveyed so keen a pleasure in the sheer act of singing; and her enunciation, in several languages, was extremely vivid. Her many gramophone records, though sometimes adding a falsely strident quality to her louder tones, convey very well the vivacity, charm and intimacy of her style.

Conchita Supervia in the title role of Bizet's 'Carmen'

*

I. Newton: 'Conchita Supervia', *Recorded Sound*, no.52 (1973), 205–29 [with discography by H. M. Barnes, D. Cattanach, V. Girard and others]

DESMOND SHAWE-TAYLOR

Suppan, Jakob. *See* ZUPAN, JAKOB.

Suppé [Suppè], **Franz** (**von**) [Francesco Ezechiele Ermenegildo Cavaliere Suppé Demelli] (*b* Spalato [now Split], Dalmatia, 18 April 1819; *d* Vienna, 21 May 1895). Austrian composer and conductor of Belgian descent. His father and grandfather were Austrian civil servants working in Dalmatia, his mother Viennese. Despite paternal opposition Suppé showed his musical talent at an early age, encouraged by the bandmaster Ferrari and the cathedral choirmaster Cigalla. He was sent to study law at Padua, but he heard and made much music, visiting Milan and meeting Rossini, Donizetti and Verdi as well as hearing their operas.

After his father's death in 1835 he and his mother went to Vienna. He considered studying medicine but he took up music in earnest, taught and encouraged by Seyfried and Sechter; although the former's testimonial of 14 March 1840 emphasizes Suppé's abilities in serious composition, he helped secure him a post, initially unpaid, as third Kapellmeister at the Theater in der Josefstadt in autumn 1840. There his first complete score was very successfully given on 5 March 1841; under the title of *Jung lustig, im Alter traurig, oder Die Folgen der Erziehung* it received a favourable review in the *Theaterzeitung*, being praised for qualities associated with his later masterpieces:

> Melodious, rich in tender ideas [and] fine nuances, clearly and effectively orchestrated and containing such surprising modulations and transitions, that the overture and most of the songs and choruses had to be encored ... The whole composition has traces of the Italian style but now and then goes in for thoroughly vernacular, simply handled themes.

Suppé is reported to have said later that much of the success was due to his having unconsciously (owing to his very limited knowledge of German) treated a *Jodler* in the style of a sentimental Donizettian farewell, through misunderstanding the text. Donizetti, a distant relative, encouraged Suppé during one of his visits to Vienna (probably in the early 1840s) when the young man showed him the score of an opera, *Gertrude della valle*, that he was then writing, and Donizetti was probably instrumental in bringing about Suppé's later visits to Italy.

Until 1845 Suppé wrote well over 20 scores for the Theater in der Josefstadt (and for the director Pokorný's other theatres in Baden, Ödenburg [Sopron] and Pressburg [Bratislava], in which he was mainly employed in and around 1843); among them were *Ein Morgen, ein Mittag und ein Abend in Wien* and *Nella die Zauberin* (both 1844), and a score for *A Midsummer Night's Dream*; he also appeared with success as a singer on the provincial stages, making his début in that capacity as Dulcamara (in *L'elisir d'amore*) at Ödenburg on 2 May 1842.

In 1845 Suppé moved to Pokorný's newly acquired Theater an der Wien, where for the next 17 years he was Kapellmeister, sharing the duties with Lortzing in 1846–8 and with Adolf Müller from 1848. Apart from a string of more or less successful theatre scores, he conducted many important operatic performances – for instance the productions of Meyerbeer's *Die Gibellinen in Pisa* (*Les Huguenots*) in May 1846, with Jenny Lind and Tichatschek, and *Vielka* (*Ein Feldlager in Schlesien*) with Lind and Staudigl in February 1847.

In 1860 Suppé's *Das Pensionat* was the first successful attempt at a genuine Viennese operetta in answer to the French product, which since October 1858 (the Carltheater production of Offenbach's *Le mariage aux lanternes*) had been gaining a firm hold on the Viennese repertory. In 1862 Suppé moved to the Kaitheater and in 1865 to the Carltheater (formerly the Theater in der Leopoldstadt). Year after year he turned out a series of theatre scores, ranging from overtures and incidental music to operettas, opera parodies and even the occasional opera. Among his greatest successes were *Gervinus* (1849), *Flotte Bursche* (1863) and *Fatinitza* (1876), each of which received 100 or more performances in a few years; and, above all, *Boccaccio* (1879), which he referred to as 'the greatest success of my life'. In the late 1870s he purchased an estate in Lower Austria, and his increasing fame was reflected in invitations to visit the first Bayreuth festival in 1876, and Paris, Brussels, Germany and Italy (1879). In 1881 he was given the freedom of the City of Vienna. In 1882 he retired from his post as Kapellmeister to the Carltheater, though he continued to compose until the end of his life, enjoying successes in Germany in 1883 when he conducted his latest operetta, *Die Afrikareise*. Although he was working on another operetta, *Das Modell*, at the time of his death, his last works were mainly sacred.

Suppé is the earliest Viennese composer of musical farces whose works still survive as viable stage scores (and popular overtures), and later in his career he became the first master of the classical Viennese operetta in the train of the acclimatized scores of Offenbach. His light, fluent style includes the ability to vary a phrase length or melodic and rhythmic figure in a personal and immediately effective way. Though now remembered mainly as the composer of overtures such as *Poet and Peasant*, *Light Cavalry* and *Morning, Noon and Night in Vienna*, his ambitions extended to the composition of large-scale sacred works and operas. He is at his best and most characteristic in the series of famous operettas from *Die schöne Galathee* (1865) to *Boccaccio* (1879). Numbers like 'Hab ich nur deine Liebe', 'Mia bella Fiorentina' and 'Holde Schöne' from *Boccaccio* have an irresistible elegance and élan, and his scoring is worthy of the finest orchestras rather than the bands that so often seize upon the overtures in particular. The song 'O du [Das ist] mein Österreich' of 1849 has become virtually Austria's second national song.

See also BOCCACCIO; FATINITZA; and SCHÖNE GALATHEE, DIE.

WC – *Vienna, Carltheater*
WJ – *Vienna, Theater in der Josefstadt*
WW – *Vienna, Theater an der Wien*

1841: Jung lustig, im Alter traurig, oder Die Folgen der Erziehung (komisches Gemälde, 3, C. Wallis), WJ, 5 March, *A-Wgm**; Die Wette um ein Herz, oder Künstlersinn und Frauenliebe (Original-Lebensbild, 3, K. Elmar), WJ, 10 March, *Wn*; Stumm, beredt, verliebt (Lustspiel, 2, F. X. Told), Ödenburg, 1 May, *Wgm**; Die Bestürmung von Saida (historisches Gemälde, 3, Told), Baden, Arena, 3 or 10 Sept, collab. Binder and Titl, *Wn*; Der Pfeilschütz in Lerchenfeld, die Hochzeit am Neubau und das Testament in der Josefstadt, oder Der Mulatte (Original-Charaktergemälde, 3 Bilder, Told), WJ, 27 Oct, incl. music by J. Lanner, *Wgm**; Der Komödiant, oder Der Narr und Bräutigam, oder Eine Lektion in der Liebe (Zauberspiel, 3, Elmar), WJ, 14 Dec, *Wgm* (?autograph), *Wn*

1842: Der Mulatte (Lustspiel, 3, T. Hell), Pressburg, 12 Feb, *Wgm**; Das grüne Band (romantisch-komisches Zauberspiel, 2, Elmar, H. Levitschnigg, J. H. Mirani, J. Seydl, Told and W. Vogel), WJ, 2 July, *Wgm**; Die Hammerschmiedin aus Steiermark, oder Folgen einer Landpartie (Localposse, 2, J. Schickh), WJ, 14 Oct, *Wn* (part autograph); Der Musikant und sein Liab' (Lebensbild, A. von Klesheim), Baden bei Wien, *Wgm**

1844: Ein Morgen, Mittag und Abend in Wien (lokales Gemälde, 2, Told), WJ, 26 Feb; Nella die Zauberin, oder Der Maskenball auf Hochgiebel (romantisch-komisches Gemälde, 4, Elmar), WJ, 11 May, *Wgm**; Ein Sommernachtstraum (phantastisches Märchen, 3, E. Straube, after W. Shakespeare), WJ, 31 Aug, *Wgm**; Der Krämer und sein Kommis (Posse, 2, F. Kaiser), WJ, 28 Sept, *Wgm**, *Wn*; Dolch und Rose, oder Das Donaumädchen (romantisch-komisches Zauberspiel, 3, Told), WJ, 30 Nov, *Wn**; Zum ersten Mal im Theater, WJ, 31 Dec; Der Jahreswechsel (dramatische Szene, W. Just), WJ, 31 Dec

1845: Die Champagner-Cur, oder Lebenshass und Reue (Posse, 3, K. Gruber), WJ, 2 or 20 Feb; Die Müllerin von Burgos (vaudeville, 2, J. Kupelwieser), WJ, 8 March, *Wgm**, *Wn*; Der preussische Landwehrmann und die französische Bäuerin (Szene), Vienna, Kärntnertor, 20 April, *Wn*; Die Preussen in Oesterreich, oder Landmädchen, Volontär und Trompeter (Original-Charaktergemälde, 2, Nachspiel, Elmar), WJ, 29 April, *Wgm**; Der Nabob (Lokalposse, 3), WJ, 5 May, *Wgm**; Die Industrie-Ausstellung (Volksstück, 2, Kaiser), WJ, 1 Aug, *Wgm*, *Wn*; Wanderers Ziel (Festspiel, 1, K. Meisl), WW, 28 or 30 Aug, *Wgm**; Der verkaufte Schlaf, oder Reich an Geld, arm an Schlaf (phantastisches Märchen, 2, Told, after Saphir), WW, 17 Sept, *Wgm**, *Wn* (part autograph); Das Lustspiel in Hietzing (Original-Lustspiel, F. Blum, after Molière), WW, 26 Sept; Sie ist verheirathet (romantisch-komisches Charakterbild, 3, Kaiser), WW, 7 Nov, *Wn** (?inc.), *Wst*

1846: Er ist verheirathet (komisches Lokalgemälde, 3, Schickh), WJ, 10 Jan, *Wn*; Die Gänsehüterin, oder Hans und Gretchen (romantisches Lustspiel, 3, G. Ball), WW, 11 Feb, *Wn**; Der Sohn der Heide (romantisch-komisches Lebensbild, 3, Kaiser), WW, 15 June, *Wgm** (inc.); Dichter und Bauer (Lustspiel, 3, Elmar), WW, 24 Aug, *Wn**, vs (Berlin, 1968)

1847: Caricaturen (Posse, 2, Kaiser), WW, 8 Feb; Die Reise nach Grätz, oder Die Räuber auf dem Semmering (localer Schwank, 3, Schickh), WJ, 24 Feb; Das Menschenherz (Phantasie-Gemälde, 3, F. X. Lang [Told]), WW, 15 March; Liebeszauber, oder Ein Wunder in den Bergen (dramatisch-komisches Gemälde, 3, Elmar), WW, 21 April, *Wn* (?autograph); Zwei Pistolen (Posse, 2, Kaiser), WW, 8 May, *Wn*; Ein Feen-Märchen (Lustspiel, 3, Kupelwieser), WW, 25 May; Das Mädchen vom Lande (grosse Oper, 3, Elmar), WW, 7 Aug, *Wn* (part autograph), *Wst* (?autograph); Tausend und eine Nacht (romantisch-komisches Zauberspiel, 3, Told), WJ, 20 Aug, *Wn*; Die Schule der Armen, oder Zwei Millionen (Original-Gemälde, 4, Kaiser), WW, 26 Oct, *Wn**; Was eine Frau einmal will, oder Der Friedrichsd'or (vaudeville, 3, H. Börnstein, after Duvert and Lauzanne), WW, 23 Nov or 30 Dec, collab. Proch; Hier, da, dort ein Schmied (Posse, 3, Elmar and Mirani), WW, 30 Dec

1848: Männerschönheit (Original-Charaktergemälde, 3, Kaiser), WW, 6 Feb, *Wn*; Unter der Erde, oder Freiheit und Arbeit (Charakterbild, 3, Elmar), WW, 30 May, *Wn*, *Wst*; Der ewige Jude (dramatisches Gemälde, 5, K. Schmidt, after E. Sue), pt 1, WW, 24 June, pt 2, WW, 1 July, both pts, WW, 6 Sept 1853, *Wn** (inc.); Eine Petition der Bürger, WW, 12 July; Wie die Reactionäre dumm sind (Schwank, 1, Elmar), WW, 3 Aug; Der Bandit, oder Ein Abenteuer in Spanien (Schauspiel, 5, A. C. Ambo), WW, 13 Aug, *Wn*; Der wirkliche, überzählige, unbesoldete Wirtschaftspraktikant (Original-Posse, 3, G. Schönstein), WW, 13 Sept; Ein Traum, kein Traum, oder Die letzte Rolle einer Schauspielerin (Posse, 2, Kaiser), WW, 2 Dec, *Wn*; Martl, oder Der Portiunkulatag von Schnabelhausen (parodistische Posse, 3, A. Berla), WW, 16 Dec, *Wgm**; Nacht und Licht (melodramatische Parabel, 1, Kaiser), WW, 31 Dec

1849: Des Teufels Brautfahrt, oder Böser Feind und guter Freund (Original-Zauberposse, 3, Elmar), WW, 30 Jan, *Wgm**, *Wn*; Ein Fürst (Charakterbild, 3, Kaiser), WW, 13 March, *Wn*; Gervinus der Narr von Untersberg, oder Ein patriotischer Wunsch (Posse, 3, Berla), WW, 1 July, *Wn*; Die Räuber auf dem Semmering, WW, 1 Sept; Der Edelstein, oder Drei Proben (Märchen, Berla), WW, 9 or 17 Sept; Ein Blatt der Geschichte [der Weltgeschichte] (dramatisches Gedicht, 4 Bilder, O. Prechtler), WW, 3 or 30 Oct; Unterthänig, unabhängig (Zeitgemälde, 3, Elmar), WW, 13 Oct,

*Wgm**, *Wn*; s'Alraundl [s'Alraunl] (romantisches Märchen, 3, Klesheim), WW, 13 Nov, *Wgm**, *Wn*

1850: Die Philisterschule, oder Alles auf einmal (Posse, 3, Elmar), WW, 17 Jan; Gentil Bernhard, oder Die Kunst zu lieben (vaudeville, 5, J. Schuselka-Brüning), WW, 26 Feb, *Wn*, collab. A. Müller; Liebe zum Volke, oder Geld-Arbeit-Ehre (Charaktergemälde, 3, Elmar), WW, 18 March, *Wn*; Bürger und Soldat, oder Liebe zum Vaterland (J. K. Böhm), WW, 26 April; Die beiden Fassbinder, oder Reflexionen und Aufmerksamkeiten (Posse, 3, L. Feldmann), WW, 16 May, collab. Binder, *Wn*; Der Dumme hat's Glück, oder Tolle Streiche (Posse, 3, Berla), WW, 29 June, *Wgm**, *Wn*; Der Mann an der Spitze, oder Alles aus Freundschaft (Charaktergemälde, 2, A. Bittner), WW, 19 Aug; Der Vertrauensmann, oder Wahrheit und Lüge (Charaktergemälde, 3, Berla), WW, 19 Sept, *Wgm**

1851: Dame Valentin, oder Frauenräuber und Wanderbursche (romantisch-komisches Spl, 3, Elmar), WW, 9 Jan, *Wgm**; Die Industrie-Ausstellung (Gelegenheitsposse, 3, Feldmann), WW, 25 May; Waldmärchen (Zauberposse, 3, Berla), WW, 30 July, *Wn**; Angeplauscht (Posse, 2, L. Wysber), WW, 20 Aug

1852: Tannenhäuser (dramatisches Gedicht, 2, Levitschnigg, after a Ger. legend), WW, 27 Feb, *Wn**, *Wst*; Jungfer Mahm aus Gmunden, oder Einen muss sie nehmen (Schwank, 3, J. Nikola), WW, 20 May, *Wgm**; Das Beispiel (ländliches Gemälde, F. Nissel and S. Schlesinger), WW, 2 May or 2 Oct; Ein Filz als Prasser (Posse, 3, Feldmann and T. Flamm), WW, 30 June, *Wn*; Pech (Lokalposse, 3, Berla), WW, 31 July, *Wn*; Der Grabsteinmacher (Charakterbild, 3, Wysber), WW, 6 Nov, *Wn*

1853: Die Heimkehr von der Hochzeit (Faschingsposse, 3, Feldmann), WW, 8 Jan, *Wn**; Der Baum des Lebens (Festspiel, 1, Feldmann), WW, 3 Feb or 1 March; Irrfahrt um's Glück (romantisch-komisches Zaubermärchen, 3, Elmar), WW, 24 April, *Wn*; Österreichs Eiche (Festspiel, 1, Feldmann), WW, 13 May; Die weiblichen Jäger (Posse, 3, Feldmann), WW, 30 July, *Wgm**

1854: Die Bernstein-Hexe (Schauspiel, 5, H. Laube, after Schweidler), WW, 5 Jan, *Wn*; Trommel und Trompete (Posse, 3, Elmar), WW, 1 April, *Wgm*; Im Bauernhaus, im Herrenhaus (Festspiel, 1, J. L. Deinhardstein), WW, 24 April; Der Biberhof (Dorfgeschichte, 3, Feldmann and Märzroth, WW, 25 May, *Wn*; Wo steckt der Teufel (komisches Märchen, 3, J. Grün, after E. Breier), WW, 28 June, *Wgm**, *Wn*; Mozart (Künstler-Lebensbild, 4, L. Wohlmuth), WW, 23 Sept, *Wn*, 3-act version with prol. *Wst**; Nur romantisch! (Posse, 1 or 3, Kaiser), WW, 18 Nov, *Wn*; Der Juwelier, oder Der Festmarkt auf Kronborg (historisch-romantisches Lustspiel, 5, F. von Holbein, after Blumenhagen), WW, 6 Dec; Bum, bum, oder Zwei Schlauköpfe und ein Dummkopf (Posse, 2, Bittner), WW, 9 Dec

1855: Das Bründl bei Siefring [Sievering] (Volksmärchen, 4, H. Merlin), WW, 14 April, *Wn* (part autograph); Der Teufel hol' die Comödie (Quodlibet), WW, 17 May; Das Höllen-Ross (romantisch-komisches Märchen, 3, K. Bruno), WW, 23 May; Die G'frettbrüder (Posse, 3, Berla and Bittner), WW, 28 June, *Wn*; Kinder-Märchen [Märchen, Prinz Liliput und Das Schneiderlein] (Märchenbilder, 3, Klesheim), WW, 20 Oct, *Wgm**; Judas im Frack [Judas von anno Neun] (Volksstück, 3, A. Langer), WW, 20 Dec, *Wn*

1856: Nur keine Verwandten (Posse, 3, Feldmann), WW, 12 April, *Wn*, *Wst*; Lord Byron (dramatische Bilder, 3, Levitschnigg), WW, 8 June, *Wn*; Ein Musikant, oder Die ersten Gedanken (komisches Charakterbild, 3, L. Gottsleben), Vienna, Sommerarena Braunhirschen, 8 June, *Wgm**, *Wn* (autograph frag.); Die Wahrheit auf Reisen (komisches Zaubermärchen, 3, O. F. Berg), WW, 24 June, *Wgm**, *Wn*; Der Schuster von Sievring (Volksmärchen, 3, Merlin), WW, 16 July; Die Weingeister [Ein alter Tarokspieler] (komisches Zauberspiel, prol., 3, J. Bernhofer and A. Blank), WW, 10 Aug, *Wn*; Eine ungarische Dorfgeschichte, oder Der Liebeszauber (Charaktergemälde, 3, Berla and Bittner), WW, 31 Aug, *Wgm**, *Wn*; Die schöne Leni (Volksstück, 3, J. Findeisen), WW, 4 Oct, *Wn*; Die Kreuzköpfeln (Posse, 3, Berg and Grün), WW, 22 Oct, *Wgm**, *Wn*; Ein Bergvolk (Schauspiel, 5, K. Liebold), WW, 5 Nov; Vertrauen (Charakterbild, 3, M. Grandjean), WW, 22 Nov; Der gefährliche Mensch, oder Das Vertrauen (komisches Charakterbild, 3, Berla and W. Tesko), WW, 7 Dec, *Wgm**, *Wn*

1857: Der Faschings-Teufel (Zauberposse, 3, Berla, after A. Pokorny), WW, 13 or 23 Feb, *Wgm**; Eine Schlange (Original-Charakterbild, 3, K. Gründorf), WW, 18 April; Kopf und Herz (Original-Lebensbild, 3, Flamm), WW, 9 May, *Wn*; Der Comet von 1857 [Der Komet 1857] (Posse, 3, Feldmann and Weyl), WW, 23 May, *Wn*; Ein desparater Kopf (Posse, 2, Nachspiel, L. Karl), WW, 20 June; Die Wäschermädeln (Wiener Lokalbild, 3, Berg), WW, 29 June, *Wgm**, *Wn*; Eine Landparthie (Lokalposse, 3, Findeisen), WW, 17 July, *Wgm**

1858: Paragraf drei (grosse Oper, 3, Grandjean), Vienna, Hof, 8 Jan, *Wn**; Die Mozart-Geige, oder Der Dorfmusikant und sein Kind (Charakter-Gemälde, prol., 3, Elmar), WW, 27 Feb, *Wgm**, *Wn*; Das tägliche Brod (Charakterbild, 3, Berla), WW, 13 March, *Wgm**, *Wn*; Der Werkelmann und seine Familie (Lebensbild, 3, Langer), WW, 10 or 17 April, *Wn*, *Wst**; Die Firmgodl (Volksstück, 3, Elmar), WW, 21 May, *Wn*; Die Kathi von Eisen (Lokalposse, 3, Berla), WW, 19 July, *Wn*; Nach der Stadterweiterung (Original-Zukunfts-Charaktergemälde, 2, Gans and Schlesinger), WW, 11 Dec, *Wn*, *Wst**

1859: Ein Fasching-Kugelhupf (Quodlibetburleske, prol., 2, Jocosus Juxinger [Langer]), WW, 5 March, collab. Müller, *Wn*; Etwas zum Lachen, oder Keine Politik (Posse, 3, Feldmann), WW, 11 June, *Wgm**, *Wn*; Eine Wienerin (Lebensbild, 3, Flamm), WW, 23 July, *Wgm**; Der Waldteufel, oder Der Fex aus dem Höllenthal (komisches Charakterbild, 3, Berla and Tesko), WW, 5 Aug, *Wn**; Über Land und Meer, oder Abenteuer eines Glücklichen (Zauberspiel, 3, Blank), WW, 21 Aug, collab. Müller; Eine Judenfamilie (Originalcharaktergemälde, 4, Mirani), WW, 22 or 23 Oct, *Wgm**; Fanny, die schieche Nuss (Charaktergemälde, 4, Findeisen), WW, 23 Nov, collab. Müller, *Wn*; Die Zauberdose, oder Um zehn Jahre zu spät (Märchenposse, 3, Elmar), WW, 19 Dec, *Wgm**, *Wn*

1860: Meister Winter (komisches Märchen, 3, Berla), WW, 14 March, *Wst*; Das Pensionat (komische Operette, 1, J. Kaulich), WW, 24 Nov (Vienna, *c*1865), *Wgm*, *Wn*, *Wst**; Mein ist die Welt (Charaktergemälde, 3, Kaiser), WW, 16 Dec

1861: Ein Loch in der Hölle (Zauberposse, prol., 2, J. Schönau), WW, 2 Feb, *Wgm**; Der politische Schuster (Volksstück, 3, Berg), WW, 1 June, *Wn*, *Wst*; Höllen-Candidat [Der Höllenkandidat] (komisches Märchen, 3, Blank and Bernhofer), WW, 26 July, *Wgm**, *Wn*; Wunderkinder aus Californien (Ausstattungsstück, 10 Bilder), WW, 14 Aug, *Wgm**, *Wn*; Nachtfalter [Wiener Nachtfalter] (Lebensbild, 3, Gottsleben), WW, 29 Sept, *Wgm**, *Wn*; Ein Schwindler (Charakterbild, 3, Mirani), WW, 6 or 12 Oct; Reise durch die Märchenwelt (dramatischer Bilderbogen, 5 scenes, Bittner), WW, 4 Nov, *Wgm**, *Wn*, *Wsm**

1862: Die Kartenschlägerin, oder Pique Dame (komische Operette, 1, T. Treumann), Vienna, Kai, 26 April, rev. as Pique Dame (komische Oper, 2), Graz, Thalia, 24 June 1864, *Wn* (autograph frag.), *Wst**; Zehn Mädchen und kein Mann (Operette, 1, Friedrich), Vienna, Kai, 25 Oct, vs (Vienna, ?1865), *Wn*, *Wst**; Bädekers Reisehandbuch (Schwank, 1, G. Belly), Vienna, Kai, 27 Dec, *Wn*, collab. Conradi

1863: Der Herr Vetter (Posse, 2, Berla), Vienna, Kai, 28 Feb; Flotte Bursche, oder Das Bild der Madame Potifar (komische Operette, 1, Leitermayer or J. Braun), Vienna, Kai, 18 April, vs (Vienna, ?1870), *Wn*, *Wst*; Etwas für alte Junggesellen (Posse, 3, Blank), WW, 5 Sept, collab. Müller and Hopp; Überall Geister (Posse, 1, Langer), Vienna, Carl, 23 Sept

1864: Das Corps der Rache (Operette, 1, Harisch), WC, 5 March, *Wst* (part autograph); Franz Schubert (Operette, 1, H. Max), WC, 10 Sept, *Wst**; Der Schwiegerpapa aus Krems (Posse, 3, Langer), WC, 19 Nov, *Wn*; Das Christkindl (Lebensbild, 4, Langer and/or Gottsleben), WC, 26 Dec, *Wn*

1865: Dinorah, oder Die Turnerfahrt nach Hütteldorf (burleske Oper, 3, 'Julius Caesar' [J. Hopp]), WC, 4 May; Die schöne Galathee (Operette, 1, Poly Henrion [L. Kohl von Kohlenegg]), Berlin, Meysel's, 30 June (Vienna, 1865), *Wgm*, *Wn*, *Wst**; Der Ehemann in der Baumwolle (Posse, 1), WC, 4 Nov; Die alte Schachtel (Posse, Berg), WC, 2 Dec, *Wn* (part autograph)

1866: Leichte Cavallerie (komische Operette, 2, C. Costa), WC, 21 March, vs (Vienna, 1866), *Wn*, *Wst**; Der letzte Gulden (Volksposse, 2, Berg), WC, 5 May, *Wn*, *Wst*; Der Selbstmörder (Posse, 1, Blank), Vienna, ? Fürst's Singspielhalle, ? 21 June, *Wn** (inc.), collab. K. Kleiber; Ein patriotischer Dienstbothe, WC, 18 Aug; Es wird annectirt (Gelegenheitsstück, 1), WC, 20 Sept; Die alte Schachtel (Berg), WC, 11 Oct, *Wn*; Freigeister (Operette, 2, Costa), WC, 23 Oct, *Wst**

1867: Banditenstreiche (komische Operette, 1, B. Boutonnier), WC, 27 April, vs (Leipzig, ?1865), *Wn**

1868: Die Frau Meisterin (komische Zauberoperette, 3, Costa), WC, 20 Jan, arr. as Die Pariserin, oder Das heimliche Bild (Operette, 3, Léon and Held), WC, 26 Jan 1898; Schlechte Mittel, gute Zwecke (Operette, 3, Kaiser), WC, 5 March; Tantalusqualen (komische Operette, 1, Suppé, after L. Angely: *Der Schmarotzer* *in der Klemme*), WC, 3 Oct, *Wn**

1869: Juliska (dramatisches Gedicht, 4, K. Schram), WC, 6 Oct; Isabella (komische Operette, 1, J. Weyl), WC, 5 Nov, *Wgm**, *Wn*

1870: Vineta, oder Die versunkene Stadt (Märchen, 3), Munich, Gärtnerplatz, 10 Feb, *Wn*; Lohengelb, oder Die Jungfrau von Dragant (parodistische Operette, 3, Grandjean and Costa, after J. Nestroy: *Lohengrin*), Graz, Stadt, 23 July, *Wn*, *Wst* (part autograph)

1871: Centifolie (Lebensbild, 3, Langer), WC, 9 Feb, *Wst*; Eine schöne Wirtschaft (Posse, 3, Flamm), WC, 14 Nov, *Wn*

1872: Ein weiblicher Dämon (Lebensbild, 3, Langer), WC, 13 April, *Wn*; Cannebas (komische Operette, 1, J. Doppler), WC, 2 Nov, *Wn*, *Wst**

1873: Tricoche et Cacolet (humoristisches Sittenbild aus dem Pariser Leben, 3 Bilder, H. Meilhac and L. Halévy, trans. Treumann), WC, 3 Jan; Wolfgang und Constanze (Charakterbild, 3, Langer), WC, 3 May; Additionelle Ausstellung des Carl Theaters (Quodlibet), WC, 30 Aug, *Wn*

1875: Fräulein Schwarz (Schauspiel, 3, Langer), WC, 11 March; Die Reise um die Erde in 80 Tagen (Ausstattungsstück, 5, A. Ennery, after J. Verne), WC, 28 March, *Wn*

1876: Fatinitza (Operette, 3, F. Zell and R. Genée, after E. Scribe: *La Circassienne*), WC, 5 Jan (?Hamburg, ?1877), *Wn*, *Wst**; Zahnarzt und Magnetiseur (Burleske, 1, A. Reichenbach), WC, 4 Feb; Zum Mond und unterm Meer (Phantastisch-burleskes Ausstattungsstück, Zell, after Verne), WC, 25 March, also as Die Reise nach dem Mond, *Wst*; Die treulose Witwe (Posse, 1, Berg), WC, 2 Dec; Die Baronin vom Ballet (Posse, 1, Berg), WC, 2 Dec, *Wn* (autograph frag.)

1877: Unsere Handwerker (Posse, 1, Berg), Vienna, Carl, 1 April, *Wgm**; Der Courier des Czaren, oder M. Strogoffs Reise (grosse Ausstattungsrevue, 12 tableaux, F. Csepregh, after Verne), WC, 3 May, *Wn* (autograph frag.)

1878: Der Teufel auf Erden (fantastische Operette, 3 or 4, C. Juin and J. Hopp), WC, 5 Jan, *Wn*, vs (London, 1878) [incl. musical motifs from Suppé's Das Höllenkind, inc.]; Historischer Wiener Possenabend (5 Bilder, Langer), WC, 3 Oct

1879: Boccaccio [Giovanni Boccaccio] (Operette, 3, Zell and Genée, after G. Boccaccio: *Decameron*), WC, 1 Feb (Hamburg and Stockholm, ?1880), *Wn*, *Wst**

1880: Donna Juanita (Operette, 3, Genée and Camillo Walzel [Zell]), WC, 21 Feb (Brussels, 1880), *Wn*, *Wst* (part autograph); Die Schwestern (Posse, 3, Held), WC, 19 Oct, *Wgm* (part autograph)

1881: Der Gascogner (Operette, 3, Genée and Zell), WC, 22 March, vs (Hamburg, 1881), *Wst**

1882: Herzblättchen (Operette, 3, C. Tezlaff), WC, 4 Feb, *Wn**, *Wst* (part autograph)

1883: Die Africareise (Operette, 3, Genée and M. West), WW, 17 March (Hamburg, ?1883), *Wst**

1885: Des Matrosen Heimkehr (romantische Oper, 2, Langer), Hamburg, Stadt, 4 May, vs (Hamburg, 1885), *Wgm**, *Wn**, *Wst**

1887: Bellmann (komische Oper, 3, West and L. Held), WW, 24 or 26 Feb, *Wgm*, *Wn**, *Wst* (part autograph); Joseph Haydn (biographisches Genregemälde, 3, F. von Radler), WJ, 30 April, *Wst**

1888: Die Jagd nach dem Glücke (Operette, prol., 3, Genée and B. Zappert), WC, 27 Oct, *Wst** (Hamburg, 1888)

1895: Das Modell (Operette, 3, V. Léon and Held), WC, 4 Oct, completed by J. Stern and A. Zamara (Leipzig, 1895)

Probably unperformed: Il Pomo (Operette, 4), inc. [music of Act 1 given private perf., 1834]; Virginia, 1837 (grosse Oper, 2, L. Holt), frag. *Wn*; Die beiden Blinden, *Wn*; Beim Souper (Quodlibet, Schwank, 2), *Wn*; s'ersti Buhserl, *Wn*; Ein Faschings-Abenteuer, oder Der letzte tolle Streich (Posse, C. F. Stix), *Wn*; Geltrude (tragedia lirica, 3, G. Brazanovich), *Wn*; Das Höllenkind (fantastische Operette, prol. and 3, Juin), *Wn*, *Wst** (inc.); Kinder des Regiments, *Wn*; Nur keine Verwandten (Posse, 3, Feldmann), *Wst*; Papageno und Zeitgeist, *Wn*; Robert und Bertram (Posse, 4, G. Räder), *Wn*; Schwertmayer (komische Operette, 1), *Wgm*; Spanisch und Englisch (vaudeville, B. A. Hermann), *Wn*; Die Tochter der Hölle, *Wst**

Music in: Das Armband, 1842; Rococco, 1842; Das Vaterherz, 1847; Wallensteins Lager, 1849; Durcheinander, 1854; Lumpazivagabundus; *c*1855; Die Seufzerbrücke, 1862; Wiener Vergnügungszügler, 1862; Zwei arme Blinde, 1863; Theatralischer Ausverkauf, 1866; Nagerl und Handschuh, 1870

*

WurzbachL

Theater Kompositionen von Franz von Suppé (MS, *A-Wn* s.m.5396) [Suppé's own handwritten list of his works]

G. Sabalich: *Franz Suppé e l'operetta* (Zara, 1888)

O. Keller: *Franz von Suppé: der Schöpfer der deutschen Operette* (Leipzig, 1905)

E. Rieger: *Offenbach und seine Wiener Schule* (Vienna, 1920)

O. Keller: *Die Operette in ihrer geschichtlichen Entwicklung* (Leipzig, 1926)

A. Würz, ed.: *Reclams Operettenführer* (Stuttgart, 1938, 11/1962), 9ff

J. Kromer: *Franz von Suppé: Leben und Werke* (diss., U. of Vienna, 1941)

F. Hadamowsky and H. Otte: *Die Wiener Operette* (Vienna, 1947)

A. Bauer: *150 Jahre Theater an der Wien* (Zürich, 1952)

——: *Opern und Operetten in Wien* (Graz, 1955)

——: *Das Theater in der Josefstadt zu Wien* (Vienna, 1957)

B. Grun: *Kulturgeschichte der Operette* (Munich, 1961)

G. Hughes: *Composers of Operetta* (London, 1962)

J. Hüttner: 'Baugeschichte und Spielplan des Theaters am Franz Josefs Kai', *Jahrbuch der Gesellschaft für Wiener Theaterforschung*, xvii (1970), 87–161

O. Schneidereit: *Franz von Suppé: der Wiener aus Dalmatien* (Berlin, 1977)

PETER BRANSCOMBE (work-list with DOROTHEA LINK)

Surprises de l'Amour, Les ('Cupid's Surprises'). *Opéra-ballet* in a prologue and two (later, three or four) entrées by JEAN-PHILIPPE RAMEAU to a libretto by PIERRE-JOSEPH BERNARD; Versailles, Théâtre des Petits Cabinets, 27 November 1748.

Les surprises de l'Amour had a complex performing history. Mme de Pompadour commissioned it for her private theatre and created two of the soprano roles, Uranie [Urania] and Vénus [Venus], though she was reputed to be no great lover of Rameau or his music. The work originally consisted of two entrées, 'La lyre enchantée' and 'Adonis'. These were preceded by a prologue ('Le retour d'Astrée') which, like that of Rameau's *Naïs*, celebrated the Treaty of Aix-la-Chapelle. In May 1757 the work was staged at the Paris Opéra. By now the prologue, no longer topical, was abandoned and a new overture substituted; moreover, the original two entrées were drastically revised (the second renamed 'L'enlèvement d'Adonis') and Rameau and Bernard added a new entrée, 'Anacréon' (distinct from Rameau's *acte de ballet* of the same name, to a text by Cahusac). A few weeks later 'La lyre enchantée' was replaced by a revised version of 'Les sibarites', an *acte de ballet* by Marmontel and Rameau first given at Fontainebleau in 1753. Thereafter, the various components were further reshuffled from time to time. 'Anacréon' proved the most successful, remaining in the repertory until 1771.

Each entrée involves a central struggle – between peace and aggression ('Le retour d'Astrée' and 'Les sibarites'), love and indifference ('La lyre enchantée'), love and chastity ('Adonis'), love and wine ('Anacréon'). In each, it is L'Amour [Cupid] (soprano) or his cupids who bring reconciliation, often in an unexpected way – hence the work's title. Collé thought the 1757 version 'smelt of old age' (Rameau was by then 73), yet the new and revised music is almost invariably more interesting than that of the original. The *airs de ballet* are, as always, amazingly inventive, but the score includes some routine passages. The best entrée is 'Anacréon', the plot of which is less stereotyped and provides the motivation for some attractive vocal music – for example the *air* 'Nouvelle Hébé, charmante Lycoris' for Anacréon [Anacreon] (bass) – and a ravishing, chromatic *sommeil* with pizzicatos representing the falling rain.

GRAHAM SADLER

Surtitles [supertitles]. Translations of a libretto, or excerpts from a libretto, projected above the stage during a performance. The purpose of surtitles is analogous to that of subtitles in a foreign-language film: to inform the watcher, unable to follow the text, of what is being sung (and said) on the stage.

1. History. 2. Technique.

1. History. Before the Canadian Opera Company, of Toronto, became the first to introduce surtitles, in 1983, similar devices had often been used in music-theatre presentations. Chinese opera has for centuries been accompanied by a scrolled translation for audiences unfamiliar with the dialect being sung; and in opera up to the 19th century audiences could generally follow foreign-language operas in bilingual librettos. In recent decades, the presentation of translated texts for viewing by the audiences has been attempted in Japan, at performances by foreign opera companies; on Broadway, in 1964, for the Italian musical *Rugantino*; and at Lyons, in 1976, for *L'incoronazione di Poppea*. Before the appearance of surtitles, however, no production had executed simultaneous translation of this sort with the thoroughness, consistency and sophistication that would eventually be achieved by many North American and British opera companies.

The use of surtitles was an idea conceived by Lotfi Mansouri, director of the Canadian Opera Company at the time. John Leberg, the company's director of operations, developed the basic technique and used it initially for a production of *Elektra* on 21 January 1983; the translator was Sonya Friedman, an experienced subtitler of feature films and televised opera. *Elektra*, and the surtitled *L'incoronazione di Poppea* three months later, proved successful with Toronto audiences and attracted the attention and curiosity of a wider, international operatic community.

Surtitles rapidly came to be used throughout the USA and Canada. The first surtitled performance in the USA, a production of *Elektra* using Friedman's translation, was given in the summer of 1983 by Artpark, an arts festival in Lewiston, New York. In September of the same year, the New York City Opera used, for *Cendrillon*, the first surtitle translation commissioned for a US company. After the Canadian Opera Company adopted the word 'surtitles' as a registered trademark, American companies created their own names, e.g. 'ENCAPS' (The Dallas Opera) and 'OpTrans' (Pittsburgh Opera). During the past few years, many American companies have rejected their own sobriquets in favour of 'supertitles', a term coined by San Francisco Opera. Indeed, throughout the USA 'supertitles' rather than 'surtitles' has become the word most often used, whether by the press, audiences or opera professionals. Among the leading North American companies that present opera in the original language, by 1990 only the Metropolitan Opera and the Santa Fe Opera did not give surtitled performances. The New York City Opera, the Dallas Opera and Houston Grand Opera have gone further, projecting English surtitles for certain unfamiliar operas (often world premières) even though the works were sung in English.

Surtitles arrived in Great Britain in 1984, experimentally with schools' performances of *La bohème* and *Falstaff* at Covent Garden. These performances resulted in Glyndebourne adopting them in October 1984 for their Touring Opera productions of *Così fan tutte* and *Le nozze di Figaro* and later for their festival staging of *Kát'a Kabanová*. Covent Garden has used surtitles regularly since January 1986 when they were introduced in a new production of *Jenůfa*; all performances of operas in a foreign language are now surtitled there, and they have been used to accompany Birtwistle's English-language opera, *Gawain*. In 1986, the German producer Michael Hampe took them to the Maggio Musicale Fiorentino for *Die Meistersinger von Nürnberg*. Surtitles have also been seen in several other European houses, including the Paris Bastille, and at the major opera houses in Australia and New Zealand where they are also regularly used to accompany operas sung in English.

2. Technique. In preparing a script, the surtitler begins by acquainting himself fully with the score. If possible, he attends rehearsals to make certain that nothing in his surtitles will conflict with the action as interpreted by the director. In translating the libretto, he eliminates all non-essential lines, retaining up to about three-quarters of the text; though a surtitler defeats his purpose when, by 'overtitling', he draws too much attention away from the stage. Effective surtitles do not repeat text except when the drama requires it. The language of any title should be read and understood at a glance, but at the same time it must be literate and eloquent enough to preserve the basic character of the original.

The average surtitled opera includes between 500 and 600 titles, although this number increases substantially in operas containing lengthy recitative scenes, e.g. the Mozart-Da Ponte comedies. At Covent Garden, a performance of *Duke Bluebeard's Castle* used 190 titles, *Die Entführung aus dem Serail* 373 and *Das Rheingold* 589. The standard format shows a maximum of two lines of text per title, with no more than 40 characters per line. After completing the translation, the surtitler numbers each title and marks each musical cue in his score. During performances, a music assistant cues a title at the appropriate musical moment. Surtitles can be satisfactorily timed only by listening carefully to the singers' phrasing, as if one were a conductor.

If a company's projection equipment incorporates a dissolve unit, it becomes possible to fade a title 'in' or 'out'. In general, slower fades are preferred in slow music and faster ones in fast. Fades lasting longer than one-and-one-half seconds may create excellent dramatic effects and are most successful in quiet moments, such as the last lines of Mimì in Act 4 of *La bohème*. In this case, quick 'cuts' from one title to the next (which might be appropriate for recitative or dialogue) would destroy the mood of the music.

The most common method of projection continues to be 35mm slides. Placed between protective glass mounts to prevent burning, the slides are projected on to a grey screen above the stage using powerful xenon projectors. Some major American companies, and also Covent Garden, have invested in computerized video projection systems. A computer allows the text of a title to be changed in a matter of seconds and can accommodate a variety of fade times and light intensities. Companies can also store several complete translations on a single disk, an important advantage over slides.

Specific criticism of surtitled performances generally addresses one or more of the following concerns: (*a*) too many titles, or too few; (*b*) inaccurate, grammatically incorrect or stylistically unacceptable translations; (*c*) imperfect synchronization between the projected text and what is being sung (a serious problem in comic operas); (*d*) titles that clash with the production or stage setting; (*e*) titles that twist or censor aspects of a libretto (that is, a deliberate misinterpretation of libretto text) and (*f*) faults in projection, such as slides shown upside-down or with insufficient brightness. The problems presented by passages where two or more singers have different texts simultaneously can often be solved by careful timing, following the most important line dramatically or allowing the positioning of characters on stage to dictate which text is translated.

Many objections to surtitles have been voiced, and their main sense is admirably summarized in the remarks of Rodney Milnes: 'that [surtitles] should be allowed to interpose themselves and so dilute that live, immediate, intimate yet shared communication between artists and audiences that has been the whole point of western drama for thousands of years is a prospect too horrible to contemplate'. James Levine, artistic director of the Metropolitan Opera, has declared that the company would use surtitles only 'over my dead body'. It has also been objected that their use will discourage singers in taking due care over the enunciation of their words. On the other hand, surtitles' virtues have been repeatedly and eloquently proclaimed. One of the most persuasive statements supporting the use of surtitles comes not from a performer or opera administrator, but from Isaiah Berlin in the 1986 programme of Glyndebourne Touring Opera:

> This courageous experiment alone seems to me to support strongly the thesis that opera-goers – and above all those who may either underrate the beauty and depth of operas because they cannot follow the words, or perhaps be deterred from going to see opera altogether – can be converted and illuminated and made enthusiastic by becoming able to understand the meaning, musically and emotionally, of what is going on, instead of being made to listen to mumbo-jumbo.

The critical debate over the validity of surtitles will undoubtedly continue; but it is clear that the public's enthusiastic acceptance of them, and the heightened response to opera to which they have given rise, will assure their use indefinitely among opera companies.

*

D. Henahan: 'It's Nice to Know What is Happening in an Opera', *New York Times* (2 Oct 1983)
P. Blake: '*Cendrillon* Becomes Cinderella: Subtitling a Fairy Tale at the New York City Opera', *Time* (17 Oct 1983)
G. D. Lipton: 'Everybody's Doing it', *ON*, (1984), 16, 18, 20, 67
R. Milnes: 'Sounding Board', *Opera*, xxxv (1984), 1077
I. Berlin: 'A Personal View of Super-titles', *Glyndebourne Touring Opera 1986* [programme book]; repr. as 'A Voice in Favour', *ON* (1990), 26–7
G. Heymont: 'New Software for Supertitles', *Opera Monthly* (Feb 1988), 47–50
J. Mackerras: 'The Craft of Surtitling', *About the House* (Spring 1989), 20–22
'Around the Table: Five Experts have a go at Projected Titles', *ON*, liv (1989–90), 13–16, 18
A. Steven: 'The Writing on the Wall', *Opera Now* (May 1991), 16–19
ROGER PINES

Susa, Conrad (*b* Springdale, PA, 26 April 1935). American composer. A graduate of the Juilliard School, he studied composition with Bergsma and Persichetti. He has composed numerous choral works and more than a hundred scores for the theatre, documentary films and television. He was resident composer for the Old Globe Theater in San Diego and dramaturg for the O'Neill Center in Connecticut, and in 1988 joined the faculty of the San Francisco Conservatory of Music.

Susa's first opera, *Transformations* (1973), one of the most frequently performed contemporary American operas, is a setting of nine poems from Anne Sexton's book of the same title, a highly personal retelling of the Grimms' fairy-tales. Constructed according to the principles of story theatre, Susa's narrative libretto also weaves a sub-plot dealing with Sexton's creative process, psychological growth and personal transformation. To underscore the text's many topical references, the singers and accompanying chamber ensemble parody popular musical styles, entertainers and dance forms from the 1940s and 50s. The première was given by Minnesota Opera in Minneapolis on 5 May 1973.

The same company gave the first performance of Susa's second and most conventional opera, *Black River: a Wisconsin Idyll* (1975; they also gave the revised version in 1981). The work is a meditation about the triumph of the human spirit over loss, grief and anguish. Inspired by Michael Lesy's documentary book *Wisconsin Death Trip*, which details the inexplicably profound psychic malaise that pervaded rural Wisconsin during the late 19th century, *Black River* chronicles the lives of three women against a tapestry of historical and fictional characters. This non-linear opera evokes a surrealistic, romantic dreamscape through the application of cinematic techniques such as flashbacks.

Susa's third opera, *The Love of Don Perlimplín* (performed at PepsiCo Summerfare in 1984), adapted from Lorca's play, draws inspiration from Domenico Scarlatti. Through its tale of Perlimplín's ill-fated yet redemptive love for Belisa, this sensuous work deals with the traditional concept of honour in Spanish life. Like all of Susa's witty and innately theatrical operas, it is eclectic in style and brilliantly orchestrated, uses parodies and authentic musical materials to evoke period and characterization, mixes tragic and comic elements, and exhibits textual clarity.

Transformations (operatic entertainment, 2, Susa, after A. Sexton), Minneapolis, Cedar Village, 5 May 1973
Black River: a Wisconsin Idyll (grand op, prol., 3, R. Street and Susa, after M. Lesy: *Wisconsin Death Trip*), St Paul, O'Shaughnessy Auditorium, 1 Nov 1975; rev. version, O'Shaughnessy Auditorium, 21 Feb 1981
The Love of Don Perlimplín (1, Susa and Street, after F. G. Lorca: *Amor de Don Perlimplín con Belisa en su jardín*), Purchase, NY, 2 Aug 1984

*

R. H. Kornick: *Recent American Opera: a Production Guide* (New York, 1991), 307–9
MARY LOU HUMPHREY

Susannah. Musical drama in two acts by CARLISLE FLOYD to his own libretto; Talahassee, Florida State University, 24 February 1955.

Floyd's libretto is based on the story of Susanna and the Elders from the biblical Apocrypha, transposed to the remote mountain village of New Hope Valley, Tennessee, in the 1950s. Susannah Polk (soprano), a pretty 19-year-old, has attracted the admiration of the Elders of the village church and the jealousy of their wives, as becomes clear during the opening square dance. Little Bat McLean (tenor), son of one of the Elders, sees Susannah home (Act 1 scene ii) but flees upon the arrival of her brother Sam (tenor), who brought her up after the death of their parents.

Because of their poverty the Polks are held in contempt by the villagers, who view Sam as a drunkard and Susannah as a wanton – at least potentially. When the four Elders come upon Susannah bathing in a creek near her home (Act 1 scene iii) they consider this a provocation on her part and when she goes to church that evening (Act 1 scene iv) she is snubbed by everyone there.

Little Bat, badgered by his parents into 'confessing' that Susannah has seduced him, salves his conscience by rushing to tell Susannah (Act 1 scene v). Sam, who has overheard, counsels patience, and before setting off on a trapping expedition the next morning (Act 2 scene i) urges her to show fortitude by attending the revival meeting to be led that evening by Olin Blitch (bass-baritone), an itinerant evangelist. Shocked by Susannah's rejection of his public call to repentance (Act 2 scene ii), Blitch visits her home (Act 2 scene iii) to counsel her in person. Though he does not believe her emotional denials of wrongdoing, he is attracted by her vulnerability and, emboldened by her reputation, makes advances to her. Although disgusted by the whole situation, Susannah allows him to stay the night.

The next morning (Act 2 scene iv) Blitch is stricken with remorse, because she had been a virgin. He attempts to repair Susannah's reputation among the villagers, but since he does not confess his own role, they are unmoved. When, upon Sam's return (Act 2 scene v), Susannah tells him of these events, he shoots Blitch dead. The townspeople come to drive Susannah away, but she warns them off with Sam's shotgun. She coaxes Little Bat back seductively, in order to slap his face; the curtain falls as he runs off.

Susannah was an immediate success at its New York première (September 1956) and has remained popular for its skilful and appropriate imitations of Appalachian square dances, revival hymns and folksongs.

ANDREW STILLER

Susannens Geheimnis. Opera by Ermanno Wolf-Ferrari; *see* SEGRETO DI SUSANNA, IL.

Süssmayr [Süssmayer], **Franz Xaver** [Dolcevillico, Francesco Saverio] (*b* Schwanenstadt, Upper Austria, 1766; *d* Vienna, 17 Sept 1803). Austrian composer. He studied music as a boy with his father, a teacher and choirmaster in Schwanenstadt. In 1779 he moved to the monastery school at Kremsmünster and later studied philosophy and law at the Ritterakademie there. While a student he participated in services at the cathedral as a singer, violinist and organist, and took composition lessons from local teachers. Beginning in or around 1785 he composed several operas that were performed in the monastery theatre. In the late 1780s he moved to Vienna where he taught music privately and performed in the Hofkapelle. He began studying composition with Mozart in 1790 or 1791, subsequently working for him as a copyist, almost certainly assisting him in composing the *secco* recitative for *La clemenza di Tito* and completing the Requiem at Constanze Mozart's request. After Mozart's death he studied with Salieri. Several of Süssmayr's first operatic projects in Vienna were undertaken for Schikaneder's Theater auf der Wieden; then, in 1792, he became harpsichordist and acting Kapellmeister for the Nationaltheater. Two years later, in May 1794, he was made Kapellmeister of the Viennese court's newly re-established National-Singspiel in the Kärntnertortheater. In 1798 Süssmayr applied to succeed Pierre Duttilou as court composer in Vienna but was not offered the post; he served as Kapellmeister of the National-Singspiel until his death, composing a series of German works for the national stage. He also wrote cantatas (for performance in Vienna and Kremsmünster) and other sacred and instrumental works.

Like many late 18th-century German composers, Süssmayr worked in a variety of operatic genres. He wrote a handful of Italian operas, both serious and comic, for theatres in Vienna and Prague. His German works range from modest Singspiels for Kremsmünster in the early north German vein to extravagant heroic-comic operas produced in Vienna. His most popular and best known work was *Der Spiegel von Arkadien* (1794), commissioned by Schikaneder, who wrote the libretto. Composed in the style of *Die Zauberflöte*, it features lyrical arias, folklike songs, lengthy finales and the musical depiction of ambitious scenic effects. In his *Eipeldauer Briefe* (1794), the writer Joseph Richter observed soon after the première that pieces from the opera were often sung and played in cafés and taverns around Vienna. Schikaneder and Süssmayr even filed an official protest against several Viennese music shops that were selling copies of the opera's most popular numbers without their permission. The opera's renown was not limited to Austria and south Germany; with the text revised by C. A. Vulpius, it ran successfully in many theatres in the north.

Among the works Süssmayr composed for the Kärntnertor, *Der Marktschreyer* (1799) and *Solimann der Zweite* (1799) enjoyed the most performances. The latter's success is reflected in Beethoven's set of piano variations (WoO76, 1799) on the terzetto 'Tändeln und scherzen'. Süssmayr, like most Viennese opera composers, used a wide range of national styles in his German works, including Italian *seria* and *buffa* idioms, French *comique* forms, popular German styles and melodrama. His melodic gift and formal craftsmanship show best in his solos, duets and trios; larger ensembles and choral numbers often lack intensity, with little of the contrapuntal and harmonic interest necessary to sustain long scenes. Süssmayr's fame as an opera composer faded quickly after his death, and only a few of his works found performances after the first decade of the 19th century.

See also SPIEGEL VON ARKADIEN, DER.

Die Liebe für den König, oder Karl Stuart (Spl, 5, G. Stephanie the younger and B. Planck), Kremsmünster, Stift, 25 April 1785, *A-KR*

Die Liebe auf dem Lande, *c*1785 (Spl, 3, C. F. Weisse), *Wgm*

Die Drillinge (Spl, R. Bonin and Planck), Kremsmünster, Stift, 19 Feb 1786

Der Bürgermeister (Spl, F. A. Brühl and Planck), Kremsmünster, Stift, 6 Aug 1786, *KR*

Die gar zu strenge Kinderzucht (Spl, F. X. Jann and Planck), Kremsmünster, Stift, 4 Feb 1787

Nicht mehr als sechs Schüsseln (Spl, B. Wallner, after F. W. Grossman), Kremsmünster, Stift, 10 June 1788

Die väterliche Rache (Spl, Jann and Planck), Kremsmünster, Stift, 1 July 1789

Der rauschige Hans, 1791 (Spl, M. Lindemayr), for Lambach, Stift, unperf.

Moses, oder Der Auszug aus Ägypten (grosse Oper, 2, 'von einem Theaterfreund'), Vienna, Wieden, 4 May 1792, *D-DS*

L'incanto superato (favola romanesca, 2, G. Bertati), Vienna, Burg, 8 July 1793, *A-Wn*, *H-Bn**; as Der besiegte Zauber, Prague, 1793

Piramo e Tisbe, *c*1793 (azione tragica, 2, M. Coltellini), inc., *Bn* (partly autograph)

Meister Schnaps, oder Er führt ihm's Mädchen selbst zu, ?1793 (Posse, 1), inc., *A-Wn*, *H-Bn**

Il turco in Italia [Il musulmano in Napoli] (ob, 2, C. Mazzolà), Prague, Landesständisches, 12 Feb 1794, *Bn**

Der Spiegel von Arkadien (heroisch-komische Oper, 2, E. Schikaneder), Vienna, Wieden, 14 Nov 1794, *A-Wn* (*R*1986: GOB, xvii), *D-Mbs*, *H-Bn**, vs (Vienna, 1795); rev. as Die neuen Arkadier (C. A. Vulpius), Weimar, Hof, 2 Feb 1796, *D-Bds*, vs (Mannheim, n.d.; Brunswick, n.d.)

Idris und Zenide (heroisch-komische Oper, 2, J. G. C. L. Gieseke, after C. M. Wieland), Vienna, Wieden, 9 May 1795

Die edle Rache (komische Oper, 2, F. X. Huber), Vienna, Kärntnertor, 27 Aug 1795, *A-Wn*, *D-Bds*, *H-Bn**

Die Freiwilligen (Gemälde der Zeit, 1, Stephanie), Vienna, Kärntnertor, 27 Sept 1796, *A-Wn*
Der Wildfang (komische Oper, 2, Huber, after H. von Kotzebue), Vienna, Kärntnertor, 4 Oct 1797, *Wn*, *D-Bds*, *Mbs*, *H-Bn**, *US-Wc*
Der Marktschreyer (Operette, 1, F. K. Lippert), Vienna, Kärntnertor, 6 July 1799, *A-Wgm*, *D-DS*, *H-Bn**, *US-Wc*, vs (Offenbach, n.d.)
Solimann der Zweite, oder Die drei Sultaninnen [Die Liebe im Serail] (Spl, 2, Huber, after C.-S. Favart), Vienna, Kärntnertor, 1 Oct 1799, *A-Wn*, *D-Bds*, *Dlb*, *DS*, *Mbs*, *H-Bn**, *US-Wc*, vs (Bonn, n.d.; Vienna, n.d.)
Gülnare, oder Die persische Sklavin (Spl, 1, Lippert, after B.-J. Marsollier), Vienna, Kärntnertor, 5 July 1800, *A-Wn*, *H-Bn**
Phasma, oder Die Erscheinung im Tempel der Verschwiegenheit (heroische Oper, 2), Vienna, Kärntnertor, 25 July 1801, *A-Wn*, *D-DS*, vs (Vienna, n.d.)
Das Hausgesinde, 1802 (Posse, 1), unperf., *H-Bn**
L'imbarazzo degli amanti (farsa, 1), unperf.
Gl'uccellatori (dg, after ? C. Goldoni), inc., *A-Wgm*, *Wn*, *H-Bn**
Alcidoro e Dalisa, o sia Gli amanti in Tempe, 1 scene *Bn**

Various pieces in Die Liebe macht kurzen Prozess, oder Die Heirat auf gewisse Art (1798); sections of unidentified operas and items for insertion into operas by other composers in *A-Wn*, *Wgm*, *H-Bn* (some autograph) [for details see Lehner and Kecskeméti]

Doubtful: List und Zufall (komische Oper, 2, M. Stegmayer), Vienna, An der Wien, 11 Jan 1806

W. Lehner: *Franz Xaver Süssmayr als Opernkomponist* (diss., U. of Vienna, 1927); extracts in *SMw*, xviii (1931), 66–96
C. Preiss: 'Franz Xaver Süssmayr (1766–1803)', *Heimatgaue*, xvii (1936), 21–33
O. E. Deutsch: *Das Freihaustheater auf der Wieden 1787–1801* (Vienna, 2/1937)
J. Winterberger: *Franz Xaver Süssmayr: Leben, Umwelt und Gestalt* (diss., U. of Innsbruck, 1946)
E. Komorzynski: *Emanuel Schikaneder: ein Beitrag zur Geschichte des deutschen Theaters* (Vienna, 1951)
A. Kellner: *Musikgeschichte des Stiftes Kremsmünster* (Kassel, 1956)
I. Kecskeméti: 'Süssmayr-Handschriften in der Nationalbibliothek Széchényi, Budapest', *SM*, ii (1962), 283–320; viii (1966), 297–377 [incl. thematic catalogue]
K. Marguerre: 'Mozart und Süssmayr', *MJb 1962–3*, 172–7
H. H. Hausner: *Franz Xaver Süssmayr* (Vienna, 1964) [review by O. E. Deutsch, *ÖMz*, xx (1965), 235–6]
W. Jerger: 'Mozarts Schüler und Mitarbeiter: zu Franz Xaver Süssmayrs 200. Geburtsjahr', *Acta mozartiana*, xiii (1966), 91–5
F. Giegling: 'Zu den Rezitativen von Mozarts Oper "Titus"', *MJb 1967*, 121–6
R. Angermüller: 'Süssmayr: ein Schüler und Freund Salieris', *Mitteilungen der Internationalen Stiftung Mozarteum*, xxi/1–2 (1973), 19–21

LINDA TYLER

Sutermeister, Heinrich (*b* Feuerthalen, 12 Aug 1910). Swiss composer. After preliminary studies in the humanities in Basle and Paris, he attended classes in musicology at Basle University in 1931. From 1932 to 1934 he was a pupil of Courvoisier, Röhr, Geierhaas, Pfitzner, Büchtger and Orff at the Munich Akademie der Tonkunst. He returned to Switzerland in 1934 and spent a year working as an opera coach at the Berne municipal theatre. Subsequently, he devoted himself to composition, settling at Vaux-sur-Morges on Lake Geneva in 1943. From 1963 to 1975, he directed a composition class at the Hanover Hochschule für Musik and in 1977 was elected a member of the Bavarian Academy of Arts.

Sutermeister's interest in opera was stimulated by three formative influences: a passionate enthusiasm for Debussy's *Pelléas et Mélisande*, a belief in the elemental power of Verdi's late operas and a strong admiration for the melodic and primeval simplicity of the music of his teacher Orff. He consciously rejected the complex modernistic devices adopted by some of his contemporaries, in favour of a more spontaneous diatonicism. In this respect he may be compared with Britten, Menotti and von Einem, all of whom sought to write theatre works that attracted the widest audience. Although his first opera, *Die schwarze Spinne* (composed in 1935), was initially conceived for the radio, it already demonstrates considerable evidence of a natural dramatic talent, particularly in its colourful choral writing. This potential was fully realized in *Romeo und Julia* (1938–40), which remains one of his best-known compositions. It received its highly successful première (13 April 1940) at the Dresden Opera, under Karl Böhm with Maria Cebotari in the role of Juliet. The opera is notable for the freshness of its melodic invention, and its unbridled romanticism struck a particular resonance during the war-ravaged period of the 1940s. Indeed, within a few years the opera had been heard in more than 20 different theatres. Its instant popularity secured for the composer a further commission from Dresden. However, this new work, *Die Zauberinsel* (1939–42), also based on Shakespeare (*The Tempest*), failed to make such an impact. Whereas in *Romeo und Julia* the skilled handling of theatrical effects, such as the use of offstage voices to intensify the atmosphere of the love duet, seem entirely in keeping with the spirit of the drama, in *Die Zauberinsel* such devices have become mere mannerism. Moreover, the musical substance is less convincing.

Despite the relative failure of *Die Zauberinsel*, Sutermeister was determined not to repeat the musical formulae he had so successfully exploited in *Romeo und Julia*. After the war, he continued to set himself specific challenges by tackling a wide variety of subjects in very different ways. *Niobe* (1943–5), with a libretto by the composer's brother, follows the example of some of Orff's scenic cantatas in combining elements of song and dance. In this monodrama, a solitary singer is surrounded on stage by a group of dancers, as well as a large-scale chorus. *Raskolnikoff* (1945–7), based on Dostoyevsky's novel *Crime and Punishment*, uses two separated orchestras to represent the division of the inner and the outer world. In *Der rote Stiefel* (1949–51), the composer dispensed with a chorus but introduced an offstage vocal quartet, a speaker and a dancer. All these works achieved temporary popularity, but they quickly disappeared from the repertory in the wake of the more experimental musical styles increasingly favoured during the late 1950s. Indeed, many of the composer's later works were received with less enthusiasm: *Titus Feuerfuchs* (1956–8) was criticized for understating Nestroy's biting satire, while sentimentality seemed to reduce the effectiveness of *Madame Bovary* (1967), an adaptation of Flaubert's novel that concentrates almost exclusively on the psychological portrayal of the main character. On the other hand, the composer found television opera to be extremely conducive to his dramatic talents. Thus *Seraphine* (1959) and *Das Gespenst von Canterville* (1962–3) both reached a wide and appreciative audience.

In the 1980s Sutermeister returned to conventional opera with *Le roi Bérenger* (1981–3). This composition marks a departure in that the libretto is based, for the first time, on the work of a contemporary dramatist, in this case Ionesco. The opera's central theme of fear and readiness for death is treated in a modest, almost unassuming manner. Although the composer readily matches Ionesco's surrealistic flights of fancy by writing music that is almost reminiscent of Les Six, the overall impression is one of noble restraint and economy of means.

See also ROMEO UND JULIA.

Die schwarze Spinne (radio op, 1, A. Rösler, after J. Gotthelf), Radio Beromünster, 15 Oct 1936; rev. for stage, 1948, St Gall, 2 March 1949, vs (Mainz, 1949)
Romeo und Julia (2, Sutermeister, after W. Shakespeare), Dresden, Staatsoper, 13 April 1940, vs (Mainz, 1940)
Die Zauberinsel (2, Sutermeister, after Shakespeare), Dresden, Staatsoper, 30 Oct 1942, vs (Mainz, 1942)
Niobe (monodrama, 2, P. Sutermeister), Zürich, 22 June 1946 (Mainz, 1946)
Raskolnikoff (2, P. Sutermeister, after F. Dostoyevsky), Stockholm, 14 Oct 1948, vs (Mainz, 1948)
Fingerhütchen (radio ballad, 1, Sutermeister, after C. F. Meyer), Berlin, 12 Feb 1950; stage, St Gall, 26 April 1950
Die Füsse im Feuer (radio ballad, 1, Sutermeister, after Meyer), Berlin, 12 Feb 1950
Der rote Stiefel (2, Sutermeister, after W. Hauff), Stockholm, 22 Nov 1951, vs (Mainz, 1951)
Titus Feuerfuchs, oder Liebe, Tücke und Perücke (2, Sutermeister, after J. N. Nestroy: *Der Talisman*), Basle, 14 April 1958, vs (Mainz, 1958)
Seraphine [Die stümme Apothekerin] (television op, 1, Sutermeister, after F. Rabelais), Swiss Television, 10 June 1959; stage, Munich, Cuvilliés, 25 Feb 1960, vs (Mainz, 1959)
Das Gespenst von Canterville, 1962–3 (television op, 1, Sutermeister, after O. Wilde), ZDF, 6 Sept 1964
Madame Bovary (2, Sutermeister, after G. Flaubert), Zürich, 26 May 1967, vs (Mainz, 1969)
Das Flaschenteufel (television op, R. K. Weibel, after R. L. Stevenson), ZDF, 1971
Le roi Bérenger (prol. and 18 scenes, Sutermeister, after E. Ionesco), Munich, 22 July 1985 (Mainz, 1985)

*

G. Hausswald: 'Heinrich Sutermeister: Leben, Werk, Persönlichkeit', *ZfM*, Jg.109 (1942), 433–6
H. Sutermeister: 'Essentials of Opera', *Music*, ii/4 (1953), 9–10
H. Lindlar: 'Heinrich Sutermeister', *Musik der Zeit* (1955), no.10, pp.44–5
P. Mieg: 'Heinrich Sutermeister', *40 Schweizer Komponisten der Gegenwart* (Amriswil, 1956)
H. Ehinger: 'Heinrich Sutermeisters neue Oper "Titus Feuerfuchs" ', *SMz*, xcviii (1958), 203–4
A. Briner: 'Heinrich Sutermeisters "Madame Bovary" ', *SMz*, cvii (1967), 223–5
D. Larese: *Heinrich Sutermeister* (Amriswil, 1972)
G. Birkner: *Heinrich Sutermeister: der Weg des Bühnenkomponisten* (Zürich, 1985) ERIK LEVI

Suthaus, (Heinrich) Ludwig (*b* Cologne, 12 Dec 1906; *d* Berlin, 7 Sept 1971). German tenor. He studied in Cologne and made his début at Aachen in 1928 as Walther. Engagements followed at Essen (1931–3), Stuttgart (1933–41), the Berlin Staatsoper (1941–8) and then the Berlin Städtische (later Deutsche) Oper (to 1965). He first sang at Bayreuth in 1943 as Walther, returning in 1944 in the same role and in 1956–7 as Loge and Siegmund. He sang Tristan at Covent Garden in 1953, the year of his American début as Aegisthus (*Elektra*) at San Francisco, where he also sang Tristan, Siegmund and Erik. At Vienna, where he appeared from 1948 until shortly before his death, his roles included Florestan, Otello and Hermann (*The Queen of Spades*). In 1949 he sang the Emperor in *Die Frau ohne Schatten* at the Teatro Colón and the next year sang Števa Buryja in the first South American production of *Jenůfa*. His large repertory also included Rienzi, Bacchus, Pedro (*Tiefland*), Samson, the title role in *Sadko*, which he sang at the German première in Berlin (1947), and the Drum Major (*Wozzeck*). Suthaus appeared at La Scala as Siegfried (*Götterdämmerung*) in 1954 and Siegmund in 1958. His voice, baritonal in quality, was of true Heldentenor proportions. HAROLD ROSENTHAL/R

Joan Sutherland in the title role of Handel's 'Alcina'

Sutherland, Dame **Joan** (*b* Sydney, 7 Nov 1926). Australian soprano. Her mother taught her until she was 19 when she trained formally in Sydney with John and Aida Dickens. She sang in concerts, oratorios and broadcasts throughout Australia and in August 1947 made a significant concert début in Sydney as Purcell's Dido. In 1951 she sang the title role in the world première of Eugene Goossens's *Judith* at the Sydney Conservatorium. The same year, having won Australia's most prestigious vocal competition, she went to London and studied with Clive Carey at the Opera School of the RCM. She then joined the Covent Garden company where she made her début on 28 October 1952, as the First Lady in *Die Zauberflöte*.

At Covent Garden, Sutherland sang a diversity of roles including Amelia (*Un ballo in maschera*), Aida, Frasquita and Micaëla (*Carmen*), several roles in the *Ring* cycle, Agathe, the soprano roles in *Les contes d'Hoffmann* and Eva. She created the role of Jenifer in Tippett's *A Midsummer Marriage* (1955) and sang Lidoine in the British première of Poulenc's *Dialogues des Carmélites* (1958). In 1956 she made her Glyndebourne début as Countess Almaviva in *Figaro*.

Her greatest talent, developed and encouraged by RICHARD BONYNGE, whom she married in 1954, lay in Italian bel canto opera of the 18th and 19th centuries. She was an outstanding Alcina for the Handel Opera Society in 1957 and in that year sang for the first time Gilda and Desdemona. In 1958 she made her international début as Donna Anna at the Vancouver Festival. But international recognition of her full vocal stature came with her appearance at Covent Garden, on 17 February 1959, in the title role of *Lucia di*

Lammermoor, produced by Zeffirelli. In Venice, after a performance of *Alcina*, she was hailed as La Stupenda, and it was in that role that she made her American début, in Dallas, on 16 November 1960. Her débuts as Lucia at the Paris Opéra (25 April 1960), La Scala (14 May 1961) and the Metropolitan (26 November 1961) were all highly acclaimed. In 1965 she took her own company to Australia, with Bonynge as musical director.

With a phenomenally beautiful voice of great range, power and flexibility, Sutherland could deliver fiendishly difficult coloratura with exceptional agility, clarity and mellifluous warmth. She had a vocal range from *g* to *e‴*, and was blessed with an exquisitely even trill. On the debit side, she was frequently criticized for swallowing the vowels and blurring the consonants.

As a leading exponent of bel canto Sutherland enjoyed huge success in all the major international opera houses, extending her repertory to include the Bellini roles of Amina and Elvira (both 1960), Beatrice di Tenda (1961) and Norma (1963), and reviving Rossini's *Semiramide* (1962) and Donizetti's *La fille du régiment* (1966, in which her spirited performance was long admired), *Maria Stuarda* (1971), *Lucrezia Borgia* (1972) and *Anna Bolena* (1984). Her lively championship of the early 19th-century Italian repertory did much to bring it back into favour. To her Verdi roles she added Violetta (1960), Leonora in *Il trovatore* (1975) and Amalia in *I masnadieri* (1980). She was an accomplished Handelian (Cleopatra in *Giulio Cesare* was one of her outstanding roles) and also distinguished herself in the French repertory with Marguerite de Valois in Meyerbeer's *Les Huguenots* (1962), Marguerite in *Faust* (1965), Delibes' *Lakmé* (1967) and Massenet's *Esclarmonde* (1974). Outside her normal repertory she was highly successful as Puccini's *Suor Angelica* and recorded an excellent *Turandot*.

Sutherland's concert and recital repertory is extensive and there is a vast catalogue of recorded work, including a notable two-disc set 'The Art of the Prima Donna'. In 1979 she was made a DBE. She gave her final performances in 1990 (when her farewell performance, in Sydney, was as Marguerite de Valois) and in 1991 was appointed a member of the Order of Merit.

For further illustration *see* MIDSUMMER MARRIAGE, THE.

R. Braddon: *Joan Sutherland* (London, 1962)
E. Greenfield: *Joan Sutherland* (London, 1972) [with discography]
J. B. Steane: *The Grand Tradition* (London, 1975), 383ff
B. Adams: *La Stupenda* (Hutchinson, Australia, 1980)
N. Major: *Joan Sutherland* (London, 1987) [with discography and catalogue of performances]
R. Christiansen: 'Sutherland: a Wonderful Innings', *Opera*, xli (1990), 1284–8
NORMA MAJOR

Sutherland, Margaret (Ada) (*b* Adelaide, 20 Nov 1897; *d* Melbourne, 12 Aug 1984). Australian composer. She studied the piano and composition at the conservatories in Melbourne, where her teachers included Fritz Hart. She continued her studies in Vienna and London between 1923 and 1925, then returned to Australia, where she gave recitals, taught and composed. *The Young Kabbarli*, a one-act chamber opera, was Sutherland's only theatre work. Written in 1964, it was first performed at the Festival of Contemporary Opera and Music in Hobart on 19 August 1965 and published in Sydney in 1972. The libretto, by Maie Casey, is based on the life of Daisy Bates (1863–1951), who devoted herself to the welfare of aborigines in Western and South Australia and was called by them 'Kabbarli' ('grandmother'). In *The Young Kabbarli* the sharply contrasting aboriginal and European cultures are underlined by such diverse musical material as the sounds of the didjeridu, Irish folk melody and vocal passages which recall the tumbling strains of aboriginal song. Sutherland's writing for the orchestra is effective if uncomplicated and reflects her long experience of the composition and performance of chamber music.

R. Covell: *Australia's Music: Themes of a New Society* (Melbourne, 1967)
A. McCredie: *Musical Composition in Australia* (Canberra, 1969)
J. Murdoch: *Australian Composers* (Melbourne, 1972)
LAUGHTON HARRIS

Švanda the Bagpiper [*Švanda dudák* ('Schwanda the Bagpiper')]. Opera in two acts by JAROMÍR WEINBERGER to a libretto by Miloš Kareš after an old Czech children's story; Prague, National Theatre, 27 April 1927.

The robber Babinski (tenor), hiding from foresters, is welcomed at the farmhouse of Švanda the Bagpiper (baritone) and his wife Dorota (soprano). Švanda agrees to go with Babinski to see a sad Queen (mezzo-soprano) in order to bring her happiness, see the world and become wealthy. Act 1 scene ii shows the Queen, who is in the power of an evil Magician (bass), in her palace. When Švanda arrives and starts to play the (now famous) polka on his bagpipes, she becomes happy and falls in love with him; she proposes marriage and Švanda, forgetting Dorota, accepts and kisses her. Dorota and the Magician then appear and challenge the Queen. The Queen is furious and orders Švanda to stand trial. In scene iii Švanda, awaiting execution, asks for his bagpipes as a last request, but they cannot be found. In the nick of time Babinski transforms the executioner's blade into a broom and returns Švanda's bagpipes to him; he then unlocks the gate, through which the people dance to Švanda's playing. Asked by Dorota about his relationship with the Queen, Švanda says that if he has ever kissed her, he will go to hell – and thereupon disappears amid flashes of lightning. Babinski promises Dorota that he will bring him back.

Act 2 scene i takes place in hell. The Devil (bass) orders Švanda to play, and when he refuses he takes up the bagpipes himself. He then tricks Švanda into signing away his soul to him. Babinski, however, comes to the rescue and gains Švanda's soul by beating the Devil in a game of cards. In scene ii Švanda has returned home. Babinski, wanting Dorota for himself, tells him that she is now an old woman, but as soon as she appears the couple are joyfully reunited.

Švanda the Bagpiper is the most widely known Czech opera after Smetana's *Bartered Bride* and is Weinberger's most famous work. By 1990 it had received more than 4000 performances in more than 20 languages, and the polka (Act 1) and fugue (Act 2) are staples of the light orchestral repertory. Weinberger's use of such national symbols as a bagpiper, a polka and songs in folk style (notably 'Na tom našem dvoře'), although nostalgic, is highly effective, and the music also shows his gifts for brilliant orchestration and fluent counterpoint. J. POLACEK

Svanholm, Set (Karl Viktor) (*b* Västerås, 2 Sept 1904; *d* Saltsjö-Duvnäs, nr Stockholm, 4 Oct 1964). Swedish tenor. At first a church organist and singer, in 1929 he became a pupil of John Forsell at the Stockholm Conservatory opera school. In 1930 he had made his début with the Swedish Royal Opera in the baritone roles of Silvio and Rossini's Figaro, and in 1937 he was engaged by the company. In 1936 he had made his tenor début as Radames, and he subsequently took on such heavy tenor parts as Otello, Siegmund, Parsifal and Tristan. He sang at Salzburg and Vienna (1938), Berlin, Budapest and Milan (1941–2) and Bayreuth (1942). In Sweden his repertory included Manrico, Canio, Florestan, Bacchus, Idomeneus, Tristan and the *Ring* tenor roles; in 1946 he sang Peter Grimes in the Swedish première of Britten's opera. In the same year he visited North and South America, singing Siegfried at the Metropolitan. At Covent Garden he sang regularly from 1948 to 1957. He was always reliable, and though his voice had neither the warmth nor the splendour to match that of Flagstad (with whom he often sang), his performances were admired for intelligence, musicianship and stamina. He was director of the Swedish Royal Opera, 1956–63, introducing several contemporary operas, among them *The Turn of the Screw*, *Mathis der Maler* and *The Rake's Progress*.

H. Rosenthal: 'Set Svanholm', *Opera*, vi (1955), 357–62
B. Hagman: 'Porträtt av operachef', *Musikrevy*, xii (1957), 253
H. Rosenthal: *Great Singers of Today* (London, 1966)

CARL L. BRUUN/R

Švara, Danilo (*b* Ricmanje, nr Trieste, 2 April 1902; *d* Ljubljana, 24 April 1981). Slovene composer. While at the Handelshochschule, Vienna, he studied the piano privately (1920–22). He completed studies in politics and law at Frankfurt University (1922–5), at the same time studying the piano, and conducting with Scherchen. After a period as répétiteur and conductor at the Ljubljana Opera (1925–7), he attended the Hoch Conservatory, Frankfurt (1927–30), as a composition pupil of Szekles, and also studied conducting and stage direction. He was then active as a conductor (he was director of the Ljubljana Opera, 1957–9) and a music critic, and taught conducting at the music academy in Ljubljana.

Švara reworked his first opera *Kleopatra* (composed 1937) before its première in 1940, reducing the sharpness of the dissonances and atonality in order to make it more appealing to audiences. *Veronika Deseniška* (1946), a neo-Romantic work, represents the composer at his best, and in *Slovo od mladosti* (1954), he drew even more heavily on local folklore to create a kind of 'national Romanticism'. By the end of the 1960s, Švara was once again employing expressionist atonality and 12-note technique (as in *Ocean*), but in the 1970s he returned to a more moderate style for the children's opera *Štirje junaki* ('The Four Heroes'; 1974).

Kleopatra, 1937 (2, Švara), Ljubljana, 11 May 1940
Veronika Deseniška, 1941–5 (4, Švara, after O. Župančič and J. E. Tomić), Ljubljana, 29 Dec 1946
Slovo od mladosti [Farewell to Youth], 1952 (3, L. Prennerjeva), Ljubljana, 23 May 1954
Ocean (5, Švara, after L. Andreyev), Ljubljana, 3 March 1969
Štirje junaki [The Four Heroes] (children's op, 2, Švara, after J. L. Grimm and W. C. Grimm), Maribor, 22 Dec 1974

ANDREJ RIJAVEC

Svätopluk. Opera in three acts by EUGEN SUCHOŇ to a libretto by the composer, Ivan Stodola and Jela Krčméry-Vrteľová after Stodola's tragedy *Kráľ Svätopluk* ('King Svätopluk'); Bratislava, Slovak National Opera, 10 March 1960.

In the first act King Svätopluk (bass), approaching the end of his reign, instals two of his sons, the philanthropic Mojmír (baritone) and the power-seeking Svätopluk the younger (tenor), as rulers, but their conflicting ideologies make union impossible. Záboj (tenor), the court scribe and minstrel, unguardedly reveals military plans to Lutomíra (soprano), whom he loves and who is plotting to secure the throne for her father, the leader of an enemy army.

Act 2 is set in a pagan sacrificial grove at Zemlin. Svätopluk the younger interrupts the sacrifice of a young woman and consults the oracle, which tells him that to further his ambitions he must kill his father or die. Mojmír and his troops rout the pagans, release their victim and destroy the temple. Lutomíra resolves to ruin Mojmír and the whole dynasty.

In Act 3, in a military camp, Mojmír is imprisoned, through Lutomíra's false testimony, on a charge of plotting to murder his father; Svätopluk the younger is caught when about to assassinate the king, who hands him over to the guards in despair. Záboj discovers Lutomíra's treachery and kills her as she is signalling to her father's troops. The king, in a vision, sees the bloody path he has followed culminating in the execution of Mojmír and Svätopluk. At the instigation of his third son, the exiled monk Predslav (tenor), he frees his other sons with the plea that they rule in harmony. Svätopluk the younger, however, refuses to share power and attacks Mojmír; their father, cursing them, falls unconscious and dies. Svätopluk flees and Mojmír becomes king. Záboj is left hoping for the future freedom of his people.

Svätopluk deals with actual events in 9th-century Great Moravia at the dawn of Slovak history, and the libretto draws on other literary, historical and archaeological sources besides Stodola's play. The characters in the opera are drawn in more detail and with greater historical accuracy than in Stodola's drama, so that the development is more direct and the general effect more monumental. Characters of limited psychological growth are represented by musical ideas that remain undeveloped, while the dynamic characters appear in several musical guises.

Suchoň attempted in *Svätopluk* to re-create the atmosphere of the period through careful study of early European musical styles: he incorporated elements of Teutonic music into the ceremonial singing of the chorus of Franks in Act 1; traces of Byzantine music can be heard at Mojmír's entrances and in Svätopluk's duet with his son Predslav; pentatonicism and Old Slavonic inflections appearance in Záboj's music; and Old Slavonic elements are also dominant in Act 2, where the atmosphere of the pagan sacrifical site is suggested by a scale consisting of alternating minor and augmented 2nds.

The music acquires its national character from an individual language distilled from folk music. The pagan incantations, ceremonial chants and dances are not original folk melodies but stem from ancient prototypes. Harmonically, precedence is given to expressiveness, with chords based on 5ths in exposed passages and unaccompanied wind recitatives at key points in the action. Harsh dissonances are reserved for special effect. Suchoň uses characteristic harmonic progressions as his main building-blocks, often constructing extended passages around one chord or the alternation of several chords, favouring full sonority and colour. The structure is akin to that of an enormous fugue; Act 1 is a palindrome, Act 2 a rondo, Act 3 a concisely constructed free form in which the musical ideas of the first two acts are repeated. In general, *Svätopluk* consists of organically connected numbers which together form a monumental musico-dramatic epic. IGOR VAJDA

Svéd, Sándor [Sved, Alexander] (*b* Budapest, 28 May 1904; *d* Vienna, 9 June 1979). Hungarian baritone. He studied in Budapest and later in Italy with, among others, Mario Sammarco and Riccardo Stracciari, making his Budapest début in 1928 as Count di Luna. In 1936 he first appeared at the Vienna Staatsoper and at Covent Garden, and in 1938 at La Scala as Macbeth – the first of several Milan roles that included Germont, Prince Igor, William Tell and Amfortas. After his Metropolitan début in 1940 as Anckarstroem (Renato), he sang there regularly (as Alexander Sved) until his return to Hungary in 1950, when he rejoined the Budapest Opera. From 1956 he taught in Stuttgart. Sved was a somewhat stiff actor, but he had a fine technique, ample power, and an italianate, velvety beauty of tone. He was best suited to the Italian lyric repertory but capable of other, more dramatic roles such as Rigoletto, as well as Don Giovanni, Sachs and Telramund.

GV (L. Riemens; R. Vegeto) PÉTER P. VÁRNAI

Sveinsson, Atli Heimir (*b* Reykjavík, 21 Sept 1938). Icelandic composer. He studied the piano at the Reykjavík College of Music with Rögnvaldur Sigurjónsson and composition with Günter Raphael, Rudolf Petzold and Bernd Alois Zimmerman at the Cologne Hochschule für Musik (1959–62). He encountered Stockhausen and Pousseur at Darmstadt and took a course in electronic music with Gottfried Koenig at Bilthoven in 1964. He was president of the Icelandic Composers' Society (1972–83) and has taught at the Reykjavík College of Music.

A prolific composer of orchestral, chamber and secular vocal music, with a deep sense of Icelandic tradition, Sveinsson's eclecticism often brings the bizarre and the romantic into collision. His first opera, *Silkitromman* ('The Silken Drum', 1982), to a tragi-comic libretto by Örnolfur Arnason after a 14th-century Japanese noh play, uses film, slides and tape to enhance its oriental lyricism. Its success encouraged him to write a pop-style musical, *Land míns födur* ('My Father's Country', 1985). In the television opera *Vikivaki* (1990), adapted from the surrealist novel by Gunnar Gunnarsson, ghosts of the Sagas clash with modernity in a lush, neo-Romantic score. It was the first Nordic co-production of its kind and was broadcast throughout Scandinavia.

MARTIN DREYER

Sverdlovsk. YEKATERINBURG.

Svetlanov, Yevgeny Fyodorovich (*b* Moscow, 6 Sept 1928). Russian conductor. He studied at the Gnesin Institute and with Shaporin and Alexander Gauk at the Moscow Conservatory, making his conducting début with the All-Union Radio in 1953 while still a student. From 1955 he worked at the Bol'shoy Theatre, where he became principal conductor (1962–4). His repertory includes many of Rimsky-Korsakov's operas and Dargomïzhsky's *Rusalka*, as well as Borodin and Tchaikovsky, and while at the Bol'shoy he added contemporary operas such as Shchedrin's *Ne tol'ko lyubov'* ('Not for Love Alone', 1961). He conducted the Bol'shoy Opera at La Scala, Milan, in 1964. In 1965 he was appointed principal conductor of the USSR State SO, but he has also toured widely, occasionally conducting opera, such as *Boris Godunov* at Covent Garden in 1984. He continued working at the Bol'shoy Theatre where, in 1988, he conducted the first production there for more than 60 years of Rimsky-Korsakov's *The Golden Cockerel*. He was named People's Artist of the USSR in 1968, and received the Lenin Prize in 1972 and the Glinka Prize in 1975.

I. M. YAMPOL'SKY/NOËL GOODWIN

Svetlev, Michail [Michel] (*b* Sofia, 6 March 1943). Bulgarian tenor. He studied in Sofia and made his début in 1971 at Passau as Manrico. He has sung in Sofia, Vienna, Hamburg, Berlin, Munich, Stuttgart and La Scala, Milan (1979). He made his American début as Riccardo (*Un ballo in maschera*) in Washington, DC (1980), and his Covent Garden début in 1983 as Grigory (*Boris Godunov*). His repertory ranges from Lensky, Hermann (*The Queen of Spades*) and Lïkov (*The Tsar's Bride*) to Gabriele Adorno, Radames, Chénier, Turiddu, Cavaradossi and many other Italian roles. With a powerful, keenly focussed voice, he is an exciting, committed performer. ELIZABETH FORBES

Svoboda, Josef (*b* Časlav, 10 May 1920). Czech stage designer. He was apprenticed in his father's profession of cabinet maker before studying (1941–3) to be an interior architect. It was through his hobby, painting, that he became interested in stage design. His first work was for an amateur group in Časlav (1942), after which he did designs for the Novy Soubor ('New Group'), of which he was a founder member, in Prague (1943–4). After World War II he studied architecture in Prague (1945–50), also taking over in 1945 the direction of design at the Grand Opera of 5 May, which became the Smetana Theatre in 1948. He was appointed chief designer and technical director of the National Theatre in 1951 and exercised a decisive influence on the development of Czech music theatre. His work outside Czechoslovakia from the late 1950s also considerably affected international opera.

Influenced by the architecturally plastic quality of Czech stage design in the 1930s and 40s and by the ideas of Appia and Craig, Svoboda developed the concept of a 'psycho-plastic stage' whose basic elements of space, time, rhythm and light combine to form a dynamic continuum, allowing for the development of the music drama as a homogeneous kinetic process. The emancipatory experiences of cubo-futurism, constructivism and the Bauhaus are assimilated but largely reinterpreted in a symbolist way, concentrating on the 'inner' (or 'immanent') meaning of the work and the psychology of action (e.g. the dualism of the towers in *Il trovatore*; 1966, Berlin). Svoboda's revival of the constructivist concept of the unity of art and technique campaigning 'for a theatre that truly reflects its age and its scientific spirit' opened new formal horizons to contemporary stage art: the dynamics of the visual processes are not left to stage machinery but are based on a mechanics of transformation, specially designed, and in particular the use of modern lighting techniques. Svoboda made inspired use of such effects as low-voltage light walls dividing up the stage area (*Les vêpres siciliennes*; 1969, Hamburg) or laser beams and holo-

Scene from the 1969 Hamburg production of Verdi's 'Les vêpres siciliennes', directed by John Dexter, with sets by Josef Svoboda

grams (*Die Zauberflöte*; 1970, Munich). In particular, he developed a superb projection technique, involving a complex system of colour projections which sometimes combine to animate a mobile plastic framework (*Oberon*; 1968, Munich, directed by Rudolf Hartmann) or with a transparent cyclorama, hangings, mirrors and lenses (the *Ring*; 1974–6, Covent Garden), which themselves form the variable stage area. From the combinations of slide and film projections based on collage, new forms were devised which have been used in such operas as Nono's *Intolleranza 1960* (1961, Venice; with a third medium, television, 1965, Boston) and Zimmermann's *Die Soldaten* (1969, Munich). There are formal similarities, especially in the montage technique, to the epic, distancing theatre of Piscator and Brecht. But in opposition to this, Svoboda's 'psycho-plastic' stage art is a suggestive and subjective one that seeks to lead on the spectator's imagination, vivifying 'the theatre's traditionally evocative, inherently metaphoric power' (Burian 1971).

Svoboda's career has been particularly associated with that of Václav Kašlík, the première of whose *Zbojnická balada* ('The Brigand's Ballad') he designed in 1948 for Prague, restaging it in 1986. As well as collaborating with Kašlík on numerous productions (*Die Frau ohne Schatten*, 1967; *Pelléas et Mélisande*, 1969; and *Nabucco*, 1972, all at Covent Garden; and *Idomeneo*, 1981, Ottawa), he designed the first production of Kašlík's opera *La strada* (1982, Prague). Svoboda was responsible for the opening production, *Libuše*, of the refurbished National Theatre in Prague in 1983. Although his 'trademark' staircase began to seem a formula, few other stage designers have had such a consistently influential appeal. The productions he has designed include several that have transferred from one house to another, for instance *Les vêpres siciliennes*, originally mounted in Hamburg in 1969, directed by John Dexter, which went on to the Paris Opéra and the Metropolitan in the mid-1970s and the ENO in 1984. Other notable productions include *From the House of the Dead* (1978, Zürich), *Wozzeck* (1981, Hamburg), Fibich's *Nevěsta messinská* ('The Bride of Messina'; 1985, Prague), Verdi's *Macbeth* (1985, Zürich) and *Elektra* (1986, Bonn).

For further illustration *see* INTOLLERANZA 1960; PRODUCTION, fig.23; and STAGE DESIGN, fig.26.

See also STAGE DESIGN, §7.

selective list of writings

'Nouveaux éléments en scénographie', *Le théâtre en Tchechoslovaquie: scénographie*, ed. V. Jindra (Prague, 1962), 58
'Designing for the Stage', *Opera*, xviii (1967), 631–6 [interview]
'Szenographie als Teil der Aufführung', *Bühnentechnische Rundschau*, lxii/6 (1968), 11–13

*

J. Grossman: 'Josef Svoboda', *Le théâtre en Tchechoslovaquie: scénographie*, ed. V. Jindra (Prague, 1962), 45ff
V. Jindra: *Who is Josef Svoboda?* (Prague, 1968)
Josef Svoboda: Bühnenbilder und Szenographien: eine Ausstellung des Theaterinstituts in Prag und der Akademie der Künste vom 6. September bis 12. Oktober 1969 (Berlin, 1969) [exhibition catalogue; incl. list of productions]
D. Bablet: *La scena e l'immagine: saggio su Josef Svoboda* (Turin, 1970)
——: *Josef Svoboda* (Prague, 1970) [in Eng.]
J. M. Burian: 'Josef Svoboda: Theatre Artist in an Age of Science', *Educational Theatre Journal*, xxii (1970), 123–45
——: *The Scenography of Josef Svoboda* (Middletown, CT, 1971) [incl. list of productions]
D. Mack: *Der Bayreuther Inszenierungsstil (1876–1976)* (Munich, 1976)
J. M. Burian: *Svoboda, Wagner: Josef Svoboda's Scenography for Richard Wagner's Operas* (Middletown, CT, 1983)
G. Friedrich: *Wagner Regie* (Zürich, 1983)

MANFRED BOETZKES

Swarowsky, Hans (*b* Budapest, 16 Sept 1899; *d* Salzburg, 10 Sept 1975). Austrian conductor. He studied theory with Schoenberg (from 1920) and Webern (until 1927), and conducting with Weingartner and Richard Strauss. He held appointments at the opera houses of Stuttgart, Hamburg and Berlin, but was not allowed to conduct in Germany between 1936 and 1944, and so turned to opera management (Munich,

Salzburg Festival), and sometimes worked abroad (Zürich Opera, 1937–40). In addition to making frequent guest appearances he was director of the opera house in Graz from 1948 to 1950, and in 1957 Karajan, who had recently become director of the Vienna Staatsoper, appointed him permanent conductor there. Swarowsky's interpretations, particularly in Classical works, always followed the score faithfully, an approach that he advocated in his teaching (he became director of the conducting class at the Vienna Academy of Music in 1946) and in his articles. Abbado and Mehta were among his students. A strong advocate of the works of Schoenberg, Berg and Webern, he had close links with Richard Strauss, who called him his 'secret associate' on the libretto of *Capriccio*. Swarowsky also made German translations of operas by Monteverdi, Gluck, Haydn, Verdi and Puccini; his collected writings, *Wahrung der Gestalt*, edited by M. Huss, were published in Vienna in 1979.

RUDOLF KLEIN

Swarthout, Gladys (*b* Deepwater, MO, 25 Dec 1900; *d* Florence, 7 July 1969). American contralto. She studied singing in Chicago, making her operatic début there in 1924 as the Shepherd-boy in *Tosca*; the following year she sang Carmen at Ravinia. Her début role at the Metropolitan was La Cieca (*La Gioconda*, 1929); she performed there regularly until 1945, as Siébel, Preziosilla, Adalgisa and – her most famous roles – Mignon and Carmen. She also sang in the première of Hanson's *Merry Mount* (1934). After 1954 she retired to Florence. Swarthout had a fine, well-placed voice which was admirably but not very imaginatively used. On stage, her presence was beautiful yet often placid, hampered by lack of genuine temperament. Her autobiography, *Come Soon, Tomorrow* was published in New York in 1945. MAX DE SCHAUENSEE/R

Sweden (Swed. Sverige). The first traces of operatic activity date from the mid-17th century, with the arrival in Stockholm of Vincenzo Albrici's Italian troupe (1652). The troupe was employed by Queen Christina; among its 18 members were two brothers from the famous Pistoian family, Domenico and Nicola Melani, both castratos. It is not certain that they performed complete operas; it is more likely that madrigal comedies and cantatas were sung, but pieces or scenes from operas may have been given. After Christina's abdication in 1654 the troupe was disbanded, and during Charles XI's reign the cultural life of Sweden lay fallow. Some attempts were made to produce pastoral dramas with musical elements, such as Johans Celsius's *Orpheus och Eurydice* in the 1680s, but it was not until Nicodemus Tessin contracted Claude de Rosidor's French troupe in 1699 – originally a theatre company with dancers and musicians – that the first steps towards Swedish opera were taken. To celebrate Charles XII's victory over the Russians at Narva in 1701, a member of the ensemble, Charles Louis Sevigny, was commissioned to write a text to which Anders von Düben the younger wrote the music. Düben belonged to an important German musical family that had come to Sweden at the invitation of Gustavus II Adolphus, Queen Christina's father, in about 1620. His *Ballet meslé de chants héroïques* was after French models, and is an interesting example of contemporary musical taste and culture. Because of the constant wars, political expansionism and the disbanding of Rosidor's troupe in 1706, the cultural climate did not foster further developments; the *Ballet* should therefore be seen as the beginning of Swedish opera.

During the following three decades operatic life was intermittent. Swedish composers such as Arvid Niclas von Höpken attempted operas: Höpken set two Metastasio librettos, *Il re pastore* (1752) and *Catone in Utica* (1753), and the comic intermezzo *Il bevitore* (1755). His music has both elegance and dramatic verve, and his comic characterization is outstanding in Swedish opera. It was not until 1744 and the arrival of the young Crown Princess Lovisa Ulrika, who married the future King Adolf Fredrik, that the cultural life of Stockholm dramatically changed. In 1753 she engaged a French theatre troupe and started to build up an Italian company. In 1754 the tenor Giovanni Croce and other singers arrived and in 1755 Rosa Scarlatti with her husband, the composer Francesco Uttini. He was appointed conductor of the company and composed a series of operas: *La Galatea*, *L'isola disabitata*, *Il re pastore* (all 1755) and *L'eroe cinese* (1757). Although the Italians (apart from Uttini and his wife) did not stay more than a few years, the foundations of opera were laid in Swedish musical life and favourable conditions created for the Gustavian period.

Gustavus III's accession in 1771 was the beginning of perhaps the most brilliant era in Swedish operatic life. In 1773 the new Royal Theatre in Stockholm was inaugurated with Uttini's *Thetis och Pélée*, to a libretto by Johan Wellander. This was the first opera in the Swedish language. Later that year Gluck's *Orfeo ed Euridice* was performed in its French version. Gluck was to be the musical ideal for the period and was a striking influence on the new conductors and composers imported by Gustavus, mostly from German-speaking countries: J. G. Naumann, G. J. Vogler and J. M. Kraus. The growing consciousness of history and national heritage determined the plots of the next operas. Among these were Vogler's *Gustav Adolf och Ebba Brahe* (1788), to a libretto by the poet Johan Henrik Kellgren based on a synopsis by the king, and Naumann's *Gustaf Wasa* (1786), again to a text by Kellgren, who also wrote the libretto to Kraus's *Aeneas i Cartago* (1799). Gustavian opera was formed by Kellgren, Naumann, Vogler and Kraus, but came to an abrupt end with the assassination of the king in 1792.

The first half of the 19th century was rather thin as regards opera. Swedish composers were few, and those who wrote for the theatre composed mostly incidental music modelled on French *opéra comique*. The lack of musical education was also a contributory factor. In Stockholm the Royal Theatre gave operas by Mozart, Auber, Rossini and Weber, often just a few months after the premières. The germination of Romantic nationalism, the influence of the Geatish movement and the new trend for collecting folk music resulted in such minor pieces as Edouard Du Puy's *divertissement Balder* (1818) and the unfinished opera *Björn Jernsida* (1817). But it was not until the creation of *Ryno* (1831) by the promising young Eduard Brendler, to a libretto by Bernhard von Beskow, that Sweden had its first national Romantic opera. Unfortunately, Brendler died during its composition, and it was completed by the crown prince, later Oscar I, under the direction of Adolf Fredrik Lindblad. Although *Ryno* has a clear central European influence, mostly from Spohr and Weber, Brendler's strongly personal language made it a landmark in 19th-century Swedish opera. A success at its première in

1834, it was performed 20 times during the next four years. On the initiative of the prince, Lindblad also wrote *Frondörerna* ('The Fronde Rebels', 1835), which failed to arouse lasting interest even after a revival in 1860. Lindblad, like Franz Berwald, wrote in a predominantly symphonic idiom, and their musical languages were never convincing for music drama. Nevertheless Berwald wrote several operas; he first attempted to rewrite Naumann's *Gustaf Wasa* in 1827, a project that was never fulfilled; he had a *succès d'estime* with *Estrella de Soria* in 1862, but his last opera, *Drottningen av Golconda* ('The Queen of Golconda', composed 1864–5), never had a complete performance during his lifetime.

In Ivar Hallström Sweden found an international opera composer. He was much influenced by Gounod but also embraced the Classical-Romantic style of Mendelssohn and Schumann; the result was an eclectic musical language. Hallström incorporated Swedish folk music naturally into his own style and managed to give folktunes a musico-dramatic sense. His masterpiece was *Den bergtagna* ('The Bride of the Mountain King', 1874), based on a Swedish legend, the theme of which is found in other European cultures. The opera was a great success and replaced *Gustav Wasa* as the Swedish national opera. His next opera, *Vikingarna* ('The Vikings', 1877), showed he was not untouched by Wagner, and he used that idiom to develop his own style. A certain success was also achieved by Per August Ölander's *Blenda* (1876). Like *The Bride of the Mountain King*, it is set in the early Christian era and deals with the conflict between rising Christianity and old Aesir cult; it is characterized by great lyricism and impressive strength in the dramatic scenes.

On the threshold of the new century, a new and different idiom was apparent. Wilhelm Stenhammar had shown a totally different temperament and deeper artistic expression in his first opera *Gildet på Solhaug* ('The Feast at Solhaug', composed 1892–3), based on Ibsen's play. In his next opera *Tirfing* (1898), Wagnerian influence earned him profound disfavour from Wilhelm Peterson-Berger, the leading critic of the time. The Wagnerian echo, however, is deceptive; Stenhammar's own style is to the fore and its characteristic sharpness was beyond Peterson-Berger's comprehension. As a result, however, Stenhammar abandoned the theatre. Andreas Hallén was heavily influenced by Wagner. His *Harald der Wiking* (1881) had a successful première in Leipzig, and when he was in Germany he was considered one of the most important heirs to the Bayreuth master. The opera stands wholly in the post-Wagnerian tradition, using all the resources of leitmotif, but is more a pastiche than an independent work of art. Any connection with Scandinavian tradition, except for the plot, is hard to trace. In one of Hallén's later operas, *Waldemarsskatten* ('Waldemar's Treasures', 1899), written after his return to Sweden, he treated a more local historical event, with folk music and popular dance (notably in Act 2). It is skilfully done, but lacks Hallström's naturalness.

Among Peterson-Berger's four operas only *Arnljot* (1910) is performed regularly. It is hampered by too close a relationship to Wagner's work and musical theories but contains episodes of an intense lyrical beauty that is often considered Nordic. Superficially Ture Rangström's work is also Nordic, especially *Kronbruden* ('The Crown Bride', 1915), after Strindberg's play. Although folkloristic elements are found, Rangström's style is extremely expressive and personal, freely declamatory in the manner of late Debussy, so that, like Stenhammar, he can hardly be considered a national Romantic or be easily classified. His contemporaries Kurt Atterberg and Natanael Berg are more traditional and considerably influenced by German music. Atterberg's *Härvard harpolekare* ('Härvard the Harpist', 1919) and *Bäckahästen* ('The White Horse', 1925) and Berg's *Engelbrekt* (1924–8) are examples of a post-Romantic style that tend to be fixed in a mould. The same can be said of Gunnar de Frumerie's *Singoalla* (1940), but his music is more Gallic and freely expressive.

New operas in recent decades have been rather sparse, mostly because of the limited opportunities for commissions. Sweden has an outstanding singing tradition, but musical composition is mostly non-theatrical. Yet there has been an interesting output of music dramas from contemporary composers. Hilding Rosenberg has a rich and varied oeuvre: *Resa till Amerika* ('Journey to America', 1932), the romantic *Lycksalighetens ö* ('The Isle of Felicity', 1945), *Porträttet* (1956, after Gogol) and *Hus med dubbel ingång* ('The House with Two Doors', 1970, after Calderón de la Barca) are all impressive and worthy of international interest. Some of Rosenberg's pupils created works that have become landmarks in Swedish opera: Sven-Erik Bäck's chamber work *Tranfjädrarna* ('The Crane Feathers', 1957) caused great interest at its première, as did the most famous Swedish opera, the space opera *Aniara* (1959) by Karl-Birger Blomdahl, performed more than 100 times. Another Rosenberg pupil, Ingvar Lidholm, has written *Holländaren* (1967) and a setting of Strindberg's *Ett drömspel* ('A Dream Play', 1991) for television.

The tendency to break with old traditions and move towards theatrical drama has resulted in fascinating works by Lars Johan Werle. *Drömmen om Thérèse* ('Dream about Thérèse', 1964) and *Resan* ('The Journey', 1969) reveal new concepts of staging, scenery, the use of film, electronic music and pastiche, elements also found in *Tintomara* (1973). Political satire, burlesque and consciously eclectic music characterize *Animalen* (1978), which was commissioned by the Grand Theatre in Göteborg. In *Linardo* (1987), Werle's style has developed a more intense lyrical expression, closer to romantic opera than any of his other dramatic works. With the rising popularity of opera in recent years there has been an increase in the number of commissions, for instance *Christina* (1987) by Hans Gefors (*b* 1952), commissioned by the Royal Theatre, and *Hästen och gossen* ('The Horse and the Lad', 1987) by Jonas Forssell (*b* 1957), commissioned by Norrlandsoperan. Both operas deal with Swedish themes. It is interesting that, while both use all the modern means of musical expression, their operatic idiom is still founded on a traditional base. Forssell's recent opera *Riket är ditt* ('The Kingdom is Yours'), commissioned by the Vadstena Academy in 1991, was an outstanding success. It is a comic chamber opera about a serious subject (immigrants seeking refuge in a convent), and is a real landmark in contemporary Swedish opera. Opera companies in Göteborg and Malmö and music-theatre groups in Umeå and Karlstad also indicate that, slowly but surely, a mainstream opera tradition is being created in a country that for a long time was on the periphery of the European musical tradition.

For further information on operatic life in the country's principal centres *see* DROTTNINGHOLM; GÖTEBORG; STOCKHOLM; and UMEÅ.

*

F. Dahlgren: *Anteckningar om Stockholms teatrar* [Notes on Stockholm's Theatres] (Stockholm, 1866)
N. Personne: *Svenska teatern* (Stockholm, 1913–27)
G. Nordensvan: *Svensk teater* (Stockholm, 1917–18)
G. Jaensson: 'Vår första opera och den Rosidorska teatertruppen i Sverige' [Our First Opera and the Rosidor Theatre Group in Sweden], *STMf*, i (1919), 4–39
H. Nyblom: 'Gustaf III:s opera', *Gustaf III:s opera: minnesskrift utgiven med anledning av Kungl. Teaterns 150-års jubileum* [Gustaf III's Opera: Memoir for the Royal Theatre's 150-year Jubilee] (Stockholm, 1923)
T. Norlind and E. Trobäck: *Kungl. Hovkapellets historia 1526–1926* [History of the Royal Court Choir 1526–1926] (Stockholm, 1926)
E. Kjellberg: *Kungliga musiker i Sverige under stormaktstiden* [Royal Musicians in Sweden in the Golden Age] (diss., U. of Uppsala, 1968)
ANDERS WIKLUND

Sweerts, Cornelis [Zweerts, Kornelis] (*b* Amsterdam, 20 Feb 1669; *d* Maarssen, nr Utrecht, 23 March 1742). Netherlands librettist and poet. He came from a family of established scholars, poets and publishers. Among his poems is a rhymed treatise on music (1698). His two *zangspel* (Singspiel) librettos, *De verliefde Rykaard* (?1694) and *Apollo en Dafne* (1698), were both set to music by Hendrik Anders. His verse was also set by song composers.
RUDOLF A. RASCH

Swiney [McSwiney], **Owen** (*b* Co. Wexford, 1676; *d* London, 2 Oct 1754). Irish impresario. He entered Trinity College, Dublin, in November 1694 and first became known in London in 1705 when he published his comedy *The Quacks* (after Molière). In 1706 he was associated with Christopher Rich at Drury Lane, and the same year signed the dedication of the libretto of Giovanni Bononcini's *Camilla*. The following season he became manager of the Queen's Theatre in the Haymarket, the home of Italian opera in London. He recruited the castrato Nicolini, who made his début on 14 December 1708 in Alessandro Scarlatti's *Il Pirro e Demetrio*; Swiney translated Adriano Morselli's libretto. After the second performance of Handel's *Teseo* in January 1713 Swiney fled to the Continent, leaving the singers unpaid. He went first to France and then by spring 1724 was established in Venice, where he acted as agent for the Royal Academy of Music in London, recruiting singers and recommending librettos. In this capacity he was responsible for bringing the soprano Faustina Bordoni to London in the spring of 1726. In Bologna in summer 1730 he acted as agent for the formation of Handel's new opera company. During this period he was also involved in the commission and purchase of Italian art works to be sold to English collectors. He had returned to London by 26 February 1735 when he had a benefit at Drury Lane and obtained posts in the Custom House and the King's Mews. On his death, the bulk of his estate was bequeathed to the actress Peg Woffington.

*

DNB (E. I. Carlyle)
Gentleman's Magazine, xxiv (1754), 483
O. E. Deutsch: *Handel: a Documentary Biography* (London, 1955)
J. Milhous and R. D. Hume: *Vice Chamberlain Coke's Theatrical Papers 1706–1715* (Carbondale, IL, 1982)
E. Gibson: 'Owen Swiney and the Italian Opera in London', *MT*, cxxv (1984), 82–6
J. Simon, ed.: *Handel: a Celebration of his Life and Times, 1685–1789* (London, 1985)
E. Gibson: *The Royal Academy of Music 1719–1728* (New York, 1989)
ELIZABETH GIBSON

Switzerland (Fr. Suisse; Ger. Schweiz; It. Svizzera). Opera in Switzerland lacks the distinctive national identity and depth of tradition found in neighbouring France, Germany and Italy. In the 18th and 19th centuries Switzerland had no princely courts with the kind of patronage necessary for a flourishing operatic life. Its two biggest cities, Zürich and Geneva, boasted a Protestant tradition inimical to the theatre. With a population of only six million, speaking four national languages, the country has never enjoyed a unifying linguistic thread in the arts.

The first signs of operatic life can be traced to centres where ecclesiastical music dramas were staged with the approval or support of the Catholic church. The Obrigkeitliche Comödienhaus, a theatre built by the Jesuits in Lucerne, for example, was used for opera in the 1740s, when the composer Meyer von Schauensee produced a series of Italian-influenced operas. Geneva's geographical and cultural links with France were the key to its operatic awakening in the late 18th century. In Zürich opera flourished only after the privately funded Aktientheater was built in 1833. Operatic tradition in Basle dates from the same period. In the first half of the 19th century touring ensembles gave smaller cities like St Gall their first taste of opera.

Switzerland in the 19th century was more notable for its influence on foreign composers than for a native school of composition. Wagner spent most of his years of exile in Zürich and Lucerne. Several Romantic composers chose Swiss settings for their operas, as in Cherubini's *Elisa*, Rossini's *Guillaume Tell* and Bellini's *La sonnambula*. Delius's *A Village Romeo and Juliet* was based on the Swiss pastoral idyll evoked by the Swiss author Gottfried Keller.

In the early 20th century the strong pull of linguistic ties to Switzerland's French- and German-speaking neighbours established a pattern of operatic activity that has lasted to the present day. Geneva, and to a lesser extent Lausanne, operates a stagione pattern and has traditionally taken its cue from artistic trends in Paris. Zürich and the cities of central and eastern Switzerland, on the other hand, maintain their own ensembles and have more in common with the repertory system of German houses. All Swiss theatres are financed locally through subsidies from city (and in some cases cantonal) authorities.

The early 20th century was also the period when Swiss opera composers first began to win recognition abroad. In the 1920s and 30s Othmar Schoeck was championed by Fritz Busch and Karl Böhm in Dresden, and his last opera, *Das Schloss Dürande*, received its première in Berlin (1943). Frank Martin found equal recognition in French- and German-speaking Europe. Honegger and Rolf Liebermann chose to work abroad, but their music is more frequently performed in Switzerland than in any other country.

Heinrich Sutermeister and Rudolf Kelterborn have become the most successful Swiss opera composers of the later 20th century. Sutermeister's *Seraphine* and *Le roi Bérenger* were first staged in Munich (1960, 1985), but his stage works have yet to be taken up with any enthusiasm by Swiss theatres. Kelterborn has kept up a prolific output, but the appeal of his operas has been confined to the German-speaking world. Of the middle

1. *The Sydney Opera House (completed in 1973), designed by Jørn Utzon*

and younger generation of Swiss composers, only Jost Meier has shown an aptitude for opera.

A number of conductors, singers and stage directors, including Ernest Ansermet, Silvio Varviso, Peter Maag, Lisa della Casa, Hugues Cuénod and Luc Bondy, have had distinguished operatic careers outside Switzerland.

For further information on operatic life in the country's principal centres *see* BASLE; BERNE; GENEVA; LAUSANNE; LUCERNE; ST GALL; and ZÜRICH.

*

Schweizer Theaterbuch (Zürich, 1964)
A. Briner: *Swiss Composers in the 20th Century* (Zürich, 1990)

ANDREW CLARK

Swolfs, Laurent (*b* Ghent, 8 March 1868; *d* Ghent, 4 Nov 1954). Belgian tenor. He studied in Antwerp and Brussels, making his début in 1902 in Antwerp as Merlyn in Blockx's *Herbergprinses*. In 1903 he created roles in Gilson's *Prinses Zonneschijn* and Blockx's *De kapel*. Between 1906 and 1911 at the Théâtre de la Monnaie he sang Samson, Lohengrin, Aeneas (*La prise de Troie*), Herod (*Salome*), John the Baptist (*Hérodiade*), Siegmund and the Burgomaster (*Feuersnot*). At the Paris Opéra he sang Siegmund, Samson (1910) and Loge (1913); at the Opéra-Comique he created Titus in Magnard's *Bérénice* (1911). Parsifal at Antwerp in 1914 was his last role before his retirement.

ELIZABETH FORBES

Sydney. Australian city, capital of New South Wales. The largest city in the country, it is important as a port and financial centre. Before the establishment of the Australian Opera (or Elizabethan Trust Opera) Company in 1956, Sydney had neither a permanent theatre devoted solely to opera nor a regular annual season. Here, as elsewhere in Australia, opera was intermittent, brought by visiting companies, with only the occasional, and generally unsuccessful, attempt to establish a locally based operation. The first operas presented were ballad operas and semi-operas, in fairly makeshift conditions. With the opening of the first permanent theatre, the Theatre Royal, in 1833, such works were given in addition to the more usual straight plays. The first true opera seen in Sydney was probably *Der Freischütz*, given in 1838 at the newly opened Royal Victoria Theatre. From 1845 to 1853 several operas were presented there, still alternating with drama and performed by the same casts: they included *La Cenerentola*, *La sonnambula* and *The Bohemian Girl*. The orchestration was usually adapted to suit the small theatre orchestra, and the shortage of singers meant that roles were often assigned to the wrong voices.

In the 1850s short seasons were arranged around the visiting sopranos Catherine Hayes and Anna Bishop. The 1860s and 70s saw the first extensive seasons devoted entirely to opera, presented by the Irish impresario W. S. Lyster, who took a company to Australia, and later managed others when it broke up. After his death in 1880, less regular seasons were the pattern, up to the 1950s. Companies were of two kinds: those visiting in the course of world tours, such as the Gonsalez companies in 1916–17 and 1928, and those specially imported by or on behalf of local impresarios – Martin and Fanny Simonsen (1887, 1889, 1892), George Musgrove (1901, 1907), J. C. Williamson and, after his death, the firm he founded (1893, in association with Musgrove; 1901–2, 1910, 1932, 1948–9, 1955), and Sir Benjamin Fuller (1934–5). Of particular importance in raising standards were the three Melba-Williamson seasons of 1911, 1924 and 1928. The visiting companies generally made use of local orchestras and choruses, and sometimes minor principals. The only exception was the full company brought by the Irish impresario Thomas Quinlan, which made two visits, bringing the first *Tristan und Isolde* in 1912 and the first *Ring* and *Meistersinger* in 1913. A wide variety of theatres was used, the two most important being the Theatre Royal and Her Majesty's.

From 1951 to 1955, the New South Wales National Opera Company, founded by Clarice Lorenz, presented the first consecutive seasons, though of only a few weeks' duration. Following the establishment of the Australian Elizabethan Theatre Trust in 1954, an opera company building on the foundations of the New South

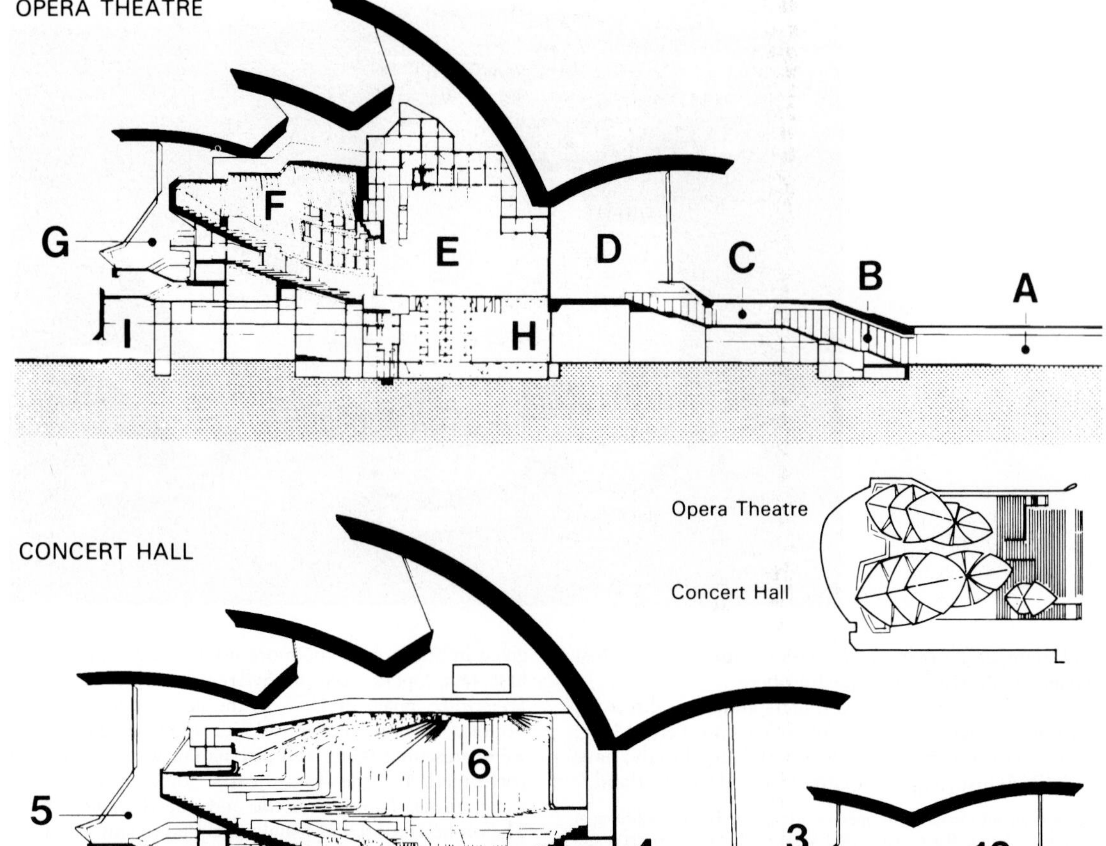

2. Longitudinal sections (with reduced plan views) of the opera theatre and concert hall forming the Sydney Opera House complex

Wales company and the Melbourne-based National Theatre Movement gave its first performances in 1956 under the title of the Australian Opera Company, changing its name to the Elizabethan Trust Opera Company in 1957 and the Australian Opera in 1970. With only a couple of gaps in the early years, the company has performed regularly since 1956. An important landmark was the formation in 1967 of an orchestra to accompany the national ballet and opera companies, the Elizabethan Trust Orchestra, subsequently expanded and split into two segments, one based in Sydney and one in Melbourne. The company's first subscription season was also in 1967.

The Australian Opera is the only full-time company in the country, giving a total of over 200 performances a year. Its charter is national but it is based in Sydney, where it increased its season from five weeks in 1967 to seven months (January–February, June–October) by the mid-1970s. Before 1973 it performed in the Elizabethan Theatre in suburban Newtown and in two city houses, the Tivoli and Her Majesty's, returning to the Elizabethan in 1970 when Her Majesty's burnt down in the middle of a season. The Australian Opera has had a permanent performing base since 1973, when the Sydney Opera House, designed by Jørn Utzon and built for $102 million, was officially opened on 28 September with a performance of Prokofiev's *War and Peace*; a double bill of two Australian operas, Larry Sitsky's *The Fall of the House of Usher* and James Penberthy's *Dalgerie*, had been staged there the previous July. This multi-purpose venue consists of two principal halls built side by side, with two (formerly three) smaller ones underneath. The Australian Opera mostly performs in the opera theatre (cap. 1547), but has also given successful productions in the concert hall (cap. 2690, without a proscenium arch), as well as in the two smaller halls. The Australian Opera also appears regularly in Melbourne (March–May) and less frequently in other state capitals, including Adelaide, where the company gave the first performance of Richard Meale's *Voss* in 1986. Joan Sutherland made her first appearances with the company in 1974 and appeared regularly, in most of her best roles, until 1990. Her husband Richard Bonynge was musical director from 1975 to 1986. Earlier musical directors have included Joseph Post, Karl Rankl and Edward Downes.

From 1968 the University of New South Wales Opera has given annual professional seasons, often of new Australian works and fringe repertory.

*

A. I. Gyger: *Opera for the Antipodes* (Sydney, 1990) A. I. GYGER

Sylva, Marguerite [Smith, Marguerite Alice Helene] (*b* Brussels, 10 July 1875; *d* Glendale, CA, 21 Feb 1957). American soprano of English parentage. She studied in Paris, making her London début in 1892 as Carmen, a role she was to sing more than 600 times and in which she was often compared to Calvé. She sang with the Opéra-Comique (1892–1907) and appeared in shows on Broadway in 1897–8, including Herbert's *The Fortune Teller*, and in 1908–9. She also sang with the Chicago Opera, Manhattan Opera, the Philadelphia-Chicago Company, and in Berlin and Vienna, in roles including Giulietta (Offenbach), Santuzza and Tosca. Later in her career, she put her spicy theatricality to good use in films and small character roles on Broadway, as well as working as a teacher and producer. Most of the recordings she made between 1901 and 1912 were unfortunately destroyed by fire in 1914.

CORI ELLISON

Synge, John Millington (*b* Newtown Little, Rathfarnham, nr Dublin, 16 April 1871; *d* Dublin, 24 March 1909). Irish playwright. Most of his plays deal with Irish peasant life and are written in an expressive prose which was Synge's rhetorical reshaping of the rhythms of ordinary Irish speech. His most famous play, *The Playboy of the Western World* (1907), caused riots at its first performance at the Abbey Theatre in Dublin, on account of its unsparing portrait of village morality. Synge's rich idiom is more purely musical in the elegiac tragedy *Riders to the Sea* (1904), in which a mother awaits the death of her last surviving son. Operatic settings of *Riders to the Sea* include those by Fritz Hart (1915), Henri Rabaud (1924, as *L'appel de la mer*) and Vaughan Williams (1937). Synge's *In the Shadow of the Glen* (1903) was the source for Pedrollo's *La veglia* (1920); *The Playboy of the Western World* was used for Klebe's *Ein wahrer Held* (1975); and settings of *Deirdre of the Sorrows* (1910) include those by Fritz Hart (1915) and J. J. Becker (1956). ANTHONY PARR

Syracuse. American town in New York State. Syracuse Opera, founded in 1974, has performed in the 2000-seat Crouse-Hinds Theatre since 1976. Originally sponsored by the Syracuse SO, it was named the Opera Theatre of Syracuse in 1976, then renamed Syracuse Opera in 1984. The company produces four operas each year between October and May, with two performances each. The repertory is generally conservative; no premières have so far been given. The Syracuse Opera's outreach and education division, the Empire State Ensemble, presents approximately 140 performances to a total audience of more than 33 000 in the central state area each year. The county-run Crouse-Hinds Theatre includes three halls; that in which the opera company performs includes a mezzanine, a balcony and three upper and lower boxes on each side. ROBERT V. PALMER

Syros [Hermopolis; Gk. Ermoupolis]. Greek city, capital of the Cyclades Islands. It was founded during the Greek War of Independence (1821–7) by refugees from the islands of Chios, Psara and Crete and from Asia Minor. It became one of the most important Greek cities in the 19th century in terms of economic activity. On 31 October 1861 the merchants formed a theatrical society to build a theatre. Designed by the Italian architect Pietro Sampo, the Apollo Theatre (cap. *c*500, with three tiers of boxes) was inaugurated in summer 1864. For the next 90 years until its closure in 1953 the Apollo saw productions staged by Italian opera companies and Greek drama companies. The opera season normally began in October and continued until the last Sunday in Carnival. Impresarios engaged Italian singers, mainly from Milan and Naples, to sing an almost exclusively Italian repertory, notably Donizetti and Verdi. Romilda Pantaleoni appeared at the Apollo in the 1869–70 season. The only Greek opera to be presented there was Pavlos Carrer's *Marcos Botsaris* in the 1866–7 season.

*

N. Bakounakis: *To fantasma tis Norma: i ipodochi tis operas stin Ellada ston 19on eona* [Norma's Phantom: the Reception of Opera in Greece in the 19th Century] (Athens, 1991)

NIKOS BAKOUNAKIS

Szantho, Enid (*b* Budapest, 1907). Hungarian contralto. She made her début in 1928 at the Vienna Staatsoper, where she was engaged until 1939. At Bayreuth (1930–37) she sang Erda, the First Norn and Waltraute in the *Ring*, and an Esquire and a flowermaiden in *Parsifal*. She made her Covent Garden début in 1936 as Erda and then sang Fricka (*Die Walküre*), the role in which she made her Metropolitan début in 1938, when she also sang Brangäne and Clytemnestra. She appeared as Mary (*Der fliegende Holländer*) with the New York City Center Opera Company (1946). Her voice, a true contralto, was strong but her small stature was unsuited to dramatically powerful roles. ELIZABETH FORBES

Szczecin (Ger. Stettin). Polish town on the mouth of the river Odra (Oder). It was formerly (1713–1945) the capital of the Prussian province of Pomerania. The first traces of operatic life appear at the end of the 18th century: J. A. Hiller's Singspiels were performed in 1773, and private opera performances were given for the city's aristocracy. The first professional opera activity was in the early 19th century: from 1794 to 1810, over 70 operas, Singspiels and vaudevilles by 35 composers (18 German, 17 French and Italian) were performed in the city's theatre (built 1794, directed by Hans Heinrich Meyer), among them Mozart's *Die Zauberflöte* (1794), *Don Giovanni* (1795), *Die Ent-*

führung, *Figaro* and *La clemenza di Tito*. There were no regular opera seasons in the city, but only occasional visits by companies from Berlin, such as the one in 1821–2 that brought Méhul's *Joseph*, Joseph Weigl's *Die Schweizerfamilie* and Weber's *Der Freischütz* (on 28 August 1821, only two months after its première). On 21 October 1849 a new municipal theatre was opened (rebuilt 1905) with Mozart's *Don Giovanni*, followed by performances of Wagner's works: *Tannhäuser* (1854), *Lohengrin* (1862), *Rienzi* (1868), *Die Meistersinger* (1870), *Der fliegende Holländer* (1878) and *Die Walküre* (1884). In the late 19th century and in the first four decades of the 20th over a third of the Stadttheater's repertory consisted of works new to the company. Wagner's operas were also a major feature. Anton Webern conducted at the theatre in 1913.

After World War II, during which it was badly damaged, the town became part of Poland. Attempts to stage opera were made only in 1956 by an amateur ensemble which gave Schubert's *Dreimädelhaus* and other operettas and musical comedies. On 25 January 1957 the Państwowa Operetka (State Operetta) was inaugurated; it was renamed the Państwowy Teatr Muzyczny (State Music Theatre) in 1965. Its repertory consisted at first mostly of standard operettas of the 19th and 20th centuries; from 1971, under the direction of Tadeusz Bursztynowicz, it also included contemporary operettas, musicals, and operas such as Nicolai's *Die lustigen Weiber von Windsor* (1978), the Kurpiński pasticcio *Henryk VI na łowach* ('Henry VI goes Hunting', 1979), Moniuszko's *Straszny dwór* ('The Haunted Manor', 1980) and Telemann's *Pimpinone* (1981). On 13 April 1978 the company found a new home in the restored castle of the Pomeranian princes. In 1985 it was again renamed the Państwowa Opera i Operetka (State Opera and Operetta), and from 1987 came under the direction of the eminent singer Urszula Trawińska-Moroz.

W. Freytag: *Musikgeschichte der Stadt Stettin im 18. Jahrhundert* (Greifswald, 1936)
B. M. Jankowski and M. Misiorny: *Muzyka i życie muzyczne na ziemiach zachodnich i północnych* [Music and Musical Life in Western and Northern Poland] (Poznań, 1968)
W. Panek: *Droga na Zamek* [The Road to the Castle: Notes on 25 Years of the Musical Stage in Szczecin, 1957–82] (Szczecin, 1982)
B. Zakrzewska-Nikiporczyk: *Życie muzyczne Pomorza w latach 1815–1920* [Musical Life in Pomerania, 1815–1920] (Gdańsk, 1982)
KORNEL MICHAŁOWSKI

Szeged. Town in southern Hungary. Its earliest music theatre was school drama, given by the Piarists; with an orchestra of town musicians they staged about 50 works in Latin from 1722 to 1758, thereafter performing in Hungarian. In 1800 a new town hall opened, incorporating a theatre equipped with machinery where Ferdinand Kauer's *Inkle und Yariko* was staged in Hungarian. Kilényi's touring company from Kolozsvár (now Cluj-Napoca) visited in 1827 and performed *Der Freischütz*, *La gazza ladra* and Méhul's *Joseph*, all with Róza Déry. Operas in Hungarian were given by itinerant troupes in 1840, 1844 (from Kolozsvár) and 1846 (from Szabadka, now Subotica), while German companies visited intermittently until 1848.

In 1856 the first permanent theatre opened, and Havi and Szabó's company staged *Ernani* and Erkel's *Hunyadi László*. A company from Temesvár (now Timişoara) played there successfully in 1860. A new theatre, built in 1883, burnt down in 1885 but was restored in 1886 and became the home of all later companies. Now called the Szegedi Nemzeti Színház (Szeged National Theatre), it holds 720. At first, seven or eight operas were performed annually but this rose to 14 or 15 in the mid-1920s. In 1949, four years after Viktor Vaszy was appointed conductor, Socialist rule forced the opera to be dissolved. It was reorganized by Vilmos Rubányi in 1950 and Vaszy returned as conductor in 1957. He was followed in 1979 by Tamás Pál and later by Géza Oberfrank. The singers József Simándy and József Gregor also began their careers there.

The Szegedi Ünnepi Játékok (an open-air festival), begun in 1931, always includes performances, of Imre Madách's drama *The Tragedy of Man* as well as other plays and operas. In 1934 Mascagni conducted *Cavalleria rusticana* with soloists from La Scala. The festival stopped in 1939 but was revived in 1959 by Vaszy, who became chief conductor before Pál. It runs for a month from mid-July and attracts an audience of about 100 000. Verdi operas receive frequent performances as do *Hunyadi László*, *Bánk bán* and *Háry János*. Works are usually given in the soloists' native language or in Italian and, less often, in French and Russian.

N. Szmollény: *A szegedi magyar nemzeti színészet százéves története* [A Hundred Years' History of Hungarian Theatre in Szeged] (Budapest, 1906)
D. Lugosi: *A szegedi színjátszás vázlatos története* [A Brief History of Theatre in Szeged] (Szeged, 1929)
B. Ostváth: *Képek a szegedi színészet történetéből* [Information on the History of Theatre in Szeged] (Szeged, 1956)
J. Farkas, ed.: *Szeged története*, ii: *1686–1849* [History of Szeged] (Szeged, 1985)
I. Simon: *A játékok krónikája* [Chronicle of the Festivals] (Szeged, 1985)
DEZSŐ LEGÁNY

Székely, Mihály (*b* Jászberény, 8 May 1901; *d* Budapest, 22 March 1963). Hungarian bass. He studied with Géza László and made his début at the Budapest Municipal Theatre in 1923 as the Hermit (*Der Freischütz*). He joined the Budapest Opera the same year and was soon singing leading bass roles such as Cardinal Brogni (*La Juive*), Gounod's Méphistophélès, Sarastro and King Mark. His international career developed after World War II: his Metropolitan début (1947) was as Hunding, after which he sang many Wagner and other bass roles in New York until 1949. At Glyndebourne (1957–61) his Sarastro, Osmin, Bartolo (*Le nozze di Figaro*) and Rocco were greatly admired. He sang Boris in Paris (1957), and Bartók's Bluebeard throughout Europe, partly transposed for his bass range by the composer (he also recorded the part). Székely was a major figure in Hungarian opera, with a voice of intrinsic beauty and wide range (his lowest notes were of particularly powerful 'black' timbre), as well as outstanding acting ability. His Philip II, Fiesco, Ochs, Dosifey and Konchak were also memorable.

P. Várnai: *Székely Mihály* (Budapest, 1967)
PÉTER P. VÁRNAI

Szeligowski, Tadeusz (*b* Lwów, 13 Sept 1896; *d* Poznań, 10 Jan 1963). Polish composer and teacher. He studied composition with Wallek-Walewski in Kraków, and then with Nadia Boulanger in Paris (1929–31). Returning to Poland, he taught composition in Poznań (1932–9, 1947–62) and in Warsaw (1951–62), and was president of the Polish Composers' Union (1951–4).

Szeligowski was arguably the most significant Polish opera composer of his generation, although he came to the genre late in life and probably under some pressure. *Bunt żaków* ('The Scholars' Revolt', 1951) was hailed as the first opera of People's Poland and set the tone for the few Polish operas to be written later during the 1950s. *The Scholars' Revolt* is based on actual events in Kraków in 1549, when unarmed peasant students at the Jagiellonian University were murdered by townsfolk, whose crime went unpunished. The opera incorporates a love story between the scholars' leader, Konopny (tenor), and Anna (soprano), the sister of one of the murderers. But the central issue was compatible with the prevailing Stalinist dogma: the community (of scholars) united against injustice and oppression, expressed through mass scenes, collective action and, musically, through the chorus (the final chorus reiterates the phrase 'Long live the Polish Republic!'). Characterization of the principals is fairly crude, as is the differentiation between good and evil. Szeligowski used derivatives of Renaissance and Baroque counterpoint and dance forms, set in a language that is primarily modal, with frequent 'antique' inflections. *The Scholars' Revolt* draws on Wagnerian leitmotif technique, while its melodic style bears the imprint of chant and the occasional folk model, often recalling Musorgsky's usage. It also cites pre-existing melodies: Act 1 opens with a well-known Kraków trumpet call (also used by Różycki in his 1921 ballet *Pan Twardowski*), Act 3 scene ii quotes a song by the Renaissance composer Wacław z Szamotuł, and Act 4 scene ii incorporates a familiar 15th-century tune from Kraków, *Breve regnum*.

Szeligowski's next opera, *Krakatuk* (1956), set in the Old Town market square in Warsaw on Christmas eve 1820, reworks the familiar Nutcracker story in Polish terms. In pitting the evil, grotesque fantasy of the fairy world against the kindness and devotion of human beings, Szeligowski was providing a contemporary model for the socialist citizen. His musical language is simple and light, and strongly recalls Prokofiev, with its harmonic sidesteps and distortions and its use of 18th-century dance forms. This tendency is even more apparent in *Teodor Gentleman* (1963), a science-fiction tale about cybernetics. Here the harmonic language becomes more chromatic and even includes the influence of the blues, although Szeligowski had by now been left behind by younger, more daring colleagues. By the time of *Odys płaczący i opuszczony* ('Odysseus Weeping and Desolate', 1962), Szeligowski had returned to the more conservative, diatonic idioms of earlier works, in which he achieved greater stylistic consistency. Although their standing today may seem marginal, his operas retain their importance within the Polish context for the range of subject matter and as an indicator of the socio-political and musical pressures of their time.

Bunt żaków [The Scholars' Revolt] (4, R. Brandstaetter), Wrocław, State, 14 July 1951 (Kraków, 1951)

Krakatuk, 1953–4 (prol., 3, K. Niżyńska, after E. T. A. Hoffmann: *Nussknacker und Mausekönig*), Gdańsk, Baltic, 30 Dec 1956

Teodor Gentleman, 1960 (2, C. Chruszczewski), Wrocław, State, 21 July 1963

Odys płaczący i opuszczony [Odysseus Weeping and Desolate], 1961 (radio opera-oratorio, Brandstaetter, after Homer), Polish Radio, 5 June 1962; stage, Poznań, 29 March 1973

*

R. Brandstaetter: 'Bunt żaków', *Muzyka* (1951), no.2, pp.15–16

Z. Lissa: 'Pierwsza opera w Polsce Ludowej: "Bunt żaków" Tadeusza Szeligowskiego i Romana Brandstaettera' [The First Opera in People's Poland: *Bunt żaków* by Tadeusz Szeligowski and Roman Brandstaetter], *Muzyka* (1951), no.10, pp.3, 29

T. Szeligowski: 'Jak komponowałem "Bunt żaków"' [How I Composed *Bunt żaków*], *Muzyka* (1951), no.12, pp.11–13

Z. Lissa: *'Bunt żaków' T. Szeligowskiego* (Kraków, 1955, 2/1957)

——: '"Bunt żaków" redivivus', *Ruch muzyczny* (1967), no.14, pp.6–7

I. Gertig: *Problem archaizacji w operze 'Bunt żaków'* (thesis, U. of Poznań, 1978)

R. Brandstaetter: 'Moja współpraca z Tadeuszem Szeligowskim' [My Partnership with Tadeusz Szeligowski], *Tadeusz Szeligowski: studia i wspomnienia* [Tadeusz Szeligowski: Studies and Reminiscences], ed. F. Woźniak (Bydgoszcz, 1987)

ADRIAN THOMAS

Szell, George [Georg] (*b* Budapest, 7 June 1897; *d* Cleveland, 29 July 1970). American conductor of Hungarian birth. He grew up in Vienna, and studied with Mandyczewski, J. B. Foerster and Max Reger. After his début with the Berlin PO as composer, pianist and conductor, he was engaged by Richard Strauss for the staff of the Berlin Staatsoper in 1915. He held appointments at the opera theatres of Darmstadt (1921), Düsseldorf (1922), and then Berlin (1924–9), where he was also professor at the Hochschule für Musik (1927–30). From 1929 to 1937 he was general musical director of the Neues Deutsches Theater in Prague. Following his move to the USA in 1939 he conducted at the Metropolitan Opera, beginning with a performance of *Salome*, from 1942 until 1946, and was noted for his performances there of Wagner and Strauss. In 1946 he was appointed musical director of the Cleveland Orchestra, a post he held until his death. During the 1950s he conducted operas at the Salzburg Festival, including the premières of Liebermann's *Penelope* (1954) and *Die Schule der Frauen* (1957) and of Egk's *Irische Legende* (1955).

PHILIP HART

Szeluto, Apolinary (*b* St Petersburg, 11/23 July 1884; *d* Chodzież, 22 Aug 1966). Polish composer. He studied successively at the conservatories in Saratov and (1902–5) Warsaw, at the latter with Noskowski and Statkowski, but made a lifelong career as a lawyer. He was a member of the group Młoda Polska ('Young Poland'), which sought to modernize Polish music, but its ideas are reflected only in his earliest compositions. Szeluto wrote prolifically in almost all genres without, however, developing an individual style or even sound compositional techniques. His earliest operas are the most substantial; representative among them are the three-act *Kalina* ('The Cranberry Tree') op.18 (composed 1918); *Faktor turecki* ('The Turkish Agent') op.71 (1930; 3 acts); *Pani Chorążyna* ('The Ensign's Wife') op.20 (1921; 4, S. Krzywoszewski); and the five-act *Karnawał* ('Carnival') op.74 (1932). Of his estimated 50 operas (autograph MSS in *PL-Wn* and *Wu*) almost without exception to his own librettos, about 40 were written between 1959 and 1965. Most of the operas were not scored, and only *Kalina* was performed (posthumously, at the State Opera, Poznań, on 29 September 1968); two arias from it were published in vocal score (Kraków, 1936).

ZOFIA CHECHLIŃSKA

Szene (Ger.). SCENE.

Szirmai [Sirmay], **Albert** (*b* Budapest, 2 July 1880; *d* New York, 15 Jan 1967). American composer of Hungarian origin. He studied the piano with Árpád Szendy and composition with Hans Koessler at the

Budapest Academy of Music, receiving the Volkmann Prize for composition, while at the same time reading political science at the university. While still a student he was second music critic of the Budapest German newspaper *Pester Lloyd*, and later he held a similar post on the Hungarian newspaper *Polgár*. In 1907 he took over the musical direction of the Budapest theatre Népszínház-Vígopera, for which he wrote some 300 songs and the music for 12 one-act plays. After the success of his first operetta *A sárga dominó* ('The Yellow Domino', 1907) he remained faithful to that genre. From 1926 until his death he lived in New York as musical director for Chappell, acting as music editor for Kern, Porter, Gershwin, Rodgers and other major show composers. Szirmai belonged, with Emmerich Kálmán, Viktor Jacobi and Huszka, to the group of composers who, at the beginning of the 20th century, raised Hungarian operetta to international status. His own operettas successfully combined the influence of German romanticism with those of Hungarian popular music and the French turn-of-the-century chanson.

operettas and musical plays, selective list; first performed in Budapest unless otherwise stated

A sárga dominó [The Yellow Domino] (operetta, 3, A. Mérei), Népszínház-Vígopera, 4 Oct 1907; Bálkirályné [The Belle of the Ball] (operetta, 2, Á. Pásztor), Népszínház-Vígopera, 16 Nov 1907; Naftalin [Naphthalene] (musical comedy, 3, J. Heltai), Vígszínház, 6 June 1908; Táncos huszárok [Dancing Hussars] (operetta, 3, F. Rajna and E. Szép), Király, 7 Jan 1909; A mexikói lány [The Mexican Girl] (operetta, 3, Rajna and A. Gábor), Király, 11 Dec 1912; The Girl on the Film (musical play, 3, J. T. Tanner and A. Ross, after R. Bernauer and R. Schanzer: *Filmzauber*), London, Gaiety, 5 April 1913, collab. W. Kollo and W. Bredschneider

Erüstpille [Silver Butterfly] (musical comedy, 3, Gábor), Vígszínház, 9 May 1914; Mágnás Miska [Magnate Miska] (operetta, 3, K. Bakonyi and Gábor), Király, 12 Feb 1916; Harangvirág [Bellflower] (ballad, 2 tableaux, T. Emőd), Royal Opera, 11 March 1918; Gróf Rinaldo [Count Rinaldo] (operetta, 3, Bakonyi and Gábor), Király, 7 Nov 1918; Mézeskalács [Honey Cake] (musical comedy, 3, Emőd), Király, 15 Dec 1923; The Bamboula (operetta, 3, H. M. Vernon, G. Bolton, D. Furber and I. Caesar), London, His Majesty's, 24 March 1925, collab. H. Rosenthal; Alexandra (operetta, 3, F. Martos), Király, 25 Nov 1925

Éva grófnő [Countess Éva] (operetta, 3, Martos), Király, 3 Feb 1928; Lady Mary (musical play, 3, F. Lonsdale, J. H. Turner and H. Graham), Southsea, King's, 13 Feb 1928 (London, Daly's, 23 Feb 1928); Ripples (musical comedy, 2, W. A. McGuire, I. Caesar and G. John), New York, New Amsterdam, 11 Feb 1930, collab. O. Levant; A ballerina [The Ballerina] (operetta, 3, Martos), Király, 7 March 1931; Tabáni legenda [The Legend of Tabán] (operetta, 3, K. Kristóf), Dérynké, Jan 1957; A Tündérlaki lányok [The Tündérlaki Sisters] (operetta, 3, E. Innocent-Vincze, after Heltai), Operett, 29 Jan 1964

*

G. S. Gál: *Weiner Leó életműve* [The Life Work of Leó Weiner] (Budapest, 1959)
F. Bónis: 'Szirmai Alberttal, emlékeiről' [Albert Szirmai: Recollections], *Magyar zene*, iv (1963), 503–9
——: 'Szirmai Albert 1880–1967', *Magyar zene*, viii (1967), 286–7
R. Traubner: *Operetta: a Theatrical History* (New York, 1983)

FERENC BÓNIS, ANDREW LAMB

Szirmay, Marta (*b* Kaposvar, *c*1939). Hungarian mezzo-soprano. She studied in Budapest and became a member of the Hungarian State Opera in 1964, singing Azucena, Amneris, Ulrica, Eboli, Fricka, Brangäne and Gluck's Orpheus. In 1976 she joined Cologne Opera and in 1977 made her Covent Garden début as Clytemnestra, returning as Erda, the Nurse (*Boris Godunov*) and Mistress Quickly. She has appeared at Vienna, Barcelona, Genoa, Venice, Florence, Naples, Basle, Hamburg, Berlin and Salzburg, where in 1985 she sang Eurycleia (*Il ritorno d'Ulisse*). Her roles include Herodias (*Salome*), Gaea (*Daphne*), the Princess (*Suor Angelica*) and Fidalma (*Il matrimonio segreto*). An exuberant actress, she has a rich voice with a strong lower register.

ELIZABETH FORBES

Szokolay, Sándor (*b* Kunágota, 30 March 1931). Hungarian composer. He studied composition with Szabó (1950–52) and Farkas (1952–7) at the Budapest Academy of Music. He worked with Hungarian Radio (1955–9) and then joined the Budapest Music Academy to teach composition. He is president of the Hungarian Kodály Society. He has won two Erkel Awards, the Kossuth Prize (1966) and the Bartók-Pásztory Award (1987).

In Szokolay's music, an unrestrained leaning towards expression and an impulsive responsiveness to various kinds of emotional challenge prevail over premeditated stylistic decisions or the raising and solving of intellectual problems of composition. The predominance of vocal music in his output can be considered the external sign of this temperament, which led him inevitably to opera. In *Vérnász* ('Blood Wedding'), his direct approach resulted in an explosive musical drama, in which intentionally primitive resources like ostinatos, ample use of brass and percussion and recurring short motifs in the voices go to form a clearcut and well-proportioned construction. A frankly realistic opera (with surrealistic touches in the third act), it was progressive enough to elicit respectful reviews, and forceful, melodious and tonal enough to reach the general public.

After decades of dramatic impotence in Hungarian opera, the emotion and sincerity of *Blood Wedding* came as an absolute novelty, and Szokolay established himself as the only professional opera composer in Hungary. In *Hamlet* he responded to the avant-garde atmosphere of the mid-1960s with a more subtle handling of musical material and with a refined leitmotif technique. The character of his hero gave him a welcome opportunity for the introduction of 12-note rows as musical symbols for hesitancy, scepticism and intellect. Thus dodecaphony remained for him not so much a means of construction as a means of expression. With *Hamlet*, it also became obvious for the first time that for Szokolay every subject invokes a specific historical type of opera; here it was the late 19th-century music drama of historical-mythological dimensions (reminders in *Blood Wedding* of *Cavalleria rusticana* were not so much musical as textural).

With *Sámson*, Szokolay wanted to create a synthesis of the philosophical quality of *Hamlet* with the musical exultation of *Blood Wedding*. His model here was late 19th-century exotic grand opera. Although he did not abandon expressive dodecaphony, a return to triadic harmony and uncompromising, glaring tonal surfaces is unmistakable.

Szokolay composed his first three operas in a single decade, but ten years elapsed before his fourth, *Ecce homo*, was completed. He condensed material from Nikos Kazantzakis's novel *Christ Recrucified* into a libretto (which he set in both Hungarian and German), to produce a musical and dramatic style. *Ecce homo* displays a simplicity of expression and a passion-like, epic dramaturgy that are new to Szokolay but not to most of his Hungarian contemporaries after 1966. The Byzantine subject inspired him to an illustrative and narrative style of writing, and a kind of transcendental realism reminiscent of Musorgsky.

See also BLOOD WEDDING.

all performed at the Hungarian State Opera House, Budapest

Vérnász [Blood Wedding] op.26 (3, Szokolay, after F. García Lorca: *Bodas de sangre*), 31 Oct 1964
Hamlet op.31 (3, Szokolay, after W. Shakespeare), 19 Oct 1968
Sámson op.41 (3, Szokolay, after L. Németh), 26 Oct 1973
Ecce homo op.92 (passion op, 3, Szokolay, after N. Kazantzakis: *Christ Recrucified*), 25 Jan 1987
Szávitri op.101, 1987–8 (3, Szokolay, after E. Illés), unperf.

*

A. Boros: *Harminc év magyar operái 1948–1978* [30 Years of Hungarian Opera 1948–1978] (Budapest, 1979)
G. Staud, ed.: *A budapesti operaház száz éve* [100 Years of the Budapest Opera House] (Budapest, 1984) TIBOR TALLIÁN

Szőnyi, Erzsébet (*b* Budapest, 25 April 1924). Hungarian composer. Between 1942 and 1947 she studied music education and composition at the Budapest Music Academy with Visky. There followed a year at the Paris Conservatoire, where she attended courses given by Aubin, Messiaen and Nadia Boulanger. From 1948 until her retirement in 1981 she taught music education at the Budapest Music Academy and played an important role in developing the Kodály method of music education. Her awards include the Liszt (1947) and Erkel (1959) prizes.

Szőnyi's output includes much vocal and pedagogical music. Her first impetus towards opera came from the neo-romantic phase in national opera around 1950, to which she responded in 1953 with the three-act *Dalma. Firenzei tragédia* ('The Florentine Tragedy', 1958) combines 'French' harmony with pentatonically coloured 'Hungarian' declamation. Szőnyi also tried her hand at lighter stage genres, including children's opera, the musical comedy *Le malade imaginaire* (1961) and the Singspiel *Vidám sirató* ('Gay Lament', 1980). With *Adáshiba* ('Break in Transmission', 1982) she dealt with a contemporary plot in an urban milieu.

Dalma, 1953 (3, after M. Jókai), unperf.
Firenzei tragédia [The Florentine Tragedy], 1958 (after O. Wilde), Meiningen, 8 March 1960
Le malade imaginaire (musical comedy, 3, after Molière), Budapest, Petőfi, 20 Oct 1961
Vidám sirató [Gay Lament] (Spl, 1, S. Weöres, after A. Sütő), Budapest, Néps, 7 March 1980
Adáshiba [Break in Transmission] (1, after K. Szakonyi), Szeged, Nemzeti, 7 May 1982

*

A. Boros: *Harminc év magyar operái 1948–1978* [30 Years of Hungarian Opera 1948–1978] (Budapest, 1979)

TIBOR TALLIÁN

Szymanowski, Karol (Maciej) (*b* Tymoszówka, Ukraine, 6 Oct 1882; *d* Lausanne, 28 March 1937). Polish composer. He was a leading figure in Polish music in the first half of the 20th century.

1. LIFE. Szymanowski was born into a family of prominent landowners in the Ukraine. He was introduced to music, literature and the fine arts at a very early age, since his home, described by the poet Iwaszkiewicz as 'un palais enchanté', was a centre for cultural events of every kind. Already in these early years at Tymoszówka he was composing sophisticated piano music indebted to Chopin and songs to texts by the 'Young Poland' poets. In 1901 he moved to Warsaw, studying composition with Noskowski and forming the group 'Young Poland in Music' with other emerging composers. His first major success was a performance of his Concert Overture op.12 at a Young Poland concert in 1906; Szymanowski's models at this time were contemporary German composers, notably Reger and Strauss, and their music left clear marks on the Concert Overture and on other major works of his early years in Warsaw, notably Piano Sonata no.2 and Symphony no.2. Strauss's *Salome* and *Elektra* were also the models for the first of Szymanowski's two major operas, *Hagith*, composed in 1912–13 partly in Tymoszówka and partly in Vienna.

Hagith was followed by a year of extensive travel (including visits to Sicily and North Africa) in the course of which Szymanowski steeped himself in the worlds of classical and oriental mythology as well as in the history and culture of the Arab lands. On his return to Poland in 1915 he found himself achieving (belatedly) full creative maturity as a composer, and began to branch out in quite new aesthetic directions, inspired both by his travels and by his extensive reading. His most prolific period followed, coinciding almost exactly with the war years (he was exempt from conscription because of a knee disability). The works composed during these years, including *Songs of a Fairy Princess*, *Myths*, *Metopes*, *Masques*, the Violin Concerto no.1 and Symphony no.3, were indebted to Debussy, Ravel and late Skryabin for certain harmonic and textural devices, yet there is no question of slavish imitation. Szymanowski's sound-world in these works is all his own, characterized by flexible, chromatically sinuous melodic lines which in turn evoke appropriately sensitive and sophisticated harmonic accompaniments.

The private world developed in the music of the war years, influenced heavily by the culture of the eastern Mediterranean, was shattered by the brutal intrusion of the real world in the form of the Russian Revolution, which razed the Szymanowski estate to the ground. The creative crisis Szymanowski experienced at this time was partly exorcised in the semi-autobiographical opera *Król Roger* ('King Roger'), begun in 1918 and completed in 1924. By then the composer had already adopted a simpler musical idiom, owing much to the folk music of the Tatra highlands of southern Poland, in an obvious response to the country's new-found independence. The works of these later years include the ballet-pantomime *Harnasie*, the Mazurkas op.50 for piano, the song-cycle *Słopiewnie*, the *Stabat mater* and Violin Concerto no.2.

In later life Szymanowski was dogged by ill-health and straitened circumstances. Following an unhappy period as director of the Warsaw Conservatory (1927–9), during which he wrote extensively about music, he was appointed Rector of the Warsaw State Academy of Music (which had replaced the conservatory), a post which did even more to fray his nerves. He was dismissed, along with others, in a controversy of monumental proportions in 1932 and spent his remaining years trying to make a living by playing at concerts. He died of tuberculosis in a Lausanne sanatorium at the age of 54.

2. WORKS. Apart from the childhood pieces *Roland* and *Złocisty szczyt* ('The Golden Summit'), which have been lost without trace, Szymanowski's first stage work was the operetta *Loteria na mężów* ('Lottery for a Husband'), composed to a libretto by Juliusz Krewiński-Haszyński in 1908–9. Undoubtedly his least happy artistic venture ('I decided to finish it with clenched teeth'), the work remains unpublished and unperformed.

His first important opera, the one-act *Hagith*, was composed to a German libretto by Felix Dörmann (Polish translation by Stanisław Baracz). Based on oriental legends of King David as well as on the Bible, its central theme is the demand for the live sacrifice of Hagith to restore youth and strength to the old king. Hagith's refusal to make the sacrifice (because of her love for the young prince) results in her being stoned to death. The libretto was modelled on Hofmannsthal and the music, on the composer's own admission, on Strauss: 'I often fall into the Straussian manner', he conceded in a letter to his friend Stefan Spiess. At times the music veers alarmingly from Straussian frenzy to banal echoes of Puccini, as in the love duet between Hagith and the young prince. Wagner is also echoed here, and again in Hagith's *Liebestod*; yet in the final duet between Hagith and the old king, the dramatic climax of the work, there is music of genuine power, foreshadowing the world of *King Roger*. *Hagith* had its first performance at the Wielki Theatre, Warsaw, on 13 May 1922 under Emil Młynarski.

Szymanowski's other stage works are the ballet-pantomimes *Mandragora* (1920) and *Harnasie* (1923–31), incidental music to Tadeusz Miciński's drama *Kniaź Patiomkin* ('Prince Potemkin', 1925) and his only other opera, *King Roger*, first given at the Wielki Theatre under Młynarski on 19 June 1926. *King Roger*, to a libretto by Jarosław Iwaszkiewicz (modified by the composer), has strong claims to be considered Szymanowski's masterpiece. Ostensibly it concerns the conflict between the Christian church in medieval Sicily and a pagan creed of beauty and pleasure proclaimed by a young Shepherd. Queen Roxana is seduced by the allurements of the Shepherd and his faith and leaves with him and his followers. King Roger at first follows the Shepherd as a pilgrim, but in the end stands alone. This provides a framework for a Nietzschean reworking of Euripides' *Bacchae*, which Szymanowski knew in Zieliński's Russian translation, where Roger (Pentheus) emerges 'strong enough for freedom', having overcome the enriching but dangerous Dionysian forces within himself.

The ending (in which Roger alone resists the Shepherd's influence) marked a crucial modification by Szymanowski himself of the original version of the libretto (where Roger follows the Shepherd as a disciple), and the change was symptomatic of a change in the composer's attitude to the hedonistic private world of his own earlier music. In *King Roger* that private world is symbolized above all by the 'Bacchic singing and dancing' of the second act, built as it is around two extended set numbers – Roxana's aria, in which she pleads for clemency for the Shepherd, and the ritual dance of the Shepherd's followers. Yet the seductions of this act are given distance and perspective by means of a gentle stylized counterpoint, arising naturally out of specific stylizations of Byzantine, Arabic and Hellenic elements in the opera. It is indeed possible to view the three acts as three vast scenic tableaux, Byzantine, oriental and Hellenic respectively. The archaisms of the first and third acts contrast with the revelries of the second act, where the attractions of Dionysus are presented without dilution in a musical language which recalls the most opulent of Szymanowski's middle-period works.

See also King Roger.

Z. Jachimecki: *Karol Szymanowski* (Kraków, 1927)
J. Iwaszkiewicz: *Spotkania z Szymanowskim* [Meetings with Szymanowski] (Kraków, 1947)
J. Rytard: *Wspomnienia o Karolu Szymanowskim* [Memories of Karol Szymanowski] (Kraków, 1947)
S. Golachowski: *Karol Szymanowski* (Warsaw, 1948)
T. Bronowicz-Chylińska, ed.: *Karol Szymanowski: Z listów* [From the letters] (Kraków, 1958)
T. Bronowicz-Chylińska, ed.: *Karol Szymanowski: Z pism* [From the writings] (Kraków, 1958)
J. M. Chomiński, ed.: *Z życia i twórczósci Karola Szymanowskiego* [On Szymanowski's Life and Works] (Warsaw, 1960)
K. Michałowski: *Karol Szymanowski: katalog tematyczny dzieł i bibliografia* [Thematic Catalogue and Bibliography] (Kraków, 1967)
J. Chomiński: *Studia nad tworczością Karola Szymanowskiego* [Studies on Szymanowski's Works] (Kraków, 1969)
A. Wightman: *The Music of Szymanowski* (diss., U. of York, 1972)
T. Bronowicz-Chylińska: *Karol Szymanowski* (Kraków, 1962, 3/1973; Eng. trans., 1973)
J. Samson: *The Music of Szymanowski* (London and New York, 1980)
T. Bronowicz-Chylińska, ed.: *Karol Szymanowski: Korespondencja* (Kraków, 1982)
C. Palmer: *Szymanowski* (London, 1983)
M. Bristiger, R. Scruton and P. Weber-Bockholdt, eds.: *Szymanowski in seiner Zeit* (Munich, 1984)
T. Bronowicz-Chylińska, ed.: *Karol Szymanowski: Pisma* [Writings] (Kraków, 1984)

JIM SAMSON

T

Tabarro, Il ('The Cloak'). Opera in one act by GIACOMO PUCCINI to a libretto by GIUSEPPE ADAMI after Didier Gold's play *La houppelande*; New York, Metropolitan Opera, 14 December 1918 (as no.1 of *Il trittico*).

Michele *a barge-owner (aged 50)*	baritone
Giorgetta *Michele's wife (aged 25)*	soprano
Luigi *a stevedore (aged 20)*	tenor
Il 'Tinca' *a stevedore (aged 35)*	tenor
Il 'Talpa' *a stevedore (aged 55)*	bass
La Frugola *Talpa's wife (aged 50)*	mezzo-soprano

Stevedores, a ballad-seller, *midinettes*, an organ-grinder and two lovers

Setting A bank of the river Seine, Paris, 1910

Il tabarro is the first item in a triple bill of contrasted one-act operas, a project which Puccini had cherished for many years but from which he had been regularly dissuaded by Giulio Ricordi as being harmful to the box office. Not until Ricordi's death in 1912 did he feel free to proceed. The first subject was found easily enough: Didier Gold's play *La houppelande*, which Puccini saw performed at the Théâtre Marigny in Paris in autumn that year and which he described to Illica as '*apache* in every sense of the word, and almost, no, more than almost, *Grand Guignol*'. But relations with his old librettist had begun to turn sour; and it was to the young playwright Giovacchino Forzano that Puccini first turned for a suitable text. Forzano, however, was unwilling to adapt someone else's work (in due course he would furnish the other two panels of the 'triptych', *Suor Angelica* and *Gianni Schicchi*, from his own invention) and suggested instead the poet and diplomat Ferdinando Martini. When after a few months he too bowed out, having decided that the profession of librettist was not for him, Puccini approached Giuseppe Adami, who accepted with alacrity his first commission from the composer. Progress was held up for a time by their joint work on *La rondine*; consequently Puccini did not begin the composition until October 1915. The opera was completed on 25 November 1916, the subjects of the companion-pieces being still unchosen. However, Puccini was sufficiently pleased with *Il tabarro* to consider giving it the following year in Rome as part of a double bill with *Le villi*; but the absence on military service of Titta Ruffo, his ideal Michele, caused him to abandon the idea. So *Il tabarro* waited to take its place in the *Trittico*, which had its première overseas in the composer's absence a month after the end of World War I. The cast included Claudia Muzio (Giorgetta), Alice Gentle (La Frugola – 'the lively one'), Giulio Crimi (Luigi), Luigi Montesanto (Michele), Angelo Bada (Tinca – 'tench') and Adam Didur (Talpa – 'mole'); the conductor was Roberto Moranzoni. The first Italian production was given at the Teatro Costanzi, Rome, on 11 January 1919, under Puccini's supervision, with Maria Labia (Giorgetta), Matilde Blanco Sadun (La Frugola), Edoardo de Giovanni (Edward Johnson) (Luigi) and Carlo Galeffi (Michele); the conductor was Gino Marinuzzi (i) and the director Tito Ricordi (ii). Late in 1921 Puccini replaced Michele's original apostrophe to the Seine ('Scorri, fiume eterno') with a brief, tauter monologue, strictly concerned with the action ('Nulla! Silenzio'), which thereafter became definitive.

A quay, with a barge moored alongside Giorgetta is on deck busy with domestic chores, while her husband stands silent, gazing at the sunset. A slow, swirling theme (ex.1) on muted strings, touched here and there

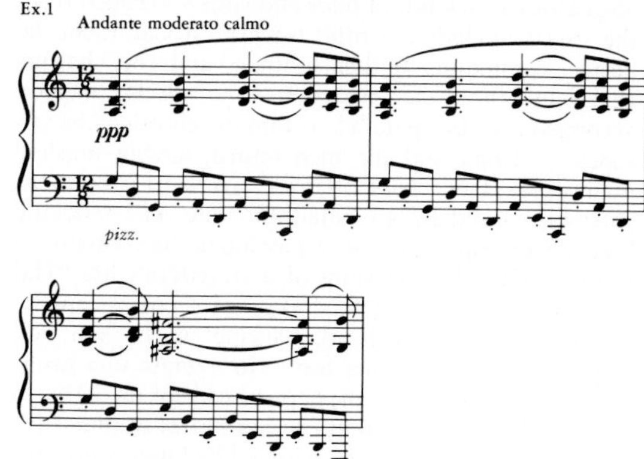

with soft woodwind notes, evokes the river Seine (it will recur constantly throughout the opera, so fixing the scene in the listener's consciousness). From time to time a ship's siren sounds. Men pass to and from the hold carrying sacks which they unload on to the quay. Below deck the strains of a shanty can be heard. Giorgetta

'Il tabarro' (Puccini): final scene from the original production at the Metropolitan Opera, New York, 14 December 1918, with Luigi Montesanto as Michele, Claudia Muzio as Giorgetta, and Giulio Crimi as Luigi

offers a glass of wine all round; Luigi, Tinca and Talpa gladly accept. Luigi calls to a passing organ-grinder, who obliges by striking up a waltz in discordant 7ths (reminiscent of Stravinsky's *Petrushka*). First Tinca, then Luigi dance with Giorgetta until the reappearance of Michele pulls them up short. He pays off the organ-grinder, who departs. A ballad-seller arrives on the quay and delights the strolling *midinettes* with 'The Story of Mimì' – a sad little ditty which contains a musical reference to *La bohème*. Giorgetta converses awkwardly with Michele, whose reserve she finds vaguely disquieting. La Frugola arrives in search of her husband, Talpa. She carries a sack full of odds and ends scavenged from the streets, including a titbit for her cat Caporale, the perfect companion of her solitude, and she chatters cheerfully about her activities to a modal melody accompanied by parallel common chords ('Se tu sapessi'). Talpa and the men return, having finished their work. Tinca goes off to a tavern to drown his sorrows, caused by an unfaithful wife. His mocking laughter prompts Luigi to a passionate 'declamato', a tirade against the hardships of a stevedore's life ('Hai ben ragione'). La Frugola dreams of a cottage in the country with her husband, basking in the sun and Caporale curled up at her feet ('Ho sognato una casetta'). Giorgetta longs for the happy bustle of the Parisian suburb where she was born. In her lyrical outburst ('È ben altro il mio sogno') she is joined by Luigi, who conjures up similar memories. Talpa and La Frugola retire still absorbed in their pastoral idyll, leaving Luigi and Giorgetta alone together.

At once the atmosphere becomes electric. A tense dialogue proceeds over a tremolando on the violins and a bass ostinato, broken off as Michele appears from the hold, surprised to find Luigi still there. The young man requests to be put off at Rouen, but Michele persuades him to remain aboard. No sooner has her husband gone than Giorgetta asks Luigi why he wanted to leave them. He replies that he cannot bear the thought of sharing her with someone else. They arrange a tryst for that night, the signal for which will be, as usual, a lighted match. The feeling of unbearable tension is heightened by recurrences of an upward-darting figure first heard on the horn. In a final access of passion Luigi declares that he would sooner stab her to the heart than lose her to another man. When he has gone Giorgetta reflects miserably on the difficulty of finding true happiness. The ostinato figure dissolves into the rocking motion of ex.1 as Michele returns, and in the course of a long *scène à deux* permeated by a new warmth, melodic and harmonic, he tries to reawaken his wife's affection for him. He recalls the child, now dead, whose cradle they used to tend, and how when the nights were cold he used to enfold them in his cloak (*tabarro*) – and here a faintly sinister motif (ex.2) is heard. He asks Giorgetta

why she now seems never to sleep at night and she replies that the air of the cabin suffocates her; she must go on deck to breathe. For the last time Michele begs her to remain with him that night, but she evades his embrace and goes below. Michele utters one word – 'Whore!' A pair of lovers are heard singing in the distance; a bugle call from the barracks sounds the last post; then all is silence. Michele wonders who the adulterer can be. Talpa? Too old. Tinca? Always drunk. Luigi? No, he asked to leave them at Rouen. Still brooding, Michele takes out his pipe and begins to light it. Seeing the flame, which he takes to be the agreed signal, Luigi hastens aboard. To a volley of action music based on ex.2, Michele seizes him by the throat, forces him to admit that he is Giorgetta's lover, then strangles him and wraps the body in his cloak. Giorgetta returns, penitent at having caused her husband pain. Timidly she begs him to take her once more within his cloak. She remembers a saying of his: 'Every one of us wears a cloak that hides sometimes a joy, sometimes a sorrow'. 'Sometimes a crime!', Michele cries, opening the garment. Giorgetta screams as Luigi's body rolls at her feet. Michele grasps her by the neck and forces her face against that of the corpse.

* * *

Of the three works that make up the *Trittico*, *Il tabarro* is the one most frequently performed today. Although it was composed long after the *verismo* movement of the 1890s had run its course, it approaches the canons of literary realism more closely than any of its Italian predecessors, if only by reason of its comparative restraint. The element of Grand Guignol, so blatant in Gold's play, with its double murder, is here softened. *Il tabarro* is arguably the best integrated of Puccini's scores. By far the greater part of it is cast in variants of triple or compound duple rhythm, thereby permitting ex.1 to surface at any point in the action without incongruity. If the lyrical moments are few, they are the more telling for their rarity.

JULIAN BUDDEN

Tableau (Fr.). SCENE.

Tableau parlant, Le ('The Talking Picture'). *Comédie-parade* in one act by ANDRÉ-ERNEST-MODESTE GRÉTRY to a libretto by LOUIS ANSEAUME; Paris, Comédie-Italienne (Hôtel de Bourgogne), 20 September 1769.

As her lover Léandre has been away for two years, Isabelle (soprano) feels unable to resist any longer the amorous advances of her tutor Cassandre (tenor). Having secured her consent, Cassandre announces that he must leave on business. Isabelle's servant, Columbine (soprano), tries in vain to make him realize that Isabelle is not in love with him. After Cassandre has left, Léandre (tenor) returns, preceded by his servant Pierrot (tenor). The two men are reconciled with the two women and the servants prepare a celebratory dinner. When the stage is empty, Cassandre emerges from a cupboard where he has been overhearing the events. He feels betrayed. He cuts out the face from a portrait of himself and takes its place. At the dinner Isabelle jokingly addresses the picture to ask Cassandre for his consent to her marriage to Léandre, and Cassandre starts to speak. After much confusion he agrees to their marriage; Columbine agrees to marry Pierrot.

The originality of Grétry's opera, emphasized by Grimm in the *Correspondance littéraire*, is founded on its witty approach to the characters: the music dovetails sudden changes in their feelings and, in particular, captures ironic and self-ironic expressions. Isabelle's *ariette*, 'Tiens ma reine, je soupire', has a quick, nonchalant accompaniment that enhances the irony of her affectedly sentimental words. The deceptive sorrow of Isabelle and Columbine at Cassandre's feigned departure is expressed in the music of their trio, 'Il faut partir', and Cassandre's individual arias reflect his anger and fear of being betrayed. The farcical side of the opera is counterbalanced by lyrical, amorous duets between the two couples. However, the funniest scene in the opera, when Cassandre speaks out of his portrait, is omitted from the music, and the ensuing quintet is set in a predominantly choral style which conveys general astonishment rather than individual feelings.

MICHAEL FEND

Tacca, Ferdinando (*b* Florence, 8 Oct 1619; *d* Florence, 24 Feb 1686). Italian architect and stage designer. He received his early artistic education from his father Pietro, sculptor to the court of Grand Duke Ferdinando II de' Medici, a post which he inherited after Pietro's death in 1640; he was later also appointed court architect. As well as designing buildings, such as the Teatro dell'Accademia degli Immobili (later della Pergola), built in Florence in 1656, he devised scenery, machines and apparatus for various performances and dynastic ceremonies, which are partly documented in engravings. Three by Stefano della Bella show images of *Proteo e la Fama*, a horseback entertainment in the Boboli gardens in 1652 for which Tacca conceived the mechanism of the *orca marina*, or sea monster (the other devices were by Alfonso Parigi). The scenery and mechanisms for Cavalli's opera *Hipermestra* (libretto by G. A. Moniglia), performed at the Teatro degli Immobili in 1658 to mark the birth of the Spanish Infanta, are known from 13 engravings by Silvio degli Alli included in the published libretto (see illustration; the costume designs, by Stefano della Bella, are in the British Museum, London). 13 engravings by Valerio Spada accompany the libretto, also by Moniglia, of Jacopo Melani's *festa teatrale Ercole in Tebe*, performed in Florence in 1661 for the wedding of Cosimo III de' Medici and Marguerite Louise d'Orléans (*see* FLORENCE, fig.3). Besides designing traditional mechanical marvels, Tacca introduced new pictorial and view effects in his exterior scenes, while in his interiors he sought structures that were harmonious and ordered without being overloaded with ornament.

*

ES (E. Povoledo)

G. A. Moniglia: *Descrizione della presa d'Argo e de gli amori di Limeo con Hipermestra, festa teatrale rappresentata dal Signor Principe Cardinal Gio. Carlo di Toscana* (Florence, 1658)

Design by Ferdinando Tacca for Act 1 (the gardens of Venus; ballet of the furies) of the original production of Cavalli's 'Hipermestra' at the Teatro degli Immobili, Florence, 12 June 1658: engraving by Silvio degli Alli

——: *Ercole in Tebe, festa teatrale rappresentata in Firenze per le reali nozze de' serenissimi sposi Cosimo terzo principe di Toscana e Margherita Luisa principessa d'Orléans* (Florence, 1661)
A. Ademollo: *I primi fasti del Teatro di via della Pergola in Firenze (1657–1661)* (Milan, 1885)
C. Molinari: 'I nuovi spettacoli di Firenze', *Le nozze degli dei: un saggio sul grande spettacolo italiano nel seicento* (Rome, 1968), 175–87
F. Decroisette: 'La construction des personnages dans deux fêtes théâtrales à la cour de Florence au XVIIe siècle', *Revue d'histoire du théâtre*, xxiv (1972), 207–22
Il luogo teatrale di Firenze: Brunelleschi, Vasari, Buontalenti, Parigi, ed. M. Fabbri, E. Garbero Zorzi and A. M. Petrioli Tofani (Milan, 1975) [exhibition catalogue]
F. Mancini and M. T. Muraro: 'Ferdinando Tacca: il fiorire della tipologia scenica', *Illusione e pratica teatrale* (Venice, 1975), 69–72 [exhibition catalogue] MERCEDES VIALE FERRERO

Tacchinardi, Nicola [Niccolò] (*b* Livorno, 3 Sept 1772; *d* Florence, 14 March 1859). Italian tenor. After playing the cello in the orchestra of the Teatro della Pergola, Florence, he studied singing, appearing in various Italian cities in 1804. In spring 1805 he made his début at La Scala in Paer's *Griselda* and Farinelli's *Odoardo e Carlotta* for the celebration of Napoleon I's coronation as king of Italy; during Carnival 1805–6 he sang at the Teatro Carcano, Milan, in Gnecco's *Le nozze di Lauretta*. He then established himself in Rome, Bergamo, Bologna (summer 1809) and Turin (Carnival 1810–11); his greatest successes were in Rome, at the Teatro Valle (1806–7) and the Teatro Argentina (1809–10) in Morlacchi's *Le danaidi*, Giuseppe Nicolini's *Traiano in Dacia* and Zingarelli's *La distruzione di Gerusalemme*. His performance of the last-named at the Paris Odéon on 4 May 1811 brought him tumultuous applause; he remained in Paris until 1814 at the Théâtre Italien, singing in Paer's *Didone*, *Don Giovanni* (with the title role transposed), Cimarosa's *Gli Orazi ed i Curiazi* and Pucitta's *Adolfo e Chiara*, and, most successfully, in Paisiello's *La molinara*. He sang in Spain, 1815–17, and in Vienna in 1816. In 1818–19 he sang at the Teatro Argentina and elsewhere in Italy, in Mayr's *Le danaide* (as *Danao*), Nicolini's *Cesare nelle Gallie* and Rossini's *Ciro in Babilonia* and *Aureliano in Palmira*. In April 1820 he sang Rossini's Otello (which became his warhorse) at the Teatro del Giglio, Lucca, and in 1820–21 appeared in *Il barbiere di Siviglia* and *La donna del lago*.

Tacchinardi was made principal singer of the grand ducal chapel in Florence in 1822, but was free to continue his operatic career; he appeared again in Vienna (1823), Barcelona (1826) and throughout Italy (1827–8); in 1825 he sang at the Teatro Ducale, Parma, in *Il crociato in Egitto*, which Meyerbeer composed for him. He retired from the stage in 1831. He wrote an essay on contemporary opera in Italy (*Dell'opera in musica sul teatro italiano e de' suoi difetti*, Florence, 2/1833). Short and stocky, though with a noble, expressive face, Tacchinardi had a voice that was mellow, powerful, extensive in compass and almost baritone in colouring. His technique was masterly, especially with regard to breathing, phrasing, agility in vocal flourishes and ease in passing from chest to head voice. A marble bust of him by Canova is in the Museo Teatrale alla Scala in Milan.

ES (R. Celletti); *MGG* (F. Bussi)
N. Jarro: *Le memorie di un impresario fiorentino* (Florence, 1892)
A. Bonaventura: *Musicisti livornesi* (Livorno, 1930)
A. Rapetti and C. Censi: *Un maestro di musica piacentino: Giuseppe Nicolini* (Piacenza, 1944)
A. Della Corte: *L'interpretazione musicale e gli interpreti* (Turin, 1951) FRANCESCO BUSSI

Tacchinardi-Persiani [née Tacchinardi], **Fanny** (*b* Rome, 4 Oct 1812; *d* Neuilly-sur-Seine, 3 May 1867). Italian soprano, daughter of Nicola Tacchinardi and wife of the composer Giuseppe Persiani. She made her début in Livorno in 1832 in the title role of Giuseppe Fournier-Gorre's *Francesca da Rimini*. Singing in *Tancredi*, *La gazza ladra*, *Il pirata* and *L'elisir d'amore* (Carnival 1832–3, Venice) and in *L'elisir*, *Beatrice di Tenda* and *La sonnambula* (summer 1833, Milan), she made a deep impression as an interpreter of Bellini and particularly of Donizetti, who wrote for her the title roles of *Rosmonda d'Inghilterra* (1834, Florence), *Lucia di Lammermoor* (1835, Naples) and *Pia de' Tolomei* (1837, Venice). She triumphed further in 1834 at the Teatro del Fondo, Naples, in Valentino Fioravanti's *Le cantatrici villane* and again in *L'elisir* and *Beatrice*, and in 1836 at the Teatro Comunale, Bologna, in Persiani's *Ines de Castro*; her frequent appearances in her husband's operas contributed to their success.

She first sang in Paris at the Théâtre Italien in autumn 1837 in *La sonnambula* and *Lucia*, and distinguished herself as Carolina in *Il matrimonio segreto*. She remained there for 13 years, appearing also in *Le nozze di Figaro*, *Don Giovanni* (as Zerlina), *Il barbiere di Siviglia*, *Linda di Chamounix* (1842) and her husband's *Il fantasma*. She sang in London almost every year between 1838 and 1849, first at the King's Theatre (where she made her début in *La sonnambula*) and later at Covent Garden, appearing in, among other operas, *Lucia* with Rubini. She also appeared in Vienna (1837, 1844) in *Torquato Tasso*, *Lucrezia Borgia*, *I due Foscari* and *Ernani*, in the Netherlands (1850) and at the Italian Opera in St Petersburg (1850–52), where in her last performances she showed signs of decline with a 'hoarseness' which, according to Fétis, had been noticeable in London in 1843.

Called 'la piccola Pasta', she had a small and delicate voice that was sweet, polished, distinct by virtue of good placement, and had a compass of *b♭* to *f‴*. Her technique was almost impeccable, with an extraordinary agility in embellishing. A lack of fullness of tone and passion was compensated for by exceptional bel canto purity and near-instrumental virtuosity. Tacchinardi-Persiani's ethereal presence and fragile build fitted her for identification with her roles of the early Romantic 'amorosa angelicata'. She was less effective in comic roles (in which she nevertheless triumphed) than as a dejected, tremulous heroine of a gloomy Romantic tragedy.

For illustration *see* LUCIA DI LAMMERMOOR.

ES ('Persiani, Fanny'; R. Celletti); *FétisB*
Chaudesaigues: *Madame Persiani* (Paris, 1839)
E. Creathorn Clayton: *Queens of Song* (New York, 1865)
G. Tebaldini: 'Giuseppe Persiani e Fanny Tacchinardi, memorie e appunti', *RMI*, xii (1905), 579–91
A. Della Corte: *L'interpretazione musicale e gli interpreti* (Turin, 1951)
T. Kaufman: 'Giuseppe and Fanny Persiani', *Donizetti Society Journal*, vi (1988), 123–51 [incl. chronology of operatic appearances] FRANCESCO BUSSI

Taddei, Giuseppe (*b* Genoa, 26 June 1916). Italian baritone. He studied in Rome and made his début there in 1936 as the Herald in *Lohengrin*. He sang regularly in Rome, where his repertory included Alberich, Germont and Rivière (Dallapiccola's *Volo di notte*), until he was conscripted into the army in 1942. Engaged in 1946 for two seasons at the Vienna Staatsoper, he scored particular successes in Verdi roles. In 1947 he sang Scarpia and Rigoletto at the Cambridge Theatre, London, and in 1948 Mozart's Figaro at the Salzburg Festival. At La Scala (1948–61) his roles included Pizarro, Malatesta, the four villains in *Les contes d'Hoffmann* and parts in operas by Nino Sanzogno and Ferrari Trecate. Elsewhere in Italy he sang (in Italian) Hans Sachs, Gunther, Wolfram and the Dutchman. Later he specialized in Mozart, singing Papageno, Figaro and Leporello. He appeared at Covent Garden between 1960 and 1967 as Macbeth, Rigoletto, Iago and Scarpia and also sang in San Francisco, Chicago and at the Bregenz Festival (1968, 1969, 1971) as Falstaff, Dulcamara and Sulpice (*La fille du régiment*). Taddei was a most versatile and gifted singer, as successful in dramatic as in comic roles. HAROLD ROSENTHAL/R

Tadeo, Giorgio (*b* Verona, 2 Oct 1929). Italian bass. He studied at the Parma Conservatory and the opera school of La Scala, Milan, then made his début in 1953 at Palermo as Méphistophélès in Gounod's *Faust.* His career flourished in the principal Italian centres, including Rome, Turin and Florence; later he specialized in *buffo* roles and toured more widely. He made his Covent Garden début in 1974 as Don Pasquale, and was described then as 'rubber-faced, round-voiced and wholly lovable', with a rich, resonant voice. He has sung at Chicago Lyric Opera and at Dallas, at the Colón, Buenos Aires, and in Mexico City, and also at major European festivals. His recordings include Mathieu in *Andrea Chénier* under Chailly (1985), Arbaces in *Idomeneo*, and roles in *Le nozze di Figaro* and *Manon Lescaut.* NOËL GOODWIN

Tadolini [née Savonari], **Eugenia** (*b* Forlì, 1809; *d* Naples, after 1851). Italian soprano. She studied with Giovanni Tadolini, whom she married, and made her début in 1828 in Florence. She first appeared in Paris at the Théâtre Italien in Rossini's *Ricciardo e Zoraide* (1830). During the next 12 years she sang at La Scala and in Venice, Vienna and Florence. Her repertory included Donizetti's Jane Seymour, Anne Boleyn, Lucia, Adina, Antonina (*Belisario*), Parisina, Fausta, Maria Padilla and Norina, as well as Bellini's Amina, Elvira and Norma. She created the title roles of *Linda di Chamounix* (1842) and *Maria di Rohan* (1843), both in Vienna. After singing Elvira (*Ernani*) in 1844, she created the title role of Verdi's *Alzira* in Naples (1846), and sang Odabella (*Attila*) at La Scala and Lady Macbeth at Naples in 1848, the year she made her London début at Her Majesty's Theatre as Linda; she also sang Leonora (*La favorita*) and Paolina in the Italian première of *Poliuto*, both at Naples. She retired in 1851. She had a large, flexible voice, which Verdi considered too beautiful for the role of Lady Macbeth.

For illustration *see* MARIA DI ROHAN.

G. Zavadini: *Donizetti: vita, musiche, epistolario* (Bergamo, 1948)
H. Weinstock: *Donizetti and the World of Opera in Italy, Paris and Vienna in the First Half of the 19th Century* (New York, 1963)
J. Budden: *The Operas of Verdi*, i: *From 'Oberto' to 'Rigoletto'* (London, 1973) ELIZABETH FORBES

Tadolini, Giovanni (*b* Bologna, 18 Oct ?1789; *d* Bologna, 29 Nov 1872). Italian composer and singing teacher. He studied with Stanislao Mattei and Matteo Babbini at the Liceo Musicale in Bologna, and became répétiteur and later chorus master at the Théâtre Italien, Paris (1811–14). He returned to Italy, where his eight operas were produced between 1815 and 1827. The soprano Eugenia Tadolini was his wife. He was a member of the Accademia Filarmonica in Bologna and *maestro di cappella* of the cathedral (1825). In 1829 he returned to Paris to become musical director of the Théâtre Italien. He is said to have composed six sections of the *Stabat mater* commissioned from Rossini which was performed in Madrid on Easter Saturday, 1833. In 1839–41 Tadolini was in Italy; he founded a singing school at Bologna, went back to the Théâtre Italien in 1841, then returned to teach singing at his school in 1848.

Le bestie in uomini (dramma, 2, A. Anelli), Venice, S Moisè, April 1815
La fata Alcina (dg, 2), Venice, 1815
La principessa di Navarra, ossia Il Gianni di Parigi (dramma serio, 5), Bologna, 1816
Il credulo deluso (dg, 2, C. Sterbini), Rome, 1817; as Il finto molinaro, Rome, Valle, 8 Jan 1820
Tamerlano, Bologna, 1818
Moctar, gran visir di Adrianopoli (dramma serio, 2, L. Romanelli), Bologna, Comunale, May 1824
Mitridate (melodramma eroico, 2, G. Rossi), Venice, Fenice, 26 Dec 1826
Almanzor (melodramma serio, 2, F. Romani), Trieste, Grande, 22 Sept 1827 ELIZABETH FORBES

Tagi-zade-Hajibeyov, Nijazi Zul'fagarovich. *See* NIJAZI.

Tagliabue, Carlo (*b* Mariano Comense, 13 Jan 1898; *d* Monza, 5 April 1978). Italian baritone. He studied with Gennai and Guidotti and made his début at Lodi in 1922 as Amonasro. After appearances at provincial theatres and in Florence, Palermo and the Verona Arena he was engaged at La Scala, where he sang regularly from 1930 to 1953. As well as the Italian repertory, his roles included Telramund, Wolfram, Gunther and Kurwenal. At the Rome Opera he created Basilio in Respighi's *La fiamma* (1934), and he sang Scedeur in the first performances at La Scala of Pizzetti's *Lo straniero.* He sang at the Teatro Colón (1934), at the Metropolitan (1937–9), where he made his début as Amonasro, and in San Francisco (1938). He made his Covent Garden début in 1938 as Rigoletto and returned in 1946 as Germont with the S Carlo company. In 1953 he sang Don Carlo (*La forza del destino*) at the Stoll Theatre. He continued to sing until 1960. Tagliabue possessed a warm, beautifully produced voice, but his acting was limited and his performances were reliable rather than inspired.

GV (R. Celletti; R. Vegeto)
G. Lauri-Volpi: *Voci parallele* (Milan, 1955)
HAROLD ROSENTHAL/R

Tagliafico, Joseph (Dieudonné) (*b* Toulon, 1 Jan 1821; *d* Nice, 27 Jan 1900). French bass of Italian parentage. He studied in Paris and made his début there in 1844 at the Théâtre Italien. In 1847 he sang Oroe (*Semiramide*) in the inaugural performance of the Royal Italian Opera at Covent Garden, and he appeared there every season until 1876. He sang Oberthal in *Le prophète* (1849), Sparafucile in *Rigoletto* and Fieramosca in *Benvenuto Cellini* (1853), Ferrando in *Il trovatore* (1855), the High Priest in *L'Africaine* (1865) and Friar Laurence in *Roméo et Juliette* (1867), all first London performances. Although his voice was neither large nor remarkable in quality, his enormous repertory of Mozart, Rossini, Bellini, Donizetti, Halévy, Meyerbeer, Gounod and Verdi operas made him invaluable.

*

H. Rosenthal: *Two Centuries of Opera at Covent Garden* (London, 1958)

ELIZABETH FORBES

Tagliavini, Ferruccio (*b* Reggio Emilia, 14 Aug 1913). Italian tenor. He studied in Parma with Brancucci and in Florence with Amadeo Bassi. He made his début in October 1938 in Florence as Rodolfo in *La bohème* and by the end of World War II had established himself as one of the leading tenors of the Italian stage; he then appeared successfully at the Metropolitan (1947–54 and 1961–2). During the visit of the La Scala company to Covent Garden in 1950, he sang Nemorino in *L'elisir d'amore*, revealing his vocal achievements as well as a considerable talent as a comic actor. He made further appearances in London as Cavaradossi and as Nadir in *Les pêcheurs de perles*.

Essentially a *tenore di grazia*, Tagliavini excelled in the bel canto operas of Bellini and Donizetti and in the title role of Mascagni's *L'amico Fritz*, which he recorded under the composer's direction, with his wife, the soprano Pia Tassinari, as Suzel. Many regarded him as the successor of Tito Schipa; Tagliavini's style, however, was less dependable. He could spin out a sustained note until it became a mere thread of tone, and he sang florid passages more accurately than was usual in the postwar period; but he also relied on abrupt transitions between *fortissimo* and *pianissimo* to the neglect of the intermediate shades, and in later years permitted his louder tones to develop a harsh quality.

*

GV (G. Gualerzi; R. Vegeto)
C. Tedeschi: *Ferruccio Tagliavini* (Rome, 1942)
A. Natan: 'Tagliavini, Ferruccio', *Primo uomo: grosser Sänger der Oper* (Basle, 1963) [with discography]
H. Rosenthal: *Great Singers of Today* (London, 1966)
H. Sanguinetti and C. Williams: 'Ferruccio Tagliavini', *Record Collector*, xxix (1984), 197–240 [with discography]

DESMOND SHAWE-TAYLOR

Tagliavini, Franco (*b* Novellara, nr Reggio Emilia, 29 Oct 1934). Italian tenor. He studied at Vercelli and made his début in 1961 at the Teatro Nuovo, Milan, as Canio. He then appeared at all the leading theatres in Europe and North America. He made his Covent Garden début in 1967 as Pollione, returning as Cavaradossi and the Duke (*Rigoletto*). At the Florence Maggio Musicale he sang Leicester (*Maria Stuarda*) in 1967 and Licinio (*La vestale*) in 1970. His repertory included Alfredo, Gabriele Adorno, Percy (*Anna Bolena*), Calaf, Pinkerton, Foresto (*Attila*), Enzo (*La Gioconda*), Maurizio (*Adriana Lecouvreur*), Faust (*Mefistofele*) and Lohengrin, which he sang in Italian at Naples (1970). His voice was robust with a ringing top register.

ELIZABETH FORBES

Tagliazucchi, Giampietro (*fl* 1749–63). Italian librettist. He was called to Berlin by Frederick II to serve as court poet on the death of Leopoldo de Villati in July 1752. At first the king sketched out in French prose the entire texts of the librettos that Tagliazucchi fashioned for the court opera. For *Il tempio d'amore* and *I fratelli nemici* his contributions grew less detailed. In the preface to his first libretto for Berlin, *Silla* (1753), Tagliazucchi related that Frederick was responsible for the substance of the text, to which he simply 'gave the adornment of Italian theatrical poetry'. With the advent of the Seven Years War in 1756 Tagliazucchi left Berlin. He worked with Jommelli on two occasional pieces for Ludwigsburg in 1763, after which nothing is known of his whereabouts.

Mario in Numidia, Rinaldo di Capua, 1749; *Silla* (drama per musica, with Frederick II, after J.-F. Duché de Vancy: *Scylla*), Graun, 1753; *Semiramide* (drama per musica, after Voltaire), Graun, 1754; *Montezuma* (tragedia per musica, with Frederick II), Graun, 1755; *Il tempio d'amore* (with Frederick II), J. F. Agricola, 1755; *Ezio* (drama per musica, after P. Metastasio), Graun, 1755; *I fratelli nemici* (tragedia per musica, with Frederick II, after J. Racine: *Les frères ennemis*), Graun, 1756; *Merope* (tragedia per musica, with Frederick II, after Voltaire), Graun, 1756; *La pastorella illustre* (azione per musica), Jommelli, 1763; *Il trionfo d'amore* (azione pastorale), Jommelli, 1763

THOMAS BAUMAN

Täglichsbeck, Thomas (*b* Ansbach, 31 Dec 1799; *d* Baden-Baden, 5 Oct 1867). German violinist and composer. After study with Molique in Munich, in 1817 he became a violinist in the Isartortheater orchestra, and, despite his youth, succeeded Lindpaintner as music director two years later. In 1822 he became a solo violinist at the Munich court, a post which allowed him more time to give concert tours and to compose; his first opera, *Webers Bild*, dates from that period. For the rest of his life he worked mainly as an orchestral violinist and a conductor; the climax of his career as a composer came with the performance of his Symphony no.1 in E♭ at the Paris Conservatoire in 1836. The opera *König Enzio*, produced in Karlsruhe in 1843, did not establish itself in the repertory.

Webers Bild (1, A. Lewald), Munich, Hof, 24 Aug 1823, rev. as Das Quiproquo; MS, Donauwörth, Cassianeum
König Enzio (2, G. Schilling), Karlsruhe, Hof, 14 May 1843, MS, Donauwörth, Cassianeum
Kaiser Heinrich IV (3, F. von Oldenburg), Karlsruhe, Hof, 1844
Der Liebesring, 1860 (2, H. Schmid), ?unperf.
Guido, oder Das Jägerhaus im Walde Sila (2, F. Ellmenreich), unperf., Act 1, Donauwörth, Cassianeum

*

StiegerO
E. Flad: 'Thomas Täglichsbeck', *Zollernheimat*, vi/8–9 (Hechingen, 1937)
C. Gruber: *Opern Uraufführungen*, ii (Vienna, 1987)

ALBERT MELL

Taglioni, Filippo (*b* Milan, 5 Nov 1777; *d* Como, 11 Feb 1871). Italian dancer and choreographer. In 1794 he became first dancer at the Teatro dei Nobili, Pisa, where his father Carlo was ballet-master. After touring throughout Italy, 1796–8, he went to Paris to study with J.-F. Coulon, making his début at the Opéra in *La caravane* (1799). He worked at the Royal Opera, Stockholm, in 1803–4, and at the Hoftheater, Vienna, in 1805, before undertaking an extended European tour; he was ballet-master or first dancer at opera houses in Kassel, Milan, Turin, Florence, Munich, Stuttgart, Berlin, London, St Petersburg and Warsaw. Taglioni's importance for opera lies mainly in his choreography for the premières, all at the Paris Opéra, of Auber's *Le dieu et la bayadère* (1830) and *Gustave III* (1833), Meyerbeer's *Robert le diable* (1831) and *Les Huguenots* (1836), and Halévy's *La Juive* (1835). That for *Robert*, including the famous 'Scène des nonnes' in which 50 dancers dressed in white wafted through the ghostly cloister, made theatrical history: the first *ballet blanc*, it proclaimed a new aesthetic, combining an airy style of dancing with the mysterious atmosphere of the spirit world. Soon afterwards, Taglioni retired from the

Marie Taglioni in Auber's 'Le dieu et la bayadère': coloured lithograph, c1834

stage to devote himself to his daughter Marie's career, choreographing ballets to display her genius.

Marie Taglioni (*b* Stockholm, 23 April 1804; *d* Marseilles, 22 April 1884), among the first ballerinas to capture the spirit of Romanticism in dance, incorporated astonishing *pointe* techniques into an individualistic style that was unusual for its modesty and spirituality. She studied with Coulon at the Paris Opéra but was assisted mainly by her father in creating a new, highly poetic style. Among her greatest operatic successes were *Guillaume Tell*, *Le dieu et la bayadère* and *Robert le diable*, though the ballet most closely identified with her was *La sylphide* (1832). Her brothers Salvatore (1789–1868) and Paul (1808–84) were also active as dancers and choreographers.

A. Levinson: *Marie Taglioni* (Paris, 1929)
A. Michel: 'Les ballets de Philippe Taglioni', *Archives internationales de la danse*, ii (1934), 122–5
I. Guest: *The Romantic Ballet in Paris* (London, 1966)
M. H. Winter: *The Pre-Romantic Ballet* (London, 1974)

MAUREEN NEEDHAM COSTONIS

Taiber. *See* TEYBER.

Taille [*haute-taille*] (Fr.). The middle of the three male voices intermediate between the *dessus* (soprano) and the *basse* in Baroque and Classical French opera, with a range *c–g'*, notated in the tenor clef (throughout that period, pitch was as much as a whole tone lower than that now used). These three voices (the others were *haute-contre* and *basse-taille*, later *baryton*) corresponded to the three *parties intermédaires* of the string orchestra.

Brossard (*Dictionaire de musique*, 1703) described the *taille naturelle* (with range normally *e–f'*) as 'the voice in which almost all men can sing'; for the *haute-taille* (or *première taille*) he extended the range upwards to *a'*. *Taille* solo roles occur rarely in French 17th- or 18th-century opera, the high tenor parts being assigned to *haute-contre* singers. Significant exceptions in Lully's operas include the role of Admetus in *Alceste* (1674) and Theseus (1675).

Notable *taille* singers included Louis-Antoine Cuvillier, 'a good musician and a good actor', who entered the Paris Opéra in 1725, deserted it briefly in 1729 during Destouches' directorship, was ordered to return by the Count of Toulouse for whom he also worked, and was still performing minor roles in 1763 (the revival of Rameau's *La princesse de Navarre* at Bordeaux). André Richer sang in operas at court, including the Spectacles du Cabinet du Roi organized by Mme de Pompadour (1747–8) and works of Rameau at Fontainebleau in 1754, while his son, Louis-Augustin Richer, also a *taille*, who had begun his career as a boy treble, was praised by the *Mercure de France* in 1768 as singing 'without the sourness of the falsetto or the aridity of voices conserved against the order of nature' (when replacing a castrato in a concert performance, and presumably singing an octave lower).

LIONEL SAWKINS

Tailleferre, Germaine (Marcelle) (*b* Parc-St-Maur, nr Paris, 19 April 1892; *d* Paris, 7 Nov 1983). French composer. A child prodigy, she began composing at the age of five; one of her first projects was an opera, *Sur les lieux de malheur*. Despite her father's opposition and her equal skills as an artist she entered the Paris Conservatoire in 1904; there she won numerous prizes and met Auric, Honegger and Milhaud in 1913. She was also introduced to Satie in 1917, who referred to her as his 'musical daughter'; he brought her to prominence first as one of his group of Nouveaux Jeunes and in 1920 as the only female member of Les Six, calling her 'our Marie Laurencin'. Although her career was successfully launched, she continued to study orchestration with Koechlin (until 1924) and Ravel (1925–30), all the while writing mostly chamber and piano music in a prolific, neo-classical manner. Her two *opéras comiques*, *Le fou sensé* (1930) and *Zoulaina* (1930–31), were never performed, and she did not see any of her operas staged until 1937, when she composed the *opéra bouffe Le marin du Bolivar* for the Paris Exhibition.

Most of Tailleferre's operas date from the 1950s, and her light, appealing approach is epitomized in the series of four short comic operas ('Du style galant au style méchant') that she wrote for French radio with Denise Centore. In these she recreated with delight and typically consummate craftsmanship the styles of the 18th century, the Romantic period, Offenbach and naturalism à la Bruneau. This renewed interest in opera (which reached a climax with her setting of Ionesco's *Le maître* in 1959) was sparked off by her 1948 collaboration with Henry Jeanson on *Il était un petit navire*. Although this was produced at the Opéra-Comique in 1951, it was not a success; the setting was considered too protracted for the slight plot to bear (as was again the case with her Soupault collaboration *La petite sirène*, based on Andersen's *The Little Mermaid*). As her talents as a musical dramatist were limited and her music uneven, Tailleferre has remained better known as a composer of ballets (such as *Le marchand d'oiseaux*, 1923), piano and chamber music; none of her operas has entered the repertory. However, much of her music has real spontaneity, freshness and charm, and revival of her shorter operatic works would prove worthwhile.

opéras bouffes unless otherwise stated

Zoulaina, 1930–31 (oc, 3, C.-H. Hirsch), unperf.
Le marin du Bolivar (1, H. Jeanson), Paris, Paris Exhibition, 1937
Dolorès (opérette), Paris, OC, 1950
Il était un petit navire (satire lyrique, 3 tableaux, Jeanson), Paris, OC, 9 March 1951
Parfums (comédie musicale, 3, G. Hirsch and J. Bouchor), Monte Carlo, Opéra, 11 April 1951
La fille d'opéra (1, D. Centore), RTF, 28 Dec 1955
Le bel ambitieux (1, Centore), RTF, 28 Dec 1955
Monsieur Petitpois achète un château (1, Centore), RTF, 28 Dec 1955
La pauvre Eugénie (1, Centore), RTF, 28 Dec 1955
Mémoires d'une bergère (1, P. Jullian), RTF, 1959
Le maître (chamber op, 1, E. Ionesco), RTF, 12 July 1960
La petite sirène (opéra, 3, P. Soupault, after H. C. Andersen), RTF, 30 Sept 1960

*

O. Pannetier: 'Avec Germaine Tailleferre', *Candide* (19 Nov 1931)
J. Bruyr: 'Germaine Tailleferre', *Musica*, xxxvi (1957), 29–33
L. Mitgang: *'La Princesse des Six': a life of Germaine Tailleferre* (thesis, Oberlin College, OH, 1982)
G. Tailleferre: 'Mémoires à l'emporte-pièce', *Revue internationale de musique française*, no.19 (1986), 5–82 ROBERT ORLEDGE

Tajemství. Opera by Bedřich Smetana; *see* SECRET, THE.

Tajikstan. For discussion of opera in Tajikstan *see* DUSHANBE.

Tajo, Italo (*b* Pinerolo, Piedmont, 25 April 1915). Italian bass. He studied with Bertozzi in Turin and made his début there as Fafner (*Das Rheingold*) in 1935. During the war he sang at the Rome Opera in a variety of roles, including the Doctor in the Italian première of *Wozzeck* (1942), and at La Scala, where he returned in the first postwar season (1946) as Don Magnifico and Ochs, and where he continued to appear until 1956. At the 1947 Edinburgh Festival he sang Figaro and Banquo with the Glyndebourne company, then appeared in London at the Cambridge Theatre (1947–8), as Don Basilio, Leporello and Don Pasquale, and at Covent Garden with the Scala company in 1950 when, as Dulcamara, he revealed his outstanding gifts as a *buffo* artist. He made his American début in Chicago as Ramfis (1946), and sang at San Francisco (1948–56) and the Metropolitan (1948–50). In Italy Tajo created roles in operas by Bucchi, Malipiero, Nono, Berio, Lualdi and Tosatti; he sang Samuel in the first performance at La Scala of Milhaud's *David* (1955) and took part in the Italian premières of *Troilus and Cressida* (1956) and *The Nose* (1964). He continued to make occasional appearances in the USA as the Sacristan and Benoit and in other character roles until the late 1980s.

*

R. Hastings: 'Italo Tajo', *Opera Annual*, vii (London, 1960), 102–10
C. Faria: 'Old Pros: Tajo and Barbieri', *ON*, xli/16 (1976–7), 9–13
HAROLD ROSENTHAL/R

Takata, Saburō (*b* Nagoya, 18 Dec 1913). Japanese composer. He was a pupil of Kiyoshi Nobutoki and Pringsheim, and graduated from the Tokyo Music School in 1939. In 1947 he joined the Japanese Society for Contemporary Music, of which he was president from 1963 to 1968, and again from 1979 to 1984. He taught composition at the Kunitachi Music College from 1953 to 1979. His early works reflect the influence of German Romanticism as well as of impressionism, but later he became more concerned with how to set Japanese words to music. He is best known for his songs and choral music, including two masses, psalms and hymns. His only opera, *Aoki ōkami* ('The Dark Blue Wolf'), in four acts, to his own libretto after the novel by Yasushi Inoue, had a successful première at the Metropolitan Festival Hall, Tokyo, on 15 October 1972. It tells the story of Temujin, a Mongolian youth who eventually became the great Genghis Khan. The music incorporates Mongolian folktunes.

MASAKATA KANAZAWA

Taktakishvili, Otar Vasil'yevich (*b* Tbilisi, 27 July 1924; *d* Tbilisi, 22 Feb 1989). Georgian composer, conductor and writer on music. He graduated in composition from the Tbilisi Conservatory in 1947, where he continued to work as a teacher. His experience as a choral conductor gained him the post of artistic director of the Georgian State Choral Kapella in 1952. He was also a deputy to the Supreme Soviets of the USSR and Georgia. Further appointments included Minister of Culture of the Georgian SSR (1965) and Secretary of the Composers' Union of the USSR. He composed in a wide variety of genres but wrote no operas until *Mindiya* (1961), whose success was partly due to his long absorption in vocal music and his developing interest in Georgian folk styles. *Mindiya* makes extensive use of Georgian folk idioms and alternates elements of the old epic narrative style with traditional lyric-dramatic scenes. He returned to opera in 1967 with a trilogy of one-act operas, *Sami novela* ('Three Stories'), which depict the sufferings of the people in pre-revolutionary Georgia in a musical style rich in rural and urban folk elements. In later operas he pursued lighter themes.

Mindiya (R. Tabukashvili, after V. Pshavela), Tbilisi, 23 July 1961
Sami novela [Three Stories] (trilogy), Tbilisi, 1967
Ori ganacheni [Two Verdicts] (1, Taktakishvili, after M. Dzhavakhishvili)
Dzhariskatsi [The Soldier] (1, Taktakishvili, after Dzhavakhishvili)
Droshebi chkara [Hold the Banners High] (1, G. Tabidze)
rev. as Tri zhizni [Three Lives] with new no.3: Chikor, 1972 (S. Tsenin, after Dzhavakhishvili)
Mtvaris motatseba [The Abduction of the Moon] (after K. Gamsakhurdia), Moscow, Bol'shoy, 1977
[The Philanderer], 1978 (after Dzhavakhishvili)
[First Love], 1980 (R. Gabriadze) STEPHEN JOHNSON

Taktakishvili, Shalva Mikhailovich (*b* Kvemo Khviti, 14/27 Aug 1900; *d* Tbilisi, 18 July 1965). Georgian composer and conductor. He studied at the Tbilisi Conservatory (1920–28) and then helped to found a music school at Batum, where he was both director and teacher of music theory. From the 1930s he was active as a conductor in Tbilisi as well as teaching the opera class at the conservatory (1937–9) and directing its opera studio (from 1951). His operas *Gantiadi* ('Daybreak', 1926) and *Deputat* ('The Deputy', 1940) were both performed in Tbilisi. He also published writings on Rimsky-Korsakov and Shalyapin and studies of several operas.

Mir tsvetov [The World of Flowers], 1922 (fairy-tale op)
Pervoye Maya [The First of May], 1924 (children's op)
Osen' [Autumn], 1925 (children's op)

Gantiadi [Daybreak] (fairy-tale op, 3, G. Taktakishvili), Tbilisi, 10 April 1926
Deputat [The Deputy] (4, G. Taktakishvili and A. Takayshvili), Tbilisi, 5 May 1940
Otarova vdova [Otar's Widow], 1942 (after I. Chavchavadze)

*

P. V. Hukua: *Shalva Taktakishvili* (Tbilisi, 1962)
S. D. Krebs: *Soviet Composers and the Development of Soviet Music* (London, 1970)

Tal [Gruenthal], **Josef** [Joseph] (*b* Pinne, nr Poznań, 18 Sept 1910). Israeli composer of Polish birth. After studying at the Berlin Hochschule für Musik with Heinz Tiessen, Hindemith and others, he went to Palestine in 1934. He was director of the Rubin (formerly Jerusalem) Academy of Music from 1948 to 1952, and from 1950 he taught at the Hebrew University, Jerusalem, becoming professor in 1971. A pioneer of electronic music, he became director of the Israel Centre for Electronic Music in 1961. He won several prizes, among them the State of Israel Prize (1971).

Many of Tal's early works were based on biblical subjects or epic events in Jewish history. However, in style he remained faithful to his European background and was not affected by the trends which dominated most Israeli compositions in the 1940s and 50s, namely Jewish folklore or eastern musical traditions (the *maqām*) of the region. By that time Tal was writing 12-note music and gradually his use of dodecaphonic elements became less constrained. A prolific composer in many genres, he also incorporated electronic music into many of his compositions.

His most successful opera, *Ashmedai*, is based on a Talmudic legend, and has been staged in Hamburg, New York and Los Angeles. *Massada*, a commission from the Israel Festival, was written for electronic sounds rather than a conventional orchestra. Israel Eliraz provided the librettos for these and for *Die Versuchung*, the story of a man from the wild adapting to civilization, *Else*, which is based on the life of Else Lasker Schüler, and *Der Garten*, the story of Adam and Eve. Tal's 1983 opera *Der Turm*, a parable concerning the political forces behind the building and destruction of the Tower of Babylon, to a libretto by Hans Keller, was commissioned by the Institute for Advanced Studies, Berlin. Unlike the five Eliraz operas, the work was not well received at its 1987 première at the Berlin Festival.

See also ASHMEDAI.

Saul at Ein Dor (op concertante, 1, Tal, after the Bible), Tel-Aviv, 1957
Amnon and Tamar, 1958 (1, R. Freier, after the Bible), Jerusalem, 1961
Ashmedai, 1968–9 (2, I. Eliraz), Hamburg, Städtische Oper, 9 Nov 1971 (in German)
Massada (15 scenes, Eliraz), Jerusalem, July 1973
Die Versuchung, 1973–4 (2, Eliraz), Munich, Staatsoper, 26 July 1976
Else (chamber scene, Eliraz), Tel-Aviv, July 1975
Scene (after F. Kafka), 1978
Der Turm, 1983 (2, H. Keller), Berlin, Kassel Opera, Sept 1987
Der Garten (chamber op, prol., 7 scenes, int, Eliraz), Hamburg, Städtische Oper, May 1988
Die Hand (dramatic scene, Eliraz), Berlin, 1988

*

J. Tal: 'Gedanken zur Oper "Ashmedai"', *Ariel*, xv (1972), 89
M. Brod and J. W. Cohen: *Die Musik Israels* (Kassel, 1976)
J. Tal: *Der Sohn des Rabbiners* (Hamburg, 1985)
W. Y. Elias: *Joseph Tal* (Tel-Aviv, 1987)

WILLIAM Y. ELIAS

Talazac, Jean-Alexandre (*b* Bordeaux, 6 May 1851; *d* Chatou, Paris, 26 Dec 1896). French tenor. He studied at the Paris Conservatoire, then in 1878 was engaged by the Opéra-Comique, singing Selim in Reyer's *La statue*and also in Auber's *Haydée*. He created the title roles of Delibes' *Jean de Nivelle* (1880) and Offenbach's *Les contes d'Hoffmann* (1881); Gérald in *Lakmé* (1883), Des Grieux in *Manon* (1884) and Mylio in Lalo's *Le roi d'Ys* (1888). He also sang Tamino, Méhul's Joseph, Alfredo (*La traviata*) and, at the Eden-Théâtre, Samson in the first staged performance in Paris of Saint-Saëns' *Samson et Dalila* (1890). At Monte Carlo (1883–9) he sang Faust, Wilhelm Meister, Fernand (*La favorite*), Donizetti's Edgardo, Noureddin (David's *Lalla-Roukh*) and Grétry's Richard the Lionheart. He appeared in Lisbon (1887) as Raoul and at Covent Garden (1889) as Alfredo, Faust and Nadir (*Les pêcheurs de perles*). His voice was of great brilliance and purity.

For illustration *see* MANON.

ELIZABETH FORBES

Tale of Tsar Saltan, The [*The Tale of Tsar Saltan, of his Son the Renowned and Mighty Bogatïr Prince Guidon Saltanovich, and of the Beautiful Swan-Princess* (*Skazka o Tsare Saltane o sïne ego slavnom i moguchem bogatïre knyaze Gvidone Saltanoviche i o prekrasnoy Tsarevne Lebedi*)]. Opera in a prologue and four acts by NIKOLAY ANDREYEVICH RIMSKY-KORSAKOV to a libretto by VLADIMIR NIKOLAYEVICH BEL'SKY after the imitation folktale in verse by ALEXANDER SERGEYEVICH PUSHKIN; Moscow, Solodovnikov Theatre (Savva Mamontov's Private Russian Opera), 21 October/3 November 1900.

Tsar Saltan	bass
Tsaritsa Militrisa *the youngest sister*	soprano
Tkachikha ('Weaver') *the middle sister*	mezzo-soprano
Povarikha ('Cook') *the eldest sister*	soprano
Matchmaker-Crone Babarikha	contralto
Tsarevich [Prince] Guidon	two boy ballet students; tenor
Swan-Princess (*at first* Swan-Bird)	soprano
Old Grandpa	tenor
Messenger	baritone
Jester	bass
Three Shipmasters	tenor, baritone, bass
Voices of Sorcerers and Spirits	male choristers

Boyars and their wives, courtiers, nursemaids, sentries, troops, boatmen, astrologers, footmen, singers, scribes, servants and maids, dancers of both sexes, crowd; 33 knights of the sea with their leader Chernomor; squirrel, bumblebee

Setting The city of Tmutarakan' and the island of Buyan

The Tale of Tsar Saltan, composed at Vladimir Stasov's suggestion, was Rimsky-Korsakov's contribution to the celebration of the Pushkin centenary (1899). Although seemingly a return to a vein he had mined exhaustively in earlier fairy-tale operas, it in fact marked a new departure, for not only the content but the form of the opera followed that of the folktale (*skazka*) on which it was based. The composer plays the part of a storyteller by prefacing each act (and the orchestral interludes as well) with a famous little fanfare that functions as a *priskazka*, the verbal flourish with which the *skazochnik* seizes the listener's attention. The listener's attention is released in the same manner, and the one time Rimsky's fanfare is actually sung comes at the very end of the opera, when the assembled *dramatis personae* step out of character to sing the audience a rhyming *envoi* in unison: 'Well, that's the whole *skazka*; there's no more to tell!' (ex.1).

Ex.1
(a) Opening fanfare (*priskazka*)

(b) Choral *envoi*

The plot of a *skazka* is usually heavily stylized by means of multiple characters and repetitive, ritualized actions: hence in *The Tale of Tsar Saltan* there are three sisters, three wishes, three wonders and three bee stings, the composer organizing the formal structure of his music around these built-in 'strophes'. There is virtually no concession to realism. The characters (making limited exception for the romantic leads and the hero's mother, Militrisa) are figures of fun, and the music exploits funny modern folk genres the composer would have spurned as trivial in his earlier period, when he was infatuated with archaic peasant music as key to a romantically idealized national mythology. Now he happily adapted children's songs, domestic lullabies (including one in memory of his children's nanny, who had died the year before), urban ditties and various genres associated with urban fairs, including the jingles of carnival barkers and peepshow operators. All this will bring *Petrushka*, the fairground ballet by Rimsky-Korsakov's most famous pupil, to mind; and indeed Stravinsky (perhaps unconsciously) drew on *Tsar Saltan* in composing that work, adapting the orchestral texture at the very beginning from his teacher's evocation of ships at sea (ex.2).

At its first performance, the opera was conducted by Mikhail Ippolitov-Ivanov; Nadeshda Zabela sang the Swan-Princess, Anton Sekar-Rozhansky was Guidon and Vasily Shkafer Old Grandpa.

PROLOGUE *A brightly lit room in a cottage in Tmutarakan', Tsar Saltan's capital, on a winter evening* Three sisters are spinning, the old witch Babarikha is sitting to one side. The elder sisters, who have been exhausting the youngest with menial chores, preen themselves (their duet is a compound of at least four folksongs, three of them from Rimsky-Korsakov's collection of 1877; the musical style, especially at the beginning, is an astute stylization of folk heterophonic polyphony, the earliest published examples of which had only recently appeared). They end by imagining

Ex.2
(a) Act 4 (Cannon-salute from Saltan's ship)

(b) Stravinsky: *Petrushka*, beginning

themselves queen (tsaritsa). The eldest says if she were queen she would prepare a feast for one and all; the middle sister says if she were queen she would weave linen for one and all. The youngest sister suddenly chimes in to say that if she were queen she would bear Tsar Saltan a hero for a son. At this the door bursts open and there is Tsar Saltan, who has overheard their conversation. He claims the youngest sister, Militrisa, for his wife and as consolation prizes names the elder sister his royal cook and the middle sister his royal weaver. (The music accompanying his speech, from Rimsky-Korsakov's anthology, will henceforth be his leitmotif.) He leaves with his bride. The jealous older sisters plot with Babarikha to ruin the lucky one.

ACT 1 *A room in the royal palace* After an entr'acte based on Saltan's royal march, heard in the prologue, the curtain goes up to show Tsaritsa Militrisa waiting disconsolately for Saltan to return from war (her short aria stylizes the 'drawn-out' genre of Russian folksong). She has long since sent a messenger with news of Prince Guidon's birth but has had no word from her husband. Voices of nursemaids are heard off stage, singing to the infant (their songs are familiar lullabies and children's songs too lowly to have been anthologized; Rimsky knew them from oral tradition). The jester tries to distract Militrisa with some jingles; an old storyteller tries a *skazka* (adapted from a folktale parody by Pushkin). What they do not know is that the wicked sisters and Babarikha have intercepted her message and substituted another, according to which Militrisa has borne 'not a son, not a daughter, not a mousie, not a froggy, but some kind of strange little monster'. A messenger from the tsar at last arrives (his greeting to Militrisa incorporates a familiar urban lyric). When the scribes have deciphered the scroll, it appears that Saltan has ordered that Militrisa and Guidon be put in a barrel and sent out to sea. Militrisa reacts in horror (ironically, to the tune of a famous wedding song in Rimsky-Korsakov's collection). Tearfully, the lamenting populace executes the order while Babarikha and the sisters exult. (In this act the fast-growing little hero Guidon is a mime role, played by two boys from ballet school, the second noticeably taller than the first.)

ACT 2 *A desert island* After an entr'acte depicting its cruise atop the waves, the barrel washes ashore on the desert island of Buyan. Militrisa and the now full-grown Guidon emerge. Hungry, Guidon fashions a bow and arrow out of a branch from a solitary oak and goes hunting. He spies a swan being chased by a kite and shoots the predator. As the kite sinks, the voices of a sorcerer and his invisible spirits are heard, bewailing their defeat. The swan thanks Guidon for saving her and promises to be his magical helper. Night falls. While Guidon and Militrisa sleep, the enchanted city of Ledenets materializes on the island. The gates open to the ringing of bells. The inhabitants greet Guidon as their saviour from the sorcerer and make him their ruler (their chorus is in part adapted to a chant from the Orthodox liturgy).

Nadeshda Zabela as the Swan-Princess, the role she created in Rimsky-Korsakov's 'The Tale of Tsar Saltan' at the Solodovnikov Theatre, Moscow, 21 October/3 November 1900: portrait by her husband Mikhail Vrubel

ACT 3.i *A desert island* After an entr'acte depicting a ship on the open sea, Guidon muses about his homesickness and his wish to meet his father. The swan shows him how to turn himself into a bumblebee so that he can fly to Tmutarakan'.

3.ii *A hall in Saltan's palace* After an entr'acte (the famous 'Flight of the Bumblebee') the curtain rises on a feast at which Saltan is entertaining some ship-masters and boatmen. They tell the tsar about the marvellous city of Ledenets, ruled by Prince Guidon, and the wonders to be seen there: a magic squirrel that eats golden nuts and sings songs, and 33 magic heroes who emerge periodically from the waves. Saltan decides to go there. Babarikha and the wicked sisters attempt to dissuade him by telling of an even greater wonder that is not in Ledenets, a princess whose beauty dims the sun by day and lights the world by night. Guidon, meanwhile, has been observing everything in the guise of a bumblebee, and stings the sisters and Babarikha in turn.

ACT 4.i *A desert island* Guidon cannot sleep, his mind haunted by the beautiful princess of Babarikha's tale. He calls the swan for help. He is ready to walk on foot to the thrice-ninth kingdom if she can tell him where to find the princess. 'Why go so far?', she answers, 'I am she!', and transforms herself into the legendary beauty. They sing a brief but exuberant love duet (soprano and tenor both leaping to high Cs). Morning arrives; Militrisa joyously greets her son and his gorgeous bride.

4.ii After a grand entr'acte depicting the three wonders of Ledenets (squirrel, knights of the sea, Swan-Princess), the curtain goes up on Tsar Saltan's arrival in Buyan. The tsar views the wonders (the music for the squirrel, both here and in the entr'acte, consists of one of the most hackneyed of all Russian tunes, 'Vo sadu li, v ogorode': 'In the garden or the vegetable patch', which has a history in written tradition, including opera, going back to the 18th century). But then, to his even greater astonishment, he sees his beloved wife Militrisa. He asks to see his son, and is surprised again when his host, the ruler of Ledenets, greets him as Papa. Babarikha flees, the wicked sisters are disgraced, and all make sail for Tmutarakan' (the homeward-bound theme being adapted from a song in the Rimsky-Korsakov anthology).

* * *

Rimsky-Korsakov's unique powers of musical illustration reached their peak in *Tsar Saltan*. The orchestra is large – triple wind, six trumpets (three on stage), xylophone, glockenspiel, celesta and tubular bells, in addition to a full complement of brass and strings – but its sounds are always airily colourful and transparent, befitting the pervasive toyshop atmosphere. The popular orchestral suite from the opera, first performed in advance of the stage première, is in fact a sequence of *Musical Pictures* op.57, including Saltan's march from Act 1, the Apparition of the City of Ledenets from Act 2 and the Three Wonders from Act 4. An additional musical picture – the 'Flight of the Bumblebee' from Act 3 – has also lived a rich and varied life of its own, popular not only in its full orchestral dress but also arranged as a display piece or *morceau de concours* for practically every conceivable instrument. The many diminutive vocal numbers, equally toylike, are rarely if ever detached from the opera.

The libretto, the first of three Vladimir Bel'sky created for Rimsky-Korsakov on *skazka* subjects, deserves honourable mention for its virtuoso literary qualities. Essentially an expansion of Pushkin's poem, incorporating most of the source's actual dialogue, it shows astonishing mastery in two difficult non-standard Russian idioms – the archaic and the peasant-poetic – altogether unexpected in a political economist, which is what Bel'sky was by profession. RICHARD TARUSKIN

Tale of Two Cities, A. Romantic melodrama in six scenes by ARTHUR BENJAMIN to a libretto by Cedric Cliffe after CHARLES DICKENS's novel; London, Sadler's Wells Theatre (New Opera Company), 23 July 1957.

The opera is a skilful condensation of the Dickens novel. The first scene forms a prologue in the Paris wine shop owned by Defarge where Lucie Manette (lyric soprano) recovers her father (tenor) after his release from the Bastille. Scene 2 finds Lucie at her engagement party in Soho, with Charles Darnay (tenor) and Sydney Carton (baritone). Scene 3 is concerned with the storming of the Bastille, and Scene 4 with the Revolutionary Tribunal at which Darnay is condemned. Scene 5 is the condemned cell and Scene 6 the foot of the guillotine. Madame Defarge (dramatic soprano) becomes the dominant character.

Benjamin's opera won an Arts Council Festival of Britain prize in 1951. Three broadcast performances by the BBC Third Programme in 1953 and one on Canadian radio in 1954 preceded the stage première by the New Opera Company, conducted by Leon Lovett and directed by Anthony Besch. The music is apt to character and situation, with effective chorus writing in the scenes of revolution and tribunal. Madame Defarge has a generously declamatory role to contrast with descriptive vocal writing for the others, though reliance is placed more on aria *parlante* than on imaginative lyrical invention. In 1958 the opera was successfully transferred to television in a BBC production by Rudolph Cartier. NOËL GOODWIN

Talich, Václav (*b* Kroměříž, 28 May 1883; *d* Beroun, 16 March 1961). Czech conductor. The son of a choirmaster and music teacher, he studied the violin at the Prague Conservatory (1897–1903) with Otakar Ševčík. He joined the Berlin PO in 1903, and soon became leader; its conductor, Nikisch, was the inspiration for his future career. In 1904 he was appointed leader at the Municipal Opera in Odessa, but in 1906 the stormy political events took him back to Bohemia and he began working in Prague as a répétiteur at a singing school. At this time he formed friendships with Josef Suk and Vítězslav Novák and attended Nikisch's lectures in Leipzig. He conducted *Rusalka* with great success in Ljubljana and after working in the Plzeň theatre from 1912 to 1915 he held a conducting post with the Czech PO. This he combined with a position as head of opera at the National Theatre in Prague from 1935 until 1944 when the theatre was closed by the Nazis. Following the liberation he conducted the opera in the 1947–8 season but thereafter devoted himself to orchestral conducting and teaching.

Talich was one of the great Czech conductors of modern times. His sensitivity, imagination and exceptional feeling for orchestral colour placed him in the forefront of international conductors between the wars. His work in opera was grounded in the classic Czech composers, Smetana, Dvořák and Janáček, whose operas he brought into the standard repertory, as well as promoting works by his contemporaries Novák and Foerster, and French impressionist composers. His personal views often provoked argument, especially in operatic productions, where they were frequently connected with his far-reaching dramaturgical changes. He made early recordings of Czech operas, and various works were dedicated to him, including Martinů's *Julietta*.

*

O. Šourek, ed.: *Václav Talich* (Prague, 1943) [incl. bibliography, discography, repertory and selection of Talich's articles]

V. Pospíšil: *Václav Talich: několik kapitol o díle a životě českého umělce* [Some Chapters on the Life and Work of a Czech Artist] (Prague, 1961)

M. Kuna: *Václav Talich* (Prague, 1980) ALENA NĚMCOVÁ

Talley, Marion (*b* Nevada, MO, 20 Dec 1907; *d* Beverly Hills, CA, 3 Jan 1983). American soprano. At the age of 15 she caused excitement as Mignon in Thomas' opera in an amateur production, and her audition for the Metropolitan the following year was much publicized. Her professional début, as Gilda (1926, Metropolitan), was eagerly awaited but fell short of expectations. She sang there regularly until 1929; among her roles were Stravinsky's Nightingale, Donizetti's Lucia and the Queen of Night. After her retirement from the Metropolitan she made occasional appearances; she returned to opera in 1940 but did not regain her previous fame. Recordings made early in her career preserve little more than a brilliant coloratura technique. RICHARD LESUEUR

Tallinn (Ger. Reval). Capital of Estonia. The first opera performance took place in 1680, when the students of Reval Gymnasium staged J. V. Meder's *Die beständige Argenia*. During the 17th and 18th centuries, under first Swedish and then Russian rule, it was visited by opera troupes from western Europe. The first opera troupe to be based in Tallinn was C. C. Agthe's Hündenberg theatre company which was active from 1776 to 1782, performing works such as Agthe's own Singspiel *Martin Velten* (1778). The Revaler Liebhaber-Theater was founded in 1784 by August von Kotzebue. The repertory included works by Kotzebue himself and various other Singspiels; Mme Tilly's troupe also performed here, presenting Singspiels and Mozart's operas (*Die Zauberflöte*, *c*1795; *Don Giovanni*, 1797). The theatre became a permanent institution with its own building in 1809. Traditions of German opera remained strong in Tallinn during the 19th century. The German soprano and teacher Gertrud Elisabeth Mara worked in the city from 1812 until her death in 1833. The latter part of the century also saw occasional performances of Wagner's operas, including *Tannhäuser* in 1860 and *Lohengrin* in 1883.

The Teatr Operï i Baleta Estoniya was founded in 1906 with funds contributed by the Estonian Choral Society and began producing operas in 1908 with Flotow's *Alessandro Stradella*, the Teatr Estoniya being completed in 1913. A permanent opera troupe was established by 1918 and staged the premières of the first important Estonian operas, including *Vikerlased* ('The Vikings', 1928) by Evald Aav and *Armastus ja surm* ('Love and Death', 1931) by Artur Lemba, during Estonia's first period as an independent nation. During the period when Estonia was incorporated into the Soviet Union, 1940–91, the theatre was renamed the State Theatre of the Estonian SSR, and the repertory emphasized Soviet opera as well as classic Western and Russian operas and operettas.

*

A. Kasemets: *Eesti muusika arenemislugu* [A History of Estonian Music] (Tallinn, 1937)

K. Krïvits, ed.: *Teatr operï i baleta 'Estoniya'* (Tallinn, 1956)

A. Mikk, ed.: *Teatr 'Estoniya'* (Tallinn, 1965)

H. Korvits, L. Tormis and M. Oja: *RAT 'Estoniya'* (Tallinn, 1969)

M. Vaitmaa, ed.: *Teatr 'Estoniya'* (Tallinn, 1974)

K. Kask, L. Tormis and V. Paalma: *Estonskiy teatr* (Moscow, 1978)

K. Krïvits: *Muzïka sovetskoy Estonii* (Tallinn, 1987)

MITCHELL MORRIS

Talma, Louise (*b* Arcachon, 31 Oct 1906). American composer. Although she studied in New York at the Institute of Musical Art, 1922–30, her most important training was at Fontainebleau, where she studied composition with Nadia Boulanger every summer from 1926 to 1939. With a Fulbright grant and two MacDowell Colony residencies, she completed the three-act opera *The Alcestiad* (1955–60), to a libretto by Thornton Wilder based on the Greek legend. It was first performed on 1 March 1962 in Frankfurt in a German translation. The opera was well received, with one critic noting 'We are surprised to find an American lady of Miss Talma's generation writing music more modern than Hindemith'. Seven performances followed. *The Alcestiad* marked the first production of an American woman's work by a major European opera house and won for Talma the Waite Award of the American Academy and Institute of Arts and Letters; she later became the first woman composer elected to that institution (1974). The opera's style combines her 1950s shift to 12-note technique with the clean lines and clear textures of her earlier neo-classical works. She used serial technique more to generate motivic ideas than to control their deployment, embellishing *The Alcestiad* with rich, curving lyrical lines. The opera requires 11 principal singers, a large chorus and orchestra and contains many 'full-throated' arias. An autograph full score is held by Carl Fischer in New York. Talma's later, smaller dramatic works, such as *Voices of Peace* (1973), *Have you Heard? Do you Know?* (1978) and *Diadem* (1979), confirm her operatic skill.

*

R. Berges: 'The German Scene: "Alcestiad" in Frankfurt: Hamburg and Munich Seasons', *Musical Courier*, clxiv/May (1962), 33–4
P. Moor: 'Louise Talma's "The Alcestiad" in Première at Frankfurt Opera', *New York Times* (2 March 1962)
'The Singing Greeks', *Time* (23 March 1962)
V. Thomson: *American Music since 1910* (New York, 1971)
J. W. LePage: *Women Composers, Conductors & Musicians of the Twentieth Century* (Metuchen, NJ, 1980), 226–40

MARJORIE MACKAY-SHAPIRO

Francesco Tamagno in the title role of Verdi's 'Otello' which he created (1887, Milan), wearing one of the costumes designed by Alfred Edel for the original production

Talvela, Martti (Olavi) (*b* Hiitola, 4 Feb 1935; *d* Juva, 22 July 1989). Finnish bass. Originally a schoolteacher, he entered the Lahti Academy of Music in 1958 and continued his studies in Stockholm, making his début at the Royal Opera House there in 1961 as the Commendatore. Shortly afterwards, an audition with Wieland Wagner resulted in his being engaged as Titurel at the Bayreuth Festival of 1962, the year he joined the Deutsche Oper, Berlin. A voice of immense size and wide range, capable of thundering grandeur and great gentleness, allied to a giant's physique and an impressive stage presence, won him international fame in Musorgsky, Verdi and all the principal Wagner bass roles. In 1974 he was Boris, which became one of his most famous roles, in the first 'original version' of the opera heard in New York, at the Metropolitan (where he had made his début in 1968 as the Grand Inquisitor). In 1973 his first Gurnemanz, at Covent Garden (where he had made his début in 1970), was remarkable for its natural nobility; he also sang Dosifey and Hunding there. He was the first director of the Savonlinna Festival, 1972–9, the first opera under his aegis being, in 1973, *Die Zauberflöte*, in which he was Sarastro. In 1978 he sang Paavo Ruotsalainen in Kokkonen's *The Last Temptations*, another of his celebrated roles. Shortly before he died he was appointed general director of the National Opera in Helsinki. MAX LOPPERT

Tamagno, Francesco (*b* Turin, 28 Dec 1850; *d* Varese, 31 Aug 1905). Italian tenor. After singing in the chorus of the Teatro Regio, Turin, he made his solo début in 1870 as Nearco in Donizetti's *Poliuto*. From 1874, when he sang Riccardo (*Un ballo in maschera*) at Palermo, he was in constant demand throughout Italy. In 1875, at La Fenice, he sang Poliuto and Edgardo (*Lucia di Lammermoor*). He made his La Scala début in 1877 as Vasco da Gama (*L'Africaine*), then sang in Verdi's *Don Carlos* and Massenet's *Le roi de Lahore*, and created Fabiano in Gomes's *Maria Tudor* (1879). In 1880 he created Azael in Ponchielli's *Il figliuol prodigo* and in 1881 he sang Gabriele Adorno in the first performance of the revised version of *Simon Boccanegra*. He also made several visits to Buenos Aires.

At La Scala, Tamagno took part in the première of Ponchielli's *Marion Delorme* (1885), and sang Radames in *Aida* (1886). In 1887 he created Verdi's Otello; he repeated the role in the first London performance of *Otello* (Lyceum Theatre) in 1889, at Chicago (where he had made his American début as Arnold in *Guillaume Tell*), at the Metropolitan (with a touring company) and in Nice (1891). He appeared in Puccini's *Edgar* at Madrid (1892) and in the first performance of Leoncavallo's *I Medici* at the Teatro Dal Verme, Milan (1893). He returned to the Metropolitan for the 1894–5 season, and made his Covent Garden début in 1895 as Otello. After creating Hélion in De Lara's *Messaline* at Monte Carlo (1899), he sang the role at La Scala and at Covent Garden, where he returned for a final season in 1901.

Tamagno's heroic voice, with its brazen, trumpet-like top notes, was heard to best advantage in the role of Otello, which displayed the magnificent strength and security of its upper register. He was a forceful, convincing actor.

B. Roosevelt: *Verdi: Milan and 'Otello'* (London, 1887)
H. Klein: *Thirty Years of Musical Life in London* (London, 1903)
M. Corsi: *Francesco Tamagno* (Milan, 1937)
W. H. Seltsam: *Metropolitan Opera Annals* (New York, 1949)
H. Rosenthal: *Two Centuries of Opera at Covent Garden* (London, 1958)
C. Gatti: *Il Teatro alla Scala nella storia e nell'arte: 1778–1963* (Milan, 1964)
ELIZABETH FORBES

Tamberg, Eino (*b* Tallinn, 27 May 1930). Estonian composer. He studied composition with Eugen Kapp at the Tallinn Conservatory, graduating in 1953. He was a sound producer and consultant for the Union of Composers of the Estonian SSR, and in 1967 was appointed to teach at the Tallinn Conservatory.

After several experiments in oratorio writing, Tamberg turned to opera and ballet. The opera *Zheleznyy dom* ('The Iron House', 1965) tells the story of a naval mutiny (the time and place of which are hypothetical). The action is continuous and the music is mainly a recitative-like arioso, though there are vocal ensembles, and choruses with Estonian folksong elements.

The three-act opera *Cyrano de Bergerac* (1976), to a libretto based on Edmond Rostand's play, is at the opposite pole of Tamberg's experiments in opera. In his preference for 'melody, tunefulness and beauty' and use of lyrical and dramatic imagery, Tamberg paid tribute to neo-romanticism, which was widespread in Soviet music of the 1970s. At the same time he used elements of Baroque style to convey the atmosphere of the period.

The two-act opera *Pareniye* ('Soaring'), composed in 1983, is by the composer's own account autobiographical; it is the story of his dreams and passions, his compromises with himself and the impossibility of overcoming his inner malaise. Two worlds are contrasted, namely that of creative sublimation, which embodies the wish to rise above the everyday level of existence, and that of the commonplace, stereotyped 'synthetic people' who fill the streets. If the heroine, the Girl (mezzo-soprano), who is capable of 'rocketing' into the air by the power of her fantasy and imagination, is a whole and complete creature, then the other main character, the Composer (baritone), is a split personality. In art, he is the creator of daydreams, but in life he is bound to ordinary everyday existence, and this brings his beloved, the Girl, to her doom.

The character of the Girl and her dream are conveyed through a lyrical melody on the bass flute which is subjected to continuous development, undergoing metamorphosis in both symphonic and vocal episodes. The music representing the callous, uniform crowd is atonal and harsh in timbre, played by an augmented triple percussion section. In the voice parts free declamation is combined with short expressive arioso sections, which usually represent the inner monologues of the characters. The best of these is the Girl's arioso from the seventh scene, akin to traditional female songs of expectation, which is intensified by a prolonged quotation from Grieg's 'Solveig's Song'. In another sequence a substantial episode from Tchaikovsky's *Swan Lake* represents the Girl's striving to soar upwards in order to free herself from the gravity of earthly life. Ballet plays an important part in the opera, where certain key episodes (such as 'Flight' and 'Love') are resolved by choreographic means; the ballet is performed by dancers doubling the characters. In the scenes of everyday life which serve as interludes, ballet and chorus unite and there is parody of the music hall and of conventional happy endings. In *Soaring* Tamberg successfully united the principles developed in his earlier theatre works.

Zhelezniy dom [The Iron House] (3, U. Lakht, after E. Tammlaan), 15 July 1965
Cyrano de Bergerac (3, Y. Kross, after E. Rostand), Tallinn, Estonia Theatre, 2 July 1976
Pareniye [Soaring] (2, A. Valton, after P. Vezhinov), Tallinn, Estonia Theatre, 30 Dec 1983

MARINA NEST'YEVA

Tamberlik [Tamberlick], **Enrico** (*b* Rome, 16 March 1820; *d* Paris, 13 March 1889). Italian tenor. He studied in Rome, Naples and Bologna, making his official début at the Teatro del Fondo, Naples, as Tebaldo (*I Capuleti e i Montecchi*) in 1841. At the S Carlo in 1843 he sang in Nicolai's *Il templario*. He made his London début in 1850 as Masaniello at Covent Garden, where he appeared regularly until 1864, singing Rossini's Otello, Arnold (*Guillaume Tell*), Florestan, Max, Pollione, Zampa, Ernani, Robert le diable, John of Leyden, Faust, Benvenuto Cellini, and Manrico in the first London performance of *Il trovatore* (1855).

Tamberlik sang at St Petersburg, creating Don Alvaro in *La forza del destino* (1862). He also appeared at Buenos Aires, Paris, Madrid and Moscow; in 1881, when over 60, he toured the Spanish provinces. His robust voice, with its ringing top notes, was marked by a fast vibrato, but his musicianship and handsome, exciting stage presence made him a superb interpreter of heroic roles.

*

H. F. Chorley: *Thirty Years' Musical Recollections* (London, 1862)
H. Rosenthal: *Two Centuries of Opera at Covent Garden* (London, 1958)
H. Weinstock: *Donizetti and the World of Opera in Italy, Paris and Vienna in the First Half of the 19th Century* (New York, 1963)

ELIZABETH FORBES

Tambor de granaderos, El ('The Grenadier Drummer'). Zarzuela in one act by RUPERTO CHAPÍ to a libretto by Emilio Sánchez Pastor; Madrid, Teatro Eslava, 16 June 1894.

The action takes place against the background of internal strife in Spain, where Bonaparte has made his brother Joseph (dubbed 'Pepe Botella' by the people) king. Gaspar (soprano), a drummer in the Grenadiers, and the charming Luz (mezzo-soprano) are in love. When he hears that she has been ordered into a convent by her half-blind, pro-French guardian, his indignation and his own patriotic sentiments (reinforced by the fact that his father, a nobleman, has been dispossessed by the invaders) lead him to refuse to take an oath of allegiance demanded by his Colonel (bass). He is sentenced to be shot, but a sympathetic friar engineers his escape from his cell, whereupon, by pretending to be a famous preacher, he gains access to Luz. However, he is caught by the Colonel, and is saved from summary execution only by the news that Joseph has fled and the army now has to swear loyalty to King Ferdinand. A military atmosphere pervades the whole work and there are frequent references to the brilliant overture, which makes much play with a side-drum figure.

LIONEL SALTER

Tamburini, Antonio (*b* Faenza, 28 March 1800; *d* Nice, 8 Nov 1876). Italian baritone. He made his début at Cento in 1818 in Generali's *La contessa di Colle Erboso*, and then sang in Piacenza, Naples, Livorno and Turin. In 1822 he appeared at La Scala in Rossini's *Matilde di Shabran*, Mercadante's *Il posto abbandonato* and the first performance of Donizetti's *Chiara e Serafina*. After singing in Trieste and Vienna, he took part in the première of Donizetti's *L'ajo nell'imbarazzo* at Rome (1824). Engaged in Palermo (1825–6), he appeared in Rossini's *L'italiana in Algeri*, *Il barbiere di Siviglia*, *Aureliano in Palmira*, *L'inganno felice* and *Tancredi* and Mercadante's *Elisa e Claudio*. In 1826 he sang in the first performance of Donizetti's *Alahor di Granata*.

At La Scala he created Ernesto in Bellini's *Il pirata* (1827), repeating it in Vienna. He sang in Bellini's *Bianca e Fernando* and in the first performance of Donizetti's *Alina, regina di Golconda* at Genoa (1828). He took part in the premières of Donizetti's *Gianni di Calais* (1828), *Imelda de' Lambertazzi* (1830), *Francesca di Foix* (1831), *La romanziera* (1831) and *Fausta* (1832) in Naples. He created Valdeburgo in Bellini's *La straniera* at La Scala (1829), a part he repeated in Naples (1830) and at the King's Theatre, London (1832).

In 1832 Tamburini appeared for the first time at the Théâtre Italien, Paris, singing Dandini (*La Cenerentola*), Assur (*Semiramide*), the title role of *Mosè in Egitto* and in *La straniera*. For a decade he sang alternately in London and Paris, where his repertory included Mozart's Don Giovanni and Count Almaviva, and Rossini's *La gazza ladra*, Otello, *La donna del lago*, *L'assiedo di Corinto* and *Guillaume Tell*. He created Riccardo in Bellini's *I puritani* and Ismaele in Donizetti's *Marino Faliero* (both 1835, Paris) and also sang in *Lucia di Lammermoor*, *Parisina*, *Roberto Devereux* and *Lucrezia Borgia*. He sang in the first Paris performance of Donizetti's *Linda di Chamounix* (1842) and created Malatesta in *Don Pasquale* (1843). After an absence from London of five years, he sang Assur at the opening of the Royal Italian Opera at Covent Garden (1847). He retired in 1855. His voice, unusually flexible for a baritone, was rich and solid throughout its range.

Antonio Tamburini as Riccardo in Bellini's 'I puritani', the role he created at the Théâtre Italien, Paris, in 1835: lithograph by R. J. Lane after A. E. Chalon

As is clear from much of the music created for him, Tamburini's compass extended unusually low for a baritone; he would today probably be classed as a bass-baritone. His talent was essentially lyrical, a far cry from the higher, more intense 'Verdian' baritones of the next generation. Henry Chorley wrote in his *Thirty Years' Musical Recollections* (1862): 'He was a singularly handsome man; his voice was rich, sweet, extensive and equal – ranging from *F* to *f'*, two perfect octaves – and in every part of it entirely under control. His execution has never been exceeded ... No one since himself has so thoroughly combined grandeur, accent, florid embellishment and solidity'.

*

J. de Biez: *Tamburini et la musique italienne* (Paris, 1877)
H. Gelli-Ferraris: *Antonio Tamburini nel ricordo d'una nipote* (Livorno, 1934)

ELIZABETH FORBES

Tamerlano ('Tamerlane'). Libretto by AGOSTIN PIOVENE after Michel Ducas' *Historia byzantina* (1649) and Jacques Pradon's play *Tamerlan, ou La mort de Bajazet* (1675, itself related to Racine's *Bajazet* of 1672), first set by Francesco Gasparini (1711, Venice); Gasparini made two further settings (*see* BAJAZET).

The defeat of Sultan Bajazet (Bayazeid; 1347–1403) by the Turko-Mongol emperor Tamerlane (Timur I Leng, Tamburlaine; 1333–1405) had been treated in Antonio Salvi's *Il gran Tamerlano*, also after Pradon, first set by Alessandro Scarlatti (1706, Florence) and subsequently by Gasparini (and two of his pupils) as *Il Trace in catena* (1717, Rome). Piovene locked his characters into a Racinian series of dilemmas: Tamerlane has defeated the Ottoman emperor Bajazet but is prevented from destroying his enemy because he loves his daughter Asteria; Bajazet desires to ennoble his defeat by committing suicide but fears for his daughter's safety at Tamerlane's hands; Asteria would like to reject Tamerlane in favour of the Greek prince Andronico [Andronicus] but is incensed by his complicity with Tamerlane and fears for her father's safety; Andronicus intends to declare openly his love for Asteria but is bound by duty to his ally Tamerlane; and Princess Irene of Trebizond wants to break off her engagement to Tamerlane but is compelled by love to dissemble and wait. Eventually Asteria, Andronicus and Bajazet defy Tamerlane who, enraged, condemns all three, creating a dramatic impasse which is resolved only by Bajazet's suicide.

Piovene's *Tamerlano* shows marked similarities with another Gasparini opera: his setting of Silvani's *La fede tradita e vendicata* (1704). Both appear to contain political allegories based on events in the War of Spanish Succession, with the defeated but haughty monarch representing Silvani's former patron Ferdinando Carlo Duke of Mantua, the barbarian Eastern conqueror representing Prince Eugene, who conquered Italy for the Habsburgs, and the genteel prince with divided loyalties representing the Duke of Savoy, whose changing alliances contributed to Prince Eugene's victory. Bajazet's suicide may refer to the Duke of Mantua's mysterious death in Venice in 1708. *Tamerlano*, like *La fede tradita*, was popular throughout the 18th century, perhaps because of its association with Habsburg victory in Italy but more importantly because its complex and ambivalent relationships mirrored the political situation in Italy, in effect providing an idealized enactment of political reality.

The libretto was reset by Gasparini in 1719 for the Este court in Reggio Emilia as *Il Bajazet*. Although most of the textual changes were by the court poet, Ippolito Zanelli, Francesco Borosini, the singer of the new title role, provided the inspiration for the revised finale. This, with its daring onstage suicide, probably served as the model for the tragic finales in Metastasio's *Didone* and *Catone*. The libretto was also set by Handel for the King's Theatre in London in October 1724; there the story also had strong political overtones (*see* TAMERLANO, below). Important later settings of the libretto include those by Porpora (1730) and Jommelli (1754) for the Teatro Regio, Turin.

For a list of settings *see* PIOVENE, AGOSTIN. KURT MARKSTROM

Tamerlano ('Tamerlane'). Opera in three acts by GEORGE FRIDERIC HANDEL to a libretto by NICOLA FRANCESCO HAYM adapted from AGOSTIN PIOVENE's *Tamerlano* (1711, Venice) and from *Bajazet* (1719, Reggio Emilia), a revised version of the same libretto prepared by Ippolito Zanelli and Francesco Borosini, after Jacques Pradon's play *Tamerlan, ou La mort de Bajazet* (1675, Paris); London, King's Theatre, 31 October 1724.

Tamerlano [Tamerlane] *emperor of the Tartars*	alto castrato
Bajazete [Bajazet] *emperor of the Turks*	tenor
Asteria *his daughter, in love with ...*	soprano
Andronico [Andronicus] *Greek prince*	alto castrato
Irene *princess of Trebizond, betrothed to Tamerlane*	contralto
Leone [Leo] *friend of Tamerlane and Andronicus*	bass
Zaida *friend of Asteria*	silent role

Setting Prusa [now Bursa], capital of Bithynia, Western Anatolia, 1402

Tamerlano opened the sixth season of the Royal Academy of Music and was Handel's sixth full-length opera for that organization. It was given 12 performances with a cast consisting of Francesca Cuzzoni (Asteria), Francesco Borosini (Bajazet), Anna Vincenza Dotti (Irene), Giuseppe Boschi (Leo) and the castratos Senesino (Andronicus) and Andrea Pacini (Tamerlane). He drafted the first version of the score, based only on Piovene's 1711 libretto, between 3 and 23 July 1724, but subjected it to extensive revision before the first performance. The revisions, almost certainly prompted by Borosini, make use of the 1719 version of the libretto. There were 12 performances in the first run, suggesting moderate success; Lady Mary Wortley Montagu's offhand verdict ('execrable') was probably untypical. The opera opened shortly before the annual performances of Nicolas Rowe's tragedy *Tamerlane* (1702) at Drury Lane and Lincoln's Inn Fields Theatre on 4 and 5 November, commemorating the birthday of William III and his landing in England. In the play the noble Tamerlane represents William, the ranting Bajazet Louis XIV. It has been suggested that the opera, by presenting Bajazet as the more sympathetic character, carried an alternative (and subversive) political message; but as Borosini's presence in the company fully accounts for the choice of libretto, and as it was normal for the operatic season to open at the end of October, the juxtaposition of opera and play was probably no more than a piquant coincidence.

Handel revived the opera at the King's Theatre on 13 November 1731, again with Senesino, but with the other parts taken over by Anna Maria Strada del Pò (Asteria), Giovanni Pinacci (Bajazet), Francesca Bertolli (Irene) and Antonio Montagnana (Leo); there were four performances. Montagnana received an expansive new aria ('Nel mondo e nell'abisso', adapted from *Riccardo Primo*) but there was no other additional music and several passages (including the Act 2 trio) were cut. An adaptation by Telemann, incorporating ballets in all three acts, was produced in Hamburg on 27 September 1725. The first modern revival, in a version by A. Rudolf and H. Roth, was given at Karlsruhe on 7 September 1924. The first modern British production was at the Barber Institute, Birmingham, on 21 March 1962, conducted by Anthony Lewis. In 1985 Opera North took its production first to Berlin and then, on Handel's 300th birthday, to Halle. The main text of Chrysander's Händel-Gesellschaft edition includes all the music of Handel's 1724 performing version, but also incorporates several elements of earlier versions without explanation; his treatment of the final scene is especially misleading (and has unfortunately influenced three recordings of the opera). Though some of the music Handel himself rejected is of high quality, its inclusion in performances of the complete opera has little artistic justification.

ACT 1 Outside Bajazet's prison house, Andronicus orders the release of Bajazet. On learning that this concession has been granted by Tamerlane, Bajazet determines to kill himself, but he relents when Andronicus suggests that the action will endanger Asteria. Tamerlane puts Andronicus in his debt by offering him the throne of Byzantium, but then reveals he fell in love with Asteria when Andronicus brought her to him to plead for her father's life. He resolves to renounce Irene and give her to Andronicus if the latter will now help him win Asteria. Tamerlane tells Asteria that he wishes to marry her and will spare her father if she consents; he adds that Andronicus is to marry Irene and is attempting to obtain Bajazet's consent to Asteria's marriage. Asteria, appalled at Andronicus's apparent perfidy, recognizes she may have to accept Tamerlane for her father's sake. Bajazet rejects Andronicus's proposal and is told by Asteria that Andronicus has changed his affections, which Andronicus denies. Bajazet tells him to defy Tamerlane and prove his love. Fearing for Bajazet, Andronicus is hesitant, and Asteria remains cold to him. Irene, arriving at Tamerlane's court in company with Andronicus's attendant Leo, finds herself barred from seeing Tamerlane. Andronicus says he will help her gain justice. He advises her to appear as one of her companions bringing a message to Tamerlane; Leo will assist her.

ACT 2 Tamerlane informs a startled Andronicus that Asteria has agreed to marry him (Tamerlane); he will do without Bajazet's consent. Asteria and Andronicus reproach each other. Andronicus vows to object to the marriage and goes to inform Bajazet. Tamerlane, with Asteria at his side, receives the disguised Irene, who upbraids Asteria for taking Irene's place; Tamerlane angrily warns her that he will embrace Irene only if Asteria becomes displeasing to him. After he has left, Asteria mysteriously assures Irene that she does indeed propose to become unpleasing to Tamerlane. Leo promises to support Irene's cause. Andronicus informs Bajazet of Asteria's decision: Bajazet determines to stop her and Andronicus says he will kill himself if Asteria proves unfaithful. In the throne room Tamerlane invites Asteria to sit beside him, but Bajazet intervenes. The guards attempt to force him to bow to Tamerlane, but Bajazet throws himself to the ground and tells Asteria to tread on his neck as she mounts the throne. Tamerlane attempts to drag Asteria to the throne over her prostrate father. She refuses but says she will join Tamerlane if the path to the throne is cleared. The guards pull Bajazet up and, in shame, he disowns his daughter.

Tamerlane offers Andronicus Irene's hand, but Irene herself appears, still disguised, and denounces Tamerlane. Bajazet makes an impassioned plea to Asteria to remember her former vow to be avenged on Tamerlane; he asks her to kill him if she now disowns it. She descends from the throne, and places a dagger before Tamerlane: it was with that weapon, she says, that she intended to murder Tamerlane at their first nuptial embrace. Her defiance enrages Tamerlane, who threatens her and Bajazet with death; but she gains admiring tributes from Bajazet, Andronicus and Irene.

ACT 3 Bajazet, imprisoned with Asteria in the seraglio, shares a poison with his daughter: he will use his portion if a rescue attempt he expects does not succeed; she must use hers rather than submit to Tamerlane. Tamerlane tells Andronicus he has relented and orders him to renew his offer to Asteria. Overheard by Asteria, Andronicus is at first reluctant, annoying both Tamerlane and Asteria, but then openly declares he is Tamerlane's rival. Asteria confirms her love for Andronicus and her hatred for Tamerlane. Tamerlane orders the decapitation of Bajazet and says Asteria shall be married to the meanest slave. On her knees Asteria begs mercy for her father, but he enters at that moment and rebukes her for kneeling to the tyrant. Tamerlane orders Bajazet and Asteria to attend him at table and Andronicus to witness their fate. Leo comes to fetch Asteria; she and Andronicus bid each other a tender farewell.

In the imperial hall, Leo urges Irene to seize the throne: Asteria can no longer take her place. Tamerlane leads in Bajazet, warning of his coming humiliation. Asteria is summoned and ordered by Tamerlane to offer him his cup on bended knees, like a slave. Despite Andronicus's objections she appears to agree, but drops her portion of poison in the cup. This action is seen by Irene, and as Tamerlane exultantly takes the cup she prevents him from drinking. She announces her true identity and Tamerlane is impressed by her concern for him. He orders Asteria to give the cup to either her father or her lover. When she attempts to drink the poison herself, Andronicus dashes the cup from her hand. Tamerlane orders her to be raped by slaves as Bajazet watches. Horrified, Bajazet vows to be free of Tamerlane. Irene and Tamerlane are reconciled. Leo approaches with Asteria, begging a final audience for Bajazet. Calmly Bajazet tells Tamerlane he has taken poison, and will soon be free of his tyranny. Asteria begs Bajazet to kill her with his sword before he dies, but he says he no longer has the power to do so. Bajazet curses Tamerlane, calling on the Furies to rip out Tamerlane's heart and drag him to hell, where Bajazet's ghost will continue to torment him. Asteria and Andronicus escort him out as he dies, Asteria saying that only her own death remains to complete Tamerlane's triumph. Tamerlane orders the guards to watch her. Andronicus prepares to kill himself, but Tamerlane declares that he is appeased: he will marry Irene, and Andronicus can take the Byzantine throne and marry Asteria. Irene, Tamerlane, Andronicus and Leo look forward to the dawn of a new day after dark night.

* * *

Tamerlano is among the most consistently serious of all Handel's operas and the only one to end with a real sense of tragedy; the drama generated by the clash of wills between conquering and conquered emperors, compounded by Bajazet's loving concern for his daughter, is sustained throughout with remarkable intensity. Though the primo uomo role is that of Andronicus, the dominant character is, exceptionally, a tenor role, that of Bajazet, a feature to which Borosini clearly made a major contribution (he had sung the role earlier in Gasparini's 1719 setting of the libretto and prompted many of the revisions to it adopted by Handel). Bajazet's death scene – stunningly realized in a series of accompanied recitatives alternating with arioso passages of varying styles and tempos – forms the climax of the work. In Handel's performing version (reached after much revision of earlier drafts) all that follows is the brief, 22-bar recitative 'Barbaro! or manca solo' and the final *coro*, in which the words anticipating a new dawn are bleakly contradicted by the sombre minor-key tonality. (Asteria is not on stage and her fate is left unclear.) The music nevertheless displays considerable variety within the prevailing mood, there being ample contrast between the calm nobility of Andronicus's most appealing arias ('Benché mi sprezzi' and 'Cerco in vano') and the spiky brilliance of Tamerlane's; Irene's arias, two spirited and one ('Par che mi nasca in seno') touchingly beautiful, similarly offset the pathos of Asteria's music. Ultimately *Tamerlano* is memorable for its great scenes of confrontation rather than for individual arias. One is the death scene; another is the throne-room scene of Act 2, the tension of which is built up and maintained in Handel's longest passage of recitative (plain and accompanied) until it explodes in a fiery trio and unwinds with brief and moving *ariette* for Bajazet, Andronicus and Irene as they acknowledge Asteria's courage. The orchestral scoring is restrained, without brass instruments, though notable for Handel's first use of clarinets (in 'Par che mi nasca in seno'; the indication of 'cornetti' in the autograph is almost certainly an error). ANTHONY HICKS

Taming of the Shrew, The. Opera by V. Y. Shebalin; *see* *UKROSHCHENIYE STROPTIVOY*.

Tams, Arthur W. (*b* Philadelphia, 7 Oct 1848; *d* Palisade, NJ, 25 June 1927). American opera manager and singer. His début as a singer was in Gounod's *Faust* in Philadelphia in 1864. He subsequently appeared with a minstrel troupe and with Caroline Richings. He was chorus master for Clara Kellogg (1876–8) and stage manager for the companies of Emily Melville (1878–9) and Emma Abbott (1879–83). During the following decade he produced and managed light opera and musical comedy, in particular at the Casino Theatre, New York. In the mid-1880s Tams began to collect scores and parts for choral works and operas; by the 1920s his hire library was one of the largest in the world. In 1925 the library was combined with that of his rival, Isidore Witmark; the collection was dispersed in 1971 and is now housed at the University of Wisconsin and the Wisconsin Historical Society, both at Madison, the Library of Congress, Princeton University and the Westminster Choir College in Princeton. Tams's business papers are in the Warshaw Collection at the Smithsonian Institution.

*

Obituary, *New York Times* (26 June 1927) WILLIAM BROOKS

Tancia, La. Opera by Jacopo Melani; *see* POTESTÀ DI COLOGNOLE, IL.

Tancrède. *Tragédie en musique* in a prologue and five acts by ANDRÉ CAMPRA to a libretto by ANTOINE DANCHET after TORQUATO TASSO's *Gerusalemme liberata*; Paris, Opéra, 7 November 1702.

The plot is a tangled web of amorous rivalries spun out against the background of the first crusade. Argante (bass), the Saracen leader, loves Clorinde (contralto), a Saracen princess and renowned warrior, who has been captured by the crusader Tancrède (baritone) and secretly loves him. Herminie (soprano), daughter of the king of Antioch, also loves Tancrède, her father's enemy, and Ismenor (bass), a Saracen magician, loves Herminie. Tancrède, declaring his love for Clorinde, frees all the Saracen prisoners. Argante calls on Ismenor to create an enchanted forest where Tancrède can be captured. Ismenor and Herminie, who now knows that Clorinde is her rival, arrive in the forest to kill the captured Tancrède, but Herminie, admitting her love, blocks Ismenor's sword. Furious, he tries again, but this time it is Clorinde who stays his hand. She confesses her passion for Tancrède, whom she releases, but duty and pride prevent her from surrendering to love. Tancrède emerges victorious from an ensuing battle in which he believes he has killed Argante. Argante enters, however, mortally wounded by Tancrède's knights, and announces that it is Clorinde, dressed in his armour, whom Tancrède has slain. Tancrède is led off the stage in suicidal despair. A new ending for the 1737 revival has the mortally wounded Clorinde exhorting Tancrède to 'forget that I am dying from your blows, but never forget my love'.

Tancrède is Campra's best-known lyric tragedy. Reputedly considered a 'chef-d'oeuvre' by Rameau, it was performed regularly until 1764. It marks the first appearance of a contralto on the French lyric stage. The role of Clorinde was composed to exploit the particular timbre of voice and histrionic abilities of the flamboyant Mlle Maupin. Clorinde's part ranges from *d'* to *f''*, which is the range more of a mezzo-soprano than of a true contralto. This suggests that voice quality, not vocal range, must have been at issue, and Maupin, in fact, later wanted to sing the role a tone lower.

Campra also broke with tradition by composing the three male roles for low voices, an innovation which Le Cerf de La Viéville, who devoted much space to *Tancrède*, found 'shocking' and 'excessive'.

Although the clean dramatic lines of a Lully-Quinault tragedy are compromised here by an over-abundance of dances (23 in *Tancrède*, compared with 13 in Lully's *Amadis*), Danchet's tragic libretto and Campra's music maintain impressive forward motion. Much of the music is of very high quality indeed. 'Suivons la fureur', the vengeance duet sung by Argante and Ismenor (Act 1 scene ii) generates much excitement; Tancrède's monologue *air*, 'Sombres forêts' (Act 4 scene i), accompanied by string orchestra, has an almost Handelian breadth of expression; and Herminie's 'Cessez mes yeux' (Act 3 scene ii), a 'tendre et plaintive' lament accompanied by violins with flute obbligato, so moved the Parfaict brothers that they assumed that Campra and Danchet had invented the genre. JAMES R. ANTHONY

Tancredi. *Melodramma eroico* in two acts by GIOACHINO ROSSINI to a libretto by GAETANO ROSSI after VOLTAIRE's *Tancrède*; Venice, Teatro La Fenice, 6 February 1813.

The work exists in two distinct editions. For the Venice *prima*, Rossini and his librettist engineered a happy ending to the drama; but the following month, for a revival in Ferrara, Rossini worked with the poet and scholar Luigi Lechi to restore the tragic ending of Voltaire's original play.

To understand the far from clear plot-lines of Rossi's text, it is necessary to know something of the drama's pre-history. The setting is the 11th-century city-state of Syracuse. Like the houses of Montague and Capulet in *Romeo and Juliet*, those of Argirio (tenor) and Orbazzano (bass) are constantly feuding. When the Orbazzani gain the upper hand, Argirio's wife and his daughter Amenaide (soprano) are exiled to the Byzantine court. There Amenaide is wooed by the powerful Saracen leader Solamir but falls in love with another Sicilian exile, the young knight Tancredi (contralto). On her deathbed, Amenaide's mother gives her blessing for a marriage with Tancredi. Meanwhile, the Syracusans, harassed by Solamir and ineptly led by Orbazzano, have put Argirio at the head of their army. As a gesture of reconciliation, he offers to Orbazzano Amenaide's hand in marriage, while agreeing to seize the Tancredi family estates and condemning Tancredi to death in his absence. Meanwhile Amenaide, largely ignorant of these events, has sent an anonymous note to Tancredi urging him to return to Syracuse.

The opera begins with Argirio and Orbazzano in the process of ratifying their various agreements; but Argirio is astonished and angered when his daughter greets with dismay the idea of marriage with Orbazzano. Tancredi's clandestine arrival is marked by his cavatina 'Tu che accendi questo core', with its buoyant cabaletta 'Di tanti palpiti' (which rapidly became a huge favourite throughout Europe). While Amenaide continues to prevaricate, she is informed by her father of the death sentence that has been passed on Tancredi. When Tancredi appears out of hiding Amenaide (somewhat implausibly) is terror-struck and begs him to go away for ever. In the Ferrara revision, Rossini removes the lovers' Act 1 duet 'L'aura che intorno spira' and brings forward their Act 2 duet 'Lasciami! non t'ascolto'. The intention is economy and added dramatic cogency, but the loss of the original Act 1 duet, spacious and lyrical, is considerable, and the brilliantly confrontational nature of the Act 2 duet makes it inappropriate as a vehicle for the lovers' first reunion. In the long and innovatory Act 1 finale, Amenaide again refuses to marry Orbazzano, but Orbazzano now has in his possession the note Amenaide sent to Tancredi. Convinced by its vague terms and anonymous nature that it is an act of collaboration with the hated Solamir, Orbazzano demands Amenaide's death as a punishment for high treason.

In Act 2 the imprisoned Amenaide is finally condemned to death by her father; but an unknown knight – in reality, Tancredi – comes to champion her cause.

Argirio, conscience-stricken over his signing of the death sentence, embraces the champion. In the combat that follows Orbazzano is slain by Tancredi and Amenaide is set free. The leaderless Syracusans now beg Tancredi to help defend them against the Saracens but Tancredi, still convinced of Amenaide's guilt over the anonymous letter and uncertain of the real object of her affections, is not to be persuaded. In the original version, Tancredi reluctantly joins the Syracusan army; the Saracens are defeated, Amenaide's innocence is established, and to repeated cries of 'felicità!' the opera ends with a vaudeville finale. In Voltaire's play, and in the revised Ferrara edition, Tancredi is mortally wounded and dies accepting Amenaide's pleas of innocence and vows of love. The Ferrara revision also brings forward Voltaire's Act 4 scene iv, the lovers' only encounter in the original drama, and shapes it into Tancredi's fine 'Perchè turba la calma', sung to Amenaide before Tancredi's departure to fight the Saracens.

* * *

Tancredi marks Rossini's coming of age as a composer of *opera seria*. Static forms and limited harmonic horizons are given a new dynamism and reach as Rossini successfully redeploys structural innovations derived from his early one-act operas. It is also one of his most purely lyrical works, a primary example of what Stendhal calls his 'candeur virginale'. The critic and poet Giuseppe Carpani wrote of the opera: 'It is cantilena and always cantilena: beautiful cantilena, new cantilena, magic cantilena, rare cantilena'. Although Rossini and his librettist, Rossi, would expand the forms and refine the dramaturgy in *Tancredi's* sequel *Semiramide* (1823, Venice) the later work cannot lay claim to the mixture of primal innocence and musical sophistication which made *Tancredi* so popular in its day and which it can still reveal when it is staged and sung with a proper degree of refinement and intimacy.

RICHARD OSBORNE

Taneyev, Sergey Ivanovich (*b* Vladimir, 13/25 Nov 1856; *d* Dyud'kovo, nr Zvenigorod, 6/19 June 1915). Russian composer and pedagogue. His biography is simple to relate: in 1866 he went to the brand-new Moscow Conservatory, where he spent his life from the age of nine to the age of 48. He studied there with Tchaikovsky, with whom he early formed an intimate relationship; he graduated in 1875 with gold medals in both piano and composition; he took over Tchaikovsky's harmony and orchestration classes on the latter's resignation from the faculty in 1878; he succeeded Nikolay Rubinstein as professor of piano in 1881, taught composition from 1883 (Skryabin, Rakhmaninov and Glier were among his pupils), and from 1885 to 1889 was the institution's director. He resigned from the faculty during the turbulent revolutionary year 1905 in protest at reprisals against student strikers. He devoted his remaining decade to composing chamber music and compiling learned treatises on counterpoint, and died of complications from pneumonia contracted after attending Skryabin's funeral in April 1915.

Often called 'the Russian Brahms', Taneyev was his country's academic musician *par excellence*. Like Brahms he was an idealist who felt little attraction to the musical stage. (His idealism was also reflected in his life outside music: he was an enthusiastic Esperantist and became an intimate of the Tolstoy family.) His one completed opera, *Oresteya* ('The Oresteia', after Aeschylus, in three acts, composed in 1887–94; St Petersburg, Mariinsky Theatre, 17/29 October 1895), stands apart, both in subject matter and musical dramaturgy, from contemporary operatic practice (parallels with certain 20th-century works on classical themes, while striking, are fortuitous). Though he found Wagner's music 'interesting in the highest degree', his final judgment on him was negative: 'From Wagner one can learn much, including how not to write an opera'. His acknowledged model was Mozart, and he regarded his *Oresteya* as an imitation of *Don Giovanni* ('in form, that is, not content, for in a contemporary opera the music must of course be contemporary').

Subtitled 'a musical trilogy', Taneyev's *Oresteya* is an extremely compressed treatment of its literary prototype, in which the three constituent tragedies of Aeschylus are each reduced to a single monumental act. In a famous letter to Tchaikovsky, with whom he was on quasi-filial terms, Taneyev described his musico-dramaturgical method as 'concentric', meaning that he first sketched the whole, establishing the length and tonal scheme of each scene in advance, before working on the individual numbers. Given this extreme commitment to 'organic' structure, it is not surprising that, when Tchaikovsky had helped secure the opera's acceptance at the Mariinsky Theatre over the objections of Nápravník, the director, Taneyev took a wholly defensive and uncompromising attitude with respect to practical matters (especially cuts), which resulted in the opera's withdrawal from the repertory after a few performances in 1895–6.

Despite Taneyev's pronouncement, the style of his one opera was not really 'contemporary'. Alexey Venkstern's very old-fashioned libretto lent a Scribe-Meyerbeer cast to the proceedings, and Taneyev's musical idiom, while uncommonly full of contrapuntal interest and virtuoso motivic development, was heavily dependent for its melodic and harmonic style on Glinka (as mediated on the one hand by Tchaikovsky and on the other by Anton Rubinstein, the opera's dedicatee). The fate motif that permeates the opera literally from its first note seems to have been fashioned unconsciously on its counterpart in *Carmen* (ex.1). The exceptional role is that of Orestes. He is a real Heldentenor (a rarity

Ex.1

(a) *Oresteya*, beginning of introduction

Allegro moderato

f *p* *f*

p *f*

etc.

(b) Bizet: *Carmen*, fate motif (from overture)

in Russian opera), and from the moment of his arrival (Act 2 scene ii) the opera takes on a heightened dramatic pressure that at climactic moments verges on expressionism. The strongest impression in Act 1 is created by Cassandra's scena with the chorus, based on a tenderly expressive romance-like leitmotif.

Before *Oresteya*, Taneyev considered a variety of other operatic projects, including Danton and Robespierre (1871), *Ephraim* (1875–6) to a libretto based on Egyptian history which Konstantin Shilovsky had prepared for Tchaikovsky, and Lope de Vega's *Fuente Ovejuna* (1884). Afterwards he again flirted with Spanish drama in Moreto y Cavaña's *El desden con el desden* (1894). His last operatic venture was on the story of Hero and Leander after Ovid, for which he accumulated sketches for nearly two decades (1895–1913), but finally shelved.

See also ORESTEYA.

ed. V. Zhdanov: *P. I. Chaykovsky, S. I. Taneyev: pis'ma* [Letters] (Moscow, 1951)

ed. L. Korabel'nikova: *Dnevniki* [Diaries] (Moscow, 1981–5)

*

H. Laroche [G. Larosh]: '"Oresteya" S. Taneyeva' [orig. pubd 1895], *Izbrannïye stat'i* [Selected Essays], iii (Leningrad, 1976), 344–6

A. Glazunov: '"Oresteya" S. I. Taneyeva (k 25-letiyu napisaniya "Orestei")' [On the 25th Anniversary of the Composition of Taneyev's *Oresteia*], *RMG* (1915), no.44

I. Glebov [B. Asaf'yev]: *'Oresteya': muzïkal'naya trilogiya S. I. Taneyeva* (Moscow, 1916)

M. D. Calvocoressi and G. Abraham: *Masters of Russian Music* (London, 1936) [incl. G. Abraham: 'Taneief', 439–49]

I. Belza, ed.: *Taneyev i russkaya opera* (Moscow, 1946)

G. Bernandt: *S. I. Taneyev* (Moscow, 1950, 2/1983)

N. Bazhanov: *Taneyev* (Moscow, 1971)

A. Gozenpud: *Russkiy opernïy teatr na rubezhe XIX–XX vekov i F. I. Shalyapin 1890–1904* [Russian Opera Theatre at the Turn of the 20th Century and Shalyapin] (Leningrad, 1974), 97–105

L. Korabel'nikova: '"Oresteya" S. I. Taneyev: antichnïy syuzhet v russkoy khudozhestvennoy kul'ture vtoroy polovinï XIX veka' [Taneyev's *Oresteia*: an Antique Subject in Russian Artistic Culture of the Second Half of the 19th Century], *Tipologiya russkogo realizma vtoroy polovinï XIX veka* [A Typology of Russian Realism in the Second Half of the 19th Century] (Moscow, 1979), 79–118

L. Korabel'nikova: *Tvorchestvo S. I. Taneyeva* [Taneyev's Works] (Moscow, 1986) RICHARD TARUSKIN

Tanglewood. Located near the towns of Lenox and Stockbridge in the Berkshire Hills of western Massachusetts, Tanglewood is the summer home of the Boston SO and the site of America's most important music festival. The Tanglewood Music Center, formerly known as the Berkshire Music Center, is the summer school for advanced musical training founded by Sergey Koussevitzky, music director of the Boston SO, in 1940.

Opera played a large part in the activity of the Berkshire Music Center during its first 20 years, in which Tanglewood became an important centre of American operatic training. Boris Goldovsky ran the innovatory and influential programme designed to make young singers self-reliant musicians and actors. Each summer there was a large-scale production featuring student singers, and in the rustic Theater-Concert Hall across the lawn from the famous Tanglewood Shed Goldovsky conducted the American premières of *Idomeneo*, *Zaide* and *La clemenza di Tito*, as well as such then unusual works as Gluck's *Iphigénie en Tauride*, Rossini's *Il turco in Italia* and *Le comte Ory*, Puccini's *La rondine* and Chabrier's *Une éducation manquée*. The most important American première was *Peter Grimes* (1946), a Koussevitzky commission conducted by his protégé Leonard Bernstein, and there were also new works by Mark Bucci, Jacques Ibert, Lukas Foss, Jan Meyerowitz and Bernstein.

The majority of the foremost American singers of several generations studied at Tanglewood – Adele Addison, Richard Cassilly, Phyllis Curtin, Justino Diaz, Mattiwilda Dobbs, Rosalind Elias, John Macurdy, Robert McFerrin, Sherrill Milnes, James Pease, Leontyne Price, George Shirley, Shirley Verrett and Claire Watson; others went on to successful careers in teaching, stage direction and conducting.

Erich Leinsdorf dissolved the opera department during his tenure as music director, although in 1964 Phyllis Curtin inaugurated a summer programme in vocal training that she was still supervising in the early 1990s. Prominent alumni of her classes include Cheryl Studer, John Aler and Dawn Upshaw. In 1971–3 the opera programme was briefly revived under the direction of Ian Strasfogel; it presented the American premières of Maderna's *Satyricon*, Birtwistle's *Down by the Greenwood Side* and Ligeti's *Aventures* and *Nouvelles aventures*, and the first performance of Robert Selig's *Chocorua*. Occasionally since then the students have been enlisted for an opera, such as *Elegy for Young Lovers* when Henze was composer-in-residence (1989).

Leinsdorf introduced concert opera to the Boston SO's summer schedule and conducted the American première of the 1806 version of *Fidelio* there, as well as a performance of *Lohengrin* that was recorded. In 1980 Seiji Ozawa inaugurated a regular series of staged performances in the Tanglewood Shed. These varied in effectiveness because singers and orchestra shared the stage, but they enabled Tanglewood audiences to experience some of the leading operatic portrayals of the day, Verrett's Tosca, Behren's Leonore and Electra, Ghiaurov's Boris, Horne's Orpheus and Freni's Lisa (*Queen of Spades*). Ozawa has announced his wish to renovate the Theater-Concert Hall and return student opera to Tanglewood. RICHARD DYER

Tango, Egisto (*b* Rome, 13 Nov 1873; *d* Copenhagen, 5 Nov 1951). Italian conductor. He first studied engineering, then music at the Naples Conservatory, making his conducting début in Venice in 1893. He was an assistant conductor at La Scala in 1895–6, and active at Berlin (Theater des Westens) from 1903 to 1908. In 1909–10 he made his American début at the Metropolitan, conducting Italian and French repertory. He returned to Europe and from 1913 to 1919 was music director at the Budapest Opera, where he conducted the première of Bartók's *Bluebeard's Castle* in 1918. From 1927 he was music director at the Royal Theatre, Copenhagen, where he then settled. NOËL GOODWIN

Tannhäuser [*Tannhäuser und der Sängerkrieg auf Wartburg* ('Tannhäuser and the Singers' Contest on the Wartburg')]. *Grosse romantische Oper* in three acts by

Richard Wagner (*see* WAGNER family, (1)) to his own libretto; Dresden, Hoftheater, 19 October 1845.

Herrmann *Landgrave of Thuringia*		bass
Tannhäuser	*knights and minstrels*	tenor
Wolfram von Eschinbach		baritone
Walther von der Vogelweide		tenor
Biterolf		bass
Heinrich der Schreiber		tenor
Reinmar von Zweter		bass
Elisabeth *the Landgrave's niece*		soprano
Venus		soprano
A Young Shepherd		soprano
Four Noble Pages		soprano, alto

Thuringian knights, counts and nobles, ladies, older and younger pilgrims, sirens, naiads, nymphs, bacchantes. In Paris version, additionally the Three Graces, youths, cupids, satyrs and fauns

Setting Thuringia at the beginning of the 13th century

Wagner's text is a conflation of two separate medieval legends: those concerning Tannhäuser, believed originally to have been a crusading knight from Franconia, and the song contest on the Wartburg – drawing on a number of 19th-century versions, notably those of Ludwig Tieck, E. T. A. Hoffmann, Heinrich Heine, Friedrich de la Motte Fouqué and Joseph Eichendorff. The anachronistic linking of the two legends was originally made by Ludwig Bechstein, in *Der Sagenschatz und die Sagenkreise des Thüringerlandes* of 1835–8 (see Spencer 1976), and reinforced by a contemporary scholar, C. T. L. Lucas.

Wagner worked out a detailed prose draft (28 June–6 July 1842) at Aussig (now Ústí nad Labem) in the Bohemian mountains, and versified it the following spring. After making a number of preliminary sketches for the musical setting, Wagner made his 'fragmentary complete draft' (so called because it survives only in fragmentary form, albeit now largely reconstructed) and a continuous complete draft, the two evolving side by side between the summer or autumn of 1843 and December 1844. The overture was completed on 11 January 1845 and the full score on 13 April. As late as the continuous complete draft, there is evidence of Wagner's conception in terms of traditional numbers, despite his suppression of such designations in the autograph score (see Abbate 1984).

The uncomprehending response of the audience at the first performance on 19 October 1845 was largely due to the inability of Joseph Tichatschek, the singer of the leading role, to grasp the principle of *melos* towards which Wagner was progressing. His abnormal vocal demands also took their toll on Wilhelmine Schröder-Devrient (Venus), his niece Johanna Wagner (Elisabeth) and Anton Mitterwurzer (Wolfram). However, by the mid-1850s the work had established itself in the repertory of more than 40 German opera houses. An invitation from Emperor Napoleon III to stage *Tannhäuser* in Paris led to one of the most celebrated débâcles in the annals of operatic history. Revenging themselves on the politically unpopular Princess Pauline Metternich, who had negotiated the invitation, the members of the Jockey Club disrupted three performances at the Opéra in March 1861 with aristocratic baying and dog-whistles before Wagner was allowed to withdraw the production.

The *Wagner Werk-Verzeichnis* (1986) identifies four 'stages' of the work: (1) the original version as given at the Dresden première in 1845; (2) the edition published by Meser in 1860, incorporating revisions made (notably to the ending of the work) between 1847 and 1852; (3) the version of 1861 (not published), as performed at the Opéra that year; and (4) the version performed under Wagner's supervision in Vienna in 1875, incorporating revisions made subsequent to 1861 (vocal score 1876, full score 1888). There is, however, no reason to abandon the convenient traditional labels of 'Dresden version' (i.e. no.2) and 'Paris version' (no.4), provided it is borne in mind that these terms refer not to what was actually heard in Dresden in 1845 or Paris in 1861 but to revised editions of those performances.

The most noticeable feature of the Paris version (the major differences are described below, and the Paris variants are usefully given in the Dover full score) is the stylistic incongruity arising from the grafting of new sections in Wagner's mature, post-*Tristan* style on to a work of the 1840s. The characterization of Venus was deepened for Paris in a manner prophetic of Kundry. Where her somewhat plain declamation was punctuated for Dresden by bare chords, her vocal line for Paris is sensually pliable, with richly scored accompaniments (ex.1).

The title role in the Opéra performance in 1861 was taken by Albert Niemann, who went on to sing it at the Metropolitan (1886–9). Tannhäuser was the role in which Lauritz Melchior made his Metropolitan début on 17 February 1926; he went on to sing it 51 times in New York, as well as in other major opera houses (144 times in all).

ACT 1.i–ii *Inside the Hörselberg near Eisenach* One of the primary changes for Paris concerned the opening of the opera. The bacchanal in the Venusberg (identified by Wagner and others with the Hörselberg in Thuringia) was extended to provide the ballet demanded by the management and patrons of the Opéra (albeit in the first rather than the traditional second act). In the original version, the stage directions prescribed a rocky grotto with bathing naiads, reclining sirens and dancing nymphs. Venus lay on a couch in a rosy light, with Tannhäuser, half-kneeling, nestling his head in her lap. Urged on by bacchantes, the dancers reached a peak of orgiastic excitement. The Paris version adds the Three Graces and cupids, while satyrs and fauns cause a riotous frenzy by chasing the nymphs. Prompted by the Graces, the cupids quell the riot by raining down love-arrows on all below (*see* DANCE, fig.4). The Paris bacchanal is both longer and more frenzied, with the addition of castanets and a third timpani. At the height of the revelry the rising chromatic four-note phrase ubiquitous in *Tristan* is much in evidence. Orchestral textures are richer, more voluptuous, and transitions are negotiated with the assurance of Wagner's mature style.

In scene ii Tannhäuser starts, as though from a dream. He is surfeited with the sensual pleasures of the Venusberg and longs for the simple joys of earthly life. Urged on by the love goddess, he sings his Hymn to Venus, the first stanza in D♭ with harp accompaniment, the second in D with added strings, both ending with a plea to be released. Venus summons a magic grotto and against an accompaniment of ethereal divided strings tempts him to surrender to ecstasy: 'Geliebter, komm!'. Tannhäuser seizes his harp again and, to a full orchestral accompaniment, drives his plea to a pitch by singing the third stanza in E♭. Venus angrily releases him ('Zieh hin! Wahnsinniger!'), prophesying that he will in desperation one day return. When Tannhäuser invokes the Virgin Mary, Venus and her domains instantly disappear. In the Paris version, the voluptuous nature of both vocal line and accompaniment is much enhanced, while two additional passages after Venus's slightly reworded outburst ('Zieh hin! Wahnbetörter!') reveal new aspects of her character as she gives vent to first angry mockery and then despair.

1. Drawing by Ferdinand Heine (copy by H. Plock) of the stage set for the original 1845 Dresden production of Wagner's 'Tannhäuser', Act 1 scene iii. Heine's drawing (top) and groundplan (bottom) follow faithfully the stage directions in Wagner's score: the Wartburg (back right), the Hörselberg in the distance (middle left), a rocky eminence for the shepherd boy (h), and a shrine to the Virgin (f); the dotted line indicates the path taken by the procession of pilgrims.

1.iii–iv *A valley below the Wartburg* Tannhäuser finds himself in a sunlit valley; sheep bells are heard from the heights and a young shepherd is playing his pipe (an irregularly phrased monody started on the clarinet and continued by an english horn on or behind the stage). His simple song, 'Frau Holda kam aus dem Berg hervor', is followed by the chant of the Elder Pilgrims, wafting from the direction of the Wartburg. The second stanza, in which anguished chromaticisms depict the oppression of sin, is a recollection in quadruple time of the corresponding strain of the overture's main theme. As the pilgrims approach, the shepherd greets them and Tannhäuser makes a pious exclamation. The procession passes and Tannhäuser takes up the guilt-oppressed strain of the pilgrims. As the chant dies away, hunting horns are heard, at first in the distance, then closer to.

The Landgrave and minstrels approach (scene iv) and, recognizing Tannhäuser, greet him warmly ('Gegrüsst sei uns'). Tannhäuser's rejection of the past leads to a brief seven-part ensemble, terminated by Wolfram's cry of 'Bleib bei Elisabeth', an invocation of talismanic force. Tannhäuser, stopped in his tracks, can only repeat the name. Wolfram goes on to reveal how in their earlier song-contests, Tannhäuser had won the heart of Elisabeth, who had subsequently retired from their company – 'Als du in kühnem Sange uns bestrittest' – followed by the aria proper, 'War's Zauber, war es reine Macht?'. The aria, though of conventional cut, has inspired many superlative performances both on stage and on record, often eclipsing those of the singer in the notoriously taxing title role. To Wolfram's pleas for Tannhäuser to stay are added those of the other minstrels in a brief sextet. Tannhäuser yields and embraces his former friends (to an orchestral accompaniment made slightly more exultant in the Paris version). He leads them in a final ensemble which brings the act to an end resounding with the blasts of hunting horns.

Act 2 *The Hall of Song in the Wartburg* The act opens with Elisabeth's joyous greeting to the Hall of Song, abandoned by her during Tannhäuser's absence, 'Dich, teure Halle, grüss' ich wieder'. The aria is conventional in phrase structure, but its introduction effectively uses repeated quaver triplets to portray Elisabeth's agitation; an oboe and clarinet also sound the ominous motif first heard when Tannhäuser was dismissed by Venus (ex.1). The aria avoids closure only by an interrupted cadence on to the flat submediant (first inversion), which chord initiates scene ii. Wolfram and Tannhäuser have entered at the back; the former remains there discreetly while the latter throws himself at Elisabeth's feet. The chords on pizzicato strings depict Elisabeth's steps (according to Mottl) and are followed by a rushing semiquaver figure illustrative of Tannhäuser's gesture.

She begs him to rise and, after regaining her composure, recalls his earlier minstrelsy, 'Der Sänger klugen Weisen', against an accompaniment of sustained, muted strings, with flowing viola and serene wind punctuations. The vocal line becomes disjointed and the accompaniment sparer as she relives the pain of

2. *'Tannhäuser' (Wagner), Act 2 (the Hall of Song in the Wartburg), as designed by Edouard-Désiré-Joseph Desplechin for the first Paris production (Opéra; Salle Le Peletier), 13 March 1861: engraving*

Tannhäuser's departure. Tannhäuser, enraptured, hails the power of love, and the two break into an ecstatic duet in the old-fashioned style, 'Gepriesen sei die Stunde' (often abridged in performance).

Tannhäuser and Wolfram depart, and an abrupt transition introduces scene iii, in which the Landgrave welcomes his niece back to the Hall but finds her unwilling to divulge her thoughts. Trumpets sound from the courtyard, heralding the arrival of the guests (knights, counts, their ladies and retinue) for the song contest (scene iv). March tunes accompany the long procession, eventually with choral parts added, first male, then female, then both together. When everybody has assembled, in a semicircle, the minstrels enter to a more lyrical theme, still in march tempo, but played *sostenuto* on strings alone. In a passage of recitative interspersed with arioso the Landgrave extols the art of song and calls on the minstrels to demonstrate it by singing in praise of love; the worthiest contender will receive his prize from Elisabeth herself. Fanfares and acclamation greet his announcement.

The first contender is Wolfram, who uses the image of a fountain to sing of the purity of love, 'Blick, ich umher'. His simple, unadorned line (which Wagner wanted sung in time, not as free recitative) is accompanied first by harp alone, to which are subsequently added the mellow tones of divided violas and cellos. His song is approved by the assembled company, but not by Tannhäuser, who retorts that the fountain of love fills him only with burning desire. This response was varied in the Paris version, because Wagner also wished to omit the following song for Walther, as the singer assigned the role was inadequate. In the original, Dresden version, Walther picked up the image of the fountain, celebrating it as chastity itself, in an aria similar to Wolfram's in its stiff, formal style and accompaniment, 'Den Bronnen, den uns Wolfram nannte'.

Another minstrel, Biterolf, voices the outraged opinions of the knights and ladies when he challenges Tannhäuser to a combat of more than vocal prowess. He is scorned by Tannhäuser for his inexperience as regards the joys of true love. Wolfram attempts to restore calm with another invocation of pure love, but Tannhäuser responds with what is, in effect, the fourth stanza of his Hymn to Venus from the previous act. The first three stanzas had winched up the tonality successively from D♭ to D to E♭. The E major tonality of the fourth stanza both continues that sequence and contrasts sharply with the E♭ of Wolfram's last utterance.

There is general consternation, and the ladies, with the exception of Elisabeth, leave the hall in shock. The knights round threateningly on Tannhäuser, but Elisabeth steps between them with the cry 'Haltet ein!', a dramatic moment strongly reminiscent of Leonore's 'Töt' erst sein Weib!' in *Fidelio*, as she protects her husband from Pizarro's knife (ex.2). The knights are taken

aback, but Elisabeth urges clemency, first with some forcefulness, then more touchingly as a woman whose heart has been broken, 'Der Unglücksel'ge'. This section, in B minor and marked Andante, gives way to an Adagio prayer in B major whose simple eloquence moves everybody. Tannhäuser himself, overcome with remorse, sinks to the ground with a cry of grief. In a double chorus the minstrels and knights take up the theme of Elisabeth's prayer, hailing this intervention by an 'angel'. Tannhäuser's interjections of 'Erbarm dich mein!' were originally intended to carry over the flood of the entire ensemble; later Wagner allowed the other voices to be omitted if necessary. Finally Elisabeth and the knights take up a melodic idea which is brought to a climax rather in the Italian style; indeed, it has been demonstrated that the whole of scene iv (that is, from the assembly of the guests to the end of the act) follows the typical pattern of a mid-19th-century italianate finale (see Abbate, 1984 and 1988).

The Landgrave steps forward to tell Tannhäuser that his only hope of salvation is to join the band of pilgrims preparing to make their way to Rome. A final chorus, once again in B major, adopts this more optimistic tone and, after the younger pilgrims are heard in the distance, the act ends with Tannhäuser's cry 'Nach Rom!', echoed by Elisabeth, minstrels and nobles.

ACT 3 *Valley below the Wartburg* The introduction, depicting Tannhäuser's pilgrimage, is built from themes already associated with the pilgrims and with Elisabeth's plea for Tannhäuser, to which is added a new, chromatically winding idea soon to form the basis of Tannhäuser's Narration. As the curtain rises, Elisabeth is praying in front of a statue of the Virgin. Both she and Wolfram, who has been observing her from a discreet distance, are alerted by the return of the pilgrims from Rome. Their chorus moves through a stanza of tortured chromaticism (a vulnerable passage in performance) to an exultant climax, after which it recedes again into the distance.

Elisabeth, seeing that Tannhäuser is not among the pilgrims, falls to her knees and sings her Prayer, 'Allmächt'ge Jungfrau' (in effect another set-piece aria). The use once again of ex.1, as she sings of 'foolish longing', invests this phrase with something of the force of a motif of reminiscence. Her prayer ended, Elisabeth notices Wolfram but indicates that he should not speak to her. She leaves; Wolfram remains for scene ii. After an introductory section of arioso, he sings his celebrated Hymn to the Evening Star, 'O du, mein holder Abendstern', a number in the old-fashioned style whose conventionality of phrasing and harmony has done nothing to diminish its evergreen popularity.

The pinched tone of stopped horns and a five-note chromatic phrase in the strings (ex.3) herald the third

scene and the reappearance of Tannhäuser; Wolfram initially fails to recognize him. On being told that he has returned from Rome impenitent and unshriven, Wolfram demands to hear the full story. Tannhäuser's Narration, 'Inbrunst im Herzen', is notable on several counts. First, it is the most advanced piece of writing in the opera, in terms of musico-poetic synthesis: that is, the vocal line reflects the natural accentuations of the verse and even changes in character as the narrator's emotional state changes. Second, its formal structure is dictated entirely by the narrative. Third, it is a clear example of the composer's growing recognition of the orchestra's potential for expressive, illustrative purposes. The Narration begins with two stanzas making prominent use of the chromatic winding theme from the act's introduction. A whirr of strings lifts the music into D♭ as Tannhäuser tells how he arrived in Rome, and a celestial wind chorus sounds the 'Dresden Amen'. He describes how he saw the Pope, and the whirring string figure sweeps on into D and E♭ major, the frenzied modulations and formal dissolution aptly reflecting Tannhäuser's state of mind. The climax is reached as he repeats the Pope's words of condemnation: if he has tasted the hellish delights of the Venusberg, he can no more be forgiven than the Pope's staff can sprout green leaves. At these words, ex.3 returns, the pinched tone of the stopped horns transmuted into the Pope's condemnation.

To Wolfram's horror, Tannhäuser declares his intention of returning to the Venusberg. The orchestral frenzy increases and Venus herself appears in a bright, rosy light, reclining on her couch. (In the original 1845 version Venus did not appear at the end, the Venusberg being suggested by a red glow in the distance; similarly, Elisabeth's death was announced only by bells tolling from the Wartburg. These revisions date from spring 1847.) A struggle ensues for Tannhäuser's soul, resolved by another emphatic enunciation of Elisabeth's name by Wolfram. An offstage chorus announces that Elisabeth has died. But her intercession has redeemed Tannhäuser and Venus disappears, vanquished. Elisabeth's bier is carried on, and Tannhäuser, calling on the saint to intercede for him, falls lifeless to the ground. The final strains of the Pilgrims' Chorus tell of a miracle: the Pope's staff has burst into leaf. Tannhäuser's soul is saved.

* * *

Tannhäuser, with its frequently abrupt contrasts and rudimentary motivic integration, falls well short of the mature Wagnerian music drama. Yet it marks a considerable advance over *Der fliegende Holländer* in the deployment of the orchestra, continues Wagner's preoccupation with the dramatic conception or 'poetic intent', and shows some awareness of what he later referred to as 'the beautiful, convincing necessity of transition'.

For further illustration *see* NIEMANN, ALBERT; and PUBLISHING, fig.9.

BARRY MILLINGTON

Tansman, Alexandre [Aleksander] (*b* Łódź, 12 June 1897; *d* Paris, 15 Nov 1986). French composer of Polish origin. After early training at the Łódź conservatory, he studied law and philosophy at Warsaw University and took lessons in composition with Rytel. Successes in the Polish National Music Competition enabled him to move to Paris, where he became acquainted with Ravel, Roland-Manuel, Milhaud and Honegger; his music was later taken up by Toscanini. During World War II he lived in the USA, where he associated with Stravinsky. He returned to France in 1946.

Tansman's earliest Parisian music was composed under the influence of Chopin, Stravinsky and Ravel, but by the early 1920s he was writing pieces of a more individual lyricism and melancholy. At this time he was close to the ideas of Les Six; he may be compared to Milhaud in his use of folk materials and his ready response to different instrumental combinations. Tansman was as adept at writing in C major as he was at composing serially and he made use at different times of atonality and polytonality. The music of his opera *Sabbataï Zévi* (1953–9), which tells of the rise and fall of the 17th-century mystic, is post-tonal in style. *Le serment* (1955) is a tale of jealousy, set in a strange garden, in which a reciter introduces the scene, links the tableaux and closes the piece, narrating over an eerie orchestral accompaniment. As well as several operas he composed ballets, incidental music (for the theatre, cinema and radio) and many instrumental and vocal works.

La nuit kurde, 1925–7 (drame lyrique, prol., 3, J.-R. Bloch), French radio, 1927; orch suite, 1927

La toison d'or, 1938 (opéra bouffe, 3, S. de Madariarga), arr. 2 pf, French radio, 1948
Sabbataï Zévi, le faux Messie, 1953–9 (fresque lyrique, 4, prol., N. Bistritzky), Paris, Champs-Elysées, 3 March 1961
Le serment (1, D. Vincent, after H. de Balzac), Brussels, Monnaie, 11 March 1955
L'usignolo di Boboli [Le Rossignol de Boboli], 1962 (M. Lambroca), Nice, 22 July 1965
Georges Dandin (oc, 3, Molière), Sarlat-la-Canéda, 25 July 1974

ANNE GIRARDOT, RICHARD LANGHAM SMITH

Tapfere Soldat, Der ('The Brave Soldier') [*The Chocolate Soldier*; *Der Praliné-Soldat* ('The Chocolate-cream Soldier')]. Operetta in three acts by OSCAR STRAUS to a libretto by RUDOLF BERNAUER and Leopold Jacobson, after BERNARD SHAW's play *Arms and the Man*; Vienna, Theater an der Wien, 14 November 1908.

While her lover Alexius (buffo) is fighting in the Serbo-Bulgarian War in 1885, the Bulgarian girl Nadina Popoff (soprano) is surprised in her bedroom by Bumerli (tenor), a fleeing Swiss mercenary who is fighting for the Serbs. He proves a harmless fellow, who keeps chocolates in his cartridge box. She is charmed by him, helps him to escape and, after the war, agrees to marry him. The score is celebrated for Nadina's exposition of the absent Alexius's charms, 'Komm', komm', Held meiner Träume', first sung by Grete Holm. The work was most successful in the USA. ANDREW LAMB

Tappy, Eric (*b* Lausanne, 19 May 1931). Swiss tenor. He studied at Geneva, Salzburg and Hilversum and in Paris with Nadia Boulanger, making his début in 1959 at Zürich in Milhaud's *Les malheurs d'Orphée*. He sang the title role of *Zoroastre* at the Opéra-Comique in 1964, during the bicentenary commemorations of Rameau's death. In 1966 he sang Monteverdi's Orpheus at Herrenhausen and created Léon in Milhaud's *La mère coupable* at Geneva. He sang Nero (*L'incoronazione di Poppea*) at Hanover the following year. In 1974 he made his Covent Garden début as Mozart's Titus and his American début as Don Ottavio in San Francisco. He also sang at Aix-en-Provence, Salzburg and Drottningholm. His repertory included Aaron (*Moses und Aron*), Pelléas, Idomeneus, Tamino, Lensky, Don Ramiro and Lysander (*A Midsummer Night's Dream*). He retired in 1982. HAROLD ROSENTHAL/R

Tarade, Théodore-Jean (*b* Paris, 1 Nov 1731; *d* La Flèche, 14 Sept 1788). French violinist and composer. He may have been a pupil of Jean-Marie Leclair. He played for the balls at the Opéra in 1750–51 and was a member of the Opéra orchestra from 1751 until he was pensioned in 1776. Between 1754 and 1757 he appeared as soloist at the Concert Spirituel on four occasions, and played in the orchestra there from 1755 to 1772. His operetta *La réconciliation villageoise* (1, A. A. H. Poinsinet, after La Ribardière; Comédie-Italienne, 15 July 1765) was well received, the *Mercure de France* finding its music 'agreeable, and extremely well suited to the light kind of spectacle to which it is adapted'. Its success was reflected by 14 performances in 1765–6, by two published editions (Paris, 1765) and by the appearance of its airs in several anthologies. His one-act *comédie La reconnaissance* (in *F-Pc*, according to Eitner) is also dated 1765. From the 1760s to the early 1780s he ran a music shop with his wife. In 1783 he moved to La Flèche, where he taught the violin at the Collège Royal.

Apart from his collection of *airs*, which preserves Gaviniès's famous *Romance* and demonstrates contemporary taste, Tarade's music, which includes instrumental works, is of slight worth. More important are his two violin treatises. NEAL ZASLAW

Tarantini, Leopoldo (*fl* 1835–45; *d* after 1875). Italian librettist. He was a distinguished Neapolitan lawyer, an advocate specializing in criminal cases, whose reputation was such that in 1875 he was elected a deputy to the Italian parliament. Between 1835 and 1845 he wrote on average two librettos a year, most of them for the royal theatres. They were well organized and fluent, giving the impression that writing them came easily. His *Lara* was an interesting attempt to develop Byron's tale for an opera, while *Don Carlos*, written for Costa for performance in London, showed a most skilled hand at work on Schiller's drama, comparing favourably with the text that Verdi was to struggle with 20 years later.

mel – *melodramma* tl – *tragedia lirica*

Il gioiello (dramma per musica), G. Lillo, 1835; *La battaglia di Lepanto* (mel serio), T. Genovés y Lapetra, 1836; *I due Savoiardi* (mel), M. Aspa, 1838 (A. Cagnoni, 1846); *Valeria* (dramma per musica), S. Sarmiento, 1838; *Alfonso d'Aragona* (azione drammatica), Sarmiento, 1838; *Antonio Foscarini* (tl), L. Pastini, 1839 (E. Coen, 1841); *Le disgrazie di un bel giovane, ossia Il zio e il nipote* (mel giocoso), Lillo, 1840; *Maria d'Arles* (tl), Aspa, 1840; *L'osteria d'Andujar* (azione comica), Lillo, 1840; *Ettore Fieramosca* (tl), M. Manzocchi, 1840; *Matilde d'Inghilterra* (mel tragico), A. de Simone, 1841; *I quindici* (azione comica), L. Bordese, 1842; *Lara* (tl), Lillo, carn. 1842 (M. Salvi, 1843); *Maria, regina d'Inghilterra* [*Maria Tudor*] (tl), G. Pacini, 1843; *Matteo l'invalido* (mel semiserio), D. Majo, 1843; *Luisetta* [*La cantatrice del molo*] (mel giocoso), Pacini, 1843; *Don Carlos* (tl), Michele Costa, 1844 (Moscuzza, 1862); *Isella la modista* (op giocosa), De Giosa, 1857

*

J. Commons: 'Giovanni Pacini and *Maria Tudor*', *Journal of the Donizetti Society*, vi (1988), 57–92 JOHN BLACK

Ţăranu, Cornel (*b* Cluj [now Cluj-Napoca], 20 June 1934). Romanian composer. He studied composition in Cluj (1951–7) and later in Paris (1966–7) with Nadia Boulanger and Messiaen and took part in the Darmstadt summer courses (1968, 1969). Since 1957 he has taught composition at the Cluj Conservatory; he is also a conductor. The experience of writing several cantatas and incidental scores for the Cluj National Theatre led to the composition in 1969 of an opera which brought him fame and popularity: *Secretul lui Don Giovanni* ('The Secret of Don Giovanni'; I. Balea, after D. Tamás), described as 'three lyrical sarcastic pieces under the pretext of an *opera buffa*' and first performed in Cluj by the group Gong 49 from the conservatory (8 July 1970). This work encompasses a multitude of styles, forms and musical techniques ranging from Gregorian chant and the Renaissance madrigal to serialism and jazz; all these elements merge into a modern formula, of astonishing invention and professionalism.

*

T. Albescu: 'Opera "Secretul lui Don Giovanni" de Cornel Ţăranu', *Muzica*, xx/8 (1970), 32–4 VIOREL COSMA

Tarare. *Opéra* in a prologue and five acts by ANTONIO SALIERI to a libretto by PIERRE-AUGUSTIN BEAUMARCHAIS; Paris, Opéra, 8 June 1787.

In a lengthy prologue that begins with a musical representation of Chaos, Nature calms the winds and creates out of the disparate elements the characters that will take part in the drama. Atar, King of Hormuz (bass), having made Tarare (tenor) general of his armies after he saved the king's life, is jealous of Tarare because he finds happiness in doing his duty and in loving his wife Astasie (soprano). Atar decides to abduct Astasie in order to make Tarare unhappy. When Atar's general Altamort (bass) has captured Astasie, Atar orders a great festivity to celebrate her entry into the harem. Atar praises Astasie's beauty; outraged, she calls on the god Brama to avenge her. Atar gives Astasie the name Irza, and orders her to be brought to the harem. When Atar is informed of Tarare's unhappiness at his wife's abduction he is finally happy. He offers Tarare a female slave in compensation for his loss, but Tarare can only praise Astasie ('Astasie est une déesse'); Atar responds with a brilliant aria mocking Tarare for his apparent weakness ('Qu'as-tu donc fait de ton male courage?'). Tarare swears vengeance on the abductor, whoever he is.

Calpigi (tenor), a eunuch who guards Atar's harem, tells Tarare where Astasie is. In a brief bravura aria, 'J'irai! Oui, j'oserai', Tarare swears that he will rescue his wife. Calpigi organizes a festival for Astasie, a 'fête européenne': gaily dressed shepherds and shepherdesses, and peasants with their farming tools, perform a series of dances and choruses. Calpigi sings a strophic romance in which the accompanying mandolin is represented by pizzicato strings and the chorus echoes the last phrase of each verse. Meanwhile Tarare finds his way into the harem.

While Atar's soldiers enter the harem in search of Tarare, Calpigi disguises him as an African. In an elaborate *scena* in F♯ minor Astasie expresses her desperation. Tarare is caught by Atar's troops before he can find Astasie; Calpigi angrily denounces Atar's abuse of power in the aria 'Va! l'abus du pouvoir suprême'. As Atar gloats over Tarare's impending execution, the slaves sing a mournful chorus in G minor in which trombones, a continuous drum roll and tremolo in the cellos and double basses contribute to the funereal effect. Tarare and Astasie are finally reunited and fall into each other's arms. After a trio for Astasie, Tarare and Atar, 'Le trépas nous attend', Calpigi enters with an army ready to defend Tarare. The soldiers and slaves declare Tarare king and Atar stabs himself. Tarare at first refuses the crown, but the soldiers persuade him to accept it. The high priest Arthénée (bass) crowns Tarare as the people celebrate the coronation with the chorus 'Quel plaisir de nos cours s'empare'.

Tarare represents in many ways the venerable tradition of *tragédie lyrique* that goes back to Lully: the elaborate, allegorical prologue; five acts; extensive use of chorus and ballet and orchestral accompaniment throughout. Yet Beaumarchais and Salieri called their work not 'tragédie lyrique' but simply 'opéra'; they seem to have been attempting to create a music drama *sui generis*, mixing tragedy and comedy, exoticism and romance, with a current of political allegory that appealed strongly to pre-Revolutionary Parisian audiences. The conflict between Tarare and Atar is a conflict between reason, nature and virtue on the one hand and violence, selfishness and hatred on the other. Salieri and Beaumarchais showed the overthrow of King Atar to be completely justified: a concept in tune with the times, two years before the French Revolution.

JOHN A. RICE

Taras Family, The. Opera by D. B. Kabalevsky; *see* SEM'YA TARASA.

Tarchi, Angelo [Angiolo] (*b* Naples, *c*1760; *d* Paris, 19 Aug 1814). Italian composer. He is said to have entered the Pietà dei Turchini conservatory, Naples, in 1771, studying with Lorenzo Fago and Sala. In 1778 his first opera, a Neapolitan dialect comedy, was performed so successfully at the conservatory that the king commanded a performance at the palace in Caserta. This was followed by three more comic operas for Neapolitan theatres in 1778–80, his last for that city except for one in 1790. From 1781 to Carnival 1785 he worked mostly in Rome and then farther north, centring his activities on Florence in 1785 and Milan in 1787–8. He produced his first serious opera *Ademira* at Milan in 1783, and from Carnival 1785 most of his work was in that genre. A remarkably fertile composer, even for the time, he usually produced from four to six operas each year; perhaps his most successful work of this period was *Ariarate* (1786, Milan), also performed at Naples and elsewhere.

The quick growth of his reputation resulted in his appointment as music director and composer at the King's Theatre in the Haymarket, London, for the seasons December 1787 to June 1788 and January to June 1789 (he had earlier composed the music for the castrato Rubinelli's part in a pasticcio, *Virginia*, performed at the King's Theatre for Rubinelli's début there on 4 May 1786, but it is not clear whether he went to London then). In 1790 his earlier opera *Il conte de Saldagna* (1787) was performed in Paris, and two new comic works were given there in 1790–91. Continuing his career in Italy, he is said by Fétis to have fallen ill on a visit to Naples in 1793, making a slow recovery and not producing a new opera until Carnival 1794–5. His output of operas had slowed somewhat in the early 1790s and now it did so still more. His last Italian works were performed early in 1797. He then went to Paris and attempted to establish himself as an *opéra comique* composer, having seven works performed between late 1798 and early 1802. But he never found the formula for success in that genre. Although some Italian influence was not distasteful to *opéra comique* audiences at this time, Tarchi's music seems to have remained too italianate to please completely. Several of his attempts were failures (Fétis called *D'auberge en auberge*, 1800, his best), and he finally abandoned the stage, remaining in Paris as a fashionable singing teacher.

During most of his career in Italy Tarchi was involved in breaking down the century-long *opera seria* conventions, although a series of Metastasian operas runs through his entire career. His work with the innovatory librettist Moretti, in Milan, yielded operas incorporating spectacular French elements such as choruses, dance and pantomime, along with early examples of *introduzioni*, scene complexes and multiple ensembles within and at the end of acts. In his two-act version of *Ifigenia in Aulide* (1785) the ensemble finale of Act 2 encapsulates all the action in Zeno's original Act 3, while in his *Adrasto* (1792) the quartet in Act 2 includes an extensive battle pantomime, and the finales, with chorus, are comparable to those in comic operas. *L'apoteosi d'Ercole* (1790), a *dramma per musica* in the French style based on a mythological subject, is progressive for the scene complexes concluding each act but is retrospective for the supernatural finale in which Hercules appears in the heavens.

Tarchi's setting of *Il conte di Saldagna* (1787, Milan) was among the first to present a murder and prolonged death scene on stage, and it was also among the first tragedies in which the hero dies rather than the villain. In his revised version of *Ifigenia in Tauride* for Florence two years earlier the death on stage of the tyrant Thoas, equally foreign to Italian audiences, paved the way for a happy ending. More shocking would have been the tragic ending of *Virginia* (1785, Florence), where, by order of the tyrant, the young heroine dies offstage at the hands of her father, who then carries the bloody dagger on stage to swear vengeance in the final scene. By the mid-1790s deaths on stage had become fashionable. Still, the excessive carnage in *Le Danaidi* (1794) required a supernatural finale in which the offending Danaus is dragged down to Hell in an inferno scene that harks back to the origins of opera.

Tarchi's comic operas, notably those on texts by G. and P. Mililotti, are sophisticated pieces usually involving conflicts between the nobility and their servants. The number of arias is reduced in order to accommodate sizeable introductions, expansive finales and many ensembles, including arias with interjections by one or two other characters. Both the introduction and the sextet in *Il rè alla caccia* (1780) are unusual for multiple entries of characters and extensive action. Tarchi wrote two operas in the French *opéra comique* style, with spoken dialogue interspersed with arias, ensembles and finales: *Dorval e Virginia*, on a serious subject set in colonial America, and *Lo spazzacamino principe*, a comedy.

The popularity of Tarchi's music is evident from the abundance of operatic excerpts in contemporary manuscripts and the number of his serious operas that were produced in more than one city. The source of his popularity lies in his smooth and facile style, especially in his talent for grateful vocal writing with accompaniments skilfully contrived to highlight the voice without obscuring it. Tarchi was also effective in writing highly-charged dramatic music intensified by chromaticism, modal contrast, wind colour and a short-breathed, often declamatory vocal line. In arias and obbligato recitatives he often scored for solo wind instruments, including bassoon, and provided individual parts for cellos and violas (sometimes *divisi*). His choral pieces are sometimes extensive, incorporating contrapuntal and antiphonal styles within the homophonic framework normally expected at this period.

See also Ademira; Ariarate; and Conte di saldagna, il.

cm – *commedia per musica* dm – *dramma per musica*
int – *intermezzo* oc – *opéra comique*

L'archetiello (cm), Naples, Conservatorio della Pietà dei Turchini, carn. 1778
I viluppi amorosi (cm, G. Mililotti), Naples, Nuovo, spr. 1778
Il barbiere di Arpino (farsa), Naples, Fondo, sum. 1779
Il re alla caccia (cm, P. Mililotti), Naples, Nuovo, aut. 1780; ? also as La caccia di Enrico IV
Le disgrazie fortunate (int), Rome, Capranica, carn. 1781
Don Fallopio (int), Rome, Valle, carn. 1782
Il guerriero immaginario (int), Rome, Valle, carn. 1783, quintet *I-Rc*
Ademira (opera seria, F. Moretti), Milan, Scala, 27 Dec 1783, *F-Pn*, *GB-Lbl* (different version), *I-Tf*
I fratelli Pappamosca (cm, S. Zini), Rome, Valle, carn. 1784
Bacco ed Arianna (festa teatrale or cantata, C. Olivieri), Turin, Regio, spr. 1784, *Gl*
Le cose d'oggi giorno divise in trenta tomi, tomo primo, parte prima (int), Rome, Capranica, 26 Dec 1784
Il matrimonio per contrattempo (cm), Livorno, Nuovo, carn. 1785
Mitridate re di Ponto (dm), Rome, Dame, carn. 1785, selections *F-Pn*, arias *I-Gl*, *Mc*, *Nc*, *PAc*, *PEsp* and *Rsc*, trio *Mc* and *Rsc*
L'Arminio (dm, Moretti), Mantua, Nuovo Regio Ducale, 8 May 1785, *D-Mbs*, selections *F-Pn*, *GB-Lbl*
Ifigenia in Aulide (dm, A. Zeno), Padua, Nuovo, June 1785, *I-I*, *P-La*
Virginia (dm), Florence, Pergola, aut. 1785, aria *Mc*, duet *Bsf* and *Nc*
Ariarate (dm, Moretti), Milan, Scala, Jan 1786, *F-Pn*, *H-Bn*, *P-La*, *US-Bp*
Ifigenia in Tauride (dm, Coltellini), Venice, carn. 1786, *D-Bds*, *F-Pn*; Florence, Pergola, aut. 1786, *I-Fc*
Publio (dm, A. Piovene), Florence, Pergola, spr. 1786
Demofoonte (dm, P. Metastasio), Crema, Nuovo, 24 Sept 1786, or Milan, Scala, 1786, duet *I-Mc* (from Crema perf.)
Il trionfo di Clelia (dm, Metastasio), Turin, Regio, 26 Dec 1786, *F-Pn*, *P-La*
Melite riconosciuta (dm, G. Roccaforte), Rome, Dame, 3 Feb 1787, duet *I-Rsc*
Il conte di Saldagna (tragedia, Moretti), Milan, Scala, 10 June 1787, *F-Pn*
Le nozze di Figaro (cm, after L. da Ponte), Monza, Villa Reale, aut. 1787, duet *I-Mc* [new Acts 3 and 4 to Mozart's op]
Antioco (dm, Moretti), Milan, Scala, 26 Dec 1787, *F-Pn*; Naples, 1788, *I-Gl*
Demetrio (dm, Metastasio), Milan, Scala, 1787
Artaserse (dm, Metastasio), Mantua, Ducale, spr. 1788, *D-Mbs*, *F-Pn*
Le due rivali (cm), Rome, Dame, 1788 or spr. 1787
Alessandro nelle Indie (dm, Metastasio), Milan, 1788, *I-Fc*; Livorno, 1791, *F-Pn*; rev. as La generosità di Alessandro (C. F. Badini, after Metastasio), London, 1789, *F-Pn*, arias, trio (London, 1789); Sienna, 1791, *Pn*; new setting, Turin, Regio, carn. 1798
Il disertore francese (cm, B. Benincasa, ? after J. M. Sedaine: *Le déserteur*), London, Haymarket, 28 Feb 1789, *D-Bds*, *F-Pn*, *I-Fc*
Ezio (dm, Metastasio), Vicenza, Eretenio, 1789, *F-Pn*, *I-Fc*; new setting, Vicenza, Nuovo, sum. 1792, *F-Pn*
Giulio Sabino (dm, P. Giovannini), Turin, Regio, carn. 1790, *P-La*
Il cavaliere errante (dramma eroicomico), Paris, Monsieur, sum. 1790
Lo spazzacamino principe (cm, G. Carpani, after M. de Pompigny: *La ramoneur prince*), Monza, Villa Reale, aut. 1790, *I-MOe*
L'apoteosi d'Ercole (dm, M. Botturini), Venice, S Benedetto, 26 Dec 1790
La finta baronessa (cm, F. Livigni), Naples, Fiorentini, 1790
Tito Manlio (dm, Roccaforte), Rome, Argentina, carn. 1791
Don Chisciotte (cm), Paris, 1791
L'Olimpiade (dm, Metastasio), Rome, Argentina, carn. 1792, selections *F-Pn*
Adrasto re d'Egitto (dm, G. De Gamerra), Milan, Scala, ?4 Feb 1792, aria *I-Mc*, *PAc*
La morte di Nerone (dm), Milan or Florence, 1792
Dorval e Virginia (dramma prosa e musica, G. M. Foppa), Venice, S Benedetto, 8 Jan 1793, aria *Gl*; also as Paolo e Virginia
Lo stravagante (cm, L. Lantini), Bergamo, Nuovo, Fair 1793
Le Danaidi (dm, G. Sertor), Milan, Scala, 26 Dec 1794, *Mr*
L'impostura poco dura (cm, ? after G. B. Neri: *Le vicende d'amore*), Milan, Scala, 10 Oct 1795, *Mr* (Act 1 and Act 2 finale)
Ciro riconosciuto (dm, Metastasio), Piacenza, Ducale, carn. 1796
La congiura pisoniana (dm, F. Salfi), Milan, Scala, Jan 1797
Le cabriolet jaune, ou Le phénix d'Angoulême (oc, J. A. de Ségur), Paris, OC, 7 Nov 1798, *F-Pn**
Aurore de Gusman (oc), Paris, OC (Favart), spr. 1799
Le général suédois (oc, T. Favart), Paris, OC (Favart), 5 May 1799
Le trente et quarante (oc, A. Duval), Paris, OC (Favart), 18 May 1799, *B-Bc*, *D-Wa*, *F-Lm*, *Pn*, *US-Bp*
D'auberge en auberge, ou Les préventions (oc, E. Mercier-Dupaty), Paris, OC (Feydeau), 26 April 1800, *A-Wgm*, *D-Bds*, *F-Pn*; as Zwei Posten, *I-Fc*, excerpts (Vienna, n.d.)
Une aventure de M. de Sainte-Foix, ou Le coup d'épée (oc, Duval), Paris, OC (Feydeau), 20 or 28 Jan or 27 Feb 1802, *B-Bc*, *F-Pn* (2 versions)
Astolphe et Alba, ou A quoi la fortune (oc, De Ségur), Paris, OC (Feydeau), spr. 1802

Doubtful: Il Pimmaglione, *D-Dlb*

Miscellaneous excerpts: *A-Wgm*; *B-Bc*, *Br*; *CH-Zz*; *D-Bds*, *Dlb*; *E-Mp*; *F-Lm*, *Pc*; *GB-Cfm*, *Lbl*, *Lcm*, *T*; *I-Bc*, *Bsf*, *Fc*, *Gl*, *Li*, *Mc*, *Nc*, *OS*, *Pca*, *PAc*, *PEsp*, *Rsc*, *Tn*, *Vnm*

*

FétisB
C. Gervasoni: *Nuova teoria di musica* (Parma, 1812)

C. A. di Rosa [Marchese di Villarosa]: *Memorie dei compositori di musica del regno di Napoli* (Naples, 1840)
F. Florimo: *La scuola musicale di Napoli ed i suoi conservatorii*, iii (Naples, 1883), 55
A. Einstein: 'Mozart and Tarchi', *MMR*, lxv (1935), 127; repr. in *Essays on Music* (New York, 1956), 187–90
C. Sartori: 'Lo "Zeffiretto" di Angelo Tarchi', *RMI*, lvi (1954), 233–40
U. Zelaschi: *L'opéra italien jusqu'en 1900* (Brussels, 1982)
M. P. McClymonds: '*La morte di Semiramide, ossia La vendetta di Nino* and the Restoration of Death and Tragedy to the Italian Operatic Stage in the 1780s and 90s', *IMSCR*, xiv *Bologna 1987*, iii, 285–92
——: 'The Venetian Role in the Transformation of Italian Opera Seria during the 1790s', *I vicini di Mozart: Il teatro musicale tra sette e ottocento: Venice 1987*, 221–40

DENNIS LIBBY, MARITA P. McCLYMONDS

Targioni-Tozzetti, Giovanni (*b* Livorno, 17 March 1863; *d* Livorno, 30 May 1934). Italian librettist and critic. He was a professional journalist who became a newspaper editor and filled a number of public appointments. His earliest libretto seems to have been *Pinotta*, written for Mascagni in the early 1880s; the score was lost for 50 years. Then came *Cavalleria rusticana*, a work which, like all of Targioni-Tozzetti's, shows a strong sense of the theatre. In this, as in a number of his subsequent librettos, he worked with Guido Menasci (*b* Livorno, 1867); it was said that while Targioni-Tozzetti was responsible for the passionate, dramatic sections, Menasci supplied the more elegant, restrained ones. Targioni-Tozzetti was responsible for the first Italian translation of Massenet's *Werther*, and the Italian version of Mascagni's *Amica*, the composer's only work to a French text. He is sometimes credited (for example by Loewenberg) with a share in the libretto of Mascagni's *Il piccolo Marat* but the libretto carries the name of Forzano alone. In 1900 Targioni-Tozzetti and Menasci published a libretto *Vistilia*, 'scene liriche per la musica di Pietro Mascagni', but nothing seems to have come of it. In it they also listed five other librettos in preparation but none of them was heard of again.

Pinotta (idillio), Mascagni, *c*1880, lost until 1932; *Cavalleria rusticana* (melodramma, with G. Menasci), Mascagni, 1890; *I Rantzau* (with Menasci), Mascagni, 1892; *Regina Diaz* (with Menasci), Giordano 1894; *Silvano* (dramma marinaresco), Mascagni, 1895; *Zanetto* (after F. Copée: *Le passant*, with Menasci), Mascagni, 1896; *La sposa di Nino* (dramma lirico), A. Biagi, 1913; *Amor vero*, O. Rossi, 1925; *Nerone* (after P. Cossa), Mascagni, 1935

*

Nascita e gloria di un capolavoro italiano: cinquantenario della 'Cavalleria rusticana' (Milan, 1940)

JOHN BLACK

Tariol-Baugé, Anna (*b* Clermont-Ferrand, 28 Aug 1872; *d* Asnières, 1 Dec 1944). French soprano. She appeared widely in leading roles of the classic light operatic repertory including the title role in *Boccaccio*, Fiorella (*Les brigands*), Gabrielle (*La vie parisienne*) and Boulotte (*Barbe-bleue*), and created such parts as Agathe in Messager's *Véronique*, Manuela in Audran's *Miss Helyett* and Gabrielle in Terrasse's *Le sire de Vergy*. In 1908 she appeared in London in Lecocq's *La fille de Madame Angot* and Offenbach's *La fille du tambour-major*, before turning to straight theatre. She returned to the musical stage in the 1920s to repeat her Agathe and to appear in several shows (Marcel Lattès's *Le diable à Paris*, Tiarko Richepin's *Venise*, Hermann's *Vouvray*) alongside her son, André Baugé, a prominent leading man of the period in comic opera and operetta.

KURT GÄNZL

Tartuffe. Opera in two acts by ARTHUR BENJAMIN to a libretto by Cedric Cliffe after the play by MOLIÈRE; London, New Opera Company at Sadler's Wells Theatre, 30 November 1964.

Benjamin completed the short score before his death in 1960, but had orchestrated only about 250 bars of the overture; the remainder was completed by Alan Boustead, who conducted the première. Cliffe's libretto is in rhyming verse, mostly free but with arias and ensembles in strict verse-forms. In a sophisticated derivation from *commedia dell'arte*, the story is set in 1660 in the house of Orgon (bass-baritone), a rich Parisian bourgeois and benefactor of Tartuffe (baritone), a religious humbug who creates domestic chaos before being exposed as a scoundrel and seducer. Cliffe's additions to Molière's play include a love duet for Mariane (soprano) and Valère (tenor), a monologue for Tartuffe, and a French folksong quoted by Molière in *Le misanthrope*, for which Benjamin found, in the library of the Comédie Française, the setting traditionally used in French theatre productions. His music wittily distinguishes between different sides of Tartuffe's nature. It is more successful in depicting comic than serious characters, and acquires Straussian overtones to convey erotic feeling. Cliffe's denouement is different from Molière's with Tartuffe brought before the curtain to seek the audience's sympathy; this refused, he is pursued offstage by his compulsory new wife in a boisterous, moral-pointing epilogue. NOËL GOODWIN

Taruskin, Richard (Filler) (*b* New York, 2 April 1945). American musicologist and critic. He studied at Columbia University (PhD 1975), where he taught from 1973 until 1987, when he became professor at the University of California, Berkeley. A wide-ranging scholar, Taruskin has written on the 15th-century chanson, the Early Music movement (of which he is a trenchant critic, seeing it more as an outcome of 20th-century taste than as truly re-creative), on theoretical aspects of Stravinsky and, above all, on Russian music, from the 18th century to the present. His writings, original and highly perceptive, include *Opera and Drama in Russia* (Ann Arbor, 1981; based on his dissertation) and a study of Stravinsky, as well as articles dealing with views of Russian musical history and textual, technical and interpretative questions in the operas of Musorgsky and Prokofiev. Taruskin is also a vigorous, forthright critic, and has contributed to *Opus* and to the *New York Times* on a wide variety of topics.

Tashkent. Capital of Uzbekistan. Popular concerts, including performances of operas and operettas, were frequent in the Russian section of the city in the latter half of the 19th century; opera companies from Italy, Russia and Tbilisi played there between 1891 and 1915. Performances were held in private homes and in public theatres until the opening in 1918 of the Russkiy Opernïy Teatr in the former circus building, the Kolizei, whose repertory consisted mainly of Russian and European classics. The first steps towards national opera came after the incorporation in 1924 of Uzbekistan into the USSR, with two 'musical dramas', G. Zafari's *Kakhalima* (1920) and *Farkhad i Shirin* (1937) by Georgy Mushel', V. A. Uspensky and S. Tsveyfeld. In 1929 the Russian Opera Theatre was renamed the Gosudarstvennïy Teatr Operï i Baleta imení Ya. M. Sverdlova (Sverdlov State Theatre of Opera and Ballet) and in 1931 became the new home of the Uzbekskiy

Muzïkal'nïy Teatr, which had been formed in Samarkand as part of an ethnographic ensemble in 1929. Under the impetus of the Uzbek composer and director M. A. Ashrafi, this company helped to produce the first Uzbek national operas: Ashrafi and Vasilenko's *Buran* (1939) and Glier's *Leyli i Mejnun* (1940).

The company received a new 1400-seat theatre (designed by A. Shchusev) in 1947 and in 1948 merged with the Russian Opera Theatre, becoming the Teatr Operï i Baleta imeni A. Navoi (Navoi Theatre of Opera and Ballet); in 1959 Academic was added to the name and in 1966 it became known as the Akademicheskiy Bol'shoy Teatr Operï i Baleta Uzbekskoy SSR imeni A. Navoi (Great Academic Navoi Uzbekistan Theatre of Opera and Ballet). The company helped to sponsor members of the Tashkent Conservatory in founding the Samarkand Theatre of Opera and Ballet, which opened in 1964 with a performance of Ashrafi's *Serdtse poeta* ('The Heart of a Poet'). Both theatres mix Russian and European classics (in the original and in translations) with national operas, including premières of the works of S. Yudakov and R. K. Khamrayev.

*

ME (R. S. Abdulayev; also 'Uzbekskiy teatr operï i baleta', T. A. Yuldashbayeva)
N. B. Sokolov: *Teatr operï i baleta v Tashkente* (Moscow, 1949)
T. N. Karï-Niyazov: *Ocherki istorii kul'turï Sovetskogo Uzbekistana* [Studies on the Cultural History of Soviet Uzbekistan] (Moscow, 1955)
A. Korsakova: *Uzbekskiy opernïy teatr* (Tashkent, 1961)
G. Bernandt: *Slovar' oper vpervïye postavlennïkh ili izdannïkh v dorevolyutsionnoy Rossii i v SSSR 1736–1959* [Dictionary of Operas First Performed or Published in Pre-revolutionary Russia and in the USSR 1736–1959] (Moscow, 1962), 551
Ya. B. Pekker: *Uzbekskaya opera: ot vozniknoveniya do kontsa shestidesyatïkh godov XX veka* [Uzbek Opera: from its Origin to the End of the Sixties] (Moscow, 1963)
Yu. V. Keldïsh, ed.: *Istoriya muzïki narodov SSSR* [History of the Music of the Soviet Peoples], i–v (Moscow, 1970–74)
T. Vïzgo: *Razvitiye muzïkal'nogo iskusstva Uzbekistana i ego svyazi s russkoy muzïkoy* [The Development of the Musical Art of Uzbekistan and its Connections with Russian Music] (Moscow, 1970)
Istoriya uzbekskoy sovetskoy muzïki (Tashkent, 1972–3)
Yu. Korev and O. Shokhman: 'Kogda tvoryat yedïnomïshlenniki' [When Like-minded People Create], *SovM* (1981), no.12, pp.47–53
V. Zarudko: 'Novaya vstrecha s uzbekskimi artistami' [A New Encounter with Uzbek Actors], *SovM* (1984), no.3, pp.61–3
Arkhitektura sovetskogo teatra (Moscow, 1986), 153
M. A. Khamidova: *Uzbekskaya muzïkal'naya drama* (Tashkent, 1987)

GREGORY SALMON

Tashko-Koço, Tefta (*b* El Faiyûm, Egypt, 2 Nov 1910; *d* Tirana, 28 or 29 Dec 1947). Albanian soprano. She studied in Montpellier and Paris (1927–35), where her teachers included André Gresse, and returned to Albania in 1935; later she studied in Italy. She gave numerous recitals throughout Albania, even in remote villages. Her combination of a classical opera repertory with Albanian folksong arrangements (and later partisan songs) endeared her to a popular audience, for many of whom she provided the first contact with foreign art-music. She appeared in Rome, Bari and other Italian cities, and in November 1945 sang Rosina and Mimì at the Belgrade Opera. In 1946 she organized singing classes at the newly-founded Jordan Misja, Albania's first teaching institution for music. Her repertory leaned towards coloratura arias. Her perfect intonation and rich, clear, sweet tone were combined with a keen sense of style, natural charm and beauty and great will-power.

GEORGE LEOTSAKOS

Taskin, (Emile-)Alexandre (*b* Paris, 18 March 1853; *d* Paris, 5 Oct 1897). French baritone. He studied in Paris, making his début in 1875 at Amiens as Roland in Halévy's *Les mousquetaires de la reine*. Engaged by the Opéra-Comique, Paris, from 1878 to 1894, he sang in the first performance of Delibes' *Jean de Nivelle* (1880); he created Lindorf, Coppelius and Dr Miracle in *Les contes d'Hoffmann* (1881), Lescaut in *Manon* (1884), Falstaff in Thomas' *Songe d'une nuit d'été* (1886) and Phorcas in *Esclarmonde*(1889). He also sang Count Almaviva (*Le nozze di Figaro*), Escamillo, Ourrias (*Mireille*), Sulpice (*La fille du régiment*), Jupiter (Gounod's *Philémon et Baucis*) and Lothario in the 1000th performance of *Mignon* at the Opéra-Comique (1894).

ELIZABETH FORBES

Tassi, Abate **Niccolò** (*b* Florence; *fl* 1763–81). Italian librettist. He was resident poet at the Cocomero Theatre in Florence during the 1770s. His first libretto was also his most popular, attaining 35 recorded productions: *La contadina in corte*. It received its première in Venice (S Moisè, Carnival 1763) in a setting by Giacomo Rust. The text has been tentatively attributed to 'G. Gozzi' (*ES*, *The New Grove*) and Goldoni (in a libretto for Warsaw, 1765), but Tassi's authorship is clearly stated by the *Gazzetta toscana* (1777). Tassi reduced his original *dramma giocoso* to an intermezzo for a new setting by Sacchini for Rome, 1765, but re-expanded it for Lucca, 1768, again for Sacchini. Anfossi composed a setting of the full *dramma giocoso* as *La contadina incivilita* for Venice, 1775, and as *Il principe di Lago Nero* for Florence, 1777. Yet another setting with the last title followed, this time by Paisiello for Casale, 1779. A ballet on the subject was presented in Cremona in 1794.

Tassi's *L'olandese in Italia* was set in 1765 by G. M. Rutini for Florence, and the opera was subsequently heard in a dozen European cities. *L'amore soldato*, set first by Felici for S Moisè, was his most typical libretto, exhibiting the moral probity and somewhat bland, sentimental comic style of Leopoldine Florence.

La contadina in corte (dg), G. Rust, 1763 (Sacchini, 1765, as int, rev. 1768 as dg; Anfossi, 1775, as La contadina incivilita (dg), and 1777, as Il principe di Lago Nero; Paisiello, 1779, as Il principe di Lago Nero); *L'olandese in Italia* (dg), G. M. Rutini, 1765 (? Piccinni, 1770); *L'amor tra l'armi* (dg), Rutini, 1768; *L'amore soldato* (dg), Felici, 1769 (Sacchini, 1778); *L'amante che spende* (dg), P. A. Guglielmi, 1770 (Caruso, 1777, as Il cavalier magnifico); *Amor per rigiro* (farsa), G. M. Rutini, 1773 (A. Gagni, 1781); *Le nozze della Bita* (dg), B. Ottani, 1778

*

StiegerO
Gazzetta toscana (1777), 54
Marcello de Angelis: *La felicità in Etruria* (Florence, 1990)
C. Sartori: *I libretti italiani a stampa dalle origini al 1800* (Cuneo, 1990–)
R. L. Weaver and N. Weaver: *Chronology of Music in the Florentine Theater 1751–1800* (Warren, MI, 1992)

ROBERT LAMAR WEAVER

Tassinari, Pia (Domenica) (*b* Modigliana, 15 Sept 1903). Italian soprano, later mezzo-soprano. She studied in Bologna with Cesare Vezzani and in Milan, making her début in 1929 as Mimì at Casale Monferrato. In 1932 she appeared at La Scala in the première of Veretti's *Il favorito del re*, and in the 1936 season she sang Elsa and Margherita and created Lucia in Zandonai's *La farsa amorosa*. After World War II she extended her career to the Americas, but continued to appear at La Scala until 1956. At the Metropolitan in 1947 she sang Tosca to the Cavaradossi of her husband,

Ferruccio Tagliavini, but her voice was by then considered too worn. From 1952 she sang principally in mezzo roles such as Carmen and Charlotte. Her best solo recordings are those of the 1930s, fresh of tone and generous without being excessive in emotion. She was also an excellent Alice Ford in the first recording of *Falstaff* (1930), and as a mezzo sang an effective Ulrica in *Un ballo in maschera* (1954). J. B. STEANE

Tasso, Torquato (*b* Sorrento, 11 March 1544; *d* Rome, 25 April 1595). Italian poet and playwright. The son of the poet Bernardo Tasso, he entered the service of Cardinal Luigi d'Este in 1565, transferring to the court of Luigi's brother, Alfonso II d'Este, Duke of Ferrara, in 1572. His precocious career as a poet was crowned by the pastoral play *Aminta* (1573) and the epic poem *Gerusalemme liberata* (first sketched in 1559; published in 1581). Tasso then succumbed to mental illness that led to incarceration by Alfonso from 1579 to 1586. He spent his last years in Naples and Rome, producing a reworking of his epic more in keeping with Counter-Reformation sensibilities (*Gerusalemme conquistata*, 1593). His fraught life later inspired numerous theatrical works, including plays by Giacometti, Goethe, Goldoni and Nota, and operas by Manuel García (*La mort du Tasse*, 1821) and Donizetti (1833).

Aminta was staged in Florence in April 1590, when Tasso was the guest of the prominent patron Jacopo Corsi – there may have been music by Emilio de' Cavalieri – and it had a direct influence on the first opera librettos by Ottavio Rinuccini. It was revived in Florence in 1616 with musical *intermedi* by Domenico Belli (*Orfeo dolente*). *Aminta* provided the basis for operas and theatrical works by Tomaso Albinoni (1703, Florence; libretto by A. Zeno), Francesco Maggiore (1742, Bologna), Alessio Prati (?1787, Ferrara; G. Muzzarelli Brusantini), and Pietro Alessandro Guglielmi (1790, Naples; C. Filomarino); incidental music was composed for it by Henry Gadsby (1898) and Ildebrando Pizzetti (1914).

Gerusalemme liberata vied with Ariosto's *Orlando furioso* as the leading epic of the century, and it offered a rich quarry of texts for madrigalists and monodists. Tasso's vibrant treatment of the first crusade also provided ample material for later operas: Monteverdi established the pattern both with his *Combattimento di Tancredi et Clorinda*, staged at the Mocenigo Palace in Venice, Carnival 1624, and with his *Armida abbandonata* (1626), now lost. Like Ariosto, Tasso was a popular source for operas and other stage works in Italy until the 1650s, then in France in the second half of the century, then in Italy and England (perhaps under French influence, and also that of the Arcadians) through the 18th century. Armida's love for Rinaldo was by far the most popular episode (*see* ARMIDA), inspiring operas by Ferrari (1639), Lully (1686), Handel (1711), Salieri (1771), Gluck (1777), Haydn (1784), Rossini (1817) and Dvořák (1904) among many others; but the tales of Sofronia and Olindo (ii:14–54), Erminia (vi:55ff; vii:1–22; xix:77ff), and Tancredi and Clorinda (xii:52–68) also reached the operatic stage (the last sometimes by way of Voltaire). Moreover, a reading of *Gerusalemme liberata* encourages the religious conversion of the heroine, Baltassara, in Antonio Maria Abbatini's *La comica del cielo* (1668, Rome; libretto by G. Rospigliosi).

A full list of operas and other dramatic works drawing (however freely) on Tasso's epic can be derived from Balsano and Walker (1988) and Carter (1990): that which follows omits works by unknown composers, ballets, oratorios, compilations, pasticcios and parodies.

ARMIDA, RINALDO

O. Vernizzi, *Armida abbandonata* (intermedi, S. Branchi), Bologna, 1623; C. Monteverdi, [*Armida abbandonata*], 1626, ?inc.; B. Ferrari, *L'Armida* (B. Ferrari), Venice, 1639; Marazzoli, *L'amore trionfante dello sdegno* (A. Pio di Savoia), Ferrara, 1641; ? Scacchi, *Armida abbandonata* (V. Puccitelli), Warsaw, 1641; Lully, *Armide* (P. Quinault), Paris, 1686; C. Pallavicino, *La Gierusalemme liberata* (G. C. Corradi), Venice, 1687, and Dresden, 1687 [as *Armida*, Hamburg, 1695]; A. Chiochiolo, *L'Armida*, Rovigo, 1694 [rev. as *Gli amori di Rinaldo con Armida*, Brescia, 1697]; Orgiani, *L'Armida* (? G. Colatelli), Mantua, 1695 [subsequent perfs. under several titles]

Eccles, *Rinaldo and Armida* (J. Dennis), London, 1698; Philippe de Bourbon, *Renaud et Armide* (? B. Requeleyne), Paris, 1705 [rev., ? collab. Gervais, as *La suite d'Armide, ou La Jérusalem délivrée*]; Ruggieri, *Armida abbandonata* (F. Silvani), Venice, 1707; Boniventi, *Armida al campo* (Silvani), Venice, 1708; Handel, *Rinaldo* (G. Rossi), London, 1711; Rampini, *Armida in Damasco* (G. Braccioli), Venice, 1711; G. M. Buini, *Armida abbandonata* (Silvani), Bologna, 1716; Sarro, *Armida al campo* (Silvani), Naples, 1718; Vivaldi, *Armida al campo d'Egitto* (G. Palazzi), Venice, 1718; Falco, *Armida abbandonata* (?Silvani), Naples, before 1719

Buini, *Armida delusa* (Buini), Venice, 1720; Desmarets, *Renaud, ou La suite d'Armide* (S.-J. Pellegrin), Paris, 1722; Schürmann, *Das eroberte Jerusalem* [*Armida und Rinaldo*] (Corradi, rev. J. S. Müller), Brunswick, 1722; Bioni, *Armida abbandonata* (Silvani), Prague, 1725; Albinoni, *Il trionfo di Armida* (Colatelli), Venice, 1726; Bioni, *Armida al campo* (Silvani), Breslau, 1726; Bertoni, *Armida* (B. Vitturi), Venice, 1746; Mele, *Armida placata* (G. Migliavacca), Madrid, 1750; Graun, *L'Armida* (L. de Villati, after Quinault), Berlin, 1751; Sarti, *Armida abbandonata* (Villati), Copenhagen, 1759; Traetta, *Armida* (G. Durazzo and Migliavacca, after Quinault), Vienna, 1761

G. Scarlatti, *Armida* (M. Coltellini), Vienna, *c*1766; Anfossi, *Armida* (J. Durandi), Turin, 1770; Jommelli, *Armida abbandonata* (F. S. de Rogatis), Naples, 1770; Manfredini, *Armida* (Durandi), Bologna, 1770; Salieri, *Armida* (Coltellini), Vienna, 1771; Sacchini, *Armida* (Durandi), Milan, 1772 [rev. as *Rinaldo*, London, 1780; rev. as *Renaud* (J. Leboeuf and Pellegrin), Paris, 1783]; Astarita, *Gli amori di Armida e Rinaldo* (Migliavacca, after Quinault), Livorno, 1773 [rev. as *Armida*, Venice, 1777]; Gazzaniga, *Armida*, Rome, 1773; J. G. Naumann, *Armida* (G. Bertati), Padua, 1773 [rev. as *Armide*, Leipzig, 1780]

L. Gatti, *Armida* (G. de Gamerra), Mantua, 1775; A. Tozzi, *Rinaldo* (after Bertati, Durandi and De Rogatis), Venice, 1775; Mortellari, *Armida* (after Durandi and De Rogatis), Modena, 1776; Cimarosa, *L'Armida immaginaria* (G. Palomba), Naples, 1777; Gluck, *Armide* (Quinault), Paris, 1777; Mysliveček, *Armida* (Migliavacca), Lucca, 1778; C. Rheineck, *Rinaldo* (C. Städele), Wolfegg, 1779; Bertoni, *Armida abbandonata* (Vitturi), Venice, 1780; Winter, *Reinhold und Armida* (J. M. von Babo), Munich, 1780; Cherubini, *Armida abbandonata* (Vitturi), Florence, 1782; V. Righini, *Armida* (Coltellini), Vienna, 1782 [rev. as *La Gerusalemme liberata, ossia Armida al campo de' Franchi* (A. Filistri de Caramandani), Berlin, 1799]

Haydn, *Armida* (N. Porta), Eszterháza, 1784; Mortellari, *Armida abbandonata*, Florence, 1785; Prati, *Armida abbandonata* (G. Sertor), Munich, 1785; Zumsteeg, *Armide* (J. C. Bock, after Bertati), Stuttgart, 1785; Sarti, *Armida e Rinaldo* (Coltellini), St Petersburg, 1786; Zingarelli, *Armida*, Rome, 1786; P. Skokoff, *Rinaldo* (Leboeuf), Naples, 1788; P. A. Guglielmi, *Rinaldo* (G. M. Foppa), Venice, 1789; Alessandri, *Armida* (Foppa), Padua, 1794; Paradis, *Rinaldo und Alcina* (L. von Baczko), Prague, 1797; André, *Rinaldo und Alcina* (Baczko), ?Dresden, 1799; G. Mosca, *Rinaldo e Armida* (F. Gonella), Florence, 1799; Haeffner, *Renaud* (Leboeuf and N. B. Sparrschöld, after De Gamerra), Stockholm, 1801

Andreozzi, *Armida e Rinaldo*, Naples, 1802; F. Bianchi, *Armida* (L. da Ponte), London, 1802; V. Righini, *La selva incantata* (Filistri de Caramandani), Berlin, 1803 [as *Der Zauberwald*, Berlin, 1811]; Rossini, *Armida* (G. Schmidt), Naples, 1817; Gläser, *Armida die Zauberin im Orient* (C. Meisl), Vienna, 1825; A. Belisario, *Armida e Rinaldo* (Bisaccia), Rovigo, 1828; G. Dabray, *Armida e Rinaldo* (Dabray), Nice, 1851; C. Tadeucci, *Armida* (G.

Tadeucci), Florence, 1868; G. des Roches, *Renaud* (Thémines-Lauzières), Boulogne-sur-mer, 1888; A. Pellizona, *Armida e Rinaldo* (Pellizona), Casale Monferrato, 1896; Zajc, *Armida* (A. Havambašić and S. Miletić), Zagreb, 1896; Dvořák, *Armida* (J. Vrchlický), Prague, 1904

CLORINDA, TANCREDI

C. Monteverdi, *Combattimento di Tancredi et Clorinda*, Venice, 1624; C. F. Pollarolo, *Gli avvenimenti di Erminia e di Clorinda* (Corradi), Venice, 1693; Campra, *Tancrède* (A. Danchet), Paris, 1702; A. Scarlatti, *Erminia, Tancredi, Polidoro e Pastore*, Naples, 1723; Apell, *Tancrède*, Kassel, 1789; Gardi, *Tancredi* (A. Pepoli), Venice, 1795; Langlé, *Tancrède*, ?1800; Pavesi, *Tancredi* (L. Romanelli), Milan, 1812; Rossini, *Tancredi* (Rossi, after Voltaire), Venice, 1813

ERMINIA

M. Rossi, *Erminia sul Giordano* (G. Rospigliosi), Rome, 1633 [also adapted from *Aminta*]; Moratelli, *Erminia ne' boschi* (G. M. Rapparini), Düsseldorf, 1687; Moratelli, *Erminia al campo* (Rapparini), Düsseldorf, 1688; C. F. Pollarolo, *Gli avvenimenti di Erminia e di Clorinda* (Corradi), Venice, 1693; A. Scarlatti, *Erminia, Tancredi, Polidoro e Pastore*, Naples, 1723; G. de Majo, *Erminia* (B. Saddumene), Naples, 1729; L. A. Calegari, *Erminia* (L. G. Buonavoglia), Venice, 1805; A. Gandini, *Erminia* (L. A. Vincenzi), Modena, 1818; L. Lucantonio, *Erminia* (G. delle Rossi), Naples, 1903

SOFRONIA, OLINDO

J. C. Hertel, *Olint und Sophronia* (J. F. Cronegk), Hamburg, 1767; Andreozzi, *Sofronia ed Olindo* (C. Sernicola), Naples, 1793; Paer, *Olinde et Sophronie*, ?1824, inc.

OTHERS

Persuis, *Godefroy de Bouillon, ou La Jérusalem délivrée* (P.-M. Baour-Lormian), Paris, 1812; Nicolai, *Gildippe ed Odoardo* (T. Solera), Genoa, 1840

*

A. Solerti: *Vita di Torquato Tasso* (Turin, 1895)
B. Pennacchietti: 'Studi Metastasiani', *Studi di letteratura italiana*, xi (1915), 155–202
L. Frati: 'Torquato Tasso in musica', *RMI*, xxx (1923), 389–400
A. Einstein: '*Orlando furioso* and *La Gerusalemme liberata* as Set to Music during the Sixteenth and Seventeenth Centuries', *Notes*, viii (1950–51), 623–30
B. Corrigan: 'Tasso's Erminia in the Italian Theater of the Seicento', *Renaissance Drama*, vii (1964), 127–50
C. Girdlestone: *La tragédie en musique (1673–1750) considérée comme genre littéraire* (Geneva, 1972)
M. P. McClymonds: 'Haydn and his Contemporaries: "Armida abbandonata"', *Bericht über den internationalen Joseph Haydn Kongress: Vienna 1982*, 325–32
L. Bianconi and T. Walker: 'Production, Consumption and Political Function of Seventeenth-Century Italian Opera', *Early Music History*, iv (1984), 209–96
M. A. Balsano and T. Walker, eds.: *Tasso, la musica, i musicisti* (Florence, 1988)
T. Carter: Review of Balsano and Walker (1988), *JRMA*, cxv (1990), 258–61

TIM CARTER

Tate, Jeffrey (*b* Salisbury, 28 April 1943). English conductor. He qualified in medicine before taking the répétiteur's course at the London Opera Centre, 1970–71, then joining the Covent Garden music staff. Boulez chose him as assistant for the Bayreuth *Ring*, 1976–80, and for the first three-act *Lulu*, in Paris, 1979. The previous year he made his conducting début at Göteborg with *Carmen*, followed by *Lulu* at the Metropolitan in 1980 and *La clemenza di Tito* at Covent Garden in 1982, where he was named Principal Conductor from 1985 (under Colin Davis, then Bernard Haitink). In that year he also had further opera débuts, at the Salzburg Festival (the première of Henze's realization of *Il ritorno d'Ulisse in patria*) and the Vienna Staatsoper (*Tito*). He conducted the première of Rolf Liebermann's *La forêt* at Geneva, 1987.

Tate has developed his career in spite of being handicapped from birth by severe spinal malformation, which obliges him to sit while conducting. It does not impair his decisive beat nor the clarity he imparts to his performances. He has conducted little Italian opera, preferring Mozart, Wagner and Strauss, whose *Arabella* was his first opera recording (1988). He was made a CBE in 1990.

*

E. Forbes: 'Jeffrey Tate', *Opera*, xxxviii (1987), 631–7

NOËL GOODWIN

Tate, Maggie. *See* TEYTE, MAGGIE.

Tate [Teate], **Nahum** (*b* Dublin, 1652; *d* London, 12 Aug 1715). Irish librettist. His first work for the theatre was the blank verse tragedy *Brutus of Alba; or the Enchanted Lovers* (1678), from which he later drew the libretto of Purcell's *Dido and Aeneas* (first performed before December 1689). Tate was fiercely loyal to Charles II and, like the poet laureate John Dryden, an extremely political writer. His adaptation of Shakespeare's *Richard II* (1680), which included a song by Purcell, was banned because of its alleged allusions to the Exclusion Crisis, the attempt to block the accession of the Catholic Duke of York. Even more overt in support of Charles is Tate's version of *Coriolanus*, re-titled *Ingratitude of a Common-wealth* (1681). But his most notorious adaptation (though not particularly political) is the *History of King Lear*, a travesty of Shakespeare (for example, it ends happily with Cordelia marrying Edgar), but effective in its own right. Tate's 1687 version of John Fletcher's *The Island Princess* formed the basis of P. A. Motteux's text for the 1699 semi-opera of the same name.

Tate's play *Brutus of Alba*, based on the *Aeneid* (book iv), was originally called *Dido and Aeneas*, but he changed the title to avoid invidious comparisons with Virgil: Aeneas became Brutus, Dido the Queen of Syracuse, and the Sorceress was re-named Ragusa. The play was a failure, but from its ruins Tate extracted *Dido and Aeneas*. Reduced from five acts to three, the plot radically simplified, the characters restored to their original names and all traces of gore removed, it is a brilliant libretto. The trochaic tetrameter, softened by artful repetitions and enjambments, proved ideal for Purcell's plastic melodies, and the terse, rapid exchanges between the lovers gave the composer ample scope for lyrical and highly expressive recitatives. Its one widely perceived weakness is the under-development of Aeneas, for whom Purcell provided no proper aria. But his cowardly and ignominious exit in Act 3, though it may seem an anticlimax, helps to focus the tragedy even more sharply on Dido.

Considering Tate's strong political instincts and the fact that the story of Aeneas at Carthage was a favourite vehicle for covert political comment throughout the 17th century, the libretto probably has a subtext. But because it could have been written any time between about 1684 and December 1689 (a period which saw the death of Charles II, the overthrow of James II and the coronation of William and Mary) it is impossible to say exactly what Tate intended. Adroitly trimming his sails and quietly transferring his allegiance to the new monarchs, he was appointed poet laureate on 24 December 1692 in succession to Thomas Shadwell, becoming historiographer royal in 1702.

*

Nicoll H
C. Spencer: *Nahum Tate* (New York, 1972)
R. D. Hume: *The Development of English Drama in the Seventeenth Century* (Oxford, 1976)

C. Price: *Henry Purcell and the London Stage* (Cambridge, 1984)
E. T. Harris: *Henry Purcell's Dido and Aeneas* (Oxford, 1987)
J. A. Winn: *John Dryden and his World* (New Haven, CT, 1987)

CURTIS PRICE

Tattermuschová, Helena (*b* Prague, 28 Jan 1933). Czech soprano. She studied singing with Vlasta Linhartová and acting with Ferdinand Pujman in Prague, and appeared at the National Theatre while still a student. After a period with the Ostrava Opera, 1954–6, she moved to the National Theatre in Prague. At first she took soubrette and boyish roles, to which she was ideally suited. Her secure lyric technique, clear diction and girlish charm then destined her for roles in Mozart, Smetana (Blaženka in *The Secret*, Jitka in *Dalibor*, Karolina in *The Two Widows*) and the Italian repertory (Rosina, Gilda, Violetta, Musetta, Liù, Butterfly). She displayed her acting ability and wide range of expression as Papagena (in Herlischka's innovatory *Zauberflöte*, 1957), the Vixen and Málinka/Etherea/Kunka in the British première of Janáček's *The Excursions of Mr Brouček* (1970, Edinburgh).

*

ČSHS
E. Kopecký: *Pěvci Národního divadla* [Singers of the National Theatre] (Prague, 1983), 291–5
Čeští koncertní umělci – pěvci [Czech Concert Artists – Singers] (Prague, 1984), 205–6
V. Procházka, ed.: *Národní divadlo a jeho předchůdci* [The National Theatre and its Predecessors] (Prague, 1988), 512–20

ALENA NĚMCOVÁ

Taube [Tauber, Täuber, Tayber]. *See* TEYBER.

Tauber [Taube], **Maria Anna** [Marianne] (*fl* 1777–9). Austrian soprano. A member of the Esterházy opera company, she probably sang the role of Markesinn Bellavita in the first performance of Ulbrich's *Frühling und Liebe* (Vienna, 8 February 1778), appearing on the playbill as 'Mlle Tauber'. She was probably also the 'Mlle Teuberin' referred to by Baron von Gebler in a letter of the same date. She was not related to Therese Teyber (*see* TEYBER family, (3)), who sang in the same performance.

Tauber, Richard (*b* Linz, 16 May 1891; *d* London, 8 Jan 1948). Austrian tenor, naturalized British. He was the illegitimate son of the actor and theatre director Richard Anton Tauber. After study at Freiburg, he first appeared in opera at Chemnitz (2 March 1913) as Tamino in *Die Zauberflöte*. He was at once engaged by the Dresden Opera, where he sang all the leading lyrical tenor roles. By 1919 he was well known throughout the German-speaking countries, and he soon became extremely popular at the Munich and Salzburg Mozart festivals. It was to lighter music, however, that he owed his world fame. He appeared with increasing frequency in the operettas of Lehár and others, charming thousands by his true tenor quality and by the grace and variety of his vocal inflections. England succumbed in 1931, when Lehár's *Das Land des Lächelns* repeated its universal success at Drury Lane. When Covent Garden first heard him he was no longer at his very best; in 1938 he sang Tamino and Belmonte, in 1939 Don Ottavio, and Hans in the German version of *The Bartered Bride*. After the war, however, he surprised even his warmest admirers by the excellence of his Don Ottavio in 1947. Tauber's first marriage was dissolved, and he married the actress Diana Napier in 1936. He wrote three operettas, music for films, and various songs.

D. N. Tauber: *Richard Tauber* (London, 1949)
——: *My Heart and I* (London, 1959)
J. Dennis, with G. O. Abell and L. E. Abell: 'Richard Tauber', *Record Collector*, xviii (1968–9), 171–272; xix (1970–71), 81–6
C. Castle and D. N. Tauber: *This was Richard Tauber* (London, 1971)

DESMOND SHAWE-TAYLOR

Tauberová [née Proskeová], **Maria** (*b* Vysoké Mýto, Bohemia, 28 April 1911). Czech soprano. She trained mainly in Vienna where she sang in 360 performances of Kreisler's operetta *Sissy*, and also studied in Milan and Prague. In 1936 she made her débuts as Gilda in Plzeň and then at the National Theatre in Prague, where she continued to sing until 1973. Tauberová was in her element in lyric roles. Her technique, accomplished and even in all registers, was effectively displayed in Mozart and as Eurydice (in Talich's interpretation of Gluck's *Orfeo*), Zerbinetta, Olympia (*Les contes d'Hoffmann*) and Rosina (*Barbiere*). A charming Vixen and a lively Karolina (in Smetana's *The Two Widows*), she was a delicate Julietta and a coquettish Mirandolina in Martinů's operas of the same names. She sang throughout Europe and in South America, frequently with her husband, Jaroslav Krombholc.

*

ČSHS
L. Šíp: *Pěvci před mikrofonem* [Singers Before the Microphone] (Prague, 1960), 70–73
E. Kopecký and V. Pospíšil: *Slavní pěvci Národního divadla* [Famous Singers of the National Theatre] (Prague, 1968), 207–12
Čeští koncertní umělci – pěvci [Czech Concert Artists – Singers] (Prague, 1984), suppl.
V. Procházka, ed.: *Národní divadlo a jeho předchůdci* [The National Theatre and its Predecessors] (Prague, 1988), 520–21

ALENA NĚMCOVÁ

Taubert, (Carl Gottfried) Wilhelm (*b* Berlin, 23 March 1811; *d* Berlin, 7 Jan 1891). German conductor and composer. He studied with Ludwig Berger (piano) and Bernard Klein (composition) and by 1831 had become assistant conductor and accompanist of the Berlin court concerts. During the 1840s he was associated with the Berlin Hofoper, serving as Generalmusikdirektor from 1845 to 1848. At that time he was also court Kapellmeister, a position he retained until 1869. As Hofkapellmeister, Taubert continued to conduct the royal orchestra until 1883.

Among his first compositions were small instrumental pieces and sets of songs which attracted the favourable notice of Mendelssohn and led to a correspondence in which Mendelssohn seems to pinpoint the lack of impetus and spirit that hindered Taubert, for all his musicianship, refined taste and immense industry, from achieving real importance as a composer. His larger works include, besides his operas, incidental music for eight plays, and a substantial quantity of orchestral and chamber music.

all performed at Berlin, Königliches Theater

Die Kirmes op.7 (komische Oper, 1, E. Devrient), 23 Jan 1832, vs (Berlin, 1832)
Der Zigeuner (4, Devrient), 14 Sept 1834
Marquis und Dieb (komische Oper, 1, L. Schneider), 15 Feb 1842
Joggeli op.100 (2, H. Klöster), 9 Oct 1853, vs (Berlin, 1854)
Macbeth op.133 (5, F. H. Eggers), 16 Nov 1857, vs (Berlin and Posen, 1857)
Cesario, oder Was ihr wollt op.188 (komische Oper, 3, E. Taubert, after W. Shakespeare), 13 Nov 1874, vs (Berlin and Posen, 1875)

*

StiegerO
R. Schumann: *Gesammelte Schriften* (Leipzig, 1854, 5/1914)

W. Neumann: *Wilhelm Taubert und Ferdinand Hiller* (Kassel, 1857)
E. Glusman: 'Taubert and Mendelssohn: Opposing Attitudes toward Poetry and Music', *MQ*, lvii (1971), 628–35
C. Gruber: *Opern Uraufführungen*, ii (Vienna, 1987)

Taucher, Curt (*b* Nuremberg, 25 Oct 1885; *d* Munich, 7 Aug 1945). German tenor. After studying in Munich, he made his début in 1908 at Augsburg as Faust. He sang at Chemnitz and Hanover, then in 1920 went to Dresden, where he was engaged at the Staatsoper until his retirement in 1934. He created the title role of Weill's *Der Protagonist* (1926), sang in the première of Graener's *Hanneles Himmelfahrt* (1927) and created Menelaus in *Die ägyptische Helena* (1928). From 1923 to 1927 he sang at the Metropolitan as Siegmund, Siegfried, Tannhäuser, Tristan and Parsifal. In 1932 he appeared at Covent Garden, as Tannhäuser and Tristan. His voice was strong and reliable, although its tone was not particularly ingratiating. ELIZABETH FORBES

Tautenhayn, Ernst (*b* Vienna, 3 April 1873; *d* Zlabing, 30 Aug 1944). Viennese bass, noted for his partnership with LOUISE KARTOUSCH.

Tavener, John (Kenneth) (*b* London, 28 Jan 1944). English composer. He studied at the RAM (1961–5) with Lennox Berkeley and David Lumsdaine. His cantata *Cain and Abel*, which won the Prince Rainier of Monaco prize in 1965, shows signs of Stravinsky's influence. In later works such as *The Whale* (1965–6), the *Celtic Requiem* (1969) and *Ultimos ritos* (1969–72) Tavener developed a highly personal style, in which mystical and ritualistic elements play a significant part. The music of the Russian Orthodox church, of which he is a member, has influenced him and can be discerned both in more recent concert works and in the operas.

His only large-scale opera, *Thérèse* (1973–6), stems from the same creative roots as the later concert works and resembles them in making bold use of the apparatus of music theatre and in its overriding concern with spiritual matters. His one-act chamber opera *A Gentle Spirit* is also more concerned with the inner life than with the outward world. The young wife (soprano) of a pawnbroker (high tenor) has killed herself by jumping from a window. Scenes from their past life are re-enacted as the husband recalls with agony the events leading up to his wife's suicide and reproaches himself for his lack of love and understanding. In a complex score, Tavener taxes both soloists and chamber ensemble to their technical and expressive limit.

Tavener's third opera, *St Mary of Egypt*, to a libretto by Mother Thekla, Abbess of the Greek Orthodox Monastery of the Assumption, deals with a meeting in the Jordanian desert of a holy ascetic (tenor) and a sinful woman (soprano): 'Father Zossima was on the road of lovelessness and death, St Mary, from the beginning, was on the road of love and life ... in his awakened love for her as a person, not an ideal, Father Zossima was roused to the clarity of vision which can only come *from* love and be directed *to* love.' The opera, scored for chamber orchestra, was given at Aldeburgh in 1992.

See also THÉRÈSE (ii).

A Gentle Spirit (chamber op, 1, G. McLarnon, after F. M. Dostoyevsky), Bath, Royal, 6 June 1977 (London, 1978)
Thérèse (1, McLarnon), London, Covent Garden, 1 Oct 1979, vs (London, 1977)
St Mary of Egypt (5, Mother Thekla), Aldeburgh, Snape Maltings, 19 June 1992

*

A. Jacobs: Review of 'A Gentle Spirit', *Opera*, xxviii (1977), 802–3
P. Griffiths: 'Thérèse: a Saint in Hell', *MT*, cxx (1979), 814–16
J. Tavener: 'Thérèse', *Opera*, xxx (1979), 944–7 HUGO COLE

Taverner. Opera in two acts by PETER MAXWELL DAVIES to his own libretto after 16th-century documents; London, Covent Garden, 12 July 1972.

The creation of *Taverner* dominated Davies's development between 1956 and 1970. He had prepared a draft outline of a large-scale opera based on the life of the Tudor composer John Taverner (1495–1545) while still a student at Manchester University in the mid-1950s. In the two Taverner Fantasias (1962 and 1964) and the *Seven in Nomine* (1963–4), all of which share

'Taverner' (Maxwell Davies): Act 1 scene i (John Taverner on trial for heresy) from the original production at Covent Garden, London, 12 July 1972 (designed by Ralph Koltai), with Ragnar Ulfung as Taverner

thematic material with *Taverner*, he refined some of the transformation techniques deployed in the opera. He began to compose *Taverner* during his years at Princeton University (1962–4) and the score was completed by 1968; part was then destroyed by fire and reconstructed from sketches in 1970.

The dramatic plan of the opera is symmetrical: each of the four scenes in the first act has its counterpart (its parodistical opposite) in the second. The opera opens in pre-Reformation England with the trial of the composer (tenor) for heresy before the White Abbot (baritone). His father, Richard (baritone), and wife, Rose Parrowe (mezzo-soprano), are called as witnesses against him. Taverner is convicted but reprieved by the Cardinal (tenor), who is then seen in debate with the King (bass), who wishes to break with the Church of Rome to rid himself of an unwanted wife. The argument is observed by the Jester (baritone), who points up the irony of their self-interest and in the final scene of the first act is revealed as Death, challenging Taverner to distinguish good from evil, Christ from Antichrist.

In Act 2, after the Reformation, it is Taverner who is prosecuting the White Abbot for heresy. But now there is no reprieve and Death is shown controlling the Wheel of Fortune. The Cardinal is recast as an Anglican archbishop, and Taverner is compelled to deny his musical past, confessing his part in the corruption of the old order. The opera ends with the White Abbot's execution and, implicitly, with the final destruction of Taverner's own creative life.

Davies's use of Taverner's own music both as the starting-point for his own transformational procedures and in direct quotation sustains the musical commentary on several planes. An onstage consort of viols playing Davies's own reworking of Tudor dances accompanies the Cardinal's and the King's dialogue in the first act, while the equivalent scene in the second replaces the strings with wind and percussion and parodies of the originals; as Taverner denies his own artistic achievement he does so against the background of his *Gloria tibi Trinitas* mass. For all their ingenuity, however, and the discreet structural use of motivic chords and pitch collections, Davies's procedures do not produce a convincing fusion of music and theatre: the ironic parodies remain within the score, quite separate from the drama. ANDREW CLEMENTS

T'avrizyan, Mik'ayel Arsen (*b* Baku, 14/27 May 1907; *d* Erevan, 17 Oct 1957). Armenian conductor. At the Leningrad Conservatory he studied the viola and conducting, and led the viola section of the opera studio. After a period in the orchestra of the Maliy Opera Theatre, Leningrad, he turned to conducting in 1935. In 1938 he was appointed principal conductor at the Erevan Opera and Ballet Theatre, where he played an important part in the development of Armenian national opera. Displaying a fine instinct for music drama and operatic character, T'avrizyan aimed at blending all the constituent elements of opera, so that the stage and musical characterizations were closely linked. Among the operas he conducted were Tchukhatjian's *Arshak II* (1945), Step'anyan's *Lusabatsin* (1938) and *Herosuhi* (1950), *David-Bek* (1956) by Armen Tigranyan and *Ardsvaberd* (1957) by Andrey Babayev. I. M. YAMPOL'SKY

Taylor, (Joseph) Deems (*b* New York, 22 Dec 1885; *d* New York, 3 July 1966). American composer and critic. He studied at New York University and with Oscar Coon before becoming the editor of *Musical America*. During the 1930s and 40s he worked for ASCAP and was opera commentator for NBC and NY Philharmonic commentator for CBS. A popular musical personality, he composed a variety of music, including an orchestral suite, *Through the Looking-Glass* (1922), which has often been performed.

Taylor's first four stage works, dating from 1908 to 1916, were light operas or musical comedies. Two of the four operas that followed, *The King's Henchman* (1927) and *Peter Ibbetson* (1931), were commissioned by the Metropolitan Opera, and with their premières Taylor became the most successful American opera composer of his era. Both received more performances at the Metropolitan than any other opera by a native composer and after its première *The King's Henchman* toured the USA and Canada, reaching 46 cities during the 1927–8 season. In spite of their initial popularity, however, neither opera remained in the repertory.

The libretto of *The King's Henchman* was fashioned by the American poet, Edna St Vincent Millay, from a 10th-century Saxon tale. Olin Downes called the opera 'poetic and glamorous', but critics and audiences alike were especially attracted to the novelty of an opera by an American in the English language. *Peter Ibbetson* is based on George du Maurier's romantic novel of 1891 and the play adapted by the actress Constance Collier for herself and the Barrymore brothers in 1917. At its 1960 revival at the New York Empire State Park, the opera was considered 'deft and elegant' but its libretto dated and old-fashioned. Taylor's style resembles aspects of Wagner, Debussy and Puccini. With its *Tristan*-like story, *The King's Henchman* employs an intricate system of leitmotifs, while *Peter Ibbetson* constructs a sensuous musical fabric with occasional arias. *Ramuntcho* (1934–8) is a lyric opera with set pieces, more like a romantic turn-of-the-century operetta. A one-act comic opera, *The Dragon* (1958), was intended for college workshops and local companies, groups that were increasing in number in the USA at the time.

first performed in New York unless otherwise stated

Cap'n Kidd & Co (comic op, 2, W. le Baron), New York U., Carnegie Lyceum, 24 April 1908, vs (New York, 1908)

The Undergraduates (musical comedy, 1, le Baron), New York U., Berkeley Theatre, 28 April 1910, vs (New York, 1910)

The Echo (musical comedy, 2, le Baron), New York U., Berkeley Lyceum, 30 April 1910; Globe, 17 Aug 1910, vs (New York, 1909)

The Breath of Scandal [The Mistress of the Seas] (operetta, 1, J. M. Flagg), Delmonico's, 28 Feb 1916, vs (New York, 1916)

The King's Henchman (lyric drama, 3, E. St Vincent Millay), Met, 17 Feb 1927, vs (New York, 1926)

Peter Ibbetson (lyric drama, 3, C. Collier and Taylor, after G. du Maurier), Met, 7 Feb 1931, vs (New York, 1930)

Ramuntcho, 1934–8 (lyric drama, 3, Taylor, after P. Loti), Philadelphia, Academy of Music, 10 Feb 1942, vs (New York, 1941)

The Dragon (lyric comedy, 1, Taylor, after A. Gregory), New York U., Hall of Fame, 6 Feb 1958

J. T. Howard: *Deems Taylor* (New York, 1927, 2/1940)

E. E. Hipsher: *American Opera and its Composers* (Philadelphia, 1927, 2/1934)

O. Thompson: 'Critical Estimate of the Score of *The King's Henchman*', *Music News* (25 Feb 1927)

O. Downes: 'An American Opera Composer's new Opera', *New York Times* (1 Feb 1931)

C. E. Watt: '*Peter Ibbetson*', *Music News* (27 Feb 1931)

F. D. Perkins: '*The Dragon* – Premiere of Deems Taylor's Opera', *New York Herald-Tribune* (7 Feb 1958)

'Ibbetson Revisited', *Time* (1 Aug 1960) ELISE K. KIRK

Taylor, Rayner (*b* London, 1747; *d* Philadelphia, 17 Aug 1825). English composer, later naturalized American. He established himself in Chelmsford, Essex, as a music teacher and organist, but during the period 1765–92 he was increasingly involved with music at Marylebone Gardens, the Apollo Gardens, the Royal Circus and the Haymarket Theatre as a singer and composer, ultimately becoming music director at Sadler's Wells. As well as in numerous songs, his dramatic talent is evident in the burletta *Buxom Joan* (1778, Haymarket), to a text by Thomas Willet. Within *galant* conventions, it displays sensitivity to English prosody, effective musical characterization and immediate projection of emotion. Though he never achieved the fame of his contemporary William Shield, with whom he may profitably be compared, Taylor was responsible in part for it, having ghosted Shield's celebrated song 'The Heaving of the Lead' (*Hartford Bridge*, 1792).

In the same year, Taylor and an *ingénue*, Miss Huntley, who had recently starred in Shield's *The Woodman* (1791), gave up their successful London careers for the uncertainties of a new life in the USA. At first, always in the hope of returning to England, he made his living as an organist and teacher, but in 1809 he became a naturalized American citizen. Intermittent calls to theatrical duty by his former pupil Alexander Reinagle, manager of the Chestnut Street Theatre, resulted in some incidental music and orchestral accompaniments for imported London shows. His only complete American theatrical score, for the Philadelphia production (1814) of William Dimond's failed London melodrama *The Aethiop* (1812), was occasioned by the unavailability of Henry Bishop's music. The surviving souvenir keyboard score shows that Taylor had kept up with the times. To the communicative musical manner of his London work he assimilated in his songs a Mozartian flair for melody, and in some noble choruses, the orchestral figurations of Haydn, as well as touches of Romantic harmony.

Taylor's position in the history of Anglo-American opera is anomalous; had he remained in London, he might have achieved a secure niche in English theatrical history. 'I made a mistake in coming to this country,' he once commented, 'for had I stayed home, I should now have occupied Shield's place at Covent Garden Theatre'. In the USA, where he had few opportunities for self-expression, he might have grown bitter. However, he always maintained a public decorum and affability, and is remembered equally as 'that scientific and valuable man' and as a 'playful' entertainer who could 'sit down to the piano forte and extemporize an Italian opera … Thus would he often in sportive mood, throw away ideas sufficient to establish a musical fame.'

*

J. R. Parker: 'Musical Reminiscences', *The Euterpeiad*, ii/21 (1822), 162; abridged in *Musical Biography* (Boston, 1825), 179ff

F. Archer: 'A Philadelphia Organist of the Past', *The Keynote*, iii/9 (1884), 7

O. G. T. Sonneck: 'Early American Operas', *SIMG*, vi (1904–5), 428–95

J. Mates: *The American Musical Stage before 1800* (New Brunswick, NJ, 1962), 198–9

J. A. Cuthbert: *Rayner Taylor and Anglo-American Musical Life* (diss., West Virginia U., 1980)

V. F. Yellin: 'Rayner Taylor', *American Music*, i/3 (1983), 43–71

——: 'Rayner Taylor's Music for *The Aethiop*', *American Music*, iv/3 (1986), 249–67; v/1 (1987), 20–47

VICTOR FELL YELLIN

Taylor, Samuel Coleridge. *See* COLERIDGE-TAYLOR, SAMUEL.

Taylor, William (*b* c1753; *d* London, 1825). English impresario and manager. A bank clerk by training and confessedly ignorant of music and all foreign languages, Taylor was deeply involved in the management of Italian opera in London from 1781 until 1815. For much of this time he was proprietor-manager of the King's Theatre in the Haymarket, sometimes running its affairs from debtors' prison. Although he was an unscrupulous businessman and was vilified by Da Ponte for cavalier treatment of artists, Taylor's policies determined the direction of Italian opera in London during a particularly chaotic period. His main achievements were the rebuilding of the King's Theatre after the 1789 fire and the recruitment of Noverre, Haydn, Da Ponte, Martín y Soler and Brigida Banti. He is chiefly remembered, however, for serious financial mismanagement which continued to plague the King's Theatre long after his death.

Taylor first became directly involved with the King's Theatre in early 1781. Its co-owner, the politician and playwright RICHARD BRINSLEY SHERIDAN, was on the verge of bankruptcy and sold his friend Taylor a part-interest in the theatre, though very little money actually changed hands. As Sheridan's debts mounted, Taylor acquired more control of the theatre and became proprietor-manager early in the 1781–2 season. In summer 1782 he undertook a major refurbishment of the theatre, which had remained virtually unaltered since Handel's day, but the remodelling proved financially ruinous. Most of the performers went unpaid at the end of the 1782–3 season, and Taylor was forced to assign the theatre to a group of trustees. They in turn appointed his arch-rival GIOVANNI ANDREA BATTISTA GALLINI as manager in 1785.

After several years out of management, much of it spent in the Fleet Prison under King's Bench orders, Taylor accomplished one of the great reversals of fortune in opera history. When the King's Theatre burnt down on 17 June 1789, he immediately raised a subscription and started constructing a new opera house designed by the former scene painter Michael Novosielski, although he had little prospect of receiving a licence; the Lord Chamberlain was determined to suppress the Haymarket in favour of his own opera house managed by a front-man, ROBERT BRAY O'REILLY. But Taylor kept his nerve and opened his large and well-equipped theatre in early 1791 with a series of free dress rehearsals, some of which were conducted by Haydn, who was engaged as house composer. Taylor had outwitted the Lord Chamberlain, who, unable to compete with the rival opera company, conceded victory. The Haymarket was officially established as London's sole Italian opera house, beginning with the 1792–3 season, with Taylor as manager. Though encumbered by an accumulated deficit and constantly criticized by all his associates, Taylor's position was only once seriously threatened during the next two decades. He did not concern himself with the day-to-day management or artistic policy of the opera house, which was placed in the hands of a series of assistant managers. In February 1782 he appointed Domenico Angelo, a riding and fencing master, as his deputy. Angelo was required to attend all opera and ballet rehearsals and to recruit performers from abroad, subject to Taylor's approval. Similar arrangements were presumably reached with Gallini in 1791 and with Michael Kelly and Stephen Storace, joint music directors in 1793.

Taylor was a colourful character whose personal life was as eventful as his professional. He married or at least cohabited with the *prima donna seria* Maria Prudom in the early 1780s and is reputed to have had an affair with Brigida Banti when she joined the King's Theatre in the mid-1790s. While watching the laying of the cornerstone of his new theatre in April 1790, he is said to have remarked that he had nothing in his pockets but his hands. He was a Member of Parliament (for Leominster, 1797–1802; for Barnstaple, 1806–12), a position he sought because it gave him immunity from arrest for debt. Artistically, Taylor had minimal influence, but his financial management contributed substantially to many decades of operatic turmoil and mediocrity in London.

*

BDA; *BurneyH*; *LS*
[W. Allen, T. Luppino and H. Reynell]: *The Case of the Opera-House Disputes Fairly Stated* (London, 1784)
R. B. O'Reilly: *An Authentic Narrative of the Principal Circumstances Relating to the Opera House in the Hay-Market* (London, 1791)
W. Taylor: *A Concise Statement of Transactions and Circumstances Respecting the King's Theatre in the Haymarket* (London, 1791)
F. H. W. Sheppard, ed.: *Survey of London*, xxix, xxx (London, 1960)
D. Nalbach: *The King's Theatre 1704–1867* (London, 1972)
C. Price, J. Milhous and R. D. Hume: 'A Royal Opera House in Leicester Square (1790)', *COJ*, ii (1990), 1–28
——: 'The Rebuilding of the King's Theatre, Haymarket, 1789–1791', *Theatre Journal*, xl (1991), 421–44

CURTIS PRICE

Tbilisi (Russ. Tiflis). Capital of Georgia. It was a cultural centre for the entire Caucasus region at least from the incorporation of Georgia into Russia in 1801, but musical theatre appeared in the form of Russian and Ukrainian musical comedies only after the opening of a 340-seat theatre in 1845. The local opera company can trace its history to the city's first opera theatre, a 700-seat house designed by the architect Skudieri which opened in 1851 with a performance of *Lucia di Lammermoor* by an Italian company. The city was frequently a tour stop, as well as a holiday retreat for Russian musicians – Tchaikovsky began several of his works there, including *The Queen of Spades*. Numerous Italian troupes played at the theatre until it was destroyed by fire in 1874 and performances were temporarily relocated to the summer theatre. A Russian troupe, formed in 1880, performed Russian classics and recent works from the capital; it moved in 1896 to a new 1200-seat theatre in Moorish style with four balconies, designed by the architect V. A. Shretter – the so-called Kazyonnïy Teatr (Public Theatre), which opened with a performance of *A Life for the Tsar*. The city still relied mostly on touring companies, until the foundation of the Tbilisi Philharmonic in 1905 enabled the production of Russian and European works in Georgian. The first Georgian operas entered the repertory in 1919: Paliashvili's *Abesalom da Eteri* ('Absalom and Etery'), Arakishvili's *Tkmuleba Shota Rustavelze* ('The Legend of Shota Rustaveli') and Dolidze's *Keto da Kote* ('Keto and Kote'), the first Georgian comic opera. In 1921 the theatre was nationalized with the establishment of the Georgian SSR. Since then, the theatre has presented a mixture of the Russian and European classics (generally performed in their original languages) with a national repertory of works first performed in the city, including further works of Paliashvili and operas by Meliton Balanchivadze and Shalva and Otar Taktakishvili. In 1937 the theatre was renamed the Tbilisskiy Gosudarstvennïy Teatr Operï i Baleta imeni Z. P. Paliashvili (Paliashvili Tbilisi State Theatre of Opera and Ballet); in 1966 'Academic' was added to the name. An affiliated theatre opened in Kutaisi in 1969.

*

ME (M. S. Kavtaradze; also 'Gruzinskiy teatr Operï i baleta')
G. D. Shavgulidze: *Dni i godï Tiflisskogo opernogo teatra* [Days and Years of Tbilisi Opera Theatre] (Tbilisi, 1936)
Iv. Dzhavakhishvili: *Osnovnïye voprosï istorii gruzinskoy muzïki* [Fundamental Aspects of the History of Georgian Music] (Tbilisi, 1938)
Sh. Kashmadze: *Tbilisskiy teatr operï i baleta: materialï dlya istorii* (Tbilisi, 1950–55)
Gruzinskaya muzïkal'naya kul'tura [Georgian Musical Culture] (Moscow, 1957)
P. Khuchua: *Tbilisskiy gosudarstvennïy ordena Lenina teatr operï i baleta im. Zakhariya Paliashvili* (Tbilisi, 1958)
G. Bernandt: *Slovar' oper vpervïye postavlennïkh ili izdannïkh v dorevolyutsionnoy Rossii i v SSSR 1736–1959* [Dictionary of Operas First Performed or Published in Pre-revolutionary Russia and in the USSR 1736–1959] (Moscow, 1962), 551–2
Yu. V. Keldïsh, ed.: *Istoriya muzïki narodov SSSR* [History of the Music of the Soviet Peoples], i–v (Moscow, 1970–74)
D. Mchelidze: *Tri pokoleniya gruzinskikh pevtsov* [Three Generations of Georgian Singers] (Tbilisi, 1968)
M. Kvaliashvili: *Po trudnomu puti* [On a Difficult Path] (Tbilisi, 1969)
A. Tsulukidze: *Gruzinskaya sovetskaya muzïka* (Tbilisi, 1971)
V. Donadze: *Essays on the History of Georgian Soviet Music*, i (Tbilisi, 1975) [in Georgian]

GREGORY SALMON

Tchaikovsky, Alexander Vladimirovich. *See* CHAYKOVSKY, ALEXANDER VLADIMIROVICH.

Tchaikovsky [Chaykovsky], **Modest Il'yich** [Il'ich] (*b* Alpayevsk, Verkhotur'yev district, Perm' province, 1/13 May 1850; *d* Moscow, 2/15 Jan 1916). Russian dramatist and librettist, brother of PYOTR IL'YICH TCHAIKOVSKY. In 1870 he graduated from the Imperial School of Jurisprudence in St Petersburg, where his brother had preceded him. After five years in the civil service he resigned his commission to devote himself to literature and to tutoring a deaf-mute boy named Kolya Konradi, who later became his ward. In the late 1870s he worked as an anonymous musical and theatrical reviewer for several newspapers. He made his début as a playwright in 1881, with the comedy *Blagodetel'* ('The Benefactor'), written the year before under the pseudonym 'Gorovoy'. Over the next dozen years he established himself as a popular fixture of the Moscow and St Petersburg stages, with *Lizaveta Nikolayevna* (1884), *Simfoniya* ('Symphony', 1890), *Den' v Peterburge* ('A Day in St Petersburg', 1892) and *Predrassudki* ('Prejudices', 1893). It was on a visit to St Petersburg to see the last that Pyotr Tchaikovsky met his untimely death. Modest Tchaikovsky's final work for the dramatic stage was a translation of Corneille's tragedy *Horace* (1894). Thereafter he devoted himself to his brother's memory, with a monumental three-volume biography (*Zhizn' Petra Il'icha Chaykovskogo*, Moscow and Leipzig, 1901–3; translated and abridged by Rosa Newmarch as *The Life and Letters of Tchaikovsky*), and as founder of the Tchaikovsky museum at Klin. He also wrote important biographical articles on the critic Hermann Laroche (1913) and on Sergey Taneyev (1916).

Tchaikovsky began his career as a librettist as a functionary of the Imperial Theatres, with a commission to turn Pushkin's novella *Pikovaya dama* ('The Queen of

Spades') into a libretto, not for his brother, but for the minor composer Nikolay Klenovsky (1857–1915), who was employed by the Bol'shoy Theatre in Moscow as conductor. It was only after both Klenovsky and Nikolay Solov'yov had turned the project down that it was offered, with spectacular result, to Pyotr Tchaikovsky. By now it is a commonplace to hold up the libretto of *The Queen of Spades* (which the composer considerably revised) as a cautionary example of operatic hackwork; it is worth noting, therefore, that when the work was new it was hailed as an epitome of theatrical craftsmanship. The Russian operatic chronicler Vsevolod Cheshikhin wrote that it was 'a singular example of its type in libretto lore: usually adapters distort and abbreviate the original, while M. Tchaikovsky managed to embellish and develop the original – and not just any original, but one by Pushkin! – into a play with seven scenes, full of dramatic and scenic variety. The libretto of *Pikovaya dama* is in its way a *chef d'oeuvre*!'.

The brothers followed up on this success with *Iolanta* (1892), a one-act adaptation of *King René's Daughter*, a popular play by the Danish playwright Henrik Hertz, as translated from the Danish by Fyodor Miller and previously adapted for the Malïy Theatre (Moscow) by Vladimir Rafailovich Zotov. At the time of the composer's death the brothers were casting about for new subjects. At the young Rakhmaninov's request Modest drew up a scenario for an opera on Friedrich de la Motte Fouqué's *Undine*, but first tried to interest his brother, who had written his second (destroyed) opera of 1869 on that subject, in setting it himself. Pyotr declined (Rakhmaninov never set it either) with a request that Modest 'find or invent a subject as *unfantastic* as possible, something along the lines of *Carmen* or *Cavalleria rusticana*'. They considered a subject out of George Eliot's *Scenes from Clerical Life*, for which a fragment of a scenario survives in the composer's hand.

After his brother's death Modest Tchaikovsky found himself much in demand as a librettist for other composers. Almost immediately he received a commission from the Imperial Theatres to turn Pushkin's novella *Dubrovsky* into a libretto for Eduard Nápravník, the chief conductor of the Mariinsky Theatre (1895). This was conceived in every way like *The Queen of Spades*, even down to casting (lead roles for Nikolay Figner and Medea Mei-Figner); it survives as a sumptuous showpiece of the old Russian 'Imperial' style, and was dusted off occasionally for gala presentations on the Soviet stage. In 1899 Tchaikovsky adapted Ivan Lazhechnikov's novel *Ledyanoy dom* ('The Ice Palace', 1835) for setting by the pianist-composer Arseny Nikolayevich Koreshchenko (1870–1921), an Arensky pupil then considered a white hope of Russian music. For Arensky himself Tchaikovsky had as early as 1891 adapted Vasily Zhukovsky's *Nal' i Damayanti*, a poetic translation from the Hindu epic Mahābharata. The opera was not completed until 1903 (first performed 1904). Tchaikovsky's last libretto was *Francesca da Rimini*, a much expanded treatment of an episode from the fifth canto of Dante's *Inferno*, set as a one-act opera by Rakhmaninov between 1900 and 1904 and first performed in 1906.

*

V. Cheshikhin: *Istoriya russkoy operï* (Moscow, 2/1905)

G. Bernandt and I. Yampol'sky: *Kto pisal o muzïke* [Writers on Music], iii (Moscow, 1979)

V. Popov: 'Modest Il'ich Chaykovsky: maloizvestnïye stranitsï biografii' [Little-known Pages from his Biography], *Muzïkal'naya zhizn'* (1981), no.12, p.17

RICHARD TARUSKIN

Tchaikovsky, Pyotr Il'yich [Chaykovsky, Pyotr Il'ich] (*b* nr Votkinsk, north-eastern Russia, 25 April/7 May 1840; *d* St Petersburg, 25 Oct/6 Nov 1893). Russian composer. Of his ten finished operas, nine survive complete and one survives in two versions. In sheer size his operatic legacy was exceeded by those of two of his countrymen, his teacher Anton Rubinstein and his near-contemporary Rimsky-Korsakov; but Tchaikovsky's is a more varied corpus than theirs. While his main historical influence was as a composer of instrumental music, in terms of enduring representation in the world repertory Tchaikovsky is surely the preeminent Russian operatic composer, despite an eclecticism of subject matter and style that has impeded critical acceptance of his work, especially in the West.

1. Life. 2. The early operas. 3. The late 1870s. 4. The later operas. 5. Aesthetic and historical position.

1. Life. The crucial facts of Tchaikovsky's creative biography are two. First, he was the earliest important academically trained Russian composer, a member of the first graduating class (1866) of Anton Rubinstein's St Petersburg Conservatory (following nine years of preparatory education at the Imperial School of Jurisprudence and an initial year studying thoroughbass at the conservatory's parent organization, the Russian Musical Society); immediately on graduation he was hired by Anton's brother Nikolay to teach harmony at the conservatory's new sister school in Moscow, the city that became his lifelong home. Secondly, from 1876 to 1890 he was supported by a patroness, Nadezhda von Meck, the widow of a Riga baron who had made a fortune in railways. This stroke of luck enabled Tchaikovsky to resign his position at the Moscow Conservatory and devote himself to composition. Thus he was during his lifetime Russia's sole professional full-time composer.

It was a status he prized, and one that conditioned his relatively traditional musical attitudes. It set him apart from his contemporaries, the Five or 'Mighty Kuchka', heirs to a long line of Russian artistic autodidactism. Professionalism, not 'nationalism', was the issue that divided them. (As Tchaikovsky put it once with somewhat uncharacteristic bravado, 'I sit down to work each morning at 9 a.m., and the muse has learnt to be on time'.) Where the 'kuchkists' adopted the viewpoint of Schumann's *Davidsbund* – a maverick, outsider's position, hostile to authority on the one hand and the philistine crowd on the other – Tchaikovsky was an establishmentarian, comfortable with official institutions and existing conventions (though he turned the latter with increasing boldness to his idiosyncratic will as his career progressed), and never unwilling to conform to the expectations of the paying public. Of all the major Russian composers, he was the most tolerant, as his perceptive occasional reviews and feuilletons reveal, of the existence of an Italian opera company in St Petersburg, though he recognized the disadvantages Russian musicians suffered and worked towards their amelioration. He was willing to learn from the Italians, though his personal tastes were strongly francophile (as well as reverentially Mozartian).

Where the kuchkists remained essentially insular talents until their belated or posthumous discovery by the French (thanks in large part to Dyagilev's promotion), Tchaikovsky saw himself, and was seen at large, as an artist on the world stage. Adept in foreign languages, he travelled frequently in western Europe, composing many of his works during extended stays abroad; he was honoured with the Cambridge MusD alongside Saint-Saëns, Boito, Bruch and Grieg (1893); and on his American tour of 1891, during which he conducted at the Carnegie Hall inaugural concert, he was repeatedly hailed as, with Brahms and Saint-Saëns, one of the three greatest living composers. This contemporary recognition contrasts poignantly with the catastrophic downturn in his critical reputation in the 20th century, even as his popularity has increased, to the point where it is difficult to write approvingly about his work without assuming a defensive tone.

Where opera was concerned, Tchaikovsky remained faithful to the 'numbers' format and always relied on lavish production values and virtuoso singers, many of whom he counted among his friends. 'In writing an opera', he wrote to Mme von Meck in 1879, 'the author must constantly keep the stage in mind, that is, remember that the theatre requires not just melodies and harmonies but also action; that one must not abuse the patience of the opera audience, which has come not only to listen but also to look; and, finally, that the style of theatrical music must correspond to that of the set-painting, which means it must be simple, clear and colourful'. These strictures, ostensibly directed at his own maiden effort, were obliquely aimed at the over-idealistic kuchkists, whose influence (exercised chiefly through the magnetic Balakirev) he was actively striving to shed. The revisions that turned the early *Kuznets Vakula* ('Vakula the Smith', 1874) into the mature *Cherevichki* (composed 1885) also constituted an implicit anti-kuchkist critique, extremely instructive for the historian.

Yet having given his operatic prescription, Tchaikovsky felt the need to add that 'these conditions paralyse the author's purely musical inspiration to a significant degree, and that is why the symphonic and chamber varieties of music stand much higher than the operatic'. This was an echo of Anton Rubinstein's teaching, and alerts the historian to the significant relationship that obtained between Rubinstein's operatic methods and ideals and those of his former pupil, however critical the pupil may eventually have become of the quality of his erstwhile mentor's work. Tchaikovsky's music was never as slapdash as Rubinstein's, and his stylistic idiosyncrasies marked him as a far more original talent than his former teacher. Yet he depended on Rubinstein for more than a general aesthetic orientation. The extraordinary last scene of *Yevgeny Onegin*, in which great dramatic power is somehow generated from what virtually amounts to a medley of drawing-room songs, is unthinkable without the parallel scene in Rubinstein's *Demon*, first performed only two years before Tchaikovsky embarked upon his masterpiece.

One might say that Tchaikovsky's operas were the operas Rubinstein would have written had he possessed the requisite genius. As works that were at once conventional in form, masterly in technique and exalted in inspiration, they made Tchaikovsky the darling of the Imperial Theatres, where his works, unlike those of the kuchkists, were always welcome. Indeed, they were often officially commissioned during his late period, roughly corresponding to the reign of Tsar Alexander III, when the staunchly monarchist and politically reactionary Tchaikovsky was something very like Russia's official court composer, and his theatrical works, both operas and ballets, defined what was known as the 'Imperial style'. For him the saving grace of opera, despite its necessary stylistic crudity, was something that actually went far beyond mere public appeal: 'Opera, and opera alone', he wrote to his patroness in 1885, 'makes you friends with the people, makes your music familiar to the real public, makes you the property not merely of separate little circles but – with luck – of the whole nation'. Alone among Russian composers, Tchaikovsky had this luck during his lifetime. His burial in St Petersburg (27 October/8 November 1893) was a public event such as no Russian musician, not even Shostakovich, has ever called forth, before or since.

And yet the private man, as we know from his exceptionally prolific correspondence and a flood of memoirs by his friends and relations, often controverted the proud public persona. The morbid self-criticism that resulted in the destruction of his two earliest operas (of which one, *Voyevoda* ('The Provincial Governor'), has been reconstructed from performance parts) is only one manifestation of a deep-rooted sense of personal inadequacy that also showed through in an extreme shyness and an impulse to withdraw from society to which the composer often referred as his 'misanthropy'. The conflicts a closet homosexual in the 19th century inevitably experienced in coming to terms with his plight may have exacerbated both the intense self-absorption that gave rise to his exhibitionistic epistolary habits, and its apparent antipode, his persistent feelings of self-alienation. In any case, they led to the one really dramatic event in his biography, a disastrous impulsive marriage (1877) that gave rise to obsessive thoughts of suicide and even a half-hearted, ineffectual attempt at it. Professionally very much the institutional insider, Tchaikovsky inwardly regarded himself as an outsider, even a social outcast.

Professional success brought with it entrée to aristocratic circles where Tchaikovsky's homosexuality was more readily tolerated; this, plus a loving and protective family (including a worshipping younger brother, Modest, who, sharing his sexual orientation, became his literary collaborator and personal confidant, later his biographer), seems to have helped the composer towards self-acceptance in his later years. At the same time, burgeoning fame made him increasingly the subject of salacious rumour, culminating in a veritable orgy of gossip following his untimely death from cholera during a visit to St Petersburg, where he stayed with Modest. The persistence of these preposterous unsubstantiated stories of pederastic affairs, threatened exposure and suicide at the behest of an honour court is symptomatic of the unfortunate climate surrounding Tchaikovsky criticism to this day, in which the art is to a sometimes childish extent read as clandestine autobiographical effusion, and the composer's artistic success (particularly in his operas) measured in terms of primitive emotional identification. The sheer amount of available data makes Tchaikovsky an obvious candidate for responsible psychobiography (such as Poznansky and Zajaczkowski have promised). Such a study cannot, however, replace critical engagement with the musical texts and a proper respect for their author's powers of sophisticated fabrication. If only as a corrective, some unreconstructed 'immanent criticism' would seem to be appropriate for this particular composer's legacy.

2. THE EARLY OPERAS. From the first Tchaikovsky was a committed musical dramatist, collaborating very actively with his librettists when he was not taking on full verbal responsibilities himself. Having set his heart while still a conservatory student on Alexander Ostrovsky's *The Storm*, the most popular play by Russia's premier playwright, he wrote the overture to a projected operatic treatment in Rubinstein's composition class (1864). When he had moved to Moscow, Tchaikovsky established friendly relations with Ostrovsky, but found to his disappointment that *The Storm* had been promised to Vladimir Kashperov. The playwright suggested *Voyevoda* as substitute, and offered to furnish the libretto himself, free of charge. Their collaboration foundered, in the first place, because Tchaikovsky managed to mislay Ostrovsky's verses to the first act of the opera, and the first scene in the second, so that the playwright had to write them twice. More serious was the fledgling composer's increasing interference in the dramaturgy, which finally cooled Ostrovsky's enthusiasm for the project, leaving Tchaikovsky 'somehow to concoct' the rest on his own. The result, in the composer's own words, was a 'very insipid', static piece of work which he eventually destroyed after cannibalizing its best parts in later works. (His second opera, *Undina* ('Undine'), suffered a similar fate; and since, unlike *Voyevoda*, it never achieved performance in its entirety, there are no performance materials in the archives from which it could be posthumously reconstructed.) Yet the habit of writing his own texts stuck, and he improved considerably as a librettist with practice. For two of his operas, *Oprichnik* ('The Oprichnik') and *Orleanskaya deva* ('The Maid of Orléans'), Tchaikovsky was sole author of the words, modelling his dramatic technique closely, and far from ineptly, on that of Eugène Scribe. He also made major contributions to the verbal texts of *Yevgeny Onegin*, *Mazepa* and *Cherevichki*.

For *Oprichnik* (1870–72), his third opera but the first to achieve repertory status and reach posterity intact, Tchaikovsky chose as literary source a gaudy costume play by Ivan Lazhechnikov about a member of the *oprichnina*, Ivan the Terrible's dreaded mercenary retinue. Though written in 1834, it had until recently been banned from the stage because of its horrifying characterization of the tsar. Yet while nominally a historical drama, Lazhechnikov's *Oprichnik* was really a drama of star-crossed love, a sort of Romeo and Juliet *à la russe*. This must have been one of its chief appeals to Tchaikovsky, who had just composed his famous concert overture after Shakespeare's play. The opera's music is in fact heavily redolent of its instrumental predecessor. Its strong melodic profile, ample scale and opulent vocalism mark a tremendous advance over the composer's previous operatic essays and laid the foundation of what is aptly called his 'Imperial' style – a style geared to the magnificent resources of the Russian Imperial Theatres at a time when opera elsewhere in Europe was being scaled back in keeping with the decline of political absolutism.

At 32, Tchaikovsky was the only composer in Russia then capable of functioning at a joint peak of inspiration and professionalism such as *Oprichnik* reveals. That the achievement made him the object of kuchkist envy is apparent both from Cui's characteristically savage press attack following the 1874 première, in which the professionalism was misrepresented as cynical routine, and from Musorgsky's scathing report, in a letter to Vladimir Stasov, on his meetings with Tchaikovsky in the autumn and early winter of 1872, when the Moscow composer was in the capital to submit the opera to the Imperial Theatres' directorate. The composer of *Boris Godunov*, recently rejected by that very directorate, derided the composer of *The Oprichniks* [*sic*] as a 'worshipper of pure musical beauty' who nevertheless wrote 'with the aim of becoming a favourite with the public and making a name for himself'.

The first of many, Musorgsky rather odiously impugned the Russianness of Tchaikovsky's hothouse muse, insinuating that his choice of a subject out of the national history and his conspicuous consumption of folksongs (mostly transferred from *Voyevoda*), for all that they might have betokened kinship with kuchkist ideals, were merely additional evidence of pandering ('the public demands Russian things of Russian artists'). The animus that informed these remarks found stentorian echo in Stasov's influential published writings, thence entering the critical tradition in the West, where Tchaikovsky was long regarded (particularly by the French) as a less authentic talent than Musorgsky, Borodin or Rimsky-Korsakov because he was less conspicuously Russian than they. The biases and contradictions informing this judgment include the equation of authentic Russian culture with peasant culture (as some Russians agreed), and the assumption that the appropriation of folksongs as thematic material confers authenticity on Russian art music (purely a Western notion, as Musorgsky's rejection of *Oprichnik* already shows). The main prejudice, often unrecognized as such, is the requirement that Russian music be exotic in order to rank as authentic.

Tchaikovsky's single comic opera, *Vakula the Smith* after Gogol's story *Christmas Eve*; composed 1874,

Title-page of the first edition of the vocal score of Tchaikovsky's 'Vakula the Smith' (Moscow: Jürgenson, 1876) revised as 'Cherevichki' (1885)

revised as *Cherevichki*, 1885), was composed to a prescribed libretto for a contest. It is often held up as a paradigm of his 'High Nationalist' phase and especially valued for its uncorrupted folkish pedigree. This exaggerated and one-sided view of the opera actually hides its chief distinctions. While it sports an attractive 'peasant' idiom and quotes Ukrainian or Russian folktunes in the opening number and in one of the dances in Act 3 (as well as in the insert aria composed for the title character, on revision), these features were mandated by the subject matter – vernacular or dialect idioms being the traditional stuff of comic opera in every country – and do not constitute evidence for conventional exotic nationalism. Nor do they set any record within Tchaikovsky's output. More interesting by far is precisely what Western writers tend to write off or deplore: the neo-classical St Petersburg music in Act 3, to which the composer also made a significant addition when revising the opera. It was the first of many such '18th-century' confections, which found their culmination in *The Sleeping Beauty* ballet and *Pikovaya dama* ('The Queen of Spades'), and which represent one of the truly idiosyncratic components of Tchaikovsky's musical voice.

Meanwhile, if there is an element of genuine 'kuchkism' in *Vakula the Smith*, it consists in the declam- atory style, the overspiced harmonies and the detail-heavy orchestral writing – that is, the very aspects of the work the composer sought to remove or ameliorate on revision. That these traits may be fairly labelled 'kuchkist' we learn from two of the opera's earliest judges. Rimsky-Korsakov, writing to Tchaikovsky at the time of the original contest, had nothing to say about 'high nationalism', but did exclaim, 'What a superb, and above all, what an original harmonist you are!'. And Herman Laroche, reviewing the opera in its first incarnation on stage, worried about his friend's 'regrettable wish to create at least in the musical forms something in the order of that pernicious substance known as dramatic truth in tones', which he identified explicitly with 'the so-called Young Russian School', meaning the Balakirev circle.

Yet when a true kuchkist got hold of Gogol's *Christmas Eve*, he made of it something altogether unlike Tchaikovsky's setting. Rimsky-Korsakov's eponymous opera, on which he embarked almost immediately on hearing the news of Tchaikovsky's death, places the emphasis where Gogol had placed it – on farce and fantasy (plus a characteristically Rimskian dose of folk ritualism) – rather than on the love intrigue. Indeed, its crowning moments, the fantastic ballets representing Vakula's aerial trip on devil-back, have no counterpart in *Vakula the Smith* or *Cherevichki*, in which the magic flight is not composed at all except for some paltry curtain music preceding and following the St Petersburg scenes.

In such later operas as *The Maid of Orléans* or *The Queen of Spades*, Tchaikovsky always presented the supernatural, whether angelic or horrific, in the context of abnormal psychology. Psychology, the exploration of the mental and emotional worlds of individual characters, was the task that increasingly interested him as a composer and the one for which he revealed a supreme aptitude. 'It seems to me', he wrote in 1891 to Vladimir Pogozhev, a theatre official, 'that I am truly gifted with the ability *truthfully, sincerely and simply* to express the feelings, moods and images suggested by a text. In this sense I am a *realist* and fundamentally a Russian' (the italics are original).

3. The late 1870s. The accuracy of this self-assessment came out for the first time in *Yevgeny Onegin* (completed 1878), the unclassifiable and in some ways virtually anti-operatic 'lyric scenes' Tchaikovsky composed on the basis of Pushkin's beloved novel in verse. To adapt a novel with a nearly contemporary setting to the musical stage already betokened a realist bent. Neither Dargomïzhsky nor Musorgsky, to cite the names more typically associated with Russian operatic realism, ever attempted any such thing. Their declamatory and 'formless' realism was one of manner rather than subject matter, and to Tchaikovsky it seemed a literalistic and anti-musical blunder: 'If there is anything more hateful and *false*', he wrote of *The Stone Guest* in his diary, 'than this unsuccessful attempt to introduce *truth* into a branch of art where everything is based on *pseudo* and where *truth* in the usual sense of the word is not demanded at all – I do not know what it is!'. Realism as he practised it had to do with a more specifically musical semiotic – the adaptation of genres and stylistic conventions to characterizational purposes – and in *Yevgeny Onegin*, based on a novel that with a famous irony explores the mutual influence of mores and literary conventions, he found the perfect subject.

Tchaikovsky clothed this tale of life among the rural landowners and petty bourgeoisie of early 19th-century Russia in the ambient sounds that accompanied their existence. (Stravinsky recognized this better than anyone when he came to write *Mavra*; Asaf'yev echoed this recognition on a scholarly level with his pioneering book on the opera's musical idiom and its sources.) The background music includes ballroom dance and domestic singing as well as the songs of serfs. More obviously than in any other work, but characteristically, Tchaikovsky relegated the folkloristic idiom in *Yevgeny Onegin* to the decorative level (compare, in the instrumental realm, the decorative folkish finales to his concertos). In the first act Mme Larina's serfs sing and dance to entertain her; they exist in the opera not as real people but literally as properties. (This servile portrayal of the peasants – wholly Tchaikovsky's idea, probably inspired by an almost exact parallel in the first act of Dargomïzhsky's *Rusalka* – offended early Soviet taste and the number was traditionally excluded from Soviet productions until after World War II.) In Act 2, even more tellingly, a chorus of berry-picking peasant girls drawn directly from Pushkin serves as decorative frame for one of the opera's turning-points: the scene in which Onegin rejects Tatyana.

Yet the music the 'real people' sing in this opera is just as authentically Russian as that sung by the decorative peasant choristers: it is modelled on the 'intonations' of the early 19th-century domestic romance. (Asaf'yev's useful coinage 'intonation' connotes something akin to the linguists' morpheme, a minimal semantic unit or semiotic marker.) Pre-eminent among these is the interval of the 6th (particularly between the fifth and third degrees). To express the passions and spontaneous reactions of the characters by means of stereotyped melodic and harmonic figures, however freshly and virtuosically recombined, makes exactly the same point Pushkin makes in his novel: feelings are never spontaneous but always mediated by the conventions and constraints, as often learnt from literature as from 'life', to which we have adapted. Therein lie both the tragedy (the constraints) and the salvation (the adaptation) of human society. These themes are all exquisitely foreshadowed in the eccentric 'quartet' for women's voices at the very start of the opera, in which a very 'sixthy' romance, sung offstage by Tatyana and Olga, accompanies a speech-song conversation between Mme Larina and Filip'yevna that begins with an invocation to the books in Larina's life ('O Grandison! O Richardson!') and ends with a modest paean to habit ('given to us from above as substitute for happiness'). Just as Tchaikovsky put it in his letter to Pogozhev, the realism and the Russianness of *Yevgeny Onegin* are equally profound and profoundly interrelated. And they are equally likely to be missed by those who equate realism with 'formlessness' and can discern national character only in folklore. Nor is it easy to fathom how a composer capable of feats of inspired calculation and shapely execution such as one finds on every page of this score can go on being described as an hysteric who achieves artistic success in direct proportion to the 'passionate sympathy' he manages to muster for his characters.

Which is not to say that the composer's biography is never critically relevant. Consider *The Maid of Orléans* (completed 1879), freely based on Schiller's Joan of Arc play: an all-out bid for international recognition, in which Tchaikovsky applied the heroic technique of *Oprichnik* to a subject of general European interest. It was an obvious emulation of Rubinstein, who had just reached the zenith of his career with *Die Maccabäer*, the single opera by a Russian composer to achieve repertory status during the 19th century both at home and abroad. In like fashion, Tchaikovsky's new work was a programmatically anti-Wagnerian reversion to the old-fashioned Parisian (Scribian) model, with echoes of outstanding musical predecessors not only by Rubinstein but by Meyerbeer (*Les Huguenots*) and Verdi (*Don Carlos*). Everything was geared to grandiose stage pictures projected in musical terms that were at once vast and elementary, and in which entertainment values were given strong emphasis. 'Symphony and opera are in all respects polar opposites', Tchaikovsky wrote to Mme von Meck while at work on *The Maid of Orléans*, attributing all the failings in his prior work for the stage to his neglect of this categorical distinction. While the instrumental genre stood unequivocally higher from the purely aesthetic point of view, opera had one powerful compensating advantage: 'An opera may be given 40 times in one season, a symphony perhaps once in ten years'.

Despite an overwhelming first-night success that established Tchaikovsky's reputation at home as premier operatic composer of his generation, *The Maid of Orléans* failed to hold the stage. In part this was sheer bad luck; Tsar Alexander II was assassinated two weeks after the première and the season was cancelled. But there is indeed something conceptually awry with the opera that impeded revival. The standard justification of its failure has been the predictable cavil that the composer could not 'identify' with his heroine. The truth is probably more nearly that he identified all too well with certain aspects of her story, as Cui, reviewing the opera in characteristically reptilian fashion, came close to divining.

Cui commented cynically that the libretto, an irremediably incoherent farrago of seemingly random bits of Schiller and historical fact, was nevertheless perfectly tailored to the composer's needs. 'Mr Tchaikovsky's talent is foreign to strength, drama, humour, merriment; his talent is mild, feminine and lyrical, with a constant tinge of care and melancholy.' These belittling remarks show to what extent reception of Tchaikovsky's music was coloured, even midway through his career, by consciousness of his sexual orientation, at the time of *The Maid of Orléans* particularly acute in the aftermath of the composer's marriage and the rumours it had set in motion. (From then on it was always as an 'unmanly' composer that Tchaikovsky was most liable to be derided by critics.)

And yet closer, more sympathetic study than Cui's confirms the impression that the opera's damaging peculiarities may perhaps be most profitably viewed through a psychosexual prism. The fairly inscrutable inconsistencies in the treatment of the title character led a Tchaikovsky biographer to charge him with 'not merely weakening the character of Joan, but debasing it' (Brown 1978, iii). In fact it was an exorcism. Unlike Schiller's Joan, Tchaikovsky's is an easy prey to her emotions. Her infatuation with the Burgundian knight Lionel, a passing episode in Schiller, becomes with Tchaikovsky the central intrigue, fatally compromising her and disqualifying her from her mission in the eyes of heaven. She is persecuted unremittingly by her father, the man who knows her best. Yet, having been repudiated in heaven and on earth, she is nevertheless finally redeemed, but only after capture and condemnation.

Horror of female sexuality as a disruptive and destructive force – one recently and balefully unleashed in the composer's own life – and belief in the necessity for its containment, provide a vantage point from which these contradictions and inconsistencies form a pattern. There have been many calls for an approach to Tchaikovsky that would admit the fact of his homosexuality as a potential critical tool. Such a critique might well begin with *The Maid of Orléans*. (For a more conventional Freudian approach to issues tangential to the opera, see Zajaczkowski 1990.)

4. THE LATER OPERAS. Tchaikovsky's next opera, *Mazepa* (completed 1883), though it drew on the national history as mediated by Pushkin's patriotic romantic epic *Poltava* (1828) and thus gave the composer a pretext for trapping out the drama with a bit of *style russe*, was actually another attempt to transcend the limits of the national with a subject of general European appeal. Ivan Mazeppa (*c*1640–1709), leader of the Ukrainian cossacks, sought independence from Russia through an alliance with Charles XII of Sweden against Peter the Great. The Russian victory at the Battle of Poltava in 1709 ruined Mazeppa and put an end to 'Little Russian' separatism until the 20th century. As the champion of a subject people he became a Romantic legend, attracting the attention of Western poets (Byron, Hugo), painters (Delacroix) and musicians (Liszt). Treatment of Mazeppa by eastern European artists became a political code: he was cast as hero or villain depending upon attitudes towards the Russian Empire. Pushkin's dramatic poem, a virtual panegyric to Peter the Great, occupied a position on the far right of this spectrum. Tchaikovsky's opera, too, was a celebration of Russian hegemony, for which purpose he appropriated the famous 'Slava', the folktune already immortalized (though in 1883 this was far from clear) by Musorgsky in the scene of Boris Godunov's coronation, to represent the victorious Russians in the big symphonic battle-piece preceding the third act.

Yet the relatively intimate scale and formal freedom of this opera – at least compared with its grandiose predecessor – suggest a reversion to the 'realist' dramaturgical ideal of *Yevgeny Onegin* (an ideal Tchaikovsky is often assumed to have opposed). Models for such a stance might have been found in the middle-period Verdi – and probably were, the masterly blend of *parlante* and full-blown ritornello-like lyric statement in the mother-daughter confrontation in Act 2 scene ii skilfully emulating the Italian master's 'dialectical' manner. Yet it is hard to shake off the thought that Tchaikovsky was more impressed by the work of Serov, and even Musorgsky, than he ever admitted. The drunken cossack whose song and dance creates a disturbance during the execution scene in Act 3 is surely a chip off the Shrovetide revellers in Serov's *Vrazh'ya sila* (and was censured by reviewers, including Cui, in precisely the same terms). And there is much besides the appropriation of the 'Slava' motif that recalls *Boris*, from the whiffs of Pimen-like service music in the role of Kochubey to the concluding 'idiot' lullaby, for the sake of which the composer overrode Victor Burenin's libretto. Tchaikovsky's incorporation of five Russian and Ukrainian folksongs as genre music was merely pro forma; far more idiosyncratic is the subtle Polish – or rather, polonaise-like – colouration of Act 1.

Most distinctive in *Mazepa*, despite all romance and local colour, is its heavy pall of morbidity. Nápravník, conductor of the St Petersburg première and an inveterate complainer, nevertheless caught the opera's special quality when he bemoaned its way of 'heaping scene upon scene, each more horrible than the last: enmity, betrayal, torture, execution, murder and madness – there is nowhere for the listener to relax'. Nápravník's worries on behalf of the audience were characteristic. His misgivings on the composer's account – 'Where will he find such a quantity of necessary colours?' – seem peculiarly misplaced and patronizing. But by then even Nápravník was feeling envious; it is precisely from *Mazepa*, fought over and finally presented in tandem by both leading Russian opera houses, that Tchaikovsky's undisputed ascendancy among Russian composers may be said to date.

Charodeyka (the title translates as 'The Enchantress', not 'The Sorceress', 1887) is another lurid melodrama, mounted against an even more gratuitous period setting. A monumentally inflated counterpart to *Mazepa*, it is at once Tchaikovsky's longest opera and possibly his least significant. It is often wondered what could have attracted Russia's greatest living composer to Ippolit Shpazhinsky's *faux-antique* farrago of sexual obsession and mayhem. Its setting gave him another magnificent opportunity for composing in national costume, but the 'Russian' music in *The Enchantress* is largely concentrated in the first act, a veritable public-house pageant. That music, although singled out by Western tourist-critics for comparison with the work of the Mighty Kuchka, or hailed as an otherwise incomprehensible opera's saving grace, is of a distinctly manufactured quality that only too faithfully reflects the ersatz character of the literary source. One melody, the main theme of the entr'acte before Act 4, is a firmly documented folktune (at first on Modest Tchaikovsky's testimony, later corroborated in the field); the main theme of the overture, repeated later in Act 1 as the title character's main set piece, has been plausibly related to another. From the little turn figure these two melodies have in common Tchaikovsky cloned a multitude of bromidic fakesongs at all structural levels from primary theme to fugitive recitative punctuation.

The best of *The Enchantress* is found, as so often with Tchaikovsky, in its erotic dimension: not only in the numerous duets and ariosos of longing (e.g. the title character's dramaturgically static but captivating 'Gde zhe tï, moy zhelannïy?' ('Where art thou, desired one?') in Act 4, the opera's most famous number) but also in the unaccompanied 'decimet' with chorus, an astonishing tour de force that signals the dramatic turning-point (the title character's sexual domination of the vicegerent) at the beginning of the Act 1 finale. This triumph of artful strangeness or strange artfulness – 'an ensemble', crowed the ardent anti-realist Laroche, 'with three voices worth more "untruth" than the unholy Meyerbeer achieved in the *Huguenots* septet' – gives a hint of the direction Tchaikovsky's muse would take him in his next, arguably his greatest, opera.

The Queen of Spades (1890), a masterpiece not of realism but of surrealism, marks the beginning of a new stage in Tchaikovsky's evolution as musical dramatist, one that, had he lived out a normal span of years, would surely have marked him as one of the guiding geniuses of the Russian 'Silver Age'. Often classified with the bombastic works preceding it because of its melodramatic alterations to the plot of Pushkin's admired novella and its reliance on virtuoso singing (for which Tchaikovsky had found a pair of remarkable protagonists in the husband-and-wife team of Nikolay Figner and Medea Mei-Figner), it has suffered many indignities at the hands of critics while gaining inexorably on *Yevgeny Onegin* in terms of audience appeal.

Audiences in this case have been right. The music in *The Queen of Spades* performs a miracle similar to the one accomplished in Tchaikovsky's other oft-maligned Pushkin opera: it keeps up a running commentary on social milieux and relations and the emotional ills they beget. But where the music to *Onegin*, like the celebrated narrative voice in its literary source, recreated 'reality' with magnificent precision, the music to *The Queen of Spades* floods the action in an atmosphere of hallucination, corresponding in tone not to the source of its plot but to another work of Pushkin's, the narrative poem *Mednïy vsadnik* ('The Bronze Horseman'), which famously portrays the Russian capital as a dream city, a will-o'-the-wisp on the northern bogs. That poem is often said to be the precocious progenitor of the Russian symbolist movement. The generalization may be extended to encompass music as well as literature if Tchaikovsky's mastery of the grotesque, and its chilling correlation with aberrant psychology, is given due recognition.

The main hallucinogen in *The Queen of Spades* is not harmony (though there are chromatic leitmotif transformations in plenty, and the whole-tone scale makes its customary spectral appearance à la Glinka) but orchestration. Tchaikovsky reveals an unparalleled genius for timbral grotesquerie, which reaches its height in the overtly hallucinatory scene of ghostly visitation, when the dead Countess reveals to Hermann, the deranged officer-protagonist, the secret of the three cards for the sake of which he had killed her one scene earlier. The prefatory entr'acte is a weirdly feverish montage of church music (the Countess's burial service) and barracks music. It juxtaposes divided violas and cellos in the pit, *pianissimo*, against snare drum and trumpet offstage, *fortissimo*, producing a sound balanced as to volume but, like Hermann's mind, grossly unbalanced in perspective. (Later the burial music is resumed by an offstage chorus singing in the wind's voice, an indistinct, distant *fortissimo*.) Even the less obviously illustrative music constantly features outré combinations of timbre seemingly at odds with expression – for example, english horn calling lyrically to bass clarinet over an accompaniment of staccato bassoons, as Hermann recalls his crimes with remorse.

Rimsky-Korsakov, nominally the past master of colouristic orchestration, could not understand Tchaikovsky's psychological grotesques: to him the music of his rival's late period was just 'written topsy-turvy: music suitable for strings had been allotted to wind instruments and vice versa, and hence it occasionally sounds downright fantastic but at altogether unsuitable moments'. This remark tellingly parallels the way in which Tolstoy's novels were misunderstood by contemporaries. Both Tchaikovsky and Tolstoy habitually violate the normal obligations of genre, but with such art-concealing art that their supreme sophistication is often misread as naivety.

The 'Mozart' idiom of the neo-classical *intermède* in *The Queen of Spades* is an excellent case in point. It is a critical commonplace to note how ineptly it imitates the Viennese master: the orchestra is all wrong, telltale harmonic anachronisms peep through everywhere, the excessively 'sensitive' dynamics and articulations are those of the late 19th century. The composer could hardly have been less aware of these 'solecisms' than his critics (just as he knew as well as they that a sarabande has three, not four, beats to a bar); they are precisely the means through which he conjures up the necessary aura of unreality, as if to say (with Hermann), 'What is our life? A game! Good and evil – only dreams!'.

Tchaikovsky's last opera, the one-act *Iolanta* (composed 1891), is another dream vision, but a benign one. Slight as it is, the work has borne a great deal of heavy critical baggage, a tale of a hidden virgin from whom the world is hidden – and how she is discovered, 'brought out' and made whole – being susceptible to any number of obvious allegorical readings from folk-religious (compare the dramatic shape and more overtly symbolic purport of Rimsky-Korsakov's *Kashchey the Deathless*) to Freudian. A clue to Tchaikovsky's own reading of the play may perhaps be gleaned by taking note of what is out of the ordinary in his musical treatment of it. The opening numbers, showing the blind Iolanta and her companions before the plot begins to thicken with the presence of men, are a consummate pre-Raphaelite pastel. Within a subdued scheme of timbres Tchaikovsky discovered myriad exquisite shades, foreshadowing devices commonly associated with 'impressionism' – divided and solo strings, measured tremolos, woodwind arabesques. At the moment of Iolanta's cure in the finale, the first rays of light reaching her newly sensitive eyes are depicted with chords of artificial string harmonics, and her momentary fright is underscored by fugitive whole-tone scales. The latter, while a Russian cliché since Glinka's time for the depiction of supernatural evil, take on a fresh aspect in the present context of nature-inspired wonder. The abundant use in these scenes of the solo violin in a concertante capacity, directly taken over from the ballet where it was *de rigueur*, adumbrates the scoring of Skryabin's more openly erotic symphonies.

5. Aesthetic and historical position. The voluptuous timbral virtuosity of his late period shows Tchaikovsky, in the years immediately preceding his untimely death, approaching the aestheticist methods and goals that would shortly crystallize around the movement known as 'The World of Art' (*Mir iskusstva*), led by Alexandre Benois and Sergey Dyagilev. It was a retrospective and nostalgic aesthetic, betokening a resurgence of aristocratic values against the challenge of a newly empowered, nationalistic bourgeoisie. These were values with which the composer increasingly identified as he sought refuge in aristocratic friendships from the oppressive Victorian judgment of his social peers.

Tchaikovsky witnessed only the earliest stirrings of Russian aestheticism. Its later phases were played out against the background of Silver Age decadence and, after the Revolution, in the West. Still, it is important to bear in mind his connections to the future of Russian music as well as to its past. It was as an avatar of the past that the composer was seized upon after World War I and claimed as model by the émigré artists surrounding Dyagilev, who were attempting a sort of vicarious Imperial restoration. It is ironic that Stravinsky, whose coming of age through the 'World of Art' and its latterday theatrical ventures in the West made him a distant but lineal descendant of Tchaikovsky, should have claimed him, however clamorously, as a mere collateral forebear by way of tendentious pastiches like *Mavra* and *The Fairy's Kiss*. In the Soviet Union Tchaikovsky's politically motivated centennial canonization in 1940 (following Pushkin's in 1937) was even more wilful and oblique – and ironic, given the composer's actual political orientation and the institutions he had served in life.

He remains a controversial, poorly understood figure in the West: explicitly designated the archetypal musician of the 19th century (see Fédorov 1970), he has been, Stravinsky's advocacy notwithstanding, perhaps the chief target of conventional modernist abuse. One can still find him written off as a purveyor of kitsch, but his friends have done his reputation hardly less harm than his foes. Attempts to assimilate him to conventional notions of 'Russian music' have diminished him, as attempts to assimilate his works to the story of his life and loves have diminished them. Lacking has been due appreciation of his technical virtuosity, his intellectual sophistication, above all his brilliant (and very 'modern') exploitation of style and genre as semiosis. A new-found willingness to confront the music on its own terms (or at least on new terms) prompts hope that his just measure may yet be taken.

See also Cherevichki; Enchantress, the; Iolanta; Maid of Orléans, the; Mazepa; Oprichnik; Queen of spades, the; Undina; Vakula the smith; Voyevoda; and Yevgeny Onegin.

Edition: *P. I. Chaykovsky: Polnoye sobraniye sochineniy* [Complete Collected Works] (Moscow and Leningrad, 1940–71) [T]
printed works published in Moscow unless otherwise stated

op.	*title*	*genre, acts*	*libretto*	*first performance*	*sources, remarks*	*T*
3	Voyevoda [The Provincial Governor]	3	A. N. Ostrovsky and P. I. Tchaikovsky, after Ostrovsky: *Son na Volge* [A Volga Dream]	Moscow, Bol'shoy, 30 Jan/11 Feb 1869, cond. E. Merten	comp. 8/20 March 1867–sum. 1868; destroyed by Tchaikovsky, reconstructed by S. Popov (1927), P. Lamm and others (1953)	i, i suppl.
	Undina [Undine]	3	V. Sollogub, after F. H. C. de la Motte Fouqué	Moscow, 16/28 March 1870, concert perf., excerpts only	comp. Jan–July 1869, destroyed by Tchaikovsky, 1873, frags. only (Moscow and Leningrad, 1950)	ii (frags.)
	Mandragora		S. Rachinsky	Moscow, 18/30 Dec 1870	comp. 27 Dec/8 Jan 1870, orchd by 13/25 Jan 1870, Chorus of Flowers and Insects only, mixed and children's vv, pf (Moscow and Leningrad, 1950)	ii
	Oprichnik [The Oprichnik]	4	Tchaikovsky, after I. Lazhechnikov: *Oprichniki*	St Petersburg, Mariinsky, 12/24 April 1874, cond. E. Nápravník	comp. Feb 1870–April 1872, vs (St Petersburg, 1874), full score (St Petersburg, 1896); entr'acte to Act 2 by V. S. Shilovsky	iii, xxxiv
14	Kuznets Vakula [Vakula the Smith]	3	Ya. Polonsky, after N. V. Gogol: *Noch' pered rozhdestvom* [Christmas Eve]	St Petersburg, Mariinsky, 24 Nov/6 Dec 1876, cond. Nápravník	comp. June–21 Aug/2 Sept 1874, vs (1876), rev. as Cherevichki	
24	Yevgeny Onegin [Eugene Onegin]	lyric scenes, 3	K. S. Shilovsky and Tchaikovsky, after A. S. Pushkin	student perf., Moscow, Maliy, 17/29 March 1879, cond. N. Rubinstein; professional première, Moscow, Bol'shoy, 11/23 Jan 1881, cond. E. Bevignani	comp. May 1877–20 Jan/1 Feb 1878, vs (1878), full score (1880)	iv, xxxvi
	with rev. Act 3			St Petersburg, Mariinsky, 19 Sept/1 Oct 1885, cond. Nápravník		
	Orleanskaya deva [The Maid of Orléans]	4	Tchaikovsky, after V. A. Zhukovsky's trans. of F. von Schiller: *Die Jungfrau von Orleans*, J. Barbier: *Jeanne d'Arc* and A. Mermet	St Petersburg, Mariinsky, 13/25 Feb 1881, cond. Nápravník	comp. late Nov 1878–late Aug 1879; rev. 1882; vs (1878), full score (1902)	v, xxxvii
	Mazepa [Mazeppa]	3	V. Burenin, rev. Tchaikovsky, after Pushkin: *Poltava*	Moscow, Bol'shoy, 3/15 Feb 1884, cond. I. Al'tani	comp. sum. 1881–28 April/10 May 1883, vs (1883), full score (1899); Act 2 aria to words by V. Kandaurov	vi, xxxviii
	Cherevichki	comic-fantastic op, 4	Polonsky (with Tchaikovsky and N. Chayev), after Gogol: *Noch' pered rozhdestvom*	Moscow, Bol'shoy, 19/31 Jan 1887, cond. Tchaikovsky	comp. Feb–22 March/3 April 1885; rev. of Kuznets Vakula (comp. 1874), vs (1885)	vii, xxxix
	Charodeyka [The Enchantress]	4	I. V. Shpazhinsky	St Petersburg, Mariinsky, 20 Oct/1 Nov 1887, cond. Tchaikovsky	comp. Sept. 1885–6/18 May 1887, vs (1887), full score (1901)	viii, xl
68	Pikovaya dama [The Queen of Spades]	3	M. I. Tchaikovsky and P. I. Tchaikovsky, after Pushkin	St Petersburg, Mariinsky, 7/19 Dec 1890, cond. Nápravník	comp. 18/30 Jan–8/20 June 1890, vs (1890), full score (1891)	ix, xli

op.	title	genre, acts	libretto	first performance	sources, remarks	T
69	Iolanta [Iolanthe]	lyric op, 1	M. I. Tchaikovsky, after V. R. Zotov's adaptation of H. Hertz: *Kong Renés Datter* ('King René's Daughter'), trans. F. Miller	St Petersburg, Mariinsky, 6/18 Dec 1892, cond. Nápravník	comp. 28 June/10 July–8/20 Nov 1891; commissioned as companion piece to *The Nutcracker* ballet, vs (1892), full score (1892)	x, xlii
	MUSIC FOR OTHER STAGE WORKS					
	Le domino noir [Auber]	recitatives and choruses		Moscow, 1868	comp. Oct 1868, lost	
	Le barbier de Séville	couplets 'Vous l'ordonnez' for Almaviva, 1v, 2 vn (1906)	P.-A. Beaumarchais, trans. M. Sadovsky	Moscow, Conservatory, 12/24 April 1872	comp. by 12/24 Feb 1872	xiv
	Le nozze di Figaro [Mozart]	recitatives		Moscow, Conservatory, 5/17 May 1876	comp. 1875, vs (1884)	

H. A. Laroche [G. Larosh]: *Chaykovsky kak dramaticheskiy kompozitor* [Tchaikovsky as a Dramatic Composer] (St Petersburg, 1895)

N. D. Kashkin: *Vospominaniya o P. I. Chaykovskom* [Reminiscences of Tchaikovsky] (Moscow, 1896, 2/1954)

M. I. Chaykovsky: *Zhizn' P. I. Chaykovskogo* (Moscow, 1900–02; Eng. trans., 1906, as *Life and Letters of Tchaikovsky*)

H. A. Laroche [G. Larosh]: *Sobraniye muzïkal'no-kriticheskikh statey*, ii: *O P. I. Chaykovskom* [Collected Critical Articles on Music] (Moscow, 1922–4)

P. I. Chaykovsky: *Dnevniki 1873–1891* [Diaries], ed. I. Chaykovsky (Moscow and Petrograd, 1923; Eng. trans., 1945, as *The Diaries of Tchaikovsky*)

V. M. Bogdanov-Berezovsky: *Opernoye i baletnoye tvorchestvo Chaykovskogo* [Tchaikovsky's Operas and Ballets] (Leningrad and Moscow, 1940)

A. I. Shaverdyan, ed.: *Chaykovsky na muzïkal'noy stsene: pervïye postanovki v godï ego zhizni* [Tchaikovsky on the Musical Stage: Premier Productions During his Lifetime] (Moscow and Leningrad, 1940)

V. V. Yakovlev, ed.: *Dni i godï P. I. Chaykovskogo: letopis' zhizni i tvorchestva* [Tchaikovsky's Days and Years: a Chronicle of his Life and Work] (Moscow, 1940)

G. Abraham: 'Operas and Incidental Music', *Tchaikovsky: a Symposium* (London, 1945), 124–83; repr. in *Slavonic and Romantic Music: Essays and Studies* (London, 1968), 116–77

B. Yarustovsky: *Opernaya dramaturgiya Chaykovskogo* [Chaykovsky's Operatic Dramaturgy] (Moscow and Leningrad, 1947)

——: 'Operas', in D. Shostakovich and others: *Russian Symphony: Thoughts about Tchaikovsky* (New York, 1947), 40–85

I. Kunin, ed.: *P. I. Chaykovsky ob opere* [Tchaikovsky on Opera] (Moscow and Leningrad, 1952)

V. V. Protopopov and N. V. Tumanina: *Opernoye tvorchestvo Chaykovskogo* [Tchaikovsky's Operas] (Moscow, 1957)

G. S. Dombayev: *Tvorchestvo P. I. Chaykovskogo v materialakh i dokumentakh* [The Art of Tchaikovsky: Materials and Documents] (Moscow, 1958)

P. I. Chaykovsky: *Literaturnïye proizvedeniya i perepiska* [Literary Works and Correspondence], v–xvii (Moscow, 1959–81)

E. E. Bortnikova and others, eds.: *Vospominaniya o P. I. Chaykovskom* [Reminiscences about Tchaikovsky] (Moscow, 1962, 4/1980)

V. Fédorov: 'Čajkovskij, musicien type du XIXe siècle?', *AcM*, xlii (1970), 59–70 [see also *AcM*, xliii (1971), 205–36]

V. Tsukkerman: *Vïrazitel'nïye sredstva liriki Chaykovskogo* [The Expressive Methods in Tchaikovsky's Work] (Moscow, 1971)

A. A. Orlova: *P. I. Chaykovsky o muzïke, o zhizni, o sebe* [Tchaikovsky on his Music, his Life and Himself] (Leningrad, 1976; Eng. trans., enlarged, 1990, as *Tchaikovsky: a Self-Portrait*) [selections from letters, diaries, feuilletons]

D. Brown: *Tchaikovsky: a Biographical and Critical Study* (London, 1978–91)

B. Anshakov: *P. I. Chaykovsky i russkaya literatura* (Izhevsk, 1980)

R. J. Wiley: *Chaykovsky's Ballets* (Oxford, 1985)

P. I. Chaykovsky: *Muzïkal'no-kriticheskiye stat'i* (Leningrad, 4/1986) [critical articles]

L. Krasinskaya: *Opernaya melodika P. I. Chaykovskogo: k voprosu o vzaimodeystvii melodii i rechevoy intonatsii* [Tchaikovsky's Operatic Melodies: on the Question of the Interaction of Melody and Vocal Intonation] (Leningrad, 1986)

H. Zajaczkowski: *Tchaikovsky's Musical Style* (Ann Arbor, 1987)

A. Poznansky: *Tchaikovsky: the Quest for the Inner Man* (New York, 1991)

Voyevoda

H. Laroche [G. Larosh]: 'Novaya russkaya opera "Voyevoda" g. Chaykovskogo' [The New Russian Opera *Voyevoda* by Tchaikovsky], *Sovremennaya letopis'* (9 Feb 1869); repr. in *Sobraniye muzïkal'no-kriticheskikh statey* [Collected Critical Articles on Music], ed. N. D. Kashkin and V. Yakovlev, ii/1 (Moscow, 1922–4), 102–5

S. Popov: 'A. N. Ostrovsky i P. I. Chaykovsky', *A. N. Ostrovsky i russkiye kompozitorï* [Ostrovsky and Russian Composers], ed. E. Kolosova and V. Filippov (Moscow, 1937), 141–71

G. Abraham: 'Tchaikovsky's First Opera', *Festschrift Karl Gustav Fellerer* (Regensburg, 1962), 12–22

A. Gozenpud: *Russkiy opernïy teatr XIX veka* [Russian Operatic Theatre in the 19th Century], iii (Leningrad, 1971), 242–7

Oprichnik

H. Laroche [G. Larosh]: '"Oprichnik"', *Muzïkal'nïy listok*, nos.21–2 (1873–4); 'Muzïkal'naya khronika: "Oprichnik", opera v chetïryokh deystviyakh: syuzhet zaimstvovan iz tragedii Lazhechnikova, muzïka P. I. Chaykovskogo' [Music Chronicle: *Oprichnik*, an Opera in 4 Acts: Subject borrowed from Lazhechnikov's Tragedy, Music by Tchaikovsky], *Golos* (17 April 1874); both repr. in *Sobraniye muzïkal'no-kriticheskikh statey* [Collected Critical Articles on Music], ed. N. D. Kashkin and V. Yakovlev, ii/1 (Moscow, 1922–4), 107–23

C. Cui: 'Muzïkal'nïye zametki: "Oprichnik", opera g. Chaykovskogo', *Sankt-peterburgskiye vedomosti* (23 April 1874)

A. Gozenpud: *Russkiy opernïy teatr XIX veka* [Russian Operatic Theatre of the 19th Century], iii (Leningrad, 1973), chap. 6

R. Taruskin: 'The Present in the Past: Russian Opera and Russian Historiography, ca.1870', *Russian and Soviet Music: Essays for Boris Schwarz* (Ann Arbor, 1984), 74–143

Vakula the Smith/Cherevichki

C. Cui: 'Muzïkal'nïye zametki: "Kuznets Vakula", opera g. Chaykovskogo' [Musical Notes: *Vakula the Smith*, an Opera by Tchaikovsky], *Sankt-petersburgskiye vedomosti* (30 Nov 1876)

H. Laroche [G. Larosh]: 'Muzïkal'nïye ocherki: opera "Vakula-Kuznets" (slova Ya. P. Polonskogo, muzïka P. I. Chaykovskogo) na Mariinskoy stsene' [Essays on Music: the Opera *Vakula the Smith* (Words by Polonsky, Music by Tchaikovsky on the Mariinsky Stage], *Golos* (2 Dec 1876); repr. in *Sobraniye muzïkal'no-kriticheskikh statey* [Collected Critical Articles on Music], ed. N. D. Kashkin and V. Yakovlev, ii/1 (Moscow, 1922–4), 125–34

——: 'Muzïkal'naya khronika' [Music Chronicle], *Russkiy vestnik* (1887), no.10; repr. in *Sobraniye muzïkal'no-kriticheskikh statey* [Collected Critical Articles on Music], ed. N. D. Kashkin and V. Yakovlev, ii/1 (Moscow, 1922–4), 146–52 [on *Cherevichki*]
V. Vanslov: *Cherevichki P. Chaykovskogo* (Moscow and Leningrad, 1949)
V. Ferman: '*Cherevichki* (*Kuznets Vakula*) Chaykovskogo i *Noch' pered rozhdestvom* Rimskogo-Korsakova (opït sravneniya opernoy dramaturgii i muzïkal'nogo stilya' [Tchaikovsky's *Cherevichki* and Rimsky-Korsakov's *Christmas Eve*: an Attempt at Comparison of Operatic Dramaturgy and Musical Style], *Voprosï muzïkoznaniya* [Problems in Musicology], i, ed. A. Ogolevets (Moscow, 1954), 205–38
A. Gozenpud: *Russkiy opernïy teatr XIX veka* [Russian Operatic Theatre in the 19th Century], iii (Leningrad, 1973), 142–52, 291–3
P. Taylor: *Gogolian Interludes: Gogol's Story 'Christmas Eve' as the Subject of the Operas by Tchaikovsky and Rimsky-Korsakov* (London and Wellingborough, 1984) [incl. trans. of Laroche's reviews]

Yevgeny Onegin

H. Laroche [G. Larosh]: 'Muzïkal'nïye ocherki: nedelya v Moskve: "Yevgeny Onegin" v konservatorii,' stsenïy P. I. Chaykovskogo' [Essays on Music: a Week in Moscow: *Yevgeny Onegin* at the Conservatory, Scenes by Tchaikovsky], *Golos* (31 Dec 1878); '"Yevgeny Onegin" Chaykovskogo v spektakle konservatorii' [Tchaikovsky's *Yevgeny Onegin* Performed at the Conservatory], *Moskovskiye vedomosti* (22 March 1879); both repr. in *Sobraniye muzïkal'no-kriticheskikh statey* [Collected Critical Articles on Music], ed. N. D. Kashkin and V. Yakovlev, ii/1 (Moscow, 1922–4), 136–45
C. Cui: 'Muzïkal'nïye zametki: "Yevgeny Onegin", liricheskiye stsenï g. Chaykovskogo' [Musical Notes: *Yevgeny Onegin*, Tchaikovsky's Lyrical Scenes], *Nedelya* (4 Nov 1884)
G. Abraham: '"Eugene Onegin" and Tchaikovsky's Marriage', *MMR*, lxiv (1934), 222–3; repr. in *On Russian Music* (London, 1935), 225–33
B. V. Asaf'yev: *'Yevgeny Onegin', liricheskiye stsenï P. I. Chaykovskogo: opït intonatsionnogo analiza stilya i muzïkal'noy dramaturgii* [*Yevgeny Onegin*: Tchaikovsky's Lyrical Scenes: an Attempt at Intonational Analysis of Style and Musical Dramaturgy] (Moscow and Leningrad, 1944)
M. Peltz: 'Seen through a Letter: Notes on Eugene Onegin', *ON*, xxii/5 (1957–8), 4–7, 34–6
E. Berlyand-Chyornaya: *'Yevgeny Onegin' P. I. Chaykovskogo* (Moscow, 1960)
A. Porter: 'Tchaikovsky's Finest Opera', *About the House*, iii/7 (1970), 32–7
J. Russell: 'Onegin – an Anti-opera?', *About the House*, iii/7 (1970), 29–31
H. McLean: 'The Tone(s) of "Eugene Onegin"', *California Slavic Studies*, no.6 (1971), 3–15
A. Gozenpud: *Russkiy opernïy teatr XIX veka* [Russian Operatic Theatre in the 19th Century], iii (Leningrad, 1973), 152–68, 288–91
C. Stanislavski and P. Rumyantsev: *Stanislavski on Opera* (New York, 1975), chap. 2
G. Schmidgall: *Literature as Opera* (Oxford, 1977), chap. 7
I. Berlin: 'Tchaikovsky, Pushkin and Onegin', *MT*, cxxi (1980), 163–8
L'avant-scène opéra, no.43 (1982) [*Yevgeny Onegin* issue]
A. Sholp: *'Yevgeny Onegin' Chaykovskogo: ocherki* [Essays] (Leningrad, 1982)
N. John, ed.: *Eugene Onegin* (London, 1988) [ENO opera guide; incl. C. Emerson: 'Pushkin into Tchaikovsky: Caustic Novel, Sentimental Opera', 7–16; R. J. Wiley: 'Tchaikovsky's "Eugene Onegin"', 17–36; N. Challis: 'An Appreciation of "Eugene Onegin"', 37–47]
C. Dahlhaus: *Nineteenth-Century Music* (Berkeley and Los Angeles, 1989)

The Maid of Orléans

C. Cui: 'Muzïkal'nïye zametki: "Orleanskaya deva", opera g. Chaykovskogo' [Musical Notes: *The Maid of Orléans*, an Opera by Tchaikovsky], *Golos* (19 Feb 1881)
I. Kunin, ed.: *P. I. Chaykovsky ob opere* [Tchaikovsky on Opera] (Leningrad, 1952) [incl. orig. scenario]
A. Gozenpud: *Russkiy opernïy teatr XIX veka* [Russian Operatic Theatre in the 19th Century], iii (Leningrad, 1973), chap. 14
M. Williamson: 'Tchaikovsky and the Maid of Orleans' (Columbia M4 33210, 1973) [record notes]
H. Zajaczkowski: 'Tchaikovsky: the Missing Piece of the Jigsaw Puzzle', *MT*, cxxxi (1990), 238–42 [see also correspondence in issues of Aug 1990 and Feb 1991]

Mazepa

C. Cui: 'Muzïkal'nïye zametki: "Mazepa", opera g. Chaykovskogo' [Musical Notes: *Mazepa*, an Opera by Tchaikovsky], *Nedelya* (5 Feb 1884)
Mazepa/Opera v 3 deystviyakh/Muzïka P. I. Chaykovskogo [*Mazepa*: an Opera in 3 Acts, Music by Tchaikovsky] (Moscow, 1934) [articles by A. Svetlov, L. Grossman, A. Groman-Solovtsov, L. Shteynberg, L. Baratov]
A. Gozenpud: *Russkiy opernïy teatr XIX veka* [Russian Operatic Theatre in the 19th Century], iii (Leningrad, 1973), 277–88
H. Babinski: *The Mazeppa Legend in European Romanticism* (New York, 1974)
D. Brown: 'Tchaikovsky's *Mazeppa*', *MT*, cxxv (1984), 696–8

The Enchantress

H. Laroche [G. Larosh]: 'P. I. Chaykovsky i muzïkal'naya drama (po povodu "Charodeyki")' [Tchaikovsky and Musical Drama (concerning *The Enchantress*)], *Moskovskiye vedomosti* (8 Feb 1890); repr. in *Sobraniye muzïkal'no-kriticheskikh statey* [Collected Critical Articles on Music], ed. N. D. Kashkin and V. Yakovlev, ii/1 (Moscow, 1922–4), 153–65
B. Asaf'yev: *Charodeyka P. I. Chaykovskogo* (Moscow and Leningrad, 1947)
A. Gozenpud: *Russkiy opernïy teatr XIX veka* [Russian Operatic Theatre in the 19th Century], iii (Leningrad, 1973), chap. 19
C. Osborne: 'Russian Opera, part II', *HiFi/MusAm*, xxv/l (1975), 37–46 [annotated discography]

The Queen of Spades

V. Meyyerkhol'd and others: *Pikovaya dama: opera v 4 deystviyakh, muzïka P. I. Chaykovskogo* [*The Queen of Spades*: an Opera in 4 Acts, Music by Tchaikovsky] (Leningrad, 1935)
I. Sollertinsky: 'Pikovaya dama', *Kriticheskiye stat'i* [Critical Essays] (Leningrad, 1963), 35–43
B. Asaf'yev: 'Pikovaya dama', *Kriticheskiye stat'i, ocherki i retsenzii* [Critical Essays, Articles and Reviews], ed. I.V. Beletsky (Moscow and Leningrad, 1967)
A. Gozenpud: *Russkiy opernïy teatr na rubezhe XIX–XX vekov i Shalyapin 1890–1904* [Russian Operatic Theatre at the Turn of the 19th Century and Shalyapin] (Leningrad, 1974), chap. 3
Yu. Vasiliyev: 'K rukopisyam "Pikovoy damï"' [On the Manuscripts of *The Queen of Spades*], *SovM* (1980), no.7, pp.114–19
L'avant-scène opéra, nos.119–20 (1989) [*Queen of Spades* issue]
L. Karagicheva: 'Dva etyuda o "Pikovoy dame"' [Two Studies on *The Queen of Spades*], *SovM* (1990), no.6, pp.46–54

Iolanta

D. Lloyd-Jones: 'A Background to Iolanta', *MT*, cix (1968), 225–6
A. Gozenpud: *Russkiy opernïy teatr na rubezhe XIX–XX vekov i Shalyapin 1890–1904* [Russian Operatic Theatre at the Turn of the 19th Century and Shalyapin] (Leningrad, 1974), chap. 4
A. Lischke: record notes, *Iolanta* (Erato NUM 75207, 1985)

RICHARD TARUSKIN

Tcherepnin, Alexander (Nikolayevich) (*b* St Petersburg, 9/21 Jan 1899; *d* Paris, 29 Sept 1977). American composer of Russian origin, son of Nikolay Tcherepnin. He played the piano and composed prolifically from an early age. With his family he fled from St Petersburg in 1918 to Tbilisi, and in 1921 to Paris, where he completed his studies. He made his début as a pianist in London in 1922 and toured the USA in 1926. In 1934–7 travels in the Far East brought him into contact with Chinese and Japanese musical ideas that were to have far-reaching consequences in his creative work. He settled in Paris, and after World War II returned to the USA, where he taught at De Paul University, Chicago; he became an American citizen in 1958 and in 1964 moved to New York.

Many elements contributed to the formation of Tcherepnin's quicksilver, cosmopolitan musical personality, which, though recognizably Russian at base, conspicuously lacked the nostalgia and melancholy of other expatriate Slavs. In his early works the influences of Prokofiev and contemporary French music are discernible, but he also began experimenting with new scales and a new species of counterpoint. Other important constituents of Tcherepnin's musical language are those derived from the various folk cultures he encountered. An important work that attests to the influence of oriental music is the opera *The Farmer and the Nymph* (1952). After this literal and metaphorical 'journey to the East' came a return to the West: the American period was one of synthesis and consummation. Although he remained unaffected by both serialism and jazz, Tcherepnin incorporated electronic elements in his incidental music to *The Story of Ivan the Fool* (1968; after L. Tolstoy) for BBC radio.

Ol-Ol op.35, 1925 (3, after L. Andreyev: *Dni nashei zhizni*), Weimar, 31 Jan 1928; rev. 1930, New York, 1934; vs (New York, 1926)

Die Hochzeit der Sobeide op.45, 1930 (3 scenes, after H. von Hofmannsthal), Vienna, 17 March 1933, vs (Vienna and Leipzig, 1931)

Die Heirat [The Marriage] op.53, 1933–5 [completion of work by M. P. Musorgsky], Essen, 14 Sept 1937

The Farmer and the Nymph op.72 (lyric legend, Siao Yu), Aspen, CO, 13 Aug 1952, vs (London, 1972)

*

W. Reich: *Alexander Tscherepnine* (Bonn, 1959, 2/1970)

CHRISTOPHER PALMER

Tcherepnin, Nikolay (Nikolayevich) (*b* St Petersburg, 3/15 May 1873; *d* Paris, 27 June 1945). Russian composer. He was a pupil of Rimsky-Korsakov at the St Petersburg Conservatory. From 1898 he appeared as a pianist and conductor with the Belyayev Symphony Concerts, at the Mariinsky Theatre and, in 1908, at the Imperial Opera. In that year he supervised the Paris première of Rimsky-Korsakov's *The Golden Cockerel* and in 1909 was engaged by Dyagilev to conduct the celebrated first season of the Ballets Russes in Paris. In 1918 he was appointed director of the National Conservatory of Tbilisi, where for three years he was also conductor of the city's opera company. In 1921 he took his family to Paris, where he assumed control of the Russian Conservatory. Paris remained his home for the rest of his life, although he conducted widely and in 1923 directed in Monte Carlo the first performance of *The Fair at Sorochintsï*, for which he completed Musorgsky's score. His revision of Sokolovsky's opera *Mel'nik-koldun, obmanshchik i svat* ('The Miller who was a Wizard, a Cheat and a Matchmaker' was first performed at the Petite Scène, Paris, on 14 June 1929.

Tcherepnin's music is basically traditional. The faery fantasy world of Rimsky-Korsakov dominates his earlier orchestral works, while compositions from after his encounter with modern French music contain elements of impressionism. The Russian note asserted itself increasingly during Tcherepnin's years of exile, particularly in his operas. *Svat* ('The Matchmaker'; 2, after A. N. Ostrovsky: *Bednost' ne porok*) was composed in 1930 and first performed in Paris in 1937; *Vanka* (9 scenes, after F. Sologub) was first performed in Belgrade in 1933. Both are more strongly nationalist in character than anything he had composed previously. His memoirs were published posthumously (Leningrad, 1976).

CHRISTOPHER PALMER

Tchukhatjian, Tigran (*b* Constantinople, 1837; *d* Smyrna, 25 Feb 1898). Armenian composer and conductor. He studied in Constantinople, then at the Milan Conservatory (1861–4). On his return to Armenia he took part in the activities of the Armenian Musical Society; he also worked with the Gusanergakan Music Theatre and with the Arevelyan T'adron, the theatre of the Constantinople Armenians. In 1868 he completed the opera *Arshak Erkrord* ('Arshak II'), to a libretto by T. T'erzian, which marked the beginning of Armenian national opera. Excerpts were performed in Constantinople, Venice, Paris and Vienna during the composer's lifetime. The score, which was thought to have been lost, was discovered in Erevan in 1942, and a version revised by Shahverdyan and Khodjia-Eynatov to a libretto by A. Gulakyan was given in 1945. In the 1870s Tchukhatjian wrote the comic operas *Arifi khardakhutyunê* (based on Gogol's comedy *The Inspector General*), *Kyose K'ehya* ('The Balding Elder') and *Leblebidji khor, khor aga* ('The Pea Seller'), and in 1880 the *opera semiseria Zemire* to a libretto from Arabian tales. His last opera, *Indiana*, was composed in 1897.

As the founder of Armenian opera, Tchukhatjian was an important figure in the cultural history of the Near East. He was the first composer to fuse the techniques of European music with the special features of eastern, and in particular Armenian, folk music. His musical ideals were interwoven with notions of patriotism and the liberation of the Armenians from Turkey and he was instrumental in arousing the Armenian liberation movement in the second half of the 19th century. His style was forged under the influence of the Italian operatic school (he has been called 'Il Verdi armeno'), French operetta (when he was giving concerts of his own music in 1891, the Paris press called him 'the eastern Offenbach') and above all Armenian urban folklore – the last is particularly noticeable in *The Balding Elder* and *The Pea Seller*. The historical-heroic opera *Arshak II* occupies an important place in Armenian music because of its high level of artistry; with a libretto based on 4th-century Armenian history it is national in its general tone, though conceived on the scale of grand opera. Its monumental proportions, especially the choral prologue and finale, present a contrast to his comic operas which, with their social awareness, stereotyped characters and references to Armenian folk music, are thoroughly local and convey a true feeling of their time. *The Pea Seller*, a satirical comedy of manners, is distinguished by lively action, precise characterization, a variety of vocal forms and the *buffo* technique of writing; the opera was instantly popular, and in 1943 was produced in a revised version under the title *Karine*. The lyrical opera *Zemire*, written in Turkish and translated into French and Italian, was remarkable for its variety of melodic forms including stylized Eastern motifs, and Act 4 included an 'Arabian ballet'.

Arshak Erkrord [Arshak II] (T. T'erzian), 1868; rev. A. Shahverdyan and L. Khodjia-Eynatov (lib. A. Gulakyan), Erevan, Spendiaryan Armenian Theatre of Opera and Ballet, 1945; arr. pf (Erevan, 1969)

Arifi khardakhutyunê (comic op, H. Adjemian, after N. V. Gogol), Constantinople, 1872

Kyose k'ehya [The Balding Elder], 1874 (comic op, G. Rshtuni), Constantinople, 1974

Leblebidji khor, khor aga [The Pea Seller] (comic op, T. Nalian), Constantinople, 1876; rev. 1943 as Karine, Erevan, Theatre of Musical Comedy

Zemire, 1880 (op semiseria, T. Galymdjian, from Arabian tales), Constantinople, A. Vardovian, 1891

Indiana, 1897

*

A. Babayan: 'Tigran Tchukhatjian ev nra *Arshak II* operan' [Tigran

Tchukhatjian and his Opera Arshak II], *Sovetakan grakanut'yun* (1942), no.8, p.69 [in Armenian]
G. Tigranov: *Armyanskiy muzikal'nïy teatr* [The Armenian Music Theatre], i (Erevan, 1956)
A. Shahverdyan: *Ocherki po istorii armyanskoy muziki XIX–XX vekov* [Essays on the History of Armenian Music in the 19th and 20th Centuries] (Moscow, 1959)
G. Geodakyan: *T. Tchukhatjian i evo opera Arshak Vtoroy* (Erevan, 1971) SVETLANA SARKISYAN

Tear, Robert (*b* Barry, 8 March 1939). Welsh tenor. He studied at Cambridge and made his début in 1963 as the Male Chorus (*The Rape of Lucretia*) with the English Opera Group, for which he created Meshach (*The Burning Fiery Furnace*, 1966), Younger Son (*The Prodigal Son*, 1968), and the title role in Crosse's *Grace of Todd* (1969), and sang Quint and Idomeneus. He sang Jaquino for the WNO and Alfredo and Belmonte for Scottish Opera. At Covent Garden he created Dov in *The Knot Garden* (1970), the Deserter in *We Come to the River* (1976) and Rimbaud in Tavener's *Thérèse* (1979). His roles there have included Lensky, Paris (*King Priam*), Prince Vasily Golitsïn, Matteo (*Arabella*), Jack (*The Midsummer Marriage*), Froh, Loge (which he also sang in Paris and Munich), Spalanzani, Tom Rakewell, Admetus (*Alceste*), Captain Vere, Peter Grimes, David (*Die Meistersinger*), Jupiter (*Semele*), Prince Shuysky (also in Paris and Brussels), Herod (also in Geneva and with the WNO), Monostatos, Valzacchi, the Emperor Altoum (also in Los Angeles), Don Basilio, Handel's Samson, Fisherman (*The Nightingale*) and the Director (British première of Berio's *Un re in ascolto*, 1989). He sang the Painter/Negro in *Lulu* (première of the three-act version, 1979, Paris), Eumaetus in *Il ritorno d'Ulisse* (1985, Salzburg) and Aschenbach in *Death in Venice* (1989, Glyndebourne tour). In 1991 he created the title role of Penderecki's *Ubu Rex* at Munich. A stylish singer, he developed into an expressive character actor.

For illustration *see* PRODIGAL SON, THE. ALAN BLYTH

Teatro (It.). For information on any particular theatre, see under the theatre's name or under the name of the city where it is situated.

Tebaldi, Renata (*b* Pesaro, 1 Feb 1922). Italian soprano. She studied at the Arrigo Boito Conservatory in Parma with Carmen Melis and made her début in 1944 as Elena in Boito's *Mefistofele* at Rovigo. In 1946 she took part in the reopening concert at La Scala, under Toscanini, and subsequently sang Mimì and Eva in the rebuilt theatre's first winter season (1946–7). She sang regularly at La Scala from 1949 to 1954; her roles included Maddalena (*Andrea Chénier*), Adriana Lecouvreur, Tosca, Desdemona and the title role of Catalani's *La Wally*. She also made frequent appearances at S Carlo, Naples and in South America, where she was compared with Claudia Muzio, especially for her interpretation of Violetta.

She made her London début at Covent Garden as Desdemona, on the opening night of the Scala company's London season in 1950, and returned to London in 1955 to sing Tosca. Her American début was in San Francisco in 1950 as Aida. She also sang in Chicago, and became a member of the Metropolitan in 1955, remaining with the company for nearly 20 years. Besides the usual *lirico spinto* repertory, she sang such rarely heard roles as Spontini's Olympia, Pamyre in Rossini's *Le siège de Corinthe*, Cleopatra in Handel's *Giulio Cesare* and the title role of Verdi's *Giovanna d'Arco*.

Tebaldi possessed one of the most beautiful Italian voices of this century. Early in her career her interpretations lacked dramatic conviction, but later they gave evidence of a heightened sense of drama.

*

F. F. Clough and G. J. Cuming: 'Renata Tebaldi Discography', *Gramophone Record Review*, new ser. (1957), no.46, p.789
W. Panofsky: *Renata Tebaldi* (Berlin, 1961)
V. Seroff: *Renata Tebaldi: the Woman or the Diva* (New York, 1961)
H. Rosenthal: *Great Singers of Today* (London, 1966)
K. Harris: *Renata Tebaldi: an Authorised Biography* (New York, 1974)
A. M. Gasparri Rossotto: *Renata Tebaldi* (Florence, 1990)
E. Forbes: 'Tebaldi: Wonderful Memories', *Opera*, xlii (1991), 883–5 HAROLD ROSENTHAL/R

Tedeschi [Amadori], **Giovanni** (*b* Ronciglione, *c*1715; *d* ?Ronciglione, ?1787). Italian alto castrato. A pupil of Bernacchi, he sang in *opera seria* from 1732 to 1738, mostly in female roles, exclusively in Rome, where he was in the service of Prior Vaini. He then sang throughout Italy; he was probably the 'Tedeschino, contralto' listed at Bayreuth in 1748–9, and his singing was admired by Metastasio in Vienna in 1750; he was in Berlin in 1754–5 and retired from the stage in 1756. He was in the Naples royal chapel from 1748 until pensioned off in 1784, retiring then to Ronciglione. A noted singing teacher, he was also impresario of the S Carlo, 1764–7 and 1769–72. His music suggests a rather ornate style of singing, perhaps reflecting Bernacchi's school. DENNIS LIBBY (with JOHN ROSSELLI)

Tedesco, Fortunata (*b* Mantua, 14 Dec 1826; *d* after 1866). Italian contralto. She studied in Milan, where she made her début in 1844 at La Scala as Isabella in the first (and only) performance of Pasquale Bona's *I Luna e i Perollo*; she also created the Queen in Salvi's *I Burgravi* and Michal in Canneti's *Saul* (1845) and sang Elizabeth (*Roberto Devereux*) and the title role of Donizetti's *Alina, regina di Golconda*. At the Park Theatre, New York, she sang Elvira in *Ernani* (1847) and Odabella in *Attila* (1851), both American premières. Engaged at the Opéra (1851), she sang Fidès, Léonor (*La favorite*), Théodora in the première of Halévy's *Le Juif errant* (1852) and Catarina in the 100th performance of *La reine de Chypre* (1854). She sang Zayda in *Dom Sébastien* at the S Carlo (1857) and also appeared in Venice and Lisbon. Returning to the Opéra (1861), she sang Venus in the disastrous Paris première of *Tannhäuser*. She last appeared at Madrid (1865–6). Her voice, powerfully dramatic and flexible, with a very wide range, was especially effective in Donizetti and early Verdi. ELIZABETH FORBES

Teheran. Capital of Iran. In the 1930s Réza Shah, the last Shah's father, who had heard much opera in Europe, planned to create an Iranian Opera Company as part of his plans to modernize his country. In 1937–8 the construction of a new National Opera House began. With the occupation of Iran in 1941 by the Russians and the English, these plans came to nothing and the building became a bank. With the influx of musical refugees from eastern Europe, a Teheran SO was formed and the Teheran Opera Group was founded in 1960. It at first performed excerpts but in May 1962 gave Bizet's

Djamileh in the Farhang Hall of the Girls' College, Nour-Bakhck. *Don Pasquale* followed in 1963 and Gluck's *Orphée et Euridice* in 1964–5. In 1967 three performances of *Così fan tutte*, sung in Italian by an all-Iranian cast, were given at the Ministry of Culture and Arts. The Shah and his wife attended one of these performances. The soprano was Monir Valiki, who had studied at the Paris Conservatoire and in Boston; Heshmat Sanjari conducted the Teheran SO.

The Shah decided to build a new opera house, modelled on those in Munich and Vienna; seating 1200, with a private box and entrance, it was inaugurated in October 1967 during the Shah's coronation ceremonies (25 years after his actual accession). It was named the Rudaki Hall after a famous Iranian poet, and its first director was Farhad Mechkat (who had worked with Leonard Bernstein in New York). In 1968 the company opened the Teheran Festival of the Arts with an opera by the Iranian composer Ahmad Pezhman, *The Hero of Sahaud*; the Shah was present. Other productions included *Madama Butterfly* (1968) and (in 1969) *Il trovatore*, *Die Zauberflöte* and *Il barbiere di Siviglia*. About one performance of opera was now being given each week from September to June, and the repertory was gradually extended. The 14th new production, in 1970, was *La bohème*, with the leading Iranian soprano, Monir Vakili. In 1973, Lotfi Mansouri returned to Teheran to produce *Carmen* with Pari Samar in the title role. Alberto Erede spent several seasons with the company as chief guest conductor.

Five new operas in Farsi (Persian) took their place in the repertory: *Zal and Roudabeh* (based on Persian mythology) by Samin Baghtcheban, *Dehgan's Fete* ('The Beginning of Autumn') by Ahmad Pejman, *Khosrow and Shirin* (a Persian Romeo and Juliet story) by Hossein Dehlavi, *Delavar Sahand* ('The Brave Warrior Sahand') by Pejman and *Atossa* ('The Daughter of Cyrus') by the Austrian conductor and composer Thomas Christian David. In 1976 Alun Francis was appointed musical director. His 1978–9 season proposed *Die lustige Witwe*, *Der Rosenkavalier*, *Otello*, *Pardis and Parisa* by the Iranian composer Tcheknavarian, *Lulu*, *La traviata*, *Macbeth*, *Werther*, *La bohème* and *Die Zauberflöte*; but after the Shah fled in January 1979, the season collapsed and the government that eventually succeeded had no interest in opera, with women not allowed to perform in public. The Rudaki Hall continued in use as a playhouse.

CHARLES PITT

Teiber [Teuber]. *See* TEYBER.

Teixeira, António (*b* Lisbon, 14 May 1707; *d* Lisbon, after 1770). Portuguese composer. He was sent to Rome as a royal scholar at the age of nine and remained there until 1728, when he returned to Lisbon. Sacred music formed the bulk of his output, but he also wrote operas on the Singspiel-type Portuguese librettos of António José da Silva, *Guerras do alecrim e manjerona* and *Os encantos de Medeia*; he may also have written the music for the remaining six operas with text by this Brazilian-born Jewish lawyer, who was burnt at the stake by the Inquisition in 1739. All but two of these operas are on mythological subjects and were performed by large-size puppets at the Teatro do Bairro Alto in Lisbon between 1733 and 1739. Teixeira's extant theatrical and sacred music shows him to be a very competent practitioner of the contemporary Italian style.

first performed at Lisbon, Teatro do Bairro Alto

Os encantos de Medeia (2, A. J. da Silva), May 1735, only lib. extant

Guerras do alecrim e manjerona (ópera joco-séria, 2, Silva), carn. 1737, *P-VV*

Doubtful: As variedades de Proteu (2, Silva), May 1737, *VV*

*

M. de Sampayo Ribeiro: *A música em Portugal nos séculos XVIII e XIX* (Lisbon, 1936), 28–9, 64

J. Mazza: 'Dicionário biográfico de músicos portugueses', *Ocidente*, xxv (1945); also pubd separately (Lisbon, 1944–5)

M. C. de Brito: *Opera in Portugal in the Eighteenth Century* (Cambridge, 1989)

MANUEL CARLOS DE BRITO

Te Kanawa, Dame **Kiri** (*b* Gisborne, Auckland, 6 March 1944). New Zealand soprano. Winner of many prizes in New Zealand and Australia, she later studied at the London Opera Centre with Vera Rozsa. In 1969 her singing of Elena in *La donna del lago* at the Camden Festival marked her as a singer of exceptional promise, and this was confirmed with her first major role at Covent Garden, Mozart's Countess Almaviva (1971). In the same year she repeated the role at the Lyons Opéra and in her American début at Santa Fe. Further roles at Covent Garden have included Amelia (*Simon Boccanegra*), Donna Elvira, Violetta, Desdemona, Marguerite, Mimì, Fiordiligi, Manon Lescaut, Arabella and the Marschallin. She made her Metropolitan début at three hours' notice as Desdemona in 1974; she has reappeared there regularly. She sang at Glyndebourne in 1973, with further débuts in Paris (1975), Milan and Sydney (1978), Salzburg (1979) and Vienna (1980). In 1982 she gave her only stage performances as Tosca in Paris, and in 1989 added Elisabeth de Valois to her repertory at Chicago. She was made DBE in 1982. Her voice, vibrant but mellow, ample but unforced, impressed from the first with its freshness and warmth. Less remarkable are her interpretative powers, though her stage presence has both beauty and dignity. Her recordings sometimes lack animation, yet many are unsurpassed as examples of the lyric soprano's art.

*

D. Fingleton: *Kiri te Kanawa* (London, 1983)

A. Simpson and P. Downes: *Southern Voices: International Opera Singers of New Zealand* (Auckland, 1992), 218–31

J. B. STEANE

Tel-Aviv. City in Israel, the centre of the country's musical life; it incorporated the ancient port of Jaffa in 1950. In 1923 the immigrant Russian conductor Mordechai Golinkin inaugurated the city's first opera company, the Palestine Opera, with *La traviata* at the Eden Cinema. 120 performances of standard repertory works (all translated into Hebrew) followed until 1927, when Golinkin left for the USA on a fund-raising mission. Performances resumed in 1931, the company (still under Golinkin's baton) now renamed the New Palestine Opera Corporation and with a larger orchestra. But these performances were sporadic, and the company survived less than five years. From 1935 to 1940 the Chamber Opera Group put on shows in the Heifetz and Ohel-Shem theatres with two pianists in place of an orchestra, bridging the gap until the birth of the Palestine Folk Opera in 1941 (with *Die Fledermaus*) at the Mugrabi Theatre. But this company too was short-lived, and closed its doors in 1946. 1948 saw the foundation of the state of Israel; in the same year the Israeli National Opera was founded by the soprano Edis de Philippe, who had emigrated there after many years on the operatic stages of North America and Europe. The first night was on 15 April 1948 (*Thaïs*, with De

Philippe in the title role) at the Habimah Theatre. The company folded in 1953, re-opening in 1957 in its own home (the former parliament building). Its repertory consisted of standard opera and operetta, with premières of works by native composers. Placido Domingo was a member of the company from 1962 to 1965. After the death of De Philippe in 1978 the company declined, the curtain coming down for the last time in 1982. Opera in Tel-Aviv has also been given by the Israel Philharmonic, initially in concert, though the move to the Mann Auditorium in 1957 enabled works to be staged. Zeffirelli's prestigious La Scala *Falstaff* was seen there in 1959 (conducted by Giulini), and this paved the way for a new production in most seasons, with international soloists and conductors. From 1965 less familiar operatic fare was provided by the Israel Chamber Ensemble (from 1975, Israel Chamber Orchestra) under Gary Bertini, with the emphasis on 20th-century works. In 1985 the New Israel Opera was founded (with the Israel Chamber Orchestra as its orchestra), opening with *Dido and Aeneas*. In 1988 the company moved to its permanent home, the new Noga Theatre in Jaffa, and in 1990 the Rishan LeZion SO became its orchestra. Most of the singers are local, and all productions are in the original language with Hebrew surtitles. Between 1989 and 1991 the wave of immigrants from the USSR brought 2000 musicians to the country, greatly enriching the reservoir of singers in the city.

*

M. Golinkin: *Meheikhalei Yefet Le'Oholei Shem* [From the Mansions of Japhet to the Tents of Shem] (Tel-Aviv, 1948)
P. Domingo: *My First Forty Years* (London, 1983)
J. Olitzky: *Edis: Chapters in the Life of Edis de Philippe* (Tel-Aviv, 1983)
Y. Fischer, ed.: *Tel-Aviv: 75 Years of Art* (Tel-Aviv, 1984)

WILLIAM Y. ELIAS

Telemachus. Libretto subject popular in the 18th century. The story of Telemachus, son of Odysseus and Penelope, is recounted in the first four books of HOMER's *Odyssey*, in which Telemachus learns from Menelaus that his father is a prisoner of Calypso on a distant island; Odysseus later returns and they are reunited. The Telemachus legend takes various forms; it is frequently held that he later married Circe, and from this union Latinus was born. François de Salignac de la Mothe-Fénelon's version of the myth, in his novel *Aventures de Télémaque* (1699), aroused considerable controversy during the 18th century. Often parodied and criticized, the work became a political pawn in the dispute between Fénelon (Archbishop of Cambrai and champion of an anti-cartesian Christianity) and Jacques Bénigne Bossuet, Bishop of Meaux. A didactic novel, it was designed to demonstrate to Fénelon's pupil, the Duke of Burgundy (heir apparent to the French throne), the right way to govern. Fénelon expanded on the classical account, passing Telemachus through dozens of adventures and trials as he sought his father. In the seventh book, Telemachus is shipwrecked on the island of the goddess Calypso, who falls in love with him, though he is enamoured of a shepherdess, Eucharis. Calypso, jealous, tries to detain him and his tutor (Minerva in disguise) by burning the ship that is to provide their escape; at the last moment the tutor pushes Telemachus into the sea from a rock and together they swim to a passing ship.

A series of productions throughout the 18th century followed this tradition, and most acknowledge their debt to Fénelon: in Paris (1704; Pellegrin, with music by Destouches, 1714), Florence (C. L. Rossi, music by Meucci, 1773), Pisa (C. L. Rossi, music by Gazzaniga, 1776), Venice (Pindemonte, music by Bertoni, 1776), Munich (Serimann, music by F. P. Grua, 1780), Naples (music by Cipolla, 1785), Paris (P. Dercy, music by Le Sueur, 1796) and Venice (Sografi, music by Mayr, 1797). In Capece's *Telemaco* for Alessandro Scarlatti, the shepherdess's name is Erifile and she is revealed in the end to be Antiope, the daughter of Idomeneus of Crete, whom Telemachus is destined to marry. Other librettos, based on different episodes in Telemachus's travels, include Sografi's *Telemaco in Sicilia* (Padua; music by Calegari, 1792), and various accounts of Telemachus's alliance with Circe (such as Coltellini's *Telemaco, ossia L'isola di Circe* for Gluck, Vienna, 1765; librettos entitled *Circe* follow a different portion of her adventures).

See also CALYPSO AND TELEMACHUS [Galliard] and TELEMACO [Gluck].

DALE E. MONSON

Telemaco [*Telemaco, ossia L'isola di Circe* ('Telemachus, or Circe's Island')]. *Dramma per musica* in two acts by CHRISTOPH WILLIBALD GLUCK to a libretto by MARCO COLTELLINI after CARLO SIGISMONDO CAPECE; Vienna, Burgtheater, 30 January 1765.

At the end of the Trojan War, Ulysses (tenor) and his army are being held captive by the sorceress Circe (soprano) on her island Aeaea. Ulysses' son Telemachus (alto castrato) has recently been shipwrecked on the island while searching for his father.

In Act 1, Telemachus learns from another of Circe's captives, her maid Asteria (soprano), that Circe has been holding an army of shipwrecked warriors prisoner for seven years and has transformed them into trees. Asteria also tells him that Circe has fallen in love with their leader; Telemachus, realizing that this is probably his father, sets off with his companion Meriones (son of the King of Crete, but originally sung by a female soprano) to rescue him. Circe eventually frees Ulysses as a gesture of her passionate but unrequited love for him. Ulysses and Telemachus are reunited and the act ends with Circe giving in to their pleas and releasing Ulysses' followers.

Although Circe has freed her prisoners she will not help them escape from her magic island, and in Act 2 she invokes her evil spirits to help her. Meriones announces that his followers have nearly finished building a fleet of ships, but Telemachus will not leave without Asteria, whom he loves. Ulysses refuses to allow this, but when Asteria shows him a token of her birth, a jewelled necklace, Meriones realizes that Asteria is his long-lost sister, the daughter of Idomeneus and Telemachus's intended bride. As they all embark Circe arrives and pursues them in a magic chariot, vowing to destroy them all.

* * *

Telemaco is Gluck's most important opera between his first two 'reform' operas, *Orfeo ed Euridice* (1762) and *Alceste* (1767), and stylistically it shows a partial assimilation of his reform principles into the world of the conventional Italian *opera seria*. *Telemaco* was composed for the wedding celebrations of the future Austrian Emperor Joseph II and Princess Maria Josepha of Bavaria. Coltellini shared the ideals of Calzabigi, Gluck's librettist for his reform operas, but there is little evidence of them in *Telemaco* with its complicated plot in two acts, each so self-contained that they could stand as one-act operas. But the ending is a far cry from the world of *opera seria*, and the central villainous character of Circe anticipates Gluck's treatment of a similar heroine and theme 12 years later in *Armide*. Gluck drew on *Telemaco* for his later operas, including *Alceste*, *Armide* and both the *Iphigénie* settings; but as an opera in its own right *Telemaco* contains some remarkable music, including much orchestrally accompanied recitative, many fine ensembles and short arias, and sequences of open-ended numbers. The chorus plays a major part in *Telemaco*, for example in the opening scene in Act 1, where with a succession of striking choruses, ensembles and ballets we are plunged into the world of Gluck's 'reform' operas. JEREMY HAYES

Telemann, Georg Philipp (*b* Magdeburg, 14 March 1681; *d* Hamburg, 25 July 1767). German composer. Although known today principally for his instrumental music, Telemann was the most important composer of German-language opera in the first half of the 18th century. His works include at least 29 operas for which there is documentary evidence, though the actual number may exceed 50, if his own accounts are to be believed. Only nine complete works are extant.

1. LIFE. In his two autobiographies Telemann reports that his career as an opera composer began at the age of 12 with *Sigismundus*, possibly based on a libretto by Postel (Hamburg, 1693). The composer himself sang the title role in what was apparently a street performance on a makeshift stage. As a youth, Telemann heard his first professional opera performances at the court at Brunswick, travelling there from his boarding-school in nearby Hildesheim some time between 1697 and 1700. In 1702 and 1704 he visited Berlin specifically to hear opera performances. One of the two works he heard was Giovanni Bononcini's *Polifemo* (1702), and the other may have been *Les amours de Procris et Céphale* (1702 or 1704), also by Bononcini. For the latter performance, Telemann reports that he was 'concealed by friends, since admission was granted to few outsiders'.

Soon after beginning his university studies at Leipzig in 1701, Telemann became director of the civic opera there. It is uncertain how many works he composed before leaving Leipzig in early 1705. He himself reports having written a total of 'several and twenty' operas for the Leipzig stage, but this number includes works composed *in absentia* between 1705 and 1720. While in Leipzig, Telemann also composed as many as four operas for the nearby court at Weissenfels, though no trace of these remains. There is documentary evidence for the performance of only eight operas by him in Leipzig, but records from this period are very incomplete. The sole extant Leipzig opera is *Die Satyren in Arcadien* (1719), but only in the Hamburg version of 1724. Fragments of six or seven other early Telemann operas survive in various contemporary manuscripts. He claims to have written the librettos of many of his Leipzig operas himself, a believable assertion given his not inconsiderable talent as a poet. In many instances, however, his role may simply have been that of a translator, as was certainly the case with *Die Satyren*. He also appeared on the Leipzig stage as a singer. This brought an admonition from the city's ecclesiastical authorities that he should 'keep away from the theatre, and give up acting' as a condition of receiving a church post.

After holding court and civic positions in Sorau (1705–8), Eisenach (1708–12) and Frankfurt (1712–21), during which time he continued to deliver operas to Leipzig, Telemann settled permanently in Hamburg in 1721. Although employed principally as director of music at the city's five main churches, he may have been drawn to Hamburg by its famous Gänsemarkt opera, the first public opera house in Germany. His first work for it, *Der geduldige Socrates*, was given its première on 28 January 1721, almost six months before his appointment as head of the city's musical establishment. In 1722, within a year of his arrival, he was named musical director at the Gänsemarkt theatre, a position he held until the opera's demise in 1738. As director he received an annual salary of 300 Reichsthaler, which accounted for about one-third of his regular income. Of the 35 operas he claimed to have composed for the Gänsemarkt opera there is evidence of 18. Seven of these have survived, along with individual pieces from six others. All but two of his Gänsemarkt operas date from before 1730; the declining fortunes of the Hamburg Opera in the early 1730s evidently precluded his writing further operas. He returned to opera only once in his later career, with the one-act comic 'Serenade' *Don Quichotte auf der Hochzeit des Comacho*, presented in a concert performance in 1761.

In addition to composing works for Hamburg, Telemann also supplied operas to the courts of Eisenach and Bayreuth, where he was employed during the 1720s as 'Capellmeister von Haus aus' (composer *in absentia*). In his 1739 autobiography, Telemann mentions three 'Operetten' sent to Eisenach and two operas composed for Bayreuth. Of the Eisenach works, two librettos survive from 1729 and 1730, but no music. From one of the Bayreuth operas, *Adelheid* (1725), there survive 14 comic arias which Telemann published in 1728.

Although Telemann wrote no original librettos for himself in Hamburg, as he had done in Leipzig, he sometimes acted as a translator or reviser of his librettos. He translated the texts of *Omphale* (1724) and *Flavius Bertaridus* (1729) and also wrote the German verse for the former. He adapted the texts of *Sieg der Schönheit* (1722) and *Orpheus* from 17th-century German librettos. Apart from these, a number of his other Hamburg operas show signs of his having made changes to the libretto during the process of composition. The librettos are nearly always polyglot, with recitatives in German and arias in both German and Italian.

Telemann's involvement with the opera in Hamburg was not just as a composer of his own works but also as an arranger and performer of operas by other composers, especially those of his longtime friend Handel. About a dozen of Handel's operas were given in more than a hundred performances under Telemann's direction between 1722 and 1738 – the first systematic cultivation of Handel's works in Germany. Most of the Hamburg performances came shortly after their London premières, suggesting direct contact between the two men during this period. Telemann revised at least five Handel operas, sometimes extensively, for performance in Hamburg. The recitatives were translated into German and recomposed, castrato roles were transposed, new arias were substituted or added, and the plot might be substantially altered (as with *Riccardo Primo*). In accordance with a longstanding Hamburg tradition, comic characters were sometimes introduced as well (e.g. Isaurus in *Ottone*).

As well as reworking Handel operas, Telemann made additions to operas by Orlandini, Porpora, Keiser,

Chelleri and Campra. He also provided about a dozen prologues to other operas; these usually celebrated political events (e.g. coronations, royal births and marriages) and were commissioned by foreign ambassadors resident in Hamburg. None of these prologues is extant, though some of their stage settings are depicted in Thomas Lediard's *Eine Collection Curieuser Vorstellungen* (Hamburg, 1730).

2. WORKS. Little can be said about the musical style of Telemann's early operas, since virtually nothing has survived. In his 1718 autobiography, he relates that he had first cultivated the French operatic style but had recently turned more towards the Italian style. The few extant arias from his Leipzig operas before 1710 show a mixture of styles – a characteristic of Telemann's music generally. They are basically italianate, but their use of regular periods, predominantly conjunct melodic motion and frequent passages in parallel 3rds and 6ths may derive from the contemporary French style. In his choice of librettos Telemann seems to have favoured historical and mythological plots.

Most of Telemann's Hamburg operas are comedies, and he may be regarded as a pioneer of German-language comic opera. Among the surviving operas, two are full-length comedies (*Die Satyren in Arcadien*, 1719, 1724; *Der geduldige Socrates*, 1721) and one is an Italian-style intermezzo (*Pimpinone*, 1725). Furthermore, two of the serious operas contain substantial comic elements (*Sieg der Schönheit*, 1722; *Emma und Eginhard*, 1728), while the extant comic arias from the Bayreuth opera *Adelheid* (1725) are so numerous that they nearly form a self-contained work – only the recitatives are lacking. The librettos to the comic operas are usually quite sophisticated, anticipating the social criticism of later 18th-century *opera buffa*. The subject matter often deals with class conflicts, in which lower-class persons are presented as morally superior to the aristocracy (as in *Emma und Eginhard* and *Don Quichotte*). Not all of Telemann's humour is high comedy; Hamburg tradition demanded the presence of slapstick elements as well, and these are sometimes carried to extremes (e.g. the absurd and repetitious 'bat-face' joke in *Socrates*).

Stylistically, Telemann's comedies also anticipate later developments. The Italian *buffo* style is present as early as 1721 in *Socrates* and appears fully developed in *Pimpinone* (1725), eight years before Pergolesi's *La serva padrona*. Apart from the *buffo* style, Telemann cultivated a simple melodic idiom which is often reminiscent of German folksong. He reserved a more virtuoso *opera seria* style for the serious characters who typically appear in the full-length comedies (e.g. Melito in *Socrates*). He was a pioneer in the use of the bass voice in comic roles, as exemplified by the title character in *Pimpinone*. Also notable is his extensive use of ensembles; most are duets, but trios, quartets and even quintets appear occasionally.

Telemann's surviving serious operas are commonly in an italianate style comparable to contemporary works by Handel; this is not surprising, given his familiarity with Handel's music. The serious operas from the early and mid-1720s depart from the *opera seria* tradition largely through their inclusion of comic characters, usually servants or rustics. In the late 1720s Telemann composed several works (e.g. *Miriways* and *Flavius Bertaridus*) which belong more strictly to the category of *opera seria*. An exceptional work is the recently discovered *Orpheus* (1726), which is essentially a *tragédie lyrique* incorporating many elements from *opera seria*. Comic scenes are excluded, and there is no *lieto fine*. The work contains French-style choruses (with French texts), and the arias are alternately in Italian, French and German styles, corresponding to the language of the text.

A feature of Telemann's operas generally is the substantial role of the orchestra, which he usually handled in a highly varied and colourful fashion. The orchestra at Hamburg's Gänsemarkt opera boasted a large complement of wind instruments, and Telemann took full advantage of this with frequent concertante writing for winds (as in *Socrates*). Only in the later 1720s did he generally simplify his orchestration, undoubtedly influenced by contemporary developments in Italian *opera seria*. Thus, the orchestra in *Miriways* and *Flavius Bertaridus* usually consists of three sounding parts, dominated by the outer voices, a texture found in much of *Orpheus* as well.

Although the surviving operas are of high quality, Telemann's undeserved reputation as a second-class composer has prevented them from gaining wide recognition. The most significant revivals have been at the 'Telemann-Festtage' held in Magdeburg from the early 1960s.

See also GEDULDIGE SOCRATES, DER and PIMPINONE (ii).

Catalogue: W. Menke: *Thematisches Verzeichnis der Vokalwerke von Georg Philipp Telemann*, ii (Frankfurt, 1983) [TWV]

Ferdinand und Isabella TWV21:2 (5), Leipzig, spr. 1703

Der lachende Democritus TWV21:1 (3, after N. Minato), Leipzig, 1703

Cajus Caligula TWV21:3 (3), Leipzig, Easter 1704

Adonis TWV21:4 (3), Leipzig, Easter 1708, 1 aria *D-SHs*

Narcissus TWV21:5 (3), Leipzig, ?1701 and [?rev.] Easter 1709, 3 arias *SHs*

Mario TWV21:6 (3), Leipzig, Easter 1709, 2 arias *SHs*

Jupiter und Semele TWV21:7 (3), Leipzig, 1716 or 1718, lib. ed. W. Hobohm, Magdeburger Telemann-Studien, x (1987)

Die Satyren in Arcadien [Damon] TWV21:8 (3, Telemann, after P. Pariati), Leipzig, 1719; rev. as Der neumodische Liebhaber Damon, Hamburg, Gänsemarkt, 30 Aug 1724, *B*; ed. in *G. P. Telemann: Musikalische Werke* (Kassel and Basle, 1950–), vol.xxi

Der geduldige Socrates TWV21:9 (komisches Spl, 3, J. U. [von] König, after Minato: *La pazienza di Socrate*), Hamburg, Gänsemarkt, 28 Jan 1721, *Bds**, *F*; ed. in *Musikalische Werke*, xx

Sieg der Schönheit TWV21:10 (3, C. H. Postel, rev. Telemann and C. F. Weichmann), Hamburg, Gänsemarkt, 13 July 1722; as Gensericus, Brunswick, 1725 and 1732; 1732 version *B* and *SWl*

Belsazar, oder das Ende der babylonischen Monarchie TWV21:11 (3, J. Beccau), Hamburg, 19 July 1723; a second pt perf. ?22 Sept 1727; 3 arias *SWl*, Telemann, *Der getreue Music-Meister* (Hamburg, 1728–9)

Alarich, oder Die Straf-Ruthe des verfallenen Roms [Stilico] TWV21:12 (3), Bayreuth, 2 Aug 1723

Omphale TWV21:14 (5, Telemann, after A. H. de Lamotte), Hamburg, Gänsemarkt, 24 April 1724

Pimpinone, oder Die ungleiche Heirat, oder Die herrschsüchtige Cammer-Mädgen TWV21:15 (int, 3 scenes, J. P. Praetorius, after Pariati), Hamburg, Gänsemarkt, 27 Sept 1725 (Hamburg, 1728), *B*, *F*, ed. in EDM, 1st ser., vi (1936)

La caprizziosa e il credulo [Die geliebte Eigensinnige und der leichtgläubige Liebhaber] TWV21:16 (3, Praetorius), Hamburg, 1725, 4 arias *Bds*

Adelheid, oder Die ungezwungene Liebe TWV21:17 (3, ?Praetorius, after P. Dolfino), Bayreuth, 1725, 14 arias (Hamburg, 1728, 2/1733)

Orpheus, oder Die wunderbare Beständigkeit der Liebe TWV21:18 (musicalisches Drama [Serenate], 3, Telemann, after F. C. Bressand), ?concert perf., Hamburg, Gänsemarkt, 9 March 1726; as Die rachgierige Liebe, oder Orasia, verwittwete Königin in Thracien TWV21:31, 15 Oct 1736; 2 MS scores, private collection

Calypso, oder Sieg der Weisheit über die Liebe TWV21:19 (Spl, 3, Praetorius), Hamburg, Gänsemarkt, 18 Aug 1727, 1 chorus in *Der getreue Music-Meister* (Hamburg, 1728–9)

Sancio, oder Die siegende Grossmuth TWV21:20 (3, König), Hamburg, Gänsemarkt, 6 Oct 1727, 4 arias *Bds*, *Der getreue Music-Meister* (Hamburg, 1728–9)

Buffonet und Alga, oder Die Mans-Tolle alter Jungfer TWV21:21 (int, C. G. Wend), Hamburg, Gänsemarkt, 14 June 1727

Die Amours der Vespetta, oder Der Galan in der Kiste TWV21:22 (Nachspiel, C. W. Haken), Hamburg, Gänsemarkt, 1 Oct 1727

Die verkehrte Welt TWV21:23 (oc, Praetorius, after A. R. Lesage), Hamburg, Gänsemarkt, 1728, 1 aria, 3 canonic pieces in *Der getreue Music-Meister* (Hamburg, 1728–9)

Miriways TWV21:24 (Spl, 3, J. S. Müller), Hamburg, Gänsemarkt, 26 May 1728, *B*, *Mbs*

Emma und Eginhard, oder Die Last-tragende Liebe TWV21:25 (3, Wend), Hamburg, Gänsemarkt, 12 Nov 1728, copy of 18th-century MS in *US-Wc*; orig. in *D-Hs* lost 1943

Aesopus bei Hofe TWV21:26 (3 or 5, trans. from It. by J. Mattheson), Hamburg, Gänsemarkt, 28 Feb 1729, 3 arias in *Der getreue Music-Meister* (Hamburg, 1728–9)

Der Weiseste in Sidon, oder Abdolonimus TWV21:30 (3, J. G. Hamann), Hamburg, Gänsemarkt, ?10 Oct 1729; ? revived or first perf., 4 Feb 1733

Flavius Bertaridus, König der Longobarden TWV21:27 (3, Wend and Telemann, after S. Ghigi), Hamburg, Gänsemarkt, 23 Nov 1729, *Bds**

Margaretha, Königin von Castilien TWV21:29 (3 or 5, Hamann), Hamburg, Gänsemarkt, 10 Aug 1730

Don Quichotte auf der Hochzeit des Comacho TWV21:32 (serenade, 1, D. Schiebeler), concert perf., Hamburg, Konzertsaal, 3 Nov 1761, *Bds**, *B*, *LEm*, *Mbs*; ed. in RRMBE, lxiv–v (1991)

Frags., undated, ? first perf. Leipzig: Adam und Eva TWV21:33 (operette, prol., 3, C. Richter), *F*; Hercules und Alceste TWV21:34 (Comödie), *F*; Herodes und Marianne TWV21:35 (op/oratorio, ? J. S. Müller), ? *c*1715, *F*; 43 arias and duets TWV21:101–43, *F*

*

C. Ottzenn: *Telemann als Opernkomponist: ein Beitrag zur Geschichte der Hamburger Oper* (Berlin, 1902)

P. Merbach: 'Das Repertoire der Hamburger Oper von 1718 bis 1750', *AMw*, vi (1924), 354–72

W. Schulze: *Die Quellen der Hamburger Oper (1678–1738): eine bibliographisch-statistische Studie zur Geschichte der ersten stehenden deutschen Oper* (Hamburg and Oldenburg, 1938)

H. C. Wolff: *Die Barockoper in Hamburg* (Wolfenbüttel, 1957)

——: 'G. Ph. Telemann und die Hamburger Oper', *Beiträge zu einem neuen Telemannbild: 1. Magdeburger Telemann-Festtage: Magdeburg 1962*, 38–49

B. Baselt: 'Zum Typ der komischen Oper bei Georg Philipp Telemann', *Ein bedeutender Meister der Aufklärungsepoche: 3. Magdeburger Telemann-Festtage: Magdeburg 1967*, i, 73–87

W. Hobohm: 'Zum Stil einiger Jugendwerke Telemanns', ibid, i, 61–72

D. Litt: 'Einige Erfahrungen mit der "opera buffa" G. Ph. Telemanns', ibid, i, 92–100

R. Pečman: 'Zur Interpretation der Opern des 18. Jahrhunderts unter besonderer Berücksichtigung von Telemanns "Pimpinone"', ibid, i, 88–91

M. Peckham: *The Operas of Georg Philipp Telemann* (diss., Columbia U., 1972)

300 Jahre Oper in Hamburg: 1678–1978 (Hamburg, 1977)

B. Baselt: 'Georg Philipp Telemann und die Opernlibrettistik seiner Zeit', *Telemann und seine Dichter: 6. Magdeburger Telemann-Festtage: Magdeburg 1977*, i, 31–51

G. Fleischhauer, W. Siegmund Schulze and E. Thom, eds.: *Georg Philipp Telemann: Autobiographien – 1718, 1729, 1739* (Blankenburg, 1977)

A. Koch: 'Telemanns Bearbeitung der Händel-Oper "Ottone" in bezug auf Sujet, Libretto und Rezitativstil', *Telemann und seine Dichter: 6. Magdeburger Telemann-Festtage: Magdeburg 1977*, i, 58–67

R. Pečman: 'Zur Typologie der Operngestalten Telemanns und ihrer Beziehung zur italienischen Librettistik', ibid, i, 52–7

E. Thom: 'Telemann und Praetorius', ibid, ii, 41–50

B. Baselt: 'G. Ph. Telemanns Serenade "Don Quichotte auf der Hochzeit des Comacho": Beiträge zur Entstehungsgeschichte von Telemanns letztem Hamburger Bühnenwerk', *HJbMw*, iii (1978), 85–100

K. Zelm: 'Die Sänger der Hamburger Gänsemarkt-Oper', ibid, 35–74

R. Lynch: *Opera in Hamburg, 1718–1738: a Study of the Libretto and Musical Style* (diss., New York U., 1979)

B. Baselt: 'Zu einigen Aspekten des Opernschaffens von Georg Philipp Telemann', *Georg Philipp Telemann: Leben–Werk–Wirkung* (Berlin, 1980), 35–49

——: 'Telemann und die deutsche Oper', *Musik und Gesellschaft*, xxxi (1981), 140–46

M. Ruhnke: 'Komische Elemente in Telemanns Opern und Intermezzi', *GfMKB, Bayreuth 1981*, 94–107

K. Harnisch: 'Telemann als Bearbeiter von Händels Oper "Riccardo I"', *Die Bedeutung Georg Philipp Telemanns für die Entwicklung der europäischen Musikkultur im 18. Jahrhundert: 8. Magdeburger Telemann-Festtage: Magdeburg 1981*, i, 114–20

A. Koch: 'Telemanns Auseinandersetzung mit der Charakterisierungskunst und dem Wort-Ton-Verhältnis im Opernschaffen Händels', *ibid*, ii, 15–26

G. Rienäcker: 'Oper als Organ bürgerlicher Selbstverständigung: Notate zum Lustspiel "Der geduldige Sokrates" von Georg Philipp Telemann', ibid, i, 94–103

K. Zelm: 'Georg Philipp Telemann und Reinhard Keiser: zur Konzeption der Opernarie um 1730', ibid, ii, 3–14

——: 'Reinhard Keiser und Georg Philipp Telemann: zum Stilwandel an der frühdeutschen Oper in Hamburg', ibid, i, 104–13

B. Stewart: *Georg Philipp Telemann in Hamburg: Social and Cultural Background and its Musical Expression* (diss., Stanford U., 1985)

BRIAN D. STEWART

Telephone, The [*The Telephone, or L'amour à trois* ('The Eternal Triangle')]. *Opera buffa* in one act by GIAN CARLO MENOTTI to his own libretto; New York, Heckscher Theatre, 18 February 1947.

The action takes place in Lucy's apartment somewhere in the USA in the present time. After a lively introduction Lucy (soprano) opens a package just given to her by Ben (baritone). He says he has something to ask her before his train leaves, but the telephone rings. She has a little refrain, repeated for each of the ensuing telephone conversations: 'And how are you? And how is ...' etc. Ben tries again to ask his question but is interrupted by a wrong number. Mention of time prompts Lucy to telephone for the speaking clock: 'four-fifteen and three-and-a-half seconds'. Another call – this time a boyfriend with whom she has an argument. Lucy, upset, leaves to get a handkerchief. Ben, enraged, is about to cut the telephone cord when it rings again loudly. Lucy returns just in time to save it from destruction. She must call her friend Pamela. A duet follows with Lucy on the telephone and Ben cursing the machine to himself. He exits and a small side stage reveals a telephone booth. Ben calls Lucy and proposes; she accepts. But he must promise one thing: never to forget her telephone number, which she then dictates to him.

This 22-minute 'skit with music', as it has been called, was written as a lightweight curtain-raiser for performances of *The Medium*, a dark and tragic contrast. The latter had received its première the year before and was revised for the 1947 performances at the Heckscher Theatre (18 to 20 February). The directors Chandler Cowles and Efrem Zimbalist jr were impressed and moved the production to the Ethel Barrymore Theatre on Broadway where on 1 May 1947 it began an unprecedented run of 211 performances. In 1951 the two works toured Europe, sponsored by the State Department. *The Telephone* has cheerful, witty and bright tonal music. The scoring is light. Lucy's part is frequently coloratura in style, at one point with a trill on *a''* followed by a slide up to *d'''*.

BRUCE ARCHIBALD

Television. Opera has been transmitted by television since the inauguration of the medium in the mid-1930s, and many operas have been composed with the specific capacities of television in mind. The transmission of traditional opera by television raises special problems because of the conflicts between two media with recognized conventions of their own, one highly stylized, the other naturalistic; the static character of operatic arias or ensembles of a contemplative character is alien to a medium that thrives on movement and action.

This article discusses the history and presentation of opera on television. For a discussion of the techniques of filming opera, *see* FILMING, VIDEOTAPING; *see also* FILM.

1. History. 2. Presentation.

1. HISTORY. Opera on television emanates from three sources: relays (live or recorded) from opera houses and festivals, studio productions and films. In the earliest days of the television medium, the primitive technical equipment ruled out the first of these, and up to the outbreak of World War II in 1939 almost all opera presentations came from the studio. The first regular TV service in the world (initially of one and a half hours three times a week, then daily) was operated by the small Paul Nipkow Sender in Berlin, which began transmissions in March 1935; but it was the BBC, whose daily television programmes started in November 1936, which was the pioneer in scheduling opera. Within 11 days of its inauguration it broadcast scenes from Albert Coates's *Pickwick*, which was to receive its première at Covent Garden a week later; this was followed by abbreviated versions (because of the limited airtime) of Blow's *Venus and Adonis*, Arne's *Thomas and Sally* and other smaller-scale works. The first opera to be given in its entirety was Pergolesi's *La serva padrona* (September 1937), and the same year also saw isolated acts from *Faust*, *La traviata* and *Aida* from the BBC. It experimented with mimed opera in *Hänsel und Gretel* and Act 2 of *Tristan und Isolde*; and an extension of transmission hours allowed complete performances of Falla's *El retablo de maese Pedro*, *Gianni Schicchi*, *Pagliacci* and Busoni's *Arlecchino*. Between 1938 and 1940 the Paul Nipkow Sender showed a film of Mozart's *Der Schauspieldirektor* nine times, but its sole studio productions were of Mozart's *Bastien und Bastienne* (with Schwarzkopf as Bastienne) and Lortzing's *Die Opernprobe* in 1939. The only other station to present opera on TV in the early days was NBC in New York, starting in 1940 with a shortened version of *Pagliacci*.

There was then a gap until after the war, when the BBC resumed televising opera and again led the field: by 1947 it was able to include theatre relays of several repertory operas. The USA was next off the mark in 1948 with a relay by station WJZ (New York) of *Otello* from the Metropolitan Opera, and then *Les contes d'Hoffmann* and Paisiello's *Il barbiere di Siviglia* in college productions screened by WRGB (Schenectady, NY). In 1949 NBC began again with scenes from standard operas and complete productions of Menotti's *The Old Maid and the Thief* and Weill's *Down in the Valley*. During the early 1950s the Canadian Broadcasting Corporation and several European stations came on air and included opera in their schedules, usually beginning with tried and trusted favourites although RAI was bolder in starting with Chiarini's *Il geloso schernito*. The first opera transmitted in colour was NBC's *Carmen* in October 1953.

NBC set a valuable example not only by commissioning Menotti's *Amahl and the Night Visitors* – the first American opera composed for television, transmitted on Christmas Eve 1951 and eagerly taken up by numerous other TV stations in ensuing years – but also by proceeding to commission works from other composers, among them Martinů's *The Marriage* (1953), Lukas Foss's *Griffelkin* (1955), Hollingsworth's *La grande Bretèche* (1957) and Menotti's *Maria Golovin* (1958) and *Labyrinth* (1963). Other countries began to follow suit: from 1956 the BBC commissioned about a dozen operas, of which the most notable were Bliss's *Tobias and the Angel* (1960) and Britten's *Owen Wingrave* (1971); Sutermeister wrote *Seraphine* (1959) and *La croisade des enfants* (1969) for Swiss stations and *Das Gespenst von Canterville* (1964) for the German Zweite Deutsche Fernsehen; for Nederlande Televisie Stichting Badings wrote the first entirely electronic score, *Salto mortale* (1959), and Ton de Leeuw composed *Alceste* (1963).

The institution in 1959 of the triennial Salzburg Opera Prize for new TV operas provided a further incentive to TV organizations and composers, since besides the cash prize the winning work was assured of showings in other countries: among the prizewinners have been Paul Angerer's *Passkontrolle* (1959, Österreichischer Rundfunk) and Lidholm's *Holländarn* (1967, Sveriges Radio Television); Vlad's *La fantarca* (1967, RAI) was awarded a special mention. In the music category of the prestigious annual Prix Italia other new operas attracted attention, including Riccardo Malipiero's *Battono alla porta* (1962, RAI), Prodromides' *Les Perses* (1961, RTF) and Phyllis Tate's *Dark Pilgrimage* and Edwin Coleman's *Christmas Carol* (both 1962, BBC). There has been general agreement that new TV operas should have a strong, well-told plot which is not too static, a smallish cast and a duration of not more than 90 minutes.

A number of the television operas mentioned have been adapted for stage presentation, though the greater concision of the television medium has sometimes necessitated small modifications, such as the lengthening of transition passages to allow for scene changes (which on TV could be immediate). This possibility of further usage, with the payment of extra performing rights fees, has naturally been an inducement to composers (such as does not exist in the case of radio operas). Nevertheless, new works for the medium represent only a minute fraction of TV operatic output, which in the main concentrates on works originally intended for the stage. By theatrical standards, TV audiences are immense: for example, a single performance of *Carmen* by the BBC was watched by vastly more than the total number who had ever seen that work on the stage in Britain since its composition in 1875; or, to put it another way, equivalent to a full house at Covent Garden every night for over five years. Yet the range of operas that have been shown has been extremely wide, from the most popular to the recherché. A tally of productions by European stations is kept by the Internationales Musikzentrum (IMZ) in Vienna.

2. PRESENTATION. The most idiomatic form of opera presentation on television is, generally speaking, the studio production. Its great advantage is that it can draw the spectator closer to the characters and involve

The final scene of the BBC television production of Richard Strauss's 'Salome', 26 September 1957: soldiers can be seen crushing Salome under their shields while the cameraman (front) lines up a camera on the closing caption

him in the drama. (By the use of stereophonic effects in the theatre, Nono in *Intolleranza 1960*, Zimmermann in *Die Soldaten* and Werle in *Drömmen om Thérèse* have swept their audiences into the heart of the action.) Some traditionalists have objected to this intimate view and demanded that, as in the theatre, the spectator be kept at some distance, which is analogous to insisting that a translation of a book should be so literal as not to be idiomatic in the new language. The intimacy of the medium enables the director to dispense with unwanted stage areas and to concentrate on a single person or group of persons who are of special importance at that moment, or on some significant action (such as the Count in *Figaro* pricking his finger on the pin – a detail scarcely noticeable in the theatre – or Michele in *Il tabarro* striking a match). There is greater scope for variety of decor, which may be suggested by the aid of back projection and the incorporation of filmed sequences: one might see the coach caught in the storm in *Cenerentola*, the menacing revolutionary mob in *Dialogues des Carmélites* or the band marching past the window in *Wozzeck*. Settings can range in style from the fantastic to the naturalistic, though open-air scenes in the latter call for some caution if there is to be no conflict with the element of stylization that every opera contains. The cameras' mobility in the studio also allows for variety of images from different angles, distances and heights. Supernatural scenes, such as the appearance of Banquo's ghost in *Macbeth*, can call special effects (superimposition and the like) into play; but in general it is considered best to keep electronic trickery to a minimum.

Studio productions can be made in one of three ways: performed live (even if the result is recorded for later transmission); by the 'playback' method, where the music is pre-recorded and the singers then devote their attention to acting, in synchronization with the recorded track; and (an extension of this) by 'doubling', i.e. with actors chosen for their physical suitability to the role miming to pre-recorded track by singers who do not appear in vision. This last method has attracted directors for operas in which the composer wrote music for a youthful, sometimes frail, heroine that is singable only by a mature-voiced leading lady, or in which actresses impersonate children (as in *Hänsel und Gretel*, *L'enfant et les sortilèges* and *Pelléas et Mélisande*), or in which it may be desirable to have ethnically authentic faces which will look convincing in close shot (as in *Madama Butterfly*). But it is rarely very successful and its artifice is too often apparent.

In recent years, because of the sense of occasion created and the appearance of star singers, programme chiefs have tended to favour relays from opera houses, particularly since international exchanges have brought to the screen productions from centres in other countries. Relays are the least idiomatic to the new medium, restricted as they are by the tyranny of the proscenium arch and the conventional ideal of 'a view from the best seat in the house, with a pair of opera-glasses'. Opera-house relays may flatten out perspectives and emphasize the conflict of pace between the forward thrust of the dramatic action and the retarding tendency of lyrically expressive music; the larger vista of the stage invites a slower unfolding of the action and relatively static production, which in studio circumstances can in some degree be mitigated by sympathetic treatment, in particular through discreet changes of shot.

Television production is detailed and demanding in quite a different sense from stage production. Every image on the screen has to be planned so as to parallel and enhance the musico-dramatic intent. Working from the score (not only from the libretto), the director has at every moment to ask himself a number of vital questions: what do I want to see here? does my layout allow me to do so? is the shot musically or dramatically motivated, or does it just make a good picture? is it well composed? on which camera should it be taken, from what position, from what height and with which lens? As with all musical programmes on television, certain basic rules of 'grammar' apply. The frequency and rhythm of image changes should accord with the pace and rhythm of the musical flow and the atmosphere, with few changes in calm passages and more at moments of excitement. The practice of coupling opera on television with a simultaneous radio broadcast of the work in stereo undoubtedly improves the received sound quality, but dictates that only frontal shots can be used, since otherwise the fixed left-and-right sound channels may not match the positioning of the singers and produce a contradiction between vision and sound.

*

H. Graf: *Opera for the People* (Minneapolis, 1951)
Opera in Radio, TV and Film (Salzburg, 1956) [pubn of Internationales Musikzentrum]
K. A. Wright: 'Television and Opera', *Tempo*, new ser., no.45 (1957), 8–14
L. Salter: 'Opera on Television', *Opera*, viii (1957), 673–9
R. Cartier: 'Producing Television Opera', ibid, 679–84
L. Salter: 'The Presentation of Music', *Journal of the Royal Society of Arts*, cix/Nov (1961), 954–67
E. G. M. Alkin, C. L. S. Gifford and L. Salter: *The Broadcasting of Music in Television* (London, 1962)
R. C. Burke: *A History of Televised Opera in the United States* (Ann Arbor, 1963)
K. Blaukopf, ed.: *IMZ Report: Music in TV* (Vienna, 1964)
L. Salter: 'Gedanken über die Fernsehoper', *IMZ Bulletin* (1964), no.1, pp.1–5
——: 'Opera at Home', *EBU Review*, no.96*b* (1966), 12–18
B. Paulu: *Radio and Television Broadcasting on the European Continent* (Minneapolis, 1967)
J. Bornoff, ed.: *Music Theatre in a Changing Society* (Paris, 1968)
H. Bertz-Dostal: *Oper im Fernsehen* (Vienna, 1970–71)
'Die Fernsehoper und ihre Probleme', *Kunst und Literatur*, xviii (1970), 653
J. Bornoff and L. Salter: *Music and the 20th-century Media* (Florence, 1972)
L. Salter: 'The Birth of TV Opera', *Opera*, xxviii (1977), 234–9
——: 'The Infancy of TV Opera', ibid, 340–44
IMZ Symposium: Opera in Television (Vienna, 1978) [pubn of Internationales Musikzentrum]
M. Andersen: 'Opera and Television', *EBU Review*, xxxiii/6 (1982), 17–18
R. Stromberger: 'New Forms of Dramatic Musical Work', ibid, 19–21

LIONEL SALTER

Tello, Rafael (*b* Mexico City, 1872; *d* Mexico City, 1946). Mexican composer. He was director of the Mexican National Conservatory (1914–15), where he also lectured in piano and composition, teaching among others Silvestre Revueltas. He was also director of the Free Conservatory (1917–30). His output consists of about a hundred works, including a *Triptico mexicano* for orchestra and the symphonic poem *Patria heroica*. He was one of the first Mexican composers to realize the need for a distinctive national opera free from the heavy influence of Italian and French Romantic models. His ideas led him to the creation of his most important opera, *Nicolas Bravo*, based on the life of the hero of the Independence war of 1810–21 who was also president of Mexico during several short periods. The opera was first performed in 1910 as part of the celebrations of the first centenary of independence. The libretto, by Ignacio Mariscal, a well-known politician and writer who made the first Hispano-American translation of Poe, centres on the time when Bravo takes command of the Mexican army during the last stage of the war. Other operas include *Juno* (1896), still unperformed, *Due amori*, produced in 1916 and *El oidor* (1924), set during the years following the Spanish conquest. Tello's music remains largely in manuscript because of a ban on publication established by his family after his death. His style has been described as rhapsodic and discursive, and if his first works betray a major influence of pre-impressionistic music, his later ones show a move towards a more modern language, often of a desolate nature. When dealing with national and historical subjects, Tello used elements of folklore to lend an air of authenticity to his operas and symphonic poems. Rather complex harmonic textures and marked dynamic contrasts at climactic points also characterize his work.

Juno, 1896, unperf.
Nicolas Bravo (drama lirico, 2, I. Mariscal), Mexico City, Arbeu, 27 Aug 1910
Due amori (E. Trucco), 1916
El oidor, 1924 (2, J. Péon-Contreras), ?unperf.

*

N. Slonimsky: *Music of Latin America* (New York, 1972)
J. Estrada, ed.: *La música de México* (Mexico City, 1989)

RICARDO MIRANDA-PÉREZ

Telva [Toucke], **Marian** (*b* St Louis, MO, 26 Dec 1897; *d* Norwalk, CT, 23 Oct 1962). American mezzo-soprano. As a protégée of Ernestine Schumann-Heink in New York she made her début in 1920 as the Singer in *Manon Lescaut* at the Metropolitan, where she remained till 1931. Appearing at first in small parts such as Lola (*Cavalleria rusticana*) and Marthe (*Faust*), she graduated to Mistress Quickly and Marina (*Boris Godunov*) with Shalyapin. Occasionally the big Verdi roles (Eboli and Azucena) came her way and she also sang Fricka (*Die Walküre*) but the true climax to her career came in 1927 when she sang Adalgisa to Rosa Ponselle's Norma. Recurrent in press comments on her work is the word 'capable', and this is borne out by the recording for which she is chiefly remembered, the duet 'Mira, o Norma' with Ponselle, a model of sympathetic, carefully rehearsed work by both singers. J. B. STEANE

Temirkanov, Yury (*b* Nal'chik, 10 Dec 1938). Russian conductor. He studied the violin at the Leningrad Conservatory School for Talented Children, and then conducting at the conservatory, graduating in 1965. He began conducting at the Malïy Opera Theatre, Leningrad, making his début with *La traviata*. After winning the Soviet All-Union Conductors' Competition in 1968 he became music director of the Leningrad SO the next year. From 1977 he was artistic director and chief conductor of the Kirov Opera and Ballet Theatre in Leningrad, and he made his Covent Garden début with the Kirov company in 1987, conducting his own productions of *The Queen of Spades*, *Yevgeny Onegin* and *Boris Godunov*. In 1980 he became principal guest conductor of the RPO in London and in 1988 principal conductor of the Leningrad PO, in succession to Mravinsky. Temirkanov's conducting style has drawn adverse comment for its balletic movement and fondness for bold instrumental colours, but its emotional charge has been shown to vitalize operatic performance. He has declared his uncompromising mistrust of 'producer's opera' as an encroaching threat to the lyric theatre. NOËL GOODWIN

Temistocle ('Themistocles'). Libretto by PIETRO METASTASIO, first set by Antonio Caldara (1736, Vienna).

Fearful of his power and fame, the people of Athens have driven Themistocles from the city. He believes that his daughter, Aspasia, dispatched to Argos for safety, has perished in a shipwreck, and with his son, Neocle [Neocles], has taken refuge in the land of his enemy, Serse [Xerxes], King of Persia, where he remains unrecognized. Meanwhile, Aspasia, rescued from the sea,

*'Temistocle', Act 1 scene ix (*XERXES*: 'This object of my loathing, where is he?'* THEMISTOCLES*: 'He stands already before you'.* XERXES*: 'Who is he?'* THEMISTOCLES*: 'It is I'.): engraving from the 'Opere' of Pietro Metastasio (Paris: Hérissant, 1780–82)*

has become attendant to the Princess Rossana [Roxana], now residing in Susa.

ACT 1 Aspasia learns from Sebaste [Sebastes], confidant of Xerxes, that there is a price on her father's head, information that she conveys to him when the two meet and recognize each other. She is in love with Lisimaco [Lysimachus], the Athenian ambassador, who arrives in Susa in search of Themistocles. A friend of Themistocles, but bound by patriotic duty, Lysimachus entreats Xerxes to return the fugitive to Athens to stand trial, but Xerxes refuses and Lysimachus departs. Unexpectedly, Themistocles reveals himself to the king who, admiring his courage, befriends him and offers him refuge. Roxana, in love with Xerxes, suspects Aspasia of being a rival and joins with Sebastes, now resentful of the king's new friendship, in a conspiracy against the throne.

ACT 2 Hoping to win Aspasia's love, Xerxes offers Themistocles honours and threatens Lysimachus, who has returned with new demands for Themistocles' return. Believing Aspasia dead, Lysimachus is surprised to find her in Susa but resists her pleas to choose friendship for Themistocles over patriotic duty, despite his conflicting feelings. To test his loyalty, Xerxes commands Themistocles to lead an army against Athens. He refuses, and Xerxes renounces his friendship in anger; but he is moved when Aspasia offers him her hand in marriage, a safeguard against Themistocles' extradition. Sebastes and Roxana are further spurred to revenge.

ACT 3 Unable to betray Xerxes, whom she still loves, Roxana gives him a document that reveals the conspiracy and incriminates Sebastes. Meanwhile, Themistocles, ordered by Xerxes to take an oath renouncing Greece, plans suicide in preference to betrayal of country and honour. Impressed by this stand and the virtue of Aspasia and Lysimachus, Xerxes grants general pardons, unites the lovers, and makes peace with Athens.

* * *

The coincidence of names as well as events suggests Metastasio's chief classical source for this drama to have been the Plutarch *Vitae* (Themistocles). Other early sources include Diodorus Siculus, *Bibliotheca* (book 11); Thucydides, *Historiae* (book 1); Justin's epitome of the Trogus, *Historiae* (book 2); and Cornelius Nepos, *Vitae* (Themistocles). The action of a *Thémistocle* by Pierre Du Ryer (published 1648) contains, within a web of amorous intrigues, several points of coincidence with Metastasio's plot, which has even closer parallels with Adriano Morselli's libretto for Giannettini's *Temistocle in bando* (1682, Venice) and Zeno's *Temistocle*, first set by Marc'Antonio Ziani for Vienna in 1701. Zeno has his title character take refuge with Artaxerxes who, according to Thucydides, had just ascended the throne. Nepos conforms, but Plutarch, Metastasio's source, corrects Thucydides and insists upon Xerxes. In Caldara's setting, *Temistocle* was first performed on the name day of the Austrian Emperor, Charles VI. The opera was well received, but Metastasio had found it difficult to write because of fundamental problems in the plot and a sense of lacklustre about his own writing style, the result of excessive forced productivity. *Temistocle* achieved only moderate popularity, but in 1772 a particularly successful setting by Johann Christian Bach (libretto adapted by Mattia Verazi) was given a sumptuous presentation in Mannheim with a strong cast and with a score that exploited the capability of the orchestra. Metastasio's libretto was also set as *Artaserse Longimano* (1737, by Pampini). A French, *tragédie lyrique* version related to Metastasio's libretto was set by F.-A. D. Philidor and first given at Fontainebleau in 1785.

For a list of settings *see* METASTASIO, PIETRO. DON NEVILLE

Temistocle ('Themistocles'). *Opera seria* in three acts by JOHANN CHRISTIAN BACH to a libretto by PIETRO METASTASIO (*see* TEMISTOCLE above) with alterations and additions by MATTIA VERAZI; Mannheim, Hoftheater, 5 November 1772.

In the first of his two operas for the court of the Elector Palatine Carl Theodor, Bach, responsive as ever to local fashions, broadened his musical style to accommodate the Mannheim taste. He also took advantage of the exceptional orchestral and vocal resources at his disposal to produce a score which demanded great virtuosity from all concerned. The cast included the veteran tenor Anton Raaff, who had created the title roles in Bach's two operas for Naples, and the sopranos Dorothea and Elisabeth Wendling, all three of whom were subsequently to create major roles in Mozart's *Idomeneo* (1781, Munich). There are extended arias with bassoon (at the end of Act 1) and oboe obbligato. A trio of clarinetti d'amore appears twice. However, not all of the music was new: the outer movements of the overture came from *Carattaco* (1767, London).

The recasting of Metastasio's 1736 libretto, undertaken at the command of the elector by his private secretary and court poet, Mattia Verazi, is extensive. Verazi cut, rearranged and supplemented Metastasio's recitatives in radical fashion. Only ten of the original arias remain, and two of these are partly rewritten. To these Verazi added six of his own and a duet. More importantly, he provided for the ends of Acts 2 and 3 texts calling for lengthy and complex musical structures with orchestral accompaniment of a kind then still rare in *opera seria*. Nonetheless, the use of dal segno form in all but four of the arias shows that *Temistocle* was firmly rooted in the *opera seria* tradition.

ERNEST WARBURTON

Tempelbrand, Der. Opera by Toshirō Mayuzumi; *see* KINKAKUJI.

Temperley, Nicholas (Mark) (*b* Beaconsfield, 7 Aug 1932). English musicologist. He studied at the RCM, London, and at King's College, Cambridge, where he took the PhD (1959) and later lectured, 1961–6. Having been a postdoctoral Fellow at the University of Illinois (1959–61), he then returned, becoming full professor in 1972. Temperley has done much to promote a reassessment of English 19th-century music in its social and historical context. He has worked particularly on opera in England, 1700–1900, especially Romantic English opera, and edited Loder's opera *Raymond and Agnes* (given at Cambridge, 1966). His realization of the *Beggar's Opera* was given at the University of Illinois in 1986 by Illinois Repertory Theatre. In November 1991 Illinois Opera Theatre staged his completion and orchestration of the one act of *L'oca del Cairo* for which Mozart left music.

Tempest [née Etherington], **Marie (Susan)** (*b* London, 15 July 1864; *d* London, 15 Oct 1942). English soprano. She was a pupil of Manuel García the younger at the RAM in London. At 21, she succeeded Florence St John in the title role of *Erminie*, but it was a second take-over, as *Dorothy* in Henry Leslie's revised production of Cellier's long-running comedy opera, which made her into a West End star. She played the title roles of *Doris* and *The Red Hussar* for Leslie, and repeated the latter with great success in the USA where she also appeared in Zeller's *Der Vogelhändler* and De Koven's *The Fencing Master*. On her return, George Edwardes hired her as prima donna for Daly's Theatre where she starred in the Sidney Jones musicals *An Artist's Model*, *The Geisha*, *A Greek Slave* and *San Toy*, which established that theatre as the bulwark of substantial modern musical theatre. The combination of a strong, unaffected soprano and a superior acting talent made Tempest arguably the finest of all musical players of the Victorian era. She later had a distinguished career in drama, her roles including Judith Bliss in Noël Coward's *Hay Fever*.

*

H. Bolitho: *Marie Tempest* (London, 1936)

KURT GÄNZL

Tempest, The (i) [*The Tempest, or The Enchanted Island*]. Semi-opera probably by JOHN WELDON to a text by WILLIAM DAVENANT, JOHN DRYDEN and Thomas Shadwell after WILLIAM SHAKESPEARE; London, Theatre Royal, Drury Lane, ? 7 January 1712.

Uncertainty surrounds both the dating and the authorship of this *Tempest* setting. A modern edition of the music is in vol.xix of the Purcell Society Edition; it is attributed to Purcell in the earliest printed version of the music (1786) and in most 18th-century manuscript sources. It was long regarded as Purcell's last major stage work, and only in 1964 was Purcell's authorship seriously questioned (see M. Laurie: 'Did Purcell set '*The Tempest*?', *PRMA*, 1963–4, pp.43–57) and John Weldon's claims – now generally accepted, though unproven – advanced.

Shakespeare's play was first adapted by Davenant and Dryden in 1667, with further revisions by Shadwell in 1674. The main story is retained, but some subplots are omitted or rearranged and new characters and subplots introduced; the play is made more comic, with several characters gaining new partners. Shakespeare's language is largely rewritten, or 'modernized', though occasional lines remain intact. New songs were introduced and a masque of devils inserted into Act 2; Shakespeare's fourth-act masque was cut and replaced by a grand fifth-act masque of Neptune and Amphitrite. The usual elaborate stage machinery and splendid costumes and scenery were all present in the 1674 production, for which music was contributed by Locke, Pelham Humfrey, John Banister, Pietro Reggio and G. B. Draghi.

Weldon's *Tempest* contains more music than the 1674 setting, since his style is more ornate and weightier than the earlier composers', using more repetition of text, more florid melismas and longer instrumental interludes in songs. The final masque, in particular, is more substantial than Humfrey's of 1674. Weldon's much longer masque, in contrast with Humfrey's predominantly arioso-style setting, is a series of short recitatives followed by more demanding songs, three of them full-blown da capo arias; there are also two choruses. The masque of devils, however, is written in a faster-moving, more syllabic style, with an important chorus part. Nevertheless, the song 'Arise ye subterranean winds', sung by a devil, is a virtuoso number. Ariel's songs are in a more direct, lyrical manner, except for 'Dry those eyes', which is a substantial ground bass.

The Davenant-Dryden version of *The Tempest*, popular on the stage, was given in London most years up to 1750. It is unclear, however, when the Weldon setting replaced the 1674 music, and whether it did so all at once. Purcell's 'Dear pretty youth', found in the Weldon setting, was composed in 1695, almost certainly as an addition to the 1674 music. The dances in the Weldon setting were, Laurie suggests, not composed by Weldon but hangovers from the earlier setting (one comes from Lully's *Cadmus et Hermione*). Ariel's 'Come unto these yellow sands' and 'Full fathom five' were probably composed independently of, and probably before, the two masques, and their authorship remains an open question.

Weldon's music, although it undoubtedly enhances the drama (especially where, as in the masque of devils, it reflects and explores the dramatic situation), is mostly dramatically inessential: the play makes sense without it. Even when music is dramatically desirable, such as a celebratory masque in Act 5, it is the music's function that is important, rather than its specific identity linked with specific lyrics. Accordingly, other music was sometimes substituted for this final masque (for example Purcell's masque from *Timon of Athens* in 1706 and 1707). Further, cuts were often made. Weldon's setting seems to have been used most years until 1750, by when some of its songs had been replaced with songs by Arne. After further *Tempest* settings by J. C. Smith, Boyce and Thomas Linley the younger, some of it – now attributed to Henry Purcell – found itself back on the London stage, in a production by J. P. Kemble in 1789. Several songs persisted in *Tempest* performances until 1821 when Henry Bishop finally replaced all previous *Tempest* settings with his own compositions and arrangements. IRENA CHOLIJ

Tempest, The (ii). Grand opera in three acts by JOHN C. EATON to a libretto by ANDREW PORTER after WILLIAM SHAKESPEARE's *The Tempest*; Santa Fe, Opera Theater, 27 July 1985.

Porter's libretto retains Shakespeare's language but excises descriptions, expressions of feeling and the like, thereby preserving these functions for the music. All the essential action of the original is present, compressed into three acts of unequal length. The first, the longest (lasting more than an hour), opens with a dramatic staging of the shipwreck and introduces the main characters: Prospero (baritone), Miranda (soprano), Ariel (mezzo-soprano), Caliban (female jazz singer), Ferdinand (tenor), Alonso (baritone), Gonzalo (bass), Sebastian (tenor), Antonio (tenor), Trinculo (countertenor) and Stephano (baritone). The second act, the shortest, positions the three main groups of characters (Miranda and Ferdinand; the royal party; and Caliban, Trinculo and Stephano) on three separate levels of the stage, representing different parts of the island, while Prospero observes all from above. Throughout most of the act the scene shifts back and forth among the three groups, following the characters' attempts to find their bearings on the mysterious island. Ultimately all are brought together in a final, climactic ensemble. The last act opens with the play's Masque and Antimasque ('magic shows' staged by Prospero to reward the two lovers and to punish the Caliban trio, respectively), followed by the resolution of the various conflicts and reconciliations among the characters. The opera closes with Prospero's final monologue.

To differentiate musically the various characters and dramatic levels, Eaton employs a varied stylistic palette and draws upon the full resources of a large orchestra, augmented by electronic synthesizers and two small instrumental ensembles. The 'aery spirit' Ariel, for example, is treated as something of a show-off. She sings in an elaborate coloratura manner, except when performing the set songs from the play ('Full fathom five', etc.), when her voice is modified by electronic manipulations. While carrying out Prospero's magic she is accompanied by a 'Renaissance ensemble' (recorder, shawm and lute), which plays Eaton's own highly unorthodox brand of 'early music'. The low-tessitura part of Caliban is heavily influenced by traditional blues and is accompanied by a jazz trio (alto saxophone, electric guitar and double bass). Miranda and Ferdinand sing music of an intensely lyrical nature, always associated with solo string instruments. Indeed, since the opera, like the play, turns upon matters of personal separation and individual identity, Eaton gives all the characters their own key, tempo and harmonic identity. Only Prospero commands the full range of musical resources. This aspect of the score reaches its fullest expression during the ensemble that closes the second act, when 15 solo voices, each with its own music and tempo, but coordinated by Prospero's all-embracing musical presence, join forces to produce a contrapuntal texture of remarkable richness and complexity. ROBERT P. MORGAN

Tempesta, La ('The Tempest'). Opera in a prologue and three acts by FELICE LATTUADA to a libretto by ARTURO ROSSATO after WILLIAM SHAKESPEARE's play; Milan, Teatro Dal Verme, 23 November 1922.

After a brief orchestral introduction, the opera opens with a prologue in which the King of the Island (baritone) unleashes the sea against the ships of the Usurper (bass) and watches with satisfaction the resulting shipwreck. His plan to take vengeance by bringing the Usurper and his court alive to the island is revealed in a dialogue between Ariel (soprano) and the King at the opening of the first act. Amid the cries of the shipwrecked coming ashore, the King tells his daughter Miranda (soprano) how the Usurper had robbed him of his kingdom and cast him into the sea with his child. Meanwhile the Usurper and his courtiers are bewailing the disappearance in the storm of the Usurper's son, Prince Fernando [Ferdinand] (tenor); he, however, is safe, meets Miranda and falls in love with her but is imprisoned by the King. The King kills Calibano [Caliban] (bass), who has conspired against him, and completes his revenge by compelling the Usurper to acknowledge him as king; he forgives the Usurper and the marriage between Miranda and Fernando can take place.

Lattuada interprets Shakespeare's ambiguous and subtle text in accordance with his late-Romantic sensitivity, stressing the natural setting with an accompaniment that often becomes comment on the action, and giving emphatic expression to the emotional elements. The musical and dramatic structure confirm his links with the Italian operatic tradition of the late 19th century. RAFFAELE POZZI

Tempestad, La ('The Storm'). Zarzuela in three acts by RUPERTO CHAPÍ to a libretto by MIGUEL RAMOS CARRIÓN after ERCKMANN-CHATRIAN's *Le Juif polonais*; Madrid, Teatro de la Zarzuela, 11 March 1882.

Simón (baritone), the innkeeper in a Breton coastal village, has such a horror of storms that he locks himself in his room whenever one is raging. Because of his avarice he is hated by all the neighbourhood: his sole benevolent deed has been to adopt Angela (soprano), whose father was robbed and murdered while waiting to board a ship during a storm. Simón endeavours to stop her marrying a brave but impecunious fisherman, Roberto (soprano), but is foiled when Beltrán (tenor), a rich man returning home after many years, gives Roberto a handsome reward for having saved his life. Simón accuses Beltrán of having been Angela's father's assassin, and when the dates seem to fit Beltrán is arrested, despite his protestations of innocence. But that night a storm breaks out again, and Roberto, intent on freeing Beltrán, overhears Simón having the nightmare he always suffers during tempests and confessing that he himself was the murderer. Proof is also found in a letter he has left to be read after his death. He replaces Beltrán in prison, and the wedding of the lovers can go ahead.

The major numbers in this work, Chapí's most melodramatic and one of his greatest successes, are Simón's monologue '¿Por qué temblar?', Beltrán's romance 'Salve, costa de Bretaña', and Angela's Act 3 solo 'Dardo cruel'. As in several zarzuelas of the period, the role of the hero is a 'breeches part' for soprano.

LIONEL SALTER

Tempête (Fr.: 'tempest'). A scene-type in late 17th-century and in 18th-century French opera. Usually, *tempêtes* make use of both instrumental and vocal forces in the portrayal of the wilder forces of nature. The first example is in Collasse's *Thétis et Pélée* (1689): the outer string parts feature long rushes and flourishes in very short note values (no fewer than six beams at one point) and there is an instruction for the addition of a *batterie de tambour*, conceived as a sound effect. The other important musical element is the exploitation of bass sonorities: this is particularly evident in the most celebrated of all *tempêtes*, that in Marais' *Alcyone* (1706). The complexities of the *tempête* mark one of the most radical departures from the Lullian model of opera in the decades after his death, and show the use of the orchestra as a unifying force in the construction of large-scale scenes.

C. Wood: 'Orchestra and Spectacle in the *tragédie en musique*, 1673–1715: oracle, *sommeil* and *tempête*', *PRMA*, cviii (1981–2), 25–46

CAROLINE WOOD

Temple, Richard [Cobb, Richard Barker] (*b* London, 2 March 1847; *d* London, 19 Oct 1912). English bass-baritone. Following several amateur singing appearances, he made his professional début as Rodolfo in *La sonnambula* in the inaugural production at the Crystal Palace Theatre, London (31 May 1869). He was first engaged by Richard D'Oyly Carte to play Sir Marmaduke Pointdextre in Gilbert and Sullivan's *The Sorcerer* (1877). For the next decade he was intimately identified with D'Oyly Carte's opera company, appearing in the principal bass-baritone roles from *HMS Pinafore* (1878) to *The Yeomen of the Guard* (1888). He then withdrew from the stage, but returned several years later in operatic roles at Covent Garden and several West End theatres; he later appeared in musical comedy.

Temple's voice was of a higher calibre than was usual in comic opera, and he was praised for the dignity and versatility of his acting, particularly for his 'suave and oily Mikado' (E. MacGeorge: *The Life and Reminiscences of Jessie Bond*, London, 1930). In 1910 he was appointed to the RCM, where he directed many student productions. In about 1902–3 he recorded several light operatic numbers for the Gramophone and Typewriter Company.

FREDRIC WOODBRIDGE WILSON

Temple de la Gloire, Le ('The Temple of Glory'). *Opéra-ballet* in five acts by JEAN-PHILIPPE RAMEAU to a libretto by VOLTAIRE; Versailles, La Grande Ecurie, 27 November 1745.

It had long been Voltaire's belief that opera could be both entertaining and edifying. Commissioned to write a libretto for the court celebration of the Battle of Fontenoy (1745), he produced one which concerned itself not with the traditionally all-important romantic love but with the nature of kingship. To the Temple of Glory come in turn three kings of markedly different character. Bélus [Belus] (bass), the power-hungry Assyrian, is judged unworthy to enter because of his bloodthirsty and unjust nature. The self-indulgent Bacchus (*haute-contre*), having enslaved the Indies with strong drink, is refused because of his unbridled debauchery. Only the Roman Emperor Trajan (*haute-contre*) proves worthy: after quelling a revolt, he shows magnanimity in victory and receives the crown of laurels.

In its original form the work devoted one act to each king. These were framed by a prologue-like Act 1 and an epilogue-like Act 5 in which the Temple of Glory was transformed at Trajan's request into the Temple of Happiness. By the time the work was given at the Paris Opéra (19 April 1746), it had been extensively reworked to conform with the conventional format of *opéra-ballet*: Act 1 became the prologue, 'La caverne de l'Envie'; Act 2 (almost entirely rewritten) and Act 3 became respectively the entrées 'Bélus' and 'Bacchus', while Acts 4 and 5 were combined as the entrée 'Trajan'. It is this version that virtually all musical sources preserve. The score, which became a rich source of self-borrowings, is full of interest, notably for the pastoral music of Act 1 and other ballet music, which includes the composer's elaborate reworking of his harpsichord piece 'La Cupis'. In the prologue, the monologue for L'Envie [Envy] (bass), 'Profonds abîmes du Ténare', was justly famous in Rameau's day (it may have originated in the still-born *Samson* and was cited admiringly in Diderot's *Le neveu de Rameau*). Yet Trajan's final evocation of birdsong, superb though it is, was criticized as inappropriate for a Roman emperor, especially one widely taken to represent Louis XV.

GRAHAM SADLER

Templer und die Jüdin, Der ('The Templar and the Jewess'). *Grosse romantische Oper* in three acts by HEINRICH AUGUST MARSCHNER to a libretto by Wilhelm August Wohlbrück after various plays, themselves based on WALTER SCOTT's novel *Ivanhoe*; Leipzig, Stadttheater, 22 December 1829.

Maurice de Bracy	*Norman knights*	tenor
Brian de Bois-Guilbert	*Norman knights*	baritone
Rowena of Hargottstandstede	*ward of Cedric of Rotherwood*	soprano
Cedric of Rotherwood	*Saxon knight*	bass
Wamba	*a fool in Cedric's service*	tenor
Friar Tuck	*the Hermit of Copmanhurst*	bass
The Black Knight (King Richard I, 'the Lionheart')		bass
Rebecca	*daughter of Isaac of York*	soprano
Wilfred of Ivanhoe	*son of Cedric*	tenor
Locksley	*captain of a band of outlaws*	baritone
Lucas de Beaumanoir	*Grand Master of the Knights Templars*	bass
Conrad	*a squire of Malvoisin*	choral roles
Oswald	*a steward in Cedric's service*	choral roles
Elgitha	*Rowena's maid*	choral roles
Isaac of York	*a Jew*	choral roles
Walter	*outlaws*	choral roles
Willibald	*outlaws*	choral roles
Albert Malvoisin	*Norman knight and Precept of Templestowe*	choral roles
Robert	*squires of Bois-Guilbert*	choral roles
Philip	*squires of Bois-Guilbert*	choral roles

Normans, Saxons, outlaws, townspeople, Knights Templars

Setting English forests and countryside in the neighbourhood of the Castle of Torquilstone and the Templars' Preceptory at Templestowe in 1194

After reviewing a performance of J. F. von Auffenberg's play *Der Löwe von Kurdistan*, based on Sir Walter Scott's *The Talisman*, Marschner decided – with his librettist Wohlbrück – to write an opera based on one of Scott's novels. They chose *Ivanhoe*. By eliminating non-essential characters and simplifying the plot, Wohlbrück developed the libretto from J. R. Lenz's play *Das Gericht der Templer* (Breslau, 7 May 1824), which Lenz had based on one or more of several English plays, particularly W. T. Moncrieff's *Ivanhoe! or, The Jewess* (London, 24 January 1820), that were performed in England after the publication of Scott's book.

Universally considered during the 19th century as Marschner's most popular opera, *Der Templer und die Jüdin* was performed more than any of the others – over 200 times in Germany alone. Additional performances took place in Denmark, Holland, Russia, England, the USA, and Hungary. Towards the end of the century, both Mottl and Kleinmichel simplified the libretto, eliminating several minor roles; the latter published a new edition of the vocal score in 1896. In 1912, Pfitzner overhauled the work again and published an even newer edition. A few performances using it were given, including those in Lübeck (1912), Strasbourg (1912), and Cologne (1913). Since that era, however, escalating costs and censorship have combined to discourage further productions, although a significant revival was heard at the Wexford Festival in 1989.

The cast at the Leipzig première included W. Pögner (Cedric), Ubrich (Ivanhoe), S. Löwe (Rowena), Hammermeister (Bois-Guilbert), Schütz (Black Knight), A. Wiedemann (Wamba), F. Fischer (Tuck) and F. Franchetti-Walzel (Rebecca).

ACT 1.i *A wild, romantic glen in the forest* De Bracy and his Norman knights emerge from cover to ambush Bois-Guilbert's party of Templars, but shortly after the fight starts Bois-Guilbert calls a halt to it. Each leader confesses that he intends to win a particular woman. Bois-Guilbert names the lovely Jewess Rebecca and De Bracy, relieved that Bois-Guilbert has no interest in Cedric's ward, agrees to help the Templar capture her. As they leave, Cedric and Rowena enter with Saxon knights. Cedric curses the tournament at Ashby from which he has just come because his disinherited son Ivanhoe was the victor there; Rowena, who is in love with Ivanhoe, chides him for his harshness. Cedric hates the idea of Ivanhoe marrying Rowena, but Wamba urges him in the lied ''S wird besser geh'n', nevertheless, to leave the lovers alone. Oswald rushes in to report that Isaac, Rebecca and Ivanhoe have been captured; the Saxons march off to avenge the wrong, singing their battle song 'Wer Kraft und Muth in freier Brust'. Wamba's lied, not at all the rustic folksong its title suggests, has the compound time, guitar-like accompaniment, and melodic contour characteristic of the Italian bel canto style popular at that time. But the opening and closing sections of the scene each feature a different chorus of knights singing in the more triadic and tonally conservative German style.

1.ii *Inside Friar Tuck's hut in the forest* Tuck serves wine to a mysterious guest, known as the Black Knight, while singing the drinking song, 'Der barfüssler Mönch seine Zelle verliess, Ora pro nobis!' (in performance, the piece was often censored because of the juxtaposition of texts devoted to drinking and prayer). The style here is completely German and in the final verses Tuck's refrain, 'Ora pro nobis!', is set first against a laughing counterpoint provided by the Black Knight and is then taken up by a band of outlaws who have wandered in to listen. Their leader, Locksley, recognizes the Black Knight and asks if he will help rescue an unidentified Englishman and his niece. The Black Knight readily agrees.

1.iii *An apartment in a castle turret* Locked inside the turret, Rebecca prays. Bois-Guilbert enters and claims her as his property because he won her in battle, but she wrenches herself free when Saxon soldiers attack the castle. Bois-Guilbert rushes off to join the fight and Rebecca escapes to the bedside of the wounded Ivanhoe, who convinces her that she must flee. As she leaves, the Black Knight dashes in to help Ivanhoe escape. Unlike previous scenes, this one is cast almost entirely as a series of small ensemble sections that permit maximum simultaneous interaction among characters and propel the drama forward at the frenetic pace its content demands. (This kind of musical construction enabled Marschner to break away from such of his contemporaries as Lortzing, who continued to pursue in their number operas the older and simpler style of Singspiel. Later, in *Hans Heiling*, Marschner used this new design to enhance the psychological development of characters, thereby paving the way for Wagner.)

1.iv *A courtyard inside the castle* Frenziedly seeking an escape route, Rebecca stumbles into Bois-Guilbert, who is staggering from wounds. When she refuses to elope with him, he carries her off. The fight reaches the stage and the Saxons win.

ACT 2.i *A forest clearing* The morning after the battle, Tuck, the Black Knight and a band of outlaws praise the great outdoors in a rousing Germanic hunting chorus calculated to relieve some of the tension built up in the previous act. Having discovered their merry-making, Ivanhoe enters with the Black Knight, who reveals himself to be King Richard the Lionheart, back from the Crusades.

2.ii *The hall of justice at Templestowe* The Templars enter, Beaumanoir presiding, followed by Bois-Guilbert, the victim of Rebecca's supposed powers of witchcraft. Ordered to stand trial by ordeal, Rebecca must name a champion to face a representative of the Templars. When Bois-Guilbert offers to fight on her behalf, the knights pick him as their representative. He sinks to the ground in despair.

ACT 3.i *Richard's throne room* The king listens as Ivanhoe extends his praise for Richard to all of England in the stirring patriotic *Romanze* 'Wer ist der Ritter hochgeehrt' (a piece that became so popular that audiences would join in at the anthem-like refrain, 'Du stolzes England, freue dich', as they do in *Iolanthe*). Wamba provides a facetious commentary on their seriousness in his equally famous lied 'Es ist doch gar köstlich, ein König zu sein'.

3.ii *A dungeon in Templestowe* In a fervent prayer (preghiera) with ethereal harp-like accompaniment, 'Herr, aus tiefen Jammersnöthen', Rebecca begs for deliverance from an unjust fate. Bois-Guilbert knocks on the door and offers to undergo the scourging of a dishonoured knight if she will only love him, but she refuses as guards take her away.

3.iii *The tournament grounds* The Templars march in to join Rebecca, who stands in chains. Bois-Guilbert begs her to escape with him, but she prefers the stake. Ivanhoe appears unexpectedly as her champion, and the duel begins. Initially, Bois-Guilbert seems to be winning, but as he is about to deal Ivanhoe a crushing blow, he drops dead. The king enters and asserts his authority over the land as the Templars bear off Bois-Guilbert's body.

* * *

As a Schilleresque historical drama, *Der Templer und die Jüdin* is close in structure to Weber's *Euryanthe* (as opposed to *Der Freischütz*, the model for *Der Vampyr*, which is more a Gothic romance) and embodies a mixture of German and Italian elements. There are extended sections of *secco* recitative; but there are also sections of choral writing that draw on the traditions of the German choral society (to one of which Marschner belonged), with its direct, diatonic writing. More forward-looking are the flexibly constructed scenes, some of them using ensemble sections that permit maximum interaction between characters and help to propel the drama forward. A. DEAN PALMER

Templeton, John (*b* Riccarton, nr Kilmarnock, 30 July 1802; *d* New Hampton, nr London, 2 July 1886). Scottish tenor. After appearances in the provinces (1828–30), he made his London début at Drury Lane in 1831 as Belville in William Shield's *Rosina*. In 1832 he sang Raimbaut in the British première of *Robert le diable* and the following year scored a brilliant success as the first British Don Ottavio. In 1833 he appeared with Malibran in *La sonnambula* and later sang with her in *Fidelio* and Balfe's *The Maid of Artois*. He took the leading tenor roles in the first performances in English of Auber's *Le cheval de bronze* (1836), *Zampa* (1836), *Le siège de Corinthe* (1836), *Die Zauberflöte* (1838) and *La favorite* (1843).

*

J. Templeton: *A Musical Entertainment* (Boston, MA, 1845)
W. H. Husk: *Templeton and Malibran* (London, 1880)
HAROLD ROSENTHAL/R

Tempo d'attacco (It.: 'movement of *attacco*', i.e. of the opening). In Italian opera of the 19th century, the first, fast movement of a closed number following the recitative or scena (slow cantabile sections are never so qualified). It is most commonly applied to duets, whether in two movements or the more usual three. In finales that lack an initial chorus the 'cinetic' movement that precedes the *pezzo concertato* may be described as a 'tempo d'attacco', e.g. 'Teco sperai combattere' (*Alzira*, Verdi, 1845). 'La mia spada è la più fida' (*La donna del lago*, Rossini, 1819) unusually provides the material for the concluding stretta. The term can also be used for the opening movement of a triple aria, e.g. 'Ah sì, per voi già sento' (*Otello*, Rossini, 1816). JULIAN BUDDEN

Tempo di mezzo (It.: 'middle movement'). In Italian opera of the 19th century, a fast transitional passage that separates a cantabile from a cabaletta or a *pezzo concertato* from a *stretta*. It is generally free in form and varies in length according to the dramatic situation, its prime function being to effect the required change of mood. In an aria this may involve the entrance and departure of a secondary character, e.g. Foresto in the case of Ezio's 'Dagli immortali vertici' (*Attila*, Verdi, 1846), whose news of an ambush causes the Roman general to break out in exultation. In the duet 'Il pallor funesto orrendo' (*Lucia di Lammermoor*, Donizetti, 1835) the *tempo di mezzo* consists mainly of a flourish of offstage horns announcing the arrival of Arturo, whose marriage to Lucia will save her brother from financial ruin. The *tempo di mezzo* of a central finale is often very complex and may contain a reprise of *parlante* material from the 'cinetic' movement that precedes the *pezzo concertato*, as happens in the Act 1 finale of Rossini's *Tancredi* (1813) and the Act 2 finale of *Lucia di Lammermoor*. For a *tempo di mezzo* of unique dramatic importance see the dialogue of the two queens in the Act 2 finale of Donizetti's *Maria Stuarda* (1834), a *parlante* of 199 bars whose climax seals the heroine's fate. JULIAN BUDDEN

Tempranica, La ('The Headstrong Girl'). Zarzuela in one act (three scenes) by JERÓNIMO GIMÉNEZ to a libretto by Julián Romea; Madrid, Teatro de la Zarzuela, 19 September 1900.

Don Luis (baritone), a young nobleman, was once injured in the mountains near Granada and tended by a gypsy family whose young daughter, Maria (soprano), nicknamed 'La tempranica', fell passionately in love with him and was heartbroken when he returned home. Now, some years later, he is again in the area with a hunting party. Among its members is an Englishman who wants to hear genuine folk music; a youngster (mezzo-soprano) entertains the company with a brilliant *zapateado*. He is Maria's brother and, recognizing Luis, informs her of his presence. Despite being about to marry a young gypsy, Maria pleads passionately with Luis, but he tells her that he is married. She cannot bring herself to believe him, and only a visit to Granada, where she sees his wife and little son, forces her to realize that she must stay with the gypsies to whom she belongs.

The first production of this zarzuela, whose text makes much use of Andalusian modes of speech, ran for three whole years. Federico Moreno Torroba later made an operatic version of it. LIONEL SALTER

Tenaglia [Tanaglia, Tanaglino], **Antonio Francesco** (*b* Florence, *c*1610–20; *d* Rome, after 1661). Italian composer. By 1644 he was in Rome in the service of Donna Olimpia Aldobrandini, wife of Camillo Pamphili. In September of that year he became a musician in Cardinal Antonio Barberini's household and thus an associate of Giovanni Lotti (whose poetry he set) and Luigi Rossi, whom he emulated and whom he acknowledged in his cantata *Che volete ch'io canti*. By 1648 he had left Rome to work abroad; he may have served the cardinal during his exile in Lyons.

In 1654 Tenaglia was again in Rome, as a keyboard virtuoso and lutenist. In 1656, when the Roman aristocracy organized splendid festivities in honour of Queen Christina of Sweden, he seems to have been connected with the Pamphili: his opera *Il giudizio di Paride* (G. Lotti) was performed at the Palazzo Pamphili during Carnival in honour of the queen. Another theatrical work by him, the *favola musicale Il Clearco* (L. Cortesi), was performed in 1661. Both operas are lost, but Tenaglia's many solo cantatas, widely known and much appreciated in his day, show him to have been a composer of powerful and audacious imagination and extraordinary musicality.

*

A. Ademollo: *I teatri di Roma nel secolo decimosettimo* (Rome, 1888)
H. Prunières: 'Les musiciens du Cardinal Antonio Barberini', *Mélanges de musicologie offerts à M. Lionel de La Laurencie* (Paris, 1933), 117–22
ELEANOR CALUORI

Tender Land, The. Opera in three acts by AARON COPLAND to a libretto by Horace Everett [Erik Johns] after James Agee's book *Let us now Praise Famous Men*; New York, City Center Theater, 1 April 1954.

Copland's second opera was commissioned by Richard Rodgers and Oscar Hammerstein II through the League of Composers for the society's 30th anniversary. Set in the American Mid-west in the mid-1930s during harvest time, the plot concerns a farm family: Ma Moss (contralto), her daughter Laurie (soprano), about to graduate from high school, Laurie's ten-year-old sister Beth (spoken) and Grandpa Moss (bass). Two drifters, Martin (tenor) and Top (baritone), appear at the farmhouse asking for odd jobs. Grandpa and Ma Moss are reluctant, since they have heard reports of two men molesting young girls in the area, but with Laurie's urging, the men are hired. Martin and Top are accused of being the molesters. Although the accusations are soon proved false, the men are asked to leave in the morning. At the party the evening before graduation, Laurie and Martin fall in love and plan to run away together. Top convinces Martin that the road is no place for Laurie. When Laurie discovers that Martin has gone without her, she decides to leave home anyway. Ma Moss looks to her younger daughter as the continuation of the family legacy.

In *The Tender Land* Copland combines traditional operatic set pieces and recitative with a naturalistic language appropriate for college students and opera workshops. The music is diatonic, in the style of his popular ballet music, with only occasional dissonances for dramatic purposes. The score incorporates several folksongs and is written in a simple style for small orchestra. Commissioned as a television opera, the work was rejected by NBC but accepted by the New York City Opera. Jerome Robbins was director and Thomas Schippers conducted. Norman Treigle created the role of Grandpa Moss. Originally the opera was in two acts, but following the première, which received mixed reviews, Copland and Johns turned it into a full-length three-act work; this version was first performed at Oberlin, Ohio, by the Oberlin College opera workshop (20 May 1955). It has rarely been produced since, though a concert version was given at the Lincoln Center (31 July 1965) from which excerpts were recorded. A recording of the complete opera was released by Virgin Classics in 1990. For a 1987 revival at the Long Wharf Theatre, New Haven, Connecticut, the conductor Murry Sidlin revised the score for 13 instruments. Soon after the original production, Copland arranged an orchestral suite and prepared choral settings of 'The Promise of Living' and 'Stomp Your Foot', which may be used alone or with the suite. These two sections were arranged also for piano duet, and the aria 'Laurie's Song' exists in a version for high voice and piano.

VIVIAN PERLIS

Tenducci, Giusto Ferdinando (*b* Siena, *c*1735; *d* Genoa, 25 Jan 1790). Italian soprano castrato and composer. He made his début in Cagliari in 1750, during the wedding festivities of the Duke of Savoy. After appearing both in minor roles and in comic opera in Milan, Naples, Venice, Dresden and Munich, in 1758 he went to London, where he spent two seasons at the King's Theatre and sang in Cocchi's *Il ciro riconisciuto* as secondo uomo. His extravagant living led to a short spell in a debtors' prison in 1760, but in 1762 he created Arbaces in Arne's *Artaxerxes*, subsequently appearing in the première of J. C. Bach's *Adriano in Siria* (1765). He visited Dublin in 1765 and the following year (despite some scandal) married Dora Maunsell, the daughter of a Dublin lawyer. According to Casanova the couple had two children (though a castrato, his nickname was 'Triorchis', or 'triple-testicled'). Tenducci spent a year or more in Edinbugh before returning in 1770 to London, where he sang in a pasticcio of Gluck's *Orfeo* and was responsible for popularizing 'Che farò'. Impressed with 'Scotch' songs, he persuaded his friend J. C. Bach to arrange some for insertion into English operas, a practice which was then widely adopted by other composers, notably Linley in *The Duenna*. Tenducci sang in ten Italian cities (repeating *Orfeo* in Florence) up to 1776 and then appeared in London (1777–85), Paris (1777) and Dublin (1783–4). Smollett described his voice as particularly lyrical and the *ABCDario Musico* (Bath, 1780) compared him with Gioacchino Conti; he was widely known as another Seresino. He adapted several operas, but none was very successful; his singing tutor *Instruction of Mr Tenducci to his Scholars* (London, 1782) is of more lasting value.

all first performed in Dublin

Amintas (R. Rolt, after P. Metastasio), July 1765 [all-sung adaptation of G. Rush: The Royal Shepherd]; with addns by S. Arnold, London, CG, 15 Dec 1769, Act 2 (London, 1769)

The Revenge of Athridates, 1767 [trans. and adaptation of D. Perez: Il Farnace]; Favourite Songs (London, 1767)

Il castello d'Andalusia, 1783 [? adaptation of Arnold: The Castle of Andalusia]

The Campaign (afterpiece with spoken dialogue, Jephson), 1784; arr. W. Shield, London, CG, 1785

*

J. C. Hadden: *George Thomson, Friend of Burns* (London, 1898)
C. S. Terry: *Johann Christian Bach* (London, 1929, 2/1967)
A. Heriot: *The Castrati in Opera* (London, 1958)
T. J. Walsh: *Opera in Dublin, 1705–1797* (Dublin, 1973)
D. E. Monson: 'Galuppi, Tenducci, and Motezuma: a Commentary on the History and Musical Style of Opera Seria after 1750', *Galuppiana 1985: studi e ricerche: Venice 1986*, 279–300

ROGER FISKE, DALE E. MONSON

Tenerife. Island in the Canary Islands; for a discussion of operatic activity *see* SANTA CRUZ DE TENERIFE.

Tennstedt, Klaus (*b* Merseburg, 6 June 1926). German conductor. He studied at the Leipzig Conservatory and began his career as a violinist, leading the orchestra at Halle from 1948 and becoming principal conductor there. He made his operatic début in 1952 conducting Wagner-Régeny's *Der Günstling*. He moved to Chemnitz and then to Dresden in 1958; there he was Generalmusikdirektor at the Landestheater, where he gave several modern works (including operas by von Einem, Liebermann and Weill), and he conducted at the Dresden Staatsoper. From 1962 he was music director at Schwerin, and appeared at the East Berlin Staatsoper and Komische Oper, where he worked with Felsenstein. He settled in the West in 1971, as music director at Kiel Opera and as guest conductor at major opera houses including Munich and the Deutsche Oper, Berlin; he gave the first German performance of von Einem's *Der Besuch der alten Dame* there in 1972, following its Vienna première. His reputation rapidly spread after his American début with the Boston SO in 1974, taking him to the Metropolitan for *Fidelio* in 1983, but he has since worked chiefly in the symphonic repertory. He is most admired for his command of form and depth of perception in major classics of the Romantic repertory.

NOËL GOODWIN

Tenor (from Lat. *tenere*: 'to hold'; Fr. *ténor*, *taille*; Ger. *Tenor*). The highest natural male voice, usually written for in the range *c–a′*, which may be extended at either end. In medieval and Renaissance polyphony the word signified a 'holding' part, often written in long notes, to which other parts sung by male voices, a 'contratenor altus' and 'contratenor bassus', were added; the term came to refer to a part occupying a particular vocal range in a three-voice male ensemble, with an alto part above it and a bass part below, and hence to the voice pitched in that range.

1. Up to 1750. 2. 1750–1800. 3. After 1800: voice types: (i) Introduction (ii) The tenor in Romantic opera. 4. Singers and roles: the 19th century: (i) Italian, French and Russian opera (ii) German opera. 5. Singers and roles: the 20th century.

1. UP TO 1750. The tenor voice was the most important for solo and virtuoso singing in the 16th century, and many writers on music and singing were themselves tenors (notably Giulio Caccini, one of the earliest opera composers). During the first decades of opera it retained this position; the role of Orpheus in the *Euridice* operas of Peri and Caccini is a tenor one, as is Monteverdi's in his *Orfeo*, where the role was probably sung by Francesco Rasi; the title role in his *Il ritorno d'Ulisse in patria* (1640) is also for tenor, but the principal male part of *L'incoronazione di Poppea* (1643), that of Nero, is for a castrato, as are other secondary roles. Several operas by Cavalli have principal parts for tenors (Ormindo and Egisto, for example); but during the remainder of the 17th century heroic roles and those of lovers were increasingly assigned to castratos, and tenors came to be allotted only small or comic roles, as servants, grotesques (for example Irus in *Il ritorno d'Ulisse*) or even, in travesty, old women, especially nurses. Tenors were also often cast as kings and fathers, particularly tyrants and heavy fathers, the stereotypes to which they were largely confined in the early 18th century. In the operas of Alessandro Scarlatti the tenor is normally subordinate to the castrato; in his *Tigrane*, for example, 11 of the 52 arias go to the castrato hero, in the title role, while the principal tenor has only four.

By the second decade of the 18th century tenors were beginning to be assigned more significant roles, though still only rarely the central heroic ones. Handel wrote for several tenors of distinction. Francesco Borosini, the son of another Italian tenor who had performed in operas by Steffani and Caldara, went to London in 1724 and sang Handel's first important tenor role, Bajazet in *Tamerlano* (1724), a role he had earlier sung in a setting of the same story by Francesco Gasparini; he also created Grimoaldo (*Rodelinda*, 1725) and Handel rewrote for him with much new music the part of Sextus in *Giulio Cesare*, originally for soprano. Borosini was a composer, as too was Annibale Pio Fabri, a tenor who sang widely in Italy in the 1720s and created several important Handel roles, Berengario (*Lotario*, 1729), Emilio (*Partenope*, 1730) and Alexander (*Poro*, 1731), as well as several that the composer adapted for him; Burney wrote that 'the merit of this tenor was often sufficient in Italy to supply the want of it in the principal soprano'. He later pursued his career in Italy, Spain and Portugal. The English tenor John Beard sang in ten Handel operas, creating roles in several of them including Lurcanio in *Ariodante* and Oronte in *Alcina* (both 1735). He later sang all the main tenor parts in Handel's oratorios and appeared in English operas, notably in works by J. C. Smith and in Arne's *Artaxerxes* (1762).

In France, where the castrato voice was not normally used in opera (it was occasionally heard in sacred music), most heroic roles were assigned not to the true tenor but to the HAUTE-CONTRE, a very high tenor voice (with resemblances to the English countertenor); the true tenor voice, known as the TAILLE before the term *ténor* came into general use, was little used for important solo parts, though there are occasional examples in the operas of Lully and Rameau. When Gluck's Viennese operas calling for castrato soloists were arranged for Paris he rewrote these parts for *haute-contre*.

2. 1750–1800. During the later part of the era of Metastasian opera the principal tenor began to assume an importance only one step below that of the prima donna and the primo uomo (who was a castrato). In Mozart's *Mitridate, re di Ponto* (1770), in fact, the tenor (Guglielmo d'Ettore, again himself a composer) sang the title role, and was assigned five arias, more than the principals, though his are shorter; the pattern of tenors as kings is sustained throughout Mozart's serious Italian operas (*Mitridate*, *Lucio Silla*, *Idomeneo*, *La clemenza di Tito*), as in those of his contemporaries. In *opera buffa* or *dramma giocoso* of the Goldoni era, however, there was normally no place for a castrato and the roles of young lovers are almost invariably sung by tenors.

Casting patterns were of course dependent on circumstances; Mozart's Count Almaviva in *Le nozze di Figaro* (1786) might well have been a tenor had the Viennese company had a suitable one at the time (the only tenor was Michael Kelly, a *tenore buffo* and a composer, who created Don Basilio and Don Curzio). The leading Viennese tenor in Mozart's time was the German, Valentin Adamberger, who created Belmonte in *Die Entführung aus dem Serail* (1782) and sang in a number of Gluck revivals; but most of Mozart's tenor roles in his Viennese years were created by singers of no great reputation: Antonio Baglioni (Don Ottavio in *Don Giovanni*, 1787, and the title role in *La clemenza di Tito*, 1791), Vincenzo Calvesi (Ferrando in *Così fan tutte*, 1790) and Benedikt Schack (Tamino in *Die Zauberflöte*, 1791, once more a composer).

The most famous tenor for whom Mozart composed was his first Idomeneus, Anton Raaff, who in 1781 was close to the end of his career, in Munich; he had been a pupil of the famous castrato Bernacchi in Bologna, who emphasized legato singing and *portamento*, and had sung in many German centres, in Venice, Vienna, Lisbon and Madrid, in Naples and Florence (where he was a leading figure in the 1760s), and finally at Mannheim and Munich. He was probably the foremost tenor in serious opera in the age of Hasse, Jommelli and J. C. Bach, creating many roles; according to Kelly, he still retained his fine *voce di petto* and pure style when he was 73.

3. AFTER 1800: VOICE TYPES.

(i) Introduction. The changes in opera, and indeed in society, around the turn of the century affected the ways the tenor voice was treated. The earlier idea that an opera was created for one particular occasion (or series of occasions), and accordingly that each role should be composed to suit the capacities of a particular singer, though it survived (especially in Italy) well into the 19th century, began to fade as a consolidated repertory gradually came into existence and singers increasingly had to perform music not specifically composed for them. This inevitably led to some degree of classification

of different types of the tenor voice, role types and singers. In terms of power and weight the categories begin with the lyric tenor, with roles such as Rossini's Almaviva, Elvino in *La sonnambula* and Nadir in *Les pêcheurs de perles* (the *tenore di grazia* is a special category of this, meaning a high voice apt to the florid writing of the serious operas of Rossini and his contemporaries; another is the *ténor leger*). The lyric-dramatic is represented by Rodolfo, the Duke and Faust, and the *lirico spinto* by Don Alvaro in *La forza del destino*, Chénier and perhaps Lohengrin (the term *tenore di forza* or *fort-ténor* is also sometimes used, generally for the more dramatic roles of Donizetti and French grand opera). The *tenore robusto* or heroic tenor, a sturdier voice, often more baritonal in timbre, serves for the more vigorously dramatic roles of Verdi – Ernani, Manrico and in particular Otello – and is the counterpart of the German *Heldentenor*, usually identified with Wagner, especially Tristan and Siegfried (Wagner complained about tenors who were 'unmanly, soft and completely lacking in energy'). This type is already foreshadowed by the heroic roles of the late 18th century and the early 19th, of which Beethoven's Florestan (*Fidelio*, 1805) is the most familiar. A quite different aspect of the tenor voice, in what might be called anti-heroic roles, was exploited especially by Wagner in his characterization of the dwarf Mime (*Siegfried*), chattering, sly, would-be ingratiating, sometimes snarling with malice; a variant of this comes in Loge (*Das Rheingold*). This can be seen as a development of the type represented by Monostatos (*Die Zauberflöte*); other types of *comprimario* tenor are found in smaller character roles such as Goro the marriage broker (*Madama Butterfly*) or the elderly Emperor Altoum (*Turandot*). A highly specialized type of tenor is the *tenor altino* (or *contraltino*) which extends into the treble region without breaking into falsetto; an example (though here the composer did expect falsetto) is the Astrologer in Rimsky-Korsakov's *The Golden Cockerel*.

National differences have been notable, too, with the Russians specializing in a high, penetrative tone which other nationalities sometimes regard as 'white' or colourless, while the Germans have tried to meet their own need for heavy voices, frequently at the expense of grace or sweetness. The traditional French tenor is lyrical in manner, possibly a shade reedy in timbre, and an elegant stylist; there also exist two types of French character tenor, the 'Laruette' (comic old men) and the 'Trial' (nasal in timbre, suitable for simpletons), named after particular singers of the 18th century. The Italian tenor has for so long been famous as a species throughout the world, with Enrico Caruso, then Beniamino Gigli and most recently Luciano Pavarotti as popular figures in their time, that there may be too limited an awareness of the loss opera is likely to sustain now at a time when the supply seems to be decreasing. A remarkable feature in recent years has been the prominence of foreign tenors in Italian theatres; and possibly the least anticipated development has been the resurgence of a practical interest in the bel canto repertory, when scholars and enthusiasts have been promoting the revival of many forgotten works in opera houses and at festivals.

(ii) The tenor in Romantic opera. The tenor voice gained pre-eminence on the operatic stage with the rise of Romantic opera. As composers and librettists turned away from the grand passions of classical tragedy, the characters in their operas increasingly became 'ordinary' human beings. They graduated through the monarchy, aristocracy and attendant deities to the middle classes (as for example in *La traviata*), eventually to embrace the more artistic elements in lower-class life (as in *La bohème* and *Louise*). A love story was almost invariably central to the plot, most frequently involving a soprano and tenor, since there seems to have been a general disposition to believe that youth is best represented by the higher voice-ranges and that these are also the voices most appropriate to the conducting of a love affair on stage. One may object that depth of voice is no very reliable indication of age (or indeed of the capacity for romance); but it would have been thought remiss of Verdi had he cast *La traviata* with the son as a baritone and a tenor for his father, while the mature wisdom of Hans Sachs in *Die Meistersinger* would not be suitably voiced by a tenor any more than it would be thought proper were a bass-baritone to have won the singing competition and Eva with it.

Verdi and Wagner did most to define the scope of the modern operatic tenor. Earlier in the 19th century, Rossini and his contemporaries required a high degree of accomplishment in florid work, and in many of their operas, as in some of Bellini's, great demands are made on the upper range of the voice. Rossini's *Semiramide* and Bellini's *I puritani*, for instance, show the ready availability of notes above the staff to have been taken for granted, and in *I puritani* the solo 'Credeasi misera' notoriously rises to an *f″* (though this, written for G. B. Rubini, is exceptional). Opinions differ in analysis of the historical implications of such writing. It may be that these high notes were habitually taken in the head-voice (*voce di testa*), or in some kind of fortified falsetto, or by means of a production which was neither quite one nor the other (variously referred to, with differing connotations, as the *voce finta*, the 'feigned voice', the pharyngeal voice and the mixed voice).

Prominent in the evidence adduced for this belief is the overnight sensation caused at the Paris Opéra in 1837 when Gilbert Duprez sang a *c″* in *Guillaume Tell* with the full chest-voice (*ut de poitrine*). What caused this to become such a famous event was not so much the quality of the note, which some considered highly disagreeable, as the fact that it could be sung in this way at all. Duprez's predecessor in the role, Adolphe Nourrit, had sung these notes in the head-voice, which, according to Rossini, was how they should be sung. Nourrit also took the tenor lead in the premières of *Le comte Ory*, *Les Huguenots*, *Robert le diable* and *La Juive*, so it may well be that the top notes in these too were originally taken with the head-voice rather than in the full-bodied tenor tone we expect today. Some historians and students of the voice conclude that tenors with the ringing type of high notes familiar to us on records from the time of Francesco Tamagno (creator of Verdi's Otello) onwards are a relatively modern phenomenon, dating from roughly the 1840s, when singers began to emulate Duprez. Others claim that, whatever the practice at the Opéra, there is no evidence that Italian tenors sang with falsetto or 'mixed' tone, but rather that the Italian tradition was against it, and that there was probably no need for it as the orchestration of the time allowed a lighter kind of voice production so that such tenor roles as Rossini's and Bellini's could be managed successfully, as they have been in recent times by tenors properly trained to that end.

From the mid-century onwards tenors were called upon to meet increasing demands for vocal and dramatic power. The last great exponent of the elegant style associated with operas of the so-called bel canto school in the earlier part of the century was Giovanni Rubini, who was widely considered to be an anachronism in the musical world well before his death in 1854. His successor, the tenor G. M. Mario, endowed with exceptional beauty of tone, did less for the status of the tenor as virtuoso but more for his acceptability as the hero of romance. Even so, the most significant developments in opera were such as to create the need for a type of tenor voice that could hold its own against the ever more ample and important orchestra, while having sufficient stamina to come through one performance of the great Wagnerian music dramas with enough voice left for the next. The prototypes here were Enrico Tamberlik, creator of Don Alvaro in *La forza del destino*, and the Bohemian Joseph Tichatschek, who was the original Rienzi and Tannhäuser. The process culminated in the *Heldentenor* roles of Tristan and Siegfried and, in Italian opera, Verdi's Otello. The romantic tenor reached his apogee shortly afterwards in the operas of Puccini, Mascagni, Leoncavallo and their school. The later 20th century has brought diversification, with operas such as Stravinsky's *The Rake's Progress* and Walton's *Troilus and Cressida* making fairly traditional use of the lyric-dramatic type, 'romantic' though in different senses, while Berg's *Wozzeck* and *Lulu* deromanticize the voice altogether and *Peter Grimes* gives the tenor dramatic opportunities comparable to the bass-baritone's in *Boris Godunov*.

4. SINGERS AND ROLES: THE 19TH CENTURY.

(i) Italian, French and Russian opera. Among the tenors for whom Rossini composed were two pupils of Giacomo Davide (himself a famous tenor): his son Giovanni Davide and Andrea Nozzari. In 1813 Rossini wrote Narciso in *Il turco in Italia* at La Scala for Giovanni Davide, then 23; this was the first of six Rossini premières in which he took part. At Naples, where Rossini's *Elisabetta, regina d'Inghilterra* (1815) marked the start of a group of serious operas for Isabella Colbran, Davide found Nozzari already installed. They complemented one another perfectly: Davide's voice was very flexible, with a compass of three octaves, especially strong at the top, while the main strength of Nozzari's voice, baritonal in quality, lay in the middle register. Nozzari sang Leicester in *Elisabetta*; he took the title role of *Otello* with Davide as Rodrigo; they both sang in *Ricciardo e Zoraide*, *Ermione* and *Zelmira*, as well as *La donna del lago*, in which Nozzari sang Roderick Dhu and Davide was James; Nozzari also took part in the premières of *Armida* (as Rinaldo), *Mosè in Egitto* and *Maometto II*. He later created the title role of Donizetti's *Alfredo il grande* (1823).

Another tenor associated with Rossini was Manuel García, who created Norfolk in *Elisabetta* and also Almaviva in *Il barbiere di Siviglia* (1816) at Rome; he was greatly admired for his Otello, which he sang at the London première of Rossini's opera. Rubini also scored many triumphs as Otello: his voice, with a very powerful falsetto extension up to *f''* or *g''*, inspired several composers, in particular Donizetti and Bellini. Between 1822 and 1835 he sang in the premières of eight Donizetti operas, including *L'esule di Roma*, *Alina, regina di Golconda*, *Gianni di Calais*, *Anna Bolena* (in which he sang Percy) and *Marino Faliero*. During the period 1826–35 Rubini created Bellini's Gernando in *Bianca e Gernando*, Gualtiero in *Il pirata*, Elvino in *La sonnambula* and Arturo in *I puritani*. These roles, with their very high tessitura and long, flowing vocal lines, were tailored to Rubini's special talents. One need only compare them with Bellini's roles for other tenors – Arturo (*La straniera*, 1829) for Domenico Reina, Pollione (*Norma*, 1831) for Domenico Donzelli (earlier the creator of two Rossini roles), Orombello (*Beatrice di Tenda*, 1833) for Alberico Curioni, all with heavier and lower voices – to realize the care Bellini took in writing for individual singers.

In the Paris première of *Marino Faliero* at the Théâtre Italien, when Rubini sang Fernando, the Russian tenor Nikola Ivanoff, a protégé of Glinka, sang the offstage Gondolier's Barcarolle. As Ivanoff passed his whole career in Western Europe, the tenor roles in Glinka's operas, Sobinin in *A Life for the Tsar* (1836) and Finn in *Ruslan and Lyudmila* (1842), fell to Leon Leonov, whose basically lyrical voice could encompass roles as different as Almaviva and Robert le diable. Feodor Komissarzhevsky, a tenor of stronger but still lyrical timbre, created roles in operas by four distinguished Russians: Don Juan in Dargomïzhsky's *The Stone Guest* (1872), Grigory in *Boris Godunov* (1874), Sinodal in Rubinstein's *The Demon* (1875) and the title role of Tchaikovsky's *Vakula the Smith* (1876). In *Cherevichki* (1887), the revised version of Tchaikovsky's opera, Vakula was first sung by Dmitry Usatov, who sang Lensky in the first professional performance of *Yevgeny Onegin* (1881) and created Andrey in *Mazepa* (1884); he was also a notable exponent of Sobinin and Finn. Nikolay Figner, after singing in Italy and at Covent Garden, where his roles were Ernani, Elvino and the Duke, went back to Russia to sing in two Tchaikovsky premières, creating Hermann in *The Queen of Spades* (1890), and Vaudémont in *Iolanta* (1892); later he became a powerful Radames and Otello. Hermann was sung in the British première of *The Queen of Spades* by Vladimir Rosing, while Dmitry Smirnov, whose voice was the most typical as well as the finest of all Russian tenors heard in Western Europe before the Revolution, sang Grigory in the first performance at the Paris Opéra of *Boris Godunov*; he also sang the Prince in Dargomïzhsky's *Rusalka* at Monte Carlo and Levko in the British première of Rimsky-Korsakov's *May Night*. Other notable Russian tenors, of the next generation, include Ivan Yershov and Ivan Kozlovsky.

In Paris during the 1820s and 30s the leading tenor at the Opéra-Comique was Jean Baptiste Chollet, for whom Auber wrote several roles, including Fritz in *La fiancée* (1829) and Fra Diavolo (1830). Hérold wrote Henri in *Marie* (1826) and Zampa (1831) for Chollet, and Halévy composed Lionel in *L'éclair* (1835) for him; but his best and most popular creation was Chapelou in Adam's *Le postillon de Lonjumeau* (1836), in which he could display his magnificently strong and secure *d''*s. The tenor roles in Rossini's works for the Opéra (1826–9), *Le siège de Corinthe*, *Moïse et Pharaon*, *Le comte Ory* and *Guillaume Tell*, were all adapted for the voice of Adolphe Nourrit, who combined the flexibility, range and tonal brilliance of Davide with the strength of Nozzari. Particularly successful as Arnold in *Guillaume Tell*, he had no difficulty with the high tessitura. Auber wrote Masaniello in *La muette de Portici* (1828) for him and he also created Eléazar in Halévy's *La Juive* (1835), Meyerbeer's Robert le diable and Raoul in *Les Huguenots*. Nourrit was replaced as principal tenor at the Opéra by Gilbert Duprez.

Although French by birth, Duprez studied in Italy and sang there for several years, creating Ugo in Donizetti's *Parisina* (1833), Henry II in *Rosmonda d'Inghilterra* (1834) and, scoring an enormous personal success, Edgardo in *Lucia di Lammermoor* (1835). His voice, though less trumpet-toned, was similar in quality and range to that of Nourrit, many of whose roles he took over on his appointment to the Opéra. He created the title role of *Benvenuto Cellini* (1838) and sang in the premières of three of Donizetti's French operas: as Polyeucte (*Les martyrs*, 1840), Fernand (*La favorite*, 1840) and Dom Sébastien (1843). He also sang Gaston in Verdi's *Jérusalem* (1847), the French adaptation of *I Lombardi*.

Many Italian tenors had to adapt their vocal styles to the demands of Verdi's early operas. Lorenzo Salvi, who took part in five Donizetti premières (1830–41) – *Il diluvio universale*, *Il furioso all'isola di San Domingo*, *Betly*, *Adelia* and *Gianni di Parigi* (written for Rubini though he never sang it) – created Riccardo in Verdi's first opera, *Oberto* (1839), and Edoardo in his second, *Un giorno di regno* (1840), both lyrical roles. Carlo Guasco, having sung Riccardo, Count de Chalais in Donizetti's *Maria di Rohan* (1843), created Oronte in *I Lombardi* (1843), the title role of *Ernani* (1844) and Foresto in *Attila* (1846), still relatively lyrical roles. Gaetano Fraschini, the first Zamoro in *Alzira* (1845), Corrado in *Il corsaro* (1848), Arrigo in *La battaglia di Legnano* (1849) and Stiffelio (1850), had a more powerful voice than Salvi or Guasco and was able to dominate Verdi's increasingly heavy orchestration.

By mid-century tenors who appeared at the Italian Opera in London were required to take on roles of very varied weight and character, from Mozart to Meyerbeer. After the retirement of Rubini, Mario, by nature a lyric tenor, who had created Ernesto in *Don Pasquale* (1843), added a falsetto extension to his voice to allow him to sing the Rubini roles of Bellini and Donizetti. At the same time he embarked on the heavier Verdi repertory, singing Oronte and Jacopo Foscari (Verdi wrote a new cabaletta rising to *f''* for him) and later the Duke, Alfredo, Riccardo (*Un ballo in maschera*) and Manrico. Manrico was first sung in London by Enrico Tamberlik, a tenor more robust in voice than Mario, although they shared many roles; a much admired and forceful exponent of Rossini's Otello, Tamberlik created Don Alvaro in *La forza del destino* at St Petersburg (1862) and was an early exponent of the *ut de poitrine*, carrying the chest voice up to *c''*.

Mario and Tamberlik both sang (in Italian) the French role of John of Leyden in *Le prophète*, a role created at the Opéra (1849) by G.-H. Roger, whose career had begun at the Opéra-Comique, where he had taken part in the premières of Auber's *La sirène* (1844) and *Haydée* (1847) and Halévy's *Les mousquetaires de la reine* (1846). Roger's voice was also basically lyrical; Louis Guéymard, the tenor who created Jonas in *Le prophète*, had a more substantial voice and soon graduated to John of Leyden, Robert le diable, Masaniello and Raoul. He created roles in three of Gounod's earlier operas, *Sapho* (1851), *La nonne sanglante* (1854) and *La reine de Saba* (1862), and sang Henri at the première of *Les vêpres siciliennes* (1855) at the Opéra.

During the 1870s and 80s the presence again of several fine tenors at the Opéra-Comique encouraged composers to write interesting roles. Paul Lhérie, who created Charles II in *Don César de Bazan* (1872), Massenet's second opera, and Benoit in Delibes' *Le roi l'a dit* (1873), achieved immortality by singing Don José in the première of *Carmen* (1875). Shortly afterwards he became a baritone. Jean-Alexandre Talazac created Offenbach's Hoffmann (1881), Massenet's Des Grieux (1884), Gérald (*Lakmé*, 1883) and Mylio (*Le roi d'Ys*, 1888); he was also the first Paris Samson (at the Eden-Théâtre) and a fine Nadir, in spite of Shaw's observation that 'his figure offered a terrible temptation to a hungry shark'.

The finest tenor in the French repertory at the turn of the century was the Polish-born Jean de Reszke, who had begun as a baritone. Massenet persuaded him to pursue a career as a tenor and sing John the Baptist in the Paris première of *Hérodiade*; he went on to create Rodrigue in *Le Cid* (1885) and became a marvellous interpreter of Des Grieux and Werther, and of Faust, Romeo, Raoul and Don José.

The outstanding Italian tenor of this period was Francesco Tamagno, who created roles in two Ponchielli operas, Azael (*Il figliuol prodigo*, 1880) and Didier (*Marion Delorme*, 1885) and sang Gabriele Adorno in the revised version of *Simon Boccanegra* (1881) and the title role of *Don Carlos* in the première of its revised Italian version (1884), both at La Scala, where Verdi chose him to create the title role of *Otello*. Tamagno repeated his Otello at many other theatres, including Covent Garden, the Metropolitan and the Opéra. The very high natural placement and limitless power of his voice have caused problems ever since for singers of the role; few tenors have both the vocal range and the strength that Tamagno could so easily command.

(ii) German opera. The specialization that so sharply categorized the tenor from about 1850 onwards was not apparent at the beginning of the century. Joseph Demmer, Florestan at the première of the first version of *Fidelio* (1805) in Vienna, was a lyric tenor. So was Heinrich Stümer, who created Max in *Der Freischütz* (1821); his repertory included Belmonte and Almaviva as well as Florestan and Gluck's Pylades, Achilles, Admetus, Renaud (*Armide*) and Orpheus. Anton Haizinger, the Austrian tenor who first sang Adolar in *Euryanthe* (1823), was a notable Don Ottavio; later he became the first Paris Florestan, Max and Huon (*Oberon*). John Braham, who created Huon at Covent Garden in 1826, had earlier sung in Italy, creating a role in Cimarosa's *Artemisia* (1801), and had pursued a career in English as well as Italian opera; he sang Sextus in the first London performance of *La clemenza di Tito* in 1806, in place of the usual mezzo-soprano.

The advent of Wagner did not at first necessitate a special kind of tenor: Joseph Tichatschek, the Bohemian tenor who created Rienzi and Tannhäuser, had earlier sung Tamino at Dresden; when he had difficulty in singing a passage in the Act 2 finale of *Tannhäuser* Wagner, who held him in high regard, obligingly cut it before the première (1845). Aloys Ander, who sang Lohengrin when Wagner heard his opera for the first time (1861), had introduced Raoul, John of Leyden, Faust and Arnold to Vienna; when *Tristan und Isolde* was under consideration there it was proposed that Ander should sing Tristan, but he lost his voice and his nerve and stood down, despite Wagner's offer to shorten Act 3.

When the Paris version of *Tannhäuser* was given (with disastrous consequences) at the Opéra in 1861,

Albert Niemann, having often sung the title role, as well as Rienzi and Lohengrin, in Germany, refused to accept Wagner's suggestions on performance or interpretation. Ludwig Schnorr von Carolsfeld, who created Tristan at Munich in 1865, was a different type of artist, who considered it an honour to work with the composer; Wagner in turn admired his Lohengrin, Tannhäuser (in which he restored the cut made for Tichatschek) and Tristan and thought them vocally and dramatically excellent. Schnorr however died, at the age of 29, five weeks after the *Tristan* première.

The search for singers in general and tenors in particular continued to preoccupy Wagner. Max Schlosser, an actor and singer of operetta, was engaged as David for the première of *Die Meistersinger* in Munich (1868) and, when he proved successful, as Mime in the première of *Das Rheingold* (1869). Schlosser also sang Mime in *Siegfried* in the first complete *Ring* at Bayreuth (1876). The first Walther and Froh in Munich was Franz Nachbaur, also a fine Lohengrin, much admired by King Ludwig II; he sang Loge, Siegmund and Tannhäuser during his long career in the Bavarian capital. Heinrich Vogl, who created Loge and Siegmund in Munich, sang the former role at Bayreuth but was replaced as Siegmund by Albert Niemann; he later sang that role as well as Tristan and Parsifal at Bayreuth.

Wagner's main casting difficulty before the first Bayreuth *Ring* was to find a suitable Siegfried. He refused to accept Niemann, ostensibly because he did not want the same singer as Siegmund and Siegfried, or Vogl, for reasons more obscure, and chose Georg Unger, whom he coached in the role. Unger was no great success, but Niemann and Vogl both became legendary interpreters of Siegfried. Ferdinand Jäger, another of Wagner's protégés and one of three tenors who first sang Parsifal in 1882 at Bayreuth, was also a disappointment, though he sang Siegfried in Berlin and Vienna.

The other tenors engaged for Parsifal, Hermann Winkelmann and Heinrich Gudehus, were both renowned for their magnificent interpretations of Tristan, Walther and, in Winkelmann's case, Tannhäuser. Max Alvary, a second-generation Wagner singer and the first Metropolitan Siegfried and Loge, sang all four chief tenor roles under Mahler in the first Covent Garden *Ring* cycle (which began with *Siegfried* so that Alvary could make his début in a star part). At Covent Garden in the early 1890s the more lyrical Wagner roles, Walther and Lohengrin, were shared by Ernest Van Dyck, the Belgian who created the title role of *Werther* in Vienna, and de Reszke. By the end of the century Van Dyck was singing Tannhäuser, Loge and Siegmund at the Metropolitan, while de Reszke had taken on Tristan and Siegfried, in London and New York. Both tenors continued to sing the French repertory in which they excelled.

5. Singers and roles: the 20th century. If Tamagno was the major Italian tenor of the last two decades of the 19th century, in the first two decades of the 20th the field was dominated by Enrico Caruso. Having already created Loris in *Fedora* at Milan, in 1902 Caruso burst on to the international scene at Covent Garden, causing a sensation with the beauty and power of his voice and the ebullience of his personality; the following year, having returned to Milan to create Maurizio in *Adriana Lecouvreur* (1902), he made his début at the Metropolitan, where he sang until 1920. Early in his career Caruso sang such lyrical roles as Edgardo, Nemorino and Nadir; later he took on heavier ones, mainly French, including Samson, John of Leyden, Don José and Eléazar (*La Juive*). If Canio, Radames and Enzo (*La Gioconda*) headed the list of parts he sang most often, the backbone of his repertory was Puccini: the composer wrote only one part, Dick Johnson, for him, but the major tenor roles in his earlier operas fitted Caruso's voice perfectly and in these he has never been surpassed.

Giovanni Zenatello took on the heavier tenor roles at Covent Garden when Caruso did not sing there for six years. He had made his début as a baritone but when substituting for a sick colleague as Canio (*Pagliacci*) he met with such success that he remained a tenor. He created Vassili in Giordano's *Siberia* (1903) and sang Pinkerton in both the two-act and three-act premières of *Madama Butterfly* (1904). He lacked Caruso's mellowness of tone but had a gloriously rich and powerful voice. He caused a sensation on his New York début as Enzo, a Caruso role, with the Manhattan Opera Company, winning praise for his finished style and his 'brilliant, pealing and thoroughly musical' upper notes. His finest role was Otello, which he sang more than 300 times.

Richard Strauss was notoriously unkind to tenors; in his first opera, *Guntram*, the title role was created by Heinrich Zeller, who must have found Tannhäuser, which he sang at Bayreuth a few years later, easy by comparison. Herod, a part now often delegated to tenors nearing the end of their careers, was originally entrusted to Carl Burrian (1905), who also sang it at the Metropolitan in the American première of *Salome*; the Bohemian tenor was an admired Tristan, Lohengrin and Tannhäuser. The first Herod at Covent Garden and in Berlin was Ernst Kraus, who had sung Dalibor there in the German première of Smetana's opera and was a notable Siegmund and Siegfried. Lucien Muratore, the first Herod at the Opéra, created three dramatic roles in works by Massenet, Theseus (*Ariane*, 1906), Bacchus (1909) and Lentulus (*Roma*, 1912).

Strauss's Bacchus (*Ariadne auf Naxos*, 1912) was first sung by the Latvian tenor Hermann Jadlowker, who had created the King's Son – another role calling for both lyricism and dramatic strength – in Humperdinck's *Die Königskinder* at the Metropolitan (1910). He had a voice of unusual flexibility as well as power: though he sang Raoul and other florid roles, he was more often heard as Florestan, Lohengrin and Parsifal. These last two roles were also in the repertory of K. A. Oestvig, the Norwegian tenor who created the Emperor in *Die Frau ohne Schatten* (1919), as well as Giovanni in Schillings's *Mona Lisa* (1915), a work greatly influenced by Strauss.

Two heroic Danish-born Wagnerian tenors, who had begun their careers as baritones, spanned the first half of the century. Erik Schmedes, after making his début as the King's Herald (*Lohengrin*), made his tenor début in 1898 as Siegfried at the Vienna Staatsoper, where he continued to sing until 1924. Lauritz Melchior, after several years as a baritone in Copenhagen, made his tenor début there as Tannhäuser in 1918; his international fame dated from 1924 when he sang Siegmund at Covent Garden and Parsifal at Bayreuth. He gradually acquired all the major Wagnerian tenor roles (apart from Rienzi and Walther) and for 25 years lavished his large, resplendent voice and exercised his superb breath control on them at the Metropolitan. Other baritones to become heroic tenors included Set Svanholm, who sang Siegmund and Siegfried in Stockholm, London and New York during the 1940s and 50s, and became the first Swedish Peter Grimes; and Ramón Vinay, the Chilean whose finest role was Otello.

After Caruso's death there were various contenders for succession at the Metropolitan. The lyrical roles devolved on Beniamino Gigli, who sang Rodolfo, Chénier, Enzo, Cavaradossi and Des Grieux (both Massenet and Puccini) as well as Alfredo and the Duke. His tone was like liquid gold, but his style was apt to be lachrymose. Many of his Metropolitan roles were inherited by Jussi Björling, whose timbre was equally golden but whose taste was impeccable; a notable interpreter of Verdi, he was an elegant Duke, Manrico, Riccardo and Don Carlos. Giovanni Martinelli, who took on Caruso's heroic roles, first appeared as Dick Johnson, at Rome, Brescia, Naples, Genoa, Monte Carlo and La Scala; he sang at the Metropolitan for 32 seasons in a repertory that ranged from Gérald in *Lakmé* to Otello, but was based on Radames, Don José, Manrico and Canio. His voice grew somewhat in power and, returning to Covent Garden in 1937 after many years, he was much admired for his style and dignity. Among this generation the most notable *tenore di grazia* was Tito Schipa, who in a long career at Chicago and the Metropolitan shone in the lyrical Italian roles and in French opera.

Calaf was sung in the posthumous première of *Turandot* (1926) at La Scala by Miguel Fleta, the Spanish tenor who also created Romeo in Zandonai's *Giulietta e Romeo* (1922). His voice was lighter and more lyrical than that of Giacomo Lauri-Volpi, the first Calaf at the Metropolitan, who with his trumpet-like top notes was a magnificent Arnold (*Guillaume Tell*). At the opening of the Rome Opera he sang the title role of Boito's *Nerone*, originally sung at La Scala (1924) by Aureliano Pertile, Toscanini's favourite tenor, who also created the title roles of Mascagni's *Nerone* (1935) and Wolf-Ferrari's *Sly* (1927). The first Calaf at the Opéra was Georges Thill; although he sang other Italian parts, including Radames, and the lighter Wagner roles (Lohengrin, Parsifal and Walther), he was above all a superb exponent of French style. With a repertory ranging from Gluck to Massenet, he was at his best as Aeneas in *Les Troyens à Carthage*, where his eloquent diction was allied to a firm, even voice.

Thill never sang in the complete *Les Troyens*, but growing interest in Berlioz's great work after World War II, especially in Britain, led to the search for a dramatic tenor capable of singing Aeneas's role. Jon Vickers, the Canadian tenor equally at home in Italian, German and French opera, filled the bill admirably, more through the sheer energy and dramatic conviction of his performance than for elegance of style. Other roles in which Vickers excelled – Florestan, Siegmund, Otello, Don José, Samson and Peter Grimes – benefited from this intense commitment.

Vickers and a number of other heroic tenors scored triumphs as Peter Grimes, but the role was originally intended for a quite different type of voice. Britten composed roles in nine operas (12 including the church parables) for Peter Pears, a lyric tenor whose highly placed, flexible voice had a peculiar individuality of timbre: between 1945 and 1973 he created Grimes, Male Chorus (*Rape of Lucretia*), Albert Herring, Captain Vere (*Billy Budd*), Earl of Essex (*Gloriana*), Quint (*Turn of the Screw*), Flute and Thisbe (*A Midsummer Night's Dream*), Sir Philip (*Owen Wingrave*) and Aschenbach (*Death in Venice*). Grimes apart, these are lyric or character roles and tenors who have subsequently sung them (such as Robert Tear and Philip Langridge) have tended to sound uncannily like Pears himself.

Richard Lewis, a fine Grimes and an even finer Vere, was vocally heavier than Pears but lighter than Vickers; he created roles in two Tippett operas, Mark (*The Midsummer Marriage*, 1955) and Achilles (*King Priam*, 1962). Lewis also sang Aaron in the British stage première of Schoenberg's opera (1965) and included Tom Rakewell, the Captain (*Wozzeck*) and Alwa (*Lulu*) among his most effective roles.

Wagnerian tenors were in short supply in the 1950s, when Bayreuth reopened after World War II. For some seasons Wolfgang Windgassen, by nature a Lohengrin and Parsifal, held the fort virtually alone, singing every tenor role from Erik to Siegfried; his Tristan was especially memorable. Then a new generation of heroic tenors, mainly American, began to appear: Ramón Vinay and Jean Cox, both able to take on any role; Jon Vickers, superb as Parsifal and Siegmund; Jess Thomas, a fine Siegfried and Lohengrin; James King, another excellent Lohengrin and a sturdy Siegmund. King, among the best interpreters of Bacchus, sang the very high-lying role of Apollo in *Daphne*, revived in 1964, on Strauss's centenary.

As the use of original languages has become increasingly prevalent internationally, singers fluent in Russian or Czech have come to be in demand. The multilingual tenor Nicolai Gedda, of Swedish-Russian parentage, made his début in Stockholm as Chapelou (*Le postillon de Lonjumeau*) and sang the equally high-lying role of Huon (*Oberon*) at the Paris Opéra. He was a notable Lensky, created Anatol in Samuel Barber's *Vanessa* at the Metropolitan (1958) and made a spectacular Cellini at Covent Garden; his elegant singing in French opera has been specially admired. Beno Blachut was the leading Czech tenor of his generation; among his many roles were the Prince (*Rusalka*), Smetana's Dalibor, Boris Grigorjevič (*Kát'a Kabanová*), Mr Brouček, Filka Morozov (*From the House of the Dead*) and Simonson (Cikker's *Resurrection*).

Italian opera in the postwar period was dominated by two tenors with great vocal gifts but insufficient technique to make full use of them. Mario del Monaco, a heroic tenor with a voice of unlimited power, was magnificent as Otello, but sang too loudly in most other roles. Giuseppe di Stefano, whose voice possessed great beauty of timbre, at first sang lyrical roles such as Nemorino, Edgardo, Almaviva and Alfredo, but later moved on to a heavier repertory, including Cavaradossi, Rodolfo, Don Alvaro and Radames, when the tonal bloom on his voice disappeared. Carlo Bergonzi, who over a career of 40 years never sang a role too heavy for his perfectly placed, mellow-toned voice, began his career as a baritone; as a tenor, he became an extremely stylish Verdi specialist, who could sing Riccardo, Radames, Don Alvaro and Manrico (though not Otello) as easily as the more lyrical roles of Rodolfo (*Luisa Miller*), Gabriele Adorno and Ernani. Another supreme stylist is the Spanish tenor Alfredo Kraus, whose voice has lasted over 35 years; he excels in bel canto roles such as Arturo (*I puritani*), Tonio (*La fille du régiment*) and Gennaro (*Lucrezia Borgia*), as well as in French opera (Werther, Des Grieux and Hoffmann).

Placido Domingo, also Spanish, began his career as a baritone and has developed from a lyric to a dramatic tenor; he too is admired in the French repertory and sings Don José, Rodrigue (*Le Cid*), Henri (*Les vêpres siciliennes*), Hoffmann and Vasco da Gama (*L'Africaine*) as well as Puccini and Verdi: Dick Johnson and Otello are among his finest roles, while he has also attempted Lohengrin and Parsifal (1991) with success. Another Spanish tenor of distinction is José Carreras, primarily an interpreter of the more lyrical Verdi roles. At the beginning of his career, Luciano Pavarotti sang Bellini's Elvino and Arturo and Donizetti's Tonio and Edgardo, with other bel canto roles, but his voice has since grown commensurate with his frame and Verdi and Puccini figure more largely in his repertory. A number of tenors from South America have been active in Europe, among them the Peruvian Luigi Alva, possessor of a graceful style specially apt for the comic Rossini roles and for Mozart. The tradition of lyrical Mozart singers is however largely a German one; Fritz Wunderlich was a leading figure until his early death and Peter Schreier became its main representative in the 1970s and 80s.

The revival of interest in Rossini's serious operas has required tenors capable of singing the florid roles composed for Davide, Nozzari and Nourrit; the most successful of these, the American Chris Merritt, has sung in *Ermione*, *Mosè in Egitto*, *Maometto II*, *Elisabetta, regina d'Inghilterra*, *Otello*, *La donna del lago*, *Tancredi* and *Semiramide*; his finest role is Arnold in *Guillaume Tell.*

Burney H

M. Kelly: *Reminiscences of the King's Theatre* (London, 1826, 2/1826); ed. R. Fiske (London, 1975)

H. Killer: *Die Tenorpartien in Mozarts Opern: ein Beitrag zu Geschichte und Stil des Bühnengesanges* (Kassel, 1929)

E. Carducci: 'The Tenor Voice in Europe', *ML*, xi (1930), 318–23

K. Spaswald: *Die Rolle des Helden-Tenor in den Werken Richard Wagners bis zum 'Lohengrin'* (diss., U. of Berlin, 1940)

E. F. Herbert-Caesari: *Tradition and Gigli, 1600–1955* (London, 1958, 2/1973)

H. Matheopoulos: *Bravo: Today's Great Tenors, Baritones and Basses Discuss their Roles* (London, 1986)

For further bibliography *see* SINGING: A BIBLIOGRAPHY.

OWEN JANDER, J. B. STEANE, ELIZABETH FORBES

Tenor, The. Opera in one act by HUGO WEISGALL to a libretto by Karl Shapiro and Ernst Lert after FRANK WEDEKIND's play *Der Kammersänger*; Baltimore, MD, Peabody Opera Company, 11 February 1952.

The Tenor is the first opera that Weisgall wrote as a mature composer. Its dramatic action focusses on the self-centred tenor, Gerardo (tenor), whose dramatic characterizations on stage, particularly in Germanic opera, win him many female admirers. Amorous involvements with several of these admirers give him a reputation offstage as well, if only in his own mind. As the opera begins, Gerardo, as a prelude to rehearsals for Tristan, is entertaining his valet (baritone) and bellboy (buffo tenor) by identifying his admirers from their perfumed calling cards. Left alone to rehearse, Gerardo discovers a young girl (lyric soprano) hiding in his room and offering a gift of roses. The arrival of the tenor's manager, Maurice (baritone), interrupts this impromptu liaison, and the young girl exits. Maurice urges Gerardo to end his current affair with Helen (dramatic soprano), the wife of a prominent town citizen. Although this would be in his best interest, Gerardo is upset and threatens to cancel his contract. Maurice's assurance that a rival replacement is now available quickly changes Gerardo's mind. He agrees to stop seeing Helen. When Helen enters, she is prepared to leave husband and children to devote herself to the tenor. Attractive as this sounds to Gerardo, a telephone call from Maurice reminds him of his promise. Since Gerardo's career means more to him than Helen's love, he packs to leave. Helen, overcome with love and the thought of losing him, shoots herself and falls, blocking his exit from the room. As the telephone begins to ring again, a dazed Gerardo steps over Helen's lifeless body and leaves the room.

The musical style of this work may be characterized as basically atonal with a free use of chromaticism. The score shows the influence of Richard Strauss, Berg and Janáček. Varied in mood and style, the music is sustained, held together by the use of similar musical material. The inherent dissonance is actually based on concordant intervals, usually 3rds and 6ths, which Weisgall skilfully combines to produce a score of immense expressiveness. The vocal writing employs frequent leaps into upper registers. There are smooth transitions between song and speech and several quotes from Wagner's *Tristan und Isolde* are used. The tremendous dramatic sensibilities of the composer are exemplified by the smooth development from the superficiality of the work's opening to its tragic ending. The serviceable libretto remains true to the original despite several changes, the most significant of which is the expansion of the minor role of Maurice in the play into the seminal dramatic force of the opera.

JAMES P. CASSARO

Tenor altino [tenor-contraltino]. A very high tenor voice, capable of moving into treble regions, supposedly without using falsetto. In the best-known operatic use of the voice, however, for the role of the Astrologer in Rimsky-Korsakov's *The Golden Cockerel* (1909), falsetto is specified.

See also TENOR, §3(i).

Tenore di forza (It.: 'tenor of force'; Fr. *fort-tenor*). Term used for tenors of the early–middle 19th century, to some extent corresponding with the modern *lirico spinto* – a sturdier voice than the lyric tenor, but not as powerful or baritonal as the *tenore robusto*. The term is mostly applied to singers of the more dramatic Donizetti roles or the roles in French *grand opéra*. Domenico Donzelli, Adolphe Nourrit and Gilbert Duprez were tenors of this type.

See also TENOR, §3(i).

Tenore di grazia (It.: 'graceful tenor'). The lighter kind of Italian lyric tenor. He is heard in the comic operas of Rossini and Donizetti; the Duke in *Rigoletto*, Alfredo in *La traviata* and Fenton in *Falstaff* are his main roles in Verdi. He is useful in the French repertory for operas such as *Les pêcheurs de perles*, *Lakmé* and *Mignon*. In Mozart, the roles of Ferrando, Don Ottavio and Tamino come within his scope, and he may find parts in earlier 18th-century opera, back to Handel and further to Monteverdi. The preferred timbre is clear and free of the throat and of any baritonal admixture. The 'grace' ('grazia') will be partly inherent in the voice quality, but also in the style, which ideally should be equally proficient in legato and florid singing. An admired *tenore di grazia* in the first half of the 20th century was Tito Schipa, whose pupil, Cesare Valletti, had comparable qualities. In more recent times the Argentinian Raul Gimenez has aroused interest as a gifted tenor working successfully within the agreed limits. If these limits are the subject of a slighting reference, or if the singer in question has a very small voice indeed, the word 'tenorino' may be used.

See also TENOR, §3(i). J. B. STEANE

Tenore robusto (It.: 'robust tenor'). The robust or heroic tenor in Italian opera, a voice type that came to prominence during the first half of the 19th century (its German counterpart is the HELDENTENOR). Typical roles are Manrico in *Il trovatore* and Radames in *Aida*; while these are the ultimate roles for most tenors of the 'spinto' type, they will be home ground to the 'robusto', who will then go on to sing Otello. From the last decades of the 19th century to the first half of the 20th, Italian tenors within this category were also likely to be recruited for performances (in Italian) of Wagner. At La Scala from 1900 to 1937 the major tenor roles in Wagner were taken by Giuseppe Borgatti, Fiorello Giraud, Amadeo Bassi, Isidoro Fagoaga and so forth; only rarely was a German *Heldentenor* called in. In the 1950s a genuine *tenore robusto* emerged in the person of Mario del Monaco whose style, lacking grace and subtlety, met with critical resistance. The next generation has preferred to see a gradual extension from the lyric-dramatic to the *robusto* in the career of Placido Domingo.

See also TENOR, §3(i). J. B. STEANE

Tenore spinto (It.: 'pushed tenor'). Although this category of tenor is quite respectable in Italy, the term is not a happy one and to the observer it may seem that the whole concept has much to answer for. Two Italian tenors who come within the category have been Giovanni Martinelli and Giuseppe di Stefano. Both had voices that originally impressed their hearers through the exceptional beauty of their tone, but Martinelli's style and temperament drew him immediately into a strenuous repertory, lessening his ease of production and freshness of tone, while Di Stefano involved himself increasingly in parts such as Don Alvaro, Radames and Canio, suffering similar losses and with less in the way of artistry to compensate. The 'spinto' voice at best has an excitement of its own, a brilliance and concentration that convey a sense of risk and dramatic tension: that can be the only justification for a term which otherwise suggests an incitement to excess.

See also SPINTO and TENOR. J. B. STEANE

Teodorini [de Monzunu], **Elena** (*b* Craiova, 25 March 1857; *d* Bucharest, 27 Feb 1926). Romanian singer. She studied the piano and theory in Craiova and Milan, and singing with Stephănescu at the Bucharest Conservatory. In 1877 she made her début in Cuneo as Gondì (*Maria di Rohan*). She sang mezzo-soprano roles at the Teatro Dal Verme, Milan, before appearing at La Scala in 1880 as Gounod's Marguerite; she remained until 1893, creating the title role in Smareglia's *Bianca di Cervia* (1882). In 1886 she sang Gioconda, Valentine and Donna Anna at Covent Garden. She toured widely in Europe, Africa and South America until her retirement in 1904, and was a leading singer in the Italian opera company and the Romanian Opera in Bucharest. Her repertory included *Norma*, *Aida*, *Il trovatore* and *Un ballo in maschera*; with her exceptional range, she was equally at ease in lyric and dramatic soprano, mezzo and contralto roles. Her stage presence was imbued with her passionate dramatic temperament.

GV (R. Celletti, with discography)
V. Cosma: *Cîntăreaţa Elena Teodorini* (Bucharest, 1962)

VIOREL COSMA

Teofane ('Theophano'). *Dramma per musica* in three acts by ANTONIO LOTTI to a libretto by STEFANO BENE-

Stage and orchestra pit of the Dresden court theatre during the first performance of Lotti's 'Teofane' (13 September 1719) in celebration of the wedding of the Prince Elector Friedrich August II and the Archduchess Maria Josepha of Austria: pen and ink drawing with wash by Carl Heinrich Jacob Fehling

DETTO PALLAVICINO; Dresden, Neues Opernhaus, 13 September 1719.

Teofane was performed to celebrate the wedding of the Prince Elector Friedrich August II of Saxony to the Archduchess Maria Josepha of Austria (see illustration; *see also* DRESDEN, fig.2). The plot, loosely based on history, was especially appropriate for the occasion, since it deals with the wedding of a prominent Saxon ruler, Ottone II (alto castrato) (Holy Roman Emperor, 973–83), to an emperor's daughter, the Byzantine princess Teofane (soprano). Names and relationships were changed and events were transposed and conflated. Teofane, believing she is being led to her betrothed, falls into the hands of Adelberto (soprano castrato) and his mother Gismonda (soprano), who hope to gain control over Italy. The Greek prince Isauro (tenor) also declares his love for Teofane. Emireno (bass), Teofane's brother, lives the life of a pirate while in exile from Constantinople. Eventually Ottone wins his bride; Adelberto is re-united with his betrothed, Matilda (contralto), Ottone's cousin; and all are reconciled. The opera consists of 34 arias and two duets; each act ends with a spectacular allegorical scene with ballet.

Lotti wrote for a superb cast, including Senesino (Ottone), Giuseppe Boschi (Emireno) and Margherita Durastanti (Gismonda). Handel probably attended a performance of this work while travelling on the continent in search of singers for the Royal Academy of Music in London, and in 1723 the above-mentioned singers repeated their original roles in Handel's *Ottone*, based on Pallavicino's libretto and adapted by Nicola Haym. In two Brunswick productions of Handel's *Ottone* (August 1723 and February 1725) several arias from Lotti's setting were substituted.

HARRIS S. SAUNDERS

Teplice (Ger. Teplitz). Czech town. The first theatre was a private one built in the palace of the Clary-Aldringen family in 1751. A new 'Comoedien Haus' was built in 1789, since when it has been hired to various theatre companies for the summer season only. Although the date of the first opera production in Teplice is not recorded (the oldest poster is from 1807), it is known that Anton Grams's company from Prague first went to Teplice in 1794 to give Singspiels there.

In 1856 a new summer stage was built in Trnovany Park. A civic theatre was built during the period 1872–4, but it burnt down in 1919 and a new theatre on the same site was opened in 1924. Productions were at first given in German, but from 1925 the theatre was shared by German and Czech companies. It became a Czech house only after 1945, and from 1958 presented only operettas. In the post-war years its name changed several times; it is now known as Krušnohorské Divadlo Teplice (The Erzgebirge Theatre Teplice). Up to 1968 it was jointly administered with the opera house in Ústí nad Labem.

ČSHS

J. Boehm: 'Zámecké divadlo v Teplicích' [The Teplice Palace Theatre], *Revue Teplice*, xii (1980), 2–3

B. Plevka: *Severočeské hudební kapitoly* [Chapters from the History of Music in North Bohemia] (Ústí nad Labem, 1983)

——: *Krušnohorské divadlo Teplice: cesty 1945–1985* [The Erzgebirge Theatre Teplice: the Paths of Development 1945–1985] (Teplice, 1985)

MICHAELA FREEMANOVÁ

Teraminta. Opera in three acts by JOHN STANLEY to a libretto by HENRY CAREY; composed about 1754, probably unperformed during Stanley's lifetime, though broadcast on BBC radio in the 1950s.

The opera is set in Cuba. Prince Xarino (countertenor) abandons court to pursue the shepherdess Teraminta (soprano). He is accompanied by Cratander (tenor), a secret rival. Acts 1 and 2 centre on Cratander's scheme to woo Teraminta. He convinces each lover that the other has been unfaithful, while promoting himself as a suitor. Teraminta rejects him and is rescued from threats of force by the intervention of Ardelia (soprano). Cratander repents, and resolves to love Ardelia and help re-unite Teraminta and Xarino. Act 3 witnesses Xarino's rescue of his captured father Gozanes (bass) and his reconciliation with Teraminta. Gozanes recognizes Teraminta as the daughter of the late Cuban king whom he had deposed. He relinquishes his throne in favour of Xarino and Teraminta, and the opera ends joyously with a double wedding for the two pairs of lovers.

Teraminta is a fine work, though of uncertain origin. It survives in a single source (*GB-Lcm*) bearing Stanley's name, yet there is no other evidence that Stanley composed *Teraminta*. Carey's libretto was, however, set by J. C. Smith and performed at Lincoln's Inn Fields in November 1732. Smith's opera is now lost – a factor which prompted Roger Fiske (1973, pp.135–7) to speculate that the London manuscript is in fact by Smith rather than Stanley. A thorough investigation of the score, however, shows that the work is, after all, by Stanley (see Williams 1979), and the Handelian style is certainly consistent with Stanley's music of the time.

A. GLYN WILLIAMS

Terfel, Bryn (*b* Pwllheli, Gwynedd, 9 Nov 1965). Welsh baritone. He studied at the GSM and made his début in 1990 as Guglielmo with the WNO; with that company he then sang Mozart's Figaro, a role he repeated at Santa Fe, with the ENO (1991) and in Hamburg. In 1992 he made his Covent Garden début as Masetto and sang the Spirit Messenger (*Die Frau ohne Schatten*) and John the Baptist at Salzburg, Almaviva at the Vienna Staatsoper and Donner in Chicago. A fine actor with a good stage presence, he has a large, flexible and warm-toned voice.

ELIZABETH FORBES

Ternina [Trnina], **Milka** (*b* Doljnji, Moslavina, 19 Dec 1863; *d* Zagreb, 18 May 1941). Croatian soprano. She studied in Zagreb and Vienna and, while still a student, made her début in 1882 at Zagreb as Amelia (*Un ballo in maschera*). In the following year she was engaged at Leipzig, where she sang Elisabeth (*Tannhäuser*). After performances at Graz and Bremen, in 1889 she sang in Munich as Valentine (*Les Huguenots*), Amelia and Elisabeth, and in 1890 she inaugurated her engagement there as Leonore (*Fidelio*). She made her Covent Garden début as Isolde in 1898, later singing Sieglinde, Brünnhilde (*Siegfried* and *Götterdämmerung*) and Leonore. In 1899 she sang Kundry at Bayreuth and, returning to Covent Garden, she sang both Elsa and Ortrud, and Tosca in the first London performance of Puccini's opera (1900). In 1896 she sang Brünnhilde and Isolde in Boston with the Damrosch Opera Company, and she first appeared at the Metropolitan in 1900 as Elisabeth. Her later Metropolitan roles included Tosca, which she sang at the American première (1901), and Kundry, in the first staged performance of *Parsifal* outside Bayreuth (1903). In 1906 she made her Covent

Milka Ternina as Elisabeth in Wagner's 'Tannhäuser'

Garden farewell as Elisabeth, and her final stage appearance at Munich as Sieglinde. She had a superb voice whose warmth and plenitude were heard to best advantage in Wagner.

*

H. Klein: *Thirty Years of Musical Life in London* (London, 1903)
W. H. Seltsam: *Metropolitan Opera Annals* (New York, 1949)
I. Kolodin: *The Story of the Metropolitan Opera* (New York, 1951)
H. Rosenthal: *Two Centuries of Opera at Covent Garden* (London, 1958)
H. Wagner: *200 Jahre Münchner Theaterchronik* (Munich, 1958)

ELIZABETH FORBES

Terradellas, Domènech [Domingo; Terradeglias, Domenico] **Miguel Bernabé** (*b* Barcelona, bap. 13 Feb 1713; *d* Rome, 20 May 1751). Spanish composer. He probably received his initial music education from Francisco Valls, the choirmaster of Barcelona Cathedral. In 1732 he moved to Naples and on 23 May registered as a student in the Conservatorio dei Poveri di Gesù Cristo, committing himself to stay for six years, until 1738. His career as an opera composer began in Rome in 1739 with the production of *Astarto* at the Teatro delle Dame. About that time he came to the attention of the Neapolitan envoy to the papal court, Cardinal Acquaviva d'Aragona, who invited him to write a celebratory composition for the birthday of the King of Naples on 20 January 1740. During the same carnival season he also composed a comic opera for the Teatro dei Fiorentini in Naples. Neither production led immediately to further commissions, and in fact a break of three years occurred before the presentation of his next opera, *Merope*, once more at the Teatro delle Dame in Rome.

Merope is generally thought to have been the first of Terradellas's operas to gain unqualified public approval. Acquaviva was so impressed by it that he wrote a strong recommendation for the composer to the court authorities in Naples, claiming that *Merope* had obtained a success in Rome 'the like of which no one can remember for many years'. Since the Neapolitan court took no interest, Terradellas remained in Rome, where he secured an appointment at the church of S Giacomo de' Spagnoli.

In 1746 he went to London as musical director of the King's Theatre for the winter–spring season of 1746–7. This was the one period of his life when he wrote two complete operas in one season for the same theatre and the same singers. Burney commented, however, that the singers were poor and blamed them, rather than Terradellas, for the financial losses the theatre sustained. What happened to the composer during the next few years is unclear. Rousseau wrote in his *Lettre sur la musique française* as though he had conversed with Terradellas on at least one occasion. (The two probably met some time during 1747–9.) The next definite news of him is during Carnival 1750, when his *Didone abbandonata* was performed in Turin. *Sesostri re d'Egitto*, his last work, was produced with great success in Rome during Carnival 1751. The following May he died; the circumstances are still a mystery. The lurid report in the *Allgemeine musikalische Zeitung* of 12 March 1800 (cols.430–31) that, following a period of intense rivalry between him and another rising composer, Niccolò Jommelli, he was murdered and his body thrown into the Tiber, is nowadays discounted.

Although Terradellas was Spanish by birth, his musical style and taste were thoroughly italianate. His reputation rests on his *opere serie*. Burney judged his operatic output to be unusually well written and musically even in quality. His laudatory remarks have often been quoted by later critics as evidence that Terradellas was among the most gifted opera composers of his generation. From what survives, it is apparent that much of Terradellas's music contains strong contrasts created by changes of colour and texture, of dynamic, of key (from major to minor and back again), and of time signature and speed. The absence of elaborately decorated melodies, and of long passages in slow tempos, are other aspects of style distinguishing his music from that of some of his important Neapolitan contemporaries such as Porpora and Jommelli. A particular ferocity of expression, caused in part by the vigorous orchestral accompaniment, marks many of his arias in fast time. Terradellas used accompanied recitative sparingly but always to good advantage in moments of heightened dramatic intensity, and often increased its effectiveness by introducing wind instruments in addition to the strings. Before the 1740s, composers had usually supported such recitatives with strings and continuo, and Terradellas was among the first to popularize use of the wind.

See also MEROPE.

dm – *dramma per musica*

Astarto (dm, 3, A. Zeno and P. Pariati), Rome, Dame, carn. 1739
Romolo (dm, 3), Rome, Dame, carn. 1739 [music, according to the orig. lib., by Latilla; according to Burney, by Latilla and Terradellas]
Cerere (componimento per musica, 2), Rome, 20 Jan 1740
Gl'intrichi delle cantarine (commedia per musica, 3, A. Palomba), Naples, Fiorentini, carn. 1740
Merope (dm, 3, Zeno), Rome, Dame, 3 Jan 1743, *A-Wn*, *GB-Cfm* (17 items), *I-Bc*; (Barcelona, 1951)
Artaserse (dm, 3, P. Metastasio), Venice, S Giovanni Grisostomo,

carn.1744, *Vnm*, 7 arias in *Vqs*; 5 arias and duet in Dudici arie e due duetti (London, *c* 1747)
Semiramide riconosciuta (dm, 3, Metastasio), Florence, Pergola, carn. 1746
Mitridate (dramma, 3, F. Vanneschi), London, King's, 6 Dec 1746, 12 arias in The Favourite Songs in the Opera call'd Mitridate (London, 1746–7)
Bellerofonte (dramma, 3, Vanneschi), London, King's, 24 March 1747, 6 arias in The Favourite Songs in the Opera call'd Bellerofonte (London, 1747)
Didone abbandonata (dm, 3, Metastasio), Turin, Regio, carn. 1750, 10 arias in *Rsc*
Imeneo in Atene (componimento drammatico, 3, S. Stampiglia), Venice, S Samuele, 6 May 1750
Sesostri re d'Egitto (dm, 3, Pariati), Rome, Dame, carn. 1751, *D-MÜs* (*R*1978: IOB, xliii), *I-Rsc*

*

BurneyH; *GiacomoC*; *MGG* (H. Bloch)
J.-J. Rousseau: *Lettre sur la musique française* (Paris, 1753)
J. R. Carreras y Bulbena: *Domènech Terradellas, compositor de la xviii centuria* (Barcelona, 1908)
H. Volkmann: 'Domenico Terradellas', *ZIMG*, xiii (1911–12), 306–9
U. Prota-Giurleo: *Nicola Logroscino 'il dio dell'opera buffa'* (Naples, 1927)
J. Subirá: *Historia de la música*, ii (Barcelona, 1947, 3/1958)
R. Gerhard: Introduction to D. M. B. Terradellas: *La Merope*, Publicaciones de la Departamento de Música de la Biblioteca de Catalunya, xiv (Barcelona, 1951), p.vii MICHAEL F. ROBINSON

Terrades [Terrade, Terades, Terradis], **(Giovanni) Antonio** [Jean Antoine] (*fl* 1755–92). French choreographer and dancer. His activities were concentrated in Venice, where he produced ballets for more than three dozen operas between 1755 and 1792. Much of his work was for the Teatro S Moisè during the 1770s and 80s, in operas by Traetta, Guglielmi, Bertoni, Astarita and Anfossi, among others, but he also created ballets for the S Samuele (1755–6, 1760, 1780–81), S Benedetto (1760, 1768–9), S Cassiano (1765, 1791–2), and S Salvatore (1767) theatres. In addition he worked as a dancer and choreographer in a number of other Italian cities, including Pistoia (1755, 1767), Rome (1757, 1761, 1778), Parma (1761), Reggio Emilia (1763), Milan (1766) and Turin (1778–9). About 1760 he married the ballerina Anna Conti-Nadi de Sales (detta la Russiene), and apparently adopted her son Federico Nadi. Federico worked at opera houses in Italy from the mid-1760s to the early 90s, often in productions with his parents; in 1795 he went to Stockholm, where he worked as a dancer and choreographer, retired from the stage in 1812, and died in 1824.

*

F. A. Dahlgren: *Förteckning öfver Svenska Skådespel* (Stockholm, 1866)
K. K. Hansell: 'Il ballo teatrale e l'opera italiana', *Storia dell'opera italiana*, v (Turin, 1988), 175–306 IRENE ALM

Terrasse, Claude (Antoine) (*b* Grand-Lemps, Isère, 27 Jan 1867; *d* Paris, 30 June 1923). French composer. He studied the organ at the Lyons Conservatory and then entered the Ecole Niedermeyer in Paris. His teacher was Eugène Gigout, organist of St Augustin, with whom his studies continued privately after Gigout left the Niedermeyer in 1883. After a period in the army and as a piano teacher at Arcachon (Gironde), Terrasse returned to Paris in 1895. He began to compose incidental music for the theatre, notably for Alfred Jarry's *Ubu-Roi* (1896) and Ferdinand Hérold's *Savitri* (1898). He had previously written only piano music and a few religious works, but he now found his métier in *opéra bouffe*; his works formed a conspicuous part of the renaissance of this genre which followed the last examples by Audran and Strauss, and was contemporary with Lecocq's last pieces. Debussy, reviewing *Le sire de Vergy* (1903), acknowledged Terrasse's success and praised his invention and orchestration.

The appeal of Terrasse's works over more than 30 years came partly from the distinction of his librettists, who were active contributors to a vintage period of French light comedy; they included De Flers and De Caillavet, Tristan Bernard and Franc-Nohain. Jarry himself was a co-librettist. Terrasse also wrote incidental music for Georges Courteline's *Godefroy*, *L'expulsion d'Antoine* and *Panthéon-Courcelles*.

opéras bouffes, first performed in Paris, unless otherwise stated

La p'tite femme de Loth (2, T. Bernard), Mathurins, 1 Oct 1900; Les travaux d'Hercule (1, R. de Flers and G.-A. de Caillavet), Bouffes-Parisiens, 7 March 1901; On demande des chanteuses (bouffonerie, A. Verse), Royan, 6 July 1901; La fiancée du scaphandrier (1, Franc-Nohain [M.-E. Legrand]), Mathurins, 8 Jan 1902; Chonchette (1, Flers and Caillavet), Capucines, 11 April 1902; Au temps des croisades (1, Franc-Nohain), Liège, Pavillon de Flore, 21 Dec 1902; La botte secrète (1, Franc-Nohain), Capucines, 27 Jan 1903
Le sire de Vergy (3, Flers and Caillavet), Variétés, 16 April 1903; Péché-Véniel (opérette, 1, Franc-Nohain), Capucines, 14 Nov 1903; Monsieur de la Palisse (3, Flers and Caillavet), Variétés, 2 Nov 1904; Le Manoir de Cagliostro (opérette, 1, A. Jarry and E. Demolder), Salle rue Murillo, 10 Jan 1905; Paris, ou 'Le bon juge' (opérette, 2, Flers and Caillavet), Capucines, 18 March 1906; Eglé, ou L'enfant de la vache (opérette, E. Moreau, Clairville and E. Depré), Moulin Rouge, 7 May 1907
L'ingénu libertin (opérette, 3, L. Artus), Bouffes-Parisiens, 11 Dec 1907; Le coq d'Inde (opérette, 2, Rip), Capucines, 6 April 1908; Le troisième larron (opérette, 1, H. Gauthier-Villars), Folies Pigalle, 13 April 1908; Le mariage de Télémaque (oc, 5, J. Lemaître and M. Donnay), OC (Favart), 4 May 1910; Pantagruel (5, Jarry and Demolder), Lyons, Grand Théâtre, 30 Jan 1911; Les transatlantiques (comédie musicale, 3, A. Hermant and Franc-Nohain), Apollo, 20 May 1911
Cartouche (opérette, 3, H. Delorme and F. Gally), Trianon Lyrique, 6 March 1912; Le tiers porteur, ou L'honneur de Desirée (?opérette, 1, J. Kolb and A. de Fourquières), Michel, 27 April 1912; Miss Alice des P. T. T. (comédie musicale, 3, Bernard and M. Vaucaire), Cigale, 14 Dec 1912; L'amour patriote (opérette, 3, Gally and Kolb), Royan, 12 Aug 1913; La farce du poirier (oc, 1, A. F. Hérold), Bouffes-Parisiens, 29 July 1916
Le cochon qui sommeille (opérette, 2, Rip and R. Dieudonné), Michel, 24 Dec 1918; Le muphti (opéra, 1, P. Millet), Monte Carlo, 10 April 1919; Un mari sans sa femme (?opérette, E. Adenis), Alhambra, 1 Nov 1920; Chamouche (?opérette, M. de Féraudy), 23 March 1923; Faust en ménage (fantaisie lyrique, 1, A. Carré), Potinière, 5 Jan 1924; Le manoir enchanté (?opérette), Radio-Paris, 1936

*

R. Dumesnil: *Portraits de musiciens* (Paris, 1938)
F. Lesure, ed.: C. Debussy: *Monsieur Croche et autres écrits* (Paris, 1971) DAVID CHARLTON/R

Terteryan, Avet [Al'fred] **Ruben** (*b* Baku, 29 July 1929). Armenian composer. In 1957 he graduated from Erevan Conservatory, where in 1967 he completed advanced studies in composition with E. Mirzoyan. He was appointed to the conservatory staff and later was made professor there. He received the Armenian State Prize in 1977. The individualization of his musical style coincided with the appearance of his two-act opera *Krakē ōghakum* ('In the Ring of Fire'; Erevan, Spendiaryan Opera and Ballet Theatre, 1967) to a libretto by V. Shahnazaryan, based on B. Lavrenyov's story *Sorok perviy* ('The Forty-first') and poems by Eghishe Tcharents. The composer synthesizes archaic Armenian melodies (*sharakan*: spiritual hymn) and untempered folk instruments with contemporary sonorities. In its structure, the opera is a musical interpretation of Brecht's ideas of 'epic theatre'. The speaker, who directs the work declaiming Tcharents's poetry, the chorus, resolute in oratorio style and arranged like statues around the stage, and the chamber lyricism of the two main characters represent three distinct lines of development. Terteryan revised the work in 1978 as *Navstrechu solntsu* ('Towards the Sun'); this version was first performed that year at the Spendiaryan theatre in Erevan.

In the two-act opera *Das Erdbeben* (1984), there is a reflection of the experience Terteryan gained in his earlier work, the ballet *Monologi Richarda III* ('Soliloquies of Richard III', 1979). The opera's libretto, written (in German) by G. Strecher, is based on Heinrich von Kleist's story *Das Erdbeben in Chili*. Wide use is made of ostinatos and static and glissando block-clusters; an electronic tape accompanies the orchestra. The scenic structure of the opera is enriched by elements of a medieval miracle-play, slapstick clowning and religious symbolism. Although instrumental sonority predominates over vocal line, the two are united by motivic structures, which are often rotated. The work has not been performed.

*

K. Khudabashyan: 'Romanticheskaya epopeya' [A Romantic Epic], *SovM* (1967), no.9, pp.32–5

G. Tigranov: *Armyanskiy muzïkal'nïy teatr*, iii (Erevan, 1975), 26–40; iv (Erevan, 1988), 70–77

M. Sabinina: 'Opera-oratoriya i monoopera', *Sovetskiy muzïkal'nïy teatr* (Moscow, 1982)

S. Sarkisyan: *Voprosï sovremennoy armyanskoï muzïki* [Problems of Contemporary Armenian Music] (Erevan, 1983), 62–100

N. Paronyan: 'Avet Terteryans Oper "Das Erdbeben"', *Kunst und Literatur* (1989), no.3, p.409

S. Sarkisyan: 'Zhanrovo-stilisticheskiye sintezï v teatral'nom tvorchestve armyanskikh kompozitorov' [Stylistic and Genre Synthesis in the Stage Works of Armenian Composers], *Muzïkal'nïy teatr: sobïtiya, problemï*, ed. M. Sabinina (Moscow, 1990), 109–20

SVETLANA SARKISYAN

Terzet [terzett, terzetto]. TRIO.

Terziani, Eugenio (*b* Rome, 30 July 1824; *d* Rome, 30 June 1889). Italian conductor and composer, son of Pietro Terziani. He studied under Mercadante at the Naples Conservatory and later under Giuseppe Baini in Rome. He became a member of the Filarmonica in Rome in 1842. His first opera, *Giovanna I regina di Napoli*, was performed at Ferrara in Carnival 1845. He fought as a volunteer in the Garibaldi brigade (Legion Lipari, 1848). From 1847 to 1868 he was the conductor of the Teatro Apollo in Rome, and from 1867 to 1871 at La Scala. The Milanese did not like him, but Verdi admired him and entrusted him with the revised *La forza del destino* (1869). From 1871 to 1875 he was again at the Apollo, but his stay was marred by critical opprobrium. Nevertheless, he was considered by many one of the most illustrious and learned of Roman musicians. From 1875 he held the composition chair at the Liceo Musicale di S Cecilia; he also taught singing.

The last of Terziani's three operas, *Niccolo de' Lapi*, owes much to Verdi: the short Prelude with two motifs; the texture of tremolo chords under a melody doubled by voice and orchestra, as in *Aida*; and a scena and monologue for the tenor. The musical style is more interesting than that of most Italian operas of the day. Among his other works are two ballets, sacred pieces and occasional items.

Terziani's son Raffaele (1860–1928) composed an opera, *Aman*; although never performed, it won a prize in the first Sonzogno competition (1889).

Giovanna I regina di Napoli (3, C. Giuliani), Ferrara, Comunale, 26 Dec 1844

Alfredo (4, G. Cencetti), Rome, Apollo, 21 Feb 1852

Niccolo de' Lapi [L'assedio di Firenze, ossia Palleschi e Piagnoni] (dramma lirico, 4, F. Guerrazzi), Rome, Apollo, 24 Feb 1883, vs (Milan, n.d.)

MARVIN TARTAK

Terziani, Pietro (*b* Rome, 1765; *d* Rome, 5 Oct 1831). Italian composer. He was a pupil of G. B. Casali in Rome and Insanguine in Naples. In 1784 he was admitted to the Bologna Accademia Filarmonica and at about the same time also became a member of the Rome Accademia di S Cecilia. In the early years of his career he composed two operas, *Il geloso imprudente* (1785, Rome) and *Creso* (1788, Venice). After the French invasion of Italy he went to Vienna, where he composed the opera *I campi d'Ivri* (1805); he remained there until the end of the Napoleonic wars. He then returned to Rome and in 1816 became *maestro di cappella* at St John Lateran, devoting himself to sacred music.

Il geloso imprudente (int, M. Bernardini [M. da Capua]), Rome, Capranica, carn. 1785

Creso (dramma per musica, ? G. Pizzi), Venice, S Samuele, 1788, *P-La*

I campi d'Ivri, Vienna, 1805

SIEGFRIED GMEINWIESER

Teschemacher, Margarete (*b* Cologne, 3 March 1903; *d* Bad Wiessee, 19 May 1959). German soprano. She studied in Cologne, where she made her début in 1923 as Ruth in *Die toten Augen*. Her first great success came the following year as Micaëla, also at Cologne. Engagements followed at Aachen (1925–7), Dortmund (1927–8), Mannheim (1928–31), Stuttgart (1931–4), Dresden (1935–46) and Düsseldorf (1947–52). At Dresden she created the title role in Strauss's *Daphne* (1938) and Miranda in Sutermeister's *Die Zauberinsel* (1942); she was also the first Dresden Countess in *Capriccio* (1944). She sang Pamina and Elsa at Covent Garden in 1931 and Countess Almaviva and Donna Elvira during the Dresden Staatsoper's visit to London in 1936. In 1934 she appeared at the Teatro Colón, as Arabella, Senta, Sieglinde and Mařenka. Teschemacher's roles also included Jenůfa, Minnie, Kundry and Zandonai's Francesca da Rimini. Her warm lyric-dramatic voice was one of the best of its kind, especially during her Dresden days.

HAROLD ROSENTHAL/R

Teseo ('Theseus'). Opera in five acts by GEORGE FRIDERIC HANDEL to a libretto by NICOLA FRANCESCO HAYM adapted from PHILIPPE QUINAULT's *Thésée* (1675, Paris); London, Queen's Theatre, 10 January 1713.

Teseo – the standard modern Italian pronunciation of 'Teseo' has the accent on the second syllable, but in Handel's time the older form with the accent on the first syllable was still current – was Handel's third opera for London and in its combination of heroic and magical elements was clearly designed to repeat the success of *Rinaldo*, the deviation into the pastoral with *Il pastor fido* the previous year having proved unpopular. It is nevertheless a weaker piece, some of its deficiencies deriving from the libretto's French origins (which account for its five-act form, unique in Handel). Haym dedicated the libretto to the Earl of Burlington, and Handel may well have composed the music while staying in Burlington House. The final page of the autograph is dated 19 December 1712. There was a run of 15 performances between 10 January and 16 May 1713, with a cast including the castratos Valeriano Pellegrini and Valentino Urbani (Theseus and Egeo [Aegeus]), Elisabetta Pilotti-Schiavonetti (Medea), Margherita de l'Epine (Agilea), Maria Gallia (Clizia) and the contralto Jane Barbier (Arcane [Arcanes]). The opera seems to have had mixed success and Handel never revived it. Its first modern revival was at Göttingen on 29 June 1947, conducted by Fritz Lehmann; the first in Britain was at the Royal Northern College of Music, Manchester, on 26 March 1985, conducted by Stephen Cleobury. A production conducted and directed by Nicolas McGegan at Boston College Theatre Arts Center, Boston, Massachusetts, on 30 May 1984, using imitation Baroque sets, showed the effectiveness of the opera in performance when the prescribed scenic transformations are integrated into the action (*see* HANDEL, GEORGE FRIDERIC, fig.5).

The action takes place in Athens in mythical times. As the opera begins a battle is in progress offstage, in which Theseus (soprano castrato) is fighting on behalf of the Athenian king Aegeus (alto castrato). (He is in fact Aegeus's son, sent away as a child to Troezen, but he has returned disguised as a foreign prince.) Agilea (soprano), a princess under Aegeus's guardianship, and her confidante Clizia (soprano) are anxious for Theseus's safety, because he saved their lives earlier in the war. Clizia tells her lover Arcanes (alto) to join the battle to prove his love for her, but as he agrees to do so Aegeus enters and announces victory. He declares that Agilea shall be his wife, despite his former promise to marry the princess and enchantress Medea (soprano). Agilea is in love with Theseus, however, and resolves to be faithful to him. When Aegeus proposes to Medea that she should wed Theseus she swiftly accepts the situation, being already in love with him. Theseus enters Athens in triumph and, to Aegeus's annoyance, is acclaimed as king. He reveals his love for Agilea to Medea. In jealous rage Medea attempts to break Agilea's love for Theseus and, failing, causes her spirits to abduct Agilea. She brings Theseus, asleep, to Agilea and threatens him with death unless Agilea rejects him. When Theseus awakes, Agilea begs him to leave her. Medea, with an apparent change of heart, interrupts and approves their union. Her intention to be avenged on Theseus remains unaltered, however, and, knowing that Theseus is unrecognized by Aegeus, she plans to cause the king to kill his own son. She gives Aegeus a poisoned drink so that he may eliminate the man he believes is attempting to usurp him. But Theseus draws his sword as he takes the cup and Aegeus recognizes it as one he gave his son when he sent him away. He gladly agrees to allow Theseus to marry Agilea and Arcanes is permitted to marry Clizia. Her plans thwarted, Medea flies over the palace in a chariot drawn by dragons, threatening to set it on fire. The goddess Minerva descends to avert the danger and her Priest (bass) promises that she will always be a defence against infernal powers.

* * *

Haym was faced with considerable difficulties in fashioning an Italian *opera seria* from Quinault's libretto for Lully's *Thésée*, which conforms to an entirely different set of conventions; he was only partly successful in overcoming them. Several scenes are structured so that characters remain on stage after singing full-scale arias, thereby inhibiting the function of the arias in discharging emotional tension. Haym's efforts were further subverted by the heavy cutting of the recitative before first performance, causing obscurities in plot and motivation. (The cuts included all the lines for an extra character, Medea's confidante Fedra [Phaedra], though she remains present in the stage directions.) As might be expected, the most powerful music is that for Medea, especially in the scenes which close Acts 2 and 3, though Agilea also has some fine arias, notably the lovely 'Vieni, torna' in Act 3. A solo trumpet is the only brass instrument in the score, but Handel's use of the woodwind (oboes, bassoons, recorders and flutes all appear) often adds subtle touches of colour. ANTHONY HICKS

Vittoria Tesi: caricature by Anton Maria Zanetti (1680–1767)

Tesi (Tramontini), Vittoria ['La Moretta'] (*b* Florence, 13 Feb 1700; *d* Vienna, 9 May 1775). Italian contralto. A pupil of Francesco Redi and Campeggi, she first appeared as an opera singer in 1716, in Parma (*Dafni*) and Bologna (*Il sogno avverato*). In 1718–19 she was in Venice, as *virtuosa di camera* to Prince Antonio of Parma, and in Dresden, where she sang in Lotti's *Giove in Argo* and appeared as Matilda in his *Teofano* (1719). She was based in Florence from 1721 until 1747, visiting all the great theatres of Italy between Naples, Venice and Milan, and made a guest appearance in Madrid (1739–40). Her career reached a peak at the opening of the Teatro S Carlo in Naples in 1737; she was again a success there in Giuseppe de Majo's *Il sogno d'Olimpia* (text by Calzabigi) in 1747. She took the title roles in Gluck's *Ipermestra* in Venice (1744) and in his *Semiramide riconosciuta* in Vienna (1748), where she also appeared successfully in title roles in Jommelli's *Achille in Sciro* and *Didone abbandonata* (1749) and in Gluck's *Le cinesi* (1754). She was working as 'costume director' for the Vienna court theatres in 1751. After retiring from the stage she devoted herself to teaching, and lived in Maria Theresa's palace in Vienna. Many of her contemporaries, including Quantz, Mancini,

Metastasio, Dittersdorf and Burney, found her incomparable in expression and stage bearing, though her actual singing was sometimes criticized.

A Faustini Tesi, who combined the names of the famous singers Faustina Bordoni and Vittoria Tesi, may be related to the latter; she was active from 1765 at various Italian theatres, including Venice (1765), Piacenza (1775) and Naples (1777).

*

A. Ademollo: 'Le cantanti italiane celebri del secolo decimottavo: Vittoria Tesi', *Nuova antologia di scienze, lettere ed arti*, 33rd ser., xxii (1889), 308–27

B. Croce: *Un prelato e una cantante del secolo XVIII* (Bari, 1946)

GERHARD CROLL

Tess(arolo) [Tessi, Tessaroli], **Giulia** (*b* Milan, 9 or 19 Feb 1889; *d* Milan, 17 March 1976). Italian soprano and director. She studied in Verona and made her début as a mezzo-soprano at Prato in 1904; in 1909 she sang Mignon at La Fenice, Venice. After appearances in Prague, Vienna, St Petersburg and other centres as Adalgisa, Léonor (*La favorite*), Amneris and Charlotte, she became a soprano and a leading exponent of the *verismo* repertory. She created Jael in Pizzetti's *Dèbora e Jaéle* at La Scala (1922) and continued to appear in Milan until 1936 in roles that included Salome, Electra and Orsola in the première of Wolf-Ferrari's *Il campiello*. She was the first Italian Composer in *Ariadne auf Naxos* (1925, Turin), and sang the title role in the Italian première of Honegger's *Judith* (1937, Naples). She left the stage in 1940 and worked as a director in Florence, Bologna and Milan, then returned to sing Orsola in her own production of *Il campiello* in Cagliari (1949) and Palermo (1950). HAROLD ROSENTHAL/R

Tessitura (It.: 'texture'). Term used in reference to the 'lie' of a role in terms of the voice range of a singer who might be cast in the part. If a tessitura is said to be high, this may not mean that any individual note is particularly high but rather that the part as a whole tends to lie in the upper area of the voice. Thus the role of Rigoletto has no written note which is outside the compass of most baritones, but it exploits the upper half of the voice so persistently that many baritones find it uncomfortable to sing. The role of Siegfried in the *Ring* ranges from *c*♯ to *c''*, but its tessitura is high because the tenor is required to sing in the range *c'*–*a'* with great frequency. OWEN JANDER, J. B. STEANE

Testagrossa [Testa Grossa, Teste Grosse], **Gaetano.** *See* GROSSATESTA, GAETANO.

Testament de la tante Caroline, Le [*Testament Tety Karoliny*] ('Aunt Caroline's Will'). *Opéra bouffe* in three acts by ALBERT ROUSSEL to a libretto by Nino (pseudonym of Michel Veber); Olomouc, 14 November 1936.

Composed in 1932–3, this lightweight operetta bears little resemblance to Roussel's more serious operas. He claimed the success of the operettas of Honegger and Ibert as encouragement to try a work of this nature. He described it as 'a sort of *opérette-bouffe* whose characters are almost entirely grotesque and who should be played without any fear of exaggerating their effect'.

In the mainstream tradition of the French operetta the plot has an ironic twist at the end. It opens in a Paris apartment where the expectant heirs to Aunt Caroline's fortune await the opening of her will. Her nieces, the two sisters Naomi (soprano) and Christine (spoken), with their husbands Ferdinand (baritone) and Jobard (baritone), dream about what they will do with their inherited money. However, the will bequeaths her money not to her nieces, but rather to their first-born sons. She has imposed a time limit of one year, and if neither has produced a son within the given time the money will go to the Salvation Army. In the end the chauffeur, Noël, is claimed as the illegitimate son of one of the nieces and the opera ends as he prepares to inherit the fortune, much to the chagrin of the others.

Roussel's intention was to be 'clear, pleasant and accessible' but the work was coolly received. One anonymous newspaper critic perceptively remarked that Roussel had difficulty in 'adapting himself to simplicity'. In reaction to the cool reception the published scores make considerable cuts, reducing the number of acts from three to one. Following its first production, in Czech, the opera received its French première at the Opéra-Comique on 11 March 1937.

RICHARD LANGHAM SMITH

Testi, Flavio (*b* Florence, 4 Jan 1923). Italian composer. He studied with Giulio Gedda and Luigi Perrachio at the Turin Conservatory, and graduated in arts at Milan University (1951). He worked for Suvini Zerboni and Ricordi while also composing, pursuing his interest in music history and working on various radio projects for the RAI. From 1972 he devoted himself to educational activities, teaching music history at the Padua Conservatory and then taking up teaching posts at the Milan and Florence conservatories. In his work for the stage Testi realized his ability to write in a style that even in his vocal and instrumental works is often implicitly dramatic; his operas evolve towards junctures of violent scenic-musical realism. *L'albergo dei poveri* (1966) displays a clearly characteristic attitude of rough dramatic purpose, confirmed in *Il sosia* (1981) and *Riccardo III* (1987), which are characterized by intense probing into characters' psychological depths. Here the musical language re-elaborates and reflects, not without eclecticism, certain crucial 20th-century achievements, from Stravinsky and Bartók to early Schoenberg.

Il furore di Oreste op.3 (Testi, after Aeschylus), Bergamo, 2 Oct 1956

La Celestina op.10 (R. Prinzhofer, after F. de Rojas), Florence, 28 May 1963

L'albergo dei poveri op.16 (Testi, after M. Gorky), Milan, 21 March 1966

Il sosia op.36 (after F. Dostoyevsky), Milan, 5 Feb 1981

Le chat op.38 (azione mimata, after C. Baudelaire), Turin, 1982

Riccardo III op.40 (Testi, after W. Shakespeare), Milan, Scala, 27 Jan 1987

*

DEUMM (R. Zanetti)

P. Rattalino: 'Flavio Testi', *Ricordiana*, viii/3 (1963), 6

G. Zaccaro: *Flavio Testi* (Milan, 1976) RAFFAELE POZZI

Testo (It.: 'text'). A term commonly used in 17th-century Italian oratorio for the narrative portions of the text and, by extension, the role of the narrator. In the 18th century, when narrative was almost entirely dropped in favour of continuous dramatic dialogue, the term fell into disuse. The *testo* part was normally set as recitative with continuo accompaniment and sung either by one or more soloists or (less often) by a group of soloists forming a *coro*. In secular music the term was occasionally used for the narrator in dramatic dialogues and similar works. Monteverdi used a solo tenor for the *testo* in his dramatic madrigal, *Combattimento di Tancredi e Clorinda* (1624).

Tetide in Sciro ('Thetis in Scyros'). *Dramma per musica* in three acts by Domenico Scarlatti (*see* SCARLATTI family, (2)) to a libretto by CARLO SIGISMONDO CAPECE; Rome, Queen Maria Casimira's private theatre in the Palazzo Zuccari, ?10 January 1712.

The plot is based on the classical story of how Ulysses on the island of Scyros discovered the love of Achilles for Deïdameia. Achille [Achilles] (soprano) has been detained on Scyros and dressed as a girl ('Arminda') by his mother Thetis (soprano), who knows that he will die if he leaves for Troy. Ulisse [Ulysses] (soprano) has been sent there by Agamemnon to seek the hand of Deidamia (contralto), daughter of King Licomede [Lycomedes] (contralto), for his son, Orestes. Antiope (soprano) arrives on Scyros disguised as a man ('Filarte') to avenge her father, who, she believes, was murdered by Lycomedes, to whom she was betrothed. The complications of the plot turn on the misunderstandings and jealousies occasioned by the various disguises, but all is resolved, as usual, in the final scene of the opera, in which Achilles is united with Deidamia, and Lycomedes (shown to be guiltless of murder) is reunited with Antiope.

The arias of *Tetide in Sciro* are well suited to their dramatic contexts, and Scarlatti makes inventive use of a small orchestra of flutes, oboes, strings and continuo. Some of the most dramatically effective music is found in the two trios of Act 1. In both of these, Scarlatti ignores the da capo indication of the libretto, and in the second, 'Amando, tacendo', he characterizes each singer with a particular instrumental line. MALCOLM BOYD

Luisa Tetrazzini in the title role of Donizetti's 'Lucia di Lammermoor'

Tetrazzini, Luisa [Luigia] (*b* Florence, 29 June 1871; *d* Milan, 28 April 1940). Italian soprano. She studied at the Istituto Musicale in Florence and with her elder sister Eva, also a soprano. She made her début in Florence in 1890, toured Italy, and sang in St Petersburg, Madrid, Buenos Aires and Mexico. Her Covent Garden début as Violetta (2 November 1907) caused a sensation, and she returned every summer until 1912, also singing Lucia, Gilda, Rosina, Amina, Lakmé, Léïla (*Les pêcheurs de perles*) and Marguerite de Valois (*Les Huguenots*). Immediately after her Covent Garden début she was engaged by Hammerstein for his Manhattan Opera House, where, on 15 January 1908, she repeated her London triumph, again as Violetta. There, and briefly also at the Metropolitan and in Chicago and Boston, she appeared successfully in most of her London roles, as well as in several others, including Bellini's Elvira, Donizetti's Linda, Adina and Marie, and Thomas' Ophelia and Philine. After these pre-1914 triumphs she made many lucrative concert tours until her final appearances in New York (1931) and in London (1934). Tetrazzini possessed technical gifts of the highest order, a dazzling ease and agility in virtuoso passages, and a tone of warm, clarinet-like beauty, qualities vividly present in the best of her many recordings.

*

L. Tetrazzini: *My Life of Song* (London, 1921)

——: *How to Sing* (New York, 1923); repr. as *The Art of Singing* (New York, 1975)

J. B. Richards: 'Luisa Tetrazzini', *Record Collector*, iv (1949), 123–39 [with discography by P. H. Wade]

DESMOND SHAWE-TAYLOR

Teufelsmühle am Wienerberge, Die ('The Devil's Mill on the Wienerberg'). *Volksmärchen mit Gesang* in four acts by WENZEL MÜLLER to a text by Leopold Huber and KARL FRIEDRICH HENSLER; Vienna, Theater in der Leopoldstadt, 12 November 1799.

Die Teufelsmühle was one of the most successful of the series of Singspiels in a mixed genre that made use of local legends about knights and ladies, robbers and murderers, and good-hearted comic servants, landlords and peasants. The 'devil's miller' of the title, Kilian (spoken), pays with his life for his crimes, while the noble hero, Günther von Schwarzenan (spoken), triumphs over difficulties to win the heart of Mathilde (spoken). The loosely constructed plot contains important minor roles for ghosts, benign spirits and minstrels, and offers abundant comic opportunities for Käsperle (bass), the hero's timorous squire. Müller's score (which survives in *A-Wn*) contains 21 vocal numbers, mainly comic songs and duets, though there are medieval romances and a five-part canon, and two of the four acts end with extensive musical numbers. There are also numerous instances of melodrama and atmospheric Harmoniemusik. Müller's six-year-old daughter Therese enjoyed great success as the guardian spirit Jeriel, with a song in each act. *Die Teufelsmühle* was staged in many European cities (and in New York in 1858 and 1873) and was translated into several languages; it long outlived most of the products of the *Volkstheater*, achieving 163 performances in the Leopoldstadt up to 1860 and surviving in the repertory of the Theater an der Wien until 1881. *Die Teufelsmühle* left its mark on many later Singspiels, most notably its offshoot by the same authors, *Der Teufelsstein bey Mödling* (1800). PETER BRANSCOMBE

Te Wiata, Inia (*b* Otaki, 10 June 1915; *d* London, 26 June 1971). New Zealand bass. In 1947 he obtained a government scholarship to study in London, under Charles Kennedy Scott and Sir Steuart Wilson and at the Joan Cross Opera School. He was appointed to the resident company at Covent Garden, making his début as the Speaker in *Die Zauberflöte* in 1951. For the next three years he sang a wide range of roles there, creating Dansker in *Billy Budd* (1951) and the ballad-singer in *Gloriana* (1953). After three years he began a freelance career, making frequent guest appearances at Covent Garden as well as with Sadler's Wells, Scottish Opera and other companies. He also took leading roles in a number of musicals. He returned to New Zealand several times for concerts and for two highly successful engagements with the New Zealand Opera Company, as Porgy (1965) and Osmin (1968–9). In 1969 he sang at Covent Garden the dual roles of the Ghost and the Player King in the première of Searle's *Hamlet* and the following year, along with the title roles in *Boris Godunov*, *Don Carlos* and *Falstaff*, he sang Schomberg in the London, Berlin and Munich premières of Richard Rodney Bennett's *Victory*. He was taken ill during rehearsals of *Boris* at Covent Garden in 1971 and died soon after.

*

B. Te Wiata: *Most Happy Fella – a Biography of Inia Te Wiata* (Wellington, 1976)

A. Simpson and P. Downes: *Southern Voices: International Opera Singers of New Zealand* (Auckland, 1992), 64–75

PETER DOWNES

Teyber [Deiber, Taiber, Taube, Tauber, Täuber, Tayber, Teiber, Teuber]. Austrian family of musicians.

(1) **Elisabeth Teyber** (*b* Vienna, bap. 16 Sept 1744; *d* Vienna, 9 May 1816). Soprano. After study with Hasse and Tesi and a series of Vienna performances in the 1760s, including Hasse's *Partenope* (1767), she made her career mainly in Italy, where she sang with great success in Naples, Bologna, Milan and Turin. She is said to have sung in Russia in the 1770s and in Vienna in 1778 and 1788.

(2) **Franz Teyber** (*b* Vienna, bap. 25 Aug 1758; *d* Vienna, 21 or 22 Oct 1810). Composer, brother of (1) Elisabeth Teyber. After receiving musical instruction from his father, the Viennese violinist and court musician Matthäus Teyber (*c*1711–85), and Wagenseil, he undertook extensive tours of Swabia, Switzerland and Baden. Then, in or about 1786, he joined Schikaneder's travelling troupe as conductor and composer, having been in Vienna again the previous season. Leopold Mozart, discussing the company's Salzburg season of 1786, refers to Teyber as 'my very good acquaintance from Vienna; a thorough, excellent musician, good composer, organist, and violoncellist' (letter of 5 May 1786). In 1788–9 Teyber was in Karlsruhe, from 1791 to 1793 in Cologne, and then in Regensburg and Augsburg. From 1796 until 1798 he was at Berne and then returned to Vienna. He was honoured with the task of writing the opera for the opening performance at the new Theater an der Wien on 13 June 1801 – *Alexander*, to a libretto by Schikaneder, which was given 44 times in less than three years. None of his later works for this theatre enjoyed much success, and his name disappears from the repertory list after a setting of Huber's *Der Zerstreute* in January 1805. He moved to the Leopoldstadt Theatre in 1807, and on 13 August 1810 was appointed court organist (from the previous year he had been organist at St Stephen's Cathedral). Despite his honours and successes, he died in penury.

first performed in Vienna unless otherwise stated

Laura Rosetti (3, ? G. Stephanie the younger, after B. C. d'Arien), Pressburg, Aug 1785, *A-Wgm*

Die Dorfdeputierten (komische Oper, 3, G. E. Heermann, after C. Goldoni), Kärntnertor, 18 Dec 1785, *Wn*

Adelheid von Veltheim (Spl, 3, G. F. Grossmann), Karlsruhe, 26 Nov 1788

Fernando und Jariko, oder Die Indianer (Spl, 3, K. von Eckartshausen), Wieden, 5 Sept 1789, ov. arr. kbd (Vienna, 1802)

Alexander (grosse heroische Oper, 2, E. Schikaneder), An der Wien, 13 June 1801

Der Schlaftrunk (Spl, 2, C. F. Bretzner), An der Wien, 12 Nov 1801

Der Neuigkeitskrämer, oder Der Telegraph (Spl, 2, F. Gewey), An der Wien, 12 May 1802

Pfändung und Personalarrest (Spl, 2, Schikaneder), An der Wien, 7 Dec 1803

Der Zerstreute (komische Oper, 3, F. X. Huber), An der Wien, 29 Jan 1805

Andrassek und Jurassek (pantomime, 2, F. Kees), Leopoldstadt, 20 Feb 1807

Der Schiffmeister von Straubing (Lustspiel mit Gesängen, 3, Schikaneder), Leopoldstadt, 23 May 1807

Ruthards Abenteuer, oder Die beiden Sänger (romantisch-komische Oper, 3, W. Neubauer), Leopoldstadt, 26 July 1808

Pumphia und Kulikan (Karikaturoper, 2, J. Perinet, after J. F. von Kurz [Kurz-Bernardon]), Leopoldstadt, 8 Oct 1808

Der bezauberte Blumenstrauss (pantomime, 2, J. Worelly), Leopoldstadt, 29 Aug 1809

Der lebendige Postillonstiefel, oder Die Luftreise des Arlequin und der Columbina (pantomime, 2, Kees), Leopoldstadt, 7 July 1810

(3) **Therese Teyber** (*b* Vienna, bap. 15 Oct 1760; *d* Vienna, 15 April 1830). Soprano, sister of (1) Elisabeth Teyber. A pupil of Bonno and Tesi, she made her début at the Vienna court theatre as Fiametta in Ulbrich's *Frühling und Liebe* (1778). A popular portrayer of young lovers and artless girls, she created the role of Blonde in *Die Entführung* (1782) and appeared with success in many other operas and Singspiels; the charm of her acting and singing was praised in contemporary reviews. She and her husband, the tenor Ferdinand Arnold, are reported to have performed together with much success at Hamburg, Berlin, Warsaw and Riga, though the chronology of these appearances is confused. Therese probably appeared as Zerlina in the later Viennese performances of *Don Giovanni* (1788) and is certainly the 'Mad:elle täuber' ('Teyber') referred to in Mozart's letter of 29 March 1783.

*

StiegerO; *WurzbachL*

F. Teyber: [autobiographical sketch] (MS, *A-Wgm*)

R. Haas: *Wiener Musiker vor und um Beethoven* (Vienna, 1927)

F. Hadamowsky: *Das Theater in der Wiener Leopoldstadt 1781–1860* (Vienna, 1934)

O. E. Deutsch: *Das Freihaus-Theater auf der Wieden* (Vienna, 1937)

E. Anderson, ed.: *The Letters of Mozart and his Family* (London, 1938, 3/1985)

E. von Komorzynski: *Emanuel Schikaneder: ein Beitrag zur Geschichte des deutschen Theaters* (Vienna, 2/1951)

H. Vogg: *Franz Tuma (1704–1774) als Instrumentalkomponist nebst Beiträgen zur Wiener Musikgeschichte des 18. Jahrhunderts (Die Hofkapelle der Kaiserin-Witwe Elisabeth Christine)* (diss., U. of Vienna, 1951), esp. 58–87

A. Bauer: *150 Jahre Theater an der Wien* (Zürich, 1952)

O. E. Deutsch, ed.: *Mozart: die Dokumente seines Lebens* (Kassel, 1961; Eng. trans. as *Mozart: a Documentary Biography*, 1965, 2/1966)

W. A. Bauer and O. E. Deutsch, eds.: *Mozart: Briefe und Aufzeichnungen* (Kassel, 1962–75)

O. Michtner: *Das alte Burgtheater als Opernbühne* (Vienna, 1970)

PETER BRANSCOMBE

Maggie Teyte as Mélisande in Debussy's 'Pelléas et Mélisande'

Teyte [Tate], Dame **Maggie** (*b* Wolverhampton, 17 April 1888; *d* London, 26 May 1976). English soprano. She studied in London, then with Jean de Reszke in Paris. After appearances there in the 1906 Mozart Festival organized by Reynaldo Hahn and Lilli Lehmann, at Monte Carlo (notably as Zerlina), and at the Opéra-Comique in Paris, she was selected by Debussy to succeed Mary Garden in the role of Mélisande, for which he coached her. In England she sang Mélisande and many other roles, notably Cherubino and Butterfly, with the Beecham Opera Company and its successor, the British National Opera Company; with the latter she was the first Princess in Holst's *The Perfect Fool* at Covent Garden in 1923. In the USA she sang with the Chicago Grand Opera (1911–14) and in Boston (1914–17). A rare Chicago occasion had united her, as the heroine of Massenet's *Cendrillon*, with the Prince Charming of Mary Garden; her Mélisande, however, was not heard in the USA until 1948 (New York City Opera). Between the wars she performed a good deal in operetta and musical comedy; after 1937 she devoted herself mainly to recitals and recordings of French song with Gerald Moore. The exquisite purity and perfect placement of her tone, together with her spontaneity and distinction as an interpreter, secured for her a unique position, which was recognized when she was made a Chevalier of the Légion d'honneur in 1957 and DBE in 1958.

*

D. Tron: 'Maggie Teyte', *Record Collector*, ix (1954), 129–38 [with discography by J. Dennis]

M. Teyte: *Star on the Door* (London, 1958) [with discography by D. Tron]

G. O'Connor: 'Maggie Teyte and Beecham', *Opera*, xxx (1979), 312–17

——: *The Pursuit of Perfection: a Life of Maggie Teyte* (London, 1979)

DESMOND SHAWE-TAYLOR

Thaïs. *Comédie lyrique* in three acts and seven scenes by JULES MASSENET to a libretto by LOUIS GALLET after the novel of the same title by Anatole France (1890); Paris, Opéra, 16 March 1894.

Thaïs *actress and courtesan*	soprano
Athanaël *a coenobite monk*	baritone
Nicias *a young sybarite philosopher*	tenor
Palémon *an old coenobite monk*	bass
Crobyle } *slaves*	soprano
Myrtale } *slaves*	mezzo-soprano
Albine *abbess*	mezzo-soprano
La Charmeuse *ballet dancer*	soprano
Servant of Nicias	baritone

Actors, philosophers, monks, nuns, citizens of Alexandria

Setting The Thebaid and Alexandria, 4th century AD

The legend of the courtesan-turned-saint Thaïs was written down in the 10th century by the German nun Hrostwitha; a French translation published in the 19th century inspired the Nobel Prizewinner Anatole France (1844–1924) first to a poem (1867) and later to a novel, originally entitled *Paphnuce* after the name of the monk who brings the courtesan back to the bosom of the faith (changed in the opera to Athanaël). The novel was published first as a serial in the *Revue des deux mondes* (1889) and in book form the following year as *Thaïs*. An anti-clerical satire of Voltairean irony, it was savagely attacked by the church. Massenet and Gallet were granted permission to turn it into an opera in 1892. At first France expressed disappointment at the quality and selectiveness of Gallet's libretto (one of the earliest unrhymed examples in France, a 'poème mélique', in the author's words) but after seeing the opera he wrote to Massenet in flattering – and one must assume sincere – terms.

The opera was written for the Californian soprano Sibyl Sanderson, for whom Massenet had a deep *tendresse*. She had sung Manon successfully in France, Belgium and London, and enjoyed a personal success in *Esclarmonde* (1889). *Thaïs* was destined for the Opéra-Comique, but just as Massenet was finishing it, in the spring of 1893, Sanderson signed a contract with the Opéra after a dispute with Léon Carvalho over performance fees, and *Thaïs* was adapted to follow its protagonist to the Palais Garnier; Massenet composed the obligatory ballet during the summer. Despite the controversial nature of the subject matter and the fact that Sanderson 'accidentally' exposed her bust, the première was not a success; there were only 14 performances at the Opéra before Sanderson retired into married life in 1897.

Also in 1897, Massenet revised *Thaïs*, adding the scene at the Oasis (Act 3 scene i), suppressing the original ballet and the second-act interlude ('Symphonie des amours d'Aphrodite') and supplying a new ballet for the end of Act 2. It was first given in this form at the Opéra on 13 April 1898, again without conspicuous success. Massenet himself attended the Italian première in Milan with Lina Cavalieri in the title role (1903, Teatro Lirico) – or rather was in earshot, since he seldom actually 'assisted' at his premières – and reported a triumph in a letter to his wife. Cavalieri repeated her success at the 69th performance at the Opéra in 1907, after which the work's popularity was assured: it remained in the repertory of the Palais Garnier until 1956, falling just short of 700 performances. It was popular in the USA in the early part of the century, thanks mainly to Mary Garden and Geraldine Farrar; other famous protagonists include Maria Jeritza, Maria Kousnetsov, Aïno Ackté, Lilian Berthon, Ninon Vallin, Fanny Heldy and Géori Boué; notable Athanaëls have included its first interpreter, Jean-François Delmas (also the first French Wotan), Vanni Marcoux, John Brownlee and Roger Bourdin. There is a substantial discography. *Thaïs* has never entirely lapsed from the repertory but – undeservedly – has never achieved the popularity of *Werther* or *Manon*.

ACT 1.i *Monks' cells in the Thebaid* Led by Palémon, the monks prepare their evening meal and pray for Athanaël, who has been absent. He enters, scandalized by the life of the courtesan Thaïs in Alexandria, and recalls how as a young man ('Hélas! Enfant encore') he went to her house but was saved by God's intervention on the threshold. He sees her activities as an affront to religion, and despite Palémon's warning ('Ne nous mêlons jamais, mon fils, aux gens du siècle') is determined to win her soul for God. The monks retire to bed. Athanaël is tormented by visions of Thaïs at work, wakes, and in a confident C major outburst sees this as a sign from God to go at once to convert her ('Toi qui mis la pitié dans nos âmes'). Palémon repeats his warning as Athanaël strides off into the desert.

1.ii *The terrace of Nicias's house in Alexandria* Athanaël greets the city of his birth in a three-part aria ('Voilà donc la terrible cité'), recalling how he has rejected its beauty and its learning, and praying for the protection of angels on his mission. The angels who answer his prayer are Crobyle and Myrtale, who enter with their master Nicias, a friend of Athanaël's youth who greets him affectionately. On learning of his mission, Nicias reveals that he has hired Thaïs's services for a week and that this is his last day: she is even now on her way from the theatre. He advises the monk to change into less forbidding clothes, and in a wittily teasing quartet ('Ne t'offense pas') the slaves fail to remove his habit but at least slip a robe over it and comb and perfume him. Thaïs enters with actors and philosophers. She takes a gentle farewell of Nicias ('C'est Thaïs, l'idole fragile qui vient pour la dernière fois') before inquiring after the stranger with the fierce glances. Nicias warns that he has come to convert her, and she asks Athanaël with lazy mockery why he denies his true nature and the love-light in his eyes ('Qui te fait si sévère'). As she prepares to disrobe, he rushes away, to general amusement, threatening to come to her house. She accepts the challenge.

Sibyl Sanderson as Thaïs in Massenet's opera, the role she created at the Paris Opéra, 16 March 1894

ACT 2.i *Thaïs's house* Suddenly conscious of the emptiness of her life, Thaïs seeks reassurance from her mirror ('Dis-moi que je suis belle et que je serai belle, éternellement') but in growing panic sees signs of approaching old age. She regains her composure as Athanaël enters, and warns him against loving her. He responds with the offer of a type of love unknown to her. She replies that he comes too late: she already knows 'toutes les ivresses'. With growing ardour, he promises that his love will lead to eternal life, which interests her. In preparation, she prays to Aphrodite (and he to God). He suddenly flings aside his robe to reveal his habit, and curses the sins of the flesh. As she cowers, fearful for her life, he repeats his offer of eternal life ('Je l'ai dit: tu vivras') to a rolling, rapturous 9/8 tune. The voice of Nicias off-stage reminds her of her past, and as Athanaël promises to wait on her doorstep for her repentance, she collapses in hysteria.

2.ii *Outside Thaïs's house* After the 'Méditation' intermezzo describing her conversion, Thaïs enters humbly, saying that prayer and Athanaël's words have shown her the light. Athanaël promises to take her to Mère Albine's settlement, but orders her first to burn her house and all traces of her past. She pleads, in vain, to keep only an ivory statuette of Eros ('L'amour est une vertu rare') before returning to her house to carry out his orders. Nicias and his companions enter for an elaborate ballet. As it ends, Athanaël announces Thaïs's conversion, and the crowd threaten to stone them both while flames lick at the windows. Nicias saves them by throwing gold to the crowd.

ACT 3.i *An oasis, near Mère Albine's settlement* Thaïs, exhausted, begs to be allowed to rest, but Athanaël drives her on, rejoicing in the mortification of her flesh. The sight of blood on her feet eventually moves him to pity, and he goes to fetch water. She praises his kindness ('O messager de Dieu') and blesses him for having brought her to salvation (duet, 'Baigne d'eau mes mains'). Mère Albine and the sisters receive Thaïs, and she bids farewell to Athanaël 'pour toujours'. The significance of the words sink in, and to the tune of the Méditation Athanaël realizes with horror that he will never see her again.

3.ii *The Thebaid* A storm threatens. In the 20 days since he returned Athanaël has neither eaten nor drunk. He tells Palémon that no amount of self-flagellation brings peace. Palémon merely repeats his warning. Further visions of pre-conversion Thaïs are interrupted by distant voices proclaiming the imminent death of St Thaïs of Alexandria. With the sole thought of seeing and possessing her, Athanaël rushes headlong into the storm.

3.iii *The garden of Mère Albine's settlement* Albine and the sisters pray at Thaïs's deathbed, welcome the distraught Athanaël, and withdraw. The final duet ('Te souvient-il du lumineux voyage') is based on the Méditation and the hymn Athanaël sang as he set out on his journey. She tenderly and gratefully remembers his part in her redemption, sees angels waiting to greet her at the gates of heaven, and at the moment of death is granted a vision of God. Athanaël can only sing of his long repressed desire for her physical beauty, renounce heaven, and passionately admit his love to her unhearing ears. The curtain falls on his agonized cry of 'Pitié!'.

* * *

Thaïs has never entirely been taken seriously, sadly, since it is one of Massenet's most successful and troubling works. An aura of spurious naughtiness has surrounded it ever since Sanderson's 'accident' at the première, through to when Carol Neblett became the first full-frontally nude opera singer when she sang Thaïs in New Orleans in 1973. There are countless photographs of Andrée Esposito dressed as if for the Folies Bergère, or of Beverly Sills lounging seductively in an elaborate hammock with mirrors suspended above. Then there is the famous Méditation, submitted over the years to all manner of Palm Court indignities but in fact a marvellous example of self-generating, potentially endless melody and – as no less an authority than Ernest Newman has argued – not inappropriate to the dramatic context. Many, after all, are the *grandes horizontales* – Liane de Pougy, Hortense Schneider – who have found solace in sentimental religiosity after retirement. In the theatre, well played, its effect is extremely powerful even, or perhaps especially, with the optional offstage humming-chorus backing.

Gallet's adaptation of France's anti-clerical tirade is skilful. Obviously the *Symposium*-style discussion of religion at its centre defied operatic setting in 19th-century terms, but otherwise he does justice to the central situation based on two characters whose spiritual journeys in opposite directions meet briefly before passing on – the prostitute finding God, the repressed monk being forced to recognize his true nature. Their brief meeting in the Oasis scene is indeed the emotional centre of the work – it is hard to imagine the effect of the piece as a whole before Massenet added it for the 1897 revival. The only important thing missing from the adaptation is the pre-history of the principals. Athanaël's can be surmised on internal evidence: a well-to-do, educated young man who foreswore luxury and education and embraced monasticism. But from the novel we learn of Thaïs's slum childhood, her early Christian baptism, her equally early recourse (Lulu-like) to prostitution and her rise to the top of her profession. Her 'conversion', then, is no such thing; it is rather the classic Roman Catholic 'twitch of the thread', and in the light of that the central duet takes on considerable dramatic truth.

At the end of France's novel, the nuns mistake the deranged monk for a vampire preying on their dead sister and run screaming into the desert; the last words are: 'he had become so repulsive that, passing his hands over his face, he recognized his own repulsiveness'. That is also how Massenet originally ended the opera, but shortly before the première he substituted the simple, abrupt cry of 'Pitié!'. That is symptomatic, because what he adds to the novel is compassion for France's deluded coenobite, most notably at the moment of realization at the end of the Oasis scene. From the very start, the music reveals the truth behind Athanaël's stern moralistic posturing: as he piously recounts his narrow escape when as an adolescent he went to Thaïs's place of work, the interval of the 7th that tends to denote desire in the language of music is prominent. That conflict between words and notes is maintained throughout the writing for the baritone, especially in the rapture with which he greets Alexandria before remembering himself with a sour little woodwind chord and ritually cursing its luxury, beauty and learning.

The characterization of Thaïs through music suggests a figure far removed from the vamp traditionally represented on stage: there is a cool, calm, teasing confidence to her public persona in the first act; only when she is alone in the second are disillusion and panic at the approach of old age heard, and she is easy prey by the time Athanaël enters. In the third act her childlike simplicity and trust are all the more touching in that the audience already knows that the object of her trust is unworthy of it.

Massenet's musical painting reaches full maturity in *Thaïs*, from the open 5ths that portray the vastness of the desert through the coenobite community's chaste diatonic accompaniments and the chromaticism that obviously but effectively suggests the pleasures of the flesh to the carefree hedonistic melodies of Nicias and his companions. The cross-referencing of the thematic material achieves a new subtlety far transcending the bland reminiscences of the earlier works: the Méditation derives both from Athanaël's erotic visions and part of his hymn, which in turn is also derived at one remove from the visions; another vision-fragment is transformed into the lightly sensuous quartet when the slaves tease Athanaël while attempting to undress him, and it turns up in adapted form in Thaïs's Mirror aria. By the time the finale is reached, there is a web of interconnected motifs, chaste and erotic, that starts to match through the music the irony at the heart of France's novel, albeit in gentler, more compassionate form. The human truths contained in *Thaïs* have yet to be revealed either on stage or indeed on record; it is, in many ways, an opera still awaiting its first serious production.

RODNEY MILNES

Thalberg, Sigismond (Fortuné François) (*b* Paquis, nr Geneva, 8 Jan 1812; *d* Posillipo, nr Naples, 27 April 1871). German or Austrian pianist and composer. He studied theory with Sechter and the piano with Hummel in Vienna. While his career as a virtuoso flourished, his compositions never fulfilled their first promise. However, with his technical skill and taste for elegant decoration, Thalberg played a seminal role in the development of the piano fantasy on operatic themes. He established the pot-pourri structure of an introduction followed by several of the opera's themes, first varied and then combined for a grand finale. His choice of operas for the piano fantasies highlighted his preference for the Italian style; the most famous was his fantasy on Rossini's *Moïse*. Thalberg himself wrote two operas to Italian texts – *Florinda* (opera seria, 4, E. Scribe; London, 1851; vs pubd Paris, 1854) and *Cristina di Svezia* (1855, Vienna) – but neither achieved any success.

piano works based on opera themes
(many with orch accompaniment ad lib)

Fantasias and variations on: Euryanthe op.1; Robert le diable op.6; La straniera op.9; I Montecchi ed i Capuleti op.10; Norma op.12; Don Giovanni op.14; Les Huguenots opp.20 and 43; Moïse op.33; Benedict's The Gipsy op.34; Oberon op.37; La donna del lago op.40bis; Serenade and Minuet from Don Giovanni op.42; Andante finale from Lucia di Lammermoor; Beatrice di Tenda op.49; Lucrezia Borgia op.50; Semiramide op.51; Auber's La muette de Portici op.52; Hérold's Zampa op.53; Triumphal March from Berlioz's L'apothéose op.58; Il barbiere di Siviglia op.63; Don Pasquale op.67; La fille du régiment op.68; Il trovatore op.77; La traviata op.78; 1 variation in Hexaméron, variations on a theme from I puritani (1837), collab. Liszt and others

Other works: Impromptu on Le siège de Corinthe op.3; Mélange on Guillaume Tell op.5bis; Les soirées musicales, divertimento on favourite themes by Rossini op.18; Caprice, on La sonnambula op.46; Caprice, on Halévy's Charles VI op.48; Decaméron, 10 pieces [based on opera themes] op.57; L'art du chant appliqué au piano [arrs. of operatic arias] op.70; Six morceaux originaux, on Thalberg's Florinda op.71; Souvenir de Un ballo in maschera op.81; Souvenir de Rigoletto op.82

*

A. Marmontel: 'Sigismond Thalberg', *Les pianistes célèbres* (Paris, 1878), 157–67

E. Mühsam: *Sigismond Thalberg als Klavier-Komponist* (diss., U. of Vienna, 1937)

G. Puchelt: *Verlorene Klänge: Studien zur deutschen Klaviermusik 1830–1880* (Berlin, 1969)

C. R. Suttoni: *Piano and Opera: a Study of the Piano Fantasies Written on Opera Themes in the Romantic Era* (diss., New York U., 1973)

AMANDA GLAUERT

Thalberg, Zaré [Western, Ethel] (*b* Derbys., 16 April 1858; *d* London, 1915). English soprano. A pupil of the pianist Sigismond Thalberg, she adopted his name professionally. After studying in Paris and Milan, she made her début at Covent Garden in 1875 as Zerlina (*Don Giovanni*). During the five seasons that she appeared in London, she also sang Cherubino, Zerlina (*Fra Diavolo*), Adina (*L'elisir d'amore*), Lady Harriet (*Martha*), Mrs Ford (*Die lustigen Weiber von Windsor*) and Elvira (*Ernani*). At the age of 22 she lost her singing voice and became an actress under her real name of Ethel Western.

ELIZABETH FORBES

Theatre (Fr. *théâtre*; Ger. *Theater*; It. *teatro*). For information on any particular theatre, see under the theatre's name or under the name of the city where it is situated.

Théâtre à machines [*Théâtre en machines*] (Fr.). A term used for French plays, mostly from the middle third of the 17th century, which require complicated machinery for special effects, such as scenes of hell and descents of gods and goddesses. Their authors most often called them *tragédies*, but occasionally *tragédie en machines* was used. (Modern literary scholars prefer *tragédie* or *théâtre à machines*.) Sometimes the title refers to the importance of this aspect of staging (as in Chapoton's *La grande journée des machines, ou Le mariage d'Orphée et d'Eurydice*, 1648); reviews and published texts often cite the *machiniste*, supervisor of stage effects, by name; in prefaces authors (for example, Pierre Corneille in *Andromède*, 1650) offer a commentary on aesthetic justification for the practice; and finally, the theatre where many of them were performed, the Théâtre du Marais, was known for a while as the 'Théâtre des Machines'. Music had an even more extensive role than in other spoken theatre, for instrumental music was often used to accompany the scenic effects, and vocal pieces, including choruses, were also prominent, although (as Corneille insisted) they were not allowed to convey the dramatic action. Both for their use of *spectacle* and the place of music as entertainment and embellishment the *théâtre à machines* served as a significant source for later French Baroque opera.

See also PIÈCE À MACHINES.

*

E. Gros: 'Les origines de la tragédie lyrique et la place des tragédies à machines dans l'évolution du théâtre vers l'opéra', *Revue d'histoire littéraire*, xxxv (1928), 161–93

J. R. Anthony: *French Baroque Music from Beaujoyeulx to Rameau* (London, 1974, 2/1978; Fr. trans., 1981)

M. ELIZABETH C. BARTLET

Theatre architecture.

1. The Renaissance theatre. 2. The proscenium arch. 3. Seating patterns. 4. Capacity. 5. Social distinctions. 6. Opera houses and other theatres. 7. Acoustics.

1. THE RENAISSANCE THEATRE. Although theatres for the performance of revived classical plays (chiefly comedies of Terence) and song-and-dance *intermezzi* were set up in academies and court banquet halls in the late 15th century, these were of an occasional nature. The earliest permanent theatre may have been one in Ferrara, Italy, which supposedly burnt down in 1532. The Teatro Olimpico in Vicenza, the oldest permanent Renaissance theatre still standing, opened on 3 March 1585 with a production of Sophocles' *Oedipus tyrannus*, translated into Italian, with choral and incidental music by Andrea Gabrieli. The original architect, Andrea Palladio, designed the Olimpico as a scaled-down and indoor Roman theatre, with an elliptical seating area of 13 tiers of bench-like structures and a wide, narrow stage with five entrances in an elaborate scenic façade (for illustration *see* VICENZA). The theatre was completed by Vincenzo Scamozzi, who added permanent built-perspective vistas behind the doors. The theatre was not originally planned as an opera house, though only works of an operatic nature can hold their own there against the spectacular façade and perspectives. By the time the theatre opened, however, changeable scenery had been developed, and theatres equipped for such changes were better suited to musical theatre works.

The largest and most lavishly equipped permanent theatre of the late Renaissance was the Gran Teatro dei Farnese in Parma (fig.1), which was designed by Giovanni Battista Aleotti (1546–1636) for Ranuccio Farnese I. Though completed in 1618 (some sources give 1619), the theatre was not used for ten years. It was the first surviving theatre with a permanent proscenium arch (*see* PARMA, fig.1), a hallmark of opera houses everywhere, and the opening performance set a standard for magnificence that has rarely been equalled. It also confirmed operatic entertainments as lavish playthings of the wealthy. This practice of men and women of power and substance supporting extravagant theatrical productions was not new; well-to-do Greeks in the 5th century BC had provided financial support for dramatic competitions.

The Duke of Parma spared nothing. Designed as a tournament and festival hall, the theatre was on the second floor of the Farnese Palace and measured 87×32 metres; the stage was 41 metres deep and the proscenium opening 12 metres wide (Mullin 1970, p.23). The spectators, some 3500, were seated on U-shaped *gradi* (tiered benches) well above the auditorium

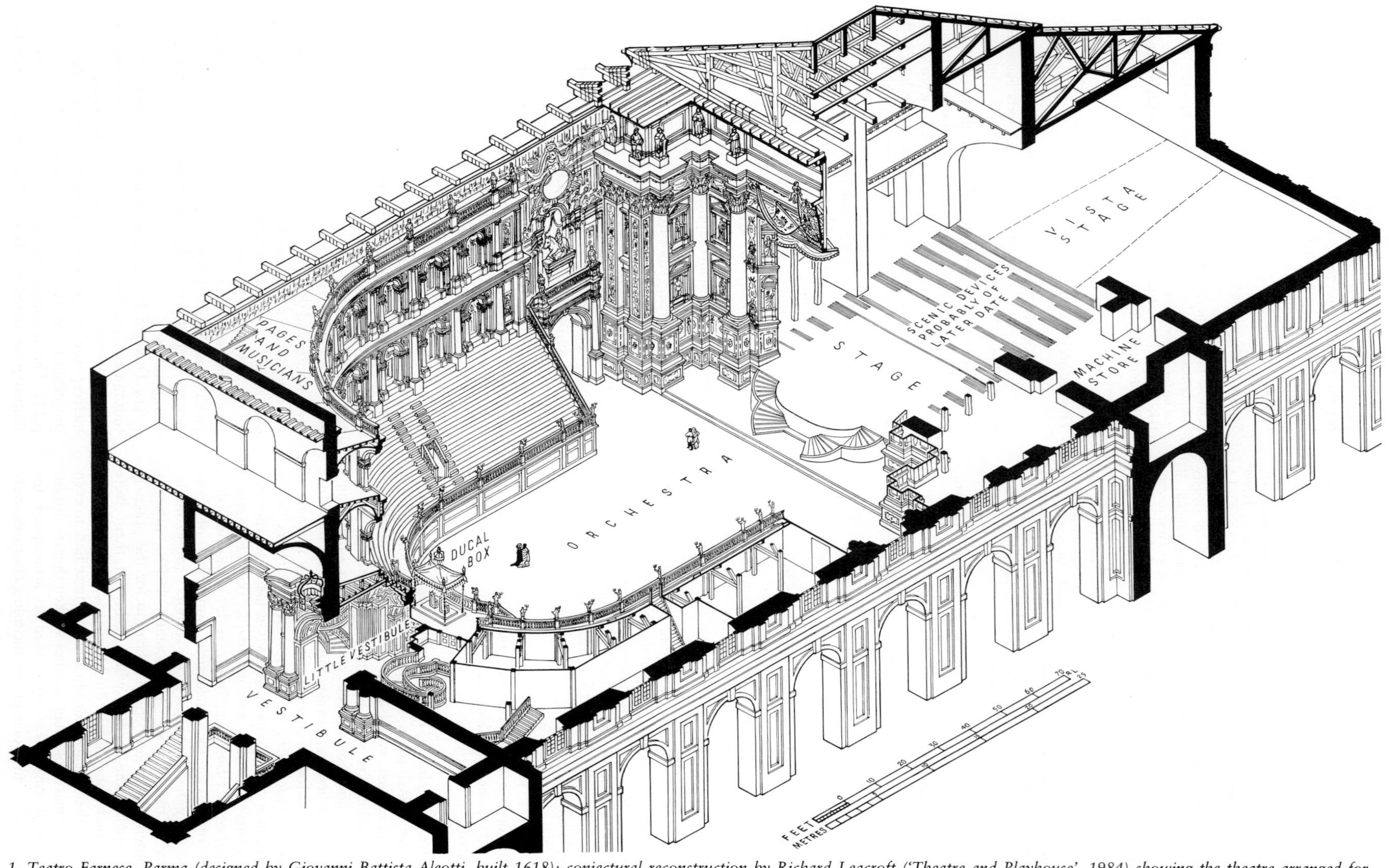

1. *Teatro Farnese, Parma (designed by Giovanni Battista Aleotti, built 1618): conjectural reconstruction by Richard Leacroft ('Theatre and Playhouse', 1984) showing the theatre arranged for the inaugural production, 1628*

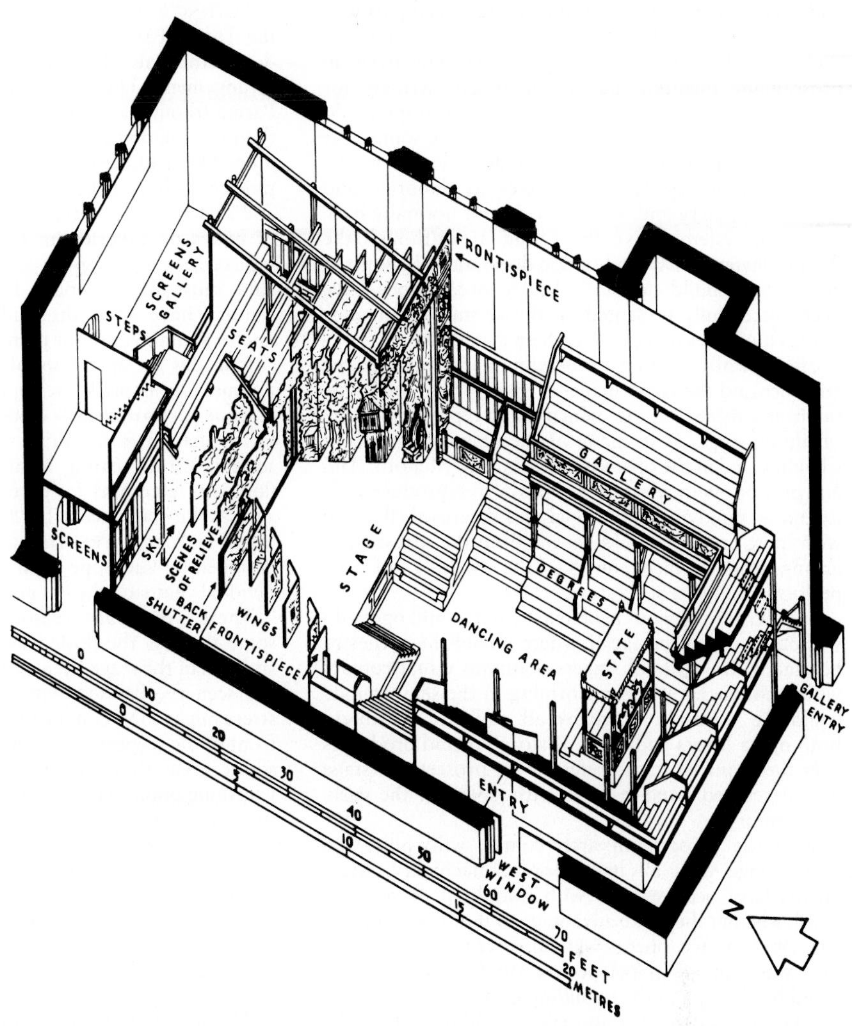

2. The Tudor Hall, Whitehall, arranged for a production of the masque 'Florimene' in 1635: conjectural scale reconstruction by Richard Leacroft ('The Development of the English Playhouse', 1973), based on drawings in the British Library (Lansdowne MS 1171) and the Chatsworth Collection

floor, which was flat and designed as a performance area. Sightlines for the onstage action were not good for those sitting along the sides of the U, but neither are they good for opera patrons in side boxes near the stage in most houses to this day. Behind the highly embellished proscenium arch was a stage fully equipped with the latest scenes and machines.

The opening production on 21 December 1628 celebrated the wedding of Odoardo Farnese and Margherita de' Medici. Marcello Buttigli in 1629 described the spectacular show. The performance was of Claudio Achillini's *Mercurio e Marte*, a *torneo regale* with music by Claudio Monteverdi. Among other things, the evening featured five orchestras and two organs scattered around the theatre (but not in front of the stage), elaborate cloud and sea machinery, magical appearances from below and above the stage, and the flooding of the auditorium floor with real water to the depth of 30 cm so that fabricated islands and sea monsters could float in (Carrick, pp.13–14; Nagler 1964, pp.153–61).

2. THE PROSCENIUM ARCH. Certain characteristics of the Parma theatre can be found in most opera houses down to the present. Most important, perhaps, is the proscenium arch. Its purpose is practical: to mask the backstage and above-stage areas from the view of the audience. It also serves as a picture frame that separates the make-believe world of the performance from the real world of the spectators in the auditorium. The arch is not necessarily shaped in the form of an arch but can be a half circle, a square, or a rectangle (upright or on its side). The English architect-designer Inigo Jones (1573–1652) in the early 17th century called it, appropriately, a frontispiece (see fig.2). The arch creates a very clear division between the stage and the auditorium, and rarely in an opera house do singers break out of the frame, even though the orchestra, which is part of the opera, is usually on the audience side of the arch. In the 19th century Richard Wagner solved that by concealing the pit, adding a second proscenium arch, and creating a 'mystic gulf' between the spectators and the performance. (Ironically, at the Teatro Farnese, where the highly decorated proscenium opening clearly divides the stage from the auditorium, much of the opening performance took place on the auditorium floor.)

In spoken theatre the performance and audience are not always separated. The theatres of Sophocles and Shakespeare (and imitations of their shape today, like Stratford, Canada, and Chichester, England) provide an important performing space that thrusts into the audience area, and the spectators are wrapped part way around the action. It was found that plays written for these 'thrust' stages could be performed effectively in proscenium theatres, but often pieces written for proscenium theatres – operas being good examples – do not work well on thrusts. Thrust stages have some clear advantages: they bring more spectators closer to the stage, they do not lend themselves to elaborate and expensive scenery and, since they do not normally have a rigging system above the acting area (though the recent Olivier Theatre in London does), they do not cost as much to build. Musical theatre productions have been successfully presented on thrust stages, but most opera companies do not use such an arrangement.

Theoretically, putting a proscenium arch between the audience and the performance is appropriate for realistic theatre pieces – those which try to reproduce a slice of life on stage, as in many of the plays of Ibsen and Chekhov and in the operas of Puccini and Menotti. And any play or opera which does not try to reproduce reality but is frankly presentational and theatrical (the case with most operas) should benefit from the thrust stage arrangement, which merges the worlds of the performers and the spectators.

But there are obvious problems: what would opera do without its stage spectacle? where would the orchestra be placed? how would singers maintain visual contact with a conductor while performing in the semi-round? could the voices be heard by all audience members? Both opera lovers and opera performers and producers over the centuries have preferred the proscenium stage that developed hand-in-hand with opera in the early 17th century.

With the proscenium arch comes, willy-nilly, the scenic stage with all its elaborate machinery. Most operas have been written with that kind of stage in mind, whether they take advantage of it or not. Until the late 19th century, operas were also written for scenery that was painted in perspective on flat surfaces and could be changed in the twinkling of an eye – the wing-and-border system. Composers and librettists in the 17th, 18th and 19th centuries knew they could ask for multiple locales, quick shifts and elaborate special effects (flying through the air, simulation of oceans, fire etc) and so, especially in the 19th century, they did. Opera-goers have come to expect such visual spectacle.

With the proscenium arch also comes, usually, an orchestra pit, but the orchestra's position has varied over the years. In a 1635 English court masque designed by Inigo Jones the musicians may have been on seats at the rear of the stage; they could be lifted out of sight behind borders or lowered into the view of the audience. On 8 May 1663 Samuel Pepys wrote in his diary that he was disappointed to find the musicians 'below' at the new Bridges Street Theatre; he said the music sounded 'under the very stage'. Presumably in earlier theatres the music room had been somewhere above or in a side gallery. When the Dorset Garden Theatre opened in 1671 in London the musicians were in a room just above the proscenium arch (*see* LONDON, fig.1). But in the vast majority of theatres the place for the musicians is just in front of the stage, with a parapet separating the 'pit' from the audience. At first the musicians were on the same level as the first row of seats, but by the late 19th century a sunken pit was common. Now most opera houses have pits on lifts so the height can be adjusted.

3. SEATING PATTERNS. A second architectural feature of the Teatro Farnese can also be found in opera houses down through the centuries: the U-shaped seating arrangement. The U was sometimes elongated, as at Parma (though a semicircle had originally been planned there), sometimes splayed, sometimes shallower and more like a horseshoe, sometimes ovoid (fig.4), sometimes bell-shaped (fig.3) or squared (*see* MONTE CARLO and VIENNA, fig.2). To provide for more spectators, tiers of boxes or galleries or a combination of both soon replaced the single *gradi* arrangement found at Parma. And most public opera houses since the mid-17th century have used the auditorium floor for seating and/or standing, not for performing.

In its day the open floor of the Teatro Farnese was not unique. On a smaller scale, early 17th-century English masque performances – elaborate song-and-dance spectacles of an operatic nature – were given in halls with a squared-off U seating arrangement, and the flat hall floor was left empty for performers. Court opera houses such as the magnificent 1748 Markgräfliches Opernhaus (fig.5; *see also* BAYREUTH, fig.1) in Bayreuth, the interior designed by Giuseppe Galli-Bibiena, had removable individual chairs on the flat auditorium floor.

There were many reasons for this arrangement. In some theatres the floor was a more useful performing space than the stage because of the forced perspective in the scenery. Painted wings depicting buildings on a street might look convincing if the performers stayed in front of the scenery, but if they stepped upstage, into the scenic area, they dwarfed the buildings. In time the vanishing point in the scenery, instead of being placed at the back of the scenic area, was moved far behind the back wall of the theatre building. (By 1711 the designer Ferdinando Galli-Bibiena recommended a vanishing point 30 metres behind the scenic area.) The perspective was thus less forced, and performers were able to move into the scenic area without causing distortion. When they could do that, the hall floor was less necessary as a performing space.

Also affecting the use of the floor was the position of the 'state' or seat of honour for the leading dignitary in the audience (the king, queen, duke, etc.). The ideal position in any auditorium for viewing scenery painted in perspective was at the point of distance – a spot in the hall corresponding to the vanishing point in the scenery. Wherever the seat of honour was, no other spectator would be so impolite as to sit in front of it (for illustration *see* INTERMEDIO; SEATING, fig.1, and SOCIOLOGY OF OPERA, fig.1). This left an empty floor area between the state and the stage, and the performers made use of it, especially for their greetings to the leading dignitary and for dancing. Indeed, the floor of a banquet hall would have been much more suitable for dancing than the more rough-hewn stage floor.

When the vanishing point was moved further backstage, the point of distance moved to the rear of the auditorium. At some time in the 17th century the standard vanishing point in the scenery was raised on the horizon so the seat of honour could be raised in the auditorium. Aleotti anticipated this at the Teatro Farnese, for the state there (and all seating) was raised well above the hall floor to provide the tournament space that could be flooded. By the end of the 17th century in most European theatres the 'Royal' box had been fixed at the rear centre of the auditorium, in the first tier – the best viewing place (see fig.5; *see also* MUNICH, fig.1 and VIENNA, fig.3).

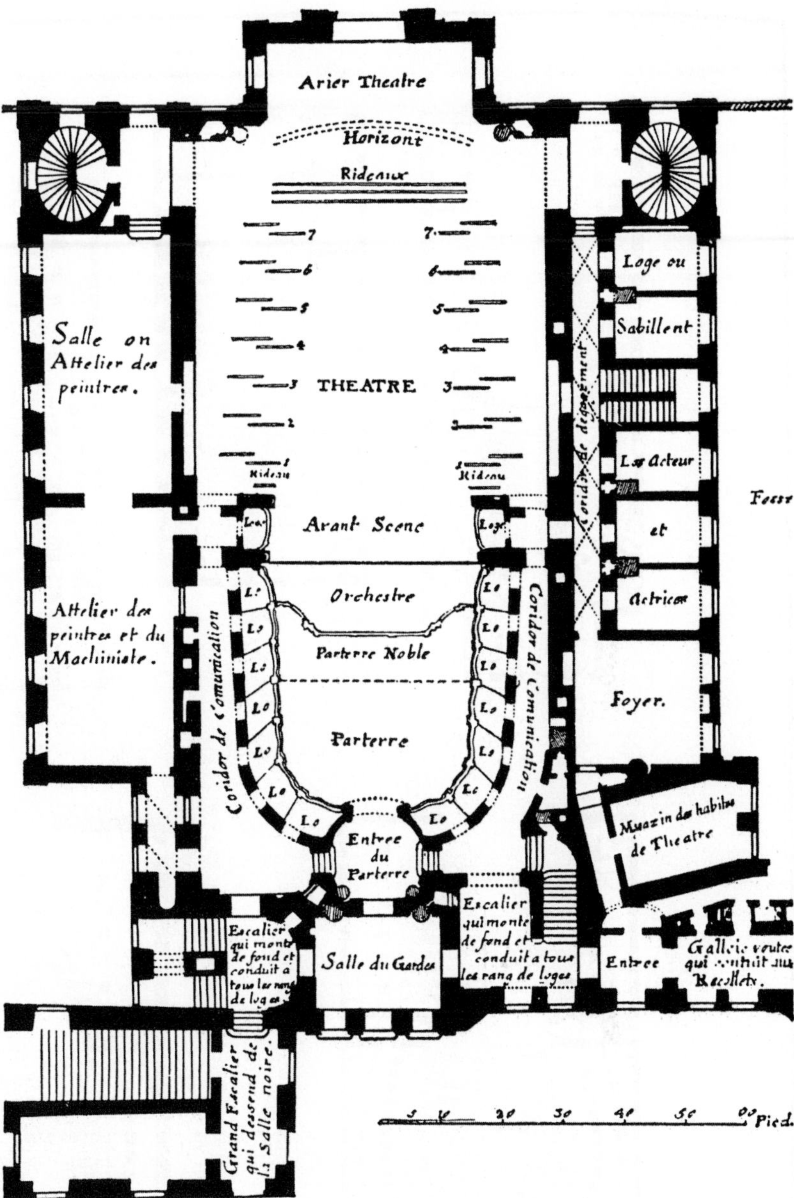

3. *Plan of the Cuvilliéstheater (1753) in the Residenz, Munich (note the bell-shaped auditorium)*

Today in some houses the seat of honour is at the side of the auditorium and near the stage. In England this arrangement dates from as early as 1705, when the architect John Vanbrugh built the Queen's Theatre opera house (fig.6). The view of the stage from there is poor, but dignitaries are there not so much to see a performance themselves as to be on display to the rest of the audience. In any case, now that wing-and-border painted perspective scenery is not normally used, viewing stage settings from the side is acceptable if not ideal.

The Teatro Farnese's *gradi* seating, borrowed from classic Greek and Roman amphitheatres and also used in the Teatro Olimpico, did not become standard. Aleotti himself, about 1606, had drawn plans for a theatre with tiers of boxes instead of open *gradi*; such tiers are found in most opera houses today, though the upper ones at the back are usually open balconies or galleries instead of segregated boxes. The tiers of seating along the sides of an auditorium are less suitable for seeing than for being seen, but for some opera patrons this is not only acceptable but preferred.

The open, flat auditorium floors at the Farnese theatre and in Jones's banquet hall usually gave way in the 17th century to sloping floors and places for spectators – in most houses, benches (usually backless) filling the whole 'pit' area (see fig.6; *see also* LONDON, fig.13, and PARIS, fig.4). Public theatres began installing benches with backs in the 18th century, and by the time Richard Wagner built his Festspielhaus in Bayreuth in 1876 individual chairs were provided (see fig.12). Wagner used 'Continental' seating (no aisles except at the sides of the auditorium), but not many opera-house architects have followed that plan (see fig.7; *see also* BAYREUTH, fig.3, and SEATING, fig.10).

For ideal sightlines all seats should be orientated towards the stage. A fan-shaped arrangement, as in Wagner's theatre but at hardly any other opera house, is

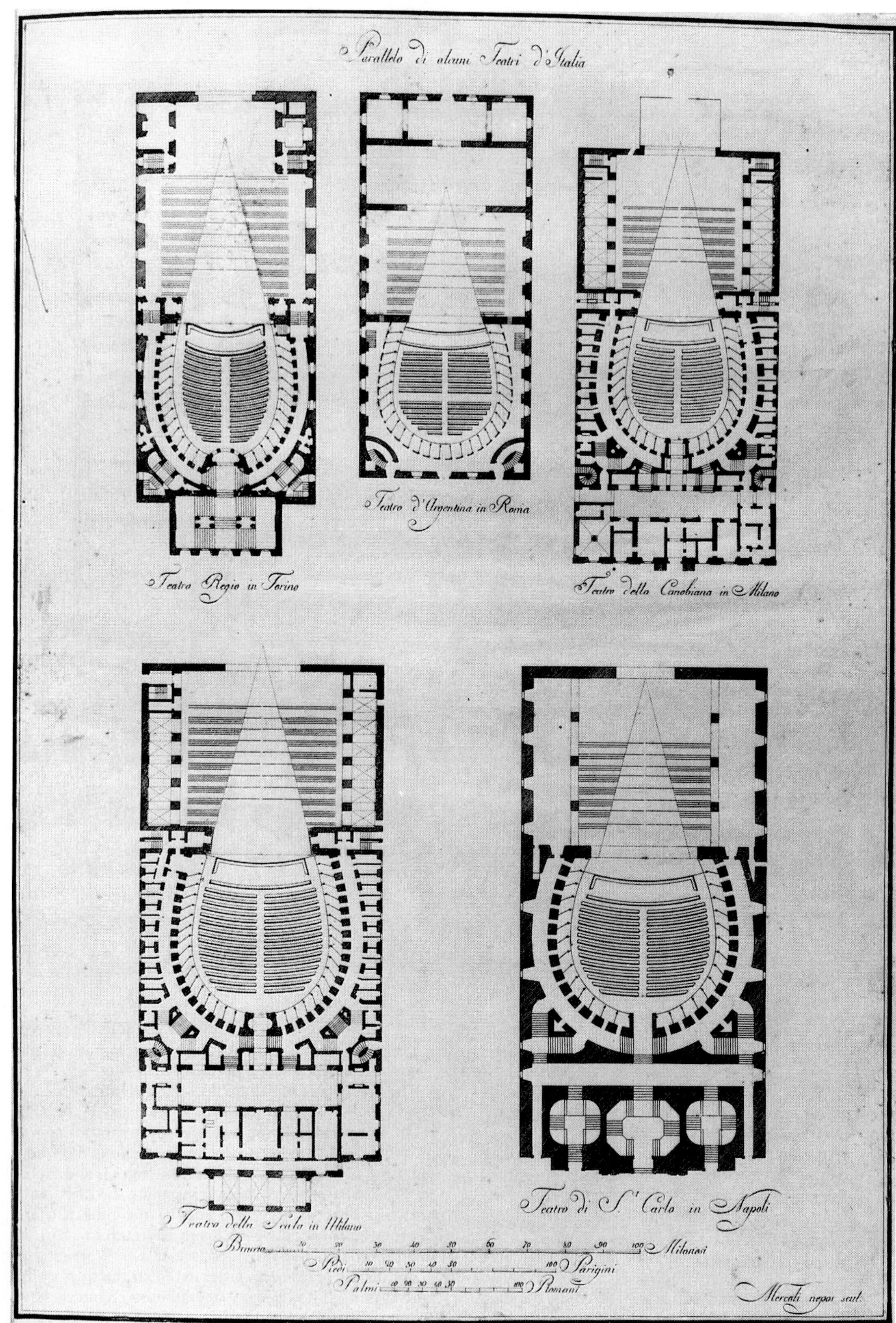

4. Comparative ground plans of five major Italian theatres: (left to right, above) Teatro Regio, Turin, Teatro Argentina, Rome, and Teatro Cannobiana, Milan, and (below) Teatro alla Scala, Milan, and Teatro S Carlo, Naples; engraving after G. Piermarini

5. Auditorium of the Markgräfliches Opernhaus, Bayreuth (built by Joseph Saint-Pierre, 1745–8, with interior decoration by Giuseppe and Carlo Galli-Bibiena); see also BAYREUTH, *fig.1*

splendid for viewing the stage. Wagner's seats 1925 (according to Hartmann; Forsyth gives 1800). But if economics demand a capacity of 3000 or more, the alternative is to have tiers of balconies with many seats at a great distance from the stage, or tiers of seating along the sides of the auditorium, or both.

Architects have sometimes tried to create something close to fan-shaped seating even with a U or horseshoe. The English in the 18th century tried widening the horseshoe, bringing the rear seating closer to the stage and cutting down the number of seats on the sides. In recent years architects have orientated the side seats (whether arranged in boxes or as balcony arms) towards the stage, giving spectators along the sides a good view (fig.8). The Salzburg Grosses Festspielhaus has all of its 2200 seats facing the unusually wide stage (fig.9).

4. CAPACITY. It is worth noting the capacities of some Baroque-style opera houses that have the horseshoe shape: the Royal Opera House, Covent Garden, holds 2186; the Vienna Staatsoper 1642 (2209 with standing room); La Scala, Milan, 2289 (Forsyth; Hartmann gives 3600); and the Paris Opéra 2131 (*see* SEATING). The Metropolitan Opera House has a total capacity of almost 4000, including standing room. Most opera houses, grand though some of them are, hold only about half as many people as the Metropolitan. The reason, of course, is the European tradition of government support of national opera companies, making immense capacities unnecessary. (The variant capacity figures above can be explained by different seating configurations that reporters do not always explain; standing areas can sometimes be increased considerably by the removal of barriers or rows of seats.)

By the end of the 18th century some theatres built for spoken drama had become opera houses in size, with capacities of over 3000 (the new Drury Lane in 1794, for instance, could hold 3600). But most plays, even those of Shakespeare, get lost in such large houses. Opera can hold its own in the vastness of a house seating 3000 or more, and such large capacities are necessary to help defray the enormous cost of most opera productions.

The capacity of the first public opera house, the Teatro Cassiano in Venice (1637), is not known, but the *Mercure galant* in 1683 (according to Worsthorne) said the auditorium had five levels of boxes with 31 boxes on each tier. That suggests a capacity in the boxes alone of about 800, so the total capacity may have been as much as 1500 or 2000. Most court opera houses, on the other hand, held far fewer people even if they were designed on a grand scale. Forsyth, for example, lists five European 18th-century court theatres with capacities under 500. The Eszterháza opera house (1769) had a volume of 9486 cubic metres but a capacity of only 400. By comparison, the Paris Opéra (1875) has 9968 cubic metres of space and a capacity of 2131.

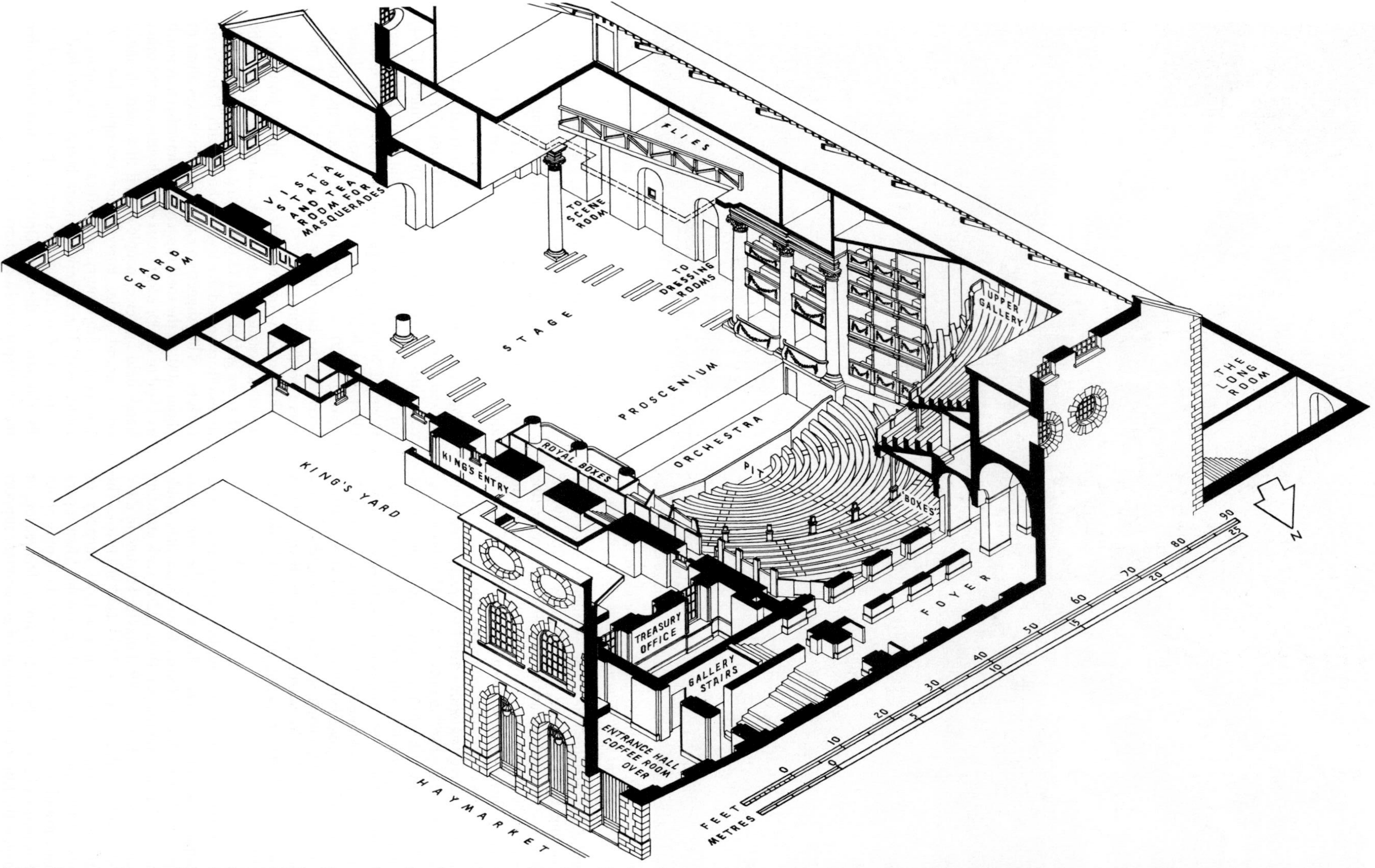

6. The Queen's Theatre (King's from 1714), Haymarket, London (designed by John Vanbrugh, opened 1705) after the alterations of 1709: conjectural scale reconstruction by Richard Leacroft ('The Development of the English Playhouse', 1973), based on G. Dumont, 'Parallèle de plans des plus belles salles de spectacles d'Italie et de France' (Paris, 1764); originally planned as a playhouse, it proved better for music than speech and became the principal London opera house; see also LONDON, *fig.16*

7. *Festspielhaus, Bayreuth: longitudinal perspective showing a reconstruction of Paul von Joukowsky's set for the Grail Scene in the original production of Wagner's 'Parsifal' in 1882, from George Izenour, 'Theater Design' (1977); the fan-shaped continental seating, deeply sunken orchestra pit and double proscenium arch are still unusual features in opera houses*

8. Auditorium of the Deutsche Oper, Berlin, 1961, with all seats orientated towards the stage (an unusual arrangement for an opera house)

5. SOCIAL DISTINCTIONS. Some theatres began to be democratized in the 19th century; in many the partitions separating the boxes were removed, creating what amounted to open balconies (*see* PARIS, fig.16). Some token, ceremonial boxes were usually left near the stage on perhaps two levels, with the worst sightlines in the house. In opera houses this democratization was pointless. Opera patrons for centuries have been, for the most part, upper class. The Earl of Mount Edgcumbe in 1834 remembered audiences at the King's Theatre opera house in London before it burnt down in 1789 (Nalbach, p.65):

Both of these [the pit and boxes] were filled exclusively with the highest class of Society, all, without exception, in the full dress then universally worn. The audiences thus assembled were considered as indisputably presenting a finer spectacle than any other theatre in Europe, and absolutely astonished the foreign performers to whom such a sight was entirely new. At the end of the performance the

9. Grosses Festspielhaus, Salzburg, 1960: longitudinal perspective showing a reconstruction of Günther Schneider-Siemssen's setting for Wagner's 'Ring', from George Izenour, 'Theatre Design' (1977); the rear projection cove was blasted out of solid rock, and the proximity of the site to the mountain required the architects Clemens and Holzmeister to design an unusually wide building

company of the pit and boxes repaired to the coffee room, which was then the best assembly in London, private ones being rarely given on opera nights and all the first society was regularly to be seen there. Over the front box was the five shilling gallery, then resorted to by respectable persons not in full dress: and above that an upper gallery to which the admission was three shillings.

The least expensive seats in opera houses – in the top gallery and in slips on the top level along the sides – were generally thought of as being for poor students (*les enfants du paradis*) or servants of the aristocrats sitting below in the boxes. The top level of seating, indeed, was often referred to as the footmen's gallery.

In previous centuries the idea of partitioning (even curtaining) boxes was to give opera-goers privacy to enjoy whatever they came to the theatre to enjoy, which was not necessarily the opera. George Saunders in his *Treatise* of 1790 (p.64) noted that 'It is the fashion in Italy to receive visitors in the boxes, to play at cards, and often sup there; this doubtless first gave occasion for enclosed boxes, which from thence were adopted in other countries' (fig.10).

From the 16th century to the 19th most theatres separated access to the different seating areas. While box patrons might come in through the main theatre entrance, those sitting in the top gallery would not. One still finds this at many opera houses today. (The reasons arise from concern with safety as well as from snobbery; theatres must have multiple exits in case of fire. Before electricity was used in theatres, beginning in the 1880s, the danger of fire was very real: Sachs and Woodrow in *Modern Opera Houses* counted more than 1100 auditorium fires between 1797 and 1897.)

6. OPERA HOUSES AND OTHER THEATRES. Opera houses are similar to theatres built for play productions, the chief differences being size and splendour. The typical opera house façade is grand, if not grandiose, the magnificent Paris Opéra designed by Charles Garnier (1825–98) being a good example (fig.11; *see also* PARIS, figs.18–20). Since there is no functional reason for this splendour, or for the elaborate staircases that one almost invariably finds inside, it is clear that opera architects for centuries have provided these elegant façades and foyers to make a social statement. That statement is then reinforced by the spectacle of the auditorium; it is usually grand not only in size but in richness (if not ostentatiousness) of decor. The wealthy feel at home in this environment; the poor feel out of place. Under these circumstances, the common man, if he comes to the opera at all, might be expected to be happier entering by a side door and climbing an ordinary stairway to the top gallery, where he will be too far from the splendour below to be intimidated by it.

The stage and backstage areas of the opera houses are also similar to those of other theatres, but there are important differences, and not only in size. Opera companies almost invariably work in repertory (a different opera every day) and their theatre must be capable of handling multiple stage settings for several operas at once (fig.12). Ideally, an opera house should also contain all of the necessary supporting shops – for costumes, scenery, properties, wigs, electrical equipment and the like. Unfortunately, many opera companies must (as Covent Garden does) store most of their belongings elsewhere and have things built in shops scattered around the city. The new Metropolitan, like most recently-built opera houses, has virtually all its shops under one roof. In addition to supporting shops, any house should have an assortment of large and small rehearsal and dressing rooms; dance studios; storage areas for scenery, properties, lighting and projection equipment and musical instruments; machine rooms for stage lifts and wagons; intercommunications and television monitoring systems; control areas for lights, sound, rigging, wagons and lifts; a library; lounge, cooking and eating areas – the list seems endless. Opera is a gigantic and complex operation and stage and backstage areas need to be huge.

By contrast, commercial theatres designed for spoken plays (apart from university theatres) usually consist of little more than the stage and auditorium, owned and operated by people who rent it out to producing groups, who bring in not just a play but virtually everything necessary to produce it: lighting instruments and control boards, scenery, costumes, properties, crews. Such theatres are usually much smaller than even modest opera houses. Ironically, on Broadway until recently, commercial theatres were not parts of larger buildings and had income only from stage productions – hence high ticket prices for productions that were usually far less elaborate than operas.

10. Interior of a box at La Scala, Milan: engraving (1844) after A. Focosi

7. ACOUSTICS. An opera house without good acoustics is doomed. Designing a stage and auditorium with the necessary combination of reflecting and absorbing surfaces to make the sound of an orchestra and singers clear but mellow is a science in itself, and not a very perfect one even today. Some older theatres, with their plethora of ornament breaking up the sound, have remarkably good acoustical properties, sometimes better than more recent houses with their cleaner designs and harder surfaces.

The acoustics at Wagner's Festspielhaus have been much discussed. The unusual hood over the orchestra pit throws the sound toward the stage, where it blends with but does not overwhelm the singers' voices. A blurred effect that is sometimes remarked on may be

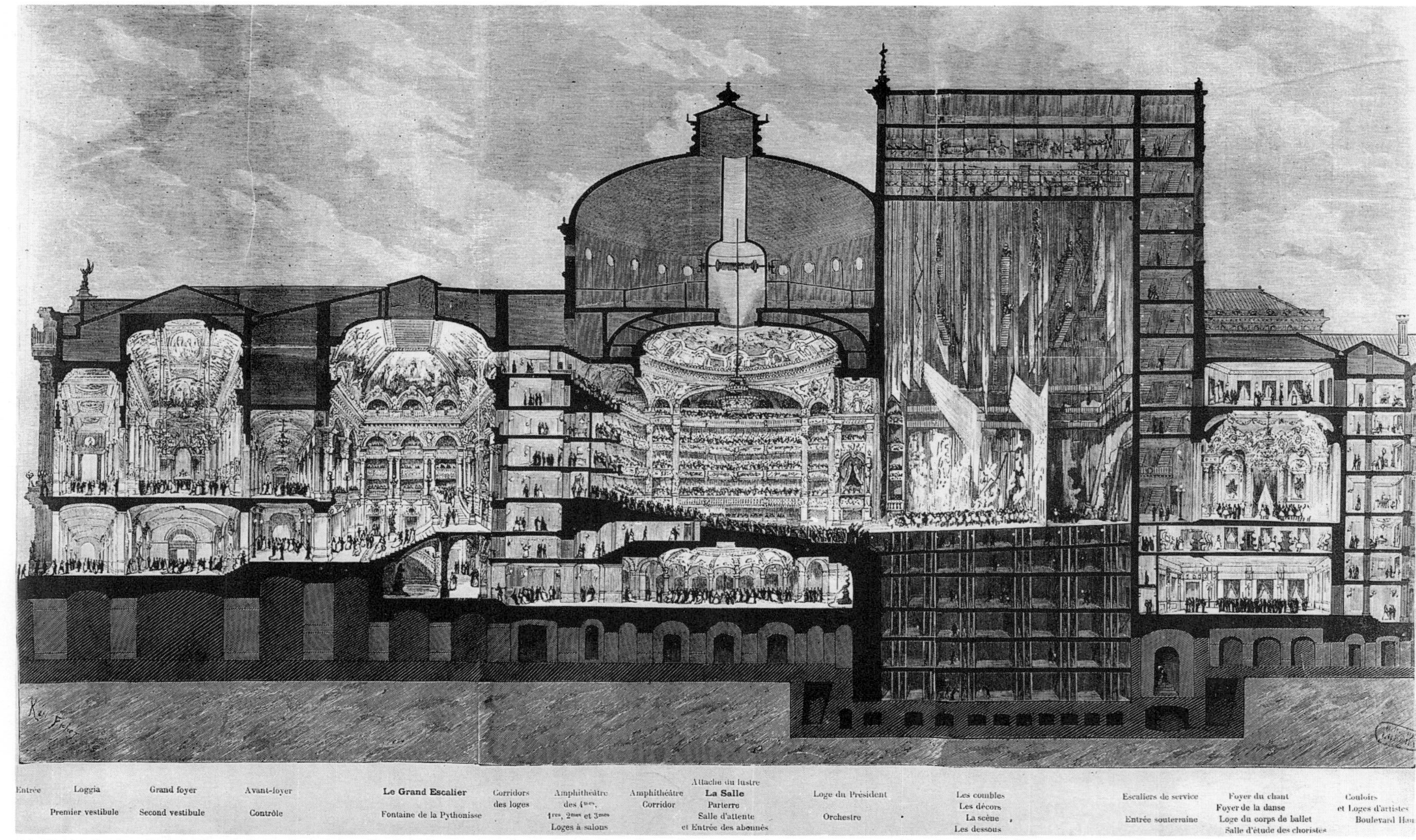

11. *Paris Opéra (Palais Garnier), designed by Charles Garnier, and inaugurated in 1875: longitudinal section, engraved by F. Méaulle after Karl Fichot and Henri Meyer, from 'Le journal illustré' (February 1875)*

12. The Metropolitan Opera House, New York: cut-away drawing of the backstage area, by Donald A. Mackay, 1966

caused not so much by the blending as by the fact that the conductor and instrumentalists cannot hear the singers and the music as clearly as they would in a concert-hall arrangement. Pierre Boulez said that it is like trying to conduct under water (Fay and Wood, p.97). It is perhaps significant that Wagner's orchestra pit, having been designed to meet the requirements of a particular repertory, has not been copied elsewhere.

Forsyth (p.8) is particularly attentive to the acoustics of the old Baroque theatres. 'Filled with sound-absorptive, elaborately costumed spectators and heavy drapery, and with low cubic volume relative to the audience size (with a consequently short reverberation time, tending towards 'open air' conditions), the Italian opera house had characteristically clear, intimate acoustics, which allowed the rich ornamentation of baroque arias to be revealed to splendid effect.'

Even the large Teatro Farnese in Parma was much admired by the visiting English author Joseph Addison for its acoustics. The architect, Aleotti, evidently understood how the proper use of wood and plaster affected acoustics. The auditorium was ceiled with light fir, and all of the interior structure was of wood, the colonnade and proscenium façade being faced with plaster (Leacroft and Leacroft, p.63). Perhaps the old theatre, which has other features that have influenced today's buildings, can still teach us something.

See also LIGHTING; MACHINERY; SEATING; and STAGE DESIGN.

*

Pianta, e spaccato del nuovo Teatro di Bologna (Bologna, 1763); Eng. trans., ed. T. Ault, in 'Ground Plan and Elevation of the New Theatre of Bologna [1763]', *Theatre Design & Technology*, xxiii/3 (1987), 19–26

F. Algarotti: *Saggio sopra l'opera in musica* (Bologna, 1755; Eng. trans., 1767)

G. Saunders: *A Treatise on Theatres* (London, 1790)

E. O. Sachs and E. A. E. Woodrow: *Modern Opera Houses and Theatres* (London, 1896–8)

A. Nicoll: *The Development of the Theatre* (New York, 1927, 5/1966)

E. Carrick: 'Theatre Machines in Italy, 1400–1800', *Architectural Review*, lxx/416 (1931), 9–14, 34–6

A. Beijer: *Court Theatres of Drottningholm and Gripsholm* (Malmö, 1933)

A. M. Nagler, ed.: *Sources of Theatrical History* (New York, 1952)

S. T. Worsthorne: *Venetian Opera in the Seventeenth Century* (Oxford, 1954, enlarged 2/1968)

'The Haymarket Opera House', *Survey of London*, xxix/1, ed. F. H. W. Sheppard (London, 1960)

A. M. Nagler: *Theatre Festivals of the Medici: 1539–1637* (New Haven, CT, 1964)

M. Baur-Heinhold: *Theater des Barock* (Munich, 1966; Eng. trans., 1967)

D. C. Mullin: 'The Queen's Theatre, Haymarket: Vanbrugh's Opera House', *Theatre Survey*, viii/2 (1967), 84–105

Theatre Architecture and Stage Machines (New York, 1969) [engravings from the *Encyclopédie*, 1762–72]

D. C. Mullin: *The Development of the Playhouse: a Survey of Theatre Architecture from the Renaissance to the Present* (Berkeley, CA, 1970)

'The Theatre Royal Drury Lane and the Royal Opera House Covent Garden', *Survey of London*, xxxv, ed. F. H. W. Sheppard (London, 1970)

'Notes on the Salzburg Festival Theatre', *Theatre Design & Technology*, no.27 (Dec 1971), 17–20

H. Schubert: *Moderner Theaterbau: internationale Situation, Dokumentation, Projekte, Bühnentechnik* (Stuttgart, 1971; Eng. trans., 1971)

F. Lesure: *L'opéra classique français XVIIe et XVIIIe siècles* (Geneva, 1972)

D. Nalbach: *The King's Theatre 1704–1867* (London, 1972)

R. Leacroft: *The Development of the English Playhouse* (London, 1973, 2/1988)

S. Orgel and R. Strong: *Inigo Jones: the Theatre of the Stuart Court* (Berkeley, CA, 1973)

S. Tidworth: *Theatres: an Architectural and Cultural History* (New York, 1973)

R. Hartmann, ed.: *Opera* (New York, 1977)

G. C. Izenour: *Theater Design* (New York, 1977)

L. L. Secchi: *1778/1978 Il Teatro alla Scala* (Milan, 1977)

The Italian Baroque Stage: Documents by Giulio Troili [1672], Andrea Pozzo [1693–1700], Ferdinando Galli-Bibiena [1711, 1732], Baldasarre Orsini [1773, 1785], trans. D. H. Ogden (Berkeley, CA, 1978)

E. Langhans: 'The Theatres', *The London Theatre World, 1660–1800*, ed. R. D. Hume (Carbondale, IL, 1980)

D. C. Mullin: 'Theatre Structure and its Effect on Production', *The Stage and the Page*, ed. G. W. Stone jr (Berkeley, CA, 1981), 73–89

E. Craig: *Baroque Theatre Construction: a Study of the Earliest Treatise on the Structure of Theatres by Fabrizio Carini Motta Architect and Scene Designer at the Court of Mantua 1676* (n.p., 1982)

A. Saint and others: *A History of the Royal Opera House Covent Garden 1732–1982* (London, 1982)

F. Shelton: 'Bayreuth's "Invisible Orchestra" ', *Strad*, xciii (1982), 496–9

M. Mayer: *The Met* (New York, 1983)

L. Tamburini: *L'architettura dalle origini al 1936*, Storia del Teatro Regio Torino, iv (Turin, 1983)

S. Fay and R. Wood: *The Ring* (London, 1984) [on 1983 Bayreuth production]

E. Gábor: 'The Re-Opening of the Budapest Opera House', *Hungarian Quarterly*, xxv/wint. (1984), 189–94

R. Leacroft and H. Leacroft: *Theatre and Playhouse* (London, 1984)

P. Nicolin and others: 'Project for the Bastille Opera House in Paris', *Lotus International*, xliii (1984), 88–93

G. Staud: 'One Hundred Years of the Budapest Opera House', *The New Hungarian Quarterly*, xxv/wint. (1984), 194–206; xxvi/spr. (1985), 194–200

M. Forsyth: *Buildings for Music* (Cambridge, 1985)

S. McCarthy: 'Gottfried Semper and the Development of the Theatre Form', *Theatrephile*, ii/6 (1985), 48–53

J. Näther: 'The Dresden Semper Opera Restored to its Old Splendour', *Theatrephile*, ii/6 (1985), 38–47

Arkhitektura sovetskogo teatra [Soviet Theatre Architecture] (Moscow, 1986)

'Architecture 87', *Theatre Crafts*, xxi/10 (1987) [special issue]

O. K. Larson: *The Theatrical Writings of Fabrizio Carini Motta* (Carbondale, IL, 1987)

J. Moatti and others: *The Paris Opéra* (New York, 1987)

A. Seebohm, ed.: *Der Wiener Oper: 350 Jahre Glanz und Tradition* (Vienna, 1986; Eng. trans. 1987)

A. Clark: 'The Bastille – "Vision fugitive"?', *Opera*, xl (1989), 406–12

R. Hughes: 'Paris à la Mitterand', *Time* (18 Sept 1989)

S. Sadie, ed.: *History of Opera* (London, 1989), chaps. 6, 12, 19 and 20

'Architechture 91: the Opera House', *Theatre Crafts*, xxv/5 (1991) [whole issue]

S. Williams: 'Bayreuth Festspielhaus: Enchaining the Audience', *Theatre Survey*, xxxiii/1 (1992), 65–73

EDWARD A. LANGHANS

Theatre Royal. Designation originally used for a British theatre enjoying the privileges of a royal charter or patent. In 18th-century London there were three such theatres, Covent Garden, Drury Lane and, from 1766, the Little Theatre in the Haymarket. The same applies to the Theatre Royal in Crow Street, Dublin. Privileges arising from possession of a royal patent ceased in 1843 and the term has since been freely appropriated.

Théâtres de la Foire. The name by which troupes performing at the Foires St Germain and St Laurent in Paris, during the 17th and 18th centuries, were commonly known. They became, in 1714, the Opéra-Comique, and merged with the Comédie-Italienne in 1762; *see* PARIS, §§2(iii) and 3(i).

Thebom, Blanche (*b* Monessen, PA, 19 Sept 1918). American mezzo-soprano. In New York she studied with Margarete Matzenauer and Edyth Walker. She made her first appearance with the Metropolitan on tour in Philadelphia as Brangäne in 1944 and her New York début with the company as Fricka in *Die Walküre* in the same year; she remained with the Metropolitan until the 1966–7 season, singing much Wagner as well as Marina, Herodias, Orlofsky and Amneris. In 1950 she sang Dorabella at Glyndebourne, and in 1957 she had considerable success at Covent Garden as Dido in the first English professional staged performance of *Les Troyens*. Other roles included Azucena and Carmen. In 1967–8 she was artistic director of Atlanta Opera. Thebom had a wide-ranging mezzo-soprano of generally fine quality, not a great voice, but one capable of most pleasing effect. Her handsome presence and gracious manner served her well as did her secure musicianship. Her article 'Singing or Acting?' was published in *Opera News* (xxix/21, 1964–5, pp.9–11).

MAX DE SCHAUENSEE/R

Theile, Johann (*b* Naumburg, 29 July 1646; *d* Naumburg, bur. 24 June 1724). German composer. He received his first musical training in Magdeburg, and studied law at the University of Leipzig; some time between 1666 and 1672 he was a pupil of Schütz. In 1673, after a period in Lübeck, he was appointed Kapellmeister at Gottorf. There he may have written his first operas or opera-like works, as Duke Christian Albrecht's expenses included 'musical entertainments' as well as plays. The renewed territorial dispute between Schleswig-Holstein and Denmark soon interrupted the duke's promising reign: he fled to Hamburg in 1675. Theile was released from service when the Kapelle was dissolved but went with his patron. In Hamburg his first opera, *Adam und Eva, oder Der erschaffene, gefallene und auffgerichtete Mensch*, inaugurated the new Theater am Gänsemarkt on 2 January 1678; his opera *Orontes* was given there the same year, and *Die Geburth Christi* three years later. Though Theile remained on good terms with Christian Albrecht he left the city to become Kapellmeister at Wolfenbüttel (1685–91), after which he entered the service of Duke Christian I at Merseburg. Later he may have been connected with the Prussian court in Berlin; by 1718 he had moved to Naumburg. Mattheson paid him this simple tribute in *Critica musica*: 'he was an especially pious, honest man and thoroughly understood the harmonious arts'.

A skilful contrapuntist, Theile is particularly important for his sacred music, which forms the majority of his surviving output. Of his three known operas, only the librettos survive (in *D-Hs*). Five strophic arias from *Orontes* survived in manuscript until World War II; they were transcribed before being lost, and were later published (Wolff 1957). They are simple, syllabic, folk-like in style and moderate in range. Indeed, the poetry in all three librettos suggests uncomplicated music. *Adam und Eva*, to a text by Christian Richter, expands the Biblical account of creation with a prologue by the four elements, and closes with the appearance of the Saviour and a chorus of thanksgiving from Adam and Eve, Mercy, Justice and the angels; *Die Geburth Christi*, which is in rather strict poetry by an unidentified author, opens with a prologue for priests of Apollo declaring that their gods have no more power. *Orontes*, based on a story of love and disguise, is longer and more complex in poetic structure and staging requirements.

J. Mattheson: *Critica musica*, ii (Hamburg, 1725), 57–8, 282–3
W. Maxton: *Johann Theile* (diss., U. of Tübingen, 1927)
B. Engelke: 'Die Gottorfer Hofkapelle unter Joh. Theile und M. Colerus', *Kieler Blätter* (1943), 93
H. C. Wolff: *Die Barockoper in Hamburg* (Wolfenbüttel, 1957)

JOCELYN MACKEY

Théobalde. *See* GATTI, THEOBALDO DI.

Thérèse **(i).** *Drame musical* in two acts by JULES MASSENET to a libretto by Jules Claretie; Monte Carlo, Opéra, 7 February 1907.

Thérèse, whose two acts stretch to no more than an hour of music, was based on an original idea by the composer, and both written for and dedicated to the creator of the title role, the mezzo-soprano Lucy Arbell (under her real name of Georgette Wallace). She had created the role of Persephone in Massenet's *Ariane* (1906, Paris Opéra) and the aging composer was infatuated with her. He was later to write the role of Dulcinée in *Don Quichotte* for her.

Thérèse is set in 1792 (Act 1) and 1793 (Act 2). The heroine is married to the Girondin André Thorel (baritone), former employee and now owner of a chateau near Paris. As he leaves to pursue his duties as a Deputy, a shadowy figure enters the park: it is Armand de Clerval (tenor), the dispossessed owner of the chateau, boyhood companion to André and former admirer of Thérèse. The pair recall happier times and Armand presses his claims to her love, which are rejected. Thérèse may have married André out of friendship rather than love, but she vows to stand by him. André returns with a troop of soldiers: the suspicious stranger is passed off as André's brother and invited by the unsuspecting husband to take refuge with him and his wife.

The second act is set in a house in Paris eight months later. Armand is still lodging with the Thorels. André sings of the friendship that has led him to acquire a safe-conduct for Armand, and again goes off to work. The jealous Armand refuses to leave Thérèse, and begs her to flee with him. After token resistance she agrees. News is brought of André's arrest. Armand escapes, Thérèse promising to follow him in due course. But when she sees her husband in the tumbril in the street outside, remorse leads her to change her mind. She cries out 'Vive le roi!', and is dragged by the mob to join André at the guillotine.

Thérèse is one of Massenet's least successful operas, and joins *Andrea Chénier* (1896), an obvious inspiration, in the graveyard of works set during the French Revolution. Claretie's libretto is greatly inferior to the one he collaborated on for the analogous *La Navarraise*, and there is something curiously distasteful about the way this shallowly conceived eternal triangle is set against political events of such moment. Characterization and motivation are at the level of romantic fiction, and the way the three have lived together for eight months without either anything happening or the husband's suspecting beggars belief. Ever the craftsman, the composer brings a certain autumnal charm to the love music ('Au loin ... là-bas', Thérèse's vision of an imaginary refuge, is vintage Massenet), which only serves to underline the banality of the revolutionary passages, but at too many crucial moments he is content to rely on well-tried formula, with many a pale echo of *Manon* and *Werther*.

The first Paris performance on 19 May 1911 shared a double bill at the Opéra-Comique with the world première of *L'heure espagnole*. *Thérèse* survived in the French repertory until 1930 and has only occasionally been revived. RODNEY MILNES

Thérèse **(ii).** Opera in one act by JOHN TAVENER to a libretto by Gerald McLarnon; London, Covent Garden, 1 October 1979.

The opera traces the spiritual growth of St Thérèse of Lisieux (1873–97). The poet Rimbaud (tenor) guides Thérèse (soprano) through purgatory and hell, forcing her to question her childlike faith. She encounters the triple murderer Pranzini (low bass) and comes to accept that even he must be loved and cherished. Christ (tenor), who is later identified with Thérèse's father, then leads her to the Flanders trenches and the concentration camps of the 20th century. These visions strengthen her flagging faith, and the opera ends with a serene song of ecstasy, in which Christ joins.

Thérèse calls for a heroine who, as Paul Griffiths (1979) has suggested, 'can range from childish babbling to the depths of despair and then to elevated grandeur, one who can, in Tavener's words, "sing a Berio score with the same ease as she could sing Salome" '. The problem of portraying onstage the inward life of a character whose outward life is entirely uneventful was not solved at the first production. *Thérèse* has more in common with Tavener's larger-scale concert works than with any existing opera, and it seems not impossible that it will eventually make more of a mark in the concert hall, where the listener can give unfettered rein to his imagination, than onstage. HUGO COLE

Thern, Károly [Karl] (*b* Iglau, 13 Aug 1817; *d* Vienna, 13 April 1886). Hungarian composer of German birth. His early years were spent in Miskolc, where he founded a music society (1832) and an orchestra (1834). In 1837 he entered the University of Pest and four years later was made assistant conductor of the National Theatre. In this capacity he wrote the operas *Gizul* (1841), *Tihany ostroma* (1845) and *A képzelt beteg* (1855). From 1853 he taught at the National Conservatory. In 1864 Thern moved to Leipzig to secure a better education for his sons; he returned to Pest in 1868 but spent his last years in Vienna.

Thern's music shows a sound theatrical inventiveness but does not rise above the level of most Hungarian operatic music of the time. He was most successful in adapting folksongs for use in popular stage works such as *Hortobágyi pusztán* ('On the Hortobágy puszta').

Gizul (grand op, Lengyel), Pest, 1841
Tihany ostroma [The Siege of Tihany] (grand op), Pest, March 1845
A képzelt beteg [The Imaginary Invalid] (comic op), Pest, Oct 1855

Thésée ('Theseus'). *Tragédie en musique* in a prologue and five acts by Jean-Baptiste Lully (*see* LULLY family, (1)) to a libretto by PHILIPPE QUINAULT after Ovid's *Metamorphoses*; St Germain-en-Laye, court, 11 January 1675.

The aging King Egée [Aegeus] (baritone) wishes to marry his ward, the princess Eglé [Aegle] (soprano). The magician princess Médée [Medea] (soprano) wants to marry Theseus (*haute-contre*), the young hero who has led the king's victorious army. Theseus and Aegle, however, love each other. A subplot involves the confidants of Aegeus, Aegle and Medea in a love triangle. Medea unleashes her magical powers in an unsuccessful attempt to force Aegle to relinquish Theseus, transporting her first to a dreadful desert where the 'inhabitants of hell' torment her, then to an enchanted island where she must lie to Theseus about her feelings if she wishes his life to be spared. Unable to vanquish the lovers, Medea pretends to honour them and turns to the king for vengeance: she persuades Aegeus to regard Theseus as a potential threat to the throne and to poison him during a festival in his honour. At the last moment the king recognizes Theseus' sword and realizes what the others already know – that the young hero is his son who has been raised in a faraway place. Aegeus stops Theseus from drinking the poison and gladly gives him Aegle's hand. Medea's final act of vengeance – the destruction of the festive setting – is undone by the goddess Minerve [Minerva] (soprano).

The orchestra and chorus are used with brilliant effect in several *divertissements*, but especially in the evocation of battle throughout Act 1. Medea's role (like that of Lully's final lovesick sorceress, Armide) is replete with expressive monologue *airs*: 'Doux repos', 'Dépit mortel', 'Sortez, Ombres' and 'Ah! faut-il me venger'. *Thésée* was part of the standard repertory at the Paris Opéra from 1675 until 1767; in addition, it was selected to represent Lully when, in 1779, the Opéra presented an historical survey of French operatic styles. Lully's score was substantially modernized by editors for productions from 1754 onwards. LOIS ROSOW

Thessaloniki. SALONICA.

Thétis et Pélée ('Thetis and Peleus'). *Tragédie en musique* in a prologue and five acts by PASCAL COLLASSE to a libretto by BERNARD LE BOVIER DE FONTENELLE; Paris, Opéra, 11 January 1689.

The Nereid Thetis (soprano) is wooed by two gods, Jupiter (bass) and Neptune (bass), and a mortal, Peleus (*haute-contre*). A celebration ordered by Jupiter in her honour is disrupted by a storm whipped up by Neptune. An oracle consulted about the outcome of this rivalry declares that Thetis's husband will one day be less powerful than his son. Dismayed, Neptune and Jupiter withdraw their claims, and the wedding of Thetis and Peleus is duly celebrated. Although the plot is rather thin and padded out with spectacular interventions and effects, musically these afford considerable interest; Collasse expands the model of the temple scene inherited from Lully (e.g. *Bellérophon*) and develops the use of the orchestra for dramatic effects. The *tempête* in Act 2 scenes vii–ix is the first of many going by way of Marais' *Alcyone* (1706) to Rameau. CAROLINE WOOD

Thetis och Pelée ('Thetis and Peleus'). Opera in five acts (later revised in three) by FRANCESCO ANTONIO BALDASSARE UTTINI to a libretto by Johan Wellander after a sketch by Gustavus III based on BERNARD LE BOVIER DE FONTENELLE's *tragédie lyrique Thétis et Pelée*; Stockholm, Bollhuset, 18 January 1773.

The opera begins with Pelée [Peleus] (tenor), King of Thessaly, expressing his love for the naiad Thetis (soprano), though he fears competition from both Neptune (bass) and Jupiter (baritone). Thetis encourages his suit and persuades him of her constancy. Neptune then declares his love but is interrupted by Jupiter, who angrily orders Eolus (bass) to attack Neptune's realm with storms, forcing him to leave. In Act 2 the naiad Doris (soprano), who believes that

Peleus loves her, confides in Echo (soprano). Peleus, unsure of his fate, asks Doris's advice. Thetis finds the two together and upbraids Peleus for his faithlessness. Jupiter gives a celebration in Thetis's honour complete with Olympic Games. In Act 3 the oracle tells Peleus that he may marry Thetis but that his son will be greater than he, leaving Peleus uneasy. In Act 4 Thetis comes to realize Peleus's constancy. Peleus, however, is discovered by Jupiter, who chains him to a cliff. He is freed by Neptune, who takes his side. In Act 5 Neptune takes Peleus to Olympus to argue his complaint before the gods. Eros (soprano) and Mercury (tenor) both state that Thetis is to marry the most sensitive suitor. Neptune withdraws his suit and Jupiter, afraid of the oracle, graciously sanctions the marriage of Thetis and Peleus.

Thetis och Pelée was the first of a series of operas commissioned by King Gustavus III to encourage the development of Swedish opera; he provided sketches for both the plot and the staging. The première was such a success that J. Ehrensvärd proclaimed a renaissance of the Swedish stage. It also marked the début of Carl Stenborg, who with the soprano Elisabeth Olin dominated the Royal Opera for more than a decade. In 1775 Wellander and Uttini revised the opera heavily, reducing the five acts to three and making cuts in the ballet music; the opera remained in the repertory into 1781. In 1791 it was revived in a five-act version, reorchestrated (possibly by Kraus) and heavily edited. This was performed with renewed success until 1792, with excerpts published in the *Musikaliskt tidsfördrif*.

The musical style of Uttini's original is a blend of French and Italian operatic idioms. There are large segments of *secco* recitative and occasional da capo arias, interspersed with choral interludes and ballet. The melodies are often quite lyrical and Uttini's orchestration uses much woodwind colour. The expanded orchestration of the 1791 version adds a distinctive modern harmonic language that contrasts with the simplicity of the original. BERTIL H. VAN BOER

Thévenard, Gabriel-Vincent (*b* Orleans or Paris, 10 Aug 1669; *d* Paris, 24 Aug 1741). French singer. He went to Paris in 1690 and was a pupil of Destouches, who wrote several roles for him including Hylas in *Issé* (1698) and Amadis in *Amadis de Grèce* (1699). A member of the Académie Royale de Musique, he performed for over 30 years in some 80 *tragédies* and ballets, including premières of works by Campra, Collasse, Desmarets and Marais, as well as revivals of works by Lully. He frequently took the role of a king, a god or a grand priest (his *basse-taille* range was approximately *G* to *e'*) and was particularly admired for his ability to declaim recitative in a speech-like manner. He excelled at tragic roles in which, especially in the works of Destouches, he often performed an emotional lament as a monologue. In 1729 he married a young girl and retired from opera.

*

J. B. Durey de Noinville: *Histoire du théâtre de l'Académie royale de musique en France* (Paris, 1757)

E. Campardon: *L'Académie royale de musique au XVIIIe siècle* (Paris, 1884)

MARY CYR

Thieving Magpie, The. Opera by Gioachino Rossini; *see* GAZZA LADRA, LA.

Thill, Georges (*b* Paris, 14 Dec 1897; *d* Paris, 17 Oct 1984). French tenor. He studied in Paris and in Naples with de Lucia, making his début at the Opéra in 1924 as Nicias (*Thaïs*). He continued to sing there for 16 years, graduating from Marouf, Jean (*Hérodiade*), Roland (*Esclarmonde*), Raoul (*Les Huguenots*), Berlioz's Faust and Gluck's Admetus to Walther, Lohengrin, Tannhäuser, Parsifal, Arnold (*Guillaume Tell*), Aeneas (*Les Troyens à Carthage*), Samson and Calaf. At the Opéra-Comique his roles included Don José, Des Grieux, Werther and Cavaradossi. He sang Calaf at La Scala, Verona and Buenos Aires, where he also sang Don Carlos and Boito's Faust. He made his Covent Garden début in 1928 as Samson, returning as Don José (1937). At the Metropolitan (1931–2) his first role was Romeo, followed by Radames, Gounod's Faust and Sadko. He made his farewell to the stage in 1953 as Canio at the Opéra-Comique. With his brilliant, robust tone, spirited phrasing and aristocratic enunciation, he was the most distinguished heroic French tenor of his time. He recorded a complete *Werther* and made several films, including Abel Gance's *Louise* with Grace Moore.

*

D. Shawe-Taylor: 'A Gallery of Great Singers, 16: Georges Thill (1897–1984)', *Opera*, xxxvi (1985), 741–7

ANDRÉ TUBEUF/ELIZABETH FORBES

Thillon [née Hunt], **Sophie Anne** [Anna] (*b* Calcutta or London, 1819; *d* Torquay, 5 May 1903). English soprano. She studied in France and sang in the provinces before being engaged in 1838 for the Théâtre de la Renaissance, Paris (Salle Ventadour), where she made her début in the title role of Grisar's *Lady Melvil*. In 1840 she first appeared at the Opéra-Comique as Mathilde in Auber's *La neige*; she created Catarina in his *Les diamants de la couronne* (1841) and repeated the role for her English début in 1844 at the Princess's Theatre, London; in 1845 and 1846 she sang at Drury Lane, where she created Stella in Balfe's *The Enchantress*. From 1851 to 1854 she sang in the first San Francisco opera seasons. She made her final stage appearance at the Lyceum Theatre, London, in 1855.

Thoma, Therese. *See* VOGL, THERESE.

Thomas. Opera in three acts by EINOJUHANI RAUTAVAARA to his own libretto; Joensuu, 21 June 1985.

Thomas was a commission from the Joensuu Song Festival in eastern Finland. On one level the opera deals with the conflict between the old, withering pagan religion of the Finns and the new Christian religion that was overpowering it in the early 13th century. It is also a study in human ambition and its consequences.

The Thomas of the title (baritone) is the first Christian Bishop of Finland (according to history, probably an Englishman by birth). In old age he recollects his turbulent life in a dreamlike vision. Bishop Thomas assembles a great crusade against Russian Novgorod. He has ambitions of creating his own church-state; to this end he is not above deceit. At the same time he is beset by sinful thoughts: when he imagines that he sees the Virgin, it is in fact a Maiden (soprano) embodying temptation. The Western army is confronted by the Russians, led by Alexander Nevsky. In spite of Thomas's brutal attempts to stem the rout, the crusaders are annihilated. Thomas retires to a monastery, where, in his vision as an old man, he must now answer for his actions.

In *Thomas* Rautavaara combines aleatory and serial procedures, gently lyrical tonality and even Gregorian chant to create a logically coherent, dramatically charged and, at the same time, mystical work.

ERKKI ARNI

Thomas, (Charles Louis) Ambroise (*b* Metz, 5 Aug 1811; *d* Paris, 12 Feb 1896). French composer. He brought a fresh lyricism to *opéra comique* and, with *Mignon*, composed one of the most popular works in the history of opera.

1. LIFE. The son of a musician, Thomas began to play the piano at an early age and in 1828 entered the Paris Conservatoire, where his teachers included Pierre-Joseph-Guillaume Zimmermann for piano and Le Sueur for composition. In 1832 he won the Prix de Rome with a cantata, *Herman et Ketty*, and subsequently spent three years in Italy. His first opera, the one-act comedy *La double échelle*, produced by the Opéra-Comique in 1837, scored a considerable success and received 247 performances before it was dropped from the repertory. His next three operas, produced at the rate of one a year, made little mark, although *Le panier fleuri* (1839), another one-act piece, was adapted as *The Fox and the Goose, or The Widow's Husband* and performed at the Adelphi Theatre, London, in 1844.

Meanwhile in 1841 Thomas, who had already made his début at the Opéra with the second act of the ballet *La gipsy* in 1839, presented there a two-act opera, *Le comte de Carmagnola*. In spite of an excellent cast that included Prosper Dérivis in the title role, Julie Dorus-Gras and Eugène Massol, it received only eight performances, probably because of the poor libretto by Scribe. His next work for the Opéra, *Le guerillero*, did little better, and Thomas returned to the Opéra-Comique, for whom he continued to compose without much success. Then, after a gap of over four years, in 1849, he wrote his first undisputed triumph, *Le caïd*. T. M. F. Sauvage's libretto, a mixture of *Il barbiere di Siviglia* and *L'italiana in Algeri*, was better than average, while in his sparkling score Thomas also drew on the Rossinian style to excellent comic effect. By 1900 *Le caïd* had received over 400 performances.

Le songe d'une nuit d'été (1850), Thomas' next work for the Comique, was also a considerable success. The text owes nothing to *A Midsummer Night's Dream*, but Shakespeare is one of the characters, as also are Queen Elizabeth I and Sir John Falstaff, the governor of 'Richemont', where the action takes place. *Raymond, ou Le secret de la reine* (1851), based on the legend of The Man in the Iron Mask, was not much liked except for the overture, which quickly became popular; nor was *La Tonelli* (1853) a success, despite the presence in the cast of the young baritone Jean-Baptiste Faure, who had made his début with the Opéra-Comique a few months previously.

On the death of Spontini in 1851 Thomas had inherited his chair in the Académie des Beaux Arts; the following year he became professor of composition at the Conservatoire. For the next 14 years he continued to write for the Comique without any particular success. The protagonist of *La cour de Célimène* (1855), a lady with no fewer than 14 suitors, was sung by Marie Miolan-Carvalho; *Psyché* (1857) was, with some justification, considered an inferior copy of Gounod's *Sapho*; and in *Le carnaval de Venise* (also 1857) he was accused of imitating Massé, whose light operas were popular during the 1850s. *Le roman d'Elvire* (1860) was a total fiasco.

Meanwhile, the success of Gounod's *Faust* (1859) had set librettists throughout Europe searching the works of Goethe for suitable operatic subjects. Barbier and Carré, the librettists of *Faust*, took an episode from *Wilhelm Meisters Lehrjahre* as a basis for the text that they wrote for Thomas; it proved an inspired choice. *Mignon* (1866) follows Goethe only a little more closely than *Faust* does, but it is a great deal nearer its original in spirit. With Galli-Marié (who nine years later would create Carmen) in the title role, *Mignon* was an instant success, achieving 500 performances in its first dozen years of life, and 1200 by the end of the century. A work perfectly tailored to the talents of the composer and undoubtedly his masterpiece, *Mignon*, despite the happy ending tacked on to placate family audiences at the Opéra-Comique, offers its original author no disrespect.

The same cannot be said of *Hamlet* (1868), with which Thomas finally scored a triumph at the Opéra, in emulation of Gounod's *Roméo et Juliette* the year before. Barbier and Carré, in their adaptation of Shakespeare's tragedy, not only provided *Hamlet* with a happy ending but trivialized the most famous drama in the English language to an unpardonable degree. However, they provided Thomas with a melodramatic but effective libretto on which he could lavish some of his finest music. Thomas had originally conceived the title role for tenor but, as no suitable tenor was available, he transposed it for the baritone Faure, who achieved a tremendous personal triumph as Hamlet.

Mignon and *Hamlet* formed the climax of Thomas' career as a composer. Leaving aside *Gille et Gillotin*, written in 1859 but not performed at the Opéra-Comique until 1874, he wrote only one more opera: *Françoise de Rimini* (1882), based on canto v of Dante's *Inferno*, received 41 performances at the Opéra over a period of 18 months before disappearing for ever from the repertory. In 1871 Thomas succeeded Auber as director of the Conservatoire, a post he held until his death. He no longer had time for composition, no pressing financial need to write operas, nor, one may presume, any artistic stimulus to continue doing so.

2. WORKS. Thomas was an eclectic composer who seemed able to write in almost any style. Hérold and Auber are clear influences on his earlier works for the Opéra-Comique; it was not until *Le caïd* (1849) that Thomas showed any true originality in his music. Even then, the debt to his predecessors – in this case chiefly to Rossini – remained considerable, but the music of *Le caïd* has a charm of its own that transcends the conventionality of the text. *Le songe d'une nuit d'été*, though less successful as a whole, also contains much delightful and individual music, while the orchestration is often quite ravishing.

The classical subject of *Psyché* (1857) did not inspire Thomas at all deeply, but *La cour de Célimène* (1855) and *Le carnaval de Venise* (1857), although derivative in style, point the way towards *Mignon*. The ensemble music of *La cour de Célimène* has a new fluency and expressiveness, while *Le carnaval* includes some extremely florid music for the heroine Sylvia, written for Marie Cabel, the coloratura soprano who nine years later sang Philine in *Mignon*. *Gille et Gillotin*, dating from 1859 but not produced until 15 years later, is a throwback to *Le caïd*, with Donizetti rather than Rossini as the chief model. The composer tried, without success, to prevent its performance in 1874, when the opera, not surprisingly, failed dismally.

In *Mignon* the various stylistic influences on Thomas all combine harmoniously together. A completely new ingredient is the dramatic strength of the characters: Mignon herself has no predecessor in the composer's oeuvre; Olivia, in *Le songe d'une nuit d'été*, shows similar traits, but no other Thomas heroine displays the complexity of Mignon, in whom love, affection, pathos and loyalty are mixed with a very human jealousy; after all, no other Thomas heroine is based on an original drawn by Goethe. Wilhelm Meister, the student, and the elderly minstrel Lothario, who turns out to be a nobleman and father of Mignon, are also well characterized in their music.

In *Hamlet* the prince springs to strong dramatic life, despite his conventional drinking song and the happy ending. Baritones from Faure and Maurel to Sherrill Milnes and Thomas Allen have found Hamlet a rich and rewarding role. Claudius and Gertrude are less three-dimensional, but the Closet Scene between Hamlet and his mother is the most dramatically effective in the opera. Ophelia is descended from a long line of recognizable Thomas heroines, including La Tonelli, Célimène, Sylvia and Philine. It is significant that Christine Nilsson, who created Ophelia, always refused to sing Philine, the obvious choice of role for a singer of her vocal accomplishments, but took the part of Mignon, insisting that the music should be adapted for soprano.

If Thomas had written no stage works except *Mignon* and *Hamlet* he would probably be more widely recognized as one of the most influential and important of French 19th-century operatic composers.

See also HAMLET and MIGNON.

published and first performed in Paris; opéras comiques unless otherwise stated

La double échelle (1, F. A. E. de Planard), OC (Nouveautés), 23 Aug 1837 (1837)
Le perruquier de la régence (3, de Planard and P. Dupont), OC (Nouveautés), 30 March 1838 (n.d.)
Le panier fleuri (1, A. de Leuven and Brunswick [L. Lhérie]), OC (Nouveautés), 6 May 1839 (1839)
Carline (3, de Leuven and Brunswick), OC (Nouveautés), 24 Feb 1840, vs (1840)
Le comte de Carmagnola (opéra, 2, E. Scribe), Opéra, 19 April 1841 (1841)
Le guerillero (opéra, 2, T. Anne), 22 June 1842, vs (1842)
Angélique et Médor (1, T. M. F. Sauvage), OC (Favart), 10 May 1843, vs (1843)
Mina, ou Le ménage à trois (3, de Planard), OC (Favart), 10 Oct 1843, vs (1843)
Le caïd (2, Sauvage), OC (Favart), 3 Jan 1849 (1849)
Le songe d'une nuit d'été (3, J. B. Rosier and de Leuven), OC (Nouveautés), 20 April 1850 (1850)
Raymond, ou Le secret de la reine (3, Rosier and de Leuven), OC (Favart), 5 June 1851 (*c*1851)
La Tonelli (2, Sauvage), OC (Favart), 30 March 1853 (*c*1853)
La cour de Célimène (2, Rosier), OC (Favart), 11 April 1855, vs (1855)
Psyché (3, J. Barbier and M. Carré), OC (Favart), 26 Jan 1857, vs (1857); rev. 21 May 1878
Le carnaval de Venise (3, Sauvage), OC (Favart), 9 Dec 1857 (1857)
Gille et Gillotin (opéra, 1, Sauvage), OC (Favart), 22 April 1874 (1874) [written in 1859 as Gillotin et son père, unperf.]
Le roman d'Elvire (3, A. Dumas *père* and de Leuven), OC (Favart), 4 Feb 1860 (1860)
Mignon (3, Barbier and Carré, after J. W. von Goethe: *Wilhelm Meister*), OC (Favart), 17 Nov 1866, (n.d.), vs (1866)
Hamlet (opéra, 5, Barbier and Carré, after W. Shakespeare), Opéra, 9 March 1868 (1869)
Françoise de Rimini (opéra, 5, Barbier and Carré, after Dante: *Inferno*, v:97–142), Opéra, 14 April 1882 (1882)

L. Escudier: *Mes souvenirs* (Paris, 1863, 2/1863)
E. Hanslick: *Die moderne Oper*, ii: *Musikalische Stationen* (Berlin, 1880, 6/1911); viii: *Am Ende des Jahrhunderts* (Berlin, 1899, 3/1911)
H. Sutherland Edwards: *The Lyrical Drama* (London, 1881)
A. Jullien: *Musiciens d'aujourd'hui* (Paris, 1892–4)
A. Soubies and C. Malherbe: *Histoire de l'Opéra-Comique* (Paris, 1892–3)
A. Hervey: *Masters of French Music* (London, 1894)
H. Delaborde: *Notice sur la vie et les oeuvres de M. Ambroise Thomas* (Paris, 1896)
A. Jullien: 'Ambroise Thomas', *RMI*, iii (1896), 358–66
J. Simon: 'Ambroise Thomas', *Revue de Paris*, iii/2 (1896), 98–111
H. Berlioz: 'Le caïd', *Les musiciens et la musique* (Paris, 1903)
A. Pougin: *Musiciens du XIXe siècle* (Paris, 1911)
J. Combarieu: *Histoire de la musique*, iii (Paris, 1919, 3/1947, rev. R. Dumesnil, 1955)
C. Le Senne: 'Période contemporaine: Ambroise Thomas (1811–1896)', *EMDC*, I/iii (1921), 1697–1706
A. Luzio, ed.: *Carteggi Verdiani* (Rome, 1935–47)
P. Landormy: *La musique française* (Paris, 1943–8, 19/1948)
M. Cooper: 'Charles Louis Ambroise Thomas', *The Music Masters*, ed. A. L. Bacharach, ii (London, 1950); pubd separately (London, 1957–8)
M. Curtiss: *Bizet and his World* (New York, 1958)
W. Dean: 'Shakespeare and Opera', *Shakespeare in Music*, ed. P. Hartnoll (London, 1964), 89–175
H. R. Cohen, ed.: *The Original Staging Manuals for Twelve Parisian Operatic Premières/Douze livrets de mise en scène lyrique datant des créations parisiennes* (Stuyvesant, NY, 1991) [incl. production book for *Mignon*]

ELIZABETH FORBES

Thomas, Arthur Goring (*b* Ratton Park, Sussex, 20 Nov 1850; *d* London, 20 March 1892). English composer. He studied in Paris for two years from 1873; this was a formative period and most of his compositions show strong traces of French influence. From 1877 to 1880 he studied with Sullivan and Prout at the RAM, London, where he twice won the Lucas Medal for composition; later he received orchestration lessons from Max Bruch. In 1879 his opera *The Light of the Harem* was performed in part at the RAM; the success of this performance led to a commission from Carl Rosa, which Thomas fulfilled with *Esmeralda* (1883). The libretto, based on Victor Hugo's *Notre-Dame de Paris*, was described as 'a flow of doggerel' which stripped the story of all drama and passion (following the example of Gounod's *Faust*, the librettists gave *Esmeralda* a happy ending). This emasculated libretto was well suited to Thomas's graceful and elegant music, which only occasionally achieved the degree of passion displayed in the climactic love duet in the third act. Complicated scenes with several principals and chorus severely taxed his powers of dramatic invention, but some of the single, lyrical numbers are more successful. Although Thomas felt that he had never mastered the art of setting English words, the recitatives were considered 'advanced' and praised for their naturalness and flexibility. *Esmeralda* was later given in a German version at Cologne, Hamburg and Berlin, and in a French version (with a tragic ending) at Covent Garden in July 1890.

In 1885 the Carl Rosa Company produced a second opera by Thomas, *Nadeshda*, with a libretto adapted from a Russian story. The subject was more serious than that of *Esmeralda*, and Thomas found some difficulty in producing music of sufficient dramatic power. Critics remarked that the music did not grow naturally out of the drama, but merely accompanied it, although the recitatives were again singled out for praise and several of the more lyrical passages were commended. *Nadeshda* was also given in a German version, at Breslau in 1890. An unfinished comic opera, *The*

Golden Web, was completed by S. P. Waddington and performed with some success in 1893.

Thomas never found an individual musical style; as Shaw said, he 'always seems to be dreaming of other men's music'. Turns of phrase or chord progressions, particularly in the operas, constantly recall pieces by Gounod, Bizet, Delibes or Ambroise Thomas. Yet much of his lighter music has an infectious sparkle or a refined charm that is worthy of the French school at its best.

MSS in GB-Lbl, Lcm

Don Braggadocio (3, C. I. Thomas), inc.
The Light of the Harem (3, C. Harrison, after T. Moore), London, RAM, 7 Nov 1879 (London, 1913)
Esmeralda (4, T. Marzials and A. Randegger, after V. Hugo: *Notre-Dame de Paris*), London, Drury Lane, 26 March 1883 (London, 1883); rev. CG, 12 July 1890
Nadeshda (4, J. Sturgis), London, Drury Lane, 16 April 1885 (London, 1885)
The Golden Web (3, F. Corder and B. C. Stephenson), Liverpool, Royal Court, 15 Feb 1893 (London, 1893), completed by S. P. Waddington

*

DNB (R. H. Legge)
G. B. Shaw: *Music in London 1890–94* (London, 1932)
J. W. Klein: 'English Opera Abroad', *MO*, lxvi (1942–3), 44–6, 78–9
——: 'Tragic, Forgotten Pioneer: Arthur Goring Thomas', *MR*, xxxvi (1975), 180–86 JENNIFER SPENCER

Thomas, David (*b* Orpington, Kent, 26 Feb 1943). English bass. He studied at King's College, Cambridge, where he was a choral scholar, and quickly established himself in the Baroque and Classical repertory. He made his British operatic début in 1981 with Kent Opera, as Pluto in Monteverdi's *Il ballo delle ingrate*, and his American début in 1988 at Los Angeles as the Devil in Stefano Landi's *Il Sant' Alessio*. Thomas has performed with many of the leading period instrument ensembles in opera and choral works. He has appeared in concerts throughout the world and has broadcast frequently. His recordings include Rameau's *Zaïs* (1979), Purcell's *Dido and Aeneas* (1981) and *The Fairy-Queen* (1982), Monteverdi's *Orfeo* (1986) and Handel's *Orlando* (1991). His singing is distinguished by a wide-ranging, well-focussed and strongly projected voice which lends authority to his characterizations. NICHOLAS ANDERSON

Thomas, Jess (Floyd) (*b* Hot Springs, SD, 4 Aug 1927). American tenor. After studying psychology at Stanford University, he was encouraged by his singing teacher, Otto Schulman, to pursue an operatic career. He made his début in 1957 at San Francisco and then went to Germany, where he sang at the Karlsruhe Opera for three years. He soon began to make guest appearances with larger German companies, and in 1961 Wieland Wagner cast him as Parsifal in Bayreuth and Radames in Berlin. He returned to the USA and made his Metropolitan début in 1962 as Walther (the role of his Covent Garden début in 1969). Although his repertory at first included such relatively lyrical parts as Lensky and Cavaradossi, he later began to concentrate on the heavy Wagnerian roles such as Siegfried (which he sang in the Bayreuth centenary *Ring* in 1976) and Tristan. Some listeners have felt that the strain of these challenges robbed his voice of freshness and ease; nevertheless, his intelligence and histrionic credibility remained uncommon assets. Other roles included Samson, Florestan and the Emperor in *Die Frau ohne Schatten*; he also sang Caesar in the première of Barber's *Antony and Cleopatra* (1966). MARTIN BERNHEIMER

Thomas, John Charles (*b* Meyersdale, VA, 6 Sept 1891; *d* Apple Valley, CA, 13 Dec 1960). American baritone. He studied in Baltimore and, after singing in musical comedy and Gilbert and Sullivan, made his operatic début in 1924 at Washington, DC as Amonasro. Engaged at La Monnaie, he made his début there in 1925 as Herod (*Hérodiade*) and sang Amfortas, Hamlet, Escamillo, Zurga, and Orpheus in the première of Milhaud's *Les malheurs d'Orphée* (1926). He made his Covent Garden début in 1928 as Valentine, also singing Amonasro. In 1930 he sang John the Baptist at San Francisco and Tonio in Chicago, where he later sang Falstaff (1940). He made his Metropolitan début in 1934 as Germont, and remained with the company until 1943, also singing Rossini's Figaro, Athanaël (*Thaïs*) and Scarpia. His recordings display a voice of great power and intensity.

RICHARD LESUEUR/ELIZABETH FORBES

Thomas, Michael Tilson (*b* Hollywood, CA, 21 Dec 1944). American conductor. He studied at the University of Southern California, Los Angeles, and began conducting orchestras there, with further study at Bayreuth masterclasses (1966) and at Tanglewood, where he won the Koussevitsky conducting prize in 1968. Orchestral appointments at Buffalo, Boston, Los Angeles, and with the LSO (principal conductor since 1988) have been the main focus of his work, with widespread guest engagements in Europe and the USA. Appearances in opera have been occasional rather than regular. They include the first American production of the three-act *Lulu* (1979, Santa Fe), *The Cunning Little Vixen* with New York City Opera (1981), *Fidelio* at Houston (1984), *La bohème* at the Hollywood Bowl (1985) and with the Chicago Lyric Opera (1987), and *Tosca* (also at Chicago, 1988), which he later recorded in Hungary with Eva Marton. He made a strong case for Rimsky-Korsakov's neglected *Mlada* in concert excerpts at Chicago and Pittsburgh, and an almost full performance – the first in Britain – with the LSO at the Barbican, London, in 1989. He is also an eloquent advocate of Gershwin (he conducted a semi-staged double-bill of *Of Thee I Sing* and *Let 'em eat Cake* at Brooklyn Academy of Music, 1987). His conducting is vigorous and demonstrative, stressing sharpness of detail sometimes at the expense of lyrical line, and he has acquired a reputation for popular verbal communication in expository musical television programmes. NOËL GOODWIN

Thomas, Theodore (Christian Friedrich) (*b* Esens, East Friesland, 11 Oct 1835; *d* Chicago, 4 Jan 1905). American conductor of German birth. His family came to New York in 1845. More than any other individual he disseminated symphonic culture in the USA. Beginning in 1869, he toured widely with his own orchestra. He later conducted the New York PO and Chicago Orchestra (later the Chicago SO), which he helped to found. His influential credo was 'a symphony orchestra shows the culture of a community, not opera'. Thomas also played a crucial role in the American Wagner cult of the late 19th century. He gave the first American performances of the overture to *Der fliegende Holländer* and the preludes to *Tristan und Isolde* and *Die Meistersinger*, among other Wagner extracts. For the 1876 Philadelphia Centennial Exhibition he also commissioned and gave the première of Wagner's *Grosser Festmarsch*. A figure of unimpeachable respectability, he was the composer's indispensable American champion before the coming of Anton Seidl in 1885. He legitimized Wagner for genteel audiences and intellectuals of the period.

Though not a natural theatre conductor, Thomas occasionally conducted opera, most notably for Jeannette Thurber's American Opera Company. In 1886 and 1887 the company went on tour with lavish English-language productions; its collapse was a striking setback for America's efforts to establish a tradition of opera in the vernacular.

*

GroveAM (E. Schabas)
E. Schabas: *Theodore Thomas – America's Conductor and Builder of Orchestras, 1835–1905* (Chicago, 1989)
J. Horowitz: *Wagner Nights* (in preparation)

JOSEPH HOROWITZ

Thomas and Sally [*Thomas and Sally, or The Sailor's Return*]. Dramatic pastoral in two acts by THOMAS AUGUSTINE ARNE to a libretto by ISAAC BICKERSTAFF; London, Covent Garden, 28 November 1760.

Sally (soprano), the milkmaid, laments the loss of her love Thomas, who has gone to sea. Dorcas (mezzo-soprano), the matron, bids her enjoy the pleasures of youth, and the Squire (tenor) attempts to woo her but is rebuffed. In Act 2 Thomas (tenor) returns from sea, his language loaded with nautical terms. The Squire, encouraged by Dorcas, again attempts to force his attentions on Sally. Their dialogue 'Well met, pretty maid' recalls the words of the folksong 'Sweet nightingale'. Thomas arrives in the nick of time, puts the Squire to flight and claims Sally as his bride. The Squire is left to vent his annoyance on Dorcas.

Thomas and Sally can claim to be the first all-sung English comic opera. It is noteworthy as well for the introduction of clarinets into the orchestra. In the opening scene the Squire (played originally by John Beard) sings a rousing hunting song, 'The echoing horn', accompanied on stage by horns and clarinets alone. Sally's songs are simple and melodious, avoiding excessive display, although Charlotte Brent, who created the role, had a brilliant coloratura technique. The opera was the most successful afterpiece of the period and remained in the repertory until the end of the century; it has been successfully revived in recent years. The full score was published by the composer in 1761.

JOHN A. PARKINSON

Thomé, Francis [François Luc Joseph] (*b* Port Louis, Mauritius, 18 Oct 1850; *d* Paris, 16 Nov 1909). French composer. He was taken as a child to Paris, where he studied at the Conservatoire with Duprato and Thomas. Soon after leaving the Conservatoire he became well known as a composer of salon pieces and was in demand as a teacher. His music was particularly successful in the French provinces, and two of his operas were first performed outside Paris.

Although Thomé's music has generally fallen into oblivion, it was formerly much appreciated. Pougin's obituary describes the composer as 'a neat, refined artist, gifted with an attractive melodic vein ... and enriched by solid learning'. Thomé's stage music encompassed various genres, including ballet, pantomime, incidental music (for a wide range of plays) and *bleuettes*.

Martin et Frontin (oc, 2, Grimault and P. Dubois), Eaux-Bonnes, Aug 1877
Le baron Frick (opérette, 1, E. Depré and C. Clairville), Paris, Cercle artistique et littéraire, 19 Dec 1885, collab. A. Duvernoy, Guiraud, Joncières and Pfeiffer
Caprice de reine (oc, 1, A. Brisson C. Foley), Cannes, 1892
Le château de Koenigsberg (légende, 3, A. Silvestre), Paris, Bodinière, 22 April 1896
Chaperon rouge (conte, 3, Lefebvre-Henri), Paris, Odéon, 7 April 1900
Le conversion de Pierrot (oc, 1, H. and M. Jacquet), Paris, Salle d'horticulture, 27 Jan 1901

*

Obituary, *Le courrier musical* (1 Dec 1909)
A. Pougin: Obituary, *Le Ménestrel* (20 Nov 1909)

DAVID CHARLTON

Thompson, Mrs. *See* POITIER, JANE.

Thompson, Randall (*b* New York, 21 April 1899; *d* Boston, 9 July 1984). American composer. He graduated in 1920 from Harvard University, where he had studied with A. T. Davison, Edward Burlingame Hill and Walter Spalding; he also studied with Ernest Bloch. In 1922 he was awarded a three-year fellowship at the American Academy in Rome, and in 1929 and 1930 he was awarded Guggenheim fellowships. He was particularly distinguished as a teacher, working at various institutions before being appointed to the faculty of music at Harvard (1948–65), where his pupils included Adler, Bernstein and Foss. Thompson is best known for his sensitive and rewarding choral music.

Thompson's opera, *Solomon and Balkis*, was written for radio. In one act and based on *The Butterfly that Stamped* by Rudyard Kipling, *Solomon and Balkis* is scored for five soloists, female chorus and orchestra. It was first broadcast by CBS on 29 March 1942 and staged two weeks later in Cambridge, Massachusetts (14 April). The music is almost consistently merry and often puckish. The one sustained lyric moment in the opera comes when Balkis sings her lovely song, 'A butterfly has made complaint'. Thompson describes his other staged dramatic work, *The Nativity according to Saint Luke*, as 'A Musical Drama in Seven Scenes'. Composed in honour of the 200th anniversary of the dedication of Christ Church, Cambridge, Massachusetts, the first performance took place there on 13 December 1961. The directions for lighting and stage action show Thompson's usual care for the dynamics of performance.

ELLIOT FORBES

Thomson, Brian (*b* Sydney, 5 Jan 1946). Australian stage designer. He trained as an architect in Perth and Sydney but left the course in 1966, before graduating. His early influences include the imagery and techniques of Pop Art. He designed an Australian production of the rock opera *Tommy* in 1970, and this led to a full-time career as a stage and production designer in theatre, opera, film and television. In London he was set designer for Lloyd Webber's record-breaking *Jesus Christ Superstar* (1972) and Richard O'Brien's *The Rocky Horror Show* (1973). He also designed *Rocky Horror Show* productions in Los Angeles, New York and Tokyo as well as the film version (1974). His first opera designs were for the State Opera of South Australia's production of Britten's *Death in Venice* (1980) and the Adelaide Festival of the Arts' production of Janáček's *The Makropulos Affair* (1982). For the Australian

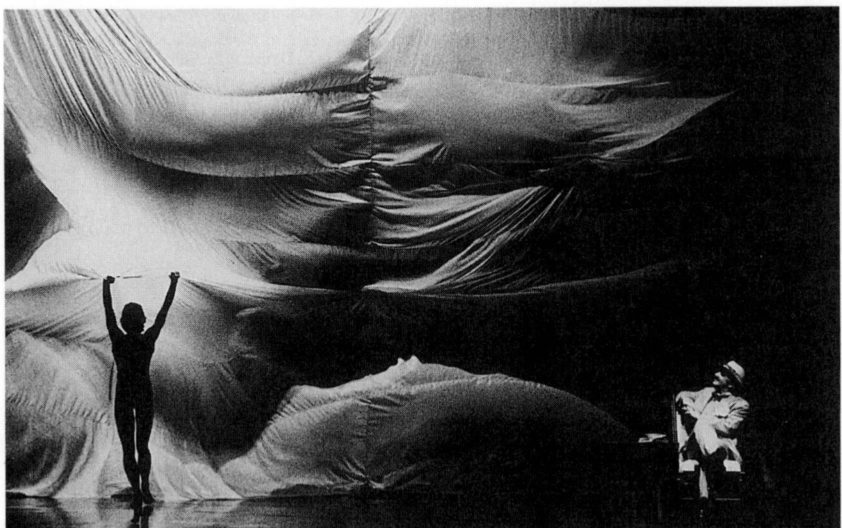

Scene from the State Opera of South Australia's production of Britten's 'Death in Venice' at the Festival Theatre, Adelaide, 1980, designed by Brian Thomson

Opera, he designed sets for Richard Meale's *Voss* (1986), *Death in Venice* (1989) and *Tristan und Isolde* (1990). He is considered the most exciting of the younger Australian designers. The grand scale of his sets and the freedom he gives to his idiosyncratic ideas reflects his early training as an architect. He uses modern materials and technology and often creates powerful visual metaphors that challenge director and audience alike.

DAVID J. HOUGH

Thomson, John (*b* Sprouston, Roxburgh, 28 Oct 1805; *d* Edinburgh, 6 May 1841). Scottish composer. Having trained first as a solicitor, he began work on *Vallery* in 1829, an Arabian opera with text by the poet C. D. Sillery (1807–37), but the opera was never completed. In December, his musical play *The House of Aspen* was performed in Edinburgh. With a letter of introduction from Mendelssohn, whom he had met earlier that year, Thomson left for Berlin. He subsequently studied with Schnyder von Wartensee in Leipzig, and later visited Paris. More theatrical works followed: the opera *Hermann* (1834), which revealed the influence of Mozart and Weber, and the musical play *The Shadow on the Wall* (1835). While both were well received and Thomson's musical invention praised, it was felt that he had not succeeded in integrating the music with the emotions in the librettos. In October 1839 Thomson was elected the first Reid Professor of Music at Edinburgh, having been recommended by Mendelssohn and Balfe. His tenure of the post was short-lived. Four months after presenting the first Reid Concert, in 1841 (he is credited with being one of the first in Britain to write analytical programme notes), he died from dropsy. Some of his correspondence is in Edinburgh University Library.

Vallery, inc. (C. D. Sillery), excerpt perf. 16 May 1829, *GB-Er**

The House of Aspen (play with music, 3, W. Scott), Edinburgh, Royal, 17 Dec 1829, *Er**, vs (Edinburgh, 1829)

Hermann, or The Broken Spear (musical drama, 2), London, Lyceum, 27 Oct 1834, *Er**, vs (London, 1834)

The Shadow on the Wall (musical play, 2, T. J. Serle), London, Lyceum, 20 April 1835, *Er** (London, 1835)

*

S. Hensel: *Die Familie Mendelssohn, 1729–1847*, i (Berlin, 1879), 243; Eng. trans., i (London, 1881), 197–8

G. H. Farmer: *A History of Music in Scotland* (London, 1947), 495–7

P. A. Scholes: *The Mirror of Music 1844–1944*, ii (London, 1947), 662

R. Elvers, ed.: *Mendelssohn-Briefe. Eine Auswahl mit Kommentaren und Abbildung* (Frankfurt, 1984)

MICHAEL T. R. B. TURNBULL

Thomson, Virgil (Garnett) (*b* Kansas City, MO, 25 Nov 1896; *d* New York, 30 Sept 1989). American composer and critic. He was educated in Kansas City schools, at Harvard College and with Nadia Boulanger in Paris, where he was among the first in the line of American composers to study with that formidable teacher. He lived in Paris between 1925 and 1940, cultivating a wide circle of artistic friends, chief among them the American writer Gertrude Stein, whom he met in 1926. Paris also provided his principal musical inspiration, in the works of Satie. Before and shortly after his first meeting with Stein, Thomson had set several of her poems, and the two then collaborated on *Four Saints in Three Acts*, first performed in Hartford, Connecticut, in 1934; its fashionable success established Thomson's reputation. Returning to New York in 1940, he became chief music critic of the *New York Herald Tribune* until his retirement in 1954. As such, he was perhaps the most influential of all American music critics, delighting a sophisticated readership with his 'sassy but classy' prose style, and gathering around him a distinguished group of fellow composer-critics.

Musically, he spent the 1930s and 40s expanding his technical facility, concentrating on music for strings and other instrumental writing, and on a variety of dance and film projects. Before her death in 1946, however, Stein provided Thomson with another libretto, *The Mother of Us All*, which was first performed in 1947. It counts as Thomson's richest statement of Americana, both in its evocations of the vernacular and also in its cavalcade of American historical figures: the 'mother' is Susan B. Anthony, who fought for the women's vote. His two collaborations with Stein are among the boldest, most original of all 20th-century operas.

Thomson concentrated on composition after 1954, his principal effort being the opera *Lord Byron* (1972). This had a more conventional libretto, epic and Romantic, by Jack Larson, and has been less warmly received, although Thomson cherished it. His death in 1989 occasioned widespread notice among American composers and intellectuals, who appreciated his witty criticism and his long-held place in American letters.

Although he composed only three operas in his long career, Thomson wrote inherently dramatic music, with the bulk devoted to text-settings (operas, choral works, songs), ballets, film scores and solo piano 'portraits', whose subjects 'sat' for him as before a painter with brush and easel. His characteristic musical style knits short phrases with rich indigenous inspiration (above all the Baptist hymns and the white and black folk music of his Missouri youth) into a mosaic full of repetition. His music anticipated both minimalism and the blends of cultivated and vernacular music so common late in the 20th century. In his influential critical writings he concentrated on specific problems in the dramatic setting of texts and helped shape American taste in opera, pointing away from Germanic masterpieces and toward a lighter, wittier idiom.

See also FOUR SAINTS IN THREE ACTS; LORD BYRON; and MOTHER OF US ALL, THE.

Four Saints in Three Acts, 1927–8 [orchd 1933] (prol., 4, G. Stein), Hartford, CT, Wadsworth Atheneum, 8 Feb 1934 (New York, 1948)

The Mother of Us All (2, Stein), New York, Columbia University, Brander Matthews Hall, 7 May 1947 (New York, 1947)

Lord Byron, 1961–8 (3, J. Larson), New York, Juilliard, 20 April 1972 (New York, 1975) [ballet from Act 3 pubd as Symphony no.3]

*

A. Copland: 'Our Younger Generation: Ten Years Later', *MM*, xiii/4 (1935–6), 3–11

S. Barlow: 'American Composers, XVII: Virgil Thomson', *MM*, xviii (1940–41), 242–9

R. F. Eyer: 'Virgil Thomson', *MusAm*, lxiv/7 (1944), 7, 25

C. Smith: 'Gertrude S., Virgil T., and Susan B.', *Theatre Arts*, xxxi/7 (1947), 17–20

F. W. Sternfeld: 'Current Chronicle', *MQ*, xxxv (1949), 115–21

C. Smith: 'Thomson's Four Saints Live again on Broadway', *MusAm*, lxxii/7 (1952), 7

M. G. Field: 'Virgil Thomson and the Maturity of American Music', *The Chesterian*, xxviii (1953–4), 111–4

H. R. Garvin: 'Sound and Sense in Four Saints in Three Acts', *Bucknell Review*, v/1 (1954), 1–11

E. Helm: 'Virgil Thomson's Four Saints in Three Acts', *MR*, xv (1954), 127–32

K. Hoover and J. Cage: *Virgil Thomson: his Life and Music* (New York, 1959)

R. Jackson: *The Operas of Gertrude Stein and Virgil Thomson* (diss., Tulane U., 1962)

H. C. Schonberg: 'Virgil Thomson: Parisian from Missouri', *HiFi/Stereo Review*, xiv/5 (1965), 43–56

'Thomson, Virgil (Garnett)', *CBY 1966*

D. Henahan: 'And Now, Virgil's Odyssey', *New York Times* (21 March 1971), 15, 26

P. J. Smith: 'Musician of the Month: Virgil Thomson', *HiFi/MusAm*, xxi/11 (1971), 8–9

M. Dulman: 'Independent Spirit: Virgil Thomson Speaks Out', *ON*, xli/1 (1976–7), 16–18

G. Freedman: 'Everbest, Virgil Thomson', *Musical Journal*, xxv/3 (1977), 8–10, 71

K. M. Ward: *An Analysis of the Relationship between Text and Musical Shape and an Investigation of the Relationship between Text and Surface Rhythmic Detail in 'Four Saints in Three Acts' by Virgil Thomson* (diss., U. of Texas, 1978)

'Yale Music Library Receives Thomson Papers', *Notes*, xxxvi (1979–80), 78

H. Gleason and W. Becker: 'Virgil Thomson', *20th-century American Composers*, Music Literature Outlines, ser. iv (Bloomington, IN, 2/1981), 170 [incl. bibliography]

D. J. Soria: 'Artist Life: Virgil Thomson', *HiFi/MusAm*, xxxii/2 (1982), 8–9, 38–41

R. H. Kornick: *Recent American Opera: a Production Guide* (New York, 1991), 313–15 JOHN ROCKWELL

Thorborg, Kerstin (*b* Venjan, 19 May 1896; *d* Hedemora, Dalarna, 12 April 1970). Swedish mezzo-soprano. She studied at the Royal Conservatory, Stockholm, and sang small roles at the Royal Opera in 1923, graduating to principal roles in 1924 as Ortrud. With the company until 1930, she also made appearances elsewhere, notably as Amneris in Göteborg to Flagstad's Aida, in Dresden (Waltraute, 1929) and in Prague. She was engaged at the Städtische Oper, Berlin (1932–5) and the Vienna Staatsoper (1935–8); her roles at Salzburg (1935–7) included Brangäne, Magdalene and Donna Mercedes in *Der Corregidor*. From 1936 to 1939 she made annual appearances at Covent Garden in the Wagner mezzo roles and was greatly acclaimed; Ernest Newman, after her Kundry, described her as 'the greatest Wagnerian actress of the present day'. Also in 1936 she began a Metropolitan Opera career (début as Fricka in *Die Walküre*) which lasted 15 years. Although her rich and ample tones were most admired in Wagner, her repertory also included Gluck's Orpheus, Marina, Ulrica, Strauss's Herodias and Clytemnestra, and Delilah.

*

E. H. Palatsky: 'Goddess in Retirement', *ON*, xxvii/16 (1962–3), 32–3

B. Berthelson: 'Kerstin Thorborg', *Musikrevy*, xxii (1967), 345–7

CARL L. BRUUN/R

'The 1st Great Flat Scene': drawing in pen, ink and wash by James Thornhill, possibly representing the proscenium of the Queen's/King's Theatre, Haymarket, London, built by John Vanbrugh, early 18th century

Thornhill, Sir **James** (*b* Melcombe Regis, Dorset, 25 July 1675 or 1676; *d* Thornhill, Dorset, 13 May 1734). English architect and decorator. He studied under Thomas Highmore, the serjeant painter whom he succeeded in 1720. He was engaged as scenographer for Clayton's opera *Arsinoe* at Drury Lane in 1705, sketches for which are extant in the Victoria and Albert Museum, London. The style is simple and not as ornamental as that of baroque contemporaries. Other sketches for unknown productions are in a sketchbook in the British Museum, and for a great flat scene in baroque style in the Art Institute of Chicago (see illustration).

For further illustration *see* ARSINOE.

J. Laver: *Drama: its Costume and Décor* (London, 1951), 139–93
S. Rosenfeld: *Georgian Scene Painters and Scene Painting* (Cambridge, 1981), pls. 1–4

SYBIL ROSENFELD

Thornton, Edna (*b* Bradford, 1875; *d* Worthing, 15 July 1964). English contralto. She was a pupil of Charles Santley and made her début in the musical comedy *Ib and Little Christina* at Daly's Theatre, London, in 1899. At Covent Garden she first appeared in 1905, singing with Caruso in *Un ballo in maschera* and *Rigoletto*. She took part in the English première of Franchetti's *Germania* in 1907, and the following year made an impression as Erda in the first *Ring* cycle given in English under Hans Richter. In one performance of *Götterdämmerung* she undertook three roles: Waltraute, Flosshilde and First Norn. Other roles in the pre-war seasons included Brangäne (*Tristan und Isolde*), Geneviève (*Pelléas et Mélisande*) and Giulietta (*Les contes d'Hoffmann*). She sang with the Beecham company at Drury Lane and the Aldwych, and was later a mainstay of the British National Opera Company, singing a wide range of parts including Amneris and Azucena, Delilah and Marfa (*Khovanshchina*). After tours in Canada, Australia and New Zealand with the Quinlan Company in 1924 she retired to teach. 'Regal' was a favourite word of critics to describe her acting and bearing on stage, while records confirm that she had an exceptionally strong, resourceful contralto voice to match.

J. B. STEANE

Thornton, Margaret. *See* MARTYR, MARGARET.

Thorpe Davie, Cedric (*b* London, 30 May 1913; *d* Dalry, Scotland, 18 Jan 1983). Scottish composer. He studied at the Scottish National Academy of Music (later the Royal Scottish Academy of Music), Glasgow, at the RAM and later at the RCM, where his teachers included Vaughan Williams. He was also a pupil of Kodály in Budapest and Kilpinen in Helsinki. Thorpe Davie taught at the Scottish National Academy of Music from 1936 and in 1945 was appointed master of music to St Andrews University; he founded the department of music there (1947) and later became professor (1973–8).

In 1936 Thorpe Davie wrote a one-act opera, *Gammer Gurton's Needle* (W. Stevenson), based on the anonymous Elizabethan play (1575). Later he began to rewrite it, but it has not been performed. Also in 1936 he composed the first of two one-act children's operettas, *The Kingdom of King Winter* (B. Waddell). The second, *Sea Tangle*, was produced in Glasgow and Belfast in 1937 and had a Command Performance at Buckingham Palace. Thorpe Davie reset Pepusch's *The Beggar's Opera* in 1942 for performances at St Andrews, retaining the original overture but providing new settings for the songs. He made a realization of Allan Ramsay's 1726 ballad opera *The Gentle Shepherd* in 1949 for the Edinburgh Festival, and another of Joseph Mitchell's 1731 imitation of it, *The Highland Fair*, in 1952. Much his most successful undertaking was his realization of Burns's dramatic cantata *The Jolly Beggars* for the Scottish Festival at Braemar in 1954, which has been performed throughout Scotland, broadcast on radio and television and commercially recorded. His music, traditional in tonality, shows the influence of Kilpinen, Sibelius and Scots folksong.

MAURICE LINDSAY

Thrane, Waldemar (*b* Christiania [now Oslo], 8 Oct 1790; *d* Christiania, 30 Dec 1828). Norwegian composer and violinist. He studied in Paris briefly with Anton Reicha and F. A. Habeneck and returned to Christiania in 1818. He worked as a teacher and as a conductor, and gave violin recitals. His main compositions are a Concert Overture (1818) and the first Norwegian opera, *Fjeldeventyret* ('Mountain Adventure'; 1824), a Singspiel based on a libretto by the Norwegian poet H. A. Bjerregaard. It was first given on 9 February 1825 at the Musikalske Lyceum and immediately became a great success; it has from time to time been taken up by various theatres and is in the repertory of the Norwegian National Opera. The story is simple, as in a folk comedy, and Thrane retained the spoken dialogue. The music conforms more or less to the taste of its time; it contains reminiscences of Mozart and Weber, but is still more in the popular style of the French *opéras comiques* of the late 18th century. In some sections, however, Thrane shows a musical individuality, particularly in the scenes which are of a folkloristic nature, e.g. in 'Aagots fjeldsang' ('Aagot's mountain song'). This beautiful melody became internationally known through Jenny Lind, who often performed it at her recitals. *Mountain Adventure* has a strong national flavour, and includes imitations of Norwegian folktunes, so convincing that later generations have imagined them genuine. Thrane made use of specific intervals and motifs and also rhythmic peculiarities of the instrumental peasant dances. His use of folk music idioms in art music set the model for Norwegian composers who followed him: this may be regarded as his greatest achievement.

FINN BENESTAD

Threepenny Opera, The. Play with music by Kurt Weill and Bertolt Brecht; *see* DREIGROSCHENOPER, DIE.

Through-composed (Ger. *durchkomponiert*). A term used primarily to describe a song or aria in which the music for each stanza is different (i.e. not strophic); it is applied particularly to the lied repertory though is occasionally used in opera. It has also been used, in opera, to refer to a work that is continuous in texture, with no individual 'numbers'.

Thuille, Ludwig (*b* Bozen [now Bolzano], Tyrol, 30 Nov 1861; *d* Munich, 5 Feb 1907). Austrian composer of Savoyard ancestry. He won acclaim in Munich as a composer, chamber music pianist and professor of theory and composition at the Königliche Musikhochschule. As an opera composer, he eschewed the prevalent taste for dramatic music in the Wagnerian idiom by favouring lighthearted and whimsical subjects. Though his first opera *Theuerdank*, on a text by Alexander Ritter, was awarded a prize in 1896, its première under Richard Strauss proved unsuccessful. Thuille accordingly published only its attractive overture. *Lobetanz*, which followed, was heard from Riga to New York after its first performance. Its success, though transient, stimulated another collaboration with the same librettist, Otto Julius Bierbaum, on a similar fairy-tale subject: *Gugeline*, a five-act opera. This, though a failure as a stage work, contains music of ingratiating lyricism, especially in Act 3, and of dramatic intensity.

Thuille's final operatic endeavour, *Der Heiligenschein*, to a libretto by Elsa von Wolzogen, was abandoned by the composer in 1905 after one act. The fragment was orchestrated by Walter Courvoisier and given in concert by Felix Mottl, but without success.

See also LOBETANZ.

Theuerdank, 1893–5 (3, A. Ritter), Munich, 12 Mar 1897, ov. (Leipzig, 1899)
Lobetanz op.10, 1896 (Spl, 3, O. J. Bierbaum), Karlsruhe, 6 Feb 1898 (Berlin, 1897)
Gugeline op.18, 1898–1900 (5, Bierbaum), Bremen, 4 March 1901 (Mainz, 1900)

*

W. Mauke: *Gugeline*, Opernführer, liii (Leipzig, 1901)
E. Istel: 'Ludwig Thuille', *Monographien moderner Musiker*, i, ed. C. F. Kahnt (Leipzig, 1906), 35–45
R. Louis: *Die deutsche Musik der Gegenwart* (Munich, 1909)
E. Istel: *Lobetanz*, Opernführer, cxiv (Berlin, 1910)
F. Munter: *Ludwig Thuille* (Munich, 1923)
E. Istel: 'Ludwig Thuille', *MQ*, xviii (1932), 463–70

EDWARD F. KRAVITT

Thurm zu Babel, Der [*Vavilonskoye stolpotvoreniye*] ('The Tower of Babel'). Sacred opera in one act by ANTON GRIGOR'YEVICH RUBINSTEIN to a libretto by Julius Rodenberg after *Genesis* xi.1–9; Königsberg [now Kaliningrad], 9 February 1870 (concert performance).

The first of Rubinstein's so-called sacred operas, a hybrid genre midway between opera and oratorio (but usually performed, because of contemporary censorship conditions, in concert), *Der Thurm zu Babel* exhibits features of each of its antecedent genres. At its dramatic centre is an invented wisp of plot involving a conflict between bold Nimrod (bass) and timorous Abram (tenor), two vaguely defined leaders of the people, as to whether the tower should be completed. The monumental choruses, meanwhile, are its musical centre of gravity. Those involving the 'children of Sem, Ham and Japhet', nations rent asunder by the confusion of tongues, are full of characteristic 'oriental' colour: the 'Semites' have augmented 2nds; the 'Hamites' sing in unison against drone 5ths; the 'Japhetic' chorus strongly resembles the 'Turkish Dance' in Act 4 of *Ruslan and Lyudmila*. Another chorus, depicting a heaven-sent fire, is cast in a Glinka-esque 5/4 time. The opera ends with an ambitious triple chorus in a broad compound metre, its three levels representing the world's peoples, the heavenly host and the demons of hell. As usual, the last-named get the most imaginative music.

RICHARD TARUSKIN

Tibaldi, Giuseppe (Luigi) (*b* Bologna, 22 Jan 1729; *d* *c*1790). Italian tenor. He studied singing with Domenico Zanardi, and also with Padre Martini with whom he continued to correspond (letters in *I-Bc*). In 1747 he was admitted to the Accademia Filarmonica as a singer. After a few years as *maestro di cappella* at S Giovanni in Monte, Bologna, he decided to devote himself to a career as an operatic tenor and sang in the most important European opera houses, taking leading roles in the premières of Gluck's *Alceste* (1767, Vienna) and Mozart's *Ascanio in Alba* (1771, Milan). His few extant compositions are vocal pieces. His son, Ferdinando Tibaldi (*c*1750–1785), was also a singer and composer.

HOWARD BROFSKY

Tibbett [Tibbet], **Lawrence** (*b* Bakersfield, CA, 16 Nov 1896; *d* New York, 15 July 1960). American baritone. After beginning his career as an actor and as a singer in church and light operas, he studied with Joseph Dupuy and Basil Ruysdael in Los Angeles and with Frank La Forge and Ignaz Zitomirsky in New York, which led to his Metropolitan début as Lewicki in *Boris Godunov* (1923). A week later he sang Valentin in *Faust*, but recognition did not come until 1925 when he sang Ford in *Falstaff*, eclipsing Antonio Scotti in the title role; he eventually succeeded Scotti in the leading Italian roles and remained a principal with the company for 27 seasons, noted, in his prime, for his legato and vivid acting. He sang in the premières of Gruenberg's *The Emperor Jones* (1933), Taylor's *The King's Henchman* (1927) and *Peter Ibbetson* (1931), Hanson's *Merry Mount* (1934) and Seymour's *In the Pasha's Garden* (1935). He also took part in the first Metropolitan performances of *Jonny spielt auf*, *Peter Grimes*, Hageman's *Caponsacchi*, *Simon Boccanegra* and *Khovanshchina* (in which he made his last Metropolitan appearance in 1950, as Ivan). He also sang in San Francisco, Chicago, Paris, Vienna and Prague, and at Covent Garden created the title role in Goossens's *Don Juan de Mañara* (1937). His dark, pliant voice and matinée-idol appearance made him popular in films as well as light opera, and he was a significant force in early American radio. In 1950 he appeared on Broadway in *The Barrier*; his last stage role was in *Fanny* (1956). He is perhaps best represented by his *Otello* recordings, which reveal him as an Iago of sly wit, his ample fervour in the 'Credo' counterbalanced by a silken *pianissimo* in 'Era la notte'. He published an autobiography, *The Glory Road* (Brattleboro, VT, 1933).

*

GV (R. Celletti; S. Smolian)
R. Whelan: 'Lawrence Tibbett Discography', *Record News* [Toronto], v (1960–61), 165–70
J. B. Steane: *The Grand Tradition* (London, 1974), 295ff

MARTIN BERNHEIMER

Tichatschek, Joseph [Ticháček, Josef] **(Aloys)** (*b* Ober-Weckelsdorf [now Teplice, nr Broumov], 11 July 1807; *d* Blasewitz, nr Dresden, 18 Jan 1886). Bohemian tenor. He had lessons with Ciccimarra while studying medicine in Vienna, and in 1830 he joined the chorus of the Kärntnertortheater. He soon progressed to comprimario parts, and sang as a principal in Graz in 1837. He sang in Vienna that year and made his Dresden début on 11 August in the title role of Auber's *Gustavus III*; the following year he was appointed to the Dresden Hofoper. With Wilhelmine Schröder-Devrient and Anton Mitterwurzer, Tichatschek helped the company set new standards of singing. In 1841 he sang at Drury Lane (as Adolar, Tamino and Robert le diable) and elsewhere in England. He was pensioned in 1861 but continued to appear until 1870, his voice being remarkably well preserved. His repertory included the principal tenor roles in *Idomeneo*, *Die Zauberflöte*, *Fernand Cortez*, *I Capuleti e i Montecchi*, *La muette de Portici* and *La dame blanche*. His range included lyric and dramatic tenor parts, but he was also the prototype of the Wagner Heldentenor, creating the title roles of *Rienzi* in 1842 and *Tannhäuser* in 1845.

Opinions agree on the beauty and brilliance of Tichatschek's voice. Sincerus praised his range of expression, even production, intonation, and enunciation, although he had reservations about his coloratura. In 1840 Nicolai called him the greatest German tenor, and Cornelius was deeply moved by his Lohengrin in 1867. Berlioz described him in the role of Rienzi as

Joseph Tichatschek in the title role of Wagner's 'Tannhäuser' which he created at Dresden in 1845: engraving

'brilliant and irresistible ... elegant, impassioned, heroic, his fine voice and great lustrous eyes marvellously effective'; Wagner, however, while admiring his 'glorious voice and great musical talent', found him unable to portray the character's 'dark, gloomy, demonic strain'. Tichatschek's simple devotion to his voice, appearance and costumes was exclusive of any fuller dramatic perception, and he horrified Wagner at the première of *Tannhäuser* by addressing his outburst in praise of Venus with great passion to Elisabeth.

A. Sincerus: *Das Dresdner Hoftheater und seine gegenwärtigen Mitglieder* (Zerbst, 1852)

M. Fürstenau: *Joseph Tichatschek* (Dresden, 1868)

H. Berlioz: *Mémoires* (Paris, 1870; Eng. trans., 1969)

R. Wagner: 'Über Schauspieler und Sänger', *Gesammelte Schriften und Dichtungen*, ix (Leipzig, 1873; Eng. trans., 1896)

E. Kloss: 'Joseph Tichatschek', *NZM*, lxxiv (1907), 613–16

A. Kohut: 'Aus Joseph Tichatscheks Nachlass', *Bühne und Welt*, ix/2 (Berlin, 1907), 418–23

E. Newman: *The Life of Richard Wagner* (London, 1933–47)

M. Gregor-Dellin, ed.: R. Wagner: *Mein Leben* (Munich, 1963), 943

JOHN WARRACK

Ticket (Fr. *billet*; Ger. *Billet, Eintrittskarte*; It. *biglietto, bolletino, tessera*). A pass giving admission to a theatre or hall; stamped or engraved on metal (sometimes silver, regularly copper, bronze, brass, lead or tin), engraved on ivory or bone, or printed on thin card or paper. Research into this topic is still at a preliminary stage.

It is known that the first public opera house, the Teatro S Cassiano in Venice, had from 1637 both a subscription system and admission by single ticket, but no example of a ticket appears to survive. In London, the earliest known theatre tickets were circular metal 'checks'. Bronze or brass checks are extant from two theatres on Bankside, the Bear Garden (in use *c*1585–1682) and Swan (*c*1595–*c*1632), and the Red Bull at Clerkenwell (*c*1605–63); none is dated, but the Red Bull checks state the parts of the theatre to which they give admittance. A silver check dated 1668 survives from the Theatre Royal (in Bridges Street, the original Drury Lane theatre), while the first Restoration checks that specify areas of the house are dated 1671, for Dorset Garden Theatre and the Theatre Royal. The latter, of brass, are about 2.5 cm in diameter, the obverse stamped with a bust of Charles II and 'Theatre Royal', the reverse with the part of the theatre, e.g. 'Upper Gallerie', and the year of issue. The evidence suggests that right from the reopening of the theatres in 1660 checks were purchased at the door of the theatre and then given up to a collector on entering the specified area of the house. Checks for some theatres could also be purchased at certain coffee houses and inns – a custom that lingered on at several of the smaller British theatres at least until the end of the 18th century.

Opera in London had relied from the start on subsidy and subscription, and subscribers' tickets for the pit and boxes were instituted in the first decade of the 18th century; these were at first made of metal (often silver) but later (from the 1760s to the 1880s) more usually of ivory or bone. Subscription as well as other longer-term tickets would normally be engraved with the name of the holder. In the 19th century subscription and season tickets were also issued on card.

Except for subscription and benefit performances, it was the 18th-century custom in London that only boxes could be booked in advance; box checks were normally delivered at the stage door (from the 1790s at the 'box office'). Other checks were purchased within the theatre at ticket offices positioned at the doors admitting the public to each area of the house. For benefit performances there was a different system: advance tickets were sold by the beneficiaries themselves, either at their own house or lodgings, or at coffee houses, or by peddling them at the houses of influential patrons.

While metal checks of various shapes and sizes remained the regular means of admission well into the 19th century, London theatres soon introduced paper tickets for special purposes, early references to them being made in Drury Lane advertisements of 1702 and 1703, when they could be purchased at White's Chocolate House and Tom's or Will's Coffee House. The earliest one extant, for 5 May 1716 (Sarah Sophia Banks Collection, *GB-Lbl*), is in fact for an opera, *Hydaspes* (see illustration), given for the benefit of Elizabetta Pilotti Schiavonetti at the King's Theatre (the date of the performance was subsequently changed to 9 May). In Britain throughout the 18th century paper tickets were issued when reusable checks would not have been appropriate, primarily for benefits and 'orders'. At the Paris Opéra they were in regular use for the boxes at least as early as 1790.

A typical 18th-century benefit ticket might include the name of the theatre and of the beneficiary, the address where tickets could be obtained, the date (often without the year), the part of the house to which admission was given, the beneficiary's signature, initials, stamped monogram or wax seal (for authentication), a serial number, and the price of the ticket. It was uncommon for details of the programme to be stated, though occasionally the mainpiece would be named or a general

(a)

(b)

(d)

THEATRE ROYAL, DRURY-LANE.
Admit Two to the BOXES. 1819
J. November M Kelly
Admitted only at the Free Privilege Office, where a Cheque will be given.
Not admitted after Half-past 7.

(e)

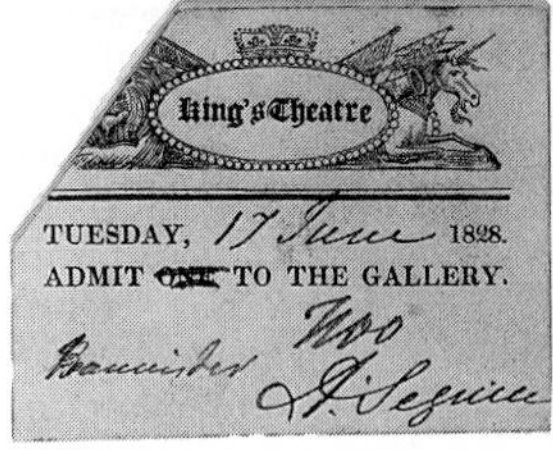

(f)

(c)

Théâtre Royal Italien.

BALCON.

Stalle No 20 côté gauche.

Représentation de Puritani

Paris, le 30 Mars 1835

Le Préposé à la location des Loges,

S'il y avait changement de Spectacle, ce billet serait nul et on en rendrait le prix, pourvu qu'il soit présenté au remboursement au bureau à l'entrée de la salle, entre 7 heures et 7 heures et demie.
Le présent restera entre les mains du locataire, pour lui servir de contremarque d'entrée et de sortie.

(g)

ROYAL ITALIAN OPERA
Carati Esq
DRURY LANE

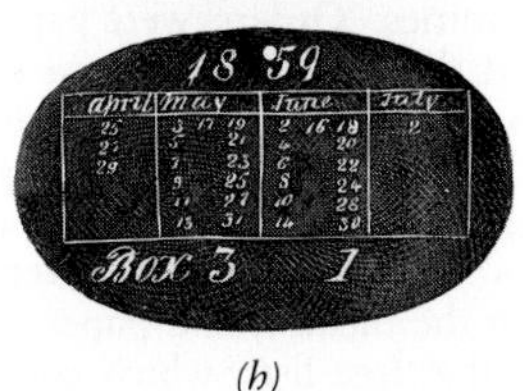

(h)

(i)

Examples of opera tickets, 1716–1861 (all reduced to 50% of original size): (a) the earliest known paper ticket for a British theatre, for a performance of Francesco Gasparini's 'Hydaspes' (for the benefit of Elizabetta Pilotti Schiavonetti) at the King's Theatre, London, May 1716; (b) metal ticket for Covent Garden, London, the reverse stamped 'first gallery 1755'; (c) paper ticket for one of Giusto Ferdinando Tenducci's London benefits, engraved by Francesco Bartolozzi (c1770), stamped with Tenducci's monogram and numbered in ink; (d) subscriber's bone ticket for the King's Theatre, London, 1794 (obverse and reverse); (e) free pass for the Drury Lane theatre, London, 1819, signed by Michael Kelly; (f) free pass for the King's Theatre, London, 17 June 1828; (g) paper ticket for a performance of Bellini's 'I puritani' at the Théâtre Italien, Paris, 1835 (the year of the original production), an early example of a numbered seat; (h) bone ticket, stained blue, obverse engraved 'Carati Esq', for the Royal Italian Opera, at Drury Lane, London (the reverse is engraved with the diary of performances for April to July, 1859); (i) bone season ticket for Covent Garden, 1861 (obverse and reverse) indication, such as 'a serious opera', given. The purpose of authentication was to prevent forgeries, which were touted outside the theatres and presented a problem to managers and beneficiaries everywhere. Another device was to commission an elaborately engraved ticket that would be difficult to forge; those designed by William Hogarth, John Devoto and Francesco Bartolozzi are especially celebrated. From as early as the 1720s, warnings against the purchase of tickets outside the theatres and from irregular sources were made in newspapers and on playbills.

A widespread custom – one that assisted the forgers – was that until the mid-19th century (earlier in Paris) tickets allowed admission to an area of the house but not to specific seats (apart sometimes from in the boxes). This led to the practice, possibly initiated in France, of the upper classes sending footmen or engaging 'place-keepers' to occupy seats and then exchanging places with them shortly before curtain time. The fact that seats were not numbered meant that, especially at benefits (for which the part of the house was often not stipulated), it was common for more tickets to be in circulation than there were seats in the theatre. By about 1710 both Drury Lane and the Haymarket opera were on occasions attempting to exercise some control by advertising that the number of tickets issued would be limited, in order to avoid overcrowding. But it seems to have been the French who initiated the system of numbering seats and restricting tickets to the capacity that each area of the house could accommodate, for a notice in the *Thespian Magazine* in 1793 implies that the current French practice differed from the one known to English theatregoers. However, while the box tickets in France certainly designated seat numbers, and while seats throughout the house were numbered, it may not have been until somewhat later (the 1830s at the latest) that specific seats outside the boxes could be reserved. At the Opéra the benches in the stalls were not numbered until 1831, and a slightly higher price was thereafter paid for tickets purchased in advance than for those bought on the night – a convention that applied to many of the major Parisian theatres, certainly in the 1850s. At Her Majesty's all seats except those in the stalls were numbered by the mid-1840s, while at Covent Garden numbering began probably in 1858.

In addition to the tickets for sale, there were various categories of free ticket in the London theatres of the 18th and early 19th centuries. 'Orders' were paper tickets given to actors and theatre servants for a specific night (whence the origin of the phrase 'papering the house'); 'bones' were ivory or bone tickets, engraved with the actor's name, allowing repeated access over a period of time; 'renters'' tickets, usually of silver, were held by stockholders in the theatre; and paper or card tickets were issued to the 'free list', which comprised critics, authors and composers of new pieces, and friends of both the proprietor and the actors.

In Italy there was a different system. Everyone entering the theatre building was required to buy a pass or *ingresso* (*see* VENICE, fig.3). In many theatres this did not give right of entry into the auditorium, for which the additional purchase of a seat was required; in others (e.g. La Scala from 1800) an *ingresso* gave admittance to the stalls, but possibly only to stand. During the 19th century the numbering of seats was gradually introduced, though the gallery at La Pergola, Florence, was still unnumbered as recently as 1949.

The type of ticket generally in use today, with perforated counterfoils and admitting to numbered seats, was a mid-19th-century innovation, certainly in use by the 1850s. Drury Lane adopted it by 1863, and the Bayreuth tickets for the first complete *Ring* cycle in 1876 were of this type, with the numbers of the seats and entrance doors specified on them (*see* BAYREUTH, fig.4). Covent Garden introduced computer-generated tickets in 1987: these give admission details on one half and the purchaser's name and address on the other.

See also ADMISSION; BENEFIT; and SEATING.

*

ES ('Biglietto')
R. Blum, G. K. R. Herlosssohn and H. Marggraff: 'Billet', *Allgemeines Theater-Lexikon, neue Ausgabe* (Altenburg and Leipzig, 1846)
A. Pougin: 'Billet', 'Billet à droit', 'Billet d'auteur', 'Billet de faveur de service', *Dictionnaire historique et pittoresque du théâtre* (Paris, 1885)
A. Oppenheim and E. Gettke: 'Billet', *Deutsches Theater-Lexikon* (Leipzig, 1889)
W. J. Davis and A. W. Waters: *Tickets and Passes of Great Britain and Ireland, Struck or Engraved on Metal, Ivory, etc. for Use at Theatres, Public Gardens* (Leamington Spa, 1922)
Catalogue of the Montague Guest Collection of Badges, Tokens and Passes, Presented in 1907 to the Department of British and Mediaeval Antiquities (London, 1930)
V. C. Clinton-Baddeley: *All Right on the Night* (London, 1954)
W. van Lennep and others, eds.: Introductions to *The London Stage 1660–1800* (Carbondale, IL, 1960–68), pt 1, pp.lxx–lxxiv; pt 2, pp.lvi–lxii; pt 3, pp.lxix, cxv–cxvi; pt 4, pp.xlviii–l, ci–civ; pt 5, pp.xx–xl
St. V. Troubridge: *The Benefit System in the British Theatre* (London, 1967), 106ff
J. Rosselli: *The Opera Industry in Italy from Cimarosa to Verdi: the Role of the Impresario* (Cambridge, 1984)
R. Macnutt: 'The Earliest Paper Theatre Ticket', *Theatre Notebook*, xlvi (1992), 160–61
RICHARD MACNUTT

Tieck, (Johann) Ludwig (*b* Berlin, 31 May 1773; *d* Berlin, 28 April 1853). German poet and dramatist. Although he was not musically talented, his friendship with the writer Wilhelm Wackenroder and acquaintance with Reichardt encouraged his awareness and understanding of music. In 1798 Tieck wrote the libretto *Das Ungeheuer und der verzauberte Wald* for Reichardt, to whom he had become related by marriage. Reichardt failed to set it, however, and their collaboration on another opera, *Sakuntula* (1811–12), was ended by the composer's death. Tieck settled in Dresden in 1819 and in 1825, following his appointment as dramatic adviser to the German opera there, became friendly with Weber. From 1842 he lived at Potsdam and in Berlin, as adviser to the Berlin theatre. Although illness prevented him from taking up Spohr's invitation to write a libretto, his Berlin years saw some important stage productions and collaborations, notably with Mendelssohn.

Apart from his writings, in which music (especially song) plays an important part, Tieck's lyrics were frequently set to music. In his highly individual plays *Der gestiefelte Kater* (1797), *Die verkehrte Welt* (1798) and *Prinz Zerbino* (1799) he satirized contemporary theatrical conditions and parodied its authors and styles. His love for Mozart's operas is apparent in numerous direct and indirect references and quotations. The librettos of Schumann's *Genoveva*, Spohr's *Pietro von Abano* and Bialas's *Der gestiefelte Kater* are based on his works.

*

K. Schönewolf: *Ludwig Tieck und die Musik* (diss., U. of Marburg, 1925)
R. Paulin: *Ludwig Tieck: a Literary Biography* (Oxford, 1985)
PETER BRANSCOMBE

Tiefland ('The Lowlands'). *Musikdrama* in a prologue and two acts by EUGEN D'ALBERT to a libretto by Rudolph Lothar [Rudolph Spitzer] after Angel Guimerá's Catalan drama *Terra baixa*; Prague, Neues Deutsches Theater, 15 November 1903.

Sebastiano *a rich landowner*		baritone
Marta	*in Sebastiano's employment*	soprano
Pepa		soprano
Antonia		soprano
Rosalia		contralto
Pedro *a shepherd*		tenor
Tommaso *the village elder*		bass
Moruccio *a miller*		baritone
Nuri *a little girl*		soprano
Nando *a shepherd*		tenor
	Villagers and peasants	

Setting The Pyrenees and the Catalan Lowlands in the early 20th century

Tiefland was d'Albert's seventh opera; after the success of the première, the work spread rapidly from Prague to other major cities in Europe and America, reaching Berlin in 1907, Vienna in 1908 and the Metropolitan, New York the same year, when the cast included Emmy Destinn as Marta and Erik Schmedes as Pedro. The London première, conducted by Sir Thomas Beecham, was on 5 October 1910, when the girl Nuri was sung by Maggie Teyte, who was making her Covent Garden début. *Tiefland* has remained in the repertory of opera houses in German-speaking countries, but receives only infrequent revivals elsewhere.

PROLOGUE *Outside a shepherd's hut, high in the Pyrenees* Pedro greets Nando, another shepherd and the first person he has spoken to for six months. He claims to enjoy his solitary life, though sometimes he prays for a wife. Sebastiano, the local landowner, arrives, accompanied by Tommaso and Marta. He is about to make an advantageous marriage, and intends to give Marta, his mistress, to the unsuspecting Pedro as wife. They can run the mill together. Pedro is overjoyed, though Nando warns him that life in the lowlands is more complicated than the simple existence up in the mountains.

ACT 1 *The main room inside the mill* Pepa, Antonia and Rosalia gossip and question Moruccio about Marta's impending marriage. Marta drives the women out, although she welcomes the child Nuri. Marta, in effect a slave owned by Sebastiano, expresses her misery and shame at being forced to marry a country bumpkin. Moruccio demands to know how Tommaso, the respected village elder, could have got involved in such a wicked arrangement. Cries of 'The bridegroom!' can be heard as Pedro arrives. While Pedro is getting dressed for the wedding, Sebastiano assures Marta that nothing will change between them as a result of her marriage; that evening, if she sees a light in her room, it means that he will be there, waiting for her. Pedro and the villagers come to fetch Marta and they all go off to the church. Tommaso accuses Sebastiano of dishonourable behaviour, but the latter denies it. The wedding procession can be heard returning and Marta and Pedro re-enter. She makes it quite clear to Pedro that he cannot sleep in her room. Upset and bewildered, Pedro offers Marta a wedding present, a silver thaler that he earned, as he explains in 'Wolfserzählung', for killing a wolf that had been preying on the sheep. Although she is touched by his generosity, Marta remains adamant. Suddenly Pedro notices a light in her room; he is about to investigate when it goes out. Marta denies having seen anything, but she agrees to spend the night on a chair in the main room, while Pedro lies down to sleep on the floor.

ACT 2 *The same room in the mill, the following morning* Marta is awoken by Nuri's singing and goes to her room. Nuri wakes Pedro, who decides to leave, certain now that there was a man in Marta's room the previous night. When Nuri artlessly says she is sorry that everyone is laughing at him, Pedro at last understands the situation; he knows everything but the name of the man who has dishonoured him. He goes out with Nuri just as Marta, about to follow them, is stopped by Tommaso. Accused by the old man of involving him in the plot to trick Pedro, Marta tells him her story, 'Ich weiss nicht, wer mein Vater war'. She never knew her father; penniless, she and her mother begged for their living. They were joined by a cripple and after the death of her mother she remained with him, earning money by dancing in the street. One day, when she was 14, they came to this valley and she was noticed by Sebastiano. Installing the cripple as miller, he forced Marta to become his mistress. Now she would give anything to be free and worthy of Pedro, whose simplicity has won her heart.

The three women try to question Tommaso as he leaves, but he tells them nothing. When Pedro returns, he demands to know why they are laughing at him, but the women only laugh the more. Pedro, aware that he ought to kill Marta to save his honour but unwilling to hurt the woman he loves, prepares to leave. Marta tells him the wedding guests were laughing at him because they knew she had belonged to another man. Furiously Pedro seizes a knife and stabs her in the arm. Marta, in tears, begs him to kill her. Finally, avowing their mutual love, they plan to go together to the mountains. On Sebastiano's entry, Pedro tells him that he and Marta no longer want the mill as they are leaving. Sebastiano takes no notice and orders Marta to dance; Pedro orders her to go with him. Realizing that it was Sebastiano in Marta's room the previous night, Pedro attacks the landowner. The villagers drag him away as Marta faints and Tommaso informs Sebastiano that his marriage has been called off; he has told the bride's father all about his prospective son-in-law. Sebastiano and Marta quarrel violently and he is about to take her by force when Pedro comes back. There is a fight and Pedro strangles Sebastiano. Calling in the villagers to view the corpse, Pedro tells them that they can laugh now, if they like. Together with Marta he is leaving the hated lowlands to return to his beloved mountains.

* * *

The violent events of *Tiefland* inspired d'Albert to compose his most effective dramatic work, in which he used an Italian *verismo* idiom to achieve a near-perfect balance between content and style, a balance that he never quite achieved in his other operas. At the same time, the German element of his cultural heritage ensures that the characters and their motivation are drawn with unusual subtlety for a work written in the *verismo* tradition, while the underlying, linked themes of the opera, innocence and guilt (themes again tackled by d'Albert in *Die toten Augen*), are demonstrated to be opposite sides of the same coin.

Marta's complex personality, with the dawning realization that her only chance of happiness lies in the country bumpkin whom she dismissed so derisively at first, is most skilfully mirrored in her music. Though Pedro appears impossibly naive in the earlier scenes, he acquires compassion and understanding as his illusions are shattered one by one. The happy ending, so unlikely at first glance, becomes a genuine possibility as Pedro and Marta discover a new tolerance of each other's weaknesses. The least interesting of the three principals is undoubtedly Sebastiano, a cardboard villain who learns nothing from his experiences, but even he is described in music of an appropriately inflexible strength, while Tommaso, venerable in years but innocent, and the child Nuri, innocent but naturally wise, are sketched with respect and affection by the composer.

ELIZABETH FORBES

Tietjen, Heinz (*b* Tangier, 24 June 1881; *d* Baden-Baden, 30 Nov 1967). German Intendant, director and conductor. He was born of Anglo-German parents and after a brief career in business he worked as conductor and director at Trier in 1904, becoming Intendant in 1907. He held similar posts in Saarbrücken (1921), Breslau (1922) and Berlin (1925), where at the Städtische Oper he had a notable partnership with Bruno Walter. Both men favoured modestly innovatory stagings of an essentially mainstream repertory centred on Mozart, Wagner and Strauss. In 1927 Tietjen was appointed director of all the Prussian state theatres, including those at Hanover, Kassel, Wiesbaden and the Staatsoper and Kroll Oper, Berlin.

In 1931 Tietjen was invited by Siegfried Wagner's widow, Winifred, to become artistic director of the Bayreuth Festival – the first holder of that position not to be a member of the Wagner family. He brought to Bayreuth many leading singers from Berlin, the conductor Wilhelm Furtwängler and the designer Emil Preetorius. He also continued a policy of conservative revolution; by 1943 he had mounted new productions of every work in the hitherto rather moribund festival repertory, departing markedly from the received traditionalism of Cosima's stagings. Here also Tietjen resumed his conducting career with performances of *Lohengrin* and the *Ring*; recordings reveal a lighter, swifter approach to the music dramas than that of many contemporaries.

After the war Tietjen was recalled to his old post at the Berlin Städtische Oper (1948–54), where his work of rebuilding a company helped launch the career of the young Hungarian conductor Ferenc Fricsay and secured the reputation of the composer Werner Egk. Tietjen's last permanent post was in Hamburg (1956–9); in his last year there he was invited back to Bayreuth by Wieland Wagner to conduct performances of *Lohengrin*.

Tietjen's multi-faceted career owed much to his diplomatic gift for self-promotion and lack of rigorous political scruples. His work as a director was hardly in the vanguard of contemporary European staging, but his choice of design collaborators (notably Preetorius) often gave an imaginative stimulus to his own conventional epic stagings. The wide range of his activities set a precedent for contemporary German Intendanten, whose role could no longer remain purely administrative.

MIKE ASHMAN

Tietjens [Titiens], **Therese (Carolina Johanna Alexandra)** (*b* Hamburg, 17 July 1831; *d* London, 3 Oct 1877). German soprano. She studied in Hamburg and Vienna, making her début at Altona in 1849 as Donizetti's Lucrezia Borgia. Engaged at Frankfurt, she created Louise in Lortzing's *Opernprobe* (1851). After appearances at Brno and Vienna, she made her London début at Her Majesty's Theatre in 1858 as Valentine (*Les Huguenots*), then sang in London every year until her death. At Drury Lane she sang Hélène in *Les vêpres siciliennes* (1859), at the Lyceum Theatre Amelia in *Un ballo in maschera* (1861), at Her Majesty's Marguerite in *Faust* (1863), Mrs Ford in *Die lustigen Weiber von Windsor*, Gounod's Mireille (1864), Cherubini's Medea (1865) and Leonora in *La forza del destino* (1867), all first London performances. Her extensive repertory included Gluck's Iphigenia, Mozart's Countess Almaviva, Donna Anna, Konstanze and Pamina, Leonore (*Fidelio*), Weber's Agathe and Reiza, Semiramide, Anne Boleyn, Norma, Elvira (*Ernani*), Giselda (*I Lombardi*), Leonora (*Il trovatore*), Meyerbeer's Alice and Fidès and Wagner's Ortrud. She sang in Paris and Naples and made her Covent Garden début in 1868 as Lucrezia Borgia, the role of her final appearance at Her Majesty's in 1877. The power and flexibility of her voice made her a magnificent interpreter of Norma, Medea and Lucrezia.

L. Arditi: *My Reminiscences* (London, 1896)
H. Klein: *Thirty Years of Musical Life in London* (London, 1903)
H. Rosenthal: *Two Centuries of Opera at Covent Garden* (London, 1958)
P. Forster: 'Titiens – the Earnest Prima Donna', *Opera*, xxxi (1980), 224–31

ELIZABETH FORBES

Tiflis (Russ.). TBILISI.

Tigers, The. Burlesque opera in a prologue and three acts by HAVERGAL BRIAN to his own libretto; BBC broadcast, 3 May 1983 (concert performance of extracts, London, St John's, Smith Square, 29 January 1976).

Brian sketched his unusual first opera in 1917–19; scoring was delayed until 1928–9, though he orchestrated extracts in 1922. The vocal score was published in 1932, but Fritz Busch's proposed production for the 1933–4 Dresden season was aborted; the full score was lost for many years and came to light only in 1977 (Brian re-scored the opening of the prologue in 1969, at the age of 93).

Brian's libretto refracts his 1914–15 experiences in the Honourable Artillery Company, with a blend of music-hall humour and absurdist fantasy. A Bank Holiday carnival on Hampstead Heath is interrupted by the declaration of war. Then follow the misadventures of the Tigers, an incompetent infantry regiment in training. Their elderly colonel, Sir John Stout (baritone), is visited by the ghosts of great generals and is wooed by Mrs Pamela Freebody (soprano), a supporter of good works; there is also a large cast of minor characters. The tone is flippant, anarchic and anti-authoritarian, every situation dissolving into anticlimax. The real horrors of war are hinted at in symbolic ballet sequences, which make staging problematic.

The lavish scoring includes two vibraphones – innovatory for 1929. Humble themes receive elaborate and colourful treatment (much of the prologue consists of symphonic variations on the tune 'Has anybody seen Kelly?', further developed elsewhere), and there are several parodic references to *Die Walküre* and *Ein Heldenleben*; Brian himself said the work was 'as serious as *Die Meistersinger*'. He extracted an orchestral version of the 'Kelly' variations for concert performance, as well as five symphonic dances: 'Shadow Dance', 'Wild Horsemen', 'Green Pastures', 'Gargoyles' and 'Lachryma'. MALCOLM MACDONALD

Tigrane [*Il Tigrane, o vero L'egual impegno d'amore e di fede* ('Tigranes, or The Dual Allegiance to Love and Loyalty')]. *Dramma per musica* in three acts by Alessandro Scarlatti (*see* SCARLATTI family, (1)) to a libretto by DOMENICO LALLI; Naples, Teatro S Bartolomeo, 16 February 1715.

The account in *Herodotus* (book 1, 253–71) of how Thomyris, Queen of the Massagetae, took bloody revenge on the Persian emperor Cyrus the Great, who had taken her son captive and refused to release him, was used by Lalli as a springboard for the totally fictitious plot of *Tigrane*. In the opera, Tomiri [Thomyris] (soprano) has two sons, the first of whom, Archinto, was kidnapped in infancy and reared as Tigranes (soprano castrato) by the Prince of Armenia, whom he has now succeeded. Thomyris has promised to marry either King Policare of Lydia (contralto) or King Doraspe of Damascus (tenor) in return for their help in overcoming Cyrus, but her love for Tigranes (whom she does not recognize) makes her hesitate. When Tigranes' betrothed, Meroe (soprano), daughter of King Cyrus (now dead), arrives in disguise to avenge her father's death, Tigranes is caught in the *egual impegno d'amore e di fede* typical of heroic opera plots of the period. The succeeding imbroglio, which occasionally involves also the two comic characters, Dorilla (contralto) and Orcone (bass), is resolved only in the last scene when Tigranes' true identity is brought to light. Thomyris is then free to marry Policare, and the other main characters, except for the unlucky Doraspe, are also suitably paired off in the customary *lieto fine*.

Tigrane was among the most successful of Scarlatti's late operas, and within a year it had been revived at Innsbruck and Livorno. Modern critics have valued it highly too, and D. J. Grout described it as 'one of the greatest, if not the very greatest, of Scarlatti's operas', but its notoriety in the history books is based on the erroneous claim that it was the first opera to include horns in the orchestra. The instrumentation is nevertheless of particular interest, and includes obbligato parts for oboe, trumpet and viola, as well as the ubiquitous violins. Scarlatti's lyricism is at its most inspired, not least in Meroe's darkly expressive Act 3 aria 'Sussurrando il venticello', accompanied by muted strings. MALCOLM BOYD

Tigranyan, Armen Tigran (*b* Alexandropol [now Gyumzi], 14/26 Dec 1879; *d* Tbilisi, 10 Feb 1950). Armenian composer. The artistic side of his character was strongly influenced by his home environment in an area steeped in the traditions of folk craft and of the *ashughner*, or *gusanner*, the Armenian folk minstrels. He studied in Tbilisi from 1894, and after returning to Armenia he worked as a school music teacher and choirmaster, staged his own dramatized arrangements of national songs, and wrote songs on Armenian texts. His first opera, *Anush*, was performed with success in amateur workshops in various Transcaucasian towns in 1912. In the next year he settled in Tbilisi, where he was a manager of the Tbilisi Armenian Music Society. *Anush* was republished in the 1930s and revived in Erevan.

With this work Tigranyan laid the foundations of an Armenian national operatic style. The lyrical, everyday nature of the text – concerning the love of Anush and Saro, who perish as a result of social prejudice – is matched in Tigranyan's music, which achieves its national qualities by approaching folksong intonation, though there is only one direct quotation, and using folksong forms (*ashugh* improvisations, ceremonial and wedding songs etc.). The use of the chorus, important in *Anush*, was developed further in *David-Bek*, a five-act heroic opera concerning the Armenians' struggle against Persian invaders in the 18th century; but the folklike melody remained, and here Tigranyan employed more quotations, notably from the song 'I ninj maned ark'ayakan' by the celebrated *ashugh* Paghdasar Dpir. Various nationalities presented in the opera – Russians, Georgians and Persians – are characterized by material approaching their respective folk music. On a large scale, *David-Bek* is organized along symphonic lines, linking it with Spendiaryan's *Almast*.

See also ANUSH.

Anush, 1908–12 (4, Tigranyan, after H. T'umanyan), Alexandrapol, People's City Hall, 4/17 Aug 1912 [orchd G. Ya. Burkovich]; rev. (5), Erevan, Spendiaryan Armenian Theatre of Opera and Ballet, 27 March 1935 [reorchd S. A. Shatiryan]; rev. version, Moscow, Bol'shoy (Spendiaryan Armenian Theatre of Opera and Ballet), 22 Oct 1939 [partly reorchd A. G. Ter-Gevondyan]

Leyli ev Mejnun [Leyli and Mejnun], 1915 (Spl, Tigranyan, after H. Voskanyan), Tbilisi, Armenian Comedy Theatre, 1918

Kyer-ogli, 1936 (Tigranyan), inc.

David-Bek, 1940–49 (os, 5, Tigranyan, after Raffi [H. Melik-Hakobyan]); rev. version (A. Ter-Hovhanyan), Erevan, Spendiaryan Armenian Theatre of Opera and Ballet, 3 Dec 1950 [orchd L. Khodja-Eynatov]

*

K. Melik-Vrt'anesyan: *Armen Tigranian* (Moscow, 1939)

R. A'tayan and M. Muradyan: *Armen Tigranyan* (Erevan, 1955)

G. Tigranov: *Armyanskiy muzikal'niy teatr*, i (Erevan, 1956), 221–70; ii (Erevan, 1960), 41–68

Sh. Talyan: *Depk'er, demk'er, mtk'er* [Events, Figures, Thoughts] (Erevan, 1973)

M. Ter-Simonyan: '"Anushi" ev "Leyli ev Mejnuni" anmahout'yun' [Immortality of "Anush" and "Leyli and Mejnun"], *Sovetakan arvest* (1981), no.5, pp.13–16

SVETLANA SARKISYAN

Tijardović, Ivo (*b* Split, 18 Sept 1895; *d* Zagreb, 19 March 1976). Croatian composer. He studied music in Split and Vienna and graduated from the Zagreb drama school in 1922. He then worked as conductor and stage designer at the Split Municipal Theatre (1922–9) before joining the music department of the Edison Bell Penkala recording company in Zagreb (1929–33). Returning to Split, he worked as director-conductor of the opera and as stage manager at the Municipal Theatre (1933–41); he was later stage manager of the National Theatre in Zagreb (1945–9). As a theatre composer Tijardović was primarily active in the lighter genres; of his operettas, *Mala Floramye* ('Little Floramye', 1926), written to his own libretto, had an enormous success and has remained in the Yugoslavian operetta repertory. In this work he succeeded in conveying the local colour of Split, and showed his gift for dramatic development and effective ensembles. Tijardović's musical style is traditional, with an attractive, Mediterranean melodiousness enriched with folk elements.

operettas unless otherwise stated

Pierrot Illo, Split, Municipal, 31 Dec 1922

Mala Floramye [Little Floramye], Split, Municipal, 14 Jan 1926
Kraljica Lopte [The Queen of the Ball], Split, Municipal, 21 Aug 1926
Splitski akvarel [A Water-Colour of Split], Split, Municipal, 5 March 1928
Zapovijed Maršala Marmonta [The Order of Marshal Marmont], Split, Municipal, 30 April 1929
Jurek i Štefek, Zagreb, National, 24 June 1931
Dimnjaci uz Jadran [Chimneys on the Adriatic], 1949 (op, 3, I. Tijardović), Zagreb, National, 20 Jan 1951
Marko Polo, 1955 (op, prol., 3, epilogue, V. Rabadan), Zagreb, National, 3 Dec 1960
Doživljaji u Šangaju [The Adventures in Shanghai], 1933 (musical comedy, A. S. Dale); as Min, Osijek, 6 June 1958
Katerina Velika [Catherine the Great], 1956 (musical), Zagreb, Komedija, 9 April 1960
Dioklecijan, 1966 (op, 4, B. Radica)

*

M. Logar: 'Ivo Tijardović: *Marko Polo*', *Zvuk*, nos.47–8 (1961), 45–6
A. Tomašek: 'Stvaralaštvo u znaku kazališta: povodom 75-godišnjice rođenja I. Tijardovicá' [Creative Work under the Heading of Theatre: on the Occasion of the 75th Anniversary of the Birth of I. Tijardović], *Zvuk*, nos.111–12 (1971), 28–31
J. Andreis: *Music in Croatia* (Zagreb, 1974) KORALJKA KOS

Tikhiy Don. Opera by I. I. Dzerzhinsky; *see* QUIET FLOWS THE DON.

Tikotsky [Tsikotski], **Yevgeny Karlovich** (*b* St Petersburg, 13/25 or 14/26 Dec 1893; *d* Minsk, 23 or 24 Nov 1970). Russian composer of Polish origin. He studied the piano and theory with Volkova-Bonch-Bruyevich in St Petersburg (1912–14), but in composition he was largely self-taught. He began to compose at the age of 14, including some operas on Russian literary subjects, in consultation with his friend, the composer Deshevov. At his father's insistence he began studying at the St Petersburg Psychoneurological Institute in 1911 but left in 1914 to study physics and mathematics at St Petersburg University. After war service (1915–24) he taught in a music school in Bobruysk (1927–34), where his first contacts with Belorussian folk music stimulated more intensive creative activity; his output shows wide use of this music, treated entirely in a 19th-century manner. His earliest major works included music for stage productions in Minsk, where he taught at the music school (1934–41) and was a staff composer for Belorussian Radio. *Mikhas' Podgorniy* was one of the first Belorussian operas, and during World War II he wrote the first version of *Alesya* to a libretto by P. Brovka. He received many honours and awards, including the title People's Artist of the USSR (1955). Together with Churkin, Aladov and Turenkov, Tikotsky was a founder of Belorussian art music; his cultivation of opera and the symphony was of particular importance.

Kukhnya svyatosti [Kitchen of Sanctity] op.6 (musical comedy, G. Gradov and V. Orlov), Bobruysk, 1931
Mikhas' Podgorniy op.18 (P. Brovka), Minsk, 10 March 1939
Alesya op.31 (Brovka), Minsk, 24 Dec 1944; rev. 1947; rev. 1949; rev. as Devushka iz Poles'ya [The Girl from Poles'ye] op.46 (Brovka and E. Romanovich), Minsk, 7 Feb 1952; rev. 1953; rev. as Alesya, 1967
Anna Gromova, 1970

*

G. Tsitovich and I. Nisnevich: *Belorusskaya SSR* (Moscow, 1957)
B. Smol'sky: *Belorusskiy muzïkal'nïy teatr* (Minsk, 1963)
I. L. Gusin: *Yevgeny Karlovich Tikotsky* (Moscow and Leningrad, 1965) L. M. BUTIR

Tilla, La. *See* PINI, MARIA DOMENICA.

Timbre d'argent, Le ('The Silver Bell'). *Opéra fantastique* in four acts by CAMILLE SAINT-SAËNS to a libretto by JULES BARBIER and MICHEL CARRÉ; Paris, Théâtre Lyrique, 23 February 1877.

Saint-Saëns' first opera was a significant link between Gounod's *Faust* and Offenbach's *Les contes d'Hoffmann*, in all three of which the same librettists, Barbier and Carré, explored the hero's dependence on a sinister older man enforced by a diabolic pact. In *Le timbre d'argent* Conrad (tenor), an artist, has a fatal appetite for gold, and is also entranced by his own portrait of Circe, personified in real life by the ballerina Fiametta. Dr Spiridion (bass) gives Conrad a silver bell: when he strikes it he will get all the gold he could desire, but at the price of someone's death. Conrad is a strikingly Hoffmannesque figure, while Spiridion-Polycastre-Pippo is clearly an extension of Lindorf-Coppélius-Dapertutto-Dr Miracle.

Composed in 1864–5 for the Théâtre Lyrique, Paris, the opera was kept from the stage first by the theatre's bankruptcy, then by the Franco-Prussian War, and was not played until 1877. In the meantime Saint-Saëns had recomposed the dialogue to form a grand opera version, which was not played until 1913. The music is enormously fluent and versatile, but the mimed part of Fiametta presents some difficulties on stage, and the conclusion (that the events have all taken place in Conrad's feverish imagination) is a little weak. There are some bold scenic ideas, including a theatre seen from the back of the stage and some fanciful transformations. It seems no coincidence that the opera's 18 performances in 1877 exactly coincided with Offenbach's first concentrated labours on *Les contes d'Hoffmann*.

HUGH MACDONALD

Timişoara (Hung. Temesvár). Town in western Romania (Transylvania). The first theatre was built in the town in 1781 (cap. 600). Visiting opera companies appeared in the late 18th century – Mozart's *Die Zauberflöte* was presented in 1796, and Salieri's *La fiera di Venezia*. Hungarian-language troupes performed there in the 1830s, though opera in German was generally favoured. The company, under F. Strampfer, flourished particularly in the 1850s and 60s. A peak of activity was reached between 1863 and 1870, when under Eduard Reimann the most important works in the standard repertory were presented. A new theatre in the Italian Renaissance style (built by the architects Helmer and Fellner) was opened on 22 September 1875; on 10 December 1882 a second theatre was inaugurated. Bruno Walter conducted here (*Les Huguenots*, *Il barbiere di Siviglia*, *Pagliacci*, *Cavalleria rusticana*). Destroyed by fire in 1921, the theatre was rebuilt by the Romanian architect Duiliu Marcu, and it became the Opera de Stat (State Opera) on 30 March 1946. The 1989 revolution began on the steps of the opera house.

Besides Gluck, Cimarosa, Mozart, Rossini, Wagner and Puccini, the repertory includes works by Carl Orff, Liang-Han-Kuan, Sabin Drăgoi, Brediceanu, Negrea, Doru Popovici, Liana Alexandra and others. Romanian soloists, together with the Vienna SO under Silvia Voina, gave the world première of Schubert's *Sakuntala* in Vienna in 1971. Among the singers who have appeared in Timişoara are Cornelia Creţu-Hollósy, Irina Arkhipova, Giuseppe di Stefano, Kim Borg, Pavel Lisitsyan, Aldo Protti, Titus Moraru, Iuliu Marc, Gabriela Ganea, Traian Nicolau and Elena Gaja; conductors have included Mircea Popa, Hermann Klee and

Nicolae Boboc. The Timişoara company has toured in Bulgaria, Italy, the Netherlands, Yugoslavia and Austria.

*

M. Fekete: *A temesvári színészet története* [History of the Theatrical Art of Temesvár] (Temesvár, 1911) VIOREL COSMA

Tindaridi, I [*I tindaridi, o Castore e Polluce* ('The Heavenly Twins, or Castor and Pollux')]. *Opera seria* in five acts by TOMMASO TRAETTA to a libretto by CARLO INNOCENZO FRUGONI after PIERRE-JOSEPH BERNARD's *Castor et Pollux*; Parma, Teatro Ducale, April 1760.

Pollux (tenor), immortal son of Giove [Jupiter] (tenor), and his mortal half-brother Castor (soprano castrato) both love Telaira (soprano). Pollux steps aside in favour of Castor, whom Telaira prefers. Her sister Febe [Phoebe] (soprano) induces Linceo [Lynceus] to direct his army against Castor, who is killed in battle. Pollux gains permission from Jupiter to take Castor's place in Hades. Jupiter then restores both to immortal life and reunites the couple forever.

Frugoni's text closely follows Bernard's, though he omits the role of Lynceus. The principal departures from Italian dramaturgical practices are the many cavatinas and choruses (some combined with soloists) and the incorporation of pantomime, dance and spectacle within and between acts. Pollux's visits to Mount Olympus and the underworld feature magical scene changes and scene complexes involving chorus, soloists, pantomime and dance. Phoebe, Pollux and Mercurio [Mercury] (tenor) sing a confrontational trio during the inferno scene, and a duet for Castor and Telaira precedes the final chorus of rejoicing.

Traetta provided a variety of *dal segno* arias and through-composed cavatinas. His choruses are substantial, with music suited to diverse roles ranging from soldiers to demons; the most complex one, which includes programmatic battle music, uses imitative textures, but most choruses are predominantly homophonic with occasional antiphonal entrances. Dance music is conspicuously absent and was probably left to another composer. Most of the action proceeds in simple recitative. Traetta used effective dramatic obbligato recitative for a few select moments; here he often employed wind instruments in a variety of accompaniment styles – obbligato commentary, sustained *accompagnato* and measured arioso. He used programmatic obbligato recitative for the appearance of Jupiter in Act 3, where the sinfonia includes a part for piccolo.

MARITA P. McCLYMONDS

Tinsley, Pauline (Cecilia) (*b* Wigan, 23 Nov 1928). English soprano. She studied in Manchester at the Northern School of Music and in London, making her début in 1961 as Desdemona (Rossini's *Otello*) at St Pancras Town Hall, London, where she also sang Amalia (*I masnadieri*), Elvira (*Ernani*), Gulnara (*Il corsaro*) and Irene (*Rienzi*). For the WNO (1962–72) she sang Elsa, Susanna, Lady Macbeth, Sinaïde, Donna Elvira, Abigail, Aida and Turandot. At Sadler's Wells (1963–74) she sang Gilda, the Queen of Night, Fiordiligi, Countess Almaviva, Leonora (*La forza del destino*), Leonore (*Fidelio*, both versions) and Elizabeth (*Maria Stuarda*), which she had already sung for the New York City Opera. At Santa Fe she sang Anne Boleyn (1971) and Senta. She made her Covent Garden début in 1965 as the Overseer (*Elektra*) returning as Amelia (*Ballo*), Santuzza, Mother Marie (*Dialogues des Carmélites*) and Lady Billows, which she also sang in St Louis and Rome, at Reggio Emilia and at Glyndebourne. Returning to the WNO (1975–81) she sang the Kostelnička; Electra, a role she repeated at San Diego, Mannheim, Düsseldorf, Basle and Amsterdam; the Dyer's Wife, which she also sang at La Scala and Barcelona (1986); and Tosca. She created Candace (Paulus's *The Village Singer*, 1979, St Louis). Later roles included Isolde, Ortrud, Kundry, Brünnhilde (*Die Walküre*), the Witch (*Königskinder*) at Wexford, Fortune-Teller (*The Fiery Angel*) at Geneva, Fata Morgana for Opera North, Mother/Witch (*Hänsel und Gretel*) and Kabanicha for the ENO. She was an idiosyncratic actress with a flexible voice, brilliant in tone, of great stamina and penetration.

*

E. Forbes: 'Pauline Tinsley', *Opera*, xxxiii (1982), 258–67

ALAN BLYTH

Tintner, Georg (Bernhard) (*b* Vienna, 22 May 1917). Australian conductor of Austrian birth. He was a member of the Vienna Boys' Choir, which he also conducted before studying with Weingartner at the Vienna Academy. In 1938 he joined the Vienna Volksoper as coach and conductor, then emigrated to New Zealand, where he at first worked as a choral conductor. He moved to Australia as conductor for the Elizabethan Theatre Trust (later the Australian Opera; 1954–63), and introduced the televising of opera in Australia. He was music director of the New Zealand Opera Company in 1964. In 1969 he made his British opera début with Sadler's Wells Opera at the London Coliseum with *La vie parisienne* and *Die Zauberflöte* (to marked lack of critical approval), and returned to Australia as music director of West Australian Opera, Perth (1971–2). He was resident conductor again with Australian Opera (1973–6), then music director of the Queensland Theatre Orchestra, Brisbane (which included opera performances), from 1977 to 1987, returning there for *La bohème* in 1991 while holding an orchestral appointment in Nova Scotia, Canada. He has conducted elsewhere in Canada and in South Africa and the Far East. ANN CARR-BOYD, NOËL GOODWIN

Tintomara. Opera in three acts (revised in two) by LARS JOHAN WERLE to a libretto by Leif Söderström, after Carl Jonas Love Almqvist's *Drottningens juvelsmycke* ('The Queen's Jewel'); Stockholm, Royal Opera, 18 January 1973 (revised version, Göteborg, Stora Teatern, 7 March 1976).

Written to celebrate the bicentenary of the Stockholm Royal Opera and beginning where Verdi's *Un ballo in maschera* ended, *Tintomara* deals with the political intrigues that followed the assassination of King Gustavus III (tenor) at a masked ball in the opera house. Tintomara (mezzo-soprano), the mysterious hermaphrodite who signifies happiness to the other characters, is executed at the end. A quartet of young lovers, oblivious to anyone but themselves – Amanda (soprano), Adolfine (mezzo-soprano), Claes-Henrik (tenor) and Ferdinand (baritone) – are contrasted with the conspirators, including the king's brother Prince Carl (tenor) and Baron Reuterholm (bass), the virtual dictator of Sweden after the king's death. The plot, condensed to the point of inscrutability, is narrated by a speaker.

In *Tintomara* Werle reverts to a more conventional style than that of his previous operas, dividing the music into arias and ensembles, but he displays all his habitual technical mastery of orchestration as well as a new wealth of melodic invention in his writing for the voice.

ELIZABETH FORBES

Tippett, Sir **Michael (Kemp)** (*b* London, 2 Jan 1905). English composer. His reputation as one of the most significant and original composers of the 20th century was hard won and established at an unusually late stage in his singleminded career. His five mature operas (all to his own librettos) are in many ways the most important pillars of his extensive compositional development and enshrine the wide-ranging musical and extra-musical concerns of a creative lifetime.

1. Early years. 2. Mature operas. 3. Style.

1. EARLY YEARS. Tippett grew up at Wetherden in the Suffolk countryside, where his father, a lawyer and business man of Cornish descent, had retired early. His mother trained as an artist, wrote novels and was closely involved with the suffragette movement. Educated at first by a governess, and also given piano lessons, Tippett was sent in 1914 to a preparatory school in Dorset and in 1918 to Fettes College, Edinburgh, but after two unhappy years he was transferred to Stamford Grammar School, Lincolnshire. Although he knew from an early age that he wanted to be a composer, he received no formal musical training at school. In 1923 he entered the RCM, where he studied composition with Charles Wood and C. H. Kitson, the piano with Aubyn Raymar and conducting with Malcolm Sargent and Adrian Boult. He acted as répétiteur for a student performance of *Parsifal* and came across operas as diverse as *Pelléas et Mélisande* and *Hugh the Drover*.

In 1924 Tippett started to conduct a small choir at Oxted, Surrey, and on leaving the RCM in 1928 he settled at Oxted, where he remained until 1951. He had already persuaded a local dramatic society, the Oxted and Limpsfield Players, to join forces with his choir with a view to performing operas; their first venture, in 1927, was the first amateur production of Vaughan Williams's *The Shepherds of the Delectable Mountains*. In 1928 Tippett's own realization of the 18th-century ballad opera *The Village Opera* was given, followed in 1930 by Stanford's *The Travelling Companion*. In the same year Tippett wrote the incidental music for their production of Flecker's *Don Juan*.

In 1929 Tippett became conductor of the operatic society of the Music School of the Hackney Institute in London, where he directed Holst's *The Perfect Fool*, followed by *Martha*, *Ruddigore* and *The Emerald Isle* (Sullivan, completed by German). He was at this time dissatisfied with his own compositional efforts and between 1930 and 1932 he again studied at the RCM, with R. O. Morris and Gordon Jacob. In 1933 he organized the music at a work-camp for unemployed ironstone miners at Boosbeck, North Yorkshire, and produced a version of *The Beggar's Opera*. This was followed in 1934 by an original folksong opera, *Robin Hood* (music from which survives in the Suite for the Birthday of Prince Charles), which he produced again a few years later with the London Labour Choral Union. Tippett was by now deeply if temporarily involved with radical Trotskyist politics in London and sought to give musical expression to his social ideals. A plan for an opera based on the 1916 Easter Rising in Ireland came to nothing, though the motivation behind it spurred the writing in 1935 of a revolutionary play, *War Ramp*, which was produced with the support of the Labour League of Youth. In the same year he completed the first composition he now acknowledges and the first in which he found his individual musical voice, the String Quartet no.1.

Tippett's next operatic projects, though produced at a cooperative hall in Peckham Rye, London, in 1938 and 1939 respectively, were non-political. These two 'plays for children' to words by his friend the playwright Christopher Fry – *Robert of Sicily* (after Longfellow's poem) and *Seven at One Stroke* (based on a fairy-tale by Grimm) – were subsequently withdrawn. In 1939, however, the hitherto unfocussed concern with notions of war and pacifism which lay behind the idea of an Irish opera and *War Ramp* crystallized in Tippett's mind under the impact of recent events, for example the horrific pogrom of the Jews in 1938, which led to the notorious *Kristallnacht*, precipitated by the shooting of a Nazi diplomat in Paris by Herschel Grynspan.

Tippett sketched a scenario for an oratorio and asked his mentor T. S. Eliot if he would write the text. Eliot asked for a very detailed outline, and eventually responded that Tippett should take it one stage further and complete it himself. His advice was based partly on Tippett's not inconsiderable literary skill but it also gave practical support to the natural affinity which Tippett already felt for the marriage of action, words and music. He was advised, in Eliot's words, not to 'let the poets loose on your librettos; because they are going to do with the words what your music should do'. Tippett followed the advice not only in the oratorio *A Child of our Time* but also in the five operas of his maturity, as well as such works as *The Vision of St Augustine*, *Songs for Dov*, Symphony no.3 and *The Mask of Time*.

2. MATURE OPERAS. An earlier plan for writing a neo-classical *opera buffa* was significantly affected by the composition of *A Child of our Time*, completed in 1941 but not performed until 1944. Tippett planned a new comic opera as a relaxation after work on the oratorio, but having drafted a scenario (*The Man with the Seven Daughters*) he realized that the implications of the oratorio demanded dramatic treatment. The Jungian perspective of *A Child of our Time* (Tippett had himself undergone Jungian analysis in 1938–9) was summed up in a statement: 'I would know my shadow and my light, so shall I at last be whole'. The aspiration to portray this vision on stage was the genesis of *The Midsummer Marriage*, which preoccupied Tippett as the war drew to a close (and during which he had been sentenced to three months in Wormwood Scrubs for his pacifist belief). Provisionally called *Aurora Consurgens, or The Laughing Children*, the opera took shape as a visionary comedy. Tippett began work on libretto and music in 1946 and was occupied with the opera until 1952, with no real prospect of commission or production. From 1940 he was director of music at Morley College and a leading figure in London's musical life, though he relinquished the post in 1951 in order to concentrate on composition. The sequence of Ritual Dances from *The Midsummer Marriage* was arranged as a suite and performed in 1953 by Paul Sacher in Basle, and in 1955 the opera was first produced at Covent Garden, where it was received with general incomprehension.

Unlike his friend and contemporary Benjamin Britten who, after the success of his first opera, *Peter Grimes*, in 1945 had embarked on his stated ambition to be a professional opera composer, Tippett knew that his operas would, because of the long gestation period they required, be balanced in his canon between periods of abstract writing. Thus *The Midsummer Marriage* was separated from *A Child of our Time* by the second and third string quartets and the First Symphony and itself gave rise to the Corelli Fantasia, the Piano Concerto and the Second Symphony, which all share the opera's musical world. Following the production of *The Midsummer Marriage* Tippett reacted by assessing its strengths and shortcomings from a dramatic standpoint as a preparation for a second opera. Seeing Paul Claudel's *Christophe Colomb* drew him towards the world of Brecht's epic theatre, and he heeded the advice of the producer Peter Brook to take a well-known story rather than invent his own myth as he had in *The Midsummer Marriage*. So he turned to the Greek world and chose the history of King Priam from Homer's *Iliad*. His declared aim in this tragedy was to focus on the 'mysterious nature of human choice'. A commission from the Koussevitzky Foundation in 1957 for a choral and orchestral work gave shape to this new impulse, and the commission was suitably adapted for an opera. (A project for chorus and orchestra called *The Windrose* mentioned in a letter of 1950 had by now evaporated.) *King Priam* was begun in 1958, completed in 1961 and first performed in 1962 at the Belgrade Theatre, Coventry, by the Royal Opera, during a festival to celebrate the building of the new cathedral, replacing the one destroyed during World War II.

Between 1963 and 1965 Tippett shaped the scenario of his third opera, *The Knot Garden*, which he started to compose in 1966; he completed it in 1969, and it received its première at Covent Garden in 1970. A notable offshoot of this intense psychodrama, which has Shakespeare's *The Tempest* as a notional backdrop (Tippett wrote incidental music for a production of the play at the Old Vic in 1962), was the orchestral song cycle *Songs for Dov*. In this work Tippett developed one of the opera's characters independently as he had done earlier, but on a smaller scale, with *Songs for Achilles* following *King Priam*.

In 1965 Tippett visited the USA for the first time, and his experiences there directly influenced the scenario of his fourth opera, *The Ice Break*, composed during 1973–6 and first staged at Covent Garden in 1977, when it was described as his last. The opera's brutal conflicts of race and generation issuing in qualified optimism found a broader contemplative platform in *The Mask of Time* (1980–82), and this huge 'epiphany' for voices and orchestra in turn spurred Tippett to the composition of a fifth opera during 1985–8, concerned with aspirations and dreams. This was *New Year*, first given in October 1989 by Houston Grand Opera, which had commissioned it jointly with Glyndebourne Festival Opera, which gave the European première in July 1990, and the BBC, which mounted a special television production in 1991.

3. STYLE. Even though each of Tippett's operas is deliberately different from the others, he has succeeded in creating a unique and immediately recognizable world of richness and resonance. Moreover, the frequently radical changes in Tippett's musical style seem largely to have been dictated by the course of his operatic development. *The Midsummer Marriage* was consciously the culmination of his first mature period of composition and the completion of a strategy in which he tackled all the major genres. His individual method of generation of rhythmic buoyancy through madrigalian 'sprung rhythm' and the energetic deployment of contrapuntal textures within a Classical framework here reaches a peak, matched by an unprecedented enrichment of his innate lyricism. At the same time the glowing harmonic fabric of the music and its unequivocal tonal foundation also embody precisely the opera's visionary goal of spiritual and psychic unity and balance.

With the appearance of *King Priam* in 1962 it seemed that Tippett had almost entirely changed his musical personality. The instrumental expression is spare and angular, counterpoint has gone, the tonal foundation is fragmented, and the lyricism is now highly rhetorical. This sea-change in Tippett's style mirrors profoundly the tragic nature of this second opera. The hard-hitting idiom immediately inhabits the brutal world of the Greek epic. In *The Knot Garden* the style is not so much fragmented as splintered, and the infiltration of the language by a number of jazz and blues idioms curiously revitalizes a strand in Tippett's music from the late 1930s and early 1940s – the use of spirituals and folk elements. The opera's anguished psychodrama is very much a product of its period but the Shakespearean backdrop allows Tippett to cast his musical net wide in pursuit of an expressionist vein and to include haunting quotations of Schubert and Ives.

The broader canvas of *The Ice Break* and its wider terms of reference inspired Tippett to a musical style which expands the gestures of *The Knot Garden* but paradoxically on a more concentrated scale to match the cinematic speed of presentation. The music shows Tippett at his most violent, but it seems to release a renewed stream of lyricism, which finds its fulfilment in his fifth opera, *New Year*. Here Tippett manages to maintain the regeneration of his language, even to the point of incorporating 'rap' rhythms, but alongside an enriching synthesis of his wide-ranging operatic gestures. This flow continued (with a tiny reference) into the expansive setting of W. B. Yeats's *Byzantium*, which, together with *The Mask of Time* and *New Year*, forms the crown of Tippett's achievement in terms of a recapturing of the lyrical rapture of *The Midsummer Marriage*.

See also ICE BREAK, THE; KING PRIAM; KNOT GARDEN, THE; MIDSUMMER MARRIAGE, THE; and NEW YEAR.

title	*composition*	*genre, acts*	*libretto*	*first performance*	*sources*
The Village Opera	1927–8	ballad op, 3 [realization with addl music of orig. by C. Johnson, 1729]		1928	MS private collection, unpubd

title	composition	genre, acts	libretto	first performance	sources
Robin Hood	1934	folksong op, 2	D. M. Pennyless [pseud. of Tippett, D. Ayerst and R. Pennyman]	1934	MS private collection, unpubd
Robert of Sicily	1938	play for children, 1	C. Fry, after H. W. Longfellow	1938	MS private collection, unpubd
Seven at One Stroke	1939	play for children, 1	Fry	1939	MS private collection, unpubd
The Midsummer Marriage	1946–52	op, 3	Tippett	London, Covent Garden, 27 Jan 1955	*GB-Lbl**, vs (London, 1954), full score (London, 1976)
King Priam	1958–61	op, 3	Tippett, after Homer: *Iliad*	Coventry, Belgrade Theatre, 29 May 1962	*Lbl**, *US-Wc**, vs (London, 1962)
The Knot Garden	1966–9	op, 3	Tippett	London, Covent Garden, 2 Dec 1970	*GB-Lbl**, *US-Eu**, vs (London, 1970)
The Ice Break	1973–6	op, 3	Tippett	London, Covent Garden, 7 July 1977	*GB-Lbl**, vs (London, 1977)
New Year	1985–8	op, 3	Tippett	Houston, Grand Opera, 27 Oct 1989	*Lbl**, vs (London, 1989)

A. E. F. Dickinson: 'Round about "The Midsummer Marriage"', *ML*, xxxvii (1956), 50–60

M. Tippett: 'King Priam: Some Questions Answered', *Opera*, xiii (1962), 297–9

R. Donington: 'Words and Music', *Michael Tippett: a Symposium on his 60th Birthday* (London, 1965), 87–113

W. Mann: 'The Operas: an Allegory and an Epic', ibid, 114–34

J. Warrack: 'The Knot Garden', *MT*, cxi (1970), 1092–5

T. Sutcliffe: 'Tippett and the Knot Garden', *Music and Musicians*, xix/4 (1970–71), 52–4 [interview]

D. Cairns: 'The Midsummer Marriage', *Responses: Musical Essays and Reviews* (London, 1973), 33–45

J. Agar: *An Approach to the Operas of Michael Tippett* (diss., U. of East Anglia, 1976)

D. Fingleton: 'The Ice Break', *Music and Musicians*, xxv/11 (1976–7), 28–30

'The Composer as Librettist', *Times Literary Supplement* (8 July 1977) [conversation between Tippett and P. Carnegy]

R. E. Jones: *The Operas of Michael Tippett* (diss., U. of Wales, Cardiff, 1977)

Michael Tippett: a Man of our Time (London, 1977) [exhibition catalogue]

G. N. Odam: *Michael Tippett's Knot Garden: an Exploration of its Musical, Literary and Psychological Construction* (diss., U. of Southampton, 1977)

J. Warrack: 'The Ice Break', *MT*, cxviii (1977), 553–6

E. W. White: *Tippett and his Operas* (London, 1979)

D. Matthews: *Michael Tippett* (London, 1980)

M. Bowen: *Michael Tippett* (London, 1982)

F. Sternfeld and D. Harvey: 'A Musical Magpie: Words and Music in Michael Tippett's Operas', *Parnassus: Poetry in Review*, x/2 (1982), 188–98

B. V. Vaughn: *The Hope of Reconciliation: a Stylistic Characteristic ... Culminating in The Ice Break* (diss., Ohio State U., 1982)

A. Whittall: *The Music of Britten and Tippett: Studies in Themes and Techniques* (Cambridge, 1982, 2/1990)

I. Kemp: *Tippett: the Composer and his Music* (London, 1984)

A. Clements: 'Tippett at 80', *Opera*, xxxvi (1985), 16–24

R. Furness: 'Goethe and Tippett: Lila and "The Knot Garden"', *Michael Tippett O.M.: a Celebration* (Tunbridge Wells, 1985), 161–6

N. John, ed.: *Operas of Michael Tippett* (London, 1985) [ENO Opera Guide]

R. E. Jones: 'Ritual, Myth and Drama', *Michael Tippett O.M.: a Celebration* (Tunbridge Wells, 1985), 59–72

M. Bowen: '*New Year*', *Opera Cues*, xxx/1 (1989), 15–19

G. Lewis: '"New Year" in the New World', *MT*, cxxx (1989), 665–9

M. Bowen: '*The Ice Break*', *Henry Wood Promenade Concerts 1990*, 3–9 [programme book]

——: '*New Year*', *Opera Now* (June 1990), 30–31 [interview with Tippett]

D. Clarke: *Language, Form and Structure in the Music of Michael Tippett* (New York, 1990)

——: '*New Year*', *ML*, lxxi (1990), 468–72 [review of vocal score]

G. Lewis: 'New Year is Here', *MT*, cxxxi (1990), 355–7

S. Pettitt: 'New Worlds in "New Year"', *Opera*, xli (1990), 672–6

M. A. Scheppach: *Dramatic Parallels in Michael Tippett's Operas: Analytical Essays on the Musico-Dramatic Techniques* (Lewiston, NY, 1990)

GERAINT LEWIS

Tirana [Tiranë]. Capital of Albania. An Italian touring company, the Carro di Tespi Lirico, first brought staged opera to Albania in the 1940s (*Rigoletto*, *La traviata*, *Tosca* and *La bohème* in 1942–3). The earliest step towards a systematic organization and development of music and dance was the founding, formalized in 1950, of the Filarmonia Shqiptare (Albanian Philharmonia), embracing the Radio Tirana SO, the State Chorus, a ballet company and a number of opera singers. The organization had in fact been active earlier, with *Dasma Shqiptare* ('Albanian Wedding'), a 'musical tableau' in a prologue and three scenes by Konstandin Trako (1919–86), being given at the stadium in 1947. The earliest opera production with an Albanian cast was Darghomïzhsky's *Rusalka*, given by the newly founded Teatri i Operës dhe i Baletit (Theatre of Opera and Ballet; TOB) on 27 November 1953.

The first indoor performances of the Albanian Philharmonia were given at the Teatri Kombëtar Dramatik (National Theatre for Drama), formerly a cinema, with some 500 seats. With Smetana's *The Bartered Bride* (19 May 1956) the company transferred to the conservatory theatre, constructed by the Italians, with excellent acoustics and 560 seats. Finally, with Vangjo Nova's opera *Heroina* ('The Heroine', 17 June 1967), it settled in the modern theatre (cap. 865) of the Palace of Culture in Skanderbeg Square. Usually two opera or ballet performances are given weekly, from September to May or June; the theatre is also used for concerts and recitals. Ticket prices are low as the enterprise is state-funded. The early achievements of the Albanian Philharmonia and the TOB owed much to native pioneers of opera in Albania.

The work of the TOB is almost equally divided between opera and ballet. From 1966 a change of cultural policy encouraged national creativity while generally disallowing the presentation of foreign works. As well as *The Heroine*, the following operas and operettas by Albanian composers were given their first performances by the TOB: Daija's *Pranvera* ('Spring',

1960) and *Vjosa* (1980); Gaci's *Përtej mjegullës* ('Beyond the Mist', 1971) and *Toka jonë* ('Our Land', 1981); Harapi's *Zgjimi* ('The Awakening', 1976); Jakova's *Gjergj Kastrioti-Skënderbeu* (1968); Kono's *Lulja e kujtimit* ('The Flower of Remembrance', 1961); Llazar Morcka's *Brigada e grave* ('Women's Brigade', 1969); Mula's *Karnavalet* ('Carnivals', 1978), *Borana* (1984) and *Trimat* ('The Valiant Ones', 1987); Agim Prodani's *Dhëndrri u transferua* ('The Bridegroom was Transferred', 1974); and Zoraqi's *Komisari* ('The Commissar', 1975) and *Paja* ('The Dowry', 1989).

The TOB is probably the only company in the world to employ librettists on a permanent basis with a full salary (since 1980). It also houses an extensive archive, which embraces all the events held at the Tirana Palace of Culture and the greater part of Albania's musical life.

*

S. Kalemi: *Arritjet e artit tonë muzikor: vepra dhe krijues të muzikës Shqiptare* [Achievements of our Musical Art: Creations and Creators of Albanian Music] (Tirana, 1982)

'Muzike skenike' [Music for the Stage], *Historia e muzikës Shqiptare* [History of Albanian Music] (Tirana, 1983), i, 150–52; ii, 273–327 [pubn of Superior Institute of Arts, Tirana]

J. Emerson: *Albania: the Search for the Eagle's Song* (Studley, Warwicks., 1990) GEORGE LEOTSAKOS (with JUNE EMERSON)

Titiens, Therese. *See* TIETJENS, THERESE.

Titl [Tittl], **Antonín Emil (František Seraf)** (*b* Pernštejn, 2 Oct 1809; *d* Vienna, 2 Jan 1882). Moravian composer. He started his career in Brno as a double-bass player in the theatre, and as a composer of incidental music. He wrote his first opera, *Die Burgfrau an dem Schlosse Pernstein*, based on a story by A. Boček, by 1825; it was first performed in 1832 in Brno and repeated later that year in Olomouc, where Titl had moved. By 1833 he had moved again, to Prague, where he became famous as a military-band Kapellmeister and a composer of military and dance music. In 1837 the overture to his second opera, *Der Leichenräuber*, was first performed at a charity concert.

From 1840 to 1849 Titl was the Kapellmeister of the Theater in der Josefstadt in Vienna. At that time he wrote much incidental music (particularly for plays by F. X. Told) and several operas and Singspiels. He was employed as a 'Speziell Opernkomponist' by the Theater an der Wien (1847–9). He was appointed Kapellmeister of the Hofburgtheater in Vienna (1850–70) and composed incidental music and overtures, such as *Ouvertura dle slovanských nápěvů* ('Overture on Slavonic Melodies'), for the first Czech theatre performance in Vienna. Titl's works were very successful, especially *Der Zauberschleier*, which was performed in Vienna alone more than 375 times up to 1850 and also to great acclaim in Prague, though their artistic merit is questionable.

Die Burgfrau an dem Schlosse Pernstein (3, A. Boček), Brno, 28 May 1832

Der Leichenräuber, ov. perfd, Prague, 22 Feb 1837

Der Zauberschleier, oder Maler, Fee und Wirtin (Spl, 3, F. X. Told, after E. Scribe: *Le lac des fées*), Vienna, 11 Feb 1842 (Vienna, n.d.)

Der Totentanz (ballet-opera, 2, Told), Vienna, 18 Nov 1843

Das Wolkenkind (2, Told), Vienna, 14 March 1845, vs (Vienna, *c*1865)

*

J. Trojan: 'Opera o Bílé paní pernštejnské: k první opeře na lokální námět z Moravy' [An Opera Entitled The White Lady from Pernštejn Castle: the First Opera with a Moravian Theme], *Program* [Brno State Theatre pubn], lviii/4 (1986–7), 124–5

MICHAELA FREEMANOVÁ

Tito ('Titus'). *Melodramma* in three acts by ANTONIO CESTI to a libretto by NICOLÒ BEREGAN; Venice, Teatro di SS Giovanni e Paolo, 13 February 1666.

Beregan probably formed the outline of his plot from Flavius Josephus's account of the Jewish War and C. Suetonius Tranquillus's account of Emperor Titus in *The Lives of the Twelve Caesars*. The opera deals with the future Roman emperor's conquering of Jerusalem in AD 70, and his subsequent love for the conquered Palestinian princess Berenice. After numerous complications, woven into the plot by a cast of 15 characters, Polemone, whom Berenice has claimed as her brother, is revealed to be her husband, and Titus abandons his quest for love in favour of his former militaristic ways. Three characters, Titus (soprano castrato), Berenice (soprano) and Domitian (soprano castrato), are drawn from history and another, Polemone (tenor), portrayed as the King of Licea, is probably the equivalent of Polemon, the priest-king of Olba in Cilicia. The fictional character Martia Fulvia (soprano) may have been inspired by the historical Marcia Furnilla, daughter of a noble Roman family, whom Titus married but subsequently divorced. The remaining cast of generals, servants, pages and sorceresses remind us of Racine's famous dictum 'Toute l'invention consiste à faire quelque chose de rien'.

17 letters from Cesti to the impresario Marco Faustini (11 March 1665–16 May 1666, in *I-Vas*) shed light on the composition and performance preparation of *Tito* in a way virtually unprecedented for mid-17th-century Italian opera. These letters discuss how and when the music was composed, casting and production problems, and how the opera was received. *Tito* is the only extant Cesti opera which lacks a prologue, and for which the opening sinfonia is put together from music taken from his own earlier works, *Argia* (1655) and *La magnanimità d'Alessandro* (1662). Among the work's dozens of arias, three particularly fine ones ('Cieca diva in esorabile', 'Quanto vale quanto puo' and 'Berenice ove sei') were published by P. & J. Blaeu in Amsterdam in 1691 (*RISM* 1691[4]). Printed librettos exist for revivals between 1668 and 1676. CARL B. SCHMIDT

Tito Manlio ('Titus Manlius'). Libretto by GAETANO ROCCAFORTE, first set by Gennaro Manna (1742, Rome).

The libretto is based on a story found in Livy's history of Rome, book 8. Having shared the hardships of war, the Latins, allies of the Romans, want representation in government; the Roman Senate refuses the request, whereupon the Latins declare war on the Romans. The Roman consul, Titus Manlius, commands his son Manlio [Manlius] to enter the Latin camp to determine the army's strength, but gives him explicit orders not to engage in any fighting. In the camp Manlius is challenged to a duel by Geminio [Geminius], the Latin leader, whom he kills. Manlius returns in triumph, but his father harshly reminds him of his violated orders. To uphold the authority of the Senate and to maintain discipline in the army, Titus Manlius condemns his son to execution.

The libretto expands the story by introducing three more characters. Sabina is the sister of Manlius and Geminius's secret lover. Lucio [Lucius] is a Latin but also a friend of Manlius, secretly in love with Sabina. Servilia, the sister of Geminius, is also Manlius's intended wife. Manlius is sent on his mission at the end of Act 1. The encounter with Geminius takes place off stage, and Act 2 begins with Manlius's return to Rome. In the final scene, Lucius rouses the army in support of Manlius, whereupon Titus is obliged to recognize the voice of the people and pardon his son.

The libretto has been confused with the identically entitled one by Matteo Noris, first set by C. F. Pollarolo in 1696. They differ in their treatment of the material. In Noris's libretto, Geminius is seen interacting with the women and Manlius in the Latin camp. In Roccaforte's, the entire action takes place in Rome and Geminius does not appear; the focus is firmly on the conflict between happiness and duty. The comic servant in Noris's version does not appear in Roccaforte's; this reflects the change in taste brought about by the reform movement of Zeno and Metastasio. (In Jommelli's setting of Noris's libretto – the last known, in 1746 – the comic character is excised.) Manlius's sister Sabina is called Vitellia by Noris. The scene structure and verses of the two librettos are entirely different.

For a list of settings *see* ROCCAFORTE, GAETANO. DOROTHEA LINK

Tito Manlio ('Titus Manlius'). *Dramma per musica* in three acts, RV738, by ANTONIO VIVALDI to a libretto by MATTEO NORIS; Mantua, Teatro Arciducale 'detto il Comico', Carnival 1719.

The libretto was first set by C. F. Pollarolo for Florence in 1696. The Roman consul Titus Manlius (bass) swears an oath of hatred against the rebellious Latins; he is followed in this by his son Manlio [Manlius] (soprano), the captain Decio [Decius] (contralto), and even the Latin knight Lucio [Lucius] (soprano), since he is in love with Titus's daughter Vitellia (contralto). Vitellia refuses to swear the oath, however, for she is in love with the Latin captain Geminio [Geminius] (tenor). Sent to spy on the enemy camp, Manlius encounters Geminius; he is provoked by Geminius and, ignoring his father's express orders not to engage in armed combat, he fights and kills his opponent. When Titus hears of his son's disobedience, he sentences him to death, despite the pleas of Manlius's betrothed, Servilia (contralto), Geminius's sister. Lucius offers to free Manlius, who is not prepared to betray Rome even for his own safety. However, Decius and his forces arrive to rescue him, father and son are reunited, and the hostilities between Romans and Latins cease.

Vivaldi's opera was written to celebrate the forthcoming wedding (which never actually took place) of the governor of Mantua, Prince Philipp of Hessen-Darmstadt, with Princess Eleanora of Guastalla, to whom the opera is dedicated. From the autograph score, which Vivaldi headed 'Musica Del Vivaldi fatta in 5 giorni', it is apparent that he originally set Noris's 1696 libretto but then made various alterations to it. These included the addition of several arias and the expansion of the minor role of the servant Lindo [Lindus] into a substantial comic part for the Mantuan bass Giovanni Battista Calvi. Calvi specialized in comic roles, and his four arias present a unique example of Vivaldi's writing in the style of the contemporary intermezzo.

The celebratory nature of the production of *Tito Manlio* was reflected in the use of expensive fashionable costumes, usually worn for public ceremonies, and in the work's elaborate orchestration. One of Vivaldi's most colourful scores, it calls for pairs of oboes, horns, trumpets and *flauti grossi* (tenor recorders) in addition to a *flautino* (sopranino recorder), bassoon, timpani, strings and continuo (the original version of one aria also contains an elaborate part for viola d'amore written in scordatura). The music for Tito emphasizes his stern aspect by means of strong rhythmic figures in the orchestra and firm leaps in the voice, while Lucio's haunting 'Non ti lusinghi la crudeltade' from the opening of Act 2 is a fine example of Vivaldi's treatment of a solo instrument (here an oboe) in partnership with the voice. Several arias are taken from earlier operas, and the atmospheric sinfonia for muted instruments in Act 3, as Manlio is led in for his execution, shares material with the *Concerto funebre* RV579.

As well as the Mantuan setting of *Tito Manlio*, Vivaldi also provided music for Act 3 of a Roman *Tito Manlio*, RV Anh.56, produced at the Teatro della Pace on 8 January 1720. The other acts were written by Gaetano Boni and Giovanni Giorgi. ERIC CROSS

Titov, Alexey Nikolayevich (*b* St Petersburg, 12/23 July 1769; *d* St Petersburg, 8/20 Nov 1827). Russian composer and violinist, from a family of high-born musical dilettantes (he was a cavalry officer by profession). The cultured host of a major St Petersburg salon, he maintained a wide circle of literary acquaintances from among whom he drew his collaborators, the most constant being Alexander Yakovlevich Knyazhnin (1771–1829), son of the chief librettist of the 18th-century Russian musical stage. Of Titov's Singspiels, the most significant were the so-called Yam trilogy (1805–9), depicting typical if romantically sentimentalized scenes of country life and peasant ritual. (In *Yam*, a stationmaster's daughter triumphs over her father's plan to marry her off to a rich fool; in *Posidelki*, her younger sister does the same; in *Devishnik*, the rich fool finally finds a suitable bride.) The somewhat clumsy, gypsy-tinged music to these spectacles, which remained in repertory for several decades, laid a foundation for the so-called *rossiyskaya pesnya* (imitation-folksong romance) of the early 19th century, a genre cultivated by A. N. Titov's son Nikolay Alexeyevich (1800–75) and his nephew Nikolay Sergeyevich (1798–1843). Filatka, the 'rich old fool' of the Yam trilogy, lived on until the 1830s as a stock character in endless Singspiels, comedies and vaudevilles. *Muzhestvo kiyevlyanina*, written in the aftermath of the Napoleonic wars, was more overtly patriotic. It contains a choral paean to the 10th-century Prince Svyatoslav that is based on the same folksong ('Slava!') that Musorgsky employed in the Coronation Scene in *Boris Godunov*. Titov also composed many melodramas, ballets and much incidental music.

all first performed in St Petersburg; MSS in RU-SPtob

La statue, ou La femme avare (opéra-féerie, 1, Hofman), 1803
Yam, ili Pochtovaya stantsiya [Yam, or The Postal Station] (comic op, 1, A. Y. Knyazhnin), Maliy, 16/28 June 1805, 1 no. in IRMO, ii
Tatiana, ou La jeune paysanne des montagnes de Vorobyoff (opera-vaudeville, 2, D. Claparède), May 1806 (French court players); revived 1825 (in Russ.), Maliy
Emeric, ou Les hongrois (heroic op, 1, Claparède), Bol'shoy, 4/16 Feb 1807; revived 1814 (in Russ.), Moscow, Apraksin's
Nurzakhad, ili Neschastiye ot bessmertiya [Nurzakhad, or Misfortune from Immortality] (4, Knyazhnin), 24 (?26) May/5 (?7) June 1807
Posidelki, sledstviye Yama [Winter Gatherings, a Sequel to Yam] (comic op, 1, Knyazhnin), 20 April/2 May 1808, 1 no. in IRMO, ii
Devishnik, ili Filatkina svad'ba [The Bridal Party, or Filatka's Wedding], 1808 (comic op, 1, Knyazhnin), Bol'shoy, 13/25 April 1809, 1 no. in IRMO, ii
La caverne orientale, ou Une aventure du Calif de Bagdad, 1808

Minutnoye zabluzhdeniye [A Momentary Delusion], 1809 (1, Knyazhnin), German, 13/25 Sept 1812
Legkoverniye [Gullible Types] (comic op, 1, Knyazhnin), German, 28 June/10 July 1812
Maslenitsa [The Shrovetide Fair] (intermediya-divertisment, 1, P. Titov), German, 23 Feb/7 March 1813
Muzhestvo kiyevlyanina, ili Vot kakovï russkiye [The Courage of a Kievan, or That's what Russians are Like] (comic op, 2, Knyazhnin), Maliy, 1/13 May 1817
Prazdnik Mogola, ili Torzhestvo Olimara [Mogol's Holiday, or Olimar's Triumph] (3, A. Bjork, after a Fr. source), Bol'shoy, 3/15 Sept 1823

*

A. Rabinovich: *Russkaya opera do Glinki* [Russian Opera Before Glinka] (Moscow, 1948)
M. Druskin: 'Teatral'naya muzïka' [Theatre Music], *Ocherki po istorii russkoy muzïki 1790–1825*, [Studies in the History of Russian Music 1790–1825], ed. M. Druskin and Yu. V. Keldïsh (Leningrad, 1956), 217–62
A. Gozenpud: *Muzïkal'nïy teatr v Rossii ot istokov do Glinki* [Musical Theatre in Russia from its Origins up to Glinka] (Leningrad, 1959)
L. Orlova: 'A. N. Titov', *Istoriya russkoy muzïki v desyati tomakh* [A History of Russian Music], ed. Yu. V. Keldïsh, iv (Moscow, 1986), 168–83 RICHARD TARUSKIN

Titov, Sergey Nikolayevich (*b* St Petersburg, 1770; *d* St Petersburg, 24 March/5 April 1825). Russian composer and cellist, brother of Alexey Titov. He was a military officer by profession. Besides the popular ballet *Noviy Verter* ('The New Werther'), he is remembered for *Krest'yane, ili Vstrecha nezvannïkh* ('The Peasants, or Meeting the Uninvited', 1813), an opera-vaudeville to a text by Alexander Shakhovskoy commemorating the very recent events of the Patriotic War of 1812. It was a benchmark of realism in its day for its treatment of contemporary themes, and for its heroic portrayal of peasant characters, paving the way toward the Ivan Susanin operas of Cavos and Glinka. First performed on 23 November/5 December 1814 at the German Theatre in St Petersburg, it remained a repertory item for decades to come. The simple score chiefly consists of arranged folktunes after the fashion of the 18th-century Russian Singspiels composed *na golosï*.

RICHARD TARUSKIN

Titta, Ruffo Cafiero. *See* RUFFO, TITTA.

Titus, Alan (*b* New York, 28 Oct 1945). American baritone. He grew up in Denver, studying dance as well as singing (with Aksel Schiøtz at the Colorado School of Music). At the Juilliard School he became a pupil of Hans J. Heinz and attracted attention as Figaro in *Il barbiere*. He took part in the première of Hoiby's *Summer and Smoke* (1971, St Paul) and in the American television premières of Pasatieri's *The Trial of Mary Lincoln* and Henze's *La cubana*. He made his European début in Amsterdam as Pelléas in 1973, and engagements followed at Marseilles, Aix-en-Provence and Strasbourg. In 1975 he made his début at San Francisco as Papageno and the following year made his Metropolitan début as Harlequin in *Ariadne auf Naxos*. Titus's high, soft-grained baritone, exceptional vitality on the stage and boyish appearance have proved useful in a lyrical repertory ranging from Monteverdi to Dallapiccola. He has also sung more dramatic roles, such as Don Giovanni, and comic parts such as Eisenstein (1982, Santa Fe), Ford (1985, San Francisco) and Belcore (1985, Dallas). MARTIN BERNHEIMER

Tkmuleba Shota Rustavelze ('The Legend of Shota Rustaveli'). Opera in three acts by DIMITRI IGNAT'YEVICH ARAKISHVILI to a libretto by A. Khakhanashvili after a Georgian folk legend; Tbilisi, Opera Theatre, 5 February 1919.

Shota Rustavelze was a Georgian poet, probably in the late 12th or early 13th century, whose exploits became legendary. In the first act, Rustavelze (tenor) sets off from his home to study, leaving behind his childhood sweetheart Nina (soprano). In Act 2 he learns that in his absence Nina has married, and he himself takes a wife. When one of his poems wins him honour from Queen Tamara, there is a great celebration; in the midst of it he is told by a mysterious young man that he must return home. In the final act he surprises his wife in the arms of an Arab servant, and subsequently discovers, to his amazement, that the mysterious youth is in fact Nina in disguise. He leaves in high dudgeon and Nina commits suicide. It is a little surprising that Arakishvili should have chosen this variant against the legend's more common ending, where Rustavelze in his fury kills the nameless youth, only then to discover that it is Nina.

Tkmuleba Shota Rustavelze had its triumphant première just before Paliashvili's now more highly regarded *Abesalom da Eteri*, and it thus enjoys significance as Georgia's first national opera. Like Paliashvili, Arakishvili used a number structure, largely in separate ballads and choruses, with a hint of leitmotif. Arias tend to reflect urban folk styles; the choruses employ rural elements, including unusual characteristic harmonies, although the polyphonic style Arakishvili so much admired is absent in this largely monodic work.

STEPHEN JOHNSON

Toch, Ernst (*b* Vienna, 7 Dec 1887; *d* Santa Monica, CA, 1 Oct 1964). Austrian, later American composer. He was entirely self-taught as a composer, using the string quartets of Mozart as his models. He moved to Germany on winning the Mozart Prize of the City of Frankfurt in 1909 and he was awarded the Berlin Mendelssohn Prize for composition in 1910; from 1913 he taught at the Mannheim Musikhochschule. At this time he also won the Austrian State Prize in composition for four years in succession and was active as a pianist.

During the 1920s Toch emerged as a major figure in German modernism; 34 of his works were published by Schott in a 15-year period. His first opera, *Die Prinzessin auf der Erbse*, a *Märchenoper* in one act, was composed for the 1927 Baden-Baden festival and first performed with works of Hindemith, Milhaud and Weill. The next year he wrote a short, topical chamber opera, *Egon und Emilie*, set for coloratura soprano, speaker and woodwind.

In 1929 Toch moved to Berlin, where he composed a full-length *Opern-Capriccio*, *Der Fächer*, a satirical treatment of contemporary culture. He also wrote scores for radio and stage plays and became interested in music for film. Fleeing Germany in 1933, he went to London and New York, and finally settled in California, where he taught at the University of Southern California and composed film and concert music. He became an American citizen in 1940. In 1956 he won the Pulitzer and Huntingdon-Hartford prizes and was elected to the American National Institute of Arts and Letters. He composed his final opera, *The Last Tale* (formerly *Scheherazade*), also a one-act *Märchenoper*, between 1960 and 1962.

Toch's musical style is rooted in German Romanticism but frequently displays a neo-classical clarity of design and linearity of texture. He experimented increasingly with a highly chromatic idiom, but at the same time maintained an overriding lyricism. Both traditional aria style and spoken narration are used in his vocal works.

Die Prinzessin auf der Erbse op.43 (Märchenoper, 1, B. Elkan, after H. C. Andersen: *The Princess on the Pea*), Baden-Baden, Kurhaus, 17 July 1927 (Mainz, 1927)
Egon und Emilie [Edgar and Emily] op.46 (kleines Familiendrama, 1, C. Morgenstern), Mannheim, National, 21 Oct 1928, vs (Mainz, 1928)
Der Fächer op.51 (Opern-Capriccio, 3, F. Lion), Königsberg, 8 June 1930
The Last Tale [Das letzte Märchen] op.88, 1960–62 (Märchenoper, 1, M. Lengyel), unperf., vs (New York, 1965)

CHARLOTTE ERWIN

Toczyska, Stefania (*b* Grudziadz, 19 Feb 1943). Polish mezzo-soprano. She studied in Gdańsk, making her début there in 1973 as Carmen. After appearing in Warsaw, Copenhagen and the USSR, in 1977 she sang Ulrica in Vienna. In 1979 she sang Eboli in Munich and Laura (*La Gioconda*) in San Francisco. She made her Covent Garden début in 1983 as Azucena, returning for Venus, Marina and Amneris, a role she sang in Rome in 1990; she has also sung in Hamburg, Geneva, Zürich and Chicago. Her repertory includes Isabella, Rosina, Mary Stuart and Jane Seymour (*Anna Bolena*). Her voice, rich-toned and flexible, is particularly well suited to Russian roles such as Marina, which she sang at the Metropolitan in 1990, and Lyubasha (*The Tsar's Bride*).

ELIZABETH FORBES

Toda, Kunio (*b* Tokyo, 11 Aug 1915). Japanese composer. After graduating in law from Tokyo University in 1938, he entered the Japanese foreign ministry and was sent to Berlin and then to Moscow. Returning to Tokyo in 1941, he became a composition pupil of Saburō Moroi. At the end of World War II he was in Saigon, where he remained a prisoner for three years, during which time he came across Leibowitz's *Schönberg et son école* and wrote what was probably the first 12-note piece by a Japanese. On his repatriation in 1948, he introduced Leibowitz's book to Japan and this inspired the rise of the country's dodecaphonic school and the formation of the Shinseikai group by Irino, Minao Shibata and Toda. In his first opera, *Akemi* (1956), Toda described scenes of postwar Japan, contrasting three different compositional styles: tonal (inside the Akemi bar), dodecaphonic (the street outside) and *musique concrète* (a construction site in the background). The music of *Shito Paolo* ('St Paul', 1973), an 'oratorio-mystery play', is almost exclusively based on a 12-note row, but it incorporates traditional noh prosody in the vocal parts. His most ambitious opera, *Kyara monogatari* ('The Story of Kyara City', 1973), the legendary history of a doomed city and of an orphan maiden who saves it, again combines serial and tonal music, each representing different characters in the drama. Toda was a professor at the Tōhō Gakuen School of Music (1964–76), then at the Senzoku Gakuen College (1977–88).

Akemi (1, F. Ariga), Tokyo, NHK Hall, Uchisaiwaicho, 7 Aug 1956
Shito Paolo [St Paul], 1961–4 (oratorio-mystery play, 1, Z. Toki), Tokyo, Yubin Chokin Hall, 15 Feb 1973
Kyara monogatari [The Story of Kyara City] (3, Toda), Tokyo, Metropolitan Festival Hall, 11 Oct 1973
Jochū no Anna [Anna, The Maid] (monodrama, 1, Toda, after J. Cocteau), Tokyo, Zōjōji Hall, 14 Nov 1978
Kesa to Moritō [Kesa and Moritō] (chamber op, 1, Toda, after R. Akutagawa), concert perf., Tokyo, Aoyama Tower Hall, 26 Nov 1980; stage, Tokyo, Mozart Salon, 23 April 1990

MASAKATA KANAZAWA

Todesca, La. *See* EBERHARD, GIUSTINA MARIA.

Todi [née d'Aguiar], **Luisa** [Luiza] **(Rosa)** (*b* Setúbal, 9 Jan 1753; *d* Lisbon, 1 Oct 1833). Portuguese mezzo-soprano. In 1769 she married the Italian Francesco Saverio Todi (*d* 1803), leader of the Bairro Alto theatre orchestra in Lisbon; the next year she made her opera début in Lisbon in Scolari's *Il viaggiatore ridicolo*. In 1777–8 she was engaged for comic opera at the King's Theatre, London, making her first appearance in Paisiello's *Le due contesse*. Her international fame was established at the Concert Spirituel, Paris, in 1778 and confirmed by her change to serious parts; in the following years she sang in Germany and Austria, at Turin, and at the Berlin Opera. In 1784 she joined a brilliant company at St Petersburg headed by Sarti, in whose *Armida e Rinaldo* and *Castore e Polluce* she sang with enormous success in 1786. She made her last Russian appearance at Moscow in her own *festa teatrale*, *Pollinia*, in 1787. She sang in Berlin, Mainz and Hanover, 1788–9, and at the Teatro S Samuele, Venice, 1790–91, where the season was declared 'anno Todi'. In 1791–2 she appeared in Padua, Bergamo, Prague, Turin and Parma, then sang at the Madrid Opera (1792–3 and 1794–5, including comic roles) and at Lisbon in Leal Moreira's *Il natale augusto* (1793). Her last major engagement was at S Carlo, Naples, 1797–9; from 1803 she lived in retirement in Portugal. According to Choron and Fayolle, Todi's voice was 'large, noble, sonore, intéressante', with an extensive lower register. She was best known for her sensibility and ability to evoke tears in pathetic roles, but also acquired considerable skill in the bravura style.

DBP
'Madame Todi in Berlin', *Musikalische Monatsschrift*, ii (1792), 48–50
A. Choron and F. Fayolle: *Dictionnaire historique des musiciens* (Paris, 1810–11)
J. Ribeiro Guimarães: *Biographia de Luiza de Aguiar Todi* (Lisbon, 1872)
J. de Vasconcellos: *Luiza Todi: estudo critico* (Oporto, 1873, 2/1929)
M. de Sampayo Ribeiro: *Luisa de Aguiar Todi* (Lisbon, 1934)
R.-A. Mooser: *Annales de la musique et des musiciens en Russie au XVIIIe siècle*, ii (Geneva, 1951), 422ff, 435f, 509; iii (Geneva, 1951), figs.78, 80, 96

ROBERT STEVENSON

Todisco, Nunzio (*b* Torre del Greco, *c*1942). Italian tenor. Self-taught as a singer, he made his début in the early 1970s and has sung at Bergamo, Naples, Florence, Verona, Trieste, Zürich, Lisbon, Rome, Turin, Barcelona and Orange. He made his American début at San Francisco in 1978 as Pollione. His repertory includes Erik, Don José, Licinius (*La vestale*), Turiddu, Canio, Enzo (*La Gioconda*), Cavaradossi, Dick Johnson and Luigi (*Il tabarro*), but his strong, bronze-coloured voice and fierce attack are best displayed in Verdi: as Ernani, Manrico, Radames, Carlo (*I masnadieri*), Foresto (*Attila*), Gabriele Adorno, Ishmael (*Nabucco*), Arrigo (*La battaglia di Legnano*) and Jacopo Foscari.

ELIZABETH FORBES

Luisa Todi (wearing a crown) singing in the salon of a nobleman's home, accompanied by violin and harpsichord: satirical engraving, by I. Colombo after Jacopo Leonardis, produced in response to the declaration of 'anno Todi' during the 1790–91 season at the Teatro S Samuele, Venice (the figure fourth from the right represents Envy)

Tofts, Catherine (*b* c1685; *d* Venice, 1756). English soprano. The first English prima donna, she appeared in subscription concerts in the winter of 1703–4. Rivalry between her and Margherita de L'Epine was fostered by their supporters (respectively Whigs and Tories) and at Drury Lane on 5 February her maid hissed and threw oranges at L'Epine. Mrs Tofts played the title roles in the first English operas in the Italian style, Clayton's *Arsinoe* (1705) and Bononcini's *Camilla* (1706). She was the Queen in Clayton's *Rosamond* and then, still singing in English, had leading parts in the mixed language productions which followed the introduction of the castratos. Cibber admired the 'Beauty of her fine proportion'd Figure, and exquisitely sweet, silver Tone of her Voice'. She was proud and mercenary, involved in opera house intrigues and demands for more money and more elaborate costumes. On 26 May 1709 the *Tatler* hinted that 'the unfortunate Camilla' had had a nervous breakdown. She left England for Venice, where she sang at fashionable assemblies and married a wealthy British resident, Joseph Smith.

*

BDA; *DNB* (L. M. Middleton); *LS*
D. Arundell: *The Critic at the Opera* (London, 1957)
M. Sands: 'Mrs Tofts, 1685?–1756', *Theatre Notebook*, xx (1966), 100–13
R. Fiske: *English Theatre Music in the Eighteenth Century* (London, 1973, 2/1986)
J. Milhous and R. D. Hume: *Vice Chamberlain Coke's Theatrical Papers 1706–1715* (Carbondale, IL, 1982)

OLIVE BALDWIN, THELMA WILSON

Togni, Camillo (*b* Gussago, nr Brescia, 18 Oct 1922). Italian composer. He first encountered Schoenberg's music when he was in his early twenties; the experience, followed up by intensive study, was to have a lasting impact on his work. Although he was one of the first Italian composers to explore the new directions in the postwar Darmstadt summer schools, his strong roots in the expressionist tradition remain a dominant feature of his distinctive style. From the mid-1950s Togni has repeatedly made his mark with vivid chamber settings of the poetry of 15th-century France and, crucially, of Georg Trakl. He first encountered Trakl's *Blaubart* in 1956; although he did many preparatory studies for an operatic setting of the text, the project was not completed for another two decades. Written between 1972 and 1975, *Blaubart* was first performed (in a double bill with Bartók's *Bluebeard's Castle*) at La Fenice, Venice, on 14 December 1977. It is typical of the concentration that Togni imposed upon himself that all the music in this hypersensitive setting derives from a single series. Trakl also provided him with the materials for a second one-act opera, *Barrabas*, intended with *Blaubart* to constitute two parts of a trilogy. Written between 1981 and 1985, it has as yet received only concert performances of some of its sections.

DAVID OSMOND-SMITH

Tokatyan, Armand (*b* Plovdiv, 16 June 1894; *d* Pasadena, CA, 12 June 1960). Armenian tenor. His parents settled first in Bulgaria and then in Egypt, where he made his début in 1914. After studying in Milan he appeared there in 1921 as Chevalier des Grieux (*Manon Lescaut*). Later that year he travelled to the USA, inaugurating a substantial career with Antonio Scotti's touring company and from 1923 to 1946 he appeared frequently at the Metropolitan. He sang mostly in lyric roles such as Nicias in *Thaïs* (with Jeritza) and Corentin in *Dinorah* (with Galli-Curci). House premières included Falla's *La vida breve* (1926) and Puccini's *La rondine* (1928), in which he took the light baritone role of Prunier. During the 1930s he travelled widely in Europe, appearing at Covent Garden in 1934 as Calaf. His few recordings show a bright, well-defined voice rather than a rich one, with adequate rather than distinctive powers of characterization.

J. B. STEANE

Tokody, Ilona (*b* Szeged, 27 April 1953). Hungarian soprano. She studied in Budapest, making her début there in 1976. Engaged in Vienna since 1979, she has sung in the USSR, Prague, Munich, Frankfurt, Cologne, Berlin, Naples and at La Scala. In 1986 she made her Covent Garden début as Mimì and sang Desdemona in San Diego. Her repertory includes Pamina, Fiordiligi,

Violetta, Leonora (*Il trovatore* and *Forza*), Amelia (*Simon Boccanegra*), Aida, Giselda, Maddalena de Coigny, Nedda and Asteria (*Nerone*). Her creamy voice and delicacy of phrasing are particularly well displayed in Puccini, as Tosca, Suor Angelica, Lauretta, Liù, Butterfly and Mimì. ELIZABETH FORBES

Tokyo. Capital of Japan. The earliest record of Western opera there dates from 1876, when a French group gave a performance of *La Périchole* with piano accompaniment. A scene from Gounod's *Faust* performed at the Tokyo Music School in 1894 used an orchestra for the first time, while the earliest performance by an exclusively Japanese cast, Gluck's *Orfeo*, was given at the same institution in 1903.

The Tokyo Music School, renamed the Tokyo Geijutsu Daigaku (the Tokyo National University of Fine Arts and Music) in 1949, has trained a considerable number of Japanese opera singers, including the sopranos Tamaki Miura and Michiko Sunahara (*b* 1923). There was no genuine opera house; performances were often given at the traditional Kabuki Theatre or the Imperial Theatre (built in 1911). The impresario G. V. Rosi's attempt, from 1916 to 1918, to maintain regular opera seasons at the Akasaka Royal Theatre failed, but it did inspire successful productions of operettas by Offenbach, Suppé and Sullivan, as well as of *Carmen* and *Aida*, at theatres in the Asakusa district from 1918 to 1925.

After World War I, a number of European opera companies visited Tokyo, while there were more performances by native artists and attempts to produce works by Japanese composers such as Kósçak Yamada. In 1934 the Fujiwara Opera Company, the first major opera company in Japan, was founded by the tenor Yoshie Fujiwara; it maintains a broad, standard repertory.

Since the end of World War II, opera productions in Tokyo have become increasingly frequent. In addition to the Fujiwara Opera, several groups have set up their headquarters in Tokyo: the more important are the Nagato Miho Opera Company (founded in 1946), the Niki Kai (1952), the Nihon Opera Kyōkai (Japan Opera Society, 1958) and the Tokyo Shitsunai Kagekijō (Tokyo Chamber Opera, 1969), producing a wide range of works, including opera by Japanese composers. Performances are on an occasional basis, without a fixed opera season. There is still no proper opera house, in spite of frequent discussions and proposals to build one; operas are performed in concert halls or drama theatres, such as the Tokyo Bunka Kaikan (Tokyo Metropolitan Festival Hall), the NHK (National Broadcasting System) Hall, the Nissei Gekijō (Nissei Theatre) and the Bunkamura Orchard Hall. MASAKATA KANAZAWA

Toldrá, Eduardo (*b* Villanueva y Geltrú, Barcelona, 7 April 1895; *d* Barcelona, 31 May 1962). Catalan composer. He studied the violin and composition at the conservatory in Barcelona, and began his career as an orchestral musician, founding in 1912 the Quartet Renaixement in which he played first violin. From 1916 he was increasingly active as a soloist, especially after his appearance with the Orquestra Casals in 1921. After the Spanish Civil War he conducted the new Spanish National Orchestra and in 1944 he became director of the newly founded Barcelona Municipal Orchestra. He also conducted in France and Portugal. On 24 November 1961 he conducted the first concert performance of Manuel de Falla's *Atlántida* at the Gran Teatre del Liceu in Barcelona.

Toldrá's chief work is the one-act comic opera, *El giravolt de maig*, to a libretto by Josep Carner, first performed on 27 October 1928 at the Liceu, Barcelona. An attempt to revive the conventions of *opera buffa*, it is in Catalan and contains subtle allusions to the Catalan nationalist ideals of the time. Melodic lyricism, naturalness of vocal writing, transparent harmonization and bright orchestral colour are skilfully used to support the action on stage. Despite its brevity, the psychological introspection of the four principal characters is effectively conveyed. The staging of the opera presents problems because, although the action takes place at an inn, a large amount of empty stage is required to create a 'magical' ambience (undoubtedly influenced by Shakespeare). Toldrá's output also includes instrumental works and songs.

*

M. Capdevila Massana: *Eduardo Toldrá* (Barcelona, 1964)
A. Fernández Cid: *Eduardo Toldrá* (Madrid, 1977)

XOÁN M. CARREIRA

Toledo. American city, in Ohio. An audience for opera was cultivated at recitals and concerts in the Peristyle (1800 seats) at the Toledo Museum of Art. Built in 1933 to a design by Clifford Swan that featured a curving row of 28 Ionic columns surrounding the main seating area, the Peristyle was tuned by Leopold Stokowski, whose pencil punctures can still be seen in the canvas and hair-felt covered walls. Singers who performed there included Kirsten Flagstad (1936), Lotte Lehmann (1937), William Warfield (1955) and Lily Pons (1956). The Toledo Opera was founded in 1959 by Lester Freedman, who presented *Aida* to a full house in the Paramount Theatre (3500 seats). Soon after, Freedman formed the Dayton Opera, which shared production costs. In 1962 the company moved to the Peristyle, where performances included *Tosca* with Placido Domingo (1966) and Robert Ward's *The Crucible* (1971). Freedman's retirement in 1972 led to a succession of directors. By 1974 competition for bookings at the Peristyle, coupled with its inadequate wing and fly space, compelled the company to move to the Masonic Auditorium (2433 seats), built in 1969. The Toledo Opera gives between six and eight performances of three or four repertory operas throughout the season.

NANCY MALITZ

Tolomeo [Tolomeo re di Egitto ('Ptolemy, King of Egypt')]. Opera in three acts by GEORGE FRIDERIC HANDEL to a libretto by NICOLA FRANCESCO HAYM adapted from CARLO SIGISMONDO CAPECE's *Tolomeo et Alessandro* (1711, Rome); London, King's Theatre, 30 April 1728.

Tolomeo was Handel's 13th and last full-length opera for the Royal Academy of Music, and the last of the five operas in which the leading female roles were designed for the rival sopranos Francesca Cuzzoni and Faustina Bordoni, who sang Seleuce and Elisa. The other singers were the alto castratos Senesino (Ptolemy) and Antonio Baldi (Alessandro), and the bass Giuseppe Boschi (Araspe).

Handel revived *Tolomeo* twice, subjecting it to drastic revision each time. For the production at the King's Theatre on 19 May 1730 the castrato Antonio Bernacchi took over the title role and Anna Strada del Pò sang Seleuce, while the other roles were adapted for changed voices: the contraltos Antonia Merighi and Francesca Bertolli sang Elisa and Alessandro, and the tenor Annibale Pio Fabri sang Araspe. Handel replaced 12 of the original numbers (including the final *coro*) by others from earlier Academy operas; three arias were simply omitted. Senesino returned to the title role for the revival on 2 January 1733, when the roles of Elisa and Araspe reverted to their original voice types, sung by Celeste Gismondi and Antonio Montagnana. One of the original arias and the *coro* were restored, but six other arias were again replaced. *Tolomeo* was not performed again until 19 June 1938, when an arrangement by Fritz Lehmann was produced at Göttingen; the first modern British revival was at the Unicorn Theatre, Abingdon, on 8 September 1973. Chrysander's score shows the 1728 performing version of the opera, but gives little information about Handel's revivals; his appendix includes only two of the replacement arias (originally written as additions to *Giulio Cesare* and *Floridante*).

The title role is the historical Ptolemy Lathyrus (Ptolemy IX Soter II), joint ruler of Egypt with his mother Cleopatra III in 116 BC, but deposed by her in favour of his younger brother Ptolemy X Alexander (Alessandro in the opera) and exiled to Cyprus around 108 BC, at which period the action of the opera may be supposed to take place. The setting is 'a maritime country of Cyprus, near a delightful village'. Ptolemy (alto) is disguised as the shepherd Osmin. His wife Seleuce (soprano) is also on the island, disguised as the shepherdess Delia. Cyprus is ruled by the tyrannical king Araspe (bass), whose sister Elisa (soprano) is in love with Ptolemy though unaware of his identity.

The plot deals with Ptolemy's banishment, his estrangement from his brother Alessandro, his separation from Seleuce and the attempts of Araspe to win her. Fraternal and marital loyalty prevail, in spite of intrigues and deceptions; at the end of the opera Ptolemy, in prison, drinks what he supposes to be a cup of poison, given him by Elisa, and falls senseless, but it was only a sleeping draught, and when he awakens Alessandro unites him with Seleuce and declares him King of Egypt.

* * *

Despite the quasi-Arcadian setting and the modest demands of the score – horns are used only as reinforcing instruments in the overture and the final *coro* – the opera does not have a particularly pastoral feel, most of the arias being decent but unexceptional examples of Handel's Royal Academy manner. Each act ends strongly, however. 'Torna sol', closing Act 1, is one of Handel's deeply felt E♭ major arias, aptly expressing Ptolemy's yearning for his wife. The woodland scene concluding Act 2 begins with the attraction of an aria ('Dite, che fa, dov'è') accompanied by muted upper strings and pizzicato basses which becomes a duet as Ptolemy echoes Seleuce's musings; but the mood swiftly changes to near-tragedy with Araspe uttering threats in a forceful aria of anger ('Piangi pur') and husband and wife exchanging farewells in a poignant duet. The final scene of Act 3 has a striking *scena* for Ptolemy as he takes the supposed poison, including 'Stille amare', an aria remarkable for its halting accompaniment and B♭ minor tonality. The most famous item in the opera is nevertheless 'Non lo dirò col labbro', Alessandro's brief cavatina in Act 1: it became a familiar recital piece after 1928, when an arrangement was published with a new English text ('Did you not see my lady') by Arthur Somervell, under the title 'Silent Worship'.

ANTHONY HICKS

Tolstoy, Lev [Leo] **Nikolayevich** (*b* Yasnaya Polyana, 28 Aug/9 Sept 1828; *d* Astapovo railway station, 7/20 Nov 1910). Russian writer, distinguished hater of opera. He had some musical education: he could play the piano after a fashion and even composed waltzes. Sensitive not only to the pleasures of music but also to its 'hypnotic' influence and hence its power to uplift or corrupt, he maintained that there could be no aesthetic judgment without an ethical component. Good art was art that communicated simple ideas and emotions directly and intelligibly, uniting artist and audience in accord with Christian teachings. For Tolstoy opera, with its mongrel mixture of media, its needless complexity, its irreality and its reliance on flamboyant convention, epitomized the falsity of art at its most debased and stood as metaphor for falsity in social relations. The scene of Natasha Rostova's moral downfall in his novel *Voyna i mir* ('War and Peace', 1869) is set fittingly against the background of an opera performance, in detailing which Tolstoy employed the (actually extremely artful) device of outwardly naive description – what critics of a later age would call *ostraneniye* ('strange-making') – to unmask and condemn the absurdity of such perverted 'counterfeit art'.

Tolstoy used this technique again in his late aesthetic tract *Chto takoye iskusstvo?* ('What is Art?'), with its memorable, if fundamentally obtuse, exposure of Wagnerian pretence and its angry rejection of Beethoven's Ninth Symphony. (Beethoven had previously come under suspicion in *Kreytserova sonata*, 'The Kreutzer Sonata', a novella in which his purportedly 'erotic' music precipitated the break-up of a marriage and a murder.) *What is Art?* opens with a rollicking satire of an opera in rehearsal, followed by some chilly moralizing on the unworthiness of the enterprise and the un-Christian attitudes that must necessarily infect those who devote their lives to the frivolous perfectionism art demands. After describing a harangue administered by the exasperated conductor, Tolstoy notes:

> I have seen one workman abuse another for not supporting the weight piled upon him when goods were being unloaded, or at haystacking, the village Elder scold a peasant for not making the rick right, and the man submitted in silence. And however unpleasant it was to witness the scene, the unpleasantness was lessened by the consciousness that the business in hand was necessary and important and the fault for which the Elder scolded the labourer was one which might spoil a necessary undertaking.
>
> But what was being done here? For what, and for whom?

It is grandly ironical to imagine the scoldings that have been administered over the years by directors and conductors immersed in the task of staging one of the operas that have been based on the works of Tolstoy. Pride of place among them, of course, goes to Prokofiev's magnum opus, *War and Peace*, in which the irony is compounded by the fact that, while he did not show the imaginary opera Tolstoy described (evidently compounded out of stock elements remembered from *Lucia*, *Robert le diable*, *Rigoletto*, *Trovatore* and other operas popular in Tolstoy's – not Natasha's – time), Prokofiev devoted practically the whole first half of his opera ('Peace') to the episode that the night at the opera sets in motion: Natasha's infatuation and planned elopement with the rake Anatole Kuragin.

Prokofiev had been anticipated, in fashioning an opera out of Tolstoy's sprawling fictional chronicle, by two obscure composers. One was an Italian resident in Moscow, Scipione Fenzi (1823–1914): his *Prodi di*

Mosca was produced in Taganrog in 1872. The other, even more shadowy, was a certain Aël, who published the vocal score of a work entitled *Sozhzhyonnaya Moskva* ('Moscow reduced to Ashes') at his own expense (Kiev, 1914); it is based partly on Tolstoy (the war council at Fili) but mainly on the eponymous novel by Grigory Danilevsky (1886). The most recent operatic adaptation of Tolstoy's epic is by the Romanian composer Ervin Junger (1961, Cluj).

Tolstoy's most popular novel among opera composers has been *Anna Karenina* (1877), which concerns the quintessential operatic theme – ungovernable passion. There have been ten settings, in addition to an unrealized project of Janáček's. The remaining operatic derivations from Tolstoy's fiction are largely by Czechoslovak composers.

Voyna i mir [War and Peace] (novel, 1869): S. Fenzi, 1872, as Prodi di Mosca; Aël, as Sozhzhyonnaya Moskva (pubd 1914); Prokofiev, comp. 1941–52; E. Junger, 1961, as Razboi si pace

Anna Karenina (novel, 1877): S. Sassano, 1905; E. I. Granelli, 1906; Janáček, 1907, sketches; E. Malherbe, 1914, as Anna Karénine; Hubay, 1923, as Karenina Anna; I. Robbiani, 1924; S. Goldbach, 1930; V. I. Anpilogov, 1943; Hlobil, 1963; Meytus, comp. 1969–70; I. Hamilton, 1981

Pervïy vinokur [The First Distiller] (drama, 1884): V. N. Paskhalov, comp. c1885, inc.

Dorogo stoit [It Costs Dearly] (fable, after G. de Maupassant): Joubert, 1973, as The Prisoner

Chem lyudi zhivut [What Men Live by] (story, 1886); Martinů, 1953, as Čim člověk žije

Rabotnik Yemel'yan i pustoy baraban [The Worker Yemel'yan and the Empty Drum] (story, 1888): R. Réti, 1933, as Iwan und die Trommel

Skazka ob Ivane-durake i ego dvukh brat'yakh: Semyone-voine i Tarase-bryukhane i nemoy sestre Malan'ye i o starom d'yavole i tryokh chertenyatakh [Tale of Ivan the Fool and his Two Brothers, Semyon the Warrior and Taras the Paunchy, and their Dumb Sister Malan'ya and the Old Devil and the Three Little Devils] (story, 1888): Ostrčil, 1934, as Honzovo království; J. B. Foerster, 1936, as Bloud; A. Tcherepnin, 1968

Voskreseniye [Resurrection] (novel, 1899): Alfano, 1904, as Risurrezione; Cikker, 1962, as Vzkriesenie

Zhivoy trup [The Living Corpse] (story, 1902): Leroux, 1912; Janáček, 1916, sketches

Za chto? [What For?] (story, 1906): N. M. Strel'nikov, 1933, as Beglets

*

A. Maude, ed. and trans.: *L. Tolstoy: What is Art? (1898) and Essays on Art* (London, 1930)

N. Gusev and A. Gol'denveyzer: *Tolstoy i muzïka* (Moscow, 1953)

R. Taruskin: 'Current Chronicle', *MQ*, lxii (1976), 105–15 [on Tolstoyan aesthetics]

B. Shteynpress: 'Russkaya literatura v zarubezhnoy opere' [Russian Literature in Foreign Opera], *SovM* (1985), no.6, pp.83–8

R. Rischin: 'Allegro Tumultuosissimamente: Beethoven in Tolstoy's Fiction', *In the Shade of the Giant: Essays on Tolstoy*, ed. H. McLean (Berkeley and Los Angeles, 1989), 12–60

D. Lowe: 'Natasha Rostova Goes to the Opera', *OQ*, vii/3 (1990), 74–81

RICHARD TARUSKIN

Tomášek, Václav Jan Křtitel [Tomaschek, Wenzel Johann] (*b* Skuteč, 14 April 1774; *d* Prague, 3 April 1850). Bohemian composer. A self-taught musician, he studied history, aesthetics and philosophy, then law, at Prague University. In 1806 he became music tutor and composer to Count Georg Buquoy and his family, with whom he remained for 16 years. Thereafter his reputation was sufficiently established for him to work as a freelance composer and teacher in Prague and in 1824 he founded his own music school. He became a dominant figure in Prague musical life, attracting a circle of friends and pupils that included J. B. Kittl, J. V. Voříšek and Eduard Hanslick, though he never held an official position.

Tomášek completed one surviving opera, *Seraphine, oder Grossmut und Liebe* op.36 (2, J. H. Dambek, after an older Italian libretto, *L'amore per l'amore*; 15 December 1811, Prague, Estates Theatre). The second, *Alvaro* op.114 (2, after C. A. Herbst), remained unfinished. A libretto for a third, *Sakontala*, was written for him in 1825 by C. E. von Ebert, but nothing is known about the music, or about that of a projected fourth opera, *Božena, česká kněžna* ('Božena, Bohemian Princess'), on a libretto by Václav Hanka. *Seraphine*, written in the Classical operatic style, was successful at its première, but did not stay in the repertory. Tomášek's other dramatic works are operatic settings of various scenes from Schiller's plays (*Maria Stuart* op.99; *Piccolomini* op.100; *Die Braut von Messina* op.104) and Goethe's *Faust* (opp.102 and 103).

*

K. Emingerová: 'Dramatická díla' [The Dramatic Works], *Hudební dílo Václava Jana Tomáška* [The Music of Tomášek] (Prague, 1925), 36–40

Z. Němec, ed.: *Vlastní životopis Václava Jana Tomáška* [Tomášek's Autobiography] (Prague, 1941)

M. Tarantová: *Václav Jan Tomášek* (Prague, 1946)

E. Holubová: 'Václav Jan Tomášeks Oper "Seraphine" als Quelle und Werk', *Sborník prací filosofické fakulty brněnské university*, H8 (1973), 51–8

J. Tyrrell: *Czech Opera* (Cambridge, 1988)

MICHAELA FREEMANOVÁ, ADRIENNE SIMPSON

Tomasi, Giovanni Battista (*fl* c1656–1692). Italian composer. He served the Duke of Mantua as an organist for 23 years from about 1656, and from 1679 to 1685 was *maestro di cappella di camera* of the court; for a time he also worked at S Andrea, Mantua. As well as many oratorios he wrote two operas: *Il gran Costanzo* (A. Lanzoni; 1670, Mantua, pubd lib. in *I-Bc*) and *Sesto Tarquinio* (C. Badoaro; 1678–9, Venice, pubd lib. in *US-Wc*). The music of both is lost.

*

AllacciD; *EitnerQ*; *RicordiE*; *SchmidlD*; *SchmidlDS*

A. Bertolotti: *Musici alla corte dei Gonzaga in Mantova dal secolo XV al XVIII* (Milan, 1890)

P. Besutti: *La corte musicale di Ferdinando Carlo Gonzaga ultimo duca di Mantova: musici, cantanti e teatro d'opera tra il 1665 e il 1707* (Mantua, 1989)

THOMAS WALKER

Tomasi, Henri (*b* Marseilles, 17 Aug 1901; *d* Paris, 13 Jan 1971). French composer and conductor of Corsican descent. A pupil of Gaubert and others at the Paris Conservatoire, he won the Prix de Rome in 1927 and the Grand Prix de la Musique Française in 1952. During the 1930s he was one of the founders, alongside Prokofiev, Poulenc, Milhaud and Honegger, of the contemporary music group 'Triton'. He divided his career equally between composing and conducting, and he conducted at many opera houses throughout the world. As a composer, his orchestral music is important, but he was attracted above all to the theatre, and it was two of his operas, *L'Atlantide* and *Miguel Mañara*, that established his reputation. *Miguel Mañara* is based on the work of a Lithuanian poet and tells of a mystical Don Juan who has renounced debauchery. The composer's own origins are reflected in *Sampiero Corso*, which deals with the oppression of Corsica by the Genoese in the 16th century. In *Ulysse*, Ulysses is demystified, returning amid ordinary sailors. Tomasi's postwar works reflect a disillusionment with mankind; *L'éloge de la folie*, which he described as a cross between opera and ballet, includes references to Nazism and napalm. Tomasi also composed several ballets; before his death he had been working on an operatic version of *Hamlet*.

His music is intensely direct in feeling, occasionally dissonant and highly coloured; he absorbed influences from his French contemporaries (chiefly Ravel) while retaining an individual voice.

L'Atlantide (drame lyrique et choréographique, 4, F. Didelot, after P. Benoît), Mulhouse, Municipal, 26 Feb 1954, vs (Paris, 1959)
La triomphe de Jeanne (op-oratorio, Tomasi and P. Soupault), concert perf., excerpts, Rouen, 23 March 1956; concert perf., complete, Paris, 7 Oct 1957
Miguel Mañara [Don Juan de Mañara], 1941–4 (drame lyrique, 4, Tomasi, after O. V. de Milosz), Munich, Prinzregenten, 29 March 1956, vs (Paris, 1952)
Sampiero Corso, 1953–4 (3, R. Cuttoli), Bordeaux, Grand, 6 May 1956, vs (Paris, 1957)
François d'Assise [Le petit pauvre], 1957 (drame lyrique, 2, A. Bonheur), concert perf., Paris, 30 Dec 1960
Le colibri (féerie radiophonique, 1, Didelot), ORTF, 20 June 1961
Princesse Pauline, 1958–61 (opéra-mascarade, 2, Didelot), ORTF, 11 Jan 1962; stage, Paris, OC (Favart), 22 June 1962
Le silence de la mer, 1959–60 (drame lyrique, 1, Tomasi, after Vercors), concert perf., Strasbourg, 15 June 1963; stage, Toulouse, Capitole, 3 April 1964
L'élixir du Révérend Père Gaucher, 1962 (oc, 2, L. Bancal, after A. Daudet), Toulouse, Capitole, 3 April 1964
Ulysse, ou Le beau périple, 1962 (jeu littéraire et musical, 2, Tomasi after J. Giono), Mulhouse, Municipal, 22 Jan 1965
L'éloge de la folie (jeu satirique, symphonique et chorégraphique, prol., 2 scenes), concert perf., Paris, 11 June 1968

*

F. Ducros: 'Les opéras d'Henri Tomasi', *Le théâtre lyrique français, 1945–1985*, ed. D. Pistone (Paris, 1987), 299–308
'Hommage à Henri Tomasi', *L'avant-scène opéra*, no.109 (1988), 108–39 ARTHUR HOÉRÉE/RICHARD LANGHAM SMITH

Tombeau (Fr.). A scene-type in late 17th- and 18th-century French opera. The frequent appearances of oracles and the spirits of the departed (*ombres*) in the opera plots of this period are handled using identifiable musical characteristics which, although not individually restricted to such scenes, produce in combination a recognizable genre. The scoring is usually low in pitch; a recurring rhythmic motif is often used; the usually flexible rhythm of the recitative is suspended in favour of regular note values; monotones are used in the voice and/or accompaniment; and an 'extreme' key is selected (C minor for Lully, more often F minor or B♭ minor for later composers). Several of these elements are already present in Lully's *Amadis* (1684); nearly 100 years later, when Mozart set an adaptation of Danchet's libretto for Campra's *Idomenée*, the oracle scene in the last act features monotone declamation, the key of C minor, and a low-lying accompaniment.

*

C. Wood: 'Orchestra and Spectacle in the *tragédie en musique*, 1673–1715: oracle, *sommeil* and *tempête*', *PRMA*, cviii (1981–2), 25–46 CAROLINE WOOD

Tomeoni [Tomeoni Dutillieu], **Irene** (*b* 1763; *d* Vienna, 12 Oct 1830). Italian soprano. She was married to the French composer Pierre Dutillieu. Her earliest public performances were given in Florence in 1784. In 1787 she went to Naples and sang there almost exclusively during the next three years in comic operas by Cimarosa, P. A. Guglielmi, Anfossi, Sarti and others. In 1791 she succeeded Adriana Ferrarese as *prima buffa* of the Italian opera troupe in Vienna, making her début as Dorinda in Guglielmi's *La bella pescatrice* (a role she had created in Naples in 1789). She sang in Vienna throughout most of the following decade, specializing in sentimental heroines and creating, among others, the roles of Carolina in Cimarosa's *Il matrimonio segreto* (1792) and Mrs Ford in Salieri's *Falstaff* (1799). She retired from the stage around the turn of the century.

Tomeoni was not a singer of outstanding virtuosity. In writing for her, composers avoided coloratura and rarely exceeded an octave in range. She was noted for the simplicity of her singing, her ingenuous charm and her playfulness. An engraving of her as Paisiello's Nina evokes something of her appeal to late 18th-century audiences (for illustration *see* NINA).

*

O. Michtner: *Das alte Burgtheater als Opernbühne* (Vienna, 1970)
J. A. Rice: *Emperor and Impresario: Leopold II and the Transformation of Viennese Musical Theater, 1790–1792* (diss., U. of California, Berkeley, 1987) JOHN A. RICE

Tomeoni, Pellegrino (*b* Lucca, *c*1729; *d* Lucca, ?1816). Italian composer. He held a series of posts as *maestro di cappella* in or near Lucca and was also an organist. According to Schmidl he was *maestro al cembalo* at the public theatre in Lucca for a performance of *Zenobia* in 1761 (text by Metastasio, composer unknown), to which he added some pieces and perhaps also the recitatives. He contributed at least three operas (all *drammi serie*, music now lost) to Lucca's *funzioni delle Tasche*, a three-day local festival held every 30 months to elect the city's government: *Dione siracusano* (Giglio, 15 December 1750), *Il Narsete, generale di Giustiniano imperatore* (3rd day of *Tasche*, 1770) and *Marzio coriolano* (3rd day of *Tasche*, 1773). Most of his works, however, were for the church.

*

FlorimoN; *SchmidlD*; *SchmidlDS*
L. Nerici: *Storia della musica in Lucca* (Lucca, 1879)
JAMES L. JACKMAN

***Tom Jones* (i).** *Opéra comique* in three acts by FRANÇOIS-ANDRÉ DANICAN PHILIDOR to a libretto by Antoine Alexandre Henri Poinsinet and Bertin Davesne after HENRY FIELDING's novel; Paris, Comédie-Italienne (Théâtre de l'Hôtel de Bourgogne), 27 February 1765 (revised version with alterations to the libretto by MICHEL-JEAN SEDAINE, Théâtre de l'Hôtel de Bourgogne, 30 January 1766).

In *Tom Jones* Poinsinet and Philidor expanded the scale of *opéra comique* while presenting a realistic story without farce. With Davesne (who is credited with Act 2) Poinsinet produced a well-turned plot, using only early scenes from Fielding and imitating the novelist's earthy dialogue. The initial poor reception led to comprehensive revision. Sedaine's dialogue is shorter and more decorous; Philidor lengthened two arias and changed the position of another. Three arias and a trio were omitted and appear to be lost, but two new arias were composed. Philidor rewrote the final vaudeville; the original setting survives in the 1765 libretto with a verse in which Sophia begs indulgence ('Notre seul but est de vous plaire'). In the 1766 libretto the verse 'Jone [*sic*] au malheur fut livré dès l'enfance' alluded to the opera rather than the hero. This libretto corresponds closely (though not in every detail) to the published score. A deserved success in 1766, *Tom Jones* was soon performed all over Europe, and in Philidor's lifetime was translated into German, Russian and Swedish. It has been revived in modern times in England and France.

In the house of Squire Western (bass) his daughter Sophia (soprano) and her companion Mrs Honour (soprano) discuss Tom Jones (tenor), a handsome youth of unknown birth, ward of a neighbour, Allworthy

'Tom Jones' (Philidor), Act 3 (in the inn at Upton): drawing by Willie fils

(baritone). Tom enters with Western, who sings of their hunting achievements ('D'un cerf dix cors', a *tour de force* with horns and final chorus). Western and his sister, Mrs Western (mezzo-soprano), want Sophia to marry Allworthy's nephew Blifil (tenor); through a misunderstanding she reveals her love for Tom and is roundly abused by her aunt. Act 2 takes place in the garden. Tom sings of his love and Western assumes he is after Mrs Honour. Sophia cannot hide her distaste for Blifil; her father commands obedience. Tom bids Sophia a tender farewell ('Vous voulez que je vous oublie?'). They are surprised by the entire company and Tom is banished by Allworthy; the act ends with a magnificent septet. Act 3, set in the inn at Upton, opens with a drinking chorus (unaccompanied, starting as a canon). Sophia has run away; she feels guilty and afraid (orchestral recitative and aria, 'O toi qui ne peux m'entendre'). Tom appears in time to rescue her from the drunks. The families arrive in pursuit but the Quaker Dowling (speaking role) reveals that Tom is also a nephew of Allworthy and that Blifil, entrusted with the evidence, has tried to destroy it. Blifil is denounced and the young couple united.

Philidor's music matches the development of the libretto; the love music is touching rather than elevated, the comedy well handled, and the ensembles are among his finest. Tom is tamely portrayed, but the Western family, including Sophia and Mrs Honour, comes vividly to life. The obbligato recitative and aria for Sophia represent a significant step in the assimilation of a serious style into *opéra comique*. JULIAN RUSHTON

***Tom Jones* (ii).** Operetta in three acts by EDWARD GERMAN to a libretto by Alexander M. Thompson and Robert Courtneidge (lyrics by Charles H. Taylor) after HENRY FIELDING's novel; Manchester, Prince's Theatre, 30 March 1907.

The neat adaptation omits much of Fielding's extensive narrative to concentrate on the romance of Tom (baritone) and Sophia (soprano), daughter of Squire Weston (baritone) who initially has other matrimonial plans for her. Tom's dalliance with Lady Bellaston (mezzo-soprano) is retained, but the raciness of the novel was necessarily subdued for Edwardian audiences.

As in *Merrie England*, German drew on his popular 'olde English' style to good effect, especially in the dance music which gained independent success. The most celebrated vocal number is the glittering waltz-song 'For tonight', but others achieved popularity, including 'Dream o' day Jill' (a late addition), 'West country lad', 'Tonight my spinet' and 'If love's content'. The pseudo-madrigal 'Here's a paradox for lovers' exemplifies the high standard of ensemble writing. A particular subtlety of the music is the distinct sense of time and locale it evokes within each act. Although arguably one of the finest English operettas, German's richest and most satisfying lyric score retains a place only in the amateur repertory. DAVID RUSSELL HULME

Tomlinson, John (*b* Oswaldtwistle, Lancs., 22 Sept 1946). English bass. He studied in Manchester, then in 1972 he sang Colline for Glyndebourne Touring Opera and Leporello for Kent Opera, as well as Monteverdi's Seneca. He sang Reede in Goehr's *Arden Must Die* (New Opera Company, 1974). Joining the ENO in 1975, he sang Talbot (*Maria Stuarda*), Masetto, King Mark, Fasolt, Pogner, Bartók's Bluebeard,

Méphistophélès, Rossini's Moses, Sparafucile, the Padre Guardiano, Ochs and Fiesco. He made his Covent Garden début in 1979 as Colline, later singing Mozart's Figaro, Leporello and the Commendatore, Don Basilio and Timur. He has sung Ramfis, Hunding and Hagen at San Francisco; Pimen and Banquo in Paris; Claggart for Scottish Opera; and Boris and Attila (1991) for Opera North. At Bayreuth he has sung Wotan (1988–91) and the Wanderer (1989–91). A superb actor, he has a dark, resonant voice with a wide range, powerful in both the upper and lower registers.

*

H. Finch: 'John Tomlinson', *Opera*, xli (1990), 770–77

ELIZABETH FORBES

Tommasini, Vincenzo (*b* Rome, 17 Sept 1878; *d* Rome, 23 Dec 1950). Italian composer. He studied music at the Liceo di S Cecilia, Rome, and classics at Rome University, after which he spent some time in Berlin, where he attended Bruch's class at the Hochschule für Musik. But his sympathies soon gravitated more towards the French tradition, especially Debussy, and the instrumental works of his early maturity include some of the best Italian (and italianized) examples of post-Debussian impressionism. His compositions from 1926 onwards often show neo-classical tendencies, paralleling those in Casella's music; yet even his more formalized pages usually retain melodic and harmonic characteristics from his earlier period. Despite the youthful post-Wagnerian aspirations revealed in *Medea*, opera was never central to Tommasini's output, and only three of his contributions to the genre seem ever to have reached the stage. However, the unperformed *Dielja* has been praised by Domenico de' Paoli, who saw the score; and *Il tenore sconfitto*, which won considerable though ephemeral success just before the composer's death, reveals a flair for ironic comedy, such as had been only partly developed in the early, rather Wolf-Ferrarian *Uguale fortuna*. Tommasini also helped Toscanini to complete four of the projected five acts of Boito's *Nerone*, and published a series of articles on Wagner's operas (*RMI*, ix, 1902, pp.113–47, 422–41, 694–716) as well as one on Debussy (*RMI*, xiv, 1907, pp.157–67).

Medea, 1902–4 (3, Tommasini), Trieste, Verdi, 8 April 1906, unpubd
Amore di terra lontana, 1907–8 (Tommasini), unperf., unpubd
Uguale fortuna, 1911 (scherzo lirico, 1, Tommasini, after F. de Nion), Rome, Costanzi, 20 Feb 1913
Dielja, 1930s (G. Denis), unperf., unpubd
Il tenore sconfitto, ovvero La presunzione punita (1, V. Brancati), Rome, Eliseo, 24 Oct 1950

*

G. Barini: 'Uguale fortuna di Vincenzo Tommasini', *Nuova antologia*, no.248 (1913), 148–52
M. Zanotti-Bianco: 'Vincenzo Tommasini', *The Chesterian*, new ser., no.29 (1923), 133–8
D. de' Paoli: *La crisi musicale italiana* (Milan, 1939), esp. 72, 184, 307–8
G. M. Gatti: 'Vincenzo Tommasini (1878–1950)', *RaM*, xxi (1951), 48–9
M. Rinaldi: 'Vincenzo Tommasini', *RMI*, liii (1951), 323–36

JOHN C. G. WATERHOUSE

Tomowa-Sintow, Anna (*b* Stara Zagora, 22 Sept 1941). Bulgarian soprano. Her mother was an opera chorus singer and she was involved in opera from an early age as Butterfly's child. Her studies were at the Sofia Conservatory with Gyorgy Zlatew-Tscherkin; she then sang small roles at Leipzig, where she made her main début as Abigaille in 1967. She built her repertory mainly on Italian roles, and in 1972 became a member of the Berlin Staatsoper. The next year she was engaged at Salzburg for the première of Orff's *De temporum fine comoedia* under Karajan, who helped promote her international career and developed her Mozart and Strauss repertory. She made her American début at San Francisco as Donna Anna in 1974, and played the same role at the Metropolitan in 1978, following débuts at Covent Garden as Fiordiligi (1975) and at the Vienna Staatsoper as Countess Almaviva (1977); she returned to Covent Garden in 1990 as Yaroslavna (*Prince Igor*). Her beautifully moulded spinto soprano with its creamy tone may be heard on recordings in roles including Donna Anna, Countess Almaviva and Elsa, all under Karajan, and Ariadne under Levine (1987).

*

T. Lanier: 'Divided Loyalty', *ON*, xlix/11 (1984–5), 17–19
H. Rosenthal: 'Anna Tomowa-Sintow', *Opera*, xxxviii (1987), 250–53

NOËL GOODWIN

Tomyris [*Die grossmüthige Tomyris* ('The Magnanimous Tomyris')]. Singspiel in three acts by REINHARD KEISER to a libretto by JOHANN JOACHIM HOË after DOMENICO LALLI's *L'amor di figlio non conosciuto*; Hamburg, Theater am Gänsemarkt, July 1717.

Tomyris (soprano), Queen of the Messagetes, has just defeated the Persian king Cyrus. Although she had promised to marry one of her two allies, Policares (tenor), King of Lydia, and Doraspe (bass), King of Damascus, she keeps postponing a choice because she secretly loves her general, Tigranes (tenor). Meroë (soprano), Cyrus's daughter and Tigranes' betrothed whom he believes dead, arrives disguised as a soothsayer, seeking to avenge her father's death on Tomyris. She prevails on Tigranes to write a letter to the Persian commander betraying Tomyris, but out of loyalty to the queen he also writes a second letter revoking it. An attempt by Meroë to stab the sleeping Tomyris is foiled by Tigranes, who, in order to protect his beloved, lets Tomyris believe it was he who meant to kill her. Discovery of his first letter appears to confirm his treachery, but in the end Meroë reveals herself, and the second letter comes to light, proving Tigranes' faithfulness. It is also disclosed that he is Tomyris' long-lost son. Recognizing at last why she loves him, Tomyris forgives Meroë and chooses Policares as her husband.

Despite the conventionality of the libretto, *Tomyris* ranks high among Keiser's operas for the richness of its musical inspiration and the varied colouring of its orchestration. The title role, with its extremely difficult coloratura writing, was composed for Margaretha Susanna Kayser.

JOHN H. ROBERTS

Tonadilla (Sp., diminutive of *tonada*: 'song'). An intermezzo sung between the acts of a play or (more rarely) an opera or *auto sacramental* in 18th-century and early 19th-century Spanish theatre. The name was used originally for a strophic song usually preceding a dance, which is why the theatrical *tonadilla* is sometimes referred to as a *tonadilla escénica*. The genre developed from about 1750 in Madrid, where it became a customary part of the miscellaneous fare in the playhouses, along with dances, songs and the main entertainment. The first *tonadilla* was once thought to have been written in 1757 by the Catalan composer Luis Misón, who was then active in Madrid, but Subirá showed that Antonio Guerrero (*c*1710–76) had included *tonadillas* in many of his plays a few years earlier. His early *tonadillas* include *Los señores fingidos* and *Los náufragos*.

The *tonadilla*, which dealt mainly with lower-class characters (peasants, innkeepers, gypsies, barbers etc.), soon found popular acceptance, first in Madrid and then elsewhere in Spain and in Latin America, and developed into a kind of short comic opera akin to the Neapolitan intermezzo. Some *tonadillas* were for one singer only, others for two, three, four or more; a *tonadilla* with more than four characters was sometimes called a *tonadilla general*. The most complex example ever performed seems to have been Jacinto Valledor's *La Plaza de Palacio de Barcelona* (1774), which required 12 singers and was performed, as the printed libretto informs us, on King Charles III's name-day (4 November) in Barcelona's Teatre de la Santa Creu. Some *tonadillas* required a chorus, but such works were not common.

Subirá's painstaking research into the history of the *tonadilla* has perhaps elevated the genre to a rank of importance it never actually occupied. He described the earliest type, from about 1751–7, as usually a short piece which, like the SAINETE or ENTREMÉS, served to separate the acts of a play. It reached its maturity between 1771 and 1790, when it developed a kinship to Italian opera, with the Catalan Pablo Esteve y Grimau and the Navarrese Blas de Laserna as its most distinguished composers. During the following years (1791–1810) it suffered a kind of hypertrophy, becoming longer and more complicated. A contest announced by the Spanish government in the *Gaceta de Madrid* in 1791 was for a *tonadilla* for one to four characters with a length of between 10 and 22 minutes. Leandro Fernández de Moratín, a well-known playwright and sometime theatrical censor, frowned on the *tonadilla* of this period as 'cheap and low'. In the years between 1810 and 1850 the *tonadilla* slowly declined; a few remained in the repertory for a time, often with an admixture of well-known numbers from other pieces, but the Romantic theatre found no place for them.

The spirit of Spanish music is evident in the *tonadilla* above all in its melodies and rhythms (specifically those of the *fandango*, *folia*, *jota*, *seguidilla*, *tirana* and other Spanish dances) and in the use of some typically Spanish instruments such as the guitar and castanets. Italian influence is present too in the musical style, the aria form, the titles of set numbers ('quartetto', 'arietta' etc.) and even in Italian texts or subjects concerning Italian music or life. The song, or aria, usually to be found at the beginning has a simple binary form (*AA'*) or the typical aria form *ABA*; the two sections of the *AA'* type were often separated by a few spoken lines. A chorus, if present, would sometimes sing a refrain once or twice at the end of a number. In the mature *tonadilla* the first aria was usually introduced by a ritornello, sometimes entitled 'introducción', 'preludio' or even 'obertura'.

Up to 1760 most *tonadillas* had only three numbers, the middle one consisting of *coplas* (verses) which told the story, but in the 1760s it became customary to have four sections, the second and fourth being normally *seguidillas*, with the *coplas* placed third. However, no regular pattern was established, and several different numbers could be included under cover of a single one; for instance, a *seguidilla* could include other popular dances such as the *jota* or (more likely) the *tirana*. The verses sung with a *seguidilla* were usually repeated many times, making it an item of some length. Some of the musical numbers might be preceded by recitative, as in Italian opera.

Despite Subirá's efforts to underline the importance of the genre as a remarkable part of Spain's musical past, the *tonadilla* repertory remains today largely unexplored and unperformed.

*

LaborD

F. Pedrell: *El teatro lírico anterior al siglo XIX* (La Coruña, 1896–8)

J. Gómez: 'Don Blas de Laserna: un capítulo de la historia del teatro lírico español visto en la vida del último tonadillero', *Revista de la Biblioteca, archivo y museo [de ayntamiento de Madrid]*, ii (1925), 406–30, 531–48; iii (1926), 88–104, 222–40

J. Subirá: *La tonadilla escénica* (Madrid, 1928–30)

——: *Tonadillas teatráles inéditas* (Madrid, 1932)

——: 'Les influences françaises dans la tonadilla madrilène du XVIIIme siècle', *Mélanges de musicologie offerts à M. Lionel de la Laurencie* (Paris, 1933), 209–16

——: *La tonadilla escénica: sus obras y sus autores* (Barcelona, 1933)

M. N. Hamilton: *Music in 18th Century Spain* (Urbana, 1937)

N. González Ruiz: *La Caramba* (Madrid, 1944)

J. Subirá: 'El "cuatro" escénico español, sus antecedentes, evoluciones y desintegración', *Miscelánea en homenaje a Monseñor Higinio Anglés*, ii (Barcelona, 1961), 895–921

ROGER ALIER

Tonality. A term, first coined by Castil-Blaze in 1821, and now primarily used to denote a system of relationships between a series of pitches having a tonic, or central pitch, as its most important element. The present article is concerned with the use of tonalities as an element in opera, particularly as regards the large-scale articulation of the drama.

1. Before 1800. 2. Since 1800.

1. BEFORE 1800. From the earliest operas, tonality has been used to colour and to enhance the effect of dramatic incident; a familiar example is the use by Monteverdi in Act 2 of *Orfeo* (1607) of E major in juxtaposition with G minor when the Messenger announces Eurydice's death to Orpheus. Within individual arias or other discrete items, in Baroque opera, tonality is used as in instrumental movements of the time. It is difficult to determine, in the absence of any regularity of procedure or support from theoretical sources, whether larger-scale use of tonality can be found in Baroque opera or, when it appears to be found, whether it represents intentional tonal planning or is fortuitous. The rewritings and transpositions that were taken for granted in Baroque and pre-Classical opera, not to mention the substitutions of new music (often the work of different composers) that were normal at every revival or change of cast, must imply that tonal planning, if used at all in this era, represented a very low priority when it came to the practical business of putting an opera on the stage. Yet scholars have occasionally noted what seem to be tonal schemes of some sort applied in the compositional process, for example in Handel's *Agrippina* (1709), *Rinaldo* (1711) and possibly *Giulio Cesare* (1724) (see Dean and Knapp 1987, pp.127–8, 180 and 500).

In such cases, however, it is not always easy to distinguish between tonal planning for dramatic purposes, as such, or for unifying ones, and tonal usage for other, more practical reasons. Thus if an act or a scene calls for the use of trumpets at the beginning and the end, the choice of the most probable key of D major at those points might seem to suggest its planning as a closed unit. The association of particular characters in the drama with particular kinds of emotion may lead to their music being cast in a group of related keys. It is indeed possible to argue that in one sense tonal planning resides in nothing more than the use of such conventions. In Metastasian *opera seria*, and in opera of the Classical era more generally, the association of particular keys with specific emotions was strong. Arias of rage were commonly in D minor and of anxiety or yearning in G minor, while D major served for bravura or military prowess, E♭ for warm and pathetic feeling (especially the heroine's climactic *aria d'affetto*), A major for amorous sentiment, and G major (sometimes F major) for rural or pastoral feeling. The use of particular instruments to colour an aria immediately affected the choice of key. It is therefore normal for a character drawn with reasonable consistency to acquire *ipso facto* some measure of tonal identity, although composers were generally careful to give singers at least one aria in a contrasted key. Other factors, however, influenced tonal organization. Strong or favourable emotion, or aggression, was normally reflected in recitative by a move towards the sharp or dominant side, while tenderness or unfavourable emotion would dictate a move to the flat or subdominant side (or to the minor); this would inevitably have some effect on the probable or available keys for the ensuing number. Further, the convention that successive arias should generally be in contrasted 'affects', and that keys of more than three accidentals should be used only rarely, also influenced the choice. It is clear that composers in the Classical period took some care about the key relationships between successive arias or scenes, using sharply marked ones (tritonal, semitonal) only for a decisive articulation or some other special effect, steps of a 4th or 5th when moving in the appropriate direction towards the sharp or flat side of the previous tonality, and steps of a 3rd to avoid any strongly directed tonal movement of that kind.

In his recorded notes on his professional career, Salieri described the process of setting a libretto to music (see Heartz 1990, pp.139 and 154–5); his description refers to a comic opera of 1770, but there is no reason to think that the relevant parts of it would not apply equally to a serious one. At an early stage he decided, following the practice of his teacher, Gassmann, 'on the key appropriate to the lyric character of each number'; a little later he planned the key scheme of the first finale, which would be extended and sectional. By the Classical period it had become common, but by no means invariable, for composers to end operas in the key of the overture. That Mozart did so in his seven mature operas has led commentators to suggest that each opera is in some sense 'in' a particular key and that the relationships between other keys used in the opera and this tonic should be seen as serving some dramatic function (Levarie went so far as to suggest that *Figaro* could be seen as a progression I – ♭II – V – I). In considering such factors, however, it is important to realize the constraints on a composer's choice, traditional (in the assignment of particular keys to numbers of a particular character) and practical. The latter, for example, affected the act finales if, as was normal, trumpets were to play: it would be unusual for a key other than C, D or E♭ major to be chosen. One of these would begin or end the opera, and others would serve to end the intermediate finale or finales. Further, the legitimacy of considering a large series of tonal relationships in terms of perceptibility, or supposing that composers so considered them (at any level of creative consciousness), across entire, eventful evenings of music, cannot be taken for granted.

Long, sectional finales normally began and ended in the same key, and it is clear that some degree of tonal planning was involved, although it is doubtful whether this is different in kind from the normal Classical tonal planning which dictated that a symphony or a string quartet should begin and end in the same key. A section of a work could be defined as such by its use of a single tonal space: the same applies, for example, to the *divertissements* or *fêtes* of the French *tragédie en musique*. The special kinds of tonal usage found in Mozart's operas, such as the conscious choice of A minor as a sharp (but not too sharp) contrast with F major to portray Osmin's rage in *Die Entführung aus dem Serail* (1782), or in *Idomeneo* (1781) the tendency to move to G major at references to Electra in the course of orchestral recitative (one of her three arias is in that key), represent a particular use of tonality for dramatic purposes. As opposed to such local devices, the concept of large-scale tonal planning in opera before 1800 needs to be approached with caution and within the broader context of 18th-century tonal usage generally.

2. Since 1800. The richness of Romanticism in music lay in the degree to which, while resisting Classical constraints, it sought to preserve concepts of unity and integration – if only because the lure of the unexpected, the immediate and the fragmentary was so great. As instrumental design developed, and equal temperament came to prevail, it was no longer necessary to emphasize keys with relatively few sharps or flats, and as the formalities of the number opera were more decisively eroded there was less adherence to the convention that particular keys had special associations with particular expressive states. By the time Wagner composed *Parsifal* (1877–82) it was not only possible to begin and end the work in A♭ major but also to use that key during very different phases of the drama, and for very different musical materials – the knights of the Grail at their most spiritual (Acts 1 and 3), the flowermaidens at their most seductive (Act 2).

Because 19th-century composers tended to think thematically, while composing harmonically, and were also loath to theorize about technical specifics, later commentators on their operas have been left with special difficulties (*see* Analysis). There has never been any credible demonstration that a 19th- or 20th-century opera is 'purely musical', with the text simply another aspect of the material for the composer to fit into an absolute musical plan. Yet the relations between structure and symbolism, form and expression, text and music are so complex that the argument that tonal identities and relations are consciously used as ways of integrating musical and textual aspects of the drama usually depends as much if not more on the willingness of readers to be convinced as on the ability of commentators to provide definitive proof. In general, commentators have learnt circumspection, since only rarely does musicological detective work provide conclusive evidence of conscious planning of larger and smaller-scale tonal relations. In the case of Richard Strauss's *Elektra*, for example, Bryan Gilliam has deduced from the sketches that the tonal basis was established before any significant thematic invention took place.

There are few today who would endorse Alfred Lorenz's argument (1924) that the whole of *Tristan und Isolde* coheres around E major – the key which, Lorenz believed, was associated by Wagner with that idea of love which is more fundamental to the work than any other idea. Even if it would be no less improbable to claim that the various tonal assertions and allusions in *Tristan* were totally random or accidental, the more integrated the scheme proposed, with a single 'tonic' to which all other key areas are functionally subordinate, the less plausible it seems. In writing of Weber's *Euryanthe* that it 'manifests a network of tonal relationships in which the keys of individual pieces are determined not only by the logic of musically convincing relationships, but also by a well-developed system of symbolism, according to which keys act as signs for elements of the drama', Tusa (1991) chose his words carefully. Such 'networks' may even be flexible enough to survive last-minute transpositions agreed by the composer at the request of a singer, though the knowledge that Verdi willingly transposed the Act 2 quartet from *Otello* down a semitone from B to B♭ after the work was complete indicates the caution with which arguments about tonal integration and symbolism need to be presented.

Another kind of tonal planning might involve the reservation of a particular key for the climax of an opera, as with the culminating E♭ major of Janáček's *Jenůfa*. More generally, the use of strong tonal contrasts to symbolize dramatic conflicts is a more common (and more audible) procedure than the use of close tonal relationships to give operas a 'symphonic' dimension. In Debussy's *Pelléas et Mélisande*, for example, 'a key-scheme ... was in Debussy's mind from an early stage', and this included 'the sharp-ward procedure to a "goal" key of C sharp, and the use of keys from the opposite side of the circle-of-fifths to represent forces pulling against this forward progression' (Langham Smith 1989). Similar parallels between dramatic tensions and tonal oppositions were often used by Britten, and most explicitly in *Billy Budd*, where B minor and B♭ major are uneasily combined in the Prologue and Epilogue, and the ultimate resolution, apparently in favour of B♭, is undermined by the final vocal phrases, matching the doubts that remain about the validity of Captain Vere's expressions of serenity. It might be expected that the more neo-classical 20th-century operas would seek to avoid far-reaching systems of tonal symbolism. But it has been pointed out that in Stravinsky's *Oedipus rex* there is a clear sense in which 'dramatic form' is defined by tonal symbolism (Walsh 1988).

It would be surprising if tonal relations, as well as functional harmony, were not used as an organizing principle in through-composed opera, rather than just as an unavoidable, structurally insignificant side effect of the composer's musical language. Debates about how extensive, systematic and symbolic such structuring may be – how much in the mind of the composer as well as of the analyst – will rarely be decisively resolved. Yet keys as such provide only the foundation for the harmonic, melodic and colouristic components of the musical material. In the end it is tonalities as supportive of musical ideas which composers use as structuring and symbolic devices. Opera has easily survived the loss of tonality as a structuring principle, but the importance of that principle when opera is tonal is of the first order.

*

BEFORE 1800

H. Abert: Preface to miniature score of W. A. Mozart: *Le nozze di Figaro* (London, n.d.) [Eulenburg edn]

S. Levarie: *Mozart's 'Le nozze di Figaro': a Critical Analysis* (Chicago, 1952)

'Tonartenplan und Motivstruktur in Mozarts Musik', *MJb 1973–4*, 82–144

R. Steblin: *A History of Key Characteristics in the Eighteenth and Early Nineteenth Centuries* (Ann Arbor, 1983)

W. Dean and J. M. Knapp: *Handel's Operas, 1704–1726* (Oxford, 1987)

D. Heartz: *Mozart's Operas* (Berkeley and Los Angeles, 1990)

J. Webster: 'Mozart's Operas and the Myth of Musical Unity', *COJ*, ii (1990), 197–218

SINCE 1800

A. Lorenz: *Das Geheimnis der Form bei Richard Wagner* (Berlin, 1924)

A. Whittall: 'The Music', *Richard Wagner: Parsifal*, ed. L. Beckett (Cambridge, 1981), 61–86

——: 'The Challenge from Within: Janáček's Musico-Dramatic Mastery', *Jenůfa/Katya Kabanova*, ed. N. John (London, 1985), 21–30 [ENO Opera Guide]

J. A. Hepokowski: *Giuseppe Verdi: Otello* (Cambridge, 1987)

S. Walsh: *The Music of Stravinsky* (London, 1988)

C. Abbate and R. Parker: 'Introduction', *Analyzing Opera: Wagner and Verdi* (Berkeley and Los Angeles, 1989), 1–24

R. Langham Smith: 'Tonalities of Darkness and Light', *Claude Debussy: Pelléas et Mélisande*, ed. R. Nichols and R. Langham Smith (Cambridge, 1989), 107–39

A. Whittall: '"Twisted Relations": Method and Meaning in Britten's *Billy Budd*', *COJ*, ii (1990), 145–71

B. Gilliam: *Richard Strauss's Elektra* (Oxford, 1991)

M. C. Tusa: *Euryanthe and Carl Maria von Weber's Dramaturgy of German Opera* (Oxford, 1991)

STANLEY SADIE (1), ARNOLD WHITTALL (2)

Tonarelli, Lorenzo (*b* ?Iesi; *fl* 1747–71). Italian soprano castrato. He sang a female role in a comic opera in Rome in Carnival 1747 but did not begin a sustained career until Carnival 1753 at Bologna as secondo uomo in *opera seria*. From 1753 he was primo uomo at the Mannheim court, singing in operas by Holzbauer, Traetta and Majo, and he also appeared in Rome in Carnival 1759. From 1768 to 1771 he was primo uomo in leading Italian theatres, although at Naples he did not please the audiences and was replaced. DENNIS LIBBY

Tonina, La. *See* PELLIZARI, ANTONIA.

Tonnelier, Le ('The Cooper'). *Opéra comique* in one act by FRANÇOIS-JOSEPH GOSSEC and others to a libretto by NICOLAS-MÉDARD AUDINOT and Antoine-François Quétant; Paris, Comédie-Italienne (Théâtre de l'Hôtel de Bourgogne), 16 March 1765.

Colin (tenor) is in love with Fanchette (soprano), but she hesitates to show her feelings for him because she fears her stepfather Martin (baritone), a cooper, who intends to remove Colin from the village and marry Fanchette himself. In despair, Colin makes his uncle Gervais (baritone) demand back the money Martin owes him. Martin can escape from prison only by consenting to the marriage between Fanchette and Colin.

According to a handwritten note in a copy of the score (in *F-Pn*), this *opéra comique*, variously attributed to Audinot or Gossec, is in fact a pasticcio by Gossec, Alexandre, Philidor, Schobert, J.-C. Trial, Kohaut and Ciapalanti. This work was preceded by another *opéra comique* of the same title (1761), for which Audinot wrote both text and music. Gossec successfully turned a predictable plot into a fast-paced, lively and popular opera. There are a variety of musical forms, including *airs*, *romance*, vaudeville, accompanied recitative, duet, trio and a four-part canon with four different texts; in the duets the principal characters quickly follow each other in short phrases, as in Italian *opera buffa*. The dialogues are interspersed with additional *airs*, possibly using popular tunes. The score was printed by two publishers, in about 1767 and 1770; individual *airs* continued to appear between 1770 and 1785.

MICHAEL FEND

Tooley, Sir **John** (*b* Rochester, 1 June 1924). English administrator. He was educated at Repton and at Magdalene College, Cambridge. From 1952 to 1955 he was secretary of the Guildhall School of Music and Drama. In 1955 he went to Covent Garden as assistant to David Webster, being appointed assistant general administrator in 1960 and succeeding Webster as general administrator in 1970; from 1980 to 1988 he was general director. He played an important role in arranging regular meetings between the directors of the leading European and American opera houses in an attempt to stabilize artists' fees and make possible the exchange of productions. He was largely responsible for establishing 'promenade' opera performances at Covent Garden in an attempt to bring in a new and younger audience. He was knighted in 1979.

*

J. Higgins: 'John Tooley', *About the House*, iii/7 (1970), 5–7 [incl. interview with Tooley]

HAROLD ROSENTHAL/R

Töpfer, Der ('The Potter'). *Komische Oper* in one act by JOHANN ANDRÉ to his own libretto; Hanau, Fürstliches Theater, 22 January 1773.

The potter's wife Marthe (soprano), reckoning on winning a large lottery prize, opposes the projected marriage of her daughter Hannchen (soprano) to the peasant Gürge (tenor); she relents only after the other candidate for the prize, the Jew Amschel (bass), wins the draw.

Der Töpfer, André's first opera, earned wide critical and popular acclaim. Goethe praised the ingredients others also applauded – a simple, effective melodic style and a fully developed but unobtrusive orchestral accompaniment (including in one number a C clarinet). Despite the title, the potter's trade plays no role in the opera; rather, attention centres on his family, their healthy rustic milieu and the foolishness of Marthe's pretensions to wealth and station. It was one of only a few German comic operas to be printed in full score during the 18th century (Offenbach, 1773).

THOMAS BAUMAN

Töpper, Hertha (*b* Graz, 19 April 1924). Austrian mezzo-soprano. She studied at Graz, where she made her début in 1945 as Ulrica and remained until 1952, singing leading mezzo-soprano roles and also Lady Macbeth. At Bayreuth she sang Flosshilde and Siegrune (1951) and the Third Norn (1952), later returning as Brangäne and Fricka (1960). She sang Octavian at the Staatsoper in Munich in 1952 and remained there for 20 years. She sang Clairon at Covent Garden in 1953 when the Munich company gave the British première of *Capriccio*; later she returned as Octavian, also the role of her San Francisco (1960) and Metropolitan (1962) débuts. In Munich she created roles in *Die Harmonie der Welt* (1957) and Yun's *Sim Tjong* (1972). Her repertory included, in addition to the Verdi, Wagner and Strauss mezzo roles, Judith (*Duke Bluebeard's Castle*), Jocasta (*Oedipus rex*) and the Secretary (*The Consul*). She brought a warm, well-schooled voice and an attractive stage presence to all her roles.

HAROLD ROSENTHAL/R

Toradze, David Alexandrovich (*b* Tbilisi, 14 April 1922; *d* Tbilisi, 7 Nov 1983). Georgian composer. He studied at the Tbilisi Conservatory, and at the Moscow Conservatory with Glier. From 1948 to 1951 he did postgraduate work at the Tbilisi Conservatory, where he taught from 1952 and became professor in 1973. From 1962 to 1968 he was first deputy chairman of the Georgian Composers' Union, and he received several awards and honours.

Toradze displayed an active interest in the theatre from the time of his first opera *Suramis tsikhe* ('The Surami Fortress', 1942), which tells of the people's struggle for freedom and of patriotic self-sacrifice. Patriotism and heroic-romantic ideas remained major concerns in his next opera, *Mtebis dzakhili* ('The Call of the Mountains', 1947), and in subsequent works including the ballet *Gorda* (1949), which earned Toradze widespread recognition. His opera *Chrdiloetis patardzali* ('Bride of the North', 1958) relates the tragic story of the love of the poet Griboyedov for the young Princess Nina which unfolds against a broad panorama of Russian and Georgian life in the first half of the 19th century.

Suramis tsikhe [The Surami Fortress], 1942, unperf.

Mtebis dzakhili [The Call of the Mountains] (I. Noneshvili), Tbilisi, 20 Nov 1947

Natel (musical comedy, D. Taktakishvili), Tbilisi, 10 Jan 1948

Shurismadziyebelni [The Avengers] (musical comedy, P. Gruzinsky and G. Svani), Tbilisi, 20 Dec 1952

Chrdiloetis patardzali [Bride of the North] (3, Noneshvili), Tbilisi, 1958 (1964)

*

O. Egadze: '10 tseli – 200 spektakli' [10 Years – 200 Shows], *Sabchota khelovneba* (1959), no.11, p.22

YEVGENY MACHAVARIANI

Tordinona. First Venetian-style theatre established in Rome, with the patronage of Queen Christina and Maria Mancini Colonna, opened in 1671. *See* ROME, §§1(iii), 2 and 3(i).

Torelli, Giacomo [Jacopo] (*b* ?Fano, 1 Sept 1608; *d* Fano, 17 June 1678). Italian stage designer, engineer and architect. He was probably trained as an architect and engineer, but he may also have been a pupil of the stage designers Niccolò Sabbatini and Francesco Guitti. He was working as an engineer in the Venice Arsenal around 1640, when he designed the Teatro Novissimo, Venice's fourth public opera house, built in 1641. He invented a new system of stage machinery which for the first time enabled the whole set to be changed in one operation: the wings were supported on undercarriages running on rails beneath the stage, and were moved by turning a central roller to which the undercarriages were attached by ropes. In the next few years Torelli designed the sets for all the operas staged in the Teatro Novissimo, and occasionally worked for the Teatro di SS Giovanni e Paolo as well. Summoned to Paris in 1645, he installed new stage machinery in the theatres of the Hôtel du Petit Bourbon (1645) and the Palais Royal (1647) and designed sets for the Italian opera troupe which enjoyed Mazarin's protection, for the spectacular staging of Corneille's *Andromède* (1650) and for numerous *ballets de cour*. Falling into disfavour after Mazarin's death, he returned to Fano in 1661, where he designed the Teatro della Fortuna (1677), on a plan much discussed in 17th- and 18th-century treatises on theatre architecture.

Design by Giacomo Torelli for the final scene (a chamber of the royal palace) of Sacrati's 'Bellerofonte' performed at the Teatro Novissimo, Venice, in 1642

The stage techniques pioneered by Torelli are recorded in some detail in the librettos of the Teatro Novissimo. The ability to change the entire setting in a single operation, tested for the first time in Sacrati's *La finta pazza* (1641), considerably enhanced the pace of events on the stage and had a lasting influence on the dramatic construction of operas in the second half of the 17th century.

Torelli's sets created a concrete, clearly defined area which, whatever its symbolic significance, attempted to represent a milieu with a particular character. Such a conception was appropriate to the small ensemble scenes of Venetian opera and met the increasing preference for historical subjects and the realistic tendencies fostered by the growing influence of middle-class audiences. The rhythmic articulation of the stage by the transverse and longitudinal lines of the sets, an approach shared by other Venetian designers such as Giovanni Burnacini, focussed attention on the acting zone and enhanced the development of the design of interiors. An almost completely enclosed room appeared for the first time in a production of Sacrati's *Bellerofonte* (1642; see illustration), the starting-point of the architectural visions of operatic production in the late Baroque period.

See also STAGE DESIGN, §3(i, ii). For further illustration *see* DANCE, fig.1; *FINTA PAZZA, LA*; STAGE DESIGN, fig. 2; and VENICE, fig.7.

*

Il cannocchiale per La finta pazza drama dello Strozzi (Venice, 1641)

Il Bellero fonte drama musicale del Sigr Vincenzo Nolfi (Venice, 1642) [with 10 engravings]; extract trans. in S. T. Worsthorne: *Venetian Opera in the Seventeenth Century* (Oxford, 1954)

M. Bisaccioni: *Apparati scenici per lo Teatro novissimo* (Venice, 1644) [with 12 engravings from Sacrati's *Venere gelosa*]

G. C. Bianchi: *Feste theatrali per La finta pazza drama* (Paris, 1645) [with 5 engravings]

Andromede tragedie (Rouen, 1651) [with 6 engravings]

A. Amalteo: *Scene e machine preparate alle Nozze di Teti balletto reale* (Paris, 1654) [with 11 engravings]

Descrizione de gli apparati, et intramezzi nel dramma Il trionfo della Continenza (Fano, 1677)

S. Tomani-Armani: *Del teatro antico della Fortuna in Fano* (Sanseverino, 1867)

H. Prunières: *L'opéra italien en France avant Lulli* (Paris, 1913), 68ff

A. Tessier: 'Giacomo Torelli a Parigi e la messa in scena delle "Nozze di Peleo e Teti" di Carlo Caproli', *RaM*, i (1928), 573–90

A. Mabellini: 'L'antico Teatro della Fortuna in Fano: il suo architetto Giacomo Torelli e Ferdinando Galli Bibiena', *Studia picena*, vii (1931), 161–74

F. Torrefranca: 'Il "grande stregone" Giacomo Torelli e la scenografia del seicento', *Scenario*, iii (1934), 473–9

A. G. Bragaglia: *Nicola Sabbatini e Giacomo Torelli: scenotecnici marchigiani* (Pesaro, 1952), 95–150

P. Bjurström: *Giacomo Torelli and Baroque Stage Design* (Stockholm, 1961, 2/1962)

M.-F. Christout: *Le ballet de cour de Louis XIV: 1643–1672* (Paris, 1967), 40ff, 170ff, 227ff

C. Molinari: *Le nozze degli dei: un saggio sul grande spettacolo italiano nel seicento* (Rome, 1968), 137ff, 163ff

F. Mancini, M. T. Muraro and E. Povoledo: *Illusione e pratica teatrale: proposte per una lettura dello spazio scenico dagli intermedi fiorentini all'opera comica veneziana* (Vicenza, 1975)

F. Battistelli: 'Giacomo Torelli: note biografiche e bibliografiche', *Fano: studi dedicati a Giacomo Torelli nel III centenario della morte* (Fano, 1978), 7–26

H. Leclerc: *Venise et l'avénement de l'opéra public à l'âge baroque* (Paris, 1987)

MANFRED BOETZKES

Torino (It.). TURIN.

Tormis, Velio (*b* Kuusalu, nr Tallinn, 7 Aug 1930). Estonian composer. He studied at the Tallinn Music Institute (1943–51), the Tallinn Conservatory (1951), and with Shebalin at the Moscow Conservatory (1951–6). He then taught at the Tallinn Music Institute (1956–60) and acted as a consultant to the Estonian Composers' Union (1956–69 and from 1972). In 1967 he received a first-class diploma at the All-Union Musical Stage Works Competition for his chamber opera *Luigelend* ('Swan Flight', E. Vatemaa, after O. Tooming), which was first performed at the Vanemuine Theatre, Tartu, on 20 April 1966. The opera has three singing characters and a female offstage choir, which personifies the voice of Nature and is treated as an instrument of the orchestra. The laconic style of the libretto is reflected in the controlled combination of orchestral colour and in the small number of leitmotifs, which are subject to intensive elaboration. The vocal sections are basically recitative. MARINA NEST'YEVA

Torneo (It.). *See* OPERA-TORNEO.

Torneo notturno ('Nocturnal Tourney'). *Sette notturni* in one act by GIAN FRANCESCO MALIPIERO to his own libretto, using old Italian texts by Angelo Poliziano and others; Munich, Nationaltheater, 15 May 1931.

Malipiero claimed that this perplexing yet singularly haunting work, written in 1929, embodied (for him) 'the quintessence of all I ever hoped to achieve, from *Sette canzoni* onwards, in "my" theatre'. His use of dream-like symbolism – which in his previous operas *Filomela e l'Infatuato* (written 1925) and *Merlino mastro d'organi* (1926–7) had sometimes seemed merely confused or even unintentionally comic – here achieved a strange power. Massimo Bontempelli, one of the composer's most eloquent advocates, aptly compared *Torneo notturno* to 'a lugubrious gyration of anguished faces within the walls of a bleak city'.

Like *Sette canzoni* before it, *Torneo notturno* is constructed as a series of seven dramatic episodes, linked by extensive orchestral interludes and making some use of old Italian texts. Unlike the earlier work, however, it has at least the rudiments of a unifying plot. The same pair of symbolic characters, described simply as Lo Spensierato and Il Disperato (baritone and tenor), recur throughout, seemingly representing two irreconcilable facets of the human spirit. They confront each other in a succession of situations: outside a lady's window; in a forest; in 'la taverna del buon tempo'; in a deserted room; in 'il castello della noia'; and finally in prison, where Il Disperato kills Lo Spensierato and seems to regain his freedom. But his triumph is illusory. The callboy (sic) comes forward and tells the audience, in a spoken interlude: 'It is not finished! ... Perhaps you believe that revenge and regained liberty have given peace to Il Disperato, but instead he has returned to his endless wanderings'; then, against quiet drums: 'Do you hear the rhythm of a funeral procession? It is Life passing, waving the banner of Death. Listen.' There follows a long, sombre orchestral epilogue.

The exact significance of this 'lugubrious gyration' is hard to define conceptually. Repeatedly, it is true, the two principal characters are in conflict over a lady, the individual and circumstances varying from episode to episode: these ladies may seem to represent some ideal that ultimately eludes them both, although the brutal, unscrupulous Spensierato has his share of superficial successes. In the last analysis, however, Piero Santi was probably right in calling the work 'a phantom drama, whose meaning is defined exclusively by the music'; if it were spoken, he continues, 'the action would be disconnected and senseless. Because of the musical discourse, however, each episode acquires an exact meaning ... while the symbolic personages, otherwise inexplicable, are precisely defined.'

Be that as it may, it is indeed mainly through the music that the opera achieves its extraordinary effectiveness. While it is not Malipiero's most perfect work (the free interplay of musical shapes leads to occasional hiatuses and arbitrary juxtapositions), very few of his other scores have quite so potent an expressive aura. The style is sometimes darkly neo-Monteverdian (since 1926 Malipiero had been working on his complete edition of Monteverdi's music); but there are also many flashes of intensely poignant imagery which, despite the obvious differences, invite comparison with Janáček. Most memorable of all is the insidious, obsessional main melody which runs through the score like a curse, recurring – at least in part, and with many variations of detail – in all seven episodes: the *Canzone del tempo*, which includes words by Poliziano, one of Malipiero's favourite poets. This song is the supreme expression of one of the composer's most fundamental preoccupations: Time the destroyer, constantly opposing our attempts to grasp hold of life and beauty. Usually (though not always) it is sung by Lo Spensierato, and Il Disperato takes it over after the killing.

Torneo notturno presents a major challenge to directors: not only must they make something visually convincing from the enigmatic action, but the substantial stretches of purely orchestral music necessarily throw them back on their own resources. This is particularly the case with the disconcertingly long orchestral epilogue; yet Sylvano Bussotti's Venice production of 1976 has shown how strikingly that problem can be solved. Perhaps, despite the relatively numerous Italian stage productions, the most satisfactory medium for this extraordinary opera is the radio: significantly, there have been more different RAI performances of *Torneo notturno* than of any other Malipiero theatre work. JOHN C. G. WATERHOUSE

Toronto. Canadian city, capital of Ontario. The company from Rochester, New York, that introduced opera to Toronto in 1825 had to perform in Mr Frank's Assembly Rooms, as there was no theatre; the works given were C. E. Horn's *The Devil's Bridge*, Samuel Arnold's *The Mountaineers* and Storace's *No Song, No Supper*. Bishop's *The Miller and his Men* was produced in 1843; ten years later *Norma* was staged at the Royal Lyceum Theatre by the Artists' Italian Opera with Rosa de Vries in the title role, conducted by Arditi. From 1867 the Holman English Opera Troupe presented several seasons at the Royal Lyceum, with a repertory including *Il trovatore*, *La sonnambula* and *Der Freischütz*; in 1874 the theatre burnt down and the Grand Opera House was built. During the 1880s Emma Abbott's opera company visited Toronto; in 1883 Emma Albani made her first operatic appearance in Canada in *Lucia di Lammermoor* with Her Majesty's Italian Opera, which also performed *Il trovatore*. In the 1890–91 season *Lohengrin*, *Rigoletto*, *Carmen*, *Les Huguenots* and some 20 operettas were staged. In 1892 a company from the Metropolitan Opera accompanied Patti in an abridged version of *Semiramide*; in 1899 the Metropolitan presented six operas at the Grand Opera House.

The Henry Savage Grand Opera Company gave the Canadian première of *Parsifal* in Toronto in 1905; the Montreal Opera Company first visited Toronto in 1911; and the Boston Grand Opera Company made four visits (1915–17), bringing *La bohème* and *Faust* with Maggie Teyte, as well as Montemezzi's *L'amore dei tre re*. Between the two world wars there were many visits from Fortune Gallo's San Carlo Opera Company as well as the Metropolitan Opera. Other companies heard there included Antonio Scotti's troupe (1921), while the Russian Grand Opera Company (1922–3) presented

Boris Godunov, *Yevgeny Onegin*, *The Snow Maiden* and *The Tsar's Bride*. Local groups in this period included the Toronto Conservatory Opera Company (1928–30), which gave *Hänsel und Gretel*, *Dido and Aeneas* and *Hugh the Drover*; and the Opera Guild of Toronto, together with the Canadian Grand Opera Association (1936–9), which put on *Faust*, *Cavalleria rusticana*, *Pagliacci*, *Aida*, *Tosca*, *Rigoletto*, *Tannhäuser* and *Lohengrin*.

The founding in 1946 of the Royal Conservatory Opera School (later the Opera Division) was of major significance for operatic life in Toronto. The first production, *The Bartered Bride* (1947), was followed by the world première of Pannell's *Aria da capo* (1963), the English-language première of Searle's *Hamlet* (1969), the stage première of Willan's *Deirdre* (1965) and the Canadian premières of Orff's *Die Kluge*, Holst's *The Wandering Scholar*, *Il turco in Italia*, Bennett's *The Mines of Sulphur*, and *Kát'a Kabanová*. There were also productions of *Angélique*, *Riders to the Sea*, *Sir John in Love*, Moore's *Gallantry*, *Dialogues des Carmélites*, *Les mamelles de Tirésias*, *L'heure espagnole*, *Iolanthe* and in 1989 Massenet's *Le portrait de Manon*.

The Opera school generated the roots of the Canadian Opera Company (COC). The school presented a festival in 1950, giving *Don Giovanni*, *Rigoletto* and *La bohème*. In the same year the festival's organizers formed the Opera Festival Association of Toronto, which took over responsibility for the financial and administrative planning of the annual festival. In 1954 the association began to mount its own productions under the name Opera Festival Company of Toronto, employing professional singers but including students in its productions; official links with the school were gradually severed. The company began using the name 'Canadian Opera Company' in 1958 (Canadian Opera Association is its legal name). It performs five or six operas each season, mainly at the O'Keefe Centre (3200 seats); the Elgin Theatre (1500 seats) is used for smaller-scale productions. From the beginning the repertory was more adventurous than those of other Canadian opera companies; during its first 15 years it gave the world premières of Somers's *Louis Riel* and Raymond Pannell's *The Luck of Ginger Coffey* (both 1967) and Charles M. Wilson's *Heloise and Abelard* (1973), and the Canadian premières of *The Maid of Orléans* and *Lulu*, as well as productions of *Salome*, *Elektra*, *Die Walküre*, *Siegfried*, *Götterdämmerung*, *Don Carlos*, *Boris Godunov* and *Peter Grimes*. It was also among the companies that performed at Expo 1967 in Montreal. Hermann Geiger-Torel, a co-founder of the COC, was succeeded as general director in 1976 by Lotfi Mansouri, whose successor in 1989 was Bryan Dickie.

Other companies active in Toronto include the Ukrainian Opera Society, which presented Anatol' Vakhnyanin's *Kupalo* in 1979 and Gulak-Artemovsky's *Zaporozhets za Dunayem* ('A Cossack Beyond the Danube') in 1981; and the Toronto Cosmopolitan Opera Association, which performed *Falstaff*, *Don Pasquale* and *Tosca* the same year. The repertory of the COC since 1976 has included *Turandot*, Thomas' *Hamlet*, *Anna Bolena*, *Lady Macbeth of the Mtsensk District*, *The Queen of Spades*, *Andrea Chénier*, *Wozzeck*, *Der Rosenkavalier*, *Otello*, *Simon Boccanegra*, *Falstaff*, *Jenůfa*, *The Makropulos Affair* and *Tristan und Isolde*. Its touring company has visited virtually every town in Canada, while the main company also tours to larger cities. The COC Ensemble, a group of young Canadian singers founded in 1980, has staged *Les contes d'Hoffmann*, *Il ritorno d'Ulisse in patria* and other operas. The COC gave the premières of John Oliver's *Guacamayo's Old Song and Dance* (1991) at the Imperial Opera Theatre and Somers's *Mario the Magician* (1992) at the Elgin Theatre.

ELIZABETH FORBES

Torquato Tasso. *Melodramma semiserio* in three acts by GAETANO DONIZETTI to a libretto by JACOPO FERRETTI after Giovanni Rosini's *Torquato Tasso*, and to a lesser degree CARLO GOLDONI's *Tasso*, JOHANN WOLFGANG VON GOETHE's *Tasso* and BYRON's *The Lament of Tasso*; Rome, Teatro Valle, 9 September 1833.

Donizetti was drawn to the subject because of Tasso's connections with his native Bergamo. Unfortunately, *Tasso* is compromised by the *semiseria* genre, here involving an odd deployment of vocal types: tenor rival, *buffo* villain and baritone hero. Tasso's moving death scene, written for Giorgio Ronconi and a favourite with baritones of the Battistini ilk, survived more hardily than the rest of the opera. Recent revivals have revealed Donizetti's effective treatment of the figures of Tasso and Eleonora d'Este, but the viability of this work has yet to be established.

The plot deals with Tasso (baritone) at the Ferrarese court of Alfonso d'Este. He loves his patron's sister Eleonora (soprano), but when his passion is revealed the Duke (bass) declares the poet mad and orders him to be confined. After seven years Tasso learns that he is to be crowned poet laureate, but this vindication means little because Eleonora has died and cannot share his glory.

Ferretti's libretto contains a number of quotations from Tasso's texts as well as some allusions to them. Eleonora's expressive *sortita*, 'Io l'udia nei suoi bei carmi', and her duet with the poet that follows, 'Colei Sofronia', are notable passages. The finest music in the score, however, comes in the last act with Tasso's Larghetto, 'Perché dell'aure in sen', leading into a touching dialogue with chorus; this culminates in a mournful cantabile to form the lyric section of the *tempo di mezzo*, and is followed by an elegiac cabaletta in C major. As in *Anna Bolena*, Donizetti here expanded the structure of the aria-finale to fill out an entire scene.

WILLIAM ASHBROOK

Torre del Lago. Hamlet near Viareggio, on the shore of Lake Massaciuccoli in Tuscany, central Italy. Puccini had a villa and composed most of his operas there; it is now a Puccini museum. In his honour, operas were performed there in 1930 (*La bohème*, conducted by Mascagni), 1931 (*La bohème* and *Butterfly*) and 1949 (*La fanciulla del West*, performed by the Rome Opera). Since 1952 an opera festival has been staged in July and August, in a purpose-built, open-air structure by the lake seating 3500. The works performed are almost exclusively by Puccini; singers who have taken part include Maria Chiara, Fedora Barbieri and Giuseppe Taddei.

ARRIGO QUATTROCCHI

Torregrosa, Tomás López [López Torregrosa, Tomás] (*b* Alicante, 24 Sept 1868; *d* Madrid, 23 June 1913). Spanish composer. He studied first in his native town and then at the Madrid Conservatory. Thanks to the influence of Chapí, he then became musical director at the Teatro Apolo at the age of 19. He thereafter became a prolific composer of zarzuelas, generally styled *sainete* *lírico*, indicating an example of the lighter one-act *genero chico*. He is credited with over 100 such works, many in collaboration with the younger Valverde. His fluent, lively music is exemplified by his two most successful individual pieces, *El santo de la Isidra* and *La fiesta de San Antón* (both 1898).

unless otherwise stated, zarzuelas, in one act, first performed in Madrid

¡Victoria! (C. Arniches), Tívoli, 19 Aug 1891; Los puritanos (pasillo cómico-lírico, Arniches and C. Lucio), Eslava, 31 March 1894, collab. Valverde *hijo*; Las amapolas (Arniches and Lucio), Apolo, 21 June 1894; Tabardillo (Arniches), Apolo, 14 March 1895; El príncipe heredero (Arniches), Romea, 9 Jan 1896; El jefe del movimiento (Arniches), Maravillas, 31 July 1896; Los bandidos (Arniches), Zarzuela, 24 Dec 1896; La banda de trompetas (Arniches and Lucio), 25 Dec 1896; Arco Iris (Arniches), Eslava, 14 May 1897

La madre abondesa, Cordoba, July 1897, collab. A. Brull; El primer reserva (E. Sánchez Pástor), 14 Oct 1897, collab. Valverde *hijo*; Los camarones (Arniches and Lucio), Zarzuela, 4 Dec 1897, collab. Valverde *hijo*; Los cocineros (E. García Alvarez and A. Paso), Eslava, 1897, collab. Valverde *hijo*; El pobre diablo (apropósito-revista, Lucio), Eldorado, 1897, collab. Valverde *hijo*; El santo de la Isidra (Arniches), Apolo, 19 Feb 1898; Las niñas de la Villagarda (J. Jackson Veyán), March 1898, collab. Valverde *hijo*

Las castañeras picadas (C. Fernández Shaw), Apolo, 28 May 1898, collab. Valverde *hijo*; La fiesta de San Antón (Arniches), Apolo, 24 Nov 1898; Los mineros (S. Delgado), Barcelona, 11 March 1899; El trabuco [Pepet, Nelet y Tonet] (E. Sánchez Pástor), Apolo, 1 April 1899, collab. Valverde *hijo*; Instantáneas (Arniches and López Silva), Eldorado, 28 June 1899, collab. Valverde *hijo*; Las flamencos (Sánchez Pástor), Eldorado, 13 July 1899, collab. Valverde *hijo*; El último chulo (sainete lírico, Arniches and Lucio), Eslava, 7 Nov 1899, collab. Valverde *hijo*

Ligerita de cascos (Delgado), Romea, 24 April 1900; Los niños llorones (Arniches, Paso and García Alvarez), 4 July 1901, collab. Barrera and Valverde *hijo*; El debut de la Ramirez (G. Merino), 11 Nov 1901, collab. Valverde *hijo*; Plantas y flores (Lucio), Nov 1901, collab. Valverde *hijo*; Chispita [El barrio de Maravillas] (Jackson Veyán and Rodriguez), 14 Dec 1901, collab. Valverde *hijo*; La muerte de Agripina (Arniches), Zarzuela, 5 April 1902; San Juan de Luz (Arniches), Eldorado, 9 July 1902; Los granujas (Arniches), Cómico, 8 Nov 1902

El cuñao de Rosa (apropósito, Merino and Candela), Apolo, Feb 1903; El terrible Pérez (humorada trágico-cómico-lírico, Arniches and García Alvarez), Apolo, 1 May 1903, collab. Valverde *hijo*; Colorín, colorao (Arniches), Eldorado, 11 July 1903; Los chicos de la escuela (Arniches), Moderno, 22 Dec 1903; La perla negra (Trayzon), Moderno, 9 Feb 1904; El ciego de Buenavista (Dominguez and Toral), 1 July 1904; El pobre Valbuena (humorada-lírica, Arniches and García Alvarez), Apolo, 1 July 1904, collab. Valverde *hijo*; La guarda barrera, Jan 1905

El moscón, Apolo, April 1906, collab. Valverde *hijo*; La pena negra (Arniches), Gran, 30 Oct 1906; Los falsos dioses, Cómico, Oct 1907; La brocha gorda (revista, J. Capella and González Pastor), Gran, 1907, collab. R. G. Calleja; El palacio de cristal (J. Jackson Veyán and Capella), 1907; Los niños de Tetuán (A. Ramos Martín), Apolo, April 1908, collab. Calleja; El hurón y Felipe II (Arniches), Cómico, 9 May 1908; El brasero, Gran, Jan 1909; La moza de mulas (drame lyrique, 2), Cómico, May 1910; Los perros de presa, Cómico, Oct 1910; La misa del gatto, Gran, Feb 1913; La última película (revista), Sept 1913, collab. Valverde *hijo*

Undated: Adivina quien te dió; La divisa; El gran capitán; La maja desnuda

*

StiegerO

'López Torregrosa, Tomás', *Enciclopedia universal ilustrada europea-americana* (Barcelona, 1907–30)

A. Fernández-Cid: *Cien años de teatro musical en España (1875–1975)* (Madrid, 1975)

J. Arnau and C. M. Gómez: *Historia de la zarzuela* (Madrid, 1979)

ANDREW LAMB

Torrejón y Velasco, Tomás de (*b* ?Villarrobledo, nr Albacete, bap. 23 Dec 1644; *d* Lima, 23 April 1728). Spanish composer. The son of Miguel de Torrejón, huntsman to King Philip IV, he began his career in about 1658 as a page in the household of the Count of Lemos. As a gentleman of the chamber, he travelled to Peru in 1667 when Lemos was appointed 19th Viceroy of Peru. Having held administrative civil and military positions, he became *maestro de capilla* of Lima Cathedral in 1676, even though he was not a cleric. Through his pupils and the wide diffusion of his vernacular and Latin sacred pieces, he became the most celebrated and influential composer of his age in the Spanish New World.

The opera *La púrpura de la rosa* (1, P. Calderón de la Barca; Lima, Viceregal Palace, 19 October 1701; now held in the Lima National Library; ed. in Stevenson 1976, and in Cardona, Cruickshank and Cunningham 1990) is the sole surviving secular work by Torrejón, although contemporary writers indicate that he composed for other theatrical productions as well. Commissioned by the Count of Monclova (viceroy 1689–1705) to honour King Philip V's 18th birthday and the first year of Bourbon rule in Spain, it was the earliest opera composed and performed in the New World. The libretto was first set by the Spanish court composer Juan Hidalgo and performed in Madrid (probably in 1660) to celebrate the Peace of the Pyrenees. The choice of libretto for the Lima celebrations in 1701 was a natural one given the popularity of Calderón's works in the New World and the association between the libretto and a Spanish-French alliance. Musical trends and conventions in Madrid were closely followed in Lima, such that sections of Torrejón's opera include quotations from Spanish theatrical music. Formally and stylistically, this setting has much in common with Hidalgo's surviving opera *Celos aun del aire matan*, although a Peruvian writer compared Torrejón not to Hidalgo (whose music he may have heard before he left Madrid) but to Sebastián Durón, a more direct contemporary. (For a note on Torrejón y Velasco's setting *see* Hidalgo's LA PÚRPURA DE LA ROSA.)

*

R. Stevenson: 'Opera Beginnings in the New World', *MQ*, xlv (1959), 8–25

——: 'The First New-World Opera', *Americas*, xvi (1964), 33–5

——: *Renaissance and Baroque Musical Sources in the Americas* (Washington DC, 1970)

S. Claro: 'La música secular de Tomás de Torrejón y Velasco (1644–1728)', *Revista musical chilena*, no.117 (1972), 3–23

R. Stevenson, ed.: *Tomás de Torrejón y Velasco: La púrpura de la rosa* (Lima, 1976) [incl. commentary]

J. C. Estenssoro: *Música y sociedad coloniales, Lima 1680–1830* (Lima, 1989)

A. Cardona, D. Cruickshank and M. Cunningham, eds.: *Pedro Calderón de la Barca and Tomás de Torrejón y Velasco: La púrpura de la rosa* (Kassel, 1990)

LOUISE K. STEIN

Torresella, Fanny (*b* Tbilisi, 1856; *d* Rome, 2 May 1914). Italian soprano. She studied with her father, who was conductor at the Tbilisi Opera House and later chorus master at Trieste, where she made her début in 1876 as Fenena in *Nabucco*. Though she sang at La Scala, most of her career was spent as a touring artist, part of it with Edoardo Sonzogno's company which specialized in the new *verismo* school. She was Musetta in the first Buenos Aires performance of *La bohème*, and in 1901 she sang in the Turin première of Mascagni's *Le maschere*, one of six simultaneous productions. A favourite soprano at the S Carlo, Naples, she appeared there from 1886 to 1904, often in lyric roles, and sometimes in relatively unfamiliar operas (Massenet's *Cendrillon*, Puccini's *Le villi* and Leoncavallo's *I Medici*). Her repertory also included coloratura parts such as Lucia, Marguerite de Valois in *Les Huguenots* and Gilda in *Rigoletto*, which she sang at her single appearance in London at Drury Lane in 1887. Her few and rare recordings, made in 1900, display her fluent technique and fresh, clear tone, without perhaps quite explaining Tullio Serafin's remark that he had heard three great sopranos in his life: Maria Callas, Rosa Ponselle and Fanny Torresella. J. B. STEANE

Torri [Torri Cecchi], **Anna Maria** ['La Beccarina'] (*b* Bologna; *fl* 1684–1708). Italian soprano. She is first mentioned in 1684 in the role of Flora in Alessandro Melani's *La calma fra le tempeste, overo Il prencipe Roberto fra le sciagure felice* in Reggio Emilia. On 20 May 1688 she was granted the designation 'virtuosa' and an annual salary by Duke Ferdinando Carlo Gonzaga of Mantua. With that title she sang in Genoa, Piacenza, Venice and, in 1690, in Parma, where she contributed to the festivities for the wedding of Odoardo Farnese by taking part in Bernardo Sabadini's *Il favore degli dei*. She entered the service of the ducal court of Parma on 1 May 1691, remaining there until 15 February 1695. Between 1701 and 1708 she sang in Florence, where she performed in 11 operas, including Handel's *Vincer se stesso è la maggior vittoria* (or *Rodrigo*); in 1704 she sang in Venice in *Da la virtute ha la bellezza onore* (probably by C. F. Pollarolo). She was last mentioned in Florence, where she sang the title role in *La Statira* (possibly by Francesco Gasparini) in 1708. She may have been the sister of the composer Pietro Torri (*c*1650–1737).

*

P. Besutti: *La corte musicale di Ferdinando Carlo Gonzaga ultimo duca di Mantova: musici, cantanti e teatro d'opera tra il 1665 e il 1707* (Mantua, 1989) PAOLA BESUTTI, COLIN TIMMS

Torri, Pietro (*b* Peschiera, Lake Garda, *c*1650; *d* Munich, 6 July 1737). Italian composer. He is first mentioned as organist and *maestro di cappella* at the court of the Margrave of Bayreuth in 1684 (though Junker contended that he joined the court as organist in 1667 and succeeded J. P. Krieger as Kapellmeister in 1672). He left the court in 1684 and may have spent the next five years travelling in Italy. In 1689 he joined the court of Maximilian II Emanuel, Elector of Bavaria, in Munich as organist, and the next year his first stage work, the serenata *Gli oracoli di Pallade e di Nemesi*, was performed to celebrate a visit by Emperor Leopold I. Thereafter he regularly prepared operas and serenatas for the court theatre.

Torri followed Maximilian to Brussels in 1692 and was guest Kapellmeister at Hanover in 1696. He then returned to Munich and in 1701 was named director of chamber music. As a result of the War of the Spanish Succession Maximilian was forced to return to Brussels in exile, together with part of his chapel, including Torri. No operas were produced because of the war, and Torri took the additional position of *maître de chapelle* at the church of Ste Gudule; some of his sacred works and the oratorio *La vanità del mondo* date from this time. In 1715 Maximilian finally returned to Munich with his court, and Torri, with the title of Hofkapell-Direktor and a salary of 2000 gulden, entered his most creative period, producing operas almost at the rate of one a year until his death. Although the scale of his duties was somewhat reduced after 1726 by Maximilian II Emanuel's successor Karl Albrecht, Torri's salary was increased on the death of Bernabei in 1732, and he was finally named Hofkapellmeister.

The style of Torri's operas and instrumental music is founded in the late Venetian school but shows the strong influence of Alessandro Scarlatti. Torri, however, lacked Scarlatti's skill of characterization and (according to Kaul) his coloratura arias lack dramatic accent, and his lyric arias are merely graceful; his ensembles, for the most part, fail to delineate the different emotions of the characters involved. During Torri's first stay in Brussels the operas of Lully were performed with great success under the direction of Fiocco, and their influence can be seen in Torri's late operas, which use ballet, accompanied recitative, declamation, instrumentation and chorus in the French manner.

Le peripezze della Fortuna (6), ?Brussels, ? Jan 1695, *D-Mbs* [for wedding of Maximilian II Emanuel and Therese Kunigunde]
Untitled torneo, Munich, Schloss Leuchtenberg, 30 Jan 1702, *Mbs* (pts)
Enone (pastorale), Brussels, ? 12 Oct 1705, *Mbs* (frag.)
Le réciproque (divertissement), Valenciennes, 1714, *Mbs*
L'innocenza difesa dai numi [Ismene] (dramma, 6), Munich, Hof, Aug or Oct 1715, *Mbs**
Astianatte (A. Salvi), Munich, Hof, 12 Oct 1716, *Mbs*; as Andromacca, Munich, Hof, wint. 1717, *Mbs*
La Merope (A. Zeno), Munich, Hof, 12 Oct 1719, *Mbs*, rev. 24 Jan 1723
Eumene (dramma per musica, Zeno), Munich, Hof, 14 July 1720, *Mbs* (pts)
Lucio Vero (dramma per musica, Zeno), Munich, Hof, 12 Oct 1720; rev. version, Munich, Hof, 3 Jan 1723; *Mbs* (pts)
L'amor d'amico vince ogni altro amore [Pirro e Demetrio] (3), Munich, Hof, 12 Oct 1721, *Mbs*
Adelaide (dramma per musica, Salvi), Munich, Hof, 18 Oct 1722, *Mbs* (pts) [for wedding of the Prince-Elector Karl Albrecht and Maria Amalia]
Griselda (dramma per musica, Zeno), Munich, Hof, 12 Oct 1723, *Mbs*
Amadis aus Griechenland (trans. of P. di Perozzi: *Amadis in Grecia*), Munich, Hof, Oct 1724, *Mbs*
Venceslao (dramma per musica, Zeno), Munich, Hof, 12 Oct 1725, *Mbs* (score, pts)
L'Epaminonda (dramma per musica, D. Lalli), Munich, 1727, *Mbs* (score, pts)
Nicomede (dramma per musica, Lalli), Munich, 1728, *Mbs**, *Mbs* (pts)
Edippo (tragedia per musica, Lalli), Munich, 1729, *Mbs* (pts)
L'Ippolito (tragedia per musica, Lalli), Munich, 1731, *Mbs* (pts)
Ciro (dramma per musica, L. de Villati), Munich, 1733, *Mbs* (pts)
Catone in Utica (tragedia per musica, P. Metastasio), Munich, 1736, *Mbs**, *Mbs* (pts)

Doubtful: L'ambizione fulminata (? D. L. Orlandi), Munich, 1691 [cited in Junker]; Briseide (dramma per musica, 3, F. Palmieri), Hanover, carn. 1696, *A-Wn*, *D-B*, *Bds*, *Mbs*, *GB-Lbl* [previously attrib. Steffani; partly ed. in DTB, xxi, Jg. xxi/2 (1911); 3 arias ed. in SCMA, xi (1951)]

*

EitnerQ; *FétisB*; *GerberNL*; *HawkinsH*; *MGG* (O. Kaul)
F. M. Rudhart: *Geschichte der Oper am Hofe zu München* (Freising, 1865)
H. Junker: Preface to *P. Torri: Ausgewählte Werke*, DTB, xxxi, Jg.xix–xx (1920)
T. Kroyer and M. Zenger: *Geschichte der Münchner Oper* (Munich, 1923)
R. Schaal: 'Ein unbekanntes Inventar der Müncher Hofkapelle aus dem Jahre 1753', *Convivium musicorum: Festschrift Wolfgang Boetticher* (Berlin, 1974), 309–24
R. Münster: *Bayern und Europa um 1700*, i: *Die Musik am Hofe Max Emanuels, Kurfürst Max Emanuel* (Munich, 1976) [exhibition catalogue at Schloss Schleissheim, 1976]
——: 'Neu aufgefundene Opern, Oratorien und szenische Kantaten von Pietro Torri', *Musik in Bayern*, xiii (1976), 49–58
GORDANA LAZAREVICH

Torvaldo e Dorliska ('Torvaldo and Dorliska'). *Dramma semiserio* in two acts by GIOACHINO ROSSINI to a libretto by CESARE STERBINI after J.-B. de Coudry's *Vie et amours du chevalier Faubles* (1790) and the *Lodoiska*

librettos derived from it; Rome, Teatro Valle, 26 December 1815.

In the opening act, the tyrannical Duke of Ordow (bass, a role created by Filippo Galli) traps Torvaldo (tenor) and his wife Dorliska (soprano) in a wood at night. His motive is his love for Dorliska, but in the darkness and confusion Dorliska escapes and Torvaldo, contrary to Ordow's belief, is not left dead. The next day Dorliska unwittingly takes refuge in Ordow's castle, taken in by the genial Carlotta (mezzo-soprano), wife of the equally genial custodian of the castle, Giorgio (*buffo* baritone). It is the presence of these two *buffo* characters that gives the work its *semiserio* nature; indeed, Giorgio is generally thought to be its most effectively drawn character. Torvaldo effects entrance to the castle disguised as a woodsman. He carries a letter, purportedly written by the dying Torvaldo, but though this secures him access to Dorliska, her surprise at seeing him betrays them both. The second act deals with the imprisonment and rescue of Torvaldo and Dorliska, the rescue plan set in train by Giorgio and Carlotta and completed by Ormondo (bass), the Duke's turncoat henchman, and the local villagers who demand and eventually secure the Duke's overthrow and execution. Torvaldo's Act 1 cavatina, 'Fra un istante e te vicino', is notable, as is his Act 2 aria 'Ah, qual voce d'intorno rimbomba', which Rossini later used for parts of the vengeance duet in *Otello*.

Sterbini's libretto, a 'rescue opera' of the type popular at the time of the French Revolution, must be held responsible for the low esteem in which this work has been held by commentators in Rossini's time and later. The opera does, however, contain some notable music and was widely performed in Italy and elsewhere up to 1840.

RICHARD OSBORNE

Tosatti, Vieri (*b* Rome, 2 Nov 1920). Italian composer. He studied with Dobici, Ferdinandi, Jachino and Petrassi at the Rome Conservatory until 1942, and with Pizzetti between 1942 and 1945. He taught composition in Rome from 1966 to 1986, although after 1970 he virtually gave up composing for writing. His theatre music consists of an early work, which he considered a failure, and five others. Though his style was initially eclectic (showing the influence of Wagner, Ravel, Prokofiev, Stravinsky, Puccini and Wolf-Ferrari), he made a step towards a more personal inspiration in *Il giudizio universale* (1955), based on Bonacci. *La fiera delle meraviglie* (composed 1959–61) satirizes artistic practices of the time: two opposing entertainments take place side by side before an audience which is increasingly amused by the failures of both. The components and underlying themes – irony, hallucination, passion – of Tosatti's theatre music come together in his last opera, *Il paradiso e il poeta* (composed 1964–5), in which the leading figure, the Poeta maledetto, may be taken to be Edgar Allan Poe.

Antagonistic towards *verismo*, Tosatti adopted the Wagnerian concept of music drama as the only authentic practice of musical theatre. His work – which seems to embrace the aesthetics of Pizzetti (who championed dramatic continuity in opera) – remained a largely solitary and conservative approach in Italy; it is as far removed from the avant garde as it is from post-*verismo*.

Dioniso, 1945–6 (dramma musicale, 3, Tosatti), unperf., unpubd

Il sistema della dolcezza (opera paradossale, 1, Tosatti, after E. A. Poe: *The System of Dr Tarr and Professor Fether*), Bergamo, Donizetti, 25 Oct 1951 (Milan, 1953)

Il giudizio universale (dramma musicale, 3, C. V. Ludovici, after A. Bonacci), Milan, La Scala, 2 April 1955 (Milan, 1955)

L'isola del tesoro (dramma musicale, 3, Tosatti, after R. L. Stevenson), concert perf., Rome, RAI auditorium, 22 June 1958; stage, Bologna, Comunale, 20 Nov 1958 (Rome, 1958)

La fiera delle meraviglie, 1959–61 (dramma musicale, 3, Tosatti), Rome, Opera, 30 Jan 1963 (Rome, 1962)

Il paradiso e il poeta, 1964–5 (dramma musicale, 3, Tosatti), concert perf., Turin, RAI auditorium, 3 Dec 1971 (Rome, 1969)

*

F. Abbiati: '*La Madre* di Donato di Veroli e *Il sistema della dolcezza* di Vieri Tosatti', *Corriere della sera* (26 Oct 1951)

N. Costarelli: 'Vieri Tosatti e "Il sistema della dolcezza"', *Il diapason* (1952), 10–13

G. M. Gatti: 'L'isola di Tosatti', *Tempo* (Nov 1958)

M. Mila: 'Spazza via lirici ed elettronici', *L'espresso* (10 Feb 1963)

V. Carratoni: 'Un intervista a Vieri Tosatti: melodramma e rumori', *La fiera litteraria* (17 Feb 1963)

F. L. Lunghi: 'Il paradiso e il poeta', *Il giornale d'Italia* (7–8 Dec 1971)

RAFFAELE POZZI

Tosca. *Melodramma* in three acts by GIACOMO PUCCINI to a libretto by GIUSEPPE GIACOSA and LUIGI ILLICA after VICTORIEN SARDOU's play *La Tosca*; Rome, Teatro Costanzi, 14 January 1900.

Floria Tosca *a celebrated singer*	soprano
Mario Cavaradossi *a painter*	tenor
Baron Scarpia *Chief of Police*	baritone
Cesare Angelotti *former Consul of the Roman republic*	bass
A Sacristan	bass
Spoletta *a police agent*	tenor
Sciarrone *a gendarme*	bass
A Gaoler	bass
A Shepherd-boy	alto
Roberti *the executioner*	silent role

Soldiers, police agents, noblemen and women, townsfolk, artisans

Silent: cardinal, judge, scribe, officer, sergeant

Setting Rome, June 1800

In May 1889, less than a month after the première of *Edgar*, Puccini wrote to the publisher Ricordi begging him to obtain Sardou's permission to set his play, 'since in this *Tosca* I see the opera that I need: one without excessive proportions or a decorative spectacle; nor is it the kind that calls for a superabundance of music' – by which he meant that it did not conform to the genre of 'grand opera' which had been in vogue in Italy since the 1870s. For the time being matters went no further and Puccini turned his attention to other subjects. In 1895, however, he saw the play performed in Florence with Sarah Bernhardt (for whom it was written) in the title role. The following year, with *La bohème* behind him, he returned to his idea. Unfortunately Sardou had by now granted the rights to Alberto Franchetti, and Luigi Illica had already written him a libretto, to which Verdi had given his unqualified approval. However, Illica and Ricordi had no difficulty in persuading Franchetti to relinquish it and so leave the field open for their favourite composer. As usual the versification was entrusted to Giuseppe Giacosa, who to begin with was against the project. There was too much plot, he argued, and too little room for lyrical expansion, and, as so often, he continually threatened to withdraw from the partnership. However, by the beginning of 1898 Puccini had the entire libretto in his hands and was able to begin work on the first act. In June of that year he visited Sardou in Paris, who encumbered him with various suggestions ('a fine fellow', Puccini wrote, 'all life and fire and full of historico-topo-panoramic inexactitudes'). Sardou gave his blessing to the libretto, however; and Puccini himself considered it an improvement on the original play.

As always, Puccini was much concerned with authenticity of detail. His friend Father Pietro Panichelli supplied him with information regarding the plainsong melody to which the *Te Deum* was sung in Roman churches, the correct order of the cardinal's procession and the costumes of the Swiss Guard. From Meluzzi, an elderly musician in the employ of the Vatican, he learnt the exact pitch of the great bell of St Peter's; and he made a special journey to Rome to hear for himself the effect of the matins bells from the ramparts of the Castel Sant'Angelo. The Roman poet Luigi Zanazzo provided a suitable text for the song of the Shepherd-boy featured in the prelude to Act 3, the last piece to be composed. By the time the opera was completed in October 1899 two important changes had been made to the libretto. In Act 2 Puccini rejected an aria sung by Cavaradossi under torture which developed into a quartet with Tosca, the Judge and Spoletta, on the grounds that it reverted to the static *pezzo concertato* convention of a bygone age. Likewise he would have none of a 'Farewell to Art and Life' to be sung by the painter as he awaits execution, despite Verdi's avowed admiration for it. Instead he insisted on a lover's anguished lament built around the words 'Muoio disperato'. And, as usual, after much argument with his librettists, he had his way. More disturbing was a letter from Giulio Ricordi complaining of the lack of a transcendental love duet in Act 3 which should form the climax of the drama – doubtless he had in mind the concluding scene of Giordano's highly successful *Andrea Chénier* (1896). Ricordi found the existing dialogue between the lovers intolerably perfunctory, and he regretted the musical quotation from the original version of *Edgar* ('Where indeed is the Puccini of noble, warm and vigorous inspiration?'). The composer stood firm. Tosca, he maintained, would be far too preoccupied with the outcome of events to be able to indulge in a time-wasting effusion. In this, as so often, his theatrical instinct had not betrayed him.

Presumably it was the opera's Roman setting that led Ricordi to arrange the première in the Italian capital. The cast included Hariclea Darclée (Tosca), Emilio de Marchi (Cavaradossi) and Eugenio Giraldoni (Scarpia); the conductor was Leopoldo Mugnone. The sets were by Adolfo Hohenstein, chief stage designer of La Scala, and the production was in the hands of the younger Tito Ricordi, Giulio's son. Although the critical reception was mixed – several reviewers took exception to the brutality of the plot – the opera ran for 20 evenings to packed houses. Its success was confirmed two months later in Milan, at La Scala, where it was conducted by Toscanini with Giuseppe Borgatti as Cavaradossi and the other principals as at Rome. The first foreign performance was given at Buenos Aires in June the same year, followed on 12 July by the London première, at Covent Garden, with Milka Ternina as Tosca ('a true creation' according to Puccini), Fernando de Lucia as Cavaradossi and Antonio Scotti as Scarpia (a role in which he specialized until the end of his career 33 years later). He and Ternina appeared in the New York première (4 February 1901), together with Giuseppe Cremonini (Puccini's first Des Grieux) as Cavaradossi. Since then outstanding Toscas have included Geraldine Farrar, Maria Jeritza (who sang 'Vissi d'arte' lying prone), Maria Caniglia and, later, Maria Callas, whose performances with Tito Gobbi as Scarpia became legendary.

ACT 1 *Interior of the church of S Andrea della Valle* The curtain rises to a progression of three very loud, heavy chords based on the whole-tone scale (ex.1,

a motif that will connote the villainous police chief Scarpia throughout the opera). The fugitive Angelotti hurries into the church, searches frantically for a key concealed in a shrine of the Madonna and slips into the private chapel of the Attavanti family. The Sacristan enters to a characteristic *buffo* motif (ex.2). He carries a

Ex.2

Allegretto grazioso

bundle of paintbrushes which he proceeds grumblingly to wash. They belong to Cavaradossi, who arrives to put the finishing touches to his portrait of the Magdalen. He contemplates his canvas, in which he has succeeded in blending the dusky, southern charms of his beloved Tosca with the blonde beauty of an unknown woman whom he has often observed at prayer in the church ('Recondita armonia'). The aria is punctuated by asides from the Sacristan. A quiet orchestral postlude follows as the Sacristan leaves, whereupon Angelotti emerges from hiding; he is recognized by a shocked Cavaradossi, who hastily locks the church door. Angelotti explains that he has just escaped from the Castel Sant'Angelo, where he had been imprisoned by order of Scarpia.

Their conversation is interrupted by the sound of Tosca's voice outside the church. Angelotti again retreats into the chapel, while Cavaradossi admits the singer, who enters in a mood of jealous suspicion – she is sure she heard voices – though her accompanying motif (ex.3) conveys a dignified and beautiful presence. Reassured with some difficulty by Cavaradossi, she suggests that they should go to his villa in the country after her evening performance. Cavaradossi, his mind on Angelotti, responds absently. Tosca is further disturbed by the painting, with its resemblance to someone other than herself – the Marchesa Attavanti. For the moment she accepts the painter's explanation and joins

him in a tender love duet whose principal theme, occurring at the words 'Mia gelosa', functions as the motif (ex.4) for their mutual passion. Their conversation is not set as a conventional duet until, at the words 'Qual' occhio al mondo', a typically long-arched Puccini melody leads to a brief unison passage (four bars), but immediately the conversational form returns as Tosca leaves, to a 'leggerissimo' wind and harp accompaniment.

When she has left, Cavaradossi and Angelotti plot the latter's escape. After dark he must make for Cavaradossi's villa in female disguise and in the event of danger hide in a well in the garden. A cannon shot from the Castel Sant'Angelo warns that Angelotti's flight has been discovered. At the same time the Sacristan re-enters with the news (false, as it turns out) of Napoleon's defeat at Marengo. The church fills with a joyous throng. At the height of the tumult Scarpia himself appears with Spoletta and other police agents. His first utterance is sung unaccompanied (marked 'con grande autorità'); his next phrases are accompanied by a low E played by double bassoons, a growling sound that seems to characterize his cruelty. He rebukes the crowd for desecrating the atmosphere of a church and orders the Sacristan to make ready for a *Te Deum* in honour of the victory. Meanwhile he orders his men to look for clues to Angelotti's presence, which are soon found: a key, a basket empty of provisions which Cavaradossi, the Sacristan tells him, had left untouched; and a fan belonging to the Marchesa Attavanti, Angelotti's sister. When Tosca returns, Scarpia uses the fan to arouse her jealousy. She hurries away to the villa to surprise the guilty pair. Her exit is to a repeat of the phrases heard at the end of the love duet, only now for the full orchestra, marked 'crescendo molto'. Scarpia gives orders for her to be followed, and in a monologue, over a characteristically obsessive pattern of alternating chords, accompanied by bells, organ, drum-beats to simulate cannon-fire and again the growling bassoons, gloats at the prospect of capturing the fugitive and enjoying the prima donna's favours; as the *Te Deum* swells to a climax he exclaims, 'Tosca, you make me forget God!'.

ACT 2 *Scarpia's apartment in the Palazzo Farnese* Scarpia is dining alone, while below at an entertainment given by Queen Caroline a gavotte is being danced. Spoletta enters to report on his fruitless search of Cavaradossi's villa for traces of Angelotti. Scarpia's fury is mollified when he hears that his men have arrested Cavaradossi himself and brought him to the palace. During the singing of a cantata in the queen's honour, led by Tosca, Scarpia interrogates the painter in the presence of the executioner, Roberti, and a judge of the criminal court. The choir, with Tosca's voice rising above it, provides an occasionally dissonant, tense background to Scarpia's opening interrogation, accompanied only by low strings and woodwind. As the cantata finishes Scarpia becomes more insistent, then, at Tosca's entrance sings, 'con forza e sostenuto', 'Mario Cavaradossi, the Judge awaits your testimony'. Cavaradossi denies all knowledge of Angelotti, at which Scarpia gives orders for him to be tortured in an adjoining room. Tosca also refuses to reveal Angelotti's whereabouts (her words 'Non so nulla' are echoed by the strings), until, overcome by Cavaradossi's groans she mentions the well in the garden. Scarpia suspends the torture. Apprised of her betrayal Cavaradossi curses her for her weakness. Sciarrone comes in with the news that the Battle of Marengo had in fact been won by Napoleon.

Cavaradossi breaks out in a paean to liberty, for which Scarpia has him again put under arrest and marched to prison to be shot at dawn. In a monologue in which he laments his unfinished supper, 'La povera mia cena fu interrotta', which ends with a drum tattoo suggesting the march to the scaffold, he then promises to have the painter set free on condition that Tosca yield to his embraces. This prompts from Tosca the aria 'Vissi d'arte', into which Puccini wove the motif that accompanied her first appearance. Spoletta enters and announces that Angelotti has killed himself. Scarpia turns to Tosca and she accepts his terms; he then bids Spoletta set up a mock-execution 'as in the case of Palmieri'. Tosca insists that he write her and Cavaradossi a safe-conduct. While he does so she catches sight of a knife lying to hand. A sinister motif on the strings (ex.5) indicates the thought going through

her mind. No sooner has Scarpia finished writing than she stabs him and as he expires the 'knife' theme is played on full strings. Before leaving with the safe-conduct she places candles at his head and feet and a

'Tosca' (Puccini), scenes from the original production at the Teatro Costanzi, Rome, 14 January 1900, from 'L'illustrazione italiana' (28 January 1900): (top vignette) Act 3, Cavaradossi's execution; (lower left) Act 1, Tosca joins Cavaradossi in the church of S Andrea della Valle; (lower right) Act 2, Cavaradossi is interrogated by Scarpia in the Palazzo Farnese; (below) the final scene in Act 2, Tosca has placed candles beside the body of Scarpia

crucifix on his breast in conformity with her religious upbringing, and sings on a repeated middle C (although the words are often spoken instead) 'E avanti a lui tremava tutta Roma!' ('And before him all Rome trembled!').

ACT 3 *A platform in the Castel Sant'Angelo* A prelude evokes the breaking of dawn. A Shepherd-boy is heard singing as he drives his flock. The sound of sheep-bells gives way to the mingled chimes of matins. Cavaradossi enters accompanied by the melody of the aria he will sing, heard here for the first time, 'con molta anima', on the strings. To a reminiscence of ex.4 played on solo cellos Cavaradossi asks for pen and paper with which to write a farewell letter to Tosca. His anguish at leaving her for ever is expressed in the aria 'E lucevan le stelle', a recollection of past bliss before the final darkness, with a mournful clarinet taking the main line before he sings it at the words 'O dolci baci, languide carezze'. Spoletta arrives with Tosca, then retires. Tosca produces the safe-conduct and explains to a suspicious Cavaradossi how she obtained it and how she repaid the giver. Cavaradossi is astonished and delighted. Their tender exchanges are continually overshadowed by Tosca's concern for her lover – will he be able to act his part convincingly during the mock-execution? But when the firing squad arrives he plays his part all too well, for the rifles are loaded, and Tosca finds herself addressing his lifeless body. Meanwhile the news of Scarpia's murder has broken. Spoletta, Sciarrone and the other agents are heard calling for Tosca's blood. She climbs on to the battlements and, crying that she and Scarpia will meet before God, Tosca leaps to her death, to an orchestral peroration of Cavaradossi's 'E lucevan le stelle'.

* * *

None of Puccini's operas has aroused more hostility than *Tosca*, by reason of its alleged coarseness and brutality; yet its position in the central repertory has remained unchallenged. Not only is it theatrically gripping from start to finish: it presents the composer's most varied and interesting soprano role, hence its perennial appeal for the great operatic actress. In contrast to Sardou's heroine, against whose ignorance and simplicity the playwright can never resist tilting, Puccini's Tosca is a credible woman of the theatre, lacking neither intelligence nor humour, and capable of genuine dignity. Nowhere is she more moving than in Act 3, in which she imagines herself to be in command of the situation and that all she has to do is to teach

Cavaradossi how to act. All the more heart-rending is her discovery of the truth.

Tosca is the most Wagnerian of Puccini's scores in its use of motifs, every one of which refers to a single object, person or idea, though none of them is developed or modified. But, like Wagner, he sometimes used them to give us information about a character's unexpressed thoughts. An instance of this occurs in Act 1 where Tosca asks Cavaradossi to meet her that evening. 'This evening?', he queries in alarm, and the orchestra plays a snatch of the motif associated with Angelotti. Likewise Scarpia's interrogation of the painter is punctuated by a motif connoting the well, which Cavaradossi refuses to mention, but of which he is obviously thinking. The only weakness in the drama is Puccini's inept handling of the political element; but issues of this kind held no interest for the composer of *La bohème*, *Tosca* and *Madama Butterfly*. JULIAN BUDDEN

Toscanini, Arturo (*b* Parma, 25 March 1867; *d* New York, 16 Jan 1957). Italian conductor. He became famous when, at the age of 19, he took over a performance of *Aida* in which he had been playing the cello (Rio de Janeiro, 30 June 1886). From 1886 to 1898 he worked in various Italian theatres, conducting the premières of *Pagliacci* (1892), *La bohème* (1896) and operas by Catalani, championing Wagner ('the greatest composer of the century') and waging war on shoddy traditions of performance. In 1898 he was appointed artistic director of La Scala, where he built the repertory on Wagner, Verdi, new works and Italian premières (including *Yevgeny Onegin* and *Pelléas et Mélisande*). From the outset he concerned himself with every aspect of operatic performance, down to the smallest detail of staging, and coached his singers himself, even for minor roles. Standards rose dramatically; but it was a fierce struggle, not only to eradicate singers' bad habits and the administrative cutting of corners, but also to educate the audience to a serious attitude towards opera. Toscanini had the house lights lowered, got the ladies to remove their hats, and abolished the obligatory concluding ballet. Encores were harder to suppress. On the last night of the 1902–3 season, when the audience was insisting on one in *Un ballo in maschera*, he walked out in the middle of the performance.

Toscanini stayed away from La Scala for three years, and, only two years after his return, the former La Scala manager Giulio Gatti-Casazza invited him to New York in 1908 as artistic director of the Metropolitan Opera. There for seven years, Toscanini ruled over a dazzling constellation of singers (Caruso, Scotti, Farrar, Destinn, Martinelli and others) and to a remarkable extent imposed his will on them. In 1915, frustrated at the impossibility of fully realizing his operatic ideals, in growing disagreement with the administration and restless at being away from his country in wartime, he resigned and went back to Italy.

In 1920 Toscanini was made artistic director of a reorganized La Scala, with unprecedented powers. The culmination of his regime came in 1929, when he took the company on a triumphant tour to Vienna and Berlin. In the same year, however, dissatisfied with his own achievements, hampered by the management's financial troubles and increasingly at odds with the Fascists, he finally left La Scala. From then until his retirement 25 years later he never entered an opera house to direct opera except as a guest at the festivals of Bayreuth (1930–31) and Salzburg (1934–7) – both of which he broke with on political grounds. The final period of Toscanini's career was dominated by symphonic music, which he had cultivated from the first with a passion rare in an Italian conductor of his time and in which he had long been regarded as an interpreter of unrivalled clarity and intensity. But opera was not entirely neglected. Concert performances, especially of Verdi, figured in his programmes with the NBC SO. In particular, the recording of *Falstaff* made in New York in 1950 remains a classic and a monument to his exceptional vitality and interpretative insight.

*

A. Della Corte: *Toscanini* (Vicenza, 1946)
A. Segre: 'Toscanini: the First Forty Years', *MQ*, xxxiii (1947), 149–77
F. Sacchi: *Toscanini* (Milan, 1951; Eng. trans., abridged, as *The Magic Baton*, 1957)
A. Della Corte: *Toscanini visto da un critico* (Turin, 1958)
S. Hughes: *The Toscanini Legacy* (London, 1959, enlarged 2/1969) [with discography by W. Toscanini]
F. Sacchi: *Toscanini: un secolo di musica* (Milan, 1960)
H. Sachs: *Toscanini* (New York, 1978)
D. Matthews: *Arturo Toscanini* (New York, 1982)
G. Nello Vetro and V. Vaccaro: *Il giovane Toscanini* (Parma, 1983)
J. Horowitz: *Understanding Toscanini* (London, 1987)

DAVID CAIRNS

Tosi, Adelaide (*b* Milan, *c*1800; *d* Naples, 27 March 1859). Italian soprano. She studied with Crescentini and made her début in 1821. In the opening season of the Teatro Carlo Felice, Genoa (1828), she sang Pamira in Rossini's *Le siège de Corinthe* and Bianca in Bellini's *Bianca e Fernando* (the revised version of *Bianca e Gernando*). She created roles in three operas by Donizetti at S Carlo, Naples: Argelia in *L'esule di Roma* (1828), Neala in *Il paria* and the title role of *Elisabetta al castello di Kenilworth* (both 1829).

ELIZABETH FORBES

Tosi, Giuseppe Felice (*b* Bologna; *fl* 1677–93). Italian composer. According to Fétis he was a founder member of the Bolognese Accademia Filarmonica in 1666 and organist at S Giovanni in Monte, Bologna. He was *principe* of the academy in 1679. From 1680 to 1683 he was *maestro di cappella* of the Accademia della Morte, Ferrara, and in 1682–3 of Ferrara Cathedral as well. He was assistant organist at Bologna Cathedral (S Petronio), 1692–3.

The description of *Il Celindo* (1677) as his 'first musical work' must mean that he came late to composition. It shows a competent hand, albeit with a trace of awkwardness in the vocal writing. Like many operas of the 1670s it makes prominent use of a solo trumpet in dialogue with the voice.

Il Celindo (? G. B. Neri), Cento, Accademico del Sole, 6 Sept 1677, *I-Vnm*
Atide [Act 1] (3, T. Stanzani), Bologna, Formagliari, 23 June 1679, lib. (Bologna, 1679) [Act 2 by P. Degli Antoni, Act 3 by G. A. Perti]
Erismonda (Stanzani), Bologna, Formagliari, 27 Jan 1681
Traiano (M. Noris), Venice, SS Giovanni e Paolo, ? Jan 1684
Aladario, Ferrara, Bonacossi, 20 Jan 1685
Il Giunio Bruto (P. P. Seta), Bologna, Formagliari, 4 Jan 1686
Orazio (V. Grimani), Venice, S Giovanni Grisostomo, 16 Jan 1688 [attrib. Tosi by Bonlini]
Amulio e Numitore (A. Morselli), Venice, S Giovanni Grisostomo, 1689, *A-Wn*
L'incoronazione di Serse (Morselli, after P. Corneille: *Rodogune*), Venice, S Giovanni Grisostomo, 26 Dec 1690

L'idea di tutte le perfezioni (L. Lotti), Piacenza, Nuovo, 1690 [introduction to a ballet]
Pirro e Demetrio (Morselli), Venice, S Giovanni Grisostomo, 1690
L'Alboino in Italia (G. C. Corradi), Venice, SS Giovanni e Paolo, 1691 [attrib. Tosi and C. F. Pollarolo by Bonlini]

Arias in C. Pallavicino: Il Vespasiano (Corradi), Ferrara, Bonacossi, carn. 1682, aria *I-MOe*; 6 arias, dated 'Ferrara 1686', probably from an opera, *MOe*

*

G. C. Bonlini: *Le glorie della poesia e della musica* (Venice, 1730)
C. Ricci: *I teatri di Bologna nei secoli XVII e XVIII* (Bologna, 1888)

THOMAS WALKER

Tosi, Pier Francesco (*b* Cesena, 13 Aug 1654; *d* Faenza, on or just after 16 July 1732). Italian castrato, teacher and writer. He was the author of a highly influential treatise on singing (*Opinioni de' cantori antichi e moderni*, 1723). He was not (as stated in earlier works of reference) the son of the Bologna composer G. F. Tosi. He sang in a Rome church in 1676–7, made his one recorded appearance in opera at Reggio Emilia in 1687, in Giovanni Varischino's *Odoacre*, and was based in Genoa before going in 1693 to London, where he gave weekly public concerts and taught. From 1701 to 1723 he travelled extensively as musical and diplomatic agent of Emperor Joseph I and the Elector Palatine. From 1724 he again taught in London for some years; in 1730, back in Italy, he became a priest. A number of cantatas and arias are among his works.

Though Tosi claimed some originality, his treatise codified past teaching and was itself drawn upon by later writers. Opera for him was only one of three types of singing (along with church and chamber) for students to master. They were to practise (untempered) scales, unite chest and head registers, and seek all-round attainment in music, acting and civility. With this went a polemic in favour of expressive pathos and against new-fangled display, but Tosi avoided identifying any eminent singers with either the 'old' or the 'new'; he shared in a 'general compromise by which he said singers and composers presided over the development of musical trends and tastes which were rejected in theory as much as they were pursued in practice' (Durante). His book in fact had much to say about ornamentation, which he said should be worked out by the singer rather than written down; it is still informative about Baroque performing practice.

See also MANCINI, GIOVANNI BATTISTA.

Opinioni de' cantori antichi e moderni o sieno Osservazioni sopra il canto figurato (Bologna, 1723, repr. in Della Corte; Dutch trans., 1731; Eng. trans. as *Observations on the Florid Song*, by J. E. Galliard, London, 1742; Ger. trans., ed. J. F. Agricola, Berlin, 1757; Fr. trans., 1874)

*

ES (L. F. Tagliavini)
A. Della Corte: *Canto e bel canto* (Turin, 1933) [incl. repr. of *Opinioni*]
B. Ulrich: *Die altitalienische Gesangsmethode* (Leipzig, 1933)
R. Celletti: 'La vocalità al tempo del Tosi', *NRMI*, i (1967), 676–84
——: *Storia del belcanto* (Fiesole, 1983; Eng. trans., 1991)
S. Durante: 'Theorie und Praxis der Gesangsschulen zur Zeit Händels: Bemerkungen zu Tosis "Opinioni de' cantori antichi e moderni"', *Händel auf dem Theater*, ed. H. J. Marx (Karlsruhe, 1988), 59–72
J. Rosselli: 'The Castrati as a Professional Group and a Social Phenomenon, 1550–1850', *AcM*, lx (1988), 143–79, esp. 171

JOHN ROSSELLI

Toten Augen, Die ('The Dead Eyes'). *Bühnendichtung* in a prologue and one act by EUGEN D'ALBERT to a libretto by Hanns Heinz Ewers and Marc Henry (Achille Georges d'Ailly-Vaucheret) after Henry's play *Les yeux morts* (1897); Dresden, Hofoper, 5 March 1916.

The opera is set in Jerusalem on Palm Sunday. The previous evening, as the reapers return home at dusk from the fields, a Shepherd (tenor) discovers that one of his lambs is missing; despite the darkness he goes at once to look for it.

In the courtyard of the house of Arcesius (baritone), special envoy of the Roman Senate to Jerusalem, his wife, the beautiful Myrtocle (soprano), laments that she is blind and unable to see the tall and handsome husband of her imagination. Many famous doctors, including the Egyptian Ktesiphar (tenor), have failed to cure her, so she hopes for a miracle. Arsinoe (mezzo-soprano), her slave, tells her of the prophet Jesus (tenor), a miracle worker whom she has overheard the Jewish women mention as they fetch water from the well. Jesus will come to Jerusalem that day and Myrtocle determines to ask his help. Arcesius, in reality misshapen and ugly, does not want his wife cured, believing that she will no longer love him if she discovers his true appearance. Summoned to a council in Jerusalem by Pontius Pilate, Arcesius departs with the handsome young Roman captain, Aurelius Galba (tenor), who is secretly in love with Myrtocle.

The procession led by Jesus passes by the house on its way to Jerusalem. Mary Magdalen (contralto) narrates the parable of the Good Shepherd. The miracle occurs: Myrtocle is enabled to see. As she expresses her gratitude, the voice of Jesus is heard, warning her that she will curse his name before sunset. When Arcesius and Galba return they are greeted with the news that Myrtocle is cured. Arcesius watches from behind the well as Myrtocle comes into the courtyard and, mistaking Galba for her husband, throws herself into his arms. Unable to hide his love, Galba embraces her warmly. Arcesius, in a fit of jealous rage, kills Galba, and Myrtocle, understanding the truth, curses the name of Jesus, as he had predicted. She stares into the setting sun until she loses her sight once more. As she goes inside the house with the repentant Arcesius, the Shepherd, the lost lamb in his arms, crosses the courtyard.

The first performance of *Die toten Augen* was strongly cast, with Helena Forti as Myrtocle, Curt Taucher as Aurelius Galba and Friedrich Plaschke as Arcesius, but the opera, with its rather heavy mixture of mysticism, symbolism and realism, was only moderately successful. The most Wagnerian of all d'Albert's stage works, it derives much of its style from *Parsifal*. It also shows the influence of Richard Strauss (the ensembles of Jewish men and women inevitably recall *Salome* and *Elektra*) and, in the orchestration, of Debussy. While Myrtocle and Arcesius, both firmly characterized by their music, carry dramatic conviction, the unfortunate Aurelius Galba, less well drawn, remains a cipher, a symbol of Myrtocle's illusions. ELIZABETH FORBES

Tote Stadt, Die ('The Dead City'). Opera in three acts, op.12, by ERICH WOLFGANG KORNGOLD to a libretto by Paul Schott [Julius and E. W. Korngold] after Georges Rodenbach's novel *Bruges la morte*; Hamburg and Cologne, 4 December 1920.

Korngold's fourth and most celebrated work for the stage came about at the suggestion of Siegfried Trebitsch, who had recently completed a translation of Georges Rodenbach's play *Le mirage*, itself an adaptation of a novel by the same author. Korngold quickly drafted a one-act scenario, before seeking the advice of Hans Müller, the librettist for his earlier one-act work *Violanta*. Müller urged the composer to turn it into a full-scale opera and began work on the libretto, but other commitments obliged him to withdraw, and in the end the libretto was provided by Korngold and his father, working under the pseudonym of Paul Schott. A number of factors held up progress on the opera, but it was eventually completed on 15 August 1920. Its simultaneous premières later that year in Hamburg (under Egon Pollak) and Cologne (under Klemperer) were successful, and during the next decade the work received performances in Vienna, New York, Prague, Zürich, Antwerp, Berlin, Budapest, Lwów and Amsterdam. Among the singers who took part were Maria Jeritza, Lotte Lehmann, Richard Tauber and Richard Mayr.

Bruges la morte was a symbolist-inspired work showing the influence of Maeterlinck and, beyond that, of Poe. Essentially it is a dream-tale in which the images of death and decay are uppermost; throughout, the image of the dead city is no mere backdrop but a living presence, a protagonist that controls and determines the actions of those who live in her. The Korngolds wrought profound changes, however, by pushing the city into the background and concentrating on greater realism and dramatic characterization.

The action of *Die tote Stadt* takes place in Bruges at the end of the 19th century. In Act 1 Paul (tenor) mourns the death of his young wife Marie. The decaying city is a constant reminder to him both of her and of the past, and in a room in his house he keeps a 'temple of memories', a museum of all the objects that remind him of her, the most precious of which is a braid of her golden hair. Paul's friend Frank (baritone) arrives to find him in an excited state; he has recently met a woman who bears a striking resemblance to Marie, and now he has invited her to his house so that he can see her walk through his wife's room, thereby returning death to life. Eventually the woman, a dancer called Marietta (soprano), arrives. She so arouses Paul's passions that he tries to embrace her. As she pulls away she uncovers a picture of Marie, and is surprised to see what appears to be a portrait of herself. But it is time for her to go to a rehearsal; she is playing Hélène in Meyerbeer's *Robert le diable*. Paul stays behind, and as he wrestles with the contradicting emotions of loyalty to his dead wife and desire for Marietta, he witnesses an apparition: Marie (her part taken by the same singer as Marietta) steps from her portrait, and as she tells him to live his own life she is transformed into the dancing figure of Marietta.

Act 2 takes place a few weeks later. Paul's vision is continuing; he imagines himself outside Marietta's house, tormented by guilt and inner turmoil. He sees Brigitta, his housekeeper (contralto) – who has left him because of his infidelity to Marie's memory – and falls out with Frank, who has also succumbed to Marietta's charms. Marietta and her friends now approach and, watched from hiding by Paul, rehearse Hélène's scene from *Robert le diable*. As Marietta acts out Hélène's rise from the tomb, Paul rushes forward, outraged at this mockery of resurrection. She sends her friends away, and he hurls accusations at her, telling her that the strength of his passion was only because in her he saw his dead wife. Marietta decides to confront the challenge of her dead rival, and again seduces Paul. She suggests that they spend the night at his house, there to banish the ghost for ever.

Act 3 opens in Marie's room. It is the following morning, and Marietta is standing triumphantly in front of Marie's portrait. A holy procession is passing and Marietta and Paul watch it from the window. Paul is absorbed in the ceremony, and when the bishop appears he falls to his knees. Marietta, disgusted by Paul's piety, decides to test it against her erotic powers. She insists that Paul kiss her but he refuses and the two of them begin to argue, Paul defending his faith in loyalty and Marietta accusing him of hypocrisy and weakness. She taunts him with her dancing, and when she mockingly drapes the lock of Marie's hair around her neck, Paul strangles her. Now she is exactly like Marie. At this point the vision ends. Paul awakes and sees the lock of hair untouched. The housekeeper announces that the lady who visited him, Marietta, has returned for her umbrella and roses. Marietta enters, but to her suggestion that this is an omen for her to stay Paul says nothing; he has been disillusioned by his dream. Marietta shrugs her shoulders and leaves, and Paul decides to leave Bruges, the city of death. The past cannot be recaptured, and those who have departed cannot be brought back.

The musical material is organized in terms of short, pregnant motifs rather than fully-fledged themes, with the interval of a 4th (and its inversion, a 5th) as the strongest connecting thread: they are always associated with the past and their constant recurrence symbolizes the omnipresence of the 'dead city'. Korngold was one of the finest orchestrators of his day, and the vivid, sumptuous sound of the Straussian-sized orchestra – with triple woodwind, bass trumpet, two harps, celesta and piano, harmonium, pipe organ and bells – is one of the major splendours of the opera. The other is the vocal writing, which permits the grandest opportunities for bel canto brilliance and display yet is carefully woven into the orchestral tissue; Korngold was a composer who thought and wrote in the grand manner. Sometimes the lyric poet briefly takes precedence over the epic dramatist. But the emotional voltage is consistently high, above all because of the elastic nature of Korngold's rhythm: the music exists in a constant state of ferment but with a basically regular four-square pulse, leading to tensions quite different from those that result from a conflict of metres and which, wedded to his orchestral sound, give rise to considerable reserves of expressive power. CHRISTOPHER PALMER

Tóth, Aladár (*b* Székesfehérvár, 4 Feb 1898; *d* Budapest, 18 Oct 1968). Hungarian director and critic. He studied philosophy at the Péter Pázmány University of Budapest, graduating in 1925 with a dissertation on the aesthetics of Mozart's operas. He worked as a critic in the 1920s and 30s and from 1940 to 1946 lived in exile in Sweden with his wife, the pianist Annie Fischer. He returned to Hungary in 1946 and took over the direction of the Hungarian State Opera House, a post he held until 1956.

Tóth was the most important music critic in Hungary between the two world wars. He fought for the recognition of Bartók and Kodály, and also for the works of earlier composers not widely known in Hungary, such as Schütz, Purcell, Bach, Handel, Mozart and Verdi. As director of the Opera he championed the same ideals in difficult circumstances. After the war Tóth had to rebuild operatic life in Hungary, a task he achieved with the cooperation of Klemperer, who was engaged at the Budapest Opera from 1947 to 1950. The second half of

Tóth's period as director of the Opera coincided with a period of increasingly harsh political and artistic dictatorship (Bartók's *The Miraculous Mandarin* was dropped from the repertory of the Opera House). The closing of state borders forced Tóth to work solely with Hungarian artists. With the limited resources, he nevertheless managed to create one of the most brilliant epochs in the history of opera in Hungary, overseeing the premières of Kodály's *Czinka Panna* (1948), Kadosa's *A Huszti kaland* ('The Adventure at Huszt', 1951), Ferenc Farkas's *Csinom Palkó* (1951) and Tibor Polgar's *A kérők* ('The Suitors', 1954), and the Hungarian premières of *Peter Grimes* (1947), Musorsky's *The Fair at Sorochintsï* (1949) and Meytus's *Moloda hvardiya* ('The Young Guard', 1953), as well as the premières of many ballets. Tóth's final triumph as director of the Opera was the restoration of *The Miraculous Mandarin* to the repertory in 1956.

Tóth's writings include *Mozart: Figaro lakodalma* ('The Marriage of Figaro', Budapest, 1928), *Verdi művészi hitvallása* ('Verdi's Artistic Credo', Budapest, 1941) and *Válogatott zenekritikái* ('Selected Criticisms on Music', ed. F. Bónis, Budapest, 1968).

FERENC BÓNIS

Totila. *Dramma per musica* in three acts by GIOVANNI LEGRENZI to a libretto by MATTEO NORIS; Venice, Teatro SS Giovanni e Paolo, Carnival 1677.

The libretto has two historical characters – Totila, King of the Ostrogoths (soprano), and the Byzantine General Belisarius (tenor) – but the plot is largely fanciful and very complex, encompassing a broad emotional range and alternating quickly between pathos and farce. The main historical element is the chaos that ensues from Totila's laying waste to Rome. Two patrician families are torn asunder by the amorous appetites of Totila and his general, Vitige (mezzo-soprano). Misdirected letters, disguise and madness add to the general confusion. The opera ends happily and improbably with the patrician daughter Marzia (soprano) putting country before love and consenting to marry Totila. There are 12 named human characters; nine gods and allegorical figures appear in the concluding spectacular scene.

The score has staves for five-part strings (two violins, alto and tenor violas and violoncello), two trumpets and continuo. (From halfway through the score, the staves for violins and violas are largely left blank.) Trumpets are used in four arias: two trumpets join with strings in the opening ritornello of Totila's entrance aria 'Arda Roma' and in his 'Snodate i fremiti, o trombe e timpani', while a single trumpet is used in Belisario's aria concluding Act 2, 'Coronato di verdi allori', and in the aria sung by Peace at the end of the opera, 'Il mondo festeggi'. The *Mercure galant* (August 1677) praised the spectacular stage effects of the original production.

HARRIS S. SAUNDERS

Totis, Giuseppe Domenico de. *See* DE TOTIS, GIUSEPPE DOMENICO.

Tottola, Andrea Leone (*d* Naples, 15 Sept 1831). Italian librettist. The place and date of his birth are unknown. An agent for the impresario Barbaia and poet to the royal theatres (reputedly without salary), he began writing librettos in 1802. Most of these were for Naples; over half were for the Nuovo theatre, with *buffo* roles in dialect. He has had a worse press than he deserves; although he wrote some verse of appalling clumsiness and vacuity and much of his serious work is monotonous and prolix, his comedies contain sharply observed situations and witty, theatrically effective dialogue. Given a good subject he could write a first-class libretto: for instance *Il vascello L'occidente* (Carafa, 1814), *Gabriella di Vergy* (Carafa, 1816), *L'ultimo giorno di Pompei* (Pacini, 1825, for which he received a royal merit award) or, probably his best, *Imelda de' Lambertazzi* (Donizetti, 1830). Stendhal referred to the curious mixture of burlesque and pedantry in his makeup, qualities reflected in the extraordinary range of his work.

drammi per musica unless otherwise stated
cm – *commedia per musica*   mel – *melodramma*

Siface e Sofonisba, P. A. Guglielmi, 1802; *L'impostore* (cm), L. Mosca, 1802; *Le nozze per impegno* (dramma giocoso), Capotorti, 1802; *Obeide ed Atamare*, Capotorti, 1803; *La riedificazione di Gerusalemme* (tragedia sacra), pasticcio, incl. music by Cimarosa, 1804; *Olimpia* (dramma serio per musica), E. Paganini, 1804 (C. Conti, 1826); *Camilla* (azione drammatica serio-giocoso per musica), Valentino Fioravanti, 1804; *I matrimoni in maschera* (farsa per musica), G. Chioggia, 1805; *I vecchi delusi* (farsa per musica), Trento, 1805

Il servo trappoliere (cm), D. Cercià, 1806; *La contadina fortunata* (cm), Paer, 1807 (Vincenzo Fioravanti, 1820); *L'inganno del festino* (farsa per musica), G. B. De Luca, 1807; *L'appuntamento notturno per burla* (farsa per musica), De Luca, 1808; *I due policarpi* (cm), De Luca, 1810; *Semplicità ed astuzia* (cm), Valentino Fioravanti, 1810; *Amor dal naufragio* (farsa per musica), G. Prota, 1810; *Amore ed avarizia* (burletta per musica), Valentino Fioravanti, 1811; *Raoul signore di Crequi* (mel eroi-comico), Valentino Fioravanti, 1811; *Amalia e Carlo* (mel), P. C. Guglielmi, 1812

La foresta di Hermanstadt (mel eroi-comico), Valentino Fioravanti, 1812; *Adelaide maritata* (mel), Valentino Fioravanti, 1812; *Il califfo di Bagdad* (mel), M. Garcia, 1813; *Una follia* (cm), Cordella, 1813; *Don Gregorio nell'imbarazzo* (commedia in musica), G. Mosca, 1813; *Elena*, S. Mayr, 1814 (Carnicer, 1821 and Coccia, 1822, as Elena e Costantino); *Il vascello L'occidente* (mel), Carafa, 1814; *Il blondello* (mel eroi-comico), C. Ceccarini, 1814 (Radicati, 1816; P. Fabrizi, 1830); *Carlotta ed Errico* (mel), G. Mosca, 1814; *Ernesta e Carlino* (mel), Capotorti, 1815

La gelosia corretta (cm), Carafa, 1815; *I solitari di Scozia* (mel), Vaccai, 1815; *La casa da vendere* (cm), Chelard, 1815 (D. Pagliani-Gagliardi, 1823); *L'azzardo fortunato* (cm), Cordella, 1815; *Adelson e Salvini*, Valentino Fioravanti, 1816 (Bellini, 1825); *Gabriella di Vergy* (azione tragica), Carafa, 1816; *Il solitario di Posilippo*, Valentino Fioravanti, 1816; *La morte d'Adelaide* (azione tragi-comica), Valentino Fioravanti, 1817; *Mosè in Egitto* (azione tragico-sacra), Rossini, 1818; *Gli amori di Adelaide e Comingio* (mel), Valentino Fioravanti, 1818; *Berenice in Siria* (azione tragica), Carafa, 1818

Ermione (azione tragica), Rossini, 1819; *La donna del lago* (mel), Rossini, 1819 (J. Hoven, 1830, as Elena); *Solimano II*, L. Carlini, 1820; *Violenza e costanza*, Mercadante, 1820; *Eugenia degli Astolfi*, Pavesi, 1820; *Chiara di Rosembergh* (mel eroi-comico), P. Generali, 1820; *Adelaide di Baviera*, Carlini, 1721; *La testa meravigliosa*, Generali, 1821; *Elena ed Olfredo*, Generali, 1821; *Zelmira*, Rossini, 1822; *La zingara*, Donizetti, 1822; *Ines di Almeida*, Pavesi, 1822; *Gli sciti*, Mercadante, 1823; *Le nozze fra nemici* (dramma semiserio per musica), Generali, 1823

Alfredo il grande, Donizetti, 1823; *Il fortunato inganno* (dramma giocoso), Donizetti, 1823; *Costanzo ed Almeriska*, Mercadante, 1823; *Ogni eccesso è vizioso* (dramma giocoso), Valentino Fioravanti, 1824; *Sansone* (azione tragico-sacra), F. Basili, 1824; *Alessandro nell'Indie*, G. Pacini, 1824; *Tamerlano*, A. Sapienza, 1824; *Fatima e Selim* (mel), Pagliani-Gagliardi, 1824; *Il disertore* (mel), P. Raimondi, 1825; *Zadig e Astartea*, Vaccai, 1825; *La cena frastornata* (commedia lirica), L. Ricci, 1825; *Il sogno avverato* (azione teatrale), L. Ricci and Pagliani-Gagliardi, 1825

Amina (mel sentimentale, after F. Romani), C. Valentini, 1825; *Gl'italici e gl'indiani* (dramma), Carafa, 1825; *L'ultimo giorno di Pompei*, Pacini, 1825; *Aladino* (dramma comico), L. Ricci, 1825; *Il langravio di Turingia* (mel), Pagliani-Gagliardi, 1826; *Il solitario ed Elodia*, Pavesi, 1826; *Niobe* (dramma eroico-mitologico), Pacini, 1826; *Un bizzarro inganno* (cm), Pagliani-

Gagliardi, 1826; *Il diavolo condannato nel mondo a prender moglie* (azione comico-favelosa), L. Ricci, 1827; *Giuditta* (azione tragico-sacra), P. Raimondi, 1827

Un cestellino di fiori (mel), Raimondi, 1827; *Margherita regina d'Inghilterra*, Pacini, 1827; *Gli aragonesi in Napoli* (mel buffo), C. Conti, 1827 (Valentini, 1830, as Il muratore di Napoli; L. Gordigiani, 1841); *Robinson Crosuè nell'isola deserta*, Vincenzo Fioravanti, 1828; *Amalia di Reaumur* (mel), N. Fornasini, 1828; *L'antiquario e la modista* (mel comico), Pagliani-Gagliardi, 1828; *Alexi* (azione tragica), Conti and Vaccai, 1828; *L'infanzia accusatrice* (mel comico-sentimentale), Raimondi, 1828; *Selim e Zulima* (mel), A. Cipullo, 1829; *Il castello di Kenilworth* (mel), Donizetti, 1829

Il diavolo color di rosa (opera buffa), E. Petrella, 1829; *Il giorno di nozze* (cm), Petrella, 1830; *Imelda de' Lambertazzi* (mel tragico), Donizetti, 1830; *Il figlio del signor padre* (mel comico), Valentini, 1830 (Zanetti, 1839); *La strega di Dernecleugh* (mel), Pagliani-Gagliardi, 1830; *La gioia de' sudditi* (azione teatrale), G. Moretti, 1830; *La portentosa scimmia del Brasile con Pulcinella* (comico mel), Vincenzo Fioravanti, 1831; *I litiganti senza la lite* (mel comico), Aspa, 1831; *A mezza notte* (mel comico), Raimondi, 1831; *La burla* (mel giocoso), Aspa, 1832

*

L. Miragoli: *Il melodramma italiano nell'ottocento* (Rome, 1924)
Stendhal: *Vie de Rossini* (Paris, 1824, 2/1922; Eng. trans., 1956)
A. C. Ramelli: *Libretti e librettisti* (Milan, 1973)
W. Ashbrook: *Donizetti and his Operas* (Cambridge, 1982)

JOHN BLACK

Toulon. Town in southern France, a port and important naval base. The first opera heard there was Lully's *Phaëton* on 28 January 1681. The first permanent theatre was built in 1765 in the rue de la Comédie (now rue Denfert Rochereau); the entrance can still be seen. In 1855 the municipality decided to build the Grand Théâtre Municipal in the rue Louis Napoleon (now Boulevard de Strasbourg). It was inaugurated on 12 October 1862 with a performance of Halévy's *Les mousquetaires de la reine*. With 1797 seats (increased to 1926 seats in 1916), it was one of the largest of the French provincial opera houses, and was run by impresarios with its own company and orchestra and guest singers from Paris. From 1959 to 1982 it was run by the impresario who ran the Nice Opera, before returning to independence. The present season lasts from October to April, during which eight operas are each given two performances. CHARLES PITT

Toulouse. Town in southern France, historically the capital of Languedoc. A theatre has stood on or near the same site adjoining the town hall since the 16th century, when it was called the Logis de l'Ecu. Louis XIV was present at a *divertissement* here in 1659. The *Mercure galant* mentions performances of ballets during the 17th century; the Jesuits also presented *tragédies en musique*, including *La paix de retour* (1678), *Codre, roy d'Athènes* (1682), *La naissance de Mercure* (1683), *Agrippine* (1685), *Mars guéri* (1687) and Aphroidise's *Les bergers heureux* (1710). In 1687, Francine, Lully's son-in-law, was authorized to open a competing opera house. In 1736 the Capitouls, the 12 city councillors, decided on the construction of a new theatre. Called the Théâtre du Capitole (cap. 1550), it was designed by Guillaume Cammasand and opened in 1737. From the 1750s the company employed 31 singers and actors and an orchestra of 20; it presented mainly *opéra comique* and *opera buffa*, including Grétry's *La fausse magie* (1777) and Pergolesi's *La serva padrona* (1785). The building gradually fell into disrepair and was closed in 1807. A new Capitole was built in 1817–18; transformed and partly rebuilt in 1835 and again in 1880, it burnt down in 1917. Rebuilt in 1923 by the 80-year-old Paul Pujol, it was inaugurated with *Les Huguenots*. It was modernized in 1950 and again in 1973, when the orchestra pit was enlarged to hold up to a hundred players and the seating capacity reduced to 1200 (of which only some 800 have perfect visibility). Since the theatre lacks space, operas have often since 1978 been given 'in the round' in the Halles aux Grains, a 19th-century industrial building transformed into a multi-purpose concert hall and opera house that can seat up to 3000.

The Capitole was reputed in the 19th and early 20th centuries to have one of the most difficult publics in France. One of its directors, the bass Pierre Gailhard, also became a famous director of the Paris Opéra. After a period of decline, the theatre again found a certain glory, particularly in its Wagner presentations with Lorenz, Flagstad, Mödl and Hotter under the artistic direction of the tenor Louis Izar (1948–68). Michel Plasson has been musical director since 1972. In a season that runs from October to May, the Toulouse company mounts seven or eight productions, each given four to six performances (Friday evenings and Sunday matinées plus some in midweek), from a judicious mixture of the French, Italian and German repertories. Five or six operetta productions are given slightly more performances. The singing competition founded in 1954 is held annually in the Capitole.

*

A. Rivière and A. Jouffray: *Le théâtre du Capitole 1542–1977* (Toulouse, 1978)
L. J. Brote: 'A propos du répertoire lyrique des théâtres français', *Le théâtre lyrique français 1945–1985*, ed. D. Pistone (Paris, 1987), 51–73

CHARLES PITT

Toupin, Jacques. *See* JANSEN, JACQUES.

Tourangeau, Huguette (*b* Montreal, 12 Aug 1938). French-Canadian mezzo-soprano. She studied at the Quebec Conservatory with Ruzena Herlinger. Her début was as Cherubino at the Stratford Festival in Ontario in 1964. The same year she was a finalist in the Metropolitan Opera Auditions, which led to an engagement with the Metropolitan's touring company. A protégée of Sutherland and Bonynge, she has performed, toured and recorded with them frequently. Her Metropolitan Opera début was in 1973 as Nicklausse, and she has sung in major North American opera houses as well as in Amsterdam, Hamburg and Sydney. The essentially lyric element in her voice befits her for a repertory that includes several Mozart roles, Adalgisa, Carmen, Julius Caesar, Mignon, Gluck's Orpheus, Rosina and Suzuki. CORI ELLISON

Tourcoing. Town in northern France. The Théâtre Municipal in the boulevard Gambetta is unique among European opera houses in that it was built by a philanthropic industrialist as a theatre for his factory, in 1892; the present gateway to the theatre is the original gateway to the factory. Seating 850 in stalls and two galleries, the house was acquired by the municipality in 1920 and let out on a concession basis with a small municipal subsidy. Marcel Féru was the first impresario to make his mark when in 1972 he founded his Théâtre d'Action Lyrique, presenting not only repertory works but those of Menotti, Britten, Bartók and Landowski and even world premières of commissions, all on a commercial basis. In 1981 Tourcoing became part of the short-lived Opéra du Nord, grouped with Lille (the

Grand Opéra) and Roubaix (ballet): Tourcoing provided the Atelier Lyrique (opera workshop), first under the direction of Féru, then of Jean-Claude Malgoire, whose personality is stamped on the company. He brought with him his Baroque orchestra, Le Grand Ecurie et la Chambre du Roi (founded in 1967). With the break-up of the Opéra du Nord in 1985, Tourcoing and its Atelier Lyrique became autonomous. The repertory consists of contemporary, Baroque and Classical works, many of them little known – Campra's *Tancrède*, Piccinni's *Didon*, Domenico Scarlatti's *Narciso*, Rameau's *Platée* and Kreutzer's *Paul et Virginie*, together with innovations such as Astor Piazzolla's tango opera *María de Buenos Aires* and the jazz opera *La baraque rouge*, given by promising young singers and directors. There are about five productions a year, usually performed twice in Tourcoing (Friday evenings and Sunday matinées) before being taken throughout France. Several of these productions have been recorded. CHARLES PITT

Tourel [Davidovich], **Jennie** (*b* Vitebsk, Belorussia, 9/22 June 1900; *d* New York, 23 Nov 1973). American mezzo-soprano. A refugee with her family from the Revolution, she eventually settled in Paris, where she studied with Reynaldo Hahn and Anna El Tour (in later years Tourel denied that her stage name was chosen as an anagram of her teacher's). She made her American début at the Chicago Civic Opera in Ernest Moret's *Lorenzaccio* (1930) and subsequently sang at the Opéra-Comique in Paris as Carmen (1933) and, later, Cherubino and Charlotte (*Werther*). Her career at the Metropolitan was brief: she made her début as Mignon in 1937 and appeared for a few seasons in the 1940s as Rosina, Adalgisa and Carmen.

Considered peerless as an interpreter of French music, she also specialized in the Italian coloratura mezzo-soprano repertory. In 1951, in Venice, she created Baba the Turk in *The Rake's Progress*. She taught at the Juilliard School and at the Aspen Music School. Her reputation, supported by many recordings, rests on her enormous versatility, both musical and linguistic, her stylistic elegance, her sensitivity to textual nuance and tone colour, and a remarkable technique.

*

E. Burns: 'Teacher Tourel', *ON*, xxxiv/27 (1969–70), 20
A. Hughes: Obituary, *New York Times* (25 Nov 1973)
R. Offergeld: 'Some Notes on the Future of Jennie Tourel', *Stereo Review*, xxxv/5 (1975), 78
P. L. Miller: 'Recorded Tributes to Jennie Tourel and Richard Tucker', *Journal* [Association of Recorded Sound Collections], viii/1 (1976), 43 MARTIN BERNHEIMER

Tournemire, Charles (Arnould) (*b* Bordeaux, 22 Jan 1870; *d* Arcachon, 3 Nov 1939). French composer and organist. After early training at the Bordeaux Conservatoire he entered the Paris Conservatoire in 1887. Although he won a *premier prix* in Widor's class, it was Franck's teaching which had a lasting effect on him as a composer. He was organist at Ste Clotilde, Paris, from 1898 until his death and from 1919 was a professor at the Paris Conservatoire. His best-known work is *L'orgue mystique*, a series of 51 organ suites, though his major works are orchestral and vocal, and include four operas – all sadly neglected, partly because he became a recluse in his later years. Much of his music was composed on (and sometimes inspired by) the remote island of Ouessant; an individual Christian mysticism is always evident, and harmonically he bridged the gap between the world of Franck and that of Messiaen, whose musical language bears interesting comparison with that of Tournemire's mature works. As a teacher he inspired a generation of composers, including Maurice Duruflé and Daniel-Lesur.

Tournemire's first opera, *Nittetis*, a love story set in ancient Egypt, has never been performed. *Les dieux sont morts*, staged at the Paris Opéra in 1924, deals with a favourite theme of the composer: that the pagan gods died at the birth of Christ – the moment that provides the work's climax. Its harmonies are often reminiscent of Debussy and less daring than in the later operas. In his next operatic work, *La légende de Tristan*, the use of leitmotifs is ideal for the fragmentary style that Tournemire favoured in his maturer works. Distorted and deliberately obscure thematic hints give his treatment of the legend a subtle intensity. Completed shortly before his death, *Il poverello di Assisi* focusses on the spiritual journey of St Francis and his transcendence of worldly values. The work develops from a series of harmonically ambiguous musical ideas expressed at the opening, which gain clarity as St Francis increases in spiritual stature.

Nittetis op.30, 1905–7 (tragédie lyrique, 3, after P. Metastasio), unperf.
Les dieux sont morts [Chryséis] op.42, 1910–12 (drame antique, 2, E. Berteaux), Paris, Opéra, 19 March 1924
La légende de Tristan op.53, 1925–6 (3, A. Pauphilet), unperf.
Il poverello di Assisi [Le petit pauvre d'Assisi] op.73, 1937–9 (5 épisodes lyriques, J. Péladan), unperf. NICHOLAS KAYE

Tourney. *See* OPERA-TORNEO.

Tours. Town on the Loire in western central France. The Grand Théâtre, situated in the rue de la Scellerie, is the third theatre to stand on that site. The first was the church of the convent of the Cordeliers, converted into a theatre in 1796; in spite of its inconvenient layout an impressive list of plays and operas was presented there over 70 years. After numerous proposals the city council in 1867 decided to demolish it and build a new theatre. Designed by the young architect Léon Rohard, it was inaugurated on 8 August 1872 with a comedy coupled with Victor Massé's *Les noces de Jeannette*. This theatre, except for the façade, burnt down in August 1883. A new, slightly larger theatre with four galleries seating 1300 was built behind the existing façade by the local architect François Hardion; the ceiling, foyer and grand staircase were decorated by Clairin, who also worked at the opera houses in Paris and Monte Carlo. The new theatre was inaugurated in 1889. Principally an opera house, the Grand Théâtre also accommodates touring drama companies, its own ballet company and orchestral concerts. The season, which runs from October to May, typically consists of productions of six operas and six operettas, the operas being performed twice only (Friday evenings and Sunday matinées), the operettas more frequently. One opera by a contemporary composer is commissioned each season: recent commissions include *La parisienne* by Jack Ledru (1982), *Annapurna* by Clostre (1989) and works by Bécaud and Aznavour.

*

L. J. Brote: 'A propos du répertoire lyrique des théâtres français', *Le théâtre lyrique français 1945–1985*, ed. D. Pistone (Paris, 1987), 51–73 CHARLES PITT

Toussaint [*Toussaint, or The Aristocracy of the Skin*]. Opera in three acts by DAVID BLAKE to a libretto by Anthony Ward; London, Coliseum, 29 September 1977.

A chronicle of Haiti's struggle for freedom from French dominion and exploitation between 1791 and 1803, the opera is a bold and largely successful confrontation of the problems involved. Far from being restricted to the activities of Toussaint (baritone) and his family, its focus expands to include a cast of several dozen, more than 20 scenes in places as far apart as Port-au-Prince and Paris, and a history of political idealism and corruption ending in Toussaint's imprisonment in France and the ruthless triumph of Dessalines (bass), his successor as leader of the slave revolt in Haiti.

Making use of voodoo drum rhythms and other authentic Haitian material, as well as French Revolutionary songs and stylistic allusions ranging from neoclassical to music hall, Blake's music is vivid in atmosphere, powerfully dramatic in some scenes and romantically lyrical in others, above all those featuring Toussaint's wife Suzanne (mezzo-soprano). The score is remarkable more for its variety of colour than for structural coherence, despite recurring motifs and a cyclical relationship between the first chorus and the last.

Because of weaknesses in the construction and pacing of the opera, when the ENO production was revived in 1983 it was heavily cut, not least in those passages involving the ironic agent of Brechtian alienation, Mars Plaisir (tenor). Since then Blake has further revised the work in the light of those problems. GERALD LARNER

Tower of Babel, The. Opera by Anton Rubinstein; *see THURM ZU BABEL, DER.*

Toye, (John) Francis (*b* Winchester, 27 Jan 1883; *d* Florence, 31 Oct 1964). English writer on music. Intended for the diplomatic service, he turned to music and in 1922 joined the *Daily Express*, first as leader writer, then music critic. He was music critic on the *Morning Post* from 1925 to 1937. In 1939 he became director of the British Institute in Florence, where he eventually retired. He is best known for his gracefully written, discerning and authoritative studies *Giuseppe Verdi: his Life and Works* (London, 1931, 2/1962) and *Rossini: a Study in Tragi-Comedy* (London, 1934, 2/1954).

Toye, (Edward) Geoffrey (*b* Winchester, 17 Feb 1889; *d* London, 11 June 1942). English conductor, brother of Francis Toye. After studying at the RCM he conducted in London theatres until World War I interrupted his career. From 1919 to 1924 he conducted the D'Oyly Carte Opera Company in three seasons and was musically responsible in 1920 (Glasgow) and 1921 (London) for the first revival since 1887 of *Ruddigore*: the rewritten overture and other alterations are mainly Toye's work, although not acknowledged as such in the edition of the vocal score published in association with that revival.

From 1925 Toye was associated with Lilian Baylis at the Old Vic as conductor and a member of the governing body; he was her co-director at Sadler's Wells Theatre, 1932–4, where the opera and ballet came to be located. He shared with Lambert the conducting of Vic-Wells Ballet performances, including the fledgling company's first foreign tour to Copenhagen in 1932. In 1935 he also became managing director of the Royal Opera House Co. Ltd, which had acquired the lease of Covent Garden; but his insistence on engaging the American singer Grace Moore for *La bohème* there led to a quarrel with Beecham (as artistic director) and to Toye's departure later the same year. He renewed his association with the D'Oyly Carte company, and was adapter-producer as well as conductor for the film version of *The Mikado* first shown in 1939. His own works include an operetta, *The Red Pen* (words by A. P. Herbert), broadcast in 1927. ARTHUR JACOBS

Tozzi, Antonio (*b* Bologna, *c*1736; *d* Bologna, after 1812). Italian composer. He studied with Padre Martini and became a member of the Accademia Filarmonica at Bologna in 1761; in 1769 he was elected a *principe* of the academy. His first operas, *Tigrane* and *La morte di Dimone, o sia L'innocenza vendicata*, were performed in Venice in May 1762 and autumn 1763. *La morte di Dimone*, Bertati's first libretto and an early *opera semiseria*, is an extravaganza involving 16 characters, including four deities. It incorporates multiple ensembles, chorus, dance, magical transformations, sudden scene changes and gods in machines. In 1764 Tozzi was invited to conduct opera at the court of Carl I, Duke of Brunswick, in association with the Venice-trained Kapellmeister J. G. Schwanenberger. Tozzi's wife, Marianna Bianchi, sang in his *Andromaca* (1765, Brunswick) and *Zenobia* (1773, Munich). In 1774 he was appointed Hofkapellmeister at Munich, where seven performances of his opera *Orfeo ed Euridice* were given between 9 January and 27 February 1775. His liaison with the Countess von Törring-Seefeld caused a scandal which resulted in his leaving Munich shortly before 1 March 1775, when Leopold Mozart wrote to his wife: 'You may tell everyone the story of Tozzi and Countess Seefeld, so that people may realize that Italians are knaves the world over'. By late spring Tozzi was back in Venice for the première of his *Rinaldo*, another spectacle opera whose libretto was to be the principal textual source for Haydn's *Armida* (1784). In February 1776 he headed an Italian company hired to perform at the Reales Sitios (Carlos III's seasonal homes around Madrid). From 1781 he directed opera performances in Barcelona, conducting local premières of works by Paisiello, Cimarosa, Martín y Soler, Guglielmi, Anfossi and others, and his own compositions, including *I due gemelli Castore e Polluce*, which celebrated the birth of twins to the future Carlos IV. He spent the 1790–91 season in Madrid conducting at the Academias Místicas (similar to the Parisian Concert Spirituel). His cantata *El triunfo de Venus* was performed in October 1802 to welcome the royal court to Barcelona, and he was often termed the leading local composer in the *Diario de Barcelona*. He left Barcelona in 1805 and returned to Italy.

Tozzi was a gifted melodist with a strong sense of drama. His orchestrations often involve full four-part textures in which each string part plays a separate role, such as marking the beat with repeated notes, providing support with motivic figures, doubling the voice, moving in parallel 3rds, or supplying a countermelody or melodic elaboration. He used chromaticism sparingly, achieving emotional expression instead through the use of wind instruments, modal and dynamic contrasts, and appropriate vocal and instrumental gestures.

Tigrane (dramma, 3, C. Goldoni, after F. Silvani: *La virtù trionfante dell'amore e dell' odio*), Venice, S Angelo, 19 May 1762, *I-Bc*

La morte di Dimone, o sia L'innocenza vendicata (serio-giocoso, 3, G. Bertati, after J. von Kurz), Venice, S Cassiano, aut. 1763
Andromaca (dramma serio, 3, A. Salvi), Brunswick, Hof, spr. 1765, *D-Bds*, *Wa*, *I-Nc**
Arcifanfano (dg, Goldoni), Brunswick, ?1766–7
Il re pastore (dramma serio, ? P. Metastasio), Brunswick, ?1766–7, *D-Wa*
Siroe (dramma serio, Metastasio), Brunswick, ?1766–7, *Wa*
Adriano in Siria (dramma serio, 3, Metastasio), Modena, Ducale, 17 Jan 1770
Il paese della cuccagna (dg, 2, Goldoni), Bologna, Formagliari, carn. 1771
Zenobia (dramma, 3, Metastasio), Munich, Hof, Jan 1773, *Mbs*, *F-Pn*
Orfeo ed Euridice (tragedia, 3, M. Coltellini, after R. de' Calzabigi), Munich, Hof, 9 Jan 1775, *B-Bc*, *D-DS*, *Mbs*, *F-Pn*
Rinaldo (dramma, 3, after Bertati, J. Durandi and F. de Rogatis), Venice, S Salvatore, Ascension 1775, *A-Wgm*; (Venice, 1775; lacks simple recits.)
Le due gemelle (dg, 3, G. Tonioli), Madrid, Real Sitio de S Ildefonso, sum. 1776
La serva astuta (dg, 2), Munich, Hof, sum. 1776
I due gemelli Castore e Polluce (favola), Barcelona, 8 Dec 1783
Lo scherzo della magia, ossia La casa incantata (dg, 3), Barcelona, *c*1785, MS in Palacio Liria, Madrid
La caccia di Enrico IV (ob, 3, G. Palomba), Barcelona, S Cruz, 4 Nov 1788
Zemira ed Azor (dg, 3, L. da Ponte), Barcelona, S Cruz, 4 Nov 1791
El amor a la patria, o sea Córdoba liberada (os, 2), Barcelona, S Cruz, 21 Jan 1793
I due ragazzi savoiardi (ob), Barcelona, S Cruz, 27 Jan 1794
Angelica e Medoro (dramma eroico-pastorale, 2, G. Sertor, after L. Ariosto), Barcelona, S Cruz, Jan 1805

*

F. M. Rudhart: *Geschichte der Oper am Hofe zu München* (Freising, 1865), 156, 162–3
R. Engländer: 'Zu den Münchener Orfeo-Aufführungen 1773 und 1775', *Gluck-Jb*, ii (1915), 26–55
E. Cotarelo y Mori: *Orígines y establecimiento de la ópera en España* (Madrid, 1917), esp. 320–30
J. Subirá: *La música en la casa de Alba* (Madrid, 1927), 224
A. Par: 'Representaciones teatrales en Barcelona durante el siglo XVIII', *Boletín de la Real academia española*, xvi (1929), 492–513, 594–614
E. Anderson, ed.: *The Letters of Mozart and his Family* (London, 1938, 3/1985), 255–6, 263–4
J. Subirá: *La ópera en los teatros de Barcelona* (Barcelona, 1946), 40–53, 56
M. McClymonds: 'Haydn and his Contemporaries: "Armida abbandonata"', *Joseph Haydn: Vienna 1982*, 325–32
U. Zelaschi: *L'opéra italien jusqu'en 1900* (Brussels, 1982)

ROBERT STEVENSON, MARITA P. McCLYMONDS

Tozzi, Giorgio [George] (*b* Chicago, 8 Jan 1923). American bass. After vocal study with Rosa Raisa, Giacomo Rimini and John Daggett Howell, he made his professional début as Tarquinius in the Broadway production of *The Rape of Lucretia* (1948). He studied further in Milan with Giulio Lorandi, and made the transition from baritone to bass. His Italian début was in 1950 as Rodolfo in *La sonnambula* at the Teatro Nuovo. His La Scala début followed in 1953 (in Catalani's *La Wally*), and in 1955 he made his Metropolitan début as Alvise (*La Gioconda*). He then appeared with remarkable success in Salzburg, San Francisco, Florence, Frankfurt, Munich and Lisbon. His notable roles included Philip II, Boris, Don Giovanni and Hans Sachs. He created the Doctor in Barber's *Vanessa* at the Metropolitan in 1958, and took part in the celebrated La Scala revival of *Les Huguenots* with Corelli, Sutherland and Simionato in 1962. He has also been active in musical comedy. At his best, Tozzi was an imposing figure on the stage and a singer of uncommon versatility, warmth and intelligence.

MARTIN BERNHEIMER

Tracey, Edmund (*b* Preston, 14 Nov 1927). English administrator, translator and librettist. After working as music critic for *The Observer* (1958–65), he became a director of the Sadler's Wells (later English National) Opera, with responsibilities for repertory planning and literary texts. He became one of the company's most prominent translators with such works as *Les contes d'Hoffmann* (1970), *Aida* (1978) and *Manon* (1979). He also translated Mozart's *La finta giardiniera* (as *Sandrina's Secret*) for English Music Theatre's production at Sadler's Wells (1976). These translations generally found favour for their clarity and directness, winning a success denied to Tracey's collaboration with Malcolm Williamson on *Lucky-Peter's Journey* (after Strindberg; 1969), a Sadler's Wells Opera commission.

ARTHUR JACOBS

Traetta [Trajetta], **Tommaso** (**Michele Francesco Saverio**) (*b* Bitonto, nr Bari, 30 March 1727; *d* Venice, 6 April 1779). Italian composer. He was trained between 1738 and 1748 at the Conservatorio di S Maria di Loreto, Naples, where his teachers were Porpora (until 1742) and Durante. In accordance with local custom, he presumably proved his talents for the stage by writing comic operas for the smaller Neapolitan theatres before receiving a commission to write *Il Farnace* for S Carlo in 1751. He continued to write both serious and comic opera throughout his life. In Rome and Naples during the early 1750s he came into contact with the commanding figure of Jommelli, to the production of whose *Ifigenia in Aulide* at S Carlo in 1753 he contributed four arias. In 1757–8 he had no fewer than five Metastasian operas performed.

The crucial phase of Traetta's career began with his appointment in 1758 to the court at Parma, where the intendant Du Tillot proposed to unite some features of French *tragédie lyrique* with the reigning ideals of Italian aria opera, and to this end had the text of Rameau's *Hippolyte et Aricie* translated and adapted by the court poet C. I. Frugoni. The work was conceived mainly as a vehicle for the prima donna, Caterina Gabrielli, who inspired Traetta to his best efforts here and on several later occasions. Frugoni introduced choruses and spectacle into *Ippolito ed Aricia* but was unable to integrate them with the drama. He was also hard pressed to extract suitable scenes and aria texts from the model, so he used Racine's *Phèdre* as well. The result, for all its weaknesses, was deemed epochal, even by Algarotti, who attended the performances. Within six months Ignaz Holzbauer, who probably saw the production at Parma, took the libretto back to Mannheim and set it, almost certainly using some of Traetta's music, thus presaging the day when Traetta himself would be called to Mannheim. During 1760 Frugoni reworked French models for the texts of *I Tindaridi* (after *Castor et Pollux*) and a wedding serenata *Le feste d'Imeneo*.

Traetta had Rameau's scores at his disposal when composing these works, as is evident from his occasional borrowings, which are restricted to dance music and, more rarely, pictorial effects such as the storm music in *Hippolyte*. What he did not borrow is more significant. Whereas Rameau had set the scene around Castor's urn as a choral *tombeau*, grief being expressed through descending chromatic lines in imitation, Traetta made it a solo scene for Telaira (sung by Gabrielli). During the scene's initial obbligato recitative the orchestra depicts several phases of emotion: grief, terror, resignation and consoling hope. The set piece that follows, a cavatina addressed to the shade of the departed, is a tender Andante in E♭, a type of Italian opera aria to which Traetta gave a new degree of sensuous expression. The writer J. J. W. Heinse declared that this scene alone was worth an entire opera; while little else in the work equals it, audiences in 1760 were unprepared for more than a few scenes of such intensity. These scenes placed Traetta in the vanguard of the young opera composers who, following Jommelli's example, increasingly extended the range of orchestral colour and developed an arsenal of effects for the dramatic ballets, melodramas (in the specific sense) and other peculiarly *Sturm und Drang* phenomena that came to flourish in Germany during the 1770s.

Parma broadened Traetta's view of the dramatic possibilities of musical theatre; writing for Gabrielli strengthened his already powerful gifts as a melodist. Pleased with the fame of his *maestro di cappella*, the duke allowed him to fulfil commissions for other courts, and between 1760 and 1763 he composed operas for Turin, Vienna and Mannheim. *Armida* (1761, Vienna) again involved Gabrielli in the title role; the libretto, adapted by the intendant Durazzo and the court poet Migliavacca from Quinault's *Armide*, was designed to display her talents. Although the score is full of marches, choruses, ensembles and dances, *Armida* is still dominated by the da capo aria in the longwinded Neapolitan style of the mid-century. The orchestra is skilfully used to depict Armida's turning from hatred to pity, then to love in the scena and aria 'Mori, si mori' (Act 2 scene ix) – the very point in the drama about which Rousseau and Rameau had disagreed, the one attacking and the other defending Lully's setting. Most of the recitatives are orchestrally accompanied, and Traetta often took pains to connect them not just to the beginnings of the set pieces, but also, by means of transitions, to their endings. He was evidently intent upon building large scene complexes, and began to take more account of tonal planning.

Sofonisba (1762, Mannheim) carried these advances further. The commission brought Traetta again into contact with Jommelli, who then directed opera at the neighbouring court of Stuttgart. Verazi, Jommelli's frequent collaborator and Mannheim court poet, provided the libretto. Apparently the event was an attempt by the Elector Palatine Carl Theodor to outshine Carl Eugen of Württemberg in lavishness of spectacle and brilliance of musical effect. With the famous Mannheim orchestra at his command, Traetta wrote the most symphonic of his operas, and certainly his best operatic sinfonia. He himself wrote the ballet music. The pomp of ancient Rome comes to life in such scenes as the gladiatorial games, a ballet with chorus in the middle of Act 1, and the march and obbligato recitative for the equestrian procession and entry of Scipio. The ways of achieving grand scenic effects learnt from Rameau had more scope here than in the Parma operas; but it was again the heroine of the piece who inspired Traetta to his highest achievement. Sophonisba was played by the young Dorothea Wendling, the future Ilia of Mozart's *Idomeneo*. Heinse commented at length on Sophonisba's suicide and the final quintet of lament, likening them to classical tragedy.

Goldschmidt underestimated *Sofonisba*, although he chose to edit most of it, omitting only some routine arias for the secondary characters. His judgment was swayed by a mistaken dating of Traetta's second Viennese opera, *Ifigenia in Tauride*, which he assigned to 1759 instead of 1763. The earlier dating is historically and stylistically implausible, whereas if the later date is accepted *Ifigenia* can be seen to follow and intensify the bold advances made in *Armida* and *Sofonisba*. The text was the most direct, uncluttered and 'classical' that Traetta had yet been given. The opera was written one year after Gluck's *Orfeo ed Euridice* and for the same forces, and profited much from its predecessor. The castrato Gaetano Guadagni, for whom the role of Orpheus had been created, was the first Orestes, and his scene with the Furies compares favourably with, and is indebted to, Gluck's similar scene in *Orfeo*. Artistic relations between the two composers went further: Gluck directed a performance of Traetta's *Ifigenia* at Florence in 1767, and he had not forgotten its music when he came to write his own *Iphigénie en Tauride* at the end of his career. When Burney visited him in 1772 Gluck had his niece sing arias by Traetta which he accompanied. Traetta was stimulated by Gluck's dramatic vision. The impression made on him by *Orfeo* is evident in his *Antigona* (1772), particularly in Antigone's lament and invocation of the Furies at the beginning of Act 2; the structure and versification of the text are themselves derivative. In his revision of *Stordilano* (as *Il cavaliere errante*) of the late 1770s Traetta paid Gluck the compliment of parodying 'Che farò'.

With his Viennese *Ifigenia* (1763) Traetta had gone further in the direction of classical tragedy than would have been possible on any other operatic stage outside Paris. For his setting of the people's compassion for Orestes ('O come presto a sera', Act 1 scene v), emboldened not only by Gluck's example but also by Rameau's chromaticism in the laments for Castor, Traetta returned to the sombre colours of his *Stabat mater* (1750) for a long and difficult chorus, producing an effect of grandeur which equalled Gluck's highest aspirations and achievements. *Ifigenia* became Traetta's best-known serious opera and was frequently revived; Haydn chose to stage it (with his own additions) as late as 1786.

Declining enthusiasm and lack of funds for opera at Parma made it expedient for Traetta to accept the post of director of the Conservatorio dell'Ospedaletto at Venice in 1765. This position gave scope to his talents for sacred music and prompted the oratorio *Rex Salomone* for women's voices. He also wrote two comic operas which were later widely appreciated during his Venetian stay: *Le serve rivali* and *Amore in trappola*. His serious operas for the public theatres of Venice incurred no financial risk for their promoters; they were conventional aria operas after the Metastasian formula. The tragic opera he was capable of writing was possible only at court theatres, and then only when directors like Durazzo and Du Tillot or princes like Carl Theodor and Carl Eugen enforced their wills, whereas Maximilian III Joseph of Munich commissioned and received from Traetta a perfectly ordinary setting of Metastasio's *Siroe* (1767).

In 1768 Traetta accepted another court position, as successor to Galuppi in the service of Catherine II of Russia, arriving at St Petersburg late in the year. Besides giving singing lessons to his princely patrons (a task he had fulfilled in his previous posts as well), he became musical director of the opera. At first he revived some of his conventional aria operas, embellishing them with a few choruses and with arias reorchestrated to take advantage of newly fashionable instruments such as the clarinet. He must have felt the need to test reactions at a court that was accustomed to hearing operas in the best Italian tradition – a tradition that Galuppi had maintained. But in 1772 he produced a major new work, *Antigona*, stimulated by his reunion with the librettist Coltellini, a refugee from Vienna, and with Caterina Gabrielli. The opera has been considered his masterpiece ever since Heinse acclaimed it; Goldschmidt pronounced it the culmination of *opera seria*. In dedicating the libretto to Frederick the Great, Coltellini claimed that he had eliminated sententious comparisons (referring to Metastasio) and substituted the real 'pity' and 'terror' of his classical model, Sophocles' drama, at the king's suggestion (advice which saw strangely little application at Berlin). In fact the libretto has some dramatic ineptitudes and banal dialogue, which is however mitigated by the force of Traetta's music, especially in the scenes dominated by the heroic central figure and in the great choral pantomimes. *Antigona*, like *Sofonisba*, is flawed by having to serve too many singers. If its creators had gone one step beyond eliminating simile arias and had eliminated all but the three central characters, they could have avoided anticlimactic scenes such as the one at the end of the first act. Traetta partly compensated for an excessively prolix drama by concentrating on a few emotions and restricting his tonality to a few constantly recurring keys. The most effective tonal shock of the opera is that of the E minor choruses of Act 3, which powerfully challenge the flat keys of the neighbouring solo scenes; they suggest the futility of the struggle by trapped individuals against tragic destiny. Traetta was particularly conscious here of building scene complexes through tonal planning. He also advanced beyond the most adventurous aspects of his earlier tragedies by the repeated use of a few easily identified motifs, such as rushing ascending and descending scales to suggest the Furies of Hell, and the sobbing figure at the beginning of Act 2, which appears many times later, most impressively to introduce Antigone's final aria in E♭ (the figure is also used within the aria). Research may show that such motivic repetition was an operatic commonplace of the early 1770s; certainly it anticipates techniques used by Benda in his melodramas from the middle of the decade, and by Mozart (in *Idomeneo*) at its end.

Traetta left Russia in ill-health during the summer of 1775. He tried his fortunes for a time in London, among other places, with a serious opera, *Germondo*. Burney related that the great English success of Sacchini at the time prevented Traetta from becoming popular. By 1777 he had settled again in Venice, where his son Filippo (also a composer) was born; his last two completed works were comic operas for the Venetian carnivals of 1778 and 1779. By the latter date he was already suffering from his final illness. He was a celebrated man at his death, and was buried with honours near the Ospedaletto. Arteaga summed up his achievements by speaking of the 'talents and the learning of the always beautiful and sometimes sublime Traetta'.

See also ANTIGONA; ARMIDA (i); IFIGENIA IN TAURIDE (i); IPPOLITO ED ARICIA; SERVE RIVALI, LE; SOFONISBA; and TINDARIDI, I.

Buovo d'Antona (dg, 3, C. Goldoni), ?Florence, ?1750; Venice, S Moisè, 27 Dec 1758, *A-Wn*, *D-Dlb*, *US-Wc*

Il Farnace (os, 3, A. M. Lucchini, after A. Zeno: *Mitridate*), Naples, S Carlo, 4 Nov 1751, *I-Vnm*; Act 1.xii ed. in DTB, xxv, Jg.xiv/i (1914)

La Costanza (ob, A. Palomba), Naples, Fiorentini, wint. 1752

I pastori felici (ob, 2), Naples, 1753

Le nozze contrastate (ob, 3), ?Naples, ?1753; Rome, Dame, carn. 1755

Ezio (os, 3, P. Metastasio), Rome, Dame, ?1754; Rome, Dame, 1757, *I-MAav*, *P-La*; Padua, Fiera, 1765, *La*

L'incredulo (ob, 2, P. Mililotti), Naples, Fiorentini, aut. 1755

La fante furba (ob, 2, Palomba), Naples, Nuovo, aut. 1756

Nitteti (os, 3, Metastasio), Reggio Emilia, Pubblico, 29 April 1757, *F-Pn* (inc.), *I-MAav* (inc.), *P-La*

Didone abbandonata (os, 3, Metastasio), Venice, S Moisè, aut. 1757, *D-B* (Act 1), *P-La* (2 copies), *US-Wc*; Naples, 20 Jan 1764, *I-Nc*, *P-La*

Olimpiade (os, 3, Metastasio), Verona, Accademia Filarmonica, aut. 1758; Florence, Pergola, aut. 1767, *F-Pn*, *I-Fc*, *P-La*, *US-Wc*; St Petersburg, 10/21 April 1769, *B-Bc*, *D-Dlb*, *F-Pn*, *RU-SPtob*

Demofoonte (os, 3, Metastasio), Mantua, Vecchio, carn. 1758, *I-MAav* (inc.)

Solimano (os, 3, G. A. Migliavacca), Parma, Ducale, carn. 1759, *MAav*

Ippolito ed Aricia (tragedia, 5, C. I. Frugoni, after S.-J. Pellegrin and J. Racine), Parma, Ducale, 9 May 1759 [some music after Rameau], *D-B* (*R*1982: IOB, lxxviii), *I-Bc*, *BGc*, *P-La* (2 copies)

Enea nel Lazio (os, 3, V. A. Cigna-Santi), Turin, Regio, carn. 1760, *D-Bds*, *P-La* (2 copies)

I Tindaridi [Tintaridi], o Castore e Polluce (os, 5, Frugoni, after P.-J. Bernard), Parma, Ducale, April 1760, *A-Wn*, *D-B*, *I-Fc*, *P-La*, *US-Wc*; Act 2.iii ed. in DTB, xxv, Jg. xiv/i (1914); Florence, 3 Jan 1768, *I-Fc* (with pts)

Stordilano, principe di Granata (semiseria e bernesca, 3, ? G. Bertati), Parma, Ducale, spr. 1760; rev. as Il cavaliere errante (dramma eroicomico, 2, Bertati), ?Naples, ?1777, *F-Pn*; Venice, S Moisè, spr. 1778, *I-Mc* (with pts), *D-Dlb*, *F-Po*, *US-Wc*; as Il cavaliere errante nell'isola disabitata, Vienna, Kärntnertor, 1779; Eszterháza, Feb 1782, *H-Bn*

Le feste d'Imeneo [Il trionfo d'amore] (serenata, prol., 3, Frugoni, after L. de Cahusac), Parma, Ducale, 3 Sept 1760, *P-La*; Act 2.vi ed. in DTB, xxv, Jg.xiv/i (1914)

Armida (azione teatrale, 1, G. Durazzo and Migliavacca, after P. Quinault), Vienna, Burg, 3 Jan 1761, *A-Wn*, *D-B*, *Dlb*, *Mbs*, *F-Pn*, *I-Fc*, *Mc*, *Tn*; Naples, 1763, *Nc*, *P-La*

Enea e Lavinia (os, 3, J. A. Sanvitale, after B. le B. de Fontenelle), Parma, Ducale, spr. 1761, *I-Tn*, *P-La* (2 copies)

Zenobia (os, 3, Metastasio), Lucca, aut. 1761, *I-Tn*, incl. recits. and arias from other operas by Traetta

Alessandro nell'Indie (os, 3, Metastasio), Reggio Emilia, Pubblico, spr. 1762, *MOe*, *P-La*

Sofonisba (os, 3, M. Verazi, after A. Zanetti and G. Zanetti), Mannheim, Hof, 4 Nov 1762, *D-B*, *US-Wc*; excerpts ed. in DTB, xxv, Jg.xiv/1 (1914); xxix, Jg.xvii (1916)

La francese a Malaghera (dg, 3, P. Chiari), ?Parma, ?1762; Venice, S Cassiano, aut. 1764, *I-Gl*, *US-Wc*

Ifigenia in Tauride (os, 3, M. Coltellini), Vienna, Schönbrunn, 4 Oct 1763, *A-Wgm*, *Wn*, *B-Bc*, *D-B*, *Bhm*, *DS*, *I-Fc* (*R*1978: IOB, xlvii), *Nc*, *US-Wc*; excerpts ed. in DTB, xxv, Jg.xiv/i (1914); Eszterháza, 26 July 1786, *H-Bn* (with addns by Haydn)

Antigono (os, 3, Metastasio), Padua, Nuovo, 16 June 1764; *D-DS* (MS copy *US-Wc*), *F-Pn*, *I-Mc*, *P-La* (2 copies); rev. (2), St Petersburg, court, 11/22 Sept 1770, *RU-SPtob*

Semiramide (os, 3, Metastasio), Venice, S Cassiano, carn. 1765, *I-Mc*, *Nc*, *P-La* (2 copies)

Le [due] serve rivali [La serva scaltra; I capricci del sesso] (burletta, 3, Chiari), Venice, S Moisè, aut. 1766, *A-Wn*, *D-B*, *Dlb*, *DS*, *F-Pn*, *I-Fc*, *MOe*; Lisbon, Ajuda, 1768, *P-La* (2 copies and pts)

Siroe, re di Persia (os, 3, Metastasio), Munich, Hof, carn. 1767, *A-Wgm*, *D-Bds*, *Dlb*, *Mbs*

Amore in trappola (dg, 3, Chiari), Venice, S Moisè, carn. 1768

L'isola disabitata (azione drammatica, 1, Metastasio), Bologna, Nuovo Pubblico, 26 Dec 1768, *P-La*; St Petersburg, court, carn. 1769, *RU-SPtob*

Fetonte (os, 3), Vienna, court, 1768

Il tributo campestra (pastorale, 1, G. B. Baganza), Mantua, Ducale Nuovo, 1768

Astrea placata (azione teatrale, Metastasio), St Petersburg, court, 1770

Antigona [Antigone] (os, 3, Coltellini), St Petersburg, court, 31 Oct/11 Nov 1772, *D-DS*, *RU-SPtob*, *US-Wc*; ed. A. Rocchi (Florence, 1962); excerpts ed. in DTB, xxv, Jg.xiv/i (1914)

Amore e Psiche (os, 3, Coltellini), St Petersburg, court, 29 Sept 1773

Lucio Vero (os, 3, Coltellini, after Zeno), St Petersburg, court, 17/28 Nov 1774, *D-DS*, *F-Pn*, *GB-Lbl*, *RU-SPtob*

Germondo (os, 3, Goldoni), London, King's, 21 Jan 1776, Favourite Songs (London, *c*1776)
La Merope (os, 3, Zeno), Milan, Ducale, 25 Jan 1776, ov. *I-Mc*
Telemaco (os, 3, Z. de Seriman), London, King's, 15 March 1777
La disfatta di Dario (os, 3, A. Morbilli), Venice, S Benedetto, Feb 1778, *D-Bds*
Gli eroi dei Campi Elisi (dg, 3), Venice, S Samuele, carn. 1779, completed by G. Astarita, ov. *I-Gl*
Artenice, unfinished

Music in: Ifigenia in Aulide, 1753; La Rosmonda, 1755; I disturbi, 1756; La virtuosa ritornata da Londra, 1757, doubtful; L'Issipile, 1763; Zophilette, 1765; Olimpiade, 1768, *GB-Lbl*; Olimpiade, 1769, Favourite Songs (London, *c*1769); Antigono, ?1775, Favourite Songs (London, 1776)

*

FlorimoN
V. Capruzzi: *Traetta e la musica* (Naples, 1873)
H. Goldschmidt: 'Traettas Leben und Werke', DTB, xxv, Jg.xiv/1 (1914); xxix, Jg.xvii (1916)
A. Nuovo: *Tommaso Traetta* (Rome, 1922)
——: *Tommaso Traetta: grande musicista* (Bitonto, 1938)
R.-A. Mooser: *Annales de la musique et des musiciens en Russie au XVIIIe siècle*, ii (Geneva, 1951)
'Tommaso Traetta, Leonardo Leo, Vincenzo Bellini: notizie e documenti', *Chigiana*, ix (1952)
E. Saracino: *Tommaso Traetta: cenni biografico-artistici* (Bitonto, 1954)
A. Yorke-Long: *Music at Court* (London, 1954)
B. Cantrell: *Tommaso Traetta and his Opera 'Sofonisba'* (diss., U. of California, Los Angeles, 1957)
F. Casavola: *Tommaso Traetta di Bitonto (1727–1779): la vita e le opere* (Bari, 1957)
H. Bloch: 'Tommaso Traetta's Reform of Italian Opera', *CHM*, iii (1963), 5–13
D. Heartz: 'Operatic Reform at Parma: "Ippolito ed Aricia" ', *Convegno sul settecento parmense nel 2º centenario della morte di C. I. Frugoni: Parma 1968*, 271–300
G. Massera: 'L'incontro Traetta-Frugoni: riforma o novità', *I teatri di Parma dal Farnese al regio*, ed. I. Allodi (Milan, 1969), 117–22
S. Martinotti: 'Traetta, o il musicista di un'impossibile "riforma" ', *Chigiana*, xxix–xxx (1975), 343–56
M. Cyr: 'Rameau e Traetta', *NRMI*, xii (1978), 166–82
D. Heartz: 'Traetta in Vienna: *Armide* (1761) and *Ifigenia in Tauride* (1763)', *Studies in Music from the University of Western Ontario*, vii (1982), 65–88
M. McClymonds: 'Mattia Verazi and the Opera at Mannheim, Stuttgart, and Ludwigsburg', *Studies in Music from the University of Western Ontario*, vii (1982), 99–136
N. Morea: *Tommaso Traetta: riformatore del melodramma* (Bitonto, 1982)
U. Zelaschi: *L'opéra italien jusqu'en 1900* (Brussels, 1982)
S. Henze: 'Opera seria am kurpfälzischen Hofe: Traettas "Sofonisba", de Majos "Ifigenia in Tauride", Bachs "Temistocle" ', *Mannheim und Italien: zur Vorgeschichte der Mannheimer: Mannheim 1983*, 78–96

DANIEL HEARTZ, MARITA P. McCLYMONDS

Tragédie en musique [tragédie lyrique] (Fr.). The most important species of French opera in the period from Lully to Rameau (1673–1764). In its internal organization and musical character it shares many features with lesser genres like the *pastorale-héroïque*. It is nevertheless distinguished by its consistent five-act structure (others usually had fewer acts) and by a greater dramatic intensity and seriousness of tone. In the later 18th century the *tragédie en musique* profoundly influenced the operatic reforms of Jommelli, Traetta and, above all, Gluck. In their turn the French tragedies of Gluck, Piccinni, Sacchini and Salieri, produced in the 1770s and 80s, represent a transformation and final flowering of the genre.

1. Terminology. 2. History, 1673–1773. 3. The lyric tragedy as a 'regular' genre. 4. Dramatic and musical characteristics, 1673–1773. 5. Reform and regeneration.

1. TERMINOLOGY. During the greater part of the Lully-Rameau period, the term 'tragédie lyrique' is rarely encountered. For the first 85 years of the genre's existence, this expression was scarcely ever employed by librettists or composers. Almost without exception, librettos printed before 1760 use the terms 'tragédie' or 'tragédie en musique'. On printed scores the same terms are found with similar consistency, together with such variants as 'tragédie mise en musique' or (after the mid-18th century, when old librettos began to be recycled) 'remise en musique' (e.g. Dauvergne's *Enée et Lavinie*, 1758). Among writers on music, Le Cerf de la Viéville is typical of his time in referring to 'nos Opéra que nous appelons des Tragédies en Musique' (*Comparaison de la musique italienne et de la musique françoise*, 1704–6, iii, 3). During the 18th century, as other genres grew in stature and popularity, writers found the need to invent additional makeshift terms (e.g. 'tragédie-opéra', 'opéra tragédie').

It was in literary circles, and not until the mid-18th century, that the expression 'tragédie lyrique' first became fashionable. Rémond de Saint-Mard (1741), for example, uses 'tragédie lyrique' and 'tragédie en musique' interchangeably; Cahusac (1751, 1754) is more consistent in employing the former to distinguish lyric from spoken tragedy. During the 1760s the new term is found sporadically on title-pages (e.g. Dauvergne's *Hercule mourant*, 1761). But only in the following decade, particularly after the arrival in Paris of Gluck's operas, does it appear at all frequently in this context.

For much of the present century 'tragédie lyrique' has been the preferred term among musicologists. Yet

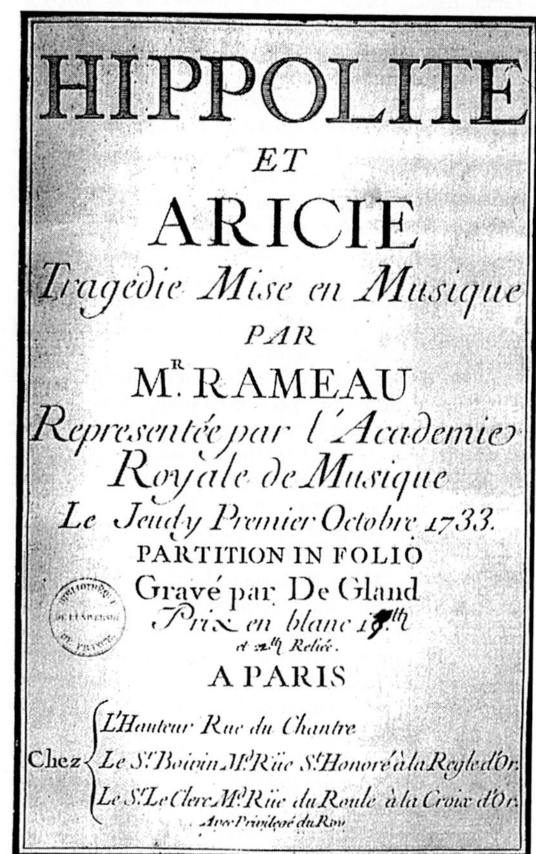

1. *Title-page of the first edition of Rameau's 'Hippolyte et Aricie' (Paris, 1733)*

nowadays scholars are increasingly following Girdlestone's lead in returning to the terms used by librettists and composers, at least for the Lully-Rameau period.

2. History, 1673–1773. A year after seizing control of the Académie Royale de Musique and hence acquiring a total monopoly of French opera, Lully produced the first of his *tragédies*, *Cadmus et Hermione* (1673). Thus was born the genre that was to dominate the composer's output and bear his imprint for many years to come: between them, Lully's 13 *tragédies*, all but two to librettos by Quinault, set the dramatic and in some respects the musical tone of the genre for almost a century.

The *tragédie en musique* emerged more or less fully fledged. Although various developments may be traced through Lully's subsequent works, *Cadmus* already includes most features characteristic of the genre. The Lullian *tragédie* is, in fact, an extraordinary amalgam of pre-existing elements. From the tragedies of Corneille and Racine come the five-act structure and the use, if no longer exclusive, of alexandrines, while the 'déclamation enflée et chantante' of the *tragédienne* C. C. La Champmeslé influenced Lully's conception of recitative. From the *ballet de cour* come the panegyrical prologues, stage spectacle, dances, *symphonies* and choruses. From the *tragédie à machines*, the *pastorale* and pre-Cornelian tragedy, the *comédie-* and *tragédie-ballet* come various other elements, both musical and dramatic. Lully's supreme achievement is to have synthesized all these into an art-form in which everything – music, drama, dance, staging – was subservient to an overriding dramatic unity: a true *Gesamtkunstwerk* 'avant la lettre'.

This eclectic mixture proved astonishingly popular at all levels of society, from Louis XIV down. Having created a taste for the *tragédie en musique*, Lully used his monopoly to ensure that only his operas could satisfy that taste. In any year after 1673, audiences could see a new Lully *tragédie* (they appeared at the rate of about one per year) and at least one revival of his existing operas, but no others. Given that devotees could buy season tickets and that the season lasted most of the year, it is hardly surprising that audiences got to know these works by heart; there are, indeed, reports of their joining in with the actors.

Lully's unexpected death in 1687 left something of a vacuum. Because of his monopoly, few French composers had first-hand experience of composing opera. (Marc-Antoine Charpentier was a rare exception, having written music for various private productions, including biblical operas for the Jesuits.) To fill the vacuum, the practice of reviving Lully's *tragédies* continued, reinforcing their dominant position in the public's affections. Many went on to be revived for 60, 70 or 80 years after their creation; *Thésée* lasted an astonishing 104 years, until 1779.

Not surprisingly, such new works as appeared in the remaining years of the 17th century were almost all *tragédies* in the Lullian mould. Among the composers were Lully's son, Louis, and former colleagues or pupils, Collasse, Marais and Desmarets. The works of these years are not without originality or musical interest. Indeed, Charpentier's *Médée* (1693) is one of the finest in the repertory. But almost all were judged unsatisfactory by comparison with the works of the revered Lully – Charpentier's because of its too-adventurous harmonic idiom, others because they seemed pale imitations. Only Collasse's *Thétis et Pélée* (1689) enjoyed a success comparable with the master's.

Almost half a century separates the last of Lully's *tragédies* (1687) and the first of Rameau's (1733). During this time several librettists emerged, among them Danchet, Lamotte and Roy, who came near to equalling the great Quinault without deviating much from his style. Yet even composers of the calibre of Campra, Destouches, Marais and Montéclair seldom managed the musical ingredients in a manner that carried dramatic conviction. Such men often seemed more comfortable in the lighter genres of opera. The gaps between successful *tragédies* became steadily wider: A. C. Destouches' *Omphale* (1701), Campra's *Tancrède* (1702), Desmarets and Campra's *Iphigénie en Tauride* (1704), Marais' *Alcyone* (1706), Gervais' *Hypermnestre* (1716), Montéclair's *Jephté* (1732). By the late 1720s, indeed, the Opéra had become 'a veritable graveyard of the *tragédie lyrique*' (Anthony).

Yet for Rameau the *tragédie* clearly remained the most esteemed genre. In all, he devoted to it about a third of his operatic output. Few others now showed the same commitment. In the 20-year period 1739–58, the Académie Royale de Musique presented only six new *tragédies*. (A similar period between 1718 and 1737 included three times as many.) If Rameau's first operas initially appeared controversial, that was not through any radical break with tradition: most elements of his style are at least hinted at in 'pré-ramiste' operas of the 1720s and early 30s. The Lulliste–Ramiste dispute had more to do with the complexity and intensity of Rameau's idiom. Once audiences had accepted this, they readily placed *Castor* and *Dardanus* on a level equal to, or even higher than, Lully's masterpieces.

From its beginnings, the *tragédie en musique* had been inseparably linked with the court and the Académie Royale de Musique (which inherited Lully's monopoly). It was thus highly institutionalized and firmly identified with the political and social hierarchy. Inevitably, therefore, the genre found itself attacked in the 1750s by the anti-establishment intellectuals of the new Enlightenment, prominent among them F. M. Grimm and J.-J. Rousseau. The resulting Querelle des bouffons, as much political as artistic in its motivation, succeeded in undermining the whole aesthetic basis of serious French opera and hastened the search for alternatives. There were those who clung to the *tragédie*: if anything, the Querelle led to an upsurge of activity. Between 1758 and 1773 a dozen new *tragédies* appeared, including such anticipations of Gluck as Philidor's *Ernelinde* (1767) and Gossec's *Sabinus* (1773). Dauvergne's *Enée et Lavinie* (1758) is one of several to take the hitherto unthinkable step of re-using librettos from the golden age; Mondonville (1765) even had the temerity to reset Quinault's *Thésée*. Yet few were successful enough to merit a revival, and it was gradually conceded that the genre was moribund. Moribund but not dead, for the arrival of Gluck's operas in Paris in 1774 was to provide a massive and invigorating transfusion. Gluck's work was 'at once a blow to French opera and a renewal of it' (Einstein, *Gluck*, 1936, p.138).

3. The lyric tragedy as a 'regular' genre. Opera in France emerged at a time when the native spoken theatre was at its peak. This fact, and the fact that the 'classic' French theatre of Corneille and Racine was governed by a strict code of rules ultimately derived from Aristotle's *Poetics*, explains many characteristics

2. *'Phaëton' (Lully), the final scene in Act 5 (Jupiter causes Phaethon's chariot to crash to the ground): wash drawing after J. Berain, engraved by J. Le Pautre for the frontispiece to the first edition of the libretto (1683); see also* MACHINERY, fig.8

of the *tragédie en musique*. Even before the birth of the genre, the poet Pierre Perrin had insisted that opera, to be taken seriously, must be accommodated within the Aristotelean system of poetics; not only should the three genres Perrin envisaged – *pastorale*, comedy, tragedy – be regarded as lyric counterparts to the 'regular' genres of spoken theatre, but they should be governed by the same code of rules. For a century thereafter, in the often intense debates concerning opera, the place of lyric tragedy within the *système poétique* was widely conceded, even by those hostile to the genre or the system itself.

Yet although the *tragédie en musique* shares features with spoken tragedy (most obviously the five-act structure), it was never conceived of as merely an adaptation of the existing genre. Spoken tragedy, it was widely believed, had reached a state of perfection: to graft music on to it would be both impractical and inappropriate. Far better that lyric tragedy should aim at a perfection equal to that of Corneille or Racine without directly imitating it. Indeed, lyric tragedy came to be seen not only as the counterpart but also the inverse of spoken tragedy. This idea was first put forward by Perrault in 1674, only a year after the emergence of the genre; during the next 80 years the theory was developed at greater length, notably by the Abbé de Mably (1741), Batteux (1746) and Cahusac (1751, 1754).

The inversion applies first to the subject matter. Whereas spoken tragedy preferred to treat historical figures, such subjects were considered inappropriate for opera. What rational mind could tolerate the idea of a Brutus or a Pompey expressing himself solely through singing? But if opera restricted itself to a world inhabited by gods, demigods, magicians and allegorical or legendary figures, the problem disappeared. Hence the preponderance of *tragédies* based on classical myth or legend (Lully, *Alceste*; Marais, *Alcyone*; Rameau, *Castor et Pollux*), Italian epic (Lully, *Armide*; Campra, *Alcine*) or Spanish romance (Lully, *Amadis*; Destouches, *Amadis de Grèce*). For the same reasons, librettists turned very occasionally to the Old Testament (Montéclair, *Jephté*) or other ancient religious sources (Rameau, *Zoroastre*).

Almost by definition, then, opera made extensive use of supernatural elements, collectively known as *le merveilleux*. In spoken tragedy this had been marginalized; certainly it played no part in the denouement. In the *tragédie en musique*, conversely, the supernatural was considered not only desirable but essential. Indeed, for many writers *le merveilleux* was the key feature – 'la pierre fondamentale de l'édifice' (Cahusac 1751) – that distinguished lyric from spoken tragedy. If it was pointless to imitate what spoken tragedy did perfectly, Cahusac argued, lyric tragedy was bound to explore what the theatre could not do or was forbidden from doing. In this way *tragédie en musique* became the antithesis of its spoken counterpart. *Le merveilleux* provided justification for this inversion. Where spoken tragedy eschewed stage machinery, the supernatural happenings in opera cried out for elaborate effects – divine descents, transformations, aerial battles. Where violent events in spoken tragedy were perforce enacted offstage or merely recounted, they happened in full view in lyric tragedy (compare the treatment of the sea monster in Racine's *Phèdre* and in Rameau's *Hippolyte*). Where dance was seldom required in spoken tragedy, it was justified within the supernatural milieu of opera in the same way that music was. Even the balance of elements in the plot was inverted: whereas love interest in the theatre was usually secondary to themes of a political nature, overtly political themes were generally thought ill-suited to opera. Rather, the typical *tragédie en musique* adopted one of a number of formulae involving a pair of lovers and one or more rivals. Significantly, the rivals often included at least one divinity or magician.

Similar inversions may be seen to apply to the Cornelian unities. In lyric tragedy, unity of place was routinely ignored: it was usual for each act to be set in a different location, and individual acts might include further scene changes. Such infringements were positively encouraged by La Bruyère ('il faut des changements') though discouraged by the Abbé de Mably. Unity of time was likewise generally ignored. In Rameau's *Zoroastre*, 'the librettist ... has had to make it day and night two or three times in each act so that it might be day at the end of the play' (Grimm, exaggerating as usual). Most librettos are merely vague concerning the passage of time. Certainly there was little attempt to make a virtue of observing this unity. As for unity of plot, the episodic nature of a genre so devoted to *divertissement* and spectacle made this difficult to respect.

Cahusac goes on to develop what earlier writers had merely stated – that the lyric tragedy, once these inversions were made, remained governed by the rules of spoken tragedy: (1) *nécessité*, whereby each aspect of the work, whether it concerned actors, situations, actions, subplots, dance, entrances or exits, must justify

3. *'Castor et Pollux' (Rameau): drawing, possibly by Jean-Louis Fesch (1738–73), of the characters Telaira and Castor (above) and Phoebe and Pollux (below) in a revival at the Paris Opéra; gouache on vellum*

itself as 'necessary' by the criterion that its removal or displacement would somehow damage the harmonious disposition of the work; (2) *propriété* or *convenance*, whereby each of those same elements must receive only those attributes that were 'appropriate' or 'suitable' to it; and (3) *vraisemblance*, whereby each element must be managed in such a way as not to offend the audience's sense of what was 'probable' or 'likely'. While the desirability of such rules might seem obvious enough, Cahusac showed that they could even be (and had in practice always been) applied to *le merveilleux*. The 'necessity' of the supernatural in lyric tragedy had been established from the outset: how else could one justify a drama that was sung throughout? This did not, however, give the librettist free rein to introduce magical effects in any way he pleased. Recourse to *le merveilleux* was permissible only when all human means had been exhausted. Likewise the rule of 'propriety' applied as much to the supernatural elements as to all others. The attributes and conduct of gods, magicians and the like had to conform with what was known about them (or could reasonably be inferred) from classical sources; moreover, the supernatural beings must behave in keeping with their status. Thus, in *Hippolyte et Aricie* (Prologue), a dispute between Diana and Cupid cannot be settled except by a divinity of superior rank – Jupiter; in Act 2, a conflict of interests between Pluto and Neptune cannot be resolved by a direct confrontation but only by an intermediary – Mercury, a lesser god, acting as ambassador.

The 'credibility' (*vraisemblance*) of the supernatural might seem hardest to justify but was at least as important. Although audiences wanted to see marvels at the Opéra, they could not be expected to accept anything. A supernatural event, once it was justified by the law of necessity, would seem more credible if its execution conformed to the laws of the natural world. Hence the preponderance of storms, earthquakes, shipwrecks and dream-sequences. By the same argument, the descent of a supernatural being would be more acceptable if it took place either in a 'natural' manner (e.g. on a cloud) or in a way that did not stretch the audience's credulity (on a chariot supported by cupids or other winged beings).

It was by such means that the lyric tragedy could be justified as a 'regular' genre within the *système poétique* (not to everyone's satisfaction: for Le Brun it remained 'une tragédie irregulière, à la vérité'). While it is clear that what Cahusac and others describe is a theoretical model (necessarily simplified here; fully discussed in Kintzler 1991), it is equally clear from empirical evidence that this model was widely accepted by librettists and composers of the Lully-Rameau period. True, not all works conform to all aspects of the model. Rebel and Francoeur's *Scanderberg* (1735), for instance, is based not on legend, romance or ancient religion but on a 'real' life – that of the 15th-century Albanian hero Iskander-Beg. Lully's *Atys* is likewise exceptional in observing the unity of time: the action begins before dawn and takes place within the regulation 24 hours. Moreover, the list of works including features that are neither necessary, appropriate nor probable is long indeed. Yet it is important to remember that individual works were often criticized on precisely those grounds, prompting librettists and composers to make extensive revisions – whole acts in the case of Rameau's *Dardanus* or *Zoroastre*. In short, it is only in the light of the above theories that much contemporary criticism becomes fully comprehensible. While individual aspects of the theory apply to other operatic genres, the whole theoretical model applies only to the *tragédie en musique*.

4. Dramatic and musical characteristics, 1673–1773. The object of both lyric and spoken tragedy was, in Aristotle's phrase, to excite pity and terror. Yet this was never the sole or main aim of the *tragédie en musique*. The prevailing tone, at least until the time of Rameau, was more elegiac than tragic. Such pity and terror as is engendered was quickly dissipated by scenes of calm and joy.

For La Bruyère, indeed, the essential characteristic of the genre was not so much to plumb the depths of human experience as 'to hold the spirit, the eyes and the ears in an equal enchantment'. This was a view echoed many times in the 18th century to justify the mixture of drama, spectacle, singing and dancing. In order to accommodate the competing demands of these elements, Lully and Quinault established a convention whereby the action would give way at some point in each act to *divertissement* or (in tragedy, as opposed to *pastorale* or ballet) *fête*. Whereas the *scènes*, as the former were known, would be declaimed predominantly in recitative, the *fêtes* would involve *airs*, choruses, ballet and spectacle in continuous sequences that between them might make up a third of the whole work or more.

These *fêtes* still had to satisfy the laws of necessity, propriety and probability. Thus in any given act the plot might require a religious ceremony, wedding, occult conjuration or victory celebration. *Fêtes* could help further the action: the goddess Cybèle uses a dream-sequence to apprise Atys of her love and warn him of the consequences if he spurns her (*Atys*, Act 3). Moreover, *fêtes* were often effective in preparing for what Aristotle calls *peripeteia* – unexpected reversals of fortune. It is during pre-nuptial rejoicings that Roland learns with horror of the betrothal of Angélique to his rival Médor (*Roland*, Act 3). Such *fêtes* may even generate a degree of dramatic irony, where the audience knows that the celebration is premature (e.g. *Hippolyte et Aricie*, Act 4). Significantly, the contrast between action and *fête* is often reflected in a work's tonality, which will be in a state of flux during the former but static during the latter.

In Lully's day the *scènes* consisted largely of declamatory, French-style recitative, with painstakingly notated rhythms, fluctuating time signatures and active bass lines. This was periodically relieved by binary or rondo *petits airs* usually expressing some sententious maxim, or – less often, and only in passages of high emotion – by accompanied recitative, elegiac monologues or laments. During the 18th century the recitative changed remarkably little: Rameau could genuinely claim to have taken as guide 'la belle déclamation & [le] beau tour du Chant qui regnent dans le Récitatif du Grand Lully'. Steadily, however, the proportion of recitative to set piece decreased, while that of accompanied to unaccompanied recitative grew. Likewise there was greater musical involvement in the *scènes*: accompaniments of *petits airs* became more elaborate, while the monologue, in the hands of Destouches, Campra and, above all, Rameau, could generate an intensity undreamt of by Lully. Nevertheless, the primacy of the action outside the *fêtes* was seldom forgotten: however intricate the accompaniments, the vocal line remained predominantly syllabic and the transition from recitative to set piece flexible. Monologues often lack a final ritornello, so that the ensuing recitative immediately follows the singer's last words; they are usually placed at the beginnings of acts so as not to interrupt the action.

Indeed, the principal differences between Lullian and Ramellian *tragédie* have little to do with dramatic structure and much more with musical expansion. Campra may have thought Rameau's *Hippolyte* contained enough music to make ten operas; but Campra himself, with Destouches, Montéclair and others, had contributed much to this expansion. It affected every aspect, including choruses, dramatic *symphonies*, dances and *ariettes*. These last, unknown to Lully, were fully-developed da capo arias, the only movements to allow extensive vocal display. Characteristically, though, their role was purely decorative. As such, they were confined to the *fêtes* and, in many *tragédies*, limited to a single example. The *ariette* was French Baroque opera's most obvious debt to Italian opera; yet in the course of the 18th century, the *tragédie* gradually succumbed to the general influence of italianate music, even if most composers contrived to disguise it with a French accent.

For the first 75 years of its existence, the *trágedie en musique* was prefaced by a prologue, roughly the length of a single act. In Lully's day the prologue had a political function – to focus attention on the monarch: Louis XIV's achievements, real or imagined, were allegorized in a brief action usually independent of the ensuing *tragédie*. During the 18th century, and especially after

4. 'Atys' (Niccolò Piccinni): scene from a production by the Stockholm Opera in 1784: painting by Pehr Hillström

1715 when such panegyric became unfashionable, the subject matter of prologues varied widely: some (for example that in Campra's *Idomenée*) act as general introductions to the ensuing drama; others (*Hippolyte et Aricie*) justify the treatment of the source material; one (Campra's *Achille et Déïdamie*) even makes a polemical point in the Lulliste–Ramiste dispute. With Rameau's *Zoroastre* the prologue was decisively abandoned. In his preface, the librettist Cahusac argued that the time devoted to the prologue would be better spent on the main plot; instead, 'the overture serves as prologue'. Indeed, for some time (and several decades before Gluck) Rameau had been experimenting with ways of linking overture and drama.

5. Reform and regeneration. When Gluck published his preface to *Alceste* (1769), many of the reforms he advocated for Italian *opera seria* had long been established practice in France – not just the integration of the overture but the avoidance of excessive vocal display, irrelevant ritornellos, da capos, superfluous ornament, too sharp a contrast between recitative and aria. In fact, Gluck's librettist Calzabigi (possible author of the *Alceste* preface) had long appreciated the potentiality of French opera. Meanwhile, Diderot, D'Alembert and others advocated a simplification and humanizing of the *tragédie* and the adoption of an international musical language. Thus Gluck, disappointed with his lack of success in Vienna, was well aware of the advantages of moving to Paris. His six French *tragédies* (*Iphigénie en Aulide*, *Orphée et Euridice*, *Alceste*, *Armide*, *Iphigénie en Tauride* and *Echo et Narcisse*) exactly capture the ideals of all those reformers and others, among them Algarotti and Noverre. In these works he preserves the best of French practice – the structural flexibility and the subordination of aria, ballet, chorus, *symphonie* to the requirements of the drama – but subjects it to a rigorous simplification. Although *le merveilleux* is not eliminated, it is never allowed to detract from the sincere expression of human feelings. The traditional French musical idiom was now decisively abandoned; Gluck's claim that 'I have found a musical language fit for all nations, and hope to abolish the ridiculous distinctions between national styles of music' (*Mercure de France*, February 1773) was to some extent justified.

There were many who nevertheless found such operas too severe. As a rival to Gluck, the Italian composer Piccinni was brought to Paris and especially championed by the librettist Marmontel. Piccinni's 'tragédies lyriques' have the structural flexibility and even something of the musical style of Gluck's French operas; insipid as they now seem, they control and integrate the ballet, chorus and spectacle in a way that would satisfy the Encyclopedists. Piccinni's scoring is fuller than Gluck's, and he no longer confines long arias to soliloquy. Works like *Roland* (1778) and *Atys* (1780) are based on Quinault librettos, albeit 'Marmontelized' (Grimm's term) into three acts; they thus make extensive use of the supernatural. In the subsequent development of *tragédie lyrique* by Lemoyne, Gossec, Sacchini, Salieri, J. C. Bach and others, it was generally Piccinni rather than Gluck who was taken as a model. As well as further resettings of Quinault and other venerable old librettos, operas of the 1780s include adaptations of Corneille (e.g. Sacchini, *Chimène*, 1783), Greek tragedy (Lemoyne, *Electre*, 1782; Salieri, *Les Danaïdes*, 1784) and historical subjects (Sacchini, *Arvire et Evelina*, 1788).

DOCUMENTARY MATERIALS

Recueil général des opéra représentés par l'Académie royale de musique depuis son établissement (Paris, 1703–46)

F. and C. Parfaict: *Histoire de l'Académie royale de musique depuis son établissement jusqu'à présent* (MS, 1741, *F-Pn*)

J.-B. Durey de Noinville: *Histoire du théâtre de l'Académie royale de musique en France* (Paris, 1753, 2/1757)

A. de Léris: *Dictionnaire portatif des théâtres* (Paris, 1754, 2/1763)

Mémoires pour servir à l'histoire de l'Académie royale de musique vulgairement l'opéra depuis son établissement en 1669 jusqu'en l'année 1758 (MS Amelot, *Po*)

L.-C. Lavallière: *Ballets, opéra, et autres ouvrages lyriques, par ordre chronologique depuis leur origine* (Paris, 1760)

L.-F. Beffara: *Dictionnaire de l'Académie royale de musique* (autograph MS, 1783–4, *Po*)

17TH- AND 18TH-CENTURY THEORY AND CRITICISM

C. Perrault: *Critique de l'opéra, ou Examen de la tragédie intitulée 'Alceste ou Le triomphe d'Alcide'* (Paris, 1674)

J. de La Bruyère: *Les caractères, ou Les moeurs de ce siècle* (Paris, 1699)

J. L. Le Gallois, Sieur de Grimarest: *Traité du récitatif: dans la lecture, dans l'action publique, dans la déclamation et dans le chant* (Paris, 1707)

A. L. Le Brun: *Théâtre lyrique; avec une préface où l'on traite du poëme de l'opéra, et la réponse à une épitre satyrique contre ce spectacle* (Paris, 1712)

J.-B. Dubos: *Réflexions critiques sur la poésie et sur la peinture* (Paris, 1719, 7/1770)

G. Bonnot de Mably: *Lettres à Madame la marquise de P*** sur l'opéra* (Paris, 1741)

T. Rémond de Saint-Mard: *Réflexions sur l'opéra* (The Hague, 1741)

C. Batteux: *Les beaux-arts réduit à un même principe* (Paris, 1746, 3/1773)

P. C. Roy: 'Lettre sur l'opéra', in E. C. Fréron: *Lettres sur quelques écrits de ce temps* (Geneva, 1749), ii, 7–22

L. de Cahusac: 'Enchantement', *Encyclopédie, ou Dictionnaire raisonné des sciences, des arts et des métiers*, ed. D. Diderot and J. le Rond d'Alembert (Paris, 1751–65)

——: *La danse ancienne et moderne, ou Traité historique de la danse* (The Hague, 1754)

F. Algarotti: *Saggio sopra l'opera in musica* (Bologna, 1755, 2/1763; Eng. trans., 1767)

R. de Calzabigi: *Dissertazione su le poesie drammatiche del sig. Abate Pietro Metastasio* (Paris, 1755)

M.-P.-G. de Chabanon: *De la musique considérée en elle-même et dans ses rapports avec la parole, les langues, la poésie et le théâtre* (Paris, 1785)

J.-F. Marmontel: *Eléments de littérature*, in *Oeuvres complètes* (Paris, 1819–20), xii–xv

F. M. Grimm: 'Du poème lyrique (1765)', *Correspondance littéraire, philosophique et critique par Grimm, Diderot, Raynal, Meister, etc.*, ed. M. Tourneux (Paris, 1877–82), xvi, 363–405

D. Launay, ed.: *La querelle des bouffons* (Geneva, 1973) [facs. of 61 pamphlets pubd 1752–4]

B. Durand-Sendrail, ed.: *Denis Diderot: Ecrits sur la musique* (Paris, 1987)

MODERN STUDIES

J. Ecorcheville: *De Lulli à Rameau, 1690–1730: l'esthétique musicale* (Paris, 1906)

E. Gros: *Philippe Quinault* (Paris, 1926)

P.-M. Masson: *L'opéra de Rameau* (Paris, 1930)

C. Girdlestone: *Jean-Philippe Rameau: his Life and Work* (London, 1957, 2/1969)

P. Howard: *Gluck and the Birth of Modern Opera* (London, 1963)

D. Heartz: 'From Garrick to Gluck: the Reform of Theatre and Opera in the Mid Eighteenth Century', *PRMA*, xciv (1967–8), 111–27

J. Rushton: *Music and Drama at the Académie Royale de Musique 1774–1789* (diss., U. of Oxford, 1969)

C. Girdlestone: *La tragédie en musique, considérée comme genre littéraire (1673–1750)* (Geneva, 1972)

H. Lagrave: *Le théâtre et le public à Paris de 1715 à 1750* (Paris, 1972)

J. R. Anthony: *French Baroque Music from Beaujoyeulx to Rameau* (London, 1973, 2/1978)

R. M. Isherwood: *Music in the Service of the King* (Ithaca, 1973)

G. Cowart: *The Origins of Modern Musical Criticism: French and Italian Music 1600–1750* (Ann Arbor, 1981)

L. Rosow: *Lully's 'Armide' at the Paris Opéra: a Performance History, 1686–1766* (diss., Brandeis U., 1981)
C. Wood: *Jean-Baptiste Lully and his Successors: Music and Drama in the 'tragédie en musique' 1673–1715* (diss., U. of Hull, 1981)
H. Schneider: 'Tragédie et tragédie en musique: querelles autour de l'autonomie d'un nouveau genre', *Komparatistische Heft*, nos. 5–6 (Bayreuth, 1982), 43–58
C. Kintzler: *Jean-Philippe Rameau: splendeur et naufrage de l'esthétique du plaisir à l'âge classique* (Paris, 1983, 2/1988)
J. de La Gorce: 'Documents de critique musicale et théâtrale: dix lettres extraites de la correspondance entre Ladvocat et l'abbé Dubos', *XVIIe siècle*, xxxv (1983), 267–82
L. E. Brown: 'Departure from the Lullian Convention in the *tragédie lyrique* of the *préramiste* Era', *Recherches sur la musique française classique*, xxii (1984), 59–78
R. Fajon: *L'Opéra à Paris du Roi Soleil à Louis le Bien-Aimé* (Geneva, 1984)
W. Weber: '*La musique ancienne* in the Waning of the Ancien Régime', *Journal of Modern History*, lvi (1984), 58–88
L. Auld: *The 'Lyric Art' of Pierre Perrin, Founder of French Opera* (Henryville, 1986)
J. Hajdu-Heyer, ed.: *Studies on Jean-Baptiste Lully and the Music of the French Baroque: Essays in Honor of James R. Anthony* (Cambridge, 1989)
P. Howard: 'The Influence of the Précieuses on Content and Structure in Quinault's and Lully's tragédies lyriques', *AcM*, lxiii/1 (1991), 57–72
C. Kintzler: *Poétique de l'opéra français de Corneille à Rousseau* (Paris, 1991)
GRAHAM SADLER

Tragédie lyrique. *See* TRAGÉDIE EN MUSIQUE.

Trăilescu, Cornel (*b* Timişoara, 11 Aug 1926). Romanian composer and conductor. He studied at the Timişoara Conservatory (1945–9) with Sabin Drăgoi and Vasile Ijac and at the Bucharest Conservatory (1949–53) with Mihail Andricu (composition), Theodor Rogalski (orchestration), George Georgescu and Constantin Silvestri (conducting). After a period as a répétiteur with the State Opera in Timişoara (1946–51), he spent a year with the Bucharest State Opera as chorus master (1951–2), before becoming music director of the Romanian Opera there in 1953. His operas, based on traditional or historical themes, often quote from old popular songs and ballads: *Bălcescu* uses the tune 'Mioriţa' as a leitmotif throughout the work, culminating in its appearance in the finale. Trăilescu's lyrical arias and dramatic choral climaxes are supported by subtle yet lively orchestration.

all first performed at Bucharest, Romanian Opera House
Motanul încălţat [Puss-in-Boots] (children's op, 3, T. Muşatescu and N. Stoiceva), 22 March 1964 (Bucharest, 1972)
Bălcescu (3, V. Sandulescu), 20 Aug 1974
Dragoste şi jertfă [Love and Sacrifice] (3, D. Tărchilă), 28 Aug 1977

VIOREL COSMA

Trajetta, Tommaso. *See* TRAETTA, TOMMASO.

Trambitsky, Viktor Nikolayevich (*b* Brest, 12 Feb 1895; *d* Leningrad [now St Petersburg], 13 Aug 1970). Russian composer. He studied the piano in Vilnius and in 1915 became a pupil of Kalafati in Petrograd (from 1917 at the conservatory). Subsequently he worked as an editor and concert organizer with the People's Commissariat for Education (1917–19), as conductor and pianist with travelling theatre troupes (from 1919) and, after moving to Sverdlovsk (now Yekaterinburg) in 1930, as an editor at Sverdlovsk Radio (1930–33); he then taught at the Sverdlovsk Conservatory, becoming director of theory and composition in 1944. He settled in Leningrad in 1961. Trambitsky wrote nine operas over a period of nearly 50 years; four of them were given in Sverdlovsk. His compositions show the influence of the folk music of the Urals and, according to Goldstein, of Musorgsky.

Karnaval zhizni [Carnival of Life] (Bianca), Krasnodar, Mobile Theatre, 1921
Ovod [The Gadfly] (Trambitsky, after E. Voynich), Sverdlovsk, 1929
Gnev pustïni [Anger of the Deserts] (Trambitsky), 1930
Velikiy put' [The Great Way] (Trambitsky), broadcast, Sverdlovsk, 1932
Orlyona (I. Keller), Sverdlovsk, 13 Nov 1934; rev. as Za zhïzn' [For Life], Sverdlovsk, 1938
Groza [The Storm] (5, Keller, after A. N. Ostrovsky), Sverdlovsk, 1942; rev. 1957, vs (1959)
Dni i nochi [Days and Nights] (V. Grishev, after K. Simonov), 1950
Kruzhevnitsa Nastya [Nastya the Lacemaker] (3, K. Paustovsky and Trambitsky), Leningrad, Kirov, 1963
Pamyat' serdtsa [Memory of the Heart], excerpts perf. 1968

*

MGG ('Trambizkij'; M. Goldstein)
B. I. Pevzner: 'Opernoye tvorchestvo V. Trambitskogo' [Trambitsky's Operatic Works], *Nauchno-metodicheskiye zapiski ural'skoy konservatorii*, iii (Sverdlovsk, 1957)
——: 'Kompozitor Trambitsky', *Ural* (1959)
——: 'V. Trambitsky, B. Gubalin, N. Puzey', *Kompozitorï Urala* (Sverdlovsk, 1968)
DETLEF GOJOWY

Trame deluse, Le [*Le trame deluse, ossia I raggiri scoperti* ('The Foiled Schemes, or The Tricks Discovered')]. *Commedia per musica* in three acts by DOMENICO CIMAROSA to a libretto by GIUSEPPE MARIA DIODATI; Naples, Teatro Nuovo, 7 December 1786.

The cunning and astute Ortensia (soprano) and her partner, the Neapolitan vagabond and trickster Don Nardo Fionza (bass), have worked their way into the house of Don Artabano (bass), a rich but foolish, uneducated simpleton. In order to steal Artabano's fortune Nardo has led him to believe that Ortensia is willing to be his bride. Artabano's niece, Olimpia (soprano), is in love with the Bolognese gentleman Clicerio (tenor). Both Clicerio and Dorinda (soprano), who was originally of noble rank but is now a gardener at Artabano's house, have already been exposed to the tricks of Ortensia and Nardo: on a previous occasion Clicerio was betrayed by Ortensia, while Dorinda is in her present situation because she has been betrayed and robbed by Nardo. The gullible Artabano allows himself to be manipulated by the thieves, but Clicerio decides to avenge his and Dorinda's honour by exposing them. Justice prevails when Artabano comes to his senses, recognizing the true motives of Ortensia and Nardo, and Olimpia and Clicerio celebrate their impending wedding.

This excellent opera is suffused with simple, folklike melodies, already evident in the lilting 6/8 section of the overture. As with most of Cimarosa's operas, witty characterization occurs in the fast-paced ensembles (e.g. the quintet in Act 1 scene viii) and there are some clever *basso buffo* 'patter' passages, as in Artabano's aria 'A me tal sfregio in faccia' (1.xiv). GORDANA LAZAREVICH

Tranchell, Peter (**Andrew**) (*b* Cuddalore, India, 14 July 1922). English composer and teacher. Educated at King's College, Cambridge (BA 1946, MusB 1949), he returned to teach at the university (1950) and was Fellow and director of music at Gonville and Caius College from 1960 to 1989. He has composed a large quantity of dramatic works, among them 'concert entertainments' which may be staged, and much of his music is direct, eclectic and harmonically sophisticated. His first opera, *The Mayor of Casterbridge* (3, Tranchell and P. S. Bentley; Cambridge, Arts, 30 July 1951), was a compressed version of Thomas Hardy's novel. In the style of a ballad opera and including some Scottish folktunes, it enjoyed a modest success, critics commenting on the impressive choral writing, complex orchestral scoring and balanced structure of the solos, ensembles and choruses. A second work, the musical comedy *Zuleika* (J. Ferman, after Max Beerbohm), was given at the Cambridge Arts Theatre on 25 October 1954. Tranchell has subsequently written, for dramatic presentation with pre-recorded tapes, a number of classical settings: *Bacchae* (1956), *Troades* (1957) and *Antigone* (1959).

Translation.

1. Definition. 2. History. 3. General aesthetic. 4. Problems in English translation.

1. DEFINITION. 'Opera translation' is usually taken to mean the provision of a singable text designed for performances of an opera. For this function some modern Italian published scores use the designation 'versione ritmica' rather than an equivalent of 'translation' in its literary sense, and in Britain Edward J. Dent and several of his successors have preferred the credit 'English version by' rather than 'translated by'. Spaeth (1915) particularized the task as 'translating to music'.

Apart from singing translations, there is a long history of translations made to be read, in order to help the auditor comprehend a foreign-language text in performance. An Italian translation of Lully's *Armide* was published in Rome in 1690, when this work became the first French opera to be performed in Italy. Booklets (which is what *libretti* literally means) providing the Italian original and an English translation were normally issued during the Handelian era in London. Such translations were not always literal but could interpret the text with poetic licence; Samuel Humphreys, translating *Orlando* (1733), expanded three non-rhyming Italian lines to make two English rhyming couplets. Similarly, the English prose translations issued for early and later 19th-century Italian performances might occasionally break into verse in independent metre:

Astounded by the din that broke
Upon my vision, I awoke,
Vexed that a dream at first so fair
At last should vanish into air.

(Dual-language word-book for Rossini's *La Cenerentola*, King's Theatre, 1828; end of Act 1.)

Until the late 19th century the retention of lighting in the auditorium during performances permitted such texts to be followed during performance. By the mid-20th century the provision of 'reading' (non-singing) versions chiefly answered the demands of record-buyers listening to complete operas in the original language. Many translations issued with such recordings cultivated an extreme literalism, subjugating all other considerations to the goal of enabling the listener to follow a foreign text almost word for word. The present article is concerned with translation not for reading but for performance.

2. HISTORY. The earliest operas listed by Loewenberg as being performed in a foreign-language translation within or near the lifetime of the composer are Lully's *Acis et Galatée* (1686, Paris; in German in 1695 at Hamburg, and in 1698 at Stuttgart) and Pallavicino's *La Gierusalemme liberata* (1687, Venice; likewise in 1695 at Hamburg). From a date even earlier (see White 1983, pp.54–5) there exists an English singing version of Cavalli's *Erismena*, an opera originally given in Venice in 1655 and revised in 1670. Whether this English version was actually produced – and whether such an event corresponds to the entry in Evelyn's diary on 5 January 1674 ('I saw an *Italian Opera* in musique, the first that had been in *England* of this kind') – remains conjectural.

In any case such occurrences were wholly exceptional in the 17th century. The first time that translated opera became a serious issue in the musical life of a major city was when Bononcini's *Camilla* was performed in London. Originally given at Naples at the end of 1696, this Italian opera was mounted at Drury Lane Theatre in April 1706 in an English translation by Owen Swiney. From December 1707 the performances were given in mixed English and Italian (to accommodate the participation of non-British singers), but the revivals at Lincoln's Inn Fields in 1717, 1719 and 1726 were wholly in English. 'There were no less than 113 performances between 1706 and 1728, which is by far the greatest number an Italian opera reached in London in the course of the 18th century; most of the performances, it is true, were wholly in English' (Loewenberg).

The objections to mixed-language opera, the failure of original English operas in the Italian style, and the triumph of Italian castratos and other singers in their own repertory and language then combined to halt the demand for translated opera. None of Handel's operas was translated for complete performance during the century, though some were given in Hamburg with German recitatives linking the arias in the original Italian. To transfer Gluck's Italian-language *Orfeo ed Euridice* and *Alceste* into a French-language repertory required not mere translation but recomposition to accommodate them to French taste. A pattern was established which was henceforth to prevail, subject to local modifications, all over Europe and the Americas: Italian opera was exported in Italian and performed by companies of (mainly) Italian singers either on tour or with stable theatres and regular seasons of their own.

Exceptionally, Pergolesi's *La serva padrona* (1733) was widely performed in translation. Likewise some French *opéras comiques* of the mid-18th century, particularly Grétry's, achieved sufficient fame to be translated. Two such works, performed in Italian, formed the only non-Italian component in the repertory which Haydn mounted (with a company mainly of Italian singers) for his princely employers at Eszterháza. French *opéras comiques* also achieved performance in German in Vienna. But only from the mid-1780s and with Mozart's works did translation take root as a regular mode of musical exchange. Barely six years after its première in Vienna (1786), *Le nozze di Figaro* had been given in German in at least 15 locations, including Vienna itself; *Don Giovanni* in German was seen in well over 60 locations up to 1802. In their total history, these works must have been performed far more often in German (and other) translations than in the original. Mozart himself encouraged the making and touring of a German version of *La finta giardiniera* (this German version, with spoken dialogue replacing recitatives, became for a long time the only full score available in complete form) and had also hoped to present *Idomeneo* in German.

The converse happened with *Die Zauberflöte*, which

(described as a *dramma eroicomico*) became *Il flauto magico* for a production by an Italian company visiting Leipzig in 1794. The reaction of a local newspaper was one of gratification that a German work had been so singled out: 'It is no small triumph for us Germans that at last the all-conquering Italians have had recourse to *us*' (quoted in Schuh 1963). Two decades later the success of Rossini (particularly *Il barbiere di Siviglia*, 1816) led to the diffusion of his works both by the export of the Italian original and in translations: *Il barbiere* was produced in English in 1818, in German in 1819 and in French in 1821. The process was thereafter accelerated: to be translated was an opera's infallible mark of international success. Meyerbeer's *Les Huguenots* (1836) had three German-language productions in the first year of its life, and it spread much less in the original French than in German (1842, London; 1850, St Petersburg) and Italian (1848, London; 1866, Constantinople).

As these examples make clear, translated versions did not exclusively serve a native vernacular but also formed the diet of an operatic 'outpost', whether a small touring company or a resident institution such as the Royal Italian Opera in London (at Her Majesty's, later at Covent Garden) or the Théâtre des Italiens in Paris. In general, however, translation meant popularization via the native tongue. In regions where a national culture formerly suppressed was allowed to emerge, the point was clearly made: in Prague *Rigoletto* was given as early as 1853 in German but not until 1864 in Czech, and in Latvia the opera house opened its initial season (1919) with the first-ever performance in Latvian of *Tannhäuser*.

Translated librettos, or individual numbers from them, could be popular enough to generate almost a proverbial force, in such English phrases as 'Home to our mountains' (*Il trovatore*), 'All hail, thou dwelling pure and lowly' (*Faust*), 'On with the motley' (*Pagliacci*) and 'One fine day' (*Madama Butterfly*). In both French and German the translated title is much more often used even in scholarly discourse (*Der Troubadour* or *Le trouvère* instead of *Il trovatore*) than is the case in English. Even the Breitkopf edition of the full score of *Le nozze di Figaro* (1869), which gives the opera text in both Italian and German, indexes the actual numbers by their German first words only. In the standard Russian one-volume musical encyclopedia (B. S. Shteynpress and I. M. Yampol'sky 1969) Mozart's opera titles, including *Così fan tutte*, are listed only in Russian translation.

In German-speaking countries and in France and Italy, opera in the native language became the norm and enjoyed the prestige of performance at the highest level, with original operas in that language providing the basic repertory to which translated works were added. Composers lent not only their sanction but their active participation to the process of translation, and were ready to provide such musical modification as was thought necessary. Wagner with the French-language version of *Tannhäuser* (1861, Paris), Gounod with the English-language *Faust* (1864, London) and Verdi with the French version of *Otello* (1894, Paris) afford well-known examples, and Massenet's *Werther* (1892) was actually first given, in German translation, at Vienna. Works commissioned with French texts from Italian composers (Rossini, Donizetti, Verdi) became without exception better known and indeed standardized in their subsequent Italian versions; Donizetti himself was credited with the Italian translations of *Betly* and *La fille du régiment*.

The crucial application of translation to Czech opera is exemplified by both Smetana and Janáček. The universal fame of *The Bartered Bride* (1866) did not begin until after it had been given in Max Kalbeck's German version at Vienna in 1892 – and indeed the common English title follows the German (*Die verkaufte Braut*) rather than the Czech original (*Prodaná nevěsta*, 'The Sold Fiancée'). The opera of 1904 which Janáček entitled *Její pastorkyňa* ('Her Foster-Daughter') began to win international recognition only from 1918 – retitled as *Jenůfa*, in Max Brod's German translation, also at Vienna. Later composers as diverse as Strauss, Prokofiev, Britten and Henze encouraged the translation of their work in print and on the stage, Henze even providing his own German translation to appear in the score with the original English text of *Elegy for Young Lovers* (1961), with many divergences in sense from it.

Practices in 19th-century Britain and the USA differed sharply from those on the European mainland. No tradition of first-class native opera composers establishing itself, opera in foreign languages (not necessarily the original languages) reflected the preferred repertory and the provenance of the most admired singers, and opera in translation achieved only a secondary esteem. British touring companies invariably sang in English but no English-singing company took firm root in London before that of the post-1918 Old Vic. Covent Garden's mounting of the *Ring* in English in 1908, at the direct urging of Hans Richter, remained exceptional. Whereas the Old Vic enterprise led ultimately to the English National Opera, attached exclusively to the native language, the equivalent second company in New York, the City Opera, divides its repertory between the vernacular and the original. For obvious theatrical reasons, however, operetta in English-speaking countries as elsewhere enjoyed its preponderant success in the native language.

An attempt to base the post-1945 Covent Garden company on English-language performances foundered in the face of a change in the international aspect of opera itself. As late as 1947, the Vienna Staatsoper, visiting London with three of Mozart's Italian operas, performed two of them in German. But from the 1950s the proliferation of European festivals and, even more, the increasingly dominant economic role of the record companies built a bias in favour of a single, internationally accepted language for each opera, usually the original language (but Italian for Verdi's *Don Carlos*!), with universally accepted stars repeating their performances on a travel schedule of a hitherto unknown scale. The major houses not only in London and New York but in Paris, Vienna and Milan began to base their repertory on such original-language performances.

Countries outside the circulating-star system, or only partly within it, adhered more strongly to translation for reasons of popularization still considered valid. In the republics that formed the USSR performances of opera have been given almost entirely in Russian (with some mixed-language performances to accommodate foreign soloists) or in local languages; a production of Handel's *Imeneo* in Italian, given by the Moscow Chamber Opera in 1989, was noted as a rare exception.

3. GENERAL AESTHETIC. The art of operatic translation is often assumed to be *sui generis* but is not so. Parallel aesthetic and practical problems arise with the transla-

tions of oratorio and similar texts (the cases of Bach, Handel, Haydn and Mendelssohn furnish some well-discussed examples); and within operas there are self-contained songs of a purely lyrical nature, without narrative or characterizing feature (such as 'Deh vieni, non tardar' in *Le nozze di Figaro* or 'Elle a fui, la tourterelle' in *Les contes d'Hoffmann*), where the translator's role is the same as it would be for the preparation of a concert edition. At the other extreme, as in the treatment of spoken dialogue, the opera translator's role approaches that of the translator of spoken drama, for whom the goal of the dramatic counterpart may override literal equivalence.

The perception of translated opera as essentially a debasement of the original, thus inevitably imparting a secondary status to performances, is fairly common among lay writers in English. In the words of Covent Garden's former chairman of directors, 'I wanted to hear works given as the composer originally intended: I mean the actual vowel and consonant sounds or as near to them as we could get' (Drogheda 1976, p.234). Apart from its assumption as to 'intention', this view hypothesizes a one-for-one equivalence between notes and words which is not common practice in composition (where a given musical phrase often recurs to different words) and is not sustained by citation from composers' practice. Composers' own encouragement of translation (see above) has at times sanctioned alterations of both verbal sense and actual notes to a surprising extent, as in the French score of Verdi's *Otello* (where the original librettist, Boito, is jointly credited with the translation).

British and American translators themselves have often felt impelled to defend the legitimacy of their work in principle. By contrast, the German literature on opera translation, in which Kurt Honolka as a leading modern translator is prominent, concentrates on matters of better or worse in translation, the importance or non-importance of rhyme, etc. In such matters, taste changes. The inbuilt obsolescence of the task was noted by the leading British translator of his day, Edward J. Dent (1938): 'Thomas Oliphant's version of *Fidelio* (1833) is a model of good style. Unfortunately it sounds too elegant for the present day: owing to changes in literary convention translations, like accompaniments to folksongs, must sooner or later become out of date, and have to be rewritten.' It remains arguable, however, that a period flavour coinciding with that of the music and the original words may be appropriate.

Alteration of note values in translation is obviously to be minimized, if not altogether to be avoided. Dent noted (1945) that 'rhythm is what gives character to all music, vocal and instrumental, and musical rhythms very often are strongly influenced by those of a spoken language'. He claimed that English had an elasticity which accommodated Russian, Hungarian and other rhythms, whereas 'German translators are ruthless in altering them'. The extent to which earlier German translators altered and even re-composed the recitatives in Mozart was noted by Honolka (1976) in introducing his new translation of *Le nozze di Figaro*. But Honolka acknowledged the necessity of compromise, noting the difficulty of navigating between 'the Scylla of belying the original and the Charybdis of leathery, convulsed or unmusical German'.

Elsewhere (1968) Honolka disparages the flowery, 'bombastic' (*schwülstig*) flavour of what he calls typical *operndeutsch*. The corresponding English 'flowery' style may be seen at its worst in Chorley's long-surviving translation (1871) of *Faust*, though an even worse feature of that translation is its phrasing *against* the music and the original text. Marguerite's unbroken melodic line over the original 'de me voir si belle [en ce miroir]' cannot be sensibly sung to '[Oh, the joy,] *past compare*, *These jew*-els [bright to wear]'.

The call made by the composer-conductor Gustav Brecher (1911) to get rid of rhyme altogether in German translation has not been generally followed, for the obvious reason that in most (not all) cases the rhymed verse is paralleled, or significantly and deliberately misparalleled, in musical setting. A later conductor, Gotthold Ephraim Lessing (1957), condemned the practice of putting translation in the hands of mere 'rhyme-smiths' who could only count syllables and stresses, instead of musicians who could 'hear' how the words would sound in their musical setting. That the translator should be a score-reader is treated as a prerequisite by Auden (1957, one of the few examples of opera translation by a leading poet), but he and his collaborator Chester Kallman claimed a bold poetic freedom as well:

> The goal of the translator, however unattainable, must be to make audiences believe that the words they are hearing are the words which the composer actually set, which means that a too-literal translation of the original text may sometimes prove a falsification ... In doing an aria, for example, it is often better, once he has grasped its emotional mood and general tenor, to put the actual words out of his mind and concentrate upon writing as good an English lyric as possible.

Declamation, in the sense of the correct allocation of verbal stress to musical stress, is recognized either explicitly (Spaeth 1915) or implicitly as the first principle to be observed by the translator. It merges into the principle of compatibility with the musical phrase. Once these principles are satisfied, the translator must balance the various demands of suitability to the voice, fidelity to the original meaning and an appropriate sense of period and genre. The stipulation by Andrew Porter (1976) that a sung translation should make 'audible sense at first hearing, without needing to be "worked out" by a puzzled listener' was made with special reference to the *Ring* but may be applied generally. It follows that, since many original texts may be considered awkward or obscure either inherently or through historical distance, the translator may 'improve' the text with the present-day listener in mind. There is no call to write 'I hear footprints' as a literal translation of 'Sento l'orme de' passi spietati' (*Un ballo in maschera*). Common sense may similarly override a composer's lapses: 'O namen-, namenlose Freude' (*Fidelio*) is not to be preserved (even if scansion would permit it) as 'Oh name-, nameless joy'.

To all these desiderata it might seem that 'a good literary style' should be added, but the achievement of style is better thought of as a by-product, the result of attention to the other qualities (Dent 1938, pp.vi–vii):

> After all [such] conditions are fulfilled, there is not much chance left for 'poetry'. The reader is asked to remember that the words of these English versions have been written to be sung and acted, not to be read. Stage scenery is not meant to be hung in a private house; the scene-painter is satisfied if it looks reasonably well on the stage. If the reader discovers in these pages any line he can call poetry, he may be sure that it has been stolen from a more respectable – and, I hope, non-copyright – author.

The reason why no general theory of opera translation has been evolved perhaps lies in the incommensurability of the material. The presence of *secco* recitative in Italian opera raises its own problem; many translators would rate its literal meaning more important, and its metrical values less important, than those in other parts of an opera. (Indeed, in some early performances in English as well as German the *secco* recitative was replaced by speech – and could be again.) But the diversities do not end there. To translate an opera text which is basically a spoken play (*Pelléas et Mélisande*, *Salome*, *Lulu*) is as different from the task of translating *Le nozze di Figaro* as the translating of Chekhov is from the translating of Racine.

4. PROBLEMS IN ENGLISH TRANSLATION. Opera in English, according to Porter (1976), has the reputation of 'sounding awful'. Or, according to Procter-Gregg (*Opera*, 1974–5): 'When read or spoken well and thoughtfully, how beautiful it [English] can sound! Sung, how clipped its wings or painfully stretched its noble tendons, how often hymnally ridiculous!'. Problems for the operatic translator accordingly arise partly from the nature of the English language as it is perceived in song by English-speakers themselves; partly from its differences from other languages in vowel-values, accent and other measurable qualities; and partly from the traditions which have been inherited by the English-language stage.

The apprehension of the correct 'tone', as an English-speaking audience would perceive it, demands particular sensitivity on the translator's part. A deliberate echo of past poetic styles is rare, though Auden and Kallman in translating *Die Zauberflöte* were bold enough to substitute for the matter-of-factness of Papageno's 'Ein Mädchen oder Weibchen' a version of English pastoral:

> Could I but once discover
> Some soft congenial She,
> How kindly I would love her
> And how happy I should be.

'Tone' and vocabulary were topics raised in the long and diverse symposium of 1974–5 by various translators in the magazine *Opera*, restating from a current point of view the arguments expressed by others years before. One contributor (Jacobs) preferred to keep vocabulary and verse conventions within the boundaries of the composer's period (unless for deliberate comic purpose). Such constraints are considered pedantic and irrelevant by some other modern translators, who rhyme 'together' and 'for ever' in *La traviata* even though English poets of Verdi's time would not have done.

Spaeth (1915) was perhaps the last to propose that operatic English required the deliberate substitution of a 'poetic' for a 'commonplace' vocabulary, but the dangers of banality continue to be recognized. In song, difficulties arising from the phonetic constitution of English words, particularly its short vowels and its consonant-clusters, have often been noted. Dent even gave his lecture audience (1935–6) a list of 'English words beloved of poets, and all more or less unsingable – that is, unsingable to long-sustained notes, or to high notes', beginning:

> abominable, battle, brother, cherish, death, deity, divinity, dream, forest, horror, image, innocent, jealousy, king, kiss, lily, listen, love, mariner, melody, memory, minute, miserable …

The restrictiveness of polysyllabic rhymes in English has also been noted. Very common and easily marshalled in Italian (the rhymes in *-ato* and *-ito* are virtually limitless), such rhymes in English tend to be grasped as cunningly artificial (Browning) or comic (Gilbert). Their use may advisedly be curbed except in places where they would actually be missed.

If Gilbert's ingenuities in his operettas with Sullivan constitute a comparison too easily recalled for English-speaking audiences encountering 'serious' opera, then a comparison of a rather different kind arises with non-English operas based on Shakespeare. Such operas may stick more closely or less closely to the original plots, and may make many or few contacts with well-remembered lines; but what is certain is that their librettists will not have presented the composer with a text wholly line-by-line in the original metre (as E. von Bauernfeld did when providing *Was ist Silvia?* for Schubert). The translator will therefore need to decide whether to use as much Shakespeare as possible, perhaps supplemented by pseudo-Shakespeare, or to eschew such things altogether and start anew.

Two further recurrently problematic points may be raised: proper names and repetition. In classical English verse tradition 'Eurydice' has a second-syllable accent: in translating from Gluck, and not wishing to alter note values, is the translator to accept the standard Italian (and French) third-syllable stress, or substitute other words and lose the composer's identification of the name with a rhythmic sequence of notes? Dent (1935) considered it 'absolutely necessary to alter the music in order to accent the names properly' when he was translating *Les Troyens*. But it might be considered excessively bold to alter the rhythmic utterance of Mozart's Statue to accommodate 'Don Juan' instead of 'Don Giovanni'. Again, can the invariable second-syllable stress which Massenet gives to 'Werther' be reconciled with our knowledge that, except in French, it is wrong?

As regards repetition, a distinction may be made between a composer's deliberate repetition of sentences for formal purposes, for example in da capo arias, and the mere reiteration of words, phrases and sentences to fill out an autonomous musical structure – reiterations most obvious in Rossini, Donizetti and others of their period. In such cases the translator may well, in contemplation of a modern English-speaking audience's thresholds of interest and boredom, provide new words. The songs in *The Bartered Bride* provide another place where there simply seem not enough words to span the musical length in the theatre.

It is also to be noted that differences between British and North American speech are sufficient to have erected a partial barrier in the acceptance of translations. Ruth and Thomas Martin's standard American versions have been seldom heard in Britain, and even more rarely Edward J. Dent's in the USA.

See also LIBRETTO (ii) and SURTITLES.

*

LoewenbergA
R. Batka: 'Opernitalienisch und Operndeutsch', *Der Merker*, i (1909), 101–5
G. Brecher: *Opernübersetzung* (Berlin, 1911)
A. Kalisch: 'The Tribulations of a Translator', *PMA*, xl (1914–15), 145–61
S. Spaeth: 'Translating to Music', *MQ*, i (1915), 191–8
E. Istel: 'Opernübersetzung', *Der Merker*, vii (1916), 673–8
H. Abert: 'Vom Operübersetzen', *Festschrift Hermann Kretzschmar* (Leipzig, 1918), 1–5
H. F. Peyser: 'Some Observations on Translation', *MQ*, viii (1922), 353–71
'Translating for Music', *Sunday Times* (22 June 1924)
R. L. Stuart: Introduction to libretto, *Orpheus* [Monteverdi] (Oxford, 1925)

H. Creuzberg: 'Zur Frage: Operübersetzung', *Die Musik*, xxvii (1934–5), 356–8
G. C. Lempert: 'Opern-Übersetzungen', *Die Musik*, xxvii (1934–5), 258–60
E. J. Dent: 'The Translation of Operas', *PMA*, lxi (1935–6), 81–104
——: Introduction to libretto, *Fidelio* (London, 1938)
G. Schünemann: Introduction to score, *Le nozze di Figaro* (Leipzig, 1941)
E. J. Dent: 'The Future of British Opera', *Opera in English*, ed. E. Crozier (London, 1945), 26–41
——: Introduction to libretto, *Don Pasquale* (London, 1946)
J. A. Westrup: 'Dent as Translator', *MR*, vii (1946), 198–204
W. H. Auden and C. Kallman: Introduction to libretto, *The Magic Flute* (London, 1957)
J. Kerman: 'Auden's *Magic Flute*', *Hudson Review*, x (1957), 309–16
G. E. Lessing: 'Opernübersetzungen', *NZM*, cxviii (1957), 214–17
A. Porter: 'Opera in English', *Opera*, viii (1957), 78–81, 279–82
W. Schuh: 'Il flauto magico', *Festschrift Friedrich Blume zum 70. Geburtstag* (Kassel, 1963), 327–39
B. Jičínský: 'K. Brodové interpretaci Janáčkových operních textů', *Sborník Janačkovy akademie muzickych umění*, v (1965), 81–8
J. Procházka: 'Brods Übersetzung des Librettos der Jenůfa und die Korrekturen Franz Kafkas', *Operní dílo Leoše Janáčka: Brno 1965*, 109–13
D. Bartha: 'Haydn's Italian Opera Repertory at Eszterháza Palace', *New Looks at Italian Opera: Essays in Honour of Donald J. Grout* (Ithaca, NY, 1968), 172–219
K. Honolka: Introduction to libretto, *Manon* (Kassel, 1968)
F. Oeser and W. Zimmer: Introduction to score, *Margarete* [Gounod: *Faust*] (Kassel, 1972)
R. Milnes and others: 'The Translator at Work', *Opera*, xxv (1974), 951–62, 1056–64; xxvi (1975), 242–50, 738–42
K. Honolka: 'Zur deutschen Übersetzung', introduction to vocal score, *Le nozze di Figaro* (Kassel, 1976)
A. Porter: 'Translating The Ring', *Richard Wagner: The Ring* (Folkestone, 1976)
Lord Drogheda: *Double Harness* (London, 1978)
J. E. Ellison, ed.: *Norman Tucker, Musician* (London, 1978)
K. Honolka: *Opernübersetzung: Zur Geschichte und Kritik der Verdeutschung musiktheatralischer Texte* (Wilhelmshaven, 1978)
S. Dudley: 'Les premières versions françaises du Mariage de Figaro de Mozart', *RdM*, lxix (1983), 55–83
E. W. White: *A History of English Opera* (London, 1983)
J. Machlis: 'On Translating a Russian Opera', *Russian and Soviet Music: Essays for Boris Schwarz* (Ann Arbor, 1984) [on trans. of Prokofiev's *War and Peace*], 221–7

ARTHUR JACOBS

Transposed Heads, The. Opera in six scenes by PEGGY GLANVILLE-HICKS to a libretto adapted by the composer, with THOMAS MANN, from the latter's novella; Louisville, KY, Columbia Auditorium, 3 April 1954.

The plot is based on an incident from the Hindu epic *The Ramayana*. An ascetic young Brahmin, Shridaman (tenor), and his low-caste friend Nanda (baritone) approach a temple in the forest. Shridaman enters to pray, is entranced by the goddess of death, Kali (speaking role), and offers himself as a sacrifice, cutting off his own head with a sword. Nanda, seeing the disaster and blaming himself because of his secret love for Shridaman's wife, Sita (soprano), also cuts off his own head. Sita prays to Kali who empowers her to restore life to husband and lover, but in assembling the bodies Sita transposes the heads. Unable to achieve happiness in this life and wishing to be together in the next, the men fight a duel to the death in order to make Sita a legal widow, who can now commit suttee on their funeral pyre. All are consumed in the flames.

The through-composed score uses rhythms derived from Hindu sources. The sinuous melodic lines and static ostinatos, sometimes referred to as pulseless, make for music which, for all its artificiality, is readily accessible.

THÉRÈSE RADIC

Trantoul, Antonin (*b* Toulouse, 21 Feb 1887; *d* Marseilles, 31 Aug 1966). French tenor. He made his début at Nîmes in 1911; this was as Des Grieux in *Manon*, which was also his first role at the Opéra-Comique. A member of the company from 1920 to 1924, he sang mostly lyric parts such as Almaviva, Werther and Gluck's Orpheus, also creating the role of Hippias in Henri Busser's *Les noces corinthiennes*. At the Opéra his repertory included Lohengrin, a solid preparation for the career that lay ahead as a dramatic tenor. Toscanini's engagement of him for La Scala in 1925, first as Faust and Radames, then Don Carlos, Max (in *Der Freischütz*) and Boito's Nero the following year, all leading to the coveted role of Otello in 1927, caused great controversy, some comparing him with Tamagno, others deriding any such claim. In 1928 he sang Otello at Naples and elsewhere in Italy, but he was heard no more after Toscanini's departure from Milan. After appearances mostly in the French repertory at New York in 1929 and an unsuccessful season at Buenos Aires, he returned to France, retiring in the mid-1930s. He was one of the few prominent singers of his time who did not make gramophone recordings.

J. B. STEANE

Traubel, Helen (Francesca) (*b* St Louis, 20 June 1899; *d* Santa Monica, CA, 28 July 1972). American soprano. From the age of 13 she studied singing with Vetta Karst. She made her concert début in 1923 in St Louis, but refused an offer to sing at the Metropolitan in 1926, returning instead to St Louis for further study. Her Metropolitan début was in Damrosch's *The Man without a Country* (1937); but her first important role was Sieglinde (1939), which initiated her career as the foremost American Wagnerian since Nordica, with whom she was frequently compared. When Flagstad left the Metropolitan in 1941 Traubel became her successor, as Brünnhilde, Elisabeth, Elsa, Kundry and, above all, Isolde. Her statuesque presence, vocal grandeur and expressive warmth made her unrivalled in Wagner until Flagstad's return. The two sopranos shared the *Ring* cycles for one season (1951), and Traubel added the Marschallin to her rather limited repertory. In 1953 she left the Metropolitan after a disagreement with Bing over her appearances in other entertainments. At the time, despite some loss of freedom at the top, her voice was virtually unimpaired. Thereafter she concentrated on films and television, and appeared in a Broadway show, *Pipe Dream* (1955). Although she had sung in South America, Mexico and very briefly in London, Traubel remained essentially an American phenomenon.

GV (L. Riemens; S. Smolian)
H. Traubel: *St Louis Woman* (New York, 1959)

MARTIN BERNHEIMER

Traubmann, Sophie (*b* New York, 17 May 1867; *d* New York, 16 Aug 1951). American soprano. The daughter of immigrants from Prague, she won a scholarship to the National School of Music, New York, where she studied with Fursch-Madi. She was among the first American-born singers to have trained solely in the USA, though later, as an established artist, she pursued studies in Europe with Mathilde Marchesi, Cosima Wagner and Pauline Viardot. After appearing with the National Opera Company in New York, she became one of the first American artists to sing at the Metropolitan Opera, making her début as Helmwige in

Die Walküre in 1888. She performed with the company until 1902, singing in 79 performances of 15 different operas, including the American premières of *Das Rheingold*, *Götterdämmerung* and Cornelius's *Der Barbier von Bagdad*, as well as roles such as Aida, Leonora (*Il trovatore*), Marzelline, Micaëla and Venus. She also sang in European cities including Cologne, Hamburg, London, Munich and Vienna. She commanded a repertory of some 53 parts as diverse as Brünnhilde, Marguerite, Norma and Zerlina. After retiring, she taught in New York. Contemporary accounts describe her as an artist of charm and emotional immediacy, with a sweet, lush and powerful voice.

CORI ELLISON

Traumgörge, Der ('Görge the Dreamer'). Opera in two acts and a Nachspiel by ALEXANDER ZEMLINSKY to a libretto by Leo Feld; Nuremberg, Opernhaus, 11 October 1980.

Zemlinsky's third opera, *Der Traumgörge* (1904–6) depicts the progress of a naive and idealistic dreamer, a kind of latter-day Parsifal, who renounces revolution in favour of idyllic married life with the princess of his dreams. It is a kind of epithalamium for his first wife, Ida, whom he married in 1907. Feld's libretto, a conflation of various sources including Richard Volkmann-Leander's fairy-tale *Vom unsichtbaren Königreich* and Hermann Sudermann's novel *Der Katzensteg*, is marred occasionally by some incoherent symbolism. The music is characterized by a propensity to total thematicism, and the density of the leitmotivic web and some of the harmonic and thematic material reflect the influence of Schoenberg's *Pelleas und Melisande*. Mahler accepted *Der Traumgörge* for the Hofoperntheater and suggested a number of improvements. Although the rehearsals (with Erik Schmedes in the title role) were far advanced when Mahler left Vienna, Felix Weingartner, his successor, refused to honour a promise to perform the work, thus dealing a major blow to Zemlinsky's career. The specifically *Jugendstil* subject matter of *Der Traumgörge* militated against later attempts to secure performances of the opera, though to the end of his life Zemlinsky continued to believe that it was one of his best works.

Act 1 is set in a village in the early 19th century. Görge (tenor), an introspective orphan, is seen musing over his books. He longs to experience the fairy-tales that fire his imagination. Grete (soprano), his bride-to-be, tries to instil in him a sense of reality. Her marriage has been arranged for financial reasons, and Görge's nature compares unfavourably with the ruddy good humour of her former sweetheart Hans (baritone), who now appears. Görge is lulled to sleep by a murmuring brook, which evokes memories of childhood. In a dream a princess passionately urges him to pursue his quest in the world that lies beyond the confines of the village. He awakens, acutely conscious of the prosaic nature of rural life. At the end of the act he rushes out in pursuit of his dreams.

Act 2 is set in another village three years after Act 1. A group of unruly villagers led by Kaspar (bass) is seen planning an uprising. Görge's quest has ended in failure, drunkenness and despair, although he has found a kindred spirit in Gertraud (soprano), the daughter of a dispossessed nobleman, who is suspected by the villagers of witchcraft and arson. Kaspar attempts to secure Görge's oratorical gifts for the planned uprising, but when the latter learns of the peasants' bloodthirsty plans his initial enthusiasm for their insurrection evaporates. Concurrently Gertraud has lost all hope, and contemplates suicide. Now, with the red glow of the distant Whitsun bonfires, they reveal their love for each other. In a thrilling final scene the villagers attempt to lynch Gertraud. She is saved by Görge, who at last awakens from his introspection to engage in purposeful action.

The Nachspiel is set in the village of Act 1. Görge has returned to claim his inheritance, and he and Gertraud have done much to improve the villagers' lot. Görge's quest has led him to realize that the truth of the fairy-tales resides in life itself, and Gertraud is revealed to be the princess of his dreams. The opera concludes with a magical duet that, appropriately, ends on an unresolved added 6th chord symbolizing an unending state of bliss.

ALFRED CLAYTON

Travelling Companion, The. Opera in four acts, op.146, by Sir CHARLES VILLIERS STANFORD to a libretto by Henry Newbolt after the story by HANS CHRISTIAN ANDERSEN; Liverpool, David Lewis Theatre, 30 April 1925.

John (tenor), a young wayfarer left homeless and alone after the death of his father, shelters from a storm in a church, where he loses even his money to two ruffians in order to prevent them from plundering a corpse lying there on a bier. The corpse reappears as his Travelling Companion (baritone) and helps him to woo a fair but cold princess (soprano) who, like Turandot, has executed all previous suitors for failing to answer her riddle. He kills the wizard (bass) to whom she is in thrall and wins her hand. In the moving final scene the Travelling Companion departs from the wedding feast and becomes a corpse again.

Stanford's score, tuneful and dignified, succeeds as fairy-tale narrative in the manner of Humperdinck, but his best passages, for John and the Companion, add a dimension of spiritual rhetoric echoing Wagner's *Parsifal* and Elgar while remaining syntactically simple.

STEPHEN BANFIELD

Travelling troupes. Since the earliest days of opera it has been economically more practical, in many sets of circumstances, for opera to be presented by travelling troupes rather than by resident companies. Such troupes have been active in various European countries throughout the history of opera; in the USA they flourished particularly during the second half of the 19th century, largely because of the huge distances and isolated communities hungry for cultural entertainment.

The present article aims to give a broad view of the activities of travelling troupes in Europe and Australasia; fuller information on the more important companies will be found in individual entries, for which cross-references are indicated. The much larger phenomenon of travelling troupes in the USA is treated more extensively.

The present article deals with touring companies rather than companies that tour. It generally excludes the consideration of companies that undertake tours from an established, home performance base; such companies are treated within the relevant city entry.

1. Italy. 2. France. 3. The German-speaking lands. 4. Great Britain. 5. The USA: (i) English companies to 1860 (ii) English companies, 1860–1900 (iii) French companies (iv) Italian companies to 1860 (v) Italian companies, 1860–1900 (vi) German companies. 6. Latin America. 7. Australia and New Zealand.

1. ITALY. Although Italy in about 1600 had a model for a travelling opera troupe, the new genre never fully adopted it, save for a few decades at the very start. The model was that of the theatrical company headed by a *capocomico*, or actor-manager, who contracted with theatre owners to provide its services, received a fee or a proportion of the takings, and paid the company. Each player had one of an array of stereotyped functions (first lover, second lover, 'tyrant' etc.) and could be slotted into most of the plays in an extensive repertory; often some of the players were related, typically to the actor-manager. The troupe went throughout Italy, sometimes appearing in very small towns, and on occasion abroad.

Members of such troupes could often sing, and some appeared in early operas that called for dramatic expression at least as much as for vocal qualities, for example Virginia Andreini, who with her husband was a member of the Comici Fedeli troupe. Two series of early opera company, those centred on the family of Francesco Manelli and the slightly later ones called Febiarmonici, approximated to the theatrical troupes in their organization; according to a Jesuit commentator (1652) they had a leader-manager and moved about either as a self-sufficient body or as a core troupe, recruiting in each city the extra singers and musicians they needed. The Manelli appeared in the first public opera house, in Venice (1637), with previous and later appearances in Padua and Bologna, while the Febiarmonici, mainly Roman artists, took early operas to a number of Italian cities, so helping to establish the 'Venetian' style as the norm.

As the new genre became established, the usual arrangement emerged of a local opera season run by an impresario or a group of impresarios who engaged singers specifically for it. By the period 1684–1710 groups of singers went round the same theatres, but this resulted from exchanges among their princely patrons rather than their own organization as cohesive troupes. As ties of patronage loosened, engagements became still more individual. Elements of the troupe, however, persisted in comic opera. The comic intermezzos of the early 18th century were typically performed by a male and a female singer who travelled everywhere together. The more developed comic opera of the period *c*1740–1820 was often performed by a small family group (husband, wife and wife's brother; or father, daughter and son-in-law) in which one of the men might be the composer or impresario (or both) and the other the leading comic bass, while the woman was the leading *buffa*. In their travels – and they went to towns just as small as those visited by the old theatre troupes – these little groups picked up other singers and kept them on only as long as they needed them. One or two of the better-known families of *opera seria* singers such as the Mombelli occasionally followed this model.

With the decay of comic opera this form of organization seems to have vanished from Italy, though it persisted for a time abroad and in children's opera troupes. Late 19th-century operetta, whose personnel in Italy (unlike Germany) was separate from that of opera, followed the *capocomico* model. In the 1930s, the Carro di Tespi, well-organized summer touring companies arranged by Nicola de Pirro, gave open-air performances throughout Italy. During the imperial days of Italy in the late 19th century, touring Italian companies periodically brought opera to colonial theatres for the colonists and armed forces, visiting Somaliland, Asmara in Eritrea, and Tripoli and Cyrenaica (now Benghazi) in Tripolitania (now Libya).

See also ANDREINI, VIRGINIA; COMMEDIA DELL'ARTE; DE PIRRO, NICOLA; FEBIARMONICI; MANELLI, FRANCESCO; and MOMBELLI, DOMENICO.

2. FRANCE. The French influence on the music of late 17th- and early 18th-century European opera, often commented upon, has mystified historians, for French opera was rarely performed outside France. The explanation usually given is that a number of musicians visited Paris to study Lully's operas and ballets, that Lully operas were published (unlike Italian opera), and that suites of instrumental music from those works were widely performed. Largely overlooked, however, is an additional factor: troupes of French *comédiens* travelled throughout Europe in this period, appearing in Amsterdam, Basle, Bayreuth, Berlin, Bonn, Brunswick, Brussels, Cologne, Copenhagen, Danzig, Dresden, Dublin, Düsseldorf, Florence, Frankfurt, Ghent, Geneva, Haarlem, The Hague, Hamburg, Kassel, Kraków, Leipzig, Leyden, Livorno, London, Lübeck, Mannheim, Mantua, Milan, Moscow, Munich, Naples, Parma, Pisa, Prague, Vienna, Warsaw and elsewhere. The repertory of these troupes consisted mostly of spoken plays with generous amounts of music – *airs*, dances and instrumental numbers. This repertory comprises one of the ancestors of the *opéra comique* in France and of the Singspiel in Germany.

Although most of the travelling French troupes of this early period presented plays with incidental music abroad, at least one company toured with operas and ballets in France. After Lully had secured control of the Académie Royale de Musique in Paris, he also arranged that that institution would enjoy a monopoly on musical theatre throughout France. This was enforced until the mid-18th century, and both touring and resident companies had to be licensed by Lully or his successors. Nicolas Le Vasseur signed a contract with Lully's son-in-law Jean-Nicolas de Francine on 16 December 1690, which gave him the exclusive right to produce opera in Lyons (where he was based), Marseilles, Aix, Montpellier, Grenoble, Dijon, Chalon-sur-Saône and Avignon; the contract was soon expanded to include Toulouse, Bordeaux and Arles and then all opera in the French provinces. In 1696 the right to produce opera in Lyons, Grenoble and Arles was assigned to Jean-Pierre Leguay for three years and in 1699 extended for six more years. As these entrepreneurs travelled to Paris to negotiate their contracts, for which they paid dearly, it can be assumed that they exercised their rights, but details are few. In January 1700 the Lyons troupe received permission to tour to Marseilles, Toulon, Aix, Arles and Nîmes, probably also visiting Avignon. In March 1702 they again performed in Marseilles. In 1703 their visit to Dijon is documented. The repertory in these years included *Alceste*, *Le temple de la paix*, *Persée*, *Isis*, *Armide* and *Phaëton* by Lully; *Les amours de Momus* and *Didon* by Desmarets; *L'Europe galante* by Campra; and other works.

3. THE GERMAN-SPEAKING LANDS. For all of the 17th century and most of the 18th, a troupe of itinerant actors was far more characteristic of theatrical life in German-speaking lands than a standing company at a single private or public stage. Troupes travelled by necessity rather than inclination, forced to seek out new audiences scattered among relatively small population centres at which repertories and interest were soon exhausted. Travel was not only arduous and unpleasant,

but also linked actors in public consciousness with disreputable bands of roving entertainers, mountebanks and charlatans. Official disapproval of the professional actor in Germany, most often voiced from the pulpit, diminished only when conditions made it possible for the better companies to establish relatively permanent bases at large cities or at theatre-loving courts.

A German theatrical company was normally organized under an impresario, called its *Prinzipal*, who ran the enterprise at his or her own risk and profit. A privilege obtained from a court or city council was usually needed to perform publicly, and often carried exclusive rights. Arrangements varied from simple permission to the concession of a theatre or opera house, together with its appurtenances, and possibly even a subvention from a court wishing to secure a troupe's services for its own entertainment. Events that drew large crowds of potential spectators, such as the annual fairs held at Leipzig and Frankfurt, were especially attractive and the object of heated competition among troupes.

Following the example of the strolling bands of English comedians, who brought their crude but entertaining verse comedies and farces to German stages in the 16th century, German travelling companies found it necessary to cater to their public's often unrefined taste, which ran in the direction of rough humour, pranks, physical violence and the improvisatory spirit familiar from the *commedia dell'arte.* These features continued throughout the 18th century in the popular theatres of Austria, southern Germany, Bohemia and the Czech lands, most notably in the person of a great actor-principal such as Josef Stranitzky (1676–1726), who created a local replacement for Harlequin as the Salzburg peasant Hanswurst.

In northern Germany the traits on which Stranitzky and his successors continued to trade began to disappear towards the mid-18th century, beginning with the reforms of Caroline Neuber (1697–1760), who collaborated with the Leipzig professor J. C. Gottsched in banishing Harlequin and his excesses from her stage. One of her actors, J. F. Schönemann (1704–82), left Neuber to form his own company in 1739. Four years later at Berlin his troupe performed an English ballad opera in translation, Charles Coffey's *The Devil to Pay* (1728). The experiment remained an isolated one, but Schönemann along with other principals steadily built up his musical offerings in the form of ballet and pantomime. In 1751 his company was taken under court subvention at Schwerin for three years, the first such venture in Germany. Another landmark came in 1755 when Konrad Ernst Ackermann (1712–72), who had left Schönemann in 1741, completed a new playhouse at Königsberg, the first privately built commercial theatre in Germany.

After the disruptions of the Seven Years War (1756–63), the transformation of the German theatre into an institution of high culture envisaged by Neuber and others became a reality. National theatres were created at Hamburg, Mannheim, Vienna and Mainz. Enlightened courts extended favourable terms to the best of the travelling companies as a way of establishing standing theatres. Joseph II founded not only a National Theatre at Vienna (1776) but a subsidiary enterprise devoted to German opera, the National-Singspiel (1778). Through exemplary deportment and high professional ideals the greatest German actors of the era, Konrad Ekhof (1720–78) and Friedrich Ludwig Schröder (1744–1816), did much to elevate the social standing of players.

During this same era, the Singspiel was born at Leipzig in 1766. Its early history is unthinkable outside the motivations and constraints that governed Germany's travelling companies. It was at the instigating of the principal Heinrich Gottfried Koch (1703–75) that C. F. Weisse and J. A. Hiller brought the new genre to life, and it was Koch's prodding for a steady supply of new comic operas that made it possible for the Singspiel to flourish. As was the case on most German stages, operas could be repeated far more often in a given city than spoken plays, and to full houses. Their popularity saved Koch from financial ruin, and did the same for other principals who embraced them later on.

The Singspiel, with its extensive spoken dialogue and modest musical demands, took account of the limited abilities of the executants most travelling companies were able to muster. These actor-singers stood in striking contrast to the outstanding virtuosos in many wandering Italian companies dedicated to performing *opera seria* and *opera buffa*; such a troupe under Pietro Mingotti had worked the same annual fairs at Leipzig in the 1740s that Koch's company worked in the 1760s and early 1770s. Excellent singers of German opera and new repertory pieces to serve their talents tended to be found mostly in troupes attached to stabler court and civic stages.

In Austria and the Rhineland, opera had always played a central role in the repertories of the more successful travelling companies, such as those of T. H. Marchand at Mainz, Strasbourg, Frankfurt and Mannheim, and J. F. von Kurz, who at Vienna and elsewhere made his reputation as Bernardon, a less boorish version of his godfather Stranitzky's Hanswurst. By the last decades of the 18th century, most of the important northern companies had also developed considerable musical resources. The possibility of setting German opera on a high artistic footing had first been realized by the most distinguished private company of the era, that of Abel Seyler, which mixed its years of travel, 1769–79, with extended court appointments at Weimar (1771–4) and Gotha (1774–5). Other companies notable for their operatic repertories were those of G. F. W. Grossmann in the Rhineland, the troupe of Pasquale Bondini (*c*1737–1789) operating out of Dresden, and many of the companies that visited cities in southern Germany and Austria, notably those of Johann Böhm and Emanuel Schikaneder.

By the 19th century the travelling company had become a subsidiary feature of German theatrical life, whose characteristic institution was now the more prestigious and accomplished standing theatres established at most German cities of any size. Travel was most commonly undertaken in the form of the *Kunstreisen*, or artistic journeys, of leading actors and singers.

See also BÖHM, JOHANN; BONDINI, PASQUALE; GROSSMANN, GUSTAV FRIEDRICH WILHELM; KURZ, JOSEPH FELIX VON; MARCHAND, THEOBALD HILARIUS; MINGOTTI, PIETRO; SCHIKANEDER, EMANUEL; and SEYLER, ABEL.

4. GREAT BRITAIN. The history of travelling opera in Great Britain effectively dates from 1875 when Karl August Nikolaus Rose founded the Carl Rosa Opera Company to promote opera in English. By 1891 three Carl Rosa touring companies had been established, though they were reduced to two at the end of World War I. In 1924 H. B. Phillips took over as general

manager and completely reorganized the company, which performed most of the opera heard outside London before World War II.

1875 also marked the establishment of Gilbert and Sullivan opera under the management of Richard D'Oyly Carte. In 1881 the D'Oyly Carte Opera Company, which already toured the provinces, moved to the newly built Savoy Theatre in London. After Carte's death in 1901 it evolved into a travelling company and survived as such until 1982. The New D'Oyly Carte Opera Company was launched in 1988.

The Moody-Manners Company was founded in 1898 to promote grand opera in English. Though at first successful, by 1910 it had run into financial difficulties. It closed in 1916, having provided the principal training ground for British artists before World War I along with the Denhof Opera Company, founded in 1910 to give performances of the *Ring* in English. In 1913 the latter was rescued by Beecham and became the Beecham Opera Company; in 1922 it was refounded as the British National Opera Company. It gave the first European radio broadcast of a complete opera (*Hänsel und Gretel* from Covent Garden, 6 January 1923). Both Barbirolli and Sargent had their first important operatic engagements with the company. In 1928 it went into voluntary liquidation, but was taken over by the Royal Opera House and survived as the Covent Garden English Opera Company until 1931.

The establishment of the Arts Council of Great Britain after World War II, along with the new Covent Garden and Sadler's Wells operas, created difficulties for existing travelling companies. The Carl Rosa company lost its public grant in 1957 when it refused to merge with Sadler's Wells, and closed in 1960. One company that successfully adapted to postwar conditions by commissioning works from young composers was Intimate Opera, founded in 1930 by Frederick Woodhouse to revive unknown opera of the chamber type. The English Opera Group, founded by Benjamin Britten, John Piper and Eric Crozier in 1947, also promoted chamber opera; in 1975 it was expanded and reformed as the English Music Theatre Company, having previously established an Opera Studio in London that eventually became the London Opera Centre. By 1980 the London Opera Centre had become the mainstay of Opera for All, originally established in 1949 by the Arts Council to bring live opera to small towns and villages. In 1981 it was refounded as Opera 80, operating on a larger scale than its predecessor; in 1992 it took the name English Touring Opera.

The later 20th century has seen the inception of several new ventures: Phoenix Opera (1965–75) and Kent Opera (1969–90) both toured southern England; English Touring Opera (1986–7, formerly the Cambridge Opera Group) was a medium-sized company based in the Midlands which then merged with Birmingham Music Theatre to form the highly successful City of Birmingham Touring Opera; Travelling Opera Show (1987–9) concentrated on updated versions of mainstream works. Despite the diversity of their repertories, all these companies eventually became victims of the increasingly adverse economic situation and the advent of televised opera. Today British travelling opera embraces chiefly the touring activities of the ENO (from London), Opera North (Leeds), the WNO (Cardiff), Scottish Opera (Glasgow) and Glyndebourne Touring Opera.

See also CARL ROSA OPERA COMPANY; CARTE, RICHARD D'OYLY; DENHOF OPERA COMPANY; ENGLISH OPERA GROUP; INTIMATE OPERA COMPANY; KENT OPERA; LONDON, §II, 1; MOODY-MANNERS COMPANY; OPERA FOR ALL; and PHOENIX OPERA.

5. THE USA. The history of opera performance in the USA during the 19th century is for the most part a history of itinerant opera companies. Except for works mounted by theatrical stock companies and by the resident companies in New Orleans (founded 1790) and New York (Metropolitan Opera, founded 1883), the vast majority of opera productions witnessed by North Americans at this period were given by touring troupes. As a consequence, performances were much more numerous and geographically widespread than the rather chequered history of resident companies would seem to indicate. The repertory of the various companies (English, French, Italian and German) further reveals that American operatic tastes closely mirrored those on the Continent and in England.

(i) English companies to 1860. English comic and ballad operas, performed first by itinerant players and later by the stock companies of theatres in larger cities, were an indispensable part of the American theatrical repertory in the 18th century. The general adoption of the star system as a style of theatrical management in the early 19th century, however, eventually changed both the repertory and the method of opera production in the USA, taking opera away from singing actors and actresses and putting it into the hands of trained singers. This system meant that British vocal stars could travel to North America not to join the resident company of a particular theatre but to perform for short-term engagements in theatres around the country, commanding high wages; the first important itinerant singers arrived in 1817. Since they tended to form themselves into small troupes of two, three or four singers, they could cover the principal roles in most operatic productions mounted by local stock companies. The assignment of principal operatic roles to specialized singers significantly improved the quality of opera performance during the 1820s, 30s and 40s, resulting in a gradual elevation in the musical expectations of American audiences; raised expectations, in turn, created a demand for the importation of even better singers.

During these three decades a number of British singers visited the USA and Canada. Some elected to settle in North America, while others returned to Great Britain; all of them, however, toured widely in the east and south, appearing in concerts, and in opera productions in cities as far removed geographically as Quebec City and New Orleans. Singers of particular importance during the 1820s and 30s include Elizabeth Austin (1828–35), Joseph and Mary Anne Paton Wood (1833–6, 1840–41), Jane Shirreff and John Wilson (1838–40), William F. Brough (arrived in 1833) and Anne and Edward (better known as Arthur in England) Seguin (arrived 1838). All these stars (especially Austin and the Woods) had a significant impact on the development of opera appreciation in the USA; in particular, they helped to foster Americans' love for Italian melody by introducing works by Rossini (*La Cenerentola*, in M. R. Lacy's pastiche, retitled *Cinderella, or The Fairy Queen and the Little Glass Slipper*) and Bellini (*Norma* and *La sonnambula*), which became extraordinarily popular. Their repertory also included adaptations of other foreign-language operas (Auber's *Fra Diavolo*, Weber's *Der Freischütz*, Donizetti's *L'elisir d'amore* and

La fille du régiment) as well as operas originally written in English (Rooke's *Amilie*, Balfe's *The Bohemian Girl*, Wallace's *Maritana*).

During the 1840s the Seguins, who settled in the USA, helped pave the way for the proliferation of English opera companies by forming small touring troupes of six to eight singers; they toured widely with these expanded vocal-star companies (all known as the Seguin Opera Company) until Edward Seguin's death in 1852. Despite the company's success, however, by the late 1840s the halcyon days of vocal-star troupes had ended, and small groups of itinerant singers were replaced by moderate-sized English troupes that were less dependent on stock companies. To a great extent this change was a response to the appearance of large, high quality, completely self-sufficient Italian companies in the late 1840s. English opera companies varied in size, but usually included principal and secondary singers and the nucleus of a chorus; for instrumental accompaniment they still relied on resident theatre orchestras. Their repertory was similar to that of the vocal stars: *The Enchantress* and *The Bohemian Girl* (Balfe), *Les diamants de la couronne* (as *Crown Diamonds*) and *Fra Diavolo* (Auber), *Cinderella* (Rossini, arr. Lacy), *La sonnambula* and *La fille du régiment* (as *The Daughter of the Regiment*); in the 1850s English translations of more current Italian operas, in particular *Il trovatore* and *La traviata*, also became standard fare. Anna Bishop, who arrived in 1847, toured the east, south and far west of the country until 1855, sometimes as the star of the Anna Bishop Opera Company, sometimes as part of a smaller concert ensemble formed from the ashes of her various opera companies, which tended to disintegrate in mid-tour. In August 1855 she left for Australia, returning to the USA only in 1858. Anna Thillon toured as the star of her own opera company from 1851 to 1854. This troupe, although small, was popular and widely travelled; Thillon performed in cities on the east coast, in the Mid-west (St Louis, Memphis, Cincinnati), and the far west (San Francisco).

Among the many other English opera troupes that toured the country in the 1850s were the Manvers, Durand, Cooper, New Orleans, Escott and Miranda and Richings companies. But by far the most popular and successful English troupe of the decade was the Pyne-Harrison Opera Company, an ensemble formed around Louisa Pyne and William Harrison, two strong proponents of English opera from Covent Garden. Between 1854 and 1857 they travelled throughout the eastern half of the continent, performing in cities from Montreal to New Orleans and St Louis. After their departure English opera lost ground to Italian as the fashionable or 'proper' style of operatic performance. Despite an increasing anti-English bias, however, opera in the vernacular continued to be extremely popular, particularly in areas away from the eastern seaboard.

(ii) English companies, 1860–1900. Some of the English opera companies active in the antebellum period (in particularly the Richings and Bishop troupes) continued to tour after the Civil War. Others were formed in the 1860s, 70s and 80s, and a selfconscious movement towards English opera 'for the people' flourished. Among the important English troupes of this period were the Richings Opera Company (1859–early 1870s); the Parepa-Rosa Opera Company, a large and very successful troupe formed around the soprano Euphrosyne Parepa (1867–71); the Max Strakosch English Opera Company (1877–80); the Emma Abbott English Opera Company, active principally in the American west (1878–91); the Emma Juch Opera Company, which toured in the USA, Canada and Mexico (1889–91); and the American Opera Company, founded by Jeannette Thurber and led by Theodore Thomas, which was established in 1885 in an ill-fated attempt to encourage the performance of opera in English by American singers (the company disintegrated on the road in 1887 and disbanded during the 1887–8 season). Perhaps the most successful and influential English company of the period was that founded and managed by the American soprano Clara Louise Kellogg. The Kellogg English Opera Company, founded in 1873, toured throughout the country (including the far west) until Kellogg retired in 1887, and performed a large repertory of old and new operas in English translation. Kellogg was a tireless proponent of opera 'for the people' and she encouraged young American singers, including Emma Abbott.

Many other English opera companies were active in the USA in the 1880s and 90s, a number of them exploiting the new American passion for operetta, especially the works of Gilbert and Sullivan. Little is known about the itineraries or histories of most of these troupes; a few of the many include the McCaull Opera Company, Ford's Opera Company, Alice Oates Opera Company, Emelie Melville Company, Norcross Fifth Avenue Opera Company, William Lyster's English Opera and Opera Bouffe Company, Templeton Opera Company, Alcazar Opera Company and the Castle Square Opera Company. The Boston Ideal Opera Company (later the Bostonians) was formed to present 'ideal' productions of Gilbert and Sullivan operettas, but also gave the premières of several works by Victor Herbert and became closely associated with Reginald de Koven's *Robin Hood*.

(iii) French companies. The New Orleans Opera Company, under the direction of the impresario John Davis, was the first opera troupe to mount a tour of the USA. From their base at the French-language Théâtre d'Orléans, they made six tours to the east coast, presenting operas by Adam, Isouard, Boieldieu, Auber, Rossini and others in New York, Philadelphia, Boston and Baltimore (1827–33). During the 1840s various versions of the French Opera Company of New Orleans toured the north-east; although not as important as Davis's companies, these troupes kept French-language opera before the American public. In 1859 the French Opera House opened in New Orleans in competition with the Théâtre d'Orléans. This theatre's resident company, which included such singers as Julie Calvé, Me St Urban, Lecourt, Mathieu, Victor and Genibrel, appeared in other parts of the country; during the 1840s and 50s troupes featuring Calvé, in particular, mounted acclaimed performances on the east coast. The first American performance of Offenbach's *La Grande-Duchesse de Gérolstein* in 1867 marked the beginnings of an *opéra bouffe* craze in the USA that persisted throughout the 1870s. The troupes most frequently mentioned in secondary sources include the Aimée French Opera Company (formed around the French soubrette Marie Aimée and under the management of Maurice Grau), the DeBeauplan Grand French Opera Company of New Orleans and the Maurice Grau French Opera Company.

(iv) Italian companies to 1860. From 1825 until 1847 the history of Italian opera performance is a chronicle of fits and starts. No company active in this period lasted longer than a year or two before going bankrupt; many remained intact for a shorter length of time. There were also stretches of years during which no Italian companies were active, and opera was known to Americans only through the presentations of English and French troupes. To the mid-1840s the performance of opera in Italian was a novelty because most Americans preferred to hear Italian opera sung in English. Until 1847 both New York and New Orleans acted as headquarters for visiting Italian opera troupes; companies visited nearby towns and cities only after exhausting the market in one or the other of these two centres.

The first Italian troupe to perform in the USA was a travelling company only in the broadest terms: Manuel García's Italian Opera Company performed at the Park Theatre in New York from November 1825 until September 1826, then left for Mexico. This brief introduction to the Italian style, coupled with the growing American taste for Italian melody as performed by such vocal stars as Austin and the Woods, resulted in several attempts to establish Italian opera in New York during the 1830s. The Montresor Opera Company, recruited from Italy by Lorenzo da Ponte, mounted two seasons in New York and one in Philadelphia during the winter–spring of 1832–3. When it disbanded, many of the singers travelled to Havana, where they sang with Francesco Brichta's Havana Opera Company for the 1833–4 season. Two other short-lived troupes were attempted on the east coast: the Rivafinoli Company (New York and Philadelphia, 1833–4) and the Porto-Sacchi Company (New York and Albany, 1834–5). In 1836 the Montresor company resurfaced in New Orleans, where the De Rosa Company (1836–7) and Brichta's Havana Opera Company (1837) also appeared. Italian opera production then ceased in the country for five years because of depressed economic conditions. In 1842 a new version of the Havana company visited New Orleans. This troupe, which numbered 57 (including principal singers, chorus and orchestra), had been assembled by the Cuban businessman Marti y Torrens. After further performances in the city in spring 1843, the troupe embarked on the first extended tour of the USA undertaken by an Italian troupe, in nine months visiting Cincinnati, Pittsburgh, Philadelphia, New York, Baltimore, Washington and (again) New Orleans. Their repertory included principally works by Bellini and Donizetti, and their success was marked.

Italian opera performance entered a new phase during the period 1847–60, when between three and six Italian troupes were performing somewhere in the USA in any single year. The activities of over 70 different troupes have been documented for this period; itineraries of these companies expanded significantly – away from the east coast and the towns and cities on the Ohio and Mississippi rivers, and ever deeper into the interior of the country. This sudden escalation was the result of three factors: renewed economic prosperity, a realization by European performers that an American tour would bring enormous riches and the appearance of the impresarios Bernard Ullman, Max Maretzek and Maurice Strakosch.

It is almost impossible to ascertain clearly the names, personnel, itineraries and repertories of all the troupes active during this time. Italian companies formed, broke down, reformed and merged with a dismaying frequency; furthermore, each company is typically referred to in the contemporary press by a variety of names. A broad summary of the activities of some of the most important troupes should suffice to suggest the wealth of activity. The Havana Opera Company of Marti y Torrens made extended tours of the eastern and southern United States during 1847, 1848 and 1850 with troupes that sometimes numbered more than a hundred musicians (including principal and secondary singers, chorus and orchestra). Companies from the Astor Place Opera House in New York (from 1849 under the management of Maretzek) toured widely (principally on the east coast, but also including New Orleans and Mexico) from 1847 until 1853. Maurice Strakosch managed a variety of troupes from 1848 until 1861, Bernard Ullman was active as a manager from the early 1840s until 1862, and Maretzek continued to act as an impresario after the ultimate failure of the Astor Place House; all three managed troupes under their own names (e.g. the Strakosch Opera Company, the Maretzek Italian Opera Company) and occasionally embarked on joint endeavours (the Ullman-Strakosch Opera Company). These companies toured as far as the Mid-west as well as in the south and north. In addition, companies named for visiting European celebrities were numerous and highly visible as they toured throughout the eastern half of the continent and as far west as California (via Panama); these troupes took the names of such artists as Henriette Sontag, Marietta Alboni, Balbina Steffanone, Catherine Hayes, Grisi and Mario, Teresa Parodi, Adelaide Cortesi, Anna de LaGrange and Luigi Arditi. The Academy of Music companies, nominally resident at the opera house of that name in Manhattan, also toured regularly, appearing principally in east coast cities. The repertory of the 1850–51 Astor Place company is fairly representative of that performed by most of these Italian troupes; it included operas by Bellini (*Norma*, *La sonnambula* and *I Capuleti e i Montecchi*), Donizetti (*Lucia di Lammermoor*, *Gemma di Vergy*, *Parisina*, *Lucrezia Borgia* and *La favorite*), Rossini (*Semiramide* and *Il barbiere di Siviglia*), Verdi (*Ernani*) and Mozart (*Don Giovanni*).

(v) Italian companies, 1860–1900. The performance of Italian opera greatly accelerated in the years after the Civil War. The expansion of the American railroad system made longer and more distant tours an economic proposition, while continued growth of the American population and the unceasing expansion westward meant that there were more towns of a size large enough to support a two- or three-night visit by an itinerant company. Large cities along the rivers had been visited by itinerant troupes for years; now it was also economically feasible for companies to stop at many of the smaller towns in between. The completion of the transcontinental railroad in 1869 and the subsequent settling of the western interior opened a vast market for itinerant performers of all types; opera houses opened in such small towns as Ogden City, Utah; Central City, Colorado; and Grand Forks, North Dakota.

During the 1880s and 90s uncounted numbers of Italian opera companies travelled throughout the United States. The two most important Italian companies active in the postwar period were those of James Mapleson and the Metropolitan Opera. Mapleson took over management of the New York Academy of Music in

1878; his company performed from mid-October to December in New York, then toured for three months, appearing in Chicago, Boston, St Louis, Cincinnati, Washington, Baltimore and Philadelphia. His troupes continued to perform successfully in New York and elsewhere (Detroit, Indianapolis, Syracuse, Albany, Buffalo, Pittsburgh and Cleveland) for the next three seasons, but with the establishment of the Metropolitan Opera in 1883, Mapleson's company was faced with serious competition. After two debilitating tours in the far west Mapleson abandoned the contest.

The Metropolitan Opera Company, although firmly based in New York, was an itinerant troupe from its first season (1883–4), when the manager, Henry Abbey, took the company on the road for four months. Seasons were then mounted almost every year in Boston, Philadelphia, Chicago, St Louis, Cincinnati, Washington and Baltimore, and during the next decade tours were extended to include San Francisco and Mexico as well as small towns in the eastern states. For a fuller account of the touring company's activities *see* METROPOLITAN OPERA COMPANY.

(vi) German companies. The performance of opera by German companies in the USA was sporadic at best during the first half of the 19th century; the few troupes that were formed (usually in New York) were not sufficiently successful to mount tours. A company organized around Mme Johannsen (presumably from New York) gave a season at the Philadelphia Academy of Music in 1857, and other somewhat peripatetic companies (associated with Carl Anschütz and Mme Johannsen) performed works such as *Martha*, *Der Freischütz*, *Fidelio*, *Die lustigen Weiber von Windsor* and *Tannhäuser* for several seasons in New York and Philadelphia in the early 1860s. Other companies mentioned in the secondary literature (but about which little is known) include Grau's German Opera Company (1869), an unnamed German opera company (1876) and Marie Geistinger's Grand Opera Company (1881). German opera first flourished in the USA during the 1880s, when the New York Metropolitan Opera adopted a completely German format in its second season (1884–5), under the direction of Leopold Damrosch, and went on to give several entirely German tours. When the company resumed Italian and French productions, opera in German was essentially banished, and to fill the void Leopold's son Walter Damrosch organized the Damrosch Opera Company in 1894. In its first season the troupe performed exclusively Wagner, making a five-month tour that extended as far west as Kansas City. During the next season Damrosch added several non-Wagner operas and the troupe toured in the south. By the late 1890s it had become clear that Americans were interested in German as well as French and Italian opera and both the Met and the Damrosch company adopted the wing system of opera production, obviating the need for a separate German company; in 1896–7 and 1897–8 the German wing of the Damrosch troupe performed in Boston, Chicago, Cincinnati, Cleveland, Buffalo and Detroit.

See also ABBOTT, EMMA; AUSTIN, ELIZABETH; BISHOP, ANNA; BROUGH, WILLIAM FRANCIS; DAMROSCH, WALTER; GRAU, MAURICE; HARRISON, WILLIAM; JUCH, EMMA; KELLOGG, CLARA; LAMBARDI, MARIO; MAPLESON, JAMES HENRY; MARETZEK, MAX; METROPOLITAN OPERA COMPANY; PAREPA, EUPHROSYNE; PYNE, LOUISA; SEGUIN, ANNE; SEGUIN, ARTHUR; SHIRREFF, JANE; STRAKOSCH, MAURICE; THILLON, SOPHIE ANNE; ULLMAN, BERNARD; WILSON, JOHN; and WOOD, MARY ANNE.

6. LATIN AMERICA. In the early 19th century the first European opera singers to reach Latin America arrived along two main routes. One began in New York and went by water (either down the coastline via Charleston, South Carolina, or down the Ohio and Mississippi rivers via Cincinnati and St Louis) to Havana, New Orleans, possibly Mexico or the Caribbean islands and coasts; thus a troupe headed by Manuel García and his family reached Mexico in 1825. The other began in Brazil (where the refugee Portuguese court had established opera in 1808) and went on, also by water, to Montevideo and Buenos Aires, eventually to other Argentine towns and (rounding the Horn) to Chile and Peru, possibly to Central America and, after the 1849 gold rush, to California.

The early visiting troupes were Italian, French and Spanish; each nationality kept almost wholly to itself and to its own brand of (mainly comic) opera. The French had an early monopoly of opera in New Orleans and kept a base there until 1919, but to about 1860 small French groups travelled many parts of Latin America. The Spaniards specialized in *tonadillas*, later in zarzuela. The Italians to about 1860 were mainly small family groups of the kind that had given comic opera throughout Italy, or else a mixture of beginners and superannuated singers who had had at best modest engagements at home; the family groups picked up extra singers and players in each city as they needed them.

Rio de Janeiro and Havana had theatres and audiences able to cope with complete operas before most other parts of Central and South America, which at first made do with extracts. By 1860 the focus had shifted to Buenos Aires and Montevideo, both of which had lately built handsome new opera houses. This led to regular visits by opera companies, mainly Italian, of much higher quality than the early troupes. But although these companies travelled (typically to Rio, Montevideo, Buenos Aires and Santiago), they were formed by an impresario for a season of six months at most and had no inner cohesion. From the 1920s French and German companies followed suit. More lasting – and much more modest – Italian troupes still travelled Central America, for example the Lambardi Opera Company. Stranded in Costa Rica in 1910, it appealed for help to Fortune T. Gallo; taking it to California set him on his long North American career as a touring impresario.

See also AZZALI, AUGUSTO; BRACALE, ADOLFO; GONSALEZ, GIUSEPPE; and LAMBARDI, MARIO.

7. AUSTRALIA AND NEW ZEALAND. Although intermittent operatic activity took place in both countries before the gold rushes of the 1850s and 60s, these provided the catalyst for a number of adventurous artists and entrepreneurs to seek fame and fortune in Australasia. The most important pioneer was an Irish-born impresario, W. S. Lyster, who brought a company from San Francisco to Melbourne in 1861. He quickly extended his activities to Sydney, and then to other Australian centres; in 1864 he crossed the Tasman Sea to tour the major towns of New Zealand. From a base in Melbourne, Lyster's travelling operatic companies became an almost permanent feature of Australasian cultural life for nearly two decades, presenting an eclectic repertory of works by French, German, Italian and English composers.

The majority of artists in these travelling troupes were Anglo-Saxon in origin. However, the colonial preference for Italian opera sung in the original language encouraged a number of mainly second-rank singers from Italy to seek stardom in the Antipodes. Augusto Cagli brought an Italian company through India and the East in the late 1860s, later joining forces with Lyster for a period. The connection with the East remained strong, and some Australian-based travelling troupes extended their activities into this area.

Touring the Antipodes presented great difficulties. Population centres in Australia, and particularly New Zealand, were small, and the distances between them vast by European standards. Although modern theatres were soon built in major towns, some troupes regularly ventured to smaller settlements performing, even in the 1890s, in makeshift venues lit by oil lamps. Companies travelled with the nucleus of an orchestra and chorus as well as their solo singers, since they could seldom rely on more than a handful of competent local performers being available outside major towns.

After Lyster's death in 1880 the travelling opera tradition was maintained in more sporadic fashion, most notably by the husband-and-wife team of Fanny and Martin Simonsen. The Pollard juvenile operatic troupes took light opera throughout Australasia with great success. However, by the end of the century, locally based companies had been virtually superseded by companies recruited overseas for limited and specific tours. In 1893 George Musgrove (1854–1916) and J. C. Williamson (1845–1913) consolidated this trend with a specially selected company of Italian artists with which they introduced *verismo* opera to Australia. Musgrove later recruited two further companies (1901 and 1907), but it was Williamson and, after his death, the theatrical organization he had founded, which came to dominate all aspects of stage life in Australasia. Eight opera companies toured under the Williamson banner in all.

Although the imported companies brought by Musgrove and Williamson included some Antipodean singers – indeed the 1911 Williamson company was created as a vehicle for Melba to perform in her homeland – costs decreed that they could visit only the larger cities. Many towns that had regularly received travelling companies now found themselves bypassed, and opera, established on an almost permanent footing in the heyday of Lyster and his immediate successors, became available only on rare occasions to a small proportion of the population.

Notable among later travelling troupes were those of Thomas Quinlan, who in 1913 staged the first *Ring* cycle in Australasia. The Williamson organization mounted two more tours in conjunction with Melba (1924 and 1928), and brought out an Italian company in 1932 that included New Zealand in its itinerary. The Gonsalez company's tours (1916 and 1928) marked a reversion to the 19th century, in that the company was a largely family one presenting pared-down productions throughout both countries. By contrast, Williamson's 1965 company, built around Joan Sutherland, was analogous with the earlier, lavish Melba-Williamson seasons. By this time permanent regional companies were becoming consolidated in Australia. In New Zealand the tradition of the travelling opera troupe was maintained until 1971 by the New Zealand Opera Company. However, the Australian Opera, which is based in Sydney, still gives regular seasons in Melbourne and occasionally travels to other centres, thus keeping the Antipodean touring tradition alive.

See also CAGLI, AUGUSTO; LYSTER, W. S.; NEW ZEALAND OPERA COMPANY; POLLARD; POMPEI, GIOVANNI; and SIMONSEN, MARTIN.

*

EUROPE

Indice de' teatrali spettacoli (Milan, Venice and Rome, 1764–1823) [annual]

J. C. Brandes: *Meine Lebensgeschichte* (Berlin, 1799–1800)

F. J. Reden-Esbeck: *Caroline Neuber und ihre Zeitgenossen: ein Beitrag zur deutschen Kultur- und Theatergeschichte* (Leipzig, 1881)

J.-J. Olivier: *Les comédiens français dans les cours d'Allemagne au XVIIIe siècle* (Paris, 1901–5)

E. Devrient: *Geschichte der deutschen Schauspielkunst* (Berlin, 1905)

J. A. Christ: *Schauspielerleben im achtzehnten Jahrhundert* (Munich and Leipzig, 1912)

A. von Weilen: *Carl Ludwig Costenoble's Tagebücher von seiner Jugend bis zur Übersiedlung nach Wien (1818)* (Berlin, 1912)

L. Vallas: *Un siècle de théâtre et de musique à Lyon, 1688–1789* (Lyons, 1932)

L. Pietsch-Ebert: *Die Gestalt des Schauspielers auf der deutschen Bühne des 17. und 18. Jahrhunderts* (Berlin, 1942)

M. Fuchs: *Lexique des troupes de comédiens au XVIIIe siècle* (Paris, 1944)

H. Kindermann: *Theatergeschichte der Goethezeit* (Vienna, 1948)

H. Knudsen: *Deutsche Theatergeschichte* (Stuttgart, 1959)

C. Sartori: 'Profilo di una cantante della fine del secolo XVII: Barbara Riccioni', *Festschrift K. G. Fellerer zum 60. Geburtstag* (Regensburg, 1962), 454–60

P. Petrobelli: 'Francesco Manelli – documenti e osservazioni', *Chigiana*, new ser., xxiv (1962), 43–66

L. Bianconi and T. Walker: 'Dalla *Finta pazza* alla *Veremonda*: storie di Febiarmonici', *RIM*, x (1975), 379–454

R. L. Weaver and N. W. Weaver: *A Chronology of Music in the Florentine Theater* (Detroit, 1978), 41, 62–9, 71

G. Mongrédien and J. Robert: *Les comédiens français du XVIIe siècle: dictionnaire biographique, suivi d'un inventaire des troupes, 1590–1710, d'après des documents inédits* (Paris, 1961, 3/1981)

S. Maurer-Schmoock: *Deutsches Theater im 18. Jahrhundert* (Tübingen, 1982)

F. Piperno: 'Buffe e buffi (considerazioni sulla professionalità degli interpreti di scene buffe ed intermezzi)', *RIM*, xviii (1982), 241–84

L. Bianconi and T. Walker: 'Production, Consumption and Political Function of Seventeenth-Century Opera', *Early Music History*, iv (1984), 209–96, esp. 274–82

T. Bauman: *North German Opera in the Age of Goethe* (Cambridge, 1985)

R. Verti: 'The *Indice de' teatrali spettacoli*, Milan, Venice, Rome, 1764–1823: Preliminary Research on a Source for the History of Italian Opera', *Periodica musica*, iii (1985), 1–7

C. B. Schmidt: 'The Geographical Spread of Lully's Operas during the Late Seventeenth and Early Eighteenth Centuries: New Evidence from the Livrets', *Jean-Baptiste Lully and the Music of the French Baroque*, ed. J. H. Heyer (Cambridge, 1989), 183–211

THE AMERICAS

M. Maretzek: *Crotchets and Quavers* (New York, 1855)

R. G. White: 'Opera in New York', *Century Magazine*, xxiii (1881–2), 686–703, 865–82; xxiv (1882–3), 31–43, 193–210

J. H. Mapleson: *The Mapleson Memoirs* (New York, 1888); ed. H. Rosenthal (London, 1966)

M. Maretzek: *Sharps and Flats* (New York, 1890)

S. E. Martin: *The Life and Professional Career of Emma Abbott* (Minneapolis, 1891)

H. E. Krehbiel: *Chapters of Opera* (New York, 1908, 3/1911)

K. Hackett: *The Beginnings of Grand Opera in Chicago (1850–1859)* (Chicago, 1913)

C. L. Kellogg: *Memoirs of an American Prima Donna* (New York, 1913)

G. C. D. Odell: *Annals of the New York Stage* (New York, 1927–49)

W. G. Carson: *The Theatre on the Frontier: the Early Years of the St. Louis Stage* (Chicago, 1932)

L. Gafford: *A History of the St. Charles Theatre in New Orleans, 1835–1843* (Chicago, 1932)

Works Progress Administration: *The History of Opera in San Francisco*, San Francisco Theatre Research, vii–viii (San Francisco, 1938)

N. Smither: *A History of the English Theatre in New Orleans* (New York, 1944)
W. G. Carson: *St. Louis Goes to the Opera, 1837–1941* (St Louis, 1946)
W. S. Hoole: *The Ante Bellum Charleston Theatre* (Montgomery, AL, 1946)
G. E. Schiavo: *Italian Music and Musicians in America* (New York, 1947)
S. Chevalley: 'La première saison théâtrale française de New-York', *French Review*, xxiv (1950–51), 471–9
S. Chevalley: 'Le Théâtre d'Orléans en tournée dans les villes du nord, 1827–1833', *Comptes rendus de l'Athénée louisianais* (New Orleans, 1955), 27–71
H. A. Kmen: *Music in New Orleans: the Formative Years, 1791–1841* (Baton Rouge, LA, 1966)
L. Lerner: *The Rise of the Impresario: Bernard Ullman and the Transformation of Musical Culture in Nineteenth Century America* (diss, U. of Wisconsin, 1970)
J. A. Belsom: *Reception of Major Operatic Premières in New Orleans during the Nineteenth Century* (diss., Louisiana State U., Baton Rouge, 1972)
Q. Eaton: *Opera Caravan: Adventures of the Metropolitan on Tour, 1883–1956* (New York, 1978)
O. Albrecht: 'Opera in Philadelphia, 1800–1830', *JAMS*, xxxii (1979), 499–515
C. Hamm: *Yesterdays: Popular Song in America* (New York, 1979)
J. F. Cone: *First Rival of the Metropolitan* (New York, 1983)
P. D. Wolz: *Opera in Cincinnati before 1920* (diss., U. of Cincinnati, 1983)
D. Cooper: *Opera in Montreal and Toronto: A Study of Performance Traditions and Repertoire* (diss., U. of Toronto, 1984)
T. G. Kaufman: 'The Arditi Tour: the Midwest gets its First Real Taste of Italian Opera', *OQ*, iv/4 (1986), 39–52
V. B. Lawrence: *Strong on Music: the New York Music Scene in the Days of George Templeton Strong, 1836–1874*, i: *Resonances (1836–1850)* (New York, 1988)
K. K. Preston: *Travelling Opera Troupes in the United States, 1825–1860* (diss., CUNY, 1989)
J. Rosselli: 'The Opera Business and the Italian Immigrant Community in Latin America, 1820–1930: the Example of Buenos Aires', *Past and Present*, no.127 (1990), 155–82

AUSTRALIA AND NEW ZEALAND

F. C. Brewer: *The Drama and Music in New South Wales* (Sydney, 1892)
H. Love: *The Golden Age of Australian Opera: W. S. Lyster and his Companies, 1861–1880* (Sydney, 1981)
A. Gyger: *Opera for the Antipodes* (Sydney, 1990)
A. Simpson, ed.: *Opera in New Zealand: Aspects of History and Performance* (Wellington, 1990)
K. Brisbane, ed.: *Entertaining Australia* (Sydney, 1991)
R. Holmes, ed.: *Through the Opera Glass: a Chronological Register of Opera Performed in South Australia 1836–1988* (Adelaide, 1991)

JOHN ROSSELLI (1, 6), NEAL ZASLAW (2), THOMAS BAUMAN (3), NIGEL BURTON (4), KATHERINE K. PRESTON (5), ADRIENNE SIMPSON (7)

Travesty (It. *travesti*: 'disguised'). Any role played by a member of the opposite sex (*see also* BREECHES PART). The term is commonly applied to men who play elderly females in the manner of the pantomime dame. Such parts are frequent in early Venetian opera, for example the Nurse in Monteverdi's *L'incoronazione di Poppea* (1643) or Linfea in Cavalli's *Calisto* (1651). The age of Zeno and Metastasio banished such parts as distasteful, but the custom persisted in early Neapolitan comic operas; and in Rome, where women were at many periods barred from singing on the stage, travesty parts prevailed well into the 18th century. French opera offers an amusing specimen in the title role of Rameau's *Platée* (1745). A solitary instance in 19th-century Italian opera is Mamm' Agata in Donizetti's *Le convenienze ed inconvenienze teatrali* (1827), the hectoring mother of a seconda donna. In Humperdinck's *Hänsel und Gretel* (1893) the Witch is sometimes played as a travesty role. Notable examples from the present century are the Cook in Prokofiev's *The Love for Three Oranges* (1921) and, following the tradition of the Japanese noh play, the Madwoman in Britten's *Curlew River* (1964).

Several of Gilbert and Sullivan's unattractive middle-aged women, though sung by contraltos, have the attributes of the travesty dame, for example Lady Jane in *Patience* (1881) or the Fairy Queen in *Iolanthe* (1882).

JULIAN BUDDEN

Traviata, La ('The Fallen Woman'). Opera in three acts by GIUSEPPE VERDI to a libretto by FRANCESCO MARIA PIAVE after ALEXANDRE DUMAS (ii)'s play *La dame aux camélias*; Venice, Teatro La Fenice, 6 March 1853.

Violetta Valéry *a courtesan*	soprano
Flora Bervoix *her friend*	mezzo-soprano
Annina *Violetta's maid*	soprano
Alfredo Germont	tenor
Giorgio Germont *his father*	baritone
Gastone, Vicomte de Letorières *friend of Alfredo*	tenor
Baron Douphol *Violetta's protector*	baritone
Marchese D'Obigny *friend of Flora*	bass
Doctor Grenvil	bass
Giuseppe *Violetta's servant*	tenor
Flora's Servant	bass
Commissioner	bass

Ladies and gentlemen, friends of Violetta and Flora, matadors, picadors, gypsies, servants of Violetta and Flora, masks etc.

Setting In and around Paris, about 1700

By April 1852 Verdi had agreed to write a new opera for the Carnival 1853 season at the Teatro La Fenice in Venice, with Francesco Maria Piave as librettist. But even as late as October no subject had been decided upon: the unusually tight schedule was due in part to Verdi's continuing work on *Il trovatore*, whose première in Rome eventually took place less than two months before that of *La traviata*. By the beginning of November, however, Verdi and Piave had elected to base their opera on Dumas *fils'* play, which had first been performed in Paris earlier that year. The working title of the opera, later changed at the insistence of the Venetian censors, was *Amore e morte* ('Love and Death'). As Verdi wrote to his friend Cesare De Sanctis on 1 January 1853, it was 'a subject of the times. Others would not have done it because of the conventions, the epoch and for a thousand other stupid scruples'. The composer even proposed that, contrary to custom, the opera should be performed in modern costume; but again the Venetian authorities would not agree, and the period was put back to the beginning of the 18th century.

La traviata, it seems, was written in something like record time. Even though the above-quoted letter to De Sanctis dates from just over two months before the première, it is primarily concerned with compositional problems surrounding the still unfinished *Trovatore*; it is clear that *La traviata* was largely unwritten at the time. The première cast included Fanny Salvini-Donatelli as Violetta, Ludovico Graziani as Alfredo and Felice Varesi, creator of Rigoletto and Macbeth, as Giorgio Germont. It was the most celebrated fiasco of Verdi's later career, a circumstance probably attribut-

'La traviata' (Verdi): design by Giuseppe and Pietro Bertoja for the original production at La Fenice, Venice, 6 March 1853

able more to the singers – Salvini-Donatelli was physically unsuited to Violetta and Varesi was too far past his prime to tackle such an exposed role – than to problems the audience may have had with the musical style. Verdi was reluctant to allow further performances until he could find a more suitable cast, but eventually allowed a second staging (on 6 May 1854) at the Teatro S Benedetto, Venice, making various alterations to the score, the most important of which were to the central Act 2 duet between Violetta and Germont. This time success was unequivocal, and the opera soon became one of the composer's most popular works. It has retained this position into modern times, in spite of the fact that the heroine's role is one of the most feared in the soprano repertory.

The prelude to *La traviata* is a curious narrative experiment: it paints a three-stage portrait of the heroine, but in reverse chronological order. First comes a musical rendering of her final decline in Act 3, with high, chromatic strings dissolving into 'sobbing' appoggiaturas; then a direct statement of love, the melody that will in Act 2 become 'Amami, Alfredo'; and finally this same melody repeated on the lower strings, surrounded by the delicate ornamentation associated with Violetta in Act 1.

ACT 1 *A salon in Violetta's house* It is August. In a festive atmosphere, the action underpinned by a sequence of lively orchestral dances, Violetta and friends greet their guests, among whom is Alfredo Germont, a young man who has loved Violetta from afar for some time. Eventually all sit down to supper and Violetta calls for a toast. Alfredo takes up the cup to sing the famous brindisi 'Libiamo ne' lieti calici', a simple, bouncing melody repeated by Violetta and finally (with judicious transposition) by the entire chorus. A band in an adjoining room now starts up a succession of waltzes and the guests prepare to dance; but Violetta feels unsteady (the symptoms suggest she is consumptive) and begs the others to go on without her. Alfredo remains behind and, with the dance music still sounding, warns Violetta that her way of life will kill her if she persists. He offers to protect her and admits his love in the first movement of the duet: 'Un dì felice, eterea' begins hesitantly but builds to the passionate outpouring of 'Di quell'amor ch'è palpito', a melody that will reappear later as a kind of emblem of Alfredo's devoted love. Violetta answers with an attempt to defuse the situation, telling him he will soon forget her, and surrounding his passionately insistent melody with showers of vocal ornamentation. The dance music (which unobtrusively disappeared during the duet) now returns as Violetta playfully gives Alfredo a flower, telling him to return when it has faded. To round off the scene the returning guests, seeing dawn approaching, prepare to leave in the concluding stretta, 'Si ridesta in ciel l'aurora'.

Left alone, Violetta closes the act with a formal double aria. She muses fondly of her new conquest in the Andantino 'Ah fors'è lui', which – like Alfredo's declaration – begins hesitantly but then flowers into 'Di quell'amor'. This sequence is then literally repeated (in the style, that is, of a French *couplet* rather than an Italian cantabile) before Violetta violently shrugs off her sentimental thoughts and resolves that a life of pleasure is her only choice. She closes the act with the cabaletta 'Sempre libera degg'io', full of daring, almost desperate coloratura effects. But in the closing stages her melody is mixed with 'Di quell'amor', sung by Alfredo from below the balcony.

ACT 2.i *A country house near Paris* It is the following January; three months have passed since Violetta and Alfredo set up house together in the country. Alfredo sings of his youthful ardour in 'Dei miei bollenti spiriti', an unusually condensed Andante with no repetition of the initial melodic phrase. Annina then hurries in to inform Alfredo that Violetta has been selling her belongings to finance their country life together. Alfredo immediately decides to raise money himself and rushes off to Paris after expressing his remorse in the conventionally structured cabaletta 'Oh mio rimorso!' (often cut in modern performances).

Violetta appears and is joined by Giorgio Germont. Their ensuing grand duet is unusually long; typically for Verdi, the formal expansion is concentrated on the opening section of the conventional four-movement structure, the so-called *tempo d'attacco*. After an initial passage of recitative this first movement involves three main subsections: a kind of lyrical dialogue between the principals. First comes an Allegro moderato ('Pura siccome un angelo') in which Germont describes the plight of his daughter, whose forthcoming marriage is threatened by Alfredo's scandalous relationship with Violetta. After a brief transition, Violetta reveals the seriousness of her illness and protests that Alfredo is all she has in the world (the breathless 'Non sapete quale affetto'). But Germont is adamant and in 'Bella voi siete, e giovane' assures Violetta that she will find others to love. Eventually Violetta capitulates: the second movement of the duet, 'Dite alla giovine', begins with her heartbroken agreement to leave Alfredo, and gives ample opportunity for the voices to interweave. The final two movements are relatively brief and conventional: Violetta agrees to break the news to Alfredo in her own way, begging Germont to remain to comfort his son; and then in the cabaletta 'Morrò! la mia memoria' she asks Germont to tell Alfredo the truth after her death.

As Germont retires, Violetta begins to write a letter to Alfredo, but cannot finish before her lover appears. He is disturbed by her agitation, but she answers his questions with a simple, passionate declaration of love, 'Amami, Alfredo' (the melody that served as the basis for the opera's prelude) before rushing out. The remainder of the scene might well, of course, focus on Alfredo, but operatic convention requires a formal double aria for the baritone (who has no other opportunity for an extended solo), so Alfredo's reactions are sandwiched into the transition passages. Soon after Violetta has left, a servant brings Alfredo her letter saying that she must leave him forever, and his anguished reaction is immediately countered by Germont's lyrical Andante, 'Di Provenza il mar, il suol', which conjures up a nostalgic picture of their family home. But Alfredo will not be consoled and at the end of Germont's cabaletta, 'No, non udrai rimproveri', his anger boils over: knowing that she has received an invitation to a party in Paris, he assumes that Violetta has deserted him to return to her old friends.

2.ii *A salon in Flora's town house* A boisterous orchestral opening, over which Flora and her new lover discuss the separation of Violetta and Alfredo, is followed by a two-part *divertissement* as a chorus of gypsies (with more than an echo of the musical world of *Il trovatore*) and then of matadors, dance and sing. Alfredo enters and, to an obsessively repeated motif on the lower strings and wind, begins playing recklessly at cards, apparently uncaring when Violetta appears on the arm of Baron Douphol. As Alfredo and the Baron bet against each other with barely concealed hostility, Violetta repeatedly laments her position in an anguished rising line. Supper is served, and Violetta manages to see Alfredo privately. In answer to his accusations she desperately claims that she now loves the Baron, at which Alfredo calls the guests together and, in a declamatory passage of rising fury, denounces Violetta and throws his winnings in her face as 'payment' for their time together. This precipitates the concertato, which begins with a rapid passage of choral outrage before Germont, who has just arrived, leads off the main Largo. This large-scale movement depicts the contrasting moods of the main characters: Germont reproachful and lyrically contained; Alfredo distressed and remorseful with a fragmentary line; and Violetta, privately begging Alfredo to understand her distress with a line which eventually dominates through its simplicity and emotive power. Such is the charge of the movement that the act can end there, without the conventional concluding stretta.

ACT 3 *Violetta's bedroom* It is February. The orchestral prelude opens with the idea that began the entire opera, and then develops into an intense solo for the first violins, full of 'sobbing' appoggiaturas. In the spare recitative that follows we learn from a doctor that Violetta is near death. To a restrained orchestral reprise of 'Di quell'amor', Violetta reads a letter from Germont, telling her that Alfredo (who fled abroad after fighting a duel with the Baron) now knows the truth about her sacrifice and is hurrying back to her. But she knows that time is short, and in the aria 'Addio, del passato' bids farewell to the past and to life, the oboe solo adding poignancy to her painfully restricted vocal line. A chorus of revellers heard outside underlines the gloom of Violetta's isolation, but then, to a sustained orchestral crescendo, Alfredo is announced and arrives to throw himself into Violetta's arms. After the initial greeting Alfredo leads off the Andante movement of the duet, 'Parigi, o cara': a simple waltz-time melody reminiscent of Act 1, in which the lovers look forward to a life together away from Paris. It is significant, though, that Violetta's attempts at Act 1-style ornamentation are now severely restricted in range. Violetta decides that she and Alfredo should go to church to celebrate his return, but the strain even of getting to her feet is too much and she repeatedly falls back. This painful realization of her weakness precipitates the cabaletta 'Gran Dio! morir sì giovane', in which Violetta gives way to a despair that Alfredo can do little to assuage. Germont appears, and a brief but passionate exchange between him and Violetta leads to the final concertato, 'Prendi: quest'è l'immagine', in which Violetta gives Alfredo a locket with her portrait, telling him that, should he marry, he can give it to his bride. The movement begins with an insistent full-orchestra rhythmic figure, similar to that used in the 'Miserere' scene of *Il trovatore* and clearly associated with Violetta's imminent death; later, Violetta develops the simple, intense vocal style that has characterized her in this act. A last orchestral reprise of 'Di quell'amor' sounds as the final blow approaches. Violetta feels a sudden rush of life, sings a final 'Oh gioia!', but then collapses on to a sofa.

* * *

As we have seen, *La traviata* was written in great haste and its genesis was thoroughly entangled with the creation of Verdi's previous opera, *Il trovatore*. Perhaps not surprisingly, there are a series of startling musical resemblances between the two operas. But these similarities are on what one might call the musical surface; in dramatic structure and general atmosphere the two works are remarkably different, in some senses even antithetical. *La traviata* is above all a chamber opera: in spite of the 'public' scenes of the first and second acts, it succeeds best in an intimate setting, where there can be maximum concentration on those key moments in which the heroine's attitude to her surroundings are forced to change. Perhaps for this reason, the cabalettas, those 'public' moments which are so inevitable and essential to the mood of *Il trovatore*, tend to sit uneasily; we remember *La traviata* above all for its moments of lyrical introspection.

It is nevertheless easy to see why *La traviata* is among the best loved of Verdi's operas, perhaps even *the* best loved. In many senses it is the composer's most 'realistic' drama. The cultural ambience of the subject matter and the musical expression are very closely related: no suspension of disbelief is required to feel that the waltz tunes that saturate the score are naturally born out of the Parisian setting. And, perhaps most important, this sense of 'authenticity' extends to the heroine, a character whose psychological progress through the opera is mirrored by her changing vocal character: from the exuberant ornamentation of Act 1, to the passionate declamation of Act 2, to the final, well-nigh ethereal qualities she shows in Act 3. Violetta – Stiffelio, Rigoletto and Gilda notwithstanding – is Verdi's most complete musical personality to date.

For a page of autograph sketches, *see* VERDI, GIUSEPPE, fig.1.

ROGER PARKER

Travis, Roy (Elihu) (*b* New York, 24 June 1922). American composer. His principal teachers were Otto Luening, Bernard Wagenaar and Felix Salzer; he also studied with Milhaud in Paris on a Fulbright scholarship (1951–2). After teaching at the Mannes College (1952–7), he joined the faculty of UCLA in 1957 and became professor in 1968. His honours include a Gershwin Award, a Martha Baird Rockefeller Award (1968), a Guggenheim Fellowship (1972–3), a Ford Foundation grant (1975) and two NEA grants (1976, 1978). Travis's works are characterized by a strong rhythmic impulse and an expanded tonality. He has written two operas, both to his own librettos, on Greek subjects. *The Passion of Oedipus* (2, after Sophocles) was composed in 1965 and first performed in Los Angeles on 8 November 1968. *The Black Bacchants* (2; composed 1982), based on *The Bacchae* of Euripides, fuses mythology and Greek drama with traditional West African dance rhythms, emphasized by the inclusion of African instruments in the score. In 1987 he published a monograph on Britten's *Death in Venice*.

LAWRENCE STARR

Traxel, Josef (*b* Mainz, 29 Sept 1916; *d* Stuttgart, 8 Oct 1975). German tenor. He studied at the Darmstadt Conservatory, but was conscripted into the army before properly beginning his career, except for his début as Don Ottavio at Mainz in 1942 while on sick-leave. After internment in Britain as a prisoner of war he returned to take up his career at the Nuremberg Stadttheater in 1946, moving to Stuttgart in 1952. In that year he sang Mercury in the première of Strauss's *Die Liebe der Danae* at the Salzburg Festival, and he first appeared at Bayreuth in 1953 as Walther. His lyrical, finely poised tenor, unusually high for a German singer, was also admired in the roles of Belmonte and Siegmund, but his recordings were mostly confined to arias and excerpts and to the smaller roles in *Der fliegende Holländer* under Fricsay and *Das Rheingold* under Knappertsbusch, in both of which his best qualities are heard. From 1963 he taught at Stuttgart. NOËL GOODWIN

Trebelli, Zélia [Gillebert, Gloria Caroline] (*b* Paris, 1838; *d* Etretat, 18 Aug 1892). French contralto. She studied with Wartel, and made her début in 1859 at Madrid as Rosina, also singing Azucena, Arsace (*Semiramide*), Urbain (*Les Huguenots*) and Federica (*Luisa Miller*). In 1860 she sang at the Berlin Hofoper and in 1861 at the Théâtre Italien, Paris. She made her London début at Her Majesty's Theatre in 1862 as Orsini (*Lucrezia Borgia*), and returned to London regularly for the next 25 years. She sang Siébel in *Faust* (1863), Taven in *Mireille* (1864) and Preziosilla in *La forza del destino* (1867), all first London performances. At Drury Lane she sang Cherubino, Maddalena (*Rigoletto*) and Frédéric in the first London performance of Thomas' *Mignon* (1870); she first appeared at Covent Garden in 1868. In 1878 she toured the USA with Mapleson's company. She made her Metropolitan début in 1883 as Azucena, and then sang in *Mefistofele*, *Carmen* and Flotow's *Martha*. She retired in 1888. Her voice, which could easily encompass both mezzo-soprano and contralto roles, was particularly strong and resonant in the lower register. She was a fine actress and at 50 was still convincing in the travesty roles which had won her fame. She was married to the tenor Alessandro Bettini.

J. H. Mapleson: *The Mapleson Memoirs* (London, 1888); ed. H. Rosenthal (London, 1966)
A. Ehrlich: *Berühmte Sängerinnen der Vergangenheit und Gegenwart* (Leipzig, 1895)
I. Kolodin: *The Story of the Metropolitan Opera* (New York, 1953)
H. Rosenthal: *Two Centuries of Opera at Covent Garden* (London, 1958) ELIZABETH FORBES

Treble (from Lat. *triplum*, 'third [voice]'). A high voice; the term normally refers to the unbroken singing voice of a boy, but is occasionally also applied to that of a girl. In opera, a treble rather than a soprano may be called upon to sing parts such as Yniold in *Pelléas et Mélisande* or the Shepherd-boy in Act 3 of *Tosca*; boys' voices are commonly specified for use in the chorus, as in Act 1 of *Carmen*. Britten's operas frequently involve children; the most rewarding part for a treble is probably that of Miles in *The Turn of the Screw*. J. B. STEANE

Trecate, Luigi Ferrari. *See* FERRARI TRECATE, LUIGI.

Tre commedie goldoniane ('Three Goldoni Comedies'). Triptych of one-act operas by GIAN FRANCESCO MALIPIERO, consisting of *La bottega da caffè* ('The Coffee Shop'), *Sior Todero brontolon* ('Grumpy Sior Todero') and *Le baruffe chiozzotte* ('Quarrels in Chioggia'), to librettos by the composer, condensed and freely adapted from the comedies of the same (or similar) names by CARLO GOLDONI; Darmstadt, Hessisches Landestheater, 24 March 1926.

Malipiero's decision to base these operatic miniatures on so 'normal' a source as Goldoni may seem surprising, in view of the uncompromising eccentricity of most of his other theatre works of the period. Yet, far from emulating the straightforwardly Goldonian operas of Wolf-Ferrari, his reinterpretations of three of the playwright's best-known comedies are so high-handed that only the first of them refers more than intermittently to the original plot. Malipiero was interested less in Goldoni's dramas as such than in some of his characters and, still more, in their Venetian setting: in *La bottega da caffè* he was concerned, he said, to evoke 'the life of the Venetian streets'; *Sior Todero brontolon* similarly evokes 'the life of intimate domesticity' and *Le baruffe chiozzotte* 'that of the lagoons'. (*Le baruffe chiozzotte*, though normally performed as the third opera in the triptych, was composed in 1919–20 – before the other two, which were added in 1922.)

The operas centre on three well-known Goldonian figures: the mischievous gossip Don Marzio (baritone), surrounded, outside a coffee shop, by a colourful assembly of wayward husbands, suspicious wives and gambling cheats; the crusty old miser Sior Todero (baritone), who sings a love song to his treasure-chest and is determined that his granddaughter should marry in such a way that no dowry leaves the house; and the long-suffering 'rappresentante della giustizia' Isidoro (baritone), who copes as best he can with quarrelsome women and with men who brandish knives and throw stones. Malipiero sometimes lifted episodes and phrases from other Goldoni comedies as well as inventing many details himself. The highly stylized approach, with many mute or almost mute characters and a compressed, unrealistically rapid action, is less far removed from the composer's previous theatrical methods than one might suppose.

Malipiero did, however, go back on at least one principle that was fundamental in *Pantea* and *Sette canzoni*: unlike those earlier works, the *Commedie* contain a number of unabashed recitatives, sometimes even approaching 18th-century *recitativo secco* in their rapid 'parlato' delivery, although the accompanying harmonies are thoroughly 20th-century and sometimes acutely dissonant. In the orchestra the influence of *Petrushka* is unmistakable – transformed, however, in quintessentially Italian terms. The music's vitality is enhanced by a continuous stream of bright, kaleidoscopic instrumental imagery and by many suggestions of the spirit (rather than the letter) of Venetian popular melodies.

The extreme brevity of these operatic miniatures – their combined length being less than that of many a one-act opera – has stood in the way of frequent performances. They would perhaps be more at home in a festival than in a normal repertory. But with singers who have mastered the appropriate acting style they could prove extremely effective: the effervescent *Le baruffe chiozzotte* surely remains the supreme expression of the comic side of Malipiero's genius.

JOHN C. G. WATERHOUSE

Tree, Ann Maria (*b* London, Aug 1801; *d* London, 17 Feb 1862). English mezzo-soprano. She studied with T. S. Cooke and sang first in the chorus at Drury Lane. In 1819 she made her début at Covent Garden as Rosina in *The Barber of Seville*, adapted from Rossini by Bishop; Leigh Hunt reported that 'her rich and easy tones smack most delightfully of taste and tenderness'. For the next six years she was one of the leading singers on the London stage. Among her most famous roles were Luciana in Bishop's setting of *The Comedy of Errors* (1819), and the title role in his *Clari* (1823), in which she launched the popular song 'Home, Sweet Home'. In 1825 she married the politician James Bradshaw and afterwards appeared only in concert performances. Chorley called her 'a singer with a cordial, expressive mezzo-soprano voice and much real feeling'.

*

DNB ('Bradshaw, Ann Maria'; J. Knight); *GSL*
T. Fenner: *Leigh Hunt and Opera Criticism: the 'Examiner' Years, 1808–1821* (Lawrence, KS, 1972)
——: *Opera in London: Views from the Press, 1785–1830* (Carbondale, IL, forthcoming)

THEODORE FENNER

Treemonisha. Opera in three acts by SCOTT JOPLIN to his own libretto; Atlanta, Symphony Hall, 28 January 1972.

The action of *Treemonisha* is set in September 1884, on and near a remote Arkansas plantation that has been abandoned to its former slaves following the Civil War. Ned (bass) and Monisha ([mezzo-]soprano) have a foundling daughter, named after the tree under which she was discovered. They have been at great pains to give Treemonisha (soprano) a proper education, and she, now adult, comes into conflict with the local 'conjur men' who cater to the superstitions of her people. The conjurors kidnap her, but she is rescued (Act 2) by her friend Remus (tenor) and brought home. At Treemonisha's insistence (Act 3) the kidnappers are let off with 'a severe lecture'. The people proclaim her as their leader (see illustration overleaf) and she joins them in the celebratory dance 'A Real Slow Drag', in which ragtime is raised to a level of unequalled power and grandeur.

Except for an unstaged public reading with piano in 1915, the opera, completed and published in 1911, was not produced until the ragtime revival of the 1970s renewed interest in its composer. It then proved so successful that it won for him a posthumous Pulitzer prize (1974). Joplin's orchestration (1915) is lost. Conflicting legal and musicological interests resulted in the appearance of three competing modern orchestrations (by T. J. Anderson, William Bolcom and Gunther Schuller) and impeded full dissemination of the opera before the expiry of copyright in 1986.

ANDREW STILLER

Tréfeu (de Tréval), Etienne (Victor) (*b* Saint-Lô, Manche, 25 Sept 1821; *d* Paris, June 1903). French librettist. He achieved attention in Paris as an author of words for popular songs; he is credited with more than 500 songs in total, of which one (*Vive la France*) was specially popular in the *cafés-concerts* in about 1855. In that year he was first associated with Offenbach, whose close friend he became. He wrote several librettos for Offenbach and in 1873 was appointed by him as administrator of the Théâtre de la Gaîté in Paris. Tréfeu's librettos were usually written in collaboration, most often with Charles Nuitter. Mostly they were of the shorter, more farcical kind and served their contemporary purpose well.

Le rêve d'une nuit d'été (opérette), Offenbach, 1855; *Le violoneux* (opérette, with E. Mestépès), Offenbach, 1855; *Les trois troubadours* (opérette), Nargeot, 1855; *Croquefer, ou Le dernier des paladins* (opéra bouffe, with L.-A. Jaime), Offenbach, 1857; *Les petits prodiges* (opérette, with Jaime), E. Jonas and Offenbach, 1857; *Geneviève de Brabant* (opéra bouffe, with H. Crémieux), Offenbach, 1859; *Les échos de Rosine* (opérette), A. Thys, 1862; *Il Signor Fagotto* (opérette, with C. Nuitter), Offenbach, 1863; *Le fifre enchanté, ou Le soldat magicien* (opéra bouffe, with Nuitter), Offenbach, 1864; *Jeanne qui pleure et Jean qui rit* (opérette, with Nuitter), Offenbach, 1864; *Coscoletto, ou Le Lazzarone* (opérette, with Nuitter), Offenbach, 1865

'Treemonisha' (Joplin): scene from the Houston Grand Opera Association's production, conducted by Gunther Schuller, at the Uris Theatre, New York, 1975

En manches de chemise (opérette, with Mendel), E. Ettling, 1868; *Un bal à la souspréfecture* (opérette), Villebichot, 1868; *La princesse de Trébizonde* (opéra bouffe, with Nuitter), Offenbach, 1869; *La romance de la rose* (opéra bouffe, with J. Prével), Offenbach, 1869; *Boule de neige* (opéra bouffe, with Nuitter), Offenbach, 1869; *Javotte* (opéra bouffe), Jonas, 1871; *Le nain* (opérette), Ettling, 1872; *Le tigre* (opérette), Ettling, 1873; *Le chignon d'or* (opéra bouffe, with E. Grangé), Jonas, 1873; *Whittington* (féerie, with Nuitter), Offenbach, 1874, later as Le chat du diable; *Monsieur de Floridor* (opéra, with Nuitter), Lajarte, 1880; *Le marché aux domestiques* (opérette), L. Bordèse, 1889; *Chien et chatte* (opérette, with P. Pittaud de Forges, Hubert), G. Bornier, 1892; *Le gaudriole* (opéra, with Nuitter), A. Vizentini, 1897 ANDREW LAMB

Treigle, Norman (*b* New Orleans, 6 March 1927; *d* New Orleans, 16 Feb 1975). American bass-baritone. He studied with the contralto Elizabeth Wood and after a brief career in New Orleans, where he made his stage début in 1947, joined the New York City Opera in 1953, singing Colline in *La bohème*. For the next 20 years he was a mainstay of that company, singing the major bass-baritone roles of the standard repertory. With a vivid, even flamboyant stage personality, he achieved his greatest successes in such parts as Mephistopheles (Boito and Gounod), Boris, Don Giovanni, Reverend Olin Blitch (Floyd's *Susannah*), and Handel's Julius Caesar.

In 1973 he left the City Opera to broaden his international activities with appearances in Hamburg, London (Covent Garden, *Faust*, 1973) and Milan. A singer who often sacrificed musical fidelity to a broad theatrical effect, he resembled Shalyapin in many respects but vocally was less generously endowed. His voice was well schooled and serviceable but limited by its dry, throaty and occasionally raspy timbre. PETER G. DAVIS

Treitschke, Georg Friedrich (*b* Leipzig, 29 Aug 1776; *d* Vienna, 4 June 1842). German librettist and translator. He went to Vienna in 1800 to pursue a career as an actor at the Hofoper, where two years later he was raised to the position of poet and stage manager. During the French invasion of 1809 he took over the management of the Theater an der Wien, where he remained until 1814 despite his reappointment to the Hofoper in 1811.

Treitschke wrote, translated and revised many opera and Singspiel librettos for performance in Vienna. In 1814, Beethoven asked him to revise the libretto of FIDELIO for the opera's revival; Treitschke not only agreed to perform this task but also left a substantial written record of what he saw, because of his close connections with the Theater an der Wien, as a 'pious duty'. His changes shift the emphasis away from the personal drama of Florestan and Leonore and strengthen the opera's universal moral dilemma. Treitschke's improvements inspired Beethoven 'to rebuild the ruins of an old castle'. He also translated many French operas into German, including Cherubini's *Les deux journées* (as *Der Wasserträger*) and *Médée*, as well as works by Spontini, Isouard and Boieldieu, for performances in the Habsburg capital; and he made German translations of Mozart's *Idomeneo* (1806) and *Così fan tutte* (as *Die Zauberprobe*, 1814). Beethoven contributed music for two of his Singspiels, *Die gute Nachricht* (1814) and *Die Ehrenpforten* (1815), and set his poem *Ruf vom Berge*.

Mitgefühl (Liederspiel), Lichtenstein, 1800 (Wranitzky, 1804); *Des Dichters Geburtstag* (Liederspiel), Bergt, 1802; *Die Neger*, Salieri, 1804; *Das Singspiel auf dem Dache* (after T. M. Dumersan), A. Fischer, 1807; *Die Junggesellen-Wirtschaft* (komisches Singspiel, trans. from the French), Gyrowetz, 1807; *Adrian von Ostade* (Singspiel), Weigl, 1807; *Das Milchmädchen von Bercy* (after C. A. Sewrin), A. Fischer, 1808; *Das Waisenhaus* (Singspiel), Weigl, 1808; *Clementine, oder Die Felsen von Arona*, J. J. Rösler, 1809; *Der Einsiedler auf den Alpen*, Weigl, 1810; *Der Geburtstag* (Operette), C. W. Häser, 1814

Die gute Nachricht (Singspiel), various composers, 1814; *Die Jugend Peter des Grossen* (Singspiel, after J. N. Bouilly), Weigl, 1814; *Fidelio* (rev. of Bouilly, Sonnleithner and Breuning), Beethoven, 1814; *Die Ehrenpforten* (Singspiel), various composers, 1815; *Romulus und Remus*, Fusz, 1816; *Die Nachtigall und der Rabe* (after C. G. Etienne), Weigl, 1818; *Edmund und Caroline* (after B.-J. Marsollier des Vivetières), C. F. Kreubé and Weigl, 1821; *Die musikalische Akademie* (Operette, after Marsollier des Vivetières), H. Payer, 1822; *Die beiden Figaro* (komisches Oper, after J. F. Jünger), C. Kreutzer, 1840

*

G. F. Treitschke: 'Die Zauberflöte, Der Dorfbarbier, Fidelio: Beitrag zur musikalischen Kunstgeschichte', *Orpheus: Musikalisches Taschenbuch für das Jahr 1841*, ed. A. Schmidt (Vienna, 1841), 239–64
T. Frimmel: 'Treitschke, Georg Friedrich', *Beethoven-Handbuch*, ii (Leipzig, 1926), 332–6
A. Bauer: *150 Jahre Theater an der Wien* (Zürich, 1952)
——: *Opern und Operetten in Wien* (Graz and Cologne, 1955) [includes complete worklist]
A. Sandberger: 'Léonore von Bouilly und ihre Bearbeitung für Beethoven durch Joseph Sonnleithner', *Ausgewählte Aufsätze zur Musikgeschichte*, ii (Munich, 1924), 141–53, 283–365
M. Ruhnke: 'Die Librettisten des Fidelio', *Opernstudien: Anna Amalie Abert zum 65. Geburtstag* (Tutzing, 1975), 121–40

KRISTIN M. KNITTEL

Trekel-Burckhardt, Ute (*b* Pirna, Saxony, 3 Nov 1939). German mezzo-soprano. She studied in Berlin and in 1963 was engaged at the Komische Oper, making her début as the Page in *Salome*. She joined the Berlin State Opera in 1978, and has sung in Dresden, Vienna, Cologne, Madrid, Brussels, Basle and Bonn. Her repertory includes Cherubino, Sextus, Ortrud, Venus, Fricka, Kundry, Ulrica, Preziosilla, Amneris, Eboli, Octavian, the Nurse, the Composer, Róza (*The Secret*), Carmen and Frasquita (*Der Corregidor*). She also sings many modern roles, including Renata (*The Fiery Angel*), Geschwitz (*Lulu*), Begbick (*Mahagonny*) and Queen Marguerite in Sutermeister's *Roi Bérenger*, which she created in Munich in 1985. An extremely effective singing actress, she has a voice which is always responsive to the music's emotional and dramatic requirements.

ELIZABETH FORBES

Tremolo (It.). For the use of tremolo in singing *see* VIBRATO and ORNAMENTATION.

Trenti, Mme. *See* CORNELYS, THERESA.

Trentini, Emma (*b* ? Milan, 1885; *d* Milan, 12 April 1959). American soprano of Italian birth. She was discovered singing in a Milan cabaret by Oscar Hammerstein, who took her to America in 1906 to sing with his Manhattan Opera Company. She remained with the troupe until Hammerstein sold out in 1910. He subsequently cast her in the title role of *Naughty Marietta* (1910), in which she introduced 'Italian Street Song' and 'Ah, Sweet Mystery of Life'. His son gave her the lead in *The Firefly* (1912), in which she sang 'Giannina Mia'. Unfortunately, her fiery temper and growing arrogance alienated her associates, and after some lesser assignments in New York and London she returned to her homeland, where she died in poverty and obscurity.

GERALD BORDMAN

Trento, Vittorio (*b* Venice, *c*1761; *d* ?Lisbon, 1833). Italian composer. After studying under Bertoni at the Conservatorio dei Mendicanti in Venice, he began writing music for ballets to be performed between the acts of an opera, composing about 50 of these, mostly before 1803, for various theatres in Venice. There he became *maestro al cembalo* first at the Teatro S Samuele and later at La Fenice. His most successful ballet, and his best-known work, was *Triumph of Love* (or *La forza dell'amore*), composed in 1797 for Drury Lane at the invitation of Dragonetti.

Trento's earliest opera seems to have been *Orfeo negli Elisi*, an *azione teatrale* performed privately in Verona in 1789, followed in 1791 by *Le cognate in contesa* for Padua. Thereafter he specialized in comic subjects and farces, his one great success being the *farsa Quanti casi in un sol giorno* (1801), which for 20 years was performed all over Europe under different titles and in various forms. Meyerbeer heard it in Florence as late as 1818, describing it in his diary as a piece of 'good old-fashioned music'. Trento's first attempt at *opera seria* dates from 1797 (*Bianca de' Rossi*), and from 1804 he returned increasingly to the genre, though with only moderate success. In 1806 he went to Amsterdam as *maestro concertatore* of the Italian opera company of Nicola Miarteni; three years later he probably visited Lisbon, and in 1811–12 he was in London, where his opera *Climene* had its première as a benefit for Angelica Catalani. He seems to have contributed one opera each in Munich and Lisbon in 1815, and he was in Italy again from 1817 producing several works, mostly unsuccessful, for Naples, Rome and Venice. He was then music director of the Lisbon opera house from 1821 until 1823. Back in Italy in September 1823, he failed in his attempt to rescue his declining fortunes with a last revival of *Quanti casi in un sol giorno* at La Scala. He wrote two more operas before abandoning the composition of stage works.

Trento's output includes at least 45 operas, but despite his tireless activity and his not inconsiderable reputation at home and abroad, he never achieved prominence among his fellow Italian opera composers. He could turn his hand to a wide variety of subjects but seems to have been at his best in the lighter genres and in dance music. His more ambitious serious operas, judging from what remains, suffer from a certain dramatic inconsistency and lack of coherence due partly to his submission to the demands of the singers. In his later years his works, like those of many of his contemporaries, were overshadowed by those of Rossini, and he was soon forgotten.

VB – *Venice, Teatro S Benedetto*

Orfeo negli Elisi (azione teatrale, 1), private perf., Verona, Accademici Riuniti, 1789
Le cognate in contesa (dg, C. Lanfranchi Rossi), Padua, Obizzi, aut. 1791
Gli innamorati [Act 2] (dg, 2, G. M. Foppa, after C. Goldoni), VB, 4 Feb 1793, *I-Tf* (Act 2 only), *Mc* (excerpts) [Act 1 by Nasolini]
La finta ammalata (dg, 2, G. Squilloni), Florence, Pallacorda, spr. 1793, *Bc*
La gabbia dei matti (dg, 2), VB, 3 March 1794
La morte di Semiramide (tragedia per musica, S. A. Sografi, after P. Giovannini: *La vendetta di Nino*), Verona, Accademia filarmonica, carn. 1794
I capricci (farsa, 1, Foppa), Trieste, S Pietro, 5 Feb 1795
La serva padrona (int, G. A. Federico), private perf., Venice, Sala di Bartolomeo Cambi, carn. 1795
Il cucù scopre tutto (commedia, 2, G. Artusi), Florence, Pallacorda, 1796, *Mr**
Bianca de' Rossi (os, 3, M. Botturini), VB, 14 Jan 1797
Amore e paura [Il conte Pimpinella] (farsa, 1, G. Rossi), VB, 8 Dec 1798
L'uomo di quarant'anni (farsa, 1, Sografi), Venice, S Moisè, aut. 1799
Lucrezia romana in Costantinopoli (farsa, 2, Artusi, after Goldoni), Venice, S Moisè, carn. 1800, *Mc* (excerpts)
Lidia (os, 2, ?Foppa, after Marmontel), Florence, Pallacorda, spr. 1800, *OS* (sinfonia)
Il segreto (farsa, 1, Foppa), Padua, Nuovo, 13 June 1800
L'impossibile nel possibile (farsa, 1, Foppa), Venice, S Angelo, sum. 1800
Il ritorno di Serse (os, 2, F. G. Ferrari), Vicenza, Eretenio, sum. 1800
I due cognomi (farsa, 1, Rossi), Venice, S Samuele, aut. 1800

Quanti casi in un sol giorno, ossia Gli assassini (farsa, 1, Artusi), VB, Dec 1801; rev. (commedia per musica, 2, with some Neapolitan dialect by G. Palomba), Naples, Fiorentini, sum. 1817; *Fc, Mc*, Nc, Pl, PAc, Rmassimo* [also perf. as Gli assassini, Roberto l'assassino, Roberto capo d'assassini, La foresta di Nicobar]
Teresa vedova (farsa, 1, Artusi), VB, 13 Jan 1802, *F-Pc, I-Fc*
Elvira di Vitry, ossia Il cappello parlante (farsa, 1, Artusi), VB, Feb 1802
Le nozze dei Morlacchi (os, 2), Padua, Nuovo, June 1802, excerpts in *Fc* and *Vnm*
Ines de Castro (os, 2, A. Gasperini), Livorno, Avvalorati, 9 Nov 1803, *Fc* (excerpts)
La baronessa immaginaria (dg, 2), Rome, Capranica, carn. 1804, *Fc*
Crescono gli anni e scema il giudizio, ossia I due sindaci (farsa), Venice, S Moisè, 9 April 1804, *Vc* (excerpt)
Robinsone secondo (dg, 2, parody of D. Defoe: *Robinson Crusoe*), Milan, Carcano, 9 June 1804
Il primo giorno dell'anno (farsa, 1, L. Buonavoglia), VB, 8 Sept 1804, *F-Pc* (as Il capo d'anno)
Ifigenia in Aulide (os, 2, G. Pagliuca), Naples, S Carlo, 4 Nov 1804, *I-Nc*
Semira, regina di Cambaja (os, F. Tarducci), Rome, Argentina, 5 Feb 1805
Andromeda (os, 2, G. Schmidt), Naples, S Carlo, 30 May 1805, *Nc*
I vecchi delusi, ossia La burla (farsa, 1, A. L. Tottola, after Palomba), Naples, Nuovo, aut. 1805, *Nc*
Le astuzie di Ficchetto (farsa, 1, ? F. Ballani), Rome, Jan 1806
Odonte (os, 2, M. Rispoli), Rome, Dame, carn. 1806, *Rsc* (excerpts)
La donna giudice (ob), Amsterdam, Italiano, Dec 1806
Arsinoe (os), Amsterdam, Italiano, Jan 1807
Climene (op eroi-comica, 2, G. Caravita), London, King's, 25 April 1811, *GB-Lbl* (partly autograph), excerpts (London, 1811)
L'addio e il ritorno trionfale di Ettore (azione drammatica, 2), Munich, Hof, Jan 1815, collab. others
Tutto per inganno (ob, 2), Lisbon, S Carlos, 1815
Emilia di Laverpaut (dramma sentimentale, 2), Naples, Fiorentini, sum. 1817, *I-Nc* (as Il ritiro, ossia Emilia)
L'equivoco dei due anelli (dg, 2, M. A. Prunetti), Rome, Valle, 26 Dec 1817
I sette Maccabei (dramma sacro, 3, F. Tarducci), Rome, Valle, 25 May 1818, *Fc, PAc*
Il principe della nuova China (dg, 2, Tarducci), VB, 26 Dec 1818
La clemenza d'Entragues (os, 2, F. Romani), Venice, Fenice, 6 Feb 1819
La conquista delle nuove Amazzoni (op semiseria, 2, Tarducci), Rome, Valle, 22 Jan 1821
Le gelosie villane [La comunità di Castel Formicolone] (ob, 2, ?J. Ferretti, after T. Grandi: *Le gelosie villane*), Livorno, Carlo Lodovico, carn. 1824; as Le gelosie villane, Florence, Cocomero, 2 Nov 1825; *Gl*
Giulio Sabino in Langres (os), Bologna, Comunale, spr. 1824

Music in: Der Kampf im Vorzimmer, 1816

*

AMZ, vii (1805), 763; x (1808), 404–5
A. Cametti: *Un poeta melodrammatico romano: appunti e notizie in gran parte inediti sopra Jacopo Ferretti e i musicisti del suo tempo* (Milan, 1898), 135ff
ANDREA LANZA

Treptow, Günther (Otto Walther) (*b* Berlin, 22 Oct 1907; *d* Berlin, 28 March 1981). German tenor. He studied in Berlin, where he made his début at the Deutsche Oper in 1936 as the Italian Tenor in *Der Rosenkavalier*. Despite being on the 'forbidden' list of non-Aryan musicians, he managed to remain a member of the company until 1942, by which time he was singing such parts as Florestan, Pedro (*Tiefland*), Max and Otello. In 1942 he joined the Staatsoper in Munich, where he was heard chiefly in the Wagner repertory. After the war he returned to Berlin, first to the Staatsoper and then to the Deutsche Oper, where he created La Rocca in *Der junge Lord* (1965). He made regular guest appearances in Vienna. He sang Siegmund at Bayreuth in 1951 and 1952; Siegmund, Florestan and Tristan at the Metropolitan, 1951; and Siegfried at Covent Garden in 1953. His repertory included Adolar (*Euryanthe*), Tannhäuser and Parsifal. Treptow's voice was not intrinsically beautiful but was capable of great dramatic intensity. HAROLD ROSENTHAL/R

Treu [Trew], **Daniel Gottlob** [Fedele, Daniele Teofilo] (*b* Stuttgart, 1695; *d* Breslau, Aug 1749). German composer. What is known of his life comes largely from an autobiography in Mattheson's *Grundlage einer Ehren-Pforte*. Early in his childhood, after he had learnt to sing and to play the violin and keyboard instruments, he was taught double counterpoint and other aspects of composition by his uncle, J. S. Kusser. His first compositions were published when he was 12; at about the same time he composed several German operas to his own librettos, but these were not performed. At 21, he was given financial support to study in Venice with Vivaldi and Antonio Biffi.

In 1725 Treu was employed as Kapellmeister to an Italian opera company which went to Breslau, where he had four of his own operas performed: *Astarto* (libretto by A. Zeno and P. Pariati, 1725), *Caio Martio Coriolano* (1726), *Ulisse e Telemacco* (D. Lalli, 1726) and *Don Chisciotte* (1727). In 1727 he moved to Prague and served as Kapellmeister, composer and performer to a number of noble families there as well as in Vienna and at Silesian courts. According to Mattheson he later lived in Breslau again, with a family of several children, but nothing further is known of his career. Treu was a prolific composer but almost all his music is apparently lost. Mattheson praised him highly as a performer and composer.

*

J. Mattheson: *Grundlage einer Ehren-Pforte* (Hamburg, 1740); ed. M. Schneider (Berlin, 1910)
R. Brockpähler: *Handbuch zur Geschichte der Barockoper in Deutschland* (Emsdetten, 1964)
GEORGE J. BUELOW

Treumann, Louis [Pollitzer, Ludwig] (*b* Vienna, 1 March 1872; *d* Theresienstadt, 1942). Austrian tenor. He gravitated from businessman, via member of the claque at the Carltheater in Vienna and tenor *buffo* in provincial theatres, to be a member of the Carltheater company from 1899, creating the role of Josef in the Strauss-Müller *Wiener Blut* (1899). There, at the Theater an der Wien and elsewhere, he formed a successful partnership with Mizzi Günther, creating the role of Danilo in *Die lustige Witwe* (1905) and other leading roles in Ziehrer's *Die drei Wünsche* (1901), Lehár's *Der Rastelbinder* (1902), *Der Göttergatte* (1904), *Das Fürstenkind* (1909) and *Eva* (1911), and Fall's *Die Sirene* (1905) and *Die Dollarprinzessin* (1907). Without Günther he also created leading roles in Lehár's *Der Sterngucker* (1916) and Kálmán's *Die Bajadere* (1921). His appeal lay as much in his stage presence and magnetic personality as in his light *buffo* tenor voice.

For illustration *see* LUSTIGE WITWE, DIE.

*

GSL
ANDREW LAMB

Trèves (Fr.). TRIER.

Treviso. Italian city in the Veneto. The first theatre for opera, the S Margherita, was built by the Bensi-Zecchini family, and was in use from 1678 until *c*1693; in 1692 the Onigo family built a larger one (in use until 1714), which was in turn replaced by the smaller Dolfin (1721; still used in the 19th century for plays). These were all of the Venetian type, with boxes, and managed by an impresario; the principal season was in autumn when the audience included Venetian aristocrats. The repertory depended on that of Venice (at the Dolfin Vivaldi revived *Ottone in villa* in 1729 and *Farnace* in 1737), though some premières were also given, such as Albinoni's *Il più fedel tra gli amanti* in 1731. The Onigo, redesigned by Antonio Galli-Bibiena, reopened in 1766 with the première of P. A. Guglielmi's *Demofoonte*; in 1844 the management passed to a company of box-holders and it was renamed the Teatro Sociale. In 1868 it was destroyed by fire and rebuilt in its present form, becoming municipal property as the Teatro Comunale in 1931; it is distinguished for the modernity of its repertory and the quality of the performers. From 1858 the Teatro Emeronitio (later Garibaldi: rebuilt in 1887, bombed in 1944 and rebuilt as a cinema) also staged many operas, with a more popular repertory of Italian works mixed with operetta and variety. More recently the autumn season of the Teatro Comunale (which also stages concerts and plays) has seen the return of pre-Verdi *melodramma* as well as some important premières (for example Malipiero's *Il marescalco*, 1969; Bussotti's *Le rarità, potente*, 1979).

*

B. Bassan: *I teatri di Treviso fino alla caduta della Repubblica Veneta* (diss., U. of Padua, 1969)
C. Martinelli Roscioni: *Cronologia del Teatro Comunale di Treviso* (Treviso, 1972–)
L. de Piccoli: 'Il Teatro Comunale nelle origini e nella storia', *Autunno musicale trevigiano* (1981) [programme booklet]
L. Zoppelli: 'Opera al Garibaldi (1850–1915)', *Studi trevisani*, v (1987), 67–91
F. Mancini, M. T. Muraro and E. Povoledo: *I teatri del Veneto*, ii (Venice, 1990) LUCA ZOPPELLI

Trial (i). French family of musicians.

(1) **Jean-Claude Trial** (*b* Avignon, 13 Dec 1732; *d* Paris, 23 June 1771). Composer. A precocious violinist and composer of violin music, he went to Paris to ask Rameau's advice, intending to return to the south as music master for the province of Languedoc. Parisian musical life enticed him, however, and he became first violin at the Opéra-Comique, then second violin and later director of the Prince of Conti's private orchestra. On 1 April 1767 he was named co-director of the Opéra, with Pierre Berton. Although their administration achieved successful reorganization of the orchestra and choruses, they were badly received by critics and the public, and in 1769, during a financial crisis, the city assumed administrative control.

At least one of Trial's compositions for the theatre, *Silvie*, had considerable success. He also wrote overtures, chamber music, *ariettes*, religious music and cantatas, in which he is said to have been the first French composer to have written for the female contralto voice (the *bas-dessus*).

all printed works published in Paris

Le tonnelier (oc, 1, N.-M. Audinot and A.-F. Quétant, after La Fontaine: *Le cuvier*), Paris, Comédie-Italienne (Bourgogne), 16 March 1765 (*c*1767), collab. Alexandre, Ciapalanti, Gossec, Kohaut, F.-A. D. Philidor and J. Schobert
Renaud d'Ast (cmda, 2, P.-R. Lemonnier), Fontainebleau, 12 Oct 1765, ov., arr. 2 vns (n.d.), collab. P. Vachon
Silvie (opéra, prol., 3, P. Laujon), Fontainebleau, 17 Oct 1765 (1767), collab. P.-M. Berton
Esope à Cythère (cmda, 1, L.-J.-H. Dancourt), Paris, Comédie-Italienne (Bourgogne), 15 Dec 1766, excerpts (n.d.), collab. Vachon [according to Brenner, perf. Bordeaux, 1762]
Théonis, ou Le toucher (pastorale-héroïque, 1, A.-A.-H. Poinsinet), Paris, Opéra, 11 Oct 1767, *F-Pc*, *Po*; (n.d.), collab. Berton and L. Granier [2nd entrée of Poinsinet: *Fragments nouveaux*]
La fête de Flore (pastorale-héroïque, 1, J.-P.-A. Razins de Saint-Marc), Fontainebleau, 13 Nov 1770 (n.d.)
La chercheuse d'esprit (C.-S. Favart), after 1756
Linus (5, C.-A. La Bruère), inc., *Pn*, collab. Berton and A. Dauvergne

(2) **Antoine Trial** (*b* Avignon, 1737; *d* Paris, 5 Feb 1795). Tenor and actor, brother of (1) Jean-Claude Trial. He first appeared in provincial theatres. Antoine followed his brother to Paris and joined the troupe of the Prince of Conti. On 4 July 1764 he made his début with the Comédie-Italienne as Bastien in Philidor's *Le sorcier*. Despite his thin, nasal voice, he achieved success, mostly through his acting, and interested himself from then on in the interpretation of peasants' and simpletons' roles; his name remained associated with this genre, qualified sometimes as 'singer without voice' or more usually 'singer Trial'. His most famous roles were Bertrand in *Le déserteur* (Monsigny), Ali in *Zémire et Azor* (Grétry), André in *L'épreuve villageoise* (Grétry) and Crispin in *La mélomanie* (Champein). During the Revolution he sided with Robespierre and was an active agent of the Terror; after Robespierre's fall (1794) he had to renounce the theatre because of public hostility, and ultimately he poisoned himself.

Antoine's wife, Marie-Jeanne Trial (1746–1818), was a soprano and actress. She made her début at the Théâtre Italien, Paris, in 1766 under the stage name Félicité Mandeville. Her ability was particularly remarkable in vocalises and roulades; she is remembered as an interpreter of Grétry and Monsigny.

(3) **Armand-Emmanuel Trial** [*fils*] (*b* Paris, 1 March 1771; *d* Paris, 9 Sept 1803). Composer, son of (2) Antoine Trial. At the age of 17 he attracted attention with an *opéra comique*, *Julien et Colette*, presented by the Comédie-Italienne. A remarkable accompanist, he became director of singing at the Théâtre Lyrique in 1797. He married the actress Jeanne Rigorey-Méon, who left him, allegedly because of his debauchery, a primary cause of his early death. His music for several stage works did not fulfil the promise of *Julien et Colette*; it was found banal, though occasionally redeemed by well-written choruses.

all first performed in Paris

Julien et Colette, ou La milice (cmda, 1, P.-G. Parisau), Comédie-Italienne (Favart), 3 March 1788 (Paris, n.d.)
Adélaïde et Mirval, ou La vengeance paternelle (J. Patrat), Comédie-Italienne (Favart), 6 June 1791
Les deux petits aveugles (oc, 1, Noël), Comédie-Italienne (Favart), 28 July 1792
Cécile et Julien, ou Le siège de Lille (cmda, 3, Joigny), OC (Favart), 21 Nov 1792
La cause et les effets, ou Le réveil du peuple (oc, Joigny), OC (Favart), 17 Aug 1793
Le congrès des rois (cmda, 3, Desmaillot [A. F. Eve]), OC (Favart), 26 Feb 1794, collab. Dalayrac, Grétry, Méhul and 8 others

*

ES (F. Serpa)
A. Choron and F. Fayolle: *Dictionnaire historique des musiciens* (Paris, 1810–11)
G. Vauthier: 'Deux joyeux directeurs de l'Opéra', *Revue musicale*, xi (1911), 417–20
C. D. Brenner: *A Bibliographical List of Plays in the French Language 1700–1789* (Berkeley, 1947) ROGER J. V. COTTE

Trial (ii). French term for a tenor with a thin, nasal voice, suitable for simpletons' and peasants' roles. It is derived from Antoine Trial (*see* TRIAL (i) family, (2)). The comic tenors in *Les contes d'Hoffmann* and in Ravel's operas are examples.

Trial by Jury. Operetta in one act by ARTHUR SULLIVAN to a libretto by W. S. GILBERT; London, Royalty Theatre, 25 March 1875.

Through-composed and lasting little over half an hour, the piece is set in a court of justice, where Angelina (soprano) is suing Edwin (tenor) for breach of promise. The Judge (baritone), whose song 'When I, good friends, was called to the bar' became the best-known number, proposes a novel and wholly acceptable solution: he will marry Angelina himself. In lampooning the establishment the libretto is typically Gilbertian. Sullivan, too, reveals his humour in clever stylistic burlesque, especially in the ensemble 'A nice dilemma', modelled on Bellini.

Trial by Jury had its genesis when Richard D'Oyly Carte, manager of the Royalty Theatre, needed an afterpiece to Offenbach's *La Périchole*. Recalling that Sullivan and Gilbert had collaborated in *Thespis* (1871), he persuaded them to work together again. Gilbert suggested expanding an idea he had published in *Fun* in 1868. Sullivan was delighted with it and within weeks the 'dramatic cantata', as the operetta was described, was playing to enthusiastic houses, Sullivan's brother Frederic scoring a personal triumph as the Judge. The work's success encouraged Sullivan, Gilbert and Carte to pursue their creative relationship.

DAVID RUSSELL HULME

Tribou, Denis-François (*b* c1695; *d* Paris, 14 Jan 1761). French *haute-contre*. He made his début at the Paris Opéra as the Sun in the 1721–2 revival of Lully's *Phaëton*, and during the same run was promoted to sing the title role in place of Muraire. He created the title role in Desmarets' *Renaud* (1722) and in Lully revivals sang Attis (1725), Bellerophon (1728), Amadis (1731, to the rapturously received Oriane of Mlle Lemaure) and Mercury (*Isis*, 1732), before creating Ammon in Montéclair's *Jephté* (1732). In 1734 he took Pylades (Desmarets and Campra's *Iphigénie en Tauride*) while the role of a Triton was sung by the young Jélyotte, whose meteoric rise to prominence overtook the end of Tribou's career. Yet Tribou sang Perseus in 1737, before retiring in 1741 to become a theorbist in the *musique de la chambre du roi*.

*

Mercure de France (Oct 1731), 2413ff; (Feb–March 1737), 355, 359, 562–76

E. Campardon: *L'Académie royale de musique au XVIIIe siècle* (Paris, 1884), ii, 326–32

PHILIP WELLER

Tricarico, Giuseppe (*b* Gallipoli, nr Lecce, 25 June 1623; *d* Gallipoli, 14 Nov 1697). Italian composer. He received his early training at Naples. The libretto of his first opera, *L'Endimione* (1655), identifies him as *maestro di cappella* of the Accademia dello Spirito Santo at Ferrara. His reputation was already established; his sacred music and madrigals had been published, separately and in collections, in Rome, beginning in 1649. He was *maestro di cappella* at the court of the Dowager Empress Eleonora in Vienna by 1658, and provided the annual birthday opera for her stepson, Emperor Leopold I, from 1659 to 1662. Because no scores of his operas survive, his style can be ascertained only from his other compositions, notably his arias and two sacred dramatic works, and the type of librettos he set. His writing is flexible, clearly indebted to monodic influences, but with greater vocal and structural formality (e.g. the nine da capo arias in *La virtù guerriera*). By 1663 Tricarico had probably returned to Gallipoli to teach, having played an important part in the transmission of Italian operatic style and practice to the Viennese court.

L'Endimione (prol., 3, A. Passarelli), Ferrara, 1655, lib. (Ferrara, 1655)

La virtù guerriera (inventione dramatica, prol., 3, A. Aureli), Vienna, Favorita, 9 June 1659, lib. (Vienna, 1659)

L'Almonte (componimento dramatico, prol., 3, A. Draghi), Vienna, Favorita, 9 June 1661, lib. (Vienna, 1661)

La generosità d'Alessandro (prol., 3, F. Sbarra), Vienna, Favorita, 15 June 1662, lib. (Vienna, 1662)

L'Edmiro [Endimero] creduto Uranio (P. Russo), Naples, S Bartolomeo, 1670, lib. (Naples, 1670)

*

E. Wellesz: 'Die Opern und Oratorien in Wien, 1660–1708', *SMw*, vi (1919), 5–138

G. A. Pastore: 'Giuseppe Tricarico da Gallipoli, musicista del secolo XVII', *Studi salentini*, v–vi (1958), 143–68; vii (1959), 88–130

H. Seifert: *Die Oper am Wiener Kaiserhof im 17. Jahrhundert*, Wiener Veröffentlichungen zur Musikgeschichte, xxv (Tutzing, 1985)

RUDOLF SCHNITZLER

Nicolò Tricarico: caricature by Anton Maria Zanetti (1680–1767)

Tricarico, Nicolò [Nicola] (*fl* 1685–1727). Italian singer (alto or soprano). He came from Gallipoli where his brother, Bonaventura, was a cathedral canon and a singing teacher; they may have been the sons of the composer Giuseppe Tricarico, who was also from Gallipoli. In his early career Nicolò seems to have sung comic parts, appearing at Modena in 1685 in M. A. Ziani's *Alcibiade*; a contemporary caricature of him by A. Zanetti (reprinted in *COJ*, i, 1989, p.31) clearly shows him as a comic singer. In 1687 and again in 1694 he was paid for occasional appearances at St Mark's,

Venice. Three years later he sang in Perti and Sabadini's *Furio Camillo* at Parma, and between 1711 and 1716 he performed, apparently as primo uomo, in four operas at Venice. He was described there as a 'virtuoso' of the Duke of Mantua, and it was at Mantua that he made his last known appearance – in Vivaldi's *Scanderbeg* (given as *Climene*) in June 1722 on the occasion of a visit by Prince Francesco of Modena.

*

V. Tardini: *I teatri di Modena* (Modena, 1898–1902), iii, 863, 1273
O. Termini: 'Singers at San Marco in Venice: the Competition between Church and Theatre (*c*1675–1725)', *RMARC*, no.17 (1981), 65–96
J. Rosselli: 'Il sistema produttivo dall'unità a oggi', *SOI*, iv (1987), 300
L. Cataldi: 'L'attività operistica di Vivaldi a Mantova', *Nuovi studi vivaldiani: edizione e cronologia critica delle opere*, ed. A. Fanna and G. Morelli (Florence, 1988), i, 131–45, esp. 135
J. Rosselli: 'The Castrati as a Professional Group and a Social Phenomenon, 1550–1850', *AcM*, lx (1988), 152

COLIN TIMMS, JOHN ROSSELLI

Tri-Cities Opera. American company based in BINGHAMTON.

Triebensee [Trübensee], **Josef** (*b* Wittingau, 21 Nov 1772; *d* Prague, 22 April 1846). Bohemian composer. He studied composition with Albrechtsberger and the oboe with his father. In 1791, as second oboist at the Theater auf der Wieden in Vienna, he took part in the première of *Die Zauberflöte* under Mozart's direction; he frequently performed as a soloist in the Tonkünstler-Sozietät concerts in Vienna. After a succession of orchestral and court posts he composed for the theatre in Brno, and in 1816 he succeeded Weber as director of the Prague Opera, a post he held until his retirement on 31 December 1836. A prolific composer, he also wrote two notable sets of Harmoniemusik (which included some arrangements) and a number of vocal pieces, orchestral and chamber works.

Der rote Geist im Donnergebirge [1 act] (heroische Oper, 2, M. Stegmayer), Vienna, Wieden, 5 June 1799, duet in *D-Rp* [1 act by I. Seyfried]
Männertreue (komische Oper, 1, J. von Seyfried), Vienna, 1815
Der Feuergeist, Brno, 18 Jan 1816
Die wilde Jagd (S. W. Schiessler), Prague, Stände, 8 March 1820
Die Ehemänner nach der Mode (komische Oper, 3, Seyfried), Prague, Stände, 31 Jan 1821
Der Genius Böhmens (Festspiel, Schiessler), Prague, Stände, 12 Feb 1822
Telemach auf der Insel Ogygia (2, K. J. Schikaneder), Prague, Stände, 10 Jan 1824, *Bds*
4 others, 1792–1828

Music in: Die Liebe macht kurzen Prozess, oder Heirat auf gewisse Art, 1798

*

Allgemeine musikalische Zeitung mit besonderer Rücksicht auf den österreichischen Kaiserstaat, iii (Vienna, 1819), 205; v (Vienna, 1821), 503
C. d'Elvert: *Geschichte des Theaters, der Musik, in Mähren und Oesterreichisch Schlesien* (Brno, 1852)
C. Gruber: *Opern-Uraufführungen*, ii (Vienna, 1987)

ROGER HELLYER

Trier (Fr. Trèves). City in western Germany, and the oldest German city. Now over 2000 years old, it was the Roman settlement of Augusta Treverorum. In 1802–5 the Stadttheater was installed in the secularized Capuchin monastery on the initiative of the French (who occupied Trier in 1794). German and French operas, operettas, vaudevilles and Viennese farces were performed in preference to plays. The building assumed its final form with the extensions of 1815 and 1816, remaining basically the same until it was destroyed in World War II. An important period in the history of opera in the city was that during which Heinz Tietjen (later famous in Berlin, Bayreuth and Hamburg) was Intendant (1907–22); at this time the celebrated baritone Francisco D'Andrade made a guest appearance as Don Giovanni, his famous role. Interim arrangements were made after the war, and the present Theater der Stadt Trier opened in 1964 with *Fidelio*. The modern building, its auditorium a single, sloping arena without balconies, has seating for 622. The opera season comprises some 55 performances and runs from mid-September to the end of June. Five operatic works, including a modern piece and a *Spieloper*, are produced every season and the company makes regular guest appearances in the vicinity, including Luxembourg. The theatre is financed by the city, with assistance from the *Land* of the Rhineland Palatinate. GÁBOR HALÁSZ

Trieste. Italian city, capital of the Friuli-Venezia Giulia region. During the Middle Ages it was ruled by the count-bishops and enjoyed a degree of autonomy, and in 1382 it placed itself under the protection of Leopold III of Austria. In 1719 it was made a free port by imperial decree, and remained so until 1891. The economic prosperity and importance of the city as a commercial and industrial centre increased almost continuously (in 1913 it had 247 000 inhabitants, as against 20 000 at the end of the 18th century). Apart from two periods of French occupation during Napoleonic times, Trieste remained part of the Habsburg empire until it was united with the kingdom of Italy at the end of World War I. During World War II it was occupied by the Germans, then by the Yugoslavs and finally by the Allies. After nine years of uncertainty it became part of the Italian Republic in October 1954, when much of the surrounding territory passed to Yugoslavia. The particular character of Trieste as a meeting point of Italian, German and Slav cultures, especially during the 19th and early 20th centuries, made it a distinctly cosmopolitan city and a meeting-place for different linguistic communities.

Regular operatic activity developed later in Trieste than in most other Italian centres of comparable size. This was probably because of the relative proximity of Venice by sea; local performances at the beginning of the 18th century were largely dependent on Venetian theatres for both repertory and performers. It is possible, however, that Trieste was more active than was previously thought. It is known that intermezzos were performed in 1721 (*La contadina*, possibly by J. A. Hasse) and 1730 (G. M. Orlandini's *Serpilla e Bacocco*; libretto printed in Venice), the latter at the Teatro di S Pietro for the S Lorenzo fair instituted by the Viennese government in 1729. (The municipality had agreed to the construction of a theatre in 1705, but there is no earlier record of its having been used for opera.)

The next 20 years are sparsely documented, but from the middle of the century mainly *opera buffa* was performed, either on the occasion of the fair, which brought spectators from Venice and Vienna, or during Carnival (Galuppi's *Le virtuose ridicole* in 1753, Cocchi's *La maestra* in 1755). In 1763 the Teatro di S Pietro acquired the title 'cesareo regio', and in the same year there was a production of *Amore in libertà* by Giacomo Notte, perhaps the first opera written specifically for Trieste. In 1785 Bertoni's *Quinto Fabio* was particularly successful, with Pacchierotti, Banti and Maffoli in the cast. The following period was characterized by a higher proportion of *opera seria*. In spring 1787 two recent operas to librettos by Ferdinando Moretti were staged, Sarti's *La vergine del sole* and Tarchi's *Ariarate*, and in the following year *Nitteti*, the first opera by Sebastiano Nasolini. Nasolini lived for some years in Trieste, where he also composed *Ercole al Termodonte* to Sografi's libretto in 1791. At the end of the 18th century Trieste seems to have acquired particular fame as a theatrical centre: the Viennese productions of Da Ponte and Martín y Soler arrived there early, *Una cosa rara* and *L'arbore di Diana* in 1788 and 1789 respectively. Da Ponte wrote his spoken tragedy *Il Mezenzio* for Trieste in 1791, and a version of *L'ape musicale* with music by various composers.

The construction of the Teatro Nuovo, originally planned to seat 1300 with five rows of boxes, was completed in 1799 or 1800; Antonio Selva designed the exterior, Matteo Pertsch the interior. It was inaugurated in spring 1801 with two new operas, Mayr's *Ginevra di Scozia* (21 April) and Salieri's *Annibale in Capua* (April). In 1821 it took the name of Teatro Grande, and after it had been bought by the municipality in 1861 it became the Teatro Comunale. During the 19th century the auditorium underwent alterations which enlarged its capacity to 2000 seats. Its fortunes, however, declined in the early years of the century as a result both of the Napoleonic invasions and of a certain mediocrity in the repertory. The production of operas by Rossini marked a decided revival of interest, from *Otello* in 1818. Productions of Mozart, on the other hand, were less successful, sometimes because of poor performances (the case with *Le nozze di Figaro* in 1819 and *Don Giovanni*, for the centenary of the composer's birth in 1856), but they revealed an interest in Mozart himself greater than in most other Italian cities, possibly because of the local fondness for Viennese Classical music. In the middle of the 19th century Trieste shared the taste and preferences of the major centres: Bellini's operas were successful and to a lesser extent those of Donizetti, and among other successes was Alberto Mazzucato's *Esmeralda*. Local initiative commissioned two operas from Verdi, *Il corsaro* (25 October 1848) and *Stiffelio* (16 November 1850). There were less fortunate productions from minor composers, such as Ruggero Manna's *Il profeta velato* (1846), Francesco Chiaromonte's *Armando il gondoliero* (1851), Francesco Cortesi's *Il trovatore* and Nicolò Stermich's *La madre slava* (1865), whereas others had a good reception: Giuseppe Sinico's *I moschettieri* (1859), A. K. Lickl's *La disfida di Barletta* and *Aurora di Nevers* (1861) and Lionello Ventura's *Alda* (1869).

The major operas of the international repertory reached Trieste with some regularity, and among the most important were Auber's *La muette de Portici* (1832), Hérold's *Zampa* (1841), the novelty of whose music was acclaimed, Meyerbeer's *Robert le diable* (1842, at the Teatro Mauroner, later La Fenice), Balfe's *The Bohemian Girl* (1854, for the first time in Italian), Flotow's *Martha* (1863), Gounod's *Faust* (1864) and Halévy's *La Juive* (1866).

Spring 1878 saw the inauguration of a second important theatre, the Politeama Rossetti, seating 3000 and intended for varied use (alterations were made in 1928 and again in 1969). Despite a long period of inactivity it staged all kinds of musical and theatrical entertainments, from symphony concerts to operetta, opera and plays, and in the 20th century it was also used as a cinema. At the turn of the century operas were frequently and well performed at the Rossetti; the complete *Ring* was staged in German in 1883 by Angelo Neumann's company under the direction of Anton Seidl, who had taken part in the first production at Bayreuth. Wagner's music had been heard before at the Comunale, in orchestral concerts (the overtures to *Rienzi* and *Tannhäuser* were played there in 1870 and 1873) and stage performances (*Lohengrin* in 1876 and *Tannhäuser* in 1878, the latter being particularly successful). Italo Svevo (under the pseudonym Ettore Samigli) and Ferruccio Busoni (who sometimes signed himself with the anagram Bruno Fioresucci) were writing for the local newspaper, *L'indipendente*, at the time. Among the lesser theatres the Armonia staged the first performance in Trieste of *Carmen* (1884, transferred to the Rossetti after a few performances).

After a century of impresarial management, the Teatro Comunale Giuseppe Verdi (as it was renamed in 1901) became one of the 'Enti Lirici Autonomi', a national company with a permanent orchestra (since 1944) and chorus, and a ballet company of international standard. Its main activities are an operatic season and a symphonic season, and (since 1950) an operetta festival remarkable for the high quality of its productions. The municipality, which shares in the administration and choice of events at the Verdi and Rossetti theatres, also supports the important Civico Museo Teatrale named after the scholar, publisher and administrator Carlo Schmidl, whose large library forms one of its historical centres.

*

DEUMM (P. Derossi)

G. Righetti: *Cenni storici, biografici e critici degli artisti ed ingegneri di Trieste ovvero del progresso fatto nelle arti e mestieri dalla metà del sec. XVIII fino ad oggi* (Trieste, 1865)

F. Danziger: *Memorie del Teatro Comunale di Trieste dal 1801 al 1876 raccolte da un vecchio teatrofilo* (Trieste, ?1877)

A. Hortis: 'Delle rappresentazioni sceniche in Trieste prima del Teatro di San Pietro', *Archeografo triestino*, viii (1881), 144–60

G. C. Bottura: *Storia aneddotica documentata del Teatro Comunale di Trieste* (Trieste, 1885)

G. Caprin: *Il Teatro Nuovo* (Trieste, 1901; repr. 1970, with introduction by V. Levi)

G. Schiroli: *Memorie teatrali 1820–1855* (MS, *I-TSmt*)

A. Boccardi: *Memorie teatrali triestine (1820–1855)* (Trieste, 1913)

M. Nordio: *Il Politeama Rossetti: storia di cinquant'anni, 1878–1928* (Trieste, 1928)

R. Kraus: 'Grandezza e decadenza di un teatro scomparso (Teatro "Armonia", poi "Goldoni") di Trieste', *Porta orientale*, i (1931), 672–90

C. L. Curiel: *Il Teatro S Pietro in Trieste* (Milan, 1937)

G. Cesari: *Il Teatro Comunale di Trieste Giuseppe Verdi: memorie e date 1801–1941* (MS, *TSmt*)

A. Boccardi: *Memorie teatrali triestini 1820–1855* (Trieste, 1943)

G. Stefani: *Il Teatro Verdi di Trieste, 1801–1851* (Trieste, 1951)

I. Bremini: *Il Politeama Rossetti di Trieste dalla sua inaugurazione ai giorni nostri: cenni storici e statistici* (MS, 1957, *TSmt*)

V. Levi, G. Botteri and I. Bremini, eds.: *Il Comunale di Trieste* (Udine, 1962)

B. M. Favetta: 'Vita musicale nella Trieste settecentesca e ottocentesca', *Porta orientale*, xxxiii (1963), 305–20

——: 'Il Verdi: mito di un teatro', *Porta orientale*, xli (1971)

G. Botteri and V. Levi: *Il Politeama Rossetti 1878–1978: un secolo di vita triestina nelle cronache del teatro* (Trieste, 1978)

A. Dugulin: 'Mahler a Trieste', *Atti dei civici musei di storia ed arte [di Trieste]*, xi (1980), 143–60

A. Dugulin, G. Pavan, D. Riccesi and D. Tamburini, eds.: *Disegni per il Teatro Comunale di Trieste* (Trieste, 1988)

G. Radole: *Ricerche sulla vita musicale a Trieste (1750–1950)* (Trieste, 1988)

P. Ugolini Bernasconi: *Il Teatro 'G. Verdi' di Trieste: le origini neoclassiche e i restauri attraverso due secoli* (Trieste, 1988)

SERGIO DURANTE

Trilogia das barcas ('Trilogy of the Boats'). Opera in two acts by JOLY BRAGA SANTOS to a libretto by M. J. B. Santos after Gil Vicente's plays *Barca do inferno*, *Barca do purgatório* and *Barca da glória*; Lisbon, Fundação Calouste Gulbenkian, 8 May 1970.

The plot deals with the evaluation of human behaviour at the moment of death. On a river bank some 20 characters representing the different social classes, from an artisan to the pope, are about to take one of three boats to eternity; the Devil (bass) and the Angel (soprano) organize the voyage and direct the souls' boats to hell, to purgatory or to heaven. The composer, in attempting to maintain the dramatic rhythm of the original plays, wrote in a mixture of styles, incorporating spoken dialogue and recitative into the voice parts. The harmony is also treated freely and uses both chromaticism and madrigalian diatonic passages. The opera calls for two choirs and a large orchestra with a strong percussion section.

ADRIANA LATINO

Trimarchi, Domenico (*b* Naples, 21 Dec 1940). Italian bass-baritone. He began as an actor, and then studied singing at the Naples Conservatory and with Gino Campese, making his début in 1964 at La Fenice, Venice, as Belcore (*L'elisir d'amore*). Other engagements quickly followed, including La Scala and S Carlo, and he first sang abroad with the Scala company in Moscow and Leningrad. His British début was at the 1972 Edinburgh Festival, with the Teatro Massimo company from Palermo, as Baron Valdeburgo in *La straniera*, followed by Bartolo and Melitone at Covent Garden in 1975. He has appeared at the New York Metropolitan, Chicago Lyric Opera and San Francisco, and sang the Salieri and Verdi Falstaffs in the same season at Parma (1986–7). He is admired for musicality as well as comedy in *buffo* roles, and has recorded roles in nearly 20 operas, notably Dulcamara in *L'elisir d'amore* and Taddeo in *L'italiana in Algeri*, both under Scimone (1986, 1988); Buonafede in *Il mondo della luna* (one of his four Haydn roles) under Dorati, and Lindus in *Tito Manlio* (Vivaldi) under Negri.

NOËL GOODWIN

Trinchera, Pietro [Partenio Chriter; Terentio Chirrap] (*b* Naples, 11 June 1702; *d* Naples, 12 Feb 1755). Italian librettist. He wrote prose comedies, librettos for comic operas and texts for *cartelli* (carnival songs). A notary by profession, Trinchera began his literary career with the prose comedy *La moneca fauza* in 1726 (the existence of three modern editions suggests a revival of interest in the work). Influenced probably by Gerolamo Gigli's *Don Pilone* and Molière's *Tartuffe*, this attack on religious hypocrisy was taken up again in the comic opera *La tavernola abentorosa* (1741), whose protagonist roams the countryside in the guise of the hermit Fra Macario. The opera incurred the displeasure of the ecclesiastical authorities, and Trinchera was imprisoned. After his release in January 1742, he did not resume his theatrical activity until 1744, with *Ciommetella correvata*. In 1747 Trinchera became impresario of the Teatro dei Fiorentini, and while the ensuing years were productive for his writing, the theatre continued to lose money, forcing him to declare bankruptcy. He was again imprisoned, and committed suicide in 1755. Setting aside the cloak of martyrdom with which some writers have clothed him, critics now tend to regard Trinchera as one of the finest Neapolitan comic opera librettists of the early 18th century. He himself claimed that 'lo stile mio è de scrivere ncoppo a lo naturale' (*Elmira generosa*, 1753); this naturalistic approach to characterization, along with a seriousness in his satire, helps to distinguish him from his contemporaries.

Li 'nnammorate correvate (commeddeia acconciata, e fenuta), ? d'Ambrosio, 1732 (G. Ventura, 1732, as Prizeta correvata); *Don Pasquino* (chelleta pe mmuseca), Brunetti, 1735; *Lo corrivo* (pazzia pe mmuseca), Brunetti, 1736; *Le mbroglie p'ammore* (commeddea pe mmuseca), Carasali, 1736; *La simpatia del sangue* (melodramma), Leo, 1737; *L'amante impazzito* (melodrama), Capranica, 1738; *La Rosa* (mmenzeone musajeca), ? di Fiore, 1738; *Lo secretista* (pazzia pe mmuseca), Cecere, 1738; *Il barone di Zampano* (melodrama), Porpora, 1739

L'incanti per amore (comedia per musica), Palella, 1741; *La tavernola abentorosa* (melodrama), Cecere, 1741; *Ciommetella correvata* (mmenzione musajeca), Logroscino, 1744 (as Lo Cicisbeo, 1751); *Le fenzeune abbentorate* (commeddea pe mmuseca), Gomes, 1745; *Li zite* (commesechiamma), Logroscino, 1745; *Don Paduano* (mmenzeone pe' mmuseca), Logroscino, 1745; *Il concerto* (melodrama per musica), Latilla, 1746; *La finta vedova* (commedia per musica), Conforto, 1746; *L'Emilia* (commedia per musica), Capranica, 1747

La vennegna (commeddea), Gomes, 1747 (A. Corbisiero, 1751, as Lo finto 'nnammorato); *L'Aurelio* (commedia per musica), Capranica, 1748; *L'abate Collarone* (commesechiamma), Fischietti, 1749 (Fischietti, Logroscino and Maraucci, 1754, as Le chiajese cantarine); *Lo tutore nnammorato* (commeddea pe mmuseca), Calandro, 1749; *Il mercante innamorato* (invenzione per musica), Corbisiero, 1750; *La vecchia mmaretata* (commeddea), Latilla, 1750; *Il finto cieco*, Cocchi, 1752; *Lo finto Perziano* (commeddia), Logroscino, 1752; *Il pazzo per amore*, Fischietti, 1752; *Elmira generosa*, Logroscino and Barbella, 1753

*

P. Martorana: 'Trinchera, Pietro', *Notizie biografiche e bibliografiche degli scrittori del dialetto napoletano* (Naples, 1874)
M. Scherillo: *L'opera buffa napoletana durante il settecento: storia letteraria* (Naples, 1883, 2/1917), 229–79
E. Mele: 'Monzù Moliero', *Flegrea*, iv (1900), 139–44
U. Prota-Giurleo: *Nicola Logroscino, 'il dio dell' opera buffa': la vita e le opere* (Naples, 1927), 64–78
V. Viviani: *Storia del teatro napoletano* (Naples, 1969), 312–39

GRAHAM HARDIE

Trio [terzet] (Fr. *trio*; Ger. *Trio*, *Terzett*; It. *terzetto*). An ensemble for three voices; the term 'terzet' is sometimes preferred, in vocal music, to 'trio'.

Trios have been used throughout the history of opera. An early example is the item for Seneca's *famigliari* in Monteverdi's *L'incoronazione di Poppea* (1643); there are also trios in two Cavalli operas (*Rosinda*, 1651, and *Eliogabalo*, composed 1668) and in some of Alessandro Scarlatti's late Roman operas. Handel used the trio several times, notably in *Tamerlano* (1724), *Orlando* (1733) and *Alcina* (1735), and Vivaldi used one to close Act 2 of his *Griselda* (1735). In Italian opera after 1720, short trios could appear at any point in the action; it was not unusual to find one closing an act or at the end of the opera, although the use early in the 18th century of a *coro* for all the characters to end the opera tended to displace it. Since intermezzos tended to include only two characters, the appearance of the trio became relatively rare. From the 1730s, however, intermezzos for three or even four characters were composed and some, for example Jommelli's *Don Chichibio* (1742) and *Don Trastullo* (1749), included trios (the latter has two). In French opera the trio maintained a continuous presence, as one of the textural options in the *divertissements* and other concerted pieces and as a foil for the simultaneous expression of contrasting emotions among the three principals (e.g. in Rameau's *Castor et Pollux* and Lully's *Alceste*). Often, in both French and Italian opera, the participants were a pair of lovers and an adversary, usually the prima donna, the castrato and a tenor or bass; often the composer used musical means to establish the situation, having (for example) the lovers sing in 3rds or 6ths with the adversary singing music of a strongly contrasting texture and rhythm. A familiar example from the English repertory is 'The flocks shall leave the mountains', from Handel's *Acis and Galatea* (1718).

By the middle of the century trios in comic opera, like other types of ensemble, were beginning to incorporate action, to fluctuate in the number of participants (that is, reduce to a duet or a solo or build up from them) and to be through-composed, eventually taking the form of the multi-sectional, action-ensemble finales of the kind used in comic opera for the rest of the century. In *opera seria* they became increasingly prevalent, led, it seems, by Galuppi and Jommelli. A trio was often formed by combining the emotions expressed in the final scenes and arias of one of the first two acts in an *aria a terza* or *terzetto*, an effective way of cutting down the number of arias. Metastasio placed a trio at the end of Act 2 of his *Nitteti* (1756); Jommelli has one at the end of Act 1 of Metastasio's *Ezio* in his settings of 1741 and 1758, and they appear regularly in his Stuttgart operas of the 1760s. Galuppi used trios, to close one of the first two acts, in several operas of the 1760s, and a sprinkling appear in other Venetian operas, particularly those of Sacchini (*Alessandro nell'Indie*, 1763; and an early ensemble incorporating action in *Nicoraste*, 1769). As in the Baroque period, trios usually follow the same forms as arias of the time. Each principal section tends to move from long solos for each participant to short, sometimes imitative comments. Imitative entries initiate a final homophonic section, broken with repeats back to the short comments and building up to florid sections for all three singers.

In French *opéra comique* during the third quarter of the 18th century, trios account for a fifth of all ensembles. There are examples of duets developing into trios in the operas of Egidio Duni, Philidor and Monsigny, as in Monsigny's *Le roi et le fermier* (1762, Act 1 finale). Trios begin to include action and plot development, as in Philidor's *La nouvelle école des femmes* (1770), where in Act 2 a wife and mistress confront one another in the presence of a servant. There are trios for three female voices in Duni's *Mazet* (1761) and Monsigny's *Le roi et le fermier* (where three separate solos are gradually blended in free counterpoint) and for male voices in Philidor's *Le maréchal ferrant* (1761), this last including one for three drunkards in a cellar. Trios in Monsigny's *Rose et Colas* (1764) and *Le déserteur* (1769) have fugal textures.

During the 1770s it became usual for the first act of an Italian *opera seria* to end with a duet and the second with a trio; trios in two or more tempos began to appear at the end of the decade, as in the trios of farewell 'Prendi un paterno amplesso' (*Adriano in Siria*, Anfossi, 1777) and 'Pria di partir, o Dio!' (*Idomeneo*, Mozart, 1781); in the 1780s they started to incorporate action and to have duet or solo sections, as in 'Ah, mio bene' (*Arbace*, Francesco Bianchi, 1781), where a lovers' duet is interrupted by an angry third character. The trio became increasingly popular in the last decade of the century. Mozart's operas show a wide variety in the use of the trio. There is a notable example in *Zaide* (1780) where two lovers are opposed to a tyrant, while in *Le nozze di Figaro* (1786) the Act 1 trio incorporates a recitative during which the Count uncovers the concealed Cherubino, and in *Don Giovanni* (1787) the trio opening Act 2 sees an elaborate pantomime where Giovanni and Leporello, in each other's clothes, dupe Elvira with false pleas of love. *Così fan tutte* (1790) begins with three trios; there are trios for the Three Ladies and the Three Boys in *Die Zauberflöte* (1791), notable for their pellucid scoring, and in *La clemenza di Tito* (1791) there are two that are essentially solos with commentary from two secondary characters.

Among Rossini's most memorable trios are several that imply dramatic action. In 'Ah! qual colpo' (*Il barbiere di Siviglia*, 1816) Figaro is trying desperately to cut short the endearments of Almaviva and Rosina to secure their escape; in 'A la faveur de cette nuit' (*Le comte Ory*, 1828), the Countess is being wooed at night by Ory and his page, neither aware of the other's presence; and in the grandiose three-movement 'Quand l'Helvétie est un champ de supplices' (*Guillaume Tell*, 1829) Arnold learns of the death of his father. A still more elaborate scheme, which Rossini humorously labelled 'terzettone' ('a great big trio'), is to be found in *Maometto II* (1820), not only incorporating a preghiera for the heroine with choral support but also bridging a change of scene ('Ohimè, qual fulmine'). In his revision of the opera as *Le siège de Corinthe* (1826) Rossini reduced the original length by more than half. Other action trios in French opera include the 'duel' trio 'Que voulez-vous, messieurs?' from Gounod's *Faust* (1859) and Bizet's card-playing scene for Carmen and two gypsy girls in *Carmen* (1875), 'Mêlons! coupons!'

The trio as central finale was (by his own account) pioneered by Donizetti in *L'esule di Roma* (1828); his ensemble was followed up by Bellini in *Norma* (1831) as well as by Donizetti himself in *Lucrezia Borgia* (1833). Several of Verdi's last-act finales take the form of a trio, from 'Solo, errante, misero' in *Ernani* (1843) to 'Non imprecare, umiliati' in *La forza del destino* (revised version, 1869). There are three terzets in his *Un ballo in maschera* (1859). Trios that witness a struggle for the soul of a hero or heroine include 'Que faut le faire' from Meyerbeer's *Robert le diable* (1831) and 'Oui, c'est toi, je t'aime', the finale of Gounod's *Faust*, in which the main melody ('Anges purs, anges radieux') is stated three times, each time a whole tone higher than the last – a device imitated in 'Ah, mon ange comme autrefois', the trio that concludes the Antonia episode of Offenbach's *Les contes d'Hoffmann* (1881). Outstanding among contemplative trios is the one in the closing scene of Richard Strauss's *Der Rosenkavalier* (1911), 'Hab' mirs gelobt, ihm liebzuhaben', which achieves a unique synthesis of vocal and instrumental writing.

See also FINALE.

MARITA P. MCCLYMONDS, ELISABETH COOK, JULIAN BUDDEN

Trionfi. The title of Carl Orff's theatrical triptych comprising *CARMINA BURANA*, *CATULLI CARMINA* and *TRIONFO DI AFRODITE*.

Trionfo dell'onore, Il ('The Triumph of Honour'). *Commedia* in three acts by Alessandro Scarlatti (*see* SCARLATTI family, (1)) to a libretto by FRANCESCO ANTONIO TULLIO; Naples, Teatro dei Fiorentini, 26 November 1718.

The action takes place in Pisa. Flaminio (tenor), a rich merchant with his eye on an equally rich (and elderly) landowner, Cornelia (tenor), is visited by his nephew Riccardo (soprano castrato), a dissolute young army officer, and his servant Rodimarte (bass). Riccardo plans an elopement with Cornelia's niece, Doralice (soprano), but his designs are thwarted by Erminio (soprano castrato), who is also in love with Doralice, and by Erminio's sister, Leonora (contralto), one of Riccardo's earlier conquests who still loves him. A series of complications and misunderstandings is brought to a head when Riccardo, wounded in a sword fight with Erminio, comes to his senses, realizes the error of his ways and asks forgiveness of the others. Honour triumphs: Riccardo is united with Leonora, Erminio with Doralice, Flaminio with Cornelia and Rodimarte with Cornelia's maid, Rosina (contralto).

Although Scarlatti's operas had regularly included comic scenes in accordance with the prevailing taste in Naples and elsewhere, *Il trionfo dell'onore* was his first and, as it turned out, his only true comedy. That the situations and to a considerable extent the language are akin to those of an *opera seria* enhances the satirical nature of Tullio's libretto, since the characters, far removed from the unreal stereotypes of the pastoral and the cardboard figures of heroic opera, are recognizable as the librettist's contemporaries: soldiers, merchants and their families. Similarly, the musical components are those of Scarlatti's serious operas – a three-movement sinfonia, recitative (more extensive than usual because of the rapid twists and turns in the plot), da capo arias and ensembles, and a final *coro*. Some of the arias would not be out of place in a serious *dramma*, but the music as a whole is characterized by a lightness and vivacity that set it apart from Scarlatti's other operas.

Although the opera was a notable success (it was performed 18 times during the 1718–19 season at the Fiorentini), it seems never to have been revived during Scarlatti's lifetime. MALCOLM BOYD

Trionfo di Afrodite ('Triumph of Aphrodite'). *Concerto scenico* in seven scenes by CARL ORFF to poems by Catullus, Sappho and EURIPIDES; Milan, Teatro alla Scala, 13 February 1953.

In the first section, a setting of a poem by Catullus, a group of young girls and boys await the arrival of a bride (soprano) and groom (tenor), and in alternation sing a hymn of praise to the evening star. A brief chorus (words by Sappho) welcoming the couple leads to a third section comprising their ecstatic love duet (Sappho). The chorus sing an invocation and hymn of praise (Catullus) to Hymenaios, the god of marriage, that rises to a passionate and dramatic climax. The fifth section, 'Wedding Games and Songs outside the Bridal Chamber' (Catullus), is divided into three parts. First, the chorus summons the bride to the chamber: she remains hesitant and is afraid to enter. Then, she is led into the chamber and the chorus's leader sings a coarse rhythmic song which makes fun of the groom. Finally, the groom enters the bridal chamber as the leader and the chorus exhort the couple to use their flourishing youth. The doors close and the sixth section, 'The Song of the Newlyweds in the Bridal Chamber' (Sappho), follows. This is a love duet with the words of love sung only by the tenor while the soprano responds with an ecstatic coloratura line. The final section for both chorus and soloists (Euripides) describes how the goddess Aphrodite descends from the heavens to bless the union.

Trionfo di Afrodite is the final part of Orff's theatrical triptych *Trionfi*, the first two parts being *Carmina burana* and *Catulli carmina*. It represents an exploration of divine and worldly love. Although the score demands a lavish orchestral accompaniment, including a vast array of percussion instruments, the idiom attains a pagan simplicity of expression largely through its uninhibited exploitation of expressive melody.

ERIK LEVI

Trionfo di Camilla, regina de' Volsci, Il ('The Triumph of Camilla, Queen of the Volscians'). *Dramma per musica* in three acts by GIOVANNI BONONCINI to a libretto by SILVIO STAMPIGLIA; Naples, Teatro di S Bartolomeo, 27 December 1696.

Camilla *disguised as Dorinda, a shepherdess*	soprano
Prenesto *son of Latino*	soprano
Lavinia *daughter of Latino*	soprano
Turno *King of the Rutilians, disguised as Armidoro, a blackamoor slave*	soprano castrato
Latino *King of Latium*	tenor
Linco *Camilla's servant*	bass
Mezio *a Volscian knight*	tenor
Tullia *Lavinia's servant*	tenor

Setting Piperno, an ancient city in the realm of the Volscians

No other Italian opera produced during the late Baroque (*c*1680–*c*1720) equalled *Camilla*'s remarkable series of 'triumphs'. The text received 38 known productions by 1767, and Bononcini's score was conjecturally the basis for 27 of them. After 13 performances the first production was still receiving 'the greatest applause' from 'an infinite concourse', but the most successful productions were the three in London, which resulted in 111 performances between 1706 and 1728 (a number surpassed only by *The Beggar's Opera* in early 18th-century London). The joint creators were in charge of the productions at Naples in 1696 and Rome in 1698, but they presumably had nothing to do with any others. Passages deleted by adapters were most frequently those for the elders (the three tenors and the bass) rather than the young lovers. All five comic scenes were often excised. Some editors, including Nicola Haym in London, replaced a little of Bononcini's music; others, such as the anonymous editor at Venice in 1698, replaced a great deal. The title was sometimes changed to *La rinovata Camilla* (1698, Rome), *Camilla* (1698, Florence and elsewhere), *La fede in cimento* (1704, Udine and elsewhere) or *Amore per amore* (1709, Bologna). There have been two modern revivals in English, one edited and directed by Anthony Ford (1980, University of Hull) and one edited by Piero Weiss (1988, Peabody Conservatory, Baltimore).

In the original production Turno was the only castrato (Domenico Cecchi), and was clearly the star, for he was given the final arias in Acts 1 and 2 and sang in all four duets for noble characters. Travesty roles were taken by Maddalena Musi (Prenesto) and Antonio Predieri (Tullia). Camilla was sung by Vittoria Tarquini, Lavinia by Barbara Riccioni, Linco by Giovanni Battista

Cavana, Mezio by Giuseppe Scaccia and Latino by Francesco Sandri.

ACT 1 In a rugged landscape near Piperno the disguised Camilla laments her sad fate, then courageously spears a wounded and rampaging boar in order to save the life of the disarmed and fleeing hunter. He is Prenesto, son of King Latino, who has cruelly usurped the Volscian territory (which is hers by right of birth). Prenesto's admiration for her bravery quickly turns to love. By this surprising turn of events Fortune has at last smiled on Camilla, who ends the first *action* (i.e. group of scenes) with the first coloratura aria in the opera, 'Mi lusingo e l'alma spera'. Like the other 56 arias it is brief, but the music is clearly distinct from the tunefulness and tender affect of most of them.

At Latino's court the king interrupts a love duet between his daughter Lavinia and the disguised Turno and orders her to marry any prince who will help him conquer his enemy Turno. He then rewards Camilla's noble deed by ordering his Volscian troops, led by Mezio, to help her overcome her tyrannical usurper (not realizing, of course, that the tyrant is himself). With the noble characters' goals firmly established, the comic characters provide relief with a scene of tomfoolery in which Camilla's middle-aged servant, Linco, is pursued by Lavinia's superannuated nurse, Tullia. Such comic scenes are placed at breaks between the scenes, usually allowing a lapse of time between a noble character's appearance in one setting and reappearance in another; they are distinctive in musical structure: an aria for each character is followed (in three of the scenes) by a duet.

The king cuts short a conversation between his daughter and Armidoro in order to learn her choice of a marriage partner. When she names his enemy Turno, the king confines her to a horrid chamber to choose between another prince or death. Only Armidoro will be allowed access to her. The king has thus unwittingly delivered his troops and his daughter into the hands of his disguised rivals. In London performances he 'never failed to make all that beheld him merry at his Appearance', according to Richard Steele in *The Spectator* (26 March 1711). Turno ends the act by praising Lavinia's fortitude in 'Mai non si vide ancor', 'that celebrated Air ... which is the softest and most tender of any in the World, and yet its Symphony is as lively and piercing as ever was composed' (Raguenet 1709).

ACT 2 In the gallery of the palace Camilla raves, in three accompanied recitatives, when she sees the portraits of her parents, and then calls for revenge in an aria interrupted by the arrival of Prenesto in search of his beloved Dorinda. Latino orders Armidoro to bring the intractable Lavinia poison and a dagger so that she can choose her means of death; left alone, Turno sings 'Consiglio ed aita', depicting his anguish in affective modulations and a truncated da capo, in which the first section of text is restated in complete disorder. After a comic scene Latino enters to see his command carried out by Armidoro, who boldly reveals himself as Turno and thereby shocks Latino into friendship. Elsewhere in the city Camilla reveals her true identity to the Volscian troops just before Prenesto inopportunely arrives; after the troops leave she tells Prenesto that she loves the son of her usurper, a statement he misunderstands and therefore bewails. After another comic scene Camilla encounters Turno in the palace, and Lavinia overhears, misinterprets and interrupts their conversation. She icily dismisses Camilla and jealously rages at Turno ('Vanne a seguire chi t'innamora'), who himself ends the act with his most elaborate aria, 'Tiranna gelosia'.

ACT 3 After a peaceful duet for Turno and Prenesto the plot moves swiftly: the jealous Lavinia tells Tullia to observe Turno closely; Linco pretends to return Tullia's love; Dorinda tells Prenesto that she loves him; Tullia overhears Dorinda ask Turno to join in Camilla's planned coup; Latino therefore orders the immediate imprisonment of Dorinda, then sings his only aria, the bellicose 'Non vanti amor di regno'. Mezio and Prenesto swear to rescue Dorinda; Linco and Tullia 'philosophize'; Lavinia and Turno sing a love duet; then Prenesto and Mezio forcibly enter Camilla's prison with their troops. She surprisingly imprisons the brave Prenesto in her cell, and he responds with the most turbulent aria in the opera, 'Tutte armate di flagelli'. Meanwhile Lavinia and Turno vow eternal fidelity at their festive wedding celebration, which is interrupted by a skirmish between the forces of Camilla and Latino. The heroine triumphs and, because she reciprocates Prenesto's love, forgives even Latino, who is at last moved to reply: 'Amore ha vinto'.

* * *

Stampiglia's structure is designed to heighten the excitement from act to act, in that the number of *actions* progresses from five to seven to nine. The result is increased activity by contrasting groups of characters on the stage during acts that are approximately equal in number of arias (18 + 19 + 20) and of stage sets (4 + 5 + 5). Bononcini's score has ten arias (all of them non-exit pieces) without any treble accompaniment, 25 with thematically related four-part ritornellos and 22 with instrumental accompaniment in two, three or four parts. Strings alone may have been used in all but two: the final solos in Acts 2 and 3, which include a brilliant cornetto part. The pace is rapid, for eight arias are marked 'andante' (a moderate speed), 11 are slower and 38 are faster. Such rapid pieces feature 'vigorous, incisive rhythms ... to which even a viceregal foot could quite easily beat time' and even 'an irresistible swing', so 'one cannot wonder at the immense popularity which the composer's music enjoyed' (Dent 1905 and 1910–11). LOWELL LINDGREN

Trionfo di Clelia, Il ('The Triumph of Cloelia'). Libretto by PIETRO METASTASIO, first set by Johann Adolf Hasse (1762, Vienna).

In league with Tarquinio [Tarquinius, Tarquin], who seeks restoration to the throne, Porsenna [Porsena], King of the Etruscans, lays siege to Rome. The Romans, however, obtain a truce and, as a sign of their good faith, present Porsena with a group of young hostages, among whom is the noblewoman Cloelia.

ACT 1 Cloelia, betrothed to Orazio [Horatius], the Roman ambassador, refuses Tarquinius when he offers her both throne and marriage, reminding him that the throne is not his to give and that he is already promised to Larissa, daughter of Porsena. Learning from Larissa that Porsena knows nothing of Tarquinius's duplicity, Cloelia begs Horatius to flee with her, but soon realizes that such an action would betray Rome. She is comforted, however, to learn from Mannio [Manius], Prince of the Veientes and in love with Larissa, that he is bent on proving Tarquinius's unworthiness. When negotiations between Horatius and Porsena fail, Tarquinius plays upon the ambassador's patriotism by offering to relinquish all claims to the throne in exchange for Cloelia.

ACT 2 Horatius bids Cloelia a hasty farewell before rushing to the aid of his countrymen against an attack, mounted by Tarquinius, on the bridge leading to Rome. Larissa tells her father of her aversion to Tarquinius, and is interrupted by Cloelia, who accuses Porsena of treachery. Innocent and offended, he chastises her, believing that it was the Romans who broke the truce. Meanwhile, Horatius recaptures the bridge and orders his followers to set fire to the Roman end of it, himself escaping into the river as the routed enemy flees. Tarquinius, afraid that Porsena will release Cloelia, determines to abduct her and advises his cohorts in a letter.

ACT 3 Manius intercepts the letter and gives it to Cloelia, who escapes with it to Rome. Believing this escape to be yet another sign of treason, Porsena bids Horatius prepare for war. He is soon assured of Roman loyalty, however, when Cloelia makes a timely return and offers Tarquinius's letter as proof of his perfidy. Tarquinius flees and Porsena, overwhelmed by the honourable conduct of Cloelia and Horatius, liberates Rome.

* * *

Porsena's siege of Rome and Cloelia's involvement in it are described in some detail in Livy, *Ab urbe condita libri [Historiae]* (book 2) and Dionysus of Halicarnassus, *Antiquitates* (book 5). Other early sources include Silus Italicus, *Punica* (book 10); Florus, *Epitomae* (book 1); Victor, *De viris* (no.13); and Plutarch, *Vitae* (Publicola). Closer to Metastasio's time, the story was popularized with the publication of *Clélie* (1654–60), a ten-volume romance by Madeleine de Scudéry. Subsequent librettos, with love intrigues centred on Cloelia, include Nicolò Minato's *Mutio Scevola* (1665), Friedrich Bressand's *Clelia* (1695), Silvio Stampiglia's *Muzio Scevola* (1695), Agostino Piovene's *Porsenna* (1712) and Giovanni Pasquini's *Clelia*, a *festa teatrale* which, in a setting by Ignazio Conti, Metastasio could have seen in Vienna in 1733. Set by Hasse, Metastasio's drama served to celebrate the confinement of the Archduchess Isabella, consort to the Archduke Joseph, soon to be Joseph II of Austria. A late libretto for Metastasio, *Il trionfo di Clelia* did not prove popular, even though Hasse's initial setting was well received. So also was Jommelli's version for Lisbon in 1774. Gluck, the first to set the text after Hasse, wrote his opera for the opening of the Teatro Comunale in Bologna in 1763.

For a list of settings *see* METASTASIO, PIETRO. DON NEVILLE

Trionfo di Clelia, Il ('The Triumph of Cloelia'). *Opera seria* in three acts by JOHANN ADOLF HASSE to a libretto by PIETRO METASTASIO (see TRIONFO DI CLELIA, IL, above); Vienna, Burgtheater, 27 April 1762.

The opera tells how the Roman noblewoman Cloelia (soprano), taken hostage by the Etruscan king Porsenna [Porsena] (tenor), regains her city's liberty through patriotism, courage, faith and honesty. The other roles are those of Orazio [Horatius] (alto), the Roman ambassador; Larissa (soprano), Porsena's daughter, secretly in love with Mannio [Manius] (soprano), Prince of the Veienti, but betrothed to Tarquinio [Tarquinius] (soprano), Cloelia's lover.

One of a series written by the imperial poet for Hasse in the 1760s, the work was composed to celebrate the birth of a child to the Archduchess Isabella, consort of Archduke Joseph. The working relationship between Metastasio and Hasse was especially cordial, and over the years their ideals of *dramma per musica* had moved progressively closer. The music of *Il trionfo di Clelia* demonstrates that the conservatism and alleged rigidity of the composer have long been exaggerated by scholars and commentators, beginning with Burney, who contrasted the approach of Hasse and Metastasio with that of Gluck and Calzabigi to the detriment of the former (Burney, *The Present State of Music in Germany*). Both in this work and in *Ruggiero* (1771) Hasse gave increasing independence to the oboes, and the underlying harmonic rhythm is rather slower than was usual for him; another noteworthy feature of *Il trionfo di Clelia* is the precision and careful graduation of the dynamic indications. ERIC D. WEIMER

Tristan und Isolde ('Tristan and Isolde'). *Handlung* (drama) in three acts by Richard Wagner (*see* WAGNER family, (1)) to his own libretto; Munich, Königliches Hof- und Nationaltheater, 10 June 1865.

Tristan	tenor
König Marke [King Mark]	bass
Isolde	soprano
Kurwenal *Tristan's servant*	baritone
Melot *a courtier*	tenor
Brangäne *Isolde's maid*	soprano
A Shepherd	tenor
A Steersman	baritone
A Young Sailor	tenor

Sailors, knights and esquires

Setting At sea, in Cornwall and Brittany during the Middle Ages

The ancient Tristan legend, probably of Celtic origin, achieved its first literary form in the 12th century. The version used by Wagner as the basis for his drama was that of Gottfried von Strassburg (*fl* 1200–20). Wagner conceived the idea of writing an opera on the Tristan subject in the autumn of 1854, but the earliest dated surviving sketch (an elaboration of two fragments) is from 19 December 1856, at which point he was still engaged on Act 1 of *Siegfried*.

Wagner began his prose scenario the following summer, on 20 August 1857, and the poem was completed on 18 September. Like *Siegfried* – but unlike all the other music dramas – each act was drafted and elaborated, in sequence, the full score being reached before the next act was embarked on in sketch. Indeed, because Breitkopf & Härtel were eager to have the new work ready for public consumption, the score was actually engraved one act at a time. The fair copy of the full score of Act 1 was completed on 3 April 1858 in Zürich, of Act 2 on 18 March 1859 in Venice, and of Act 3 on 6 August 1859 in Lucerne.

Epoch-making as *Tristan* proved to be, the work had some notable antecedents. There are frequent pre-echoes in the sultry chromaticism of Spohr's *Jessonda*, while the rising chromatic phrase that opens *Tristan* is prominent in Liszt's song *Die Lorelei*. The celebrated '*Tristan* chord' (see ex.1) is presaged (though never given in that precise form) in the Liszt song, as well as by composers as various as Mozart (K428, slow movement), Spohr (String Quartet in C op.4 no.1 and *Der*

Alchymist) and Gottschalk (*The Last Hope*). Berlioz's *Roméo et Juliette*, of which Wagner was a staunch admirer, contains a number of melodic inspirations that found their way into *Tristan*, in particular a theme which was developed into that of the so-called Liebestod; the sighing chromatic phrases and general atmosphere of the 'Scène d'amour' from *Roméo et Juliette* foreshadow the love scene in Act 2 of *Tristan*. A further remarkable antecedent of *Tristan* is Hans von Bülow's orchestral fantasy *Nirwana*, the score of which Wagner was studying at precisely the time of his conception of *Tristan* (autumn 1854). When he came to compose the opera three years later, he took over from *Nirwana* (possibly unconsciously) several ideas, both general and specific. *Nirwana* provides not only another, more immediate, source for the rising chromatic phrase that opens *Tristan*, but also a parallel sublimation of it at the close (see Spencer and Millington 1987).

The prelude to *Tristan* (with Wagner's own concert ending) was included in a series of three concerts in Paris early in 1860, intended to pave the way for a possible performance of the opera in France by German singers. That scheme came to nothing, as did plans to produce the work in Karlsruhe and Vienna. The day eventually fixed for performance in Munich, 15 May 1865, was the day chosen by Wagner's creditors to send in the bailiffs; in the afternoon his Isolde, Malvina Schnorr, lost her voice. The long-delayed première finally took place on 10 June, with three subsequent performances. Uncomprehending hostility in some quarters was matched by unbridled enthusiasm in others; the work was to exert an extraordinary influence over future generations (see Zuckerman 1964).

The conductor at the Munich première was Hans von Bülow; Tristan was sung by Malvina Schnorr's husband, Ludwig Schnorr von Carolsfeld, who died only three weeks after the final performance. Felix Mottl conducted the first performance at Bayreuth in 1886, which was also the year of the first production in the USA (Seidl conducting at the Metropolitan, with Niemann and Lilli Lehmann). The first production in England was at the Theatre Royal, Drury Lane, in 1882. Notable exponents of the role of Tristan have included Jean De Reszke, Melchior, Lorenz, Svanholm, Suthaus, Vinay, Windgassen, Vickers and Peter Hofmann. Isolde has been sung by Nordica, Fremstad, Turner, Leider, Lubin, Flagstad, Varnay, Mödl, Nilsson, Ligendza, Gwyneth Jones and Behrens. Notable conductors of the work, in addition to Mottl and Seidl, have included Mahler, Nikisch, Walter, Beecham, Coates, Erich Kleiber, Furtwängler, Böhm, Kempe, Solti, Karajan, Goodall, Carlos Kleiber and Barenboim.

The titles of Prelude and Liebestod for the opening and closing sections of the work are firmly established by tradition, though Wagner referred to them as respectively Liebestod and [Isolde's] Transfiguration. The prelude introduces several of the work's principal motifs. The descending chromatic phrase that begins it (ex.1*x*) is typical in that, although it has been given such labels as 'Tristan', 'Tristan's suffering', 'grief' and 'the confession', it ultimately defies categorization. Its inversion, the rising four-note phrase with which it is combined (ex.1*y*), is ubiquitous in *Tristan* and a potent musical image of the work's preoccupation with yearning. The chord occurring at their conjunction in bar 2 is known as the '*Tristan* chord'; returning at various points of significance in the drama, the chord has elicited much analytical discussion (see Bailey 1985).

ACT 1 *At sea, on the deck of Tristan's ship, during the crossing from Ireland to Cornwall* The curtain rises to reveal a construction like a tent on the foredeck of a ship (scene i); Isolde is seen on a couch, her face buried in the cushions. A young sailor sings, 'as if from the masthead', an unaccompanied song about the Irish lover he has left behind in the west ('Westwärts schweift der Blick'). Isolde, who is being brought from Ireland to Cornwall by Tristan to be the bride of his uncle, King Mark, starts up, assuming that the reference to an 'Irish maid' is an insult to her. When her maid and confidante Brangäne tells her that they are soon to land in Cornwall, Isolde launches into a furious outburst against her own 'degenerate race' who have succumbed so easily to the enemy. Brangäne attempts in vain to calm her.

For the second scene the whole length of the ship becomes visible; in the stern stands Tristan, thoughtfully, with folded arms, his faithful retainer Kurwenal reclining at his feet. The young sailor strikes up again, this time accompanied by a tremolando in the bass. Her eyes fixed on Tristan, Isolde sings the enigmatic words 'Mir erkoren, mir verloren' ('Chosen to be mine, lost to me') to motif ex.1*y*, followed by 'Todgeweihtes Haupt! Todgeweihtes Herz!' ('Death-devoted head! Death-devoted heart!') to a chord change from A♭ to A major, the poignant effect of which is enhanced by the switch from woodwind to brass (ex.2), a switch repeated on subsequent occurrences of the motif.

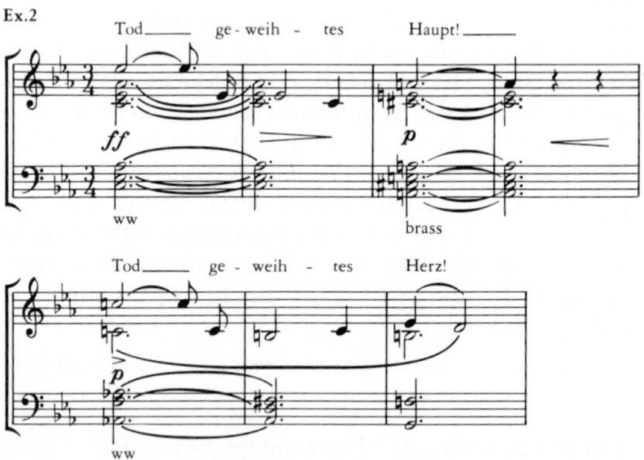

['Death-devoted head! Death-devoted heart!']

Isolde tells Brangäne to instruct Tristan to attend on her. Brangäne's timid request to Tristan is courteously turned aside by him, but when she repeats Isolde's command – to the same imperious chord sequence as her mistress used – Kurwenal makes his own bluntly negative reply, in the firmly diatonic idiom that is to characterize him. He goes on to revel in the slaying by Tristan of Morold, Isolde's betrothed, who came from Ireland to exact tribute from Cornwall. The mockery of Kurwenal's song is reinforced by its self-contained, ballad-like nature; its refrain is picked up by the sailors. Brangäne returns in confusion to Isolde who is barely

'Tristan und Isolde' (Wagner): model of Angelo Quaglio (ii)'s design for Act 1 (the deck of Tristan's ship) of the original production at the Königliches Hof- und Nationaltheater, Munich, 10 June 1865

able to control her anger (scene iii). With both (*x*) and (*y*) of ex.1 repeatedly in attendance, Isolde's Narration tells how the wounded Tristan, disguised as 'Tantris', came to her to be healed and how she recognized him as Morold's killer: 'Wie lachend sie mir Lieder singen'. The names Tantris and Tristan are offset not only melodically (rising 5th/falling 5th) but also harmonically (the fateful A♭–A major juxtaposition of ex.2). Isolde's determination to slay Tristan in revenge dissolved as he looked pitifully into her eyes – (*y*) is meltingly transformed here – but now she bitterly regrets that she let the sword drop. With heavy irony she mimics Tristan's 'insulting' offer to Mark to collect her as bride, and (*x*) undergoes an angry metamorphosis as she curses Tristan.

Brangäne's response makes much use of a tender appoggiatura figure – derived from (*y*); after another gnomic utterance from Isolde, Brangäne switches to triple time in an even more lyrical attempt to console her mistress. The opening bars of the prelude are recalled as Brangäne reminds Isolde of her mother's magic potions. But Isolde has only vengeance in mind (ex.2 intervenes) and she selects the draught of death, at which point the tension suddenly rises as the sailors are heard again, preparing to land.

Kurwenal boisterously calls the ladies to make ready (scene iv), but Isolde insists on speaking to Tristan before they land, in order to 'forgive' him. Her excited farewells to Brangäne, however, and the death-portending motif (ex.3) in the bass (heard previously

Ex.3

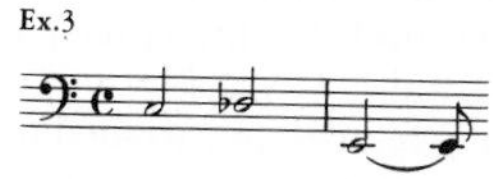

when she selected the draught) betoken her real intention. Brangäne's pleas are in vain, as is confirmed by the close succession of exx.3 and 2.

Tristan's approach is awaited (scene v) with a striking instrumental passage consisting of a new idea (ex.4)

Ex.4

answered by a series of *martellato* chords on full strings; ex.4 has been variously labelled 'Tristan's honour', 'Morold' and 'Isolde's anger' – an indication of the flexibility Wagner allowed himself in the deployment of motifs in *Tristan.* The ominous ex.3 is heard as Tristan approaches. Isolde tells him that she saw through his disguise as 'Tantris' and demands vengeance (exx.2 and 4). Tristan offers her his sword, but Isolde signals to Brangäne for the potion, ex.3 and the offstage sailors' cries again raising the tension. After more ironic mimicry (reflected in the accompaniment by a jauntily repeated dotted figure), Isolde hands Tristan the cup (exx.4 and then 2 are prominent). Tristan lifts the cup and drinks. Fearing further betrayal, Isolde wrests the cup from him and drinks in her turn: Brangäne, in desperation, has substituted the love for the death potion. The climactic chord, played by the full orchestra, is the '*Tristan* chord'. Its association with betrayal, as the obverse of faithful love, resonates beyond *Tristan*, occurring at Brünnhilde's discovery of her betrayal by Siegfried (*see* GÖTTERDÄMMERUNG, Act 1.iii); in *Parsifal* the ambivalent properties of the chord are exploited by its dual association with temptation and redemption. After they have both drunk, they are seized with a succession of conflicting emotions, all portrayed in the music: rapt wonderment by the prolongation of the '*Tristan* chord', agitation by tremolando cellos with muffled drum roll, breathless frenzy by a brief, snatched phrase on unison winds and strings, and finally yearning for each other by the music from the beginning of the prelude. Tristan and Isolde embrace ecstatically, offstage salutations to King Mark again raising the emotional temperature, while Brangäne looks on in horror. The lovers express their passion, first in alternating fragments of phrases, then, in defiance of Wagner's earlier theoretical principles, in conjunction. Only half jolted back to reality by Kurwenal's innocent breeziness and by the jubilant shouts of the onlookers, Tristan and Isolde struggle to comprehend what has happened to them. The act comes to an exhilarating end with the impassioned rising chromatic motif, ex.1(*y*), threading its way through exultant brass fanfares.

ACT 2 *In Mark's royal castle in Cornwall* The orchestral introduction to Act 2 introduces several new principal motifs: exx.5, 6 and 7, each of which resists

definitive categorization, though ex.5 is generally associated in the ensuing act with 'day' (in Schopenhauer's terms the outer material world of phenomena, as opposed to the noumenal sphere of inner consciousness represented by 'night'). Ex.1(*y*) also assumes a more urgent form: the lovers' yearning has intensified. The curtain rises to reveal a garden with high trees; Isolde's chamber is to one side and a burning torch stands at the open door. A volley of horn calls gradually receding into the distance signifies the departing hunt of King Mark and his courtiers. The cautious Brangäne warns her mistress that the horns are still audible, but all Isolde can hear are the sounds of the balmy summer night: the horn calls are transmuted into a shimmering orchestral texture by clarinets, second violins and violas, a sweet sound to the lovers ('Nicht Hörnerschall tönt so hold').

Brangäne further warns Isolde that in her impatience to see Tristan she should not be oblivious to the devious Melot, Tristan's supposed friend, who, she alleges, has arranged the nocturnal hunt as a trap. Isolde brushes these fears aside and requests Brangäne to extinguish the torch: the signal for Tristan to approach. Brangäne demurs, bewailing her fateful switching of the potions (exx.1 and 3, with a hint of 2). Over glowing orchestral colours, Isolde extols the powers of the love goddess, Frau Minne, which are then celebrated in a new theme (ex.8), the second bar of which includes the shape

characteristic of Wagner's main love themes (cf DIE WALKÜRE, ex.3). This new theme is developed sequentially, its ever-intensifying repetitions finally finding release in Isolde's expansive phrase 'dass hell sie dorten leuchte', before her extinguishing of the torch; the climactic power of that phrase is enhanced by the sudden cessation of rhythmic and harmonic motion.

Isolde throws the torch to the ground and, sending Brangäne to keep watch, waits impatiently for Tristan. Her agitated expectation is depicted by ex.6 (with a breathlessly syncopated accompanimental figure); together with another brief figure, that motif is subjected to remorseless sequential repetition, building to a frenzied climax as Tristan finally bursts in (scene ii). They greet each other ecstatically, his perfect 4th and her augmented one recalling in linear form the two intervals that make up the '*Tristan* chord'. A breathless exchange follows, in which each brief, snatched phrase (both musical and textual) of Isolde is impetuously appropriated by Tristan: 'Bist du mein?/Hab' ich dich wieder?' After further rapturous effusions, both in alternation and conjunction, against frenetically repeated sequential figures, their minds turn to the long-delayed extinction of the torch, a train of thought which soon enters the metaphysical realm of the night–day, noumenon–phenomenon polarity. (An extensive cut (324 bars) is often made at this point, from 'bot ich dem Tage Trutz!' to 'wahr es zu sehen tauge'.) Ex.5, the motif associated with 'day', is prominent here, but most of the others already cited also appear in one form or another.

Tristan draws Isolde to a flowery bank for their central love duet: 'O sink hernieder, Nacht der Liebe', approached by a masterly transition passage that effects a gradual reduction in tension by dynamic, harmonic and rhythmic means. The tonality of A♭ gradually establishes itself out of the tonal flux of the preceding duet, but the transition to some extent disguises the fact that 'O sink hernieder' has aspects of the traditional operatic duet (the singers sharing phrases of music and text, sometimes moving in step, at one point even in 6ths, together with the slow rate of harmonic change).

An interlude is provided by Brangäne's Watchsong from the tower: 'Einsam wachend in der Nacht'. Ravishingly scored, this passage also exemplifies a trait new in *Tristan*: syllables of the text become so distended that the vocal line is treated as an instrument rather than as the carrier of semantic meaning. The exquisitely prolonged dominant 7th cadence of Brangäne's Watchsong resolves on to ex.9 (an elaboration of an idea heard

earlier in the duet) on hushed strings alone, for Isolde's 'Lausch, Geliebter!'. Ex.9 is much developed, leading to a new melodic idea (ex.10), taken up first by Tristan,

then by Isolde, to the thought of union in death ('So stürben wir, um ungetrennt'); this theme is to provide the main material both for the latter part of this duet and for the Liebestod.

Brangäne's song returns, in curtailed form, leading to a restatement of ex.9, now in G major, at which point Tristan echoes Isolde's earlier words with 'Soll ich lauschen?'. From this point the duet gathers momentum. The final stage is launched with 'O ew'ge Nacht', the two singing in harmony of eternal night. The long approach to the final climax is shaped by a series of peaks; sequential repetitions and a sustained dominant pedal raise the tension to an unbearable level, which eventually reaches the point of no return.

The cadence, like the coitus, is *interruptus* (scene iii). A savage discord on the full orchestra (topped by shrieking piccolo) is accompanied by a scream from Brangäne, as King Mark, Melot and the courtiers burst in on the scene. The orchestra graphically depicts the subsiding of the lovers' passions as morning dawns (ex.5). King Mark, much moved, addresses Tristan and receiving no direct answer, embarks on his long monologue of questioning reproach: would Tristan do this to him ('Mir dies?')? His new motif, ex.11, announced on his

characteristic instrument, the bass clarinet, is an inverted form of the motif sometimes described as 'Tristan's honour' (ex.4). To King Mark's questions there can be no reply, Tristan responds. His feeling that he no longer belongs to this world is captured in a magical enharmonic modulation from the music of the opera's opening to ex.9 (on to a second inversion in A♭). He invites Isolde to follow him into the realm of night; she assents and he kisses her on the forehead. At this, Melot, whose actions (according to Tristan) have been motivated by his jealous love for Isolde, draws his sword. Tristan also draws, but allows himself to be wounded. The act ends with ex.11 pealing out on brass instruments in D minor.

ACT 3 *Tristan's castle in Brittany* The prelude to the final act opens with a doleful, diatonic transformation of ex.1(*y*) in a desolate F minor. When the curtain rises, Tristan is seen lying asleep under a lime tree, with Kurwenal bending over him, grief-stricken. A melancholy shepherd's song is heard on the english horn, offstage. The shepherd appears over the castle wall. Kurwenal tells him to play a merry melody if Isolde's ship should come into sight. The sea is empty and desolate ('Öd und leer das Meer!'), responds the shepherd, continuing with his mournful tune. To the joy of Kurwenal, expressed in his characteristically hearty rhythms and melodic lines, Tristan revives and asks where he is. Kurwenal replies that he is in his family castle, Kareol.

Tristan's slow, painful return to consciousness is reflected in his fragmented vocal line. He is dimly aware that he has been brought back from the distant realm of endless night, where he had glimpsed oblivion. Isolde remains in the bright light of day (ex.5) but he looks forward to the final extinction of the torch and their union. This first phase in Tristan's delirium is reflected in the wild lack of control in his music: the complexity of the chromatic harmony, the lurching tempo changes and the undisciplined line.

Kurwenal tells him that he has sent for Isolde, and Tristan, in his fevered imagination, sees the ship approaching; a motif (ex.12) first heard in a sombre

form in the prelude to the third act returns here in obsessive sequential repetition. Tristan's frantic cries to Kurwenal to look for the ship are answered by the english horn playing the mournful shepherd's song. In the next phase of his delirium, Tristan remembers how he heard that song ('Du alte ernste Weise') in his childhood, when his mother and father died. The strains of the song are now woven into a fantasy, to be joined by the falling chromatic phrase heard in Act 1 as Isolde recalled her tending of the sick Tristan. Another frenzied climax follows, in which Tristan curses the love potion, for which he senses he is somehow responsible.

He sinks back in a faint. Kurwenal listens anxiously for signs of life. Tristan revives and the music moves to E major for the final, sublime phase of his delirium, in which he imagines Isolde coming to him across the water: 'Wie sie selig'. Tristan's vocal line, introduced by the mellow ex.9 on horns, is now infinitely, ecstatically protracted – sometimes to ten slow-moving bars. Gradually the lines begin to fragment as Tristan again imagines he sees the ship approaching. This time a sprightly C major tune on the english horn confirms that it has been sighted. Kurwenal rushes to the watchtower and reports on its progress. He sees Isolde come ashore and goes down to assist (scene ii). Tristan, meanwhile, anticipates her arrival in feverish excitement, tearing the bandages from his wounds.

Isolde enters in haste (ex.7) but Tristan, to a recapitulation of music from the opera's prelude, expires in her arms. Isolde is distraught, her fragmented line accompanied by various themes including the opening of ex.10, subsequently to form the basis of the Liebestod.

The music becomes reanimated as the shepherd tells Kurwenal that a second ship is arriving (scene iii); they try to barricade the gate. Brangäne appears, and then Melot, whom Kurwenal strikes dead. King Mark and his followers also appear and, oblivious to the king's pleas, Kurwenal sets upon them, sustaining a fatal wound; he dies at Tristan's feet. King Mark, who had come to yield Isolde to Tristan, laments the scene of death and destruction. The Liebestod, or Isolde's Transfiguration, now begins, with ex.10: 'Mild und leise' ('Gently and softly'). In its latter stages, the conclusion of the Act 2 love duet is also recalled, but passion is now sublimated and the climax of the Liebestod is insistent rather than frantic. Isolde sinks, as if transfigured, on to Tristan's body, mystically united with him at last. A final statement of ex.1(*y*), achieving its long-awaited resolution on to a chord of B major, brings the opera to a radiant close.

* * *

Tristan und Isolde is regarded as a milestone in the history of music, largely on account of its pervasive emancipation of the dissonance. The far-reaching influence of the work in technical terms is matched by the overwhelming effect the extremity of its emotional expression has had on generations of artists in all media. On one level, *Tristan* is the ultimate glorification of love: 'a monument to this loveliest of all dreams', as Wagner put it. But on another level, the work goes beyond emotional experience and enters a metaphysical realm. Human existence and the outer material world of phenomena are ultimately transcended and salvation found in the embrace of the noumena, the ultimate reality.

For further illustration *see* STAGE DESIGN, fig.15 (Angelo Quaglio (ii)'s design for Act 3); and SCHNORR VON CAROLSFELD, LUDWIG.

BARRY MILLINGTON

Trittico, Il ('The Triptych'). The collective title given to Giacomo Puccini's three one-act operas *IL TABARRO*, *SUOR ANGELICA* and *GIANNI SCHICCHI*.

Tritto [Tritta], **Giacomo** (**Domenico Mario Antonio Pasquale Giuseppe**) (*b* Altamura, nr Bari, 2 April 1733; *d* Naples, 16 or 17 Sept 1824). Italian composer. He studied at the Pietà dei Turchini conservatory, Naples, with Cafaro, whose assistant he later became. While a *maestrino* there, he had his first opera performed (1754), but it had no immediate successors. In 1764, however, he also embarked on an abortive stage career. A comic opera performed at the Teatro Nuovo was followed by an intermezzo at a Naples convent in Carnival 1765. In Carnival 1766 he directed the production of Sacchini's *Lucio Vero* at the S Carlo. In 1777 he tried again, addressing petitions to the king and prime minister begging permission to compose an *opera seria* for the S Carlo. This request was denied, with Tritto's lack of experience and reputation given as reasons. He turned to the secondary theatres of Naples and in the summer of 1780 began to provide them with a series of 24 comic operas that lasted until 1798. During the same period he produced ten others in Rome, and in the 1790s four in Madrid, Vienna and Venice. In May 1783 he directed the production of Sarti's *Medonte* at the S Carlo and in 1784 was finally given his own opportunity there with *Artenice*, for which he was paid only the minimum fee of 200 ducats. During this period he wrote three more *opere serie*, performed in Rome (1786), the Fondo theatre at Naples (1786) and Milan (1795). However, seven of his last nine operas (1799–1810) were *opere serie*, all performed in Naples and Rome, four at the S Carlo.

In 1799 Tritto succeeded Sala as *primo maestro* at the Pietà dei Turchini conservatory, and in 1806 he became, with Fenaroli and Paisiello, one of the three joint *maestri* of the new Collegio Reale di Musica. Later he was named *maestro* of the royal chapel and chamber under the restored Bourbon monarchy. As a teacher he was influential in the formation of several generations of Neapolitan composers, but as a composer he was rather pedestrian and of only local significance in Naples and, to some extent, Rome. That his *opere serie* achieved some prominence in the first decade of the 19th century is an indication less of their own merit than of the impoverishment of the Neapolitan scene by the death or the silence of the leading older figures such as Cimarosa, Paisiello and P. A. Guglielmi. Lippmann emphasized the modern tendencies in Tritto's last opera, *Marco Albino in Siria* (1810, Naples), pointing to the use of the chorus in the arias and to the multi-tempo forms. However, these were hardly innovatory in 1810, and a slightly earlier work, *Cesare in Egitto*, which was very successful in Rome in 1805 and was also performed in Naples, makes a rather old-fashioned impression, especially in style, but also in its range of forms. While exhibiting an attempt to cater to the Roman taste in the prominence given to wind passages, it is timid in its use of the new formal possibilities and of the chorus and accompanied recitative.

According to Florimo, Tritto also worked for several Neapolitan churches, and he composed a considerable amount of church music. His 18 children included Domenico Tritto (1776–1851), Neapolitan church musician and dramatic composer who sold his father's manuscripts, including scores (mostly autograph) of nearly all his operas, to the conservatory. Other libraries also possess scores of some operas. Michael Costa was a grandson of Giacomo Tritto.

Le nozze contraste (ob), Naples, Fiorentini, 1754
La fedeltà in amore (ob, F. Cerlone), Naples, Nuovo, 1764, *I-Nc*
Li furbi (int), Naples, Convento S Chiara, carn. 1765, *Nc**
Il principe riconosciuto (ob, 1, Cerlone), Naples, Nuovo, sum. 1780, *Nc**
La marinella (farsetta, Cerlone), Naples, Nuovo, sum. 1780, *F-Pc**
La francese di spirito, o La viaggiatrice di spirito (ob, G. M. Mililotti), Rome, Argentina, carn. 1781, *I-Nc** (inc.)
La Bellinda, o L'ortolana fedele (ob, 3, Cerlone), Naples, Nuovo, carn. 1781, *H-Bn*, Act 1 *Nc**
Don Procopio in corte del Pretejanni (ob, 3), Naples, Nuovo, carn. 1782, *Nc** (inc.)
Don Papirio (ob, G. Palomba), Naples, Nuovo, 1782
I due gemelli (ob, G. Lorenzi), Naples, Fiorentini, carn. 1783, *F-Lm* (Paris, n.d.)
Il convitato di pietra (op semiseria, 2, Lorenzi), Naples, Fiorentini, carn. 1783, *I-Fc*, *Nc**
La sposa stramba (ob), Naples, Fondo, spr. 1783, *Nc**
La scuola degli amanti (ob, 3, Palomba), Naples, Nuovo, ?aut. 1783, *Nc*
La scuffiara (ob, 1, Lorenzi), Naples, Fiorentini, carn. 1784, *Nc**; perf. with I due gemelli
Il matrimono negli Elisii, ovvero La sposa bizzarra (ob, C. G. Lanfranchi Rossi), Rome, Valle, carn. 1784, *Nc**
L'Artenice (os, 3), Naples, S Carlo, 13 Aug 1784, *Nc**, *P-La*
L'Arminio (os, F. Moretti), Rome, Argentina, Jan 1786, *I-Nc** (inc.)
Le gelosie, ovvero I due fratelli burlati (farsetta, 2), Rome, Valle, carn. 1786, *Nc**
Li raggiri scoperti (ob, 2), Rome, Valle, carn. 1786, *Nc**, *P-La*
La vergine del sole (os, 3, Lanfranchi Rossi), Naples, Fondo, 26 Dec 1786, *I-Nc**
Armida (os), Naples, Fondo, 1786, aria *PS*
Le vicende amorose (dg, 2, P. A. Timido), Rome, Valle, April 1787, *F-Pn*, *P-La*; also as Le avventure galanti; I raggiri d'amore; Li disprezzatori delle donne o sia Le vicende amorose, *D-Dl*
La molinara spiritosa (ob, F. S. Zini), Naples, Fondo, sum. 1787, Act 2 *I-Nc**
La bella selvaggia (op semiseria, ?after C. Goldoni), Rome, Valle, carn. 1788, *Nc**
La scaltra avventuriera (ob, 2, Palomba), Naples, Fiorentini, ?carn. 1788, *Nc**
Il giuocatore fortunato (ob, G. Petrosellini), Naples, Nuovo, 1788
I finti padroni (farsa, 2), Rome, Valle, carn. 1789, *Nc**
La pruova reciproca [L'inganno fortunato, ossia La prova reciproca] (ob, 2, Palomba), Naples, Fiorentini, sum. 1789, *Fc*, *Nc**
I servi padroni (farsetta), Rome, Valle, carn. 1790, duet *PAc* (Modena, 1791), aria *MC*
La cantarina (ob, 2, Goldoni), Rome, Valle, carn. 1790, *Nc**
Il cartesiano fantastico (ob, 2, G. M. Diodati), Naples, Nuovo, carn. 1790, *Nc**
Le astuzie in amore (ob, 2, Diodati), Naples, Nuovo, carn. 1790, *Mc*, *Nc**, *Tn*
L'inganno amoroso (ob), Madrid, Caños del Peral, 30 Dec 1790
L'equivoco (ob, 2, C. Fiori), Naples, Fondo, carn. or spr. 1791, *Nc**
La creduta selvaggia (farsetta), Rome, Valle, carn. 1792
Gli amici rivali (ob), Vienna, Burg, 5 Nov 1792
Le trame spiritose (commedia, 2, Palomba), Naples, Nuovo, 1792, *Gl*, *Nc** (1787), *PAc*
La fedeltà nelle selve [La fedeltà tra le selve] (ob, M. Prunetti), Venice, S Moisè, carn. 1793, *Nc** (inc.), also complete copy
Le nozze in garbuglio (op semiseria, 1, Diodati), Naples, Nuovo, aut. 1793, *Nc**
L'ordine dal disordine (ob), Naples, S Ferdinando, aut. 1793
L'impostore smascherato (ob, Diodati), Naples, Nuovo, spr. 1794, *Nc**
Gli amanti in puntiglio (ob, 2, Diodati), Naples, Nuovo, sum. 1794, *Nc**
Apelle e Campaspe (os, 3, A. S. Sografi), Milan, Scala, 26 Dec 1795, *Nc*; also as Alessandro in Efeso; ?Campaspe e Apelle, *Fc*
Il barone in angustie (ob, 2, Palomba), Naples, Fondo, 1 Feb 1797, *Nc**; also as Il barone di Terragialla in angustie
La donna sensibile, o sia Gli amanti riuniti (ob, D. Piccinni), Naples, Fondo, sum. 1798, *Nc**
?La morte di Cesare (os, G. Sertor), Brescia, Nazionale, sum. 1798
Nicaboro in Jucatan (os, 2, Piccinni), Naples, S Carlo, 12 Jan 1799, *Nc**

I matrimoni in contrasto (op semiseria, 3, ?G. Checcherini), Rome, Valle, carn. 1800, *Nc**; also as I matrimonj contrasti
Ginevra e Ariodante (os, 2, Piccinni), Naples, S Carlo, 13 Aug 1801/1803, *Nc**
Gli americani [Gonzalvo, ossia Gli americani] (os, 2, G. Schmidt), Naples, S Carlo, 4 Nov 1802, *Fc*, *Nc*
Cesare in Egitto (os, Schmidt), Rome, Dame, 8 Jan 1805, *F-Pn*, *I-Nc** (inc.), *US-Bp*
Lo specchio dei gelosi (ob), Rome, Valle, carn. 1805
Elpinice e Vologeso (os, 2, Piccinni), Rome, Alibert delle Dame, carn. 1806, *I-Nc**
Andromaca e Pirro (os), Rome, Argentina, carn. 1807, ?*GB-Lbl*; Act 1 *I-Nc**
Marco Albino in Siria (os, 2), Naples, S Carlo, 15 Aug 1810, *Nc**
Impresario in angustie, sextet *Mc*; Sesostri, aria *Nc*

*

EitnerQ; *FétisB*; *FlorimoN*; *MGG* (U. Prota-Giurleo)
G. de Napoli: *La triade melodrammatica altamurana: Giacomo Tritto, Vincenzo Lavigna, Saverio Mercadante* (Milan, 1931)
F. Lippmann: 'Vincenzo Bellini und die italienische opera seria seiner Zeit', *AnMc*, no.6 (1969), esp. 96

DENNIS LIBBY (text), JAMES L. JACKMAN, MARITA P. McCLYMONDS (work-list)

Trneček, Hanuš [Jan] (*b* Prague, 16 May 1858; *d* Prague, 28 March 1914). Czech composer and conductor. In 1882 he appeared as an operetta conductor in Franzensbad (now Františkovy Lázně), and from that year until 1888 he played the harp in the orchestra of the Grossherzogliches Hoftheater in Schwerin, where his first opera, *Die Geigenmacher von Cremona*, was staged in 1886. Returning to Prague in 1888, he attained an important position in the city's musical life (which probably influenced the acceptance of his operas for staging at the Prague National Theatre): he was a prominent pianist, harpist and teacher, and was chairman of the Umělecká Beseda (Artists' Society). His *Amaranta* was performed only four times (1890), and *Andrea Crini* only five (1900). Trneček was a well-educated but self-taught composer. In his operas he often used superficial theatrical effects, most of them taken over from French *grand opéra*. He also made many operatic transcriptions for harp and piano.

Die Geigenmacher von Cremona (2, L. Günther, after F. Coppé), Schwerin, Grossherzogliches Hof, 16 April 1886, *CS-Pnm** [orig. in 1 act]
Amaranta, 1884–9 (prol., 3, D. Harnicke, after O. Redwitz), Prague, National, 16 Nov 1890, vs excerpts *Pnm**
Smytá vina [The Expiated Guilt], 1896 (2, A. Rostran), unperf., ?lost
Andrea Crini, 1898 (3, B. Beneš), Prague, National, 2 Feb 1900, vs *Pnd*

*

L. D. [L. Dolanský]: 'Jan Trneček', in D. Harnicke: *Amaranta* (Prague, 1890)
Hda. [F. K. Hejda]: 'Národní divadlo v Praze: Amaranta' [The National Theatre in Prague: *Amaranta*], *Dalibor*, xii (1890), 350–51, 362–3
K. Hoffmeister: 'Andrea Crini: úvodem k opeře Hanuše Trnečka' [*Andrea Crini*: an Introduction to the Opera by Hanuš Trneček], *Dalibor*, xxii (1900), 17–20
V. A. J. Hornové [V. Horn, A. Horn and J. Horn]: *Česká zpěvohra* [Czech Opera] (Prague, 1903)
Z. Nejedlý: *Dějiny Národního divadla*, iii: *Opera Národního divadla do roku 1900* [History of the National Theatre, iii: Opera at the National Theatre up to 1900] (Prague, 1935, 2/1949)

MARTA OTTLOVÁ, MILAN POSPÍŠIL

Troia* [Troja] *distrutta ('The Destruction of Troy'). *Opera seria* in three acts by MICHELE MORTELLARI to a libretto by MATTIA VERAZI; Milan, Teatro alla Scala, 1 September 1778.

One of three operas based on texts by Verazi for the opening of La Scala, *Troia distrutta* was designed to exploit the spectacular capabilities of the new theatre. After an introductory Allegro the curtain opens on a temple scene; an ensemble with chorus functions as the Andante of the sinfonia; the second Allegro, a *sinfonia strepitosa*, is heard as the earth trembles and lightning flashes from a sacred cavern. Paride [Paris] (alto castrato), Prince of Troy, has captured Elena [Helen] (soprano) and brought her to Troy from Greece, where she was promised to King Menelaus. Cassandra, sister of Paris, warns that his actions will bring ill-fortune to Troy, which their brother Deifebo [Deiphobus] (tenor) governs. Creusa (soprano) leads the priestesses of Pallas in a solo with chorus lamenting the fruits of love's madness, 'Dagli amorosi lacci'. A terrible spectre appears and a trio with choral response closes the scene. The finale of Act 1 spans four scenes, in which the terrified Trojans react to the battle with the Greeks (off stage) and the death of Hector, their champion. Act 2 deals with efforts to appease the Greeks, and concludes with an aria for Cassandra with chorus, 'Non si fidi chi ha prospero il vento'. The first three scenes of Act 3 are entirely in pantomime, as the Trojans wheel the horse into the city and the Greeks burn, sack and pillage. The stage is filled with death, fire and destruction for the remainder of the opera, the action moving freely through recitative, cavatina, ensemble and chorus. At the climax Paris and Helen throw themselves into the flames together. Cassandra and Deiphobus remain behind with the Trojan women and their Greek captors, and the opera concludes with an ensemble and chorus. Mortellari's conservative harmonic language proved unequal to Verazi's challenging text; his vocal lines are too long, smooth and flowing to dramatize the emotional extremes expressed in the text. MARITA P. McCLYMONDS

Troilus and Cressida. Opera in three acts by WILLIAM WALTON to a libretto by CHRISTOPHER HASSALL after Geoffrey Chaucer and other sources; London, Covent Garden, 3 December 1954.

Act 1 opens in the citadel of Troy after ten years of war between the Trojans and Greeks. Calkas, the High Priest (bass), tells a group of Trojans that the Delphic Oracle has advised surrender to the Greeks. They are bewildered by this news, as is a young officer, Antenor (baritone), who accuses Calkas of forgery and of being in the Greeks' pay. The crowd turns on Calkas, who takes refuge in the temple just as Prince Troilus (tenor), son of Priam, the Trojan king, drives them back. He rebukes Antenor and supports Calkas. Antenor ascribes this defence to Troilus's interest in Calkas's daughter Cressida (mezzo-soprano), who keeps the altar candles burning.

Troilus admits to himself that Antenor is right and sings of his love for Cressida ('Child of the wine-dark wave'). Cressida enters, a crimson scarf round her neck. She is a war widow and knows that Calkas is preparing to desert to the Greeks. Her only peace of mind comes from tending the altar.

She is overheard by her uncle, Pandarus (tenor), a wealthy, dandyish schemer. He tells Troilus he will intercede with Cressida on his behalf. He is about to enter the temple when Calkas emerges with Cressida and her servant Evadne (mezzo-soprano). He admits he is deserting, and when he has gone Cressida recalls the doubts of her childhood ('Slowly it all comes back'). News comes that Antenor has been taken prisoner. Troilus vows to buy him back or to recapture him by force and seeks Calkas to ask him to bless his sword.

'Troilus and Cressida' (Walton): scene from the original production at Covent Garden, London, 3 December 1954, with Magda László as Cressida (left) and Richard Lewis as Troilus

Thus he discovers Calkas's treachery. Meanwhile Pandarus has persuaded Cressida to leave her scarf as a token of her regard for Troilus.

Act 2 is set in a room in Pandarus's luxurious house. Cressida is playing chess after supper. A thunderstorm breaks. This suits Pandarus's plans and he sends a servant to fetch Troilus. He then persuades Cressida to stay the night. Troilus arrives, angry at first, but the inevitable follows after a love duet. An orchestral interlude describes the storm and the lovers' passion. Next morning the lovers' bliss is interrupted by the arrival of the Greek prince Diomede (baritone), who says that the price of Calkas's services is that Cressida will join him in exchange for Antenor. When Diomede sees Cressida, he is struck by her beauty. Troilus vows to disrupt the exchange, and promises meanwhile to send her daily messages and to bribe the Greek sentries so that they can meet. He gives her back her scarf before she is escorted away.

Act 3 is set in the Greek camp, ten weeks later. Cressida has not heard from Troilus and sends Evadne to the palisade in the hope that there might be a message at last. Evadne advises her to forget Troilus and encourage Diomede. Calkas also urges her to love Diomede, to whom Cressida is attracted. She yields to him and gives him her scarf as a token of her promise to marry him. On overhearing this, Evadne burns the latest of the messages from Troilus which, on Calkas's orders, she has intercepted and concealed.

During an hour's truce, Troilus and Pandarus enter the Greek camp seeking Cressida. Troilus explains that in his latest message he warned Cressida to be ready to return to Troy, as he had arranged her ransom. Cressida comes from her tent in her wedding attire. Distraught on seeing Troilus, she asks why he has sent no message. At this moment, voices acclaim her as Diomede's bride. When Troilus sees Cressida's scarf on Diomede's helmet, he claims her as his own. Cressida kneels by Troilus, disobeying Diomede's order to denounce him. In a sextet ('Troy, false of heart, yet fair'), each of the main characters comments on the situation. Diomede throws the scarf to the ground and is attacked by Troilus, who is stabbed in the back by Calkas. Diomede, horrified, orders Calkas to be returned in chains to Troy but insists that Cressida shall remain as a whore for the Greek soldiers. She picks up Troilus's sword and kills herself.

Walton began to compose *Troilus and Cressida* in 1948. It was revised and cut in 1963 and again in 1972–6, when the heroine's role, originally composed with Elisabeth Schwarzkopf in mind, was changed from dramatic soprano to mezzo. Walton said he wanted to write an English bel canto opera, and he designed the work on a grand, heroic scale that was regarded by many commentators as already out of date when the opera was first performed in 1954; but outdatedness is merely a question of fashion and ultimately may be held to be of little account. More crucial is the quality of the music itself, and this is distinctly uneven. Some of the love music is of luminous beauty, colourfully scored, and the characterization of the epicene Pandarus is in Walton's lightest vein (almost parodying Britten, perhaps because Peter Pears created the role), but the heroic style that was needed to make Troilus and Cressida credible and compelling tragic lovers was not forthcoming, part of the fault lying in Hassall's libretto.

MICHAEL KENNEDY

Trois fermiers, Les ('The Three Farmers'). *Comédie mêlée d'ariettes* in two acts by NICOLAS DEZÈDE to a libretto by Jacques Marie Boutet de Monvel; Paris, Comédie-Italienne (Hôtel de Bourgogne), 24 May 1777.

Louise Desvignes (soprano) eagerly awaits her marriage to her cousin Louis (tenor) scheduled for the next day. Her sister Babette (soprano) confesses to Louise that she is in love with the 16-year-old Blaise (tenor) who has encouraged her affection. Louise's parents, Jacques (bass-baritone) and Alix (soprano), express their delight at the closer family ties to be created by the marriage of the cousins. Grandfather Mathurin (baritone) has unexpectedly arrived to attend the wedding. When the family sits down to eat and drink, the landlord, M. de Belval (baritone), announces that since he expects to lose a legal case, he is forced to sell the estate to Le Comte (bass). While the women show the new proprietor round, the peasant farmers offer to repay Belval's debts. Clearly touched, Belval accepts the offer and the farmers rejoice in having kept their landlord.

This is a drama with insertion pieces rather than an *opéra comique*; most of the musical numbers deal with love or drinking in a general sense instead of relating it to the plot. Apart from composing a musical caricature of Alix's fury ('Hein? quoi? que veux tu dire?', 1.vi), Dezède wrote in a simple fashion with little employment of the wind instruments, using mainly short instrumental phrases in imitative style. The entertaining quality is enhanced by his rendering, in spoken dialogue, of Belval's announcement to sell the estate. The most popular number was the overture, which appeared in arrangements for duo, trio and string quartet. Defending the surprising end of the opera against public criticism, Monvel disclosed that there was a historical source for the drama published in an economics journal, *Ephémérides du citoyen* (1769). MICHAEL FEND

Trois souhaits, Les [*Les trois souhaits, ou Les vicissitudes de la vie* ('The Three Wishes, or Life's Vicissitudes' [*Trojí přání*])]. Film opera in a prelude, three acts and a postlude by BOHUSLAV MARTINŮ to a libretto by Georges Ribemont-Dessaignes; Brno, State Theatre, 16 June 1971.

Les trois souhaits was Martinů's second collaboration with Ribemont-Dessaignes. Composed between autumn 1928 and the end of May 1929, largely in Paris, it was one of the composer's most experimental works, blending film with stage action. An orchestral entr'acte now entitled *Le départ* exists independently.

Essentially, the opera works on two levels. The film element is apparent at the beginning and end of the work and reinforces the impression of fantasy and reality held in balance. The three wishes are the blessings of riches, youthfulness and love, offered by a fairy (contralto) to a middle-aged couple, Nina (soprano) and Arthur (bass-baritone). The opera opens in a studio where the story, a fairy-tale film entitled 'The Three Wishes', is being shown. The three wishes are granted in the succeeding acts in a series of fantastic, dream-like situations, some of which are projected on film. After a showing of the film which is the *raison d'être* of the opera, the postlude reveals the true emptiness of the participating couple.

The music reflects the eclectic practices of Martinů's first decade in Paris: a strong jazz element is enhanced by the use of saxophones and banjo, and besides the techniques of contemporary popular music, Martinů also made use of barbershop vocal style and accordion playing. The result, as the first production in Brno in 1971 and a later one in Prague (1988) revealed, is a mature drama of considerable ingenuity and power, comparable in theatrical impact to many of Martinů's later operas. JAN SMACZNY

Trojan, Václav (*b* Plzeň, 24 April 1907; *d* Prague, 5 July 1983). Czech composer. At the Prague Conservatory he studied conducting with Ostrčil (1923–7) and continued his studies in the composition masterclasses of Josef Suk and Novák until 1929; he also attended Hába's classes in quarter-tone and sixth-tone music. Trojan worked as a music teacher, music manager for Prague Radio (1937–45), composer for the State Cartoon Film Company (1945–6) and, from 1949, lecturer in theatre and film music at the Prague Academy. His early compositions were mainly entertainment music, dances and incidental scores; after World War II he concentrated on music for puppet films, a field which gave full expression to his fresh melodic invention, dramatic gift and wit; he received many awards, including the K. Gottwald State Prize (1960) for *Sen noci svatojanské* ('A Midsummer Night's Dream', composed 1958). In 1940 he received the Czech National Prize for his remarkable children's opera *Kolotoč* ('The Merry-go-round', 1936–9; 6, M. Charousová-Gardavská; Ostrava, Zdeněk Nejedlý, 13 Feb 1960), in which some children fall asleep on their favourite merry-go-round cars and, accompanied by a kindhearted moon, participate in four imaginary adventures with an African gorilla, an Australian gold-digger, an Indian white elephant and a small Hollywood duck. Trojan also composed the successful operetta *Paní Marjánka, matka pluku* ('Mrs Marjánka, Mother of the Regiment'; 6, F. Rachlík, after J. K. Tyl), first performed at the Karlín State Theatre, Prague, in 1951.

MILAN KUNA, HELENA HAVLÍKOVÁ

Trojí přání. Opera by Bohuslav Martinů; *see* TROIS SOUHAITS, LES.

Trompeter von Säkkingen, Der ('The Trumpeter of Säckingen'). Opera in a prologue and three acts by VIKTOR E. NESSLER to a libretto by Rudolf Bunge after J. V. von Scheffel's poetic epic; Leipzig, 4 May 1884.

When the Baron von Schönau (bass) learns that his trumpeter Werner Kirchhofer (tenor) seeks the hand of his daughter Maria (soprano), he banishes Werner and consigns Maria to marriage with the cowardly but noble-born Damian (tenor). Werner then returns with troops to save the Baron from a peasant uprising. A mark on Werner's arm reveals that he is of noble birth after all, and his union with Maria is permitted. Nessler combined stock characters with formula-composed numbers, some of which, like Werner's Act 2 farewell to Maria, 'Behüt dich Gott, es wär so schön gewesen', became popular. The opera's success was attributed by critics to Scheffel's well-known poem, with its mixture of German history and romantic sentimentality, rather than to the deliberate 'Volkstümlichkeit' of Nessler's score. PETER FRANKLIN

Tron. Family of Venetian nobles. Successive generations of the family owned, and at times managed, the S Cassiano theatre situated in the Venetian parish of the same name. The original theatre, of wood, was erected by Ettore Tron in 1580. After its destruction by fire in 1629 the family built a new theatre of stone on the same site. In Carnival 1637 S Cassiano became the first public theatre anywhere to offer opera when it staged Manelli's *Andromeda*. With this production the Tron family also pioneered the practice, which soon spread to other Venetian opera houses, of renting out a theatre to an independent impresario (on this occasion, Manelli himself). Opera at S Cassiano flourished between 1637 and 1651, when Cavalli was the dominant composer, and again between 1696 and 1716, when M. A. Ziani, Francesco Gasparini and Lotti were prominent. At other times the theatre was frequently closed or limited its activity to spoken comedy. Comic intermezzos regularly partnered *opere serie* in the early part of the 18th century, but full-length comic operas were introduced only in 1744. The reputation of S Cassiano, once high, declined greatly in the second half of the century; the theatre passed through marriage to Zuanne Veronese in 1779, so bringing to an end the family's involvement with opera.

*

N. Mangini: *I teatri di Venezia* (Milan, 1974) MICHAEL TALBOT

Tronsarelli, Ottavio (*d* Rome, 31 Aug 1646). Italian librettist. According to Erythraeus (1648), he was educated by the Jesuits and patronized by Cardinal Alessandro Ludovisi of Bologna, later Pope Gregory XV. He belonged to the famous Accademia degli Umoristi in Rome (along with J. H. Kapsberger and Pietro Della Valle), which he left to join the rival Accademia degl'Ordinati. He published eight volumes of lyric poetry and two heroic poems, in addition to his librettos. The *Drammi musicali* (Rome, 1631) contains 30 of his works, ranging from five-act music dramas to prologues and other occasional pieces, often designed to include spectacular machines, costumes and danced choruses (balli). His dedicatees include members of the Aldobrandini and Barberini families and other leading Roman patrons. The composers for four of his librettos are known – Domenico Mazzocchi (two), Kapsberger and an unidentified Cignani – but music survives only for Mazzocchi's *La catena d'Adone*, performed with great success at the house of Evandro Conti, Duke of Poli, during Carnival 1626. Tronsarelli adapted the text from Giovanni Battista Marino's *Adone*, which was placed on the Index by Urban VIII the following year. Tronsarelli generally preceded his collections with a disclaimer of any non-Christian intent in the use of pagan names and themes; he provided a detailed, moralizing explanation of *La catena* and altered the tragic ending of the fable of Marsyas (1628) at the behest of Cardinal Francesco Barberini. Pirrotta (1984) saw in the character of Arsete in *La catena* a precursor of Seneca in Monteverdi's *L'incoronazione di Poppea*. Tronsarelli's last libretto, *Il martirio de' Santi Abundio prete …*, was also the last opera by Mazzocchi, who commissioned it for performance in his native city of Civita Castellana in 1641. Mazzocchi also set three of Tronsarelli's lyrics as madrigals (1638, 1640).

La catena d'Adone (favola boschereccia), D. Mazzocchi, 1626; *La sirena* (cantata musicale), 1627; *Il giudizio di Venere* (scherzo musicale), 1627; *La mensa di Nettuno*, 1624–7; *Il ritorno d'Angelica nell'India* (dramma musicale), Cignani, 1628; *Marsia*, 1628; *Fetonte* (dramma musicale), Kapsberger, 1630; *Il ballo de' segni celesti*, comp. unknown, 1630; *Il martirio de' Santi Abundio prete, Abundantio diacono, Marciano, e Giovanni suo figliuolo cavalieri romani*, Mazzocchi, 1641

Datable before 1631: *L'amante sospettoso*; *Amore*; *Gli applausi Urbani*; *L'augurio felice*; *Belisario*; *La contesa delle virtù*; *La creatione del mondo*; *La danza di Diana*; *L'essequie di Cristo*; *L'età dell'oro*; *Faraone sommerso*; *La filia di Iefte*; *L'humiltà trionfante*; *Ifigenia*; *La nascita di Romolo*; *Il natale dell'anno*; *Parthenope*; *Rinaldo prigioniero*; *Silvio amante*; *Il trionfo di primavera*; *La vendetta*

J. N. Erythraeus [pseud. of G. V. Rossi]: *Pinacotheca imaginum illustrium … virorum*, iii (Cologne, 1648)
S. Reiner: '"Vi sono molt'altre mezz'Arie … "', *Studies in Music History: Essays for Oliver Strunk* (Princeton, 1968), 241–58
F. Testi: *La musica italiana nel seicento* (Milan, 1970)
M. Murata: *Operas for the Papal Court 1631–1668* (Ann Arbor, 1981)
N. Pirrotta: 'Falsirena and the Earliest *Cavatina*', *Music and Culture in Italy from the Middle Ages to the Baroque* (Cambridge, MA, 1984), 335–42
F. Hammond: 'More on Music in Casa Barberini', *Studi musicali*, xiv (1985), 235–62
FREDERICK HAMMOND

Troppau (Ger.). OPAVA.

Trost, Johann Baptist Matthäus (*fl* 1714–26). German composer. He was one of a group of German musicians of the early 18th century who wrote operas for the court of Margrave Karl Wilhelm of Baden-Durlach. According to archival material (*D-KA*), Trost was born in Württemberg. He became a *Hofmusicus* in autumn 1714 and also served as tutor for singers of the court opera at Durlach. All Trost's operas seem to be lost, including *Rhea Sylvia* (1716) and *Ademarus* (1718). Two other works attributed to him are *Die bestürzte Königin in Schottland Maria Stuart* and *Die enthauptete Königin in Schottland Maria Stuart* (1716). In 1715 Trost was sent on court business to Stuttgart and Nürtingen, but he returned to Durlach the following year. His name continued to appear in court documents until July 1726.
GEORGE J. BUELOW

Troszel [Troschel], **Wilhelm** (*b* Warsaw, 26 Aug 1823; *d* Warsaw, 2 March 1887). Polish bass. He studied with August Freyer and others. He made his début at Warsaw on 17 April 1843 as Rodolphe in Auber's *Le lac des fées* and sang at the Warsaw Opera until 1865. Particularly noted for his interpretations of bass roles in operas by Moniuszko, Münchheimer and Dobrzyński, and in German and Italian operas, he was also a fine recital singer. After retiring from concert and operatic work in 1866, Troszel devoted himself to composition and teaching. He wrote a tutor, *Szkoła do śpiewu na głos sopranowy i mezzosopranowy* (Warsaw, 1860), and a book of vocal exercises for women's voices (Warsaw, n.d.), as well as composing over 50 songs and some church music.

Echo muzyczne, teatralne i artystyczne, iv (1887), 135–6
S. Barbag: 'Polska pieśń artystyczna' [Polish Art Songs], *Muzyka*, v/10 (1927), 95
IRENA PONIATOWSKA

Trouble in Tahiti. Opera in one act by Leonard Bernstein to his own libretto; Waltham, Massachusetts, Brandeis University, 12 June 1952. In 1984 it was incorporated in the revision of A QUIET PLACE.

Trouillon-Lacombe, Louis. *See* LACOMBE, LOUIS.

Trouser role. *See* BREECHES PART.

Troutbeck, John (*b* Blencowe, Cumberland, 17 Nov 1832; *d* London, 11 Oct 1899). English translator. A clergyman, ordained in 1856, and a church musician, he translated many sacred works. Though his opera translations have now been superseded, they served Victorian audiences well and were published in vocal score by Novello. His translation of Goetz's *Der Widerspänstigen Zähmung*, an operatic version of Shakespeare's *The Taming of the Shrew*, was used for the first London productions of that work (1878, 1880) and contributed to its success. Other works he translated include Gluck's *Iphigénie en Tauride* and *Iphigénie en Aulide* (1876), and Wagner's *Der fliegende Holländer*.

J. Troutbeck: 'Precentor of Westminster', *MT*, xl (1899), 297–301
ARTHUR JACOBS

Trovatore, Il ('The Troubadour'). *Dramma* in four parts by GIUSEPPE VERDI to a libretto by SALVADORE CAMMARANO (with additions by Leone Emanuele Bardare) after ANTONIO GARCÍA GUTIÉRREZ's play *El trovador*; Rome, Teatro Apollo, 19 January 1853 (revised version, *Le trouvère*: Paris, Opéra, 12 January 1857).

Verdi was still in Venice enjoying the success of *Rigoletto* (in March 1851) when he wrote to Cammarano suggesting García Gutiérrez's play (first performed in 1836) as a subject for his next opera. It is clear from his early letters that he saw the drama as a sequel to *Rigoletto*, this time with an unconventional female character, the gypsy Azucena, at the centre of the action. Azucena, like Rigoletto, was to be fired by two opposing passions: filial love and a desire for vengeance. More than this, it is clear that Verdi wished to develop further the formal freedoms he had experimented with in parts of *Rigoletto*. In an early letter to Cammarano, for example, he urged:

> As for the distribution of the pieces, let me tell you that when I'm presented with poetry to be set to music, any form, any distribution is good, and I'm all the happier if they are new and bizarre. If in

Count di Luna *a young nobleman of Aragon*	baritone
Leonora *a lady-in-waiting to the Princess of Aragon*	soprano
Azucena *a gypsy*	mezzo-soprano
Manrico *an officer in the army of Prince Urgel, and the supposed son of Azucena*	tenor
Ferrando *a captain in the Count's army*	bass
Ines *Leonora's confidante*	soprano
Ruiz *a soldier in Manrico's service*	tenor
An Old Gypsy	bass
A Messenger	tenor

Leonora's female attendants, nuns, servants and armed retainers of the Count, gypsies, followers of Manrico, etc.

Setting Biscay and Aragon, in 1409

operas there were no more cavatinas, duets, trios, choruses, finales, etc. etc., and if the entire opera were, let's say, a single piece, I would find it more reasonable and just.

But, as so often with Verdi, his revolutionary statements in his writings were considerably toned down when it came to practical matters. Cammarano's draft libretto turned out to be fashioned along conventional lines, and Verdi made little objection.

In part owing to personal difficulties, work on the new opera moved along rather slowly. Verdi, who could by now write for more or less whichever theatre he chose in Italy, considered a number of places for the première, being particularly concerned with the availability of a first-rate Azucena. Eventually, in the middle of 1852, the Teatro Apollo in Rome was decided upon. But then, in July 1852, Cammarano died, leaving a draft of *Il trovatore* with many details in need of attention. Leone Emanuele Bardare was brought in, and was particularly involved in the expansion of Leonora's role, which Verdi had originally wished to minimize but now fashioned as a dramatic equal to Azucena, thus forming a symmetry with the pair of opposed male roles, Manrico and the Count. The première cast included Giovanni Guicciardi (Luna), Rosina Penco (Leonora), Emilia Goggi (Azucena) and Carlo Baucardé (Manrico), and the opera was a huge success. It very soon became the most popular of Verdi's works, both in Italy and around the world. In the mid-1850s Verdi created a revised version for a performance at the Paris Opéra, in part to ensure his French rights to the score. This revision, in a translation by Emilien Pacini, and entitled *Le trouvère*, included a ballet (placed after the opening chorus of Part 3), omitted Leonora's Part 4 cabaletta, 'Tu vedrai che amore in terra', and involved a substantial rewriting of the end of the opera (during which the 'Miserere' music returns in a lengthy coda).

PART 1: 'The Duel'

1.i *A hall in the Aliaferia palace* There is no overture or formal prelude, merely a series of martial arpeggios and horn calls to set the scene. Ferrando bids the sentries and servants keep alert: the Count fears that the troubadour who has sometimes been seen in the garden is his rival in love. At the chorus's bidding, Ferrando narrates the story of Garzia, the Count's brother. One day, when still a baby, Garzia was found with an old witch at his cradle. She was driven off, but the boy sickened and was thought to have been given the evil eye. The witch was sought out and burnt at the stake, but her daughter exacted a terrible revenge: on the day of the execution young Garzia disappeared, and the charred remains of a baby were found in the embers of the witch's funeral pyre. All this is told in a two-stanza narrative, each stanza divided into a relatively free introductory passage ('Di due figli'), and then a more formal 'aria' ('Abbietta zingara') in which violins double the voice in octaves (a typical trait of 'gypsy' style). The chorus rounds off each stanza with horrified comments. In freer recitative, run through with a good deal of winding chromaticism, Ferrando continues his narration. The old Count fell into a decline and died; nothing more was heard of the gypsy's daughter, though the old witch herself is said still to roam the skies at night. The chorus joins Ferrando in 'Sull'orlo dei tetti', a rapid stretta that conjures up the ghostly forces around them. At the climax, the chiming of the midnight bell causes universal panic, and all hurriedly disperse.

1.ii *The palace gardens* Leonora, restlessly wandering, tells her maid Ines how she met a mysterious knight at a tournament and how he vanished when civil war broke out. This is for the most part delivered in the spare, functional recitative typical of the opera, a style that makes the moments of arioso all the more effective. Leonora continues her story in the formal mould of a two-stanza Andante, 'Tacea la notte placida', a piece that moves from minor to major, flowering into an angular rising line as she describes how her lover has now returned as a troubadour to serenade her with melancholy songs. Ines suggests that Leonora should forget her lover, but in a highly ornamental cabaletta, 'Di tale amor', Leonora swears that she will die rather than lose him.

The ladies depart and the Count enters to declare his consuming passion for Leonora. He is about to climb up to her apartment when he hears a distant serenade: Manrico's 'Deserto sulla terra', a simple two-stanza canzone. Leonora hurries down to greet the troubadour, mistakenly addresses the Count, and is then accused of treachery by Manrico. The three principals finish the act with a two-movement trio, first an Allegro agitato ('Qual voce!') dominated by a breathless, disjointed figure from the violins, and then – ignoring the usual lyrical slow section – straight to a furious stretta ('Di geloso amor sprezzato'). The final curtain sees the Count and Manrico striding off to fight a duel as Leonora falls senseless to the ground.

PART 2: 'The Gypsy'

2.i *A ruined hovel on the lower slopes of a mountain in Biscay* The tonality, rhythms and melodic gestures of the orchestral introduction bring us back to the musical world of Part 1 scene i as the gypsies celebrate their return to work with the famous 'anvil' chorus, 'Chi del gitano i giorni abbella?' This is immediately juxtaposed with Azucena's canzone, 'Stride la vampa', an invocation of fire and destruction that hovers obsessively around the note *b'*. The gypsies retire (to a muted reprise of their chorus); Azucena tells Manrico of her mother's death at the stake, and of how she planned to take revenge by casting the old Count's son on to the embers of the fire. Her *racconto*, 'Condotta ell'era in ceppi', starts out formally controlled, with a repeating accompaniment figure and regular melodic periods; but as the tale unfolds the music breaks from its tonal and rhythmic confines, coming to an intense declamatory climax as Azucena admits that she mistakenly threw her own baby on to the fire.

'Il trovatore' (Verdi), Part 2 scene i (a ruined hovel on the lower slopes of a mountain in Biscay): Giuseppe and Pietro Bertoja's design for the production at La Fenice, Venice, 1853–4 season

Manrico asks whether he is, then, Azucena's son, but the gypsy diverts him with assurances of love and encourages him, in turn, to tell a story. Manrico's 'Mal reggendo' recounts his duel with the Count and how a strange voice commanded him not to deal the fatal blow; but with Azucena's answer it turns into the first lyrical movement of a 'dissimilar' duet. They are interrupted by Ruiz, who bears a letter telling Manrico that Leonora, thinking him dead, is about to enter a convent. Manrico resolves to go to her immediately, and so begins the duet cabaletta, 'Perigliarti ancor languente', in which Azucena begs him in vain not to court danger yet again.

2.ii *The cloister of a convent near Castellor* The Count is resolved to steal Leonora away from the convent and apostrophizes her in 'Il balen del suo sorriso', an 'aristocratically' graced Largo that exposes the baritone's full expressive range. A bell from the convent urges action, and the Count and his followers disperse to hide, the male chorus's 'Ardir, andiam' serving as a frame for the Count's vigorous cabaletta of expectation, 'Per me ora fatale'. A chorale-like chant from offstage nuns, which mingles with a restrained reprise of the chorus's 'Ardir, andiam', introduces Leonora. Her affecting arioso is cut short by the Count and then, to general amazement, by Manrico, whose sudden appearance precipitates the main lyrical section of the concertato finale, 'E deggio e posso crederlo?' Led off by a breathless Leonora, continued by the patterned opposition of the two male principals, the movement comes to a magnificent climax with Leonora's rising line, 'Sei tu dal ciel disceso, o in ciel son io con te?'. Action once more boils up as Manrico's followers surround the Count's men. With a final reprise of 'Sei tu dal ciel' (whose lyrical power functions in place of the usual stretta movement), Leonora rushes off with Manrico.

PART 3: 'The Gypsy's Son'

3.i *A military encampment* The Count's men are eager to mount an attack on Castellor and when Ferrando tells them they will move at dawn the next day they celebrate with the famous chorus 'Squilli, echeggi la tromba guerriera'. The Count is still in agony over his loss of Leonora when Ferrando brings in Azucena, who has been captured nearby. To divert attention under interrogation, Azucena lapses into her 'gypsy' mode, singing 'Giorni poveri vivea', a simple minor-mode song that unexpectedly flowers into the major as she mentions the love she has for her son. But Ferrando has guessed her true identity and in a concluding stretta, 'Deh! rallentate, o barbari', she begs for mercy, the Count exults and Ferrando and the chorus look forward to her death at the stake.

3.ii *A room adjoining the chapel at Castellor, with a balcony at the back* We move to the rival camp, where Leonora and Manrico are about to be married. Manrico calms his bride's fear with the Adagio 'Ah sì, ben mio, coll'essere', in which the tenor approaches most closely the 'aristocratic' musical world of Leonora and the Count, and which follows a 'progressive' tonal plan, beginning in F minor and finishing in D♭ major. The lovers indulge in a brief duet before Ruiz interrupts to inform Manrico of Azucena's capture. Manrico immediately summons his followers and prepares to mount a rescue operation, pausing only to sing the cabaletta 'Di quella pira'. This movement, which rudely casts Manrico back into the more direct musical world of the gypsies and is probably best known for its (unauthentic) high C's, hides within its blunt exterior a good number of those subtle harmonic and orchestral gestures that Verdi seemed so effortlessly to integrate with his most energetic music.

PART 4: 'The Execution'

4.i *A wing of the Aliaferia palace* It is now too late in the drama for even brief narratives, and we must grasp by deduction that Manrico's attack has failed and that he is now a prisoner of the Count. Leonora arrives to try to save him, and from outside the prison sings of her love in the Adagio 'D'amor sull'ali rosee', which retains her 'aristocratic' ornamental style, but now colours it with dark instrumental sonorities and a predominantly falling line. The ensuing *tempo di mezzo*, perhaps the most famous in Italian opera, magnificently combines three contrasting musical ideas: a solemn 'Miserere' sounding from within; Leonora's fragmented response, underpinned by a quiet yet insistent 'death' rhythm from the full orchestra; and Manrico's farewell to his beloved, 'Ah che la morte ognora', a simple melody that recalls his Act 1 serenade. The number concludes with Leonora's reiteration of her love in the cabaletta 'Tu vedrai che amore in terra' (often omitted in performance for fear of overtaxing the soprano).

The Count appears, determined to execute both Manrico and Azucena. The arrival of Leonora initiates a conventionally structured though powerfully condensed four-movement duet. The first movement involves rapid dialogue over an orchestral melody; then the opponents move to a formally fixed statement of their positions (the Andante mosso 'Mira di acerbe lagrime'), Leonora begging for the life of Manrico, the Count obstinate in his desire for revenge. But then, in the third movement, Leonora strikes a Tosca-like bargain: herself in exchange for her lover's life. The Count jubilantly agrees, failing to see that Leonora has secretly taken poison. They join in the celebratory cabaletta 'Vivrà! ... Contende il giubilo'.

4. ii *A grim prison* The Finale ultimo finds Manrico and Azucena languishing in prison. Azucena has a frightening vision of the death that awaits her, the orchestra recalling her 'Stride la vampa' of Part 2. With reassurances from Manrico, sleep gradually overcomes her. They join in the narcotic duet 'Sì, la stanchezza', which begins in the minor but moves to the parallel major for Manrico's 'Riposa, o madre' and Azucena's picture of the simple gypsy life, 'Ai nostri monti'. Leonora appears, telling Manrico that he is free to go; but he quickly guesses the nature of her bargain with the Count. He accuses her in the concertato 'Parlar non vuoi?', which includes Leonora's frantic attempts to defend herself and, in the later part, Azucena's somnolent reprise of 'Ai nostri monti'. Leonora collapses at Manrico's feet as the ensemble finishes; the poison begins to take effect, and soon the truth is out. In a second formal ensemble, 'Prima che d'altri vivere', Manrico and Leonora bid a tender farewell, the Count entering to add his comments in the later stages. As Leonora dies, the Count assumes control: Manrico is led off to the scaffold, and Azucena is forced to watch his execution. As the fatal blow falls, she tells the Count that he has just killed his own brother, and brings down the curtain with a final, exultant cry: her mother has been avenged.

* * *

Il trovatore, though without doubt one of the two or three most popular Verdi operas, has until recently fared rather badly with critics and commentators, mostly because of its unabashedly formalistic exterior in comparison with the works on either side of it, *Rigoletto* and *La traviata*. This attitude at last shows signs of changing, perhaps as our criteria for judging Verdi's musical dramas alter with time. Indeed, many of the most important stages in the critical rehabilitation of this opera have concentrated attention on just those aspects that were earlier castigated. The libretto, for example, with its immovable character types and 'unrealistic' stage action, has recently been seen as one of the work's great strengths, its economy of dramatic means and immediacy of language forming the perfect basis on which to build Verdian musical drama. Similarly, the extreme formalism of the musical language has been seen as serving to concentrate and define the various stages of the drama, above all channelling them into those key confrontations that mark its inexorable progress.

But if one trait can be singled out that best accounts for the opera's success, it is probably the sheer musical energy apparent in all the numbers. Time and again we find a relentless rhythmic propulsion in the accompaniment, and a tendency for the melodic lines to be forced into a restrictive compass, freeing themselves rarely but with consequent explosive power. This internal energy often runs through entire numbers, making a sense of progress across the various formal stages – from arioso to cantabile to cabaletta – that is just as convincing as the more radical, 'external' experiments with form encountered in the surrounding operas. ROGER PARKER

Trowell, Brian (Lewis) (*b* Wokingham, Berks., 21 Feb 1931). English scholar, director and translator. He studied at Cambridge and a distinguished academic career (largely as a medievalist) led to professorships at King's College, London (1974), and at Oxford (1988). He has shown both a scholarly and a practical concern with opera, as director of opera at the GSM (1963–7) and as head of BBC radio opera (1967–70). For the Barber Institute, University of Birmingham, he translated Rameau's *Hippolyte et Aricie* (1965) and Haydn's *Orfeo* (*L'anima del filosofo*, 1967). His translation of Handel's *Giulio Cesare*, also for the Barber Institute and subsequently given by the ENO, displays his combined literary and musical strengths. Other works he has translated include Handel's *Imeneo*, *Tamerlano* (both with Nigel Fortune), *Ariodante* and *Orlando*. As a director, he was responsible for a wide variety of productions at the GSM, including the first London performance of Peter Wishart's *The Captive* (1963). His fine essay '*Acis, Galatea and Polyphemus*: a "serenata a tre voci"?' appeared in *Music and Theatre: Essays in Honour of Winton Dean* (Cambridge, 1987, pp.31–93). ARTHUR JACOBS

Troyanos, Tatiana (*b* New York, 12 Sept 1938). American mezzo-soprano. She studied at the Juilliard School with Hans J. Heinz, making her début in 1963 as Hippolyta in the New York première of Britten's *A Midsummer Night's Dream* with the City Opera. After two seasons with the company, during which she sang Marina, Stravinsky's Jocasta, Cherubino and Carmen, in 1965 she made her European début as Preziosilla at Hamburg, where she remained for ten years; her roles there included Elisetta (*Il matrimonio segreto*), Dorabella and Baba the Turk, and she created Jeanne in Penderecki's *The Devils of Loudun* (1969). She has sung the Composer at the Aix-en-Provence, Munich and Edinburgh festivals, and Octavian at Salzburg, Covent Garden and the Metropolitan (where she made her début in 1976). Her other roles include Handel's Ariodante (which she sang at the inauguration of the Kennedy Center, Washington, in 1971), Charlotte, Poppaea, Adalgisa (in which she made her La Scala début in 1977), Romeo (*I Capuleti*), Eboli, Geschwitz, Santuzza, Berlioz's Dido and Brangäne. She has a warm, flexible voice of wide range and is a highly emotional actress.

*

M. Mayer: 'Tatiana Troyanos', *Opera*, xxxvi (1985), 268–72

HAROLD ROSENTHAL/R

Troyens, Les ('The Trojans'). *Opéra* in five acts by HECTOR BERLIOZ to his own libretto after VIRGIL's *Aeneid*; Paris, Théâtre Lyrique, 4 November 1863 (Acts 3–5, as *Les Troyens à Carthage*); Karlsruhe, 6–7 December 1890 (complete).

Enée [Aeneas] *Trojan hero, son of Venus and Anchises*	tenor
Chorèbe [Coroebus] *Asian prince, Cassandra's fiancé*	baritone
Panthée [Panthous] *Trojan priest, friend of Aeneas*	bass
Narbal *minister to Dido*	bass
Iopas *Tyrian poet to Dido's court*	tenor
Ascagne [Ascanius] *15-year-old son of Aeneas*	soprano
Cassandre [Cassandra] *Trojan prophetess, Priam's daughter*	mezzo-soprano
Didon [Dido] *Queen of Carthage, widow of Sichée [Sychaeus] Prince of Tyre*	mezzo-soprano
Anna *Dido's sister*	contralto
Hylas *a young Phrygian sailor*	tenor/contralto
Priam *King of Troy*	bass
A Greek Chieftain	bass
Ghost of Hector	bass
Helenus *a Trojan priest, Priam's son*	tenor
Two Trojan Soldiers	basses
Mercure [Mercury]	baritone/bass
A Priest of Pluto	bass
Polyxène [Polyxena] *Cassandra's sister*	soprano
Hécube [Hecuba] *Queen of Troy*	soprano
Andromaque [Andromache] *Hector's widow*	silent
Astyanax *her 8-year-old son*	silent

Trojans, Greeks, Tyrians, Carthaginians, nymphs, satyrs, fauns, sylvans, invisible spirits

Setting Troy (Acts 1 and 2) and Carthage (Acts 3–5) in classical antiquity

Berlioz was encouraged to undertake an opera on the *Aeneid* by Liszt's mistress, the Princess Carolyne Sayn-Wittgenstein, during his visits to Weimar in 1855–6. His *Mémoires*, compiled for the most part between 1848 and 1854, trace the lure of Virgil to the 'budding imagination' of his childhood. The scene of Dido on her funeral pyre was but the most vividly remembered of these 'epic passions for which instinct had prepared me'. In his writings Berlioz often cites the *Aeneid*, in Latin and from memory (and often, therefore, with errors). Yet his correspondence lacks the references to compositional ferment over *Les Troyens* that exist for the funeral and Napoleonic works, the Shakespearian compositions and *Faust*. The implication is that until then he had considered Virgil too hallowed for operatic setting, especially in view of the shoddy treatment an operatic *Aeneid* might receive in production. In any case it was the sort of project best reserved for one's seniority. When in 1856 he began to compose the libretto and some of the music, Berlioz had just been elected to the Institute and was enjoying the pinnacle of his success as a conductor. His domestic situation was stable at last. His health, on the other hand, had begun its long decline: anything he wrote he might not live to see performed. Conditions favoured a valediction.

Les Troyens was completed for the most part by April 1858. Berlioz devoted much of the next half-decade, unsuccessfully, to securing its production at the Opéra. Even the three acts staged as *Les Troyens à Carthage* at the Théâtre Lyrique in 1863 lasted unadulterated but a single night, following which number after number was trimmed away, beginning with the Royal Hunt and Storm. Transmission of the source materials was compromised accordingly. Only 15 copies of the complete vocal score were made – at the composer's expense – before the mutilations began. In successive generations *Les Troyens* circulated in the flawed, misordered and incomplete vocal scores of *La prise de Troie* and *Les Troyens à Carthage* published by Choudens in conjunction with the 1863 production. In his will of 29 July 1867 Berlioz complained bitterly of Choudens' unmet contractual obligation to engrave the full score (and that of *Benvenuto Cellini*), but left to his executors the responsibility of seeing that it 'be published without cuts, without modifications, without the least suppression of the text – in sum, exactly as it stands'. The firm was subsequently enjoined by lawsuit to meet the provisions of the contract. Full scores of *La prise de Troie* and *Les Troyens à Carthage*, along with orchestral parts and an improved vocal score, appeared in the late 1880s. Of these only the vocal score was offered for sale, access to the more significant sources being limited to short-term hire.

Such chaos inevitably meant the slow assimilation of *Les Troyens* into the canon of the century's great operas. A more or less complete version was presented in Karlsruhe in December 1890 under Felix Mottl and elsewhere in Germany in the decade following; shortened versions began to be presented in Paris in 1921. Momentum towards a serious performance tradition for *Les Troyens* was established by the 1957 Covent Garden production under Rafael Kubelík, an event which in many respects fostered the renaissance in Berlioz studies of the 1960s. The Berlioz centennial year, 1969, saw the publication of a definitive score, a new production at Covent Garden and the release of a now famous recording, part of the Colin Davis Berlioz cycle. The 1973 production at the Metropolitan Opera, New York, was televised nationally and later issued as a video. In March 1990 a *Les Troyens* billed as 'intégrale', but in fact lacking the ballets, opened the new Opéra Bastille in Paris.

ACT 1 *The site of the former Greek encampment on the Trojan plain* The Greeks have lifted their siege of ten years, and the Trojans rejoice near the tomb of the Greek hero Achilles, discovering on the plain the debris of battle and, offstage, the enormous horse that has been left behind. Three shepherds perched on the tomb play their 'antique flutes' (the same as the 'flutes of Dindymus' called for elsewhere in the score), their recurring motif rendered by the orchestral oboes. There has been no overture, and the accompaniment of the first scene is primarily for winds, such that use of the full string choir is delayed for Cassandra's entry. Alone, she is agitated by dark premonitions; she has seen the ghost of Hector wandering the ramparts of Troy. Neither King Priam nor the Trojan people, she complains in her aria 'Malheureux roi!', will heed her warnings of the disaster to befall that very night. Even her suitor Coroebus thinks she has lost her reason. His tender *cavatine* implores her to abandon her visions of catastrophe and return to her senses, but to no avail.

Nor is she able, in their frantic duet, to convince him to flee the city. Instead she gives Coroebus her hand and the chaste kiss of a bride. Death will prepare their nuptial bed.

A march and solemn hymn of thanksgiving signal the processional entry of the Trojan court. The wrestling and games that follow are interrupted by the appearance of Hector's widow, Andromache, and their son, Astyanax, each dressed in the white mourning costume of Trojan tradition. A dolorous clarinet solo accompanies their mute progress downstage. Astyanax, heir to the throne of Troy, lays a basket of flowers at the altar as his mother kneels and prays; she then presents the frightened child to Priam and Hecuba. Andromache, overcome with emotion, lowers her veil to hide her tears. The crowd parts before them and, as they disappear, murmurs a mournful sigh. Descended in spirit from the trombone invocation of the *Symphonie funèbre* and the concluding bars of the *Marche funèbre pour la dernière scène d'Hamlet*, this pantomime is one of Berlioz's most ravishing passages.

Aeneas bursts in with news of Laocoön's death. (This is an error of stagecraft – Aeneas had already entered during the processional march and hymn.) Laocoön, having hurled his javelin into the horse and exhorted the Trojans to set it afire, was set upon and devoured live by two monstrous sea-serpents. The horrified company reacts in a majestic fugal octet and double chorus: such awful chastisement of Laocoön, a priest, is taken to be the vengeance of Pallas, to whom it is now imagined the Greeks must have offered the horse as an act of contrition. Priam and Aeneas, to beg pardon of the goddess for Laocoön's sacrilege, order the huge idol to be brought through the city gates to the Palladium. Cassandra weeps at the thought of her proud nation charging mindlessly towards its destruction. In the distance begins the Trojan march, sacred hymn of Ilium; the *cortège* eventually reaches the stage, but in neither Berlioz's libretto nor the autograph score is there an indication that the horse is seen by the audience. Suddenly there is confusion: the rattle of arms is heard inside the horse. But the people regard this as a good omen, and the helpless Cassandra at length follows the procession into Troy – there, she knows, to die in its ruins.

ACT 2.i *A room in the palace of Aeneas* Aeneas has fallen asleep in his armour. Ascanius, terrified by the sounds of battle, hurries towards his father, but when the din subsides he is embarrassed to wake him and runs away. Out of the darkness materializes the bloody and dishevelled ghost of Hector. The collapse of a building rouses Aeneas. In cadaverous recitative Hector announces that the Greeks have taken the walls of Troy and begun to burn the city. To Aeneas are entrusted his nation's children and sacred idols; in Italy, after long wanderings at sea, he will establish a mighty empire and die a hero's death. Panthus brings the idols, and he and Aeneas are soon joined by Ascanius, Coroebus and their warriors. Together they go off to defend the citadel protecting Priam's palace.

2.ii *A gallery in the palace* The sack of Troy is under way. The Trojan women pray before the sacred flame of Vesta-Cybele, their incantations penetrated from time to time by the trumpets of encroaching battle. Aeneas, Cassandra tells them, has liberated those trapped at the citadel and taken Priam's treasure; his force is marching towards Mount Ida, called by destiny to Italy, the new Troy. Coroebus has been killed. When the women cry that nothing can save them from the Grecian rape, Cassandra proffers her dagger and indicates as similar instruments of suicide the silken belts of their garments and a parapet over the square. The women take lyres and begin an ecstatic hymn, 'Complices de sa gloire'; a few cowards are driven away in shame. Cassandra, too, takes a lyre, and it is during this awesome bacchanale that Greek soldiers enter to demand the treasure. Scorning them, Cassandra stabs herself and Polyxena follows suit. As the Greeks discover that Aeneas and his band have escaped with the treasure, the women turn towards Mount Ida and salute the retreating Trojans with the prophetic 'Italy! Italy!'. Some leap from the parapet; others stab themselves or draw the silken belts around their necks. Cassandra, unable to reach the parapet, falls dead on the last cry of 'Italy!'.

ACT 3 *Dido's throne-room at Carthage* The Carthaginians celebrate the return of good weather and sunshine after a violent tempest. Dido and her retinue arrive during the Carthaginian national anthem, her subjects waving palm fronds and tossing flowers towards their queen. In her recitative and aria we learn that seven years have passed since Dido fled with her people from Tyre and the tyrant who murdered her husband. Now their city flourishes, but they must prepare for war, for the arrogant Numidian Iarbas seeks to impose marriage on her. The multitude, aroused, vow to drive the Numidians back to the desert. Dido, however, has commanded this festival to celebrate the works of peace, and builders, sailors and farmers come forward to receive gifts. Resolved to become military heroes, they leave Dido and Anna to themselves.

In their duet Dido confesses to feelings of uneasiness she cannot understand. Anna, sensing the issue at hand, assures her she will again be loved and suggests that Carthage needs a king. But Dido's marriage vows require her fidelity to the memory of Sychaeus, whose ring remains on her finger. Iopas interrupts them to announce that representatives of an unidentified fleet, driven towards Carthage during the recent storm, seek an audience. Dido extends them welcome. The Trojan March, now in the minor mode, accompanies the entry of Ascanius, Panthous and the Trojan chieftains. Among them is Aeneas, disguised as a sailor. In exchange for shelter Ascanius brings Dido tribute: Iliona's sceptre, Hecuba's crown, Helen's veil – proof that they are Trojans.

Dido instructs the youth to assure Aeneas that his band may take refuge in her city. But the promised repose must wait, for the Numidian invasion has begun. The Carthaginians, though valorous, are short of weapons, and the odds are against them. Aeneas, casting off his cloak, identifies himself and offers his men and arms to Carthage. Dido is smitten at once by this legendary hero, now dazzling in his tunic and breastplate. Pausing to embrace Ascanius and entrust him to Dido's care, Aeneas summons the new allies to battle. The Carthaginians trade their scythes and slings for Trojan armament as the curtain falls.

ACT 4.i *A forest near Carthage* In the Royal Hunt and Storm, a ballet-pantomime, water nymphs dart about the pool, and then are frightened by sounds of the hunt. Hunters enter with their dogs, but disperse when a storm gathers; their calls echo through the forest. Dido, dressed as Diana the huntress, and Aeneas enter on foot and take refuge in a cave. In the tumult one can

1. 'Les Troyens' (Berlioz): design by Philippe Chaperon for the grand floral hall in Dido's palace at Carthage (the throne-room) in the original production of 'Les Troyens à Carthage' ('Les Troyens', Acts 3–5) at the Théâtre Lyrique, 4 November 1863

distinguish voices and then cries of 'Italy! Italy!'. The stream overflows and waterfalls form; a tree is struck by lightning and catches fire. The storm abates. The clouds disperse.

4.ii *Dido's garden on the shore* Since the defeat of the Numidians, Narbal observes, Dido has neglected the enterprises of her kingdom in favour of hunting and feasting. The Trojans, moreover, stay on. Anna responds that in conflicts between destiny and the heart the greater of the gods is Love. Narbal's fears of impending disaster contrasted with Anna's delight in the state of things come together in a typically Berliozian *réunion des thèmes*. As the orchestral winds play a restrained version of the national anthem over unsettling figuration in the violins, Dido takes her seat for the evening's *divertissement* by Egyptian girls, slaves and Nubian slave women. Unimpressed, she reclines on her couch and directs Iopas to sing a simple song of the fields.

Dido's anxieties are unrelieved, and she turns to Aeneas, asking him to finish his sad tale of the miseries of Troy and to tell her the fate of the beautiful Andromache. Andromache, he begins, was taken in slavery by Pyrrhus, but at length succumbed to her captor and married him. Startled by this precedent of remarriage, Dido senses circumstance conspiring to make her abandon her grief for her late husband. Here begins the great quintet: Ascanius, leaning against his bow like a statue of Cupid, draws the wedding ring from Dido's finger as Anna, Iopas and Narbal look on. Aeneas, rising, turns Dido's attention from melancholy stories to the enchanted Mediterranean night, and in following him she leaves the ring behind on the couch. A shimmering, palpitating magic settles over the scene. During the nocturne for septet and chorus, 'Tout n'est que paix et charme autour de nous', the company slips away. In the celebrated love duet, 'Nuit d'ivresse', Dido and Aeneas compare their love to other epic passions just as Jessica and Lorenzo do in *The Merchant of Venice*. Towards the end they retire, arm in arm, their last refrain heard from the wings. Suddenly Mercury appears in a ray of moonlight, crosses to the column where Aeneas's breastplate hangs, and strikes it with his caduceus. Stretching his arm towards the sea, he intones the now familiar, and suddenly urgent, 'Italy! Italy! Italy!', and vanishes.

ACT 5.i *The Trojan camp at the harbour* It is night. While two sentinels patrol the shore, the Phrygian youth Hylas sings wistfully of the homeland to which he will never return. Panthous and the Trojan captains, preparing to leave, note the parallels with that fatal night in Troy: once again the ghost of Hector has been seen, now followed by a retinue of shades. A ghostly chorus of 'Italy! Italy! Italy!' sends them hurrying into their tents. The sentries continue their watch, grumbling to each other at having to leave Carthage for the boredom of the sea. They withdraw before Aeneas, who in his single extended recitative and aria, 'Inutiles regrets', determines to postpone his sacred mission long enough to exchange a last, supreme adieu with his beloved queen. Yet when the ghosts of Priam, Coroebus, Hector and Cassandra command him to delay no longer, he wakes the Trojans and hurries them to their ships to embark before daybreak. He directs a terse but noble farewell towards the palace, then turns to answer his destiny. A thunderstorm rises as the ships begin to move. In the confusion Dido rushes frantically onstage, powerless to arrest this sudden and, to her, inexplicable turn of events. Over strains of the Trojan March she curses Aeneas and the Trojan gods, then flees. From Aeneas and the Trojans comes a last, lusty chorus, 'Italy! Italy! Italy!'.

5.ii *A room in Dido's palace at dawn* Some of the vessels have reached the high sea. Dido's first thought is of sending Anna and Narbal to beg Aeneas to grant her a few days more; then, enraged, she gives the futile order to pursue and burn his ships. Finally she dismisses her attendants to construct a pyre on which the hateful souvenirs of their love might melt in flames. In her monologue, 'Je vais mourir', she resolves to die as well. She bids adieu to her proud city, to Anna, to Africa, the music and text momentarily recalling the love duet.

5.iii *The palace gardens* A pyre has been erected; on its platform are a bust of Aeneas, his toga, helmet and sword, and the bed he had shared with Dido. The priests of Pluto enter with Narbal and Anna, who, in the ritual of sacrifice, loosens Dido's hair and removes her left shoe. Dido climbs to the platform and throws Aeneas's toga and her own veil – symbols of an unhappy love – on to the bundles of wood, but at the sight of Aeneas's armour swoons on the bed. With the prophetic gifts of those about to meet their death, she foresees her memory avenged by the Carthaginian hero Hannibal. Thereupon she draws Aeneas's sword from the scabbard and stabs herself. She rises three times, now seeing all too clearly Carthage vanquished by eternal Rome. At the moment of her death the people curse Aeneas and his race, but the music is that of the Trojan March and in the distance one perceives an apotheosis: at the Roman Capitol victorious legions pass in review before the emperor, his poets and his artists.

* * *

Berlioz intended from the beginning that *Les Troyens* should be on an epic scale, but he was equally determined to limit its length to four and a half hours. In its duration, therefore, the opera is not especially unusual. The question of length did, however, lead Berlioz to adopt the short and rather abrupt finale that replaces the more ambitious tableau he had originally written.

Les Troyens is technically speaking a number opera, yet within the scenes the advance of the long, intricate story is aggressive and seldom interrupted. Berlioz crafts the seams between the movements with particular finesse, often using shifts of tonality (for instance, the rise from F to G♭ between the septet and love duet) and texture (the sudden *a cappella* fugue for 'Châtiment effroyable') to articulate new turns of dramatic intent. And while *Les Troyens* has strong roots in past operatic practice, Berlioz is less interested in traditional recitative and aria than in freer structures such as monologue, *scène* and pantomime. Dialogue and narrative often seem to be set down over primarily orchestral movements: the sentinels' march in Act 5, for example, and much of the *cérémonie funèbre*, a dirge with mournful winds. The prominent role the orchestra can play in establishing imagery had, of course, been a lesson of the dramatic symphonies; in some respects Berlioz's practice is not so different from Wagner's of the same period.

Orchestral commentary enriches the dramatic impact of *Les Troyens* at every turn. One of its threads is the kind of thematic recall common in Romantic music: the frequent allusion to, and transformation of, the Trojan March, for example, or the surging string figures that convey Cassandra's distress, or the semitone oscillations of the flutes of Dindymus (recalled, from the opening scene, in both the finale of Act 1 and the Royal Hunt and Storm). In the closing bars of Act 3, conversely, Berlioz foreshadows the opening of the Hunt and Storm. Orchestral representations of heartbeats, sighs and other agitations of the spirit are as typical of *Les Troyens* as of the *Fantastique* and *Faust*. Stopped horns

2. 'Aeneas telling Dido of the Misfortunes of Troy': painting (1815) by Pierre-Narcisse Guérin which inspired the Act 4 quintet of 'Les Troyens' (letter from Berlioz to his sister, Adèle, 12 March 1857)

and ghostly string harmonics evoke the supernatural world. In the Hunt and Storm virtually every stage action has an orchestral equivalence, and here, too, occurs a mixture of mythical, sexual and atmospheric symbolism that shows Berlioz's Romanticism at its most vivid.

In short, Berlioz's understanding of sonority as a poetic device is profound, beginning with the choice of the mezzo-soprano voice for each of the heroines. The clarinet solo for the pantomime of Andromache and Astyanax is of wrenching loneliness, as is the two-bar reference to it when, in Act 3, Ascanius begins to weep while bidding his father farewell; of similar impact is the singular appearance of the bass clarinet during the funeral ceremony. Percussion, oboes and harps approximate what Berlioz understood to be the sounds of classical antiquity. Antiphonal and offstage effects lace the work and lend it its epic size; of these the most substantial is in the finale of Act 1, with its three offstage bands placed to suggest the long, slow approach of the Trojan Horse. The orchestra is typical of the large Berlioz force, with piccolos, english horn, four bassoons, trumpets and piston cornets, a large battery, a half-dozen or more harps, and another two dozen players offstage – and, of course, the immense chorus. Yet, as in the Requiem, the full complement is summoned only now and again: it is in the division and permutation of his legions that Berlioz most revels.

A central tenet of his artistic creed was that the union of music and poetry held incomparably greater power than either art alone. In writing his own libretto, he gave himself the freedom to perfect both the story and the lyrics as part of the compositional process. (The poetry, though *passé* for the 1860s, is always serviceable and often lovely, and both writing it and setting it certainly stimulated his imagination more than anything a professional librettist had ever provided for him.) By *Les Troyens* he had become a master of design, imagery and multi-dimensional architecture, and what resulted from his particular sense of the composer as hero was a marked solidarity of overall structure. It is not just Aeneas who elides Cassandra's world and Dido's, but the Trojan March, the chorus, the ghosts and the gods – too much, in short, for *Les Troyens* to survive being divided in two. *Les Troyens à Carthage* was after all a compromise, accepted as a necessity by a composer who imagined his weeks to be numbered; *La prise de Troie* was never more than a title of convenience. To imagine *Les Troyens* as a succession of two self-contained operas is not merely to embrace a historical accident but to miss the opera's point entirely. D. KERN HOLOMAN

Trübensee, Josef. *See* TRIEBENSEE, JOSEF.

Truinet, Charles-Louis-Etienne. *See* NUITTER, CHARLES-LOUIS-ETIENNE.

Tsar Saltan. Opera by N. A. Rimsky-Korsakov; *see* *TALE OF TSAR SALTAN, THE.*

Tsar's Bride, The [*Tsarskaya nevesta*]. Opera in four acts by NIKOLAY ANDREYEVICH RIMSKY-KORSAKOV to a libretto by Il'ya Fyodorovich Tyumenev based on a scenario by the composer after the drama by Lev Alexandrovich Mey; Moscow, Solodovnikov Theatre (Savva Mamontov's Private Russian Opera), 22 October/3 November 1899.

Vasily Stepanovich Sobakin *Novgorod merchant*	bass
Marfa *his daughter*	soprano
Grigory Grigor'yevich Gryaznoy (*oprichniki*)	baritone
Grigory Luk'yanovich Malyuta-Skuratov (*oprichniki*)	bass
Ivan Sergeyevich Lïkov *nobleman*	tenor
Lyubasha	mezzo-soprano
Elisa Bomelius *the tsar's physician*	tenor
Domna Ivanovna Saburova *a merchant's wife*	soprano
Dunyasha *her daughter, Marfa's friend*	contralto
Petrovna *the Sobakins' housekeeper*	mezzo-soprano
The Royal Oven-Stoker	bass
An Immured Maiden	mezzo-soprano
Young Lad	tenor
'Two Noble Horsemen' (Ivan the Terrible and an *oprichnik* companion)	silent roles

Oprichniki, singers and dancers, nobles, immured maidens, servants, crowd

Setting Alexandrovskaya sloboda (Ivan the Terrible's personal headquarters), autumn 1572

Although usually described as a historical opera, *The Tsar's Bride* is based on a wholly fictional drama that conjures an imaginary tragedy out of the tantalizing documentary vacuum surrounding Ivan the Terrible's brief third marriage, to a commoner named Marfa Sobakina. A lurid compound of jealousy, murder, potions and madness, Mey's play was from the first an opera in search of a composer, and before Rimsky set it Borodin (at Balakirev's urging) had considered it. Rimsky's first inclination towards the play dates from 1891, a period of disillusion and creative blockage following the failure of *Mlada*. The demonstrative traditionalism of his eventual setting surely reflects the consequences of that crisis.

The première was conducted by Mikhail Ippolitov-Ivanov, with Nadeshda Zabela as Marfa, Anton Sekar-Rozhansky as Lïkov and Vasily Shkafer as Bomelius.

ACT 1: 'The Banquet'

A large reception room in Gryaznoy's house
Gryaznoy, a high-ranking member of the tsar's special retinue known as the *oprichniki*, broods over his failure to win the hand of Marfa, who has been promised by her father Sobakin to the young nobleman Ivan (Vanya) Lïkov, her childhood sweetheart. He vows that their wedding shall not come to pass. His guests, including Lïkov, his fellow-*oprichnik* Malyuta and the tsar's German physician Bomelius, arrive for a banquet. Lïkov describes the wonders he has seen in Germany. Entertainers are brought out. They first sing a toast to the tsar to the famous folk melody (the only such quotation in the score) familiar to all operagoers from the Coronation Scene in Musorgsky's *Boris Godunov* (though its earliest use in Russian opera goes back to Franz Xaver Blyma's *Old-Time Yuletide* of 1798); thereafter the melody functions in the opera as one of the tsar's leitmotifs. Next the entertainers perform a choral dance-song; Gryaznoy shows off the singing of his mistress, Lyubasha, whose melancholy strophic song in the style of a traditional Russian *protyazhnaya* ('drawn-out song') is set unaccompanied except for ritornellos, and with melismas on the repeat. The guests leave. Gryaznoy calls Bomelius aside; Lyubasha, noticing this, hides and eavesdrops on their conversation. Pretending he is acting on another's behalf, Gryaznoy requests a love

potion; Bomelius agrees to supply it; Lyubasha realizes Gryaznoy wants it for his own use because he no longer loves her. When Bomelius leaves, Lyubasha confronts Gryaznoy, imploring him to love her; he leaves impatiently for matins. Crazed with jealousy, Lyubasha swears revenge on her unknown rival.

ACT 2: 'The Baleful Potion'

A street at evening in the Alexandrovskaya sloboda; the houses of Sobakin and Bomelius are visible People streaming from the monastery after vespers chatter about the weather and the latest news; a band of aggressive *oprichniki* passes by, filling the crowd with alarm; two boys, leaving Bomelius's house with medicine, are persuaded by the superstitious crowd to throw away the package they have received from the 'evil sorcerer'. The stage empties. Marfa enters with Dunyasha and expresses her joy at being reunited with Lïkov after his foreign campaign. Two noble horsemen suddenly appear; one of them gazes intently at Marfa – the orchestral music, compounded of the 'Slava' melody and Ivan the Terrible's leitmotif from Rimsky's first opera, *The Maid of Pskov*, identifies him as the tsar. Marfa does not recognize him but feels great foreboding. Sobakin and Lïkov join Marfa and Dunyasha, who greet them affectionately. They all enter the Sobakin residence. An orchestral intermezzo based on Lyubasha's song from Act 1 accompanies her sinister entrance; she peers through the window of the Sobakin house, espies the beautiful Marfa and despairingly divines that she is her rival. She calls Bomelius out of his house and demands from him a potion that will cause a person to lose her beauty, offering her jewels in payment. Bomelius demands her love; she rejects him, but he threatens to expose her. Lïkov, leaving the Sobakins' house, promises to bring Gryaznoy with him the next day. Lyubasha is beside herself; in a passion, she runs to Bomelius's house, receives the potion, and is dragged inside. The *oprichniki* reappear, vowing to destroy any who oppose the tsar.

ACT 3: 'The Best Man'

The receiving room in the Sobakin home Sobakin, Lïkov and Gryaznoy are discussing Marfa's wedding to Lïkov, at which Gryaznoy will be the best man. But the betrothal cannot be announced until the tsar has chosen his bride. It seems he has assembled 2000 girls from all over Russia for inspection, and has narrowed the search down to 12, among them both Marfa and Dunyasha. Lïkov is apprehensive; the dissembling Gryaznoy lightly reassures him. Saburova, Dunyasha's mother, enters boasting to Sobakin that the tsar seemed to favour her daughter at the inspection; Lïkov breathes easier (his aria was inserted at Sekar-Rozhansky's request after the first performance). The nuptial pair is toasted, Gryaznoy having slipped his potion into Marfa's cup (sextet with chorus), and a traditional wedding song is sung in their praise. Suddenly Petrovna announces Malyuta, with word from the tsar: he has chosen Marfa to be his bride.

ACT 4: 'The Bride'

A hall in the tsar's palace Sobakin, now a boyar, laments the mysterious illness that has befallen his daughter, now the tsarina-elect. A messenger from the tsar is announced: it is Gryaznoy, with news that Lïkov has confessed to having tried to poison Marfa and has been executed, Gryaznoy himself having carried out the sentence. Marfa faints (quintet with chorus, 'Zagublena stradalitsa tsarevna!': 'Our afflicted princess is ruined'); when she revives, delirious, she mistakes Gryaznoy for Lïkov (scena and aria, 'Ivan Sergeyevich, khochesh' v sad poydyom?': 'Ivan Sergeyevich, shall we go to the garden?'). Gryaznoy is overcome with remorse; he confesses that he is responsible for Marfa's illness because Bomelius had given him poison instead of a love potion. But now Lyubasha rushes in, confessing that it was she who made the substitution. She asks to be killed; Gryaznoy, in a frenzy, stabs her with his dagger. He is led away prisoner, but first takes tender leave of the demented Marfa, who, to general horror, looks on him fondly and whispers, 'Come again tomorrow, Vanya'.

* * *

The vocal idiom of *The Tsar's Bride* is essentially that of the magnified romance, and for this reason the opera is a natural counterpart not to anything else in Rimsky-Korsakov's oeuvre but to Tchaikovsky's *Enchantress* or (for a better-known comparison) his *Queen of Spades*. In its extremely effective exploitation of opulent vocal display Rimsky's opera is an emulatory tribute to his late rival's 'Imperial style' (though its first performances took place under private sponsorship at a time when Rimsky was *persona non grata* on the Imperial stage).

Traces of the 'old' Rimsky-Korsakov inhere in the archaic setting, which required, or gave pretext for, some decorative numbers in 'neo-Russian' style; there is also a tendency to employ harmonic progressions based on circles of major or minor 3rds (formerly the exclusive property of his 'fantastic' characters) at moments of high drama or suspense (e.g. the orchestral prelude to Act 4, recalling Lyubasha's spying in Act 2; or Marfa's concluding mad scene, recalling her first aria). Some of the music – particularly the unaccountably fugal chorus of *oprichniki* at the Act 1 banquet, or the excessively decorous genre scene at the beginning of Act 2 – may compare unfavourably with 'kuchkist' tradition, but most of it is dramatically apt and economical, the work of a seasoned master taking justifiable pride in his mastery.

In the fourth act, with its extended quintet with chorus, the synergy between formal control and dramatic tension is undeniable. Here Rimsky proved wholly worthy of his models, which despite the many leitmotifs no longer included Wagner. With the exception of the unseen tsar's, these are of the 'recalling' rather than the 'identifying' variety, the kind of which Verdi, not Wagner, was the past master.

For placing greater emphasis on mastery than on stylistic adventure (and especially for doing so at a time when stylistic adventure was elsewhere reaching the stage of an obsession), Rimsky-Korsakov has been much maligned by modernist critics (including his erstwhile pupil Stravinsky) who identify with Musorgsky. But in context the composer of *The Tsar's Bride* is better seen in his late phase as a representative of a self-conscious classicism – an excellent Salieri if not a Mozart – in whom his musical countrymen have taken enormous pride, both for what he was and for what he came to represent. RICHARD TARUSKIN

Tsarskaya nevesta. Opera by N. A. Rimsky-Korsakov; *see* TSAR'S BRIDE, THE.

Tsarskoye Selo [now Pushkin]. Town in Russia, outside St Petersburg. The name means 'royal village'; it was renamed Detskoye Selo ('Children's Village') in 1918 and renamed for Pushkin, who had lived there, on his centenary in 1937. The suburban residence of Catherine the Great, it is the site of a magnificent complex of palaces and gardens. Two operas by Paisiello were produced there: *Demetrio* (13/24 June 1779, in a revised version), to a libretto by Metastasio; and *Lo sposo burlato*, a *dramma giocoso* in two acts to a libretto by G. B. Casti, presented later that same summer. The main significance of Tsarskoye Selo for the history of opera in Russia lies in its being the site of the first performance of *Anyuta*, the first comic opera in Russian (26 August/6 September 1772). The text, by the actor Mikhail Popov, was modelled on Favart's *Annette et Lubin*, and the score (now lost), like that of its model, was probably a compilation of popular tunes. The composer or arranger is not named in the printed libretto (St Petersburg, 1772). RICHARD TARUSKIN

Tsikotski, Yevgeny Karlovich. *See* TIKOTSKY, YEVGENY KARLOVICH.

Tsintsadze, Sulkhan Fyodorovich (*b* Gori, 23 Aug 1925). Georgian composer. A member of the State Quartet of Georgia (1944–6), he studied the cello at the conservatories of Tbilisi and later Moscow, where he was also a composition pupil of Bogatïryov. From the early 1960s he taught at the Tbilisi Conservatory, of which he was rector from 1965. In 1968 he was appointed to the board of the Composers' Union of the USSR, and he has received many honours and awards. Tsintsadze's output includes works in various genres, although in the earlier part of his career he concentrated particularly on music for string quartet. His opera *Okros verdzi* ('The Golden Fleece') was produced in 1952 and the one-act *Gandegili* ('The Hermit') in 1972. Tsintsadze's many film scores have earned him popularity throughout the USSR.

Okros verdzi [The Golden Fleece] (G. G. Gelovani and G. Tsagareli), 1952
Ablabuda [The Spider's Web] (musical comedy), Tbilisi, 1960
Simgera tkeshi [A Song in the Forest] (musical comedy), Tbilisi, 1967
Gandegili [The Hermit] (1, P. Gruzinsky, after I. G. Chavchavadze), Tbilisi, 20 Dec 1972
Shvejki Franc Josefis tsinaagmdeg [Schweik against Franz Joseph] (musical comedy), Tbilisi, 1976

*

I. Bakhtadze: 'Akhali kartuli opera' [A New Georgian Opera], *Sabchota khelovneba* (1973), no.1, p.78
M. Pichkhadze: 'Opera Sulkhana Tsintsadze', *SovM* (1974), no.5, pp.40–43 YEVGENY MACHAVARIANI

Tubin, Eduard (*b* Kalaste, 5/18 June 1905; *d* Stockholm, 17 Nov 1982). Estonian composer. He studied composition at the Tartu Academy (1924–30) and was then conductor of the Vanemuine Theatre Orchestra (1930–44) in the same city. Keenly interested in new music, he conducted Stravinsky's Symphony of Psalms in Tallinn in 1936, and two years later he met Kodály in Budapest and became acquainted with Bartók's work. In 1944 he moved to Sweden. He composed two operas, *Barbara von Tisenhusen*, which was first performed in Tallinn on 4 December 1969, and *Reigi Ōpetaja* ('The Priest of Reigi', 1971), whose première was in Tartu on 10 June 1979. Both are tragic and violent love stories based on historical events, and are adapted from short stories by Aino Kallas. *Barbara von Tisenhusen*, a psychological drama in three acts and nine scenes to a libretto by Jaan Kross, was commissioned by the Estonia Theatre. The opera is set in Estonia in 1551; a noble maiden Barbara (soprano), after a love affair with the socially inferior Franz Bonnius (tenor), is drowned by her brothers in an ice-covered pond as punishment. The symphonic development of the opera is based on a chaconne. *The Priest of Reigi*, to a libretto by Kross and Kallas, is notable for its court scene in which the accused lovers, brought to trial by the woman's husband (the priest) are the only singers, while the others on stage speak over a fughetta in the orchestra. Tubin admired Alfred Hitchcock's methods of creating suspense. His expressively orchestrated music often combines propulsive rhythm with expansive melody. HARRY OLT

Tucci, Gabriella (*b* Rome, 4 Aug 1929). Italian soprano. After studying at the Rome Academy, she continued her vocal training with Leonardo Filoni, whom she later married. In 1951 she made her début in *La forza del destino* opposite Gigli. She sang throughout Italy (her La Scala début was as Mimì in 1959), and made guest appearances internationally, notably at the Teatro Colón and the Bol'shoy Theatre. She made her London début at the Adelphi Theatre as Mimì in December 1959 and first appeared at Covent Garden in the next year, as Aida and Tosca. Her American début, in San Francisco, was as Maddalena (*Andrea Chénier*) in 1959; the following October, as Butterfly, she began a close association with the Metropolitan which lasted until 1973. Her repertory included most of the standard Italian spinto roles and she also successfully undertook the challenge of such florid parts as Elcia (*Mosè*), Luisa Miller and Elvira (*I puritani*), as well as Mozart, Gluck and Gounod roles. Tucci was an uneven singer but her best performances were notable for communicative warmth, taste and lustrous tone. A poignant actress, she was especially effective in the final acts of *Otello* and *La traviata*. MARTIN BERNHEIMER

Tuček [Tuczek, Tutschek], **Jan** (*b c*1743; *d* Prague, 19 Sept 1783). Bohemian composer. He made his career in Prague as a choirmaster and band conductor. He wrote incidental music to a number of plays which have taken on a particular significance because they were some of the earliest productions in the professional theatre to use the Czech language and, as such, provide an important link with the pioneering work of František Škroup. He is credited with the music for the pantomime-intermezzo *Der verliebte Nachtwächter* which, despite its German title, is in Czech, and probably the first Czech play to be professionally staged. The date of its first performance may have been as early as 1763, but the first documented performance was in Brno on 11 January 1767. Another of Tuček's early works, the burlesque *Verbování na koňském trhu* ('Recruiting at the Horse Fair'), was probably first performed in 1769. For another play, *Opilý muž* ('The Drunken Man'), he composed an overture, seven arias, six duets and five recitatives; Tomášek, in his autobiography, mentioned that this piece was performed in his home town of Skuteč, which gives evidence of its continuing popularity in 18th-century Bohemia.

Tuček's significance in the tentative beginnings of Czech opera lies in his bringing the provincial tradition of Czech Singspiel into an urban setting, where it competed with the attractions of Italian opera and violated the dictates of aristocratic taste. From then on Czech Singspiel always held a place, however tenuous, in Prague's theatres, particularly at U Hybernů, the

Patriotic Theatre, where it alternated with German Singspiel and Italian *opera buffa*.

*

Z. Němec, ed.: *Vlastní ž ivotopis V. J. Tomášeka* [Tomášek's Autobiography] (Prague, 1911)
F. Batha: 'K otázce skladatelů Tučků' [The Issue of Tuček's Compositions], *Zprávy Bertramky*, xx (1960), 3
F. Černý and A. Scherl: *Dějiny českého divadla* [History of Czech Theatre], i (Prague, 1968)
ADRIENNE SIMPSON

Tuček, Vincenc (Tomáš Václav) [Tuczek, (Franz) Vinzenz (Ferrerius)] (*b* Prague, 2 Feb 1773; *d* Pest, 1821 or later). Czech composer, conductor and singer, son of Jan Tuček. In 1794 he sang Tamino in the first Czech performance of *Die Zauberflöte*. From 1794 to 1796 he was harpsichordist at the Patriotic Theatre and composed half a dozen Singspiels for it; some of them were given in Czech and in German. In 1797 he became Kapellmeister to Duke Peter of Courland, and staged *Don Giovanni* at the castle theatre at Náchod (east Bohemia). In 1800 he moved to Breslau, and in March 1801 to Vienna, where he had been known as early as 1794 as having set Gieseke's *Der travestierte Hamlet*, performed at the Theater auf der Wieden (10 July) and presumably commissioned by Schikaneder. He joined the Leopoldstädter Theater in 1801, making his début in Wenzel Müller's *Die Schwestern von Prag* (he had earlier written music for the Prague première of this work), and later became Kapellmeister there. He resigned in September 1809 and spent the remainder of his life in Budapest.

Tuček achieved more than a passing success with the opera *Lanassa*, the melodrama *Samson, Richter in Israel* and the Singspiel *Dämona, das kleine Höckerweibchen* (56 performances in the Leopoldstädter Theater, 1806–15, revived in the Theater in der Josefstadt, 1822). Most popular of all were the Singspiel *Honza Kolohnát z Přelouče* (1795 or 1796) and its sequel *Die zwei Klacheln*. His output for the theatre also includes ballets, pantomimes and incidental music.

all Vienna operas performed at Leopoldstädter Theater

Pražšti sládci [Die Prager Bräuer] (P. Šedivého), Prague, Hibernian, 28 Sept 1795
Honza Kolohnát z Přelouče [Hanns Klachl von Przelautsch, oder Das Rendezvous in der neuen Allee] (Spl, 2, F. G. Quolfinger von Steinsberg), Prague, Hibernian, 31 Jan 1796 or earlier; as Hans Dachel, oder Der Bräutigam von Kakran, Teplitz, 1797
Die zwei Klacheln von Przelautsch (2, Steinsberg), Prague, 6 Jan 1797 [sequel to Hanns Klachl]; as Die beiden Dacheln (2, Tuček), Pest, Stadt, 5 Aug 1811
Rübezahl [Ripheus; Typhon] (3, S. G. Bürde), Breslau, National, 1801
Dämona, das kleine Höckerweibchen (Spl, 3, J. Bullinger), Pest, Stadt, 29 May 1805, *Bc*, vs (Leipzig, n.d.)
Lanassa, oder Die Eroberung von Malabar (3, Tuček), Pest, Stadt, 13 Dec 1805
Der Zauberkuss, oder Die Stunde der Erlösung [Le charme du baiser] (grosse heroisch-komische Oper, 2, J. Hofmüller), 26 May 1807, *B-Bc*
Die Polterhexe von Lichtenstein, oder Die Zwogenhöhle (komisches Volksmärchen mit Gesang, 3, J. Einweg), Vienna, 3 Oct 1807
Idas und Marpissa (travestierte Dekorations-Oper, 3, J. Perinet), Vienna, 19 Dec 1807 [parody of opera by Stegmayer and Seyfried]
Die neue Semiramis (grosse heroisch-komische Travestie-Oper, 3, Perinet), Vienna, 25 June 1808
Samson, Richter in Israel (melodrama, 3, J. A. Schuster), Vienna, 13 Aug 1808, *Bc*
Der Durchmarsch, oder Der Alte muss bezahlen (komische Oper, 3, Perinet), Vienna, 30 Nov 1808 [based on J. Panek: Die christliche Judenbraut, 1788]
Alarich und Zaïde, oder Die bezauberte Leyer (komische Zauberoper, 3, J. A. Gleich), Vienna, 5 Jan 1809
Die vier Heymonskinder (komisches Volksmärchen mit Gesang, 4, Gleich), Vienna, 4 Feb 1809
Die schöne Melusine, Vienna, 6 May 1809
Das Laternenfest (3, Perinet), 1809
Israels Wanderung (3, Girzik), Pest, Stadt, 22 Dec 1810
Der Papillonfänger auf den blauen Gebirgen (heroisch-komische Oper, 2, M. Fenzl), Vienna, 7 Nov 1812
Moses' Tod (3, Tuček), Pest, Stadt, 22 Dec 1812
Der Kosak und der Freywillige (1, A. von Kotzebue), Pest, Stadt, 8 Nov 1814
Der Canarienvogel (1, Tuček), Pest, Stadt, 11 Feb 1816
Ruderich der Grausame (3, Tuček), Pest, Stadt, 18 Nov 1816
Fürstin Wlasta, oder Der Amazonenkrieg (4, Tuček), Pest, Stadt, 8 July 1817
Laïs und Amindas, oder Der Kampf für Vaterland und Liebe (3, Tuček), Pest, Stadt, 29 Dec 1817; ? as Doris und Amindas, oder Verrat aus Liebe (3, J. Jung), Pest, 23 March 1829
Arabella, oder Die Schreckensfolgen der Eifersucht (3), Pest, Stadt, 26 Oct 1818

*

J. Kádár: *A Pesti és Budai német színészet története 1812–1847* [A History of German Actors in Pest and Buda] (Budapest, 1923)
J. Pulanszky-Kádár: *Geschichte des deutschen Theaters in Ungarn* (Munich, 1933)
F. Hadamowsky: *Das Theater in der Wiener Leopoldstadt 1781–1860* (Vienna, 1934)
P. Branscombe: 'Some Viennese *Hamlet* Parodies and a Hitherto Unknown Musical Score for One of Them', *Festschrift Otto Erich Deutsch* (Kassel, 1963), 337–44
F. Černý and A. Scherl: *Dějiny českého divadla* [History of Czech Theatre], i (Prague, 1968)
W. Binal: *Deutschsprachiges Theater in Budapest* (Vienna, 1972)
PETER BRANSCOMBE

Tucker, Norman (*b* Wembley, 24 April 1910; *d* London, 10 Aug 1978). English administrator and translator. He was educated at St Paul's School, London, Oxford and the RCM. From 1936 to 1940 and after World War II he was a concert pianist. In 1947 James Robertson invited him to join Sadler's Wells Opera as joint director with himself and Michael Mudie. From 1953 to 1954 he was joint director with Robertson, and from 1954 to 1966 sole director. He translated *Simon Boccanegra*, *Luisa Miller* and *Don Carlos* (with some drastic rearrangements), as well as *Werther*, *Kát'a Kabanová*, *The Cunning Little Vixen*, *The Makropulos Affair* and Sutermeister's *Romeo und Julia*, all of which were performed during his time at Sadler's Wells. In 1972 he translated Gottfried von Einem's *Der Besuch der alten Dame* for Glyndebourne. Tucker's disappointment at the decision not to build an opera house on the South Bank and differences with the Sadler's Wells Trust led to his resignation in March 1966. His autobiography, *Norman Tucker, Musician*, was published in London in 1978.

*

N. Goodwin: 'Norman Tucker', *Opera*, xii (1961), 565–71
HAROLD ROSENTHAL/R

Tucker, Richard [Ticker, Reuben] (*b* Brooklyn, NY, 28 Aug 1913; *d* Kalamazoo, MI, 8 Jan 1975). American tenor. He studied with Paul Althouse and, after a spell in business, made his stage début as Alfredo with the Salmaggi Opera, New York, in 1943. He made his European début in 1947 at the Verona Arena as Enzo to Callas's La Gioconda (her Italian début) and later appeared in London, Vienna, Milan and Florence. America in general and the Metropolitan in particular, however, remained the focal point of his extraordinary career, which spanned three decades of leading roles and frequently brought him public comparisons with Caruso. Tucker's singing was never notable for finesse, and his acting, though energetic, remained primitive.

But he had few peers in the projection of italianate passions, or in fervour, ease, evenness and vocal security. He gave over 600 performances in 30 leading roles at the Metropolitan, first lyric and later dramatic, beginning with *La Gioconda* in 1945 and ending with *Pagliacci* a few weeks before his sudden death. Tucker was a deeply religious man; his wish to sing Eléazar in *La Juive* at the Metropolitan remained unfulfilled, though he did undertake the role elsewhere (1973, New Orleans). He was the brother-in-law of a rival tenor, Jan Peerce.

*

GV (G. Gualerzi; S. Smolian)
J. B. Steane: *The Grand Tradition* (London, 1974), 426
J. A. Drake: *Richard Tucker: a Biography* (New York, 1984) [with discography by P. A. Kiser]

MARTIN BERNHEIMER

Tucson. American city, in Arizona. The Arizona Opera Company, which was founded in 1972 as Tucson Opera, stages four productions each year at the Convention Center Music Hall (1750 seats), with two performances of each production. The company takes the same productions to Phoenix and is based in both cities. Glynn Ross has directed the company since 1983.

Tudoran, Ionel (*b* Bărăştii de Vede, 24 June 1913). Romanian tenor. He studied in Iaşi and made his début there in 1936 as Robert in Ziehrer's operetta *Die Landstreicher*. He was the leading tenor at Cluj from 1937, and sang at the Bucharest Opera from 1948 to 1963, notably as Faust, Cavaradossi and Otello. Considered the finest Romanian tenor of his generation, he appeared in Prague, Dresden, Berlin and Budapest. He toured Russia in 1957 and 1962. He retired in 1963 and taught at the Bucharest Conservatory until 1972.

DAVID CUMMINGS

Tulebayev, Mukhtan Tulebayevich (*b* Karshagan, Burlyu-Tyubinsky, Kazakhstan, 28 Feb/13 March 1913; *d* Alma-Ata, 2 April 1960). Kazakh composer. He studied at the Kazakh opera studio attached to the Moscow Conservatory, 1938–44. He continued composition lessons with E. G. Brusilovsky until 1946 and then with V. G. Fere and Myaskovsky at the Moscow Conservatory, graduating in 1951. He taught at the Alma-Ata Conservatory from 1953, and was president of the governing body of the Composers' Union of Kazakhstan from 1956 to 1960. He was made a National Artist of the USSR in 1959. His first opera, *Amangel'dï*, to a libretto by G. Muzrenov, was written in collaboration with Brusilovsky in 1945; his second, *Birzhan i Sara* ('Birzhan and Sara'), followed a year later: both had their first performances at the Kazakh Theatre of Opera and Ballet. *Birzhan i Sara* won a USSR State Prize in 1949. Tulebayev was also the composer of the official Kazakh anthem.

*

A. Zhubanov: *Mukhtan Tulebayev* (Alma-Ata, 1963)

STEPHEN JOHNSON

Tullio, Francesco Antonio (*b* Naples, 1660; *d* Naples, 7 March 1737). Italian librettist. Names under which he is known (or wrote) include: Col'Antuono Feralintisco, Col'Antuono Ferlentisco, Tertulliano Fonsaconico and Filostrato Lucano Cinneo. Nothing is known of the activities of this most influential and prolific of the librettists of the Neapolitan comic opera before his first recorded comedy in dialect, *La Cilla*, performed privately in 1707. Tullio's theatrical activity began in earnest in 1717–19, with three comedies in dialect, followed by three in Tuscan – the latter presumably at the order of the impresario. It is a measure of the esteem in which Tullio was held that he was commissioned to provide six of the nine comedies of those years, when the Teatro dei Fiorentini was beginning to devote its attention almost exclusively to comic opera. After the experiments of 1718–19, Tullio wrote entirely in dialect until *La Rosilla* (1733); his last comedy, *Angelica ed Orlando* (1735), has six parts in Tuscan and only two in dialect.

La Cilla (commeddia pe' museca), Faggioli, 1707; *Le fenzejune abbenturate* (commeddeja pe' museca), N. Fago, 1710; *Li viecchie coffejate* (commeddeia pe museca), ? Falco, 1710; *La Cianna* (commeddeia pe museca), Fago, 1711; *Lo finto Armeneio* (commedeia), A. Orefice, 1717; *Le fente zingare* (commeddeia), Orefice, 1717 (rev. Leo, 1724); *Retella e Chiarchia* (int), Orefice, 1718; *La fenta pazza co la fenta malata* (commeddeia), Orefice, 1718; *Il gemino amore* (commedia), Orefice, 1718

Il trionfo dell'onore (commedia), A. Scarlatti, 1718; *La forza della virtù* (commedia), Feo, 1719; *La festa de Bacco* (commeddeja), Vinci, 1722; *Li stravestemiente affortunate* (commeddeia pe' museca), Domenico, 1722; *La Locinna* (traggecommeddeia), Orefice, 1723 (Leo and Orefice, 1733, as La Rosilla); *Le pazzie d'ammore* (commeddeia), Falco, 1723; *Le fente zingare* (commeddeja), comp. unknown, 1724; *Lo 'ngiegno de le femmene* (commeddeia), Corradini, 1724

L'aracolo de Dejana (commeddeia boscareccia), Corradini, 1725; *La Donna Violante* (commeddeia), Leo, 1726; *Lo viecchio avaro* (commeddeia pe' museca), G. de Majo, 1727; *La vecchia trammera* (commeddeia pe' museca), Leo and Orefice, 1732; *La finta pellegrina* (commedia per musica), Orefice and Sarro, 1734; *Il trionfo del glorioso patriarca S Francesco di Paola*, 1734; *Angelica ed Orlando* (commedia per musica), Latilla, 1735

*

CroceN; *ES* (U. Prota-Giurleo); *FlorimoN*
M. Scherillo: *L'opera buffa napoletana durante il settecento: storia letteraria* (Naples, 1883, 2/1916), 95–124
U. Prota-Giurleo: *Nicola Logroscino, 'il dio dell'opera buffa': la vita e le opere* (Naples, 1927), 50–51

GRAHAM HARDIE

Tulsa. American city, in Oklahoma. In 1904 (three years before statehood) *Faust* was presented at the Epperson Opera House, a hall above a store. Over the next 40 years touring companies such as the Ellis Grand Opera, Scotti Grand Opera, San Carlo Opera, Chicago Civic and Grand operas and the Boston Ideal Opera were brought to the city by the Hyechka Club (named for the Creek Indian word for music), also founded in 1904. Performances were given at the Grand Opera House (opened in 1906) and later at the Convention Hall (1914; renamed Tulsa Municipal Theatre in 1953), which housed the Tulsa Opera until the opening in 1977 of the 2450-seat Chapman Music Hall at the Performing Arts Center. In 1948 the Tulsa Opera Club was founded by the tenor Ralph Sassano and his wife, the soprano Ione Sanger, who was born in Tulsa; they presented *La traviata* in modern dress. Five years later the club became the Tulsa Opera, which has since maintained its commitment to its original three goals: to present musical theatre of the highest quality by bringing in international stars, to encourage the talents of local performers and to provide educational programmes. The company presents three productions annually (three performances each). Nicholas Muni has been artistic director since 1988.

*

M. Craig: 'Tulsa's Answer to the Opera Problem in America', *Musical Courier*, cliv/4 (1956), 2
——: 'Superlative: the Word for Tulsa Opera', *Musical Courier*, clvi/1 (1957), 2
D. Wright: 'Opera in Oklahoma', *Opera Journal*, iii/2 (1970), 5–12
E. Davidson: 'Tulsa's Brand', *ON*, xxxviii/20 (1973–4), 30–31

M. H. Markham, ed.: *Tulsa Opera, Inc., Dec 4, 1948–March 17, 1973* (Tulsa, 1974)
J. Kestner: 'Oklahoma, O.K.!', *ON*, l/5 (1985–6), 28–30, 62–3, 66

MELODY LAYTON McMAHON

Tumanyan, Barseg (*b* Erevan, 3 Aug 1958). Armenian bass. He studied in Erevan, where he made his début with the Spendiaryan Opera in 1980 in the title role of Armen Tigranyan's *David-Bek*. After further study at La Scala and in Moscow with Yevgeny Nesterenko, he won the Busseto Verdi Prize (1983). He has appeared in Lisbon, Boston, Los Angeles, Melbourne and Monte Carlo, and at the Verona Arena, the Metropolitan and the Bol'shoy. He made his Covent Garden début in 1990 as Colline, returning as Attila and Don Basilio. His repertory includes Don Giovanni, Ramfis, Philip II, Boris, Gounod's Méphistophélès, Escamillo, Tigran Chukhadjian's Arshak Erkrord and Nadir (Alexander Spendiaryan's *Almast*). A convincing, subtle actor, he has an agile voice of warmth and amplitude.

I. Bel'skaya: 'Barseg Tumanyan', *Muzykal'naya zhizn'* (1987), no. 19, pp.17–18

SVETLANA SARKISYAN

Tunisia. From 1881 to 1956 Tunisia was a French protectorate, but even before the arrival of the French administration it had been settled by many Italians, Maltese and French, who provided a clientèle for opera. The first theatre built in the capital, Tunis, in about 1830, was the Théâtre Tapia. An Italian company performed *La traviata* there in 1856 and *Un ballo in maschera* in 1859. Adelina Patti stayed on her way to Cairo in 1864 and sang in Marchetti's *Ruy Blas*.

In 1875 a local theatre lover, David Cohen-Tanugi, built the Théâtre Cohen; there were 400 seats and all the local European bourgeois élite had boxes there. *Faust* (in Italian) and *La favorita* were given, followed in 1879 by the first French operetta, Lecocq's *Giroflé-Girofla*, Audran's *La mascotte* and Hervé's *Le petit Faust*. This theatre later became a music hall before being demolished in 1904. The all-wooden Théâtre Brulat was built in 1880, and *Mignon* was given its local first performance there. In 1884 the troupe Portalier-Le Gall played a season of operettas by Lecocq, Hervé and Audran. The theatre burnt down in 1889, and opera was transferred to the Théâtre Français. Here all lyric styles, from vaudeville to operetta, from *opéra comique* to grand opera, were given for the following 13 years. The orchestra numbered only 25 plus piano, but that did not stop the company performing works such as *La Juive*, *L'Africaine*, *Hérodiade* and *Aida*. Italian companies, often on their way to Cairo, performed for a six-week season each year.

Around 1900 three casino theatres on the outskirts of Tunis – the Casino d'Hamman-Lif, the gardens of the Khereddine Palace, and the Rotonde Daïda built on the water at La Goulette – mounted performances on a smaller scale (orchestras of eight or ten) of many popular operas and operettas, including *Lucia di Lammermoor*, *Otello* and *Robert le diable*. In 1902 the rather larger Casino Municipal was opened with a performance of *Manon*; *Grisélidis*, *Louise* and *Samson et Dalila* were included in the season. The musical director was Gaston Coste from Nice. In 1912 the Casino Municipal was completely renovated and reopened as the Théâtre Municipal (seating 1150) under the direction of Coste, who with artists from the Opéra-Comique gave a season of French favourites such as *La dame blanche*, *Carmen*, *Louise*, *Roméo et Juliette* and *Le jongleur de Notre-Dame*. The theatre was closed during the 1914–18 war, but annual seasons of opera continued until the French left. The Théâtre Municipal still stands, and opera has once again begun to be performed there. During the French administration, théâtres municipaux were also built at Sfax Bizerta and Garbès, where opera seasons were given. During the summer months opera is sometimes performed in the Antique Theatre at Carthage and in the Roman coliseum at El Jem.

R. Damon: 'Un "presque siècle" de théâtre à Tunis', *Bulletin économique et social de Tunisie*, no.52 (1951), 42–51
K. Bornac: *'La Bonbonière de Tunis': histoire du Théâtre municipal* (Tunis, 1992)
C. Pitt: 'L'opéra en Tunisie', *Opéra international* (May 1992)

CHARLES PITT

Turandot (i). *Chinesisches Fabel* in two acts by FERRUCCIO BUSONI to his own libretto after CARLO GOZZI's dramatic fairy-tale; Zürich, Stadttheater, 11 May 1917.

After his father's defeat in battle, Kalaf (tenor) flees to Peking in search of adventure. He is recognized by his former servant, Barak (baritone). The latter tells him of the Emperor's daughter Turandot (soprano) and of her cruel decree – that every contender for her hand must undergo a trial by riddles and that those who fail are to be beheaded. The narrative is interrupted by the entrance of the Queen Mother of Samarkand (soprano), who bewails the execution of her son. She hurls a portrait of Turandot to the ground. Kalaf picks it up, is fired with love and storms off to the imperial palace.

In scene ii Truffaldino (tenor), chief eunuch, orders his servants to prepare the great hall for a new trial. Neither the Emperor Altoum (bass) nor his ministers, Pantalone (bass) and Tartaglia (bass), are able to dissuade Kalaf, who steadfastly refuses to reveal his identity and insists on 'death or Turandot'. Turandot's confidante Adelma (soprano) recognizes him as the man she once vainly loved, but she remains silent. The riddle ceremony begins. Before reading the third riddle, Turandot unveils herself, nearly dazzling Kalaf with her beauty. He triumphs, but when Turandot refuses to fulfil her pledge of marriage he counters with the riddle of his name.

As the second act opens, neither song nor dance can soothe Turandot's rage. Truffaldino recounts an unsuccessful attempt to bewitch the sleeping prince into revealing his name; Altoum announces that a secret messenger has brought him the coveted information; finally Adelma, hoping to win Kalaf for herself, whispers the name to the princess. In scene ii Turandot, dressed in mourning, reveals Kalaf's name to the assembled citizens. But she surprises and delights them by proclaiming her marriage. Only Adelma remains disconsolate. The opera ends with a jubilant choral dance in praise of Buddha.

Busoni composed incidental music for Gozzi's *Turandot* in 1905, perhaps with a view to celebrating the centenary of the playwright's death the following year. In 1911 Max Reinhardt staged a production of the play in a new translation by Karl Vollmoeller, using Busoni's complete score of incidental music, at the Deutsches Theater, Berlin. After a further stage production in London, which was by all accounts a travesty, Busoni resolved to transform the work into an opera. He eventually put this plan into effect in 1917, reducing the original scoring and adding several new passages, including arias for Kalaf, Turandot and Altoum. Thus in just three months he devised an apt companion piece for his one-act opera *Arlecchino*.

Like *Arlecchino*, *Turandot* is a number opera with spoken dialogue; otherwise the works have little in common apart from the participation of *commedia dell'arte* characters. They form an exotic and amusing double bill, which was well received at the première. Gustav Brecher, Otto Klemperer and Leo Blech were among the first conductors to champion both works. In recent times each has more often been performed separately, coupled with shorter operas by other composers.

Much of the melodic material in Busoni's score is taken from the *Geschichte der Musik* by A. W. Ambros. In an effort to illustrate the earliest developments in non-European music, the historian cites allegedly Chinese, Arabic, Byzantine, Indian and Nubian themes. The notation (and sometimes harmonization) of these musical examples often implies a superficial similarity to Western music. Ambros's synthetic cultural link supported Busoni's own theories of melody, as expounded in the *Entwurf einer neuen Ästhetik der Tonkunst*: 'The myriad strains that once shall sound have existed since the beginning, ready, afloat in the ether'. Nor did Busoni stop at Ambros, for in his *Turandot* music he also quotes *Greensleeves* in a delicate arrangement for two flutes and two harps.

In 1911 Puccini saw a performance of Max Reinhardt's production of *Turandot*, which later prompted him to use the story for his own opera of the same name. He accentuated the exoticism and cruelty latent in the fable, while underplaying the *commedia dell'arte* element. Where Busoni's Emperor is wise and warm-hearted, a Chinese counterpart to Sarastro, Puccini depicts him as a weak and feeble old monarch. Puccini characterizes Turandot as a 'princess of ice' while Busoni follows Goethe in finding her 'highly subtle'. The slave girl Liù was Puccini's invention and bears virtually no resemblance to Gozzi's Adelma. Above all, Puccini's opera is a tragedy, calling for every musical and theatrical resource of a major opera house, whereas Busoni's work is a comedy, using modest orchestral and choral forces. ANTONY BEAUMONT

Turandot (ii). *Dramma lirico* in three acts by GIACOMO PUCCINI to a libretto by GIUSEPPE ADAMI and RENATO SIMONI after CARLO GOZZI's dramatic fairy-tale; Milan, Teatro alla Scala, 25 April 1926.

Princess Turandot	soprano
The Emperor Altoum *her father*	tenor
Timur *the dispossessed King of Tartary*	bass
Calaf *his son*	tenor
Liù *a young slave-girl*	soprano
Ping *Grand Chancellor* (Masks)	baritone
Pang *General Purveyor* (Masks)	tenor
Pong *Chief Cook* (Masks)	tenor
A Mandarin	baritone
The Prince of Persia	silent role
The Executioner (Pu-Tin-Pao)	silent role

Imperial guards, the executioner's men, boys, priests, mandarins, dignitaries, eight wise men, Turandot's handmaids, soldiers, standard-bearers, musicians, ghosts of suitors and a crowd

Setting Peking, in legendary times

The notion of basing an opera on Gozzi's most celebrated *fiaba* (fairy-tale) – one that should 'modernize and bring human warmth to the old card-board figures' – arose during a meeting in Milan between Puccini, Adami and Simoni in winter 1919–20. Adami supplied the composer with a copy of Schiller's adaptation of the play in the Italian translation of Andrea Maffei. Puccini returned it to him with the instruction to make it the basis of the libretto, adding 'but on it you must rear another figure; I mean – I can't explain!' (clearly he was groping his way towards the conception of the slave-girl Liù). His first instinct was to exclude Gozzi's 'masks' but almost immediately afterwards he wrote: 'It is just possible that by retaining them *with discretion* we should have an Italian element which, in the midst of so much Chinese mannerism ... would introduce a touch of our life and, above all, of sincerity.' By August 1920 the poets' original scheme had been reworked to Puccini's temporary satisfaction. Of the three acts, the first was to end with Calaf's solving of the riddles and his offer to release Turandot from her obligation provided she could find out who he is. The second would begin with her attempts to do so, including the interrogation and torture of Liù, and end with a long duet, at the climax of which Calaf would reveal his name and thus apparently seal his own fate. Act 3 would open with the preparations for Calaf's execution. At the last moment Turandot would deny all knowledge of his identity and proclaim her love for him. By the beginning of 1921 Puccini had already begun sketching the music with the help of a Chinese musical box belonging to his friend Baron Fassani and some folk music supplied by the firm of Ricordi.

Meanwhile, of the two librettists Adami seems to have assumed the usual role of Illica, working out the dialogue, and Simoni that of Giacosa, versifying the result. By September Puccini was convinced that the last two acts should be run together, so as to avoid a slackening of interest after the riddle scene. The librettists, however, were against a two-act format; and in December it was decided to bring down the curtain on Act 1 at the point where Calaf, not dissuaded by Timur, Liù and the masks, strikes the gong that announces his challenge. During the early months of 1922 Puccini worked on a new scene for the masks which would open the second act. In October he was engaged with Turandot's aria, 'In questa reggia', which follows. In November, after briefly reverting to the idea of an opera in two acts, Puccini took the unfortunate decision to have Liù die under torture. For the next two years the final duet between Calaf and Turandot proved the great obstacle. None of the versions supplied by Simoni satisfied him. By the time of his death on 29 November 1924 only a few scarcely legible sketches for it existed. At Toscanini's suggestion these were handed over to Franco Alfano for completion. But at the première 17 months later with an outstanding cast that included Miguel Fleta (Calaf), Rosa Raisa (Turandot), Maria Zamboni (Liù), Carlo Walter (Timur) and Giacomo Rimini (Ping), Toscanini laid down his baton after the death of Liù, the last music composed by Puccini. The score was published with Alfano's ending, shortened in a second edition (the one in regular use). Alfano's conclusion (which has since been given in full in concert performance) fails to redeem the inevitable anticlimax. Clearly the man who can persist in his wooing of a woman of whom he knows nothing, and whom he has every reason to dislike, immediately after a slave-girl has killed herself for his sake, is bound to forfeit our sympathy. Puccini hoped that the librettists would be able to solve the problem for him; but even if they had succeeded it is likely that, as in *Suor Angelica*, he would not have found the appropriate note of transfiguration on which to end.

The title role is one of the supreme challenges for a dramatic soprano. Outstanding exponents have included Claudia Muzio, Lotte Lehmann, Maria Jeritza, Maria Németh, Eva Turner and, later, Maria Callas, Birgit Nilsson and Gwyneth Jones.

ACT 1 *A public square in Peking beneath the city ramparts, with the imperial palace to one side* From a bastion a Mandarin proclaims the Emperor's decree: the Princess Turandot shall wed the first suitor of royal lineage who succeeds in solving her three riddles; all who fail will be executed. The Prince of Persia 'whom fortune has not favoured' is due to be beheaded when the moon rises. The crowd surges forward in eager anticipation, only to be brutally repulsed by the imperial guards. As their shouts turn to groans and lamentations, the stark, bitonal flourishes of the orchestra give way to a broad, characteristically Puccinian, drooping melody. In the scrimmage an old blind man is knocked to the ground. The girl accompanying him calls for help. Their rescuer is the disguised Prince Calaf, who recognizes the old man as his father, Timur, exiled King of Tartary. Both are in flight from their country's enemies. Timur's companion is the slave-girl Liù, who decided to share the family's sufferings when Calaf bestowed a smile on her long ago. The hectic motion is resumed as the Executioner's men arrive and begin sharpening the axe. The general blood-lust is conveyed in a fierce ostinato of varied phrase-lengths (ex.1), yielding to a mood of rapt

Ex.1

reverie as all pray for the moon to appear. Slowly the scene fills with a silvery light, reflected in a diaphanous tissue of harmony and scoring. As the culminating cry of 'Pu-Tin-Pao' (the Executioner's name) subsides, a chorus of boys is heard approaching. Their chant ('Là, sui monti dell'est') is a version of the Chinese folksong 'Moo-Lee-Vha' and will stand for Turandot in her official capacity (ex.2). Next comes the procession that

Ex.2

['There on the eastern mountains']

escorts the Prince of Persia to the scaffold (here Puccini uses a modal idiom with sharpened 4th). The young man's looks and dignified bearing move the crowd to pity and they call on the Princess to spare his life, but she confirms his sentence with a silent gesture. Timur, Calaf and Liù are left alone in the square. From far off the Prince of Persia invokes the name of Turandot as the axe falls. But Calaf has been so overwhelmed by the Princess's beauty that he is determined to try his fortune with her, despite his father's remonstrances. He is about to strike the gong and issue his challenge when the masks, Ping, Pang and Pong, rush in and restrain him. To fragments of the Chinese national hymn set out in alternations of duple and triple time, they try to deflect Calaf from his purpose. From the balcony the Princess's handmaidens call for silence – their mistress is sleeping. The masks pay no heed and continue their persuasions. The ghosts of former suitors materialize on the battlements, each bewailing his unrequited love. The masks point to where the Executioner appears bearing the Prince of Persia's severed head. Timur joins his plea to theirs. In her pentatonic arietta ('Signore, ascolta') Liù makes a last appeal, to which Calaf, deeply moved, replies ('Non piangere, Liù'), recommending Timur to her care should he himself fail the test. As he continues to hold out, the music develops into a broadly swaying tug-of-war based on alternating chords and reinforced by the full chorus singing offstage. At the climax Calaf strikes the gong three times. Liù and Timur are in despair.

ACT 2.i *A pavilion* Ping, Pang and Pong are preparing for either eventuality – a wedding or a funeral. They reflect on China's misery ever since Turandot came to power. From ministers of state they have become servants of the Executioner. In an andantino of nostalgia ('Ho una casa nell'Honan') each recalls his home in the peace of the countryside. Memories of Turandot's past victims, evoked by ex.1 sung by an unseen chorus, give way to hopes that the man has been found who can tame her and restore tranquillity to the land. To the sound of trumpets the palace wakes to life, and the music continues without a break into scene ii.

2.ii *The palace courtyard* Gradually a crowd assembles. The various dignitaries take their places, among them the eight wise men, each bearing three scrolls. High up on an ivory throne sits the Emperor Altoum. In an old man's quavering voice he tries in vain to dissuade Calaf from his enterprise. A solemn choral hymn wishes him 10 000 years of life. Once again the Mandarin reads aloud the imperial decree regarding the Princess; and again the boys' chorus (ex.2) is heard, a prelude to the appearance of Turandot herself. Her aria 'In questa reggia' tells the story of her ancestress Lo-u Ling, who was ravished and murdered by a foreign army, and whose memory she has sworn to avenge on any man foolhardy enough to woo her. A pattern of three chords introduces each of her riddles, to which Calaf gives the correct answers ('Hope', 'Blood' and 'Turandot'). The music of ex.2, entrusted to full chorus and orchestra, now celebrates Calaf's victory. Turandot begs Altoum to release her from her vow, but he refuses. It is Calaf who offers her a way of escape. If by the following dawn she can discover his name, he will consent to be beheaded. Everyone hails Altoum, who hopes to be able to welcome Calaf as his son-in-law.

ACT 3.i *The palace gardens, at night* Distant heralds repeat the Princess's command that none shall sleep on pain of death until the Prince's name be revealed. In his *romanza* 'Nessun dorma', whose principal strain (ex.3)

'*Turandot' (Puccini), final scene of Act 1 (a public square in Peking beneath the city ramparts; Calaf strikes the gong) of the original production at La Scala, Milan, 25 April 1926: from 'L'illustrazione italiana' (May 1926)*

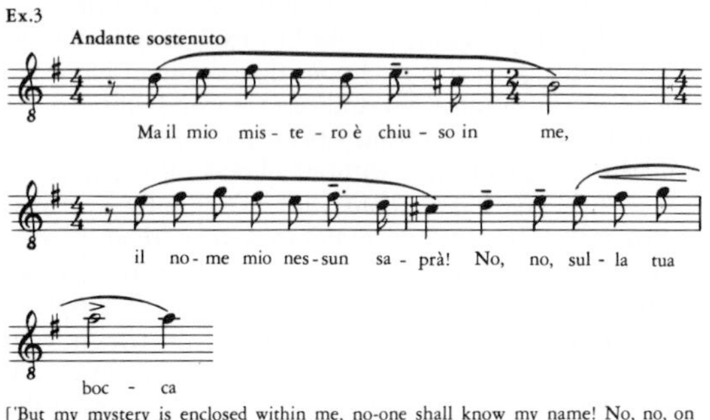

['But my mystery is enclosed within me, no-one shall know my name! No, no, on your lips (I will speak it).']

testifies to Puccini's undiminished lyrical gifts, Calaf echoes their words, resolving that his secret shall never be disclosed. The three masks emerge from the shrubbery and offer Calaf various bribes – young half-naked girls, jewels, promises of renown – but he rejects them all. The crowd that has meantime gathered menace him with their daggers, when suddenly the imperial guards appear dragging in Timur and Liù. The Princess is summoned. She orders the interrogation of Timur, but it is Liù who steps forward, claiming that she alone knows the Prince's name. Turandot has her bound and Ping tries to make her talk. In words of Puccini's own devising Liù tells the mystified Princess that love has given her the power to resist ('Tu che di gel sei cinta'). Her mournful melody (ex.4) continues throughout the painful scene that follows with an insistence that recalls the roll-call of the prostitutes in *Manon Lescaut.* The Executioner arrives; he and his men torture Liù. At the end of her strength she snatches a dagger from one of the guards and stabs herself. Timur, being blind, has to be told of her death; he joins the lugubrious procession that bears her body away. At this point Alfano's reconstruction takes over, beginning with a duet ('Principessa di morte') between Calaf and Turandot, in which the Princess, at first haughty and unyielding, succumbs when Calaf embraces her. Humiliated, she begs him to leave, taking his secret with him. But he now feels sufficiently confident to tell her that he is Calaf, son of Timur. At once she recovers her pride, realizing that she still holds his life in her hands. A female chorus punctuated by brass flourishes leads into the final scene.

3.ii *The palace courtyard* Once again the Emperor, his courtiers and the people have assembled. Advancing with Calaf, Turandot declares that at last she knows his name – it is 'Love'. Chorus and orchestra unite in a triumphant reprise of ex.3.

* * *

Despite its unfinished state *Turandot* is rightly regarded as the summit of Puccini's achievement, bearing witness to a capacity for self-renewal unsurpassed by that of still greater composers. The style remains true to the composer's 19th-century roots, but it is toughened and amplified by the assimilation of uncompromisingly modern elements, including bitonality and an adventurous use of whole-tone, pentatonic and modal harmony. The resulting synthesis commands a new range of expression (the pentatonic scale, no longer a mere orientalism as in *Madama Butterfly*, conveys the full depth of Liù's pathos in 'Signore, ascolta'). The music is organized in massive blocks, each motivically based – a system which shows to particular advantage in Act 1, arguably the most perfectly constructed act in Puccini's output; while the scoring shows a rare imagination in the handling of large forces (the writing for xylophone alone immediately attracts the attention). These attributes, combined with Puccini's unfailing ability to communicate directly with an audience, have established *Turandot* as a classic of 20th-century opera.

JULIAN BUDDEN

Turcano, Lucia (*b* Bucharest, 1913). Romanian soprano. She studied at the Bucharest Conservatory with Elena Saghin and Demetru Baziliu. From 1939 she sang at the Bucharest Opera as Marguerite, Leonora (*Il trovatore*), Tosca, Elsa, and Rachel in *La Juive*. After wartime appearances at the Vienna Volksoper she opened the 1946–7 season at La Scala, as Abigaille in *Nabucco*. Other roles in Milan (until 1949) and in Naples, Bologna, Venice and Rome included La Gioconda, Turandot, Aida and Norma. She sang in North America during the 1950s, notably in New York (City Opera) and Philadelphia. After returning to Romania in 1963 she gave concerts and taught.

DAVID CUMMINGS

Turchi, Guido (*b* Rome, 10 Nov 1916). Italian composer. He took diplomas in piano and composition at the Rome Conservatory, where he was a pupil of Cesare Dobici and Alessandro Bustini, and then of Pizzetti at the Accademia di S Cecilia. He taught for many years at the Rome Conservatory and was director of the conservatories of Parma and Florence (1967–72), and artistic director of the Accademia Filarmonica Romana (1963–6) and the Teatro Comunale in Bologna (1968–70). Without belonging to a specific school or trend, his experiments show awareness of the major European innovations of the first half of the 20th century, with Petrassi, Hindemith and Bartók as his principal points of reference. He is an experienced composer of incidental music but has written only one opera: the two-act *Il buon soldato Svejk* (5 April 1962, La Scala) was the result of ten years' work and occupies a central place in his output.

See also BUON SOLDATO SVEJK, IL.

PAOLO PETAZZI

Turco in Italia, Il ('The Turk in Italy'). *Dramma buffo* in two acts by GIOACHINO ROSSINI to a libretto by FELICE ROMANI after CATERINO MAZZOLÀ's *Il turco in Italia*, set by FRANZ SEYDELMANN (1788, Dresden); Milan, Teatro alla Scala, 14 August 1814.

The poet Prosdocimo (bass) is in search of a subject for a comedy drawn from real life. At a gypsy camp near Naples he encounters Zaida (soprano) who, as a slave girl in the Erzèrum harem, once loved the prince Selim (bass) but was forced to flee after slanders by jealous rivals had led Selim to sentence her to death. The poet tells Zaida that a Turkish prince will soon arrive and that news of her continued fidelity to Selim can then be sent to Turkey. In fact, the prince is Selim himself. To the delight of the poet, whose plot is badly in need of incident and intrigue, the first girl Selim sees and falls for is the shrewish Fiorilla (soprano), wife of the irascible and frustrated Don Geronio (bass), whose skirmishes with Fiorilla are abetted by his friend, the lady-killing Don Narciso (tenor). During the remainder of the first act the poet takes increasing delight in events: the flirting of Selim and Fiorilla, the anger of Geronio and Narciso, the bedlam that ensues when Selim and Zaida finally meet, recognize one another, and are discovered in an affectionate embrace by the remainder of the company.

In Act 2, Selim offers to buy Fiorilla from her husband but Geronio indignantly refuses. Fiorilla and Zaida confront Selim, who manages to insult both ladies by his indecision: he has, in fact, laid plans to abduct Fiorilla at a masked ball, a ploy the all-knowing poet reveals to Zaida, who resolves to go to the ball disguised as Fiorilla. Meanwhile, the poet advises Geronio to masquerade as Selim in order to forestall the abduction. To add to the confusion Narciso, overhearing the plotting, decides to attend in Turkish guise as he too wishes to make off with Fiorilla. There follows confusion on a grand scale; and though Selim and Zaida do eventually find one another and set sail for Turkey, leaving the various Italian parties decently reconciled, the comedy, particularly at the expense of the hapless Geronio, is often tinged with cruelty. This is particularly the case in the Act 2 quintet, 'Oh, guardate che accidente', with the bemused Geronio involved in a sinister game of ballroom hide-and-seek with two Selims and two Fiorillas.

That quintet is representative of Rossini's preoccupation here with ensembles as opposed to solo numbers. What solo numbers there are occur mainly in Act 2 and are largely 'arias of obligation' written, not always by Rossini, to satisfy the demands of individual singers. (The aria for Selim's henchman, the tenor Albazar, is not by Rossini.) Even Fiorilla, cavilling hussy and sophisticated woman of the world, is characterized more by her role-playing in ensembles than by either of her cavatinas. Significantly, the poet – the detached Rossinian observer – has no aria or duet. He sings only in recitatives, the fine Act 1 trio and in the ensembles within the Act 1 finale where Rossini has cheekily scrawled on the autograph manuscript: 'Well, at least you have a chance to do something here!'. As Gian Carli Ballola has observed, the opera is dominated by ensembles and conversations, etched in with the most delicate strokes, in a style entirely appropriate to the drawing-room chatter of a piece full of 'double meanings, hypocrisy, smothered anger, forced smiles, and asides through clenched teeth'.

RICHARD OSBORNE

Turcotti, Maria Giustina (*b* Florence, *c*1700; *d* after 1763). Italian mezzo-soprano. She sang in opera at Florence and Siena in 1717 but began a sustained career only in 1720, appearing in all the main centres and commanding a large salary; she sang in Venice in 1721–2, 1731–2 and 1742–3, and in Naples in 1727 and 1732–5. She seems to have been primarily a dramatic singer in a mostly syllabic style (range approximately *b*♭ to *g*″), without much brilliance or bravura; evidence from arias written for her by G. B. Pescetti and

Maria Giustina Turcotti: caricature by Anton Maria Zanetti (1680–1767)

Francesco Corselli, however, shows that she could master elaborate coloratura, rhythmically complex divisions and wide pitch leaps. Her last Italian engagements in 1745–6 were in secondary centres (Crema, Ferrara), suggesting vocal decline; she then sang with the Mingotti company in Germany and Copenhagen and was described as 'a monstrous mass of flesh, who accompanies every syllable with a grimace or emphatic gesture'. She was a member of the Bayreuth court opera (1750–58, 1760–63). DENNIS LIBBY, CARLO VITALI

Turenkov, Alexey Evlampiyevich (*b* St Petersburg, 9/21 Jan 1886; *d* Minsk, 27 Sept 1958). Belarusian composer. He studied with A. K. Lyadov and N. A. Sokolov at the St Petersburg Conservatory, 1911–14, and in 1918 took up residence in Gomel' (Belarus'), where he was one of the organizers and teachers of the music school and worked as director of several amateur choirs. He moved to Minsk in 1934 and wrote Belarusian national songs and choral works. He was made an Honoured Artist of the Belarusian SSR in 1940. His first opera, *Tsvetok schast'ya* ('Flower of Happiness', 1940), one of the earliest Belarusian operas, was first performed at the Belarusian Theatre of Opera and Ballet in Minsk, as was its successor, *Yasnyïy rassvet* ('Bright Dawn', 1958); the latter was revised in 1963 by the composer G. M. Vagner and the poet A. Bachil. STEPHEN JOHNSON

Turgenev, Ivan Sergeyevich (*b* Oryol, 28 Oct/9 Nov 1818; *d* Bougival, nr Paris, 3 Sept 1883). Russian writer. He was the first representative of his country's literature to gain an outstanding reputation in the West. One of the reasons for his frequent periods of residence abroad – principally in France and Baden-Baden – was his lifelong passion for Pauline Viardot, conceived in 1843 during her first season with the Italian Opera in St Petersburg. Turgenev's preference for bel canto opera over the Russian (and also over Meyerbeer and Verdi) was typical of his aristocratic class. He gave it voice in a number of critical articles published between 1847 and 1860, debated it heatedly in letters with Vladimir Stasov (published by the latter after Turgenev's death) and memorialized it in his novel *Dïm* ('Smoke', 1867) through the character of Potugin, the consummate 'Westernizer', whose sarcastic remarks on Russian dilettante musicians and their diehard proponents offended many. Musorgsky's own private performance of excerpts from *Boris Godunov* and *Khovanshchina* in the spring of 1874 did, however, impress Turgenev greatly; and his early collection *Zapiski okhotnika* ('Notes of a Hunter') contained many lyrical evocations of folksinging (e.g. 'Pevtsï', 'The Singers', from which derived a one-act opera by Alexander Goldenweiser, 1945).

Turgenev wrote a number of librettos in French for Viardot's *operettes* (of which one, *Le dernier sorcier*, reached the Weimar stage in 1869), and even took part in private performances alongside her pupils. Acquainted with Brahms through Viardot, he became one of the many who broached operatic projects to that most resistant prospect. Turgenev's fiction and plays have been mined for operas by a number of minor Russian and non-Russian composers, from Mikhail Ippolitov-Ivanov (*Asya*, 1900), Giacomo Orefice (*Il pane altrui*, 1907, after *Chuzhoy khleb*, 'Another's Bread') and Vladimir Rebikov (*Dvoryanskoye gnezdo*, 'A Nest of Gentlefolk', 1916) to Lee Hoiby (*Natalia Petrovna*, 1964, after *Mesyats v derevne*, 'A Month in the Country'). The great church musician Alexander Kastal'sky's most extended secular work was an opera after Turgenev (*Klara Milich*, 1916, Moscow).

*

I. S. Turgenev: 'Sovremennïye zametki', *Sovremennik*, no.1 (1847); repr. in *Sobraniye socheneniy*, ii (Moscow, 1956), 280–90 [on Verdi, Rossini, Meyerbeer, Berlioz, F. David etc.]
——: 'Neskol'ko slov ob opere Meyerbera "Prorok"' [A Few Words on Meyerbeer's *Le prophète*], *Otechestvennïye zapiski*, lxvii (1850); repr. in *Sobraniye socheneniy*, ii (Moscow, 1956), 291–4
——: 'Ob opere "Mariya Tyudor" Kashperova', *Sankt-peterburgskiye vedomosti* (8 Feb 1868)
——: 'Pervoye predstavleniye operï g-zhi Viardo v Veymare' [The First Performance of Viardot's *Le dernier sorcier*], *Sankt-peterburgskiye vedomosti* (21 April 1869); repr. in *Russkiye propilei*, iii (Moscow, 1916)
V. Stasov: 'Dvadtsat' pisem Turgeneva i moyo znakomstvo s nim' [Twenty Letters of Turgenev and My Acquaintance with Him], *Severnïy vestnik* (1888), no.10, pp.145–67
M. Alekseyev: *Turgenev i muzïka* (Kiev, 1918)
N. Bernshteyn: *I. S. Turgenev i muzïka* (Leningrad, 1933)
B. Asaf'yev: 'Turgenev i muzïka', *Izbrannïye trudï*, iv (Moscow, 1955), 157–64
A. FitzLyon: *The Price of Genius: a Biography of Pauline Viardot* (London, 1964)
R. Olivier: 'Operettï Turgeneva', *Literaturnoye nasledstvo*, lxxiii/1 (1964), 69–207 [also incl. note on performances of *Le dernier sorcier* by G. Shvirts, p.208]
A. Rozanov: *Polina Viardo-Garsia* (Leningrad, 1969)

RICHARD TARUSKIN

Turin (It. Torino). Italian city, capital of Piedmont. Opera at the Savoy ducal court began in the context of court celebrations and plays performed with musical accompaniment. These forerunners of opera included the stage performance of G. B. Guarini's *Il pastor fido* in 1585 at the command of Carlo Emanuele I and the intermezzos composed by Pietro Veccoli, some of them true stage music, for the tragicomedy *Adelonda di Frigia* by the playwright Federigo della Valle (1595). Court entertainment in this period tended towards *ballets de cour* rather than melodrama, in accordance with the tastes of an aristocracy which had strong connections with France and was inclined by military requirements towards jousting and tourneys; but in spite of this preference the second half of the 17th century saw sporadic performances of operas by P. A. Ziani, Antonio Cesti and Cavalli on celebratory occasions.

In 1681 the Salone delle Feste of the old Palazzo di S Giovanni was adapted as a modern theatre with boxes, the city's first permanent theatre and a first sign of the theatrical interests of Vittorio Amedeo II (see fig.1). He was then 14; he later succeeded to total control of the dukedom, which was made a kingdom in 1720 by the peace treaties following the wars of the Austrian and Spanish Successions. A strong and ambitious personality, Vittorio Amedeo II aimed to make Turin a modern city, as did his successor Carlo Emanuele III. The work of architects and painters such as Guarini, Juvarra and Carl van Loo was matched by a serious 'politica operistica'. Paris was no longer the model to be followed (although musicians and dancers were still exchanged with France), and Vittorio Amedeo himself searched Italy and corresponded with the Venetian Vincenzo Grimaldi in order to enrol famous singers.

The court moved towards the establishment of a regular operatic season, from 26 December to the end of Carnival, helped by two important factors: the princes of Carignano modernized the old Teatro Trincotto, inaugurating it in 1715 as the Teatro Carignano; and in 1727 the Nobile Società dei Cavalieri was established, with an annual subsidy from the king, replacing impresario management and assuming absolute control of all forms of theatrical activity in the city, including that of the Teatro Carignano. At the wish of Carlo Emanuele III the construction of a new Teatro Regio (cap. 2500) was begun in 1738 near the royal palace (*see* OPERA SERIA, fig.1). This became an operatic centre of European importance. Among the composers who wrote for the Regio were Jommelli, Leo, Galuppi, Gluck, J. C. Bach, Piccinni, Traetta, Paisiello and Cimarosa. The most illustrious virtuosos sang there and important contributions were made by the stage designs of Fabrizio and Bernardino Galliari (see fig.2; *see also* STAGE DESIGN, fig.7), the splendour of the ballets and the excellence of the orchestra, conducted from 1770 by Gaetano Pugnani. In that year Charles Burney was in Turin, as was the young Mozart with his father. The economic rigours imposed by the upheavals of 1789 brought this brilliant period to an end. With Turin ruled by the French and the Teatro Regio renamed the Nazionale, G. D. Boggio adapted old librettos, giving them a Jacobin slant, and also wrote new ones, such as *I veri amici repubblicani*, for N. A. Zingarelli; normal seasonal activity was not resumed until the Restoration.

Carlo Felice, the first Savoy ruler to return to the city in 1815, was an opera enthusiast, taking a great interest in librettos, scenery and costumes and attending rehearsals as well as performances. The Teatro Regio resumed the custom of producing two *opere serie* each year, while the Carignano turned increasingly to *opera buffa* and plays. Nostalgic feeling led to the reconstitution in 1824 of the old Società dei Cavalieri. In 1831 the violinist G. B. Polledro returned to Turin from European travels and proposed various reforms to allow the leader of the orchestra greater control over the number of rehearsals and appointments and dismissals, heralding the modern concept of musical director. His suggestions were rejected as the Società dei Cavalieri was afraid of losing its authority, but in 1833 Carlo Alberto, the new king, dissolved the Società and handed over management of the Turin theatres to private impresarios; unlike his predecessor he had little interest in the opera and wished to separate the theatre from the court. In the 1830s Turin fell behind the times in comparison with other Italian centres where Bellini and Donizetti were paramount, remaining faithful to Rossini, Vaccai and Mercadante. The first Bellini opera to be given in Turin was *La straniera* in 1832, and in 1834 Polledro conducted *Norma* in a production which won the composer's approval. The librettist Felice Romani, whom Carlo Alberto had invited to become editor of the *Gazzetta ufficiale piemontese* (1834–49), also played an important part in the debates over Classicism versus Romanticism and Italian versus foreign music; but in spite of Romani's dislike of early Verdi, Verdi's operas were successfully performed in Turin throughout the century. Ballet also continued to enjoy

1. Interior of the theatre in the Palazzo di S Giovanni, Turin, during the inaugural performance (Pagliardi's 'Lisimaco', 1681): watercolour by Tomasco Borgonio

2. Design by Bernardino and Fabrizio Galliari for Galuppi's festa teatrale 'La vittoria di Imeneo', first performed on 7 June 1750 at the Teatro Regio, Turin, as part of the celebrations in honour of the wedding of Maria Antonietta Ferdinanda of Spain to Vittorio Amedeo, heir to the throne of Piedmont

popular favour: Marie Taglioni visited Turin from Milan for seven nights in the winter of 1845, and the ballet school of the Regio theatre had a European reputation.

In the mid-19th century the organization of the Turin theatres was all in private hands. The war with Austria, in which Piedmont was in the front line, followed by the grave social and economic problems resulting from the proclamation of the Kingdom of Italy in 1861 (of which Turin was the first capital), made things hard for the theatres. There was a marked improvement with the appointment of Carlo Pedrotti as director of the Teatro Regio orchestra in 1868 and with the arrival in 1876 of the impresario Giovanni Depanis, who made the Regio, for the second time in a century, one of the pivots of Italian musical life. In 1876 Wagner's *Lohengrin*, which had failed at La Scala three years previously, was a great success there; in 1888, on the other hand, a revival of *Carmen* spurred a member of the audience, Friedrich Nietzsche, to extol Mediterranean art at the expense of Wagner. At the Teatro Carignano Arturo Toscanini made his Italian début with Catalani's *Edmea*, and in 1895, at the Teatro Regio, he conducted the local première of *Götterdämmerung*. The last years of the century included the first performances of Puccini's *Le villi* (1884 revision), *Manon Lescaut* (1893) and *La bohème* (1896). In 1906 Richard Strauss conducted *Salome* at the Regio; in 1914 the first performance of Zandonai's *Francesca da Rimini* was given there, and new opera houses were built, including the Vittorio Emanuele and the Politeama Chiarella. In 1925 the old Teatro Scribe was renamed the Teatro di Torino and until 1931 it was used for opera; under the artistic direction of G. M. Gatti and with the collaboration of Vittorio Gui and Alfredo Casella it brought back into the repertory neglected operas such as Rossini's *L'italiana in Algeri* and Gluck's *Alceste*, and staged the first Italian performances of Strauss's *Ariadne auf Naxos*, Malipiero's *Sette canzoni* and Ravel's *L'heure espagnole*. Compared with these 'European' occasions, the other seasons pursued a dignified routine. The Fascist regime showed only a moderate interest in opera, preferring the new art for the masses. Nonetheless, among the first Italian films made (1909–10) were *Manon Lescaut* and *Lucia di Lammermoor*, produced and directed by Giovanni Pastrone, which were shown at the Odeon theatre synchronized with gramophone recordings. Lodovico Rocca, the composer of *Il Dibuk*, was a director of the conservatory (1940–66).

In 1936 the Teatro Regio burnt down, and almost all the other theatres were destroyed or damaged by bombing during World War II. After 1945 opera took second place to orchestral concerts and chamber music, and the Carignano was used solely for plays. Productions of the Ente Autonomo Teatro Regio were performed at the Teatro Nuovo until 1973 when a new Regio was built; this was inaugurated on 10 April 1973 with Verdi's *I vespri siciliani*, rehearsed by Gui and directed by Maria Callas with choreography by Serge Lifar. Operas by Sandro Fuga, Rocca's successor as director of the conservatory, performed in Turin were *Otto Schnaffs* (1950), *Confessione* (1971) and *L'imperatore Jones* (1976); in 1984 Azio Corghi's *Gargantua* was commissioned by the Regio. In the late 1980s the Teatro Regio passed through a financial crisis; some rare and foreign operas were given concert performances.

G. Papini: *Il Teatro Carignano dal 1608 ai giorni nostri* (Turin, 1935)

A. Basso, ed.: *Storia del Teatro Regio di Torino* [i, M.-T. Bouquet: *Il teatro di corte dalle origini al 1788*; ii, A. Basso: *Il teatro della città dal 1788 al 1936*; iii, M. Viale Ferrero: *La scenografia dalle origini al 1936*; iv, L. Tamburini: *L'architettura dalle origini al 1936*; v, M.-T. Bouquet, V. Gualerzi and A. Testa: *Cronologie*] (Turin, 1976–88)

M.-T. Bouquet-Boyer: *Turin et les musiciens de la cour 1619–1775: vie quotidienne et production artistique* (Paris, 1987)

P. Bassi: *Storia del Teatro Carignano di Torino dalle origini al 1799* (diss., U. of Turin, 1989)

V. Gualerzi, G. Gualerzi and G. Rampone: *Momenti di gloria – Il Teatro Regio di Torino 1740–1936* (Turin, 1990)

A. Basso, ed.: *Il nuovo Teatro Regio di Torino* (Turin, 1991)

GIORGIO PESTELLI

Turina (Pérez), Joaquín (*b* Seville, 9 Dec 1882; *d* Madrid, 14 Jan 1949). Spanish composer. He was the son of a painter of Italian descent. Music played a large part in his life from his early childhood, and although in deference to his family's wishes he began to study medicine, he soon abandoned everything that interfered with music, for which he showed a strong aptitude. His serious study began with piano lessons from Enrique Rodriguez and composition lessons from Evaristo García Torres, choir master of Seville Cathedral.

He soon became well known in Seville as a composer and, from 1897, as a pianist. His early successes prompted him to go to Madrid with the intention of arranging to have his opera *La sulamita*, which treats a biblical subject in a very traditional style, performed at the Teatro Real. This was an impossible ambition for an unknown provincial composer; but Turina gradually became well known in artistic circles and his friendship with Falla influenced his ideas on the proper character of Spanish music. In 1902 he began to study the piano at the Royal Conservatory with José Tragó. He was more affected by orchestral and chamber music than by the opera performances at the Teatro Real. Almost the only way for a composer to earn a living in Madrid, however, was as a composer of zarzuelas of the *género chico* type. But the failure of a short zarzuela, *Fea y con gracia* ('Ugly but Witty'), discouraged him, and the première in Seville of *La copla* ('The Verses') was no more successful. He accordingly turned to more ambitious forms.

In 1905 Turina moved to Paris, where he studied the piano with Moritz Moszkowski for a time and worked at composition at the Schola Cantorum under d'Indy – though it was hard to escape the influence of Debussy and other antagonists of the Schola. Albéniz, however, now joined Falla in advising him to seek inspiration in popular Spanish music. After returning to Spain with Falla in 1914 he produced his best piano and chamber music. He was elected to the Academia de Bellas Artes de San Fernando, and appointed Comisario General de la Música in 1941; he tried unsuccessfully to rebuild the ruined Teatro Real.

The picturesque local colour of Turina's music is modified by a subtle elegance, grace and humour characteristic of his native Seville. His best music, however, is not to be found in his stage works. Apart from his youthful operatic ventures, which arose from the desire, common at the time, to create Spanish opera as well as symphonic music, and the unsuccessful zarzuelas, he is remembered for his music for the lyric comedy *Margot* and the short opera *Jardín de Oriente*, conventionally exotic but based on authentic themes he had collected in Morocco. These works are however handicapped by the flawed librettos of Gregorio Martínez Sierra (or more probably Martínez Sierra's wife María who collaborated on them); indeed their dramatic weakness was remarked on at the time. Turina's theatre music is perhaps heard to best advantage in the concert hall.

See also JARDÍN DE ORIENTE.

La sulamita (3, P. Balgañón, after the Bible), *c*1900
La copla (zar, 1, J. Labios and E. Lucuix), Seville, Cervantes, 24 March 1904
Fea y con gracia (zar, 1, S. and J. Alvárez Quintero), Madrid, Moderno, 3 May 1905
Margot (lyric comedy, 3, G. Martínez Sierra), Madrid, Zarzuela, 10 Oct 1914
Jardín de Oriente op.25 (1, Martínez Sierra), Madrid, Real, 6 March 1923, prelude (Madrid, 1931)
Pregón de flores, 1939–40 (1, S. and J. Alvárez Quintero)

*

F. Sopeña: *Joaquín Turina* (Madrid, 1943, 2/1956)
A. Fernández-Cid: *Cien años de teatro musical en España* (Madrid, 1975)
J. L. García del Busto: *Joaquín Turina* (Madrid, 1981)
T. Marco: *Historia de la musica española: el siglo xx* (Madrid, 1983)
A. Morán: *Joaquín Turina a bravés de sus escritos* (Madrid, 1983)

CARLOS GÓMEZ AMAT

Turkey. Turkish interest in opera began in 1675 when the Grand Vizier Koprulu Fazil Ahmet Pasha sought the assistance of the Venetian ambassador, Giacomo Guerini, in bringing an opera company to Istanbul for the festivities on the circumcision of the Sehzade Mustafa (later Sultan Mustafa II). The project was never realized, so it was through the reports of ambassadors in various European capitals that the Turks began to learn about opera. The first such report was sent from Paris by Celebi Mehmet Efendi, describing in detail the performances he attended in Paris at the invitation of Louis XV. Information on opera could also be gleaned from the reports sent by Mustafa Hatti from Vienna in 1748, by Ahmet Resmi, again from Vienna, in 1797, by Ahmet Aziz from Berlin in 1797, by Rasih Efendi from St Petersburg and Seyit Mehmet from Paris. Selim III was the first Sultan to attend an opera performance in Turkey; this, in 1797, in the courtyard of Topkapi Sarayi, would appear to have been given by artists invited by the French Embassy.

The abolition of the Janissary Corps in 1826 was followed by the introduction of military bands in the Western style, and this westernization movement was further accelerated by a decree issued by Sultan Mahmut II in 1839. Western-type music was taught in the palace and performances were given by an Italian operatic company brought to Turkey by a Venetian, Giustiniani. In 1840 Bosco, another Italian, built a theatre for an audience of 400 in the Beyoglu (Pera) district of Istanbul, where he initiated a series of performances by an Italian company. Giuseppe Donizetti, brother of Gaetano and teacher of music in the palace, was the company's musical director. Apparently the first opera presented was Donizetti's *Belisario*, of which a Turkish translation was distributed to the audience. These performances continued for two years; when Bosco returned to his own country the theatre was taken over by Mihail Naum, a businessman with an interest in the theatre. The first piece performed under his management was Donizetti's *Lucrezia Borgia*, which was followed by Rossini's *Il barbiere di Siviglia* and a number of other Italian operas, including some by Verdi. An Italian, Lanzoni, was in charge of production, while Guatelli, a tutor in the palace, took over the musical direction. Naum's theatre burnt down in 1846 but was restored with the assistance of Sultan Abdulmecid and reopened with Verdi's *Macbeth*, followed by a large number of operas including Verdi's *Giovanna d'Arco* and *I due Foscari*, Donizetti's *Don Pasquale* and Bellini's *Norma*. The theatre again burnt down in 1870, during a performance of Auber's *La muette de Portici*; this time Naum was not in a position to undertake further initiatives.

While the new Dolmabahce Palace was under construction, Sultan Abdulmecid decided that an opera theatre should be built in the immediate vicinity: the Dolmabahce Palace Theatre was completed in 1859. A number of operas were presented, mostly by Italian companies. Some of the leading roles were taken by the tenor Mehmet Zeki, the first Turkish opera singer. The theatre burnt down in 1864, but works from the French and Italian repertory were performed by Italian artists under Italian direction in the theatre opened by Sultan Abdulhamit II in Yildiz Palace in 1889, continuing until 1908.

Armenian and Italian operas and French operettas were given in the Opera Tiyatrosu (Opera Theatre), opened in 1874, in the Gullu Agop Tiyatrosu and in the

Osmanli Opera Tiyatrosu, opened in 1883. A significant figure in the establishment of a national operatic tradition was the Armenian composer Tigran Tchukhatjian (1837–98). During World War I companies from Germany and Austria performed operettas in Turkey, and some Turkish works were seen in Vienna (such as Radeglia's *Shaban* and Saba's *Kenan Çobanlari*). Operetta continued to flourish, at the Şehir Tiyatrosu, between the wars, notably works by Cemal Rey and Sabahattin.

With the establishment of the Turkish republic in 1923, a more planned approach to opera became possible. Talented students were sent to Europe for training and in 1936 an opera and drama school connected with the State Conservatory in Ankara was set up under the direction of Carl Ebert; operatic life in the country began to approach European standards.

The first true Turkish opera was commissioned in 1934, by Kemal Atatürk, on the occasion of a state visit by the Shah of Persia; Atatürk himself chose the story (a Turkish-Persian legend) and engaged Münir Hayri Egeli to write the libretto and Ahmed Adnan Saygun to compose the music (in six months). *Özsoy* was triumphantly given at the Halkevi, Ankara; this and Saygun's later operas, *Kerem* (1953, Ankara) and *Köroğlu* (1973, Istanbul), became the basis of a national repertory, to be joined later by three operas of Okan Demiriş, *Murat IV* (1980, Istanbul), *Karyağdi Hatun* (1985, Istanbul) and *Yusuf ile züleyha* ('Joseph and his Brethren', 1990, Istanbul). Other Turkish composers whose works feature in the Ankara and Istanbul repertories include Sabahattin Kalender (*b* 1919) with *Nasrettin Hoca*, Nevit Kodalli with *Gilgameş*, Ferit Tüzün with *Midas in kulaklari* ('The Ears of Midas'), Cetin Isiközlü (*b* 1944) with *Gülbahar Agri Dagi Efsanesi* ('Gülbahar, the Legend of Mount Ararat') and *Ask ve baris* ('Love and Peace'), Selman Ada (*b* 1952) with *Ali Baba ve kirk haramiler* ('Ali Baba and the 40 Thieves'), and Turgay Erdener (*b* 1957) with *Istanbulname*.

The Turkish government has for some time had a policy of generous opera subsidy; box office proceeds are expected to cover only one per cent of the running costs and tickets are cheaper than those for the cinema. Besides the opera companies in Ankara, Istanbul and Izmir, a new one was established at Mercen in 1992 (with a company of 184 artists and a new house seating 588) and others were projected for Samsun, Gaziantep and Van as well as a new house for Ankara.

FARUK YENER, CHARLES PITT

Turkmenistan. For discussion of opera in Turkmenistan *see* ASHKHABAD.

Turnage, Mark-Anthony (*b* Grays, Essex, 10 June 1960). English composer. He studied at the RCM from the age of 14, first with Oliver Knussen and later with John Lambert. In 1981 he was awarded the Guinness Prize for his orchestral work *Night Dances*, and in a series of instrumental works over the following five years continued to develop a distinct and eclectic style. In these pieces a variety of 20th-century influences, especially those of Stravinsky and Britten, are mingled with elements taken over from rock and jazz idioms.

Study with Henze at Tanglewood in 1983 led to a continuing association, and eventually to an opera commission for the first Munich Biennale, for which Henze was artistic director. The resulting two-act work, *Greek*, to a libretto by the composer and Jonathan Moore after Steven Berkoff's play, pulled together the strands of Turnage's early development. In the wide expressive range of its vocal writing and violent orchestral interludes *Greek* revealed a distinctive dramatic flair. The première took place in Munich, at the Carl-Orff Saal on 17 June 1988.

See also GREEK. ANDREW CLEMENTS

Turner [Haas], **Claramae** (*b* Dinuba, CA, 28 Oct 1920). American contralto. She studied at San Francisco, making her début there in 1942 as the voice of a boy in *L'amore dei tre re*. In 1946, after further study in New York, she created Baba (Madame Flora) in *The Medium* at Columbia University and made her Metropolitan début as Marthe (*Faust*), returning as La Frugola (*Il tabarro*), Zita (*Gianni Schicchi*), the Princess (*Suor Angelica*) and Amneris. At New York City Opera she sang Baba (1952) and took part in the première of Copland's *The Tender Land* (1954). Her roles at Chicago (1955–7) included the Matron from Milwaukee (Banfield's *Lord Byron's Love Letter*), Fricka, Azucena and Ulrica. She sang Madame de Croissy in *Dialogues des Carmélites* at San Francisco (1957) and Baroness Grünwiesel in *Der junge Lord* at San Diego (1967), both American premières, and created Diana Orsini in *Bomarzo* at Washington, DC (1967). Her repertory included Delilah, Herodias (*Salome*), Mistress Quickly and Little Buttercup (*HMS Pinafore*). With an opulent voice, fine musicianship and an impressive stage presence, she was equally effective in 19th- and 20th-century operas. ELIZABETH FORBES

Turner, Dame **Eva** (*b* Oldham, 10 March 1892; *d* London, 16 June 1990). English soprano. She studied in Bristol, and with Albert Richards Broad. She made her début in 1916 as a Page in *Tannhäuser* with the Carl Rosa company, with which she remained until 1924, singing such roles as Santuzza, Tosca, Aida, Brünnhilde and Butterfly. In the last role she was heard by Ettore Panizza, who sent her to Milan to sing for Toscanini. She made her La Scala début as Freia (*Das Rheingold*) in 1924 and soon established herself as a leading dramatic soprano, singing Aida, Leonora (*Il trovatore*) and other roles with an Italian company touring Germany in 1925. In 1926 at Brescia she sang her first Turandot, a role with which she was closely associated for the next 20 years, and in which Alfano, who completed the opera after Puccini's death, considered her ideal (see illustration).

Turner first sang at Covent Garden with the Carl Rosa company in 1920 and then, when established internationally, between 1928 and 1939 and in 1947–8, as Turandot, Aida, Santuzza, Sieglinde, Isolde, Agathe and Amelia (*Ballo*). She also appeared in Chicago, Buenos Aires, Lisbon and elsewhere. Her voice, of enormous proportions in its prime, ranging from *g* to *d‴*, and her generous personality, were admirably suited to the dramatic soprano roles in Verdi and Wagner. She was created DBE in 1962.

T. English: 'Eva Turner', *Opera*, i/6 (1950), 29–35

J. B. Richards: 'Eva Turner', *Record Collector*, xi (1957), 29–57 [with discography], 71, 183–4, 231–3

I. Cook: 'This is Eva Turner', *ON*, xxiv/4 (1959–60), 7, 30–31

R. Crichton and others: 'Eva Turner, 1892–1990', *Opera*, xli (1990), 920–28 HAROLD ROSENTHAL/R

Eva Turner in the title role of Puccini's 'Turandot', Brescia, 27 January 1927

Turn of the Screw, The. Opera in a prologue and two acts, op.54, by BENJAMIN BRITTEN to a libretto by MYFANWY PIPER after HENRY JAMES's tale; Venice, La Fenice, 14 September 1954.

The Prologue	tenor
The Governess	soprano
Miles } *children in her charge*	treble
Flora } *children in her charge*	soprano
Mrs Grose *the housekeeper*	soprano
Miss Jessel *a former governess*	soprano
Peter Quint *a former manservant*	tenor

Setting Bly, a country house, about the middle of the 19th century

This chamber opera – the orchestra comprises 13 players – was the result of a commission for the Venice Biennale of 1954 and at the première the cast included Peter Pears as Quint, Jennifer Vyvyan as the Governess and the young David Hemmings as Miles. The subject had been in Britten's mind for some years, after a suggestion by Myfanwy Piper, and her ideas for its operatic treatment encouraged Britten to request a libretto from her rather than from William Plomer, whom he had initially thought of approaching. A complete scenario was arrived at during the summer of 1953 and the libretto began to reach Britten from early in 1954. However, it was the end of March before he was able to begin composing the music, less than six months before the date fixed for the première. The opera was completed in full score by the beginning of August, but various changes were introduced at relatively late stages, notably the addition of the Prologue and of material to the closing scene.

Like its predecessor, *Gloriana*, though for totally different reasons, *The Turn of the Screw* takes risks, not least with the demands it makes on young singers: Miles must be sung by a treble, even if Flora is rarely sung by a young girl. The première had a mixed reception, though the predominant reaction was that the work was one of Britten's finest to date, and remarkably successful in its use of small forces to create memorable dramatic effects. It has received a substantial number of productions worldwide: the first independent production was in Darmstadt in 1958; the American première was in New York in 1958; the ENO staged a successful new production in 1979. *The Turn of the Screw* was the first of Britten's operas to be recorded complete, relatively soon after the première, under the composer's own direction (1955); a second recording, under Colin Davis (1984), was associated with a television performance.

PROLOGUE Though not part of the original plan, and added for the mundane reason that the opera risked being too short, the Prologue now seems the ideal way to create an expectant, uneasy atmosphere. On paper it may look like little more than a prosaic, convenient means of filling in the background, telling how the Governess – whose name we never learn – finds out about, and finally decides to accept, the post at Bly, despite the curious circumstance that the uncle of the two children to be in her charge is an absentee guardian and insists that she shall not bother him once she is installed. Britten's musical shaping of the prose text into an arioso (for tenor and piano – the tenor often doubles as Prologue and Quint) balances justified apprehensiveness and unjustified calm to perfection; the vocal line is too shapely and expressive to be termed recitative. Above all, the way in which the orchestra unobtrusively enters at the Governess's moment of decision produces one of those powerful dramatic frissons with minimal means of which Britten is a master.

ACT 1.i (Theme) *On the journey* Each of the relatively brief, separate scenes is linked to its predecessor by the statement or variation of a 12-note theme, whose intervals rotate in screw-like fashion. This, and the organization of the work's tonal centres around a sequence from A to A♭ for Act 1, which is intervallically inverted for Act 2, reaching A at the end by a different route, suggests a high degree of structural control. The work loses nothing of vividness or vitality through this framework, and indeed it has a remarkable variety of form and mood to balance its evident coherence. In Act 1.i the Governess is travelling to Bly, and the music that depicts the rattling motion of her coach also reflects her deep anxiety about the task she has undertaken. The most ornate phrase, a melodic shape that will recur as one of the opera's principal motifs, is set to the words 'O why did I come?'.

1.ii (Variation 1) *The welcome* As they wait on the porch at Bly, the children chant exuberantly, teasing the Housekeeper. After all three greet the Governess, Britten weaves the four high-register voices into a ravishing ensemble. The Governess is completely at her ease, and declares that 'Bly is now my home'.

1.iii (Variation 2) *The letter* After a fleet-footed variation that continues the lively mood of scene ii, the first signs of trouble appear. The Housekeeper gives the Governess a letter stating that Miles has been expelled from school: the 'Why did I come?' theme, with its anxious chromaticism, returns, but the two women cannot accept that Miles is at fault. As the children sing an innocent nursery rhyme, 'Lavender's blue', the women add countermelodies whose poised shape and dissonant harmony encapsulate their hopes and fears.

1.iv (Variation 3) *The tower* All is peaceful and serene on a warm summer evening. The Governess walks in the grounds, expressing her contentment and claiming to have conquered her fears in a miniature da capo aria. Suddenly, on the tower of the house, she sees the shape of a man, and the change of mood is total. She is agitated, afraid, not knowing who he is.

1.v (Variation 4) *The window* The linking variation leads from the music of the Governess's agitation to the children's most strident and sinister rhyme, 'Tom, Tom, the piper's son'. As they move away the Governess again sees the menacing male figure, and Britten's use of celesta and harp to represent the apparition is chillingly apposite. The Governess describes the man to Mrs Grose and gradually, to music of eerie, implacable power, the Housekeeper explains her realization that the man must be Peter Quint, the former valet of the house's absent master, who was sent away for his association with the previous governess, Miss Jessel, and for his evil influence on the children: moreover – as the music settles into numb patterns of horror – both Quint and Miss Jessel are dead. Despite the horror, the Governess rallies, declaring that she must protect the children and, as instructed, not trouble their guardian. Even at this stage it is clear that her precarious sense of confidence is misplaced.

1.vi (Variation 5) *Lessons* Like scene iv, scene vi embodies a single, extreme change of mood. First Miles and Flora sing a nursery-rhyme-like list of Latin nouns. But when the Governess, after praising Miles, asks him what else he remembers, he sings a very different song, each line giving a new translation of the Latin word 'malo', and expressing his longing for change. The boy's sudden, gloomy remoteness is poignant in its simplicity, though the music, as usually with Britten, balances motivic economy and rhythmic clarity with harmonic ambivalence.

1.vii (Variation 6) *The lake* Walking with Flora in the grounds, the Governess encourages her to name as many seas as she can (to a variant of the previous scene's Latin list), then to sing a lullaby to her doll. The association between death (the Dead Sea) and sleep is underlined in both the lullaby's text and its uncannily 'limp' music. The Governess does not ask Flora where she learnt such a strange song, but the probable answer arises in the apparition of Miss Jessel, whom the Governess suddenly sees across the lake. In despair she urges Flora to run back to find Miles, and, alone, she pours out her anguished recognition that she can do nothing to save the children. Here the verbal repetitions, packed into a small-scale musical form, show Britten relishing the unavailability of large forces and of an extended time scale to create and sustain a mood.

1.viii (Variation 7) *At night* In the act's final scene the music is more expansive, though tightly focussed both in form and texture by the emphasis on relatively high voices – tenor, treble, soprano. Now the ghosts are not only seen but also heard, and the full extent of their malign power over the children is revealed. Quint's highflown poetic imagery is scarcely realistic for a corrupt valet, but it has expressive truth, an otherworldly fantasy suggesting that he is the mouthpiece for deep-seated forces of evil. There is an appropriately ornate quality to the melodic lines of Quint and Miss Jessel, especially in their duet 'On the paths'. Eventually the voices of the ghosts and the children, who have come to their call, coalesce into a haunting ensemble of incantation and response, with the Governess and the Housekeeper joining in as they approach. When they enter, the ghosts suddenly disappear, and Miles tells the Governess, using the perfect-4th interval basic to much of the work's material, especially the 'screw' theme and the 'malo' song, that he is, indeed, 'bad'. This disconcerting blend of innocence and knowingness gives a strong ending to the act.

ACT 2.i (Variation 8) *Colloquy and soliloquy* The story is not so neatly symmetrical that it can end with the restoration of the situation with which it began. But the opera underlies the complementary relationship between the acts by beginning Act 2 with the scene most similar to that which ends Act 1.

Quint and Miss Jessel reappear; their purpose now is not to display their control over the children but to explain their own motives, their desire for a power that will compensate for their previous servile status, a power that will reach its culmination when, in Yeats's line used by Myfanwy Piper, 'the ceremony of innocence is drowned', and the children are destroyed. (The setting of the Yeats line to a version of the 'Why did I come?' motif also indicates the Governess's involuntary complicity in the corruption of Miles and Flora.) The scene ends with a short aria for the Governess, 'Lost in my labyrinth', that lends strength to the confidence of the ghosts in its expression of despair and failure; she has no idea how to save the children.

2.ii (Variation 9) *The bells* This scene does much to explain the Governess's continued, crippling indecision. On the surface the children are 'charming', singing a modified *Benedicite* that never slips into outright mockery. Mrs Grose tells the Governess that if she believes the children are really in danger she should write to their uncle, and although the Governess is at first unwilling, still insisting that the uncle is not to be bothered, her unnerving exchange with Miles as the others leave for church spurs her into action. The bells that dominate the scene now seem more brazen than celebratory, and the Governess's instinct is to flee from Bly.

2.iii (Variation 10) *Miss Jessel* The Governess returns to the schoolroom, still intent on escape, but she finds Miss Jessel there, lamenting her own tragedy and threatening revenge. This assertion of possession – over the room, but also over the children – drives the Governess to retaliate, to abandon her selfish plan of flight and take the only step she believes will help the children. She writes to their guardian, accompanied by agitated music that is heard in a calmer version as she reads the letter over. Some commentators have seen this as a declaration of love as much as a plea for help; more obviously, it simply confirms the Governess's crippling ineffectiveness. She is still unable to take the children away. Somehow, as the darker interpretations of the story suggest, there is a part of her that also wills their destruction.

2.iv (Variation 11) *The bedroom* Miles is singing his 'malo' song when the Governess comes in to see if he is ready for bed. She reproaches him for failing to confide in her, and he still refuses to answer her questions about what happened at school, or at Bly before her arrival. Instinctively she knows that a frank confession will free Miles from Quint's power. She tells him that she has written to his guardian, but he hears only the seductive calls of Quint, and refuses to respond to her. The scene is crucial in its psychological insight, and the music, with the nocturnal musing of alto flute and bass clarinet disturbed by occasional flickers and shudders, is highly atmospheric.

'The Turn of the Screw' (Britten): scene from the original production at La Fenice, Venice, 14 September 1954, with Peter Pears as Quint, David Hemmings as Miles and Jennifer Vyvyan as the Governess (designed by John Piper)

2.v (Variation 12) *Quint* To music of febrile intensity and sinister charm, Quint urges Miles to steal the letter from the Governess's desk before it can be posted. After brief resistance, Miles does so.

2.vi (Variation 13) *The piano* Miles is playing the piano, the music a skilful parody of a classical sonata, to the praise of the Governess and Mrs Grose. Flora sings a cat's-cradle rhyme, lulling Mrs Grose to sleep. Flora then slips away, and the Governess quickly wakes the Housekeeper, convinced the girl has gone in search of Miss Jessel. As the scene ends, Miles continues to play the piano with increasing flamboyance. The women hurry off to find Flora.

2.vii (Variation 14) *Flora* The Governess and Housekeeper find Flora by the lake, and Miss Jessel promptly appears; Mrs Grose does not see her, and seeks to comfort Flora as the girl rails at the Governess in foot-stamping, bad-tempered music. The Governess realizes that it is Miss Jessel who has taught Flora to hate her.

2.viii (Variation 15) *Miles* Mrs Grose approaches the Governess, convinced that Flora is possessed by evil, having heard her pour out 'things I never knew nor hoped to know' in her sleep. The women agree that Mrs Grose should take Flora to her uncle, though the Housekeeper says that he will not have had the letter: it was not where the Governess had left it. Now the Governess is alone with Miles, and the passacaglia that underpins the rest of the final scene begins. It is a form that ensures a gradual increase of tension and momentum, and the rhythmic profile of the opera's recurring theme expresses the Governess's resolution. The theme also brings with it a degree of harmonic stability, in the 'home' key of A major, which is suddenly and severely disrupted as Quint begins his last attempt to prevent Miles from betraying him by speaking his name. The progress of the confrontation is brilliantly managed by Britten, though this was not achieved without some trial and error, as surviving sketches reveal. The combined lines of Quint and the Governess were not originally included, but they increase the dramatic and musical tension to breaking point. The crux is reaches as Miles at last cries out 'Peter Quint, you devil!' Quint is defeated, and his voice dies away on a restatement of his most seductive melisma; but Miles, despite the Governess's immediate, optimistic reaction – 'you are saved, now all will be well' – collapses and dies. As she realizes what has happened, the Governess sings the 'malo' song as a lament. Her final question, 'What have we done between us?', is rhetorical to the extent that the consequences of her actions (and those of the children's guardian) are all too evident – if we assume that with proper care the children need never have been exposed to the corrupting influence of Quint and Jessel. But there are larger doubts – about whether evil forces, when unleashed, can ever be contained – and the music underlines the doubt to the very end, the vocal line fading on a chromatic dissonance.

* * *

With its tightly-controlled response to James's tale, Britten's opera runs the risk of seeming to shirk depth of expression as decisively as it shuns technical elaboration. Yet there is a spontaneity and naturalness in the musical ideas, and a compact solidity in the form-schemes of each scene, which give the lie to arguments that Britten's response was thin or inhibited. Above all, the music reveals its absolute rightness in the way it brings to convincing life the extraordinary Jamesian blend of starchy social conventions and turbulent emotional forces which those conventions promote, while seeking their suppression. Britten gives substance to James's psychological insights without in any way distorting them. *The Turn of the Screw* marked a decisive change in Britten's development. After it, chamber opera would be his main concern, and the chromatic intensity obtainable from the acknowledgment of some aspects of 12-note principles a central technique. What did not change, in essence, was the type of subject Britten favoured in his dramatic works.

ARNOLD WHITTALL

Turnovský, Martin (*b* Prague, 29 Sept 1928). Czech conductor. He studied at the Prague Academy with Karel Ančerl and Robert Brock, and made his début in 1952 with the Prague SO. He won the 1958 international conductors' competition at Besançon, and took up orchestral appointments at Brno and Plzeň, then became music director at the Dresden Staatsoper (1967–8). Afterwards he embarked on a freelance career in Europe and the USA, becoming music director of the Norwegian Opera Company, Oslo (1975–80), and at the Theater der Stadt, Bonn (1979–83), and he was frequently admired for supportive understanding of singers' needs. He has conducted in Australia and New Zealand (including *L'elisir d'amore* for Canterbury Opera, 1987), and made his British opera début in *Yevgeny Onegin* with the WNO at Swansea in 1988, when he was praised for the combination of passion and sensitivity in his performance. He continues an active concert career. LESLIE EAST, NOËL GOODWIN

Turp, André (*b* Montreal, 20 Dec 1925; *d* Montreal, 25 Feb 1991). Canadian tenor. He studied in Montreal with Edouard J. Woolley and Frank H. Rowe, and was later awarded a scholarship to Italy. He made his stage début in 1950 singing operettas with the Montreal Variétés Lyriques company. In 1956 he sang in New Orleans and in 1959 appeared with the Montreal SO in Cherubini's *Médée* opposite Eileen Farrell. His New York début was also that year, in Offenbach's *La Grande-Duchesse de Gérolstein*. He made his Covent Garden début in 1960 as Edgardo in *Lucia di Lammermoor* opposite Joan Sutherland. He sang a wide variety of roles there, mainly French and Italian, and also performed elsewhere in Britain, in France, Spain, Portugal, Switzerland, Belgium, South America and Canada. Among his most successful roles were Don José, Don Carlos, Werther and Hoffmann, which he sang in 1973 with the New York City Opera. His voice had an appealing lyric quality and he was also a fine dramatic singer. From 1979 to 1989 he taught at the Conservatoire de Musique in Montreal. GILLES POTVIN

Turski, Zbigniew (*b* Konstancin, nr Warsaw, 28 July 1908; *d* Warsaw, 6 Jan 1979). Polish composer. He studied with Rytel at the Warsaw Conservatory and was later music producer for Polish Radio (1936–9) and conductor of the Baltic PO in Gdańsk (1945–6). Turski is perhaps best known as an early victim of socialist realism when his dark-hued Second Symphony (1948) was criticized at a composers' conference in Łagów in 1949. His subsequent output includes not only symphonic and chamber works but also theatre music and several ballets. Turski's musical language remained relatively immune to contemporary Polish developments in the late 1950s and 60s. His one operatic venture shows him in a light vein: the radio opera *Rozmówki* ('Chats', 1966) is a setting of a sequence of four little stories by S. Grodzieńska ('The Husband and the Television Set', 'The Dentist', 'Thin Soup' and 'The Bicycle'). ADRIAN THOMAS

Tutino, Marco (*b* Milan, 30 May 1954). Italian composer. After completing his education at the Milan Conservatory, he first came to international attention at the 1976 Gaudeamus Festival in Amsterdam. Within a few years he had established himself, alongside Lorenzo Ferrero, as one of the leading figures in a highly eclectic generation of Italian neo-romantic composers.

Tutino's willingness to respond to tastes shared by a wide range of listeners has made him a natural candidate for operatic commissions. His fluent revitalization of 19th-century convention (for instance the death scene, rich in pathos, that ends *Cirano*), combined with echoes of more recent sources such as film music and disco, has triggered lively debate among critics, and enthusiasm among operagoers.

Pinocchio (2, L. Brunetta, after C. Collodi), Genoa, Opera, 23 May 1985

Cirano (commedia lirica, 2, D. Bramati, after E. Rostand), Alessandria, Comunale, 18 Sept 1987

La lupa (1, G. di Leva, after G. Verga), Livorno, Gran Guardia, 4 Sept 1990

Le vite immaginarie (chamber op, 2, di Leva, after M. Schwob), Modena, Storchi, 16 Oct 1990 DAVID OSMOND-SMITH

Tutti in maschera ('Everyone in Disguise'). *Commedia lirica* in three acts by CARLO PEDROTTI to a libretto by M[arco] M[arcelliano] Marcello after CARLO GOLDONI's comedy *L'impresario delle Smirne*; Verona, Teatro Nuovo, 4 November 1856.

The action takes place in Venice in 1780 and centres on the intrigues of a small opera company. Two rival prima donnas compete for the professional attentions of Abdalà (baritone), a rich merchant from Damascus who has come to Venice to engage his own opera company. He flirts with one, but the *billet doux* he sends her is unfortunately picked up by the husband of the other, who assumes it is intended for his wife. The second act ends in an atmosphere of some suspicion which is not dispelled by Abdalà's invitation to the entire company to return with him to Turkey.

The third act takes place on the first night of Carnival. Everyone is in disguise (*tutti in maschera*) and the two men, still suspicious of their respective ladies, appear dressed as Turks in imitation of Abdalà. The usual misunderstandings follow, but in the end true love will out: Abdalà returns to Turkey with part of his company at least, leaving the lady with whom he first flirted to the joys of married life in Venice.

The opera is Pedrotti's best: skilfully written, vivacious and tuneful as befits the subject, it is one of the last examples of the tradition that had its origins in Neapolitan *opera buffa*, before Verdi and Puccini transformed the genre for ever. MICHAEL ROSE

Tüzün, Ferit (*b* Istanbul, 24 April 1929; *d* Ankara, 21 Oct 1977). Turkish conductor and composer. He studied the piano with U. C. Erkin and composition with Necil Akses at the Ankara State Conservatory. In 1950 he became assistant professor there, and in 1954 he left Turkey for Munich to study at the Hochschule, where he completed a four-year course in orchestral conducting under Fritz Lehmann and Adolf Mennerich. Later he worked as a répétiteur at the Prinzregententheater. In 1959 he became assistant conductor at the Ankara State Opera; he was appointed general director shortly before his death. Tüzün's music is characterized by a skilful use of folk music and modal systems, combined with a keen but refined satirical approach. Besides piano, chamber and orchestral pieces, he composed one opera, *Midas in kulaklari* ('The Ears of Midas', based on a play by the Turkish writer Güngör Dilmen), first performed in 1969. FARUK YENER

Tvrdé palice. Opera by Antonín Dvořák; *see STUBBORN LOVERS, THE.*

Twardowski, Romuald (*b* Vilnius, 17 June 1930). Polish composer. He studied the piano and composition with Julius Juzeliūnas at the Vilnius Conservatory (1952–7) and was then a pupil of Bolesław Woytowicz at the Warsaw Conservatory. In 1963 a French government scholarship took him to Paris to study medieval polyphony and Gregorian chant with Nadia Boulanger. He has received many awards, including first prize in the Prince Rainier of Monaco competition at Monte Carlo in 1973, for *Lord Jim*. His early writing, marked by sharply dissonant counterpoint and rich harmony, gave way in the 1960s to a more avant-garde manner akin to that of other Polish composers of his generation.

Twardowski is committed to music drama as a principal forum for bridging the divide between contemporary writing and its audiences. His musical idiom is spare and contrapuntal, and he tends to adopt a specific style for each opera that reflects his interest in synthesizing older music, particularly medieval and Renaissance polyphony, and modern compositional practices. That concern is furthered by his choice of subjects, which cover a wide historical range, from *Tragedyja, albo rzecz o Janie i Herodzie* ('Tragedy, or A Piece on John and Herod'), based on a 17th-century drama but set in AD 29, through *Historia o św. Katarzynie* ('The History of St Catherine') with its 4th-century setting, *Maria Stuart*, *Cyrano de Bergerac* (17th century) and *Lord Jim* (19th century) to *Pieśń bez słów* ('Song without Words'), an 'operatic humoresque' for television set in Warsaw and Rome in the 1920s. In *Tragedy*, material that draws on 17th- and 18th-century Polish sacred music is juxtaposed with folk-derived idioms, while in *Maria Stuart*, based on the play by Stefan Zweig, stylized Renaissance music is used to lend period colour. *Upadek Ojca Suryna* ('The Fall of Father Suryn'), which concerns illicit sex in the monastic orders, was composed before Penderecki's more famous opera on a similar subject, *The Devils of Loudon*. It features three different systems of notation for the vocal parts, allowing a gradual transition from speech to singing.

Lord Jim, based on the novel of the same name by Joseph Conrad, is arguably Twardowski's masterpiece. It is set in the Far East in the late 19th century, and the composer adopted an 'exotic' idiom for the Patusan scene. The dialogue is constructed in a manner consonant with the narrative style of the author, for whom the narrator in the prologue serves as a spokesman. In the portrayal of the individual against society, a deft combination of the lyrical and the explosively violent gives the music a strong expressive edge; this also holds true for *Maria Stuart* and the morality opera *The History of St Catherine*. Besides opera Twardowski has written three ballets and a large quantity of choral music.

all librettos by the composer

Cyrano de Bergerac (4, after E. Rostand), Bytom, Silesian Opera, 6 July 1963

Tragedyja, albo rzecz o Janie i Herodzie [Tragedy, or A Piece on John and Herod], 1964 (mystery op, 2, epilogue, after J. Gawatowic), Łódź, Wielki, 26 April 1969

Upadek Ojca Suryna [The Fall of Father Suryn] (radio op, 1, after J. Iwaszkiewicz: *Matka Joanna od Aniołów* [Mother Joan of the Angels]), Polish Radio, 3 Dec 1969

Lord Jim, 1970–73 (music drama, 3, after J. Conrad), Łódź, Wielki, 14 Feb 1976, prol. and 2nd interlude (Kraków, 1976)

Pieśń bez słów [Song without Words], 1976 (operatic humoresque for TV, 1, after S. Żeromski: *Pavoncello*), broadcast, Warsaw, 1985

Maria Stuart, 1976–8 (music drama, 3, after S. Zweig), Łódź, Wielki, 12 April 1981

Historia o św. Katarzynie [The History of St Catherine], 1981 (mystery op, 2, with J. Lewański, after J. P. Cichoński), Warsaw, Wielki, 14 Dec 1985

T. Marek: 'A New Opera by Romuald Twardowski: *Tragedy or A Tale of John and Herod*', *Polish Music* (1970), no.1, pp.28–9

R. Twardowski: 'Composer's Workshop: Progress Reports on the Opera *Lord Jim*', *Polish Music* (1970), no.4, pp.20–23

——: 'A Composer's Reflection on "Mary Stuart"', *Polish Music* (1981), no.3–4, p.24

D. Szwarcman: 'After the Premiere of Romuald Twardowski's "The Story of St. Catherine"', *Polish Music* (1986), no.1–2, p.19

MIECZYSŁAWA HANUSZEWSKA, JIM SAMSON, ADRIAN THOMAS

Twilight of the Gods. Opera by Richard Wagner, the fourth part of *Der Ring des Nibelungen*; *see* GÖTTERDÄMMERUNG.

Twin Cities Opera. Opera company founded in 1930 in MINNEAPOLIS AND ST PAUL. In 1933 it re-formed as the St Paul Civic Opera.

Two Widows, The [*Dvě vdovy*]. Comic opera in two acts by BEDŘICH SMETANA to a libretto by EMANUEL ZÜNGEL after P. J. F. Mallefille's play *Les deux veuves*; Prague, Provisional Theatre, 27 March 1874 (with spoken dialogue); Prague, Provisional Theatre, 15 March 1878 (with recitatives and extra numbers).

Karolina *a rich widow*	soprano
Anežka *a rich widow, recently bereaved*	soprano
Ladislav Podhajský *a landowner in love with Anežka*	tenor
Mumlal *Karolina's gamekeeper*	baritone
Toník *a country lad*	tenor
Lidunka *a country girl engaged to Toník*	soprano

Young countryfolk

Setting Karolina's country estate

Mallefille's one-act comedy was known to Prague audiences from Alexander Bergen's German translation (Estates Theatre, 24 June 1862), and from Emanuel Züngel's Czech translation (Provisional Theatre, 25 August 1868), based not on the original French, but on Bergen, who muted the French satire and wit. Züngel then adapted his version as an opera libretto for Smetana. According to his pencil sketch, Smetana began *The Two Widows* on 14 July 1873 and finished it on 30 August 1873. The scoring of Act 1 was completed by 18 November 1873 and that of Act 2 by 15 January 1874. At this stage the work was an 'opéra comique' with spoken dialogue, four soloists and chorus, and 13 numbers including the two preludes. Smetana himself conducted the première.

Dissatisfaction with this version after its production in Prague in 1874 led to a second, in which the spoken dialogue was replaced by recitatives and two minor parts (Toník and Lidunka) were added. There was also a new finale to Act 1 and two new numbers in Act 2: Ladislav's aria and the trio for Lidunka, Toník and Mumlal. This version, completed on 13 July 1877, is regarded as definitive despite the additions that Smetana reluctantly conceded in 1882, after the Hamburg production of December 1881. The Hamburg version (published in 1893 – an authentic Czech edition appeared only in 1914) added a cabaletta to Anežka's aria and a new trio for Karolina, Anežka and Mumlal, within a much-altered libretto in three acts in which the action was relocated to France.

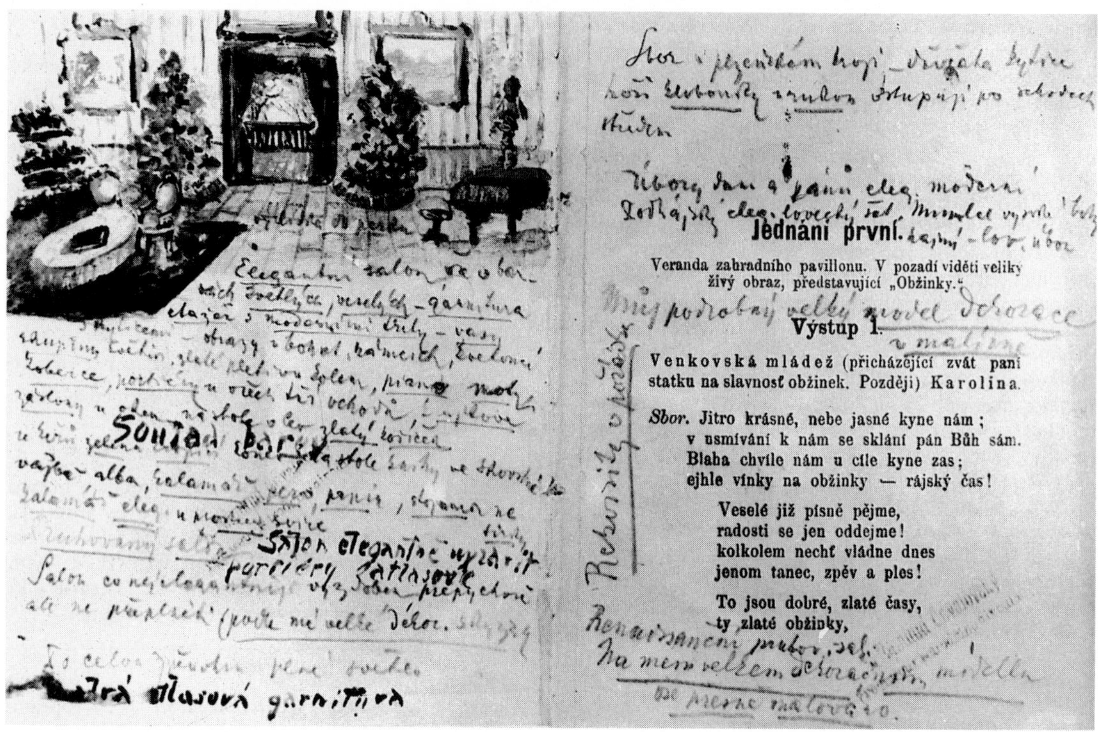

Edmund Chvalovský's production notes for the première of the definitive version of Smetana's 'The Two Widows' at the Provisional Theatre, Prague, 15 March 1878

Apart from two brief episodes (Andante, 6/8) and a four-bar introduction, the separate overture is a vigorous Alla breve, its opening theme a *moto perpetuo* that suggests the brisk pace of much of what follows.

ACT 1 *The veranda of a garden pavilion* Young countryfolk greet the lady of the manor, Karolina, their 3/4 chorus breaking into a 2/4 polka, one of the most characteristic musical features of the opera. Karolina thanks them and after a further chorus welcomes her cousin Anežka, seen in deep mourning. In her aria 'Samostatně vládnu já' ('I rule independently') Karolina tries to cheer up Anežka by describing her own life as a widow. Again the initial 3/4 soon moves into 2/4, Karolina's carefree attitude reflected by the coloratura flourishes at the end. The entrance of her gamekeeper Mumlal injects a comic element: his ponderous self-importance (in the tradition of Kecal in *The Bartered Bride*) is the frequent butt of Karolina's humour. As usual he is complaining, first about Karolina's undermining his efforts to catch poachers, and then about a strange new poacher who mocks him and seems almost as if he wants to be caught. This long number concludes with a repeated structure consisting of Mumlal's description of the poacher with a trio refrain. The women withdraw to observe Mumlal's encounter with the poacher, set to the *moto perpetuo* from the overture. Ladislav (the poacher) is indeed anxious to be caught and it is only Mumlal's timidity that prevents it. When eventually Mumlal plucks up his courage, the two men are heard in simultaneous duet in which Ladislav's slow, lyrical lines are contrasted with Mumlal's triplet patter.

Mumlal brings his captive before the ladies and Karolina decides that he must be tried – by Anežka. Anežka's reaction makes clear that she knows him: he is an old admirer, anxious to gain an entrée. Reactions are summed up in a quartet, a slow 6/8 in which Anežka's misgivings and Ladislav's joy are prominent. Ladislav freely admits his motives and in a 6/8 ballad, 'Aj, vizte lovce tam' ('Ah, you see the hunter there'), tells the sad story of a hunter searching vainly for a beautiful water nymph (who has evaded his efforts by turning into a deer). His tale is rounded off by a quartet: the ladies are affected. Ladislav is then formally interrogated (he comes across as a most eligible bachelor) and fined. This provokes a sparkling 6/8 trio; recitative discussions of how the criminal is to be locked into the former master's room lead to a further verse with Mumlal's voice added to make a quartet.

In the finale the chorus returns and makes fun of Mumlal (all in 2/4 polka music). Lidunka and Toník are observed in a compromisingly tender duet, which broadens out into an ensemble for chorus and all six soloists about the power of love. As the curtain falls Mumlal leads off Ladislav for his 'sentence'.

ACT 2 *A large room with a veranda* The separate prelude (a *moto perpetuo* polka in quavers) is followed by Ladislav's 'song', 'Kdy zavítá máj' ('When May welcomes the time of love'), sung from his 'prison' to an empty stage. It was one of the 1874 additions, and its strophic structure and variable metre at the beginning suggest a folk imitation – an odd notion in view of its aristocratic singer. Anežka enters and listens. Karolina joins her and declares that he must be in love with one of them. If Anežka doesn't want him, Karolina will take him. This recitative leads into the best-known number of the opera, the duet 'Rozhodnuto, uzavřeno' ('It's decided, concluded'), based on the Act 2 prelude. It is sung in turn and then together by the two women. In the middle section Anežka ironically recalls Karolina's

'Samostatně vládnu já' and, before the polka duet is recalled, warns her to be careful.

Karolina leaves her. Against an orchestral background of disconnected phrases harmonized with a chromatic poignancy unparalleled elsewhere in the opera, Anežka silently reads a letter from Ladislav. He enters; Anežka tries to leave. Their long confrontation shows the depth of Anežka's feeling and her unsuccessful attempts at suppressing it. Anežka admits that she has received Ladislav's letter, saying however that she has 'burnt' it without reading it. Ladislav insists on reading a copy (a melodrama against the orchestra) and Anežka betrays herself by declaring that his speech was not in the letter. But she wishes to remain faithful to the memory of her husband and the couple bid each other a painful farewell. Ladislav is about to leave when Karolina enters in a ball-gown and insists on dancing (a waltz now strikes up). Anežka should go and mourn, she declares, as she goes off with Ladislav. Left alone, Anežka gives full vent to her feelings. She acknowledges that she drove Ladislav away herself; her multi-tempo aria culminates in an Allegro con fuoco of self-pity.

Light relief is provided by numbers for the comic characters: a strophic song for Mumlal (with much unsuitable coloratura) and a trio in which Mumlal intercepts Toník and Lidunka every time they try to kiss but is finally bettered by them.

Karolina pursues her 'conquest' of Ladislav until Anežka enters, now also in a ball-gown. All are surprised, Anežka herself by the rate at which Karolina's advances seem to be progressing; a quartet (which includes Mumlal) prolongs this moment into an expressive Andante. Karolina tells Anežka that her change of mind has come too late but finally confesses that her own behaviour was simply a ploy to bring about this change of mind. Thus Anežka and Ladislav are finally united. Mumlal announces a banquet. The opera concludes with a polka to which chorus voices are added.

* * *

After his most nationalist operas, *Dalibor* and *Libuše*, Smetana wrote this opera, sometimes considered to be his least nationalist. This is perhaps because of the French provenance of the text (unique for a Smetana opera – all his other completed operas are based on Czech subjects), and the conversational style (much admired by Richard Strauss). And yet Züngel's mostly trochaic text, the basis for the ubiquitous polkas, and Smetana's new-found sensitivity to Czech word-setting, meant that in its musical language *The Two Widows* is no less obviously Czech than any other of Smetana's operas. It provided the model for a new genre of Czech conversational operas such as Ostrčil's *Poupě* ('The Bud'). JOHN TYRRELL

Tyl Theatre [Tylovo Divadlo]. Opera house in Prague, until 1945 known as the Estates Theatre; in 1991 it reverted to the name Estates Theatre. *See* PRAGUE, §IV, 1.

Tyrén, Arne (*b* Stockholm, 27 Feb 1928). Swedish bass. After studying in Stockholm, he made his début in 1955 as Bartolo with the Royal Swedish Opera, of which he was a member for 30 years. He created the commander Chefone in Blomdahl's *Aniara*, repeating the part at Edinburgh (1959) and Covent Garden (1960), the title role of Blomdahl's *Herr von Hancken* (1965) and Reuterholm in Werle's *Tintomara* (1973). He sang frequently at Drottningholm and his repertory included many comic roles, such as Buonafede (*Il mondo della luna*), Don Alfonso, Leporello, Don Magnifico, Don Pasquale, Rocco, Daland, Falstaff and Ochs; but he sang Seneca, Sarastro, Wotan, King Mark, Gurnemanz, the Grand Inquisitor and the four villains (*Les contes d'Hoffmann*) with equal success. A superb actor with a moderate-sized but well-projected voice, he excelled in characterizations such as the Doctor in *Wozzeck* or Kolenatý in *The Makropulos Affair*. ELIZABETH FORBES

Tyroler Wastel, Der ('Wastel the Tyrolese'). *Komische Oper* in three acts by JAKOB HAIBEL to a libretto by EMANUEL SCHIKANEDER; Vienna, Theater auf der Wieden, 14 May 1796.

One of the best and most successful of Schikaneder's *Lokalstücke* – Singspiels set in Vienna and characterized by 'realistic' depiction of local characters – *Der Tyroler Wastel*, with music by Mozart's posthumous brother-in-law Haibel (he married Sophie Weber in 1807), was performed 66 times in 1796 and in October was followed by a more briefly popular sequel, *Östreichs treue Brüder, oder Die Scharfschützen in Tirol*. These plays helped establish the popularity of Tyrolese characters and costumes in Vienna, by emphasizing the simple, outspoken nature of the honest countryman faced by the duplicity and selfishness of city manners. Wastel (bass) visits Vienna with his wife, but stays only long enough to help cure his vain sister-in-law's social aspirations and help his niece secure the hand of the young baker with whom she is in love. The extensive score (like *Die Zauberflöte* it has an overture and 21 numbers) includes two trios and three duets as well as two extended finales; the best-loved numbers, especially the dance-duet 'Tyroler sand often so lustig, so froh' and the harpist's song 'Ihr Männer, nehmt euch mit die Weiber in acht', became virtual folksongs. The work was widely performed in Austria and Germany until well into the 19th century and reached St Petersburg and Paris. A vocal score arranged by Joseph Strobl has been published (Vienna and Munich, 1969).

PETER BRANSCOMBE

Tyrrell, John (*b* Salisbury, Southern Rhodesia [now Harare, Zimbabwe], 17 Aug 1942). British musicologist. He studied at the University of Cape Town (BMus 1963) and at Oxford (DPhil 1969: *Janáček's Stylistic Development as an Operatic Composer as Evidenced in his Revisions of the First Five Operas*). He served as associate editor of *The Musical Times* and worked on the editorial staff of *The New Grove Dictionary of Music and Musicians* before becoming lecturer at Nottingham University (1976; Reader in Opera Studies, 1989). He has written widely on Janáček's operas, in books, in learned journals and in many lucid, informative record notes and programme notes; his writings include a monograph *Leos Janáček: Kát'a Kabanová* (Cambridge, 1982), a valuable study of Czech opera (Cambridge, 1988) and *Janáček's Operas: a Documentary Account* (London, 1992).

Tzveych, Biserka. *See* CVEJIĆ, BISERKA.

U

Uber, Christian Friedrich Hermann (*b* Breslau [now Wrocław], 22 April 1781; *d* Dresden, 2 March 1822). German composer. While studying law in Halle he came to the attention of D. G. Türk. He conducted some of his own works in Halle in 1801, including the Violin Concerto op.3. In 1804 he turned to a career in music and travelled with Prince Radziwiłł to Berlin, where he performed at the opera and entered the service of Prince Louis Ferdinand. After serving briefly as a violinist in Brunswick, in 1808 he took over the directorship of the Kassel opera, for which he wrote his stage work *Moses*. He left in 1814 to become theatre conductor at Mainz, where he composed an opera, *Der frohe Tag* (1815); in 1816 he became director of the Seconda company in Dresden. After it was dissolved he worked briefly in Leipzig as a teacher, lecturer and author, then in 1818 returned to Dresden to take up a career in church music. He wrote another opera, *Les marins* (the overture of which appeared in print), a melodrama *Der Taucher*, an intermezzo *Der falsche Werber*, an overture to *Le Juif errant* (published as op.6), some incidental music and several cantatas and violin concertos.

His father, Christian Benjamin Uber (1746–1812), a lawyer and amateur musician, was a virtuoso glass-harmonica player. He composed a comic opera, *Clarissa, oder Das unbekannte Dienstmädchen* (3, J. C. Bock; vs, Breslau, 1772), which was performed in Breslau in 1771.

FRITZ FELDMANN

Uccellatrice, L' ('The Bird-Catcher'). Intermezzo in two parts by NICCOLÒ JOMMELLI; Venice, Teatro S Samuele, 6 May 1750 (revised as *Il paratajo*, to a libretto by Charles-François Clément, Paris, Opéra, 25 September 1753).

The original Italian version involves only two singing characters and a silent role. While hunting, Don Narciso (tenor) spies the bird-catcher Mergellina (soprano). Thinking her a woodland goddess, he falls in love. She teases him unmercifully, then relents, and they join the rest of the hunting party. The intermezzo was reworked as *Il paratajo* (in French, *La pipée* – the libretto includes the French translation), acquiring another pair of characters and several new arias. This opera, along with works like Pergolesi's *La serva padrona*, presented in Paris during 1753, fuelled the Querelle des Bouffons and led to the introduction of italianate elements into French opera.

Jommelli's music is in the graceful, lightly ornamented mid-century *buffo* style. Arias are brief, and melodies, built on simple harmonic progressions, are short-breathed, repetitious of words and music, and periodic. As a whole the work is playful and charming. The woodland setting calls forth musical references to birds, and terror elicits nonsense syllables and rapid parlando. A duet concludes each of the two parts, and there is a string obbligato to accompany Don Narciso's recitative when he believes he is losing his 'Diana'.

MARITA P. McCLYMONDS

Udbye, Martin Andreas (*b* Trondheim, 18 June 1820; *d* Trondheim, 10 Jan 1889). Norwegian composer. He was largely self-taught, but scholarships enabled him to study composition with Hauptmann in Leipzig (1851) and to make a study trip to Berlin, Leipzig, Dresden, Vienna and London (1858–9). He held appointments as organist at churches in Trondheim and was for a time singing master at the cathedral school.

Udbye's impressive output of diverse and complex works belies his limited formal training. His compositions include the opera *Fredkulla* ('The Peacemaker', 1858) and the operettas *Hr. Perrichons reise* (1861), *Hjemve* ('Homesickness', 1862; Christiania [now Oslo], 8 April 1864) and *Junkeren og flubergrosen* ('The Squire and the Rose of Fluberg', 1867; Christiania, 7 January 1870). These dramatic works in particular show the influence of Weber, among others, and his attempts to create a personal style were only partly successful. His affinity for drama is apparent, however, in his other vocal works, from his choice of texts and his musical expression.

T. Wisth: 'Komponisten Martin Andreas Udbye og de musikalske miljø i Trondhjem omkring 1850', *Trondhjemske samlinger*, 3rd ser., ii/4 (Trondheim, 1967), 304

KARI MICHELSEN

Udine. City in Friuli, north-east Italy. Opera was first performed in 1651 by a travelling company led by G. G. Arrigoni. For Carnival 1672 G. B. Spinelli's company gave Draghi's *Iphide greca*, and for the occasion he equipped a theatre with boxes in the Sala della Loggia (via Mercatovecchio), named Teatro Contarini. After the performance of an *Argia* there during Carnival 1673–4 the theatre was dismantled, and the municipality decided to construct a new Teatro Contarini in a building of its own. The work was however suspended in 1677 or 1678, when a private citizen, Carlo Mantica, equipped a hall with two rows of boxes;

the resulting Teatro Mantica was opened for Carnival 1680 with the Spinelli company, and remained in use until 1754. Between 1730 and 1755 opera was also staged in the theatre of the Barnabite College. In 1754 Giacomo Cicogna had two tiers of boxes installed in the Sala della Racchetta, and operas were performed there until 1769. Work also started on the Teatro Nobile, or Teatro dei Nobili Associati, so called because the interior of the building had been furnished with 68 boxes in three tiers by a group of nobles. It was inaugurated on 9 August 1770 with *Eurione* (the season lasted until 10 September). Renovated in the 19th century, it presented seasons of some 23 performances at Carnival and for the S Lorenzo fair (10 August), and occasionally minor seasons of comic opera for S Caterina (25 November). It became the Teatro Sociale in 1852. During the early 20th century the number of boxes was gradually reduced, and between the wars the building was renamed Teatro Puccini. After World War II it was used as a cinema; it was finally demolished in 1964.

*

DEUMM (F. Piperno)
A. Battistella: *I vecchi teatri udinesi* (Udine, 1929)
M. Fior Sartorelli: 'Il Teatro sociale di Udine', *'Ce fastu?', Rivista della Società filologica friulana*, xxix (1953), 83–91; xxx (1954), 125–40
G. Pressacco: 'La musica nel Friuli storico', *Enciclopedia monografica del Friuli Venezia Giulia*, iii: *La storia e la cultura* (Udine, 1981), 2011ff

PAOLO FABBRI

Udinskoye. ULAN-UDE.

Ufa. Capital of Bashkortostan, in western central Russia, on the western slope of the Urals. Formed in 1938 with soloists chosen from new graduates of the Moscow Conservatory, the Bashkirskiy Teatr Operï i Baleta opened with a performance of Paisiello's *La molinara*. During World War II the theatre served as a temporary home for the Shevchenko State Academic Opera and Ballet, evacuated from Kiev. Premières at the theatre have included the first Bashkir national opera, M. M. Valeyev's *Kakmar* (1940), N. K. Chemberdzhi's *Karlugas* (1941), and a number of works by Ismagilov.

*

ME ('Bashkirskiy teatr operï i baleta'; N. Sh. Gubaydullin)
N. A. Shumskaya: 'Muzïkal'naya kul'tura bashkirskoy ASSR', *Muzïkal'naya kul'tura avtonomnïkh respublik RSFSR* (Moscow, 1957), 88
G. Bernandt: *Slovar' oper vpervïye postavlennïkh ili izdannïkh v dorevolyutsionnoy Rossii i v SSSR 1736–1959* [Dictionary of Operas First Performed or Published in Pre-Revolutionary Russia and in the USSR 1736–1959] (Moscow, 1962), 552
R. Khayrullin: *Mastera opernogo iskusstva Bashkirii* [The Masters of Opera in Bashkir] (Ufa, 1963)
Yu. V. Keldïsh, ed.: *Istoriya muzïki narodov SSSR* [History of the Music of the Soviet Peoples], i-v (Moscow, 1970–74)

GREGORY SALMON

Ugalde [née Beaucé], **Delphine** (*b* Paris, 3 Dec 1829; *d* Paris, 19 July 1910). French soprano. She studied in Paris with Cinti-Damoreau and made her début in 1848 at the Opéra-Comique as Angèle in Auber's *Le domino noir*, a role created by her teacher. In 1851 she sang at Her Majesty's Theatre, London, as Delilah in Auber's *L'enfant prodigue*. In 1858 she sang Leonora (*Il trovatore*) at the Paris Opéra and was then engaged at the Théâtre Lyrique. In 1863 she moved to the Bouffes-Parisiens, where in 1867 she sang in her own operetta, *Halte au moulin*. She retired in 1871. Her daughter, Marguerite Ugalde (1862–1940), was a mezzo-soprano who sang with the Opéra-Comique; in 1881 she created Nicklausse in the company's production of *Les contes d'Hoffmann*.

ELIZABETH FORBES

Ugarte, Floro M(elitón) (*b* Buenos Aires, 15 Sept 1884; *d* Buenos Aires, 11 June 1975). Argentine composer. He showed an early interest in music, and later studied composition at the Paris Conservatoire. On completing his education in 1913, he returned to Buenos Aires, where he held various teaching positions, including a professorship at the Conservatorio Nacional de Música. He had a longstanding association with the Teatro Colón. As a member of its Board of Directors (1924–6), he presided over the formation of resident orchestral, choral and ballet troupes. He also served as the Technical Director (1930) and General Director (1936–43, 1946, 1956) of the theatre.

Ugarte is recognized as one of the leading Argentine composers of his generation. His early works show traces of French impressionism; later he infused his style with melodic, rhythmic and harmonic suggestions derived from Argentine folk music. He composed a one-act fairy-tale opera, *Saika*, to his own libretto, which was first performed at the Teatro Colón on 22 July 1920. Critics praised its colourful orchestration and predicted a bright future for the young composer.

*

M. Kuss: 'La contribución de Floro Ugarte a la formación del teatro lírico argentino', *Heterofonía*, vii/6 (1974), 17–21
——: *Nativistic Strains in Argentine Operas Premiered at the Teatro Colón (1908–1972)* (diss., UCLA, 1976)

DEBORAH SCHWARTZ

Ugo conte di Parigi ('Hugo, Count of Paris'). *Tragedia lirica* in four parts by GAETANO DONIZETTI to a libretto by FELICE ROMANI after HIPPOLYTE-LOUIS-FLORENT BIS's *Blanche d'Aquitaine*; Milan, Teatro alla Scala, 13 March 1832.

The plot concerns Ugo [Hugues Capet] (tenor) and his loyalty to Louis V of France (contralto). The royal fiancée Bianca (soprano) loves Hugues, whose engagement to Bianca's sister Adelia (soprano) is announced by Louis. The plot is resolved when Bianca drinks the poison she had originally intended for Louis.

Ugo was important to Donizetti's career as his first major engagement at La Scala (not counting the anaemic *Chiara e Serafina* of 1822). It put him once more in direct opposition to Bellini, who had opened that season with *Norma*. Donizetti's score, designed for the same historic cast, headed by Pasta and Giulia Grisi, ran into such problems with the censors that the opera had to be extensively revised, rendering the plot almost incomprehensible and causing Romani to repudiate his libretto. The première was delayed until the end of the season, and though the opera failed Donizetti's music won a *succès d'estime*.

WILLIAM ASHBROOK

Uhde, Hermann (*b* Bremen, 20 July 1914; *d* Copenhagen, 10 Oct 1965). German baritone. He studied as a bass at Philipp Kraus's opera school in Bremen, where he made his début as Titurel in *Parsifal* (1936). After some years at Freiburg and Munich he first appeared in baritone roles at The Hague in 1942. A prisoner-of-war from 1944 to 1947, he then sang regularly at Hamburg, Vienna and Munich. He scored a great success at Covent Garden with the Munich company as Mandryka in *Arabella* (1953), and later in Munich itself as Gunther and Telramund, roles in which he was generally recognized as unsurpassed in his lifetime. He sang at Bayreuth and Salzburg, and made a particular impression at the Metropolitan with his Wozzeck, sung in English. He created many roles, including Creon in Orff's *Antigonae* (which, like his performance of Wagner's Dutchman, is still impressive on record). He died during a performance of Bentzon's *Faust III*.

A. Williamson: 'Hermann Uhde', *Opera*, xii (1961), 762–9

J. B. STEANE

Uhl, Alfred (*b* Vienna, 5 June 1909; *d* Vienna, 8 June 1992). Austrian composer. A pupil of Schmidt, he studied at the Vienna Hochschule für Musik and from 1945 taught there. Awards made to him include the Austrian State Prize (1960), the Vienna Music Prize (1961) and the Viennese Gold Medal of Honour (1969). His comic opera *Der mysteriöse Herr X* (3, T. Lingen) was first performed at the Theater an der Wien, Vienna, on 8 June 1966. Uhl avowedly sought to preserve the best of the Austrian heritage in this *buffo*-style piece, constructed as theatre within the theatre.

CHARLOTTE ERWIN

Uhl, Fritz (*b* Matzleinsdorf, nr Vienna, 2 April 1928). Austrian tenor. After study with Elisabeth Rado in Vienna, he made his début at Graz in 1950. Appearances in Lucerne and Oberhausen were followed by an engagement at the Munich Opera, where he sang from 1957. He made his début at the Bayreuth Festival in 1958 and sang there until 1968 as Erik, Loge and Siegmund. During the 1960s he appeared in Paris, Buenos Aires, Vienna, San Francisco and London (Walther in *Die Meistersinger* under Kempe, 1963). He appeared in the première of Sutermeister's *Le roi Bérenger* at the 1985 Munich Festival. His forthright, even unsubtle, style can be heard in his recording of Tristan under Solti.

DAVID CUMMINGS

Uhlig, Theodor (*b* Wurzen, nr Leipzig, 15 Feb 1822; *d* Dresden, 3 Jan 1853). German theorist, critic and composer. The illegitimate son of King Friedrich August II of Saxony, he studied with Friedrich Schneider in Dessau (1837–40) and joined the Dresden orchestra in 1841. Although he was initially hostile to Wagner, study of *Tannhäuser* and of the essay on Beethoven's Ninth Symphony turned him into one of the earliest, most loyal and most articulate of Wagner's defenders. His 'great seriousness and his quiet but unusually firm character' attracted the attention of Wagner, who also wrote in his autobiography that Uhlig 'had grasped with clear understanding and perfect agreement those very tendencies of mine which many musicians of apparently wider culture than his own regarded with almost despairing horror, as being dangerous to the orthodox practice of their art'. He remained a close friend of Wagner, whose correspondence with him is filled with enlightening personal and professional details. He attacked Meyerbeer and *Le prophète* in 1850–51 in the *Neue Zeitschrift für Musik*, at the same time defending *Tannhäuser*, *Lohengrin* and Wagner's operatic practice in general. He allowed his sympathies for Berlioz, Weber, Mendelssohn and Schumann to be diminished by his devotion to Wagner; but he is important for being one of the first critics to write about music, with reference to the issues raised by Wagner, as not merely a limited aesthetic sensation or a matter for technical theory but part of the cultural life of a country and an epoch. Most of his published writings appeared in an edition by L. Frankenstein in Regensburg in 1914.

Uhlig's compositions include Singspiels, symphonies, chamber music and songs. His three-act Zauberposse, *Ein Prophet, oder Johannes Leiden und Freuden*, to a text by G. Räder, was given at Dresden in 1850.

M. Ahrend: *Theodor Uhlig* (Bayreuth, 1904)
M. Gregor-Dellin, ed.: *Richard Wagner: Mein Leben* (Munich, 1963)
G. Strobel and W. Wolf, eds.: *Richard Wagner: Sämtliche Briefe*, iii-v (Leipzig, 1975–89)
S. Spencer and B. Millington, eds.: *Selected Letters of Richard Wagner* (London, 1987)

JOHN WARRACK

Ukraine. The operatic history of Ukraine falls neatly into two periods: before and after 1917 (for Kiev and other cities of eastern and southern Ukraine, Kharkiv, Odessa and Donets'k; the break falls in 1939 for L'viv, in western Ukraine, since it was incorporated into the Ukrainian Soviet Socialist Republic only at that date). The beginnings of operatic activity were essentially an extension of the operatic life of the dominant political force occupying the country, whether tsarist Russia, Austro-Hungary or Poland. The colonial powers did however develop a thriving operatic life, building fine theatres and inviting the best singers, directors and conductors. As provincial capitals, Kiev, L'viv, Odessa and Kharkiv had extensive and important operatic lives, but Ukraine as such lacked the economic and territorial integrity to develop an independent operatic culture until after the 1917 revolutions. The national aspirations of the 19th century were dealt with harshly by the tsarist regimes, culminating in the Ems Ukase of 1876, which essentially forbade the development of Ukrainian culture. Thus by the end of the 19th century, any Ukrainian national operatic life was confined to travelling troupes with a repertory reflecting peasant life – in short, musical comedies of the vaudeville variety.

The operatic life of the principal cities did not lack superior productions, international singers, conductors or the latest repertory. But until the 20th century no national school of composers or performers could develop. The earliest important Ukrainian operatic composers are Maxim Berezovsky (1745–77) and Dmitry Bortnyansky (1751–1825); Berezovsky's *Demofoonte* was the first opera by a 'Russian' to be performed in Italy (1773, Livorno). Both are usually referred to as Russians because Ukraine was part of the Russian empire, and both worked outside Ukraine (Berezovsky in Bologna and St Petersburg; Bortnyansky, after completing his musical education in Venice, in St Petersburg from 1779). Bortnyansky's operas are based on Italian models but incorporate elements of Ukrainian monophonic chant and Ukrainian and Russian folk music.

Ukrainian national opera began with Semyon Gulak-Artemovsky's *Zaporozhets za Dunayem* ('A Cossack Beyond the Danube'; 1863, St Petersburg). Spoken dialogue is used rather than recitative. The Italian tradition provides a basis, but there is a marked Ukrainian colour, in the harmonic and melodic structure as well as in the use of folk tunes; this lively and clever work manages to combine musical sophistication and Ukrainian vaudeville. In the late 19th century Petro Sokal's'ky composed *Mazepa* (1858–9), *Mays'ka nich* ('May Night', 1876) and *Osada Dubno* ('The Siege of Dubno', 1878); although not professionally produced, these works attempted to create a musical language distinctively Ukrainian though with strong European roots. The models were Czech as well as Russian. Other significant

Ukrainian opera composers include Mykola Arkas (1852–1909; *Kateryna*, 1899), Anatol' Vakhnyanin (1841–1908; *Kupalo*, 'St John the Baptist Day', 1870), Borys Pidhorets'ky (1873–1919; *Kupal'na iskra*, 'The Spark of Kupalo', 1901), Denis Sichyns'ky (1865–1909; *Roksolyana*, 1908) and Kyrylo Stetsenko (1882–1922; the miniatures *Ivasyk-Telesyk*, *Lesychka kotyk i pivnyk*, 'A Fox, a Cat and a Cockerel' and *Ifheniya v Tavrydi*). In all these the material is based on Ukrainian history or on plots drawn from works by Taras Shevchenko or Nikolay Gogol (Mykola Hohol in Ukrainian), and there is the almost obligatory use of folktunes to establish Ukrainian identity.

A central role in the development of a national style belongs to Mykola Lysenko, who further developed the operetta in such works as the folksy *Natalka Poltavka* (1889) and the satirical *Eneida* (1910), based on the great parody-epic by Kotlyarevs'ky. *Taras Bulba*, (composed 1880–91, after Gogol) became the cornerstone of Ukrainian grand opera and a model for Ukrainian national opera tradition. As reworked in the 1920s by Levko Revuts'ky, it is still seen on the Ukrainian stage. Lysenko's style, with its lines based on Ukrainian melody and a harmonic tradition of 19th-century Romanticism, became one that composers either continued to emulate (such as Mykhaylo Verykivsky, 1896–1962, and Kostyantyn Dan'kevych, 1905–84) or rejected (such as Boris Lyatoshyns'ky, 1895–1968). Lysenko established a national school which tried during the late 19th century and the early 20th to create a Ukrainian version of what was being done in Russia, Poland and what became Czechoslovakia. He and others were hampered by the impossibility of professional productions; until the creation of a Ukrainian state and Ukrainian opera companies, the composers tended to work in a vacuum.

During the early 20th century, subject matter as well as style began to move from historical and peasant themes to the fantastic and impressionistic. The musical style also began to show impressionistic tendencies and greater refinement of Ukrainian folk melody. A work of considerable originality is Mykola Leontovych's unfinished *Na Rusalchyn Velykden'* ('On Rusalka's Easter', or 'On the Mermaid's Holiday', 1921, edited and given its première in 1977); it pioneered a genre of 'ritual' opera that reached its most complete development in Yevhen Stankovych's folk opera *Tsvit paporoti* ('The Fern's Bloom', 1977: see below). After the establishment of the Ukrainian Republic in 1917, 19th-century works were revived and new works written in an essentially grand operatic tradition, culminating in Dan'kevych's *Bohdan Khmel'nyts'ky* (1951) and an expressionist tradition, established with Lyatoshyns'ky's masterpiece *Zolotyy obruch* ('The Golden Ring'; 1930, rev. 1970). This was a Ukrainian music drama of the first order, with a strong, modern harmonic language and expressionistic staging and decor. Unfortunately, it came at a time close to the establishment of the 'socialist realism' dogma, which forbade such developments and encouraged the Lysenko line.

Until the 1970s, operatic life was forced to follow the Russian model. Little new ground was broken but the concept of a distinctive Ukrainian sound was legitimized. The style of Romantic vitalism was directed towards the composition of operas on revolutionary themes (Volodymyr Femelidi's *Rozlom*, 'The Split', 1929; Yuly Meytus's *Moloda hvardiya*, 'The Young Guard', 1947; Heorhy Mayboroda's *Arsenal*, 1960; Vitaly Hubarenko's *Zahybel' Eskadry*, 'The Destruction of the Squadron', 1967), on peasant life (Meytus's *Ukradene shchastya*, 'Stolen Happiness', 1960) and on historical figures (Lyatoshyns'ky's *Shchors*, 1938; Mayboroda's *Taras Shevchenko*, 1964). The more recent operatic works reflect a many-sided stylistic coin: from Volodymyr Zahortsev's extremely contemporary and experimental *Maty* ('Mother', 1983) to Mayboroda's traditional grand opera *Yaroslav mudryy* ('Yaroslav the Wise', 1975) and Valentin Bibik's highly personal musical style in *Byeg* ('Flight', completed 1983). A significant achievement of the mid-1970s was the folk opera *Tsvit paporoti* by Stankovych. The original commission by a French company had been for an opera on Gogol's *Taras Bulba*, but that was forbidden by the communist party censors and instead a folk opera was created, its outer acts dealing with traditions of the Zaporozhian Cossacks, while Act 2, on Gogol's *The Eve of Ivan Kupalo*, became an investigation and celebration of the Ukrainian rites of St John's Eve. The significance of the work was the mystical folkloristic imagery created by Stankovych as an expression of a still suppressed Ukrainian renaissance that exposed the oldest traditions of the Ukrainian mythopoetic imagination in words and music. After one private rehearsal however, it was banned. The style is eclectic; the most original feature was the use of the folk vocal tradition rather than the academic operatic style, surrounded by a sophisticated Western orchestra. This particular direction was pursued by Volodymyr Zubyts'ky (*b* 1953), a prolific and talented composer, in *Chumats'kyy shlyakh* ('The Galaxy', literally 'Ox-Cart Driver's Way', 1983), dramatic frescoes based on Ukrainian legends, dumas and historical songs. The independence of Ukraine in 1991 offered new opportunities for the exploration of subjects and styles formerly neglected or forbidden.

For further information on operatic life in the country's principal centres *see* DONETS'K; KHARKIV; KIEV; L'VIV; and ODESSA.

*

M. Hrinchenko: *Istoriya ukraïns'koï muzyky* (Kiev, 1922, 2/1961)
V. Kubijovyč, ed.: *Entsyklopediya ukraïnoznavstva* (Paris and New York, 1955–84)
A. Rudnyts'ky: *Ukraïns'ka muzyka: istorychno-krytychnyy ohlyad* [Ukrainian Music: a Historic and Critical Outline] (Munich, 1963)
O. Ya. Shryeyer-Tkachenko, ed.: *Istoriya ukraïns'koï dozhovtnevoy muzyky* [History of Ukrainian Music before the October Revolution] (Kiev, 2/1969)
L. Arkhimovych: *Shlyakhy rozvytku ukraïns'koï radyans'koï opery* [Paths of Development of Ukrainian Soviet Opera] (Kiev, 1970)
Yu. Stanyshevs'ky: *Operniy teatr radyans'koï ukraïny* [The Opera Theatre of Soviet Ukraine] (Kiev, 1988) VIRKO BALEY

Ukroshcheniye stroptivoy ('The Taming of the Shrew'). Comic opera in four acts by VISSARION YAKOVLEVICH SHEBALIN to a libretto by ABRAM AKIMOVICH GOZENPUD after Shakespeare's comedy; Kuybïshev (now Samara), Opera and Ballet Theatre, 25 May 1957 (previously performed in concert, Moscow, Central House of Art Workers, 1 October 1955).

Shebalin initially contemplated *The Taming of the Shrew* as a musical comedy in 1942, but during its long gestation the work gradually evolved into a comic opera. Shebalin continued to adapt and rework it for various productions: between the first staged performance in Kuybïshev and the production by the Bol'shoy Theatre two months later, for instance, he completely rewrote the penultimate scene, between Katherine and Petruchio.

To condense Shakespeare's comedy to its operatic essence many of the secondary characters and complex plot lines were eliminated and scenes were added or re-arranged. What was retained was the pact between two suitors – Liuchentsio [Lucentio] (tenor) and Gortenzio [Hortensio] (bass) – for Bianka [Bianca] (soprano), the younger daughter of the rich Paduan merchant Baptista Minola (bass), and Petruchio (baritone), a nobleman from Verona, who undertakes to marry Minola's 'shrewish' elder daughter, Katarina [Katherine] (soprano), and to tame her within a month. By the end of the opera, not only has this goal been brilliantly achieved but the young couple have fallen deeply in love. Little of Shakespeare's text was retained. In his versified libretto, however, Gozenpud remained close to the spirit of the original, finding an equivalent for Shakespeare's adroit blend of coarse and lofty styles and a vehicle for his trenchant wit as well as the genuine ardour of the lovers' passions.

In his musical treatment, Shebalin did not aim for novelty; rather he emphasized classic operatic values. The structure of the opera retains aria, ensemble and choral numbers, and the styles of recitative range from cantilena to parlando. The composer made little attempt to imitate period musical styles, although the dance music for the wedding in Act 3 is a suite consisting of Menuet, Sarabande and Tarantella. Use of leitmotifs helps to unify the drama. A sophisticated command of polyphonic textures and orchestral colour does not detract from the strong melodic focus of the opera. The lyrical warmth of the score, its memorable melodies and infectious rhythms, the satisfying balance between the good-natured comic elements and the human emotion and sympathetic characterization of the strong-willed lovers as their romance unfolds, all contributed greatly to the work's success. The opera has received numerous productions and revivals both in Soviet cities and abroad. LAUREL E. FAY

Ulaanbaatar [Ulaan Baatar; Ulan Bator]. Capital of the Mongolian People's Republic. In 1922 a music and theatrical circle was formed to stage musical plays. In 1942 B. Damdinsurem wrote the first national opera, *Uchirtai gurvan tolgoi* ('Three Fateful Hills'), to a libretto by D. Natsagdorj, the founder of modern Mongolian literature. Mongolia's first symphony orchestra gave its first public performance in 1945, and the State Opera and Ballet Theatre (cap. 800) in Sukhe Baatar Square was opened at this time. The company performs mainly Russian operas and ballets, though there is also a number of Mongolian operas in the repertory. These include *Three Fateful Hills* (performed there over 2000 times) and the same composer's *Amongst those Mountains* and *Jargalyn zam* ('Way of Happiness'); *Ünen* ('Truth'), written in the late 1950s by S. Gonchigsumlaa (Merited Artist of the Republic and chairman of the Mongolian Composers' Union); *Khukhu Namdjil* ('"Cuckoo" Namdjil') by L. Mördorj; *Cloudy Fate* (1988) by Ts. Natsagdorj; and *Lambugain nulims* ('A Lama's Tears'; 1989) by H. Bilegjargal.
CHARLES PITT

Ulan-Ude. Capital of Buryatiya, south-eastern Russia, formerly known as Udinskoye (1666–1783) and Verkhne-Udinsk (1783–1934). The history of professional music for the stage began with a performance on 3 July 1938 of P. M. Berlinsky's *Bair* in the Dramaticheskiy Teatr. The theatre was reorganized for musical-dramatic works the following year, and the group performed the first fully-fledged Buryat opera, Frolov's *Enkhe – Bulat-bator* ('Enkhe, the Steel Hero'), in 1940. The musical group became independent of the dramatic in 1948 and was renamed the Buryatskiy Teatr Operï i Baleta, receiving a new 718-seat theatre in 1952. Premières have been almost exclusively of Buryat national operas such as Knipper's *Na Baykale* ('At Baikal', 1948), S. N. Riauzov's *Medegmasha* (1949) and works by V. V. Yampilov.

*

ME ('Buryatskiy teatr operï i baleta')

L. S. Khodorovskaya: *Buryat-Mongol'skiy teatr* (Moscow, 1954)

Iskusstvo Buryatskoy ASSR [The Art of the Buryat Republic] (Ulan-Ude, 1959)

G. Bernandt: *Slovar' oper vpervïye postavlennïkh ili izdannïkh v dorevolyutsionnoy Rossii i v SSSR 1736–1959* [Dictionary of Operas First Performed or Published in Pre-Revolutionary Russia and in the USSR 1736–1959] (Moscow, 1962), 552

P. S. Gurevich: *Operniy teatr Buryatii* (Ulan-Ude, 1964)

Yu. V. Keldïsh, ed.: *Istoriya muzïki narodov SSSR* [History of the Music of the Soviet Peoples], i–v (Moscow, 1970–74)
GREGORY SALMON

Ulbrich, Maximilian (*b* Vienna, 16 January 1743; *d* Vienna, 20 Sept 1814). Austrian civil servant and composer. He attended the Jesuit seminary in Vienna and studied harmony and composition with G. C. Wagenseil and the organ and sacred music with J. G. Reutter. He entered the service of the Lower Austrian *Stände* (estates of the realm) in 1770 and was pensioned in 1804. Between 1778 and 1786 he composed two Singspiels – the earlier of which, *Frühling und Liebe* (1778), survives in manuscript – and a 'heroisch-komische Oper', *Der blaue Schmetterling* (1782). Ulbrich was repeatedly invited to perform as a bass singer, cellist and pianist in chamber music at the court of Emperor Joseph II. As a composer he is best known for the oratorio *Die Israeliten in der Wüste*; besides operas he also wrote church music and a number of instrumental works.

all performed in Vienna

Frühling und Liebe (Spl, 2, J. F. Schmidt, after C. Gozzi), Burg, 8 Sept 1778, *A-Wn*

Der blaue Schmetterling, oder Sieg der Natur über die Schwärmerei (heroisch-komische Oper, 2, Ulbrich, after C. M. Wieland), Burg, 2 April 1782

Die Schnitterfreude (Spl, 3, K. F. Hensler), Leopoldstadt, 6 July 1786

*

StiegerO

L. von Köchel: *Die kaiserliche Hof-Musikkapelle in Wien von 1543–1867* (Vienna, 1869)

E. Hanslick: *Geschichte des Concertwesens in Wien* (Vienna, 1869–70), 32–3
OTHMAR WESSELY

Ulfung, Ragnar (Sigurd) (*b* Oslo, 28 Feb 1927). Norwegian tenor. He studied at Oslo and Milan, making his début in 1952 at Oslo as Magadoff (*The Consul*). He sang Faust at Bergen and in 1955 went to Göteborg, where he sang Jeník, Don Ottavio, the Duke, Fra Diavolo and Don José. In 1958 he was engaged at the Royal Opera, Stockholm, where he created the Deaf Mute in Blomdahl's *Aniara* (1959) and sang Canio, Hoffmann, Alfredo, Cavaradossi, Tom Rakewell, Lensky and Gustavus III, which he also sang in Edinburgh (1959) and on the company's visit to Covent Garden (1960). There he returned as Don Carlos (1963), Mime and Herod, and created the title role in *Taverner* (1972). At Hamburg he sang Turiddu, Erik and Števa (also on the company's visit to New York in 1967) and created

Christopher in Werle's *Resan* (1969). He made his San Francisco début as Chuck (Schuller's *The Visitation*), returning for Riccardo, Valzacchi and Mime, the role of his Metropolitan début (1972). His repertory included Fatty (*Aufstieg und Fall der Stadt Mahagonny*), Captain (*Wozzeck*), Loge, Aegisthus (1972, La Scala), Otello (1983, Stockholm) and Jadidja (American première of Penderecki's *Die schwarze Maske* at Santa Fe, 1988). A brilliant actor with an incisive voice, he excelled as Herod and Mime. He also directed many operas.

*

N. Benvega: 'Ragnar Ulfung', *Opera*, xxvi (1975), 837–42

ALAN BLYTH

Ulisse [Ulysses]. Opera in a prologue, two acts and an epilogue by LUIGI DALLAPICCOLA to his own libretto after HOMER's *Odyssey*; Berlin, Deutsche Oper, 29 September 1968.

The prologue consists of three episodes. In the first, the goddess Calypso (soprano) gazes out to sea from the island of Ogygia, lamenting that Ulysses (baritone) has left her, even though she offered to make him immortal. The second episode, depicting Poseidon's angry persecution of Ulysses, is for orchestra alone. As the sound of the stormy sea dies away, the scene changes to a wooded beach on the island of Phaeacia, where a group of young girls are playing as they wait for their washing to dry. Only the princess Nausicaa (high soprano) sits apart. She is remembering a dream, a vision of a bridegroom who came to her from the sea. The girls resume their game, but break off suddenly when a man appears from the wood, wearing only a few twigs and leaves. They throw a robe round his shoulders, and Nausicaa, without knowing his identity, welcomes him as the bridegroom of her vision. The stranger is overcome with wonder at Nausicaa's beauty, and kneels at her feet. She tells him to rise and accompany her to the palace of her father, King Alcinoo [Alcinous] (bass-baritone).

Act 1 consists of five scenes: the first and last take place in the King's palace, and they act as a frame for the inner three, in which Ulysses narrates some of his past adventures. Alcinous is holding court in the great hall of his palace when Ulysses enters with Nausicaa. The bard Demodoco [Demodocus] (tenor) sings of what befell the Greek heroes after the fall of Troy and then begins musing on Ulysses' fate. As Demodocus becomes more impassioned, Ulysses can restrain himself no longer and breaks down. The King, noticing his tears, asks his name. Ulysses identifies himself, and agrees to tell them his story. The first scene immediately dissolves, revealing Ulysses' ship about to drop anchor off the island of the Lotus-eaters (boys' voices). His crew are near to mutiny, but they agree to beach the ship when they hear the sound of the Lotus-eaters in the distance. The islanders then appear, drugged into euphoric lassitude through eating the blossoms and fruits of the lotus. They offer these to Ulysses' crew, some of whom, despite his exhortations to the contrary, accept. When Ulysses finally re-embarks, only a few of his companions go with him.

After an orchestral interlude, scene iii opens on the island of Aeaea, home of the enchantress Circe (mezzo-soprano). Ulysses has spent more than a year with her, and he is anxious to move on. At first she refuses to let him, and when finally she does give way, she revenges herself by pointing out that all the horrors he encountered on his wanderings were reflections of his own inner nature. He will eventually return to Ithaca, she assures him, but he will find no repose there; his heart – unquiet to the last – will crave the sea again.

Following a brief interlude depicting the sirens' song, scene iv opens on a desolate riverbank in Hades where the souls of the damned wander for eternity in torment. Ulysses has come to Hades to question the ghost of the seer Tiresia [Tiresias] (tenor; often doubling Demodocus) about his future destiny. But first, to his horror, the shade of his mother Anticlea (soprano) appears. She reproaches him for leaving Ithaca: his long absence broke her heart, and her existence in the afterlife is a continual torment. Ulysses tries to embrace her, but she vanishes before he can do so. Tiresias then appears, to tell Ulysses that he will see Ithaca and his

'Ulisse' (Dallapiccola): scene from the original production at the Deutsche Oper, Berlin, 29 September 1968, with Erik Saedén as Ulysses

wife and son again, but his homecoming will be a bloody one. Tiresias goes on to confirm Circe's prophecy: even after Ulysses has returned to Ithaca, he will set out again on his wanderings. Scene v reverts to Alcinous's palace where Ulysses winds up his narrative, briefly indicating his other adventures. Alcinous promises to help him, and Act 1 ends as Nausicaa bids him farewell, asking him not to forget her.

In the first scene of Act 2 the suitors of Penelope, Ulysses' wife, have set a trap for Telemaco [Telemachus] (countertenor), Ulysses' son, who is returning by sea from Sparta. Antinoo [Antinous] (baritone), Eurimaco [Eurymachus] (tenor) and Pisandro [Peisander] (baritone), together with their whore, the maidservant Melanto (mezzo-soprano; often doubling Circe), are waiting on a clifftop on Ithaca, to see whether their plans have succeeded. After a while the suitors depart, and Ulysses arrives, disguised as an old beggar, asking the shepherd Eumeo [Eumaeus] (tenor) for hospitality. His eyes frighten Melanto, and when she sees beacons (announcing Telemachus's safe arrival) flare up on the neighbouring hill, she rushes, terrified, back to the palace. Telemachus then runs in, describing his escape, and he too, like everyone else, fails to recognize the disguised Ulysses.

In scene ii Ulysses is standing outside the royal palace, listening to Penelope (soprano; often doubling Calypso) singing as she weaves. Inside, the suitors are holding a banquet, but Melanto is worried because she feels that some terrible danger threatens. She leaves the palace, and re-enters only when Antinous assures her that all will be well.

As scene iii opens, the feast is in full progress. The suitors make Melanto dance, giving her the bow of Ulysses as inspiration. Her savage dance is interrupted by the arrival of Telemachus, whom the suitors believed to be dead. They have not recovered from their surprise when Ulysses enters, and reveals his identity. He orders the guards to hang Melanto, strings the great bow that only he can use and strikes down the suitors one by one. As the crowd disperse Penelope appears.

The epilogue follows after a symphonic intermezzo. Once more at sea and far from Ithaca, Ulysses contemplates the stars, knowing that his knowledge and experience have not brought him repose or wisdom. He prays for some word that will make everything clear. The opera ends as he is vouchsafed a prophetic vision of God. He is alone no more.

With this ending Dallapiccola hoped to answer the question posed at the end of his earlier opera *Il prigioniero*. His understanding of the Ulysses myth, while following the outline of Homer's narrative, owes much to subsequent, more philosophical, less dramatic interpretations of the *Odyssey*, e.g. those of Dante, Pascoli, Tennyson and of course Joyce. The music is in Dallapiccola's late, very refined style and uses 12 closely related 12-note rows that are leitmotifs in themselves and from which a large range of symbols is derived. Dallapiccola's earlier theatre pieces took as their central idea the struggle of man against a force stronger than he, but Ulysses' struggle is above all a struggle against himself, inasmuch as he aspires to penetrate the mystery of the world. The opera is structured as a large, symmetrical arch. In the centre is Ulysses' descent into Hades where, gazing into the abyss, he realizes that he is utterly alone. On either side of this, through his encounters with women and with the Homeric monsters, Ulysses is made to search into himself – an attitude encapsulated in the words 'Guardare, meravigliarsi, e tornar a guardare' ('To search, to wonder, and to search again and again'), with which the opera opens. The vision of God which Ulysses is vouchsafed at the end of the opera enables him to put aside his doubts. It also enabled Dallapiccola to do the same, and to express the certainty in God which had often eluded him throughout his own life. In this respect, Dallapiccola conceived *Ulisse* as the summation of his life's work, and he incorporated into it fragments of many of his earlier scores.

ANTHONY SELLORS

Ullman [Ullmann, Ulman, Uhlman], **Bernard** (*b* Budapest, ?1817; *d* 2 Oct 1885). Hungarian impresario active in the USA. He arrived in America in about 1842 and from 1846 managed American tours by various important instrumentalists and singers, including Henriette Sontag and her opera troupe (1852–4). In 1857 he was awarded the lease to the New York Academy of Music; his opera company (co-managed by Maurice Strakosch) was backed by Sigismund Thalberg. Ullman kept the lease on the Academy for five seasons; his troupes, known variously as the Academy of Music, the Ullman and the Ullman-Strakosch opera companies, featured such singers as Anna de la Grange, Elena d'Angri, Erminia Frezzolini, Edouard Gassier, Carl Formes, Marietta Piccolomini and Adelina Patti. Conductors included Carl Anschütz and (in 1859) Theodore Thomas. The 1859–60 season suffered financial losses, but was saved from complete ruin by the operatic début of Adelina Patti (24 November 1859). In spring 1862 Ullman returned to Paris, where he managed Carlotta Patti (1865–9) and Christine Nilsson (1876–7). He was one of the first impresarios to measure success commercially rather than artistically.

L. M. Lerner: *The Rise of the Impresario: Bernard Ullman and the Transformation of Musical Culture in Nineteenth Century America* (diss., U. of Wisconsin, 1970)

R. A. Lott: *The American Concert Tours of Leopold de Meyer, Henri Herz, and Sigismund Thalberg* (diss., CUNY, 1986)

K. K. Preston: *Travelling Opera Troupes in the United States, 1825–1860* (diss., CUNY, 1989)

R. A. Lott: 'Bernard Ullman: Nineteenth-Century American Impresario', *A Celebration of American Music: Words and Music in Honor of H. Wiley Hitchcock* (Ann Arbor, 1990), 174–91

WILLIAM BROOKS, KATHERINE K. PRESTON

Ullmann, Viktor (*b* Těšín, 1 Jan 1898; *d* Auschwitz, 17 Oct 1944). Austro-Czech composer. He grew up in Vienna where he was accepted into Schoenberg's advanced courses for the 1918–19 academic year. Through Schoenberg he was invited to join Zemlinsky's conducting assistants at the New German Theatre in Prague in 1920, his duties including preparation of choruses and solo singers. He occasionally substituted for Zemlinsky (notably in Schoenberg's *Gurrelieder* in 1921) and his own productions were favourably reviewed. In 1927 he became 'first Kapellmeister' in Aussig, where he directed operas of his own choice, among them *Tristan und Isolde*, *Ariadne auf Naxos*, *Jonny spielt auf* and *Le nozze di Figaro*. After one season Ullmann left Aussig and spent several years in Stuttgart where, as a follower of Rudolf Steiner, he worked in the anthroposophical bookstore. Following a visit to Dornach and a brief stay in Zürich, in 1933 he returned to Prague, where he taught privately, lectured, worked for the radio and wrote articles for *Der Auftakt* and other German-language periodicals. He studied with Alois Hába for two years, receiving instruction in quarter-tone music, and maintained contact with other members of the Schoenberg circle, especially those in the Prague section of the Society for Private Musical Performances. The German occupation in 1939 prevented Ullmann from leaving Prague and in September 1942 he was deported to Theresienstadt (Terezín), the Nazi concentration camp. He continued to compose, organized concerts, lectured and served as music critic there until his transport to and immediate death in Auschwitz in October 1944.

Ullmann's music, which includes piano, chamber and orchestral works and songs, is eclectic: besides his admiration for Mahler, it echoes both Debussyan and Schoenbergian textures and sonorities. It is always intensely expressive, and the mixture of chromatic harmony, variation techniques and frequent polyphonic structures displays a strong individuality, also felt in his stage works. He began his first opera, *Peer Gynt* (after Ibsen), in 1928 but it was not performed and the music is lost. In 1935 he finished *Der Sturz des Antichrist*, a setting of the anthroposophical drama by Albert Steffen, with whose aesthetic and philosophical outlook he identified. Although the opera is highly chromatic, it does not exceed the bounds of an extended tonality. His one-act opera, to Kleist's *Der zerbrochene Krug*, was written in about 1940. In Terezín Ullmann wrote a libretto for the play *Der 30. Mai 1431*, about St Joan, but apparently did not begin the music. In 1943, however, he did complete *Der Kaiser von Atlantis, oder Der Tod dankt ab*. In four scenes, it is an often grotesque portrayal of a king, who forces humanity to indulge in senseless slaughter as part of a universal war, and of Death, who refuses to allow people to die; the music contains echoes of Weill, Hindemith and Viennese expressionism. The work was rehearsed in September 1944, but the obvious allusion to Hitler, together with the removal to Auschwitz of most of the participants, prevented its performance at that time; its première was on 16 December 1975 in Amsterdam.

See also KAISER VON ATLANTIS, DER.

*

E. Steinhard: 'Deutsche Tondichter der Tschechoslowakei', *Der Auftakt*, iv (1924), 149

M. Brod: 'Junge deutsch-Prager in der Musik', *Der Auftakt*, xiii (1933), 39–40

E. Steinhard and V. Helfart: *Die Musik in der Tschechoslowakischen Republik* (Prague, 1938)

M. Bloch: 'Viktor Ullmann: a Brief Biography and Appreciation', *Journal of the Arnold Schoenberg Institute*, iii (1979), 151–77

J. Ludvová: 'Nezhámý Rozbitý Džbán' [The Broken Jug], *HRo*, xxxii (1979), 470–73 [on *Der zerbrochene Krug*]

——: 'Viktor Ullmann (1898–1944)', *HV*, xvi (1979), 99–122

J. Karas: *Music in Terezin 1941–1945* (New York, 1985)

DAVID BLOCH

Ulm. German town on the Danube. The Wengenstift, a house of Augustinian canons, began to stage Singspiels in the early 1500s. During that century, at the height of the city's importance as a centre of commerce, its Meistersinger school provided occasional theatre performances, some with music. Touring troupes used the Binderhof, the city's first purpose-built theatre (1641), and the Komödienhaus im Kutschenhaus (1781, later the Stadttheater); the latter saw the local premières of operas by Mozart, Wagner and Richard Strauss. In 1920 the theatre established its own orchestra (until then a military band had served that function), and in 1928 it was granted municipal status. Herbert von Karajan conducted there from 1929 to 1934, and the mezzo-soprano Margarete Klose made her début there in 1927. The house was closed in 1944 and destroyed in March 1945, but in September of the same year a provisional theatre opened at the former gymnasium of the Wagnerschule, and was used until 1969 when the newly built Ulmer Theater opened. It has two stages and two auditoriums, with capacities of 815 and 200 seats. Giancarlo del Monaco was stage director there from 1970 to 1973. Since then Ulm has presented a wide repertory, and commissioned Kurt Schwertsik's *Der lange Weg zur grossen Mauer* (1975). HORST KOEGLER

Ulmar, Geraldine (*b* Boston, 23 June 1862; *d* 13 Aug 1932). American soprano. She began her career in autumn 1879 as a leading soprano with the Boston Ideal Opera Company, where her repertory included roles in Gilbert and Sullivan operas. Her connection with D'Oyly Carte's opera company began in July 1885, when she auditioned for Sullivan and was engaged to play Yum-Yum in Carte's New York *Mikado*. She remained with the company on its return to England and subsequent visit to Berlin. In May 1887 she replaced Leonora Braham at the Savoy Theatre as Rose Maybud in *Ruddigore*, making a favourable impression. Thereafter Ulmar sang leading soprano parts at the Savoy, including Elsie Maynard in *The Yeomen of the Guard* (1888) and Gianetta in *The Gondoliers* (1889). She left Carte in 1890 to appear in Audran's *La cigale et la fourmi* at the Lyric Theatre, where she was re-engaged to play Teresa in Gilbert's *The Mountebanks* (music by A. Cellier, 4 January 1892). In 1894 she married the composer Ivan Caryll, then musical director at the Gaiety Theatre; her second husband was the songwriter Jack Thompson. FREDRIC WOODBRIDGE WILSON

Ultimo giorno di Pompei, L' ('The Last Day of Pompeii'). *Opera seria* in two acts by GIOVANNI PACINI to a libretto by ANDREA LEONE TOTTOLA; Naples, Teatro S Carlo, 19 November 1825.

Pacini considered this opera to have been the 'greatest triumph' of his first artistic period. It centres on a love triangle in which the tribune Appio Diomede (tenor) is rejected by Ottavia (soprano), wife of Sallustio (bass), the First Magistrate of Pompeii. Seeking revenge, Appio conspires with Pubblio (tenor), custodian of the public baths, to accuse her of seducing Pubblio's young son Clodio (soprano). Since his wife is unable to refute their charges, Sallustio must sentence her to be buried alive. Before she can be entombed, however, Vesuvius rumbles ominously, leading Pubblio and Clodio to confess their role in Appio's intrigue. Ottavia's salvation is only momentary, because the volcano then erupts, killing everyone (for illustration *see* MILAN, fig.5).

L'ultimo giorno is typical of the Neapolitan machine operas of its time in incorporating a final cataclysm (like the one in Rossini's *Mosè in Egitto*). In his memoirs Pacini discussed innovations in his treatment of several cabalettas in the opera, and his formal experimentation is evident on a larger scale in the Act 1 ensemble 'Ecco la man di Astrea'. An unsuccessful effort at mounting the opera in Paris (1830) began a series of failures that affected Pacini profoundly and led eventually to his temporary withdrawal from the operatic scene in 1835.

SCOTT L. BALTHAZAR

Ulysse ('Ulysses'). *Tragédie lyrique* in a prologue and five acts by JEAN-FÉRY REBEL to a libretto by HENRY

GUICHARD after HOMER; Paris, Opéra, 23 January 1703.

The libretto recounts the return of Ulysses (bass, originally sung by Thévenard) to Ithaca where the sorceress Circé [Circe] (soprano, Desmatins), still in love, follows him and tries to win him back with guile and magic. The gods play an active part in thwarting Circe's designs: Junon [Juno] (soprano, Loignon) prevents Pénélope [Penelope] (soprano, Maupin) from succumbing to her suitor Urilas [Urylaos] (bass, Hardouin); Mercure [Mercury] (*haute-contre*, Boutelou) releases Ulysses' companions from darkness; Minerve [Minerva] (soprano, D'humé) saves Télémaque [Telemachus] (*haute-contre*, Cochereau), the last pawn of Circe's Machiavellian plot. The opera ends with true love triumphing over evil.

In *Ulysse* Rebel followed the framework of Lully's *tragédies lyriques* and included scenes which lent themselves to the 'merveilleux'. There are certain pre-Ramiste elements, such as 'high-lying textures' (G. Sadler) in which the lowest part lies in violin range; in addition, the orchestra is used as an expressive tool, especially in battle, earthquake and storm scenes. Although *Ulysse* was never revived, Campra and Danchet included selections in *Télémaque, ou Les fragmens des modernes* (1704), a pastiche of both text and music drawn from *tragédies lyriques* that had been staged only once at the Opéra between 1691 and 1703.

VLADIA KUNZMANN

Ulysses (i). *Musicalisches Schau-Spiel* in a prologue and three acts by REINHARD KEISER to a libretto by Friedrich Maximilian Lersner after HENRY GUICHARD's *Ulysse*; Copenhagen, Court Theatre, ?November 1722.

After a prologue acclaiming King Frederick IV of Denmark on his birthday, the opera tells the story of Ulysses' return to Ithaca in a version very different from that in the *Odyssey*. During the long years of his absence, his wife Penelope (soprano) has remained constant in her love. One of her disappointed suitors, Urilas [Urylaos] (bass), seeks the aid of the sorceress Circe (soprano), who has come to Ithaca in hopes of again seducing Ulysses with her magical powers. She summons infernal spirits to make Penelope love Urylaos, but Penelope succeeds in resisting their charms. The returning Ulysses (bass) first encounters Circe, who tells him that Penelope is planning to kill him and gives him a magic sword that causes him to believe he loves her instead. When Penelope joyfully welcomes him he accuses her of treachery. Ulysses' lieutenant, Eurilochus (tenor), discovering what has happened, takes the sword away from him, breaking the spell. The enraged Circe tries to stab Penelope, but Mercury (tenor) intervenes and drives Circe away. Having put down a rebellion fomented by Urylaos, Ulysses is happily united with Penelope, and the opera ends with more praise of Frederick and his queen.

Though virtually unknown today, *Ulysses* is one of Keiser's most impressive achievements. Along with moments of intense dramatic expression, such as Ulysses' homecoming aria 'Mit Freudenthränen in den Augen' and Penelope's anguished 'Liebster Schatz, ich muss dich lassen', it offers some charming lighter songs and, in the prologue and conclusion, a generous share of courtly pomp (the overture calls for four trumpets). Unfortunately Margaretha Susanna Kayser, for whom the role of Penelope was composed, fell ill shortly before the first performance, and her role was taken by another singer who apparently insisted on the insertion of four Italian arias in the previously all-German score, two of them by Giuseppe Maria Orlandini ('Usignuol tra rami ascoso' and 'Tu che scorgi').

JOHN H. ROBERTS

Ulysses (ii). Opera in three acts by JOHN CHRISTOPHER SMITH to a libretto by Samuel Humphreys after HOMER's *Odyssey*, books 16–24; London, Lincoln's Inn Fields Theatre, 16 April 1733.

Humphreys provided a weak libretto, almost entirely without incident – every event of substance, including the slaughter of the suitors, is merely reported. Smith could do little to counter its effects. While much of the music is interesting and some of it is of high quality, the whole does not add up to the sum of its parts. The score (in *D-Hs* MA/279), shows Smith's predilection for the da capo aria, and an unsurprising Handelian influence. However, the arias and the choruses are small-scale – the middle sections of the former, for example, are usually short, as are the choruses. The opera was performed with 'the Habits and the Scenes proper to the Subject', and the original performers included Jane Barbier (Ulysses), Cecilia Young (Penelope) and Michael Kelly (Telemachus).

Ulysses was the seventh work in the series of English operas given at the Little Theatre in the Haymarket and at the theatre in Lincoln's Inn Fields during the 1731–2 and 1732–3 seasons; it was performed only once. These seasons were the idea of the elder Thomas Arne; Smith, then only 20, and John Frederick Lampe were also involved. They were not a success probably, as Roger Fiske (1973, p.142) suggests, because 'those who worshipped at the shrine of Italian Opera saw no reason to dent their idols, while those besotted with the easy attractions of ballad operas found the all-sung variety tedious'.

MICHAEL BURDEN

Umeå. Town in northern Sweden. In 1974 it became the home of Sweden's newest permanent opera company, Norrlandsoperan (Opera North), created to fill a need in an area which is sparsely populated and has never had regular visits from opera troupes. The company was formed from a group of new graduates of the Opera School in Stockholm, with Arnold Östman as general and music director; the first production was Rossini's *L'italiana in Algeri*. Experiment and revitalization of musical drama are important aims of the company, the model being the Vadstena Academy which in 1974 was also conducted by Östman. Swedish composers were commissioned almost from the beginning, and the company also made extensive tours from an early stage, creating an appetite for opera rivalling that in Stockholm and Göteborg. Opera North has been the only company to revive forgotten Swedish operas of the 19th century: such a work was Hallström's *Den bergtagna* ('The Bride of the Mountain King', 1874), taken to England and performed in York in 1988. The Umeå Sinfonietta, an orchestra of 40 young musicians, plays for the company. Opera North gives regular performances from September to June and is housed in the old fire station, which has been converted into a fine musical theatre. Productions are occasionally given in the Idunteatern, inaugurated in 1986.

ANDERS WIKLUND

Umlauf [Umlauff], **Ignaz** (*b* Vienna, 1746; *d* Meidling, nr Vienna, 8 June 1796). Austrian composer. His name first appears as a viola player in the Vienna court orchestra in 1772, the year of his Singspiel *Die Insul der Liebe*. By 1775 he was principal viola player in the German Theatre orchestra, and in 1778 he was given the commission to write *Die Bergknappen*, the first work for Joseph II's new 'German National Singspiel'. Umlauf was appointed Kapellmeister to the new venture at a modest 600 florins a year, less than some of the singers received. Four further works by him were given before the closure of the Singspiel company in 1783, including *Die schöne Schusterinn* (1779), which had over 60 performances in 23 years and was staged in at least four other Vienna theatres, and *Das Irrlicht* (1782), which also exceeded the 30 repetitions of *Die Bergknappen*. By 1782 Umlauf had advanced to the position of Salieri's deputy Kapellmeister. On the occasion of Leopold's coronation at Frankfurt in 1790 Umlauf made his only lengthy journey from Vienna, as a member of the official entourage of the emperor. He died shortly after his appointment as music teacher to the imperial children.

Umlauf was the most successful Viennese Singspiel composer before Dittersdorf began to establish himself in this popular genre in the mid-1780s. He was studious and careful and had a striking melodic gift (his air 'Zu Stephen sprach im Traume' from *Das Irrlicht* was a particular favourite, as witness Eberl's set of variations long attributed to Mozart). His tendency to juxtapose such stylistic features as Italian coloratura arias and homely Austrian songs and dances is characteristic but by no means original; the best of his operas would still prove viable for their effective orchestration, but also because, despite the occasionally jerky effect of rapid key change, they reveal sufficiently marked gifts of dramatic timing and musical characterization to make Mozart's comments (e.g. the letters of 21 December 1782 and 5 February 1783, admittedly discussing *Welche[s] ist die beste Nation?*, one of his least successful works) seem rather intolerant. It was no doubt mainly through lack of resilience and power of development, however, that his last success dates from his 36th year, a few months before the première of Mozart's *Die Entführung aus dem Serail*: none of Umlauf's last three Singspiels achieved double figures in the repertory lists, and at the time of his death only *Die schöne Schusterinn* and *Das Irrlicht* were still being performed.

See also BERGKNAPPEN, DIE; IRRLICHT, DAS; and SCHÖNE SCHUSTERINN, DIE.

all Singspiels; first performed in Vienna unless otherwise stated

Die Insul [Insel] der Liebe (J. H. F. Müller), Burg, 22 Aug 1772
Die Bergknappen (Original-Spl, 1, P. Weidmann), Burg, 17 Feb 1778, *A-Wn*, *KR*; ed. in DTÖ, xxxvi, Jg.xviii/1 (1911)
Die Apotheke (2, J. J. Engel), Burg, 20 June 1778, *Wn*
Die schöne Schusterinn, oder Die pücefarbenen Schuhe (2, G. Stephanie the younger, after Ferrières), Burg, 22 June 1779, *Wn*
Das Irrlicht, oder Endlich fand er sie (3, Stephanie, after C. F. Bretzner), Burg, 17 Jan 1782, *Wn*
Welche[s] ist die beste Nation? (2, C. H. von Ayrenhoff), Burg, 13 Dec 1782
Die glücklichen Jäger (3, Stephanie), Kärntnertor, 17 Feb 1786
Der Ring der Liebe, oder Zemirens und Azors Ehestand (3, P. Weidmann or J. Weidmann), Kärntnertor, 3 Dec 1786 [sequel to A.-E.-M. Grétry: Zémire et Azor], extracts *Wgm*
Melide (4), ?unperf., *Wgm* (?autograph)

MGG (E. Badura-Skoda); *StiegerO*; *WurzbachL*
J. H. F. Müller: *Theatralische Neuigkeiten* (Vienna, 1773)
G. Nottebohm: *Beethoveniana* (Leipzig, 1872)
O. Teuber and A. von Weilen: *Die Theater Wiens*, ii/2/1 (Vienna, 1903)
R. Haas: Introduction to *I. Umlauf: Die Bergknappen*, DTÖ, xxxvi, Jg.xviii/1 (1911)
B. Glossy and R. Haas: *Wiener Comödienlieder aus drei Jahrhunderten* (Vienna, 1924) [incl. 2 vocal numbers from Umlauf Singspiels]
L. H. Skrbensky: 'Drei deutsche Tonkünstler: Christian Umlaufft, Ignaz Umlauff, Michael Umlauff', *Mitteilungen zur Geschichte der Familien Umlauff*, ii (Prague, ?1926)
R. Haas: *Wiener Musiker vor und um Beethoven* (Vienna, 1927)
F. Hadamowsky: *Das Theater in der Wiener Leopoldstadt* (Vienna, 1934)
A. Bauer: *Opern und Operetten in Wien* (Graz and Cologne, 1955)
O. E. Deutsch, ed.: *Mozart: die Dokumente seines Lebens* (Kassel, 1961)
R. Reuter and E. Wächtler: 'Die künstlerische und historische Bedeutung des Singspiels "Die Bergknappen" von Ignaz Umlauf am Beginn der Geschichte der deutschen Nationaloper', *Freiburger Forschungshefte*, xlviii (1965)
F. Hadamowsky: *Die Wiener Hoftheater (Staatstheater), 1776–1966*, i (Vienna, 1966)
O. Michtner: *Das alte Burgtheater als Opernbühne* (Vienna, 1970)

PETER BRANSCOMBE

Umlauf [Umlauff], **Michael** (*b* Vienna, 9 Aug 1781; *d* Baden, nr Vienna, 20 June 1842). Austrian composer, conductor and violinist, son of Ignaz Umlauf. At an early age he became a violinist in the Vienna court orchestra; the first of a series of ballet scores for the court theatres dates from 1804. He is listed in the theatre almanac of 1809 as Kapellmeister Gyrowetz's deputy, and by the 1815 almanac he had advanced to fourth of the six Kapellmeister at the court theatres. Umlauf retired in 1825, when Barbaia took over the court opera, and applied without success for the post of second Kapellmeister at St Stephen's. It was 1840 before he again came to the fore, this time as music director at the two court theatres, but his lengthy absence had left him quite out of touch and he soon retired again, dying not long after.

Umlauf's name is most familiar from his connections with Beethoven, whose works he several times conducted. In 1814 it was he who, at the revival of *Fidelio*, directed the performance; on other occasions, too, it was Umlauf whom the orchestra and singers followed, rather than the deaf and impetuously conducting composer. As a composer Michael Umlauf enjoyed less esteem than his father, but his ballet scores (especially *Paul und Rosette*, which was played 65 times in the court theatres and was also given in the Leopoldstadt Theatre) were popular in their day. He wrote three Singspiels.

all Singspiels

Das Fest der Liebe und der Freude (2, J. Perinet), Eisenstadt, 12 April 1806
Der [deutsche] Grenadier, oder Die Medaille (1, ? F. J. M. Babo), Vienna, Kärntnertor, 8 July 1812, *A-Wn*
Das Wirtshaus von Granada, *c*1812, ?unperf., vs (Vienna, n.d.)

For bibliography *see* UMLAUF, IGNAZ.

PETER BRANSCOMBE

Undina. Opera in three acts by PYOTR IL'YICH TCHAIKOVSKY to a libretto by Count Vladimir Sollogub after Friedrich Heinrich Carl de la Motte Fouqué's story *Undine* (formerly used by Alexey L'vov).

Composed very quickly (January–July 1869), Tchaikovsky's treatment of the ubiquitous water-nymph legend never achieved performance. It was refused by the Imperial Theatres (owing, according to a notice by César Cui, to its 'ultracontemporary style, careless instrumentation and absence of melody'). Three numbers from Act 1 – the orchestral introduction, Undine's song ('The waterfall, my uncle') and the choral finale (storm) – were extracted for concert performance

'Undine' (E. T. A. Hoffmann): design by Karl Friedrich Schinkel for the final scene of Act 3 of the original production at the Königliche Schauspiele, 3 August 1816: gouache

in Moscow (16/28 March 1870) and therefore escaped destruction when the despairing composer burnt the score in 1873. Five years later he considered setting the libretto again, but reconsidered in favour of *Romeo and Juliet* (also unrealized).

Of the three surviving fragments, the introduction and the song were reused in Tchaikovsky's incidental music to Ostrovsky's *Snegurochka* (1873). In addition, it is known that the wedding march from Act 3 became the second movement (Andantino marziale, quasi moderato) of the Second Symphony and that the culminating love duet for Undina (soprano) and Hulbrand (tenor) in Act 2 formed the basis for the great pas de deux (Odette's Adagio) in Act 2 of *Swan Lake*, the singers' voices being replaced by solo violin and cello (the duet was reconstructed from the ballet number by Sergey Popov in 1920). The one number known only in connection with *Undina* – the storm finale – contains a bit of experimental horror harmony of a kind more often found in the work of Dargomïzhsky and the Five.

RICHARD TARUSKIN

Undine **(i).** *Zauberoper* in three acts by E. T. A. HOFFMANN to a libretto by Friedrich Heinrich Carl de la Motte Fouqué after his own story *Undine* (1811); Berlin, Königliche Schauspiele, 3 August 1816.

Act 1 opens on a stormy night. Undine (soprano) has fled from the hut of her poor foster-parents, a fisherman (bass) and his wife (mezzo-soprano). As the knight Huldbrand (baritone) shelters from the storm, he learns how Undine was adopted in infancy when the fisherman's own daughter disappeared into the waters. Surrounded by other water spirits, the powerful spirit Kühleborn (bass) warns Undine against humankind. But she meets Huldbrand, and the couple fall in love. They are blessed by Heilmann (baritone), a priest, to Kühleborn's annoyance. Undine reveals to Huldbrand that she too is a spirit; moreover, she will return to the waters, or even kill Huldbrand, if he loses faith with her. But they decide to be married.

In Act 2 Undine has become friends with Berthalda (soprano), supposed daughter of the local duke and duchess. Kühleborn meets Undine and imparts to her the secret of Berthalda's origins. During the latter's birthday celebrations, Undine announces publicly that Berthalda is the daughter of the fisherman and his wife. Huldbrand does not take this action lightly: after general consternation, and Berthalda's mortified exit, he goes to her assistance. Some time later, water spirits intervene directly, succeeding in turning Huldbrand against Undine; he curses her. She is drawn back into the waters, finally warning him to brick up the garden fountain.

At the beginning of Act 3, a love duet between Huldbrand and Berthalda is ended by Kühleborn's threatening interruptions. Against the advice of Heilmann, Huldbrand becomes engaged to Berthalda. Undine's voice is heard when the fisherman remembers her with affection. During the celebrations Berthalda impetuously has the fountain unstopped. Undine appears in its waters, embraces Huldbrand and draws him with a kiss back into her element.

Undine, the crowning work of Hoffmann's composing career, embodies his highly developed theories of Romantic opera both musically and dramatically. As a Romantic myth it perfectly symbolizes 'the influence of higher natures on our lives' – its depiction was a condition of Romantic opera for Hoffmann. Although some spoken dialogue is employed, the opera stands at the opposite extreme from domestic Singspiels of the time, and at a great distance from comic magic ones like Ferdinand Kauer's *Das Donauweibchen*. Hoffmann himself influenced the dramatic plan constructed by Fouqué, although the latter did not escape contemporary criticism. The music, influenced in different ways by Gluck, Mozart and Cherubini, sharply contrasts the milieux of the fisherfolk, the court and the water spirits. But through its extraordinary structural continuity it succeeds in blending and confounding the human and supernatural worlds. The score also uses several reminiscence motifs, for example for Kühleborn's realm, for Heilmann and for various human relationships. DAVID CHARLTON

Undine **(ii).** *Romantische Zauberoper* in four acts by ALBERT LORTZING to a libretto by the composer after Friedrich Heinrich Carl de la Motte Fouqué's story *Undine*; Magdeburg, Nationaltheater, 21 April 1845.

Act 1 takes place in the hut of the old fisherman Tobias (bass), where Hugo von Ringstetten (tenor) and his squire, Veit (tenor), have taken refuge after a flood. Hugo is in love with the fisherman's adopted daughter Undine (soprano), found by the river just after the fisherman's own baby daughter had disappeared. During preparations for the wedding feast Undine's real father, the powerful prince of the water-spirits Kühleborn (baritone), arrives in disguise to find out about Hugo's background. The act ends with the departure of the newly married pair for Hugo's homeland.

Act 2 is set in the court of the recently deceased Duke Heinrich, with whose daughter Bertalda (soprano) Hugo had previously been in love. At the end of the act Kühleborn, who has appeared in another disguise as an ambassador from Naples, asserts that Bertalda is not really the daughter of the duke, but of the fisherman, and this is borne out by the opening of the duke's will. To the horror of the onlookers Kühleborn then reveals himself as the prince of the water-spirits. In Act 3, which takes place near Hugo's castle, Bertalda succeeds in displacing Undine in Hugo's affections. The distraught Undine is taken back into the water by Kühleborn. Act 4 begins in the courtyard of the castle while preparations are under way for Hugo and Bertalda's wedding. Hugo is troubled by a dream in which Undine opened her arms to him. After a comic scene between Veit and the cellarer Hans (bass), Undine emerges weeping from a well in the centre of the court and enters the castle. In the great hall, wedding guests are celebrating. On the last stroke of midnight Undine appears; Hugo rushes into her arms and falls insensible at her feet. As the guests flee, the room fills with water and the scene changes to reveal Kühleborn's palace. Undine and Hugo kneel at his feet; at Undine's request he pardons Hugo's unfaithfulness.

With *Undine* Lortzing attempted a type of opera different from his earlier successes, all comic operas, and his choice of subject may have been prompted by the death of Fouqué in 1843, which aroused new interest in that writer's almost forgotten stories. As with most of his other works Lortzing wrote his own libretto. He made several significant additions and alterations to Fouqué's original. In order to create a comic element he introduced two entirely new characters, the squire Veit and the cellarer Hans; under persuasion from colleagues and friends, he also modified the ending. Perhaps influenced by criticisms of his comic opera *Hans Sachs* for its inappropriate mixture of the comic and the serious, Lortzing confined the comic elements in *Undine* to specific scenes and characters; the principal roles of Hugo, Undine, Kühleborn and Bertalda are treated entirely as serious characters. In keeping with the subject of the opera, the music is in many respects more serious and substantial than in Lortzing's earlier operas. He retained some of the number types that had been so popular in previous works, but in general the ensembles and finales are musically weightier, and, in addition, he made considerable use of musical reminiscence and leitmotif to give coherence to the whole. After early performances, Lortzing made several changes to the opera's structure, composing new endings for the overture and for the second and fourth acts as well as making many other smaller modifications. CLIVE BROWN

Ungarelli [Ungherelli, Ongarelli], **Rosa** (*b* Bologna; *fl* 1709–32). Italian soprano. She was the wife of Antonio Maria Ristorini, with whom she achieved international fame as an interpreter of comic intermezzos. She began as a singer of *opera seria*, appearing in three productions at Florence in winter 1709–10; but in spring 1714 she performed intermezzos at Parma with Giovanni Battista Cavana and by 1716 had formed a partnership with Ristorini which was to last for at least 17 years.

Their performance of Orlandini's *Il marito giocatore e la moglie bacchettona* at Pistoia in 1725 is described at length by the diarist Giovanni Cosimo Rossi-Melocchi. He particularly admired Ungarelli's acting: she used 'gestures that would have moved a stone' and 'words that would have liquefied bronze ... her gestures and manner on the stage are something that cannot be believed by one who has not seen them. For this reason I gave her the name "Man-killer". And she really is not pretty; God help us if she were'.

*

C. E. Troy: *The Comic Intermezzo: a Study in the History of Eighteenth-Century Italian Opera* (Ann Arbor, 1979)

F. Piperno: 'Appunti sulla configurazione sociale e professionale delle "parti buffe" al tempo di Vivaldi', *Antonio Vivaldi: teatro musicale, cultura e società: Venice 1981*, ii, 483–97

COLIN TIMMS

Unger, Georg (*b* Leipzig, 6 March 1837; *d* Leipzig, 2 Feb 1887). German tenor. He first studied theology, but made his opera début in Leipzig in 1867 with such success that he was soon engaged in other cities. Hans Richter heard him in Mannheim and recommended him to Wagner to create Siegfried at Bayreuth (1876). In 1877 Unger went to London for the series of Wagner concerts in the Albert Hall, but his frequent failure to appear caused the composer to take a dislike to him; he returned to Leipzig that year, singing at the Opera there until 1881. He is an early example of the Wagnerian Heldentenor.

*

E. Newman: *The Life of Richard Wagner*, iv (London, 1947), 410–11

H. Pleasants: *The Great Singers* (London, 1967), 233

Unger, Gerhard (*b* Bad Salzungen, Thuringia, 26 Nov 1916). German tenor. He studied in Eisenach and in 1947 was engaged at Weimar, where he sang lyric roles such as Tamino, Alfredo and Pinkerton, and David, his most popular role at that period of his career, at Bayreuth (1951–2). In 1952 he moved to the Berlin Staatsoper and in 1961 to Stuttgart, where he remained until 1982. A member of the Hamburg Staatsoper (1962–73), he appeared at the Vienna Staatsoper, La Scala, the Paris Opéra, the Metropolitan and in Salzburg, where in 1961 he sang Pedrillo, another favourite role, which he repeated over 300 times. In the 1970s and 80s he specialized in character roles, such as the Captain (*Wozzeck*), Skuratov (*From the House of the Dead*), Brighella (*Ariadne auf Naxos*), the Italian Singer (*Der Rosenkavalier*) and, above all, Mime in both *Das Rheingold* and *Siegfried*, which he sang widely in Europe and North and South America: in Stuttgart, Munich, Vienna, Chicago, Milan, Cologne, Buenos Aires, Florence and Dallas (1984). His highly placed, bright, clear-toned voice hardly changed as he grew older, so that in 1980 (aged 64) he could still carry conviction as Pedrillo at Bregenz. He has recorded Pedrillo and also David and Alwa (*Lulu*).

WOLFRAM SCHWINGER/ELIZABETH FORBES

Unger [Ungher, Unger-Sabatier], **Karoline** [Caroline, Carolina, Carlotta] (*b* Stuhlweissenburg [now Székesfehérvár], 28 Oct 1803; *d* Florence, 23 March 1877). Austrian contralto. She studied with Aloysia Weber and J. M. Vogl and with D. Roncini in Milan, made her début in Vienna in 1821 as Tancredi, and went on to sing Dorabella there. In 1825 she was engaged by the impresario Domenico Barbaia in Italy; she sang there for many years, creating Pacini's Niobe (1826), Marietta in Donizetti's *Il borgomastro di Saardam* (1827), Isoletta in *La straniera* (1828), Parisina (1833), Antonina in *Belisario* (1836), the title role in *Maria di Rudenz* and Bianca in Mercadante's *Le due illustri rivali* (1838). In October 1833 she sang at the Théâtre Italien in Paris; it was perhaps on this occasion that Rossini spoke of her as possessing 'the ardour of the south, the energy of the north, brazen lungs, a silver voice and a golden talent'. Meyerbeer went to Dresden in September 1841 to hear her and Mariani in *Lucia di Lammermoor* and *Belisario*. In that year she married the French writer François Sabatier; she continued her career until 1843, when she retired from the stage.

One of the few 19th-century Austrian singers to enjoy her greatest triumphs on the Italian stage, Unger had great dramatic ability and intelligence as well as a remarkable voice with a range of *a–d‴*. According to Fétis she was large and attractive and had a fine, broad tone except in her upper register, in which there was some harshness and forcing. Besides singing in operas, she was an outstanding interpreter of Mozart and Schubert songs.

*

ES (R. Celletti); *FétisB*

'Karoline Unger', *Dresdener Abendzeitung* (1 March 1826)

'Karoline Unger in Padua', *Allgemeine Theaterzeitung*, xxv (1832), nos.174–6

F. Liszt: 'Karoline Unger', *Allgemeine Theaterzeitung*, xxxii (1839), no.76, pp.47–54

Trionfi melodrammatici di Carolina Ungher in Vienna (Vienna, 1839)

E. Pirchan: *Henriette Sontag* (Vienna, 1946)

Union of Soviet Socialist Republics [USSR; Soviet Union]. Federation of 15 republics, brought together beginning in 1917 and dissolved in 1991. Operatic activity in the former Soviet Union is discussed under the names of the individual republics and their principal cities in the cases of ESTONIA, LATVIA, LITHUANIA, RUSSIA and UKRAINE, and in addition under the following cities: ALMA-ATA, ASHKHABAD, BAKU, BISHKEK, DUSHANBE, EREVAN, KISHINEU, MINSK, TASHKENT and TBILISI.

United States of America. For more than two centuries American operatic practices have blended many diverse elements – vernacular and cultivated, comic and serious, indigenous and foreign, conservative and avant-garde – into a multi-faceted artistic expression reflecting the nation's unique democratic spirit. During the 18th and 19th centuries, Americans welcomed all the latest operatic styles brought by talented immigrants from England, France, Italy and Germany. From these influences arose four main traditions that shaped the course of musical drama in the USA: English comic opera, which led to the Broadway and Hollywood musicals; foreign-language opera, which gave rise to more formal 'grand opera' traditions, social customs and institutions such as the Metropolitan Opera; 'Americanized' or popularized foreign opera, which enlarged the audience for opera and expanded its role in American life; and American opera, which, drawing on all these traditions, discovered a strong creative voice of its own. With the economic, cultural and technological advances of the 20th century, a vital indigenous operatic culture reached throughout the nation.

1. English influences. 2. Continental influences. 3. The dissemination of opera. 4. The search for an American identity. 5. Trends of the 1920s–50s. 6. After 1960: the democratization of opera.

1. ENGLISH INFLUENCES. From its earliest decades American theatrical activity was primarily musical in nature. Religious dramas with music played an active part in the life of Spanish and French settlers as early as the 16th century. The many secular plays presented in eastern seaboard cities throughout the 18th century almost always contained music, and the term 'opera' was applied to musical shows both with and without dialogue or central plot. The English ballad opera, a type of light, satiric play interspersed with strophic songs set to traditional or popular tunes, was especially popular. This genre and its related forms – pasticcio, comic opera, farce, pantomime, extravaganza, opera-ballet, interlude, afterpiece and olio – dominated American entertainment until the early 19th century when Italian opera began to rise in popularity. Even foreign-language operas fell under the spell of the entertaining ballad opera. They were often translated into English, shortened and interspersed with dialogue and popular tunes; Egidio Duni's *opéra comique Les deux chasseurs*, for example, was staged as a pantomime in New York on 9 November 1790.

As early as the 1730s ballad operas were modestly rendered in New York and in Williamsburg, Virginia, which from 1718 had a theatre measuring 26 by 9 metres with five windows. Productions increased after the Murray-Kean troupe and the Hallam Company (later the American Company) arrived in these cities in the 1750s. The earliest advertised performance of a ballad opera took place in Charleston, South Carolina, in 'the Courtroom'. With text by Colley Cibber and musical interpolations arranged by John Hippisley, *Flora, or Hob in the Well* was produced on 18 February 1735, with the pantomime *Harlequin and Scaramouche* as an afterpiece. Rather than a single work, two or more theatrical amusements (sometimes performed between the acts of an opera) were common on an evening's programme. As the century progressed, English comic operas with somewhat more elaborate musical settings became especially popular, such as Thomas Arne's *Love in a Village* (1761) with its complex duets and brilliant finales, and O'Keefe and Shield's *The Poor Soldier* (1784). Staged as far west as Detroit in 1799, *The Poor Soldier* was one of the most widely performed English operas of the time.

The first documented American ballad opera was composed in England by a former American resident, James Ralph. Performed in 1730 at the Theatre in

Goodman's Fields, London, Ralph's *The Fashionable Lady; or Harlequin's Opera*, was produced after the composer had emigrated from Philadelphia in 1724. Another ballad opera, *The Disappointment, or The Force of Credulity* by Andrew Barton (a pseudonym; his real identity is unknown), is the first extant opera composed by an American for an American stage, although its early production history remains obscure. The libretto, first published in 1767, is a two-act satire on Philadelphia social life, with well-known personalities depicted in the roles of Hum, Washball, Racoon and Rattletrap; it calls for some 18 identifiable tunes ranging from 'Yankee Doodle' to the airs of Thomas Arne.

Although the Revolutionary War, together with religious objections (mainly in the northern and middle colonies), temporarily curtailed opera performance, the late 18th and early 19th centuries witnessed a thriving new cultural era as gifted immigrants became composers, entrepreneurs, teachers and performers. The Englishman Alexander Reinagle, whose opera-melodrama *Columbus* enjoyed at least ten performances in Philadelphia during 1797, expertly managed this city's elegant, 2000-seat Chesnut Street Theatre. In 1792 with the English actor Thomas Wignell he formed the New Company, offering operatic productions of a highly professional quality. By about 1800 pure ballad opera had been largely superseded by works in which the majority of the music was newly written by a single composer. Raynor Taylor's overwhelmingly successful 'Grand Romantick Drama' *The Aethiop* represents the transition from ballad opera to a new romantic operatic style. It was produced in Philadelphia on New Year's Day 1814 'in a style of splendour never exceeded on the American stage', according to *Poulson's American Daily Advertiser*. Like Philadelphia, New York rapidly became an important operatic centre and saw the premières of two of the earliest operas composed in the USA: James Hewitt's *Tammany, or The Indian Chief* (3 March 1794), to a libretto by Anne Julia Hatton, and Benjamin Carr's *The Archers, or The Mountaineers of Switzerland* (18 April 1796). With its anti-Federalist propaganda and Indian protagonist, *Tammany* inaugurated a long line of operas on specifically American subjects.

2. Continental influences. While English comic opera provided the mainstay of American theatrical repertory in the northern and middle colonies, foreign-language opera began to achieve prominence in areas further south, such as Baltimore, Charleston, Savannah, Georgia and New Orleans, with their numerous French-speaking residents. French operas were performed occasionally in the original language in Charleston by professional entertainers from Paris and Santo Domingo. The troupe included Louis Douvillier, Alexandre Placide from La Scala and Jean Baptiste Francisqui, a noted dancer from the Paris Opéra, who directed operas, ballets and pantomimes in Boston, New York and New Orleans, 1793–1808. In New Orleans the *Barbiere di Siviglia* of both Paisiello (in 1805) and Rossini (in 1823) were produced in French.

With a permanent opera company by 1810, New Orleans established the first tradition of lyric opera in the USA. Through its graceful sentiment, romantic parody, intellectual radicalism and powerful humanitarian ideals, late 18th-century *opéra comique* transferred to American shores the spirit of the French Revolution, and with it the first waves of European Romanticism. Settlers came to New Orleans not only from Paris, but also from Santo Domingo in the West Indies, where a thriving passion for opera existed among the wealthy planters whose large theatres were destroyed during the slave uprisings of 1791.

No other city in America and few in Europe could match the fecund outpouring of opera that took place in New Orleans between 1796 and 1810 at the city's first theatre, the Spectacle de la rue St Pierre. During the years 1806–10, for example, there were at least 351 performances of 76 different operas by 32 composers who represented the entire range of *opéra comique* style and development. Especially popular were the light romantic comedies, such as Dezède's *Blaise et Babet* (1783) and Devienne's *Les visitandines* (1792), or operas that showed the darker side of human nature, such as Grétry's *Richard Coeur-de-lion* (1784) and Monsigny's *Le déserteur* (1769). Méhul's intense *Euphrosine* (1790) was also frequently performed, as were Dalayrac's *Nina* (1786) and Berton's *Le délire* (1799), with their mentally deranged protagonists. As at the Comédie-Italienne in Paris, operas were often coupled with plays by Corneille, Molière, Beaumarchais or Sedaine, forming double or even triple bills. Elaborately staged, they used skilled professional singers, both spoken dialogue and recitative, and an orchestra of about 25.

The earliest documented performance of an opera in New Orleans was that of Grétry's *Silvain* (1770), produced on 22 May 1796 at the St Pierre. With its libretto by Marmontel, *Silvain* contains three of the period's most popular themes: a pastoral setting, a moral lesson and the question of the common rights of peasants. New Orleans also boasted a prominent composer of its own, Philip Laroque, whose operas *La jeune mère*, *Nicodème dans la lune* and *Pauvre Jacques* were performed often before 1810. Between 1827 and 1833, the latest French works were introduced to audiences in Baltimore, Philadelphia, New York, Boston and other eastern cities by John Davis and his touring company from the Théâtre d'Orléans.

French opera was not as well received in the eastern cities, however, as Italian, which was often Anglicized and popularized. Henry Bishop's English version of *Don Giovanni* (as *The Libertine*) was produced at the Park Theatre in New York on 7 November 1817. Another successful adaptation was of *La Cenerentola*, in a version by the Irishman Michael Rophino Lacy called *Cinderella, or The Fairy-Queen and the Glass Slipper*. The opera was first given in the USA on 24 January 1831, less than a year after its London première, and rapidly became one of the most popular works in American theatrical history. Italian opera in the original language made its American début with Rossini's *Barbiere*, staged at the Park Theatre in New York on 29 November 1825 by the family company of Manuel García. Rosina was sung by García's brilliant 17-year-old daughter Maria (later Malibran), who became one of the century's most celebrated singers.

Operatic activity increased rapidly as the 19th century progressed, with Italian opera taking the lead and German works coming to the fore around the middle of the century. The new florid Italian operas with their bel canto arias, recitatives and ensembles sung by agile professional singers became enormously popular. Favourite selections from these operas appeared in countless arrangements, from sheet music for the home pianist to transcriptions for the village band. Some of the most popular operas, moreover, were produced in the USA only a few years after their world premières, among them *La sonnambula* (1831, Milan; 1835, New York), *Norma* (1831, Milan; 1836, New Orleans) and *La fille du régiment* (1840, Paris; 1843, New Orleans). To house these and many other productions, new buildings were constructed, especially in New York, where the Italian Opera House was built with the support of Lorenzo da Ponte in 1833, the Astor Place Opera House in 1847 and the 4600-seat Academy of Music in 1854. The mystique of foreign-language opera and fashionable new theatres with private boxes encouraged a new upper-class audience, creating a social custom – and a power base – that would shape the nation's important operatic institutions, notably the Metropolitan Opera, in the decades to come.

American composers during the middle and later 19th century seemed to be striving for an identity which they found more often in European models than in original American ones. For William Henry Fry, composing an opera in English in the style of Bellini or Donizetti, and sung throughout, was a new venture and a tribute to the bel canto tradition. Fry's *Leonora*, the first grand opera by an American-born composer to be publicly performed, had its première in Philadelphia at the Chesnut Street Theatre on 4 June 1845. A decade later, the German Romantic spirit began to take hold as opera in the German language was produced with increasing frequency: *Fidelio* (1805) and *Tannhäuser* (1845) were staged at the Stadt Theater in New York in the 1850s. Eventually, native stories and legends provided inspiration for American composers, such as George F. Bristow, whose *Rip Van Winkle*, based on a tale by Washington Irving, was produced at Niblo's Garden, New York, on 27 September 1855. Others who composed operas to English-language librettos, though with varying levels of success, were Charles Hopkins, Dudley Buck, Frederick Grant Gleason, Silas G. Pratt and Max Maretzek, whose *Sleepy Hollow, or the Headless Horseman* (1879) was also inspired by Irving.

3. THE DISSEMINATION OF OPERA. In the 19th century countless performances were given by itinerant troupes whose numbers increased as the railroads pushed westward. Before the Civil War these troupes were mainly English in origin, such as the Pyne-Harrison Opera Company, or Italian, such as the Havana Opera Company, which in 1850 had more than a hundred performers. Among the most noted impresarios were Luigi Arditi, Max Maretzek, Bernard Ullman and Maurice Strakosch; other foreign troupes were formed around such stellar divas as Teresa Parodi, Henriette Sontag and Anna Bishop. After the Civil War American troupes became prominent, such as the Andrews Opera Company, a family of nine, and two troupes run by enterprising prima donnas – in the 1870s, Clara Louise Kellogg from South Carolina, and the following decade, Emma Abbott from Chicago. Abbott not only edited and translated her company's repertory of 19 operas (mainly Italian), but during her tours opened 35 opera houses across the country.

Between 1872 and 1882 a unique all-black troupe, the Colored American Opera Company from Washington, DC, toured with a wide-ranging repertory including Julius Eichberg's *The Doctor of Alcantara* (1862) and Gilbert and Sullivan's *HMS Pinafore* (1878). The latter had been given its first American performance only six months after the London première, initiating a dynamic Gilbert and Sullivan craze in the USA that would last until the end of the century. One of the largest, most ambitious itinerant companies of the era, however, was the American Opera Company founded by Theodore Thomas in 1886. It specialized in presenting grand opera sung in English by American performers, and toured from coast to coast with a repertory of works by Wagner, Mozart, Verdi, Meyerbeer, Delibes and Gluck, whose *Orfeo ed Euridice* (1762) and *Alceste* (1767) were given their American premières. Among its 300 members were a chorus of 100, a ballet company of 80 and 25 principal singers, all of whom travelled with a ton of electrical apparatus, 500 separate pieces of scenery, 4000 costumes and even a live goat for one of the ballets. Requiring two trains for its transport, the American Opera Company not surprisingly disbanded after two seasons (1886–8) for lack of funds.

4. THE SEARCH FOR AN AMERICAN IDENTITY. The second half of the 19th century saw the rise of many small regional opera companies, such as Chicago's Swedish Theatre (1868–1950) or its highly active Lithuanian Opera Company, reflecting the theatrical life of urban immigrant communities. In New York, the first Yiddish theatre was established in 1882, offering light operas and plays, and from 1879 to 1883 James Henry Mapleson produced opera on a grand scale at the Academy of Music. With the opening of the 3625-seat Metropolitan Opera House in New York on 22 October 1883, however, a new era of American operatic history began. Through the backing of the Morgans, Vanderbilts and other wealthy patrons, this famous institution reflected the nation's changing face of finance and industry. Rapidly achieving international eminence, the Metropolitan was unrivalled in the USA. Its first production, Gounod's *Faust*, was given in Italian, but from its second season (under Leopold Damrosch) until 1891, the operas were sung mainly in German, with Wagner accounting for nearly half the repertory. Under Anton Seidl, the complete *Ring* cycle (with extensive cuts) was produced for the first time in the country, during the 1888–9 season. As the adulation of Wagner increased, several American operas were composed under his influence, such as Walter Damrosch's *The Scarlet Letter* (1896; called by Seidl a 'New England Nibelung Trilogy'), John Knowles Paine's *Azara* (1900), George Chadwick's *Judith* (1901) and Deems Taylor's *The King's Henchman* (1927). Both *Henchman* and Taylor's *Peter Ibbetson* (1931) received their premières at the Metropolitan and, though achieving fewer than 20 performances each, are still the longest-running American operas in the company's history.

During the era of Giulio Gatti-Casazza, director of the Metropolitan, 1908–35, 17 new American operas were produced, beginning with Frederick S. Converse's *Pipe of Desire* in 1910; the company also gave early performances of Victor Herbert's *Natoma* (1911), Horatio Parker's *Mona* (1912), Charles Wakefield Cadman's *Shanewis* (1918), Henry Hadley's *Cleopatra's Night* (1920), Louis Gruenberg's *The Emperor Jones* (1933) and Howard Hanson's *Merry Mount* (1934). These were received with enthusiasm and acclaim, but while audiences had high hopes for 'the great American opera', only foreign-language works remained in the repertory. Gatti-Casazza also brought several young American singers into the company at a time when native singers were still a rarity, among them Rosa Ponselle, Lawrence Tibbett, Grace Moore, Gladys Swarthout and John Charles Thomas. Although black artists such as Julia E. Rhea and Caterina Jarboro made their débuts with opera companies in the USA during the 1930s, Marian Anderson was the first black singer to perform at the Metropolitan (as Ulrica in *Un ballo in maschera*, 7 January 1955).

Some early 20th-century American composers, including Deems Taylor, viewed opera as an international art form demanding a universal, rather than a specifically American, setting. 'We love Italian opera, not because it is so Italian, but because it is so singable', he said. Others, however, turned to indigenous American themes; Mary Carr Moore's four-act grand opera *Narcissa* (1912) has a heroic protagonist from the American North-west, and Indian settings provided inspiration for several other works. But unlike Hewitt's *Tammany* or John Bray's opera melodrama *The Indian Princess* (1808), 'Indianist' operas of the early 20th century began to acquire a certain authenticity as musical, rather than merely dramatic, significance occupied composers. Arthur Nevin, whose *Poia* was the first American opera of real consequence to receive its première in Berlin (23 April 1910), had spent two summers on a Blackfoot Indian reservation studying indigenous melodies and rhythms, which he then incorporated into his opera. Cadman's *Shanewis* uses four authentic Indian chants, one a Cheyenne melody that appears in the opera's most famous aria, 'Spring Song of the Robin Woman'.

5. TRENDS OF THE 1920S–50S. Popular music, jazz, Broadway, regional Americanism and social and political thought all interacted within opera as it reached out to a broader artistic community during the period surrounding World War II. Composers met the challenges of the 1930s and 40s with vigour, imagination and individuality. Haitian settings were popular with black composers, for example Clarence Cameron White (*Ouanga*, 1932) and William Grant Still (*Troubled Island*, 1941). Set in New Orleans, Amy Marcy Beach's *Cabildo* (1932) employs Creole folk melodies, and George Gershwin brought jazz and folk elements to the European grand opera tradition with his enduring *Porgy and Bess* (1935). Though at first having only moderate success, *Porgy* is now one of the most frequently performed American stage works and perhaps the nation's most successful musical export. But it remained for Virgil Thomson and Marc Blitzstein to break the ubiquitous European spell. In his *Four Saints in Three Acts* (1934) to a libretto by Gertrude Stein, and *The Mother of Us All* (1947), Thomson created a new musical language, effective in both narrative and lyrical passages, that closely follows the natural accents and inflections of American speech. Marc Blitzstein's *The Cradle Will Rock* (1937) and *Regina* (1949) deal with social issues, the latter combining elements from jazz, black spirituals and Broadway musicals in a distinctive texture fluctuating between song and speech.

The newest, most significant avenues for the dissemination of opera during this period came from radio and television. In autumn 1927 Deems Taylor's *The King's Henchman* was the first opera to be aired on the newly opened CBS radio network. Broadcasts from the Metropolitan Opera were heard as early as 1910, and the current Saturday afternoon Metropolitan broadcasts were begun on 25 December 1931; since 7 December 1940 they have been sponsored by Texaco. Recognizing the potential of this new medium, composers such as Louis Gruenberg (*Green Mansions*, 1937) and Gian Carlo Menotti (*The Old Maid and the Thief*, 1939) began to write operas expressly for radio. In 1948 Verdi's *Otello* made history as the first live telecast from the Metropolitan Opera. A few years later Menotti's *Amahl and the Night Visitors* (1951) became the first American opera to be commissioned for television (NBC) and ranks among the most frequently performed operas of all time. Menotti's influence is seen in the television operas of his pupils Stanley Hollingsworth (*La grande Bretèche*, 1957) and Lee Hoiby (*Beatrice*, 1959). The growing popularity of televised opera, moreover, resulted in the use of surtitles in American opera houses from the early 1980s.

Opera workshops, scattered across the nation on college and university campuses, offered a type of opera similar to the early radio operas – short, often one-act, works that are simple to stage and have appealing stories, such as Aaron Copland's *The Second Hurricane* (1937). Eleanor Everest Freer, whose life was dedicated to making opera accessible to all, wrote 11 such works during the 1920s and 30s. Kurt Weill's *Down in the Valley* (1947) was composed for Indiana University and later performed by countless colleges, clubs, high schools and churches throughout the nation. Many academic workshops were established by enterprising émigrés who had fled Europe during or shortly after the war. By the early 1950s the ratio of college workshops to professional organizations had jumped from one in five to two out of three. The training they provided for young singers and composers, as well as the development of a new 'grass roots' audience, proved invaluable for the course of opera in the USA. The workshops, moreover, less dependent on box-office receipts and full houses, tended to programme more innovatory works. During the 1940s and 50s several hundred American and world premières, many of operas by prominent American composers in the early stages of their careers such as Dominick Argento, Leonard Bernstein, Carlisle Floyd, Gian Carlo Menotti and Jack Beeson, took place at academic institutions. The academic workshops also encouraged the rise of regional opera companies, notably Kentucky Opera (1952), Tulsa Opera (1953), Santa Fe Opera (1956) and Seattle Opera (1962). Significantly, a number of other regional companies, including Minnesota Opera (1964), Michigan Opera Theater (1971) and Opera Theatre of St Louis (1976), have emphasized the production of contemporary works.

6. AFTER 1960: THE DEMOCRATIZATION OF OPERA. Opera in the USA since 1960 has shown remarkable vitality and growth both as an art and a business. Between 1964 and 1989, for example, the number of American opera companies with annual budgets exceeding $100 000 increased from 27 to 209. By 1989 six companies reported annual budgets of over $10 million: the Metropolitan Opera (founded 1883), San Francisco Opera (1923), New York City Opera (1943), Lyric Opera of Chicago (1954), Houston Grand Opera (1955) and the Los Angeles Music Center Opera (1986). Completing this roster of the nation's ten largest companies are the Washington, DC, Seattle, Dallas and Santa Fe operas. During the 1980s, moreover, both opera production and attendance increased dramatically, with the 1988–9 season showing the biggest growth ever for any one

season. Several factors have contributed to this extraordinary phenomenon, among them more skilful managerial and marketing approaches, a wider variety of financial support, expansion of the repertory and greater visibility through the broadcast media, especially television. (More than a hundred operas are available for home video.) Indeed it is in the USA rather than in Europe that opera has experienced its greatest popularity in recent times.

Unlike European opera companies, American ones rely more on private than on public support. From a 1986–7 survey of the total income of 51 professional opera companies, 56.4% came from earned income (performances, broadcasts, other), 37.9% from private support (foundations, corporate, guild, private, other) and 5.8% from public support (federal, state, other). Financial support, especially for new works, is creative and diverse. Founded in 1965, the National Endowment for the Arts (NEA) provides grants in three separate phases: commissioning, development and production. Opera America's programme 'Opera for the 80s and Beyond' offers pre-commissioning or 'team-building' grants to encourage collaboration on new works by composers, designers, librettists and directors, while other agencies give 'workshopping' grants, which allow a new opera to be tried out in whole or part before its actual première. The Meet the Composer Commissioning Program, launched by *Reader's Digest* in 1988, is a kind of life-support system for carrying new operas beyond opening night. To cut costs, moreover, opera companies have experimented with shared commissioning and production. Bernstein's *A Quiet Place* (1983) was jointly commissioned by Houston Grand Opera, Teatro alla Scala and Kennedy Center for the Performing Arts, and *Porgy and Bess* was co-produced in 1987 by 13 opera companies from across the nation, sharing expenses as well as profits.

Opera in the 1980s reached wider audiences than ever before through performances in recreation areas, hospitals, schools, homes for the elderly and office buildings. Effective community outreach is reflected in such programmes as San Francisco's 'Brown Bag Opera', designed to bring opera to parks and shopping malls, and Dallas Opera's 'Frito-Lay Night', which drew 700 employees of that corporation to a dress rehearsal, encouraging both corporate and community support. The USA is a world leader in opera production for children, too. New one-hour children's operas such as *Charlotte's Web* by Charles Strouse (Opera Delaware, 1988–9 season) are being commissioned with increasing frequency.

With more than a thousand organizations presenting opera in one form or another, young American artists now have increased opportunities to make their careers in their own country. College and university workshops, and small regional companies such as the Summer Opera Theatre Company, Washington, DC (founded 1978), continue to provide professional opportunities for young artists, but many major opera companies now have apprentice programmes; these include San Francisco Opera Center, Chicago Lyric Opera's Center for American Artists and the Metropolitan Opera's Young Artists Development Program, among others. Not only are more American singers, administrators, conductors, orchestral musicians and stage directors now established as professionals in American companies, but they are in demand throughout the world. One of the most important organizations for promoting younger artists, especially Americans, has been the New York City Opera, recognized also for its frequent production of new and little-known works. With the composer conducting, it staged Thea Musgrave's *The Voice of Ariadne* (1972–3) on 30 September 1977 – the first opera by a woman to be performed by a major opera company since the Metropolitan Opera's production of Ethel Smyth's *Der Wald* in 1902–3.

With the expansion of repertory characteristic of the 1970s and 80s came a renewed interest in reviving operas from earlier periods and creating new stagings for traditional works. Several Baroque operas were given large-scale American premières, such as Handel's *Rinaldo* (1975), Vivaldi's *Orlando furioso* (1980) and Lully's *Atys* (1989), as were historic American operas such as Scott Joplin's *Treemonisha* (1976) and William Grant Still's *A Bayou Legend* (1981). The conceptual approach to production (usually involving scenic reinterpretation) has afforded new prominence to stage directors, notably John Dexter, Robert Wilson and Peter Sellers, who staged a contemporary realization of the Mozart-Da Ponte operas. Repeated performances of more recent American works, on the other hand, is a barometer of their durability. During the 1988–9 season alone Floyd's *Susannah* (1954), Ward's *The Crucible* (1961), Moore's *The Ballad of Baby Doe* (1956), Hoiby's *Summer and Smoke* (1971), Argento's *Postcard from Morocco* (1971), Copland's *The Tender Land* (1954), Pasatieri's *The Seagull* (1974) and Paulus's *The Postman always Rings Twice* (1982), among others, were produced.

But the single most significant trend in American opera during the late 1980s and into the 1990s was the surge of interest in new works. John Corigliano's *The Ghosts of Versailles* (1991) was the first work to be specially commissioned and performed by the Metropolitan Opera since the opening of Lincoln Center. Composers employed a wide variety of musical and theatrical styles, from the traditional lyricism of Menotti (*Goya*, 1986), Pasatieri (*Three Sisters*, 1986) and Argento (*The Aspern Papers*, 1988), to the minimalist works of Philip Glass (*Akhnaten*, 1984) and John Adams (*Nixon in China*, 1987), which also weave American dance rhythms and neo-romantic harmonies into a kaleidoscopic texture. Films, abstract projections and other cinematic effects have figured in the works of Eric Salzman, Stanley Silverman, Laurie Anderson, Libby Larsen and others, and experiments in 'theater of images' have offered a visually orientated alternative to traditional operatic forms. Many new musicals, including Sondheim's *Sweeney Todd*, point towards the structure, scale and sweep of opera, in what critics call the 'crossover phenomenon'. In the words of David Gockley, president of Opera America, 'Composers are moving back to writing for audiences, using attractive melodies, harmonies, seeking emotional payoffs, and conceiving fantastic tonal-visual images'. Opera in the USA, in other words, is far more than merely 'grand'.

For further information on operatic life in the country's principal centres *see* AMARILLO; ANCHORAGE; ASPEN; ATLANTA; AUGUSTA; AUSTIN; BALTIMORE; BATON ROUGE; BINGHAMTON; BLOOMINGTON; BOSTON; CARMEL; CENTRAL CITY; CENTRAL OPERA SERVICE; CHARLESTON; CHARLOTTE; CHAUTAUQUA; CHICAGO; CINCINNATI; CLEVELAND; COLORADO SPRINGS; COLUMBUS; COOPERSTOWN; COSTA MESA; DALLAS; DAYTON; DENVER; DETROIT; EUGENE; FORT LAUDERDALE; FORT WORTH; GREENSBORO; HARTFORD; HONOLULU; HOUSTON; INDIANAPOLIS; INDIANOLA; JACKSON; KANSAS CITY; KNOXVILLE; LAWRENCEVILLE; LEWISTON; LITTLE ROCK; LONG BEACH; LOS ANGELES; LOUIS-

VILLE; MEMPHIS; METROPOLITAN OPERA COMPANY; MIAMI; MILWAUKEE; MINNEAPOLIS AND ST PAUL; NEWARK; NEW ORLEANS; NEW YORK; NORFOLK; OBERLIN; OMAHA; OPERA AMERICA; ORLANDO; PALM BEACH; PHILADELPHIA; PHOENIX; PITTSBURGH; PORTLAND; PURCHASE; QUEENSBURY; RALEIGH; RENO; ROCHESTER; SACRAMENTO; ST LOUIS; SALT LAKE CITY; SAN DIEGO; SAN FRANCISCO; SAN JOSE; SANTA CRUZ; SANTA FE; SARASOTA; SEATTLE; STAMFORD; SYRACUSE; TANGLEWOOD; TOLEDO; TRAVELLING TROUPES, §5; TUCSON; TULSA; WASHINGTON, DC; WILMINGTON; WINSTON-SALEM; WOLF TRAP; and WOOSTER.

*

M. Maretzek: *Crotchets and Quavers* (New York, 1855)
M. Strakosch: *Souvenirs d'un impresario* (Paris, 1887)
J. H. Mapleson: *The Mapleson Memoirs* (New York, 1888); ed. H. Rosenthal (London, 1966)
M. Maretzek: *Sharps and Flats* (New York, 1890)
L. Arditi: *My Reminiscences* (New York, 1896)
H. C. Lahee: *Grand Opera in America* (Boston, 1902)
O. G. Sonneck: 'Early American Operas', *SIMG*, vi (1904–5), 428–95
H. E. Krehbiel: *Chapters of Opera* (New York, 1908, 3/1911)
O. G. T. Sonneck: *Early Opera in America* (New York, 1915)
H. E. Krehbiel: *More Chapters of Opera* (New York, 1919)
E. E. Hipsher: *American Opera and its Composers* (Philadelphia, 1927, 2/1934)
Opera News (1936–)
G. Gatti-Casazza: *Memories of the Opera* (New York, 1941)
H. Graf: *The Opera and its Future in America* (New York, 1941)
H. W. Hitchcock: 'An Early American Melodrama: *The Indian Princess* of J. N. Barber and John Bray', *Notes*, xii (1954–5), 375–88
J. Mates: *The American Musical Stage before 1800* (New Brunswick, NJ, 1962)
J. Mattfeld: *A Handbook of American Operatic Premieres, 1731–1962* (Detroit, 1963)
H. E. Johnson: *Operas on American Subjects* (New York, 1964)
L. M. Aufdemberge: *An Analysis of the Dramatic Construction of American Operas on American Themes, 1896–1958* (diss., Northwestern U., 1965)
L. M. Lerner: *The Rise of the Impresario: Bernard Ullman and the Transformation of Musical Culture in Nineteenth Century America* (diss., U. of Wisconsin, 1970)
E. I. Zimmerman: *American Opera Librettos, 1767–1825: the Manifest Result of the Imitative Principle in American Literary Form* (diss., U. of Tennessee, 1972)
J. Layng: 'America's First Opera', *Opera Journal*, ix/3 (1976), 3–7
K. E. Gombert: *Leonora by William Henry Fry and Rip Van Winkle by George Frederick Bristow: Examples of Mid-Nineteenth-Century American Opera* (diss., Ball State U., 1977)
S. Porter: *Performance Practice in American Opera at the Turn of the Nineteenth Century as seen in 'Children of the Wood', a Representative Musical Entertainment* (diss., U. of Colorado, 1977)
C. Ammer: 'Opera Conductors and Composers', *Unsung: a History of Women in American Music* (Westport, CT, 1980), 163–80
P. H. Virga: *The American Opera to 1790* (Ann Arbor, 1982)
C. Rabson: '*Disappointment* Revisited: Unweaving the Tangled Web', *American Music*, i/1 (1983), 12–27; ii/1 (1984), 1–28
I. Heskes: 'Music as Social History: American Yiddish Theater Music, 1882–1920', *American Music*, ii/4 (1984), 73–87
C. A. Hoover: 'Music in Eighteenth-Century American Theater', *American Music*, ii/4 (1984), 6–18
V. B. Lawrence: 'First Fling: When Italian Opera Stepped Ashore in New York with the Garcías', *ON*, liii/3 (1988–9), 20–23
K. K. Preston: *Travelling Opera Troupes in the United States, 1825–1860* (diss., CUNY, 1989)
E. Borroff: *Operas by Composers of the United States: an Exploratory Checklist* (Warren, MI, 1992)

AMERICAN THEATRE AND CULTURE

W. Dunlap: *A History of the American Theatre* (New York, 1832)
T. A. Brown: *History of the American Stage, containing Biographical Sketches of nearly every Member of the Profession that has appeared on the American Stage, from 1733 to 1870* (New York, 1870)
G. O. Seilhamer: *History of the American Theatre: New Foundations* (Philadelphia, 1891)
G. C. D. Odell: *Annals of the New York Stage* (New York, 1927–49)
F. Leuchs: *The Early German Theatre in New York, 1840–72* (New York, 1928)
B. G. Henneke: *The Playgoer in America (1752–1952)* (diss., U. of Illinois, 1956)
R. Moody: *The Astor Place Riot* (Bloomington, IN, 1958)
H. F. Rankin: *The Theater in Colonial America* (Chapel Hill, NC, 1960)
D. Grimsted: *Melodrama Unveiled: American Theatre and Culture, 1800–1850* (Chicago, 1968)
M. Sellen, ed.: *Ethnic Theatre in the United States* (Westport, CT, 1983)
W. B. Durham, ed.: *American Theatre Companies, 1749–1887* (New York, 1986)
——: *American Theatre Companies, 1888–1930* (New York, 1987)
S. L. Porter: *With an Air Debonair: Musical Theatre in America 1785–1815* (Washington DC, 1991)

OPERA IN AMERICAN CITIES

W. G. Armstrong: *A Record of the Opera in Philadelphia* (Philadelphia, 1884)
J. C. Baroncelli: *L'opéra français de la Nouvelle Orléans* (New Orleans, 1914)
E. Willis: *The Charleston Stage in the XVIII Century with Social Settings of the Time* (Columbia, SC, 1924)
J. Mattfeld: *A Hundred Years of Grand Opera in New York, 1825–1925* (New York, 1927)
E. C. Moore: *Forty Years of Opera in Chicago* (New York, 1930)
I. Kolodin: *The Metropolitan Opera* (New York, 1936, enlarged 4/1966)
R. L. Davis: *A History of Opera in the American West* (Englewood Cliffs, NJ, 1965)
——: *Opera in Chicago: a Social and Cultural History, 1850–1965* (New York, 1966)
H. A. Kmen: *Music in New Orleans: the Formative Years, 1791–1841* (Baton Rouge, LA, 1966)
R. H. Cowden: *The Chautauqua Opera Association, 1929–1958: an Interpretive History* (Commerce, TX, 1974)
J. R. Teran: *The New York Opera Audience, 1825–1974* (diss., New York U., 1974)
A. Bloomfield: *The San Francisco Opera, 1922–1978* (Sausalito, CA, 1978)
O. E. Albrecht: 'Opera in Philadelphia, 1800–1830', *JAMS*, xxxii (1979), 499–515
R. L. Brubaker: '130 Years of Opera in Chicago', *Chicago History*, viii/3 (1979), 156–69
C. Cassidy: *Lyric Opera of Chicago* (Chicago, 1979)
J. F. Cone: *First Rival of the Metropolitan Opera* (New York, 1983)
M. Mayer: *The Met: One Hundred Years of Grand Opera* (New York, 1983)
D. McKay: 'Opera in Colonial Boston', *American Music*, iii/2 (1985), 133–42
T. G. Kaufman: 'The Arditi Tour: the Midwest gets its First Real Taste of Italian Opera', *OQ*, iv/4 (1986), 39–52
B. A. McConachie: 'New York Operagoing, 1825–50: Creating an Elite Social Ritual', *American Music*, vi/2 (1988), 181–92
G. Fitzgerald, ed.: *Annals of the Metropolitan Opera* (Boston and New York, 1989)

MODERN AMERICAN OPERA PRODUCTION

Central Opera Service Bulletin (1959–)
C. Hamm: 'Opera and the American Composer', *The American Composer Speaks*, ed. G. Chase (Baton Rouge, LA, 1966), 284–97
'Opera in America: Performance and Musicology', *CMc*, no.26 (1978) [whole issue]
M. Mayer: *Sound Ambitions, Unsteady Resources: Opera Companies in the '80s* (Washington DC, 1985)
R. Hansen: 'Opera on Campus: an Interdisciplinary Approach', *Opera Journal*, xx/2 (1987), 11–17
R. H. Kornick: *A Guide to New American Operas: Performance Requirements and Critical Appraisals of Operas Published, Premiered and Reviewed from 1972 to 1986* (diss., Northwestern U., 1987)
Opera Monthly (1988–)

B. Cartland: 'Targeting the Opera Consumer', *Opera Monthly*, i/8 (1988), 59–62

Profile 1988: The Guide to Opera America and the Professional Opera Companies (Washington DC, 1988)

J. B. Clark, ed: 'The Composer and Performer and Other Matters: a Panel Discussion with Virgil Thomson and Philip Glass, Moderated by Gregory Sandow', *American Music*, vii/2 (1989), 181–204

G. Heymont: 'Land of Plenty: Opera has Established Itself across the Nation', *ON*, liv/9 (1989–90), 20–21

M. F. Rich: 'US Opera Survey 1988–89: Broadening the Base', *ON*, liv/5 (1989–90), 44–52

ELISE K. KIRK

Unities. An important issue in dramatic, and hence operatic, criticism from the late 16th to the late 18th centuries. Severe classicistic and rationalistic critics, beginning with Castelvetro (*Poetica d'Aristotele*, 1576), felt that they had the revered Aristotle's authority for preaching two 'unities', of plot and of time-scale, for drama. A proper play, they held, must contain just one coherent action, to which everything manifestly contributes; and this action must work itself through in a single fictive day. Various factors, such as the shortness of the distances characters could be expected to travel in one day, and the existence on several 16th-century Italian court stages of permanent or semi-permanent Vitruvian sets representing a single street in perspective, made it attractive to add a third prerequisite: that the action of the play should be set throughout in one place. From all this emerged the Rule of the Three Unities – action, time, place – which, if followed with skill, was thought by many to be capable of ensuring a verisimilitude both classical and natural.

There were disputes, however. Among the writers and critics of spoken drama some 'unitarians' (for example D'Aubignac and Boileau) were strict rigorists, while others (for example Corneille and Martello) had a broader and more indulgent view where the definition of terms and any infringements of the strict letter were concerned. And other people, especially in Spain and England, were sceptical or downright dismissive of the whole concept, in the name of common sense, artistic liberty, anticlassical modernity or simply the pressing need to divert an audience at any cost. Lope de Vega, George Farquhar and Samuel Johnson were in their different ways notable dismissers of 'unitarianism'.

Opera as sung play was as much involved as spoken drama in the critical wars surrounding the unities. One might expect early opera, as a child of Renaissance humanism, to be severely unitarian from birth, particularly if, as Gagliano put it in his preface to *Dafne* (1608), it was aiming for a perfection 'to approach the celebrated Greek and Latin tragedies'. However, it was born into the only-half-classical genre of pastoral tragicomedy. This placed it outside the domain of strict classicizing rules, though its most notable manifestation, the Monteverdi-Striggio *Orfeo* (1607), does have an action from which it would be difficult to displace or remove anything without dislocation, a time-span in which each act seems to be separated from the next by only a few hours, and two basic locales (the fields of Thrace and the depths of Avernus) which are apparently within walking – and ferrying – distance of each other.

Still, the librettos of early opera came quite quickly to be written by dramatists who were influenced by the more freely-formed Spanish drama à la Lope de Vega or by a Baroque reaction against all 'mechanical' rules. Precepts were read but then locked away with six keys, in Lope's phrase. By the 1640s the prefaces to Venetian operas are making the point insistently: 'this opera is ... not made according to the prescriptions of the ancient rules; in accord with Spanish usage it represents years and not hours' (Busenello, *Didone*, 1641); 'I wanted ... to beat a path not trod by others, sure that, if Aristotle lived in these days, he would adjust his *Poetics* to the inclinations of this century' (Badoardo, *Ulisse errante*, 1644); 'I freely confess that ... I observed no other precepts than the desires of the inventor of the machines, nor had I any other aim than the pleasure of the audience' (Nolfi, *Bellerofonte*, 1642). It is a nice irony that the spectacular machine effects which Nolfi here mentions as anti-Aristotelian derive from the tradition of inserting eruptions of spectacle into 16th-century spoken plays as *intermedi*, where, as the younger G. B. Strozzi pointed out in his memorandum on *intermedi* (?1600), they were in part 'invented ... to preserve the verisimilitude of time in the action' of the play proper by symbolizing time passing at a greater speed in the inter-act gaps. In fact on several occasions, as in the Florentine *intermedi* of 1539 (*Il commodo*) and 1566 (*Il granchio*), they allude specifically to times of day appropriate to the plot.

Some observers well into the 18th century went on feeling that Italian opera, with its elaborate and often rambling Spanish-Venetian plots and its cavalier way (on occasion) with time and space, was outside the neo-Aristotelian pale. The opera's laws the opera's patrons gave. According to Mr Primcock, pseudonymous author of *The Touchstone* (1728), 'those merry gentlemen [who] would reduce operas to the standards of Aristotle and Rapin' are 'carrying the cause into as wrong a court of judicature as trying a pirate for murder in chancery' (compare Farquhar's disdain for the assumption 'that Aristotle's criticisms may give rules to Drury Lane'). According to the ironic Marcello in his *Teatro alla moda* (*c*1720), the librettist should fill his preface with learned allusions to ancient rules and critics but then announce 'the place as *this or that theatre*, the time as *from seven to eleven o'clock at night*, and the action as *the ruin of the impresario*'. Yet the high fashion for the unities in the French spoken drama of the later 17th century had its effect on opera: at first directly, when the ideas and achievements of D'Aubignac, Rapin, Boileau, Corneille and Racine helped to shape the librettos Quinault wrote for Lully in the 1670s and 80s, with their careful *liaison de scènes*, their synchronizing within each act (battles and the like excepted) of stage-time and audience-time, their Racinian vagueness as to the time elapsed between acts, their restriction of place-changes (magical visions excepted) to neighbouring locales, and their domination by one heroic action so impressive – or oppressive – that *tragédie lyrique* soon generated a counter-form in *opéra-ballet*, which (as Pierre-Charles Roy put it in his *Lettre sur l'Opéra*, 1749) 'pleases by its variety and sympathizes with French impatience'.

Further, a taste for the unities became part of the general feeling among the 'Arcadian' reformers of the late 17th century and beyond that opera in Italy could learn some useful things about dramatic order and decorum from recent French trends, even if it had to accommodate the Italian passion for arias much as Quinault had to accommodate the French passion for *divertissements*. Hence Calzabigi was able to say half a century later, in his *Dissertazione* prefacing Metastasio's collected librettos (1755), that Zeno and Metastasio were to be praised for reducing Italian opera to a regular, unified form, making it a strict imitation of

Greek and Latin tragedy except for the striking incidence of scene-changing: something which modern stage-machinery allowed and which was anyway a necessary correction to an over-restrained unity of place in the classics. Unlike their Venetian predecessors of the 1640s, but like Milton and Racine, Zeno and Metastasio sometimes use their prefaces to point up which aspects of their plots (aspects often involving modification of their sources) show deference to one unity or another. Thus Metastasio's *argomento* to his *Semiramide* (1729) highlights a significant recognition – an Aristotelian *anagnorisis* – as the libretto's principal action; it establishes a particular city (Babylon) as a reasonable place for the coming together of all the characters contributing their elements of intrigue to the action; and it sets that action on a particular day which has proper verisimilitude because it is the one on which a proclamation will precipitate the grand recognition. Not averse to decorous spectacle, however, Metastasio allows the action to be backed by six neighbouring scenic locales, the Hanging Gardens among them.

This sort of regularity, in the observation of the unities among other things, was enough even to impress Voltaire (in the preface to *his* 1748 *Sémiramis*) that Metastasian opera, arias and all – and for Voltaire arias took some swallowing – was a just image and recreation of the theatre of the ancients. But Metastasio himself was no pedantic antiquarian. His view, as expounded with some autobiographical reflections in the section on dramatic unity of his *Estratto dell'Arte Poetica d'Aristotele* (1773), was as broad and unfussy as Corneille's, Racine's and Martello's. His idea of a moderately free unity of place finds echoes in the thought of younger men such as Antonio Planelli (*Dell'opera in musica*, 1772); but Planelli's Gluckiste contemporaries are all for extreme unitarian rigour if this will raise the operatic temperature, though their use of the unities cuts radically across the complexities of intrigue generated by Metastasio's. Thus Calzabigi's libretto for *Orfeo ed Euridice* (1762) – far severer than Striggio's for Monteverdi – is an instance of the new sublime simplicity fuelled by 200-year-old rules. A puritanical unity of action is foregrounded; the time-frame falls within a natural day; and, as Calzabigi points out in his preface to the 1764 Paris score, the locales of earth and hell are cunningly unified as far as they can be through having Eurydice's funeral in Act 1 take place by Lake Avernus itself.

Another Gluck librettist, François du Roullet, insists on 'the sacred rule of the unity of time, even more necessary to observe in opera than in any other kind of dramatic poem', in his *Lettre sur les drames-opéra* of 1776 – the year of La Porte and Chamfort's *Dictionnaire dramatique*, with its magisterial 17-page entry on *les unités*. But by the 1770s the twilight of the unities as a hot theoretical issue in opera and in spoken drama is beginning. In spoken drama the representative voice of advanced thought in the next generation could be taken to be Coleridge, influenced significantly by the *Vorlesungen über dramatische Kunst* (1809) of A. W. von Schlegel. In his notes on *Romeo and Juliet* (?1810), Coleridge not only dismisses the unities of time and place as 'mere inconveniences attached to the local peculiarities of the Athenian drama', but would also prefer to replace the less ephemeral unity of action with a concept of 'homogeneity, proportionateness, and totality of interest' which will rise above 'the shaping skill of mechanical talent' and only be possible to 'the creative, productive life-power of inspired genius'. In opera at about the same time, this creative, productive life-power begins to be associated with the unifying genius of the composer rather than the unity-obeying (or -disobeying) skill of the librettist; and the way is open to Wagner's *Oper und Drama* (1851), where 'unified artistic form can only be conceived as a manifestation of unified content'. For Wagner, space and time, the past and the future, drama and poetry, reason and feeling are to be unified through pure music: 'the orchestra is the grand agent which constantly completes the unity of expression'. Sung play has become music drama.

R. Bray: *La formation de la doctrine classique en France* (Paris, 1927)
T. M. Raysor: 'The Downfall of the Three Unities', *Modern Language Notes*, xlii (1927), 1–9
B. Weinberg: *A History of Literary Criticism in the Italian Renaissance* (Chicago, 1961)
R. S. Freeman: *Opera without Drama: Currents of Change in Italian Opera, 1675–1725* (Ann Arbor, 1981)
M. Carlson: *Theories of the Theatre: a Historical and Critical Survey* (Ithaca, 1984)
M. Collins: 'Dramatic Theory and the Italian Baroque Libretto', *Opera and Vivaldi*, ed. M. Collins and E. K. Kirk (Austin, 1984), 15–40

ROGER SAVAGE

Uno dei Dieci ('One of the [Council of] Ten'). Opera in one act by GIAN FRANCESCO MALIPIERO to his own libretto; Siena, Teatro dei Rinnuovati, 28 August 1971.

Written, astonishingly, in 1970, when Malipiero was 88, this terse little opera (lasting barely 16 minutes) has been regarded by many as a caricatured self-portrait. The chair-bound, irascible old aristocrat Almorò da Mula (baritone) certainly has traits in common with the octogenarian composer – ranging from his physical disability to his obsession with his city's glorious past. A former member of the 18th-century Venetian Consiglio dei Dieci, Da Mula has lived on into the Napoleonic period, yet stubbornly refuses to recognize that the Venetian republic no longer exists. Those around him have at first tried to humour his illusions by surrounding him with an anachronistic environment (a situation comparable to that in Luigi Pirandello's *Enrico IV*). However, the truth eventually gets through to him, whereupon he tears off his bandages, proudly dresses up as a Procuratore di S Marco, dismisses everyone and calmly awaits death.

Although narrower in range than *Il marescalco* (the secondary characters are mere ciphers compared with the all-dominating protagonist), *Uno dei Dieci* is perhaps the most movingly personal of Malipiero's postwar operas. Composed mainly in the tense yet poignant chromatic idiom that he had been using since the 1950s, the work nevertheless has an atmosphere of its own, with occasional appropriately nostalgic allusions to 18th-century styles.

JOHN C. G. WATERHOUSE

Unruhige Nacht, Die. Opera by F. L. Gassmann; *see* NOTTE CRITICA, LA.

Unterbrochene Opferfest, Das [*Il sacrifizio interrotto*; *Le sacrifice interromptu* ('The Oracle, or The Interrupted Sacrifice')]. Opera in two acts by PETER WINTER to a libretto by FRANZ XAVER HUBER; Vienna, Kärntnertortheater, 14 June 1796.

One of Winter's first works composed for Vienna, this opera proved a notable success there and beyond. Performed throughout Europe well into the 19th century, it was translated and published in several foreign languages. The action takes place in prehistoric Peru. An Inca village prepares for the sacrifice to the sun-god. Elvira (soprano) and Villacuma (bass), desiring revenge on Murney (tenor), imitate the voice of the sun-god during the preparatory ceremony and call for Murney to be the sacrificial victim. Despite his longing to stay alive to be with Myrha (soprano), Murney resolves to face death bravely. During the ceremony of sacrifice, however, the deception is unveiled, and Murney is saved. Several comic characters, including the servants Pedrillo (bass) and Balisa (soprano), provide humorous episodes to lighten the serious tone of the work. Over half of the musical numbers in the work are for ensemble or chorus. Winter draws on a variety of polyphonic and homophonic styles to build several large-scale scenic tableaux, and on an array of idioms in the arias: *seria* bravura and coloratura, lighter italianate lyricism and square-cut German song. LINDA TYLER

Uppman, Theodor (*b* San Jose, CA, 12 Jan 1920). American baritone. He received his vocal training at the Curtis Institute, Stanford University and the University of Southern California. He won praise as Pelléas in a concert performance of the opera by the San Francisco SO under Monteux in 1947, with Maggie Teyte as Mélisande. Uppman's light, high baritone and boyish appearance made him a particularly suitable choice, and he repeated the role in his débuts with the New York City Opera (1948) and the Metropolitan (1953); he also made a speciality of Papageno. In London he sang the title role in the première of Britten's *Billy Budd* (1951, Covent Garden), and also created roles in Carlisle Floyd's *The Passion of Jonathan Wade* (1962, New York City Opera), Villa-Lobos's *Yerma* (1971, Santa Fe), and Pasatieri's *Black Widow* (1972, Seattle). Uppman's Metropolitan repertory included Guglielmo, Piquillo (*La Périchole*), Eisenstein (*Die Fledermaus*), Taddeo (*L'italiana in Algeri*), Harlequin (*Ariadne auf Naxos*) and Marcello. MARTIN BERNHEIMER/R

Upshaw, Dawn (*b* Nashville, TN, 17 July 1960). American soprano. While at the Manhattan School of Music in 1983 she took the title role of Hindemith's *Sancta Susanna* and at the 1984 Spoleto Festival USA she sang Echo in Strauss's *Ariadne*. Engaged at the Metropolitan under the Development of Young Artists Program, she has progressed from Countess Ceprano, Frasquita and a Lady in Waiting (*Francesca da Rimini*) to Sophie (*Werther*), Sister Constance (*Dialogues des Carmélites*), Ilia, Zerlina (1990) and the Woodbird. She sang Mary (William Mayer's *A Death in the Family*) at St Louis (1986); Pamina in Amsterdam, Despina at Aix-en-Provence (1988); Servilia in Chicago (1989); Susanna at Salzburg (1991) and Anne Trulove at Aix-en-Provence (1992). With a charming appearance and a beautiful, vibrant voice, she excels in Mozart's soubrette and lyric-soprano roles. ELIZABETH FORBES

Urban, Josef (*b* Vienna, 26 May 1872; *d* New York, 10 July 1933). American architect and stage designer of Austrian birth. He was educated at the Vienna Academy of Fine Arts and the polytechnic, and he became a member of the Viennese Secessionists. A number of architectural commissions (a khedive's palace in Egypt, the remodelling of an Esterházy castle in Vienna, and a tsar's bridge over the River Neva in St Petersburg) preceded work with Mahler and Alfred Roller at the Vienna Opera (1897–1907). He designed the *Ring* for Budapest before going to Boston Opera as artistic director in 1911.

Urban moved from Boston to Broadway in 1915 and designed 12 *Ziegfeld Follies*; he also designed the Ziegfeld Theatre (no longer in existence), which opened with Kern's *Show Boat* (1927). He designed many musicals for Romberg, the Gershwins and Richard Rodgers. Harry Tierney's *Rio Rita* (1929), with Urban's exceptionally lavish settings, was one of the first musical comedies on screen.

Urban designed *Faust* for the Metropolitan Opera (1917), the first of more than 50 intelligent productions under Giulio Gatti-Casazza's management (1908–35); these included *Parsifal* (1920, described as 'poetically atmospheric'), *Tristan und Isolde* (1920), *Don Carlos* (1920), *Così fan tutte* (1922), *Pelléas et Mélisande* (1924, the first at the Metropolitan), *Turandot* (1926, first performance in the USA), *Norma* (1927) and *Don Giovanni* (1929). In Krenek's *Jonny spielt auf*, Urban's designs 'set the audience on their ear' (1929). He designed an opera house for Otto Kahn (1927), but it was never built. His many innovative features were included, however, in the Radio City Music Hall, built in 1932.

Urban, described as a 'Rabelaisian gentleman', created imaginative, three-dimensional settings that integrated architectural understanding with modern painting techniques and sophisticated lighting, the closest the Metropolitan ever came to realizing the principles of Adolphe Appia and Gordon Craig.

*

ES (J. Landy)
M. Kreuger: *Show Boat: the Story of a Classic American Musical* (New York, 1977) DAVID J. HOUGH

Urbanec, Bartolomej (*b* Krompachy, Slovakia, 12 Nov 1918; *d* Bratislava, 2 July 1983). Slovak composer. He studied at the Bratislava conservatory. A prominent representative of the so-called retrospective or neo-Secessionist school of Slovak opera, he completed two operas and sketched two others. *Tanec nad plačom* ('Dance over Tears'), first performed at the Slovak National Opera, Bratislava, on 26 May 1979, oscillates between Baroque and Classical influences, but also includes jazz elements in its depiction of the interwar years. *Majster Pavol* ('Master Pavol'), first performed at the Banská Bystrica Opera on 25 October 1980, draws on Slovak Renaissance music; its subject is the conflict between family and work (it focusses on the death of one of the builders of the world's highest altar at Levoča). *Pani úsvitu* ('Lady of Daybreak') and *Velúrove sako* ('The Suede Jacket') were not completed.

*

I. Vajda: *Slovenská opera* (Bratislava, 1988), 136–45, 238
IGOR VAJDA

Urbani, Valentino. *See* VALENTINI.

Urlus, Jacques [Jacobus] (*b* Hergenrath, 9 Jan 1867; *d* Noordwijk aan Zee, 6 June 1935). Dutch tenor. He studied in Amsterdam with Cornelie van Zanten and others and made his operatic début in Utrecht in 1894 as Beppe (*Pagliacci*). He sang with the Netherlands National Opera, 1894–9, then in Leipzig, 1900–14. One by one he mastered the leading Wagnerian parts, for which his robust voice and declamatory gifts well fitted him. He made his London début at Covent Garden in spring 1910 as Tristan during the Beecham opera season. In 1911 he was called to Bayreuth, where his first part was Siegmund. He sang regularly at the Metropolitan Opera, 1913–17, becoming its foremost Wagnerian tenor. From 1917 onwards he accepted no fixed engagements, but settled in the Netherlands and toured extensively in Europe and the USA. He was also an excellent concert singer. He made many records and published an autobiography, *Mijn loopbaan* ('My Career'; Amsterdam, 1930).

*

GV (R. Celletti; T. Kaufmann)
O. Spengler: *Jacques Urlus* (New York, 1917)
L. Riemens: 'Jacques Urlus', *Gramophone*, xv (1937–8), 405–8 [with discography]
CARL L. BRUUN/R

Ursuleac, Viorica (*b* Czernowitz [Cernăuţi, now Chernovtsy], 26 March 1894; *d* Ehrwald, Tyrol, 23 Oct 1985). Romanian soprano. She studied in Vienna and made her début at Agram in 1922 as Charlotte. She sang at Cernăuţi, the Vienna Volksoper and the Frankfurt Opera, whose conductor, Clemens Krauss, she later married. In 1930 she moved to Vienna, in 1935 to the Berlin Staatsoper and finally to the Staatsoper in Munich (1937–44). She created the leading soprano roles in Strauss's *Arabella* (1933, Dresden), *Friedenstag* (1938, Munich) and *Capriccio* (1942, Munich) and sang the title role in the public dress rehearsal of *Die Liebe der Danae* (1944, Salzburg). She also appeared in *Elektra*, *Der Rosenkavalier*, *Die Frau ohne Schatten*, *Ariadne auf Naxos* and *Die ägyptische Helena*, giving in all 506 performances of 12 Strauss roles.

Ursuleac also created the leading soprano roles in Sekles's *Die zehn Küsse* (1926, Frankfurt), Krenek's *Der Diktator* (1928, Wiesbaden) and d'Albert's *Mister Wu* (1932, Dresden). She appeared regularly at Salzburg, 1930–34 and 1942–3. She made her only Covent Garden appearance in 1934, when she sang in the English premières of *Arabella* and *Švanda the Bagpiper* and as Desdemona. She sang at the Teatro Colón in 1948 as Brangäne; her other Wagner roles included Senta and Sieglinde. She was a notable Tosca and Turandot, and a fine Elisabeth de Valois. There were 83 roles in her repertory.

*

I. Cook: 'Viorica Ursuleac, the First Arabella', *ON*, xix/16 (1954–5), 6–8
O. von Pandor: *Clemens Krauss in München* (Munich, 1955)
S. von Scanzoni: *Richard Strauss und seine Sänger* (Munich, 1961)
I. Cook and A. Frankenstein: 'Remembering Viorica Ursuleac', *Opera*, xxxvii (1986), 22–8
HAROLD ROSENTHAL/R

Uruguay. For discussion of opera in Uruguay *see* MONTEVIDEO.

USA. UNITED STATES OF AMERICA.

Usandizaga [Soraluce], **José Maria** (*b* San Sebastián, 31 March 1887; *d* San Sebastián, 5 Oct 1915). Basque composer. He showed early signs of musical talent and at the age of nine began his studies at the conservatory of his native town; when he was 14, on the instigation of the pianist Francis Planté, who had heard him play, he was accepted at the Schola Cantorum in Paris, where d'Indy took a personal interest in him and he formed a lasting friendship with his fellow-Basque Guridi. Ill-health turned his ambitions from the piano (for which Grovlez was his professor) to composition. In 1906, after winning first prize in composition at the Schola, he returned to San Sebastián, where in each of the next three years he won composition competitions, making much use of Basque folk music in his own pieces. The Basque scene and its music also formed the basis for his opera *Mendi mendiyan* ('High in the Mountains'), written in the Basque language: this was received with acclamation in Bilbao in 1910 and was repeated elsewhere. Three years later he composed, in only two months, the zarzuela *Las golondrinas*, a score of fecund invention and distinguished craftsmanship, which won him national fame on its production in Madrid in 1914 and has remained in the repertory. In October 1915, while at work on *La llama*, he died of consumption. The opera was completed by his brother Ramón (later director of the San Sebastián Conservatory) and performed in his native town; in 1929 his brother also converted *Las golondrinas* into an opera. In his brief life Usandizaga wrote, besides his stage works, a number of orchestral, choral and chamber compositions.

Viorica Ursuleac as Countess Madeleine in Richard Strauss's 'Capriccio', the role she created at the Staatsoper, Munich, in 1942

See also GOLONDRINAS, LAS.

Mendi mendiyan [High in the Mountains] (Basque lyric pastoral, 3, epilogue, J. Power), Bilbao, Campos Elíseos, 21 May 1910
Las golondrinas (drama lírico, 3, G. Martínez Sierra, after his *Teatro del ensueño*), Madrid, Price, 5 Feb 1914; rev. R. Usandizaga, 1929
La llama, 1915 (drama lírico, 3, Martínez Sierra), inc.; completed by R. Usandizaga, San Sebastián, 1918

*

J. M. de Arozamena: *Jesús Guridi* (Madrid, 1967)
LIONEL SALTER

Usatov, Dimitri Andreyvich (*b* 10/22 Feb 1847; *d* Yalta, 10/23 Aug 1913). Russian tenor. He studied in St Petersburg and in 1880 was engaged at the Bol'shoy Theatre,

Moscow. He sang Lensky in the first professional performance of *Yevgeny Onegin* (1881); he created Andrey in *Mazepa* (1884) and Vakula in *Cherevichki* (1887), and sang lyric roles such as Sobinin (*A Life for the Tsar*), Finn (*Ruslan and Lyudmila*), Gounod's Faust, Raoul and Alfredo. From 1890 he taught in Tbilisi, where he was teacher and mentor to Shalyapin. 'I always had an affection for this man', Shalyapin wrote, 'who raised me out of the gutter. He was so generous with his time, his energy, his immense knowledge.'

ELIZABETH FORBES

Usiglio, Emilio (*b* Parma, between 8 and 18 Jan 1841; *d* Milan, 7 or 8 July 1910). Italian composer and conductor. He began piano lessons at the age of five, later studying harmony and counterpoint in Pisa and Florence. He had a predilection for comic opera, considering it 'the most spontaneous and creative product of Italian music'. In an attempt to revive this spirit his operas were all comedies, but their success rarely survived their own time. The most famous, *Le educande di Sorrento* (1868, Florence), was revived in Berlin in 1911. In the 1870s Usiglio seemed destined to succeed Mariani as Italy's most important conductor. He was known for his quick, secure conducting style, his memory, intelligence and eclectic tastes. However, he was given to excessive drinking. In Perugia in 1874 he abandoned a performance of *Aida*; consequently, he lost the confidence of many impresarios. In later years he grew deaf and eventually retired to Milan with his wife, the singer Clementine Brusa. Brusa died four months before him, leaving him a legacy to found a competition for Italian composers of comic opera.

La locandiera (1861, Turin), the first of Usiglio's six operas, was based on Goldoni's comedy. It is in an old-fashioned, Rossinian style, relieved by many dances (waltzes, polacca) and thematic reminiscences, but the tunes are trivial, and the work was considered too close to operetta. Next came *L'eredità in Corsica* (1864, Milan) and *Le educande di Sorrento* (1868, Florence), which is more up-to-date: the model is Verdi (the score has a rataplan, a temporale and a brindisi), but there is no occasion for love music, and a trivial tone again prevails. After *La scommessa* (1870, Florence) there followed *Le donne curiose* (1879, Madrid), again taken from Goldoni. Although its harmonies are more modern than Rossini's, and certain of its forms slightly more contemporary (as in the 'Congiura delle donne' and the thematic repetitions spread across the opera), the quick, square melodies and fast, *staccatissimo* ensembles sound almost like parodies of a style over 50 years old. His last opera was *Le nozze in prigione* (1881, Milan).

La locandiera (ob, 4, G. G. Barilli, after C. Goldoni), Turin, Emanuele, 5 Sept 1861

L'eredità in Corsica (ob, 3, R. Berninzone), Milan, Radegonda, 17 June 1864

Le educande di Sorrento [La figlia del generale] (ob, 3, R. Berninzone), Florence, Alfieri, 1 May 1868

La scommessa (ob, B. Prato), Florence, Principe Umberto, 6 July 1870

La secchia rapita (ob, A. Anelli, after A. Tassoni), Florence, Goldoni, April 1872, collab. C. Bacchini, E. de Champs, R. Felici, G. Gialdini and G. Tacchinardi

Le donne curiose (ob, 3, A. Zanardini, after Goldoni), Madrid, Real, 11 Feb 1879

Le nozze in prigione (ob, Zanardini, after Labiche: *La mariée du mardigras*), Milan, Manzoni, 23 March 1881, *I-Mr*

*

A. Galli: 'Emilio Usiglio', *Teatro illustrato*, xii (1881)

MARVIN TARTAK

Uspensky, Viktor Alexandrovich (*b* Kaluga, 19/31 Aug 1879; *d* Tashkent, 9 Oct 1949). Russian composer and ethnomusicologist. He studied composition and the harp at the St Petersburg Conservatory (1908–13), and in 1918 was a co-founder of the Tashkent Conservatory, where he served as director and lecturer. From 1925 he took part in ethnographical expeditions to Turkmenistan, and to the Fergana Basin, where he made a further visit, as well as to Uzbekistan to collect folk music. He held posts at the Uzbek Music Technical School from 1928 and, in addition, from 1932 worked at the academic research institute for the arts in the folklore department and in the laboratory for the reconstruction of Uzbek folk instruments. His music drama *Farkhad i Shirin* ('Farkhad and Shirin') was first performed in Tashkent on 2 February 1936; a second version, revised in collaboration with Georgy Mushel' and S. Tsveyfeld, received its première at the Bol'shoy Branch Theatre in Moscow in May 1937. Uspensky and Mushel' further revised *Farkhad and Shirin* in 1940 as an opera (Sh. Khurshid, after A. Navoi), which was first performed at the Navoi Theatre of Opera and Ballet, Tashkent, on 15 May 1957.

DETLEF GOJOWY

USSR. UNION OF SOVIET SOCIALIST REPUBLICS.

Ústí nad Labem (Ger. Aussig). Czech town. The neo-Baroque Stadttheater was built in 1907–8 by the architect Alexander Graf, with decorations by Eduard Veit; it was modernized in 1947, and a further reconstruction started in 1987. From 1918 and the independence of Czechoslovakia, there was a two-month Czech opera season alongside the eight-month German one; the Czech seasons consisted mostly of performances by groups from Olomouc and České Budějovice.

In 1945 the Divadlo Severu (Theatre of the North) operated for a short time from Teplice. It performed the first postwar Czech opera in Ústí nad Labem, Smetana's *Bartered Bride*. The Ústecko-Karlovarská Zpěvohra (Music Theatre of Ústí and Karlovy Vary) represented a further phase in the development of Czech opera in northern Bohemia, opening its season with Smetana's *Dalibor* in Karlovy Vary (1946–7). The Divadlo Zdeňka Nejedlého (Zdeněk Nejedlý Theatre), the only independent theatre for opera and ballet in the country, was founded in 1952. Its opera group organized regular tours to Most, Teplice and elsewhere, and established a relationship with the Dresden Staatsoper. It has a diverse and attractive repertory, ranging from Baroque to contemporary works and including many Romantic ones, among them several Czech operas. It has also presented *Boris Godunov* (1967) and *Tristan und Isolde* (1972, the first performance in Czechoslovakia since 1945). In 1990 the theatre's name was changed to the Státní Divadlo Ústí nad Labem (State Theatre of Ústí nad Labem).

*

Almanach Městské oblastní divadlo v Ústí nad Labem, 1948–1949 [Almanac of the Town Regional Theatre in …] (Ústí nad Labem, 1949)

Kronika 20 let práce Divadla Z. Nejedlého v Ústí nad Labem, 1945–1965 [The Chronicle of 20 Years of Work of the Nejedlý Theatre in …] (Ústí nad Labem, 1965)

25 let Státního divadla Z. Nejedlého v Ústí nad Labem, 1946–1971 [25 Years of the State Nejedlý Theatre in …] (Ústí nad Labem, 1971)

EVA HERRMANNOVÁ

Utah Opera. Company based in SALT LAKE CITY.

Uthal [*Malvina*]. *Opéra* in one act by ETIENNE-NICOLAS MÉHUL to a libretto by Jacques M. B. Bins de Saint-Victor after James Macpherson's Ossianic poem *Berrathon*; Paris, Opéra-Comique (Théâtre Feydeau), 17 May 1806.

Malvina (soprano) is torn between her love for her father, King Larmor (baritone), and her husband Uthal (*haute-contre*), who has deposed Larmor. Larmor takes comfort from her support, and they are soon joined by Fingal's warriors. As they plan their attack, Malvina worries about the outcome. Shortly after they leave, Uthal arrives. At first not recognized by his wife, he rejects her pleas to watch over her father. Larmor and his allies defeat Uthal's troops, and Uthal is exiled in spite of Malvina's urging clemency. When she announces, to the surprise of those present, that she will follow her husband, Uthal is moved to ask Larmor's forgiveness and the king is reconciled with his son-in-law.

Uthal is best known as 'the opera without violins', a description that does not do justice to Méhul's sensitivity to orchestration as a means of establishing atmosphere. The Ossianic subject prompted him not only to remove these brighter tones from the orchestra, but also to reinforce the middle register: the viola section is increased (by the addition of those who would normally play violin, according to the composer's instructions) and divided into first and second parts throughout. Other instruments are used imaginatively; the woodwinds, for example, are more prominent than usual. Méhul gave particular attention to the sonority of the horns and bassoons, sometimes joined by the harp (for its bardic symbolism), as in the opening of the overture and several ensembles. The male chorus is also remarkable: for example, in the bards' *hymne au Sommeil*, 'O de Selma la gloire et l'espérance' in the *morceau d'ensemble*, 'Vers le palais de tes nobles ancêtres', and, in a later ensemble, their *chant* 'Près de Balva, sur le nuage'. That there is only one straightforward solo (Uthal's *récitatif et romance* 'Quoi! je la recherche en vain! ... Tel que l'on voit sur nos montagnes') is indicative of the composer's intention to translate the drama into integrated tableaux in which all contribute. *Uthal* is exceptional in its orchestration and, for its time, it is also effective in its dramatic and musical translation of the mists and passion of the Ossian epic.

M. ELIZABETH C. BARTLET

Uttini, Francesco Antonio Baldassare (*b* Bologna, 1723; *d* Stockholm, 25 Oct 1795). Italian composer and conductor active in Sweden. He received his musical education from Padre Martini and, according to Fétis, from Perti and Sandoni in Bologna. In 1743 he was elected to membership in the Accademia Filarmonica and produced his first opera, *Alessandro nelle Indie*, in Genoa. During the next ten years he achieved some fame as a composer of both operas (mostly *opere serie*) and oratorios throughout Italy, joining the Mingotti theatre troupe in 1752 as resident composer. It was in that troupe that he met his first wife, the singer Rosa Scarlatti. His first tour to northern Europe (1752) resulted in the opera *Siroe*, performed in Hamburg, and in the following years he directed *L'olimpiade* and *Zenobia* in Copenhagen; he also presented numerous pasticcios in Rostock and elsewhere, of which only one, *Armide*, survives (1754; *D-ROu*).

In 1755 members of the Mingotti troupe including Uttini were invited by Queen Lovisa Ulrika to visit Stockholm and perform operas for the court. For the newly built theatre at Drottningholm he composed the opera *Il re pastore*, which was later printed in score. After the troupe disbanded, Uttini remained in Stockholm as the court *kapellmästare*, writing mostly Italian *opere serie* until 1762, when he turned his attention to settings of French *opéra comique* texts, such as Favart's *Soliman II* and Quinault's *Psyché*. In 1772 he was commissioned by Gustavus III to provide the music for the first Swedish grand opera, *Thetis och Pelée*, which was successfully performed the following year. During the next ten years he turned towards larger works such as *Birger Jarl och Mechtilde* (1774, with H. P. Johnsen) and *Aline, drottning uti Golconda* ('Aline, Queen of Golconda', 1776); he added choruses to Swedish versions of Racine's *Athalie* (1776) and *Iphigénie* (1777), and wrote ballet music and prologues to Gluck's operas. After 1778 his role as principal conductor of the *hovkapell* was mainly taken over by other musicians and he gradually retired from concert life. By 1788, when he retired, he had largely ceased to compose; he married his second wife, the singer Sophia Liljegren (1765–95), in the same year. Uttini's early musical style conforms to the *opera seria* style of the period; his operas of 1766 onwards, however, tend to show a greater reliance on the orchestral accompaniment, often resulting in colourful scores. In his Swedish operas, the use of folk melodies is occasionally noticeable.

See also BIRGER JARL OCH MECHTILDE and THETIS OCH PELÉE.

Alessandro nelle Indie (os, 2, P. Metastasio), Genoa, 1743
Astianatte (dramma seria, 3, A. Salvi), Cesena, 1748
Demofoonte (os, 2, Metastasio), Ferrara, 1750, 1 aria *B-Bc*
Siroe (os, 2, Metastasio), Hamburg, 1752
L'olimpiade (os, 2, Metastasio), Copenhagen, Royal Opera, 1753, 1 aria *GB-Lbl*
Zenobia (os, 2, Metastasio), Copenhagen, Feb 1754
La Galatea (os, 2), Drottningholm, 1755
L'isola disabitata (dramma per musica, 1, Metastasio), Drottningholm, 1755
Il re pastore (dramma per musica, 2, Metastasio), Drottningholm, 1755, *S-Skma* (The Hague, 1757)
L'eroe cinese (os, 2, Metastasio), Drottningholm, 1757, *Skma*
Adriano in Siria (os, 2, Metastasio), Drottningholm, 1757
Cythère assiégée (oc, 2, C.-S. Favart), Stockholm, 1762, *St*
Il sogno di Scipione (dramatic serenade, 1, Metastasio), Stockholm, 1764
Soliman II, ou Les trois sultanes (oc, 2, Favart), Stockholm, 1765, *Skma* (Act 1)
Le gui de chène (oc, 2, La Junquières), Stockholm, 1766, *St*
Psyché (tragédie lyrique, 5, P. Quinault, after Molière), Drottningholm, 1766
L'aveugle de Palmyre (oc, 2, F.-G. Desfontaines), Drottningholm, 1768, *St*
Thetis och Pelée (5, J. Wellander, after B. B. de Fontenelle and Gustavus III), Stockholm, Bollhuset, 18 Jan 1773, *F-Pc, S-Skma*; rev. (3), 1775; rev. and reorchd (5), 1791, *St*
Aeglé (opera-ballet, 1, G. G. Adlerbeth, after P. Laujon), Stockholm, Bollhuset, 8 July 1774, collab. H. P. Johnsen
Birger Jarl och Mechtilde (drama with divertissements, 3, G. F. Gyllenborg, after Gustavus III), Stockholm, Rikssalen, 8 July 1774, collab. Johnsen
Aline, drottning uti Golconda [Aline, Queen of Golconda] (3, C. B. Zibet, after M.-J. Sedaine), Stockholm, Bollhuset, 11 Jan 1776, *Skma, St*

Prologues (all *St*) to C. W. Gluck: Orfeo ed Euridice, Stockholm, 25 Nov 1773; P.-M. Berton: Silvie, Stockholm, 13 July 1774; Gluck: Iphigénie en Aulide, Stockholm, 28 Dec 1778

*

FétisB
F. Dahlgren: *Anteckningar om Stockholms teatrar* (Stockholm, 1866)
H. Nyblom: 'Tryckning av ett operapartitur på 1750-talet', *STMf*, iv (1922), 53–7

E. Sundström: 'F. A. Uttini och Adolf Fredriks italienska operatrup', *STMf*, xiii (1931), 5–44
——: 'Francesco Antonio Uttini som musikdramatiker', *STMf*, xlv (1963), 33–93
A. Beijer: *Les troupes françaises à Stockholm 1699–1792: listes de répertoire* (Uppsala, 1989)
M. Tegen: 'Uttini's *Thetis och Pelée*', *Gustavian Opera 1770–1809* (Stockholm, 1991), 236–52

BERTIL H. VAN BOER, MARTIN TEGEN

Uzbekistan. For discussion of opera in Uzbekistan *see* TASHKENT.

Uzunov, Dimitar (*b* Stara Zagora, 10 Dec 1922; *d* Vienna, 11 Dec 1985). Bulgarian tenor. He studied in Sofia, making his début there in 1947 as Werther. Early roles included Rodolfo, Don José, Lensky and Grigory. He appeared at the Bol'shoy (1952), the Paris Opéra, La Scala and the Metropolitan (1959), where he sang Radames and Canio. He made his Covent Garden début in 1960 as Othello, returning as Calaf. Engaged at the Vienna Staatsoper (1962–9), he sang Bacchus at Aix-en-Provence (1963) and Dmitry at Salzburg (1965). He continued to appear at the Staatsoper until 1980, mainly in character roles. His repertory included Chénier, Florestan, Manrico and Turiddu. His voice was not truly heroic, but a strong presence and good diction allowed him to triumph as Otello, his favourite role.

ELIZABETH FORBES

V

Vaccai, Nicola (*b* Tolentino, 15 March 1790; *d* Pesaro, 5 or 6 Aug 1848). Italian composer and singing teacher. Though he was born into a family of doctors, his first inclination was towards poetry; by the age of 17 he had written four verse tragedies in the style of Alfieri, one of which was performed by a professional company in Pesaro. Not until he left for Rome in 1807 to read law did he become aware of his true vocation: he began to take regular music lessons from Giuseppe Janacconi, later *maestro di cappella* of St Peter's, and by 1811 had been awarded the *diploma di maestro* of the Accademia di S Cecilia. He then went to Naples, where he studied dramatic composition with Paisiello, gaining his first practical experience by writing church music and insert arias for opera revivals in Neapolitan theatres. Encouraged by his début at the Teatro Nuovo with *I solitari di Scozia* (1815), Vaccai left for Venice in search of opera commissions. But there success eluded him; *Malvina* (1816) was removed after one night, while *Il lupo di Ostenda* (1818) was criticized as imitation Rossini. Four ballets, written for La Fenice between 1817 and 1821, fared better. Meanwhile, his literary training bore fruit in an Italian translation of the libretto of Méhul's *Joseph*.

During this period Vaccai was much in demand in Venetian high society as a singing teacher. In this capacity he went to Trieste in 1821, spending three months in 1822 at Frohsdorf, near Wiener Neustadt, in the establishment of Murat's widow. Still hoping for operatic fame in Italy, he turned down an offer to be Kapellmeister at Stuttgart. After leaving Trieste for good in 1823 he secured a commission for the Teatro Ducale, Parma, resulting in *Pietro il grande* (1824), in which Vaccai himself substituted for one of the singers; this inaugurated a brief period of theatrical glory for him, to which belong *Zadig e Astartea* (1825, Naples) and his masterpiece *Giulietta e Romeo* (1825, Milan), the only one of his operas to achieve frequent performance outside Italy.

With the advent of Bellini, Vaccai's fortunes declined rapidly. *Saladino e Clotilda* (1828, Milan) was received so badly that his commission to compose an opera for the opening of the Teatro Carlo Felice in Genoa was revoked in Bellini's favour. A quarrel with Felice Romani – Vaccai had failed to ensure full payment to him for the libretto of *Saul* – undoubtedly played its part in the decision by Romani and Bellini to recoup their losses over *Zaira* with the hastily written *I Capuleti e i Montecchi*, which inevitably eclipsed Vaccai's slighter opera on the Romeo and Juliet story. But the older composer was avenged at a Paris performance in 1832 when Malibran, at Rossini's suggestion, interpolated the penultimate scene of Vaccai's opera into Bellini's. From then on this became a regular option for contraltos such as Marietta Alboni who essayed the role of Bellini's Romeo, originally written for the soprano Giuditta Grisi; hence its inclusion as an appendix in all later printed editions of *I Capuleti e i Montecchi*.

In 1830 Vaccai renounced the stage for the second time and went to Paris as a teacher. A visit to England in that year was unexpectedly prolonged until 1833, while he enjoyed a highly successful career as a teacher and composer of salon pieces. During that time he published his *Metodo pratico di canto italiano per camera* (London, 1832), still a standard work. On the death of his father in 1833 he returned to Italy to settle down, marry and raise a family. Once again the lure of the theatre proved strong. But in spite of the presence of Malibran in the title role, his *Giovanna Gray* (1836, Milan) was a failure.

Compensation came in the offer of a post at the Milan Conservatory. After succeeding Basili as *censore* in 1838, he reorganized the study of singing, inaugurated opera performances among his students on the Neapolitan model and began a new choir school. He also enlarged the repertory to include the German classics. However, the reversal in 1843 of his decision to include Handel's *Messiah* in the conservatory's celebration of Holy Week determined him to resign the following year, and he returned to manage his family estates at Pesaro. In 1845 his operatic activity came to an end with *Virginia*, performed at Rome. Even in retirement he continued teaching and composing with an industry that is thought to have hastened his death.

In a famous letter of 1851 Rossini paid tribute to Vaccai as a teacher and a composer 'in whom sentiment was allied to philosophy'. Yet as a theatre composer he was an honourable failure. Very few of his operas were ever printed in their entirety. *Zadig e Astartea* and *Giulietta e Romeo* owed their success to a delicate, personal inflection of the current Rossinian style, but they were not proof against the much higher emotional charge of Bellini's music. Two of the later works achieved a certain *succès d'estime*: *Marco Visconti* (1838, Turin) shows an attempt to come to terms with the dramatic style of Donizetti, but the best of it is to be found in isolated, often purely episodic pieces of a refined charm and workmanship; *Virginia* is a full-blown Risorgimento opera with plentiful choruses and two stage bands, whose intermittent grandeur recalls Spontini rather than Vaccai's contemporaries. Both operas show a regard for academic values unusual at the time. It is, however, as a singing teacher that Vaccai left his chief mark. His *Metodo pratico* is not only an excellent primer for the amateur but also a valuable document for the study of 19th-century performing practice.

See also GIULIETTA E ROMEO (ii).

I solitari di Scozia (melodramma, 2, A. L. Tottola, after G. De Gamerra), Naples, Nuovo, 18 Feb 1815, *I-TOL**
Malvina (op di sentimento, 2, G. Rossi), Venice, S Benedetto, 8 June 1816, *TOL** (inc.)
Il lupo di Ostenda, ossia L'innocenza salvata dalla colpa (op semiseria, 2, B. Merelli), Venice, S Benedetto, 17 June 1818, *TOL**
Pietro il grande, ossia Un geloso alla tortura (dramma buffo, 2, Merelli), Parma, Ducale, 17 Jan 1824, excerpts (Milan, 1824)
La pastorella feudataria (op semiseria, 2, Merelli), Turin, Carignano, 18 Sept 1824, *US-Wc*, excerpts (Milan, 1826; London, n.d.)
Zadig e Astartea (dramma per musica, 2, Tottola, after Voltaire), Naples, S Carlo, 21 Feb 1825; rev. version, Trieste, 1826; as L'esiliato di Babilonia, Venice, 1832; *I-TOL* (with autograph annotations), *US-Wc*, excerpts (Milan, 1826 or 1827/*R*1989: IOG, xlv; Paris, ?1825)
Giulietta e Romeo (tragedia, 2, F. Romani), Milan, Cannobiana, 31 Oct 1825, *I-Mr**, copy *Mc*, vs (Milan, 1826/*R*1989: IOG, xlv); rev. version (3), Milan, 1835, *Mc*
Bianca di Messina (os, 2, L. Piossasco), Turin, Regio, 20 Jan 1826, *TOL*, excerpts (Milan, 1826)
Il precipizio, o Le fucine di Norvegia (melodramma semiserio, 2, Merelli), Milan, Scala, 16 Aug 1826, *Mr**, copy *TOL* (with autograph annotations), excerpts (Milan, 1826 or 1827)
Saul, 1826 (azione sacra, 2, Romani), unperf.; rev. version (tragedia lirica, Tottola), Naples, S Carlo, 11 March 1829; rev. version, Milan, 1829; *Mr**, *TOL**, copy *TOL*, excerpts (Milan, n.d.)
Giovanna d'Arco (melodramma romantico, 4, Rossi, after F. von Schiller), Venice, Fenice, 17 Feb 1827; rev. version, Naples, 1828; *Mr**, copy *TOL*, excerpts (Milan, 1827)
Saladino e Clotilda (melodramma tragico, 2, L. Romanelli), Milan, Scala, 4 Feb 1828, *TOL**, excerpts (Milan, 1828)
Alexi (azione tragica, 2, Tottola), Naples, S Carlo, 6 July 1828, begun by C. Conti
Giovanna Gray (tragedia lirica, 3, C. Pepoli), Milan, Scala, 23 Feb 1836, *TOL**, copy *TOL*, excerpts (Milan, 1836)
Marco Visconti (dramma lirico, 2 acts [4 giornate], L. Toccagni), Turin, Regio, 27 Jan 1838, *TOL**, vs (Milan, 1839)
La sposa di Messina (melodramma, 3, J. Cabianca, after Schiller), Venice, Fenice, 2 March 1839, *TOL*
Virginia (tragedia lirica, 3, C. Giuliani), Rome, Apollo, 14 Jan 1845; rev. version, Pesaro, 1846; *Mr**, copy *TOL*, vs (Milan, 1846)

*

G. Vaccai: *La vita di Nicola Vaccaj scritta dal figlio Giulio con prefazione del professore A. Biaggi* (Bologna, 1882)
L. Orrey: *Bellini* (London, 1969), 100ff

JULIAN BUDDEN

Vacchi, Fabio (*b* Bologna, 19 Feb 1949). Italian composer. A pupil of Giacomo Manzoni and Franco Donatoni at the Bologna Conservatory and the Accademia Chigiana, Siena, he has taught in conservatories, notably that in Vicenza. His compositional style is characterized by attention to detail, a concern with melody and strict techniques of organization, and a conception of sound that does not exclude euphonic mellowness or anguished oscillations. Such euphony is to be found in the best passages of *Girotondo* (Florence, Teatro della Pergola, 16 June 1982), an opera in two acts to a libretto by Roberto Roversi based on a play by Arthur Schnitzler. The apparent frivolity of Schnitzler's comedy is treated by the composer with a profound melancholy. The virtuoso writing for voice, exemplified in the parts written for Dorothy Dorow, is intended to convey an effect of futile effort, like a bird fluttering in a cage or a maddened butterfly spiralling and making sudden rushes, soaring in frenzied movement. The libretto is designed to allow allusion to traditional 'closed' forms such as arias and duets.

In the eight years that separate *Girotondo* from his second opera, *Il viaggio*, Vacchi explored ways of achieving greater economy of material. In *Il viaggio* (Bologna, Teatro Comunale, 23 January 1990) the slender action of the five scenes, narrated in verse by Tonino Guerra, concerns an elderly couple from Romagna who leave their little village to go for once to see the sea, no more than 30 km away. They arrive on a day so misty that they can see nothing, after a journey that has been the occasion for many thoughts, memories, dreams and meetings. In spite of the use of Romagnolo dialect in the choral episodes, the movement in *Il viaggio*, shifting between reality, memory and dream, between external facts and internal reflection, is conceived in universal rather than local terms. Vacchi calls for a type of vocal utterance as close as possible to natural speech, with many nuances amplified by microphones. From the point of view of harmony and timbre his writing achieves simplicity and a new translucency through use of prolonged harmonic fields and immediately recognizable gestures. PAOLO PETAZZI

Vacek, Miloš (*b* Horní Roveň, nr Pardubice, 20 June 1928). Czech composer. He studied in Prague, at the Conservatory (1942–7) and then at the Academy of Musical Arts (1947–51). His style is traditional, based on clear melodic lines with close links between music and text, and is often pictorial. For his operas he has drawn on successful literary works. The 'historical fresco' *Jan Želivský*, in which a clash between rich burghers and the poor in a Hussite revolutionary camp is contrasted with a love story, shows the influence both of the cultural trends of the 1950s and of Romantic opera. *Bratr Žak* ('Brother Žak') depicts the attractive milieu of a circus, with its clowns who long for freedom and respect but are faced with harassment and bureaucracy. *Romance pro křídlovku* ('Romance for the Bugle') sets to music one of Hrubín's works about the vulnerable inner life of a student who simultaneously experiences his first love and the death of a close relative. The children's opera *Kocour Mikeš* ('Mikeš the Tomcat') describes the adventures of a talking tomcat and his friends, a piglet and a billy-goat. Vacek has also written ballets, musicals and music for film, television and radio.

Jan Želivský, 1956–8 (historical fresco, 6, M. Kroha); rev. 1974 (N. Mauerová), Olomouc, O. Stibor State, 15 April 1984
Bratr Žak [Brother Žak], 1977–8 (2, Mauerová and Vacek, after I. Olbracht), Ostrava, State, 12 June 1982
Romance pro křídlovku [Romance for the Bugle], 1980–81 (lyric chamber op, 2 scenes and epilogue, Mauerová, after F. Hrubín), České Budějovice, South Bohemian, 19 Dec 1987
Kocour Mikeš [Mikeš the Tomcat], 1981–2 (comic children's op, 2, Mauerová, after J. Lada), Brno, Janáček, 28 March 1986

*

V. Tašlová: 'Bratr Žak a moderní opera' [Brother Žak and a Modern Opera], *Scéna*, viii/9 (1983), 4
V. Pospíšil: 'Vackova operní premiéra v Českých Budějovicích' [Vacek's Opera Première in České Budějovice], *HRo*, xli (1988), 167–8

HELENA HAVLÍKOVÁ

Vachon [Vasson, Waschon], **Pierre** (*b* Arles, June 1731; *d* Berlin, 7 Oct 1803). French composer. According to Fétis he went to Paris to study the violin in 1751. He may be the Vasson who in 1754 was a violinist in the orchestra of the Comédie-Italienne, with which Vachon later had connections as a composer. He played at the Concert Spirituel in 1756 and 1758, and in 1761 became first violinist in the orchestra of the Prince of Conti. With Jean-Claude Trial, Vachon gave concerts for the court at Fontainebleau (1765) and composed two operas, *Renaud d'Ast* (1765) and *Esope à Cythère* (1766). These and his next two stage works were not successful, but his last work in this genre, *Sara* (1773), enjoyed a certain popularity in Paris. (The opera *Le meunier*, attributed to Vachon by Fétis, is identical with *Renaud d'Ast*, its title being a misspelling of the name of the librettist, Lemonnier.) Vachon spent some ten years from about 1774 in London, then went to Germany and by 1786 was leader of the royal orchestra at Berlin. His skill as a conductor was praised by Dittersdorf in his account of the 1789 performance of his Singspiel *Doktor und Apotheker* at Charlottenburg. Vachon retired from his post in Berlin in 1798.

Vachon's instrumental works – he was one of the first French musicians to compose string quartets, and wrote symphonies that reveal a variety of national influences – are more important than his operas, which are simply collections of pleasant melodies and occasional ensembles, interspersed throughout the dialogue without dramatic continuity.

Renaud d'Ast (cmda, 2, P.-R. Lemonnier), Fontainebleau, 12 Oct 1765, ov., arr. 2 vns (Paris, n.d.), collab. J.-C. Trial

Esope à Cythère (cmda, 1, L. J. H. Dancourt), Paris, Comédie-Italienne (Bourgogne), 15 Dec 1766, excerpts (Paris, n.d.), collab. Trial [according to Brenner, perf. Bordeaux, 1762]

Les femmes et le secret (comédie, 1, A.-F. Quétant), Paris, Comédie-Italienne (Bourgogne), 9 Nov 1767 (Paris, 1768)

Hippomène et Atalante (ballet-héroïque, P.-N. Brunet), Paris, Opéra, 8 Aug 1769

Sara, ou La fermière écossaise (comédie, 2, J.-B. Collet de Messine), Paris, Comédie-Italienne (Bourgogne), 8 May 1773 (Paris, 1773)

*

FétisB

C. D. Brenner: *A Bibliographical List of Plays in the French Language 1700–1789* (Berkeley, 1947)

JEAN HARDEN

Vadé, Jean-Joseph (*b* Ham, Picardy, 17 Jan 1719; *d* Paris, 4 July 1757). French composer and dramatist. For much of his life he held various tax-collecting posts, notably in the *bureau du vingtième* in Paris from 1745. After an unsuccessful début at the Comédie-Française in 1749, he turned to the Opéra-Comique at the invitation of the new director, Jean Monnet. The huge success of *La fileuse* (1752), Vadé's first *opéra comique*, helped to put the newly reopened theatre on a sound financial basis; most of his subsequent works staged there were equally well received.

Despite a large and varied literary output, Vadé is now mainly remembered as the creator of the *genre poissard*, or 'fishmarket style', found in many of his chansons and *opéras comiques*. This style developed from a close study of the behaviour of Parisian market folk, giving his writing a new realism and earthy humour which made it immensely popular at all levels of society until long after his death. It was the spontaneity and liveliness of his work for the Fair Theatres that caused him to be chosen as librettist for *Les troqueurs* (1753), produced at the height of the Querelle des Bouffons and modelled on *opera buffa*. The combination of Vadé's simple plot and Dauvergne's italianate music was highly successful and did much to establish a style of *opéra comique* in which newly composed music replaced the traditional vaudevilles.

Vadé's remaining *opéras comiques*, however, are all of the earlier type, which enjoyed a final flowering in the 1750s. Prominent among them are the ever-popular parodies of contemporary Opéra productions. Although most of the music for these consists of standard vaudeville melodies, Vadé composed some of the *airs* himself (exactly which is difficult to establish, since many of the 'Airs de M. Vadé' included in editions of the plays turn out to be well-known tunes). They are written in a simple but attractive style, strongly influenced by the Italian music of the Bouffons. Only the melodic lines survive. As well as those included in editions of the librettos, others were printed in the *Recueil noté de chansons de M. Vadé* (Paris, 1758) and in the various editions of *Oeuvres de M. Vadé* (Paris, 1755, enlarged 2/1758; The Hague, 1759, 1785).

opéras comiques unless otherwise stated; first performed in Paris

PSG – *Foire St Germain* PSL – *Foire St Laurent*

La fileuse, PSG, 8 March 1752 [parody of Destouches: Omphale]

Le poirier, PSL, 7 Aug 1752

Le bouquet du roi, PSL, 24 Aug 1752, collab. J. Fleury and Lattaignant

Le suffisant, ou Le petit maître dupé, PSG, 12 March 1753

Le rien, PSG, 10 April 1753 [parody of parodies of Mondonville: Titon et l'Aurore]

Le trompeur trompé, ou La rencontre imprévue, PSG, 18 Feb 1754

Il était temps, PSG, 28 June 1754 [parody of Ixion from Destouches and Lalande: Les élémens]

La nouvelle Bastienne, PSL, 17 Sept 1754, collab. Anseaume

Compliment de clôture, PSL, 6 Oct 1754

Les troyennes en Champagne, PSG, 1 Feb 1755 [parody of Chateaubrun: Les Troyennes]

Jérôme et Fanchonette, ou La pastorale de la grenouillière, PSG, 18 Feb 1755 [parody of Mondonville: Daphnis et Alcimadure]

Compliment de clôture, PSG, 6 April 1755

Le confident heureux, PSL, 31 July 1755

Folette, ou L'enfant gâté, PSL, 6 Sept 1755 [parody of Destouches: Le Carnaval et la Folie]

Compliment de la clôture, PSL, 6 Oct 1755

Nicaise (comédie poissarde), PSG, 7 Feb 1756 [parody of Destouches: Le Carnaval et la Folie]

Les raccoleurs, PSG, 11 March 1756

Compliment de clôture, PSG, 6 April 1756

Compliment pour la clôture de l'Opéra-comique, PSL, 6 Oct 1756

L'impromptu du coeur, PSG, 8 Feb 1757

Compliment pour la clôture de l'Opéra-Comique, PSG, 3 April 1757

Le mauvais plaisant, ou Le drôle de corps, PSL, 17 Aug 1757

La folle raisonnable, unperf.

Librettos: *Le paquet de mouchoirs* (monologue) (Paris, 1750), also attrib. Duke of Valentinois; *Les troqueurs* (opéra bouffon), Dauvergne, 1753; *La veuve indécise* (oc), Duni, 1759

*

E. C. Fréron: *L'année littéraire*, iv (1757), 350

J. A. J. Desboulmiers: *Histoire du théâtre de l'Opéra-comique*, ii (Paris, 1769), 33, 54f, 70, 78, 224, 260, 333, 364ff, 408, 546

J. Monnet: *Supplément au roman comique, ou Mémoires*, ii (London, 1772), 57, 61ff, 74ff

L. G. Michaud: *Biographie universelle* (Paris, 1811–28)

H. Bonhomme, ed.: *Journal et mémoires de Charles Collé* (Paris, 1868)

G. Lecocq: 'Notice sur la vie … de Vadé', *Poésies et lettres facétieuses de Joseph Vadé* (Paris, 1879), i–xxxvi

L. de La Laurencie: 'Deux imitateurs des Bouffons', *L'année musicale*, ii (1912), 65–125

F. J. Carmody: *Le répertoire de l'Opéra-Comique en vaudevilles de 1708 à 1764* (Berkeley, CA, 1933)

A. P. Moore: *'Le genre poissard' and the French Stage in the 18th Century* (Columbia, SC, 1935)

H. Lagrave, ed.: *René Louis de Voyer de Paulmy, marquis d'Argenson: notices sur les oeuvres de théâtre* (Geneva, 1966)

GRAHAM SADLER

Vadstena. Town in south-central Sweden. Its only operatic activity involves the Stiftelsen Internationella Vadstenaakademien (International Vadstena Academy Foundation), begun by Ingrid Maria Rappe in 1964. In 1969 the Academy was converted into a foundation with the aim of promoting young opera singers who are not yet professionals. It also commissions new chamber operas, mainly from young Nordic composers; an exception was Ian McQueen's *The Line of Terror* (1987), an opera that had enjoyed success both in Sweden and internationally. The activities, which include a synthesis of study, research and production, take place in summer. Students are instructed in both singing and operatic acting; and the resulting productions now form the most prominent opera festival in Sweden. The research, including the making of critical editions, centres on unfamiliar operas of the 17th and 18th centuries, mostly Italian; some are connected with Vadstena through Queen Christina, who sponsored many operas during her time in Italy – a number of these have been given their first modern productions in the town. Performances take place in the Wedding Hall of Vadstena Castle and in the Old Theatre situated near the former convent of St Birgitta. The theatre is the oldest provincial one in Sweden, built in 1825. The academy's director during the formative period was Arnold Östman (1970–82); the artistic director from 1990 was Clas Persson. Many international singers and directors received their first operatic experience in Vadstena, among them Anne-Sofie von Otter, Helena Döse and Göran Järvefelt. ANDERS WIKLUND

Vaëz, Gustave [Nieuwenhuysen, Jean-Nicolas Gustave van] (*b* Brussels, 5 Dec 1812; *d* Paris, 12 March 1862). Belgian librettist and translator. Abandoning a possible career in law, he enjoyed a few minor successes as a dramatist before going to Paris; there he was to write some 30 plays, *comédies-vaudevilles* and librettos, often in collaboration with ALPHONSE ROYER. Together they translated a number of Italian opera librettos into French, including those of Rossini's *Otello* (1844), Donizetti's *Lucia di Lammermoor* (1839) and *Don Pasquale* (1843) and Verdi's *Jérusalem*, after *I Lombardi* (1847). They also devised the librettos for *Robert Bruce* (1846), re-using music by Rossini. Their most important original work was the libretto for Donizetti's *La favorite* (1840), and Vaëz also provided the libretto for the same composer's *Rita, ou Le mari battu*, composed in 1841 and first performed in 1860. He collaborated with Eugène Scribe on the librettos of two three-act *opéras comiques* for D. F. X. Boisselot, *Ne touchez pas à la reine* (1847) and *Mosquita la sorcière* (1851), and with Sardou on *Le capitaine Henriot*, an *opéra comique* by Gevaert (1864). Vaëz was awarded the Belgian Ordre de Léopold in 1846 and became deputy director of the Théâtre de l'Odéon in Paris in 1853. From 1856, the year in which he was made a member of the Légion d'honneur, until 1860 he was deputy director of the Paris Opéra. CHRISTOPHER SMITH

Vaison la Romaine. Town of Roman origins in the Rhône Valley, south-eastern France. The festival, held each summer from 1952 to 1989, used the Théâtre Antique, a Roman amphitheatre (4000 seats), for plays, ballets and usually one large-scale opera with internationally known singers. Smaller productions, principally of 18th-century operas, often put on by visiting opera companies, were given in the adjoining Nymphée (1000 seats), where the staging took advantage of the natural decor. In 1985 the first performance in France of Haydn's *L'anima del filosofo* (*Orfeo ed Euridice*) was given. The artistic quality of the productions varied greatly over the years; some visiting companies did not appreciate the acoustical difficulties of a theatre with no back wall. In 1989 the municipal council withdrew their subsidy and the festival was abandoned. CHARLES PITT

Vakula the Smith [*Kuznets Vakula*]. Opera in three acts by PYOTR IL'YICH TCHAIKOVSKY (composed 1874) to a libretto by Yakov Polonsky after NIKOLAY VASIL'YEVICH GOGOL's story *Noch' pered rozhdestvom* ('Christmas Eve'); St Petersburg, Mariinsky Theatre, 24 November/6 December 1876. Tchaikovsky later revised the work as *CHEREVICHKI*. (For illustration of the first edition *see* TCHAIKOVSKY, PYOTR IL'YICH.)

Valdengo, Giuseppe (*b* Turin, 24 May 1914). Italian baritone. After studying in Turin, he made his début in 1936 at Parma as Rossini's Figaro, then sang Sharpless at Alessandria. Though engaged at La Scala in 1939, he did not sing there (because of military service) until 1941, when he made his début as Baron Douphol. In 1946 he performed at the New York City Opera, then in 1947 made his San Francisco début as Valentin, returning as Escamillo, Sharpless, Iago, Amonasro and Rigoletto. At the Metropolitan (1947–54) he sang Tonio, Marcello, Germont, Count Almaviva, Belcore, Ford, Paolo (*Simon Boccanegra*) and Puccini's Lescaut. In 1955 he sang Don Giovanni and Raimbaud (*Le comte Ory*) at Glyndebourne, and in 1961 he created the Lawyer in Rossellini's *Uno sguardo dal ponte* in Rome. His recordings of Iago, Amonasro and Falstaff, deriving from NBC broadcasts (1947–50) conducted by Toscanini, are vividly and firmly sung, with an even, flexible line. He wrote an autobiography, *Ho cantato con Toscanini* (Como, 1962). ALAN BLYTH

Valencia. Spanish city and provincial capital. In 1584 the Teatro de l'Olivera was inaugurated as the property of the Hospital de Caridad, which had a monopoly of theatrical activity. There are indirect references to a performance of Francesco Manelli's *Andromeda* (1710), but the first fully documented performance is that of *El amor más fino y constante* (27 January 1729) by Francesco Corradini, *maestro de capilla* to the viceroy Prince of Campoflorido, Captain General of Valencia; Corradini's *Amado y aborrelido* followed (24 November 1729). In 1731 there were two performances of Italian opera and in 1734 *Argene y Artaserse* was sung in Italian; in 1738 *Por amor y por lealtad*, probably G. B. Mele's Spanish version of Metastasio's *Demetrio*, was heard in Madrid in 1736. The Teatro Público was closed in 1748 by the archbishop Andrés Mayoral, whose distaste for theatrical activity led to its demolition in 1750.

In 1760 the Hospital opened the Botiga de la Balda, a theatre converted from a warehouse; in 1763–4 at least three operas were performed in the Casa de la Cofradía de Zapateros by the company of Petronio Setti, the most important travelling company in the Iberian peninsula until after 1779. Between 1768 and 1770 the company of Francisco Creus and Luigi Marescalchi performed Italian operas in the theatre of the palace of the dukes of Gandia. Companies from Barcelona, Cartagena, Mallorca, Murcia, Orihuela and other Mediterranean cities performed in the Botiga de la Balda (1774–8). Between 1789 and 1797 a company led by the Spaniard Antonio Solis, with occasional performances by other minor companies, presented comedies, dramatic *tonadillas* and Italian operas there. *Il barbiere di Siviglia* was a great success between 1789 and 1791, and *La Isabela* in the 1796–7 season. The company's bankruptcy was followed by a serious crisis in the musical life of the city which continued for many years, even after the inauguration in 1831 of the Teatro Cómico (Teatro Principal from 1853). Opera performances, mainly of Italian works, were limited to travelling companies and alternated with zarzuelas, revues and other kinds of entertainment. More recently short festivals of opera have been provided by private initiative through the Asociación de Amigos de la Opera, centred on the traditional repertory but with some attention given to Valencian composers such as Vicente Martín y Soler and Matilde Salvador.

*

E. Cotarelo y Mori: *Orígenes y establicémiento de la ópera en España hasta 1800* (Madrid, 1917)
A. Zabala: *La ópera en la vida teatral valenciana del siglo XVIII* (Valencia, 1960)
XOÁN M. CARREIRA

Valente, Benita (*b* Delano, CA, 19 Oct 1934). American soprano. The daughter of Swiss and Italian immigrants, she began vocal studies with Chester Hayden and later worked with Lotte Lehmann in Santa Barbara. She attended the Curtis Institute (1955–60), where she was a pupil of Singher, and from 1968 studied with Harshaw. In 1960 she won the Metropolitan Opera Auditions and two years later made her début in Freiburg as Pamina, a role which also served for her débuts in Santa Fe, Strasbourg, Zürich and at the Metropolitan Opera (1973). She subsequently appeared at the Metropolitan as Susanna, Countess Almaviva, Nannetta, Ilia, Gilda (on tour) and Almirena in *Rinaldo*. Though best known as an interpreter of Mozart and Handel, she has also enjoyed success as Anne Trulove, Antonia, Eurydice, Liù, Marguerite, Mélisande, Mimì and Violetta in Boston, Dallas, Philadelphia, Pittsburgh, San Diego, Washington, DC, and elsewhere. Her European engagements have included *Rinaldo* in Parma and other Italian cities and seasons in Freiburg (1962–3) and Nuremberg (1966–7). Valente is admired for her pure but warm tone, flawless technique, sympathetic presence and impeccable musicianship. CORI ELLISON

Valentina, La. *See* AZZOLINI, CATERINA.

Valentini [Urbani, Valentino] (*b* Udine; *fl* 1690–1722). Italian alto castrato. He was a pupil of Pistocchi and later in the service of the Duke of Mantua. His first known appearances were in 1690 in Venice (in Perti's *Brenno in Efeso*) and Parma (Sabadini's *Il favore degli dei*). He sang at Bologna in 1691 and 1695, Rome in 1694 and Venice in 1695, in two operas by C. F. Pollarolo. In 1697–1700 he was in the service of the Electress of Brandenburg in Berlin, where he sang the title role in *La festa del Himeneo* by Ariosti and others (1700). In 1703 he was at Mantua in Caldara's *Gli equivoci del sembiante*. He was the first castrato to sing regularly in London, making his début at Drury Lane in Haym's version of *Camilla* (1706) and returning in 1707–11 and 1712–14. He sang in many of the early Italian operas in London, most of them pasticcios and some bilingual – *Thomyris* (1707), *Love's Triumph* and *Pirro e Demetrio* (1708), *Clotilda* (1709), *Almahide* and *Idaspe fedele* (1710), *Dorinda* (1712, 1714), *Ernelinda* (1713), *Creso* and *Arminio* (1714) – and in the first performances of Handel's *Rinaldo* (1711, Eustazio), *Il pastor fido* (1712, Silvio), *Teseo* (1713, Aegeus), and probably the title role in *Silla* (1713). He adapted the music of *Love's Triumph* from a pastoral with music by Cesarini, Gasparini and perhaps others, adding French-style choruses and dances and commissioning English words from P. A. Motteux, but it was a failure. After leaving London he sang in five operas in Venice (1717–19) and Conti's *Don Quixotte* in Hamburg in 1722. Valentini's Handel parts were restricted in compass (*a* to *e*♭″) and not remarkable for inspiration or virtuosity, but his powers seem to have been on the decline. Burney reported that 'his voice was feeble, and his execution moderate', adding of his part in *Teseo* that Valentini 'seems to have been gifted with very limited powers ... It seems manifest that Handel was obliged, in writing for this performer, to ride Pegasus with a curb-bridle'. Others who heard him (which Burney never did) described him as a fine actor and 'more chaste in his singing' than Nicolini. WINTON DEAN

Valentini, Carlo (*b* Lucca, *c*1790; *d* Lucca, 1 April 1853). Italian composer. He studied with Pacini. From 1827 to 1835 he conducted at the opera house in Messina, during which period he wrote several operas. Later he taught singing at Lucca. The rest of his output consists mainly of sacred vocal works.

Amina, ossia L'orfanella di Ginevra (3, A. L. Tottola, after F. Romani), Naples, Nuovo, 2 Oct 1825
I falsi galantuomini (1, M. A. Prunetti), Milan, Re, sum. 1827
Il capriccio drammatico (G. Bertati), Messina, 1827
Ines de Castro (3), Oporto, S João, 1827
Lo spettro parlante, ossia La figlia del sicario (2, F. Livigni), Naples, Nuovo, Feb 1829
Ildegonda (2, P. Giannone), Palermo, Carolino, spr. 1829
Il figlio del signor padre (2, Tottola), Naples, Fondo, Nov 1830
Ferdinando II granduca di Toscana, Naples, Nuovo, 1831
Il sonnambulo (Romani), Lucca, Pantera, 22 Jan 1834
Gli avventurieri (Romani), Lucca, Pantera, 1836
Gli aragonesi in Napoli (Tottola), Rome, 1838

Valentini, Giovanni (*b* ? Naples or Rome, *c*1750; *d* ? Naples, 1804). Italian composer. He might have been born in Rome and educated in Naples: some librettos describe him as *maestro di cappella napoletano*, others as *romano*. He wrote several comic operas in Venice between 1779 and 1786. The success of two of his early operas, *Le nozze in contrasto* (1779) and *La statua matematica* (1780), made his name known in many Italian opera centres and in some cities beyond the Alps; according to Gerber (1790–92), *Le nozze* was performed in Leipzig in 1784. By the summer of 1784 Valentini had been elected a member of the Accademia Filarmonica of Verona, and by 1786 he was serving as music director at the Ospedaletto, Venice.

all first performed in Venice

Le nozze in contrasto (dg, 2, G. Bertati), S Moisè, aut. 1779
L'isola della luna (dg, 2, A. Piazza), S Samuele, aut. 1780
La statua matematica (dg, 2, Bertati), S Moisè, 26 Dec 1780, *P-La*
Rosina consolata, o sia L'innocenza protetta (int, 2, P. A. Bagliacca), S Cassiano, aut. 1781
I castellani burlati (dg, 2, F. Livigni), S Moisè, carn. 1785
La Quakera spiritosa (dg, 2, G. Palomba), S Moisè, carn. 1786
Il capriccio drammatico [pt 1] (dg, 2, after Bertati: *La novità*), S Moisè, 5 Feb 1787; collab. with others [pt 2 set by G. Gazzaniga as Don Giovanni, o sia Il convitato di pietra] JOHN A. RICE

Valentini, Giuseppe (*b* Florence, 14 Dec 1681; *d* Rome, Nov 1753). Italian composer, violinist and poet. In a sonnet published in his *Rime* (1708) he writes that he was taught music by Giovanni Bononcini, probably around 1695 when both composers are known to have been active in Rome. Like Corelli, Alessandro Scarlatti and Pasquini he was a member of the Arcadian Academy, where he bore the name Euginaspe Leupinto. As well as publishing many sets of violin sonatas and concertos, he wrote cantatas and oratorios (some preserved in *I-Rps*) which are the only surviving examples of his vocal writing. He composed the first act of an opera, *La finta rapita*, performed on 17 January 1714 at the theatre in Cisterna of Michelangelo Caetani, Prince of Caserta (the other two acts were by N. Romaldi and C. Cesarini and the libretto by D. Renda). The following year *La costanza in amore*, which he composed to a libretto by A. Rossi, was performed in the same theatre. No other stage works by him are known.

*

M. Talbot: 'A Rival of Corelli: the Violinist-Composer Giuseppe Valentini', *Nuovissimi studi corelliani: Fusignano 1980*, 347–65
E. Careri: 'Giuseppe Valentini (1681–1753): documenti inediti', *NA*, ser.2, v (1987), 69–125 ENRICO CARERI

Valentini [Valentino], **Michelangelo** [Michele Angelo] (*b* Naples, *c*1720; *d* after 1768). Italian composer. He called himself a student of Leonardo Leo, but no attendance has been traced at either Neapolitan conservatory where Leo taught. Like many other young composers of the time, he first brought himself to public notice with the production of comic operas, *Il Demetrio* (1745) and *La villana nobile* (1748). From the production of his next four operas it can be assumed that he was in north Italy a good deal in the following ten years. *La clemenza di Tito* and *Adriano in Siria* were written for Bologna (both 1753), *Andromaca* for Milan (1754) and *Solimano* for Turin (1756). *La clemenza*, probably rewritten for the opening of the Teatro Nuovo di Corte in Modena in 1768, and *Solimano*, rewritten for Naples, were particularly successful. For a not very prolific composer, an unusual amount of Valentini's music survives, although the score of an opera *La statua matematica* in Lisbon is misattributed to him; it was written by the later composer Giovanni Valentini.

The well-known opera singer Regina Mingotti was Michelangelo Valentini's sister. Prota-Giurleo speculated that he travelled with her on tour.

Il Demetrio (ob, A. Palomba), Naples, Nuovo, wint. 1745
La villana nobile (ob, Palomba), Naples, Fiorentini, spr. 1748
La clemenza di Tito (os, P. Metastasio), Bologna, Formagliari, 3 Jan 1753; Modena, Nuovo di Corte, 26 Dec 1768
Adriano in Siria (os, Metastasio), Bologna, Formagliari, carn. 1753, 7 arias *GB-Lbl*
Andromaca (os, A. Zeno), Milan, Ducale, 26 Dec 1754; collab. A. Salvi
Solimano (os, G. Migliavacca), Turin, Regio, 1756; rev., Naples, S Carlo, 4 Nov 1756; *I-Tf*, *P-La*
La sconfitta di Dario (os, S. A. Morbilli), Genoa, S Agostino, carn. 1757
Viriate (os, after Metastasio: *Siface*), Pavia, Omodeo, carn. 1761
Arias in *GB-Lbl*, *I-Gl*, *Mc* and *P-La*

*

MGG (U. Prota-Giurleo) JAMES L. JACKMAN

Valentini, Pier Francesco (*b* Rome, bap. 1 Nov 1586; *d* Rome, 21–24 March 1654). Italian composer and librettist. Best known for his sacred music and theoretical writings, he composed *La Metra, favola greca* to his own libretto (music and text lost). Allacci lists the publication (Rome, 1654) of what was probably only the text. In 1646 Valentini noted that the opera had 23 roles for five singers in *recitativo scenico* (that is, not in the affective chamber style) and was performed in Rome in 1628. It must have been in three acts, since it was published with two *intermedi* (also with text and music by Valentini). His libretto *La trasformatione di Dafne, favola morale* (*I-Rvat*) was also published in 1654. The publisher's note suggests that Valentini set its three acts and two *intermedi* to music, but no performances have been documented.

*

AllacciD
M. C. Cortesi: 'P. F. Valentini: profilo di un musicista barocco', *NRMI*, iii-iv (1983), 531–2 MARGARET MURATA

Valentini-Terrani, Lucia (*b* Padua, 28 Aug 1948). Italian mezzo-soprano. She studied at the Padua Conservatory and in Venice (Accademia Benedetto Marcello). Her début was at Brescia in 1969 as Angelina (*La Cenerentola*), a role that also introduced her at La Scala (1973) and at Covent Garden (1976) with the Scala company in the Ponnelle production conducted by Abbado. She toured with the company to Washington, Moscow and Tokyo, and first sang at the Metropolitan in 1974 as Isabella; she appeared with the Royal Opera at Covent Garden in 1982 as Mistress Quickly in *Falstaff*, conducted by Giulini. Her bright, fluent tone, buoyant rhythm and control of *fioriture* are allied to inward expressiveness in lyric roles, notably Rossini, but also including Massenet's Dulcinée and Charlotte and Musorgsky's Marina. Frequent engagements at the Rossini Festival, Pesaro, have included *La donna del lago* and *Il viaggio a Reims*, both of which are among her recordings, as are roles in *L'italiana in Algeri*, *Aida*, *Don Carlos*, *Nabucco* and Vivaldi's *Orlando furioso*.
NOËL GOODWIN

Valentino, Francesco [Frank; Dinhaupt, Francis] (*b* Denver, CO, 6 Jan 1907; *d* New York, 14 June 1991). American baritone. He studied in Denver and Milan, making his début in 1930 at Parma as Germont. He sang at La Scala and the Rome Opera and in 1938 was Verdi's Macbeth at Glyndebourne. He took part in the first performances of Frazzi's *Re Lear* (1939) and Dallapiccola's *Volo di notte* (1940) at Florence. At the Metropolitan, where he was engaged from 1940 to 1961, his roles included Enrico Ashton, Malatesta, Count Almaviva, Valentin, Rigoletto, Luna and Scarpia. At San Francisco (1943–52) he also sang Rossini's Figaro, Dapertutto (*Les contes d'Hoffmann*), Barnaba (*La Gioconda*) and Escamillo. He had a flexible voice, not large but well focussed. ELIZABETH FORBES

Valeri, Gaetano (*b* Padua, 21 Sept 1760; *d* Padua, 13 April 1822). Italian composer. He served for nearly 35 years at Padua Cathedral, first as organist and then as *maestro di cappella*. He was also an excellent pianist. Most of his output consists of liturgical works and keyboard sonatas. Although he composed little for the theatre, his short *azione lirica Il trionfo di Alessandro sopra se stesso* (A. Meneghelli; Padua, Nuovo, 18 May 1792; music lost) is unusual: its libretto, recalling that of Rousseau's *Pygmalion*, not only gives the dialogue and describes the stage actions of the singers but also indicates the length (from a few seconds to several minutes) of 40 passages of music and characterizes the music as it changes during the opera's 11 scenes. Valeri's other music for the stage was an *introduzione* and *primo finale* for a revival of Ferdinando Robuschi's 1786 *dramma giocoso, Li Castrini padre e figlio* (G. Greppi; Padua, Obizzi, aut. 1791; ov. *I-Vnm*).

*

EitnerQ; *GerberNL*
A. Pallerotti: *Spettacoli melodrammatici e coreografici rappresentati in Padova ... 1751–1892* (Padua, 1892), 70
B. Brunelli: *I teatri di Padova* (Padua, 1921), 288, 295

SVEN HANSELL

Valeriani, Giuseppe (*b* Rome, before 1708; *d* St Petersburg, 7/18 April 1762). Italian stage designer. According to some writers he was born in 1708, but that is impossible because by 1721 he and his brother Domenico (*b* Rome, before 1708; *d* Rome, *c*1770) were official stage designers at the Teatro S Angelo, Venice, for G. M. Orlandini's *Antigona*. From 1722 to 1731 they worked at the Teatro S Giovanni Grisostomo, where they designed Nicola Porpora's *Ezio* (1728). In October 1724 they provided the scenery for Pietro Torri's festive entertainment *Amadis di Grecia* in Munich. They were summoned to Turin by Filippo Juvarra to help decorate the salon in the royal hunting lodge at Stupinigi (1731–3). In 1735–9 they were in Rome, where Giuseppe worked at the Teatro delle Dame (Domingo Terradellas's *Astarto*, 1739). In 1742 Giuseppe went to St Petersburg, where he was appointed court 'theatre engineer'. In 1750 he designed the new imperial opera house, which was inaugurated on 9 December. Among the many productions he designed were Francesco Araia's *Alessandro nell'Indie* (1755 and 1759), *Amor prigioniero* (1755) and *Bellerofonte* (1757). Several of his theatrical drawings are preserved in St Petersburg (the Hermitage and other collections); they show the influence of Filippo Juvarra and Giuseppe Bibiena, as well as an intensely individual style, characterized by brilliant colours.

*

J. von Stählin: 'Nachrichten von der Musik in Russland', in J. Haigold: *Beylagen zum neuveränderten Russland* (Riga and Leipzig, 1769–70), ii, 37–192, esp. 96
M. S. Konopleva: *Teatral'niy zivopisez: Dzhuseppe Valeriani* (Leningrad, 1948)
R.-A. Mooser: *Annales de la musique et des musiciens en Russie au XVIIIe siècle*, i (Geneva, 1948), 206–7
M. T. Muraro, ed.: 'Teatro di San Giovanni Grisostomo', *I teatri pubblici di Venezia (secoli XVII–XVIII)* (Venice, 1971), 138–9 [exhibition catalogue]
A. Schiavo: 'Veduta di Giuseppe Valeriani del S Lorenzo in Damaso', *Studi romani*, xx (1972)

MERCEDES VIALE FERRERO

Valero, Fernando (*b* Écijha, 6 Dec 1852 or 1854; *d* St Petersburg, Feb 1914). Spanish tenor. Sometimes known as 'the little Gayarre', he studied with Julián Gayarre's teacher, Melchiorre Vidal, and later with the younger Manuel Garcia. He made his début at the Teatro Real, Madrid, in 1878, his first roles there including Lorenzo in *Fra Diavolo* and Nadir in *Les pêcheurs de perles*, which he also sang at the opera's Italian première. After two years in the Italian provinces he appeared at La Scala as Faust in 1883. Guest performances in Berlin, St Petersburg and London followed, and the great event of his career occurred at Florence in 1890 when he sang Turiddu in the première of *Cavalleria rusticana*. From then on he was in demand wherever the opera was given, and sang in the premières in Milan, Palermo, New York and other American cities. At Covent Garden he appeared in his most famous role for a single performance, in 1901. Illness compelled him to retire from the stage in the following year, and he then taught in St Petersburg. His few and rare recordings include excerpts from *Cavalleria rusticana*: these have some stylistic delicacies, take considerable freedom, and show a voice of good quality but past its best.

J. B. STEANE

Valesi [Vallesi], **Giovanni** [Walleshauser, Johann Evangelist] (*b* Unterhattenhofen [now Hattenhofen], Upper Bavaria, 28 April 1735; *d* Munich, 10 Jan 1816). German tenor. A pupil of Camerloher, he held posts as a court singer in Munich and was a member of the Munich Hofkapelle, 1770–94. He also sang in Amsterdam and Brussels (1755), in Italy (after 1757, when he assumed the name Valesi, and 1770–75) and in Prague, Dresden and Berlin (1777–8). He sang in the first performance of Mozart's *La finta giardiniera* (1775) in Munich, where he also created the part of the High Priest of Neptune in the first performance of *Idomeneo* (1781). He trained over 200 singers, among them his children Anna (1776–92), Joseph (1778–1807), Magdalena (*b* 1781), Crescentia (*b* 1785) and Thekla (1789–1868), Valentin Adamberger and Carl Maria von Weber.

*

R. Münster: 'W. A. Mozarts "Bernrieder Kanon": die Geschichte einer Legende', *MJb 1962–3*, 178–84
——: 'Mozart "... beym Herzoge Clemens ..."', *MJb 1965–6*, 133–41
H. Schmid: 'Zur Biographie des bayerischen Hofsängers Giovanni Valesi (Walleshauser)', *Musik in Bayern: Halbjahresschrift der Gesellschaft für bayerische Musikgeschichte*, x (1975), 28–30

HANS SCHMID

Valis. Opera in two continuous parts by TOD MACHOVER to his own libretto (with contributions from others) after the novel by Philip K. Dick; Paris, Centre Pompidou, 1 December 1987.

Valis had a long and difficult gestation that makes credit for the libretto hard to assign. The Centre Pompidou commissioned the work in 1985, having suggested it two years earlier. The original, French libretto was a collaboration between Machover, the video artist Catherine Ikam and the director Bill Raymond. Following the controversial première, Machover revised the opera, shortening it by one third (to 75 minutes) and recasting it, on his own, into English. Even this version contains small text contributions by Patrick Mason, Julie Machover and Arnaud Petit. The revised ('definitive, final') version was commercially recorded in 1988 and first performed in concert form in Boston on 16 June 1989.

In the opera's final form Dick's bizarrely autobiographical science-fiction novel has been so severely compressed that neither the order nor the meaning of events is entirely clear; but that is part of the point. The action takes place in southern California in 1974. Horselover Fat (baritone), whose name is an etymological translation of 'Philip Dick', is transfixed through the head by a beam of pink light. This transmits to him a huge, incoherent mass of information, including the revelation that human minds are part of a larger 'computer-like thinking system' that has, however, failed to function properly. Fat's friend Gloria (mezzo-soprano) has been stockpiling barbiturates with an eye to eventual suicide; Fat attempts to dissuade her, but is so preoccupied that he succeeds only in making her feel guilty. Indeed, Fat has troubles of his own, for he has recurrent dreams of an alternative existence so superior to his own that he is made miserable by comparison. After attempting suicide himself, he consults a psychiatrist, Dr Stone (bass), who insists that only he, Fat, can explain the universe to himself. Still distraught, he confronts his *alter ego* Phil Dick (the same actor, appearing on massed video monitors), who counsels patience while Gloria, unnoticed in the background, finally succeeds in killing herself. Help appears in the form of two rock musicians, Eric and Linda Lampton (baritone and soprano), who are mysteriously well-informed about Fat's pink-light revelation and its source, which they call VALIS, for 'Vast Active Living Intelligent System'. Their silent, Svengali-like composer-associate Mini (the conductor, who climbs out of the orchestra pit) materializes a godlike child, Sophia (soprano), who temporarily heals the Phil/Fat duality, but is herself then apparently destroyed by Mini. Nonetheless, she later bids Phil goodbye in a dream (in Gloria's voice), and Phil sits down before his television set to await instructions in calm readiness.

For the instrumentation of *Valis*, *see* ORCHESTRA, fig.18.

ANDREW STILLER

Välkki, Anita (*b* Sääksmäki, nr Vakeakoski, 25 Oct 1926). Finnish soprano. She studied in Helsinki, making her début there with the National Opera in 1955. She sang in Stockholm, Prague and London, where she made her Covent Garden début in 1961 as Brünnhilde. She sang the same role at the Metropolitan (1962), at Bayreuth (1963–4) and with Scottish Opera (1966). She has also appeared in Vienna, Mexico City and Philadelphia. Her roles included Santuzza, Aida, Turandot and Kundry, but it was the young Brünnhilde that best displayed her strong, bright-toned voice and engaging stage personality. In 1983 she sang Mary in *Der fliegende Holländer* at the Savonlinna Festival, and in 1986 she sang in Merikanto's *Juha* in Helsinki.

ELIZABETH FORBES

Vallandri, Aline (*b* Paris, 1878; *d* Paris, 30 May 1952). French soprano. She studied at the Paris Conservatoire with Jacques Isnardon and made her début in the title role of Gounod's *Mireille* in 1904 with the Opéra-Comique. This company remained at the centre of her career, though she also sang in Brussels, Lisbon, Cologne and London (in Jean Nouguès' *Quo vadis?* during Oscar Hammerstein I's 1911 season). At Monte Carlo in 1907 she was 'an excellent and graceful Elvira' in *Don Giovanni*, and another great success was in the open-air *Mireille* production at Arles. Her roles for the Opéra-Comique included Pamina, Manon, Ensoleidad (*Chérubin*), Louise and Mélisande. In 1906 she appeared in the première of Henry Février's *Le roi aveugle* and in 1920 as Dorabella in the first Opéra-Comique performances of *Così fan tutte*. Her recordings show a firm voice of beautiful quality used with charming art.

J. B. STEANE

Valle. Theatre in Rome, built in 1726. *See* ROME, §3(i, ii).

Valle d'Itria Festival. Summer opera festival instituted in 1975 in MARTINA FRANCA, Italy.

Valleria [Lohman; Schoening], **Alwina** (*b* Baltimore, 12 Oct 1848; *d* Nice, 17 Feb 1925). American soprano. She studied in London at the RAM and, after further instruction from Arditi, made her concert début in 1871 and was promptly engaged for Italian opera in St Petersburg, where she made her stage début on 23 October in *Linda di Chamounix*. She sang next in Germany and Milan, later in London at the Drury Lane Theatre (1873–5), Her Majesty's Theatre (1877–8), where she was highly successful as Micaëla, and, in a large number of parts, at Covent Garden (1879–82).

On 22 October 1879 Valleria made her début in New York as Gounod's Marguerite, adding Aida to her repertory in the same season. In 1882–3, back in England, she sang under Carl Rosa in productions in English of *Der fliegende Holländer* and *Tannhäuser*; in 1883 she was praised for her spirited creation of Mackenzie's Colomba. She made her Metropolitan Opera début on 26 October 1883 as Leonora (*Il trovatore*). Having returned to London, she created the principal parts in Goring Thomas's *Nadeshda* (1885) and Mackenzie's *The Troubadour* (1886) and then retired. Her voice, which extended from *b♭* to *d‴* (in her earlier years to *f‴*), was of considerable flexibility, fair power and volume and pleasing quality, and she was an admirable actress.

Valletti, Cesare (*b* Rome, 18 Dec 1922). Italian tenor. After studying privately he made his début at Bari in 1947 as Alfredo. In 1950 he took part in *Il turco in Italia* at the Teatro Eliseo, Rome, with Callas and Stabile; that autumn he sang Fenton (*Falstaff*) with the Scala company at Covent Garden. He sang regularly at La Scala, as Nemorino, Almaviva, Filipeto (*I quatro rusteghi*), Lindoro and other *tenore di grazia* roles. In 1953 he made his American début at San Francisco as Werther, and from 1953 to 1962 sang regularly at the Metropolitan, where he was especially admired as Don Ottavio (a role he also sang at the Salzburg Festival), Des Grieux, Ferrando and Ernesto.

He returned to Covent Garden in 1953 to sing Alfredo opposite Callas. In 1968 he sang Nero (*L'incoronazione di Poppea*) at the Caramoor Festival in Katonah, New York. Although his voice was not large, Valletti sang with rare style and elegance.

GV (R. Celletti, with discography)
H. Rosenthal: *Great Singers of Today* (London, 1966)

HAROLD ROSENTHAL/R

Vallin, Ninon [Vallin-Pardo, Eugénie] (*b* Montalieu-Vercieu, 8 Sept 1886; *d* Lyons, 22 Nov 1961). French soprano. She studied in Lyons and made her début in 1912 as Micaëla with the Opéra-Comique, where she continued to sing throughout her career, in a repertory that included Mimì, Mignon, Louise, Manon, Carmen, Nedda, Rozenn (*Le roi d'Ys*), Salud (*La vida breve*), Charlotte and St Mary in the French première of Respighi's *Maria Egiziaca* (1934). At La Scala (1916–17) she sang Mignon, Wolf-Ferrari's Susanna and the Princess (*Marouf*). She first appeared at the Teatro Colón, Buenos Aires, in 1916 as Gounod's Marguerite, returning there regularly for 20 years. In 1920 she made her Opéra debut as Thaïs and she also sang Boito's Marguerite there. She appeared at San Francisco (1934) and Monte Carlo (1943). Her repertory also included the three *Hoffmann* heroines, as well as Alcestis, Mélisande and Countess Almaviva, which she sang in 1946 at the Opéra-Comique. A versatile and stylish singer, she had a distinctive timbre, cool and clear, with a forward production, which can be admired in many fine recordings, especially a complete *Werther* with Georges Thill.

*

GV (R. Celletti; R. Vegeto)
H. M. Barnes: 'Vallin, Ninon', *Record Collector*, viii (1953), 53–65 [with discography]
R. de Fragny: *Ninon Vallin, princesse du chant* (Lyons, 1963)

MARTIN COOPER/ELIZABETH FORBES

Valsini, Frencasco. *See* SILVANI, FRANCESCO.

Valverde, Joaquín [*padre*] **(i)** (*b* Badajoz, 27 Feb 1846; *d* Madrid, 17 March 1910). Spanish composer and conductor. He began his musical studies in his native city, and as a boy he played the piccolo in a military band. He later studied at the Madrid Conservatory, where he won first prize for flute in 1867 and composition in 1870. In 1871 his *Sinfonía Batilo* was awarded a prize by the Sociedad Fomento de las Artes. He composed flute studies and in 1882, during an unsuccessful attempt to become flute teacher at the Madrid Conservatory, wrote a pamphlet *La flauta: su historia, su estudio* (Madrid, 1886), which was later adopted by the conservatory as a text. In all he composed over 200 instrumental works, but his prime preoccupation was with the theatre. He was a theatre conductor throughout the 1870s and 80s and composed many zarzuelas, often in collaboration. Of these the best-known are those with Chueca, including *La canción de la Lola* (1880), *La gran vía* (1886), *Cádiz* (1886) and *El año pasado por agua* (1889). Others were with Bretón, Caballero, Romea and Rogel, as well as with his son.

selective list of zarzuelas, usually in one act and first performed in Madrid

Las ferias (sainete lírico, 1, M. Barranco y Caro), Madrid, Buen Retiro, 3 July 1878, collab. F. Chueca; ¡A los toros!, 1878, collab. Chueca; Majas y toreros (1), ?1878, collab. Chueca; La función de mi pueblo, 1879, collab. Chueca; La canción de la Lola (sainete lírico, 1, R. de la Vega), Madrid, Alhambra, 25 May 1880, collab. Chueca; El centenario en la aldea, Madrid, Oct 1881; Luces y sombras (gacetilla cómico-lírico, S. Lastra, A. Ruesga and E. Prieto), Madrid, Variedades, 1882, collab. Chueca

Fiesta nacional (acontecimiento cómico-lírico, T. Luceño and J. de Burgos), Madrid, Variedades, 25 Nov 1882, collab. Chueca; De la noche a la mañana (sueño cómico-lírico, Lastra, Ruesga and Prieto), Madrid, Variedades, Dec 1883, collab. Chueca; Caramelo (juguete cómico-lírico, Burgos), 1883/4, collab. Chueca; Vivitos y coleando (pesca cómico-lírica, Lastra, Ruesga and Prieto), Madrid, Variedades, March 1884, collab. Chueca; Agua y cuernos (revue, Burgos and M. Pina), Madrid, Buen Retiro, July 1884, collab. Chueca; Medidas sanitarias, collab. Chueca

En la tierra como en el cielo, collab. Chueca; Niña Pancha (3, C. Gil), Madrid, Larra, April 1886, collab. J. Romea; Pasar la raga (1, F. Pérez y González), Madrid, April 1886, collab. Romea; La Gran Vía (revista madrileña cómico-lírico-fantástico-callejera, 1, Pérez y González), Madrid, Felipe, 2 July 1886, collab. Chueca; Cádiz (episodio nacional cómico-lírico-dramático, 2, Burgos), Madrid, Apolo, 20 Nov 1886, collab. Chueca; El año pasado por agua (Vega), Madrid, Apolo, 1 March 1889, collab. Chueca

De Madrid á Paris (viaje cómico-lírico, J. Jackson Veyán and E. Sierra), Madrid, Felipe, 12 July 1889, collab. Chueca; La magasin de musique (Prieto and Barbera), Lisbon, Aug 1889, collab. Chueca; La baraja francesa (1, S. Delgado), Madrid, Felipe, 1890; De Madrid á Barcelona (Perillán y Buxó), 1890, collab. Chueca; La caza del oso, ó, El tendero de comestibles (viaje-cómico-lírico, Jackson Veyán and Sierra), Madrid, Apolo, 6 March 1891, collab. Chueca; El directór (C. Gil), Madrid, Oct 1891

Retolondrón (Pina), Madrid, Tivoli, 18 June 1892; Los coraceros (D. Jiménez Prieto), Madrid, Sept 1896; Padre Benito (E. Sánchez Pástor and A. Paso), Seville, June 1897; Portfolio madrileño (revue, E. Montesinos and P. Frutos), Madrid, Romea, Dec 1897, collab. Valverde *hijo*; La batalla de Tetuán (G. Perrín and M. de Palacios), Madrid, Eldorado, 22 July 1898, collab. Valverde *hijo*; Sangre moza (1, J. López Silva and J. Pellicer), Madrid, Apolo, 10 April 1907, collab. Valverde *hijo*; La isla de los suspiros, Madrid, Popolario, June 1910; Los barrios bajos, collab. Chueca and J. Rogel; El bautiza de Pepín, collab. T. Bretón and Chueca

Other zarzuelas: ¡Adios, Madrid!; La cruz de Mayo; La fiesta del hogar; La fiesta de San Isidro; El gallo de la pasión (1), collab. Valverde *hijo*; Música celestial; La noche de San Juán, collab. Valverde *hijo*; El primer desliz; La redoma encantada; Salón Eslava (apropósito cómico-músical, 1, C. Navarro); La segunda tiple, collab. Romea

*

F. Pazdírek: *Universal-Handbuch der Musikliteratur* (Vienna, 1904–10) [incl. list of pubd works]
'Valverde (Joaquín)', *Enciclopedia universal ilustrada europeo-americana* (Barcelona, 1907–)
E. Cotarelo y Mori: *Historia de la zarzuela, o sea el drama lírico* (Madrid, 1934)
M. Muñoz: *Historia de la zarzuela española y del género chico* (Madrid, 1946)
A. Fernández-Cid: *Cien años de teatro musical en España (1875–1975)* (Madrid, 1975)
J. Arnau and C. Gomez: *Historia de la zarzuela* (Madrid, 1979)
R. Alier and others: *El libro de la zarzuela* (Barcelona, 1982, 2/1986 as *Diccionario de la zarzuela*)

ANDREW LAMB

Valverde (y Sanjuán), Joaquín [*hijo*; 'Quinito'] **(ii)** (*b* Madrid, 2 Jan 1875; *d* Mexico City, 4 Nov 1918). Spanish composer, son of Joaquín Valverde. He was taught by his father and Irache. His first zarzuela, *Con las de Caín*, produced when he was only 15, was a great success, and during a short but prolific career he composed over 200 theatre works, some in collaboration. Among the most successful was *La marcha de Cádiz* (Madrid, Eslava, 11 October 1896), based on his father's and Chueca's *Cádiz* (1886), composed with Ramón Estellés and produced also in Paris, where his music became popular. Other collaborations were with his father, with Tomás López Torregrosa, Rafael Calleja, Ruperto Chapí and José Serrano.

zarzuelas, selective list from over 200 works, mostly in one act and first performed in Madrid

Con las de Caín, *c*1890; Los puritanos (pasillo cómico-lírico, 1, C. Arniches and C. Lucio), Madrid, Eslava, 31 March 1894, collab. T. L. Torregrosa; Los lunes de 'El Imparcial' (T. Luceño), 1894; La fantasía de Carmen (Arniches and Lucio), Madrid, Sept 1896; La marcha de Cádiz (zarzuela cómico-lírica, 1, Lucio and E. García Alvarez), Madrid, Eslava, 10 Oct 1896, collab. R. Estellés; La torre de Babel (D. Jiménez Prieto), Madrid, Romea, Sept 1897

El primer reserva (E. Sánchez Pástor), Madrid, 14 Oct 1897, collab. Torregrosa; Las camarones (Arniches and Lucio), Madrid, Zarzuela, 4 Dec 1897, collab. Torregrosa; Portfolio madrileño (revue, E. Montesinos and P. Frutos), Madrid, Romea, Dec 1897, collab. Valverde *padre*; Los cocineros (García Alvarez and A. Paso), Madrid, Eslava, 1897, collab. Torregrosa; El pobre diablo (apropósito-revista, Lucio), Madrid, Eldorado, 1897, collab. Torregrosa

El alcalde de Corneja (L. Olona), Madrid, 5 Jan 1898; Las niñas de la Villagarda (1, J. Jackson Veyán), Madrid, March 1898, collab. Torregrosa; Toros de Galtillo (J. Prieto), Madrid, 29 April 1898; Las castañeras picadas (C. Fernández Shaw), Madrid, Apolo, 28 May 1898, collab. Torregrosa; Las campesinas (Villegras), Madrid, 25 June 1898; La batalla de Tetuán (G. Perrín and M. de Palacios), Madrid, Eldorado, 22 July 1898, collab. Valverde *padre*

La chiquita de Nájera (Jackson Veyán), Madrid, 27 July 1898; El sueño de una noche de verano (Lucio and G. Merino), Madrid, 2 Aug 1898; La estatua de Don Gonzalo (Meyrán and Rufino), Madrid, 29 Aug 1898; La magia negra (opereta-revista, M. Gullón), Madrid, 24 Sept 1898, collab. Caballero; Los tres millones (Jackson Veyán), Madrid, 24 Dec 1898; Bettina (Perrin and Palacios), Madrid, 13 Jan 1899; La Mari-Juana (Jackson Veyán), Madrid, 14 Feb 1899

¡Citrato, de ver será! (parodía-opereta, Merino and Lucio), Madrid, 24 March 1899, collab. Caballero; El trabuco, ó Pepet, Nolet y Tonet (Sánchez Pástor), Madrid, Apolo, 1 April 1899, collab. Torregrosa; Concurso Universal (García Alvarez, Paso and A. López Monis), Madrid, Maravillas, 3 June 1899, collab. R. Calleja; Instantáneas (J. López Silva and Arniches), Madrid, Eldorado, 28 June 1899, collab. Torregrosa

Las buenas formas (opereta-revista, Jackson Veyán), Madrid, Apolo, 12/13 July 1899, collab. A. Rubio; Los flamencos (Sánchez Pástor), Madrid, Eldorado, 13 July 1899, collab. Torregrosa; La reina de la fiesta (Sánchez Pástor and S. Delgado), Madrid, 28 Oct 1899; El último chulo (sainete lírico, 1, Lucio and Arniches), Madrid, Eslava, 7 Nov 1899, collab. Torregrosa; Los besugos (Merino and J. Abati), Madrid, Comedía, Dec 1899, collab. A. Saco del Valle

La señora capitána (Jackson Veyán), Madrid, Romea, 21 March 1900, collab. T. Barrera; El fondo del baúl (Jackson Veyán), Madrid, 18 Sept 1900, collab. Barrera; La tremenda (López Silva and Jackson Veyán), Madrid, Moderne, June 1901, collab. Barrera; Los niños llorones (Arniches, Paso and García Alvarez), Madrid, 4 July 1901, collab. Barrera and Torregrosa; El género infimo (pasillo, S. Alvarez Quintero and J. Alvarez Quintero), Madrid, Apolo, 17 July 1901, collab. Barrera

El debut de la Ramirez (Merino), Madrid, 11 Nov 1901, collab. Torregrosa; Plantas y flores (Lucio), Madrid, Nov 1901, collab. Torregrosa; Madrid–Valencia (revue), Valencia, Nov 1901; Chispita [El barrio de Maravillas] (Jackson Veyán and Rodríguez), Madrid, 14 Dec 1901, collab. Torregrosa; El código penal (E. Sierra and Abati), Madrid, Cómico, 24 Dec 1901, collab. Barrera; Pluma y capis (revista, R. Asensio Más), Madrid, Oct 1902

El terrible Pérez (humorada trágico-cómico-lírico, 1, Arniches, García Alvarez), Madrid, Apolo, 1 May 1903, collab. Torregrosa; La inclusera (1, L. de Larra), Madrid, 19 Nov 1903, collab. Caballero; San Juan de Luz, Madrid, Cómico, 1903; El trébol (Paso and Abati), Madrid, 19 Feb 1904, collab. J. Serrano; El pobre Valbuena (humorada-lírica, 1, Arniches and García Alvarez), Madrid, Apolo, 1 July 1904, collab. Torregrosa

Las estrellas (Arniches), Madrid, 31 Dec 1904, collab. Serrano; Pasacalle (M. Rámos Carrión and A. Ramos Martín), Madrid, 3 March 1905; La mulata, Madrid, Eslava, 23 March 1905; La galerna (Larra), Madrid, Apolo, April 1905; El perro chico (Arniches and García Alvarez), Madrid, Apolo, 5 May 1905, collab. Serrano; La reja de la Dolores, Madrid, Apolo, 26 Sept 1905, collab. Serrano

El iluso Cañizares (Arniches, García Alvarez and A. Casero), Madrid, Apolo, Dec 1905, collab. Calleja; El vals de las sombras (Dicenta), Madrid, Eslava, March 1906; El moscón, Madrid, Apolo, April 1906, collab. Torregrosa; La pena negra (Arniches), Madrid, Gran, 30 Oct 1906; La ola verde, 1906, collab. Calleja; El pollo Tejada (Arniches and García Alvarez), 1906, collab. Serrano; Sangre moza (1, López Silva and J. Pellicer), Madrid, Apolo, 10 April 1907, collab. Valverde *padre*

Los bárbaros del norte (1, Delgado), Madrid, Apolo, 1907, collab. R. Chapí; La rose de Grenade (opérette, 2, Hannaux and Frédoff), Brussels, Variétés, March 1911; La reluquera (opérette, 1, Joullot and Adams), Paris, Européen, 17 Nov 1911; El fresco de Goya (Arniches, García Alvarez and Dominguez), Madrid, Apolo, 24 April 1912; La última película (zarzuela-revista), Madrid, Sept 1913, collab. Torregrosa; Las mujeres guapas, Madrid, Apolo, Jan 1914, collab. L. Foglietti

La feria de abril, Madrid, Cómico, Feb 1914, collab. Foglietti; A versicuidas de Amalia, Madrid, Eslava, June 1914, collab. Foglietti; El potro salvaje, Madrid, Cómico, June 1914, collab. P. Luna; El amigo Melquíades (1, Arniches), Madrid, Apolo, 1914, collab. Serrano; La gitanada, Madrid, Cómico, 1914, collab. Foglietti; Las pildoras de Hercules (vaudeville, 3, R. Blasco), Madrid, Eslava, 1914, collab. Foglietti; El príncipe carnaval (operetta-revue, J. J. Cadenas and Asensio Más), Madrid, Reina Victoria, Dec 1920, collab. Serrano

Other works: La boda de Serafín [El zapaterin]; Caretas y capuchones; Charito; La de vámonos; El doctor Paletilla (juguéte, 1, S. López); Entrar en la casa; El gallo de la pasión (1), collab. Valverde *padre*; Los escopetas; La fuente de los milagros; Gente menuda; El gran capitán, collab. Torregrosa; Los invasores; Madrid petit; La maison de danses (5), Paris; El mirlo blanco; La noche de San Juán, collab. Valverde *padre*; El ratón; El paso de Judas; El señor Pérez, collab. Estellés; Serafína la Rubiales; El titirimundi; La tonta de Capirote; Las venecianas; Y no es noche de dormir

*

F. Pazdírek: *Universal-Handbuch der Musikliteratur* (Vienna, 1904–10) [incl. list of pubd works]

'Valverde y San Juan (Joaquín)', *Enciclopedia universal ilustrada europeo-americana* (Barcelona, 1907–30), lxvi, 869

E. Cotarelo y Mori: *Historia de la zarzuela, o sea el drama lírico* (Madrid, 1934)

M. Muñoz: *Historia de la zarzuela española y el género chico* (Madrid, 1946)

A. Fernández-Cid: *Cien años de teatro musical en España (1875–1975)* (Madrid, 1975)

J. Arnau and C. Gomez: *Historia de la zarzuela* (Madrid, 1979)

R. Alier and others: *El libro de la zarzuela* (Barcelona, 1982, 2/1986 as *Diccionario de la zarzuela*)

ANDREW LAMB

Vampuka, ili Nevesta afrikanskaya ('Vampuka, or The African Bride'). Opera parody in one act by VLADIMIR GEORGIYEVICH EHRENBERG to his own libretto after a scenario by Anchar Mantsenilov (Prince Mikhaíl Volkonsky); St Petersburg, Krivoye Zerkalo, 19 January/1 February 1909.

A send-up of every grand-opera stereotype, this famous parody (chiefly of *Aida* and *L'Africaine*), subtitled 'a model opera in every way', was first performed at Nikolay Yevreynov's theatrical cabaret 'Krivoye zerkalo' ('The Fun-House Mirror') and had countless professional and amateur productions up until 1927. The title is reputed to stem from a line in the Russian translation of Scribe's libretto for *Robert le diable*, as repetitively enunciated in the opera: 'Vam puk, vam puk, vam puk tsvetov podnosim' ('We bring you a bunch, you a bunch, you a bunch of flowers'). 'Vampuka' became a common noun in Russian theatrical and operatic slang, meaning any sort of false grandiloquence, and even gave rise to a verb, *vampuchit'*, meaning to affect any sort of pretentious or melodramatic pose. Stravinsky in particular enjoyed using these words as part of his general polemic against opera in the period of his early fame.

RICHARD TARUSKIN

Vampyr, Der **(i)** ('The Vampire'). *Grosse romantische Oper* in two acts by HEINRICH AUGUST MARSCHNER to a libretto by Wilhelm August Wohlbrück after plays based on John W. Polidori's story *The Vampyre*, itself a revision of Lord BYRON's *Fragment of a Novel*, sometimes called *Augustus Darvell*; Leipzig, Stadttheater, 29 March 1828.

The original literary source for Marschner's *Vampyr* was the fragment of a novel that Byron's doctor, John W. Polidori, worked up from sketches Byron had abandoned. Attributed to Byron and published in 1819 in the *New Monthly Magazine* under the title *The Vampyre*, the story created a sensation. Plays on the vampire theme became popular in France. The most favoured among them proved to be *Le vampire* (Paris, 13 June 1820) by P. F. A. Carmouche, C. Nodier and A. de Jouffroy, but when J. R. Planché transplanted the action to Scotland, added fresh intrigue, and adapted the work for English audiences as *The Vampire, or The Bride of the Isles* (London, 9 August 1820), he achieved equal success. The same may be said of *Der Vampyr, oder Die Todten-Braut* (Karlsruhe, 1 March 1821), by the elusive H. L. Ritter, who lengthened but simplified the drama and modified the cast. While Ritter's work appears to have been Wohlbrück's immediate model, the latter interpolated additional material, mainly from Ritter's predecessors.

Although the vampire craze spread quickly in the realm of the novel and spoken play, it was slow to creep into opera. Before Wohlbrück's effort, only two one-act works enjoyed any popularity: S. di Palma's *I vampiri* (1812, Naples), based on G. Davanzati's *Dissertazione sopra i vampiri*, and M. J. Mengal's *Le vampire* (1826, Ghent), based on a play Eugène Scribe adapted from

Lord Ruthven *Earl of Marsden, the vampire*	baritone
Sir John Berkley *Laird of the House of Berkley*	bass
Janthe *his daughter*	soprano
Sir Humphrey Davenaut *Laird of the House of Davenaut*	bass
Malwina *his daughter*	soprano
Edgar Aubry *member and employee of the House of Davenaut*	tenor
The Vampire Master	spoken
John Perth *superintendent on the Marsden estate*	spoken
Emmy *his daughter, George Dibdin's fiancée*	soprano
George Dibdin *a servant of Davenaut*	tenor
Berkley's Manservant	bass
James Gadshill } *peasants on the Davenaut estate*	tenor
Richard Scrop }	tenor
Robert Green }	bass
Toms Blunt }	bass
Suse Blunt *Toms's wife*	mezzo-soprano

Demons, witches, hobgoblins and other creatures from the underworld; hunters and servants of Berkley and Davenaut; peasants from the estates of Davenaut and Marsden; ladies and gentlemen of the nobility

Setting The castle of Sir Humphrey Davenaut and its grounds, in Scotland in the 18th century

Polidori. Contemporary with the Marschner-Wohlbrück work was another opera entitled *Der Vampyr* (Stuttgart, 21 September 1828) with music by Lindpaintner and a libretto by C. M. Heigel. Though less tightly constructed dramatically and less convincing psychologically, Lindpaintner's work (*see* VAMPYR, DER (ii)) did have a following and effectively prevented Marschner's from reaching certain stages, notably those in Vienna, until late in the century.

During the century after its première, nonetheless, Marschner's *Vampyr* spread to most major centres in Europe, including Moscow, St Petersburg, Copenhagen, London, and Budapest. In a 1924 revision of the score, Pfitzner turned the first half of the first act into a prologue, similar to those found in the work by Carmouche, Nodier and Jouffroy and the works of Planché and Ritter, in order to avoid an awkward scene change. This is the version used in performances today, of which there were a number in the 1970s and 80s, primarily in the UK, Germany and the USA.

The cast at the Leipzig première included Köckert (Davenaut), W. Streit (Malwina), W. Höfler (Aubry), E. Genast (Ruthven), Vogt (Dibdin), D. Devrient (Emmy), F. Fischer (Blunt) and Madame Köckert (Suse).

ACT 1.i *A deserted clearing in the forest on the Berkley estate, with the vampires' cave on the left* Summoned by a chorus of witches and hobgoblins, the Vampire Master appears with Lord Ruthven, a newly created vampire. Ruthven has petitioned for another year on earth before being dragged into hell for eternity. The Vampire Master consents, provided Ruthven can sacrifice three young brides by the following midnight. As Ruthven sings his opening aria, 'Ha! welche Lust!', full of sinister chromatic writing, about the delights of divesting his victims of their blood, the unsuspecting Janthe, his latest conquest, collapses into his arms. Ruthven escorts her into the vampires' cave and sucks her veins dry. Immediately afterwards, Berkley's search party enter the cave to drag out Ruthven, whom Berkley stabs and leaves for dead. On his way back from London, Aubry sees the almost lifeless Ruthven, who asks to be taken to a plateau above the cave to be healed by the rays of the moon. In a melodrama, similar to Weber's Wolf's Glen scene, Aubry accedes to his wishes. Aubry now realizes that Ruthven must be a vampire, and is aghast; but Ruthven, who once saved Aubry's life, swears him to secrecy. As Ruthven's body slowly revives, Aubry runs off in terror. Sparse at first, the musical fabric becomes more agitated, and more chromatic, as Ruthven recovers.

1.ii *A tastefully decorated hall in the castle of Davenaut* From an upstairs window, Malwina sees her sweetheart Aubry approaching; she rushes out to meet him. Sir Humphrey, unaware of his daughter's love for Aubry, announces plans for her to marry before midnight the Earl of Marsden, laird of a neighbouring estate. Malwina implores him to reconsider, but Davenaut is adamant. When the Earl of Marsden enters, Aubry pales as he recognizes Ruthven; the vampire quietly reminds him of his oath of silence.

The most significant characteristic of this half of Act 1 is that the music is almost entirely in ensemble. The action is swift, involves close interaction among several characters, and individuals are rarely allowed to impede the dramatic flow with arias that concentrate on a single topic or emotion. Marschner's tendency to integrate the action musically in this way, an important departure from his predecessors' procedures, was to become even more pronounced in *Hans Heiling* (1833).

ACT 2.i *A square in front of the castle of Marsden* Guests have arrived for the wedding in the afternoon of the peasants George and Emmy and, as if summoned by Emmy's allegorical *Romanze* about vampires, 'Sieh, Mutter, dort den bleichen Mann', Ruthven appears and begins to woo her. Unable to talk the vampire out of his hideous plans, Aubry resigns himself to hopelessness in the aria 'Wie ein schöner Frühlingsmorgen' (to which Wagner appended a stretta in 1833) and leaves in despair as Ruthven leads Emmy off to claim her as his second victim. The tipsy Scrop, Blunt, Green and Gadshill shuffle in to provide some comic relief with their quartet 'Im Herbst da muss man trinken'. Incensed at their drunken lethargy, Suse jumps on to a table to castigate them, but a shot offstage interrupts her. George runs in to relate that he found Emmy murdered by the vampire, whom he has shot.

Marschner continues here to emulate Weber but provides new effects of his own. The dramatic digression provided by Emmy's *Romanze* matches in general musical style that of Ännchen in *Der Freischütz*, although Marschner does not accompany her with the exotic instrumental countermelody that characterizes the genre in the works of Mozart, Kreutzer and Weber. The spontaneous men's drinking quartet, an operatic innovation of Marschner's (it was encored at all early performances), comes directly from the German *Gesangverein* tradition and was calculated to appeal to the popular taste of audiences as well as to provide some relief from the gruesome, emotionally charged narrative.

2.ii *A hall in the castle of Davenaut* It is now evening. Guests assemble for Malwina's wedding. Although despondent, she has resigned herself to marrying Ruthven; but she has no idea that he is a vampire. As midnight nears Davenaut orders the ceremony to begin,

'Der Vampyr' (Marschner), the final scene of Act 2 (Ruthven is dragged down to hell): engraving by C. A. Schwerdgeburth after H. Ramberg from the 'Orphea-Taschenbuch' (Leipzig, 1831)

but Aubry, prepared to sacrifice himself, divulges Ruthven's identity. Immediately, the vampire is dragged into hell amid the raucous laughter of its unholy denizens. Davenaut gives his consent for his daughter to marry Aubry.

* * *

Marschner's aim in 1828 was to continue the tradition of German Romantic opera established by Weber in *Der Freischütz* and he therefore created *Der Vampyr* in its image. The intermingling of mortals with supernatural characters from native folklore (rather than Greek mythology), an inheritance from Singspiel, matched Weber's practice as did the general musical construction of the work, and though *Der Freischütz* is more expertly crafted musically and more tightly constructed dramatically than *Der Vampyr*, Marschner advanced structurally, harmonically and dramatically beyond what Weber had achieved. Both works possess a tripartite overture (placed at the end of Act 1 scene i in Pfitzner's revision of *Der Vampyr*) that associates a lyrical second theme with the heroine (Agathe in *Freischütz*, Malwina here). While Weber favoured a predominantly diatonic harmonic idiom closely allied with folksong, Marschner began to introduce chromatic progressions and melodic lines (partly inherited from Spohr) to produce a feeling of foreboding and to increase dramatic tension. The effect of this chromaticism is immediately apparent in such movements as Ruthven's opening aria and in the untitled melodrama that accompanies Aubry's placement of Ruthven's body in the moonlight. A. DEAN PALMER

Vampyr, Der (ii) ('The Vampire'). *Romantische Oper* in three acts by PETER JOSEPH VON LINDPAINTNER to a libretto by Cäsar Max Heigel after John W. Polidori's story *The Vampyre*; Stuttgart, Hoftheater, 21 September 1828.

The story is based on a French melodrama by C. Nodier, P. F. A. Carmouche and A. de Jouffroy (translated into German by H. L. Ritter). The plot follows the main lines of Marschner's opera of the same title (*see* VAMPYR, DER (i)), given in the same year, whose libretto by Wohlbrück is based on the same sources; most of the cast, however, were given different names since the action was transferred by Heigel to the south of France. Marschner's Malwina is here Isolde (soprano), his Ruthven becomes Hypolit (tenor) and his Davenaut Port d'Amour (bass); the only name in common is Aubry, here Aubri (bass). The influence of Spohr and Weber is apparent in the use of polacca rhythms and chromatic harmony and in the character of various numbers. A cavatina and a Bridesmaids' Chorus seem indebted to *Der Freischütz*, while the collapse of the palace recalls the destruction of Sir Gulf's castle in Spohr's *Faust*. *Der Vampyr* was the most successful of Lindpaintner's operas. In 1850 he revised it, replacing the original dialogue with recitatives. CLIVE BROWN

Van Allan, Richard (*b* Clipstone, Notts., 28 May 1935). English bass. He studied at the Birmingham School of Music with David Franklin and made his début in 1964 in the chorus at Glyndebourne, where he has subsequently sung many roles, creating Jowler in Nicholas Maw's *The Rising of the Moon* (1970). He made his Covent Garden début in 1971 as the Mandarin (*Turandot*) and sings with the WNO and the ENO; he has also sung at the Paris Opéra, Wexford, Nice, Bordeaux, Boston and the Metropolitan. His repertory includes Mozart's Figaro, Don Giovanni, Leporello, Don Alfonso and Osmin (roles to which he brings resonance as well as wit), and Verdi's Zaccaria, Banquo, Procida, Silva, Padre Guardiano, Philip II and Grand Inquisitor, as well as King Henry (*Lohengrin*), Pizarro, Boris, Berlioz's Méphistophélès, Colline and Ochs, which he first sang at San Diego in 1976. His voice is not large but is well focussed and intelligently used, while his dramatic ability is effectively demonstrated in roles such as Claggart (*Billy Budd*), Collatinus (*The Rape of Lucretia*) and Tiresias, which he created in Buller's *Bakxai* (1992). ELIZABETH FORBES

Vanbrugh, Sir **John** (*b* London, Jan 1664; *d* London, 26 March 1726). English architect, playwright and theatre manager. After achieving literary celebrity with *The Relapse* (1696) and *The Provok'd Wife* (1697), in 1703 he obtained financial backing from the nobility and began construction of the Queen's Theatre in the Haymarket, which was to be London's principal opera house in the 18th century. The theatre was intended for use by a combined theatre and opera company that would stage plays and English semi-operas. It opened in April 1705 with Greber's *Gli amori d'Ergasto*, a dismal failure. In 1705–6 Vanbrugh tried both semi-opera and all-sung italianate opera in English, again without much success. On 31 December 1707 he engineered a royal order granting him an opera monopoly at the Haymarket. His company featured Valentini (singing in Italian) and mounted *Love's Triumph*, a new pasticcio, but expenses were far higher than receipts and within four months Vanbrugh was functionally bankrupt. He blamed the Lord Chamberlain for setting salaries too high, and the town for refusing to 'come into any Subscription'. Because of the preservation of Vice Chamberlain Coke's papers, the financial details of this venture are better documented than those of any other early 18th-century London opera company. Vanbrugh transferred his licence to Owen Swiney in May 1708, retaining only his rent on the theatre, and occupied himself with building Blenheim Palace and other architectural projects. He invested in the Royal Academy of Music in 1719 but seems to have taken no active part in its management. He was knighted in 1714.

*

LS
B. Dobreé and G. Webb, eds.: *The Works of Sir John Vanbrugh* (London, 1927–8) [incl. a volume of *Letters*]
L. Whistler: *Sir John Vanbrugh, Architect and Dramatist* (London, 1938)
——: *The Imagination of Vanbrugh and his Fellow Artists* (London, 1954)
P. Olleson: 'Vanbrugh and Opera at the Queen's Theatre, Haymarket', *Theatre Notebook*, xxvi (1971–2), 94–101
R. Leacroft: *The Development of the English Playhouse* (London, 1973)
J. Milhous: 'The Financial Plan for a United Theatre Company in P.R.O. LC 7/3', *Maske und Kothurn*, xxi (1975), 81
——: 'New Light on Vanbrugh's Haymarket Theatre Project', *Theatre Survey*, xvii (1976), 143–61
C. A. Price: 'The Critical Decade for English Music Drama, 1700–1710', *Harvard Library Bulletin*, xxvi (1978), 38–76
J. Milhous and R. Hume, eds.: *Vice Chamberlain Coke's Theatrical Papers, 1706–1715* (Carbondale, IL, 1982)
R. Hume: 'Opera in London, 1695–1706', *British Theatre and the Other Arts, 1660–1800*, ed. S. S. Kenny (Washington DC, 1984), 67–91
J. Milhous: 'The Capacity of Vanbrugh's Theatre in the Haymarket', *Theatre History Studies*, iv (1984), 38–46
K. Downes: *Sir John Vanbrugh: a Biography* (London, 1987)
G. F. Barlow: 'Vanbrugh's Queen's Theatre in the Haymarket, 1703–9', *EMc*, xvii (1989), 515–21

ROBERT D. HUME

Vancouver. City in Canada. The Vancouver Opera House opened in 1891 with the Emma Juch Opera Company (from the USA) performing *Lohengrin*. In 1906 Henry Savage's troupe gave *Lohengrin*, *Tannhäuser*, *Rigoletto*, *La bohème* and *Faust*. In 1919 Fortune Gallo's San Carlo Opera paid the first of several visits. There was no serious attempt to produce opera in the city until 1958, when the Vancouver International Festival staged *Don Giovanni*; for a decade thereafter it incorporated one opera a year, including the North American première of Britten's *A Midsummer Night's Dream* (1961) as well as *Die Zauberflöte*, *Hänsel und Gretel* and *La fanciulla del West*. The Vancouver Opera Association, formed in 1959, opened in 1960 with *Carmen* at the Queen Elizabeth Theatre. Irving Guttman was artistic director until 1974, followed by Richard Bonynge until 1978. At first the repertory consisted mainly of popular Italian works, but also included Joan Sutherland's first *Norma* (1963) and her first *Lucrezia Borgia* (1972), as well as *Le roi de Lahore*, *Roméo et Juliette* and *Les contes d'Hoffmann*. After Brian McMaster was appointed artistic director in 1984 the repertory became more adventurous: *Yevgeny Onegin*, *I puritani*, *Così fan tutte*, *Fidelio*, *From the House of the Dead*, *The Cunning Little Vixen*, *The Turn of the Screw*, *The Rake's Progress* and *Ariadne auf Naxos* were introduced. Guus Mostart succeeded McMaster in 1989.

ELIZABETH FORBES

Vančura [Wanžura, Wanczura, Wanskura], **Arnošt** [Ernest] (*b* Vamberg [now Vamberk], Bohemia, *c*1750; *d* St Petersburg, Jan 1802). Russian composer and musical entrepreneur of Czech birth. After a short career as a lieutenant in the Austrian army, he arrived in Russia in 1783, passed himself off as a noble dilettante (Russian sources still occasionally refer to him as 'Baron Vančura'), and took part in the reorganization of the St Petersburg theatres. After resettling in Moscow, he attempted to found a theatre of his own, but was outmanoeuvred by Michael Maddox, the established Moscow impresario, and spent a couple of years instead directing the music school attached to Maddox's Petrovsky Theatre. By Feburary 1786 Vančura was back in St Petersburg, where he served until 1796 as a lavishly remunerated official in the directorate of the Court (later Imperial) Theatres, also appearing as 'court fortepianist' in a quartet with violin, cello and harp (he also specialized in imitating animal cries and human bodily functions at the keyboard). After the failure of Fomin's setting of Catherine II's second opera libretto, *Novgorodskiy bogatïr' Boyeslavich* ('Boyeslavich, Champion of Novgorod'), the fast-talking newcomer was entrusted with her third, written in collaboration with her literary secretary, Alexander Khrapovitsky: *Khrabroy i smeloy vityaz' Akhrideich* ('The Brave and Bold Knight Akhrideich'), a comic opera in five acts, also known as *Ivan-Tsarevich* (St Petersburg, Hermitage, 23 September/4 October 1787; *RU-SPtob*, ov. in Findeyzen 1968). 'Baron Vančura's' pastiche of folktunes was successful and remained in the repertory until 1810.

As an official of the Imperial Theatres, Vančura may have had a hand in revising the music of the popular folktune-based comic opera *THE MILLER* for its St Petersburg performances. (Contrary to widespread supposition, he could not have assisted Fomin in this task, as the latter was out of favour at court until the accession of Paul I.) This would help explain how the first movement of Vančura's 'Russian' Symphony (*Rossiyskaya simfoniya*, subtitled 'Sinfonie russe, composée d'airs ukraïniens') became attached to *The Miller* as an overture; in the original vocal score (Moscow, 1884), the whole opera is misattributed to Fomin (as in Tcherepnin 1966). An attractive if elementary composition in its own right, the symphony was originally published in keyboard reduction in the October 1790 issue of Vančura's *Journal de musique pour le clavecin ou pianoforte dédié aux dames par B. W. Amateur*; the first movement is reprinted in Ginzburg (1968).

*

N. F. Findeyzen: *Ocherki po istorii muzïki v Rossii s drevneyshikh vremyon do kontsa XVIII veka* [Studies in the History of Music in Russia from Ancient Times to the End of the 18th Century], ii (Moscow and Leningrad, 1929)
R.-A. Mooser: *Annales de la musique et des musiciens en Russie au XVIIIme siècle*, ii (Geneva, 1951)
M. S. Druskin and Yu. V. Keldïsh, eds.: *Ocherki po istorii russkoy muzïki 1790–1825* [Studies in the History of Russian Music 1790–1825] (Leningrad, 1956)
A. Tcherepnin, ed.: *Russische Musik-Anthologie* (Bonn, 1966), 49–54
S. L. Ginzburg: *Istoriya russkoy muzïki v notnïkh obraztsakh* [History of Russian Music in Examples], ii (Moscow, 1968), 477–83
Yu. Keldïsh and others: *Istoriya russkoy muzïki v desyati tomakh* [History of Russian Music in Ten Volumes], iii (Moscow, 1985)

RICHARD TARUSKIN

Vanda. Grand opera in five acts by ANTONÍN DVOŘÁK to a libretto by Václav Beneš-Šumavský and František

Zákrejs after a story by Julian Surzycki; Prague, Provisional Theatre, 17 April 1876.

The opera is based on the myth of the Polish queen Vanda (soprano), who drowned herself in the River Vistula in fulfilment of an oath to lay down her life if her people were delivered from the German invader. A major feature of the plot is Vanda's love for the valiant, though not nobly born, Slavoj (tenor). The villain is the German prince Roderich (baritone), who courts Vanda in Act 2, is found to be in league with dark forces in Act 3 and is defeated by a Polish army led by Slavoj in Act 4. The fifth act deals with Vanda's farewell and suicide.

Vanda was written in 1875 as Dvořák was approaching his first maturity as a composer. The musical style owes something to Meyerbeer, Gounod and Wagner, but throughout Dvořák's musical personality is clear. With its fine melodic writing, *Vanda* is one of the composer's most rewarding operas. The handling of recurring motifs, transformed and used as reminiscences, is dramatically effective; and the larger structures, particularly those involving chorus, generate considerable tension. While the work represents a clear development of Dvořák's operatic style, it is built on a series of distinct numbers and remains within the confines of 19th-century grand opera. After the first performance, because of the limited resources of the Provisional Theatre, which was inadequate for the conjuration scene in Act 3, the work was given in four acts rather than five. For a revival in 1880 (also in four acts) Dvořák provided a new, extensive overture.

The success of Dvořák's next grand opera, *Dimitrij*, has always tended to overshadow *Vanda*. Nevertheless, the earlier work shows theatrical instinct and originality, while Vanda's aria 'Bohové velcí' anticipates arias in *Rusalka* and *Armida*, and the concluding pages anticipate the finales of *Dimitrij* and *Armida*.

JAN SMACZNY

Van Dam, José [Van Damme, Joseph] (*b* Brussels, 25 Aug 1940). Belgian bass-baritone. He studied in Brussels, making his début in 1960 at Liège as Don Basilio. From 1961 to 1965 he was engaged at the Paris Opéra and Opéra-Comique, singing minor roles. After two seasons at Geneva, where he sang in the première of Milhaud's *La mère coupable* (1966), he joined the Deutsche Oper, Berlin. His roles there included Mozart's Figaro, Leporello and Don Alfonso, Attila, Prince Igor and Rangoni (*Boris Godunov*). He has appeared at the Salzburg, Aix-en-Provence and Athens festivals. Equally at home in the French, German or Italian style, he has a repertory encompassing Golaud, Balducci (*Benvenuto Cellini*), the four villains (*Les contes d'Hoffmann*), Caspar (*Der Freischütz*), Wozzeck, Amfortas and Boccanegra. He is a notable Escamillo, a role he sang for his San Francisco (1970), Covent Garden (1973) and Metropolitan (1975) débuts. At the Théâtre de la Monnaie, Brussels, he has sung Boris, Philip II, the Dutchman, Hans Sachs, Don Giovanni and Falstaff. He created the title role of Messiaen's *Saint François d'Assise* at the Paris Opéra in 1983 and sang William Tell at Geneva in 1991. He has a magnificent resonant and expressive voice and is an excellent actor.

ELIZABETH FORBES

Vandenbroek [Brock, Vandenbrock, Vandenbrask, Vanderboeck, Vanderbrock, Van der Broeck], **Othon-Joseph** (*b* Ieper, 20 Dec 1758; *d* Passy, nr Paris, 18 Oct 1832). Flemish composer. After studying at The Hague and Amsterdam, he joined the French theatre of Maastricht as a violinist, and his first operas were produced there. He made his Parisian début at the Concert Spirituel in 1784; in the same year, the Théâtre des Beaujolais opened, and it may be assumed that Vandenbroek had some function there, since two of his operas were staged at that theatre. He subsequently played the horn first at the Théâtre de Monsieur and then at the Opéra, from 1793 to 1816. Besides several instrumental works, Vandenbroek published two pedagogical treatises, which brought him an appointment as professor at the Conservatoire in 1795. The only one of his operas to acquire a certain notoriety was *Le codicile* (1793), because its music was considered too obviously influenced by the *charmant* style of Dezède. His compositions for the Cité-Variétés and the Ambigu-Comique are more in the nature of theatre music than genuine opera.

first performed in Paris unless otherwise stated

Tircis et Céphise, ou Le lotto de l'amour (3, Vallier), Maastricht, 6 July 1782

Les étrennes de la nouvelle année (comédie-vaudeville, 1, Vallier), Maastricht, 1783

Colin et Colette, ou Le milicien (opéra bouffon, 1), Beaujolais, 8 June 1786

La ressemblance supposée (opéra bouffon, 1), Beaujolais, 26 July 1788

Le codicile, ou Les deux héritiers (comédie mêlée de chants, 1, J. G. A. Cuvelier), Montansier, 5 Aug 1793, incl. music by Cuvelier, Haydn and I. Pleyel; *F-A*

La fête à l'Etre Suprême (scènes patriotiques mêlées de chants, pantomimes et danses, Cuvelier), Cité-Variétés, 9 June 1794

La fille hermite (oc, 1, Cuvelier), Amis de la Patrie, 23 Oct 1795

Le génie Assouf, ou Les deux coffrets (pantomime, ?Cuvelier), Cité-Variétés, 25 Dec 1795

C'est le diable, ou La bohémienne (drame à grand spectacle, 5, Cuvelier), Ambigu-Comique, 18 Nov 1797, collab. Cuvelier

Les Incas, ou Les Espagnols dans la Floride (mélodrame), Cité-Variétés, 1797

L'anniversaire, ou La fête de la souveraineté (scène lyrique et mélodramatique, Mittié and Cuvelier), Ambigu-Comique, 20 March 1798

La fontaine merveilleuse, ou Les époux musulmans (pantomime-féerie, 5, Loaisel de Tréogate), Ambigu-Comique, 13 Sept 1799

*

StiegerO

F. Faber: *Histoire du théâtre français en Belgique* (Brussels and Paris, 1878–80), ii, 51; iv, 102, 335

C. Pierre: *Histoire du Concert spirituel 1725–1790* (Paris, 1975), 215

MICHEL NOIRAY

Vandenburg, Howard (*b* Buffalo, NY, 18 May 1918). American tenor and baritone. He studied in Philadelphia, making his début as a baritone as Count Almaviva. Later he became a tenor and in 1952 joined the Bayerische Staatsoper in Munich; he sang Midas with the Staatsoper in the British première of *Die Liebe der Danae* (1953, Covent Garden). He sang at Florence, Naples, Zürich and Vienna and his tenor roles included Idomeneus, Florestan, Radames, Lohengrin, Don José, the Emperor (*Die Frau ohne Schatten*), Matteo (*Arabella*), Calaf and Laca. Reverting to baritone, he sang the title role in the German première of *King Priam* at Karlsruhe (1963), created Michael in Steffens's *Eli* (1967) and sang Adam Brant in the European première of Levy's *Mourning Becomes Electra* (1969), both at Dortmund. He was a powerful actor with an expressive voice whose baritone repertory included Scarpia, the Dutchman and Telramund. He was married to the soprano Anna Green.

ELIZABETH FORBES

Van der Walt, Deon. *See* WALT, DEON VAN DER.

Van Durme, Jef. *See* DURME, JEF VAN.

Van Dyck [van Dijck], **Ernest (Marie Hubert)** (*b* Antwerp, 2 April 1861; *d* Berlaer-lez-Lierre, 31 Aug 1923). Belgian tenor. He studied in Paris, making his début in 1887 at the Eden-Théâtre. He sang Parsifal at Bayreuth in 1888, returning there in the same role until 1912, and as Lohengrin in 1894. From 1888 to 1900 he was engaged at the Vienna Hofoper, where he sang Des Grieux in Massenet's *Manon* (1890). He made his London début in that role at Covent Garden (1891), where he also sang Faust, Lohengrin, Tannhäuser, Siegmund, Mathias in Kienzl's *Der Evangelimann*, Loge and Tristan. In Vienna he created Massenet's Werther (1892), and sang Marcello in Leoncavallo's *La bohème* (1898). He made his début at the Paris Opéra as Lohengrin (1891) and at the Théâtre de la Monnaie, Brussels, in the same part (1894), becoming a regular visitor to the latter house in Wagner and Massenet roles. He made his Chicago and Metropolitan débuts in 1898 as Tannhäuser. He returned to the Paris Opéra in 1908 as Siegfried (*Götterdämmerung*) and finally, in 1914, as Parsifal. His voice, both powerful and sweet-toned, not only encompassed the heavy Wagnerian roles, but also the more lyrical French repertory.

For illustration *see* WERTHER.

*

H. de Curzon: *Ernest Van Dijck, une gloire belge de l'art lyrique* (Brussels, 1933)
W. Beetz: *Das Wiener Opernhaus 1869 bis 1945* (Vienna, 1949)
S. Wolff: *L'Opéra au Palais Garnier (1875–1962)* (Paris, 1962)
G. Skelton: *Wagner at Bayreuth* (London, 1965)
J. Sales: *Théâtre royal de la Monnaie 1856–1970* (Nivelles, 1971)

ELIZABETH FORBES

Vāne, Alīda (*b* Sarkanmuiža, Ventspils district, 11 Oct 1899; *d* Riga, 27 Feb 1969). Latvian soprano. She studied in Milan, making her début at Genoa in 1925 in Franchetti's *Asrael*. During the next five years she appeared at Bologna, Turin, Naples, Milan (La Scala), Venice (La Fenice), Parma and Trieste, singing Aida, Amelia (*Ballo*), Gounod's Marguerite, Boito's Helen of Troy, Mascagni's Isabeau and Elsa. She toured the USA with the San Carlo Opera Company (1931–3), then sang Abigaille (*Nabucco*) and Thaïs in the Netherlands, and Elisabeth, Tosca and Sieglinde in Buenos Aires (1935–6). She also sang Leonora (*Il trovatore*), Desdemona and Santuzza. Engaged at the Latvian National Opera, Riga (1937–44), she made a final appearance as Amelia in 1950. Her powerful, brilliant-toned voice was equally effective in Italian and German music. ELIZABETH FORBES, ARNOLDS KLOTIŅŠ

Vaness, Carol (*b* San Diego, 27 July 1952). American soprano. She studied at California State University and in 1977 made her début in San Francisco as Vitellia in Mozart's *La clemenza di Tito*; she first appeared at the New York City Opera in 1979 in the same role. In 1982 she made her official European début as Donna Anna at Glyndebourne, having already sung Mimì and Vitellia at Covent Garden in emergencies. Other roles at Covent Garden include Rosalinde and Countess Almaviva. She made her Metropolitan début in 1984 as Armida (*Rinaldo*). Her repertory includes Handel's Alcina, Cleopatra (*Giulio Cesare*) and Delilah (*Samson*). Her bright, well-focussed voice, with its facility for coloratura, is shown to splendid advantage as Fiordiligi (*Così fan tutte*) and Electra (*Idomeneo*), the role of her La Scala début (1990). In the mid-1980s she began to sing more dramatic roles: Massenet's Manon, Verdi's Violetta, Amelia (*Un ballo in maschera* and *Simon Boccanegra*) and Leonora (*Il trovatore*), as well as Tatyana, which she sang in Toronto (1990), and the title roles of *Anna Bolena* (1991, Seattle) and *Iphigénie en Tauride* (1992, La Scala).

*

E. Forbes: 'Carol Vaness', *Opera*, xl (1989), 418–24

ELIZABETH FORBES

Vanessa. Opera in four acts, op.32, by SAMUEL BARBER to a libretto by GIAN CARLO MENOTTI; New York, Metropolitan Opera, 15 January 1958.

Inspired by Isak Dinesen's *Seven Gothic Tales*, *Vanessa* is set in a country manor in an unnamed 'northern country about 1905'. The story unfolds about two women, Vanessa (soprano), 'a lady of great beauty', and her beautiful young niece, Erika (mezzo-soprano). Vanessa has for 20 years awaited the return of her only love, Anatol. In a sombre gothic dreamscape, in which chandeliers are dimmed and mirrors draped against the reflection of Vanessa's advancing age, the wizened Baroness (contralto), Vanessa's mother, condemns her daughter's withdrawal from life through her silence. Another Anatol (tenor), the errant lover's fatally charming son, a bounder and opportunist, enters the manor. Vanessa, mistaking the young man for his father, passionately inquires if he still loves her; she is devastated upon realizing the visitor is not her lover. Erika entreats the impostor to leave, but he refuses.

Act 2 begins a month later; Erika confesses to the Baroness that she was seduced by Anatol on the night of his arrival but has refused his offer of marriage because he cannot promise eternal love. Her grandmother advises: 'Love never bears the image that we dream of; when it seems to, beware the disguise!'. Vanessa and Anatol, radiantly returning from ice-skating, announce to the Old Doctor (baritone) plans for a New Year's Eve ball reminiscent of earlier celebrations. Aware that her aunt is blindly in love with Anatol, Erika confronts him and bitterly rejects him.

At the ball (Act 3), Anatol and Vanessa declare their love and their engagement is announced by the bibulous Doctor. Erika, dazed and carrying Anatol's child, stumbles into the bitter cold towards the lake to attempt an abortion. Unaware of the reason for, and disturbed by, her beloved niece's behaviour, Vanessa marries Anatol (Act 4). As they prepare to leave for Paris, they are joined by Erika, the Baroness and the Doctor; their quintet ('To leave, to break, to find, to keep') provides a brilliant and highly dramatic climax to the work. As her aunt had earlier, Erika withdraws from the world: 'Now it is my turn to wait', she declares to the silent Baroness.

In *Vanessa*, Barber used conventional forms and genres of the grand opera tradition but in an unstylized manner: set-piece arias, love duets, a glimpsed ball scene requiring a waltz, a folkdance ballet (reminiscent of *Yevgeny Onegin*) and a coloratura skating aria (cut from the revised version). Simultaneous musical representation of different threads of action supports psychological undercurrents of the drama. Predominantly neo-romantic, the music is imbued with many elements of Barber's compositional strengths: metric flexibility that supports the natural rhythms of the text, a fluent use of harmonic colour to underscore the bittersweet poetry and an abundance of accessible melody.

'Vanessa' (Barber): set design by Cecil Beaton for the original production at the Metropolitan Opera, New York, 15 January 1958

Several arias and one orchestral interlude (the intermezzo between Acts 1 and 2) are well known as independent pieces: Erika's poignant ballad 'Must the winter come so soon'; Vanessa's dramatic aria 'Do not utter a word, Anatol'; a simulated ländler 'Under the willow tree', which, in the opera, is used as a solo, a trio, a chorus and lastly as a dance; and the final act's quintet, a canon.

Eleanor Steber, in one of the great challenges of her career, stepped into the role of Vanessa six weeks before opening night when Sena Jurinac unexpectedly withdrew from the cast. Rosalind Elias's portrayal of Erika was considered a vocal and dramatic triumph, and Giorgio Tozzi stopped the show with his remarkable characterization of the Doctor in Act 1.

Lang viewed Barber's mastery of operatic language in *Vanessa* as 'remarkable and second to none on the Salzburg-Milan axis'; Sargent extolled it as 'by far the finest and most truly "operatic" opera ever written by an American, as well as one of the most impressive things of its sort to appear anywhere since Richard Strauss's more vigorous days'. *Vanessa* won Barber a Pulitzer Prize in 1958; that same season, it was produced in Salzburg – the first American opera performed at the festival, as well as the first time in Salzburg history that an opera was sung in English and produced by an outside organization. In 1964 Barber revised *Vanessa*, consolidating four acts to three by merging Acts 1 and 2. The new, shorter version was performed for the first time at the Metropolitan Opera on 13 March 1965, conducted by William Steinberg. There have been subsequent performances in 1978 (Spoleto Festival, Charleston, South Carolina) and 1988 (Opera Theater, St Louis, Missouri).

BARBARA B. HEYMAN

Van Gilse, Jan. *See* GILSE, JAN VAN.

Van Hoof, Jef. *See* HOOF, JEF VAN.

Vanini [Boschi], **Francesca** (*b* Bologna; *d* Venice, 1744). Italian contralto. She was in the service of the court of Mantua. Between 1695 and 1699 she appeared in operas in Bologna, Florence, Venice and Mantua. She sang in Naples in 1701 and in Caldara's *Gli equivoci del sembiante* at Mantua in 1703, at Genoa in 1706 and Vicenza in 1707. Between 1707 and 1709 she appeared with her husband, the bass GIUSEPPE BOSCHI, in 12 operas in Venice (including Handel's *Agrippina*) and Bologna, often playing male parts. She accompanied him to London (1710–11), singing in Alessandro Scarlatti's *Pirro e Demetrio*, Giovanni Bononcini's *Etearco* and Handel's *Rinaldo* (Goffredo). Her voice was then on the decline, but earlier she had been an outstanding artist: Tosi praised her for following Pistocchi's method 'of introducing Graces without transgressing against Time'. Handel's two parts for her, Otho in *Agrippina* and Goffredo, have a limited compass of *g* to *e″*; the tessitura of the former is exceptionally low.

WINTON DEAN

Vanloo, Albert (*b* Brussels, 10 Sept 1846; *d* Paris, 1920). French librettist of Belgian origin. He spent his childhood in Paris where his family had some contact with Alexandre Dumas *père*, and where he developed an early passion for the theatre. Bored with legal studies he began writing little plays and *opéra comique* librettos with Eugène Leterrier. Their collaboration was very productive, including Chabrier's *L'étoile* (1877) and *Une éducation manquée* (1879), and lasted for nearly 20 years until Leterrier's premature death (1884). Vanloo later found new partners in William Busnach (1832–1907), a nephew of Fromental Halévy and manager of the Théâtre de l'Athénée, in Henri Chivot and, most importantly, in Georges Duval (1847–1919). Anecdotes of Parisian theatrical life of the period, as well as some account of the friendly but essentially subservient relationship of a craftsman librettist to such composers as Offenbach and Lecocq, are to be found in

Vanloo's book *Sur le plateau: souvenirs d'un librettiste* (Paris, 1913).

Le Petit Poucet (opéra bouffe, with E. Leterrier), F. A. Laurent de Rillé, 1868; *Madeleine* (oc, with Leterrier), H. Potier, 1869; *La nuit du 15 octobre* (opérette, with Leterrier), G. Jacob, 1869; *Nabucho* (opéra bouffe, with Leterrier), A. de Villebichet, 1871; *Giroflé-Girofla* (opéra bouffe, with Leterrier), Lecocq, 1874; *Le voyage dans la lune* (opéra féerie, with Leterrier and A. Mortier), Offenbach, 1875; *La petite mariée* (oc, with Leterrier), Lecocq, 1875; *La marjolaine* (opéra bouffe, with Leterrier), Lecocq, 1877; *L'étoile* (opéra bouffe, with Leterrier), Chabrier, 1877; *La Camargo* (oc, with Leterrier), Lecocq, 1879; *Une éducation manquée* (opérette, with Leterrier), Chabrier, 1879; *La jolie Persane* (oc, with Leterrier), Lecocq, 1879; *Le beau Nicolas* (oc, with Leterrier), P. Lacome, 1880; *Le droit de l'aînesse* (opéra bouffe, with Leterrier), F. Chassaigne, 1883

Le roi de carreau (oc, with Leterrier), Lajarte, 1883; *La Béarnaise* (oc, with Leterrier), Messager, 1885; *Ali-Baba* (opérette, with W. B. Busnach), Lecocq, 1887; *La gamine de Paris* (opéra bouffe, with Leterrier), G. Serpette, 1887; *La gardeuse d'oies* (oc, with Leterrier), Lacome, 1888; *L'oeuf rouge* (opérette, with Busnach), Audran, 1890; *La fée aux chèvres* (opérette, with P. Ferrier), Varney, 1890; *Le pays d'or* (opérette, with H. Chivot), Vasseur, 1892; *Le bonhomme de neige* (opérette, with Chivot), Banès, 1894; *Les p'tites Michu* (opérette, with G. Duval), Messager, 1897; *Véronique* (opérette, with Duval), Messager, 1898; *La belle au bois dormant* (opérette, with Duval), Lecocq, 1900; *La soeur de Jocrisse*, Banès, 1901; *Les dragons de l'impératrice* (opérette, with Duval), Messager, 1905

CHRISTOPHER SMITH

Vannarelli [Vanarelli], **Francesco Antonio** (*b* Rome, *c*1615; *d* ?Padua, after 1676). Italian composer. A Franciscan friar, he was a *maestro di cappella* in Rome before taking similar posts at Spoleto (1649–65, intermittently), Terni, Orvieto and Padua. He was an able composer of the Roman school, held in high esteem by his contemporaries. His music is mainly sacred, but includes one opera, *La Fedra* (D. Montio; 1661, Spoleto; *I-Nc*).

JOHN HARPER

Vanneschi, Francesco (*b* ?Florence, early 18th century; *d* ?London, *c*Aug 1759). Italian librettist and impresario. His most frequently performed comic opera was *La commedia in commedia*, incorrectly attributed to Giovanni Barlocci, first performed in 1731 at the Cocomero in Florence by the company of Pietro Pertici with music by Chinzer. A new score by Rinaldo di Capua for Rome, 1738, was used for a tour by the same company through northern Italy. In 1741 he moved to England and was employed by Charles Sackville, the Earl of Middlesex, as poet and impresario at the King's Theatre, London. He wrote at least two new librettos for his patron: *Scipione in Cartagine* (1742) and *Fetonte* (1747). His seasons were dominated by revivals which he reworked to a greater or lesser extent. He was instrumental in bringing the Pertici company, with which he had earlier been associated, to London from November 1748 to May 1750. The company performed nine comic operas, five of which had been staged previously in Florence (1731–43). This introduction of Italian comic opera into England is comparable with the more famous Parisian seasons of 1752–4 directed by Eustache Bambini. Vanneschi's management of the King's Theatre intermittently from 1741 to 1759 was marred by scandals, thefts, disputes (notably with the prima donna, Regina Mingotti) and financial distress resulting in his incarceration briefly in debtors' prison. His lack of success may partly explain why his season of Italian comic opera did not have the lasting impact in England that Bambini's did in France.

Although the language is sometimes crude, hasty and inappropriate, Vanneschi's librettos are nevertheless important as a bridge between the 17th-century Tuscan classic librettos of Moniglia and Villifranchi and the more sentimental Leopoldine ones of Casorri, Coltellini, Somigli and Tassi in the late 18th century.

blt – *burletta* dm – *dramma per musica*
sd – *scherzo drammatico*

La vanità delusa (blt), Chinzer, 1731; *La commedia in commedia* (blt), Chinzer, 1731 (Rinaldo di Capua, 1738, rev. as L'ambizione delusa, 1745; Latilla, 1747, as Il vecchio amante); *L'Enrico* (dm), 1731 (Galuppi, 1743); *La serva padrona* (blt), Predieri, 1732; *La moglie accorta* (sd), various composers, 1735; *Pimpinone* (sd), Chinzer, 1735; *Alessandro in Persia* (dm), Paradies, 1738 (pasticcio, 1741); *Scipione in Cartagine* (dm), Galuppi, 1742; *Fetonte*, Paradies, 1747

Doubtful: *L'inconstanza delusa*, pasticcio with some music by Count St-Germain, 1745; *Artamene*, Gluck, 1746; *Caduta de' giganti*, Gluck, 1746; *Bellerofonte*, Terradellas, 1747

*

LS

F. Sbigoli: *Tommaso Crudeli e i primi frammassoni in Firenze* (Milan, 1884)

W. B. Squire: 'Gluck's London Operas', *MQ*, i (1915), 398–400

W. S. Lewis and others, eds.: *Horace Walpole's Correspondence with Sir Horace Mann* (New Haven, CT, 1954–71)

R. Fiske: *English Theatre Music in the Eighteenth Century* (London, 1973, 2/1986)

R. L. Weaver and N. W. Weaver: *A Chronology of Music in the Florentine Theater 1590–1750* (Detroit, 1978)

C. Taylor: 'From Losses to Lawsuit: Patronage of the Italian Opera in London by Lord Middlesex, 1739–45', *ML*, lxviii (1987), 1–25

ROBERT LAMAR WEAVER

Vanni-Marcoux [Marcoux, Vanni; Marcoux, Jean Emile Diogène] (*b* Turin, 12 June 1877; *d* Paris, 22 Oct

Vanni-Marcoux in the title role of Massenet's 'Don Quichotte'

Set design by Luigi Vanvitelli for Dido's palace (probably for a setting of Metastasio's 'Didone abbandonata') framed by the proscenium of the theatre at Caserta: drawing in pen, ink and wash by an unknown artist, c1775

1962). French bass and baritone. His father was French and his mother Italian; the 'Vanni' which he incorporated into his professional name was originally an abbreviation for 'Giovanni'. He made early appearances both in Bayonne (début 1889 as Gounod's Friar Laurence) and in Turin (1894, as Sparafucile in *Rigoletto*); but the timbre of his voice was always characteristically French. He was engaged in 1905 by Covent Garden, where he first appeared as Rossini's Don Basilio, returning every summer until 1912 in a wide variety of roles, both baritone and bass. Exceptionally, he gravitated towards the higher range as his career developed, moving for example from the bass role of Arkel in *Pelléas* (1909, London) to the baritone Golaud (1914, Paris; 1937, London). Before World War I he was predominantly a bass, singing even Hunding and Fafner; and it was as Gounod's Méphistophélès that he first appeared at the Paris Opéra in 1908. For nearly 40 years he was a familiar and much admired figure in Parisian musical life, mainly at the Opéra, but also at the Opéra-Comique, where he was particularly famous as the Father in *Louise* and in the title role of Massenet's *Don Quichotte*. He was also director of the Grand Théâtre at Bordeaux from 1948 to 1951. His American career centred on Chicago, where he sang frequently between 1913 and 1932. He was a fine actor as well as an accomplished singer; his recordings from *Don Quichotte* and Verdi's *Don Carlos* are especially treasurable.

D. Shawe-Taylor: 'Vanni Marcoux', *Opera*, xiv (1963), 156–62; rev. in *Recorded Sound*, nos. 29–30 (1968), 266–272 [with discography by H. Barnes]

DESMOND SHAWE-TAYLOR

Van Rooy, Anton. *See* ROOY, ANTON VAN.

Vanvitelli, Luigi (*b* Naples, 26 May 1700; *d* Caserta, 1 March 1773). Italian scene designer and inventor of stage machinery. The son of the landscape painter Gaspar Van Wittel, he trained with his father in Rome. He was, however, strongly influenced by Filippo Juvarra, whom he met in 1715 and perhaps again in 1726, when Juvarra was responsible for some revolutionary productions in which the scenography, in contrast to the tradition established by the Galli-Bibiena family, was concerned more with creating a dramatic atmosphere than with appealing to the audience's imagination. In 1720 Vanvitelli made a series of sketches for the theatre (now in the Palazzo Reale, Caserta), five of which – 'Atrio', 'Carcere', 'Appartamenti', 'Giardino' and 'Sala con trono' (the last marked 'Scenes from the Teatro della Pace in Rome') – are connected with Gaetano Boni's *Tito Manlio*. The rejection of any attempt at illusion, the vibrant chiaroscuro, the concentration of space, the structural solidity of the scenery and above all the establishment of a relationship with the architecture of the auditorium – already obvious in the proscenium frame limiting the composition – demonstrate links with Juvarra's ideas. A harbour scene (Naples, Museo di S Martino) and the scenery panels from the Caserta theatre (New York, Metropolitan Museum) confirm that Vanvitelli retained an interest in stage settings in his maturity; his last work was his festive machinery for the birth of a first child to Queen Maria Carolina (1772).

L. Vanvitelli the younger: *Vita dell'architetto Luigi Vanvitelli* (Naples, 1823)
F. Mancini: *Scenografia napoletana dell'età baroca* (Naples, 1964)
C. de Seta: 'Disegni di Luigi Vanvitelli architetto e scenografo', *Luigi Vanvitelli*, ed. R. di Stefano (Naples, 1973), 273–311

FRANCO MANCINI

Van Vlijmen, Jan. *See* VLIJMEN, JAN VAN.

Van Zandt, Marie (*b* New York, 8 Oct 1858; *d* Cannes, 31 Dec 1919). American soprano. Her mother, a member of the Carl Rosa company, was her first teacher; she also received encouragement from Patti and further training from Francesco Lamperti. After a successful début in Turin in January 1879 as Zerlina, she was engaged for Her Majesty's Theatre, London, as Amina (*La sonnambula*). Her voice was already well developed and pleasant, if not powerful, while her execution was competent and her acting graceful and charming. These gifts contributed to her success as Mignon at the Opéra-Comique in March 1880, and to her popularity in Paris during the next five years. Her interpretations of Mignon, Dinorah and Cherubino found such favour with the critics that Delibes entrusted her with the creation of the title role in *Lakmé* (1883). Her voice did not stand the strain of constant work, and she left the Opéra-Comique in March 1885. She made her American début in Chicago as Amina in November 1891, a month later repeating the role at the Metropolitan Opera. She continued to make guest appearances at various houses until her marriage in 1898.

*

H. de Curzon: *Croquis d'artistes* (Paris, 1898)
O. Thompson: *The American Singer* (New York, 1937), 184

Vanzo, Alain (Fernand Albert) (*b* Monte Carlo, 2 April 1928). French tenor. A boy chorister in Monte Carlo, he later studied at Aix-les-Bains. He made his Paris Opéra début in 1954 (a Pirate in *Oberon*). Following a period of small roles at both Paris houses, in 1956 he undertook the Duke at the Opéra and Gérald (*Lakmé*) at the Opéra-Comique, and then won renown throughout France and Belgium in French lyric parts – Berlioz's Cellini, Gounod's Faust (a role he also sang in Philadelphia in 1984), Lalo's Mylio (*Le roi d'Ys*), Massenet's Des Grieux and Werther – and in Donizetti, Verdi and Puccini. He appeared at Covent Garden as Edgardo (1961) and Rodolfo (1963), and in Wexford as well as in the USA; it is somewhat surprising that, in a time of shortage, a French tenor of his elegant, clean style and well-formed vocal timbre should not have received wider international acclaim. His recordings include *Lakmé* with Joan Sutherland and Massenet's *La Navarraise*. MAX LOPPERT

Vanzo, Vittorio Mario (*b* Padua, 29 April 1862; *d* Milan, 13 Dec 1945). Italian conductor and composer. He studied at the Milan Conservatory and developed an early interest in Wagner, whom he got to know in Palermo in 1882. He conducted Wagner's works in Italy, giving the Italian première of *Die Walküre* in Turin in 1891. He conducted Italian works in Moscow (1897) and in 1900 visited Buenos Aires. As a pianist he undertook many concert tours and he opened a singing school in Milan. His opera *Edipo re* was composed in 1893; his two other operas, *Fosca* and *Pamela*, were not completed.

*

A. Toni: *Vittorio Mario Vanzo* (Milan, 1946) [with work-list]

Varady, Julia (*b* Oradea, 1 Sept 1941). Romanian soprano. She studied in Bucharest with Arta Florescu, joining the Cluj State Opera at 22. Guest engagements took her to Italy and Cologne, where she soon became known as a Mozart soprano of passionate intensity, vocal warmth and technical smoothness, as Donna Elvira, Fiordiligi and Vitellia. After two years at Frankfurt she was engaged at Munich in the 1972–3 season; her roles there included Offenbach's Antonia, Verdi's Leonoras (*Trovatore* and *Forza*), Violetta, Elisabeth de Valois and Butterfly; in 1977 she sang the title role in Strauss's *Arabella* there. She later added to her repertory dramatic roles such as Abigaille and Senta, which she sang at Covent Garden in 1992. Her recordings include Mozart's *Lucio Silla* (as Cecilius) and *Idomeneo* (Electra, a role she sang in Milan in 1984) as well as Bartók's *Bluebeard's Castle* (Judith) with Dietrich Fischer-Dieskau, whom she married in 1978.

*

A. Blyth: 'Julia Varady', *Opera*, xliii (1992), 646–51

MAX LOPPERT

Varesco, (Girolamo) Giovanni Battista [Gianbattista] (bap. Trent, 26 Nov 1735; *d* Salzburg, 25 Aug 1805). Italian cleric, poet and musician. He was educated at the Jesuit college in his home town from 1753 to 1756. In 1766 he became a chaplain to the Archbishop of Salzburg, serving also as a musician in the archbishop's orchestra. When Mozart received the commission for *Idomeneo* (1781) from the Munich court, he turned not to an established theatrical poet but to Varesco, who, as an Italian educated by the Jesuits in the liberal arts, was as capable as more prolific librettists. Furthermore, his presence in Salzburg allowed Mozart to work closely with him during the preparation of the libretto and the early stages of composition. Varesco translated and reworked Danchet's *tragédie lyrique Idoménée* (1712) under Mozart's supervision, producing a libretto in which the grand choruses, spectacular effects and supernatural elements reflect its French origins and probably the influence of Gluck's *Alceste*. Varesco's work is fluent and theatrical, with moments of great beauty, both poetic and dramatic.

Although Varesco was offended by Mozart's persistent attempts to alter the libretto of *Idomeneo*, that did not keep him from a second collaboration with Mozart. When Joseph II organized an *opera buffa* troupe in Vienna in 1783, Mozart, eager to display his abilities as a composer of Italian comic opera, set to work with Varesco on *L'oca del Cairo*. Most of the first act had been completed when, in early 1784, they abandoned the project, possibly because Mozart was dissatisfied with Varesco's work. After *L'oca del Cairo*, Varesco collaborated with Michael Haydn on the *opera seria Andromeda e Perseo* (1787). Having survived Mozart by 14 years, Varesco died in poverty in his adopted city.

*

P. von Waldersee: 'Varesco's *L'oca del Cairo*, nach der Originalhandschrift herausgegeben', *AMZ*, xvii (1882), cols. 693, 710, 728, 745
H. F. Redlich: '*L'oca del Cairo*', *MR*, ii (1941), 122–31
D. Heartz: 'The Genesis of Mozart's *Idomeneo*', *MJb 1967*, 150–64; repr. in *MQ*, lv (1969), 1–19; repr. in *Mozart's Operas* (Berkeley, 1990)
K. Kramer: 'Antike und christliches Mittelalter in Varescos *Idomeneo*, dem Libretto zu Mozarts gleichnamiges Oper', *Mitteilungen der Internationalen Stiftung Mozarteum*, xxviii/1–2 (1980), 6–20
——: 'Frauengestalten in Varescos *Idomeneo*', *Mitteilungen der Internationalen Stiftung Mozarteum*, xxviii/3–4 (1980), 16–24
——: 'Giovanni Battista Varesco: Versuch einer Biographie', *Acta Mozartiana*, xxvii (1980), 2–14
——: 'Das Libretto zu Mozarts *Idomeneo*', *Wolfgang Amadeus Mozart: Idomeneo 1781–1981*, ed. R. Münster (Munich, 1981), 7–43

JOHN A. RICE

Varèse, Edgard [Edgar] **(Victor Achille Charles)** (*b* Paris, 22 Dec 1883; *d* New York, 6 Nov 1965). American composer of French origin. He studied with d'Indy and Roussel at the Schola Cantorum in Paris (1904–5) and with Widor at the Conservatoire (1905). Late in 1907 he moved to Berlin, where he became a close acquaintance of Busoni and met Hofmannsthal and Strauss. When he returned to Paris in 1913, he left most of his manuscripts (including an opera) in Berlin, where they were destroyed in a warehouse fire. Though active in artistic circles he was unable to secure a permanent position and in 1915 emigrated to the USA.

In 1921 he and Carlos Salzedo founded the International Composers' Guild, which promoted important contemporary works. There followed a long stay in Paris (1928–33), where he was soon involved again in the artistic milieu. Several of his works were performed, but he also worked continuously on projects that came to nothing. Before leaving Paris again he tried to raise interest in a centre for electric-instrument research; his failure to obtain funds or facilities was the principal reason for the lengthy depression which caused him to stop composing for almost two decades (1936–53). During this time he taught sporadically. In 1953 he received, from an anonymous donor, an Ampex tape recorder, which enabled him to begin concrete work on the plans he had nurtured for 40 years.

The last years of Varèse's life brought him honour and renown; Boulez and Craft made recordings of his works, and performances became much more frequent. In terms of new compositions the period was less rich: he laboured with several projects on themes of night and death, but none of these was ever completed.

Varèse composed two operas, both of them early works which are now lost. As a schoolboy he wrote *Martin Pas* (*c*1895) for his friends, based on a story by Jules Verne and scored for boys' voices and mandolin. Between 1909 and 1913 in Berlin he set, with Hofmannsthal's permission, *Oedipus und die Sphinx*; this was the score destroyed by fire. Some 15 years later he also spent much time on a dramatic project, first mooted as *The One-all-alone* (1927), to a text by his wife Louise on an American Indian subject. This appears to have been transformed into *L'astronome* (1928–9), for which he sketched a scenario concerning an astronomer who makes contact with the inhabitants of a distant solar system, provokes the anger of the mob and is finally annihilated by the star's rays. He collaborated with several writers on this work, including Antonin Artaud, Carpentier, Desnos and Giono. The project was never completed and no music survives. Ultimately Varèse left only 12 self-sufficient compositions: pieces for large or chamber orchestra which make striking use of wind and percussion, and two of the first major works with sound on tape. PAUL GRIFFITHS

Varesi, Felice (*b* Calais, 1813; *d* Milan, 13 March 1889). Italian baritone. He made his début at Varese in 1834, and then sang at Faenza, Florence, Modena, Rome, Perugia and Genoa in Donizetti roles. He first appeared at La Scala in 1841 as Publius in Mercadante's *La vestale*, and then sang in Luigi Ricci's *Le nozze di Figaro* and the first performance of Federico Ricci's *Corrado d'Altamura*. From 1842 to 1847 he was a frequent visitor to the Kärntnertortheater, Vienna, where he created Antonio in Donizetti's *Linda di Chamounix* (1842) and also appeared in the same composer's *Alina, regina di Golconda* (1843), *Roberto Devereux* (1844) and *Maria Padilla* (1847). His first Verdi role was Don Carlo (*Ernani*), which he sang at Padua in 1844, and the following year he sang the Doge (*I due Foscari*) at Bergamo. In 1847 he created the title role of *Macbeth* at the Teatro alla Pergola, Florence. At the S Carlo, Naples, he sang Francesco (*I masnadieri*) and Alphonse in Donizetti's *La favorite*, and at the Argentina, Rome, he appeared as Malatesta (*Don Pasquale*). At La Fenice, Venice, he created the title role in *Rigoletto* (1851) and Germont in *La traviata* (1853). He sang in Madrid (1856–7) and was engaged at Her Majesty's Theatre, London, in 1864, making his début as Rigoletto. Varesi was a prototype of the dramatic baritone that evolved from the operas of Donizetti and of early- and middle-period Verdi. Though he made a powerful Macbeth, Rigoletto was undoubtedly his finest role.

Felice Varesi in the title role of Verdi's 'Rigoletto', which he created at La Fenice, Venice, in 1851

G. Cesari and A. Luzio, eds.: *I copialettere di Giuseppe Verdi* (Milan, 1913)

L. A. Garibaldi, ed.: *Giuseppe Verdi nelle lettere di Emanuele Muzio ad Antonio Barezzi* (Milan, 1931)

H. Weinstock: *Donizetti and the World of Opera in Italy, Paris and Vienna in the First Half of the 19th Century* (New York, 1963)

Bolletino [quadrimestriale] dell'Istituto di Studi Verdiani, iii, (1969–73)

J. Budden: *The Operas of Verdi*, i: *From 'Oberto' to 'Rigoletto'* (London, 1973) ELIZABETH FORBES

Variétés. Theatre opened in Paris in 1790, becoming in 1807 one of the four secondary theatres established in Paris by imperial decree; *see* PARIS, §4(vii).

Varischino, Giovanni (*fl* Venice, 1680–92). Italian composer. He composed two operas for Venice: *L'Odoacre* (N. Bonis; S Angelo, 1680; *I-Vnm*) and *L'amante fortunato per forza* (P. d'Averara; S Angelo, 29 November 1684; lost). They are his only known works apart from six MS cantatas (*A-Wn*) which may themselves be excerpts from operas.

The libretto of *L'Odoacre* describes Varischino as a nephew and pupil of Giovanni Legrenzi. The score shows the hand of a competent and at times graceful composer with no great fund of imagination. Most arias are written-out da capos with extended reprise, typical in form of the period *c*1675–85. A trumpet joins the string ensemble several times, as in the strikingly imitative opening symphony.

EitnerQ; *FétisB*
H. C. Wolff: *Die venezianische Oper in der zweiten Hälfte des 17. Jahrhunderts* (Berlin, 1937, 2/1975) THOMAS WALKER

Varna. City in Bulgaria. It is the largest Bulgarian port and resort city on the Black Sea coast. Once the ancient Greek colony of Odessos, Varna is the centre of operatic activity in north-eastern Bulgaria. The first performances of opera scenes date from the founding of a choir at St Michael's Church in 1893 and of the Gusla Music Society in 1899. In 1920, 1928 and 1930 attempts were made to organize a permanent theatre; from the period 1926–37 the first Bulgarian musical festivals began to be organized.

After the socialist revolution in 1944, Varna became the home of the Varnensko Lyato (Varna Summer), an international music festival. A symphony orchestra was founded in 1946, and the Varnenska Narodna Opera (Varna National Opera) in 1947, housed in the National Theatre. The first opera performance was Smetana's *The Bartered Bride*. The repertory is predominantly Italian and German, with special emphasis on Mozart and modern European and Bulgarian music (especially that of Parashkev Hadjiev). Operas staged for the first time in Bulgaria include *Così fan tutte*, Britten's *Albert Herring* and his version of *The Beggar's Opera*, *Il turco in Italia* and Prokofiev's *Betrothal in a Monastery*. The regular season starts in September and ends in August, with between four and eight new productions a year. The theatre, built by N. Lazarov in 1932 in a mainly classical style, holds about 600; it was renovated during the 1980s and reopened with *Die Zauberflöte* (1989). The company presents four opera performances weekly in addition to those staged as part of the summer festival.

R. Biks: *Balgarski operen teatr* [Bulgarian Opera Theatre] (Sofia, 1976–85) MAGDALENA MANOLOVA

Varnay, Astrid (Ibolyka Maria) (*b* Stockholm, 25 April 1918). American soprano of Swedish birth. Her family emigrated in 1920 to the USA, where she studied with Paul Althouse and Hermann Weigert. She made her début at the Metropolitan in 1941 as Sieglinde, a last-minute replacement for Lotte Lehmann; six days later she replaced Helen Traubel as Brünnhilde. She also sang Elsa, Elisabeth, and Telea in the première of Menotti's *The Island God*. In 1948 she attempted her first Italian roles (La Gioconda, Tosca, Aida, Santuzza) in Mexico City and made her European début at Covent Garden as the *Siegfried* Brünnhilde; she also sang Isolde and returned to London as a powerful Kostelnička. In 1951 she sang Lady Macbeth at the Florence Maggio Musicale and first appeared at Bayreuth, returning every year until 1967, as Brünnhilde, Isolde, Ortrud, Kundry and Senta. In the 1950s and 60s Varnay sang mostly in Munich, Düsseldorf, Berlin and Vienna. In 1959 she created Jocasta in Orff's *Oedipus der Tyrann* at Stuttgart. In 1962 she began to take mezzo roles, including Strauss's Herodias and Clytemnestra, Begbick (*Aufstieg und Fall der Stadt Mahagonny*) at the Metropolitan in 1979 and Claire (*Der Besuch der alten Dame*). Although her vocal technique was imperfect, her intense, passionate singing and committed acting made her a superb Wagnerian soprano.

B. W. Wessling: *Astrid Varnay* (Bremen, 1965) [with discography]
H. Rosenthal: *Great Singers of Today* (London, 1966)
R. Jacobson: 'Varnay Revisited', *ON*, xxxix/8 (1974–5), 24–6
A. Tubeuf: 'Astrid Varnay', *Le chant retrouvé* (Paris, 1979), 77–101
HAROLD ROSENTHAL/R

Varney, Louis (*b* New Orleans, 30 May 1844; *d* Paris, 20 Aug 1908). French composer. The son of Alphonse Varney, conductor at and sometime manager of the Bouffes-Parisiens, he followed his father into the theatre, becoming in 1876 musical director at the Athénée-Comique in Paris, where he conducted and supplied music for the theatre's productions. In 1880 Louis Cantin of the Bouffes-Parisiens commissioned a full-length work from him, to a libretto by Paul Ferrier and Jules Prével, and the resulting *opérette*, *Les mousquetaires au couvent*, proved an enormous success, hoisting the composer immediately to the top of his profession. It is a remarkable work, full of melodious and lilting numbers and featuring some fine ensembles. Hurriedly completed, with some assistance from the director of the Bouffes-Parisiens, Achille Mansour, it was revised for a second season and the role of Brissac, originally played by a singing actor, was rewritten with two added solos for a star baritone, 'Gris, je suis gris' and 'Pour faire un brave mousquetaire'; these proved to be the hits of what became the definitive, if dramatically lopsided, version.

Over the next 25 years, Varney composed nearly 40 *opérettes* of varying kinds without repeating the triumph of *Les mousquetaires*, but a good many of his pieces, including *Fanfan-la-tulipe* (1882), *Babolin* (1884), *Les petits mousquetaires* (1885), *L'amour mouillé* (1887) and *Dix jours aux Pyrénées* (1887), all written with Ferrier and/or Prével, and the later *La falote* (1896) and *Le papa de Francine* (1896) had initial successful runs in Paris. *Les mousquetaires au couvent* and *L'amour mouillé* won some success outside France, but although several of his works have been revived in France, only *Les mousquetaires* has survived in the repertory.

Varney was a bright-hearted and extremely melodious composer, particularly in his earliest years, and his best works profited from stronger librettos than was often the case. *Les mousquetaires* well deserves its place among the most enjoyable *opérettes* of its time. He also wrote ballets, pantomimes, revues and dance music.

all opérettes, first performed in Paris unless otherwise stated; most published (vocal score) in Paris at the time of the first performance

PBP – *Paris, Bouffes-Parisiens* PC – *Paris, Théâtre de Cluny*
PFD – *Paris, Folies-Dramatiques* PV – *Paris, Théâtre des Variétés*

Il signor Pulcinella (4, L. Beauvallet and M. S. Leprévost), Athénée, Sept 1876; Les mousquetaires au couvent (3, P. Ferrier and J. Prével, after V. de Saint-Hilaire and P. Duport: *L'habit ne fait pas le moine*), PBP, 16 March 1880; La reine des Halles (3, A. Delacour, V. Bernard and P. Burani), Comédie-Parisienne, 4 April 1881; Coquelicot (3, A. Silvestre), PBP, 2 March 1882; Fanfan-la-tulipe (3, Ferrier and Prével), PFD, 21 Aug or Oct 1882

La petite reinette (3, W. Busnach and C. Clairville), Brussels, Galeries St Hubert, 11 Oct 1882; Joséphine (1, A. Millaud), Trouville, Casino, Aug 1883; Babolin (3, Ferrier and Prével), Nouveautés, 19 March 1884; Les petits mousquetaires (3, Ferrier and Prével), PFD, 5 March 1885; L'amour mouillé (3, Prével and A. Liorat), Nouveautés, 25 Jan 1887; Dix jours aux Pyrénées (5, Ferrier), Gaîté, 22 Nov 1887; Divorcée (1, R. Toché), Cabourg, 11 Aug 1888

La japonaise (3, Millaud and E. de Najac), PV, 23 Nov 1888; La Vénus d'Arles (3, Ferrier and Liorat), Nouveautés, 30 Jan 1889;

Riquet à la houppe (3, Ferrier and Clairville), PFD, 20 April 1889; La fée aux chèvres (3, Ferrier and A. Vanloo), Gaîté, 18 or 19 Dec 1890; La fille de Fanchon la vielleuse (3, Liorat, Busnach and A. Fonteny), PFD, 3 Nov 1891; La femme de Narcisse (3, F. Carré), Renaissance, 11 or 14 April 1892

Le brillant Achille (3, Clairville and F. Beissier), Renaissance, 21 Oct 1892; Miss Robinson (3, Ferrier), PFD, 17 Dec 1892; Cliquette (3, Clairville and Busnach), PFD, 11 July 1893; Les forains (3, M. Boucheron and A. Mars), PBP, 9 Feb 1894; La fille de Paillasse (3, Liorat and L. Leloir), PFD, 20 April 1894; Les petites Brebis (2, Liorat), PC, 5 June 1895; Mam'zelle Bémol (4, A. Delilia and H. Raymond), PC, 7 Sept 1895

La belle épicière (3, P. Decourcelle and H. Kéroul), PBP, 16 Nov 1895; La falote (3, Liorat and M. Ordonneau), PFD, 16 or 17 April 1896; Le papa de Francine (4, V. de Cottens and P. Gavault), PC, 5 Nov 1896; Le pompier de service (4, de Cottens and Gavault), PV, 18 Feb 1897; Pour sa couronne (1, A. Fordyce), PBP, 17 April 1897; Les demoiselles des Saint-Cyriens (3, Gavault and de Cottens), PC, 28 Jan 1898; La tour de bois (2, J. Oudot and H. de Gorsse), PV, 3 June 1898

Les petites Barnett (3, Gavault), PV, 8 Nov 1898; La fiancée de Thylda (3, de Cottens and R. Charvay), PC, 26 Jan 1900; Frégolinette (1, de Cottens), Mathurins, 25 April 1900; Mademoiselle George (3, de Cottens and P. Véber), PV, 2 Dec 1900; Princesse Bébé (3, Decourcelle and G. Berr), PC, 18 April 1902; Le chien du régiment (4, Decourcelle), Gaîté, 24 Dec 1902; L'âge d'or (3, G. Feydeau and M. Desvallières), PV, 1 May 1905

*

R. Traubner: *Operetta: a Theatrical History* (New York, 1983)

KURT GÄNZL (text), ANDREW LAMB (work-list)

Varona, José Luciano (*b* Mendoza, 14 Aug 1930). Argentine stage and costume designer. After studying at the Escuela Superior de Bellas Artes in Buenos Aires, he made his operatic début at the Teatro Colón in 1959 with designs for *The Love for Three Oranges*. He began working with Tito Capobianco, director of the Colón, in 1961 with *L'italiana in Algeri*, and went to the USA in 1962. Then began a long, successful association with Capobianco and the New York City Opera, with costumes for *Giulio Cesare* (1966), *The Golden Cockerel* (1967), *Manon* (1968), *Lucia di Lammermoor* (1969) and the 'Tudor Ring' – Donizetti's *Roberto Devereux* (1970), *Maria Stuarda* (1972) and *Anna Bolena* (1973). He also designed Handel's *Ariodante* for the opening of the Kennedy Center in Washington, DC, in 1971.

After designing *Norma* for the San Francisco Opera's 50th-anniversary season (1972), he created for the Vancouver Opera Association a sumptuous *Lucrezia Borgia* (1973) and an *art nouveau Merry Widow* (1976). He also designed Capobianco's production of *Les contes d'Hoffmann* (1974); it was a spectacular success. West Berlin audiences, however, were shocked by the 'old-fashioned' Capobianco-Varona productions of *Attila* in 1971 and *Aida* in 1972, and audiences in the Netherlands were unimpressed with *Rodelinda* in 1973 and *La traviata* in 1974.

During the 1980s Varona worked mostly with the Teatro Colón, designing lavish productions of *Roméo et Juliette* (1981), *Zauberflöte* (1983) for Margherita Wallmann, *Carmen* (1985) and *Entführung* (1988). His designs are notable for their visual appeal and authenticity more than for their innovation. His distinctive Latin American perspective is realized most fully in his many Baroque productions. DAVID J. HOUGH

Varviso, Silvio (*b* Zürich, 26 Feb 1924). Swiss conductor. The son of a singing teacher, he studied in Zürich and began his career as an accompanist, making his conducting début in *Die Zauberflöte* at St Gall in 1944. He worked at the Basle Opera, 1950–62 (music director from 1956), made débuts at Berlin and Paris in 1958, and with the San Francisco Opera in 1959; there, the next year, he conducted the first American production of Britten's *A Midsummer Night's Dream*. He made his Metropolitan début in 1961 with *Lucia di Lammermoor* and was frequently engaged there subsequently. His British début was at Glyndebourne in 1962 with *Le nozze di Figaro*, and his Covent Garden début followed with *Der Rosenkavalier* later the same year; he returned often in operas ranging from *La bohème* and *Arabella* to *Lohengrin* and *Pelléas et Mélisande*.

Varviso was music director of the Stockholm Royal Opera, 1965–71 (with the title of Court conductor from 1970), and became a frequent guest at the Vienna Staatsoper, the Bayerische Staatsoper in Munich and the Hamburg Staatsoper. His first appearance at Bayreuth was in *Der fliegende Holländer* in 1969; his conducting of *Meistersinger* there in 1974 was issued as a live recording. He was music director at the Stuttgart Staatsoper (1972–80) and at the Paris Opéra (1980–85). In 1989 he conducted *Rigoletto* with West Berlin Opera at Wiesbaden. He continued active into the 1990s as a conductor of buoyant sensitivity in the Italian repertory, and of expressive character and zestful clarity in Mozart, Wagner and Strauss. His other recordings include *L'italiana in Algeri* (1963) and *Il barbiere di Siviglia* (1964), both with Berganza; *Norma* (1967) and *Anna Bolena* (1970), both with Souliotis, and several discs of operatic arias, choruses and interludes. NOËL GOODWIN

Vasilenko, Sergey Nikiforovich (*b* Moscow, 18/30 March 1872; *d* Moscow, 11 March 1956). Russian composer. He began systematic music studies in 1888, taking lessons with Richard Nokh, then with Grechaninov and others. From 1891 to 1896 he studied law at Moscow University and attended the conservatory (1895–1901), where he was a pupil of Taneyev and Ippolitov-Ivanov. He conducted at the Mamontov Private Opera, Moscow, 1903–5, and from 1907 organized and conducted the Historic Concerts in Moscow; in 1925 he helped organize music broadcasting there. He taught orchestration and composition at the Moscow Conservatory (1906–41, 1943–56). In 1939 he worked in Tashkent on *Buran*, the first Uzbek opera.

Vasilenko's early works reflect his enthusiasm for Russian folk music, *kryuk* (neume notation) and Old Believer song. After 1906 he produced orchestral works and songs that show a connection with Russian symbolist poetry, and between 1910 and 1920 he was attracted by eastern exoticism; an interest in oriental folk music, particularly that of central Asia, remained with him in the post-revolutionary period. His music is distinguished by masterly orchestration.

Skazaniye o grade velikom Kitezhe i tikhom ozere Svetoyare [Legend of the Great City of Kitezh and the Quiet Lake Svetoyar] (op-cantata, 1, N. Manïkin-Nevstroyev), concert perf., Moscow, 16 Feb/1 March 1902; stage, Moscow, 2/15 April 1903, vs (Moscow, 1902)

Sïn solntsa [Son of the Sun] op.62 (4, M. Gal'perin), Moscow, Bol'shoy, 23 May 1929, vs (Moscow, 1930)

Khristofor Kolumb op.80, 1933 (4, A. Argo and S. Antimonov), concert perf., extracts, Moscow, Actors' House, 28 Jan 1939, unpubd

Buran (4, K. Yashen), Tashkent, 12 June 1939, aria (Tashkent, 1950); collab. M. Ashrafi

Velikiy kanal [The Grand Canal] (4, Yashen and M. Rakhmanov), Tashkent, 12 Jan 1941, unpubd, collab. Ashrafi
Suvorov op.101 (4, S. Krzhizhanovsky), Sverdlovsk, 21 Feb 1942; Moscow, Stanislavsky–Nemirovich-Danchenko Music Theatre, 23 Feb 1942, aria (Moscow, 1952), aria (Moscow, 1962)

*

ME (G. Polyanovsky)
G. Polyanovsky: *S. N. Vasilenko: zhizn' i tvorchestvo* [Vasilenko: Life and Work] (Moscow, 1964), 104–42
Notograficheskiy sprarochnik: S. N. Vasilenko (Moscow, 1973)
S. N. Vasilenko: *Vospominaniya* [Memoirs] (Moscow, 1979)

INNA BARSOVA

Vasilyev [Kyrilov], **Vladimir** (*b* St Petersburg, 1828; *d* St Petersburg, 24 Aug/6 Sept 1900). Russian bass. He studied in St Petersburg, where he made his début in 1856 at the Bol'shoy. In 1860 he was engaged at the Mariinsky, where he sang in the première of Serov's *Rogneda* (1865), created Pimen in *Boris Godunov* (1874), Prince Zhemchuzhny in *Oprichnik* (1874) and the King in *The Maid of Orléans* (1881). His repertory included Ivan Susanin, Leporello and Bertram (*Robert le diable*). He retired in 1881. ELIZABETH FORBES

Vasoli, Pietro (*fl* Milan, 1812–14). Italian bass. He took part in three premières of Rossini operas at La Scala: as Pacuvio in *La pietra del paragone* (1812), as Licinius in *Aureliano in Palmira* (1813) and as Prosdocimo in *Il turco in Italia* (1814). Apart from an unflattering reference by Stendhal, who heard him in 1812, nothing else is known about this 'ex-grenadier of Napoleon's army in Egypt'. ELIZABETH FORBES

Vasseur, Léon (Félix Augustin Joseph) (*b* Bapaume, Pas-de-Calais, 28 May 1844; *d* Paris, 25 May 1917). French composer. The son of an organist, he moved to Paris at the age of 12 to study at the Ecole Niedermeyer and began his musical career at 20 as organist at Saint-Symphorien, Versailles. In 1872 his first *opérette*, *Un fi, deux fi, trois figurants*, was produced at L'Alcazar, and shortly afterwards his *La timbale d'argent*, hastily written to a libretto by Jaime and Noriac to fill a gap at the Bouffes-Parisiens, proved an enormous success. Its success in other countries was limited because of its risqué libretto, but it established Vasseur's popularity in France. It remained his most successful piece, even though *La cruche cassée* (1875), *Le droit du seigneur* (1878), *Le billet de logement* (1879) and his pasticcio *Le voyage de Suzette* (1890) had good runs in Paris, and others, including *La famille Trouillat* (1874), *La blanchisseuse de Berg-op-Zoom* (1875) and *Madame Cartouche* (1886), won foreign productions.

In the 1880s and 90s Vasseur began to write for the spectacular productions and 'comedies with music' that were challenging the established *opérette* style. He became conductor at the Folies Bergère in 1890 but in 1897 retired from the theatrical scene where his attractive if unexceptional style of light music was finding little acceptance.

opérettes, first performed in Paris unless otherwise stated; most published (vocal score) in Paris at the time of first performance

PBP – *Paris, Bouffes-Parisiens* PFD – *Paris, Folies Dramatiques* PFP – *Paris, Fantasies-Parisiennes*

Un fi, deux fi, trois figurants (1), Alcazar, 1 April 1872; La timbale d'argent (3, L.-A. Jaime and J. Noriac), PBP, 9 April 1872; Mon mouchoir (1, Jaime), PBP, 9 May 1872; La petite reine (3, Jaime and Noriac), PBP, 9 Jan 1873; Le grelot (1, V. Bernard and E. Grangé), PBP, 20 May 1873; Le roi d'Yvetot (3, H. Chabrillat and E. Hemery), Brussels, 25 Oct 1873; Les parisiennes (4, J. Moinaux and V. Koning), PBP, 20 March 1874; La famille Trouillat ou La rosière d'Honfleur (3, H.-J. Crémieux and E. Blum), PFD, 10 Sept 1874; La blanchisseuse de Berg-op-Zoom (3, H. C. Chivot and A. Duru), PFD, 17 Jan 1875
La cruche cassée (3, Noriac and Moinaux), Taitbout, 27 Oct 1875; La Sorrentine (3, Moinaux and Noriac), PBP, 24 March 1876; L'Opoponax (1, W. Busnach and C. Nuitter), PBP, 2 May 1877; Le droit du seigneur (3, P. Burani and M. Boucheron), PFP, 13 Dec 1878; Le billet de logement (3, Burani and Boucheron), PFP, 15 Nov 1879; Le petit Parisien (3, Burani and Boucheron), PFP, 16 Jan 1882; Royal amour (1, Lagrange and C. de Tragoff), PFD, 1 Nov 1884; Le mariage au tambour (3, Burani, after A. Dumas *père*, de Leuven and Brunswick), Châtelet, 4 April 1886
La brasserie (ballet-pantomime, 1, C. Narrey), Eden, 18 Sept 1886; Madame Cartouche (3, P. Decourcelle and Busnach), PFD, 19 Oct 1886; Ninon de Lenclos (3, E. Blavet and Burani), Nouveautés, 23 Oct 1887; Mam'zelle Crénom (3, Jaime and P. Duval), PBP, 19 Jan 1888; Le prince soleil (4, H. Raymond and Burani), Châtelet, 27 Jan 1889; Le voyage de Suzette (3, Chivot and Duru), 1890; La famille Vénus (3, Clairville and R. Bénédite), Renaissance, 2 May 1891; Le pays de l'or (3, Chivot and A. Vanloo), Gaîté, 20 Jan 1892
Le commandant Laripète (A. Silvestre, Burani and A. Valabrigue), Nouveautés, 3 March 1892; La prétentaine (4, P. Ferrier and Bénédite), Nouveau, 10 Oct 1893; Au premier hussard (1, M. Ordonneau), St Malo, 6 Aug 1896 [? first perf. 1883]; Le royaume d'Hercule (1, C. Guinel and R. Dubreuil), Cigale, 20 Nov 1896; Au chat qui pelote (1, Oudot and H. de Gorsse), Scala, 28 Aug 1897; La souris blanche (3, Chivot and Duru), Déjazet, 9 Nov 1897, collab. de Thuisy; Dans la plume (1, Kok), Eldorado, 17 Oct 1898 ANDREW LAMB

Vasson, Pierre. *See* VACHON, PIERRE.

Vaucorbeil, Auguste Emmanuel (*b* Rouen, 15 Dec 1821; *d* Paris, 2 Nov 1884). French theatre administrator and composer. He was the son of a famous French actor known as Ferville. He entered the Paris Conservatoire in 1835, studied under Marmontel, Victor-Charles-Paul Dourlen and Cherubini and took the *second prix* for solfège in 1838. In 1871 he became professor of vocal ensemble at the Conservatoire, in 1872 government commissioner of subsidized theatres, in 1878 Inspector General for the Arts, and from 1879 director of the Opéra. Works seen there for the first time during his term of office included *Aida*, Gounod's *Le tribut de Zamora*, Thomas' *Françoise de Rimini* and Saint-Saëns' *Henri VIII*.

His compositions included the *opéra comique Bataille d'amour* (Paris, Opéra-Comique, Salle Favart, 13 April 1863), the *scène lyrique La mort de Diane* (performed at the Conservatoire by Gabrielle Krauss in 1870), the opera *Mahomet* (of which only a few excerpts were performed), songs and orchestral and chamber music.

ANDREW LAMB

Vaudeville (i) (Fr.). A French song in popular, often dance-like, style and usually in strophic form with texts frequently comic, epigrammatic or satirical; by extension, a French stage work with spoken dialogue and primarily or exclusively using pre-existing tunes (which may be newly arranged or adapted).

Developing from the traditions of the Renaissance *vau de vire* and *voix de ville*, the vaudeville became the favourite vehicle for satire (as in the *mazarinades* hostile to Cardinal Mazarin, first minister of Louis XIV), social and political commentary (as in the repertory of street singers during the Revolution) and witty entertainment (as in 19th-century singing societies). Often authors expected their audiences to recognize the tune and remember its original text (identified by its incipit or refrain, known as a *timbre*) in order to interpret fully the meaning of the new one. Occasionally a vaudeville

Scene from 'Annette et Lubin' by Charles-Simon Favart and others (1762): engraving by De Bucourt after his own original

became so popular that it was later used as the reference in other vaudevilles (a *faux timbre*). As with the folk-song, oral transmission played an important role in the dissemination of the vaudeville.

The earliest example of a stage work making extensive use of existing songs is *La comédie en chansons* by C. de Beys (1640): it was in fact an experiment in which the author fashioned a play by quoting songs, changing the words as little as possible. Music, however, has a limited place; it is most prominent in a serenade scene where Beys specified the tune to be used to a new text. The arrival of the *comédiens italiens* in 1680 marked the true beginning of the vaudeville as a popular form of entertainment. Gherardi's selections of their French repertory show an increasing use of music. Among the few *airs* in *Arlequin Mercure galant* (1682) is one to a tune by Lully (whose operas subsequently became a major source for vaudevilles). In 1697, just before their expulsion from France, the *comédiens* presented *Les fées, ou Les contes de ma mère l'oye* (1697), in which the role of music is more extensive, particularly in scenes of magic. Then the Fair Theatres (*see* PARIS, §2(iii)) took up this now popular form and gave a much more substantial place to the *airs* – much to the annoyance of the Académie Royale de Musique, which soon had the right to sing on stage forbidden to the Fair Theatres as an infringement of its monopoly. They retaliated by displaying the text on rolls or placards while the orchestra played, thus inviting the audience to sing along (helped by the placing of actors among the public). Soon, in return for an annual fee to the Académie, the Opéra-Comique received permission to use singing actors. Not only were the Fair Theatres successful, but a significant part of their repertory was made up of parodies of the works at the Académie and the Comédie-Française or more general attacks on the rival theatres, witty and often malign critiques not always accepted with good grace by the authors of the originals or their institutions (as in *L'Opéra-Comique assiégé* by A.-R. Le Sage and D'Orneval, which commented vigorously on a current lawsuit filed by the Comédie-Française, performed at the Foire St Germain, 1730). Works set in exotic or mythical places were also favourites. Le Sage's *Arlequin, roi de Sérendib* (Foire St Germain, 1713), entirely made up of short vaudevilles, is a fine example. In general, slapstick and sexual innuendo were important ingredients of the humour.

With very few exceptions, *opéras comiques* in 18th-century terminology were, in fact, *opéras comiques en vaudevilles* (e.g. C.-S. Favart's very popular *Acajou*, 1744). In the mid-century there were two dominant trends: sentimental village love (e.g. Favart's *Les amours champêtres*, 1751; and *Annette et Lubin*, 1762) and *poissard*, caricatures of lower-class Parisians (e.g. Vadé's *Les raccoleurs*, 1756). Parodies and fairy-tales remained popular. With Favart the tone of the vaudeville became less vulgar, more moralizing. After the middle of the century (and the Querelle des Bouffons), works with newly composed music, *comédies mêlées d'ariettes*, began to dominate the repertory of the Comédie-Italienne (which had absorbed the Opéra-Comique in 1762); by the time of the Revolution vaudevilles had become rare there and they had virtually disappeared by the time of the Empire (except for an occasional *pièce de circonstance*).

But the genre continued to flourish at the Théâtre du Vaudeville (founded in 1792 by two prolific authors, J. de Piis and P.-I. Barré), the Ambigu-Comique and other smaller theatres of the boulevards and the Palais Royal. A variety of phrases replaced *opéra comique en vaudevilles*: *comédie-vaudeville*, *pièce mêlée de vaudevilles*, *comédie en vaudevilles* and so on. As well as traditional songs, the Opéra-Comique's 18th-century repertory became an important musical source. While the *féerie* and *arlequinade* declined in popularity, parodies, dramatizations of anecdotes, stories set in exotic places and *pièces de circonstance* remained staples. Eugène Scribe, among many others, achieved early dramatic successes with his vaudevilles (such as *L'ours et le pacha*, 1820, an oriental fantasy with an outlandish plot) and continued to write them throughout his career, even after the popularity of his *grand opéra* librettos.

Stock figures (like the grotesque Mme Angot, a fishwife who wants a dissolute chevalier for a son-in-law rather than an honest worker), burlesque situations (travesties and mistaken identities are common) and frank humour appealed to audiences. The element of caricature was strong. Social critique (often in an anti-bourgeois vein) and political commentary – sometimes tolerated by the censors in this genre, considered a 'frivolous' one, when forbidden in 'higher' theatre – were important ingredients in some works, while others sought only to entertain.

About 1860–70 the vaudeville lost its music. The term came to be applied to theatre works whose plots are lighthearted and rapid and whose comedy relies on witty dialogue. The prime examples are in the works of Georges Feydeau (e.g. *La dame de chez Maxim*, 1899). Among 20th-century authors Louis Verneuil (who also wrote for Broadway) was one of the most popular. The technique of forming an evening's entertainment on songs, some re-using familiar tunes or tunes written in similar style, survives in the *café-concert*.

*

Grove6 (C. Barnes)
E. Gherardi, ed.: *Le théâtre italien, ou Le recueil de toutes les scènes*

françoises qui ont esté jouées sur le théâtre italien de l'hôtel de Bourgogne (Paris, 1694, 2/1695)
——: *Le théâtre italien, ou Le recueil général de toutes les comédies et scènes françoises jouées par les comédiens italiens du Roy* (Paris, 1700)
A.-R. Le Sage and D'Orneval, eds.: *Le théâtre de la foire, ou L'opéra comique contenant les meilleures pièces qui ont été représentées aux foires de S. Germain et de S. Laurent* (Paris, 1721–37)
C. Parfaict and F. Parfaict: *Mémoires pour servir à l'histoire des spectacles de la foire* (Paris, 1743)
L. de Jaucourt: 'Vaudeville', *Encyclopédie, ou Dictionnaire raisonné des sciences, des arts et des métiers*, ed. D. Diderot and others (Paris, 1751–80)
J.-J. Rousseau: 'Couplets', 'Vaudeville', *Dictionnaire de musique* (Paris, 1768)
P. J. B. Nougaret: *De l'art du théâtre* (Paris, 1769)
P. Capelle: *La clé du caveau* (Paris, 1811)
J. Doche: *La musette du vaudeville* (Paris, 1822)
E. Campardon: *Les spectacles de la foire* (Paris, 1877)
J. Tiersot: *Histoire de la chanson populaire en France* (Paris, 1889)
A. Font: *Favart, l'opéra-comique et la comédie vaudeville aux XVIIe et XVIIIe siècles* (Paris, 1894)
M. Albert: *Les théâtres de la foire (1660–1789)* (Paris, 1900)
——: *Les théâtres des boulevards (1789–1848)* (Paris, 1902)
C. Pierre: *Les hymnes et chansons de la Révolution: aperçu général et catalogue* (Paris, 1904)
G. Cucuel: *Les créateurs de l'opéra-comique français* (Paris, 1914)
F. J. Carmody: *Le répertoire de l'opéra-comique en vaudevilles de 1708 à 1764* (Berkeley, 1933)
D. J. Grout: *The Origin of the Opéra-Comique* (diss., Harvard U., 1939)
C. R. Barnes: *The 'Théâtre de la Foire' (Paris, 1697–1762): its Music and Composers* (diss., U. of Southern California, 1965)
N. Wild: 'Aspects de la musique sous la Régence: les foires, naissance de l'opéra-comique', *RMFC*, v (1965), 129–41
C. R. Barnes: 'Vocal Music at the "Théâtres de la foire"', *RMFC*, viii (1968), 141–60
D. S. Packer: '"La Calotte" and the Eighteenth-Century French Vaudeville', *JAMS*, xxiii (1970), 61–83
A. Verchaly and M. Honegger: 'Vaudeville', *Dictionnaire de la musique: science de la musique*, ed. M. Honegger (Paris, 1976)
L. Matthes: *Vaudeville: Untersuchungen zu Geschichte und literatursystematischem Ort einer Erfolgsgattung* (Heidelberg, 1983)
C. Pré: *Le livret d'opéra-comique en France de 1741 à 1789* (diss., U. of Lille III, 1984)
M. M. Root-Bernstein: *Boulevard Theater and Revolution in Eighteenth-Century Paris* (Ann Arbor, 1984)
H. Gidel: *Le vaudeville* (Paris, 1986)
R. M. Isherwood: *Farce and Fantasy: Popular Entertainment in Eighteenth-Century Paris* (New York and Oxford, 1986)

M. ELIZABETH C. BARTLET

Vaudeville (ii). Theatre founded in Paris in 1792, becoming in 1807 one of the four secondary theatres established in Paris by imperial decree; *see* PARIS, §4(vii).

Vaudeville final (Fr.). A type of finale used originally in French vaudevilles and some *opéras comiques*, and later more widely: it is in strophic form and most often has verses of seven or eight relatively short lines with a refrain in which all may join. Generally different characters take turns. The first verse sums up the moral of the work, subsequent ones frequently refer to key moments in the plot and point to the character's sentiments or reform because of the action, and the final one is traditionally a compliment to the public, asking their indulgence. The works of Favart and other authors for the Fair Theatres, Opéra-Comique and Comédie-Italienne offer numerous examples of this classic format during the 18th century. The repertory of several boulevard theatres continued this tradition into the first decades of the 19th century.

In vaudevilles, pre-existing tunes were most often used, but occasionally the theatre's resident composer (who was usually a violinist in the orchestra and responsible for arrangements and revisions of *airs*) would write a new setting, although his contribution might remain unacknowledged publicly. In *opéras comiques* of the mid-18th century composers wrote new music but deliberately imitated the style and spirit of the model and labelled the piece 'vaudeville'. Philidor's 'Ne donnons jamais à nos femmes' (the *vaudeville final* in *Les femmes vengées*, libretto by Sedaine, 1775) is typical. The moral of the opera is to beware the dangers of jealousy and false assumptions and to practise tolerance: 'don't look too closely' is the refrain. A simple melody in duple metre has a folklike quality. A largely three-part string accompaniment is entirely subordinate to the voice. Subsequent verses cite examples of foibles forgiven, and finally there is a plea to the public to remember the moral as they judge the work. Philidor's treatment differs from the standard one only in his repetition of the text of the first verse in a new, more extended setting to bring his opera to a more impressive close than a straightforward vaudeville would permit. Associated with broad comedy, the *vaudeville final* gradually went out of fashion during the reign of Louis XVI, when sentimental and *drame*-influenced works increased in popularity; they were rare at the Comédie-Italienne (from 1793 on called the Opéra-Comique) after the Revolution. (Then and later the custom was to conclude with a brief chorus of all characters; occasionally one-act works have a longer ensemble containing the plot's denouement.)

The *vaudeville final* is rarely found in works for the Académie Royale de Musique and the Comédie-Française, and the few examples are in comedies: J.-J. Rousseau's *Le devin du village* (1752) at the former and Beaumarchais' *Le mariage de Figaro* (1784) at the latter are representative of these exceptions.

The idea of the *vaudeville final* was borrowed for other, non-French works. Familiar examples are Gluck's *Orfeo ed Euridice* (1762) and Mozart's *Die Entführung aus dem Serail* (1782) – in each of which one verse differs musically from the others, in *Die Entführung* conspicuously and comically so, to point up that one of the characters (Osmin) remains unaffected by any moral expounded in the opera. Later examples include Rossini's *Il barbiere di Siviglia* (1816), Verdi's *Falstaff* (1893), Ravel's *L'heure espagnole* (1911) and Stravinsky's *The Rake's Progress* (1951).

M. ELIZABETH C. BARTLET

Vaughan, Denis (Edward) (*b* Melbourne, 6 June 1926). Australian conductor and musicologist. He studied in Melbourne and London, where he made his conducting début in 1953 as assistant to Beecham with the RPO, and worked with Knappertsbusch at Bayreuth. As a scholar he became absorbed by textual inaccuracies between autograph and published texts of operas by Verdi and Puccini, and was drawn into dispute with the Ricordi publishing house. He published papers on Verdi (*La Scala*, no.104, 1958, pp.11–15, 71–2) and on Puccini's orchestration (*PRMA*, lxxxvii, 1960–61, pp.1–14), and the article '"Tradition" in Verdi and Puccini' (*Opera*, xii, 1961, pp.301–5). He became adviser to UNESCO on musical copyright and its abuses (1962–7) and was largely responsible for the 1967 Stockholm revision of the Berne International Copyright Convention.

Vaughan was music director for the Elizabethan Trust Opera Company, Sydney, in 1966, and in the 1970s he worked at the Munich and Hamburg opera houses. He returned to Australia as music director of the State Opera of South Australia at Adelaide (1981–4), where his repertory included Musgrave's *A Christmas Carol* (1981) and Janáček's *The Makropulos Affair* (with Söderström, 1982). His American opera début was with *I Capuleti e i Montecchi* at the Juilliard American Opera Center, New York (1983), in an edition based on his own research. Besides numerous orchestral works he recorded Mozart's *Il re pastore* (1967).

NOËL GOODWIN

Vaughan, Elizabeth (*b* Llanfyllin, Montgomeryshire, 12 March 1937). Welsh soprano. She studied with Olive Groves at the RAM. In 1960 she first appeared as Abigaille in *Nabucco* with the WNO: her success led to her joining the Royal Opera. Her many Covent Garden roles since 1961 have included Mimì, Liù, Britten's Tytania, Teresa (*Benvenuto Cellini*), and both Andromache and Hecuba (Tippett's *King Priam*). She has also sung with the ENO, notably as Penelope Rich in *Gloriana* (1984) and as Fidelio. Above all in Verdi roles – Gilda, Violetta, Amelia (*Simon Boccanegra*), a brilliant Abigaille (1973) – her lyric soprano has most happily displayed its rhythmic vitality, flexibility and reserves of power; and although her vibrant tone sometimes lacks sweetness her phrasing is always musically sensitive. A diminutive figure lends credibility to her touching Butterfly, seen with the ENO and in Johannesburg, Vienna and Montreal. She made her Metropolitan début as Donna Elvira (1972). In the 1980s she took on mezzo roles such as Laura (*La Gioconda*) and Herodias, which she sang with Scottish Opera in 1990.

MAX LOPPERT

Vaughan Williams, Ralph (*b* Down Ampney, Gloucs., 12 Oct 1872; *d* London, 26 Aug 1958). English composer. He was educated at Charterhouse and the RCM, where his teachers included Parry and Stanford. He then read history at Trinity College, Cambridge, and returned to the RCM as Stanford's pupil, remaining until 1897. In 1903 Vaughan Williams responded to Cecil Sharp's call for a concerted effort to collect English folksongs: during the next decade he collected over 800 songs and variants. From 1904 to 1906 he edited the music of *The English Hymnal* and in 1908, dissatisfied with his compositions, went to Paris for three months of intensive study with Ravel. On his return, he began to compose in an individual style and moved rapidly to the forefront of composers of the post-Elgar generation.

Although primarily regarded as a symphonist and composer of choral works, film music, church music and songs, Vaughan Williams wrote five operas and left one unfinished. As a child he wrote operas for his toy theatre and when he was 17 went for his summer holidays to Munich, where he heard *Die Walküre* and became a lifelong Wagnerian. He spent his honeymoon in Berlin the following year so that he could attend *Der Ring des Nibelungen*. Stanford, who had wanted him to go to Italy to hear opera in Milan, and whose operas had been taken up in Germany, was undoubtedly responsible for the ambition to compose operas that was shared by his pupils Vaughan Williams, Gustav Holst and Rutland Boughton. With Joseph Holbrooke, they alone of their generation had any abiding interest in the stage.

Operatic outlets for a struggling young English composer at the beginning of the 20th century were virtually non-existent, so Vaughan Williams's first musical connections with the stage were through the medium of incidental music for plays, notably for the Cambridge Greek Play of 1909, *The Wasps* of Aristophanes. In 1913 he was director of music for Frank Benson's company at the Stratford-upon-Avon Shakespeare Festival, arranging music for five of the historical plays and for Bernard Shaw's *The Devil's Disciple*. By this date he was already far into the composition of his first opera, *Hugh the Drover*. In 1910, saying he wanted 'to set a prize fight to music', he was put in touch with Harold Child, a leader-writer on *The Times*, to whom he outlined his ideas for an English *Bartered Bride*. The result was a love story set in a Cotswold village during the Napoleonic wars (and it does contain a prize fight). Most of the music was composed contemporaneously with *A London Symphony* and both works reflect the nationalism expressed in his 1912 article 'Who Wants the English Composer?': 'Have we not all about us forms of musical expression which we can take and purify and raise to the level of great art ... the children dancing to a barrel-organ ... the cries of the street pedlars ... ?'.

In the case of *Hugh the Drover*, it was the salesmen's cries at a village fair, a ballad-seller's song and the singing of the villagers as they went a-maying in the dawn that became the 'forms of musical expression' to be 'purified'. Several folksongs are quoted in the score, and there are songs, such as 'Cold blows the wind in Cotsall', which sound like folksongs but are original compositions. The score is unpretentious, fresh and lyrical, with a Puccinian warmth in the love duet that will surprise only those who do not know some of Vaughan Williams's early songs, with their deep Romanticism. The opera was completed in August 1914, but was laid aside when Vaughan Williams joined the army and was not performed until 1924.

After the experiences of the war, Vaughan Williams never attempted to recapture the early-morning dew of his ballad opera and his most picturesque symphony. They belonged, it seemed, to a vanished age – what Wilfrid Mellers has called Vaughan Williams's 'vision of Albion' – which is part, now, of their claim on our affections. He began to think about writing another opera in 1924, whether spurred by the production of *Hugh the Drover* or by his friend Holst's work on *At the Boar's Head* we do not know. At any rate, he drew his own Falstaff libretto from Shakespeare's *The Merry Wives of Windsor* and called the resulting opera *Sir John in Love*. Like Holst, he used English folktunes in the texture of the music, the most famous being 'Greensleeves' which, as sung by Mistress Ford in Act 3, is the opera's 'hit number'. Altogether ten folksongs are quoted in the score; and lyrics from other Shakespeare plays and Elizabethan poets are interpolated into the libretto.

The score of *Sir John in Love* is a rich compendium of the main stylistic threads in Vaughan Williams's music between 1925 and 1935. Some of the hieratic splendour of the oratorio *Sancta civitas* is there, together with foreshadowings of the Scherzo of the Fourth Symphony and of the luminous beauty of the Fifth (begun in 1938). The word-setting is fluent and often so natural that one scarcely notices it. This is particularly true of the recitatives in Act 2 which remind us that in 1925, while at work on *Sir John in Love*, Vaughan Williams also began his one-act setting of J. M. Synge's play about Irish fisherfolk, *Riders to the Sea*. Together with the masque for dancing, *Job* (1927–30), this is Vaughan Williams's masterpiece for the stage. The text is set almost verbatim and the story of the woman Maurya who has lost all her sons and male relatives to the sea has an element of Greek tragedy. The vocal writing, like Debussy's in *Pelléas et Mélisande*, is a kind of speech-song, at times rising to lyrical outbursts, as in Maurya's beautiful final aria in E major. The music is entirely characteristic of Vaughan Williams's style at this date as exemplified by *Sancta civitas* and the Violin Concerto. Fluctuations between major and minor 3rds (or between diminished 4ths and minor 3rds) occur throughout his mature output and are a principal feature of the structure of the Sixth Symphony (1944–7). *Riders to the Sea* anticipates the symphony's bleak epilogue, with its 'whiffs of theme' drifting about a lunar landscape or, as to composer would have preferred to say, 'an agnostic's *Paradiso*'; and in its depiction of a vain human struggle against the implacable force of Nature it also anticipates the *Sinfonia antartica* (1949–52), Vaughan Williams's elegy for Scott's last journey to the South Pole. The keening of the women in *Riders to the Sea* became the disembodied voices heard in the polar winds of the symphony.

Riders to the Sea was completed in 1932 but not performed for another five years. In 1927, although he had two other operas and the masque on the stocks, Vaughan Williams also began to compose his 'romantic extravaganza' with spoken dialogue, *The Poisoned Kiss*, to a libretto by Cecil Sharp's sister Evelyn. This was the only score he never showed to Holst who, he feared, would never have understood why 'I considered it unimportant yet wanted to write it' (this of the composer of *The Perfect Fool*!). Although the music, with its waltzes, foxtrots and tangos, is witty and tuneful, the libretto, in spite of attempts to improve it, remains its weakness. *The Poisoned Kiss*, strangely, was the first Vaughan Williams opera to be given its première by a professional cast (in Cambridge in 1936 and a week later at Sadler's Wells Theatre, London). Although *Hugh the Drover* was performed in 1924 by the British National Opera Company, its first five performances were by students at the RCM, where Vaughan Williams was teaching composition, and this was where *Sir John in Love* and *Riders to the Sea* were also first staged. His only opera to reach the stage at Covent Garden was *The Pilgrim's Progress*, during the 1951 Festival of Britain.

John Bunyan's book was a lifetime's obsession for Vaughan Williams, not because he shared its religious outlook but because he saw it as a universal myth of man's struggle towards a spiritual goal of some kind. In adapting it for the stage, significantly he altered the hero's name from Christian to Pilgrim, not wishing to tie it to any one religion. His own musical pilgrimage to the heart of this work began in 1904 when he wrote a tune for the *English Hymnal* version ('He who would valiant be') of the song Bunyan gives to Christian. Two years later he wrote incidental music for a private dramatization of the book in which he used his own hymn tune and also the Roundhead hymn tune 'York' which eventually became the prelude and epilogue to the 1951 opera.

In 1921 Vaughan Williams composed the one-act 'pastoral episode' *The Shepherds of the Delectable Mountains* (produced at the RCM in 1922) as his next encounter with Bunyan. It was always his intention that this should be part of a larger scheme on which he worked fitfully from about 1925 to 1936, adapting the libretto himself. He then seems to have decided to abandon the idea and in 1938 began to compose the Fifth Symphony, in which some of the themes intended for the opera were used. But the Pilgrim would not go away. In 1942 Vaughan Williams set Mr Valiant-for-Truth's great speech as a motet and used much of his operatic material for a BBC dramatization of Bunyan's book by Edward Sackville-West, first broadcast in 1943 with John Gielgud as Christian. This rekindled his interest in the opera, which he completed between 1944 and 1949 while also working on his Sixth Symphony. Covent Garden produced it shoddily and, although amends were made with a Cambridge production in 1954, the work's failure deeply wounded Vaughan Williams, who usually had a philosophical attitude to the fate of his works, almost affecting indifference whatever his inner feeling. He knew it was not a conventional opera; indeed, he called it a 'morality' and insisted that 'it is to be acted almost like a ritual and not in the ordinary dramatic sense'. The clue is that the opera, like the book, is 'in the similitude of a dream'.

Musically and emotionally, *The Pilgrim's Progress* is central to the whole of Vaughan Williams's creative life. It is linked, sometimes thematically, always stylistically, to the major works of his career, from the *Tallis Fantasia* of 1910 to the Mass in G minor, *Sancta civitas*, *Job*, *Riders to the Sea*, the Fourth, Fifth and Sixth Symphonies, and even to the *Sinfonia antartica*, with the icy, glittering orchestration that marked the composer's final phase. If it is thus a mixture of styles, it is also bound together by the strength and individuality of the composer's musical personality, which remained constant. Whatever its dramatic shortcomings – and these seem not to matter in an imaginative production – the music has a radiance and splendour which were described by Eric Blom as characterized by 'unworldly nobility'. For those who, as we say today, are 'on its wavelength', *The Pilgrim's Progress* has a unique and lasting appeal.

Although it is now customary to believe that British opera began in 1945 with Britten's *Peter Grimes* – and without that masterpiece the immense burgeoning of operatic life in Britain in the last half of the 20th century could scarcely have happened – it is still true that the torch was kept burning, or perhaps only flickering, by composers before Britten who then handed it to him and to those he inspired. Of these, Vaughan Williams was far from being the least effective, and was also probably the greatest composer. Yet none of the professional companies which now exist in London and the regions and which could not have been remotely foreseen when *Hugh the Drover* was composed has even contemplated staging a Vaughan Williams opera since Sadler's Wells dropped that work from its repertory.

Advocates of Vaughan Williams's operas have to ask themselves yet again if the criticism that he had no dramatic flair is a sustainable blow to his standing as an opera composer, or whether he added to the risk of staging British works by choosing subjects with built-in resistance points. For example, *Sir John in Love* has Verdi's *Falstaff* to contend with; *The Poisoned Kiss* inhabits a no-man's-land between operetta and musical comedy; *Riders to the Sea* lasts 35 minutes and needs to be part of a triple bill; *The Pilgrim's Progress* is difficult and expensive to stage and for some tastes belongs outside the opera house. Yet to ignore these works is to ignore some of the finest and most beautiful music written by an Englishman. He himself was not disheartened by the neglect of his operas, not even by the failure of *The Pilgrim's Progress*, for he spent the last year of his life on a three-act opera, *Thomas the Rhymer*, left completed in a voice and piano version but otherwise unrevised and unscored. His admirers can only share his own faith in his operas and await a day when it may yet be justified.

See also HUGH THE DROVER; PILGRIM'S PROGRESS, THE; POISONED KISS, THE; RIDERS TO THE SEA; and SIR JOHN IN LOVE.

first performed in London unless otherwise stated

The Shepherds of the Delectable Mountains (pastoral episode, 1, Vaughan Williams, after J. Bunyan), RCM, 11 July 1922 (London, 1925) [incorporated into The Pilgrim's Progress]

Hugh the Drover, or Love in the Stocks, 1910–14 (romantic ballad op, 2, H. Child), RCM, 4 July 1924, vs (London, 1924); new scene (now opt.) inserted 1933; final rev. 1956

Sir John in Love, 1924–8 (4, Vaughan Williams, after W. Shakespeare: *The Merry Wives of Windsor*), RCM, 21 March 1929, vs (London, 1930); prologue [later withdrawn], episode and interlude added 1933, vs (London, 1936)

The Poisoned Kiss, or The Empress and the Necromancer, 1927–9 (romantic extravaganza, 3, E. Sharp, after R. Garnett: *The Poison Maid* and N. Hawthorne: *Rapaccini's Daughter*), Cambridge, Arts, 12 May 1936, vs (London, 1936); rev. 1934–5, 1936–7, 1956–7 [with spoken dialogue by U. Vaughan Williams]

Riders to the Sea, 1925–32 (1, Vaughan Williams, after J. M. Synge), RCM, 1 Dec 1937 (London, 1972)

The Pilgrim's Progress, 1909–49 [song added 1951] (morality, prol., 4, epilogue, Vaughan Williams, after Bunyan, the Bible and U. Vaughan Williams), CG, 26 April 1951, vs (London, 1952); rev. 1951–2, Cambridge, Guildhall, 1954

*

S. Goddard: 'The Operas of Vaughan Williams', *The Listener* (27 Oct 1938), 917

——: '"The Poisoned Kiss"', *The Listener* (27 Nov 1941), 737

N. Suckling: 'Vaughan Williams and the Fat Knight', *The Listener* (23 May 1946), 693

H. J. Foss: *Ralph Vaughan Williams* (London, 1950)

S. Wilson: '"Hugh the Drover"', *Opera*, i (1950), 29–31

M. Mullinar: '"The Pilgrim's Progress"', *RCM Magazine*, xlvii (1951), 46–9

H. Murrill: 'Vaughan Williams's Pilgrim', *ML*, xxxii (1951), 324–7

C. Smith: '"The Pilgrim's Progress"', *Opera*, ii (1951), 373–7

H. J. Foss: '"The Pilgrim's Progress" by Vaughan Williams', *Music 1952*, ed. A. Robertson (Harmondsworth, 1952), 38–50

H. Ottaway: '"Riders to the Sea"', *MT*, xciii (1952), 358–60

P. M. Young: *Vaughan Williams* (London, 1953)

S. Pakenham: *Ralph Vaughan Williams: a Discovery of his Music* (London, 1957)

J. Warrack: 'Vaughan Williams and Opera', *Opera*, ix (1958), 698–703

J. Day: *Vaughan Williams* (London, 1961, 2/1975)

A. E. F. Dickinson: *Vaughan Williams* (London, 1963)

M. Kennedy: *The Works of Ralph Vaughan Williams* (London, 1964, 2/1980)

U. Vaughan Williams: *R. V. W.: a Biography* (London, 1964)

H. Ottaway: *Vaughan Williams* (London, 1966)

M. Hurd: *Vaughan Williams* (London, 1970)

U. Vaughan Williams: 'Vaughan Williams and Opera', *Composer*, no.41 (1971), 25–7

G. Bush: 'Hugh the Drover Rides Again', *Records and Recordings*, xxii/9 (1978–9), 12

M. Kennedy: *A Catalogue of the Works of Ralph Vaughan Williams* (London, 1982)

W. Mellers: *Vaughan Williams and the Vision of Albion* (London, 1989)

MICHAEL KENNEDY

Vavilonskoye stolpotvoreniye. Opera by Anton Rubinstein; *see* THURM ZU BABEL, DER.

Vaynberg [Weinberg], **Moisey Samuilovich** (*b* Warsaw, 8 Dec 1919). Russian composer of Polish origin. After completing the piano course at the Warsaw Conservatory in 1939, he continued his studies at the Minsk Conservatory, graduating in 1941. He settled in Moscow in 1943 and by 1948 he had produced some 40 compositions. The musical drama *Mech Usbekistana* ('The Sword of Uzbekistan'), written in collaboration with a team of composers, was first performed in Tashkent on 29 April 1942. He subsequently wrote seven operas. His style is terse and intense, alternating between driving vitality and lyric introspection, his harmonic language contemporary though essentially tonal, his orchestration skilful and sonorous, and his knowledge of various solo instruments remarkable. Occasionally influences of Bartók and Shostakovich as well as Hindemith can be discerned.

Passazhirka [The Lady Passenger] op.97, 1967–8 (2, A. Medvedev and Y. Lukin, after Z. Posmysz)

Madonna i soldat [Madonna and the Soldier] op.105, 1970 (3, Medvedev)

Lyubov' d'Artanyana [D'Artagnan in Love] op.109, 1972 (comic op, 3, Y. Galerina, after A. Dumas *père*)

Ledi Magneziya [Lady Magnesia] op.112, 1975 (1, Vaynberg, after G. B. Shaw)

Pozdravlyayem! [Congratulations!] op.111, 1975 (2, Vaynberg, after S. Aleichem), Moscow, Chamber Opera Theatre, 13 Sept 1985

Portret [The Portrait] op.128, 1980 (3, Medvedev, after N. V. Gogol)

Idiot [The Idiot] op.144, 1986 (4, Medvedev, after F. M. Dostoyevsky), Moscow, Chamber Opera Theatre, 19 Dec 1991

BORIS SCHWARZ/LAUREL E. FAY

Vázquez, José (*b* Guadalajara, 1895; *d* Mexico City, 1961). Mexican composer. Active as a conductor and teacher, he wrote three symphonies, four piano concertos, a violin concerto and numerous chamber works, in addition to six operas, four of which were performed in Mexico City. His style was largely influenced by the late German Romantics, and is characterized by precise and accurate notation.

Citlali (1, M. Bermejo), Mexico City, Esperanza Iris, 19 Dec 1922

El mandarin (comedia lírica, 1, Bermejo, after Clemenceau: *Le voile du bonheur*), Mexico City, Arbeu, 3 April 1927

El rajah (drama lírico, 2, Bermejo), Mexico City, Arbeu, 14 June 1931

El ultimo sueño (opera-ballet, 3, Bermejo), Mexico City, Arbeu, July 1935

Los mineros (1, A. Molina), unperf.

Monna Vanna (3, A. Michel), unperf.

*

N. Slonimsky: *Music of Latin America* (New York, 1972)

J. Estrada, ed.: *La música de México* (Mexico City, 1989)

RICARDO MIRANDA-PÉREZ

V buryu ('Into the Storm'). Opera in four acts, op.8, by TIKHON NIKOLAYEVICH KHRENNIKOV to a libretto by Alexey Fayko and Nikolay Virta after Virta's novel *Odinochestvo* ('Loneliness'); Moscow, Nemirovich-Danchenko Music Theatre, 10 October 1939; revised version, Moscow, Stanislavsky–Nemirovich-Danchenko Music Theatre, 12 October 1952.

After the condemnation of Shostakovich's *Lady Macbeth of the Mtsensk District* in 1936, Soviet theatres were in pressing need of operas that fulfilled the political and aesthetic requirements of Socialist Realism. Khrennikov, a promising 23-year-old who had demonstrated a flair for the theatre, was approached by V. I. Nemirovich-Danchenko with a request for an opera on a contemporary theme, and the latter – to whom Khrennikov dedicated the opera – participated with composer, author and librettist in bringing the work to the stage. *Into the Storm* achieved signal success as a model Stalinist 'song opera': on a plot that combined an unambiguous patriotic impulse with a human dimension, it wove accessible folk and popular music idioms into a tuneful and effective drama. It also marked the first appearance of Lenin as a character – albeit in a cameo speaking role – on the operatic stage.

The action takes place in 1920–21 in a rural Russian village. Rumours of the approach of the counter-Revolutionary gang led by Antonov (tenor) strike terror into the villagers. The Party organization orders the local communists to withdraw from the village, which draws the scorn of Frol Bayev (bass). His daughter Natal'ya (soprano) is in love with Lyon'ka (baritone), a labourer for the landowner Storozhev (bass), who joins Antonov's forces with his employer while his brother Listrat (tenor) departs with the communists. Their mother, Aksin'ya (mezzo-soprano), laments the enmity between her sons. In a secret meeting at her hut, Lyon'ka's allegiance begins to waver under Listrat's arguments, and when Storozhev takes the whip to him, he decides to join the partisans with his brother.

To bolster the flagging support of the disillusioned villagers, Storozhev proposes that Antonov display the bodies of murdered peasants while blaming the communists. He also suggests to Natal'ya that Lyon'ka has abandoned her for another, but the lovers are eventually reconciled. At the head of a group of peasants, Frol Bayev pleads with Antonov to defend the villagers from Storozhev's plundering, but is himself offered punishment instead. Confused by the conflicting claims, Frol Bayev resolves to turn for the truth to Lenin. In Moscow, Listrat tells Frol Bayev and Andrey (tenor) about the victories of the Red Army. Lenin (spoken) invites them into his study for discussions.

In the now liberated village, Frol Bayev and Andrey tell the villagers of their meeting with Lenin and go off to spread the news. Antonov's gang has been defeated and only stragglers hide out in the forest, led by Storozhev. Storozhev captures Frol Bayev and, unable to intimidate him, kills him. Captured himself, he is guarded by Lyon'ka, whom he manages to trick and wound before he escapes. Realizing what has happened, Natal'ya runs off in pursuit of Storozhev. Shots are fired; Storozhev is killed. The people celebrate their victory. LAUREL E. FAY

Veasey, Josephine (*b* Peckham, London, 10 July 1930). English mezzo-soprano. She studied with Audrey Langford. In 1949 she joined the Covent Garden chorus, returning in 1955, after a spell with Opera for All, to make her solo début as Cherubino. Later roles included Magdalene, Rosina, Marina, Emilia, Dorabella, Carmen, Waltraute, Fricka, Amneris, Preziosilla, Berlioz's Dido and Cassandra, Eboli, the title role of *Iphigénie en Aulide*, Brangäne, Venus and the Emperor in the première of Henze's *We Come to the River* (1976). She first appeared at Glyndebourne in 1957 as Zulma (*L'italiana in Algeri*), then sang Cherubino, Clarice (Rossini's *La pietra del paragone*), Octavian and Charlotte. She sang Fricka (*Das Rheingold*) at the Salzburg Easter Festival and for her Metropolitan début in 1968. Having made her Paris Opéra début in 1969 as Dido, she returned for Kundry in 1973, then sang Eboli in San Francisco. In 1980 she sang Gertrude (*Hamlet*) at Buxton and in 1982 made her final appearance, at Covent Garden, as Herodias. Later she became vocal consultant at the ENO. She had a rich, vibrant voice of wide range and dramatic power, highly effective in roles such as Dido, which she recorded for Colin Davis.

*

A. Blyth: 'Josephine Veasey', *Opera*, xx (1969), 759–63

ALAN BLYTH

Vécla, Djemma. *See* GRANDI, MARGHERITA.

Věc Makropulos. Opera by Leoš Janáček; *see* MAKROPULOS AFFAIR, THE.

Vedernikov, Alexander (Filippovich) (*b* Mokino, nr Kirov, 23 Dec 1927). Soviet bass. After study in Moscow and Milan he made his début at the Bol'shoy in 1957, as Ivan Susanin in Glinka's *A Life for the Tsar*. He sang in Moscow, Leningrad, Kiev and Tbilisi, most notably as Dosifey (*Khovanshchina*), Konchak (*Prince Igor*), Boris and Varlaam. With the Bol'shoy he appeared in Milan, Paris and New York as King Philip, the Grand Inquisitor and Massimiliano (*I masnadieri*). He sang Boris with the Bol'shoy on a tour of West Germany in 1987. Other successful roles were Kutuzov in *War and Peace*, Prince Gremin, Méphistophélès and Daland. Rimsky-Korsakov's *The Snow Maiden* and Dargomïzhsky's *The Stone Guest* are among his recordings. DAVID CUMMINGS

Vedova scaltra, La ('The Cunning Widow'). Comic opera in three acts by ERMANNO WOLF-FERRARI to a libretto by Mario Ghisalberti after CARLO GOLDONI's play of the same name (1748); Rome, Teatro Reale dell'Opera, 5 March 1931.

This fourth of Wolf-Ferrari's five Goldoni operas is based on one of the Venetian playwright's earlier and slighter plays – a rather simplistic study in contrasted national temperaments, as represented by four rival suitors for the hand of the young widow Rosaura (soprano). Monsieur Le Bleau and the Conte di Bosco Nero (tenors), Milord Runebif and Don Alvaro di Castiglia (baritones) are all supposed to typify the nationalities evident from their names. Rosaura eventually manages to choose between them by disguising herself, in turn, as a lady compatriot of each suitor: catching them at moments when they are off their guard, she tempts all but one of them to prove himself less than wholly committed to her. The lucky exception is the impulsive but fundamentally sincere Italian.

The slightness of the original play helps to explain the rather slender effect of this opera, when compared with *I quatro rusteghi* (1906) on the one hand and *Il campiello* (1936) on the other: only intermittently does the work match the abundant vitality of those two greatest of Wolf-Ferrari's Goldoni comedies. There are just occasional signs (notably at the end of Act 2) of that expansion in his harmonic vocabulary which had been much more evident in *L'amore medico* (1913), while in some respects *La vedova scaltra* comes unprecedentedly close to the mannerisms of real 18th-century *opera buffa*: there are even some brief examples of *recitativo secco* with harpsichord accompaniment. The harpsichord also figures prominently in Rosaura's superb Act 2 aria 'Nella notturna selva'; and at the other end of the work's stylistic spectrum stands the colourful 'Spanish' music associated with Don Alvaro, the most tellingly characterized of the four suitors. Highlights such as these help to justify the revivals that the opera still sometimes receives. But it can scarcely be ranked among Wolf-Ferrari's masterpieces.

JOHN C. G. WATERHOUSE

Veerhoff, Carlos (*b* Buenos Aires, 3 June 1926). German composer of Argentine origin. He studied composition at the Berlin Hochschule für Musik with Blacher and Hermann Grabner and conducting with Scherchen in Cologne. In 1948 he returned to Argentina and taught at the University of Tucumán, but in 1951 he went back to Berlin as assistant to Fricsay; he settled in Munich the following year.

Veerhoff has composed in a wide range of genres, eschewing avant-garde tendencies in developing his own creative language. His first opera, *Targusis*, is an ambitious, dramatically charged work, calling for eight principal and seven supporting solo singers. It was followed by *Tanz des Lebens*, a puppet opera in lighter vein, for which the music is pre-recorded. In *Die goldene Maske* Veerhoff adopted serial procedures. Two chamber operas date from the early 1970s: *Es gibt doch Zebrastreifen*, which includes spoken dialogue and exists in two versions, one fully orchestrated, the other with accompaniment of chamber proportions; and *Die Grünen*, a chamber opera.

*

Targusis, 1955–8 (musical tragedy, 7 scenes, Veerhoff), unperf.
Tanz des Lebens, oder Der letzte Gast (puppet op, 1, F. Schneckenburger), Zürich, 1963
Die goldene Maske, 1962–6 (2, Veerhoff), unperf.
Es gibt doch Zebrastreifen (chamber op, 1, E. Sartorius), Ulm, 20 Jan 1972
Die Grünen (chamber op) ALFRED GOODMAN

Vega, Félix Lope de. *See* LOPE DE VEGA, FÉLIX.

Veichtner, Franz Adam (*b* Regensburg, 10 Feb 1741; *d* Klievenhof, Courland [now Kalnciems, Lithuania], 3 March 1822). German composer. He studied the violin with Franz Benda at Potsdam and music theory with Joseph Riepel before entering the service of Count Hermann von Keyserling; in 1763 he travelled to Königsberg (now Kaliningrad), where he met and taught the young J. F. Reichardt. Veichtner was appointed Konzertmeister to the Courland court at Mitau (now Jelgava) in 1765 and about that time wrote his first published compositions. He wrote about 60 symphonies for the chamber orchestra and composed three Singspiels for the court's amateur theatre: *Scipio* (C. F. Neander; Mitau, 30 June 1778), *Cephalus und Prokris* (K. W. Ramler; Mitau, 16 February 1779; published Berlin, 1779) and *Cyrus und Cassandana* (2, Ramler; Libau, 15 February 1784; MS, Jelgava, Muzei); the last earned him much praise (*Journal von und für Deutschland*, Ellrich, April 1784, p.460). He became one of the leading figures in the musical life of Courland during the late 18th century.

*

J. Döring: ['Biographische Notizen über den herzoglichen Konzertmeister Franz Adam Veichtner'], *Sitzungs-Berichte der kurländischen Gesellschaft für Literatur und Kunst* (Mitau, 1870), 43–8
R.-A. Mooser: *Annales de la musique et des musiciens en Russie au XVIIIme siècle* (Geneva, 1948–51)
E. Gercken: 'Franz Adam Veichtner und das Musikleben am kurländischen Hof', *Baltische Hefte*, xi (Hanover and Döhren, 1965), 99–129 GEOFFREY NORRIS

Veiga, José Augusto Ferreira, Visconde do Arneiro (*b* Macau, 22 Nov 1838; *d* San Remo, 7 June 1903). Portuguese composer. A member of a business family, he studied music in Lisbon. His operetta *A questão do oriente* was performed in Coimbra, at the Teatro Acadêmico (1859). In 1866 his ballet *Ginn* was performed in Lisbon with great success, and in 1871 his *Te Deum* was given there. His opera-ballet *L'elisir di giovinezza* (4, J. J. Magne), to an Italian text, was performed at the S Carlos theatre on 31 March 1876, but was not popular with the public, and he decided to present it in Italy. Given in Milan, at the Teatro Dal Verme (1877), the work still failed to win public favour. Veiga adapted the music to a new libretto by Rudolfo Paravicini, based on an English novel by Ann Radcliffe. The new version, a *melodrama tragico* entitled *Dina la derelitta* (S Carlos, 14 March 1885), was finally accepted by audiences. Veiga wrote another opera, *Don Bibas*, based on Alexandre Herculano's previously unknown novel *O Bobo*, which drew him into the Portuguese nationalist movement; the opera has never been performed.

*

F. F. Benevides: *O Real theatro de S Carlos de Lisboa desde a sua fundação em 1793 até à actualidade* (Lisbon, 1883)
——: *O Real theatro de S. Carlos de Lisboa: memórias 1883–1902* (Lisbon, 1902)
'Arneiro, Visconde do', *Grande enciclopédia portuguesa brasileira* (Lisbon and Rio de Janeiro, *c*1936–60) LUISA CYMBRON

Veitsi ('The Knife'). Opera in two acts by PAAVO HEININEN to a libretto by Veijo Maeri after his dramatic poem *Runoilijan kuolema* ('The Death of a Poet'); Savonlinna, Olavinlinna Castle, 3 July 1989.

Veitsi was commissioned as a part of the celebrations of the 350th anniversary of the city of Savonlinna. The central character, a young Poet (tenor), earns his living as a pianist in a sleazy Turkish café frequented by a gang of dubious characters. He is in love with Hildur (mezzo-soprano), a middle-aged saleswoman and former beauty queen who encourages his poetry, although he is spurned by the literary establishment. Thinking his love for Hildur hopeless, the Poet commits suicide by cutting his throat.

Heininen's opera is conceived on a grand scale, with a large number of characters whose lives impinge on each other. The music is skilfully crafted and dense in texture, its idiom and structure reminiscent of Berg.

ERKKI ARNI

Vejzovic, Dunja (*b* Zagreb, 20 Oct 1943). Croatian mezzo-soprano. She studied in Zagreb, where she made her début. She joined the Frankfurt Opera in 1978 and the same year sang Kundry at Bayreuth, Venus at the Metropolitan and the Woman in *Erwartung* in Florence. She has appeared in Vienna, Hamburg, Düsseldorf, Bologna, Paris, Geneva, Basle, Brussels and Salzburg and at La Scala. Her wide range, encompassing soprano and mezzo-soprano roles, allows her to sing Senta, Brünnhilde, Abigaille and Marie (*Wozzeck*) as well as Azucena, Massenet's Herodias, Bartók's Judith, Stravinsky's Jocasta and Dido (*Les Troyens*). In 1990 she sang Ortrud in Vienna. The harsh quality of her voice is offset by the intensity of her performances.

ELIZABETH FORBES

Velikaya druzhba ('The Great Friendship'). Opera in four acts by VANO IL'ICH MURADELI to a libretto by G. D. Mdivani; Stalino (now Donets'k), Opera and Ballet Theatre, 28 September 1947.

The Great Friendship, Muradeli's first opera, was begun in 1940 under the title *Chrezvïchaynïy komissar* ('The Extraordinary Commissar') and completed in 1947, when it received its definitive title. It deals with historical events of the Civil War period in the region of the northern Caucasus and with the role of the Communist Party in unifying the feuding peoples into a single nation. The hero of the opera, the 'extraordinary commissar', was modelled on Sergo Ordzhonikidze, Stalin's Georgian compatriot and close revolutionary comrade, who died in 1937.

The political credentials of the composer and the opera were solid enough to persuade many Soviet theatres to mount productions timed to coincide with the 30th anniversary of the revolution. Although it received its première in Stalino, the most illustrious of the productions was unveiled on the actual date of the anniversary, 7 November 1947, at the Bol'shoy Theatre, Moscow. By the end of the year, productions had been mounted in no fewer than 13 Soviet theatres, sometimes under the title *Druzhba narodov* ('The People's Friendship').

In January 1948, after Muradeli's opera had been viewed by Party functionaries, a conference of Soviet musicians was convened in Moscow by Andrey Zhdanov, Stalin's notorious cultural commissar. On 10 February 1948 *The Great Friendship* served as the pretext for a resolution issued by the Central Committee of the Communist Party condemning the formalistic distortions of the country's leading composers, including Shostakovich, Prokofiev, Myaskovsky and Khachaturyan. In vitriolic language reminiscent of the *Pravda* editorial attacking Shostakovich's *Lady Macbeth of the Mtsensk District* in 1936, Muradeli's opera was savaged on both musical and historical grounds. But the charges were merely the preamble to a broad-based attack on the composers, critics and institutions responsible for Soviet musical life. The repressive effects began to be felt immediately: *The Great Friendship* vanished from the repertory, and Muradeli publicly accepted the censure.

The opera was not an obvious candidate as a scapegoat. Its conventional, tonal language hardly warranted the charge of musical formalism, and the subject and treatment seemed beyond reproach. After Stalin's death, however, it was revealed that Ordzhonikidze's death in 1937, originally attributed to a heart attack, was in fact suicide. Although the rumours that Stalin had him murdered have not been substantiated, it is at least evident that Stalin was not without guilt in the matter; thus the heroic leader Muradeli had chosen to immortalize was one of the dictator's victims.

In May 1958 a declaration which 'amended and cancelled' the resolution of 10 February 1948 was issued by the Central Committee. It noted that, while Muradeli's opera had merited some criticism, the label 'formalistic' was not justified. Specific reference was made to the charge of historical inaccuracy, the blame for which was laid on Stalin's 'subjective' approach. Although Muradeli subsequently revised the work, first performed at the North Ossetian Musical-Dramatic Theatre, Ordzhonikidze (now Vladikavkaz), on 22 April 1970, it failed to enjoy even a trace of its initial success.

LAUREL E. FAY

Velis, Andrea (*b* New Kensington, PA, 7 June 1932). American tenor. He studied in Pittsburgh and at the Accademia di S Cecilia in Rome and made his début at Pittsburgh in 1954, subsequently appearing with the Chicago Lyric Opera and the Cincinnati Summer Opera. He became a member of the Metropolitan Opera in 1961 and has since given over 1500 performances in more than 50 comprimario roles. These include the Witch in *Hänsel und Gretel*, the four comic parts in *Les contes d'Hoffmann*, a Spy in *Andrea Chénier*, Mime in the *Ring*, Triquet in *Yevgeny Onegin* and Squeak in *Billy Budd*.

CHARLES JAHANT

Vellisani Buini, Cecilia. *See* BELISANI BUINI, CECILIA.

Velluti, Giovanni Battista (*b* Montolmo [now Corridonia], Ancona, 28 Jan 1780; *d* Sambruson di Dolo, Venice, 22 Jan 1861). Italian soprano castrato. He studied in Bologna, then for six years with Calpi in Ravenna, and made his début in Forlì in 1801. Two years later he was in Naples, singing in the première of P. C. Guglielmi's *Asteria e Teseo* and in Andreozzi's *Piramo e Tisbe*. He appeared in Rome from 1805 to 1808 in Nicolini's *La selvaggia nel Messico* and *Traiano in Dacia* (première), Tritto's *Andromaca e Pirro* and Cimarosa's *Gli Orazi ed i Curiazi*. At La Scala he sang in Nicolini's *Coriolano* (1808), Federici's *Ifigenia in Aulide* and Lavigna's *Orcamo* (1809), and Mayr's *Raùl di Créqui* and Pavesi's *Arminio* (1810). He also sang in Venice and in 1811 he appeared in Turin in Nicolini's *Angelica e Medoro*. The following year he visited Vienna and Munich. Returning to Milan, he created Arsace in Rossini's *Aureliano in Palmira* (1813).

Over the next three years he sang in Nicolini's *Quinto Fabio* (1814, Milan), *Carlo Magno* (1814, Sinigaglia) and *Balduino* (1816, Padua), and also sang in Turin in Bonfichi's *Abradate e Dircea*; after a tour of Germany and a visit to St Petersburg, he sang again in Turin in Nicolini's *Eroe di Lancastro* (1821), an opera he repeated in Bergamo. Tebaldo, in Morlacchi's *Tebaldo e Isolina*, which he sang in Venice, Reggio Emilia, Parma and Verona, became his favourite role. In 1823 he returned to Venice to sing in Mercadante's *Andronico*, and in 1824 he created Armando in Meyerbeer's *Il crociato in Egitto*.

Engaged at the King's Theatre, London, he made his début there in 1825, arousing curiosity and, later, enthusiasm. He made his final appearance in London in 1829. The last of the great castrato singers, Velluti was without rival during the greater part of his career; his retirement marked the end of an era in operatic history.

*

C. Parolari: 'Giambattista Velluti, ultimo dei sopranisti sulle liriche scene', *RMI*, xxxix (1932), 263–98

A. Heriot: *The Castrati in Opera* (London, 1956)

ELIZABETH FORBES

Veltri, Michelangelo (*b* Buenos Aires, 18 Aug 1940). Argentine conductor. He studied in Argentina and conducted widely in South America before moving to Europe in 1970, initially working with the Stuttgart Opera and in Milan. He has been artistic director of the Liceu theatre, Barcelona, and music director of the Avignon Opera. Best known for his vigorous performances of operas by Verdi, he has conducted *Giovanna d'Arco* at Parma (1980), *Macbeth* and *Un ballo in maschera* at Avignon (1980–81), *Don Carlos* at Macerata and Marseilles (1983–4) and *Aida* at Orange (1983). He has returned regularly to South America, giving *Otello* and *La forza del destino* in Buenos Aires and *I due Foscari* and *La traviata* in Santiago. His repertory includes *Francesca da Rimini* (1982, San Diego) and *Tosca*, *Samson et Dalila* and *Andrea Chénier* (1983–5, Santiago). He conducted *Lucia* at Covent Garden in 1986 and *La traviata* in the 1989–90 season at the Metropolitan.

DAVID CUMMINGS

Vendetta di Nino, La ('The Revenge of Nino'). Libretto subject used in the 18th and 19th centuries. Its source is VOLTAIRE's *Sémiramis* and it deals with different incidents from those treated in Metastasio's SEMIRAMIDE RICONOSCIUTA. Operas on the subject are also entitled *Semiramide* and *La morte de Semiramide*.

Semiramide, who has murdered her husband Nino and plans an incestuous marriage, is fatally stabbed by their son, unwitting agent of his father's vengeful ghost. Angiolini and Gluck's ballet for Vienna, 1765, preceded by 20 years the first opera on the subject by an Italian composer. In Ferdinando Moretti's libretto *Semiramide*, set by Michele Mortellari (1784, Milan), Nino's ghost is satisfied with the assassination offstage of Semiramide's lover and the establishment of a new generation on the throne; in this version Semiramide is innocent of her husband's death, and the matricide is thus avoided.

The libretto for Alessio Prati's opera (1786, Florence), though attributed to Moretti, is the work of Pietro Giovannini. It led the way towards an abrogation of the century-long taboos surrounding the staged depiction of murder and death in Italian *opera seria*. Here the parricide, in itself a bold challenge to the precepts of verisimilitude, becomes the more offensive because the deed takes place on stage. Heretofore deaths (preferably suicides) took place offstage and were reported, as in Moretti's version. Even the reappearance of the dying Semiramide in Voltaire's and Gluck's versions would have been viewed as objectionable.

Francesco Bianchi's setting of Giovannini's text (1790, Naples) is notable for extensive scenes in obbligato recitative: at the appearance of Nino's ghost an extended, dramatic obbligato recitative employing a variety of accompaniment styles (including the use of a *voce umana* as the ghost demands vengeance) links the opening celebratory chorus of the scene with the trio finale; at the staged matricide in the last scene, obbligato recitative coloured with double-reed timbres moves into a duet and then a final solo with chorus. The opera also includes an aria with choral interpolations, then a novel construction. In the same year a revised version of Prati's setting was given in Venice, the matricide still intact; Emperor Leopold II, Archduke of Tuscany at the time of the Florence première in 1786, chose Prati's opera to initiate his efforts to re-establish *opera seria* in Vienna.

Simeone Sografi's libretto for Sebastiano Nasolini, *La morte di Semiramide* (1790, Padua), also set by G. B. Borghi (1791, Milan), was one of several 'la morte' operas of the period. It tempers the parricide: Semiramide dies when she steps between her son and Assur, the object of his vendetta, thus committing suicide. Sografi's remained the preferred version for the rest of the century. All the librettos contain ghost scenes and make extensive use of chorus. Sografi's was the first Milanese production containing elements the poet had pioneered in his *Gli argonauti in Colco* (1789, Venice): freely constructed introductions, ensembles and scene complexes, the last incorporating dance and casting the chorus as a character. A setting of Sografi's libretto for Venice in 1791 under the title *La morte di Semiramide*, with music attributed to Prati, seems to be a composite of the Florentine, Paduan and Milanese versions with new additions. A French setting of the story is Catel's *Sémiramis* (1802, Paris Opéra).

See also SEMIRAMIDE [Rossini]. For a list of operas based on Voltaire's *Sémiramis see* VOLTAIRE.

MARITA P. McCLYMONDS

Vendramin. Family of Venetian nobles. For over 250 years members of the S Fosca branch of the Vendramin family were proprietors of the Venetian theatre known both as S Salvatore after a neighbouring church and as S Luca after the parish in which it was situated. The original house was built in 1622 but was substantially reconstructed after a fire in 1653 and again in 1776. Under Andrea Vendramin (*d* 1684) S Luca at first presented only spoken comedy, but between 1661 and 1700 it was turned over to opera during Carnival, achieving a level of activity surpassed only by S Giovanni Grisostomo. After Andrea's death, control passed successively to his son Alvise (*d* 1733) and grandson Antonio (*d* 1756). During the 18th century S Luca reverted largely to comedy, although between 1753 and 1769 it presented serious operas during Ascension. In the 19th century opera and comedy enjoyed greater parity. The family's connection with S Luca ended in 1880 on the death of the widow of Domenico Vendramin (*d* 1844). Content to entrust the management of S Luca to impresarios, the Vendramin were not innovators in artistic matters, but their family archive (in *I-Vcg*) sheds precious light on the general condition of Venetian opera in the 17th and 18th centuries.

N. Mangini: *I teatri di Venezia* (Milan, 1974) MICHAEL TALBOT

Venere prigioniera ('Venus the Prisoner'). *Commedia musicale* in two acts and an intermezzo by GIAN FRANCESCO MALIPIERO to his own libretto after Emmanuel Gonzales's novella *Giangurgolo*; Florence, Teatro della Pergola, 14 May 1957.

Gonzales's 19th-century French novella is a tortuous tale about a disgraced 18th-century count who commits murder, then wins the secret love of the Queen of Spain by twice saving her life, before vengeance resulting from his previous crime catches up with him. Malipiero's adaptation of this melodramatic story is characteristically capricious: whereas the first and last scenes have readily intelligible story lines – even quoting much of Gonzales's dialogue word for word – the intervening portions of the opera have only intermittent points of contact with the original, using fragments of the tale as a loose framework into which settings of old Italian texts are arbitrarily slotted. The resultant sequence of events is often incomprehensible if one has not read the novella, the identity of which the composer never revealed in public; and the opera's three middle scenes thus acquire something of the enigmatic, dream-like fascination of his extraordinary 'symbolic' operas of the later 1920s, notably *Torneo notturno*.

Musically *Venere prigioniera* (composed in 1955) is of uneven quality; yet it contains some of the most intensely dramatic passages in any of Malipiero's postwar works, marking a major point of arrival in his development. The new, highly personal chromatic manner (with occasional dodecaphonic tendencies), which during the previous few years had been gradually superseding the dissonant diatonicism he had preferred in the 1930s and 40s, here came to full maturity. The opening scene in particular – in which the count (known in the opera as Don Giovanni Mediana (tenor)) comes face to face with Melchiorre (baritone), the father of the man he has murdered – has a dark, obsessive forcefulness which led Piero Santi to speak of 'una sorta di *Forza del destino* malipieriana'. JOHN C. G. WATERHOUSE

Veneziano, Giovanni (*b* Naples, 11 March 1683; *d* Naples, 13 April 1742). Italian composer. Son of the composer Gaetano Veneziano, he is said to have studied under his father at the Neapolitan conservatory S Maria di Loreto. He was one of three musicians, the others being Francesco Mancini and Domenico Scarlatti, appointed to the salaried position of organist of the Neapolitan court chapel on 26 December 1704; like his father, however, he lost his position on 31 August 1707 when the Spanish regime was ousted by the invading Austrians. In 1716 he was appointed second *maestro di cappella* at the Loreto, and he held this position for the rest of his life. In 1735, a year after the expulsion of the Austrians from Naples, he applied to the new regime of Charles Bourbon for readmission to the court chapel, claiming that he had been unfairly dismissed by the Austrians in 1707. His petition was successful and he was granted a supernumerary position in the chapel, but he was never readmitted on a salaried basis.

Veneziano is nowadays chiefly remembered as being among the earliest Neapolitan musicians to compose comic operas in the local dialect. These works are *Lo mbruoglio de li nomme* and *Patrò Tonno d'Isca*, both with text by 'Agasippo Mercotellis' and both produced at the Teatro dei Fiorentini in 1714, and *Lo Pippo*, text by 'Persio Segisto', produced at the Fiorentini in 1715. The music of these operas does not survive. Veneziano's chief extant music appears to be Acts 1 and 2 of a sacred opera *Giuseppe Giusto*, composed in 1733 for performance by the students of the Loreto (in *I-Nc*): it is not a distinguished work, possessing little of the ingratiating lyricism of the best Neapolitan operas of the period and providing no evidence that its composer was an outstanding musical figure. A *Componimento per musica sopra il felice arrivo in Macerata dell'ill.mo ... monsignore Ignazion Stelluti* for which no score survives was performed in Macerata on 29 May 1736.

Patrò Tonno d'Isca (commedia marenaresca, 3, A. Mercotellis), Naples, Fiorentini, Sept 1714, lib. *I-Bu*, *Nc*, *Nn* (as Lucchesi Palli), *US-NYp* and *Wc*

Lo mbruoglio de li nomme (ob, 3, Mercotellis), Naples, Fiorentini, 26 Sept 1714, lib. *I-Bn* and *Nc*

Lo Pippo (ob, 3, P. Segisto), Naples, Fiorentini, 1715, lib. *Bu*

Componimento per musica sopra il felice arrivo in Macerata dell'ill.mo ... monsignore Ignazion Stelluti, Macerata, 29 May 1736, lib. *D-Mth*, *I-MAC* and *Nn*

*

U. Prota-Giurleo: *Nicola Logroscino 'il dio dell'opera buffa'* (Naples, 1927)

——: *Breve storia del teatro di corte e della musica a Napoli nei secoli xvii–xviii* (Naples, 1952)

M. F. Robinson: 'The Governors' Minutes of the Conservatory S Maria di Loreto, Naples', *RMARC*, no.10 (1972), 38, 45, 95

MICHAEL F. ROBINSON (with DALE E. MONSON)

Venezuela. For discussion of opera in Venezuela *see* CARACAS.

Venice (It. Venezia). Italian city of the greatest historical and cultural importance, capital of the Veneto. The home of the first public opera house (opened in 1637), it was a major centre of operatic activity and development throughout the 17th and 18th centuries.

1. Before 1637. 2. The birth of public opera. 3. The stabilization of the system. 4. The comic intermezzo and Neapolitan influence. 5. The spread of comic opera. 6. The Napoleonic era and the Restoration. 7. The Romantic age. 8. The disappearance of the minor theatres. 9. From the unification of Italy to World War II. 10. The postwar years.

1. BEFORE 1637. From the late 16th century pastoral and mythological entertainments with musical accompaniment were staged in Venice to celebrate important religious and secular events. When Marino Grimani was doge (1596–1605) these followed a regular pattern of four performances a year which took place in the doge's palace for the feasts of St Mark, the Assumption, St Vitus and St Stephen. Pastoral and allegorical entertainments with intermezzos were also organized by academies (the Tredici Nobili, Murano, Immobili) in places adapted for the occasion. Court musical performances on the Florentine and Mantuan models seem to have appeared somewhat later: Girolamo Mocenigo commissioned Monteverdi to compose *Combattimento di Tancredi e Clorinda* (1624 or 1625) and *Proserpina rapita* (1630), which were staged at his palace. If the *Combattimento* was not true opera as far as length and scenic demands were concerned, *Proserpina*, written for the wedding of Mocenigo's daughter Giustiniana, certainly was. Contemporary witnesses relate that it was performed 'in music (which has never been seen before) with most perfect voices and instruments, with aerial apparitions, changes of scene and so on', to the admiration of the noble audience. This was the first 'court' opera performed in Venice, but it remained an isolated instance.

Meanwhile the popularity of the *commedia dell'arte* had spread. Noble families, in competition, began to build theatres on their vacant properties in the city, initially of wood but often rebuilt in stone, accommodating a socially mixed paying public: in the parish of San Cassiano the Michiel and Tron theatres, in San Moisè the Giustinian-Zane, in San Salvador (San Luca) the Vendramin, in Santi Giovanni e Paolo (San Zanipolo) the Grimani. Little is known of their shape but they probably contained several rows of boxes (or loggias with partitions); the previously widespread assumption that they were built in levels, without boxes, now appears to be unfounded; the possibility of leasing boxes eventually constituted the most important source of finance for public opera. The exterior, to the astonishment of travellers and in contrast with the architectural splendour of the city, was almost always plain, without any attempt at adornment. These theatres constituted the infrastructure for the growth of public music drama in Venice.

2. THE BIRTH OF PUBLIC OPERA. The decisive event for the introduction of opera in the city was the performance in 1636 of Sances's *Ermiona* in neighbouring Padua, as the prelude to a tourney organized by the Marquess Pio Enea degli Obizzi, who wrote the libretto, in a theatre constructed for the purpose. The opera was of the courtly type, but the audience was socially mixed. The performers, mostly from Rome but with others who were singers in the choir of St Mark's, sought to capitalize on its success, and in 1637 in Venice they joined a company led by Benedetto Ferrari to present *Andromeda*, with music by Francesco Manelli to a text by Ferrari, at the newly opened Teatro Tron in the parish of S Cassiano, the first opera house ever opened to the public; admission was by payment as for *commedia dell'arte* performances. In 1638 the group returned to perform *La maga fulminata*, by the same two authors. In 1639 a second theatre, the Teatro di SS Giovanni e Paolo (fig.1), was adapted and opened for opera, initiating a long tradition of dominance by the

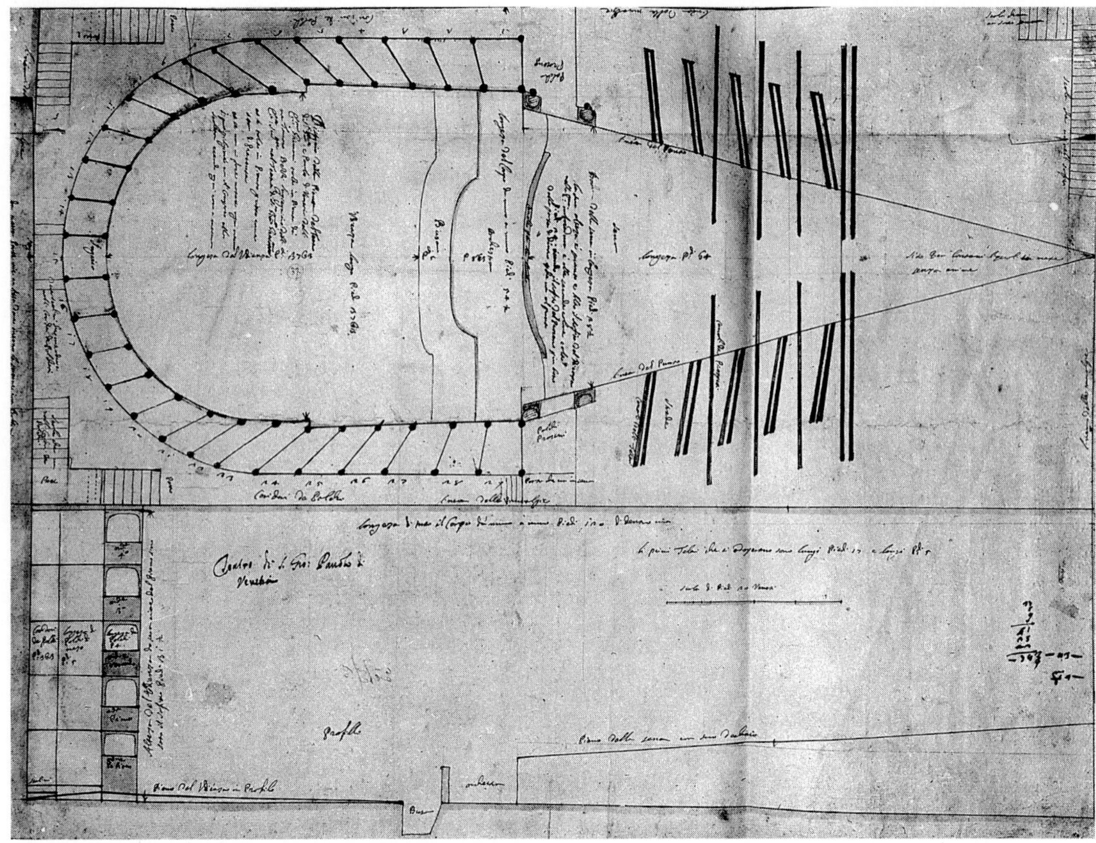

1. Plan (with longitudinal section below) of the Teatro di SS Giovanni e Paolo, Venice, opened in 1639

Grimani family in Venetian operatic life. In the first year the Ferrari company performed there, but in 1640 they moved to the new Teatro S Moisè, having abandoned the S Cassiano to a company headed by Francesco Cavalli. In 1641 the Teatro Novissimo, in the same parish as the SS Giovanni e Paolo, was built for a group of nobles whose aims were academic and recreational rather than strictly commercial. Monteverdi was one of the chief composers at the theatres of SS Giovanni e Paolo and S Moisè during their first few years.

Production costs were borne collectively by the members of the companies: in the introduction to the libretto of *La maga fulminata* the cheapness (and implicitly the profitability) of such operations, 'which cost an infinite amount of money to princes', was underlined. In a few years, however, it became clear that the business of musical drama was intrinsically a loss-making one, and the companies of artists assumed the role of mere performers of opera hired by an impresario who was answerable to the owners of the theatre. Often the role of impresario was undertaken by the librettist, who had usually received a humanist education with some legal training. In the early decades it was not unusual for families who owned theatres (the Zane at S Moisè, the Grimani at SS Giovanni e Paolo) to be involved in the business in various ways, but direct management remained more frequently the case for plays, which required less investment (a theatre often had different managements for the two kinds of entertainment). It must be observed that taxes on opera theatres in favour of the poor and of charitable institutions, widespread in Europe in the 17th and 18th centuries, never came into use in the Republic of Venice.

For about 15 years there was feverish activity, with frequent changes of artistic personnel among the different theatres. The Novissimo, which closed before 1647 and was demolished soon after, was graced by the splendid stage machinery of Giacomo Torelli, with its transformation scenes, the first appearances of Anna Renzi, and the music of Francesco Sacrati (it was here that his *La finta pazza* began the career which was to carry it to many Italian cities and to Paris). The S Cassiano was used only sporadically (especially after the 1650s), although Cavalli worked there regularly. The SS Giovanni e Paolo became the most illustrious and constantly used theatre of this first phase, employing the stars of the Novissimo, such as Renzi and Torelli, and staging masterpieces by Cavalli (*Xerse*, 1655) and Cesti (*Tito*, 1666). When the Grimani family handed over management to an impresario, from 1660 to 1668, they appointed the able Marco Faustini, from the S Cassiano, whose network of international contacts allowed him to engage the best Italian and European virtuosos. The smaller S Moisè theatre was less regularly used. For about ten years there was a Teatro Sant'Apollinare (Sant'Aponal), built in 1651 by a company led by Giovanni Faustini (then by his brother Marco), where operas by Cavalli and P. A. Ziani were performed. From 1660 the Teatro Vendramin in S Luca also regularly staged musical dramas, and the librettist Nicolò Minato was long active there.

The main opera season was that of Carnival, from 26 December to Shrove Tuesday: it is normally indicated in sources by reference to the year in which the greater part of the season lay (for example, the marking 'Carnevale 1668' could include an opera performed on 26

December 1667). Moreover, the official Venetian calendar had the year starting from 1 March, with January and February still dated in the old year: so in some sources the marking 'Carnevale 1672' may be a *more veneto* reference to the 1673 season. Nevertheless, the Venetian repertory of the time tends to follow international usage, and dating *more veneto* (abbreviated to *m.v.*) is less common, though the correct interpretation of a date may sometimes be questionable. Seasons of secondary importance took place in the autumn and (from the 18th century) during the feast of the Ascension.

3. THE STABILIZATION OF THE SYSTEM. After the initial enthusiasm, operatic activity tended to decrease; from the end of the 1640s to the mid-1670s Venice rarely had more than two theatres open in the same season, each presenting one or two operas, making a total for the city of three or four productions a year (on average each opera was performed about 20 times). Some established composers were conspicuously represented, Cavalli at their head, and only slowly did productions by the next generation emerge, by Ziani, G. A. Boretti, Antonio Sartorio and Carlo Pallavicino. In 1674 the impresario Francesco Santurini (the younger), who had revived the S Moisè theatre, decided to reduce drastically, by just over a half, the price of an entrance ticket, which at all theatres from the outset had been around 4 lire (about half a ducat, an extremely high figure which gradually appreciated in value over 40 years of steady deflation). It seems likely that the theatres were not often filled to capacity (in 1659 the S Cassiano had an average attendance of 272 an evening, the highest being 533, still below capacity) and that a potential middle-class section of the audience had been excluded by economic considerations.

Santurini's move was decisive. The other theatres had to follow suit, and that this provided a strong stimulus to the market is shown by the subsequent proliferation of active theatres. Santurini left S Moisè and in 1677 founded the Teatro Sant'Angelo, which was to put on productions continuously (though of mediocre quality) until the mid-18th century. The S Cassiano began again to provide opera from time to time, and a number of minor halls opened. In the last 20 years of the century an average of eight or ten operas was produced each year in four or five theatres, more than double the number in the previous period, and these figures remained more or less constant until the mid-18th century, when the spread of comic opera led to more and cheaper productions. The Grimani, while continuing to maintain the SS Giovanni e Paolo (abandoned in 1699), responded to this increased demand by building the San Giovanni Grisostomo theatre (1678; see fig.2), elaborately decorated, with lavish stage equipment and engaging singers of the highest quality for its productions; in this élite theatre the price of admission remained high. It was there more than anywhere that the social function of the opera house as an 'official' meeting-place of the ruling classes was evident; in a situation where profit was expected the probable loss that was made by the entertainment was of minimal importance from the standpoint of the political patronage of the controlling family, which kept the management firmly in hand.

For Venice, a city in decline, the splendour of the productions in the carnival season was a means of attracting rulers from all over Europe, especially the German territories, and of forging advantageous relationships and alliances; even the gazette writers, referring to these visits 'for pleasure', did not fail to stress the number of soldiers that the visitors provided for the Venetian Republic in its wars against the Turks. Librettos were increasingly dedicated to the princes of northern Europe: where the Roman and Trojan music dramas of the 1640s had alluded to the republican tradition of Venice, the vogue now was for subjects relating to the north. The librettists of the S Giovanni Grisostomo were often amateur noblemen of 'reformed' literary tendencies, but the most frequently produced composers (above all C. F. Pollarolo and Antonio Lotti) guaranteed a continuity of style that was scarcely innovatory: on the other hand, thanks to the international contacts of the Grimani family, it was here that the Venetians heard Alessandro Scarlatti (*Il Mitridate Eu-*

2. Interior of the Teatro Grimani a S Giovanni Grisostomo, built by Tomaso Bezzi for Giovanni Carlo and Vincenzo Grimani and opened in 1678: engraving

patore, *Il trionfo della libertà*, 1707; both unsuccessful) and Handel (*Agrippina*, 1709). In the first decades of the 18th century the S Cassiano, S Moisè and S Angelo generally shared the services of Francesco Gasparini, Albinoni and Vivaldi (who also acted as impresario at the S Angelo and directed operatic activity on the mainland, where it was dependent on the Venetian repertory); in 1710 the Grimani also opened the San Samuele theatre for opera, which in spite of its imposing dimensions had previously been used only for plays.

4. THE COMIC INTERMEZZO AND NEAPOLITAN INFLUENCE. From 1706 onwards at the S Cassiano and S Angelo the traditional dances at the ends of acts were habitually replaced with comic intermezzos, the texts of which were printed in separate librettos (unlike the practice in Naples); the composer was rarely indicated but was usually that of the opera, and included Lotti, Gasparini and Albinoni, whose *Pimpinone* (S Cassiano, 1708, to a libretto by Pietro Pariati) was to have a great success. From 1706 to 1709 the S Cassiano exploited the presence of the bass Cavana, the most highly esteemed Italian *buffo* of the time. Only the S Giovanni Grisostomo avoided – though not entirely – this kind of spectacle as too 'popular' for its aristocratic audience. It was, however, the first theatre to stage a 'tragicomedy' (Pollarolo's *La fortuna per dote*, 1704), the first example of this genre which was initially intended to parody heroic opera. Although they appeared only

3. A ticket for the Teatro Grimani a S Giovanni Grisostomo, Venice, 18th century

rarely, these works (also called *comidrama*, *drama melolepido* and later *divertimento comico* and *opera bernesca*) were the beginnings of a comic tradition which enjoyed considerable success in the period 1725–45, especially with the music of G. M. Buini. Another development of the parodic vein, but with a more marked satirical purpose and sometimes a far-reaching critical effect as in Benedetto Marcello's pamphlet *Il teatro alla moda* (*c*1720), was the *dramma per musica* performed after 1726 by actors without professional singers, especially at the Grimani's S Samuele theatre (it is not known what music was used); this tradition was also destined to fade away with the arrival of the Neapolitan type of comic opera.

Meanwhile, from about 1715, the S Giovanni Grisostomo, always eager to enlist the services of the greatest virtuosos, began to present the stars of the new style of singing: Faustina Bordoni in 1716 and Francesca Cuzzoni in 1718 (the year in which the two sang together in Pollarolo's *Ariodante*, and in which Vittoria Tesi sang at the S Angelo). At that time the Neapolitan presence, represented among others by Nicola Grimaldi, was only sporadic, but it soon increased: between 1725 and 1735 the Grisostomo audience applauded Farinelli, Caffarelli (together in Giacomelli's *Merope* in 1734), Paris, Tolve and others. The same applied to composers: from 1725 almost half the works performed were by Neapolitans, such as Leonardo Vinci, Nicola Porpora, Leonardo Leo and Johann Adolf Hasse. Two Metastasio librettos had their premières at the S Giovanni Grisostomo at this time: *Siroe* (1726, music by Vinci) and *Ezio* (1728, music by Porpora); others were staged there immediately following their premières at Naples or Rome. Thenceforward Venice was no more than an important part of an international circuit, exchanging not only artists but also operas for production elsewhere, without developing a style of its own.

5. THE SPREAD OF COMIC OPERA. Neapolitan comic opera reached the S Angelo and the S Moisè in 1743, and the S Cassiano in the following year. The leader of this conquest was Gaetano Latilla, whose *La finta cameriera* was performed three years running, in the three different theatres. Goldoni and Baldassare Galuppi began their series of comic masterpieces at the S Angelo in 1749 (*L'Arcadia in Brenta*), then at the S Moisè and the S Samuele, which had burnt down and been rebuilt in 1747. From the late 1740s productions of *opera seria* grew rarer: in a financially critical period the Grimani abandoned the S Giovanni Grisostomo to comedy (1752) and built the new San Benedetto theatre, equally elegant and exclusive but smaller; in 1766, however, the crisis compelled them to sell it to a company of boxholders (the theatre burnt down and was rebuilt in 1774). In the 1760s, therefore, *opera seria* was performed at the S Benedetto and sometimes at the S Luca (one opera a year at Ascensiontide) and comic opera at the S Moisè, with occasional productions of both kinds at other theatres. In the 1770s and 80s, however, *opera seria* was confined exclusively to the S Benedetto (three or four productions a year), while the S Moisè (where the librettist Giovanni Bertati was director for a long period) and the S Samuele each staged four or five comic operas a year; at the S Cassiano a one-act work or a *farsa* was often performed 'after the play'. Although the collapse of the Venetian Republic was not far off, the average number of operas produced each year reached its historical maximum, around 15 or 20 productions.

6. THE NAPOLEONIC ERA AND THE RESTORATION. In 1787, after a lawsuit, the company that owned the S Benedetto had to cede it to the proprietors of the site on which it stood. In a short time the company, having raised considerable capital and applied political pressure, had succeeded in building a large new theatre, designed by Gian Antonio Selva – the Teatro La Fenice (1792), inaugurated with the première of Paisiello's *I giuochi d'Agrigento*. It was the first Venetian theatre to proclaim its status from the outside, its elegant architecture symbolizing an 'enlightened' relationship with the city, whose theatre *par excellence* it soon became (see figs. 5 and 6; *see also* SOCIOLOGY OF OPERA, fig.2). Originally intended solely for *opera seria*, the Fenice staged the first operas of Mayr (*Saffo*, 1794; *Lodoiska*, 1796) and in succeeding years many works by Zingarelli, Paisiello, Cimarosa (*Gli Orazi ed i Curiazi*, 1796) and later by Stefano Pavesi, Francesco

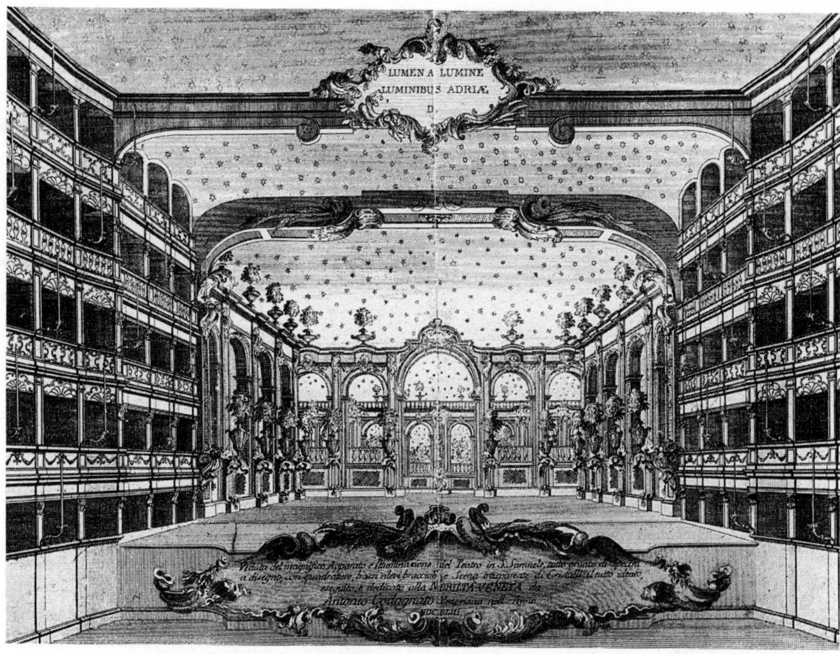

4. Interior of the Teatro S Samuele, Venice (designed by Alessandro (i) and Romualdo Mauro), with a set by Antonio Codognato for a production of Galuppi's 'Il mondo alla roversa' in 1753

Basili and Carlo Coccia. In 1813 Rossini's first work for the Fenice, *Tancredi*, was given; he wrote *Sigismondo* (1814) and *Semiramide* (1823) for it, while Meyerbeer's *Il crociato in Egitto* was staged there in 1824.

Unable to withstand the competition, the S Benedetto turned increasingly to comic opera: it staged the premières of Rossini's *L'italiana in Algeri* (1813) and *Edoardo e Cristina* (1819). The outstanding phenomenon in the various minor theatres in Venice at this time, and especially after 1797, was, however, the growing popularity of one-act *farse*, many to librettos by Giuseppe Foppa; only La Fenice remained impervious, though not entirely, to this trend. With the fall of the republic and the subsequent political domination by Austria, France (the kingdom of Italy) and again Austria, the city's economic crisis had a severe effect on the theatres: the S Angelo finally closed in 1803, the S Cassiano in 1804 and the S Moisè in 1818, soon after staging the first *farse* by Rossini (*La cambiale di matrimonio*, 1810; *L'inganno felice*, *La scala di seta*, *L'occasione fa il ladro*, 1812; *Il signor Bruschino*, 1813). The successive occupying powers, moreover, attempted to rationalize theatrical activity, not least to control public order; during the time of the kingdom of Italy it was proposed to reduce to four the official number of theatres, and the Austrians prohibited the construction of others (in practice no more were built).

7. THE ROMANTIC AGE. Until the unification of Italy the Fenice was one of the principal theatres in the peninsula, staging important premières and early revivals of operas produced elsewhere, with performances of a high standard. The company that owned it elected a

5. Teatro La Fenice, Venice: pen and ink drawing with wash by Francesco Guardi (1712–93)

6. Interior of the Teatro La Fenice, Venice, rebuilt after the fire of 1837, following Gian Antonio Selva's original design (1792): lithograph (1854)

triumvirate of presidents for three-year periods, one of whom was appointed *presidente agli spettacoli* ('head of entertainments'), worked in collaboration with the Podestà (the chief officer of the municipality, which contributed financially to the running of the theatre) and was naturally subject to Austrian censorship. In some seasons the company managed the theatre directly, without the intervention of impresarios (1823, 1831, 1843–4, 1847). For example, it was Alvise Francesco Mocenigo who, as president, dealt with Verdi over the production of *Ernani*, overcoming the reluctance of the members of the company to pay the young musician the sum he asked, suggesting Victor Hugo's play as its subject and helping Piave draft the first libretto (Piave later worked at La Fenice, as a stage director, from 1848 to 1859). Most seasons, however, were left to impresarios, but in many cases the company used them simply as agents, giving them fairly detailed instructions. The difficult negotiations with Verdi over *Rigoletto*, *La traviata* and *Simon Boccanegra* were conducted by the presidents Carlo Marzari and G. B. Tornielli and the secretary Guglielmo Brenna, and not by the impresarios G. B. Lasina and the Marzi brothers. The great impresario Alessandro Lanari (at the Fenice in 1830, 1832–3, 1837–9 and 1845–6) was given greater independence, in spite of disagreements with the company; he was responsible for securing two Bellini premières, two out of three by Donizetti and one by Verdi.

Among the premières staged at that period were operas by Mercadante, Nicola Vaccai and Francesco Morlacchi; the Bellini works were *I Capuleti e i Montecchi* (1830) and *Beatrice di Tenda* (1833), and those by Donizetti *Belisario* (1836) and *Pia de' Tolomei* (1837). In 1837 the Fenice burnt down and the season took place instead at the Teatro di Apollo (formerly S Luca). Rebuilt by the Medunas without altering much of Selva's original design, the Fenice reopened at the end of the year with Giuseppe Lillo's *Rosmunda in Ravenna*, judiciously chosen to avoid jealousy between Mercadante (who had composed *Le due illustri rivali*) and Donizetti (whose *Maria di Rudenz* was badly received). Other premières of importance were Pacini's *Il duca d'Alba* (1842), Giuseppe Apolloni's *L'ebreo* (1855) and, notably, five works by Verdi (more than at any other theatre except La Scala): *Ernani* (1844), *Attila* (1846), *Rigoletto* (1851), *La traviata* (1853) and *Simon Boccanegra* (1857). The last two, especially *Simon Boccanegra*, were unsuccessful. The subject of *I due Foscari* was rejected by the presidents for fear of offending the descendants of the Loredan and Barbarigo families. The Fenice was of course involved in the political vicissitudes of the time: it did not stage melodramas in the tragic year of 1849; in 1859, after the treaty of Villafranca had upheld the cession of the Veneto to Austria, the company decided to close the theatre until the situation had changed, and it reopened only in October 1866, when the Veneto had been reunited with Italy.

8. THE DISAPPEARANCE OF THE MINOR THEATRES. In the first decades of the 19th century the general decline in

operatic activity also affected the four smaller theatres. At the S Benedetto, bought by Giovanni Gallo in 1821, productions were continuous but routine (an exception was the première of Federico and Luigi Ricci's *Crispino e la comare*, 1850). The best it could do was to secure the first Venetian performances of various operas produced elsewhere (*I due Foscari*, 1845; *La forza del destino*, *Mefistofele*, *La Gioconda*, 1876). Renamed in honour of Rossini in 1868, and used increasingly for a variety of other entertainments, it finally became a cinema (and was rebuilt as one in 1951). The S Luca, renamed the Apollo (after restoration in 1833) and later Teatro Goldoni (1875), was primarily a theatre for plays but also put on operatic works from time to time (Giuditta Pasta performed there in 1834). It stood in for La Fenice when that theatre was closed in 1837 and again from 1859 to 1866 (under pressure from the Austrian government, which wanted a regular operatic season in Venice in spite of the protest closure of the Fenice). It then remained closed for a long time until it was acquired by the Comune of Venice and reopened in 1974 (with almost all the boxes replaced by stalls); it became the city's principal theatre for plays, sometimes also staging productions for the Fenice, especially chamber operas for which its smaller dimensions were more suitable. The S Samuele, reduced to a ruin, was acquired in 1853 by Giuseppe Camploy, who restored it with the intention of using it for opera, but it soon reverted to more popular forms of entertainment (comedies, operettas, variety) and was demolished in 1894. The S Giovanni Grisostomo, which remained the largest theatre in Venice, was also acquired by Gallo in 1819 and in 1835 was renamed in honour of Maria Malibran, who had appeared there after its restoration the previous year; there were ambitious plans for it, but it soon became a theatre mainly for all kinds of popular entertainment, from operetta to acrobatics. It was restructured in 1919 (with an imposing operatic season including *Otello*, *La traviata* and *Lohengrin*) but soon became a cinema. It was also used for La Fenice productions and symphony concerts.

In the vicissitudes experienced in the 19th and 20th centuries by the minor theatres, which turned to popular audiences in order to survive – a change often emphasized by the substitution of stalls for boxes – opera thus played a role as a prestigious entertainment with which to mark a change of ownership or restoration, but could never constitute the staple fare offered to a more widely based middle-class public.

9. From the unification of Italy to World War II. In the context of a general economic crisis for opera in Italy, Venice, which had suffered severely from historical events and was isolated from the main industrial and commercial developments of the age, was no longer capable of supporting the Teatro La Fenice at the level of quality it had previously enjoyed, and for many years its activity was no more than second-rate and provincial (even relative to the tastes of its audiences). This critical situation was frequently marked by seasons when nothing was produced there, not only in the years affected by war (1915–20), and not only because of the physical condition of the building. New European works came late: although the Italian première of the entire *Ring* cycle was given there in 1883 by the travelling company of Angelo Neumann, the city where Wagner died was slow to accept his music (*Tristan* only in 1909, the year in which, however, Strauss's *Salome* was given, with Gemma Bellincioni). But Venice was isolated too as regards the 'young school' of Italian composers: only premières by Leoncavallo (*La bohème*, 1897) and Mascagni (*Isabeau*, 1912, after Buenos Aires) were given. Even more significant was the fact that Wolf-Ferrari and Malipiero, two composers who had a long association with Venice as directors of the conservatory and were to some extent heirs to the city's cultural tradition, hardly ever had first performances of their works given there. The operatic scene was imbued with a degree of liveliness by the revival, especially as led by Wolf-Ferrari, of old masterpieces: *La serva padrona* (1906, conservatory); *Il filosofo di campagna* (1907, conservatory); *Orfeo* (1910, Fenice, a concert performance in the revised version by Giacomo Orefice, after Milan); and Marcello's *Arianna* (1913, conservatory, concert performance). The growing conception of the city – excluded from modern economic processes – as a museum, the custodian of the artistic glories of its past, resulted in increased attention to early Venetian opera: in 1907 the publisher Ricordi suggested the Fenice as the site for an annual festival of early Italian operas (which never materialized). In 1935 the increasing difficulties of the Fenice finally led the owners to donate it to the Comune, and its management was entrusted to a limited company (on the model of other Italian theatres, primarily La Scala). After restoration work, concluded in 1937, the first manager of the new company was Goffredo Petrassi (until 1941), who, in spite of the shortsighted cultural policies of the Fascist regime, secured for Venice the Italian première of Busoni's *Arlecchino* in 1940.

10. The postwar years. While the activity at the Fenice and the quality of its productions returned Venice to the circuit of the principal opera houses of Italy (the adoption of new open-air spaces such as the courtyard of the doge's palace was also important), the most illustrious regular event of the postwar decades became the Festival of Contemporary Music, linked with the Biennale of Contemporary Art; in spite of the difficulties imposed by the xenophobic and conservative cultural policy of the Fascist regime, some seasons took place before the war (it had been founded in 1930 by Mario Labroca and Alfredo Casella, the première of whose *La favola d'Orfeo* was given in 1932). In keeping with the city's new role as a tourist centre of the highest importance and a stage for world-class performances, from 1946 the September Festival became, thanks to the artistic direction of Guido Ballo and Alessandro Piovesan, an important event in the world of modern music. Productions were staged at the Fenice, where the technical and artistic contribution was always fundamental, especially when the artistic aims of both festival and opera house were united by Mario Labroca. Among the most important world premières were Stravinsky's *The Rake's Progress* (1951), Britten's *The Turn of the Screw* (1954), Prokofiev's *The Fiery Angel* (1955, first complete stage performance), Nono's *Intolleranza 1960* (1961), Maderna's *Hyperion* (1964), G. F. Malipiero's *Le metamorfosi di Bonaventura* (1966), Bussotti's *Lorenzaccio* (1972) and many first Italian performances. After a period of crisis the festival (renamed Biennale Musica) achieved a leading position under the direction of Mario Messinis (1979–82) and Carlo Fontana (1983–6), and included the premières of Salvatore Sciarrino's *Cailles en sarcophage* (1979, at the Malibran), Francesco Carluccio's *Prometeo liberato*

7. 'La finta pazza' (Sacrati): scene from the 1987 production by Alan Curtis (Campo Pisani, 7 July 1987) with sets based on the original scenography by Giacomo Torelli (c1641)

(1979), Niccolò Castiglioni's *Oberon, the Fairy Prince/ The Lords' Masque* (1981) and Nono's *Prometeo* (1984; for this production Renzo Piano designed a set in the deconsecrated church of S Lorenzo). There have also been festivals devoted to historical avant-garde movements, and revivals of old operas (Sartorio's *L'Orfeo*, 1979; Pergolesi's *Il Flaminio*, 1981). The activity of the Fenice, especially under the artistic direction of Italo Gomez (1979–87), was distinguished for revivals of rare operas, especially in the bel canto tradition, and the introduction of musicological projects. Notable among these were the first *Don Carlos* to include the material suppressed at the Paris première (1973), various works by the 'serious' Rossini and by Handel (*Agrippina*, *Orlando*, *Rinaldo*), Donizetti's *Maria di Rudenz* (1980), the first version of Puccini's *Madama Butterfly* (1982), Verdi's *Stiffelio* (performed with *Aroldo*), the Ricci brothers' *Crispino e la comare* (1985) and in the same year the 'stage' performance of Bach's *St John Passion* directed by Pier Luigi Pizzi. In 1987 Sacrati's recently discovered *La finta pazza* was staged by La Fenice in an open-air production based on the original scenography by Torelli. Some important premières of contemporary works should also be mentioned, such as Camillo Togni's *Blaubart* (1977) and Aldo Clementi's *ES* (1981).

*

AllacciD; *ES* (M. T. Muraro)

C. Ivanovich: *Minerva al tavolino* (Venice, 1681)

G. Bonlini: *Le glorie della poesia e della musica* (Venice, 1730)

A. Groppo: *Catalogo di tutti … fin all'anno presente 1745 drammi per musica recitati ne' teatri di Venezia dall'anno 1637c* (Venice, 1745)

——: *Notizia generale de' teatri della città di Venezia* (Venice, 1766)

R. Arrigoni: *Notizie e osservazioni intorno all'origine ed al progresso dei teatri in Venezia* (Venice, 1840)

F. Caffi: *Storia della musica teatrale in Venezia* (Venice, 1854–5)

A. M. Fabris: *La Fenice* (Padua, 1868)

E. Uberti: *I teatri di Venezia* (Venice, 1868)

L. Lianovosani [G. Salvioli]: *La Fenice, gran teatro di Venezia: serie degli spettacoli dalla primavera 1792 a tutto il carnovale 1876* (Milan, 1876)

G. Salvioli: 'Saggio di drammaturgia veneziana', *Archivio veneto*, xii (1876), 193–202, 432–40; xiii (1877), 451–67

L. N. Galvani [G. Salvioli]: *I teatri musicali di Venezia nel secolo XVII (1637–1700)* (Milan, 1879)

B. Cecchetti: 'Carte relative ai teatri di S. Cassiano e dei SS. Giovanni e Paolo', *Archivio veneto*, xvii (1887), 246

T. Wiel: *I codici musicali contariniani del secolo XVII nella R. Biblioteca di S. Marco in Venezia* (Venice, 1888)

H. Kretzschmar: 'Die venetianische Oper und die Werke Cavallis und Cestis', *VMw*, viii (1892), 1–76

M. Scherillo: 'La prima commedia musicale a Venezia', *Giornale storico della letteratura italiana*, i (1893), 230

T. Wiel: *I teatri musicali veneziani nel settecento* (Venice, 1897)

L. C. Borghi: *La polizia sugli spettacoli nella Repubblica Veneta e sulle produzioni teatrali nel primo governo austriaco* (Venice, 1898)

A. Solerti: 'Le rappresentazioni musicali di Venezia dal 1571 al 1605', *RMI*, ix (1902), 503–58

R. Rolland: 'L'opéra populaire à Venise: Francesco Cavalli', *Mercure musical*, ii/1 (1906), 60–70, 151–60

H. Kretzschmar: 'Beiträge zur Geschichte der venetianischen Oper', *JbMP 1907*, 71–81; *1910*, 61–71; *1911*, 49–61

E. Wellesz: 'Cavalli und der Stil der venetianischen Oper 1640–1660', *SMw*, i (1913), 1–103

G. Pavan: *Il Teatro S. Benedetto (ora Rossini): catalogo cronologico degli spettacoli* (Venice, 1916)

Various authors: *Il Teatro Malibran di Venezia* (Venice, 1919)

A. Sandberger: 'Zur venetianischen Oper', *JbMP 1924*, 61–70; *1925*, 53–63

M. Nani Mocenigo: *Il Teatro la Fenice: note storiche e artistiche* (Venice, 1926)

V. Malamani: 'Il teatro lirico a Venezia nel secolo XVIII', *Archivio veneto*, 5th ser., i (1927), 191–220

H. Prunières: *Cavalli et l'opéra vénitien au XVIIe siècle* (Paris, 1931)

H. C. Wolff: *Die venetianische Oper in der zweiten Hälfte des 17. Jahrhunderts* (Berlin, 1937)

B. Brunelli: 'L'impresario in angustie', *Rivista italiana del dramma*, v (1941), 311–41

P. De Pità: *Origini e curiosità del Teatro Goldoni* (Venice, 1945)

S. T. Worsthorne: 'Venetian Theatres, 1637–1700', *ML*, xxix (1948), 263–75

——: *Venetian Opera in the Seventeenth Century* (Oxford, 1954)

N. Pirrotta: 'Commedia dell'arte and Opera', *MQ*, xli (1955), 305–24

E. Povoledo: 'Tendenze della scenografia veneziana del seicento in rapporto agli altri centri dell'Italia settentrionale', *Venezia e l'europa: Venice 1955*, 329–33

G. Cozzi: 'Appunti sul teatro e i teatri a Venezia agli inizi del '600', *Bollettino dell'Istituto di storia della società e dello stato veneziano*, i (1959), 187–92

G. Damerini: 'Cronache del Teatro Vendramin', *Il dramma*, no.291 (1960), 101–15; no.294 (1961), 49–58; no.296, pp.41–52; no.298, pp.41–52; no.302, pp.55–66

P. Bjurström: *Giacomo Torelli and Baroque Stage Design*

(Stockholm, 1961)
W. Osthoff: 'Maske und Musik: die Gestaltwerdung der Oper in Venedig', *Castrum Peregrini*, lxv (1964), 10–49
P. Petrobelli: 'L'"Ermiona" di Pio Enea degli Obizzi e i primi spettacoli d'opera veneziani', *Quaderni della RaM*, iii (1965), 125–41
P. Bjurström: 'Unveröffentliches von Nicodemus Tessin d.J.: Reisenotizen über Barock-Theater in Venedig und Piazzola', *Kleine Schriften der Gesellschaft für Theatergeschichte*, xxi (1966), 14–41
N. Pirrotta: 'Il caval zoppo e il vetturino: cronache di Parnaso 1642', *CHM*, iv (1966), 215–26
R. Giazotto: 'La guerra dei palchi: documenti per servire alla storia del teatro musicale a Venezia come istituto sociale e iniziativa privata nei secoli XVII e XVIII', *NRMI*, i (1967), 245–86, 465–508
P. Petrobelli: 'Francesco Manelli: documenti ed osservazioni', *Chigiana*, xxiv (1967), 43–66
M. Velimirović: 'Cristoforo Ivanovich from Budva, the First Historian of the Venetian Opera', *Zvuk*, nos.77–8 (1967), 135–45
S. Dalla Libera: 'L'archivio del Teatro la Fenice', *Ateneo veneto*, vi (1968), 135–46
C. Sartori: 'La prima diva della lirica italiana: Anna Renzi', *NRMI*, ii (1968), 430–52
R. Giazotto: 'Nel CCC anno della morte di Antonio Cesti: ventidue lettere ritrovate nell'Archivio di Stato di Venezia', *NRMI*, iii (1969), 496–512
N. Pirrotta: 'Early Venetian Opera Librettos at Los Angeles', *Essays in Musicology in Honor of Dragan Plamenac* (Pittsburgh, 1969)
M. T. Muraro, ed.: *Studi sul teatro veneto fra Rinascimento ed età barocca* (Florence, 1971)
L. Zorzi and others: *I teatri pubblici di Venezia (secoli XVII–XVIII)* (Venice, 1971)
M. L. Padoan: *La scenografia al Teatro 'La Fenice' nell'ottocento* (diss., U. of Padua, 1972)
Venezia e il melodramma nel seicento: Venice 1972
Venezia e il melodramma nel settecento: Venice 1973–5
N. Mangini: *I teatri di Venezia* (Milan, 1974)
L. Bianconi and T. Walker: 'Dalla *Finta pazza* alla *Veremonda*: storie di Febiarmonici', *RIM*, x (1975), 379–454
J. Glover: *The Teatro S. Apollinare and the Development of 17th-Century Venetian Opera* (diss., U. of Oxford, 1975)
——: 'The Peak Period of Venetian Public Opera: the 1650s', *PRMA*, cii (1975–6), 67–82
G. Verardo Tieri: 'Il Teatro Novissimo: storia di "mutationi macchine e musiche"', *NRMI*, x (1976), 555–95; xi (1977), 3–25
L. Zorzi: *Il teatro e la città* (Turin, 1977)
F. Degrada and M. T. Muraro, eds.: *Antonio Vivaldi da Venezia all'Europa* (Milan, 1978)
C. B. Schmidt: 'An Episode in the History of Venetian Opera: the "Tito" Commission (1665–66)', *JAMS*, xxxi (1978), 442–66
M. Lavagetto: *Un caso di censura: il 'Rigoletto'* (Milan, 1979)
C. E. Troy: *The Comic Intermezzo* (Ann Arbor, 1979)
E. Rosand: 'In Defense of the Venetian Libretto', *Studi musicali*, ix (1980), 271–85
O. Termini: 'Singers at San Marco in Venice: the Competition between Church and Theatre', *RMARC*, no.17 (1981), 65–96
Antonio Vivaldi: teatro musicale, cultura e società: Venice 1981
M. De Angelis: *Le carte dell'impresario: melodramma e costume teatrale nell'ottocento* (Florence, 1982)
A. L. Bellina and T. Walker: 'Il melodramma: poesia e musica nell'esperienza teatrale', *Storia della cultura veneta*, ed. G. Arnaldi and M. P. Stocchi, iv/1 (Vicenza, 1983), 409–32
M. Conati: *La bottega della musica: Verdi e la Fenice* (Milan, 1983)
S. Mamy: *L'influence des chanteurs napolitains sur l'évolution de l'opéra baroque tardif vénitien au théâtre San Giovanni Grisostomo (1701–1755)* (diss., U. of Paris-Sorbonne, 1983)
A. L. Bellina: 'Metastasio in Venezia: appunti per una *recensio*', *Italianistica*, xiii (1984), 145–73
S. Benedetti: 'Il teatro musicale a Venezia nel '600: aspetti organizzativi', *Studi veneziani*, viii (1984), 185–221
L. Bianconi and T. Walker: 'Production, Consumption and Political Function of Seventeenth-Century Opera', *Early Music History*, iv (1984), 209–96
T. Walker: '"Ubi Lucius": Thoughts on Reading *Medoro*', *DMV*, iv (1984), pp.cxxxi–clxiv
P. Weiss: 'Venetian Commedia dell'Arte "Operas" in the Age of Vivaldi', *MQ*, lxx (1984), 195–217
A. L. Bellina and B. Brizi: 'Il melodramma', *Storia della cultura veneta*, ed. G. Arnaldi and M. P. Stocchi, v/1 (Vicenza, 1985), 337–400
B. Glixon: *Recitative in Seventeenth-Century Venetian Opera: its Dramatic Function and Musical Language* (diss. Rutgers U., 1985)
H. S. Saunders: *The Repertoire of a Venetian Opera House (1678–1714): the Teatro Grimani di San Giovanni Grisostomo* (diss., Harvard U., 1985)
E. Selfridge-Field: *Pallade veneta: Writings on Music in Venetian Society 1650–1750* (Venice, 1985)
T. Bauman: 'The Society of La Fenice and its First Impresarios', *JAMS*, xxxix (1986), 332–54
A. L. Bellina and B. Brizi: 'Il melodramma e la musica strumentale', *Storia della cultura veneta*, ed. G. Arnaldi and M. P. Stocchi, vi (Vicenza, 1986), 429–60
L. Zoppelli: 'Il rapto perfettissimo: un'inedita testimonianza sulla "Proserpina" di Monteverdi', *Rassegna veneta di studi musicali*, ii–iii (1986–7), 343–5
L. Bianconi and G. Pestelli, eds.: *Storia dell'opera italiana* (Turin, 1987–)
M. Brusatin and G. Pavanello: *Il Teatro la Fenice* (Venice, 1987)
H. Leclerc: *Venise et l'avénement de l'opéra public à l'âge baroque* (Paris, 1987)
G. Morelli: '"Il filo di Poppea": il soggetto antico-romano nell'opera veneziana del seicento: osservazioni', *Venezia–Roma* (Milan, 1987), 245–63
I vicini di Mozart: Venice 1987
N. Dubowy: '"I trionfi della costanza": sulle fonti dell'opera veneziana: una partitura ritrovata di Marc'Antonio Ziani', *Rassegna veneta di studi musicali*, iv (1988), 113–22
M. G. Miggiani: 'Giovanni Bertati impresario al S Moisè', *Rassegna veneta di studi musicali*, iv (1988), 153–75
L. Trezzini: 'Venezia, la Fenice, la Biennale nell'Europa musicale', *L'Europa musicale*, ed. A. L. Bellina and G. Morelli (Venice, 1988)
M. Girardi and F. Rossi: *Il Teatro la Fenice: cronologia degli spettacoli* (Venice, 1989–)
E. Rosand: 'The Opera Scenario, 1638–1655: a Preliminary Survey', *In canto et in sermone: for Nino Pirrotta on his 80th Birthday* (Florence, 1989), 335–46
M. G. Miggiani: 'Il teatro di S. Moisè (1793–1818): con cronologia degli spettacoli', *Bollettino del Centro rossiniano di studi*, xxx (1990), 5–213
E. Rosand: *Opera in Seventeenth-Century Venice: the Creation of a Genre* (Berkeley, 1991)
F. Mancini, M. T. Muraro and E. Povoledo: *I teatri del veneto*, i (Venice, 1992)
B. L. Glixon and J. E. Glixon: 'Marco Faustini and Venetian Opera Production in the 1650s: Recent Archival Discoveries', *JM*, x (1992–3), 48–73
F. Piperno: 'L'opera buffa fra Napoli e Venezia: i cantati e il repertorio', *Il teatro musicale a Venezia e a Napoli nel settecento*, ed. F. Degrada (Florence, forthcoming) LUCA ZOPPELLI

Vénitienne, La ('The Venetian'). *Ballet* in a prologue and three acts by MICHEL DE LA BARRE to a libretto by ANTOINE HOUDAR DE LAMOTTE; Paris, Opéra, 26 May 1705.

The story is set in Venice, in a cellar and an apartment near St Mark's Square. The inconstant Octave deserts Isabelle in order to court Léonore; but, after intervening in a magic ceremony, hiding in the darkness, then appearing in disguise at a ball, Isabelle finally succeeds in winning the heart of the one she loves. The third act proved the most popular: it was revived in 1711 as the last *entrée* of *Les nouveaux fragments* (a work composed of extracts of operas by Lully, Campra and Destouches) and in 1726 as the third *divertissement* of *Le ballet sans titre* (extracts of operas by Stuck, Mouret and Campra). The libretto, which shows the influence of that for *Le Carnaval et la Folie* by Lamotte for Destouches (1703), calls for sung dialogue throughout, in a humorous tone that mocks the magical scenes of *tragédies en musique*. With its Venetian subject, then very fashionable, its lively marches, *branle* and *forlane*, and its symphony of sleep, however, the work is most closely related to Campra's *Le carnaval de Venise* of 1699, another ballet with continuous action.

JÉRÔME DE LA GORCE

Ventadour [Salle Ventadour]. Theatre used by the Opéra-Comique, Paris (1829–32), the Théâtre Italien (1841–78) and other companies; *see* PARIS, §4(iii, v).

Ventaglio, Il ('The Fan'). *Commedia per musica* by PIETRO RAIMONDI to a libretto by DOMENICO GILARDONI after CARLO GOLDONI's play; Naples, Teatro Nuovo, 22 January 1831.

Although Gilardoni transferred the setting from Lombardy to Naples, the broad outlines of Goldoni's plot are respected. Don Evaristo (tenor), in love with Donna Candida (mezzo-soprano), secretly purchases a new fan to replace the one she has accidentally broken. The busybody shopkeeper Susanna (mezzo-soprano) is curious to know for whom the fan is intended, but Evaristo evades her questions; later, observed from a distance by Susanna, he entrusts it to the peasant girl Palmetella (soprano), asking her to present it to Candida. Concluding that the fan was intended for Palmetella, Susanna rushes to report what she has witnessed to the innkeeper Coronato (bass) and the cobbler Crespino (tenor), whose bitter rivalry over Palmetella constitutes the principal subplot of the opera; they now direct their ire towards Evaristo. Susanna also spreads the rumour to Palmetella's brother Moracchio (bass), who forbids her to leave their house, thus thwarting her mission, and to Candida, who is devastated by Evaristo's apparent betrayal. Further complications arise when the Count (baritone) offers both to mediate in the Crespino-Coronato rivalry over Palmetella (only to decide that he wishes to marry her himself) and to intercede with Candida's aunt Geltrude (contralto) on behalf of his friend the Baron (tenor), who wishes to marry Candida. The fan runs like a connecting thread through all the twists and turns of the complicated plot, arriving finally in the hands of Candida. Evaristo is united with Candida, Palmetella with Crispino, Coronato with Susanna and the Count with Geltrude; all join in a chorus of praise for the fan, which has been the source of such confusion and hilarity.

Written in a gracious, tuneful style reminiscent of Paisiello but with Rossinian touches, *Il ventaglio* was the most frequently performed comic opera in Naples during the mid-19th century. It calls for a high degree of ensemble work; there is only one aria and even that rapidly develops into an ensemble piece. The opera's most celebrated numbers are both in the second act, the trio 'Due casette di campagna', sung by Geltrude, the Count and the Baron, and the quartet 'Leggi, leggi, via fà presto', sung by the Count, Moracchio, Coronato and Crespino. Animated arguments and misunderstandings, exacerbated by near deafness or blindness, figure prominently in each piece. For a Milanese production in 1834 the parts in Neapolitan dialect (Palmetella, Moracchio, Coronato and Susanna) were translated into Italian, and the spoken dialogues were reduced, versified and set to recitatives of unknown authorship. In this guise the opera spread throughout Italy and as far afield as Athens and Odessa, enjoying sporadic revivals into the 20th century. Though increasing the potential audience for the work, a translation considerably weakens the comic effect of scenes in which Raimondi deftly juxtaposed the dialect- and Italian-speaking characters.

JESSE ROSENBERG

Venth, Carl (*b* Cologne, 16 Feb 1860; *d* San Antonio, TX, 29 Jan 1938). American composer of German birth. He studied with Henryk Wieniawski at the Brussels Conservatory and served as leader of the symphony orchestra in Utrecht and of the Opéra-Comique orchestra in Paris. In 1884 he became leader of the Metropolitan Opera orchestra in New York. From 1908 he lived in Texas, where he founded symphony orchestras at both Dallas and Fort Worth, and in 1931 he became Dean of Fine Arts at Westmoorland College (later the University of San Antonio).

Venth composed several short operas that combine dance, pantomime and pageantry. *Golden Bells* is based on an oriental subject; *Cathal* and *The Fisherman* use a Wagnerian system of leitmotifs. His four short 'scherzo plays', composed for two or three voices and small orchestra, resemble light Viennese operettas. In 1923 his 'lyric dance drama' *Pan in America* received the National Federation of Music Clubs prize. Performed by the New York PO, conducted by Venth, it involved soloists from the Metropolitan Opera and a children's chorus of several hundred voices. His last work, *La vida de la misión*, was written for the Texas Centennial of 1936 and tells the story of an Indian uprising in 1785 against the San Jose Mission in San Antonio.

The Rebel, 1900 (fairy op, 5 scenes, Venth), Fort Worth, 29 May 1926
Cathal, or Monk of Iona, 1908 (music drama, 1, F. McLeod)
Fair Betty (extravaganza, 2, Venth), Texas, vs (1916)
The Fisherman [Jack] (music drama, 1, H. E. Hard, after E. Phelps)
Golden Bells (dramatic scene, 1, Venth)
Lima Beans (scherzo play, 1, A. Kreymborg), Dallas, May 1922
Mannekin and Minnekin (scherzo play, 1, Kreymborg), Texas
Alexander's Horse (scherzo play, 1, M. Baring), Dallas, April 1923
Pan in America (operatic pageant, prol., 3 scenes, epilogue, R. F. Allen), Asheville, NC, National Federation of Music Clubs Convention, 13 June 1923, vs (Boston, 1924)
The Juggler (scherzo play, 1, Venth), Fort Worth, Feb 1926
Don Juan of the Dolls (operatic pantomime, 1, Venth)
Grand Duke and Duchess, or Ozone (comic op, 2, Venth)
La vida de la misión, 1935 (grand op, 2, Venth), San Antonio, Municipal Auditorium, 28 Oct 1959

E. E. Hipsher: *American Opera and its Composers* (Philadelphia, 2/1934), 416–18
C. Venth: *My Memoirs* (San Antonio, TX, 1939)
G. Gibbs: *Carl Venth (1860–1938): Texas's Master Musician – his Life, his Music, his Influence* (diss., U. of Texas, 1990)

ELISE K. KIRK

Vento, Mattia (*b* Naples, 1735; *d* London, 22 Nov 1776). Italian composer. His early musical training at the Conservatorio di S Maria di Loreto in Naples was followed by a number of operatic successes in Rome, Venice and Milan. In 1763 Giardini brought him to London, where he composed operas until his death. In the pasticcio *Leucippo e Zenocrita* (1764) he made his first contribution to the London stage. In 1765 his first complete London opera, *Demofoonte*, was given concurrently with J. C. Bach's *Adriano in Siria*; the greater success of Vento's opera was a triumph for the Italians in London. *Demofoonte* was given 14 times during the 1764–5 season and six the next season. The following two seasons at the King's Theatre saw the premières of two more complete operas, *Sofonisba* (1766) and *La conquista del Messico* (1767). After a mysterious hiatus of seven years, Vento's final operas, *Il bacio* and *La vestale* (his only comic opera for London), were given at the King's Theatre in 1776.

Vento's operas were popular with London audiences. Between 1765 and 1776 five operas were given a total of

68 performances at the King's Theatre. Many arias found their way into pasticcios, both Italian and English, and into 18th-century song anthologies. Burney explained the popularity of his music: 'Vento's genius never approached the sublime; however, his melody was totally free from vulgarity, and, though not new, was always pleasing and graceful'. Another critic, writing in the *Public Advertiser* (19 March 1766), was more enthusiastic: '[*Sofonisba*] is most beautifully heightened by the harmonious sounds of Signor Vento ... the song *Che bramate o giusti Dei*, heightened by Mr Vincent's hautboy, worked powerfully on every one as was evident from the high applause'. This da capo aria for strings, bassoons, horns and obbligato oboe does have some beautiful moments. The constant interplay of soprano and oboe, as well as the modulation to the relative minor in the middle section, produce a hauntingly tragic atmosphere for this death scene.

arias from London productions published in Favourite Songs

Le deluse accortezze di Don Gianserio (int), Rome, 1756
La finta semplice (? C. Goldoni), Rome, 1759
L'egiziana (dg, F. Ronzi), Venice, 1763, *A-Wn*; arr. F. L. Gassmann as Zingara, Vienna, 1769
Demofoonte (3, P. Metastasio), London, King's, 2 March 1765
Sofonisba (op eroica, 3, G. G. Bottarelli), London, King's, 21 Jan 1766, *US-Wc*; as pasticcio, 1772–3
La conquista del Messico [La conquista del vello d'oro] (Bottarelli), London, King's, 4 April 1767, ov., arias *GB-Mp*
Artaserse (?Metastasio), London, 1771
Il bacio (comic op, 3, C. F. Badini), London, King's, 9 Jan 1776
La vestale (serious opera, Badini), London, King's, 6 Feb 1776

Music in: Leucippo e Zenocrita (1764); Ezio (1764); Berenice (1765); Daphne and Amintor (1765); Solimano (1765); [The Revenge of] Arthridates (1766); Love in the City (1767); Lionel and Clarissa (1768), rev. as School for Fathers (1770); The Captive (1769); La sposa fedele (1775); Antigono (1776); The Castle of Andalusia (1782)

*

BurneyH
F. Torrefranca: 'Intermezzo di date e documenti', *RMI*, xxvi (1919), 140–67, 291–331, esp. 322–31
——: 'Influenza di alcuni musicisti italiani vissuti a Londra su W. A. Mozart (1764–65)', *Kongressbericht: Basel 1924*, 336–62
C. S. Terry: *John Christian Bach* (London, 1929, 2/1967)
F. Petty: *Italian Opera in London, 1760–1800* (Ann Arbor, 1980)

FREDERICK PETTY

Ventura, Giuseppe (*b* Naples, ?1702; *d* after 1751). Italian composer. He provided one of the settings for Pietro Trinchera's earliest dialect comedy *Prìzeta correvata* (Aversa, nr Naples, Nuovo, autumn 1732), an adaptation from an unknown author. The other setting, *Li 'nnamorate correvate* (Angri, nr Salerno, August 1732), was by 'Jacovo d'Ambrosio', probably Giacomo d'Ambrosio, the principal *buffo* singer at the Naples Teatro dei Fiorentini between 1728 and 1741; it is not known which performance was first.

In collaboration with Logroscino, Ventura also wrote the comic opera *Amore figlio del piacere* (A. Palomba; Naples, Nuovo, Carnival 1751). The intermezzo *Le deluse accortezze di Don Gianserio* (1756, Rome), sometimes attributed to him, was written by Mattia Vento.

*

FlorimoN
M. Scherillo: *L'opera buffa napoletana durante il settecento: storia letteraria* (Naples, 1883, 2/1916), 229–30

JAMES L. JACKMAN

Venturini, Clarice Beni (*b* Parma; *fl* 1686–97). Italian soprano. She is first mentioned in Milan in 1686 in the role of Julia in Antonio Sartorio's *Antonino e Pompeiano*. She was already designated a 'virtuosa' of the Duke of Parma, whose service she entered officially on 15 June 1687, remaining until 15 February 1695. In 1687 she was again in Milan, in Carlo Pallavicino's *Galieno*, and she was then active principally in Parma (1688–90, 1692, 1696–7) and Piacenza (1688, 1692, 1694). She also sang in Modena, Venice, Bergamo, Crema and Lodi (1692–3, 1695). She married Giuseppe Venturini, chief violinist at the court of Parma.

PAOLA BESUTTI

Venus and Adonis **(i).** Tragic opera in a prologue and three acts by JOHN BLOW; London or Windsor, court, *c*1683.

Cupid	soprano
Venus	soprano
Adonis	baritone
Shepherd	alto
Shepherdess	soprano
Huntsman	alto

Choruses of shepherds, shepherdesses, huntsmen, little cupids, courtiers

Setting Venus's palace

One of the early manuscript scores describes *Venus and Adonis* as 'A Masque for the entertainment of the King', that is, Charles II. It was presumably mounted privately at court, though there is no record of the venue and the identity of the librettist remains unknown; the suggestion that, because of its feminist overtones, the poem might have been written by Aphra Behn, with whom Blow later collaborated on a play, is intriguing but unproven. The same early manuscript also records that the actress-singer Mary (Moll) Davies, the king's former mistress, took the part of Venus, while their illegitimate daughter, Lady Mary Tudor (about ten years old at the time), sang the part of Cupid. This unusual casting tends to confirm the private nature of the first production. The opera is to some extent a satire on the liberal sexual mores of King Charles's court, and the fact that from September 1683 Lady Mary was granted an annuity of £1500 suggests that the entertainment was designed as a gentle reminder to the king of his extramarital responsibilities.

A recently discovered printed libretto of *Venus and Adonis* shows that the opera was revived on 17 April 1684 at Josias Priest's boarding-school at Chelsea, the same institution that mounted Purcell's *Dido and Aeneas* some time later. Blow's original score was apparently arranged for all-female performance, since Priest's daughter acted Adonis (a baritone in the main sources), with Misses Baker and Helsham as Venus and Cupid respectively. No other public or private production is recorded during Blow's lifetime, but the existence of several contemporaneous manuscript scores shows that the opera possibly enjoyed further revivals, first in the early 1690s and then around 1700.

Venus and Adonis is the earliest surviving English opera and served as the model for Purcell's *Dido and Aeneas*. It is further remarkable for being through-composed (with no spoken dialogue) and for having a tragic ending. While the musico-dramatic structure is *sui generis*, Blow was indebted to Matthew Locke for the basic style of the recitative: a measured arioso, always in duple metre, in which expressive words are set melismatically and sometimes repeated. *Venus and Adonis* also resembles Lully's *tragédies en musique* in its reliance on dance to articulate and relieve the drama and for the inclusion of a French overture. But to Blow alone should go the credit for creating large, coherent structures in which recitative, ariettas and choruses constantly alternate to impel the story to its tragic conclusion.

Purcell's debt to Blow is everywhere to be seen in *Dido and Aeneas*. Both works are three-act miniatures with an active and dramatically multifarious chorus; both include scenes of comic relief (the Cupids' spelling lesson in Blow, the sailors' scene in Purcell); each ends with the death of one of the lovers. Purcell borrowed many melodic details from Blow and even alluded to the earlier work in Act 2 scene i, where Aeneas enters with a 'monster's head' impaled on his spear: Adonis's death by the Aedalian boar is thus avenged. The most obvious difference between the two operas is Blow's almost total avoidance of arias or other set pieces. The music is virtually continuous from beginning to end.

PROLOGUE *The grove* After a rather brash French overture, Cupid addresses the shepherds and shepherdesses (actually Venus's courtiers) in his traditional posture ('Behold my arrows and my bow'). They are inclined to make love; he at first deplores their general faithlessness ('At Court I find constant and true/ Only an aged lord or two'), then invites them to seek the sweetest pleasures of the grove.

ACT 1 *A room in Venus's palace* Venus and Adonis are discovered embracing on a couch; an obbligato recorder is added to the sensuous recitative; she toys with his sexual frustration ('Adonis, thy delightful youth') and is about to let him have his way when hunting music is heard ('Hark, hark the rural music sounds'). Adonis vows not to join the chase, but Venus (in a departure from the myth) urges him to leave ('Absence kindles new desire'), and Blow underscores the line 'I would not have my lover tire' with witty, descending chromatic lines. Adonis responds indignantly to her teasing, but the huntsmen burst in to describe a mighty boar that is wreaking havoc. Unable to resist the challenge, he leaves for the hunt.

ACT 2 *A room in Venus's palace* Cupid is taking instruction in the art of love from Venus, his mother, who sings the arietta 'Fit well your arrows when you strike'. Cupid in turn teaches the Little Cupids, a children's chorus, to spell the word 'mercenary', a few letters at a time. Cupid responds with the only proper aria of the opera, 'Choose for the formal fool' (in binary form). When he humorously advises his mother to treat Adonis badly to assure his constancy, Blow writes out Venus's terrifying laugh note-for-note. The rest of this act is occupied by an incidental scene for the Graces who sing the chorus 'Mortals below, Cupids above' and offer a series of dances, culminating in a long chaconne.

ACT 3 *The same room* The curtain opens to show Venus standing 'in a melancholy posture. A mourning Cupid goes across the stage and shakes an arrow at her'. The recitative which opened Act 1 is transformed into a portentous wail ('Adonis, uncall'd for sighs'). Adonis, gored by the wild boar, is led in mortally wounded. After a passionate exchange, he sings his final ironic lines, 'Let me on your soft bosom lie/There I did wish to live, and there I beg to die'. Struggling to regain her composure, Venus begins a funeral march ('With solemn pomp') and is joined by her courtiers. The finest piece in the opera is the final G minor chorus, 'Mourn for thy servant', whose elegiac counterpoint does not suffer from comparison with the similar final chorus of *Dido and Aeneas*.

* * *

The tragedy of *Venus and Adonis* is born of circumstance rather than inner conflict, as in Purcell's opera. But Blow has drawn a vivid picture of pastoral indolence, sexual impetuosity and grief, all of which are visited upon real characters. That the score includes only one outstanding piece ('Mourn for thy servant') is less a comment on Blow's inspiration than an indication of his desire for true *dramma per musica* in which nothing is allowed to impede the action. CURTIS PRICE

Venus and Adonis **(ii).** Masque in two interludes by JOHANN CHRISTOPH PEPUSCH to a libretto by Colley Cibber after OVID's *Metamorphoses*, book x; London, Drury Lane, 12 March 1715.

Pepusch composed no original dramatic music before accepting the position of music director at Drury Lane in 1714. Though he remained there for only two seasons, he composed four musical afterpieces, the first and most substantial of which is the masque of *Venus and Adonis*. The piece has only three principal characters: Venus (soprano), Adonis (soprano, sung as a travesty role) and Mars (tenor, but reset for bass for a revival in 1718–19 at Lincoln's Inn Fields). The scene is a rural setting near Mount Ida in Crete. The first interlude involves only Venus and Adonis in an amusing tale of amorous pursuit. The second interlude is in vivid contrast: Cibber introduces the truculent Mars, whose jealousy of Adonis, occasionally presented under a thin veil of humour, is useful for the purposes of dramatic and musical contrast, but obtrudes strangely into Ovid's original story.

Pepusch's music is distinctly italianate. The piece begins with an Italian overture scored for strings and woodwind, highlighted by virtuoso treatment in concertato style. All but one of the 15 arias are in da capo form, and each is introduced by parlando recitative. One of the more elaborate and dramatic arias is 'Cupid, bend thy bow', which has forceful orchestral comments contrasted with an oboe obbligato imitating the voice. The dramatic climax of the masque is Adonis's poignant lament, 'O welcome gentle death', scored for strings and transverse flute. Though called a masque, the work is essentially a miniature italianate opera.

Venus and Adonis received only four contemporary performances after 1719 and was last performed for Jane Barbier's benefit night on 16 March 1730. A modern revival was staged at Holme Pierrepont Hall, Nottingham, on 17 September 1980. The full score and instrumental parts survive in manuscript (in *GB-Lcm*); the songs were printed by Walsh (London, 1715).

D. F. COOK

Vêpres siciliennes, Les [*I vespri siciliani* ('The Sicilian Vespers')]. *Opéra* in five acts by GIUSEPPE VERDI to a libretto by EUGÈNE SCRIBE and Charles Duveyrier after their libretto *Le duc d'Albe*; Paris, Opéra, 13 June 1855.

After the performances of *Jérusalem* at the Opéra in 1847 Verdi had intended to produce an entirely new opera for the first theatre of Paris, but the revolutions of 1848 caused the plan to be shelved. He renewed negotiations with the Opéra, however, in 1852, and a

Guy de Montfort (Montforte) *Governor of Sicily under Charles d'Anjou, King of Naples*		baritone
Le Sire de Béthune	*French officers*	bass
Count de Vaudemont	*French officers*	bass
Henri (Arrigo) *a young Sicilian*		tenor
Jean Procida *a Sicilian doctor*		bass
Duchess Hélène (Elena) *sister of Duke Frédéric of Austria*		soprano
Ninetta *her maid*		contralto
Daniéli *a Sicilian*		tenor
Thibault (Tebaldo)	*French soldiers*	tenor
Robert (Roberto)	*French soldiers*	baritone
Mainfroid (Manfredo) *a Sicilian*		tenor

Sicilian men and women, French soldiers, monks, *corps de ballet*

Setting In and around Palermo, 1282

contract was drawn up for a full-scale French grand opera in five acts, with a libretto by Eugène Scribe, the acknowledged poetic master of the genre. After various subjects had been proposed, poet and composer eventually agreed to use a revised version of an existing libretto, *Le duc d'Albe*, written by Scribe and Charles Duveyrier for Halévy (who did not use it) and partly set to music by Donizetti in 1839. Verdi spent most of 1854 working at the score, making a reluctant Scribe undertake some important revisions and complaining about the sheer length demanded by audiences at the Opéra. The première, which included Marc Bonnehée (Montfort), Louis Guéymard (Henri), Louis-Henri Obin (Jean Procida) and Sophie Cruvelli (Hélène), was well received, even by such severe critics as Berlioz, but the work failed to enter the standard repertory of the Opéra. Its revolutionary subject caused difficulties with the Italian censors and it was first performed in Italian in a bowdlerized version translated by Eugenio Caimi and entitled *Giovanna de Guzman*. Later performances as *I vespri siciliani* retained most aspects of Caimi's translation and it is almost invariably in this Italian version that the opera is encountered today. For a revival at the Opéra in 1863, Verdi replaced 'O jour de peine' with the tenor *romance* 'O toi que j'ai chéri'.

The overture, the longest Verdi wrote and still sometimes revived in the concert hall, follows convention in being made up of themes drawn from the opera. It falls into two movements: a Largo, full of rhythmic 'death' figures, even in its more lyrical, major-mode section; and an Allegro agitato, whose main theme is taken from the Henri-Montfort duet in Act 3 and is repeated twice before a noisy Prestissimo brings the piece to a close.

ACT 1 *The main piazza in Palermo* The opening chorus, 'Beau pays de France!' ('Al cielo natio'), musically juxtaposes the victorious French soldiers with the resentful Sicilian people and includes a brief episode in which a drunken soldier, Robert, looks forward to claiming his share of the vanquished Sicilian women.

Hélène enters dressed in mourning; Béthune explains to Vaudemont that she is a hostage of Montfort and has come to pray for her brother Duke Frédéric, executed by Montfort a year ago. Robert staggers up, asking her for a song; she complies with a freely structured aria made up of three brief episodes (recitative, cantabile and linking Allegro), and a closing cabaletta, 'Courage! ... du courage!' ('Coraggio, su, coraggio'), in which she rallies the Sicilians around her. As the cabaletta draws to a close, the Sicilians advance on the French; but they are interrupted by the appearance of Montfort, who precipitates a largely unaccompanied quartet 'Quelle horreur m'environne!' ('D'ira fremo all'aspetto'), in which Hélène and Montfort explore their conflicting positions. Henri now arrives and, unaware of who Montfort is, explains to Hélène that he has inexplicably been released from prison by the Governor of Sicily but would dearly love to meet the tyrant face to face. At this Montfort reveals his identity and dismisses the women, thus preparing the ground for the closing duet finale. Like Hélène's aria, the duet passes through a number of short contrasting sections (as Montfort learns of Henri's history, offers him a commission in the French army and advises him to avoid Hélène) before closing with a cabaletta, 'Téméraire! téméraire!' ('Temerario! qual ardire!'), in which the characters' mutual defiance is reflected in a clash of strongly contrasting individual themes.

ACT 2 *A delightful valley near Palermo* An orchestral introduction suggesting the movement of a boat accompanies Procida's disembarkment. He greets his homeland in a brief recitative before beginning the famous Andante, 'Et toi, Palerme' ('O tu, Palermo'), fashioned in ternary form with a striking level of orchestral detail in the middle section. Procida's followers appear and together they sing the cabaletta 'Dans l'ombre et le silence' ('Nell'ombra e nel silenzio'), in which a stealthy, staccato choral passage precedes the main solo melody. Henri and Hélène arrive and are told by Procida that Spanish forces have agreed to aid the Sicilian cause, but that the Spaniards will not act unless there is a local uprising. Procida departs, to allow Henri and Hélène a two-movement duet – the first half of the traditional four-movement Italian model. In the first movement, the Allegro 'Comment, dans ma reconnaissance' ('Quale, o prode'), rapid dialogue precedes Henri's declaration of love; in the second, 'Près du tombeau peut-être' ('Presso alla tomba'), the couple sing together (though with highly differentiated lines), Hélène agreeing to accept Henri if he will avenge her brother's death.

Béthune appears, summoning Henri to a ball at Montfort's house that evening; when Henri refuses he is surrounded and dragged away. Hélène explains to Procida what has happened, but he is nevertheless determined to continue his plan of attack. To the strains of a festive tarantella, the stage fills with young Sicilian men and women, among them 12 brides and their prospective husbands. Some French soldiers arrive and Procida encourages them to take advantage of the local women – to such good effect that at the end of the dance the soldiers abduct the young brides at swordpoint. The chorus of outrage that follows, 'Interdits, accablés' ('Il rossor mi coprì!'), again obsessively repeating rhythmic 'death' figures, is interrupted by offstage voices singing a barcarolle: a boat is seen in the distance carrying French officers and Sicilian women. In a brief interlude, Procida decides that Montfort will be assassinated that very night; and the two very different choruses join in cleverly worked counterpoint to bring the act to a close.

ACT 3.i *A study in Montfort's palace* A brief orchestral prelude introduces Montfort, alone and brooding on his past: the woman he abducted many

Title-page (showing the Act 4 quartet) of the first edition of the vocal score of Verdi's 'Giovanna de Guzman' (Milan: Ricordi, 1855/6), the title under which 'Les vêpres siciliennes' was first performed in Italy

years ago has died, but she brought up their son Henri (who does not know his father's identity) to hate Montfort. The governor summons Henri to his presence before singing the famous 'Au sein de la puissance' ('In braccio alle dovizie'), a freely structured aria full of surprising harmonic excursions, in which he muses on his outward power and inward emptiness. Henri, entering, begins a lengthy duet, 'Quand ma bonté toujours nouvelle' ('Quando al mio sen'), which departs notably from standard Italian formal practice. There is a rapid alternation of tempos and moods in which Montfort presents Henri with proof of their relationship and, to a statement of the main theme of the overture (a melody that also dominates the final section of the duet), rejoices in his revelation. Henri is shocked, fears he must now lose Hélène and, in spite of Montfort's continued pleading, rejects the embrace of his father.

3.ii *A magnificent hall laid out for a grand ball* The long ballet that begins this scene is entitled 'Les quatre saisons' ('Le quattro stagioni') and, at least at the first production, entailed an elaborate mixture of mime and dance, with gods, zephyrs, naiads, fauns and a final dance to Bacchus. Verdi's succession of brief contrasting movements shows the requisite instrumental invention and rhythmic vitality, though it is perhaps too one-dimensional to be of much interest outside its immediate context.

The Act 3 finale is a large choral tableau, typical of French grand opera in its setting of private emotions within a public frame. The festive opening chorus, 'O fête brillante' ('O splendide feste!'), is interrupted by various dance tunes as Procida and Hélène approach Henri to tell him of the plot to murder Montfort. Henri warns Montfort of the danger but still refuses to side with his father. However, when Hélène tries to stab Montfort, Henri defends him and the conspirators are immediately arrested. The ensuing Adagio concertato, 'Coup terrible' ('Colpo orrendo'), which closes the act, is made up of two contrasting musical segments: first, a section of stunned surprise in which a tiny rhythmic motif is isolated and repeated; and then, its antithesis, a long lyrical melody in which all participants join to effect a stirring close.

Act 4 *The courtyard of a fortress* A robust orchestral introduction presents Henri, who shows a pass allowing him to visit the prisoners. He laments his position in 'O jour de peine' ('Giorno di pianto'), a strophic aria whose angular melodic arch and harmonic underpinning are quite unlike the Verdian norm and which ends with a fast coda. Hélène then arrives to precipitate the first movement of the grand duet, 'De courroux et d'effroi' ('O sdegni miei'), in which fragmentary responses coalesce into a patterned melody as Henri begs for understanding, the melody momentarily breaking into recitative when Henri admits the identity of his father. The second movement, 'Ami! ... le coeur d'Hélène' ('Arrigo! ah parli a un core'), is a miniature minor-major *romanza* for Hélène, in which she reconciles herself to Henri, though with no hope of their union; and the duet closes with a curtailed cabaletta, 'Pour moi rayonne' ('È dolce raggio').

Procida enters to announce that Spanish forces are ready to aid the revolutionaries; he is quickly followed by Montfort, who orders the prisoners' immediate execution. Procida then leads off the quartet, 'Adieu, mon pays' ('Addio, mia patria'), in which the principals explore their differing emotions. Montfort offers clemency if only Henri will call him 'father'. A *de profundis* is heard offstage, the place of execution is revealed and eventually, to a slow, high violin melody,

Henri submits. The prisoners are released and all join in a final stretta.

ACT 5 *Luxurious gardens in Montfort's palace in Palermo* The final act begins with three 'atmospheric' numbers in which the plot is barely advanced but local colour is richly explored. First comes the chorus 'Célébrons ensemble' ('Si celebri alfine'), quickly followed by Hélène's *sicilienne*, 'Merci, jeunes amies' ('Mercè, dilette amiche'), a *couplet* form entailing considerable virtuosity. Finally, there is Henri's lightly scored *mélodie* 'La brise souffle au loin' ('La brezza aleggia'), a song in praise of the evening breezes. Procida enters to announce the imminent uprising, which will begin at the sound of the wedding bells. He upbraids Hélène when he sees her love for Henri, who leads off the first movement of the terzetto finale, 'Sort fatal!' ('Sorte fatal!'). In spite of Hélène's pleading, Henri refuses to leave the scene and in the closing stretta of the trio, 'Trahison! imposture!' ('M'ingannasti, o traditrice'), the principals' conflicting positions are again explored. Montfort enters and signals for the wedding bells to sound. The Sicilians rush in with daggers drawn and fall on Montfort and the French.

* * *

Les vêpres siciliennes, in common with almost all French grand operas, has fallen from the repertory, its sheer length and the complexity of its vocal and scenic demands placing severe pressure on modern opera-house economics. There may also be purely musical reasons for the opera's comparative neglect: with a very few exceptions, its main lyrical numbers lack the melodic immediacy of the trio of Italian operas (*Rigoletto*, *Il trovatore* and *La traviata*) that immediately preceded it. However, for those wishing to understand Verdi's musical development during the 1850s, *Les vêpres siciliennes* is of enormous importance. In both strictly formal terms and in larger matters of operatic structure, it marks a decisive turn away from the language of the middle-period Italian operas and the emergence of many stylistic features we associate with the later Verdi. There is no subsequent Verdi opera in which the experience of *Les vêpres* will not be recalled and refined.

For a page from the *livret de mise en scène* based on the original Paris production, *see* PRODUCTION, fig.17. ROGER PARKER

Veprik, Alexander Moiseyevich (*b* Balta, nr Odessa, 11/23 June 1899; *d* Moscow, 13 Oct 1958). Russian composer and musicologist. He studied at Leipzig Conservatory with Reger and others and with D. V. Zhitomirsky at the Petrograd Conservatory (1918–21), then at the Moscow Conservatory under N. Y. Myaskovsky (1921–3), where he subsequently taught until 1943. In the controversy surrounding Shostakovich's *Lady Macbeth* in 1936 he was among the leaders of the Composers' Union who supported the work, for which he was sent to a prison camp. His works, in their emotional, ornamental style, represent the national Jewish school. He was among the group of Russian composers sent to the Central Asian Republics, going to Kirghizia (now Kïrgïstan), where his opera *Toktogul* to a libretto by D. Bokombayev was given at the opera house in Frunze (now Bishkek) in 1940; it was revised, in collaboration with A. Maldibayev, and revived in 1949.

Vera, Edoardo [Odoardo] (*b* Rome, Feb 1821; *d* Rome, March 1889). Italian composer. He studied music with his mother, the singer Charlotte Häser, and appeared as a pianist in concerts in London and Paris. His first opera, *Anelda da Messina*, was given at La Scala on 17 October 1843. He went to London, where he published a quantity of vocal music, including songs dedicated to Pauline Viardot. His sister, the soprano Sofia Vera-Lorini (*d* Livorno, 8 January 1882), was much admired for her interpretations of Gluck, Mozart and Beethoven; his other operas were both written for her. *Adriana Lecouvreur* (dramma lirico, 4, A. de Lanzières) was first given during the carnival season at Florence in 1859, and *Valeria* (tragedia lirica, 4, A. Ghislanzoni) at the Teatro Comunale, Bologna, on 16 March 1869. Adriana and the dual roles of Valeria/Licisca (a Greek courtesan) require a singer capable of both coloratura and dramatic declamation. In *Adriana* the passionate duet between the eponymous heroine and her rival, the adulterous Duchess of Bouillon (created by Maria Talvò), includes the fierce assertion by Adriana 'In mia mano è la tua fama' (anticipating the better-known Cilea setting, as does Adriana's fourth-act aria 'Cari fior'); she dies on a high B♭, exclaiming 'T'aspetto in ciel'. With their sextet finales in two sections modelled on those of Donizetti, Vera's operas must have seemed old-fashioned even in the 1860s. *Valeria* contains a mad scene for the emperor, Claudio (baritone), created by Antonio Cotogni. PATRICK O'CONNOR

Veracini, Francesco Maria (*b* Florence, 1 Feb 1690; *d* Florence, 31 Oct 1768). Italian composer and violinist. He was born into a family of musicians and artists and received his early training from his uncle Antonio Veracini, a violinist and composer. His other instructors included G. M. Casini and (apparently) G. A. Bernabei, with whom he may have studied in 1715 when he was in southern Germany. From 1711 (or earlier) his centre of activity was Venice, though he also performed in London and elsewhere. From 1717 to 1722 he served at the Dresden court.

After a period in Italy Veracini returned in 1733 to London, where he frequently appeared as a soloist. Perhaps he began immediately to play for the Opera of the Nobility, Handel's rival, which presented Veracini's first opera, *Adriano in Siria*, for a run of 20 performances beginning on 26 November 1735, with the composer leading. The same company gave his second opera, *La clemenza di Tito*, its four performances, 12–23 April 1737, as well as his third, *Partenio*, 14 March–6 June 1738. There being no opera in London for the season of 1738–9, Veracini returned briefly to Florence. But by 28 February 1741 he was back in London, playing a concerto between the acts of Handel's *Acis and Galatea*. During autumn 1742 he played concertos as entr'acte music at 21 dramatic performances at Drury Lane. A run of ten performances of his last opera, *Rosalinda*, an Italian adaptation by Paolo Rolli of Shakespeare's *As you Like it*, began on 31 January 1744. Veracini's inclusion of the popular ballad tune *The Lass of Paties Mill* in this opera greatly annoyed Burney, who condemned Veracini's own arias as 'wild, aukward, and unpleasant; manifestly produced by a man unaccustomed to write for the voice, and one possessed of a *capo pazzo*'. Though he may have shown signs of madness, Veracini was certainly not inexperienced in vocal music. At least half of his known output is for the voice. He spent his last years as a church musician in Florence.

Veracini's operas, composed only for London theatres, are outnumbered by his instrumental works and by his other vocal pieces. They resemble those of his Italian colleagues in London in their general musical style, but contain more strongly expressive arias, particularly of the *parlante* type. Consistent and contrasting character development, traced in the arias, is a notable feature of Veracini's operas.

all first performed in London, King's Theatre

Adriano in Siria (A. M. Cori, after P. Metastasio), 26 Nov 1735, *GB-Mp*, arias *Lbl* and *I-Rsc*, arias (London, 1736)

La clemenza di Tito (Cori, after Metastasio), 12 April 1737

Partenio (P. A. Rolli), 14 March 1738, ov. *GB-DRc*, arias *Lgc* and *I-Mc*

Rosalinda (Rolli, after W. Shakespeare: *As you Like it*), 31 Jan 1744, arias *D-Dlb*, arias (London, 1744)

*

BurneyH

J. Mattheson: *Critica musica*, i (Hamburg, 1722), 153, 224, 287

C. F. Cramer, ed.: *Magazin der Musik*, ii (1785), 373ff

M. Fürstenau: *Zur Geschichte der Musik und des Theaters am Hofe der Kurfürsten von Sachsen und Könige von Polen* (Dresden, 1862)

I. Becker-Glauch: *Die Bedeutung der Musik für die Dresdener Hoffeste bis in die Zeit Augusts des Starken* (Kassel, 1951)

F. C. Ricci: 'Appunti per una biografia di Francesco Maria Veracini nel bicentenario della morte (1690–1768)', *Annuario dell'Accademia nazionale di Santa Cecilia* (1968), 155–94

M. G. White: 'The Life of Francesco Maria Veracini', *ML*, liii (1972), 18–35

J. W. Hill: *The Life and Works of Francesco Maria Veracini* (Ann Arbor, 1979)

JOHN WALTER HILL

Vera costanza, La (i) ('True Constancy'). *Dramma giocoso* in three acts by PASQUALE ANFOSSI to a libretto by Francesco Puttini; Rome, Teatro delle Dame, 2 January 1776.

The opera is a *comédie larmoyante* which connects the archetypes of the quasi-folktale of the patient Griselda and Samuel Richardson's *Pamela, or Virtue Rewarded*. The fishergirl Rosina (soprano) has secretly married Count Errico (tenor) and has borne him a child. He has since rejected her. His aunt, Baroness Irene (soprano), wants to marry the Cavaliere Ernesto (tenor), but she believes that her nephew Errico's suspected interest in Rosina will tarnish the family reputation. The buffoon Villotto (bass) is brought in to marry Rosina, but in the end Errico rediscovers his love, the Baroness relents and all ends happily. The text is akin to that set by Haydn in 1779; Anfossi's music is perhaps too uniformly mellifluous and sweet. The opera received well over 20 productions in its first five years, travelled as far afield as London and Copenhagen by 1778 and remained in the repertory until the early 1790s.

MARY HUNTER

Vera costanza, La (ii) ('True Constancy'). *Dramma giocoso* in three acts by JOSEPH HAYDN to a libretto by Francesco Puttini; Eszterháza, 25 April 1779.

There is insufficient evidence to prove that Haydn wrote this opera to fulfil an imperial commission, as claimed by his early biographers. It represents a considerably shortened version of Puttini's libretto for Anfossi (1776, Rome), already somewhat condensed, especially in Act 3, for performances later that year in Venice (as *La pescatrice fedele*) and in Vienna (1777). Andrea Totti, who sang Count Errico in Venice, also sang the role in Haydn's opera at Eszterháza. Barbara Ripamonti, the talented soprano for whom Haydn tailored three difficult arias, played Rosina. Also in the cast were Vito Ungricht (Ernesto), Marianna Zannini (Lisetta), Benedetto Bianchi (Villotto), Catharina Poschva (Baroness) and Leopold Dichtler (Masino) – the last three had also appeared in Haydn's *Il mondo della luna*. The sets were by Pietro Travaglia, the resident designer who studied with Bernardino and Fabrizio Galliari in Milan.

Count Errico *an eccentric and inconstant young man, secret husband of Rosina*	tenor
Rosina *a virtuous fisherwoman*	soprano
Baroness Irene *Count Errico's aunt, beloved of Ernesto*	soprano
Marquis Ernesto *friend of the Count*	tenor
Villotto *a wealthy but doltish gentleman, Rosina's intended husband*	baritone
Lisetta *maidservant of the Baroness*	soprano
Masino *head fisherman, brother of Rosina*	tenor
Rosina's small son	spoken

Setting A fishing village, on the riviera near Genoa

Two original cast members, Bianchi and Ripamonti, were at Eszterháza when the opera was revived in April 1785. Since the earlier performance materials were apparently destroyed when the opera house burnt down in late 1779, Haydn probably recreated the score from memory and from a few extant materials, including a concert version of the overture issued in a set of six by Artaria (Vienna, 1782–3), manuscript copies of certain numbers and fragmentary sketches. A comparison between the 1785 score (most of which is autograph) and corresponding sketches reveals that six recitatives were completely rewritten, while arias and ensembles transmit much the same content. Haydn apparently sanctioned the insertion of Anfossi's solo scene for Count Errico in Act 2, even though an undated sketch of his own survives. The opera was subsequently performed as *Der flatterhafte Liebhaber, oder Der Sieg der* (or *Die wahre*) *Beständigkeit* in Pressburg (now Bratislava, 1786–7), Budapest (1789), Vienna (1790) and Brno (1792), and (with numerous changes) as *Laurette* in Paris (1791). Recent productions in Italian have been given in Lyons (1980), Assisi (1982) and at Schönbrunn, Vienna (1982).

ACT 1 *A seashore stretching to the horizon cluttered with trees, rustic cottages and fishing huts* The overture leads directly into the opening sextet, a storm scene in which Baroness Irene, Ernesto, Lisetta and Villotto, shipwrecked near the shore, are rescued by Rosina and Masino. The Baroness has come in search of her nephew, Count Errico, whom she hopes to dissuade from marrying Rosina. However, the Count married Rosina secretly five years earlier, only to abandon her soon afterwards; the couple have a son, but neither the Count nor, of course, the Baroness and her retinue know of the child's existence. In her only aria, 'Non s'innalza', the Baroness, whose direct vocal expression suggests nobility and strength, assures Rosina that her love for Villotto, her betrothed, will grow. Villotto's foolish advances only deepen Rosina's inner torment, initiated by the Count's long absence and indifference towards her. The Count suddenly appears, threatening to kill his rival with a pistol. This so unnerves Villotto that when the Baroness tries to solicit his consent to the marriage, the buffoon can only reply in broken phrases, directed alternately to the Count and the Baroness, in the two-tempo aria 'Non sparete ... mi disdico'. Masino, whom Ernesto has threatened with a dagger, remains unchanged by Lisetta's consoling words offered in her only aria ('Io son, poverina'), a lyrical piece in the key (G major) and compound time common to servants.

In their first encounter, the Count reveals himself to be a victimizer; he rebuffs Rosina, turning his attention to Villotto who has decided to go off to war rather than take a wife. In a bold and extended accompanied recitative and aria, the Count instructs Villotto in the art of war. 'A trionfar t'invita' – a four-part aria with horns and timpani and set in contrasting tempos, metres and keys corresponding to the changes in textual expression – seems dramatically unmotivated until its battle metaphors are interpreted as the Count's inopportune advice on how to win a wife. In the last section ('Oimè, che smania orribile'), the confused Count appears surprised by his own inconsistencies of character and somewhat frightened at his present predicament, a reading underscored by the violent C minor setting. Rosina and the Count meet again in the finale where they sing a strained love duet, but Rosina's earlier pain returns when the Baroness lures the Count away with a picture of his designated wife.

ACT 2.i *A courtyard in Belmonte castle* Baroness Irene informs Ernesto that she will consent to their own marriage only after Count Errico is suitably wed. Fearing that the clever Rosina might seduce the Count, Ernesto surmises that it would be to his advantage to secure Rosina and Villotto's marriage. But his words to Rosina are misinterpreted by the others as a profession of love, prompting each of the five to attack the poor young woman in succession. Alone, Rosina laments her fate in the recitative 'Misera, chi m'aiuta', followed by her outpourings in the aria 'Dove fuggo'. Rosina's desperation is apparent in the driving quality of the opening F minor theme.

2.ii *A room* Count Errico and Villotto express their mutual disgust with Rosina, but the wayward Count once more threatens to kill his rival. Before taking his leave, Villotto makes a verbal will in 'Già la morte in mante nero'. Lisetta intercedes for Rosina, prompting the now delirious Count, in a scene borrowed from Anfossi, to compare himself to Orpheus in search of his wronged Eurydice.

2.iii *Landscape with Rosina's rustic cottage and adjoining tower, partly in ruins* Having escaped to her hiding-place, an exhausted and defeated Rosina clutches her son and expresses her resignation in 'Care spiagge', a farewell to life. Over the course of the finale everyone searches for her. The Count meets a small boy for whom he feels an extraordinarily strong affection and, with Rosina's entrance, the family is united. The Count, now a repentant husband and father, joins Rosina in a love duet. From a distance, the others express their shock in a *poco adagio* homophonic tutti. The finale concludes with a canonic chorus.

ACT 3 *A room* In a last attempt to break the bonds between the Count and Rosina, Baroness Irene sends each of them a forged letter, which only succeeds in setting up the traditional Act 3 love duet. In 'Rosina vezzosina', the couple express their mutual and boundless love. The Baroness admits defeat, embraces Rosina and promises to marry Ernesto. All rejoice in a chorus in praise of virtue and constancy.

* * *

Rosina is a sentimental heroine in the tradition of Cecchina (Piccinni's *La Cecchina, ossia La buona figliuola*, 1760) and Nina (Paisiello's *Nina*, 1789). Spurned by an aristocratic husband, she endures insufferable torment; her steadfast patience, fortitude and high moral character inform the entire work. The opera has often been compared to Mozart's *Le nozze di Figaro*, another 'commedia tenera' ('tender comedy') full of intense human drama, but *La vera costanza* lacks the intrigue of Mozart's opera. If these two operas share any deep affinities it is in the artistry the composers brought to their respective scores. Haydn's finales for Acts 1 and 2 in particular aspire to the Mozartian ideal in their attention to details of textual structure, characterization, location and stage events. Within the 651 bars of the Act 2 finale, thematic and tonal relationships among sections 4–5 and 7–8 serve to isolate the onlookers in the unexpected tutti in section 6. Many other structural features of these mature finales point to Haydn's capable dramatic technique. CARYL CLARK

Vera-Lorini, Sofia. Italian singer, sister of EDOARDO VERA.

Vera storia, La ('The True Story'). Opera in two acts by LUCIANO BERIO to a libretto by Italo Calvino; Milan, Teatro alla Scala, 9 March 1982.

The principle of establishing a 'text', whether musical or verbal, which is subsequently reworked so as to generate new levels of meaning, is widely established in Berio's music. Here it receives its most monumental and grimly impressive application. The first act sets out multiple levels of material; the second resynthesizes them into a more urgent and immediate statement. A framework for the first act is provided by four choral sections that embody different aspects of the popular feast, or *festa* (in part inspired by the work of the Russian critic Mikhail Bakhtin). They reveal the ambiguities of the collective psyche: anarchic ebullience, contrasted with sadistic relish of a public execution, and rebellion against repressive authorities, followed by resignation and the resumption of 'the long wait' once that rebellion is crushed. A common reservoir of eight notes generates the basic harmonic materials for all four Festas.

Within this frame, soloists act out through individually titled 'numbers' a skeletal sequence of situations that were the stock-in-trade of 19th-century Italian opera (though a particular reference to *Il trovatore* is clearly intended). In the first act, the characters bear a name, but such psychological attributes as they display derive entirely from their interactions: 'characterization' is scrupulously avoided. A quartet of voices assume the main roles, with two other male voices for minor roles. The soprano (Leonora) and the tenor (Luca) are ill-starred lovers: their vocal lines are the most florid (and the most directly indebted to the work's eight-note nucleus), their texts the richest in poetic imagery. The baritone (Ivo) is Luca's brother and rival in love. Independent of this classic triangle is the mezzo-soprano (Ada), who both unleashes the action and comments upon it. Both of these characters are agents rather than victims of fate, and their style is accordingly more direct. In revenge for the public execution that follows on from the first Festa, Ada, 'perhaps the daughter of the condemned man', steals the youngest son of Ugo, the Commandant (tenor) who ordered the killing ('Il ratto'). Grief-stricken, the Commandant collapses and dies,

'La vera storia' (Berio): scene from the original production at La Scala, Milan, 9 March 1982

demanding reprisals from his eldest son, Ivo, who succeeds him ('La vendetta'). Ivo and Luca, represented by dancers, fight for the love of Leonora: Ivo is wounded, and Luca arrested ('Il duello'). Leonora and Ada agonize over his fate ('Il grido'): Luca has in effect assumed the role of the heroic victim of oppression ('La prigione'). After the general rebellion of the third Festa he, too, is led towards the firing squad ('Il sacrificio'), but his fate dissolves into the collective resignation of the fourth Festa. Ada closes the act, insisting that though the advent of a just world may be in perennial doubt, we must keep faith by refusing to forget past evil ('Il ricordo').

A telling commentary on the action, both private and public, is provided by street singers (Berio's models were the *cantastorie* of Sicily), who perform six ballads in differing popular styles, both urban and rural, at appropriate points in the action. At first detached and harshly or whimsically ironic, these interpolations acquire great intensity in the final two ballads – the last a lament for the dead after the rebellion of the third Festa has been crushed.

The separate numbers of Act 1 have set out the materials, verbal and musical, that Berio now takes up and mixes into the continuous flow of Act 2. The action follows analogous outlines, so that those elements of the text preserved from Act 1 generally appear in the same sequence as before. But they now combine with musical materials of quite different provenance to provide a fluid network of new associations. On stage, the operatic story-telling of the first act has dissolved into the nightmare of the modern city. There are no longer named roles, only anonymous 'passers-by' hurrying through the street. The chorus, which in Act 1 assumed its traditional role as 'the people' in action, is here reduced to abject passivity and semi-silence: disembodied voices sound from the orchestra pit. The authorities control attempts at urban guerilla warfare with ruthless efficiency. In a gesture of desolate irony, it is left to the named roles of Act 1 – 'characters' from an imaginary opera – finally to re-enter and sing the message of stoic humanist resignation that concluded the fourth Festa, whereupon Ada steps forward to conclude Act 2 as she did Act 1, exhorting us to refuse to forget.

DAVID OSMOND-SMITH

Verazi, Mattia (*b* ?Rome, *c*1730; *d* Munich, 20 Nov 1794). Italian librettist. Librettos refer to him as 'Romano'. Niccolò Jommelli composed the music for his first known opera libretto, *Ifigenia in Aulide*, for Rome in 1751. The work was unusually successful for an *opera seria*, with two more Italian productions in 1753 (Livorno and Naples) and several outside Italy: Mannheim (1751), Barcelona (1755), Prague (1762) and Kassel (1766). It initiated a lifelong friendship between the composer and the librettist and a series of collaborative efforts spanning 20 years. In *Ifigenia* Verazi already showed innovatory tendencies that challenged the conventions of Italian *opera seria*: Iphigenia's main aria without subsequent exit, Eriphile's suicide and the extensive final ensemble all break with mid-century practice. Jommelli, admired for the passion and eloquence of his music, may have influenced Verazi to write dramatic aria texts of a generous length, often closely tied to the plot. For Jommelli too he provided an unusually large number of impassioned solo scenes suitable for obbligato recitative. Verazi's tendencies to emphasize horror and terror and to build to great climaxes at the end of each act are also apparent in this early work.

Verazi's association with Jommelli drew him to the attention of the Stuttgart and Mannheim courts. He was called to Stuttgart in 1755 to provide two French-inspired operas, *Enea nel Lazio* and *Pelope*, for Jommelli, who had become *maestro di cappella* there in 1754. Catering to Duke Carl Eugen's taste for French opera, these works, based on mythological subjects and involving deities, machine spectacle, chorus, pantomime and possibly dance, antedate similar works by Traetta in Parma (1759) and Gluck's *Orfeo* for Vienna in 1762. Verazi follows established practice when placing a piece of spectacle in the middle of each act, but in *Enea* his first big ensemble, a quintet near the end of Act 3, replaces the traditional succession of exit arias with dynamic simultaneous expressions of conflicting emotions, and the opening scene complex with chorus replaces the usual intimate scenes for a few characters.

A year later Verazi became court poet for the Palatinate at nearby Mannheim. By 1762 he had also become private secretary to the Elector Carl Theodor.

He held both posts until the court moved to Munich in 1778, when he retired. After his début libretto for Mannheim, the *festa teatrale Le nozze d'Arianna* for Holzbauer (1756), the *maestro di cappella*, Verazi is credited with no new *opera seria* until *Cajo Fabrizio* (1760). His extensive correspondence with Jommelli and with the Württemberg court in the 1770s (*D-Sl*) suggests that he may have been responsible for revisions in Metastasian texts for Jommelli in Stuttgart and Ludwigsburg as well as for Holzbauer and others composing operas on pre-existing librettos for Mannheim. Unusually, two librettos revised by Verazi for J. C. Bach in 1772 and 1774 acknowledge his services. Indeed, Metastasian and other librettos produced in both Mannheim and Stuttgart (or Ludwigsburg) during the 1760s and 70s frequently have ensembles at the close of Acts 1 and 2 some 20 years before these became common in Italian theatres. Verazi's reworking of Metastasio's *Temistocle* for Bach was designed to tighten the action and direct it towards the ensemble finales.

Verazi provided new librettos at two-year intervals for a succession of three guest composers, beginning in 1760 with the dramatic but formally conventional *Cajo Fabrizio* for Jommelli (who must have been unable to complete the work since Giuseppe Colla is credited with half the arias). Verazi's operas for Mannheim contain the spectacular staging and the choruses and ballets associated with French opera, but at the same time adhere to an important principle of the Italian Arcadian reform that proscribed the participation or intervention of mythological deities. As a result the lavish spectacle depicts either natural phenomena or human activities. The arrival of Traetta from Parma, where he had composed several Italian operas based on French models as part of an effort to reform Italian opera, must have inspired Verazi to undertake unique and bold challenges to conventional Italian dramaturgy. In their collaborative effort, *Sofonisba* for Mannheim in 1762, Verazi introduced a number of characteristic innovations: the opera opens with a programmatic sinfonia accompanying a battle pantomime, and later a pantomime and chorus depict gladiatorial games. Fragments of recitative invade Sofonisba's declamatory aria, 'Crudeli, aimè! Che fate?', and footnotes specify extensive actions. For the end of Act 2 Verazi wrote an action ensemble of diminishing forces – a trio that becomes a solo when two of the participants leave the stage. This construction parallels the conclusion to the first or second act in a conventional opera where, one after another, the characters sing arias and depart, leaving the stage to a single character who brings the act to a close with a solo scene and aria. Most significant of all, Verazi challenged the dramaturgical laws of verisimilitude by staging unmodified Sofonisba's tragic suicide and prolonged death during a period when audiences expected tragedies to be revised to end happily.

This libretto enjoyed unusual success outside Mannheim. Two years later, Galuppi set Verazi's libretto for Carnival in Turin (1764). In accordance with Turinese taste, the opening battle scene and the triumphant procession remained, but the choruses along with the gladiatorial games were cut. Many of Verazi's declamatory aria texts were replaced with more conventional poetry, and the aria and cavatina for the child as well as the final quintet disappear. Boroni's setting of this revised libretto for Venice later the same year was revived for Prague in 1766. Here the spectacle scenes and the child's part were omitted, the trio of diminishing forces became a conventional duet, and two scenes were added to Act 1 in order to give Sofonisba the final aria. Bottarelli's libretto for Vento (1766, London) appears to be heavily indebted to Verazi as well.

Verazi's *Ifigenia in Tauride*, set by Majo two years later, continued the advances of *Sofonisba*. In contrast with the stark classicism of Coltellini's version of this fable as set by Traetta (1763, Vienna), Verazi's libretto was full of typical Italian intrigue and placed strong emphasis on the tormented and terrifying aspects of the plot. (Guillard borrowed the programmatic sinfonia for Gluck's Paris opera on the same subject.) Verazi suspends the exit-aria convention, producing lengthy scene complexes that incorporate spectacle, obbligato recitative, cavatina, aria and programmatic battle music. An unconventional duet for two men contains a second novelty, an interjection from a third character. The chorus functions both as supernumeraries and as characters in the drama. In the final scene the tyrant Thoas dies, not at the hands of Iphigenia but in his burning temple, much as Dido departed in Metastasio's earliest and highly successful drama.

After these two innovatory works for Mannheim, Verazi was called to provide new and revised operas for Duke Carl Eugen's enormous new theatre at Ludwigsburg, which had been constructed to accommodate French spectacle. In 1766 Verazi again collaborated with Jommelli, revising *Enea nel Lazio* and substantially reworking Zeno's *Lucio Vero* as *Vologeso* (which Jommelli considered among his most emotionally compelling operas). Two years later they worked together on the most radical opera of Jommelli's career, *Fetonte*, a tour de force combining a complex italianate plot with spectacle based on French models, which C. F. D. Schubart extolled for the perfect blending of music, drama, stagecraft, poetry and dance and for its impact on the audience. Formally, Verazi made use of cavatinas and ensembles of diminishing personnel to avoid the traditional succession of recitative and exit arias, and the opera's impressive and tragic conclusion takes place within the first freely constructed action ensemble finale ever appended to an *opera seria*.

In 1778 Verazi was called to Milan to provide spectacle opera for the opening of La Scala. In prefaces to *Europa riconosciuta* (Salieri) and *Troia distrutta* (Mortellari), he claimed to have taken the path of innovator in order to reform longstanding abuses and to add variety, verisimilitude and action in his librettos, which he termed *dramma in azione*, while at the same time adhering to Metastasian models in shunning crude, unseemly language and in striving for purity, elegance and sweetness. Metastasio himself described *Europa* as 'happy, clear and rich in that enviable fertility of fancy which constitutes the principal merit of dramatic poetry'. *Europa* is among the first *opere serie* in only two acts. In *Europa* and *Troia* Verazi abolished the hierarchy of roles and drastically reduced the number of exit arias, replacing them with introductions, ensembles, action finales and cavatinas embedded in great scene complexes incorporating chorus, pantomime and machine spectacle. The librettos contain detailed, almost line-by-line footnotes specifying action and even giving instructions to the composer regarding instrumentation and musical effects. Aegisthus is slain on stage in *Europa* and *Troia* ends tragically. Pietro Verri, who saw *Europa*, commented in a letter to his brother Alessandro:

The drama was written by a certain Signor Verazi, a Roman, who is a man, not of poetry, or of letters, but of the theatre. He has an imagination and skill developed outside Italy. He seems to have genius, and with this he has outdone and put to shame all of the heroes of stagecraft by finally putting a decent operatic production on the stage.

Few other critics were so generous. Public outrage over these two works led Verazi to present a revival of his *Calliroe* and a far less controversial *Cleopatra*. Here all spectacle, ballet and chorus have disappeared; arias remain free of action. Of Verazi's innovations only the ensembles remain. *Calliroe* returns to life when the potion she has drunk proves harmless, but events in *Cleopatra* are allowed to proceed to a staged double suicide. Disappointed at the reception of his reforms, Verazi returned to Mannheim where he wrote *Laodamia*, an *azione teatrale*, set by his son in 1780. He also provided several theatrical pieces for Poli and Zumsteeg in Stuttgart in 1781 and 1782. The final ten years of his life are undocumented.

Verazi returned to Germany having lost all hope of a favourable reception for his innovations in his native land. But during the early 1780s composers and librettists began cautiously to incorporate them into more conventional works, and by the 1790s a new genre of opera can be said to have supplanted the old.

See also CALLIROE.

Ifigenia in Aulide (os), Jommelli, 1751 (with arias by Traetta, 1753); *Pelope* (os), Jommelli, 1755; *Enea nel Lazio* (os), Jommelli, 1755; *Le nozze d'Arianna* (festa teatrale), Holzbauer, 1756; *Cajo Fabrizio* (os), Jommelli and Colla (6 arias), 1760; *Sofonisba* (os), Traetta, 1762 (Galuppi, 1764; Boroni, 1764); *Ifigenia in Tauride* (os), Majo, 1764 (Monza, 1766, as *Oreste*; reworked for Jommelli, 1771); *Vologeso* (os, after P. Zeno), Jommelli, 1766; *Alessandro* (os), Majo, 1766; *Fetonte* (os), Jommelli, 1768; *Calliroe* (os), Sacchini, 1770 (G. Rust, 1776; Mysliveček, 1778; F. Alessandri, 1778; Nasolini, 1792); *Catone in Utica* (os, after P. Metastasio), Piccinni, 1770; *Ezio* (os, after Metastasio), Jommelli, 1772; *Temistocle* (os, after Metastasio), J. C. Bach, 1772; *Lucio Silla* (os, after G. de Gamerra), Bach, 1775; *Europa riconosciuta* (os), Salieri, 1778; *Troia [Troja] distrutta* (os), Mortellari, 1778; *Cleopatra* (os), Anfossi, 1779

*

StiegerO

C. Burney: *Memoirs of the Life and Writings of the Abate Metastasio*, iii (London, 1796), 219

C. Schubart: *Gesammelte Schriften und Schicksale*, i (Stuttgart, 1839), 83

J. Sittard: *Zur Geschichte der Musik und des Theaters am Württembergischen Hofe 1458–1793* (Stuttgart, 1890)

F. Walter: *Geschichte des Theaters und der Musik am kurpfälzischen Hofe* (Leipzig, 1898)

R. Krauss: *Das Stuttgarter Hoftheater von den ältesten Zeiten bis zur Gegenwart* (Stuttgart, 1908)

P. Verri: *Carteggio di Pietro e Alessandro Verri dal 1 luglio 1778 al 29 dicembre 1779*, x (Milan, 1939), 42–3, 51

C. Vianello: *Teatri, spettacoli, musiche a Milano nei secoli scorsi* (Milan, 1941)

B. Cantrell: *Tommaso Traetta and his opera 'Sofonisba'* (diss., U. of California, Los Angeles, 1957)

K. Kuzmick Hansell: *Opera and Ballet at the Regio Ducal Teatro of Milan, 1771–1776: a Musical and Social History* (diss., U. of California, Berkeley, 1980), ii, 267–75

M. McClymonds: *Niccolò Jommelli: the Last Years, 1769–1774* (Ann Arbor, 1980)

——: 'Mattia Verazi and the Opera at Mannheim, Stuttgart and Ludwigsburg', *Studies in Music from the University of Western Ontario*, vii (1982), 99–136

S. Henze: 'Opera seria am kurpfälzischen Hofe: Traettas "Sofonisba", De Majos "Ifigenia in Tauride", Bachs "Temistocle"', *Mannheim und Italien: zur Vorgeschichte der Mannheimer*, ed. R. Würtz (Mainz, 1984), 78–96

M. McClymonds: 'The Venetian Role in the Transformation of Italian Opera Seria during the 1790s', *I vicini di Mozart: Venice 1987*, 221–40

——: 'Verazi's Controversial *drammi in azione* as Realized in the Music of Salieri, Anfossi, Alessandri and Mortellari for the Opening of La Scala 1778–1779', *Omaggio a Claudio Sartori* (forthcoming)

MARITA P. MCCLYMONDS

Verbena de la paloma, La ('The Festival of the Dove'). *Sainete lírico* in one act by TOMÁS BRETÓN to a libretto by Ricardo de la Vega; Madrid, Teatro Apolo, 17 February 1894.

In a residential district of Madrid the inhabitants prepare for the evening's celebrations of the annual Festival of the Dove. Julián (baritone) laments his unrequited love for the brunette Susana (soprano), while further down the street the old chemist Don Hilarión (comic tenor) looks forward to spending the evening with a pair of young ladies – a brunette and a blonde. When evening comes, Julián arrives outside Susana's home and is surprised to see her emerge on one arm of Don Hilarión. The upshot is a brawl in a local dance hall, but when the police arrive to arrest the participants Susana finally repents of her treatment of Julián. A classic of the *género chico*, portraying Madrid low life, the work is appropriately lighthearted and tuneful, and full of local colour. Its highlight is the *habanera concertante* '¿Dónde vas con mantón de Manila?', with which Julián greets Susana when she emerges on Don Hilarión's arm.

ANDREW LAMB

Verdi, Giuseppe (Fortunino Francesco) (*b* Roncole, nr Busseto, 9 or 10 Oct 1813; *d* Milan, 27 Jan 1901). Italian composer, by common consent recognized as the greatest Italian musical dramatist.

1. Introduction. 2. Life, 1813–39. 3. Life, 1839–53. 4. Operas: *Oberto* (1839) to *La traviata* (1853): (i) Composition (ii) Dramatic forms (iii) Lyric prototype (iv) Harmony, *tinta*, local colour (v) Reception and politics. 5. Life, 1853–71. 6. Operas: *Les vêpres siciliennes* (1855) to *Aida* (1871): (i) Composition (ii) Dramatic forms (iii) Lyric prototype (iv) Harmony, *tinta*, local colour (v) Reception and politics. 7. Life, 1871–1901. 8. The last style: *Otello* (1887) and *Falstaff* (1893). 9. Reputation, scholarship: (i) Late reception and posthumous reputation (ii) Verdi scholarship and editions.

1. INTRODUCTION. A month after Verdi's death, a solemn procession through Milan accompanied by hundreds of thousands of mourners assisted the transfer of his remains to their final resting place. At one point during this procession the crowd, aided by the chorus and orchestra of La Scala, apparently sang a moving rendition of 'Va pensiero', the chorus of Hebrew slaves from one of Verdi's earliest operas, *Nabucco*.

It is easy to see why this event has captured the imagination and assumed significance. By the time of his death, Verdi had established a unique position among his fellow countrymen: although many of his operas had disappeared from the repertory, he had nevertheless become a profound artistic symbol of the nation's achievement of statehood. Parts of his operatic legacy had entered into a kind of empyrean, divorced from the checks and balances of context and passing fashion. The fact that 'Va pensiero', written some 60 years earlier, could express contemporary Italians' feelings for their departed hero demonstrated the extent to which Verdi's music had been assimilated into the national consciousness.

However, nearly a hundred years after Verdi's death, such an event is likely to take on other meanings, and it can serve here as a cautionary note on which to introduce an account of the life and works. To begin at the end of Verdi's long life is a timely reminder of our present perspective: Verdi's story has continually been written backwards, the early events and achievements accruing narrative force and meaning through the powerful attraction of our sense of their ending. Such is of course true of all critical biography, but the extent to which it has influenced our perception of Verdi makes his an exceptional case. In an attempt to revalue (rather than evade) that perspective, the present survey will follow much recent scholarship in attempting to place Verdi's operas more firmly in the context of their time; and, perhaps more important, it will treat their reception as a separate historical phenomenon, so far as is possible disentangled from present-day critical opinion.

After an outline of Verdi's early years, his life and operas will be discussed within three unequal periods. This particular grouping of works is unusual, though as defensible as any other on artistic grounds; it is, however, made primarily for practical reasons and should not be taken to imply the kind of hierarchy of value traditionally signalled by subheadings such as 'youth' or 'maturity'. The first period takes in the 19 operas from *Oberto* (1839) to *La traviata* (1853). Claims are frequently made for a qualitative leap to a 'second period', beginning some time in the late 1840s or early 1850s, with *Macbeth*, *Luisa Miller* or *Rigoletto* as the watershed; but the entire period is probably best seen as a gradual unfolding within the Italian operatic tradition. A second period, during which the influence of French grand opera is of great importance, includes the seven operas from *Les vêpres siciliennes* (1855) to *Aida* (1871). After the compositional hiatus of the 1870s, a final period, that of Verdi's last style, includes the revisions to *Simon Boccanegra* and *Don Carlos*, and the operas *Otello* (1887) and *Falstaff* (1893).

2. LIFE, 1813–39. Verdi was born in Roncole, a small village near Busseto in the Duchy of Parma. His exact birth date is uncertain. The baptismal register of 11 October records him as 'born yesterday', but as days were sometimes counted as beginning at sunset, that could mean either 9 or 10 October. The birth register describes his father Carlo (1785–1867) as an 'innkeeper', his mother Luigia Uttini (1787–1851) as a 'spinner'; both belonged to families of small landowners and traders, certainly not the illiterate peasant class from which Verdi later liked to present himself as having emerged.

In typically middle-class fashion, Carlo Verdi was energetic in furthering his son's education. Before the age of four, Verdi began instruction with the local priests, probably in music as well as other subjects; his father bought him an old spinet when he was seven, and he was soon substituting as organist at the local church of S Michele, taking the position permanently at the age of nine. In 1823 he moved to Busseto, and at the age of 11 he entered the *ginnasio* there, receiving training in Italian, Latin, humanities and rhetoric. In 1825 he began lessons with Ferdinando Provesi, *maestro di cappella* at S Bartolomeo, Busseto, and director of the municipal music school and local Philharmonic Society. The picture emerges of youthful precocity eagerly nurtured by an ambitious father and of a sustained, sophisticated and elaborate formal education – again something Verdi tended to hide in later life, giving the impression of a largely self-taught and obscure youth.

In 1829 Verdi applied unsuccessfully for the post of organist at nearby Soragna. He was becoming increasingly involved in Busseto's musical life, both as a composer and as a performer. As he later recalled:

> From the ages of 13 to 18 I wrote a motley assortment of pieces: marches for band by the hundred, perhaps as many little *sinfonie* that were used in church, in the theatre and at concerts, five or six concertos and sets of variations for pianoforte, which I played myself at concerts, many serenades, cantatas (arias, duets, very many trios) and various pieces of church music, of which I remember only a *Stabat mater*.

In May 1831 he moved into the house of Antonio Barezzi, a prominent merchant in Busseto and a keen amateur musician. Verdi gave singing and piano lessons to Barezzi's daughter Margherita (*b* 4 May 1814; *d* 18 June 1840) and the young couple became unofficially engaged.

At about the same time it became clear that the musical world of Busseto was too small, and Carlo Verdi applied to a Bussetan charitable institution (the Monte di Pietà e d'Abbondanza) for a scholarship to allow his son to study in Milan, then the cultural capital of northern Italy. The application, bolstered by glowing references from Provesi and others, was successful; but no scholarship was available until late 1833. However, Barezzi guaranteed financial support for the first year and in May 1832, at the age of 18, Verdi travelled to Milan and applied for permission to study at the conservatory. He was refused entry, partly for bureaucratic reasons (he was four years above the usual entering age and was not resident in Lombardy-Venetia), partly on account of his unorthodox piano technique. It was an 'official' rejection that Verdi felt keenly until the end of his life. Barezzi agreed to the added expense of private study in Milan, and Verdi became the pupil of Vincenzo Lavigna, who had for many years been *maestro concertatore* at La Scala.

According to Verdi's later recollections, lessons with Lavigna involved little but strict counterpoint: 'in the three years spent with him I did nothing but canons and fugues, fugues and canons of all sorts. No one taught me orchestration or how to treat dramatic music.' This insistence was probably a further attempt to fashion his own image as a 'self-taught' composer. Contemporary evidence suggests that Lavigna encouraged Verdi to attend the theatre regularly, and his letters of recommendation specify study in 'composizione ideale' (free composition) as well as in counterpoint. Lavigna also helped his pupil into Milanese musical society; in 1834 Verdi assisted at the keyboard in performances of Haydn's *Creation* given by the Milan Philharmonic Society directed by Pietro Massini, and a year later co-directed with Massini performances of Rossini's *La Cenerentola*.

By the time Verdi had completed his studies with Lavigna, in mid-1835, Busseto had again claimed his attention. Provesi had died in 1833, leaving open the post of musical director there; by June 1834 one Giovanni Ferrari had been appointed organist at S Bartolomeo but, encouraged by Barezzi, Verdi was eventually appointed to the post of *maestro di musica* (that is, to the secular portion of Provesi's post) in March 1836, though not before a prolonged struggle between rival factions in the town. On 4 May 1836 Verdi married Margherita Barezzi and settled in Busseto, directing and composing for the local Philharmonic Society and giving private lessons. He held the post for nearly three years, during which time he and Margherita had two children, Virginia (*b* 26 March

1837; *d* 12 Aug 1838) and Icilio Romano (*b* 11 July 1838; *d* 22 Oct 1839).

Verdi's provincial existence is best seen as an irritating delay in his professional career, and there is evidence that he was actively pursuing more ambitious plans. In April 1836 he renewed his contact with Massini's Milanese society by composing for them a cantata, to words by Count Renato Borromeo, in honour of the Austrian Emperor Ferdinand I. A series of letters to Massini informs us that during 1836 Verdi composed an opera entitled *Rocester*, to a libretto by the Milanese journalist and man of letters, Antonio Piazza. During 1837 he tried unsuccessfully to have the opera staged at the Teatro Ducale in Parma. But eventually, again with Massini's help, Verdi arranged for a revised version of the opera, now entitled *Oberto, conte di San Bonifacio*, to be performed at La Scala. In October 1838 he resigned as *maestro di musica* of Busseto and in February 1839 left for Milan. Nine months later his first opera received its première in the Lombard capital's most famous theatre.

3. LIFE, 1839–53. From the première of *Oberto* until at least the midpoint of his long career, the outward progress of Verdi's life is inseparable from that of his professional activities: a continual round of negotiations with theatres and librettists, of intense periods of composition and of exhausting preparations for and direction of premières and revivals. Much of this activity is summarized in the introductory sections to the entries in this dictionary on individual operas; certain general matters, however, are best mentioned here.

The success of *Oberto* apparently encouraged BARTOLOMEO MERELLI, impresario at La Scala, to offer Verdi a contract for three more operas, to be composed over two years. The first was the comic opera *Un giorno di regno*, which failed disastrously on its first night in September 1840. Verdi's later autobiographical glosses (which are notoriously unreliable) state that this professional failure, together with the tragic loss of his young family (his wife Margherita died in June 1840; they had lost their two children in the previous two years), caused him to renounce composition. This may be partly true: his next opera, *Nabucco*, appeared some 18 months later, an unusually long delay. However, Verdi certainly continued a level of professional activity by writing new music for, and supervising revivals of, *Oberto*.

After *Nabucco*, whose public success in Milan was unprecedented, the round of new operas was virtually unremitting: in the 11 years from March 1842 (the première of *Nabucco*) to March 1853 (the première of *La traviata*), Verdi wrote 16 operas, an average of one every nine months. He also supervised numerous revivals, on occasion writing new music to accommodate a star performer. During the first part of this period he moved almost continually from one operatic centre to another, dividing what little time remained between Milan and Busseto. The years 1844–7 were particularly arduous (eight operas appearing in less than four years); his health broke down frequently and more than once he vowed to renounce operatic composition once he had achieved financial security and fulfilled outstanding contracts. His gathering fame did, however, have its advantages. The success of *Nabucco* opened doors in Milanese society and Verdi soon made some longstanding friendships, notably with Clara Maffei, whose artistic salon he frequently attended. It is likely that during these early years of success he formed a lasting attachment to the soprano GIUSEPPINA STREPPONI, who was to become his lifelong companion.

Apart from a brief visit to Vienna in 1843, Verdi remained within the Italian peninsula until March 1847 when he undertook a long foreign expedition, initially to supervise the premières of *I masnadieri* in London and *Jérusalem* in Paris. He then set up house with Strepponi in Paris, staying there about two years, although with a visit to Milan during the 1848 uprisings and a trip to the short-lived Roman Republic to supervise the première of *La battaglia di Legnano* in early 1849. Verdi returned with Strepponi to Busseto in mid-1849, and in 1851 they moved to a permanent home at the nearby farm of Sant'Agata, land once owned by Verdi's ancestors.

4. OPERAS: 'OBERTO' (1839) TO 'LA TRAVIATA' (1853).

(i) Composition. The genesis of a Verdian opera of this period follows a fairly predictable pattern, one that can teach us a good deal about the composer's artistic priorities and aims. The first step almost always involved negotiations with a theatre, an agreement of terms and deadlines. Unlike most of his Italian predecessors, Verdi was reluctant to deal through theatrical agents, preferring to negotiate fees for the première performance directly with the theatre management. Even though copyright protection was not fully established, he would supplement this income with rental fees and sales of printed materials; indeed, as his career progressed, Verdi's publishers (almost always the Milan firm of RICORDI) took a more active part in commissioning new works. The eventual contract with the theatre often included stipulations about the cast of the première, and Verdi chose operatic subjects with a direct eye to the available performers. The subject itself was then decided upon either by Verdi or his librettist, although – as success brought a new level of artistic freedom – Verdi became increasingly likely to reserve for himself this crucial decision. He favoured works that had already proved their worth as spoken dramas, and he had a fondness for foreign subjects, in particular Romantic melodramas set in the Middle Ages, by famous authors such as Byron, Schiller and Hugo, or by their more obscure contemporaries. In searching for new subjects he constantly stressed the need for unusual, gripping characters and for what he called 'strong' situations: scenes in which these characters could be placed in dramatic confrontation.

The first stage in fashioning an opera from the source text would typically involve a parcelling of the action into musical numbers such as arias, duets and ensembles. This was often done by annotating a prose summary of the source, and would typically be a collaborative effort between Verdi and his librettist. Once the work's essential formal outlines had been fixed, the librettist would prepare a poetic text in which the configuration of verse forms would reflect in detail the various musical forms agreed upon. Verdi frequently played an active part in this stage, particularly when working with his most common librettist of this period, FRANCESCO MARIA PIAVE. He might, for example, require certain sections to be cut down (Verdi was in general anxious to avoid long passages of recitative), might ask for changes of poetic metre in fixed forms, or even for line by line rewording to clarify the dramatic effect.

Finally came composition of the score, which typically occurred in at least three stages. First Verdi drafted

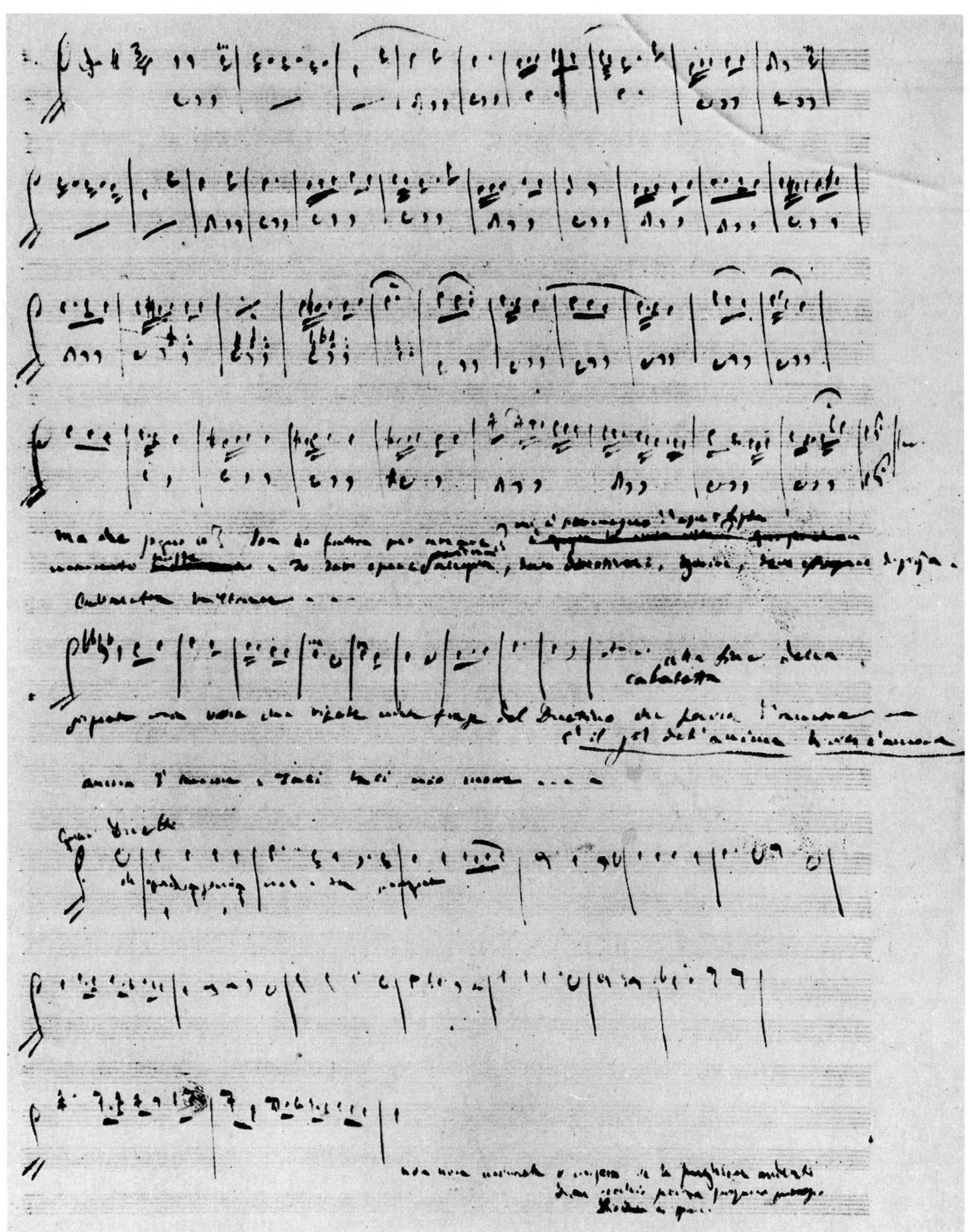

1. Verdi's preliminary sketches (possibly from late 1852) for Violetta's double aria at the end of Act 1 of 'La traviata': 'Ah fors'è lui' (top four systems) and 'Sempre libera degg'io' (central system); the passage marked 'Gran Duetto' was not used in the definitive version. The fact that there is no text underlay, and that the melodies are connected by a prose commentary, suggests that Verdi had not yet received the final version of the libretto.

the opera in short score, usually on just two staves (only one of these drafts, for *Rigoletto*, is currently available, although we can infer from the structure of Verdi's autographs that similar documents existed from at least the time of *Nabucco*). In writing this short-score draft, Verdi differed from predecessors such as Rossini and Donizetti, who typically composed straight on to the autograph; the practice gives an indication of the care and time he was willing to spend on each new work. The second stage of composition involved transferring the draft version to the autograph, adding essential instrumental lines (usually the first violin and bass) to create what has been termed a 'skeleton score'. From this skeleton score, vocal parts would be extracted by copyists and given to the singers of the première. Pressure of time dictated that only when Verdi arrived at the venue of the first performance, and had heard his singers in the theatre, would he complete (often in extreme haste) the orchestration.

(ii) Dramatic forms. It is clear from the preceding summary that various fixed forms were at the basis of Verdian musical drama; and these forms, geared as they mostly were to the individual expression and patterned confrontation of the major characters, arose from an awareness of the overwhelming importance of the principal performers in the success of an opera. The basic forms, inherited by Verdi from his Italian predecessors, are fairly simple to outline. The normative structure was the solo aria, called 'cavatina' if it marked the first entrance of a character, and typically made up of an introductory scena or recitative followed by three 'movements': a lyrical first movement, usually slow in tempo, called 'cantabile' or (preferably) 'adagio'; a connecting passage, often stimulated by some stage event – the entrance of new characters or the revelation of new information – and called the 'tempo di mezzo'; and a concluding cabaletta, usually faster than the first movement. The grand duet was identically structured, though with an opening movement before the Adagio, commonly employing patterned exchanges between the characters and called the 'tempo d'attacco'. Large-scale internal finales followed the pattern of the grand duet, though often with a more elaborate *tempo d'attacco*; the Adagio in ensembles was often called 'largo' or 'largo concertato', and the final movement was called a 'stretta'. Ranged around these large, multi-sectional units were shorter, connecting pieces, notably various purely choral movements and shorter, one-movement arias, often called 'romanza'. There is a close parallel between musical and poetic forms, each 'movement' tending to be in a different type of *versi lirici* (rhyming stanzas of fixed line length and syllable count). Given the nature of an opera's genesis, this parallel is of course unremarkable; the fact that it has occasioned so much detailed discussion of late is perhaps as much due to the possibilities it furnishes for formal abstraction as to the dramatic insights it occasionally offers.

In discussing Verdi's individual approach to these fixed forms, there has been a tendency to paint a romantic picture, one that equates release from formal 'constraints' with 'progress', and that celebrates the composer's gradual emancipation from formal 'tyranny'. According to this interpretation Verdi is a formal revolutionary, constantly striving towards a more naturalistic mode of musical drama. There is some truth in this image: as the 19th century progressed, opera in all countries turned to looser, less predictable musical forms. However, Verdi is perhaps better seen as a conservative influence within this broad trend, especially when viewed in the context of his immediate predecessors in Italy. The operas up to *La traviata* are at least as easy to codify in formal terms as those, for example, of Donizetti.

True, Verdi sometimes radically altered or ignored traditional forms. There are classic examples: the introduction of Macbeth by means of an understated duettino, 'Due vaticini', rather than a full-scale cavatina; the curious Act 1 duet between Rigoletto and Sparafucile, which is a kind of free conversation over an instrumental melody; the stretta-less grand finales of *Nabucco* Act 2, *I due Foscari* Act 2, *Attila* Act 1, *Luisa Miller* Act 1 and *Il trovatore* Act 2; the complete absence of a concertato finale in *I masnadieri* and *Rigoletto*. Other moments are less often mentioned: the grand duets of *La battaglia di Legnano* Act 1 and *Stiffelio* Act 3 follow the fluctuations of character confrontation so minutely that they are extremely difficult to parcel out into the traditional four 'movements'; the Act 1 duet in *Alzira* moves from *tempo d'attacco* straight to cabaletta, a process repeated in the Act 1 trio finale of *Il trovatore*.

However, much more often Verdi chose to manipulate forms from within, preserving their boundaries but expanding or condensing individual movements as the drama dictated. Famous examples include the Violetta-Germont duet in *La traviata* Act 2, which boasts a vastly expanded and lyrically enriched *tempo d'attacco*; or Leonora's aria in *Il trovatore* Act 4, in which the usually fugitive *tempo di mezzo* expands to become the famous 'Miserere' scene. Equally important in this enrichment is Verdi's tendency to focus musical weight on ensemble numbers and to concentrate in these numbers on the opposition between characters. In this respect the almost complete absence in his works of the 'rondò finale' (a favourite Donizettian form in which a soloist, usually the soprano, closes the opera with an elaborate, two-movement aria) is significant, as is its replacement by ensemble finales such as those of *Ernani* and *Il trovatore*. The lyrical movements of Verdi's ensembles, particularly of the grand duets, tend to establish at the outset a vivid sense of vocal difference and often retain that sense until the last possible moment. The extended passages of parallel 3rds or 6ths so well-known in Donizetti and Bellini are rare and are usually reserved as coda material.

Certain operas, particularly those written in collaboration with TEMISTOCLE SOLERA, are notable for a dynamic new use of the chorus. While choruses in the earlier 19th century had typically served a neutral, scene-setting function, Verdi's chorus frequently appears in the vocal forefront, offering powerful sonic enrichment to ensemble numbers and even intruding into the soloist's domain. *Nabucco* offers many early examples: the dramatic incursion of the chorus in both the slow movement and the cabaletta of Zaccaria's Act 1 aria; their climactic appearance in the Act 2 canonic ensemble, 'S'appressan gl'istanti'; and of course 'Va pensiero' in Act 3, where the chorus sings mostly in unison, with a directness and simplicity of emotional appeal that had traditionally been heard only from soloists.

(iii) Lyric prototype. In attempting to summarize the smaller-scale level of Verdi's lyrical movements, many critics have again appealed to a traditional norm, though one more abstractly analytical than the set-piece forms and one whose limitations and partiality need to be remembered. This is the 'lyric prototype', a four-phrase pattern usually represented by the scheme *AA'BA"* or (its common variant) *AA'BC*. Such a model could also include subscript numbers to indicate phrase length – the normative phrase would be four bars – and poetic lines can also be incorporated, as the usual consumption of text exactly parallels the musical periodicity, with two poetic lines matching one four-bar period. The prototype does, however, ignore harmonic movement, which can vary significantly within pieces that would have an identical letter scheme. What is more, in its 'pure' form the scheme appears only rarely,

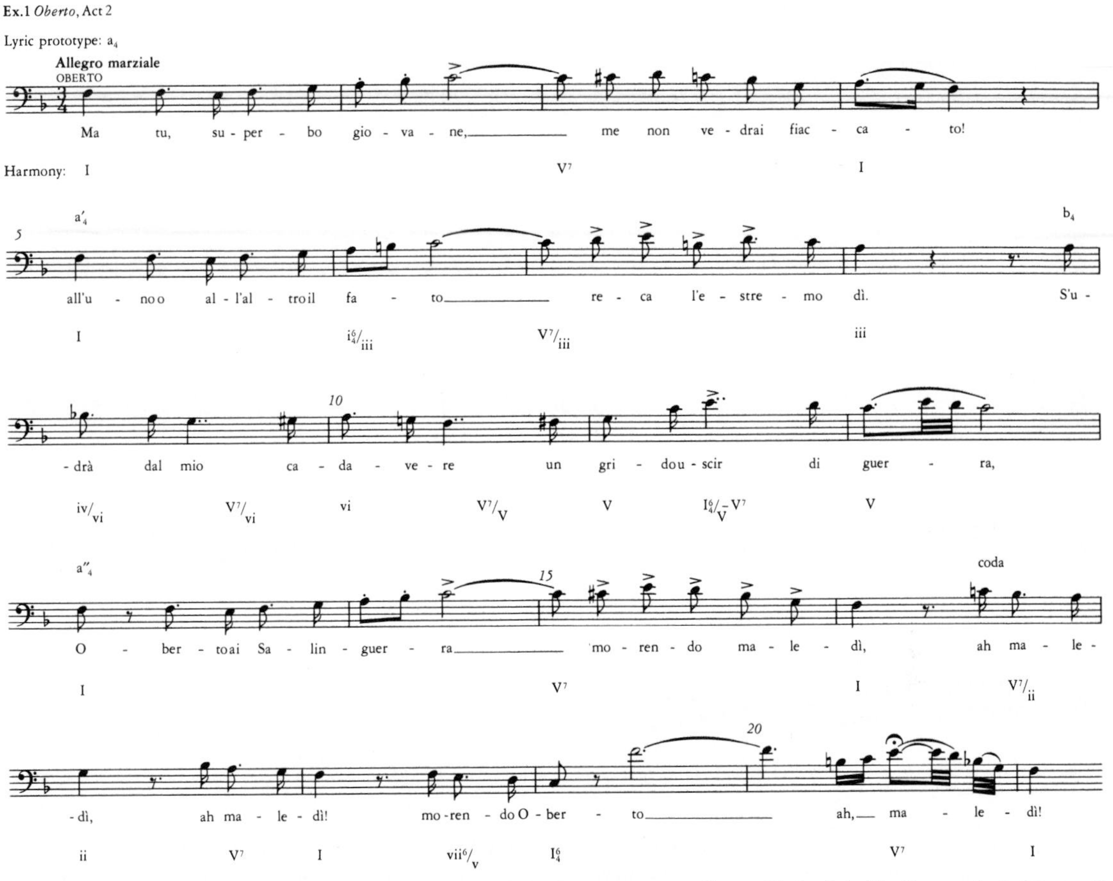

Ex.1 *Oberto*, Act 2

['But you, proud youth, you will not exhaust me! For one of us, this day will be the last. From my corpse, a war-like cry will be heard: the dying Oberto, cursing the Salinguerra!']

usually as one character's solo statement in an ensemble movement; in solo arias, some level of expansion, typically in coda material, is clearly necessary to achieve adequate length. These limitations notwithstanding, the prototype has proved the most reliable and flexible method of codifying Verdi's basic lyric shapes.

A very early example of the model, close to its basic form, comes in the cabaletta of the protagonist's aria in Act 2 of *Oberto* (ex.1). Even at this early stage, a Verdian novelty can be discerned in the comparative restriction of the formal scheme. In the hands of Verdi's predecessors, the prototype tended to dissolve after the *B* section into looser periods of ornamental vocal writing and word repetition, especially in a solo aria. Verdi did occasionally write arias of that kind: for Riccardo in Act 1 of *Oberto*, or – significantly, as the part was expressly written for the 'old-fashioned' virtuosa Jenny Lind – for Amalia in both Acts 1 and 3 of *I masnadieri*. However, his typical practice, even when writing a bravura aria, was to bind the ornamentation strictly within a periodic structure, even as the aria reached its final stages.

As with his conservatism in larger formal matters, this self-imposed restriction had the effect of channelling Verdi's invention into manipulations of the prototype from within, into expansions, contractions and enrichments of the lyric form. Elvira's *Andantino* in Act 1 of *Ernani*, for example, contains an expansion of the *B* section which injects a new sense of dialectic tension into the aria. More than that: far from 'dissolving' into ornamental writing at the end, the aria continues to subordinate, or rather harness, the ornamentation, containing it within a strictly controlled periodicity (ex.2). Such an example, which could easily be multiplied, demonstrates at least a part of how the energy so typical of Verdi's music is created.

As the 1840s unfolded, Verdi's lyrical forms increasingly show the influence of French models, especially after his prolonged stay in Paris in 1847–9. *Il corsaro*, for example, opens with two slow arias that, if in very different ways, are organized into two strophes (a typically French design). Later, more famous examples include the *couplet* forms (so called because of the shorter, refrain line that ends each stanza) found in Rodolfo's 'Quando le sere al placido' (*Luisa Miller* Act 2) and Germont's 'Di Provenza il mar, il suol' (*La traviata* Act 2). However, none of these examples entirely abandons the lyric prototype; indeed, in one sense it is more pervasive, tending to appear in miniature in each stanza. As we move to the early 1850s, the variety of internal structures that can be generated proliferates, giving rise to such startling experiments as Gilda's 'Caro nome' (*Rigoletto* Act 1), in which the second half of an initial *AA′ BA″* form, remarkable for its simplicity, is subjected to an elaborate series of surface variations.

(iv) Harmony, tinta, local colour. Verdi's small-scale harmonic language is for the most part simple and direct, following general patterns that can easily be summarized within the lyric prototype. The opening *A* sections concentrate on tonic and dominant harmonies, sometimes ending with a modulation to a near-related

['Ernani! . . . Ernani, spirit me away from this horrible embrace. Let us fly. . . if love allows me to live with you, I will follow you through caves and barren lands. Those caves will be for me an Eden of delights.']

key; the *B* section is comparatively unstable; the final *A* (or C) section returns to a stable tonic. Secondary modulations within an aria are frequently to keys a 3rd apart, thus allowing a new harmonic underpinning for important vocal sonorities. In large set pieces, notably in the Largo concertato, there is often a dramatic plunge into a distant key area near the end, a gesture from which Verdi occasionally found some difficulty in extricating himself. A few pieces show that Verdi was fully capable of an advanced, colouristic chromaticism – the Act 1 'Salve Maria' from *I Lombardi* is an early example, the prelude to Act 3 of *La traviata* a later, more persuasive one; but for the most part his liking for strict periodic structures made elaborate chromatic effects difficult to employ except at moments of high relief.

The extent to which organized, directed tonality may be traced at a larger level of structure is still a matter for debate. Unlike most of his Italian predecessors, Verdi seemed indifferent to tonal closure at levels larger than the single 'movement': most arias, duets and ensembles begin in one key and end in another; nor do individual acts, let alone entire operas, often display any obvious tonal plan. It seems likely that Verdi chose the tonality of movements within set pieces primarily with a view to the vocal tessituras he wished to exploit, and various last-minute transpositions he effected to aid individual singers would seem to support this theory. There is, though, evidence in some operas of an association between certain keys and certain characters or groups of characters. *Il trovatore* is an obvious example: the flat keys are linked with the aristocratic world of Leonora and Count di Luna, while sharp keys tend to accompany Manrico, Azucena and the world of the gypsies. *Macbeth* shows a similar binary divide (Macbeth and Lady Macbeth on the flat side, the witches on the sharp side). Such associations may also attend other harmonic recurrences, such as the occasional repetition of large-scale tonal progressions. But these rather loose juxtapositions – by no means rigidly maintained – probably represent the ultimate point of tonal organization in Verdi: there have been no convincing demonstrations of 'tonal motion' across large spans of Verdian musical drama.

More important than harmony as a means of establishing what Verdi called the *tinta* or *tinte* (identifying colour or colours) of a given opera are various recurring melodic shapes. These should not be confused with recurring motifs, which Verdi occasionally used to great effect by association with an important element of the drama (the horn-call in *Ernani* is a classic early example), and which gain their effect by means of straightforward semantic identification and a sense of isolation from the basic musical fabric. Nor are they connected with the proto-leitmotivic experiment of *I due Foscari*, in which the main entrances of certain characters or groups are marked by the repetition of a 'personal' instrumental theme (an interesting case in that the curiously undramatic tone of these recollections illustrates, as Carl Dahlhaus has suggested, that leitmotivic technique is basically incompatible with Italian opera's constant tendency to create a vivid sense of the affective present). On the contrary, these recurring shapes will tend to hover on the edge of obvious reminiscence, thus contributing to a sense of musical cohesion without accruing semantic weight. The rising 6th that begins so many lyric pieces in *Ernani*, the 'bow shape' of *Attila*, perhaps even the stepwise rising line of *Oberto* are possible examples, ones that could cautiously be multiplied.

At least until the later part of this period, the fixing of an opera within a specific ambience, the use of what is often called 'local colour', was sporadic and often routine. The single gesture towards the exotic ambience of *Nabucco*, for example (the chorus that opens Act 3), is probably the opera's least inspired number, and one reason why *Nabucco* is more successful than *I Lombardi* (Verdi's next opera, and one that resembles *Nabucco* in many ways) is that the later opera's frequent changes of locale and ambience necessitate a larger amount of this rather pallid, 'colouristic' music. By the end of the 1840s, however, particularly after his exposure to the French stage, Verdi's attitude changed. In *Luisa Miller*, the rustic ambience is an important element of the opera's *tinta*, joining with the recurring shapes (in this case as much rhythmic ideas as melodic ones) to give the work a pronounced individuality. This merging of local colour with other recurring elements is also evident in *Il trovatore*, where the 'Spanish' atmosphere is intimately bound to the musical sphere inhabited by Azucena. It reaches a pinnacle with *La traviata*, in which much of the drama unfolds against telling refractions of the waltz-laden social world so vividly depicted in the opening scene.

(v) Reception and politics. By the early 1850s, Verdi had become the most famous and frequently performed Italian opera composer in Europe, having wrested the former epithet from Rossini, the latter from Donizetti. He commanded unprecedented fees for new operas (although he lagged some way behind the most famous singers in earning potential), could choose more-or-less freely which theatres were to launch his latest works, and had begun to acquire substantial assets in farm land and buildings. Admittedly, Verdi's 'noisy' instrumentation (perhaps in particular his favouring of the middle to low register of the orchestra), his often extreme demands on singers and his taste for extravagant melodramatic plots had on occasions brought him criticism in the press during the 1840s; and several of his operas failed to find a place in the 'repertory' that was rapidly forming during this period. However, despite the occasional critical attack, and the occasional public failure such as that which initially greeted *La traviata*, opponents of Verdi (at least within Italy) were becoming an eccentric minority.

On occasion it seemed that the composer's most serious opposition came from those elaborate and multifarious organs of state censorship which controlled artistic expression in most parts of Italy. Librettos could be subject to modification on religious, moral or political grounds; and in Milan and Naples (perhaps elsewhere) the censor would also attend the dress rehearsal, to ensure that the music and staging produced no improprieties. However, severity varied greatly from state to state, and because censorship in the northern states (in which Verdi concentrated his early career) was far more easygoing than that in Rome or Naples, the composer encountered few difficulties with his early operas. The Zaccaria of *Nabucco*, for example, ended his Act 1 cabaletta with the words 'Che dia morte allo stranier' ('That gives death to the foreigner') without censorial interference in a huge number of early productions, and even the 'revolutionary' *Ernani* encountered only minor obstacles in the north. After 1848 the situation worsened, and it is significant that Verdi's most severe bouts with the censor occurred in the austere, counter-revolutionary atmosphere of the late 1840s and 50s, over the religious subject matter of *Stiffelio* and over many aspects of *Rigoletto* and *Un ballo in maschera*.

The business of government censorship, imposed by foreign nations and the local governments that controlled Italy, inevitably leads to a consideration of Verdi's political status during this period and of the extent to which his operas served to heighten the Italian people's national consciousness. Verdi was undoubtedly a staunch patriot, as can be seen from many of his letters, from his return to Milan during the 1848 uprising, and from his one unambiguously 'patriotic' opera, *La battaglia di Legnano* (1849, Rome). However, before 1846 there is hardly any evidence that his operas were regarded as especially dangerous politically or that they excited patriotic enthusiasm in their audiences. In the period between the liberal reforms of Pius IX in 1846 and the revolutions of 1848, the theatre increasingly became a focus of political demonstrations, but Verdi's operas seem to have accompanied such outbursts no more often than those of other composers. It is also significant that, during the months of mid-1848 in which the Milanese governed their own city, neither the newly-liberated theatrical press nor the public seemed especially interested in Verdi or his music. This is not to deny the stirring force of Verdi's early music, in particular his treatment of the chorus as a dynamic new expressive power; but connections between his music and political events were for the most part made later in the century, some time after the revolutionary atmosphere had cooled.

5. LIFE, 1853–71. After the première of *La traviata* in March 1853, the pace of Verdi's operatic production slowed considerably. The 11 years up to *Traviata* had produced 16 operas; the 18 years that followed saw only six new works: *Les vêpres siciliennes*, *Simon Boccanegra*, *Un ballo in maschera*, *La forza del destino*, *Don Carlos* and *Aida*. Admittedly, such a comparison gives a slightly exaggerated picture. Two of the operas (*Vêpres* and *Don Carlos*) were written for the Paris Opéra: they are thus both considerably longer than any other of Verdi's scores and required the composer's presence in Paris during extended rehearsal periods. Furthermore, Verdi devoted much time and creative energy to revising various works: there were relatively minor adjustments to *La traviata* and *Simon Boccanegra* after unsuccessful first performances, and to *Il trovatore* for its Paris version; a thorough overhaul of *Macbeth*, again for Paris; the refashioning of *Stiffelio* as *Aroldo*; and substantial revisions to *La forza del destino* for its La Scala première. Such efforts notwithstanding, however, Verdi now spent an increasing amount of time away from the theatre, and on at least one occasion – in the more than three-year gap between finishing *Un ballo in maschera* (early 1858) and starting *La forza del destino* (mid-1861) – he seems to have decided to stop composing altogether.

His three most extensive foreign expeditions were all related to professional engagements: a two-year period in Paris (1854–5) saw the completion and performance of *Les vêpres siciliennes*; *La forza del destino* required two trips to Russia, with visits en route to Paris, London and Madrid (1862–3); and the production of *Don Carlos* kept him in Paris for nearly a year (1866–7). When not travelling, Verdi divided his time between periods of intense activity on his farmlands at Sant'Agata and visits to friends in other cities, notably

2. Verdi rehearsing 'Un ballo in maschera' in Naples in 1858, with the soprano Fioretti (seated) and the tenor Gaetano Fraschini (standing, left): caricature by Melchiorre Delfico

Naples and Venice. In 1859, after more than ten years together, Verdi and Giuseppina Strepponi were finally married; in 1866 they set up permanent winter quarters in Genoa, finding the climate of Sant'Agata too hostile. As early as 1845, Verdi had quarrelled with the directors of La Scala over what he considered the unacceptable production standards. Not long after, he broke completely with Milan, which had been his centre of operations in the early to mid-1840s; after his dramatic return during the 1848 revolutions, he did not enter the city again for 20 years, losing touch with most of his Milanese friends. But the late 1860s saw a rapprochement. In 1868 he returned to the city to visit Clara Maffei and to meet for the first time Alessandro Manzoni, whom he had long revered. A year later he re-established contacts with La Scala, supervising there the première of the revised *Forza del destino*. On hearing of the death of Rossini (in November 1868), Verdi suggested to Ricordi that a *Messa per Rossini* be written jointly by the most famous Italian composers of the day. The Mass was duly completed, Verdi supplying the 'Libera me', but there was much bitter wrangling over administrative problems and the work was never performed.

6. Operas: 'Les vêpres siciliennes' (1855) to 'Aida' (1871). *(i) Composition.* The genesis, and thus to a certain extent the aesthetic premises, of a Verdi opera of this period had changed a little from those operating earlier in his career, the principal difference being that the composer's burgeoning reputation allowed him greater artistic freedom. He was besieged by offers from the major theatres of Italy, Europe and beyond, and could choose the venue and the subject of any new opera. He was also free to refuse commissions much more often than he had in the hectic 1840s, as he could live from accumulated wealth for long periods. However, when he did work the old patterns remained. Verdi was still wary of committing himself to a subject before the principal singers had been engaged, refusing, for example, to sign a contract for *La forza del destino* until the company had been fixed. He still composed by way of a prose scenario to clarify the musical forms, a libretto to reflect those forms, a draft and then a 'skeleton score', and finally an orchestration of that score. He continued to compose with great facility and, allowing for the vastly increased length of several of these operas, probably took no longer drafting music than he had when writing his earliest works.

On the surface, at least, the types of subject he chose were also unchanged: he remained loyal to Schiller and also to the lesser lights of romantic melodrama. Towards the end of the period, however, there is evidence of a decisive move away from melodramatic extremes. In revising *Macbeth* in 1865, for example, he replaced the final, onstage death scene with a Victory Chorus; more telling still, in the 1869 revision of *La forza del destino* he replaced the bloody denouement with an ensemble of religious consolation. This move towards a broader canvas is part of a larger change, a gradual expansion in the stylistic and dramatic scope of his operas. Verdi now repeatedly called for more variety in his operatic subjects and he castigated his earlier operas as one-dimensional. He strove to blend or boldly juxtapose comic and tragic scenes and genres (notably in *Un ballo in maschera* and *La forza del destino*) and to explore greater extremes of musical and dramatic ambience, sacrificing the dramatic cohesion of his best earlier work in an effort to bring Italian opera into line with an increasingly dominant French fashion.

(ii) Dramatic forms. Were we to judge solely from Verdi's correspondence, it would seem that this period saw the composer seeking radical alternatives to the fixed dramatic forms that had characterized his early operas. In negotiations over a possible setting of *King Lear*, for example, he more than once voiced his need for entirely new structures, and in discussing *Un ballo in maschera* he warned the Neapolitan impresario Torelli that Scribe's libretto 'has the conventional modes of all operas, a thing that I have always disliked and now find

insufferable'. However, these radical epistolary statements are better taken as hortatory rather than prescriptive: a way of encouraging his librettists not to lapse into the merely routine. When it came to the discussion of concrete detail, Verdi continued to think along traditional lines, and the eventual librettos for both *Re Lear* and *Ballo* are largely constructed in the conventional manner. As in the earlier period, the bulk of Verdi's operatic music remains definable within traditional formal types, although his tendency to manipulate these types according to the dramatic situation became ever more extreme.

The most fragile unit of the old, multi-movement structure was the cabaletta (which, in its ensemble form as stretta, had already disappeared from certain finales of the 1840s). Verdi was inclined to shorten it, sometimes (for example in the Henri-Montfort duet of *Les vêpres siciliennes* Act 3) making it nothing more than a fast coda section with no independent thematic ideas, or even to omit it entirely, ending the number with some stage action or portentous utterance (as in the Boccanegra-Fiesco duet in the prologue of *Simon Boccanegra*), or with a final, climactic melody (as in Riccardo's aria in Act 3 of *Un ballo in maschera)*. But, in particular with the earlier movements of set pieces, his usual practice was to continue those complex expansions and manipulations found in the Germont-Violetta duet from *La traviata* Act 2; the multi-movement form became extremely flexible, but could nevertheless articulate important stages in the dramatic development. The classic illustration of this internal renewal of form is in the last opera of this period, *Aida*, which boasts a magnificent series of grand duets, each traceable to traditional patterns but each offering a profoundly individual solution to the dramatic situation it underpins.

It is entirely in keeping with Verdi's ambivalent position towards formal conventions that, even as the various 'movements' of set pieces became less and less predictable, he sought ever more vivid ways of using the moment of transition between one movement and the next to articulate dramatic turning points. One outward manifestation of this search was his coining of the term 'parola scenica', which, as he wrote to ANTONIO GHISLANZONI, the librettist of *Aida*, 'sculpts and renders clear and evident the situation'. 'Parole sceniche', utterances such as Amonasro's 'Dei Faraoni tu sei la schiava!' in his Act 3 duet with Aida, typically occur immediately before the start of a new movement, signalling with a violent injection of musical prose that a new stage of the dramatic conflict, and a new lyrical stage of the set piece, is about to ensue.

Although examples in which traditional structures can still be found constitute the main stylistic line there are, especially in the French operas, passages where we see an emerging new aesthetic. Arias such as Philip II's 'Elle me n'aime pas' (*Don Carlos* Act 4) show comparatively little tendency to formal partition, and are better regarded as descendants of the great ariosos of Verdi's youth, especially those for Macbeth and Rigoletto. In numbers such as the Don Carlos-Elisabeth de Valois duet in Act 2 of *Don Carlos* it may even be nugatory to search for the remnants of traditional forms: the musical discourse follows in minute and constantly changing configuration the ebb and flow of the confrontation, creating the kind of 'musical prose' (or, as Verdi would call it, musical *dramma*) that was rapidly becoming the norm in European opera.

(iii) Lyric prototype. The proliferation of lyrical types towards the end of the previous period continues into this one, with the influence of French operatic forms increasingly evident. While solo statements within duets and ensembles frequently retain the old $AA'BA''$ form, full-scale aria movements commonly show a typically French ternary form, with larger A sections (often themselves based on the old 'lyric prototype') flanking a looser, declamatory B section. Amelia's 'Come in quest'ora bruna' (*Simon Boccanegra* Act 1) is a fine example of this form at its most extended; the classic condensed example is Radames' 'Celeste Aida' (*Aida* Act 1), which brings back elements of the B material to fashion a delicate coda.

When Verdi chose to retain the old-fashioned Italian model, he usually did so for characters in old-fashioned melodramatic situations: Posa's 'C'est mon jour' in *Don Carlos* Act 4 is an obvious example. And frequently he made telling changes, ones indicative of a general shift in his lyric language. In Don Carlo's 'Urna fatal' (*La forza del destino* Act 3) the harmonic openness at the start of each lyric segment undermines the $AA'BC$ form, encouraging us to hear the first two sections as one limb, and thus as the first part of a larger structure.

While the move towards larger, looser periods underlies much of Verdi's music during this period, he also continued to experiment in the opposite direction: following the example of 'Caro nome', he was occasionally encouraged by the dramatic situation to construct lyric movements of extreme formal simplicity. The final section of the Aida-Radames duet (*Aida* Act 4) is a most telling example (ex.3). This passage, first sung by Aida,

Ex.3 *Aida*, Act 4

Lyric prototype: a_2

AIDA Meno mosso

O ter-ra ad - di-o; ad - di - o val - le di pian - ti, so - gno di gau - dio che in do - lor sva - nì. A noi si schiu - de, si schiu - de il ciel, si schiu-de il ciel e l'al-me er - ran - ti vo - la-no al rag - gio del - l'e - ter - no dì.

['Farewell, earth; farewell valley of tears, dream of joy that vanished in sorrow. Heaven opens to us, and our wandering spirits to the beams of eternal day.']

is repeated literally by Radames and then repeated again by both characters in unison. The energy is, as it were, turned inwards, the extreme angularity and sheer difficulty of the vocal line forming an uncanny complement to the wellnigh obsessive formal repetition.

(iv) Harmony, tinta, local colour. In comparison with that of his French and German contemporaries, Verdi's harmonic language remained for the most part within a simple diatonic framework. However, the musical surface of his operas became increasingly complex. Devices

seen only exceptionally in the early operas – passages of rootless chromaticism, sudden shifts into remote keys (notably by way of unprepared 6-4 chords), a tendency to add surprising harmonic colour to much-used vocal sonorities – now become the norm. Nor are such devices so frequently subordinate to a firmly diatonic melody. Even in conventional arias such as Posa's 'C'est mon jour', the voice part may now be co-opted into a colouristic chromatic shift, creating a melodic line that makes little sense without its harmonic underpinning (ex.4).

Ex.4 *Don Carlos*, Act 4

['Death has its attractions, oh my Carlos, for one who dies for you.']

The effect, out of context, may sound wildly empirical; but, unlike some parallel moments in the earlier operas, these daring harmonic shifts are often carefully prepared (in the present case by a tonicization of G minor in the preceding *B* section). What is more, as set pieces expanded so too did the extent of chromatic interruption: in many arias and ensembles, the chromatic shifts expand to control entire phrases or even sections.

There remains little evidence of control over spans larger than a single number, whether harmonic or motivic; indeed, the relative broadness of dramatic scope and looseness of construction among these operas work against even that patterned juxtaposition of tonal regions or melodic types found in operas such as *Il trovatore*. Occasionally a key centre or motif may briefly shoulder the burden of semantic weight (the 'death associations' of D♭ in *Ballo*, for example, or certain recurring motifs in *Don Carlos* or *Aida*), but – as he had learnt much earlier, in the experiment of *I due Foscari* – the continuing formal fixity of Verdi's musical language militates against the sustained use of such techniques, and they never approach a level of 'structural' significance.

On the other hand, local colour becomes an ever more important connecting device, perhaps as a necessary corrective to the expansion of dramatic scope and mood. Each of the operas is shot through with particular colours intimately associated with its setting: the sea images of *Simon Boccanegra*, the Gallic poise of *Un ballo in maschera*, the Spanishness of *La forza del destino* and *Don Carlos*. And with the musical orientalism of *Aida* local colour takes up a central position it will nearly always occupy in *fin-de-siècle* opera. Clearly this added dimension is intimately bound up with Verdi's increasingly sophisticated use of the orchestra. By the time of *Aida*, Verdi was capable of setting up a classic 'nature' scene such as the prelude to Act 3, in which the elements of harmony, melody and rhythm are all subsumed under a mantle of evocative orchestral colour.

(v) Reception and politics. As the 1850s unfolded, Verdi's pre-eminence in Italian music, and his international reputation, became ever more secure; although many of the early operas had been forgotten, *Rigoletto*, *Il trovatore* and *La traviata* quickly became cornerstones of the newly-emerging Italian operatic repertory. Each new Verdian opera generated enormous interest both in the national and the foreign press.

It gradually became clear, however, that Verdi's more recent works were not duplicating his successes of the early 1850s. Neither *Les vêpres siciliennes* nor *Don Carlos* established themselves at the Opéra, and both had difficulties in transplanting to the Italian stage. *Simon Boccanegra* was poorly received and *Un ballo in maschera* and *La forza del destino* made their way comparatively slowly. Part of the problem undoubtedly lay in the seeming conservatism of Verdi's new creations. Although operas such as *Il trovatore* had quickly attained 'classic' status, a new generation of Italians was emerging, with young artistic revolutionaries such as Arrigo Boito calling for an end to the insular, 'formulaic' musical dramas of the past. Italian intellectuals began to read Wagner, and Italian theatres began to open their doors to French (and later to German) operas.

The paradox of this uncertain Italian reaction to Verdi's 'new manner' was that it went hand-in-hand with his institution as a national figure beyond the operatic world. In 1859, his name was apparently taken up as an acrostic message of Italian nationalistic aspirations ('Viva VERDI' standing for 'Viva *V*ittorio *E*manuele *R*e *D*'*I*talia); in 1861, during the first shaky months of Italian statehood, he agreed, at the personal insistence of Cavour, to serve as a member of the newly-formed Italian parliament. And it was precisely during these years that Verdi's early music began to be consistently associated with the revolutionary struggles of the 1840s. The famous choruses of his first operas, in particular 'Va pensiero' from *Nabucco*, gradually assumed something like iconic status, all the more so as the economic collapses and social tensions of the new Italian state engendered nostalgia for a past age in which Italians had been united against a foreign enemy.

In the face of these momentous cultural and political developments, and despite periodic bursts of professional and social activity, Verdi chose strategic withdrawal: physically behind the walls of Sant'Agata, mentally into an image of himself as a rough, untutored

3. *Giuseppe Verdi: photograph, late 1870s*

man of the soil, the peasant from Roncole, an 'authentic' Italian willing to set himself against the tide of cosmopolitan sophistication he saw washing around him. It was overwhelmingly this image that he offered to those first biographers who now began to pester him for information on his early life, and the resulting self-portrait was one he sedulously cultivated (along with his farm lands) for the rest of his long life.

7. LIFE, 1871–1901. After *Aida* in 1871, there was to be no Verdi operatic première for 16 years: in the 30 years that were left him, he composed just two more dramatic works, *Otello* and *Falstaff*. The creative tally was not, of course, quite so modest. In 1874 came the *Messa da Requiem*, composed in honour of Alessandro Manzoni; in the early 1880s Verdi made important revisions to *Simon Boccanegra* and, a little later, to *Don Carlos*; there are various sacred vocal pieces, some of them later collected under the title *Quattro pezzi sacri*. But the fact remains that the 1870s and early 80s, years in which we might imagine Verdi to have been at the height of his creative powers, saw no new operas.

The 1870s did, though, see an increase in what might be called Verdi's 'social' energy. He travelled widely to supervise and direct performances of *Aida* and the *Requiem*, in 1875 undertaking a veritable European tour with the latter work, conducting in Paris, London and Vienna. Perhaps not incidental to this new burst of energy was a close attachment to the soprano TERESA STOLZ, who was to remain a lifelong friend. More direct creative encouragement came later in the decade from Giulio Ricordi and Boito, whose careful planning and extreme diplomacy seem largely responsible for tempting Verdi back to operatic composition.

Apart from professional tours, Verdi divided his life mostly between Milan, Genoa and Sant'Agata, continuing to oversee his lands and add to his property. In his last years he devoted a considerable amount of money and energy to two philanthropic projects, the building of a hospital at Villanova sull'Arda Piacenza and the founding of a home for retired musicians, the Casa di Riposo, in Milan. Giuseppina Strepponi died in 1897. In December 1900 Verdi made arrangements for his youthful compositions (including, one assumes, those 'marches for band by the hundred') to be burnt after his death. He died in Milan a month later, and was buried next to his wife in the Casa di Riposo.

8. THE LAST STYLE: 'OTELLO' (1887) AND 'FALSTAFF' (1893). In spite of the chronological gap, critics have tended to see Verdi's last two operas as a logical continuation (and almost always as the 'culmination') of his previous work, thus stressing stylistic continuity across his entire career. There is much to be said for such an approach. Although Verdi was now firmly established as an international figure who could – and did – dictate his own terms, he continued to compose in the old manner, carefully tailoring his music to the singers at his disposal, for example, and altering or transposing passages that were not suited to them. In choosing to work with Boito, he secured librettos of unprecedented linguistic and prosodic sophistication; but he nevertheless continued an unshakeable allegiance to certain operatic conventions, fashioning for *Otello*, *Falstaff* and the revised *Boccanegra* magnificent examples of the grandest of the traditional set pieces, the Largo concertato.

However, the strain and difficulty with which a suitable concertato was eventually accommodated into *Otello* indicates a fundamental change in Verdian dramaturgy. At some time between *Aida* and *Otello* we might hazard that Verdi passed an intangible divide, and now saw the basis of his musical drama residing in continuous 'action' rather than in a patterned juxtaposition of 'action' and 'reflection'. (It was precisely the difficulty of embedding comprehensible 'action' into the Act 3 concertato of *Otello* that continued to pose problems, even causing Verdi to revise the piece for the opera's Parisian première in 1894.) The long Act 2 duet between Otello and Iago is a good example of how the new hierarchy worked. The duet itself cannot usefully be parsed as a central set piece of contrasting 'movements'; and the true set pieces – the Credo, Homage Chorus, quartet and *racconto* – are embedded within the larger structure.

This tendency for the music to react minutely and spontaneously to the constant changes typical of spoken dialogue brought about an inevitable decrease in periodic structures and a loosening of some of the traditional links between prosody and music. On rare occasions, Verdi may have sought to replace these losses with purely musical structures (the sonata-form subtext of the opening scene in *Falstaff*, or its closing comic fugue, are likely examples). The necessary level of purely musical coherence (always less important in opera than in music without text) was, however, usually supplied by local increases in harmonic, motivic and orchestral activity. Passages such as the Act 3 orchestral prelude to the revised *Don Carlos* (1884) show how a short motivic fragment is now sufficient to construct large spans of music, so extensive is Verdi's control over orchestral nuance and chromatic detail. But such moments are strictly local. The occasions on which Verdi used musical recurrence to make long-range connections between dramatic events are rare and, as anyone who has experienced the final minutes of *Otello* will

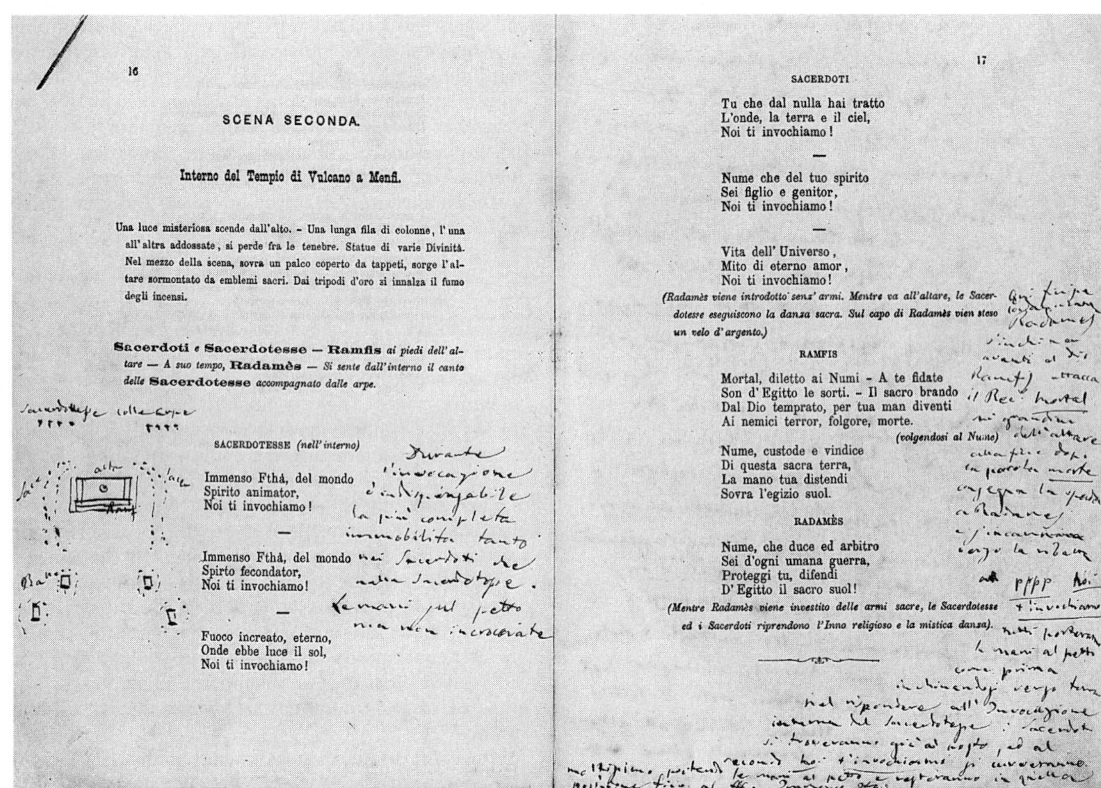

16

SCENA SECONDA.

Interno del Tempio di Vulcano a Menfi.

Una luce misteriosa scende dall'alto. – Una lunga fila di colonne, l'una all'altra addossate, si perde fra le tenebre. Statue di varie Divinità. Nel mezzo della scena, sovra un palco coperto da tappeti, sorge l'altare sormontato da emblemi sacri. Dai tripodi d'oro si innalza il fumo degli incensi.

Sacerdoti *e* **Sacerdotesse** — **Ramfis** *ai piedi dell'altare — A suo tempo,* **Radamès** — *Si sente dall'interno il canto delle* **Sacerdotesse** *accompagnato dalle arpe.*

SACERDOTESSE *(nell'interno)*

Immenso Fthà, del mondo
Spirito animator,
Noi ti invochiamo!

—

Immenso Fthà, del mondo
Spirto fecondator,
Noi ti invochiamo!

—

Fuoco increato, eterno,
Onde ebbe luce il sol,
Noi ti invochiamo!

17

SACERDOTI

Tu che dal nulla hai tratto
L'onde, la terra e il ciel,
Noi ti invochiamo!

—

Nume che del tuo spirito
Sei figlio e genitor,
Noi ti invochiamo!

—

Vita dell' Universo,
Mito di eterno amor,
Noi ti invochiamo!

(Radamès viene introdotto senz' armi. Mentre va all'altare, le Sacerdotesse eseguiscono la danza sacra. Sul capo di Radamès vien steso un velo d'argento.)

RAMFIS

Mortal, diletto ai Numi – A te fidate
Son d'Egitto le sorti. – Il sacro brando
Dal Dio temprato, per tua man diventi
Ai nemici terror, folgore, morte.
(volgendosi al Nume)
Nume, custode e vindice
Di questa sacra terra,
La mano tua distendi
Sovra l'egizio suol.

RADAMÈS

Nume, che duce ed arbitro
Sei d'ogni umana guerra,
Proteggi tu, difendi
D'Egitto il sacro suol!

(Mentre Radamès viene investito delle armi sacre, le Sacerdotesse ed i Sacerdoti riprendono l'Inno religioso e la mistica danza).

4. *'Aida': the first Italian edition of the libretto by Antonio Ghislanzoni (Milan, c1872), showing the beginning of Act 1 scene ii (in the temple of Vulcan in Memphis), in which Verdi has sketched out details of the production. On p.16 Verdi sketched the altar and positions of the priests and priestesses, with the comment: 'During the invocation, complete immobility is necessary, both of the priests and priestesses. The hands on the chests but not crossed'. On p.17 he wrote: 'At this point the dancing stops. Radames bows before the god. Ramfis begins the recitative "Mortal" on the steps of the altar. At the end, after the word "morte", he hands the sword to Radames and walks downstage. At the pppp "Noi t'invochiamo" all put their hands on their chests, as before, bowing to the ground. In replying to the offstage invocation of the priestesses, the priests are already in position, and on the second "Noi t'invochiamo" they move about extensively, put their hands on their chests, and remain in this position until the fff "Immenso Fthà"'.*

know, such moments gain their extraordinary power from the distinctiveness and simplicity of the musical material involved. Verdi's music, here as ever, continues to serve the drama, never to usurp it.

9. Reputation, scholarship. *(i) Late reception and posthumous reputation.* By the time Verdi wrote his last operas, he had become a national monument: the premières of *Otello* and *Falstaff* were cultural events of almost unprecedented importance, occasioning a flood of publicity all over Europe. Both works, inevitably in the circumstances, were heralded as brilliant successes, but – like so many of the operas after *La traviata* – neither established a place at the centre of the Italian repertory. The operatic times had changed and, in an era when Wagner and the Italian *veristi* were making the headlines, *Otello* and *Falstaff*, for all their 'modernity', were seen as *sui generis*, unsuitable for the common round of smaller theatres in particular. (It is a strange fact that, despite his pre-eminent position in our present operatic repertory, Verdi's influence on the next generation of composers was very slight.)

Far more important in the development of Verdi's reputation was the consolidation of his national status: as 'vate del Risorgimento' (bard of Italy's struggle towards national unity) and as the self-made man, the 'authentic' product of an emerging nation. As mentioned earlier, this image was encouraged by Verdi himself, whose press interviews and autobiographical statements exaggerated the lowliness of his upbringing and the trials of his early life, and also fashioned for particular musical numbers (notably the chorus 'Va pensiero') an iconic significance within the unfolding of his career. As mentioned at the start of this survey, the singing of that chorus at his burial procession in 1901 was a confirmation that, by the time of his death, Verdi's preferred self-image was firmly embedded in the minds of the Italian people.

So far as performances and purely musical reputation were concerned, the years around the turn of the century represented a low point in Verdi's fortunes. In the sophisticated, cosmopolitan atmosphere of *fin-de-siècle* Italy, it became commonplace to find Verdi's musical personality too simple and direct, and although *Rigoletto*, *Il trovatore* and *La traviata* remained staples of smaller opera houses, they were rarely granted the prestige of important revivals.

Signs of a general change in attitude began in the 1920s, during which a Verdi Renaissance was fostered in Germany by Franz Werfel (who wrote a novel based on the composer's life) and by several notable revivals, in particular a 1926 Dresden production of *La forza del destino*. By the 1930s, performances of 'forgotten' works such as *Nabucco* and *Ernani* were springing up all over Europe and the USA. Appropriated by fascists and anti-fascists alike, Verdi's music survived World War II relatively untarnished. Since then the boom has shown no signs of losing momentum, and more of Verdi's operas are in the repertory today than ever before. The works continue to provoke fresh interpretations and renewed energies. It is hard to imagine an operatic world in which they will cease to enrich and inspire.

(ii) Verdi scholarship and editions. Although there continue to be lingering pockets of resistance, it is rare these days to meet with easy dismissals of Verdi's art. One reflection of this new standing is that scholarly attention to his music is now fully respectable. The first 60 years of our century saw an indispensable series of biographical and epistolary publications: the *Copialettere* of 1913, and books by Gatti, Luzio, Abbiati and Walker. Since the 1960s, the most important stimulus has come from the Istituto Nazionale di Studi Verdiani in Parma, which has assembled a considerable archive and has published a vast amount of biographical and critical writing. In the 1970s, an American Institute of Verdi Studies was formed at New York University. Much of this activity was brought to a larger audience, and magnificently synthesized, by Julian Budden's three-volume commentary on the operas. The inauguration of a complete edition of Verdi's correspondence (by the Istituto Nazionale) and of a critical edition of his complete works (by the University of Chicago Press and Ricordi) is new testimony to the seriousness with which the man and his music are now treated.

No critical edition of Verdi's librettos exists, and the most satisfactory editions remain those published by Ricordi. Most modern printings of the texts obscure important information by ignoring the lineation, verse forms and indentations of the original. *Tutti i libretti di Verdi* (ed. L. Baldacci, Milan, 1975), which contains Italian librettos of all the operas except *Stiffelio*, has some useful facsimile pages and other illustrations, but also ignores details of the verse layout.

Vocal scores usually appeared near the time of the operas' first performances (an exception is that of *Un giorno di regno*, issued *c*1845). Most were first published by Ricordi, the exceptions being *Attila*, *I masnadieri* and *Il corsaro* (by Lucca), *Stiffelio* (by Blanchet, Paris, 1850; by Ricordi, 1852) and the French operas *Jérusalem*, *Les vêpres siciliennes* and *Don Carlos* (by the Bureau Central de la Musique/Escudier, Paris, and, often almost simultaneously and in Italian translation, by Ricordi). Vocal scores of most of the Italian operas up to *La forza del destino* were also published in Paris (*Nabucco* by Schonenberger, *Il corsaro* by Chabal and the rest by the Bureau Central de la Musique/ Escudier or by Blanchet), often within a year of the Italian editions. In 1981 Ricordi published a vocal score of *Don Carlos* containing all versions of the opera.

Full scores at first circulated in manuscript copies. Ricordi printed (for hire only) *La traviata* (*c*1855) and (later in the century or during the first half of this century) all the operas except *Oberto*, *Un giorno di regno*, *Alzira*, *I masnadieri*, *Jérusalem*, *Il corsaro*, *Stiffelio* and the first versions of *Macbeth*, *Simon Boccanegra* and *Don Carlos*. The first printed full score on public sale was Del Monaco's *La traviata* (Naples, *c*1882). In 1913–14 Ricordi published 'study scores' of *Rigoletto*, *Il trovatore*, *La traviata*, *Un ballo in maschera*, *Aida*, *Otello* and *Falstaff*; in the 1950s, revised editions of these; and in the 1980s a study score of *La forza del destino*. All but three (*I Lombardi*, *I due Foscari* and *Attila*) of the full scores printed by Ricordi have been reprinted by Kalmus (New York). Ricordi published a facsimile of the *Falstaff* autograph in 1951. The complete critical edition, published jointly by the University of Chicago Press and Ricordi under the general editorship of Philip Gossett, is in progress.

See also AIDA; ALZIRA; AROLDO; ATTILA; BALLO IN MASCHERA, UN; BATTAGLIA DI LEGNANO, LA; CORSARO, IL; DON CARLOS; DUE FOSCARI, I; ERNANI; FALSTAFF (ii); FORZA DEL DESTINO, LA; GIORNO DI REGNO, UN; GIOVANNA D'ARCO; JÉRUSALEM; LOMBARDI ALLA PRIMA CROCIATA, I; LUISA MILLER; MACBETH (ii); MASNADIERI, I; NABUCCO; OBERTO, CONTE DI SAN BONIFACIO; OTELLO (ii); RIGOLETTO; SIMON BOCCANEGRA; STIFFELIO; TRAVIATA, LA; TROVATORE, IL; and VÊPRES SICILIENNES, LES.

Edition: *The Works of Giuseppe Verdi*, ed. P. Gossett and others (Chicago and Milan, 1983–) [V]

Genre and librettist (when not in square brackets) are as stated on the libretto of the first performance (except for 'I masnadieri', which the London libretto describes as a 'tragic opera' and 'Macbeth', 'Il corsaro', 'Stiffelio', 'La traviata', 'Simon Boccanegra' and 'Aroldo', in which the libretto gives no genre).

title	*genre, acts*	*libretto*	*first performance; remarks*	*V; autograph*
Oberto, conte di San Bonifacio	dramma, 2	T. Solera, from A. Piazza's lib. *Rocester*	Milan, Scala, 17 Nov 1839	*I-Mr*
Un giorno di regno [Il finto Stanislao]	melodramma giocoso, 2	F. Romani, [? rev. Solera], from Romani's lib. for A. Gyrowetz's Il finto Stanislao (1818), after A. V. Pineu-Duval: *Le faux Stanislas* (play, 1808)	Milan, Scala, 5 Sept 1840; alternative title first used 1845	*Mr*
Nabucodonosor [Nabucco]	dramma lirico, 4 pts	Solera, after A. Anicet-Bourgeois and F. Cornu: *Nabuchodonosor* (play, 1836) and A. Cortesi: *Nabuccodonosor* (ballet, 1838)	Milan, Scala, 9 March 1842	1/iii; *Mr*
I Lombardi alla prima crociata	dramma lirico, 4	Solera, after T. Grossi (poem, 1826)	Milan, Scala, 11 Feb 1843	*Mr*
Ernani	dramma lirico, 4 pts	F. M. Piave, after V. Hugo: *Hernani* (play, 1830)	Venice, Fenice, 9 March 1844	1/v; *Mr*
I due Foscari	tragedia lirica, 3	Piave, after Byron: *The Two Foscari* (play, 1821)	Rome, Argentina, 3 Nov 1844	*Mr*
Giovanna d'Arco	dramma lirico, prol., 3	Solera, in part after F. von Schiller: *Die Jungfrau von Orleans* (play, 1801)	Milan, Scala, 15 Feb 1845	*Mr*
Alzira	tragedia lirica, prol., 2	S. Cammarano, after Voltaire: *Alzire, ou Les Américains* (play, 1736)	Naples, S Carlo, 12 Aug 1845	*Mr*
Attila	dramma lirico, prol., 3	Solera [and Piave], after Z. Werner: *Attila, König der Hunnen* (play, 1808)	Venice, Fenice, 17 March 1846	*Gb-Lbl*

title	genre, acts	libretto	first performance; remarks	V; autograph
Macbeth	opera, 4	[Piave and A. Maffei], after W. Shakespeare (play, 1605–6)	Florence, Pergola, 14 March 1847	*I-Mr*
rev. version	opéra, 4	Piave, from 1847 lib.; Fr. trans. by C. Nuitter and A. Beaumont	Paris, Lyrique, 21 April 1865	*F-Pn* (part autograph)
I masnadieri	melodramma, 4 pts	[Maffei], after Schiller: *Die Räuber* (play, 1781)	London, Her Majesty's, 22 July 1847	*I-Mr*
Jérusalem	opéra, 4	A. Royer and G. Vaëz, from Solera's 1843 lib. *I Lombardi alla prima crociata*	Paris, Opéra, 26 Nov 1847	*F-Pn*
Il corsaro	opera, 3	Piave, after Byron: *The Corsair* (poem, 1814)	Trieste, Grande, 25 Oct 1848	*I-Mr*
La battaglia di Legnano	tragedia lirica, 4	Cammarano, after J. Méry: *La bataille de Toulouse* (play, 1828)	Rome, Argentina, 27 Jan 1849	*Mr*
Luisa Miller	melodramma tragico, 3	Cammarano, after Schiller: *Kabale und Liebe* (play, 1784)	Naples, S Carlo, 8 Dec 1849	*Mr*
Stiffelio	opera, 3	Piave, after E. Souvestre and E. Bourgeois: *Le pasteur, ou L'évangile et le foyer* (play, 1849)	Trieste, Grande, 16 Nov 1850; autograph used for Aroldo, 1857	*Mr*
Rigoletto	melodramma, 3	Piave, after Hugo: *Le roi s'amuse* (play, 1832)	Venice, Fenice, 11 March 1851	1/xvii; *Mr*
Il trovatore	dramma, 4 pts	Cammarano [and L. E. Bardare], after A. García Gutiérrez: *El trovador* (play, 1836)	Rome, Apollo, 19 Jan 1853	*Mr*
La traviata	opera, 3	Piave, after A. Dumas *fils*: *La dame aux camélias* (play, 1852)	Venice, Fenice, 6 March 1853	*Mr*
Les vêpres siciliennes	opéra, 5	E. Scribe and C. Duveyrier, after their lib. *Le duc d'Albe* (1838)	Paris, Opéra, 13 June 1855	*F-Pn*
Simon Boccanegra	opera, prol., 3	Piave [and G. Montanelli], after García Gutiérrez: *Simón Bocanegra* (play, 1843)	Venice, Fenice, 12 March 1857	*I-Mr*
rev. version	melodramma, prol., 3	Piave [rev. A. Boito], from 1857 lib.	Milan, Scala, 24 March 1881	*Mr*
Aroldo	opera, 4	Piave, from his lib. *Stiffelio* (1850)	Rimini, Nuovo, 16 Aug 1857	*Mr*
Un ballo in maschera	melodramma, 3	A. Somma, from Scribe's lib. for Auber's Gustave III, ou Le bal masqué (1833)	Rome, Apollo, 17 Feb 1859	*Mr*
La forza del destino	opera, 4	Piave, after A. de Saavedra, Duke of Rivas: *Don Alvaro, o La fuerza del sino* (play, 1835) with a scene from Schiller: *Wallensteins Lager* (play, 1799), trans. by Maffei	St Petersburg, Imperial, 10 Nov 1862	*Mr*
rev. version	opera, 4	Piave [rev. A. Ghislanzoni], from his 1862 lib.	Milan, Scala, 27 Feb 1869	*Mr*
Don Carlos	opéra, 5	Méry and C. Du Locle, after Schiller's dramatic poem (1787)	Paris, Opéra, 11 March 1867	*F-Pn*
rev. version, Don Carlo	opera, 4	[rev. Du Locle] from Méry's and Du Locle's 1867 lib.; It. trans. by A. de Lauzières and A. Zanardini	Milan, Scala, 10 Jan 1884	*I-Mr*
Aida	opera, 4	Ghislanzoni, from A. Mariette's scenario	Cairo, Opera, 24 Dec 1871	*Mr*
Otello	dramma lirico, 4	Boito, after Shakespeare: *Othello, or the Moor of Venice* (play, 1604–5)	Milan, Scala, 5 Feb 1887	*Mr*
Falstaff	commedia lirica, 3	Boito, after Shakespeare: *The Merry Wives of Windsor* (play, 1600–01) and *King Henry IV* (plays, 1597–8)	Milan, Scala, 9 Feb 1893	*Mr*

For alternative or additional numbers in *Oberto*, *Nabucco*, *I Lombardi*, *Ernani*, *I due Foscari*, *Giovanna d'Arco* and *Attila*, see D. Lawton and D. Rosen: 'Verdi's Non-definitive Revisions: the Early Operas', *III° congresso internazionale di studi verdiani: Milan 1972*, 189–237.

BIBLIOGRAPHICAL

MGG (Ho Kühn)

L. Torri: 'Saggio di bibliografia verdiana', *RMI*, viii (1901), 379–407

C. Vanbianchi: *Nel I° centenario di Giuseppe Verdi, 1813–1913: Saggio di bibliografia verdiana* (Milan, 1913)

C. Hopkinson: 'Bibliographical Problems concerned with Verdi and his Publishers', *I° congresso internazionale di studi verdiani: Venice 1966*, 431–6

D. Lawton: 'Per una bibliografia ragionata verdiana', ibid, 437–42

M. Pavarani: 'Per una bibliografia e documentazione verdiana', ibid, 446–51

O. Strunk: 'Verdiana alla Biblioteca del Congresso', ibid, 452–7; Eng. orig. in *Essays on Music in the Western World* (1974), 192–200

G. Tintori: 'Bibliografia verdiana in Russia', ibid, 458–63

D. Kämper: 'Das deutsche Verdi-Schrifttum: Hauptlinien der Interpretation', *Verdi – Wagner: Rome 1969*, 185–99 [*AnMc*, no.11 (1972)]

M. Conati: 'Bibliografia verdiana: aspetti, problemi, criteri per la sistemazione della letteratura verdiana', *III° congresso internazionale di studi verdiani: Milan 1972*, 546–68

M. Mila: *La giovinezza di Verdi* (Turin, 1974), 501–17

E. Surian: 'Lo stato attuale degli studi verdiani: appunti e bibliografia ragionata (1960–1975)', *RIM*, xii (1977), 305–29

A. Porter: 'A Select Bibliography', *The Verdi Companion*, ed. W. Weaver and M. Chusid (New York, 1979), 239–54

M. Conati: 'Bibliografia verdiana', *Studi verdiani* (1982–) [each vol. carries an extensive list of publications, covering the following years: i (1977–9), ii (1980–82), iii (1983–4), iv (1985–6), v (1987–8), vi (1988–9)]

——: 'Fonti verdiane: i giornali dell'ottocento', *Nuove prospettive nella ricerca verdiana: convegno internazionale in occasione della prima del 'Rigoletto' in edizione critica: Vienna 1983*, 130–37

CATALOGUES

D. Lawton and D. Rosen: 'Verdi's Non-Definitive Revisions: the Early Operas', *III° congresso internazionale di studi verdiani: Milan 1972*, 189–237

C. Hopkinson: *A Bibliography of the Works of Giuseppe Verdi, 1813–1901*, i (New York, 1973) [vocal and instrumental works excluding operas]; ii (New York, 1978) [operas]

M. Chusid: *A Catalog of Verdi's Operas* (Hackensack, NJ, 1974)

M. Chusid, J. Nadás and L. Jensen: 'The Verdi Archive at New York

University: Part I' [catalogued and uncatalogued material in the collection], *Verdi Newsletter*, no.7 (1979) [whole issue]
M. Chusid, L. Jensen and D. Day: 'The Verdi Archive at New York University: Part II (A List of Verdi's Music, Librettos, Production Materials, Nineteenth-Century Italian Periodicals, and other Research Materials)', *Verdi Newsletter*, nos.9–10 (1981–2) [whole issue]
S. Casale: *A Catalogue of Letters from Verdi and Giuseppina Strepponi Verdi to the Escudiers* (thesis, New York U., 1983)
M. A. Bacherini Bartoli: 'Aggiunte, integrazioni e rettifiche alla *Bibliography of the Works of Giuseppe Verdi* di Cecil Hopkinson: edizioni verdiane nella Biblioteca nazionale centrale di Firenze', *Studi verdiani*, iv (1986–7), 110–35
L. B. Fairtile: 'The Verdi Archive at New York University: a List of Verdi's Music', *Verdi Newsletter*, nos.17–18 (1989–90) [whole issue; incl. more details of sources and the music than nos.9–10]

ICONOGRAPHICAL

G. Monaldi: *Saggio d'iconografia verdiana* (Bergamo, n.d.)
G. Bocca: 'Verdi e la caricatura', *RMI*, viii (1901), 326–59
H. Schultz: *Giuseppe Verdi 1813–1901: sein Leben in Bildern* (Leipzig, 1938)
C. Gatti: *Verdi nelle immagini* (Milan, 1941) [incl. sketches, pp. 64–5, 184, 186–7]
H. Kuehner: *Giuseppe Verdi in Selbstzeugnissen und Bilddokumenten* (Reinbek bei Hamburg, 1961)
R. Petzoldt: *Giuseppe Verdi 1813–1901: sein Leben in Bildern* (Leipzig, 1961)
W. Weaver: *Verdi: a Documentary Study* (London, 1977)
Con Verdi a Casa Barezzi [photographs and essays] (Busseto, 1985)
Giuseppe Verdi: vicende, problemi e mito di un artista e del suo tempo (Colorno, 1985) [exhibition catalogue; incl. essays by P. Petrobelli, G. Marchesi, M. Conati, G. Guccini, F. Benedetti and M. Dall'Acqua, E. Baker]
Verdi: album per un maestro, ed. Istituto nazionale di studi verdiani (Florence, 1991)

LETTERS AND DOCUMENTS

I. Pizzi: *Ricordi verdiani inediti* (Turin, 1901)
A. Pascolato: *Re Lear e Ballo in maschera: lettere di Giuseppe Verdi ad Antonio Somma* (Città di Castello, 1902)
T. Costantini: *Sei lettere inedite di Verdi a Giovanni Bottesini* (Trieste, 1908)
G. Cesari and A. Luzio: *I copialettere di Giuseppe Verdi* (Milan, 1913; Eng. trans., much abridged, as *Letters of Giuseppe Verdi*, ed. C. Osborne, 1971)
J. G. Prod'homme: 'Unpublished Letters from Verdi to Camille Du Locle', *MQ*, vii (1921), 73–103; *ReM*, x (1928–9), no.5, pp.97–112, no.7, pp.25–37
——: 'Verdi's Letters to Léon Escudier', *ML*, iv (1923), 62–70, 184–96, 375–7; It. orig., *RMI*, xxxv (1928), 1–28, 171–97, 519–52
A. Damerini: 'Sei lettere inedite di Verdi a G. C. Ferrarini', *Il pianoforte*, vii/Aug–Sept (1926)
A. Della Corte: 'Lettere a Maria Waldmann', *Il pianoforte*, vii/Feb (1926)
F. Werfel and P. Stefan: *Das Bildnis Giuseppe Verdis* (Vienna, 1926; Eng. trans., enlarged, as *Verdi: the Man in his Letters*, 1942)
A. Luzio: 'Il carteggio di Giuseppe Verdi con la contessa Maffei', *Profili biografici e bozzetti storici*, ii (Milan, 1927), 505–62
G. Morazzoni and G. M. Ciampelli: *Verdi: lettere inedite: le opere verdiane al Teatro alla Scala (1839–1929)* (Milan, 1929)
A. Alberti: *Verdi intimo: carteggio di Giuseppe Verdi con il conte Opprandino Arrivabene (1861–1886)* (Verona, 1931)
L. A. Garibaldi: *Giuseppe Verdi nelle lettere di Emanuele Muzio ad Antonio Barezzi* (Milan, 1931)
R. De Rensis: *Franco Faccio e Verdi: carteggio e documenti inediti* (Milan, 1934)
A. Luzio: *Carteggi verdiani*, i–ii (Rome, 1935); iii–iv (Rome, 1947)
C. Bongiovanni: *Dal carteggio inedito Verdi-Vigna* (Rome, 1941)
A. Oberdorfer: *Giuseppe Verdi: autobiografia dalle lettere* (Verona, 1941 [under pseud. C. Graziani; censored], complete, 2/1951, enlarged M. Conati, 3/1981)
F. Walker: 'Verdi and Francesco Florimo: some Unpublished Letters', *ML*, xxvi (1945), 201–8
——: 'Four Unpublished Verdi Letters', *ML*, xxix (1948), 44–7
'Cinque lettere verdiane', *RaM*, xxi (1951), 256–61
F. Schlitzer: 'Inediti verdiani nella collezione dell'Accademia musicale chigiana', *Bollettino dell'Accademia musicale chigiana* [special issue] (1951), 30–36; enlarged as *Inediti verdiani nell'archivio dell'Accademia chigiana*, Quaderni dell'Accademia chigiana, xxvii (Siena, 1953)
F. Walker: 'Verdi and Vienna: with some Unpublished Letters', *MT*, xcii (1951), 403–5, 451–3
——: 'Verdian Forgeries', *MR*, xix (1958), 273–82; xx (1959), 28–37; It. trans., *RaM*, xxx (1960), 338–49
J. W. Klein: 'Verdian Forgeries – a Summing-up', *MR*, xx (1959), 244–52
T. Jauner: *Fünf Jahre Wiener Operntheater, 1875–1880: Franz Jauner und seine Zeit* (Vienna, 1963)
U. Günther: 'Documents inconnus concernant les relations de Verdi avec l'Opéra de Paris', *III° congresso internazionale di studi verdiani: Milan 1972*, 564–83
A. Di Ascoli: *Quartetto milanese ottocentesco* (Rome, 1973) [letters of Verdi, Strepponi, A. Maffei, C. Maffei, C. Tenca and others]
G. N. Vetro: 'Giuseppe Verdi Maestro di Musica in Busseto: il giudizio inedito di Alinovi e altre carte dell'archivio di stato di Parma', *Verdi: Bollettino dell'Istituto di studi verdiani*, iii/8 (1973), 1142–9, 1503–15
E. Zanetti: 'La corrispondenza di Verdi conservata a S. Cecilia', *Verdi: Bollettino dell'Istituto di studi verdiani*, iii/8 (1973), 1131–41, 1485–1502
M. Conati: 'Le lettere di Giuseppe Verdi e Giuseppina Verdi a Giuseppe Perosio', *Nuova rassegna di studi musicali*, i (1977), 47–67
M. Medici and M. Conati: *Carteggio Verdi-Boito* (Parma, 1978)
G. Marchesi: *Verdi, merli e cucù: cronache bussetane fra il 1819 e il 1839* (Busseto, 1979)
M. Conati: *Interviste e incontri con Verdi* (Milan, 1980; Eng. trans. as *Interviews and Encounters with Verdi*, 1984)
F. Cella and P. Petrobelli: *Giuseppe Verdi-Giulio Ricordi: corrispondenza e immagini 1881–1890* (Milan, 1981)
E. Baker: 'Lettere di Giuseppe Verdi a Francesco Maria Piave, 1843–1865: documenti della Frederick R. Koch Foundation Collection e della Mary Flagler Collection presso la Pierpont Morgan Library di New York', *Studi verdiani*, iv (1986–7), 136–66
C. M. Mossa: 'Le lettere di Emanuele Muzio alla Casa Ricordi', ibid, 167–201
P. Petrobelli, M. Di Gregorio Casati and C. M. Mossa, eds.: *Carteggio Verdi-Ricordi 1880–1881* (Parma, 1988)
L. Jensen: *Giuseppe Verdi and Giovanni Ricordi, with Notes on Francesco Lucca: from 'Oberto' to 'La Traviata'* (New York, 1989)

PUBLICATIONS OF THE ISTITUTO NAZIONALE DI STUDI VERDIANI, PARMA

Verdi: Bollettino dell'Istituto di studi verdiani, i/1–3 (1960) [mainly on *Un ballo in maschera*]
Verdi: Bollettino dell'Istituto di studi verdiani, ii/4–6 (1961–6) [mainly on *La forza del destino*]
Atti del I° congresso internazionale di studi verdiani: Venice 1966 (Parma, 1969)
Verdi: Bollettino dell'Istituto di studi verdiani, iii/7–9 (1969–82) [mainly on *Rigoletto*]
Atti del II° congresso internazionale di studi verdiani: Verona 1969 (Parma, 1971)
Atti del III° congresso internazionale di studi verdiani: Milan 1972 (Parma, 1974)
Studi verdiani (1982–)
Ernani: ieri e oggi: Modena 1984 [*Bollettino dell'Istituto di studi verdiani*, no.10 (1987; Eng. trans., 1989)]
Nuove prospettive nella ricerca verdiana: atti del convegno internazionale in occasione della prima del 'Rigoletto' in edizione critica: Vienna 1983 (Parma and Milan, 1987)
Quaderni dell'Istituto di studi verdiani, i: *Il corsaro* (1963); ii: *Gerusalemme* (1963); iii: *Stiffelio* (1968); iv: *Genesi dell'Aida* (1971); v: *Messa per Rossini: la storia, il testo, la musica* (1988)

SPECIAL PERIODICAL NUMBERS AND COMMEMORATIVE VOLUMES

**article titles listed in M. Mila: 'La giovinezza di Verdi' (Turin, 1974), 514–15*

La farfalla (1896)
**Gazzetta musicale di Milano*, lvi (1901), March
Natura ed arte (1901)
**RMI*, vii/2 (1901)
**Nuova antologia*, clxvii (16 Oct 1913)
Die Musik, xiii (1913–14) [incl. articles by A. Weissmann, E. Istel, R. Specht]
Illustrazione italiana (26 Jan 1941)
**Aurea Parma*, xxv (1941), Jan–Feb
Verdi, Studi e memorie a cura del Sindacato nazionale fascista musicisti nel XL anniversario della morte (Rome, 1941)
**La regione Emilia-Romagna* (1950), nos. 9–12

Verdiana: bollettino di notizie (1950–51) [12 issues]
**ZfM*, Jg.112 (1951), Jan
**Il diapason* (1951), Feb
**Melos*, xviii (1951), Feb
**Das Musikleben*, iv (1951), Feb
**Opera*, ii/2 (1951)
**La fiera letteraria* (22 April 1951)
**RaM*, xxi (1951), July
**Giuseppe Verdi* (Milan, 1951) [pubn of Teatro alla Scala, ed. F. Abbiati]
Per il cinquantenario della morte di Giuseppe Verdi (Naples, 1951) [pubn of Teatro S Carlo]
Collana di saggi verdiani nel primo cinquantenario della morte di Giuseppe Verdi, ed. A. Zecchi (Bologna, 1952)
M. Hinrichsen: 'Anno verdiano', *HMYB*, vii (1952), 494–509
HiFi, xiii (1963), Oct [incl. articles by A. Moravia and W. Weaver and on early New York productions]
Verdi–Wagner: Rome 1969 [*AnMc*, no. 11 (1972); incl. essays by A. A. Abert, K. Hortschansky, D. Kämper, L. Finscher, E. Zanetti, F. D'Amico, W. Witzenmann, R. Celletti]
19th Century Music, ii/2 (1978–9) [incl. articles by A. Porter, G. A. Mendelsohn, S. Levarie and D. Coe]
OQ, v/2–3 (1987) [incl. articles by H. Busch, W. Ducloux, M. Chusid, J. Ardoin, G. Martin, M. Valente and R. Parker]

BIOGRAPHY, LIFE AND WORKS

G. Demaldè: *Cenni biografici* (MS, *c*1853, archives of Monte di Pietà, Busseto) [pubd in *Newsletter of the American Institute for Verdi Studies*, nos.1–2 (1976) and *Verdi Newsletter*, no.3 (1977)]
H. Cavalli: *Biografias artisticas contemporaneas de los célebres José Verdi, maestro de música y Antonio Canova escultor* (Madrid, 1867)
M. Lessona: 'Parma: Giuseppe Verdi', *Volere è potere* (Florence, 1869), 287–307
G. Monaldi: *Verdi e le sue opere* (Florence, 1878)
A. Pougin: *Giuseppe Verdi: vita aneddotica* (Milan, 1881) [trans. and annotated by 'Folchetto' (pseud. of J. Caponi) from articles in *Le ménestrel*, 1878]; repr., ed. M. Conati (Florence, 1989); Fr. orig., incorporating Caponi's additions, 1886; Eng. trans., 1887)
G. Monaldi: *Verdi: la vita e le opere* (Turin, 1899, 4/1951)
G. Bragnolo and E. Bettazzi: *La vita di Giuseppe Verdi narrata al popolo* (Milan, 1905)
F. Werfel: *Verdi: Roman der Oper* (Berlin, 1925, 2/1930; Eng. trans., 1947) [novel]
F. Bonavia: *Verdi* (London, 1930)
B. Barilli: *Il paese del melodramma* (Lanciano, 1931)
C. Gatti: *Verdi* (Milan, 1931, 2/1951; Eng. trans., abridged, as *Verdi: the Man and his Music,* 1955)
F. Toye: *Giuseppe Verdi: his Life and Works* (London, 1931)
H. Gerigk: *Giuseppe Verdi* (Potsdam, 1932)
D. Hussey: *Verdi* (London, 1940, 5/1973)
G. Cenzato: *Itinerari verdiani* (Parma, 1949, 2/1955)
F. Walker: 'Vincenzo Gemito and his Bust of Verdi', *ML*, xxx (1949), 44–55
M. Mila: *Giuseppe Verdi* (Bari, 1958)
F. Abbiati: *Giuseppe Verdi* (Milan, 1959)
F. Walker: *The Man Verdi* (London, 1962)
G. Martin: *Verdi* (New York, 1963, 2/1964)
M. J. Matz: 'The Verdi Family of Sant'Agata and Roncole: Legend and Truth', *I° congresso internazionale di studi verdiani: Venice 1966*, 216–21
——: 'Verdi: the Roots of the Tree: an Examination of Unexplored Verdi Documents of the Bassa Parmense', *Verdi: Bollettino dell'Istituto di studi verdiani*, iii/7 (1969), 333–64
C. Sartori: 'La Strepponi e Verdi a Parigi nella morsa quaratottesca', *NRMI*, viii (1974), 239–53
W. Weaver: 'Verdi the Playgoer', *Musical Newsletter*, vi/1 (1976), 3
P. Southwell-Sander: *Verdi: his Life and Times* (Tunbridge Wells, 1978)
G. A. Mendelsohn: 'Verdi the Man and Verdi the Dramatist', *19th Century Music*, ii (1978–9), 110–42; iii (1979–80), 214–30
M. Baroni: *Il declino del patriarca: Verdi e le contraddizioni della famiglia borghese* (Bologna, 1979)
G. Marchesi: *Giuseppe Verdi: l'uomo, il genio, l'artista* (Milan, 1979)
W. Weaver and M. Chusid, eds.: *The Verdi Companion* (New York, 1979)
M. Mila: *L'arte di Verdi* (Turin, 1980)
D. R. B. Kimbell: *Verdi in the Age of Italian Romanticism* (Cambridge, 1981)
M. De Angelis: *Le carte dell'impresario: melodramma e costume teatrale nell'ottocento* (Florence, 1982)
W. Marggraf: *Giuseppe Verdi: Leben und Werk* (Leipzig, 1982)
R. Parker: 'Verdi and the *Gazzetta privilegiata di Milano*', *RMARC*, no.18 (1982), 51–65
A. Porter: 'Giuseppe Verdi', *The New Grove Masters of Italian Opera*, ed. S. Sadie (London, 1983), 193–308
J. Rosselli: 'Verdi e la storia della retribuzione del compositore italiano', *Studi verdiani*, ii (1983), 11–28
R. Parker: '"Classical" Music in Milan during Verdi's Formative Years', *Studi musicali*, xiii (1984), 259–74
J. Rosselli: *The Opera Industry in Italy from Cimarosa to Verdi: the Role of the Impresario* (Cambridge, 1984; It. trans., enlarged, as *L'impresario d'opera: arte e affari nel teatro musicale italiano dell'ottocento*, 1985)
J. Budden: *Verdi* (London, 1985)
C. Osborne: *Verdi: a Life in the Theatre* (New York, 1987)
G. Martin: *Aspects of Verdi* (New York, 1988)
R. Parker: *Studies in Early Verdi 1832–1844: New Information and Perspectives on the Milanese Musical Milieu and the Operas from 'Oberto' to 'Ernani'* (New York, 1989)

LOCATIVE STUDIES AND ANNALS

**article titles listed in M. Mila: 'La giovinezza di Verdi' (Turin, 1974), 514–15*
F. Resasco: *Verdi a Genova* (Genoa, 1901)
Giuseppe Verdi, Chigiana, no.8 (1951)
La passione verdiana di Trieste (Trieste, 1951)
G. Steffani: *Verdi e Trieste* (Trieste, 1951)
**Verdi e la Fenice* (Venice, 1951)
**Verdi e Roma* (Rome, 1951)
Verdi e Firenze (Florence, 1951)
P. P. Várnai: 'Verdi in Hungary', *Verdi: Bollettino dell'Istituto di studi verdiani*, ii/5 (1962), 949–1030, 1429–503; iii/7 (1969), 246–332, 718–89; iii/8 (1973), 1038–130, 1409–84
M. Labroca: 'Verdi e Venezia', *I° congresso internazionale di studi verdiani: Venice 1966*, 367–74
R. Massarani: 'Giuseppe Verdi a Rio de Janeiro', *I° congresso internazionale di studi verdiani: Venice 1966*, 383–412
G. Gualerzi and C. M. Roscioni: 'Il Verdi "minore" dal 1945 al 1971', *La Fenice, Venice 1970*, 335 [programme book; list of perfs. in Italy]
K. Hortschansky: 'Die Herausbildung eines deutschsprachigen Verdi-Repertoires im 19. Jahrhundert und die zeitgenössische Kritik', *AnMc*, no.11 (1972), 140–84
M. Chusid: 'Casts for the Verdi Premières in the U.S. (1847–1976)', *Newsletter of the American Institute for Verdi Studies*, no.2 (1976), 16–18; *Verdi Newsletter*, no.3 (1977), 11–12
G. Marchesi: *Giuseppe Verdi e il Conservatorio di Parma (1836–1901)* (Parma, 1976)
M. Conati: 'Saggio di critiche e cronache verdiane dalla *Allgemeine musikalische Zeitung* di Lipsia (1840–48)', *Il melodramma italiano dell'ottocento: studi e ricerche per Massimo Mila* (Turin, 1977), 13–43
M. Chusid: 'Casts for the Verdi Premières in London (1845–1977)', *Verdi Newsletter*, no.5 (1978), 13–17; no.6 (1979), 15–19
U. Dauth: *Verdis Opern im Spiegel der Wiener Presse von 1843 bis 1859: ein Beitrag zur Rezeptionsgeschichte* (Munich, 1981)
M. Conati: *La bottega della musica: Verdi e la Fenice* (Milan, 1983)
L. Sartoris: *Verdi a Genova, 1841–1901* (Genoa, 1983)
M. Conati: 'Verdi per Napoli', *Il Teatro di San Carlo 1737–1987*, ed. B. Cagli and A. Ziino (Naples, 1987), iii, 179–223
T. Kaufman: *Verdi and his Major Contemporaries: a Selected Chronology of Performances with Casts* (New York, 1990), 263–564

LIBRETTO STUDIES

U. Rolandi: *Il libretto per musica attraverso i tempi* (Rome, 1951), 126ff
L. Baldacci: 'I libretti di Verdi', *Il melodramma italiano dell'ottocento: studi e ricerche per Massimo Mila* (Turin, 1977), 113–24
M. Lavagetto: *Quei più modesti romanzi: Il libretto nel melodramma di Verdi: techniche costruttive, funzioni, poetica, di un genere letterario minore* (Milan, 1979)
F. Portinari: *Pari siamo! Io la lingua, egli ha il pugnale: storia del melodramma ottocentesco attraverso i suoi libretti* (Turin, 1981)
J. N. Black: 'The Libretto of *La creazione del mondo*, Milan – April 1834: a Note', *Studi verdiani*, ii (1983), 147–9
——: *The Italian Romantic Libretto: a Study of Salvadore Cammarano* (Edinburgh, 1984)

D. Goldin: *La vera fenice: librettisti e libretti tra sette e ottocento* (Turin, 1985)
M. Girardi: 'Verdi e Boito: due artisti fra tradizione e rinnovamento', *Arrigo Boito musicisti e letterato*, ed. G. Tintori (Milan, 1986), 97–106

MUSICAL STUDIES

A. Basevi: *Studio sulle opere di Giuseppe Verdi* (Florence, 1859); repr. in Studi e testi verdiani, iii (1978)
H. F. Chorley: *Thirty Years' Musical Recollections* (London, 1862, 2/1926)
E. Hanslick: *Die moderne Oper*, i (Berlin, 1875), 217–55
F. Filippi: *Musica e musicisti: critiche, biografie ed escursioni* (Milan, 1876)
G. B. Shaw: 'A Word More about Verdi', *Anglo-Saxon Review*, vii/ March (1901), 221–9; repr. in *London Music in 1888–89* (London, 1937), 386–97
A. Soffredini: *Le opere di Verdi: studio critico analitico* (Milan, 1901)
L. Torchi: 'L'opera di Giuseppe Verdi e i suoi caratteri principali', *RMI*, viii (1901), 279–335
C. Bellaigue: *Verdi* (Paris, 1912)
D. Alaleona: 'L'evoluzione della partitura verdiana', *Nuova antologia*, clxvii (1913), 521–8
G. Roncaglia: *Giuseppe Verdi: l'ascensione dell'arte sua, con uno studio di Alfredo Galletti sui libretti musicati dal Verdi e il dramma romantico* (Naples, 1914)
M. Mila: *Il melodramma di Verdi* (Bari, 1933)
P. Bekker: *Wandlungen der Oper* (Leipzig, 1934; Eng. trans., 1935), 110–26
J. Loschelder: *Das Todesproblem in Verdis Opernschaffen* (Cologne and Stuttgart, 1938)
G. Roncaglia: *L'ascensione creatrice di Giuseppe Verdi* (Florence, 1940)
——: 'Il "tema-cardine" nell'opera di Giuseppe Verdi', *RMI*, xlvii (1943), 218–29
A. Della Corte: *Le sei più belle opere di Giuseppe Verdi: Rigoletto, Il trovatore, La traviata, Aida, Otello, Falstaff* (Milan, 1947, 3/ 1958)
M. Mila: 'Verdi e Hanslick', *RaM*, xxi (1951), 212–24
I. Pizzetti: 'Contrappunto ed armonia nell'opera di Verdi', ibid, 189–200
R. Vlad: 'Anticipazioni nel linguaggio armonico verdiano', ibid, 237–45
G. Roncaglia: 'Il cammino e l'insegnamento di Giuseppe Verdi', *RMI*, liv (1952), 114–20
E. T. Cone: 'The Old Man's Toys: Verdi's Last Operas', *Perspectives USA*, vi (1954), 114–33; repr. in E. T. Cone: *Music: a View from Delft* (Chicago, 1989), 159–75
A. Porter: 'Verdi and Schiller', *Opera Annual*, no.3, ed. H. Rosenthal (London, 1956), 52–63
F. I. Travis: *Verdi's Orchestration* (Zürich, 1956)
G. Roncaglia: *Galleria verdiana: studi e figure* (Milan, 1959)
W. Siegmund-Schultze: 'Gedanken zum Verdischen Melodie-Typus', *Verdi: Bollettino dell'Istituto di studi verdiani*, ii/4 (1961), 255–84, 671–710
L. Dallapiccola: 'Parole e musica nel melodramma', *Quaderni della RaM*, ii (1965), 117; Eng. trans., in *The Verdi Companion*, ed. W. Weaver and M. Chusid (New York, 1979), 193–215
M. Chusid: 'The Organization of Scenes with Arias: Verdi's Cavatinas and Romanzas', *I° congresso internazionale di studi verdiani: Venice 1966*, 59–66
J. Kovács: 'Zum Spätstil Verdis', ibid, 132–44
F. Lippmann: 'Verdi e Bellini', ibid, 184–96
P. P. Várnai: 'Contributo per uno studio della tipizzazione negativa nelle opere verdiane: personaggi e situazioni', ibid, 268–75
P. Pinagli: *Romanticismo di Verdi* (Florence, 1967)
L. K. Gerhartz: *Die Auseinandersetzungen des jungen Giuseppe Verdi mit dem literarischen Drama: ein Beitrag zur szenischen Strukturbestimmung* (Berlin, 1968)
S. Hughes: *Famous Verdi Operas* (London, 1968)
J. Kerman: 'Verdi's Use of Recurring Themes', *Studies in Music History: Essays for Oliver Strunk* (Princeton, 1968), 495–510
M. Mila: 'L'unità stilistica nell'opera di Verdi', *NRMI*, ii (1968), 62–75
A. A. Abert: 'Über Textentwürfe Verdis', *Beiträge zur Geschichte der Oper*, ed. H. Becker (Regensburg, 1969), 131–8
L. Finscher: 'Wort und Ton in den Opern Verdis', *Colloquium Verdi–Wagner: Rome 1969*, 255–71 [*AnMc*, no.11 (1972)]
C. Osborne: *The Complete Operas of Verdi* (London, 1969)
G. Baldini: *Abitare la battaglia: la storia di Giuseppe Verdi* (Milan, 1970; Eng. trans., as *The Story of Giuseppe Verdi: 'Oberto' to 'Un ballo in maschera'*, 1980)
P. Petrobelli: 'Osservazioni sul processo compositivo in Verdi', *AcM*, xliii (1971), 125–42
A. A. Abert: 'Leidenschaftsausbrüche zwischen Recitativ und Arie', *III° congresso internazionale di studi verdiani: Milan 1972*, 56–70
C. Casini: 'L'analogo sintattico: sul recitativo del primo Verdi', *Spettatore musicale*, vii/4 (1972), 38
W. Dean: 'Some Echoes of Donizetti in Verdi's Operas', *III° congresso internazionale di studi verdiani: Milan 1972*, 122–47
F. Noske: 'Verdi and the Musical Figure of Death', ibid, 349–86; repr. in F. Noske: *The Signifier and the Signified: Studies in the Operas of Mozart and Verdi* (The Hague, 1977)
G. Pestelli: 'Le riduzioni del tardo stile verdiano', *NRMI*, vi (1972), 372–90
J. Budden: *The Operas of Verdi*, i: *From Oberto to Rigoletto* (London, 1973); ii: *From Il trovatore to La forza del destino* (London, 1978); iii: *From Don Carlos to Falstaff* (London, 1981)
D. Lawton: *Tonality and Drama in Verdi's Early Operas* (diss., U. of California, Berkeley, 1973)
F. Lippmann: 'Der italienische Vers und der musikalische Rhythmus: zum Verhältnis von Vers und Musik in der italienischen Oper des 19. Jahrhunderts, mit einem Rückblick auf die 2. Hälfte des 18. Jahrhunderts', *AnMc*, no.12 (1973), 253–369; no.14 (1974), 324–410; no.15 (1975), 298–333 (It. trans., rev., as *Versificazione italiana e ritmo musicale: i rapporti tra verso e musica nell'opera italiana dell'ottocento*, 1986)
F. Noske: 'Ritual Scenes in Verdi's Operas', *ML*, liv (1973), 415–39; repr. in F. Noske: *The Signifier and the Signified: Studies in the Operas of Mozart and Verdi* (The Hague, 1977)
M. Mila: *La giovinezza di Verdi* (Turin, 1974, 2/1978)
F. Lippman: 'Verdi und Donizetti', *Opernstudien: Anna Amalie Abert zum 65. Geburtstag* (Tutzing, 1975), 153–73
V. Godefroy: *The Dramatic Genius of Verdi: Studies of Selected Operas*, i: *'Nabucco' to 'La traviata'* (London, 1975); ii: *'I vespri siciliani' to 'Falstaff'* (London, 1977)
R. A. Moreen: *Integration of Text Forms and Musical Forms in Verdi's Early Operas* (diss., Princeton U., 1975)
F. Noske: *The Signifier and the Signified: Studies in the Operas of Mozart and Verdi* (The Hague, 1977)
R. Dalmonte: 'Da *Oberto* a *Rigoletto*: precisazione di una formula', *Ricerche musicali*, iii (1979), 53–69
P. Ross: *Studien zum Verhältnis von Libretto und Komposition in den Opern Verdis* (diss., U. of Berne, 1980)
G. Tomlinson: 'Verdi after Budden', *19th Century Music*, v (1981–2), 170–82
P. Weiss: 'Verdi and the Fusion of Genres', *JAMS*, xxxv (1982), 138–56
J. Budden: 'Problems of Analysis in Verdi's Works', *Nuove prospettive nella ricerca verdiana: convegno internazionale in occasione della prima del 'Rigoletto' in edizione critica: Vienna 1983*, 125–9
S. Balthazar: *Evolving Conventions in Italian Serious Opera: Scene Structure in the Works of Rossini, Bellini, Donizetti, and Verdi, 1810 to 1850* (diss., U. of Pennsylvania, 1985)
P. Weiss: '"Sacred Bronzes": paralipomena to an Essay by Dallapiccola', *19th Century Music*, ix (1985), 42–9
M. Beghelli: *Atti performativi nella drammaturgia verdiana* (diss., U. of Bologna, 1986)
A. Roccatagliati: *Drammaturgia romantica verdiana: 'Luisa Miller', 'Stiffelio' e 'Rigoletto'* (diss., U. of Bologna, 1986)
M. Baroni: 'Le formule d'accompagnamento nel teatro del primo Verdi', *Studi verdiani*, iv (1986–7), 18–64
G. Tomlinson: 'Italian Romanticism and Italian Opera: an Essay in their Affinities', *19th Century Music*, x (1986–7), 43–60
M. Beghelli: 'Per un nuovo approccio al teatro musicale: l'atto performativo come luogo dell'imitazione gestuale nella drammaturgia verdiana', *Italica*, lxiv (1987), 632–53
H. S. Powers: '"La solita forma" and "The Uses of Convention"', *AcM*, lix (1987), 65–90 [also in *Nuove prospettive nella ricerca verdiana: Vienna 1983*, 74–109]
D. Rosen: 'How Verdi Operas Begin: an Introduction to the Introduzioni', *Tornando a 'Stiffelio': popolarità, rifacimento, messinscena, effettismo e altre 'cure' nella drammaturgia del Verdi romantico*, ed. G. Morelli (Florence, 1987), 203–21; repr. in *Verdi Newsletter*, no.16 (1988), 3–18
S. Balthazar: 'Rossini and the Development of the Mid-Century Lyric Form', *JAMS*, xli (1988), 102–25
M. Engelhardt: *Die Chöre in den frühen Opern Giuseppe Verdis*

(Tutzing, 1988)
E. Lendvai: *Verdi and Wagner* (Budapest, 1988)
R. Parker: 'On Reading Nineteenth-Century Opera: Verdi through the Looking-Glass', *Reading Opera*, ed. A. Groos and R. Parker (Princeton, 1988), 288–305
G. Tomlinson: 'Opera and *Drame*: Hugo, Donizetti, and Verdi', *Music and Drama*, Studies in the History of Music, ii (New York, 1988), 171–92
W. Osthoff: 'Dante beim späten Verdi', *Studi verdiani*, v (1988–9), 35–64
C. Abbate and R. Parker, eds.: *Analyzing Opera: Verdi and Wagner* (Berkeley, 1989)
S. Balthazar: 'The *Primo Ottocento* Duet and the Transformation of Rossinian Code', *JM*, vii (1989), 471–97
G. de Van: *Théâtre et musique dans les opéras de Giuseppe Verdi* (diss., U. of Paris, 1989)
M. Girardi: 'Per un inventario della musica in scena nel teatro verdiano', *Studi verdiani*, vi (1990), 99–145
P. Gossett: 'Becoming a Citizen: the Chorus in *Risorgimento* Opera', *COJ*, ii (1990), 41–64
G. de Van: 'Musique et narration dans les opéras de Verdi', *Studi verdiani*, vi (1990), 18–54
M. Engelhardt: *Verdi und andere: 'Un giorno di regno', 'Ernani', 'Attila', 'Il corsaro' in Mehrfachvertonungen* (Parma, 1992)
A. Gerhard: *Die Verstäderung der Oper* (Stuttgart, 1992)

TEXTUAL STUDIES

D. Vaughan: 'Discordanze tra gli autografi verdiani e la loro stampa', *La Scala* (1958), no.104, pp.11–15, 71–2
G. Gavazzeni: 'Problemi di tradizione dinamico-fraseologica e critica testuale, in Verdi e in Puccini', *RaM*, xxix (1959), 27–41, 106–22; repr. with Eng. trans., 1961 [see also D. Vaughan and G. Gavazzeni, *RaM*, xxx (1960), 60–67; *Musica d'oggi*, iv (1961), 65–8]
D. Vaughan: 'Meeting Verdi on his Own Ground', *Verdi: Bollettino dell'Istituto di studi verdiani*, i/2 (1960), pp.lxvii–lxxviii
——: 'The Inner Language of Verdi's Manuscripts', *Musicology*, v (1979), 67–153; abridged as 'Markings and Meanings in Verdi', *World of Opera*, i/1 (1978–9), 43–54
Nuove prospettive nella ricerca verdiana: convegno internazionale in occasione della prima del 'Rigoletto' in edizione critica: Vienna 1983 [incl. essays by P. Gossett, D. Lawton, C. Gallico, U. Günther and M. Chusid]
D. Lawton: 'Why Bother with the New Verdi Edition?', *OQ*, ii/4 (1984–5), 43–54
J. A. Hepokoski: 'Compositional Emendations in Verdi's Autograph Scores: *Il trovatore, Un ballo in maschera*, and *Aida*', *Studi verdiani*, iv (1986–7), 87–109
P. Gossett: 'Censorship and Self-Censorship: Problems in Editing the Operas of Giuseppe Verdi', *Essays in Musicology: a Tribute to Alvin Johnson* (Philadelphia, 1990), 247–57

PERFORMING PRACTICE AND STAGING

Disposizioni sceniche (contemporary production books) exist for the following operas: *Les vêpres siciliennes* (1856, Paris); *Giovanna de Guzman* [It. version of *Les vêpres siciliennes*] (?1856, Milan); *Le trouvère* [Fr. version of *Il trovatore*] (?1857, Paris); *Un ballo in maschera* (1859, Milan); *La forza del destino* (?1863, Milan); *Don Carlos* (1867, Milan, 3/1886); *Aida* (1873, Milan); *Simon Boccanegra* (1883, Milan); *Otello* (1888, Milan) [photocopies available at the Istituto nazionale di studi verdiani, Parma]

M. T. Muraro: 'Le scenografie delle cinque "prime assolute" di Verdi alla Fenice di Venezia', *I° congresso internazionale di studi verdiani: Venice 1966*, 328–34
D. Rosen: 'The Staging of Verdi's Operas: an Introduction to the Ricordi *Disposizioni sceniche*', *IMSCR*, xii: *Berkeley 1977*, 444–53
R. H. Cohen (with S. l'Ecuyer Lacroix and J. Léveillé): *Les gravures musicales dans 'L'Illustration', 1843–1899* (Quebec, 1982–3)
W. Crutchfield: 'Vocal Ornamentation in Verdi: the Phonographic Evidence', *19th Century Music*, vii (1983–4), 3–54
R. H. Cohen: 'A Survey of French Sources for the Staging of Verdi's Operas: "Livrets de mise en scène", Annotated Scores and Annotated Libretti in two Parisian Collections', *Studi verdiani*, iii (1985), 11–44
G. W. Harwood: 'Verdi's Reform of the Italian Opera Orchestra', *19th Century Music*, x (1986–7), 108–34
R. Meucci: 'Il cimbasso e gli strumenti affini nell'ottocento italiano', *Studi verdiani*, v (1988–9), 109–62
N. Cipriani and M. Stefanoni: *Verdi dal vivo: antologia di edizioni discografiche* (Parma, 1989)
M. Chusid: 'A Letter by the Composer about *Giovanna d'Arco* and some Remarks on the Division of Musical Direction in Verdi's Day', *Performance Practice Review*, iii (1990), 7–57
H. R. Cohen, ed.: *The Original Staging Manuals for Twelve Parisian Operatic Premières/Douze livrets de mise en scène lyrique datant des créations parisiennes* (Stuyvesant, NY, 1991) [incl. production books for *Le trouvère* and *Les vêpres siciliennes*]
L. Jensen: 'The Emergence of the Modern Conductor in 19th-Century Italian Opera', *Performance Practice Review*, iv (1991), 34–63

INDIVIDUAL WORKS

Oberto

C. Sartori: '*Rocester*, la prima opera di Verdi', *RMI*, xliii (1939), 97–104
M. Conati: 'L'*Oberto, conte di San Bonifacio* in due recensioni straniere poco note e in una lettera inedita di Verdi', *I° congresso internazionale di studi verdiani: Venice 1966*, 67–92
D. R. B. Kimbell: 'Poi ... diventò l'*Oberto*', *ML*, lii (1971), 1–7
P. D. Giovanelli: 'La storia e la favola dell'*Oberto*', *Studi verdiani*, ii (1985), 29–37
L. Jensen: 'The Early Publication History of *Oberto*: an Eye Toward Nabucco', *Verdi Newsletter*, no.13 (1985), 6–20
R. Parker: 'The Autograph Score of Oberto, conte di San Bonifacio', *Studies in Early Verdi (1832–44)* (New York, 1989), 63–82

Un giorno di regno

R. Parker: '*Un giorno di regno*: from Romani's Libretto to Verdi's Opera', *Studi verdiani*, ii (1983), 38–58
M. Engelhardt: 'Nuovi dati sulla nascita dell'opera giovanile di Verdi *Un giorno di regno*', *Studi verdiani*, iv (1986–7), 11–17

Nabucco

P. Petrobelli: 'Nabucco', *Associazione Amici della Scala: Milan 1966–7*, 17–47
D. Lawton: 'Analytical Observations on the *Nabucco* Revisions', *III° congresso internazionale di studi verdiani: Milan 1972*, 208–20
L'avant-scène opéra, no.86 (1986) [*Nabucco* issue]
R. Parker: 'The Critical Edition of *Nabucco*', *OQ*, v (1987), 91–8

I Lombardi

'Gerusalemme', *Quaderni dell'Istituto di studi verdiani*, ii (1963) [whole issue]
D. R. B. Kimbell: 'Verdi's First Rifacimento: *I Lombardi* and *Jérusalem*', *ML*, lx (1969), 1–36

Ernani

L. K. Gerhartz: *Die Auseinandersetzungen des jungen Giuseppe Verdi mit dem literarischen Drama: ein Beitrag zur szenischen Strukturbestimmung der Oper* (Berlin, 1968), 30–82, 453–4
J. Kerman: 'Notes on an Early Verdi Opera', *Soundings*, iii (1973), 56–65
G. Paduano: 'Turbamenti del triangolo: il sistema delle autorità e delle tenerezze nell'*Ernani*', in G. Paduano: *Noi facemmo ambedue un sogno strano: il disagio amoroso sulla scena dell'opera europea* (Palermo, 1982), 22–59
R. Parker: 'Levels of Motivic Definition in Verdi's *Ernani*', *19th Century Music*, vi (1982–3), 141–50
Ernani: ieri e oggi: Modena 1984 [*Bollettino dell'Istituto di studi verdiani*, no.10 (1987; Eng trans., 1989)]
M. Spada: '*Ernani* e la censura napoletana', *Studi verdiani*, v (1988–9), 11–34
P. Gossett: 'The Composition of *Ernani*', *Analyzing Opera: Verdi and Wagner*, ed. C. Abbate and R. Parker (Berkeley, 1989), 27–55

I due Foscari

C. Simone: 'Per la cabaletta de *I due Foscari*', *Nuova antologia*, ccclxxv (1934), 327–34
G. Biddlecombe: 'The Revision of "No, non morrai, chè i perfidi": Verdi's Compositional Process in *I due Foscari*', *Studi verdiani*, ii (1983), 59–77

Alzira

M. Mila: 'Verdi minore: lettura dell'*Alzira*', *RIM*, i (1966), 246–67
P. Petrobelli: 'Pensieri per *Alzira*', *Nuove prospettive nella ricerca verdiana: convegno internazionale in occasione della prima del 'Rigoletto' in edizione critica: Vienna 1983*, 110–24

Attila

M. Noiray and R. Parker: 'La composition d'*Attila*: étude de quelques variantes', *RdM*, lxii (1976), 104–24

M. Mila: 'Lettura dell'*Attila* di Verdi', *NRMI*, xvii (1983), 247–76

Macbeth

G. Cora Varesi: 'L'interpretazione del *Macbeth*', *Nuova antologia* (1932), 433–40

L. K. Gerhartz: *Die Auseinandersetzungen des jungen Giuseppe Verdi mit dem literarischen Drama: ein Beitrag zur szenischen Strukturbestimmung der Oper* (Berlin, 1968), 82–193, 465–75

W. Osthoff: 'Die beiden Fassungen von Verdi's *Macbeth*', *AMw*, xxix (1972), 17–44

F. Noske: 'Schiller e la genesi del *Macbeth* verdiano', *NRMI*, x (1976), 196–203

F. Degrada: 'Lettura del *Macbeth* di Verdi', *Studi musicali*, vi (1977), 207–67; repr. in *Il palazzo incantato: studi sulla tradizione del melodramma dal Barocco al Romanticismo*, ii (Fiesole, 1979), 79–141

E. Antokoletz: 'Verdi's Dramatic Use of Harmony and Tonality in *Macbeth*', *In Theory Only*, iv/6 (1978–9), 17–28

D. Goldin: 'Il *Macbeth* verdiano: genesi e linguaggio di un libretto', *AnMc*, no.19 (1979), 336–72; repr. in D. Goldin: *La vera fenice: librettisti e libretti tra sette e ottocento* (Turin, 1985), 230–82

M. Conati: 'Aspetti della messinscena del *Macbeth* di Verdi', *NRMI*, xv (1981), 374–404

L'avant-scène opéra, no. 40 (1982) [*Macbeth* issue]

D. Rosen and A. Porter, eds.: *Verdi's 'Macbeth': a Sourcebook* (New York, 1984)

M. Chusid and T. Kaufman: 'More about the Performance History of *Macbeth*', *Verdi Newsletter*, no.13 (1985), 38–41

N. John, ed.: *Macbeth* (London, 1990) [ENO opera guide]

Jérusalem: see *I Lombardi*

Il Corsaro

'Il corsaro', *Quaderni dell'Istituto di studi verdiani*, i (1963) [whole issue]

M. Mila: 'Lettura del *Corsaro* di Verdi', *NRMI*, v (1971), 40–73

S. Town: 'Observations on a Cabaletta from Verdi's *Il corsaro*', *CMc*, no.32 (1981), 59–75

D. Lawton: 'The Corsair Reaches Port', *ON*, xlvi/20 (1981–2), 16, 18, 42

La battaglia di Legnano

J. Budden: '*La battaglia di Legnano*: its Unique Character, with Special Reference to the Finale of Act I', *III° congresso internazionale di studi verdiani: Milan 1972*, 71–80

F. Noske: 'Verdi und die Belagerung von Haarlem', *Convivium amicorum: Festschrift Wolfgang Boetticher* (Berlin, 1974), 236–45

Luisa Miller

L. K. Gerhartz: *Die Auseinandersetzungen des jungen Giuseppe Verdi mit dem literarischen Drama: ein Beitrag zur szenischen Strukturbestimmung der Oper* (Berlin, 1968), 193–270, 475ff

Stiffelio

V. Levi: '*Stiffelio* e il suo rifacimento (*Aroldo*)', *I° congresso internazionale di studi verdiani: Venice 1966*, 172–5

'Stiffelio', *Quaderni dell'Istituto di studi verdiani*, iii (1968) [whole issue]

G. Morelli, ed.: *Tornando a 'Stiffelio': popolarità, rifacimento, messinscena, effettismo e altre 'cure' nella drammaturgia del Verdi romantico* (Florence, 1987)

Rigoletto

C. Gatti: Introduction to *L'abbozzo del Rigoletto di Giuseppe Verdi* (Milan, 1941) [sketches]

G. Roncaglia: 'L'abbozzo del *Rigoletto* di Verdi', *RMI*, xlviii (1946), 112–29; repr. in G. Roncaglia: *Galleria verdiana* (Milan, 1959), 87–100

P. Petrobelli: 'Verdi e il *Don Giovanni*: osservazioni sulla scena iniziale del *Rigoletto*', *I° congresso internazionale di studi verdiani: Venice 1966*, 232–46

C. Gallico: 'Ricognizione di *Rigoletto*', *NRMI*, iii (1969), 855–901

Verdi: Bollettino dell'Istituto di studi verdiani, iii/7–9 (1969–82)

M. Lavagetto: *Una casa di censura: il 'Rigoletto'* (Milan, 1979)

N. John, ed.: *Rigoletto* (London, 1982) [ENO opera guide]

M. Conati: *'Rigoletto' di Giuseppe Verdi: guida all'opera* (Milan, 1983)

W. Osthoff: 'Verdis musikalische Vorstellung in der Szene III, 4 des *Rigoletto*', *Nuove prospettive nella ricerca verdiana: convegno internazionale in occasione della prima del 'Rigoletto' in edizione critica: Vienna 1983*, 57–73

C. Danuser: *Studien zu den Skizzen von Verdis 'Rigoletto'* (diss., U. of Berne, 1985)

S. Döhring: 'Le roi s'amuse – Rigoletto: vom "drame" zum "melodramma"', *Oper als Text: romanistische Beiträge zur libretto-Forschung*, ed. A. Gier (Heidelberg, 1986), 239–47

L'avant-scène opéra, nos. 112–13 (1988) [*Rigoletto* issue]

U. Günther: '*Rigoletto* à Paris', *L'opera tra Venezia e Parigi*, ed. M. T. Muraro (Florence, 1988), 269–314

M. Chusid: 'The Tonality of *Rigoletto*', *Analyzing Opera: Verdi and Wagner*, ed. C. Abbate and R. Parker (Berkeley, CA, 1989), 241–61

Il trovatore

P. Petrobelli: 'Per un'esegesi della struttura drammatica del *Trovatore*', *III° congresso internazionale di studi verdiani: Milan 1972*, 387–400; repr. as 'Towards an Explanation of the Dramatic Structure of *Il trovatore*', *Music Analysis*, i (1982), 129–40

W. Drabkin: 'Characters, Key Relations and Tonal Structure in *Il trovatore*', *Music Analysis*, i (1982), 143–53

R. Parker: 'The Dramatic Structure of *Il trovatore*', *Music Analysis*, i (1982), 155–67

J. Black: 'Salvadore Cammarano's Programma for *Il trovatore* and the Problems of the Finale', *Studi verdiani*, ii (1983), 78–107

N. John, ed.: *Il trovatore* (London, 1983) [ENO opera guide]

L'avant-scène opéra, no. 60 (1984) [*Il trovatore* issue]

D. Lawton: '*Le trouvère*: Verdi's Revision of *Il trovatore* for Paris', *Studi verdiani*, iii (1985), 79–119

J. Greenwood: 'Musical and Dramatic Motion in Verdi's *Il trovatore*', *JbO*, ii (1986), 59–73

J. Rosenberg: 'A Sketch Fragment for *Il trovatore*', *Verdi Newsletter*, no. 14 (1986), 29–35

M. Chusid and T. Kaufman: 'The First Three Years of *Trovatore*', *Verdi Newsletter*, no. 15 (1987), 30–49

La traviata

M. Chusid: 'Drama and the Key of F major in *La traviata*', *III° congresso internazionale di studi verdiani: Milan 1972*, 89–121

J. Budden: 'The Two *Traviatas*', *PRMA*, xcix (1972–3), 43–66

D. Rosen: 'Virtue Restored', *ON*, xlii/9 (1977–8), 36–9

N. John, ed.: *La traviata* (London, 1981) [ENO opera guide]

L'avant-scène opéra, no.51 (1983) [*La traviata* issue]

F. Della Seta: 'Il tempo della festa: su due scene della *Traviata* e su altri luoghi verdiani', *Studi verdiani*, ii (1983), 108–46

C. Dahlhaus: 'Realism in Italian Opera', in C. Dahlhaus: *Realism in Nineteenth-Century Music* [trans. of *Musikalischer Realismus: zur Musikgeschichte der 19. Jahrhunderts* (1982)] (Cambridge, 1985), 63–71

J. A. Hepokoski: 'Genre and Content in mid-century Verdi: "Addio, del passato" (*La traviata*, Act III)', *COJ*, i (1989), 249–76

Les vêpres siciliennes

P. Bonnefon: 'Les métamorphoses d'un opéra: lettres inédites d' Eugène Scribe', *Revue des deux mondes*, xli/4 (1917), 877–99

J. Budden: 'Varianti nei *Vespri siciliani*', *NRMI*, vi (1972), 155–81

M. Mila, R. Celletti and G. Gualerzi: *Opera: collana di guide musicali*, 1st ser., i (Turin, 1973) [essays with Fr./It. lib.]

R. Vlad: 'Unità strutturale dei *Vespri siciliani*', *Il melodramma italiano dell'ottocento: studi e ricerche per Massimo Mila* (Turin, 1977), 45–90

A. Porter: '*Les vêpres siciliennes*: New Letters from Verdi to Scribe', *19th Century Music*, ii (1978–9), 95–109

F. Noske: 'Melodia e struttura in *Les vêpres siciliennes* di Verdi', *Ricerche musicali*, iv (1980), 3–8

J. Budden: 'Verdi and Meyerbeer in relation to *Les vêpres siciliennes*', *Studi verdiani*, i (1982), 11–20

M. Conati: 'Ballabili nei *Vespri*: con alcune osservazioni su Verdi e la musica popolare', *Studi verdiani*, i (1982), 21–46

L'avant-scène opéra, no.75 (1985) [*Les vêpres siciliennes* issue]

A. Gerhard: '"Ce cinquième acte sans intérêt": preoccupazioni di Scribe e di Verdi per la drammaturgia de *Les vêpres siciliennes*', *Studi verdiani*, iv (1986–7), 65–8

Simon Boccanegra

F. Walker: 'Verdi, Giuseppe Montanelli and the Libretto of *Simon Boccanegra*', *Verdi: Bollettino dell'Istituto di studi verdiani*, i/3 (1960), 1373–90

W. Osthoff: 'Die beiden *Boccanegra*-Fassungen und der Beginn von Verdis Spätwerk', *AnMc*, no.1 (1963), 70–89

L'avant-scène opéra, no.19 (1979) [*Simon Boccanegra* issue]

E. T. Cone: 'On the Road to *Otello*: Tonality and Structure in *Simon Boccanegra*', *Studi verdiani*, i (1982), 72–98

J. Kerman: 'Lyric Form and Flexibility in *Simon Boccanegra*', ibid, 47–62

P. P. Várnai: 'Paolo Albiani: il cammino di un personaggio', ibid, 63–71

M. Conati: *Il 'Simon Boccanegra' di Verdi a Reggio Emilia (1857): Storia documentata: alcune varianti alla prima edizione dell'opera* (Reggio Emilia, 1984)
D. Goldin: 'Il *Simon Boccanegra* da Piave a Boito e la drammaturgia verdiana', in D. Goldin: *La vera fenice: librettisti e libretti tra sette e ottocento* (Turin, 1985), 283–334
N. John, ed.: *Simon Boccanegra* (London, 1985) [ENO opera guide]
D. Puccini: 'Il *Simon Boccanegra* di Antonio García Gutiérrez e l'opera di Giuseppe Verdi', *Studi verdiani*, iii (1985), 120–30
H. Busch: *Verdi's 'Otello' and 'Simon Boccanegra' (revised version) in Letters and Documents* (Oxford, 1988)
A. Sopart: *Giuseppe Verdis 'Simon Boccanegra' (1857 und 1881): eine musikalisch-dramaturgische Analyse*, [whole issue] *AnMc*, no.26 (1988)
H. Powers: '*Simon Boccanegra* I. 10–12: a Generic-Genetic Analysis of the Council Chamber Scene', *19th Century Music*, xiii (1989–90), 101–28

Aroldo: see *Stiffelio*

Un ballo in maschera

A. Pascolato: *Re Lear e Ballo in maschera: lettere di Giuseppe Verdi ad Antonio Somma* (Città di Castello, 1902)
Verdi: Bollettino dell'Istituto di studi verdiani, i/1–3 (1960)
S. Levarie: 'Key Relations in Verdi's *Un ballo in maschera*', *19th Century Music*, ii (1978–9), 143–7; see also J. Kerman, 'Viewpoint', ibid, 186–91, and G. A. Marco and S. Levarie, 'On Key Relationships in Opera', ibid, iii (1979–80), 83–9
L'avant-scène opéra, no.32 (1981) [*Un ballo in maschera* issue]
S. Levarie: 'A Pitch Cell in Verdi's *Un ballo in maschera*', *Journal of Musicological Research*, iii (1981), 399–409
R. Parker and M. Brown: 'Motivic and Tonal Interaction in Verdi's *Un ballo in maschera*', *JAMS*, xxxvi (1983), 243–65
P. Ross: 'Amelias Auftrittsarie im *Maskenball*: Verdis Vertonung im dramaturgisch-textlichem Zusammenhang', *AMw*, xl (1983), 126–45
N. John, ed.: *Un ballo in maschera* (London, 1990) [ENO opera guide]

La forza del destino

Verdi: Bollettino dell'Istituto di studi verdiani, ii/4–6 (1961–6)
E. Rescigno: *La forza del destino di Verdi* (Milan, 1981)
N. John, ed.: *The Force of Destiny* (London, 1983) [ENO opera guide]
J. Nadás: 'New Light on Pre-1869 Revisions of *La forza del destino*', *Verdi Newsletter*, no.15 (1987), 7–29
L'avant-scène opéra, no.126 (1989) [*La forza del destino* issue]
W. C. Holmes: 'The earliest revisions of *La forza del destino*', *Studi verdiani*, vi (1990), 55–98

Don Carlos

II° congresso internazionale di studi verdiani: Verona 1969
A. Porter: 'A Sketch for *Don Carlos*', *MT*, cxi (1970), 882–5
——: 'The Making of *Don Carlos*', *PRMA*, xcviii (1971–2), 73–88
U. Günther: 'La genèse de *Don Carlos*', *RdM*, lviii (1972), 16–64; lx (1974), 87–158
——: 'Zur Entstehung der zweiten französischen Fassung von Verdis *Don Carlos*', *IMSCR*, xi: *Copenhagen 1972*, 396–402
A. Porter: 'A Note on Princess Eboli', *MT*, cxiii (1972), 750–54
U. Günther and G. Carrara Verdi: 'Der Briefwechsel Verdi–Nuitter–Du Locle zur Revision des *Don Carlos*', *AnMc*, no.14 (1974), 1–31; no.15 (1975), 334–401
A. Porter: 'Preamble to a New *Don Carlos*', *Opera*, xxv (1974), 665–73
M. Clémeur: 'Eine neu entdeckte Quelle für das Libretto von Verdi's *Don Carlos*', *Melos/NZM*, iii (1977), 496–9
F. Degrada: '*Don Carlos*: il teatro musicale e la funzione critica', in F. Degrada, ed.: *Il palazzo incantato: studi sulla tradizione del melodramma dal Barocco al Romanticismo*, ii (Fiesole, 1979), 143–54
G. Paduano: 'Noi facemmo ambedue un sogno strano', in G. Paduano: *Noi facemmo ambedue un sogno strano: il disagio amoroso sulla scena dell'opera europea* (Palermo, 1982), 60
U. Günther: 'Wagnerism in Verdi's *Don Carlos* von 1867?', *Wagnerliteratur – Wagnerforschung*, ed. C. Dahlhaus and E. Voss (Mainz, 1985), 101–8
P. Robinson: 'Realpolitik: Giuseppe Verdi's *Don Carlo*', in P. Robinson: *Opera and Ideas: from Mozart to Strauss* (Ithaca, NY, 1985), 155–209
L'avant-scène opéra, nos.90–91 (1986) [*Don Carlos* issue]
U. Günther: 'La genèse du *Don Carlos* de Verdi: nouveaux documents', *RdM*, lxxii (1986), 104–77
D. Rosen: 'The Operatic Origins of Verdi's "Lacrymosa"', *Studi verdiani*, v (1988–9), 65–84
N. John, ed.: *Don Carlos* (forthcoming) [ENO opera guide]

Aida

A. Luzio: 'Come fu composta l'*Aida*', *Carteggi verdiani*, iv (Rome, 1947), 5–27
E. Lendvai: 'Verdis Formgeheimnisse', *I° congresso internazionale di studi verdiani: Venice 1966*, 157–71
'Genesi dell'*Aida*', *Quaderni dell'Istituto di studi verdiani*, iv (1971) [whole issue]
U. Günther: 'Zur Entstehung von Verdis *Aida*', *Studi musicali*, ii (1973), 15–71
P. Gossett: 'Verdi, Ghislanzoni, and *Aida*: the Uses of Convention', *Critical Inquiry*, i (1974), 291–334
L'avant-scène opéra, no.4 (1976) [*Aida* issue]
J. Humbert: 'A propos de l'égyptomanie dans l'oeuvre de Verdi: attribution à Auguste Mariette d'un scénario anonyme de l'opéra *Aida*', *RdM*, lxii (1976), 229–56
L. Alberti: 'I progressi attuali [1872] del dramma musicale: note sulla *Disposizione scenica per l'opera "Aida"*', *Il melodramma italiano dell'ottocento: studi e ricerche per Massimo Mila* (Turin, 1977), 125–55
H. Busch: *Verdi's 'Aida': the History of an Opera in Letters and Documents* (Minneapolis, 1978)
N. John, ed.: *Aida* (London, 1980) [ENO opera guide]
P. Petrobelli: 'Music in the Theatre (a propos of *Aida*, Act III)', *Themes in Drama*, iii (1980), 129–42
G. de Bosio: *Aida 1913, 1982: diario pe, una regia all'Arena* (Milan, 1982)
M. Conati: 'Aspetti di melodrammaturgia verdiana: a proposito di una sconosciuta versione del finale del duetto Aida–Amneris', *Studi verdiani*, iii (1985), 45–78
D. Lawton: 'The Autograph of *Aida* and the New Verdi Edition', *Verdi Newsletter*, no. 14 (1986), 4–14
G. Erasmi: '*Norma* ed *Aida*: momenti estremi della concezione romantica', *Studi verdiani*, v (1988–9), 85–108
D. Lawton: 'Tonal Systems in *Aida*', *Analyzing Opera: Verdi and Wagner*, ed. C. Abbate and R. Parker (Berkeley, 1989), 262–75
R. Parker: 'Motives and Recurring Themes in *Aida*', ibid, 222–38
K. A. Jürgensen: 'Le coreografie originali di "Aida" (Paris, Théâtre de l'Opéra, 1880)', *Studi verdiani*, vi (1990), 146–58

Otello

F. Busoni: 'Verdi's *Otello*: eine kritische Studie', *NZM*, liv (1887), 125–7
Otello: dramma lirico in quattro atti ... Giudizi della stampa italiana e straniera [2nd edn; suppl. to *Gazzetta musicale di Milano*, no. 13] (Milan, 1887)
Verdi e l'Otello [special issue of *Illustrazione italiana*] (Milan, 1887)
V. Maurel: 'A propos de la mise-en-scène du drame lyrique Otello' [1888], *Dix ans de carrière* (Paris, 1897; repr. New York, 1977), 1–148
J. Kerman: 'Verdi's *Otello*, or Shakespeare Explained', *Opera as Drama* (New York, 1956, 2/1988), 100–39
W. Dean: 'Verdi's *Otello*: a Shakespearean Masterpiece', *Shakespeare Survey*, xxi (1968), 87–96
L'avant-scène opéra, no.3 (1976) [*Otello* issue]
D. Lawton: 'On the "Bacio" Theme in *Otello*', *19th Century Music*, i (1977–8), 211–20
D. Coe: 'The Original Production Book for *Otello*: an Introduction', *19th Century Music*, ii (1978–9), 148–58
F. Degrada: '*Otello*: da Boito a Verdi', *Il palazzo incantato: studi sulla tradizione del melodramma dal Barocco al Romanticismo*, ii (Fiesole, 1979), 155–66
J. Budden: 'Time Stands Still in *Otello*', *Opera*, xxxii (1981), 888–93
N. John, ed.: *Otello* (London, 1981) [ENO opera guide]
R. Parker and M. Brown: '"Ancora un bacio": Three Scenes from Verdi's *Otello*', *19th Century Music*, ix (1985–6), 51–62
J. A. Hepokoski: *Giuseppe Verdi: Otello* (Cambridge, 1987)
K. Bergeron: 'How to Avoid Believing (While Reading Iago's "Credo")', *Reading Opera*, ed. A. Groos and R. Parker (Princeton, 1988), 184–99
H. Busch: *Verdi's 'Otello' and 'Simon Boccanegra' (revised version) in Letters and Documents* (Oxford, 1988)
J. A. Hepokoski: 'Boito and F.-V. Hugo's "Magnificent Translation": a Study in the Genesis of the *Otello* Libretto', *Reading Opera*, ed. A. Groos and R. Parker (Princeton, 1988), 34–59
——: 'Verdi's Composition of *Otello*: the Act II Quartet', *Analyzing Opera: Verdi and Wagner*, ed. C. Abbate and R. Parker (Berkeley, 1989), 125–49
J. A. Hepokoski and M. Viale Ferrero: *Otello di Giuseppe Verdi*,

Collana di disposizioni sceniche, ed. F. Degrada and M. Viale Ferrero (Milan, 1990)

Falstaff

Verdi e il Falstaff [special issue of *Illustrazione italiana*] (Milan, 1893)

H. Gál: 'A Deleted Episode in Verdi's *Falstaff*', *MR*, ii (1941), 266–72

E. T. Cone: 'The Stature of *Falstaff*: Technique and Content in Verdi's Last Opera', *Center*, i (1954), 17–23

G. Barblan: *Un prezioso spartito di Falstaff* (Milan, 1957)

D. Sabbeth: 'Dramatic and Musical Organization in *Falstaff*', *III° congresso internazionale di studi verdiani: Milan 1972*, 415–42

W. Osthoff: 'Il sonetto nel *Falstaff* di Verdi', *Il melodramma italiano dell'ottocento: studi e ricerche per Massimo Mila* (Turin, 1977), 157–83

D. Linthicum: 'Verdi's *Falstaff* and Classical Sonata Form', *MR*, xxxix (1978), 39–53

J. A. Hepokoski: *The Compositional History of Verdi's 'Falstaff': a Study of the Autograph Score and Early Editions* (diss., Harvard U., 1979)

——: 'Verdi, Giuseppina Pasqua and the Composition of *Falstaff*, *19th Century Music*, iii (1979–80), 239–50

N. John, ed.: *Falstaff* (London, 1982) [ENO opera guide]

J. A. Hepokoski: *Giuseppe Verdi: Falstaff* (Cambridge, 1983)

——: 'Under the Eye of the Verdian Bear: Notes on the Rehearsals and Première of *Falstaff*', *MQ*, lxxi (1985), 135–56

T. Bauman: 'The Young Lovers in *Falstaff*', *19th Century Music*, ix (1985–6), 62–9

L'avant-scène opéra, nos. 87–8 (1986) [*Falstaff* issue]

Il re Lear

A. Pascolato: *Re Lear e Ballo in maschera: lettere di Giuseppe Verdi ad Antonio Somma* (Città di Castello, 1902)

M. Medici: 'Lettere su Re Lear', *Verdi: Bollettino dell'Istituto di studi verdiani*, i/2 (1960), 767–78, 1039–56

L. K. Gerhartz: 'Il *Re Lear* di Antonio Somma ed il modello melodrammatico dell'opera verdiana: principi per una definizione del libretto verdiano', *I° congresso internazionale di studi verdiani: Venice 1966*, 110–15

——: *Die Auseinandersetzungen des jungen Giuseppe Verdi mit dem literarischen Drama: ein Beitrag zur szenischen Strukturbestimmung der Oper* (Berlin, 1968), 277–8, 497–8

G. Martin: 'Verdi, *King Lear* and Maria Piccolomini', *Columbia Library Columns*, xxi (1971), 12–20

G. Schmidgall: 'Verdi's *King Lear* Project', *19th Century Music*, ix (1985–6), 83–101

ROGER PARKER

Verdier, Marie (*fl* 1675–80). French soprano. The little we know about her career comes from the Parfaict brothers in their manuscript *Histoire de l'Académie royale de musique* (in *F-Pn*). Esteemed for her performances of confidantes and other secondary parts, she created the following roles in Lully's operas: a priestess of Minerva in *Thésée* (1675); Flora in *Atys* (1676); and La Renommée and a syrinx in *Isis* (1677). Durey de Noinville (*Histoire du théâtre de l'Académie royale de musique*, Paris, 1757) in his discussion of her 1676 performance in *Atys* claimed that Verdier sang in spectacles 'from the age of 15 to the age of about 60'. She left the stage in 1680; in 1698 she was receiving an opera pension of 500 livres. She was described by the Parfaicts as having been a 'rather good actress, tall and thin with chestnut-brown hair and with a delicate temperament'.

JAMES R. ANTHONY

Veretti, Antonio (*b* Verona, 20 Feb 1900; *d* Rome, 14 July 1978). Italian composer. He studied the piano and composition with Guglielmo Mattioli and Alfano at the Bologna Conservatory, graduating in 1921. After working in Milan as music critic of the *Fiera letteraria*, he moved to Rome where he founded the Conservatorio Musicale della Gioventù Italiana; thereafter he directed the conservatories of Pesaro (1950–52), Cagliari (1953–5) and Florence (1956–70). Introduced to the literary circle Ronda by his librettist Riccardo Bacchelli, and having absorbed some of the trends towards renewal expressed by the 'eighties generation', Veretti distanced himself in his music-theatre works from the dominant realist taste by his interest in pre-19th-century musical culture. This explains, for example, the attempt in his first theatrical work, the comedy *Il medico volante* (1923), to re-introduce the verbal quickness of the *commedia dell'arte*. He was also, however, attracted by the new, and in the 1950s adopted 12-note methods, these being present in *I sette peccati capitali* (1956).

Il medico volante, 1923 (farsa, 3, R. Bacchelli, after Molière: *Le médecin volant*), unperf.

Il favorito del re (comic op, 3, A. Rossato), Milan, Scala, 17 March 1932; rev. as Burlesca (opera-ballet, 1), Rome, Opera, 29 Jan 1955, vs (Milan, 1932)

Il galante tiratore (azione coreografica, Bacchelli, after C. Baudelaire), Sanremo, Casino, 11 Feb 1933

Una favola di Andersen (azione mimo-sinfonica, Veretti, after H. C. Andersen), Venice, Sept festival, 1934

I sette peccati capitali (mistero musicale e coreografico), Milan, Scala, 24 April 1956, vs (Milan, 1956)

*

F. Brusa: '"Il favorito del re" di Antonio Veretti', ed. Arturo Rossato, *RMI*, xxxix (1932), 15–9

M. Mila: 'Sette peccati senza penitenza', *Cronache musicali 1955–1959* (Turin, 1959), 179–82

G. Vigolo: 'I peccati dodecafonici', *Mille e una sera all'opera e al concerto* (Florence, 1971)

RAFFAELE POZZI

Verga, Giovanni (*b* Catania, 2 Sept 1840; *d* Catania, 27 Jan 1922). Italian writer. His short story *Cavalleria rusticana* was based on an actual event, originally fictionalized as part of his novel *I Malavoglia* but later published separately. The young Eleonora Duse read it and encouraged him to turn it into a play, which he did, heightening the dramatic impact and developing the part of Santuzza as a tragic heroine, played by Duse.

Altogether three operas were based on the story. The first, set to music by Stanislao Gastaldon, with a libretto by Bartocci Fontana, was performed in 1888 under the title *Mala Pasqua*; all that survives is a serenade, revived by Beniamino Gigli with the title 'Musica proibita' ('Forbidden Music'). Verga gave permission for the librettists Giovanni Targioni-Tozzetti and Guido Menasci to adapt his play for the opera by Mascagni (1890), but trouble arose over royalties and Verga took the publisher Sonzogno to court and won. In revenge, Sonzogno saw to it that Verga's name appeared only in small lettering on the published score and finally removed it altogether. The third setting, by Domenico Monleone with a libretto by his brother Giovanni, was performed in 1907 in Amsterdam, Budapest and Turin. In response, Mascagni and Sonzogno brought an action alleging unlawful imitation, which they won.

Monleone's music was later used for a new opera based on another short story by Verga, *Mistero* (1921). Giulio Ricordi, who, to his lasting regret, had originally rejected Mascagni's score, suggested to Puccini that he might make an opera of yet another of Verga's stories, *La lupa*, which had already been turned into a play. Puccini set to work with enthusiasm and even went to Catania to meet Verga, but he lost interest and later made use of the music he had composed in *La bohème*.

*

Cavalleria Rusticana and Other Stories (London, 1928) [incl. Eng. trans. by D. H. Lawrence]

J. W. Klein: 'Pietro Mascagni and Giovanni Verga', *ML*, xliv (1963), 350–57

A. Alexander: *Giovanni Verga* (London, 1972) [incl. Eng. trans. of *Cavalleria rusticana* as a short story, pp.100–05]

BARBARA REYNOLDS

Vergine del sole, La ('The Virgin of the Sun'). Libretto subject used in the 18th century. Its source is JEAN FRANÇOIS MARMONTEL's *Les Incas, ou La destruction de l'empire du Pérou*. Operas on the subject were also entitled *Alonso e Cora*, *Cora och Alonzo* and *Idalide*.

Alonso, a conquistador, has assisted the Inca ruler Ataliba in vanquishing his enemies; as a reward, Ataliba bestows his sister's hand on the Spaniard. Alonso, however, has fallen in love with Cora, a virgin of the sun. A volcanic eruption destroys the temple of the sun, threatening Cora's life; in saving her, Alonso carries her from the temple. But in leaving the temple she has broken a sacred law and must die by burial alive. Alonso resolves to die with her. They are saved when the ancient law is abrogated.

Gudmund Göran Adlerbeth prepared a Swedish version of this plot, *Cora och Alonzo*, set by J. G. Naumann for the inauguration of the Royal Opera House, Stockholm, on 30 September 1782 (a concert version had been given in 1780 using a German translation by J. L. Neumann). Ferdinando Moretti prepared the first Italian version, *Idalide, o sia La vergine del sole*, for Milan in 1783, with music by Giuseppe Sarti. Here Alonso becomes Enrico and Cora becomes Idalide. Cherubini set the libretto for Florence in 1784 and Rispoli for Turin in 1786; Sarti revised his version for Florence in 1788 and Cimarosa provided a setting for Bologna in 1790. Sarti's settings enjoyed a number of revivals, sometimes under its alternative title. The libretto is noteworthy for the temple scene with dancing in Act 1 and the volcanic eruption, which destroys the temple in Act 2.

Carlo Lanfranchi Rossi's version for Naples, *Le vergine del sole*, set by Giacomo Tritto (1786), though based on Moretti's libretto, names the principals Alonso and Cora. Rossi reduces the text from three acts to two, moving the temple scene forward and replacing the dancing with a cavatina and a military procession. The volcanic eruption is incorporated into a multisectional action-ensemble finale to Act 1; the resolution of the drama takes place within a similar finale to Act 2. These are very early examples of the use in *opera seria* of the multisectional action-ensemble finale, formerly an exclusively *buffa* form. This work anticipates by one year Paisiello's *opera seria*, *Pirro*, also for Naples, which is often cited for its early and extensive usage of the same form. Gaetano Andreozzi set versions of the Rossi libretto for Palermo in 1797 and Livorno in 1799. In Giuseppe Foppa's *Alonso e Cora*, which Francesco Bianchi set for Venice in 1786, Ataliba has no sister and there is no complication of an unwanted betrothal; Cora must be sacrificed to appease the angry gods and bring peace, but her people save her.

See also ALONSO E CORA [Foppa] and CORA OCH ALONZO [J. G. Naumann].
MARITA P. McCLYMONDS

Vergnet, Edmond(-Alphonse) (*b* Montpellier, 4 July 1850; *d* Nice, 15 Feb 1904). French tenor. He studied in Paris, making his début at the Opéra in 1874 as Raimbaut (*Robert le diable*). He also sang Faust, Léopold (*La Juive*), Ruodi (*Guillaume Tell*), Laertes (*Hamlet*), Don Ottavio, Fernand (*La favorite*), Max (*Der Freischütz*), Alim (*Le roi de Lahore*), John of Leyden, Vasco da Gama, Samson and Lohengrin. At the Théâtre de la Monnaie, Brussels, he created John the Baptist in Massenet's *Hérodiade* (1881) and Shahabarim in Reyer's *Salammbô* (1890). He sang at Covent Garden (1881–2) as Radames, Faust, Belmonte and Wilhelm Meister. In 1883 he created Admetus in Catalani's *Dejanice* at La Scala. At Monte Carlo (1884–9) he sang Riccardo (*Ballo*), Fra Diavolo, Raoul, Donizetti's Edgardo, the Duke, Gérald (*Lakmé*) and Florestan. He created Zarastra in Massenet's *Le mage* at the Opéra (1891) and Dominique in Bruneau's *L'attaque du moulin* at the Opéra-Comique (1894).
ELIZABETH FORBES

Verheyen, Pierre Emmanuel (*b* Ghent, *c*1750; *d* Ghent, 11 Jan 1819). South Netherlands composer. A tenor, he first sang in Ghent and then in Bruges in the cathedral choirs. Attracted by the theatre, he became a member of the Vlaamse Opera, a travelling company directed by J. Neyts, and performed in France and the Netherlands. Later he joined the Brussels Théâtre de la Monnaie; the conductor there, Ignaz Vitzthumb, gave him his first composition lessons. He was later *compositeur ordinaire* to Prince Ferdinand Lobkowitz, Bishop of Ghent. In about 1788 he took a conducting post in Maastricht, but from 1790 worked in Ghent, as *maître de chapelle*, as organist and finally as an administrator; he was pensioned by the Ghent Société des Beaux-Arts. Among his compositions are three operas and many sacred works.

Les chevaliers, Ghent, 20 Jan 1779
De Jaghtpartij van Hendrik IV, Ghent, 1794
Le jardin de l'amour [?Arlequin magicien] (oc), Ghent, 1795

*

BNB (R. Vannes); *FétisB*
P. van Duyse: 'Notice biographique sur Pierre Verheyen', *Messager des sciences historiques de Belgique* (Ghent, 1841), 429–38
E. G. J. Gregoir: *Galerie biographique des artistes-musiciens belges* (Brussels, 1862)
JACQUES VAN DEUN

Verismo (It.: 'realism'; Fr. *vérisme*). A movement in Italian literature, and subsequently in opera, which developed in the 1870s as a result of the innovatory drive of the SCAPIGLIATURA and the influence of French naturalism. Its major literary representatives are the Sicilian writers Giovanni Verga (1840–1922) with the collection of stories *Vita dei campi* (1880) and the novels *I Malavoglia* (1881) and *Mastro-don Gesualdo* (1889), Luigi Capuana (1839–1915), theorist and critic of the movement, and Federico De Roberto (1861–1927) with the novel *I Viceré* (1894).

Although sharing certain characteristics with naturalism – an impersonal style of narration, a deep interest in the lower social strata, a true-to-life approach in dealing with contemporary reality – *verismo* developed distinctive traits that marked it out as an original trend in the literature of a newly unified country. In particular, the *veristi* gave a markedly regional character to their works; they reassessed the link between art and science, established by Zola as a fundamental aesthetic premise, so as to allow greater freedom to the imagination; and they arrived at an objectivity that implied total consistency of form and content. In fact, stylistic verisimilitude became a crucial problem for the *veristi*, which no one solved more successfully than Verga. In his quest for impersonality, he evolved a language capable of conveying the idioms, metaphors and turns of phrase peculiar to the actual vernacular of Sicilian fishermen and peasants. His self-effacing, highly expressive prose style remains a unique achievement in veristic literature. Considering that Italy lacked a modern narrative tradition (Manzoni's novel *I promessi sposi* remained an isolated case), *verismo* made a significant contribution to the renewal of literary prose by annexing new areas of subject matter (the life of the lower classes in the southern regions) and developing a flexible, realistic language.

Verismo also had a regenerating effect on the Italian theatre with the introduction of regional milieux, local customs and lower-class idioms. The repertory of romantic and bourgeois comedies was enriched and a new acting style evolved in order to portray the unsophisticated characters of the 'scene popolari' (as veristic plays were described). However, the emphasis on environmental elements was to turn the characteristic regionalism of *verismo* into mere picturesqueness. Veristic plays rarely matched up artistically to the prose works from which most of them were derived. Such is the case with Verga's 'scene popolari siciliane' *Cavalleria rusticana* (1884) and his 'scene drammatiche' *La lupa* (1896), both of which were dramatized versions of earlier short stories. The same is true of minor authors like the Neapolitan Salvatore Di Giacomo whose colourful 'scene popolari napoletane' *Malavita* (1889) in the local dialect was derived from a short story written in standard Italian.

Verismo entered opera through the 'scene popolari' rather than the narrative works. *Cavalleria rusticana* was the first text to be turned into an opera. In 1888 the publisher Edoardo Sonzogno advertised his second competition for a one-act opera to be written by a young Italian composer. Mascagni had no innovatory intentions in his choice of a veristic subject. Verga's play had a one-act format and already enjoyed public favour. The libretto by Giovanni Targioni-Tozzetti and Guido Menasci preserved the vividness of the dialogue and the rapid pace of the action; but, in spite of apparent structural similarities, the operatic version was distanced from the veristic play by a distortion of the social characteristics of the original story and a dilution of its down-to-earth language with traditional high-flown libretto jargon. The opera's unprecedented success, however, at the Teatro Costanzi in Rome, on 17 May 1890, led to *Cavalleria rusticana* becoming the prototype of a new genre. The term *verismo* was adopted, to designate not only the subject of the libretto but also the musico-dramatic structure of the work. The 1890s witnessed a brief flowering of operas on veristic subjects, both in Italy and abroad, as well as a large number of mediocre imitations.

Under the auspices of Edoardo Sonzogno and the first interpreters of *Cavalleria*, Gemma Bellincioni and Roberto Stagno, a 'Neapolitan' brand of operatic *verismo* was launched with Umberto Giordano's *Mala vita* (Rome, Teatro Argentina, 21 February 1892). The three acts were arranged by Nicola Daspuro from Di Giacomo's 'scene popolari'. The libretto marked an appreciable advance on the *Cavalleria* prototype as regards its relationship with the prose play. Daspuro, the librettist of Mascagni's *L'amico Fritz*, treated Di Giacomo's text with scrupulous respect for layout, characterization and environment. The sordid conditions prevailing in the alleys of a big city and the *mala vita* ('wretched life') of a prostitute were transposed without softening their crude reality. The play featured the traditional Piedigrotta festival, and this was put to effective use in the opera. Di Giacomo himself contributed vernacular lines for the ritual 'new song' of the festival. Both the song and the tarantella written by Giordano have the ring of authenticity. *Mala vita* actually sounds Neapolitan; its musical idiom can be traced back to one of the most popular Neapolitan operas of the mid-19th century, Luigi Ricci's *commedia per musica*, *La festa di Piedigrotta* (1852, Naples). The unmitigated *verismo* of *Mala vita*, however, accounts for the opera's disastrous failure on its first and only performance in Naples (S Carlo, 26 April 1892). The display of the miseries of the urban proletariat raised outraged protests from the public and the local press. Away from its natural milieu, *Mala vita* enjoyed a decent but ephemeral success. In September 1892, when the opera was presented in Vienna together with *Cavalleria* and *Pagliacci*, Eduard Hanslick wrote: 'In its merciless truthfulness to life *Mala vita* is both gripping and revolting at the same time, like most of these realistic pieces.'

The second most famous veristic opera, Leoncavallo's *Pagliacci* (Milan, Teatro Dal Verme, 21 May 1892), is a sensational and more complex work. Leoncavallo wrote both libretto and music. The explicit violence of the double murder committed by the white-faced clown is usually seen as the dramatization of an actual incident remembered from the composer's childhood. The operatic 'slice of life' so skilfully contrived by Leoncavallo is in fact the result of a subtle blending of various ingredients: a village murder, the device of the play-within-a-play with *commedia dell'arte* masks, the Pierrot pantomime as revived in Paris in the 1880s (when Leoncavallo was living there), and the open-air revels associated with a religious festival as exemplified by the Easter celebrations in *Cavalleria*.

In the following years, the customs and folkloric peculiarities of Italy's poor regions – the South, Sicily and Sardinia – were exploited by the opera industry for the production of plebeian stage works. The tendency to lapse into picturesqueness and sensationalism, inherent in the veristic theatre, became an irreversible trend. As for the music, popular songs accompanied by guitars and mandolins, tarantellas, saltarellos or other local dances, drinking songs, litanies and religious hymns, were inserted on the slightest pretext. The vocal style and the musico-dramatic structures had three main references: the scrapyard of romantic opera, the contemporary 'veristic' manner of the *giovane scuola*, and the drawing-room song style. The one-act format of the *Cavalleria* prototype was in most cases discarded in favour of two or three acts. Feeble stories with colourful vignettes were thus inflated and sustained by violent vocal outbursts, heavy orchestration, big unison climaxes, agitated duets and mellifluous intermezzos, a tendency that culminated in Wolf-Ferrari's *I gioielli della Madonna* (1911, Berlin).

The veristic fashion spread to other countries. In France, the mature Massenet composed *La Navarraise* (1894, London), a two-act opera closely modelled on *Cavalleria*, on which Bernard Shaw commented: 'He has not composed an opera: he has made up a prescription.' In Germany, Eugen d'Albert wrote *Tiefland* (1903, Prague), a two-act opera set in Catalonia. Frédéric d'Erlanger composed *Tess*, a four-act 'dramma' by Illica derived from Hardy's novel *Tess of the D'Urbervilles* (1906, Naples). Bretón's *La Dolores* (1894), Janáček's *Jenůfa* (1904) and Smyth's *The Wreckers* (1906), should also be mentioned.

The constant presence of low-life subjects and the high concentration of quotations (popular songs, dances, street cries) in Italian operas following *Cavalleria* have been taken to justify the general designation 'operatic *verismo*' for this minor genre. The

'Mala vita' (Giordano), a scene from Act 1 of the original production at the Teatro Argentina, Rome, 21 February 1892: engraving from 'Il teatro illustrato' (May 1892)

genre itself petered out in the early years of the 20th century, leaving *Cavalleria* and *Pagliacci* as its best contributions to the musical theatre.

The term *verismo*, however, has proved misleading and inadequate as a synonym for turn-of-the-century Italian opera, and it has been applied to such a variety of genres as to become practically meaningless. Derogatory implications were attached to its generalized use: *verismo* implied sensationalism, excess and triviality when applied to such operas as Mascagni's *Iris* (1898), Puccini's *Tosca* (1900) or Leoncavallo's *Zazà* (1900). This literary concept of realism, in choice of subject matter and stylistic treatment, interfered with the defining of the new kind of musical dramaturgy that arose after the decline of the old Romantic *melodramme*, irrespective of the veristic movement in Italian literature. Already by 1890 *verismo* in literature had given way to other trends that in turn influenced the evolution of opera, among them symbolism, exoticism and expressionism.

Verismo as a general description of the musical style of the *giovane scuola* is characterized by a new emotional rhetoric influenced partly by Massenet and, to a lesser degree, by Wagner: passionate tension alternates with sentimental languor, delicacy with violence, especially in the vocal lines; recitatives, solo pieces and ensembles enjoy equality of status, textural cohesion being supplied by the use of orchestral motifs; and there is a total absence of bel canto coloratura. All such features need to be viewed in the context of a steady trend in late 19th-century opera towards dramatic continuity, in which the canons of musical and spoken drama draw ever closer together, so allowing the possibility of *Literaturoper* such as Mascagni's *Guglielmo Ratcliff* (1895), Montemezzi's *L'amore dei tre re* (1913) and Zandonai's *Francesca da Rimini* (1914), settings respectively of plays by Heine (in a translation by Maffei), Sem Benelli and D'Annunzio; hence, too, a new rapidity of action, especially notable in Act 1 of Giordano's *Fedora* (1898) and the whole of Mascagni's *Il piccolo Marat* (1921). It was left to Puccini in his operas from *Manon Lescaut* (1893) onwards to achieve the most satisfactory synthesis and, by enriching a highly personal idiom with elements derived from his younger European contemporaries, to lead Italian opera into the 20th century.

*

E. Hanslick: *Fünf Jahre Musik (1891–1895)* (Berlin, 1896)

L. Torchi: 'The Realistic Italian Operas', *Famous Composers and their Works*, new ser., i, ed. P. Hale and E. Elson (Boston, 1900), 183

L. Laloy: 'Le drame musical moderne: les véristes français: Gustave Charpentier', *Mercure musical*, i (1905), 169–77

G. Bastianelli: *Pietro Mascagni* (Naples, 1910)

M. Rinaldi: *Musica e verismo* (Rome, 1932)

R. Dumesnil: 'Réalistes et naturalistes', *Histoire de musique*, iv (Paris, 1958)

J. W. Klein: 'Pietro Mascagni and Giovanni Verga', *ML*, xliv (1963), 350–57

M. Morini, ed.: *Pietro Mascagni* (Milan, 1964)

G. Ugolini: '*La traviata* e i rapporti di Verdi con l'opera verista', *I° congresso internazionale di studi verdiani: Venice 1966*, 261–7

G. Abraham: 'Realism in Janáček's operas', *Slavonic and Romantic Music* (New York, 1968), 83–98

M. Morini, ed.: *Umberto Giordano* (Milan, 1968)

S. Ferrone: *Il teatro di Verga* (Rome, 1972)

A. Barsotti: *Verga drammaturgo* (Florence, 1974)

R. Mariani: *Verismo in musica* (Florence, 1976)

R. Tedeschi: *Addio fiorito asil: il melodramma italiano da Boito al verismo* (Milan, 1978)

E. Voss: 'Verismo in der Oper', *Mf*, xxxi (1978), 303–13

J. Davies: *The Realism of Luigi Capuana* (London, 1979)

J. Nicolaisen: *Italian Opera in Transition, 1871–1893* (Ann Arbor, 1980)

F. Nicolodi: 'Parigi e l'opera verista: dibattiti, riflessioni, polemiche', *NRMI*, xv (1981), 577–623

C. Dahlhaus: *Musikalischer Realismus: zur Musikgeschichte des 19. Jahrhunderts* (Munich, 1982; Eng. trans., 1985)
G. Favre: *Musique et naturalisme: Alfred Bruneau et Emile Zola* (Paris, 1982)
R. Taruskin: 'Handel, Shakespeare, and Musorgsky: the Sources and Limits of Russian Musical Realism', *Studies in the History of Music*, i (1983), 247–68
C. Casini, F. Cella, F. Nicolodi and G. Salvetti: *Mascagni* (Milan, 1984)
M. Kelkel: *Naturalisme, vérisme et réalisme dans l'opéra d'1880 à 1930* (Paris, 1984)
L. Baldacci: 'I libretti di Mascagni', *NRMI*, xix (1985), 395–410
M. Sansone: *Verismo: from Literature to Opera* (diss., U. of Edinburgh, 1987)
——: 'Verga, Puccini and *La lupa*', *Italian Studies*, xliv (1989), 63–76
——: 'The 'verismo' of Ruggero Leoncavallo: a Source Study of *Pagliacci*', *ML*, lxx (1989), 342–62
——: 'Verga and Mascagni: the Critics' Response to *Cavalleria rusticana*', *ML*, lxxi (1990), 198–214 MATTEO SANSONE

Verlobung in San Domingo, Die ('The Betrothal in San Domingo'). Opera in two acts with a prologue and interlude by WERNER EGK to his own libretto after HEINRICH VON KLEIST's story; Munich, Nationaltheater, 27 November 1963.

The action takes place on the island of San Domingo during the slaves' violent uprising of 1803. Christoph von Ried (tenor), an officer in the French army, seeks food and shelter for himself and his relatives at a settler's lonely house. He is welcomed with feigned friendliness by the mulatto Babekan (contralto) and her light-skinned daughter Jeanne (soprano) who have been instructed to detain him there until the return of the Negro house-owner Hoango (baritone). Then Christoph is to be brutally murdered, a fate that has befallen other white people who have come to the house. However, Jeanne, enamoured of Christoph, plans to save him. Surprised by the premature return of Hoango, she is forced to bind the sleeping Christoph to his bed and then claim that she is trying to prevent him from escaping. In answer to a secret summons by Jeanne, Christoph's relatives take over the house and free him. Believing that he has been treacherously deceived by Jeanne, Christoph shoots her as she rushes towards him.

In addition to the dramatic scenario, which follows the outlines of Kleist's story but leaves out the episode of Christoph's subsequent suicide in order to maximize the impact of the opera's final tragic pages, Egk introduces two newly created sections, a prologue in Act 1 and an interlude in Act 2. Both feature a violent argument between a present-day White man (baritone) and a Black man (tenor). Shadows of the four main characters witness this altercation and make the apposite comment that 'people must learn to live together or else they will kill each other as we did'. The opera was written on the suggestion of Rudolf Hartmann for the reopening of the Munich Nationaltheater and combines Egk's customary mixture of swiftly moving arias, duets and ensembles with more lyrical elements. The exotic orchestral accompaniment with prominent use of bongos and congas and its blues episodes often attains a film-like realism. ERIK LEVI

Vermeersch, Jef (*b* Bruges, 7 Feb 1928). Belgian baritone. He studied at Bruges and Ghent, then in 1960 he joined the Koninklijke Vlaamse Opera, Antwerp, making his début as Wotan (*Das Rheingold*). In 1966 he moved to Gelsenkirchen and in 1973 to the Deutsche Oper, Berlin. He sang Kurwenal at Salzburg (Easter 1973) and Köthner at Bayreuth (1981–8). He appeared at Brussels, Vienna, Amsterdam and in Germany, France and Italy. His wide repertory included Boris, Pizarro, Amonasro, Falstaff, John the Baptist, Orestes, Golaud, Amfortas and Hans Sachs. He also sang Keppler (*Die Harmonie der Welt*), King Fisher (*The Midsummer Marriage*), Saint-Just (*Dantons Tod*) and Lopakhin (Kelterborn's *Der Kirschgarten*). A member of the Wuppertal Opera from 1984, he sang the secret police agent (*The Consul*) there in 1991. With his strong, serviceable voice and a fine stage presence, he made a particularly convincing Wotan.

ELIZABETH FORBES

Vérnász. Opera by Sándor Szokolay; *see* BLOOD WEDDING.

Verni, Andrea (*b* Rome, *c*1765; *d* Parma, Aug 1822). Italian bass. He made his début about 1790. From 1800 to 1816 he sang at La Scala, where in 1814 he took the part of Don Magnifico in Pavesi's *Agatina* (a version of the Cinderella story). In 1817 he sang the same role in the first performance of Rossini's *La Cenerentola* at the Teatro Valle, Rome. His cousin Pietro Verni created Gilberto in Donizetti's *Enrico di Borgogna* (1818) at the Teatro S Luca, Venice, and several other members of his family were also singers. ELIZABETH FORBES

Vernon, Mrs. *See* POITIER, JANE.

Vernon, Joseph (*b* Coventry, *c*1737; *d* London, 19 March 1782). English tenor and actor. He studied under William Savage and first sang at Drury Lane in December 1750 as Puck in *Queen Mab*, a pantomime with music by Charles Burney. He was Thyrsis in Boyce's *The Shepherd's Lottery* and built up a repertory of minor acting and singing roles. His Savoy Chapel marriage in June 1755 to the singer Jane Poitier was declared invalid and Vernon had to give evidence against the officiating clergyman; as a result he was repeatedly hissed off stage the next season. He spent four years at the Crow Street Theatre, Dublin (1758–62) and then remained at Drury Lane until a few months before his death; together with Michael Arne he wrote the music for a short interlude by Garrick, *Linco's Travels*, first performed at Drury Lane in 1767. He sang leading roles in the English operas *Almena* by Arne and Battishill (1764) and *Pharnaces* by William Bates (1765) and was Leander in Dibdin's *The Padlock*. The *Theatrical Review* praised the delicacy and exquisite taste of his singing, his acting was universally admired and Boaden wrote that 'his look was an invitation to be happy'.

*

BDA; *DNB* (L. M. Middleton); *LS*
'Mr. Vernon', *Theatrical Review*, i (1763), 36
C. Dibdin: *A Complete History of the English Stage*, v (London, 1800)
C. H. Wilson: *The Myrtle and Vine* (London, 1802)
M. J. Young: *Memoirs of Mrs Crouch*, i (London, 1806)
J. Boaden: *Life of Mrs Siddons*, i (London, 1827)
R. Fiske: *English Theatre Music in the Eighteenth Century* (London, 1973, 2/1986) OLIVE BALDWIN, THELMA WILSON

Vernoy de Saint-Georges, Jules-Henri. *See* SAINT-GEORGES, JULES-HENRI VERNOY DE.

Verocai, Giovanni (*b* Venice, *c*1700; *d* Brunswick, ? 13 Dec 1745). Italian composer and violinist. Apparently a pupil of Vivaldi, he was recruited in 1727 by the theatre director Santo Burigotti to travel from Venice to Breslau and join the orchestra at the new Stadttheater. His first known compositions are arias that he contributed to the pasticcio *Griselda* (Breslau, summer 1728). In 1729 he entered the service of Friedrich August, Prince-Elector of Saxony and King of Poland, at the Dresden court. He was one of a group of 22 musicians chosen by Friedrich August who travelled to Moscow in 1731; here he composed his only known cantata, for the first anniversary of the coronation of the Empress Anna Ivanova. When the Dresden musicians were recalled home, Verocai stayed on as a member of the Russian court orchestra and later moved with the court to St Petersburg, where he was involved in the first opera production in the city, *La forza dell'amore e dell'odio* by Francesco Araia (1736). He married the singer Sophie Amalia Kayser. Verocai left St Petersburg in June 1738 and travelled to Brunswick, where he became Kapellmeister and director of the Opera. He remained in Brunswick until his death and all his operas were produced there. Although Mooser reported the date of his death as 13 December 1745, Loewenberg pointed out that his operas were produced regularly until 1747, with no indication in the librettos that the composer had died, and Jackman contends that it is unlikely that Verocai composed four operas long before they were to be produced, as he would not have known what singers his music would have to suit.

first performed Brunswick, Hoftheater, unless otherwise stated

Venceslao (os, 5, after A. Zeno), 1739
Penelope (os, ? P. Pariati), 1740
Demofoonte (os, 3, P. Metastasio), Feb 1742
Zenobia und Radamistus (os, 3, G. Schürmann, after Metastasio: *Zenobia*), sum. 1742
Cato (os, 3, after Metastasio: *Catone in Utica*), spr. 1743
Hissifile (os, 3, after Metastasio: *Issipile*), 1743
La forza dell'amore e dell'odio (os), 1744
Sesostri (os, 3, after Pariati), 1744
Die getreue Emirena (os, 3, Schürmann, after Metastasio: *Adriano in Siria*), Candlemas 1745
Il Ciro riconosciuto (os, 3, Metastasio), Feb 1746
Achille in Sciro (os, 3, Metastasio), Aug 1746
Apollo fra i pastori (pastoral), 1746
Temistocle in bando (os, 3, after Metastasio), 1747

*

EitnerQ; *ES* ('Breslavia', §2, W. Boetticher); *FétisB*; *Grove5* (A. Loewenberg); *Grove6* (J. Jackman); *LaMusicaD*; *MGG* (C. Sartori); *RicordiE*
J. Mattheson: *Grundlage einer Ehren-Pforte* (Hamburg, 1740); ed. M. Schneider (Berlin, 1910), 376–7
R.-A. Mooser: 'Violinistes-compositeurs italiens en Russie au XVIIIe siècle: I. Giovanni Verocai', *RMI*, xlii (1938), 309–449
——: *Annales de la musique et des musiciens en Russie au XVIIIe siècle*, i (Geneva, 1948), 55ff
E. Thiel and G. Rohr, eds.: *Verzeichnis der bis 1800 erschienenen Textbücher* (Frankfurt, 1970), 31, 165, 357
R. Zanetti: *La musica italiana nel settecento*, i (Milan, 1978), 374

CAROLYN V. RICKETTS

Veroli, Giacomo [Jacopo] (*b* Arezzo, *c*1730; *d* Florence, after 1797). Italian soprano castrato. He first sang *innamorato* roles in comic operas, appearing at the Teatro dei Nobili in Perugia in 1751 while in the service of Duke Salviati, and in Pietro Pertici's famous comic company at the Cocomero, Florence, in 1752 and 1753. Later in 1753 he turned to serious opera at the Teatro delle Dame, Rome (Publius in Jommelli's *Attilio Regolo* and Masinissa in Galuppi's *Sofonisba*). Over the next few years he sang in the major houses of Italy, most frequently at S Carlo in Naples, the Grande in Siena and the Pergola in Florence; at the last he sang the title role in Galuppi's *L'arrivo d'Enea nel Lazio* to celebrate the arrival in Florence of the new grand duke, Pietro Leopoldo (14 November 1765). The following year the grand duke appointed him 'virtuoso della Real Cappella, e di Corte', and at his direct command Veroli sang at the Pergola in Tommaso Traetta's *Ifigenia in Tauride*, conducted by Gluck during the carnival of 1767. Later the same year he was called to Naples to sing in Hasse's *Partenope* for the wedding of Ferdinando IV of Naples and Maria Carolina, Pietro Leopoldo's sister. These occasions firmly established his reputation, and he was much in demand throughout Italy. He retired from the grand ducal chapel in 1797.

ROBERT LAMAR WEAVER

Véron, Louis (*b* Paris, 5 April 1798; *d* Paris, 27 Sept 1867). French theatre director. Displaying a keen eye for a lucrative venture, early in his career he procured the rights for a medicinal chest paste and marketed it as a cure for the common cold. He applied the same flair for publicity to the post of director of the Paris Opéra, to which he was appointed in 1831. He was the first director to be permitted to operate the institution as a private enterprise, albeit with a large state subsidy and surveillance by a government commission. With the financial backing of the Spanish banker Alexandre Aguado and new business strategies that included increasing the number of long-term subscribers, Véron amassed a considerable fortune during his four-year directorship. He steered the Opéra to a position of renewed prominence in Parisian society by creating a meeting ground for the aristocracy and upper castes of the bourgeoisie. His early triumph with the première of Meyerbeer's *Robert le diable* in 1831 was followed by the successes of the ballet *La sylphide* (1832) and Halévy's *La Juive* (1835). A revival and refashioning of *Don Giovanni* in 1834, with the title role sung by Adolphe Nourrit, fared less well. Following Véron's period at the Opéra, this self-styled 'bourgeois de Paris' went on to acquire a major interest in the newspaper *Le constitutionnel* and to participate in French political life as a parliamentarian during the Second Empire. His *Mémoires d'un bourgeois de Paris* were published in Paris (1856–7).

STEVEN HUEBNER

Verona. City in the Veneto, in northern Italy. In the first half of the 17th century there was a continual series of spectacular entertainments with instrumental and vocal music: dancing, jousting, feasts, and drama of various kinds, often on mythological subjects. The first public theatre for musical works, called the Teatro dell'Isolo from the name of a ward of the city, was founded in 1651 by a priest, a dancer, a carpenter and a musician (a Roman, Paolo Cornetti), but after a few performances of the opera *Endimione* (libretto by Antonio Cariola, music probably by Cornetti) the enterprise failed and the small theatre was demolished. In 1656 the Accademia dei Temperati (amateur actors) built another theatre for plays and opera, which opened with *La regia pescatrice* (verse by Giacomo Casatoreo). The Teatro dei Temperati, which moved in about 1677 to the Palazzo del Capitanio (and was then called Teatro di Palazzo, Prefettizio or del Capitanio), had 108 boxes in four tiers. It closed in 1715, under pressure from the Accademia Filarmonica which started building its new Teatro Filarmonico in that year. The more than 80 known librettos performed there indicate considerable activity with a repertory largely deriving from the Venetian theatres, but with some interesting premières,

1. Interior of the Teatro Filarmonico, Verona (designed by Francesco Galli-Bibiena; built 1715–c1729) during a rehearsal for the inaugural performance of Vivaldi's 'La fida ninfa' on 6 January 1732: wash drawing by Francesco Galli-Bibiena and Giuseppe Chamant

for example *Agripina minore* (1673) by the impresario Alessandro Spinazzari, who was active in both Verona and Vicenza; C. F. Pollarolo's *La Costanza gelosa negli amori di Cefalo e Procri* (1688) and *Alarico, re de gotti* (1689); and Bassani's *Gli amori tra gli odi* (1693).

The Teatro Filarmonico (140 boxes in five tiers), a splendid example of Baroque architecture (see fig.1), was built between 1715 and about 1729 and designed by Francesco Galli-Bibiena, who was brought to Verona by Marchese Scipione Maffei, an illustrious literary figure and member of the Accademia. It was inaugurated in Carnival 1732 with Vivaldi's *La fida ninfa*, to a libretto by Maffei. The theatre was managed directly by the Accademia Filarmonica; the repertory almost always centred on *opera seria* by Vivaldi (who also acted as impresario), Hasse and Chiarini. The theatre was destroyed by fire in January 1749. In that year the Teatro del Capitanio opened for a few months and in 1750–53 the small Nuovo Teatro, behind the Arena, staged *drammi giocosi* by Goldoni and others. The Filarmonico reopened in 1754 with *Alessandro nell'Indie* by Hasse and *Lucio Vero* by Pérez. Other notable performances were Traetta's *Olimpiade* (1758), Sarti's *Antigono* (1765), P. A. Guglielmi's *Ruggiero* (1770, with Mozart in the audience), Salieri's *La scuola dei gelosi* (1780), Bertoni's *Artaserse* and Francesco Bianchi's *Il disertore* (1785, with an enthusiastic reception for the soprano Gasparo Pacchierotti), but especially the lavish *Giunio Bruto* by Cimarosa in autumn 1781, with pantomime ballets by Gasparo Angiolini.

Between 1722 and 1731 the little Teatro dell'Accademia in Via Nova, which belonged to an innkeeper, staged *opera buffa* and intermezzos by G. M. Buini, G. M. Orlandini and G. A. Ristori. It was enlarged and re-opened in 1760 with the name Teatro dell'Accademia Vecchia, and successfully specialized in *opera buffa* or *bernesca*. In 1783 it was leased to the Accademia Filarmonica which thus maintained a monopoly on music theatre in the city. The Teatro dell'Accademia Vecchia continued to be used for opera sporadically until 1826, and then until 1873 predominantly for plays and puppet shows. From about 1797 to 1806 a society of theatre-lovers ran the Teatro del Territorio, where an early performance of Paer's *Griselda* was given (1797 or 1798).

In the 19th century, in spite of political events, the control of the Austrian authorities and frequent patriotic demonstrations, a great deal of opera was performed. The Filarmonico continued to be the most prestigious theatre. Giuditta Pasta sang there in 1830 and Giuseppina Strepponi in 1844 in *Nabucodonosor*, the first appearance of Verdi's work at the Filarmonico. The theatre was closed from 1858 to 1866 and was used as a military storehouse. After the unification of Italy, apart from the dominance of the Verdi canon, there were the first productions in Verona of Boito (1878, *Mefistofele*), Ponchielli (1883, *La Gioconda*), Wagner (1884 and 1894, *Lohengrin*), Bizet (1887, *Les pêcheurs de perles* and *Carmen*, conducted by Toscanini) and Puccini (1890, *Le villi*).

In the course of the 19th century other theatres had full operatic seasons, and local enthusiasm produced accomplished artists such as the singers Adelaide Malanotte, Maria Spezia, Gottardo Aldighieri and Domenico Conti, and the composers Carlo Pedrotti (whose operas had their premières at the Filarmonico and the Nuovo) and, in the early 20th century, Italo Montemezzi.

The Teatro Morando was first installed in the deconsecrated church of S Tomio (reconsecrated in 1837), where it opened in 1814 with works mostly by Rossini and Pacini; it then moved to the 'Beverara', from 1837 to about 1869, and staged amateur dramatics. The Teatro Sardi (later Valle, then Ristori) was

2. *The 100th performance of Verdi's 'Aida' at the Verona Arena, 1968, designed by Attilio Colonello*

active from 1844, and in 1851 opened for light opera, melodrama and vaudeville; until 1943 many kinds of entertainment were put on there, including Mascagni's *Amica* conducted by the composer in 1908. After World War II a long period of decline reduced it to a cinema, and for many years it was abandoned.

The Teatro Nuovo (known also in the 20th century as the Teatro Drammatico), designed by Enrico Storari and later modified, opened in 1846 with Verdi's *Attila*, and like the Ristori often competed with the Filarmonico, engaging artists of high quality such as Rosina Storchio, Gilda Dalla Rizza, Aureliano Pertile, Toti Dal Monte and Gina Cigna. It was restored in 1946 and used for plays, films and concerts.

The Filarmonico has staged some important operas in this century: *Tosca* (1900, the first performance in the Veneto), *Aida* (1907) with Giovanni Zenatello and Lucia Crestani, both Veronese, Zandonai's *Giulietta e Romeo* (1922), *Lohengrin* (1914) and *Tristan und Isolde* (1938). On 23 February 1945 the theatre was completely demolished by bombing. Rebuilding was begun by the Accademia in 1961 and it reopened for opera in 1975 with Salieri's *Falstaff*. It now has regular spring and autumn seasons organized by the Ente Lirico Arena di Verona. In the 1950s the Piccolo Teatro dell'Opera, connected with the Liceo Musicale F. E. Dall'Abaco (now the State Conservatory), gave chamber opera performances.

The most important musical event in Verona is the annual open-air season in the Arena (the amphitheatre dating from the first century AD where there had been a small theatre for comedy since the 17th century), inaugurated in 1913 with *Aida* to mark the centenary of Verdi's birth. Since then, except during the World Wars, the productions in the Arena have attracted tens of thousands of spectators every summer. In 1934 the Ente Lirico was formed, which has remained faithful to the traditional repertory: *Aida*, the Arena spectacle *par excellence*, is almost always on the programme, often with *Carmen*, *Turandot*, *La Gioconda*, *Cavalleria rusticana*, *La forza del destino*, *Il trovatore* and regular ballet performances and concerts.

ES (N. Mangini); *MGG* (E. Paganuzzi)

G. Gagliardi: *Attori e spettatori a Verona nel settecento* (Verona, 1907)

V. Cavazzocca Mazzanti: 'Rossini a Verona durante il congresso del 1822', *Atti dell'Accademia di Verona*, 4th ser., xxiv (1922), 53–112

——: 'Un teatro veronese anteriore al Filarmonico', *Atti dell'Accademia di Verona*, ci (1924), 77–91

C. Garibotto: 'Teatrini privati a Verona nel '700', *Atti dell'Accademia di Verona*, civ (1928), 113–22

V. Cavazzocca Mazzanti: 'L'Accademia Filotima e i teatri a Verona nel XVIII secolo', *Atti dell'Accademia di Verona*, cxii (1935), 153–222

C. Garibotto: 'Spettacoli lirici al Filarmonico nel settecento', ibid, 27–72

T. Lenotti: *I teatri di Verona* (Verona, 1949)

A. Gajoni Berti: *Cronistoria del teatro Filarmonico (1732–1938)* (Verona, 1963)

A. Zecchinato: *Il teatro Filarmonico di Verona: due secoli di spettacoli lirici 1732–1938* (Verona, 1956)

1913–1963: Cinquant'anni di melodramma all'Arena di Verona (Verona, 1963)

Arena di Verona dal 1913 al 1977 tra musica e cronaca (Verona, 1977)

Aida di Giuseppe Verdi dal 1913 al 1972 (Verona, 1972)

E. Paganuzzi and others: *La musica a Verona* (Verona, 1976)

P. Rigoli: 'Teatri per musica a Verona nella seconda metà del XVII secolo', *Atti dell'Accademia di Verona*, clvi (1979–80), 215–37

——: 'Tre teatri per musica a Verona nella prima metà del settecento: cronologie e documenti', *Atti dell'Accademia di Verona*, clviii (1981–2), 239–85

Arena di Verona: la sua storia dal 1913 al 1982 (Verona, 1982)

E. Paganuzzi, ed.: *L'Accademia Filarmonica di Verona e il suo teatro* (Verona, 1982)

G. Rigobello: 'Il dramma per musica a Verona nel XVIII secolo (abbozzo di cronologia teatrale dal 1700 al 1715)', *Vita veronese*, xxxv (1982), 27–35

F. Mancini, M. T. Muraro and E. Povoledo: *I teatri del Veneto: Verona Vicenza Belluno e il loro territorio* (Venice, 1985) [with further bibliography]

P. Rigoli: 'L'architettura effimera: feste, teatri, apparati decorativi', *L'architettura a Verona nell'età della Serenissima*, ii (Verona, 1988), 5–86

E. Negri: *Il fondo musicale Malaspina nell'Archivio di Stato di Verona* (Rome, 1989)

P. Rigoli: 'Feste, spettacoli, apparati per il congresso di Verona', *Il Veneto e l'Austria* (Milan, 1989), 466–9

C. Vitali: 'Vivaldi e il conte bolognese Sicinio Pepoli: nuovi documenti sulle stagioni vivaldiane al Filarmonico di Verona', *Informazioni e studi vivaldiani*, x (1989), 25–55
E. Paganuzzi: 'Per la storia del secondo settecento musicale a Verona', *L'Accademia Filarmonica di Verona per il bicentenario mozartiano* (Verona, 1991), 53–84
PAOLO RIGOLI

Verona, Bartolomeo (*b* Andorno, nr Biella, May 1744; *d* Berlin, 1813). Italian stage designer. He was the nephew of Bernardino and Fabrizio Galliari and their pupil and collaborator at the Teatro Regio, Turin and the Regio Ducal Teatro, Milan. In 1767 he went to Vienna for the production of Gluck's *Alceste* designed by his uncles, and remained there until 1772. He then followed Bernardino to Berlin and settled there, becoming designer at the royal opera house and making journeys to Italy (1784), Paris (1784), Hanover (1785) and Kassel (1791).

An important collection of his drawings survives in the Kunstbibliothek, Berlin, and in some cases the operas for which they were intended have been identified, including C. H. Graun's *Alessandro e Poro* (1784) and *Orfeo* (1785), *Gerusalemme liberata* (1803) and *Deodata* (1810). Verona often used the compositional structures of the Galliaris but just as often (and increasingly over the years) he elaborated the stylistic forms and created new effects with the use of 'aerial perspective'. He was also active as a decorator (among the few surviving examples of his work is the Chinese Gallery in Charlottenburg Castle).

*

C. Denina: *La Prusse littéraire sous Frédéric II*, iii (Berlin, 1791)
H. Tintelnot: *Barocktheater und Barocke Kunst* (Berlin, 1939)
R. Amerio: 'Il pittore Bartolomeo Verona', *Bollettino della società piemontese di archeologia e di belle arti*, new ser., xii–xiii (1958–9), 173–8
M. Viale Ferrero: 'Scenografia', *Mostra del barocco piemontese* (Turin, 1963), 39–41 [exhibition catalogue]
A. Baudi di Vesme: 'Bartolomeo Verona', *Schede Vesme: l'arte in Piemonte dal XVI al XVIII secolo*, iii (Turin, 1968), 1089
MERCEDES VIALE FERRERO

Veronelli, Ernesto (*b* Milan, 30 Jan 1938). Italian tenor. He studied in Milan, and has sung in Dublin, Cologne, Verona Arena, Paris, Barcelona, Vienna, Berlin, Zürich and Detroit. In 1983 he made his début with the Royal Opera at Manchester as Pinkerton and sang Roland de Blois (*Esclarmonde*) at Covent Garden. He made his Metropolitan début in 1985 as Canio. His roles include Don Carlos, Manrico, Riccardo (*Ballo*), Radames, Carlo (*Giovanna d'Arco*), Macduff, Chénier, Cavaradossi and Calaf. He has a fine natural voice, strong in the upper register, but is not a very convincing actor.
ELIZABETH FORBES

Véronique. *Opéra comique* in three acts by ANDRÉ MESSAGER to a libretto by Georges Duval and ALBERT VANLOO; Paris, Théâtre des Bouffes-Parisiens, 10 December 1898.

The plot is based around the relationship between Viscount Florestan de Valiancourt (baritone) and Hélène de Solanges (soprano) and takes place during the reign of Louis-Philippe. Florestan's lifestyle has left him crippled with debt and, in a last attempt to reform him, the king has given him the options of marriage (to Hélène) or life in a debtors' prison. Florestan is meanwhile having an affair with Mme Agathe Coquenard (soprano), wife of a captain in the National Guard: the Coquenards also keep a flower shop in Paris. Hélène unexpectedly arrives at the Coquenards' shop on the day the marriage contract is to be signed, and overhears Florestan taking his leave of Mme Coquenard; he expresses regret that he must leave her for a simple girl from the provinces whom he has yet to meet. Hélène vows revenge and, taking the name of Véronique, she and her aunt Ermerance (mezzo-soprano) (who becomes 'Estelle') take employment as shop assistants in the Coquenards' business. Shortly afterwards, Florestan invites the whole of the staff to join him at a party at Romainville, given to celebrate his last day as a bachelor. At Romainville he falls in love with 'Véronique', while M. Coquenard takes a liking to

Design by Bartolomeo Verona for Pluto and Proserpina's palace in the underworld for a performance of Graun's 'Orfeo' at the Royal Opera House, Berlin, in 1785

'Estelle'; but following a donkey ride (inspiration for the famous Donkey Duet in Act 2) and a ride on the swings (the 'Duo de l'escarpolette') Véronique and Estelle flee to the Tuileries, where the marriage is to take place. In Act 3, Florestan and Hélène come face to face, and the deception is revealed; but Florestan, feeling dishonoured by Hélène's trickery (in spite of his own previous bad behaviour) wishes the marriage to be called off. Reconciliation follows, however, with a joyful marriage ceremony.

The piece was an immediate success in both France and England, and enjoyed many revivals in Paris between 1920 and the late 1940s. There were productions in Spain in 1921 and Switzerland in 1923; and the work was also produced in Germany in the 1920s, under the title *Brigitte*. After the ballet *Les deux pigeons*, *Véronique* is Messager's most enduring work, and one of the very few of his compositions to have been recorded in its entirety (1953, to celebrate the centenary of the composer's birth). Jean Périer, who played Florestan in the first production, also recorded extracts in 1905, as did Anna Tariol-Baugé, the original Agathe. The title role was created by Mariette Sully. Later interpreters on disc included Yvonne Printemps, and Anne Ziegler and Webster Booth. *Véronique* was Messager's second successful collaboration with Vanloo and Duval, following *Les p'tites Michu* the previous year; their subsequent (and last) collaboration, on *Les dragons de l'impératrice* in 1905, met with less success.

For the front cover of the 'programme illustré' for the original production *see* PROGRAMME, fig.3. JOHN WAGSTAFF

Verrall, John (Weedon) (*b* Britt, IA, 17 June 1908). American composer. He studied composition with R. O. Morris in London (1929–30) and Kodály in Budapest (1931–2), and continued his studies with Copland, Roy Harris and Frederick Jacobi. From 1948 to 1973 he taught at the University of Washington in Seattle. In addition to chamber and orchestral works he has composed three operas, all of which have been produced and directed by Stanley Chapple at the University of Washington. *The Cowherd and the Sky Maiden* and *The Wedding Knell* make use of Verrall's nine-note scale, adapted from the Phrygian mode. *The Wedding Knell* has been particularly praised for its evocation of mood; it won the Seattle Centennial Opera Award in 1952.

all first performed at Seattle, University of Washington

The Cowherd and the Sky Maiden (2, E. Shepherd, after a Chinese legend), 17 Jan 1952
The Wedding Knell (chamber op, 1, after N. Hawthorne), 5 Dec 1952
Three Blind Mice (chamber op, 1, G. Hughes), 22 May 1955

*

EwenD RICHARD SWIFT

Verratene Meer, Das ('Treacherous Oceans'). *Musikdrama* in two parts by HANS WERNER HENZE, to a libretto by Hans-Ulrich Treichel, after Yukio Mishima's *Gogo no eiko*; Berlin, Deutsche Oper, 5 May 1990.

Das verratene Meer was Henze's ninth full-length opera and the third (after *König Hirsch* and *Der junge Lord*) commissioned by the Deutsche Oper. Working to a libretto that Treichel had prepared to his specifications, Henze composed the opera between 1986 and 1989. The première was conducted by Markus Stenz in a production by Götz Friedrich; Stephanie Sundine was scheduled as Fusako, but was ill and only walked

Fusako Kuroda *a 33-year-old widow*	high soprano
Noboru *her 13-year-old son, known as Number Three*	tenor
Ryuji Tsukazaki *a merchant navy officer*	baritone
The youth gang, friends of Noboru:	
Number One	baritone
Number Two	tenor
Number Four	baritone
Number Five	bass-baritone
Ship's mate	bass-baritone

Ship's officer, sailors, harbour master, boutique manager, three shop assistants

Setting Yokohama in the 1950s

through the role on the first night while it was sung offstage by Beverly Morgan. Clemens Bieber was Noboru and Andreas Schmidt Ryuji. A second production opened at the Hessisches Staatstheater, Wiesbaden, on 30 June 1990, conducted by Ulf Schirmer and directed by Alois Michael Heigl with Sigune von Osten, Roberto Saccà and Espan Fegran in the cast. Stenz conducted the Italian première at the Teatro Lirico, Milan, on 21 March 1991 in a production by Philippe Piffaut: the cast was led by Morgan, Saccà and Lenus Carlson. The US première in San Francisco on 8 November 1991 used the Milan production: Stenz conducted and Ashley Putnam, Craig Estep and Tom Fox took the leading roles.

PART 1 *Summer*

Scene i *Fusako's house* Fusako, owner of a Europeanized boutique in Yokohama, is putting her son Noboru to bed; she tells him that the next day they are going to visit a merchant ship in the harbour. Fusako locks his bedroom door to prevent him going out during the night to meet his friends; she has been a widow for eight years and in her own room fantasizes about a new lover. As she undresses for bed Noboru watches her through a hole in the wall and is overwhelmed by her beauty, but he is torn between love for her and a desire to rid himself of all family ties. His dream of a free, 'heroic' future, perhaps in the navy, is depicted in the orchestral interlude that follows.

Scene ii *The harbour at Yokohama* Fusako and Noboru are shown around the *Rakuyo-Maru* by its second officer, Ryuji Tsukazaki. He is most impressed by the boy's knowledge of life at sea, while in her turn Fusako is much taken with Ryuji. When Noboru hurries on to view the ship's engine room, the couple take the opportunity to shower each other with compliments in a duet that follows the outline of a musette. Fusako invites the seaman out to dinner.

Scene iii *Two days later. A park overlooking the sea* The interlude that follows the second scene continues the dance-like mood of the duet; against the background of a bourrée, it depicts Ryuji's dreams and their lack of fulfilment in his career at sea. He tells Fusako of his failed aspirations and loneliness when they pause on their return from dinner.

Scene iv *Fusako's bedroom* Fusako and Ryuji make love, watched through the wall by Noboru; their declarations are entwined in a trio with the boy's commentaries as his admiration for the seaman's 'heroism' begins to wane. The following orchestral interlude is a highly charged *Nachtspiel* as Fusako and Ryuji fall asleep and Noboru stays motionless in his room.

Scene v *Midnight the same evening. A warehouse near the harbour* Noboru reports on domestic events to the members of the gang in which he is known as Number Three. He portrays Ryuji in glowing terms, but the others sceptically refuse to believe that the seaman is different from any other adult and any more willing to take youth or its views seriously. The gang has its own power to exercise and makes detailed plans for the ritual execution of a cat.

Scene vi *The park overlooking the sea* In a long sustained aria Ryuji regrets that his shore leave will soon be over, but consoles himself with the idea that he will be able to think of Fusako during his long hours at sea. When he goes to cool off at a spring he is spotted by the gang, who ridicule him when he wets his shirt; Noboru is left alone with the seaman and tries hard to make Ryuji portray his life as adventurous and heroic, full of exotic encounters. He is unsuccessful: Ryuji's descriptions remain sober and detached, and quite lacking in excitement.

Scene vii *The harbour* The sounds of ships' whistles are heard on pre-recorded tape as Fusako and Ryuji say their fond farewells, watched by Noboru who hopes desperately that the seaman will remain in the service. Ryuji patronizes him as though he were a child, and Noboru feigns friendliness.

Scene viii *The warehouse by the harbour* The gang meets to carry out its ritual killing of the cat; the youths assume absolute moral authority – they can determine who shall live and who die.

PART 2 *Winter*

Scene ix *New Year's Day. A winter landscape in a park* As they wait for the sun to rise, Ryuji proposes to Fusako; he will give up life at sea and settle down, investing his savings in Fusako's boutique. They contemplate the future as the orchestra outlines the rhythms of a tango, which are gradually submerged during the following orchestral interlude.

Scene x *The warehouse by the harbour* The boys discuss their parents and the ways in which they might be rid of them. It is fathers who trouble them most and, though Noboru attempts to defend Ryuji, the others make fun of all his claims: the seaman's decision to give up life at sea and to settle down is taken as the final proof that he is just as much a coward as all the others. But Number One, the leader of the gang, points out that there is still one way in which Ryuji could be saved and restored as a hero again.

Scene xi *Fusako's house: the dining room, the bedrooms of Fusako and Noboru* Ryuji is learning the business of Fusako's boutique, as she is keen for him to become a department manager. Fusako tells Noboru that she and Ryuji are to be married; though Noboru will shake his future stepfather by the hand, he baulks at calling him father. When Noboru goes to bed, Ryuji insists that the bedroom door remain unlocked. While working at his English primer Noboru falls asleep at his spyhole; as Fusako and Ryuji prepare for bed they notice a gleam of light and discover Noboru's secret. Yet Ryuji will not allow the boy to be punished, and Noboru remembers a saying of Number One: 'There are worse punishments than a beating'.

Scene xii *The following day. The warehouse* The gang puts Ryuji on trial and condemns his failure to be a hero. Number One demands ultimate vengeance, as the seaman has become just another pathetic father figure. The plans for execution are laid: Noboru is to lead Ryuji to a deserted place where the sentence will be carried out.

Scene xiii *Midday. Fusako's boutique* In a large-scale aria of wide vocal range Fusako plans her bridal gown and imagines her new life with Ryuji and Noboru. She hopes her son will become a linguist and study at Oxford, and that he will grow to love his stepfather. But in the closing passage of her aria Ryuji is seen in the background being led by the youths to what they claim is a dry dock. A pre-recorded assemblage of machine noises takes the place of an orchestral interlude before the final scene.

Scene xiv *An industrial wasteland* Confronted by his accusers, Ryuji once again refuses to glamorize life at sea; in a lyrical and increasingly impassioned aria he reveals his disillusionment. He went to sea because he hated life ashore, but he now realizes his aspirations were false and longs for what once he hated. He becomes so preoccupied with his declaration that he fails to notice the gang preparing itself for a strange ritual, just as it had with the cat. The opera ends with a brief *fff* tutti, dominated by tuned percussion.

* * *

Though it incorporates clearly defined and labelled set pieces within its schemes, the through-composed structure of each part of *Das verratene Meer* relates more clearly to Henze's stage works of the 1960s (and to *The Bassarids* in particular) than to its immediate predecessors such as *The English Cat*. In the integration of vocal set pieces, the dramatic function of the orchestral interludes and the vocal characters of the protagonists, Berg's operas appear to have been a significant model, and the demanding writing for Fusako, from *Sprechgesang* to coloratura over a wide compass, invites comparison with that for Lulu. Henze allots distinctive instrumental sounds to each of the main characters – the music for Fusako is predominantly coloured by strings, that for Ryuji by a chorus of wind – an identification, the composer has revealed, taken over from his work on an orchestration of Monteverdi's *Il ritorno d'Ulisse in patria*, performed in 1985. Noboru and the remainder of the gang are represented primarily by the piano and also by other tuned percussion. Each character also has its characteristic collection of thematic material, derived from separate note rows and harmonic aggregates.

ANDREW CLEMENTS

Verrett [Verrett-Carter], **Shirley** (*b* New Orleans, 31 May 1931). American mezzo-soprano and soprano. She studied in Los Angeles and at the Juilliard School, New York, making her début in 1957 at Yellow Springs, Ohio, as Britten's Lucretia. In 1958 she joined the New York City Opera, singing Irina in Weill's *Lost in the Stars*, then in 1959 made her European début in Cologne as the Gypsy in Nabokov's *Rasputin's End*. At Spoleto in 1962 she sang Carmen, repeating the role at the Bol'shoy (1963), at the New York City Opera (1964), for her La Scala (1966) and Metropolitan (1968) débuts, and at Covent Garden (1973), where she had first sung in 1966 as Ulrica, returning there as Amneris, Eboli, Azucena, Gluck's Orpheus, Norma and Delilah. She sang Elizabeth (*Maria Stuarda*) in Edinburgh (1968) and Léonor (*La favorite*) at Dallas (1971). In San Francisco she sang Sélika (1972) and Lady Macbeth (1986). Her Metropolitan roles include Bartók's Judith, Cassandra and Dido (*Les Troyens*), Néocles (*Le siège de Corinthe*), Adalgisa and, as she undertook soprano parts, Norma, Tosca, Madame Lidoine (*Dialogues des Carmélites*), Aida and Leonore (*Fidelio*). In 1990 she sang Dido at the opening of the Opéra Bastille, Paris. She has a burnished, wide-ranging voice that she uses with the utmost intelligence, and a magnetic stage presence.

S. Jenkins: 'Shirley Verrett', *Opera*, xxiv (1973), 585–9
J. B. Steane: *The Grand Tradition* (London, 1974), 418–19

ALAN BLYTH

Versailles. Royal palace, 16 km west of Paris, used for theatrical performances from the 17th century onwards; *see* PARIS, §§2(ii), 3(ii) and 6(ii).

Verschwender, Der ('The Spendthrift'). *Zaubermärchen* in three acts by CONRADIN KREUTZER to a libretto by FERDINAND RAIMUND; Vienna, Theater in der Josefstadt, 20 February 1834.

The last of Raimund's eight magic plays with music, *Der Verschwender* has the most distinguished score composed for the Vienna popular theatre since *Die Zauberflöte*. Julius Flottwell (spoken), the spendthrift of the title, forfeits the love of the fairy Cheristane (spoken), woos, marries and loses the heiress Amalie (spoken) and finally learns from his bitter experiences, and from the selfless devotion of his former servant Valentin (tenor), the true values of life. The piece is more remarkable for its depiction of life below stairs – Rosa (soprano) is anything but the conventional charming servant – than for that of the aristocratic and fairy milieux, though the Beggar (bass), sent by Cheristane to beseech alms from Flottwell against his own future penury, is a hauntingly effective figure, endowed by Kreutzer with a nobly elegiac cantilena (offset by the tipsy jollity of Flottwell's false friends) not unworthy of Schubert. The extensive music includes three choruses, five ensembles and four songs as well as numerous melodramas and pieces of incidental music. The best-known numbers, widely familiar although their composer is usually unrecognized, are the songs of Valentin (Raimund's own role): 'Heissa lustig ohne Sorgen', the hunting song 'Wie sich doch die reichen Herrn', and especially the carpenter's song – *Hobellied*, or 'planing song' – 'Da streiten sich die Leut' herum'. The duet for Valentin and Rosa, 'Ein Schlosser ist mein' schwache Seit'', is another favourite. *Der Verschwender*, widely performed in the mid-19th century, has never lost its popularity in Vienna.

PETER BRANSCOMBE

Verschworenen, Die ('The Conspirators') [*Der häusliche Krieg* ('Domestic Warfare')]. Singspiel in one act by FRANZ SCHUBERT to a libretto by Ignaz Castelli after ARISTOPHANES' plays *Lysistrata* and *Ecclesiazusae*; Frankfurt, 29 August 1861.

Die Verschworenen dates from 1822–3, the period between Schubert's two grand romantic operas *Alfonso und Estrella* and *Fierrabras*. At the end of 1823 the rejection of each of his latest operas and the failure of the play *Rosamunde*, for which he had written incidental music, led Schubert to abandon composing for the theatre for several years; and in fact he completed no other opera. Ironically, after its first performance in a concert version in Vienna, in March 1861, it became immensely popular in the theatre and was widely performed throughout Europe. The humour of Castelli's text, of a kind in vogue in Austria about 1820, is too naive for modern audiences, but the play is well-structured and the Singspiel is still occasionally performed.

The libretto, which has long stretches of spoken dialogue, was the work of an able poet and playwright who wrote the piece as a challenge to composers of German opera who were deploring the inferior quality of opera texts. It is based on the *Lysistrata* and *Ecclesiazusae* tales, transposed into a medieval German setting. The wives of returning knights, tired of their husbands' long absences at war, decide to withhold their favours until their menfolk promise to give up fighting and remain at home. The conclusion is a happy one after a certain degree of humbling on both sides.

Schubert's music is lively, imaginative, often humorous, embodying some witty parody and showing traces of Rossini's influence. The musical characterization is excellent, both of the two choruses (male and female) and of the solo roles, notably of the central figure, the Countess (soprano). There are some effective choruses, though they are apt to be repetitive. Outstanding is the Romance, no. 2, for the young wife Helene (mezzo-soprano), 'Ich schleiche bang' und still herum', a lament for her absent husband, with obbligato clarinet. The opening duet 'Sie ist's! Er ist's!' for Isella, the Countess's maid (soprano), and Udolin, the Count's page (soprano or tenor), is one of Schubert's happiest Singspiel creations with its easy-flowing melodies, warm harmonies and immense charm. And the short parodistic arietta sung first by the Count (bass) in C (no.9) and then repeated (but in A) by the Countess (as no.10), with the emphasis on his 'für dich' and her 'für mich', is a small gem of economically written music of high spirits.

ELIZABETH NORMAN McKAY

Versification. This article considers verse structure in librettos in the chief languages of the opera repertory; for a fuller discussion of words and music, *see* LIBRETTO (ii), §I.

1. Italian. 2. French. 3. German. 4. English. 5. Slavonic languages.

1. ITALIAN. Two issues concern the analysis of Italian verse: the number of syllables in a given line and the position of the final accent. Accordingly, this verse is essentially qualitative rather than quantitative – insofar as such terms have any meaning – although the issue was always a matter of some debate among Italian theorists, especially in periods drawn to classical antiquity. In general, a given line can be from three to eleven syllables in length (thus *ternario*, *quaternario*, *quinario*, *senario*, *settenario*, *ottonario*, *novenario*, *decasillabo* and *endecasillabo*): the *endecasillabo* is the 'classic' norm, with its chief component, the *settenario*, in second place. Syllable counts are affected by elisions (*sinalefe*) and diphthongs (*sineresi*): respectively, the fusion of the final and initial vowels of two consecutive words in a given line into one syllable, and the similar fusion – permitted in specific contexts – of consecutive vowels in a single word. Thus

Ve-/drò, / men-/tre io / so-/spi-/ro
(*Le nozze di Figaro*, Act 3.iii)

is a *settenario*, with the diphthong 'io' read as one syllable and further elided with the end of 'mentre': were 'io' ('mio', 'lui', 'due', 'sia', 'quei' etc.) at the end of the line, it would almost invariably be two syllables. In practice, elisions and diphthongs can be handled with some flexibility by the poet, and also by the composer, as required.

That line is a conventional *verso piano*, with the final accent on the penultimate syllable ('so-*spi*-ro'). An accent on the final syllable produces a *verso tronco* ('truncated') – 'Notte e giorno fati*car*' – and on the antepenultimate syllable a *verso sdrucciolo* ('sliding'): 'La donna è *mo*bile'. *Versi tronchi* and *sdruccioli* are counted as modified *versi piani*. For example,

Me-/tà / di / voi / qua / *va*-/da/no
e / gli al-/tri / va- / dan / *là*
(*Don Giovanni*, Act 2.iv)

presents a *settenario sdrucciolo* and a *settenario tronco* (albeit with eight and six syllables respectively). The position of internal accents is to some extent free, although each line-length has standard patterns (and lines with even numbers of syllables – *versi parisillabi* – tend to be particularly clearcut), with longer lines more than one: the *endecasillabo* is the most flexible of all. These patterns produce characteristic rhythms associated with specific line lengths: this, together with questions of genre, prompted periodic attempts to identify a specific ethos for each type of line. All this has obvious ramifications for musical setting; it further helps explain the obvious differences between music for Italian verse and for verse in some other language.

The *verso piano* is the standard form: *versi sdruccioli* and *tronchi* can be used for special effects. For example, in librettos *versi sdruccioli* often invoke pastoral resonances (on the precedent of Sannazaro's *Arcadia* of 1504); they also have a long history of association (often in *quinari*) with infernal, demonic or magic scenes – Medea's 'L'armi apprestatemi' in Cavalli's *Giasone* (1649), Act 3.ix; the infernal chorus 'Chi mai dell'Erebo' in Gluck's *Orfeo ed Euridice* (1762), Act 2.i; the witches' 'Tre volte miagola' at the opening of Act 3 of Verdi's *Macbeth* (1847). The *verso tronco* can be comic (and it is sometimes associated with nonsense syllables), but on a structural level, it becomes most significant as an articulative device to indicate closure: the result has strong musical implications, given the greater suitability of *versi tronchi* (with a masculine ending, weak–strong) over *versi piani* (with a feminine ending, strong–weak) for musical perfect cadences.

Italian opera librettos draw only rarely upon the standard poetic forms of Renaissance Italian (Tuscan) hendecasyllabic verse: for example, Dante's *terza rima* (rhyming *aba bcb cdc* ...), Petrarch's 14-line sonnet (with two quatrains – *abba abba* – and two tercets, e.g. *cdc dcd*) and the *ottava rima* stanzas of Ariosto and Tasso (*abababcc*). When they do, it is often for special (archaic, moralizing etc.) effect, as with Orpheus's 'Possente spirto, e formidabil nume' in *terza rima* in Act 3 of Monteverdi's *Orfeo*, Don Alfonso's *ottava rima* 'Tutti accusan le donne, ed io le scuso' in Mozart's *Così fan tutte*, Act 2.xiii, and the sonnets in Verdi's *Falstaff*, Act 3.ii, and Act 3 of Puccini's *Tosca*. The same applies, *mutatis mutandis*, to line-lengths and forms invoking 'popular' poetry, such as the *novenario* – historically, always a special case – and in some contexts, *endecasillabi* in rhyming couplets (compare Susanna's 'Deh vieni non tardar, oh gioia bella' in *Figaro*, Act 4.x).

Instead, the basis of early librettos – as of the late Renaissance pastoral plays that provided their most immediate precedent – was a mixture of free-rhyming *endecasillabi* and *settenari*, producing *versi sciolti* ('loose' or 'free' verse): more regular rhymes and/or metric consistency could define structural units within this flow; and lines could be divided between characters to enhance the effect of dialogue. However, one major exception – and it is a crucial one – is the strophic canzone/canzonetta, generally in other than seven- or eleven-syllable lines, that appears even in the first operas. Ottavio Rinuccini, for example, introduced strophic groupings of *ottonari* (sometimes with *quaternari*), *quinari* etc., in various rhyme-schemes, in *Dafne* (1597–8) and *Euridice* (1600) specifically for the end-of-'scene' choruses (the strophic quatrains in *endecasillabi* in his prologues are a somewhat different case; *see* PROLOGUE). His model was the strophic arrangement characteristic of some such choruses in Renaissance drama, tempered by the anacreontic verse introduced (in part, on French precedent) by the poet Gabriello Chiabrera, who said that he was catering specifically for composers of the 'new music' and their 'arias'. In *Orfeo*, the librettist Alessandro Striggio took such structures into the acts themselves – as with Orpheus's 'Vi ricorda, o boschi ombrosi' (*ottonari*) in Act 2 – producing formal songs (often distinguished as such, whether dramatically or structurally) that stand apart from the prevailing *versi sciolti* for the recitative. It was a distinction of profound significance.

The history of such issues of versification is, in effect, the history of the libretto itself, and one that variously reflects shifting relationships (whether collusion or collision) between composers and librettists. Eleven- and seven-syllable *versi sciolti* remained standard for recitative (and variants thereof) through the 19th century and beyond: their fluidity and flexibility were well suited to its dramatic function and musical style. However, the style of arias (choruses, ensembles etc.) favoured shorter lines in clearcut patterns with regular rhymes. From early opera onwards, such dramatic and structural shifts were essentially cued by the librettist, whom the composer could ignore only with potential prejudice (which may or may not find compensation) to the musical outcome.

The 17th century reveals a fluid situation as the canons of opera were forged by developing social, political and even literary contexts. Lodovico Zuccolo (*Discorso delle ragioni del numero del verso italiano*; Venice, 1623) showed clear contempt for the new canzonetta, claiming it to be a mere sop to musicians. Even more sympathetic theorists of the second quarter of the century such as G. B. Doni and the anonymous author of *Il corago* felt ambivalent about shifts away from *versi sciolti*: they approved the variety thereby achieved but warned against anti-classical improprieties and the threat to dramatic verisimilitude posed by song, rather than sung speech. But as opera entered the public domain, the rising fortunes of the aria could scarce be resisted.

In his Venetian operas, Monteverdi was often willing (admittedly, somewhat exceptionally) to fashion shorter or longer aria-style passages from *versi sciolti*, responding at times to more regular metrical, rhyming and refrain groupings in the verse, and even to specific words (much later, similar issues are involved in shifts to accompanied recitative). The practice of extracting ('cavare'; the passage thereby extracted is an '[aria] cavata'; *see* CAVATA and CAVATINA) arias from recitative verse continued through the century. But Cavalli and his favoured librettist, Giovanni Faustini, confirmed the principle that arias should on the whole be set apart in poetic terms by a change in line-length and/or by the use of regular metrical and rhyming structures. Two stanzas are common but by no means universal, and these structures could be strophic or could involve a refrain (*ritornello* or *intercalare*): in fact, the patterns that emerged through the 17th century are strikingly varied.

Metastasio rationalized aria forms (with only a few exceptions) into a standard pattern: two isometric strophes, usually of four or three lines each (*settenari*, sometimes with concluding *quinari*, or *ottonari* tend to be preferred) with regular (and generally parallel) rhyme-schemes and each often ending with a *verso tronco* rhyming with its counterpart. This reflected his classicizing programme for purifying the libretto of perceived earlier abuses. It also meshed with the then preferred musical structure, the da capo aria (a strophe each for the *A* and *B* sections), with the regular poetic patterns also favouring the kind of consistent motivic development typical of the High Baroque musical style.

18th-century comic opera could make freer play of these aria forms, albeit within the same broad parameters, for dramatic or humorous effect. For example, Goldoni and his successors stretched to longer aria texts with, say, one or two strophes stating a position, a longer middle section containing comic 'patter', and a final couplet or quatrain rounding off the argument: the musical implications are obvious. Such arias might also include one or more changes of line-length; and the recurring *verso tronco*, generally rhymed, grew increasingly important for structure and unification.

This extendible technique proved particularly useful for the ensembles that were fast becoming a characteristic of *opera buffa*, and still more for the sectional chain-finales. In the work of Da Ponte, these movements can generate complex verse structures (though simple ones are still possible) that nevertheless present clear instructions to the composer, with shifts of poetic metre, etc. (themselves responding to dramatic shifts) prompting changes of musical style, tempo, key and the like. Mozart, for example, broadly followed the various structural implications of Da Ponte's verse, and where he chose not to do so it was presumably for some musical or dramatic reason: intriguing examples are the sextet 'Riconosci in questo amplesso' in *Le nozze di Figaro*, Act 3.v, with a text shifting from *ottonari* to *senari* (this prevents the opening theme being recapitulated in the voice); Elvira's 'Ah! chi mi dice mai' (in *settenari*) in *Don Giovanni*, Act 1.v, where Don Giovanni and Leporello's interjections (in *versi sciolti*) are brought in from a succeeding recitative; and the quintet 'Di scrivermi ogni giorno' in *Così fan tutte*, Act 1.v, fashioned entirely from recitative verse.

In *opera seria*, the standard two-strophe aria text fell victim to the influence of *opera buffa*, and also to complaints about anti-naturalism that lay at the heart of the reform movement. Musical factors may also have been an issue. In *Idomeneo*, Mozart could fashion 'sonata form' arias from two-strophe texts (in one model, the second strophe is set as the 'second subject' in the dominant, and the development, where present, repeats parts of both strophes before each is recapitulated regularly, the second strophe now in the tonic). But three-strophe texts began to find favour – they also became characteristic of the RONDÒ, often in *ottonari* – as did other more flexible forms, also with changing metres: comparing Caterino Mazzolà's reworking of *La clemenza di Tito* for Mozart (1791) with Metastasio's original (1734) reveals some important trends.

The shift to 'through-composed' opera in the 19th century had surprisingly little effect on approaches to versification in librettos, at least initially. Thus recitatives, arias and ensembles can still be distinguished in conventional poetic ways, and formal subdivisions within arias and ensembles (for example, cantabile–*tempo di mezzo*–cabaletta combinations) are generally matched by shifts in poetic metre (but the persistent *ottonari* in the Act 1 finale of Bellini's *La sonnambula* are a not untypical exception). The continued significance of these structures is clear from Verdi's correspondence with his librettists: the composer had an acute sense of what was necessary in his texts in terms of both metre and rhyme, often requesting particular line-lengths and exhorting regularity upon his collaborators (see for example the letters to Antonio Somma on *Un ballo in maschera*).

However, a change can be discerned from *Aida* (1871) onwards (some hints are found earlier). Verdi's former preference for clear structures (and often for *versi parisillabi*) disappears in favour of longer lines, including *versi doppi* – 'double' verses, for example of two *settenari*, treated as a single metrical unit – and the 14-syllable *verso martelliano* (named after the early 18th-century theorist and librettist Pier Jacopo Martello). This, coupled with a tendency towards irregular groupings of lines and flexible changes of line-length (and polymetric structures to distinguish characters in ensembles), produces a striking asymmetry that reflects a changing musical style, but also the search for greater naturalism on the stage: Verdi's correspondence with Ghislanzoni on *Aida* and with Boito on *Otello* and *Falstaff* makes both points clear (Boito had already experimented in a similar vein in his *Mefistofele* of 1868). Similarly, the libretto of Puccini's *La bohème*, for example, certainly falls into regular (if highly flexible) groupings of conventional line-lengths – this is by no means prose – but their effect on the musical flow often seems exiguous.

Puccini was fond of creating nonsense rhymes to indicate to his librettists the metres and structures required for particular – and pre-conceived – musical moments. The situation had been satirized over a century before in Salieri's *Prima la musica e poi le parole* ('First the Music and then the Words') of 1786. Certainly a composer's respect for the chief tools of the librettist's trade – metre and rhyme – has varied through the history of opera, itself a function of the shifting dialectic between word and music. But a poet's verse was almost always the starting point for any musician's venture on to the operatic stage. Historical and critical approaches to Italian opera that fail to take account of these issues are seriously impoverished.

2. FRENCH. Since the 16th century, spoken French has developed a rhythmic character distinct from that of any other European language. On the one hand it makes only slight difference between long and short syllables; on the other, it has largely eliminated word-stress in favour of group-stress: a word will normally be accented only if it is the last of a group. Hence French poetry has traditionally made limited use of metre as a primary principle of organization. Rather, individual poetic lines (*vers*) are classified according to the number of pronounced syllables they contain.

When French opera emerged in the 1670s, the pre-eminent *vers* for dramatic and narrative poetry was the 12-syllable alexandrine: indeed the classical tragedy of Corneille and Racine employed little else. French librettists, however, realized from the outset that a predominance of alexandrines would provide an unsatisfactory basis for opera. They thus established the custom of writing librettos in *vers libres*, a fluid mixture of lines of different length. In recitative the alexandrine remained an important component, but no more so than the *décasyllabe* or the *octosyllabe*; in *airs* and choruses a wider variety of line-lengths was deployed, as in earlier lyric poetry. To calculate the number of syllables, a distinction must be made between masculine and feminine endings: the former end with a strong syllable (e.g. 'froid'), while the latter have a so-called *e muet* ('mute e') after the last strong syllable (e.g. 'froi-*de*'). Although this final *e muet* – like all those in French poetry – was customarily pronounced, it was not included in the syllable count. Elsewhere in the line, however, all *e muets* were counted, unless elided with the following vowel. In ex.1, the + indicates the uncounted *e muet* at the

Ex.1 Lully/Quinault: *Isis*, Act 1 scene iii

1	2	3	4	5	6	| 7	8	9	10	11	12	+
La	dou -	*ce* il -	lu -	si -	on	| d'u -	*ne* es -	pe -	ran -	*ce*	vai -	*ne*
1	2	3	4	5	6	| 7	8	9	10	11	12	
Ne	les	fait	point	tom -	ber	| du	fai -	*ste*	du	bon -	heur	

feminine ending; the remaining *e muets* are either included in the syllable count (line 1/11, line 2/9) or elided as shown.

Another long-established principle of French prosody adopted in the libretto involves end-accentuation. Here, the last strong syllable received a stress. In the longer lines – *décasyllabes* and alexandrines – a further, secondary accent was produced by the caesura (medial pause, indicated in ex.1 with a vertical line). This divided the alexandrine into two six-syllable *hémistiches*, each ending with a stress; a further accent occurred in each *hémistiche*, though the fact that these had no fixed position afforded the poet great rhythmic flexibility. In the *décasyllabe* the caesura fell after the fourth (or occasionally the sixth) syllable. Such accentuation could at times produce a semblance of regular metrical organization. The alexandrine in ex.2 is

Ex.2 Rameau/Pellegrin: *Hippolyte et Aricie*, Act 1 scene iv

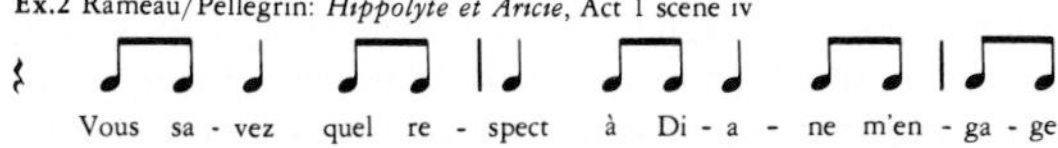

typical of many in Baroque librettos in comprising a series of anapaests; indeed both Lully and, to a lesser extent, Rameau have been criticized for the unvarying rhythm with which they tended to set such lines.

Until the 19th century, French librettos normally observed the integrity of the poetic line. The ends of most *vers*, particularly alexandrines, coincided with the end of a syntactical unit; when enjambement occurred from time to time, the sense would usually be completed at the end of the next line. There would also be a syntactical break at the caesura, though admittedly composers from Lully onwards did not always observe this.

From the start, French librettos adopted not only the tradition of rhymed lines but also the long-established custom of alternating masculine and feminine rhymes, the latter distinguished by their final *e muet*. Lines were most often arranged as *rimes plates* (*aabb*), *rimes croisées* (*abab*) or *rimes embrassées* (*abba*). Such alternation was sometimes disrupted, however, by the widespread practice of parodying – in this context, adding words to pre-existing music. Here the composer would provide the poet with a *canevas* ('outline') showing the number of syllables per line and the position of musical accents. Whether the resulting rhyme was masculine or feminine would thus depend on the nature of the pre-existing music: the more italianate the musical style, the more likelihood of a preponderance of feminine rhymes. In the following *parodie* (from Voisenon/Mondonville, *Titon et l'Aurore*, 1753) six out of seven endings are feminine: 'La tourterel-*le*/ Tendre et fidel-*le*/ Pour notre coeur/ Est un modè-*le*./ Vous que l'Amour appel-*le*,/ Aimez comme el-*le*;/ Que votre ardeur soit éternel-*le*'.

These conventions remained in force not only throughout the Baroque and Classical periods but also to a large extent during the Romantic era. True, echoes of Victor Hugo's experiments with versification – including the use of multiple enjambements and a new freedom in the positioning of the caesura – may be found in Berlioz's librettos (e.g. 'Laocoon, voyant quelque trame perfide / Dans l'ouvrage des Grecs, a d'un bras intrépide / Lancé son javelot sur ce bois, excitant / Le peuple indécis et flottant / A le brûler', *Les Troyens*, Act 2.iii). But on the whole mid-19th-century librettists, as typified by Scribe, remained conservative in such matters. Around the turn of the century, however, the influence of the *vers libérés* and *le vers libre* introduced by the Symbolist poets in the 1880s began to be felt. The former abandoned the conventions governing line-length (e.g. that a *vers* could include no more than 12 syllables), hiatus (that a word ending with a vowel could not be followed without elision by one beginning with a vowel or mute *h*), the value of the *e muet*, the alternation of rhymes, and other rules of classical versification. The latter was freer still, abandoning the twin pillars of French prosody – syllabism and obligatory rhyme – in favour of a highly personal, wholly individual approach to verbal rhythm. For example, the librettos of Louis Gallet – among them that for Massenet's *Thaïs* (1894) – are written in what he called *poésie mélique*, in which short lines, lacking rhyme or fixed length, are run together with dashes. The result resembles poetic prose. Indeed, such experiments heralded the way for the prose libretto, the most famous French example of which is Debussy's adaptation (1902) of Maeterlinck's *Pelléas et Mélisande*.

3. GERMAN. The first German-language opera, Heinrich Schütz's *Dafne* (1627; the music is lost), was a setting of a translation of the very first libretto, Rinuccini's for Peri's *Dafne* (1597–8). The translation by Martin Opitz, the leading poetic theorist and practitioner of the day, reveals greater freedom and variety of metre, rhyme-scheme and line-length than is to be found in most contemporary German poetry, in which classical patterns (ill-equipped for transposition into a language which, in its literary infancy, was dependent on stress rather than length of syllables) were predominant – Weckherlin and Opitz both favoured the alexandrine as the standard line for their verse. Fortunately, the emerging regional schools of German poets soon preferred shorter lines and freer patterns for verse intended for musical purposes.

Opitz's *Dafne* is basically in rhyming iambic pentameters, with a liberal infusion of shorter line-lengths and the occasional 12-syllable line; telling use is made of trochees. In what is self-confessedly a pastoral, intended as an epithalamium, the librettist created no opportunities for dramatic effects. Even Schütz with his powerful talent for the dramatic must have been exercised to make much of the famous transformation: in consecutive lines the fleeing Daphne begs that her body may be changed into something that can withstand violence – and Apollo apostrophizes the harsh bark of the laurel tree. The limitations of the idiom are most marked in the series of no fewer than ten six-line units of iambic tetrameters that makes up the closing choral dance of nymphs and shepherds.

The librettos of the Hamburg operas tend to appeal to the reader the more they descend the social scale: the hand of a Bostel or Praetorius is at its surest in the lyrics for peasant and servant scenes, couched in light, witty rhymes of a kind that, with little development, continued to serve German librettists through the 18th century and well into the 19th.

In the 17th century several influential poetic societies flourished, after the pattern of the Italian *accademie* founded in the previous century. Of these, the Fruchtbringende Gesellschaft of Nuremberg has a special place in the history of German opera owing to the fact that one of its members, G. P. Harsdörffer, provided Sigmund Staden with the text for the earliest extant German Singspiel, *Das geistliche Waldgedicht oder Freudenspiel genant Seelewig*, 'vocal line set in the Italian manner'. *Seelewig* was published complete with its music in Harsdörffer's *Frauenzimmer Gesprächspiele* (vol.iv, 1644). The text is a somewhat uncomfortable blend of stiff alexandrines and more flexible and fluent shorter lines in which dactyls, spondees, and occasionally other metrical devices, break up the symmetry; from time to time Staden's musical line contradicts the expected accentuation. Strophic patterns are common, and a sonnet is built into the action (a forerunner of Tamino's aria in Act 1 of *Die Zauberflöte* which, however, Mozart set more freely).

Owing mainly to the fact that, even in places where German-language operas were performed in the 17th and early 18th centuries, poets of distinction were seldom involved, a certain level of competence was rarely exceeded. If this criticism is less marked with respect to Hamburg and Vienna, the two centres in which vernacular performances were regularly given, even here there was no traditional pattern for the opera book. The first important figure in the emergence of the libretto as a literary form is C. F. Weisse (1726–1804). His librettos contain no startling technical advances by comparison with his better predecessors, and his rhymes and metres are often dependent on particles and verbal repetitions, yet Weisse's skill in placing the lyrics for musical setting within the context of the developing dramatic situation, and his abilities as a versifier – neat rhymes, fairly normal word order, appropriately straightforward imagery, lively rhythms that assist the musical setting – set new standards for the German language as operatic vehicle. The preponderance of strophic settings, sometimes with several verses, and of iambic metre, impede the creation of dramatic situations. The solution adopted by the librettists who worked for and with Mozart was to concentrate not on verbal felicities but on introducing a far wider range of quasi-poetic forms, especially in extended ensembles and finales. No one would call Schikaneder's libretto for *Die Zauberflöte* a distinguished literary achievement, but within its wide variety of verse forms and dramatic contrasts it is, as Goethe recognized, an ideal vehicle for Mozart's setting.

Goethe's Singspiel librettos, for all their lyric excellence, failed to inspire a single setting of true distinction (apart, that is, from individual lieder based on lyrics included in the librettos, such as 'Ein Veilchen', 'Es war ein Buhle frech genung' and 'Wer reitet so spät'). Indeed, with the exception of Hugo von Hofmannsthal, German opera has largely lacked poetic eminence. The clumsy but effective verse of the *Fidelio* libretto, the texts of Weber's last two German operas, and the texts that Schubert strove to turn in operas, are symptomatic of the obstacles in the path of German opera as it emerged in the Romantic era. In comparison with these, the decent linguistic and dramatic standards of practitioners such as Eduard Devrient (Marschner's *Hans Heiling*) and W. Friedrich (pseudonym of F. W. Riese, author of the librettos for Flotow's *Alessandro Stradella* and *Martha*) stand out as well suited to operatic treatment. No wonder that composers like Lortzing and Cornelius wrote their own librettos, or that later composers (Berg is an obvious example) set prose dramas with minimal alteration (though with cuts in *Wozzeck* and hefty condensation in *Lulu*).

The outstanding example of the self-help composer as librettist is of course Wagner, who from the conventional beginnings of *Die Feen* (with traditional motifs of Romantic opera, but also with a new freedom in verse-patterns, line-lengths, metres and sparing use of rhymes) moved on to create an almost entirely new musico-poetic language, characterized most obviously by the use of assonance (*Stabreim*), the greatest freedom in matters of prosody, inversion, the invention of a new-old poetic vocabulary, and the avoidance of conventional operatic repetition (such as provokes exasperation in, for instance, the Act 2 terzetto in *Der Freischütz*). This is not to deny that Wagner continued to make telling use of older poetic forms, whether one thinks of the Dutchman's opening monologue (musically one of the outstandingly original passages in the work, though largely couched in irregularly rhyming iambic pentameters and tetrameters), or of the use of varied line-lengths and metres, occasional rhyme, stichomythia, historicizing vocabulary and extended monologue, in *The Ring* and *Parsifal*. A line of Hans Sachs sums up Wagner's own achievement as poet and musician, in which he muses on Walther's Spring Song: 'es klang so alt, und war doch so neu' ('it sounded so old, and yet was so new').

From the immense shadow cast by Wagner as poet as well as composer his successors struggled with varying degrees of success to emerge. The outstanding German-language librettist after Wagner is his self-confessed antipode, Hofmannsthal. Though Richard Strauss set *Salome* and *Elektra* largely as they were written (in the former case, as translated), the Hofmannsthal-Strauss operas, from *Der Rosenkavalier* to *Arabella*, set new standards for the libretto as collaborative venture, which after Hofmannsthal's sudden death only Stefan Zweig, with cunning mixture of varied-length rhymed lines and heightened prose, managed to approach. The essence of Hofmannsthal's skill as technician is to be sought in his particular form of poetic prose, occasionally suffused by brief, shorter-lined, more traditional lyric verses, so subtle and incantatory that on two occasions Strauss found that he had set stage-directions to music.

Foreign influences, especially from France in the Napoleonic and Romantic periods, and from Italy thereafter, were very important. The influence on the emerging form of operetta was most clearly French, through Offenbach and his Parisian collaborators, though the taut Italian verses of the operas that dominated both sides of the Alps also left their mark. The team of Richard Genée and F. Zell (pseudonym of Camillo Walzel) set the pattern for the early years of the Viennese operetta; for *Die Fledermaus* Genée had the cooperation of the well-known *Volksdramatiker* Karl Haffner. These operettas, with their mixture of crisp dialogue and closed musical numbers, alternately mock-serious and dashingly dactylic or anapaestically ambiguous, and with great variety of other spiky rhythms, as well as in line-lengths, show what could be achieved in a language often considered to be heavy and unwieldy.

Like the operetta, the earlier comic Singspiel and *Spieloper* are mainly light in tone, with swift-moving and basically undemanding librettos. Hermann Mosenthal's libretto for Nicolai's *Die lustigen Weiber von Windsor* is typical of the genre: frequently changing rhyme-patterns, line-lengths and metres, with a tendency to rely overmuch on features like recurrent short-breathed masculine lines ('Mann / an / dran / kann'), and more notably feminine lines ('graben / haben / geschlagen / wagen / Betragen'. By comparison there are 14 consecutive rhymes on 'ieren' in van Bett's aria in Lortzing's *Zar und Zimmermann*, a number comfortably exceeded by Blind in *Die Fledermaus*). Quite extensive poetico-musical forms occur for instance in Nicolai's masterpiece, where we find a *Romanze* (Fenton's 'Horch, die Lerche singt im Hain!'), with its alternating trochaic tetrameters and trimeters, embedded in a chain of movements within an extended ensemble (no.7).

20th-century composers who have followed the example of Lortzing and Wagner and provided their own librettos include the Strauss of *Intermezzo* (complete with sonnet in the closing scene), Pfitzner (whose *Palestrina* alternates between dignified poetic prose and lyrical verses in irregular line-lengths), Busoni (most obviously in his reshaping of disparate sources for his *Doktor Faust*) and Hindemith, whose *Mathis der Maler* is mainly in prose, even prosaic, yet with rhymes for some of the lyrical or more dramatic moments. Other notable or notorious contributions to the history of the German libretto in the 20th century have been made by Kokoschka, Kaiser and Brecht.

4. English. The philosopher Hobbes declared in 1650 that if narrative and dramatic works were to be sung, the words needed to be in verse, as mere prose could never be 'made commensurable to the voice or instruments'. The earliest English opera librettists, writing their first texts later that same decade, seem to have shared Hobbes's view, for versification became a *sine qua non* of libretto-writing: versification which, for 150 years or more, was to be in the 'accentual-syllabic' manner *de rigueur* in almost all English art-poetry from the Renaissance to the Enlightenment.

The new operatic genre's airs and choruses presented no special problems to the versifier. Their metres and rhyme-schemes could be adapted from the stanza-forms of the long-established solo song and madrigal: an adaptation foreshadowed in the texts for the court masques of the earlier 17th century. But some difficulty was posed by the new-fangled *stile recitativo* (though even here the rhetorical sung monody of the early Stuart period offered solutions). One possibility for recitative was the ten-syllable five-pulse line which, as blank verse or rhymed couplet, was the staple metre for heightened dialogue and soliloquy in the century's spoken drama. But generally this seems to have been thought unwieldy by the early librettists. So Davenant and Flecknoe pioneered a kind of Baroque *vers libre* for recitative. This comprised fluid arrangements of lines with 2, 3, 4, 5 and occasionally 6 pulses, the lines always rhyming in some way or other (often as couplets), each metrical pulse forming the stressed syllable of a two-syllable 'foot' ('iambic' or 'trochaic'). 'My numbers', said Davenant of his versification, are 'so often diversified and fall into short fractions [because] frequent alterations of measure ... are necessary to recitative music'.

This pioneering work of appropriation and invention was very influential. For the next two centuries, during the whole time that opera in English was a matter of distinct arias, ensembles, choruses and dances separated either by recitative or (more often) by spoken dialogue, there was little basic change in the general approach to the versification of the sung sections of an English libretto.

Recitative in the later 17th and early 18th centuries largely followed the rhymed quasi-*vers libre* principle, though with a strong tendency to make a particularly extensive use of four-pulse couplets (iambic or trochaic or mixed), as in Tate's text for Purcell's *Dido and Aeneas*. Congreve in his *Semele* for Eccles, while sharing this penchant, also experiments with a *vers libre* without rhyme (though still made up of iambic or trochaic feet), so furthering his concept of recitative as 'only a more tunable speaking ... a kind of prose in music'. As the 18th century drew on, however, the taste developed (perhaps under the influence of the recitative texts in Handel's oratorios) for a less fluid versification in recitative, to be seen, for example, in Bickerstaff's formal five-pulse 'heroic couplets' for Arne's *Thomas and Sally* and the very precise blank verse of Arne's own libretto for his *Artaxerxes*. Indeed, when an English opera as late as the mid-19th century aspired unusually to be a 'grand opera seria' with dialogue 'entirely in recitative' (as did *The Daughter of St Mark* by Balfe and the poet Bunn), the recitatives are all five-pulse couplets, though decidedly unheroic ones.

Meanwhile, from Dryden, Shadwell and Tate after the Restoration to Bunn and Fitzball under Queen Victoria, there were two basic modes for the versification of arias, ensembles and choruses in operas that had new scores: (i) sequences of rhyming couplets, and (ii) fairly simple rhyming stanzas of various sorts – in both cases most often comprising lines of three or four pulses. Variety was achieved in these by the occasional use of 'feminine' line endings (that is, with unstressed syllables) and of double rhymes ('fountains/mountains' and the like); also by the replacement throughout certain arias and choruses of the standard two-syllable iambic or trochaic foot by feet of three syllables ('dactyls' and 'anapaests'), which generated a metrical buoyancy that until the mid-18th century tended only to be called on in lighthearted contexts, though thereafter its contexts widened.

All this, together with the conscious keeping simple of images and sentence structures, was done to ensure a singability that would serve the needs of composer and performer. As Dryden put it in connection with his *Albion and Albanius* for Grabu, 'the *songish* part must abound in the softness and variety of numbers'; even if that meant that the poet had sometimes to compromise 'the purity of English', behave like 'some doggerel rhymer who makes songs to tunes', and be obliged (as he later put it of his collaboration with Purcell on *King Arthur*) 'to cramp my verses and make them rugged to the reader that they may be harmonious to the hearer'.

Within two generations of Dryden, making lyrics to pre-existing tunes was becoming one of the principal occupations of the English librettist through the great vogue for ballad opera and burletta, where the challenge was to fit arresting new words neatly to old melodies. The versification used in song texts on these occasions could be looser and more adventurous than that in texts which were completed 'correctly' before any composer came near them. John Gay, for example, would probably not have printed a lyric as difficult to scan as his 'Let us take the road' (in the very influential *Beggar's Opera*) if he had not the excuse that it exactly fitted Handel's 'March in *Rinaldo*'. Such ad hoc versifying could also be more virtuoso than the prosody of pre-written lyrics, as Kane O'Hara shows flamboyantly in the texts for his burlettas of the 1760s and 70s, *Midas* and *The Golden Pippin*.

It was perhaps this loosening and sophisticating of metre and rhyme in solo airs, together with experiments at the end of the century (in such poems as Coleridge's *Christabel*) with accentual metres which did not demand a consistent syllable-count, that allowed a librettist like Planché in the 1820s to provide Weber in *Oberon* with something as metrically advanced as the Mermaid Scene, remarkable for its iamb-dactyl oscillations. Foregrounding of versification almost for its own sake also gave licence for the brilliances of some of Gilbert's 'Savoy' lyrics for Sullivan in the later 19th century, such as the apotheosis of the dactyl in his Lord Chancellor's Song from *Iolanthe*.

The ballad opera/burletta/Savoy Opera tradition contributed to the 20th-century development in Great Britain and the USA of operetta, musical comedy and the 'musical': forms in which the versification of sung numbers could range from the quite unobtrusive to the very highly profiled, in rhyme especially (e.g. in the lyrics of Cole Porter, Ira Gershwin and Stephen Sondheim). But a musical development in the opposite direction, the English adoption in the 1880s of fully 'through-composed' opera with continuous orchestral music – something which softened the distinction between recitative and 'number' or even made such categories irrelevant – had a marked effect on the versification of librettos. Though some librettists at the time extended by-now-traditional metrical devices, others began to write texts wholly or largely in blank verse (e.g. Joseph Bennett's *Jeanie Deans* for McCunn) or, since this was the age of Morris and Swinburne, to put an emphasis on even longer-lined metrics and on experiments with quasi-Nordic ones (as in Bennett's text for Cowen's *Thorgrim*).

But non-theatrical poetry had recently, in the work of Whitman, made space for an unrhymed *vers libre* that was totally accentual, i.e. freely varying both the number of syllables per pulse and the number of pulses per line. This soon invaded the libretto, as in Holst's rarely rhymed two-, three- and four-pulse accentual text for his own *Sāvitri* (composed 1908–9). It was not difficult to move from that to what would have been unthinkable to Hobbes in 1650: the libretto wholly or largely in prose, at first either in connection with low-life plots (as in Ethel Smyth's text for her own *Boatswain's Mate*) or in borrowings of classic prose texts that had their own kind of rhythmic richness (e.g. Vaughan Williams's adaptations from Shakespeare's *Merry Wives of Windsor*, John Bunyan and J. M. Synge).

Subsequent prose pieces in English (for – and sometimes by – composers as varied as Virgil Thomson, Barber, Menotti, Britten, Tippett, Henze, Maxwell Davies and Turnage) are of course unconcerned with versification, though an exception might be made in the case of Thomson's collaborations with Gertrude Stein, since Stein's circling modernist prose is so close to verse in its effects. But other 20th-century through-composed operas have made prose the foil for highly wrought verse by using it for bread-and-butter quasi-recitative 'talk' and keeping verse for lyrical passages, as in DuBose Heyward and Ira Gershwin's text for George Gershwin's *Porgy and Bess* (where it is noteworthy that about half the best-known lyrical numbers were set to pre-written stanzas by Heyward, while the words of the other half were – in the best ballad-opera manner – post-written by Ira Gershwin to fit 'pure' melodies by his brother George: a procedure not unknown elsewhere in 20th-century opera, if rarely on this scale).

Many 20th-century librettos, however, have been written wholly or very largely in verse of one sort and another. Outside the Shakespeare adaptations by Britten and Barber, the staple since mid-century at least has rarely been the five-pulse line. W. H. Auden (whose librettos with Chester Kallman for Stravinsky and Henze are highly virtuoso metrically) suspected that this had 'something to do with musical tempi being generally slower than speech tempi'. More often a range of pulses has been used, with a fondness for two-, three-, or four-pulse lines, the lines either loosely accentual or more tightly traditional in their syllable patterns. Not only have some librettists (Crozier, Raine, Harrison etc.) preferred fairly tight systems; composers have sometimes insisted on them. Thus Stravinsky required a corseted neo-classical number opera from Auden and Kallman in *The Rake's Progress*, and Alice Goodman knew that John Adams wanted an 'opera to be written in rhymed couplets' before she knew that it was to be about *Nixon in China*. (The couplets she supplied were basically iambic, two-pulse and four-pulse, with full- and half-rhyme.) Even tighter metrically have been texts like Pruslin's for Birtwistle's *Punch and Judy*: a mosaic of ritualized jingles, spells, doggerel fragments and riddle rhymes.

However, alongside these rigours there has been a broad church of later 20th-century librettists who would probably find Plomer's account of his text for Britten's *Gloriana* more congenial: 'The libretto is partly in verse and partly in prose. The verse is mostly irregular, with an intermittent use of rhyme. In general the lines have been kept short, often with only two or three stresses, and the language fairly direct and colloquial ... Dramatic unity was the general aim, not metrical uniformity.' Flecknoe and Davenant in the 1650s would not perhaps have been very greatly surprised.

5. SLAVONIC LANGUAGES. Versification largely depends on the nature of language and particularly on word

stress or accentuation. Of the three main Slavonic languages in terms of opera composition, Czech with constant first-syllable stress and Polish with unchanging penultimate stress differ fundamentally from Russian with its strong but strictly single mobile stress. Of these, only Czech has the added complication of long and short vowels, but all three tongues share the advantages of inflective word endings and relatively flexible word order. An additional factor influencing versification has been the source of librettos: whether written especially (before or after the music) or taken from an existing work of literature. Here the heavy reliance of Russian composers not only on themes but also on words drawn (sometimes *in toto*) from the classics of their national literature introduces an added element to be considered in reviewing the versification of many Russian librettos.

Modern Russian opera begins with Glinka, whose two works in this genre are very different, not least in terms of libretto. That of *A Life for the Tsar* was the work of several poets, including Vasily Zhukovsky, Nestor Kukol'nik and Fedor Sollogub, although the final version was prepared by the minor poet Yegor Rozen in response to the melodies Glinka had composed, adding the metrical accents for the verses Rozen was to write. The result is often far from regular rhythmic patterns, though the majority of arias and choruses are in basically (syllabo-tonic) trochaic metres. Antonida's Act 1 aria is in free trochees, but the Oarsmen's Chorus and the Chorus of the Villagers from the same act are in a characteristic folk rhythm: trochaic trimeters with a tendency to accentual verse. Throughout the opera, rhyme (masculine, feminine and, rarely, dactylic) is intermittent with occasional cross-rhymes (mostly FMFM) but with a preference for rhyming couplets. Glinka's second opera, *Ruslan and Lyudmila*, was not only, as the composer recalls in his memoirs, planned by a drunken nonentity, but the libretto was written by a number of very minor poets in collaboration with the composer (many later Russian composers also wrote, in whole or in part, their own librettos). Pushkin's poem had been written entirely in iambic tetrameters (iambs constituted 84% of all his verse output) and this metre is widespread in the opera, but also to be found are a range of other syllabo-tonic metres. They include a mixture of anapaests and amphibrachs in Farlaf's Act 2 Rondo; prosodically degenerating trochaic trimeters for Ratmir's waltz-time aria in Act 3 ('Chudnyy son'); the rolling rhythm of amphibrachic dimeters for Lyudmila's Act 4 aria 'Bezumnyy volshebnik' preceded by straight iambic tetrameters in her 'Ne nuzhno mne tvoikh darov'; trochaic tetrameters for the duet preceding the finale to Act 5. In both Glinka's operas the words are strictly subservient to the music, and in neither does the metre restrict the melody or injure (by artificial accents) the nature of the language, although in the case of *Ruslan* almost nothing of Pushkin's early tour de force remains.

Tchaikovsky's two best-known operas were also inspired by Pushkin, but in each case go right against the spirit of the original, substituting passionate drama for sceptical wit. The libretto of *Yevgeny Onegin* was almost all written by the composer himself (apart from the French verses in Act 2) in mixed iambs, mostly tetrameters, not divided into any stanzaic pattern. Pushkin had created a very distinctive 14-line stanza for his novel in verse, abandoned only for Tatyana's letter (ostensibly translated from French), and it is precisely in the Letter Scene, the high point of the opera, that Tchaikovsky uses Pushkin's words (in iambic tetrameters, like the rest of the novel) almost verbatim. The libretto as a whole, like the Letter, is in a mixture of alternate rhymes (mainly FMFM) and rhyming couplets. The words of *The Queen of Spades* were written by Tchaikovsky's brother Modest before the music was begun. Like *Onegin*, it is mainly in mixed iambs with cross-rhymes and couplets, as applies to several other of Tchaikovsky's operas like, for instance, the earlier *Voyevoda*, based on a verse play by Ostrovsky; *Mazepa* is almost all in iambic tetrameters, like Pushkin's poem *Poltava*, on which it was based. *The Queen of Spades*, however, is distinctive in its pastiches of earlier and contemporary Russian poets (Tomsky's ballad in Act 3 recalls the clumsy rhythm of Derzhavin, the duet of Lisa and Pauline in Act 1.ii echoes Batyushkov) and there are several direct quotations, both verbal and musical. The opening Chorus of Nannies is in the typically folk metre of trochaic trimeters with a dactylic clausula.

Pushkin's inspiration for Musorgsky's *Boris Godunov* (based also on Karamzin's *History of the Russian State*) is reflected in some of the words, originally in a combination of blank iambic pentameters and prose in imitation of Shakespeare, but when he turns to them the composer makes very free use of Pushkin's lines, changing the metre or putting the verse into prose. Pimen's arias are prosodically and verbally closest to Pushkin's play; the added 'Polish' scenes are nearly all in verse, with a predominance of feminine endings, echoing the fixed penultimate stress of the Polish language. Musorgsky's *Boris Godunov*, unlike Pushkin's, contains far more prose than verse. Dargomïzhsky in *The Stone Guest* had earlier followed Pushkin's poem of the same name verbatim, but destroyed the rhythm of the blank iambic tetrameters by constant recitative. Rimsky-Korsakov, who with Cui completed Dargomïzhsky's pioneering score, was fortunate to work with V. I. Bel'sky on many of his operas. In two of them, based on Pushkin's verse tales, he successfully imitated the trochaic tetrameters and rhyming couplets of the poet's *The Golden Cockerel* and *Tsar Saltan* in witty recreations of the originals, which introduce variety (for instance, the Queen of Shemakha's first aria in Act 2 of *The Golden Cockerel* is set to iambic tetrameters) without losing Pushkin's panache. The words of Borodin's *Prince Igor*, which was of course completed by Rimsky-Korsakov, are in a combination of mixed trochees and, predominantly, prose. Rakhmaninov was not lucky with opera librettos. Modest Tchaikovsky adapted Nemirovich-Danchenko clumsily for *Aleko*, based on Pushkin's *The Gypsies*, and *Francesca da Rimini* after Dante, but in *The Miserly Knight* he adhered almost verbatim to the blank iambic pentameters of Pushkin's play, omitting only about 40 lines and making a tiny addition. Later Russian operas, notably those of Prokofiev and Shostakovich, preferred prose.

The same applies to the most famous Polish opera, Szymanowski's *King Roger*; but one much earlier composer, the Silesian Joseph Xaver Elsner in 1818 went so far as to publish a treatise on the rhythms of metre in the Polish language with special reference to Polish verse from the point of view of music. Modern Polish opera began with Stanisław Moniuszko, a Polonized Belarusian from Minsk, one of whose early works (now lost) was *Sielanka* ('An Idyll') set to a Polono-Belarusian text in irregular rhymed syllabic verse and prose by the Belarusian writer Vikentsi

Dunin-Martsinkevich (Marcinkiewicz). Moniuszko's first grand opera, *Halka*, based on *Halszka* by Włodzimierz Wolski, is in syllabic lines, mostly between eight and 12 measures in length, with some very uneven couplets (for instance, of a 12-syllable and a four-syllable line). Alternate rhymes predominate, and most are feminine, with a few masculine endings and an occasional dactylic tendency, as, for instance, in Janusz's aria in Act 1.iii. In the 19th century, Polish versification as a whole was moving from syllabic towards syllabo-tonic metres, but in *Halka* rhyme is undoubtedly the main organizing factor. The same may be said of *The Haunted Manor*, where alternate rhymes also predominate. There is, however, less rhyme altogether than in the earlier opera, with more semi-recitative and the rhythm very subject to the measures of Polish folk dances rather than classical prosodic patterns.

In Czech versification from the middle of the 19th century the old system of *časomíra* based on vowel length was largely superseded by syllabo-tonic verse, particularly iambic, trochaic and dactylic metres. Smetana's first opera, *The Brandenburgers in Bohemia*, begins in almost regular iambs (iambic pentameters were by then standard – imitating Shakespeare, as in Russia – for high-style drama), but soon degenerates into prosodic indeterminacy. Although predominantly trochaic librettos are rare in Czech opera, Smetana used just such in two of his comedies, *The Bartered Bride* and *The Two Widows*. In the latter, the librettist Emanuel Züngel varies the trochaic metre with iambs and dactyls for about 15% of the opera; in the former the trochees are interspersed with prose, but (as Tyrrell has noted) the verse of the librettist Karel Sabina occasionally clashes with Smetana's setting, sometimes for comic purposes, sometimes perhaps because of the German-educated composer's imperfect grasp of his own very complex language. Dvořák always seemed happy to sacrifice word-setting to melody, but the librettists of his last operas received detailed instructions as to the metres and rhymes he wanted. In *Rusalka* the libretto combines iambs, trochees and dactyls with alternate rhymes and couplets, and masculine, feminine and dactylic line-endings. Janáček in his first mature opera, *Jenůfa*, seemed uncomfortable setting the prose of Gabriela Preissová, and attempted to turn some of it into metrical lines and even set pieces. In *Osud* he asked Fedora Bartošová for 'Pushkinian' syllabo-tonic (iambic) verse, but overrode it so thoroughly with his music that little of the metre remains. Janáček liked to have full control over his librettos, and his discovery of 'speech melodies' soon made prosody redundant.

*

CZECH

J. Král: *O prosodii české*, i: *Historicky vývoj české prosodie* [The Historical Evolution of Czech Prosody], ed. J. Jakuba (Prague, 1923)

J. Tyrrell: 'Czech, Metre and Word-Setting', *Czech Opera* (Cambridge, 1988), 253–98

ENGLISH

G. Saintsbury: *A History of English Prosody from the Twelfth Century to the Present Day* (London, 1906–10)

D. Attridge: *The Rhythms of English Poetry* (London, 1982)

J. Hollander: *Rhyme's Reason* (New Haven, CT, 2/1989)

FRENCH

A. Tobler: *Vom französischen Versbau alter und neuer Zeit: Zusammenstellung der Anfangsgründe* (Leipzig, 2/1883; Fr. trans., 1885, as *Le vers français, ancien et moderne*)

L. E. Kastner: *A History of French Versification* (Oxford, 1903)

G. Lote: *Histoire du vers français* (Paris, 1949)

M. Grammont: *Petit traité de versification française* (Paris, 14/1952)

W. T. Elwert: *Traité de versification française des origines à nos jours* (Paris, 1965)

GERMAN

H. G. Atkins: *A History of German Versification* (London, 1923)

A. Heusler: *Deutsche Versgeschichte, mit Einschluss des altenglischen und altnordischen Stabreimverses* (Berlin, 1925–9)

W. Kayser: *Kleine deutsche Versschule* (Berne, 1946)

K. von See: *Germanische Verskunst* (Stuttgart, 1967)

D. Breuer: *Deutsche Metrik und Versgeschichte* (Munich, 1981)

C. Wagenknecht: *Deutsche Metrik: eine historische Einführung* (Munich, 1981)

L. L. Albertsen: *Neuere deutsche Metrik* (Berne and New York, 1984)

ITALIAN

W. T. Elwert: *Italienische Metrik* (Munich, 1968); It. trans., 1973, as *Versificazione italiana dalle origini ai giorni nostri*)

F. Lippmann: 'Der italienische Vers und der musikalische Rhythmus: zum Verhältnis von Vers und Musik in der italienischen Oper des 19. Jahrhunderts, mit einem Rückblick auf die 2. Hälfte des 18. Jahrhunderts', *AnMc*, no.12 (1973), 253–369; no.14 (1974), 324–410; no.15 (1975), 298–333

R. Strohm: 'Italienische Opernarien des frühen settecento (1720–1730)', *AnMc*, no.16 (1976) [whole volume]

S. Leopold: '"Quelle bazzicature poetiche appellate ariette": Dichtungsformen in der frühen italianischen Oper (1600–1640)', *HJbMw*, iii (1978), 101–41

L. Castelnuovo: *La metrica italiana* (Milan, 1979)

J. Whenham: *Duet and Dialogue in the Age of Monteverdi* (Ann Arbor, 1982), esp. 17–47

C. Di Girolamo: *Teoria e prassi della versificazione* (Bologna, 1983)

M. Ramous: *La metrica* (Milan, 1984)

D. Goldin: *La vera fenice: librettisti e libretti tra sette e ottocento* (Turin, 1985)

H. S. Powers: '"La solita forma" and "The Uses of Convention"', *AcM*, lix (1987), 65–90

P. Fabbri: 'Istituti metrici e formali', *SOI*, vi (1988), 163–233 [with details of theoretical sources]

RUSSIAN

B. O. Unbegaun: *Russian Versification* (Oxford, 1956)

SPANISH

R. Baehr: *Spanische Verslehre auf historischer Grundlage* (Tübingen, 1912; Sp. trans. as *Manuel de versificación española*)

T. Navarro Tomás: *Métrica Española: reseña histórica y descriptiva* (Syracuse, NY, 1956)

TIM CARTER (1), GRAHAM SADLER (2), PETER BRANSCOMBE (3), ROGER SAVAGE (4), ARNOLD McMILLIN (5)

Verstovsky, Alexey Nikolayevich (*b* Seliverstovo estate, Michurin region, Tambov district, south central Russia, 18 Feb/1 March 1799; *d* Moscow, 5/17 Nov 1862). Russian composer and theatrical official. His operas, particularly those written in collaboration with the novelist Mikhail Zagoskin, known as 'the Russian Scott' (by which token Verstovsky might be called 'the Russian Weber'), were significant manifestations of Romanticism in Russia and the most highly developed native contributions to the operatic repertory before Glinka's.

1. Life. 2. Early stage works. 3. Later operas.

1. LIFE. Like Glinka, his somewhat younger contemporary and rival, Verstovsky was born into a wealthy landowning family that maintained a serf orchestra on its hereditary estate. Initially bent on a career in civil engineering, he attended the Institute of the Corps of Engineers in St Petersburg, from which he graduated in 1817. At the same time he studied the piano with Daniel Steibelt and John Field, the violin with Ludwig Maurer and thoroughbass with Karl Zeuner. Steibelt and Maurer, employees of the Imperial Theatres, steered their talented pupil towards theatrical composition; by the time he turned 20, Verstovsky was heavily involved in the local music factory, turning out romances and patter songs (couplets) for the burgeoning 'opera-vaudeville'. This was a genre specially meant for

the musical theatre, consisting of situation comedies in verse (often adapted from the French and usually involving mistaken identities), fitted out with an overture (often very elaborate), entr'actes and simple musical numbers. These last were normally meant for ordinary actors' voices, but specially composed rather than arranged from folk or popular songs and somewhat more arty in style and continuous in form (e.g. in finales) than the music then normally interpolated into spoken dramas. The opera-vaudeville had its specialist librettists (the chief ones being Nikolay Khmel'nitsky and Alexander Pisarev) and a cadre of salaried staff composers, of which Maurer was a member, along with the Silesian-born Fyodor Shol'ts (Friedrich Scholz) and Verstovsky's somewhat older contemporary Alexander Alyab'yev. Most of Verstovsky's early opera-vaudevilles were written in collaboration with this group. (For plot summaries of several, see Karlinsky 1985.)

Verstovsky's later claim to have originated the opera-vaudeville may be doubted, but his pre-eminence in the field was widely acknowledged and recognized officially in his assignment to Moscow (1823) and his appointment in 1825 as 'inspector of music' for the reorganized Imperial Theatres in Russia's second city, including the newly opened Bol'shoy. He held administrative posts involving the supervision of casts and crews, and eventually responsibility for repertory, until 1860, when he retired after almost four decades as Moscow's most powerful musical bureaucrat. His official position enabled him to control his own competition, frustrating Alyab'yev's operatic career and staving Glinka off the Moscow stage until 1842.

2. EARLY STAGE WORKS. Verstovsky's most ambitious solo effort in Moscow was a farce *en travesti*, *Kto brat, kto sestra* ('Which is the Brother, Which the Sister), to a libretto by two major Moscow literati, Prince Pyotr Vyazemsky (1792–1878) and Alexander Griboyedov (1795–1829), author of the classic Russian comedy *Gore ot uma* ('Woe from Wit'). Its main character, a young Polish noblewoman, poses as her own brother in order to cure her husband's brother of misogyny and xenophobia. With its marked reliance on contemporary popular dance genres – mazurkas, polonaises, waltzes – and its exceptional variety of vocal numbers, including many ensembles, Verstovsky's score has been called 'a unique encyclopedia of vaudeville music'. It is the sole representative of its genre to have been published in its entirety (albeit 125 years after its run). A few of its numbers were adapted from earlier opera-vaudevilles, and practically all of them were re-used in later ones. This was normal practice, abetted by the fact that for all its latterday celebrity *Which is the Brother, Which the Sister* was a notorious flop, mocked as such later the same year by Pisarev in the libretto of *Khlopotun* ('Mr Bustle'), another opera-vaudeville for which Verstovsky composed music. That will serve to show both how topical these entertainments tended to be, and how detached the professionalism of their perpetrators.

The line between Verstovsky's vaudevilles and his operas is a fine one. The latter, even those written long after Glinka broke the recitative barrier for Russian opera, continued (except for the very last) to rely on spoken dialogue, and as Serov pointed out in his obituary, Verstovsky's musical facture was always on the petty side, never too far from the couplet style. The chief differences were of size (of formal amplitude and especially of orchestra), vocal resources, subject matter and social setting. Where the vaudevilles always concerned the contemporary urban (i.e. cosmopolitan) upper crust, the operas had archaic settings and combined preoccupation with fantastic stage spectacle and with the broadly 'national'. It is a recipe that calls *Der Freischütz* to mind, and Weber's opera, first performed in Moscow in 1824, was a powerful stimulant to Verstovsky's creative imagination, even if actual musical correspondences are slim.

Pan Tvardovsky (or *Pan Twardowski*, 1828), on a libretto (begun by the novelist Sergey Aksakov and completed by Zagoskin) pertaining to a legendary Polish Faust-figure who also inspired Mickiewicz and Kraszewski, combines elements of rescue opera and Romantic spectacle. The title character imprisons Krasicki, a rival for the hand of Julia, the woman he loves. The gypsy Giksha rescues Krasicki, who then rescues Julia. The opera ends with a spectacular fire in which the evildoer's castle, and Twardowski himself, are consumed. There is also a forest storm and a flood as well as spectral visions and colourful scenes of gypsy life (the latter, according to Aksakov, included at the composer's specific request). Krasicki's first-act aria (quoted in NOHM, viii, 534) is a good example of the romance-flavoured lyric style that passed ultimately to Tchaikovsky. Its Russian quality is pronounced, if entirely urban, while the remaining published numbers show an effort to capture an equally vivid Polish-Ukrainian or gypsy quality (see especially Giksha's *Fra Diavolo*-esque strophic song with chorus at the beginning of Act 2; printed in IRMO, iii, 61). The emphasis on a distinctively East European local colour prompted one critic to exclaim, 'This is *ours*, this is the *first Russian opera*'.

Verstovsky's second opera, *Vadim* (1832), in which the questing, Parsifal-like title character is a speaking role, was based on a Russian fairy-tale and strove for a specifically antique Russian colouring. Its literary source, Vasily Zhukovsky's ballad on the Twelve Sleeping Maidens, was parodied by Pushkin in *Ruslan and Lyudmila* (compare the efforts to rouse the hypnotized heroine in the fifth act of Glinka's opera). Again, the formula of rescue-cum-spectacle provided the essential kernel. The libretto, a confused committee product, ensured the opera's failure. The music is not without historical interest: Verstovsky's scenes of folk-wedding ritual and feasting point towards famous counterparts in Glinka (*Ruslan*) and Rimsky-Korsakov (*Sadko*, *Kitezh*) and in particular towards Serov's *Rogneda*, deliberately modelled on Verstovsky in preference to Glinka.

3. LATER OPERAS. It was Verstovsky's third opera, *Askol'dova mogila* ('Askold's Grave', 1835), that brought him a measure of immortality. Set, like *Vadim*, in Kievan Russia, and based again on the theme of rescue (with Toropka the gudok player a near counterpart to Giksha in *Pan Tvardovsky*), it was, in terms of longevity and sheer number of performances, the most popular Russian opera of the 19th century. Thereafter Verstovsky's career went into a decline; unwilling to renovate his style, the old vaudevillian appeared trivial and superannuated next to the more truly operatic native work that began to play in Moscow in the 1840s. In fact he rejected the newer, more serious dramaturgy of Glinka, dismissing the 'oratorical' premises of *A Life*

for the Tsar with a haughty remark: 'Every musical genre has its own forms, its own limits; one does not go to the theatre in order to pray to God'.

After a disastrous attempt to break the antique-spectacular mould in *Toska po rodine* ('Homesickness', 1839), a feeble comic opera about Russians in Spain, Verstovsky tried to recapture the success of *Askold's Grave* with a return to ancient Kievan pageantry. *Son nayavu* ('A Waking Dream'), on which he laboured for three years (1840–43), again had a plot reminiscent of *Ruslan and Lyudmila* and again featured elaborate scenes of wedding ritual. In its more continuous music, its enhanced orchestra, its bravura arias and its sumptuous mermaid ballet it gave evidence of a wish to emulate Glinka's magic opera, but Verstovsky was hopelessly outclassed.

His last opera, *Gromoboy* (produced 1857), which revisited the literary source of *Vadim* (successfully revived in 1850), had a slow birth. A through-composed opera at last, it marked the peak of the composer's attempt, as he put it, 'to invest the character of Russian national music in European form'. Though it was given a production of unsurpassed opulence (as was only the theatre director's due), it failed to hold the stage, and to the composer's great disappointment was never mounted in St Petersburg, where the star-studded Italian opera troupe by then held sway. Its Faustian theme, reminiscent of *Pan Tvardovsky*, concerns a pact with the devil for the sake of revenge. Its most memorable scene, in the opinion of reviewers and historians alike, was the lament of Askold's widow Rogneda, who eight years later became the title character of the one opera (Serov's) that could be said to rival *Askold's Grave* for popularity in 19th-century Russia.

Despite the continuing success of his third opera, Verstovsky ended his career an embittered man, intensely resentful of Glinka's reputation as founder of the Russian national school. 'I am the number-one worshipper of Glinka's magnificent talent', he protested in a letter to Count Odoyevsky, 'but I will not and cannot yield the claim of precedence'. To the end he insisted that 'the Dawn of Russian Music took place in Moscow, and not in St Petersburg'.

See also ASKOLD'S GRAVE.

Edition: *A. Verstovsky: Askol'dova mogila* [Askold's Grave], arr. B. V. Dobrokhotov (Moscow, 1963) [vocal score] [AM]

all first performed at Moscow, Bol'shoy Theatre; MSS mainly at RU-SPsc and SPtob

Pan Tvardovsky [Twardowski] (romantic magic op, 3, S. Aksakov and M. Zagoskin), 24 May/5 June 1828, excerpts in IRMO, iii, and AM, ov. (condensed) in Rabinovich

Vadim, ili Probuzhdeniye dvenadtsati spyashchikh dev [Vadim, or The Awakening of the 12 Sleeping Maidens] (magic-romantic op, prol., 3, S. Shevïryov, A. Shakhovskoy, Aksakov and Zagoskin, after V. Zhukovsky: *Gromoboy, or The Twelve Sleeping Maidens*), 28 Nov/10 Dec 1832, excerpts in IRMO, iii, Rabinovich, and AM

Askol'dova mogila [Askold's Grave] (romantic op, 4, Zagoskin, after his novel), 16/28 Sept 1835, vs (St Petersburg, 1836), AM, excerpts in IRMO, iii

Zheleznoye pero [The Iron Quill], 1836–7 (N. Polevoy), inc.

Toska po rodine [Homesickness] (comic op, 3, Zagoskin, after his novel), 21 Aug/2 Sept 1839, 1 no. in AM

Son nayavu, ili Churova dolina [A Waking Dream, or Chur's Valley] (magic op, 3, Shakhovskoy, after Cossack Lugansky [V. I. Dahl]: *A Night at the Crossroads* and Slavonic legends), 28 Nov/10 Dec 1844, excerpts in AM

Gromoboy, 1853–4 (grand fantastic op, 4, D. T. Lensky after Zhukovsky: *Gromoboy*, i), 24 Jan/5 Feb 1857, vs (Moscow, 1857), excerpts in IRMO and AM

OPERA-VAUDEVILLES

Edition: *A. Verstovsky: Romansï, pesni i kupletï iz muzïki k vodevilyam i p'yesam* [Romances, Songs and Couplets for Music to Vaudevilles and Plays], ed. A. V. Voynova (Moscow, 1971) [RPK]

MOB – *Moscow, Bol'shoy Theatre*
MOM – *Moscow, Theatre on the Mokhovaya*
SPB – *St Petersburg, Bol'shoy Theatre*
SPML – *St Petersburg, Malïy Theatre*

Sentimental'nïy pomeshchik [voyazhyor] v stepnoy derevne [A Sentimental Landowner (Voyager) in a Village in the Steppe] (vaudeville with Russ. divertissement, after a Fr. source), SPML, 12/24 Nov 1817

Babushkinï popugai [Grandma's Parrots] (1, N. Khmel'nitsky, after a Fr. source), SPB, 29 July/10 Aug 1819, excerpts in RPK

Karantin [Quarantine] (1, Khmel'nitsky, after a Fr. source), SPB, 26 July/7 Aug 1820, excerpts in RPK; collab. L. W. Maurer

Syurprizï, ili Vsyakaya vsyachina i vse v khlopatakh [Surprises, or Everything at Once and Everyone in an Uproar] (N. V. Sushkov), SPB, 1/13 June 1821, collab. C. Cavos and others

Novaya shalost', ili Teatral'noye srazheniye [A Novel Prank, or A Theatrical Battle] (1, Khmel'nitsky), SPB, 12/24 Feb 1822, excerpts in RPK; collab. A. Alyab'yev and Maurer

Dom sumasshedshikh, ili Strannaya svad'ba [The Madhouse, or A Queer Wedding] (1, Verstovsky, after a Fr. source), SPB, 16/28 Oct 1822, excerpts in RPK

Kto brat, kto sestra, ili Obman za obmanom [Which is the Brother, Which the Sister, or Trick upon Trick] (1, A. Griboyedov and P. Vyazemsky), MOM, 24 Jan/5 Feb 1824, vs (Moscow, 1949), excerpts in IRMO, iii, and RPK

Vospitaniye, ili Vot pridanoye [Good Breeding, or There's a Dowry for You] (comedy-vaudeville, F. F. Kokoshkin), MOM, 24 Jan/5 Feb 1824

Uchitel' i uchenik, ili V chuzhom piru pokhmel'ye [Teacher and Pupil, or Your Carousing, my Hangover] (1, A. I. Pisarev, after a Fr. source), MOM, 24 April/6 May 1824, excerpts in RPK; collab. Alyab'yev and F. E. Shol'ts

Prositel' [The Petitioner] (1, Pisarev), MOM, 29 May/10 June 1824, excerpts in RPK; collab. Alyab'yev, M. I. Wielhorski and Shol'ts

Pritchi, ili Esop u Ksanfa [Fables, or Aesop at Xanthë's] (Shakhovskoy, after a Fr. source), SPB, 3/15 Nov 1824, 1 no. in RPK

Khlopotun, ili Delo mastera boyitsya [Mr Bustle, or Work Fears the Master] (1, Pisarev, after a Fr. source), Moscow, Malïy, 4/16 Nov 1824, excerpts in IRMO, iii, and RPK; collab. Alyab'yev

Vstrecha dilizhansov [The Stagecoaches Meet] (1, Pisarev, P. Arapov and M. A. Dimitriyev), MOB, 23 Jan/4 Feb 1825, excerpts in RPK; collab. Alyab'yev

Tridtsat' tïsyach chelovek, ili Nakhodka khuzhe poteri (Thirty Thousand People, or Finding is Worse than Losing] (Pisarev, after a Fr. source), MOB, 29 Jan/10 Feb 1825

Zabavï kalifa, ili Shutki za odni sutki [The Caliph's Amusements, or Jokes Around the Clock] (3, Pisarev), MOB, 9/21 April 1825, excerpts in RPK [Act 1 by Shol'ts, Act 2 by Alyab'yev]

Opït artistov, ili Avos' udastsya [An Actors' Experiment, or What if it Succeeds?] (A. M. Saburov, after a Fr. source), MOB, 23 April/5 May 1825; collab. Wielhorski and I. Genishta

Volshebnïy nos, ili Talismanï i finiki [The Magic Nose, or Talismans and Dates] (magical-whimsical op-vaudeville, Pisarev, after a Fr. source), MOB, 8/20 Oct 1825

Tri desyatki, ili Novoye dvukhdnevnoye priklyucheniye [The Three Tens, or A New Two-Day Adventure] (3, Pisarev, after a Fr. source), MOB, 19 Nov/1 Dec 1825, excerpts in RPK

Dve zapiski, ili Bez vinï vinovat [The Two Chits, or Guilty though Innocent] (1, Pisarev, after a Fr. source), MOB, 27 Jan/8 Feb 1827; collab. Alyab'yev

Shkola suprugov [The School for Husbands] (F. F. Kokoshkin, after A. Murphy: *The Way to Keep Him*), MOB, 4/16 Feb 1827, 1 no. in RPK

Stranstvuyushchiye lekari, ili Iskusstvo probuzhdayet myortvïkh [The Wandering Physicians, or Art Wakes the Dead] (Pisarev, after a Fr. source), MOB, 4/16 Feb 1827

Pastushka, starushka, volshebnitsa, ili Chto nravitsya zhenshchinam [Shepherdess, Crone and Sorceress, or What Women Like] (3, Pisarev, after C.-S. Favart), MOB, 20 May/1 June 1827; collab. Alyab'yev

Moya zhena vïkhodit zamuzh [My Wife is Getting Married] (2, N. I. Malïshev, after a Fr. source), MOB, 6/18 Oct 1827, collab. Alyab'yev

Luchshiy den' v zhizni, ili Urok bogatïm zhenikham [The Best Day of Your Life, or A Lesson to Rich Bridegrooms] (2, Malïshev, after a Fr. source), MOB, 21 Dec 1827/2 Jan 1828, 1 no. in RPK; collab. Alyab'yev and Shol'ts
Pyat' let v dva chasa, ili Kak dorogi utki [Five Years in Two Hours, or How Costly the Tattle] (Pisarev, after a Fr. source), MOB, 20 Jan/1 Feb 1828
Sredstvo vïdavat' docherey zamuzh [How to Give your Daughters Away] (Pisarev, after a Fr. source), MOB, 27 Jan/8 Feb 1828, excerpts in RPK
Utro posle bala [The Morning after the Ball] (Pisarev, after a Fr. play), MOB, 27 Jan/8 Feb 1828, excerpts in RPK
Svad'ba Figaro [The Marriage of Figaro] (5, D. N. Barkov, after Beaumarchais), SPB, 18 Feb/2 March 1829, 1 no. in RPK
Diplomat (N. V. Pavlov and Shevïryov, after a Fr. source), MOB, 21 June/3 July 1829
Novïy Paris [The New Paris] (Khmel'nitsky), MOB, 21 June/3 July 1829, excerpts in RPK; collab. Alyab'yev and Maurer
Stanislav, ili Ne vsyakiy eto sdelayet [Stanislav, or Not Everyone will Do it] (N. V. Vsevolozhsky, after a Fr. source), MOB, 29 July/10 Aug 1829, 1 no. in RPK; mostly adapted from Kto brat, kto sestra
Vecher pod Novïy god [New Year's Eve] (Pisarev), 1829
Muzh i zhena [Man and Wife] (1, Lensky, after a Fr. source), MOB, 23 May/4 June 1830; collab. Alyab'yev, Maurer and Shol'ts

*

GENERAL

N. Findeyzen: *Aleksey Nikolayevich Verstovsky* (St Petersburg, 1898) [originally suppl. to *EIT 1896–7*]
A. S. Rabinovich: *Russkaya opera do Glinki* [Russian Opera before Glinka] (Moscow, 1948)
B. V. Dobrokhotov: *A. N. Verstovsky: zhizn', teatral'naya deyatel'nost, opernoye tvorchestvo* [Verstovsky: Life, Theatrical Activities and Operatic Works] (Moscow and Leningrad, 1950)
B. Asaf'yev: 'Kompozitor iz pleyadï slavyano-rossiyskikh bardov – Aleksey Nikolayevich Verstovsky' [A Composer from the Galaxy of Slavic-Russian Bards: Verstovsky], *Izbrannïye trudï* [Selected Works], ed. T. N. Livanova and others, iv (Moscow, 1955)
A. N. Serov: 'Verstovsky i ego znacheniye dlya russkogo iskusstva' [Verstovsky and his Significance for Russian Art; orig. pubd 1862], *Izbrannïye stat'i* [Selected Essays], ed. G. N. Khubov, ii (Leningrad, 1957)
A. Gozenpud: *Muzïkal'nïy teatr v Rossii* (Leningrad, 1959)
——: *Russkiy opernïy teatr XIX veka 1836–1856* [Russian Operatic Theatre of the 19th Century (Leningrad, 1969)
S. Ginzburg: IRMO, iii (Moscow, 2/1970)
A. V. Voynova: Introduction and commentaries to A. Verstovsky: *Romansï, pesni i kupletï iz muzïki k vodevilyam i p'yesam* [Romances, Songs and Couplets for Music to Vaudevilles and Plays] (Moscow, 1971)
G. Abraham: 'The Operas of Verstovsky', *19th Century Music*, vii (1983–4), 326–35
S. Karlinsky: *Russian Drama from its Beginnings to the Age of Pushkin* (Berkeley and Los Angeles, 1985)
Yu. Keldïsh: 'A. N. Verstovsky', *Istoriya russkoy muzïki*, v (Moscow, 1988), 97–131

OPERAS

Which is the Brother, which the Sister

A. Voynova: Introduction to A. N. Verstovsky: *Kto brat, kto sestra* (Moscow, 1949) [vocal score]

Askold's Grave

B. V. Dobrokhotov: *A. N. Verstovskiy i ego opera 'Askol'dova mogila'* [Verstovsky and his Opera *Askold's Grave*] (Moscow, 1962)
B. V. Dobrokhotov and N. Biryukov: Introduction to A. N. Verstovsky: *Askol'dova mogila* (Moscow, 1963) [vocal score]
M. Shcherbakova: Introduction to A. N. Verstovsky: *Askol'dova mogila* (Leningrad, 1983) [vocal score]

RICHARD TARUSKIN

Vert (y Carbonell), Juan (*b* Onteniente, Valencia, 22 April 1890; *d* Madrid, 16 Feb 1931). Spanish composer. He received his initial musical education from his father and from Enrique Casanova, the local organist and municipal bandmaster, and then studied harmony and composition at the Valencia Conservatory before completing his musical education at the Madrid Conservatory. He began writing zarzuelas, and finally achieved real success in his many collaborations with Reveriano Soutullo, especially three zarzuela classics, *La leyenda del beso* (1924), *La del soto del parral* (1927) and *El último romántico* (1928).

zarzuelas, first performed in Madrid; selective list

Las virgenes paganas (1, E. García Alvarez and F. Garzo), Zarzuela, May 1915; El Versalles madrileño (García Alvarez and Muñoz Seca); El capricho de una reina (2, A. Paso *hijo* and J. Vidal), Apolo, 13 May 1919, collab. R. Soutullo; Justicias y ladrones (S. Delgado), Apolo, 1919/20, collab. Soutullo; Guitarras y bandurrias (Paso and F. García Pacheco), Centro, 1920, collab. Soutullo; La esnigotina (2, Paso and García Pacheco), Apolo, 30 Dec 1921, collab. Soutullo; La leyenda del beso (2, E. Reoyo, Paso and S. Aramburu), Apolo, 18 Jan 1924, collab. Soutullo; Encarna, la misterio (2, F. Luque and Calonge), Apolo, 8 May 1925, collab. Soutullo; La del soto del Parral (2, A. Carreño and L. Fernández Ardavín), Latina, 26 Oct 1927, collab. Soutullo; El último romántico (2, J. Tellaeche), Apolo, 9 Mar 1928, collab. Soutullo; about 30 other zarzuelas

*

A. Fernández-Cid: *Cien años de teatro musical en España (1875–1975)* (Madrid, 1975)
J. Arnau and C. M. Gomez: *Historía de la zarzuela* (Madrid, 1979)
R. Alier and others: *El libro de la zarzuela* (Barcelona, 1982, 2/1986 as *Diccionario de la zarzuela*)

ANDREW LAMB

Verurteilung des Lukullus, Die ('The Trial of Lucullus'). Opera in 12 scenes by PAUL DESSAU to a libretto by BERTOLT BRECHT from his radio play *Das Verhör des Lukullus*; Berlin, Deutsche Staatsoper, 12 October 1951.

Brecht suggested that Dessau might set his radio play (written shortly before the outbreak of World War II) as a libretto in the mid-1940s, during their exile in the USA, but the composer did not begin work on it until 1948, after his return to Berlin. Presenting a staged version of the radio play meant that changes were necessary, and there were also to be topical references to the collapse of the Nazi regime and, in the parable, to the Nuremberg war trials. Set in the kingdom of the dead, the opera concerns Lukullus [Lucullus] (tenor), a Roman general and epicure, whose destiny is being decided by a *Schattengericht* ('shadow court'). Characters from his life testify to his military actions, which caused the death of thousands of soldiers, though set against this are his culinary achievements: bringing back a variety of cherry tree from Asia and introducing a new method of cooking. In the radio play judgment is left to the audience but in the opera Lucullus is damned ('Ins Nichts mit ihm').

At the time of the proposed 1950 première the Cold War was at its height, and the work became the focus of the Stalinist debates on formalism instigated by Zhdanov. It became a political affair, and was criticized for pacifism and artistic decadence (because of the function of the parable, the epic structure and the allegedly unpopular 'dissonant' music). After a 'trial performance' conducted by Scherchen on 17 March 1951 at the Deutsche Staatsoper, Berlin, when the work still bore the title of the radio play, some alterations were made as a result of discussions involving leading figures in the government. The purpose of the changes was chiefly to distinguish (by means of additions to the text) between wars of aggression and wars of defence. The course of the drama itself and the musical style were not affected. The title was changed to *Die Verurteilung des Lukullus* at its official première later that year, but the work was still regarded as suspect and did not receive many performances; its time came only after the period of political thaw in the mid-1950s, and after its 1957 revival in Leipzig it was produced many times in both East and West Germany. The music seeks to avoid what Brecht attacked as the 'culinary' operatic style and follows his recommendation to reduce orchestral forces, also avoiding such expressive instruments as violins (which Brecht disliked), oboes, clarinets and horns. Instead of an unending flow of music in the Wagnerian manner it employs techniques of dovetailing, a structure of contrasts and division into sections; the basic principle is that of the number opera. In the characterization and the relationship between words and music Dessau follows Brecht's principles in emphasizing the display of 'social gesture', and in offering a commentary by means of dialectical contrast (*Verfremdung*, or the 'alienation effect').

FRITZ HENNENBERG

Verwandelten Weiber, Die [*Die verwandelten Weiber, oder Der Teufel ist los, erster Theil* ('The Metamorphosed Wives, or The Devil to Pay, Part 1')]. *Comische Oper* in three acts by JOHANN ADAM HILLER to a libretto by CHRISTIAN FELIX WEISSE, based on Charles Coffey's ballad opera *The Devil to Pay, or The Wives Metamorphos'd* (1728) and MICHEL-JEAN SEDAINE's *opéra comique* from the same source; Leipzig, Theatre in Quandt's Court, 28 May 1766.

The gruff cobbler Jobsen Zeckel lords it over his long-suffering wife Lene, while in the manor Frau von Liebreich plagues her husband and servants. The itinerant magician Mikroskop, out of pity for Lene, transforms each wife into the other. After a violent collision of wills, Jobsen and 'Lene' (Frau von Liebreich) repent and Mikroskop undoes the spell.

Hiller's first operatic triumph at Leipzig, composed as a favour to the theatre principal Heinrich Gottfried Koch, adapted the most popular German musical farce of the mid-century, *Der Teufel ist los*, set by Johann Standfuss; he retained some of Standfuss's tunes, but his own music assured the popularity of the work for the rest of the century. Lene's 'Ohne Lieb und ohne Wein' (by Hiller) became a virtual folksong throughout Germany.

For illustration *see* LEIPZIG, fig.1. THOMAS BAUMAN

Verykivs'ky, Mykhaylo [Verikovsky, Mikhail Ivanovich] (*b* Kremenets, Ternopol', 8/20 or 9/21 Nov 1896; *d* Kiev, 14 June 1962). Ukrainian composer. He completed his studies at the Kiev Conservatory in 1923. He was conductor of the opera companies at Kiev (1926–8) and Kharkiv (1928–35) and director of the opera studio at the Kharkiv Music and Drama Institute (1934–5). He returned to Kiev, where in 1946 he was appointed professor at the conservatory. His *Pan Kanyovsky* (1930) was the first Ukrainian ballet.

Dila nebesni [Heavenly Things], 1934 (O. Vishin)
Sotnyk [The Cossack Lieutenant] (after T. G. Shevchenko), Odessa, 1939
Naymychka [The Hireling] (Verykivs'ky and K. Gerasimenko, after Shevchenko), Irkutsk, 1943, vs (Kiev, 1964)
Batrachka [The Farm Maid], 1935–40 (Gerasimenko and Verykivs'ky, after Shevchenko)
Viy (musical comedy, Verykivs'ky, after N. V. Gogol), 1946
Bayka prochortopolokha i rosu [The Fable of the Thistle and the Rose], 1948
Begletsï [Fugitives], 1948 (op-étude, M. Kotsyubinsky); as Utikachi, Kiev Radio, 1957
Slava [Glory], 1961

DETLEF GOJOWY

Veselohra na mostě ('The Comedy on the Bridge'). Radio opera in one act (six scenes) by BOHUSLAV MARTINŮ to his own libretto after Václav Kliment Klicpera's play; Prague, Czech Radio, 18 March 1937; staged in Ostrava, State Theatre, 9 January 1948.

Popelka *the village beauty*	soprano
Sykoš *a fisherman, her fiancé*	baritone
Bedroň *a brewer*	bass
Eva *his wife*	contralto
Schoolmaster	tenor
Friendly Sentry	spoken
Enemy Sentry	spoken
Friendly Officer	spoken

Setting A bridge across a river separating two opposing armies, in the first half of the 19th century

Martinů's two operas for radio, *Hlas lesa* ('The Voice of the Forest') and *The Comedy on the Bridge*, arose as a result of commissions from Czech Radio. By 1935 Czech Radio had made a number of studio broadcasts of opera, including Dvořák's *Šelma sedlák* ('The Cunning Peasant') in 1931, and was beginning to commission works designed for transmission. Martinů's first opera commission for radio was *The Voice of the Forest*, composed in April–May 1935 to a libretto by Vítězslav Nezval, and its success led to a second commission. Martinů discovered Klicpera's comedy during summer 1935, which he spent at his family home in Polička, and was attracted by the spatial separation implicit in the drama as a suitable device for radio. He completed work on the opera on 10 December 1935; the première, conducted by Otakar Jeremiáš, was given by Czech Radio 15 months later. The stage première of the work took place on 9 January 1948 at the State Theatre in Ostrava conducted by František Jílek. A staged English-language performance was given at the Mannes School in New York on 28 May 1951. This last was a great success, winning for Martinů the New York Critics' Award for opera of the year. Since then, the opera has proved extremely popular with professional, student and amateur companies alike, its success being further advanced by an effective orchestral suite arranged by the composer from the work.

The opera opens with a short orchestral introduction – the instrumental ensemble comprises single woodwind, piano, percussion and strings – parodying military marches and neo-classical in style.

SCENE 1 Popelka, coming from the battlefield, has a permit that allows her on to the bridge, past the enemy sentry, but she is refused entry to the side where her mother and fiancé live since she only has a pass away from the battlefield. Lamenting her fate, she makes to return to the other side but is prevented by the enemy sentry because her pass allows her away from the battlefield but not back to it. Thus she remains stuck on the bridge.

SCENE 2 Approaching from the friendly side, Bedroň is admitted on to the bridge with a pass but is caught in the same way as Popelka, not having a pass off the bridge to the other side or back. The unfortunate pair sing a duet at the end of which Bedroň, finding Popelka increasingly attractive, kisses her.

SCENE 3 The embrace is seen by Popelka's fiancé, Sykoš. Possessing a pass, he gains access to the bridge and, fearing the worst, accuses Popelka of playing fast and loose with both the enemy and the brewer. At last he calms down, only to find that he too is unable to leave the bridge.

SCENE 4 Bedroň's wife, Eva, appears and becomes trapped on the bridge in the now familiar manner. Sikoš tells her that Bedroň and Popelka were caught kissing. Eva accuses her husband of philandering and demands an explanation for his presence there. Bedroň maintains that his business is secret, which leads to further recriminations: Eva resolves to be rid of Bedroň and Sikoš to do likewise with Popelka.

SCENE 5 The schoolmaster appears, holding forth in Latin. Trapped along with his fellows, he tells them that he is trying to find the answer to a riddle, posed by an officer, which is driving him mad: how can a stag escape from a field surrounded by an impenetrable wall? The company attempts to solve the riddle but fails. The sound of battle begins again, and the little group experiences a change of heart: Eva and Bedroň forgive each other, and Popelka reveals to Sikoš that she went to the enemy side to find her brother, who she had heard had been killed in action. Bedroň reveals that he has passed a secret to their own side which will lead to victory over the enemy. As they all contemplate their fate and Sikoš tells Popelka that he once kissed another girl, the sounds from the battlefield increase in volume and intensity.

SCENE 6 A cry of 'Victory' is heard. A return to the music of the opening heralds the arrival of the friendly, victorious army. An officer congratulates Bedroň on his useful information and reveals to Popelka that her brother is still alive. Finally, the schoolmaster recognizes the officer who posed the riddle and asks him the answer. The answer is that the stag cannot escape; the company celebrates the victory, and a triumphal march concludes the work.

* * *

At a performance of the opera in New York in 1951 Martinů noted that the opera was 'Czech, in folk style, simple, informal'. While the musical style contains elements of neo-classicism, as do the ballet *Špalíček* and *Hry o Marii* ('The Plays of Mary'), it also shows Martinů's renewed interest in national traits. These may be seen in the use of balanced melodic phrases, as in the greeting to the Schoolmaster at the start of Scene 5, and in the occasional use of polka rhythm. Martinů's interest in theatrical experiment may be discerned in the freely flowing alternation of spoken and sung parts, and his love of parody in the instrumentation of the military march and the irreverent quotation of the Rákóczi march in Scene 3 when Sikoš sings of the delightful life of a girl who wanders from one regiment to another sampling the soliders. The success of the work is largely due to Martinů's brisk treatment of the text and effective comic timing. JAN SMACZNY

Vespasiano, Il ('Vespasian'). Drama in three acts by ATTILIO ARIOSTI to a libretto by NICOLA FRANCESCO HAYM, after GIULIO CESARE CORRADI's libretto; London, King's Theatre, 14 January 1724.

Tito [Titus] (mezzo-soprano) spends the opera avoiding his faithful wife Arricida [Arrecina] (soprano) so that he can dally with his new sweetheart Gesilla (alto). Meanwhile, his villainous brother Domiziano [Domitian] (soprano) is attempting to usurp the imperial throne from their father Vespasian (bass) and obtain Arrecina for himself. Sergio (alto), a Roman general, foils the villain in Acts 1 and 3, and his surprising circumventions of Domitian's wicked designs, together with attempted and onstage murders, provide an extraordinarily exciting stage spectacle, but the love intrigues suffer from total inertia.

Ariosti's arias (but not his recitatives) survive; a large portion of them are syllabically set dance-like tunes of a gentle, languishing, pre-classical character. They suit the infatuated Titus and Gesilla, but not Arrecina or the fierce Domitian, and the audience judged *Vespasiano* inferior to Ariosti's two previous London operas, *Tito Manlio* (1717) and *Coriolano* (1723), which exhibit far greater rhythmic drive. Burney nevertheless discussed *Vespasiano* as his example of Ariosti's style. He printed Titus's 'Ah traditore spirar vorrei' as 'an exhibition of all the furbelows, flounces and vocal fopperies of the time', but it is far from typical of the opera as a whole. The published aria collection and libretto of 1724 have been reprinted (IOB, xxvi and lx). LOWELL LINDGREN

Vesque von Püttlingen, Johann (*b* Opole, Poland, 23 July 1803; *d* Vienna, 30 Oct 1883). Austrian composer. He studied law and worked in the civil service from 1827 to 1872. His music teachers included Sechter and Moscheles. In Vienna his house was a focal point of cultural activity, and he did much to further the musical life of the city as an artist and patron and through his active interest in the building of the conservatory and his support of the Gesellschaft der Musikfreunde.

Vesque's works were published under the pseudonym J. Hoven. He belonged to the generation between Schubert and Loewe, and Mendelssohn and Schumann, and had personal connections with all of these. His operas, both serious and comic, met with limited success; their characterization is weak and their expression inconsistent. But among Austrian song composers he was perhaps the most significant in the period between Schubert and Wolf.

La donna del lago (after W. Scott), Vienna, 1830, private perf.
Turandot, Prinzessin von Schiras (2, J. Zerboni, after F. von Schiller's trans. of C. Gozzi), Vienna, Kärntnertor, 3 Oct 1838, vs (Mainz, n.d.)
Johanna d'Arc (3, O. Prechtler, after Schiller), Vienna, Kärntnertor, 30 Dec 1840, vs (Vienna, 1840)
Liebeszauber (4, Prechtler, after H. von Kleist), Vienna, Kärntnertor, 8 March 1845, vs (Mainz, n.d.)
Burg Thaya, *c*1844–5 (3, A. von Perger), inc.
Ein Abenteuer Carl des Zweiten (komische Oper, 1, S. H. Mosenthal), Vienna, Kärntnertor, 12 Jan 1850, vs (Leipzig, *c*1850)
Der lustige Rath (komische Oper, 2, Mosenthal), Weimar, Hof, 12 April 1852
Lips Tullian, oder Die Ente (komische Oper, 1, Mosenthal), Weimar, Hof, Dec 1855

*

StiegerO
E. Hanslick: *Musikalisches Skizzenbuch* (Berlin, 1888)
H. Schultz: *Johann Vesque von Püttlingen* (Regensburg, 1931)
H. Ibl: *Studien zu Johann Vesque von Püttlingens Leben und Opernschaffen* (diss., U. of Vienna, 1950) REINHOLD SIETZ/R

Vestale, La (i) ('The Vestal Virgin'). *Tragédie lyrique* in three acts by GASPARE SPONTINI to a libretto by ETIENNE DE JOUY; Paris, Opéra, 15 December 1807.

Jouy was unable to interest any of the famous composers (Méhul, Boieldieu or Cherubini) in his libretto, and in 1804 he offered it to Spontini, who had just made his mark in Paris with his first *opéras*

'La vestale' (Spontini), Act 3, finale: Alexandrine Branchu as Julia, the role she created at the Paris Opéra, 15 December 1807

Licinius *a Roman general*	tenor
Cinna *commander of the legion*	tenor
The Pontifex Maximus	bass
The Chief Soothsayer	bass
A Consul	bass
Julia *a young Vestal virgin*	soprano
The High Priestess	mezzo-soprano

Vestal virgins, priests, matrons, young women, senators, consuls, lictors, warriors, gladiators, children, prisoners

Setting Ancient Rome

comiques. Jouy quoted as his source only an account given by J. J. Winckelmann of an event in the year 269 BC. But the plot agrees in significant details with an anonymous pantomime of 1786, *Julia, ou La vestale*, adapted from Jean-Gaspard Dubois-Fontanelle's verse tragedy *Ericie, ou La vestale* (1767). This was the origin of a remarkably concentrated *tragédie lyrique*, with no subplots at all, looking back to the era of Gluck in many external details, but bearing the mark of entirely new dramatic principles.

The opera, mostly composed in 1805 but repeatedly revised, was performed only after the intervention of the Empress Josephine. However, it turned out to be not only the most successful work of Spontini's unsteady career but also the one serious French opera to achieve lasting and international fame between 1789 and 1826. The first performance, with Etienne Lainez (Licinius), François Lays (Cinna), Henri-Etienne Dérivis (the Pontifex Maximus), Alexandrine Caroline Branchu (Julia) and Marie-Thérèse Davoux Maillard (the High Priestess) was a great success; the work had its 100th performance at the Opéra in 1816 and its 200th in 1830. In the years that followed, it was performed in most foreign opera houses (the Neapolitan première, with Colbran as Julia, was particularly noteworthy) before interest in it waned after 1850. *La vestale* has occasionally been revived in the 20th century, notably for Ponselle (at the Metropolitan in 1925 and at the Florence Festival of 1933) and for Callas at La Scala (1955). Gencer (1969, Palermo), Caballé (1982, Barcelona) and Kabaivanska (1984, Genoa) have also sung the title role.

ACT 1 The victorious general Licinius talks to Cinna, commander of his legions, confessing that he dreads his triumph in the Roman Forum, for among the Vestal virgins he will see his former betrothed, Julia, whom he still loves. Julia herself has never been able to forget Licinius, and after the *Hymne du matin* sung by the Vestal virgins she is warned by the High Priestess of the dangers of love, but finds herself hopelessly torn between love and duty. Julia is the Vestal chosen to crown Licinius with laurels after the triumphal procession. He makes use of this moment, which occurs in a succession of marches and dances, to tell Julia of his plan to abduct her that night, when she will be keeping watch alone on the sacred flame in the Temple of Vesta.

ACT 2 After a *Hymne du soir* Julia is left alone with her fears. Licinius arrives, and in her joy Julia does not notice the flame in the temple go out. At her insistence, Licinius is just in time to flee from the crowds demanding vengeance for this sacrilege. Julia, refusing to name the intruder, is condemned to death by the Pontifex Maximus.

ACT 3 In desperation, Licinius devises a bold ruse to save Julia. Cinna assures him that he is ready to fight at his side, but persuades him to ask the Pontifex Maximus for mercy first. The pontiff, however, remains inflexible. Julia is led to the place of execution in a procession. Deeply moved, she bids the Vestal virgins farewell, and devotes her last thoughts to Licinius, who now confesses his guilt. But Julia claims not to know him, and allows herself to be buried alive. At this point a thunderstorm darkens the stage and a flash of lightning rekindles the Vestal flame. All interpret this event as a sign of divine grace, Julia and Licinius are happily united, and their union is celebrated with choruses and dances.

* * *

The symmetry of the three-act construction, concentrated into a neo-classical simplicity, allowed Spontini to create a build-up in each act, from intimate solo scenes to the monumental final *tableaux*. The contrasts in the second act, described by Berlioz as a single *crescendo gigantesque* are particularly impressive. The cantilenas of Julia's first aria ('Toi que j'implore avec effroi') are expressive enough, but are exceeded in intensity by her dramatic second aria, the march-like refrain of the love duet, Julia's prayer, and finally the powerful death sentence pronounced by the Pontifex Maximus.

Elsewhere too the dynamics of the musical drama as it moves towards its triumphant close are reinforced by effective contrasts. In the first act, the lovers' confessions are interrupted by the High Priestess's aria 'L'amour est un monstre barbare', and in the third act the duet 'Adieu, mes tendres soeurs', a scene of touching intimacy, comes immediately after a chorus in the form of a funeral march, its gloomy character emphasized by trombones and drums playing *pianissimo*. The complete avoidance of any picturesque representation of the storm which acts as *deus ex machina* in the finale of the third act, however, shows that Spontini was not concerned simply with tone-painting, even when using features such as choral hymns and instrumental effects typical of the kind found in the works of Méhul and Le Sueur. Instead, the subtle psychological depiction of the characters is dominant, and a variety of musical forms are used in this characterization. There are several extremely concise numbers in Gluck's manner, side by side with longer *récitatifs obligés* written in arioso style, and a preghiera by Julia in the second finale ('O des infortunées, déesse tutélaire'), with a soaring melodic line over an extremely sparse accompaniment which anticipates Italian opera of the 1830s. However, Spontini preserved the conventions of the *ancien régime* not only in several unadorned recitatives but especially in the *lieto fine* (happy ending) and the extensive *divertissements* at the ends of the first and third acts, and, although after long revision of the last finale he managed to convey serenity in the final chorus, it lacks the dramatic intensity of the two other closing *tableaux*.

ANSELM GERHARD

Vestale, La **(ii)** ('The Vestal Virgin'). *Tragedia lirica* in three acts by SAVERIO MERCADANTE to a libretto by SALVADORE CAMMARANO; Naples, Teatro S Carlo, 10 March 1840.

This is one of Mercadante's most consistently interesting works, and has been regarded by some as his masterpiece. The story is much as in Spontini's opera, but Cammarano was able to ignore the happy ending forced on Jouy by French convention. A modern audience, however, will probably be reminded more of Verdi's *Aida* (1871) than Spontini's *La vestale*.

The opera opens in the Sacred Grove, where the Chief Vestal (soprano) announces the return of Decio [Decius] (tenor), a military hero formerly believed to have been killed in the Gallic wars. Among the Vestal virgins is Emilia (Spontini's Julia, mezzo-soprano), who was in love with Decius but became a Vestal on hearing of his death; his unexpected reappearance throws her into a torment of emotion, which turns to agony when, in a triumph scene of Verdian splendour, it is she who has to crown him as victor. In Act 2 Emilia is entrusted by the Chief Vestal with the guardianship of the sacred flame, but Decius has concealed himself in the temple and, during the passionate love duet which follows, the flame is allowed to go out. Decius escapes, but Emilia is left to face the wrath of the High Priest (bass). The last act concerns Emilia's trial. While the women of the populace plead for mercy, the priests, in chorus, call inexorably for her execution: she is led in, there is a brief, affecting mad scene and she is buried alive. Decius, who has raised a revolt in an attempt to save her, arrives too late and kills himself on her tomb. (It is characteristic of Mercadante's attitude to the drama throughout this work that, after stabbing himself, Decius is allowed only eight bars of a final aria before breaking off and dying in a few fragments of recitative.)

The parallels with *Aida* are evident: the triumph scene with the crowning of the returned hero, the role of the priests in the last act, the entombment alive of the chief character. There are musical echoes too, and even one literal quotation: the Chief Vestal's 'Decio ritorna, de' Galli vincitor', to a rising phrase virtually identical, even in key, to the famous 'Ritorna vincitor!' of Amneris (and Aida) in the first act of Verdi's opera. There is no question here of plagiarism, but it is certainly relevant that Verdi attended one of the first performances of *La vestale* at Genoa in 1841 and was living and working in Milan when it achieved a resounding success at La Scala that autumn.

MICHAEL ROSE

Vestris [née Bartolozzi], **Lucia Elizabeth** [Eliza Lucy] (*b* London, 3 Jan or 2 March 1797; *d* London, 8 Aug 1856). English contralto, actress and theatre manager of Italian descent. From 1813 to 1817 she was married to the French dancer Auguste-Armand Vestris (1788–1825), ballet-master at the King's Theatre, where she made her début (20 July 1815) in the title role of Winter's *Il ratto di Proserpina*; this was highly successful although her acting and singing abilities were limited. Further appearances in 1816 met with less success, her faults becoming more apparent with familiarity. That winter she appeared in Paris at the Théâtre Italien and various other theatres, including the Théâtre Français, where she played Camille in *Les Horaces*. On returning to London, she made her début at Drury Lane Theatre on 19 February 1820. Her success was immediate, and she remained an extraordinary favourite in opera, musical farces and comedies until her retirement in 1854. At the King's Theatre she sang in the English premières of many Rossini operas: *La gazza ladra* (as Pippo, 1821), *La donna del lago* (as Malcolm Graeme, 1823), *Ricciardo e Zoraide* (as Zomira, 1823), *Matilde di Shabran* (as Edoardo, 1823), *Zelmira* (as Emma, 1824) and *Semiramide* (as Arsace, 1824). She sang there again in 1825, and in 1826 created the role of Fatima in *Oberon* at Covent Garden (see illustration). She also appeared in Dublin (1824–47), but after 1830 she was more important as a theatre manager, leasing the Olympic (1831–8), Covent Garden (1839–42) and the Lyceum

Lucia Elizabeth Vestris as Fatima in Weber's 'Oberon', a role she created at Covent Garden, London (12 April 1826): hand-coloured lithograph

(1847–55); at Covent Garden she occasionally mounted fine opera productions in English. She was influential in developing the more naturalistic style of the 1860s and 70s. But Chorley (1862), among others, never quite forgave her for not becoming the greatest English operatic contralto of her age:

If she had possessed musical patience and energy, she might have queened it, because she possessed (half Italian by birth) one of the most luscious of low voices ... great personal beauty, an almost faultless figure, which she adorned with consummate art, and no common stage address. But a less arduous career pleased her better; and so she could not – or perhaps would not – remain on the Italian stage.

*

DNB (J. Knight)
H. F. Chorley: Obituary, *The Athenaeum* (17 Aug 1856)
——: *Thirty Years' Musical Recollections* (London, 1862, abridged E. Newman, 2/1926), 155
J. R. Planché: *Recollections and Reflections* (London, 1872)
C. E. Pearce: *Madame Vestris and her Times* (London, c1923)
L. Waitzkin: *The Witch of Wych Street: a Study of the Reforms of Madame Vestris* (diss., Harvard U., 1933)
W. W. Appleton: *Madame Vestris and the London Stage* (New York and London, 1974)

Vētra, Mariss (*b* Tirza, Gulbene, 19 July 1901; *d* Toronto, 24 Dec 1965). Latvian tenor. He studied in Riga, making his début in 1922 at Liepāja as Faust. In 1923 he sang Cavaradossi with the Latvian National Opera, Riga, then went to Italy for further study. On returning to Riga in 1926, he sang the Duke, Werther, and Giosta in Zandonai's *I cavalieri di Ekebù*. He created Laimons in Jāzeps Mediņš's *Vaidelote* ('The Priestess') in 1927 and Edgars in Jānis Kalniņš's *Ugunī* ('In the Fire') in 1937. He also appeared in Germany and Russia. His repertory included Lohengrin, Tannhäuser, Parsifal, Riccardo, Manrico, Radames, Otello, Don José, Pedro (*Tiefland*) and the title role of Kalniņš's *Hamlets*. His voice was strong and rich-toned; his characterizations combined psychological insight with dramatic power. In 1946 he went to live in Halifax, where he taught and, in 1949, founded the Nova Scotia Opera Association.

ELIZABETH FORBES, ARNOLDS KLOTIŅŠ

Veysberg [Weissberg, Rimskaya-Korsakova], **Yuliya Lazarevna** (*b* Orenburg, 25 Dec/6 Jan 1880; *d* Leningrad [now St Petersburg], 1 or 4 March 1942). Russian composer. From 1903 to 1905, when she was sent down for participating in a strike, she studied at the St Petersburg Conservatory with Rimsky-Korsakov and Glazunov. She was a pupil of Humperdinck and Reger in Germany (1907–12), and took an external examination in St Petersburg in 1912. Thereafter she worked on the editorial board of the periodical *Muzïkal'nïy sovremennik* ('The Musical Contemporary', 1915–17) and as choral director at the Young Workers' Conservatory (1921–3). Her translation of the musical writings of Rolland was published in Moscow in 1938. She was married to Rimsky-Korsakov's son, Andrey Nikolayevich.

Rusalochka [The Little Mermaid] (S. Parnok, after H. C. Andersen), 1923
Gyul'nara (Veysberg and Parnok), 1935, excerpts pubd
Zaykin dom [A Little Rabbit's House] (children's op, W. Weltmann), Moscow, 1937 (Moscow, 1938)
Gusi-lebedi [Geese-Swans] (children's op, Veysberg and S. Marshak), Moscow, 1937 (Moscow, 1938)
Myortvaya tsarevna [The Dead Princess] (radio op, after A. S. Pushkin), broadcast, 1938

DETLEF GOJOWY

Vézina, Joseph (*b* Québec City, 9 June 1849; *d* Québec City, 5 Oct 1924). Canadian composer. Except for instrumental lessons with his father François Vézina and six months of studies in harmony with Calixa Lavallée, Vézina was self-taught in music. However, in the course of his career he played and taught most wind instruments and became one of the leading musical figures in Québec City and the surrounding area, as a bandmaster, organist, teacher and conductor (he founded the Société Symphonique de Québec, later the Québec SO). He was involved in the establishment of the School of Music at Laval University in 1922 and taught harmony there until 1924; he was awarded an honorary DMus in 1922.

Vézina composed numerous marches and light concert pieces for the ensembles he conducted, and he also wrote for orchestra, voice and piano. His three complete operas were first performed by the Société Symphonique de Québec with soloists and a choir from Laval University. The plots of *Le lauréat* and *Le fétiche* are set in Canada. Godfrey Ridout used several tunes from Vézina's operas in his orchestral suite *Frivolités canadiennes*.

Le lauréat (oc, F.-G. Marchand), 1906
Le Rajah (opéra bouffe, B. Michaud), 1910
Le fétiche (oc, A. Plante and A. Langlais), 1912
La grosse gerbe (oc), inc.

RUTH PINCOE

Vezzani, Cesare (*b* Bastia, Corsica, 8 Aug 1886; *d* Marseilles, 11 Nov 1951). Corsican tenor. Brought up in Toulon, he studied in Paris and made his début at the Opéra-Comique in the title role of Grétry's *Richard Coeur-de-lion* (1911); his voice impressed more favourably than his artistry. He appeared with the company in *Dinorah*, Erlanger's *La sorcière*, *Manon* and *Carmen*. A disagreement with the management arose in 1914, after which his career was largely confined to the provinces, though he also sang in Brussels, Switzerland and Algiers and continued as principal tenor at Toulon until 1948. He seems to have been one of those whose gifts exceeded his attainments, for recordings (which include a complete *Faust*) show an exceptional voice, heroic and ringing in quality, admirably suited to such operas as Reyer's *Sigurd* and Meyerbeer's *L'Africaine* and *Le prophète*.

J. B. STEANE

Viaggiatori felici, I ('The Happy Travellers'). *Dramma giocoso* in two acts by PASQUALE ANFOSSI to a libretto by FILIPPO LIVIGNI; Venice, Teatro S Samuele, autumn 1780.

Giannetto (tenor) and Bettina (soprano) have eloped to an inn in Milan, where they are in desperate need of money. They disguise themselves as a French couple to avoid detection. Giannetto's father Pancrazio (bass) had arranged for him to marry Donna Isabella (soprano), an agreement which Giannetto has now broken. The stiff and haughty Spaniard Don Gastone (baritone) is also a guest at the inn; he has been jilted by Donna Isabella but is not too grief-stricken to turn his attentions to Bettina. The innkeeper Lauretta (soprano) and the servant Pasquino (bass) complete the cast. Pancrazio and Donna Isabella arrive at the inn looking for Giannetto; the plot is finally resolved by Giannetto's clever use of notaries and documents which everyone but Bettina misinterprets. The plot is a slender series of excuses for a number of comic episodes; one of these, in Act 2, involves a comparison of French and Italian music, with references to Le Gros and a quotation from Metastasio. One of Anfossi's liveliest and most varied comic works, it was also one of his most successful, receiving almost 40 productions up to the early 1790s. MARY HUNTER

Viaggio a Reims, Il [*Il viaggio a Reims, ossia L'albergo del giglio d'oro* ('The Journey to Reims, or The Hotel of the Golden Lily')]. *Dramma giocoso* in one act by GIOACHINO ROSSINI to a libretto by Luigi Balocchi derived in part from Mme de Staël's novel *Corinne, ou L'Italie*; Paris, Théâtre Italien, 19 June 1825.

Prepared as an entertainment for the coronation of Charles X, this *cantata scenica* is one of Rossini's most elaborate and most consistently inspired compositions, though its status as a *pièce de circonstance*, parts of which he later used in *Le comte Ory*, makes it an unlikely candidate for a place in the traditional operatic repertory. It is, however, a repository of some of Rossini's most brilliant vocal writing, while the musical structures take the ensemble writing of the later Neapolitan operas to new levels of length and sophistication, notably the sextet and the 'Gran pezzo concertato a 14 voci', which appears in *Le comte Ory* only in radically slimmed-down form.

The work's subtitle refers to the hotel at Plombières where the resident staff, marshalled by Madama Cortese (soprano), are preparing their international clientèle for a journey to the coronation at Reims. The principal guest is Corinna (soprano), a celebrated Roman improvising poetess (*improvisatrice*). In her entourage there is an orphaned Greek girl, symbol of Corinna's philhellenic sympathies at a time of crisis in the cause of Greek Independence, and representative of the libretto's preoccupation with the ideal of pan-European harmony in the post-Napoleonic period. Other followers of Corinna include a lover of antiquities, Don Profondo (bass), and the English colonel, Lord Sidney (bass), whose tribute to the poetess is a fine *opera seria* number with dazzling flute obbligato. The fashion-crazy Contessa di Foleville (soprano), a widow despite her years, is much admired by the gallant young French officer, the Cavalier Belfiore (tenor). Another eligible widow is the Marchesa Melibea (contralto): the Polish widow of an Italian general, she is admired both by the jealous Russian Conte di Libenskof (tenor) and the Spanish naval officer Don Alvaro (bass). The various antagonisms between the characters help energize Balocchi's plot, though when international solidarity is called for these are to some extent subjugated, as in the massive sextet, a number launched by the German Barone di Trombonok (bass), a retired major of no party who is a passionate proponent of harmony in all its forms, musical and political.

The first part of the entertainment is in eight movements. In the extended finale a spectacular evening of dance and song is announced for the residents before their departure for more festivities in Paris. There is a ballet in a lavish garden setting and toasts in the form of national songs provided by the principal guests. The entertainment is crowned by the reappearance of Corinna for a second, richly elaborated improvisation, 'All'ombre amena', before the final spectacular tableau in honour of the French royal family.

RICHARD OSBORNE

Vianesi, Auguste Charles Léonard François (*b* Legnano, 2 Nov 1837; *d* New York, 4 Nov 1908). Italian conductor, later naturalized French. He went to Paris in 1857 for further musical training with a letter of introduction to Rossini from Giuditta Pasta. Following engagements at Drury Lane, London, in 1858–9 he travelled to New York and later conducted regularly at the Imperial Theatre, Moscow, and at St Petersburg. He returned to London in 1870 and for ten years conducted at Covent Garden, directing the first London performances of *Lohengrin* (1875) and *Tannhäuser* (1876). Klein commented on the latter that 'Vianesi ... knew little or nothing of Wagner's intentions as to the reading of the score ... It satisfied curiosity without affording a true idea of the opera'. Vianesi also directed works from the Italian and French repertories, including Cherubini's *Médée* and Meyerbeer's *L'Africaine*.

On 22 October 1883 Vianesi conducted the opening night of the first season of the Metropolitan Opera, New York, returning there in 1891–2. In July 1887 he succeeded Ernest-Eugène Altès as chief conductor of the Paris Opéra, where he commanded a broad repertory and directed the first performances of Saint-Saëns' *Ascanio* (1890) and Massenet's *Le mage* (1891). A manuscript score (probably autograph) of a three-act opera by Vianesi, *Una fortuna in prigione*, signed London, 20 October 1858, was listed in Liepmannssohn's catalogue 185, no.1236.

*

H. Klein: *The Golden Age of Opera* (London, 1933)
H. Rosenthal: *Two Centuries of Opera at Covent Garden* (London, 1958)
W. Brockway and H. Weinstock: *The World of Opera* (New York, 1962)
S. Wolff: *L'Opéra au Palais Garnier (1875–1962)* (Paris, 1962)
F. Patureau: *Le Palais Garnier dans la société parisienne 1875–1914* (Liège, 1991)

DAVID CHARLTON

Viardot [née García], **(Michelle Ferdinande) Pauline** (*b* Paris, 18 July 1821; *d* Paris, 18 May 1910). French mezzo-soprano, composer and teacher, of Spanish origin; daughter of the elder Manuel García and sister of Maria Malibran. Although her father died when she was 11, she absorbed much of his teaching. She studied the piano with Meysenberg and Liszt and composition with Reicha. She made her stage début as Rossini's Desdemona in London (9 May 1839) and repeated the role in Paris (8 October 1839). Her musical and dramatic gifts were immediately acclaimed, particularly by intellectuals, to whom she was always to appeal more than to the general public. In 1840 she married the writer Louis Viardot; their house became a centre for writers, musicians and artists. In 1843 she first visited Russia, where she sang the Italian repertory, and Russian music (Glinka, Dargomïzhsky) in Russian – the first foreigner to do so. From then on she became one of the principal channels through which Russian music reached the West.

In 1849 she appeared with immense success at the Paris Opéra as Fidès in *Le prophète*, which was specially written for her. Her performance provoked Berlioz to write: 'Madame Viardot is one of the greatest artists ... in the ... history of music'. The summit of her career was in Paris in 1859, when she sang the title role in Berlioz's edition of Gluck's *Orfeo*; all who witnessed those performances (some 150 in three years) agreed that in them she reached tragic heights rarely seen on the stage. They marked the virtual end of her stage career, although she appeared later in *Alceste* and *Fidelio*, in oratorio and in concerts. In 1863 she went to live in Baden-Baden; she sang there and at Jena and Weimar until 1870, when she visited London. She returned in 1871 to Paris, where she continued to compose and teach.

Pauline Viardot helped to launch Gounod (*Sapho*), Massenet (*Marie-Magdeleine*) and Fauré in their careers. She gave the first performance of several extracts from *Les Troyens*, and a private hearing in Paris of Act 2 of *Tristan* (1860). Her voice, a mezzo-soprano artificially extended when young into the soprano register, and later into the contralto register, was not faultless; but she concealed its defects with great artistry. She never had the operatic success of her sister in the Italian repertory, and she never sang in Italy. But in highly dramatic parts, in the works of Meyerbeer, Halévy (*La Juive*) and Gluck, she had no equal. Her intellectual approach to her art and her artistic integrity did much to raise the status of singers.

Viardot's compositions included operettas, some to librettos by Turgenev (most notably *Le dernier sorcier* performed at Weimar in 1869). Among her pupils were Désirée Artôt, Aglaja Orgeni, Marianne Brandt and Antoinette Sterling. She published an *Ecole classique du chant* in Paris in 1861.

For illustration *see* ALBONI, MARIETTA.

*

F. Liszt: 'Pauline Viardot-Garcia', *NZM*, i (1859), 49–54

H. Berlioz: *A travers chants* (Paris, 1862; Eng. trans., 1913–18); ed. L. Guichard (Paris, 1971)

La Mara: *Pauline Viardot-Garcia* (Leipzig, 1883)

——: 'Pauline Viardot-Garcia', *Liszt und die Frauen* (Leipzig, 1911)

T. Baker, trans.: 'Pauline Viardot to Julius Rietz – Letters of Friendship', *MQ*, i (1915), 350–80, 526–59; ii (1916), 32–60

T. Marix-Spire: 'Gounod and his First Interpreter', *MQ*, xxxi (1945), 193–211, 299–317

T. Marix-Spire, ed.: *Lettres inédites de George Sand et de Pauline Viardot 1839–49* (Paris, 1959)

'Pis'ma Polinï Viardo k russkim znakomïm' [Pauline Viardot's Letters to Russian Friends], *SovM* (1960), no.8, pp.89–98

A. FitzLyon: *The Price of Genius: a Biography of Pauline Viardot* (London, 1964)

R. Olivier: 'Operettï Turgeneva', *Literaturnoye nasledstvo*, lxxiii/1 (1964), 62–224

A. Rozanov: *Polina Viardo-Garsia* (Leningrad, 1969, 2/1982)

A. FitzLyon: 'Pauline Viardot: 150th Anniversary Tribute', *Opera*, vii (1971), 582–8

APRIL FITZLYON

Vibrato (It., from Lat. *vibrare*: 'to shake'). A regular fluctuation of pitch and/or intensity, either more or less pronounced and either more or less rapid. The Italian term 'tremolo' is also used in connection with singing. The terminology used in vocal music is not constant (French terms include *flattement*, *flatté*, *balancement* and *balancé*; German ones *Tremolo*, *Trilletto*, *Bebung* and *Schwebung*); terminological uncertainties arise because vibrato is regarded not as a single ornament but rather as a complex of 'quivering' ornaments which might be modified in performance depending on the desired expression or the emotion to be aroused. Neither intensity nor tempo, therefore, can be clearly determined, and many Baroque or Classical kinds of vibrato are only distantly related to our present concept. 'Wobble', i.e. excessively pronounced or slow or irregular vibration of the singing voice, is not to be regarded as vibrato.

1. Before 1800. 2. Since 1800.

1. BEFORE 1800. Even in the early experiments with theatrical music and sung recitative, vibrato could be employed as a means of expression (see Doni 1633–5 and Della Valle). It is doubtful whether it was a regular component of singing technique. During the late Renaissance vibrato is occasionally mentioned as a vocal ornament, as something practical, if not absolutely essential, for instance when launching into coloratura (Zacconi 1592). Hence the expression 'ardire', sometimes used for bravura vibrato. However, monodic singing dissociated itself from this style very early, giving expressiveness precedence over a singer's dexterity and agility. The idea that vibrato easily becomes continuous – 'di natura tale, che usandolo, sempre usar si deve' (Zacconi, f.60*r*) – was not taken up again until a much later date, and should not be seen as applying to singers of early 17th-century dramatic music.

As in instrumental music, vibrato was very much a part of the soft, gentle, 'feminine' musical area and had no place in heroic or 'masculine' music. Rapid, wild vibrato, however, might also represent more violent emotions (such as agitation or anger; *see* STILE CONCITATO). Even here, however, it remained an ornament. There were certainly some singers who always used vibrato – building their amazing skill in coloratura on it, 'con applauso del volgo ignorante' (Doni) – but genuine recitative singers employed it only for ornamentation, sensibly enough, since constant vibrato is incapable of any intensification of expression.

Closely related to vibrato is the soft variety of the so-called Caccini *trillo* or *trilletto* in which there is no *coup de glotte* ('strike of the glottis') – the *trillo* itself has a *coup de glotte* and is thus not a vibrato but a staccato repetition. A different version of the trill or mordent is the *chevrotement* ('goat's trill'), against which many treatises on singing issue stern warnings ('il caprino fa ridere'). Many writers believe that the *chevrotement*, which arises from a poorly shaken, over-rapid trill, sets in with advancing age in the case of inferior or untrained singing voices. French singers were known and mocked throughout the rest of Europe for their tendency towards *chevrotement*. The nasal sounds of the French language do in fact encourage a particular kind of vibrato, still heard today in French popular singing. The 18th-century habit of using vibrato on every long note intensified this expressive device. The fact that many French singing teachers expressly warned against using vibrato on every beat is in itself an indication that such a practice existed.

The more dogmatic the music, the less vibrato was tolerated outside its own areas of expression. On the whole there seem to have been few problems with vibrato after the advent of the prima donna/primo uomo convention. Tosi's treatise on singing does not mention vibrato either as a substantial element in the production of sound or (explicitly) as an ornament. Like every good treatise on singing, it warns against 'wobble' (or 'flutt'ring'). Other treatises on vocal music describe vibrato as an ornament similar to that of instrumental music; that is to say, the starting-point is a tone production without vibrato.

It is impossible now to establish firmly whether vibrato-free production denotes a sound wholly without vibrato in the modern sense; statements that the singing voice differs from the speaking voice in that it contains an almost inaudible vibrato rather suggest that it does not. Dodart (1706) began by discussing the almost inaudible fluctuation of the voice, which he compares with the vibrato of viol and lute; however, he did not link this 'natural vibrato' to an observation elsewhere in his essay that the singing voice carries better than the speaking voice. Moreover, some treatises speak of a sound wholly without vibrato as an ornament (Bernhard, Montéclair), which would support the hypothesis that a well-trained Baroque voice normally had minimal vibrato. This would be comparable to unornamented instrumental sound, upon which an ornamental vibrato could be constructed. It is not however clear what a Baroque theorist considered inaudible. Looking at the 'artificial' instrumental vibratos of the period, the fluctuations of which are more or less determined – for instance, finger vibrato on woodwind instruments, two-finger vibrato on the viola da gamba, or the (gentle) tremulant or shaking stop (*tremblant doux*) of the organ – it is clear that fluctuations of amplitude in many ornamental vibratos are not very great and indeed tend to be small. It is accordingly logical to conclude that the natural vibrato of singers was also rather small.

Mozart provides support for this idea in a letter to his father of 12 June 1778 ('The human voice quivers of itself – but in such a way, and to such a degree, that it is beautiful – that is the nature of the voice ... As soon as you overdo it, it is not beautiful any more – because it is against nature'). Remarks from several German sources on natural vibrato in singers (the first are in a 1609 translation of Lodovico Viadana's *Cento concerti ecclesiastici*) refer not to opera singers but to a certain quality of sound in boys' voices. According to investigations, it is stated, about 5% of boys have a natural vibrato. It is not clear what artistic use was made of it – again it was described as small, 'with particular moderation'. It probably served only as a description of the voice or as a criterion for selecting a good one.

The associations of vibrato in this period are all concerned with feminine notions of softness and sweetness, and then proceed to sleep and death. The link with coloratura constructed on the rapidity of vibrato (still known today) – where vibrato, so to speak, serves as the entry to coloratura – is typical of singers. There are few early references to such a use of vibrato, and these date from the late 16th and early 17th centuries. If more violent emotions are to be expressed, they are often to do with fear or anguish (the fear of death, for instance) and, deriving from those ideas, with awe and trembling. In such cases the instrumental accompaniment is often marked by bowed vibrato or measured-breath vibrato, which may be indicated in several ways (see ex.1).

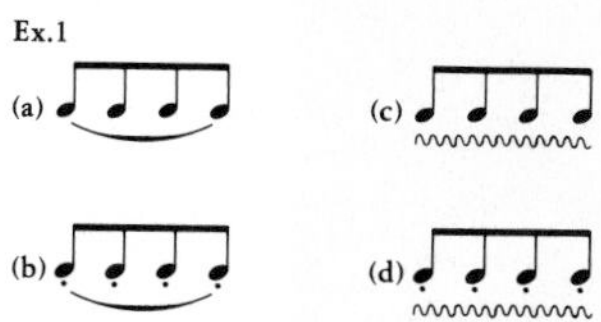

Examples of this practice in vocal music extend from the 17th century to the late 19th. There are famous examples, for instance, both vocal and instrumental, in the frost scene of Henry Purcell's *King Arthur* (1691), modelled on the 'Scène des trembleurs' from Lully's *Isis* (1677); but the figure is still used relatively frequently as late as Verdi, and very much in the traditional way, to express fear, quaking, trembling or awe (there is an example in *Rigoletto*, Act 1 scene iv; *andante sostenuto*). Technically, a measured vibrato is used; its periodicity follows the notation. The same applies to singing. There are special cases in both vocal and instrumental music; in ensemble music of the 17th and 18th centuries the figure often replaces individual vibrato and is thus a prescribed orchestral vibrato, its technique guaranteeing absolute regularity: string players apply it with the bow, wind players use a measured-breath vibrato. This is a very satisfactory solution, particularly for small instrumental groups. Such a vibrato, described in the 17th and 18th centuries as an imitation of the tremulant of the organ, is also found in operatic music. Occurrences are particularly frequent towards the end of the 18th century; there is a familiar example in the overture to Gluck's *Orfeo ed Euridice* (1762), and it appears in his *Alceste* (1767) in various gradations, from measured vibrato to staccato dots to be taken in a single bow. This imitation of the tremulant is used for dramatic effect in operatic writing.

While this and other kinds of orchestral vibrato were clearly on the increase towards the end of the 18th century, so that in some circumstances vibrato seems to be applied for the sake of the sound itself, orchestral vibrato was still used in a restricted manner in opera – only where appropriate, and not solely for its sound-quality. This use of instrumental vibrato for its dramatic significance was retained throughout the 19th century, and indeed increases in the Italian repertory from Bellini to the *verismo* operas. From the beginning of the 20th century it gradually disappeared from composition and performance, and it is discussed in treatises on instrumental playing only up to that period. Recently, probably under the influence of the revival of an early repertory, this imitation tremulant has sometimes been used in compositions referring back to early music (e.g. Philip Glass's *Einstein on the Beach*).

2. Since 1800. Vibrato was not a part of the singer's normal tone in the 19th century (see García 1847) but was still used as an ornament. As in earlier times, therefore, there are no treatises discussing vibrato as such. Vibrato was used less often in early Romantic opera than in the opera of the late 18th century. Only when orchestras became larger, and were thus better able to reinforce the strength of the singer's voice, did vibrato gradually and progressively establish itself. The way in which singing technique developed to cope with larger orchestras and concert halls resulted in more powerful singing, which in turn often produced a clearly audible and continuous vibrato. In several cases this development also led to uncontrolled wobble.

The new demands being made on singers, of whom less agility and virtuosity was required as the 19th century progressed, while parlando and clear enunciation of the libretto became more important, led to a new kind of dramatic art in singing (in the operas of Wagner and the late Verdi) which found worthy exponents in the great singers of the *verismo* operas. They too made increasing use of vibrato. Today, a singing tone without vibrato is used at most as an ornament, for special effect, or as a particular feature in the performance of early music.

This development continued into the 20th century. The agile singers of the old school generally used vibrato in a rather limited way, purely as ornament. It was also assumed that good singing technique and a well-trained voice ruled out uncontrolled or very pronounced vibrato. In the 19th century, therefore, people spoke of correct singing technique and not of continuous vibrato. Vibrato continued to be an ornament, and its use was not felt to present any problems. Continuous vibrato was neither discussed nor taught.

In the 20th century, as with a string player, a total lack of vibrato in a singer's voice came to be regarded as something special, an effect to be employed for the sake of character representation. Only when constant vibrato began to establish itself did treatises or 'tutors' of vibrato singing begin to appear. (The same phenomenon occurs in instrumental music; there are no treatises on the subject until the 20th century.) Not until then did 'incorrect' vibrato begin to be seen as a problem; earlier, it had simply been considered the result of a generally poor singing technique. Continuous vibrato is a 20th-century phenomenon, a fact that in itself indicates that the older ornament has lost its expressive power; since vibrato that always remains the same cannot suggest different passions, regular vibrato can only be an element of sound-production for its own sake. Accordingly, it becomes an important component of singing technique and indeed of voice training.

*

Grove5 ('Voice-Training'; F. Kelsey)
L. Zacconi: *Prattica di musica utile et necessaria si al compositore per comporre i canti suoi regolatamente, si anco al cantore per assicurarsi in tutte le cose cantabili* [i] (Venice, 1592)
G. Caccini: *Le nuove musiche* (Florence, 1601/2); ed. and Eng. trans. in RRMBE, ix (1970)
M. Praetorius: *Syntagma musicum*, iii (Wolfenbüttel, 1618, 2/1619)
G. B. Doni: *Trattato della musica scenica* (MS, 1633–5); ed. A. F. Gori: *De' trattati di musica di Gio. Batista Doni*, ii (Florence, 1763) [incl. P. della Valle: *Della musica dell'età nostra che non è punto inferiore, anzi è migliore di quella dell'età passata*, pp.249–65]
C. Bernhard: *Von der Singe-Kunst oder Maniera* (MS, 1648–64); ed. J. Müller-Blattau, in *Die Kompositionslehre Heinrich Schützens in der Fassung seines Schülers Christoph Bernhard* (Kassel, 1926, 2/1963)
D. Dodart: 'Supplément au Mémoire sur la voix et sur les tons', *Histoire et mémoires de l'Académie royale des sciences* (1706), 136–48
P. F. Tosi: *Opinioni de' cantori antichi, e moderni, o sieno Osservazioni sopra il canto figurato* (Bologna, 1723; Eng. trans. by J. E. Galliard, 1742, 2/1743 as *Observations on the Florid Song*)
M. Pignolet de Montéclair: *Principes de musique* (Paris, 1736)
M. P. R. García: *Ecole de Garcia: Traité complet de l'art du chant* (Paris, 2/1847; Eng. trans., enlarged, 1894)
C. Field-Hyde: *Vocal Vibrato, Tremolo and Judder* (New York, 1942)
A. Machabey: *Le bel canto* (Paris, 1948)
F. Husler and Y. Rodd-Marling: *Singing: the Physical Nature of the Vocal Organ, a Guide to the Unlocking of the Singing Voice* (London, 1965, 2/1975)
W. Vennard: *Singing: the Mechanism and the Technique* (New York, 2/1967)
R. Celletti: 'Il vocalismo italiano da Rossini a Donizetti', *AnMc*, no.6 (1968), 267–94; no.7 (1969), 214–47
L. Manén: *The Art of Singing: a Manual* (London, 1974, 3/1987 as *Belcanto: the Teaching of the Classical Italian Song-Schools, its Decline and Restoration*)
J. B. Steane: *The Grand Tradition: Seventy Years of Singing on Record* (London, 1974)
F. Neumann: *Ornamentation in Baroque and Post-Baroque Music with Special Emphasis on J. S. Bach* (Princeton, 1978)
G. Moens-Haenen: *Das Vibrato in der Musik des Barock: ein Handbuch zur Aufführungspraxis für Vokalisten und Instrumentalisten* (Graz, 1988)

GRETA MOENS-HAENEN

Vicenza. City in the Veneto, in northern Italy. The 16th and 17th centuries saw a number of dramatic and spectacular events with music, including performances of tragedies, pastoral dramas, and aristocratic tourneys and banquets, often in connection with the Accademia Olimpica and its celebrated theatre, the Teatro Olimpico, designed by Andrea Palladio and built between 1580 and 1585 by Vincenzo Scamozzi (see figs. 1 and 2). This was the site of the famous performance in 1585 of Sophocles' *Oedipus tyrannus* with choral music by Andrea Gabrieli (*see* PRODUCTION, fig.1); also worthy of mention are a tourney of 1612 with stage machinery and music, the *Intermedio delle forze d'Ercole* (April 1628) for Ferdinand II de' Medici, *La mensa degli dei alle dame di Vicenza* (1656, a strange banquet devised by P. P. Bissari) and the *intermedi* for *L'origine di Vicenza* by Lodovico Aleardi (1612) for the Accademici Inviati.

The first public opera house was the Teatro Castelli or Teatro delle Garzerie, built on the initiative of ordinary citizens and opened in 1656. Bissari provided texts for at least three operas, including *La Romilda* (1659), with music by the violinist Carlo Grossi, a native of Vicenza; later Alessandro Spinazzari, from Verona, was active as impresario and composed two operas for the theatre. The theatre (also called Teatro di Piazza) was destroyed by fire in 1683, rebuilt by local noblemen and reopened in 1689 with Domenico Freschi's *L'incoronazione di*

1. Interior of the Teatro Olimpico, Vicenza, designed by Andrea Palladio (1579) and built by Vincenzo Scamozzi (1580–85), who also designed the fixed stage scenery with diminishing diagonal perspectives seen in plan view in fig.2

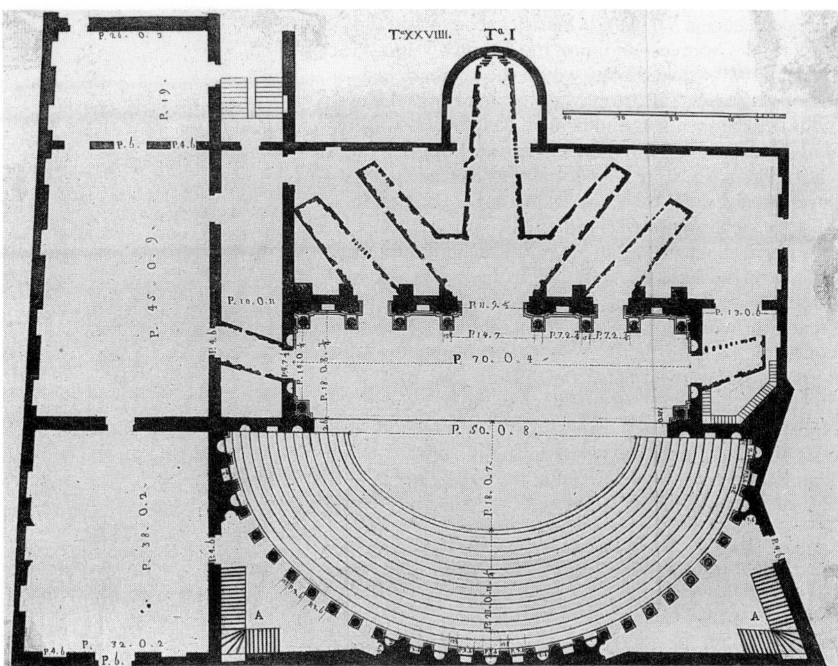

2. Plan view of the Teatro Olimpico, Vicenza, drawn and engraved by Antonio Mugnoni (1788)

Dario. It had important seasons in the early 18th century which included premières of C. F. Pollarolo's *La ninfa riconosciuta* (1709) and Vivaldi's *Ottone in Villa* (1713). The theatre was used until about 1779, with fluctuating fortunes but a successful repertory that included Galuppi, Scarlatti and Gassmann. In 1711 the Teatro delle Grazie was built, designed by Giuseppe Marchi and inaugurated in 1712 with Pollarolo's *Peribea in Salamina* and the intermezzo *Pimpinone* (some scholars believe that it opened in 1713 with his *La pazzia degli amanti* and *La violenza d'amore*). Its first 20 years of activity saw performances of works by Pollarolo, Vivaldi, Giovanni Porta, Galuppi and Albinoni, and many *opere buffe* by Paisiello, Anfossi and Astarita. The Teatro Eretenio, designed by Antonio Mauro at the order of a group of nobles, was inaugurated on 10 July 1784 with *Olimpiade* by Cimarosa, whose works, together with those of Paisiello, were frequently performed there until the end of the century. Between 1788 and 1821 the small Teatro Berico (later Teatro Garibaldi) successfully staged *opera buffa*, and continued in use until 1907.

In the first half of the 19th century the Teatro Eretenio offered full and varied seasons with works by Valentino Fioravanti, Mayr, Pavesi, Portugal and Nicolini, and later Rossini, Bellini, Donizetti and Verdi. It was closed for restoration, and also for political reasons, between 1847 and 1850 and between 1859 and 1866, and had few important seasons after that. From the end of the century a repertory of Mascagni, Ponchielli, Leoncavallo and Puccini dominated without much opposition and continued between the two world wars. The Teatro Diurno in Campo Marzio (1821–60), catering for a more popular audience, was replaced in 1861 by the Arena Pamato, which was renamed the Politeama Comunale in 1866 and Teatro Verdi in 1901 and was demolished in 1921. Local composers in the 19th century include Giuseppe Apolloni and the three Coronaro brothers. The new Teatro Verdi, inaugurated in 1923 with *Otello*, maintained a fair level of performance, with some productions by the La Scala company and singers such as Aureliano Pertile, Toti Dal Monte, Giacomo Lauri-Volpi and Beniamino Gigli. Like the Eretenio it was destroyed by bombing in 1944. Operatic activity in Vicenza has been kept alive by the Comitato Spettacoli of the Teatro Olimpico and more recently by the Vicenza Festival (June to September), which has presented operas by Monteverdi and Mozart and Italian 18th-century works, staged in the Palladian theatre.

F. D. Formenton: *Storia del Teatro Eretenio di Vicenza* (Vicenza, 1868)

S. Rumor: *Accademie in Vicenza* (Vicenza, 1892)

G. Mocenigo: *I teatri moderni di Vicenza dal 1650 al 1800, o dei due distrutti Teatri di Piazza e delle Grazie* (Bassano, 1894)

G. B. Crovato: *La drammatica a Vicenza nel cinquecento* (Turin, 1895)

G. Cogo: *Vita teatrale vicentina 1866–1922* (Vicenza, 1922)

——: *Nei teatri di Vicenza (storia, personaggi, curiosità, avvenimenti 1585–1948)* (Vicenza, 1949)

L. Puppi: *Il Teatro Olimpico* (Vicenza, 1963)

R. Schiavo: *Luci sull'Eretenio* (Vicenza, 1978)

V. Bolcato: 'L'ambiente musicale a Vicenza e a Verona ai tempi del Palladio', *Palladio a Verona* (Vicenza, 1980), 18–31

R. Schiavo: *Guida al Teatro Olimpico* (Vicenza, 1980, 2/1986)

A. L. Bellina and T. Walker: 'Il melodramma: poesia e musica nell'esperienza teatrale', *Storia della cultura veneta*, iv/1, ed. G. Arnaldi and M. P. Stocchi (Vicenza, 1983), 409–32

R. Schiavo: *Il Teatro Eretenio tra cronaca e storia: nel bicentenario dell'inaugurazione (1784)* (Vicenza, 1983)

F. Mancini, M. T. Muraro and E. Povoledo: *I teatri del Veneto: Verona Vicenza Belluno e il loro territorio* (Venice, 1985) [with further bibliography]

B. Brizi: 'Vivaldi a Vicenza: una festa barocca del 1713', *Informazioni e studi vivaldiani*, vii (1986), 35–53

F. Zanzotto: 'L'"Olimpiade" inaugurale del Teatro Eretenio', *Rassegna veneta di studi musicali*, ii–iii (1986–7), 173–93

R. Zironda: 'Il teatro a Vicenza in età napoleonica', *Il vicentino tra rivoluzione giacobina ed età napoleonica 1797–1813* (Vicenza, 1989), 183–7

PAOLO RIGOLI

Vichy. Town in central France. A spa town, it was the seat of government during the German occupation in World War II. The opera house (1450 seats in stalls and two galleries) was inaugurated in 1902, the work of the architects Lucien Vogg and Charles Lecoeur. It stands in the Parc des Sources adjoining the Grand Casino. From 1902 to 1940, when the spa was at the height of fashion, the opera season ran from May to October and had its own orchestra, chorus and troupe. Many great singers – Shalyapin, Vanni-Marcoux, Germaine Lubin, Georges Thill, Ninon Vallin, Raoul Jobin and Régine Crespin – have been heard there under famous conductors – Gustave Charpentier, Saint-Saëns, d'Indy, Richard Strauss, Weingartner, Paul Paray, Beecham and Krips. The season now runs as a festival from mid-July to mid-August, with productions generally given by one of the French provincial companies, Strasbourg, Rouen or Bordeaux. In 1989 the Warsaw Opera brought productions of *Macbeth* and *Fidelio* with John Rawnsley, Kristine Ciesinski, Alberto Remedios, Sigmund Cowan and Norman Bailey as guest artists. Numerous recitals, concerts and opera films are given during the festival, while chamber operas are performed in the Salle Napoléon III of the Casino.

*

J. Millet-Alviset: 'Le théâtre lyrique au festival de Vichy entre 1952 et 1963', *Le théâtre lyrique français 1945–1985*, ed. D. Pistone (Paris, 1987), 401–10

CHARLES PITT

Vick, Graham (*b* Liverpool, 30 Dec 1953). English director. After a period as director of productions for Scottish Opera, 1984–7, he became artistic director of the City of Birmingham Touring Opera in 1987. He is one of the leading directors of his generation; his imaginative, occasionally provocative stagings have been seen throughout Europe and in the USA. His *Madama Butterfly* for the ENO (1984) was alert to the issues of sexual and cultural imperialism, while his realization of Berio's *Un re in ascolto* (1989, Covent Garden), staged as a riotous theatrical rehearsal with acrobats and trapeze artists in full swing, was hailed as a brilliant success. His commitment to community-based work is exemplified in his *West Side Story* project involving 300 non-professionals at Saltaire, near Bradford (1988), and in his series of productions for CBTO, beginning with *Falstaff* (1987), *Zauberflöte* (1988) and the *Ring* (1990), which presented the works in scaled-down versions ideal for touring to unconventional venues.

*

H. Canning: 'Graham Vick', *Opera*, xlii (1991), 1267–72

BARRY MILLINGTON

Vickers, Jon(athan Stewart) (*b* Prince Albert, Sask., 29 Oct 1926). Canadian tenor. He studied at the Royal Conservatory of Music, Toronto. After appearances in Canada as the Duke, Don José and the Male Chorus in *The Rape of Lucretia* he joined the Covent Garden Opera in 1957, making his début as Gustavus III; he also sang Don José and Aeneas (*Les Troyens*). In 1958 he added Radames to his repertory, sang Don Carlos in Visconti's production of Verdi's opera to celebrate the centenary of the theatre and made his Bayreuth début as Siegmund; he also sang Samson in Handel's oratorio staged by Covent Garden and, in Dallas, Jason to Callas's Medea.

In 1959 Vickers appeared at the Vienna Staatsoper, made his San Francisco début as Radames, and sang Parsifal at Covent Garden. He joined the Metropolitan Opera in 1960, making his début as Canio, and sang there for more than 25 years; his roles included Florestan, Saint-Saëns' Samson, Hermann (*Queen of Spades*), Tristan, Otello, Alvaro, Laca (*Jenůfa*) and Grimes (see

Jon Vickers in the title role of Britten's 'Peter Grimes'

illustration). He sang Herod and Pollione at Orange (1974), took the title role in *Benvenuto Cellini* at Boston (1975) and sang Monteverdi's Nero in Paris (1978). He repeated Handel's Samson at Covent Garden and the Metropolitan for the composer's tercentenary (1985–6). He is considered one of the finest heroic tenors of his day, both vocally and physically suited to such parts as Tristan, Siegmund and Otello.

*

N. Goodwin: 'Jon Vickers', *Opera*, xiii (1962), 233–9
D. Cairns: *Responses* (London, 1973)
J. Ardoin: 'Jon Vickers', *The Tenors*, ed. H. H. Breslin (New York, 1974), 43–82
H. Ludwig: 'Von der Nibelungentreue in Salzburg: Heinz Ludwig sprach mit Jon Vickers', *OW* (Oct 1975), 18–19

HAROLD ROSENTHAL/R

Vico, Diana (*b* Venice; *fl* 1707–26). Italian contralto. She was in the service of the Elector of Bavaria from 1720. She first sang in her native city in Girolamo Polani's *Vindice la pazzia della vendetta* in 1707, and returned there in 1709, 1713, 1717–21, 1723 and 1726, appearing in 16 operas by Gasparini, Lotti, C. F. Pollarolo, Antonio Pollarolo, Porta and Orlandini among others, the last of them Porpora's *Melide e Selinunte*. She sang at Padua in 1712 and Vicenza (Vivaldi's *Ottone in villa*) in 1713. For the 1714–16 seasons she was a member of the King's Theatre company in London, making her début in a revival of the pasticcio *Ernelinda* in 1714. She sang Rinaldo in the 1714–15 revival of Handel's opera, Dardano in the first production of his *Amadigi* (1715), and in the pasticcio *Lucio Vero* (1715, 1716), revivals of *Arminio* and Mancini's *Idaspe fedele* (both 1715) and Alessandro Scarlatti's *Pirro e Demetrio* (1716). She was in constant demand in Italy, singing in Bologna, Padua and Genoa in 1718, Florence (1718–19), Turin (1719), Reggio (1719 and 1720) and Modena (1720). In 1720 she was engaged for Munich and probably sang there in later seasons. She appeared in Milan in 1722 and Genoa in

1724 and sang in seven operas at Naples (two by Vinci) during the period 1724–6 and one at Parma in 1726. She was a specialist in male roles; all her London parts were of this kind. In 1726 Swiney dismissed her with Merighi as 'some He-she-thing or other'. Her compass in *Amadigi* was narrow (*b*♭ to *e*♭″), but the richness of the music suggests that Handel admired her gifts.

WINTON DEAN

Victoria State Opera. Australian company founded in 1962 in MELBOURNE as the Victorian Opera Company.

Victory. Opera in three acts by RICHARD RODNEY BENNETT to a libretto by Beverley Cross after Joseph Conrad's novel; London, Covent Garden, 13 April 1970.

The action takes place in the Dutch East Indies in 1895, and centres on the reclusive Heyst (bass-baritone) and the eventually tragic outcome of his love for Lena, a singer (mezzo-soprano). The list of named characters includes a further 11 sung roles, three spoken and two silent; the large cast is completed by two choruses and an on-stage 'Ladies' Orchestra'.

The music of *Victory*, composed in 1968–9 and scored for large orchestra, vividly reflects the increasingly dramatic tensions of the story in a freely serial style that easily absorbs elements of tonality, both overt and implied.

SUSAN BRADSHAW

Victory, Gerard (*b* Dublin, 24 Dec 1921). Irish composer. He took the BMus degree at Dublin University and was awarded the MusD in 1972. From 1948 he held various posts in Irish Radio and Television (RTE), becoming director of music from 1967 until his retirement in 1982. His long career as a composer in many genres has brought him international recognition and commissions from European festivals and music bodies.

Victory's earlier operas, two of which are in Irish, are written in a light neo-classical style; *Chatterton*, his first full-length work (1968–70), mixes romantic lyricism with a free use of the 12-note idiom. This combination is taken further, and electronic tape effects are introduced, in *Eloise and Abelard* and the works that followed it. *Chatterton* was produced by the ORTF, Paris, in 1971; others have been staged in Europe, and *Circe* and *An Evening for Three* have been broadcast in both Europe and the USA.

Nita [Hungarian Summer] (operetta, 2, P. Delahunty and Victory), Dublin, Father Matthew Hall, Dec 1944
The Drummer, 1949 (ballad op, 2, R. Leech, after J. Addison)
Once Upon a Moon (2, B. Roach), Dublin, Phoenix Hall, June 1950
An fear a phós balbhán [The Silent Wife] (1, T. MacAna, after F. Rabelais), Dublin, Abbey, 20 April 1953; trans. H. W. Rosen as Das goldene Schweigen
The Two Violins, 1955 (operetta, 1, Victory, after F. Coppée)
Iomrall Aithne [Mistaken Identity] (1, Victory), Dublin, Abbey, Aug 1956
The Stranger, 1958 (2, Victory, after G. Griffin: *The Coiner*)
The Music hath Mischief (radio op, 1, Victory), RTE, 20 Oct 1967; stage, Dublin, Grand Opera Society, 3 Dec 1968
The Magic Trumpet, 1970 (musical fairytale for children, Victory), Dublin, 1972; rev. 1983
Chatterton, 1968–70 (3, Victory, after A. de Vigny), concert perf., ORTF, 28 Jan 1971
Circe, 1971–2 (radio op, 1, Victory), RTE, 22 Sept 1972
Eloise and Abelard (3, Victory), RTE, 1973 (excerpts)
An Evening for Three (1, Victory, after L. Ingrisch), RTE, 19 July 1976; concert perf., Dublin, Carroll's, 17 May 1980 [text in Eng. and Ger.]
The Rendezvous, 1984 (1, Victory, after M. Renard), Dublin, St Stephen's Church, 2 Nov 1989
The Tree of Life, 1991 (children's op)

ALOYS FLEISCHMANN

Vida breve, La ('The Short Life'). Lyric drama in two acts and four scenes by MANUEL DE FALLA to a libretto by CARLOS FERNÁNDEZ SHAW; Nice, Municipal Casino, 1 April 1913 (in French).

Set in Granada at the beginning of the century, Act 1 scene i takes place in the gypsy quarter on the Albaicín hill. A young gypsy, Salud (soprano), is anxiously awaiting her lover Paco, who has promised to marry her. Her grandmother (mezzo-soprano) tries to console her, warning her against loving too much. The scene is punctuated by voices from a nearby forge lamenting the lot of those born to be anvils rather than hammers. Paco (tenor) arrives, protesting eternal faithfulness. The couple sing a rapturous duet. Unnoticed by them, the old lady's brother tío Sarvaor (bass) enters, in threatening mood. In the town he has heard a rumour that Paco is about to marry a girl of his own prosperous class. The grandmother calms him down. Salud and Paco arrange to meet next day. Scene ii is an orchestral intermezzo, with wordless chorus, depicting night falling over Granada. It is played with the curtain up.

The first scene of the second act is set in a street in town at night. In the background is the front of a house with an illuminated patio visible through grilles. A *fiesta* is in progress to celebrate the wedding of Paco and his bride, Carmela (mezzo-soprano). A *cantaor* sings in their honour. A *jota* is danced, during which Salud appears in the street, sees Paco in the courtyard, and voices her misery and longing for death. She is joined by the grandmother and Sarvaor.

In the second scene, the guests on the patio, well-to-do townspeople in their best clothes, are engaged in a second dance. Carmela and her brother (and host) Manuel (baritone) are puzzled by Paco's nervousness – he has recognized Salud's voice. Sarvaor and Salud appear. As a gypsy, Sarvaor offers to dance and sing for the wedding guests. Salud holds back, then gathers courage to accuse Paco. As she moves towards him she falters and falls dead.

Falla and the poet and dramatist Fernández Shaw, a practised author of zarzuela librettos, had been discussing collaboration before the competition for which they entered *La vida breve* was announced. They had decided on Granada as a setting. Falla, though Andalusian-born, had at that time never visited the city. Even so, because the date for submission was so close, they had to work fast. The libretto oscillates uneasily between spurts of emotional drama and a detailed picture of the life of Granada. Falla's score is fresh, colourful, appealing and, in the music for Salud (the only character depicted in any depth), touching and full of character. The score as a whole transcends both the libretto and its own eclecticism. The first of the two dances is familiar in arrangements as 'Spanish Dance no.1'.

RONALD CRICHTON

Vidal, Paul (Antonin) (*b* Toulouse, 16 June 1863; *d* Paris, 9 April 1931). French conductor and composer. He attended the Toulouse Conservatoire and later the Paris Conservatoire, where he was in Massenet's composition class. He achieved a formidable record, winning the Prix de Rome in 1883. During his subsequent stay in Rome he became a particular friend of Debussy. He began his conducting career at the Paris Opéra in 1889, and directed performances there from

1894, beginning with Chabrier's *Gwendoline*. Apart from the standard repertory, he conducted the Paris premières of Massenet's *Ariane* and *Roma* and d'Indy's *L'étranger*. With Georges Marty he founded the Concerts de l'Opéra (1895–7) and was musical director of the Opéra-Comique, 1914–19.

One of Vidal's most successful compositions was the light opera *Eros*. *Guernica* and *La Burgonde* were unsuccessful; extensive critiques of the libretto and music of each are printed in Clément and Larousse's *Dictionnaire lyrique*. His musical style, perhaps not surprisingly for a pupil of Massenet, is professionally finished and pleasingly lyrical. The early cantata, *Le gladiateur*, shows the influence of both *Parsifal* and French grand opera, but the sweetness and artifice in parts of *Eros* rather prefigure Poulenc. Vidal wrote music for a number of mixed-genre stage works, as well as incidental music for plays. In collaboration with the writer Maurice Bouchor he wrote *Noël* (1890) and *Les mystères d'Eleusis* (1894) for a marionette theatre, and music to Bouchor's *légende dramatique*, *Saint-Georges* (1896).

Vidal's elder brother, Joseph Bernard Vidal (*b* Toulouse, 15 Nov 1859; *d* Paris, 18 Dec 1924), was a conductor and composer; his works include operettas, notably *Le mariage d'Yvette* (1, Sutra; Paris, Bodinière, 27 May 1893) and *Le chevalier de Fontenoy* (1, Le Pointe; Orléans, 11 Dec 1910).

all first performed and published in Paris

Eros (fantaisie lyrique, 3, J. Noriac, A. Jaime and M. Bouchor), Bouffes-Parisiens, 22 April 1892, vs (1892)

Guernica (drame lyrique, 3, P. Gailhard and P. B. Gheusi), OC, 7 June 1895, vs (1895)

La Burgonde (opéra, 4, E. Bergerat and C. de Sainte-Croix), Opéra, 23 Dec 1898, vs (1898)

*

A. Hoérée: 'Nécrologie: hommage à Paul Vidal', *ReM*, xii (1931), 463–4

Obituary, *Le ménestrel* (17 April 1931) DAVID CHARLTON

Video. Opera on film has existed for many decades but its commercial potential as a domestic entertainment has been recognized only since the 1980s. The wide adoption of video recorder-players as a standard system for home use has encouraged the retail selling of filmed opera for domestic viewing. The 1980s saw the emergence of a number of companies which, in collaboration with television broadcasting organizations, introduced video into the market. Productions seen at principal opera houses, and filmed by radio or television authorities for live or delayed broadcast, would be marketed by an associated business concern.

Alongside the video cassette another format, which has had a somewhat chequered career (having been launched and relaunched three times), has been the video disc. After an unsuccessful initial release, the video disc system was withdrawn in 1986 and succeeded by the compact disc video (CDV) or the laser disc (LD), launched in 1991. The LD is closely related to the standard audio compact disc, which it resembles; it carries a digital soundtrack and offers picture quality considerably superior to anything offered by the videotape system. Available in a number of sizes (though the standard format, like the LP, is a 30 cm disc) and accepted in Japan and the USA, it has been slow to establish itself in Europe, and especially Great Britain, as an alternative video medium (owing in part to the extraordinary market penetration of the VHS system in Great Britain, the relative paucity of titles offered and the minimal availability of disc-playing equipment).

Along with filmed concerts and recitals, opera forms the core of the record companies' music programmes. The addition of the visual medium has been accepted by the record industry (which has entered the market as a distributor of usually licensed films) with reluctance, though with growing enthusiasm throughout the era of digital recording (from 1983). Many record companies had been involved in 'marriages of convenience' with video for many years before the advent of commercially issued videos (Deutsche Grammophon and Unitel had long collaborated in the recordings by Herbert von Karajan and Leonard Bernstein before issuing the video equivalents of their audio recordings). It became commonplace for major opera recording sessions to be themselves recorded for release on video as a supplement (or occasionally alternative) to the audio version. Humphrey Burton's documentary *The Making of West Side Story*, a film about the recording of Bernstein's musical, achieved the status of a minor classic and established a precedent for similar productions which, however uneasily they sit between promotional material and dispassionate documentary, have proved commercially successful. Opera on video has proved as compelling in its 'raw' as in its finished state.

Until 1992 no record company attempted to undertake its own production for video, choosing rather to enter into a collaboration with an established production company or broadcasting network, but Philips Classics, the record-making wing of the large Dutch-based hardware manufacturer, then began to record productions at the Kirov Opera for both audio and video formats.

The relaunch of the laser disc in autumn 1991 saw a collaboration between leading record companies to ensure the widespread acceptance of the new system. BMG (formerly RCA) issued a number of historic films of Toscanini's NBC television programmes (including a concert performance of *Aida*); PolyGram (Deutsche Grammophon, Decca and Philips) drew on a number of large video production companies (including Unitel, RM Associates and broadcasting networks) and continued to license productions from leading opera houses such as the Metropolitan and Bayreuth (as a result they issued two complete *Ring* cycles, the Boulez/Chéreau cycle from Bayreuth and the Levine/Schenk cycle from the Metropolitan); EMI Classics Vision released film of Maria Callas as well as the Sawallisch/Lehnhoff *Ring* from Munich; Teldec (part of the Warner group) issued productions from Savonlinna and Bayreuth; and Sony Classical, having acquired the rights to the video legacy of Karajan (an assiduous devotee of music on film), offered a *Don Giovanni* from Salzburg. The future of filmed opera, and its availability for domestic viewing, is therefore set, with considerable investment on the part of the record industry.

See also FILMING, VIDEOTAPING. JAMES JOLLY

Videotaping. *See* FILMING, VIDEOTAPING.

Vidošić, Tihomil (*b* Boljun, Istria, 1 Aug 1902; *d* Zagreb, 24 Jan 1973). Croatian composer. After graduating from the Zagreb Academy of Music, where his teachers included Odak and Bersa, he worked as a military band conductor and as a teacher at the 'Pavao Markovac' music school in Zagreb. Vidošić developed a pleasing, communicative musical style incorporating elements of Istrian folk music. Of his three operas, only *Stari mladić* ('The Old Lad', 1960) was performed; in it he succeeded in depicting the regional atmosphere, using the short motifs characteristic of Istrian folk music.

Karnevalski capriccio [The Carnival Caprice], 1956 (musical comedy, 1, T. Vidošić), unperf.
Stari mladić [The Old Lad] (comic op, Vidošić), Rijeka, 11 May 1960
Čempresi i sunce [The Cypresses and the Sun], 1961, lost

*

K. Kovačević: *Hrvatski kompozitori i njihova djela* [Croatian Composers and their Works] (Zagreb, 1960), 494–9
J. Andreis: *Music in Croatia* (Zagreb, 1974) KORALJKA KOS

Vienna (Ger. Wien). Capital of Austria, formerly also of the Austro-Hungarian monarchy and the Holy Roman Empire. It has been a great European centre of opera (Italian and French as well as German) since Cesti's *Il pomo d'oro* was given there in 1668, throughout the Viennese Classical period when most of Gluck's and Mozart's mature operas and Beethoven's *Fidelio* had their premières there, and throughout the 19th and early 20th centuries, though by that time less as a centre for new music (two Strauss operas apart) than as one where performances of high prestige were given. The Viennese court opera became in 1919 the Staatsoper, with its splendid house on the Ring built in 1869 and rebuilt in 1955; it is widely regarded as a centre of excellence, though its activities and its personalities have rarely been far from controversy. Vienna has also been a famous centre of more popular operatic entertainments, from the Singspiels of Mozart's contemporaries to the operettas of Johann Strauss and his followers.

1. Up to 1740. 2. 1740–92. 3. 1792–1830. 4. 1830–1945: (i) Hofoper (later Staatsoper) (ii) Other opera (iii) Operetta. 5. Since 1945.

1. Up to 1740. In 1612 the famous tenor Francesco Rasi, who had sung leading roles in most of the important operas in Florence and Mantua in the first decade of the 17th century, gave a recital to the Emperor Matthias in Prague. In 1619 the new emperor, Ferdinand II, saw the opera *Orfeo* (probably by Monteverdi) in Salzburg, and in 1622 his wife Eleonora Gonzaga of Mantua arranged an 'invenzione in musica' with ballet; during a visit to Regensburg the following year Ferdinand himself organized a similar entertainment. In these same two years Francesco Campagnolo, another renowned opera singer from Mantua associated with Monteverdi, was active at the imperial court; and on the emperor's birthday in 1625 court musicians performed an Italian verse drama, possibly G. B. Andreini's *La Ferinda*, which was at least partly set to music. These were the events that led to the performance, in November 1627, of the first genuine opera given at the court, albeit when it was in Prague – the pastoral *Calisto e Arcade* with a libretto by Cesare Gonzaga, Prince of Guastalla, who also wrote the texts of the next known operas performed at the court, this time in Vienna, in 1629 and 1631. Of these, *La caccia felice* (1631) is the earliest Viennese libretto still extant. Probably Andreini's sacred opera *La Maddalena* was also staged in Vienna in 1629, with music either by the Kapellmeister Giovanni Valentini or by the tenor Ludovico Bartolaia, the title role being sung by Lucia Rubini from Mantua.

In the years that followed, several operatic court entertainments were mounted during Carnival or for imperial birthdays; the poet Prospero Bonarelli and Bartolaia provided text and music respectively for some of them. Ferdinand III continued the same practice after 1637, and especially after the end of the Thirty Years War in 1648. But there is no evidence that any of Monteverdi's operas were performed at the imperial court, although the two dramatic *balli* from his eighth book of madrigals, dedicated in 1638 to Ferdinand III, were intended to be. Neither is there any reason to believe earlier historians of Viennese opera who say that Cavalli's *Egisto* and *Giasone* were revived there in 1642 and 1650. Contacts with Venice did exist, but indirectly: Benedetto Ferrari, who served in Vienna as a lute player (1651–3), wrote the librettos for the carnival opera of 1652, *Dafne in alloro*, and that of 1653, *L'inganno d'amore*. This last was performed at the Regensburg Imperial Diet with music by Antonio Bertali, who in 1656 also set *Theti*, a five-act libretto imported from Mantua.

Under the reign of Leopold I (1658–1705) operas, or at least serenatas, were regularly performed during Carnival and on birthdays, weddings and (from 1669) name-days. Such attempts by the emperor to bolster his authority were not always looked on favourably because of the great expense involved; the Habsburg court of Spain and ambassadors from Venice were at times very critical of them. The emperor was encouraged and supported by his stepmother, another Princess Eleonora Gonzaga, whose singers and instrumentalists reinforced his own musicians. He used himself to compose single arias or scenes for almost all the operas and wrote the music for *Creso* (1678) and probably also for *La simpatia nell'odio, overo Le amazoni amanti* (1664). The performance of Antonio Draghi's *Chi più sa manco l'intende, overo Gli amori di Clodio e Pompea* during Carnival 1669 was not only sung and played by noblemen and ladies of the court but also directed by the emperor from the harpsichord. Leopold's younger son, Charles VI, later directed Fux's *Elisa* (1719) and Caldara's *Euristeo* (1724).

In 1665, when the Tyrolean branch of the Habsburg family died out, Leopold engaged the successful partnership of Antonio Cesti and Francesco Sbarra from Innsbruck, together with some opera singers. They worked in Vienna for only a few years until Sbarra's death and Cesti's departure for Florence in 1668, but contributed substantially to the operatic entertainments for the emperor's first wedding, especially with Cesti's elaborately staged *Il pomo d'oro*, performed in two parts in July 1668 (for illustration *see* Pomo d'oro, Il and Stage design, fig.4). Until then operas had been composed mostly by Bertali and P. A. Ziani; afterwards Draghi dominated the Viennese operatic scene for more than 30 years, together with the court poet Nicolò Minato, the stage designer L. O. Burnacini, the choreographers S. and D. Ventura and the ballet composers Johann Heinrich Schmelzer and his son Andreas Anton. Venetian influence pervaded the subjects and plots of the librettos as well as the music, but there was no systematic importation of complete operas from Italy, Alessandro Scarlatti's *Gli equivoci nel sembiante*, performed in Vienna in 1681 as *L'amor non vuol inganni*, being the sole exception.

Towards the end of the 17th century this team of opera producers was replaced. When Minato and Draghi died Donato Cupeda and P. A. Bernardoni took over as librettists and Carlo Agostino Badia, Giovanni Bononcini, Fux and M. A. Ziani as composers; the younger Schmelzer was succeeded in 1694 by J. J. Hoffer. The ballets were designed by Francesco Torti, Claudio Appelshoffer and S. P. Levassori Della Motta. During the short reign of Joseph I (1705–11) Cupeda (*d* December 1704) was replaced by Silvio Stampiglia, and Burnacini (*d* 1707) by Antonio Maria Beduzzi; Alessandro Phillebois joined the dancing-masters. More changes took place when Charles VI arrived from Barcelona in 1712. He brought the stage designers Ferdinando and Giuseppe Galli-Bibiena with him, favoured F. B. Conti and Caldara as composers and employed as librettists Pietro Pariati and Apostolo Zeno, in the late 1720s Giovanni Claudio Pasquini and, most important, Pietro Metastasio. At that time Giuseppe Porsile and Georg Reutter supported Conti, Caldara and Fux with smaller operas and especially serenatas; they were joined by Giuseppe Bonno in 1736. The younger Nicola Matteis replaced Hoffer as ballet composer in 1714.

Operas were performed by members of the imperial Hofkapelle, who also performed church music, oratorios and *Tafelmusik*. Most of the main roles, male and female, were sung by male singers from Italy, those for high voices by well-paid castratos; sometimes guest singers appeared, including Domenico Cecchi ('Il Cortona') in 1697 and Valeriano Pellegrini in 1698–9. Before 1700 it was exceptional for women to appear on the stage, and even after this date they were in a minority. Some performances were sung by men and women of the nobility.

Operas at court were staged in various rooms and halls both in the imperial palace in the city (the Hofburg) and at the court's secondary and summer residences, including the Favorita (also known as the Neue Favorita) and the palace at Laxenburg, and also in their gardens and on lakes. The ballroom (Tanzsaal) of the Hofburg, built in 1630 as its largest hall, was several times refurbished for use as a theatre: in 1658, in 1666 and, in a totally different style, from 1698 to 1700 by Francesco Galli-Bibiena. It was used for operas and dramas until 1744 (sometimes referred to as the Teatro Grande). In 1666–7 Burnacini built the Hoftheater auf der Cortina (the theatre on the city wall) for *Il pomo d'oro*; this was probably used only until 1679 and for only four operas, and was demolished during the Turkish siege of 1683. The audience for the imperial opera was restricted to members of the court, foreign ambassadors and high-ranking visitors, but from 1728 it was possible for common citizens to see operatic adaptations, billed as intermezzos, at the privately run Kärntnertortheater (built in 1709, on the site now occupied by the Hotel Sacher behind the present opera house, but at first used mostly for spoken theatre, and demolished in 1870). Only rarely are the names of the composers known in addition to the titles, but operas by Hasse and Vinci were given there in 1734 and 1735.

Viennese opera scores are extant only from 1660 onwards; for earlier operas librettos are the only sources. The most frequent aria forms are those with repetition of the last part (*ABB*) or the first (*ABA*, the da capo aria); until the late 1690s they usually have more than one stanza. Although common in 17th-century Italian operas, basso ostinato is rarely found in Viennese operas

1. Set designed by Ferdinando Galli-Bibiena for the open-air performance of Fux's 'Angelica vincitrice di Alcina' at the Favorita, Vienna, 14 September 1716: engraving by F. A. Dietel

2. Interior of the Hoftheater auf der Cortina, Vienna (built 1666–7) during the performance of Cesti's 'Il pomo d'oro' (1668) for which it was specially designed by Ludovico Burnacini: engraving by Franz Geffels

of the period. Laments, with chordal accompaniment on violas, were frequent only until 1670, after which prologues also became rare, but the *licenza* as a final scene in honour of the ruler or a patron remained in use for all but carnival operas during the whole period. After about 1700 many stylistic changes took place: plots often lacked comic elements, which from 1714 were sometimes reserved for independent intermezzos; scenes consisted schematically of recitative and a final aria in mature da capo form; and the orchestra became more important, with longer overtures and ritornellos and the inclusion in arias of obbligato instruments such as the violin, theorbo, trombone and chalumeau. Frequently two choirs of trumpets and timpani were employed in works for imperial festivities, possibly as an allegorical allusion to Charles's motto 'Constantia et Fortitudine' and the two columns of Hercules. Ostinato basses began to be more frequently employed, especially by Bononcini.

2. 1740–92. For most of the first decade of her reign Maria Theresa, Charles VI's daughter, was preoccupied with maintaining her throne in the face of invasion and consequently gave little attention to local spectacle. *Opera seria* productions at court became rare despite the presence of Metastasio, ceasing altogether after his and Hasse's *Ipermestra* of 1744. Italian opera continued in the Burgtheater in the Michaelerplatz (managed by impresarios; originally a tennis court, it was refurbished as a theatre in 1741). Works by court composers such as

3. Auditorium of the Hoftheater, Vienna, designed by Francesco Galli-Bibiena: engraving (1704) by J. A. Pfeffel and C. Engelbrecht

4. Performance of Gluck's 'Il Parnaso confuso' at Schönbrunn, 24 January 1765 (Archduke Leopold is at the harpsichord): painting by Johann Franz Griepel

Bonno and Wagenseil alternated with pieces by foreign composers, notably Jommelli, Hasse and Galuppi. In 1747 the Galli-Bibiena opera house in the Hofburg (fig.3) was converted into two (still extant) Redoutensäle, for balls (the rooms were, however, occasionally used again for opera performances in the 19th century and the early 20th). The Burgtheater was renovated to designs by Nicolas Jadot, and reopened with Gluck's first work for Vienna, his *Semiramide riconosciuta* of 1748 (in whose title character the victorious empress could easily be recognized). Despite several remodellings, the Burgtheater was to retain its small dimensions and intimate acoustics up to its demolition in 1888. The year 1747 saw the first performances in a new theatre in the Schönbrunn palace (the Schlosstheater), and in 1753 a small theatre was constructed in the garden of the Laxenburg palace to the south. In the Kärntnertortheater during this period a German-language troupe performed heroic-comic dramas and farces, often improvised and featuring local versions of *commedia dell'arte* characters. Some of these works included music (commissioned at a florin an aria) by the young Joseph Haydn. Viennese ballet during the 1740s and 50s was mainly in the hands of the choreographer Franz Hilverding, who, starting during the period of court mourning for Charles VI, undertook a reform of theatrical dance which soon had consequences for opera.

In 1752, prompted by the impresario Lo Presti's bankruptcy and the frequent indecencies in German comedies, the empress reconstituted the Viennese theatres under court control. She banned improvised pieces (only temporarily as it turned out) and, in a reflection of Austria's political rapprochement with France, substituted a company of French actors for the planned Italian opera company at the Burgtheater. This troupe's repertory soon came to include *opéras comiques* from Paris, arranged by Gluck. A resident of Vienna since 1750, he was made musical director of the Burgtheater in about 1754 by the theatre Intendant, Giacomo Durazzo. Gluck's own *opéras comiques*, as well as French imports (procured after 1759 through the playwright Favart), supplanted the expensive Italian opera during much of the Seven Years War. Several formal and stylistic features of this modest genre were of use to Gluck in composing his 'reform' works during the next decade.

Italian opera returned with the itinerant Mingotti troupe in 1759, but far more significant were the works celebrating the marriage in 1760 of Archduke Joseph to Isabella of Parma, in both Parma (an *opéra-ballet* by Traetta) and Vienna (operas by Hasse and Gluck). There was much interchange of personnel between the two courts' theatrical forces, both of which were headed by persons sympathetic to French spectacle. Isabella's birthday in 1761 was celebrated in Vienna with Traetta's *Armida*, based on Durazzo's prose adaptation of Quinault's libretto for Lully, and the next year the reform continued with Calzabigi and Gluck's *Orfeo ed Euridice*. Calzabigi was the focal point of the anti-Metastasian 'sect' described by Burney, which valued dramatic truth, theatrical illusion and continuity over poetic niceties and purely musical display. The abundant use of both chorus and ballet in *Orfeo*, unusual in *opera seria*, was a result of Durazzo's ability to combine at will the resources of the Burgtheater and the Kärntnertortheater (for which he was also responsible, both before the fire of 1761 and after the rebuilding in 1763). Metastasio's principal ally was Hasse, a special favourite of the empress, but there is also considerable evidence of support for Gluck from the imperial family. The German theatre, though benefiting from the example of the French actors, suffered financial neglect during this period. Musical plays were few, and translations of *opéras comiques* began only about 1764.

Durazzo was dismissed in 1764 during Archduke

Joseph's coronation in Frankfurt as King of the Romans, and with Emperor Francis's death in 1765 the French troupe had to leave as well. (Subsequent French companies, patronized by Chancellor Kaunitz and the high nobility, rarely performed *opéras comiques.*) The theatres were closed during the empress's protracted grief, and when they reopened it was again under a series of luckless impresarios. The bankruptcy of Giuseppe d'Afflisio in 1770 seriously affected the finances of Gluck, one of his associates. Opera reform continued with Calzabigi and Gluck's *Alceste* of 1767, which paid tribute to Maria Theresa as loving widow. But circumstances generally favoured neither *opera seria* nor experimentation. Musical theatre was now dominated by large-scale pantomime ballets, presented by Jean-Georges Noverre between 1767 and 1773, and by *opere buffe*, directed by Gluck's successor Florian Gassmann and after 1774 by Gassmann's pupil Antonio Salieri. Local librettists included both Calzabigi and his protégé Coltellini, but by 1773 Calzabigi had left Vienna in frustration and long-term subscribers such as Prince Khevenhüller were relinquishing their boxes on account of the shabbiness of theatrical offerings under the management of Count Koháry. Characteristically taking quick and drastic action, in 1776 Emperor Joseph II suspended the agreement with the bankrupt Koháry's trustee, dismissed the Italian singers and their orchestra and installed the German actors in the Burgtheater, henceforth called a 'Nationaltheater'. At the same time, he declared a 'Schauspielfreiheit' (an end to the court's monopoly on spectacles), allowing other companies or individuals to use the Kärntnertortheater – known as the Kaiserlich-königliches Hofoperntheater nächst dem Kärntnertor from 1776 – and (on free evenings) the Burgtheater, as well as other venues. Joseph and his new *Musikgraf*, Count Orsini-Rosenberg, managed the theatres directly, without an impresario.

At first Joseph's main concern was the spoken repertory; indeed, Lessing praised the lack of musical distractions at Vienna's Nationaltheater. But audiences soon clamoured for opera, and Joseph accordingly sent his troupe's director, J. H. F. Müller, on a long recruiting trip for German singers capable of performing in *opéra comique* and *opera buffa*, not mere 'Liedsänger' as in much north German opera. The first Singspiel presented (in 1778) was *Die Bergknappen* by Ignaz Umlauf. Subsequent repertory consisted largely of translations from the French or Italian, but other local composers such as Franz Asplmayr and Salieri contributed as well. Dancers were lacking until a 1779 production of the pointedly chosen *Zémire et Azor* by Grétry showed the need for them. Also in 1779 the talented Gottlieb Stephanie ('the younger') replaced Müller as house poet and director of the Singspiel.

For the 1781–2 visit of the Russian Archduke Paul and his wife, the emperor and Chancellor Kaunitz decided on revivals of three major operas by Gluck as representing the best in Viennese musical theatre. Around the same time performances of a translation of Gluck's *opéra comique La rencontre imprévue* delayed and also influenced the closely related Singspiel *Die Entführung aus dem Serail* (1782) by Mozart, newly arrived in Vienna. Despite the phenomenal success of the latter work and nationalist sentiment against foreign spectacles, Joseph and the Viennese critics found that the Nationaltheater offered too few Singspiels of too meagre a quality (musical and literary), especially when compared to French or Italian originals they remembered, and in 1783 Joseph ended the experiment and engaged an *opera buffa* company. The once-disgraced Count Durazzo, now imperial ambassador in Venice, was instrumental in recruiting these singers, who included the tenor Michael Kelly, *prima buffa* Nancy Storace and *primo buffo* Francesco Benucci, around whose comic talents the repertory was chosen or created. The singers quickly brought their acting into line with the recently raised standards of the German players, and were remembered by Caroline Pichler as the finest *buffo* company in Europe.

As his theatre poet Joseph engaged Lorenzo da Ponte, who at first collaborated with Salieri. The failure of their *Il ricco d'un giorno* and rivalry with Count Rosenberg's protégé Giambattista Casti led to a falling-out, and Da Ponte next worked with Vicente Martín y Soler, notably in *Una cosa rara* (1786), from which Mozart quoted in *Don Giovanni.* Casti collaborated with the visiting Paisiello in 1784 on *Il re Teodoro in Venezia*; influences from this work and the same composer's *Il barbiere di Siviglia* (performed 1783) are to be found in Mozart and Da Ponte's three operas. In his struggle to be heard in the Burgtheater Mozart suffered from cabals organized by Rosenberg's clique, notably in connection with *Le nozze di Figaro.* His three great comedies (including *Don Giovanni*, written for Prague) nevertheless won the approval of the Burgtheater Mozart suffered from cabals organized by Rosenberg's Viennese

5. Interior of a Viennese theatre, probably the Burgtheater: engraving from P. Hilarion, 'Bildgalerie weltlicher Misbrache' (Vienna, 1785)

audiences, though performances of *Così fan tutte* (1790) were cut short by the emperor's death.

The *opera buffa* ensemble did not enjoy the undivided support of Viennese high society, or even of the emperor. In 1785 Joseph installed a 'Deutsche Opéra Comique' in the Kärntnertortheater as healthy competition for the Italians. Their performances quickly dwindled, ending in February 1788 with Mozart's *Entführung*, after which the theatre closed down. That same year, preoccupied by a Turkish war and irritated by singers' misbehaviour and greed, Joseph for a while contemplated dismissing the entire Italian company and making do with local talent. Advocates of German culture urged such an action, but were disappointed.

Joseph's successor, Leopold II, was initially aloof from theatrical affairs and concentrated on restoring order to his realms. But in 1791 he turned to opera in earnest, drawing on his experience as regent in Tuscany and in several ways returning to practices and genres of his mother Maria Theresa's reign. Leopold and his new *Musikgraf*, Johann Wenzel Ugarte, removed control of the theatres from the bureaucracy and made a fresh start on personnel, dismissing Da Ponte and his mistress, the soprano Adriana Ferrarese; Joseph Weigl replaced Salieri as director of the opera. Although plans to build a larger theatre were not realized, Leopold did reopen the Kärntnertortheater. He re-established both ballet and *opera seria* among the offerings, the latter in alternation with comic operas mostly less complex than those of Mozart and Da Ponte. Leopold first hired Caterino Mazzolà (adapter of Metastasio's *La clemenza di Tito* for Mozart) as theatre poet and then Giovanni Bertati, whose first libretto for Vienna was *Il matrimonio segreto* (set by Cimarosa, 1792).

Mozart, having received no preferment from the new emperor, in 1791 accepted an opera commission at his fellow freemason Emanuel Schikaneder's suburban Theater auf der Wieden (built 1787). *Die Zauberflöte* displays both masonic ideals and features typical of the popular musical and machine comedies dominating the fare at that theatre, which, like Karl Marinelli's Theater in der Leopoldstadt (founded 1781), owed its existence to Joseph's 'Schauspielfreiheit'.

Of the later 18th-century operas that have survived into the modern repertory, a disproportionate number were created in Vienna, despite widely varying tastes and forms of theatrical management. An explanation is suggested by Calzabigi, who in 1790 described the city's audiences as 'the distillation of all nations' and on the whole far more cultivated than their Italian counterparts. As the capital of a large and polyglot empire, Vienna was perhaps uniquely capable of producing such a golden age of opera.

3. 1792–1830. The period of nearly four decades from the death of Mozart to the July Revolution of 1830 was, with a few notable exceptions, anything but a time of splendour in Vienna's operatic history. Apart from isolated local achievements, such as Beethoven's *Fidelio* and (on a much lower level) Singspiels by Weigl and Gyrowetz, and a few commissioned scores such as Weber's *Euryanthe* (1823), the repertory of the Hofoper (court opera) was dominated by three types of work, none of them ideally suited to the place and the age: survivals from the previous era, *opéras comiques* and a few grand Romantic operas from France, and imports from south of the Alps.

Vienna's other theatres were of only brief and limited importance. Schikaneder maintained a valuable operatic repertory in the Theater auf der Wieden, but his new Theater an der Wien, to which he moved his company in 1801, only intermittently aspired to musical distinction (notably with *Fidelio* and the concerts Beethoven gave in the theatre); it also lacked consistent artistic direction. The Theater in der Leopoldstadt rarely staged full operas, though its innumerable Singspiels and farces contained a quantity of light, attractive music by Wenzel Müller and other composers. The third regular suburban theatre, in the Josefstadt, did not gain importance as an operatic stage until the 1830s.

Not surprisingly, the focus shifted several times during this period. In the early 1790s the Italian school continued to dominate, with Cimarosa strengthening his hold, above all with *Il matrimonio segreto* (1792), and Salieri continuing to maintain a prominence that few of his later works would have won had he not been Hofkapellmeister. Other Italians enjoyed successes with one or more operas. Paisiello, who in the 1780s had had almost as many performances as any two other composers combined, added to his laurels only with *Nina*, which began a lengthy run in May 1794. Zingarelli, Silvestro Palma, Piccinni, Guglielmi and Portugal had one or two successes at the court opera, but it is significant that very few of their works were actually commissioned for Vienna. Composers who were Viennese by birth or adoption, including Winter and Joseph Weigl, also contributed Italian operas to the repertory; Weigl's *L'amor marinaro* (1797) amassed nearly a hundred performances in 24 years, but his greatest successes were to come later with German Singspiels.

By the mid-1790s Singspiel was beginning to reappear at the court opera: Süssmayr's *Die edle Rache*, first performed in August 1795, was given nearly 40 times in six years; it was followed in 1796 by his arrangement of Sedaine and Grétry's *Colinette à la cour, ou La double épreuve* which, as *Die doppelte Erkenntlichkeit*, was often performed, though a regular victim of the Viennese proclivity for giving only one act of a longer work. Winter's *Das unterbrochene Opferfest* and J. B. Schenk's *Der Dorfbarbier* also entered the repertory in 1796; the latter proved the liveliest and most enduring of the one-act Singspiels, with more than 330 performances in the court opera alone until 1891. Other works in the vernacular that enjoyed extended popularity were Süssmayr's *Der Marktschreyer* and *Soliman der Zweite* (both of 1799) and Schenk's *Der Fassbinder* (1802). Gyrowetz had a number of successes, above all with *Der Augenarzt* (given nearly a hundred times between 1811 and 1817), but it was Weigl who enjoyed the greatest popularity, with *Die Uniform* (1805; 62 performances), *Ostade* (1807; 124 performances in 15 years), *Das Waisenhaus* (1808; 107 performances) and *Die Schweizerfamilie* (1809; 221 performances by 1836).

By the turn of the century Paer, Mayr and Dutillieu were beginning to establish a place in the repertory with Italian operas (which, like most foreign works, were usually translated into German for performance in Vienna), and Fioravanti and Zingarelli also had considerable success with one or two pieces. At this time, however, there was a swing in taste towards French works. Grétry had never lost his popularity in Vienna, but the 'rescue opera' now began to make an impact, above all with Cherubini's *Les deux journées* (staged in Vienna from 1802 under a variety of German titles); by

6. *Interior of the Theater an der Wien: lithograph (1830)*

1830 it had already achieved 172 performances at the court opera alone. Other 'rescue operas' staged in Vienna included Grétry's *Richard Coeur-de-lion*, LeSueur's *La caverne* (*Die Räuberhöhle*, 1803), Paer's *Camilla* (1799) and *Leonora* (1809) – and, of course, in its three versions, Beethoven's *Fidelio*. Cherubini had further successes with *Médée* and *Faniska* (his only Viennese commission), which shared around 120 repetitions at the court opera; *Lodoïska*, however, despite numerous performances at the Theater an der Wien from 1802, had only a *succès d'estime* when it was mounted at the Kärntnertortheater in 1814. Dalayrac's *Les deux petits Savoyards* enjoyed much esteem for a decade from 1804, and Devienne, Della-Maria, Catel, Solié, Isouard and, especially, Boieldieu and Méhul all enjoyed conspicuous success in Vienna. Spontini made an impact mainly with three works, *Milton*, *La vestale* and *Fernand Cortez*. A quite different type of French product enjoyed a period of success in the mid-1820s when the Kleine Redoutensaal was taken over, from September 1826, for a long series of vaudevilles and *divertissements* in French.

A date that was to prove important was 26 November 1816, when *L'inganno felice* heralded the craze for Rossini's operas that was to hold sway in Vienna for years to come. By the time Domenico Barbaia was appointed director of the court opera in 1821 seven of Rossini's works were already in the repertory, including *Tancredi*, *Otello*, *La gazza ladra* and *Il barbiere di Siviglia*; in 1822, when Rossini himself was in Vienna, *La donna del lago*, *La Cenerentola* and three further operas entered the repertory, to be followed by yet six more in the next three years. *Le comte Ory* followed in 1829 (a rare failure, with a mere eight repetitions) and *Guillaume Tell* in 1830. By then the next generation of Italian composers had appeared on the scene, Donizetti's *L'ajo dell'imbarazzo* making little impression in 1827 and Bellini's *Il pirata* gaining rapid popularity in 1828. By the last year of the period under review Meyerbeer was establishing a name with *Il crociato in Egitto* and Auber was confirming the success of earlier works such as *Le maçon* (as *Maurer und Schlosser*), *La muette de Portici* and *Fra Diavolo*.

All this time the native repertory was being sustained to a considerable extent by two composers of previous generations, Mozart and Gluck. The latter's *Orfeo* was not given at the court opera between 1782 and 1882 and revivals of *Armide* and *Iphigénie en Aulide* in 1808 had only limited success, as was the case with *Alceste* two years later; *Iphigénie en Tauride*, however, was given 84 times between 1808 and 1819 and was revived several times later in the century. Mozart's fate was very different. Absent from the repertory after his death, except in Schikaneder's theatre, his operas began to reappear in the late 1790s. *Le nozze di Figaro* and *Don Giovanni* (as *Don Juan*) were given in 1798 (the former received four performances in Italian in 1807 and a few more in 1824–5, but German was the normal language for Mozart's Italian operas in Vienna in the 19th century, as it was for Gluck's works). *Die Entführung* was revived in 1801, and in the same year *Die Zauberflöte* was staged at the court opera for the first time, in a production so inept that Schikaneder parodied its deficiencies in his own performances; with a new production in 1812 it became an established cornerstone of the repertory. *La clemenza di Tito* (as *Titus der Gütige*) and *Così fan tutte* (as *Mädchentreue*) shared about a hundred performances between 1804 and 1830, but *Idomeneo* (*Idomeneus, König von Creta*) disappeared after five performances in 1806 and was no more successful when put on again in 1819–20. *Fidelio* slowly established its place at the court opera; by 1823, when it dropped from the repertory for eight years, it had already been given 68 times since the première of its final version on 23 May 1814.

4. 1830–1945.

(i) Hofoper (later Staatsoper). The Hofoper (court opera) continued in the old Kärntnertortheater (by now called the Kaiserlich-königliches Hofoperntheater nächst dem Kärntnertor). The Habsburgs solved the intricate problem of running the Kärntnertortheater by leasing it and by paying a subsidy to various impresarios, mostly Italians, who in their *stagioni* favoured (not unexpectedly, especially as public taste still had a strong Italian bias) operas of their own country at the expense of German works. Even after the loss of the Italian provinces in 1866, the taste for Italian singers and operas persisted, and the custom of Italian *stagioni* continued to the end of the century.

In 1854 Karl Eckert became the Hofoper's first permanent conductor and three years later was made director (until 1860), the first musician to hold the post. This became a general policy for many years and culminated in the appointment of Mahler and the co-directorship of Richard Strauss and Franz Schalk. Eckert, who introduced Wagner's operas to the Hofoper (*Lohengrin*, 1858; *Tannhäuser*, 1859), was followed by a triumvirate of conductors; one of them, Heinrich Esser, was a friend of Wagner's and was responsible for the Vienna production of *Der fliegende Holländer* (1860). The next permanent director (1861–7) was an Italian, Matteo Salvi, whose appointment was effectively a stop-gap, since the building of a new opera house as part of the reconstruction of Vienna as a modern city had been planned as early as 1860, and a clause in Salvi's contract stipulated that he was engaged only for the old house. He was further restricted by an imperial commission, whose guidelines for the artistic administration of the opera include the following remarks:

> The artistic director of the Vienna Opera must constantly bear in mind that this court theatre is primarily devoted to the cause of German opera, which is therefore to be cultivated with the utmost diligence. But this does not mean that performances, in German translations, of Italian and French operas are to be excluded; only they must not be given too frequently, otherwise for long periods there might be nothing but Italian music, to which a considerable part of the year is already given up.

In 1857 the court decreed that Vienna's medieval fortifications were to be razed, and an impressive boulevard, the Ringstrasse, was designed, to be flanked by such new buildings as the Parliament, the Rathaus, the university and the Opera. The Opera, in neo-Renaissance style, was begun in 1861 and completed in early 1869 (initially called the Kaiserlich-königliches Hofoperntheater im neuen Hause, and from 1871 known as the Kaiserlich-königliches Hofoperntheater); its architects were August von Siccardsburg and Eduard van der Nüll, neither of whom lived to see the opening performance on 25 May. Their imposing edifice reflects the splendour of the Habsburg Empire, which had by then recovered from its losses in Italy and its defeat by the Prussians in 1866. The new house was inaugurated with *Don Giovanni* (sung in German), in which the famous J. N. Beck sang the title role, Louise Dustmann-Meyer sang Donna Anna and Hans von Rokitansky was Leporello. The new director of the Hofoper was Franz von Dingelstedt (1867–70), under whom the transfer from the old Kärntnertortheater to the new house went smoothly. His successor, Johann Herbeck (1870–75), was a brilliant conductor and director who had previously staged the first Vienna *Meistersinger* (in the 19th century conductors were frequently their own directors). During his highly successful first three years in the post he mounted magnificent productions of *Der fliegende Holländer* and *Rienzi*, but after the disastrous Vienna stock market crash in December 1873 he was faced with empty houses and a constantly mounting deficit. Herbeck was followed by Franz Jauner (1875–80), a non-musician who had, however, been successful with the management of the Carltheater in the Leopoldstadt. One of Jauner's first coups at the Hofoper was his successful production of *Carmen* in 1875, a few months after its disastrous première in Paris. Jauner brought Verdi to Vienna to conduct *Aida* and the Requiem, and engaged Hans Richter as his principal conductor as a gesture of goodwill towards Wagner, with whom Jauner was on excellent terms. He further obliged the composer by his loan to Bayreuth of some of his most celebrated singers, including Amalie Materna and Emil Scaria. As a *quid pro quo* he obtained from Wagner the performing rights for the entire *Ring*, which in May 1879 was given as a complete cycle. After that Jauner's fortunes quickly declined, and in 1880 he took over the direction of the Ring-Theater am Schottentor.

The longest tenure of office was that of Wilhelm Jahn, director from 1881 to 1897. He was an extremely able conductor who specialized in Italian and French operas while Richter excelled in the German repertory. The two

7. Interior of the Hofoper, Vienna, at the inaugural performance (Mozart's 'Don Giovanni', 25 May 1869): engraving after L. E. Petrovits

8. Alfred Roller's design for the beginning of Act 2 of Wagner's 'Tristan und Isolde' in the production directed by Mahler at the Hofoper, Vienna, in 1903

men were also complementary in temperament and, aided by the general prosperity of the Habsburg monarchy in the 1880s, they made the Vienna Hofoper one of the foremost musical institutions in Europe: the works of Wagner and Verdi were actively promoted; Mascagni came to conduct his *Cavalleria rusticana* (1891); Massenet's *Manon* and *Werther* (1892) were produced, the latter a world première, as well as Smetana's *Bartered Bride* (1896) and *Dalibor* (1897); and the Vienna opera was the heart of the great International Exhibition of Music and Theatre in 1892. Strauss's *Die Fledermaus* was the first operetta to be performed in the house (October 1894). Jahn had a flair for spotting talented singers in the provincial theatres of Austria and Germany and, in addition to the singers mentioned above, his artistic personnel included Marie Renard, Ernest van Dyck, Bianca Bianchi and Antonie Schläger, all of whom specialized in French and Italian operas.

During the second half of Jahn's directorship a new mood began to assert itself in Vienna – a malaise and disenchantment which seemed to spring from a profound uncertainty about the monarchy's future. Yet, paradoxically, the growing feeling of Austria's slow political disintegration seemed to act as a stimulus to the capital's cultural, artistic and intellectual life. The period from about 1890 to the outbreak of the war saw an extraordinary flourishing in Vienna of music, literature, painting and architecture, as well as psychology and philosophy. A new spirit of adventure and exploration prevailed in the pre-war Vienna of Mahler and Schoenberg, of Schnitzler, Hofmannsthal, Zweig and the brilliant satirist Karl Kraus, of Kokoschka, Schiele and Klimt of the Secession, of the architects Otto Wagner and Adolf Loos, of Freud, Mach and the Vienna circle of philosophers. At no other period in its history did the city display such an accumulation of diverse talents. At the same time, Vienna was *par excellence* the city of gaiety which well knew how to conceal the sense of impending collapse behind a façade of waltzes, operettas and *bals parés*. No other city was so deeply pervaded by a hedonistic attitude to life as the capital of the Habsburg monarchy.

This was the background for Gustav Mahler's directorship of the Hofoper, which lasted ten years (1897–1907). Appointed over the head of Jahn by the *Obersthofmeister*, Count Liechtenstein, Mahler surpassed the achievements of his predecessor and made Vienna's opera the finest in Europe. In the Wagner works he did away with most of the cuts to which even Richter had consented, and he conducted the five great Mozart operas in a stylistically more faithful manner, accompanying the recitatives on the piano and, later, the harpsichord. In addition to some 30 contemporary works (including Leoncavallo's and Puccini's *La bohème*, *Madama Butterfly*, Saint-Saëns' *Samson et Dalila*, Bizet's *Djamileh*, Strauss's *Feuersnot*, Charpentier's *Louise*, Wolf's *Corregidor*, Pfitzner's *Rose vom Liebesgarten* and Tchaikovsky's *Yevgeny Onegin*) he created new productions of older operas such as *Fidelio* and *Tristan und Isolde* in which he was assisted by Alfred Roller, a stage designer of genius, whose strength was the exploitation of space, colour and light in the exclusive service of the drama. Mahler engaged as his assistants the young Bruno Walter and Franz Schalk, and built up an ensemble of first-rate singers like Anna Bahr-Mildenburg, Selma Kurz, Marie Gutheil-Schoder, Leo Slezak, Erik Schmedes and Richard Mayr; and, since direction at that time was still the responsibility of the conductor, he also trained his ensemble in acting. He got rid of the obnoxious claque system and ruled that no latecomer be admitted after the beginning of the act. In his search for perfection and truth of interpretation he demanded of his artists the same total dedication that he demonstrated himself; but in pursuing this aim he could be inconsiderate to the point of ruthlessness, which inevitably made him many enemies. This, combined with a simmering anti-Semitism inside and outside the company, finally induced him to resign. Furthermore, he felt that, after ten years of raising the Hofoper to unprecedented heights, his task had been accomplished.

Mahler was succeeded by Felix Weingartner (1908–11), who was a better conductor than director. Under his regime Vienna first heard Strauss's *Elektra* (1909), he himself directed Berlioz's *Benvenuto Cellini* and he also accepted into the repertory and conducted Johann Strauss's *Zigeunerbaron* (1910). From Cologne he obtained in Wilhelm von Wymetal a gifted director. He also insisted that the conductor's name, previously not mentioned on posters, appear on them. Weingartner was followed by Hans Gregor (1911–18), a non-musician but a man of great business acumen; under him the Hofoper opened its own scenery workshops. Gregor introduced to Vienna *Der Rosenkavalier* (1911), *Parsifal* (1914), the second (or Vienna) version of *Ariadne auf Naxos* (1916), and *Salome* (October 1918), which until then had been banned from the Hofoper. He was also a very able director, as he showed with his staging of *Pelléas et Mélisande* in 1911 and of *La fanciulla del West* in 1913. Outstanding singers engaged by Gregor were Maria Jeritza ('The Duse of opera'), Lotte Lehmann, Alfred Piccaver, Emil Schipper and Hans Duhan.

After World War I Austria was reduced to a small republic, whose first few years were a period of harsh economic struggle caused largely by the catastrophic depreciation of its currency. Yet cultural life in Vienna was as active as before the war, and in particular the Staatsoper (as the Hofoper was renamed) reached another peak of excellence, under the co-directorship of Richard Strauss and Franz Schalk (1919–24). As with Mahler, the almost continuous presence of a vital creative intelligence brought a renewed strength and splendour to the house, and in addition to the normal repertory there were a number of new works, including Strauss's own *Die Frau ohne Schatten* (1919), Schreker's *Die Gezeichneten* (1920) and *Der Schatzgräber* (1922), and Puccini's *Trittico* (1920). The Grosser Redoutensaal in the Hofburg was also used for opera in the interwar years, mostly for older works such as *Le nozze di Figaro* and *Don Pasquale*. Because of increasing differences of an artistic as well as personal nature, Strauss resigned and left Schalk in sole command (1924–9). Though a first-rate musician, Schalk was a traditionalist, averse to giving modern and experimental works at an institution that was subsidized by the taxpayer and therefore needed a repertory with wide general appeal. Nevertheless, he wanted to maintain ties with contemporary opera, and for this he engaged Robert Heger (1925–33), who was put in charge of most of the new works produced (Hindemith's *Cardillac*, 1927; Krenek's *Jonny spielt auf*, 1927; Korngold's *Das Wunder der Heliane*, 1927; Stravinsky's *Oedipus rex*, 1928; Ravel's *L'enfant et les sortilèges*, 1929). Also under Schalk began a revival of Verdi's lesser-known operas such as *La forza del destino* (1926) to a new libretto by the Austrian poet Franz Werfel. 1927 saw splendid new productions of *Fidelio*, for the Beethoven centenary, and *Der Rosenkavalier*, which the Staatsoper took to Paris in 1928. Schalk had a galaxy of eminent singers at his disposal; in addition to those already mentioned, they included Marie Olczewska, Vera Schwarz, Maria Németh, Rosette Anday, Elisabeth Schumann, Josef von Manowarda and Alfred Jerger. There were also many guest appearances, notably by Richard Tauber.

In 1929 Schalk was succeeded by Clemens Krauss (1929–34), who was the next best choice after abortive attempts had been made to engage Wilhelm Furtwängler. Krauss, previously assistant conductor at the Staatsoper (1922–4), was warmly recommended by his friend Strauss for the directorship. It was during his regime that Vienna first heard Berg's *Wozzeck* (1930) and Strauss's *Arabella* (1933), and he continued the Verdi revival with *Macbeth*, *Don Carlos* and *Simon Boccanegra* in collaboration with his highly talented director, Lothar Wallerstein. Owing to a change in taste after the war, the Staatsoper began regularly to produce Viennese classical operetta – Heuberger's *Der Opernball* (1931), Suppé's *Boccaccio* (1932) and Millöcker's *Der Bettelstudent* (1936). Lehár's fondest ambition was realized when his quasi-operatic *Giuditta* was given its première at the Staatsoper in January 1934, to be followed four years later by performances of his operetta *Das Land des Lächelns*.

The rise to power of the Nazis in Germany in January 1933 gradually cast an ominous shadow over Vienna. Krauss resigned suddenly in December 1934 to become opera director in Berlin. The Viennese considered this a shameless betrayal, especially because Krauss took most of his singers with him, including the sisters Anny and Hilde Konetzni, Helge Roswaenge and Viorica Ursuleac (Krauss's wife). The post went to Weingartner (1935–6) and then to Erwin Kerber (1936–40), a non-musician who called on Bruno Walter (1936–8) as his musical adviser. Walter brought new life to the Staatsoper through excellent new productions of *Djamileh*, *Carmen* and *Dalibor*, using the revolving stage built during Krauss's tenure, and he introduced new works such as Respighi's *La fiamma* and Weinberger's *Wallenstein*.

After the Anschluss in March 1938 the Staatsoper, like every other public institution, was *gleichgeschaltet* (Nazified), with the new race laws affecting every department, including the orchestra. All state theatres were made subject to the authority of the Generalintendant, Lothar Müthel, and during the war H. K. Strohm (1940–41) and E. A. Schneider (1941–3) were the directors. In addition to three permanent conductors (Wilhelm Loibner, Leopold Ludwig and Rudolf Moralt), there were a number of guest conductors, such as Furtwängler, Hans Knappertsbusch and Vittorio Gui. Knowing how greatly the Viennese were attached to their opera, the Nazi authorities granted it exceptional status in declaring virtually all its artists unfit for military service. During this period there were several special festivals at the Staatsoper – for Mozart (1941), for Verdi (1943), and for Strauss and Pfitzner (1944). The younger generation of Austrian and German opera composers was represented by Franz Salmhofer, Rudolf Wagner-Régeny, Werner Egk (*Columbus*) and Carl Orff (*Carmina burana*), and as relief from the harsh reality of the war the repertory included a great number of operettas, with Lehár the leading composer (his *Die lustige Witwe* was a favourite of Hitler's). With the appointment of Karl Böhm (1943–5) the Staatsoper was again under a first-rate musician, whose singers included Irmgard Seefried, Sena Jurinac, Hilde Gueden, Maria Cebotari, Elisabeth Schwarzkopf, Christel Goltz and Peter Klein. Because of the 'total war effort' the house was closed after a complete performance of the *Ring* in autumn 1944. On 12 March 1945, a month or so before the end of the war, the opera house received a direct hit during an Allied air raid, which destroyed the entire building except for its façade, the loggia and the great staircase.

(ii) Other opera. Next in importance to the Kärntnertortheater in the 19th century was the Theater an der Wien. Its repertory included spoken drama and opera – many of the *Zauberspiele* and farces of Nestroy (mostly with music by Adolf Müller) were first performed there – and it also served as a concert hall. In 1845–6 Berlioz conducted four concerts there and in

1862–3 Wagner gave three concerts with excerpts from his operas. In 1846 Lortzing became its chief conductor, after having introduced himself with his *Waffenschmied*; in the period after 1848 the theatre was much troubled by financial difficulties and almost brought to the point of bankruptcy, which it avoided by turning in the mid-1860s to the Offenbach operetta and its progeny, the classical Viennese operetta. Under the directorship of the famous actress Marie Geistinger (1869–75) and her partner and successor, Maximilian Steiner (1875–80), the theatre enjoyed an immense popularity. It became the home of Viennese operetta, where 13 of Johann Strauss's 15 operettas had their first performances between 1871 and 1897. But it also continued to give the occasional opera, sometimes in Vienna premières, as with Puccini's *La bohème* (1897). Its principal conductor from 1907 was Robert Stolz, a prolific composer of light music, who directed early performances of Lehár's *Die lustige Witwe* and *Der Graf von Luxemburg* as well as Oscar Straus's *Der tapfere Soldat.* Another outstanding period for the theatre came between the two world wars when Hubert Marischka, originally an operatic tenor, was its director and promoted in particular the music of Lehár. During World War II the theatre was closed.

The Volksoper, a plain but large house (1710 seats) on the Gürtel, Vienna's outer Ring, was opened in 1898 in commemoration of the 50th anniversary of Franz Joseph's reign. During its first five years (as the Stadttheater) it was devoted exclusively to spoken drama and boulevard comedy, but in 1903 it was leased by Rainer Simons and transformed into a people's opera house with popular works in the repertory and reduced ticket prices. The new form of management could allow itself greater flexibility than that of the Hofoper, and it also proved itself more enterprising and adventurous in the choice of new operas. Thus in 1907 the Volksoper staged *Tosca* and in 1910 *Salome* (both rejected by the censors to whom all productions of the Hofoper had to be submitted), and in 1910 it also produced *Kleider machen Leute* by Alexander von Zemlinsky, who was conductor of the Volksoper from 1906 to 1911 (except for the 1907–8 season). Simons had a talent for spotting promising singers, such as Maria Jeritza, Emil Schipper, Josef von Manowarda and Hans Duhan, all of whom later became prominent at the Hofoper. Simons was followed by Raoul Mader and then by Weingartner (1919–24), whose regime coincided with the co-directorship of Richard Strauss and Schalk at the Staatsoper. More and more large-scale works, including those of Wagner, were taken into the repertory. After intermittent financial difficulties, the theatre was taken over, in 1938, by the Vienna municipality as the Städtische Volksoper.

Other Viennese theatres gave operas in the 19th century. For the reopening of the Theater in der Josefstadt in 1822 Beethoven wrote and conducted the overture *Die Weihe des Hauses*. Despite its diminutive stage, grand opera was produced there, including Meyerbeer's *Robert le diable* and *Les Huguenots*, as well as *Tannhäuser* (Vienna's first Wagner production), staged in 1857 at the Thaliatheater, a summer theatre owned by the Theater in der Josefstadt, and then taken over into the main house. Conradin Kreutzer, who was its Kapellmeister from 1833 to 1835, wrote for it the opera *Das Nachtlager in Granada* and incidental music to *Der Verschwender*. In 1858 it all but ceased giving opera and began to specialize in spoken drama and comedy. During the interwar period the most famous of its directors was Max Reinhardt.

The Carltheater, reconstructed by Karl Carl (von Bernbrunn) in 1847 on the site of the old Leopoldstädter-Theater in Vienna's second district, confined itself to performing operettas and comic plays with music. It was there that Offenbach's operettas achieved the success that led to the development of the new indigenous genre. Many operettas had their premières there, including Oscar Straus's most successful piece, *Ein Walzertraum*, in March 1907. The Carltheater was bombed in World War II and demolished in 1951.

The Raimundtheater was opened in 1893 for the production of popular plays by Ludwig Anzengruber, Raimund and Nestroy. Later it turned to serious modern drama, but owing to its precarious finances ended up giving operettas; during World War I its continuing existence was ensured by the enormous success of the operetta *Das Dreimäderlhaus* (*Lilac Time*), put together from Schubert's music.

The Komische Oper am Schottentor was founded in 1874 (known as the Ring-Theater am Schottentor from 1878) in imitation of the Paris Opéra-Comique. It played a wide repertory of operas (Grétry, Dittersdorf, Rossini, Lortzing, Bellini, Offenbach) and counted among its singers Adelina Patti, Pauline Lucca and Minnie Hauk. During a performance of *Les contes d'Hoffmann* on 8 December 1881 a fire broke out, destroying the building and causing the loss of several hundred lives. From that day, except for a guest performance by the Budapest Opera in 1883, Offenbach's opera was banned from Vienna until Mahler, ignoring the widespread superstition, restored it to the repertory of the Hofoper in November 1901.

(iii) Operetta. During the 19th century and until World War I Vienna was renowned for its popular music and operettas. Dance music (waltzes, polkas etc.) could be heard in the city's coffee houses and dance locales, where the bands of Michael Pamer, Josef Labitzky and Philipp Fahrbach attracted a wide public. The waltz is an important feature of the Viennese operetta (as in the waltz finale to Act 2 of Strauss's *Die Fledermaus*), which arose as a hybrid from the operettas of Offenbach and the popular Viennese Singspiels and farces with music. The first composer to succeed with this amalgamation was Franz von Suppé (*Flotte Bursche*, 1863; *Die schöne Galathee*, 1865; *Boccaccio*, 1879). Johann Strauss soon followed, with 15 operettas of which *Die Fledermaus* (1874) and *Der Zigeunerbaron* (1885) represent the peak of the genre. Successful later Viennese operetta composers include Carl Millöcker (*Der Bettelstudent*, 1882; *Der arme Jonathan*, 1890), Richard Heuberger (*Der Opernball*, 1898), Carl Zeller (*Der Vogelhändler*, 1891; *Der Obersteiger*, 1894), Leo Fall (*Der fidele Bauer*, 1907; the one-act *Brüderlein fein*, 1909) and Edmund Eysler (*Bruder Straubinger*, 1903). Two of Franz Lehár's finest operettas are *Die lustige Witwe* (1905) and *Der Graf von Luxemburg* (1909), but his subsequent works, as well as those of his contemporaries (Oscar Straus, Emmerich Kálmán, Robert Stolz and Ralph Benatzky) show a gradual decline of this popular art form, largely because of increasing sentimentality in both texts and music. Most Viennese operettas were first given at the Theater an der Wien. After World War I Berlin became the chief centre for

operetta in German. For further discussion of the Viennese operetta *see* OPERETTA, §§ 1 and 3.

5. SINCE 1945. The Staatsoper entered a period of great achievement after the war, despite the fact that its building had been destroyed. Productions were staged in the Theater an der Wien and the Volksoper, with Egon Hilbert overseeing the combined administration and guiding the artistic development of both houses. The Viennese Mozart style became famous throughout the world, represented by the conductors Josef Krips and Karl Böhm, the director Oscar Fritz Schuh and singers such as Sena Jurinac, Hilde Konetzni, Wilma Lipp, Emmy Loose, Irmgard Seefried, Elisabeth Schwarzkopf, Ljuba Welitsch, Anton Dermota, Hans Hotter, Erich Kunz, Julius Patzak, Paul Schöffler and Ludwig Weber. Mozart's Italian operas, as well as most foreign works, were sung in German.

The rebuilding of the house on the Ring was undertaken by the architect Erich Boltenstern, the renovated auditorium having a balcony, gallery and three tiers of boxes, with seating for 1642 and standing room for 567. Böhm conducted *Fidelio* at the reopening on 5 November 1955 and became the new director. The following year he conducted one of the Staatsoper's rare premières, that of Frank Martin's *Der Sturm*. He resigned the same year after being reproached for excessive absences, and Herbert von Karajan was appointed to replace him. In the six years of Karajan's single-handed direction an exceptional number of 20th-century operas (Egk's *Der Revisor*, Hindemith's *Mathis der Maler*, Orff's *Trionfi* and *Oedipus der Tyrann*, Pizzetti's *Assassinio nella cattedrale*, Poulenc's *Dialogues des Carmélites*, Stravinsky's *Oedipus rex*) and ballets were performed. A feature of Karajan's years as director was the exchange of productions with La Scala, whereby Italian casts performed some of the Verdi and Puccini operas in Vienna, and Viennese casts took Mozart and Wagner works, and *Pelléas et Mélisande*, to Milan. From 1962 Karajan was assisted by an associate director, which left him more time for purely artistic concerns: he directed more operas himself (*Tristan und Isolde*, *Tannhäuser*, *Die Frau ohne Schatten*), introduced the singing of works in their original language and conducted some remarkable performances, including the *Ring*, Monteverdi's *L'incoronazione di Poppea* and operas by Verdi and Puccini. In 1963 Hilbert was appointed his associate, but personal tensions led to Karajan's resignation the following year. Until his retirement in 1967 Hilbert attempted to fill the gap by engaging leading directors: in the last years of his life Wieland Wagner staged memorable performances of *Lohengrin*, *Salome* and *Elektra*. Singers of worldwide reputation contributed to the Staatsoper's success in the era of Karajan and Hilbert, among them Mimi Coertse, Leontyne Price, Birgit Nilsson, Leonie Rysanek, Gundula Janowitz, Lucia Popp, James King, Fritz Wunderlich, Walter Berry, Eberhard Waechter, Peter Schreier, Nicolai Ghiaurov and some of the most famous Italian singers of the time, including Mirella Freni, Giulietta Simionato, Renata Tebaldi and Giuseppe di Stefano.

In the years that followed, the Staatsoper was placed in the charge of administrative directors, Heinrich Reif-Gintl and Rudolf Gamsjäger, who were unable to prevent a gradual deterioration in artistic standards. This was reflected in the steadily falling numbers of premières, increasingly rare performances of modern operas (not forgetting, however, the revival of Berg's *Lulu* and the successful première of Gottfried von Einem's *Der Besuch der alten Dame*, as well as the first inclusion of Schoenberg's *Moses und Aron* in the repertory of the Staatsoper) and a growing number of productions of limited artistic value. After 1966 the occasional appearance of Leonard Bernstein conducting *Falstaff*, *Rosenkavalier* and *Fidelio* was an attraction. In autumn 1976 the directorship of the Staatsoper was taken over by Egon Seefehlner and in 1979 Lorin Maazel's appointment as conductor was announced with effect from 1982.

Maazel resigned after only two years and Seefehlner continued the directorship temporarily until 1986. From then until 1991 the director was Claus Helmut Drese, who brought with him from Zürich Claudio Abbado as music director. During these years Abbado secured excellent performances of the Italian repertory, including *Simon Boccanegra* with Giorgio Strehler as stage director, followed by works such as *Wozzeck*, *Pelléas et Mélisande* and *Khovanshchina* and, later, operas by Wagner and Mozart. The repertory was extended with more unusual operas by Dvořák, Massenet, Bartók, Schreker (*Der ferne Klang*) and others. Some elaborate performances have been rehearsed in collaboration with the Salzburg Festival and presented in Vienna immediately after their summer premières in Salzburg. There thus appeared in the 1981 programme Cerha's *Baal*, in 1984 Berio's *Un re in ascolto* and in 1986 Penderecki's *Die schwarze Maske*. Giuseppe Sinopoli, Colin Davis, Václav Neumann and Riccardo Muti were among the outstanding conductors, and the directors included Harry Kupfer, Ken Russell and Götz Friedrich. In 1988 Abbado conducted Schubert's rarely performed *Fierrabras* in a production by Ruth Berghaus. After the success of Jean-Pierre Ponnelle's Monteverdi cycle in Zürich with Nikolaus Harnoncourt conducting, Drese engaged Harnoncourt for a Mozart cycle, but this was far less successful. The demanding Viennese audiences, used to star casts, preferred to follow series of performances by their favourite singers – the celebrated trio of tenors, Carreras, Domingo and Pavarotti, and also Agnes Baltsa, Edita Gruberová and Jessye Norman.

The enormous budget of the Staatsoper, unequalled by any comparable institution in the world and borne by means of taxes levied on the whole Austrian nation, is justified by its reputation and by its international influence. The high standard of performances owes much to the employment of Vienna PO players for the orchestra. The repertory comprises some 45 to 50 standard operas, and except for July and August the company plays daily for the entire year. The number of new productions each season has varied between five and eight, of which one or two are first performances of ballets.

Beginning in the 1991–2 season a new team assumed the management of the Staatsoper: Eberhard Waechter, who also continued as director of the Volksoper, and Joan Holender. The new team declined for the time being to mount new productions, dropped repeat stagings of several recent productions and employed a number of young, less well-known singers. In October 1991 Claudio Abbado laid down his musical directorship of the Staatsoper, apparently in connection with this development; and Waechter died in 1992.

The Volksoper, Vienna's second resident opera company, like the Staatsoper is open ten months of the year. Although for the first ten years after the war the theatre was used by the Staatsoper for half its productions, from 1955, expensively redecorated, it housed a largely successful attempt to revive the Viennese operetta and, to a lesser extent, to re-create the American musical in spectacular style. When the great popularity of these subsided, the Volksoper concentrated on offering competition to the Staatsoper with standard repertory works in German and presenting musical comedy and operetta. The reforms of the mid-1970s entailed, for both the Volksoper and the Staatsoper, far-reaching autonomy and independence from the state which, as the assign of the former court government, controlled the allotment of the budget.

The Theater an der Wien, used from 1945 to 1955 for Staatsoper productions, was closed as unsafe in 1955, but was rescued and reopened in 1962 by Hilbert, then director of the Vienna Festival. Since then it has been financed by the city and used for stage productions during the festival (May and June; begun in 1951) and for musicals and operetta during the rest of the year. The Raimundtheater remains true to its traditional fare of Viennese operetta. The Schönbrunn Schlosstheater is used as a rehearsal stage for chamber operas performed by students of the Hochschule für Musik und Darstellende Kunst. Since its foundation in 1952 the Wiener Kammeroper, under the artistic direction of Hans Gabor, has played an important part in reviving older works, especially Viennese operas and Singspiels of the 18th and 19th centuries, performing in its own attractive house in the Fleischmarkt, and also in the Schlosstheater at Schönbrunn.

*

GENERAL

J. Oehler: *Geschichte des gesammten Theaterwesens zu Wien, von den ältesten, bis auf die gegenwärtigen Zeiten* (Vienna, 1803)
R. Wallaschek: *Das k. k. Hofoperntheater* (Vienna, 1909)
R. Haas: *Die Wiener Oper* (Vienna and Budapest, 1926)
O. Deleglise: *Das Schönbrunner Schlosstheater* (Vienna, 1947)
L. Ferrari: 'Per la bibliografia del teatro italiano in Vienna', *Studi di bibliografia e di argomento romano: in memoria di Luigi de Gregori* (Rome, 1949), 136–49
E. Pirchen, A. Witeschnik and O. Fritz: *300 Jahre Wiener Operntheater* (Vienna, 1953)
A. Bauer: *Opern und Operetten in Wien: Verzeichnis ihrer Erstaufführungen von 1629 bis zur Gegenwart* (Graz and Cologne, 1955)
H. Kralik: *Die Wiener Oper* (Vienna, 1963)
F. Hadamowsky: *Die Wiener Hoftheater (Staatstheater) 1776–1966* (Vienna, 1966–75)
R. Klein: *Die Wiener Staatsoper* (Vienna, 1967, 2/1969; Eng. trans., 1967)
O. E. Deutsch: 'Das Repertoire der höfischen Oper, der Hof- und der Staatsoper', *ÖMz*, xxiv (1969), 369–70, 379–421
M. Dietrich, ed.: *Das Burgtheater und sein Publikum* (Vienna, 1976)
F. Hadamowsky: *Wien: Theater Geschichte, von den Anfängen bis zum Ende des Ersten Weltkriegs* (Vienna, 1988)

UP TO 1740

A. von Weilen: *Geschichte des Wiener Theaterwesens von den ältesten Zeiten bis zu den Anfängen der Hoftheater* (Vienna, 1899)
——: *Zur Wiener Theatergeschichte: die vom Jahre 1629 bis zum Jahre 1740 am Wiener Hofe zur Aufführung gelangten Werke theatralischen Charakters und Oratorien* (Vienna, 1901)
E. Wellesz: 'Die Opern und Oratorien in Wien 1660–1708', *SMw*, vi (1919), 5–138
——: *Der Beginn des musikalischen Barock und die Anfänge der Oper in Wien* (Vienna and Leipzig, 1922)
R. Haas: 'Die Musik in der Wiener deutschen Stegreifkomödie', *SMw*, xii (1925), 3–64
E. C. Salzer: *Rivista italiana del dramma*, ii–iii (1938–9) [six articles on Italian theatre at the Viennese court during the Baroque era]
F. Hadamowsky: 'Barocktheater am Wiener Kaiserhof, mit einem Spielplan (1625–1740)', *Jb der Gesellschaft für Wiener Theaterforschung 1951–2*, 7–117
E. Schenk: *Die Anfänge des Wiener Kärntnertortheaters (1710–1748)* (diss., U. of Vienna, 1969)
R. A. Griffin: *High Baroque Culture and Theatre in Vienna* (New York, 1972)
N. Hiltl: *Die Oper am Hofe Kaiser Leopolds I. mit besonderer Berücksichtigung der Tätigkeit von Minato und Draghi* (diss., U. of Vienna, 1975)
H. Seifert: *Die Oper am Wiener Kaiserhof im 17. Jahrhundert* (Tutzing, 1985)

1740–1830

BurneyGN
Répertoire des théâtres de la ville de Vienne depuis l'année 1752 à l'année 1757 (Vienna, 1757)
J. H. F. Müller: *Genaue Nachrichten von beyden kaiserlich-königlichen Schaubühnen und andern öffentlichen Ergözlichkeiten in Wien* (Vienna, 1772)
F. Nicolai: *Beschreibung einer Reise durch Deutschland und die Schweiz, im Jahre 1781* (Berlin and Stettin, 1783–96)
C. Ditters: *Karl von Dittersdorfs Lebensbeschreibung: seinem Sohne in die Feder diktirt* (Leipzig, 1801)
A. P. C. Favart, ed.: *Mémoires et correspondances littéraires, dramatiques et anecdotiques de C. S. Favart* (Paris, 1808) [with a 'notice historique' by H.-F. Dumolard]
L. da Ponte: *Memorie di Lorenzo Da Ponte da Ceneda scritte da esso* (New York, 1823–7, enlarged 2/1829–30); ed. C. Pagnini (Milan, 1971); Eng. trans. ed. L. A. Sheppard (London, 1929), ed. A. Livingston and E. Abbott (Philadelphia, 1929)
M. Kelly: *Reminiscences of Michael Kelly* (London, 1826, 2/1826); ed. R. Fiske (London, 1975)
O. Teuber: *Das k. k. Hofburgtheater seit seiner Begründung* (Vienna, 1896)
R. Graf Khevenhüller-Metsch and H. Schlitter, eds.: *Aus der Zeit Maria Theresias: Tagebuch des Fürsten Johann Joseph Khevenhüller-Metsch, kaiserlichen Obersthofmeisters 1742–1776* (Vienna, Leipzig and Berlin, 1907–25)
C. Pichler: *Denkwürdigkeiten aus meinem Leben* (Munich, 1914)
R. Smekal: *Das alte Burgtheater 1776–1888* (Vienna, 1916)
R. Payer von Thurn, ed.: *Joseph II. als Theaterdirektor* (Vienna, 1920)
R. Haas: *Gluck und Durazzo im Burgtheater* (Zürich, Leipzig and Vienna, 1925)
——: 'Die Musik in der Wiener deutschen Stegreifkomödie', *SMw*, xii (1925), 3–64
F. Hadamowsky: *Das Theater in der Wiener Leopoldstadt 1781–1860* (Vienna, 1934)
O. E. Deutsch: *Das Freihaustheater auf der Wieden 1787–1801* (Vienna, 1937, 2/1937)
W. Scheib: *Die Entwicklung der Musikberichterstattung im Wienerischen Diarium 1703–1780 mit besonderer Berücksichtigung der Wiener Oper* (diss., U. of Vienna, 1950)
O. E. Deutsch: 'Die Orangerie im Schloss Schönbrunn', *ÖMz*, xii (1957), 384–6
O. Michtner: *Das alte Burgtheater als Opernbühne* (Vienna, 1970)
P. Branscombe: 'Music in the Viennese Popular Theatre of the Eighteenth and Nineteenth Centuries', *PRMA*, xcviii (1971–2), 101–12
G. Zechmeister: *Die Wiener Theater nächst der Burg und nächst dem Kärntnertor von 1747 bis 1776* (Vienna, 1972)
E. Badura-Skoda: 'The Influence of the Viennese Popular Comedy on Haydn and Mozart', *PRMA*, c (1973–4), 185–99
G. Croll: 'Neue Quellen zu Musik und Theater in Wien 1758–1763: ein erster Bericht', *Festschrift Walter Senn* (Munich, 1975), 8–12
F. Hadamowsky: 'Die Schauspielfreiheit, die "Erhebung des Burgtheaters zum Hoftheater" und seine "Begründung als Nationaltheater" im Jahr 1776', *Maske und Kothurn*, xxii (1976), 5–19
O. Schindler: 'Der Zuschauerraum des Burgtheaters im 18. Jahrhundert', *Maske und Kothurn*, xxii (1976), 20–53
F. Hadamowsky: *Die Josephinische Theaterreform und die Spielzeit 1776/77 des Burgtheaters* (Vienna, 1978)
J. Joly: *Les fêtes théâtrales de Métastase à la cour de Vienne (1731–1767)* (Clermont-Ferrand, 1978)
M. Dietrich: 'Theater am Hofe – zwischen Tradition und Wandel', *Maria Theresia und ihre Zeit*, ed. W. Koschatzky (Salzburg and Vienna, 2/1980), 393–403
F. Hadamowsky: '"Spectacle müssen sein": Maria Theresia und das Theater', ibid, 387–92
D. Heartz: 'Haydn und Gluck im Burgtheater um 1760: Der neue

krumme Teufel, Le diable à quatre, und die Sinfonie "Le Soir" ', *GfMKB: Bayreuth 1981*, 120–35
——: 'Nicolas Jadot and the Building of the Burgtheater', *MQ*, lxviii (1982), 1–31
C. Kirk: *The Viennese Vogue for opéra-comique 1790–1819* (diss., U. of St Andrews, 1984)
F. Karro: 'De la Querelle des Bouffons à la réforme de Gluck: les lettres du Comte Giacomo Durazzo à Charles-Simon Favart conservées à la Bibliothèque de l'Opéra', *Mitteilungen des Österreichischen Staatsarchivs*, xxxviii (1985), 163–96
B. A. Brown: 'Gluck als Hauskomponist für das französische Theater in Wien', *Gluck in Wien: Vienna 1987*, 89–99
G. Croll: 'Der "alte Gluck" und Mozart in Wien', ibid, 158–65
J. A. Rice: *Emperor and Impresario: Leopold II and the Transformation of Viennese Musical Theater* (diss., U. of California, Berkeley, 1987)
F. Hadamowsky: *Wien: Theater Geschichte, von den Anfängen bis zum Ende des Ersten Weltkriegs* (Vienna, 1988)
B. A. Brown: *Gluck and the French Theatre in Vienna* (Oxford, 1991)

SINCE 1830

R. Smekal: *Das alte Burgtheater 1776–1888* (Vienna, 1916)
E. Rieger: *Die gute alte Zeit der Wiener Operette* (Vienna, 1922)
F. Hadamowsky: *Das Theater in der Leopoldstadt 1781–1860* (Vienna, 1934)
F. Hadamowsky and H. Otte: *Die Wiener Operette* (Vienna, 1947)
R. Holzer: *Die Wiener Vorstadtbühnen* (Vienna, 1951)
A. Bauer: *150 Jahre Theater an der Wien* (Zürich, Leipzig and Vienna, 1952)
——: *Das Theater in der Josefstadt zu Wien* (Vienna and Munich, 1957)
R. Klein and E. Werba: 'Sternstunden im Theater an der Wien', *ÖMz*, xvii (1962), 262–325
P. Branscombe: 'Music in the Viennese Popular Theatre of the Eighteenth and Nineteenth Centuries', *PRMA*, xcviii (1971–2), 101–12
Jb der Wiener Staatsoper (Vienna, 1991) [pubn of Freunde der Wiener Staatsoper]
Österreichischer Bundestheaterverband, 1990–91 (Vienna, 1991) [annual report] HERBERT SEIFERT (1), BRUCE ALAN BROWN (2), PETER BRANSCOMBE (3), MOSCO CARNER, RUDOLF KLEIN (4), RUDOLF KLEIN, HARALD GOERTZ (5)

Vienna, La. *See* MELLINI, VIENNA.

Vie parisienne, La ('Parisian Life'). *Opéra bouffe* in five (later four) acts by JACQUES OFFENBACH to a libretto by HENRI MEILHAC and LUDOVIC HALÉVY; Paris, Théâtre du Palais-Royal, 31 October 1866.

The work was written in anticipation of the crowds visiting Paris for the 1867 Exhibition and proved one of the hits of the season. It was composed not for Offenbach's usual company, but for that of the Palais-Royal, which comprised actors as much as singers – strengthened for the occasion by one of Offenbach's favourite players, Zulma Bouffar, as the glovemaker Gabrielle. The piece recognizes the company's limitations with music that is vocally less extensive and demanding than that Offenbach wrote for the Théâtre de la Gaîté. The musical strength lies rather in the sparkling orchestral melodies – above all, waltzes, galops and can-cans which, allied to a humorous libretto that was Meilhac and Halévy at their best, has made the work a perpetual favourite as a symbol of Second Empire gaiety. By the time the piece was revived at the Théâtre des Variétés on 25 September 1873 the fourth of the five acts had been dropped, but it is still sometimes included, as for instance at Sadler's Wells Theatre in 1961.

ACT 1 At the Gare de l'Ouest in Paris, foreign tourists are awaited. Two young dandies, Raoul de Gardefeu (tenor) and Bobinet (baritone), are there to meet the courtesan Métella (mezzo-soprano), for whose favours they are rivals. However, when her train arrives from Trouville, she has another escort and affects not to know them. Companions in misfortune, they determine to give up such women and return to the fashionable ladies of the Boulevard Saint-Germain ('Elles sont tristes, les marquises'). Then Gardefeu comes across his former valet Joseph (spoken), who is now employed by the Grand-Hôtel as a guide. Joseph is there to meet the Swedish Baron and Baroness de Gondremarck (baritone and soprano). Struck by the Baroness's charms, Gardefeu bribes Joseph to let him take his place. Meanwhile, foreign tourists are pouring in, among them a wealthy Brazilian (baritone) determined to spend as lavishly as he can ('Je suis Brésilien, j'ai de l'or').

Poster (c1886) by Jules Chéret for Offenbach's 'La vie parisienne', first performed at the Théâtre du Palais-Royal, Paris, in 1866

ACT 2 Gardefeu has brought the Swedes to his own villa, which he pretends is an annexe of the Grand-Hôtel. The Baron is determined to enjoy himself in Paris ('Dans cette ville toute pleine de plaisir') and is therefore not too worried by Gardefeu's efforts to get the Baroness to himself; he readily accepts the idea of separate rooms and an invitation to a party the following evening. For the first evening, assisted by handy tradespeople, Gardefeu lays on a table d'hôte; the bootmaker Frick (baritone) poses as a major ('Pour découper adroitement') and the glovemaker Gabrielle (soprano) as a colonel's widow ('Je suis veuve d'un colonel') who brings the act to an end with an outrageous Tyrolienne.

ACT 3 Gardefeu has entrusted to Bobinet the task of arranging the party for the Baron's second evening. Bobinet happens to have been left in charge of his aunt's villa, and he enrols the servants of the house to masquerade as fashionable guests. He himself acts as host, disguised as a Swiss admiral, with the chambermaid Pauline (soprano) detailed to seduce the Baron ('L'amour, c'est une échelle immense'). Gabrielle is there, too, in a frilly dress ('Sa robe fait frou, frou, frou, frou') and, as the wine flows in abundance, the fun increases. Bobinet's costume splits ('Votre habit a cracqué dans le dos') and, as the guests start to dance ('Tout tourne, tout tourne'), the pace becomes ever more hectic, culminating in a breathless can-can ('Feu partout!').

Act 4 Back in his villa, Gardefeu has prepared an intimate supper for the Baroness, who arrives full of the sights of Paris ('Je suis encore toute éblouie, toute ravie'). However, his plans are upset by the arrival of Bobinet's aunt, Madame de Quimper-Karadec (mezzo-soprano), and her niece, Madame de Folle Verdure (soprano). The aunt has returned unexpectedly to Paris and, having discovered her house taken over by the servants, has decided to seek accommodation at the hotel of her niece's friend, the Baroness. Gardefeu manages to deposit her in the Baron's room – much to the consternation of the latter when he returns from his party completely tipsy.

Act 5 At the Hôtel Anglais the Brazilian is spending some of his millions on a masked ball, and Alfred, the head waiter (baritone), instructs his staff to close their eyes as much as possible to what goes on ('Avant toute chose il faut être mystérieux et réservés'). Métella is there, assisting in the enjoyment to one of Offenbach's loveliest slow waltzes ('A minuit sonnant commence la fête'). In so doing she contrives to be reunited with Gardefeu, thereby restoring the Baroness safely to the Baron. At the same time the Brazilian finds happiness with Gabrielle, leaving all thoroughly contented with Parisian life ('Par nos chansons et par nos cris célébrons Paris!'). ANDREW LAMB

Vier Grobiane, Die. Opera by Ermanno Wolf-Ferrari; *see* *QUATRO RUSTEGHI, I.*

Vieru, Anatol (*b* Iaşi, 8 June 1926). Romanian composer. He studied at the Bucharest Conservatory with Leon Klepper and others (1946–51), then with Khachaturian at the Moscow Conservatory (1951–4); later he participated in a Darmstadt summer course (1967). He won the Queen Marie José, Koussevitsky and Herder prizes. After a period as a conductor at the Bucharest National Theatre, 1947–50, he worked as a musicologist and taught at the Bucharest Conservatory. His compositions include the dramatic madrigal *Scène nocturne* (1964), the dadaist comedy *Sita lui Eratostene* ('The Sieve of Eratosthenes', 1969) and the multi-media piece *Orologii* ('Clocks', 1970). Vieru came to public attention with the operas *Iona* (1, after M. Sorescu and engravings by M. C. Escher; concert perf., Bucharest, 31 Oct 1976) and *Praznicul Calicilor* ('The Feast of the Beggars', 1980; after M. Sorbul; concert perf., Bucharest, 24 June 1984). His virtuoso technique allows him to make economical use of vocal and instrumental resources: in 1982–3 he composed three micro-operas for two singers and five instrumentalists, to texts by Ion Luca Caragiale, which show his strong sense of irony. He is a master of modern sonorities, with a lucid, original style. VIOREL COSMA

Vietnam. The French occupied Saigon in 1859 and by the Treaty of Saigon (1862) obliged the Emperor Tu Duc to concede eastern Cochin China to them. It was annexed as a French colony in 1867. According to Loewenberg (*Annals of Opera*), Offenbach's *Les deux aveugles* was the first opera performed in Saigon, in autumn 1864. By 1865 the French troupe that performed there was also appearing in Manila and Batavia. As the only resident opera company in the Far East, they toured for many years, performing in China, Japan, the Philippines, the Dutch East Indies and elsewhere.

Opera in Saigon was first given in a government hangar at the Hôtel en Bois des Amiraux on the place de l'Horloge. The idea of building a theatre took root in 1883, and in 1894 the architect Ferret began the construction. Guichard completed the work in 1900, and the Nouveau Théâtre (cap. 738) was inaugurated, in an unfinished state, on 17 January with a gala performance – in honour of the visiting Prince Valdemar of Denmark – including Act 1 of *Mignon* and extracts from other French works. The theatre later became known as the Grand Théâtre, or Théâtre Municipal, and was run, with a government subsidy, by French impresarios who brought troupes from France. The first contract still existing in the French Colonial Archives dates from 1884–5: in it, M. Pontet (formerly director of the Grand Théâtre, Dijon) agreed to bring a company of ten male artists (six singers) and seven female (six singers), a chorus of nine, a conductor and six orchestral musicians (a further eight were to be engaged locally) from France to perform vaudevilles, comedies, operas and operettas; the colonial administration paid their travelling expenses, put the theatre at their disposal and provided a subsidy to meet performance costs.

By 1907 the company had grown considerably. There were virtually separate troupes for vaudevilles and comedies on the one hand and operas and operettas on the other; the orchestra was augmented to 30, the chorus to 24. The season lasted from October to April, each month seeing a minimum of five operas, five operettas and two comedies or vaudevilles; the contract insisted on five works that had not been performed in Saigon during the preceding three years. The list of works presented between, for example, 1901 and 1907 is impressive. It included over 40 operettas and as many operas, including not only all the French favourites of the day – *Carmen*, *Faust*, *La favorite*, *La fille du régiment*, *Guillaume Tell*, *Hamlet*, *Hérodiade*, *Lakmé*, *Mignon*, *Manon*, *Roméo et Juliette*, *Samson et Dalila* and *Werther* – but also *Lohengrin*, *La traviata*, *Il trovatore*, *Tosca*, *La bohème* and *L'amico Fritz*.

Tonkin and Annam were added to form French Indo-China after the French had stormed Hanoi in 1873 and forced the emperor to accept a French protectorate in 1888. In 1889 De Gréff, a co-director of the Saigon theatre, took a company of 15 artists to perform operetta in Hanoi and its port, Haiphong. A request for an annual subsidy for opera in these cities was refused by the Protectorate Administration in 1893 but finally accorded in 1896 for a company of 30 artists (orchestral musicians included). The Théâtre Municipal of Hanoi was inaugurated in 1911, in the rue des Nattes en Bambous (now Trang Tien Street). It held 737: 320 in the parterre, 181 in the first gallery and 236 in the second. The theatre at Haiphong was built shortly afterwards. The two theatres were administered by one impresario as the Théâtres de Hanoi et Haiphong Réunis, with the company appearing in alternate months in each city for six months of the year, i.e. three months in each.

Each of the five leading singers of the company was required to sing three début roles during the first month of each season in Hanoi, and the subscribers voted on whether they could stay or be returned to France (at the impresario's expense). The repertory was similar to that in Saigon but with a higher proportion of operetta. As in Saigon, fines were levied on impresarios for what were considered sub-standard performances. The importance of opera in the life of the colony can be judged by the fact that in 1920 it was estimated that altogether 10 000–12 000 Europeans (children included) lived in Saigon, Hanoi and Haiphong. The theatres at Saigon, Hanoi and Haiphong continued as French provincial opera houses up to World War II.

When the French left Indo-China in 1954, Vietnam was divided politically between the Communist north, including Hanoi and Haiphong, and the south. The Grand Théâtre de Saigon was then pressed into service as the Parliament House of South Vietnam.

*

C. Pitt: 'L'opéra au Vietnam', *Opéra international* (forthcoming)

CHARLES PITT

Vieuille, Félix (*b* Saugeon, 15 Oct 1872; *d* Saugeon, 28 Feb 1953). French bass. After study at the Paris Conservatoire he made his début at Aix-les-Bains in 1897 as Leporello. He became the leading bass with the Opéra-Comique in 1898, his first major role being Arkel in the première of *Pelléas et Mélisande* (1902). He also created roles in Charpentier's *Louise* (1900), Rabaud's *La fille de Roland* (1904) and *Mârouf* (1914), *Ariane et Barbe-Bleue* by Dukas (1907), Bloch's *Macbeth* (1910) and Milhaud's *Le pauvre matelot* (1927). He appeared at the Manhattan Opera House in the 1908–9 season and sang in the Paris premières of Fauré's *Pénélope* and Rimsky-Korsakov's *Snow Maiden*. DAVID CUMMINGS

Viganò [Braglia], **Onorato (Rinaldo Giuseppe Maria)** (*b* Milan, 6 Sept 1739; *d* ?Venice, 1811). Italian choreographer, dancer and impresario. From the 1750s he danced mostly in Rome, Vienna, Venice and Naples, becoming active as a choreographer from at least 1773 and as an impresario from at least 1783. One of the best-known choreographers in Italy, he often worked in collaboration with the composer Marescalchi. His career as an impresario, notably at the Teatro Argentina in Rome (1783–8), the S Benedetto in Venice (from 1786) and the Teatro Nuovo, Padua (1809), was, however, chequered, plagued by financial difficulties.

Many members of the Viganò family were dancers and musicians. Onorato's daughter Vincenza danced from at least 1782, mostly in serious parts, and married the tenor Domenico Mombelli. She is remembered for having written the libretto of Rossini's first opera, *Demetrio e Polibio*, in which her husband and their two famous daughters, Ester and Anna, sang. Among Onorato's sons, Salvatore (*b* Naples, 25 March 1769; *d* Milan, 10 Aug 1821) became a celebrated choreographer, working in Venice, Vienna (notably 1799–1803, during which time he choreographed Beethoven's *Die Geschöpfe des Prometheus*) and Milan (from 1811 at La Scala, where he created innovatory dramatic ballets known as *coreodrammi*). A composition pupil of Luigi Boccherini (his uncle), Salvatore Viganò also had a *farsetta*, *La credula vedova*, performed in Rome in summer 1786.

*

C. Ritorni: *Commentarii della vita e delle opere coreodrammatiche di Salvatore Viganò* (Milan, 1838)
H. Prunières: 'Salvatore Viganò', *ReM*, iii/2 (1921–2), 71–94

Vigarani, Carlo (*b* Reggio Emilia, *c* Dec 1623; *d* ?Paris, before 1713). Italian theatre architect and scene designer, son of Gaspare Vigarani. With his brother Lodovico, he accompanied his father to Paris in 1659, at Cardinal Mazarin's invitation, and participated in the design of the Salle des Machines in the Tuileries and the production of Cavalli's *Ercole amante* in 1662. In 1663 he was invited back by Louis XIV to design court entertainments and, as part of a triumvirate with Lully and Molière, he was responsible for the three *fêtes d'amour* at Versailles in 1664, 1668 and 1674. These rank among the most exquisite and sumptuous theatrical entertainments of the period. Each consisted of several plays, operas and ballets commissioned for the occasion, including *La princesse d'Elide*, *Les fâcheux*, *Le mariage forcé*, *Les fêtes de l'Amour et de Bacchus*, *Alceste* (Quinault-Lully) and *Le malade imaginaire*. With the success of the first *fête d'amour*, he was established as the principal court theatre designer; in 1673 he received French citizenship and a monopoly as 'inventor of machines for theatres, ballets and royal festivities'. With Lully, he founded the Académie Royale de Musique et de Danse (the origin of the Paris Opéra) with the famous 'Act de Société' of 1672. Although he broke with Lully in 1675, Vigarani continued to provide the sets and machinery for the composer's operas until 1680 (for illustration *see* ATYS (i)). He also designed the first theatre used by the Opéra, the Salle Jeu de Paume, and renovated the Théâtre du Palais-Royal, the official court theatre. His designs combine Italian schemes derived from Torelli with the highly ornamented, allegorical decor demanded by the French court. Although he was still in the pay of the court in 1709, his influence apparently waned after 1680.

*

ES (W. Savini Nicci and others)
A. G. Messori Roncaglia: *Documenti e notizie sulle opere di Carlo Vigarani, architetto insigne del XVII secolo* (Modena, 1879)
A. Pougin: *Les vrais créateurs de l'opéra français* (Paris, 1881)
G. Bapst: 'La décoration théâtrale à la cour de Louis XIV', *Gazette des beaux arts*, iii (1892), 484–95
H. Prunières: *L'opéra italien en France avant Lulli* (Paris, 1913)
G. Rouchés: *Inventaire des lettres et papiers manuscrits de Gaspare, Carlo et Lodovico Vigarani, conservés aux Archives d'Etat de Modena (1634–1688)* (Paris, 1913)
G. Piccinini: *Alcune notizie su Gaspare e Carlo Vigarani, architetti del sec. XVII* (Reggio Emilia, 1934)
A. Nagler: 'Lully's Opernbühne', *Kleine Schriften der Gesellschaft für Theatergeschichte*, xvii (1960), 19–45 PAUL SHEREN

Vigarani, Gaspare (*b* Reggio Emilia, 1586–8; *d* Modena, *c*1663). Italian theatre architect and scene designer. He was active as a designer of machinery for festivities at Reggio Emilia by 1618, and took part in the design of theatres there and at Modena and Carpi. From the 1630s, if not before, he was employed by the Duke of Modena, and in 1635 was promoted to 'engineer and general superintendent of buildings'. In 1659 Cardinal Mazarin invited him, with his sons Carlo and Lodovico, to Paris to supervise the entertainments planned for the marriage of Louis XIV; for this occasion they constructed the Salle des Machines in the Tuileries Palace and designed the inaugural production there, Cavalli's *Ercole amante* (with additional ballets by Lully), performed, after considerable delay, in 1662. This production, with its spectacular stage machinery and scenic effects, was a major factor in the prominence enjoyed by Italian theatrical art in France for the next century. The theatre itself marked the transition from the pre-Baroque amphitheatre auditorium, which then prevailed in Paris, to the Italian opera house with perspective wing-stage and horseshoe auditorium. G. L. Bernini criticized it (1665) as disproportionately long, and inconvenient in its seating arrangement. Neither the theatre nor the production was widely acclaimed, and Vigarani returned disillusioned to Italy in 1663.

For bibliography *see* VIGARANI, CARLO. PAUL SHEREN

Viglione-Borghese, Domenico (*b* Mondovi, 3 July 1877; *d* Milan, 26 Oct 1957). Italian baritone. He studied in Milan with Cotogni and in Pesaro and made his début in 1899 at Lodi as the Herald in *Lohengrin*. On a South American tour (1905–6) he sang Rigoletto, Germont and Enrico Ashton opposite Tetrazzini. An engagement in 1906 at Parma launched him on an Italian career that lasted until 1940. He first appeared at La Scala in 1910 as Nélusko and returned several times until 1930. He sang in the première of Leoncavallo's *Maja* (1910, Rome) and the Italian première of *The Golden Cockerel* (1925, Turin) as Dodon. His most famous role was Jack Rance, which he first sang in Brescia in 1911 and for the last time in Rome in 1940. His large repertory included Michele (*Il tabarro*), Scarpia, Napoleon (*Madame Sans-Gêne*) and Boris. He had a powerful, resonant and beautiful voice, capable of every shade of expression.

HAROLD ROSENTHAL/R

Vignas, Francesco. *See* VIÑAS, FRANCISCO.

Vignati, Giuseppe (*b* ? Bologna, end of the 17th century; *d* Milan, 1768). Italian composer. Recent scholarship has not confirmed his Bolognese origin; it has been conjectured that he died shortly before G. B. Sammartini succeeded him as *maestro* of the ducal chapel on 8 November 1768. The earliest substantiated references to him date from 1713 when he was *maestro di cappella* of the Accademia dei Faticosi, Milan, and wrote a cantata for the canonization of Andrea Avellino. Between 1719 and 1727 he wrote a series of operas for the ducal theatre. The libretto for the first of these, *Ambleto*, names him as *maestro di cappella* of S Gottardo, the ducal chapel. Documents of the state archive disclose, however, that he was merely Paolo Magni's assistant there from 1718 until 4 March 1737 (Magni died on 21 February 1737). Serving in the court chapel without pay until 12 July 1735, Vignati concurrently drew a salary as *maestro di cappella* of S Nazzaro Maggiore (from 1726) and as harpsichordist at the ducal theatre. Although he played the second harpsichord in 1748 and 1749 to allow the composers of operas to direct from the first, he is listed as the *maestro di cappella* and first harpsichordist for the entire seasons of 1720, 1738, 1739 and 1743. His opera scores are lost, but their quality is suggested by the renown of his singers: Faustina Bordoni, Francesca Cuzzoni, Antonio Bernacchi and others. The large size of his orchestra – 30 players in 1720, including many wind instrumentalists – implies rich orchestrations.

first performed in Milan, Ducale, unless otherwise stated

Ambleto [Act 1] (A. Zeno and P. Pariati), 28 Aug 1719 [Act 2 by C. Baliani, Act 3 by G. Cozzi]
Porsena (3, A. Piovene), 26 Dec 1719
Aquilio in Siracusa (2), 28 Aug 1720
Nerone (3, Piovene), 26 Dec 1724
I rivali generosi (3, Zeno), Venice, S Samuele, Ascension Fair 1726
Girita (3, C. N. Stampa), Jan 1727

Doubtful: Amor per virtù (3, D. Cupeda), Turin, Regio, carn. 1702, cited in *EitnerQ*

J.-B. de La Borde: *Essai sur la musique* (Paris, 1780), 242
A. E. Choron and F. J. Fayolle: *Dictionnaire historique des musiciens* (Paris, 1810–11), ii, 406
G. Barblan: 'Il teatro musicale in Milano nei secoli XVII e XVIII', *Storia di Milano*, xii (Milan, 1958), 972, 976

SVEN HANSELL

Vignola, Giuseppe (*b* Naples, 5 Feb 1662; *d* Naples, Nov 1712). Italian composer. He studied at the Conservatorio S Maria della Pietà dei Turchini, Naples, when Francesco Provenzale was its *maestro ordinario*. He became known as a composer first of semi-dramatic sacred works (*La nave della redenzione*, 1696; *La regina Ester*, 1699; and *Il Gedeone geroglifico*, 1701) and later also of operatic music. In 1706 he was engaged by Andrea del Pò, the impresario of the Teatro S Bartolomeo, to compose additional arias for a performance of Giuseppe Aldrovandini's opera *Mitridate*. During the following years, Vignola played a significant role in the operatic life of Naples by providing new arias and *buffo* scenes for performances of operas by other composers, particularly Venetians. With these adaptations and three successful operas of his own, he was the most frequently performed opera composer in Naples between 1706 and 1712. He also continued to write oratorios, spiritual cantatas and other sacred music (*Il giudizio universale*, 1710, *I-Nf*). In 1707 he was appointed organist of the royal chapel in Naples; he remained in that post until his death, and was succeeded by Pietro Filippo Scarlatti, the eldest son of Alessandro Scarlatti.

all performed in Naples

Il Tullo Ostilio (dramma per musica, C. de Petris, after A. Morselli), S Bartolomeo, carn. 1707, *I-Mc*, arias *Nc*
La Rosmene ovvero L'infedeltà fedele (dramma, N. Pagano, ?after G. D. de Totis), Fiorentini, 26 Jan 1709
Teodora Augusta (dramma, Morselli), Fiorentini, 27 April 1709

Arias and scenes in: Aldrovandini: Mitridate, 1706; F. Gasparini: La fede tradita e vendicata, 1707; Gasparini: Le regine di Macedonia, 1708; A. Scarlatti: L'humanità nelle fiere, 1708; Lotti: L'inganno vinto dalla ragione, 1708; Gasparini: Ambleto, 1711; Lotti: La forza del sangue, 1712

*

FlorimoN
M. Scherillo: *L'opera buffa napoletana durante il settecento: storia letteraria* (Naples, 2/1916), 60
R. Strohm: *Italienische Opernarien des frühen settecento*, *AnMc*, no.16 (1976), ii, 288–96 HANNS-BERTOLD DIETZ

Viimeiset kiusaukset ('The Last Tempatations'). Opera in two acts by JOONAS KOKKONEN to a libretto by Lauri Kokkonen; Helsinki, Finnish National Opera, 2 September 1975.

In the late 1950s and early 60s Kokkonen became interested in a play by his cousin Lauri Kokkonen about a 19th-century revivalist preacher, Paavo Ruotsalainen (1772–1852). After a long period of gestation the opera was completed in 1975.

On his deathbed Paavo Ruotsalainen (bass) reviews in a series of flashbacks key events in his life as a wandering evangelist. He sees his first wife Riitta (soprano), long since dead, and they reminisce over their life together. They meet the stern blacksmith Högman (baritone), who inspired Paavo to spread his fundamentalist gospel, and they come across their son Juhana (tenor), tragically slain in a brawl. Paavo and Riitta have a furious quarrel, because his wanderings often leave the family destitute. Time and again Paavo finds that he does not have the strength to open the 'barrier of heaven' – not even when Riitta on her deathbed calls him to the island of their first happiness. He must go on preaching, even when mocked by unbelievers or rejected by the learned bishops in a great ceremony in Helsinki. Humbly he prays for forgiveness, and hears the blacksmith, Riitta and Juhana all giving thanks to the Lord. At last he is ready to go through the 'barrier of heaven'. Paavo awakes to find that a group of people who had been tormenting him are in fact members of his family. Tired, but at peace at last, he bids them farewell; and as they sing a hymn, he calmly and quietly expires.

Viimeiset kiusaukset was an immediate success, and the Finnish National Opera broke all local records by giving it a run of 166 performances. Apart from the opera's straightforward dramatic and musical appeal, the role of Paavo found an intense and majestic interpreter in Martti Talvela. Another contributing factor was the work's religious content, including the familiar hymn tunes woven into the texture of the score. (It has even been said that the piece demonstrated to the Finnish public, somewhat to its surprise, that opera was not after all 'a sinful entertainment'.) The score is unashamedly tonal, though the lyricism is often coloured with dissonance. After its première it came to be regarded as the 'national opera' of Finland, replacing Leevi Madetoja's *Pohjalaisa*. ERKKI ARNI

Vilar, José Teodoro (*b* Barcelona, 10 Aug 1836; *d* Barcelona, 21 Oct 1905). Spanish composer. He studied in Barcelona with the composer and organist Ramón Vilanova and in 1859 went to further his studies at the Paris Conservatoire with Henri Herz (piano) and Bazin and Halévy (composition). On his return he published a pamphlet *Apuntes de historia musical, o resumen de historia de la música* (Barcelona, 1863) and began a career as a concert pianist. He also dedicated himself to the composition of zarzuelas to Catalan librettos, in which field he was something of a pioneer. Of these, his *L'ultim rey de Magnolia* (1868) contains abundant references to the revolution which that year deposed Queen Isabel II. He was also chorus master and later conductor at the Teatro Principal in Barcelona. In later years he devoted himself exclusively to teaching and composition. Despite their Catalan settings, costumes and dialogue, Vilar's zarzuelas show the strong Italian influence prevalent at the time. As a skilful orchestrator, he was able to make intelligent use of musical colour to further the dramatic situations of his librettos.

all zarzuelas, first performed in Barcelona unless otherwise stated

La romería de Recasens (2), 1867; L'ultim rey de Magnolia (1, S. Pitarra), Romeo, Dec 1868; Els pescadors de San Pol (2), Tivoli, June 1869; Una prometensa, 1870; La Rambla de las Flores (J. Feliú y Codina), 1870; Pot més que pinta, 1870; La lluna en un cove, 1870/71; L'esca del pecat, 1871; La torre del amor, Santa Cruz, 1871; Un joes de cartas, Madrid, Oct 1881; La jupa blanca (Riera and Bertran), Dec 1881

*

A. Peña y Goñi: *La ópera española y la música dramática en España en el siglo XIX* (Madrid, 1881; abridged E. Rincón, as *España desde la ópera a la zarzuela*, 1967) ANDREW LAMB

Vil'boa [Villebois], **Konstantin Petrovich** (*b* St Petersburg, 17/29 May 1817; *d* Warsaw, 4/16 July 1882). Russian composer. A military man by training and early occupation, he left the service in 1860 to devote himself to music. After two false starts – *Taras Bulba* after Gogol and *Tsïganka* ('The Gypsy Girl') after Yevgeny Baratïnsky – he managed to complete a three-act opera, *Natasha, ili Volzhskiye razboyniki* ('Natasha, or The Volga Brigands', libretto by V. Krestovsky; Moscow, Bol'shoy, 19/31 October 1861; vs, St Petersburg, 1861). The plot, set in the 17th century, involves a romantic situation often depicted in folksongs (especially 'robbers' songs') of the Volga region: a maiden is abducted by brigands and brought to their chieftain, who falls in love with her before recognizing her as his own sister. The music, following Glinka's example in *A Life for the Tsar*, is redolent of the famous folksong *Vniz po matushke po Volge* ('Downstream on Mother Volga'). Otherwise it is standard operatic entertainment, often compared with Flotow. It had a cool critical reception but rapturous success with the public, and was quickly taken up by the Mariinsky Theatre in St Petersburg, opening there on 11/23 January 1863 under the composer's direction. Its folklike songs and choruses were often reprinted in anthologies and some of them entered the oral tradition, whence they were on occasion unwittingly collected by folklorists.

*

V. Kiselyov: 'A. N. Ostrovsky i K. P. Vil'boa', *A. N. Ostrovsky i russkiye kompozitorï*, ed. E. Kolosova and V. Filippov (Moscow and Leningrad, 1937), 44–52

A. A. Gozenpud: *Russkiy opernïy teatr XIX veka (1857–1872)* [Russian Operatic Theatre of the 19th Century] (Leningrad, 1971), chap.2 RICHARD TARUSKIN

Vilda, Maria. *See* WILT, MARIE.

Villafranchi, Giovanni Cosimo. *See* VILLIFRANCHI, GIOVANNI COSIMO.

Village Romeo and Juliet, A [*Romeo und Julia auf dem Dorfe*]. Lyric drama in six pictures (or scenes) by FREDERICK DELIUS to his own libretto after GOTTFRIED KELLER's novel; Berlin, Komische Oper, 21 February 1907.

Manz	*rich farmers*	baritone
Marti	*rich farmers*	baritone
Sali	*son of Manz as a child*	soprano
Sali	*son of Manz as a man*	tenor
Vreli	*daughter of Marti*	soprano
The Dark Fiddler	*rightful heir to the wood*	baritone
Two Peasant Men		baritone
Three Peasant Women		soprano, soprano, contralto
Gingerbread Woman		soprano
Wheel of Fortune Woman		soprano
Cheap Jewellery Woman		mezzo-soprano
Showman		tenor
Merry-go-round Man		baritone
The Slim Girl	*vagabonds*	soprano
The Wild Girl	*vagabonds*	mezzo-soprano
The Poor Horn-player	*vagabonds*	tenor
The Hunchbacked Bass-player	*vagabonds*	bass
Three Bargees		baritone, baritone, tenor

Vagabonds, peasants, bargees

Setting In and around Seldwyla, Switzerland, in the middle of the 19th century

Work on the libretto for Delius's fourth opera began in 1897. Delius first asked Charles Keary to produce an English text. Unhappy with the result, he turned to Karl-August Gerhardi in 1898 for a draft in German. He then resumed negotiations with Keary before deciding to attempt an English libretto himself. This was completed in 1899. The German translation for the first edition of the vocal score (*c*1906), with piano part by Florent Schmitt, was by Jelka Delius.

Keller based his story on a report in the *Zürcher Freitagszeitung* of 3 September 1847. It told how a young man of 19 and girl of 17 had fallen in love but failed to win their parents' consent because of mutual enmity. The young couple had danced one evening in a local inn; the next day they were found dead in a nearby meadow. Keller elaborated the story, making much of the parents' quarrel over land belonging rightfully to an illegitimate fiddler who could not inherit under Swiss law. Delius used the parental enmity only in so far as it made the marriage of the young couple impossible. The Dark Fiddler was given an altogether more sinister role, as embodiment of the cruel fate that brings about the suicide of the lovers. At the end Delius has unseen bargemen emphasize the frailty of earthly happiness. Delius did concentrated work on the music during 1900–01, but the orchestral 'Walk to the Paradise Garden', often played separately, was composed in 1906 for the Berlin performance.

The première was directed by Hans Gregor and conducted by Fritz Cassirer; the main singers were Willi Merkel (Sali), Lola Artôt de Padilla (Vreli) and Desider Zador (Dark Fiddler). The London première (Covent Garden, 22 February 1910) was conducted by Thomas Beecham, with Walter Hyde, Ruth Vincent and Robert Maitland; the Beecham recording (1948) had René Soames, Lorely Dyer and Gordon Clinton. Performances in Bradford, London and Manchester to mark the Delius centenary (1962) were conducted by Meredith Davies, with John Wakefield, Elsie Morison and Neil Easton. The Davies recording (1973) was with Robert Tear, Elizabeth Harwood and John Shirley-Quirk. The American première was in Washington, DC, at the John F. Kennedy Center on 26 April 1972, directed by Frank Corsaro and conducted by Paul Callaway, with John Stewart, Patricia Wells and John Reardon. The Swiss première was at the Zürich Opernhaus, 20 December 1980, conducted by Charles Mackerras, with Gösta Winbergh, Ursula Reinhardt-Kiss and Jozsef Dene.

SCENE 1 *September; a piece of woodland luxuriously overgrown on a hill* Manz and Marti are out ploughing on either side of the disused land. Marti decides to take in an extra furrow from the waste ground, sure that Manz will be doing the same. Sali and Vreli, son and daughter of the farmers, come with lunch and go off to play in the wood while the farmers eat. The children return when they hear a distant voice. It is a lame man with a violin, the Dark Fiddler, rightful owner of the waste ground who cannot inherit because of his doubtful parentage. The children fear him, but he assures them they can play in safety on his land so long as it remains unploughed. If it is ever worked, they must beware. Perhaps time will avenge him, he tells the farmers. The land is to be sold; at once the farmers wrangle about the extra furrows, and with rising tempers drag the children apart and forbid their play.

SCENE 2 *Six years later. Outside Marti's house; around it everything has run wild with neglect* The farmers' feud led to a lawsuit which ruined them both. Sali enters, now a young man, drawn irresistibly to see again where Vreli lives. Together they lament the hatred that has wrought such havoc. Sali asks if he may stay awhile, but Vreli fears her father may soon return. They realize their childhood friendship is turning to love and agree to meet that evening on the waste land.

SCENE 3 *The wild land overgrown with poppies in bloom, surrounded by cornfields; snow mountains in the distance* Sali lies waiting, and Vreli enters unnoticed. She calls him and hides; he runs eagerly after her. They forget their cares in the delight of being together again. The Dark Fiddler limps down from his ground, reminding them of his former appearance in their lives and the troubles caused by the disputed land. They are all beggars now, and the young people can join his wanderings if they wish. He assures them they will meet again. Sali comforts Vreli in her anxiety and they resume their play. This is interrupted by Vreli's father Marti, who has been spying on her and angrily confronts the young couple. Sali strikes him to the ground, and the scene ends in despair with Vreli imagining her father dead.

SCENE 4 *Interior of Marti's house; everything is bare: only a bedstead and a bench are left* Vreli is alone. Marti has lost his reason, and she has taken her father away; the house is to be sold. Sali comes in, having heard the news. The young lovers agree they must never part; they will wander together like larks in springtime. Quietly they settle by the fire and sleep in each other's arms. They dream they are being married in the old church at Seldwyla. As dawn breaks they realize they have shared the same dream. Now they long for a happy day together. Peasants yodel in the distance, and Sali remembers it is the day of the Berghald fair. Vreli must forget her worries and join him in the merrymaking.

SCENE 5 *The fair; an inn in front of which booths are erected* The hucksters cry their wares as the town bells peal. A show is about to begin in a tent, and the crowd sings as the circus band strikes up. Sali and Vreli enter, enchanted by all they see. Sali would buy everything for her and bewails his lack of money. As they wander past the inn, a man and woman recognize them as the children of Manz and Marti, now poor and friendless. Sali purchases a cheap ring for Vreli, but more and more they are embarrassed by the insistence of the hucksters. Sali decides this is no place for them and suggests they make for the Paradise Garden, where they can be alone and no one will know them. As the crowd emerges from the tent, the young lovers make their escape and begin their walk, hand in hand, towards the garden.

SCENE 6 *The Paradise Garden. An old dilapidated house, with snow mountains in the distance, is now used as an inn; a river flows by, with a hay barge moored to the bank* Vagabonds are drinking round a table, and the Dark Fiddler stands gazing at the mountains. He joins his companions and continues the tale of his dispossessed lands: the parents hate, the children love, and no one knows the end. At that moment Sali and Vreli enter. The Dark Fiddler urges them to join his friends, who extol the vagabond life. The lovers wonder whether happiness might not lie that way. One of the women eyes Sali intently, pointing out that there will be many alternatives when they tire of each other. The Dark Fiddler suggests they think it over, but Sali and Vreli know they will find no contentment there. A bargeman is heard afar on the river, singing of passing strangers drifting by. Sali understands the meaning of the song, and they decide to drift away for ever. They sing their love-death: the hay barge shall be their marriage bed and, as the Dark Fiddler plays a wild accompaniment,

'A Village Romeo and Juliet' (Delius): set design by Adrian Allinson for the final scene for a revival conducted by Thomas Beecham at Covent Garden, London, 1920: gouache

Sali casts off, removes the plug from the barge and falls into Vreli's arms. The Fiddler points to the bend in the river as the boat sinks and the young travellers pass out of sight.

* * *

By the time of *A Village Romeo and Juliet*, Delius was musically fully formed and his idiom had become idiosyncratic and personal. The calm and diatonic opening of the work gradually clouds to the harsh chromatics of the quarrelling farmers. The lovers' duet in Scene 4 is as touching a tribute as any to the influence of Wagner, impossible to conceive without *Parsifal* and 'Ich sah das Kind'. Yet the descending semitones of the bass are a Delian hallmark and give the passage an almost unbearable poignancy. Delius employs a handful of leitmotifs, using them with masterly flexibility until he gathers the most important of them to form the magical tone poem of 'The Walk to the Paradise Garden'. In his libretto Delius played down the immediacy of the Keller story, so that the young Sali and Vreli are distanced from reality and act out their ill-starred love in trance-like isolation. The Dark Fiddler, too, is an outsider figure such as Delius himself was. The result is an operatic masterpiece with drama and music marvellously integrated, a *Tristan und Isolde* for the young and innocent.

ROBERT ANDERSON

Villa-Lobos, Heitor (*b* Rio de Janeiro, 5 March 1887; *d* Rio de Janeiro, 17 Nov 1959). Brazilian composer. He was born just two years before a revolution turned Brazil from a monarchy to a republic, and he grew up in an artistic environment which echoed and, to a certain extent, shaped the political and social changes instigated by successive governments. He was self-taught as a cellist, and almost so as a composer, eschewing any formal musical training. He earned his living first as a cellist, travelling through Brazil in the first decade of the century to give recitals and concerts in provincial venues, and then returning to Rio, where he worked in theatre and opera orchestras. On his travels he absorbed the influences of indigenous and popular musical styles.

Villa-Lobos's experiences in theatre orchestras prompted him to write several youthful operas, out of which he rescued material for his first major stage work, *Izaht* (composed 1912–14). He claimed to have written this work to confound his critics, who at the time were objecting to the influx of nationalistic traits in his music, and to demonstrate that opera need not be tedious. The huge and unwieldy work received partial and concert performances before its first complete staging a year before Villa-Lobos's death. *Izaht*'s mixture of neo-romantic and proto-nationalistic language and its unpredictable instrumental writing were typical of Villa-Lobos's music at this time.

Villa-Lobos continued to compose prolifically in all genres, including opera, and established himself as the leading exponent of modernism in Brazilian music. He was skilled at emulating the improvised music of Rio's street serenaders (*chorões*), and conversely uncomfortable when writing music requiring dramatic interplay and formal coherence. For this reason his series of *Chôros* succeeds, while his operas written around 1920 failed totally.

Busy years spent working in Paris and, after 1930, implementing musical education schemes in Brazil under the dictatorial governments of Getúlio Vargas, meant that Villa-Lobos temporarily abandoned opera composition in favour of developing his own highly charged Brazilian style, writing propaganda music, working as an administrator, conducting and broadcasting. After World War II his extensive travels as a conductor stimulated a large number of commissions, including three operas. *Magdalena* (1948) is more musical than opera, and, after its Los Angeles première, it ran at the Ziegfeld Theatre on Broadway to great critical acclaim; several songs became popular and were issued separately. *A menina das nuvens* (composed 1952–8) and *Yerma* (composed 1955–6) were both performed posthumously. *Yerma* is a significant summation of all the important elements in Villa-Lobos's style, consolidating his interests in Hispanic folklore and in human destiny. At the time of his death he was at work on a one-act opera, *Perpetual*, to a libretto by Ellen Terry, and another work, called *Amerindia*, based on an idea by Dora Vasconcellos.

See also IZAHT and YERMA.

music lost unless otherwise stated; all MSS in Rio de Janeiro, Museu Villa-Lobos

Femina, *c*1908
Aglaia, 1909 (2)
Elisa, 1910 (1)
Untitled 'comédia lírica', 1911 (3, O. F. Machado)
Izaht, 1912–14 (4, A. Júnior and Villa-Lobos), concert perf., Rio de Janeiro, Municipal, 6 April 1940; stage, Rio de Janeiro,

Municipal, 13 Dec 1959; autograph vs and full score [based on material from Aglaia and Elisa]
Jesus, 1918 (3, G. de Andrade); MS frag.
Zoé, 1920 (3, R. Viana), MS frag. (perc part); 2 dances for pf solo (Rio de Janeiro, 1920)
Malazarte, 1921 (3, G. Aranha)
Magdalena (aventura musical, 2, R. Wright, G. Forrest, F. H. Brennan and H. Curran), Los Angeles, 26 July 1948, autograph vs and full score
A menina das nuvens, 1952–8 (aventura musical, 3, L. Benedetti), Rio de Janeiro, Municipal, 29 Nov 1960, vs and autograph full score
Yerma, 1955–6 (3, after F. García Lorca), Santa Fe, 12 Aug 1971, autograph vs and full score
Perpetual (1, E. Terry), inc.
Amerindia (after D. Vasconellos), inc.

*

O. Guanabarino: Review of *Izaht*, *Jornal do comércio* (16 Aug 1918)
S. Demarquez: 'Villa-Lobos', *ReM*, x/10–11 (1929), 1–22
L. M. Peppercorn: 'Uma opera de H. Villa-Lobos', *Música viva*, i/3 (1940), 6
——: 'A Villa-Lobos Opera', *New York Times* (28 April 1940)
V. Mariz: *Heitor Villa-Lobos* (Rio de Janeiro, 1949, 5/1977; Eng. trans., 1970)
A. Faro: 'Izaht', *Opera*, x (1959), 161
C. Maul: *A glória escandalosa de Heitor Villa-Lobos* (Rio de Janeiro, 1960)
Presença de Villa-Lobos (Rio de Janeiro, 1965–73)
E. Nogueira Franca: *Villa-Lobos: síntese crítica e biográfica* (Rio de Janeiro, 1970, 2/1973)
M. Oakes: 'Villa-Lobos Opera', *Music and Musicians*, xix/12 (1970–71), 12
J. Ardoin: 'Posthumous Villa-Lobos', *Opera*, xxii (1971), 98–104
L. Guimarães and others: *Villa-Lobos visto da platéia e na intimidade 1912–1935* (Rio de Janeiro, 1972)
L. M. Peppercorn: *Heitor Villa-Lobos: Leben und Werk des brasilianischen Komponisten* (Zürich, 1972)
Villa-Lobos: sua obra (Rio de Janeiro, 1972, 3/1989)
S. Wright: 'Villa-Lobos: the Formation of his Style', *Soundings*, ix [recte viii] (1979–80), 55–70
E. Tarasti: *Heitor Villa-Lobos ja Brasilian sielu* (Helsinki, 1987)
D. P. Appleby: *Heitor Villa-Lobos: a Bio-Bibliography* (New York, 1988)
S. Wright: 'Villa-Lobos at the South Bank', *Music and Musicians*, xxxvii/10 (1988–9), 13–18
L. M. Peppercorn: *Villa-Lobos* (London, 1989)
S. Wright: *Villa-Lobos* (Oxford, 1992)

SIMON WRIGHT

Villanella rapita, La ('The Abducted Country Girl'). *Opera giocosa* in two acts by FRANCESCO BIANCHI to a libretto by GIOVANNI BERTATI; Venice, Teatro S Moisè, autumn 1783.

In the *introduzione* Biaggio oversees the wedding banquet his two daughters Ninetta and Giannina are preparing for their sister Mandina and her bridegroom Pippo. The Count, enamoured of the young bride, arrives with his friend Paulino. The Count offers 'out of fondness' to make the young girl's fortune. Pippo is suspicious, but Biaggio insists the Count means no harm. When Mandina agrees to live with him in the city, the Count gives her a purse of money. Having overheard the Count's dishonourable plan, Pippo confronts him in a trio with Biaggio. During the finale of Act 1 the Count drugs the wine and departs into the night with Mandina. It is clear the next morning that she has been abducted, and Biaggio resolves to go to the Count's palace and bring her back. Meanwhile Mandina, though thrilled with her beautiful new clothes, tells the Count that she loves only Pippo and wishes to return to him and to her father. When Pippo and Biaggio arrive they assume that her new clothing is a sign of her disgrace and reject her pleas in a trio, which becomes a quartet when the Count enters. But Mandina returns to her peasant dress and succeeds in convincing Pippo of her innocence. In the finale her family welcomes her back in the village; the Count appears to reclaim her, but is confounded to learn that she has already married Pippo.

Mozart wrote two duets (K479 and 480) for a performance of the opera in 1785 at the Burgtheater, Vienna.

MARITA P. McCLYMONDS

Villani [Villano], **Antonio** (*fl* Naples 1744–67). Italian librettist, also known by the anagram Liviano Lantino. One of a host of less important librettists working in Naples, he is known to have written eight comic opera librettos between 1744 and 1767. According to Albert Schatz, quoted in Sonneck's *Catalogue of Opera Librettos Printed before 1800*, Villani's *Lo stravagante* was revised by Goldoni as *Il pazzo glorioso* for Venice.

Le innocenti gelosie (commedia per musica), Sellitto, 1744; *Il Leandro* (commedia per musica), Logroscino, 1744; *La moglie padrona* (ob), T. Prota, 1748; *Lo stravagante* (commedia per musica), A. Costa, 1748 (N. Piccinni, 1761, 1764, 1781; Tarchi, 1793); *Il pazzo glorioso* (dg, ? rev. Goldoni), G. Cocchi, 1753; ? *La moglie imperiosa*, P. A. Guglielmi, 1759; *L'equivoco* (commedia per musica), N. Piccinni, 1764; *Li burlati*, A. Festa, 1767; *Il medico* (commedia per musica), Festa, 1767

REBECCA GREEN

Villanis, Angelo (*b* Turin, 1821; *d* Asti, 7 Sept 1865). Italian composer and conductor. He received his musical education in Turin, studying with Luigi Rossi. He suffered from the frustration that although his operas were generally received with favour, none of them enjoyed many productions. The superficial attractiveness of his music could not long conceal his lack of real originality. Like a number of other Italian opera composers of his generation who found success elusive, he supported himself by conducting opera orchestras. In 1856 he became director of the Orchestra Ducale of Parma. He wrote many songs and vocal chamber works.

I saltimbanchi di Spagna (ob, 2), Turin, Gerbino, spr. 1849
La spia, ossia Il merciaiuolo americano (F. Romani, after J. F. Cooper: *The Spy*), Turin, Sutera, 5 March 1850
La regina di Leone, ovvero Una legge spagnola (opera semiseria, 3, G. Giachetti), Venice, Apollo, 22 Feb 1851
La figlia del proscritto (melodramma, 4, A. Codebò), Turin, Carignano, 22 Nov 1851
Alina, o Il matrimonio di una cantante (opera semiseria, 2, Giachetti), Turin, Nazionale, 19 Oct 1853
La vergine di Kent (dramma, 4, G. Prati), Turin, Regio, 1 March 1856; rev. as Giuditta di Kent, Senigallia, Fenice, Aug 1857
Vasconcello (os, 3, T. Solera), Venice, Fenice, 18 March 1858
Una notte di festa (os, 3, Solera), Venice, Fenice, 15 Feb 1859; rev. as Emmanuele Filiberto, 1863
Bianca degli Albizzi (tragedia, 3, Marcello), Milan, Scala, 18 March 1865

WILLIAM ASHBROOK

Villate, Gaspar (*b* Havana, 27 Jan 1851; *d* Paris, 9 Oct 1891). Cuban composer. His first music studies were with Nicolas Ruiz Espadero. In 1874 he went to France, where he attended the Paris Conservatoire as a pupil of Bazin, Joncières and Adolf L. Dannhauser. He spent much of his life in Paris and other European cities. His greatest ambition was to be a composer of operas; and he obtained a degree of success with three, in a Romantic vein influenced by Meyerbeer and early Verdi; all were given in European theatres. He also wrote sacred and light music. His style bears little trace of Cuban musical nationalism.

most MSS in Havana, Museo Nacional de la Música

I primi armi di Richelieu (4), unperf.
Zilia, ossia Odio ed amore (4, T. Solera), Paris, Italien, 1 Dec 1877

La czarine (4, A. Sylvestre), The Hague, Royal, 2 Feb 1880
Baldassare (4, C. d'Ormeville, after G. Gomez de Avellaneda), Madrid, Real, 28 Feb 1885
Cristoforo Colombo, 1884–6 (prol., 3, epilogue, A. Lauzières-Themines), lost
Ines de Castro (4, d'Ormeville), lost
Lucifer, 1887–9 (5), inc., frags. *CU-Hn*

*

S. Ramirez: *La Habana artística* (Havana, 1891)
J. Ardevol: Introduction to *Cuba: la música* (1969)
A. Carpentier: *La música en Cuba* (Havana, 1979)
J. A. González: *La composición operística en Cuba* (Havana, 1986)

JORGE ANTONIO GONZÁLEZ

Villati, Leopoldo de (*b* 1701; *d* Berlin, 9 July 1752). Italian librettist active in Austria and Germany. After writing several oratorio texts in Vienna, 1725–9, he supplied librettos to G. B. Ferrandini and Pietro Torri in the early 1730s for the Munich court. He was called to Berlin by Frederick II in 1747 at a salary of 400 thalers to replace G. G. Bottarelli, who had been dismissed earlier that year. Between then and his death in 1752 Villati supplied Frederick's Kapellmeister, Carl Heinrich Graun, with 13 librettos. G. E. Lessing's *Nachricht von dem gegenwärtigen Zustand des Theaters in Berlin* found 'little invention, order or verisimilitude' in Villati's texts, and his satire on *opera seria*, *Tarantula* (Berlin, 1749), used Villati's name for a facetious imprimatur on its title-page.

Berenice (dramma per musica), Ferrandini, 1730; *Ciro* (dramma per musica), Torri, 1733; *Le feste galanti* (festa teatrale, after J.-F. Duché de Vancy), Graun, 1747; *Il re pastore* (pastorale), Graun, Frederick II, Quantz and C. Nichelmann, 1747; *Cinna* (dramma per musica), Graun, 1748 (also at Brunswick, as Die Gütigkeit des Augustus); *L'Europa galante* (festa teatrale), Graun, 1748; *Galatea ed Acide* (pastorale), Hasse and others; *Ifigenia in Aulide* (dramma per musica, with Frederick II), Graun, 1748

Angelica e Medoro (dramma per musica), Graun, 1749; *Coriolano* (tragedia per musica, with F. Algarotti and Frederick II), Graun, 1749; *Fetonte* (dramma per musica, with Algarotti), Graun, 1750 (Jommelli, 1753); *Il Mitridate* (tragedia per musica), Graun, 1750; *L'Armida* (dramma per musica), Graun, 1751; *Britannico* (tragedia per musica), Graun, 1751; *Orfeo* (tragedia per musica), Graun, 1752; *Il giudicio di Paride* (pastorale per musica, with Algarotti), Graun, 1752

THOMAS BAUMAN

Villeneuve, Louise [Luisa, Luigia]. Soprano. In 1787–8 she sang in Venice in operas by Guglielmi and Martín y Soler; in Milan in 1788 her roles included Amore in Martín's *L'arbore di Diana*. She spent 1789–90 and 1790–91 in Vienna, making her début on 27 June 1789 as Amore, when she was admired for 'her charming appearance, her sensitive and expressive acting and her artful, beautiful singing' (*Wiener Zeitung*, lii (1789), 1673). Mozart supplied arias for her in Cimarosa's *I due baroni* (K 578) and Martín's *Il burbero di buon cuore* (K 582–3), and wrote for her Dorabella in *Così fan tutte* (26 January 1790), alluding in her Act 2 aria to her role as Amore (see D. Link: '*Così fan tutte*: Dorabella and Amore', *MJb 1991*, 888–94). There is no evidence that, as is often stated, she was the sister of Adriana Ferrarese, who sang Fiordiligi. Zinzendorf noted in his diary (11 February 1791) that she caught the fancy of Leopold II. She appeared in Livorno in 1794.

DOROTHEA LINK

Villi, Le ('The Willis'). *Opera-ballo* in two acts by GIACOMO PUCCINI to a libretto by FERDINANDO FONTANA after Alphonse Karr's short story *Les Willis*; Milan, Teatro Dal Verme, 31 May 1884 (revised version, Turin, Teatro Regio, 26 December 1884).

In the Black Forest villagers are celebrating the engagement of Roberto (tenor) and Anna (soprano), daughter of the head forester, Guglielmo (baritone). Roberto is about to leave for Mainz to collect an inheritance. Anna brings him a posy of forget-me-nots to keep him mindful of their vows ('Se come voi piccina'). In their duet 'Tu dall'infanzia mia' he tells her to doubt the existence of God himself rather than his own constancy. All join in a prayer ('Angiol di Dio') to speed him on his way.

At the beginning of Act 2 a verse of poetry describes how Roberto has fallen into the clutches of a siren and forgotten Anna, who died of grief. During an intermezzo ('L'abbandono') her body is borne across the stage behind a gauze curtain to an unseen chorus of mourners. A second intermezzo ('La tregenda'), preceded by more poetry, depicts the dance of the Willis, ghosts of jilted maidens. Outside his cottage Guglielmo grieves for his daughter and inveighs against her faithless lover ('Anima santa della figlia mia'). Roberto returns penniless and devoured by remorse, recalling his love for Anna ('Torna ai felici dì'). The Willis appear, among them Anna, who taunts him with his treachery. They dance until Roberto falls dead at her feet.

Le villi, Puccini's first stage work, was originally entered for a competition for a one-act opera announced in 1883 by the publisher Sonzogno in his periodical *Il teatro illustrato*; but it failed to achieve even an honourable mention. However, friends and well-wishers, among them Boito, subscribed to a performance which took place under the baton of Achille Panizza with Rosina Caponetti (Anna), Antonio D'Andrade (Roberto) and Erminio Pelz (Guglielmo) and an orchestra that included Pietro Mascagni among the double basses. The reception was sufficiently encouraging for Ricordi to purchase the score. He persuaded Puccini and Fontana to enlarge the opera (originally described as a 'leggenda in due quadri') into its present form, adding Anna's cavatina in Act 1 and a dramatic scena for Roberto in Act 2, inserting the invisible chorus into the first intermezzo and converting what had originally been an aria finale for the soprano into a duet for her and the tenor. The final addition was the tenor *romanza* 'Torna ai felici dì', composed during the course of a revival at La Scala, Milan in January 1885 under Franco Faccio with Romilda Pantaleoni (who later created Verdi's Desdemona) as the heroine. Further modifications followed in the editions of 1888 and 1892, the latter being the one in general use today.

Like many a beginner's work *Le villi* shows a number of influences, from Ponchielli and Catalani (notably in the tenor *romanza*) to Gounod and Bizet in the dance movements, Massenet in the solos, and even the Weber of *Der Freischütz* in the final scene. At the same time Puccini's individual voice can be heard in the atmospheric prelude whose opening theme, a motif that will connote Roberto's vow of fidelity, is taken from a *romanza*, *Melanconia* (1881), since lost; in Anna's cavatina and subsequent duet with Roberto – in the variety of phrase-structure and flexible articulation of the verbal text; in the preghiera, based on an earlier song, *Salve del ciel regina*; in the first intermezzo, with its languishing melodies that incline towards the subdominant, its prolonged suspensions and yearning insistence on variants of the dominant 9th; and in the abundance of thematic reminiscence towards the end of the work. The second intermezzo, a miniature 'Walkürenritt', is the only instrumental piece in a Puccini opera that will bear transplantation from its original context. But for all its vitality *Le villi* is not so much a drama as a story. There is no interplay of character, no one to react to Guglielmo's grief or Roberto's remorse; hence the opera's virtual exclusion from the Puccini canon. On the rare occasions when it is performed the snatches of poetry are declaimed by a narrator; but it would seem that they were intended merely to be read by the audience. JULIAN BUDDEN

Villifranchi [Villafranchi], **Giovanni Cosimo** (*b* Volterra, 1646; *d* Florence, 12 March 1699). Italian librettist. His first dramatic work, *Amore e politica* (1677), which exists only in manuscript (in *I-Sc*), was a forerunner of the melodrama, a spoken play with incidental music organized in introductory and final scenes. His first published libretto, *Amore è veleno e medicina degl'intelletti* (Bologna, 1679), was a poetic version of G. B. Ricciardi's prose comedy *Il Trespolo tutore* (Bologna, 1669). Villifranchi's publication of his libretto was intended to counter a gross plagiarism that had been set by Bernardo Pasquini and performed at the Palazzo Colonna in Rome in 1677. Stradella composed a score for the authentic version (retaining *Il Trespolo tutore* as the title) for a performance in Genoa in 1678 or 1679 and probably for Modena in 1686.

Villifranchi wrote most of the comic librettos staged in the Villa di Pratolino by Prince Ferdinando de' Medici, whom he also served as personal physician, altogether writing five such works beginning with *Lo speziale di villa* (1683) and concluding with *L'ipocondriaco* (1695). He wrote only one serious opera, *Filippo Macedone*, which has not survived. His comic librettos enjoyed revivals in Florence and Bologna as late as 1743 in settings by G. M. Buini, Chinzer, G. Lirone and other, unknown, composers.

His importance as a comic-opera librettist has been obscured by the lack of any surviving scores except those of Pasquini and Stradella for *Il Trespolo tutore*. He was nevertheless the most productive and creative Italian comic librettist in the second half of the 17th century, and also deserves attention as an advocate of simple and natural language. As he wrote in his introduction to *L'ipocondriaco*, he wished to make 'verse appear to be prose and music a natural discourse'.

dm – *dramma per musica*

Amore e politica (tragicommedia/melodrama), 1677; *Il Trespolo tutore* (dramma giocoso), B. Pasquini, 1677 (Stradella, 1679); *Lo speziale di villa* (dm), 1683 (?Orlandini, 1730); *Il finto chimico* (dm), 1686; *La serva favorita* (dm), ? A. Scarlatti, 1689 (Chinzer, 1727); *Trespolo oste* (opera buffa), 1692; *L'ipocondriaco* (dm), Bitti, 1695 (Buini, 1718; G. Lirone, 1743); *Filippo Macedone* (dm), 1698

*

G. C. Villifranchi: *Raccolta di opuscoli del Dr. G. C. V.* (Florence, 1737) [incl. at least 8 prols. for music]

R. Maffei: *Tre volterrani: Enrico Ormanni, Giovanni Cosimo Villifranchi, e Mario Guarnacci* (Pisa, 1881)

C. Gianturco: '*Il Trespolo tutore* di Stradella e di Pasquini', *Venezia e il melodramma nel settecento: Venice 1973–5*, i, 185–98

R. L. Weaver and N. W. Weaver: *A Chronology of Music in the Florentine Theater*, i: *1590–1750* (Detroit, 1978); ii: *1751–1800* (Warren, MI, 1993) ROBERT LAMAR WEAVER

Vilnius (Russ. Vilna; Pol. Wilno). The present capital of Lithuania. It has at various times been under Polish and Russian dominion. Opera was first heard there in 1634, at the court of the King of Poland and Grand Duke of Lithuania (*Il ratto di Helena*, probably by Marco Scacchi). There are no further records of operatic activity after 1648 until the late 18th century, when the city was visited by operatic companies such as those of W. Bogusławski and D. Morawski. A permanent theatre was established in 1827, directed by K. Sibinski; it moved to the city hall in 1845, giving operas and lighter fare, mostly Italian. There was also a German company in the city from 1835 to 1844.

Moniuszko, born in Vilnius, worked in the city from 1840 to 1858; his opera *Halka* had its première there in 1848 (in concert form; stage première, 1851). During the 1860s the Polish influence gave way to Russian, and in 1869 a Russian theatre was opened; there were visits from companies from Italy, France and Ukraine, and singers en route to Moscow or St Petersburg often stopped and performed there.

The cultural movement in Vilnius intensified when, in 1904, the ban on the Lithuanian language was lifted. The musical society Vilniaus Kanklės gave a performance on 6 November 1906 of Mikas Petrauskas's *Birutė*, often counted as the first Lithuanian opera (though in fact a play with incidental music). During the first period of Lithuanian independence, 1919–40, Kaunas was the capital and most operatic activity shifted there. An opera company functioned in the city, in difficult conditions under the Germans, from 1941 to 1944. Vilnius became the capital again during the Soviet annexation and the theatre was relocated, as the Litovsky Teatr Operï i Baleta (1948). The theatre now gives a season from September to June each year, with 15 to 17 operas, from the standard (and especially Russian) repertory. The first Lithuanian work, Račiūnas's *Maritė*, was given in 1956; others include Klova's *Pilėnai* (1956); Dvarionas's *Dalia* (1959); Barkauskas's *Legenda apie meilę* ('A Legend about Love', 1975); Juzeliūnas's *Sukilėliai* ('The Rebels', 1977) and *Žaidimas* ('The Game', 1991); and Balsys's *Kelionė į Tilžę* ('A Journey to Tilsit', 1980). Notable conductors have been Rimas Geniušas, Vytautas Viržonis and Jonas Aleksa. The company, which has visited Moscow and elsewhere, and has received many visiting companies in its house, performed at the Vilniaus Miesto Teatras (Vilnius Town Theatre) up to 1974, then in the newly opened Operos ir Baleto Teatras in the city centre, seating 1150.

The Vilnius Theatre and Music Museum, founded in 1964, houses materials concerning Lithuanian theatrical history.

*

ME (Yu. Gaudrimas; also 'Litovskïy Teatr Operï i Baleta')

A. Miller: *Teatr i muzika na Litwe 1745–1865* (Vilnius, 1935)

J. Būtėnas: *Lietuvių teatras Vilniuje* [Lithuanian Theatre in Vilnius] (Kaunas, 1940)

J. Banaitis: *Tarybinė lietviu muzika 1940–1950* [Soviet Lithuanian Music] (Vilnius, 1950)

S. Yla, ed.: *Lietuvių nacionalinė opera* (Vilnius, 1960)

Yu. Gaudrimas: *Muzïkal'naya kul'tura Sovetskoy Litvï* (Leningrad, 1961)

V. Mažeika: *Opera* (Vilnius, 1967)

A. Tauragis: *Lithuanian Music: Past and Present* (Vilnius, 1971)

J. Bagdanskis: *The Lithuanian Musical Scene* (Vilnius, 1974)

V. Nakas: 'Gražina: the First Lithuanian National Opera', *Lituanus*, xxi/1 (1975), 45–62

A. Szweykowska: *Drama per musica w teatre Wazów 1635–1648* (Kraków, 1976)

V. Venkus: 'Muzïkal'nïy teatr: operï i operettï', *Iz istorii litovskoy muzïki*, iii (Leningrad, 1978), 19–44

J. Bruveris: 'Operos ir baleto teatras mūsų kultūroje' [Opera and Ballet Theatre in our Culture], *Kultūros barai*, xxvi/12 (1990), 7–11 ADEODATAS TAURAGIS, MITCHELL MORRIS

Vil'yam Ratklif. Opera by César Cui; *see* WILLIAM RATCLIFF.

Vinaccesi [Vinacesi, Vinacese], **Benedetto** (*b* Brescia, *c*1666; *d* Venice, 25 Dec 1719). Italian composer. He came from a Brescian family of Tuscan origins; one member was the 'universal savant' Fortunato Vinaccesi (1631–1713), whose salon Benedetto probably attended in his youth. He received his musical training from Pietro Pelli, *capo musico* of Brescia Cathedral, and first came to notice in 1687 with a set of sonatas dedicated to the wife of Ferdinando Gonzaga, Prince of Castiglione delle Stiviere, who employed him as his *maestro di cappella*. Other instrumental and vocal chamber works followed. During the 1690s he is known to have written four oratorios, of which only *Susanna* (1694, Modena) survives. In early 1697 his pastoral *Chi è causa del suo mal pianga sé stesso*, which borrows its title (but not its content) from Filippo Acciaiuoli's *Chi è cagion del sua mal pianga se stesso*, was performed in Rome at the Court of Cardinal Pietro Ottoboni; this may be identical with an unnamed pastoral that Vinaccesi presented in 1702 to Georg Friedrich, Margrave of Brandenburg-Ansbach. In an expanded version for the public stage G. B. Neri's libretto later enjoyed great success under various titles (*L'enigma disciolto*, *Gli amici rivali*, *Amor indovino*, *Le vicende amorose*), but it appears that the original music was not retained. In 1698 Vinaccesi competed successfully for the post of *maestro di coro* at the Ospedaletto (Derelitti), one of Venice's four *ospedali grandi*; on 7 September 1704 he was appointed second organist at St Mark's. He held the first position until 1715, the second until his death.

Between his arrival in Venice and his admission to the *cappella marciana* Vinaccesi wrote two operas for the Venetian stage. The first, *L'innocenza giustificata* (3 acts; S Salvatore, December 1699), was the original setting of an extraordinarily popular drama by Francesco Silvani revived at least 33 times up to 1740 (its alternative titles included *L'innocenza difeso*, *Carlo, re d'Allemagna*, *La Giuditta di Baviera* and *Feraspe*). Vinaccesi's music was retained for productions in Genoa (1699), Mantua (1700), Florence (1700), Crema (1701) and possibly Milan (1711). *Gli amanti generosi* (3 acts; S Angelo, 5 January 1703) was less successful. The preface to the libretto by its author, Giovanni Pietro Candi, indicates that Vinaccesi had decided to write no more operas but relented under pressure from the theatre's patrons. He continued, however, to compose serenatas, of which there survives only the libretto of *Sfoghi di giubilo*, performed on 21 July 1704 at the French embassy to celebrate the birth of the Duke of Brittany (a work described in some modern sources as *Gli sponsali di giubilo* is the same with its title garbled).

Except for one aria from *L'innocenza giustificata* (in *GB-Lbl*), the pastoral (in *F-Pn*) is all that remains of Vinaccesi's operatic music. It exemplifies Ellen Harris's description of the sub-genre as 'simplified and concise'. Its three acts contain 32 closed vocal numbers, distributed almost equally among the four characters. Many of its da capo arias include in their *A* section only one vocal period, rather than the two that were becoming more normal; most areas are accompanied only by continuo, though they usually have an introductory or concluding orchestral ritornello; the *Devise* is used only sparingly. Vinaccesi's flair for counterpoint emerges in the five duets, one of which anticipates the 'quarrelling' style of the comic intermezzo. Many numbers betray the composer's (and Ottoboni's) attachment to the French style; several feature gavotte or minuet rhythm, and the sinfonia is even cast in the form of a miniature French overture. Although Vinaccesi cultivated opera only as a sideline, his pastoral reveals a real talent for dramatic music.

*

V. Zaccaria: 'Benedetto Vinaccesi (Brescia 1670c.–Venezia 1719): profilo bio-bibliografico', *Musica sacra*, 2nd ser., vii (Milan, 1962), 12–15, 86–9, 119–25

H. J. Marx: 'Die Musik am Hofe Pietro Kardinal Ottobonis unter Arcangelo Corelli', *AnMc*, no.5 (1968), 104–77

M. Talbot: *A Musician in Brescia and Venice in the Age of Corelli: the Life and Works of Benedetto Vinaccesi* (in preparation)

MICHAEL TALBOT

Viñas, Francisco [Viñas, Francesc; Vignas, Francesco] (*b* Moya, nr Barcelona, 27 March 1863; *d* Moya, 14 July 1933). Spanish tenor. He studied in Barcelona and made an outstanding début as Lohengrin at the Liceu theatre (1888), after which he was presented by Julián Gayarre with his own Lohengrin costume. The following year he sang the role at La Scala, where he was last heard, in Franchetti's *Germania*, in 1904. He sang Turiddu in the first London performance of *Cavalleria rusticana*, at the Shaftesbury Theatre (1891), and in 1893 made his Covent Garden début as Lohengrin, returning for the seasons of 1895, 1904 and 1907 as Edgardo, Radames, Tannhäuser, Cavaradossi and Mascagni's Fritz. Though the *Musical Times* felt that his Lohengrin 'scarcely came up to expectation' (1895) he was generally credited in London with the virtues of a sincere artist. At the Metropolitan in 1893 he sang with Calvé in *Cavalleria rusticana* and with Melba in *Lucia di Lammermoor*. For many years he appeared regularly in Spain and Italy, and in 1910 at the Colón, Buenos Aires. In that year, too, he added Tristan to his repertory and in 1913 Parsifal, achievements which marked the summit of the latter part of his career. He retired in 1918, publishing a book on the art of singing in 1932. Recordings, made between 1903 and 1912, are not faultless but reveal a compact and ringing voice, expressively used.

*

L. Gregori: *Francesc Viñas* (Barcelona, 1935)

L. Lustig and C. Williams: 'Francisco Viñas', *Record Collector*, xxxiv (1989), 106–38

J. B. STEANE

Vinay, Ramón (*b* Chillán, 31 Aug 1912). Chilean baritone, later tenor. He studied with José Pierson in Mexico City, where he made his début as Alphonse (*La favorite*) in 1931. For several years he sang baritone roles, including Rigoletto, Luna and Scarpia, and then, after further study, he made his tenor début in Mexico City in 1943 as Don José, following it in 1944 with Otello. In 1945 Vinay made his New York début at the City Center as Don José and then sang at the Metropolitan (1946–61). He inaugurated the 1947–8 season at La Scala as Otello, a part he also sang at Salzburg and Covent Garden and recorded under Toscanini. From 1952 to 1957 he sang at Bayreuth, as Tristan, Parsifal, Tannhäuser and Siegmund. In 1962 he resumed baritone roles, singing Telramund at Bayreuth, and also Iago, Falstaff, Scarpia, Dr Bartolo and Dr Schön.

In his prime Vinay sang with ease and a full, splendid tone. His artistry, intelligence and musicianship were always in evidence, and his acting was distinguished by pathos and nobility.

*

GV (R. Celletti; S. Smolian)

H. Rosenthal: 'Ramón Vinay', *Opera*, vi (1958), 335–9
——: *Great Singers of Today* (London, 1966)
HAROLD ROSENTHAL/R

***Vincent* (i).** Opera in ten scenes by RAINER KUNAD to his own libretto after Alfred Matusche's play *Van Gogh*; Dresden, Staatsoper, 22 February 1979.

The opera depicts key scenes from the last two years of Van Gogh's life, leading to his suicide. It is not, however, intended as a musically illustrated biography; instead, the subject is the relationship between society and an individual who is not without some responsibility for his own downfall. On his way through life Vincent (baritone) encounters his (fictitious) lover Jacky (soprano), a drop-out with a lust for life, his fellow-painter Gauguin (bass), his brother Theo (tenor) and Dr Gachet (baritone). He meets with a mainly hostile reception from various briefly characterized figures of Arles society, who join in a nightmare chorus in passacaglia rhythm in the central sixth scene, driving Vincent into the lunatic asylum. In contrast to Berg's *Wozzeck*, which *Vincent* resembles in many ways despite occasional linguistic weaknesses, Kunad avoids large-scale musical forms and attempts, with the aid of serial technique, to let 'things themselves' speak, though without resorting to musical illustration. The music is organized around three suggestive sound patterns, employed in the manner of leitmotifs; these are easily perceived by the hearer, as is the basic series forming the tonal centres of the work, which is strictly dodecaphonic in structure. Despite being written for a small, almost conventional orchestral ensemble, with notably sparing use of special effects, the opera makes a strong impression; first staged in a sensational production by Harry Kupfer, it had been given nine productions in German-speaking countries by 1991. JOCHEN SCHÖNLEBER

***Vincent* (ii).** Opera in three acts by EINOJUHANI RAUTAVAARA to his own libretto; Helsinki, Finnish National Opera, 17 May 1990.

Vincent, an expressionistic study of Vincent van Gogh, takes the form of a long flashback. Towards the end of his life at the sanatorium of St Rémy, Vincent (baritone) recalls his work as a lay preacher in the mining village of Borignage, his stormy life with the prostitute Maria Hoornik (mezzo-soprano) and his tense friendship with Paul Gauguin (bass). He finds inspiration from the appearance of a girl, Gaby (high soprano), whom he sees as his muse. However, at a wild party with Paul's friends Vincent becomes unbalanced and cuts off his earlobe. The final scene reverts to St Rémy; but instead of leading to Vincent's suicide, the opera ends with his paean to sunshine and life.

Certain of Van Gogh's paintings ('Starry Night', 'Crows over a Wheatfield', 'The Church at Auvers') are used as visual waymarks. In a number of attempts to subjugate Vincent, four grotesques appear in different guises: as staff at the sanatorium, as the authorities at Borignage and as a group of art critics. However, his brother Theo (tenor) offers support in his tribulations. The musical language of *Vincent* encompasses both serialism and tonality, and Rautavaara's orchestration is signally colourful. The opera's subject was suggested by the baritone Jorma Hynninen, who sang the title role at the première. ERKKI ARNI

Vincent [née Burchell; Birchell], **Isabella** (*b* 1735; *d* London, 9 June 1802). English soprano. She sang at Vauxhall Gardens from 1751 and, after her marriage to the violinist Richard Vincent (*d* 1766), made her stage début as Polly in *The Beggar's Opera* in September 1760. She created the role of Zaida in Smith's *The Enchanter*, was in the new English operas *Almena* and *Pharnaces* and played the title role in Arne's reworking of his *Rosamond* (1765). Dibdin remembered that she sang 'songs of ease and sweetness with great delicacy', but the prompter Hopkins noted that her speaking in the musical version of *A Midsummer Night's Dream* was 'beyond Description bad'. After leaving the stage in 1767 she married Captain Mills, a survivor of the Black Hole of Calcutta, and went with him to India.

*

BDA; *LS*
J. Churchill: *The Rosciad* (London, 1761)
H. Kelly: *Thespis*, i (London, 1767)
C. Dibdin: *A Complete History of the English Stage*, v (London, 1800)
Gentleman's Magazine, lxxii (1802), 687
M. Sands: *The Eighteenth-Century Pleasure Gardens of Marylebone* (London, 1987)
OLIVE BALDWIN, THELMA WILSON

Vincent, Ruth (*b* Yarmouth, 22 March 1878; *d* London, 8 July 1955). English soprano. She studied singing with Hermann Klein and was educated for the stage by Jacques Brohy in Paris. Her début was in London as Gretchen in the original production of Gilbert and Sullivan's *The Grand Duke* (1896). Within a year she became principal soprano at the Savoy Theatre, where she appeared in several Gilbert and Sullivan revivals and in the original productions of Mackenzie's *His Majesty* (1897) and Caryll's *The Lucky Star* (1899). She made a particularly strong impression as the blind heroine Laine in Sullivan's *The Beauty Stone* (1898), but left the company abruptly during the run.

From about 1900 Vincent was in demand in both comic and grand opera, as much for her extraordinary beauty as for her notable lyric soprano voice. She appeared regularly at Covent Garden, her repertory including principal roles in *Hänsel und Gretel*, *Carmen*, *Les contes d'Hoffmann* and *Don Giovanni*, and was Vreli in the London production of Delius's *A Village Romeo and Juliet* (1910). In May 1904 she sang the title role in Messager's *Véronique* at the Apollo Theatre, returning there in 1907 in German's *Tom Jones*. From about 1912 until her retirement in 1930 she sang with increasing frequency at the Palladium and variety theatres. FREDRIC WOODBRIDGE WILSON

Vinci, Leonardo (*b* Strongoli, Calabria, *c*1696; *d* Naples, 27 or 28 May 1730). Italian composer. His music exerted a direct influence on many of the Neapolitan composers of the next generation, notably Pergolesi and Hasse, who were described as his disciples. He also influenced older composers such as Handel, whose pasticcios are dominated by Vinci's music, and whose later works are indebted to the style of Vinci and his colleagues.

1. LIFE. No birth or baptismal records have been found. The year of birth traditionally given, 1690, is based on the death register of S Maria della Neve, Naples, which describes Vinci as 40 years old in 1730. Another death register, however, that of S Giovanni Maggiore, describes him as 'about 34', placing the year of his birth at about 1696. This supports Dent's speculation about the composer's age and would seem to tally more closely with subsequent events in his life. Vinci entered the Con-

servatorio dei Poveri di Gesù Cristo, Naples, on 14 November 1708 as a 'convittore', paying 36 ducats a year, but after three years this fee was waived; apparently he was now earning his keep as a 'mastricello' or student teacher. At the conservatory he studied composition with Gaetano Greco. After ten years of study he left and for a short time served as *maestro di cappella* to Prince Sansevero.

Vinci made his operatic début on 19 April 1719 at the Teatro dei Fiorentini in Naples with the *commedia per musica Lo cecato fauzo*. The enthusiastic review in the *Avvisi di Napoli* made particular mention of the music, which 'contributed each night to the nobility' of the production. Vinci's second opera followed immediately in July, and for the next three years he was virtual house composer at the Fiorentini; not until Piccinni in the 1760s would another composer dominate the comic stage in Naples to the same extent. During Carnival 1722 Vinci produced *Li zite ngalera*, important for being the earliest score of a *commedia per musica* to survive complete. His first operas were of this type, full-length comic operas with texts primarily in Neapolitan dialect. He produced his first serious opera, *Publio Cornelio Scipione*, at the Teatro S Bartolomeo in Naples on 4 November 1722; it was so successful that after the production of *Lo labborinto* during Carnival, he turned primarily to the *dramma per musica*. Only on one subsequent occasion, the inauguration of the Teatro della Pace in Naples in May 1724, did he return to the comic genre (though most of his *drammi per musica* for Naples contain comic intermezzos). Whereas the Neapolitan dialect of the *commedie* restricted them to Naples, the use of standard literary Tuscan in the *drammi* made them a cosmopolitan commodity.

In 1724 Vinci secured his first commission outside Naples, the setting of Lucchini's *Farnace* for the Teatro delle Dame in Rome. According to Burney, 'so great was the success of this drama, that [Vinci] was called upon to furnish at least one opera every year till 1730, when he composed two'. Although the theatres in Rome were closed for the Holy Year in 1725, Vinci wrote two new operas for the Teatro S Giovanni Grisostomo in Venice that year; it was undoubtedly their success that led to a commission for a new opera at Parma in the spring involving the same composer, poet and principals. Vinci's activity reached a peak during the winter of 1725–6 when three new operas were produced: *Astianatte* in Naples in December, *Didone abbandonata* in Rome in January and *Siroe re di Persia* in Venice in February. The last two were the first of a series of successful collaborations between Vinci and Metastasio. Vinci set all but one of Metastasio's early librettos, and except in the case of *Didone* these were first settings. This collaboration was cited as the ideal by Algarotti, who urged composers to 'keep up such a dependence and friendly intercourse as subsisted between Lully and Quinault, Vinci and Metastasio'. Vinci's success seems to have been challenged by his older colleague Porpora. Simultaneous productions of operas by the two men in Venice early in 1726 and Rome in 1727, and of *Semiramide riconosciuta* in 1729 by Vinci in Rome and Porpora in Venice, fuelled a rivalry which, according to Burney, dated back to their youth.

Following the death of Scarlatti in October 1725, Vinci was appointed organist and pro-vice-*maestro* at the royal chapel in Naples. On his taking up the position in spring 1726, his activity was virtually restricted to Naples and Rome; each year he composed two operas, one for the Teatro S Bartolomeo during the autumn and one for the Teatro delle Dame during Carnival. In 1728 he took on further commitments: in spring he collaborated with C. I. Frugoni on the opera *Medo*, and on the equestrian ballet *Le nozze di Nettuno* for the wedding of the Duke of Parma; he served during the summer as *maestro di cappella* at his former conservatory, where Pergolesi was among his pupils; and in autumn he became a lay brother with the Congregation of the Rosary at the monastery of S Caterina a Formiello, where he also served as *maestro di cappella*. The culmination of his career came in winter 1729–30, when he collaborated with Metastasio on three major works: the serenata *La contesa de' numi*, performed at the palace of the French ambassador on 26 November in celebration of the birth of the dauphin (*see* ROME, fig.3), and the dramas *Alessandro nell'Indie* and *Artaserse* at the Teatro delle Dame the following January and February. During the same season, Porpora presented two operas at the Teatro Capranica; according to Marpurg, Vinci, fearful of Porpora's challenge, resorted to sabotage in an attempt to crush his rival. Vinci's machinations were hardly necessary, as both his operas became celebrated examples of the *dramma per musica*. According to De Brosses, the Italians did not 'want to see again any piece ... that they have already seen another year, unless it is some excellent opera by Vinci'. Unfortunately, Vinci did not live to enjoy his success. He died in Naples amid rumours that he had been poisoned because of an illicit love affair. When Metastasio heard of his death, he wrote: 'Poor Vinci! Now that merit will be known, which during his life, was blasted by his enemies'.

2. OPERAS. During the 18th century Vinci was regarded as one of the originators of the new style. The rivalry between him and Porpora was probably a major factor in its development, as each tried to outdo the other in writing *à la mode*. Vinci's early works *Silla* and *Farnace* (first setting) are written in the style of his immediate predecessors in Naples, particularly Sarro. The influence of Scarlatti is less important, even in operas based on original Scarlatti librettos such as *Eraclea* and *La caduta de' Decemviri*. In Vinci's early work three basic approaches to melody are discernible: continuous, based on Baroque *Fortspinnung*, and favoured in heroic and bravura arias; fragmented, based on declamation, and favoured in agitated and pathetic arias; and periodic, based on dance rhythms, and favoured in amorous and 'mezzo carattere' arias. During Vinci's short career there is a gradual fusion of these, with the periodic style taking on the declamatory quality of the fragmented and the dynamic quality of the continuous. This resulting 'dynamic periodicity', one of the hallmarks of the Classical style, was recognized by F.-J. Chastellux, who contrasted it with the static, dance-based periodicity of contemporary French music. Marmontel in his *Essai sur les révolutions de la musique en France* considered Vinci to be the originator of this new periodicity:

> But the true moment of its glory was when Vinci first traced the circle of periodic song which in the pure elegant and polished design presented to the ear, as a period to the wit, the development of a thought completely rendered. Therefore this was when the great mystery of melody was revealed.

Whether or not Vinci was actually the first to trace 'the circle of periodic song', he was the first composer of international repute to cultivate the style consistently, to such an extent that it became associated with him and those who continued in this vein were regarded as his disciples.

Vinci's new melodic style led Burney to single him out as one of the most innovatory and influential composers of the century:

Vinci seems to have been the first opera composer who ... without degrading his art, rendered it the friend, though not the slave to poetry, by simplifying and polishing melody, and calling the attention of the audience chiefly to the voice-part, by disintangling it from fugue, complication, and laboured contrivance.

In Vinci's arias each line or couplet is usually given its own musical phrase delimited by a caesura or cadence. The predominance of feminine endings in the internal lines of the aria strophes is matched by feminine caesuras for the internal musical phrases. Burney's reference to disentangling melody 'from fugue, complication, and laboured contrivance' refers to Vinci's simple homophonic accompaniments. The contrapuntal obbligato-style accompaniments of the late Baroque aria give way to accompaniments for four-part string orchestra which can be reinforced by the addition of oboes, horns or trumpets. The transparency of the accompaniment is further enhanced by doublings; during the ritornellos the violins play in unison, while in the vocal sections the violas double the basses at the octave and the first violins frequently double the voice. The most important aspect of this simplification is the increasing use of *Trommelbass* (steady repeated notes in the bass during periods of harmonic stasis). While this occurs sporadically in Vinci's early operas, in his later ones it is used to a greater or lesser extent in almost all the arias. The device is primarily responsible for the slowing of harmonic rhythm, an important aspect of the Classical style.

The simplified accompaniments also allowed for a greater rhythmic diversification of the melody, heightening its polished elegance through the use of dotted and lombardic rhythms, triplets and sextuplets, appoggiaturas and ornaments, and various types of syncopation. This rhythmic flexibility is responsible for breaking down the motoric rhythms of late Baroque music. Although the *Trommelbass* gives the singer greater flexibility, and may be exploited for the sake of virtuosity, vocal pyrotechnics are not an important element in Vinci's music. Coloratura is almost completely absent in the surviving comic arias, and in the heroic arias it is often relegated to a single passage at the end of each vocal period as a means of extending and intensifying the final phrase.

From a modern dramatic viewpoint Vinci is inconsistent in matching music to drama, particularly in the arias. This was noticed even in the late 18th century by Grétry, who in *Semiramide* praised Arbace's 'Vò solcando' because 'the melody, and above all the accompaniments, absolutely match the words', but dismissed Semira's 'Torna innocente' as 'a gay dance air to express fury ... like the anger of Pulcinella'. This inconsistency, found to a greater or lesser extent in all Vinci's operas, was not considered problematic by contemporaries. Martello's *Della tragedia antica e moderna* (1713–14) contains advice on aria construction that, although intended for librettists, could also be applied by composers:

Keep in mind that in the aria, the more general the propositions, the more they will please the people .... Avoid generalities [only] in the *arie di azione* ... that are in spirit adapted to one action and no other .... [Therefore] do yourself honour in the recitative, and in one or two arias in each act.

Vinci follows this principle: apart from one or two arias per act, usually the *arie di azione*, the arias tend to be tuneful and dance-like or simple and declamatory. They can be very attractive, and undoubtedly accomplished what they were intended to do, namely to 'please the people'. On the other hand Vinci indeed did himself 'honour in the recitative'; his accompanied recitative in particular attracted considerable attention during the 18th century. His mastery of this technique is apparent as early as his first setting of *Farnace*, and culminates in the recitative finales of *Didone abbandonata* and *Catone in Utica*. Moreover, some of the simple recitative, though it tends to be in long stretches (frequently extending to ten or more pages in score), contains affecting passages just as fine as the more celebrated accompanied recitatives.

There are two fine caricatures of Vinci by the Roman artist Pier Leone Ghezzi, the first drawn in 1724, the second probably originating from the production of *La contesa de' numi* in November 1729. In the latter Vinci is depicted conducting (presumably a rehearsal) according to the modern fashion before a lectern with a piece of manuscript paper. To the earlier caricature Ghezzi appended a description of Vinci's death: 'he died in Naples on 28 May 1730 on Sunday at the 17th hour, from a colic pain in an instant without even being able to confess' – a description that gives the rumours of poisoning greater substance. Ghezzi was apparently a friend of the composer, providing rare information about Vinci's personality: 'he was a man who would have gambled his eyes [away]; he was a "valentuomo" in music who composed with much spirit, but his behaviour was diverse from the talent that he had. May God give him paradise for his talent'.

See also ARTASERSE (i); *DIDONE ABBANDONATA* (i); and *ZITE 'NGALERA, LI*.

NB – *Naples, Teatro di S Bartolomeo*
NFI – *Naples, Teatro dei Fiorentini*
RD – *Rome, Teatro delle Dame*
VGG – *Venice, Teatro S Giovanni Grisostomo*

cm – *commedia per musica* dm – *dramma per musica*
int – *intermezzo*

Lo cecato fauzo (cm, 3, A. Piscopo), NFI, 19 April 1719, 11 arias *I-Nc*

Le ddoie lettere (invenzione per musica, 3, A. Birini), NFI, 9 July 1719

Lo scassone (capriccio per musica, 3), NFI, ?carn. 1720, 1 aria *Nc*

Lo scagno (fantasia marenaresca, 3), NFI, mid-1720

Lo castiello saccheato (cm, 3, F. Oliva), NFI, 26 Oct 1720, collab. Falco

Lo barone de Trocchia (cm, 3), NFI, 25 Jan 1721

Don Ciccio (cm, 3, B. Saddumene), NFI, 6 Sept 1721

Li zite 'ngalera (cm, 3, Saddumene), NFI, 3 Jan 1722, *Nc**

La festa de Bacco (cm, 3, F. A. Tullio), NFI, 29 Aug 1722, 10 arias *D-MÜs*

Publio Cornelio Scipione (dm, 3, Saddumene, after A. Piovene), NB, 4 Nov 1722, 3 arias *F-Pc*; with Bacocco e Ermosilla (int)

Lo labborinto (cm, 3, Saddumene), NFI, carn. 1723, 3 arias *D-MÜs*

Silla dittatore [Il tiranno eroe] (dm, 3, V. Cassani), Naples, Real Palazzo, 1 Oct 1723, *I-Nc*; with Albino e Plautilla (int), *Nc*

Farnace [1st version] (dm, 3, A. M. Lucchini), RD, 8 Jan 1724, *D-MÜs*

La mogliere fedele (cm, 3, Saddumene), Naples, Pace, 14 May 1724

Eraclea (dm, 3, S. Stampiglia), NB, 1 Oct 1724, *I-MC*

Ifigenia in Tauride (tragedia, 5, B. Pasqualigo), VGG, carn. 1725, arias in *GB-Lbl* and *I-Vnm*

La Rosmira fedele [Partenope] (dm, 3, Stampiglia), VGG, carn. 1725, *GB-Lbl**

Il trionfo di Camilla (dm, 3, C. I. Frugoni, after Stampiglia), Parma, Ducale, spr. 1725, 4 arias *F-Pc*, 2 arias *US-BE*

Astianatte (dm, 3, A. Salvi), NB, 2 Dec 1725, *I-Nc*, Acts 2 and 3 *B-Bc* (from a pasticcio, 1728, Florence); with Urania e Clito (int)

Didone abbandonata (dm, 3, P. Metastasio), RD, 14 Jan 1726, *D-MÜs*, *US-Cn* (*R*1977: IOB, xxix), Acts 1 and 2 *A-Wn*; arr. Handel, 1737, *GB-Lbl*
Siroe re di Persia (dm, 3, Metastasio), VGG, Feb 1726, *D-MÜs*, *GB-Cfm*, *Lam*, *Lcm*
L'Ernelinda [La fede tradita] (dm, 3, F. Silvani), NB, 4 Nov 1726, *Lcm*, *I-MC*, Act 2 *B-Bc* (from a pasticcio, 1728, Florence); with Erighetta e Don Chilone (int, after Salvi: L'ammalato immaginario), *MC*
Gismondo re di Polonia [Il vincitor generoso] (dm, 3, F. Briani), RD, 11 Jan 1727, *D-MÜs*, Acts 2 and 3 *B-Bc*, Act 1 *D-Hs*
La caduta de' Decemviri (dm, 3, Stampiglia), NB, 1 Oct 1727, *I-MC*, Act 3 *GB-Lbl*; with Flacco e Servilia (int, after Stampiglia)
Catone in Utica (tragedia per musica, 3, Metastasio), RD, 19 Jan 1728, *D-B*, *MÜs*, *I-Mc* (pasticcio, 1732), *Nc*, *US-Wc*, Acts 1 and 2 *GB-Lcm*
Medo (dm, 3, Frugoni), Parma, Ducale, May 1728, *A-Wn* (as Medea risconosciuta, pasticcio, 1735), *B-Bc*, *F-Pc*
Flavio Anicio Olibrio (dm, 3, P. Pariati and A. Zeno), NB, 11 Dec 1728, 5 arias *D-MÜs*, trio *GB-Lbl*; with Il corteggiano affettato (int), aria *I-Nc*
Semiramide riconosciuta (dm, 3, Metastasio), RD, 6 Feb 1729, *D-MÜs*, *I-MC*, *Nc*, Acts 2 and 3 *D-Hs*; arr. Handel, 1733, *Hs*
[Il] Farnace [2nd version] (dm, 3, Lucchini), NB, 28 Aug 1729, arias in *I-MC* and *Nc*; with L'amante geloso (int)
Alessandro nell'Indie (dm, 3, Metastasio), RD, 2 Jan 1730, *GB-Lbl*, *I-MC*, *Nc*, *US-Wc*, Acts 2 and 3 *B-Bc*; arr. G. B. Ferrandini, 1735, *D-Mbs*(*R*1984: IOB, lxxii)
Artaserse (dm, 3, Metastasio), RD, 4 Feb 1730, *A-Wn*, *B-Bc*, *D-B*, *GB-Lbl*, *Lcm*, *Lgc*, *I-MC*, *Nc*, *Vnm*, *US-Wc*; Fano, 1731, *I-FAN* (pasticcio); Rome, 1731, *GB-Lcm*; as Arbace, arr. Handel, 1734, *D-Hs*
Pasticcios arr. Vinci: Turno Aricino (1725); Stratonica (1727), 2 arias *I-Mc*, *Rc*

*

BurneyH; *CroceN*; *FlorimoN*; *RosaM*
F. Algarotti: *Saggio sopra l'opera in musica* (Bologna, 1755, 2/1763; Eng. trans., 1767); extract repr. in O. Strunck: *Source Readings in Music History* (New York, 1950), 657–72
F. W. Marpurg: *Kritische Briefe über die Tonkunst* (Berlin, 1760), i, 225–7
A.-E.-M. Grétry: *Mémoires, ou essais sur la musique* (Paris, 1789, enlarged 2/1797), i, 256–8
C. Burney: *Memoirs of the Life and Writings of the Abate Metastasio* (London, 1796)
C. de Brosses: *Lettres familières écrites d'Italie: à quelques amis en 1739 et 1740* (Paris, 1858), letter l
N. d'Arienzo: 'Origini dell'opera comica', *RMI*, vi (1899), 473–95 [pt 3 of 4]
E. J. Dent: 'Notes on Leonardo Vinci', *MA*, iv (1912–13), 193–201
A. Cametti: 'Leonardo Vinci e i suoi drammi in musica al Teatro delle Dame 1724–30', *Musica d'oggi*, vi (1924), 297–9
K. Geiringer: 'Eine Geburtstagskantate von Pietro Metastasio und Leonardo Vinci', *ZMw*, ix (1926–7), 27–83
H. Benedikt: *Das Königreich Neapel unter Kaiser Karl VI* (Vienna, 1927)
A. de Angelis: *Il Teatro Alibert o Delle Dame (1717–1863)* (Tivoli, 1951)
H. Hucke: 'Die neapolitanische Tradition in der Oper', *IMSCR*, viii *New York 1961*, 253–76
U. Prota-Giurleo: 'Leonardo Vinci', *Convegno musicale*, ii (1965), 3–11
R. B. Meikle: *Leonardo Vinci's 'Artaserse': an Edition, with an Editorial and Critical Commentary* (diss., Cornell U., 1970)
H. Hell: *Die neapolitanische Opernsinfonie in der ersten Hälfte des 18. Jahrhunderts* (Tutzing, 1971)
M. F. Robinson: *Naples and Neapolitan Opera* (Oxford, 1972)
R. Strohm: 'Italienische Opernarien des frühen Settecento (1720–1730)', *AnMc*, no.16 (1976)
——: *Die italienische Oper im 18. Jahrhundert* (Wilhelmshaven, 1979)
——: 'Leonardo Vinci's *Didone abbandonata* (Rome 1726)', *Essays on Handel and Italian Opera* (Cambridge, 1985), 213–24
——: 'Metastasio's Alessandro nell'Indie and its Earliest Settings', ibid, 232–48
P. Weiss: 'Ancora sulle origini dell'opera comica: il linguaggio', *Studi pergolesiani*, i (1986), 124–48
J. H. Roberts: 'Handel and Vinci's *Didone abbandonata*: Revisions and Borrowings', *ML*, lxvii (1987), 141–50
K. S. Markstrom: *The Operas of Leonardo Vinci* (diss., U. of Toronto, 1992)

KURT MARKSTROM

Vingança da cigana, A ('The Gypsy's Revenge'). *Drama joco-sério* in one act by ANTÓNIO LEAL MOREIRA to a libretto by Domingos Caldas Barbosa; Lisbon, Teatro de S Carlos, 1794.

The libretto, by the Brazilian mulatto poet Caldas Barbosa, paints a vivid social picture of late 18th-century Portugal. The opera is set in the working-class Ribeira district of Lisbon, near the river Tagus, and the characters include the gypsy Pepa (soprano), the fishmonger Tarelo (bass), the sergeant Chibante (baritone), the servant Lambisca (soprano), the barber Grilo (bass) and his black friend Cazumba (bass). There are only two middle-class characters, the French-Italian hairdresser Monsieur Pierre (tenor) and the widow Camila (soprano). The peaceful co-existence of the three couples is momentarily disturbed by a row between the two suitors for the hand of Pepa. The opera follows contemporary trends in its extensive use of vocal ensembles, and it also alternates spoken dialogue with arias, duets and recitatives. The general style of the music betrays the influence of Paisiello and Cimarosa; Monsieur Pierre's picaresque aria in which he recounts his travels in a mixture of different languages recalls Figaro's similar aria in Paisiello's *Il barbiere di Siviglia.* But there is an interesting stylistic compromise in that several numbers are written in a more popular, national or even exotic vein. This is the case with Cazumba's song, accompanied on the *canzá*, a Brazilian rattle or scraper, and Pepa's *modinha.* The work was first sung at the benefit night of the castrato 'prima donna' Domenico Caporalini by an all-Italian cast, the female parts being taken by castratos as by then women were not allowed on stage in Lisbon. MANUEL CARLOS DE BRITO

Vinzing, Ute (*b* Wuppertal, 9 Sept 1936). German soprano. She studied with Martha Mödl, making her début in 1967 as Mařenka at Lübeck. She was engaged at Wuppertal (1971–6), and she has appeared at Düsseldorf, Hamburg, Vienna, Munich, Berlin, Geneva, Paris, Barcelona, Buenos Aires and Seattle, where she sang Brünnhilde in complete cycles of the *Ring* (1975–84). She made her Metropolitan début in 1984 as Electra. Her repertory includes Leonore, Senta, Ortrud, Kundry, Isolde and the Dyer's Wife (*Die Frau ohne Schatten*), which she sang at Bonn in 1990. A talented actress, she has a very powerful voice which is particularly strong in the upper register.

ELIZABETH FORBES

Violanta. Opera in one act, op.8, by ERICH WOLFGANG KORNGOLD to a libretto by Hans Müller; Munich, Staatsoper, 28 March 1916.

Violanta is Korngold's third stage work, and was first presented in a double bill with its immediate predecessor *Der Ring des Polykrates*. The composer's father, in collaboration with the librettist Hans Müller, was responsible for the choice of subject, described by the former as 'a red-hot Renaissance drama'. Korngold's first attempt at tragedy was a success, and in the following few years received further performances in Germany and abroad. It is a work of great harmonic, melodic and formal discipline, but it also has a remarkable eloquence and authority of expression, particularly in the depiction of physical passion, which belie its composer's tender years.

The opera is set in 15th-century Venice. Simone Trovai (baritone), is angry that his wife Violanta has been indifferent to him ever since her sister was seduced by Alfonso, Prince of Naples. Violanta (soprano) appears, saying that she has arranged a meeting with Alfonso, and that Simone must avenge her sister by murdering him. Reluctantly, Simone agrees. Violanta's nurse (contralto) sings a soothing lullaby as her mistress awaits Alfonso. Eventually Alfonso (tenor) arrives and declares his love. Violanta warns Alfonso that he is about to die, but as he describes his unhappy childhood Violanta realizes that she has loved him all along. Simone rushes in to find the couple embracing. He attempts to stab Alfonso, but instead mortally wounds Violanta, who dies in his arms. CHRISTOPHER PALMER

Violins of Saint-Jacques, The. Opera in a prologue and three acts by MALCOLM WILLIAMSON to a libretto by William Chappell based on Patrick Leigh Fermor's novel; London, Sadler's Wells, 29 November 1966.

Steamy foreboding and hectic pleasure aptly characterize this drama of a small colonial Caribbean island on the eve of a volcanic explosion that buries it in the ocean, leaving only the ghostly echoes of its carnival violins to frighten away the superstitious fishermen of the prologue. Two leading St-Jacques families hope to reconcile their differences in a grand carnival night party and ball. The son of one family, Marcel (baritone), woos the daughter, Josephine (mezzo-soprano), of the other and makes plans to elope with her that night. Josephine's cousin Berthe (soprano) mistrusts Marcel and, for the moment, rejects the declarations of her own suitor, Josephine's brother Sosthène (tenor). The night's events include disclosure of Marcel's existing marriage and Berthe's discovery that Sosthène has grown into the man she might marry. All of this is nullified by the volcano's catastrophic explosion. Because Berthe has rowed out to sea to try to forestall the eloping lovers she is the only person on the island to survive. Her scena in a small boat on a featureless ocean ends the opera.

The relationships of the principal characters are shadowed by general tropical premonitions and such incidents as Sosthène's charming of the snake (Act 1), the summoning of a sinister carnival figure at the party, the accurate prophecies of a Voodoo Priestess (mezzo-soprano), the highly effective incursions of voodoo dancers and, above all, the music for the rumblings and spoutings of the volcano throughout the night. The actual eruption is less impressive musically than the warnings of its imminence (heavy wind chords and pedal points); but Williamson's control of mood on an extended scale represents his most impressive operatic achievement. The 19 principal parts (most of them substantial) and elaborate use of chorus are matched by triple wind, organ, two harps and varied percussion in the orchestra, supplemented by a stage band of about 15. ROGER COVELL

Viozzi, Giulio (*b* Trieste, 5 Aug 1912; *d* Verona, 29 Nov 1984). Italian composer. He studied the piano and composition at the Verdi Conservatory in Trieste, and began his career as a concert pianist after winning a competition in 1936. From 1939 he taught the piano at the Trieste Conservatory, where he was appointed to the chair in composition in 1956. He began composing piano and chamber works during the early 1930s, but produced his first work for the theatre, the opera *Allamistakeo*, only in 1954. Based on Poe, the typically macabre story of an unfaithful husband who dreams of a mummy threatening a group of egyptologists with destruction is treated with a sure sense of theatre and in a musical idiom that shows the influence of Stravinsky. Apart from a successful encounter with the literary world of Dino Buzzati in *La giacca dannata* of 1967, Viozzi's most important theatrical work is the three-act opera of 1962, *Il sasso pagano* (based on a Friulian novella). This relates the struggle of a country priest to overcome his peasant congregation's superstitious veneration of an ancient pagan tablet. The work exemplifies an eclecticism that combines influences from Bartók to Stravinsky and Prokofiev but is attentive to the popular culture of Trieste-Friuli, a stylistic feature that distances Viozzi from the more radical avant garde.

all librettos by the composer

Allamistakeo (1, after E. A. Poe: *Some Words with a Mummy*), Bergamo, Novità, 26 Sept 1954
La parete bianca (radio op, 1), RAI, 1954
Un intervento notturno (1, after R. A. Bowen), Trieste, Verdi, 26 Jan 1957
Il sasso pagano (3, after O. von Leitgeb), Trieste, Verdi, 10 March 1962
La giacca dannata (1, after D. Buzzati), Trieste, Verdi, 1967
Elisabetta (1, after G. de Maupassant), Trieste, Verdi, 1971
L'inverno (1, after N. Spazzali), unperf.

*

C. de Incontrera: 'Giulio Viozzi', *Pagine istriane*, 4th ser., xi/1–2 (1960), 130–31
V. Levi: *La vita musicale a Trieste: cronache di un cinquantenario 1918–1968* (Milan, 1968)
B. Bidussi: 'Teatro di Giulio Viozzi', *Umana*, xix/1–4 (1970), 16–18
G. Radole: *Giulio Viozzi: una vocazione musicale* (Trieste, 1986)
RAFFAELE POZZI

Virgil [Vergil; Publius Vergilius Maro] (*b* Andes [? now Pietole], nr Mantua, 15 Oct 70 BC; *d* Brundisium [now Brindisi], 21 Sept 19 BC). Latin poet. He was educated at Cremona, Mantua and Milan, was of delicate health and took no part in military or political life. He won the patronage of Maecenas, became a friend of Octavian (the future emperor Augustus), the historian Pollio, the poet and general Cornelius Gallus and the literary critic Varus. The *Eclogues* (42–37 BC) take as their background the Sicily of Theocritus. The *Georgics* (*c*36–29 BC) hymn the glories of the Italian countryside and give instruction for right and pleasurable farming; book 4 ends with a superb retelling of the story of Orpheus and Eurydice.

The *Aeneid* occupied Virgil for the rest of his life, and he was planning further revision when he died. The epic owes much to Homer. Books 1–6 can be described as Virgil's *Odyssey*, books 7–12 as his *Iliad*. The subject is the foundation of Rome as a new Troy, a project planned by destiny but only realized through great human suffering. The future grandeur of Rome is touched on in book 6, when Aeneas interviews his father Anchises in the underworld. But it is book 4 that has caught the operatic imagination – the account of the growing love between Dido and Aeneas in Carthage and its eventual doom. It is in Dido's capital that Aeneas recounts (books 2 and 3) the destruction of Troy and the story of his wanderings. From Cavalli and Purcell to Berlioz the tale has often been told in music, and Metastasio's first original libretto, one of the most frequently set, was *Didone abbandonata*. Aeneas in Latium and with his future wife Lavinia has also attracted composers, for example Collasse (*Enée et Lavinie*) and Guglielmi (*Enea e Lavinia*).

*

U. Rolandi: *Nel bimillenario virgiliano: Virgilio fonte di libretti per musica* (Monza, 1930)
D. Cairns: 'Berlioz and Virgil: a Consideration of *Les Troyens* as a Virgilian Opera', *PRMA*, xcv (1968–9), 97–110; repr. in idem,

Responses: Musical Essays and Reviews (New York, 1973), 88–110, and in *Hector Berlioz: Les Troyens*, ed. I. Kemp (Cambridge, 1988) ROBERT ANDERSON

Virginia. *Tragedia lírica* in three acts by JOSÉ ANGEL MONTERO to a libretto by Domenico Bancalari (in Italian); Caracas, Teatro Caracas, 27 April 1873.

The plot, drawn from Roman history, centres on Appius Claudius (baritone), a member of the Decemviri, the commission drawn up to formulate a code of laws known as the Twelve Tables. After its completion in 450 BC Appius Claudius heads a reign of terror to quash an uprising by the plebeians, among whom is Virginia (soprano), daughter of the centurion Virginio (bass), who stabs her to save her from becoming the lover and slave of Appius Claudius. The moral corruption and abuse of power among the Decemviri eventually precipitate their downfall in 449 BC.

The themes of popular defiance against political despotism and of heroic personal sacrifice to the cause of human dignity and freedom appealed to Montero who, like his librettist Bancalari in the pre-unified Italy of Garibaldi's day, was a committed liberal. The expression of lofty, archetypal emotion pervades the score. The impact of Italian operatic tradition is evident: in accordance with conventions established some 50 years earlier, Montero condensed the traditional scena, cantabile, *tempo di mezzo* and cabaletta to build unrelenting dramatic tension within each act. His restraint with sparse and thematically integrated coloratura passages reflects Bellini, and there is effective use of the chorus and orchestration to articulate textural contrasts; in addition, martial choruses appeal to patriotic emotions in the manner of Verdi's early works.

Virginia was considered the earliest Venezuelan opera until the discovery in 1977 of Osorio's *El maestro Rufo zapatero* (1847). *Virginia* was first given in Italian, but a Spanish translation of the libretto was also issued. It was revived at the Teatro Municipal, Caracas, in 1969 and recorded (with the same cast) in 1976; in his review of the recording Turró claimed that among 19th-century Latin American composers only Carlos Gomes could compete as regards musico-dramaturgical craftsmanship. For *Virginia*, Montero was awarded the Busto del Libertador (Bolívar) by the president of Venezuela.

MALENA KUSS

Virginia Opera. American company based in NORFOLK.

Virgin Prophetess, The [*The Virgin Prophetess, or The Fate of Troy*]. Semi-opera in five acts by GOTTFRIED FINGER based on the play by Elkanah Settle; London, Drury Lane, 2 May 1701.

This was the last of Finger's English stage works, performed shortly before he left the country for good. The virgin prophetess was Cassandra, and the work, a spoken play with music, deals with the fall of Troy; as in Purcell's semi-operas, the main characters do not sing. Finger's contribution consists of a suite of incidental music (London, 1701) and self-contained musical interludes in each act (in *GB-Cfm* and *Lcm*), scored for soloists, chorus and a large orchestra including five-part strings and three trumpets. In Act 1 the Trojans celebrate 'The Triumph of Paris'; Act 2 contains a 'Procession Song in the Temple of Diana', invoking the protection of the goddess; in Act 3 a masque of Cupid (soprano) celebrates Cassandra's release by the Greeks; in Act 4 Cassandra conjures up masques to warn Paris of Troy's fall; and in Act 5 the Trojans drink their cares away before the final catastrophe. PETER HOLMAN

Virineya. Opera in three acts by SERGEY MIKHAYLOVICH SLONIMSKY to a libretto by Sergey Tsenin after the story by Lidiya Seyfullina; Leningrad, Malïy Opera and Ballet Theatre, 30 September 1967; revised version, Leningrad, Malïy Opera and Ballet Theatre, February 1976.

Slonimsky composed his first opera on a commission from the Stanislavsky–Nemirovich-Danchenko Music Theatre in Moscow. Although the première eventually took place at the Malïy Theatre in Leningrad, the opera was produced simultaneously in Moscow and in Kuybïshev (now Samara) and hailed as one of the best works honouring the 50th anniversary of the Russian Revolution.

The story by Seyfullina on which the opera was based was written in 1924 and dealt with the complex relationship between peasant groups in the years immediately following the Revolution. The opera portrays a social drama, within all too human emotional dimensions, against the backdrop of historical events. Its distinctive musical profile owes much to the fusion of Russian folk styles with contemporary expressive devices, as well as to the composer's innate gift for eloquent solo and choral writing.

The action takes place in a Russian village in 1917. In the introduction Virineya (dramatic soprano) sings a sad song on a folk text, 'Akh tï, matushka' ('O you, mother'), with choral accompaniment. Responding to the alarm bell, the simple villagers gather in confusion, unable to comprehend the upheavals in their country and the conflicting claims on their loyalties. The local 'prelate', Magara (bass), describes his vision of his impending Assumption; when it fails to take place, he loses his faith. Against Virineya's wishes, her common-law husband, Vasily (tenor), departs with an Engineer (baritone) in pursuit of money. She sings of her frustrated capacity for love in an impassioned aria, 'A vesna na poroge!' ('And spring is on the threshold'). No love is lost between Vasily's mother, Mokeikha (mezzo-soprano or contralto), and Virineya; after Vasily's return the tension finally reaches breaking-point and Virineya runs away.

In Act 2 Vasily tries to persuade Virineya to return, but they argue, and she succumbs with indifference to the persistent advances of the Engineer. The drunken Magara is persuaded by the jealous Vasily to murder the Engineer. Pavel (low bass-baritone), an idealistic Bolshevik, declares his love for Virineya and touches a responsive chord in her.

In the final act, the chaos of conflicting ideologies is resolved by the villagers as they vote in favour of the Bolsheviks, symbolized through the strains of a revolutionary march which gradually gains momentum. Virineya and Pavel express their love in a duet, 'Vsyo na zemle dlya schast' ya roditsya' ('Everything on earth is born for love'), but their idyll is short-lived: news comes that kulaks (rich peasants) are fighting the Bolsheviks in the next village. Pavel leaves to join his comrades, and the kulaks demand to know where he has gone. When Virineya refuses to answer they kill her. LAUREL E. FAY

Visconti, Caterina (*b* ?Milan; *fl* 1729–54). Italian soprano. Her earliest known appearances were in operas at Florence and Venice in 1729 and 1731. From 1734 to 1754 she performed regularly in the opera houses of Parma, Reggio Emilia, Florence, Naples,

Turin and Milan, but not, apparently, in Venice or Rome. Her repertory was not exclusively operatic, for she also sang in a serenata in honour of the Empress Maria Theresa (1748, Parma) and a cantata before the King of the Two Sicilies (26 July 1752, Naples).

She may have been the Signora Visconti who sang in London in 1741 (*Alessandro in Persia*), 1743 (Galuppi's *Enrico*) and 1753–4. If so, she was paid 1000 guineas for her first visit, according to Horace Walpole, and described by Burney on her third visit as 'first woman, now *Passeè* [*sic*]' – an observation which makes it unlikely that she was the Signora Visconti engaged for London in 1765–6. COLIN TIMMS

Visconti (di Modrone), Count **Luchino** (*b* Milan, 2 Nov 1906; *d* Rome, 17 March 1976). Italian director and designer. His family was musical and had a long association with the La Scala theatre, where he was at home from an early age, but he approached opera only after considerable successful experience as a director and designer in the spoken theatre and as a film director. This step was in part prompted by his admiration for Maria Callas, who sang in his first production, Spontini's *La vestale* (1954, La Scala). In successive years, also with Callas, he staged *La sonnambula*, *La traviata* (for illustration *see* DE NOBILI, LILA), *Anna Bolena* and *Iphigénie en Tauride*, all at La Scala (he wrote on Callas in *Opera*, xxi, 1970, pp.806–19 and 911–21). In 1958 he directed his first opera outside Italy, the highly successful *Don Carlos* at Covent Garden, and inaugurated the Spoleto Festival with *Macbeth*. He worked frequently at Spoleto (Donizetti's *Il duca d'Alba* was an important revival) and ended his opera career there in 1972 with a much admired *Manon Lescaut*.

Visconti's career in the opera house coincided with and fostered the renewed interest in neglected works by the leading 19th-century Italian composers. His profound love and knowledge of music, his visual taste, his familiarity with the styles of various periods, gave his finest productions an unrivalled authenticity. His influence on opera production in Italy and elsewhere was vast. Before him, most Italian opera houses were content with routine productions, in a tired tradition; with his insistence on the individual character of each work, he renewed, indeed revolutionized, the approach to opera staging. He had a strong influence also on younger directors and designers such as Franco Zeffirelli, Piero Tosi and Filippo Sanjust, many of whom were his assistants. In collaboration with Sanjust and Enrico Medioli, he wrote the libretto for Franco Mannino's opera *Il diavolo in giardino* (1963, Palermo), which he also staged.

*

ES (G. C. Castello)
W. Weaver: 'Luchino Visconti', *Opera*, ix (1958), 289–92
M. Estève, ed.: *Luchino Visconti: l'histoire et l'esthétique* (Paris, 1963)
Y. Guillaume: *Luchino Visconti* (Paris, 1966)
G. N. Smith: *Luchino Visconti* (London, 1967)
P. Baldelli: *Luchino Visconti* (Milan, 1973)
G. Servado: *Visconti* (London, 1979) WILLIAM WEAVER

Vishnevskaya, Galina (Pavlovna) (*b* Leningrad [now St Petersburg], 25 Oct 1926). Russian soprano. She studied privately with Vera Garina in Leningrad, and made her début in operetta in 1944. In 1952 she joined the Bol'shoy Theatre. A versatile and fascinating artist, she was one of the outstanding Russian singers. Her expressive, rich-hued voice of highly individual timbre, her polished technique and strong dramatic talent allowed her to appear in a wide variety of roles. Her notable array of stage portraits included Tatyana and Lisa, Kupava (*The Snow Maiden*) and Marfa, Aida, Violetta, Tosca, Leonore and the solo part in Poulenc's *La voix humaine*. She gave the first Bol'shoy performances of Katherine in Shebalin's *Ukroshcheniye stroptivoy* ('The Taming of the Shrew', 1957), Natasha in *War and Peace* (1959), Marina in Muradeli's *Oktyabr'* ('October', 1964) and Sof'ya in Prokofiev's *Semyon Kotko* (1970). She first sang at the Metropolitan, as Aida and Butterfly, in 1961, at Covent Garden (Aida) in 1962 and at La Scala (Liù) in 1964. London critics praised her artistry, her warm, liquid tone and excellent legato, and her passionate and intense style, though some found her acting a little exaggerated. She appeared in the film of Shostakovich's *Katerina Izmaylova* (1966). Vishnevskaya has also turned to directing (e.g. Rimsky-Korsakov's *The Tsar's Bride*, Washington, DC, 1987). Married to the cellist and conductor Mstislav Rostropovich, she left the USSR for political reasons in 1974 and eventually settled in the USA. She has written an autobiography, *Galina: a Russian Story* (London, 1984; Russ. orig., Moscow, 1991). I. M. YAMPOL'SKY

Visitation, The [*Die Heimsuchung*]. Opera in three acts by GUNTHER SCHULLER to his own libretto after Franz Kafka's novel *Der Prozess*; Hamburg, Staatsoper, 12 October 1966.

Carter Jones (baritone), a black student, is persecuted by the white citizens of a small town. As the opera begins, Jones daydreams about events in the history of his race: a 'coloured' Baptist church service of the 1880s and early 19th-century slave auctions. His visions are interrupted by the entrance of three white men who threaten and interrogate him and advise him to stay out of trouble. After a brief but unconsummated flirtation with his white neighbour Miss Hampton (soprano), Jones is summoned before an impromptu tribunal, accused of aspiring to the rights that belong only to whites. The court wants to hang him but is interrupted before the sentence can be carried out. Jones, disillusioned, seeks help from several sources, but to no avail. Not even the Church can provide him with solace from persecution. In the end, Jones, badly beaten, is taken to a remote area and brutally murdered.

Schuller's musical setting of his own libretto is experimental. Combining jazz idioms and serial techniques in a manner referred to by the composer as 'third stream', the music relies heavily on aleatory devices juxtaposed with sections in improvisational style. The final scene of the opera experiments with quarter-tone effects. Use of electronic tape is also employed, including Bessie Smith's recording of 'Nobody knows you when you're down and out', which opens and closes the work. The vocal writing employs wide ranges and high tessitura, especially for Miss Hampton. Although *The Visitation* has been highly acclaimed musically, the libretto has received some harsh criticism: Schuller based it on Willa and Edwin Muir's 1937 English translation of Kafka's novel (applying the theme of the individual against bureaucracy to racial problems in the USA), but critics found it trite and naive, with too much expository dialogue. Schuller subsequently wrote an orchestral suite based on the opera, first performed in Chicago in 1970.

In Germany the opera has been performed under the title *Die Heimsuchung* in a translation by the composer.

JAMES P. CASSARO

Vismarri [Vismari], **Filippo** (*b* before 1635; *d* Vienna, ?1706). Italian soprano castrato and composer. He sang at the Vienna court, probably from 1649. In 1660 he sang in Leopold I's *Il sagrificio d'Abramo*, and his own *Orontea* was produced. About 1679 he took holy orders. His setting of *Orontea* (in *A-Wn*), in a prologue and three acts, closely follows the famous libretto of G. A. Cicognini (earlier set by Cesti). His gift for characterization is evident in the use of appropriate vocal and instrumental motifs and his recitatives are distinguished by their concise, dramatic style. Nevertheless, Holmes (1972) has demonstrated that Vismarri's *Orontea* compares unfavourably with Cesti's version in aspects such as melodic invention, structural variety and sensitivity to the text. He also composed cantatas and other vocal works.

E. Wellesz: 'Die Opern und Oratorien in Wien von 1660–1708', *SMw*, vi (1919), 5–138
——: *Essays on Opera* (London, 1950), 40
F. Hadamowsky: 'Barocktheater am Wiener Kaiserhof', *Jb der Gesellschaft für Wiener Theaterforschung 1951–52* (1955), 7–117
W. C. Holmes: 'Yet Another "Orontea": Further Rapport between Venice and Vienna', *Venezia e il melodramma nel seicento: Venice 1972*, 199–225
——: Introduction to *A. Cesti: Orontea*, WE, xi (1973)

LAWRENCE E. BENNETT

Visse, Dominique (*b* Lisieux, 30 Aug 1955). French countertenor. At the age of 13 he became a chorister at the maîtrise of Notre Dame in Paris. Later he studied the organ and flute at the Versailles Conservatory. As an instrumentalist he specialized in medieval and Renaissance music, occasionally singing as a countertenor. Between 1976 and 1978 he was a pupil of Alfred Deller and René Jacobs, became acquainted with Nigel Rogers, and decided to specialize in singing. In 1978 he founded the Ensemble Clément Janequin and joined the newly formed group Les Arts Florissants under William Christie. In 1980 Visse began to study with Jean Laurens. He made his opera début at Tourcoing in 1982 in *L'incoronazione di Poppea*. He sang Flora in Vivaldi's *L'incoronazione di Dario* at Grasse (1984); the title role of Charpentier's *Actéon* at Edinburgh (1985); Annius in Gluck's *La clemenza di Tito* at Tourcoing (1987) and at Lausanne (1991). At the Opéra he sang Cupid in *Orphée aux enfers* and Nirenus in *Giulio Cesare* (1987), and at Innsbruck he sang Delfa in Cavalli's *Giasone* (1988). He created Geronimo in Claude Prey's *Le rouge et le noir* at Aix-en-Provence in 1989, then sang Octavia's Nurse (*L'incoronazione di Poppea*) at Montpellier. His voice has a distinctive clarity which, with a forceful projection and a lively dramatic sense, lends colour and presence to his stage performances. Besides *Poppea* he has recorded Cavalli's *Xerse* and *Giasone*; Charpentier's *Actéon*, *Les arts florissants*, *David et Jonathas* and *Le malade imaginaire*; Campra's *Tancrède*, Rameau's *Anacréon* and Hasse's *Cleofide*. He married the soprano Agnès Mellon.

NICHOLAS ANDERSON

Vitale, Edoardo (*b* Naples, 29 Nov 1872; *d* Rome, 12 Dec 1937). Italian conductor. He made his début at the age of 14 conducting operetta at the Teatro Metastasio, Rome, and then studied at the Accademia di S Cecilia as a student of Eugenio Terziani. He taught harmony at the Accademia from 1893 but was advised by Giulio Ricordi to leave teaching and devote himself to conducting. In 1896 he conducted the first *La bohème* in Florence, then did a season at the Argentina in Rome before undertaking numerous engagements elsewhere in Italy and abroad, including Madrid and Cairo. He replaced Toscanini at La Scala (1908–10), where he conducted the first Italian performances of *Médée* (Cherubini), *Boris Godunov* and *Elektra*, all in 1909. He spent the 1910–11 season at the Colón, Buenos Aires, and toured other South American cities before returning to Italy as music director of the Rome Opera (1913–26). There he broadened the repertory with the introduction of new works, including *Le maschere* (Mascagni), *La via della finestra* (Zandonai), *Mirra* (Alaleona) and *Canossa* (Malipiero). From 1932 he directed the Carro di Tespi, a travelling theatre company.

In 1897 Vitale married the soprano Lina Pasini; their son Riccardo (*b* 17 Oct 1903) was artistic director of the Rome Opera (1958–62).

NOËL GOODWIN

Vitali, Filippo (*b* Florence; *d* after March 1653). Italian composer. Little is known of his life except that he became a priest before 1631 and held various chapel positions from the 1630s, including 14 years as a tenor in the Sistine Chapel choir. At least 13 volumes of his secular vocal chamber music were published between 1616 and 1647, as well as two of his three known theatrical works: the *favola in musica Aretusa* (Rome, 1620) and the *intermedi* for an academy play (Florence, 1623). His music for O. Persiani's *Narciso et Ecco immortalati* is lost. This opera was given at the Teatro SS Giovanni e Paolo in Venice in 1642, reportedly as reworked by Marco Marazzoli (libretto published Venice, 1642).

Aretusa reflects Florentine origins – not only of opera and of the composer, but also of the librettist, Ottavio Corsini, a prelate at the court of Rome, in whose house the work was performed from 8 February 1620. Based on Ovid's *Metamorphoses* (lib. in *I-Rvat*), the opera is in a prologue and three acts. Clear, simple harmonies, word-sensitive rhythms and frequent cadences characterize the recitative. The ensemble pieces employ the irregular rhythms and restricted harmony typical of pastoral stage music, and, in the classical manner, each act closes with an extended choral ensemble. The few brief solo tunes of the nymphs and shepherds are outbalanced by their emotional recitatives. The lovesick 'villain' Alfeo [Alphaeus] (tenor), originally sung by Pompeo Caccini (who also painted the sets), has two formal monologues. In a classical messenger scene Aminta [Amyntas] (contralto), first sung by Lorenzo Sances, reports Alphaeus's pursuit of Arethusa and her fearful end. Arethusa herself (soprano), created by Gregorio Lazzarini, appears in only three scenes; in fact Lazzarini also doubled as the goddess Diana, who presents the prologue and announces Arethusa's final transformation in the closing scene. Corsini offered nine performances of the work, which was praised for its brevity, fine singing and charming style.

C.-F. Menestrier: *Des représentations en musique anciennes et modernes* (Paris, 1681), 210–14
H. Goldschmidt: *Studien zur Geschichte der italienischen Oper im 17. Jahrhundert*, i (Leipzig, 1901), 7–8
A. Solerti: *Le origini del melodramma* (Turin, 1903), 90–97
——: *Gli albori del melodramma* (Milan, 1904), iii, 341–84

——: *Musica, ballo e drammatica alla corte medicea dal 1600 al 1637* (Florence, 1905), 393–408
R. Rolland: *Histoire de l'opéra en Europe avant Lully et Scarlatti* (Paris, 2/1931), 127–9
J. W. Pruett: *The Works of Filippo Vitali* (diss., U. of North Carolina, Chapel Hill, 1962)
D. J. Grout: 'The Chorus in Early Opera', *Festschrift Friedrich Blume* (Kassel, 1963), 151–61
N. Pirrotta: 'Early Opera and Aria', *New Looks at Italian Opera: Essays in Honor of Donald J. Grout* (Ithaca, 1968), 100–01; rev. in N. Pirrotta and E. Povoledo: *Music and Theatre from Poliziano to Monteverdi* (Cambridge, 1981), 276
T. Walker: 'Gli errori di "Minerva al tavolino" ', *Venezia e il melodramma nel Seicento: Venice 1972*, 7–20
S. Leopold: 'Quelle bazzicature poetiche, appellate ariette: Dichtungsformen in der frühen italienischen Oper (1600–1640)', *HJbMw*, iii (1978), 101–41
C. Gianturco: 'Nuove considerazioni su *Il tedio del recitativo* delle prime opere romane', *RIM*, xviii (1982), 212–39
P. Fabbri: *Il secolo cantante: per una storia del libretto d'opera nel seicento* (Bologna, 1990)
MARGARET MURATA

Vittadini, Franco (*b* Pavia, 9 April 1884; *d* Pavia, 30 Nov 1948). Italian composer and conductor. From 1903 he studied at the Milan Conservatory, but left prematurely because of a disagreement with the director, Giuseppe Gallignani. After a short period as organist and *maestro di cappella* in Varese, he spent the rest of his life in Pavia, where he directed the Istituto Musicale from 1924 to his death. He won his biggest success with the charming and imaginative though firmly traditional *Anima allegra*, which was performed in several foreign countries as well as in Italy. Among his other stage works only the ballet *Vecchia Milano* (1928) was comparably successful, whereas the later operas circulated very little after their first productions. In *Caracciolo*, which he himself regarded as his masterpiece, he attempted a more grandiose, tragic manner which seems to have made quite a strong impact on the work's first audience; but the gentle, playfully sentimental *Fiammetta e l'avaro* was probably a more natural expression of his talent – too conservative, however, to arouse more than passing interest at its posthumous première. Outside the theatre Vittadini attracted most attention with his large output of religious music. The poignant choral work *L'agonia del Redentore* (1933) shows his church style at its best, while *Nazareth* forms a bridge between the religious and dramatic sides of his achievement.

See also ANIMA ALLEGRA.

Il mare di Tiberiade, *c*1912–14 (L. Illica), unperf.
Anima allegra, 1918–19 (3, G. Adami and L. Motta, after S. and J. Alvarez Quintero), Rome, Costanzi, 15 April 1921
Nazareth (visione lirica, 1, Adami), Pavia, Fraschini, 27 May 1925
La Sagredo (4, Adami), Milan, Scala, 29 April 1930
Caracciolo (3, A. Rossato), Rome, Opera, 9 Feb 1938
Fiammetta e l'avaro, begun 1942 (3, Adami and G. Forzano), Brescia, Grande, April 1951
? 1 other opera, unpubd

*

A. Baratti: *Vita del musicista Franco Vittadini* (Milan, 1955)
JOHN C. G. WATERHOUSE

Vittori, Loreto (*b* Spoleto, bap. 5 Sept 1600; *d* Rome, 23 April 1670). Italian singer, composer and librettist. His early training was probably in Spoleto, where he was engaged as a soprano by the cathedral chapter from 1614 to 1617, and then in Rome, where he was taken by Maffeo Barberini, and finally in Florence. There he enjoyed the favour of Cosimo II de' Medici and embarked on a successful singing career, taking part in the performance of Marco da Gagliano's *Medoro*, among other works. In 1621 he entered the service of Cardinal Ludovico Ludovisi, nephew of Pope Gregory XV, and on 23 January 1622 he was admitted to membership of the papal choir. He participated in performances of Gagliano's *La regina Sant'Orsola* (1624, Florence) and *Flora* (1628) and Domenico Mazzocchi's *La catena d'Adone* (1626, Rome), as well as in the musical celebrations for the marriage of Odoardo Farnese and Margherita de' Medici in 1628. He also sang in Luigi Rossi's *Il palazzo incantato* in 1642, and probably in other operas commissioned by the Barberini family after 1630 as well. He was in the service of Cardinal Antonio Barberini in 1637 (and quite possibly earlier than that), and remained with him for the rest of his life, taking part as singer, poet and composer in vocal chamber music, oratorios and other sacred music, as well as in opera.

In 1639 the score of Vittori's three-act *dramma in musica Galatea*, for which he wrote both words and music, was published in Rome with a dedication to Cardinal Barberini; it was probably written to win back the Barberini's favour after Vittori had been involved in the abduction of a young woman in December 1637 and been exiled to Spoleto the following year. Apparently however, the opera was never performed in Rome, although there is evidence for a performance in Naples in February 1644 at the palace of Prince Cariati. The libretto published in Spoleto in 1655 is a revised version of the original text. In 1640 Vittori set to music the sacred drama *Sant'Ignazio* (text probably by Giano Nicio Eritreo). Contemporary accounts describe its elaborate staging on 7 July in the Gesù church for the centenary of the founding of the Jesuit order; the music does not survive. It is not known whether Vittori himself set his other dramatic texts to music. The first of these, *La Santa Irene* (1644, Rome) was intended to be sung throughout, but it was performed in the palace of the Marchese de' Nobili as a combination of speaking and singing; in *La pellegrina costante*, a sacred verse drama (1647, Rome), the choruses concluding each act are explicitly intended to be sung. The two comedies *La fiera* (lib. in *I-Rvat*; suggested by an intermezzo with the same title in Mazzocchi and Marazzoli's *Chi soffre speri*) and *Le zittelle cantarine* (1663, Genoa), both in prose, have various musical numbers.

See also GALATEA.

*

C. A. Rau: *Loreto Vittori: Beiträge zur historisch-kritischen Würdigung seines Lebens, Wirkens und Schaffens* (Munich, 1916)
L. Fausti: 'Un'autobiografia poetica di Loreto Vittori', *Atti dell'Accademia spoletina, 1920–22*, 158–68
N. Pirrotta: 'Early Opera and Aria', *New Looks at Italian Opera: Essays in Honor of Donald J. Grout* (Ithaca, 1968), 39–107; repr. in N. Pirrotta and E. Povoledo: *Music and Theatre from Poliziano to Monteverdi* (Cambridge, 1981), 237–80
F. Hammond: 'Musicians at the Medici Court in the Mid-Seventeenth Century', *AnMc*, no.14 (1974), 151–69
B. M. Antolini: 'La carriera di cantante e compositore di Loreto Vittori', *Studi musicali*, vii (1978), 141–88
M. Murata: *Operas for the Papal Court, 1631–1668* (Ann Arbor, 1981)
D. A. d'Alessandro: 'La musica a Napoli nel secolo XVII attraverso gli *avvisi* e i giornali', *Musica e cultura a Napoli dal XV al XIX secolo: Naples 1982*, 145–64
BIANCA MARIA ANTOLINI

Vitturi, Bartolomeo (*fl* Venice, 1731–53). Italian librettist. He wrote mainly *opera seria* texts, which were set for Venetian theatres by Albinoni, Galuppi, Giuseppe Scarlatti and Bertoni, among others. His plots derive from ancient history and are often set in Persia or the

Middle East. In the early works the stanzas of aria texts have irregular numbers of lines, but the later works have the rhymed double quatrains typical of aria texts for the rest of the century. Most conform to the strictest standards of the Arcadian reform libretto: a succession of recitatives and exit arias and perhaps a duet for the principal couple. Occasional irregularities can be found, however. *Il trionfo della costanza* of 1731 has an aria with interruptions by *pertichini* (one or more other characters). Two operas have more than one ensemble. *Ergilda* (1736) has a duet and a quintet, both in Act 2, and *Candalide* (1734) has two duets in Act 2. In Vitturi's works of 1740 onwards, ensembles occur at the ends of Acts 1 and 2, where they remained in librettos of this type until the 1790s. *Candalide* is also unusual for the use in its opening and closing scenes of a chorus which in the latter momentarily assumes a dramatic persona. Vitturi's *Armida* is his most distinctive work. The pastoral quality and fictional origins of the story perhaps invited the deviations from the Arcadian ideal: multiple choruses (one incorporating pairs of principals in duos), a strange trio in which each participant sings and then exits, and liberal theatrical display – a battle, a storm at sea and naval scenes. The abandoned Armida, a thoroughly tamed witch, cannot even conjure up enough venom to destroy her palace and fly off in her winged chariot. Instead she throws herself into the sea as Rinaldo sails safely away.

Both of Vitturi's *drammi giocosi* are sophisticated parodies. *I rigiri delle cantarine* is a spoof involving an opera company, and *Chi tutto abbraccia nulla stringe* has a parody of an *opera seria* monologue with three cavatinas. Both have ensembles at the ends of Acts 1 and 2. The ensemble that closes Act 1 of *Chi tutto abbraccia* has the fluid construction of Goldoni's finales, but lacks the action.

Il trionfo della costanza in Statira vedova d'Alessandro (dramma), A. Galeazzi, 1731; *L'Ardelinda* (dramma), Albinoni, 1732; *Tamiri* (os), B. Galuppi, 1734; *Candalide* (dramma), Albinoni, 1734; *Mandane regina di Persia* (os), Fiorillo, 1736; *Ergilda* (os), Galuppi, 1736; *Gli amori sfortunati d'Armido* (serenata), Galuppi, 1738; *Candaspe regina di Sciti* (dramma), Casali, 1740; *Artamene* (dramma), Albinoni, 1741; *La forza del sangue* (pastorale), Paganelli, 1743; *La gara per la gloria* (divertimento teatrale), Latilla, 1744; *Pompeo in Arminia* (dramma), G. Scarlatti, 1744; *Nicoraste re di Tracia* (dramma), G. B. Pattoni, 1745 (Sacchini, 1769); *I rigiri delle cantarine* (dg), Maggiore, 1745; *Armida* (os), Bertoni, 1746 (Bertoni, 1780, as Armida abbandonata; Cherubini, 1782, as Armida abbandonata); *Berenice* (dramma), Bertoni (recits.) and others (arias), 1748 (S. Perillo, 1759); *Chi tutto abbraccia nulla stringe* (dg), Scolari, 1753 (Scarlatti, 1756) MARITA P. McCLYMONDS

Vitzthumb [Fitzthumb, Witzthumb], **Ignaz** [Ignace] (*b* Baden, nr Vienna, 20 July 1720; *d* Brussels, 23 March 1816). South Netherlands composer, conductor and impresario of Austrian birth. According to Fétis, he first studied with the 'Scottish' Oratorians in Vienna and settled early in Brussels as a singer in the chapel of the Governor of the Netherlands. He was later court timpanist and apparently a violinist at the Théâtre de la Monnaie in Brussels (then also known as the Grand Théâtre). In 1766 Vitzthumb was nominated as *chef d'orchestre* at the theatre, but the musicians refused him because of his severity and he did not take the post until 1769. In 1771 he and Louis Compain Despierrières were licensed as directors of the theatre for ten years from Easter 1772. Some months later Burney, passing through Brussels, stated that the opera there was 'one of the most elegant ... on this side of the Alps ... the orchestra ... is celebrated all over Europe. It is, at present, under the direction of M. Fitzthumb, a very active and intelligent *maestro di capella*'.

Under Vitzthumb La Monnaie had one of its finest periods, and works by Grétry (*Zémire et Azor*, *Les mariages samnites*, *La fausse magie*), F.-A. Philidor (*Ernelinde*) and Gluck (*Iphigénie en Aulide*, *Alceste*) were performed there. His reputation spread to Paris and Vienna, although he fell out with Grétry, whose *La fausse magie* he had 'corrected'. In 1775 he launched a new opera house for works in Flemish, at first in Brussels (in a temporary theatre in the Place St Michel) and later at Mechelen (Salle des Jésuites) and Antwerp. His daughters Anne (1757–77) and Marie-Françoise (*b* 1758) made their débuts in this project, as did his future son-in-law, Henri Mees. After a failure in Brussels, he undertook a long tour in the Netherlands in summer 1776. But the financial management of La Monnaie occupied him increasingly. He closed the theatre in 1777 and was imprisoned for debt. Nevertheless he became director of the Ghent theatre for two years from Easter 1779 and in 1785 he again became *chef d'orchestre* of La Monnaie. On 27 December 1786 he was appointed *maître de musique* of the royal chapel, but was dismissed in 1791 for his opposition to Joseph II. After his dismissal he settled in the Netherlands, where he became director of music and stage manager for an opera company in Amsterdam. Shortly afterwards he returned to Brussels and tried, unsuccessfully, to resume his career; according to Fétis he spent his last years in poverty.

A skilful composer (his output includes six stage works, sacred music and symphonies), Vitzthumb was also an excellent teacher. Besides his children, such prominent musicians as Henri Mees (1757–1820), who became principal baritone at La Monnaie, and the composer P. E. Verheyen were among his pupils.

all first performed in Brussels

Le temple des arts (prol.), Concert Bourgeois, 30 May 1761

L'éloge de la vertu, ou Le tribut des coeurs (pastorale, L. Compain Despierrières), La Monnaie, 4 Nov 1761

Le soldat par amour (opéra bouffon, 2, J.-F. de Bastide), La Monnaie, 4 Nov 1766, collab. P. van Maldere

Céphalide, ou Les autres mariages samnites (oc, 3, F. de Ligne), La Monnaie, 30 Jan 1777, collab. G. Cifolelli

La foire de village (comédie pastorale avec vaudevilles, 2), ?1786

La cohorte d'Amour, ou Le siège de Cythère (ballet-pantomime), La Monnaie, 21 April 1813

*

BNB (S. Clercx); *BurneyGN*; *FétisB*

Almanach nouveau ... ou Le guide fidèle (Brussels, 1758–75)

Gazette des Pays-Bas (Brussels, 1759–86)

A. Choron and F. Fayolle: *Dictionnaire historique des musiciens* (Paris, 1810–11)

E. vander Straeten: *La musique aux Pays-Bas avant le XIXe siècle*, i, ii, iv, v (Brussels, 1867–80)

C. Piot: 'Quelques lettres de la correspondance de Grétry avec Vitzthumb', *Bulletin de l'Académie royale des sciences, des lettres et des beaux-arts de Belgique*, 2nd ser., xl (1875), 408–35

F. Faber: *Histoire du théâtre français en Belgique* (Brussels, 1878–80)

H. Liebrecht: *Histoire du théâtre français à Bruxelles au XVIIe et au XVIIIe siècle* (Paris, 1923), 253–96

G. de Froidcourt: *La correspondance générale de Grétry* (Brussels, 1962)

C. M. Carroll: 'The History of "Berthe" – a Comedy of Errors', *ML*, xliv (1963), 228–39 PAUL RASPÉ

Vivaldi, Antonio (Lucio) (*b* Venice, 4 March 1678; *d* Vienna, 27/28 July 1741). Italian composer and violinist. Although most celebrated for his 500-odd concertos, he was one of the most successful opera composers in the Italy of his day.

1. LIFE. Vivaldi was the first son of Giovanni Battista Vivaldi, a Brescian barber who became a professional violinist at St Mark's, Venice, in 1685, and Camilla Calicchio, a tailor's daughter. Giovanni Battista was a leading violinist in the city and was often styled 'Rossi' on account of his red hair, a characteristic inherited by his son. He was involved in theatre management and may even have been the Giambattista Rossi who composed *La fedeltà sfortunata* in 1688.

Antonio was baptized by the midwife immediately after birth (his full baptism was on 6 May), since she feared his life was in danger, probably from the 'strettezza di petto' (bronchial asthma) that was to affect both his physical health and his character, making him prone to paranoia, throughout his life. He trained for the priesthood from 18 September 1693 and was ordained on 23 March 1703, although soon afterwards he ceased to say Mass, later claiming his illness as the reason. In September 1703 he was appointed violin teacher at the Pio Ospedale della Pietà, one of the four Venetian charitable institutions specializing in the musical training of girls. Vivaldi was associated with the Pietà on and off for the rest of his life.

The year 1713 was an important one for Vivaldi's vocal music. It marked the beginning of a period during which he stood in for the Pietà's absent *maestro di coro* Francesco Gasparini by supplying sacred vocal works, and it also saw the production of the 35-year-old composer's first opera. On 30 April 1713 the Pietà granted him permission to leave Venice for one month, and in May *Ottone in villa* was given its première at the Teatro delle Garzerie, Vicenza.

The following November Vivaldi made his operatic début on the Venetian stage with *Orlando finto pazzo* at the Teatro S Angelo. This was one of the smaller Venetian theatres and one with which Vivaldi was to be connected, as both composer and impresario, throughout his career. He was already managing it jointly with his father, and his close involvement with the theatre over the next few years, together with the Teatro S Moisè, resulted in several successful productions of his own operas. In 1715 Johann Friedrich von Uffenbach, an amateur musician from Frankfurt, visited the S Angelo, where he admired Vivaldi's spectacular violin playing as well as the singing of Anna Maria Fabbri.

Shortly after Carnival 1718 Vivaldi left Venice for Mantua, taking with him his latest opera, *Armida al campo d'Egitto*, and two of its singers. For the next three years he served as *maestro di cappella da camera* to the governor of Mantua, Prince Philipp of Hesse-Darmstadt. Vivaldi was in charge of secular music, and between 1718 and 1732 a total of seven operas by him were performed at Mantua. Initially joint impresario, he gained full control of the theatre for the 1719 productions of *Teuzzone* and *Tito Manlio*. His operas were also produced elsewhere, including Florence, which he visited in summer 1718 for the reopening of the Teatro Pergola with *Scanderbeg*. By the following carnival season he was no longer impresario and provided only one opera; when the death of the Empress Eleonora von Neuburg in January 1720 caused the theatres to close, Vivaldi was forced to look elsewhere.

Vivaldi's excursions outside Venice must have boosted his growing reputation, for he continued to travel far from his native city. Although he returned to the S Angelo for the 1720–21 opera season, his *dramma pastorale Silvia* was produced in Milan on 28 August 1721, and it was four years before he returned to the Venetian stage. By Carnival 1723 he was in Rome for the staging of *Ercole su'l Termodonte* at the Teatro Capranica, as the famous cartoon by Ghezzi indicates, and this was followed the next year by *Giustino* and Act 2 of the composite *Tigrane*. The dating of a third carnival season in Rome, referred to in a letter of 1737, has caused much speculation: although the Roman theatres were closed for 1725, Vivaldi may have stayed on to provide other music, for he also composed instrumental and vocal music for one of the Capranica's patrons, Cardinal Pietro Ottoboni.

For the next three years Vivaldi was again at the S Angelo, and on 13 October 1726 he signed a contract as 'direttore delle opere' with the singer Lucrezia Baldini. A few weeks later *Dorilla in Tempe* saw the first appearance in a Vivaldi opera of the young mezzo-soprano Anna Girò. Described in cast-lists as 'mantovana' (Vivaldi may have met her in Mantua during his three years there), she frequently took prima donna roles in productions under his control. According to Goldoni, she was a fine actress, although her voice was limited in range and lacked power. Both she and her sister Paolina frequently accompanied the composer on his travels, something which inevitably led to gossip.

Vivaldi continued to receive commissions from outside Venice, including Reggio Emilia and Florence. A series of letters from Antonio Conti reveals the success of *Ipermestra* (1727, Florence), as well as Vivaldi's unfulfilled ambition to become impresario of Venice's renowned S Giovanni Grisostomo. His next Florentine opera, *L'Atenaide* (29 December 1728), however, was not so well received, and criticism was particularly aimed at Girò.

On 30 September 1729 Giovanni Battista Vivaldi was granted a year's leave from St Mark's in order to accompany a son, presumably Antonio, to 'Germania'. The exact itinerary is unknown: it almost certainly included Vienna and Prague, although Vivaldi was back in Venice by the following summer. He had met the Emperor Charles VI in September 1728 at Trieste, where, according to Conti, the emperor 'talked to him alone more in a fortnight than he talks to his ministers in two years'. Charles VI was also the dedicatee of Vivaldi's op.9 concertos *La cetra* published the previous year, while his op.8 set (1725), which includes 'The Four Seasons', had been dedicated to the Bohemian Count Wenzel von Morzin, to whom the composer styled himself 'maestro di musica in Italia'. In addition to Morzin, another link with Prague was through Antonio Denzio, a Venetian impresario and tenor who had created the role of Artabanus in Vivaldi's *La costanza trionfante* in 1716. Denzio directed a travelling opera company which mounted a series of Venetian operas in Prague between 1724 and 1734 for Count Franz Anton von Sporck. The years 1730–32 saw five operas in Prague set completely or in part by Vivaldi, and several of these impressed another Bohemian nobleman, Count Johann Joseph von Wrtby, who noted that *Farnace* and *Argippo* were very well received.

Over the next few years Vivaldi divided his time between Venice and the mainland. On 6 January 1732 the grand opening of the Teatro Filarmonico in Verona was celebrated with his setting of Scipione Maffei's youthful libretto *La fida ninfa* (for illustration *see* VERONA, fig.1), and he returned there for two carnival operas in 1735 and one in spring 1737. In Carnival 1736 *Ginevra principessa di Scozia* was produced in Florence, though plans for a summer season at Lucca came to nothing, and those for Ferrara between 1737 and 1739 met with mixed success.

Back in Venice Vivaldi's control of the S Angelo was waning, and his music was beginning to go out of fashion. An increasing number of works from this period are pasticcios using arias from the younger generation of composers such as Hasse, Leo and Giacomelli. Vivaldi was in charge of the S Angelo for the 1733–4 season, but, apart from Carnival 1738, that was his last season there. In spring 1735 he was commissioned to provide the Ascensiontide opera for the Grimani-owned S Samuele theatre. The text for *Griselda* was specially arranged by the young playwright Carlo Goldoni, who left two slightly different accounts of how he convinced the sceptical composer of his abilities by reworking an aria text on the spot.

The years 1736–9 are documented by a substantial correspondence with the Marquis Guido Bentivoglio d'Aragona in Ferrara. The initial letters deal with detailed arrangements for operas the following Carnival, which ended up being versions of works by Hasse instead of the intended Vivaldi originals *L'Olimpiade* and *Ginevra*, along with attacks on his fellow impresarios and financial complaints marked by Vivaldi's characteristic mixture of arrogance and self-pity. In November 1737 the Archbishop of Ferrara, Cardinal Ruffo, who regarded opera as an inappropriate activity for a priest, banned him from entering the city. Although two further productions were planned for Carnival 1739, Vivaldi's fortunes did not improve: *Siroe* was such a failure that the projected performance of *Farnace* never took place, and a legal dispute ensued. In Venice, though, his services were still required, and in May 1739 he received payments from the Pietà for supplying psalms, motets and antiphons. Yet fashions were changing rapidly, and the French visitor Charles de Brosses was surprised that Vivaldi's music was no longer highly prized in his native city.

Between spring 1739 and Carnival 1740, Anna Girò sang in a series of operas at Graz, possibly involving music by Vivaldi, and this may have encouraged him to visit Austria. His last Venetian opera, *Feraspe*, was produced in autumn 1739, and by 24 May 1740 he had left Venice for Vienna, where he took a house near the Kärntnertortheater. But any hopes of operatic performances in Carnival 1741 would have been dashed by the death of the Emperor Charles VI in October 1740. In February 1741 Vivaldi made two unsuccessful attempts to see Anton Ulrich von Sachsen-Meiningen, a collector of librettos and patron of the Kärntnertor, possibly about proposed productions. On 28 June he signed a receipt for the sale of instrumental music to Count Vinciguerra von Collalto, but exactly one month later he was dead, being given a cheap, unceremonious funeral at the Spitaler Gottesacker. Maybe the years of travel had finally taken their toll on the invalid musician, but, by an ironic twist, his final journey was not totally fruitless: *L'oracolo in Messenia* was produced posthumously at the Kärntnertortheater in Carnival 1742.

2. WORKS. It is impossible to say exactly how many operas Vivaldi wrote. In a letter of 1739 he claimed '94 opere da me composte', but he was prone to exaggeration, and doubtless this figure also included pasticcios and rearrangements of his own and other composers' works. Nevertheless a large number of surviving printed librettos have now been traced, and around 20 scores survive in varying degrees of completeness. The works all fall more or less within the typical 18th-century mould of the three-act Italian *opera seria*, made up primarily of simple recitative accompanied by continuo alone (strings are occasionally added for moments of dramatic intensity), and da capo arias, with the occasional duet or larger ensemble and a brief concluding *coro* sung by the soloists. Although this pattern remains relatively constant throughout his career, there are slight variations: *Tito Manlio*, written for the court at Mantua, has a comic bass role for a local singer; the Roman *Giustino* concludes with a substantial choral chaconne (probably borrowed from *La verità in cimento*); and the *melodramma eroico-pastorale Dorilla in Tempe* contains several choruses as well as dances. In addition to the music which survives in Vivaldi's scores, many operas were performed with comic intermezzi by other composers inserted between the acts, and sometimes ballets were also added to the later works.

Vivaldi tended to prefer older librettos: a number of his works use arrangements of 17th-century texts, and although some of his later operas set librettos by Zeno and Metastasio, he seems to have been less drawn to the newer literary styles than many other composers. The subjects of several operas reflect the fashion for the exotic (*Teuzzone*, for example, takes place in China, and several works are set in the Middle East).

The opening sinfonias are generally unconnected with the main opera; in the manuscript scores they normally precede the title-pages and were sometimes re-used for a different opera. One interesting exception is the sinfonia to *Dorilla in Tempe*, whose finale, based on the opening of the 'Spring' concerto RV269, is linked thematically with the opening chorus of Act 1.

By his operatic début in 1713, Vivaldi had already established an international reputation as an instrumental composer. His operas of the 1710s are in a typical Venetian style, showing many of the 'faults' attacked by Benedetto Marcello in his satire *Il teatro alla moda* (1720). Throughout his career his arias reflect the popular preference for major keys, though short passages often shift suddenly into the tonic minor. His melodies often use unexpected intervals, particularly the augmented 2nd or diminished 3rd, to depict emotional words in the text. Phrase lengths are sometimes highly irregular, as in the middle section of the aria 'Gemo in un punto' from *L'Olimpiade*, where the phrase structure of 3+4+2+4+5 bars emphasizes Lycidas' distraught feelings.

Although Vivaldi's harmony is strongly orientated towards tonic and dominant, chromatic chords (particularly diminished 7ths and Neapolitan and augmented 6ths) are often used for dramatic purposes. In *Griselda*, for example, diminished seventh harmonies are particularly associated with Griselda's plight (ex.1).

Ex.1 *Griselda*, Act 1 scene x

['Ah husband! Ah son! Ah my cruel fate.']

Vivaldi's treatment of recitative varies little throughout his career. Although some passages seem routine, others reveal sensitivity to their dramatic content. Rising chromatic basses, often modulating to the sharp side of the tonal spectrum, create a sense of mounting excitement; falling chromatic basses depict sorrow; and sudden increases in the rate of harmonic change generate emotional tension (ex.2). Much of Vivaldi's

Ex.2 *Orlando finto pazzo*, Act 1 scene iii

accompanied recitative falls into three basic styles: the first surrounds the vocal line in a 'halo' of held string chords with slowly changing harmonies and is particularly appropriate for an atmosphere of magic or ritual; the second also uses four-part harmony but is more suited to aggressive emotions with its short crotchet chords interspersed with rests and swifter harmonic rhythm; and the third also consists of sharp crotchets, this time in unison. Occasionally the boundaries between recitative, arioso and aria are treated more flexibly for dramatic purposes. This is most apparent in the Orlando operas, where the hero's madness is matched by a musical unpredictability, fluctuating rapidly between different styles.

Unlike the recitatives, Vivaldi's arias show stylistic change during his career. The arias of the 1710s are notable for their melodic interest, not just in the voice but also in the accompanying parts. The latter frequently contain considerable contrapuntal interest, employing imitation and sometimes even canon, as in the opening of 'Chi seguir vuol la costanza' (*Ottone in villa* 1.v and *Tito Manlio* 3.ii; ex.3).

Ex.3 *Ottone in villa*, Act 1 scene v, 'Chi seguir vuol la costanza'

Although Vivaldi's basic orchestra is of four-part strings, many arias employ lighter two- and three-part textures, sometimes omitting the bass line for long sections, and it is not until around 1720 that four-part writing becomes dominant. Effects such as pizzicato and mutes are also used (the former represents falling teardrops in *Giustino* 2.i).

In addition to varying string textures, Vivaldi's early arias use many different obbligato instruments. Strangely enough, the violin rarely appears as a concertante soloist, although the cello is used several times, and there are even florid solos for the viola d'amore (*Tito Manlio* 3.i) and its near relation the *viola (all')inglese* (*L'incoronazione di Dario* 1.xv). Recorders, oboes, horns and trumpets all appear – often in pairs – the last two being predictably associated with hunting and martial arias respectively. The scoring of solo bassoon and violone in Nicenus's 'Non lusinghi il core amante' from *L'incoronazione di Dario* emphasizes the comical side of the old philosopher. More unusual obbligato instruments include harpsichords (*Arsilda regina di Ponto* 1.xv) and a psaltery (*Giustino* 2.xiii).

In Vivaldi's operas after the mid-1720s this variety of instrumental colour gives way to a dominance of four-part string textures with the occasional addition of one or two horns. As in the works of his Neapolitan contemporaries, the emphasis is placed firmly on the voice and its display of virtuosity: the strings tend to repeat short figures and the violins often double the vocal line. The so-called 'Lombardic rhythms' (ex.4), which

Ex.4 Lombardic rhythms

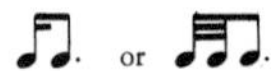

Quantz claimed had 'been introduced in Rome by Vivaldi through one of his operas', appear frequently in the works of this period. Formally, too, the later arias are less varied. The da capo aria becomes totally dominant, and its form undergoes changes: the short instrumental interjections within vocal sections often found in the earlier works disappear, as does the brief ritornello sometimes found within the *B* section.

Some features of Vivaldi's arias, however, remain unchanged, not least their tremendous rhythmic vitality. Normally the opening ritornello sets the mood for an aria, and this is frequently based on a key word or phrase from the text. Individual word-painting is also important, sometimes taken to extremes to display a singer's vocal prowess as in *Catone in Utica* 3.ix on the word 'resound' (ex.5). Vivaldi was particularly attracted

Ex.5 *Catone in Utica*, Act 3 scene ix, 'Nella foresta'

by the pictorial possibilities of 'simile arias', in which a character likens his or her situation to some natural phenomenon such as a ship tossed by stormy seas.

Ensembles tend to be more important in Vivaldi's later works, although *La verità in cimento* (1720) contains a fine quintet making use of tempo changes between Allegro and Andante. In many cases ensembles are placed at the ends of acts to create a sense of climax, something which in earlier operas may be achieved by unusual instrumentation.

As with his instrumental and sacred vocal music, Vivaldi's operas frequently use borrowed material. This can involve re-using whole arias from earlier works, or reworking material from a concerto movement into an aria. Although Vivaldi normally borrowed from himself, the pasticcios from the later part of his career contain arias by other composers: this may have been the easiest way to keep up with the latest musical fashions.

While Vivaldi's reputation as a violinist was generally acknowledged, his ability as a composer was often disputed. Avison and Quantz were critical of his vocal music, but Mattheson claimed that he 'had the sense to keep violin-leaps out of his vocal compositions so completely that his arias have become a thorn in the flesh to many an experienced vocal composer'. There are many reports of the success of his operas, and the sheer volume of his output is a clear indication of public approval. Although he was not a great innovator in the opera house, as he was in the field of the concerto, this does not imply that the music is inferior. One of his most important assets as an instrumental composer was his sense of the dramatic – something clearly apparent from his operatic scores.

See also DORILLA IN TEMPE; GRISELDA (iv); ORLANDO (i); OTTONE IN VILLA; and TITO MANLIO.

Catalogue: P. Ryom: *Verzeichnis der Werke Antonio Vivaldis: kleine Ausgabe* (Leipzig, 1974, 2/1979) [RV]

drammi per musica, in three acts, unless otherwise stated; list includes pasticcios arranged by Vivaldi

† – later versions, or revivals under different titles

RV	*title*	*libretto*	*performances*	*principal MS sources; remarks*
729	Ottone in villa	D. Lalli, after F. M. Piccioli: *Messalina*	Vicenza, Garzerie, May 1713	*I-Tn** (*R*1983: *DMV*, xii); passed by censor 21 April 1713
727	Orlando finto pazzo	G. B. Braccioli	Venice, S Angelo, Nov 1714	*Tn**; ded. 10 Nov 1714
	Orlando furioso	Braccioli, after L. Ariosto	Venice, S Angelo, aut. 1714	*Tn* (partly autograph of Acts 1 and 2); ded. 17 Dec 1714; extensive rev. of Ristori: Orlando furioso, 1713
724	Nerone fatto Cesare	M. Noris	Venice, S Angelo, carn. 1715	pasticcio arr. Vivaldi, containing 12 arias by him; passed by censor 12 Feb 1714 [=1715]
			Brescia, Accademia, carn. 1716	? adaptation of 1715 version, many new arias, but 6 of Vivaldi's aria texts the same
706	La costanza trionfante de gl'amori, e de gl'odii	A. Marchi	Venice, S Moisè, carn. 1716	ded. 18 Jan 1715 [=1716]; passed by censor 21 Jan 1715 [=1716]
701	†Artabano, re de' Parti		Venice, S Moisè, carn. 1718	revival of La costanza trionfante, 1716; passed by censor 5 Jan 1718
Anh.57	†Die über Hass und Liebe siegende Beständigkeit, oder Tigranes, König von Armenien		Hamburg, Gänsemarkt, 5 May 1719	6 arias *D-B*; int Dorimena e Tuberone; almost all arias are from Artabano, 1718
Anh.51	†L'odio vinto dalla costanza	B. Vitturi, after Marchi	Venice, S Angelo, carn. 1731	? pasticcio arr. A. Galeazzi; int Melinda; passed by censor 24 Jan 1731
708	†Doriclea		Prague, Sporck, carn. 1732	adapted from 1st version of La costanza
700	Arsilda, regina di Ponto	Lalli	Venice, S Angelo, 27 or 28 Oct 1716	*I-Tn* (1 autograph working score, 1 copy), 16 arias *D-Dlb*; int L'alfier fanfarone; passed by censor 18 Oct 1716; same sinfonia as Teuzzone, 1718
719	L'incoronazione di Dario	A. Morselli	Venice, S Angelo, 23 Jan 1717	*I-Tn**; passed by censor 15 Jan 1716 [=1717]
737	Tieteberga	A. M. Lucchini	Venice, S Moisè, 16 Oct 1717	2nd version made during 1717 season, with 9 arias by other composers
Anh.58	Il vinto trionfante del vincitore	Marchi: *Zenobia regina de' Palmireni*	Venice, S Angelo, aut. 1717	pasticcio, ? with some music by Vivaldi; ded. 22 Nov 1717
699	Armida al campo d'Egitto	G. Palazzi, after T. Tasso	Venice, S Moisè, carn. 1718	*Tn* (Acts 1 and 3 autograph; partly rev. with non-autograph addns for 1738 perf.); same sinfonia as Ercole, 1723
720	†Gli inganni per vendetta	? arr. Lalli	Vicenza, Grazie, 1720	passed by censor 12 May 1720
	†Armida al campo d'Egitto		Venice, S Margherita, carn. 1731	int Lidia ed Ircano; rev. (not by Vivaldi himself)
			Venice, S Angelo, 12 Feb 1738	pasticcio arr. Vivaldi, based on 1718 version with several new arias, incl. 2 from Leo: Farnace
732	Scanderbeg	A. Salvi	Florence, Pergola, 22 June 1718	4 arias, 2 recits *Tn*
736	Teuzzone	A. Zeno	Mantua, Arciducale, 28 Dec 1718	*D-B* (copy of final version), *I-Tn* (working score, partly autograph); aria 'Ritorna a lusingarmi' probably by Orlandini, possibly other foreign arias; same sinfonia as Arsilda, 1716
738	Tito Manlio	Noris	Mantua, Arciducale, carn. 1719	*I-Tn* (1 autograph headed 'musica del Vivaldi fatta in 5 giorni', 1 copy); 8 arias *Tn*

RV	title	libretto	performances	principal MS sources; remarks
704	La Candace, o siano Li veri amici	F. Silvani, rev. Lalli, after P. Corneille: *Héradius empereur d'Orient*	Mantua, Arciducale, carn. 1720	11 arias, 1 qt *Tn*
Anh.56	Tito Manlio [Act 3]	Noris	Rome, Pace, carn. (? 8 Jan) 1720	10 arias *F-Pc*, 9 arias, 1 chorus *D-WD*; a few of Vivaldi's arias correspond with 1719 version; Act 1 by G. Boni, Act 2 by G. Giorgi; int Breno e Dina
739	La verità in cimento	Palazzi and Lalli	Venice, S Angelo, aut. (? 26 Oct) 1720	*I-Tn**, 12 arias *D-Mbs*, 6 arias, 1qt *I-Tn*; int L'avaro by F. Gasparini; passed by censor 3 Oct 1720
715	Filippo re di Macedonia [Act 3]	Lalli	Venice, S Angelo, 27 Dec 1720	Acts 1 and 2 by G. Boniventi; passed by censor 17 Dec 1720; int Melinda e Tiburzio
734	La Silvia	E. Bissarri	Milan, Regio Ducale, 28 Aug 1721	9 arias *I-Tn*; dramma pastorale
710	Ercole su'l Termodonte	G. F. Bussani	Rome, Capranica, Jan 1723	23 arias, 1 duet *D-MÜs*, 6 arias, sinfonia *F-Pc*; same sinfonia as Armida, 1718
740	La virtù trionfante dell'amore, e dell'odio, overo Il Tigrane [Act 2]	Silvani	Rome, Capranica, 1st op in carn. 1724	Act 2 *I-Tn**; Act 1 and int by B. Micheli, Act 3 by N. Romaldo; also known as Mitridate
717	Giustino	P. Pariati, after N. Beregan	Rome, Capranica, 2nd op in carn. 1724	*Tn**, ed. R. Strohm (Milan, 1991)
721	L'inganno trionfante in amore	? G. M. Ruggieri, after Noris: *Laodicea e Berenice*	Venice, S Angelo, aut. 1725	? pasticcio arr. Vivaldi
707	Cunegonda	A. Piovene: *La principessa fedele*	Venice, S Angelo, 29 Jan 1726	? pasticcio arr. Vivaldi; passed by censor 22 Jan 1726
712	La fede tradita e vendicata	Silvani	Venice, S Angelo, 16 Feb 1726	passed by censor 10 Jan 1726
Anh.45	†Ernelinda		Venice, S Cassiano, carn. 1750	? pasticcio (with music by Vivaldi, Gasparini and Galuppi); int La preziosa ridicola
Anh.55	La tirannia gastigata	Silvani: *La fortezza in cimento*	Prague, Sporck, carn. 1726	ded. 20 Feb 1726; arr. A. Denzio using arias from La costanza trionfante; recits. by A. Guerra
709	Dorilla in Tempe	Lucchini	Venice, S Angelo, 9 Nov 1726	melodramma eroico-pastorale
			Venice, S Angelo, *c* 2 Feb 1734	*Tn* (partly autograph); pasticcio arr. Vivaldi, based on 1726 version, with arias by Hasse, Giacomelli and Leo
722	Ipermestra	Salvi	Florence, Pergola, 25 Jan 1727	3 arias *US-BE*
711	Farnace	Lucchini	Venice, S Angelo, 10 Feb 1727	passed by censor 5 Feb 1727; revived in aut. 1727 with several new arias by Vivaldi; *I-Tn* (partly autograph; 1731, Pavia); *Tn* (autograph, dated 1738, Acts 1 and 2; ? 1739, Ferrara)
735	Siroe re di Persia	P. Metastasio	Reggio Emilia, Pubblico, Ascension 1727	ded. 29 April 1727
			Ancona, Fenice, sum. 1738	incl. many arias from Vivaldi's other operas
			Ferrara, Bonacossi, 1st op in carn. 1739	? pasticcio arr. Vivaldi
728	Orlando [Orlando furioso]	Braccioli, after L. Ariosto	Venice, S Angelo, aut. (? 10 Nov) 1727	*Tn* (working score, mainly autograph); lib. similar to, but music largely different from, 1714 version; passed by censor 5 Nov 1727; int Il marito giocatore
			Brno, Taverna, carn. 1735	music by Vivaldi 'a riserva di alcune arie'; perfs. of Orlando furioso in Bergamo and Vicenza 1738, Este 1740 and Bassano 1741 may be pasticcios with Vivaldi's arias
730	Rosilena ed Oronta	Palazzi	Venice, S Angelo, carn. 1728	passed by censor 15 Jan 1728; ded. 17 Jan 1728
702	L'Atenaide	Zeno	Florence, Pergola, 29 Dec 1728	*Tn*, 6 arias *D-Dlb*
697	Argippo	Lalli	Prague, Sporck, aut. 1730	
696	Alvilda regina de' Goti	Zeno: *L'amor generoso* and G. C. Corradi: *L'amazzone corsara*	Prague, Sporck, spr. 1731	only some arias by Vivaldi, probably from other operas
733	Semiramide	Silvani	Mantua, Arciducale, carn. 1732	6 arias in *Dlb*; ded. 26 Dec 1731

RV	title	libretto	performances	principal MS sources; remarks
714	La fida ninfa	S. Maffei	Verona, Filarmonico, carn. 1732	*I-Tn**, ed. R. Monterosso (Cremona, 1964); 8 arias, 1 trio *D-Dlb*; written for opening of new theatre; ded. 6 Jan 1732
	† Il giorno felice		Vienna, 1737	? some music by Vivaldi
723	Montezuma	G. Giusti	Venice, S Angelo, 14 Nov 1733	
725	L'Olimpiade	Metastasio	Venice, S Angelo, 17 Feb 1734	*I-Tn**
703	Il Tamerlano [Il Bajazet]	Piovene	Verona, Filarmonico, carn. 1735	*Tn* (partly autograph); tragedia per musica; pasticcio arr. Vivaldi using arias by Hasse, Giacomelli, Porpora and R. Broschi
695	L'Adelaide	? Salvi	Verona, Filarmonico, carn. 1735	
718	Griselda	Zeno, rev. C. Goldoni, after G. Boccaccio: *Il decamerone*	Venice, S Samuele, 18 May 1735	*Tn** (*R*1978: IOB, xxxv), ed. R. Fasano (Palermo, 1985)
698	Aristide	? Goldoni	Venice, S Samuele, aut. 1735	drama eroi-comico per musica, 1 act; ded. signed by Domenico Lalli; ? not by Vivaldi; int Il filosofo
716	Ginevra principessa di Scozia	Salvi, after L. Ariosto	Florence, Pergola, 17 Jan 1736	
705	Catone in Utica	Metastasio	Verona, Filarmonico, May 1737	*Tn** (Acts 2 and 3)
731	Rosmira [Rosmira fedele]	S. Stampiglia: *Partenope*	Venice, S Angelo, 27 Jan 1738	*Tn* (partly autograph); pasticcio arr. Vivaldi
726	L'oracolo in Messenia	Zeno: *Merope*	Venice, S Angelo, 30 Dec 1737	passed by censor ? 27 Dec 1737
713	Feraspe	Silvani [lib. orig. *L'innocenza giustificata*]	Venice, S Angelo, 7 Nov 1739	

Arrs. of Hasse: Demetrio, 1737; Alessandro nell'Indie, 1737

CATALOGUES AND DOCUMENTATION

AllacciD

[G. C. Bonlini]: *Le glorie della poesia e della musica contenute nell'esatta notitia de teatri della città di Venezia* (Venice, 1730)

A. Groppo: *Catalogo purgatissimo di tutti li drammi per musica recitatisi ne' teatri di Venezia dall'anno MDCXXXVII sin oggi* (*I-Vnm*, 1741 but updated to 1767)

——: *Catalogo di tutti i drammi per musica recitatisi ne' teatri di Venezia dall'anno 1637 ... sin all'anno presente 1745* (Venice, 1745)

Catalogo de drammi musicali fatti in Venezia (*I-Mb* Racc. Dram. Corniani-Algarotti, 1778)

T. Wiel: *I teatri musicali veneziani del settecento* (Venice, 1897)

G. Gentili Verona: 'Le collezioni Foà e Giordano della Biblioteca nazionale di Torino', *Accademie e biblioteche d'Italia*, xxxii (1964), 405–30; repr. with Eng. summary in *Vivaldiana*, i (1969), 31–56

P. Damiliano: 'Inventario delle composizioni musicali manoscritte di Antonio Vivaldi esistenti presso la Biblioteca nazionale di Torino', *RIM*, iii (1968), 109–79

P. Ryom: *Antonio Vivaldi: table de concordances des oeuvres* (Copenhagen, 1973)

——: 'Inventaire de la documentation manuscrite des oeuvres de Vivaldi, i: Biblioteca nazionale di Torino (première partie: le fonds Foà)', *Vivaldi Informations*, ii (1973), 61–112

——: *Verzeichnis der Werke Antonio Vivaldis: kleine Ausgabe* (Leipzig, 1974, 2/1979)

E. Garbero: 'Drammaturgia vivaldiana: regesto e concordanze dei libretti', *Antonio Vivaldi da Venezia all'Europa*, ed. F. Degrada and M. T. Muraro (Milan, 1978), 111–53

O. Landmann: 'Katalog der Dresdener Vivaldi-Handschriften und -Frühdrucke', *Vivaldi-Studien: 3. Dresdner Vivaldi-Kolloquium: Dresden 1978*, 102–67

A. Girard and G. Rostirolla: 'Catalogo delle opere di Antonio Vivaldi', *RMI*, xiii (1979), 210–89

P. Ryom: 'Les catalogues de Bonlini et de Groppo', *Informazioni e studi vivaldiani*, ii (1981), 3–30

A. L. Bellina, B. Brizi and M. G. Pensa: *I libretti vivaldiani: recensione e collazione dei testimoni a stampa* (Florence, 1982)

P. Ryom: 'Deux catalogues d'opéras', *Informazioni e studi vivaldiani*, iii (1982), 13–44

M. G. Pensa: 'La felicità delle lettere, ossia l'edizione veneziana della "Drammaturgia" di Leone Allacci', *Informazioni e studi vivaldiani*, iv (1983), 20–40

E. Selfridge-Field: 'Dating Vivaldi's Venetian Operas', *Informazioni e studi vivaldiani*, v (1984), 53–65

SPECIALIST PERIODICALS AND COLLECTIONS

Antonio Vivaldi: note e documenti sulla vita e sulle opere, ed. S. A. Luciani, Chigiana, i (1939)

La scuola veneziana (secoli XVI–XVIII): note e documenti, Chigiana, iii (1941)

Vivaldiana (Brussels, 1969)

Vivaldi Informations (Copenhagen, 1971–)

F. Degrada and M. T. Muraro, eds.: *Antonio Vivaldi da Venezia all'Europa* (Milan, 1978)

Vivaldi-Studien: 3. Dresdner Vivaldi-Kolloquium: mit einem Katalog der Dresdner Vivaldi-Handschriften und -Frühdrucke: Dresden 1978

Vivaldi veneziano europeo: Venice 1978

NRMI, xiii/1 (1979) [Vivaldi issue]

Informazioni e studi vivaldiani: Bollettino dell'Istituto italiano Antonio Vivaldi (Milan, 1980–)

Antonio Vivaldi: teatro musicale, cultura e società: Venice 1981

M. Collins and E. K. Kirk, eds.: *Vivaldi & Opera* (Austin, 1984)

A. Fanna and G. Morelli, eds.: *Nuovi studi vivaldiani: edizione e cronologia critica delle opere* (Florence, 1988)

GENERAL

[B. Marcello]: *Il teatro alla moda* (Venice, 1720); Eng. trans., *MQ*, xxxiv (1948), 371–403, and xxxv (1949), 85–105

E. Wright: *Some Observations Made in Travelling through France, Italy, etc., in the Years 1720, 1721, and 1722* (London, 1730)

J. Mattheson: *Der vollkommene Capellmeister* (Hamburg, 1739)

C. Avison: *An Essay on Musical Expression* (London, 1752)

J. J. Quantz: *Versuch einer Anweisung die Flöte traversiere zu spielen* (Berlin, 1752, 3/1789; Eng. trans., 1966)

——: 'Lebenslauf', in F. W. Marpurg: *Historisch-kritische Beyträge zur Aufnahme der Musik*, i (Berlin, 1754), 197–250

C. Goldoni: Introduction to *Commedie*, xiii (Venice, 1761)

——: *Mémoires de M. Goldoni pour servir à l'histoire de sa vie, et à celle de son théâtre*, i (Paris, 1787), 286

C. de Brosses: *Lettres historiques et critiques sur l'Italie*, i (Paris, 1799), 297

F. Stefani: *Sei lettere di Antonio Vivaldi veneziano* (Venice, 1871)

R. G. Pauly: 'Benedetto Marcello's Satire on Early 18th-Century Opera', *MQ*, xxxiv (1948), 222–33

E. Preussner: *Die musikalischen Reisen des Herrn von Uffenbach* (Kassel and Basle, 1949)

W. Kolneder: *Aufführungspraxis bei Vivaldi* (Leipzig, 1955, 2/1973; Eng. trans., 1979)

M. Pincherle: *Vivaldi* (Paris, 1955; Eng. trans., 1958)
R. Giazotto: *Vivaldi* (Milan, 1965)
W. Kolneder: *Antonio Vivaldi: Leben und Werk* (Wiesbaden, 1965; Eng. trans., 1970)
P. Kneidl: 'Libreta italské overy v Praze v 18. století, 1', *Strahovská knihovna*, i (1966), 97–131
R. de Candé: *Vivaldi* (Paris, 1967)
A. Cavicchi: 'Inediti nell'epistolario Vivaldi–Bentivoglio', *NRMI*, i (1967), 45–79
T. Volek and M. Skalická: 'Vivaldis Beziehungen zu den böhmischen Ländern', *AcM*, xxxix (1967), 64–72
A. Cavicchi: 'Fac-similé et traductions de cinq lettres de Vivaldi à Bentivoglio', *Vivaldiana*, i (1969), 117–41
R. Giazotto: *Antonio Vivaldi* (Turin, 1973) [with catalogue of works by A. Girard and discography by L. Bellingardi]
W. Kolneder: *Melodietypen bei Vivaldi* (Zürich, 1973)
F. Fano: 'Una traccia prossima alla prima origine della raccolta di musiche vivaldiane conservata alla Biblioteca nazionale di Torino', *Medioevo e umanesimo*, xxiv (1976), 83–93
P. Ryom: *Les manuscrits de Vivaldi* (Copenhagen, 1977)
T. Antonicek: 'Vivaldi in Österreich', *ÖMz*, xxxiii (1978), 128–34
C. Gallico: 'Vivaldi dagli archivi di Mantova', *Vivaldi veneziano europeo: Venice 1978*, 77–88
W. Kolneder: 'Musikalische Symbolik bei Vivaldi', ibid, 13–23
L. Moretti: 'Dopo l'insuccesso di Ferrara: diverbio tra Vivaldi e Antonio Mauro', ibid, 89–99
——: 'Le inconvenienze teatrali: documenti inediti su Antonio Vivaldi impresario', *Antonio Vivaldi da Venezia all'Europa*, ed. F. Degrada and M. T. Muraro (Milan, 1978), 26–9
E. Selfridge-Field: 'Vivaldi's Esoteric Instruments', *EMc*, vi (1978), 332–8
R. Strohm: 'Bemerkungen zu Vivaldi und der Oper seiner Zeit', *Vivaldi-Studien: 3. Dresdner Vivaldi-Kolloquium: Dresden 1978*, 81–105
M. Talbot: 'Ungewöhnliche Tonleiterformen bei Vivaldi', ibid, 73–80, 176–9
——: *Vivaldi* (London, 1978, 2/1984)
W. Kolneder: *Antonio Vivaldi: Dokumente seines Lebens und Schaffens* (Wilhelmshaven, 1979)
M. Talbot: *Vivaldi* (London, 1979)
G. Corti: 'Il teatro La Pergola e la stagione d'opera per il carnevale 1726–1727: lettere di Luca Casimiro degli Albizzi a Vivaldi, Porpora ed altri', *RIM*, xv (1980), 182–8
F. Della Seta: 'Documenti inediti su Vivaldi a Roma', *Antonio Vivaldi: teatro musicale, cultura e società: Venice 1981*, 521–32
R. Wiesend: 'Vivaldi e Galuppi: rapporti biografici e stilistici', ibid, 233–55
P. Ryom and M. Talbot: 'Antonio Vivaldi', *The New Grove Italian Baroque Masters*, ed. S. Sadie (London, 1984), 271–323
P. Weiss: 'Venetian Commedia dell'Arte "Operas" in the Age of Vivaldi', *MQ*, lxx (1984), 195–217
L. Cataldi: 'I rapporti di Vivaldi con il "Teatro detto Il Comico" di Mantova', *Informazioni e studi vivaldiani*, vi (1985), 88–110
B. Brizi: 'Vivaldi e Vicenza: una festa barocca del 1713', *Informazioni e studi vivaldiani*, vii (1986), 35–54
L. Cataldi: 'Alcuni documenti relativi alla permanenza di Vivaldi a Mantova', *Informazioni e studi vivaldiani*, viii (1987), 13–23
P. Everett: 'Towards a Chronology of Vivaldi Manuscripts', ibid, 90–107
M. Talbot: 'Vivaldi and the Empire', ibid, 31–51
A. Fanna and G. Morelli, eds.: *Nuovi studi vivaldiani: edizione e cronologia critica delle opere* (Florence, 1988) [incl. W. C. Holmes: 'Vivaldi e il Teatro La Pergola a Firenze: nuove fonti', 117–30; L. Cataldi: 'L'attività operistica di Vivaldi a Mantova', 131–46; S. Durante and F. Piperno: 'Cantanti settecenteschi e musicologia vivaldiana: lo stato degli studi', 535–62; C. Vitali: 'Di alcune zone d'ombra nella biografia vivaldiana', 667–80; M. Stegemann: 'Vivaldi und Wien', 681–8; P. Everett: 'Towards a Vivaldi Chronology', 729–57]
O. Bentheim and M. Stegemann: 'Vivaldi und Böhmen: wenige Fakten, viele Fragen', *Informazioni e studi vivaldiani*, ix (1988), 75–89
M. Talbot: *Antonio Vivaldi: a Guide to Research* (New York and London, 1988)
——: 'Vivaldi and Rome: Observations and Hypotheses', *JRMA*, cxiii (1988), 28–46
R. Eller: 'Vier Briefe Antonio Vivaldis', *Informazioni e studi vivaldiani*, x (1989), 5–23
C. Vitali: 'Vivaldi e il conte bolognese Sicinio Pepoli: nuovi documenti sulle stagioni vivaldiane al Filarmonico di Verona', ibid, 25–56
P. Everett: 'Vivaldi's Italian Copyists', *Informazioni e studi vivaldiani*, xi (1990), 27–86
G. Vio: 'Alla ricerca della data dell'ultimo addio di Vivaldi a Venezia', ibid, 89–97
K. Heller: *Vivaldi: cronologia della vita e dell'opera* (Florence, 1991)
C. Vitali: 'I fratelli Pepoli contro Vivaldi e Anna Girò: le ragioni di un'assenza', *Informazioni e studi vivaldiani*, xii (1991), 19–46

OPERAS

V. Mortari: '*L'Olimpiade* e il teatro musicale di Antonio Vivaldi', *Antonio Vivaldi: note e documenti sulla vita e sulle opere*, ed. S. A. Luciani, Chigiana, i (1939), 23–6
L. E. Rowell: *Four Operas of Antonio Vivaldi* (diss., U. of Rochester, 1958)
M. Bruni: 'Letture vivaldiane: "Arsilda regina di Ponto"', *I volti musicali di Falstaff*, ed. A. Damerini and G. Roncaglia (Siena, 1961), 95–110
W. Kolneder: 'Vivaldis Aria-Concerto', *DJbM*, ix (1964), 17–27
V. Malaj: 'L'opera "Scanderbeg" dell'Abate Vivaldi', *Shêjzat (Le Pleiadi)* [Rome], xii (1968), 40–43
H. C. Wolff: 'Vivaldi und der Stil der italienischen Oper', *AcM*, xl (1968), 179–86
M. Bruni: 'Postille ed appunti sulla *Griselda* di Vivaldi', *Quadrivium*, xii (1971), ii, 267–77
R. Strohm: 'Vivaldis Opern in Mantua', *Vivaldi Informations*, i (1971–2), 84–7
——: 'Eine neuentdeckte Mantuaner Opernpartitur Vivaldis', *Vivaldi Informations*, ii (1973), 104–6
H. Maurer: *The Independent Arias of Antonio Vivaldi in Foà 28* (diss., Indiana U., 1974)
N. Mangini: 'Sui rapporti del Vivaldi col teatro di Sant'Angelo', *Venezia e il melodramma nel settecento: Venice 1975*, 263–70
P. Ryom: 'Antonio Vivaldi: les relations entre les opéras et la musique instrumentale', ibid, 249–62
R. Strohm: 'Zu Vivaldis Opernschaffen', ibid, 237–48
H. C. Wolff: 'Vivaldi's Operas', *Opera and Church Music 1630–1750*, ed. A. Lewis and N. Fortune, NOHM, v (London, 1975), 99–107
R. Strohm: *Italienische Opernarien des frühen Settecento (1720–1730)*, *AnMc*, no.16 (1976) [2 vols.]
E. Cross: 'Vivaldi as Opera Composer: "Griselda"', *MT*, cxix (1978), 411–16
——: 'Vivaldi's Operatic Borrowings', *ML*, lix (1978), 429–39
J. W. Hill: 'Vivaldi's Griselda', *JAMS*, xxxi (1978), 53–82
R. Strohm: 'Bemerkungen zu Vivaldi und der Oper seiner Zeit', *Vivaldi-Studien: 3. Dresdner Vivaldi-Kolloquium: Dresden 1978*, 81–105
Vivaldi veneziano europeo: Venice 1978 [incl. F. Degrada: 'Vivaldi e Metastasio: note in margine a una lettura dell'*Olimpiade*', 155–81; B. Brizi: 'Domenico Lalli librettista di Vivaldi?', 183–204; G. Folena: '"Prima le parole, poi la musica": Scipione Maffei poeta per musica e la *Fida ninfa*', 205–33; M. T. Muraro and E. Povoledo: 'Le scene della *Fida ninfa*: Maffei, Vivaldi e Francesco Bibiena', 235–52]
M. Rinaldi: 'Dati certi su Vivaldi operista', *NRMI*, xiii (1979), 150–59
——: *Il teatro musicale di Antonio Vivaldi* (Florence, 1979)
R. Strohm: *Die italienische Oper im 18. Jahrhundert* (Wilhelmshaven, 1979)
E. Cross: *The Late Operas of Antonio Vivaldi, 1727–1738* (Ann Arbor, 1981)
Antonio Vivaldi: teatro musicale, cultura e società: Venice 1981 [incl. R. Strohm: 'Vivaldi's Career as an Opera Producer', 11–63, repr. in *Essays on Handel and Italian Opera* (Cambridge, 1985), 112–63; K. Heller: 'Anmerkungen zu Vivaldis Opernsinfonien', 207–16; B. Brizi: 'Gli *Orlandi* di Vivaldi attraverso i libretti', 315–30; M. G. Pensa: 'L'*Atenaide* di Apostolo Zeno adattata per la musica di Vivaldi', 331–44; F. Fido: 'Le tre *Griselde*: appunti su Goldoni librettista di Vivaldi', 345–63]
F. Tammaro: 'Contaminazioni e polivalenze nell'*Orlando finto pazzo* di Vivaldi', *RIM*, xvii (1982), 71–108
K. Heller: 'Über die Beziehungen zwischen einigen Concerto- und Sinfonia-Sätzen Vivaldis', *Informazioni e studi vivaldiani*, iv (1983), 41–60
J. W. Hill: 'Vivaldi's "Ottone in Villa" (Vicenza, 1713): a Study in Musical Drama', *DMV*, xii (1983), pp.vii–xxxvii
K. Hortschansky: 'Arientexte Metastasios in Vivaldis Opern', *Informazioni e studi vivaldiani*, iv (1983), 61–75
R. Wiesend: 'Die Arie "Già si sa ch'un empio sei": von Vivaldi oder

von Galuppi?', ibid, 76–81
M. Collins and E. K. Kirk, eds.: *Opera & Vivaldi* (Austin, 1984) [incl. E. Cross: 'The Relationship between Text and Music in the Operas of Vivaldi', 279–307; K. Kropfinger: 'Vivaldi as Self-Borrower', 308–26; J. W. Hill: 'Vivaldi's *Orlando*: Sources and Contributing Factors', 327–46; M. Collins: 'Grazio Braccioli's *Orlando furioso*: a History and Synopsis of the Libretto', 367–77]
F. Tammaro: 'Il "Farnace" di Vivaldi: problemi di ricostruzione', *Studi musicali*, xv (1986), 213–56
——: 'Il "Farnace" fiorentino del 1733', *Informazioni e studi vivaldiani*, vii (1986), 55–61
L. Cataldi: 'La rappresentazione mantovana del "Tito Manlio" di Antonio Vivaldi', *Informazioni e studi vivaldiani*, viii (1987), 52–89
R. Strohm: 'Vivaldi's and Handel's Settings of "Giustino"', *Music and Theatre: Essays in Honour of Winton Dean* (Cambridge, 1987), 131–58
A. Fanna and G. Morelli, eds.: *Nuovi studi vivaldiani: edizione e cronologia critica delle opere* (Florence, 1988) [incl. M. Steinebrunner: '*Orlando furioso*: vom Epos zur Oper: Stationen des Wandels literarischer Bilder zwischen Mittelalter und Barock', 45–82; P. Mioli: '"Non più reggina, ma pastorella": sulla drammaturgia vocale medio e tardo-barocca nella "Griselda", da Scarlatti a Vivaldi', 83–116; F. Tammaro: 'I pasticci di Vivaldi: "Dorilla in Tempe"', 147–84; A. L. Bellina, B. Brizi and M. G. Pensa: 'Il pasticcio Bajazet: la "favola" del Gran Tamerlano nella messinscena di Vivaldi', 185–272; M. Collins: 'L'orchestra nelle opere teatrali di Vivaldi', 285–312; R.-C. Travers: 'L'exhumation des opéras de Vivaldi au XX siècle', 313–54; R. Strohm: 'The Critical Edition of Vivaldi's "Giustino" (1724)', 399–416; J. W. Hill: 'A Computer-Based Analytical Concordance of Vivaldi's Aria Texts: First Findings and Puzzling New Questions about Self-Borrowing', 511–34; D. E. Monson: 'The Trail of Vivaldi's Singers: Vivaldi in Rome', 563–90; L. Lindgren: 'Venice, Vivaldi, Vico and Opera in London, 1705–17: Venetian Ingredients in English Pasticci', 633–66]
R. Strohm: '"Tragédie" into "Dramma per Musica"', *Informazioni e studi vivaldiani*, ix (1988), 14–25; x (1989), 57–102; xi (1990), 11–26; xii (1991), 47–75
K. Vlaardingerbroek: 'Thematic Links to Other Works in the "Confitebor", RV 596: their Nature and Context', *Informazioni e studi vivaldiani*, ix (1988), 47–63
U. Roseman: *Antonio Vivaldi's 'Orlando finto pazzo': an Analysis and Critical Edition* (diss., UCLA, 1989)
G. Vio: 'Una satira sul teatro veneziano di Sant'Angelo datata "febbraio 1717"', *Informazioni e studi vivaldiani*, x (1989), 103–30
M. Talbot: 'Vivaldi in the Sale Room: a new Version of "Leon feroce"', *Informazioni e studi vivaldiani*, xii (1991), 5–16
D. E. Freeman: *The Opera Theater of Count Franz Anton von Sporck in Prague (1724–35)* (New York, forthcoming)

ERIC CROSS

Vives [Roig], **Amadeo** (*b* Collbató, nr Barcelona, 18 Nov 1871; *d* Madrid, 2 Dec 1932). Spanish composer and writer. He studied under Ribera and, later, Felipe Pedrell in Barcelona. With his fellow-pupil Luis Millet he founded in 1891 the Orfeó Català, which was to become the leading Catalan choir, and for which he wrote a number of compositions and arrangements. For a short time he was organist and choirmaster at a convent of Loreto nuns, but an attack of infantile paralysis, complicated by a badly set fractured shoulder, left him with an almost useless right arm. Nevertheless, in 1896 he became chorus master at the Novedades theatre in Barcelona, where his first opera *Artus* (on the Arthurian legend) was produced with some success the following year. This led him to move to Madrid and to devote the rest of his life, with the exception of a brief period of teaching at the Madrid Conservatory, to composing operas, operettas and zarzuelas, in which last sphere he was as much appreciated by discriminating musicians as by the general public, since he markedly raised standards by the finesse of his harmony and orchestration and by his superior taste. He was a prodigious worker, in 35 years composing over 100 stage pieces, about a quarter of them in collaboration with others, as was common practice (three unperformed zarzuelas were written with the young Falla); he also contemplated further operas to librettos by the Quintero brothers. An extremely well-read man with a mordant tongue, he took a cynical view of his own popularity and hankered after more serious status. Of his operas, *Euda d'Uriac* (written in Catalan) owed some of its success to its incorporation of Catalan folksongs; but his only real triumph was the sentimental *Maruxa*. His reputation today rests largely on this, the operetta *La generala*, and zarzuelas such as *Bohemios* and, particularly, *Doña Francisquita*, considered his masterpiece.

See also BOHEMIOS; DOÑA FRANCISQUITA; and MARUXA.

all first performed in Madrid unless otherwise stated

Artús (4, S. Trullol y Planes), Barcelona, Novedades, 19 May 1897
Euda d'Uriac (4, A. Guimerá, after his *Los monjes de Sant Ayman*), Barcelona, Novedades, 17 Oct 1900
Colomba (2, C. Fernández Shaw and L. Ballesteros, after P. Mérimée), Real, 15 Jan 1910
Maruxa (egloga lírica, 2, L. Frutos), Zarzuela, 28 May 1914
Balada de carnaval (1, L. Ardavín and J. Montero), Gran, 5 July 1919

Operettas: La favorita del rey (1, G. Perrín and M. Palacios), Apolo, 27 July 1905; La reina Mimí (3, Perrín and Palacios), Apolo, 8 July 1910; La generala (2, Perrín and Palacios), Gran, 14 June 1912; La veda del amor (1, Perrín and Palacios), Gran, 5 Dec 1912; El pretendiente (1, M. Echegaray), Apolo, 27 June 1913; El duquesito (3, Frutos), Reina Victoria, 16 April 1920

Zarzuelas: La primera del barrio (1, S. M. Granés and J. G. Rufino), Zarzuela, 1898; Don Lucas del Cigarral (3, T. Luceño and C. Fernández Shaw, after F. de Rojas: *Entre bobos anda el juego*), Parish, 18 Feb 1899; La preciosilla (1, D. Prieto), Romea, 25 April 1899; La luz verde (1, F. Iráyzoz), Apolo, 16 June 1899; La fruta del tiempo (1, G. Merino), Martín, 22 Nov 1899, collab. G. Mateos; El rey de la Alpujarra (1, A. Paso and F. Locatelli), Eslava, 23 Dec 1899
Campanas y cornetas (1, E. Sellés), Apolo, 14 Feb 1900; El escalo (1, C. Arniches and C. Lucío), Eslava, 28 Feb 1900; Viaje de instrucción (1, J. Benavente, after C. M. Donnay: *L'éducation du prince*), Eslava, 7 April 1900; La balada de la luz (1, Sellés), Zarzuela, 12 June 1900; Polvorilla (1, Iráyzoz and Fernández Shaw), Eslava, 31 Dec 1900, collab. M. Quislant; La buenaventura (1, Fernández Shaw and Ballesteros, after M. de Cervantes: *La gitanilla*), Apolo, 30 April 1901, collab. J. Guervós
A estudiar a Salamanca (1, Luceño), Apolo, 10 May 1901, collab. Guervós; Doloretes (1, Arniches), Apolo, 28 June 1901, collab. Quislant; El coco (1, J. F. Rodríguez and J. J. Veyán), Apolo, 24 Oct 1901; La nube (1, Sellés), Zarzuela, 8 Jan 1902; El tirador de palomas (1, Fernández Shaw and R. A. Mas), Apolo, 22 Jan or 27 Feb 1902; Sueño de invierno (1, Merino), Cómico, 29 March 1902, collab. Mateos; El curita (1, V. de la Vega), Eslava, 2 April 1902
La caprichosa (1, Frutos and A. L. Monis), Zarzuela, 25 April 1902, rev. as Sangre torera, Eslava, 6 Dec 1906; Lola Montes (1, Iráyzoz), Zarzuela, 11 June 1902; El ramo de azahar (1, Iráyzoz), Zarzuela, 19 Feb 1903; Su Alteza Imperial (3, S. Delgado), Price, 14 March 1903, collab. Morera; El parador de las Golondrinas (1, A. Rovira y Sierra), Zarzuela, 13 Oct 1903; Patria nueva (1, Iráyzoz and Merino), Zarzuela, 19 Dec 1903; La vendimia (1, J. Prieto and J. Guerra), Cómico, 12 March 1904, collab. Calleja
Bohemios (1, Perrín and Palacios), Zarzuela, 24 March 1904, rev. C. del Campo (op), Real, 26 Feb 1920, rev. R. Ferrer (zarzuela, 3, J. L. Rubio), 1965; El húsar de la guardia (1, Perrín and Palacios), Zarzuela, 1 Oct 1904, collab. J. Giménez; La familia de don Saturio [El Salvador y los Evangelistas] (1, R. de la Vega), Apolo, 6 Dec 1904; El cochero (1, R. Rocabert), Cómico, 21 Jan 1905; Sangre roja (1, M. L. Rivas), Apolo, 23 March 1905
La máscara duende (1, Fernández Shaw), Apolo, 12 April 1905; El dinero y el trabajo (1, Veyán and Rocabert), Cómico, 15 April 1905, collab. Saco del Valle; El príncipe ruso (1, L. Boada and M. de Castro Tiedra), Moderno, 18 May 1905; El arte de ser bonita (1, Paso and Prieto), Cómico, 7 Sept 1905, collab. Giménez; Las granadinas (1, Perrín and Palacios), Cómico, 29 Sept 1905, collab. Giménez; El amigo del alma (1, F. Torres), Eslava, 16 Nov 1905, collab. Giménez

La gatita blanca (1, Veyán and J. Capella), Cómico, 23 Dec 1905, collab. Giménez; La Libertad (1, Perrín and Palacios), Price, 30 Dec 1905, collab. Giménez; La marcha real (3, Paso and J. Abati), Zarzuela, 7 Feb 1906; El golpe de estado (1, Melantuche y Oria), Eslava, 3 May 1906, collab. Giménez; La Machaquito (1, L. M. Larra), Eslava, 29 May 1906, collab. Giménez; El guante amarillo (1, Veyán and Capella), Cómico, 5 Oct 1906, collab. Giménez

El diablo verde (1, Perrín and Palacios), Zarzuela, 11 Oct 1906, collab. Giménez; La chipén (1, R. Monasterio and F. Limendoux), Cómico, 16 Feb 1907; Las tres cosas de Jerez (3, Fernández Shaw and P. Muñoz Seca), Eslava, 30 April 1907; La rabalera (1, Echegaray), Zarzuela, 23 May 1907; Pepe Botella (2, M. Ramos Carrión), Zarzuela, 17 March 1908, collab. Lleó; Episodios nacionales (1, M. Thous and E. Cerdá), Zarzuela, 30 April 1908, collab. Lleó

El talismán prodigioso (1, Delgado), Apolo, 6 Nov 1908; El becerro de oro (1, Capella), Eslava, 10 April 1909; Viva la libertad! (1, Iráyzoz), Eslava, 8 May 1909; A la vera der queré (1, P. Pérez Fernández and G. de la Cruz), Cómico, 10 July 1909; La viuda mucho más alegre (1, Frutos), Cómico, 17 July 1909; Abreme la puerta (1, Iráyzoz), Eslava, 30 Oct 1909; La muela del rey Farfán (1, S. and J. Alvarez Quintero), Apolo, 28 Dec 1909; Juegos malabares (1, Echegaray), Apolo, 4 Feb 1910

Así son todas (1, E. de la Vega), Apolo, 25 May 1910; La fresa (1, Veyán and J. L. Silva), Eslava, 22 June 1910; El alma del querer (1, Pérez Fernández), Gran, 27 July 1910, collab. T. Barrera; Gloria in excelsis (1, Delgado), Apolo, 26 Oct 1910; El palacio de los duendes (1, Delgado), Apolo, 28 Dec 1910, collab. J. Serrano; La casa de los enredos (3, J. Lorenzo), Apolo, 31 Jan 1911; Los viajes de Gulliver (3, Paso and Abati), Cómico, 21 Feb 1911, collab. Giménez; Agua de noria (1, Echegaray), Apolo, 4 March 1911

La canción española (1, Mihura and G. del Toro), Gran, 14 Dec 1911, collab. Barrera; La gallina de los huevos de oro (2, Paso and Abati), Lara, 23 Dec 1911; Anita la risueña (2, S. and J. Alvarez Quintero), Apolo, 23 Dec 1911; El carro del sol (1, Thous), 1911; El gran simpático (1, del Toro), Martín, 7 Nov 1913; Miss Australia (1, Perrín and Palacios), Gran, 11 April 1914; La cena de los húsares (1, Paso and Abati), Apolo, 22 Oct 1915; La ley del embudo (1, Delgado), Apolo, 19 Jan 1916

Los pendientes de la Trini [No hay mal que por bien no venga] (1, A. Asenjo and T. del Alamo), Apolo, 1 Feb 1916; La guitarra del amor (1, Perrín and Palacios), Zarzuela, 16 May 1916, collab. 6 others; El señor Pandolfo (3, Pérez Fernández and Ardavín), Apolo, 27 Dec 1916; La mujer de Boliché (2, M. F. de la Puente), Zarzuela, 8 Feb 1917; El tesoro (3, de la Puente), Zarzuela, 7 April 1917; Todo el mundo en contra mía (2, de la Puente), Apolo, 19 Jan 1918; Trianerías (2, Seca and Pérez Fernández), Apolo, 23 Jan 1919

Las Verónicas (3, Seca and Pérez Fernández), Reina Victoria, 25 April 1919; Pepe Conde [El mentir de las estrellas] (3, Frutos), Apolo, 5 Jan 1920; El parque de Sevilla (2, Seca and Pérez Fernández), Apolo, 23 Jan 1921; El sinvergüenza en Palacio (3, Seca and Pérez Fernández), Apolo, 28 Oct 1921, collab. Luna; El ministro Giroflar (3, G. del Castillo and J. J. Cadenas), Reina Victoria, 14 Oct 1922; Doña Francisquita (3, F. Romero and G. Fernández Shaw, after F. Lope de Vega: *La discreta enamorada*), Apolo, 17 Oct 1923

La villana (3, Romero and G. Fernández Shaw, after Lope de Vega: *Peribañez y el comendador de Ocaña*), Zarzuela, 1 Oct 1927; Los flamencos (2, Romero and G. Fernández Shaw), Apolo, 15 Nov 1928; Noche de verbena (2, L. de Vargas), Eslava, 21 Dec 1929; El talismán (3, Romero and G. Fernández Shaw, after Guillen de Castro: *La fuerza de la costumbre*), Calderón, 6 Dec 1932; El abanico (E. Marquina, after C. Goldoni: *Il ventaglio*), inc.

Unperf., collab. M. de Falla: El cornetin de órdenes, *c*1903 (3), lost; La cruz de Malta, *c*1903, lost; Prisionero de guerra, *c*1903–4

*

J. Subirá: 'Ideario estético y ético de Amadeo Vives', *Revista musical catalana* (1933), Jan [Vives issue]; pubd separately as *Ideario estético de Amadeo Vives* (Barcelona, 1933)

'Chispero': *El Teatro Apolo* (Madrid, 1953)

G. Fernández Shaw: *Un poeta de transición: Carlos Fernández Shaw* (Madrid, 1969)

A. Sagardía: *Amadeo Vives: vida y obra* (Madrid, 1971)

LIONEL SALTER

Vivetières, Benoît-Joseph Marsollier des. *See* MARSOLLIER DES VIVETIÈRES, BENOÎT-JOSEPH.

Viviani, Elena Croce. *See* CROCE, ELENA.

Viviani, Giovanni Buonaventura (*b* Florence, 15 July 1638; *d* after 1692). Italian composer. He was a violinist at the court of Innsbruck at least between 1656 and 1660. From 1672 until 1676 he was director of the court music there; after the extinction of the Tyrolean Habsburgs in 1665, Innsbruck had come under the control of the emperor, Leopold I. In publications of 1678 Viviani still described himself as holding this position, although he had resigned on 31 May 1676 and seems to have gone to Venice, where in the 1676–7 season his opera *Astiage* and his arrangement of Cavalli's *Scipione affricano* were performed at the Teatro SS Giovanni e Paolo. During Lent 1678, on 25 March, he conducted a performance of a Latin oratorio at the Oratorio dell'Arciconfraternità del Ss Crocifisso at S Marcello in Rome, in which Corelli and Pasquini participated as instrumentalists. He was probably elevated to the nobility in the same year, since he subsequently designated himself 'Nobile del Sacro Romano Imperio' and in contracts 'D(on)' precedes his name.

For the 1678–9 season Viviani was engaged as director of a troupe of opera singers at the Teatro S Bartolomeo in Naples, where his duties included arranging the operas and conducting them from the harpsichord. He did not fulfil a contract for the following season because the impresario had to flee Naples, being unable to pay his debts. Viviani probably went to Milan, where in autumn or winter 1679 his *Astiage* was revived. The impresario of the Teatro dei Fiorentini in Naples summoned him in October 1681; his opera *Mitilene, regina delle Amazoni* was performed in the royal palace in November, then transferred to the theatre. Late in 1682, the newly rebuilt S Bartolomeo was inaugurated with his already successful *Astiage*. In this year as well two of his oratorios were performed in Naples, so he may have been there throughout the year; he probably stayed several years, for in 1686 he was *maestro di cappella* to the Prince of Bisignano and wrote an opera, *Elidoro*, for wedding festivities at his residence Saponara (in Grumento Nova). In January 1687 Viviani applied for and received the position of *maestro di cappella* at Pistoia Cathedral. He resigned at the end of 1692; in this year an oratorio by him was performed in Florence, and the next year he signed the dedication of his last work, also printed in Florence. The place and date of his death are unknown.

Viviani's vocal style follows that of Antonio Cesti, notably in his use of dotted rhythms at recitative cadences and in his smoothly flowing arias in 3/2 time, which may imply that he studied with Cesti during his Innsbruck years; in any case he certainly knew Cesti's works, probably from playing the violin during their performances. His arias are most often in an *ABB* or the early, short version of da capo form. Some of them begin with a motto, and some are built over a *basso ostinato*. The melodic style is often similar to Italian folksong, the rhythms following the text metres closely. Viviani's task in modernizing Cavalli's *Scipione affricano* apparently consisted mainly of composing new arias to replace recitative passages. The ritornellos and instrumental accompaniments in his operas for Naples are for two violins, in *La vaghezza del fato* sometimes with an additional viola. The overture of this last opera is in four movements and identical with Sonata no.10 of his *Suonate a 3* (Venice, 1673). Leopold I kept a copy of the opera in his personal library.

Besides operas, Viviani composed single arias, solo cantatas and five oratorios, and published nine collections, including motets, cantatas, *solfeggi* and solo and trio sonatas.

Astiage (3, M. Noris, after G. F. Apolloni), Venice, SS Giovanni e Paolo, wint. 1677, 21 arias *I-Vqs*, pubd lib. *Bc*; rev. Naples, S Bartolomeo, Dec 1682, *Mc*, *Nc*
Scipione affricano (3, T. Fattorini, after N. Minato), Venice, SS Giovanni e Paolo, carn. 1678, 5 arias *Vqs*, pubd lib. *Vnm* [rev. of Cavalli's 1664 opera]
Mitilene, regina delle Amazoni (3, Count G. Barbò), Naples, Palazzo Real, 13 Nov 1681; Fiorentini, 1681–2, *Nc*
L'Elidoro, o vero Il fingere per regnare (3, after J. B. de Villegas), Saponara, 15 June 1686, pubd lib. *Nn*
La vaghezza del fato (3, P. Guadagni), ?unperf., *A-Wn*

*

U. Prota-Giurleo: 'Breve storia del Teatro di corte e della musica a Napoli nei secoli XVII–XVIII', *Il Teatro di corte del Palazzo Reale di Napoli* (Naples, 1952), 36
——: 'Notizie inedite intorno a G. B. Viviani', *Archivi d'Italia*, 2nd ser., xxv (1958), 225–38
L. Bianconi: 'Funktionen des Operntheaters in Neapel bis 1700 und die Rolle Alessandro Scarlattis', *Colloquium Alessandro Scarlatti: Würzburg 1975*, 13–111
H. Seifert: *Giovanni Buonaventura Viviani: Leben, Instrumentalwerke, vokale Kammermusik* (Tutzing, 1982)

HERBERT SEIFERT

Vivier, Claude (*b* Montreal, 14 April 1948; *d* Paris, 7 March 1983). Canadian composer. He studied at the Conservatoire de Musique du Québec in Montreal (1967–71) and subsequently in Europe under G. M. Koenig, H. U. Humpert, Paul Méfano and Stockhausen. His work with Stockhausen led to a predilection for monody and vocal writing. His travels to Asia and the Middle East (1977) profoundly influenced him and helped him refine his musical language, in which melody became the primary focus. At the time of his death in Paris (he was found strangled in his apartment), he was on a Canada Council Grant to compose an opera on the death of Tchaikovsky.

Vivier's only extant opera is *Kopernikus: rituel de mort* (the manuscript and fragments of two others are in the library of Montreal University). *Kopernikus* is in two acts and scored for seven soloists, eight instruments and tape; it was first performed at the Monument National, Montreal, on 8 May 1980 and subsequently (on 5 July 1985) at the Almeida International Festival, London. Vivier wrote his own multi-lingual libretto drawing on Buddhist and Hindu cosmology and including a language of his own invention. The opera's historical and mythological figures include Copernicus, Mozart, the Queen of Night from *Die Zauberflöte* and Lewis Carroll; the work is like a journey through ritual trials in search of the reality beyond earthly life. It shows Vivier's fascination with Far Eastern music and incorporates elements from such disparate sources as Gregorian chant, Mozart and Stockhausen. Its success lies in its powerful simplicity and the trance-like state it induces, together with Vivier's unique way of fusing the elements into a distinctive vocal line.

*

M. Loppert: Review of 'Kopernikus', *Opera*, xxxvi (1985), 1084

GAYNOR G. JONES

Vix [Brouwer], Geneviève (*b* Le Havre, 31 Dec 1879; *d* Paris, 25 Aug 1939). French soprano. After study at the Paris Conservatoire she made her début at the Opéra-Comique in 1906. Her first roles included Louise, Chrysis in Camille Erlanger's *Aphrodite* and the title role in the première of Hillemacher's *Circe*. In 1911 she sang Concepcion in the world première of *L'heure espagnole*, and in the same year took the part of Antonia in the first complete performances of *Les contes d'Hoffmann*. 1915 brought her a notable success in Buenos Aires where she appeared as Jean in *Le Jongleur de Notre Dame*, which she adapted, as Mary Garden had done, for the soprano. She later performed the part in Chicago, and with the Chicago Company on tour at the Lexington Theatre, New York, sang a much admired Manon. In Madrid in 1922, as Thaïs and Strauss's Salome, an 'adorable nonchalance' combined with her good looks and capricious sense of rhythm to fascinate her audiences. By 1925 her voice was in poor condition, and after some performances of her old roles, such as Louise (Rome) and Concepcion (Monte Carlo), she retired from opera for a brief spell of concert work and then to teach. Deprived of her physical presence, her recordings generally fail to charm the ear though they show something of her power of characterization.

J. B. STEANE

Vlaamsoper. Opera association based in ANTWERP and GHENT.

Vlachopoulos, Michalis (*b* Athens, *c*1873; *d* Athens, 24 July 1956). Greek bass and stage designer. He was self-taught as a singer, and trained as a painter. In 1900 he was a founder-member of the third Elliniko Melodrama (Hellenic Opera Company), in which he sang leading bass roles, among them Colline (on the company's début), Mephistopheles (both Gounod and Boito), Sparafucile, Rossini's Dr Bartolo and Don Basilio, and reportedly also Scarpia; he created bass roles in operas by Lavrangas, Kalomiris and Sakellaridis. He toured with the company in Russia (1913–14) and later in the USA (1924). His voice was sonorous and highly expressive, with a certain greyness of timbre. He was married to the soprano Eleni Vlachopolou (*b* Odessa, 1884; *d* Athens, 8 March 1935; under her maiden name Theodoridi, she has been confused with the Romanian soprano Elena Theodorini), who joined the same company in 1905 and sang such roles as Norma, Leonora (*Il trovatore*) and Léonor (*La favorite*), Aida, Tosca and La Gioconda and created roles in operas by Lavrangas, Samaras and Kalomiris; she was noted for her luminous upper register and a darker lower one.

GEORGE LEOTSAKOS

Vlad, Roman (*b* Cernăuţi, 29 Dec 1919). Italian composer and writer on music of Romanian birth. In 1938 he moved to Italy, where he continued his studies with Casella at the Accademia di S Cecilia. He made his career as a pianist, composer and teacher, and among the various administrative posts he has held is that of artistic director of the Accademia Filarmonica Romana (1955–8, 1966–9). He served as co-editor of the *Enciclopedia dello spettacolo* (1958–62) and has written a notable book on Stravinsky (Turin, 1958, 2/1973; Eng. trans., 1960, enlarged 3/1979). His first operatic work was the one-act *Storia di una mamma*, described as 'a fairy-tale for grown-ups', after Andersen. The music is based on the 12-note system modified by a degree of tonality: in the finale, F major is used to assert a superior and stronger spiritual approach. The radio opera *Il dottore di vetro* (1960) has a plot typical of 18th-century *opera buffa*; one of its features is the identification of the characters with different groups of instruments, as in Prokofiev's *Peter and the Wolf*. Vlad also uses electronic tape to represent the Doctor's glassy voice after his pretended transformation, his only venture in this direction. The television opera *La fantarca* (1967) is a satire on the cold war. *Il gabbiano* (1968), to the composer's own libretto based on Chekhov, takes the form of variations on material from Tchaikovsky: in a kind of opera-ballet, sung and dance sections alternate, with the characters doubled between singers and dancers. *Il sogno* explores the musical, architectural and scenic implications of Strindberg's original play. Whereas in *Il dottore di vetro* Vlad associated groups of instruments with a character, here he creates links between characters by having them sung by the same voice type. As in *Il gabbiano* there is also doubling between a singer and a dancer, but song remains the primary element, and even the orchestral sections that function as 'curtains' between one scene and another underline its dominance.

Vlad's theatre music confirms the eclectic tendencies that characterize all his work; he has not made strict use of serial techniques, despite his study of them. Whenever he draws on avant-garde methods, it is always as a means to specific musical ends.

Storia di una mamma (fiaba musicale, 1, G. da Venezia, after H. C. Andersen), Venice, 5 Oct 1951, vs (Milan, 1953)
Il dottore di vetro (radio op, 1, M. L. Spaziani, after P. Quinault), RAI, 26 Feb 1960; rev. (ob, 6 scenes), Berlin, 1961; vs (Milan, n.d.)
La fantarca (television op, G. Berto), RAI, 1967, vs (Rome, n.d.)
Il gabbiano (variazioni danzate e cantate, 4, R. Vlad, after A. P. Chekhov), Siena, Comunale dei Rinnovati, 5 Sept 1968, vs (Milan, 1970)
Il sogno (azione musicale, Vlad, after A. Strindberg), Bergamo, Donizetti, 3 Oct 1973, vs (Milan, n.d.)

RAFFAELE POZZI

Vladigerov, Pancho (*b* Zürich, 13 March 1899; *d* Sofia, 8 Sept 1978). Bulgarian composer. From 1910 to 1912 he studied at the Sofia Music School, then went to the Berlin Hochschule, where he later attended masterclasses in composition. He won the Mendelssohn Prize in 1918 and in 1920. He worked for Max Reinhardt at the Deutsches Theater, Berlin, as a pianist, composer and conductor (1921–32) before returning to Bulgaria to teach at the Sofia Academy of Music; he remained there until his retirement in 1972.

A spontaneous, expansive musician, Vladigerov composed a large quantity of music in almost all genres. It is distinguished above all by a virtuoso compositional technique, and is high-spirited, colourful, lustrous, while yet abounding in pathos, and increasingly influenced by the rhythms, metres and melodic and tonal features of Bulgarian folk music. Vladigerov wrote one opera, *Tsar Kaloyan* (to a libretto by Nikolaj Liliev and Fani Popova-Mutafova), in which he enriched the tradition of Bulgarian historical opera of the 1930s, and demonstrated a new approach to grand opera style. The action takes place in the 13th century in the old Bulgarian capital Turnovo. The main dramatic and lyrical episodes depict the victory of the Bulgarians over the Latins, the love story of Maria (Kaloyan's wife) and the death of Baldwin (Latin emperor), interspersed with scenes from the everyday life of the people. *Tsar Kaloyan* was first performed at the National Opera in Sofia on 20 May 1936.

*

L. Sagaev: *Kniga za operata* [Book about the Opera] (Sofia, 1967), 183
E. Pavlov: *Pancho Vladigerov* (Sofia, 1965; Ger. trans., abridged, 1973)

LADA BRASHOVANOVA, MAGDALENA MANOLOVA

Vlasov, Vladimir Alexandrovich (*b* Moscow, 25 Dec/7 Jan 1903; *d* Moscow, 7 Sept 1986). Russian composer and conductor. He studied at the Moscow Conservatory (1924–31) and was founder and artistic director (1936–42) of the Musical-Dramatic Theatre in Frunze (now Bishkek); he was manager and artistic director of the Moscow PO, 1942–9. Many of his numerous operas were written in collaboration with Vladimir Fere and Abdïlas Maldïbayev, with whom he also composed the Kirghiz national anthem.

all first performed at the Frunze State Opera House; until 1966 written in collaboration with V. Fere and A. Maldïbayev

Altïn kïz [The Golden Girl] (music drama, D. Bokombayev), 12 May 1937
Adzhal orduna [Not Death but Life] (3, Y. Tursubekov), 26 March 1938
Aychurek [Moon Beauty] (4, Bokonbayev, K. Malikov and Tursubekov, after folk epic: *Manas*), 15 April 1939
Za schast'ye naroda [For the People's Happiness] (V. Vinnikov), 1 May 1941
Patriotï [Patriots] (Malikov and A. Kuttubayev), 6 Nov 1941
Aldar Kose (operetta), 1943
Manas (Malikov and A. Tokombayev), 3 March 1946; rev. 1966
Sïn naroda [A Son of his People] (Vinnikov), 8 Nov 1947
Na beregakh Issïkh-kulya [On the Banks of Lake Issïk] (K. Bayalinov and Vinnikov), 1 Feb 1951; rev. 7 Feb 1952
Toktogul (2), 6 July 1958
Ved'ma [The Witch], 1958 (after A. P. Chekhov), TV broadcast, 1961; stage, 1966
Pyat' millionov frankov [Five Million Francs] (operetta, G. Fere, after I. Ilf and Y. Petrov), Sverdlovsk, 1965
Za chas do rassveta [An Hour before Dawn], 1969
Zolotaya devushka [The Golden Maiden], 1973

*

V. Vinogradov: *A. Maldïbayev, V. Vlasov, V. Fere* (Moscow, 1958)
L. Ginzburg: 'Obrashchyonnoye k sovremenniku' [Addressed to Contemporaries], *SovM* (1973), no.1, pp.28–33

DETLEF GOJOWY

Vlijmen, Jan van (*b* Rotterdam, 11 Oct 1935). Dutch composer. He studied composition with Kees van Baaren. He taught music theory at the Utrecht Conservatory, and in 1967 he was appointed deputy director of the Royal Conservatory at The Hague (director, 1971). From 1985 to 1988 he was general manager of the Netherlands Opera, and in 1991 he became director of the Holland Festival.

Van Vlijmen's earliest compositions show the influence of Schoenberg and, particularly, Berg; his later compositional techniques were affected by the continuing development of 12-note serialism into expanded serial techniques. Van Vlijmen collaborated with four other Dutch composers and two Dutch writers on the 'morality' *Reconstructie*, and worked with Reinbert de Leeuw on *Axel*, first performed at the Holland Festival on 10 June 1977. The complex mythological story is full of mystical double characters, and centres on Axel von Auersperg, who is hiding a fabulous and mysterious 'golden treasure' in his castle. Athanasius, the alchemist, who urges Axel to keep his secret, has at the same time predestined Sara Emmanuèle de Maupers to discover the treasure. The music of the opera is generally post-serial with many references to the music of Satie and Wagner.

To commemorate the centenary of the death of Vincent van Gogh in 1990, van Vlijmen was commissioned to write an opera based on his last years. The libretto of *Un malheureux vêtu de noir*, by the Belgian critic Johan Thielemans, incorporates correspondence between Vincent and his brother Theo. The opera was first performed on 16 November 1990.

See also RECONSTRUCTIE.

Reconstructie (music theatre, 2 parts, H. Claus and H. Mulisch), Amsterdam, Carré, 29 June 1969, collab. L. Andriessen, R. de Leeuw, M. Mengelberg and P. Schat
Axel, 1975–7 (3, H. Mulisch, after F. Villiers de l'Isle-Adam), Scheveningen, Circus, 10 June 1977, collab. R. de Leeuw
Un malheureux vêtu de noir (3, J. Thielemans), Amsterdam, Stadsschouwburg, 16 Nov 1990

*

W. Markus: 'Axel or The Rejection of Life', *Key Notes*, vi (1977), 19–32
I. Fabian: 'Gelungene Annäherung an van Gogh (Un malheureux vêtu de noir, eine neue Oper von Jan van Vlijmen in Antwerpen)', *OW*, xxxii/2 (1991), 22 MICHAEL VAN EEKEREN

Vocalise (Fr.). A textless vocal exercise or concert piece to be sung to one or more vowels. The vocalise derives from two traditions. One dates from the early 19th century, when it became customary to perform and publish *solfeggi* and *esercizi* with piano accompaniment (e.g. Domenico Corri, *The Singer's Preceptor*, 1810; Manuel García, *Traité complet de l'art du chant*, 1840); by the middle of the century there were numerous such publications (the idea was that with a piano accompaniment even the most mechanical exercises would be performed more artistically). The other tradition involved using existing compositions as vocal exercises without words. In 1755 Jean-Antoine Bérard provided, with his *L'art du chant*, 20 compositions by Lully, Rameau and others selected for the technical problems they offered ('pour les sons tendres, légers, maniérés, majestueux' etc.), adding instructions as to how these problems were to be solved. In the 19th century most instruction manuals for the voice included pieces specially composed for the purpose: 'melodies without words, offering the pupil a union of all the difficulties of song' (García).

The term 'vocalization' has been reserved by composers and singing teachers for the singing of vocalises (e.g. in the title of Crescentini's *Raccolta di esercizi per il canto all'uso del vocalizzo*, *c*1810), but it is often used more generally for the singing to vowel sounds or with closed lips (*see* BOCCA CHIUSA).

OWEN JANDER

Vogel, Charles-Louis-Adolphe (*b* Lille, 17 May 1808; *d* Paris, 11 Sept 1892). French composer, grandson of Johann Christoph Vogel. He first studied in Lille, then in Paris, where his teachers included Kreutzer and Reicha, and a patriotic song 'Les trois couleurs' won immediate fame. Apart from chamber music and numerous songs and *romances*, Vogel devoted himself to the theatre. Though most of his works were produced in Paris, and one of them, *Le podestat* (1831), achieved a revival two years later, he won considerable popularity outside France: the Royal French Opera of The Hague commissioned and produced *Le siège de Leyde* in 1847 and revived it in 1854; his comic opera *Le nid de cigognes* was first performed in Baden-Baden (translated into German) in 1858; and *La filleule du roi* (1875) gained more approval in Brussels than in Paris. His success in the theatre can be attributed to his sense of drama, careful word-setting and attractive melodies. The style of his *opéras comiques* resembles Hérold's and his instrumental music shows the influence of Hummel.

Le podestat (oc, 1, J. Laffitte), Paris, OC (Ventadour), 16 Dec 1831
Marie Stuart (opéra, 3), 1833, unperf.
Le siège de Leyde (opéra, 4, H. Lucas), The Hague, Koninklijke, 4 March 1847
La moissonneuse (drame lyrique, 4, A. Bourgeois and M. Masson), Paris, Lyrique, 3 Sept 1853 (Paris, 1853)
Rompons! (oc, 1, A.-N. Jautard and A. de Jallais), Paris, Bouffes-Parisiens, 21 Sept 1857 (Paris, 1857)
Le nid de cigognes (oc, 1, E. Cormon), in Ger., Baden-Baden, Sept 1858
Gredin et Pigoche (operetta, 1, Masson and G. Fath), Paris, Folies-Marigny, 19 Oct 1866 (Paris, 1867)
La filleule du roi (oc, 3, Cormon and R. Deslandes), Brussels, April 1875 (Paris, 1875) FRÉDÉRIC ROBERT

Vogel [Fogel], **Johann Christoph** (*b* Nuremberg, bap. 18 March 1756; *d* Paris, 28 June 1788). German composer. He studied with Joseph Riepel in Regensburg before moving to Paris. From 1776 he played the horn in the service of the Duke of Montmorency and later of the Count of Valentinois; he wrote several orchestral and chamber works. His greatest enthusiasm was for Gluck's operas. *La toison d'or* is a conscientious imitation of the master and is dedicated to Gluck, who reciprocated with praise. A three-act *tragédie lyrique*, to a libretto by P. Desriaux, was performed at the Opéra on 5 September 1786, some years after its completion; by this time taste had turned towards Sacchini and it seemed old-fashioned. It had only a dozen performances, although it was revived with a new title (*Médée de Colchos*) days before the composer's death.

A lyrical bent reflecting early studies of Hasse appears more strongly in *Démophon*, a three-act *opéra lyrique*, also to a text by Desriaux, begun in 1786. Sloth or dissipation delayed its completion, and its posthumous performance (22 September 1789, at the Opéra) followed that of Cherubini's opera on the same subject. Nevertheless *Démophon* attained the respectable total of 24 performances and was revived in 1793. Its overture, first played at the Concert de la Loge Olympique in February 1789, remained popular for a decade. Both operas reveal a master of the orchestra and bespeak a dramatic composer of considerable potential.

*

G. E. Waldau, ed.: *Vermischte Beyträge zur Geschichte der Stadt Nürnberg*, iii (Nuremberg, 1788)
C. G. von Murr: 'Frühzeitiger Tod eines geschickten Musikers aus Nürnberg', *Journal zur Kunstgeschichte*, xvii (1789), 10
A. Vogler: *Johann Christoph Vogel* (Halle, 1914)
A. Bickel: *Johann Christoph Vogel: der grosse Nürnberger Komponist zwischen Gluck und Mozart (1756–1788)* (Nuremberg, 1956)
J. G. Rushton: *Music and Drama at the Académie Royale de Musique, Paris, 1774–1789* (diss., U. of Oxford, 1970)
A. L. Ringer: 'A German Gluckist in Pre-Revolutionary France', *Music in the Classic Period: Essays in Honor of Barry S. Brook* (New York, 1985), 221–31 JULIAN RUSHTON

Vogel, Johann Heinrich (*b* *c*1670; *d* after 1726). German singer. Possibly a tenor, he seems to have been part of the Opera Company at the Hamburg Gänsemarkt as early as 1694, when he sang a minor role in Johann Kusser's *Porus*. The record for 1725–6 mentions a 'Ms Vogel' (though this could be his son) who sang in three Keiser roles there: Peter in *Hamburger Schlachtzeit*, Mercurius in *Prolog auf den Geburtstag von Friedrich Ludwig* and Die Elbe in *Mistevojus*. Vogel's daughter, Margaretha Susanna, also became famous as a singer and married the Hamburg town musician Johann Kayser in 1706.

*

K. Zelm: 'Die Sänger der Hamburger Gänsemarkt-Oper', *HJbMw*, iii (1978), 35–73, esp. 71
W. Braun: *Vom Remter zum Gänsemarkt. Aus der Frühgeschichte der alten Hamburger Oper (1677–1697)* (Saarbrücken, 1987), 133 HANS JOACHIM MARX

Vogelhändler, Der ('The Bird Seller'). Operetta in three acts by CARL ZELLER to a libretto by Moritz West and Ludwig Held, after Varin and Biéville's *Ce que deviennent les roses*; Vienna, Theater an der Wien, 10 January 1891.

In an 18th-century Rhineland village the villagers have long been hunting on the Elector's estate when, to their consternation, it is announced that the Elector is coming for a wild boar hunt. To make good the absence of any remaining wild boar, the gamekeeper Weps (baritone) accepts, for a small bribe, the villagers' offer of a couple of tame pigs. Weps needs the money to pay off the debts of his nephew Stanislaus (tenor) and, when he learns that the Elector is not coming after all, he arranges for Stanislaus to impersonate him. The disguised Stanislaus gives an audience in a hunting-lodge, where the village postmistress Christel (soubrette) visits him to seek the appointment of zoo director for her lover Adam (tenor *buffo*), a bird seller from the Tyrol. The Electress Marie (soprano), believing her husband to be in the hunting-lodge with another woman, flirts with Adam by presenting him with a red rose. When Adam sees Christel emerging from an apparent rendezvous with the Elector, he is shocked and will have nothing to do with her. Misunderstandings are, of course, eventually cleared up, and Adam and Christel reunited.

A work of considerable charm, delightful melody and winning ensemble writing, the operetta originally starred Alexander Girardi as Adam, Ilka Palmay as Christel, and Ottilie Collin as the Electress. Its principal numbers include Act 1 entrance songs for Adam ('Grüss enk Gott, alle mit einander') and Christel ('Ich bin die Christel von der Post'), the Adam–Electress duet and ensemble 'Schenkt man sich Rosen in Tirol', Adam's Act 2 solo 'Wie mein Ahnl zwanzig Jahr', and the Electress's Act 3 solo 'Als geblüht der Kirschenbaum'.

For illustration *see* GIRARDI, ALEXANDER. ANDREW LAMB

Vogelstrom, Fritz (*b* Herford, Westphalia, 4 Nov 1882; *d* Dresden, 25 Dec 1963). German tenor. He studied in Mannheim, making his début there in 1904 as Tamino. In 1909 he sang Parsifal, Lohengrin and Froh at Bayreuth. From 1912 until his retirement in 1929 he was engaged at the Dresden Hofoper (later the Staatsoper). His repertory included Max (*Der Freischütz*), Canio, Cavaradossi, Pinkerton, Don José, Bacchus (*Ariadne auf Naxos*) and the Emperor (*Die Frau ohne Schatten*). A reliable singer, he had a powerful, high-lying voice. ELIZABETH FORBES

Vogl, Adolf (*b* Munich, 18 Dec 1873; *d* Munich, 2 Feb 1961). German writer on music and composer. He was a pupil of Hermann Levi and first worked as a conductor. Later he settled in Munich and devoted himself to composing and to the study of Wagner's music, which greatly influenced his own. He composed two operas: *Maja* (2, Vogl), a 'dramatische Dichtung mit Musik', was performed in Stuttgart on 12 January 1908; *Die Verdammten* (1, H. von Gumppenberg) was performed in Leipzig on 27 January 1934. During the Nazi regime he was imprisoned and his works were banned until 1945. Of his writings on Wagner, *Tristan und Isolde: Briefe an eine deutsche Künstlerin* (Munich, 1913, 3/1922) and *Parsifal: Tiefe Schau in die Mysterien des Bühnenweihfestspiels* (Munich, 1914) show a deep understanding of Wagner's music and its philosophy.

A. Wurz: 'Im Geiste Richard Wagners: Adolf Vogl achtzig Jahre alt', *ZfM*, Jg.115 (1954), 22–3

Vogl, Heinrich (*b* Au, Munich, 15 Jan 1845; *d* Munich, 21 April 1900). German tenor. He studied with Lachner and made his début in 1865 as Max (*Der Freischütz*) at the Hofoper, Munich, where he was engaged for 35 years. Having already sung Lohengrin (1867) and Tristan (1869), he created the roles of Loge in *Das Rheingold* (1869) and Siegmund in *Die Walküre* (1870), and at Bayreuth he sang Loge in the first complete *Ring* cycle (1876). He sang Siegfried in the first Munich performances of *Siegfried* and *Götterdämmerung* (1878); Loge and Siegmund in the first Berlin *Ring* cycle, as well as both Siegfrieds in the second cycle (1881, Victoria Theatre); Loge and Siegfried in the first London *Ring* cycle (1882, Her Majesty's Theatre); and took part in the early part of Angelo Neumann's European Wagner tour (1882). He returned to Bayreuth as Tristan and Parsifal (1886), and made his Metropolitan début as Lohengrin (1890), also singing Tannhäuser, Tristan, Loge, Siegmund and both Siegfrieds. In Munich he sang in Ritter's *Faule Hans* (1885), *Otello* (1888), *Benvenuto Cellini* (1889), Franchetti's *Asrael* (1892), *Pagliacci* (1893), *Dalibor* (1894), Berlioz's *La prise de Troie* and Cornelius's *Der Cid* (1895). He created Baldur in his own opera *Der Fremdling* (1899) and made his last appearance as Canio (1900), four days before his death.

Vogl's voice was powerful and his stamina legendary (he sang Loge, Siegmund and both Siegfrieds in some *Ring* cycles on four consecutive days without apparent strain). Walther was the only major Wagnerian tenor role that he never sang.

L. Nohl: *Neues Skizzenbuch* (Munich, 1868)
H. von der Pfordten: *Heinrich Vogl* (Munich, 1900)
A. Neumann: *Erinnerungen an Richard Wagner* (Leipzig, 1907; Eng. trans., 1908)
L. Lehmann: *Mein Weg* (Leipzig, 1913; Eng. trans., 1914)
E. Newman: *The Life of Richard Wagner* (London, 1933–47)
H. Wagner: *200 Jahre Münchner Theaterchronik* (Munich, 1968)

ELIZABETH FORBES

Vogl, Johann Michael (*b* Ennsdorf, nr Steyr, Upper Austria, 10 Aug 1768; *d* Vienna, 19 Nov 1840). Austrian baritone. While studying languages and philosophy at the Gymnasium in Kremsmünster he appeared in several Singspiels by Süssmayr, a fellow pupil. The two became close friends and went together to Vienna in 1786. Vogl studied law at the university and began to practise in the city. Persuaded by Süssmayr to join the German opera company he had founded, Vogl made his début at the Vienna Hofoper on 1 May 1795. The combination of his pleasing baritone voice and dramatic and declamatory gifts made him popular with audiences. He excelled as Orestes (*Iphigénie en Tauride*), Count Almaviva and Mikéli (*Les deux journées*), and he created the part of Pizarro in the 1814 revision of *Fidelio*. He also sang the lead in the première of *Die Zwillingsbrüder* in 1820, having used his influence in the Hofoper to obtain for Schubert the commission for the work. He retired from the theatre in 1822. Vogl is remembered today for his friendship and professional relationship with Schubert, who found in the singer his ideal interpreter.

A. Stadler: 'Nekrolog auf Johann Michael Vogl', *Warte an der Donau* (30 Nov 1840), 4
E. Bauernfeld: 'Erinnerungen an Johann Michael Vogl', *Allgemeine Theaterzeitung Unterhaltungsblätter* (4–5 May 1841), 473

A. Liess: *Johann Michael Vogl: Hofoperist und Schubertsänger* (Graz and Cologne, 1954) MAURICE J. E. BROWN

Vogl [née Thoma], **Therese** (*b* Tutzing, 12 Nov 1845; *d* Munich, 29 Sept 1921). German soprano. She studied in Munich, making her début (as Therese Thoma) in 1865 at Karlsruhe as Casilda in Auber's *La part du diable*. In 1867 she was engaged at the Munich Hofoper, where she remained for 25 years. The following year she married the tenor Heinrich Vogl and in 1869 sang Isolde to her husband's Tristan. She sang Sieglinde in the first performance of *Die Walküre* (1870), and Brünnhilde in *Siegfried* (1878) and *Götterdämmerung* (1879). She sang Brünnhilde in the first London performance of *Der Ring des Nibelungen*, at Her Majesty's Theatre in 1882, and took part in Angelo Neumann's tour of the *Ring* around Europe. Her repertory included Elsa, the title role in *Fidelio*, Agathe, Eglantine (*Euryanthe*) and Gluck's Alcestis. ELIZABETH FORBES

Vogler, Georg Joseph [Abbé Vogler] (*b* Würzburg, 15 June 1749; *d* Darmstadt, 6 May 1814). German composer and teacher. He was born into a musical family; his father was a violinist and instrument maker at the court of the Prince-Bishop of Würzburg. After receiving a broad education, he was appointed almoner to the electoral court at Mannheim in 1770, and by 1772 he was court chaplain. The Elector Palatine Carl Theodor encouraged his musical talents, demonstrated in his first dramatic work, *Der Kaufmann von Smyrna* (1771), by sending him to Italy in 1773. There he met Hasse in Venice, and he studied music with Padre Martini and Francesco Antonio Valotti. In Rome Vogler was named a Knight of the Golden Spur by Pope Pius VI and became a member of the Accademia dell'Arcadia. On his return to Mannheim in 1775 he was appointed spiritual counsellor to the elector. In this influential position he founded what he called a 'public music school' and published his first theoretical writings. On 28 February 1777 he was named second Kapellmeister. He preferred to stay in Mannheim after Carl Theodor's court transferred to Munich in 1778. Between 1778 and 1780, he revised *Der Kaufmann von Smyrna* and wrote incidental music for the National Theatre as well as a melodrama and a Singspiel for Darmstadt.

In 1780 Vogler travelled to Paris, where he had the opportunity to write several dramatic works, and in 1783 he visited London. Summoned to Munich in 1784, he was appointed Kapellmeister, but his tenure was short-lived. In the following year he undertook a series of concert tours and in 1786 was appointed as Kapellmeister and music tutor at the court of Gustavus III, King of Sweden. During the next decade he travelled extensively throughout Europe and even visited north Africa. In 1799 Vogler left Stockholm and, after sojourns in various cities, arrived in Vienna in 1803, when his opera *Castore e Polluce* was revived by Schikaneder's company; *Samori* received its première there in 1804. Among his pupils in Vienna was C. M. von Weber (who made a vocal score of *Samori*). Vogler went to Munich in 1805 for an extended visit and gave a series of concerts and organ recitals. On 1 August 1807 he was appointed Kapellmeister and privy councillor for ecclesiastical affairs by the Grand Duke of Hesse-Darmstadt. In the last seven years of his life he concentrated on church music and organ building, and he also taught Meyerbeer, among others.

Vogler was one of the most colourful and original musicians of his day, but his reputation was tarnished by his abrasive personality. Mozart and Schubart were among his harshest critics, but his theories and performances had their admirers. With a network of pupils and associates that included Peter Ritter, Franz Danzi, J. M. Kraus, Peter Winter, C. M. von Weber, Gottfried Weber and Meyerbeer, it is difficult to overstate his importance. Yet his own music generally lacks the inspiration of the best members of his circle, and he was undoubtedly more influential as a theorist, teacher and performer than as a composer.

Vogler wrote for the stage in a wide variety of genres: comic and serious operas, Singspiels, melodramas, ballets and incidental music. He drew on many different traditions in his operas, often mixing disparate musical styles in a single work. His music is marked by idiosyncratic harmonies and modulations. He was a strong advocate of German opera, and his only Swedish opera, *Gustav Adolf och Ebba Brahe*, is similar in design to serious German operas (e.g. Holzbauer's *Günther von Schwarzburg*). But he was also able to combine elements of French *tragédie lyrique* and Italian *opera seria* in *Castore e Polluce*. Always sensitive to tone colour and sonority, he employed exotic melody in *Samori* with some success.

See also CASTORE E POLLUCE (ii); *KAUFMANN VON SMYRNA, DER*; *LAMPEDO*; and *SAMORI*.

Der Kaufmann von Smyrna (Spl, 1, C. F. Schwan, after N. Chamfort), Mannheim, Schauspielhaus auf dem Fruchtmarkt, sum. 1771; rev., Mannheim, 20 Feb 1778, *D-DS* (*R*1986: GOB, viii), *Mbs*; selections in *Betrachtungen der Mannheimer Tonschule*, iv (1779)

Lampedo (melodrama, 1, C. F. Lichtenberg), Darmstadt, Hof, 11 July 1779, *DS* (*R*1986: GOB, ix), *Mbs*

Erwin und Elmire (Spl, 1, J. W. von Goethe), Darmstadt, 12 Dec 1781, *DS**

Albert der Dritte von Bayern (Spl, 5, K. T. von Traitteur), Stuttgart, National, Dec 1781

Le patriotisme (grand op), Versailles, 1783

La kermesse, ou La foire flamande (oc, 2, J. Patrat), Paris, OC (Favart), 15 Nov 1783, vs (Paris, n.d.)

Castore e Polluce (tragedia lirica, 3, after C. I. Frugoni: I Tintaridi), Munich, Hof, 12 Jan 1787, *A-Wgm*, *D-B*, *DS*, *Mbs*, vs (Mannheim, *c*1788)

Gustav Adolf och Ebba Brahe (lyric drama, 3, J. H. Kellgren, after a play by Gustavus III), Stockholm, Royal Opera, 24 Jan 1788, *DS**, vs ed. in MMS, vii (1973)

Zoroastre (melodrama), ?1796

Der Koppengeist auf Reisen, oder Rübezahl (Spl, A. von Kotzebue), Breslau, 1802

Samori (heroisch-komische Oper, 2, F. X. Huber), Vienna, Wien, 17 May 1804, *DS**, *Mbs*, vs (Vienna, n.d.)

Der Admiral, oder Der gewonnene Prozess (Spl, 1), Darmstadt, 1811, *DS**

Doubtful: Epimenides (Spl, 1), ?1806, *DS*

*

C. F. D. Schubart: *Ideen zu einer Äesthetik der Tonkunst* (Vienna, 1806)

F. J. Lipowsky: *Baierisches Musiklexikon* (Munich, 1811)

J. Fröhlich: *Biographie des grossen Tonkünstlers Abt G. J. Vogler* (Würzburg, 1845)

F. M. Rudhart: *Geschichte der Oper am Hofe zu München* (Freising, 1865), 173

K. E. von Schafhäutl: *Abt Georg Joseph Vogler* (Augsburg, 1888)

M. Brenet: 'L'Abbé Vogler à Paris en 1781–83', *Archives historiques, artistiques et littéraires*, ii (1891), 150–56

F. Walter: *Geschichte des Theaters und der Musik am kurpfälzischen Hofe* (Leipzig, 1898)

E. Anderson, ed.: *The Letters of Mozart and his Family* (London, 1938; 3/1985, ed. S. Sadie and F. Smart)

H. Schweiger: 'Abt Vogler', *MQ*, xxv (1939), 156–66

I. Lenz: 'Georg Joseph Vogler: zur 150. Wiederkehr seines Todestages', *NZM*, Jg. 125 (1964), 434–40

N. Benvengal: Review of 'Gustav Adolf och Ebba Brahe', *Opera*, xxv (1974), 1093–4
R. Würtz: *Verzeichnis und Ikonographie der kurpfälzischen Hofmusiker zu Mannheim nebst darstellenden Theaterpersonal, 1723–1803* (Wilhelmshaven, 1975)
W. Lebermann: 'Zur Authentizität von Georg Joseph Voglers Geburtsort', *Mf*, xxxiv (1981), 462–3
J. Warrack, ed.: *C. M. von Weber: Writings on Music* (Cambridge, 1981)
T. Bauman: Introduction to *Der Kaufmann von Smyrna* and *Lampedo*, GOB, viii and ix (1986)
F. K. Grave and M. G. Grave: *In Praise of Harmony: the Teachings of Abbé Georg Joseph Vogler* (Lincoln, NE, 1987)

PAUL CORNEILSON

Vogt, Hans (*b* Danzig, 14 May 1911). German composer. He received his musical training in Berlin. His first professional appointment was as theatre Kapellmeister in Bielefeld (1934–5), after which he was head of opera in Detmold (1935–8), then city music director in Stralsund. He later worked in Heidelberg as a freelance composer until his appointment as professor of composition at the Mannheim Musikhochschule in 1951. His *oratorische Oper*, *Die Stadt hinter dem Strom* (3, H. Kasack), was broadcast on Hamburg radio in 1953 and staged in Wiesbaden in 1955. The *opera giocosa Athenerkomödie* ('The Metropolitans'; 1, C. Middleton, after Menander) was staged in Mannheim in 1964. Among the many awards Vogt has received are the Mendelssohn Prize of Berlin (1933), the Schumann Prize of Düsseldorf (1955) and the Stamitz Prize of Stuttgart (1967).

Voice of Ariadne, The. Chamber opera in three acts by THEA MUSGRAVE to a libretto by Amalia Elguera after HENRY JAMES's short story *The Last of the Valerii*; Snape, Maltings, 11 June 1974.

Count Marco Valerio (baritone) discovers the plinth of a statue of Ariadne during excavations in the garden of his Italian villa. He becomes obsessed with the desire to find the statue itself, neglecting his young American wife (soprano). The Marchesa Bianca Bianchi (mezzo-soprano) who is in love with the Count, tries to persuade the Countess that her husband loves another woman, while an old friend, Mr Lamb (bass-baritone), offers consolation. The Count, distracted by the voice of Ariadne (soprano) pleading for her Theseus to return to her, is persuaded by his old servant Galtiero (bass) to make a blood sacrifice and cuts his own wrist. The Countess appears and occupies the empty plinth, her voice merging with that of Ariadne as she is reunited with her husband.

Elguera and Musgrave have expanded the original story by introducing several extra characters and a sub-plot involving the busybody Mrs Tracy (alto) and the foolish Baldovino (tenor) who perpetually pursues her. The Theseus-Ariadne theme also belongs to the opera alone. A ghost story has become a psychological drama, in which the natures of real and ideal loves are explored.

Ariadne's voice is pre-recorded on a tape prepared in collaboration with Richard Rodney Bennett.

HUGO COLE

Voix humaine, La ('The Human Voice'). *Tragédie lyrique* in one act by FRANCIS POULENC to a libretto by JEAN COCTEAU after his play; Paris, Opéra-Comique (Salle Favart), 6 February 1959.

La voix humaine was conceived and written (February to June 1958) for the soprano Denise Duval. It is in a single act, has a single set and is written for a single singer. As the curtain rises we see the soloist, a young, elegant woman (frequently referred to as 'Elle') stretched out on her bed. It is, as Cocteau says, 'like the scene of a murder'. She rises and makes to leave but just as she reaches the door the telephone rings. She spends the rest of the opera, some 40 minutes, on the telephone. Mostly she is talking to her lover, but the opera opens with a wrong number and is punctuated with the various vicissitudes of a French telephone system which, even when the opera was written (28 years after Cocteau's play), was notoriously unreliable. Thus an already desperate conversation is interrupted by crossed lines, losses of connection, and panicky rediallings which only serve to exacerbate the already obvious depression and anxiety of the heroine. Indeed these frustrations seem increasingly relevant, for the couple's relationship has itself been cut off, and she can no longer, in any sense, get through to him; the fact that we can only hear her side of the conversation serves to underline the situation: having left her, he has nothing to say beyond the most banal concern for her state of mind and health. This state soon becomes clear. She lies about what she is wearing, tries unsuccessfully to conceal that she has attempted suicide, becomes by turns jealous, inquisitive, insanely anxious, self-pitying and nostalgic. It becomes evident that he is not at his home; when she hears jazzy music in the background she chooses to play along with the lie, preferring to blame his neighbours. In the end she lets the telephone take his place, wrapping the cord round her neck and taking the receiver to bed with her; when she knows that communication is impossible she begs him to ring off and is left murmuring 'Je t'aime' into an unhearing earpiece.

Poulenc's music for *La voix humaine* betrays a composer all too familiar with the pulse and pace of nervous exhaustion and depression. Much of the vocal writing is unaccompanied, often jagged, gabbled and obsessive, or more frequently punctuated with 'panicky' outbursts from the orchestra. Much of the writing is a development of the music of fear which runs throughout his previous opera, *Dialogues des Carmélites*, but the long vocal lines which are there associated with faith or strength are here signally absent. The only time melody underpins the heroine's nostalgia, its sentimentality seems to make its own comment on the heightened colour her memories have attained. This tour de force of extended recitative writing, where each outburst, change of mood, even silence is precisely notated, is held together by sumptuous and highly coloured orchestration (Poulenc insisted that the music should be 'bathed in sensuality') but can only escape monotony in the hands of a peerless performer. Denise Duval recorded the work and gave it in several places outside France; more recently Elisabeth Söderström has proved to be her equal.

JEREMY SAMS

Voketaitis, Arnold [Arnoldas] (*b* New Haven, CT, 11 May 1932). American bass of Lithuanian parentage. He studied in New York and made his début in 1958 with the New York City Opera as Vanuzzi (*Die schweigsame Frau*). His other roles with the company included Creon (*Oedipus rex*), Theseus (*A Midsummer Night's Dream*) and the Father in Douglas Moore's *Carry Nation* (the first New York performance, 1968); he also sang Don Magnifico with the Metropolitan Opera National touring company (1965). In Chicago (1968–73) his roles included the Bonze (*Le rossignol* and *Madama Butterfly*), Zuniga, Loredano (*I due Foscari*), the Magistrate

(*Werther*) and Mr Ratcliffe, which he sang in the American première of *Billy Budd* (1970). His repertory also included Don Basilio, Dr Dulcamara, Don Pasquale and Rev. John Hale in Ward's *The Crucible* (1976, Milwaukee). A strong actor, he had a powerful voice of wide range and fine timbre. ELIZABETH FORBES

Volánek [Wolanek, Wollaneck, Wollanek], **Antonín** [Anton] (**Josef Alois**) (*b* Jaroměř, 1 Nov 1761; *d* Prague, 16 Jan 1817). Czech composer. He worked in Prague as a church choirmaster, violinist and organist. He was also a violinist in several Prague theatre orchestras, serving in some as music director or répétiteur. In the same capacity he was active in Leipzig (autumn 1797 to 30 March 1798), Karlsbad (now Karlovy Vary) and Teplice. He conducted the first Prague performance of Mozart's *Die Zauberflöte* (25 October 1792), as well as the first staging of that work in Czech (October 1794). Volánek's own stage works were given mostly in Prague and Vienna; now nearly all lost, they include Singspiels, ballets, pantomimes and *divertissements*.

Der Schuster-Feierabend oder Kasperl, die fressende Schildwache (Spl, 3, G. J. Ziegelhauser), Vienna, Landstrasser, 9 Sept 1792

Die Maskerade im Serail oder Die grosse Löwenjagd (Spl, P. Heimbacher), Prague, Nostitz, 1792

Der Schuster-Feierabend (Spl, K. F. Hensler), Prague, Hibernian, 31 Dec 1793

Die Überraschung (Spl, 1, Barchielli, after K. C. Engel), Leipzig, Ranstädtertor, 20 Dec 1797

Die Hochzeit auf dem Lande oder Hanns Klachel, dritter Theil (Spl, K. F. Guolfinger von Steinsberg), Prague and Leipzig, 1798

*

ČSHS; *MGG* ('Wolanek'; K. M. Pisarowitz)

Jb der Tonkunst von Wien und Prag (Prague, 1796), 138, 149, 152

G. J. Dlabacž: *Allgemeines historisches Künstler-Lexikon*, iii (Prague, 1815), col.394

T. Volek: 'Repertoir pražské Spenglerovy divadelní společnosti v sezóně 1793–94' [The Repertory of the Spengler Theatrical Troupe of Prague in the 1793–4 Season], *MMC*, no.14 (1960), 5–26

——: 'Die erste Aufführung der "Zauberflöte" in tschechischer Sprache in Prag 1794', *MJb 1967*, 387–91 MILAN POŠTOLKA

Volga Dream, A. Opera by A. S. Arensky; *see* SON NA VOLGE.

Völker, Franz (*b* Neu-Isenburg, 31 March 1899; *d* Darmstadt, 5 Dec 1965). German tenor. Discovered by Clemens Krauss, he studied singing at Frankfurt and in 1926 was engaged at the opera there, making his début as Florestan. In 1931 he moved to Vienna, in 1935 to Berlin, and in 1945 to Munich, where he remained until 1952. He also sang at the festivals at Salzburg (from 1931) and Bayreuth (from 1933). He sang Florestan and Siegmund at Covent Garden in 1934. Admired also as Lohengrin, Don Carlos and Radames, he had in his prime the flexibility for lighter, more lyrical roles, such as Ferrando; he appeared with distinction as Max and the Emperor (*Die Frau ohne Schatten*) and, late in his career, Otello and Canio. PETER BRANSCOMBE

Volkert, Franz (**Joseph**) (*b* Vienna, 12 Feb 1778; *d* Vienna, 22 March 1845). Austrian composer, organist and conductor. Although a score by him for a *Don Juan* play is recorded for the Josefstadt theatre as early as 1798, little is known about his formative years. He was organist at the Piarist Church in the Josefstadt from 1801 at the latest, and at the Schottenstift from 1806. His name appears in the repertory lists of the Leopoldstadt theatre (from *c*1812) and the Josefstadt theatre (from 1815); he became deputy Kapellmeister to Wenzel Müller at the Leopoldstadt theatre in about 1814. Although he was replaced by Drechsler in 1824, he continued to write for this theatre: in addition to Singspiels, farces and parodies, he wrote 44 pantomimes and incidental music. Even after he had ceased writing music for Singspiels and farces he continued (at least until October 1831) to write pantomime scores for the Leopoldstadt theatre, some of which enjoyed considerable success. Of his works only *Der Eheteufel auf Reisen* (1821) seems to have been published in vocal score, though songs from many of the local plays and parodies appeared in printed series. Some of his most popular settings of Meisl (e.g. *Der lustige Fritz*, *Das Gespenst auf der Bastei*, *Die beiden Spadifankerln*) and Gleich (*Der Eheteufel*, *Der alte Geist in der modernen Welt*) notched up a large number of performances.

first performed at Vienna, Theater in der Leopoldstadt, unless otherwise stated

Der Geisterseher (Schauspiel mit Chören und Tänzen, J. Perinet), 6 Feb 1810; August und Gustavina, oder Der Kopf von Erz (Schauspiel mit Chören und Tänzen, 3, Perinet), 20 March 1810; Albrecht der Grosse, Herzog von Braunschweig (Schauspiel mit Gesang, 4, J. Schuster), 1st pt 18 Aug 1810, 2nd pt 25 Aug 1810; Johann Faust, der Erfinder der Buchdruckerkunst (Schauspiel mit Musikbegleitung, 4, Perinet), 2 March 1811; Der Perückenmacher (Posse, 1, J. F. Kringsteiner), 5 July 1811

Barthel, der reisende Schustergeselle (Quodlibet, 1, Kringsteiner), 2 Nov 1811; Theophrastus Paracelsus, oder Die Basilisken-Kluft (Zaubermärchen, 3, K. Schikaneder), 9 Nov 1811; Pigmalion, oder Die Musen bei der Prüfung (Parodie, 2, F. Gewey), 29 April 1812; Erich von Lilienstein, oder Der Geisterkampf (Schauspiel, Perinet), 16 May 1812; Mutter Irmentraud, die Wandlerin auf Fronstein (Volksmärchen, 4, Schuster), 6 June 1812

Harlekin der Apothekerjunge (Pantomime, 2, K. Hampel), 23 Jan 1813; Die drei Wunderrätsel und die Zauberbrille, oder Kaspar, der lustige Scherenschleifer (grosse komische Zauberoper, 3, M. Fenzl), 6 March 1813; Die travestierte Medea (Parodie, 2, Perinet), 13 May 1813; Herrmann, Germaniens Retter (melodrama, 3, M. Stegmayer), 2 Dec 1813; Kaffee und Surrogat (Posse, 3, A. Bäuerle), 18 Dec 1813; Die Abenteuer auf der Schlangenburg (grosse Zauberoper, 3, Volkert), 25 June 1814

Der Papagei und die Gans (Spl, 3, E. Schikaneder), 8 Aug 1814 [in part with music by Haibel]; Der siegende Amor (Pantomime, 2, K. Hampel), 15 Oct 1814; Das Linzer Schiff, oder Die Beleuchtung in der Leopoldstadt (Spl, 3, Perinet, after E. Schikaneder), 22 Oct 1814; Der Nachfasching, oder Der närrische Schmaus (Quodlibet, 1, Perinet), 11 Feb 1815; Perseus und Andromeda (Pantomime, 2, P. Rainoldi), 17 March 1815; Der Tiroler-Kasper und seine Liesel-Muhm, oder Die Räuber im Pustertale (Spl, 3, M. Fenzl), 15 April 1815

Der schöne Wiener-Sepperl, oder Die Tischlerniederlage (Posse, 3, A. Gleich), Vienna, Josefstadt, 18 May 1815; Ernst, Graf von Gleichen (heroisch-komische Oper, 2, Gleich), 28 Oct 1815; Felicia, oder Die Geretteten (Spl, 1, K. Wallner), 7 Sept 1816; Die Simandel-Bruderschaft (Posse, 3, F. Kramer), 2 Nov 1816; Blitz und Donner (Quodlibet, 3, Bäuerle), 27 Dec 1816; Der Kampf mit der Riesenschlange, oder Der Leuchtturm auf der Rubinen-Insel (Zauberoper, 3, K. Schikaneder), 17 April 1817

Die Teufelsgrube in Baiern (Volksmärchen, 3, J. S. von Menner), 14 June 1817; Die falschen Kosaken (Posse, 1, K. Meisl), 18 July 1817; Harlekins Abschied von seinen Eltern (musikalisches Prolog, 1), 24 Oct 1817; Das Mädchen von Orleans (romantische Tragödie, 3, Kachler, after F. von Schiller and Cuvellier), 14 Nov 1817; Rambsamperl (Zaubermärchen, 3, L. Stegner), 15 May 1818; Der lustige Fritz, oder Schlaf, Traum und Besserung (Märchen, Meisl), 17 June 1818

Hans Heiling (Volksmärchen, 3, Kringsteiner), 29 July 1818; Die schützende Matrone zu Festenstein (Volkssage, 3, F. Stille), 2 Oct 1818; Diogenes und Alexander (Karikatur, 2, Meisl), 17 Oct 1818; Axel und Tugendreich (Ritterstück, 3, Meisl), 5 Dec 1818; Leonhardtel und Blondinel (Parodie, 1, Hoff), 19 Jan 1819; Der Mulatte (Zauberspiel, 3), 19 Feb 1819; Der Weiberbund, oder Die Belagerung von Alencon (heroisch-komische Oper, 2, from the French), 26 March 1819, collab. Bochsa

Die beiden Spadifankerln (Quodlibet, 2, Meisl), 15 April 1819; Die Stärke und die Arbeiten des Herkules (Parodie, 2, Meisl), 28 April 1819; Die nach Norden reisende und auf eine Insel durch Sturm verschlagene Schauspieler-Gesellschaft (Quodlibet, 2, Meisl), 14 May 1819; Der Esel des Timon (satirische Karrikatur, 2, Meisl), 3 June 1819; Das Gespenst auf der Bastei (Posse, 2, Meisl), 1 Oct 1819; Die Frau Ahnl (Parodie, 2, Welling), 29 Oct 1819; Der Fasching in Wien (Posse, 2, Gleich), 26 Jan 1820

Das Gespenst in der Familie, oder Sapphos und Tobias Vermählung im Reiche der Toten (Posse, 2, Meisl), 18 May 1820, rev. as Das Gespenst im Prater, 9 June 1820; Staberl in Marocco (Zauberspiel, 3, F. Rosenau), 16 June 1820; Erster und zweiter Stock (Schwank, 1, J. Willmann), 24 Aug 1820; Die Reise in den Mond (Zauberposse, 2, L. Stegner), 16 Sept 1820; Maranterl, oder Die drei Rätsel (Zauberparodie, 2, Teischl), 7 Nov 1820

Max von Plauderbach (Posse, A. Sartory), 29 Dec 1820; Ist's was oder ist's nichts, oder Das Gespenst als Bräutigam (Spl, 1, Gleich), 30 Dec 1820; Der Waldmann in der Brühl (Volksmärchen, 2, Gleich), 16 Jan 1821; Zwei Güter und die Braut (Posse, 2, Willmann), 23 Feb 1821; Der Eheteufel auf Reisen (Zauberspiel, Gleich), 9 March 1821; Der Drache der Langeweile (Quodlibet, 2, Meisl), 31 March 1821; Der Freund in der Not auf eine andere Art (Posse, 1, W. Blum), 24 May 1821

Der alte Geist in der modernen Welt (Zauberspiel, 2, Gleich), 15 Sept 1821; Die Unterhaltung auf dem Schlosstheater (Posse, 2, Blum), 5 Oct 1821; Der Mädchenraub (Schwank, 2, Gleich), 27 Sept 1822, collab. L. Schuster; Die Heirat durch die Pferdekomödie, oder Die Räuber in den Abruzzen (Posse, 1, Herzenskron), 28 Nov 1822; Den Keller, oder Die Braut (Ritterstück, 3, Gleich), Vienna, Theater an der Wien, 1 Jan 1819, rev., Leopoldstadt, 15 Jan 1823

Narrheit und Zauberei (Zauberspiel, 2, Gleich), 4 April 1823; Die goldenen Kohlen (komische Operette, 2, Gleich), 12 May 1823; Hoangpuff (Posse, 1, M. Fink), 28 May 1823; Der wilde Mann im Prater (Posse, 2, J. Schuster), 20 May 1824; Die Nachtwandlerin (Posse, 2), 10 Dec 1824; Die Wunderbrille im Zauberwalde (Zauberspiel, 2, Gleich), 25 Feb 1825, collab. Drechsler and W. Müller; Felix und Gertrud, oder Der Bräutigam auf der Flucht (Posse, 3), Vienna, Josefstadt, 16 Sept 1826

*

ADB (A. von Weilen); *MGG* (K. M. Pisarowitz); *StiegerO*; *WurzbachL*

F. Hadamowsky: *Das Theater in der Wiener Leopoldstadt 1781–1860* (Vienna, 1934)

A. Bauer: *Das Theater in der Josefstadt zu Wien* (Vienna, 1957)

PETER BRANSCOMBE

Volksoper [Städtische Volksoper]. Theatre in Vienna (and the name of the company that performs there), opened in 1898 as the Kaiserjubiläums-Stadttheater and used for opera from 1903; *see* VIENNA, §§4(ii) and 5.

Vollerthun, Georg (*b* Fürstenau, 29 Sept 1876; *d* Strausberg bei Berlin, 15 Sept 1945). German composer and conductor. He studied in Berlin with Tappert, Radecke and Gernsheim before becoming a theatre conductor in Prague, Berlin, Barmen and Mainz. From 1908 to 1910 he was in Paris, returning to Berlin where he taught singing before the war. After 1918, he retired from teaching until 1933 when the Nazis enforced a reorganization of the Berlin Hochschule für Musik and appointed him teacher of lieder interpretation and score reading, a post he gave up in 1936.

Vollerthun's reputation as an operatic composer was entirely related to his political sympathy for National Socialism. In turn, several Nazi commentators considered his *Island-Saga* (composed 1924), which is strongly influenced by Wagner, to be the purest form of Nordic opera. Hitler apparently admired *Der Freikorporal* (1931) for its spirited inclusion of some of his favourite march motifs, which are employed in a rather banal manner to represent the confronting forces of Frederick William I of Prussia and August the Strong of Saxony. The fact that the librettist of this particular work was of Jewish origin seemed of little consequence, for the opera received several performances, especially during the early years of the Nazi regime.

Veeda (Musikdrama, 2, G. Kiesau), Kassel, 5 Nov 1916

Island-Saga (Musiktragödie, 3, B. Thiersch), Munich, National, 17 Jan 1925, vs (Berlin, 1924)

Der Freikorporal (3, R. Lothar, after G. Freytag), Hanover, 10 Nov 1931 (Berlin, 1932)

Das königliche Opfer (3, O. Schrenk), Hanover, 16 May 1942 (Berlin, 1942)

Des Königs Page (O. Schrenk, after C. F. Meyer), unperf.

*

R. C. Müschler: 'Georg Vollerthun', *ZfM*, Jg. 100 (1933), 989–92

G. Vollerthun: 'Meine Absichten in die Oper', *ZfM*, Jg.100 (1933), 844–5

E. Krieger: 'Georg Vollerthun zum 60. Geburtstag (29 September 1936)', *ZfM*, Jg. 103 (1936), 1131

——: *Georg Vollerthun, ein ostdeutscher Komponist* (Berlin, 1942)

T. W. Werner: 'Georg Vollerthun: "Das königliche Opfer"' *ZfM*, Jg. 109 (1942), 277–8

C. Niessen: *Die deutsche Oper der Gegenwart* (Regensburg, 1944)

ERIK LEVI

Volo di notte ('Night Flight'). Opera in one act by LUIGI DALLAPICCOLA to his own libretto after Antoine de Saint-Exupéry's *Vol de nuit*; Florence, Teatro della Pergola, 18 May 1940.

The action takes place at the airfield at Buenos Aires in about 1930, during the pioneering days of night flying. On the left of the stage is the office of Rivière (bass-baritone), the airfield director; on the right the office of his employees. After a brief prelude depicting the tranquillity of the aerodrome by night, Scene i opens with Employee III (baritone) telling Rivière of the imminent landing of a plane from Chile. Other flights are expected, and one is scheduled to take off for Europe at three in the morning. Everyone on duty will have a chance to sleep except Rivière, who has instituted night flights to speed up the mail, and whose passion for work permits him no sleep. Against the distant background of a blues about love (offstage soprano), Rivière muses to one of his elderly pilots, Laroux (bass), about the absence of love from his own life.

In Scene ii the first plane lands and its pilot, Pellerin (tenor), stumbles in, exhausted. The inspector, Robineau (bass), offers to buy him a drink, but Rivière, disapproving, reprimands Robineau while Pellerin tells the ground staff of the joys of flying.

Scene iii reveals the Radio Operator (tenor) receiving news that the flight from Patagonia has run into problems with the weather; the plane has only half an hour's fuel left. Despite this, Rivière insists that the plane for Europe should take off on schedule. In Scene iv Simona Fabien (soprano), wife of the pilot delayed by bad weather, arrives. No one can reassure her and she runs to Rivière, telling him that she has been married only six weeks, and that he is jeopardizing her future happiness by his insistence on night flying. As she departs at the start of Scene v, Rivière ponders on how much happiness can be destroyed in an instant. The radio operator relays the endangered pilot Fabien's messages to the ground staff. By now the plane is miles off course and over the sea. The pilot abandons hope of a safe landing and turns his plane upwards towards the stars. He tells his colleagues of the luminous light that bathes the heavens and how the beauty above transcends everything below. Suddenly contact is broken off: his plane has run out of fuel. As Scene vi opens the plane from Asunción arrives on schedule, and despite the horror that his staff feel over the death of Fabien, Rivière insists that night flying will continue. The opera ends as the plane for Europe takes off and

Rivière reflects bitterly on the heavy burden of responsibility that he feels is his.

Volo di notte was Dallapiccola's first work for the stage, written in his early style, combining simple 12-note procedures with other more traditional techniques. It is his first prolonged meditation on death. He quotes wholesale from his *Tre laudi* (1936–7), medieval religious poems in honour of the Virgin, and thus broadens, through musical allusion, the significance of the actions on stage. Rivière's feelings are those of all who work and struggle to reach an ideal. A reflective man 'condemned to solitude by his own greatness' and locked in his prison of glass, he is incapable of intimate relations with another human being. His predicament is mirrored by that of the pilot Fabien trapped in his aeroplane.

Each of the opera's scenes is preceded by an introduction. Unlike the densely symbolic leitmotif technique characteristic of his later operas, Dallapiccola secures the unity of *Volo* through his use of two principal rhythms, as well as melodic and harmonic motifs, always recognizable in their transformations. On a larger scale, the music is structured using a series of closed forms that include a rhythmic ostinato, as when the radio operator begins relating the ominous news about the Patagonia flight; a 'chorale with variation and finale'; and a 'hymn' in Scene v. ANTHONY SELLORS

Vologeso ('Vologeses'). *Opera seria* in three acts by NICCOLÒ JOMMELLI to a libretto by MATTIA VERAZI, after APOSTOLO ZENO's *Lucio Vero*; Ludwigsburg, Schlosstheater, 11 February 1766.

Lucio Vero [Lucius Verus] (tenor) has defeated Vologeses (soprano castrato), King of Parthia, and has become enamoured of his fiancée, Berenice (soprano). Although betrothed to Lucilla (soprano), the daughter of the Roman co-emperor Marcus Aurelius, Lucius Verus is obsessed with securing the hand of Berenice. In Act 1, Vologeses is placed in an amphitheatre full of wild beasts but is saved by Berenice, who throws herself into the arena, forcing Lucius Verus to give Vologeses a sword in order to save her. Later (Act 3) Berenice is presented with a basin which is supposed to hold the head of her beloved. Lucius Verus offers her the crown and sceptre, but Vologeses arrives with his army. Lucius Verus relents, and the faithful couple are reunited.

An ensemble with diminishing numbers of participants closes each of the first two acts. The ensemble at the end of Act 1 begins as a quartet for Lucius Verus, Lucilla, Berenice and Vologeses. Lucius Verus and Lucilla exit in the middle of the scene, leaving Berenice and Vologeses to conclude with a duet. Here Jommelli dispenses with the usual ritornello and long opening solos for each member of the ensemble. He moves directly from obbligato recitative into short, argumentative exchanges among the characters, who combine in confrontational duets and express themselves simultaneously in four individual musical ideas. The concluding duet has three distinct sections and could stand alone as a musical unit. The multi-sectional ensemble at the close of Act 2 begins as a confrontational trio. Berenice and Vologeses then sing a duet and exit. Lucius Verus reacts with an impassioned obbligato recitative in the key of the flattened submediant before singing a two-tempo aria.

Jommelli's music is notable for its independent use of violas, cellos, basses and wind instruments, for its rhythmic and textural complexity, for its ornamental and demanding violin and vocal parts, and for its strong, sometimes violent contrasts in tempo and dynamics. The winds in particular are featured in solo obbligato roles in both recitative and arias, adding to the sense of desperation, terror and foreboding characteristic of this work. The obbligato recitative, highly developed and often programmatic, employs a variety of textures and timbres. MARITA P. McCLYMONDS

Volpe [Rovettino, Rovetta, Ruettino], **Giovanni Battista** (*b* Venice, ?*c*1620; *d* Venice, late 1691). Italian composer. He was the nephew of Giovanni Rovetta and is sometimes referred to as 'Rovettino' or 'Ruettino' and in documentary sources as 'G. B. Rovetta', though Volpe was his family name. He became *maestro di cappella* at St Mark's, Venice, in 1690; he was also a priest and held various clerical positions there. He was associated too with the orphanage-conservatory of the Mendicanti and the St Cecilia Society (a musicians' fraternity). Reports that he taught Benedetto Marcello are unlikely to be true.

Volpe composed the music for three operas – *La costanza di Rosimonda* (1659, Venice; 1675, Milan), *Gli amori di Apollo e di Leucotoe* (1663, Venice, score in *I-Vnm*) and *La Rosilena* (1664, Venice) – all *dramme per musica* to librettos by A. Aureli and all originally presented at the Teatro SS Giovanni e Paolo; he has sometimes also been credited with *Argiope* (1649, Venice), otherwise attributed to Rovetta and Leardini. Volpe's approach to text setting was a simple one; verbs of motion and emotion are often marked by melismas. *Rosilena* appears not to have been well received. Volpe also wrote cantatas, sacred music and a treatise on keyboard playing.

I. Fragalà Data and A. Colturato: *Raccolta Mauro Foà/Raccolta Renzo Giordano* (Rome, 1987), 363–4

E. Rosand: *Opera in Seventeenth-Century Venice: the Creation of a Genre* (Berkeley, 1991), 665–7 ELEANOR SELFRIDGE-FIELD

Volpone. Opera in four acts by FRANCIS BURT to his own libretto, after BEN JONSON's play; Stuttgart, Staatsoper, 2 June 1960.

Volpone (bass) is visited by his neighbours Voltore (baritone), Corbaccio (tenor) and Corvino (bass). With the connivance of his parasite Mosca (tenor) he persuades each in turn that he is near death and that his neighbour will inherit his wealth. Voltore bribes him with costly presents, Corbaccio disinherits his son Bonario (baritone) in Volpone's favour, Corvino offers his wife Celia (soprano) to lie with him as a cure for a feigned illness. When Bonario saves Celia from ravishment and wounds Mosca he is accused and tried for the attempted murder of Volpone. To mortify his dupes yet further Volpone disguises himself and lets it be known that he has died, leaving all his possessions to Mosca. When he throws off his disguise, Mosca, hoping to retain Volpone's fortune, denounces him as an impostor. Volpone in fury reveals the whole plot. Bonario's name is cleared and Volpone and Mosca are punished for their sins.

Burt has toned down the savagery of the original, extracting from it a neat *opera buffa* plot with a light-hearted finale of his own invention in which a moralizing chorus addresses the audience. *Volpone* is a number opera with attractive arias for Mosca, Volpone and Celia and many ingeniously worked ensembles. Volpone's three servants act as clown-commentators, and the three magistrates at the trial also form a self-contained vocal unit. Burt's music, vigorous, clearcut and strongly rhythmic, well suits the theme; the more grotesque characters are sharply portrayed and the many strands of the complex plot are woven together with great skill. The opera was given in London (Sadler's Wells) in 1961 and 1964. HUGO COLE

Voltaire [Voltaire, François Marie Arouet de; Arouet, François Marie] (*b* Paris, 21 Nov 1694; *d* Paris, 30 May 1778). French author and philosopher. His works include seven librettos, only two of which were performed during his lifetime: *La princesse de Navarre* (1744) and *Le temple de la gloire* (1745), both written for celebrations at the court of Versailles. Voltaire made no claim to musical expertise and expressed little interest in orchestral music. Opera, however, like everything connected with the stage, exerted a lifelong fascination for him, although his pronouncements on it were ambivalent, varying from condemnation of its absurdities to suggestions that the kind of reforms proposed by Gluck could eventually lead to the creation of a form of music theatre worthy of comparison with Greek tragedy.

His own attempts to provide a model were ultimately disappointing. *Tanis et Zélide* (1733), not intended for performance, is a typically Voltairian propaganda piece concerning the overthrow of an evil theocracy in ancient Egypt. *Samson*, written in the same year, with Rameau as the composer, is Voltaire's nearest approach to his ideal of a musical drama capable of dealing with serious moral issues. The project was eventually abandoned owing to ecclesiastical opposition, the same obstacle which Saint-Saëns had to overcome before producing his *Samson et Dalila*, based largely on Voltaire's text. *Pandore* (1740), described by Voltaire as 'a philosophical opera worthy of being performed before Bayle and Diderot', and his two comic operas, *Le baron d'Otrante* and *Les deux tonneaux*, which he forwarded to Grétry in 1768, remained unperformed.

More important than Voltaire's comparative failure as a librettist is his indirect contribution to the development of opera, particularly during the last decade of the 18th century and the early years of the 19th. Over 70 operas dating from that time were based on his tragedies alone, and when his comedies, poems, novels and other works are taken into consideration it is clear that he inspired more operas than any other writer, with the single exception of Shakespeare. This rather surprising pre-eminence in a genre with which he is not normally associated is explained primarily by the enormous popularity of his works, including his now forgotten tragedies, in Italy as well as France during the early Romantic period. Moreover, many of his tragedies, in reality melodramas in neo-classical guise, are thoroughly operatic. Constantly striving for maximum dramatic and emotional impact, Voltaire excelled in devising extreme situations which force his protagonists to make agonizing choices, often in the context of a clash of races, religions or ideologies. He was also increasingly concerned with matters of decor and spectacle. This trend culminated in the colourful pageantry of *Olympie*, the inspiration for Spontini's opera with the same title whose performance in Paris in 1819 marked the genesis of grand opera.

Among other composers who provided musical settings for librettos derived from Voltaire are three major figures: Bellini (*Zaira*, 1829), Verdi (*Alzira*, 1845) and Rossini (*Tancredi*, 1813, and *Semiramide*, 1823, but not *Maometto II*, often incorrectly stated to be based on Voltaire's *Mahomet*). Rossini's *Semiramide* is the only Voltaire opera still performed with any frequency, but Voltaire's pervasive influence on the 19th-century lyric stage is apparent to anyone familiar with his tragedies.

Zaïre (tragédie, 1732): Nasolini, 1797; F. Federici, 1799; Portugal, 1802; Winter, 1805; V. Lavigna, 1809; P. J. Pfeffinger, comp. ?1809; M. García, 1828; Bellini, 1829; A. Gandini, 1829; Mercadante, 1831; A. Manni, 1845; Ernst II, 1846; L. Del Corona, 1863; C. E. Lefebvre, 1887; P. V. de La Nux, 1890

Samson (opéra, 1733): Rameau, comp. 1733; Saint-Saëns, 1877; Weckerlin, 1890

Adélaïde du Guesclin (tragédie, 1734): Mayr, 1799, as Adelaide di Guesclino; F. Gnecco, 1800, as Adelaide di Guesclino

Alzire, ou Les Américains (tragédie, 1736): Graun, 1755, as Montezuma; P. J. Candeille, 1785, as La conquête du Pérou; Zingarelli, 1794; F. Horzizky, 1794; G. Nicolini, 1796, as Alzira; Nasolini, 1797; F. Bianchi, 1801; Manfroce, 1810; Verdi, 1845

Pandore (tragédie lyrique, 1740): La Borde, 1767

Zulime (tragédie, 1740): G. M. Rutini, carn. 1776, as Sicotencal; Bianchi, 1782; Portugal, 1796

Mahomet, ou Le fanatisme (tragédie, 1741): Winter, 1817

Mérope (tragédie, after Maffei: *Merope*, 1743): Graun, 1756; Nasolini, 1796; Bianchi, 1797; Portugal, 1804; Pacini, 1847; L. Zandomeneghi, 1875

La princesse de Navarre (comédie-ballet, 1744): Rameau, 1745

Le temple de la gloire (opéra-ballet, 1745): Rameau, 1745

Zadig (conte philosophique, 1747): Catrufo, 1818; Vaccai, 1825, as Zadig ed Astartea

Sémiramis (tragédie, 1748): Hasse, *c*1752; Graun, 1754; M. Mortellari, 1784, as Semiramide; Prati, 1786, as La vendetta di Nino; Nasolini, 1790, as La morte di Semiramide; Bianchi, 1790, as La vendetta di Nino, o sia Semiramide; Borghi, 1791, as La morte di Semiramide; Himmel, 1795, as La morte di Semiramide; Portugal, 1801, as La morte di Semiramide; Catel, 1802; Rossini, 1823; García, 1828

Memnon, ou La sagesse humaine (conte philosophique, 1750): Ragué, 1784

Oreste (tragédie, 1750): J.-B. Lemoyne, 1782, as Electre

L'orphelin de la Chine (tragédie, 1755): Bianchi, 1787, as L'orfano cinese; Reichardt, 1800, as Tamerlan; Winter, 1802, as Tamerlan; Mayr, 1813, as Tamerlano; Nicolini, 1813, as Tamerlano; A. Sapienza, 1824, as Tamerlano

La pucelle (poem, 1755): Langlé, 1791, as Corisandre, ou Les fous par enchantment

Candide (conte philosophique, 1759): Bernstein, 1956

Tancrède (tragédie, 1760): Bertoni, 1766; Holzbauer, 1783; Apell, 1790; Gardi, 1795; Langlé, unperf.; Pavesi, 1812; Rossini, 1813

Ce qui plaît aux dames (poem, 1763): E. Duni, 1765, as La fée Urgèle, ou Ce qui plaît aux dames

Gertrude, ou L'éducation d'une fille (poem, 1763): Grétry, 1766, as Isabelle et Gertrude, ou Les sylphes supposées

Histoire de Russie sous Pierre le Grand (history, 1759–63): Grétry 1790, as Pierre le Grand

Olympie (tragédie, 1764): Horzizky, ?1770s; Prati, 1786; C. Kalkbrenner, 1798; E. Paganini, 1804; Spontini, 1819; Mercadante, 1853, as Statira

L'ingénu (conte philosophique, 1766): Grétry, 1768, as Le Huron

Charlot (comédie, 1767): Stuntz, 1820, as Heinrich IV. zu Givry

Les scythes (tragédie, 1767): Nicolini, 1799, as Gli sciti; Mayr, 1800, as Gli sciti; Mercadante, 1823, as Gli sciti

La princesse de Babylone (conte philosophique, 1768): C. Arrieu, 1960

L'éducation d'un prince (poem, before 1769): Isouard, 1813, as Le prince de Catane

La bégueule (poem, 1772): Monsigny, 1773, as La belle Arsène

*

E. vander Straeten: *Voltaire musicien* (Brussels, 1876, 2/1878)

H. Lion: *Les tragédies et les théories dramatiques de Voltaire* (Paris, 1895)

E. Bouvy: *Voltaire et l'Italie* (Paris, 1898)

L. Ferrari: *Le traduzioni italiane del teatro tragico francese nei secoli XVIIo e XVIIIo: saggio bibliografico* (Paris, 1925)

P.-M. Masson: *L'opéra de Rameau* (Paris, 1930)

H. Bédarida and P. Hazard: *L'influence française en Italie au dix-huitième siècle* (Paris, 1934)

J. Tiersot: 'Voltaire et Rameau collaborateurs', *ReM*, no.168 (1936), 217–23
M. Cornu: 'Le second Voltaire', *Europe* (1959), May–June, 136–51
R. Trousson: 'Trois opéras de Voltaire', *Bulletin de l'Institut Voltaire en Belgique*, i/6 (1962), 41–6
C. M. Girdlestone: 'Voltaire, Rameau et *Samson*', *RMFC*, vi (1965), 133–43
R. Switzer: 'Voltaire, Rousseau et l'opéra', *Studies on Voltaire and the Eighteenth Century*, no.90 (1972), 1519–28
R. S. Ridgway: *Voltaire and Sensibility* (Montreal and London, 1973)
P. Gossett: *The Tragic Finale of 'Tancredi'* (Pesaro, 1977)
D. Heartz: 'Les lumières: Voltaire and Metastasio; Goldoni, Favart and Diderot', *IMSCR*, xii: *Berkeley 1977*, 233–8
H. C. Wolff: 'Voltaire und die Oper', *Mf*, xxx (1978), 257
R. S. Ridgway: 'Voltaire's Operas', *Studies on Voltaire and the Eighteenth Century*, no.189 (1980), 119–51
——: 'Voltairian Bel Canto: Operatic Adaptations of Voltaire's Tragedies', *Studies on Voltaire and the Eighteenth Century*, no.241 (1986), 125–54 [incl. list of operatic adaptations]
C. Questa: *Semiramide redenta: archetipi, fonti classiche, censure antropologiche nel melodramma* (Urbino, 1989)
D. Charlton: 'Voltaire, Grétry, and Revolution in Opera', *Buxton International Festival 1990*, 8–17 [programme book]

RONALD S. RIDGWAY

Vomáčka, Boleslav (*b* Mladá Boleslav, 28 June 1887; *d* Prague, 1 March 1965). Czech composer. He studied the organ (1906–9), composition with Novák (1909–10) and singing at the Prague Conservatory, concurrently studying law at the university (doctorate 1913). Thereafter he worked successively as a solicitor, a judge and a civil servant. He wrote a great deal of criticism on Czech musicians of the 20th century. As a member of various organizations he had a wide influence on Bohemian musical life; he received the title Artist of Merit (1955) and the Order of Work (1957). After World War I he was in the vanguard of Czech music, achieving success in vocal works whose melodic lines were rooted in folk patterns, while his instrumental music showed a bold handling of dissonance and unusual brevity. *Vodník* ('The Watersprite', 1934–7), with its melodiousness and directness of musical expression, derives from the language of folksong, and *Boleslav I* (1953–5) demonstrates a traditionalism similar to that of Smetana.

Vodník [The Watersprite] op.29, 1934–7 (4, A. Wenig, after K. J. Erben), Prague, National, 17 Dec 1937
Boleslav I op.61, 1953–5 (4, Vomáčka, after M. Jariš), Prague, National, 8 March 1957
Čekanky [Wallflowers] op.62, 1939, 1956–7 (3, Vomáčka, after F. X. Svoboda), unperf.

*

H. Doležil: 'Boleslav Vomáčka', *České umění dramatické*, ii: *Zpěvohra* [Czech Dramatic Art: Opera], ed. J. Hutter and Z. Chalabala (Prague, 1941), 337–42

MILAN KUNA, HELENA HAVLÍKOVÁ

Vom Fischer un syner Fru ('The Fisherman and his Wife'). Dramatic cantata in one act, op.43, by OTHMAR SCHOECK to his own libretto after the Low German folktale written down by P. O. Runge for the brothers Jacob Ludwig and Wilhelm Carl GRIMM; Dresden, Staatsoper, 3 October 1930.

A poor Fisherman (tenor) tells his discontented Wife (soprano) that he has caught a turbot which informed him it was a prince under a magic spell. The fisherman thereupon put the fish back in the sea. 'Did you make a wish?' asks the wife. 'What should I wish for?' says the fisherman. The wife, longing to escape from their miserable existence in a 'pisspot' of a shack, orders him to ask for a modest hut. The fisherman goes down to the shore and does her bidding. 'Go back home' says the Fish (bass, in the orchestra), 'she has her hut'. Emboldened by this success and by long deprivation the wife asks in turn to live in a castle, to be King, to be Emperor, to be Pope. Each time the fisherman goes down, less and less willingly, to make the request, explaining that 'my good wife Ilsebill and I do not think as one', and the fish gruffly obeys. Finally the wife demands to be Almighty God. The fish is horrified. 'Go home' is his threatening reply: 'you will find her in the pisspot once again'.

The sequence of increasingly outrageous demands is paralleled in the score by a series of variations. The theme is heard as the fisherman goes to make the first request. Each subsequent journey is accompanied by a variation. As the demands grow in scope a storm gradually rises at sea and the music becomes more violent: before the final, fatal request there is a turbulent double fugue. At the end, while the wife resignedly joins the fisherman in humming a melancholy tune as he casts the nets, music and sea sink back into tranquillity.

In spite of an auspicious première conducted by Fritz Busch and given during an international music congress, the quality of Schoeck's 'dramatic cantata', combining high poetic imagination with an appropriate formal framework, eluded both conservatives and progressives until the conductor Rudolf Kempe rediscovered the work after the war.

RONALD CRICHTON

Von heute auf morgen ('From One Day to the Next'). Opera, op.32, in one act by ARNOLD SCHOENBERG, to a libretto by Max Blonda (pseudonym of Gertrud Schoenberg); Frankfurt, Opernhaus, 1 February 1930.

Schoenberg described this opera as light, cheerful and at least partly comic, but also serious in seeking to expose the danger to abiding values in life and art posed by fashion, which changes 'between today and tomorrow'. He had originally begun a libretto of his own about marital discord under the same title. Thus, although when his wife took over she devised her own quite different story, she was clearly guided by his original conception. Moreover she must have known of his reluctant partial admiration for Strauss's *Intermezzo* when she took one or two hints from it. Schoenberg composed the entire work between 25 October 1928 and 1 January 1929, and was so convinced of its immense box-office success that he decided to publish it himself, a miscalculation that cost him dear in both time and money.

There are four main characters, called simply the Wife (soprano), the Husband (bass-baritone), the Friend (soprano) and the Singer (tenor). They were played in the first production respectively by Else Gentner-Fischer, Benno Ziegler, Elisabeth Friedrich and Anton Maria Topitz, under William Steinberg. The curtain rises as the married couple return late from a party at which they have met the two other characters. The husband has been swept off his feet by a former school friend of his wife, and he snaps boorishly at his wife as she prepares for the daily round. His insulting praise of the friend's elegance and wit leads her to reveal that the singer, a famous tenor, has made advances to her, and her husband's incredulous and scornful reaction sparks off an explosion. She resolves to teach him a lesson. Unobserved she slips into some finery of her sister-in-law's which he has never seen and transforms herself into the kind of 'woman of today' that he so much admires. He is instantly reconquered; but she will not let him off lightly.

Her caprice knows no bounds: the singer will be only the first of many lovers. Her husband must dance with her now, perhaps for the last time. This wakes their child (role spoken to notated rhythms) but she takes no notice of it. When the gasman (offstage) calls, very oddly in the middle of the night, she says she has spent the gas money on her new clothes. They must move into a hotel and live on credit. She has begun to pack when the tenor rings up suggesting that the four of them should meet in a bar, with the obvious implication that the couple will be ready to swap partners. She agrees flirtatiously and at some length, and then gets ready to go out. Her husband despairs, she finally relents, and they are fully reconciled over coffee. To their great embarrassment the friend and the singer turn up, having got tired of waiting. In a series of ensembles the newcomers discover that they are not welcome after all and depart pouring contempt on the couple and their outmoded notions. The breakfasters conclude that love is a better guide than fashion. The child asks what 'modern people' are.

While the reader of the libretto may have doubts about the durability of the marital reconciliation, it is clear that Schoenberg had none. His music speaks emphatically against a cynical interpretation, which would in any case destroy the moral at the heart of the piece. The plot has sometimes been said to contain autobiographical elements, but it was unconnected with the recent, and happy, marriage of the composer and librettist: the Schreker household was its point of departure.

However extraordinary the play of wit and invention in the orchestra or the refinement of the instrumentation in this first opera to employ the 12-note method, it was conceived, as the composer once remarked, vocally from beginning to end. Aria, arioso and ensemble are connected or interrupted by recitative with the flexibility needed to capture each shift of mood in the characters' querulous altercations. Schoenberg insisted that the singers should neither shout nor sacrifice beauty of tone through exaggerated characterization: the music was self-sufficient. Nor should they play for laughs, though the audience would smile often enough at the friend's false sophistication and the tenor's conceit. The husband should also be comic to the extent that he is irascible and self-important, but the wife, though capable of real anger, is a straightforward, warm and sympathetic person. The tone of the whole should be kept light, though without obscuring the moral.

O. W. NEIGHBOUR

Vonk, Hans (*b* Amsterdam, 18 June 1942). Dutch conductor. He studied the piano and conducting at the Amsterdam Conservatory and began his conducting career in 1966 with Netherlands National Ballet. After appointments with the Concertgebouw and Netherlands Radio PO, during which he made his début at Netherlands Opera with Fortner's *Don Perlimplin* (1971), he steadily increased his operatic repertory. His American opera début was at San Diego in 1979 with *La traviata*. He was music director of Netherlands Opera from 1976 to 1985; he then became principal conductor of the Dresden Staatskapelle and artistic director of the Staatsoper at the reopened Semper Oper, Dresden. A recording of his performance there of *Der Rosenkavalier* (1985) was much praised for its lively spirit and superb orchestral playing. He remained at Dresden until 1990, and in 1991 became chief conductor of the Westdeutscher Rundfunk, Cologne (Cologne Radio Orchestra). Vonk's work in other European centres has included conducting a revival of Jommelli's *Fetonte* at La Scala in 1988.

NOËL GOODWIN

Von Stade, Frederica (*b* Somerville, NJ, 1 June 1945). American mezzo-soprano. She studied at the Mannes School, New York, making her début at the Metropolitan in 1970 as the Third Boy in *Die Zauberflöte*; later roles there have included Suzuki, Lola (*Cavalleria rusticana*), Stéphano (*Roméo et Juliette*) and Nicklausse. At Santa Fe she has sung Cherubino, Zerlina and Mélisande, and created Maria in Villa-Lobos's *Yerma* (1971). An outstanding Cherubino, notably at the Paris Opéra and Glyndebourne (both 1973) and at Salzburg (1974–5), she has also been admired as Octavian, particularly at the 1976 Holland Festival. She made her Covent Garden début in 1975 as Rosina. Her repertory includes Mozart's Sextus, Idamantes, Dorabella, Cenerentola, Adalgisa, Charlotte, Monteverdi's Penelope, Hänsel, and the Composer (*Ariadne*). In 1974 she created Nina in Pasatieri's *The Seagull* at Houston; she sang Ellen (*La donna del lago*) there in 1981 and at Covent Garden in 1985. She also created Tina in Argento's *The Aspern Papers* (1988, Dallas; see illustration overleaf). Her musicianship, well-schooled high mezzo-soprano, dramatic ability and personal charm make her one of the most gifted singers of her generation.

*

G. Morshon: 'Frederica Von Stade', *Opera*, xxxi (1980), 31–4

HAROLD ROSENTHAL/R

Vorlová, Sláva [Johnová, Miroslava] (*b* Náchod, 15 March 1894; *d* Prague, 24 Aug 1973). Czech composer. She was a singing pupil of Rosa Papier at the Vienna Conservatory and studied privately with Václav Štěpán (piano) and Vítězslav Novák (composition). From 1934 she studied composition with Jaroslav Řídky, graduating from his masterclasses at the Prague Conservatory in 1948. Her dramatic works are marked by the cultural stagnation of the 1950s, although she escaped the inflexible doctrine of mass art by exploring the genre of folk opera. Her first opera, *Zlaté ptáče* ('The Golden Bird'), was based on a fairy-tale from the Chod region. Czech dances are used as a means of characterization and as an element of motoric construction.

The folk opera *Rozmarýnka* sets the true story of love in a Czech village in the 19th century, well known from a play by the poet Vítězlav Hálek. The opera vividly portrays various folk customs and festivals, such as Shrovetide, a betrothal, a wedding, and building a maypole. *Náchodská kasace* ('Náchod Cassation') is based on a real event which took place at the Manor Theatre in Náchod in 1799 at a production of Mozart's *Don Giovanni*. *Dva světy* ('Two Worlds'), composed for the Casa Ricordi competition in 1958, concerns a recently deceased man who is judged by family portraits that are brought to life. The musical writing is witty, and each portrait sings in a style appropriate to the period of his or her lifetime; for example, the founder of the family, a Crusader knight, sings in plainsong.

Zlaté ptáče [The Golden Bird] op.27, 1949–50 (fairy-tale op, prol., 6 scenes, V. H. Roklan), unperf.

Rozmarýnka op.30, 1952 (folk op, Roklan, after V. Hálek), Kladno, 16 Jan 1955

Náchodská kasace [Náchod Cassation] op.37, 1955 (historical op, Roklan, after A. Jirásek), unperf.

Dva světy [Two Worlds] op.45, 1958 (1, Roklan, after B. V. Ron), unperf.

Frederica Von Stade as Tina (standing), Elisabeth Söderström as Juliana Bordereau and Richard Stilwell as the Lodger in the original production of Dominick Argento's 'The Aspern Papers' at the Music Hall at Fair Park, Dallas, 19 November 1988

V. Šefl: 'Rozmarýnka, lidová zpěvohra S. Vorlové', *HRo*, viii (1955), 472
J. Procházka: 'O novou národní zpěvohru v duchu tylovském' [On the New National Opera in the Spirit of Tyl], *Svět v obrazech*, xi (1955), 6, 19
V. H. Roklan: 'Konfese Slávy Vorlové', *OM*, v (1973), 155–61
A. Šerých: *Sláva Vorlová* (in preparation) ANNA ŠERÝCH

Vorob'yova, Anna Yakovlevna. *See* PETROVA, ANNA YAKOVLEVNA.

Voronezh. City in western Russia, at the confluence of the Voronezh and Don rivers. The local Teatr Muzïkal'nïy Komedii, founded in 1931, became in 1961 the basis of the new Muzïkal'nïy Teatr (cap. 1100), whose concentration on opera led to its reorganization as the Voronezhskiy Teatr Operï i Baleta in 1968. Premières have included Molchanov's *Neizvestnïy soldat* ('The Unknown Soldier', 1967) and *Russkaya zhenshchina* ('Russian Woman', 1969) and G. T. Stavonin's *Oleko Dundich* (1972).

*

ME ('Voronezhskiy teatr operï i baleta') GREGORY SALMON

Vorschlag (Ger.). APPOGGIATURA.

Vorspiel (Ger.). PRELUDE.

Voss. Opera in two acts by RICHARD MEALE to a libretto by David Malouf after the novel by Patrick White; Adelaide, Festival Centre, 1 March 1986. (The 'Garden Scene' was first performed at the Adelaide Festival in 1982.)

Act 1 of the opera is set in Sydney in 1845, Act 2 in the outback and the epilogue in Sydney in 1865. The German explorer Voss (baritone) is determined to be the first man to cross the Australian continent. He seeks the support of the rich merchant Bonner (bass) and collects together the members of his expedition. A gathering to celebrate the heroic endeavour introduces Voss to Bonner's niece, Laura Trevelyan (soprano), a young woman whose uncompromising nature he sees as the equal of his own. Although the expedition ends in disaster, Laura and Voss, defying convention and the limits of time and space, enter into a correspondence between kindred but warring spirits that is also a marriage – mystic and secret, it is the one achievement of Voss's fatal enterprise. Behind their relationship lies the interaction between the environment of the Australian outback and human culture, both aboriginal and imported.

The music, with its use of leitmotifs, strong melodic lines and bitonality, is firmly rooted in the traditions of Western opera. All the more astonishing, in view of Meale's former championing of the austere, is its post-romantic atmosphere. It is nonetheless a milestone in Australian music, a work of great integrity, intelligence and heart. THÉRÈSE RADIC

Vosstaniye Vose [*Shurishe Vose*] ('Vose's Uprising'). Opera in four acts by SERGEY ARTEM'YEVICH BALASANIAN to a libretto by A. Dekhoti and M. Tursun-zade; Stalinabad (now Dushanbe), Tajik Musical Theatre, 16 October 1939.

Conscious that he was composing the first Tajik opera, Balasanian steeped himself in the history and lore of the peasant uprising of the 1880s, the subject of his opera, visiting locations in the Bukhara khanate and studying the extensive musical folklore. He kept the style of his opera simple and accessible, emphasizing familiar couplet forms, unpretentious harmonies and transparent orchestration; in the second version, first performed at the Ayni Tajik Academic Theatre of Opera and Ballet, Stalinabad, on 13 January 1959, he introduced more complex aria, ensemble and choral writing and a more sophisticated role for the orchestra.

Peasant discontent with the Emir's usurious taxation is brought to a head when Gyulizor (soprano), the beautiful daughter of Vose (bass), is kidnapped by the tax collector for the pleasure of the Emir's governor, Khakim (baritone). When he hears of the uprising, Khakim sends for reinforcements and infiltrates a spy into Vose's camp, but he barely escapes when the fortress is captured by Vose's troops. They free Gyulizor and the other prisoners.

While many of the rebels celebrate, Khakim's spy tries to persuade them of the wisdom of concluding a peace treaty with Khakim, but Vose reveals the treachery and urges them to fight on to victory. His troops are ambushed as they emerge from their mountain camp, and Vose and Gyulizor are taken prisoner. Vose goes defiantly to his death, a martyr to his cause, but other rebels free his daughter and the revolt intensifies with renewed energy. LAUREL E. FAY

Vostřák, Zbyněk (*b* Prague, 10 June 1920; *d* Strakonice, 4 Aug 1985). Czech composer. He studied conducting at the Prague Conservatory (1939–43), taking composition lessons with Karel at the same time. From 1943 to 1945 he was a member of the Prague RO, then a professor at the conservatory (1945–8) and head of the Orchestral Association (1946–7). Thereafter he devoted himself principally to composition, but in 1959–60 directed the Ústí nad Labem opera company and from 1963 conducted the new-music ensemble Musica Viva Pragensis. In his youth he composed in an idyllic romantic style, sometimes with neo-classical and other influences. He continued in this manner until the late 1950s, when he became familiar with the works of Orff, Stravinsky and Martinů. The influence of these composers begins to show in his *Pražského nokturna* ('Prague Nocturne') and is significantly developed in *Rozbitý džbán* ('The Broken Jug'), his last opera. Contact with Webern's works brought about a profound change; his first 12-note and serial chamber pieces were written in 1962. Shortly after this he became acquainted with the work of Boulez, Cage, Stockhausen and Varèse, and from 1966 his music displays these influences.

Rohovín Čtverrohý op.12 (comic op, J. Bachtík, after V. K. Klicpera), Olomouc, 3 July 1949

Králův mincmistr [Master of the King's Mint] op.18 (Bachtík, after J. K. Tyl), Prague, 25 Feb 1955

Pražského nokturna [Prague Nocturne] op.23 (J. Wenig, after F. Kubka), Ústí nad Labem, 20 Feb 1960

Rozbitý džbán [The Broken Jug] op.25 (K. Jernek, after H. von Kleist), Prague, 8 Nov 1963

*

J. Volek: 'Králův mincmistr na Národním divadle' [*Master of the King's Mint* at the National Theatre], *HRo*, viii (1955), 343–6

P. Eckstein: 'Premiéra Vostřákova Pražského Nokturna' [The Première of Vostřák's *Prague Nocturne*], *HRo*, xiii (1960), 246–7

J. Volek: 'Krystalizace!' [Crystallization!], *HRo*, xv (1962), 914

J. Bajer: 'Rozbitý džbán v Disku' [*The Broken Jug* in Disek], *HRo*, xvii (1964), 22

V. Lébl and L. Mokrý: 'O současném stavu nových skladebných směrů u nás' [The Present State of New Compositional Trends in Czechoslovakia], *Nové cesty hudby* (Prague, 1964), 21–2

JOSEF BEK

Votre Faust ('Your Faust'). 'Fantasy in the manner of an opera' by HENRI POUSSEUR to a libretto by Michel Butor; Milan, Piccola Scala, 15 January 1969.

Votre Faust (written 1960–67) constitutes an original approach to music drama, revealing a questioning attitude towards opera and exploring concepts of open artistic form. The dramatization inherent in the interplay of musical ideas, their contribution to the action on stage and the use of realistic elements create links between the functions of singers and actors. Their respective contributions are seen as necessarily complementary within a musical and dramatic phenomenon conceived as an indissoluble unity. There is an osmosis between the verbal and musical elements in *Votre Faust* and the subject is coloured by musical preoccupations: Henri (spoken), a young composer and a reflection of the modern musician, or indeed of the artist in general with all the social, political and aesthetic problems presupposed by his situation, is approached by a Theatre Director (spoken), an incarnation of Mephistopheles, to write an opera. The only condition imposed is that it should be on the theme of Faust.

The story thus becomes that of a work yet to be written, of the circumstances of its production and the many obstacles that arise between audience and work. Depending on the audience's decisions, as signalled by vocal responses and by voting, Henri's future may develop along various lines, with positive or negative results in his professional and emotional life. However, the story is not only Henri's, anecdotally told; it also questions the limits of our investigation of society and culture. As an opera about opera, *Votre Faust*, to quote an expression used by the philosopher Ernst Bloch, constitutes a 'trial by example', using as its starting-point that favourite model of Western civilization, the Faust myth. The work is a vast quotation of some of the many versions of the theme while also relating the story to other classic subjects such as Orpheus and Don Juan. It outlines a series of questions about the validity of forms and vocabularies, principles and models, providing testimony from the successive stages of our cultural development but never attempting to impose any one ideology.

Votre Faust departs from the conventions of traditional opera in many ways: five actors are used to convey the dramatic element, while four singers (soprano, mezzo-soprano, tenor and bass) establish complex connections between the interplay of the actors and the music of the instrumentalists. The orchestra of 12 solo musicians introduces supplementary percussion and vocal interpolations in the form of fragmentary phrases and dialogues. A series of tapes shows the development of certain instrumental and vocal qualities by means of electro-acoustic distortion. *Votre Faust* thus explores novel methods of musical representation, opening up new perspectives for the serial technique which was inclined to deny music any figurative quality at the time when Pousseur began writing this opera. JEAN-YVES BOSSEUR

Votto, Antonino (*b* Piacenza, 30 Oct 1896; *d* Milan, 9 Sept 1985). Italian conductor. He studied at the Naples Conservatory and made his conducting début in 1923 with *Manon Lescaut* at La Scala, Milan, where he was engaged as répétiteur and assistant conductor to

Toscanini. He first appeared at Covent Garden in 1924, conducting *Pagliacci* and *Madama Butterfly*, and was soon admired as one of the finest conductors of Italian opera in major centres in Italy, as well as touring elsewhere in Europe and appearing at the Teatro Colón, Buenos Aires. From 1948 he worked mainly at La Scala, and for over 20 years (until 1967) was a respected teacher at the Milan Conservatory.

During the 1950s Votto conducted several of the spectacular productions at La Scala mounted for Callas by Visconti, Salvini and Wallmann, including Spontini's *La vestale* (1954), *Norma* (1955) and *La sonnambula* (1957), and the Florence production of *Don Carlos* (1956). *Norma* and *Andrea Chénier* (also with Callas) were recorded from live Scala performances in 1955; his other recordings with Callas included *Un ballo in maschera* and *La bohème* (both 1956), *La sonnambula* (1957) and *La Gioconda* (1959). Other live recordings from La Scala were *Cavalleria rusticana* with Simionato (1955) and Boito's *Mefistofele* with Siepi (1957). Votto made his American début only in 1960, at the Chicago Lyric Opera, with *Aida* and *Don Carlos*.

CLAUDIO CASINI, NOËL GOODWIN

Voyage, The. Opera in three acts by PHILIP GLASS to a libretto by David Henry Hwang after Glass's story; New York, Metropolitan Opera, 12 October 1992.

The Metropolitan Opera commissioned *The Voyage* for the 500th anniversary of Columbus's discovery of America, but Glass said in 1991:

> I was not interested in doing another portrait opera about Columbus, I'm much more interested in exploring the concept of discovery, and two aspects in particular: (a) the willingness of people to leave the world they know for a world they don't know and (b) the interfacing, the *collision*, of cultures that can take place as the result of these explorations. Instead of a prosaic costume drama about the Nina, the Pinta and the Santa Maria, I want to create an allegory, to trace the kinship between Columbus and other explorers – Noah, the Flying Dutchman, Ulysses, the Ancient Mariner.

The opera also includes a character called The Scientist that would seem to be based on Stephen Hawking, author of *A Brief History of Time*. By portraying a man who discovers new worlds without leaving his wheelchair, Glass depicts voyages of the mind and of the spirit, rather than literal geographical explorations.

The Voyage is the densest, most contrapuntal and perhaps the most complicated score that Glass has yet written; indeed, it seems positively rococo compared with the early pieces written for the Philip Glass Ensemble, although recognizably the work of the same composer. There is much use of polytonality, and pages go by without a repeat sign. Glass also seems at times to be working towards a sort of musical Esperanto: the influence of Shankar and Rakha has not been so apparent in his music since the 1960s and there is a distinctly Latin quality to some of the scenes. TIM PAGE

Voyer, Giovanni (*b* Benicarló, 28 Oct 1901; *d* Lisbon, 29 Nov 1976). Spanish tenor. After study in Milan he made his début in 1927 at the Teatro Sociale in Ostiglia, as Pinkerton. At La Scala, where he sang between 1933 and 1948, his roles included Tristan, Florestan, Herod, Parsifal and Lohengrin. His only Covent Garden appearance was as Faust in the first British stage performance of *La damnation de Faust*, conducted by Beecham (1933). He was often heard in contemporary works, notably as the Emperor in the Italian première of *Die Frau ohne Schatten* (1938, Rome) and in Frazzi's *Re Lear* (1939, Florence). He taught at the Lisbon Conservatory from 1953 until his death. DAVID CUMMINGS

Voyevoda ('The Provincial Governor'). Opera in three acts by PYOTR IL'YICH TCHAIKOVSKY to a libretto by ALEXANDER NIKOLAYEVICH OSTROVSKY and the composer after Ostrovsky's comedy (subtitled *Son na Volge*, 'A Volga Dream'); Moscow, Bol'shoy Theatre, 30 January/11 February 1869.

Ostrovsky's nominal 'comedy' was actually a sprawling drama for a cast of 60 in five acts with prologue, replete with dream visions, spirit scenes and a vivid background of 17th-century social unrest. Little of this found its way into the libretto, which, in the parched words of Herman Laroche, the opera's friendliest critic, confined itself to relating 'how a certain Nechay Shalïgin [the title character] takes Marya Vlasyevna from Bastryukov and how Bastryukov takes her back again from Nechay'. Add to that the embarrassingly pat resolution of the plot by a *deus ex machina* in the form of a new Voyevoda providentially sent by the tsar (to whom a grandiose concluding hymn is sung), and there is little wonder that, after its initial, miserably produced run was cut short after five performances, the composer withdrew the opera and (having cannibalized the best music in later works such as *Oprichnik* and *Swan Lake*) eventually destroyed the score.

Whatever its dramatic handicaps, *Voyevoda* contained some attractive decorative music in the folk style, most of which later went into *Oprichnik*. Among the numbers that were not re-used were two that were separately published at the time of the première, which was conducted by Eduard Merten, with the soprano Alexandra Men'shikova as Marya. The overture begins with an interesting essay in ostinato variation (sometimes called 'changing background' technique) at a slow tempo. The Dances of the Immured Maidens in Act 2 were based on a set of 'Characteristic Dances' Tchaikovsky had composed in 1865; they were performed in advance of the opera and earned a not unfriendly press notice by Borodin. The most direct evidence of genuine operatic flair comes near the end of Act 1 in the form of a big quartet for two sopranos and two basses – Marya, her parents, Shalïgin – that effectively monumentalizes the dramatic turning-point (the Voyevoda claims Marya for his bride). At his publisher's request, Tchaikovsky prepared a piano pot-pourri on themes from *Voyevoda*, issued in 1868 under the pseudonym 'H. Cramer'.

The opera was twice reconstructed in Soviet times from the composer's sketches and the surviving orchestral and choral parts: first by Sergey Popov in 1927, later by Pavel Lamm with the composers Vissarion Shebalin and Yury Kochurov. Their version was performed (to a Sovietized libretto by S. D. Spassky) in Leningrad (Malïy Theatre, 28 September 1949).

RICHARD TARUSKIN

Voyna i mir. Opera by Sergey Prokofiev; *see* WAR AND PEACE.

Vranický, Pavel. *See* WRANITZKY, PAUL.

Vrazh'ya sila ('The Power of the Fiend'; 'Hostile Power'). Opera in five acts by ALEXANDER NIKOLAYEVICH SEROV to a libretto by ALEXANDER NIKOLAYEVICH OSTROVSKY (Acts 1–3), Pyotr Kalashnikov and Alexander Zhokhov (Acts 4 and 5)

after Ostrovsky's play *Ne tak zhivi, kak khochetsya, a tak, kak bog velit* ('Live Not the Way you'd Like, but as God Commands', 1855), completed after the composer's death by his widow Valentina Serova and Nikolay Solov'yov; St Petersburg, Mariinsky Theatre, 19 April/1 May 1871.

Ostrovsky's play, designated a 'comedy' because of its happy ending, was valued by its contemporaries for its portrayal of the confined domestic life of the Moscow merchant class and for its sustained ironic counterpoint of dark doings against the background of the Shrovetide carnival. Pyotr (baritone, in the opera), a young merchant, bored by his wife Dasha (soprano) and oppressed by his strict father, philanders with Grunya (mezzo-soprano), the daughter of Spiridonovna (contralto) the local innkeeper, and, under the influence of a sinister blacksmith named Yeryomka (bass), briefly considers murder as a means of escape. He bethinks himself in time, however, and the play ends with an affirmation of the patriarchal order. As he often did, Ostrovsky peppered the play liberally with proverbs and quotations from folksongs. The chance of using folksongs as the bearer of the drama at every level from recitative to act-finishing ensemble, plus the broad musical possibilities inherent in the carnival background, were what attracted Serov to the play, recommended to him by his close friend the poet Apollon Grigor'yev. Ostrovsky agreed to turn his prose drama into a verse libretto.

The collaboration foundered when Ostrovsky, without warning, insisted on introducing fantastic characters into the carnival scene, and Serov, also without warning, insisted on having the opera end not with reconciliation but with Dasha's murder. The suddenness of the composer's change of heart is reflected in the music. The first three acts are for the most part cast in a lightish, popular idiom reminiscent of the vaudevilles and Singspiels of an earlier age. In Act 4, set amid the carnival, dark recitative – still incorporating folkish turns of phrase – all at once predominates and contrasts tellingly with the teeming background of choral revels and realistic genre music (vendors' cries, bear trainer, drunks, etc.) that directly foreshadows the outer tableaux of *Petrushka*. The last music he lived to write, this act is in itself surely Serov's most striking achievement, but it created a fatal stylistic unevenness in the opera. The posthumous première was conducted by Eduard Nápravník, with Yuliya Platonova as Dasha, Gennady Kondrat'yev as Pyotr, Dar'ya Leonova as Spiridonovna and Mikhail Sariotti as Yeryomka.

Had he lived to finish the work, the composer would probably have mitigated this flaw. (The fifth act, grimmer yet than the fourth, was not his work, though based to an undetermined extent on his sketches and on music his widow had heard him play.) As it is, the opera remains an erratic and tantalizing near miss, probably unrevivable (as a disastrous 1947 attempt by the Bol'shoy Theatre, in a new version completed by Boris Asaf'yev, seemed to suggest). The grisly role of Yeryomka is unquestionably a first-class conception. A favourite of Fyodor Stravinsky and later of Shalyapin, it contains two excellent numbers: the holiday song in Act 2, 'Shirokaya maslenitsa' ('Great Shrovetide'), and above all the hair-raising song to the balalaika – deftly imitated in the orchestra – in the Act 3 finale, 'Ti, kupets, so mnoyu luchshe ne branis'' ('Merchant man, you'd do better not to chide me'), where Serov, in a manner worthy of the greatest musical dramatists, was able to convey a palpable sense of horror through music that is on the surface trifling and gay.

RICHARD TARUSKIN

Vrchlický, Jaroslav [Frída, Emil] (*b* Louny, 17 Feb 1853; *d* Domažlice, 9 Sept 1912). Czech poet, librettist and dramatist. He was one of the finest Czech poets and translators of his time whose works attracted many musical settings, for instance songs by J. B. Foerster and Ostrčil and cantatas by Janáček. He is particularly associated with Fibich, for whom he wrote four librettos, and Dvořák, providing texts for the oratorio *Svatá Ludmila* and his final opera, *Armida*. Vrchlický's librettos incline to the lyrical, as is evident in those he based on Shakespeare: his Miranda is more important than his Prospero, and in his version of *The Merchant of Venice* (significantly retitled *Jessika*) the trial scene was omitted and restored only in a later revision.

LIBRETTOS

Švanda dudák [Švanda the Bagpiper], Bendl, 1881 as cantata, rev. as 'opera-ballet', 1907; *Hippodamie* (3 plays), Fibich, 1890–91, as 3 stage melodramas; *Armida* (after T. Tasso: *Gerusalemme liberata*), Kovařovic, comp. 1888–95, inc. (Dvořák, 1904); *Jessika* (after W. Shakespeare: *The Merchant of Venice*), J. B. Foerster, 1905, rev. 1906 [written orig. for Bendl]; *Bouře* [The Tempest] (after Shakespeare), Fibich, 1895; *Záboj*, E. Chvála, 1918

WORKS ON WHICH OPERAS HAVE BEEN BASED

Noc na Karlštejně [A Night at Karlštejn] (play, 1885): V. Novák, 1916, as Karlštejn

Pomsta Catullova [Catullus's Revenge] (play, 1887): Chlubna, 1921

Satanella (epic poem, 1874): Rozkošný, 1898

Bratří [Brothers] (play, 1889): E. Němeček, 1934, inc.

Trojí políbení [Three Kisses] (play, 1892): Němeček, comp. 1915, unperf.

Bar Kochba (epic poem, 1897): Suda, 1905

*

ČSHS [incl. texts used for all musical genres]

L. Kundera: 'Jaroslav Vrchlický a hudba' [Jaroslav Vrchlický and Music], *Tempo – Listy Hudební matice*, xx (1932–3), 286–95

L. Boháček: 'Jaroslav Vrchlický a dramatická hudba' [Vrchlický and Dramatic Music], *Hudební věstník*, xxx (1937), 150–52; also pubd separately

O. Šourek: 'Karel Kovařovic a Vrchlického "Armida"', *Smetana*, xxxvi (1943), 53–5

A. Rektorys, ed.: *Zdeněk Fibich: sborník dokumentů a studií o jeho životě a díle* [Zdeněk Fibich: an Anthology of Documents and Studies about his Life and Work], i (Prague, 1951) [incl. correspondence]

A. Pražák: *Vrchlický v dopisech* [Vrchlický in Letters] (Prague, 1955), 425, 460, 520

R. Šťastný: *Čeští spisovatelé desetí století* [Czech Writers of Ten Centuries] (Prague, 1974) [incl. further bibliography]

B. Balajka: *Jaroslav Vrchlický* (Prague, 1979)

K. Homolová and others, eds.: *Čeští spisovatelé 19. a počátku 20. století: slovníková příručka* [Czech Writers of the 19th and Early 20th Centuries: Handbook] (Prague, 1982)

J. Tyrrell: *Czech Opera* (Cambridge, 1988), 114–16

JOHN TYRRELL

Vreuls, Victor (Jean Léonard) (*b* Verviers, 4 Feb 1876; *d* St Josse-ten-Noode, Brussels, 27 July 1944). Belgian composer. He studied at the conservatories of Verviers and Liège and went to Paris to complete his studies with d'Indy. He taught at the Schola Cantorum and then became director of the Luxembourg conservatory (1906–26); he was elected to the Belgian Royal Academy in 1925. He wrote two operas, *Olivier le simple* (3, J. Delacre; Brussels, Monnaie, 9 March 1922) and *Un songe d'une nuit d'été* (3, P. Spaak, after W. Shakespeare; Brussels, Monnaie, 17 Dec 1925) and many other works, most of them instrumental. Of the Belgian composers of his generation, he was the closest to the Franckian tradition. He often drew material from Walloon folk music. HENRI VANHULST

Vroons, Frans [Franciscus] (*b* Amsterdam, 28 April 1911). Dutch tenor. He studied in Amsterdam and Paris, making his début in 1938 as Mozart's Don Curzio. In 1945 he became leading tenor of the newly formed Netherlands Opera, with which he sang for nearly 20 years. He made his Covent Garden début in 1948 as Don José and appeared at San Francisco in 1951 as Des Grieux (Massenet's *Manon*). His wide repertory included Tamino, Florestan, Max, Huon (*Oberon*), Hoffmann and Riccardo (*Un ballo in maschera*), and he also sang in many 20th-century operas: as Pelléas, Laca (*Jenůfa*), Aegisthus (*Elektra*), Gonzalve (*L'heure espagnole*), Stravinsky's Oedipus, Peter Grimes and Sellem (*The Rake's Progress*). In 1960 he created the title role of Henk Badings's *Martin Korda D.P.* A sturdy singer who could encompass both lyric and dramatic parts, he was an excellent actor.
ELIZABETH FORBES

V studni ('In the Well'). Comic opera in one act by VILÉM BLODEK to a libretto by KAREL SABINA; Prague, Provisional Theatre, 17 November 1867.

Lidunka (soprano), a young village girl, consults Veruna (contralto), a 'witch'. Her mother wants her to marry the wealthy widower Janek (bass); Lidunka however prefers the handsome young Vojtěch (tenor). Both men have secretly followed her to Veruna's outlying cottage and overhear the advice she gets: when the full moon rises (it is midsummer eve) Lidunka should return, cry out 'Where are you, my beloved?' and look into the well, where she will see the face of her beloved. In separate arias Vojtěch and Janek register their eagerness that Lidunka should see their faces; to make sure, Janek plans to climb into the leafy tree above the well and look down into it. After an orchestral intermezzo depicting the rising of the moon, a chorus of young people celebrate the summer solstice. Janek climbs up into the tree. He is followed by Vojtěch, who has consulted Veruna and has been told to climb the tree. Janek climbs higher, his branch breaks and he plunges into the well. Lidunka enters, calls for her beloved and looks into the well, and to her dismay sees Janek. When the chorus come to investigate, Janek emerges, covered in mud. Vojtěch takes advantage of Janek's humiliation and is united with Lidunka.

Sabina's text belongs with those he wrote for other Czech composers (Smetana, Bendl, Rozkošný) based on Czech village milieux and customs. Unlike the original version of *The Bartered Bride* it is continuously sung, with an overture, five arias, two duets, a quartet, intermezzo and three numbers involving a chorus and soloists. It is often taken to be quintessentially 'Czech', but its tuneful style and sturdy craftsmanship owe as much to Nicolai and Lortzing as to Smetana. JOHN TYRRELL

Vuataz, Roger (*b* Geneva, 4 Jan 1898; *d* Geneva, 2 Aug 1988). Swiss composer. After studying in Geneva, he played an important part in the musical life of that city, primarily in the development of music broadcasting, but also as organist, conductor, lecturer and teacher. He started work in radio in 1926 and was director of music for Radio Geneva from 1944 to 1963, becoming president of the Geneva International Competition (1963–78). His compositional output was considerable, with a preponderance of religious music. Among his dramatic works are ballets and music for the theatre, cinema and radio. His *opéra bouffe Monsieur Jabot* op.100 (1; G. Hoffmann, after R. Toepffer), first performed in Geneva at the Théâtre du Grand Casino on 28 November 1958, set out to ridicule the artificiality of grand opera. The music of Gluck influenced his second opera, the lyric tragedy *Cora, amour et mort* op.130 (1, Vuataz; Geneva, Salle Ernest Ansermet, 6 Dec 1985); the work is set in Renaissance Florence, and the vocal style is declamatory, over dramatic orchestration. Rejecting any particular school, he forged a personal idiom that uses some 20th-century developments within tonal structures. PIERRE MEYLAN

Vulpius, Christian August (*b* Weimar, 23 Jan 1762; *d* Weimar, 26 June 1827). German writer. A copyist's son from a large family, he was mostly self-educated as a youth. Later he studied law at Jena and Erlangen, then supported himself and his siblings by his pen. Goethe, who lived with and subsequently married Vulpius's sister Christiane, tried to help him secure various positions. Vulpius translated and adapted Italian and German opera texts for the Bellomo company at Weimar during the 1780s, and supplied over two dozen new versions of previously composed operas to the Weimar court theatre, under Goethe's direction from 1791 to 1817. On obtaining a position in the Weimar library in 1797, Vulpius turned to cultural-historical studies. The University of Jena conferred the PhD on him in 1809, and in 1816 he was knighted by the Weimar court. Vulpius's original librettos, like his popular novels, show a decided taste for the sentimental, picaresque and supernatural. During the 1790s his revisions of several of Schikaneder's librettos – by no means improvements – sparked a war of words between the two.

Der Trank der Unsterblichkeit (Vorspiel), Walter, 1783; *Der Schleyer* (Spl), Wolf, 1786; *Die Feyer im Reich der Feen* (allegorisches Vorspiel mit Gesang), 1787; *Das hätt' ich nicht gedacht!* (Spl), Burgmüller, 1788; *Der glückliche Tag* (Vorspiel), Tuch, 1789; *Bella und Fernando, oder Die Satire* (Operette), Kospoth, 1790; *Hokus-Pokus!* (komische Oper), Dittersdorf, 1791; *Elisinde* (Original-Operette), Dieter, 1794
THOMAS BAUMAN

Výlety páně Broučkovy. Opera by Leoš Janáček; *see* *EXCURSIONS OF MR BROUČEK, THE.*

Vyvyan, Jennifer (Brigit) (*b* Broadstairs, 13 March 1925; *d* London, 5 April 1974). English soprano. She studied at the RAM, and with Roy Henderson and Fernando Carpi. She made her début in 1948 with the English Opera Group, at Cambridge, as Jenny Diver in the première of Britten's version of *The Beggar's Opera*, and in 1951 created the Matron in Easdale's *The Sleeping Children* at Cheltenham. She sang Konstanze and Donna Anna at Sadler's Wells (1952) and Electra (*Idomeneo*) with Glyndebourne at Edinburgh (1953). She created Penelope Rich in *Gloriana* (1953, Covent Garden); the Governess in *The Turn of the Screw* (1954, Venice); Titania in *A Midsummer Night's Dream* (1960, Aldeburgh Festival); the Countess de Serindan in *The Violins of Saint-Jacques* (1966, Sadler's Wells); four roles in Williamson's *Lucky-Peter's Journey* (1969, Sadler's Wells) and Mrs Julian in *Owen Wingrave* (1971, BBC television). Her repertory included Polissena (*Radamisto*), Armida (*Rinaldo*), Achilles (*Deidamia*) and other Handel roles, while Miss Wordsworth and Lady Billows in *Albert Herring* demonstrated her comic gifts. An excellent actress, she had a voice of astonishing flexibility, sometimes edgy in tone but always secure in intonation.

For illustration *see* TURN OF THE SCREW, THE. ALAN BLYTH

Vzkriesenie ('Resurrection'). Opera in three acts by JÁN CIKKER to a libretto by the composer after LEV NIKOLAYEVICH TOLSTOY's novel; Prague, National Theatre, 18 May 1962.

Before his departure for battle Nechl'udov (baritone) meets his aunt's 16-year-old foster-daughter, Katuša (soprano) and seduces her. Pregnant, she is thrown out of the house; when the baby dies she becomes a prostitute. In a bordello, in order to escape the advances of a Merchant (tenor), she has the Waiter (baritone) give him a sleeping draught. But the waiter administers poison and Katuša is arrested for the merchant's murder.

At her trial Nechl'udov is a juror. The case against her is not proved, but she is sentenced to hard labour on account of her depravity. Stricken with remorse, Nechl'udov follows her to prison, but he is rejected by her and pilloried by the other prisoners. At a second visit he offers to marry her, but she has already promised herself to a Political Prisoner (tenor). Nechl'udov pleads to be allowed to continue to see her when he has obtained her pardon from the tsar. He gives up his estate and follows Katuša to Siberia. Exhausted, she dies in his arms as he tells her of her pardon.

The action is relayed not only by conventional means but also by the use of three intermezzos that explore the secret fears and desires of the characters. Cikker's musical language is fundamentally tonal, but makes use of bitonality and harmonies built on augmented 4ths as well as pure consonances. The vocal lines are declamatory, and often appear to be independent of the orchestral texture.

IGOR VAJDA

Waart, Edo de. *See* DE WAART, EDO.

Wachmann, Ion [Ioan] **Andrei** (*b* Budapest, 1807; *d* Bucharest, 1863). Hungarian composer and conductor active in Romania. He served as conductor for operatic troupes based in Timişoara and Bucharest before taking charge of the national theatres of Bucharest (1852–8) and Craiova (1858–60). He was a prolific composer for the stage, specializing in lighter genres and writing some 15 operettas, over 30 vaudevilles and numerous musical comedies; he also wrote the national opera *Mihai Bravul în ajunul bătăliei de la Călugăreni* ('Michael the Brave on the Eve of the Battle of Călugăreni'), concerning the revolutionary activities of the Romanian prince Michael (*d* 1601). His other substantial works included the fairy operas *Fata aerului* ('The Maid of the Air') and *Roza magică* ('The Magic Rose'). He also taught the piano and composition in Bucharest.

selective list

Braconierul [The Poachers] (3), Bucharest, 11 Nov 1833; Zamfira, 1834; Triumful amorului [The Triumph of Love] (vaudeville, 2, E. Winterhalder), Bucharest, 11 Dec 1835; Mihai Braval în ajunal bătăliei de la Călugăreni [Michael the Brave on the Eve of the Battle of Călugăreni] (I. Rădulescu), Bucharest, 1848; Zoe, or Amor romanesc (vaudeville, E. Scribe and Mélesville [A.-H.-J. Duveyrier]), Bucharest, National, 31 Dec 1852

O comoară (vaudeville, I. Caragiale); Claca tărăească (vaudeville, Caragiale); Faust şi Margareta (vaudeville, after J. W. von Goethe); Lumpatius vagabondus (vaudeville, 4, J. N. Nestroy); Îngîmfata plăpumăreasă (comedy vaudeville, 2, C. Caragiale); Ninon, Nanon şi Maintenon (vaudeville, 3, M. Théaulon, A. Dartois and Lesguillon), Bucharest, National, 7 Jan 1854; Fata aerului [The Maid of the Air] (fairy op, 5, C. T. Cognard and Raymond)

Banul Craiovei (lyric drama); Cearta e din rai (vaudeville); Bărbatul fără nume (operetta, 3); Amorul dracului (vaudeville); Doi soldaţi români (vaudeville); Fata deputatului (vaudeville, M. Millo); Soldatul român (vaudeville, 1, S. Mihalescu); Prăpăstiile Bucurąstilor (comedy vaudeville, 5, Millo); Iuditha şi Olofern (parody operetta, 2, Scribe and A. Bayard); Roza magică [The Magic Rose] (fairy op, 4, after *Pied de mouton*)

*

V. Cosma: 'Un fragment de operă românească din annul 1848', *Studii de muzicologie*, no.1 (1956)

O. Cosma: *Opera românească* (Budapest, 1962)

V. Cosma: *Muzicieni români* (Bucharest, 1970)

Wachtel, Theodor (*b* Hamburg, 10 March 1823; *d* Frankfurt, 14 Nov 1893). German tenor. He studied with Julie Grandjean and made his début at Hamburg in 1849. After singing in Hanover, Dresden and other German cities, he appeared at the Berlin Hofoper between 1862 and 1879, but could not be given a permanent engagement because of a broken contract at Kassel. He made his London début in 1862 as Edgardo (*Lucia di Lammermoor*) at Covent Garden, where he also sang Salvator Rosa in Flotow's *Alessandro Stradella* (1864) and Vasco da Gama in *L'Africaine* (1865), both first London performances. He returned to Covent Garden in 1870 and sang at Her Majesty's Theatre in 1877. His roles included Arnold (*Guillaume Tell*), Manrico (*Il trovatore*), John of Leyden (*Le prophète*), Pollione (*Norma*), Raoul (*Les Huguenots*) and Elvino (*La sonnambula*), but his favourite part, and the one he sang most often, was Chapelou in Adam's *Le postillon de Lonjumeau*, which showed off not only his stentorian top notes (he commanded a powerful chest high C), but also his ability to crack a whip.

*

J. Kapp: *Geschichte der Staatsoper Berlin* (Berlin, 1937)

H. Fetting: *Die Geschichte der Deutschen Staatsoper* (Berlin, 1955)

ELIZABETH FORBES

Wächter, Johann Michael (*b* Rappersdorf, 2 March 1794; *d* Dresden, 26 May 1853). Austrian baritone. He sang in various church choirs in Vienna and made his stage début in 1819 at Graz as Don Giovanni. Engagements at Bratislava, Vienna and Berlin followed; then in 1827 he joined the Dresden Hofoper, where he remained for the rest of his career. His roles included Mozart's Figaro, Sherasmin (*Oberon*), Mikéli (Cherubini's *Les deux journées*) and Brian de Bois-Guilbert (Marschner's *Der Templer und die Jüdin*). He sang in three Wagner premières, as Orsini in *Rienzi* (1842), as the Dutchman (1843) and as Biterolf in *Tannhäuser* (1845). Berlioz, who heard *Der fliegende Holländer* in Dresden, considered Wächter's baritone 'one of the finest I have ever heard, and he uses it like a consummate singer. It is of that rich and vibrant timbre that has such a wonderful power of expression, provided that the artist sings with soul and feeling, which Wächter does to a high degree' (*Mémoires*). His wife, the mezzo Thérèse Wächter-Wittman (*b* Vienna, 31 August 1802), also sang at Dresden; she created Mary in *Der fliegende Holländer*. ELIZABETH FORBES

Wade, Joseph Augustine (*b* Dublin, *c*1801; *d* London, 15 July 1845). Irish composer. He claimed to have been a student at Trinity College, Dublin, and the Irish

College of Surgeons, but his name is not recorded at these institutions. Having decided to devote himself to music, he moved to London in 1821, conducting opera at the King's Theatre. In 1826 his comic opera *The Two Houses of Grenada* (to his own libretto) was successfully produced at Drury Lane, and his song 'Meet me by moonlight alone' became immensely popular. His style was strongly influenced by that of Henry Bishop, though it lacks technical assurance. The two best-known numbers from *The Two Houses of Grenada*, 'Love was once a little boy' and 'I've wandered in dreams', demonstrate that Wade possessed the knack of hitting upon the kind of quasi-folktune that is immediately memorable. After these initial successes, however, he began to go downhill, 'increasing the confusion of his brain by copious potations of any fluid which at the moment might be before him' (Richardson). His obituary in *The Musical World* recalled that he would 'sit up all night with a bevy of roaring blades ... and having seen every man dispatched to his home or laid on the floor, would bawl out lustily for the landlord to come and *finish the night* with him'. A self-taught dilettante, Wade nevertheless possessed a remarkable talent, and his over-indulgence in alcohol and eventual dependence on opium are all the more regrettable for that.

The Two Houses of Grenada (comic op, J. A. Wade), London, Drury Lane, 31 Oct 1826, selections (London, 1826)
The Convent Belles (comic op, T. H. Bayly), London, Adelphi, 8 July 1833, collab. W. Hawes
The Pupil of Da Vinci (burletta, M. Lemon), London, St James's, 30 Nov 1839

*

DNB (F. G. Edwards); *Grove1* (R. P. Stewart); *Grove6* (N. Temperley)
Musical World, xx (1845), 385–6, 501
J. Richardson: *Recollections*, i (London, 1856), 231–8

NIGEL BURTON

Wadsworth, Stephen (*b* Mt Kisco, NY, 3 April 1953). American director, librettist and translator. He began his career as a journalist, then worked as a stage director and as artistic director of Skylight Opera in Milwaukee, where his first production was *L'incoronazione di Poppea* (1982), followed by *Orfeo* and *Il ritorno d'Ulisse in patria*. For Bernstein he wrote the libretto of *A Quiet Place* (1983), which he also directed at La Scala and in Vienna. His productions of Gluck's *Orphée* (1988, Seattle), and Handel's *Xerxes* (1985, Milwaukee), *Alcina* (1987, St Louis) and *Partenope* (1988, Omaha) all furthered his concern with the modern interpretation of Baroque opera. He has also translated Monteverdi's *Orfeo* and the three Handel works mentioned, and has given classes at many American colleges; he was Head of the Opera Program at the Manhattan School of Music in 1991. His work for the stage is distinguished by a concern for the clarity of story-telling, a preference for opera in English and an awareness of trends in other artistic fields. Other productions include *Fidelio* and *La clemenza di Tito* (1991, Scottish Opera), *Die Entführung* (1990, San Francisco) and *Der fliegende Holländer* (1989, Seattle). For Skylight Opera he also wrote the music-theatre pieces *Bernstein Revued* (1986), *The Telephone Show* (1989) and *Close-Harmony Holidays* (1989).

PATRICK O'CONNOR

Waechter, Eberhard (*b* Vienna, 9 July 1929; *d* Vienna, 29 March 1992). Austrian baritone. After study at Vienna University and the Akademie für Musik he took singing lessons from Elisabeth Rado. His début at the Volksoper in 1953 as Silvio in *Pagliacci* led to his engagement at the Staatsoper in 1955. His career advanced rapidly: a fine Posa in *Don Carlos* at the Staatsoper in 1956 helped to establish him. The same year he enjoyed considerable success as Count Almaviva in *Figaro* at Covent Garden; in 1958 he was heard as Amfortas and Wolfram at Bayreuth, and engagements followed at the principal houses of Europe and the USA, though his Metropolitan début in 1961 as Wolfram was his only appearance there. Although he was not always wise in his choice of parts (in 1964 he was not ready for a role such as Wotan in *Das Rheingold*), Waechter's warm, expressive voice and fine bearing brought him success in such varied roles as Escamillo, Kurwenal, Don Giovanni, Ford, Scarpia, Mandryka and Wozzeck, and Danton in von Einem's *Dantons Tod*; in 1980 he created Joseph in von Einem's controversial *Jesu Hochzeit* in Vienna. By then he was taking on character parts, such as the Music-master (*Ariadne auf Naxos*), Giovanni Morone (*Palestrina*) and Melchior (*Amahl and the Night Visitors*). He became director of the Vienna Volksoper in September 1987 and, in addition, four years later was appointed artistic co-director with Joan (Ion) Holender of the Staatsoper, where he was charged with the task of re-establishing the old ensemble system.

PETER BRANSCOMBE

Waelput, Hendrik [Henri, Henry] (*b* Ghent, 26 Oct 1845; *d* Ghent, 8 July 1885). Belgian conductor and composer. He studied at the Brussels Conservatory with Fétis and Hanssens and in 1867 won the Prix de Rome with his cantata *Het woud*. He was director of the music school at Bruges, 1869–71; for the next five years he appeared as a conductor at theatres in The Hague, Dijon, Boulogne-sur-Mer, Douai, Issoudun, Fécamp and Lille. He then became principal conductor at the Ghent Theatre and professor at the Vlaamsche Muziekschool in Antwerp. In 1884 he was made director of the Ghent Opera.

Waelput's works include three operas in a high Romantic style (all in *B-Gc*): *La ferme du diable* (V. Wilder and E. Houdet; 1865, Ghent), *Berken de diamantslijper* (K. Versnayen; 1868) and *Stella* (I. Teirlinck and R. Stijns; Brussels, Alhambra, 14 March 1881).

*

P. Bergmans: *Notice biographique sur Henri Waelput* (Ghent, 1886)
E. Callaert: *Levensschets van Hendrik Waelput* (Ghent, 1886)
E. De Vynck: *Henry Waelput* (diss., U. of Brussels, 1935)

ANNE-MARIE RIESSAUW

Waffenschmied, Der [*Der Waffenschmied von* [*zu*] *Worms* ('The Armourer of Worms')]. *Komische Oper* by ALBERT LORTZING to his own libretto after Friedrich Wilhelm von Ziegler's comedy *Liebhaber und Nebenbuhler in einer Person*; Vienna, Theater an der Wien, 30 May 1846.

The opera is set in Worms in the 16th century. Count von Liebenau (baritone), under the assumed name of Conrad, is working as an apprentice of the celebrated armourer and veterinarian Hans Stadinger (bass). The count has disguised himself in order to be near Stadinger's daughter Marie (soprano), with whom he is in love. Liebenau presents himself to Marie as his real self (she does not realize the count is the same person as Conrad) and offers his hand in marriage. Towards the end of Act 1 she struggles to decide between the humble apprentice Conrad, whom she loves, and the prospect of an exalted position as the wife of a nobleman whom she hardly knows; she decides for Conrad. In Act 2 the confusion is compounded when Stadinger, who approves neither of Liebenau (because he is an aristocrat) nor of Conrad (because he thinks him a bad worker and worthless), signifies that another of his apprentices, Georg (tenor; actually Liebenau's squire in disguise), should marry Marie. At the celebration of Stadinger's silver jubilee as a master armourer, Irmentraut (mezzo-soprano), Marie's governess, rushes in to report that the count's servants have abducted Marie. But Conrad soon appears with Marie, announcing that he has rescued her. Stadinger only gives her the option of marrying Georg or entering a convent. In the final act Stadinger eventually gives way to persuasion and allows Conrad and Marie to be married; he is furious when he discovers that she has actually married Liebenau, but grudgingly gives them his blessing.

By the time he composed *Der Waffenschmied*, Lortzing was well established as the leading German composer of comic opera, and had enjoyed considerable acclaim with his *Undine* in 1845. He conducted the première of *Der Waffenschmied* about a month after taking up his post as Kapellmeister at the Theater an der Wien. It was an instant success and soon widely performed. In procedure and character the opera is in many respects similar to *Zar und Zimmermann*. It contains folksong-like elements such as Georg's 'War einst ein junger Springinsfeld' and Stadinger's 'Auch ich war ein Jüngling mit lokkigem Haar'. It also has numbers of greater musical weight, including Marie's recitative and aria 'Er schläft!', which concludes the first act's finale. The sextet and the septet demonstrate Lortzing's continuing mastery of the comic ensemble, though it is questionable whether they or the finales reach quite the same level as the best of his earlier ensembles. Only in the orchestration, which seems to have benefited from the experience gained in composing *Undine*, does Lortzing show a significant advance on his previous comic operas.

CLIVE BROWN

Wagenaar, Johan (*b* Utrecht, 1 Nov 1862; *d* The Hague, 17 June 1941). Dutch composer. He studied composition and the organ in Utrecht and Berlin. He began his career in Utrecht as a teacher and as cathedral organist, also working as a choral conductor. In 1919 he was appointed director of the Conservatory of The Hague, where he remained until 1937. He enjoyed a great reputation as a composer, organist, choral conductor and teacher; among his pupils was Willem Pijper.

In his early years Wagenaar was strongly influenced by Brahms, though Berlioz and, in particular, Strauss also attracted him, and he was able to assimilate all of these models into an individual style. In the quasi-serious operas *De Doge van Venetie* op.20 (M. P. Lindo; Utrecht, Stadsschouwberg, 13 April 1901) and *De Cid* op.27 (Lindo; Stadsschouwberg, 14 April 1916) he chose to draw attention to the false romanticism, surface sentimentality and ridiculousness of so many Romantic operas.

*

E. W. Schallenberg: 'Joh. Wagenaar's Opera's', *Muziekhistorische perspectieven* (Amsterdam, 1939), 108–14

JOS WOUTERS

Wagenseil, Georg Christoph (*b* Vienna, 29 Jan 1715; *d* Vienna, 1 March 1777). Austrian composer. In his teens his musical accomplishments brought him to the attention of the Viennese court Kapellmeister, Johann Joseph Fux, who recommended him for a court scholarship in 1735; for the next three years he received intensive instruction from his sponsor and from Matteo Palotta. He was appointed composer to the court in 1739, and held the post until his death. He also served as organist from 1741 to 1750 in the private chapel of Empress Elisabeth Christine (widow of Charles VI), becoming *Hofklaviermeister* to the imperial archduchesses.

Wagenseil travelled to Venice in 1745 to supervise the production of his first opera, *Ariodante*, and in 1759–60 he was in Milan for a performance of *Demetrio*. From the mid-1750s he produced a flood of instrumental compositions which raised him to international prominence. Burney and the young Mozart were acquainted with his works, as was Haydn; the operas found their way to Eisenstadt. Though renowned as a keyboard virtuoso and teacher – his pupils included Johann Mederitsch, Franz Teyber and J. B. Schenk – he had to curtail his activities at court from about 1765 owing to illness.

Wagenseil contributed to most of the genres current in his day. His earliest compositions are in a late Baroque style, but after about mid-century he showed a growing command of the *galant* idiom; his symphonies and keyboard music in particular were important for the formation of the Classical style. Most of his theatrical works were written during the period 1745 to 1750 for festivities celebrating the name-day or birthday of various members of the imperial family. He soon introduced diminutive arias in folk or *galant* style, expressive accompanied recitatives and finely wrought choruses to disrupt the traditional sequence of recitatives and da capo arias to which he still adhered in his earliest works. But the most significant progressive feature is the welding of aria, ensemble, recitative and chorus into large unified tableaux, exemplified in its most mature form by the central scene between Orpheus and Eurydice which Wagenseil wrote in 1750 for the pasticcio *Euridice* and which pointed the way to Gluck's operatic reform of 1762.

unless otherwise stated, first performed in Vienna and MSS in A-Wn

Ariodante (dramma per musica, 3, A. Salvi, after L. Ariosto), Venice, S Giovanni Grisostomo, aut. 1745

La clemenza di Tito (dramma per musica, 3, P. Metastasio), Burg, 15 Oct 1746

Demetrio (dramma per musica, 3, Metastasio), Florence, Pergola, 26 Dec 1746, *I-Nc*

Alessandro nell' Indie (3, Metastasio), Burg, 11 Aug 1748

Il Siroe (dramma per musica, 3, Metastasio), Burg, 4 Oct 1748

L'olimpiade (3, Metastasio), Hof, 14 May 1749

Antigono (dramma per musica, 3, Metastasio), Schönbrunn, 14 May 1750

Vincislao (dramma per musica, 3), Burg, 8 Dec 1750

Le cacciatrici amanti (festa teatrale, 2, G. Durazzo), Laxenburg, 25 June 1755

Prometeo assoluto (serenata, G. A. Migliavacca), bei Hofe, 24 March 1762

Contribs. to: Andromeda, 1750; Euridice, 1750; Armida placata, 1750; Catone and Merope, cited in *MGG*

*

Burney GN; *MGG*

I. de Luca: 'Das Andenken Georgs Christophs von Wagnseil k. k. Hofcompositors in Wien', *Kaiserlich königliche allergnädigst privilegierte Realzeitung der Wissenschaften, Künste und Kommerzien*, xxvi (23 Sept 1777), 405

W. Vetter: 'Georg Christoph Wagenseil, ein Vorläufer Christoph Willibald Glucks', *ZMw*, viii (1925–6), 385–402

——: 'Der Opernkomponist Georg Christoph Wagenseil und sein Verhältnis zu Mozart und Gluck', *Gedenkschrift für Hermann Abert* (Halle, 1928), 165–76

——: 'Zur Entwicklungsgeschichte der opera seria um 1750 in Wien', *ZMw*, xiv (1931–2), 2–28

——: 'Der deutsche Charakter der italienischen Oper Georg Christoph Wagenseils', *Festschrift Karl Gustav Fellerer zum 60. Geburtstag* (Regensburg, 1962), 558–72
——: 'Italienische Opernkomponisten um Georg Christoph Wagenseil: ein stilkundlicher Versuch', *Festschrift Friedrich Blume* (Kassel, 1963), 363–74 JOHN KUCABA

Wagner. German family of musicians.

(1) **(Wilhelm) Richard Wagner** (*b* Leipzig, 22 May 1813; *d* Venice, 13 Feb 1883). Composer. One of the key figures in the history of opera, Wagner was largely responsible for altering its orientation in the 19th century. His programme of artistic reform, though not executed to the last detail, accelerated the trend towards organically conceived, through-composed structures, as well as influencing the development of the orchestra, of a new breed of singer, and of various aspects of theatrical practice.

1. The formative years: 1813–32. 2. Early career: 1833–42. 3. Kapellmeister in Dresden: 1843–9. 4. Zürich essays. 5. Composer in exile: 1849–63. 6. Munich and Bayreuth: 1864–77. 7. 'Regeneration' writings. 8. The final years: 1878–83. 9. Style and structure.

1. THE FORMATIVE YEARS: 1813–32. It is both fitting and psychologically congruous that a question mark should hover over the identity of the father and mother of the composer whose works resonate so eloquently with themes of parental anxiety. Richard Wagner's 'official' father was the police actuary Carl Friedrich Wagner, but the boy's adoptive father, the actor-painter Ludwig Geyer, who took responsibility for the child on Carl Friedrich's death in November 1813, may possibly have been the real father. Wagner himself was never sure, though any concern he may have had about Geyer's supposed Jewish origins would have been misplaced: Geyer was of incontrovertibly Protestant stock. Recent research has further established that Wagner's mother Johanna was not the illegitimate daughter of Prince Constantin of Saxe-Weimar-Eisenach, as previously believed, but his mistress (Gregor-Dellin 1985).

Wagner's formal education began on 2 December 1822 at the Kreuzschule in Dresden, where his mother and stepfather had moved to enable Geyer to undertake engagements for the Hoftheater. On returning to Leipzig with his mother and sisters he entered the Nicolaischule on 21 January 1828, but school studies were less enthusiastically pursued than theatrical and musical interests, which resulted in a 'vast tragic drama' called *Leubald* and conscientious perusal of Logier's composition treatise. Harmony lessons (initially in secret) with a local musician, Christian Gottlieb Müller (1828–31), were followed by enrolment at Leipzig University (23 February 1831) to study music and a short but intensive period of study with the Kantor of the Thomaskirche, Christian Theodor Weinlig (about six months from October 1831).

In his autobiographical writings Wagner later played down the significance of his musical education in order to cultivate the notion of the untutored genius. But its fruits were evident in a series of keyboard and orchestral works written by spring 1832 and particularly in the Beethovenian Symphony in C major which followed shortly after. A genuine passion for Beethoven, while confirmed by such works and the piano transcription of the Ninth Symphony made in 1830–31, was exaggerated in another typical piece of mythification: Wagner's account of a supposedly momentous portrayal of Leonore by the soprano Wilhelmine Schröder-Devrient in Leipzig in 1829 is undermined by the unavailability of any evidence that the singer gave such a performance. Yet the fable (probably a semiconscious conflation of two separate events) attests to the young composer's ambition to be proclaimed the rightful heir to the symphonic tradition embodied in Beethoven.

Wagner's first attempt at an operatic project was a pastoral opera based on Goethe's *Die Laune des Verliebten* (probably from early 1830); the work was aborted with only a scene for three female voices and a tenor aria written. His second project, *Die Hochzeit*, was conceived in October or November 1832, while he was visiting the estate of Count Pachta at Pravonin, near Prague. Based on a story from J. G. G. Büsching's *Ritterzeit und Ritterwesen*, *Die Hochzeit* was a grisly tale of dark passions, treachery and murder. The libretto, according to Wagner's autobiography, *Mein Leben*, was destroyed by him as a demonstration of confidence in the judgment of his sister Rosalie. Such music as was completed, between December 1832 and March 1833 – an introduction, chorus and septet – survives.

2. EARLY CAREER: 1833–42. Wagner's first professional appointment, secured by his brother Albert, was as chorus master at the theatre in Würzburg. There he encountered repertory works by Marschner, Weber, Paer, Cherubini, Rossini and Auber, of which composers the first two influenced him most strongly in his musical setting of *Die Feen* (1833–4), a working by Wagner himself (he was to write all his own librettos) of Gozzi's *La donna serpente*. Returning to Leipzig at the beginning of 1834 he came into contact with the charismatic radical Heinrich Laube (a family friend) and other members of the progressive literary and political movement Junges Deutschland. The writers associated with this uncoordinated grouping, including Karl Gutzkow, Ludolf Wienbarg, Heinrich Heine and Ludwig Börne, rejected not only the classicism of Goethe and Mozart but also what they regarded as the reactionary, socially irrelevant and sentimentally conceived romanticism of Weber and E. T. A. Hoffmann. They turned instead for inspiration to Italy and to the French Utopian Socialists, especially the Saint-Simonians, spurning Catholic mysticism and morality in favour of hedonism and sensuality. It was under these influences that Wagner wrote his essays *Die deutsche Oper* (1834) and *Bellini* (1837), celebrating the italianate capacity for bel canto expressiveness, as well as his next opera *Das Liebesverbot* (1834–6), relocating Shakespeare's *Measure for Measure* in a sun-soaked, pleasure-filled Mediterranean setting; the chief musical models adopted were, appropriately, Bellini and Auber.

It was carnal rather than aesthetic considerations, according to Wagner, that persuaded him to accept a post as musical director of the travelling theatre company run by Heinrich Bethmann: he had fallen instantly in love with one of the leading ladies, Christine Wilhelmine ('Minna') Planer. However, during his term with Bethmann's company (1834–6) he also gained valuable conducting experience and saw *Das Liebesverbot* on to the boards (29 March 1836) for what was to be the only performance in his lifetime.

Minna continued to pursue her theatrical career with engagements at the Königstadt Theater in Berlin and then in Königsberg. Negotiations for Wagner to secure the musical directorship of the opera in the latter city were protracted until 1 April 1837, but in the meantime he had sketched a prose scenario for a grand opera, *Die hohe Braut*, which he sent to Scribe in Paris in the hope that a libretto by him might inspire an Opéra commission. It was Wagner who eventually produced a libretto for *Die hohe Braut* (in Dresden in 1842); it was offered first to Karl Reissiger and then to Ferdinand Hiller, but was finally set by Jan Bedřich Kittl. An already tempestuous relationship with Minna was sealed by their marriage on 24 November 1836. Within months she had abandoned him in favour of a merchant called Dietrich; the rift had been healed only in part when Wagner took up a new post as musical director of the theatre in Riga (the historic capital of Livonia), which was part of the Russian Empire although colonized by Germans. He made the journey alone, arriving on 21 August 1837, but subsequently shared his cramped apartment not only with Minna, but also with her sister Amalie (who had taken up an appointment as singer at the theatre) and a baby wolf. Conditions at the small theatre were similarly constricted and the management unimaginative, though Wagner's enterprise and initiative did result in a series of subscription concerts.

In the summer of 1838 he turned his attention to a comic opera based on a tale from *The Thousand and One Nights*, calling it *Männerlist grösser als Frauenlist, oder Die glückliche Bärenfamilie*. He completed the libretto and began to set it in the manner of a Singspiel, but abandoned it in order to concentrate on a major project that had been simmering since he had read, the previous year, Bulwer-Lytton's novel about the Roman demagogue Rienzi. The poem and some of the music of the five-act grand opera *Rienzi* had been written by August 1838. The Riga appointment turned out to be as precarious for Wagner as his marriage, and after a contractual wrangle he determined to try his luck in the home of grand opera, Paris.

The departure from Riga had to be clandestine; Wagner and his wife were heavily in debt and their passports had been impounded. Under cover of night, Wagner, Minna and their Newfoundland dog, Robber, clambered through a ditch marking the border, under the nose of armed Cossack guards. Then, reaching the Prussian port of Pillau (now Baltiysk), they were smuggled on board a small merchant vessel, the *Thetis*, bound for London. The dangerous, stormy crossing and the crew's shouts echoing round the granite walls of a Norwegian fjord were later represented by Wagner as the creative inspiration for *Der fliegende Holländer*. If any ideas for text or music were jotted down at the time of the sea crossing (July–August 1839), the evidence has not survived. Crossing the channel from Gravesend to Boulogne, Wagner was received there by Meyerbeer, who listened to Wagner's reading of the libretto of *Rienzi, der Letzte der Tribunen* and promised to provide letters of introduction to Duponchel and Habeneck, respectively the director and conductor of the Paris Opéra.

Wagner spent a dismal, penurious two-and-a-half years (September 1839 to April 1842) in Paris, a victim of the sharp social divisions of Louis-Philippe's July Monarchy which reserved wealth and privilege for a bourgeois élite. He was forced to earn his keep by making hack arrangements of operatic selections and by musical journalism in which he lambasted the mediocrities perpetrated by the Opéra. In March 1840 the Théâtre de la Renaissance accepted *Das Liebesverbot*, but the theatre was forced into bankruptcy two months later. There is no evidence to support Wagner's suggestion (made subsequently in *Mein Leben*) that Meyerbeer, through whose agency the work had been accepted, was aware of the imminent bankruptcy. Nor, apparently, did Wagner so believe at the time: on 20 September 1840 he wrote to Apel, 'Meyerbeer has remained untiringly loyal to my interests'. It is psychologically more plausible that Wagner's shameless obsequiousness before an influential patron was later transmuted by frustration and jealousy into the venomous bitterness seen, for example, in *Das Judentum in der Musik*.

In May 1840 Wagner sent Eugène Scribe a copy of his sketch for *Der fliegende Holländer*, and in letters of 3 May and 4 June he mentioned it to Meyerbeer, in the hope that he might use his influence to have the work put on at the Opéra. Meyerbeer introduced him to the new director of the Opéra, Léon Pillet, who bought the story for 500F, supposedly to have it made into an opera by one of the composers under contract to him. In fact, the two librettists given the sketch, Paul Foucher and Bénédict-Henry Révoil, did not, as generally stated, base their work *Le vaisseau fantôme* primarily on it but on a variety of sources including Captain Marryat's *The Phantom Ship* and Sir Walter Scott's *The Pirate*. Wagner meanwhile proceeded to elaborate his scenario into a work of his own and initially he worked on the *Holländer* in tandem with *Rienzi*, which was completed in November 1840.

At this time Wagner was threatened with imprisonment for debt, but the available evidence strongly suggests that the threat was never executed. Partly through Meyerbeer's influence, *Rienzi* was accepted by the Dresden Hoftheater. Preparations were under way by April 1842, when Wagner, deeply disillusioned with Paris, began to make his way back to the fatherland.

3. Kapellmeister in Dresden: 1843–9. The première of *Rienzi* on 20 October 1842 was an immense success, catching as the work did the rebellious spirit of the times. The darker, introspective quality of the *Holländer*, which followed at the Hoftheater on 2 January 1843, was found less appealing. Nevertheless, Wagner was an obvious candidate for the post of Kapellmeister at the King of Saxony's court in Dresden, which had become vacant. The prospect of financial security finally outweighed any doubts he had about accepting a liveried post in the royal service. Contrary to what he had been led to believe, Wagner's status was that of second Kapellmeister, subordinate to that of Reissiger, who since his appointment as Kapellmeister in 1828 had elevated the reputation of the opera house to the highest level, but who by the 1840s was content to rest on his laurels while a younger colleague undertook the more onerous duties.

Those duties included conducting operatic, instrumental and orchestral performances and composing pieces for special court occasions. Among the latter works are numbered *Das Liebesmahl der Apostel* (1843), a biblical scene for male voices and orchestra; *Der Tag erscheint* (1843), a chorus for the unveiling of a monument to the king; *Gruss seiner Treuen an Friedrich August den Geliebten* (1844), another choral tribute to the king; and *An Webers Grabe* (1844), a chorus for the ceremony accompanying the reburial of Weber's remains in his home town (the campaign to effect which Wagner had vigorously supported).

Wagner had begun work on his next major project, *Tannhäuser*, in the summer of 1842, when a detailed prose draft was worked out at Aussig (now Ústí nad Labem) in the Bohemian mountains. It was versified by the spring of the following year and the composition occupied Wagner between July 1843 and April 1845. The first performance took place at the Hoftheater on 19 October 1845. Wagner then spent three months analysing the conditions under which court music was produced at Dresden. His proposals, including a series of winter orchestral concerts, were eminently reasonable, but after a year's delay he was informed that they had been rejected.

Wagner's library in Dresden embraced a broad range of literature, both ancient and modern, from Calderón to Xenophon and Molière to Gibbon. It also contained versions of Gottfried von Strassburg's *Tristan*, editions of the Parzival and Lohengrin epics, and a number of volumes on the medieval cobbler-poet Hans Sachs. The subjects of *Lohengrin* and each of the music dramas to follow the *Ring* are thus likely to have been germinating in his mind during these years. A first prose draft was actually made for *Die Meistersinger von Nürnberg* at Marienbad (now Mariánske Lánskě) in 1845.

An event of major importance for Wagner was his organization in 1846 of a performance of Beethoven's Ninth Symphony (then still considered an unapproachable work) for the traditional Palm Sunday concert in the old opera house. Against considerable opposition from the administration he secured a notable financial and artistic success. The existence of sketches dating from 1846–7 for at least two symphonies bears witness to the inspirational effect the preparations for the Ninth had on Wagner himself.

During these years too he was working on the composition of *Lohengrin*, as well as studying Aeschylus (*Oresteia*), Aristophanes and other Greek authors in translation. In February 1847 he conducted his own arrangement of Gluck's *Iphigénie en Aulide*. His meagre salary (1500 talers per annum) was not enough to cover essential outgoings, but Minna managed the household efficiently and enjoyed the status of Kapellmeister's wife. They remained involuntarily childless (probably as a result of an earlier miscarriage) but in general the marriage was at its most stable at this period.

The insurrectionary outbreaks in Paris in February 1848 and in Vienna the following month were greeted with zealous approbation by the ranks of middle-class German liberals, indignant at the indifference of their princely rulers to social deprivation among the working classes and motivated by fear of their own proletarianization. In Dresden barricades were erected and the king was presented with demands for democratic reform. Wagner's plan for the organization of a German national theatre, which proposed that the director of such an institution be elected, that a drama school be set up, the court orchestra expanded and its administration put under self-management, was a reflection of such democratic principles, and consequently rejected. It is mistaken to see such a proposal – or, indeed, Wagner's involvement in the revolution generally – simply as opportunist. He naturally wished to see the role of the opera house enhanced in a reconstructed society, but such a desire sprang from the conviction that art was the highest and potentially most fruitful form of human endeavour.

He threw in his lot with the insurrectionists when in June 1848 he delivered a speech to the Vaterlandsverein, the leading republican grouping, on the subject of the relation of republican aspirations to the monarchy. The evils of money and speculation were denounced as barriers to the emancipation of the human race, and the downfall of the aristocracy was predicted. The notion that the Saxon king should remain at the head of the new republic, as 'the first and truest republican of all', was not an idiosyncratic one, but in tune with the limited demands of the bourgeois liberals for constitutional government.

Wagner remained for the time being at his post, and began to set down a prose résumé of what was to become *Der Ring des Nibelungen*: *Der Nibelungen-Mythus: als Entwurf zu einem Drama* (October 1848). A prose draft of *Siegfrieds Tod* (later to become *Götterdämmerung*) was made the same month, followed (not preceded, as previously supposed) by the essay *Die Wibelungen: Weltgeschichte aus der Sage* (probably written in about mid-February 1849). Other projects of the period included *Friedrich I* (in five acts, possibly an opera), *Jesus von Nazareth* (probably also intended as a five-act opera, though only a prose draft was completed), *Achilleus* (probably a three-act opera) and *Wieland der Schmied* (a heroic opera in three acts; prose draft). *Wieland* and, in particular, *Jesus von Nazareth* espouse the ideas of Pierre-Joseph Proudhon and Ludwig Feuerbach: ownership of property as the root of evil, supremacy of love over the law, and a new religion of humanity.

Wagner's assistant conductor, August Röckel, was no less of a firebrand, and the weekly republican journal he edited, the *Volksblätter*, contained various inflammatory tirades by Wagner and others. Through Röckel, Wagner came to know Mikhail Bakunin, the Russian anarchist, who in turn was acquainted personally with Marx and Engels. The fact that no works of Marx were contained in Wagner's library at Dresden provides no proof that Wagner was unfamiliar with his ideas: radical theories would have circulated freely in a major city such as Dresden.

Wagner's active role in the Dresden insurrection obliged him to flee for his life when the Prussian troops began to gain control in May 1849. He was sheltered by Liszt at Weimar before making his way on a false passport, via Paris, to Switzerland. A warrant had been issued for his arrest.

4. ZÜRICH ESSAYS. Even after the savage crushing of the 1848–9 uprisings, Wagner continued to believe that both social and artistic reform were imminent. In the first years of his exile in Zürich – he was not to enter Germany again until 1860 – he formulated a set of aesthetic theories intended to establish opera in a radically recast form as at once the instrument and the product of a reconstructed society. In the first of this series of Zürich essays, *Die Kunst und die Revolution* (1849), written under the influence of Proudhon and Feuerbach, Wagner outlined the debasement of art since the era of the glorious, all-embracing Greek drama. Only when art was liberated from the sphere of capitalist speculation and profit-making would it be able to express the spirit of emancipated humanity. The vehicle envisaged to effect this transformation process, namely the 'art-work of the future', was elaborated, along with the concept of the reunification of the arts into a comprehensive *Gesamtkunstwerk* ('total work of art') on the ancient Greek model, in two further essays, *Das Kunstwerk der Zukunft* (1849) and *Oper und Drama* (1850–51).

In the former, Wagner argued that the elements of dance, music and poetry, harmonized so perfectly in Greek drama, were deprived of their expressive potential when divorced from one another. In the 'artwork of the future' they would be reunited both with each other (in the 'actor of the future', at once dancer, musician and poet) and with the arts of architecture, sculpture and painting. Allowance was even made for the occasional use of the spoken word. Theatres would need to be redesigned according to aesthetic criteria rather than those of social hierarchy. Landscape painters would be required to execute the sets. Above all, the new work of art was to be created, in response to a communal need, by a fellowship of artists, representative of *das Volk* ('the People').

The philosophical basis of *Das Kunstwerk der Zukunft* is multi-faceted. The *völkisch* ideology, which urged a return to a remote primordial world where peasants of pure Germanic blood lived as a true community, had evolved with the rise of national consciousness in the 18th century. Notions such as that of the *Volk*'s creative endeavours arising spontaneously out of sheer necessity – a process of historical inevitability – owe much to Feuerbach and to such revolutionary thinkers as Marx. Nor was the concept of the *Gesamtkunstwerk* new: writers such as Lessing, Novalis, Tieck, Schelling and Hoffmann had previously advocated, either in theory or in practice, some sort of reunification of the arts, while the idea of the regeneration of art in accordance with classical ideals can be identified with Winckelmann, Wieland, Lessing, Goethe and Schiller.

Oper und Drama is an immense discourse on the aesthetics of drama-through-music (*see* MUSIC DRAMA). A new form of verse-setting (*Versmelodie*) is outlined, in which the melody will grow organically out of the verse. It will use *Stabreim* (an old German verse form using alliteration) and a system of presentiments and reminiscences, functioning as *melodische Momente* ('melodic impulses'; *see* LEITMOTIF). Only rarely will one voice serve as harmonic support for another; choruses and other ensembles will be eliminated. Wagner's claim that the new ideas and techniques had 'already matured' within him before the theory was formulated is something of an exaggeration, as is suggested by his willingness to adapt the theoretical principles in the light of practical experience. Their formulation did, however, enable him to grapple with the central issue: how to reconcile his own fundamentally literary and dramatic inspirations with the Classical symphonic tradition.

Two other important essays of the period should be mentioned. *Das Judentum in der Musik* argues that the superficial, meretricious values of contemporary art are embodied, above all, in Jewish musicians. The rootlessness of Jews in Germany and their historical role as usurers and entrepreneurs has condemned them, in Wagner's view, to cultural sterility. The uncompromisingly anti-semitic tone of the essay was, in part, provoked by repeated allegations that Wagner was indebted artistically, as well as financially, to Meyerbeer. The preoccupations and prejudices of *Das Judentum* also place it in an anti-Jewish tradition, perpetuated by writers often of otherwise impeccably liberal and humanitarian credentials, going back via Luther to the Middle Ages. Even the idea that Jews should, as part of the process of assimilation, undergo a programme of re-education was not novel, though the refinement (stated elsewhere) that that programme should largely consist of the Wagnerian music drama was original.

In 1851 Wagner wrote an extensive preface to accompany the projected publication of the librettos of the *Holländer*, *Tannhäuser* and *Lohengrin*. This autobiographical essay, called *Eine Mitteilung an meine Freunde*, is of interest for the insights it offers into Wagner's own view of his life and works to that date.

5. COMPOSER IN EXILE: 1849–63. In Zürich Wagner made the acquaintance of a number of cultured individuals, some of whom provided pecuniary as well as intellectual sustenance. A pair of female admirers, Julie Ritter, a widow from Dresden, and Jessie Laussot (*née* Taylor), an Englishwoman married to a Bordeaux wine merchant, jointly offered him an annual allowance of 3000F (equivalent to 800 talers, or approximately half his Dresden salary), for an indefinite period. Such benefactors showed the kind of disinterested generosity and confidence in his artistic endeavours that he found lacking in his wife, Minna, whose constant reproaches he found increasingly hard to bear. A love affair between Wagner and Jessie (who, according to him, was also unhappily married) briefly blossomed. When, after the intervention of Jessie's mother and death threats from her husband, it ended, one source of financial support dried up. But an unexpected legacy then enabled Julie Ritter to confer the full amount herself, which she continued to do from 1851 to 1859.

Lohengrin received its world première at Weimar under Liszt, with the composer necessarily absent. A drastic water cure at nearby Albisbrunn failed to relieve the dual complaints of erysipelas (a skin disease) and severe constipation, and further depression resulted from the failure of the revolution to materialize in France, or elsewhere in Europe. Several of Wagner's letters of the period speak of a loveless, cheerless existence; more than once he contemplated suicide.

By February 1853 he was able to recite the completed text of the *Ring* to an invited audience at the Hotel Baur au Lac in Zürich; 50 copies of the poem were printed at his own expense. Financial assistance from Otto Wesendonck, a retired silk merchant to whom Wagner had been introduced early in 1852, allowed him to present and conduct three concerts of excerpts from his works (May 1853) and to make a trip to Italy. Wagner's account (in *Mein Leben*) of the dream-inspired onrush of inspiration for *Das Rheingold* while he lay half-asleep in a hotel room in La Spezia has been dismissed as a further example of mythification (see Deathridge, in Deathridge and Dahlhaus 1984), though it has been argued (see Darcy 1989–90) that the documentary evidence neither supports nor contradicts Wagner's account. The story bears witness, in any case, to the perceived importance of the new artistic phase being entered, and it was indeed in the succeeding months that the music of the *Ring* began to take shape.

In September 1854 Wagner reckoned his debts at 10 000F – by this time he was supporting not only Minna and her illegitimate daughter Natalie but also Minna's parents. Wesendonck agreed to settle most of these in exchange for the receipts from future performances of Wagner's works. Appeals for clemency made on his behalf to the new king of Saxony, Johann, were rejected, no doubt on the advice of the Dresden police, whose agents still had him under surveillance. Several of his acquaintances were regarded as dangerous political refugees, not least Georg Herwegh. Ironically, it was Herwegh who in September or October 1854 introduced him to the quietist, renunciatory philosophy that was to influence his future outlook on life: that of Arthur Schopenhauer.

Schopenhauer's influence was twofold: his Buddhist-inspired philosophy, advocating the denial of the will, and the quest for the state of nirvana (cessation of individual existence), was profoundly to affect the ideological orientation – and even the locution – of each of Wagner's remaining dramatic works. Schopenhauer's aesthetics, which elevated music above the other arts, made a similarly forceful impact. But Wagner's abandonment of the concept of the egalitarian coexistence of the arts should be seen not so much as a wholesale *volte face* from *Oper und Drama* principles as a shift of emphasis from the realization of those principles in *Das Rheingold* and *Die Walküre*.

An invitation from the Philharmonic Society to conduct a series of eight concerts in London resulted in a four-month stay in England in 1855. A hostile press campaign, uncongenial weather and the philistinism of the English combined to make the visit an unhappy one. On returning to Zürich he completed his severely disrupted work on *Walküre* (1856) and made a short prose sketch for an opera on a Buddhist subject: *Die Sieger*. The latter project was never completed, but its themes – passion and chastity, renunciation and redemption – later found a place in *Parsifal*.

Otto Wesendonck put at Wagner's disposal a small house adjacent to the villa he was having built in the Enge suburb of Zürich. Wagner and Minna moved in at the end of April 1857 and Wesendonck and his wife Mathilde to their own home in August. A love affair developed between Wagner and Mathilde, though their love – celebrated and idealized in *Tristan und Isolde* – was probably never consummated. To begin work on *Tristan* (20 August 1857) Wagner abandoned *Siegfried*, returning to sustained work on it only in 1869. An eruption of marital strife necessitated Wagner's move out of the Asyl (as, following Mathilde's suggestion, he had called the little house). In the company of Karl Ritter he travelled to Venice; the second act of *Tristan* was completed there (in draft) on 1 July 1858 and the third act in Lucerne on 16 July 1859.

Preparing another offensive against Paris, Wagner conducted, at the beginning of 1860 in the Théâtre Italien, three concerts of excerpts from his works. Through the intervention of Princess Pauline Metternich *Tannhäuser* was eventually staged at the Opéra on 13 March 1861; a politically inspired demonstration, combined with Wagner's refusal to supply the customary second-act ballet, caused a débâcle and the production was withdrawn after three severely disrupted performances. A partial amnesty (Saxony remained barred until the following March) allowed Wagner to return to Germany on 12 August 1860.

In February 1862 he took lodgings in Biebrich, near Mainz, and set to work on the composition of *Die Meistersinger von Nürnberg*, for which he had made two further prose drafts (elaborating that of 1845) the previous November. Surrounded as he now was by female admirers, he yet baulked, on compassionate grounds, at putting a decisive end to his irreparably broken marriage. Instead he installed Minna, with a not ungenerous allowance, in Dresden; they last met in November 1862 and Minna died in January 1866. In May 1863 he rented the upper floor of a house in Penzing, near Vienna, furnishing it in luxurious style, heedless of the consequences. His generosity to friends was equally unstinting and by March the following year he

1. Richard Wagner: photograph taken in Vienna during the winter of 1862–3

was obliged to leave Vienna under threat of arrest for debt.

6. Munich and Bayreuth: 1864–77. A plea for pecuniary assistance published by Wagner along with the *Ring* poems in 1863 was answered in spectacular fashion when a new monarch ascended the throne of Bavaria in March 1864. The 18-year-old Ludwig II discharged Wagner's immediate debts, awarded him an annual stipend of 4000 gulden (comparable to that of a ministerial councillor) and continued his support for many years, making possible the first Bayreuth festivals of 1876 and 1882.

A plea to Mathilde Maier to join him in the Villa Pellet, his new home overlooking Lake Starnberg, was less successful. But by now Wagner was on intimate terms with Cosima von Bülow, unsuitably married to the conductor Hans von Bülow, and their union was consummated some time between the arrival at Starnberg of Cosima (with two daughters and nurserymaid) on 29 June 1864 and that of Hans on 7 July. The child that resulted, Isolde, was born on 10 April 1865.

In October 1864 a more spacious house at 21 Briennerstrasse in Munich was made available to Wagner by Ludwig; it was decked out extravagantly, as was Wagner himself, in silks and satins supplied by a Viennese seamstress. When Ludwig summoned Gottfried Semper to Munich to design a Wagnerian festival theatre, local vested interests opposed the scheme. Difficulties were also encountered with Franz von Pfistermeister and Ludwig von der Pfordten, respectively Ludwig's cabinet secretary and prime minister, and eventually with resentment from the court circles and populace generally. Wagner's proposal for a music school to be established in Munich, appropriate for the nature of German music and drama, was seen as opportunistic, and Ludwig's support of the première of *Tristan* at the Hof- und Nationaltheater merely fuelled the hostility that accompanied the work's unveiling to a bemused public.

Castigation of Wagner for 'cynical exploitation' of Ludwig can be overplayed. It is true that he was as skilled in manipulating people in real life as in his dramas, and that he seized the opportunity to acquire the domestic comforts he had been so long denied. But his overriding concern was to obtain the best possible conditions for his art. And (as Manfred Eger, 1986, has pointed out) the total amount received by Wagner from Ludwig over the 19 years of their acquaintance – including stipend, rent and the cash value of presents – was 562 914 marks, a sum equivalent to less than one-seventh of the yearly Civil List (4.2 million marks). It is a sum that also compares modestly with the 652 000 marks spent on the bed-chamber alone of Herrenchiemsee, or with the 1.7 million marks spent on the bridal carriage for the royal wedding that never took place.

Ludwig, however, recognized that his close association with Wagner was costing him popular support, and in December 1865 reluctantly instructed him to leave Munich. Accompanied by Cosima, Wagner discovered and acquired a house called Tribschen (or Triebschen, to adopt Wagner's idiosyncratic spelling) overlooking Lake Lucerne. His cohabitation with Cosima (permanent from October 1868) was initially concealed from Ludwig, and a scandal-mongering article in the Munich *Volksbote* drove the couple to blind the king with a charade of lamentable mendacity.

From Tribschen Wagner continued to offer Ludwig the political advice with which he had always been generous. Now that Bavaria was caught up in the war between Prussia and Austria, Wagner's opinion, strongly influenced by the views of the conservative federalist Constantin Frantz, was that Bavaria should remain neutral. Bavaria, however, sided with Austria; its defeat not only enabled Prussian hegemony to be established, but also brought about the collapse of the German Confederation.

The impact on Wagner of Frantz's views was crucial to the ideological background of *Meistersinger* as it took shape during the 1860s. Schopenhauer's ethic of renunciation had by now given way to a more positive, more nationalistic outlook, reflecting the mood of optimism in the country at large arising from Germany's increasing industrial growth, national wealth and social cohesion, coupled with the rise of Bismarck. In *Was ist deutsch?* (1865), written for the private edification of the king, Wagner articulated the concern of many members of the middle class for traditional German values, apparently under threat. The divided religion effected by the Reformation, and the near-collapse of the German race, have led to an invasion by 'an utterly alien element', namely the Jews. The result is a 'repugnant caricature of the German spirit', which, according to Wagner, is beautiful and noble, not motivated by profit or self-interest.

Shortly after *Was ist deutsch?* was written, Wagner received a letter from Frantz telling him that in his music he had recognized 'the fundamental chord of German being'. A subsequent essay, *Deutsche Kunst und deutsche Politik* (1867), endorses Frantz's assertion that it is the 'mission' of Germany to forge a 'nobler culture, against which French civilization will no longer have any power', and goes on to propose that German art is a manifestation of that indomitable 'German spirit' which alone is capable of steering Germany and its politics through these difficult days. *Meistersinger* is the artistic component of Wagner's ideological crusade of the 1860s: a crusade to revive the 'German spirit' and purge it of alien elements.

The première of *Meistersinger* on 21 June 1868 was a triumph for Wagner. At Ludwig's insistence, but to Wagner's dismay when he realized how inadequate the performances would be, *Rheingold* and *Walküre* were also staged in Munich in 1869 and 1870 respectively. A second child, Eva, had been born to Wagner and Cosima on 17 February 1867, and a third, Siegfried, on 6 June 1869. Cosima had meanwhile asked her husband for a divorce, and Bülow agreed, though Cosima's marriage to Wagner could not take place until 25 August 1870.

Wagner's anti-Gallic sympathies were given their head when in July 1870 war broke out between France and Prussia (supported by the south German states, including Bavaria). His farce, *Eine Kapitulation*, making tasteless capital out of the suffering endured by the Parisians during the siege of their city, returned to a favourite theme: the swamping of German culture by frivolous French art.

In the essay *Beethoven*, published in 1870 to coincide with the centenary celebrations of the composer, Wagner completed a process of rapprochement, initiated with '*Zukunftsmusik*' ten years earlier, between the aesthetics of *Oper und Drama* and those of Schopenhauer. In '*Zukunftsmusik*' Wagner continued to elevate his own species of text-related musical discourse above pure instrumental music, but the claim is modified by a reappraisal of the worth of symphonic music, particularly that of Beethoven. In *Beethoven* he finally accepts that words and music cannot enjoy totally equal status: with Schopenhauer, he maintains that music is the ultimate vehicle of expression. However, the union of music and words does permit a range of emotional expression far wider than that yielded by each alone. With this formulation, Wagner returned (as Carl Dahlhaus has pointed out) to something akin to the traditional Romantic conception of the aesthetic of music which he had espoused about 1840, long before his encounter with Schopenhauer.

Settling on the Upper Franconian town of Bayreuth for his planned festival enterprise, Wagner began to secure the support both of the local authorities and of 'patrons' across the country. The foundation stone of the theatre was laid on 22 May 1872 (Wagner's birthday); Beethoven's Ninth Symphony was performed. Wagner and Cosima moved to a temporary home in Bayreuth, and then, in April 1874, into 'Wahnfried'. The first festival, announced for 1873, had already been postponed for lack of funds. After an unsuccessful appeal to the Reich, the enterprise was saved only by a loan of 100 000 talers from Ludwig. Admission tickets would have to be sold, however, in contravention of Wagner's original ideal of free access for the populace.

The score of *Götterdämmerung* was completed on 21 November 1874; rehearsals were initiated in the summer of the following year. The part of Siegfried went not to Albert Niemann, Wagner's Paris Tannhäuser, but to the untried Georg Unger, who required close supervision from a singing teacher. The Brünnhilde, Amalie Materna from Vienna, also had to be coached, though the Wotan, Franz Betz, having sung the Munich Hans Sachs, was more familiar with Wagner's demands. In charge of movement and gesture on the stage was Richard Fricke, with Wagner retaining

overall control of the direction; his instructions were recorded in detail by Heinrich Porges. There were three cycles, beginning on 13 August 1876, attended by musicians, critics and notables from all over Europe. The reaction, predictably, was mixed, admiration for the realization of such an enterprise being tempered by criticism of details. Wagner himself was far from satisfied with the staging, which he vowed to revise in future years; nor were the tempos of the conductor, Hans Richter, to his liking.

An intimacy with the French writer Judith Gautier continued from the time of the 1876 festival until February 1878, when it was brought firmly but diplomatically to a halt by Cosima. A scarcely less intense relationship with Friedrich Nietzsche continued from 1869, when the latter first visited Tribschen, until Nietzsche's so-called 'second period' (1876–82), when he turned against art as romantic illusion and excoriated Wagner for betraying what he had identified as his challenging, affirmative spirit.

In the hope of discharging the deficit of the festival (148 000 marks) Wagner undertook a series of concerts in the recently opened Royal Albert Hall in London. He was well received, but the net profits of £700 (approximately 14 300 marks) were disappointingly low, thanks to miscalculations by the inexperienced agents.

7. 'Regeneration' writings. In January 1878 the first issue of the *Bayreuther Blätter* appeared, a journal devoted to the Wagnerian cause, set up by Wagner under the editorship of Hans von Wolzogen. Its viewpoint was described by Wagner as 'the decline of the human race and the need for the establishment of a system of ethics'. That 'system of ethics' was expounded in the series of essays known as the 'regeneration writings', beginning with *Modern* (1878) and ending with *Heldentum und Christentum* (1881). The salient themes are as follows: the human species has degenerated by abandoning its original, natural vegetable diet, and absorbing the corrupted blood of slaughtered animals. Regeneration may be effected only by a return to natural food and it must be rooted in the soil of a true religion. Even the most degenerate races may be purified by the untainted blood of Christ, received in the sacrament of the Eucharist. The miscegenation of the pure Aryan race with the Jews has also contributed to the degeneration of the species.

The last notion Wagner owed to Count Joseph-Arthur de Gobineau, whose acquaintance in these years he greatly valued. Their respective philosophies diverged, however, in as much as Gobineau held that miscegenation was a necessary evil for the continuation of civilization, whereas in Wagner's more optimistic view the human race was redeemable by Christ's blood. Racialist philosophies of this kind were rampant in Wilhelminian Germany. With the unification finally achieved in 1871 had emerged an industrial bourgeoisie that usurped the privileged position of the former liberal nationalists who had struggled for it. Wagner was one of many such whose allegiance shifted from liberalism to a form of romantic conservatism. A new wave of anti-semitic sentiment swept Germany, if anything intensified rather than tempered by the emancipation legislation of the early 1870s. This is the ideological background against which *Parsifal* was written.

8. The final years: 1878–83. The Bayreuth deficit was eventually cleared by an agreement, dated 31 March 1878, according to which Wagner confirmed Ludwig's right to produce all his works in the Hoftheater without payment, the king voluntarily setting aside 10% of all such receipts until the deficit was discharged. In a

2. *Walther's Prize Song from 'Die Meistersinger', Act 3: Wagner's preliminary sketch (opposite), of 28 September 1866, indicating melody and bass line, and second complete draft or 'orchestral sketch' (right: beginning on the second system), of between 8 October 1866 and 5 March 1867, by which stage the harmonies had been elaborated and some details of instrumentation noted*

further clause, Wagner agreed that the first performance of *Parsifal* (either in Bayreuth or Munich) should be given with the orchestra, singers and artistic personnel of the Hoftheater, after which Munich was to have unrestricted rights over the work. It was this clause that compelled Wagner to accept the Jewish Hermann Levi as the conductor of *Parsifal* in 1882.

In August 1879 Wagner responded to an appeal for his support in a campaign against vivisection by writing a sympathetic open letter to Ernst von Weber on the subject. However, he refused to sign Bernhard Förster's 'Mass Petition against the Rampancy of Judaism', partly out of self-interest and partly out of a preference for addressing the issue in a more theoretical manner. In the early 1880s his health began to deteriorate: cardiac spasms were followed by a major heart attack in March 1882. After the second Bayreuth festival, consisting of 16 performances of *Parsifal* in July and August 1882, Wagner and his family took up residence in the Palazzo Vendramin, Venice. His final, fatal heart attack occurred there on 13 February 1883, following an uncharacteristically bitter row with Cosima, apparently provoked by the announcement of a visit from one of the *Parsifal* flowermaidens, Carrie Pringle, with whom Wagner may have been having an affair. His body was taken in a draped gondola to the railway station, whence it was conveyed to Bayreuth. The burial was a private ceremony held in the grounds of Wahnfried.

9. Style and structure. Nothing more vividly demonstrates the multiplicity of genres available to composers of opera in the first decades of the 19th century than the stylistic variety of Wagner's first three operas, *Die Feen*, *Das Liebesverbot* and *Rienzi*. In *Die Feen* the model was German Romantic opera, especially as developed by Weber and Marschner: the supernatural subject matter, the enhanced role of the orchestra and the shift away from static, closed forms towards organic growth are all evident to at least some degree. Acts 2 and 3 each contain a fine scene and aria, that in the latter, depicting the mental derangement of Arindal, being a complex in which recitative, arioso and aria are juxtaposed. One of the work's most inventive numbers, the comic duet for Drolla and Gernot in Act 2,

is untypical in its *opera buffa*-style patter. *Die Feen* is marked by the return of a few characteristic melodic ideas, but scarcely with a persistence such as to merit the term 'leitmotif'.

Das Liebesverbot has a handful of recurring motifs, of which the most prominent is that associated with Friedrich's ban on love; it occasionally returns to make an ironic comment on the dramatic situation, as when Friedrich himself is tempted by passion (Act 1 finale). Wagner's models in *Das Liebesverbot* were Italian and French opera, especially Bellini, Auber and Hérold; vestiges remain of the *opéra comique* convention of spoken dialogue. German influences should not, however, be overlooked. That Wagner was absorbed at this period in the works of, particularly, Marschner is evident, and there are direct reminiscences of Beethoven, including an imitation of Leonore's 'Töt' erst sein Weib!' at the climax of the trial scene ('Erst hört noch mich').

With *Rienzi, der Letzte der Tribunen* Wagner turned his attention to grand opera, his explicit intention being to gain a popular success at the Opéra in Paris. Meyerbeer, with his spectacular large-scale effects, was naturally a primary model, but the influence of Spontini, Auber and Halévy, all of whom Wagner admired, is also evident. In his desire to 'outdo all previous examples' with the sumptuousness of his own grand opera, Wagner imposed a grandiosity of scale on material scarcely able to support it. The powerful but empty rhetoric that results has been seen both as a reflection of the extravagant pomp with which the historical Rienzi surrounded himself and as an emblem of totalitarianism inherent in the opera. Wagner's resumption of work on *Rienzi* after his move from Riga to Paris coincided with his growing dissatisfaction with the discrete number form of conventional opera. Acts 3 to 5 begin to embody the principles of unified poetry and music enunciated in such Paris essays and novellas as *Eine Pilgerfahrt zu Beethoven* (1840); the change is subtle, but is seen in a more expressive, more poetically aware use of recitative that foreshadows the arioso of the mature style, and in the occasional use of the orchestra to comment independently on the action.

According to *Mein Leben*, Wagner's intention, in *Der fliegende Holländer*, was to sweep away the 'tiresome operatic accessories' altogether. Such an aim was not completely realized, but there is a further shift towards the kind of organic continuity that was already evident in such German Romantic scores as *Euryanthe* (1822–3) and that was to distinguish the mature Wagnerian music drama. Recitative is still present in the score of the *Holländer* and referred to as such. Arias, duets, trios and choruses are also present, but such divisions as, for example, 'scene, duet and chorus' (for Daland and the Dutchman, Act 1) have suggested the designation 'scene opera' in preference to 'number opera'. In the treatment of the duets for Erik and Senta and for the Dutchman and Senta (both in Act 2) there are already signs of the greater precedence to be accorded the setting of words, though quadratic phrase structure (i.e. in regular multiples of two or four bars) is still the norm. As for ensembles, the Sailors' Chorus at the end of Act 1 and the Spinning Chorus in Act 2, despite their clever linking by the orchestra's development of a dotted figure common to both, are not closely integrated into the work's structure; the choruses of the Norwegian and Dutch crews in Act 3, on the other hand, serve a more dramatic function in their vying for supremacy. Significantly, the fidelity to, and departure from, conventional operatic norms is related to the two strikingly contrasted worlds of the *Holländer*: the exterior world of reality to which belong Daland, Erik, the spinning girls and the sailors, and the interior world of the imagination inhabited by Senta and the Dutchman. Erik's two arias, for example, represent the most old-fashioned writing in the work, while the Dutchman's Act 1 monologue frequently manages to break free from the constraints of regular periodic structure.

A similar dualism is evident in *Tannhäuser*, where traditional operatic structures are associated with the sphere of the reactionary Wartburg court while a more progressive style is associated with the Venusberg. To the former belong, for example, the more or less self-contained arias of the song contest, Elisabeth's two set-piece arias, her conventional duet with Tannhäuser and Wolfram's celebrated aria 'O du mein holder Abendstern', highly conservative in its regular eight-bar periods and tonal scheme. Venus's music, by contrast, is more radically advanced: her contributions to the duet with Tannhäuser (Act 1) continually breach the constraints of quadratic periods (notably contrasting with Tannhäuser's own more formal utterances), and both that scene and the preceding Bacchanal are progressive in their harmonic vocabulary and rhythmic structure, especially in the Paris version. The most advanced writing in *Tannhäuser*, however, occurs in the Rome Narration (Act 3), where the expressive demands of the text are satisfied by a flexible form of dramatic recitative or arioso responsive to verbal nuance; the orchestra also assumes a major illustrative role here, bearing the burden of the dramatic argument. Another primary dualism present in *Tannhäuser* (related to that of Venusberg and Wartburg) is the traditional struggle between sensuality and spirituality – a dualism reflected in an 'associative' use of tonality. E major is associated with the Venusberg and E♭ with the pilgrims, holy love and salvation. Thus Wolfram's E♭ hymn to 'noble love' (Act 2) is abruptly interrupted by the delayed fourth verse of Tannhäuser's Hymn to Venus in E. Similarly, the Rome Narration reaches E♭ as Tannhäuser recounts how he stood before the Pope; after a series of modulations the enticements of the Venusberg reappear in E, but the final triumphant return to E♭ confirms Tannhäuser's salvation.

The 'associative' use of tonality is also evident in *Lohengrin*. Lohengrin himself and the sphere of the Grail are represented by A major, Elsa with A♭ major (and minor), while Ortrud and her magical powers are associated with F♯ minor (the relative minor of Lohengrin's tonality), and the king's trumpeters on stage with C major. In the second and third scenes of Act 1, the tonalities of Lohengrin and Elsa, a semitone apart, are deployed skilfully to symbolic and expressive effect. *Lohengrin*, like the *Holländer* and *Tannhäuser*, contains various motifs associated with characters or concepts, but in general (the motif of the Forbidden Question is an exception) these do not conform to the strict prescriptions to be laid down in *Oper und Drama*; they also tend to be fully rounded themes rather than pithy ideas capable of infinite transformation, and do not therefore serve the vital structural function of the leitmotifs in the *Ring*. For all that *Lohengrin* marks a stylistic advance over the earlier operas, it fails to fulfil several criteria of the fully-fledged music drama. Vestiges of grand opera are still present in the use of diablerie, spectacle and crowd scenes, with minster, organ, fanfares and bridal procession. Traces of old-fashioned number form are still evident, but recitatives, arias, duets and choruses (even those numbers, such as Elsa's Dream or Lohengrin's Narration, which have become celebrated as independent set pieces) are in fact carefully integrated into the musical fabric. The two latter pieces, at least after their conventional openings, display a greater propensity for irregular phrase structure than most numbers in *Lohengrin*. The quadratic phrase patterns that dominate the work, together with the virtual absence of triple time, impart a uniformity of rhythmic impulse that may be perceived as ponderousness.

Several fundamental changes characterize the musical language of the *Ring*, as Wagner began, in *Das Rheingold*, to implement the principles enunciated in the theoretical essays of 1849–51. In the first place, regular phrase patterns give way to fluid arioso structures in which the text is projected in a vocal line that faithfully reflects its verbal accentuations, poetic meaning and emotional content. On occasion in *Rheingold*, the rigorous attempt to match poetic shape with musical phrase results in pedestrian melodic ideas. But in *Walküre* the musico-poetic synthesis is found at its most ingenious, interesting melodic lines registering the finer nuances of the text with no unnatural word stresses. The Forging Song in Act 1 of *Siegfried* gives notice of a shift towards musical predominance, while Act 3 of *Siegfried* and *Götterdämmerung*, for all the fine examples of scrupulous matching of words and music, exhibit a tendency towards quick-fire exchanges, as found in *Die Meistersinger* but modified in accordance with the elevated tone of the tetralogy.

Hand-in-hand with this evolution of musico-poetic synthesis go developments in formal structure and in the use of leitmotif. The excessively rigid symmetries of Lorenz's analyses (an over-reaction to charges of formlessness in Wagner's music) have now been rejected, or rather radically modified to take account also of such elements as period and phrase structure, orchestration and tempo. Lorenz's arch (*A-B-A*) and *Bar* (*A-A-B*) forms are indeed present in Wagner, but like the other traditional forms of strophic song, rondo and variation, they are constantly adapted, often in midstream, creating new, hybrid forms notable for their complexity and ambiguity.

The leitmotif (though never actually called that by Wagner) takes on a structural role in the *Ring*, whereas in *Lohengrin* its function was purely dramatic. As Wagner suggested in his 1879 essay *Über die Anwendung der Musik auf das Drama*, motivic transformation provides a key to the analysis of his music dramas; but he went on to say that his transformations were generated according to dramatic imperatives and as such would be incomprehensible in a symphonic structure. It is the dramatic origination of the motifs that is responsible for their frequent association with specific tonalities. The Tarnhelm motif, for example, is associated with G♯ minor and that of the Curse with B minor. Modulatory passages are common in which the primary tonality of an important motif is engineered. Sometimes, too, the tonality in question becomes the determining key of a whole section or structural unit (the return of B minor for the Curse motif in Scene iv of *Rheingold*, as Fasolt is murdered by Fafner, is an example of this).

The deployment of motifs in the *Ring* underwent a change during the course of composition. In *Rheingold* the identification of motifs with specific objects or ideas is at its most unambiguous. In *Walküre* and the first two acts of *Siegfried*, motivic representation is still made according to reasonably strict musico-poetic criteria, but without quite the literal-mindedness of *Rheingold*. In Act 3 of *Siegfried* and *Götterdämmerung*, however, written after the long break in composition, the motifs frequently aspire to an independent life of their own. They are combined in such profusion and with such contrapuntal virtuosity that it is clear that the principles of *Oper und Drama* are no longer being strictly adhered to. In *Rheingold*, the thematic transformations that take place in the passages that link the scenes are not typical of the work; the score of *Götterdämmerung*, however, is characterized by congeries of motifs drawn on for a brief thematic development.

Just as certain leitmotifs are associated with specific tonalities, so groups of characters (though, unlike the earlier operas, not individual characters) are also identified with particular keys: the Valkyries with B minor, the Nibelungs with B♭ minor. The entire Nibelheim Scene (Scene iii) of *Rheingold*, for example, is dominated by B♭ minor, which even interrupts Loge's A major music as Alberich asserts himself. The B♭ minor of the Nibelheim Scene is framed by the D♭ major in which Scene ii begins and Scene iv ends. The relative key, contrasting but intimately connected, denotes the relationship of Wotan (Light-Alberich) to Alberich. If the first scene of *Rheingold* be excluded (since it is in the nature of a prelude, outside the main action and its time zone), the tetralogy both begins and ends in D♭ major; it should not be regarded as the chief tonality to which all others are related, but it does provide a framework of sorts, and at the end affords a sense of homecoming. *Rheingold* was originally conceived by Wagner as a drama in three acts with a prelude, a structure which replicates not only that of *Götterdämmerung* (three acts and a prologue) but also that of the *Ring* as a whole.

The tendency towards the non-specificity of leitmotifs in the course of the *Ring* is continued in *Tristan und Isolde*. Aptly for a work dealing in metaphysical abstractions, motifs are not used in the latter to symbolize swords and spears; nor can they generally be confined to a single concept (the motifs associated with 'death' and 'day' are exceptions). The elusiveness of the motifs and their associations is reflected in their propensity for interrelation by means of thematic transformation. And if the abstract nature of the motifs in *Tristan* enhances their flexibility, making them more conducive to 'symphonic' development, they are also more closely integrated into the harmonic structure of the work: the melodic line of the motif associated with the words 'Todgeweihtes Haupt! Todgeweihtes Herz!' (*see* TRISTAN UND ISOLDE, ex.2) is a product of the chromatic progression A♭–A, not vice versa.

The elevation of motivic interplay to an abstract level in *Tristan* is accompanied by a further shift in the balance of music and text towards the former. There are still many examples of musico-poetic synthesis that conform to *Oper und Drama* principles, but there is also an increased tendency towards vowel extension, melisma, and overlapping and simultaneous declamation of the singers, not to mention the opulent orchestration with triple wind – all of which conspire to reduce the clarity with which the text is projected. The extended vowels of Brangäne's Watchsong, for example, render her words virtually inaudible; the text is not irrelevant, but has been absorbed into the music to create an intensified line that is then reintegrated into the orchestral fabric.

The temporal values of society represented by King Mark and Melot, and the earthy humanity of Kurwenal, are often matched by four-square diatonicism. Conversely, the neurotic self-absorption of Tristan and Isolde and their unassuageable yearning are reflected in the work's prevailing mode of chromaticism; suspensions, unresolved dissonances and sequential variation are ubiquitous and chromatically heightened. Every element, poetical and musical, is geared to the generation and intensification of tension – the tension of promised but evaded fulfilment.

The vocal line undergoes a further development in *Die Meistersinger*. For much of the time it is little more than recitative, but its bareness is counteracted by the orchestra's richness of detail; the orchestra is by now firmly established as the chief commentator on the dramatic action. The improvisatory nature of the musical texture corresponds to the principle that Wagner was to codify in *Über die Bestimmung der Oper* (1871), whereby the improvisatory element in acting was to be harnessed to the essential improvisatory ingredient in musical composition, resulting in a 'fixed improvisation'.

The subject matter of the music drama – the creation of a mastersong – might seem to lend weight to Lorenz's formal analysis in terms of *Bar*-form. But this would be to reckon without the more flexible, more sophisticated structures that Wagner had been developing throughout his career, and without the element of parody that is central to the work (Voss 1981). Aspects of *Bar*-form are indeed present (*see* MEISTERSINGER VON NÜRNBERG, DIE) but often in an ironic context: the variation entailed in the *A-A-B* structure of 'Am stillen Herd', for example, is absurdly florid.

A similar distancing tendency is at work in Wagner's persistent use in *Die Meistersinger* of such traditional forms as set-piece arias, ensembles and choruses; all three acts end with a massed finale worthy of grand opera. The forms of Walther's arias or of Beckmesser's Serenade tell us as much about the characters and their dramatic predicament as the notes themselves. The irregular phrase lengths, false accentuations and disorderly progress of the Serenade depict Beckmesser's agitation and supposed artistic sterility, and should not be regarded as symptomatic of an 'advanced' musical style (unlike the Act 3 'pantomime' in Hans Sachs's study, which does look to the future in its graphic musical pictorialism).

Old and new are fused also in the musical language: the work's predominant diatonicism has an archaic tendency, largely as a result of the penchant for secondary triads with their modal flavour. If this challenge to the traditional tonic-dominant hierarchy is a musical metaphor for *Die Meistersinger*'s nostalgic retrospection, it is at the same time a means of rejuvenating tonality.

In *Parsifal*, Wagner the librettist supplied Wagner the composer with some of his freest verse, ranging from sonorous, measured lines to violently expressive ones. The vocal lines which resulted similarly range from more or less melodic arioso (though often the primary idea is in the orchestra and the vocal line functions rather as counterpoint) to a form of recitative-like declamation (for example in Gurnemanz's Act 1 Narration). There are leitmotifs which can be identified with objects or concepts, such as the Spear, the Last Supper or the Grail, but the associations are not rigidly consistent: as in *Tristan*, the function of the motifs is less representational than to provide raw material for 'symphonic' development.

Again as in *Tristan* and *Die Meistersinger*, the modes of chromaticism and diatonicism are counterposed, but whereas in those two works the signification was relatively clear, in *Parsifal* the relationship of the two is more equivocal. The realms of the Grail and of Klingsor are associated with diatonicism and chromaticism respectively, but between these two poles are many cross-currents: Amfortas's suffering, for example, conforms exclusively to neither category, confirming that his experience, while ultimately the catalyst for the redemptive process, is tainted by depravity. The propensity for tonal dissolution in *Parsifal*, for diatonicism to yield to chromaticism, is a potent metaphor for the theme of spiritual degeneration. Tritones, augmented triads and mediant tonal relationships, which all undermine the tonic-dominant hierarchy, contribute to the uncertain nature of a tonal continuum that veers between diatonicism and chromaticism, stable and unstable tonality. Ambiguity also surrounds the polarity of A♭ major and D (major and minor), which are evidently not to be viewed as irreconcilably opposing forces but as complementary spheres to be brought into resolution. The final stage in that process takes place at the setting of Parsifal's last words, 'Enthüllet den Gral', which effects a modulation from D major to the A♭ with which the work unequivocally concludes.

See also FEEN, DIE; FLIEGENDE HOLLÄNDER, DER; GÖTTERDÄMMERUNG; LIEBESVERBOT, DAS; LOHENGRIN (i); MEISTERSINGER VON NÜRNBERG, DIE; PARSIFAL; RHEINGOLD, DAS; RIENZI, DER LETZTE DER TRIBUNEN; RING DES NIBELUNGEN, DER; SIEGFRIED; TANNHÄUSER; TRISTAN UND ISOLDE; and WALKÜRE, DIE.

Editions: *Richard Wagner: Sämtliche Werke*, ed. C. Dahlhaus, E. Voss and others (Mainz, 1970–) [SW]
Richard Wagners Werke, ed. M. Balling (Leipzig, 1912–29) [B; inc.]

Catalogue: J. Deathridge, M. Geck and E. Voss: *Wagner Werk-Verzeichnis (WWV): Verzeichnis der musikalischen Werke Richard Wagners und ihrer Quellen* (Mainz, 1986) [WWV]

Dates given for MS sources refer to the beginning and end of complete drafts only, including fair copies of librettos and full scores. Dates in square brackets have been deduced from sources other than those mentioned in the same column. Full details of all autograph MSS (including single musical sketches prior to first complete drafts), copies in other hands as well as first and subsequent major prints are to be found in WWV. For a discussion of terminology see WWV (foreword) and J. Deathridge: 'The Nomenclature of Wagner's Sketches', *PRMA*, ci (1974–5), 75–83. All texts are by Wagner unless otherwise stated.

NA – Nationalarchiv der Richard-Wagner-Stiftung, Bayreuth

RWG – Richard-Wagner-Gedenkstätte der Stadt Bayreuth

Text MSS (autograph)	ps – prose sketch (outline) pd – prose draft (detailed) vd – verse draft (Subsequent prose or verse drafts are indicated by superscript numerals: pd[1], vd[2] etc.)	Music MSS (autograph)	cd – complete draft (= single existing complete draft) fcd – first complete draft (outline) scd – second complete draft (detailed) fs – full score (= single existing full score) sfs – second full score (fair copy) pm – performance material ffs – first full score (draft)	Prints	vs – vocal score fs – full score ps – piano score

Writings: *Gesammelte Schriften und Dichtungen*, i–x (Leipzig, 1871–83, 4/1907)[GS]
Sämtliche Schriften und Dichtungen, i–xvi (Leipzig, [1911–16]) [SS]
Richard Wagner's Prose Works, ed. and trans. W. A. Ellis, i–viii (London, 1892–9) [PW]
Das braune Buch: Tagebuchaufzeichnungen 1865–1882, ed. J. Bergfeld (Zürich and Freiburg, 1975; Eng. trans., London, 1980) [BB]

WWV	*title*	*genre, acts, libretto*	*composition, sources*	*première*	*publication*	*dedication, remarks*
32	Die Feen	grosse romantische Oper, 3, after C. Gozzi: *La donna serpente*	text: pd, vd (both lost), [Jan–Feb 1833, Leipzig]; rev. dialogue, *GB-Lbl*, NA, vd[1], vd[2], [sum. 1834, Leipzig] music: cd, NA, fs (lost), Feb 1833–Jan 1834, Würzburg ov. (end): cd, 27 Dec 1833; fs, 6 Jan 1834 Act 1: 20 Feb–24 May 1833; fs (end), 6 Aug 1833 Act 2 (end): cd, 27 Sept 1833; fs, 1 Dec 1833 Act 3 (end): cd, 7 Dec 1833; fs, 1 Jan 1834 Act 2 scene v (scene and aria, Ada), rev.: cd, NA, [spr. 1834], Leipzig	Munich, Kgl Hof- und National, 29 June 1888, cond. F. Fischer ov.: Magdeburg, 10 Jan 1835, cond. Wagner	lib.: Mannheim, 1888; SW 22 vs: Mannheim, 1888 fs: *c*1890 (orchestration rev. H. Levi); B xiii; SW 1	pm (not autograph), *D-Mbs*, from lost fs or copy
38	Das Liebesverbot, oder Die Novize von Palermo	grosse komische Oper, 2, after W. Shakespeare: *Measure for Measure*	text: pd (lost), vd, *GB-Lbl*, [mid June–Dec 1834, Rudolstadt and Magdeburg]; Fr. trans.: vd, *Lbl*, [aut. 1839, Paris] music: cd, NA, fs (lost), Jan 1835–[March 1836], Magdeburg Act 1 (begin): cd, 23 Jan 1835 Act 2 (end): cd, 30 Dec 1835 arrs. from nos.2, 9, 11 (in Fr.): pm, NA, [Feb–March 1840, Paris]	Magdeburg, Stadt, 29 March 1836, cond. Wagner; 2 duets from Act 1: Magdeburg, Stadt, 6 April 1835, cond. Wagner	lib.: Leipzig, 1911/*R*1981; SW 22 vs: Leipzig, 1922/*R*1982 fs: B xiv; SW 2 Karnevalslied, from no.11, vs (in Ger.): Stuttgart, 1837 Gesang der Isabella, from no.6, vs (in Ger.): Munich, 1896	copy of lost fs in Wittelsbacher Ausgleichsfonds, Munich
49	Rienzi, der Letzte der Tribunen	grosse tragische Oper, 5, after E. Bulwer-Lytton: *Rienzi: the Last of the Roman Tribunes*	text: ps, *US-PHci*, pd, vd, NA, [June/July 1837, Blasewitz and Dresden; June] – Aug 1838, Mitau and Riga; Fr. trans.: vd, NA, [sum. 1839–wint. 1839/40] music: cd, NA, fs (lost), Aug 1838–Nov 1840, Riga and Paris ov.: 1st draft (begin), 20 Sept 1840; cd (end), 23 Oct 1840; fs (end), [19 Nov 1840] Act 1: cd, 7 Aug–6 Dec 1838; fs, [8 Sept 1838]–6 Feb 1839 Act 2: cd, 6 Feb–9 April 1839; fs (end), 12 Sept 1839 Act 3: cd, 15 Feb–7 July 1840; fs, 6 June–11 Aug 1840 Act 4: cd, 10 July–29 Aug 1840; fs (begin), 14 Aug 1840 Act 5: cd, 5–19 Sept 1840 Prelude to Act 3 for perf. on 2 evenings [Jan 1843]: cd, private collection, fs, NA, *S-Smf*	Dresden, Kgl Sächsisches Hof, 20 Oct 1842, cond. K. Reissiger	lib.: Dresden, 1842; Hamburg, 1844; Berlin, 1847; SW 23 vs: Dresden, 1844 fs: Dresden, 1844 (shortened version); SW 3	Friedrich August II, King of Saxony; pm (inc., not autograph), *D-Dlb*, from lost fs or copy; for Wagner's revs. see SW 3/v and WWV 49 *Erläuterungen*

WWV	*title*	*genre, acts, libretto*	*composition, sources*	*première*	*publication*	*dedication, remarks*
63	Der fliegende Holländer	romantische Oper, 3, after H. Heine: *Aus den Memoiren des Herrn von Schnabelewopski*	text: pd (in Fr.), *F-Pn*, [2–6 May 1840]; pd (in Ger.), RWG, [early 1841]; vd (in Ger.), RWG, 18–28 May 1841, Meudon Senta's Ballad, Song of Scottish Sailors, Song of the Dutchman's Crew: vd (in Fr.), *GB-Lbl*, May–June 1840 music: cd (lost), fs, NA, July–Nov 1841, Meudon and Paris ov. (end): cd, 5 Nov 1841; fs, [19 Nov 1841] Act 1 (begin): cd, 23 July 1841 Act 2 (end of Senta's Ballad): cd, 31 July 1841 Act 2 (begin no.5): cd, 4 Aug [1841] Act 2 (end): cd, 13 Aug [1841] Act 3 (end): cd, 22 Aug 1841; fs, 21 Oct 1841 Senta's Ballad, Song of Scottish Sailors, Song of the Dutchman's Crew: cd, fs (both partly lost), NA, RWG, *US-NYp*, [May–July 1840] rev. end of ov., 1860: ffs, NA, 19 Jan 1860, sfs, *GB-Lbl*, [shortly before 16 March 1860]	Dresden, Kgl Sächsisches Hof, 2 Jan 1843, cond. Wagner	lib.: Dresden, 1843; Zürich, 1852; Munich, 1864; SW 24 vs: Dresden, 1844; Berlin, 1909 (Weingartner version) fs: Dresden, 1844; Berlin, 1896 (Weingartner version); SW 4 (orig. version with later alterations in separate vol.) ov. with rev. ending of 1860, fs: 1861	Ida von Lüttichau (née von Knobelsdorf); orig. version in 1 act; orchestration rev. 1846, 1852; ending modified 1860
70	Tannhäuser und der Sängerkrieg auf Wartburg	grosse romantische Oper, 3; 1859–60 version: Handlung, 3	text: stage 1: June 1842–April 1843, Aussig, Teplitz and Dresden; pd^{1}, NA (with orig. title 'Der Venusberg'), 28 June–6 July 1842; pd^{2}, NA, 8 July 1842 (end); vd^{1} (lost); vd^{2}, NA, [shortly before 7 April 1843 with later alterations] stage 2: [early 1847, Dresden]; pd, vd (lost) stage 3: [Sept 1859–Feb/March 1861, Paris]; vd^{1}, vd^{2} (in Ger.), NA, private collection stage 4: [Aug/Sept 1861, Vienna–early 1865, Munich]; vd^{1}, vd^{2} (both partly lost), Geheimarchiv, Munich music: stage 1: [July 1843]–April 1845, Teplitz and Dresden; preliminary sketches, private collections, *D-LEu*, *Mbs*, RWG, *S-Smf*; cd, private collection, NA; fs (destroyed during lithographing in 1845) ov. (end): cd, 11 Jan 1845 Act 1: cd, Nov 1843–27 Jan 1844 Act 2: cd, 7 Sept–15 Oct 1844 Act 3: cd, 19–29 Dec 1844, fs (end), 13 April 1845 stage 2: [Oct 1845]–May 1847, Dresden; cd, NA, 30 April 1847 (end); fs, NA, 7 May 1847 (end) stage 3: [Aug/Sept 1860–March 1861, Paris] Act 1 scene i: cd, NA, fs, NA, 28 Jan 1861 (end); Act 1 scene ii: fcd, NA, scd, NA, 18 Oct 1860 (end), fs, NA; further MSS in *A-Wn*, *D-Mbs*, NA, RWG, Wagnermuseum, Eisenach, *F-Pn*, *Po* stage 4: [probably aut. 1861, Vienna–sum. 1867, Munich]; fs (partly autograph), private collection, pm (not autograph), *D-Mbs*	stage 1: Dresden, Kgl Sächsisches Hof, 19 Oct 1845, cond. Wagner stage 2: Dresden, Kgl Sächsisches Hof, 1 Aug 1847, cond. Wagner stage 3: Paris, Opéra, 13 March 1861, cond. L. Dietsch stage 4: Munich, Kgl Hof- und National, 1 Aug 1867, cond. H. von Bülow	stage 1 lib.: Dresden, 1845; SW 25 vs: Dresden, 1846; SW 20/i fs: Dresden, 1845; B iii; SW 5 stage 2 lib.: Dresden, 1847; SW 25 vs: Dresden, 1852 fs: Dresden, 1860; B iii; SW 5 stage 3 lib.: Paris, 1861; SW 25 vs: Paris, 1861 fs: B iii; SW 6 stage 4 lib.: Munich, 1867; SW 25 vs: Berlin and Dresden, 1876 fs: Berlin, *c*1888; B iii; SW 6	Camille Erard (stage 2, 1860); see WWV 70 *Erläuterungen*

WWV	*title*	*genre, acts, libretto*	*composition, sources*	*première*	*publication*	*dedication, remarks*
75	Lohengrin	romantische Oper, 3	text: pd, NA, 3 Aug 1845, Marienbad (end); vd, private collection, 27 Nov 1845 [Dresden] (end) music: fcd (partly lost), private collections, *D-Mbs*, NA, *US-NYp*, *STu*; scd, NA; fs, NA; [May 1846]–April 1848, Dresden Prelude: scd (end), 29 Aug [1847], fs (begin), 1 Jan 1848 Act 1: scd, 12 May–8 June 1847 Act 2: scd, 18 June–2 Aug 1847 Act 3: fcd (end), 30 July 1846; scd, 9 Sept 1846–5 March 1847; fs (end), 28 April 1848 arrs. for concerts in Zürich, May 1853, (mostly lost), NA arrs. for concerts in St Petersburg and Budapest, 1863, NA, *H-Bo*, private collection	Weimar, Grossherzogliches Hof, 28 Aug 1850, cond. Liszt Act 1 finale (in concert): Dresden, Kgl Sächsisches Hof, 22 Sept 1848, cond. Wagner	lib.: Weimar, 1850; SW 26 vs: Leipzig, 1851 fs: Leipzig, 1852; B iv; SW 7	Liszt; Prelude comp. last but orchd first; orig. version of lib. in SW 26
86	Der Ring des Nibelungen	Bühnenfestspiel für drei Tage und einen Vorabend		as a cycle: Bayreuth, Festspielhaus, 13, 14, 16, 17 Aug 1876, cond. H. Richter		'Im Vertrauen auf den deutschen Geist entworfen und zum Ruhme seines erhabenen Wohlthäters des Königs Ludwig II von Bayern vollendet'
86*a*	Das Rheingold	Vorabend	text: ps, pd, vd, NA, [Oct/Nov 1851]–Nov 1852, Albisbrunn and Zürich; pd, 23–31 March 1852; vd, 15 Sept–3 Nov 1852 music: cd, NA, ffs (partly lost), NA, *US-NYp*, *PRu*; sfs (lost), Nov 1853–Sept 1854, Zürich; cd, 1 Nov 1853–14 Jan 1854; ffs, 1 Feb–28 May 1854; sfs, 15 Feb–26 Sept 1854 arrs. for concerts in Vienna, 1862–3, private collections, *A-Wgm*	Munich, Kgl Hof- und National, 22 Sept 1869, cond. F. Wüllner excerpts from scenes i, ii, iv (in concert): Vienna, Wien, 26 Dec 1862, cond. Wagner	lib.: Zürich, 1853; SW 29/ii vs: Mainz, 1861 fs: Mainz, 1873; SW 10	copy by Friedrich Wölfel of lost fs, NA; pm for 1st perf. (not autograph), *D-Mbs*
86*b*	Die Walküre	erster Tag, 3	text: ps, pd, vd, NA, [Nov/Dec 1851]–July 1852, Albisbrunn and Zürich Act 1: pd (begin), 17 May 1852; vd, 1–11 June [1852] Act 2: vd, 12–23 June [1852] Act 3 (end): pd, 26 May 1852; vd, 1 July 1852 music: cd, ffs, NA, sfs (lost), June 1854–March 1856, Zürich, London, Seelisberg and Zürich Act 1: cd, 28 June–1 Sept 1854; ffs (end), 3 April 1855; sfs (begin), 14 July 1855 Act 2: cd, 4 Sept–18 Nov 1854; ffs, 7 April–20 Sept 1855 Act 3: cd, 20 Nov–27 Dec 1854; ffs, 8 Oct 1855–20 March 1856; sfs (end), 23 March 1856 arrs. for concerts in Vienna, 1862–3, private collection, *A-Wgm*, NA, RWG, *US-NYpm*, *Wc*	Munich, Kgl Hof- und National, 26 June 1870, cond. Wüllner excerpts from Acts 1, 3 (in concert): Vienna, An der Wien, 26 Dec 1862, cond. Wagner	lib.: Zürich, 1853; SW 29/ii vs: Mainz, 1865 fs: Mainz, 1874; SW 11 'Walkürenritt': Mainz, 1876	copy by Alois Niest of lost sfs, *D-Mbs*; 'Walkürenritt', 'Winterstürme wichen dem Wonnemond', arr. pf by C. Tausig (1863, 1866) approved by Wagner but not identical with his arrs.

WWV	title	genre, acts, libretto	composition, sources	première	publication	dedication, remarks
86*c*	Siegfried	zweiter Tag, 3	text: ps, pd, NA, vd[1], private collection, vd[2], NA, May 1851–[Nov/Dec 1852]; pd, 24 May–1 June 1851; vd[1], 3–24 June 1851 [1st rev., Nov/Dec 1852, 2nd rev., 1856] music: fcd, scd, ffs, sfs (Acts 1–2 only), NA, [Sept 1856]–Aug 1857, Zürich (end scd Act 2); Dec 1864–Dec 1865, Munich (ffs Act 2); March 1869–Feb 1871, Tribschen (Act 3) Act 1: fcd (end), 20 Jan 1857; scd, 22 Sept 1856–5 Feb 1857; ffs, 11 Oct 1856–31 March 1857; sfs (begin), 12 May 1857 Act 2: fcd, 22 May–30 July 1857; scd, 18 June–9 Aug 1857; ffs, 22 Dec 1864–2 Dec 1865; sfs (end), 23 Feb 1869 Act 3: fcd, 1 March–14 June 1869; scd, 25 June–5 Aug 1869; ffs, 25 Aug 1869–5 Feb 1871 arrs. of 'Schmiedelieder' for concert in Vienna, 1863, NA, RWG, *H-Bo*	Bayreuth, Festspielhaus, 16 Aug 1876, cond. Richter 2 Schmiedelieder from Act 1 (in concert): Vienna, An der Wien, 1 Jan 1863, cond. Wagner	lib.: Zürich, 1853; SW 29/ii vs: Mainz, 1871 fs: Mainz, 1875; SW 12	
86*d*	Götter-dämmerung	dritter Tag, Vorspiel, 3	text: pd, NA, vd[1], private collection, vd[2], *CH-W*, vd[3], NA, Oct 1848–Dec 1852, Dresden and Zürich; pd (end), 20 Oct 1848 [prol. late Oct 1848]; vd[1], 12–28 Nov 1848; vd[2], [late 1848/early 1849]; vd[3] (end), 15 Dec 1852 [1st rev., 1848/9; 2nd rev., Nov/Dec 1852] music: fcd, scd, fs, NA, Oct 1869–Nov 1874, Tribschen and Bayreuth Prol. (begin): fcd, 2 Oct 1869; scd, 11 Jan 1870; fs, 3 May 1873 Act 1: fcd, 7 Feb–5 June 1870; scd (end), 2 July 1870; fs (end), 24 Dec 1873 Act 2: fcd, 24 June–25 Oct 1871; scd, 5 July–19 Nov 1871; fs (end), 26 June 1874 Act 3: fcd, 4 Jan–10 April 1872; scd, 9 Feb–22 July 1872; fs, 10 June–21 Nov 1874	Bayreuth, Festspielhaus, 17 Aug 1876, cond. Richter excerpts from prol., Acts 1, 3 (in concert): Vienna, Musikvereinssaal, 25 March, 6 May 1875, cond. Wagner	lib.: Zürich, 1853; SW 29/ii vs: Mainz, 1875 fs: Mainz, 1876; SW 13	musical sketches and 2 inc. drafts of prol. (1 dated 12 Aug 1850), 1850, *US-Wc*, private collection
90	Tristan und Isolde	Handlung, 3	text: ps, pd, vd, NA, [aut. 1854]–Sept 1857, Zürich; pd (begin), 20 Aug 1857; vd (end), 18 Sept 1857 music: fcd, scd, fs, NA, Oct 1857–Aug 1859, Zürich, Venice and Lucerne Act 1 (with Prelude): fcd, 1 Oct–31 Dec 1857; scd, 5 Nov 1857–13 Jan 1858 Act 2: fcd, 4 May–1 July 1858; scd, 5 July 1858–9 March 1859; fs (end), 18 March 1859 Act 3: fcd, 9 April–16 July 1859; scd, 1 May–19 July 1859; fs (end), 6 Aug 1859 concert ending to Prelude: Dec 1859, Paris	Munich, Kgl Hof- und National, 10 June 1865, cond. Bülow Prelude (with Bülow's concert ending): Prague, 12 March 1859, cond. Bülow Prelude (with Wagner's concert ending): Paris, Italien, 25 Jan 1860, cond. Wagner	lib.: Leipzig, 1859; SW 27 vs: Leipzig, 1860 fs: Leipzig, 1860; B v; SW 8 Prelude with Wagner's concert ending: Leipzig, 1860	earliest dated sketches 19 Dec 1856; practice of ending Prelude with conclusion of Act 3 introduced by Wagner, St Petersburg, 26 Feb 1863

WWV	title	genre, acts, libretto	composition, sources	première	publication	dedication, remarks
96	Die Meistersinger von Nürnberg	3	text: pd[1] (end), 16 July 1845, Marienbad; pd[2], pd[3], vd, NA, Schott, Mainz, Nov 1861–Jan 1862, Vienna and Paris Act 1 (end): vd, 5 Jan 1862 Act 2 (end): vd, 16 Jan 1862 Act 3 (end): pd[3], 18 Nov 1861; vd, 25 Jan 1862 music: fcd, scd, NA, fs, *D-Ngm*, April–Dec 1862, Biebrich and Vienna; Feb 1866–Oct 1867, Geneva and Tribschen Prelude: scd, 13–20 April 1862; fs (begin), [3 June 1862] Act 1 (end): fcd, [Feb 1866]; scd, 21 Feb 1866; fs, 23 March 1866 Act 2: fcd, 15 May–6 Sept 1866; scd, 8 June–23 Sept 1866; fs, 22 March–22 June 1867 Act 3: fcd, 2 Oct 1866–7 Feb 1867; scd, 8 Oct 1866–5 March 1867; fs, 26 June–24 Oct 1867 concert ending to Walther's Trial Song from Act 1: 12 July 1865, Munich	Munich, Kgl Hof- und National, 21 June 1868, cond. Bülow Prelude: Leipzig, Gewandhaus, 1 Nov 1862, cond. Wagner 'Versammlung der Meistersingerzunft' and Walther's Trial Song from Act 1: Vienna, An der Wien, 26 Dec 1862, cond. Wagner conclusion of Act 3 (from Hans Sachs's 'Verachtet mir die Meister nicht'): Linz, 4 April 1868, cond. Bruckner	lib.: Mainz, 1862; SW 28 vs: Mainz, 1868 fs: Mainz, 1868; SW 9 Prelude, fs: Mainz, 1866	King Ludwig II of Bavaria; earliest dated sketch ('Wach auf' chorus) Jan 1862; entitled 'Komische Oper' in pd[1], 'Grosse komische Oper' in pd[2] and pd[3], 'Oper' in poster for 1st perf.
111	Parsifal	Bühnenweihfestspiel, 3	text: ps (lost), pd[1], RWG, pd[2], vd, NA, April 1857, Zürich; Aug 1865, Munich; [Jan]–April 1877, Bayreuth; ps, end of April (not Good Friday, see SW 30); pd[1], 27–30 Aug [1865]; pd[2] (end), 23 Feb 1877; vd (end), 19 April 1877 music: fcd, scd, fs, NA, [Sept 1877]–Dec 1881, Bayreuth and Palermo Act 1: fcd (end), 29 Jan 1878; scd, 25 Sept 1877–31 Jan 1878; fs, 23 Aug 1879–25 April 1881 Act 2: fcd (end), 30 Sept [1878]; scd, 13 March–11 Oct 1878; fs, 6 June–20 Oct 1881 Act 3: fcd, 30 Oct 1878–16 April [1879]; scd, 14 Nov 1878–26 April 1879; fs, 8 Nov–25 Dec 1881	Bayreuth, Festspielhaus, 26 July 1882, cond. Levi Prelude: Bayreuth, 25 Dec 1878, cond. Wagner	lib.: Mainz, 1877; SW 30 vs: Mainz, 1882 fs: Mainz, 1883; SW 14	

INCOMPLETE OR PROJECTED STAGE WORKS

WWV	title	genre, acts, libretto	composition, sources	publication	remarks
1	Leubald	Trauerspiel, 5	[1826–1828, Dresden and Leipzig], vd, NA	extracts from Act 5: Leipzig, 1908; SS 16 complete: SW 31	no music survives; ? none written
6	Schäferoper	after J. W. von Goethe: *Die Laune des Verliebten*	early 1830, Leipzig		entitled 'Schäferoper' in Red Pocket-Book, 'Schäferspiel' in *Mein Leben*; inc., lost
31	Die Hochzeit	Oper, adapted from J. G. G. Büsching: *Ritterzeit und Ritterwesen*	text: pd, vd, [Oct/Nov 1832, Pravonin and Prague] music (Introduction, Chorus, Septet): cd (lost), fs, NA, Dec 1832–March 1833, Leipzig and Würzburg cd (begin): 5 Dec 1832; fs (end): 1 March 1833	B xii; SW 15	inc.; frag. 1st perf. Rostock, Stadt, 13 Feb 1933

WWV	title	genre, acts, libretto	composition, sources	publication	remarks
40	Die hohe Braut	grosse Oper, 5, after H. Koenig: *Die hohe Braut*	text: pd[1], pd[2], private collection, pd[3] (in Fr.), *GB-Lbl*, [?July 1836, Königsberg; Paris, 1840]; vd (lost), [25 July–6 Sept 1842, Dresden] music: not set; no sketches survive	Prague, 1848 (lib. to setting by J. B. Kittl); SS 11; SW 31	Wagner offered lib. to K. Reissiger, 1842, and F. Hiller, 1845; Kittl's setting (Bianca und Giuseppe, oder Die Franzosen vor Nizza) 1st perf. Prague, 19 Feb 1848
48	Männerlist grösser als Frauenlist, oder Die glückliche Bärenfamilie	komische Oper, 2, after *The Thousand and One Nights*	text: vd (lost), copy (not autograph), NA, ? sum. 1838, Riga music: lost	vd copy: SS 11; SW 31	according to *Autobiographische Skizze*, 1842–3, composition discontinued after 2 nos.
66	Die Sarazenin	Oper, 5	text: ps, private collection, pd (lost), copy (not autograph) of pd (now lost), [1841, Paris; early 1843, Dresden] music: not set; no sketches survive	ps: SW 31 pd: Bayreuth, 1889; SS 11; PW 8; SW 31	scenario only
67	Die Bergwerke zu Falun	Oper, 3	text: pd[1], *D-Dla*, pd[2] (lost), [Feb]–March 1842, Paris; pd[1] (end), 5 March 1842 music: not set; no sketches survive	pd[1], copy (not autograph) of pd[2]: Bayreuth, 1905; SS 11; *19th Century Music*, v (1981–2), 201–14; SW 31	scenario only; written for J. Dessauer; later offered to A. Röckel who did not set it
76	Friedrich I	? Oper, 5	text: ps, pd[1], pd[2] frags., NA, Oct 1846 [wint. 1848–9, Dresden]; ps (end), 31 Oct 1846 music: not set; no sketches survive	SS 11; SW 31	scenario frag.; orig. planned as an opera, not a play without music, as Wagner later claimed; see WWV 76 *Erläuterungen*
80	Jesus von Nazareth	? Oper, 5	text: pd, NA, early 1849, Dresden [? 30 March–16 April 1849, see WWV 80 *Erläuterungen*] music: not set; one sketch, *S-Smf*	pd: Leipzig, 1887; PW 8; SS 11; SW 31	scenario only; entitled 'Tragödie' and 'Drama' in *Mein Leben*
81	Achilleus	? Oper, 3	early 1849, Dresden; Feb–July 1850, Paris and Zürich	notes on 'Achilleus' (Leipzig, 1885; misleadingly described in SS 12 as 'Bruchstücke eines Dramas "Achilleus" ') probably relate to Wagner's theoretical writings 1849–50, not the projected opera	in correspondence (Feb, July 1850), orig. planned as an opera; called a 'purely dramatic poem' in a letter to Ludwig II, 1865
82	Wieland der Schmied	Heldenoper, 3	text: pd[1], pd[2], pd[3], private collection, [Dec 1849, Zürich]–March 1850, Paris; pd[2], pd[3] (end), 11 March 1850 music: not set; no sketches survive	pd[2]: GS 3; PW 1; SS 3 pd[1-3]: SW 31	scenario only; offered to Berlioz (via Liszt), A. Röckel, W. Weissheimer, but none set it; Wagner changed 'Heldenoper' to 'als Drama entworfen' in GS, cf WWV 76, 80, 81
89	Die Sieger	? Oper, 3	text: ps, NA, May 1856, Zürich; ps (end), 16 May 1856	ps: Leipzig, 1885; PW 8; SS 11; SW 31	projected only; hopes of its composition mentioned in Cosima's diaries (11 Jan 1878)
99	Luther	? Oper	text: ps, RWG, Aug 1868, Tribschen; ps (middle, end), 19 Aug, 22 Aug 1868 music: not set; no sketches survive	ps: Bayreuth, 1937; BB; SW 31	projected

WWV	title	genre, acts, libretto	composition, sources	publication	remarks
100		Lustspiel, 1	text: pd, RWG, Aug/Sept 1868, Tribschen; pd (end), 1 Sept [1868] music: not set; no sketches survive	pd: BB; SW 31	scenario only
102	Eine Kapitulation	Lustspiel in antiker Manier	text: pd, RWG, vd, NA, [Nov 1870]	pd: BB; SW 31 vd: GS 9; PW 5; SS 9; SW 31	alternative title in vd: Nicht kapitulirt!: Antikes Lustspiel in 1 Akt frei nach Aristophanes: von E. Schlossenbach: Musik von Hans Richter; according to Cosima's diaries (16 Dec 1870) Richter sketched some music

Arrs., orchestrations of excerpts from: Bellini, Il pirata [orch], comp. 1833; Bellini, Norma [revs. to orch], ? Riga, 1837; Meyerbeer, Robert le diable [transcr.], ? Riga, 1838; Weber, Euryanthe [arr.], Riga, 1839; Donizetti, La favorite [arrs.], (Paris and Berlin, 1841); Halévy, Le guitarrero [arrs.], (Paris, 1841; Paris and Berlin, 1841); Halévy, La reine de Chypre [arrs.], (Paris, 1842); Auber, Zanetta [arrs.], (Paris, 1842–3); Spontini, La vestale [inst addns], Dresden, 1844; Gluck, Iphigénie en Aulide [arr.], Dresden, 1847; Mozart, Don Giovanni [arr.], Zürich, 1850; Gluck, Iphigénie en Aulide [ov. and concert ending], Zürich, 1854

Addl music for: Marschner, Der Vampyr, Würzburg, 1833; K. Blum, Mary, Max und Michel, Riga, 1837; J. Weigl, Die Schweizerfamilie, ? Riga, 1837; Bellini, Norma, comp. 1839; Dumerson and Dupeuty, La descente de la courtille, Paris, 1841

WRITINGS, SPEECHES

This list, based on that prepared by Robert Bailey for *The New Grove Dictionary of Music and Musicians* (1980) and revised by John Deathridge for *The New Grove Wagner* (1984), includes most of Wagner's writings, reviews, speeches, open letters and letters on specific subjects published (not always with complete justification) in SS; occasional poems and dedications as well as prose drafts and texts of the stage works in GS and SS are excluded, as are certain items that appeared in obscure and now inaccessible newspapers and periodicals, and items published anonymously or pseudonymously and difficult to identify. A number of unpublished writings listed by J.-J. Nattiez in the skeleton catalogue published in his *Wagner androgyne* (Paris, 1990) are however included.

The entries are listed in chronological order (within as well as between years) according to the date of writing. The precise form of the title, which occasionally varies from edition to edition, is taken from the Volksausgabe of the writings (Leipzig, 1911–16), except that all titles of journals and musical and literary works are rendered in italics.

title, date	GS, SS	PW
Die deutsche Oper, 1834	xii	viii
Pasticcio, 1834	xii	viii
Eine Kritik aus Magdeburg, 1835	xvi	
Aus Magdeburg, 1836	xii	
Berliner Kunstchronik von Wilhelm Drach, 1836 [lost]		
Bellinis *Norma*, 1837 [review of perf. in Magdeburg; first pubd in F. Lippmann: 'Ein neu entdecktes Autograph Richard Wagners', *Musicae scientiae collectanea: Festschrift Karl Gustav Fellerer* (Cologne, 1973)]		
Der dramatische Gesang, 1837	xii	
Note for the concert of 13 November 1837		
Bellini: ein Wort zu seiner Zeit, 1837	xii	viii
Theater-Anzeige, 1837 [perf. of *Norma* in Riga]	xvi	
Wagner's announcement of the concert of 19 March 1838		
Konzert-Anzeige, 1839	xvi	
Wagner's programme for the concert of 14 March 1839		
Ein Tagebuch aus Paris, 1840	xvi	
Über deutsches Musikwesen, 1840	i	vii
Über Meyerbeers *Hugenotten*, ?1840	xii	
Stabat mater de Pergolèse, arrangé ... par Alexis Lvoff, 1840	xii	vii
Der Virtuos und der Künstler, 1840	i	vii
Eine Pilgerfahrt zu Beethoven, 1840	i	vii
Über die Ouvertüre, 1841	i	vii
Ein Ende in Paris, 1841	i	vii
9 Paris reports for the *Dresden Abend-Zeitung*, 1841	xii	viii
Pariser Amüsements, 1841	xii	viii
Der Künstler und die Öffentlichkeit, 1841	i	vii
Ein glücklicher Abend, 1841	i	vii
Der Freischütz: an das Pariser Publikum, 1841	i	vii
Le Freischütz in Paris: Bericht nach Deutschland, 1841	i	vii
Pariser Fatalitäten für Deutsche, 1841	xii	viii
Rossinis *Stabat mater*, 1841	i	vii
Bericht über eine neue Pariser Oper (*La reine de Chypre* von Halévy), 1841	i	vii
Ein Pariser bericht für Robert Schumanns *Neue Zeitschrift für Musik*, 1842	xvi	viii
Halévy und die französische Oper, 1842	xii	viii
La reine de Chypre d'Halévy, 1842	xii	
Autobiographische Skizze, 1842–3	i	i
Das Oratorium *Paulus* von Mendelssohn-Bartholdy	xii	
Zwei Schreiben an die Dresdener Liedertafel: i, Aufruf, 1843; ii, Niederlegung der Leitung, 1845	xvi	
Zwei Erklärungen über die Verdeutschung des Textes der Komposition *Les deux grenadiers*: [i], Verwahrung; [ii], Erklärung, 1843	xvi	
Rede an Webers letzter Ruhestätte, 1844 [preceded in GS by report of the reburial of Weber's remains, extracted from *Mein Leben*]	ii	vii
Die königliche Kapelle betreffend, 1846	xii	
Zu Beethovens neunter Symphonie, 1846	xii	viii
Programme note for Beethoven's Ninth Symphony, 1846 [preceded in GS by report on 1846 perf. in Dresden, extracted from *Mein Leben*]	ii	vii

title, date	GS, SS	PW
Künstler und Kritiker, mit Bezug auf einen besonderen Fall, 1846	xii	viii
Eine Rede auf Friedrich Schneider, 1846	xvi	
Notes concerning the Dresden concerts of 1847–8		
Entwurf zur Organisation eines deutschen National-Theaters für das Königreich Sachsen, 1849	ii	vii
Wie verhalten sich republikanische Bestrebungen dem Königtum gegenüber, 1848	xii	iv
Vier Zeitungs-Erklärungen [i and ii from *Dresdner Anzeige*, iii from *Europe artiste*, iv from *Ostdeutsche Post*], 1848–61	xvi	
Trinkspruch am Gedenktage des 300jährigen Bestehens der königlichen musikalischen Kapelle in Dresden, 1848	ii	vii
Der Nibelungen-Mythus: als Entwurf zu einem Drama, 1848	ii	vii
Deutschland und seine Fürsten, 1848	xii	
Zwei Schreiben aus dem Jahre 1848 [i, to Franz Wigand; ii, to Lüttichau], 1848	xvi	iv
Die Wibelungen: Weltgeschichte aus der Sage, ? mid-Feb 1849, rev. 1850	ii	vii
Über Eduard Devrients *Geschichte der deutschen Schauspielkunst*, 1849	xii	viii
Theater-Reform, 1849	xii	viii
Nochmals Theater-Reform, 1849	xii	
Der Mensch und die bestehende Gesellschaft, 1849 [incl. in SS, but possibly by Röckel]	xii	viii
Die Revolution, 1849 [incl. in SS, but authorship unproven]	xii	viii
Die Kunst und die Revolution, 1849	iii	i
Flüchtige Aufzeichnung einzelner Gedanken zu einem grösseren Aufsatze: das Künstlertum der Zukunft, 1849	xii	viii
Das Kunstwerk der Zukunft, 1849	iii	i
Zu *Die Kunst und die Revolution*, 1849	xii	viii
Das Kunstwerk der Zukunft: dedication to Feuerbach, 1850	xii	
Kunst und Klima, 1850	iii	i
Vorwort zu einer 1850 beabsichtigen Herausgabe von *Siegfrieds Tod*, 1850	xvi	
Das Judentum in der Musik, 1850, rev. 1869	v	iii
Vorwort zu der 1850 beabsichtigen Veröffentlichung des Entwurfs von 1848 *Zur Organisation eines deutschen National-Theaters für das Königreich Sachsen*, 1850	xvi	
Eine Skizze zu *Oper und Drama*, 1850	xvi	
Oper und Drama, 1850–51	iii, iv	ii
Über die musikalische Direktion der Züricher Oper, 1850	xvi	
Zur Empfehlung Gottfried Sempers, 1851	xvi	
Über die musikalische Berichterstattung in der *Eidgenössischen Zeitung*, 1851	xvi	
Beethovens *Heroische Symphonie* [programme note], 1851	v	iii
Ein Theater in Zürich, 1851	v	iii
Über die 'Goethestiftung': Brief an Franz Liszt, 1851	v	iii
Eine Mitteilung an meine Freunde, 1851	iv	i
Über musikalische Kritik: Brief an den Herausgeber der *Neuen Zeitschrift für Musik*, 1852	v	iii
Wilhelm Baumgartners Lieder, 1852	xii	
Beethovens Ouvertüre zu *Coriolan*, 1852 [programme note]	v	iii
Zum Vortrag Beethovens, 1852 [letter to Uhlig]	xvi	
Ouvertüre zu *Tannhäuser*, 1852 [programme note]	v	iii
Über die Aufführung des *Tannhäuser*: eine Mitteilung an die Dirigenten und Darsteller dieser Oper, 1852	v	iii
Vieuxtemps, 1852	xvi	

title, date	GS, SS	PW
Über die Aufführung der *Tannhäuser-Ouvertüre*, 1852	xvi	
Bemerkungen zur Aufführung der Oper: *Der fliegende Holländer*, 1852	v	iii
Vorlesung der Dichtung des *Ringes des Nibelungen*, 1853 [invitation]	xvi	
Vorwort zu der Veröffentlichung der als Manuskript gedruckten Dichtung des *Ringes des Nibelungen*, 1853	xii	
Ankündigung der im Mai 1853 zu veranstaltenden Konzerte, 1853	xii	
Ouvertüre zum *Fliegenden Holländer*, 1853 [programme note]	v	iii
Zu *Tannhäuser*: i, Einzug der Gäste auf der Wartburg; ii, Tannhäusers Romfahrt, 1853 [programme notes]	xvi	
Vorspiel zu *Lohengrin*, 1853 [programme note]	v	iii
Zu *Lohengrin*: i, Männerszene und Brautzug; ii, Hochzeitsmusik und Brautlied, 1853 [programme notes]	xvi	
Über die programmatischen Erläuterungen zu den Konzerten im Mai 1853 [prefatory remarks]	xvi	
Glucks Ouvertüre zu *Iphigenia in Aulis*, 1854	v	iii
Empfehlung einer Streichquartett-Vereinigung, 1854	xvi	
Beethovens Cis moll-Quartett (Op.131), 1854 [programme note]	xii	
Dante-Schopenhauer, 1855 [letter to Liszt]	xvi	
Bemerkung zu einer angeblichen Äusserung Rossinis, 1855	xii	
Über die Leitung einer Mozart-Feier, 1856	xvi	
Über Franz Liszts Symphonische Dichtungen, 1857 [letter to Marie Sayn-Wittgenstein]	v	iii
Metaphysik der Geschlechtsliebe, 1858 [frag. letter to Schopenhauer]	xii	
Entwurf eines Amnestiegesuches an den Sächsischen Justizminister Behr, 1858	xvi	
Nachruf an L. Spohr und Chordirektor W. Fischer, 1859	v	iii
Tristan und Isolde: Vorspiel, 1859 [programme note]	xii	
Ein Brief an Hector Berlioz	vii	iii
'Zukunftsmusik': an einen französischen Freund (Fr. Villot) als Vorwort zu einer Prosa-Übersetzung meiner Operndichtungen, 1860	vii	iii
Bericht über die Aufführung des *Tannhäuser* in Paris, 1861	vii	iii
Vom Wiener Hofoperntheater, 1861	xii	
Gräfin Egmont ballet by Rota, 1861 [review pubd under pseud. in *Oesterreichische Zeitung*, 8 Oct 1861 and in E. Kastner: *Wagner-Catalog*, 1878]		
Drei Schreiben an die Direktion der Philharmonischen Gesellschaft in St. Petersburg, 1862–6	xvi	
Vorwort zur Herausgabe der Dichtung des Bühnenfestspiels *Der Ring des Nibelungen*, 1863	vi	iii
Das Wiener Hof-Operntheater, 1863	vii	iii
Die Meistersinger von Nürnberg: Vorspiel, 1863 [programme note]	xii	
Tristan und Isolde: Vorspiel und Schluss, 1863 [programme note]	xii	
Über Staat und Religion, 1864	viii	iv
Zur Erwiderung des Aufsatzes 'Richard Wagner und die öffentliche Meinung' [by O. Redwitz], 1865	xii	
Bericht an Seine Majestät den König Ludwig II. von Bayern über eine in München zu errichtende deutsche Musikschule, 1865	viii	iv
Einladung zur ersten Aufführung von *Tristan und Isolde*, 1865 [letter to F. Uhl]	xvi	viii
Ansprache an das Hoforchester in München vor der Hauptprobe zu *Tristan und Isolde* am Vormittag des 11. Mai 1865	xvi	

title, date	GS, SS	PW
Dankschreiben an das Münchener Hoforchester, 1865	xvi	
Was ist deutsch?, 1865, rev. 1878	x	iv
Ein Artikel der Münchener *Neuesten Nachrichten* vom 29. November 1865	xvi	
Preussen und Österreich, 1866		
Zwei Erklärungen im *Berner Bund*, 1866	xvi	
Deutsche Kunst und deutsche Politik, 1867	viii	iv
Censuren, i: W. H. Riehl: *Neues Novellenbuch*, 1867	viii	iv
Censuren, ii: Ferdinand Hiller: *Aus dem Tonleben unserer Zeit*, 1867	viii	iv
Vorwort zu der Buchausgabe der Aufsätze *Deutsche Kunst und deutsche Politik*, 1868	xvi	
Zur Widmung der zweiten Auflage von *Oper und Drama*: an Constantin Frantz, 1868	viii	ii
Zum Andante der Es dur-Symphonie von Mozart, 1868 [letter to H. von Bülow]	xvi	
Meine Erinnerungen an Ludwig Schnorr von Carolsfeld (+ 1865), 1868	viii	iv
Censuren, iii: Eine Erinnerung an Rossini, 1868	viii	iv
Censuren, v: Aufklärungen über *Das Judentum in der Musik* (An Frau Marie Muchanoff, geborene Gräfin Nesselrode), 1869	viii	iii
Censuren, iv: Eduard Devrient: *Meine Erinnerungen an Felix Mendelssohn-Bartholdy*, 1869	viii	iv
Vier Erklärungen in den *Signalen für die musikalische Welt*, 1869–71 [concerning i, Hans von Bülow; ii, *Rienzi*; iii, Paris; iv, Wagner's letter to Napoleon III]	xvi	
Fragment eines Aufsatzes über Hector Berlioz, 1869	xii	
Fünf Schreiben über das Verhältnis der Kunst Richard Wagners zum Auslande, 1869–80 [i, to Judith Gautier (probably written by Cosima); ii, to Champfleury; iii, to ed. of *American Review*; iv, to Professor Gabriel Monod; v, to the Duke of Bagnara (written by Cosima)]	xvi	
Zum *Judentum in der Musik* [letter to Tausig]	xvi	
Das Münchener Hoftheater: zur Berichtigung, 1869	xii	
Über das Dirigieren, 1869	viii	iv
Persönliches: warum ich den zahllosen Angriffen auf mich und meine Kunstansichten nichts erwidere, 1869	xii	
Die Meistersinger von Nürnberg: Vorspiel zum dritten Akt [programme note; Ger. trans. of letter to Judith Gautier], 1869	xii	
Zur *Walküre*: i, Siegmunds Liebesgesang; ii, Der Ritt der Walküren; iii, Wotans Abschied und Feuerzauber, 1869 [programme notes]	xvi	
An den Wiener Hofkapellmeister Heinrich Esser, 1870	xvi	
Draft of response to *Allgemeine Zeitung* (unpubd), 1870		
Beethoven, 1870	ix	v
Ein nicht veröffentlichter Schluss der Schrift *Beethoven*, 1870		
Vorwort zu *Mein Leben*, 1870		
Offener Brief an Dr. phil. Friedrich Stade, 1870	xvi	
Über die Bestimmung der Oper, 1871	ix	v
Rede anlässlich des Banketts im Hôtel de Rome in Berlin, 1871		
Ansprache an das Orchester in der Singakademie, 1871		
Über die Aufführung des Bühnenfestspieles: *Der Ring des Nibelungen* und Memorandum über Aufführung des *Ring* in markgräflichen Opernhaus Bayreuth, 1871		
Ankündigung der Festspiele, 1871	xvi	
Aufforderung zur Erwerbung von Patronatsscheinen, 1871	xvi	
Vorwort zu Gesamtherausgabe, 1871 [foreword to GS]	i	i
Einleitung, 1871 [introduction to vol.i of GS]	i	vii
Das Liebesverbot: Bericht über eine erste Opernaufführung, ?1871 [draws on notes for *Mein Leben* about perf. of 1836]	i	vii
Einleitung, 1871 [introduction to vol.ii of GS]	ii	vii
Einleitung zum dritten und vierten Bande 1871 [introduction to vols.iii and iv of GS]	iii	
Erinnerungen an Auber, 1871	ix	v
Brief an einen italienischen Freund [Boito] über die Aufführung des *Lohengrin* in Bologna, 1871	ix	v
Epilogischer Bericht über die Umstände und Schicksale, welche die Ausführung des Bühnenfestspiels *Der Ring des Nibelungen* bis zur Veröffentlichung der Dichtung desselben begleiteten, 1871	vi	iii
Ein später fortgelassener Schluss des Berichtes an den deutschen Wagner-Verein, 1871	xvi	
Rede, gehalten in Mannheim am 20. Dezember 1871		
An den Intendanten von Loën in Weimar über die Wagner-Vereine, 1871	xvi	
Eine Mitteilung an die deutschen Wagner-Vereins, 1871	xvi	
Ankündigung für den 22. Mai 1872 [laying of foundation stone in Bayreuth]	xvi	
Ankündigung der Aufführung der Neunten Symphonie für den 22. Mai 1872	xvi	
An die Patrone, 1872		
Zirkular an die Patrone über ihre Anwesenheit bei der Grundsteinlegung, 1872	xvi	
Instruction, ?1872		
Erinnerungen an Spontini, 1872 [preceded by appreciation of 1851]	v	iii
Einleitung zum fünften und sechsten Bande, 1872 [introductions to vols. v and vi of GS]	v	iii
Censuren: Vorbericht, 1872	viii	iv
Dank an die Bürger von Bayreuth nach der Grundsteinlegung am 22. Mai 1872	xvi	
Bruchstück einer Danksagung, 1872	xvi	
Zwei Erklärungen in der Augsburger *Allgemeinen Zeitung* über die Oper *Theodor Körner* von Wendelin Weissheimer, 1872	xvi	
An Friedrich Nietzsche, 1872	ix	v
Zwei Berichtigungen im *Musikalischen Wochenblatt*, 1872–3 [i, second report of the Academic Wagner Society, Berlin; ii, Brockhaus Konversationslexikon]	xvi	
Über Schauspieler und Sänger, 1872	ix	v
Schreiben an den Bürgermeister von Bologna, 1872	ix	v
Über die Benennung 'Musikdrama', 1872	ix	v
Brief über das Schauspielerwesen an einen Schauspieler, 1872	ix	v
Ein Einblick in das heutige deutsche Opernwesen, 1872–3	ix	v
Zwei Reden gehalten anlässlich eines Banketts auf der Brühlschen Terrasse in Dresden am 14. Januar 1872		
Einleitung zu einer Vorlesung der *Götterdämmerung* vor einem ausgewählten Zuhörerkreise in Berlin, 1873	ix	v
An den Vorstand des Wagner-Vereins Berlin, 1873	xvi	
Zum Vortrag der neunten Symphonie Beethovens, 1873	ix	v
Das Bühnenfestspielhaus zu Bayreuth: nebst einem Bericht über die Grundsteinlegung desselben, 1873	ix	v
Schlussbericht über die Umstände und Schicksale, welche die Ausführung des Bühnenfestspieles *Der Ring des Nibelungen* bis zur Gründung von Wagner-Vereinen begleiteten, 1873	ix	v

title, date	GS, SS	PW
An die Patrone der Bühnenfestspiele in Bayreuth, 1873 [letter of 30 August]	xii	
An die Patrone der Bühnenfestspiele in Bayreuth, 1873 [letter of 15 September]	xvi	
Zwei Erklärungen (i, Notgedrungene Erklärung; ii, Die 'Presse' zu den 'Proben'), 1874, 1875	xii	
Über eine Opernaufführung in Leipzig: Brief an den Herausgeber des *Musikalischen Wochenblattes*, 1874	x	vi
Einladungs-Schreiben an die Sänger für Proben und Aufführungen des Bühnenfestspiels *Der Ring des Nibelungen*, 1875	xvi	
An die Orchester-Mitglieder, 1875	xvi	
Zur *Götterdämmerung*: i, Vorspiel; ii, Hagens Wacht; iii, Siegfrieds Tod; iv, Schluss des letzten Aktes, 1875 [programme notes]	xvi	
Ankündigung der Festspiele für 1876, 1875	xvi	
Über Bewerbungen zu den Festspielen, 1875	xvi	
An die Künstler, 1875	xvi	
Austeilung der Rollen, 1875		
Voranschlag der 'Entschädigungen', 1876		
Skizzierung der Proben und Aufführungen 1876, 1876		
An die Orchestermitglieder (Einladung), 1876	xvi	
An die Sänger (Einladung), 1876	xvi	
Für die Patrone, 1876	xvi	
An die Ehrenpatrone, 1876		
Verzeichnis der Ehrenpatrone und Freikarten Empfänger, 1876		
Circular, die 'Costümproben auf der beleuchteten Bühne' betreffend, 1876		
Anordnung der Proben zu den Aufführungen des Bühnenfestspieles *Der Ring des Nibelungen* in Bayreuth im Jahre 1876		
Über den Gebrauch des Textbuches, 1876	xvi	
Über den Hervorruf, 1876	xvi	
Für das Orchester, 1876	xvi	
Letzte Bitte an meine lieben Genossen! Letzter Wunsch, 1876	xvi	
Ansprache nach Schluss der *Götterdämmerung*, 1876 [authenticity uncertain]	xvi	
Abschiedswort an die Künstler, 1876 [authenticity uncertain]	xvi	
Gedanken über Zahlung des Defizits und Fortführung der Festspiele, 1876	xvi	
An die geehrten Patrone der Bühnenfestspiele von 1876, 1876	xii	
Entwürfe und Notizen zu den Programmen der (1.) 6. Konzerte in London, 1877		
Entwurf: veröffentlicht mit den Statuten des Patronatvereines, 1877 [proposal of music school for Bayreuth]	x	vi
Ansprache an die Abgesandten des Bayreuther Patronats, 1877	xii	
Aufforderung zur Anmeldung für die Stilbildungsschule, 1877		
Ankündigung der Aufführung des *Parsifal*, 1877	xii	vi
Zur Einführung (*Bayreuther Blätter*, erstes Stück), 1878	x	vi
An die geehrten Vorstände der noch bestehenden lokalen Wagner-Vereine, 1878	xvi	
Modern, 1878	x	vi
Erläuterung des *Siegfried Idylls* für S. M. den König, 1878		
Publikum und Popularität, 1878	x	vi
Das Publikum in Zeit und Raum, 1878	x	vi
Ein Rückblick auf die Bühnenfestspiele des Jahres 1876, 1878	x	vi
Metaphysik. Kunst und Religion. Moral. Christentum [frags.], 1878–82	xii	viii
Ein Wort zur Einführung der Arbeit Hans von Wolzogens *Über Verrottung und Errettung der deutschen Sprache*, 1879	x	vi
Wollen wir hoffen?, 1879	x	vi
Über das Dichten und Komponieren, 1879	x	vi
Erklärung an die Mitglieder des Patronatvereines, 1879	x	vi
Über das Operndichten und Komponieren im Besonderen, 1879	x	vi
Über die Anwendung der Musik auf das Drama, 1879	x	vi
Offenes Schreiben an Herrn Ernst von Weber, Verfasser der Schrift: *Die Folterkammern der Wissenschaft*, 1879	x	vi
Zur Einführung in das Jahr 1880, 1879	x	vi
Religion und Kunst, 1880	x	vi
An König Ludwig II. über die Aufführung des *Parsifal*, 1880	xvi	
'Was nützt diese Erkenntnis?': ein Nachtrag zu: *Religion und Kunst*, 1880	x	vi
Parsifal: Vorspiel, 1880 [programme note]	xii	viii
Zur Mitteilung an die geehrten Patrone der Bühnenfestspiele in Bayreuth, 1880	x	vi
Gedanken zur Fortführung der Festspiele, 1880		
Ausführungen zu *Religion und Kunst*: i, 'Erkenne dich selbst'; ii, Heldentum und Christentum, 1881	x	vi
Zur Einführung der Arbeit des Grafen Gobineau: *Ein Urteil über die jetzige Weltlage*	x	vi
Einladung der Sänger, 1882		
Austeilung der Partien, 1882		
Begleitschreiben zur 'Austeilung' der Partien sowie Plan der Proben und Aufführungen, 1882		
Sketch of rehearsal plan, 1882		
Brief an H. v. Wolzogen, 1882	x	vi
Offenes Schreiben an Herrn Friedrich Schön in Worms, 1882	x	vi
Rede, gehalten in Wahnfried anlässlich der Hochzeit Blandine von Bülows, 1882		
Danksagung an die Bayreuther Bürgerschaft, 1882	xvi	
Das Bühnenweihfestspiel in Bayreuth 1882, 1882	x	vi
Bericht über die Wiederaufführung eines Jugendwerkes: an den Herausgeber des *Musikalischen Wochenblattes*, 1882	x	vi
Brief an H. v. Stein, 1883	x	vi
Über das Weibliche im Menschlichen [inc.], 1883	xii	vi

ANTHOLOGIES, OTHER EDITIONS

E. L. Burlingame, ed. and trans.: *Art, Life and Theories of Richard Wagner Selected from his Writings* (New York, 1875, 2/1909)

C. F. Glasenapp and H. von Stein: *Wagner-Lexikon: Hauptbegriffe der Kunst- und Weltanschauung Richard Wagners in wörtlichen Anführungen aus seinen Schriften* (Stuttgart, 1883)

C. F. Glasenapp: *Wagner-Encyclopädie: Haupterscheinungen der Kunst- und Kulturgeschichte im Lichte der Anschauung Richard Wagners* (Leipzig, 1891)

J. Kapp, ed.: *Der junge Wagner: Dichtungen, Aufsätze, Entwürfe 1832–1849* (Berlin, 1910)

W. Golther, ed.: *Richard Wagner: Gesammelte Schriften und Dichtungen in 10 Bänden* (Berlin, 1913) [incl. prefatory life and works, suppl. vol. of notes and commentary]

E. Bücken, ed.: *Richard Wagner: die Hauptschriften* (Leipzig, 1937, abridged E. Rappl, 2/1956)

A. Lorenz, ed.: *Richard Wagner: ausgewählte Schriften und Briefe* (Berlin, 1938)

M. Gregor-Dellin, ed.: *Richard Wagner: Mein Leben* (Munich, 1963, 2/1976; Eng. trans., Cambridge, 1983) [1st authentic edn.]

A. Goldman and E. Sprinchorn, eds.: *Wagner on Music and Drama: a Compendium of Richard Wagner's Prose Works* (New York, 1964) [trans. W. A. Ellis]

C. Dahlhaus, ed.: *Wagners Ästhetik* (Bayreuth, 1972; Eng. trans.,

1964) [trans. W. A. Ellis]
C. Dahlhaus, ed.: *Wagners Ästhetik* (Bayreuth, 1972; Eng. trans., Bayreuth, 1972)
R. Jacobs and G. Skelton, eds. and trans.: *Wagner Writes from Paris: Stories, Essays and Articles by the Young Composer* (London, 1973)
C. Osborne, ed.: *Richard Wagner: Stories and Essays* (London, 1973) [rev. of Eng. trans. by W. A. Ellis]
D. Mack, ed.: *Ausgewählte Schriften* (Frankfurt, 1974) [incl. essay by Ernst Bloch]
J. Bergfeld, ed.: *Das braune Buch: Tagebuchaufzeichnungen 1865–1882* (Zürich, 1975; Eng. trans., London, 1980) [incl. frags., sketches and the 'annals' (autobiographical notes for 1846–68)]
E. Voss, ed.: *Schriften eines revolutionären Genies* (Munich, 1976)
M. Gregor-Dellin and D. Mack, eds.: *Cosima Wagner: die Tagebücher 1869–1883* (Munich, 1976–7; Eng. trans., London and New York, 1978–80)
E. Voss, ed.: *Schriften: ein Schlüssel zu Leben, Werk und Zeit* (Frankfurt, 1978)
R. Jacobs, ed. and trans.: *Three Wagner Essays* (London, 1979)
G. Strobel and W. Wolf, eds.: 'Die rote Brieftasche', *Richard Wagner: Sämtliche Briefe*, i (Leipzig, 1979), 81–92 [autobiographical notes for 1813–39]
M. Gregor-Dellin, ed.: *Mein Denken* (Munich, 1982)
D. Borchmeyer, ed.: *Dichtungen und Schriften* (Frankfurt, 1983)
K. Kropfinger, ed.: *Richard Wagner: Oper und Drama* (Stuttgart, 1984)

CATALOGUES, BIBLIOGRAPHIES, RELATED STUDIES

E. Kastner: *Wagner-Catalog: chronologisches Verzeichniss der von und über Richard Wagner erschienenen Schriften, Musikwerke etc.* (Offenbach, 1878)
N. Oesterlein: *Katalog einer Richard Wagner-Bibliothek: nach den vorliegenden Originalien zu einem authentischen Nachschlagebuch durch die gesammte, insbesondere deutsche Wagner-Litteratur bearbeitet und veröffentlicht* (Leipzig, 1882–95)
H. Silège: *Bibliographie wagnérienne française* (Paris, 1902)
Catalogue of the Burrell Collection (London, 1929)
O. Strobel: *Genie am Werk: Richard Wagners Schaffen und Wirken im Spiegel eigenhandschriftlicher Urkunden: Führer durch die einmalige Ausstellung einer umfassenden Auswahl von Schätzen aus dem Archiv des Hauses Wahnfried* (Bayreuth, 1933, 2/1934)
E. M. Terry: *A Richard Wagner Dictionary* (New York, 1939)
O. Strobel: 'Richard-Wagner-Forschungsstätte und Archiv des Hauses Wahnfried', *Das Bayernland*, lii (1942), 457–66; repr. in *Bayreuth: die Stadt Richard Wagners*, ed. O. Strobel and L. Deubner (Munich, 2/1943), 39–47
H. Barth, ed.: *Internationale Wagner-Bibliographie: 1945–55* (Bayreuth, 1956); *1956–60* (1961); 1961–6 (1968); *1967–78* (1979)
H.-M. Plesske: *Richard Wagner in der Dichtung: Bibliographie deutschsprachiger Veröffentlichungen* (Bayreuth, 1971)
H. F. G. Klein: *Erst- und Frühdrucke der Textbücher von Richard Wagner: Bibliographie* (Tutzing, 1979)
G. Bott, ed.: *Die Meistersinger und Richard Wagner: die Rezeptionsgeschichte einer Oper von 1868 bis heute* (Nuremberg, 1981) [Germanisches Nationalmuseum exhibition catalogue]
H. F. G. Klein: *Erstdrucke der musikalischen Werke von Richard Wagner: Bibliographie* (Tutzing, 1983)
Richard Wagner und die politischen Bewegungen seiner Zeit (Koblenz, 1983) [Bundesarchiv exhibition catalogue]
M. Eger, ed.: *Wagner und die Juden: Fakten und Hintergründe* (Bayreuth, 1985) [documentation accompanying exhibition in the Richard-Wagner-Museum, Bayreuth]
J. Deathridge, M. Geck and E. Voss: *Wagner Werk-Verzeichnis (WWV): Verzeichnis der musikalischen Werke Richard Wagners und ihrer Quellen* (Mainz, 1986)
S. Spencer: 'The Stefan Zweig Collection' [incl. annotated list of Wagner MSS], *Wagner*, viii (1987), 4–13
E. Voss: 'Von Notwendigkeit und Nutzen der Wagnerforschung: ein Abriss über das Wagner-Werk-Verzeichnis und die Wagner-Gesamtausgaben', *Bayreuther Festspiele: Programmheft I. Lohengrin* (Bayreuth, 1987), 16–41 [incl. Eng. trans.]

ICONOGRAPHICAL STUDIES

E. Kreowski and E. Fuchs: *Richard Wagner in der Karikatur* (Berlin, 1907)
E. W. Engel: *Richard Wagners Leben und Werke im Bilde* (Leipzig, 1913)
R. Bory: *La vie et l'oeuvre de Richard Wagner par l'image* (Lausanne, 1938; Ger. trans., 1938)
W. Schuh: *Renoir und Wagner* (Stuttgart, 1959)
M. E. Tralbaut: *Richard Wagner im Blickwinkel fünf grosser Maler* (Dortmund, 1965)
M. Geck: *Die Bildnisse Richard Wagners* (Munich, 1970)
H. Barth, D. Mack and E. Voss: *Wagner: sein Leben, sein Werk und seine Welt in zeitgenössischen Bildern und Texten* (Vienna, 1975, 2/1982; Eng. trans., 1975)
M. Gregor-Dellin: *Richard Wagner: eine Biographie in Bildern* (Munich, 1982)
E. Drusche: *Richard Wagner* (Wiesbaden, 1983)

CORRESPONDENCE

catalogues, anthologies, collected editions

W. Altmann: *Richard Wagners Briefe nach Zeitfolge und Inhalt: ein Beitrag zur Lebensgeschichte des Meisters* (Leipzig, 1905)
Helbing: auction catalogue, Munich, 11 May 1909 [25 autograph letters from collection of Hofrat Edgar Hanfstaengl]
J. N. Burk, ed.: *Letters of Richard Wagner: the Burrell Collection* (London, 1951; Ger. text and trans., 1953)
G. Strobel, W. Wolf, H.-J. Bauer and J. Forner, eds.: *Richard Wagner: Sämtliche Briefe* (Leipzig, 1967–)
Musikantiquariat Hans Schneider: catalogues 215 [Richard Wagner, ii: Documents, 1850–64], 222 ['Gruss an die Schweiz', Zürich antiquarian fair], 223 [Richard Wagner, iii: Documents, 1865–83] (Tutzing, 1978)
D. Mack, ed.: *Cosima Wagner: das zweite Leben: Briefe und Aufzeichnungen 1883–1930* (Munich, 1980)
H. Kesting, ed.: *Richard Wagner: Briefe* (Munich, 1983) [annotated edn of 206 letters]
W. Otto, ed.: *Richard Wagner: Briefe 1830–1883* (Berlin, 1986) [annotated edn of 402 letters]
S. Spencer and B. Millington, eds.: *Selected Letters of Richard Wagner* (London, 1987) [Eng. trans. of 500 letters, with orig. texts of passages omitted from existing printed edns]
H. Kesting, ed.: *Franz Liszt – Richard Wagner: Briefwechsel* (Frankfurt, 1988)

individual publications

Bisher ungedruckte Briefe von Richard Wagner an Ernst von Weber (Dresden, 1883) [several Wagner letters 1879–81]
L. Herbeck: *Johann Herbeck: ein Lebensbild* (Vienna, 1885) [letters between Wagner and J. Herbeck]
F. Hueffer, ed.: *Briefwechsel zwischen Wagner und Liszt* (Leipzig, 1887, 2/1900, enlarged E. Kloss, 3/1910; Eng. trans., 1888)
E. Wille: *15 Briefe des Meisters, nebst Erinnerungen und Erläuterungen* (Leipzig, 1887, 2/1908 W. Golther, 3/1935 C. F. Meyer)
H. von Wolzogen, ed.: *Richard Wagner's Briefe an Theodor Uhlig, Wilhelm Fischer, Ferdinand Heine* (Leipzig, 1888; Eng. trans., 1890) [see also O. Strobel: 'Unbekannte Lebensdokumente Richard Wagners: 2 unveröffentlichte Briefe Wagners an Theodor Uhlig', *Die Sonne*, x (1933), 69–77, and J. N. Burk, ed.: *Letters of Richard Wagner: the Burrell Collection* (London, 1951), 607–41]
H. S. Chamberlain, ed.: *Richard Wagners echte Briefe an Ferdinand Praeger* (Bayreuth, 1894, 2/1908)
La Mara [pseud. of M. Lipsius]: *Briefe an August Röckel von Richard Wagner* (Leipzig, 1894, 2/1912; Eng. trans., 1897)
J. Hoffmann, ed.: *Richard und Cosima Wagner an Maler Josef Hoffmann* (Bayreuth, 1896) [letters in facs.]
E. Kastner, ed.: *Briefe von Richard Wagner an seine Zeitgenossen* (Berlin, 1897)
A. Heintz, ed.: *Briefe Richard Wagner's an Otto Wesendonk* (Charlottenburg, 1898, enlarged W. Golther, 2/1905; Eng. trans., 1911)
K. Heckel, ed.: *Briefe Richard Wagners an Emil Heckel: zur Entstehungsgeschichte der Bühnenfestspiele in Bayreuth* (Berlin, 1899, 3/1911; Eng. trans., 1899)
W. Golther, ed.: *Richard Wagner an Mathilde Wesendonk: Tagebuchblätter und Briefe 1853–1871* (Leipzig, 1904, 44/1914;

Eng. trans., 1905) [see also J. Kapp: 'Unterdrückte Dokumente aus den Briefen Richard Wagners an Mathilde Wesendonk', *Die Musik*, xxiii (1930–31), 877–83, and O. Strobel: 'Ueber einen unbekannten Brief Richard Wagners an Mathilde Wesendonk und seine Geschichte', *Bayreuther Festspielführer 1937*, 152–8]

O. Kitzler: *Musikalische Erinnerungen mit Briefen von Wagner ...* (Brno, 1904)

D. Spitzer, ed.: *Briefe Richard Wagners an eine Putzmacherin* (Vienna, 1906, enlarged L. Kusche, 1967; Eng. trans., 1941)

C. F. Glasenapp, ed.: *Bayreuther Briefe von Richard Wagner (1871–1883)* (Berlin, 1907, 2/1912; Eng. trans., 1912, as *The Story of Bayreuth*)

——, ed.: *Familienbriefe von Richard Wagner 1832–1874* (Berlin, 1907; Eng. trans., 1911, enlarged J. Deathridge, 1991)

'Briefe aus sechs Jahrzehnten', *Die neue Rundschau: XIXter Jahrgang der freien Bühne* (Berlin, 1908), 858–72, 981–99

E. Kloss, ed.: *Richard Wagner an seine Künstler* (Berlin, 1908)

H. von Wolzogen, ed.: *Richard Wagner an Minna Wagner* (Berlin, 1908; Eng. trans., 1909)

E. Kloss, ed.: *Richard Wagner an Freunde und Zeitgenossen* (Berlin, 1909)

T. Apel, ed.: *Richard Wagner an Theodor Apel* (Leipzig, 1910)

W. Altmann, ed.: *Richard Wagners Briefwechsel mit seinen Verlegern: Briefwechsel mit Breitkopf & Härtel* (Leipzig, 1911); *Briefwechsel mit B. Schott's Söhne* (Mainz, 1911)

F. von Hornstein, ed.: *Zwei unveröffentlichte Briefe Richard Wagners an Robert von Hornstein* (Munich, 1911)

J. Joachim and A. Moser, eds.: *Briefe von und an Joachim*, i (Berlin, 1911)

S. Röckl: 'Zwei unbekannte Briefe Richard Wagners an Heinrich Vogl', *Rheinische Musik- u. Theater-Zeitung*, xii/51–2 (1911), 706–7

M. Huch, ed.: 'Drei unbekannte Schreiben Richard Wagners an Gustav Hölzel', *Die Musik*, xii/3 (1912–13), 171–2

L. Schemann: *Quellen und Untersuchungen zum Leben Gobineaus*, i (Strasbourg, 1914), ii (Berlin and Leipzig, 1919)

E. Förster-Nietzsche: *Wagner und Nietzsche zur Zeit ihrer Freundschaft: Erinnerungsgabe zu Friedrich Nietzsches 70. Geburtstag den 15. Oktober 1914* (Munich, 1915; Eng. trans., 1922 as *The Nietzsche–Wagner Correspondence*)

J. G. Prod'homme: 'Wagner and the Paris Opéra: Unpublished Letters (February–March, 1861)', *MQ*, i (1915), 216–31

D. Thode, ed.: *Richard Wagners Briefe an Hans von Bülow* (Jena, 1916)

S. von Hausegger, ed.: *Richard Wagners Briefe an Frau Julie Ritter* (Munich, 1920)

'Lettres inédites de Wagner à Léon Leroy et Gaspérini', *ReM*, iv/11 (1923), 139–48

W. Altmann, ed.: 'Briefe Wagners an Editha von Rhaden', *Die Musik*, xvi (1923–4), 712–32

——, ed.: *Richard Wagner und Albert Niemann: ein Gedenkbuch mit bisher unveröffentlichten Briefen* (Berlin, 1924)

L. Karpath, ed.: *Richard Wagner: Briefe an Hans Richter* (Berlin, 1924)

K. Obser, ed.: 'Unveröffentlichte Briefe Richard Wagners', *Wissen und Leben: neue Schweizer Rundschau* [Zürich], xvii (20 Jan 1924)

R. Sternfeld: 'Richard Wagner in seinen Briefen an "Das Kind"', *Die Musik*, xix (1926–7), 1–11

H. Scholz, ed.: *Richard Wagner an Mathilde Maier (1862–1878)* (Leipzig, 1930)

H. J. Moser: 'Zwanzig Richard-Wagner-Dokumente', *Deutsche Rundschau*, lvii (1931), 42–54, 133–49

E. Lenrow, ed. and trans.: *The Letters of Richard Wagner to Anton Pusinelli* (New York, 1932)

G. F. Winternitz, ed.: 'Drei unbekannte Wagner-Briefe', *Die Musik*, xxv (1932–3), 357–9

H. Ziegler: 'Wagners Briefwechsel mit seinem Verleger Fritzsch', *Die Musik*, xxvi (1933–4), 5–12

G. Kinsky, ed.: 'Fünf ungedruckte Briefe Wagners an Meyerbeer', *SMz*, lxxiv (1934), 705–16

J. Tiersot, ed.: *lettres françaises de Richard Wagner* (Paris, 1935)

W. Schuh, ed. and trans.: *Die Briefe Richard Wagners an Judith Gautier* (Zürich, 1936, enlarged, with Fr. orig., 1964 as *Richard et Cosima Wagner: lettres à Judith Gautier*, ed. L. Guichard)

O. Strobel: 'Liszt an Wagner: zwei unveröffentlichte Briefe', *Bayreuther Festspielführer 1936*, 128–9

O. Strobel, ed.: *König Ludwig II. und Richard Wagner: Briefwechsel*: Briefwechsel, v: *Neue Urkunden zur Lebensgeschichte Richard Wagners 1864–1882* (Karlsruhe, 1936–9)

C. H. N. Garrigues: *Ein ideales Sängerpaar: Ludwig Schnorr von Carolsfeld und Malwina Schnorr von Carolsfeld, geb. Garrigues* (Copenhagen, 1937) [see also O. Strobel: 'Richard Wagner und Malvina Schnorr von Carolsfeld', *König Ludwig II. und Richard Wagner: Briefwechsel*, v: *Neue Urkunden zur Lebensgeschichte Richard Wagners 1864–1882* (Karlsruhe, 1936–9), xvii–l]

A. Hedley: 'An Unpublished Wagner Letter', *ML*, xix (1938), 18–21

O. Strobel: 'Anton Bruckner huldigt Richard Wagner: ein unveröffentlichter Brief', *Bayreuther Festspielführer 1938*, 35–8

M. Becker, ed.: 'Neue Briefe Richard Wagners von seinem zweiten Pariser Aufenthalt', *Die Musik*, xxxv (1942–3), 137

P. P. Kies: 'Four New Wagner Letters', *Research Studies* (State College of Washington), xvii (1949), 209–26

H. A. Fiechtner: 'Neugefundene Wagnerbriefe', *Das Musikleben*, iii (1950), 129–35

W. Jerger, ed.: *Wagner-Nietzsches Briefwechsel während des Tribschener Idylls* (Berne, 1951)

L. Strecker: *Richard Wagner als Verlagsgefährte: eine Darstellung mit Briefen und Dokumenten* (Mainz, 1951)

A. Zinsstag, ed.: *Zur Erinnerung an Malwida von Meysenburg* (Basle, 1956) [contains 9 previously unpubd Wagner letters]

G. Marbach: 'Seien Sie ganz mein Freund – Richard Wagner an Otto Bach', *NZM*, Jg.119 (1958), 207–11

D. Härtwig: 'Ein unbekannter Wagner-Brief in Schwerin', *Musik und Gesellschaft*, x (1960), 653–60

A. Zinsstag: *Die Briefsammlungen des Richard-Wagner-Museums in Tribschen bei Luzern* (Basle, 1961)

'Richard Wagner und die arme Wiener Hofoper: ein unbekannter Briefwechsel aus dem Archiv des ehemaligen Wiener Obersthofmeisteramtes', *Musik und Gesellschaft*, xiii (1963), 283–5

W. Grupe: 'Wagner-Briefe im Deutschen Zentralarchiv, Abteilung Merseburg', *Musik und Gesellschaft*, xiv (1964), 682–4

M. Ullrichowa, ed.: 'Fünf neu aufgefundene Briefe von Richard Wagner', *BMw* (1964), suppl.

'Douze lettres inédites de Richard Wagner à Edouard Schuré', *RdM*, liv (1968), 206–21

H. Oesterheld: 'Dokumente zur Musikgeschichte Meiningens', *Neue Beiträge zur Regerforschung und Musikgeschichte Meiningens*, Südthüringer Forschung, vi (1970)[5 letters to Duke Georg II of Saxe-Meiningen and his wife]

D. Petzet and M. Petzet: *Die Richard Wagner-Bühne König Ludwigs II.* (Munich, 1970) [contains previously unpubd correspondence with Düfflipp]

U. Sautter and H. E. Onnau: *Constantin Frantz: Briefe* (Wiesbaden, 1974)

P. Slezak: 'Richard Wagner an Angelo Tessarini: ein bisher unbekannter Brief Richard Wagners', *ÖMz*, xxix (1974), 31–4

G. Colli and M. Montinari, eds.: *Nietzsche: Briefwechsel* (Berlin, 1975–)

M. Eger: 'Richard Wagner an Dr. Eduard Liszt: ein bisher unveröffentlichter Brief', *Bayreuther Festspiele: Programmheft III. Die Meistersinger* (Bayreuth, 1975), 14–17, 70–71 [incl. Eng. trans.]

K. Liepmann: 'Wagner's Proposal to America', *HiFi*, xxv/12 (1975), 70–72

R. P. Locke: *Fenway Court: annual report of the Isabella Stewart Gardner Museum* (Boston, 1975) [letters from Bayreuth]

W. Keller, ed.: *Richard Wagner: Briefe an Wilhelm Baumgartner 1850–1861* (Zürich, 1976)

J. Heyne: 'Ein unbekannter Brief Richard Wagners', *Musik und Gesellschaft*, xxviii (1978), 164–9 [to King Friedrich August II of Saxony]

E. Voss: 'Wagners "Sämtliche Briefe"?', *Melos/NZM*, iv (1978), 219–23

J. Deathridge: 'Wagner und sein erster Lehrmeister: mit einem unveröffentlichten Brief Richard Wagners', *Bayerische Staatsoper: Programmheft zur Neuinszenierung Die Meistersinger von Nürnberg* (Munich, 1979), 71–5

——: 'Wagner und Spontini: mit einem unveröffentlichten Brief Richard Wagners', *Jb der Bayerischen Staatsoper* (1979), 68–76

M. Eger: 'Der Briefwechsel Richard und Cosima Wagner: Geschichte und Relikte einer vernichteten Korrespondenz', *Bayreuther Festspiele: Programmheft IV. Das Rheingold* (Bayreuth, 1979), 1–23, 108–19; *Programmheft V. Die Walküre* (Bayreuth, 1979) 1–23, 108–32 [incl. Eng. trans.]

J. Deathridge: '"Diesen Messias glaubte und wusste ich in Ihrer Person gefunden zu haben": ein unveröffentlichter Briefentwurf Richard Wagners an den Münchener Intendanten Theodor von Küstner', *Jb der Bayerischen Staatsoper* (Munich, 1980), 75–82

S. Kohler: '"Die Welt ist mir einmal durchaus conträr!" Richard Wagner und Malwida von Meysenbug: Geschichte einer Freundschaft', *Jb der Bayerischen Staatsoper* (Munich, 1981), 61–101
S. Spencer: 'Wagner Autographs in London', *Wagner*, iv (1983), 98–114; v (1984), 2–20, 45–52 [24 previously unpubd letters, with Eng. trans., from the BL collection]
O. Pausch: 'Ein Brief Richard Wagners an Peter Cornelius über "Eine kuriose Geldangelegenheit"', *Richard Wagner 1883–1983: die Rezeption im 19. und 20. Jahrhundert*, ed. U. Müller, F. Hundsnurscher and C. Sommer (Stuttgart, 1984), 541–7
J. Marshall: 'Richard Wagner's Letter to Australia', *The Richard Wagner Centenary in Australia*, ed. P. Dennison (Adelaide, 1985), 149–65
B. Millington: 'The "Kaisermarsch" in Leipzig: an Unpublished Wagner Letter', *Wagner*, viii (1987), 2–4

PERIODICALS

Bayreuther Blätter, i–lxi (1878–1938)
Revue wagnérienne, i–iii (1885–8)
Richard Wagner-Jb, i (1886)
The Meister: the Quarterly Journal of the London Branch of the Wagner Society, i–viii (1885–95)
Richard Wagner-Jb, i–v (1906–8, 1912–13)
Tribschener Blätter: Mitteilungen der Gesellschaft Richard-Wagner-Museum Tribschen (Lucerne, 1956–)
Feuilles Wagnériennes: bulletin d'information de l'association Wagnérienne de Belgique (Brussels, 1960–)
Wagner (new ser.), ed. S. Spencer (London, 1980–)

CONTEMPORARY ESSAYS

F. Liszt: *Lohengrin et Tannhäuser de Richard Wagner* (Leipzig, 1851; Ger. trans., 1852)
J. Raff: *Die Wagnerfrage: kritisch beleuchtet*, i: *Wagners letzte künstlerische Kundgebung im 'Lohengrin'* (Brunswick, 1854) [no more pubd]
F. Liszt: 'Richard Wagner's Rheingold', *NZM*, xliii (1855), 1–3
H. von Bülow: *Über Richard Wagner's Faust-Ouvertüre: eine erläuternde Mittheilung an die Dirigenten, Spieler und Hörer dieses Werkes* (Leipzig, 1860)
Champfleury [pseud. of H. Husson]: *Richard Wagner* (Paris, 1860)
C. Baudelaire: *Richard Wagner et Tannhauser à Paris* (Paris, 1861; Eng. trans., 1964) [orig. pubd in *Revue européenne* (Paris, 1 April 1861); monograph incl. new section]
F. Nietzsche: *Die Geburt der Tragödie aus dem Geiste der Musik* (Leipzig, 1872, 2/1878, enlarged 3/1886; Eng. trans., 1967)
H. Porges: *Die Aufführung von Beethovens 9. Symphonie unter Richard Wagner in Bayreuth* (Leipzig, 1872)
E. Dannreuther: *Richard Wagner: his Tendencies and Theories* (London, 1873)
E. Hanslick: *Die Moderne Oper* (Berlin, 1875)
E. Schuré: *Le drame musical*, ii: *Richard Wagner: son oeuvre et son idée* (Paris, 1875, 4/1895; Eng. trans., 1910)
W. Mohr: *Richard Wagner und das Kunstwerk der Zukunft im Lichte der Bayreuther Aufführung betrachtet* (Cologne, 1876)
C. F. Glasenapp: *Richard Wagner's Leben und Wirken* (Kassel, 1876–7) [see 'Principal biographies']
M. Plüddemann: *Die Bühnenfestspiele in Bayreuth: ihre Gegenwart und ihre Zukunft* (Leipzig, 1877)
F. von Hausegger: *Richard Wagner und Schopenhauer* (Leipzig, 1878, 2/1892)
H. Porges: *Die Bühnenproben zu den Bayreuther Festspielen des Jahres 1876* (Chemnitz and Leipzig, 1881–96, repr. 1896; Eng. trans., 1983)
J. Gautier: *Richard Wagner et son oeuvre poétique depuis Rienzi jusqu'à Parsifal* (Paris, 1882)
R. Pohl: *Gesammelte Schriften über Musik und Musiker*, i: *Richard Wagner* (Leipzig, 1883)

PERSONAL ACCOUNTS, REMINISCENCES

H. Dorn: *Aus meinem Leben* (Berlin, 1870)
M. von Meysenbug: *Memoiren einer Idealistin* (Berlin, ?1875; Eng. trans., 1937)
F. Nietzsche: *Unzeitgemässe Betrachtungen*, iv: *Richard Wagner in Bayreuth* (Chemnitz, 1876; Eng. trans., 1910)
H. Dorn: *Ergebnisse aus Erlebnissen* (Berlin, 1877)
R. Pohl: 'Richard Wagner', *Sammlung musikalischer Vorträge*, v/53–4, ed. P. Waldersee (1883), 123–98
H. von Wolzogen: *Erinnerungen an Richard Wagner* (Vienna, 1883, enlarged 2/1891; Eng. trans., 1894)
C. Mendès: *Richard Wagner* (Paris, 1886)
K. Heckel: *Die Bühnenfestspiele in Bayreuth* (Leipzig, 1891)
F. Weingartner: *Bayreuth (1876–1896)* (Leipzig, 1896, 2/1904)
A. Lavignac: *Le voyage artistique à Bayreuth* (Paris, 1897; Eng. trans., 1898, as *The Music Dramas of Richard Wagner*)
W. Weissheimer: *Erlebnisse mit Richard Wagner, Franz Liszt und vielen anderen Zeitgenossen nebst deren Briefen* (Stuttgart, 1898)
E. Schuré: *Souvenirs sur Richard Wagner* (Paris, 1900)
L. Schemann: *Meine Erinnerungen an Richard Wagner* (Stuttgart, 1902)
M. Kietz: *Richard Wagner in den Jahren 1842–1849 und 1873–1875: Erinnerungen von Gustav Adolph Kietz* (Dresden. 1905)
H. Zumpe: *Persönliche Erinnerungen nebst Mitteilungen aus seinen Tagebuchblättern und Briefen* (Munich, 1905)
R. Fricke: *Bayreuth vor dreissig Jahren: Erinnerungen an Wahnfried und aus dem Festspielhause* (Dresden, 1906); Eng. trans. in *Wagner*, xi (1990), 93–109, 134–50, and xii (1991), 3–24 [diary kept by production assistant at first Bayreuth Festival]
E. Michotte: *La visite de Richard Wagner à Rossini (Paris 1860)* (Paris, 1906; Eng. trans., 1968)
E. Humperdinck: 'Parsifal-Skizzen: persönliche Erinnerungen an die erste Aufführung des Bühnenweihfestspieles am 25. Juli 1882', *Die Zeit* (Vienna, 1907); repr. in *Bayreuther Festspielführer 1927*, 215–29
A. Neumann: *Erinnerungen an Richard Wagner* (Leipzig, 1907; Eng. trans., 1908)
J. Gautier: *Le collier des jours: le troisième rang du collier* (Paris, 1909; rev. edn in *Mercure de France*, 1943; Eng. trans., 1910)
H. Schmidt and U. Hartmann, eds.: *Richard Wagner in Erinnerungen* (Leipzig, 1909)
J. Hey: *Richard Wagner als Vortragsmeister: Erinnerungen*, ed. H. Hey (Leipzig, 1911)
L. Frankenstein, ed.: *Theodor Uhlig: musikalische Schriften* (Regensburg, 1913)
E. von Possart: *Erstrebtes und Erlebtes: Erinnerungen aus meiner Bühnentätigkeit* (Berlin, 1916)
M. Fehr: *Unter Wagners Taktstock: 30 Winterthurer- und Zürcherbriefe aus der Zeit der Wagnerkonzerte in Zürich 1852* (Winterthur, 1922)
S. Wagner: *Erinnerungen* (Stuttgart, 1923, enlarged 2/1935)
F. Klose: *Bayreuth: Eindrücke und Erlebnisse* (Regensburg, 1929)
E. Thierbach, ed.: *Die Briefe Cosima Wagners an Friedrich Nietzsche* (Weimar, 1938–40)
W. Krienitz: 'Felix Mottls Tagebuchaufzeichnungen aus den Jahren 1873–1876', *Neue Wagner-Forschungen*, i, ed. O. Strobel (Bayreuth, 1943), 167–234
M. Gregor-Dellin and D. Mack, eds.: *Cosima Wagner: die Tagebücher 1869–1883* (Munich and Zürich, 1976–7; Eng. trans., 1978–80)
P. Cook, ed.: *A Memoir of Bayreuth: 1876* (London, 1979) [Carl Emil Doepler's account of the first Bayreuth Festival; incl. his costume designs]

PRINCIPAL BIOGRAPHIES

C. F. Glasenapp: *Richard Wagner's Leben und Wirken* (Kassel, 1876–7, enlarged 2/1882, enlarged 3/1894–1911 as *Das Leben Richard Wagners*, 5/1910–23; Eng. trans. of 3rd edn, enlarged W. A. Ellis, 1900–08, as *Life of Richard Wagner* [vols. iv–vi by Ellis alone])
M. Burrell: *Richard Wagner: his Life & Works from 1813 to 1834* (London, 1898)
M. Koch: *Richard Wagner* (Berlin, 1907–18)
E. Newman: *The Life of Richard Wagner* (London, 1933–47)
M. Fehr: *Richard Wagners Schweizer Zeit*, i [1849–55] (Aarau and Leipzig, 1934); ii [1855–72, 1883] (Aarau and Frankfurt, 1953)
C. von Westernhagen: *Richard Wagner: sein Werk, sein Wesen, seine Welt* (Zürich, 1956)
R. W. Gutman: *Richard Wagner: the Man, his Mind, and his Music* (New York and London, 1968)
C. von Westernhagen: *Wagner* (Zürich, 1968, enlarged 2/1978; Eng. trans., 1978)
J. Chancellor: *Wagner* (London, 1978)
R. Taylor: *Richard Wagner: his Life, Art and Thought* (London, 1979)
D. Watson: *Richard Wagner: a Biography* (London, 1979)
M. Gregor-Dellin: *Richard Wagner: sein Leben, sein Werk, sein Jahrhundert* (Munich, 1980, 2/1983; Eng. trans., abridged, 1983)
J. Deathridge and C. Dahlhaus: *The New Grove Wagner* (London, 1984)
B. Millington: *Wagner* (London, 1984, 2/1992)

OTHER BIOGRAPHICAL AND RELATED STUDIES

F. Hueffer: *Richard Wagner* (London, 1872, 3/1912)

A. Jullien: *Richard Wagner: sa vie et ses oeuvres* (Paris, 1886; Eng. trans., 1892, repr. 1910)
H. S. Chamberlain: *Richard Wagner* (Munich, 1896, 3/1911; Eng. trans., 1897)
E. Newman: *A Study of Wagner* (London, 1899)
W. Kienzl: *Die Gesamtkunst des XIX. Jahrhunderts: Richard Wagner* (Munich, 1903, 2/1908)
M. Semper: *Das Münchener Festspielhaus: Gottfried Semper und Richard Wagner* (Hamburg, 1906)
C. von Ehrenfels: *Richard Wagner und seine Apostaten* (Vienna, 1913)
E. Newman: *Wagner as Man and Artist* (London, 1914, 2/1924)
W. Lippert: *Richard Wagner's Verbannung und Rückkehr 1849–1862* (Dresden, 1927; Eng. trans., 1930, as *Wagner in Exile*)
J. Kniese: *Der Kampf zweier Welten um das Bayreuther Erbe: Julius Knieses Tagebuchblätter aus dem Jahre 1883* (Leipzig, 1931)
E. Newman: *Fact and Fiction about Wagner* (London, 1931)
G. de Pourtalès: *Wagner: histoire d'un artiste* (Paris, 1932, enlarged 2/1942; Eng. trans., 1932)
E. Stemplinger: *Richard Wagner in München (1864–1870): Legende und Wirklichkeit* (Munich, 1933)
E. Bücken: *Richard Wagner* (Wildpark-Potsdam, 1934, 2/1943)
K. Geiringer: 'Wagner and Brahms, with Unpublished Letters', *MQ*, xxii (1936), 178–89
W. Reihlen: 'Die Stammtafel Richard Wagners (Leipziger Abschnitt)', *Familiengeschichtliche Blätter*, xxxviii (1940), 170
——: 'Die Eltern Richard Wagners', *Familiengeschichtliche Blätter*, xli (1943), 41
O. Strobel, ed.: *Neue Wagnerforschungen* (Karlsruhe, 1943)
W. Rauschenberger: 'Die Abstammung Richard Wagners', *Familiengeschichtliche Blätter*, xlii (1944), 9
O. Strobel: *Richard Wagner: Leben und Schaffen: eine Zeittafel* (Bayreuth, 1952)
H. Mayer: *Richard Wagners geistige Entwicklung* (Düsseldorf and Hamburg, 1954)
H. Engel: 'Wagner und Spontini', *AMw*, xii (1955), 167–77
W. Vordtriede: 'Richard Wagners "Tod in Venedig"'. *Euphorion*, lii (1958–9), 378–96
H. Mayer: *Richard Wagner in Selbstzeugnissen und Bilddokumenten* (Reinbek bei Hamburg, 1959; Eng. trans., 1972)
O. Daube: *Richard Wagner: 'Ich schreibe keine Symphonien mehr': Richard Wagners Lehrjahre nach den erhaltenen Dokumenten* (Cologne, 1960)
C. von Westernhagen: *Richard Wagners Dresdener Bibliothek 1842–1849: neue Dokumente zur Geschichte seines Schaffens* (Wiesbaden, 1966)
R. Hollinrake: 'The Title-Page of Wagner's "Mein Leben"', *ML*, li (1970), 415–22
M. Gregor-Dellin: *Wagner Chronik: Daten zu Leben und Werk* (Munich, 1972)
J. Bergfeld, ed.: *Richard Wagner: Tagebuchaufzeichnungen 1865–1882: 'Das braune Buch'* (Zürich, 1975; Eng. trans., 1980)
H. Conrad: 'Absturz aus Klingsors Zaubergarten: ein biographischer Beitrag zu den letzten Lebensjahren Richard Wagners', *Fränkischer Heimatbote* [monthly suppl. to *Nordbayerischer Kurier*], xi/8 (Bayreuth, 1978)
C. von Westernhagen: 'Wagner's Last Day', *MT*, cxx (1979), 395–7
G. Skelton: *Richard and Cosima Wagner: Biography of a Marriage* (London, 1982)
S. Spencer: 'Wagner in London (1)', *Wagner*, iii (1982), 98–123 [incl. previously unpubd material]
K.-H. Kröplin: *Richard Wagner 1813–1883: eine Chronik* (Leipzig, 1983, 2/1987)
M. Gregor-Dellin: 'Neue Wagner-Ermittlungen (Das Geheimnis der Mutter)', *Bayreuther Festspiele: Programmheft II. Parsifal* (Bayreuth, 1985), 21–32 [incl. Eng. trans.]
M. Eger: 'Richard Wagner und König Ludwig II.', *Richard-Wagner-Handbuch*, ed. U. Müller and P. Wapnewski (Stuttgart, 1986; Eng. trans., 1992), 162–73
M. Kreckel: *Richard Wagner und die französischen Frühsozialisten* (Frankfurt, 1986)
U. Müller and P. Wapnewski, eds.: *Richard-Wagner-Handbuch* (Stuttgart, 1986; Eng. trans., rev. J. Deathridge, 1992)
H. Erismann: *Richard Wagner in Zürich* (Zürich, 1987)
J. Thiery and U. Tröhler: 'Zweifel am Fortschrittsglauben. Der Tierversuchsgegner Richard Wagner: seine Zeitkritik und die Reaktion seiner Zeit', *Bayreuther Festspiele: Programmheft II. Parsifal* (Bayreuth, 1987), 1–64 [incl. Eng. trans.]
E. Kröplin: *Richard Wagner: theatralisches Leben und lebendiges Theater* (Leipzig, 1989)
E. Magee: *Richard Wagner and the Nibelungs* (Oxford, 1990)
B. Millington, ed.: *The Wagner Compendium* (London, 1992)

BAYREUTH: THE FESTSPIELHAUS, ITS POLITICS AND INFLUENCE

W. Schüler: *Der Bayreuther Kreis von seiner Entstehung bis zum Ausgang der wilhelminischen Ära: Wagnerkult und Kulturreform im Geiste völkischer Weltanschauung* (Münster, 1971)
M. Karbaum: *Studien zur Geschichte der Bayreuther Festspiele* (Regensburg, 1976)
H. Mayer: *Richard Wagner in Bayreuth: 1876–1976* (Stuttgart, 1976; Eng. trans., 1976)
E. Voss: *Die Dirigenten der Bayreuther Festspiele* (Regensburg, 1976)
H. Zelinsky: *Richard Wagner – ein deutsches Thema* (Frankfurt, 1976, 3/1983)
J. Deathridge: 'Bayreuth's National Front', *Times Literary Supplement* (5 Aug 1977)
S. Grossmann-Vendrey: *Bayreuth in der deutschen Presse* (Regensburg, 1977–)
R. Hartford: *Bayreuth: the Early Years* (London, 1980)
B. W. Wessling, ed.: *Bayreuth im Dritten Reich* (Weinheim and Basle, 1983)
H. Habel: *Festspielhaus und Wahnfried* (Munich, 1985)

PRODUCTION STUDIES

A. Appia: *La mise en scène du drame wagnérien* (Paris, 1895); ed. E. Stadler, in *Theaterjb der Schweizerischen Gesellschaft für Theaterkultur*, xxviii–xxix (Berne, 1963)
——: *Die Musik und die Inszenierung* (Munich, 1899; Fr. orig., 1963; Eng. trans., 1962)
F. A. Geissler: 'Wagner und die Opernregie', *Richard Wagner-Jb*, i (1906), 251–60
A. Heuss: 'Musik und Szene bei Wagner: ein Beispiel aus "Tristan und Isolde" und zugleich ein kleiner Beitrag zur Charakteristik Gustav Mahlers als Regisseur', *Die Musik*, xii/2 (1912–13), 207–13
H. de Curzon: *L'oeuvre de Richard Wagner à Paris et ses interprètes, 1850–1914* (Paris, 1920)
D. M. Oenslager: 'A Project for the *Ring*', *Theatre Arts Monthly*, xi (1927), 35–48
F. Rühlmann: *Richard Wagners theatralische Sendung: ein Beitrag zur Geschichte und zur Systematik der Opernregie* (Brunswick, 1935)
A. Bahr-Mildenburg: *Darstellung der Werke Richard Wagners aus dem Geiste der Dichtung und Musik: Tristan und Isolde: vollständige Regiebearbeitung sämtlicher Partien mit Notenbeispielen* (Leipzig, 1936)
E. Preetorius: *Richard Wagner: Bild und Vision* (Berlin, 1942)
K. F. Richter: *Die Antinomien der szenischen Dramaturgie im Werk Richard Wagners* (diss., U. of Munich, 1956)
K. H. Ruppel, ed.: *Wieland Wagner inszeniert Richard Wagner* (Konstanz, 1960)
K. Neupert: 'Die Besetzung der Bayreuther Festspiele 1876–1960', *Internationale Wagner-Bibliographie: 1956–60*, ed. H. Barth (Bayreuth, 1961), 47–119
W. Wagner, ed.: *Richard Wagner und das neue Bayreuth* (Munich, 1962)
K. Hommel: *Die Separatvorstellungen vor König Ludwig II. von Bayern* (Munich, 1963)
D. Steinbeck: *Inszenierungsformen des 'Tannhäuser' (1845–1904): Untersuchungen zur Systematik der Opernregie* (Regensburg, 1964)
G. Skelton: *Wagner at Bayreuth: Experiment and Tradition* (London, 1965, enlarged 2/1976)
D. Steinbeck, ed.: *Richard Wagners Tannhäuser-Szenarium: das Vorbild der Erstaufführungen mit der Kostümbeschreibung und den Dekorationsplänen* (Berlin, 1968)
P. Turing: *New Bayreuth* (London, 1969, 2/1971)
M. Petzet and D. Petzet: *Die Richard Wagner-Bühne König Ludwigs II.* (Munich, 1970)
W. E. Schäfer: *Wieland Wagner: Persönlichkeit und Leistung* (Tübingen, 1970)
D. Steinbeck: 'Richard Wagners "Lohengrin"-Szenarium', *Kleine Schriften der Gesellschaft für Theatergeschichte*, xxv (Berlin, 1972), 3–44
H. Barth, ed.: *Der Festspielhügel: 100 Jahre Bayreuther Festspiele in einer repräsentativen Dokumentation* (Bayreuth, 1973, 2/1976)
L. Lucas: *Die Festspiel-Idee Richard Wagners* (Regensburg, 1973)
G. Zeh: *Das Bayreuther Bühnenkostüm* (Munich, 1973)
D. Mack: *Der Bayreuther Inszenierungsstil* (Munich, 1976)
D. Mack, ed.: *Theaterarbeit an Wagners Ring* (Munich, 1978)

C.-F. Baumann: *Bühnentechnik im Bayreuther Festspielhaus* (Munich, 1980)
O. G. Bauer: *Richard Wagner: die Bühnenwerke von der Uraufführung bis heute* (Frankfurt, Berlin and Vienna, 1982; Eng. trans., 1983)
C. Osborne: *The World Theatre of Wagner* (Oxford, 1982)
M. Srocke: *Richard Wagner als Regisseur* (Berlin, 1988)
B. Millington and S. Spencer, eds.: *Wagner in Performance* (New Haven, CT, 1992)

LITERARY AND PHILOSOPHICAL STUDIES

F. Nietzsche: *Der Fall Wagner* (Leipzig, 1888; Eng. trans., 1967)
H. Dinger: *Richard Wagners geistige Entwicklung: Versuch einer Darstellung der Weltanschauung Richard Wagners*, i: *Die Weltanschauung Richard Wagners in den Grundzügen ihrer Entwicklung* (Leipzig, 1892) [no more pubd]
J. L. Weston: *The Legends of the Wagner Drama: Studies in Mythology and Romance* (London, 1896)
H. Lichtenberger: *Richard Wagner: poète et penseur* (Paris, 1898, 5/1911; Ger. trans., 2/1904)
W. Golther: *Richard Wagner als Dichter* (Berlin, 1904; Eng. trans., 1905)
R. Sternfeld: *Schiller und Wagner* (Berlin, 1905)
P. Moos: *Richard Wagner als Ästhetiker: Versuch einer kritischen Darstellung* (Berlin, 1906)
E. Dujardin: '*La revue wagnérienne*', *ReM*, iv/11 (1923), 237–56; pubd separately (New York, 1977)
K. Hildebrandt: *Wagner und Nietzsche: ihr Kampf gegen das 19. Jahrhundert* (Breslau, 1924)
A. Drews: *Der Ideengehalt von Richard Wagners dramatischen Dichtungen im Zusammenhange mit seinem Leben und seiner Weltanschauung, nebst einem Anhang: Nietzsche und Wagner* (Leipzig, 1931)
G. Woolley: *Richard Wagner et le symbolisme français* (Paris, 1931)
K. Jäckel: *Richard Wagner in der französischen Literatur* (Breslau, 1931–2)
G. Abraham: 'Nietzsche's Attitude to Wagner: a Fresh View', *ML*, xiii (1932), 64–74; repr. in *Slavonic and Romantic Music: Essays and Studies* (London, 1968), 313–22
P. Claudel: 'Richard Wagner: rêverie d'un poëte français', *Revue de Paris* (15 July 1934); ed. M. Malicet (Paris, 1970)
E. Ruprecht: *Der Mythos bei Wagner und Nietzsche* (Berlin, 1938)
H. Schneider: *Richard Wagner und das germanische Altertum* (Tübingen, 1939)
A. Schmitz: 'Der Mythos der Kunst in den Schriften Richard Wagners', *Beiträge zur christlichen Philosophie*, iii (Mainz, 1948)
P. A. Loos: *Richard Wagner: Vollendung und Tragik der deutschen Romantik* (Berne and Munich, 1952)
W. Vetter: 'Richard Wagner und die Griechen', *Mf*, vi (1953), 111–26
A. Carlsson: 'Das mythische Wahnbild Richard Wagners', *Deutsche Vierteljahrsschrift für Literaturwissenschaft und Geistesgeschichte*, xxix (1955), 237–54
M. Gregor-Dellin: *Wagner und kein Ende: Richard Wagner im Spiegel von Thomas Manns Prosawerk: eine Studie* (Bayreuth, 1958)
E. Bloch: 'Paradoxa und Pastorale in Wagners Musik', *Merkur*, xiii (1959), 405–35; repr. in *Verfremdungen*, i (Frankfurt, 1962), and *Literarische Aufsätze* (Frankfurt, 1965); Eng. trans., 1985
E. Mann, ed.: *T. Mann: Wagner und unsere Zeit: Aufsätze, Betrachtungen, Briefe* (Frankfurt, 1963); Eng. trans., enlarged, as *Thomas Mann: Pro and Contra Wagner* (London, 1985)
F. Egermann: 'Aischyleische Motive in Richard Wagners Dichtung von "Tristan und Isolde"', *DJbM*, ix (1965), 40–48
L. Siegel: 'Wagner and the Romanticism of E. T. A. Hoffmann', *MQ*, li (1965), 597–613
B. Magee: *Aspects of Wagner* (London, 1968, enlarged 2/1988)
D. Bancroft: 'Claudel on Wagner', *ML*, l (1969), 439–52
M. Gregor-Dellin: *Richard Wagner: die Revolution als Oper* (Munich, 1973)
E. Koppen: *Dekadenter Wagnerismus: Studien zur europäischen Literatur des Fin de siècle* (Berlin and New York, 1973)
C. Dahlhaus: 'Wagners Berlioz-Kritik und die Ästhetik des Hässlichen', *Festschrift für Arno Volk* (Copenhagen, 1974), 107–24
K. G. Just: 'Richard Wagner – ein Dichter? Marginalien zum Opernlibretto des 19. Jahrhunderts', *Richard Wagner: von der Oper zum Musikdrama*, ed. S. Kunze (Berne and Munich, 1978), 79–94
H. Mayer: *Richard Wagner: Mitwelt und Nachwelt* (Stuttgart, 1978)
H. Zelinsky: 'Die "feuerkur" des Richard Wagner oder die "neue religion" der "Erlösung" durch "Vernichtung"', *Richard Wagner: wie antisemitisch darf ein Künstler sein?*, Musik-Konzepte, no.5, ed. H.-K. Metzger and R. Riehn (Munich, 1978), 79–112
A. D. Sessa: *Richard Wagner and the English* (Rutherford, NJ, 1979)
M. Tanner: 'The Total Work of Art', *The Wagner Companion*, ed. P. Burbidge and R. Sutton (London, 1979), 140–224
H. Barth, ed.: *Bayreuther Dramaturgie: Der Ring des Nibelungen* (Stuttgart, 1980)
D. Cormack: 'Thomas Mann, Hanns Eisler and the "New Bayreuth"', *Wagner*, ii (1981), 44–63
D. Borchmeyer: *Das Theater Richard Wagners: Idee – Dichtung – Wirkung* (Stuttgart, 1982; Eng. trans., 1991)
R. Furness: *Wagner and Literature* (Manchester, 1982)
R. Hollinrake: *Nietzsche, Wagner and the Philosophy of Pessimism* (London, 1982)
D. Ingenschay-Goch: *Richard Wagners neu erfundener Mythos: zur Rezeption und Reproduktion des germanischen Mythos in seinen Operntexten* (Bonn, 1982)
H. Lloyd-Jones: 'Wagner', *Blood for the Ghosts* (London, 1982), 126–42 [Greek influences on Wagner]
R. Franke: *Richard Wagners Zürcher Kunstschriften* (Hamburg, 1983)
S. Kunze: *Der Kunstbegriff Richard Wagners* (Regensburg, 1983)
B. Magee: *The Philosophy of Schopenhauer* (Oxford, 1983) [incl. substantial appx on Schopenhauer and Wagner]
A. D. Aberbach: *The Ideas of Richard Wagner* (Lanham, MD, 1984, 2/1988)
I. Gillespie: 'The Theory and Practice of "Wahn"', *Wagner*, v (1984), 79–95
M. Vogel: *Nietzsche und Wagner: ein deutsches Lesebuch* (Bonn, 1984)
J. Katz: *Richard Wagner: Vorbote des Antisemitismus* (Königstein, 1985; Eng. trans., 1986, as *The Darker Side of Genius*)
C. Suneson: *Richard Wagner och den indiska tankevärlden* (Stockholm, 1985; Ger. trans., 1989)
A. Ingenhoff: *Drama oder Epos? Richard Wagners Gattungstheorie des musikalischen Dramas* (Tübingen, 1987)
U. Bermbach: 'Die Destruktion der Institutionen: Überlegungen zum politischen Gehalt von Richard Wagners "Ring des Nibelungen"', *Bayreuther Festspiele: Programmheft III. Die Walküre* (Bayreuth, 1988), 13–66 [incl. Eng. trans.]
M. Eger: *'Wenn ich Wagnern den Krieg mache ...': der Fall Nietzsche und das Menschliche, Allzumenschliche* (Vienna, 1988), 129–67
U. Bermbach, ed.: *In den Trümmern der eigenen Welt: Richard Wagners 'Der Ring des Nibelungen'* (Berlin, 1989)
U. Müller and U. Müller, eds.: *Richard Wagner und sein Mittelalter* (Anif, Salzburg, 1989)
U. Bermbach: 'Wagner und Lukács: über die Ästhetisierung von Politik und die Politisierung von Ästhetik', *Bayreuther Festspiele: Programmheft II. Lohengrin* (Bayreuth, 1990) 1–27 [incl. Eng. trans.]
S. Corse: *Wagner and the New Consciousness: Language and Love in the 'Ring'* (Rutherford, NJ, Madison, WI, and Teaneck, NJ, 1990)
E. Lippman: 'Wagner's Conception of the Dream', *JM*, viii (1990), 54–81
J.-J. Nattiez: *Wagner androgyne* (Paris, 1990; Eng. trans., forthcoming)
L. J. Rather: *Reading Wagner: a Study in the History of Ideas* (Baton Rouge, LA, 1990)
P. L. Rose: *Revolutionary Antisemitism in Germany from Kant to Wagner* (Princeton, 1990)
——: *Wagner: Race and Revolution* (London, 1992)

ANALYSIS AND CRITICISM: GENERAL STUDIES

L. Nohl: *Das moderne Musikdrama* (Vienna, 1884)
H. Bulthaupt: 'Richard Wagner', *Dramaturgie der Oper*, ii (Leipzig, 1887, 2/1902)
W. A. Ellis: *Richard Wagner as Poet, Musician and Mystic* (London, 1887)
H. von Wolzogen: *Wagneriana: gesammelte Aufsätze über Richard Wagners Werke vom Ring bis zum Gral* (Bayreuth, 1888)
L. Torchi: *Riccardo Wagner: studio critico* (Bologna, 1890)
H. E. Krehbiel: *Studies in the Wagnerian Drama* (New York, 1891)
H. S. Chamberlain: *Das Drama Richard Wagners: eine Anregung* (Leipzig, 1892, 3/1908; Eng. trans., 1915)

A. Prüfer: *Die Bühnenfestspiele in Bayreuth* (Leipzig, 1899, enlarged, 1909, as *Das Werk von Bayreuth*)
W. J. Henderson: *Richard Wagner: his Life and his Dramas* (New York, 1901, 2/1923)
A. Seidl: *Wagneriana* (Berlin, 1901–2)
G. Adler: *Richard Wagner: Vorlesungen gehalten an der Universität zu Wien* (Munich, 1904, 2/1923)
H. von Wolzogen: *Musikalisch-dramatische Parallelen: Beiträge zur Erkenntnis von der Musik als Ausdruck* (Leipzig, 1906)
A. Seidl: *Neue Wagneriana: gesammelte Aufsätze und Studien* (Regensburg, 1914)
A. Halm: *Von Grenzen und Ländern der Musik* (Munich, 1916)
P. Bekker: *Richard Wagner: das Leben im Werke* (Stuttgart, 1924; Eng. trans., 1931)
A. Lorenz: *Das Geheimnis der Form bei Richard Wagner*, i: *Der musikalische Aufbau des Bühnenfestspieles Der Ring des Nibelungen* (Berlin, 1924); ii: *Der musikalische Aufbau von Richard Wagners 'Tristan und Isolde'* (Berlin, 1926); iii: *Der musikalische Aufbau von Richard Wagners 'Die Meistersinger von Nürnberg'* (Berlin, 1930); iv: *Der musikalische Aufbau von Richard Wagners 'Parsifal'* (Berlin, 1933)
O. Strobel: *Richard Wagner über sein Schaffen: ein Beitrag zur 'Künstlerästhetik'* (Munich, 1924)
——: 'Richard Wagners Originalpartituren', *AMz*, lv (1928), 307–11
H. Pfitzner: *Werk und Wiedergabe*, Gesammelte Schriften, iii (Augsburg, 1929)
V. d'Indy: *Richard Wagner et son influence sur l'art musical français* (Paris, 1930)
W. Engelsmann: *Wagners klingendes Universum* (Potsdam, 1933)
L. Gilman: *Wagner's Operas* (New York, 1937)
E. Newman: *Wagner Nights* (London, 1949); as *The Wagner Operas* (New York, 1949)
O. Strobel: 'Eingebung und bewusste Arbeit im musikalischen Schaffen Richard Wagners', *Bayreuther Festspielbuch 1951*, 88–95
T. W. Adorno: *Versuch über Wagner* (Berlin and Frankfurt, 1952; repr. in Gesammelte Schriften, xi, 1971; Eng. trans., 1981)
P. A. Loos: *Richard Wagner: Vollendung und Tragik der deutschen Romantik* (Berne and Munich, 1952)
H. Blümer: *Über den Tonarten-Charakter bei Richard Wagner* (diss., U. of Munich, 1958)
E. A. Lippmann: 'The Aesthetic Theories of Richard Wagner', *MQ*, xliv (1958), 209–20
W. Serauky: 'Richard Wagner in Vergangenheit und Gegenwart', *DJbM*, iii (1958), 7–34
J. M. Stein: *Richard Wagner & the Synthesis of the Arts* (Detroit, 1960)
H. von Stein: *Dichtung und Musik im Werk Richard Wagners* (Berlin, 1962)
C. von Westernhagen: *Vom Holländer zum Parsifal: neue Wagner-Studien* (Freiburg, 1962)
H. Gál: *Richard Wagner: Versuch einer Würdigung* (Frankfurt, 1963; Eng. trans., 1976)
G. Knepler: 'Richard Wagners musikalische Gestaltungsprinzipien', *BMw*, v (1963), 33–43
J. Mainka: 'Sonatenform, Leitmotiv und Charakterbegleitung', *BMw*, v (1963), 11–32
E. Arro: 'Richard Wagners Rigaer Wanderjahre: über einige baltische Züge im Schaffen Wagners', *Musik des Ostens*, iii (1965), 123–68
C. Dahlhaus: 'Wagners Begriff der "dichterisch-musikalischen Periode"', *Beiträge zur Geschichte der Musikanschauung im 19. Jahrhundert*, ed. W. Salmen, i (Regensburg, 1965), 179–87
H. Mayer: *Anmerkungen zu Wagner* (Frankfurt, 1966)
H. F. Redlich: 'Wagnerian Elements in pre-Wagnerian Operas', *Essays Presented to Egon Wellesz* (Oxford, 1966), 145–56
C. Dahlhaus: 'Eduard Hanslick und der musikalische Formbegriff', *Mf*, xx (1967), 145–53
K. Overhoff: *Die Musikdramen Richard Wagners: eine thematisch-musikalische Interpretation* (Salzburg, 1968)
M. Geck: 'Richard Wagner und die ältere Musik', *Die Ausbreitung des Historismus über die Musik*, ed. W. Wiora (Regensburg, 1969), 123–46
R. Raphael: *Richard Wagner* (New York, 1969)
Colloquium Verdi–Wagner: Rome 1969 [*AnMc*, no.11 (1972)]
C. Dahlhaus: *Die Bedeutung des Gestischen in Wagners Musikdramen* (Munich, 1970)
——: 'Soziologische Dechiffrierung von Musik: zu Theodor W. Adornos Wagnerkritik', *IRMAS*, i (1970), 137–47
——: 'Wagner and Program Music', *Studies in Romanticism*, ix (1970), 3; Ger. orig., in *Jb des Staatlichen Instituts für Musikforschung Preussischer Kulturbesitz* (Berlin, 1973)
——: 'Zur Geschichte der Leitmotivtechnik bei Wagner', *Das Drama Richard Wagners als musikalisches Kunstwerk* (Regensburg, 1970), 17–40
C. Dahlhaus, ed.: *Das Drama Richard Wagners als musikalisches Kunstwerk* (Regensburg, 1970)
S. Kunze: 'Naturszenen in Wagners Musikdrama', *GfMKB: Bonn 1970*, 199
E. Voss: *Studien zur Instrumentation Richard Wagners* (Regensburg, 1970)
C. Dahlhaus: *Die Musikdramen Richard Wagners* (Velber, nr Hanover, 1971; Eng. trans., 1979)
——: *Wagners Konzeption des musikalischen Dramas* (Regensburg, 1971)
A. Sommer: *Die Komplikationen des musikalischen Rhythmus in den Bühnenwerken Richard Wagners* (Giebing, 1971)
R. Bailey: 'The Evolution of Wagner's Compositional Procedure after Lohengrin', *IMSCR*, xi *Copenhagen 1972*, 240–46
E. Lichtenhahn: 'Die "Popularitätsfrage" in Richard Wagners Pariser Schriften', *Schweizer Beiträge zur Musikwissenschaft*, i (1972), 143
U. Jung: *Die Rezeption der Kunst Richard Wagners in Italien* (Regensburg, 1974)
J. Deathridge: 'The Nomenclature of Wagner's Sketches', *PRMA*, ci (1974–5), 75–83
K. Kropfinger: *Wagner und Beethoven: Untersuchungen zur Beethoven-Rezeption Richard Wagners* (Regensburg, 1975; Eng. trans., 1991)
S. Spencer, ed.: *Wagner 1976: a Celebration of the Bayreuth Festival* (London, 1976)
H. F. Garten: *Wagner the Dramatist* (London, 1977)
P. Petersen: 'Die dichterisch-musikalische Periode: ein verkannter Begriff Richard Wagners', *HJbMw*, ii (1977), 105–23
P. Boulez: 'Anmerkung zur musikalischen Struktur', *Theaterarbeit an Wagners Ring*, ed. D. Mack (Munich, 1978), 243
S. Kunze: 'Über den Kunstcharakter des Wagnerschen Musikdramas', *Richard Wagner: von der Oper zum Musikdrama* (Berne and Munich, 1978), 9–24
H.-K. Metzger and R. Riehn, eds.: *Richard Wagner: wie antisemitisch darf ein Künstler sein?*, Musik-Konzepte, no.5 (Munich, 1978)
D. R. Murray: 'Major Analytical Approaches to Wagner's Musical Style: a Critique', *MR*, xxxix (1978), 211–22
H. E. Renk: 'Anmerkungen zur Beziehung zwischen Musiktheater und Semiotik', *Theaterarbeit an Wagners Ring*, ed. D. Mack (Munich, 1978), 275–88
E. Voss: 'Noch einmal: das Geheimnis der Form bei Richard Wagner', *Theaterarbeit an Wagners Ring*, ed. D. Mack (Munich, 1978), 251–67; Eng. trans., *Wagner*, iv (1983), 66–79
P. Wapnewski: *Der traurige Gott: Richard Wagner in seinen Helden* (Munich, 1978)
P. Burbidge and R. Sutton, eds.: *The Wagner Companion* (London, 1979)
R. Holloway: *Debussy and Wagner* (London, 1979)
N. Josephson: 'Tonale Strukturen im musikdramatischen Schaffen Richard Wagners', *Mf*, xxxii (1979), 141–9
R. T. Laudon: *Sources of the Wagnerian Synthesis: a Study of the Franco-German Tradition in 19th-Century Opera* (Munich and Salzburg, 1979)
A. D. Sessa: *Richard Wagner and the English* (Rutherford, NJ, Madison, WI, and Teaneck, NJ, 1979)
A. Newcomb: 'The Birth of Music out of the Spirit of Drama: an Essay in Wagnerian Formal Analysis', *19th Century Music*, v (1981–2), 38–66
D. Borchmeyer: *Das Theater Richard Wagners* (Munich, 1982; Eng. trans., 1991)
R. Brinkmann: '"... einen Schluss machen!" Über externe Schlüsse bei Wagner', *Festschrift Heinz Becker* (Laaber, 1982), 179–90
——: 'Richard Wagner der Erzähler', *ÖMz*, xxxvii (1982), 297–306
M. Ewans: *Wagner and Aeschylus: the 'Ring' and the 'Oresteia'* (London, 1982)
C. Dahlhaus: 'Wagner's "A Communication to my Friends": Reminiscence and Adaptation', *MT*, cxxiv (1983), 89–92
C. Dahlhaus and E. Voss, eds.: *Wagnerliteratur – Wagnerforschung: Munich 1983*
J. Deathridge: 'Cataloguing Wagner', *MT*, cxxiv (1983), 92–6
F. W. Glass: *The Fertilizing Seed: Wagner's Concept of the Poetic Intent* (Ann Arbor, 1983)

A. Newcomb: 'Those Images that Yet Fresh Images Beget', *JM*, ii (1983), 227–45

A. Whittall: 'Wagner's Great Transition? From *Lohengrin* to *Das Rheingold*', *Music Analysis*, ii (1983), 269–80

P. Dennison, ed.: *The Richard Wagner Centenary in Australia* (Adelaide, 1985)

M. C. Tusa: 'Richard Wagner and Weber's *Euryanthe*', *19th Century Music*, ix (1985–6), 206–21

L. R. Shaw, N. R. Cirillo and M. S. Miller, eds.: *Wagner in Retrospect: a Centennial Reappraisal* (Amsterdam, 1987)

J. Warrack: 'The Influence of French Grand Opera on Wagner', *Music in Paris in the Eighteen-Thirties*, ed. P. Bloom (Stuyvesant, NY, 1987), 575–87

C. Abbate: 'Erik's Dream and Tannhäuser's Journey', *Reading Opera*, ed. A. Groos and R. Parker (Princeton, 1988), 129–67

T. S. Grey: 'Wagner, the Overture, and the Aesthetics of Musical Form', *19th Century Music*, xii (1988–9), 3–22

C. Abbate: 'Opera as Symphony, a Wagnerian Myth', *Analyzing Opera: Verdi and Wagner*, ed. C. Abbate and R. Parker (Berkeley, 1989), 92–124

——: 'Wagner, "On Modulation", and *Tristan*', *COJ*, i (1989), 33–58

A. Newcomb: 'Ritornello Ritornato: a Variety of Wagnerian Refrain Form', *Analyzing Opera: Verdi and Wagner*, ed. C. Abbate and R. Parker (Berkeley, 1989), 202–21

C. Osborne: *The Complete Operas of Richard Wagner* (London, 1990)

A. Whittall: 'Wagner's Later Stage Works', NOHM, ix (1990), 257–321

S. McClatchie: *Alfred Lorenz as Theorist and Analyst* (diss., U. of Western Ontario, in preparation)

ANALYSIS AND CRITICISM: INDIVIDUAL STUDIES

early operas: Die Hochzeit to Lohengrin

A. Smolian: *The Themes of Tannhäuser* (London, 1891)

W. Golther: 'Rienzi: ein musikalisches Drama', *Die Musik*, i (1901–2), 1833–9

F. Muncker: 'Richard Wagners Operntext "Die Hochzeit"', *Die Musik*, i (1901–2), 1824–9

W. Tappert: 'Die drei verschiedenen Schlüsse des Tannhäuser vor der jetzigen, endgültigen Fassung', *Die Musik*, i (1901–2), 1844–50

W. Altmann: 'Richard Wagner und die Berliner General-Intendantur: Verhandlungen über den "Fliegenden Holländer" und "Tannhäuser"', *Die Musik*, ii (1902–3), no.2, pp.331–45, no.3, pp. 92–109, 304–17

W. Golther: 'Die französische und die deutsche Tannhäuser-Dichtung', *Die Musik*, ii (1902–3), 271–82

F. Panzer: 'Richard Wagners Tannhäuser: sein Aufbau und seine Quellen', *Die Musik*, vii (1907–8), 11–27

H. Dinger: 'Zu Richard Wagners "Rienzi"', *Richard Wagner-Jb*, iii (1908), 88–132

E. Kloss: 'Richard Wagner über "Lohengrin": Aussprüche des Meisters über sein Werk', *Richard Wagner-Jb*, iii (1908), 132–88

E. Istel: 'Richard Wagners Oper "Das Liebesverbot" auf Grund der handschriftlichen Originalpartitur dargestellt', *Die Musik*, viii (1908–9), 3–47

H. Porges: 'Ueber Richard Wagner's "Lohengrin"', *Bayreuther Blätter*, xxxii (1909), 173–201

E. Istel: 'Wagners erste Oper "Die Hochzeit" auf Grund der autographen Partitur dargestellt', *Die Musik*, ix (1909–10), 331–51

W. Krienitz: *Richard Wagners 'Feen'* (Munich, 1910)

A. Heuss: 'Zum Thema, Musik und Szene bei Wagner: im Anschluss an Wagners Aufsatz, Bemerkungen zur Aufführung der Oper "Der fliegende Holländer"', *Die Musik*, x/1 (1910–11), 3–14, 81–95

M. Graf: 'Richard Wagner im "Fliegenden Holländer"', *Schriften zur angewandten Seelenkunde*, ed. S. Freud, ix (Leipzig and Vienna, 1911)

J. Kapp: 'Die Urschrift von Richard Wagners "Lohengrin"-Dichtung', *Die Musik*, xi/3 (1911–12), 88–93

M. Koch: 'Die Quellen der "Hochzeit"', *Richard Wagner-Jb*, iv (1912), 105–14

E. Istel: 'Autographe Regiebemerkungen Wagners zum "Fliegenden Holländer" zum ersten male veröffentlicht', *Die Musik*, xii/2 (1912–13), 214–19

E. Mehler: 'Beiträge zur Wagner-Forschung: unveröffentlichte Stücke aus "Rienzi", "Holländer" und "Tannhäuser"', *Die Musik*, xii/2 (1912–13), 195–206 and suppl.

E. Lindner: *Richard Wagner über 'Tannhäuser': Aussprüche des Meisters über sein Werk* (Leipzig, 1914)

H. von Wolzogen: *Richard Wagner über den 'Fliegenden Holländer': die Entstehung, Gestaltung und Darstellung des Werkes aus den Schriften und Briefen des Meisters zusammengestellt* (Leipzig, 1914)

J. G. Robertson: 'The Genesis of Wagner's Drama "Tannhäuser"', *Modern Language Review*, xviii (1923), 458–70

O. Strobel: 'Wagners Prosaentwurf zum "Fliegenden Holländer"', *Bayreuther Blätter*, lvi (1933), 157–60; Eng. trans., *Wagner*, ii (1981), 26–9

H. Nathan: *Das Rezitativ der Frühopern Richard Wagners: ein Beitrag zur Stilistik des Opernrezitativs in der ersten Hälfte des 19. Jahrhunderts* (diss., U. of Berlin, 1934)

A. Lorenz: 'Der musikalische Aufbau von Wagners "Lohengrin"', *Bayreuther Festspielführer 1936*, 189–98; Eng. trans., *Wagner*, ii (1981), 40–43

O. Strobel: 'Die Urgestalt des "Lohengrin": Wagners erster dichterischer Entwurf', *Bayreuther Festspielführer 1936*, 141–71; Eng. trans., *Wagner*, iv (1983), 34–49

G. Abraham: '"The Flying Dutchman": Original Version', *ML*, xx (1939), 412–19

G. Graarud: '"Sandwike ist's, genau kenn' ich die Bucht!"', *Bayreuther Festspielführer 1939*, 61–72

H. Engel: 'Über Richard Wagners Oper "Das Liebesverbot"', *Festschrift Friedrich Blume* (Kassel, 1963), 80–91

D. Steinbeck: 'Zur Textkritik der Venus-Szenen im "Tannhäuser"', *Mf*, xix (1966), 412–21

G. Abraham: 'Wagner's Second Thoughts', *Slavonic and Romantic Music: Essays and Studies* (London, 1968), 294–312 [on rev. of *Der fliegende Holländer* and *Tannhäuser*]

——: 'A Lost Wagner Aria', *MT*, cx (1969), 927–9

M. Geck: 'Rienzi-Philologie', *Das Drama Richard Wagners als musikalisches Kunstwerk*, ed. C. Dahlhaus (Regensburg, 1970), 183–97

C. Hopkinson: *Tannhäuser: an Examination of 36 Editions* (Tutzing, 1973)

P. S. Machlin: 'Wagner, Durand and "The Flying Dutchman": the 1852 Revisions of the Overture', *ML*, lv (1974), 410–28

——: *The Flying Dutchman: Sketches, Revisions and Analysis* (diss., U. of California, Berkeley, 1976)

S. Spencer: 'Tannhäuser: mediävistische Handlung in drei Aufzügen', *Wagner 1976: a Celebration of the Bayreuth Festival* (London, 1976), 40–53

R. Strohm, ed.: *Dokumente und Texte zu 'Rienzi, der Letzte der Tribunen'*, R. Wagner: Sämtliche Werke, xxiii (Mainz, 1976)

J. Deathridge: *Wagner's Rienzi: a Reappraisal based on a Study of the Sketches and Drafts* (Oxford, 1977)

R. Strohm: 'Dramatic Time and Operatic Form in Wagner's "Tannhäuser"', *PRMA*, civ (1977–8), 1–10

J. Deathridge: 'Fragmente über Fragmentarisches: zur "Lohengrin"-Kompositionsskizze', *Bayerische Staatsoper: Lohengrin – Programmheft zur Neuinszenierung* (Munich, 1978), 41

——: 'Eine verschollene Wagner-Arie?', *Melos/NZM*, iv (1978), 208–14

L. Finscher: 'Wagner der Opernkomponist: von den "Feen" zum "Rienzi"', *Richard Wagner: von der Oper zum Musikdrama*, ed. S. Kunze (Berne and Munich, 1978), 25–46

R. Strohm: 'Zur Werkgeschichte des "Tannhäuser"', *Bayreuther Festspiele: Programmheft III. Tannhäuser* (Bayreuth, 1978), 12–13, 64–76 [incl. Eng. trans.]

I. Vetter: 'Holländer-Metamorphosen', *Melos/NZM*, iv (1978), 206–8

——: 'Der "Ahasverus des Ozeans" – musikalisch unerlöst? Der fliegende Holländer und sein Revisionen', *Bayreuther Festspiele: Programmheft II. Der fliegende Holländer* (Bayreuth, 1979), 70–79 [incl. Eng. trans.]

L'avant-scène opéra, no.30 (1980) [*Der fliegende Holländer* issue]

W. Breig: 'Das "verdichtete Bild des ganzen Dramas": die Ursprünge von Wagners "Holländer"-Musik und die Senta-Ballade', *Festschrift Heinz Becker* (Laaber, 1982), 162–78

A. Csampai and D. Holland, eds.: *Rororo Opernbücher: Der fliegende Holländer* (Reinbek bei Hamburg, 1982)

N. John, ed.: *The Flying Dutchman* (London, 1982) [ENO opera guide]

I. Vetter: *Der fliegende Holländer von Richard Wagner: Entstehung, Bearbeitung, Überlieferung* (diss., Technische Universität, Berlin, 1982)

C. Abbate: 'The Parisian "Venus" and the "Paris" Tannhäuser', *JAMS*, xxxvi (1983), 73–123

B. Millington: 'Did Wagner Really Sell his "Dutchman" Story? A

Re-examination of the Paris Transaction', *Wagner*, iv (1983), 114–27

S. Spencer: '"Die hohe Braut": an Unpublished Sketch', *Wagner*, iv (1983), 13–26

C. Abbate: *The 'Parisian' Tannhäuser* (diss., Princeton U., 1984)

L'avant-scène opéra, nos. 63–4 (1984) [*Tannhäuser* issue]

R. Brinkmann: 'Sentas Traumerzählung', *Bayreuther Festspiele: Programmheft I. Der fliegende Holländer* (Bayreuth, 1984), 1–17 [incl. Eng. trans.]

'Richard Wagner: Der Venusberg', *Bayreuther Festspiele: Programmheft I. Tannhäuser* (Bayreuth, 1985), 1–14 [transcr. of previously unpubd prose draft of *Tannhäuser*] [incl. Eng. trans.]

B. Millington: '"The Flying Dutchman", "Le vaisseau fantôme" and other Nautical Yarns', *MT*, cxxvii (1986), 131–5

P. Bloom: 'The Fortunes of the Flying Dutchman in France', *Wagner*, viii (1987), 42–66

N. John, ed.: *Tannhäuser* (London, 1988) [ENO opera guide; incl. C. Abbate: 'Orpheus and the Underworld: the Music of Wagner's "Tannhäuser"', 33–50]

J. Deathridge: 'Through the Looking Glass: Some Remarks on the First Complete Draft of *Lohengrin*', *Analyzing Opera*, ed. C. Abbate and R. Parker (Berkeley, 1989), 56–91

B. Millington: 'An Introduction to the Paris "Tannhäuser"', *Tannhäuser* (DG 427 625–2, 1989), 25–33 [record notes]

Der Ring des Nibelungen

E. Koch: *Richard Wagners Bühnenfestspiel im Verhältnis zur alten Sage und zur modernen Nibelungendichtung* (Leipzig, 1875)

H. von Wolzogen: *Thematischer Leitfaden durch die Musik von R. Wagners Festspiel 'Der Ring des Nibelungen'* (Leipzig, 1876; Eng. trans., 1882)

E. Meinck: *Die sagenwissenschaftlichen Grundlagen der Nibelungendichtung Richard Wagners* (Berlin, 1892)

G. B. Shaw: *The Perfect Wagnerite: a Commentary on the Ring of the Nibelungs* (London, 1898, 4/1923)

A. Smolian: *Richard Wagner's Bühnenfestspiel Der Ring des Nibelungen: ein Vademecum* (Berlin, 1901)

C. Saint-Saëns: 'Bayreuth und der Ring des Nibelungen', *Die Musik*, i (1901–2), 751–63, 879–84

W. Golther: *Die sagengeschichtlichen Grundlagen der Ringdichtung Richard Wagners* (Berlin, 1902)

W. A. Ellis: 'Die verschiedenen Fassungen von "Siegfrieds Tod"', *Die Musik*, iii (1903–4), 239–51, 315–31

R. Petsch: 'Der "Ring des Nibelungen" in seinen Beziehungen zur griechischen Tragödie und zur zeitgenössischen Philosophie', *Richard Wagner-Jb*, ii (1907), 284–330

E. Istel: 'Wie Wagner am "Ring" arbeitete: Mitteilungen über die Instrumentationsskizze des "Rheingold" und andere Manuskripte', *Die Musik*, x (1910–11), 67–78; Eng. trans., abridged, *MQ*, xix (1933), 38–44

W. Altmann: 'Zur Geschichte der Entstehung und Veröffentlichung von Wagners "Der Ring des Nibelungen"', *AMz*, xxxviii (1911), 69–71, 101–3, 129–32, 157–9, 185–7, 217–19, 245–7

H. Wiessner: *Der Stabreimvers in Richard Wagners 'Ring des Nibelungen'* (Berlin, 1924)

L. A. Leroy: *Wagner's Music Drama of the Ring* (London, 1925)

W. Hapke: *Die musikalische Darstellung der Gebärde in Richard Wagners Ring des Nibelungen* (Leipzig, 1927)

O. Strobel: 'Die Originalpartitur von Richard Wagners "Rheingold"', *Bayreuther Festspielführer 1928*, 47–55

——: 'Die Kompositionsskizzen zum "Ring des Nibelungen"; ein Blick in die Musikerwerkstatt Richard Wagners', *Bayreuther Festspielführer 1930*, 114–22

——: *Richard Wagner: Skizzen und Entwürfe zur Ring-Dichtung, mit der Dichtung 'Der junge Siegfried'* (Munich, 1930) [see also O. Strobel, *Die Musik*, xxv (1932–3), 336–41]

——: '"Winterstürme wichen dem Wonnemond": zur Genesis von Siegmunds Lenzgesang', *Bayreuther Blätter*, liii (1930), 123–7

——: 'Aus Wagners Musikerwerkstatt: Betrachtungen über die Kompositionsskizzen zum "Ring des Nibelungen"', *AMz*, lviii (1931), 463–5, 479–82, 495–8

——: 'Vom Werden der "Ring"-Dichtung: Authentisches zur Entstehungsgeschichte des Bühnenfestspiels', *Bayreuther Festspielführer 1931*, 77–90

A. Buesst: *Richard Wagner: the Nibelung's Ring* (London, 1932, 2/1952)

O. Strobel: 'Zur Entstehungsgeschichte der Götterdämmerung: unbekannte Dokumente aus Wagners Dichterwerkstatt', *Die Musik*, xxv (1932–3), 336–41

R. Grisson: *Beiträge zur Auslegung von Richard Wagners 'Ring des Nibelungen'* (Leipzig, 1934)

E. Hutcheson: *A Musical Guide to the Richard Wagner Ring of the Nibelung* (New York, 1940)

H. Engel: 'Versuch einer Sinndeutung von Richard Wagners "Ring des Nibelungen"', *Mf*, x (1957), 225–41

W. Serauky: 'Die Todesverkündigungsszene in Richard Wagners "Walküre" als musikalisch-geistige Achse des Werkes', *Mf*, xii (1959), 143–51

R. Donington: *Wagner's 'Ring' and its Symbols: the Music and the Myth* (London, 1963, enlarged 3/1974)

C. von Westernhagen: 'Die Kompositions-Skizze zu "Siegfrieds Tod" aus dem Jahre 1850', *NZM*, Jg.124 (1963), 178–82

R. Bailey: 'Wagner's Musical Sketches for "Siegfrieds Tod"', *Studies in Music History: Essays for Oliver Strunk* (Princeton, 1968), 459–94

C. Dahlhaus: 'Formprinzipien in Wagners "Ring des Nibelungen"', *Beiträge zur Geschichte der Oper*, ed. H. Becker (Regensburg, 1969), 95–129

T. Kneif: 'Zur Deutung der Rheintöchter in Wagners *Ring*', *AMw*, xxvi (1969), 297–306; Eng. trans., *Wagner*, x (1989), 21–8

D. Coren: *A Study of Richard Wagner's 'Siegfried'* (diss., U. of California, Berkeley, 1971)

R. Brinkmann: '"Drei der Fragen stell' ich mir frei": zur Wanderer-Szene im I. Akt von Wagners "Siegfried"', *Jb des Staatlichen Instituts für Musikforschung Preussischer Kulturbesitz* (Berlin, 1972), 120–62

W. Breig: *Studien zur Entstehungsgeschichte von Wagners 'Ring des Nibelungen'* (diss., U. of Freiburg, 1973)

C. von Westernhagen: *Die Entstehung des 'Ring', dargestellt an den Kompositionsskizzen Richard Wagners* (Zürich, 1973; Eng. trans., 1976)

P. Nitsche: 'Klangefarbe und Form: das Walhallthema in Rheingold und Walküre', *Melos/NZM*, i (1975), 83–8

L'avant-scène opéra, nos. 6–7 (1976) [*Das Rheingold* issue]

W. Breig and H. Fladt, eds.: *Dokumente zur Entstehungsgeschichte des Bühnenfestspiels Der Ring des Nibelungen*, R. Wagner: Sämtliche Werke, xxix/1 (Mainz, 1976)

J. Culshaw: *Reflections on Wagner's Ring* (London, 1976)

L'avant-scène opéra, no. 8 (1977) [*Die Walküre* issue]; no. 12 (1977) [*Siegfried* issue]

D. Coren: 'Inspiration and Calculation in the Genesis of Wagner's "Siegfried"', *Studies in Musicology in Honor of Otto E. Albrecht* (Kassel, 1977), 266–87

J. Deathridge: 'Wagner's Sketches for the "Ring"', *MT*, cxviii (1977), 383–9

J. M. Knapp: 'The Instrumentation Draft of Wagner's "Das Rheingold"', *JAMS*, xxx (1977), 272–95

R. Bailey: 'The Structure of the "Ring" and its Evolution', *19th Century Music*, i (1977–8), 48–61

L'avant-scène opéra, nos. 13–14 (1978) [*Götterdämmerung* issue]

R. Brinkmann: 'Mythos – Geschichte – Natur: Zeitkonstellationen im "Ring"', *Richard Wagner: von der Oper zum Musikdrama*, ed. S. Kunze (Berne and Munich, 1978), 61–77

J. L. DiGaetani, ed.: *Penetrating Wagner's Ring: an Anthology* (Rutherford, NJ, Madison, WI, and Teaneck, NJ, 1978)

D. Cooke: *I Saw the World End* (London, 1979)

W. Breig: 'Der "Rheintöchtergesang" in Wagners "Rheingold"', *AMw*, xxxvii (1980), 241–63

W. Kinderman: 'Dramatic Recapitulation in Wagner's "Götterdämmerung"', *19th Century Music*, iv (1980–81), 101–12

L. J. Rather: *The Dream of Self-Destruction: Wagner's 'Ring' and the Modern World* (Baton Rouge, LA, 1981)

S. Spencer: '"Zieh hin! Ich kann dich nicht halten!"', *Wagner*, ii (1981), 98–120

P. McCreless: *Wagner's Siegfried: its Drama, History, and Music* (Ann Arbor, 1982)

W.-D. Schäfer: 'Syntaktische und semantische Bedingungen der Motivinstrumentation in Wagners *Ring*', *Festschrift Heinz Becker* (Laaber, 1982), 191–204

D. Coren: 'The Texts of Wagner's "Der junge Siegfried" and "Siegfried"', *19th Century Music*, vi (1982–3), 17–30

C. Dahlhaus: 'Tonalität und Form in Wagner's "Ring des Nibelungen"', *AMw*, xl (1983), 165–73

N. John, ed.: *Die Walküre* (London, 1983) [ENO opera guide]

J.-J. Nattiez: *Tétralogies – Wagner, Boulez, Chéreau: essai sur l'infidélité* (Paris, 1983)

N. John, ed.: *Siegfried* (London, 1984) [ENO opera guide]

S. Kester: *An Examination of the Themes of Love, Power and Salvation in Richard Wagner's 'The Ring of the Nibelung': a Study of a*

Failed Individuation Process (diss., U. of Western Australia, 1984)
N. John, ed.: *The Rhinegold* (London, 1985) [ENO opera guide]
——: *Twilight of the Gods* (London, 1985) [ENO opera guide]
H. R. Vaget: 'Erlösung durch Liebe: Wagners "Ring" und Goethes "Faust"', *Bayreuther Festspiele: Programmheft VI. Götterdämmerung* (Bayreuth, 1985), 14–31 [incl. Eng. trans.]
W. Darcy: 'The Pessimism of the *Ring*', *OQ*, iv/2 (1986), 24–48
D. Borchmeyer, ed.: *Wege des Mythos in der Moderne: Richard Wagner 'Der Ring des Nibelungen'* (Munich, 1987)
W. Darcy: '"Alles was ist, endet!" Erda's Prophecy of World Destruction', *Bayreuther Festspiele: Programmheft II. Das Rheingold* (Bayreuth, 1988), 67–92
D. A. White: *The Turning Wheel: a Study of Contracts and Oaths in Wagner's 'Ring'* (Selinsgrove, PA, 1988)
C. Wintle: 'The Numinous in *Götterdämmerung*', *Reading Opera*, ed. A. Groos and R. Parker (Princeton, 1988)
W. Darcy: '*Creatio ex nihilo*: the Genesis, Structure, and Meaning of the *Rheingold* Prelude', *19th Century Music*, xiii (1989–90), 79–100
H. Richardson, ed.: *New Studies in Richard Wagner's 'The Ring of the Nibelungen'* (Lewiston, NY, 1992)

Tristan und Isolde

H. von Wolzogen: *Richard Wagner's Tristan und Isolde: ein Leitfaden durch Sage, Dichtung und Musik* (Leipzig, 1880; Eng. trans., 1884)
M. Kufferath: *Guide thématique et analyse de Tristan et Iseult* (Paris, 1894)
H. Porges: 'Tristan und Isolde', *Bayreuther Blätter*, xxv (1902), 186–211; xxvi (1903), 23–48, 241–70; ed. H. von Wolzogen (Leipzig, 1906)
W. Golther: 'Zur Entstehung von Richard Wagners Tristan', *Die Musik*, v (1905–6), 3–16
L. Lehmann: *Studie zu 'Tristan und Isolde'* (n.p., *c*1906)
A. Prüfer: 'Novalis Hymnen an die Nacht in ihren Beziehungen zu Wagners Tristan und Isolde', *Richard Wagner-Jb*, i (1906), 290–304
W. Golther: *Tristan und Isolde in den Dichtungen des Mittelalters und der neuen Zeit* (Leipzig, 1907)
K. Grunsky: 'Das Vorspiel und der erste Akt von "Tristan und Isolde"', *Richard Wagner-Jb*, ii (1907), 207–84
E. Istel: 'Von Wagner angeordnete Striche und Änderungen in "Tristan und Isolde"', *Die Musik*, xii (1912–13), 173–5
E. Kurth: *Romantische Harmonik und ihre Krise in Wagners 'Tristan'* (Berlin, 1920, 2/1923)
S. Anheisser: 'Das Vorspiel zu "Tristan und Isolde" und seine Motivik', *ZMw*, iii (1920–21), 257–304
H. F. Peyser: '"Tristan", First-hand', *MQ*, xi (1925), 418–26
A. Bahr-Mildenburg: *Tristan und Isolde: Darstellung der Werke Richard Wagners aus dem Geiste der Dichtung und Musik: vollständige Regiebearbeitung sämtlicher Partien mit Notenbeispielen* (Leipzig, 1936)
G. Schünemann: 'Eine neue Tristan-Handschrift', *AMf*, iii (1938), 129–137 [on a copy by Bülow]
O. Strobel: '"Geschenke des Himmels": über die ältesten überlieferten "Tristan"-Themen und eine andere – unbekannte – Melodie Wagners', *Bayreuther Festspielführer 1938*, 157–65
H. Grunsky: '"Tristan und Isolde": der symphonische Aufbau des dritten Aufzugs', *ZfM*, Jg.113 (1952), 390–94
J. Kerman: 'Opera as Symphonic Poem', *Opera as Drama* (New York, 1956), chap. 7
V. Levi: *Tristano e Isotta di Riccardo Wagner* (Venice, 1958)
M. Vogel: *Der Tristan-Akkord und die Krise der modernen Harmonie-Lehre* (Düsseldorf, 1962)
H. Scharschuch: *Gesamtanalyse der Harmonik von Richard Wagners Musikdrama 'Tristan und Isolde': unter spezifischer Berücksichtigung der Sequenztechnik des Tristanstiles* (Regensburg, 1963)
H. Truscott: 'Wagner's "Tristan" and the Twentieth Century', *MR*, xxiv (1963), 75–85
E. Zuckerman: *The First Hundred Years of Wagner's Tristan* (New York, 1964)
W. Wagner, ed.: *100 Jahre Tristan: 19 Essays* (Emsdetten, 1965)
W. J. Mitchell: 'The Tristan Prelude: Techniques and Structure', *Music Forum*, i (1967), 162–203
R. Bailey: *The Genesis of Tristan und Isolde, and a Study of Wagner's Sketches and Drafts for the First Act* (diss., Princeton U., 1969)
E. Voss: 'Wagner's Striche im Tristan', *NZM*, Jg.132 (1971), 644–7
R. Jackson: 'Leitmotive and Form in the "Tristan" Prelude', *MR*, xxxvi (1975), 42–53
C. Dahlhaus: '"Tristan"-Harmonik und Tonalität', *Melos/NZM*, iv (1978), 215–19
J. Deathridge: '"Im übrigen darf ich wohl hoffen, dass Sie mich nicht eben gerade für einen Honorararbeiter halten ...": Zur Entstehung der "Tristan"-Partitur', *Bayerische Staatsoper: Tristan Programmheft zur Neuinszenierung* (Munich, 1980), 42
L'avant-scène opéra, nos.34–5 (1981) [*Tristan und Isolde* issue]
N. John, ed.: *Tristan and Isolde* (London, 1981) [ENO opera guide]
P. Wapnewski: *Tristan der Held Richard Wagners* (Berlin, 1981)
C. Abbate: '"Tristan" in the Composition of "Pelléas"', *19th Century Music*, v (1981–2), 117–41
A. Csampai and D. Holland, eds.: *Rororo Opernbücher: Tristan und Isolde* (Reinbek bei Hamburg, 1982) [incl. E. Voss: 'Wagners "Tristan": "Die Liebe als fruchtbare Qual"', 101–11, repr. from Bayerische Staatsoper programme book, 1980]
W. Kinderman: 'Das Geheimnis der Form in Wagners "Tristan und Isolde"', *AMw*, xl (1983), 174–88
R. Knapp: 'The Tonal Structure of *Tristan und Isolde*: a Sketch', *MR*, xlv (1984), 11–25
R. Bailey, ed.: *Richard Wagner: Prelude and Transfiguration from 'Tristan and Isolde'* (New York, 1985) [Norton Critical Score]
W. Ashbrook: 'The First Singers of *Tristan und Isolde*', *OQ*, iii/4 (1985–6), 11–23
A. Groos: 'Appropriation in Wagner's *Tristan* Libretto', *Reading Opera*, ed. A. Groos and R. Parker (Princeton, 1988), 12–33

Die Meistersinger von Nürnberg

A. M. Bowen: *The Sources and Text of Wagner's 'Die Meistersinger von Nürnberg'* (Munich, 1897)
E. Thomas: *Die Instrumentation der Meistersinger von Nürnberg: ein Beitrag zur Instrumentationslehre* (Mannheim, 1899, 2/?1907)
J. Tiersot: *Etude sur les Maîtres-chanteurs de Nuremberg de Richard Wagner* (Paris, 1899)
R. Sternfeld: 'Hans Sachsens Schusterlied', *Die Musik*, i (1901–2), 1869–75
H. Abert: 'Gedanken zu Richard Wagners "Die Meistersinger von Nürnberg"', *Die Musik*, iv (1904–5), 254–64
E. Kloss: *Richard Wagner über die 'Meistersinger von Nürnberg': Aussprüche des Meisters über sein Werk* (Leipzig, 1910)
W. Altmann: 'Zur Geschichte der Entstehung und Veröffentlichung von Richard Wagners "Die Meistersinger von Nürnberg"', *Richard Wagner-Jb*, v (1913), 87–137
K. Grunsky: 'Reim und musikalische Form in den Meistersingern', *Richard Wagner-Jb*, v (1913), 138–87
E. Mehler: 'Die Textvarianten der Meistersinger-Dichtung: Beiträge zur Textkritik des Werkes', *Richard Wagner-Jb*, v (1913), 187–233
G. Roethe: 'Zum dramatischen Aufbau der Wagnerschen Meistersinger', *Sitzungsberichte der Preussischen Akademie der Wissenschaften* (1919), 673–708
F. Zademack: *Die Meistersinger von Nürnberg: Richard Wagners Dichtung und ihre Quellen* (Berlin, 1921)
H. Thompson: *Wagner & Wagenseil: a Source of Wagner's Opera 'Die Meistersinger'* (London, 1927)
O. Strobel: '"Morgenlich leuchtend in rosigem Schein": wie Walthers "Preislied" entstand', *Bayreuther Festspielführer 1933*, 148–60
R. W. Stock: *Richard Wagner und die Stadt der Meistersinger* (Nuremberg and Berlin, 1938)
R. M. Rayner: *Wagner and 'Die Meistersinger'* (London, 1940)
W. Hess: '"Die Meistersinger von Nürnberg": ihre dichterisch-musikalische Gesamtform', *ZfM*, Jg.113 (1952), 394–7
W. E. Mcdonald: 'Words, Music, and Dramatic Development in "Die Meistersinger"', *19th Century Music*, i (1977–8), 246–60
R. Brinkmann: 'Über das Kern- und Schlusswort der "Meistersinger"', *Bayerische Staatsoper: Meistersinger Programmheft zur Neuinszenierung* (Munich, 1979), 82–91
E. Voss: 'Gedanken über "Meistersinger"-Dokumente', *Bayerische Staatsoper: Meistersinger Programmheft zur Neuinszenierung* (Munich, 1979), 76–81
A. Csampai and D. Holland, eds.: *Rororo Opernbücher: Die Meistersinger von Nürnberg* (Reinbek bei Hamburg, 1981) [incl. E. Voss: 'Wagners "Meistersinger" als Oper des deutschen Bürgertums', 9–31; Eng. trans., *Wagner*, xi (1990), 39–62]
R. Turner: '"Die Meistersinger von Nürnberg": the Conceptual Growth of an Opera', *Wagner*, iii (1982), 2–16
J. Wildgruber: 'Das Geheimnis der "Barform" in R. Wagners *Die Meistersinger von Nürnberg*: Plädoyer für eine neue Art der Formbetrachtung', *Festschrift Heinz Becker* (Laaber, 1982), 205–13

N. John, ed.: *The Mastersingers of Nuremberg* (London, 1983) [ENO opera guide]
E. Voss: 'Die Entstehung der Meistersinger von Nürnberg: Geschichten und Geschichte' (Mainz, 1983), 7–19 [facs. edn of 1862 lib.]
L'avant-scène opéra, nos. 116–17 (1989) [*Die Meistersinger* issue]
B. Millington: 'Nuremberg Trial: is there Anti-Semitism in *Die Meistersinger*?', *COJ*, iii (1991), 247–60
S. Spencer: 'Wagner's Nuremberg', *COJ*, iv (1992), 21–41

Parsifal

H. von Wolzogen: *Thematischer Leitfaden durch die Musik zu R. Wagner's Parsifal* (Leipzig, 1882; Eng. trans., 1889)
E. Hippeau: *'Parsifal' et l'opéra wagnérien* (Paris, 1883)
M. Kufferath: *Parsifal de Richard Wagner: légende, drame, partition* (Paris, 1890; Eng. trans., 1904)
E. Wechsler: *Die Sage von heiligen Gral in ihrer Entwicklung bis auf Richard Wagners 'Parsifal'* (Halle, 1898)
A. Lorenz: 'Parsifal als Übermensch', *Die Musik*, i (1901–2), 1876–82
A. Drews: 'Mozarts "Zauberflöte" und Wagners "Parsifal": eine Parallele', *Richard Wagner-Jb*, i (1906), 326–61
P. Sakolowski: 'Wagners erste Parsifal-Entwürfe', *Richard Wagner-Jb*, i (1906), 317–26
K. Grunsky: 'Die Rhythmik im Parsifal', *Richard Wagner-Jb*, iii (1908), 276–370
W. Golther: *Parsifal und der Gral in deutscher Sage des Mittelalters und der Neuzeit* (Leipzig, *c*1911)
A. Prüfer: 'Zur Entstehungsgeschichte des Bühnenweihfestspieles "Parsifal" ', *Bayreuther Festspielführer 1911*, 152–71
W. Altmann: 'Zur Entstehungsgeschichte des "Parsifal" ', *Richard Wagner-Jb*, iv (1912), 162–8
R. Petsch: 'Zur Quellenkunde des "Parsifal" ', *Richard Wagner-Jb*, iv (1912), 138–61
H. von Wolzogen: 'Parsifal-Varianten: eine Übersicht', *Richard Wagner-Jb*, iv (1912), 168–83
A. Heuss: 'Die Grundlagen der Parsifal-Dichtung', *Die Musik*, xii/13 (1912–13), 206–21, 323–33
C. Debussy: 'Richard Wagner', *Monsieur Croche antidilettante* (Paris, 1921, 2/1926; Eng. trans., 2/1962), chap.16
W. Golther: *Parzival und der Gral* (Stuttgart, 1925)
M. Unger: 'The Cradle of the Parsifal Legend', *MQ*, xviii (1932), 428–42
V. d'Indy: *Introduction à l'étude de Parsifal* (Paris, 1937)
T. W. Adorno: 'Zur Partitur des "Parsifal" ', *Moments musicaux* (Frankfurt, 1964), 52–7
M. Geck and E. Voss, eds.: *Dokumente zur Entstehung und ersten Aufführung des Bühnenweihfestspiels Parsifal*, R. Wagner: Sämtliche Werke, xxx (Mainz, 1970)
W. Keller: 'Von Meyerbeers "Robert der Teufel" zum zweiten Aufzug "Parsifal" ', *Tribschener Blätter*, xxx (1971), 6–12; Eng. trans., *Wagner*, xiii (1992), 83–90
H.-J. Bauer: *Wagners Parsifal: Kriterien der Kompositionstechnik* (Munich, 1977)
P. Wapnewski: 'Parzifal und Parsifal oder Wolframs Held und Wagners Erlöser', *Richard Wagner: von der Oper zum Musikdrama*, ed. S. Kunze (Berne and Munich, 1978), 47–60
J. Chailley: *'Parsifal' de Richard Wagner: opéra initiatique* (Paris, 1979)
L. Beckett: *Richard Wagner: Parsifal* (Cambridge, 1981)
L'avant-scène opéra, nos. 38–9 (1982) [*Parsifal* issue]
A. Csampai and D. Holland, eds.: *Rororo Opernbücher: Parsifal* (Reinbek bei Hamburg, 1982)
H.-K. Metzger and R. Riehn, eds.: *Richard Wagner: Parsifal*, Musik-Konzepte, no. 25 (Munich, 1982)
W. Seelig: 'Ambivalenz und Erlösung-Wagners "Parsifal": Zweifel und Glauben', *ÖMz*, xxxvii (1982), 307–17
B. Millington: 'Parsifal: Facing the Contradictions', *MT*, cxxiv (1983), 97–8
D. Lewin: 'Amfortas's Prayer to Titurel and the Role of D in *Parsifal*', *19th Century Music*, vii (1983–4), 336–49
N. John, ed.: *Parsifal* (London, 1986) [ENO opera guide]
M. A. Cicora: *'Parsifal' Reception in the 'Bayreuther Blätter'* (Frankfurt, Berne and New York, 1987)
B. Millington: ' "Parsifal": a Wound Reopened', *Wagner*, viii (1987), 114–20
M. Geck: 'Parsifal: a Betrayed Childhood', *Wagner*, ix (1988), 75–88
B. Millington: ' "Parsifal": a Work for our Times', *Opera*, xxxix (1988), 13–17
B. Emslie: 'Woman as Image and Narrative in Wagner's *Parsifal*: a Case Study', *COJ*, iii (1991), 109–24

other works

W. Kleefeld: 'Richard Wagner als Bearbeiter fremder Werke', *Die Musik*, iv (1904–5), 231–49, 326–37
I. Vetter, ed.: ' "Leubald: ein Trauerspiel": Richard Wagners erstes (erhaltenes) Werk', *Bayreuther Festspiele: Programmheft VII. Die Meistersinger* (Bayreuth, 1988), 1–19, 95–208 [incl. Eng. trans., and transcr. of complete text]
S. Spencer, ed.: ' "Die hohe Braut": an Unpublished Draft', *Wagner*, x (1989), 50–65

WAGNERISM

O. W. Peterson-Berger: *Richard Wagner als Kulturscheinung* (Leipzig, 1917)
K. Hildebrandt: *Wagner und Nietzsche: ihr Kampf gegen das 19. Jahrhundert* (Breslau, 1924)
J. Barzun: *Darwin, Marx, Wagner: Critique of a Heritage* (Boston, 1941, 2/1958)
E. Bentley: 'Wagner and Ibsen: a Contrast', *The Modern Theatre: a Study of Dramatists and the Drama* (London, 1948), 64–90
T. W. Adorno: *Versuch über Wagner* (Berlin and Frankfurt, 1952; Eng. trans., as *In Search of Wagner*, 1981)
H. Kirchmeyer: *Das zeitgenössische Wagner-Bild*, i–vii (Regensburg, 1967–)
B. Magee: *Aspects of Wagner* (London, 1968, 3/1988)
A. Ziino, ed.: *Antologia della critica wagneriana in Italia* (Messina, 1970)
S. Grossmann-Vendrey: *Bayreuth in der deutschen Presse*, ii: *Die Uraufführung des Parsifal* (Regensburg, 1977)
S. Martin: *Wagner to 'The Waste Land': a Study of the Relationship of Wagner to English Literature* (London, 1982)
M. Kahane and N. Wild, eds.: *Wagner et la France* (Paris, 1983)
J. Kerman: 'Wagner and Wagnerism', *New York Review* (22 Dec 1983)
D. C. Large and W. Weber, eds.: *Wagnerism in European Culture and Politics* (Ithaca, NY, 1984)
U. Müller, F. Hundsnurscher and C. Sommer, eds.: *Richard Wagner 1883–1983: die Rezeption im 19. und 20. Jahrhundert* (Stuttgart, 1984)

(2) Johanna Wagner [Jachmann-Wagner] (*b* Seelze, nr Hanover, 13 Oct 1826; *d* Würzburg, 16 Oct 1894). Soprano, adopted daughter of (1) Richard Wagner's elder brother, Albert. Through the influence of her uncle, she made her début at Dresden in 1844 as Agathe. She created Elisabeth in *Tannhäuser* (1845) and also sang in Auber's *Le maçon*. After studying in Paris with the younger Manuel García, she sang in Hamburg (1849) and was then engaged at the Hofoper, Berlin (1850–61), where she took over the part of Fidès (*Le prophète*) from Pauline Viardot. She made her London début in 1856 at Her Majesty's Theatre as Rossini's Tancredi, also singing Lucrezia Borgia and Romeo (*I Capuleti e i Montecchi*). She sang Elisabeth in the first Berlin performance of *Tannhäuser* (1856) and Ortrud in the first Berlin performance of *Lohengrin* (1859). Early in the 1860s she lost her singing voice and appeared for a decade as an actress. Her voice recovered, she sang Schwertleite and the First Norn in the first complete *Ring* cycle at Bayreuth (1876). Her voice was powerful throughout its range, clear and bright in the upper register, round and full in the lower; she had a magnificent stage presence as well as considerable dramatic ability.

*

A. Ehrlich: *Berühmte Sängerinnen der Vergangenheit und Gegenwart* (Leipzig, 1895)
J. Kapp and H. Jachmann: *Richard Wagner und seine erste 'Elisabeth'* (Berlin, 1926; Eng. trans., 1944)
E. Newman: *The Life of Richard Wagner* (London, 1933–47)
H. Fetting: *Die Geschichte der Deutschen Staatsoper* (Berlin, 1955)

(3) **(Helferich) Siegfried (Richard)** [Siegfried Helferich Richard] **Wagner** (*b* Tribschen, nr Lucerne, 6 June 1869; *d* Bayreuth, 4 Aug 1930). Composer and conductor, son of (1) Richard Wagner. He studied first with Liszt and Ernst Hausburg, and later with Humperdinck in Frankfurt. A prolific composer of opera, he also composed other vocal and symphonic works. In 1896 he was one of the conductors of the *Ring* at Bayreuth, and from 1906 until his death he was artistic director there, taking charge of every production and sometimes conducting. He was succeeded by his widow, Winifred, née Williams (1897–1980). His productions of *Tristan und Isolde* (1927), *Tannhäuser* (1930), *Parsifal* (especially Act 2, 1911, 1925 and 1927) and his special design for the Norn scene of *Götterdämmerung* (1928) were particularly important. His own compositions were heavily criticized by those who preferred his father's works, while others objected to his being director of the Bayreuth Festival. Nevertheless his first opera, *Der Bärenhäuter* (1899), was extremely successful and remained in the repertory for several years. Few of his later works matched this success, though the later and more accomplished *An allem ist Hütchen schuld*, a collage of fairy-tales composed in 1914, became famous.

Siegfried Wagner's 18 operas, for which he wrote the librettos, deal mainly with the irrational or supernatural in a historical or fairy-tale context; many could be deemed Freudian. They reveal the musical influence of Verdi, Mahler and Janáček, combining post-romantic and impressionistic harmonies with linear polyphony. The shadow of Richard Wagner is not entirely absent: *Herzog Wildfang* (1901) is a parody of the story (though not the music) of *Die Meistersinger*, while some of the music of *Der Kobold* (1904) presages Richard Strauss's impressionistic tone colours in *Die Frau ohne Schatten*. He also experimented with aleatory techniques (albeit briefly) in *Banadietrich* (1910), using them in the percussion to describe a battle scene. Almost all the plots of the operas are vivid and even disturbing and display a penchant on the part of their author for exotic historical settings (declining Byzantium in *Sonnenflammen*), *verismo* (*Der Friedensengel*) and allegory, as in *Das Flüchlein, das Jeder mitbekam*, which is based on 1920s Germany and ends with the hope of peace. *Der Schmied von Marienburg* is set among the Knights Templars, discrediting their principles and advocating a life free of dogmatism. Many of the operas tell cruel and moral tales, where witches are burnt at the stake (*Schwarzschwanenreich*) and where evil-doers are either punished (*Das Liebesopfer*) or see the error of their ways (*Walamund*). (These two operas exist only as librettos and, in the case of the latter, sketches.)

After the composer's death his family prohibited discussion of his works – it was not in their interests to encourage any possible 'artistic rivalry' between father and son – but in 1972 an international Siegfried Wagner Society was founded and some concert versions of his works were performed, beginning with *Der Friedensengel* in London in 1975; other operas were performed in Wiesbaden and Munich in the 1970s and 80s. His last and incomplete opera, *Das Flüchlein, das Jeder mitbekam*, was staged under the title *W. und die gute Frau* in Kiel in 1984, in a version completed by Hans Peter Mohr.

See also BÄRENHÄUTER, DER.

all completed works in three acts with librettos by the composer; published in Leipzig unless otherwise stated

Der Bärenhäuter op.1, Munich, Kgl Hof- und National, 22 Jan 1899 (1898)
Herzog Wildfang op.2, Munich, Kgl Hof- und National, 23 March 1901 (1901)
Der Kobold op.3, Hamburg, Stadt, 29 Jan 1904 (1903)
Bruder Lustig op.4, Hamburg, Stadt, 13 Oct 1905 (1905)
Sternengebot op.5 (prelude, 3), Hamburg, Stadt, 21 Jan 1908 (1907)
Banadietrich op.6, Karlsruhe, Hof, 23 Jan 1910 (1909)
Schwarzschwanenreich op.7, 1910, Karlsruhe, Hof, 5 Nov 1918 (1911)
Sonnenflammen op.8, 1912, Darmstadt, Hof, 30 Oct 1918 (1914)
Der Heidenkönig op.9, 1913 (prelude, 3), Cologne, Städtische, 16 Dec 1933 (Bayreuth, 1914)
Der Friedensengel op.10, 1914, Karlsruhe, Badisches Landes, 4 March 1926 (1916)
An allem ist Hütchen schuld op.11, 1914 (Märchenspiel), Stuttgart, Hof, 6 Dec 1917 (Bayreuth, 1916)
Das Liebesopfer [Wernhart] op.12, 1917 (4) [lib. only]
Der Schmied von Marienburg op.13, 1920, Rostock, Städtische Bühnen, 16 Dec 1923 (1920)
Rainulf und Adelasia op.14, prelude Rostock, 1923, rest unperf., prelude (1922), lib. (Bayreuth, 1939)
Die heilige Linde op.15, prelude Bayreuth, 1924, rest unperf., prelude (1925), lib. (1927)
Wahnopfer op.16, 1928 [only lib. and Act 1 completed], unperf., unpubd
Walamund op.17, 1928, lib. (1992) [only lib. completed]
Das Flüchlein, das Jeder mitbekam op.18, prelude Bayreuth, 1934; as W. und die gute Frau, Kiel, Bühnen der Landeshauptstadt, 29 April 1984 [completed by H. P. Mohr], vs (Bayreuth, 1983)

*

L. Karpath: *Siegfried Wagner als Mensch und Künstler* (Leipzig, 1902)
C. F. Glasenapp: *Siegfried Wagner* (Berlin, 1906)
C. Waack: *Über Dichtung und Musik von Siegfried Wagners Sternengebot* (Riga, 1908)
C. F. Glasenapp: *Siegfried Wagner und seine Kunst* (Leipzig, 1911) [essays on the operas]; new ser., as *Schwarzschwanenreich* (1913); 2nd new ser., ed P. Pretzsch, as *Sonnenflammen* (1919)
P. Pretzsch: *Die Kunst Siegfried Wagners* (Leipzig, 1919)
S. Wagner: *Erinnerungen* (Stuttgart, 1923)
O. Daube: *Siegfried Wagner und sein Werk* (Bayreuth, 1925)
P. Pretzsch and O. Daube: *Offizieller Führer der Deutschen Festspiele und Siegfried-Wagner-Festspielwoche Weimar* (Bayreuth, 1926)
K. Meier-Gesees: *Festschrift zu Siegfried Wagners 60. Geburtstag* (Bayreuth, 1929)
H. Rebois: *Lettres de Siegfried Wagner* (Paris, 1933)
H. Merian: *Der Bärenhäuter von Siegfried Wagner* (Leipzig, n.d.)
P. Sakolowski: *Herzog Wildfang von Siegfried Wagner* (Leipzig, n.d.)
O. Daube: *Siegfried Wagner und die Märchenoper* (Leipzig, 1936)
F. Stassen: *Erinnerungen an Siegfried Wagner* (Detmold, 1942)
Z. von Kraft: *Der Sohn* (Graz, 1963)
G. Skelton: *Wagner at Bayreuth: Experiment and Tradition* (London, 1965, enlarged 2/1976)
T. E. Reimers: 'Siegfried Wagner as Innovator', *Opera*, xxiii (1972), 888–94
Mitteilungsblätter der Internationalen Siegfried Wagner Gesellschaft (Munich, 1972–92)
P. P. Pachl: *Siegfried Wagners musikdramatisches Schaffen* (Tutzing, 1979)
K. Söhnlein: *Erinnerungen an Siegfried Wagner und Bayreuth*, ed. P. P. Pachl (Bayreuth, 1980)
P. P. Pachl: *Siegfried Wagner, Genie im Schatten* (Munich,1988)

(4) **Wieland (Adolf Gottfried) Wagner** (*b* Bayreuth, 5 Jan 1917; *d* Munich, 17 Oct 1966). Director and stage designer, grandson of (1) Richard Wagner and son of (3) Siegfried Wagner. Brought up to direct the Bayreuth Festival, he observed the work of Preetorius and Roller in the 1930s. His first professional work as a designer and director was at Altenburg, but he also provided designs for *Parsifal* (1937) and *Meistersinger* (1943) at Bayreuth. After World War II, with his brother (5) Wolfgang Wagner, he revived the Bayreuth Festival, in

3. Wieland Wagner's production of 'Tannhäuser' (Festspielhaus, Bayreuth, 1954), with Act 2 set on a chessboard

1951, with starkly modern, symbolist productions; he remained co-director of the festival until 1966. His productions were greatly at variance with the Romantic tradition of Wagnerian staging consolidated by Wagner's widow Cosima, who at the turn of the century had firmly rejected the symbolist projects of Adolphe Appia, an acknowledged influence on Wieland.

Wieland Wagner directed and designed all his grandfather's operas, from *Rienzi* to *Parsifal*, according to his conviction that the music did not require the old-fashioned, explicit scenery and stage action that the composer had prescribed. He used much reduced stage movements, dispensed with rainbow bridges and shattering swords, and imposed his own images on the works; in his 1954 *Tannhäuser*, Act 2 was set on a chessboard where the White Queen broke the rules by rushing forward to protect a threatened Black Knight. His productions were marked by the naked simplicity of their settings – most notably the tilted disc on which he staged the second of his three *Ring* cycles (1951) – by the importance he attached to lighting, and by their strongly defined characterizations. A political, even socialist, element was perceived by some critics in productions such as that of the *Ring* of 1965, while other critics responded only to its mythical dimensions. He continually reworked his stagings, so that many Bayreuth 'revivals' were in effect new productions.

Though usually associated with Bayreuth and his grandfather's works, he contributed important productions of works by other composers, including Gluck, Verdi, Berg and Orff, notably at the Stuttgart Staatsoper. His *Fidelio* (1954) was notorious for his removal of the spoken dialogue and rearrangement of many of the musical numbers; *Salome* (1962), a production conceived specifically for Anja Silja, was remarkable for his reversal of the style of the piece: he found stillness in the dance, and movement in the traditionally static dramatic sections. After his death the Bayreuth Festival gradually replaced all his productions (*Parsifal*, the last to survive, was retired in 1973). In 1972, however, 11 of them were still in the Stuttgart repertory.

For further illustration *see* PRODUCTION, fig.22 and STAGE DESIGN, fig.25.

W. Panofsky: *Wieland Wagner* (Bremen, 1964)
G. Skelton: *Wagner at Bayreuth: Experiment and Tradition* (London, 1965, enlarged 2/1976)
V. Gollancz: *The Ring at Bayreuth* (London, 1966)
A. Goléa: *Gespräche mit Wieland Wagner* (Salzburg, 1968)
C. Lust: *Wieland Wagner et la survie du théâtre lyrique* (Lausanne, 1969)
W. E. Schäfer: *Wieland Wagner: Persönlichkeit und Leistung* (Tübingen, 1970)
G. Skelton: *Wieland Wagner: the Positive Sceptic* (London, 1971)
D. Mack: *Der Bayreuther Inszenierungsstil 1876–1976* (Munich, 1976)
W. S. Wagner: *The Wagner Family Albums* (London, 1976)
Musique en jeu, nos. 22–3 (1976)
O. Bauer: *Richard Wagner: die Bühnenwerke von der Uraufführung bis heute* (Fribourg, 1982; Eng. trans., 1982)

(5) **Wolfgang** (**Manfred Martin**) **Wagner** (*b* Bayreuth, 30 Aug 1919). Administrator and director, grandson of (1) Richard Wagner and son of (3) Siegfried Wagner. He studied music privately in Bayreuth and received practical theatre training in Berlin with Preetorius. In 1951, with his brother (4) Wieland Wagner, he revived the Bayreuth Festival after World War II. Until Wieland's death in 1966 they were co-directors of the festival, Wolfgang assuming responsibility for administration; after that date he took over as sole director.

He began by assisting his brother with his modern, controversial productions, and later staged his own productions, beginning with *Lohengrin* in 1953; he has devoted himself almost exclusively to directing his grandfather's works. Though clearly influenced by his brother's reforms, his own productions, up to and including *Meistersinger* (1981), *Tannhäuser* (1985) and *Parsifal* (1989), have been more conservative, occasionally incorporating romantic and semi-naturalistic elements. He shares his brother's love of lighting effects, though some of his productions have been criticized as too dark. His 1973 version of *Meistersinger* won praise for its new floor projections and lush variety of colour. He is sceptical of following his grandfather's written stage directions, but his introduction of a curtain (or more exactly a shutter) closing from both the top and the bottom during the scene changes in the *Ring* was not a popular innovation. His control over production concepts has been questioned, but the basic concept of his 1970 *Ring* ranks as one of his most successful achievements. This was set on a tilted disc, like Wieland's, but in the early stages of the narrative the disc broke into fragments, to be restored whole only at the end of the epic.

Wolfgang's greatest contribution has been in maintaining the Bayreuth Festival's unique role as both a shrine to Richard Wagner and a workshop for modern opera production; in his choice of other directors, designers and musicians, he has taken chances and encouraged radical experimentation.

*

G. Skelton: *Wagner at Bayreuth: Experiment and Tradition* (London, 1965, enlarged 2/1976)
D. Mack: *Der Bayreuther Inszenierungsstil 1876–1976* (Munich, 1976)
W. S. Wagner: *The Wagner Family Albums* (London, 1976)
O. Bauer: *Richard Wagner: die Bühnenwerke von der Uraufführung bis heute* (Fribourg, 1982; Eng. trans., 1982)

BARRY MILLINGTON (1; lists with JOHN DEATHRIDGE and ROBERT BAILEY), ELIZABETH FORBES (2), PETER P. PACHL (3), PAUL SHEREN (4, 5)

Wagner, Karl Jacob (*b* Darmstadt, 22 Feb 1772; *d* Darmstadt, 24 Nov 1822). German composer. The son of a Darmstadt court musician, he was apprenticed in the Hofkapelle there in 1788 and joined the orchestra as a violinist and horn player in 1790; in 1800 he was named master of military music. From 1800 to 1805 he made frequent concert tours; he went to Paris in 1805, returning to Darmstadt to become Hofkapellmeister (1811–20). For the court theatre he composed several operas and Singspiels, and incidental music to a number of plays, including Goethe's *Götz von Berlichingen*, Schiller's *Die Jungfrau von Orleans* (both 1817) and Mahlmann's once popular parody *Herodes vor Bethlehem*. He also wrote cantatas for special occasions. His manuscripts (formerly in *D-DS*) were destroyed by fire in 1944.

first performed at Darmstadt, Hoftheater, unless otherwise stated

Pygmalion, oder Die Reformation der Liebe (grosse Oper, 2, F. Bouterweck), 1797
Der Zahnarzt (komische Oper, 1, Wagner), 9 June 1808
Die Wiedergenesung (Spl, 1, G. C. Zimmermann), 1808
Der Rückmarsch ins Vaterland (Spl, 1, Zimmermann), 1810
Siaph und Nitettis (grosse Oper, 3, J. C. Markwart), 26 Dec 1811
Adonis, oder Die Rache des Ares (melodrama, 1, C. Bauer), Mannheim, 10 Dec 1815
Chimene (grosse Oper, 3, Bauer), 16 Dec 1821

*

StiegerO
C. Gruber: *Opern Uraufführungen*, ii (Vienna, 1987)

Wagner-Régeny, Rudolf (*b* Szász-Régen, Transylvania, 28 Aug 1903; *d* East Berlin, 18 Sept 1969). German composer of Romanian origin. Born Rudolf Wagner, he later adopted the name Wagner-Régeny, after his birthplace. After attending the Schässburg Gymnasium (1916–19) he went to Leipzig to study the piano at the conservatory with Robert Teichmüller. However, neither the piano nor Leipzig appealed to him and he soon left for Berlin, where he studied at the Hochschule für Musik with Rudolf Krasselt and Siegfried Ochs for conducting, Friedrich Ernst Koch for composition and E. N. von Rezniček for orchestration. Reports that he studied composition with Franz Schreker are incorrect.

Shortly before he completed his studies in Berlin he met the painter and sculptor Léli Duperrex, ten years older than himself, and moved into her studio apartment in the Waitzstrasse. This marriage of artists provided stability for the over-sensitive Wagner-Régeny, who was almost incapable of dealing with the mundane things of life. His father's bankruptcy in 1923 obliged the young musician to look for some way of earning a living; he took work playing in dance bands and as a pianist for silent films, and fell victim to dangerous moods of depression from which he managed to escape by composing. His first short opera, written towards the end of 1923, was *Sganarelle*; it was performed in 1929 in Essen, directed and conducted by Rudolf Schulz-Dornburg and with sets by Caspar Neher, who was to become an important artistic collaborator with the composer. At the same time Wagner-Régeny joined the Berlin Grosse Volksoper, where he progressed from operating the curtain to become ballet répétiteur and then deputy chorus master. The company was dissolved in 1925, and after a number of years without permanent employment he was appointed musical director of Rudolf von Laban's chamber ballet company.

A number of short operas followed, between 1928 and 1932, by which time fascism had gained a dangerous foothold in Germany and most of Wagner-Régeny's friends and colleagues had been forced to emigrate because they were either Jews or Communists. However, it was not until 1933 that the then stateless Wagner-Régeny applied for German citizenship, a fact which was later often misunderstood and held against him. His first full-length opera, *Der Günstling*, was a sensational success in Dresden in 1935. The libretto was by Caspar Neher, who was free to provide it because Kurt Weill, with whom he had recently collaborated on *Die Bürgschaft* (1932, Berlin), had been forced to flee the country. (For a similar reason Karl Böhm replaced Fritz Busch as conductor of the première.)

After composing incidental music for Shakespeare's *A Midsummer Night's Dream* (1935) and a ballet, *Der zerbrochene Krug* (1937), Wagner-Régeny resumed his collaboration with Neher and produced *Die Bürger von Calais* for the Berlin Staatsoper in 1939 and *Johanna Balk*, commissioned by the Deutsches Opernhaus in Berlin. The Berlin authorities had wanted to replace Neher with a Nazi librettist, but the composer managed to circumvent this. Various reasons have been suggested to explain why *Johanna Balk* could not be given in Berlin but was first performed instead at the Vienna Staatsoper, on 4 April 1941. However, the subject of the opera, derived from material that Wagner-Régeny had brought back with him after a visit to Transylvania, was the rising of the citizens of Hermannstadt against the Hungarian tyrant Báthory in 1612, and the work begins with an offstage chorus singing about the fear suffered in times of totalitarian rule. After 1945 the composer was rather too quick to spread the word that it had been understood in Vienna as a resistance work (there had been uproar at its première). Baldur von Schirach, the Gauleiter and governor of Vienna, professed to allow a 'freer' artistic climate there than prevailed in Berlin under Goebbels, and he even said as much in a speech at the Burghtheater two days after the opera's controversial première. At this time Wagner-Régeny and Carl Orff were receiving regular grants to work at Klosterneuburg, near Vienna, where Wagner-Régeny planned the opera *Jeanne d'Arc*. It was never completed;

he later used those parts he had written in his opera *Prometheus*.

Heinz Hilpert, Intendant of the Schauspieltheater in Berlin, suggested to Neher and Wagner-Régeny that they write an opera for actors, but the composer was called up for military service in 1943 and the work remained unfinished until 1950, when it was completed with the help of Bertolt Brecht. It was *Persische Episode*, a comic opera in four acts based on 'The Slaughterhouse Cleaner and the Fine Lady' from the *Thousand and One Nights*. Brecht's rigorous simplification of the fourth act has been revised in more recent versions of the work, using sketches by Neher and Wagner-Régeny which are in the possession of Tilo Medek.

While a composer such as Werner Egk was able to continue his musical work in the army, Wagner-Régeny served as an ordinary private, although he was permitted not to carry a gun, which he would have found an intolerable psychological burden. In 1944 he returned to Mecklenburg to record tapes for playing in field hospitals. His wife's mortal illness made the years 1944–7 the hardest of his life, as his published correspondence with Neher eloquently shows. Shortly after his wife's death he was appointed Rektor (principal) of the Rostock Academy of Music by the Soviet Army. In some ways he found the work inspiring, in others oppressive, especially because of the political watch kept over cultural activities, and in 1950 he resigned and went to teach composition at the reorganized Hochschule für Musik in East Berlin. That year he married Gertie Foth.

In the 1950s Wagner-Régeny found only grudging acceptance from those in charge of East German cultural policy, who followed the Soviet lead and regarded him as a bourgeois formalist. It is therefore not surprising that his last two operas were written for West Germany and Austria. The Berlin Wall perceptibly isolated him when he returned from Salzburg after the première of *Das Bergwerk zu Falun* in 1961. He himself described this opera as his farewell to the musical stage, and from then on he turned his attention increasingly to the cantata, a genre which occupied him until his death in 1969.

Wagner-Régeny's childless marriages may help to account for his selfless and important work as the teacher of several well-known composers. His pupils included Reiner Bredemeyer (1929), Paul-Heinz Dittrich (1930), Friedrich Goldmann (1941) and Tilo Medek (1940).

See also BERGWERK ZU FALUN, DAS; BÜRGER VON CALAIS, DIE; GÜNSTLING, DER; and PROMETHEUS.

Moschopulos (kleine Oper, 3, Wagner-Régeny, after F. Pocci), Gera, 1 Dec 1928 (Berlin, 1928)

Der nackte König (kleine Oper, 3, V. Braun, after H. C. Andersen: *The Emperor's New Clothes*), Gera, 1 Dec 1928, vs (Berlin, 1928)

Sganarelle, oder Der Schein trügt (graziöse Oper, 1, Wagner-Régeny, after Molière), Essen, Städtische Bühnen, 12 April 1929 (Berlin, 1929)

Esau und Jakob (biblische Szene, Bible), 4 solo vv, speaker, str orch, perc, Gera, 24 May 1930 (Berlin, 1931)

La sainte courtisane (musikalische Szene, Wagner-Régeny, after O. Wilde), 4 speakers, chamber orch, Dessau, 24 Oct 1930 (Berlin, 1930)

Die Fabel vom seligen Schlächtermeister, 1931–2 (Stück für die Musikbühne, 3 scenes, H. von Savigny), Radebeul, nr Dresden, 23 May 1964 (Berlin, 1964)

Der Günstling, oder Die letzten Tage des grossen Herrn Fabiano (3, C. Neher, after V. Hugo: *Marie Tudor*), Dresden, Staatsoper, 20 Feb 1935 (Vienna, 1934)

Die Bürger von Calais (3, Neher, after J. Froissart: *Chronicles*), Berlin, Staatsoper, 28 Jan 1939, vs (Vienna, 1938)

Johanna Balk (3, Neher, after Transylvanian chronicles), Vienna, Staatsoper, 4 April 1941, vs (Vienna, 1941)

Persische Episode [Der Darmwäscher], 1940–50 (komische Oper, 4, Neher and B. Brecht, after *The Thousand and One Nights*), Rostock, Volkstheater, 27 March 1963, vs (Vienna, 1951)

Prometheus (Szenisches Oratorium, 5 scenes, Wagner-Régeny and K. Holl, after Aeschylus), Kassel, Staatstheater, 12 Sept 1959 (Berlin and Wiesbaden, 1958)

Das Bergwerk zu Falun (8 scenes, Wagner-Régeny, after H. von Hofmannsthal), Salzburg, Festspielhaus, 16 Aug 1961 (Berlin and Wiesbaden, 1960)

*

D. Härtwig: *Rudolf Wagner-Régeny, der Opernkomponist* (Berlin, 1965)

T. Medek, ed.: *Rudolf Wagner-Régeny: Begegnungen* (Berlin, 1968) [autobiographical sketches, diaries and correspondence with C. Neher]

M. Becker, ed.: *Rudolf Wagner-Régeny: an den Ufern der Zeit* (Leipzig, 1989) [writings, letters and diaries] TILO MEDEK

Wagner societies. From 1871, when Wagner chose Bayreuth for his festival, various subscription schemes came into existence with the aim of supporting the project. A system of patrons' certificates, organized initially by Karl Tausig and Countess Marie von Schleinitz, was abandoned in 1882 when, in an open letter of 16 June to Friedrich Schön, Wagner proposed a foundation to assist financially those who would benefit from a visit to the festival but who would otherwise be unable to attend. On 14 May 1883, three months after Wagner's death, the Richard Wagner-Stipendienstiftung was formed by Schön for this purpose. In 1909 the Richard Wagner-Verband was founded by Anna Held and Margarethe Strauss in order to subsidize the Stipendienstiftung. The Verband was dissolved in 1945 and re-established in Hanover in 1947 by Lotte Albrecht-Potonié. Its primary function is still to subsidize visits of young artists to the festival. In 1991 there were 45 branches in Germany and 40 internationally, affiliated in the Richard Wagner-Verband International.

Numerous Wagner societies sprang up in Germany and Austria in the last decades of the 19th century, notably in Berlin and in Vienna, where the Akademische Wagner-Verein, founded in 1872, vigorously promoted the music of Hugo Wolf and other young composers before factionalism caused a split in the movement in the last years of the century. There have been Wagner societies in England since 1872; an early one produced the magazine *The Meister* under the editorship of William Ashton Ellis between 1888 and 1895. Another was founded in 1953 to foster interest in and encourage productions of Wagner's works; its journal *Wagner* (new ser., 1980–) has made a sustained and valuable contribution to Wagner scholarship.

Wagner societies were inaugurated in various American cities in the 1870s. Their history has been a broken one, but in 1991 there were societies in New York (the Wagner Society of New York and the American Wagner Association), northern and southern California, Chicago and Dallas, most issuing a journal or newsletter.

*

W. McGrath: *Dionysian Art and Populist Politics in Austria* (New Haven, CT, 1974)

A. D. Sessa: *Richard Wagner and the English* (London, 1979)

D. Large and W. Weber, eds.: *Wagnerism in European Culture and Politics* (Ithaca, NY, 1984)

A. Glauert: 'The Reception of Wagner in Vienna, 1860–1900', *Wagner in Performance*, ed. B. Millington and S. Spencer (New Haven, CT, 1992), 120–29 BARRY MILLINGTON

Design by Georges Wakhévitch for the 1948 production of Musorgsky's 'Boris Godunov' (Act 1 scene ii) at Covent Garden, London

Wakefield [Darling], **John** (*b* Wakefield, 21 June 1936). English tenor. He qualified as a chemist, sang with the Leeds Philharmonic Society and studied at the RAM with Roy Henderson, then with Ettore Campogalliani in Mantua. Taking the name of his birthplace to avoid confusion with his elder brother Edward, also a tenor, he made his opera début with the WNO in 1961 as Levko in *May Night* (Rimsky-Korsakov) for performances at Sadler's Wells. He joined Sadler's Wells Opera, first as Alfredo but then concentrating on Mozart roles, in which he won renown for lyrical sensitivity and musical perception. A memorable Sali in *A Village Romeo and Juliet* for the Delius centenary (1962), he made débuts at Glyndebourne as Macduff (1964) and at Covent Garden as Rinuccio (*Gianni Schicchi*, 1965). He won further success in Baroque opera with Monteverdi's Orpheus for Sadler's Wells and Cavalli's Ormindo for Glyndebourne, in the Leppard edition, which he also recorded (1969). He created roles in Nicholas Maw's *The Rising of the Moon* at Glyndebourne in 1970 and the next year in the première of Villa-Lobos's *Yerma* at Santa Fe. Physical problems with his voice led to a premature retirement from singing, when he joined the teaching faculty at Trinity College of Music; but he later returned to the stage, his voice a little drier, as could be heard when he sang Janáček's Tichon at Glyndebourne (1988).

NOËL GOODWIN

Wakhévitch, Georges (*b* Odessa, 5/18 Aug 1907; *d* Paris, 11 Feb 1984). Russian stage, costume and film designer, resident in France from 1920. He studied in Paris, taking painting and sculpture at the Ecole des Arts Décoratifs and architecture at the Ecole des Beaux-Arts. In the course of a prolific career he was responsible for more than 600 productions: some 150 films (including Michel Carné's *Les visiteurs du soir*, 1942), 300 plays and 200 operas, staged in most of the leading European houses. He worked with the director Peter Brook in both opera and theatre.

Wakhévitch's designs were characterized by a bold, sometimes coarse, painterly style, the sumptuous use of strong colour, dramatic chiaroscuro lighting effects and – reflecting his architectural training – confident, if conventional, handling of complicated stage space. Typical productions were the barbarically Russian *Boris Godunov* (1948, Covent Garden; directed by Peter Brook), the dramatic, enduring *Otello* (1955, Covent Garden) and *Die Zauberflöte* (1959, Vienna), set within a false proscenium of Piranesian monumentality. *Carmen* (1959, La Scala), with the intricate, urban huddle of Act 1, the great torn hanging of Act 2 and the harsh ochre sky of Act 3, may be seen as the epitome of his style.

ES (G. C. Castello, P.-L. Mignon and U. Tani) [incl. list of designs]
Benizet: *Nuovi orientamenti della scenografia* (Milan, 1965)

MARINA HENDERSON

Wald, A. G. *See* GRÜNWALD, ALFRED.

Walder. *Ernsthafte Operette* ('serious operetta') in one act by Georg Benda (*see* BENDA family, (1)) to a libretto by FRIEDRICH WILHELM GOTTER after JEAN FRANÇOIS MARMONTEL's play *Silvain* (1770); Gotha, Schloss Friedenstein, 23 February 1776.

Walder (tenor), having married Sophie (soprano) against the wishes of his father, Dolmon Vater (tenor), lives disinherited in a hut in the forest. He confronts his arrogant brother Dolmon Sohn (bass); their father, however, is won over by Walder's family and forgives him.

An idyllic companion to Benda's *Romeo und Julie* of the same year, *Walder* is a high point of northern sobriety in dealing with Roussellian rural joys. The score deftly distinguishes the conventional characters and the unconventional spoil-sport Dolmon Sohn. It culminates in an impressive quartet in which Dolmon Sohn stoutly refuses reconciliation. By adapting Marmontel's *Silvain*, Gotter and Benda set themselves in direct competition with an opera already popular throughout Germany in Grétry's setting and in a spoken adaptation by C. F. Weisse; in consequence, *Walder* was not as widely performed as Benda's other operas. But its charming rondo, 'Selbst die glücklichste der Ehen', achieved a popularity equal to Hiller's best tunes.

THOMAS BAUMAN

Waldmann, Maria (*b* Vienna, 1842; *d* Ferrara, 6 Nov 1920). Austrian mezzo-soprano. She studied in Vienna, then with Lamperti in Milan and made her début in 1865 at St Petersburg as Pierotto (*Linda di Chamounix*). After singing in Wiesbaden, Amsterdam and Trieste, she was engaged at La Scala, where in 1872 she sang Amneris in the first Italian performance of *Aida*. After three seasons in Cairo, she sang the mezzo-soprano solo in the first performance of Verdi's Requiem (1874). Her repertory included Zerlina, Maffio Orsini (*Lucrezia Borgia*) and Preziosilla.

ELIZABETH FORBES

Wales. For discussion of opera in Wales *see* CARDIFF.

Walker, David (*b* Calcutta, 18 July 1934). English stage designer. He attended the Central School of Arts and Crafts, London (1952–6), and had his first professional commission in 1955 from Joan Littlewood's Theatre Workshop. He subsequently spent 1960 with the Workshop and designed five productions for them. Early in his career he designed costumes only, often with sets by John Bury and later by Henry Bardon. He now prefers to design both costumes and sets. Among the chief opera productions he has designed are a Velázquez-style *Don Giovanni* (costumes, 1964) at the Edinburgh Festival; *Werther* (1966) and *La bohème* (1967) for Glyndebourne; *Suor Angelica* (1965), *Così fan tutte* (1968), *Don Giovanni* (1981) and *Semele* (1982) for Covent Garden; and *La traviata* (1973) and *Der Rosenkavalier* (1975) for the ENO. His work abroad includes, for the Metropolitan Opera, *Carmen* (1972) with sets by Josef Svoboda; for the Teatro Massimo, Palermo, *Manon Lescaut* with sets by Fiorella Mariani, and the première of Nino Rota's *La visita meravigliosa* (1970); for La Fenice, Venice, *Lucia di Lammermoor* with sets by Pier Luigi Samaritani; and for the Teatro dell' Opera in Rome both sets and costumes for *Roberto Devereux* (1988).

Walker has designed drama productions as well as opera and ballet, working with leading directors and choreographers, but his visualizations – what might be called 'Covent Garden baroque' – have been more popular with audiences than with critics. Although some early work may be noted for its social realism, his reputation now rests on the painterly qualities he best expresses in productions from the Romantic and Rococo repertories.

DAVID J. HOUGH

Walker, Edyth (*b* Hopewell, NY, 27 March ?1867; *d* New York, 19 Feb 1950). American mezzo-soprano. She studied with Orgeni in Dresden, and made her opera début as Fidès in *Le prophète* at the Berlin Hofoper in 1894. She was a member of the Vienna Hofoper from 1895 to 1903. In 1900 she made her Covent Garden début as Amneris and sang Ortrud, Fricka, Erda and Waltraute in the same season. From 1903 (début as Amneris) until 1906 she was a member of the Metropolitan Opera. There she began to sing soprano roles, including Brünnhilde (*Die Walküre*), and at the Hamburg opera (1903–12) she appeared regularly both as soprano and mezzo. In 1908 she sang Ortrud and Kundry at Bayreuth and returned, as Isolde, to Covent Garden. Under Beecham, in 1910, she was the first London Electra, winning high praise for both singing and acting; she also appeared as Thirza in Smyth's *The Wreckers*. From 1912 until 1917 she sang in the Munich Festivals. After her retirement she taught singing in France and the USA. The few published recordings of her voice were made between 1902 and 1909.

ERIC BLOM, HAROLD BARNES

Walker, Norman (*b* Shaw, Lancs., 24 Nov 1907; *d* London, 5 Nov 1963). English bass. He studied at the Royal Manchester College of Music and then with Walter Hyde at the GSM, London (where he returned to teach in 1951). He appeared in the international seasons at Covent Garden, 1935–9, as the Commendatore, King Mark and Gurnemanz, among other roles; after war service he returned to the resident company there. He also appeared with Sadler's Wells Opera, with which he toured in 1946. His King Mark was regularly praised for its dignity and beauty of tone, and his roles also included Polyphemus, Pogner, King Henry, Sarastro and Colline. In 1951 he created the Evangelist in Vaughan Williams's *The Pilgrim's Progress*. At Glyndebourne he appeared in 1937 as the Commendatore and the Speaker (*Die Zauberflöte*) and in 1946 alternated with Owen Brannigan as Collatinus in the first performances of Britten's *The Rape of Lucretia*. A stroke ended his stage career in 1955.

M. Walker: 'Norman Walker: an Appreciation by his Son', *Recorded Sound*, nos.57–8 (1975), 430–35

Walker, Sarah (*b* Cheltenham, 11 March 1943). English mezzo-soprano. She studied in London and made her début in 1970 as Octavia (*L'incoronazione di Poppea*) with Kent Opera, for which she sang Poppaea, Penelope (*Il ritorno d'Ulisse*) and Andromache (*King Priam*). She sang Diana in *Calisto* at Glyndebourne (1970) and Dido in *Les Troyens* for Scottish Opera (1972), for which she later sang Mistress Quickly (1991). For the ENO she has sung Dorabella, Fricka, Mary Stuart, Herodias, the Countess (*The Queen of Spades*), Cornelia (*Giulio Cesare*) Gloriana, and Agave in the première of Buller's *Bakxai* (1992). In 1979 she made her Covent Garden début as Charlotte (*Werther*), then sang Baba the Turk, Rose Parrowe (*Taverner*), Marcellina, Mrs Sedley and Caroline with the Thick Mane in the British première of Sallinen's *The King Goes Forth to France* (1987). She has sung in Vienna, San Francisco, Chicago, Geneva and Brussels, and at the Metropolitan, where she made her début in 1988 as Cornelia. An intelligent, musical and very dramatic singer, she excels in modern opera. She was appointed CBE in 1991.

ELIZABETH FORBES

Walker, Thomas (*b* London, 5 June 1698; *d* Dublin, 5 June 1744). English singer, actor and author. He acted in London from 1715, specializing in handsome daredevil roles such as Hotspur. Although untrained as a singer, he was given the role of Macheath in *The Beggar's Opera* (1728) during rehearsals, when he was heard singing some of the airs behind the scenes. Chetwood wrote that after his success as Macheath he 'follow'd *Bacchus* too ardently, insomuch that his Credit was often drown'd upon the Stage'. He sang in a few other ballad operas and held on to his roles until 1739. His career then collapsed and he died in poverty.

His own ballad opera, *The Quaker's Opera*, was performed in 1728.

BDA; *DNB* (J. Knight); *LS*
W. R. Chetwood: *A General History of the Stage* (London, 1749)
The Thespian Dictionary (London, 1802, 2/1805)
T. Gilliland: *The Dramatic Mirror*, i (London, 1808)
R. Fiske: *English Theatre Music in the Eighteenth Century* (London, 1973, 2/1986)
OLIVE BALDWIN, THELMA WILSON

Walküre, Die ('The Valkyrie'). First day of *DER RING DES NIBELUNGEN* in three acts by Richard Wagner (*see* WAGNER family, (1)) to his own libretto; Munich, Königliches Hof- und Nationaltheater, 26 June 1870 (first performance as part of cycle: Bayreuth, Festspielhaus, 14 August 1876).

Siegmund		tenor
Hunding		bass
Wotan		bass-baritone
Sieglinde		soprano
Brünnhilde		soprano
Fricka		mezzo-soprano
Gerhilde, Ortlinde, Waltraute, Schwertleite, Helmwige, Siegrune, Grimgerde, Rossweisse	*Valkyries*	sopranos and contraltos

The first prose sketch for *Die Walküre* dates from autumn (probably November) 1851. In a letter to Uhlig of 11 November 1851 Wagner referred to the new work as *Siegmund und Sieglind: der Walküre Bestrafung*, but by 20 November (letter to Liszt) he had renamed it with the familiar title *Die Walküre*. The sketch was developed into a prose draft (17–26 May 1852) and then into a verse draft (1 June–1 July 1852). The final poem was incorporated into the private printing of the entire *Ring* text in February 1853.

The first musical sketches for *Die Walküre* date from the summer of 1852 and include an early version of the Spring Song. The first complete draft was made between 28 June and 27 December 1854. Unlike the comparable draft for *Das Rheingold*, which for the most part consisted of one vocal staff and one instrumental, that for *Walküre* shows some degree of orchestral elaboration, often with one vocal staff and two instrumental. In spite of the difficulties he experienced – on account of many delays and interruptions – in expanding that first draft into score, Wagner did not find it necessary to make a second draft as for *Rheingold* since he was now familiar with the expanded orchestral forces. Instead he went straight into a draft of the full score (January 1855–20 March 1856); the fair copy was made in parallel between 14 July 1855 and 23 March 1856.

ACT 1 *Inside Hunding's dwelling* The turbulent prelude that opens the work depicts at once a raging storm and the mental convulsions that are soon to shake the participants in the drama. A tremolo on a single repeated note is maintained by the second violins and violas for 60 bars, while underneath cellos and double basses rampage up and down a series of notes clearly intended to recall the motif of the spear (*see* RHEINGOLD, DAS, ex.5): that symbol of Wotan's power and authority is evoked because this entire act is contrived, in a sense, at the instigation of his will. The motif sung by Donner, the god of thunder, at the end of *Rheingold* to the words 'Heda! Hedo!' rings out on the brass, first on the Wagner tubas. Despite the different harmonic context it begins in B♭, exactly as in *Rheingold*; however, it is winched up sequentially through a series of modulations

'Die Walküre' (Wagner): scene from Act 1 (inside Hunding's dwelling; Sieglinde (Therese Vogl) offers Siegmund (Heinrich Vogl) a horn of mead) of the original production at the Königliches Hof- und Nationaltheater, Munich, 26 June 1870

until the tension breaks in a thunderclap, after which the storm begins to subside.

As the curtain rises and Siegmund, collapsing with exhaustion, bursts into the forest dwelling, a cello takes up the Spear motif but turns its end accommodatingly back on itself (ex.1): a hint that an alternative to sheer

Ex.1

naked power is being proposed. Sieglinde enters, and as she bends over Siegmund's sleeping figure that idea is taken up again in conjunction with a phrase expressive of her tenderness (ex.2). The two melodic ideas are

Ex.2

worked to a small climax as Sieglinde fetches him water. Then ex.1 opens out into a fully-fledged Love theme, ex.3 (derived from Freia's theme in *Rheingold*), the

Ex.3

music as yet anticipating events on the stage.

Sieglinde now fetches a horn of mead for Siegmund, to the accompaniment of an effusively lyrical passage in A major, bassoons, horns and clarinets lending a bloom to the strings. The pair gaze at each other in unspoken affirmation of love, the two halves of the Love motif sounding in reverse order. The minor triad of the Volsung motif (ex.4) evokes the ill luck that dogs

Ex.4

Siegmund; the motif is combined with ex.2 as he decides to stay and await his fate.

The arrival of Hunding (scene ii) is heralded by a sharp, abrupt motif on the Wagner tubas. He roughly extends his hospitality and asks where Siegmund has come from and what is his name. Siegmund says he should be called Woeful, describing how one day he returned from hunting with his father, Wolfe, to find their home burnt down, his mother murdered and his twin sister brutally abducted. At Sieglinde's prompting he then narrates how he went to the aid of a young woman forced into a loveless marriage, killing her savage kinsmen in the fight. Hunding now realizes that he is harbouring his kinsmen's foe. The laws of hospitality compel him to give Siegmund shelter for the night, but in the morning he will have to fight for his life.

As she prepares Hunding's night drink, Sieglinde drugs it. She leaves the room with a lingering gaze, first at Siegmund and then at a spot in the trunk of the ash tree that stands in the middle of the hut: the Sword motif sounds presciently on the bass trumpet.

In the third scene Siegmund, left alone, meditates on the fever of excitement stirred up by Sieglinde and on his weaponless plight, recalling that his father had promised that there would be a sword for him in his time of need ('Ein Schwert verhiess mir der Vater'). He calls on his father: 'Wälse! Wälse!' (the octave leaps of the Sword motif without the tail-piece are traditionally regarded, by singers and listeners alike, as a test of virility). They launch Siegmund on a heart-warming soliloquy, richly orchestrated, the rippling harp arpeggios mirroring the gleaming of the sword in the ash tree.

Sieglinde enters. She tells how an old man dressed in grey had thrust the sword into the tree at the wedding ceremony of herself and Hunding. This narration, 'Der Männer Sippe sass hier im Saal', is a choice example of the musico-poetic synthesis – the practical application of Wagner's principles of word-setting – that finds its most consistent expression in *Die Walküre*. Particularly noteworthy are the low-lying vocal line depicting the old man's low-brimmed hat, the shape of the melodic line portraying the flash of his eye and then its 'threatening glance', the falling chromatic intervals for his lingering look of yearning, the expressive appoggiatura on 'Tränen' ('tears') and the final rise to a top G for the physical act of implanting the sword in the tree. The sounding of the Valhalla motif by horns and bassoons, announcing the real identity of the stranger, is one of the classic uses of leitmotif to comment on the action.

True to Wagner's theoretical principles, the ensuing duet does not allow the couple to sing together. Even Siegmund's Spring Song, 'Winterstürme wichen dem Wonnemond', celebrated as a tenor song extracted from its context, is not as conventional as at first appears. It begins like a ternary aria, but after only nine bars of the middle section the continuation of the Love motif bursts in and disrupts the form. Incomplete and hybrid structures of this kind are typical in Wagner's music dramas (see Newcomb 1981–2). Siegmund speaks of Spring and Love as brother and sister, to which Sieglinde replies that he is the spring for whom she has so longed. The remainder of the act is an ecstatic declaration of their love, with an unashamed acknowledgment that they are also brother and sister. He admits that Woeful is no longer an appropriate name and Sieglinde renames him Siegmund ('guardian of victory'). To her delight he pulls the sword out of the tree, naming it 'Nothung' ('Needful'). They embrace rapturously and the curtain falls with decorous swiftness.

ACT 2 *A wild, rocky, mountain ridge* The music of the prelude anticipates the Ride of the Valkyries in the third act; its vitality is generated by dotted rhythms in 9/8 time, and augmented 5ths heighten the tension. Wotan instructs his daughter Brünnhilde, the Valkyrie of the title, to ensure that Siegmund wins the ensuing battle with Hunding. She revels in the Valkyrie battle cry, but warns Wotan that he has another battle on hand: his wife Fricka is furiously approaching, in a ram-drawn chariot. Brünnhilde disappears as Fricka, angrily but with dignity, tells how, as guardian of wedlock, she has been appealed to by Hunding to punish the adulterous Volsung pair. To her complaint that they have flouted the vows of marriage Wotan replies that he has no respect for vows that compel union without love. Fricka turns her attack to the twins' incest, but Wotan's reply, to the tender accompaniment of the Spring Song and Love themes, indicates that not even this breach of conventional morality shocks him. Fricka continues her indignant protest in an arioso passage in G♯ minor, in which the stock of leitmotifs momentarily gives way to new and distinctive melodic material. At first glance a reversion to an old-style form, 'O, was klag' ich um Ehe und Eid' in fact displays considerable subtlety in its variety of pace and irregular phrase-lengths.

Fricka complains that Wotan has brought disgrace on the gods by fathering these incestuous twins on a mortal woman. He replies that the gods need a hero free from their protection, who will be able to do the deed they are prevented from doing. But Fricka devastatingly exposes the flaw in the guilty god's argument: Siegmund is not able to act as a free hero so long as he is protected by Wotan. As Wotan thrashes about in despair, much use is made of a motif (ex.5) labelled 'Dejection' by Newman

but whose contorted melodic shape and kinship to the Spear motif suggest something more specific: the frustration of Wotan's will. Fricka extracts from him an oath that he will no longer protect his son.

In scene ii Wotan continues to writhe in mental agony (ex.5) and Brünnhilde reappears to receive the full brunt of his outburst of grief and frustration, 'O heilige Schmach!' A powerful climax is generated by the dissonant piling up of motifs, initiated by a new one that is primarily an inversion of ex.5, though also related to that of Wotan's authority (the Spear motif). The notes to which Wotan sings of his endless rage and grief ('Endloser Grimm! Ewiger Gram!') are in fact those of the Love motif (ex.3), a poignant reminder that it is lack of love that is the cause of his troubles.

The ensuing long narration of Wotan, 'Als junger Liebe Lust mir verblich', is a key passage in the work, and one intended not only for the information of Brünnhilde, or even of the audience, but as an act of self-revelation, in which we see Wotan in a new light. He begins by confessing how he attempted to fill the vacuum of lovelessness in his life by acquiring power. His hushed reliving of the story is the closest thing in the whole work to pure recitative, but it is by no means oblivious to the *Oper und Drama* principles of word-setting and in any case it acquires a special aura of suspense from the accompaniment – double basses alone, *pianissimo*. The characteristic motifs appear as Wotan recalls Alberich's forging of the ring, the building of Valhalla and Erda's prophecy. The prominence of ex.5 attests to Wotan's sense of frustration, and the motifs of the Curse and the Sword drive the narration to a tremendous climax: he now longs for only one thing – 'das Ende'. He instructs Brünnhilde to protect not Siegmund in the coming battle but Hunding. She tries to change his mind, but he is implacable.

The third scene opens with an orchestral interlude making a symphonic development out of agitated repetitions of the Love motif. Siegmund and Sieglinde enter breathlessly. She, tormented by guilt, begs him to abandon her, but he merely vows to avenge the wrong done her by killing Hunding. Horns are heard echoing round the forest, and Sieglinde, feverishly imagining Hunding's dogs tearing at Siegmund's flesh, falls into a faint.

There follows another scene of key significance in the cycle: the Todesverkündigung (Annunciation of Death). Brünnhilde appears, announcing to Siegmund that he must follow her to Valhalla. The Wagner tubas intone a solemn motif whose interrogatory melodic shape and unresolved dominant 7th have generally earned it a label such as 'Destiny' or 'Fate' (ex.6). It is heard throughout

the scene, as is a four-bar theme whose latter half corresponds with it (ex.7). Three distinct brass groupings are used to conjure a mood of quiet, noble heroism: Wagner tubas, trumpets and trombones, horns with bassoons. When Siegmund hears that he cannot take his sister-bride with him to Valhalla, he determines not to go. Brünnhilde tells him that his fate is unalterable but, distressed by his evident devotion to Sieglinde and his threat to kill her rather than be separated, she finally relents and promises to protect him, in defiance of Wotan's command.

Siegmund bends affectionately over the sleeping Sieglinde (scene v). Hunding's horn is heard, and in the ensuing fight Brünnhilde attempts to protect Siegmund with her shield, only for Wotan to appear and shatter Siegmund's sword with his spear. Hunding kills Siegmund, but is himself despatched by Wotan with a contemptuous wave of his hand. Wotan, enraged, then sets off in pursuit of the disobedient Brünnhilde.

ACT 3 *On the summit of a rocky mountain* In the Ride of the Valkyries that opens Act 3, the war-maidens gather, collecting heroes for Valhalla. Although hackneyed, the piece has much to recommend it, especially when sung and staged. The scoring illustrates a characteristic device of Wagner's: a brass theme in unison cutting across a dense texture, in this case of trilling, antiphonal woodwind and swirling string arpeggios. The Valkyries notice that Brünnhilde is missing; eventually she is sighted carrying on her saddle not a hero but a woman. They fearfully refuse to protect her from the fury of Wotan. Sieglinde longs to die, but on being told that a Volsung stirs in her womb, she implores Brünnhilde to protect her. She is urged to make her escape to the forest in the east and is given the fragments of Siegmund's sword from which one day his son will forge a new weapon. This announcement is made with an expansive theme (later to be associated with Siegfried's heroism) whose intrepid ring prompts Sieglinde to react with the work's most enraptured melodic inspiration, 'O hehrstes Wunder!' (ex.8). The motif

returns at the end of the cycle, where Wagner referred to it as 'the glorification of Brünnhilde'.

Wotan storms in (scene ii) and the Valkyries in vain try to shield Brünnhilde. She is told that she can no longer be a Valkyrie, and that she is to be confined in sleep on the mountain-top, a prey to the first man to find her. The Valkyries, horror-struck, protest in eight-part counterpoint, but under threat of the same punishment if they interfere, they separate and scatter.

Left alone with Wotan (scene iii), Brünnhilde begs for mercy ('War es so schmählich'); she asks whether it was so shameful if, though contravening Wotan's orders, she was in fact carrying out his inward wishes. The theme she uses is derived from that of the spear, the symbol of Wotan's authority, but its severity is turned, by octave displacement, into an eloquent melody (ex.9). She

recounts how the Volsung touched her heart, and a new melody, similarly derived from the Spear motif, blossoms forth in a transported E major: Brünnhilde's compassionate love thus stands opposed to Wotan's tyrannical wielding of power, but also, in motivic terms, grows organically out of it.

Brünnhilde pleads that at least she be spared the disgrace of an ignoble union: let her be surrounded by a circle of fire that will deter all but the bravest of heroes. Deeply moved, Wotan embraces Brünnhilde and, laying her down on a rock, he kisses her shining eyes closed. Throughout the unfolding of this scene more and more motifs are recalled from the past as emotionally charged memories are brought to the surface. Two new motifs remain to be mentioned: that of the Magic Sleep, evoked by a sinking semitonal melodic line and trance-like mediant progressions, and ex.10, which is heard in an

ominous minor key as Brünnhilde dreads being woken by a coward, but which in its major form acquires a luminous, hypnotic quality in the closing pages of the score.

The last part of this scene is a succession of carefully controlled climaxes, none of which is more affecting than that following Wotan's grief-stricken farewells to Brünnhilde: 'Leb' wohl'. Finally the god summons Loge and points with his spear to where he should blaze round the rock. The sea of fire that spreads to enclose the whole mountain in flames is depicted by a richly orchestrated texture created from the themes of Loge and others. Wotan sorrowfully departs.

* * *

Die Walküre is the music drama that most satisfactorily embodies the theoretical principles of *Oper und Drama*. A thoroughgoing synthesis of poetry and music is achieved without any notable sacrifice in musical expression. Indeed, many of the most powerful passages of the work achieve their effect precisely through the organic relationship of music and text. *Die Walküre* is generally regarded as the most approachable of the *Ring* operas and it has certainly proved the most susceptible to performance in extracts. BARRY MILLINGTON

Wallace, Ian (Bryce) (*b* London, 10 July 1919). Scottish bass. He studied privately and was engaged by the New London Opera Company at the Cambridge Theatre in 1946, making his début as Schaunard. His other roles with the company were the Sacristan (*Tosca*), Dr Bartolo, Ceprano (*Rigoletto*) and Masetto. In 1948 he sang Masetto, and in 1949 Samuel, with Glyndebourne Opera at the Edinburgh Festival; he appeared regularly at Glyndebourne itself, between 1952 and 1961, as Bartolo (Rossini and Mozart), Don Magnifico (*La Cenerentola*), Ser Matteo in the first English stage performance of Busoni's *Arlecchino* and the Tutor (*Le comte Ory*). He also sang in Rome and Venice, and at the Bregenz Festivals of 1964 and 1965. With Scottish Opera he appeared as Leporello (1961), Don Magnifico (1969–70), and the Duke of Plaza-Toro in *The Gondoliers* (1972). Wallace had great gifts as a comic actor and singer. His memoirs were published as *Promise me you'll sing Mud* (London, 1975).

HAROLD ROSENTHAL/R

Wallace, (William) Vincent (*b* Waterford, 11 March 1812; *d* Château de Haget, Vieuzos, Hautes-Pyrénées, 12 Oct 1865). Irish composer. Early in his career he became well known in many countries as a violinist and pianist. His position as a composer of operas for London was established in 1845 with the production of *Maritana*.

1. LIFE. Wallace's father was bandmaster of the 29th or Worcestershire Regiment and taught him to play many band instruments. On his father's discharge from the army in 1825, the family moved to Dublin, where Wallace became a second violinist at the Theatre Royal, deputizing on occasion for the leader. He studied the piano and the organ, and in January 1830 was appointed organist at the Roman Catholic cathedral at Thurles and Professor of Music at the Ursuline Convent there. He fell in love with one of his pupils, Isabella Kelly, whose father refused permission for their marriage because Wallace was a Protestant. Wallace was therefore baptized as a Roman Catholic in the autumn of 1830, and took the name Vincent, which he thereafter used as his principal name. In 1831 he married Isabella, rejoined the Theatre Royal band as deputy leader, and began to compose in earnest.

From 1835 to 1845 Wallace lived the life of an adventurer. During these years he appeared as a concert pianist and as a violinist, becoming more famous in the latter role. He arrived in Hobart, Tasmania, on 31 October 1835 with his wife, son and sister-in-law. In January 1836 he moved to Sydney, where he is said to have taken up sheep farming. He opened an academy of music and a music shop, but neither prospered, and when he sailed from Sydney on 11 February 1838 he left behind his wife and son, and debts of nearly £2000. According to his own testimony (as given to Berlioz) he proceeded to New Zealand, where he was hospitably received by Maori cannibals, and then to India, where he went tiger-shooting. These stories were probably exaggerated, as it is known that by June 1838 he was in Chile, where he resumed his concert career. In the next few years he visited Buenos Aires, Lima, Jamaica and Cuba, and in 1841 conducted the Italian opera season at Mexico City. By 1844 he had reached New York, via New Orleans (1841), Philadelphia (1842) and Boston (1843). After touring Germany and the Netherlands, he made his London début at the Hanover Square Rooms on 8 May 1845.

Not long afterwards, Wallace met his Dublin friend Hayward St Leger, who introduced him to Edward Fitzball. Fitzball was so impressed by Wallace's talent that he immediately gave him the newly-written first act of the libretto of *Maritana*. Wallace completed the score quickly, making use of some of his earlier compositions. The opera was performed at Drury Lane on 15 November 1845, and its success was second only to that of Balfe's *Bohemian Girl* (1843).

Though Wallace wrote five more operas, and left as many more unfinished, he was never able to repeat his initial triumph. *Matilda of Hungary* (1847, Drury Lane) was still-born, owing mainly to Bunn's libretto, which R. H. Legge called 'one of the worst ... in existence'. *Lurline* was commissioned by the Paris Opéra for August 1848 and also announced for performance at Covent Garden that same year, but an attack of ophthalmia obliged Wallace temporarily to abandon composition. In 1849 he set out on his travels again and after eight months in Brazil arrived in New York in 1850, having narrowly escaped death while travelling on a steamboat that exploded. Later that year he married Hélène Stoepel, an American pianist, after receiving the convenient advice that his marriage to Isabella was illegal, since at the time he had been underage and 'bred up a Protestant'. Wallace's movements during the next few years are uncertain, but he spent some time in Germany, 1858–9, probably revising *Lurline*, which was produced at Covent Garden on 23 February 1860. Its musical sophistication pleased the critics better than *Maritana*, but it was not a success with the public. The same reception greeted *The Amber Witch* (1861, Her Majesty's), which, according to Santley, was ruined by inept stage management. *Love's Triumph* (1862, Covent Garden) was cut to make room for the Christmas pantomime, and his last opera, *The Desert Flower* (1863, Covent Garden), was saddled with a libretto which trivialized the life of Pocahontas.

Wallace had suffered from heart attacks since 1854. In 1864 his condition deteriorated, forcing him to give up work on *Estrella*. He retired to Passy, but in September 1865 was moved to the Château de Haget in the Pyrenees, where he died. His body was returned to London, and he was buried at Kensal Green Cemetery.

2. WORKS. There is no question that *Maritana* was Wallace's masterpiece, and its music's vigorous rhythms and bright, elemental colours can exercise a powerful appeal, though the libretto seems faded. Wallace's life may have been something of an emotional outburst, but its passion finds its most authentic expression in this score. Nicholas Temperley (*The New Grove*) points out that the music's exotic qualities, particularly its Spanish elements, were quite new at the time and may well have influenced Bizet's *Carmen*; indeed, the use of Maritana's Act 1 song 'It was a knight of princely mien' as an entr'acte before Act 3 directly anticipates Bizet's methods. The opera is more through-composed than any of Balfe's works, and though Act 2 scene i degenerates into a series of ballads, the individual numbers are excellent, especially Don José's 'In happy moments' and Don Caesar's magnificent 'Yes! let me like a soldier fall'. Here Wallace's brass writing is thrilling, but if his scoring has a fault it is in his overfondness for intrusive trumpets and a combination of piccolo, triangle and bass trombone. His military band origins are sometimes a little too obvious, though the beautiful harp writing in 'Scenes that are brightest' and 'The harp in the air' acts as an emollient.

The critics considered that *Maritana* contained too wide a variety of musical styles and Wallace conscientiously set out to remedy this defect in his later operas. In *Lurline*, a transitional work, he shifted his ground in favour of German models (Weber and Mendelssohn), perhaps because of the Teutonic setting. The Meyerbeerian aspects of *Maritana* were developed; *Lurline* is an attempt at 'grand opera', but all too often, as Percy Young noted, it ends up as pantomime. The libretto, later denounced by Shaw as 'desperate trash', pushed it in that direction: lines such as 'Zeelick! up! up! thy master calls thee!/Ah! dwarfish creature, quit thy rest' burlesque Wagner.

Wallace's style reached its full maturity in *The Amber Witch*, which has been unjustly neglected. Here he at last achieved an effective structural scheme and a decent level of musical characterization. Because the heroine, Mary, has been established as a living person, her trial scene is harrowing and possesses sufficient tension to involve the audience; this is never the case in *Maritana*. The musical palette is as colourful as ever but more refined, and one has only to compare the powerful symphonic overture with the pot-pourri which precedes *Maritana* to see how far Wallace developed. There are still ballads, but they are better integrated by virtue of their longer-breathed melodic lines and motivic phrase extensions. From the singers' point of view the opera is technically as difficult as anything by Mozart or Verdi.

See also LURLINE and MARITANA.

all completed works first performed in London and published there in vocal score

Maritana (grand op, 3, E. Fitzball, after A. P. d'Ennery and P. F. Pinel Dumanoir: *Don César de Bazan*), Drury Lane, 15 Nov 1845 (1846)

Matilda of Hungary (grand op, 3, A. Bunn), Drury Lane, 22 Feb 1847 (1847)

Lurline, 1847–?1859 (grand romantic op, 3, Fitzball, after the Lorelei legend), CG, 23 Feb 1860, *B-Bc**; (1859)

The Amber Witch (romantic op, 4, H. F. Chorley, after J. W. Meinhold), Her Majesty's, 28 Feb 1861 (1861)

Love's Triumph (3, J. R. Planché), CG, 3 Nov 1862, *GB-Lbl**; (1862)

The Desert Flower (romantic op, 3, A. G. Harris and T. J. Williams, after J.-H. Vernoy de Saint-Georges and A. de Leuven: *Jaguarita l'Indienne*), CG, 12 Oct 1863 (1864)

Inc. and unperf.: The Maid of Zürich; The King's Page (J. E. Carpenter); Gulnare (lt. operetta); Olga (lt. operetta); Estrella (?Estrellita) (H. B. Farnie)

*

DNB (R. H. Legge); *Grove6* (N. Temperley)

Musical World, xx (1845), 553–5, 565–7, 577–9; xxii (1847), 129–32; xxiii (1848), 482

H. Berlioz: *Les soirées de l'orchestre* (Paris, 1853); Eng. trans. as *Evenings in the Orchestra* (London, 1963), 310–20

E. Fitzball: *Thirty-Five Years of a Dramatic Author's Life* (London, 1859)

W. Guernsey: 'William Vincent Wallace', *Musical World*, xliii (1865), 656–8

C. Santley: *Student and Singer* (London, 1892), 169–71, 185–6

G. B. Shaw: *London Music in 1888–89* (London, 1937), 54, 351–3

E. W. White: *The Rise of English Opera* (London, 1951)

J. W. Klein: 'Vincent Wallace (1812–65): a Reassessment', *Opera*, xvi (1965), 709–16

P. M. Young: *A History of British Music* (London, 1967), 468–71
N. Temperley, ed.: *Music in Britain: the Romantic Age, 1800–1914* (London, 1981)
NIGEL BURTON

Wallberg, Heinz (*b* Herringen, nr Hamm, 16 March 1923). German conductor. He studied at the Dortmund and Cologne conservatories and began his career as a violinist and trumpeter in Cologne and Darmstadt. He made his conducting début in *Le nozze di Figaro* at Münster in 1947 and worked in several German cities, serving as music director at the Augsburg Städtische Bühnen in 1954 and at Bremen, 1955–60. He was music director at Wiesbaden, 1960–65, and at the same time appeared regularly at the Vienna Staatsoper. He made his Covent Garden début in 1963 with *Der Rosenkavalier*. As music director at Essen (1975–91) he opened the new Aalto-Theater there (1988). He was also chief conductor of the Bavarian RSO, with which he recorded more than a dozen operas and operettas, including Humperdinck's *Königskinder*, Leoncavallo's *La bohème*, Lortzing's *Zar und Zimmermann*, Flotow's *Martha*, Egk's *Peer Gynt* and a much-praised version of Weinberger's *Švanda the Bagpiper*. His work in Australasia included the first production in New Zealand of *Die Meistersinger*, at Wellington in 1990. He has been awarded the German Federal Service Cross, the Austrian Cross of Honour in Science and the Arts and the Gold Medal of the City of Vienna.

NOËL GOODWIN

Wallek-Walewski, Bolesław (*b* Lwów, 23 Jan 1885; *d* Kraków, 9 April 1944). Polish composer and conductor. He studied in Lwów, at the Kraków Conservatory with Żeleński and Felicjan Szopski, and in Leipzig. In 1910 he took up a teaching appointment at the Kraków Conservatory, of which he was made director in 1938. Founder, artistic director and conductor of the Kraków choral society, Echo, he also conducted opera and orchestral concerts. He composed in a traditional Romantic style, excelling in sacred choral music. His four-act opera *Pomsta Jontkowa* ('Jontek's Revenge'), set in the southern Polish highlands in the mid-19th century, is a continuation of the life-histories of the characters in Moniuszko's *HALKA* centring on Janosik, Halka's son; it includes direct quotations from Moniuszko's opera.

Kochanek Maryli [Maryla's Lover], 1906, unfinished, unperf.
Pan Twardowski [Mr Twardowski], 1911 (A. Bandrowski), Kraków, 1915
Dola [Destiny] (Wallek-Walewski), Kraków, 1919
Żona dwóch mężów [The Wife of Two Husbands], 1920, unfinished, unperf.
Pomsta Jontkowa [Jontek's Revenge] (music drama, 4, Wallek-Walewski), Poznań, Wielki, 16 Oct 1926
Legenda o królewnie Wandzie [The Legend of the King's Daughter Wanda], 1936 (M. Jaroszanka), unperf.

*

A. Kopyciński: 'Bolesław Wallek-Walewski 1885–1944', *Ruch muzyczny* (1945), no.3, pp.11–13
MIECZYSŁAWA HANUSZEWSKA, JIM SAMSON

Wallmann, Margarita [Margarethe] (*b* Vienna, 22 June 1904; *d* Monaco, 2 May 1992). Austrian director. She studied in Berlin, Vienna and Paris, and originally worked as a dancer and choreographer. She first staged an opera at Salzburg in 1936 (*Orfeo ed Euridice*), and worked at the Teatro Colón (1937–48). After 1952, she worked regularly at La Scala and during the 1950s and 60s in almost every house in Europe and the USA.

One of the first woman directors with an international career, she directed operas across the whole of the lyric repertory, from Monteverdi to Puccini, including Callas in *Norma* and *La Gioconda*, but tended to specialize in modern compositions. She thus worked with Richard Strauss, Stravinsky, de Falla, Milhaud and others, and with Nicola Benois, Dali and Wakhevitch among designers. Wallmann was responsible for premières of Poulenc's *Dialogues des Carmélites* (La Scala, 1957, later staged at Covent Garden) as well as operas by Pizzetti, Frank Martin (*Le mystère de la Nativité*, Salzburg Festival, 1960), and Rossellini. Her style was representational, flamboyant and luxurious, requiring elaborate scenery. By the mid-1970s it had gone out of fashion and, as a consequence, her activity was severely reduced.

*

M. Wallmann: *Les balcons du ciel* (Paris, 1976)
ALAN BLYTH

Wallnöfer, Adolf (*b* Vienna, 24 April 1854; *d* Munich, 9 June 1946). Austrian baritone, later tenor. He studied in Vienna and made his début in 1878 as Count di Luna. From 1880 he sang tenor roles, specializing in Wagner and the heroic German repertory. He joined Angelo Neumann's touring Wagner Theatre (1882–3), then sang in Bremerhaven and Prague. Engaged at the Metropolitan for the 1895–6 season, he sang Siegmund, Siegfried and Tristan. Later he appeared at Breslau and Nuremberg and at the Vienna Volksoper (1906–8). He had a strong but not very individual voice.

ELIZABETH FORBES

Wally, La. *Dramma musicale* in four acts by ALFREDO CATALANI to a libretto by LUIGI ILLICA after Wilhelmine von Hillern's story *Die Geyer-Wally*; Milan, Teatro alla Scala, 20 January 1892.

The action takes place in the Tyrol in about 1800. In the village of Hochstoff the rich landowner Stromminger (bass) taunts Haghenbach (tenor), from the rival village of Sölden, on his return from a hunting expedition. Stromminger's daughter Wally (soprano) tries to make peace between them and sends away the young huntsman, for whom she shows an obvious partiality; this in turn annoys the factor Gellner (baritone), secretly in love with her, who reveals his feelings to the still angry Stromminger. When her father insists that she must marry Gellner, Wally refuses and he banishes her. She goes off into the mountains with her friend Walter (light soprano), and a year later returns to claim the estate she has inherited from her now deceased father. She goes to Sölden for a festival and in a fit of jealousy over Haghenbach insults Afra (mezzo-soprano), a tavern owner, having been wrongly led to believe by Gellner that Afra is betrothed to the man Wally loves. To avenge the insult, Haghenbach consents to dance with Wally and gives her a kiss, swearing falsely that he loves her. The mockery of the bystanders makes Wally aware of the truth, and she promises to marry Gellner if he will kill Haghenbach. The same evening Haghenbach, who realizes that he loves Wally, goes to Hochstoff to see her but is attacked by Gellner, who hurls him into a ravine. Wally, overcome by remorse, rushes to save him and returns him to Afra, to whom she leaves all her wealth. She goes away before the young man recovers, returning to her refuge in the mountains, and is eventually joined by Haghenbach, who tells her of his love. The couple are finally reconciled, but as they seek the path back the young man is carried away by an avalanche. Calling his name in vain, Wally flings herself into the abyss.

In this work, recognized as his masterpiece, Catalani shows himself halfway between *verismo* opera and Puccini (who was to triumph with *Manon* the following year) and in harmony with Italian decadentism, in particular the poetry of Giovanni Pascoli and Guido Gozzano. From the strictly musical point of view the opera's merits lie in its good control of orchestration and expressive melodies, and at some points the musical characterization is very successful. Its weakness is a lack of dramatic interest in the plot, the development of which is too protracted and lacking in intensity. Although it has no great or unforgettable character, dramatic intuition or linguistic craftsmanship such as there is in Puccini, the small world of *La Wally* is real and finely chiselled, and this microcosm becomes a creation worthy of a place among the operas that characterize European *fin-de-siècle* music drama. MICHELE GIRARDI

Walpurgis. *See* MARIA ANTONIA WALPURGIS.

Walsh, T(homas) J(oseph) (*b* Wexford, 20 Nov 1911; *d* Wexford, 8 Nov 1988). Irish writer on opera and co-founder of the Wexford Festival. He was educated in Wexford and at University College, Dublin, where he graduated in medicine in 1944. In Dublin he also studied singing. In autumn 1950 two young collectors of opera records came to him with the idea of forming an opera study group. With the active support of the novelist Compton Mackenzie, they mounted a production of Balfe's *Rose of Castille* in October 1951, which initiated the annual Wexford Festival. While still working as an anaesthetist at the Wexford County Hospital, Walsh undertook the artistic direction of the festival, personally recruiting the principal singers and organizing the training of the local amateur chorus until his retirement after the 1966 season. His devoted enthusiasm helped ensure the international fame of the festival, an achievement recognized by the award of an honorary MA from the University of Dublin in 1956, and the Freedom of the Borough of Wexford in 1976. A member of the Irish Arts Council, 1973–83, and occasionally on the jury of the Concours International du Chant de Toulouse, 1967–80, Walsh wrote six books on the history of opera in Dublin, Monte Carlo and Paris. His publications earned him a PhD from the University of Dublin in 1972 and a LittD in 1983.

Opera in Old Dublin, 1819–1838 (Wexford, 1952)
Opera in Dublin, 1705–1797 (Dublin, 1973)
Monte Carlo Opera, 1879–1909 (London, 1975)
Second Empire Opera: the Théâtre Lyrique, Paris, 1851–1870 (London, 1981)
Monte Carlo Opera, 1910–1951 (London, 1985)
Frederick Jones and Opera in Dublin, 1798–1820 (Kilkenny, 1991)

BRIAN BOYDELL

Walt, Deon van der (*b* Cape Town, 28 July 1958). South African tenor. He studied singing at the University of Stellenbosch, and made his operatic début as Jaquino in 1981 at the Nico Malan Opera House in Cape Town. Since 1982 he has been attached to a number of opera houses in Europe, principally in Stuttgart and Zürich, where he sang Tonio in *La fille du régiment* (1989). He made his début at Covent Garden in 1985 as Almaviva and at the Vienna Staatsoper in 1989 as Tamino. In 1989 he also sang Belmonte at Salzburg. The lyric quality of his voice makes him an ideal interpreter of the works of composers such as Donizetti, Mozart and Rossini. JAMES MAY

Walter, Bruno [Schlesinger, Bruno Walter] (*b* Berlin, 15 Sept 1876; *d* Beverly Hills, CA, 17 Feb 1962). German conductor. He studied at the Stern Conservatory in Berlin and became a coach at the Cologne Opera (1893), where he made his conducting début with Lortzing's *Der Waffenschmied* in 1894 before moving to the Hamburg Opera to work under Mahler. After a season each at Breslau, Pressburg and Riga, he returned in 1900 to Berlin and conducted the first performance there of *Der arme Heinrich* by Pfitzner, whose operas he championed. In 1901 Walter rejoined Mahler, now at the court opera in Vienna. He was invited to Prague, to London (where in 1910 he conducted *Tristan* and Smyth's *The Wreckers* at Covent Garden), to Moscow and to Rome. From 1913 to 1922 he was musical director of the Munich Opera where he conducted the première of Pfitzner's *Palestrina* in 1917. In London, Walter was chief conductor of the German seasons at Covent Garden from 1924 to 1931. In 1925 he returned to Berlin as musical director at the Städtische Oper, Charlottenburg (*see* BERLIN, §3(ii)); that year he began his long association with the Salzburg Festival. He directed a Mozart cycle at the Champs-Elysées Theatre in Paris in 1928.

In 1933, when the political situation became impossible for him, Walter left Germany for Austria. At the Vienna Staatsoper he was guest conductor from 1935 and artistic adviser from 1936. He conducted a notable revival of *Carmen*, with Ebert as producer, in 1937. Following the Anschluss Walter was granted French citizenship. In 1939 he settled in the USA where he conducted at the Metropolitan Opera for several seasons between 1941 and 1957. From 1947 onwards he made return visits to Europe, appearing notably at Edinburgh, Salzburg, Vienna and Munich.

Walter was a conductor of superior endowments and great experience, who obtained results with a moderate range of gesture. His memoirs, *Erinnerung und Gedanken eines Musikers* (Stockholm, 1947; Eng. trans., New York, 1947), reveal an urbanity bordering on unctuousness. But this trait no doubt helped him in the opera house where, failing the dictatorial methods unsuited to a man of his temperament, diplomacy and self-control are essential. His interpretations of Mozart were poised and elegant without mannerisms; a generation of operagoers was nourished by his pre-war Covent Garden performances of Wagner and Strauss.

RONALD CRICHTON

Walter, Gustav (*b* Bilin, nr Prague, 11 Feb 1834; *d* Vienna, 31 Jan 1910). Bohemian tenor. He studied in Prague, first as a violinist then as a singer with Franz Vogl (not, as sometimes believed, with Schubert's friend Johann, who died in 1840). In 1855 he made his operatic début as Edgardo in *Lucia di Lammermoor* at Brno. He then joined the Vienna Staatsoper, where he sang from 1856 to 1887. One of the most admired Mozart singers of his time, he sang Don Ottavio at the opening of the new Vienna opera house in 1869. He sang Walther in the generally disastrous Viennese première of *Die Meistersinger* (1870), and other Wagnerian roles included Loge and Lohengrin. In 1875 he created the role of Assad in Goldmark's *Die Königin von Saba*. After retiring from opera he gave a famous series of lieder recitals. His three recordings include an aria from

Mignon, his last opera in Vienna; he recorded at the age of 71, but the voice is well preserved and the style both expressive and elegant. J. B. STEANE

Walter, (Johann) Ignaz (*b* Radonitz [now Radonice], Bohemia, 31 Aug 1755; *d* Regensburg, 22 Feb 1822). German composer and tenor. While a student at the University of Vienna, he studied singing and composition with Joseph Starzer. His identification with the Joseph Walter who sang for the National-Singspiel from 1780 to 1782 (and who was originally to have figured in Mozart's *Die Entführung aus dem Serail*) seems very doubtful. From 1780 to 1786 Walter earned a considerable reputation as a tenor and composer of comic operas with various German companies in Augsburg, Prague, Riga, Frankfurt and Mainz.

In 1792 Walter joined G. F. W. Grossmann's company in Lower Saxony as its music director. His operas for this troupe show his Viennese training to advantage in a fondness for wind instruments, a cheerful and popular melodic style and a fine sense of musical architecture (his tonal plans seem closely modelled on the practice of Mozart, in whose operas he frequently sang). In 1787 he completed a setting of H. G. Schmieder's *Doktor Faust*, a text cobbled from Goethe's *Faust* fragment of 1790 and other German sources. His music, according to Spitta, shows him 'wholly within Mozart's sphere of influence'. Walter himself took the part of Faust, and the Queen of Aragon was sung by his wife Juliane Browne Roberts (1759–1835), whom he had married while at Riga. In 1804 Walter assumed direction of the Hoftheater at Regensburg, where he died in 1822.

See also DOKTOR FAUST (i).

music lost unless otherwise stated

Die 25 000 Gulden, oder Im Dunkeln ist nicht gut munkeln (Spl, 3, C. H. Spiess), Dresden, Schwarze Thor, 15 Aug 1782

Der Kaufmann von Smyrna (Operette, 1, C. F. Schwan, after S. R. N. Chamfort: *Le marchand de Smyrne*), Prague, Nostitz, 1783

Der Trank der Unsterblichkeit (4, C. A. Vulpius), Prague, Nostitz, 1783

Der Graf von Waltron, oder Die Subordination (Spl, 4, J. B. Bergopzoomer, after H. F. Möller), Prague, Nostitz, 1784

Des Teufels Lustschloss (3, A. von Kotzebue), Prague, Nostitz, 1787

Der ausgeprügelte Teufel, 1790

Der gerade Weg ist der beste (Kotzebue), 1790

Der Spiegelritter (Spl, 3, Kotzebue), Frankfurt, National, 11 Sept 1791

Die Hirtin der Alpen (1, A. W. Schreiber, after J. F. Marmontel), Frankfurt, National, 1792

Die Harfe [Die Zauberharfe] (Operette, 2, Schreiber), 1793

Die böse Frau (komisches Original-Spl, 2, C. A. Herklots), Hanover, 26 Sept 1794, *D-Dlb*

Doktor Faust (Original-Oper, 4, H. G. Schmieder, after J. W. von Goethe and others), Bremen, 28 Dec 1787; 2nd version, Hanover, 8 June 1798, *Bhm*; rev. (C. A. Mämminger), Regensburg, Hof, 10 Oct 1819

Die Weinlese (after F.-C. Dancourt: *Les vendanges de Surênes*), 1799

Das Wildpret, Frankfurt, 1799

Ritter Löwensteins Geist auf Wanderungen, oder Die Teufelsmühle am Wienerberg, 2. Theil (3, C. Werner), Regensburg, Hof, 18 Aug 1809

Hass und Liebe, oder Das Fischermädchen (1, T. Körner), Regensburg, Hof, 8 Sept 1815

*

P. Spitta: 'Die älteste Faust-Oper und Goethe's Stellung zur Musik', *Zur Musik* (Berlin, 1892), 197–234

H. Pigge: *Geschichte und Entwicklung des Regensburger Theaters (1786–1859)* (Munich, 1953)

K. M. Pisarowitz: 'Mozarts Urbassa', *Mitteilungen der Internationalen Stiftung Mozarteum* xiii/3–4 (1965), 15–20 [incl. extensive bibliography]

T. Bauman: *North German Opera in the Age of Goethe* (Cambridge, 1985) THOMAS BAUMAN

Walters, Jess [Wolk, Jess] (*b* Brooklyn, NY, 18 Nov 1908). American baritone. He studied in New York, where his teachers included Frank LaForge, Mario Pagano, Luigi Giuffrida, and Holda and Luigi Rossini. His début was in 1941 with the New Opera Company, New York, in the title role of *Macbeth* (in the American première of the 1865 version). He made his European début at Covent Garden in 1947 as Count des Grieux in *Manon* and remained with that company for 12 years, singing 684 performances. He also appeared in Amsterdam, Brussels, Chicago, Miami, New Orleans and San Francisco, and with the New York City Opera. His repertory centred on the dramatic baritone roles of Verdi. CORI ELLISON

Waltershausen, Hermann Wolfgang (Sartorius), Freiherr von (*b* Göttingen, 12 Oct 1882; *d* Munich, 13 Aug 1954). German composer. He studied composition with Thuille in Munich, and in 1920 was appointed professor and assistant director of the Akademie der Tonkunst in Munich, working as its director from 1922 to 1932. During the Nazi era he inaugurated the Seminar für Privatmusiklehrer, which attained state recognition in 1948. Of his five operas only *Oberst Chabert* (1912), based on a story by Balzac set in Paris in 1817, attained any success; it was performed in Vienna, Berlin, Munich, London, Budapest and Stockholm. The work represents one of the earliest attempts at integrating elements of *verismo* with post-Wagnerian German opera and is notable for its harmonic adventurousness. Waltershausen's subsequent stage works, however, did not follow the same path. The dramatic mystery *Richardis* (1915), modelled to a certain extent on *Parsifal*, resembles a scenic oratorio rather than a music drama, while the comedy *Die Rauensteiner Hochzeit* (1919) returns to the idiom and structure of the 19th-century *Volksoper*.

Else Klapperzehen (musikalische Komödie, 2, Waltershausen), Dresden, Hofoper, 15 May 1909, vs (Munich, *c*1909)

Oberst Chabert (Musiktragödie, 3, Waltershausen, after Balzac), Frankfurt, Opernhaus, 18 Jan 1912, vs (Munich, 1911)

Richardis (romantische Oper, 3, O. Anthes), Karlsruhe, Hof, 14 Nov 1915, facs. of Act 3 introduction in *Ehrengabe: Dramatischer Dichter und Komponisten ... Nikolaus von Seebach zum zwanzigjährigen Intendanten-Jubiläum* (Leipzig, 1914), 168–9

Die Rauensteiner Hochzeit (3, Waltershausen), Karlsruhe, Landes, 21 Nov 1919

Die Gräfin von Tolosa (7 scenes, Waltershausen), Munich Radio, 18 Dec 1954

*

L. K. Mayer: 'Hermann Wolfgang von Waltershausen', *ZfM*, cxv (1954), 541–3

R. Sailer: *Waltershausen und die Oper* (diss., U. of Cologne, 1957)

K.-R. Danler: *Hermann Wolfgang Sartorius Freiherr von Waltershausen* (Tutzing, 1984) ERIK LEVI

Walther, Carolina. *See* MÜLLER, CAROLINA FREDRIKA.

Walton, Sir **William (Turner)** (*b* Oldham, 29 March 1902; *d* Ischia, 8 March 1983). English composer. He was a chorister at Christ Church Cathedral, Oxford, 1912–18, where he wrote his earliest compositions: songs and anthems. He was 'adopted' by the Sitwell family in 1919 and achieved notoriety in 1922 for his collaboration with Edith Sitwell in the entertainment *Façade*. In the 1920s and 30s he became the leading

British composer of his generation with a succession of works including concertos for viola (1929) and violin (1939), a symphony (1931–5) and the cantata *Belshazzar's Feast* (1931). His first involvement with opera was with Cecil Gray, who in 1941 wrote a libretto about the Italian composer Gesualdo, but no music was composed. In 1947 he was commissioned by the BBC to compose an opera and chose the subject of *Troilus and Cressida*, in Chaucer's version, with Christopher Hassall as librettist. This occupied him from 1948 to 1954. It was produced at Covent Garden (3 Dec 1954; pubd London, 1954) and later in San Francisco and Milan, but generally met with only a cool reception. He revised it several times, and in 1976 it was revived at Covent Garden with the role of Cressida transposed from soprano to mezzo-soprano to allow Janet Baker to sing it. In 1967 Walton composed a short one-act 'extravaganza' based on Chekhov's vaudeville *The Bear* (P. Dehn and Walton). This was commissioned by, and first performed at, the Aldeburgh Festival (Jubilee Hall, 3 June 1967; pubd London, 1967) and has enjoyed more success and popularity than its larger-scale predecessor. *Troilus and Cressida* was written in a romantic Puccinian idiom – 'an English bel canto opera', Walton himself claimed – which was regarded in 1954 as old-fashioned, but it fails chiefly because of the flowery style of the libretto and the weak characterization of the protagonists. *The Bear* is more successful because its witty parodies are in the manner of *Façade*.

See also BEAR, THE and TROILUS AND CRESSIDA.

*

F. Howes: *The Music of William Walton* (London, 1965)

MICHAEL KENNEDY

Waltz, Gustavus (*fl* 1732–59). English bass of German birth. His first known appearances were in Arne's English opera season at the Little Theatre in the Haymarket in spring 1732, when he sang in Lampe's *Amelia* and a pirated production of Handel's *Acis and Galatea* (Polyphemus). The following season (1732–3) he sang in Lampe's *Britannia*, J. C. Smith's *Ulysses* and Arne's *Opera of Operas* at Lincoln's Inn Fields and in several Handel oratorios. He then joined Handel's opera company, first at the King's Theatre, later at Covent Garden (1733–6), and took part in revivals of *Ottone*, *Sosarme* and *Il pastor fido*, the pasticcios *Caio Fabricio* and *Oreste*, and the first performances of *Arianna in Creta* (Minos), *Ariodante* (King of Scotland), *Alcina* (Melisso) and *Atalanta* (Nicander). He continued to sing in English theatre pieces, among them Lampe's *Opera of Operas* and *Cupid and Psyche* and works by Arne, chiefly at Drury Lane (1733–6, 1743–5) and Covent Garden (1739–42, 1749–51). Handel cast him as Charon in the unperformed incidental music to *Alceste* (1750).

Waltz is generally recalled for the wrong reasons. Burney and Hawkins both said he was at one time Handel's cook, which is possible but unverifiable. Burney's notorious aspersions on Waltz – 'a German, with a coarse figure, and a still coarser voice', 'Waltz had but little voice, and his manner was coarse and unpleasant' – almost certainly do him an injustice. Burney did not hear him until his later years, when he admitted that 'as an actor, [Waltz] had a great deal of humour'. Some of Handel's parts for him, notably the King in *Ariodante* and Saul, suggest not only dramatic power but majesty and pathos, with a good legato and a compass of nearly two octaves (*G* to *f*♯′).

W. C. Smith: 'Gustavus Waltz: was he Handel's Cook?', *Concerning Handel* (London, 1948), 165–94

WINTON DEAN

Walzel, Camillo. Austrian librettist and theatre director who worked under the pseudonym F. ZELL.

Walzer aus Wien ('Waltzes from Vienna'). Singspiel in three acts, using music by JOHANN STRAUSS and his father, the elder Johann Strauss, selected and arranged by ERICH WOLFGANG KORNGOLD and JULIUS BITTNER to a libretto by A. M. WILLNER, HEINZ REICHERT and Ernst Marischka; Vienna, Stadttheater, 30 October 1930.

Walzer aus Wien has been the most successful, internationally, of the more than 20 theatre works constructed by other hands from the music of Johann Strauss. Its story, a fictionalized life of the composer, centres on the struggles of the young Strauss (baritone) with his unsympathetic father, his romance with the confectioner's daughter, Resi (soprano), and his relationship with the extrovert Countess Olga (soprano), who helps his ambition to become a musician against his father's wishes. The music is tastefully, if sometimes confusingly, arranged from a number of well-known Strauss melodies, as well as some less familiar pieces, the most successful of which was the duet 'Hat ein Engelein in Himmel', for young Strauss and the Countess. The work's greatest popularity has been outside Austria, notably in France (as *Valses de Vienne*) and in the USA and Britain (as *The Great Waltz*). KURT GÄNZL

Walzertraum, Ein ('A Waltz Dream'). Operetta in three acts by OSCAR STRAUS to a libretto by Felix Dörmann and Leopold Jacobson, after Hans Müller's *Das Buch der Abenteuer*; Vienna, Carltheater, 2 March 1907.

In the principality of Flausenthurm, Princess Helene (soprano) has today married Lieutenant Niki (tenor) of the Hussars. Niki is uncomfortable with court life and when he hears that an all-female orchestra is playing Viennese music in the castle grounds, he cannot resist going there with his friend Lieutenant Montschi (baritone). Though it is his wedding night, he proceeds to fall in love with the orchestra leader, Franzi (soubrette). Undismayed, Helene invites Franzi back to the castle, where Franzi teaches her how to win back Niki with Viennese charm and Viennese comforts. A celebration of Viennese pleasures and Viennese rhythms, the operetta featured Mizzi Zwerenz as Franzi and Fritz Werner as Niki. Its principal numbers are the waltz dream duet for Niki and Montschi ('Leise, ganz leise'), the polka 'G'stellte Mäd'ln' for Franzi and her orchestra, the duet 'O, du lieber, o du g'scheiter' for Niki and Helene and the comedy duet 'Piccolo, Piccolo' for Franzi and Count Lothar (buffo). Straus added several new songs for later stage productions and for a film version, *The Smiling Lieutenant*, directed by Lubitsch in Hollywood in 1931. ANDREW LAMB

Wand, Günter (*b* Elberfeld, 7 Jan 1912). German conductor. He studied at Wuppertal and Cologne but was largely self-taught as a conductor. After a year working on a voluntary basis in the opera house at Wuppertal he made his conducting début with a Robert Stolz operetta. He then went to Allenstein in East Prussia (now Olsztyn, Poland), where he was répétiteur and conductor for four years, during which he noted that he conducted more than 600 performances of opera, operetta, ballets and concerts across the entire repertory. He later became chief conductor at Detmold, then conductor at Cologne (1939), where he was principal conductor until the opera house was destroyed in 1944. After working at the Salzburg Mozarteum and Landestheater for a year, he returned to Cologne and was largely responsible for rebuilding the city's postwar musical life, both as music director at the Cologne Opera (1945–8) and as director of concerts (Gürzenich Kapellmeister), the latter post later becoming an appointment 'for life'. From 1948 he also taught conducting at Cologne, concentrating, there and (from 1974) at Berne, on the concert repertory. During the 1980s, when he was chief guest conductor of the BBC SO, it was noted that he was among the last practitioners in a tradition of stylistic propriety and penetrating musical insight. He is particularly highly regarded for his performances of Mozart and Verdi operas. HANSPETER KRELLMANN, NOËL GOODWIN

Wandering Scholar, The [*The Tale of the Wandering Scholar*]. Opera in one act, op.50, by GUSTAV HOLST to a libretto by Clifford Bax after 'Le pauvre clerc' from Helen Waddell's *The Wandering Scholars*; Liverpool, David Lewis Theatre, 31 January 1934.

In a farmhouse in 13th-century France, Alison (soprano), the young wife of Louis (baritone), is preparing a meal with which to regale the local priest while her husband has gone to town for provisions. Father Philippe (bass) is interested in more than food and drink, but as he is about to carry Alison off to the attic the wandering scholar Pierre (tenor) appears, begging for something to eat. The priest drives him away and resumes his seduction, only to have to hide when Louis is heard returning. He has met Pierre, who tells a story which skilfully reveals first the meal Alison has been cooking and then Father Philippe himself. The priest is chased round the house and out of the door, Pierre has earned a meal, and Alison's fate hangs in the balance as Louis drives her up to the attic.

For his final opera Holst reverted to the chamber orchestra which he had used 30 years before in *Sāvitri*. This economy of means is mirrored by a spareness of texture and gesture which is a hallmark of his late music, and which serves the libretto eminently well. Holst composed the work between 1929 and 1930 but was too ill to attend the first performance, which took place only a few months before his death. It was edited for publication in 1968 by Benjamin Britten and Imogen Holst, who abbreviated Holst's original title.

COLIN MATTHEWS

War and Peace [*Voyna i mir*]. Opera in 13 'lyrico-dramatic scenes' and a choral epigraph by SERGEY PROKOFIEV to a libretto by the composer and MIRA ALEXANDROVNA MENDELSON (Prokof'yeva) after LEV NIKOLAYEVICH TOLSTOY's novel (1869); for premières see Table 2 opposite.

Prokofiev's operatic masterpiece and one of the tiny handful of post-1945 operas to achieve repertory status, *War and Peace* had an exceptionally complicated creative history that reflected not only the composer's artistic decisions and those of his close advisers, but also the extremely difficult circumstances that attended the opera's gestation. Five separate authorial versions can be distinguished, of which four have been the basis of staged performances and three exist in discrete written form.

First version: According to Prokofiev's widow Lina, as early as 1935 the composer, then living abroad, referred to an opera on Tolstoy's *War and Peace* as a plan of long standing, awaiting only the opportunity for long and concentrated work without interruption. It has been discovered, moreover, that the first theme of the overture (associated in the opera with Kutuzov) was first jotted down in a notebook dating from the early months of 1933. Nevertheless, the earliest concrete evidence of work on the opera dates from April 1941. The composer was living by then with Mira Mendelson, whom he recognized (and who has been recognized in Soviet historiography) as his second (common-law) wife. She was reading Tolstoy's novel aloud to Prokofiev, according to her memoirs, when he became enthusiastic over the operatic possibilities of the episode in which Natasha Rostova visits the bedside of the delirious Andrey Bolkonsky (Book III, Part 3, chapter 32 [III/3/32]). He drew up an initial list of scenes on 12 April 1941, as in Table 1 (numbers in brackets refer to the scenes of the final version; Scene 5 was an insertion that caused the renumbering of those succeeding):

Table 1

1	[3]	The Rostovs and their visit to old Bolkonsky.
2	[4]	Natasha meets Anatol at Hélène's (Hélène and Natasha. The Count: 'Let's go, Natasha'. Hélène distracts the Count. Anatol. The kiss. Natasha alone. The old Count.)
3	[5]	Anatol and Dolokhov before the elopement.
4	[6]	Unsuccessful elopement. Natasha's despair. Pierre.
5	[7]	Pierre shakes Anatol.
6		Vilna. Balashov informs Alexander that war has been declared [Tolstoy, III/1/4].
7		Balashov with Napoleon [Tolstoy III/1/5–7].
8	[8]	Before the Battle of Borodino. Kutuzov, Andrey. Pierre, Andrey.
9	[11]	Moscow. Execution scene. Pierre a prisoner.
10	[12]	Natasha with the wounded Andrey.
11	[13]	The French retreat. Pierre freed.

(That the main action of the first part of the opera would centre on the ill-starred elopement of Natasha and Anatol Kuragin was clear from the start. The main action of the second part, as envisaged at this early stage, centred on Pierre Bezukhov and his experiences on the fringes of battle and in the hands of the occupiers.)

There is no reason to assume that, having made this plan, Prokofiev would have immediately set to work on the music or even that the opera would have been the next he composed. The year before he had outlined a similar plan for an opera based on Tolstoy's novel *Resurrection*, and had made a far more detailed scenario for an opera on Nikolay Leskov's *The Wastrel*. What decided the matter inevitably in favour of *War and Peace* was of course the German invasion of the Soviet Union a couple of months after Prokofiev had drawn up his outline. Current events were paralleling in unexpected and uncanny fashion 'those pages [of Tolstoy's] recounting the Russian people's struggle against Napoleon's hordes in 1812', the composer wrote. He drew up a new plan. The first five scenes of the original plan became Scenes 2–6, with an ineffably peaceful initial scene based on the chapter in the novel in which Andrey and Natasha are first brought into (unwitting) conjunction (II/3/2; in the scenario it is called 'Night at the Rostov estate, Otradnoye'). The second half of the opera, depicting the French invasion and its resistance, now began more nearly to resemble its ultimate form; a scene 'At Napoleon's Headquarters', corresponding to

TABLE 2
PREMIÈRES

version	venue	date	notes
original (11 scenes)	Moscow, Actors' Club	16 Oct 1944	concert perf., 7 scenes with pf
	Moscow, Conservatory	7 June 1945	concert perf., 9 scenes, cond. S. Samosud
	Prague, National Theatre	1948	stage première
expanded (two-evening, 13 scenes)	Leningrad, Maliy Theatre	12 June 1946	Part I (8 scenes), cond. Samosud; Part II, dress rehearsals in July and Dec 1947, cancelled
abbreviated (10 scenes)	Florence, Maggio Musicale	26 May 1953	cond. A. Rodziński
	NBC TV (New York)	13 Jan 1957	cond. P. H. Adler
final (13 scenes)	Leningrad, Maliy Theatre	1 April 1955	11 scenes, much cut; cond. E. Grikurov
	Moscow, Stanislavsky–Nemirovich-Danchenko Musical Theatre	8 Nov 1957	13 scenes, many cuts; cond. A. Shaverdov
	Moscow, Bol'shoy Theatre	15 Dec 1959	first relatively complete perf., incl. Epigraph; cond. A. Melik-Pashayev

numbers refer to the scenes of the final version (see Table 1, opposite, and pp.1104–5) in which the character appears

Prince Andrey Bolkonsky (1, 2, 8, 12) — high baritone
Natasha Rostova (1, 2, 3, 4, 6, 12) — lyric-dramatic soprano
Sonya (1, 2, 4, 6) — mezzo-soprano
Host of the Ball *an old grandee of Catherine's day* (2) — tenor
Major-Domo at the ball (2) — tenor
Mariya Dmitriyevna Akhrosimova (2, 6) — powerful mezzo-soprano
Peronskaya (2) — soprano
Count Il'ya Andreyevich Rostov (2, 3, 4) — bass-baritone, soft quality
Pierre Bezukhov (2, 6, 7, 8, 11, 13) — dramatic tenor
Hélène Bezukhova (2, 4, 7) — contralto
Anatol Kuragin (2, 4, 5, 6, 7) — tenor
Dolokhov (2, 5, 6) — bass
Alexander I (2) — silent
Old Footman to the Bolkonskys (3) — baritone
Housemaid to the Bolkonskys (3) — mezzo-soprano
Valet to the Bolkonskys (3) — bass
Princess Mariya (Bolkonskaya) (3) — mezzo-soprano
Prince Nikolay Andreyevich Bolkonsky (3) — basso profondo, sarcastic quality
Balaga *a coachman* (5) — high, spirited bass
Joseph *a footman* (5) — silent
Matryosha *a gypsy girl* (5) — contralto (not very low)
Dunyasha *young housemaid to the Rostovs* (6, 11, 13) — soprano (not high)
Gavrila *Akhrosimova's footman* (6) — baritone or bass
Metivier *a French doctor* (7) — soft, velvet baritone or bass
A French Abbé (7) — tenor (no high notes)
Denisov (7, 8, 13) — bass-baritone
Tikhon Shcherbatiy (8, 13) — bass (no low notes)
Fyodor (8, 13) — tenor (no high notes)
Vasilisa *a village elder's wife* (8, 13) — mezzo-soprano
Matveyev (8, 11) — baritone
Trishka (8) — contralto (travesti)
Two German Generals (8) — spoken
Orderly to Prince Andrey (8) — low tenor
Field Marshal Mikhail Illarionovich Kutuzov (8, 10, 13) — bass
Adjutant to Kutuzov (8, 13) — tenor (shrill quality)
First Staff Officer (8) — tenor (possibly baritone)
Second Staff Officer (8) — bass or baritone
Napoleon (9, 11) — baritone
Adjutant to General Compans (9) — tenor
Adjutant to Marshal Murat (9) — contralto (travesti)
Marshal Berthier (9) — bass-baritone
Marshal Caulaincourt (9) — silent
General Belliard (9) — crude bass (no low notes)
Adjutant to Prince Eugène (9) — tenor
Offstage Voice (9) — high tenor
Adjutant from Napoleon's Suite (9) — high bass
De Beausset, Minister of the Court (9) — comic tenor
General Bennigsen (10) — bass
General Barclay de Tolly (10) — tenor
General Yermolov (10) — bass
Konovnitsin (10) — tenor
General Rayevsky (10) — baritone
Song Leader (*zapevala*) (10) — baritone
Malasha *a little girl* (10) — silent
Captain Ramballe (11, 13) — bass
Lieutenant Bonnet (11, 13) — tenor
Jacquot (11) — bass
Gerard (11) — tenor
Young Factory Hand (11) — tenor (possibly baritone)
Shopkeeper (11) — low soprano
Mavra Kuz'minichna *the Rostovs' old housekeeper* (11) — contralto
Ivanov (11) — piercing tenor
Marshal Davout (11) — bass (dark, rich, no low notes)
French Officer (11, 13) — baritone
Platon Karatayev (11, 13) — tenor (soft quality)
Three Lunatics (11) — tenor, high bass, silent
Two French Actresses (11) — soprano, mezzo-soprano
Military Escort (13) — silent

Guests at the ball, Muscovites, peasant militia men, Russian soldiers, partisans, French soldiers

Setting Russia (Otradnoye, St Petersburg, Moscow, Borodino, Fili nr Smolensk), 1805–12

the eventual ninth scene, took the place of the old Scenes 6 and 7 (a scene in the new list depicting 'a Russian outpost' was not actually set to music).

The opera was composed very quickly, between 15 August 1941 and 13 April 1942, during Prokofiev's and Mendelson's period of wartime evacuation, first at Nal'chik, near Stavropol' in the Russian Caucasus, then in Tbilisi, the Georgian capital. It consisted of an overture and 11 scenes (corresponding to the final version less the epigraph and Scenes 2 and 10). For the early scenes of aristocratic romance, Prokofiev mined an old abandoned score of incidental music to an aborted 1936 dramatization of Pushkin's *Yevgeny Onegin* for appropriate themes and leitmotifs, and drew as well upon music he was simultaneously composing for a film biography of the poet Lermontov. A copy of the vocal score in Pavel Lamm's hand survives in the Glinka Museum, Moscow. This version of the opera, though complete to the composer's satisfaction, would never be performed.

Second version ('original' in list of premières above): Lamm's piano score was dispatched to Moscow for evaluation by the All-Union Committee on Art Affairs whose approval had to precede acceptance by any Soviet theatre. After an audition in May 1942, in which the opera was read through from Lamm's manuscript by the pianists Anatoly Vedernikov and Svyatoslav Richter, Prokofiev received a list of stipulated revisions, which he finished by November. A convenient enumeration of these revisions is found in a letter the composer wrote from his third evacuation domicile (Alma-Ata, in Soviet Central Asia [now Kazakhstan]) to Yevgeny Radin, director of the Kirov Theatre in Leningrad, on 25 March 1943, shortly before completing the opera's orchestration. It is clear from their nature that the committee's chief concern was to underscore the opera's topical relevance, and to ensure that Russia's first 'Great Patriotic War' of 1812 would be memorialized in a fashion consistent with attitudes towards the second, in which the country was then engaged.

Thus, to the 11 scenes of the first version, a choral Epigraph was added, taking off from the famous opening sentence of III/3/2 ('The forces of a dozen European nations burst into Russia'), but continuing in a vein of bombast reminiscent of the jingoistic conclusion of *Alexander Nevsky* (and no wonder: Sergey Eisenstein, the director of *Nevsky*, with whom Prokofiev was then collaborating on *Ivan the Terrible*, was on hand in Alma-Ata and actively discussing the *War and Peace* revisions with the composer; he was also scheduled to direct the première at the Moscow Bol'shoy Theatre during the 1943–4 season). In his letter to Radin, Prokofiev confesses ambivalence as to whether the Epigraph should serve as prologue to the entire opera or just to the war scenes; this question was never resolved.

Except for two tiny cuts in Scene 4, all the revisions to existing music involved the war scenes. Anecdotal detail was curtailed; characteristic recitative in two instances (one involving Andrey, the other Denisov) was replaced by heroic arioso; the concluding scene reached its culmination in 'a grand choral apotheosis with military orchestra on stage'. The tendency towards impersonal monumentality in the treatment of the war is already noticeable. Most telling were the changes involving the figure of Field Marshal Kutuzov. A lighthearted exchange between the commander and Dolokhov in the scene on the Borodino battlefield was eliminated, and his joking address to the partisans in the last scene was transferred to Denisov. Instead, Kutuzov was given (in preparation for the Moscow concert première in 1945) a minuscule da capo aria to sing on the battlefield ('Zheleznaya grud' ne boitsya surovosti pogod': 'The iron breast fears no storm'), the most 'classical' piece of its kind Prokofiev had ever written, and – something absolutely unprecedented in Prokofiev's work to date – based on the melody of a folksong ('The Green Jug', originally intended for the cycle of folksong arrangements published as op.104). While the Field Marshal was not yet quite the dominating figure he would become beginning with the Third Version, he was already being divested of ordinary human qualities and transformed into a quasi-deific embodiment of the nation, exactly paralleling the way in which the image of Stalin was being promoted in the prosecution of the actual Patriotic War.

The second version was published in mimeographed vocal score in 1943. A combination of wartime conditions and backstage politics frustrated plans for a Bol'shoy production that year; and although the Metropolitan Opera had expressed interest in producing the work, the Committee on Art Affairs would not countenance a foreign première. Within Russia the second version, though definitive at the time of its completion, would have only concert performances, none complete.

Third version ('expanded' in list of premières): From the time of the original audition before the Committee on Art Affairs, the great champion of Prokofiev's opera had been the conductor Samuil Abramovich Samosud (1884–1964), a powerful figure in Soviet music, who had been chief conductor of the Bol'shoy Theatre since 1936. It was his loss of that position in 1943 that meant the cancellation of *War and Peace*. When he was appointed artistic director of the Maliy Theatre in Leningrad he made the production of Prokofiev's opera a condition. He also insisted on completeness, which created a problem, for the score exceeded the normal length of an operatic evening. Samosud's radical solution was further to expand the opera, which already fell into two relatively discrete and self-contained portions, by adding two more scenes (one to each half), and performing the resulting four-hour-plus spectacle on two evenings.

Samosud not only persuaded Prokofiev to add the scenes; he also chose the scenes to be added. For the first evening he fastened on II/3/14, the chapter in which Natasha and Andrey first 'officially' meet and fall in love. This now became Scene 2 of the opera, 'New Year's Eve Ball, 1810', a brilliant sequence of dances and choral odes against which a great deal of essential plot exposition is ingeniously superimposed. For the second evening, Samosud proposed III/3/4, describing the makeshift war council at Fili, where the decision was taken to abandon Moscow to the enemy. The idea was not only to fill a gap in the plot but to provide a pretext for giving Kutuzov (in Samosud's words) 'an aria such as in [Glinka's] *Susanin* or [Borodin's] *Igor* – central, eloquent, crucial', by means of which Kutuzov and the monumental historical and national forces he embodied, and not Pierre Bezukhov's personal fate, would become the true focus of the evening. After many tries and arguments with the conductor, Prokofiev (who had wanted to limit Kutuzov's big number to a short arioso linked up with the arioso on the battlefield by shared leitmotivic material) finally adapted a folk-epic style melody from his film score for *Ivan the Terrible*. This

'War and Peace' (Prokofiev), scene 8 (before the battle of Borodino) from the third version of the opera, performed at the Malïy Theatre, Leningrad, 12 June 1946

then provided the great leitmotif of exalted heroism for eventual apotheosis in the concluding chorus of the last scene (now the 13th).

Besides these, Prokofiev made numerous changes great and small (Anatoly Volkov enumerates 14) on the way to the monumentally expanded version of his opera. One of the most notable, for which Samosud again claimed credit, was the reprise of the Waltz theme from Scene 2 in the opera's penultimate scene, that of Andrey's reunion with Natasha. Most of the others involved a vastly expanded role for the chorus (mostly glorifying the Leader of the People), for which purpose the composer and Mira Mendelson found texts in anthologies at the Tolstoy Museum in Moscow, as well as in Soviet publications, in particular a 1938 volume, *Izgnaniye Napoleona iz Moskvï* ('The Expulsion of Napoleon from Moscow') and a 1945 collection in honour of the 220th anniversary of Kutuzov's birth (*Mikhail Illarionovich Kutuzov: k 220-letney godovshchine so dnya rozhdeniya*). Prokofiev never actually wrote out a definitive score of the expanded version. Its contents must be pieced together from Samosud's detailed memoirs and from the composer's manuscripts, now at the Central State Archives of Literature and Art in Moscow.

Part I of the new *War and Peace* enjoyed a spectacular success, becoming the crown of the Malïy Theatre repertory. It was given a total of 105 times during the 1946 and 1947 seasons. Part II met with disaster. After a fully staged dress rehearsal in July 1947 it was vetoed (in Samosud's grim recollection) by 'certain individuals, to whom it seemed that [its] historical conception was incorrect'. Just what the objections were has never been explicitly revealed, but they were known to have centred on the ninth scene ('Napoleon at the Shevardino Redoubt') and the 11th ('Moscow Aflame'). Perhaps 'fears' is a better word than 'objections'. During 1946, Party decrees, at once Draconian and arbitrary, had been issued on political education, literature and cinema, and many leading artists, including Eisenstein, had been disgraced (music's – and Prokofiev's – turn would come early in 1948). In such an atmosphere, no one dared take responsibility for approving a work dealing with a historical subject that had so many sensitive parallels with the uncertain present.

Fourth version ('abbreviated' in list of premières): By now, as Samosud bleakly recounted, 'Prokofiev's desire to see *War and Peace* was so urgent, so compelling, that he was prepared to go literally to any lengths of editorial changes, abbreviations or cuts if only it would be produced'. Accordingly, in a document dated 5 December 1948 (published for the first time in the 1958 vocal score), Prokofiev proposed a radical condensation of the opera, ostensibly to achieve a 'one-evening' spectacle, in reality to forestall ideological objections, when it was already much too late. The two scenes that had provoked the censors in 1947 were eliminated outright, along with the Epigraph and what was now the seventh scene ('Pierre shakes Anatol'). (The desperate composer also offered producers the option of deleting the overture, the scene at the Bezukhovs' soirée, and even the scene at Fili.) The mutilated ten-scene version thus proposed under duress, for all that it enjoyed a factitious authorization, should not be considered an authentic version, even though it was the form in which the opera first became known in the West (and though it carries the endorsement of some influential Western critics who mistakenly took it to represent, in the words of one, 'Prokofiev's last thoughts').

Fifth version ('final' in list of premières): Prokofiev's actual last thoughts are now represented in the published score, cited above. It is a restored 13-scene spectacle, with additions. (Yet it should not be thought that a complete performance necessarily entails two evenings: Rostropovich's recording totals four hours and five minutes in playing time, which is not longer than a complete performance of *Ruslan and Lyudmila*, or *The Snow Maiden*, to say nothing of *Les Troyens* or *Götterdämmerung*.) Among the items unique to the fifth version are the duet for Natasha and Sonya in the first scene (composed in April 1949), to the continuation of a text by Zhukovsky that Tchaikovsky had set in part as a duet for Lisa and Pauline in *The Queen of Spades*, and a new middle section for Kutuzov's grand aria in the council scene, composed in November 1952, after which Prokofiev did not return to the score. (The widely circulated conceit that this last item was composed two weeks before the composer's death is untrue.)

PART I

Epigraph (III/3/2) A choral cry of defiance against the foe, adapted from the preface to Tolstoy's account of the Battle of Borodino with all specific references to persons and locales removed so as to make the words fully applicable to World War II.

Scene 1 (II/3/2) *House and garden on the Rostov estate (Otradnoye); May; a moonlit night; Prince Andrey, visiting the Rostovs on business, is reading by the window* He muses pessimistically on a gnarled oak he had encountered that day among leafy birches and elms. His thoughts are interrupted by the sound of Natasha and her cousin Sonya, rapturously conversing and singing about the beautiful night. Andrey is solaced; he muses on Natasha's attractive qualities.

Scene 2 (II/3/14–17) *A ball at the home of an old grandee of Catherine's time* It is New Year's Eve (1809). A footman announces the arrival of Count Rostov and Natasha, Andrey Bolkonsky, Pierre and Hélène Bezukhov, Hélène's brother Anatol and his friend Lieutenant Dolokhov. Madames Akhrosimova and Peronskaya comment acerbically to Natasha about the other guests. Tsar Alexander I deigns to appear and dances a mazurka. A waltz is announced. Pierre Bezukhov, seeing Natasha ignored and disconsolate, asks Prince Andrey to dance with her. They become fatally attracted to one another. Natasha is delighted to hear her father invite Prince Andrey to visit them at home. Andrey, for his part, catches himself dreaming of making Natasha his wife.

Scene 3 (II/5/7) *A small receiving room in the old, gloomy town house of Prince Bolkonsky (the elder) in Vozdvizhenka Street, Moscow; a huge built-in mirror, ancient furniture, footmen in powdered wigs* Count Rostov and Natasha arrive to pay a call following her betrothal to Prince Andrey. The old man will not receive them, sending his daughter Mariya instead. All at once the prince barges in in nightcap and dressing-gown, offers a sarcastic pseudo-apology for the deliberate insult, and withdraws with Princess Mariya. Left alone, Natasha muses on her wounded dignity and her abiding love for Andrey.

Scene 4 (II/5/9–15) *A sitting-room in the home of Pierre and Hélène Bezukhov; in the main hall, joined to the sitting-room by an arcade, dancing couples are seen* Hélène offers congratulations to Natasha on her betrothal. She hints, to Natasha's consternation, that her brother Anatol is also in love with Natasha. Count Rostov tries to cut the evening short but Hélène spirits him off. Anatol arrives, confesses his love, boldly kisses Natasha on the lips, and presses a card into her hand, on which he has threatened to die if he cannot have her. Despite her love for Andrey and Sonya's stern advice, Natasha finds herself fascinated. (Tolstoy had set the early stages of Anatol's seduction at the Opera, prime symbol to him of all that is false.)

Scene 5 (II/5/16–17) *At Dolokhov's: a study hung with Persian rugs, bearskins and arms; Anatol Kuragin in an unbuttoned uniform is lying on a divan, leaning his head on his arm, smiling abstractedly; Dolokhov, in a quilted jacket and boots, is sitting before an open bureau, on which accounts and banknotes can be seen* Anatol tells Dolokhov of his scheme to elope with Natasha, and will not let his friend dissuade him. He exacts an oath of assistance in this exploit from his eager coachman Balaga and, bidding farewell to his gypsy girlfriend Matryosha, sets off into a blizzard.

Scene 6 (II/5/17–19, 22) *A room in Mariya Akhrosimova's town house (where the Rostovs are staying) in Staraya Konyushennaya Street, Moscow; a great glass door leads to a veranda and thence to the garden* Natasha awaits Anatol. When the latter arrives he is intercepted by a servant, Akhrosimova having been forewarned, and flees. Akhrosimova admonishes Natasha for her behaviour and her association with the likes of Hélène and her brother with their 'French' habits and morals. Pierre Bezukhov arrives and, having been told what has happened by Akhrosimova, gives Natasha the terrible news that Kuragin was married all along. Humiliated and disgraced, she knows that she has lost Andrey for ever. Pierre tells her that, were he free, he would gladly marry her himself.

Scene 7 (II/5/3, 20) *Pierre Bezukhov's study; Hélène, Anatol, the Abbé and Dr Metivier* Pierre's furious arrival home interrupts a frivolous conversation with the Frenchmen in which Dr Metivier reveals that the old Prince Bolkonsky had once taken him for a spy. The large but usually mild-mannered Pierre demands Anatol's departure from Moscow and the return of Natasha's letters, threatening violence and actually shaking his brother-in-law by the lapels. After Anatol agrees (though without repenting) and goes off, Pierre's reflections are interrupted by the arrival of Denisov with the news that Napoleon has invaded and 'it looks like war'.

PART II

Epigraph (alternative position).

Scene 8 (III/2/15, 20) *Before the Battle of Borodino; bulwarks are being prepared* Denisov (Natasha's first fiancé) meets Prince Andrey in the course of military affairs, prompting tender recollections on both sides. Pierre appears, saying he wishes to observe the battle. He and Andrey bid each other a fond farewell. The troops sing a series of choruses in praise of their commander Kutuzov, who upon arrival sings them a pair of tributes in return, 'Bespodobnïy narod' ('O matchless folk') and 'Zheleznaya grud' ne boitsya surovosti pogod' ('The iron breast fears no storm'). He asks Andrey to join his staff, but the latter requests leave to stay with his men. Another military chorus is interrupted by the first shots.

Scene 9 (III/2/35) *Shevardino Redoubt during the Battle of Borodino; Napoleon stands atop a hill, looking through his glass; not far from him stand Marshals Berthier and Caulaincourt, M. de Beausset and the emperor's entourage* Napoleon imagines being received in Moscow, but gets bad news about the progress of the battle. He is asked to send reinforcements, which he does with the greatest reluctance. He expresses perplexity at the fortitude of the Russians and his own impotence. From offstage one of the choruses in praise of Kutuzov is heard again.

Scene 10 (III/3/4) *A hut in Fili: the end of the council of war; Kutuzov, Barclay, Bennigsen, Rayevsky, Yermolov, Konovnitsïn and others; the little Malasha, whose head Kutuzov absentmindedly strokes* After each of the generals has expressed an opinion on the question of whether Moscow shall be given up, Kutuzov pronounces his decision that this extraordinary measure is required to save the army and hence the country. He dismisses the others and expresses his feelings about Moscow in a grand aria, 'Velichavaya, v solnechnïkh luchakh, mater' russkikh gorodov' ('Stately, sunlit, mother of Russian cities'). The aria is preceded and followed by another offstage chorus in praise of the commander.

Scene 11 (III/3/13, 17, 19, 24–5, 33–4; 4/1, 12–13) *A street in French-occupied Moscow* This sprawling, episodic scene takes in the most territory from the novel (some of it very freely adapted), proceeding in panoramic, non-narrative fashion. Among the events portrayed are Napoleon's arrival in vain expectation of a receiving delegation, Pierre's encounter with the Rostovs' housekeeper and his arrest under suspicion of arson, the release of the inmates of the lunatic asylum, the flight of the French actors, Pierre's encounter with the peasant soldier Platon Karatayev (the author's proxy in the novel), the outbreak of multiple fires and the inevitable patriotic chorus.

Scene 12 (III/3/32) *A dark hut by night: in the far corner is a bed, on which Prince Andrey is lying; on a stool is a candle, snuffed with a big mushroom* The mortally wounded Andrey, who has unknowingly been lodged with the evacuated Rostovs to await the inevitable, wakes from his delirium (represented by an offstage chorus chanting Tolstoy's 'pi-ti-pi-ti-pi-ti ...') to behold Natasha. She begs forgiveness; he bears no grudge. They relive happier times, evoked by a multitude of reprises.

Scene 13 (IV/3/12–14; 4/6) *The Smolensk road, in a savage blizzard: along the road the French army is retreating; a few soldiers, clothed and shod in whatever came to hand, huddle together for warmth; along the road are cast-off weapons, broken-down carriages* Ramballe and Bonnet, two French officers, assess the hopelessness of their situation. Together with the retreating convoy march some prisoners, including Pierre and Platon Karatayev. The latter, exhausted, is executed. A partisan detachment under Denisov attacks the convoy and frees the surviving prisoners. Marshal Kutuzov arrives and is greeted by all with a grandiose choral reprise of his Scene 10 aria; it is only one of many reprises that give this scene, like the one preceding it, the character of a summation.

* * *

Like many works by great but unconventional artists – indeed, like its literary forebear – Prokofiev's *War and Peace* has a perfection of form that is perhaps more readily apprehended by audiences than by critics. Just as Tolstoy's 'baggy monster' of a novel incorporates attributes of other genres (epic, chronicle, sermon, historical tract), Prokofiev's opera, like the operas of Glinka and Borodin, incorporates conspicuous elements of oratorio. Like the most famous operas of Tchaikovsky and Musorgsky, moreover, *War and Peace* is a medley of scenes from a familiar source rather than a trimly plotted drama. These traits, while typical of Slavonic operas (indeed, essential to the definition of the genre), have impeded the opera's progress in the West. Even in Part I, scenes are rarely dynamic enough to meet conventionally sophisticated notions of dramatic calibre, and this has led to misplaced allegations of naivety on the part of the composer.

The best proof that he knew better than his critics what he was about can be found in the very area that has incited the most complaint: that is, the seemingly disjointed selection and sequence of scenes. Prokofiev's decision to focus the early action on the seduction of Natasha Rostova (to the extent that in the early drafts of the libretto every one of the pre-Borodino scenes had derived from Book II Part 5 of the novel) has met with incomprehension and indignation. It has seemed one-sided, both in its representation of the novel's plot (absent, for example, is Natasha's brother Nikolay Rostov, the novel's key character according to many) and in its portrayal of the beloved heroine, who is shown behaving in reprehensibly selfish fashion.

One way of explaining Prokofiev's selection is simply to note that only a complete account of Natasha's seduction and attempted elopement can fully motivate Scene 12, the scene whose operatic potential had instigated the entire project. But that does not suffice. Prokofiev's true accomplishment was to give the two halves of his work, so often regarded as excessively discrete and even antagonistic, a hidden, mutually reinforcing correspondence. (Tolstoy himself hinted at this correspondence when once, rather enigmatically, he referred to the episode of Natasha and Anatol as the 'knot' in which all the themes of his work came together.) They are parallel parables of betrayal compounded: Natasha/Russia, having become infatuated with Anatol/France (note Akhrosimova's strictures in Scene 6) and betrayed her true love Andrey/the people, is in turn betrayed by her seducer. Even Pierre, in the words of one commentator 'a lumbering and implacable force, threatening but not given to unnecessary violence', and who refers to Natasha in Scene 2 as 'my protégée', has a place within this restricted scheme as counterpart to Kutuzov. The double denouement, with the two reprise-laden summation scenes (Natasha's forgiveness, Russia's victory) placed side by side, makes an impact even the opera's most fastidious detractors reluctantly acknowledge.

A full accounting of the opera's stylistic affinities and its musical construction would have to detail both its intricate network of leitmotifs, reminiscences and reprises, and its canny exploitation of contrasting, dramatically pertinent resonances with Russian operatic tradition. Scenes 2 and 4, played against a scintillating backdrop of ballroom music (some of it, like the common-time polonaise in Scene 2, of a calculated unreality) are in as apposite a line of descent from Tchaikovsky's Pushkin operas as are Scenes 8, 11 and 13 in Part II from Musorgsky's historical tableaux. As Prokofiev deliberately underscored the link with *The Queen of Spades* by his choice of text for the Scene 1 duet, so the epic scene of Moscow aflame is veritably a second Kromï Forest (*Boris Godunov*), replete with pointed musical allusions and with a surrogate Holy Fool in Karatayev. RICHARD TARUSKIN

Ward, David (*b* Dumbarton, 3 July 1922; *d* Dunedin, New Zealand, 16 July 1983). Scottish bass. He studied at the RCM and later in Munich with Hans Hotter. In 1952 he joined the chorus of Sadler's Wells Opera and in 1953 sang the Old Bard in *The Immortal Hour* and Count Walter in *Luisa Miller*; he created Hardy (*Nelson*) the following year and from then until 1958 sang a variety of roles with the company including Méphistophélès, Daland and the Dutchman. In 1960 he made his Covent Garden début as Pogner, sang Lord Walton (*I puritani*) at Glyndebourne and made his Bayreuth début as Titurel. At Covent Garden he sang Fasolt, Hunding, Morosus in the English première of *Die schweigsame Frau* (1961), the Wanderer (1962) and Wotan in a complete *Ring* cycle (1964), as well as Arkel, Pope Clement (*Benvenuto Cellini*), Ivan Khovansky, Rocco and Don Basilio. No less distinguished in Verdi, he sang Zaccaria, Philip II and Fiesco. His Boris with Scottish Opera was highly praised. He sang in Italy,

Germany and the USA, and in 1967 he sang Wotan in six complete *Ring* cycles in Buenos Aires. To a voice of beautiful quality and range he added a sensitivity and dignity which made his Wotan and King Mark profoundly moving. He was made a CBE in 1972.

*

A. Jefferson: 'David Ward', *Opera*, xix (1968), 540–45

HAROLD ROSENTHAL/R

Ward, Robert (Eugene) (*b* Cleveland, 13 Sept 1917). American composer. He studied with Howard Hanson and Bernard Rogers at the Eastman School of Music and began graduate study with Frederick Jacobi at the Juilliard School. During World War II he served as an army band director. Having graduated from Juilliard two months after his demobilization in 1946, Ward joined the faculty and taught there for ten years. In 1956 he left to become executive vice-president and managing editor of Galaxy Music Corporation and Highgate Press, where he remained until 1967, when he was appointed chancellor of the North Carolina School of Arts in Winston-Salem; he stepped down to become professor of composition there in 1975. He taught at Duke University from 1978 until his retirement in 1987.

Even as a student Ward had experienced no difficulty in securing performances, and by the time he and his Juilliard colleague Bernard Stambler wrote their first opera, he was already well known for his orchestral works. *Pantaloon* (1956, retitled *He who gets Slapped*, 1959) was well received, leading to a commission by the New York City Opera for *The Crucible* (1961), the work on which his reputation almost entirely rests. None of Ward's four subsequent operas has been able to duplicate its success, or even that of *He who gets Slapped*. Like other American composers who achieved operatic success in the pre-minimalist era, Ward is highly conservative. The roots of his style lie in Hindemith, Puccini and 1940s Broadway, overlaid with local colour appropriate to each opera. *The Crucible* is full of melodies evoking 17th-century Protestant hymnody, while *Abelard and Héloise* hints at medieval French idioms, and *Minutes till Midnight* (which deals with the threat of nuclear destruction) dabbles in expressionist angst. A concern with far-reaching social and political issues may be sensed in all Ward's operas, more overtly in some than in others.

MSS in US-DM(u)

He who gets Slapped (3, B. Stambler, after L. Andreyev), as Pantaloon, New York, Juilliard School of Music, 17 May 1956, vs (New York, 1961)

The Crucible (4, Stambler, after A. Miller), New York, City Center, 26 Oct 1961, vs (New York, 1962)

The Lady from Colorado (2, Stambler, after H. Croy), Central City, CO, 3 July 1964

Cladia Legare (4, Stambler, after H. Ibsen: *Hedda Gabler*), Minneapolis, Guthrie, 14 April 1978; rev. 1978

Abelard and Héloise (prol, 3, J. Hartman), Charlotte, NC, Ovens Auditorium, 19 Feb 1982; rev. 1983

Minutes till Midnight (3, D. Lang), Miami, Dade County Auditorium, 4 June 1982

*

R. L. Larsen: *A Study and Comparison of Samuel Barber's 'Vanessa', Robert Ward's 'The Crucible', and Gunther Schuller's 'The Visitation'* (diss., Indiana U., 1971)

A. Kozinn: 'American Eclectic', *ON*, xlvi/20 (1981–2), 24–8, 43

C. Lane: 'A Tuneful 70th for Robert Ward', *Symphony*, xxxviii/4 (1987), 5–7

K. Kreitner: *Robert Ward: a Bio-Bibliography* (New York, 1988) [incl. annotated work-list, discography and perf. details]

R. H. Kornick: *Recent American Opera: a Production Guide* (New York, 1991), 316–22

ANDREW STILLER

Warfield, Sandra (*b* Kansas City, MO, 6 Aug 1929). American mezzo-soprano. She studied in Kansas City and in New York. In 1950 she sang Orlofsky at the Chautauqua Festival. She made her Metropolitan début in 1953 in a minor role, then sang Madelon (*Andrea Chénier*), Marcellina, La Cieca and Ulrica, which she also sang at the Vienna Staatsoper in 1957. Engaged with her husband, the tenor James McCracken, at Zürich, she created Katerina in Martinů's *Greek Passion* (1961), also singing Azucena, Amneris and Fidès (*Le prophète*), a role she repeated in Berlin (1967). She sang Delilah at San Francisco (1963), Barcelona (1970) and the Metropolitan (1972); Santuzza at Seattle (1966) and Fricka and Azucena at Geneva (1968); other roles included Carmen, Orpheus and Léonor (*Le favorite*). She had a powerful, dramatic voice with a wide range.

*

'We Introduce: Sandra Warfield', *ON*, xviii/5 (1953–4), 11ff

J. McCracken and S. Warfield: *A Star in the Family*, ed. R. Daley (New York, 1971)

L. Levant: 'Return Engagement', *ON*, xxxvi/6 (1971–2), 31ff

RICHARD LESUEUR/ELIZABETH FORBES

Warfield, William (*b* West Helena, AL, 22 Jan 1920). American bass. He studied at the Eastman School of Music and appeared on Broadway, taking part in the première of Blitzstein's *Regina* (1949). In 1952–3 he toured Europe as Porgy (with Leontyne Price, to whom he was then married, as Bess; for illustration *see* PRICE, LEONTYNE), appearing in London, Vienna and Berlin, among other cities. He also sang Porgy in New York (1961) and at the Vienna Volksoper (1971–2). Other roles included Joe in *Showboat*. His fine, deep voice was used with great artistry and he was an excellent actor. In 1984 he was elected President of the National Association of Negro Musicians. ELIZABETH FORBES

Warnots, Elly [Elisabeth] (*b* Liège, 1857; *d* after 1881). Belgian soprano, daughter of Henry Warnots. She studied with her father in Brussels, making her début there in 1878 at the Théâtre de la Monnaie as Anna in Boieldieu's *La dame blanche* and later singing Pamina. In 1881 she was engaged at the Teatro della Pergola in Florence and made her Covent Garden début as Marguerite de Valois (*Les Huguenots*). She also sang the Queen in Hérold's *Le Pré aux Clercs*. Her voice, flexible and high-lying, was perfectly suited to such coloratura roles. ELIZABETH FORBES

Warnots, Henry (*b* Brussels, 11 July 1832; *d* Saint Josse-ten-Noode, Brussels, 27 Feb 1893). Belgian tenor. He studied at the Brussels Conservatory, and made his début in 1856 at Liège. He sang at the Opéra-Comique, in Boieldieu's *Jean de Paris* (1862), and at Strasbourg, where his own light opera *Une heure de mariage* was produced in 1865. In 1867 he appeared at the Théâtre National, Brussels, in Miry's *Frans Ackermann*. He taught at the Brussels Conservatory and in 1870 founded a school of music at Saint Josse-ten-Noode.

ELIZABETH FORBES

Warot, Victor (Alexandre) (*b* Verviers, 18 Sept 1834; *d* Bois-Colombes, April 1906). Belgian tenor. He studied in Paris, making his début in 1858 with the Opéra-Comique in Linnander's *Les monténégrins*. He sang a Harvester in the first performance of Meyerbeer's *Le pardon de Ploërmel* (1859). Engaged at the Opéra

(1861–9), he created Tebaldo in Massé's *La mule de Pedro* (1863) and Don Alvar in *L'Africaine* (1865). He also sang Don Ottavio, Count Ory, Henri (*Les vêpres siciliennes*), Masaniello and Vasco da Gama. At the Théâtre de la Monnaie (1868–76) he sang Riccardo (*Un ballo in maschera*), Manrico, Erik, Tannhäuser, Raoul, Eléazar (*La Juive*) and John of Leyden. His voice, originally a lyric tenor, later gained in dramatic strength.

ELIZABETH FORBES

Warrack, John (Hamilton) (*b* London, 9 Feb 1928). English writer on music. He studied at the RCM and worked as a freelance oboist. In 1954 he became assistant music critic to the *Daily Telegraph*, then moved to the *Sunday Telegraph* as chief music critic from 1960 to 1972. He has also been a critic for the *Gramophone*, a member of the editorial board of *Opera* and advisory editor of the *Cambridge Opera Journal*. In 1984 he was appointed lecturer in music at Oxford University.

German Romantic and Russian opera are at the centre of Warrack's interests, and he has made a judicious study of Weber. An elegant writer, with a special interest in relating music to its broader cultural context, Warrack has contributed many articles to periodicals, particularly *Opera* and *The Musical Times*, and to symposia.

with H. Rosenthal: *Concise Oxford Dictionary of Opera* (London, 1964, 2/1979)
Carl Maria von Weber (London, 1968, 2/1976)
Tchaikovsky (London, 1973)
ed.: *Carl Maria von Weber: Writings on Music* (Cambridge, 1981)
ed., with E. West: *The Oxford Dictionary of Opera* (Oxford, 1992)

Warren [Warenoff], **Leonard** (*b* New York, 21 April 1911; *d* New York, 4 March 1960). American baritone. After formal study with Sidney Dietch he entered the Metropolitan Opera Auditions of the Air and won a contract for 1938. After study in Italy, he made his stage début with the Metropolitan in 1939, as Paolo in *Simon Boccanegra*; his last complete performance in the house, 21 years later, was as Simon himself.

During his career, which was dominated by New York engagements, Warren won special acclaim in the great Verdi roles as well as for Barnaba (*La Gioconda*), Scarpia and Tonio. His voice was huge, smooth, superbly controlled and marked by special freedom in the top range (which extended to the tenor's high C). Foreign engagements took him to Rio de Janeiro and Buenos Aires (1942), Mexico City (1948), La Scala (1953) and the USSR (1958). His recorded legacy is an important one, and includes distinguished performances in *Il trovatore*, *Rigoletto*, *La traviata*, *Un ballo in maschera* and *Macbeth*. He died on the stage of the Metropolitan while singing Don Carlo in *La forza del destino*.

*

GV (L. Riemens; S. Smolian)
P. L. Miller: 'Leonard Warren 1911–1960', *Opera*, xi (1960), 397
H. Rosenthal: 'Leonard Warren', *Great Singers of Today* (London, 1966), 208
S. Milnes: 'The Warren Legacy', *ON*, xxxix/18 (1974–5), 26–7

MARTIN BERNHEIMER, DENNIS K. McINTIRE

Warren, Raymond (Henry Charles) (*b* Weston-super-Mare, 7 Dec 1928). English composer. At Corpus Christi College, Cambridge, he read mathematics before studying music with Robin Orr (1949–52), then with Tippett (1952–4) and Berkeley (1958). From 1955 he taught at Queen's University, Belfast, becoming professor of composition in 1966. He was appointed professor of music at Bristol University in 1972. His first full-length opera, *Graduation Ode* (1963), was first heard in Belfast. He also wrote pieces for Belfast schools and provided incidental music for productions of 11 of Yeats's plays at the Lyric Theatre. All Warren's operas have been devised to offer a challenge appropriate to the performers of the moment and to suit the particular conditions of performance. *Graduation Ode*, a comic opera for professional soloists and chorus with amateur chorus, was composed for a university occasion. *Let my People Go*, one of three church operas involving adults and children, amateurs and professonals, was planned simply but on a massive scale to suit the space and acoustic of the new Metropolitan Cathedral at Liverpool and to provide an exciting dramatic experience for some 500 young people. Warren believes that the fundamental condition of such works is that they should be written in the first place not for the audience but for the performers, and that the quality of the imaginative experience engendered will ultimately determine their value.

*

The Lady of Ephesus (chamber op), Belfast, 16 Feb 1959
Finn and the Black Hag (children's op, J. McNeil), Belfast, 11 Dec 1959, vs (London, 1962)
Graduation Ode (3, McNeil), Belfast, King George VI Hall, 20 Nov 1963
Let my People Go (church op, 2, Warren, after the Bible and spirituals), Liverpool, Metropolitan Cathedral, 22 March 1972
St Patrick (church op, 2, D. Selwyn), Liverpool, Anglican Cathedral, 3 May 1979
In the Beginning (church op, 2, Warren, after the Bible and J. Milton: *Paradise Lost*), Bristol, Clifton Cathedral, 22 July 1982

HUGO COLE

Warren-Smith, Neil (*b* Melbourne, 1930; *d* Sydney, 28 July 1981). Australian bass-baritone. Encouraged by the National Theatre movement, he made his début as Leporello in 1955 in Melbourne; he sang in every Australian Opera season from the first one in 1956 to 1981, and played the leading bass and bass-baritone roles there during that time. Rare guest appearances abroad took him to Sadler's Wells, London, and to New Zealand (1964) and included a well-received Ochs and Sarastro with the ENO (1974–5). Although gifted with an irresistible instinct for comedy, he also sang many serious roles. His warm, nobly ample voice, fine in focus and gently resounding in attack, and his general distinction as an actor resulted in outstanding portrayals of Philip II, Boris, Fiesco, Daland, Kutuzov (which he sang at the opening of the Sydney Opera House), Count Ribbing and Sarastro.

His autobiography, published posthumously as *25 Years of Australian Opera* (Melbourne, 1983), offers an irreverent account of operatic life in the period when it first became possible for singers to have an extended resident professional career in opera. An appendix lists most of his Australian roles.

ROGER COVELL

Warsaw (Pol. Warszawa). Capital of Poland. The first known opera performance in the city was given in 1628 at the court of Sigismund III on the initiative of his son Prince Władysław; the work, *Galatea*, may be identical with Santi Orlandi's setting given at Mantua in 1617. The production, using Italian singers, was also the first performance of an Italian opera outside Italy. As king (1632–48), Władysław IV continued to encourage opera; ten *drammi per musica* and several dramatic ballets were given between 1634 and 1648 by an Italian company with Margherita Basile (Cattaneo) as prima donna, her sister Adriana Basile and the famous castrato Baldassare Ferri. The librettos of eight of the operas were by the singer and royal secretary Virgilio Puccitelli, and the music was probably by various members of the royal chapel under the direction of Marco Scacchi. Opera became an important part of the court festivities surrounding royal weddings, visits of foreign envoys and sessions of parliament. In 1637 the Mantuan architect Bartolomeo Bolzoni built a provisional wooden theatre (cap. 1000), and later King Władysław had a permanent theatre built in the castle. Two royal architects, Agostino Locci and Giovanni Battista Gisleni, were responsible for the stage designs.

Performance of opera in Warsaw was interrupted by the death of Władysław IV and a long spell of wars and foreign invasions; it was revived only in the days of the Saxon dynasty (1697–1763). King August II, also Elector of Saxony (1697–1733), staged Italian comedies and operas in his castle from 1699. In 1700–05 foreign opera companies such as those of Louis Deschallières and Jean Fonpré performed *tragédies en musique* by Lully (*Armide*, *Atys*, *Thésée*) and *opéras-ballets* by Campra (*L'Europe galante*, *Les fêtes vénitiennes*). Tommaso Ristori's Italian troupe performed numerous operas and intermezzos in 1715–18, 1725–7 and 1729–30. During this period the theatre was open for some three to nine months a year. In 1725 a new royal theatre called the Operalnia (Opernhaus) was opened in the Saxon palace. It was later rebuilt as an independent theatre holding more than 500 spectators; it opened on 3 August 1748 as the first public opera house in Poland that played without charge to the nobility and citizenry alike. Under August III (1733–63) the capital's operatic life became still more active. From 1756 to 1763 the Dresden court opera was evacuated to Warsaw, where it presented 11 of Hasse's operas, among them *L'eroe cinese* (1754, the first opera to have its libretto printed in a Polish translation, by J. E. Minasowicz). Several operas on Metastasian texts were given in the twice-weekly performances, with an orchestra of over a hundred, under Hasse's direction; Faustina Bordoni and her rival Regina Mingotti also participated.

A more systematic encouragement of opera came with the reign of the last Polish king, Stanisław August Poniatowski (1764–95). In 1765–7 French and Italian opera companies under Karol Tomatis mounted works by Duni, Galuppi, Monsigny, Piccinni and Pugnani. After the ruined Operalnia was demolished in 1772, opera was performed in the Radziwiłł Palace by the troupes of Joseph von Kurtz (Kurz-Bernardon), August and Antoni Sułkowski, and Franciszek Ryx with the prima donna Caterina Bonafini, known in Warsaw since 1765. From 1775 the opera season lasted almost the whole year (from Easter to Easter, excepting Lent). Italian, French, German, Austrian and Polish troupes played in parallel twice a week. At least 150 foreign operas were performed in Warsaw during the last 20 years of independent Poland, up to the last partition in 1795. Among their composers were Haydn (*Der neue krumme Teufel*, 1774), Salieri (*La scuola dei gelosi*, 1779), Gluck (*Orfeo ed Euridice*, 1776), Paisiello (*La serva padrona*, 1781), and Mozart (*Die Entführung*, 1783; *Don Giovanni*, 1789; *Die Zauberflöte*, 1793).

From 1778 Polish operas and vaudevilles to Polish librettos were given in the National Theatre. At this time the company consisted almost entirely of Polish musicians and singers, with the participation and later under the direction of the singer and writer Wojciech Bogusławski, the 'father of Polish theatre'. On 11 July 1778 the first Polish opera was performed in a public theatre: *Nędza uszczęśliwiona* ('Misery made Happy') by Maciej Kamieński, to Bogusławski's libretto. Eight other works by Kamieński followed, 1779–95. On 7 September 1779 the new Teatr Narodowy (National Theatre) opened on Krasiński Place. Originally designed to hold about 800, it was rebuilt in 1791 to accommodate over 1200. Among the other Polish operas first performed in Warsaw around this time were Gioacchino Albertini's *Don Juan* (1783), Jan Dawid Holland's *Agatka* (1785), Antoni Weinert's *Donnerwetter* (1787), Kajetan Majer's *Żółta szlafmyca* ('The Yellow Nightcap', 1788) and Jan Stefani's *Król w kraju rozkoszy* ('The King of Cockaigne', 1787) and *Cud mniemany, czyli Krakowiacy i górale* ('The Supposed Miracle, or Kracovians and Highlanders'). First performed on 1 March 1794, the eve of the Kościuszko Insurrection, *Cud mniemany* was the most successful Polish operatic work of its time, and has remained popular in Poland to the present day. Bogusławski also translated Italian works into Polish (Paisiello's *La frascatana*, 1782; Salieri's *Axur, re d'Ormus*, 1793). Apart from the National Theatre, performances took place in the royal Łazienki Palace (1782–8), in the palace's amphitheatre (from 1785) and Orangery (from 1788), and in the royal Ujazdów Palace (from 1770).

Although Poland lost its independence after the third partition (1795), opera remained the focal point of musical life in Warsaw. In 1799 the National Theatre was reopened under Bogusławski, with Józef Elsner as music director until 1824. During the period of the Grand Duchy of Warsaw (1807–15) opera was closely connected with political life, and this continued into the period of the relatively independent Kingdom of Poland (1815–30), with a repertory mainly of Italian, French and Polish operas. Elsner's successor was Karol Kurpiński (1824–40), during whose directorship the opera company moved in 1833 to the newly built Teatr Wielki (Grand Theatre), designed by Antonio Corazzi to hold about 1200 people. In 1836 the smaller Teatr Rozmaitości (Variety Theatre; cap. *c*800) was opened in a wing of the main opera house.

After the unsuccessful uprising of 1830–31 the Warsaw theatres were maintained and governed by the Russian authorities with mostly Polish musical directors and conductors, including Tomasz Nidecki (1840–52), Jan Quattrini (1853–74), Stanisław Moniuszko (1858–72), Cesare Trombini (1874–81, 1891–8), Adam Minchejmer (1882–90) and Emil Młynarski (1893–1903). During this period the Warsaw Opera reached a high artistic standard and became one of the more important companies in Europe, performing not only the standard repertory but many Polish operas as well, notably by Elsner, Kurpiński, Stefani, Nidecki, Dobrzyński, Moniuszko, and later, Minchejmer, Noskowski, Żeleński, Paderewski, Melcer-Szczawiński, Statkowski, Różycki and A. Wieniawski. Less popular were operas by other Slavonic composers. Events of a special socio-political and patriotic significance were the first productions of Moniuszko's operas: *Halka* (1858), *Flis* (1858), *Hrabina* (1860), *Verbum nobile* (1861), *The Haunted Manor* (1865) and *Paria* (1869). Among the most eminent singers engaged were Julian Dobrski, the De Reszke brothers, Salomea Kruszelnicka and Marcella Sembrich.

After World War I Poland regained its independence and the Warsaw Opera, under Emil Młynarski (1919–29), developed its national character and reached its highest artistic level. The most important premières of Polish works were Szymanowski's *Hagith* (1922) and *Król Roger* ('King Roger', 1926), Różycki's *Casanova* (1923) and *Beatrix Cenci* (1927) and Joteyko's *Zygmunt August* (1925) and *Królowa Jadwiga* ('Queen Jadwiga', 1928). The standard repertory was represented by Mozart, Wagner, Strauss, Musorgsky, Ravel and Stravinsky. Poor economic conditions plagued the 1930s, but among the more important directorships were those of P. Stermich-Valcrociata (1929–30) and J. Korolewicz-Waydowa (1936–8).

In September 1939 and during the Warsaw uprising of 1944 the Wielki Theatre was completely destroyed; the opera had to resume activity in provisional accommodation (from 1949 the Roma Hall, refitted in 1953, cap. 1000). Conductors included Zdzisław Górzyński (1949–52), Walerian Bierdiajew (1954–6), Jerzy Semkow (1959–61) and Bohdan Wodiczko (1961–4). Among the most noteworthy productions of this period were Moniuszko's *Halka* and *Hrabina*, and *Boris Godunov* and *Salome*. Fundamental changes in the organization and artistic programme were made in 1961 when Wodiczko took over, introducing an unfamiliar repertory of modern works (e.g. Stravinsky's *Oedipus rex* and *Perséphone*, Honegger's *Judith*, Bartók's *Bluebeard's Castle*, Dallapiccola's *Il prigioniero* and Weill's *Aufstieg und Fall der Stadt Mahagonny*) as well as the operatic classics in brilliant productions. The purpose of the updated repertory, new production techniques and accelerated pace of work was to prepare the company for the new conditions at the fully reconstructed Wielki Theatre (cap. 2150), opened on 20 November 1965 with Witold Rowicki as artistic director. His successors were Z. Górzyński (1966–8), J. Krenz (1968–73), A. Wicherek (1973–80) and R. Satanowski (from 1982). The more important performances of this period include *King Roger* (1965), Baird's *Jutro* ('Tomorrow', 1966), Penderecki's *The Devils of Loudun* (1975), *Elektra*, *Wozzeck* (1984), *Albert Herring* (1986) and the *Ring* (1988–9). A chamber theatre (cap. 250) was opened at the Wielki Theatre in 1968, and the Warszawska Opera Kameralna (Warsaw Chamber Opera, directed by S. Sutkowski) was set up in 1972.

Operettas, including Offenbach's, had been given in the Wielki Theatre from 1859 and later in special separate theatres: Teatr Letni (Summer Theatre, from 1872), Teatr Nowy (New Theatre, 1881), Teatr Nowości (Novelty Theatre, 1901) and numerous garden theatres (from 1868). By the turn of the century, Warsaw operetta productions were reputed to be among the best in Europe. Since World War II the Komedia Muzyczna (Musical Comedy, from 1949) and the Państwowa Operetka (State Operetta) have continued the tradition of light musical theatre in Warsaw.

*

L. Bernacki: *Teatr, dramat i muzyka za Stanisława Augusta* [Theatre, Drama and Music in Stanisław August's Time] (Lwów, 1925)

E. Świerczewski, ed.: *Stulecie Teatru Wielkiego w Warszawie 1833–1933* [100 Years of the Wielki Theatre in Warsaw] (Warsaw, 1933)

E. Szwankowski: *Teatr Wojciecha Bogusławskiego w latach 1799–1814* (Wrocław, 1954)

J. Prosnak: *Kultura muzyczna Warszawy XVIII wieku* (Kraków, 1955)

W. Filler: *Rendez-vous z warszawską operetką* (Warsaw, 1961, 2/1977)

K. Wierzbicka-Michalska: *Teatr warszawski za Sasów* [Warsaw Theatre under the Saxon Kings] (Wrocław, 1964)

J. Kański, ed.: *Teatr Wielki w Warszawie* (Warsaw, 1965)

J. Targosz-Kretowa: *Teatr dworski Władysława IV 1635–1648* [The Court Theatre of Władysław IV] (Kraków, 1965)

H. Swietlicka: *Repertuar teatrow warszawskich 1832–1862* (Warsaw, 1968)

J. Szczublewski: *L'opera in Polonia* (Milan, 1969)

H. Secomska: *Repertuar warsawskich teatrow rzadowych 1863–1890* (Warsaw, 1971)

Z. Krawczykowski, ed.: *25 lat opery warszawskiej w Polsce ludowej 1945–1970* [25 Years of Warsaw Opera] (Warsaw, 1972)

J. Lewański, ed.: *Opera w dawnej Polsce na dworze Władysława IV i królów saskich* [Opera in Old Poland in the Court of Władysław IV and the Saxon Kings] (Wrocław, 1973)

P. J. Domanski: *Repertuar teatrow warsawskich 1901–1906* (Warsaw, 1976)

——: *Repertuar teatrow warsawskich 1907–1910* (Warsaw, 1977)

K. Wierzbicka-Michalska: *Teatr w Polsce w XVIII wieku* [Theatre in Poland in the 18th Century] (Warsaw, 1977)

A. Spóz, ed.: *Kultura muzyczna Warszawy drugiej połowy XIX wieku* [Warsaw Musical Culture in the Second Half of the 19th Century] (Warsaw, 1980) KORNEL MICHAŁOWSKI

Wartel, Pierre François (*b* Versailles, 3 April 1806; *d* Paris, 3 Aug 1882). French tenor. He studied briefly with Halévy at the Paris Conservatoire, then went to the Institut de la Musique Religieuse to study with Choron. He returned to the Conservatoire in 1828 to study singing with Davidde Banderali and Adolphe Nourrit, and was awarded the *premier prix* for singing the following year. He joined the Opéra in 1831 as a tenor and remained there for 15 years, creating the role of Don Gaspar (*La favorite*) in 1840. After a series of concert tours in Europe Wartel devoted himself to teaching; he was considered one of the finest teachers in France, and his pupils included Christine Nilsson and Zélia Trebelli.

Waschon, Pierre. *See* VACHON, PIERRE.

Washington, DC. Capital city of the USA. The earliest known productions of musical theatre in Washington date from 1800, when the New Company of Philadelphia (under Thomas Wignell and Alexander Reinagle) visited the city; the company, which performed mainly ballad operas, continued to give summer seasons there until at least 1814. The first European opera performed in Washington, Rossini's *Il barbiere di Siviglia* (in English), was given by the Walton Opera Company of Philadelphia in 1836. Productions in the 1830s and 40s were drawn from the standard repertory of Rossini, Bellini, Donizetti and (increasingly after the early 1850s) Verdi. Most performances were in the National Theatre.

In the second half of the 19th century most of the dramatic fare in Washington consisted of operettas, musical comedies and grand opera. The lighter repertory included works by Gilbert and Sullivan, Charles Lecocq, Carl Millöcker and Johann Strauss. Italian, German and English operas were presented by touring companies of such impresarios and performers as Strakosch, Maretzek, Mapleson, Damrosch, Emma Abbott and Clara Kellogg; troupes from New York – the Astor Place Opera House, the Academy of Music and the Metropolitan Opera – and elsewhere also appeared regularly. As early as 1872 a local black company was organized and mounted successful productions in Washington and Philadelphia. Albaugh's Opera House, established in 1884, offered summer seasons of serious opera for several years, and in the 1890s the Lafayette Square Opera House, the Academy of Music and the Columbia Theater all opened with the declared intention of providing operas to the metropolitan area.

The Washington Community Opera was founded in 1918 under the leadership of the local singing teacher Edouard Albion. Known as the Washington National Opera Association from 1923 to 1928, it gave performances in local auditoriums and theatres until 1924, when a new opera house, the Auditorium, was opened. The National Negro Opera Company, which had chapters in cities from New York to Chicago, was based in Washington from the late 1940s until the death of its director, Mary Cardwell Dawson, in 1962; it first performed in Washington around 1943. In addition to such operas as Gounod's *Faust*, *La traviata*, Clarence Cameron White's *Ouanga* (usually with all-black casts) and a staged version of R. Nathaniel Dett's oratorio *The Ordering of Moses*, the company presented an annual evening of music and dance at Griffith Stadium from 1947 to 1955.

The Opera Society of Washington was formed in 1956 to present a few unusual operas annually at a low cost. At first, performances were held at the Lisner Auditorium of George Washington University (cap. 1500). The society achieved an international reputation for daring and excellence. Among its more notable successes were the American premières of Haydn's *L'infedeltà delusa*, Delius's *A Village Romeo and Juliet* and *Koanga*, Berlioz's *Béatrice et Bénédict*, Schoenberg's *Erwartung*, Monteverdi's *Il ritorno d'Ulisse in patria*, Hindemith's *The Long Christmas Dinner* (which the composer conducted) and Cavalli's *Ormindo*, as well as world premières of Menotti's *Goya* and Ginastera's *Bomarzo* and *Beatrix Cenci*. A production of the last-named opened the company's new home at the Opera House (cap. 2200) of the John F. Kennedy Center for the Performing Arts in 1971. Ian Strasfogel became the first director in 1972; he was succeeded by George London (1976–80) and Martin Feinstein (from 1980).

The company, renamed the Washington Opera in 1977, changed its focus and grew significantly during the 1980s: by the middle of the decade its season had expanded from 16 performances to a peak of 72 (1986–7); since then the number has stabilized at around 60. Chamber operas have been given in smaller halls (in the Kennedy Center complex): from 1979 to 1987 in the Terrace Theater (cap. 550); since 1987 (because of an increase in audience size) the Eisenhower Theater (cap. 1100) has been used instead. During the 1980s the company acquired 36 productions of its own and began to engage guest conductors, among them Rafael Frühbeck de Burgos, John Mauceri, Gerard Schwarz, Nicholas McGegan and Daniel Barenboim. The casts are usually about 90% American.

The Opera House at the Kennedy Center has also been used for performances by visiting companies, including the New York City Opera (1972), Piccolo Teatro di Roma (1972), the Bol'shoy (1975); La Scala, the Paris Opéra and Houston Grand Opera (all during 1976); the Vienna Staatsoper (1979), the Beijing Opera (1980), the Metropolitan (1980–85), the Vienna Volksoper (1984) and the Berlin Deutsche Oper (1975, 1989). In 1981 the Kennedy Center commissioned and mounted Carlisle Floyd's *Willie Stark* and in 1988 was co-presenter (with Houston Grand Opera and the Brooklyn Academy of Music) of John Adams's *Nixon in China*.

The National Opera Institute (later renamed the National Institute for Music Theater) was founded in 1969 to encourage interest in all aspects of the genre; it was active until 1989. The Wolf Trap Opera Company, which performs at WOLF TRAP Farm Park for the Performing Arts, west of Washington, was established in 1971 as a two-month summer residence programme for 12 to 15 young singers who attend workshops, and perform and produce operas that are subsequently presented publicly. Two other important programmes in the Washington area involving young singers are the Summer Opera Theatre Company (in residence at the Catholic University of America since 1978), which offers professional training, new roles to more established singers, and professional opera at affordable ticket prices to the community; and the Maryland Opera Studio (part of the music department at the University of Maryland in College Park, in the city's north-eastern suburbs), which is a two-and-a-half year graduate training course for professional singers. Founded in 1987, the course is unique in the USA in its emphasis on acting, dance, improvisation and movement, in addition to vocal training; participants have presented three new American operas: Conrad Susa's *The Love of Don Perlimplin*, Lawrence Moss's *The Queen and the Rebels* and Roger Amers's *Amarantha*.

In 1976 Martin Feinstein, then artistic director of the Kennedy Center, invited the Handel Society of New York to co-produce an annual festival of Handel operas and oratorios. Since then, the Handel Festival Orchestra has presented nearly 30 oratorios and operas (in concert performances), many of them either Washington or American premières. The Washington Concert Opera, founded in 1987, has given highly successful concert performances of such works as *Les pêcheurs de perles*, *Werther*, *Ariadne auf Naxos* and *Lakmé*. The Maryland Handel Festival (founded in 1981 at the University of Maryland), which has as one of its goals the performance (in the order of composition) of all Handel's English oratorios, mounted a staged production of the opera *Tolomeo, rè di Egitto* (in the complete Italian version; 1987), under the direction of Nicholas McGegan, and the complete English version of *Agrippina* (also under McGegan) in November 1990. Numerous amateur, non-profit-making and small professional companies produce opera in the Washington area, including the Opera Theatre of Northern Virginia, the Prince George's County opera, Opera Americana (a company with a repertory of contemporary works and operas from colonial and federal-period America), the National Lyric Opera Company and the Victorian Lyric Opera Company.

M. Sewell: 'Washington and its Musical History', *Music Teachers' National Association: Proceedings*, xxvii (1932), 35–44

J. C. Haskins: *Music in the District of Columbia, 1800 to 1814* (thesis, Catholic U. of America, 1952)

G. Gelles: 'The Growing Up of the Opera Society', *The Washingtonian*, vii/9 (1972), 56–9

C. Jahant: 'Washington's Opera Houses', *The Ring*, ii/3 (1975), 11; iii/1 (1975), 5; iii/2 (1976), 18

M. Tyler: *The Contributions of the National Negro Opera Company and its Founder Mary Cadwell Dawson* (MS, 1975, U. of Pittsburgh)

K. Preston: *Travelling Opera Troupes in the United States, 1825–1860* (diss., CUNY, 1989)

——: *Music for Hire: Professional Musicians in Washington, D.C., 1875–1900* (New York, 1992)

KATHERINE K. PRESTON

Watanabe, Yoko (*b* Fukuoka, 12 July 1953). Japanese soprano. After studying in Tokyo and Milan, she made her début at Treviso in 1978 as Nedda and sang throughout Italy. Although her repertory includes Donna Elvira, Micaela, Marguerite, Amelia (*Simon Boccanegra*), Manon Lescaut, Suor Angelica and Liù, the role of her début at La Scala (1985), much of her time is devoted to Butterfly, which she has sung for the Royal Opera (1983, Manchester), at Chicago (1986), for her Metropolitan début and with Scottish Opera (1987), at Covent Garden, Torre del Lago (1989) and in many European cities as well as at Toronto, Detroit and Tokyo. Her voice, vibrant and warm-toned, is eminently suitable for Puccini's heroines. ELIZABETH FORBES

Water Bird Talk, A. Monodrama in one act by DOMINICK ARGENTO to his own libretto, freely adapted from ANTON PAVLOVICH CHEKHOV's dramatic monologue *On the Harmfulness of Smoking Tobacco* and J. J. Audubon's book *The Birds of America*; Brooklyn, New York, Brooklyn Academy of Music, 19 May 1977.

This 45-minute monodrama for medium male voice (baritone or low tenor) and 12 instruments is set in late 19th-century America at a provincial club meeting. A gentleman lecturer delivers a slide-illustrated talk on the peculiar habits of water fowl, during which parallels with his own unhappy life emerge and he spontaneously unburdens himself to his audience. At first henpecked by his wife, who censures his remarks from the wings, he shows a pathetic demeanour that gradually gives way to self-recognition and dignity in the course of the opera.

The music is organized as a theme and six variations with coda. The material to be varied consists of two 12-note rows, one vocal and one as an accompaniment, presented at the opening. In the fourth variation ('Consolation'), a quotation of the hymn 'Once to ev'ry man and nation' creates a pivotal moment of character development: it becomes clear that the lecturer, who sings and accompanies himself splendidly at the piano, does indeed possess refined qualities that have been suppressed by the vulgar existence of which he complains. The success of the work was instrumental in leading Argento to write his own librettos for later operas. VIRGINIA SAYA

Water Carrier, The. Opera by Luigi Cherubini; *see* *DEUX JOURNÉES, LES.*

Watkinson, Carolyn (*b* Preston, 19 March 1949). English mezzo-soprano. She studied at the RMCM and the Hague Conservatory. In 1978 she sang Phaedra in Rameau's *Hippolyte et Aricie* under Jean-Claude Malgoire (English Bach Festival at Covent Garden and Versailles). She has appeared as Nero in *L'incoronazione di Poppea* in Amsterdam and at the 1979 Spoleto Festival. Other Baroque repertory includes roles in Handel's *Serse*, *Rinaldo*, *Partenope* and *Ariodante*. She appeared in a staged version of *Solomon* at the 1984 Göttingen Festival. Her voice is not large but is admirably focussed throughout its range, and is well suited to such roles as Idamantes (Salzburg), Gluck's Orpheus, Cherubino and Cenerentola (Glyndebourne Tour and Festival). DAVID CUMMINGS

Watson [née McLamore], **Claire** (*b* New York, 3 Feb 1927; *d* Utting am Ammersee, 16 July 1986). American soprano. She studied at the Eastman School of Music and privately with Elisabeth Schumann. She made her début in 1951 at Graz as Desdemona. In 1955 she was engaged at Frankfurt; during her first season she sang 12 new roles, including Countess Almaviva, Pamina, Elisabeth (*Tannhäuser*), Leonora (*La forza del destino*), Aida and Tatyana. In 1957–8 she sang Fiordiligi, Elisabeth de Valois and the Marschallin, in which role she made her Covent Garden (1958) and Glyndebourne (1960) débuts. She appeared regularly in London, where her roles included Ellen Orford, Sieglinde, Eva, and, with the Munich company in 1972, Ariadne and the Countess in *Capriccio*. Her Munich association began in 1958, when she sang Countess Almaviva at the reopening of the Cuvilliéstheater; in 1963 she sang Eva at the inauguration of the rebuilt Nationaltheater. Watson made guest appearances in Vienna, Berlin, Italy and the USA, where she sang her first Arabella in New Orleans in 1969. She had a voice of considerable beauty and musicality, and projected great warmth in her performances.

*

G. Rothon: 'Claire Watson', *Opera*, xxi (1970), 1004

L. Rasponi: 'Claire Watson', *The Last Prima Donnas* (New York, 1982), 394–403 HAROLD ROSENTHAL/R

Watson, Lillian (*b* London, 4 Dec 1947). English soprano. She studied in London and made her début in 1971 as Papagena with the WNO, for whom she also sang Zerlina, Despina, Adina, Adele and Thibaut. She made her Covent Garden début in 1971 as Barbarina, later singing Frasquita, Sister Constance (*Dialogues des Carmélites*), the Fiakermilli (*Arabella*), Woodbird, Titania, Blonde, Young Girl (*Lulu*), Janáček's Vixen (1990) and the Italian Soprano in *Capriccio* (1991). She sang Susanna at Glyndebourne (1976) and has appeared in Hamburg, Munich, Vienna, Zürich, Rome, Paris, Salzburg, where she sang Blonde (1988), and Aix-en-Provence, where she sang Titania (1991–2). She is ideally suited in voice and personality to Mozart's soubrette roles, and she is a charming Sophie in *Der Rosenkavalier*. ELIZABETH FORBES

Watts, Helen (Josephine) (*b* Milford Haven, 7 Dec 1927). Welsh contralto. She studied at the RAM and made her operatic début in 1958 as Didymus in *Theodora* with the Handel Opera Society, for whom she also sang Ino and Juno (*Semele*) as well as Rinaldo, which she repeated at the Komische Oper, Berlin, and at Halle (1961). In 1964 she sang Britten's Lucretia (conducted by the composer) on the English Opera Group tour of Russia. At Covent Garden (1965–71) she sang First Norn, Erda, Sosostris (*The Midsummer Marriage*) and Mrs Sedley. For the WNO (1969–83) her roles were Mistress Quickly, Sosostris, Mrs Sedley and Larina, which she also sang at Lyons in 1984. She sang Mozart's Pharnaces at Salzburg (1971) and Monteverdi's Arnalta for Scottish Opera (1973). She recorded Ursula in *Béatrice et Bénédict*. A stylish singer with a firm technique, she had a warm, clear-toned voice, not large but well projected, admirably suited also to her oratorio and lieder work. HELEN SIMPSON/ELIZABETH FORBES

Wat Tyler. Opera in two acts with a prologue by ALAN BUSH to a libretto by Nancy Bush; Leipzig, Staatstheater, 6 September 1953.

The opera is set in 1381. The Kentish peasants, led by Wat Tyler (baritone), refuse to pay the poll tax and chase Bampton (bass-baritone), the royal tax commissioner, out of Maidstone. The peasant army frees the preacher, John Ball (bass), from prison and marches to London to beg the king to abolish serfdom.

In Act 2 King Richard II (tenor) and his counsellors conspire to deceive the peasants. The king meets Wat Tyler at Smithfield and agrees to put an end to serfdom. Bampton picks a quarrel with Tyler, and Walworth (bass-baritone), mayor of London, stabs Tyler in the back. A deputation of peasants waits on the king as he comes to Westminster Abbey for a thanksgiving service; he tears up the charter and declares that serfdom shall continue for ever. The opera ends with a chorus of hope for future freedom.

In his essay 'The Problems of Music' (1952, repr. 1980) Bush commented on the construction of *Wat Tyler*, saying

> Explanation and narrative are reduced to a minimum, occupying less than ten minutes in a whole of more than two and a half hours ... there are set pieces in the shape of solo songs, but these only occur where, in the actual circumstances of the time, the persons concerned might in reality have broken into song or found themselves plunged in meditation ... I have made deliberate efforts to delineate the characters throughout in their actual vocal lines ... thanks to the almost complete avoidance of small talk, the characters have only things to say which advance the story ... they are thus themselves in every word they sing and can be individually treated musically without interfering with a convincing effect.

HUGO COLE

Wayditch, Gabriel von (*b* Budapest, 28 Dec 1888; *d* New York, 28 July 1969). Hungarian composer. He studied at the Royal Academy of Music in Budapest, under Hans Koessler. He conducted at the Royal Orpheum Theatre in Budapest, but when his family emigrated to the USA in 1911 he became a ship's musician; he continued to compose, and was also engaged in theatrical conducting. He composed 14 operas, among which *Horus* had a single performance, financed by the composer and mounted on 5 January 1939. One other opera, *The Caliph's Magician* (1917), was recorded in 1975. *The Heretics* (1958), lasting eight hours, has been claimed as the longest opera ever written.

all librettos by the composer

Horus (grand op), Philadelphia, 5 January 1939

unperf.: Opium Dreams; The Caliph's Magician, 1917 (1); Buddha; Jesus before Herod; Maria Magdalena; Maria Tesztver; Nereida; Sahara; The Catacombs; Anthony of Padua; The Venus Dwellers; Neptune's Daughter; The Heretics, 1958

Webb [Webbe]**, John** (*b* London, 1611; *d* Butleigh, 24 Oct 1672). English architect. He studied with Inigo Jones and became his assistant. He never succeeded Jones as surveyor, being passed over in favour of Wren after the death of Sir John Denham.

He worked with Jones on some of the later masques, notably *Salmacida spolia*, so was familiar with italianate perspective scenery. Davenant engaged him for the scenes for his opera *The Siege of Rhodes*, produced at Rutland House, Charterhouse Yard, in 1656 and transferred in 1658 to the Cockpit, Drury Lane, which had the same measurements. Davenant complained about the restrictions of the stage which was only 3.4 metres high and 4.6 in depth, but Webb managed to fit in most of the features of the Italian scenery, including a proscenium arch, three pairs of unchanging wings of profiled trees and five scene changes. Drawings for these are at Chatsworth House, and a plan and section are in the British Museum (see also Southern, pls. 25*a–f* and 12–15). The scenes could not compare with the richness of Jones's masque scenes but were the first to introduce perspective scenery, which became the staple convention well into the 19th century, on to the public stage.

For illustration *see* SIEGE OF RHODES, THE.

*

R. Southern: *Changeable Scenery: its Origin and Development in the British Theatre* (London, 1952)

J. Orrell: *The Theatres of Inigo Jones and John Webb* (Cambridge, 1985)

SYBIL ROSENFELD

Webber, Andrew Lloyd. *See* LLOYD WEBBER, ANDREW.

Weber, Aloysia. *See* LANGE, ALOYSIA.

Weber, Bernhard Anselm (*b* Mannheim, 18 April 1764; *d* Berlin, 23 March 1821). German composer and conductor. In his youth he learnt keyboard playing, singing, theory and composition before studying theology and law at Heidelberg in 1781. Six years later he became musical director of Grossmann's theatre company in Hanover, where he first heard the music of Handel and also produced his first stage work, *Menöcreus*. In 1792 Weber was appointed joint musical director, with Bernhard Wessely, of the Nationaltheater in Berlin, and in 1793 he travelled to other parts of Germany, and especially to Vienna, to engage singers for the Berlin theatre. In Vienna he became acquainted with Salieri, who encouraged him in the composition of stage works and made him more familiar with Gluck's operas. On his return to Berlin, Weber arranged the first performance there of a Gluck opera. The success of the production of *Iphigénie en Tauride*, which took place under Weber's direction on 24 February 1795 with Margarete Schick singing the title role, was a factor in his appointment in 1796 as first musical director of the theatre, with a salary of 1000 thalers.

In 1800 Weber went on a concert tour to Breslau and in 1803 visited Paris, where he met Cherubini. On his return he was given the title of Kapellmeister, and he retained his position as first musical director when the German and Italian theatres were merged under August Iffland's direction in 1811. After a serious illness in 1818 he was compelled to withdraw gradually from his duties, before Spontini was appointed general musical director in 1820.

Weber's opera *Mudarra*, to a text by C. A. Herklots, was performed in Berlin in 1800 without success. He also set three Vorspiele, a monodrama, *Hero*, and a duodrama, *Sulmalle*, both by Herklots, and Schiller's spoken melodrama *Der Gang nach dem Eisenhammer*, as well as writing incidental music to plays including Schiller's *Wilhelm Tell* (1804). He was a prolific composer, but only individual songs from his stage works retained their popularity.

Menöcreus, Hanover, 1792

Hyala und Evandon (1), Berlin, 1796

Der Theaterprinzipal (lyrische Posse, C. A. Herklots), Berlin, 1796

Mudarra (grosse Oper, 4, Herklots), Berlin, Kgl, 10 March 1800

Die Wette (Spl, 1, after P. Guillet), Berlin, Kgl, 21 Jan 1805, vs (Berlin, ?1807)

Hermann und Thusnelde (heroische Oper, 3, A. von Kotzebue), Berlin, Kgl, 29 March 1819

Feodora (Spl, ?Kotzebue)

*

C. von Ledebur: *Tonkünstler-Lexicon Berlin's* (Berlin, 1861)

Weber, Carl Maria (Friedrich Ernst) von (*b* Eutin, ?18 Nov 1786; *d* London, 5 June 1826). German composer. He was a key figure in the early development of German Romantic opera.

1. Life, 1786–1816. 2. Life, 1817–26. 3. Operatic style and development.

1. LIFE, 1786–1816. Less than a year after Weber's birth, his father Franz Anton gave up his post as town musician in Eutin and moved to Hamburg, where he set about forming the Weber Theatre Company. The company consisted of Franz Anton, his second wife Genovefa (Weber's mother), his sister Adelheid and his three sons by his first marriage, together with a number of other actors. Most of Weber's childhood was spent travelling from town to town in the Bavarian region with this motley group as they performed their repertory of popular plays and Singspiels. Consequently, his education was somewhat haphazard; he received a few music lessons from his half-brother Fridolin and sporadic lessons in music and other subjects from teachers in the various towns where the troupe performed. A longer stay in Hildburghausen, necessitated by the serious illness of Weber's mother in 1796, enabled him to receive more stable tuition from a talented local musician, Johann Peter Heuschkel, who laid the foundations of Weber's pianistic virtuosity, and for whose teaching he remained grateful in later years. A planned tour in 1797 was forestalled by Napoleon's campaigns, and the Webers stayed for some time in Salzburg. There Carl Maria took lessons from Michael Haydn and published his first compositions, six fughettas, which were favourably reviewed in the *Allgemeine musikalische Zeitung*. After Genovefa's death in 1798 the company moved on to Munich, where Weber received singing and composition lessons. He also had the opportunity to become familiar with a larger repertory of Singspiels and French operas. Under the supervision of the court organist, Johann Nepomuk Kalcher, the 13-year-old Weber composed his first opera, *Die Macht der Liebe und des Weins*, the score of which seems subsequently to have been destroyed in a fire in Kalcher's house.

Shortly afterwards the restless Franz Anton moved to Freiburg, intending to set himself up as a lithographer. There, in autumn 1800, Weber rapidly composed his second opera, *Das Waldmädchen*, to a libretto by Carl von Steinsberg, by whose travelling company it was staged on 24 November. Apart from two fragments, which indicate Weber's lack of technical experience, the opera is lost, but reworked material from it is preserved in *Silvana*.

Weber's movements and activities during the next period of his life are somewhat obscure. By November 1801, however, he was back in Salzburg, where, under the supervision of Michael Haydn, he composed his third opera, *Peter Schmoll und seine Nachbarn*, based on a recent novel by Carl Gottlob Cramer which had already run to several editions. A planned production in Augsburg, where Weber's half-brother Edmund was conducting at the theatre, failed to materialize in 1802 but took place the following year, probably in March. However, the opera soon sank into obscurity. In September 1803 Weber moved to Vienna in order to study with Joseph Haydn, but instead he came under the influence of Abbé Vogler and became his devoted pupil. It is difficult to estimate Vogler's influence on Weber's musical development, but there is no doubt that Weber admired his music greatly at that time. He enthusiastically occupied himself with making a piano reduction of Vogler's opera *Samori* and was also fired by Vogler's interest in the exotic and his appreciation of the beauties of folksong. During his nine months in Vienna Weber composed little, but appears to have worked hard at improving his technique.

Vogler must have been considerably impressed by Weber's talent and by his experience of the theatre, for when he was asked to recommend a Kapellmeister for the theatre at Breslau he suggested his pupils Gänsbacher and Weber. After Gänsbacher declined the appointment it was offered to Weber, who took up the post in June 1804. He was then only 17, and the next two years in Breslau were difficult for him. He attempted to bring about a thorough reform of the musical organization in the theatre and to revitalize the repertory, but many of the older musicians resented his appointment and the changes which he tried to bring about, and he encountered considerable opposition. In the end, though, it was not this that caused him to leave Breslau; after unwittingly drinking engraving acid from a wine bottle he was ill for two months, and when he afterwards discovered that most of his reforms had been undermined in his absence, he resigned. Weber did not complete any significant compositions in Breslau. He began another opera on a libretto by the theatre's drama director, Johann Gottlieb Rhode, based on Musäus's *Rübezahl* story, but seems not to have got very far with it. Only three numbers survive and they do not indicate any significant advance in his creative power.

A sojourn in Carlsruhe, Upper Silesia (now Pokój, Poland), was unproductive of further operatic work (though Weber composed his two symphonies, J50 and 51 there), and in July 1807 he moved to Stuttgart as secretary to Duke Ludwig of Württemberg. He had no musical duties in Stuttgart but was encouraged to continue working at composition by the Hofkapellmeister, Franz Danzi, who many years earlier had also been a pupil of Vogler. During the next two years Weber worked intermittently on the opera *Silvana*, the libretto of which was a reworking by a local poet, F. C. Hiemer, of Steinsberg's *Waldmädchen* libretto of 1800. In 1809, at Danzi's request, he also wrote incidental music (J75) for a production of Schiller's reworking of Gozzi's *Turandot*. Despite stimulating musical and intellectual contacts in Stuttgart, Weber's position there was not congenial; a relationship of dislike concealed beneath a veneer of cordiality existed between him and Duke Ludwig's brother, the grotesquely obese and tyrannical King Friedrich. Finally, in February 1810, after a débâcle over some money belonging to the duke, which Weber's irresponsible father had misappropriated, Weber was banished from the state.

Weber spent the next three years travelling restlessly around Germany, giving concerts, organizing musical activities, planning and engaging in various literary and critical pursuits, socializing and, when time permitted, composing. His most significant instrumental compositions were the First Piano Concerto (J98, 1810) and the clarinet concertos (J109, 114 and 118), which he wrote for Heinrich Baermann in Munich in 1811. Shortly before leaving Stuttgart he had completed *Silvana*, and he now managed to secure its production, on 16 September 1810, in Frankfurt where, however, it was only moderately successful. Away from the somewhat stultifying atmosphere of Stuttgart, his interest in opera composition quickened. In Heidelberg in 1810 he discussed with Alexander von Dusch an opera on the *Freischütz* story, which had just been published in Apel and Laun's *Gespensterbuch*, but he got no further than the planning stage. He did, however, complete a one-act Singspiel, *Abu Hassan*, in Munich, and it received a successful première there on 4 June 1811. A well-received performance of *Silvana* in Berlin in 1812 may also have helped to encourage Weber in his belief that his real vocation lay in opera, and when, during a visit to Prague at the beginning of 1813, he was offered the directorship of the opera in succession to Wenzel Müller, he accepted despite initial misgivings.

Weber energetically involved himself in the work of revitalizing the Prague opera, paying close attention not only to the musical aspects but also to the acting, the details of staging, costumes and scenery, and even the recataloguing of the theatre library. He was concerned, too, to build up an operatic repertory which was both musically and dramatically more substantial than under the previous regime. His aim was avowedly to lead his public towards the appreciation of opera as a complete and unified work of art rather than an uneasy compromise between drama and music in which both elements were trivialized; as he stated in an article in the *Prager Zeitung* (13 October 1815), he had assumed the 'welcome task of influencing public taste and feeling by the beneficial medium of art'. Despite Weber's emphasis on the importance of promoting German opera, many of the works he produced in Prague were French, by such composers as Spontini, Cherubini, Isouard, Boieldieu, Dalayrac, Grétry, Catel and Méhul; these, together with the operas of Mozart, formed the backbone of his repertory, since there were insufficient German opera composers among Weber's contemporaries to sustain a largely German one. But where German works of real quality could be found, he was eager to promote them. Thus he introduced, among other German operas, Beethoven's *Fidelio* in 1814, Meyerbeer's *Wirth und Gast* in 1815, and Spohr's *Faust* and Poissl's *Athalia* in 1816.

Weber's conducting and literary activity in Prague left him with little leisure or energy for composition. He found time to compose a number of instrumental works and the cantata *Kampf und Sieg* (J190, celebrating the defeat of Napoleon), but although he wrote several pieces for insertion into other people's operas he did not pursue any operatic plans of his own. Nevertheless, his experience in Prague was undoubtedly of vital importance in preparing him for his next operatic endeavour. Eventually, worn down by ill-health and disagreements with the directors of the opera house, he handed in his resignation and, together with the singer Caroline Brandt, soon to become his wife, he left for Berlin in October 1816. During the autumn he busied himself with instrumental and song composition. He was also in negotiation with Count Heinrich Vitzthum, Intendant of the Dresden opera, over the post of Kapellmeister in Dresden, for which, on Christmas Day 1816, he received an official letter of appointment.

2. Life, 1817–26. Once more Weber threw himself wholeheartedly into the task of injecting new life into a moribund organization. Not only were resources meagre, but he had also to contend with active and passive opposition from the rival Italian faction headed by Kapellmeister Morlacchi, which held very much the upper hand in conservative, Catholic Dresden. The Italian opera tradition was well established and enjoyed the active patronage of the court, while German opera was considered distinctly second-class. This was reflected in the fact that Weber's title ranked lower than Morlacchi's, a situation of which Weber had been unaware when he accepted the post. When he discovered this he offered his resignation as a matter of principle, but withdrew it after Vitzthum had secured the equal ranking of the two Kapellmeisters. Nevertheless, friction between the Italian and German operas continued, with fluctuating intensity, for the rest of Weber's life.

Weber's first few years in Dresden were troubled by personal problems. His marriage to Caroline Brandt, which had taken place in November 1817, was in general a source of happiness and stability for him, despite a few early difficulties occasioned by her unreasonable jealousy; but the death of his infant daughter, Marie Caroline, and Caroline's miscarriage in 1820 caused considerable strain, while the inexorable progress of his tuberculosis was accelerated by the immense burden of work entailed by his self-imposed dedication to the cause of German opera. His mood ranged from enthusiasm to irritability and severe depression. Yet, even though he found his task at the theatre still more burdensome than in Prague and was additionally obliged to compose various occasional pieces for the court, he managed, after a break of six years, to return to serious operatic composition. Among his acquaintances in Dresden was Johann Friedrich Kind, a writer of poetry, novels and theatrical work with whom, early in 1817, he discussed the idea of an opera on the *Freischütz* story. They decided to proceed with the project, and by the beginning of March Kind had produced a draft of the complete opera, provisionally entitled *Der Probeschuss*. Work on the music, however, proceeded fitfully, interrupted by the manifold demands of Weber's duties. One interruption was a royal command for an opera, *Alcindor*, but after he and Kind had begun work on it in 1819 the commission was cancelled. In June 1819 Weber returned to work on *Der Freischütz* with renewed vigour, completing it on 13 May 1820. Shortly after this he also wrote incidental music to Pius Alexander Wolff's *Preciosa* and began work on a comic opera libretto by Theodor Hell, *Die drei Pintos*. Postponement of the staging of *Der Freischütz* in Berlin allowed him to undertake a successful concert tour of north Germany during autumn 1820, and it was not until 18 June 1821 that *Der Freischütz* began its triumphant career with a brilliant première at the Berlin Schauspielhaus.

The success of *Der Freischütz* seems to have done little to improve Weber's position in Dresden, where he was still subject to petty restrictions and irritations; but from Domenico Barbaia, lessee of the Kärntnertortheater in Vienna, it elicited a commission for a new opera 'in the style of *Der Freischütz*' for the 1822–3 season. Weber embraced the project with enthusiasm and, laying aside his work on *Die drei Pintos*, began to seek a suitable subject. His choice was to a considerable extent determined by his resolve to show that he was capable of writing a grand opera in German (i.e. without spoken dialogue). It is perhaps significant that, at the very moment when he received the commission from Vienna, on 11 November 1821, Spohr was with him; after they had toasted the project in champagne they no doubt exchanged views on the future direction of German opera in general and the nature of Weber's new opera in particular. Since Spohr (who was planning his own grand opera, *Jessonda*, at that time) and Weber were pursuing very similar paths, it seems improbable that their discussions were entirely without influence on each other's work.

Weber rapidly set about looking for a libretto. Kind's resentment over what he saw as lack of recognition for

1. 'Der Freischütz' (Weber), the Wolf's Glen scene from Act 2: design by Carl Wilhelm Holdermann for the 1822 Weimar production: aquatint by C. Lieber, with figures by C. A. Schwerdtgeburth

his part in *Der Freischütz* made a further collaboration impossible, and a setting of Rellstab's *Dido* was rejected on the grounds that it had been too frequently used. Ultimately Weber approached Helmina von Chezy, a fellow member of the Dresden literary circle known as the 'Liederkreis', and despite her protestations that she lacked experience, he persuaded her to write him a libretto. Several subjects were considered and rejected before *Euryanthe* was finally chosen. After various distractions, and serious problems over the quality of the libretto, Weber finished the opera (except for the overture) at the end of August and left for Vienna just over a fortnight later to supervise its production. Although the première was moderately successful, it fell far short of a triumph. Many, including Schubert, who attended some of the rehearsals, were sharply critical, particularly of the work's structure. Weber himself was persuaded to shorten several sections in the score, and after his departure in November the conductor, Conradin Kreutzer, made further extensive cuts. Despite this surgery, however, the opera was withdrawn after its 20th performance.

The effort of composing *Euryanthe* had sapped Weber's ever-lessening strength, both mental and physical; the progress of his tuberculosis became increasingly rapid and debilitating. Between August 1823 and the beginning of 1825 he composed almost nothing; he spent much of the summer quietly with his family at his country house and shunned any kind of creative work. His health was now so fragile that he was convinced that little time was left to him. In August 1824 he received an invitation from Charles Kemble, manager of Covent Garden, to write a new opera for London, where his fame had been boosted by a number of more or less bowdlerized versions of *Der Freischütz*. Convinced that by this means he would be able to provide for his family, he accepted the commission and, having been offered the subject of *Faust* or *Oberon*, chose the latter. He received Planché's libretto piecemeal between December and February and, having secured postponement of the production to the 1826 season, began work. But he was not without considerable misgivings over the unfamiliar style of opera demanded by the London public. As he wrote to Planché (in his recently acquired English), 'The cut of an English opera is certainly very different from a German one'. He intended, if he lived long enough, to rework the opera, replacing the dialogue with recitatives and generally remodelling it for the German stage, but fate did not allow this. He travelled to London in February 1826 for the production of *Oberon* with the

2. *Autograph score of part of the Wolf's Glen scene from Act 2 of Weber's 'Der Freischütz', composed 1817–21*

score still incomplete. The final numbers were written under great pressure, but the opera was rapturously received at its première on 12 April. However, the strain of Weber's activity in London was too great; his little remaining strength was exhausted and on 5 June, the day before he had planned to travel home, he died in his sleep.

3. Operatic style and development. Whatever disadvantages Weber's peripatetic childhood may have caused, his constant and intimate experience of the theatre undoubtedly laid the foundations of his later excellence as an opera director and sharpened his instinct for dramatic effect in his stage works.

In his earlier works his familiarity with the well-tried theatrical devices of the day often led him into a somewhat facile reliance on stereotyped treatments of situation and character, but as his artistic personality developed he was increasingly able to reach beyond the merely conventional. *Silvana* is an uncomfortable mixture of routine stagecraft and burgeoning genius, but it contains the seeds of much that was to come to maturity in *Der Freischütz* and *Euryanthe*. *Silvana* shows Weber's ready response to the picturesque and the bizarre, and by then both nature and strong emotional tensions could inspire him to create something out of the ordinary; but he was not yet able to sustain this level of inspiration throughout a full-length opera. *Abu Hassan*, a less ambitious undertaking which lacked the same opportunity for portraying strong contrasts and powerful images, shows greater cohesion and self-assurance than *Silvana*. Weber's relaxed approach to this lightweight one-act comedy seems to have encouraged his melodic invention to flourish more freely and more distinctively, though a tendency to give his vocal melodies a somewhat instrumental cast, which became more pronounced in his later works, is apparent. Weber's strong feeling for orchestral colour, already shown in *Silvana*, is observable in *Abu Hassan* as well, although on a more intimate scale.

In his early twenties Weber's musical style was a somewhat undigested mixture of influences from the Viennese Classical composers, north German Singspiel, French *opéra comique*, fashionable virtuoso instrumental music and even, despite his oft-repeated criticisms of it, Italian opera. During the ten years which separated the completion of *Abu Hassan* from that of *Der Freischütz*, however, his melodic and harmonic idioms became more coherent and individual. In his instrumental music he still found difficulties with handling larger forms; his sonata-form movements tended to be rather stiff, despite his ability to conceive striking ideas, and he was all too ready to let his linking sections degenerate into brilliant, though vapid, passage-work. But where he was inspired by an external stimulus, his imagination took fire; his vivid response to words is shown in his three volumes of Theodor Körner's *Leyer und Schwerdt* poems (two for solo voice and one for four-part male-voice chorus) and his song cycle *Die Temperamente beim Verluste der Geliebten* (J200–03). Even though he was not fruitfully engaged in operatic composition between 1811 and 1817, his contacts with other musicians such as Danzi, Poissl, Mosel and Spohr, who were similarly concerned about the future of German opera, and the steady maturing of his own ideas led him to refine and develop his conception of opera. He also cogently developed this conception in his critical writings. Thus, by 1817 he was well equipped both musically and intellectually for the composition of *Der Freischütz*.

In *Der Freischütz* Weber succeeded in striking a balance between accessibility and musical substance which made it by far the most widely popular German opera of its generation. It shows a feeling for the theatre and a vitality which none of Weber's German contemporaries was able to match. Spohr, Weber's most important rival in opera, had been working along much the same lines to promote a distinctive genre of German Romantic Singspiel; indeed, in *Faust* (1813) he had succeeded in producing a masterly work which foreshadows *Der Freischütz* in many respects. Spohr's use of motif, in particular, was more extensive and subtle than anything achieved before the mature Wagner. But while Weber's music was almost invariably generated directly by the exigencies of the drama itself, Spohr all too often favoured musical considerations at the expense of dramatic impact. *Der Freischütz* and *Faust* mark the furthest point of development of Singspiel as a vehicle for German Romantic opera. Later works, such as Marschner's *Hans Heiling*, though they possess estimable musical and dramatic qualities, add nothing of importance to its scope.

With *Euryanthe* Weber moved into a new stage in the development of German Romantic opera. He felt convinced that the next logical step was to compose grand opera in German so that the dramatic continuity of the music would not be interrupted by breaks for spoken dialogue. The attempt was not without recent precedent; two of Weber's friends, Johann Nepomuk Poissl and Ignaz von Mosel, had already written through-composed German operas. It seems likely, however, that from the musical point of view French operas, particularly Spontini's grand operas with their highly effective treatment of orchestrally accompanied recitative, were a more potent influence. The rivalry between Weber and Spohr (who remained personally on good terms) was intensified by their simultaneous work on German grand operas. Spohr's *Jessonda* was first performed in July 1823 and *Euryanthe* three months later, but whereas Spohr's opera was widely acclaimed as a masterpiece, *Euryanthe*, labouring under the weight of its impossible libretto, was seen to be fatally flawed even before the first performance. Nevertheless, Weber's positive achievements in *Euryanthe* were considerable. It contains many passages in which the dramatic power of the music banishes all thought of the feeble libretto, and the way Weber manages the transitions between set pieces and more fluid, recitative-like sections is often highly effective. Despite the obvious failings of the opera as a whole, its impressive musical qualities served as an inspiration for many later German composers.

Euryanthe hints at what Weber might have achieved had he lived longer. The tragedy of his untimely death is made all the more poignant by the lost opportunity of his last opera, *Oberon*. Weber knew from the start that he had committed himself to setting a virtually worthless libretto, but in the circumstances he felt he had no choice. Yet the music he wrote for *Oberon* is mostly of such high quality that it almost succeeds in compensating for the pantomime-like nature of the piece. He was particularly skilful in binding the work together, despite the extensive interruptions for dialogue, through the use of the horn-call motif that opens the overture. And he aptly matched the fairy-tale nature of the story with music of charm and delicacy, beautifully orchestrated, that frequently anticipates the elfin lightness of Mendelssohn. But even if Weber had lived he would have needed to do much more than replace the dialogue with recitatives to make *Oberon* stageworthy.

Weber died at a critical point in the development of Romantic opera. The rosy future for German opera that seemed to have dawned during the early 1820s with the successes of Weber and Spohr proved illusory; their increasingly ambitious aesthetic aims had begun to drive an ever-widening gulf between them and the taste and capacity of a large proportion of their audience. Had Weber lived the picture might have been different, though even he might have been unequal to the task of combining the high musical ideals of a 'German Artist' with the popular appeal necessary to fill a theatre in the complacent Biedermeier society of the post-revolutionary 1830s.

See also ABU HASSAN; DREI PINTOS, DIE; EURYANTHE; FREISCHÜTZ, DER; OBERON; PETER SCHMOLL UND SEINE NACHBARN; and SILVANA.

Editions: *C. M. von Weber: Musikalische Werke: erste kritische Gesamtausgabe*, ed. H. J. Moser; ii/1, ed. A. Lorenz (Augsburg, 1926); ii/2, ed. W. Kaehler (Augsburg, 1928) [WG]
Reliquienschrein des Meisters Carl Maria von Weber, ed. L. Hirschberg (Berlin, 1927) [HR]

J – no. in Jähns (1871); printed works published in full score unless otherwise stated

J	*title*	*genre, acts*	*libretto*	*first performance*	*sources and remarks*
Anh.6	Die Macht der Liebe und des Weins	Spl			comp. 1798; lost
Anh.1	Das Waldmädchen (Das stumme Waldmädchen; Das Mädchen im Spessarter Wald)	romantische Oper, 2	C. von Steinsberg	Freiberg (Saxony), Buttermarkt, 24 Nov 1800	comp. 1800; frags. WG ii/1
8	Peter Schmoll und seine Nachbarn	2	J. Türk[e], after C. G. Cramer	Augsburg, ?March 1803	comp. 1801–2; dialogue lost, ov. rev. 1807 as Grande ouverture à plusieurs instruments, op.8 (J57); WG ii/1
44–6	Rübezahl	2	J. G. Rhode, after J. K. A. Musäus: *Volksmärchen der Deutschen*	unperf.	comp. 1804–5; 3 nos. survive; WG ii/2
87	Silvana	romantische Oper, 3	F. C. Hiemer, after Steinsberg's Das Waldmädchen text	Frankfurt, 16 Sept 1810	comp. 1808–10; vs without ensemble scenes (Berlin, 1812), complete vs (Berlin, 1828); WG ii/2
106	Abu Hassan	Spl, 1	Hiemer, after *The Thousand and One Nights*	Munich, Residenz, 4 June 1811	comp. 1810–11; ed. W. W. Göttig (Offenbach, 1925), vs (Bonn, 1819)

J	title	genre, acts	libretto	first performance	sources and remarks
277	Der Freischütz	romantische Oper, 3	J. F. Kind, after J. A. Apel and F. Laun: *Gespensterbuch*	Berlin, Schauspielhaus, 18 June 1821	comp. 1817–21; (Berlin, *c*1849), vs (Berlin, 1822)
Anh.5	Die drei Pintos	komische Oper, 3	T. Hell, after C. Seidel: *Der Brautkampf*	Leipzig, Neues Stadt, 20 Jan 1888	comp. 1820–21; inc., completed by G. Mahler; text rev. C. Weber and Mahler (Leipzig, 1888)
291	Euryanthe	grosse heroisch-romantische Oper, 3	H. von Chezy, after *L'histoire du très-noble et chevaleraux prince Gérard ...*	Vienna, Kärntnertor, 25 Oct 1823	comp. 1822–3; ed. E. Rudorff (Berlin, 1866), vs (Vienna, 1824)
306	Oberon	romantische Oper, 3	J. R. Planché, after C. M. Wieland	London, CG, 12 April 1826	comp. 1825–6; (Berlin, 1874), vs (London, 1826)

Others: 2 numbers, Was ich da tu, Dich an dies Herz, J77–8, for Haydn pasticcio Der Freibrief, 1809, vs ed. F. W. Jähns (Berlin, 1839); scena, Ah se Edmondo, J178, for Méhul's Héléna, 1815, vs and parts (Berlin, 1826); 2 songs, Mein Weib ist capores (Berlin, *c*1838), Frau Lieser juhe! HR [arr. orch as Deutscher (Original-Walzer), J185, 1815 (Berlin, *c*1842–3)], J183–4, for A. Fischer's Spl Der travestirte Aeneas, 1815; scena and aria, Was sag ich?, J239, for Cherubini's Lodoiska, 1818, vs and parts (Berlin, 1824)

GENERAL

14 letters to F. von Mosel, 1 to Dr Jungh, *Weiner allgemeine Musikzeitung*, vi (1846), 473

R. Schumann: *Gesammelte Schriften über Musik und Musiker* (Leipzig, 1854, 4/1914)

M. M. von Weber: *Carl Maria von Weber: ein Lebensbild* (Leipzig, 1864–6, abridged 2/1912, ed. R. Pechel; Eng. trans., abridged, 1865)

F. W. Jähns: *Carl Maria von Weber in seinen Werken: chronologisch-thematisches Verzeichniss seiner sämtlichen Compositionen* (Berlin, 1871)

——: *Carl Maria von Weber: eine Lebensskizze nach authentischen Quellen* (Leipzig, 1873)

J. Benedict: *Weber* (London, 1881, 5/1899)

A. Krüger: *Pseudoromantik: Friedrich Kind und der Dresdner Liederkreis* (Leipzig, 1904)

G. Kaiser, ed.: *Webers Briefe an den Grafen Karl von Brühl* (Leipzig, 1911)

E. Kroll: 'E. T. A. Hoffmann und Weber', *Neue Musik-Zeitung*, xlii (1921), 336–7

W. Muche: 'Weber und Marschner', *Signale für die musikalische Welt*, xciv (1936), 746–7

S. Goslich: *Beiträge zur Geschichte der deutschen romantischen Oper* (Leipzig, 1937)

R. Engländer: 'The Struggle between German and Italian Opera at the Time of Weber', *MQ*, xxxi (1945), 479–91

P. R. Kirby: 'Weber's Operas in London, 1824–1826', *MQ*, xxxii (1946), 333–53

W. Becker: *Die deutsche Oper in Dresden unter der Leitung von Carl Maria von Weber, 1817–26* (Berlin, 1962)

J. Warrack: *Carl Maria von Weber* (London, 1968, 2/1976)

G. Jones: *Backgrounds and Themes of the Operas of Carl Maria von Weber* (diss., Cornell U., 1972)

S. Goslich: *Die deutsche romantische Oper* (Tutzing, 1975)

G. Jones: 'Weber's "Secondary Worlds": the Later Operas of Carl Maria von Weber', *IRASM*, vii (1976), 219–33

J. Warrack, ed.: *Carl Maria von Weber: Writings on Music* (Cambridge, 1981)

C. Brown: 'Spohr, *Faust* and Leitmotif', *MT*, cxxv (1984), 25–7

H. C. Worbs: 'Eine Manie, die alle Stände erfasste: zur frühen Rezeption der Werke Carl Maria von Weber', *NZM*, cxlvii (1986), 4–8

Musik und Gesellschaft, xxxvi/11 (1986) [Weber issue, incl. G. Schönfelder: 'Befreiung aus Enge und Zwang: Webers Schaffen im historischen Umfeld', 562–7; H. Goldschmidt: 'Und immer wieder *Freischütz*: ein Befund', 568–72; M. Becker: 'Zwischen Biedermeier, Romantik und Klassizismus: zur Ästhetik Carl Maria von Webers', 573–7; B. Bartz: 'Opernparodie als Spiegel sozialer Verhältnisse: *Die drei Pintos* von Carl Maria von Weber und Gustav Mahler', 577–81]

Weber und der Gedanke der Nationaloper: Dresden 1986 [incl. G. Schönfelder: 'Carl Maria von Webers romantische Gesinnung', 229–34; M. Zduniak: 'Webers Wirken am "Königlich priviligierten Breslauischen Theater"', 245–6; J. Warrack: 'Französische Elemente in Webers Opern', 277–90; V. Reising: 'Die Funktion phantastischer Gestalten bei Weber', 291–8; G. Rienäcker: 'Gedanken zur Wolfsschluct', 299–308; H. Seeger: 'Webers *Oberon* im Spannungsfeld der Traditionen', 309–16; R. Zimmermann: 'Glücklose Synthese: beim Lesen des *Euryanthe*-Autographs', 317–26; D. Härtwig: 'Plädoyer für eine vollendete Unvollendete: Bemerkungen zu Gustav Mahlers Bearbeitung von Carl Maria von Webers *Die drei Pintos*', 360–71]

E. Kröplin: *Wagner und Weber: der Vorgang einer Theatralisierung* (Dresden, 1987)

INDIVIDUAL OPERAS

Der Freischütz

C. Brühl: *Neuste Kostüme auf beiden königlichen Theatern in Berlin* (Berlin, 1822) [incl. *Freischütz* costumes]

F. Kind: *Freischütz-Buch* (Leipzig, 1843) [incl. first-hand account of opera's composition]

H. Berlioz: 'Le Freyschütz de Weber', *Voyage musicale en Allemagne et en Italie*, i (Paris, 1844), 369–81

J.-G. T. Grässe: *Die Quelle des Freischütz* (Dresden, 1870)

R. Wagner: 'Der Freischütz in Paris', *Gesammelte Schriften und Dichtungen*, i (Leipzig, 1871); *Prose Works*, ed. W. Ashton Ellis, vii (London, 1898)

G. Servières: *Freischütz* (Paris, 1913) [Fr. trans. of lib.; discussion of Fr. versions]

E. Hasselberg, ed.: *Der Freischütz: Friedrich Kinds Operndichtung und ihre Quellen* (Berlin, 1921)

J. Kapp: 'Die Uraufführung des Freischütz', *Blätter der Staatsoper*, i/8 (Berlin, 1921), 9–16

H. Abert: 'Carl Maria von Weber und sein Freischütz', *JbMP 1926*, 9–29; repr. in *Gesammelte Schriften und Vorträge*, ed. H. Blume (Halle, 1929, 2/1968)

T. Cornelissen: *Carl Maria von Webers Freischütz als Beispiel einer Opernbehandlung* (Berlin, 1940)

H. Schnoor: *Weber auf dem Welttheater: ein Freischützbuch* (Dresden, 1942, 4/1963)

W. Kron: *Die angeblichen Freischütz-Kritiken E. T. A. Hoffmanns* (Munich, 1957)

G. Mayerhofer: *Abermals vom Freischützen: der Münchener Freischütze von 1812* (Regensburg, 1959)

K. Pahlen, ed.: *Der Freischütz: kompleter Text und Erläuterung zum vollen Verständnis des Werkes* (Munich and Mainz, 1982)

C. Dahlhaus: 'Webers "Freischütz" und die Idee der romantischen Oper', *ÖMz*, xxxviii (1983), 381–8

L. Finscher: 'Weber's *Freischütz*: Conceptions and Misconceptions', *PRMA*, cx (1983–4), 79–90

H. Goldschmidt: 'Und immer wieder *Freischütz*: ein Befund', *Musik und Gesellschaft*, xxxvi (1986), 568–72

G. Rienäcker: 'Gedanken zur Wolfsschlucht', *Weber und der Gedanke der Nationaloper: Dresden 1986*, 299–308

L'avant-scène opéra, no. 105–6 (1988) [*Der Freischütz* issue]

Euryanthe

H. von Chezy: 'Carl Maria von Webers Euryanthe: ein Beitrag zur Geschichte der deutschen Oper', *NZM*, xiii (1840), 1–6, 9–11

A. A. Abert: 'Webers *Euryanthe* und Spohrs *Jessonda* als grosse Opern', *Festschrift für Walter Wiora* (Kassel, 1967), 435–40

Ludwig Weber as Gurnemanz in Wagner's 'Parsifal'

M. C. Tusa: *Carl Maria von Weber's Euryanthe: a Study of its Historical Context, Genesis and Reception* (diss., Princeton U., 1983)
R. Zimmermann: 'Glücklose Synthese: beim Lesen des *Euryanthe*-Autographs', *Weber und der Gedanke der Nationaloper: Dresden 1986*, 317–26

Oberon

'Oberon, or The Elf King's Oath', *Quarterly Musical Magazine and Review*, viii (1826), 84–101
L'avant-scène opéra, no.74 (1985) [*Oberon* issue]

CLIVE BROWN

Weber, (Franz) Edmund (Kaspar Johann Nepomuk Joseph Maria) (*b* Hildesheim, 19 June 1766; *d* Würzburg, 1828). German composer, half-brother of Carl Maria von Weber. He was briefly a pupil of Haydn and held appointments at Würzburg (1804–5), Berne (1812–19) and later Lübeck, among other places. In addition to masses and instrumental music, he wrote two operas: *Der Transport im Koffer* (1792, Nuremberg) and *Die Zwillinge* (1797, Salzburg).

Weber, Josepha. *See* HOFER, JOSEPHA.

Weber, Joseph Miroslav (*b* Prague, 9 Nov 1854; *d* Munich, 1 Jan 1906). Czech composer. He studied at the Prague Conservatory (1870–73) and began his career as a solo violinist at Sondershausen. He went on to hold court posts successively at Darmstadt, Wiesbaden and Munich. An unusually well-trained musician, he was a fine pianist as well as an accomplished violinist, and he enjoyed a well-deserved reputation as a composer of chamber music and operettas. His comic opera *Der selige Herr Vetter* (1, K. Schultes) was given at Wiesbaden in 1884, and *Die neue Mamsell* (Spieloper, 3, F. Leber) at Munich on 21 November 1896 (vocal score published Munich, ?1896). He also wrote incidental music to plays by Fels and Schultes.

StiegerO
Obituary, *NZM*, cii (1906), 49

ALBERT MELL

Weber, Ludwig (*b* Vienna, 29 July 1899; *d* Vienna, 9 Dec 1974). Austrian bass. He abandoned projected careers as teacher and artist when he discovered his vocal promise and began to study with Alfred Boruttau in 1919. Having sung at the Vienna Volksoper he joined some of the smaller German companies in the mid- and late 1920s. After a successful appearance at the 1931 Wagner Festival in Munich he joined the Staatsoper there in 1933 and soon began to sing abroad. He was heard in London in 1936 (Pogner, Gurnemanz, Hunding and Hagen), and later added Daland, King Mark, Osmin and Rocco to his Covent Garden roles. In 1938 he created the Holsteiner in *Friedenstag* in Munich. He joined the Vienna Staatsoper in 1945, and was heard again in London in 1947 and 1950–51 in Wagner roles and as Boris (1950). From 1951 he was a regular singer at Bayreuth, and he also appeared at Buenos Aires. He had a magnificently rich and solid bass and could darken his tones to accommodate the malevolence of Hagen as successfully as he conveyed the suffering and dignity of King Mark or Gurnemanz. In Mozart he commanded the line and agility to be a splendid Sarastro, Osmin and Commendatore; Wozzeck and Kecal were also among his roles. He lacked perhaps the boisterous high spirits of the complete Ochs, though was never less than impressive in this part (some have compared him with Mayr); his recording of this role, and of his 1951 Bayreuth Gurnemanz, are still much admired.

D. Brass: 'Ludwig Weber', *Opera*, ii (1950–51), 352–5

PETER BRANSCOMBE

Webster, Sir David (Lumsden) (*b* Dundee, 3 July 1903; *d* London, 11 May 1971). British musical administrator. After producing several operas during his undergraduate days at Liverpool University, he went into commerce. He was chairman of the Liverpool Philharmonic Society (1940–45) and of the Orchestral Employers' Association (1948–70), and general administrator of Covent Garden (1945–70) and of the London Opera Centre (1962–70). He successfully established Covent Garden as the permanent home of the Sadler's Wells (subsequently the Royal) Ballet and of the Covent Garden (subsequently the Royal Opera) companies; a skilful negotiator, he steered Covent Garden through several financial crises. He was largely responsible for the encouragement and launching of several British artists on to the international scene and for making Covent Garden one of the world's leading opera houses. He was knighted in 1961 and created a KCVO in 1970.

Lord Drogheda: 'Sir David Webster', *About the House*, iii/9 (1971), 59
M. Haltrecht: *The Quiet Showman* (London, 1975)

HAROLD ROSENTHAL/R

Webster, James (*b* Evanston, IL, 13 Sept 1942). American musicologist. He studied at Harvard (BA 1963), Vienna and Princeton, where he took the PhD (1974); he was appointed a professor at Cornell University in 1971. While most of his work has been on instrumental music and analytical issues in the Classical era, he has contributed to the literature of opera with articles treating of the application of analytical method to Mozart, notably 'To Understand Verdi and Wagner we must Understand Mozart' (*19th Century Music*, xi (1987–8), 175–93), 'Mozart's Operas and the Myth of Musical Unity' (*COJ*, ii (1990), 197–218) and 'The Analysis of Mozart's Arias' (*Mozart Studies*, ed. C. Eisen (Oxford, 1991), 101–99).

Weckerlin [Wekerlin], **Jean-Baptiste (Théodore)** (*b* Guebwiller, 9 Nov 1821; *d* Trottberg, nr Guebwiller, 20 May 1910). French scholar and composer. He abandoned his early studies of chemistry and was accepted at the Paris Conservatoire, where he studied composition (with Halévy) and singing. After leaving the Conservatoire he earned his living by teaching and in 1863 became librarian and archivist of the Société des Compositeurs de Musique. He was appointed clerk to the librarian of the Conservatoire in 1869 and was named main librarian in 1876; during his 33-year tenure he doubled the library's holdings.

Weckerlin's compositions are little known; he wrote over a dozen stage works (mostly *opéras comiques*), only a few of which were presented on the Paris stage, though *L'organiste dans l'embarras* (1853) received over 100 performances. All his theatre pieces are unambitious; employing few characters, they mostly rely heavily on musical and dramatic cliché (the slightly more original plot of *L'organiste dans l'embarras*, in which the old organist is saved by his young assistant from dismissal and humiliation, may go some way towards explaining its success with the Parisian public). Ensembles for more than three voices are rare. In *Les revenants Bretons* (1855) the composer attempted to add some local colour (there is a 'chanson bretonne' and a 'danse bretonne') and made use of simple, folklike melodies. Nevertheless, even in his own day his theatre works were probably regarded as diverting rather than remarkable, and like many such pieces are too much products of their age to have remained in vogue.

It is interesting to speculate on how much Weckerlin's experiences may have inspired his later scholarly efforts towards the revival of early French opera. Like Louis Niedermeyer, moving spirit behind the school which bore his name, he turned to academic life following the failure of his own stage works. Perhaps Weckerlin used his academic position to persuade Théodore Michaelis to undertake publication of volumes comprising the *Chefs-d'oeuvre classiques de l'opéra français* series, of which he edited the first, in view of the fact that Michaelis is otherwise scarcely known for his musical publications. Besides editing Cambert's *Pomone* for the series (Paris, 1881), Weckerlin was responsible for modern editions of Gluck's *La rencontre imprévue* (Paris, ?1890) and Lully's *Le bourgeois gentilhomme* (Paris, 1883).

La mort de Roland (drama, F. Haard), Paris, Conservatoire, 5 Dec 1847

L'organiste dans l'embarras (oc, 1, Alboize), Paris, Lyrique, 17 May 1853, vs (Paris, 1853)

Le marché aux fées, 1854 (3)

Les revenants Bretons (opéra de salon, 1, A. de Guezennec de Bréhat), concert perf., Paris, Salle Herz, ?1855, vs (Paris, 1855)

Tout est bien qui finit bien (opéra de salon, 1, J. Malherbe), Paris, Tuileries, 28 Feb 1856, vs (Paris, 1855)

La laitière de Trianon (opérette de salon, 1, J. H. A. Galoppe d'Onquaire), Paris, Rossini's House, 18 Dec 1858

Die dreifach Hochzitt im Bäsäthal (oc, 3, J. Mangold), Colmar, 17 Sept 1863, vs (Paris, 1863) [in Colmar dialect]

Le ménétrier de Meudon, 1868 (oc, 2, E. Adenis, L. Guillard)

La fête d'Alexandre (drame antique, C. J. Dorat), vs (Paris, 1875)

Après Fontenoy, ou Manche à manche (oc, 1, Galoppe d'Onquaire), Paris, Lyrique, 28 May 1877, vs (Paris, *c*1877)

D'r verhäxt' Herbst (4, Mangold), Colmar, 31 May 1879 [in Colmar dialect]

Le Sicilien (oc, 2), ?unperf., vs (Paris, *c*1886)

La journée de la princesse (opéra de salon, 1, O. de Crespy le Prince), ?unperf., vs (Paris, *c*1890)

La légende du Juif errant (drama, C. Grandmougin), vs (Paris, *c*1901)

Jobin et Nanette (oc, 1, M. Carré and L. Battu), ?unperf., vs (Paris, n.d.)

A. Pougin: 'J.-B. Weckerlin', *Le ménestrel*, lxxvi (1910), 173

ELISABETH LEBEAU/JOHN WAGSTAFF

We Come to the River. 'Actions for music' in two parts (11 scenes) by HANS WERNER HENZE to a libretto by EDWARD BOND; London, Covent Garden, 12 July 1976.

Henze's seventh full-length opera, commissioned by the Royal Opera, is much closer to his highly politicized music-theatre works of the early 1970s – *The Raft of 'The Medusa'*, *El Cimmaron*, *Der langwierige Weg in die Wohnung der Natascha Ungeheuer* – than to his preceding work for the opera house *The Bassarids* (1965). The 'actions for music' unfold on a bare stage divided into three acting areas, each with its own chamber orchestra, on which scenes may be presented simultaneously.

The story concerns a General (baritone) in an imaginary empire, celebrating his triumph in the bloody suppression of a rebellion. As he dictates a report of his victory to the Emperor, his soldiers celebrate their fortune (scene i). A Deserter (tenor) is brought before the General (scene ii); while the organist plays choral fantasies on Hassler's 'Herzlich tut mich verlangen' he is sentenced to be executed. As he waits in the condemned cell, telling his guards of his childhood and of the panic that overwhelmed him on the battlefield, the General is being fêted at a ball; the local people salute him and Rachel (soprano) sings an extravagant aria in A♭ major ('Hail Liberator') in his praise. While the sounds of mazurkas and waltzes continue from the ball the General returns to his tent to be told by the Doctor (bass-baritone) that he is suffering from an incurable condition that will lead to total blindness. As he forces himself to return to his desk, the celebrations have turned into an orgy, to the strains of the *Eton Boating Song* (scene iii).

At dawn the General goes out to the battlefield, and among the dead and dying he perceives, at last, the suffering that he has inflicted on others throughout his career. He encounters a Young Woman (soprano) and an Old Woman (mezzo-soprano) who are rifling the belongings of the dead just to survive. They are also searching for the corpse of the Young Woman's husband; he is the Deserter, at that moment being shot in the barracks. To the sounds of an onstage military band the new provincial Governor (baritone) arrives, but the General is too preoccupied with what he has witnessed on the battlefield to appreciate the message of thanks that he brings from the Emperor (scene v). When the Governor orders the Young Woman to be shot for looting, the General pleads for mercy and is himself arrested (scene vi). The Old Woman is shot as she tries to escape. The General is again helpless to intervene; he

'We Come to the River' (Henze): scene from the original production at Covent Garden, London, 12 July 1976

takes up her curses against the Governor and the oppressors (scene vii).

Part 2 opens with the General incarcerated in a mental asylum, surrounded by madmen who are building an imaginary boat to carry them away on an imaginary river to freedom (scene viii). He is visited by Soldier 2 (tenor), formerly under his command, who describes the horrors of the military state in the outside world and begs him to lead an uprising; the General refuses to help. The Governor arrives: he brings a request from the Emperor that the General take up his military duties again, to save the Empire from civil war. The General rejects this request also, believing that he will do least harm to everyone by remaining inactive. When the Governor reports on his visit to the Emperor's ministers, he is killed by Soldier 2 (scene ix); the act triggers a long cadenza from the Drummer.

At a picnic the Emperor (mezzo-soprano) is informed of the Governor's death and that his assassin had just returned from a visit to the mad General; in a long, sensuous aria of ambiguous tonality he decides that the General must be blinded (scene x). The General, too, hears of the killing and that the Soldier has returned home to kill his wife, children and then himself; now wishing that he were truly insane, he tries to blind himself but is overpowered, straitjacketed and chained. The Emperor's agents arrive and blind him, as the organist's choral fantasies are heard again. Now the General can see who are the victims of war, but the madmen suspect he is a spy and a danger to their imaginary scheme; they see their bedsheets to be a river and 'drown' the General beneath them. The Drummer launches into a massive 'metallic' cadenza and the inmates sing their hymn of hope: 'We stand by the river/If there is no bridge we will wade/ ... We have learnt to march so well that we cannot drown'.

Stage I is placed in the foreground; it is used for monologues and to depict the world of the oppressed. Its orchestra contains 'old' instruments (including a consort of viols) along with wind and percussion. Stage II holds the central action of the work: there the General is told of his imminent blindness, the Governor is assassinated and the Emperor has his picnic. Its orchestra comprises a string quintet with wind and celesta. Acts of atrocity – the Deserter's execution, the women's murders, the orgy – take place on stage III in the background, to the accompaniment of amplified string quartet and wind. The Drummer, a solo percussionist playing a vast array of instruments built into the set, is both a chorus figure and part of the action (a military drummer on the battlefield in part 1, and an inmate of the asylum in part 2). The portative organ, used only twice at climactic points, is positioned between stages I and II.

Musically, *We Come to the River* represents Henze at his most eclectic, with sections worked out through strict serial procedures juxtaposed with material that is deliberately banal and melodically simplistic, to characterize the feckless upper class. While the music of the oppressors becomes weak and rootless, that associated with the poor and oppressed develops and strengthens until it is brought together for the final hymn. Each character is allotted his or her own set of melodic shapes and chord group; those of the Deserter, for instance, comprise five short melodic tags and five longer ones, together with a set of five chords derived from them.

The Royal Opera production, directed by Henze, involved over 80 singers: Norman Welsby was the General and it was conducted by David Atherton. *We Come to the River* was staged in Berlin shortly afterwards, and the American première took place at Santa Fe in 1984.

ANDREW CLEMENTS

Wedekind, Erika (*b* Hanover, 13 Nov 1869; *d* Zürich, 10 Oct 1944). German soprano. A sister of the dramatist Frank Wedekind, she studied in Dresden, making her début there in 1894 as Mrs Ford in *Die lustigen Weiber von Windsor*. She remained at Dresden until 1909, but made guest appearances throughout Europe. At

Salzburg she sang Zerlina (1901) and Blonde (1904). She appeared at Covent Garden (1903) as Lucia. Her great facility in coloratura passages was much admired.

ELIZABETH FORBES

Wedekind, (Benjamin) Frank(lin) (*b* Hanover, 24 July 1864; *d* Munich, 9 March 1918). German poet and dramatist. He was intended for a legal career and was sent to Munich to study. There he became involved in the literary avant garde and began a peripatetic life working as a journalist, actor and cabaret singer, before the death of his father in 1899 gave him a measure of financial independence. His first major drama was *Frühlings Erwachen* (1891), a study of adolescent sexuality and morality that was not staged until 1906 because of problems with the censor. Shortly afterwards he began the Lulu plays, conceived as a portrait of the embodiment of sexual desire and fulfilment in a single woman, and charting her rise and fall in the bourgeois society of the late 19th century. They were eventually published in two parts: *Der Erdgeist* (1895) and *Die Büchse der Pandora* (1902), from which Berg prepared the libretto for *Lulu* (1929–35).

Wedekind was imprisoned in 1899 for his political poems, and in his subsequent stage works he pursued his theories of eroticism to bleak satirical extremes, where everything is subordinated to the sexual drive. His work came to be recognized as a vital link between 19th-century German naturalism and 20th-century expressionism, and even as pointing towards the theories of Brecht and the theatre of the absurd.

*

F. Wedekind: *Five Tragedies of Sex*, trans. F. Fawcett and S. Spender (London, 1952)

A. Kutscher: *Wedekind* (Munich, 1964)

G. Seehaus: *Frank Wedekind und das Theater* (Munich, 1964)

F. Wedekind: *The Lulu Plays*, trans. S. Spender (New York, 1967)

S. Gittelman: *Frank Wedekind* (New York, 1969)

F. Wedekind: *Werke in drei Bänden* (Berlin, 1969)

T. Wedekind: *Lulu: die Rolle meines Lebens* (Munich, 1969)

F. Wedekind: *Die Tagebücher: ein erotisches Leben*, ed. G. Hay (Frankfurt, 1986; Eng. trans., 1990)

ANDREW CLEMENTS

Weede [Wiedefeld], **Robert** (*b* Baltimore, 11 Feb 1903; *d* Walnut Creek, CA, 9 June 1972). American baritone. He studied at the Eastman School of Music and in Milan, and made his début at the Metropolitan in 1937 as Tonio, remaining with the company until 1947. His repertory included Scarpia, Manfredo (*Amore dei tre re*), Macbeth, Germont and Rigoletto, the role of his débuts in Chicago (1939), San Francisco (1940) and at the New York City Opera (1948). Though rather wooden as an actor, he had a smooth and full-toned voice particularly well suited to Verdi. He ended his career on Broadway, creating the title role of an Italian vineyard owner in Loesser's *The Most Happy Fella* (1956), which ran for 676 performances.

CHARLES JAHANT/ELIZABETH FORBES

Wehrli, Werner (*b* Aarau, 8 Jan 1892; *d* Lucerne, 27 June 1944). Swiss composer. He studied in Zürich, at the Frankfurt Conservatory with Knorr, and at the universities of Munich, Basle and Berlin; he won the Mozart Prize in 1914. From 1918 until his death he taught in Aarau; he was also a poet. His teaching activities gave rise to many of his compositions, in which a romantic sensitivity is expressed with a moderate use of new techniques.

Das heisse Eisen op.5 (komische Oper, Wehrli, after H. Sachs), Berne, 1918

Der Märchenspiegel op.21 (Spl, C. Günther), 1922

Das Vermächtnis op.29 (Wehrli), Lucerne, 1931

Auf zum Mond op.33 (Schuloper, Wehrli), Aarau, 1933

PETER ROSS

Weichsel, Elizabeth. *See* BILLINGTON, ELIZABETH.

Weidemann, Friedrich (*b* Ratzeburg, 1 Jan 1871; *d* Vienna, 30 Jan 1919). German baritone. After study in Hamburg and Berlin he sang in Essen, Hamburg and Riga. Invited by Mahler to join the Vienna Hofoper in 1903, he was the first local Orestes (1909), Golaud (1910) and Amfortas (1914). His Mozart roles included Count Almaviva, which he sang at Salzburg in 1906. During Beecham's season at Covent Garden in 1910 he appeared as Orestes in the London première of *Elektra*, as Kurwenal and in Ethel Smyth's *The Wreckers*.

DAVID CUMMINGS

Weidinger, Christine (*b* Springville, NY, 31 March 1946). American soprano. She studied at San Fernando State College and with Margaret Harshaw at Indiana University, Bloomington. Since 1974 she has sung at the Metropolitan and in San Francisco in a repertory including Konstanze, Musetta, Gilda, Lucia and Leonora (*Il trovatore*). Her attractive stage presence and secure phrasing have also been admired in the roles of Amenaide (*Tancredi*, 1989, Los Angeles), Mozart's Vitellia and Electra (La Scala), Norma, and Halévy's Rachel. She has appeared in Germany, most frequently in Hamburg, Bielefeld and Stuttgart. DAVID CUMMINGS

Weidmann, Josef (*b* Vienna, 24 Aug 1742; *d* Vienna, 18 Sept 1810). German actor and dramatist. The son of a poor servant, he was taught by the Jesuits along with his younger brother Paul. In 1757 he ran away from home and became a dancer, then turned to acting. He settled in Vienna in 1772 and earned great favour as a master of the low comic, especially with Joseph II, who exceptionally permitted him to extemporize in his roles at the Nationaltheater. His most popular text, *Der Dorfbarbier* (set by Johann Schenk in 1796), is an adaptation of a comedy (1785) by his far more prolific brother PAUL WEIDMANN, with whose stage works his are frequently confused. THOMAS BAUMAN

Weidmann, Paul (*b* Vienna, 1747; *d* Vienna, 9 April 1810). German playwright and librettist. He attended the Jesuit academy in Vienna with his elder brother Josef, then embarked on a career as a civil servant. From 1771 he wrote copiously for the stage, anonymously at first, which has wrought much confusion in constructing an accurate inventory of his works. Although harshly judged by posterity, Weidmann's stage works enjoyed great popularity with Viennese audiences; his one-act libretto *Die Bergknappen* was chosen to inaugurate Emperor Joseph II's National-Singspiel in 1778.

Der glückliche Schatzgräber (komisches Spl), 1773; *Doktor Faust* (Drama), Michel, 1776; *Die Bergknappen* (Originalsingspiel), Umlauf, 1778 (Kürzinger, 1782); *Der adeliche Tagelöhner* (komisches Originalsingspiel), Bartha, 1780; *Der Bettelstudent, oder Das Donnerwetter* (Originallustspiel mit Gesängen), Winter, 1785; *Der Maler von Paris* (lustiges Spl), 1785; *Der Ring der*

Liebe, oder Zemirens und Azors Ehestand (Spl), Umlauf, 1786; *Der Strazzensammler, oder Ein gutes Herz ziert jeden Stand* (Operette), Weigl, 1792; *Der Friede, oder Die Prüfung der Herzen* (Spl), pasticcio, 1797; *Der Schreiner* (Spl), Wranitzky, 1799

THOMAS BAUMAN

Weidt, Lucie [Lucy] (*b* Troppau, Silesia, *c*1880; *d* Vienna, 28 July 1940). Austrian soprano of German birth. She studied with her father, Heinrich Weidt, a minor Kapellmeister and composer, and with Rosa Papier. Most of her career was spent at the Vienna Staatsoper, of which she was a regular member from 1903 to 1926, first in succession to the retiring Sophie Sedlmair, and soon sharing the major Wagner roles with Anna Bahr-Mildenburg. She became a famous Leonore in *Fidelio* and was the first Viennese Marschallin in *Der Rosenkavalier*; she was also the first to sing the role of Kundry in Milan. She appeared in Munich between 1908 and 1910, for a few Metropolitan performances as Brünnhilde and Elisabeth in the season of 1910–11, and at Buenos Aires in 1912. At the première of Strauss's *Die Frau ohne Schatten* (1919, Vienna) she sang the part of the Nurse. Her recordings show a well-trained and strong voice of marked dramatic intensity.

DESMOND SHAWE-TAYLOR

Weigl, Joseph (*b* Eisenstadt, 28 March 1766; *d* Vienna, 3 Feb 1846). Austrian composer and conductor. His father, a cellist, and mother, an opera singer, worked first in the Esterházy court under Haydn (Weigl's godfather) and, from 1769, in the two court theatres of Vienna, his father as principal cellist of the Italian opera. Weigl began courses in medicine and law but soon turned to music, studying with Albrechtsberger and, from the age of 19, with Salieri. In 1786 the latter engaged him as a répétiteur at the Burgtheater, where Weigl worked with Mozart during the preparation of *Le nozze di Figaro* and *Don Giovanni*. In 1790 he was appointed deputy Kapellmeister and two years later Kapellmeister and composer at that theatre; from this time onwards his position in the musical establishment was assured.

Weigl wrote Italian as well as German operas, his first great success being *L'amor marinaro* (1797). When dance began to play an important role in the repertory in Vienna, he wrote music for ballets. He composed for La Scala, but in 1808 refused the directorship of that theatre and of the Milan Conservatory. In 1822, disillusioned by the frivolous tastes of theatre audiences in Vienna, he abandoned the composition of opera. While retaining his official position at the court opera, he wrote music principally for the church and, in 1827, was appointed vice-Kapellmeister of the court chapel.

Throughout his life, Weigl favoured the concise forms and many of the stylistic features learnt during his classical training. He had special affection for the music of Mozart, whose influence on his own music is often evident. His affinities, however, were increasingly with newer, romantic expression and richer orchestral colouring. In rejecting the cruder elements of contemporary Viennese Singspiels and the sparkling frivolity of Italian comic opera, he turned to sentimental but serious themes in his operas, creating a fashion for the idyllic and pastoral which, for a while, had considerable influence on the musical theatre in Austria. Of such a kind were his two most successful works, *Das Waisenhaus* (1808) and, even more popular, *Die Schweizerfamilie* (1809), performed throughout Europe. His other stage works include incidental music, a Liederspiel and many pieces added to operas by other composers. Weigl's music was especially admired for its melodiousness, freshness and charm, and for its classical purity of style.

See also SCHWEIZERFAMILIE, DIE.

principal sources: A-Wgm, Wn, D-Bds, Dlb, DS

WB – *Vienna, Burgtheater*
WK – *Vienna, Kärntnertortheater*

Die unnütze Vorsicht, oder Die betrogene Arglist (1, F. L. Schmidel), WB, 23 Feb 1783 [for marionette production]

Il pazzo per forza (2, C. Mazzolà), WB, 14 Nov 1788

La caffettiera bizzarra (komische Oper, 3, L. da Ponte, after C. Goldoni), WB, 15 Sept 1790

Der Strassensammler [Lumpensammler], oder Ein gutes Herz ziert jeden Stand (komische Oper, 1, P. Weidmann), Vienna, Leopoldstadt, 13 Oct 1792

La principessa d'Amalfi (komische Oper, 2, G. Bertati), WB, 10 Jan 1794, ov., arr. hpd (Vienna, ?1795), vs (Augsburg, n.d.)

Das Petermännchen (Schauspiel, 8, H. Spiess, rev. K. F. Hensler), Vienna, Leopoldstadt, 8 April 1794 [pt 1], ?April/May 1794 [pt 2], songs (Brunswick, n.d.)

Giulietta e Pierotto (dramma giocoso per musica, 2, G. De Gamerra), WB, 16 Oct 1794

I solitari (os, 3, De Gamerra), WB, 15 March 1797

L'amor marinaro, ossia Il corsaro (dramma giocoso per musica, 2, De Gamerra), WB, 15 Oct 1797, vs (Augsburg, n.d.); also as Der Korsar aus Liebe

Das Dorf im Gebirge (Schauspiel, 2, A. von Kotzebue), Vienna, National, 17 April 1798, vs (Breslau, n.d.)

L'accademia del maestro Cisolfaut (2, De Gamerra), WK, 14 Oct 1798

Die Herrenhuterin (Spl, L. B. Picard), WK, 26 Nov 1804, notturno (Vienna, n.d.)

Vestas Feuer (heroische Oper, 2, J. E. Schikaneder), Vienna, An der Wien, 7 Aug 1805

L'uniforme (heroisch-komische Oper, 3, G. Carpani), Schönbrunn, 1805, vs (Vienna, n.d.) [It. and Ger.]

Il principe invisibile (4, F. Foignet), ?Vienna, 4 Oct 1806

Kaiser Hadrian (grosse Oper, 3, P. Metastasio and J. von Sonnleithner), WK, 21 May 1807

Ostade oder Adrian von Ostade (1, G. F. Treitschke), WK, 3 Oct 1807, vs (Bonn, n.d.)

Cleopatra (2, L. Romanelli), Milan, Scala, 19 Dec 1807, ?lost

Il rivale di se stesso (2, Romanelli), Milan, Scala, 18 April 1808; as Liebhaber und Nebenbuhler in einer Person, Vienna, 1812

Das Waisenhaus (Spl, 2, Treitschke), WK, 4 Oct 1808, vs (Vienna, n.d.); Fr. trans., *B-Bc*

Die Schweizerfamilie (lyrische Oper, 3, I. F. Castelli, after C. G. d'Aucour de Saint Just), WK, 14 March 1809 (Vienna, n.d.); as Emmeline, ou La famille suisse, Paris, 1827, arr. Crémont (Paris, 1827)

Die Verwandlungen (Operette, 1, after Viscount de Ségur), ?Berlin, Feb 1810

Die Einsiedler auf den Alpen (1, Treitschke), WK, 13 June 1810

Franciska von Foix (heroisch-komische Oper, 3, Castelli), WK, 7 Feb 1812

Der Bergsturz (Spl, 3, A. F. Reil), WK, 19 Dec 1813, vs (Leipzig, n.d.)

Die Jugend [Jugendjahre] Peter des Grossen (3, Treitschke, after J.-N. Bouilly), WK, 10 Dec 1814, vs (Mainz, n.d.)

L'imboscata (2, Romanelli), Milan, Scala, 8 Nov 1815, duet (Leipzig, n.d.)

Margaritta d'Anjou, ossia L'orfano d'Inghilterra (melodramma eroicomico, 2, Romanelli), Milan, Scala, 26 July 1816; Ger. trans., 1819

Die Nachtigall und der Rabe (1, Treitschke), WK, 20 April 1818, vs (Vienna, n.d.)

Daniel in der Löwengrube, oder Baals Sturz (heroische Oper, 3, Reil), WK, 13 April 1820

König Waldemar, oder Die dänischen Fischer (Spl, 1, Castelli), WK, 11 May 1821

Edmund und Caroline (1, Treitschke, after B.-J. Marsollier des Vivetières), WK, 21 Oct 1821

Die eiserne Pforte (grosse Oper, 2, J. Ritter von Seyfried, after E. T. A. Hoffmann: *Das Majorat*), WK, 27 Feb 1823

Doubtful: La sposa collerica, 1786, unperf.

*

W. Bollert: 'Joseph Weigl und das deutsche Singspiel', *Aufsätze zur Musikgeschichte* (Bottrop, 1938)

A. Weinmann: *Verzeichnis der Musikalien aus dem K. K. Hoftheater-Musik-Verlag* (Vienna, 1962)

H. H. Hausner: 'Joseph Weigl ... Daten aus seinem Leben und Schaffen', *Mitteilungen der Internationalen Stiftung Mozarteum*, xiv/3–4 (1966), 9–17

R. Angermüller: 'Zwei Selbstbiographien von Joseph Weigl (1766–1846)', *DJbM*, xvi (1971), 46–85

ELIZABETH NORMAN McKAY

Weigl, Thaddäus (*b* 8 April 1776; *d* Vienna, 29 Feb 1844). Austrian composer, conductor and publisher. He studied music theory with Albrechtsberger, who acquainted him with the works of Bach and Handel; his brother Joseph introduced him to the music of Haydn and Mozart. From 1795 he worked as an arranger (especially of piano scores) for the court theatre's music publishing house, and in 1796 the firm sent him on a business journey that took him all over Europe. In 1801 he was granted a licence for a publishing firm of his own, which he founded in 1803. From that time he often stood in for his brother as vice-Kapellmeister at the Kärntnertortheater, and in 1806 he was granted the title of composer to the court theatre. Between 1799 and 1805 he wrote five operas (including *Idoly* and *Der Jahrmarkt zu Grunewald*) and 15 ballets. As vice-Kapellmeister of the court theatre he took over the direction of the musical archives and thoroughly reorganized them. Later he resigned from practical music-making to devote himself entirely to publishing. Apart from works by his brother, he chiefly published operatic arrangements and works by Viennese contemporaries.

Der Jahrmarkt zu Grünewald, oder Die Marionettenbude (comic op, 2, K. F. Hensler), Vienna, Leopoldstadt, 17 March 1795

Idoly (operetta, 2, J. Perinet), Vienna, Leopoldstadt, 12 March 1796

Armidoro, Prinz von Leon, 1799 (Baron Retzer), ?unperf.

Omar, oder Der schönste Sieg, 1801 (F. Rochlitz), ?unperf.

Das erhaltende Orakel, 1803 (Spl, Lippert), ?unperf.

*

StiegerO

RUDOLPH ANGERMÜLLER

Weikl, Bernd (*b* Vienna, 29 July 1942). Austrian baritone. He studied in Mainz and Hanover, where he made his début in 1968 as Ottokar (*Freischütz*). Engaged at Düsseldorf (1970–73), he sang Melot at Salzburg (1971) and Wolfram at Bayreuth (1972), returning for Amfortas, the Herald in *Lohengrin*, the Dutchman and Hans Sachs (1975–91). He made his Covent Garden début in 1975 as Rossini's Figaro and his Metropolitan début in 1977 as Wolfram. He sings regularly in Hamburg, Berlin, Munich and Vienna, where he created Ferdinand in Einem's *Kabale und Liebe* (1976), repeating the part in Florence. His repertory of over a hundred roles ranges from Guglielmo, Almaviva, Don Giovanni, Belcore, Luna, Posa and Ford, which he sang at La Scala in 1980, to Yevgeny Onegin, Tomsky, Zurga, Golaud, Eisenstein, Morone (*Palestrina*), John the Baptist and Mandryka. His powerful voice, warm and resonant, as well as his acting ability and fine stage presence, are superbly displayed as Hans Sachs.

ELIZABETH FORBES

Weil, Hermann (*b* Mühlburg, nr Karlsruhe, 29 May 1876; *d* Blue Mountain Lake, NY, 6 July 1949). German baritone. He studied at Karlsruhe and Frankfurt, making his début in 1901 at Freiburg as Wolfram. Engaged at Stuttgart from 1904 to 1933, he also appeared at La Scala, Madrid, Berlin, Vienna, Brussels and Bayreuth (1911–12 and 1924–5), where he sang Amfortas, Hans Sachs and Gunther. He made his Metropolitan début in 1911 as Kurwenal, then sang Faninal in the American première of *Der Rosenkavalier* in 1913, the year in which he made his only appearance at Covent Garden, as John the Baptist. Returning to the Metropolitan in 1916 he sang Gluck's Orestes. He toured the USA with the German Opera Company (1923–4). By 1939 he had left Germany and settled in New York as a teacher. His large repertory of more than a hundred roles included Wotan, Telramund and many Italian and French parts. He had a strong, expressive voice which he used to great dramatic effect.

ELIZABETH FORBES

Weill, Kurt (Julian) (*b* Dessau, 2 March 1900; *d* New York, 3 April 1950). German composer, American citizen from 1943. Few composers of the 20th century have devoted themselves as single-mindedly to musical theatre, including opera, as Weill. In his two composing careers, the first in Europe, the second in the USA, he moved from European highbrow to American middlebrow – the former an intellectual background which impinges even on such overtly 'popular' works as *Die Dreigroschenoper*, the latter a cultural context to which he adapted with apparent ease but which most of his American works ultimately transcend.

1. Apprenticeship and early career. 2. The Weill-Brecht partnership. 3. Exile in Europe. 4. The American years. 5. Posthumous reputation.

1. Apprenticeship and early career. Weill's first musical influences came from his father, a professional synagogue cantor. He studied the piano, theory and composition in Dessau with Albert Bing, through whom he gained access to the city's Hoftheater, with occasional work as répétiteur and coach. His first attempts at composing his own operas, *Zriny* (1916, based on a tragedy by Theodor Körner) and *Ninon von Lenclos* (1920, based on a play by Ernst Hardt), have not survived. Weill attended the university in Berlin, where he studied philosophy with Max Dessoir and Ernst Cassirer and even considered taking a doctorate in musicology, and he took lessons in composition briefly with Humperdinck. For five months in 1920 he was Kapellmeister in Lüdenscheid – an important apprenticeship, during which, as he wrote to his brother, 'apart from the complete classic and modern operettas, I conducted a few operas'. Lack of money prevented him from studying in Vienna with Schoenberg, whom he revered, but he was a regular member of Busoni's masterclass in Berlin for three years from 1921. To improve his financial situation he played the organ in synagogues, worked as a choral conductor and taught; Claudio Arrau, Maurice Abravanel and Nikolaos Skalkottas were among his pupils. His earliest extant opera is *Der Protagonist* op.14, completed in March 1925; with his Concerto for Violin and Winds op.12, it demonstrated the first signs of his maturity and brought him considerable public recognition.

Weill's debt to Busoni was aesthetic rather than stylistic. It is his ideas about opera, contained in numerous theoretical writings, rather than his actual compositions that show Busoni's direct influence. Those ideas also came to fruition later, in the celebrated collaborations with BERTOLT BRECHT. Busoni, in his *Entwurf einer neuen Ästhetik der Tonkunst* (first published in 1907), had sketched out a path away from the Wagnerian *Gesamtkunstwerk* towards an ideal derived from Mozartian opera. Weill, whose very formulations echo Busoni's, referred to this basic ideal as the *Urform* ('prototype'; Busoni spoke generally about 'Urmusik'). In some respects resembling a Platonic idea, it is informed by past achievements but directed towards future reform. For Weill, as for Busoni, it contained both creative and social aspects: a questioning of 19th-century dramatic conventions on the one hand, a concern about opera's social function on the other. (Both aspects were to appear in Brecht's emphatically anti-Wagnerian theories of opera.) A particularly Busonian touch in *Der Protagonist* is the inclusion of pantomime scenes, which dispense with singing altogether, thus affording the opportunity for absolute music with, as Weill would have said, 'the momentum of dramatic action'.

Der Protagonist, the first of Weill's collaborations with the expressionist playwright Georg Kaiser, is expressionist in its subject matter rather than in its music. Weill certainly employs so-called free atonality, but he does so to convey the emotional excesses of method acting displayed by the eponymous protagonist. If anything, the work as a whole is critical of expressionism, raising the same issue of artistic responsibility as did Hindemith's *Cardillac*, completed in 1926. The pantomimes (copied by Hindemith) are anything but expressionist; they employ a quite different style whose neo-classical angularity is indebted to Stravinsky rather than Schoenberg. Such mixing of idioms for dramatic ends characterizes Weill's entire output. Stylistic fingerprints remain, of course. But he was not concerned with developing a personal style so much as finding one appropriate to his needs as a composer for the stage. As his needs changed, so did his style.

Weill's next opera, *Royal Palace*, a collaboration with the surrealist poet Iwan Goll, signalled a shift towards *Neue Sachlichkeit* ('New Objectivity'). It is the first of his stage works to use popular dance music (or 'jazz', as it was then called) and the characteristic saxophone. The significance of the new idiom and sound is dramatic, too: rhythmic gestures borrowed from foxtrots and ragtime act as local colour for the fashionable contemporary setting, epitomized in the original staging by the use of film. When jazz idioms occur, as they do throughout the European works, they continue to be more or less 'defamiliarized' by quasi-surrealistic dissonance and rhythmic displacement, as if the borrowed idioms were in ironic quotation marks.

Na und? ('So What?'), a full-length comic opera, remains a mystery, the score being lost apart from a few sketches and Weill's correspondence with Schott. Weill worked on it with the Dramaturg and poet Felix Joachimson during 1926, a year which began with the composer's first marriage to Karoline Blamauer (the actress and dancer Lotte Lenya). His publisher, Universal Edition, rejected the new piece, however, as did Schott. *Royal Palace*, whose full score also disappeared, was conceived as a companion piece to *Der Protagonist*. But Weill, dissatisfied, allowed it to be superseded by *Der Zar lässt sich photographieren*, another collaboration with Kaiser. Whereas *Der Zar*, composed in 1927, still used a dualism of lyrical, 'operatic' *espressivo* on the one hand and dance idiom on the other, the Songspiel *Mahagonny* (composed in the same year)

Kurt Weill (right) with Lotte Lenya and Bertolt Brecht

saw the emergence of Weill's fully fledged 'song-style'. It also marked the beginning of the collaboration with Brecht.

2. THE WEILL-BRECHT PARTNERSHIP. If Weill looked back to Mozart for the *Urform* of the number opera, he looked forward to a time when it would no longer be the preserve of the privileged classes. His reform ideal was democratic through and through – hence his interest in the new medium of radio. For four years, from January 1925, he worked as a regular correspondent for the programme journal *Der deutsche Rundfunk*. Many of the articles were perfunctory announcements and reports; others dealt with socio-political and theoretical issues. At all times they express an intense curiosity about the artistic possibilities of the medium as well as a concern, shared by many of his contemporaries, for its democratic dissemination.

The works with Brecht thus reveal the *Neue Sachlichkeit* to be as much a sociological as an aesthetic issue. The programme booklet for the Songspiel contains the following:

> In his more recent works Weill is moving in the direction of those artists of all art forms who predict the liquidation of arts engendered by established society. The small epic piece *Mahagonny* merely takes the logical step from the inexorable decline of existing social structures. It already addresses an audience that naively demands its fun in the theatre.

Weill's partnership with Brecht is surrounded by myth. The questions it throws up are not always easy to answer. What attracted them to each other in the first place? What were their individual contributions to the collaboration? Did Brecht, as he himself claimed, really dictate melodies? What caused the separation? Commentators have been quick to supply answers even where evidence, both biographical and artistic, is flimsy. On a personal level, the relationship was cordial but never close (they always retained the formal mode of address). Politically they had a common sympathy for liberal causes, but Brecht, unlike Weill, had a marked affinity for Marxist theory and practice. What brought them together professionally was an interest in writing a full-scale opera. Yet when their ideas began to take shape, differences in conception eventually proved irreconcilable. Those differences, explicit in their respective theoretical statements on *Aufstieg und Fall der Stadt Mahagonny* (Brecht 1930; Weill 1930), did not prevent them from finishing the project, but it was a close thing.

They seemed happier together working in the mixed genres of the Songspiel *Mahagonny*, *Die Dreigroschenoper*, *Happy End*, the radio cantatas *Das Berliner Requiem* and *Der Lindberghflug* (the latter in collaboration with Hindemith), *Der Jasager* and *Die sieben Todsünden*, where the domination of music was not taken for granted – even though, in the end, the score may have been the principal ingredient of the success of the works.

Brecht's theory of 'epic theatre' necessarily connoted something different for Weill. To the playwright it meant the radical displacement of a creative category; the 'dramatic' had to give way to the 'epic', in the deliberate subversion of the Aristotelian unities and of theatrical illusion. To the opera composer the implications were far less revolutionary, requiring a reversion to the tradition of set numbers and a rapprochement with leading dramatists. To a large degree, then, the theoretical anomalies are generically specific. First, as applied to opera, the epithet 'epic' borders on the tautological, especially for a pupil of Busoni. Is not a number opera an epic structure by definition? On the other hand, given music's tendency towards emotional immediacy, the term 'epic opera' could also be seen to constitute an inherent contradiction. Jim Mahoney's big aria in the second act of *Aufstieg und Fall*, if convincingly sung, is dramatically defiant rather than epically reflective. Lastly, as a style of theatrical production, the concept 'epic theatre' suggests directorial intervention and 'production ideas' of a kind fundamentally opposed to any true commitment to opera, even a reforming one such as Weill's, but which are to be expected from Brecht, who wished ultimately to abolish the operatic form.

The break with Brecht came in December 1931, during rehearsals for the first Berlin production of *Aufstieg und Fall der Stadt Mahagonny*. For his next collaborator Weill turned to Caspar Neher, who had previously been responsible for the stage design of most of the Weill-Brecht premières, and again to Kaiser. The full-length opera *Die Bürgschaft*, for which Neher wrote his first libretto, received its première in Berlin in 1932, while Kaiser's play with music *Der Silbersee* was Weill's last composition before he left Germany in March 1933. Both works reflect a retreat, already apparent in the school opera *Der Jasager* (1930), from the mannerisms of the song-style. Weill was keen to cultivate a style less superficially contemporary, just as he wished his *Zeitopern* ('operas of the times') to address universal issues. *Die Bürgschaft*, in particular, moves towards a more classical monumentality symptomatic of the early 1930s. The relevance to 'the times' of these last German works is achieved not so much through the caustic, ironic wit of *Die Dreigroschenoper* as through idealistic parable.

3. Exile in Europe. When Weill arrived in Paris on 23 March 1933 his reputation had preceded him, through acclaimed productions there of the *Mahagonny* Songspiel and *Der Jasager* the previous December. In April he received the commission for the *ballet chanté Die sieben Todsünden*, for which the collaboration with Brecht was briefly and usefully revived.

On 18 September 1933 Weill became legally divorced from Lotte Lenya, who had sung in many of his works, including *Die sieben Todsünden*. Relations between the two remained affectionate, however, as their continued correspondence reveals. By the autumn of 1934 Weill was working on four separate projects at once. The Second Symphony and the play with music *Marie Galante* received their premières in October and December respectively. The operetta *Der Kuhhandel* and the biblical drama *Der Weg der Verheissung* have never been performed as originally conceived; in fact, Weill never completed them as such. *Der Kuhhandel* became *A Kingdom for a Cow*, the work with which he tried, unsuccessfully, to establish himself in London during the first half of 1935. *Der Weg der Verheissung* became *The Eternal Road*, a monumental Jewish pageant, for the New York production of which he and Lenya travelled to the USA in September 1935. After several delays, the work opened in January 1937. Despite critical acclaim and 153 performances, extravagant production costs caused it to become one of Broadway's biggest financial disasters.

4. The American years. It was in January 1937, too, that Weill and Lenya remarried. Weill had already established contact with the Group Theatre and completed the musical play *Johnny Johnson* with the playwright Paul Green. During the previous summer he had also taken part in the Group Theatre's summer course in Connecticut, lecturing on musical theatre.

The diversity of Weill's activities during his 14 years in the USA counteracts the widespread image of the composer who slavishly served the commercial theatre. The works themselves suggest that in his unceasing experimentation with new forms of musical theatre Weill never lost sight of the Busonian legacy. The American works – each breaking new ground, each laying claim to the status *sui generis* – are no less *Urformen* than the European. As Virgil Thomson wrote in Weill's obituary, 'every new work was a new model, a new shape, a new solution of dramatic problems' (*New York Herald-Tribune*, 9 April 1950).

Like other exiles, he soon managed to find work in Hollywood. But he found the working conditions intolerable. Composition to Weill included orchestration as an integral part of it, but Hollywood required not much more than a tunesmith – a role Weill considered a prostitution of his principles. That he was successful in implementing those principles on Broadway, where a similar division of labour between composer and orchestrator obtained, is testimony to his single-minded determination and dedication. Not following accepted practice required the fortitude of a workaholic, and the sacrifice exacted by such work was less that of his artistic integrity than of his health. The gulf separating Hollywood from Broadway is tellingly illustrated by the 1948 film version of the musical comedy *One Touch of Venus*: in its transition to the cinema, Weill's score was mutilated and reduced to the status of background music. Nor was the fate of the book by S. J. Perelman and Ogden Nash any better, with the proto-feminist ending (where the goddess of passion swiftly departs for Olympus on espying the lot of a suburban housewife) removed altogether.

Links with the European works are not only aesthetic but also palpably musical. In his attitude to material Weill can be likened to Handel. Borrowings abound. *Die Bürgschaft* furnishes material for *Der Silbersee*. Numbers from *Happy End* are reworked in *Marie Galante* and *Johnny Johnson*. Rather than let portions of *Der Kuhhandel* remain in obscurity, he recycled them in both *Knickerbocker Holiday* (1938) – including what became the evergreen 'September Song' – and *Lady in the Dark*. *Der Weg der Verheissung* was quarried for the theatre work *We will Never Die*, dedicated to 'the two million Jewish dead of Europe' and performed in March 1943 at Madison Square Garden. Borrowings within the American output also occur. The unfinished score of *Ulysses Africanus*, which Weill began in 1939 with Maxwell Anderson, formed the basis of their last collaboration, *Lost in the Stars* (1949).

In Europe and beyond, *Die Dreigroschenoper*'s infectious blend of cynicism and sentimentality had held audiences in the grip of what became known as *Dreigroschen*-fever – a craze that did not reach the USA until the mid-1950s. *Der Jasager* likewise achieved considerable popularity in Germany, thanks to hundreds of performances in schools before Hitler's seizure of power in 1933. *Der Jasager*'s closest relative from the American period is the folk opera *Down in the Valley*; originally intended for radio (like *Der Lindberghflug*), it can be seen as a key work without necessarily being one of Weill's best. It grew out of a quest to develop new forms and new outlets with a view to discovering a new audience for musical theatre. It is also an extreme manifestation of Weill's attitude to musical material. The principal melodies are not original, but folksongs – and hence familiar to the audience. The composer's creative imagination is employed elsewhere, in the skilful arrangement of the material into a dramatically convincing whole.

In 1947 Weill could see a progression in his output which had led to his *chef d'oeuvre*, the 'American opera' *Street Scene*, an achievement that embodies the best of his European and American aspirations for a popular yet authentic form of musical theatre. One will look in vain, however, for the traditional European continuity of style, with the problems posed by one work finding a solution in the next. The works do not 'progress' in any immanent way: any continuity between them, as with Busoni's influence, is aesthetic rather than stylistic. If anything, as Virgil Thomson recognized, they are all solutions to one abiding problem, which poses itself anew with every creative task. A true appreciation of Weill's compositions for the musical theatre leads less to their admittance to an imaginary museum of timeless masterpieces than to a more intimate understanding of the tasks he set himself.

5. Posthumous reputation. When Weill died of a heart attack in 1950 during work with Maxwell Anderson on a musical adaptation of *Huckleberry Finn*, he had two reputations: one in the USA, another in Europe. The American obituarists knew little of his European output, and although the authors of the European obituaries had at least a passing acquaintance with the American works, they were scarcely prepared to accept them. Theodor Adorno (*Frankfurter Rundschau*, 15 April 1950) pinpointed a problem: 'The profile of this composer, who died in America, is hardly commensurate with the concept of "composer"'. To be sure, the role Weill assumed as a composer from the mid-1920s onwards was increasingly at odds with 19th-century traditions. To that extent, his putative metamorphosis in America represented less a significant departure, as often maintained, than the continuation of a development already under way. To speak of 'two Weills' is radically to misconstrue that development. To call him 'one of music's great "might-have-beens"', as Weill's indefatigable postwar champion David Drew has done, is to ignore Adorno's point by retrospectively applying a 'concept of the composer', in this case a modernist one, that patently does not fit. More recently, Weill has been categorized as a post-modernist before his time. The considerable rise in his critical stock during the 1980s can indeed be put down to the fact that the 'post-modern condition' adumbrated in so much of his work has become a pervasive cultural force.

See also Aufstieg und Fall der Stadt Mahagonny; Bürgschaft, Die; Down in the Valley; Dreigroschenoper, Die; Happy End; Jasager, Der; Kingdom for a Cow, A; Lady in the Dark; Lost in the Stars; Mahagonny (i); Protagonist, Der; Sieben Todsünden, Die; Silbersee, Der; Street Scene; and Zar lässt sich photographieren, Der.

autograph MSS are of both the full score and the vocal score unless otherwise stated; printed full scores are for hire only, unless otherwise indicated by †

Zriny, 1916 (after T. Körner), lost

Ninon von Lenclos, 1920 (after E. Hardt), lost

Zaubernacht (ballet with song, V. Boritch), Berlin, Kurfürstendamm, 18 Nov 1922, full score lost, vs *US-NH**; arr. Weill as orch suite Quodlibet (Eine Unterhaltungsmusik) op.9, 1923

Der Protagonist op.14 (1, G. Kaiser), Dresden, Staatsoper, 27 March 1926, full score *A-Wst**; (Vienna, 1926)

Royal Palace op.17, 1925–6 (1, I. Goll), Berlin, Staatsoper, 2 March 1927, full score lost, vs (Vienna, 1926); reorch version, Nederlands Congresgebouw, The Hague, 25 June 1971

Na und?, 1926–7 (2, F. Joachimson), unperf., lost

Mahagonny (Songspiel, 3 pts, B. Brecht), Baden-Baden, Kurhaus, Grosser Bühnensaal, 17 July 1927, *US-NH**; (Vienna, 1964)

Der Zar lässt sich photographieren op.21 (ob, 1, Kaiser), Leipzig, Neues, 18 Feb 1928, full score *A-Wst**; (Vienna, 1928)

Die Dreigroschenoper (play with music, prol., 3, Brecht and E. Hauptmann, after J. Gay: *The Beggar's Opera*), Berlin, Schiffbauerdamm, 31 Aug 1928, *Wst**, vs (Vienna, 1928), full score (Vienna, 1972)†

Happy End (comedy with music, 3, D. Lane [E. Hauptmann] and Brecht), Berlin, Schiffbauerdamm, 2 Sept 1929, *Wst**, vs (Vienna, 1958), full score (Vienna, 1981)†

Aufstieg und Fall der Stadt Mahagonny (3, Brecht), Leipzig, Neues, 9 March 1930, full score *Wst**; (Vienna, 1929); derived in part from Mahagonny

Der Jasager (Schuloper, 2, Brecht, after the Jap. noh play *Taniko*), Berlin, Zentralinstitut für Erziehung und Unterricht, 23 June 1930, *Wst**; (Vienna, 1981)†

Die Bürgschaft (3, C. Neher, after J. G. Herder: *Der afrikanische Rechtspruch*), Berlin, Städtische Oper, 10 March 1932, *Wst**, vs (Vienna, 1932), full score (Vienna, 1977)

Der Silbersee: ein Wintermärchen (play with music, 3, Kaiser), simultaneous premières at Leipzig, Altes; Erfurt, Stadt; and Magdeburg, Stadt, 18 Feb 1933, *Wst**; (Vienna, n.d.)

Die sieben Todsünden (ballet chanté, 8 pts, Brecht), Paris, Champs-Elysées, 7 June 1933, full score *US-NYp**, vs (New York, 1955) [transposed version], full score (Mainz, 1968)

Der Kuhhandel, 1934 (operetta, 2, R. Vambery), inc., unperf.; rev. as A Kingdom for a Cow (musical play, 3, R. Arkell; lyrics D. Carter), London, Savoy, 28 June 1935, *NH**; (Mainz, 1989)

Der Weg der Verheissung, 1934–5 (biblical drama, 4, F. Werfel), unperf., autograph lost, copy in Weill-Lenya Research Center, New York; rev. by Weill and L. Lewisohn as The Eternal Road, New York, Manhattan Opera House, 4 Jan 1937, vs (New York, 1937)

Johnny Johnson (musical play, 3, P. Green), New York, 44th Street, 19 Nov 1936, *NH**; (New York, 1936)

Knickerbocker Holiday (musical comedy, 2, M. Anderson), New York, Ethel Barrymore Theatre, 19 Oct 1938, *NH**, vs (New York, 1938)

Davy Crockett, 1938 (musical play, 2, H. R. Hays), inc., vs *NH**

Railroads on Parade ('A Fantasia on Rail Transport', E. Hungerford), New York, World's Fair, 30 April 1939, *NH**

Ulysses Africanus, 1939 (musical play, 2, Anderson), inc., vs *NH**

Lady in the Dark (musical play, 2, M. Hart; lyrics I. Gershwin), Boston, Colonial, 30 Dec 1940, New York, Alvin, 21 Jan 1941, *NH**, vs, ed. A. Sirmay (New York, 1941), restored full score and vs, ed. D. Loud and J. Mauceri (New York, 1987)

One Touch of Venus (musical comedy, S. J. Perelman and O. Nash),

New York, Imperial, 7 Oct 1943, *NH**, vs excerpts (New York, 1984)

The Firebrand of Florence (operetta, E. J. Mayer; lyrics I. Gershwin), New York, Alvin, 22 March 1945, *NH**

Street Scene (American op, 2, E. Rice; lyrics L. Hughes), Philadelphia, Shubert, 16 Dec 1946, New York, Adelphi, 9 Jan 1947, *NH**, vs (New York, 1947), full score (New York, n.d.)

Down in the Valley (folk op, 1, A. Sundgaard), Bloomington, IN, School of Music, 15 July 1948, full score *NYp**, vs *NH**; (New York, 1948)

Love Life (vaudeville, 2 pts, A. J. Lerner), New York, 46th Street, 7 Oct 1948, *NH**

Lost in the Stars (musical tragedy, Anderson, after A. Paton: *Cry, the Beloved Country*), New York, Music Box, 30 Oct 1949; full score lost, copy of score used in first production in Weill-Lenya Research Center, vs *NH**, full score (New York, n.d., 2/1988)

Huckleberry Finn, 1950 (musical, Anderson), inc., songs (New York, 1954) [River Chanty; Apple Jack; This Time Next Year; The Catfish Song; Come in, Mornin']

*

T. W. Adorno: 'Kompositionskritik: Kurt Weill, Kleine Dreigroschenmusik für Blasorchester', *Musikblätter des Anbruch*, xi (1929), 316–17

——: 'Zur Dreigroschenoper', *Die Musik*, xxii (1929–30), 424–8

B. Brecht: 'Anmerkungen zur Oper *Aufstieg und Fall der Stadt Mahagonny*', *Versuche*, ii (Berlin, 1930); repr. in *Gesammelte Werke*, xvii (Frankfurt, 1967), 1004–16

K. Weill: 'Zur Aufführung der Mahagonny-Oper', *Leipziger Neueste Nachrichten* (8 March 1930)

T. W. Adorno: 'Zur gesellschaftlichen Lage der Musik', *Zeitschrift für Sozialforschung*, i (1932), 103–24, 356–78

C. Tolksdorf: *John Gays 'Beggar's Opera' und Bert Brechts 'Dreigroschenoper'* (Rheinberg, 1934)

E. Schumacher: *Die dramatischen Versuche Bertolt Brechts 1918–33*, Neue Beiträge zur Literaturwissenschaft, iii (Berlin, 1954)

D. Drew: 'Topicality and the Universal: the Strange Case of Weill's *Die Bürgschaft*', *ML*, xxxix (1958), 242–55

G. Hartung: 'Zur epischen Oper Brechts und Weills', *Wissenschaftliche Zeitschrift der Martin-Luther-Universität Halle-Wittenberg*, viii (1959), 659–73

J. Willett: *The Theatre of Bertolt Brecht* (London, 1959, 3/1967)

S. Unseld, ed.: *Bertolt Brechts Dreigroschenbuch* (Frankfurt, 1960, 2/1978)

D. Drew: 'Musical Theatre in the Weimar Republic', *PRMA*, lxxxviii (1961–2), 89–108

H. Kotschenreuther: *Kurt Weill* (Berlin, 1962)

D. Drew: 'The History of Mahagonny', *MT*, civ (1963), 18–24

——: 'Weill's School Opera', *MT*, cvi (1965), 934–7 [on *Der Jasager*]

E. J. Aufricht: *Erzähle, damit du dein Recht erweist* (Berlin, 1966)

T. O. Brandt: *Die Vieldeutigkeit Bertolt Brechts* (Heidelberg, 1968)

H. W. Heinsheimer: *Best Regards to Aida* (New York, 1968)

A. Hüfner: *Brecht in Frankreich, 1930–1963: Verbreitung, Aufnahme, Wirkung*, Germanistische Abhandlungen, xxii (Stuttgart, 1968)

U. Weisstein: 'Brecht's Victorian Version of Gay: Imitation and Originality in the *Dreigroschenoper*', *Comparative Literature Studies*, vii (1970), 314–35

F. Hadamowsky: *Caspar Nehers szenisches Werk: ein Verzeichnis des Bestandes der Theatersammlung der österreichischen Nationalbibliothek* (Vienna, 1972)

D. Drew, ed.: *Kurt Weill: ausgewählte Schriften* (Frankfurt, 1975)

——, ed.: *Über Kurt Weill* (Frankfurt, 1975)

G. Seidel: *Bibliographie Bertolt Brecht* (Berlin, 1975)

H. Marx, ed.: *Weill-Lenya* (New York, 1976)

N. Jacobs and P. Ohlsen: *Bertolt Brecht in Britain* (London, 1977)

R. Speirs: 'A Note on the First Published Version of *Die Dreigroschenoper* and its Relation to the Standard Text', *Forum for Modern Language Studies*, xiii (1977), 25–32

G. Wagner: *Weill und Brecht: das musikalische Zeittheater* (Munich, 1977)

M. Wyss: *Brecht in der Kritik: Rezensionen aller Brecht-Uraufführungen* (Munich, 1977)

E. Köhn: 'Das Ruhrepos: Dokumentation eines gescheiterten Projekts', *Brecht-Jb 1977* (Frankfurt, 1978)

K. H. Kowalke: *Kurt Weill in Europe* (Ann Arbor, 1979)

J. Knopf: *Brecht-Handbuch*, i: *Theater* (Stuttgart, 1980)

A. L. Ringer: 'Schoenberg, Weill and Epic Theatre', *Journal of the Arnold Schoenberg Institute*, v (1980), 77–98

——: 'Weill, Schoenberg, und die "Zeitoper"', *Mf*, xxxiii (1980), 465–72

R. Sanders: *The Days Grow Short: the Life and Music of Kurt Weill* (London, 1980)

J. Schebera: *Für Sie porträtiert: Kurt Weill* (Leipzig, 1980)

A. Sundgaard: 'Writing Folk Opera with Kurt Weill: Portrait of the Librettist as a Silenced Composer', *Dramatists Guild Quarterly*, xvi/4 (1980), 24–30

G. Rienäcker: 'Thesen zur Opernästhetik Kurt Weills', *JbMP 1980* (Leipzig, 1981), 116–34

S. H. Borwick: 'Weill's and Brecht's Theories on Music in Drama', *Journal of Musicological Research*, iv (1982), 39–67

D. Jarman: *Kurt Weill: an Illustrated Biography* (Bloomington, IN, 1982)

S. Amzoll: 'Kritik der Radioproduktion: Kurt Weill als Rundfunkpublizist', *Musik und Gesellschaft*, x (1983), 601–5

K. Palm: *Vom Boykott zur Anerkennung: Brecht und Österreich* (Vienna, 1983)

J. Schebera: *Kurt Weill: Leben und Werk, mit Texten und Materialien von und über Kurt Weill* (Leipzig, 1983)

J. Engelhardt: *Gestus und Verfremdung: Studien zum Musiktheater bei Strawinsky und Brecht/Weill*, Berliner musikwissenschaftliche Arbeiten, xxiv (Munich, 1984)

F. Hennenberg: *Das grosse Brecht-Liederbuch* (Frankfurt, 1984)

W. Ruf: 'Gebrauchsmusik in der Oper: der "Alabama Song" von Brecht und Weill', *Festschrift Hans Heinrich Eggebrecht* (Stuttgart, 1984), 411–22

U. Weisstein: 'Von reitenden Boten und singenden Holzfällern: Bertolt Brecht und die Oper', *Brechts Dramen: neue Interpretationen*, ed. W. Hinderer (Stuttgart, 1984), 266–99

A. Beaumont: *Busoni the Composer* (London, 1985)

G. S. Cahn: 'Weimar Music in America: its Reception and Impact', *Centennial Review*, xxix (1985), 186–204

A. Dümling: *Lasst euch nicht verführen: Brecht und die Musik* (Munich, 1985)

W. Hecht, ed.: *Brechts Dreigroschenoper* (Frankfurt, 1985)

F. Hennenberg: 'Weill, Brecht und die "Dreigroschenoper": neue Materialien zur Entstehung und Uraufführung', *ÖMz*, xl (1985), 281–91

S. Hosokawa: 'Distance, Gestus, Quotation: *Aufstieg und Fall der Stadt Mahagonny* of Brecht and Weill', *IRASM*, xvi (1985), 181–99

K. H. Kowalke, ed.: *A New Orpheus: Essays on Kurt Weill* (New Haven, 1986)

J. Willett: *Caspar Neher: Brecht's Designer* (London, 1986)

A. Beaumont, ed.: *Ferruccio Busoni: Selected Letters* (London, 1987)

A. Csampai and D. Holland, eds.: *Bertolt Brecht/Kurt Weill, Die Dreigroschenoper; Igor Strawinsky, The Rake's Progress: Texte, Materialien, Kommentare* (Reinbek bei Hamburg, 1987)

D. Drew: *Kurt Weill: a Handbook* (London, 1987)

H. Fetting, ed.: *Von der Freien Bühne zum Politischen Theater: Drama und Theater im Spiegel der Kritik*, ii: *1919–1933* (Leipzig, 1987)

J. Fuegi: *Bertolt Brecht: Chaos, According to Plan* (Cambridge, 1987)

F. Hennenberg: *Neue Funktionsweisen der Musik und des Musiktheaters in den zwanziger Jahren: Studien über die Zusammenarbeit Bertolt Brechts mit Franz S. Brunier und Kurt Weill* (diss., U. of Halle, 1987)

H. Marx: *Die Broadway-Story: eine Kulturgeschichte des amerikanischen Theaters* (Düsseldorf, 1987)

B. Meyer-Rähnitz: 'Drei Groschen und mehr: Werke von Brecht-Weill auf 78er Schallplatten', *Fox auf 78* (1987), 44–50; (1988), 24–8

S. C. Cook: *Opera for a New Republic: the 'Zeitopern' of Krenek, Weill, and Hindemith* (Ann Arbor, 1988)

D. Farneth: 'From the Archives: Retracing *The Eternal Road*', *Kurt Weill Newsletter*, vi/1 (1988), 10–13

S. Hinton: 'The Concept of Epic Opera: Theoretical Anomalies in the Brecht-Weill Partnership', *Festschrift Carl Dahlhaus* (Laaber, 1988), 285–94

P. W. Humphreys: *Expressions of Einverständnis: Musical Structure and Affective Content in Kurt Weill's Score for Der Jasager* (diss., U. of California, Los Angeles, 1988)

K. H. Kowalke: 'Accounting for Success: Misunderstanding *Die Dreigroschenoper*', *OQ*, vi/3 (1988), 18–38

——: 'In Trivial [?] Pursuit: Who Sings the "Barbarasong"?', *Kurt Weill Newsletter*, vi/2 (1988), 8–11

J. Lucchesi and R. K. Shull: *Musik bei Brecht* (Berlin, 1988)

J. Pritchard: 'Les Ballets 1933', *Ballet Review*, xvi (1988), 13–34
J. Willett: *The Theatre of the Weimar Republic* (New York, 1988)
S. Giles: 'From Althusser to Brecht: Formalism, Materialism and *The Threepenny Opera*', *New Ways in Germanistik*, ed. R. Sheppard (Berg, 1989), 1–25
——: 'Rewriting Brecht: *Die Dreigroschenoper* 1928–1931', *Literaturwissenschaftliches Jb 1989* (Berlin, 1989), 249–79
M. R. Mercado: *Kurt Weill: a Guide to his Works* (New York, 1989)
A. Quinones: 'Aspekte von Kurt Weills Musiktheaterkonzept', *Studien zur Berliner Musikgeschichte*, ed. T. Ebert-Obermeier (Berlin, 1989), 353–9
D. Spoto: *Lenya: a Life* (Boston, 1989)
S. Hinton, ed.: *Kurt Weill: The Threepenny Opera* (Cambridge, 1990)
S. Hinton and J. Schebera, eds.: *Kurt Weill: Musik und Theater, gesammelte Schriften* (Berlin, 1990)
B. Kortländer, W. Meiszies and D. Farneth, eds.: *Vom Kurfürstendamm zum Broadway: Kurt Weill (1900–1950)* (Düsseldorf, 1990)
K. H. Kowalke: 'Hin und Zurück: Kurt Weill at 90', *MT*, cxxxi (1990), 188–92
J. Schebera: *Kurt Weill: eine Biographie in Texten, Bildern, und Dokumenten* (Leipzig, 1990)
R. H. Kornick: *Recent American Opera: a Production Guide* (New York, 1991), 325–7
R. Taylor: *Kurt Weill: Composer in a Divided World* (London, 1991)
H. Edler and K. H. Kowalke, eds.: *A Stranger Here Myself: Kurt Weill Studien* (Hildesheim, 1992) STEPHEN HINTON

Weimar. German town in Thuringia. The first operatic endeavours took place there in the second half of the 17th century: Duke Wilhelm IV's Hofkapellmeister Adam Drese, who held the post from 1652 to 1662, wrote several stage works with music, probably including the operas *Adam und Eva* and *Die erhöhte Dienstbarkeit* to librettos by the court poet Georg Neumark. Touring troupes were performing in Weimar by the turn of the century. Beginning in 1696 they used the newly built baroque opera house in Schloss Wilhelmsburg. The Duchess Anna Amalia became regent in 1756; her enthusiastic support for music and theatre caused her entourage to become known as the Musenhof. *Jagd*, a Singspiel by J. A. Hiller to a libretto by C. F. Weisse, had its première in Weimar in 1770 and went on to become Hiller's most famous work. E. W. Wolf was appointed concert master in 1761 and Hofkapellmeister in 1772. He composed music for visiting theatrical companies including A. Seyler's troupe, which was resident at Weimar from 1771 to 1774. Seyler's company performed the first German melodrama, *Pygmalion*, in 1772, and the first German grand opera, *Alceste*, in 1773. Both were composed by Anton Schweitzer, Seyler's Kapellmeister, and were highly successful. The theatre at Schloss Wilhelmsburg burnt down in 1774 and Seyler's company left the court that year.

Goethe, who came to Weimar in 1775, formed an amateur dramatic company, the Liebhabertheater, which performed at various venues in the city, at court and on open-air stages in the castles at Belvedere and Tiefurt. The Komödienhaus, built in 1780, was visited by touring troupes bringing Italian and French comic operas. Goethe became the first director of the newly founded Weimar Staatstheater company, based at the Komödienhaus, in 1791; he shared the post with Schiller from 1799 to 1805, then continued in it alone until 1817. Under his direction the company staged plays, Singspiels and operas, notably those by Mozart (except *Idomeneo*), and toured to other cities in the region. Premières in Weimar during this period included Duchess Anna Amalia's *Erwin und Elmire* (1776) and her *Das Jahrmarktfest* (1778), both to librettos by Goethe; and K. S. von Seckendorff's *Lila* (1776), *Proserpina* (1778) and *Jery und Bätely* (1780), also by Goethe. In 1816 Beethoven's *Fidelio* appeared in the repertory for the first time. J. N. Hummel, Hofkapellmeister from 1819 to 1837, conducted works by Rossini and Gluck. He was succeeded in 1840 by the French composer H.-A.-B. Chelard, who continued to broaden the repertory, encouraged by the patronage of the Grand Duchess Maria Paulovna, a Russian Grand Princess and herself a composer. Franz Liszt had been made honorary Kapellmeister in 1842; he moved to Weimar in 1848 and through his influence the theatrical and musical life of the city expanded. In 1849 he conducted Wagner's *Tannhäuser* in its first production since its première at Dresden, and in 1850 gave the première of *Lohengrin*. He conducted the premières of Schumann's incidental music for Byron's *Manfred* in

Design by J. W. von Goethe for the first Weimar production of Mozart's 'Die Zauberflöte' at the Komödienhaus, 16 January 1794

1852, of Schubert's *Alfonso und Estrella* in 1854 and of Cornelius's *Der Barbier von Bagdad* in 1858. The last-named production provoked anti-Liszt demonstrations, causing Liszt to resign his post; he left Weimar in 1861, but returned from time to time between 1869 and 1886. Other premières in the following years included *Samson et Dalila* by Saint-Saëns (1877) and *Agnes Bernauer* by Felix Mottl (1880).

Under Eduard Lassen, music director from 1858 to 1895, Weimar gave the first production of *Tristan* (1874) after the opera's première in Munich. An opera school was added to the orchestral school in 1885, and a drama department established in 1898. The young Richard Strauss came to Weimar in 1889 and gave the first performances of Humperdinck's *Hänsel und Gretel* (1893) and his own first opera *Guntram* (1894). A new theatre building with 1084 seats was opened on 11 January 1908; in 1919 the Hoftheater was renamed the Deutsches Nationaltheater Weimar. First performances between the World Wars included Alexander Tcherepnin's *Ol-Ol* and Mark Lothar's *Tyll* (both 1928). The theatre, rebuilt in the neo-classical style in 1940 and reopened later that year, was destroyed in an air raid in 1945, but was rebuilt and opened again on 28 August 1948 with Verdi's *Otello*. Further reconstruction work was done from 1973 to 1975; the theatre now has 857 seats. First performances since the war have included Alan Bush's *Men of Blackmoor* (1956), J. K. Forest's *Die Blumen von Hiroshima* (1967) and G. Rosenfeld's *Der Mantel* (1978).

*

E. Pasqué: *Goethes Theaterleitung in Weimar* (Leipzig, 1863)
C. A. H. Burkhardt: 'Das Repertoire des Weimarischen Theaters unter Goethes Leitung', *Vom Mittelalter zur Neuzeit* (Hamburg and Leipzig, 1891)
A. Bartels: *Chronik des Weimarischen Hoftheaters 1817–1907* (Weimar, 1912)
C. Höfer: *Vom ältesten Weimarischen Hoftheater* (Leipzig, 1912)
W. Bode: *Der Weimarer Musenhof* (Berlin, 1925)
L. Schrickel: *Die Geschichte des Weimarer Theaters* (Weimar, 1928)
A. Orel: *Goethe als Operndirektor* (Bregenz, 1949)
G. Ohlhoff: 'R. Strauss' Berufung nach Weimar', *SMz*, civ (1964), 155–64
H. John: *Musikstadt Weimar* (Leipzig, 1985)

DIETER HÄRTWIG

Weinberg, Moisey Samuilovich. *See* VAYNBERG, MOISEY SAMUILOVICH.

Weinberger, Jaromír (*b* Prague, 8 Jan 1896; *d* St Petersburg, FL, 8 Aug 1967). Czech composer, later naturalized American. He was a piano pupil of Jaroslav Křička, Václav Talich, Rudolf Karel and others in Prague, and studied composition at the Prague Conservatory with Novák and in Leipzig with Reger. After a period of teaching in the USA (1922–3) he became musical Dramaturg at the Slovak National Theatre in Bratislava (1923–4) and around that time composed his first opera, *Kocourkov*; Pietro Mascagni, who attended the première, liked the music and took a personal interest in the young composer. Weinberger first entertained the idea of composing an opera entitled *Švanda dudák* ('Švanda the Bagpiper') in 1922, but it was not until 1924 that he concentrated fully on the work. He and the librettist Miloš Kareš, a personal friend, collaborated closely on it, and it was first performed at the National Theatre in Prague under Otakar Ostrčil in 1927. A tuneful folk drama in the tradition of *The Bartered Bride* and based on a Czech children's story, it was the first Czech opera since Smetana's to be widely performed internationally. Soon after the première it was published by Universal Edition in German translation as *Schwanda, der Dudelsackpfeifer* with the libretto adapted by Max Brod (Vienna, 1928), and this version was first performed in Breslau on 16 December 1928.

After the Munich première of *Švanda* (1929), the musical director Hans Knappertsbusch commissioned another opera for that city from Weinberger. This was *Milovaný hlas* (*Die geliebte Stimme*, 1931), which is set in a Yugoslav village. Neither this nor Weinberger's later operas, however, made the same impact. *Lidé z Pokerflatu* ('The People from Poker Flat', 1932) failed at its première, and *Valdštejn* (*Wallenstein*, 1937) met with only limited success. *Jarní bouře* (*Frühlingssturme*, 1933), the best of his four operettas, was well received, however. In the face of Nazi persecution Weinberger fled to Paris and in 1939 settled in the USA, first in New York and then in St Petersburg, Florida, where he eventually committed suicide.

See also ŠVANDA THE BAGPIPER.

Kocourkov, 1923–4, perf. in Vienna, MS (private collection)
Švanda dudák [Švanda the Bagpiper] (2, M. Kareš), Prague, National, 27 April 1927; as Schwanda, der Dudelsackpfeifer (lib. rev. M. Brod), Breslau, 16 Dec 1928; (Vienna and Leipzig, 1929)
Milovaný hlas [Die geliebte Stimme] (3, Weinberger, after R. Michel), Munich, National, 28 Feb 1931 (Leipzig, 1930)
Lidé z Pokerflatu [The People from Poker Flat] (5, Kareš, after B. Harte), Brno, Provisional, 19 Nov 1932
Valdštejn [Wallenstein] (6 scenes, Kareš, after F. von Schiller), Vienna, Staatsoper, 18 Nov 1937, vs (Vienna, 1937); Ger. trans. Brod

Operettas: Jarní bouře [Frühlingssturme] (G. Beer), Berlin, 1933; Na růžích ustláno [In a Bed of Roses] (B. Polach and F. Kožík), Brno, 1933; Apropó, co dělá Andula? [By the Way, What is Andula Doing?] (Polach and J. Žalman), Hradbačh, Brno, 5 Sept 1934; Císař pán na třešních [The Emperor and Lord of the Cherries] (Polach and Žalman), Prague, Velká, Nov 1936

*

O. Erhardt: 'Schwanda and the Czech Folk Opera', *Sackbut*, xi (1930–31), 23–6
A. Balatka: 'J. Weinberger, M. Brod, i M. Kareš', *Divadelni list*, viii (1932), 142, 169; ix (1933), 2, 10, 37
J. Tyrrell: *Czech Opera* (Cambridge, 1988)

J. POLACEK

Weinert [Wainert, Wajnert, Weynert, Veinert], **Antoni** (*b* Lusdorf, 2 June 1751; *d* Warsaw, 18 June 1850). Polish composer of Czech origin. He studied music in his native Bohemia, and in 1773 moved to Poland with Prince Lubomirski, teaching at his residence in Opole until 1774. He then moved to Warsaw, where he became a flautist in the theatre orchestra. From 1778 to 1795 he played in the court orchestra of King Stanisław August, and later was its director. After the fall of the Polish state he served in Rogalin (near Poznań) at the ducal court of the Raczyńskis, but in 1803 returned to Warsaw and until 1839 was first flautist at the National Theatre. Weinert composed three operas, all of which are lost, as well as choral and piano works. His son Filip (*b* Rogalin, 26 May 1798; *d* Warsaw, 15 Aug 1843) made his début at the Warsaw Opera in 1819 and sang there for a number of years.

Skrupuł niepotrzebny [Unnecessary Scruple] (Spl, Weinert), Warsaw, 1782
Donnerwetter (Spl, L. Pierożyński or J. Srokowski), Warsaw, 17 Jan 1787
Diabeł alchimista [Satan, the Alchemist] (Spl, J. Drodzowski, after M. A. le Grand: *L'amour diable*), Warsaw, 1797

*

M. Karasowski: *Rys historyczny opery polskiej* [A Historical Outline of Polish Opera] (Warsaw, 1859), 201ff

ZOFIA CHECHLIŃSKA

Weingartner, (Paul) Felix, Edler von Münzberg (*b* Zara, Dalmatia, 2 June 1863; *d* Winterthur, 7 May 1942). Austrian conductor and composer. He studied composition at Graz under W. A. Rémy and in 1881, on Hanslick's recommendation, went to Leipzig as a student of philosophy, soon joining the conservatory. In 1883 Liszt took him under his wing at Weimar; *Sakuntala*, his first opera, was produced there in 1884. Later that year he obtained his first conducting post, at the Königsberg Opera, and he subsequently conducted seasons at Danzig, Hamburg and Mannheim. From 1891 to 1898 he was court Kapellmeister of the Berlin Opera; then, after a period conducting concerts in Berlin and Munich, he succeeded Mahler at the Vienna Hofoper (1908–11). He was guest conductor at the Hamburg Opera (1912–14), principal conductor at Darmstadt (1914–19) and director of the Vienna Volksoper (1919–24); he also worked extensively abroad, with the Boston Opera Company (1912–13) and various orchestras. In 1927 he moved to Basle and until 1933 was director of the conservatory. From 1935 to 1936 he was again briefly at the head of the Vienna Opera (now the Staatsoper). He published several books on conducting.

Although Weingartner as a young man was profoundly influenced by Wagner and Liszt, his name was scarcely associated with the progressive school that followed them. He is remembered as one of the most eminent classical conductors of his day, outstanding for the clarity and economy of his beat, the lack of exaggeration in his interpretations and the precision without rigidity of his tempos. He was anxious to succeed in opera as both conductor and composer, but in the two most important posts of his career, in Berlin and Vienna, opposition led him to resign from the opera long before he gave up the concerts that normally went with it. He was at his finest in the concert hall, but while he may have been born with one skin too few for the rough and tumble of the theatre, the view that his temperament was essentially undramatic was not fully borne out by distinguished performances of *Tannhäuser* and *Parsifal* at Covent Garden in 1939. British admirers who revered him as the authority on Beethoven might have been surprised by his fondness for comic opera, which he was able to indulge in Vienna. Weingartner's operas had some success in their time, *Genesius* (1892) being quite widely performed. Yet the recognition he longed for as a prolific composer of large-scale music continued to elude him. His third wife was the singer Lucille Marcel.

all librettos by the composer

Sakuntala op.9 (Bühnenspiel, 3, after Kalidasa), Weimar, 23 March 1884 (Kassel and Leipzig, 1884)
Malawika op.10 (Komödie, 3, after Kalidasa), Munich, 3 June 1886, vs (Kassel and Leipzig, 1886)
Genesius op.14 (3, after H. Herrig), Berlin, 15 Nov 1892, vs (Berlin, 1892)
Orestes: Agamemnon, Das Totenopfer, Die Erinyen op.30 (after Aeschylus), Leipzig, Stadt, 15 Feb 1902, vs (Leipzig, 1902)
Kain und Abel op.54 (1), Darmstadt, Hof, 17 May 1914, vs (Leipzig, 1914)
Dame Kobold op.57 (komische Oper, 3, after P. Calderón de la Barca), Darmstadt, Hof, 23 Feb 1916, vs (Vienna and Leipzig, 1916)
Die Dorfschule op.64 (1, after Jap. play *Terakoya*), Vienna, Staatsoper, 13 May 1920, vs (Vienna and Leipzig, 1919)
Meister Andrea op.66 (2, after E. Geibel), Vienna, Staatsoper, 13 May 1920, vs (Vienna and Leipzig, 1919)
Der Apostat op.72 (3), unperf.

F. Weingartner: *Lebenserinnerungen* (Vienna, 1923, 2/1929; Eng. trans. as *Buffets and Rewards*, 1937)
Festschrift für Dr. Felix Weingartner zu seinem siebzigsten Geburtstag (Basle, 1933)
E. Evans: Obituary, *MR*, iii (1942), 214–18
H. C. Schonberg: *The Great Conductors* (New York, 1967)
F. Weingartner: *Weingartner on Music and Conducting* (New York, 1969)
D. Wooldridge: *Conductor's World* (London, 1970)
C. Dyment: *Felix Weingartner: Recollections and Recordings* (Rickmansworth, 1976)

RONALD CRICHTON

Weinstock, Herbert (*b* Milwaukee, 16 Nov 1905; *d* New York, 21 Oct 1971). American writer on music. He studied at the University of Chicago, then worked for the book publishers Alfred A. Knopf in New York, 1943–59 and 1963–71, notably as music editor. He was a fluent and prolific writer, especially on operatic subjects.

with W. Brockway: *The Opera: a History of its Creation and Performance* (New York, 1941, 2/1962 as *The World of Opera*)
Tchaikovsky (New York, 1943; Fr. trans., 1947; Ger. trans., 1948)
Handel (New York, 1946, 2/1959; Ger. trans., 1950)
Donizetti and the World of Opera in Italy, Paris and Vienna in the First Half of the Nineteenth Century (New York, 1963)
Rossini: a Biography (New York and London, 1968)
Vincenzo Bellini: his Life and Operas (New York, 1971)

Weir, Judith (*b* Aberdeen, 11 May 1954). Scottish composer. While at school she studied informally with John Tavener, and afterwards at Cambridge University (1973–6) with Robin Holloway. She taught at Glasgow University (1979–82), and held a creative arts fellowship at Trinity College, Cambridge (1983–5). In many of her works of the late 1970s and early 80s she explored the theatrical possibilities of instrumental genres, and two of them in particular – the 'grand opera in three acts for solo soprano', *King Harald's Saga* (1979), and the 'Chinese chamber opera', *The Consolations of Scholarship* (1985) – may be regarded as preliminary studies for her first full-length opera, *A Night at the Chinese Opera* (1987). Based in part upon a Chinese Yuan dynasty play, a realization of which makes up the second act, the work demonstrates the operatic possibilities of Weir's highly personal and accessible musical language, with its roots in Britten, Stravinsky and Messiaen, as well as the detached, wry humour of her stagecraft. In *Heaven Ablaze in his Breast* (1989), an elaborate treatment of E. T. A. Hoffmann's *The Sandman*, Weir blurred conventional distinctions between ballet and opera by requiring her dancers to sing and vocalists to dance. But *The Vanishing Bridegroom* (1990) was more conventionally 'operatic'; in bringing together three West Highland folktales, all concerned with loss and deliverance, whose stories remain distinct but share some characters, Weir maintains the detachment of *A Night at the Chinese Opera*. Despite its fond references to Scottish musical styles, her music remains adept at moving between narrative and lyricism, and in inventing arresting textures and motifs.

See also NIGHT AT THE CHINESE OPERA, A.

all librettos by the composer

King Harald's Saga ('grand opera', 2, after the Icelandic saga *Heimskringla*), Dumfries Music Club, 17 May 1979
The Black Spider (3, after J. Gotthelf: *Die schwarze Spinne*), Canterbury Cathedral, crypt, 6 March 1985
The Consolations of Scholarship (music drama, 2, after the *Yuan* dramas), U. of Durham, 5 May 1985

A Night at the Chinese Opera (3, after C. Chun-Hsiang: *The Chao Family Orphan*), Cheltenham, Everyman, 8 July 1987
Heaven Ablaze in his Breast (1, after E. T. A. Hoffmann: *The Sandman*), Basildon, Towngate, 5 Oct 1989
The Vanishing Bridegroom (3, after *Popular Tales of the West Highlands*), Glasgow, Royal, 17 Oct 1990

*

J. Weir: 'A Note on a Chinese Opera', *MT*, cxxviii (1987), 373–5
T. Morgan: 'Judith Weir', *New Music 88* (1988), 22–50
F. Maddocks: 'Highland Wedding', *Opera Now* (Oct 1990), 32–5
R. Milnes: 'The Vanishing Bridegroom', *Opera*, xli (1990), 1496–1500
ANDREW CLEMENTS

Weis [Weiss], **Karel** (*b* Prague, 13 Feb 1862; *d* Prague, 4 April 1944). Czech composer. He studied in Prague at the conservatory (1873–8) and the organ school (1878–81); he also took private lessons in opera composition with Fibich. His posts included one as violinist in the Prague National Theatre orchestra (1883–6) and another as conductor of the Švanda Theatre Company in Prague and Brno (1886–7). He later edited a musical journal and worked as an accompanist but from 1896 gave most of his attention to collecting and arranging folksongs. His writings include memoirs of Smetana and Dvořák and folklore studies.

Weis belonged to a generation influenced by Smetana and Dvořák. He identified himself with late Romanticism, his musical language being an eclectic offshoot of the Czech style which Smetana, Dvořák and Fibich had created. Though in songs and choral works he complied fully with the demand for patriotic music, he met with strong opposition from the Czech bourgeoisie for using German texts in his operas *Der polnische Jude* and *Der Sturm auf die Mühle*. Opera was at the centre of his large and varied output, but he is chiefly valued for his 15-volume folksong collection (1928–41).

Viola (comic op, 3, B. Adler, R. Schubert and V. Novohradský, after W. Shakespeare: *Twelfth Night*), Prague, National, 17 Jan 1892; rev. as Blíženci [The Twins] (lib. adapted by J. Vymětal), Prague, National, 28 Feb 1917
Der polnische Jude (folk op, 2, V. Léon and R. Batka, after Erckmann-Chatrian), Prague, Neues Deutsches, 3 March 1901; as Polský žid, Prague, Vinohradech, 1907
Die Dorfmusikanten (operetta, 3, R. Haas, after J. K. Tyl: *Švanda dudák*), Prague, Neues Deutsches, 1 Jan 1905
Der Revisor (operetta, 3, Weis, O. D. Batěk and F. Paul, after N. Gogol), Prague, Neues Deutsches, 21 April 1907
Die Sultansbraut (operetta, 3, R. Pohl, after K. Mekszathov), Berlin 1910
Der Sturm auf die Mühle [Útok na mlýn] (folk op, 3, Weis and Batka, after E. Zola), Prague, National, 29 March 1912
Big-Ben (operetta, 3), Berlin, Westens, 1912
Der Extrazug nach Nizza (operetta, 1, A. Lippshitz and M. Schönau), Berlin, 1913
Tanzmaus (operetta, 1, F. Hlavatý), Vienna, Apollo, 1 Aug 1916
Lešetínský kovář [The Lešetín Blacksmith] (folk op, 3, L. Novák and Weis, after S. Čech), Prague, National, 6 June 1920
Bojarská svatba [The Boyar's Wedding] (3, Weis, after L. Ganghofer), Prague, National, 18 Feb 1943

*

F. Pala: 'Karel Weis', *České umění dramatické*, ii: *Zpěvohra* [Czech Dramatic Art: Opera], ed. J. Hutter and Z. Chalabala (Prague, 1941), 309–14
V. Blažek: 'Život a dílo Karla Weise' [The Life and Work of Weis], *Smetana*, xxxv (1942), 53–4
OLDŘICH PUKL

Weisgall, Hugo (David) (*b* Ivançice [Eibenschütz], Bohemia, 13 Oct 1912). American composer. After emigrating to the USA with his parents in 1920, he studied the piano, harmony and composition at the Peabody Conservatory in Baltimore (1927–32), and then composition intermittently with Roger Sessions (1932–41). Studies with Fritz Reiner and Rosario Scalero at the Curtis Institute in Philadelphia earned him diplomas in conducting (1938) and composition (1939). In 1940 Johns Hopkins University awarded him the PhD for his dissertation on primitivism in 17th-century German poetry. After military service in Europe, he returned to the USA in 1947, becoming active as an administrator and teacher, as well as a composer, conductor and singer; he founded and conducted the Chamber Society of Baltimore (1948) and the Hilltop Opera Company (1952). He was director of the Baltimore Institute of Musical Arts (1949–51), and then taught at Johns Hopkins University (1951–7) and at the Juilliard School (1957–70). He was president of the American Music Center, 1963–73, and was named Distinguished Professor of Music, CUNY (1979).

Weisgall is one of America's most important composers of opera. The literary merit of his works, their original vocal style and their attention to musical and dramatic detail mark a significant contribution to the genre. They are often based on literary classics and deal with crucial philosophical, social and moral dilemmas of the 20th century. Stylistically, Weisgall's music has evolved gradually and logically, with each work being differentiated in dramatic treatment and musical structure. In his first mature opera, *The Tenor* (composed 1948–50), large symphonic structures alternate with arias; in *The Stronger* (1952) smaller musical segments follow the single character's volatile shifts of mood. *Six Characters in Search of an Author* (1953–6), commissioned by the Ditson Fund, fuses the two procedures and uses transformed recapitulations and epigrammatic musical ideas to punctuate events or sections; it is perhaps Weisgall's most theatrically successful full-length opera. *The Stronger*, only 25 minutes long, is his best-known work.

The one-act *Purgatory* (1958) breaks with previous formal techniques in employing a continuous vocal arioso. This work is also the first by Weisgall to employ 12-note procedures and to be consistently atonal. If *Purgatory* departs from preceding works in style, *Athaliah* (1960–63) does so in form. It contains rigorously dodecaphonic sections, with monumental setpieces and a skilful use of the chorus, harking back to the 17th-century *tragédie lyrique*. *Athaliah* was commissioned by Thomas Scherman and the Little Orchestra Society. *Nine Rivers from Jordan* (1964–8), a huge, cinematographic work in three acts, is about moral dilemmas raised by World War II. Real events merge with imaginary ones, emphasizing a favourite theme: illusion versus reality. Many languages, subtle quoting, parody and Weisgall's most expansive orchestral music all suggest the confusion of the war years.

Jenny, or The Hundred Nights (1975–6), commissioned by the Juilliard School and the National Endowment for the Arts, is an elaborate one-act work that transfers Yukio Mishima's modern noh play to 19th-century London; through Weisgall's sumptuous but veiled orchestral tapestry and the highly stylized poetic language of the librettist John Hollander, the mystery play unfolds as through a scrim. *The Gardens of Adonis* (1959; revised 1977–81), a full-length opera, is more transparent orchestrally; the work employs recitatives, arias and ensembles, and combines free atonality with jaunty, neo-classical rhythmic features.

Weisgall's earlier style fused non-tonal neo-classicism with Bergian rubato and opulence. His later music is closest to the Second Viennese School, though rarely completely atonal. Melodically and harmonically it revolves within small groups of pitches, often saving certain notes for contrast later on. Even in serial passages, the 12 pitches are introduced gradually so that the listener apprehends a high degree of pitch sensitivity. Weisgall's unique vocal lines delineate character and form the core of the musical fabric. His fluid prosody follows the rhythms of American speech in written-out rubato, while always retaining strong melodic direction.

Weisgall's view of the future of American opera is not an entirely optimistic one. He sees the need for more arts education in the USA, as well as a larger arena for contemporary composers of opera to see their works performed. A strong believer in opera in English, even if not the original language, Weisgall also dislikes 'new' stagings of traditional works, believing that they show a lack of faith in the work.

See also STRONGER, THE and TENOR, THE.

Night, 1932 (1, after S. Asch)
Lilith, 1934 (1, after L. Elman)
The Tenor, 1948–50 (1, K. Shapiro and E. Lert, after F. Wedekind: *Der Kammersänger*), Baltimore, 11 Feb 1952
The Stronger (1, R. Hart, after A. Strindberg: *Den starkare*), Westport, CT, White Barn, Hilltop Opera Company, 9 Aug 1952 (with pf); New York, Columbia U. Composers Forum, Jan 1955 (with orch)
Six Characters in Search of an Author, 1953–6 (3, D. Johnston, after L. Pirandello), New York, City Opera, 26 April 1959
Purgatory, 1958 (1, after W. B. Yeats), Washington DC, Library of Congress, 17 Feb 1961
The Gardens of Adonis, 1959 (3 scenes, J. Olon-Scrymgeour, after W. Shakespeare and A. Obey: *Venus and Adonis*); rev. 1977–81, Omaha, NE, Joslyn Art Museum, Witherspoon Concert Hall, 12 Sept 1992
Athaliah, 1960–63 (2 pts, R. F. Goldman, after J. Racine), New York, Concert Opera Association, 17 Feb 1964
Nine Rivers from Jordan, 1964–8 (prol., 3, Johnston), New York, City Opera, 9 Oct 1968
Jenny, or The Hundred Nights (1, J. Hollander, after Y. Mishima: *Sotoba Komachi*), New York, American Opera Center, Juilliard School, 22 April 1976
Will you Marry me? (1, C. Kondek, after A. Sutro: *A Marriage has been Arranged*), New York, 8 March 1989
Esther, 1992 (3, Kondek, after the Bible)

*

H. Cowell: 'Current Chronicle', *MQ*, xxxviii (1952), 285–7 [on *The Tenor*]
A. Shulsky: 'The Operas of Hugo Weisgall', *Etude*, lxxiv (1956), 15–40, passim
R. F. Goldman: 'Review of Records', *MQ*, xliii (1957), 132–4 [on *The Stronger*]
——: 'Current Chronicle', *MQ*, xlv (1959), 381–5 [on *Six Characters*]
H. W. Hitchcock: 'Current Chronicle', *MQ*, l (1964), 233–6 [on *Athaliah*]
A. Rich: 'Hugo Weisgall: *Athaliah*', *PNM*, iii/1 (1964–5), 156–8
A. Balkin: *The Operas of Hugo Weisgall* (diss., Columbia U. Teachers College, 1968)
J. A. Brooks: *Technical Aspects of the Music in the Major Operas of Hugo Weisgall* (diss., U. of Washington, St Louis, 1971)
M. Blumenfeld: 'Hugo Weisgall's 66th Birthday and the New *Gardens of Adonis*', *PNM*, xvi/2 (1977–8), 156–66
H. Weisgall: 'America's Opera', *Arts Review* (1988)
R. H. Kornick: *Recent American Opera: a Production Guide* (New York, 1991), 328–33

BRUCE SAYLOR, JAMES P. CASSARO

Weismann, Julius (*b* Freiburg, 26 Dec 1879; *d* Singen am Hohentweil, 22 Dec 1950). German composer and conductor. He was a pupil of Rheinberger, Dimmler, Bussmeyer, Herzogenberg and Thuille. From 1902 until 1906 he lived as a freelance composer in Munich, then returned to Freiburg where he also performed as a conductor, pianist and lieder accompanist. From 1930 he taught harmony and was director of the piano masterclass at the Freiburg Musikseminar which he founded with Erich Doflein; he retired in 1939 to devote himself to composition.

Weismann occupies a transitional position within the development of 20th-century German opera somewhat akin to that of his immediate contemporary, Walter Braunfels. His music draws upon the late Romantic styles of Strauss, Humperdinck and Schillings, but also incorporates elements of impressionistic harmony as well as a polyphonic severity related to Reger. These diverse influences are manipulated with great technical skill, but they tend to obfuscate any individual touches in his work. A more important feature is his predilection for setting established works of literature as operatic material. He demonstrated a special interest in the plays of Strindberg, three of which he made into operas between 1919 and 1930. Of these, *Schwanenweiss* (composed 1919–20) was the most performed during the 1920s and 30s. It is characterized by an effective use of leitmotif technique and a sensitive response to orchestral colouring but ultimately lacks dramatic tension. In contrast, the comedy *Leonce und Lena*, drawn from Büchner and completed at almost the same time as Berg's *Wozzeck*, reveals more flexibility and marks an advance in harmonic language. The composer attained greater recognition in his own country after 1933, especially when he accepted an official commission from the National Socialist Kulturgemeinde to write incidental music to replace Mendelssohn's *Ein Sommernachtstraum*. As a consequence his final opera, *Die pfiffige Magd* (1937–8), received an auspicious première in Leipzig in 1939 and was performed over 150 times in German theatres during the next five years. In moving away from the expressionist dramas of Strindberg to the comic milieu of Holberg, Weismann demonstrated a surer touch and a more clearly delineated approach to characterization. Moreover, he provided the German people with the necessary escapist material to help them through the traumas of war.

Schwanenweiss op.75 (3, Weismann, after A. Strindberg), Duisburg, 23 Sept 1923, vs (Mainz, 1924)
Ein Traumspiel op.83 (3, Weismann, after Strindberg), Duisburg, 23 April 1925, unpubd
Leonce und Lena op.89 (3, Weismann, after G. Büchner), Freiburg, 21 June 1925, pubd Cologne
Regina del Lago op.91, 1925–6 (3, E. Stuber, after W. Cale), Karlsruhe, 18 April 1928, unpubd
Die Gespenstersonate op.100 (2, Weismann, after Strindberg), Munich, 19 Dec 1930, vs (Karlsruhe, 1930)
Die pfiffige Magd op.125 (komische Oper, 3, after L. Holberg), Leipzig, Neues, 11 Feb 1939 (Mainz, 1939)

*

E. Doflein, ed.: *Julius Weismann: gesammelte Beiträge über Persönlichkeit und Werk* (Freiburg, 1925)
G. E. Lessing: 'Weismanns Leonce und Lena, eine Analyse', *Das Prisma*, Blätter der Vereinigten Bühnen Duisburg-Bochum, ii/7 (1925), 65–71
F. W. Herzog: 'Julius Weismann als Opernkomponist', *Neue Musikzeitung*, xlvii (1926), 6–12
——: 'Julius Weismann zum 50. Geburtstag', *AMz*, li–lii (1929)
R. Bechtold: 'Julius Weismann: zu seinem 50. Geburtstag am 26. Dezember', *Die Musik*, xxii (1929–30), 181–2
E.-L. Stahl: 'Weismanns Gespenstersonate: zu ihrer Münchner Uraufführung', *Beiblatt zum Programm des Nationaltheaters, München* (Dec 1930)
G. von Grävenitz: 'Julius Weismann', *ZfM*, xcviii (1931), 9–14
J. Müller-Blattau: 'Leben und Werk', *Julius Weismann zum 60. Geburtstag* (Freiburg, 1939), 3–11
W. Zentner: 'Julius Weismann zum 60. Geburtstag', *ZfM*, cvi (1939), 1156–8
H. Unger: *Von Wagner bis Weismann: Bildnisse neuerer deutscher Komponisten* (Cologne, 1940)

C. Niessen: *Die deutsche Oper der Gegenwart* (Regensburg, 1944)
O. Riemer: 'Julius Weismann: der Siebzigjährige', *Musica*, iii (1949), 452–3
A. Würz: 'Julius Weismann', *ZfM*, cxii (1951), 29
O. C. A. zur Nedden: 'Zu Julius Weismanns komische Oper "Die pfiffige Magd"', *108 Niederrheinische Musikfest* (Duisburg, 1954), 86–91
W. Falcke: *Verzeichnis sämtliche Werke von Julius Weismann, nebst Verzeichnis des Schriftums und der Ansprachen über Julius Weismann und seine Werke* (Duisburg, 1955)
H. J. Moser: 'Julius Weismann', *Musica*, ix (1955), 266–9
W. A. Berendsohn: *August Strindberg und die Musik* (Duisburg, 1957)
J. Müller-Blattau: 'Der Komponist Julius Weismann', *NZM*, Jg.120 (1959), 609–10
F. Herzfeld: *Julius Weismann und seine Generation* (Duisburg, 1965)
ERIK LEVI

Weiss, Karel. *See* WEIS, KAREL.

Weissberg, Yuliya Lazarevna. *See* VEYSBERG, YULIYA LAZAREVNA.

Weisse, Christian Felix (*b* Annaberg, Erzgebirge, 28 Jan 1726; *d* Leipzig, 16 Dec 1804). German poet, dramatist and librettist. He went to Leipzig in 1745 to study philology and theology and settled there permanently. In the 1750s he established his reputation as a dramatist and lyric poet. He also prepared German versions of two popular English ballad operas, *The Devil to Pay* and *The Merry Cobbler*, both set by J. C. Standfuss. During the Seven Years War Weisse travelled with the count he served to Paris, where he remained from 1759 to 1760, meeting Rousseau and being much struck by the naive and popular charm of C.-S. Favart's comic operas. When he began writing German librettos again for the Koch company at Leipzig in 1763, Weisse at first reworked his two early texts but then turned to French models.

In the settings by J. A. Hiller, Weisse's dramas of idealized rustic simplicity and virtue found immediate favour and unprecedented box-office success throughout Germany, although he never took them seriously as dramas. He continued to produce new librettos over the next decade, always at Koch's urging. After 1773, irked by professional criticism, Weisse ceased writing librettos for public performance. From 1776 to 1782 he edited a periodical for children, *Der Kinderfreund*, to which he contributed several didactic one-act comic operas, set by Hiller, Georg Benda and Michael Haydn.

Although Weisse sought to moderate the earthy tone of his English models, his first two operas remain farces tinged with sentimental touches. They were favourites throughout the century. His subsequent French-inspired librettos all turn on the familiar opposition of rustic innocence (variously plucky or saccharine) and the corrupt insincerity of the court or city. Weisse envisioned only the simplest role for Hiller's music, to which the indifferent abilities of the singers in many German companies also contributed. The musical texts are largely decorative strophic songs that stand apart from any dramatic involvement; on occasion they were simply omitted and the libretto was presented with success as a spoken drama. As later German writers were to do, Weisse published his librettos as independent works for the reading public.

Die Jagd (1770, Weimar) forms the summit of Weisse's collaboration with Hiller, both epitomizing and perfecting the features common to all their comic operas: the simple if static joys of country life, a preoccupation with sympathetic characters including a benevolent and fatherly ruler, a tearful reunion scene as the dramatic climax and lyric emphasis on the female partner of each of its three couples. With rather severe musical restructuring, Weisse's text was set as a two-act drama by Johann Schenk for Vienna in 1799. Hiller's version has remained popular in Germany into the present century.

komische Opern unless otherwise stated

Die verwandelten Weiber, oder Der Teufel ist los, erster Theil, J. C. Standfuss and J. A. Hiller, 1766; *Der lustige Schuster, oder Der Teufel ist los, zweyter Theil*, Standfuss and Hiller, 1766; *Lottchen am Hofe*, Hiller, 1767; *Die Liebe auf dem Lande*, Hiller, 1768; *Die Jagd*, Hiller, 1770 (J. B. Schenk, 1799); *Der Ärndtekranz*, Hiller, 1771; *Der Dorfbalbier*, Hiller and Neefe, 1771; *Der Krieg* (with C. F. Ramler), Hiller, 1772; *Die Jubelhochzeit*, Hiller, 1773; *Die Schadenfreude* (kleines Lustspiel für Kinder mit Liederchen), G. P. Weimar, 1776 (André, 1778); *Die kleine Ährenleserinn* (Lustspiel für Kinder), Hiller, 1778, unperf.; *Das Denkmal in Arkadien* (ländliches Schauspiel für die Jugend mit untermischten Gesängen), Hiller, unperf. THOMAS BAUMAN

Weissenfels. German town, in Saxon-Anhalt. A short but significant chapter in the story of the development of early German opera took place there at the court of the dukes of Sachsen-Weissenfels. The court opera company, famous in its day, performed German opera almost every year from the time of its formation in 1680 until about 1736 and toured to cities such as Weimar; it also provided an important stimulus to the young Handel, who visited the town with his father on many occasions. From 1685 the company performed in the opera theatre of the baroque Neu-Augustusburg palace built by Duke August to replace the citadel destroyed in the Thirty Years War. The composer J. P. Krieger, Kapellmeister from 1680, directed the company from its foundation until his death in 1725. J. A. Kobelius, probably Krieger's pupil, was court opera composer from 1715 to 1729 and wrote more than 20 German operas during that period. The flowering of German opera at Weissenfels ended in 1746 when the ducal line died out; thereafter the town was no longer a royal residence and had no theatre of its own.

MGG (A. Schmiedecke)
A. Werner: *Städtische und fürstliche Musikpflege in Weissenfels bis zum Ende des 18. Jh.* (Leipzig, 1911)
E. W. Böhme: 'Die frühdeutsche Oper in Thüringen', *Weissenfelser Bach-Gedenk Heft* (Weissenfels, 1950)
E. Rohloff: 'Weissenfels', *Bedeutende Musiktraditionen der Bezirke Halle und Magdeburg* (Halle and Magdeburg, n.d.)
DIETER HÄRTWIG

Weisse Rose, Die ('The White Rose'). Opera in eight scenes by UDO ZIMMERMANN to a libretto by Ingo Zimmermann; Dresden, Staatsoper, Oper Studio, 17 June 1967 (revised version, Hamburg, Staatsoper, 27 February 1986).

Zimmermann's first opera concerns the fate of two young Munich students, Hans and Sophie Scholl (baritone and soprano), and their friends; all were members of a resistance movement known as 'The White Rose' whose sense of Christian responsibility led them to distribute leaflets protesting against the policies of the Third Reich. In 1943 the Scholls were arrested, summarily condemned to death and executed.

The opera achieved its full effect only in its revised version of 1984–5 (subtitled 'Scenes for Two Singers and Fifteen Instrumentalists'), gaining international acclaim following the 1986 première. The libretto, revised by Wolfgang Willaschek, uses diary entries by the Scholls themselves and material by the theologian Dietrich Bonhoeffer, who was executed under the Third Reich, the German writer and critic Franz Führmann and Tadeusz Różewicz. Originally a realistic presentation with linear narrative, the emphasis in the revision is on the internal experience of the characters. Felicitas Nicolai has described it as

> a mosaic of isolated, dreamlike, reflective moments of reminiscence, in the nature of snapshots. An hour before their death, Sophie and Hans Scholl look back at their actions, thoughts and emotions under the Third Reich, in six incidents in prison and seven flashbacks. The opera thus becomes a single 75-minute unity in which time stands still, a kind of 'stationary music drama', beginning with the closing of the prison door behind the protagonists, both the first and the last 'dramatic action' on stage.

Die weisse Rose, in its revised version, has been performed frequently in Germany and in Zürich, Vienna, Paris, London and Omaha, Nebraska. DETLEF GOJOWY

Weissheimer, Wendelin (*b* Osthofen, 26 Feb 1838; *d* Nuremberg, 16 June 1910). German conductor and composer. He attended the Leipzig Conservatory in 1856 and later became a pupil of Liszt in Weimar. From 1858 he was Kapellmeister in many cities, including Mainz, Würzburg, Strasbourg, Baden-Baden and Milan. About 1893 he moved to Freiburg; he settled in Nuremberg in 1900. A close friend of Wagner, he published *Erlebnisse mit Richard Wagner, Franz Liszt und vielen anderen Zeitgenossen nebst deren Briefen* (Stuttgart and Leipzig, 1898). His 'vaterländische Oper' *Theodor Körner* (L. Otto), in a prologue and five acts, was given at the Hoftheater in Munich on 28 May 1872 (libretto published, Freiburg, 1891), the prologue previously having been performed as *Deutschlands Erhebung, oder Der Aufruf an das Volk* (1866, Düsseldorf). Another opera, the three-act *Meister Martin, der Küfner, und seine Gesellen* (A. Schricker, after E. T. A. Hoffmann), was given at the Grossherzogliches Hoftheater, Karlsruhe, on 14 April 1879 (full score published, Leipzig, 1880).

Weldon, John (*b* Chichester, 19 Jan 1676; *d* London, 7 May 1736). English composer. Educated at Eton College, he also studied with Purcell (1693–4). He was organist of New College, Oxford (1694–1702), then of two London churches; he also served at the Chapel Royal, where he succeeded Blow in 1708 and became second composer in 1715. He composed at least two extended stage works and contributed to others.

In March 1700 prizes were offered for the best settings of Congreve's masque *The Judgment of Paris*. When the resultant four settings were performed in 1701, Weldon's contribution won first prize, the others being awarded to John Eccles, Daniel Purcell and Gottfried Finger. Early in 1702 he supervised a performance given in Lincoln's Inn Fields at the Duke of Bedford's expense. In 1704 he composed the vocal music for Motteux's *Britain's Happiness*, an entertainment 'after the manner of an opera'. On 30 July 1716 a performance of *The Tempest* was advertised with 'all the musick compos'd by Mr Weldon and perform'd compleat, as at the revival of the play'. This was obviously not the first performance of Weldon's music, which may have dated from *c*1712. No score of music for *The Tempest* bearing his name is now known, but that sometimes attributed to Purcell may be Weldon's (see Laurie).

A composer of considerable talent, Weldon never quite fulfilled his early promise. His melodic range was wide, and his word-setting was often sensitive and rhythmically subtle, though he over-indulged in lengthy roulades and favourite turns of phrase. Apart from some effective use of chromatic passages and Purcellian plunges into the minor, his normal harmonic idiom was conventional and his range of modulation restricted. Italian influence is apparent in his textures and figuration. In *The Judgment of Paris* he employed not only the usual forms, but also constructed several original designs through varied repetition and recapitulation. He lacked the skill and imagination to be able to sustain his freedom of approach and was apt to over-rely on sequential and repetitive patterns. His work is uneven, at times dull and tautologous, but at its best shows charm and sincerity of feeling.

See also JUDGMENT OF PARIS, THE and TEMPEST, THE (i).

The Judgment of Paris (masque, 1, W. Congreve), London, Dorset Garden Theatre, 6 May 1701, *US-Ws*, single songs (London, 1702, *c*1710)

Britain's Happiness (musical entertainment, P. Motteux), London, Theatre Royal, 22 Feb 1704, 1 duet in Monthly Mask of Vocal Music (London, 1705)

The Tempest, or The Enchanted Island (semi-opera, W. Davenant, J. Dryden and ? T. Shadwell, after W. Shakespeare), London, Drury Lane, ? 7 Jan 1712; music possibly extant as Purcell's The Tempest in *The Works of Henry Purcell*, The Purcell Society, xix (London, 1912), 111–87

Song in Orpheus and Euridice (masque), ? Besselsleigh, Oxon., Besselsleigh School, Oct 1697, Mercurius Muscius (London, 1701) and single sheet edns

*

M. Laurie: 'Did Purcell set *The Tempest*?', *PRMA*, xc (1963–4), 43–57

S. Lincoln: 'A Congreve Masque', *MT*, cxiii (1972), 1078–81

R. Fiske: *English Theatre Music in the Eighteenth Century* (London, 1973, 2/1986)

N. Zaslaw: 'An English "Orpheus and Euridice" of 1697', *MT*, cxviii (1977), 805–8 MARGARET LAURIE

Welitsch [Veličkova], **Ljuba** (*b* Borissovo, 10 July 1913). Austrian soprano of Bulgarian birth. After studying in Vienna with Lierhammer she made her début at the Sofia Opera in 1936. She appeared at Graz (1937–40), Hamburg (1941–3) and Munich (1943–6), and then joined the Vienna Staatsoper. She first sang in England in autumn 1947 during the Staatsoper visit, dazzling London audiences with the passion, vocal purity and compelling force of her Salome – her most famous role (which she first sang under Strauss in 1944 and also at her Metropolitan début in 1949). She was a renowned Tosca, Aida and Musetta, and enjoyed great success in other such widely differing roles as Donna Anna, Jenůfa, Minnie (*La fanciulla del West*), Nadja (Salmhofer's *Ivan Tarassenko*) and Rosalinde (*Fledermaus*). Her rise to international fame was meteoric but, sadly, ill-health and insufficient care of her voice denied her continued success in her grandest roles, although she still appeared in a number of character parts in Vienna.

Welitsch's was one of the most exciting voices to appear in the years immediately after World War II. Impressive in dramatic utterance and in soft, sustained lyrical passages, she displayed a total dedication to and absorption in every aspect of her roles. Her few recordings, including versions of the closing scene from *Salome*, reveal her remarkable vocal qualities.

For illustration *see* GÉRARD, ROLF.

*

Earl of Harewood: 'Ljuba Welitsch', *Opera*, iv (1953), 72–7

PETER BRANSCOMBE

Weller, Walter (*b* Vienna, 30 Nov 1939). Austrian conductor. He studied at the Vienna Hochschule für Musik, and later with Szell and Josef Krips. At first a violinist, he formed and toured widely with the Weller Quartet, and became leader of the Vienna PO in 1961. After experience conducting amateur orchestras and choirs, he made a professional début in 1968 as replacement for an ailing Karl Böhm at a Vienna PO concert. The next year he conducted for the first time at the Vienna Staatsoper (*Die Entführung aus dem Serail*) and became a resident conductor for two years, during which he noted that he conducted 46 different operas and vowed 'never again'. He became Generalmusikdirektor at Detmold in 1971 and took guest engagements at the Deutsche Oper, Berlin, and elsewhere, conducting, for example, the première of Marcel Rubin's *Kleider machen Leute* (1973) at Vienna. His later career has been mainly in orchestral appointments (including Liverpool, 1977–80; RPO, London, 1980–85), but he conducted Scottish Opera in *Der Rosenkavalier* (1978) and the ENO in *Ariadne auf Naxos* (1983) followed by *Der fliegende Holländer* (1984); he also conducted the RPO at the 1984 Edinburgh Festival in a concert performance of Bartók's *Bluebeard's Castle* with Fischer-Dieskau and Varady. He conducted *Prince Igor* at the Deutsche Staatsoper, Berlin (1990), and became music director of the Royal Scottish Orchestra in 1992.

NOËL GOODWIN

Wellesz, Egon (Joseph) (*b* Vienna, 21 Oct 1885; *d* Oxford, 9 Nov 1974). Austrian composer and musicologist. After initial study with Carl Frühling, he attended Vienna University as a pupil of Guido Adler, under whom he began his systematic study of opera; this led to writings on Bonno, Cavalli and Fux and culminated in the mellow wisdom of his *Essays on Opera* (London, 1950). He was also a private pupil of Schoenberg, who clearly influenced his work as a composer, although Wellesz never became a doctrinaire serialist. In the years before World War I he established himself as a scholar of some importance and later became a professor at Vienna University. He was equally active as a composer and turned to writing for the operatic stage after 1918. The Anschluss in 1938 led him, on account of his partially Jewish origins, to move to England, where he settled in Oxford. There he was elected a Fellow of Lincoln College and became a much-loved and highly respected figure in the life of the university.

Wellesz was in his early twenties when, in 1907, Mahler resigned his position as director of the Hofoper in Vienna. Yet one may say that it was Mahler's conducting (and rehearsing) of operas that constituted a formative influence on the young composer's notions of musical drama; under Mahler he experienced some of the most exciting performances of opera in Europe. As a composer of stage music Wellesz was also profoundly influenced by other personalities encountered in Vienna. These included, in addition to Schoenberg, Richard Strauss and Strauss's librettist Hofmannsthal, who became Wellesz's own librettist in the 1920s. It is difficult to convey the magisterial seriousness and historical comprehensiveness with which the young men of Vienna, influenced by such figures as these, devoured world literature, from Euripides, *Everyman*, Calderón and Molière to Wilde and Rilke (with Goethe and Tolstoy in between). This response to greatness and to ideas, across centuries and national frontiers, was characteristic of Wellesz both as composer and scholar, and bound to be reflected in his choice of librettos and scenarios.

In the decade between 1921 and 1931 Wellesz had all but one of his stage works performed; these included four ballets, *Das Wunder der Diana*, *Persisches Ballet*, *Die Nächtlichen* (all first performed in 1924) and *Achilles auf Skyros* (1926), in addition to five operas. This was a period when several Austrian composers experimented with adapting ancient Greek mythology to the requirements of 20th-century opera. Wellesz's operas *Alkestis* and *Die Bakchantinnen* as well as the ballet *Achilles auf Skyros* point in that direction (as do Krenek's *Orpheus* and *Das Leben des Orest*). *Alkestis* is one of Wellesz's more impressive achievements, couched in an austere style and, like *Die Bakchantinnen*, making extensive use of the chorus. But perhaps because of its restrained subject matter and its musical idiom, the work was more esteemed than performed. The myth of Alcestis, like that of Iphigenia in Tauris, is lacking in erotic interest, and indeed Wellesz generally avoided the sensational in his librettos. Certainly in *Alkestis* the music is more concerned with psychological developments; the *lieto fine* is achieved by a numinous transfiguration rather than by a spectacular *deus ex machina*.

On the other hand, Wellesz's sense of humour is apparent both in his setting of Goethe's Singspiel *Scherz, List und Rache*, and in his *Incognita*, a charming little comedy commissioned by the Oxford University Opera Club; in spite of its adaptation to amateur resources it fulfills its task well, and forms a fitting conclusion to the dramatic output of a composer with a real flair for the theatre. Wellesz's comparative neglect in Vienna in the 1920s and 30s must be considered to be partly caused by the conservatism that pervaded the repertory of the Staatsoper there. In fact, a perusal of the first performances of Wellesz's operas makes clear that in the wake of World War I, Austrian composers stood a better chance of having their avant-garde experiments staged in Germany than in their native country.

Die Prinzessin Girnara op.27 (Weltspiel und Legende, 2, J. Wassermann), Hanover, 15 May 1921, vs (Vienna and Leipzig, 1921); rev. version, Mannheim, 2 Sept 1928

Alkestis op.35 (1, H. von Hofmannsthal, after Euripides), Mannheim, National, 20 March 1924 (Vienna and New York, 1924)

Die Opferung des Gefangenen op.40 (kultisches Drama, 1, E. Stucken, after Aztec legend), Cologne, Neues, April 1926, vs (Vienna and New York, 1925)

Scherz, List und Rache op.41 (Spl, 1, after J. W. von Goethe), Stuttgart, 1 March 1928, vs (Vienna and Leipzig, 1927)

Die Bakchantinnen op.44 (2, Wellesz, after Euripides), Vienna, Staatsoper, 20 June 1931, vs (Berlin, 1930)

Incognita (E. Mackenzie, after W. Congreve), Oxford, 5 Dec 1951

*

A. Rosenzweig: 'Das Stilproblem der *Alkestis*', *Musikblätter des Anbruch*, vi (1924), 95–100

O. F. Beer: 'E. Wellesz und die Oper', *Die Musik*, xxiii (1931), 909–12

H. F. Redlich: 'Egon Wellesz: an Austrian Composer in Britain', *MR*, vii (1946), 69–79

W. H. Mellers: 'Egon Wellesz and the Austrian Tradition', *Studies in Contemporary Music* (London, 1947), 120–35

R. Réti: 'Egon Wellesz, Musician and Scholar', *MQ*, xlii (1956), 1–5

A. Rosenthal: 'A Bibliography of Egon Wellesz', *MQ*, xlii (1956), 6–13
R. Schollum: *Egon Wellesz* (Vienna, 1964)
O. Kuhn: *Mythos – Neoplatonismus – Mystik: Studien zur Gestaltung des Alkestis-stoffes bei ... Hofmannsthal, T. S. Eliot und Thornton Wilder* (Munich, 1972)
D. Symons: 'Egon Wellesz and Early Twentieth Century Tonality', *Studies in Music*, vi (1972), 42–54
G. Schneider: *Egon Wellesz: Studien zur Theorie und Praxis seiner Musik* (diss., Innsbruck U., 1980)
D. Symons: *Tonal Organization in ... Egon Wellesz* (diss., U. of Western Australia, 1980)
E. Wellesz and E. Wellesz: *Wellesz: Leben und Werk* (Vienna and Hamburg, 1981) [autobiography]
R. Layton: '*Incognita*, an Oxford Opera', *Egon Wellesz: Graz 1982*, ed. O. Kolleritsch, 141–6
W. Ruf: 'Die Oper *Alkestis* von E. Wellesz', ibid, 128–40
C. Cepin Benser: *Wellesz: Chronicle of a Twentieth Century Musician* (Berne and New York, 1985)

FREDERICK W. STERNFELD

Wellington. Capital of New Zealand. On 11 May 1843 the immigrant actor, singer and scene painter James Marriott launched the settlement's first theatrical performances at the Ship Hotel; he was associated with numerous such ventures until his retirement. The Imperial Opera House opened on 20 May 1878 with a selection of popular operatic arias and Act 3 of *Faust*, performed by the visiting Royal Italian Opera Company conducted by Leon Caron. The theatre burnt down just over a year later and was replaced by the Te Aro Opera House (opened 1886), which also burnt down after a short time. It was rebuilt and opened in late 1888 as the Wellington Opera House with a performance of *The Mikado* by the Wellington Operatic Society. Rosina Buckman appeared there as La Zara in Alfred Hill's *A Moorish Maid* in September 1905, launching her international career. The house was converted into a cinema in 1914, the same year the Grand Opera House opened (now the State Opera House; original cap. 1700, now 1400). Meanwhile His Majesty's Theatre (cap. 2000) was inaugurated in 1912; it was renamed the St James Theatre in 1930 and is now used mainly as a cinema. Notable premières in the city have been Hill's romantic opera *Tapu*, staged by the Pollard Opera Company at the Opera House (1903), Farquhar's *A Unicorn for Christmas* at the St James (1962) and one-act *Shadow* at Victoria University Memorial Theatre (1988), and Ross Harris's *Waituhi* at the State Opera House (1984).

Donald Munro's enterprising New Zealand Opera Company (1954), which at first took smaller works on tour, was based in Wellington, as was the supportive New Zealand Opera Society founded the same year. It received a state subsidy in 1961 and became a national touring company until, after productions of *Aida* and *Figaro* in 1971, funding was withdrawn by the Arts Council. The De Lautour Wellington Regional Opera Trust performed in the Victoria University Memorial Theatre from 1979 to 1983. In 1984 its production of *Tosca* was adopted by and transferred to the Wellington City Opera Trust, which in 1985 moved into the State Opera House. Since then it has presented regular seasons there with international soloists, maintaining high musical standards under its conductor, the Australian Patrick Thomas. J. M. THOMSON

Welsby, Norman (*b* Warrington, 7 Feb 1939). English baritone. He studied at Manchester and with Otakar Kraus in London. In 1968 he joined Sadler's Wells Opera (later the ENO), making his début as Masetto. He sang Pentheus in the British stage première of *The Bassarids* (1974) and his roles included Donner, Gunther, Escamillo, Alfio, Silvio, Sharpless, Denisov (*War and Peace*), Peter (*Hänsel und Gretel*) and Sir Robert Cecil (*Gloriana*), which he sang with the company in Vienna (1975). He made his Covent Garden début creating the General in *We Come to the River* (1976) and also sang Ned Keene (*Peter Grimes*). He created the title role of Hamilton's *Tamburlaine* (1977, BBC). His vocal talents and fine musicianship were best displayed in 20th-century music. ELIZABETH FORBES

Welsh, Thomas (*b* Wells, *c*1780; *d* Brighton, 24 or 31 Jan 1848). English bass and composer, a grandson of Thomas Linley (i). At the age of six he became a chorister in Wells Cathedral and made such rapid progress that Wells soon became the resort of music lovers attracted by the beauty of his voice and the excellence of his singing. He appeared in 1792 in Bath, in concerts at the King's Theatre, London, during the rebuilding of Drury Lane, and also on the stage in Attwood's *The Prisoner*, written to display his talent. In 1795 he performed at Drury Lane in Attwood's *The Adopted Child*, Storace's *Lodoiska* and other pieces. John Kemble thought highly of his acting and taught him the role of Prince Arthur in Shakespeare's *King John*.

After his voice broke Welsh pursued his studies under C. F. Horn, John Cramer and Baumgarten. Between 1810 and 1816 he wrote music for several theatrical productions, but his greatest reputation was gained as a teacher of singing and stagecraft. Foremost among his students were John Sinclair, C. E. Horn, Catherine Stephens and Mary Ann Wilson (1802–67), whom he married; in the year after her highly successful début at Drury Lane in 1821 she earned an unprecedented £10 000 on the stage, though she soon ruined her voice from overexertion.

all first performed in London; librettos in US-SM

Twenty Years Ago! (musical play, 2, I. Pocock), Lyceum, 21 July 1810
The Green-eyed Monster, or How to Get your Money (operatic farce, Pocock), Lyceum, 14 Oct 1811
Kamtchatka, or The Slave's Tribute (musical play, C. Kemble, after A. von Kotzebue), CG, 16 Oct 1811
Up to Town (comic op, T. J. Dibdin), CG, 6 Nov 1811, collab. Reeve, Condell and Whitaker
Selima and Azor (2, G. Collier), CG, 5 Oct 1813, collab. Bishop and T. Cooke
For England, Ho! (melodramatic op, 2, Pocock), CG, 15 Dec 1813, air (London, 1815), collab. Bishop
Is he Jealous? (operetta, 1, S. Beazley), English Opera House (Lyceum), 2 July 1816

Welsh National Opera. Welsh opera company based in CARDIFF, founded in 1946.

Welting, Ruth (*b* Memphis, TN, 1 May 1949). American soprano. She studied with Daniel Ferro in New York, Luigi Ricci in Rome and Jeanne Reiss in Paris. After her début at the New York City Opera, as Blonde in *Die Entführung* (1971), she appeared in Dallas, Houston and San Francisco. Zerbinetta was the role of her Covent Garden (1975) and Metropolitan (1976) débuts. Her technically secure coloratura has been admired in such roles as Gilda, the Queen of Night, Marie in *La fille du régiment* (1983–4, Dallas and Barcelona), Mozart's Konstanze and Susanna, and Lucia (1985, Cincinnati).

DAVID CUMMINGS

Wendling [née Spurni], **Dorothea** (*b* Stuttgart, 21 March 1736; *d* Munich, 20 Aug 1811). German soprano. The daughter of a Stuttgart horn player, she was appointed a singer at the Mannheim court in 1752; on 9 January of that year she married the flautist Johann Baptist Wendling. Her first role was Hermione in Galuppi's *Antigona* (17 January 1753). In 1758 she sang the prima donna role in Holzbauer's *Nitteti* and for the next 20 years was the most celebrated soprano at Mannheim. Her salary, 1200 florins in 1759, increased to 1500 in 1778. She appeared in serious operas by Jommelli, Holzbauer, Piccinni and J. C. Bach, and took the title roles in Traetta's *Sofonisba* (1762) and Majo's *Ifigenia in Tauride* (1764). She also sang in the Italian comic operas performed at Mannheim in the 1770s, and appeared in more than 30 roles in 25 years. Mozart admired her voice and wrote the concert aria K486a/295a for her in 1778. Wieland, who heard her during rehearsals for Schweitzer's *Rosamunde*, wrote to Sophie La Roche: 'Her style of singing surpasses everything I have ever heard, even the famous Mara'. Heinse and Schubart praised her as one of the most expressive singers of the day, though the latter also mentioned an unfortunate 'warble'. She remained active after the court transferred to Munich in 1778, and created the title roles in Holzbauer's *La morte di Didone* (1779, Mannheim) and J. P. Verazi's *Laodamia* (1780, Oggersheim). She appeared as a guest in Munich, singing Calipso in Franz Paul Grua's *Telemaco* (1780) and Ilia in Mozart's *Idomeneo* (1781). After she left the stage, she continued to sing in concerts and taught singing in Mannheim and Munich. Her daughter, Elisabeth Augusta, also occasionally performed in comic operas at Mannheim and Schwetzingen.

*

J. J. W. Heinse: *Hildegard von Hohenthal* (1794) [novel]
C. F. D. Schubart: *Ideen zu einer Ästhetik der Tonkunst* (Vienna, 1806)
F. J. Lipowsky: *Baierisches Musiklexikon* (Munich, 1811)
F. Walter: *Geschichte des Theaters und der Musik am kurpfälzischen Hofe* (Leipzig, 1898)
E. Anderson, ed.: *The Letters of Mozart and his Family* (London, 1938, 3/1985)
W. Plath: 'Mozart und Galuppi: Bemerkungen zur Szene "Ah non lasciarmi, no" K295a', *Festschrift Walter Senn* (Munich, 1975)
P. Corneilson: *Opera at Mannheim, 1770–1778* (diss., U. of North Carolina, 1992)

PAUL CORNEILSON

Wendling [née Sarselli], **Elisabeth (Augusta)** (*b* Mannheim, 20 Feb 1746; *d* Munich, 10 Jan 1786). German soprano. Her parents, the tenor Pietro Sarselli and his wife Carolina, were singers at Mannheim. She accompanied her future husband to Italy in 1760 and after her return to Mannheim in 1761 was appointed a court musician. She married Franz Wendling, the violinist and brother of Johann Baptist, on 1 December 1764. Beginning with the role of Cirene in Traetta's *Sofonisba* (1762), she was cast in the seconda donna roles at the Hoftheater, singing opposite her sister-in-law, Dorothea. She accompanied the court to Munich in 1778, and there created her most famous role, Electra in Mozart's *Idomeneo* (1781). She also sang the title role in Salieri's *Semiramide* (1782); her last role was Zelmira in Prati's *Armida abbandonata* (1785).

*

F. J. Lipowsky: *Baierisches Musiklexikon* (Munich, 1811)
F. Walter: *Geschichte des Theaters und der Musik am kurpfälzischen Hofe* (Leipzig, 1898)
E. Anderson, ed.: *The Letters of Mozart and his Family* (London, 1938, 3/1985)
P. Corneilson: *Opera at Mannheim, 1770–1778* (diss., U. of North Carolina, 1992)

PAUL CORNEILSON

Wenkel, Ortrun (*b* Buttstadt, 25 Oct 1942). German contralto. She studied in Weimar and Frankfurt, making her début in 1971 at Heidelberg as Gluck's Orpheus. She has sung in Stuttgart, Munich, Cologne, Geneva, Amsterdam, Paris, Rome and Houston. She sang Erda and First Norn at Bayreuth (1976–80), performed in Landi's *Sant'Alessio* at Salzburg (1977), sang Phaedra in Rameau's *Hippolyte et Aricie* at Schwetzingen (1980) and appeared as Adriano in *Rienzi* at Prague (1991). Her roles include Azucena, Geneviève, Olga, Grandmother Buryjovka (*Jenůfa*) and Gaea (*Daphne*), but her voice, dark-toned and agile, is especially effective in Baroque music. ELIZABETH FORBES

Wenkoff, Spas (*b* Tŭrnovo, 23 Sept 1928). Bulgarian tenor. After study in Sofia and Dresden he sang in East Germany from 1965 (Döbeln, Magdeburg and Halle). He sang Tristan at Dresden in 1975, and became a member of the Berlin Staatsoper the same year. At the Bayreuth Festival (1976–83) he has appeared as Tristan and Tannhäuser. His greatest success has been at the Vienna Staatsoper in 1982, when he sang the title role in a new production of *Tannhäuser*. His Metropolitan début was in 1981, as Tristan. From 1984 he has sung at the Deutsche Oper, Berlin, at Cologne (as Tristan, 1990) and at the Munich Staatsoper. DAVID CUMMINGS

Wenzig, Josef (*b* Prague, 18 Jan 1807; *d* Turnov, 28 Aug 1875). Czech writer and librettist. Although educated as a German, he played an important part in the development of Czech national feeling: he instigated the first Czech *Realschule* (he was a schoolteacher by profession), and was the first chairman of the Umělecká Beseda (Artistic Society), where he came into contact with Smetana. His writings, mostly in German, include several plays (some of which were performed at the Prague Estates Theatre and the Provisional Theatre) and opera librettos. Smetana set two of his librettos after they had been translated into Czech by Wenzig's former pupil, Ervín Špindler (1843–1918).

Dalibor [Ger.], in Cz., Smetana, 1868; *Libušas Urtheilsspruch und Vermählung*, in Cz., Smetana, 1881, as Libuše; *Smrt krále Václava* [The Death of King Wenceslas], Skuherský, inc.

*

ČSHS [lists further bibliography and libs.]
E. Špindler: 'Několik vzpomínek na mistra B. Smetanu' [Some Recollections of Maestro Smetana], *HR*, ii (1909), 248–53
O. Fischer: 'K Smetanovým librettům: 1. K Daliboru'; '2. K. Libuši', *HR*, viii (1915), 153–62; 205–15
M. Očadlík: *Libuše: vznik Smetanovy zpěvohry* [The Origin of Smetana's Opera *Libuše*] (Prague, 1939), 34–94 passim
J. Bartoš, ed.: *Josef Wenzig-Ervín Špindler: Dalibor* (Prague, 1944) [critical edn with biographical introduction]
M. Očadlík: *Smetanovi libretisté* [Smetana's Librettists] (Prague, 1948), 24–30
J. Bartoš, ed.: *Josef Wenzig-Ervín Špindler: Libuše* (Prague, 1951) [critical edn with biographical introduction]
J. Tyrrell: *Czech Opera* (Cambridge, 1988), 104–5, 188, 266–70

JOHN TYRRELL

Werder, Felix (*b* Berlin, 24 Feb 1922). Australian composer of German origin. He was the elder son of Boaz Bischofs Werder, a composer and cantor at a Berlin synagogue. As his father's musical assistant, he was profoundly influenced by the cantor and his circle of associates, which included Schoenberg and Arno Nadel. In 1934 rising anti-Jewish feeling forced the family to leave Germany for London, where the father became cantor at a synagogue in Aldgate and the son a part-time student at various musical and architectural institutions, although his argumentative character soon obliged him to dissociate himself from these. In 1941 the father, still a German citizen, was deported to Australia. Werder accompanied him and was interned at Tatura in Victoria, where he composed music for the use of musicians imprisoned there. After the war Werder remained in Australia, working as a carpenter, music teacher and lecturer; during the 1950s his compositions began to receive performances.

From the early 1960s to 1977 he was a controversial music critic for the Melbourne newspaper *The Age*. Active in avant-garde music circles, he consistently championed new Australian compositions. By the late 1970s, however, lack of recognition of his own music in Australia led Werder to form Australia Felix, a self-funded group designed to perform his works and those of other Australian composers in former West Germany. (He has since travelled each year to Germany, where his works have been widely performed, as well as published and recorded.)

It was first as a writer of quartets and later as a chamber orchestra composer that Werder gained acceptance. His 11 operas remain largely unknown, although seven have been performed. Several were originally designated as music-theatre pieces, but as the vogue for opera grew in Australia during the 1970s and 80s, Werder reworked and recategorized them. Moreover, a number of compositions that he first conceived as operas evolved into cantatas and pseudo-oratorios when operatic performances did not materialize. The operas vary in subject matter from classical dramas, as in *Agamemnon* and *Medea*, which are based on plays of Aeschylus and Euripedes, to social irony, as in the television opera *Private*, a caricature of modern-day male-female relationships and power struggles.

Werder initially modelled his works on Hindemith, Schoenberg and Bartók and a number of his operas, including *Agamemnon* and *Private*, are constructed using serial techniques. He later abandoned atonalism and serial methods. His music is energetic, colourful and concentrated, but distanced from human response by its wayward intellectualism and its obsession with virtuosic pyrotechnics. The composer maintains that he is highly responsive to natural speech patterns, transforming them intuitively rather than mathematically into vocal and orchestral lines; yet this procedure often results in singers and orchestras straining for effect. His disjointed and jagged idiom is further characterized by arid orchestration. Despite Werder's lack of acceptance by wider audiences, he has nevertheless had a considerable influence in Australian music, as a theorist and critic, and as a teacher with the Council of Adult Education.

See also AFFAIR, THE and AGAMEMNON.

Kisses for a Quid op.39 (1, A. Marshall), Melbourne, Q Theatre, 23 March 1961

The General op.69, 1966 (1, L. Radic), unperf.

The Agamemnon of Aeschylus (mime-chant op, 1, Werder, after Aeschylus), broadcast, ABC, 1967; rev. as Agamemnon op.76, stage, Melbourne, Grant Street, 1 June 1977

The Affair op.99, 1969 (1, Radic), Sydney, Opera House, 14 March 1974

Private op.103 (television op, C. Rorke), Brussels, 1970; ABC, 7 Nov 1971

The Vicious Square op.121, 1971 (opera masque, 2, P. Rorke), unperf.

The Conversion op.138, 1973 (1, Werder, after F. Wedekind), unperf.

Bellyful op.159, 1975 (chamber op, 1, Radic, after Bible), unperf., ?lost

The Director (1, Werder), U. of Melbourne, 7 June 1980

Medea (1, Werder, after Euripides), Melbourne College of Advanced Education, 17 Sept 1985

Belsazer (1, Werder, after H. Heine), Dortmund, Gymnasium, 5 Oct 1988

F. Werder: 'Composing in Australia', *Meanjin*, xvi/2 (1957), 140–44

R. Covell: *Australia's Music: Themes of a New Society* (Melbourne, 1967), 182–91

L. Sitsky: 'New Music', *Current Affairs Bulletin*, xlvi/3 (1970), 43–4

J. Murdoch: *Australia's Contemporary Composers* (Melbourne and Sydney, 1972), 191–210

'20th Century Rococo', *Opera Australia*, no.1 (Jan 1974), 20–21 [on *The Affair*]

T. Radic: 'Felix Werder', *Australian Composition in the Twentieth Century*, ed. F. Callaway and D. Tunley (Melbourne, 1978), 91–3

E. Wood: *Australian Opera, 1842–1970* (diss., U. of Adelaide, 1979)

THÉRÈSE RADIC

Werfel, Franz (*b* Prague, 10 Sept 1890; *d* Beverly Hills, CA, 26 Aug 1945). Austrian poet and author. Performances of Italian operas in Prague during Werfel's time as a student awakened his interest in music, particularly in Verdi, whose works he did much to promote in Germany. In 1923 he began work on *Verdi: Roman der Oper* (Berlin, 1924, 2/1930), an epic novel of the expressionist period which struck at the heart of contemporary debates about modernism in music and rapidly became a best-seller (60 000 copies were sold by 1929); in 1926 he contributed the preface ('Das Bildnis Giuseppe Verdis') to Paul Stefan's translation of Verdi's letters. Werfel's first attempt to provide a new German version of a Verdi opera was his translation of *La forza del destino* (1925), whose resounding success – it was performed in Altenburg, Dresden, Vienna, Berlin, Basle and Prague – heralded a Verdi renaissance. There followed in 1929 a translation of *Simon Boccanegra* (performed in Vienna, Berlin, Prague, Basle and other centres) and eventually *Don Carlos*, in collaboration with Lothar Wallerstein. After the première at the Vienna Staatsoper in 1932, this *Don Carlos* became one of the most frequently performed of any Verdi opera in German-speaking countries. Further projected translations (including *I Lombardi*) were thwarted by political events in Germany; Werfel and his wife Alma Mahler-Werfel emigrated to the USA, where the book that he and Stefan had edited appeared in an English translation (*Verdi: the Man in his Letters*, New York, 1942).

For Krenek's one-act operatic work *Die Zwingburg* (1924, Berlin), Werfel put into verse the 'honest but ungainly attempt of an amateur' (Krenek, *Selbstdarstellung*). It may also have been Krenek whom Werfel had in mind as the model for the young composer and representative of modernist musical ideals Mathias Fischböck in his Verdi novel, as Alma Mahler claimed, though Joseph Mathias Hauer may equally have been an influence. Various composers made use of material from Werfel's poems, novels and plays. Settings include Milhaud's opera *Maximilien* (1932), after the play *Juarez und Maximilien* (1924); Lodovico Rocca's *Monte Ivnor* (1939), after the novel *Die vierzig Tage des Musa Dagh* (1933); and Giselher Klebe's *Jacobowsky und der Oberst* (1965), after the 1944 play of the same title.

*

A. Weissmann: 'Franz Werfels "Verdi-Roman": Das Problem der Oper', *Vössische Zeitung* (15 June 1924), 1
H. Kralik: '"Die Macht des Schicksals": Verdis Oper in neuer deutscher Bearbeitung von Franz Werfel', *Neues Wiener Tagblatt* (28 Nov 1926), 2–4
P. Stefan: 'Verdi erwacht', *Musikblätter des Anbruch*, viii (1926), 2–3
A. Heuss: 'Über Verdis Oper "Die Macht des Schicksals" und ihre unverglückte Bearbeitung durch Franz Werfel', *ZfM*, Jg.94 (1927), 1–10
H. Liepmann: 'Werfel oder das Opfer der Oper', *Weltbühne*, xxv (1929), 953–5
A. D. Klarmann: *Musikalität bei Werfel* (Philadelphia, 1931)
E. Decsay: 'Giuseppe Verdi – Franz Werfel – und die Kritik', *Die Musik*, xxiv (1931–2), 786–7
E. Krenek: *Selbstdarstellung* (Zürich, 1948)
H. Pringsheim: 'Glück und Ende der Verdi-Renaissance', *Melos*, xviii (1951), 46–8
H. Fähnreich: 'Verdi in der Deutung Franz Werfels', *NZM*, Jg.120 (1959), 258–61
H. Kühner: 'Franz Werfel und Giuseppe Verdi', *Bollettino dell'Istituto di studi verdiani*, i (1960), 1391
A. Mahler-Werfel: *Mein Leben* (Frankfurt, 1960)
H. Fähnreich: 'Zauber der Opfer: eine Studie zu Franz Werfels Romanen', *Musica*, xv (1961), 476–80
K. Honolka: 'Traduttore – traditore', ibid, 13–19
H. Fähnreich: 'Franz Werfels Anteil an der Verdi-Renaissance', *NZM*, Jg.124 (1963), 374–7
——: 'Die beide Fassungen von Franz Werfel's Verdi-Roman 1924/1930', *SMz*, ciii (1963), 76–80
P. Jungk: *Franz Werfel: eine Lebensgeschichte* (Frankfurt, 1987; Eng. trans., 1990)
R. S. Furness: 'A Discussion of *Verdi: Roman der Opfer*', *Franz Werfel: an Austrian Writer Reassessed*, ed. L. Huber (Oxford, New York and Munich, 1989), 139–52
N. Abels: *Franz Werfel* (Hamburg, 1990)

RUDOLF KLEIN

Werle, Lars Johan (*b* Gävle, 23 June 1926). Swedish composer. During his school years he taught himself the piano and led a jazz band. He studied musicology at Uppsala University (1948–51), singing in the choir and taking counterpoint lessons with Bäck, and from 1958 to 1970 he was a music producer for Swedish radio. Later he taught at the State Music Drama School, Stockholm (1970–76), and was resident composer at the Stora Teater, Göteborg (1976–9). He was influenced by Lidholm in his string quartet *Pentagram*, a rigorously serial composition, but soon broke away from serialism and went on to complete his first opera, *Drömmen om Thérèse* ('Dream about Thérèse'), in 1964. By seating the audience around an arena stage, with the small orchestra in groups behind it, Werle was able to generate a great sense of public involvement; the opera was also dramatically innovatory in its use of recorded material, allowing realistic action to be combined with interior monologues. The work, successfully performed many times in Sweden and abroad (including the Edinburgh Festival, 1974), won Werle the 1970 Nordic Council Music Prize. He then received a commission from the Hamburg Staatsoper for a second opera, *Resan* ('The Journey'), a work that portrays the many-layered psychological experiences of a man and a woman: the man, Christopher, is on a journey through a mental hell, grey, burning and sterile; Lilly, a housewife, lives in her own hell, a depressing, colourless suburb. Using flashback techniques, Werle repeated from his first opera the use of collages and of widely varying types of music. His third opera, *Tintomara*, is based on a lyrical mystery play about events at the time of the murder of Gustavus III during a masked ball. This sensitive, subtly shaded work was given its première on the bicentenary of the Stockholm Opera House.

The chamber opera *Medusan och djävulen* ('Medusa and the Devil') deals with the power of breakdowns and paralysis. It was followed by the mini-opera *Flower Power*, a fable based on two poems by Tage Danielsson; the work has been staged in Stockholm, Göteborg and Bayreuth and broadcast on Danish television. *Animalen* ('The Animal Congress') deals, also in fable form, with the reduction of armaments between East and West, using the Singspiel form of *Die Zauberflöte*. This musical-like opera ran for four seasons in Göteborg and has been staged abroad; several television versions have also been made. *En midsommarnattsdröm* ('A Midsummer Night's Dream') lies somewhere between opera and musical, switching from operatic to jazz and rock styles. *Gudars skymning* ('Twilight of the Gods'), based on Tage Danielsson's book *Mytologi*, is a burlesque on the quarrel between the old and new gods and on modern secularization; it has been staged in Göteborg together with *Kvinnogräl* ('Women's Quarrels'), a piece for two voices and a small instrumental group which also combines seriousness and humour. *Lionardo* depicts Leonardo da Vinci's life, problems and relationships with women, showing him finally confronted by the horrors made possible by his pioneering weapon designs, with parallels made to Einstein and N. H. Bohr. Two chamber operas have been written for the State Music Drama School in Göteborg. *Väntarna* ('The Ones who Wait'), based on Werner Aspenström's play, is about a collection of dolls who, while waiting for their (female) owner, devote themselves to a part-lighthearted, part-serious status game. In *Tavlan* ('The Painting'), one of Velasquez's most famous pictures, *Las meninas*, is brought to life on stage.

See also DRÖMMEN OM THÉRÈSE and TINTOMARA.

Drömmen om Thérèse [Dream about Thérèse] (2, L. Runsten, after E. Zola: *Pour une nuit d'amour*), Stockholm, Royal Opera, 26 May 1964
Resan [The Journey] (2, Runsten, after P. C. Jersild: *Till varmare länder*), Hamburg, Staatsoper, 2 March 1969
Tintomara (3, L. Söderström, after C. J. L. Almqvist: *Drottningens juvelsmycke*), Stockholm, Royal Opera, 18 Jan 1973; rev. (2), Göteborg, Storan, 7 March 1976
Medusan och djävulen [Medusa and the Devil] (lyrical mystery play, Werle, after E. Grave), Stockholm, State Music Drama School, 28 Nov 1973
Flower Power ('Springosjung', T. Danielsson), Stockholm, State Music Drama School, 25 July 1974
Animalen ['The Animal Congress'] (2, Danielsson), Göteborg, Storan, 19 May 1975
En Midsommarnattsdröm [A Midsummer Night's Dream] (Söderström, after W. Shakespeare), Malmö, 8 Feb 1985
Gudars skymning [Twilight of the Gods] (operatic parody, 1, Werle, after Danielsson: *Mytologi*), concert perf., Skinnskatteberg, 15 June 1985; stage, Uppsala, 18 Jan 1986
Kvinnogräl [Women's Quarrels] (K. Forsmark, after F. von Schiller: *Maria Stuart*, Molière: *Le misanthrope* and René de Obaldia), Göteborg, Lillan, 18 Oct 1986
Lionardo (prol., 2, epilogue, C. Fellbom), Stockholm, Folkopera, 31 March 1988
Väntarna [The Ones who Wait] (chamber op, I. Bergkwist, after W. Aspenström), Part 1, 1989, complete, Stockholm, May 1990
Tavlan: en eftermiddag på Prado [The Painting: an Afternoon at the Prado] (chamber op, Bergkwist), Göteborg, State Music Drama School, 2 Sept 1991

*

B. Wallner, L. Runsten and L. J. Werle: 'Drömmen om en arenaopera', *Nutida musik*, vii/7 (1963–4), 13–15
A. Thoor: 'Opera in Space and in the Round', *Musikrevy international* (1967), 45–7
G. Bergendal: 'Om Werles *Die Reise*', *Nutida musik*, xii/4 (1968–9), 34–6

S. Johansson: 'Den första arenaoperaiscensättningen: *Drömmen om Thérèse*, 1964', *Teatervetenskap* (1969), no.2, p.14
U.-B. Edberg: 'Drömmen om *Tintomara*', *Nutida musik*, xvi/2 (1972–3), 19–23
S. Hammar: 'Samkonstverket *Tintomara* växer fram' [The Multi-Media Work *Tintomara* develops], *Perspektiv på Almqvist* (Stockholm, 1973), 323
L. Runsten: 'Skaffa en tonsättare, så får vi se ...' [Try to Find a Composer, and we shall see ...], *Operan 200 år, jubelboken* (Stockholm, 1973), 203; *Operan* ... (1984), no.10, p.4 [programme book]
H. Sjögren: 'Werles *Tintomara*: en maskerad med ett skott i paradiset' [Werle's *Tintomara*: a Masked Ball with a Shot in Paradise], *Tonfallet* (1973), no.1, p.1
P.-A. Hellqvist: 'Operan lever: anteckningar kring tre dramer i folklig atmosfär' [The Opera Lives: Notes about Three Plays in Folklike Atmosphere], *Nutida musik*, xxi/3 (1977–8), 41–50
B. E. Johnson/L. J. Werle: 'Att tonsätta *Almqvist*' [To Compose *Almqvist*], *Artes* (1977–8), no.4, p.45
L. Sjöberg: 'Men musiken då', *Nutida musik*, xxiii/4 (1979–80), 33–7 [on *Animalen*]
T. Danielsson: *'Animalen': texten* (Malmö, 1980)
U. Dahlbäck-Hägglund: 'Så kom *Animalen* till' [How *Animalen* Came About], *På Operan* (1980), no.4, p.3
G. Petersén: 'Werle – vår meste', *MusikDramatik* (1980), no.6, p.18
——: 'Spännande, svensk, romantisk: om *Tintomara* och L. J. Werle' [Exciting, Swedish, Romantic: on *Tintomara* and L. J. Werle], *På Operan* (1980), no.2, p.1
——: 'Tonsättaren Lars Johan Werle', *På Operan* (1981), no.10, p.23
L. Carlquist: 'Från väglappar till *Animalen*' [Signposts to *Animalen*], *Turist* (1982), no.6, p.18
I. Fabian: 'Ein Erfolgsautor des Musiktheaters', *Opernwelt* (1984), no.4, p.21
G. Petersén: 'Tonsättaren Lars Johan Werle', *Operan* ... (1984), no.10, p.11 [programme book]
ROLF HAGLUND

Wernicke, Herbert (*b* Auggen, 24 March 1946). German director and designer. He studied the piano, flute and conducting at the Musikhochschule in Brunswick, and stage design under Rudolf Heinrich at the Munich Kunstakademie. He began his career as a stage designer for spoken theatre in Landshut and Wuppertal, and then turned to directing his own productions, and to opera. He staged Handel's *Belshazzar* at Darmstadt in 1978 and *Judas Maccabaeus* at the Staatsoper in Munich. His production of *Hippolyte et Aricie* for the Deutsche Oper, Berlin, was shown at the 1980 Schwetzingen Festival. During the 1980s a series of controversial productions, notably *Der fliegende Holländer* in Munich, *Die Meistersinger* in Hamburg and *Simon Boccanegra* at Basle, established him as one of the leading director-designers of the German avant garde. He favours dislocated modern settings, with characters often resorting to extreme behaviour and outlandish postures to illuminate situations and relationships.

ANDREW CLARK

Werther. *Drame lyrique* in four acts by JULES MASSENET to a libretto by ÉDOUARD BLAU, Paul Milliet and GEORGES HARTMANN, based on JOHANN WOLFGANG VON GOETHE's novel *Die Leiden des jungen Werthers* (1774); Vienna, Hofoper, 16 February 1892.

Werther *aged 23*	tenor
Le Bailli *aged 50*	bass or baritone
Charlotte *his daughter, aged 20*	mezzo-soprano
Sophie *her sister, aged 15*	soprano
Albert *aged 25*	baritone
Schmidt } *friends of the Bailli*	tenor
Johann } *friends of the Bailli*	bass or baritone
Brühlmann *a young man*	tenor
Käthchen *a young girl*	soprano
The Bailli's six remaining children	children's voices

Inhabitants of Wetzlar, guests, servants (silent roles)

Setting The outskirts of Frankfurt (Wetzlar, over 50 km distant, is specified); July to December 178 ...

In his ever-unreliable *Mes souvenirs*, Massenet recalls how his publisher Georges Hartmann accompanied him to Bayreuth for *Parsifal* in 1886 and gave him a copy of Goethe's novel when they stopped at Wetzlar on the return journey. With picturesque circumstantial detail the composer describes starting to read it in a noisy, smoke-filled beer hall and finding especial inspiration in the quotation from Ossian that was to form the emotional climax of the opera. In fact, the idea of a Werther opera is mentioned in a letter as early as 1880, and it was germinating even while Massenet was engaged on *Manon* in 1882. In 1885 he started composition; Hartmann had in all likelihood sketched the scenario, but the libretto was by Blau and Milliet, and the inclusion of the publisher's name on the title page had more to do with percentages than authorial responsibility. It is also possible that Hartmann's bankruptcy and the absorption of his business by Heugel the year before the première of *Werther* led both to this and to Massenet's generous, if fanciful, account of its genesis.

The score was finished in 1887. Léon Carvalho, director of the Opéra-Comique, turned it down as being too gloomy for his audiences. Shortly afterwards, the theatre burnt down. *Werther* remained in the composer's drawer while he busied himself with *Esclarmonde* and his infatuation with Sibyl Sanderson. There was a further opportunity for a première in 1889, but this was the year of another international exposition and *Esclarmonde* was thought more suitable. Following the successful Vienna première of *Manon* in 1890, the management asked for a new Massenet opera and were given *Werther*. The first performance was sung in German with a cast led by the Belgian tenor Ernest Van Dyck (a famous Parsifal and Lohengrin) and Marie Renard, a soprano who had also sung Manon in Vienna. The opera was first given in Paris on 16 January 1893 by the Opéra-Comique in its temporary home at the Théâtre Lyrique, with Guillaume Ibos and Marie Delna. It was not a conspicuous success. In 1894 it was withdrawn from the repertory; the same year saw performances in New York, Chicago, New Orleans and Milan, and throughout the French provinces. There was a single performance at Covent Garden, also in 1894; a dispute between Jean de Reszke and Sir Augustus Harris, as well as lukewarm audience response, prevented further airings. Albert Carré revived the piece at the Opéra-Comique in 1903, and its worldwide popularity dates from then – it has been performed over 1300 times in Paris alone. In recent years it has vied with *Manon* as Massenet's most popular work. In 1902 Massenet himself made a baritone arrangement of the title role for Mattia Battistini, which is still occasionally performed (as at Seattle in 1989, with Dale Duesing).

ACT 1 *The garden of the Bailli's house, July* The Bailli (roughly Mayor, or Steward) rehearses his unruly younger children in a Christmas carol. Johann and Schmidt call to encourage him to join them at the inn, to discuss the evening's ball, and in particular Charlotte's partner for the occasion, the urbane and melancholy poet Werther, who enjoys the Prince's favour and is destined for a diplomatic post. They also inquire after the return of Charlotte's fiancé, Albert, from a journey, and look forward to celebrating their wedding. When they have left, Werther enters and sings of the beauty of the surroundings ('Invocation': 'O Nature, pleine de grâce, reine du temps et de l'espace'; some commentators have noted the mild blasphemy of these lines, which echo the 'Ave Maria' and express a typical Romantic pantheism). He asks Nature to receive him as a human devotee and the sun to envelop him in its warmth. He then watches as Charlotte, dressed for the ball, gives the children their supper of bread and butter in the house. They are introduced; two others destined for the ball, the starry-eyed Brühlmann and Käthchen, can only utter the word 'Klopstock' and pass on, to the bemusement of the Bailli. As Charlotte consigns the children to Sophie's care, Werther apostrophizes (aside) this vision of ideal love and innocence. As all leave, the Bailli, encouraged by Sophie, decides to join his friends at the inn.

Albert returns unexpectedly, and asks Sophie if he is still remembered after his six-month absence. She reassures him that all the family's thoughts are of preparation for the marriage. Time passes. Charlotte and Werther return from the ball ('Clair de lune'). To a hushed, rocking melody in 12/8 Werther's fatal love is born (not insignificantly the scene's opening words are Charlotte's 'Il faut nous séparer'). She protests that he knows nothing of her, but he cites the children as witnesses to her beauty of spirit. She tells him of the burden of responsibility placed upon her by their mother's early death, and of how they still ask why 'the men in black' took *maman* away, to which Werther can only reply with a passionate declaration of love. As he asks if they may meet again, the Bailli's voice is heard proclaiming the news of Albert's return. Charlotte tells Werther that this is the man she promised her dying mother to marry, and admits that for a moment she was in danger of forgetting her oath. Werther enjoins her to keep it, knowing that it will mean his death.

Ernest Van Dyck in the title role of Massenet's 'Werther' which he created at the Vienna Hofoper, 16 February 1892

ACT 2 *The square in Wetzlar, with the church, the parsonage and the inn, autumn* From the inn, Johann and Schmidt watch townspeople on their way to church to help celebrate the Pastor's golden wedding. Albert asks Charlotte if she has any regrets after three months of marriage. She sweetly reassures him as they enter the church. Werther appears and gives vent to an outburst of jealous fury ('Désolation': 'Un autre est son époux ... J'aurais sur ma poitrine'). A disconsolate Brühlmann is assured by Johann and Schmidt that Käthchen, his fiancée of seven years, will return to him. Albert comes out of church and in a brief dialogue with Werther, in which there is much between the lines, confesses that his own happiness reminds him of the pain Werther might feel having met Charlotte when she was still free, and that he understands and sympathizes. Werther replies that if there were any bitterness in his heart, he would leave the town for ever; as it is, he feels only friendship for them both. Sophie enters with a bouquet for the Pastor, reserves Werther for the first minuet at the celebrations, and sings blithely of the happiness that has descended on the town ('Du gai soleil'). Left alone, Werther admits that he was lying to himself: the honourable course would be to leave. Charlotte enters. As Werther nostalgically recalls their first meeting – as does the music – she reminds him of her wifely duty, a duty that would make it prudent for him to depart. While he should not forget her, she continues, a trial separation would soften his pain; he could return, perhaps, at Christmas. Alone, Werther muses on the notion of suicide, using a variant of the parable of the Prodigal Son ('Lorsque l'enfant'): if a child returned unexpectedly from a journey, would not his father welcome him all the more warmly? He calls on the God he does not recognize to summon him home. Sophie enters; he tells her brusquely that he is leaving for ever and rushes out. The golden wedding procession emerges from the church. Sophie bursts into tears as she gives Charlotte and Albert the news. Both understand the significance of the words 'for ever'.

ACT 3 *The drawing-room of Albert's house; Christmas Eve* Charlotte, her heart full of love for Werther, re-reads the letters she should have destroyed ('Air des lettres'), remorseful at having suggested his exile. The third letter warns her that if he does not return at Christmas, she should weep for him. Sophie enters, laden with presents, instinctively senses her sister's distress and tries to cheer her ('Ah! le rire est béni'). When she mentions Werther, whom she plainly loves as well, Charlotte breaks down ('Air des larmes', with saxophone obbligato): tears unshed engulf and destroy the human heart. Sophie tries to persuade her to spend Christmas with their father and the children. Charlotte, alone, prays to God for strength in remembering her duty.

Werther suddenly appears. At first Charlotte and the music attempt to keep the conversation at the level of social pleasantries, about how the children look forward to seeing him, and how nothing has changed in her room, the harpsichord, the books, Albert's pistols, all in the same place. To distract him from the last-named, Charlotte fatally points out the volume of Ossian that Werther once started to translate, and he sings the 'Lied d'Ossian'. 'Pourquoi me reveiller': why answer the call of spring when it only presages the season of storms? The passionate melody forms the basis of the rest of the scene: Charlotte's reserves fail her and they fall briefly into each other's arms. But she recovers herself and leaves the room, saying they will never meet again. Shattered, his mind made up, Werther asks nature to mourn her erring son (to a reminiscence of the first-act 'Invocation') and rushes away. Albert enters, having heard of Werther's return, and grimly starts to interrogate his wife. A servant enters with a message from Werther: he is going on a long journey and asks to borrow Albert's pistols. The husband coldly orders his wife to hand them over. Once alone, she hurries away, praying that she will not be too late. An intermezzo, at once violent and full of foreboding, leads without break into the last act.

ACT 4 *Werther's study* Charlotte finds the dying Werther. He prevents her from summoning help, preferring not to be separated from her in this first moment of happiness. To a reminiscence of 'Clair de lune' she admits that she has always loved him and in an embrace they forget momentarily the pain that has intervened. From outside the children's voices are heard singing the first-act carol, and Werther asks to be buried under the lime trees at the far end of the cemetery or, if that is forbidden by the church, then in unhallowed ground, where the priests may pass by but at least one woman will weep at his grave. He dies as children's voices celebrate Christ's birth.

* * *

Goethe's novel, an early and crucial document of the Romantic movement, was both based on fact and, coincidentally, autobiographical. In 1772 the 23-year-old writer fell in love with Charlotte Buff, daughter of the Bailli of Wetzlar, who married instead Johann Christian Kestner; at the same time a mutual friend, Karl Wilhelm Jerusalem, shot himself for love of a married woman with pistols belonging to Kestner (the note he sent asking to borrow them survived and is quoted verbatim in both novel and opera). The publication of *Werther*, with its implicit condonation of suicide, caused a sensation; it is said that an entire Italian edition was suppressed – that is to say, sedulously bought up – by the church authorities. It was soon dramatized, and there were operas on it as early as 1792 (Rodolphe Kreutzer, Paris) and 1802 (Pucitta, Venice).

Quite why Massenet should have decided to set it nearly a century later, when the sensation had long passed, is something of a mystery. If he saw it as a companion piece to *Manon* – both deal with an amorous entanglement in an 18th-century setting – we may be thankful that musically they are sharply dissimilar and, more significantly, that the libretto of *Werther* is an infinitely more skilful adaptation of a novel than that of the earlier work: unnecessary detail is expunged, there is no chorus, and all is concentrated on the central relationship. The novel is cast in the form of letters, with Goethe intervening as 'editor' to describe the protagonist's suicide; for the opera a final duet was needed rather than the lonely death of the original (Werther never regains consciousness), and the text makes clever use of elements from the novel. There are other differences: in the novel, as in real life, Charlotte has not promised her dying mother to marry Albert, but does so out of choice, and similarly Albert has no idea why Werther/Jerusalem demands the pistols. The character of Sophie is much expanded in the opera, both as a musical foil and as the unfortunate victim of fallout from the central relationship.

Werther is a fine example of a middle-period opera by a composer who was able to enjoy a full life-span (*La traviata* and *Lohengrin* are useful analogues); there may be rough edges and problems of form, but there is also a fine balance between the vigour and freshness of the inspiration and the growing maturity of technique. In this respect it is interesting that, contrary to Massenet-inspired legend, *Werther* had a seven-year gestation period rather than just one year. The libretto is one of the best Massenet was given. While paying Gallic lip-service to the Romantic hyperbole of Goethe, there is a corresponding spareness of syntax that leaves the music plenty to do other than just illustrate and intensify. There is a lightly sketched-in and satisfying time-structure, from summer to winter, from lightness to dark, from the sun that Werther invokes at his first entry to the moon that sheds light on his first meeting with Charlotte and his death. Pantheism and bourgeois Christian values are interestingly enmeshed.

Werther is still basically a number opera, like *Manon*, as the titles quoted in the synopsis would suggest, but there are very few passages in which voices are heard together, and the numbers themselves are skilfully placed in the seamless flow of what is to all intents and purposes a through-composed conversation piece. There is also a spareness of orchestral texture, an overall darkness of colour in the frequent use of lower brass and woodwind that some have seen, perhaps facilely, as Wagnerian; be that as it may, Massenet never again risked so sombre a pervasive *tinta*, perhaps conscious of *Werther*'s uncertain reception in Paris both before and immediately after the first performance there.

In no other Massenet opera is the melodic inspiration so rich. The 'Invocation' may be inspired by 'Salut, demeure' in *Faust*, but it is thoroughly worthy of its model; both the 'Clair de lune', with its shy, filigree instrumentation, and the surging, neo-*verismo* 'Lied d'Ossian' are masterly, and it should be noted that when they are reprised they are slightly but significantly altered – something that does not happen in *Manon*. The sequence of Charlotte's 'Air des lettres', 'Air des larmes' and 'Prière' add up to an overwhelmingly grand *scena* for mezzo (it is hard to imagine a soprano, a Manon, coping with it at the Vienna première, since it needs a Berlioz Dido at the very least) on the scale of that for Desdemona in the last act of *Otello*, to which Massenet pays passing homage in Charlotte's *subito forte* cry of farewell to her sister. That this should be followed by the 'Lied' makes the third act one of the most inspired and powerfully sustained in all French opera, let alone in Massenet.

The violent 'Désolation', added after the completion of the score at, it has been suggested, the behest of Van Dyck, may be comparatively obvious, but the uncanonic version of the Prodigal Son later in the act is at once a supremely tactful and deeply felt setting of a potentially mawkish passage, and underlines what has been seen as a manic pattern in the protagonist's music, swinging from extremes of ecstasy to extremes of despair. It could be argued that Sophie's music is too relentlessly gay, but she is only 15 and the effect of her undeclared love for Werther as well as the instinctive understanding of a teenager for her elder sister's distress is artfully signalled in the swooning 3/4 tune that underpins the conversation on either side of the 'Air des larmes'.

Indeed, it is the psychological penetration through words and notes that impresses the most. Werther's passion noticeably intensifies once he realizes that his love for Charlotte is doomed (the whole 'Clair de lune' sequence shows extraordinary shrewdness of observation, not least in that neither character actually listens to what the other is saying) and there is something almost sinister in the way that for her own purposes Charlotte declines to release Werther from thraldom; the words 'Pourquoi l'oubli?' when she has already ordered him to leave verge on cruelty, and it is she who suggests Christmas as a possible time for meeting again. Here, one feels, are two people who in the interests of their own personal needs are determined to make each other as miserable as they possibly can, and they certainly succeed.

The significant changes to the original material show how the central misery is liberally spread around. Albert has few notes to sing, but a resourceful baritone can show how the iron enters his soul, how he is changed from a simple, virtuous man confident of his love into a husband who can order his wife to hand over the instruments of her lover's death. Similarly, young Sophie's life is blighted beyond recall by the unbridled and supremely selfish passions of her elders. *Werther* is on the surface a simple, almost commonplace story of love and death, but the composer's insights shed an uncomfortable light on the workings of the human psyche in a fashion that is, quite surprisingly, worthy of Goethe. Massenet may have matured subsequently as a composer, certainly in matters of form and technique, but he wrote nothing greater or more heartfelt than *Werther*.

RODNEY MILNES

Wessely, Carl Bernhard (*b* Berlin, 1 Sept 1768; *d* Potsdam, 11 July 1826). German composer. He came from a cultured Jewish family whose circle included Moses Mendelssohn (grandfather of Felix Mendelssohn) and the poet Karl Ramler. After studying music with J. A. P. Schultz in 1787 he went to Hamburg. He was appointed second music director of the Nationaltheater in Berlin in 1788 and eight years later Prince Heinrich of Prussia made him Kapellmeister at Rheinsberg. When the prince died in 1802 Wessely abandoned his musical career for family reasons and became a government official at Potsdam, where in 1814 he was co-founder of a society for classical music, which he conducted until his death. He was recognized by his contemporaries as an able pianist and composer. His opera *Psyche* failed in Berlin, however, partly owing to its mythological subject. Wessely published a comparison of Gluck and Mozart in *Archiv der Zeit* (November 1795, p.435) and contributed to the *Allgemeine musikalische Zeitung* (vol. ii, 1799–1800).

Psyche (Spl, 2, K. Müchler), Berlin, National, 18 Nov 1789, Act 1 *D-B*

Louis IX en Egypte (K. Gaillard), Rheinsberg, 1797

L'ogre, Rheinsberg, 1798/9

*

EitnerQ; *FétisB*; *MGG* (D. Härtwig)

G. Schilling, ed.: *Encyclopädie der gesamten musikalischen Wissenschaften* (Stuttgart, 1835–42)

C. von Ledebur: *Tonkünstler-Lexicon Berlins* (Berlin, 1861)

T. Bauman: *North German Opera in the Age of Goethe* (Cambridge, 1985)

DAVID CHARLTON

Westenholtz [Westenholz], **Ernst Carl Ludwig** (*b* Weterlingen, 24 Dec 1694; *d* Stade, 1753). German bass. According to Walther, he was engaged as a treble by the Margravine of Culmbach in 1704 before singing in the Landesschulen and royal chapels at Magdeburg (1710), Brunswick (1711) and Wolfenbüttel (1713). In 1718 he enrolled at the University of Helmstedt, but 'at the request of Gumbrecht, then director of the opera', he went to the Hamburg Gänsemarkt in 1719; apart from a spell in Copenhagen from 1721 to 1723, he remained there until 1733 as leading bass. His repertory included Handel's Curius (*Giulio Cesare*, 1725) and Tamerlane, Lucas in Keiser's *Der Hamburger Jahrmarkt* and *Die Hamburger Schlachtzeit* and roles by Porta, J. P. Kunzen, Lully, Porpora and Caldara. He sang in at least ten operas by Telemann including *Sancio*, *Das jauchzende Grossbritannien* and *Die verkehrte Welt* (Philosopher), appearing as Apollo in *Die aus der Einsamkeit zurückgekehrte Opera* (1729), under the composer's direction. He spent the last 20 years of his life at Stade, as Kantor.

*

WaltherML

W. Hobohm: 'Ernst Carl Ludwig Westenholz: ein bedeutender Sänger der deutschen Frühoper', *Jahresschrift des Kreismuseums Haldensleben*, xiii (1972), 59

K. Zelm: 'Die Sänger der Hamburger Gänsemarkt-Oper', *HJbMw*, iii (1978), 71–3

HANS JOACHIM MARX

Westergaard, Peter (Talbot) (*b* Champaign, IL, 28 May 1931). American composer. He studied with Piston at Harvard University (1951–3), Milhaud at Aspen and the Paris Conservatoire (1951–4), Sessions at Princeton University (1954–6) and Fortner in Germany (on a Fulbright grant, 1956–7). Since 1968 Westergaard has taught in the Princeton University music department. He has been director of the Princeton Opera Theatre since 1970 and has made English singing translations of all the Mozart-Da Ponte works and of *Fidelio*, *Der Freischütz* and *La Cenerentola*.

Westergaard's first opera, *Charivari*, in one act, was written in 1953 to a libretto by the composer, who describes the work as an 'irreverent neoclassical pastorale'. A Guggenheim Fellowship (1964) enabled Westergaard to begin his chamber opera *Mr & Mrs Discobbolos*, which was first performed in New York in 1966 by the Group for Contemporary Music, who later recorded the work (1971). The opera is based on Edward Lear's poem of the Discobbolos couple, who lived happily on top of a wall with their 12 children for 20 years, a month and a day, until their explosive demise. The work includes recitatives, arias and a grand duet, self-references (mini-leitmotifs) and internal puns, and instrumental commentary and interludes. The essences of tragicomic grand opera are parodistically depicted, albeit filtered and distilled (the work lasts a modest 17 minutes).

Another opera, *Tempest*, in three acts, was begun in 1970 and completed in 1990; it received its première at the June Opera Festival at Lawrenceville, New Jersey, in 1992 (although excerpts from Act 1 were given earlier, in 1985 and 1991).

Charivari (chamber op, 1, Westergaard), Cambridge, MA, Sanders, May 1953
Mr & Mrs Discobbolos (chamber op, 2, after E. Lear), New York, Columbia U., 21 March 1966, vs (New York, 1967)
Tempest, 1970–90 (3, Westergaard, after W. Shakespeare), Lawrenceville, New Jersey, 1992 ELAINE BARKIN

Westerhout, Nicola [Niccolò] **van** (*b* Mola, nr Bari, 17 Dec 1857; *d* Naples, 21 Aug 1898). Italian composer. He was born into a musical family of Dutch origin that had been settled in and around Bari for more than a century. He first studied with his father or his grandfather and from 1876 at the Naples Conservatory, where he was a pupil of D'Arienzo, De Giosa and Lauro Rossi; he also attended courses in aesthetics. He became a well-known pianist. Although not in sympathy with the academicism of contemporary Neapolitan musical culture, he became harmony teacher at the Naples Conservatory in 1897. His opera *Doña Flor* was written for the inauguration of the Teatro van Westerhout, Mola, in 1896.

Cimbelino (dramma lirico, 4, E. Golisciani, after W. Shakespeare), private perf., Naples, 1887; Rome, Argentina, 7 April 1892 [? rev. of earlier work, Una notte a Venezia; see Schmidl]
Fortunio (Scalinger), Milan, 16 May 1895, vs (Milan, n.d.)
Doña Flor (A. Colautti), Mola, Westerhout, 18 April 1896, vs (Milan, n.d.)
Colomba (Colautti), Naples, 27 March 1923
Tilde, unperf.

*

RicordiE; *SchmidlD*
A. Giovane: 'Nicola van Westerhout', *Musicisti e cantanti della terra di Bari* (Bari, 1968) SERGIO MARTINOTTI

Western, Ethel. *See* THALBERG, ZARÉ.

Western Australian Opera Company. Company established in 1967 in PERTH.

West Indies. Opera came to most of the West Indies principally through the French. In the 18th century the prosperous settlers of Martinique, Guadeloupe and Saint-Domingue (now Haiti) wanted the best of Paris fashions, including plays and opera. Over the following 150 years operatic enterprise struggled through wars, cyclones, earthquakes, volcanic eruptions, plagues and bankruptcy. The theatres were eclectic rather than specialist, giving performances of comedy, drama, vaudeville, opera, operetta and ballet, often with a mixture of different elements on the same evening.

In Saint-Domingue there were theatres at Port-au-Prince and Cap Français, where opera (mostly *opéra comique*) was given, including works by Rousseau, Monsigny, Philidor, Grétry, Duni, Paisiello, Sacchini and Gluck. The singers came from France, and at this period there was much to-ing and fro-ing by them between the West Indies and Louisiana, especially New Orleans. After Haiti became independent at the beginning of the 19th century, it ceased to be an operatic centre.

Probably the most splendid of the French colonial opera houses was built in 1786 in Martinique at St Pierre, then one of the most prosperous commercial centres of the Americas, by a syndicate of four local merchants; it held 800 in a parterre and four galleries. It was inaugurated with two plays in 1786, the first opera performed being Dalayrac's *Le corsair* on 30 July 1788. During the Revolution, the theatre became a centre of republican activities. Martinique fell to the English in 1794 and was only restored to the French in 1802, the event being celebrated with Dalayrac's *Camille, ou Le souterrain*, sung by a new troupe from France. During the performance the prima donna, Bérengère, died on stage of yellow fever, and the panic-stricken audience fled. During the following days, of the 25 artists who formed the troupe, 15 died.

Much damage was caused by the cyclone of 1813, and, with Martinique again under English occupation (1809–15), the damage was not immediately repaired. In 1816 the derelict theatre was acquired by the town council, lavishly restored and re-inaugurated in 1817. Between 1817 and 1819 the theatre staged ten works by Dalayrac, four by Grétry, four by Isouard, two by Boieldieu and Méhul's *Une folie* and his *Joseph*, the first time that an opera on so serious a subject became a hit (it had four performances). Public disorder closed the theatre in 1830. It was reopened in 1836 with no racial discrimination. Hitherto, coloured people had been relegated to the third gallery, the fourth being for slaves, an enthusiastic if not economically viable part of the audience. Black and coloured artists, however, had always been welcome as singers and instrumentalists, and some black and coloured musicians had even composed *opéras comiques* with the *airs* in Creole. The new director, Charvet, made price, not colour, the sole criterion for admission, as he had done at his theatre in Guadeloupe in 1831. Charvet also ran the private subscription theatre in the capital of Martinique, Fort Royal (later Fort-de-France), which he lavishly restored. The earthquake of 11 January 1839 which totally destroyed the town ruined him.

During the 19th century the Théâtre de St Pierre in Martinique was run by impresarios (with municipal subsidies) who presented the standard repertory of a French provincial theatre – *Carmen*, *Faust*, *Lakmé*, works by Donizetti, Meyerbeer, Verdi and others, and all the most popular operettas. A gala performance of *La Juive* was given in 1881 for Ferdinand de Lesseps on his way to Panama. Some of the best troupes were directed by Roumégoux, who was later to become the director of the theatre at Algiers. On 18 August 1891 a cyclone destroyed the theatre and activity was transferred to the salon of the Town Hall, which took the name Théâtre Bourgeois. A new theatre was built in 1900 on the model of the Grand Théâtre, Bordeaux, with a grand staircase and a cupola. A new troupe of 34 was formed by Erhard, Roumégoux's former pianist, and it presented an opening season that included *La traviata*, *Faust*, *Il trovatore*, *Robert le diable* and *La belle Hélène* and other popular operettas. It ruined him, and he was declared bankrupt in May 1901. On 8 May 1902 the volcanic Mount Pelée erupted, completely destroying St Pierre and killing all its inhabitants. The ruins of the theatre's monumental grand staircase can still be seen in a garden.

Seasons of opera are now given at the Teatro Nacional, Santo Domingo, capital of the Dominican Republic, in the Auditorium at Havana, Cuba, and in the Centro de Bellas Artes, San Juan, Puerto Rico.

See also HAVANA; PORT-AU-PRINCE; and SAN JUAN.

*

J. Fouchard: *Artistes et répertoire des scènes de Saint-Domingue* (Port-au-Prince, 1955)
——: *Le théâtre à Saint-Domingue* (Port-au-Prince, 1955)
M. Nicolas: 'Le théâtre de St Pierre au 18e siècle', *Annales des Antilles*, i (1955), 53–64
——: *Les grandes heures du théâtre de St. Pierre* (Fort-de-France, 1974) CHARLES PITT

Westrup, Sir **Jack Allan** (*b* London, 26 July 1904; *d* Headley, Hants., 21 April 1975). English scholar, teacher and conductor. He studied classics at Oxford, where he was musical director of the university Opera Club (1927). After a period of research in France he taught in London schools and at the RAM, also conducting at the London Opera Festival (1929–30), working as a critic for the *Daily Telegraph* and editing the *Monthly Musical Record* (1933–45). He was appointed university lecturer in Newcastle (1941), then Professor at Birmingham (1944) and finally at Oxford (1947–71), where he directed the Opera Club, 1947–62. A leading figure in British musicology, he was editor of *Music & Letters* and chairman of the *New Oxford History of Music* as well as president of the Royal Musical Association (1958–63). His chief interests lay in 17th-century England, but his operatic sympathies were wide. As an undergraduate he prepared an edition of Monteverdi's *Orfeo* for use at Oxford (1925, also performed in London in 1926 and 1929) and he did much to stimulate the revival of interest in Baroque opera; works he directed at Oxford include Wellesz's *Incognita*, Stravinsky's *Oedipus rex*, Ravel's *L'enfant et les sortilèges*, Berlioz's *Les Troyens* and Alessandro Scarlatti's *Mitridate Eupatore*. Purcell, Monteverdi and the recitative are among the topics treated in his scholarly writings.

West Side Story. Musical in two acts by LEONARD BERNSTEIN to a libretto by Arthur Laurents after WILLIAM SHAKESPEARE, from a conception by Jerome Robbins, with lyrics by STEPHEN SONDHEIM; Washington, DC, National Theatre, 19 August 1957 (New York, Winter Garden, 26 September 1957).

The idea of telling the Romeo and Juliet story in terms specific to New York City and its tensions had been discussed since 1949 by the choreographer Jerome Robbins, Arthur Laurents and Leonard Bernstein. The three collaborators kept changing their minds as to the proper social identity of the rival groups, but the work finally took shape, with Stephen Sondheim added to the team. Bernstein produced his own orchestrations, with Sid Ramin and Irwin Kostal. After a mixed critical reception, the musical proved only moderately successful during its initial Broadway run.

The story is set among two rival youth gangs in New York City in the 1950s, the longer-established Jets, led by Riff, and the Puerto Rican newcomers, the Sharks, led by Bernardo. Riff intends to meet Bernardo at a community dance – neutral territory – and challenge him to a fight for control of the neighbourhood. Tony (tenor), a former Jet and Riff's best friend, meets Maria (soprano), Bernardo's sister, at the dance, and they fall immediately in love. They meet that night on her fire escape, and again the next day at the shop where she works, where they enact a mock wedding ceremony. Tony tries to intervene at the rumble but succeeds only in accidentally permitting Bernardo to kill Riff; in a rage, Tony himself kills Bernardo. Maria manages to forgive him and they decide to run away together. She sends a message to Tony who is in hiding with the Jets, by Bernardo's girlfriend Anita, but the gang so abuse her that she angrily tells them Maria is dead. Tony, in despair, runs through the streets begging to be killed; he discovers that Maria is alive just as a Shark shoots him. Maria in her grief manages to persuade everyone to let the retaliation stop, giving a hint of hope for reconciliation as the play ends.

Groundbreaking among musicals in its tragic tone (death was hardly unknown in serious musicals of the 1940s and 50s, but choosing to end both acts with corpses on stage was probably unprecedented), *West Side Story* was even more innovatory in its integration of dance; indeed, Jerome Robbins must be considered an author of the work along with Laurents, Sondheim and Bernstein. Not only is he credited with the initial concept, but his ideas for its realization determined the casting and hence the style of vocal writing. All roles except for the few adults (and to some extent the two romantic leads) were cast primarily for dancing ability; where other dance-dominated musicals of the period employed separate singing and dancing choruses, *West Side Story* eliminated the former, and replaced the latter with a cast of named, individualized roles. Most of the dance sequences are separate, dramatically eventful numbers rather than appendages to songs, and were (like the dances in his earlier musicals) composed by Bernstein himself. Compiled as an orchestral piece, *Symphonic Dances from 'West Side Story'*, they are almost as well known as the songs. Now among the most familiar written for any American musical, the songs themselves achieved this status only gradually, aided by the popular film version of the musical released in 1961.

Bernstein unified his score around a single interval: the augmented 4th or tritone, often as C rising to F♯. Prominent melodically throughout the Prologue (and thus the 'Jet Song', which shares the same material), 'Something's Coming', 'Maria', 'Cool', the Rumble and 'Gee, Officer Krupke', this interval also emerges as a contrapuntal or tonal element in other numbers – for instance harmonically in the first two bars of 'Tonight' and 'I Have a Love', as figuration in the interlude of 'I Feel Pretty' and as a countermelody in 'One Hand, One Heart'. Significantly, it is absent from the idyllic dream of a better world reaching a balletic high point in the second act.

Another unifying feature is the handling of 'Tonight': it is used first as the centrepiece of the balcony scene, surrounded by underscoring recalling 'Maria' and giving a premonition of 'Somewhere', and second as part of the contrapuntal Quintet preceding the Rumble. Further attractions in the score include the fugal dance section of 'Cool' (a successful excursion into jazz idioms of the time), the contrapuntal combination of 'Somewhere' and 'I Have a Love' in the procession music, and the combination of the Mambo (from the Dance at the Gym) and 'America' as background (partly played on a radio) for the taunting of Anita.

These musical subtleties play their part in the richness of *West Side Story*, its ability to bear repeated viewings and hearings and its stature as one of the finest of all musicals. While it has weak points, some readily pointed out by its authors – dated slang, over-didactic dramaturgy, a failure to find music for Maria's final scene – these matter little compared with the effect of the work in almost any capable performance, its emotional power deriving from a truly operatic fusion of musical and dramatic impulses. JON ALAN CONRAD

Wette [née Humperdinck], **Adelheid** (*b* Siegburg, 4 Sept 1858; *d* 1916). German writer. The younger sister of the composer Engelbert Humperdinck, she contributed much to the family interest in folksong and fairy-tales; Humperdinck set song texts by his sister and father throughout his life. Adelheid married the Cologne doctor Hermann Wette, the author of two folklike librettos for Arnold Mendelssohn. Her own libretto for Humperdinck's *Hänsel und Gretel* began in 1890 as a series of folksongs, four of which she asked her brother to set. Her skill in expanding these into a fully-fledged opera, while keeping the text's unpretentious character, was recognized as an important ingredient in the work's eventual success. In 1895 she collaborated with Humperdinck on another Grimm fairy-tale, *Die sieben Geislein*, but this work remained a series of domestic songs. AMANDA GLAUERT

Wettergren [Pålson-Wettergren], **Gertrud** (*b* Eslöv, Malmö, 17 Feb 1897). Swedish contralto. She studied in Stockholm, and made her début there in 1922 as Cherubino. Engaged at the Stockholm Royal Opera for the next 27 years, she also sang thoughout Europe and in the USA, making her Metropolitan début in 1935 as Amneris, and her Chicago début the following year as Carmen. First heard at Covent Garden in 1936 as Amneris, she returned in 1939 as Azucena. Her large repertory included several Wagner roles – Brangäne, Venus, Fricka – as well as Delilah, Mignon, Herodias (*Salome*), Marina (*Boris Godunov*) and Marfa (*Khovanshchina*). She also appeared in many Swedish operas, including Peterson-Berger's *Adils och Elisiv* and *Domedagsprofeterna*, Rosenberg's *Resa till Amerika*, Atterberg's *Bäckahästen* and Gunnar de Frumerie's *Singoalla*, in which she sang the title role. She retired in 1949. Her voice, a true contralto, was firm and well projected, while her strong personality made her a fine interpreter of such roles as Carmen or Delilah.

*

I. Kolodin: *The Story of the Metropolitan Opera* (New York, 1951)
H. Rosenthal: *Two Centuries of Opera at Covent Garden* (London, 1958) ELIZABETH FORBES

Wetz, Richard (*b* Gleiwitz, Upper Silesia, 26 Feb 1875; *d* Erfurt, 16 Jan 1935). German composer. He studied at the Leipzig Conservatory, then privately with Thuille in Munich (1899–1900). He spent two years as Kapellmeister in the theatres of Stralsund and Barmen. In 1906 he moved permanently to Erfurt, where he worked as a conductor and teacher; he was elected to the Preussische Akademie der Künste in Berlin in 1928. The Richard Wetz-Gesellschaft was founded in Gleiwitz in 1943. Although best known for his choral works, Wetz composed two operas to his own librettos, *Judith* (unpublished) and the one-act *Das ewige Feuer* (19 March 1907, Düsseldorf). The latter, despite small dimensions, is Wagnerian in theme and style.

CHARLOTTE ERWIN

Wexford. Small town and fishing port in south-east Ireland. It is the home of the annual Wexford Festival of opera, founded in October 1951 by a local doctor, T. J. Walsh, at the prompting of Compton Mackenzie. As artistic director, Walsh inaugurated an enterprising policy of giving the public 'not what it knew and liked but what it might come to like', resulting in the distinctive Wexford tradition of presenting little-known and long-neglected works in a scheme of 'one for the heart, one for the head and one for fun'. In practice this turned out to be largely early 19th-century opera, by Bellini, Donizetti, Rossini and the young Verdi; the festival opened with Balfe's *Rose of Castille*.

Although Radio Telefís Éireann provided professional orchestral support from the beginning, the festival depended on considerable amateur involvement; rudimentary stagings were offset by the participation of such singers as Janet Baker, Graziella Sciutti, Ugo Benelli and Christiane Eda-Pierre at the outset of their careers. Latterly Sergei Leiferkus and Kristine Ciesinski have made noteworthy appearances. The success of *Don Quichotte* in 1965 led to a tradition of Massenet, Gounod, Delibes and Lalo, but programmes have also included Janáček (*Kát'a Kabanová*, 1972), Prokofiev (*The Gambler*, 1973), Marschner (*Hans Heiling*, 1983; *Der Templer und die Jüdin*, 1989; *Der Vampyr*, 1992), Goetz (*Der widerspänstigen Zähmung*, 1991) and Giordano (*La cena delle beffe*, 1987). The later 18th century has received attention, too, notably Haydn and early Mozart. Wexford has yet to embrace contemporary opera or commission a new work.

Three operas are performed over a period of up to two weeks in the Theatre Royal; built in the 1830s, the plain, rectangular auditorium had 440 seats until 1987 when, along with other improvements, capacity was increased to 555. Limited stage facilities remain a test of directors' ingenuity.

After Walsh's retirement in 1966 the directorship became a professional post, held successively by Brian Dickie (to 1974), Thomson Smillie (to 1978), Adrian Slack (to 1981) and, from 1982, Elaine Padmore. During the 1980s, productions have benefited from imaginative young directors and designers from all over the world; the scope of the festival has been widened, and programmes of popular operatic scenes given during the day in White's Barn. Now part of the growing international festival scene, Wexford attracts some 40% of its audiences from overseas. Happily, it retains a unique atmosphere of informal conviviality.

*

I. Fox: *100 Nights at the Opera: Wexford Festival Opera – an Anthology* (Dublin, 1991) ROBERT HARTFORD

Weyse, Christoph Ernst Friedrich (*b* Altona, nr Hamburg, 5 March 1774; *d* Copenhagen, 8 Oct 1842). Danish composer. He went to Copenhagen in 1789 to study with J. A. P. Schulz, musical director of the Kongelige Teater, and remained in the city for the rest of his life, becoming organist at the cathedral in 1805, titular professor at the university in 1816 and in 1819 court composer with the obligation to produce cantatas and operas. He was known for his excellent improvisation on the organ and piano and for his artistic taste (in musical and other matters), and in his later years he was the major authority in Copenhagen's musical life.

Weyse's musical ideals were very conservative and extended from Bach and Handel to Gluck and Haydn, but not beyond Mozart. This is particularly evident in three of his six Singspiel-type operas: the first, *Sovedrikken* ('The Sleeping-Draught', 1809) – a comedy similar in character to Dittersdorf's *Doktor und Apotheker* – whose fresh and charming music has made it the most performed of his operas, the oriental-inspired *Faruk* (1812) and *Ludlam's Hule* ('Ludlam's Cave', 1816), a melodramatic ghost story set in Scotland; each of them shows the stylistic influences of Schulz and Mozart. After these works Weyse wrote incidental music to Shakespeare's *Macbeth* (1817), which contains interesting music for the witches' choruses and banquet scene. His later operas, particularly *Floribella* (1825) and *Festen paa Kenilworth* ('The Feast at Kenilworth', 1836), are conceived on a larger scale with more extended dramatic forms – notably the big choruses of

Moors and Elves in *Floribella* and the differing ensembles and finales (with ballet) in *Kenilworth* – and with more varied harmonies. But on the whole Weyse lacked the dramatic flair of his contemporary Friedrich Kuhlau. In all his dramatic works the finest numbers are the shorter arias and ensembles, many of them examples of his attractive personal style – a lyrical, strophic song in moderate 6/8 time derived from the siciliana, with a characteristically Danish melodic structure. The latter had a lasting influence on Danish music and has made Weyse's dramatic songs, together with the other songs in his output, some of the best-loved in Denmark.

all first performed at the Kongelige Teater, Copenhagen; autograph scores in DK-Kk; printed works published in Copenhagen

Sovedrikken [The Sleeping-Draught] (Spl, 2, A. Oehlenschlaeger, after C. F. Bretzner), 21 April 1809, also in *B-Br*, vs (1815–16)
Faruk (Spl, 3, Oehlenschlaeger), 30 Jan 1812, ov. and excerpts, vs (1817–28)
Ludlams Hule [Ludlam's Cave] (Spl, 4, Oehlenschlaeger), 30 Jan 1816, vs (1821–2)
Floribella (lyrical-romantic drama, 3, entr'acte, C. J. Boye), 29 Jan 1825, vs (1837)
Et eventyr i Rosenborg Have [An Adventure in Rosenborg Gardens] (Spl, 1, J. L. Heiberg), 26 May 1827, vs (1833)
Festen paa Kenilworth [The Feast at Kenilworth] (romantic Spl, 3, H. C. Andersen, after W. Scott), 6 Jan 1836, vs (1877)

*

T. Overskou: *Den danske Skueplads*, iv–v (Copenhagen, 1862–4)
C. Thrane: *Danske komponister* (Copenhagen, 1875), 6–70
A. P. Berggreen: *C. E. F. Weyses biographie* (Copenhagen, 1876) [incl. Weyse's autobiography, originally pubd in *Hesperus*, iii, 1820, pp.140–78]
W. Behrend: 'Weyse und Kuhlau', *Die Musik*, iii (1903–4), 272–86
S. Lunn and E. Reitzel-Neilsen, eds.: C. E. F. Weyse: Breve [Letters] (Copenhagen, 1964)
K. Å. Bruun: *Dansk musiks historie*, i (Copenhagen, 1969), 126–85
D. Fog: *Kompositionen von C. E. F. Weyse: Thematisch-bibliographischer Katalog* (Copenhagen, 1979) GORM BUSK

Wheeler, Hugh Callingham (*b* London, 19 March 1912; *d* Pittsfield, MA, 27 July 1987). American lyricist and librettist of English birth. Wheeler turned to the musical stage after a successful career as an author of mysteries and as a playwright. His best-known works were his book for Sondheim's *A Little Night Music* (1973), the revisions he made in Bernstein's *Candide* for its 1974 revival, and his libretto for *Sweeney Todd* (Sondheim, 1979). He also assisted on the libretto for *Pacific Overtures* (Sondheim, 1975). Just before his death he finished a stage adaptation of the 1944 film musical *Meet me in St Louis* (songs by Hugh Martin and Ralph Blane; 1989). All his work was adapted from other men's material and developed in collaboration.

GERALD BORDMAN

Whelen, Christopher (*b* London, 17 April 1927). English composer. He studied at the Birmingham and Midland School of Music (1944–6) and later with Rudolf Schwarz. From 1951 to 1955 he was musical director of the Old Vic Theatre and in 1956 won the Sprague Coolidge Medal. He has always composed painstakingly and self-critically, and has shown considerable talent as a music dramatist. His best work – in a conservatively inclined idiom but with a distinctive and personal edge – is in the radio operas, of which *The Findings* and *Incident at Owl Creek* are outstanding.

all broadcast by the BBC

The Cancelling Dark (radio op, 1, V. Scannell), 1964
Some Place of Darkness (television op, 1, J. Hopkins), 23 Jan 1967
Incident at Owl Creek (radio op, 1, Whelen, after A. Bierce), 26 May 1969
The Findings (radio op, 1, Whelen), 16 July 1972

*

A. Jacobs: 'Some Place of Darkness', *Opera*, xviii (1967), 261–2
R. Milnes: 'The Findings', *Opera*, xxiii (1972), 945–8

CHRISTOPHER PALMER

Where the Wild Things Are. Fantasy opera in one act, op.20, by OLIVER KNUSSEN (1979–83) to a libretto by Maurice Sendak after his book; preliminary version in two acts, Brussels, Théâtre de La Monnaie, 28 November 1980; definitive version, London, National Theatre (Glyndebourne Touring Opera), 9 January 1984.

The opera concerns a six-year-old boy, Max (soprano). Sent to bed without his supper for defying his harassed Mama (mezzo-soprano), he imagines his room turning into a jungle from which he journeys by sea to the land of the Wild Things (solo quintet) who crown him king and follow him in a Wild Rumpus. Missing his creature comforts, Max escapes from the Wild Things, travelling home to his room to find his supper waiting after all. In elaborating words, designs and musical forms from what is essentially a picture book, Sendak and Knussen were consciously attempting to revive the genre of fantasy opera as represented by Stravinsky's *The Nightingale* and Ravel's *L'enfant et les sortilèges*. Scored for an orchestra of 48 (without trumpets) and running just under 40 minutes, the opera transcends the 'magic' scores in its background – Musorgsky, early Stravinsky, Debussy's *La boîte à joujoux* – in a luminous delicacy and exuberance of its own. During its composition, Knussen extracted Max's four numbers and journey to make a 17-minute concert piece for soprano and orchestra, *Songs and a Sea Interlude* op.20*a*, and later, as a four-minute orchestral item, *The Wild Rumpus* op.20*b*.

BAYAN NORTHCOTT

Whirlpool, The [*Krútňava* (*Katrena*)]. Opera in an overture and six scenes by EUGEN SUCHOŇ to a libretto by the composer and Štefan Hoza after Milo Urban's short story *Za vyšným mlynom* ('Over the Upper Mill'); Bratislava, Slovak National Opera, 10 December 1949.

Štelina	bass
Ondrej	tenor
Katrena	soprano
Zimoň } *Ondrej's parents*	bass
Zimoňka }	mezzo-soprano
Zalčíčka *Katrena's stepmother*	soprano
Školnica *Katrena's godmother*	contralto
Marka } *Katrena's friends*	soprano
Zuzka }	contralto
A Young Shepherd	soprano
Krúpa	tenor
Hríň	baritone
Oleň	bass
Bridegroom's Witness	bass
Bride's Witness	contralto
First Bridesman	tenor
A Woman	soprano
A Cook	soprano
Commander of Police	spoken
Policeman	spoken
Two Men	spoken

Villagers, wedding guests, musicians

Setting A village in Slovakia

Composed between 1941 and 1949, *The Whirlpool* was an immediate success, with 40 performances in its first two seasons. Further productions soon followed: Vajda (p.349) lists 43 up to 1985, several of them in the West (including the USA), where the work is sometimes given under the name *Katrena.* It is the most successful and most frequently performed postwar Czechoslovak opera and the foundation stone of modern Slovak opera. Suchoň enriched the genre with folk colour in his depiction of popular festivities and wedding celebrations (though only two genuine folk melodies are quoted), and reinforced the social context while attempting to invest the whole work with a statement of belief in the purifying and cathartic nature of art. The chorus not only contributes to the action but also acts as the conscience of rural society; in the words of Polyakova, 'The voice of the chorus, which Ondrej hears as that of the people, although it is in fact his own inner voice, persuades him finally to admit his crime and to give himself up willingly to justice'. In writing the libretto Suchoň and Hoza added many elements of folk poetry to Urban's text, including fragments of songs, rhymes and proverbs as well as characteristic figures of speech and turns of phrase.

OVERTURE The offstage chorus sings of the uplifting qualities of music.

SCENE 1 *A forest, sunrise* Katrena's lover, Jan, has been murdered and his body found in a clearing in the woods.

SCENE 2 *An anteroom at the village police station, a week later* Katrena laments Jan's death in an extended aria, 'Žiale bôl'ne, pálčivé' ('Burning sorrow torments my soul'). Her godmother tries to comfort her, urging her to marry Ondrej, who had courted her before Jan. The police have been unable to discover who killed Jan; his father, Štelina, recalls how he struggled alone to bring up his son and vows to avenge Jan's death by finding the culprit himself.

SCENE 3 *A decorated room in the Zimoňs' house, a month later* Against her inclinations, Katrena has allowed herself to be persuaded by the women of the village to marry Ondrej. The wedding festivities are disrupted by the bitter accusations of Štelina, against Katrena for being guilty of perjury before God and against Ondrej for taking Jan's place in her affections. Ondrej angrily orders the musicians to start playing again and, to the sounds of singing and dancing, leads Katrena victoriously away.

SCENE 4 *Katrena and Ondrej's peasant house, a year later* Katrena has given birth to a son. She confides to Zuzka that she is troubled by Ondrej's increasingly unreasonable behaviour. Štelina has become reconciled with Katrena but continues to mistrust Ondrej, who is convinced that Jan was the father of the child. Ondrej attacks both Štelina and Katrena and runs away.

SCENE 5 *In the forest that night* On his way home from the inn Ondrej, in a drunken state, finds himself at the spot where he killed Jan. He is overcome by terror and remorse and tormented by the obsession that the baby may be Jan's. He hears voices (those of the young people from the highlands on their way to the village festival) and thinks they are the voices of the dead pursuing him. After an agonized internal debate he dramatically declares himself to be Jan's murderer.

SCENE 6 *A village festival the next day* A young shepherd who works for Ondrej is found using the rifle with which Jan was killed. He says that he saw Ondrej hiding it at night in a stable. Štelina approaches Ondrej in a murderous rage, but the latter is about to give himself up to the police and makes a public confession of his crime. When Katrena discloses that Ondrej is the father of her baby, Štelina takes her and the boy to live with him.

* * *

The musical style of *The Whirlpool* is an original synthesis of developments in European music and fundamental operatic principles. Suchoň combined Romantic passion with Classical modes of construction, juxtaposing the contrapuntal technique of the high Baroque and elements of impressionism and expressionism, and blending all these with the modal structure of Slovak folksongs to create his own musical language. He rejected Wagnerian economy of thematic material in favour of a method of composition and treatment of motifs closer to those of Musorgsky and Janáček, as can be seen in his use of ostinatos, in the breaking up of a calm melodic surface with short rhythmic figures and in the portrayal of the murderer's public repentance.

Suchoň's themes represent situations, atmosphere and emotions rather than characters. The main thematic cell of *The Whirlpool*, from which almost all the music grows, is derived from a vocal figure used to great effect in Ondrej's cry 'Not I!' in Scene 5: an ascending 4th followed by a descending minor 3rd, out of which Suchoň forged a wide range of musical ideas, often distinctly contrasted. A typical example is a repeated motif played on the flute or clarinet in idyllic and love scenes but also used in altered form to represent the negative aspects of passion. The descending minor 3rd is often underpinned with closely spaced chords made up of perfect and augmented 4ths, signifying horror. The parallel movement of major 3rds has a similar function.

The harmonic basis of *The Whirlpool* is derived from the C major scale with a sharpened fourth degree and from a combination and modification of 9th, 11th and 13th chords which move away from the functional role of chords in Classical and Romantic writing. The main harmonic cell in the opera is a chord made up of two augmented 4ths a major 2nd apart (e.g. B–C♯–F–G, sometimes modified slightly). The melodic line, too, is based largely on these chords. Rhythmically, the flow of the music is often disrupted by syncopation in agitated passages, and there are frequent changes of metre and much use of contrasting rhythm patterns, generating a constant sense of forward movement heightened by the interjection of dance passages.

As well as arias and recitatives the opera makes use of spoken dialogue, both on its own and against a musical background. A notable feature of its structure is an overall symmetry of design: it is framed by introductory and concluding choruses, and the central fourth scene is similarly set off by a lullaby heard at the beginning and at the end. The opening and closing numbers of Scene 2 are also linked motivically. The groundplan is that of a sonata, the first three scenes constituting the exposition. The development unfolds in Scene 4. Scene 5 acts as an introduction to Scene 6, and the two together make up the recapitulation. These formal principles can also be detected within individual scenes. But *The Whirlpool* is not a symphonic opera: the composer consistently ensures that the voice is never swamped by over-dense orchestration. The orchestra is given full rein only in the instrumental preludes, interludes and postludes (codas).

Profoundly uplifting on many levels, *The Whirlpool* is remarkable for its vitality, broad dramatic range and vivid contrasts, and stands among the finest postwar operas. IGOR VAJDA

White, Clarence Cameron (*b* Clarksville, TN, 10 Aug 1880; *d* New York, 30 June 1960). American composer and violinist. He studied in London (summer of 1906, 1908–10) and Paris (1930–32); his teachers included Samuel Coleridge-Taylor, M. Zacharevich and Raoul Laparra. For many years he combined teaching with touring as a concert violinist. He received several awards, including two Rosenwald Fellowships, and the David Bispham Medal (1932) for his three-act opera *Ouanga* (originally entitled *Cocomagne*). To a libretto by John F. Matheus based on a Haitian historical episode, the opera was first performed on 10 June 1949 in South Bend, Indiana (the New York première was in May 1956, by the National Negro Opera Company at the Metropolitan Opera). White composed one other opera, *A Carnival Romance* (1952; in two acts, to his own libretto), besides a number of instrumental works and songs. His basically neo-romantic style was infused with the sharp rhythms and colourful melodies of Haitian and creole-American folksong. Critics noted especially his skilled orchestration and vigorous handling of the choral parts. His music manuscripts, as well as other papers, are held in the Schomburg Center for Research in Black Culture in the New York Public Library. EILEEN SOUTHERN

White, Don(ald Edwin) (*b* London, 14 Nov 1933). English translator. With Michael Scott, he made a free adaptation of Donizetti's *Le convenienze e inconvenienze teatrali* in its one-act form (as *The Prima Donna's Mother is a Drag*) for a production at the Camden Festival in 1972. The following year he provided an English version of Offenbach's *Robinson Crusoé* for the Opera Rara production at Camden (apparently the first British staged production) which was of exceptional neatness and wit. *Christopher Columbus* followed in 1976, using music from 22 little-heard Offenbach operettas. ARTHUR JACOBS

White, Eric Walter (*b* Bristol, 10 Sept 1905; *d* London, 13 Sept 1985). English writer on music and administrator. After studying at Oxford he held non-musical posts in Geneva; he then moved to arts administration, working for the British Arts Council (and its predecessor) until 1971. As a writer he concentrated on two areas: the music of Stravinsky, on whom he wrote his most important book, the climax of over 40 years of interest in the composer, and English opera, where his most valuable work was his close investigation into performances of the late 17th and early 18th centuries, as well as the music of Britten and Tippett, on which he published several articles in periodicals and symposia.

Benjamin Britten: a Sketch of his Life and Works (London, 1948, enlarged 3/1970 as *Benjamin Britten: his Life and Operas*; Ger. trans., 1948)
The Rise of English Opera (London, 1951)
Stravinsky: the Composer and his Works (London, 1966, 2/1979)
A Register of First Performances of English Operas and Semi-Operas from the 16th Century to 1980 (London, 1983)
A History of English Opera (London, 1983)

White, John (*b* Berlin, 5 April 1936). English composer. He studied composition with Lutyens and at the RCM (1954–7), and was music director of Western Theatre Ballet from 1959 to 1960. He then taught composition at the RCM (1961–6) and played the tuba with the London Gabrieli Brass Ensemble (1971–2). He has also worked extensively in commercial music. His output includes 119 piano sonatas, 21 symphonies and 30 ballets. He has composed two two-act chamber operas to librettos by Robin Barson; written for and performed by students at the Drama Centre, London, they use an accessible and eclectic tonal language that acknowledges the influence of Janáček and Busoni. *Stanley and the Monkey King*, first performed on 27 March 1975, is based on Kafka's *The Trial*; *Orpheus: Eurydice*, given on 6 April 1976, relates to initiation rites, not the well-known Orpheus legend. His third music-theatre piece, *Man/Machine Interface*, on themes from the world of design and fashion, is written for singers, dancers and fashion models, chamber ensemble and electronic instruments.

B. Dennis: Review of *Orpheus: Eurydice*, *MT*, cxvii (1976), 586–7
MICHAEL PARSONS

White, Willard (*b* St Catherine, Jamaica, 10 Oct 1946). Jamaican bass. After studying in New York, he made his début in 1974 at Washington, DC, as Trulove, then sang with New York City Opera. His British début was with the WNO in 1976 as Osmin and he then sang Massimiliano (*I masnadieri*) and Orestes (*Elektra*). For the ENO he has sung Seneca, Hunding, Achillas (*Giulio Cesare*), Golaud and Boris (*Lady Macbeth of the Mtsensk District*), and his Glyndebourne roles include the Speaker, Colline, King of Clubs (*Love for Three Oranges*) and Porgy. At Amsterdam he has sung Oroveso, Banquo, the Forester (*Cunning Little Vixen*), Prince Gremin and Pizarro. He made his Covent Garden début in 1980 as Don Diégo (*L'Africaine*), returning for Klingsor, Timur and Fafner. His repertory includes Sarastro, Leporello and Wotan, which he sang for Scottish Opera (*Das Rheingold*, 1989 and *Die Walküre*, 1991). A powerful singer with a resonant voice, he is a superb actor who has also played Shakespeare's Othello on the spoken stage.

M. Loppert: 'Willard White', *Opera*, xl (1989), 18–25
ELIZABETH FORBES

Whitehead, Gillian (*b* Hamilton, New Zealand, 23 April 1941). New Zealand composer. She studied in New Zealand with Ronald Tremain and David Farquhar, and at the University of Sydney with Peter Sculthorpe, graduating in 1966. The same year she attended Peter Maxwell Davies's composition class at the Adelaide Conservatorium and subsequently studied with him in England. Over the next decade her works attracted attention through performances and broadcasts in Europe, America and Australasia.

A longstanding interest in words, allied to student experiences of choral singing, influences her music. Many of her early successes were vocal and small-scale choral works, among them settings of ancient Babylonian texts and Maori myth and poetry. As a result of a commission from the 1978 Auckland Festival, she wrote her first chamber opera, *Tristan and Iseult*. After performances in Sydney and a BBC studio recording, the opera was awarded the Australasian Performing Rights Association's Silver Scroll in 1979.

This success encouraged her to concentrate on operas and large-scale choral works. She has collaborated with a noted children's author, Joan Aiken, in *The Tinker's Curse* (written during a period as composer-in-residence for Northern Arts, 1978–81), and with the New Zealand poet Fleur Adcock, notably in *Eleanor of Aquitaine*. The latter (begun in 1982) is incomplete, but part of Act 2 was given in an Australian Opera workshop production in 1987.

Whitehead's music is direct in expression and innovatory and sensitive in sonority. She is strongly influenced by the sounds of the natural world. Early in her career she cited as models Dufay (structure), Webern (orchestration) and Debussy (harmonic approach). As well as Maxwell Davies, a contemporary composer with whom she feels an affinity is Elliott Carter. Since 1982 she has been a lecturer in composition at the NSW State Conservatorium of Music.

chamber operas unless otherwise stated

Tristan and Iseult (1, M. Crowthers and M. Hill), Auckland, Maidment, May 1978

The Tinker's Curse, 1979 (children's op, J. Aiken), unperf.

Eleanor of Aquitaine, 1982 (F. Adcock), Act 2 scenes ii–vi, Sydney, Opera Centre, Oct 1987, inc. [2 acts completed]

The King of the Other Country (1, Adcock), Sydney, NSW Conservatorium, 5 June 1984

The Pirate Moon (1, A. M. dell'Oso), Auckland University Music Theatre, Aug 1986

Bride of Fortune, 1988 (3, dell'Oso), Perth, His Majesty's, 18 Feb 1991

*

E. Kerr: 'Gillian Whitehead in Interview', *Music in New Zealand*, no.6 (1989), 11–19 ADRIENNE SIMPSON

Whitehill, Clarence (Eugene) (*b* Marengo, IA, 5 Nov 1871; *d* New York, 18 Dec 1932). American baritone and bass-baritone. His vocal talent was discovered in Chicago in 1896 by Melba, who advised him to study in Paris; his teachers there were Giraudet and Sbriglia. He made his début in Brussels in 1898. After performing in Europe and the USA, and further study with Julius Stockhausen in Frankfurt, he undertook engagements in several German cities, studied the Wagner repertory at Bayreuth, appeared there very successfully as Wolfram (1904) and Amfortas (1908), and was also the much applauded Wotan in Richter's English-language Covent Garden *Ring* of 1908 and 1909. His début with the Metropolitan company (15 November 1909, Brooklyn) as Wolfram, and at the Metropolitan Opera House (25 November 1909) as Amfortas began a long and successful, though not entirely harmonious, association with that house, where his Hans Sachs was particularly admired. His Metropolitan career lasted until 9 April 1932, the year of his death. Whitehill was an outstanding singer and artist, notable for beauty of tone and for nobility and dignity of style. The best of his many recordings are the earlier ones, in which he sang his Wagner excerpts in the original German.

*

F. Williams: 'Clarence Whitehill', *Record Collector*, xxii (1974–5), 221–63 [with discography by W. R. Moran]

DESMOND SHAWE-TAYLOR

Wiata, Inia te. *See* TE WIATA, INIA.

Wich, Günther (*b* Bamberg, 23 May 1928). German conductor. He studied at Freiburg and made his conducting début in 1952 at the Freiburg Stadttheater, where he became chief opera conductor, remaining in that post until 1959. Thereafter he was successively appointed opera director at Graz (1959), and Generalmusikdirektor at Hanover (1961) and at the Deutsche Oper am Rhein, Düsseldorf/Duisburg (1965–80). While at Hanover, in 1963 he conducted the first production of Schoenberg's three one-act operas (*Erwartung*, *Die glückliche Hand* and *Von heute auf morgen*) as a triple bill, later taking it to the Venice Biennale. He was also professor of conducting at the Folkwang Hochschule, Essen, 1969–73. His work at Düsseldorf was distinguished by his performances of contemporary operas, notably Zimmermann's *Die Soldaten*, in addition to those of Berg and Schoenberg, and he toured with the company to leading European festivals (including the 1972 Edinburgh Festival with the British première of *Die Soldaten*). Since 1982 he has been professor of conducting at the Hochschule für Musik in Würzburg, where he also heads the orchestra and opera schools. A frequent guest conductor at other opera houses, he made his Covent Garden début in 1968 with *Die Zauberflöte*. He is an expressive conductor in the Furtwängler tradition, but with his own generation's feeling for clarity and transparency of texture (especially in Wagner). WOLFRAM SCHWINGER

Widdop, Walter (*b* Norland, nr Halifax, 19 April 1892; *d* London, 6 Sept 1949). English tenor. He studied with Dinh Gilly in London and joined the British National Opera Company in 1923, making his début as Radames at Leeds. The following year he appeared at Covent Garden as the protagonist in *Siegfried* (1924), his other Wagner roles there being Siegmund (1932) and Tristan (1933, 1937, 1938). In 1928 he sang with Leider in Gluck's *Armide* and in 1929 created Bagoas in Goossens's *Judith*; in 1936 he sang the title role in the British première of Stavinsky's *Oedipus Rex*, in a concert performance under Ansermet. He also appeared in Spain, the Netherlands and Germany; his roles on tour included Tannhäuser and Samson. The night before he died he sang Lohengrin's Farewell at a Promenade concert. Records made around 1930 show a firm resonant voice and a virile style, confirming his place among the best heroic tenors of the century.

*

A. D. Hillier and J. Jarrett: 'Walter Widdop: a Biography and Discography', *Record Advertiser*, iv/2 (1974), 2

A. Blyth: 'Koloman von Pataky and Walter Widdop', *Opera*, xl (1989), 288–95 [with discography] J. B. STEANE

Widerspänstigen Zähmung, Der ('The Taming of the Shrew'). *Komische Oper* in four acts by HERMANN GOETZ to a libretto by JOSEPH VICTOR WIDMANN after WILLIAM SHAKESPEARE'S comedy; Mannheim, Nationaltheater, 11 October 1874.

Baptista	*a rich gentleman of Padua*	bass
Katharine [Katherine]	*his daughters*	soprano
Bianka [Bianca]	*his daughters*	soprano
Hortensio	*suitors to Bianca*	bass
Lucentio	*suitors to Bianca*	tenor
Petruchio	*a gentleman of Verona*	baritone
Grumio	*his servant*	bass
A Tailor		tenor
Hortensio's Wife		mezzo-soprano

Baptista's and Petruchio's servants, wedding guests, neighbours

Setting Padua and its vicinity in the 17th century

Goetz began work on the opera in 1868, but because of his constant ill-health it was six years before it reached its première. In the field of German comic opera, *Der Widerspänstigen Zähmung* takes its place alongside Nicolai's *Die lustigen Weiber von Windsor* and Cornelius's *Der Barbier von Bagdad.* At its first performance the role of Katharine was sung by Ottilie Ottiker and Petruchio by Eduard Schlosser; Pauline Lucca and Minnie Hauk were among later interpreters of Katharine's role. The opera carried its composer's fame from Vienna (1875) and Berlin (1876) to London (1878) and New York (1886). Goetz, rejecting suggestions that he had been influenced by *Die Meistersinger*, the great German comic opera of the time, claimed that he remained loyal to the classicism of Mozart. Minnie Hauk, playing Katharine in Berlin in 1876, asked Goetz for an aria as an alternative conclusion. The aria arrived at the final rehearsal on 3 December 1876, the day of the composer's death; it was the last music he wrote and was performed only at that Berlin production.

ACT 1 *A street in Padua outside Baptista's house* It is night as the student Lucentio arrives to serenade Bianca. His song is interrupted by servants leaving the house, complaining at their treatment by Bianca's sister Katherine. Katherine appears on the balcony to chide her father Baptista, who is trying to pacify his employees. He succeeds and they return, leaving Lucentio to resume his serenading; Bianca now appears and together they sing a love duet. Bianca has another suitor in the older Hortensio, who enters with his own band of musicians. The two suitors quarrel, once again bringing Baptista out. Lucentio declares his love for Bianca, but Baptista rules that before he can give her away Katherine must first be wed, and meanwhile Bianca must be tutored to occupy her time. Each suitor plans to meet Bianca by disguising himself as a tutor. As Hortensio leaves he meets the rich Petruchio, who complains of boredom; Hortensio urges him to court Katherine, describing her as a woman who submits to no man. Petruchio takes up the challenge and resolves to win her.

ACT 2 *A room in Baptista's house* At their morning toilet Katherine mocks Bianca and her serenading men, vowing that she will give herself to no man. They go into the garden as Baptista enters with Petruchio, Hortensio (disguised as a musician) and Lucentio (as a linguist). The 'tutors' seek the girls while Petruchio stays with Baptista to ask for Katherine's hand. Baptista warns Petruchio of what awaits him, proof for which is the return of Hortensio, his smashed lute around his neck. Petruchio insists on seeing Katherine alone, and in the following duet she wonders if at last she has met her match. Baptista and the 'tutors' return, eager to know the outcome of Petruchio's suit. He announces that they are to wed, though Katherine refutes the suggestion. In the following quintet Katherine agrees to wed Petruchio, just to teach him a lesson.

ACT 3 *A room in Baptista's house* Baptista, his daughters and the two 'tutors' are awaiting Petruchio for the wedding ceremony. The guests arrive and Baptista is forced to apologize for the bridegroom's absence, to Katherine's fury. The guests depart with Katherine and Baptista, though before he goes he leaves instructions for the 'tutors' to continue teaching Bianca. As Hortensio tunes his lute, Lucentio, translating Virgil, reveals himself to his pupil. The scene ends with a trio in which Bianca realizes her father has been duped by the 'tutors', and Lucentio triumphs over Hortensio, who has conceded defeat in his bid for Bianca's hand. Baptista bursts in to say that Petruchio has arrived and the wedding can proceed. But Petruchio has not even dressed for the event, and with no apology for his unpunctuality he takes everyone off to church, leaving the servants behind to prepare the wedding feast. Hortensio returns first, dismayed at Petruchio's boorish behaviour during the service, and when all have returned Petruchio announces that he and Katherine cannot remain for the feast. Everyone pleads with him but he refuses and rides off with the furious Katherine.

ACT 4 *A room in Petruchio's country house* Things are no better here, judging by the opening chorus of servants complaining of the mood of their master and new mistress. Petruchio is now more shrewish than Katherine, chiding his servants and even rejecting a meal they have prepared. Katherine, left alone, sadly concedes that she has met her match and fallen in love. Petruchio provokes one final sequence of quarrels. He buys, then spoils, clothes offered by a tailor, then starts a dispute over the time of day. When she begs him to stop and admits defeat, Petruchio consoles her and reveals his true feelings. The opera ends with a septet as the servant Grumio announces Baptista, the newlyweds Lucentio and Bianca, Hortensio and his newly found wife and a chorus of guests. All rejoice at the taming of the shrew.

* * *

Although vigorous and forthright, the overture to the opera possesses an underlying lyricism and contrast of mood that summarizes the drama without using Wagnerian leitmotif. On the other hand, in spite of the composer's denial that he had been influenced by *Die Meistersinger*, it is hard to dismiss comparison with Wagner's work when hearing Lucentio's serenading guitar as Beckmesser's lute, comparing the central and dominating characters of Petruchio and Hans Sachs, noting Goetz's sparing but musically far less complex use of the chorus as townsfolk at the beginnings and ends of acts, and recognizing the musical climax of both operas in their respective quintets. Such ensembles form the backbone of the opera's structure. Each act is divided into several musically linked scenes, with a gradual increase from duet to septet, interspersed with occasional arioso passages and orchestrally accompanied recitative. The opera's tonal language and conventional orchestration place it in the line of German opera deriving from Weber; but instead of following the post-*Lohengrin* Wagner, Goetz attempted a parallel course of lesser impact and influence by way of Spohr, Lortzing and Marschner, tuneful but harmonically less adventurous. Katherine's lied in the second act (the only extractable aria) follows Lortzing's development of the operatic lied, which provided the means of expressing character and advancing plot using simple Classical form transformed by Romantic idiom. Much of the opera follows the style of fluent melody between aria and recitative developed by Wagner and Spohr.

CHRISTOPHER FIFIELD

Widmann, Joseph Victor (*b* Nennowitz, Moravia, 20 Feb 1842; *d* Berne, 6 Nov 1911). Swiss librettist. He was a protestant clergyman at Frauenfeld for a year before becoming head of a school in Berne (1868–80).

From 1880 he was editor of the *Berner Bund*. Of his many planned works for the musical theatre only seven librettos were completed and set to music. These reflect an idyllic and romantic view of nature, also present in his many fairy-tales. His version of *The Taming of the Shrew* (*Der Widerspänstigen Zähmung*) for Goetz idealizes the characters somewhat and lessens the farcical elements of the original. Widmann also wrote texts for lieder, cantatas and oratorios. Among his writings are *Johannes Brahms in Erinnerungen* (with Albert Dietrich, 1898) and accounts of three journeys he made with Brahms to Italy.

Die heiligen drei Königen (Spl), Goetz, 1866; *Der Widerspänstigen Zähmung*, Goetz, 1874; *Francesca da Rimini*, Goetz, 1877; *Der Sturm*, Frank, 1887; *Das steinerne Herz*, Brüll, 1888; *Manuel Venegas*, Heuberger, 1889; *Fürst und Sänger*, Mottl, 1893

*

E. Refardt: 'Die Musiktexte J. V. Widmanns', *Musik in der Schweiz: ausgewählte Aufsätze* (Berne, 1952), 134–9

Widor, Charles-Marie(-Jean-Albert) (*b* Lyons, 21 Feb 1844; *d* Paris, 12 March 1937). French organist, composer and teacher of Hungarian extraction. In addition to his organ studies he was a composition pupil of Fétis, and in 1876 went to Bayreuth for the first complete performance of the *Ring*. Although he is better known for his organ works, he had considerable success with music for the stage. In 1880 his ballet *La korrigane*, on a Breton subject, was performed at the Paris Opéra.

His first true opera, *Maître Ambros*, is concerned with an attack on Amsterdam by the Calvinist William of Orange. Widor's stage directions demand that several scenes should resemble specific paintings by Van der Helz and Rembrandt. Set in a simple declamatory style, *Les pêcheurs de Saint-Jean* takes place in St Jean-de-Luz and portrays events in the lives of the fisherfolk. Albert Carré had accepted this work for the Opéra-Comique but because his wife, the singer Marguerite Carré, was jealous of the singer Widor had selected for the leading role, the opera was nearly withdrawn. The main scenes are set by a small harbour with a jetty and a crucifix which forms the focus of attention in times of stormy weather. Rather than a continuous plot, although there are common themes, each act is a self-contained tableau. *Nerto*, written some 30 years before its first performance, was less well received; the story of the girl sold to Satan and her self-sacrifice to save the hero aroused little enthusiasm. Widor's style is colourful and his music always well orchestrated, with many appealing love themes contrasting with more vigorous leitmotifs, and all his operas show a natural feeling for the theatre.

Maître Ambros (drame lyrique, 4, F. Coppée and A. Dorchain), Paris, OC (Favart), 6 May 1886

Jeanne d'Arc (légende-mimée, 4, Dorchain), Paris, Hippodrome, 25 June 1890

Nerto, *c*1894 (drame lyrique, 4, M. Léna, after F. Mistral), Paris, Opéra, 23 Oct 1924

Le Capitaine Lys (comédie lyrique, 3, E. Noel and L. d'Hève), Lyons, Opéra, 28 March 1900

Les pêcheurs de Saint-Jean (scènes de la vie maritime, 4, H. Cain), Paris, OC (Favart), 26 Dec 1905

*

L. Schneider: 'Les pêcheurs de Saint-Jean', *Le théâtre*, no.171 (1906), 5–6

R. Dumesnil: *La musique française entre les deux guerres* (Geneva, 1946)

M. Kelkel: *Naturalisme, vérisme et réalisme dans l'opéra d'1890 à 1930* (Paris, 1984)

A. Thomson: *The Life and Times of Charles-Marie Widor* (Oxford, 1987)

RICHARD LANGHAM SMITH

Wiedemann, Hermann (*b* 1879; *d* Vienna, 1 Jan 1944). German baritone. He made his début at Elberfeld in 1904 and sang at Brno and Hamburg until 1914; in 1912 he took part in the première of Busoni's *Die Brautwahl* in Hamburg. He was a member of the Vienna Hofoper from 1916 (singing in the German language première of *Jenůfa* in 1918) and appeared at Salzburg until 1941, notably as Beckmesser in the performances of *Die Meistersinger* conducted by Toscanini in 1937. At Zoppot (now Sopot), Buenos Aires, Munich and the Berlin Hofoper he was successful as Guglielmo and Alberich, and in Italian opera. His only Covent Garden appearances were in 1913 as Faninal, in the London première of *Der Rosenkavalier*, and in 1938 as Beckmesser. DAVID CUMMINGS

Wieden [Theater auf der Wieden; Theater im hochfürstlich Starhembergischen Freyhaus; Freyhaus-theater; Wiedener-Theater]. Theatre in the Wieden suburb of Vienna, built in 1787 and used for opera until 1801. *See* VIENNA, §§2 and 3.

Wiedertäufer, Die. Opera by Alexander Goehr; *see* BEHOLD THE SUN.

Wiegand, (Josef Anton) Heinrich (*b* Fränkisch Crumbach, 9 Sept 1842; *d* Frankfurt, 28 May 1899). German bass. He studied in Paris and made his début in Zürich in 1870. He was principal bass at Frankfurt (1873–7) and moved to Leipzig in 1878, remaining until 1882. His only North American performances were with the Adams-Pappenheim Company, on tour in 1877. He sang Hunding and Hagen in the London première of the *Ring* (1882, Her Majesty's) and also appeared in the first Covent Garden *Ring*, conducted by Mahler in 1892. He appeared at Bayreuth from 1886 to 1891 as Gurnemanz, King Mark, the Landgrave and Pogner. His last engagement was at Hamburg in 1897, as King Henry in *Lohengrin*. DAVID CUMMINGS

Wieland, Christoph Martin (*b* Oberholzheim, nr Biberach, 5 Sept 1733; *d* Weimar, 20 Jan 1813). German poet, dramatist and librettist. He studied law at Tübingen and then visited Zürich. After a period as a private tutor he returned home in 1760. His novel *Geschichte des Agathon* (1766–7), with its Greek background and striking psychological insight, won him a chair of philosophy at Erfurt, and in 1772 he moved to Weimar, to take up the post of tutor to the young dukes. He founded *Der teutsche Merkur* in 1773, in imitation of the *Mercure de France*, and took a lively interest in the movement to found a German national Singspiel; his essays in *Der teutsche Merkur* include 'Briefe an einen Freund über das deutsche Singspiel Alceste' (1773, no.1, and 1774, no.1), 'Ueber einige ältere teutsche Singspiele' (1773, no.4), and 'Versuch über das teutsche Singspiel' (1775, nos.3–4). In 1780 he published one of his most successful works, the verse epic *Oberon*; this oriental tale was later the basis for operas by Wranitzky (1789), Weber (1826) and others. Novels, philosophical writings, translations (including 23 of Shakespeare's plays, 1762–6) and editorial work occupied him fully, and after a period of retirement (1797–1803) he returned to Weimar; after Schiller's death (1805) he was considered the most prominent German writer apart from Goethe.

Wieland's libretto for Schweitzer's *Alceste* (performed at Weimar in 1773) earns an honourable place in the annals of German opera, though his other texts for Schweitzer, *Aurora* (Singspiel, 1772), *Die Wahl des Herkules* (1773) and *Rosamund* (1780) are of more limited importance, and some of his other texts for music or arrangements for Singspiels are of purely antiquarian value. Easily Wieland's most influential work from a musical viewpoint is *Dschinnistan oder Auserlesene Feen- und Geister-Mährchen* (3 vols.; Winterthur, 1786–9); this work was edited by Wieland, its contents being partly new, partly translated and adapted, and stories from it gave birth to the Schikaneder-Mozart *Die Zauberflöte*, the Perinet-Müller *Kaspar der Fagottist* and several other operas and Singspiels.

*

E. Pasqué: 'Alceste von Wieland und Schweitzer, die erste deutsche Oper der neuen Zeit', *Recensionen und Mitteilungen über Theater und Musik*, vii (Vienna, 1861), 35

A. Fuchs: 'Wieland et l'aesthétique de l'opéra', *Revue de littérature comparée*, x (1930), 608–33

C. Sommer: *Christoph Martin Wieland* (Stuttgart, 1971)

PETER BRANSCOMBE

Wielki. Theatre in WARSAW, built in 1833 and destroyed in 1944; the Teatr Wielki (Grand Theatre) was reconstructed and opened in 1965.

Wiemann, Ernst (*b* Stapelburg, 21 Dec 1919; *d* Hamburg, 17 May 1980). German bass. After vocal studies with Philomena Herbst-Latour in Hamburg and Bender in Munich he made his operatic début in Kiel in 1938. His career was interrupted by World War II, but he resumed singing in 1946. He was engaged by many major German and Italian opera houses, also appearing in Barcelona, Brussels, Copenhagen, London, Paris, Vienna and Zürich. He became a member of the Hamburg State Opera in 1957 and eight years later was made a *Kammersänger*. He made his Metropolitan Opera début in 1961. His deep, ample voice was ideal for Wagner and Verdi, as well as for roles such as Barak, Don Basilio, Osmin, Pimen, Rocco and Sarastro.

CORI ELLISON

Wien (Ger.). VIENNA.

Wiener, Otto (*b* Vienna, 13 Feb 1913). Austrian baritone. At first a concert singer, he made his stage début in 1953 at Graz as Boccanegra. He sang in Düsseldorf, Frankfurt and Berlin and was engaged at the Staatsopern in Vienna (from 1957) and Munich (from 1960). At Salzburg he appeared in Pfitzner's *Palestrina* (1955) and the stage première of Martin's *Le mystère de la Nativité* (1960); at Bayreuth (1957–63) he sang Hans Sachs, Gunther and the Dutchman. He also appeared at Covent Garden and the Metropolitan (both 1962) as Sachs and at Glyndebourne (1964) as La Roche (*Capriccio*). His repertory included Amfortas, Kurwenal, Wotan, Pizarro, Faninal, Orestes and Dr Schön (*Lulu*). A reliable singer, he retired in 1976.

ELIZABETH FORBES

Wiener Blut ('Vienna Blood'). *Operette* in three acts arranged by Adolf Müller the younger from the music of JOHANN STRAUSS to a libretto by VICTOR LÉON and LEO STEIN; Vienna, Carltheater, 25 October 1899.

The operetta was arranged with the elderly composer's approval from dances published by the house of Cranz. It lacks the compositional span of Strauss's original operetta compositions, but the sparkle and brilliance of his melodies, allied to a lively plot by the librettists of *Die lustige Witwe*, has ensured its lasting popularity. Louis Treumann was the original Josef.

It is 1815 and, with everyone in Vienna for the Congress, Count Zedlau (tenor), Viennese ambassador of Reuss-Schleiz-Greiz, is trying to balance his amorous liaisons. Up from the country, his wife Gabriele (soprano) arrives at his villa in Döbling ('Grüss dich Gott, du liebes Nesterl'), unaware that his ballerina mistress Franziska Cagliari (soprano) is installed there. The Count's valet Josef (tenor *buffo*) attempts to protect his master's interests, unaware of the Count's latest interest in Josef's own girlfriend, the model Pepi Pleininger (soprano). Confusion ensues as identities are deliberately concealed, with the Prime Minister of Reuss-Schleiz-Greiz, Prince Ypsheim-Gindelbach (baritone), persuaded to pass off Gabriele as his own wife. Act 2 takes place at a ball given by the Prince. The Count arrives with Gabriele, who is delighted that the Viennese air has made her husband more fun-loving than she suspected ('Wiener Blut'). Since Pepi has taken Franzi's place as leader of the evening's ballet, the confusion over identities continues. The Count makes a date with Pepi for a fair at Hietzing, leaving Gabriele and Franzi to arrive there in Act 3 with the Prince and Josef respectively. The Count's three-timing is now revealed, but the fun of the fair is such that hard feelings are forgotten, leaving the Count reconciled to Gabriele, Pepi with Josef, and Prince Ypsheim paying court to Franzi. All diplomatically attribute confusion to the power of 'Vienna Blood'.

ANDREW LAMB

Wiesbaden. Spa town in Germany, near Frankfurt and Mainz. Records of operatic performances in the Komödienhaus go back to the second half of the 18th century. In 1810 the theatre on the Schützenhof was opened as the Herzoglich-Nassauisches Hoftheater, and in 1827 the theatre in the Wilhelmstrasse, also subsidized by the court, housed the town's first permanent theatrical company. From 1866 Wiesbaden belonged to Prussia, and the theatre was directly subject to the royal, later imperial, court of Prussia. Kaiser Wilhelm II had the neo-Baroque theatre that still serves as the Wiesbaden Opernhaus built and opened in 1894. In 1896 he founded the May Festival, the oldest music festival in central Europe after Bayreuth.

The building was damaged by fire in 1923 and partly destroyed in early 1945, but even in December 1945 the occupying Allied forces were able to use the Grosses Haus, calling it the 'Wiesbaden Opera House'; in 1947 the company of the Hessische Staatstheater began performing again in the restored building. The last major rebuilding took place in 1975–8, when the theatre was thoroughly renovated. The Wiesbaden Staatstheater can now accommodate an audience of 1041 in the Grosses Haus, 328 in the Kleines Haus and 89 in the Studio.

Many distinguished singers, including Caruso, appeared in Wiesbaden, and the administrative periods of Carl Hagemann (1920–27) and Claus Helmut Drese (1962–8) in particular were artistically successful. Music directors have included Otto Klemperer (1924–7), Karl Elmendorff (1932–6) and Wolfgang Sawallisch (1958–60). Alexander Kipnis spent five years with the Wiesbaden Opera, and Hans Werner Henze was engaged for two years as co-répétiteur and Kapellmeister in the early 1950s. The company's collaboration with Volker David Kirchner has been of major significance: his *Die Trauung* had its première in Wiesbaden during the 1974–5 season, *Das kalte Herz* was first performed there during the 1980–81 season, and *Belshazar* was given at Wiesbaden very soon after its first performance in Munich (1986).

Today the Hessisches Staatstheater gives 120–40 operatic performances a season, drawing on a repertory of some 17 works, including two modern pieces, one from the Baroque or early Classical period, and as a rule four *Spielopern*. The *Land* of Hessen provides 52% of the funds to finance the theatre, with the city of Wiesbaden providing the rest. GÁBOR HALÁSZ

Wigglesworth, Frank (*b* Boston, 3 March 1918). American composer. He graduated from Columbia University (BS 1940), where he studied composition with Ernest White, Luening and Cowell. From 1941 until 1988 he held various teaching appointments at Columbia. He was a Fellow of the American Academy in Rome (1951–4) and composer-in-residence there, 1969–70. Wigglesworth's music has its roots in the works of Lowell Mason, Billings, other early American composers and the New England chamber music tradition. His activities with the Composers' Forum (President, 1981) and the American Composers' Alliance (President, 1981–7) gave him unusual insights into 20th-century trends in American composition. Earlier, Varèse had introduced him to the works of Machaut.

Wigglesworth's compositions use sharply defined motifs that expand into phrases and melodic lines, mostly lyric in character but sometimes abstract and even harsh in their effect. Such melodic lines often develop into long linear statements with harmonies used both as punctuation and as chordal accompaniment. His works may be tonal or atonal, and sometimes polytonal and polymodal. In the atonal opera with slides, *The Willowdale Handcar* (also called *The Return of the Black Doll*), transparent contrapuntal accompaniments, sudden tempo changes, simple rhythmic contrasts and clear vocal prosody enhance the lyric-dramatic fantasy of the text and pictures. The libretto and the slides are by Edward Gorey. The work was first performed by the After Dinner Opera Company in the Bruno Walter Auditorium at Lincoln Center, New York, on 16 March 1973. The story concerns three people, Edna (soprano), Sam (countertenor) and Harry (baritone), who take a magical trip by rail through an imaginary landscape, riding on a handcar. Although the plot is non-developmental, the slides provide its continuity.

Wigglesworth's only other opera, *The Police Log of the Chronicle*, also involves the use of slides, to similar effect. The libretto is made up of excerpts from the Ipswich (Massachusetts) police log, illustrated with slides prepared by Anne Parker. The work was first performed by the New School Opera Workshop, New York, on 10 February 1984. Its plot tells of the activities of both the police and the inhabitants of a small town, and the wise and not-so-wise solutions to their problems. The opera is written in a singable quasi-madrigal style for soprano, alto, tenor and bass soloists (who sing in ensembles and duets) accompanied by piano. The music is often pompous and regal, as befits a proper police department. OTTO LUENING

Wikmanson [Wikman], **Johan** (*b* Stockholm, 28 Dec 1753; *d* Stockholm, 10 Jan 1800). Swedish composer. He received his earliest musical education from H. P. Johnsen, and then went to Copenhagen to study mathematics and music. After his return in 1772 he worked as an organist and civil servant. He continued his studies in composition with J. M. Kraus and Abbé Vogler, and in 1788 was elected a member of the Royal Swedish Academy of Music, where he later became director of education (1796). Although Wikmanson wrote music for the small musico-dramatic productions of the Palmstedt literary circle (texts by the poet Carl Michael Bellman), he was only an occasional participant in works for the larger stage, composing individual movements for pasticcio Singspiels, two of which survive: the Sacrificial Chorus from *Afventyraren* ('The Adventurer'; 3, J. M. Lannerstierna; 1791, Stockholm; *S-Skma*, *St*) and the finale to *Eremiten* ('The Hermit'; 2, G. Eurén, after A. von Kotzebue; 1798, Stockholm; *St*). These show his musical style to derive from that of Kraus.

*

C.-G. S. Mörner: *Johan Wikmanson und die Brüder Silverstolpe* (Stockholm, 1952) BERTIL H. VAN BOER

Wild, Franz (*b* Nieder-Hollabrunn, Lower Austria, 31 Dec 1791; *d* Oberdöbling, nr Vienna, 1 Jan 1860). Austrian tenor. He sang in various theatre choruses in Vienna, then in 1811 made his début at the Theater an der Wien as Ramiro (Isouard's *Cendrillon*). He then sang Tamino and Boieldieu's Jean de Paris. After engagements in Darmstadt and Kassel, in 1829 he first sang at the Vienna Hofoper, where he was engaged until 1855. His large repertory included Max, which he sang in London (1840), Florestan, Rossini's Otello, Licinius (*La vestale*), Méhul's Joseph, Hérold's Zampa, Nadori (*Jessonda*) and the title role of *Don Giovanni*.

ELIZABETH FORBES

Wildbrunn [Wehrenpfennig], **Helene** (*b* Vienna, 8 April 1882; *d* Vienna, 10 April 1972). Austrian soprano. She studied with Papier-Paumgartner in Vienna, where she sang small roles at the Volksoper in 1906. Engaged at Dortmund (1907–14) as a contralto, she sang Ortrud, Fricka, Amneris and Delilah, but at Stuttgart (1914–18) she moved over to the dramatic soprano repertory. Engaged at the Berlin Staatsoper (1918–25), the Vienna Staatsoper (1919–32) and the Berlin Städtische Oper (1926–29), she also sang Kundry at La Scala (1922); Brünnhilde, Isolde, Kundry and the Marschallin at Buenos Aires (1922–3); Donna Anna at Salzburg (1925); Leonore at Covent Garden (1927) and Isolde and Brünnhilde (*Die Walküre*) at the Opéra (1928). She also appeared in Amsterdam and Brussels. Primarily a fine Wagnerian, she also had the technique for Donna Anna and Leonore. LEO RIEMENS/ELIZABETH FORBES

Wilde, Oscar (Fingal O'Flahertie Wills) (*b* Dublin, 16 Oct 1854; *d* Paris, 30 Nov 1900). Irish writer. His plays, most notably *Lady Windermere's Fan* (1892) and *The Importance of Being Earnest* (1895), brought to the Victorian stage a wit that was both scintillating and subversive. Wilde cultivated the image of an aesthete and flouted convention at every turn. In 1892 his play *Salomé*, written in French, fell foul of the censor because it depicted a biblical subject (certain operas by Massenet, Saint-Saëns and Gounod were prohibited in England for the same reason); it was eventually produced in Paris in 1896. Two years earlier the play had been published in England in a translation by Lord Alfred Douglas, whose homosexual affair with Wilde led to the latter's imprisonment in 1895. After Wilde's premature death in exile, it was German interest in his work that revived his reputation: in 1902 Max Reinhardt mounted a very successful Berlin production of *Salomé*, and Richard Strauss's operatic version stimulated other German composers to use Wilde's texts.

The Canterville Ghost (short story, 1887): Křička, 1929, as Bílý pán; P. Hermann, 1961, as Das arme Gespenst; H. Sutermeister, 1964; Kalmanoff, 1967; Knaifel', 1974, as Kentervilskoye privedenie; Papandopulo, 1979, as Kentervilski duh
Lord Arthur Savile's Crime (short story, 1887): G. Bush, 1972
The Happy Prince (fairy-tale, 1888): Bossi, 1951; R. Vernon, 1956; W. J. Fisher, 1962; Williamson, 1965; Mannino, 1987, as Il principe felice; Kobekin, *c*1991, as Schastlivïy prints
The Nightingale and the Rose (fairy-tale, 1888): Bossi, 1938, as Rosa rossa; G. Lessner, 1943; Garwood, 1973; Firsova, comp. 1991, as Solovey i roza
The Selfish Giant (fairy-tale, 1888): Julia Perry, 1964; R. W. White, 1965; B. Cabena, 1970; F. Shaw, 1972; C. Wilson, 1973; Hollingsworth, 1981
The Birthday of the Infanta (novel, 1889): Schreker, 1908; Zemlinsky, 1922, as Der Zwerg; R. Nelson, 1956; Stoker, 1963
The Picture of Dorian Gray (novel, 1890): Orchard, 1919, as Dorian Gray; C. L. Flick-Stegner, 1930; H. Leger, 1939; R. Hanell, 1962; Kox, 1974; Mannino, 1982, as Il ritratto di Dorian Gray
The Duchess of Padua (play, 1891): J. van Etten, 1915, as Guido Ferranti
La sainte courtisane (unfinished play, 1894): Wagner-Régeny, 1930
The Importance of Being Earnest (play, 1895): Castelnuovo-Tedesco, 1973; Wilder, 1974, as Nobody's Earnest
Salomé (play, 1896): R. Strauss, 1905
De profundis (dramatic monologue, 1905): Sitsky, 1980
A Florentine Tragedy (play fragment, 1908): Zemlinsky, 1917; Szőnyi, 1960

ANTHONY PARR

Wilder, Alec [Alexander] **(Lafayette Chew)** (*b* Rochester, NY, 16 Feb 1907; *d* Gainesville, FL, 24 Dec 1980). American composer. After studying privately at the Eastman School with Herbert Inch and Edward Royce, he became active in the early 1930s as a songwriter and arranger in New York. Many of his songs were composed for leading singers such as Cab Calloway, Bing Crosby and (in the 1940s) Frank Sinatra. Wilder then turned from the world of popular song to classical music, completing several short operas (from 1946); in all he wrote 13 operas and musicals, most of which have been performed. In his best works, including chamber and orchestral music, he was able to forge a unique style, distinguished by those elements he most cherished in other composers: honest sentiment, unexpectedness, singing melodies, sinuous phrases and an absence of clutter.

The Churkendoose (children's op, B. R. Berenberg), 1946
Herman Ermine in Rabbit Town (children's op, Berenberg), 1946
The Lowland Sea (1, A. Sundgaard), Montclair, NJ, 8 May 1952
Cumberland Fair (1, Sundgaard), Montclair, 22 May 1953
Sunday Excursion (1, Sundgaard), Interlochen, MI, 18 July 1953
Miss Chicken Little (musical fable, 1, W. Engvick), CBS Television, 27 Dec 1953
Kittiwake Island (musical comedy, 2, Sundgaard), Interlochen, 7 Aug 1954
The Long Way (2, Engvick), Nyack, NY, 3 June 1955; rev. as Ellen, 1964
The Impossible Forest (2, M. Barer), Westport, CT, 13 July 1958
Racketty Packetty House (children's op, Engvick), 1967
The Opening (comic op, 1, Sundgaard), Boston, MA, 19 May 1969
The Truth About Windmills (chamber op, 1, Sundgaard), Rochester, NY, 14 Oct 1973
Nobody's Earnest (musical, 3, Sundgaard, after O. Wilde: *The Importance of Being Earnest*; lyrics E. Ayer), Williamstown, MA, June 1974; orig. entitled Jack in the Country

GUNTHER SCHULLER

Wilderer, Johann Hugo von (*b* Bavaria, 1670–71; *d* Mannheim, bur. 7 June 1724). German composer. In 1692 he was court organist at the St Andreas church in Düsseldorf. According to a court document of 1709, prepared by Giorgio Maria Rapparini, he studied with Giovanni Legrenzi, but it is not known when he may have been in Venice. Wilderer was already vice-Kapellmeister at the Düsseldorf court in 1696, and in 1703 he was advanced to court Kapellmeister. His operas were composed largely for the court between 1695 and 1713. Several years later the new Elector Karl Philipp, who had maintained a court at Innsbruck, joined together the Innsbruck and Düsseldorf musical establishments, first in Heidelberg and in 1720 in Mannheim; Wilderer was joint director with Jakob Greber, and remained active as a composer until his death. His final major work was the sacred opera *Esther*, performed as an oratorio at Heidelberg in 1723 and as an opera at Mannheim on 17 March 1724.

Wilderer's significance as a composer results in part from his fortuitous employment by the prince-electors of Düsseldorf-Mannheim. Musical activities at these courts influenced both the history of German opera in the late 17th century and the early stages of the musical developments leading to the Mannheim composers of the early Classical period. The Düsseldorf court assembled numerous talented musicians, and they in turn attracted many distinguished composers such as Steffani, who produced three of his operas at Düsseldorf: *Arminio* (1707), *Tassilone* (1709) and *Amor vien dal destino/Il turno Enea* (1709). Handel visited the court in 1710, 1711 and 1719. Wilderer's extant operas show a predictable similarity to Venetian operas of the late 17th century. Recitatives and arias are usually joined together freely without the severe contrasts of dramatic function found in operas of the later 18th century. Elements of French music are also evident in these works, as in most German operas of the period, and ballets frequently appear, especially as the conclusion to the final act (their music, as well as the independent orchestral movements such as the overtures, were composed not by Wilderer but by the court musician Georg Andreas Kraft). The arias are predominantly with continuo accompaniment and display some form of *ABA′* design, with a written-out *A′* section. Many of the arias with instrumental accompaniment show colouristic uses of solo instruments, very much in the manner of Reinhard Keiser's Hamburg operas (see Steffen for a thorough discussion).

first performed in Düsseldorf unless otherwise stated

Giocasta (3, S. B. Pallavicino), 1696, *A-Wn*
Il giorno di salute, ovvero Demetrio in Athene (3, ?Demanstein), 1697, *Wn*
Quinto Fabio Massimo (3, G. M. Rapparini), 1697, only lib. extant
La monarchia risoluta (1), ?1697, *Wn*
L'Armeno (3, Rapparini), ?1698, *D-WD*, *E-Mn*
La forza del giusto (3, Rapparini), 1700, only lib. extant
La monarchia stabilita (3), 1703, *A-Wn*
Faustolo (pastorale, 5, ?Pallavicino), 1706, only lib. extant
Amalasunta (?Pallavicino), 1713, only lib. extant
Coronide (pastorale, 3), Heidelberg, 1722
Esther (poema sacro drammatico, 2), Heidelberg, 1723, only lib. extant

*

G. Croll: 'Musikgeschichtliches aus Rapparinis Johann-Wilhelm-Manuskript (1709)', *Mf*, xi (1958), 257–64

G. Steffen: 'Wilderer, Johann Hugo von', *Rheinische Musiker*, ii, ed. K. G. Fellerer (Cologne, 1962)
R. Brockpähler: *Handbuch zur Geschichte der Barockoper in Deutschland* (Emsdetten, 1964) GEORGE J. BUELOW

Wildschütz, Der [*Der Wildschütz, oder Die Stimme der Natur* ('The Poacher, or The Voice of Nature')]. *Komische Oper* in three acts by ALBERT LORTZING to a libretto by the composer freely adapted from AUGUST VON KOTZEBUE's comedy *Der Rehbock, oder Die schuldlosen Schuldbewussten*; Leipzig, 31 December 1842.

The Count of Eberbach	baritone
The Countess *his wife*	mezzo-soprano
Baron Kronthal *her brother*	tenor
Baroness Freimann *the Count's sister, a young widow*	soprano
Nanette *her chambermaid*	mezzo-soprano
Baculus *schoolmaster on one of the Count's estates*	bass
Gretchen *his betrothed*	soprano
Pancratius *steward at the Count's castle*	bass
A Guest	bass

The Count's servants and huntsmen, peasants, schoolchildren

Setting On and near the Count of Eberbach's estate

The success of Lortzing's *Die beiden Schützen* and *Zar und Zimmermann* was followed, between 1839 and 1841, by three less highly acclaimed operas, *Caramo, oder Das Fischerstechen*, *Hans Sachs* and *Casanova*; but with the production of *Der Wildschütz* in 1842 the composer once more enjoyed a theatrical triumph. The opera was quickly taken up by other German theatres and appeared in various translations abroad. It is still a standard work in the German repertory.

ACT 1 *Outside a village inn* After the overture, in which a shot is heard during a fermata, the curtain goes up on a chorus of peasants celebrating Baculus's betrothal to Gretchen ('So munter und fröhlich wie heute'). Laughter (as in Weber's *Der Freischütz*) and a comic recitation of the alphabet are incorporated into the music. During the festivities Baculus receives a note from the Count summoning him to the castle to be dismissed from his post for having shot a buck on the estate. In a duet, 'Lass Er doch hören', Gretchen offers to intercede for him, but Baculus, knowing the Count's amorous reputation, is unwilling. Baroness Freimann, a young widow whose marriage to Baron Kronthal, a young widower, has been suggested by the Count, her brother (whom she appears not to have seen for several years), has come with her maid Nanette to observe her proposed husband; both are disguised as male students. Learning of Baculus's predicament, the Baroness offers to impersonate Gretchen and intercede for him with the Count. To the accompaniment of a Weberian hunting chorus, 'Seht dort den muntern Jäger', the Count, the Baron and huntsmen arrive. Both noblemen are attracted to the Baroness, now dressed as a peasant girl. In the finale, 'Lasset uns nach Hause gehen', the Count invites everyone up to the castle to celebrate his birthday.

ACT 2 *The Count's castle* Later the same day Baculus and the Baroness go to the castle, where, in the grand salon, Pancratius and the servants are bewildered by the Countess's readings of incomprehensible plays by Sophocles ('Nichts geplaudert!'). In the following scene the Baron is alone with his sister, the Countess, though she, having not seen him since childhood, does not know him (at the Baron's request the Count has introduced him under a false name). The Countess mistakes the Baron's lovesickness for the village girl he has just met (the disguised Baroness) for amorous feelings towards herself. During the duet and aria (cavatina) 'Bleiben soll ich und stets sie sehen' the voice of the Baroness is heard outside the window singing a phrase of the song she had sung in the Act 1 finale. Pancratius presents Baculus to the Countess, having previously provided him with a copy of Sophocles, and Baculus's quotations, together with his assertion that he can help stage her play, gain her sympathy. In the ensuing quintet 'Was seh ich!' the Count arrives in company with the Baron and, seeing Baculus, flies into a fury; after the Countess has failed to mollify him, Baculus summons the Baroness to assist him. When she enters, the Baron and Count are both carried away by their passion for her, but they are disappointed and astonished to learn that she is betrothed to the old schoolmaster. Baculus keeps forgetting who she is supposed to be and several times nearly gives the game away.

In the next scene the Baron is left alone with the Baroness; in the duet 'Ihr Weib?' he proposes that she give up the schoolmaster and marry him. They are interrupted by the return of the others. As a result of the Countess's intercession the Count is inclined to be merciful to Baculus; he gives permission for Baculus and his supposed bride to stay the night, promising to decide his fate in the morning. In the quintet 'Ich habe Num'ro eins', one of the most wittily contrived of all Lortzing's ensembles, the Baron and Count each try to prevent the other from being alone with the Baroness. They challenge each other to a game of billiards and, while the dozing Baculus periodically joins in with fragments of chorale melodies, they become increasingly annoyed with each other, eventually coming to blows using the billiard cues. They upset the lamps and in the ensuing confusion the Count, Baron, Baculus and Baroness end up in various embraces. Pancratius arrives with lights and they are discovered in their compromising positions by the Countess. In order to prevent further hanky-panky the Countess takes the Baroness into her room for the night. In a dialogue scene the Baron offers Baculus 5000 thalers to give up his bride. Left alone, Baculus, who stupidly thinks the Baron means the real Gretchen, considers the offer in a splendid *buffo* aria, 'Fünftausend Thaler'. At one point, undecided whether to accept the offer, he turns to the audience and asks their opinion; having decided to accept, he considers what he can do with the money (here Lortzing instructs the singer to modify the given text to bring in topical and local matter).

ACT 3 *In the park of the castle* The Count, out for an early morning ramble, sings of his love for pretty girls in a melodious polacca, 'Wie freundlich strahlt die holde Morgensonne'. The Baron arrives and tells him of his determination to marry the girl he believes to be Gretchen. They are interrupted by the arrival of a group of village maidens, with whom they merrily practise dancing until the Countess appears to summon them to breakfast. (The dancing practice in this scene is treated with a humour recalling the rehearsal scene in *Zar und*

Zimmermann.) The Baron declines breakfast and is soon joined by Baculus and the real Gretchen. In the trio 'Komm, liebes Gretchen, bekenne frei' Baculus learns, to his disappointment, that Gretchen is not the woman the Baron wants to marry; the Baron in his turn is horrified when Baculus tells him that the false Gretchen is really a male student, especially since he (she) has just spent the night with his sister. The arrival of the Baroness, and her disclosure of her real identity, quickly resolves the Baron's confusion. When the Count returns, the Baroness decides to teach her brother a lesson. At the beginning of the finale, just as the Countess appears on the scene, the Baroness flings herself into the Count's arms; however, everything is cleared up when the Baron explains to the Countess who 'Gretchen' is, and who he is, and the opera ends in general rejoicing. Even Baculus is given a full pardon when it transpires that he had shot his own donkey, not a buck.

* * *

There is an almost total avoidance of seriousness in *Der Wildschütz.* In his earlier comic operas, Lortzing had sometimes approached the style of German Romantic opera in his musical treatment of certain characters, such as Peter the Great and Hans Sachs. In *Der Wildschütz*, though, even the characters who do not have overtly comic roles never approach heroic status. Lortzing's musical lyricism enlists the sympathy of the listener for his characters in only brief moments; for the most part music and text are united in portraying absurdity or creating a farcical atmosphere. Yet the means by which Lortzing achieves his end are far from unsophisticated. Musical and dramatic structure, particularly in the ensembles and finales, is finely controlled. A particularly apt passage in the Act 3 finale, which occurs when everyone's identity has been revealed, is the quartet, partly unaccompanied, 'Kann es im Erdenleben wohl Schöneres noch geben'. Skilful use is made of the repetition of musical material at various points in the opera, and the orchestra is effectively used to support and enhance the action.

CLIVE BROWN

Wilkinson, Rosemond. *See* MOUNTAIN, ROSEMOND.

Willan, (James) Healey (*b* Balham, London, 12 Oct 1880; *d* Toronto, 16 Feb 1968). Canadian composer. Already established as an organist, choirmaster and composer in England, Willan moved to Canada in 1913 as head of theory (and later vice-principal) of Toronto Conservatory. Subsequently he became university organist and professor of music at the University of Toronto. Appointed organist and choirmaster of St Paul's Church, Toronto, in 1913, he became precentor of the Church of St Mary Magdalene in 1921. His influence on music in English Canada in the first half of the 20th century was far-reaching.

As a composer Willan is perhaps best known for his church and organ music; nevertheless, he wrote well in all forms and his output includes two symphonies, two operas, a piano concerto, some chamber music and over 100 art songs. Willan developed two distinct styles of writing (particularly after 1920): his 'sacred' style derived inspiration from plainsong, the Tudor composers and the Parry-Stanford tradition; his 'secular' style had its roots in Wagner, Richard Strauss, Elgar and others.

Willan's interest in dramatic music produced not only the operas but also the dramatic scene *Cleopatra*, the pageant *Brebeuf* and incidental music to some 20 plays. He wrote and assembled the music for five ballad operas and also made an arrangement of Gay's *The Beggar's Opera. Transit Through Fire* (1941–2), Willan's first true opera, was also the first opera in Canada commissioned for radio. Just under an hour in length, it was first broadcast by CBC Radio on 8 March 1942. *Deirdre* (1943–5), a full-length work in three acts, was also commissioned as a radio opera and was first produced on 20 April 1946 in that form. Nearly 20 years later Willan and his librettist, John Coulter, made extensive revisions to the work to make it suitable for subsequent stage productions.

The influence of Wagnerian music drama is evident in many of Willan's dramatic works, though his use of leitmotifs is closer to that of Elgar. Willan's musical idiom is a highly chromatic and late Romantic one, though some passages in *Transit* display a lighter, more populist style. *Transit* now seems somewhat dated, primarily because of its libretto (set in the Depression of the 1930s). The sombre yet moving *Deirdre*, based on ancient Irish legend, is timeless and worthy of continued performance.

See also DEIRDRE.

Cleopatra (dramatic scene), 1907
The Beggar's Opera (J. Gay, arr.), 1927
L'ordre du bon temps [The Order of Good Cheer] (ballad op, L. de Montigny, trans. J. Murray Gibbon), 1928
Prince Charlie and Flora (ballad op, Murray Gibbon), 1929
Transit Through Fire (radio op, prol., 4 scenes, J. Coulter), CBC Radio, 8 March 1942
Deirdre (3, Coulter), Toronto, CBC Radio, 20 April 1946; rev. Toronto, MacMillan, 2 April 1965, vs (Toronto, 1972)

Undated: The Ayrshire Ploughman (ballad op); Indian Christmas Play (ballad op), lost; Maureen (ballad op), lost

*

G. Ridout: 'Healey Willan', *Canadian Music Journal*, iii/3 (1959), 4–14
G. Bryant: *Healey Willan Catalogue* (Ottawa, 1972; suppl., 1982) [incl. bibliography]
F. R. C. Clarke: *Healey Willan: Life and Music* (Toronto, 1983)

F. R. C. CLARKE

Willemetz, Albert (*b* Paris, 1887; *d* Marnes-la-Coquette, nr Paris, 7 Oct 1964). French librettist. As a young man he worked as a civil servant, and for a while was secretary to Clemenceau. He published poetry under the name of Metzvil, and was a prolific writer of song texts. He wrote librettos for Christiné (*Phi-Phi, Dédé* and *Madame*), Tiarko Richepin (*Rapatipatoum* and *Le joli joker*), Messager (*Passionnément*) and above all Maurice Yvain, for whom he supplied the words for *Ta bouche*, *Là-haut* and *Au soleil du Mexique*. Willemetz also adapted Offenbach's *La créole* for its famous 1934 revival in Paris starring Joséphine Baker, and co-wrote the libretto for the French version of Oscar Straus's *Drei Walzer* as *Les trois valses*. His notable ability was to provide tongue-twisting rhymes that clung to the memory as much as the infectious waltzes of Christiné or Yvain.

*

StiegerO
A. Willemetz and others: *L'impromptu de Neuilly* (Paris, 1953)
C. Brunschwig, L.-J. Calvet and J.-C. Klein: *100 ans de chanson française* (Paris, 1972)
R. Traubner: *Operetta: a Theatrical History* (New York, 1983)

PATRICK O'CONNOR

Willer, Luise (*b* Seeshaupt, Bavaria, 1888; *d* Munich, 27 April 1970). German mezzo-soprano. She studied in Munich, where she sang first in the opera chorus. In

1910, on the recommendation of Bruno Walter, she appeared as Annius in *La clemenza di Tito*, and she remained closely associated with the company until her retirement, as Erda in *Siegfried*, in 1955. At Munich she sang in the première of Korngold's *Violanta* (1916) as well as in two Pfitzner premières, *Palestrina* (1917) and *Das Herz* (1931). In 1930 she sang Clytemnestra in *Iphigénie en Aulide* at Salzburg, where she reappeared in 1943 as Adelaide in *Arabella*. She also sang widely throughout Germany, and in 1926 and 1931 was at Covent Garden, considered 'extremely fine vocally' as Fricka in *Die Walküre*, her other roles being Brangäne, Erda and Magdalene in *Die Meistersinger*. Her repertory also included Dorabella, Carmen, Azucena and Delilah, and recordings show a good voice skilfully used, with characterful treatment of words.

J. B. STEANE

William Ratcliff [*Vil'yam Ratklif*]. Opera in three acts by CÉSAR ANTONOVICH CUI to a libretto by the composer and VIKTOR ALEXANDROVICH KRÏLOV drawn from Alexander Pleshcheyev's translation of the eponymous 'dramatic ballad' by HEINRICH HEINE, with additional verses by Krïlov; St Petersburg, Mariinsky Theatre, 14/26 February 1869.

William Ratcliff, composed over seven years beginning in 1861, was a failure at its première; only one revival seems ever to have taken place (1900, Moscow, Private Opera). Nevertheless, Cui's opera is important in the history of the genre in Russia, for it was the first opera by any member of the Balakirev circle to achieve production and was correctly perceived as a programmatic embodiment of their aesthetic ideals.

The plot may be sketched in a few lines. Edward Ratcliff had loved Betty and was killed by Betty's jealous husband MacGregor (bass), Betty herself dying shortly thereafter. Edward's son William (baritone) is haunted from childhood by a vision of the ill-starred lovers. Catching sight of Betty's daughter Mary (soprano), he conceives a violent passion for her, recognizing the woman of his vision; but, rejected by her, he becomes a bandit and resolves that he will kill anyone who attempts to make Mary his own. Douglas (tenor), Mary's third bridegroom, overcomes Ratcliff, who then rushes in a frenzy to MacGregor's castle and kills Mary, her father and himself. The vision of Edward and Betty now reappears, but this time they embrace; the death of their children has united them at last.

In the actual play, and the opera based on it, the events up to the denouement take place in almost precisely the reverse order, and unfold with an almost incredible tortuousness; for *William Ratcliff* is a *Schicksalsdrama*, a 'drama of fate' after the fashion of Kleist, in which the action is kept deliberately diffuse and mysterious as long as possible, with causes and motivations not stated at the outset but rather hinted at through signs and portents, and gradually revealed through narratives and flashbacks.

In one sense such a play is a natural for musical treatment, since music can easily be adapted to symbolic and portentous ends. And indeed, Cui's opera was, at least in Russia, an unprecedented essay in leitmotifs and reminiscence motifs. A Scottish ballad ('Quhy dois zour brand sae drap wi' bluid? Edward!'), first sung by mad Margaret (mezzo-soprano), Mary's senile nurse, carries the greatest oracular burden (Cui set it to his own mock-Hebridean 'modal' tune, but elsewhere he quotes real Scottish melodies, including 'Tibbie Fowler'). The play offered, in its demented and much-soliloquizing title character, plenty of opportunities for scena-writing in which Cui could exploit the flexible, madrigalian brand of lyric arioso he had appropriated from Dargomïzhsky's practice (in *The Stone Guest*) and christened 'melodic recitative'. Ratcliff's narrative in Act 2 scene i and his mad scene (Act 2 scene ii, 'At the Black Stone') are prime examples of the style, and vivid ones: they made a profound impression on Musorgsky just as he was embarking on *Boris Godunov*. The soaring, leitmotif-laden love duet that immediately precedes the bloody denouement in Act 3 shows Cui doing what he did best (and far better than his strangely asexual brother-'kuchkists'); for Rimsky-Korsakov *William Ratcliff* always remained 'a kind of Russian *Tristan and Isolde*'.

The reasons for the opera's failure (besides the fact that practically everybody in musical St Petersburg had a score to settle with the caustic critic of the *Sankt-peterburgskiye vedomosti*) evidently had to do, in the first place, with its static dramaturgy: Cui and Krïlov actually increased the preponderance of narrative over directly portrayed action in their adaptation of the play. There was also a pronounced unevenness of style resulting from the protracted gestation: what had evidently begun as a lightish number opera à la *Fra Diavolo* suddenly deepened and 'reformed' itself under the impact of Dargomïzhsky, whom Cui discovered midway through the project. The critic Herman Laroche rightly complained of increasing turgidity in the musical textures as the opera progressed, and was also correct in attributing the problem to 'a difference in maturity and a radical change of taste' that was never adequately resolved. His conclusion was kind, however, and might serve as well to conclude this brief account: 'For one who values elegant detail, for one who knows how to enjoy lyric moments expressed with talent, *William Ratcliff* will always remain a musical work that inspires both respect and affection'.

RICHARD TARUSKIN

Williams, Camilla (*b* Danville, VA, 18 Oct 1922). American soprano. She studied in Philadelphia and New York, and made her début in 1946 as Butterfly with New York City Opera; she remained with the company until 1954, singing Aida, Mimì and Nedda. She also appeared in Philadelphia and with other companies in the USA and Canada; her repertory included Ilia and Marguerite. In 1955 she sang Annina at the Viennese première of Menotti's *The Saint of Bleecker Street*. Later she taught singing. Her voice, lustrous in tone and finely projected, can be heard as Bess in the first complete recording of *Porgy and Bess* (1955).

CHARLES JAHANT/ELIZABETH FORBES

Williams, Grace (Mary) (*b* Barry, 19 Feb 1906; *d* Barry, 10 Feb 1977). Welsh composer. She was educated at Barry Grammar School and University College, Cardiff (BMus, 1926), and studied with Vaughan Williams and Gordon Jacob at the RCM and with Egon Wellesz in Vienna. She taught in London, then returned to Wales in 1946 to work on educational programmes for the BBC. Her main activity was as a composer, however, and she received commissions from the BBC and from Welsh music festivals.

Grace Williams's output is mainly for orchestra and for voices with orchestra, but includes a one-act opera, *The Parlour* (1961), for which she wrote her own libretto based on Maupassant's *En famille*. The characterization and frequently the musical style itself are reminiscent of Britten's *Albert Herring*, but the composer's inventiveness is here at its liveliest and allied to a genuine understanding of stagecraft. The opera was first performed at the New Theatre, Cardiff, on 5 May 1966 by the Welsh National Opera.

*

M. Boyd: *Grace Williams* (Cardiff, 1980) MALCOLM BOYD

Williams, Tom [Thomas] (*b* Burry Port, Llanelli, 2 Aug 1902). Welsh baritone. He studied in London at the Royal Academy of Music. From 1937 to 1945 he was engaged at Sadler's Wells Opera. In 1947 he joined the newly formed Covent Garden Opera company, making his début as Balstrode (*Peter Grimes*). In six seasons he sang a wide variety of roles, including Rigoletto, Telramund, Hans Sachs, the Dutchman, Escamillo, Amonasro, Kurwenal, Pizarro, Germont and Sharpless. When guest artists fell ill, he could be relied upon to take over at short notice. ELIZABETH FORBES

Williamson, Mrs. *See* FONTENELLE, LOUISA.

Williamson, Malcolm (Benjamin Graham Christopher) (*b* Sydney, 21 Nov 1931). Australian composer. From the age of 12 he studied at the Sydney Conservatorium with Goossens (composition) and Sverjensky (piano); he also learnt the horn and the violin. In 1950 he left the Conservatorium and went for the first time to Europe. In London he had composition lessons with Elisabeth Lutyens, and it was during this visit that he first seriously encountered the newer European music, from Schoenberg and Stravinsky to Boulez, who was just becoming known. Three years later Williamson returned to settle in London, where he has since lived; in October 1975 he was appointed Master of the Queen's Music. He took further lessons from Lutyens and from Erwin Stein, was received into the Roman Catholic Church and made an intensive study of Messiaen's music.

The course of Williamson's career as an opera composer is a curious one. He showed exceptional and immediate aptitude for the genre in his first opera, *Our Man in Havana*, brought off a difficult task with credit and resource in the revue-like chamber opera *The English Eccentrics* and then developed his aptitude towards a real control of pace and atmosphere on a large scale in *The Violins of Saint-Jacques*; at the same time, he produced in his one-act children's opera *The Happy Prince* a successful and delicately affecting piece of its kind, as well as a two-act children's opera of imaginative merit, *Julius Caesar Jones*. All of this, from impressive début to the achievement of prolific high professionalism on a large and a small scale, took just four years (1963–6). In the late 1960s Williamson seemed more firmly committed to opera and more likely to succeed in it than almost anyone among his contemporaries. A one-act opera for church or festival performance, *Dunstan and the Devil* (1967), is capably written and did nothing to disturb this estimate, though it fails to arrive at truly memorable tunes of the kind that Williamson wanted to write. His commitment to traditional kinds of theatre melody was distinctly unfashionable at the time but gave evidence of his desire to address as wide an audience as possible.

His next two operas are both derived from Strindberg. *The Growing Castle* (1968), after *A Dream Play*, is limited in its ability to project a drama, but this weakness perhaps derives from its source, and it is palliated by the intimate or festival or special chamber circumstances of performance for which it was meant. Williamson's attraction to Strindberg came from genuine and informed enthusiasm. His knowledge of the Swedish playwright goes far beyond that of a casual admirer. Sadler's Wells Opera commissioned a Christmas-style opera from him, *Lucky-Peter's Journey* (1969), based on a fairy-tale play by Strindberg and intended to fill a place in the repertory approximating that of Humperdinck's *Hänsel und Gretel*. Beginning with a suitably crisp, clear holiday frostiness of tone, this opera communicates itself as a series of picturesque incidents without narrative or circumstantial drama, in contrast with the strong dramatic schemes of Williamson's first two large-scale operas. But while some theatre works survive as idylls or dream-like enchantments, *Lucky-Peter's Journey* rather shows a failure to hit simple targets without distraction and busyness. The tunes have a very restricted method of generation: extension of short phrases by sequential repetition coupled with what come to seem predictable and glib enharmonic shifts of key. More to the point, Williamson's melodic invention seems prematurely to yearn for (and surrender to) a tonic, so making many of his longer solo or ensemble structures (unlike those of another melodically short-breathed composer, Richard Strauss) appear redundant or lacking in direction. For a composer apparently committed to tuneful appeal in his theatre works, the failure of *Lucky-Peter's Journey* to engage its audiences may well have been a serious blow. In effect, it closed his career as an opera composer, one not yet seriously resumed more than 20 years later.

The Red Sea (1972), described as an opera in one act, was a modest and adaptable exercise in festival cooperation. In 1968 Williamson had begun producing miniature operas or scenas, of the kind that call for the audience to learn its part quickly. Described by the composer as 'cassations', this series of eight pieces (1968–77) appears in retrospect like the fizzling out of an operatic career in a shower of tiny sparks. It would be disappointing, however, if a composer so alert to dramatic and literary values and so musically resourceful were not to resume his operatic career eventually with an additional discrimination in method and a firmer, less apparently improvisatory shaping of set-piece and act structure.

See also ENGLISH ECCENTRICS, THE; OUR MAN IN HAVANA; and VIOLINS OF SAINT-JACQUES, THE.

Our Man in Havana (3, S. Gilliatt, after G. Greene), London, Sadler's Wells, 2 July 1963

The English Eccentrics (chamber op, 2, G. Dunn, after E. Sitwell), Aldeburgh, Jubilee Hall, 11 June 1964

The Happy Prince (children's op, 1, Williamson, after O. Wilde), Farnham Parish Church, 22 May 1965

Julius Caesar Jones (children's op, 2, Dunn), London, Jeannetta Cochrane, 4 Jan 1966

The Violins of Saint-Jacques (prol., 3, W. Chappell, after P. Leigh Fermor), London, Sadler's Wells, 29 Nov 1966

Dunstan and the Devil (1, Dunn), Cookham, 19 May 1967

The Growing Castle (chamber op, 2, Williamson, after A. Strindberg: *A Dream Play*), Dynevor Castle, Wales, 13 Aug 1968

Lucky-Peter's Journey (3, E. Tracey, after Strindberg), London, Coliseum, 18 Dec 1969

The Red Sea (1, Williamson), Dartington College, Devon, 14 April 1972

*

S. Walsh: 'A Memory of Violins', *Opera*, xvii (1966), 851–5

M. Williamson: 'Lucky-Peter's Journey', *MT*, cx (1969), 1227–31

ROGER COVELL

Willmann, (Maria Anna Magdalena) Caroline (*b* Vienna, 25 Feb 1796; *d* Vienna, *c*1860). German soprano. She was a pupil of Felice Blangini at Kassel and performed as a soprano and pianist at theatres in Pest, Vienna (Theater an der Wien), Breslau (where she was prima donna, 1814–16), again in Vienna, Munich and Stuttgart until 1820, when Weber took her to Dresden. She returned to Kassel in 1822, then went to Berlin, remaining until 1825. By 1830 she was in Bayreuth as 'Madame Willmann-Debberton', teaching and appearing in 1831 as a guest at the margrave's opera house. She was a noted bravura singer.

*

K. M. Pisarowitz: 'Die Willmanns', *Mitteilungen der Internationalen Stiftung Mozarteum*, xv (1967), 7–12

Willner, A(lfred) M(aria) (*b* Vienna, 11 July 1859; *d* Vienna, 27 Oct 1929). Austrian librettist. He was a philosopher, musicologist and composer of piano pieces before turning to the writing of librettos for ballets, operas and, above all, operettas. One of his early operettas was Johann Strauss the younger's *Die Göttin der Vernunft*, a commitment the latter began to regret. Strauss was forced to complete the commission only by the threat of a lawsuit and declined to attend a performance. Later the libretto and score were legally separated, and Willner revised the libretto for Lehár as *Der Graf von Luxemburg*. Meanwhile Willner enjoyed a big success with the libretto for Fall's *Die Dollarprinzessin*, and he went on to write librettos for several successful Lehár operettas, particularly in collaboration with Heinz Reichert. The two also collaborated on highly successful adaptations of music by Schubert (*Das Dreimäderlhaus*) and by Johann Strauss father and son (*Walzer aus Wien*). In addition, they were the contracted librettists for the operetta libretto sought by Puccini and later adapted by Giuseppe Adami for *La rondine* (1917). Willner came to be much sought after for his careful working out of an operetta libretto.

operettas unless otherwise stated

Das Heimchen am Herd (Oper), Goldmark, 1896; *Die Schneeflocke* (Oper), H. Berté, 1896; *Der Schmetterling* (with B. Buchbinder), C. Weinberger, 1896; *Die Göttin der Vernunft* (with Buchbinder), J. Strauss, 1897; *Fräulein Hexe* (with Buchbinder), J. Bayer, 1898; *Die Debutantin* (with H. von Waldberg), A. Zamara, 1901; *Das Baby* (with Waldberg), R. Heuberger, 1902; *Die Millionenbraut* (with E. Limé), Berté, 1904; *Der schöne Gardist* (with A. Landesberg), Berté, 1907

Der kleine Chevalier, Berté, 1907; *Die Dollarprinzessin* (with F. Grünbaum), Fall, 1907; *Ein Wintermärchen* (Oper), Goldmark, 1908; *Baron Trenck* (komische Operette, with R. Bodanzky), F. Albini, 1908; *Ein Mädchen für Alles* (with Waldberg), H. Reinhardt, 1908; *Die Paradiesvögel* (with J. Wilhelm), P. Silber, 1908; *Die Glücksnarr* (with Landesberg), Berté, 1908; *Die Sprudelfee* (with Wilhelm), Reinhardt, 1909

Der Graf von Luxemburg (with Bodanzky), Lehár, 1909; *Zigeunerliebe* (romantische Operette, with Bodanzky), Lehár, 1910; *Schneeglöckchen* (with Wilhelm), G. Kerker, 1910; *Das Puppenmädel* (with L. Stein), Fall, 1910; *Die schöne Risette* (romantische Operette, with Bodanzky), Fall, 1910; *Die Sirene* (with Stein), Fall, 1911; *Der Eisenhammer* (Oper), B. Bersa, 1911, as Oganj

Der flotte Bob (with W. Sterk), K. Stigler, 1911; *Die kleine Freundin* (with Stein), Straus, 1911; *Eva* [Das Fabriksmädel] (with Bodanzky), Lehár, 1911; *Casimirs Himmelfahrt* (burleske Operette, with Bodanzky), B. Granichstaedten, 1911; *Prinzess Gretl* (with Bodanzky), Reinhardt, 1913; *Endlich allein* (with Bodanzky), Lehár, 1914; *Der Schuster von Delft* (Oper, with Wilhelm), Bersa, 1914, as Postolar iz Delfta; *Der Märchenprinz* (with Sterk), Berté, 1914

Der Durchgang der Venus (with R. Oesterreicher), E. Eysler, 1914; *Der künstliche Mensch* (with Oesterreicher), Fall, 1915; *Die erste Frau* (with Oesterreicher), Reinhardt, 1915; *Wenn zwei sich lieben* (with Bodanzky), Eysler, 1915; *Das Dreimäderlhaus* (Spl, with H. Reichert, after R. H. Bartsch: *Schwammerl*), Berté, 1916; *Die Faschingsfee* (with Oesterreicher), Kálmán, 1917; *Die schöne Saskia* (with Reichert), O. Nedbal, 1917

Hannerl [Dreimäderlhaus, 2. Teil] (Spl, with Reichert), K. Lafite, 1918; *Wo die Lerche singt* (with Reichert), Lehár, 1918; *Johann Nestroy* (Spl, with Oesterreicher), E. Reiterer, 1918; *Nimm mich mit* (with Waldberg), H. Dostal, 1919; *Der heilige Ambrosius* (Schwank, with A. Rebner), Fall, 1921; *Nixchen* (with Oesterreicher), Straus, 1921; *Frasquita* (with Reichert), Lehár, 1922; *Libellentanz* (Revue-Operette), Lehár, 1923; *Agri* (with Sterk), E. Steffan, 1924

Ein Ballroman [Der Kavalier von zehn bis vier] (with Oesterreicher and F. Rotter), Stolz, 1924; *Das Milliardensouper* (with H. Kottow), Steffan, 1925; *Der Mitternachtswalzer* (with Oesterreicher), Stolz, 1926; *Ade, du liebes Elternhaus* [Die Lori] (Spl, with Reichert), O. Jascha, 1928; *Rosen aus Florida* (with Reichert), Korngold, after Fall, 1929; *Walzer aus Wien* (Spl, with Reichert and E. Marischka), J. Bittner and Korngold, after J. Strauss and J. Strauss (the elder), 1930 ANDREW LAMB

Wilmington. American city, in Delaware. It is the home of Opera Delaware, a semi-professional company founded in 1945. It presents three productions a season in the Grand Opera House, a restored Victorian theatre (cap. 1100). With only one full-time staff member (managing director Leland Kimball), the company has given six world premières, including Alvar Henderson's *The Last of the Mohicans* (1976), Menotti's *The Boy who Grew Too Fast* (1982), Charles Strouse's *Charlotte's Web* (1989) and Libby Larsen's *A Wrinkle in Time* (March 1992), based on Madeleine L'Engle's children's book; works in preparation include Conrad Cummings's as yet untitled opera on Vietnam (libretto by Robert Jones and Thomas Byrd) which incorporates myths and musical traditions of Vietnam, planned for 1993. Opera Delaware uses a legion of volunteers, even in such key positions as general director. With their help the company is able to maintain programmes such as the Family Opera Theatre, lecture demonstrations for the disabled, signed opera for the hearing impaired, and other, multi-cultural events. DEAN SMITH

Wilson, Catherine (*b* Glasgow, *c*1936). Scottish soprano. She studied in Manchester and made her début in 1960 at Sadler's Wells as a mezzo-soprano in the title role of *La Cenerentola*. She also sang Rosina for the WNO and Second Lady at Glyndebourne. As a soprano she created Jenny in *The Mines of Sulphur* (1965) and sang Ninetta (*La gazza ladra*) and Lisa (*The Queen of Spades*) at Sadler's Wells and Mimì, Musetta and Ellen Orford for the WNO. For Scottish Opera she created Fulvia in Hamilton's *Catiline Conspiracy* (1974) and the title role of Musgrave's *Mary, Queen of Scots* (1977), also singing Countess Almaviva, Helena (*A Midsummer Night's Dream*), the Governess (*Turn of the Screw*), Female Chorus (*Rape of Lucretia*), the Marschallin and Verdi's Alice Ford. She sang Nicolai's Mrs Ford at Wexford (1976). Her attractive personality and rich, flexible voice were also of great advantage in operetta, as Rosalinde and Hanna Glawari. ELIZABETH FORBES

Wilson, Charles (*b* Toronto, 8 May 1931). Canadian composer. He studied composition with Godfrey Ridout at the Royal Conservatory of Music of Toronto and took the BMus (1952) and DMus (1956) degrees at the University of Toronto; he also studied with Foss (1951) and Chávez (1952) at the Berkshire Music Center, Tanglewood. In addition to holding teaching and conducting posts, he has been composer-in-residence with the Canadian Opera Company (from 1972) and at the University of Guelph, Ontario.

Wilson has written orchestral and chamber works, as well as vocal music and operas. His style is basically diatonic, incorporating chromatic alterations and serial techniques. His use of mixed media can be seen in *Heloise and Abelard*, which requires a prepared tape. His most important opera, it is based on the 12th-century love story. The vocal lines are declamatory in character; the chorus, placed on tiers and with painted faces and choreographed movements, assumes an important role, representing the Church – alternately hostile and sympathetic to the lovers. A seemingly eclectic work, including aleatory techniques and bi-tonal string glissandos, it shows the influence of Ginastera and Penderecki. Wilson's *Psycho Red*, an opera about a psychiatrist, is a dramatic 'mindscape' in music.

The Strolling Clerk from Paradise (chamber op, after H. Sachs), comp. *c*1952
Johnny Fibber (operetta, 2, P. J. Spensley), comp. 1970
Phrases from Orpheus (multi-media op), Guelph, Spring Festival, 10 May 1971
The Summoning of Everyman (church op, 1, E. Benson, after 14th-century morality play), Dalhousie, Arts Center, 6 April 1973
Heloise and Abelard (3, Benson), Toronto, O'Keefe Center, 9 Sept 1973
The Selfish Giant (children's op, after O. Wilde), Toronto, St Lawrence Center, 21 Dec 1973
Psycho Red (2, Benson), Guelph, Spring Festival, 16 May 1978
Kamouraska, 1975 (3, C. Wilson, after A. Hébert), concert perf., Toronto, Comus Music Theatre Studio, 3 Nov 1979

*

M. Schulman: 'Charles Wilson's Opera a Climax for a Busy Year', *Canadian Composer*, lxxxv (1973), 4, 6, 8, 10, 46
H. Chusid: 'Astonishingly, People go on Writing Operas', *Saturday Night*, lxxxix/4 (1974), 19–22 GAYNOR G. JONES

Wilson, James (*b* London, 27 Sept 1922). Irish composer of English birth. He studied at Trinity College of Music, London, and in 1948 settled in Co. Dublin. After travel in southern Europe he became interested in folksong, particularly flamenco and Balkan music, and this led to an enthusiasm for Bartók and Stravinsky. His first work to attract public attention was the children's opera *The Hunting of the Snark*, after Lewis Carroll, produced in Dublin in 1965. His next two operas, *The Pied Piper of Hamelin* and *Twelfth Night*, were staged at the 1969 Wexford Festival. Of his succeeding stage works, two are monodramas for soprano, and *Letters to Theo* is chiefly for a baritone. *Grinning at the Devil* (originally entitled *Aria to Ariel*), based on the life of the Danish writer Karen Blixen, met with particular success when it was performed in 1989 in Copenhagen.

Wilson has not adhered to any particular school but has rather adopted modal, polytonal or serial procedures according to mood or context, and any of his new compositions tends to be an experiment with forms and techniques he has not previously employed. Polytonality, for instance, is used to underline the comedy of deception in *Twelfth Night*, along with leitmotif; *Letters to Theo* uses 12-note technique and *Grinning at the Devil* variation technique based on three brief motifs, while *The King of the Golden River*, projected for performance in Copenhagen, is free-ranging in its style.

The Hunting of the Snark op.8 (children's op, 1, after L. Carroll), Dublin, Royal Irish Academy of Music, 5 Jan 1965
The Pied Piper of Hamelin op.25, 1967 (masque, 1, after R. Browning); two-act radio version, 1968, unperf.; staged, Wexford, White's Hotel, 25 Oct 1969
Twelfth Night op.30 (3, H. Moulton, after W. Shakespeare), Wexford, Theatre Royal, 1 Nov 1969
The Taín op.48 (monodrama, 1, I. Fox, after Irish saga), Dublin, Trinity College, 29 June 1972
Fand op.62 (monodrama, 1, Wilson), Kilkenny, St Canice's Cathedral, 26 Aug 1975
Letters to Theo op.92 (1, Wilson, after V. van Gogh), Dublin, St Stephen's Church, 26 Nov 1984
Grinning at the Devil [Aria to Ariel] op. 101 (2, E. Gress), Copenhagen, Riddersalen, 28 Feb 1989
The King of the Golden River op.111 (2, Wilson, after J. Ruskin)

ALOYS FLEISCHMANN

Wilson, John (*b* Edinburgh, 25 Dec 1800; *d* Quebec City, 9 July 1849). Scottish tenor. He studied with Lanza and Crivelli, and made his operatic début in Edinburgh (March 1830); subsequently he was very successful at Covent Garden and Drury Lane. His American début (15 October 1838) was with the National Theatre, New York, and he then toured for 20 highly successful months with Jane Shirreff, performing in New York, Boston, Providence, Washington, Baltimore, Philadelphia and Charleston. He returned to London in May 1840. Wilson and Shirreff were the most successful English singers to perform in the USA in the late 1830s and early 1840s; they helped to cultivate further the growing American taste for opera. One of the most successful 19th-century performers of Scottish song, Wilson published an *Edition of the Songs of Scotland* in 1842. He returned to North America for another tour in 1849, but was stricken with cholera in Quebec City.

*

J. W. Moore: *Complete Encyclopedia of Music* (Boston, 1854)
J. D. Brown and S. S. Stratton: *British Musical Biography: a Dictionary of Musical Artists, Authors, and Composers* (London, 1897)
K. K. Preston: *Travelling Opera Troupes in the United States, 1825–1860* (diss., CUNY, 1989) KATHERINE K. PRESTON

Wilson, Neil (*b* Lubbock, TX, 4 June 1956). American tenor. Making his début in 1980 at Wolf Trap as Fenton, he created Dog in Mollicone's *Starbird* for Texas Opera Theater, Houston (1981), then toured with the company. He made his European début in 1985 at Stuttgart as Werther, and has sung in Bonn, Bologna, Cologne, Hamburg, Zürich, Los Angeles and Washington; he sang Monteverdi's Nero at Glyndebourne in 1986. His roles include Don Ottavio, Tamino, Nemorino, Alfredo, the Duke, Macduff, Lensky, Jason (*Médée*), Romeo, Rodolfo and Pinkerton. His voice, light and sweet-toned, is better suited to Mozart than to Puccini. ELIZABETH FORBES

Wilson, Robert (*b* Waco, TX, 4 Oct 1941). American designer, playwright and director. He was educated at the University of Texas (1959–62), studied painting and graduated in architecture from the Pratt Institute, Brooklyn (1965). He began writing plays and directing in New York in the 1960s, winning critical acclaim especially in Europe. His own *Deafman Glance* (1971), together with his set designs for *A Letter for Queen Victoria* (1975), won several awards, as did his designs for Philip Glass's *Einstein on the Beach* (1974, Avignon; 1976, Metropolitan Opera). His stage designs include Charpentier's *Médée* (1984, Lyons); sections of the multilingual epic *The Civil Wars*, which Wilson wrote with Glass and Bryars (1984, 1985 and 1987, Rome and New York); Gluck's *Alceste* (1986, Stuttgart); *Salome*

(1987, La Scala); and *Le martyre de St Sébastien* (1988, Paris). His productions as a director have included *Die Zauberflöte* (1991, Paris, Bastille).

Wilson has been called a stage genius and one of 'the most daring and creative figures in contemporary theatre' (Harris); critical reaction to his work is mixed. His conceptions, in which design is the dominant element and in which every aspect of the production is controlled by the central artistic vision, are epic in scale, marathons of endurance for the audience and heroic challenges for actors, singers and collaborators. *The Civil Wars*, for instance, would run for 12 hours if ever performed in its entirety, and requires a singer to perform while suspended 15 feet above the stage, harnessed and chained in a rig of steel tubing. Columbia University holds a collection of 10 000 of Wilson's scripts, drawings, photographs and papers.

For illustration *see* DOKTOR FAUSTUS and EINSTEIN ON THE BEACH.

*

D. Harris: 'Creating for the Theatre on a Grand Scale', *Connoisseur*, no. 214 (1984), 100–05
J. Johnston: 'Family Spectacles', *Art in America*, lxxiv (1986), 94–107
D. Bradley and D. Williams: *Directors' Theatre* (London, 1988)
I. Valente: 'Mess in scena di Le martyre de Saint Sébastien', *Domus*, no.697 (1988), 46–51
L. Shyer: *Robert Wilson and his Collaborators* (New York, 1990)

DAVID J. HOUGH

Wilson, Thomas (Brendan) (*b* Trinidad, CO, 10 Oct 1927). Scottish composer. He was taken to Scotland when young and grew up near Glasgow, where he studied with Sir Ernest Bullock and Frederick Rimmer. He has taught at Glasgow University since 1957, holding a personal chair since 1977. His output includes three symphonies and many chamber, instrumental, vocal and choral works. All are written in a flexible chromatic idiom, perhaps most strongly influenced by Hindemith and Berg.

His first opera, *The Charcoal Burner* (1968), a radio opera commissioned by the BBC in Scotland (first broadcast 16 March 1969), was a collaboration with a university colleague, the poet Edwin Morgan. It is set in the Quantock Hills in 1789, and tells of a young man's pure affection for one girl, his sexual obsession with and murder of another, and his eventual execution. Wilson's music here is highly charged, and reaches an ecstatic lyricism in the farewell prison duet between the charcoal burner John Walford (tenor) and his true love Anne Rice (soprano).

Wilson's second opera, *The Confessions of a Justified Sinner* (3, J. Currie, after J. Hogg; York, Theatre Royal, 15 June 1976), was commissioned by Scottish Opera. The libretto effectively shapes James Hogg's early 19th-century Scottish tale of satanic possession. Wilson makes use here of a wide range of resources, from grimly Presbyterian psalm-singing (the tune 'Martyrs' appears early in the first act) through lowland Scottish folksong to taped sound effects. He creates a nightmarish atmosphere of murderous violence and religious mania.

*

K. Elliott and F. Rimmer: *A History of Scottish Music* (London, 1973)
C. Thorpe Davie: *Scotland's Music* (Edinburgh, 1980)

NEIL MACKAY

Wilt, Marie (Liebenthaler) (*b* Vienna, 30 Jan 1833; *d* Vienna, 24 Sept 1891). Austrian soprano. She studied in Vienna and made her début in 1865 at Graz as Donna Anna. In 1866–7 she sang Norma at Covent Garden (under the name Maria Vilda). From 1867 to 1877 she was engaged at the Vienna Hofoper, singing Elvira (*Don Giovanni*) at the opening of the new Opera House (1869) and Aida at the first performance of Verdi's opera in Vienna (1874). She created Sulamith in Goldmark's *Königin von Saba* (1875). Returning to Covent Garden she sang Marguerite de Valois, Lucrezia Borgia, Alice (*Robert le diable*) and Semiramide (1874–5). Moving to Leipzig, she sang Brünnhilde in one of the first complete *Ring* cycles outside Bayreuth. In 1886 she returned to Vienna and in 1887 she sang Donna Elvira at Salzburg in the centenary performance of Mozart's *Don Giovanni*. Her wide range enabled her to sing roles as disparate as the Queen of Night and the Wagnerian heroines.

ELIZABETH FORBES

Wimberger, Gerhard (*b* Vienna, 30 Aug 1923). Austrian composer. He studied at the Salzburg Mozarteum. He then became répétiteur at the Vienna Volksoper (1947–8), and conductor at the Salzburg Landestheater (1948–51); he has remained closely associated with the Mozarteum as a teacher. In 1967 he was awarded the Austrian State Prize for composition. His music for the stage includes operas and dance works; these are often rich in wit and irony, designed as anti-war protests, and have leanings towards an eclectic jazz style. The highly successful *Das Opfer Helena*, for example, uses a five-piece band and mixes jazz and popular songs with speech, recitative and pantomime.

Schaubundengeschichte (6 scenes, E. Spiess, after V. Katajew), Mannheim, National, 25 Nov 1954
La battaglia, oder Der rote Federbusch (Opernkomödie, 8 scenes, Spiess), Schwetzingen, 12 May 1960, vs (London, 1960)
Dame Kobold (musikalische Komödie, 3, Wimberger, after P. Calderón de la Barca), Frankfurt, 24 Sept 1964
Das Opfer Helena (Kammermusical, W. Hildesheimer), Frankfurt, Turm, 1968
Lebensregeln (catechism with music, 19 scenes, O. Hassencamp), Munich, Gärtnerplatz, 27 Aug 1972
Fürst von Salzburg – Wolf Dietrich (scenic musical chronicle, 2, Wimberger), Salzburg, Landes, 11 June 1987

Winbergh, Gösta (*b* Stockholm, 30 Dec 1943). Swedish tenor. He studied in Stockholm with Erik Saedén. After making his début in 1972 at Göteborg as Rodolfo, he was engaged at the Royal Opera, Stockholm. He has sung at Drottningholm, Aix-en-Provence, Geneva, Zürich, Salzburg, Florence, Vienna, San Francisco, Chicago, Houston and Berlin. He sang Belmonte at Glyndebourne (1980), and made his Covent Garden début (1982) as Titus, his Metropolitan début (1983) as Don Ottavio and his Scala début (1985) as Tamino. As Idomeneus he has appeared at La Scala (1990) and Vienna (1991); he is particularly noted for his Mozart roles, which also include Ferrando and Mithridates. In addition he sings Almaviva, Nemorino, the Duke, Alfredo, Lensky, Gluck's Admetus and Pylades, David, Faust, Des Grieux (*Manon*) and Sali (*A Village Romeo and Juliet*). He sang his first Lohengrin at Zürich (1991). Over the years his light, lyrical voice has become steadily more powerful.

ELIZABETH FORBES

Windgassen, Wolfgang (*b* Annemasse, Switzerland, 26 June 1914; *d* Stuttgart, 5 or 8 Sept 1974). German tenor and director. He studied in Stuttgart with his father, the tenor Fritz Windgassen, and Alfons Fischer. In 1941 he made his début at Pforzheim as Don Alvaro (*La forza del destino*). He was a member of the Stuttgart Opera

(1945–72), singing first in the Italian repertory and in parts like Tamino, Max, Hoffmann and Florestan; he then began to prepare Wagnerian roles and in 1950 sang his first Siegmund. In 1951 he sang Parsifal at Bayreuth; he appeared there each year until 1970, as Froh, Siegmund, Siegfried, Lohengrin, Tannhäuser, Walther, Erik, Loge and Tristan, establishing himself as the leading postwar Heldentenor. In 1972 he was appointed director of the Stuttgart Opera, where his productions included *Boris Godunov* (1972). He appeared regularly in the Wagnerian repertory at Covent Garden (1955–66). His roles included Adolar (*Euryanthe*), Rienzi, the Emperor (*Die Frau ohne Schatten*) and Otello. He made his American début at the Metropolitan as Siegmund in 1957 and sang Tristan at San Francisco in 1970. Although his voice was light by pre-war Heldentenor standards, Windgassen knew how to conserve it and use it with sensitivity. He had the requisite beauty of tone for the lyrical music of Tristan and Siegfried and could also rise to the dramatic moments.

K. Honolka: 'Wolfgang Windgassen', *Opera*, xiii (1962), 590–95
A. Natan: 'Windgassen, Wolfgang', *Primo uomo* (Basle and Stuttgart, 1963) [with discography]
H. Rosenthal: 'Wolfgang Windgassen', *Great Singers of Today* (London, 1966), 210–11
B. W. Wessling: *Wolfgang Windgassen* (Bremen, 1967)

HAROLD ROSENTHAL/R

Wolfgang Windgassen in the title role of Wagner's 'Siegfried', with Anja Silja as Brünnhilde, in Wieland Wagner's production at the Opernhaus, Cologne, 1963

Winkelmann [Winckelmann], **Hermann** (*b* Brunswick, 8 March 1849; *d* Vienna, 18 Jan 1912). German tenor. He studied singing in Paris and with Koch in Hanover before making his début in *Il trovatore* at Sondershausen in 1875. After appearances throughout Germany, in 1878 he settled in Hamburg where he sang in the local premières of *Das Rheingold* (as Loge, 1878), *Götterdämmerung* (1879), Rubinstein's *Nero* (1879) and *Tristan und Isolde* (1882). In 1882 he sang with the Hamburg company under Richter at Drury Lane, his roles including Lohengrin, Tannhäuser and Tristan. Following Richter's recommendation, Wagner chose Winkelmann to create Parsifal at Bayreuth in 1882. The next year he was engaged by the Vienna Hofoper, where he became the city's first Tristan and remained a favourite until his retirement in 1906. During this period he continued to sing at Bayreuth, and in 1884 appeared at Theodore Thomas's Wagner festivals in New York, Boston, Philadelphia, Cincinnati and Chicago. Besides Wagner his repertory included Gluck's *Alceste* and *Armide*, *Fidelio*, Auber's *La muette de Portici*, Verdi's *Otello*, Marschner's *Der Vampyr* and, in 1897, Smetana's *Dalibor* under Mahler's direction.

Winkelmann was a leading figure in the first generation of Wagner singers, and was coached by the composer. Although he possessed the ample, sonorous voice of a true heroic tenor, his fluid lyrical delivery stood in marked contrast to the declamatory style of many Bayreuth performers during the era of Cosima Wagner's hegemony.

ES (L. Riemens)

Winkler, Carl Gottfried Theodor [Hell, Theodor] (*b* Waldenburg, 9 Feb 1775; *d* Dresden, 24 Sept 1856). German poet, impresario and journalist. He displayed versatility and diligence in Dresden as lawyer, author and critic, translator and editor, and musical and theatrical organizer. He was assistant director of the court theatre and founder-editor of the *Dresdner Abendzeitung*. He was a friend of Weber and a trustee of his orphaned children. Although his translation of the libretto of Weber's *Oberon* is not of high quality, he wrote an excellent text for *Die drei Pintos* and was responsible for the first collection of Weber's writings (*Hinterlassene Schriften von C. M. von Weber*, Dresden, 1828). Winkler was also among the first Germans to recognize and appreciate the operas of Meyerbeer. He wrote under the pen name Theodor Hell.

E. Eckardt: *Chronik von Glauchau* (Glauchau, 1882)
P. Raabe: *Wege zu Weber* (Regensburg, 1942)
H. Schnoor: *Weber auf dem Welttheater* (Dresden, 1942)
K. Laux: *Carl Maria von Weber* (Leipzig, 1966)
J. Warrack: *Carl Maria von Weber* (London, 1968, 2/1976)
W. Hüttel: *Zur Musikgeschichte der Stadt Glauchau und ihrer näheren Umgebung* (Glauchau, 1986)

WALTER HÜTTEL

Winkler, Hermann (*b* Duisburg, 3 March 1924). German tenor. He studied in Hanover, making his début in 1957 at Bayreuth as Augustin Moser (*Meistersinger*) and Shepherd (*Tristan und Isolde*). Engaged at Zürich (1958) and Cologne (1960), he also sang in Frankfurt, Vienna, Berlin, Munich, Hamburg, Geneva, Madrid and Bologna. He returned to Bayreuth (1977) as Parsifal, made his American début at Chicago (1980) as Don Ottavio, created Publisher Mech in Cerha's *Baal* at Salzburg (1981) and made his Covent Garden début (1984) as the Captain in *Wozzeck*. His repertory ranges from Mozart's Idomeneus to Lohengrin, Erik, Loge and Florestan. A powerful actor and a fine musician, he excels in 20th-century roles such as the Emperor, Duke Cattaneo (Schoeck's *Massimilla Doni*), Prince/Marquis (*Lulu*), Peter Grimes (which he sang at Zürich in 1989) and Palestrina (Hanover, 1991). ELIZABETH FORBES

Winnipeg. City in Canada, capital of Manitoba. In 1883 the Hess Opera inaugurated the Princess Opera House with *Iolanthe*; until 1899, when it burnt down, the Princess housed the Winnipeg Operatic Society. In 1911 Ralph H. Horner staged his own comic opera, *The Belles of Barcelona*, and in 1919 Fortune Gallo's San Carlo Opera Company made the first of several visits to the Walker Theatre. The Manitoba Opera Association, formed in 1969, was inaugurated in 1972 with a concert performance of *Il trovatore*; the following year it staged *Madama Butterfly*, *Tosca* and *Die Fledermaus* in the Manitoba Centennial Concert Hall. Since then three and sometimes four operas a season have been performed; the repertory has included *Der fliegende Holländer*, *Salome* and *Die Zauberflöte* as well as the staple fare of Donizetti, Verdi and Puccini and Gounod, Bizet and Offenbach. The artistic director of the association is Irving Guttman, who holds the same position with the Edmonton Opera. ELIZABETH FORBES

Winston-Salem. American city, in North Carolina. It is the home of Piedmont Opera Theatre, which presents two fully staged productions a year there and organizes education and touring programmes. Founded by Norman Johnson in 1977, the company first performed in the R. J. Reynolds Auditorium; in 1983, it moved to the Roger L. Stevens Center for the Performing Arts (1360 seats), a lavish renovation of the vintage Carolina Theater and Hotel. The company started modestly with one production a year, adding a second in 1984. Its repertory tends towards the traditional: usually a tragedy in the autumn and a comedy in the spring, the first in its original language, the second in English, both with subtitles. Each production is accompanied by the Winston-Salem Symphony. In 1988 the company commissioned the composer Robert Chumbley for its first operatic première; he is collaborating with the librettist Dugg McDonough on *Ordinary People*, based on Judith Guest's novel. DEAN SMITH

Winter [von Winter], **Peter** (*b* Mannheim, bap. 28 Aug 1754; *d* Munich, 17 Oct 1825). German composer. He early demonstrated remarkable talent on the violin, and at the age of ten began playing in the Mannheim court orchestra. In 1776 he was officially named a court musician. For a short while around 1775 he took composition lessons with G. J. Vogler. In 1778 he moved with the electoral court to Munich and was named director of the court orchestra. It was then that he took up composing for the stage, beginning with several ballets and melodramas. In 1780–81, during a concert tour with the clarinettist Franz Tausch, he sojourned in Vienna and took lessons in vocal composition from Salieri. On his return to Munich he composed his first operas, several of which, including *Der Bettelstudent*, were well received in Munich and Mannheim. Named Munich's vice-Kapellmeister in 1787, he became director of court and church music and Italian opera. From 1791 to 1794 he was on extended leave from his Munich post and travelled to Italy, where he composed Italian operas for theatres in Venice and Naples. There soon followed a lengthy stay in Vienna, where he won great success with three new operas (1796–8).

After returning to Munich in 1798 he was named Kapellmeister, a post he held until his death. He undertook another compositional tour during the years 1802–5. He produced several Italian operas that met with success in London, including *Il ratto di Proserpina* (1804) and *Zaira* (1805); but his two works staged at the Paris Opéra, *Tamerlan* (1802) and *Castor et Pollux* (1806; a revised version of *Il trionfo dell'amor fraterno*, 1804), received few performances. Back in Munich, he produced a few more operas, but none was as successful as some of his earlier works. He turned increasingly to sacred music and also set up a singing school, though, as critics were quick to point out, he had little or no experience as a singer himself. He set off on a final tour in 1816, this time with his star vocal pupil, Clara Metzger-Vespermann, and up to 1820 they travelled extensively in Germany and Italy, and also went to Vienna. He composed three operas in Milan during these years.

Winter, like many late 18th-century German composers, wrote in a variety of operatic genres and styles: *opere serie*, *opere buffe*, *tragédies lyriques*, German operas, Singspiels and melodramas. He readily mastered the foreign styles and tried his hand at most of the newly developing sub-genres of German opera. While a violinist at Mannheim and Munich he encountered a wide range of operatic styles. He took part in performances of Italian works by Jommelli and J. C. Bach, French comic operas and north German Singspiels performed by the Marchand troupe, melodramas by Georg Benda and serious German operas by Holzbauer (*Günther von Schwarzburg*) and Anton Schweitzer (*Alceste*). His early stage works reflect these influences. The melodramas, including *Lenardo und Blandine* (1779), are modelled closely on Benda's experimental works. In *Der Bettelstudent, oder Das Donnerwetter* (1785), he mixes strophic lieder, light italianate arias and characteristic French forms to create a charming Singspiel that was admired for several decades. In *Helena und Paris* (1782) he followed Holzbauer's lead in composing a serious German work within the Mannheim operatic tradition, complete with ballets, prominent choral numbers, and arias featuring concertante instrumental parts.

Winter's widespread fame as an opera composer came with the three works he wrote in Vienna. In *Das unterbrochene Opferfest* (1796), his best-known work, he combined brilliant bravura arias, tender cantabile solos, comic folklike songs and powerful choral scenes to depict the story of a sacrificial ritual in ancient Peru. He was also commissioned to set Schikaneder's sequel to *Die Zauberflöte*, entitled *Das Labyrinth, oder Der Kampf mit den Elementen* (1798). In this work and another heroic-comic opera, *Babylons Pyramiden* (1797), he modelled his music closely on Mozart's *Zauberflöte* style. After these successes he tended to favour serious genres: *opere serie* for London and Italy, *tragédies lyriques* for Paris and 'ernsthafte Singspiele' for Munich.

Winter's standing as an opera composer remained high during his lifetime. In a long obituary (*AMZ*, xxviii, 1826) reflecting this, the anonymous writer wrote of his operas:

> The splendour of his choruses, an always rich orchestration ... an unprecedented handling of the brass instruments, an artistic and nuanced handling of timbre, and so much else that only the experienced artist can offer can be found throughout [his works] ... He did not, however, achieve the ideal of a genuine Italian aria ... His best arias are actually in essence only lieder raised to a higher level of pathos ... He agreeably pleased and entertained us; moved us, shocked us – never (cols. 372–3).

Indeed, though Winter worked in many different operatic styles and had a sure instinct in handling his forces, he rarely ventured beyond his models. Even so, his career as a composer included a number of successes, and his contribution to German opera, especially during the period between Mozart's death and Weber's rise to prominence, is significant.

See also BABYLONS PYRAMIDEN; BETTELSTUDENT, DER (i); LABYRINTH, DAS; LENARDO UND BLANDINE; and UNTERBROCHENE OPFERFEST, DAS.

Cora und Alonzo (melodrama, 4, J. M. von Babo), Munich, 1778, *US-Wc*
Lenardo und Blandine (melodrama, 2, J. F. von Göz, after G. A. Bürger), Munich, National, 25 June 1779, *D-Mbs* (R1986: GOB, x), *US-Wc*
Reinhold und Armida (melodrama, 3, Babo, after T. Tasso: *Gerusalemme liberata*), Munich, Altes Opernhaus, 30 March 1780, *D-DS*
Helena und Paris (3, K. J. Förg, ?after R. de' Calzabigi), Munich, National, 5 Feb 1782, *Mbs*
Das Hirtenmädchen (Spl, 1, H. Braun), Munich, National, 26 March 1784
Der Bettelstudent, oder Das Donnerwetter (Spl, 2, P. Weidmann, after M. de Cervantes: *La cueva de Salamanca*), Munich, National, 2 Feb 1785, *Bds, DS, Mbs, US-Cn*
Bellerophon (ernsthaftes Spl, 3, J. F. Binder von Krieglstein), Munich, Hof, 29 July 1785, *D-DS*
Circe (os, 2, D. Perelli), comp. for Munich, Hof, carn. 1788, but not perf.
Medea und Jason (melodrama, A. C. von Törring-Seefeld), ? Munich, Schloss Seefeld, 1789
Psyche (heroisches Spl, 2, K. F. Müchler), Munich, Hof, Oct 1790, *A-Wn*
Jery und Bäteli (Spl, 1, J. W. von Goethe), ? Munich, Schloss Seefeld, 1790
Das Lindenfest, oder Das Fest der Freundschaft, 1790 (operetta, 2), ?unperf.
Scherz, List und Rache [Scapin und Scapine] (Spl, 4, Goethe), Munich, Schloss Seefeld, 1790, *Wgm*
Catone in Utica (dramma per musica, 3, P. Metastasio), Venice, S Benedetto, May 1791
Antigona (os, 2, M. Coltellini), Naples, S Carlo, 4 Nov 1791, ? *I-Nc*
Il sacrifizio di Creta, ossia Arianna e Teseo (dg, 2, P. Pariati), Venice, S Benedetto, 13 Feb 1792
I fratelli rivali (dg, 2, M. Botturini), Venice, S Benedetto, Nov 1793, *A-Wn, B-Bc, D-DS, Mbs, US-Wc*, vs (Bonn, n.d.), Ger. trans. as Die Brüder als Nebenbühler
Belisa, ossia La fedeltà riconosciuta (dramma tragicomico, 2, A. Pepoli), Venice, S Benedetto, 5 Feb 1794, *A-Wgm*; as Elise, Gräfin von Hilburg (trans. and arr. K. L. Gieseke), Vienna, Wieden, 30 Jan 1798, *B-Bc, D-DS*
Die Thomasnacht (komische Oper, 2), Bayreuth, 1 July 1795
Ogus, ossia Il trionfo del bel sesso [Il tartaro convinto in amore] (dg, 2, G. Bertati), Prague, National, 1795, *Bds, Mbs*, vs (Leipzig, n.d.)
I due vedovi (2, G. De Gamerra), Vienna, Burg, 13 Jan 1796, *A-Wgm, Wn*
Das unterbrochene Opferfest [Il sacrifizio interrotto; Le sacrifice interromptu; The Oracle, or The Interrupted Sacrifice] (2, F. X. Huber), Vienna, Kärntnertor, 14 June 1796, *Wgm, Wn, D-Bds, Mbs, US-Bp, NYp*, vs (Bonn and Offenbach, 1798)
Babylons Pyramiden (heroisch-komische Oper, 2, E. Schikaneder), Vienna, Wieden, 25 Oct 1797, *A-Wgm, Wn, D-Bds, Mbs, US-Wc*, vs (Vienna, 1797), collab. J. Mederitsch
Das Labyrinth, oder Der Kampf mit den Elementen (heroisch-komische Oper, 2, Schikaneder), Vienna, Wieden, 12 June 1798, *A-Wgm, D-Bds*, vs (Offenbach and Bonn, n.d.)
Der Sturm (grosse Oper, 2, F. X. Kaspar, after W. Shakespeare: *The Tempest*), Munich, Hof, Oct 1798, *DS, Mbs*
Marie von Montalban (ernsthaftes Spl, 4, K. Reger, after J. N. Komarek), Munich, Hof, 28 Jan 1800, *A-Wgm, Wn, D-Bds, Mbs, US-Wc, Bp*, vs (Mainz, 1798)
Tamerlan (4, E. Morel de Chédeville, after Voltaire: *L'orphelin de la Chine*), Paris, Opéra, 14 Sept 1802, *F-Pc, Po, A-Wn* (Ger.), *US-Su* (It.); (Paris, 1802)
La grotta di Calipso (2, L. da Ponte), London, Haymarket, 31 May 1803, *A-Wgm, Wn, D-Bds*, vs (Leipzig, n.d.); in Ger., as Calypso, Munich, Hof, 17 Jan 1807, *Mbs*
Il trionfo dell'amor fraterno (os, 3, Da Ponte), London, Haymarket, 22 March 1804; as Castor et Pollux (5, P.-J. Bernard and Morel de Chédeville), Paris, Opéra, 19 Aug 1806, *A-Wgm, Wn, F-Po*
Il ratto di Proserpina (os, 3, Da Ponte), London, Haymarket, 3 May 1804, *A-Wgm, Wn, B-Bc, D-Bds, US-Wc*, vs (London, ?1815)
Zaira (2, Da Ponte, after Voltaire), London, Haymarket, 29 Jan 1805, *A-Wgm, Wn, B-Bc, Mbs*
Der Frauenbund (komische Oper, 3, Babo), Munich, Hof, 17 March 1805
Die beiden Blinden, 1807–10 (Spl, 3, F. von Holbein), ? Munich, Hof, spr. 1810 [cited in Manferrari]
Salomons Urteil (3), ? Munich, Hof, 1808, *Mbs*
Colmal (heroische Oper, 2, M. von Collin, after Ossian), Munich, Hof, 15 Sept 1809, *DS, Mbs*
Die Pantoffeln (Spl, J. F. Schink), Hamburg, April 1811
Maometto II (tragedy, 2, F. Romani, after Voltaire), Milan, Scala, 28 Jan 1817, *B-Bc, D-Bds, Mbs, US-Wc* (Ger.)
I due Valdomiri (os, 2, Romani), Milan, Scala, 26 Dec 1817
Etelinda (opera semiseria, 2, G. Rossi), Milan, Scala, 23 March 1818
Der Sänger und der Schneider (Spl, 1, F. von Drieberg), Munich, Hof- und National, 20 Jan 1820, *D-Mbs*

*

StiegerO
I. T. F. C. Arnold: *Peter Winter* (Erfurt, 1810)
Obituary, *AMZ*, xxviii (1826), 353, 369, 372–3, 465
F. Grandaur: *Chronik des königlichen Hof- und Nationaltheaters in München* (Munich, 1878)
P. Legband: 'Münchner Bühne und Literatur im 18. Jahrhundert', *Oberbayerisches Archiv*, li (1904), 1–546
E. Istel: *Die Entstehung des deutschen Melodramas* (Berlin and Leipzig, 1906)
V. E. Frensdorf: *Peter Winter als Opernkomponist* (Erlangen, 1908)
H. Kretzschmar: *Geschichte der Oper* (Leipzig, 1919)
L. Kuckuck: *Peter Winter als deutscher Opernkomponist* (diss., U. of Heidelberg, 1923)
M. Zenger: *Geschichte der Münchner Oper* (Munich, 1923)
E. Bücken: *Der heroische Stil in der Oper* (Leipzig, 1924)
O. Ursprung: *Münchens musikalische Vergangenheit von der Frühzeit bis zu Richard Wagner* (Munich, 1927)
L. Schiedermair: *Die deutsche Oper* (Leipzig, 1930, 2/1940)
F. Brukner: *'Die Zauberflöte': unbekannte Handschriften und seltene Drucke aus der Frühzeit von Mozarts Oper* (Vienna, 1934)
O. E. Deutsch: *Das Freihaustheater auf der Wieden, 1787–1801* (Vienna, 1937)
A. Bauer: 'Der "Zauberflöte" zweiter Teil', *ÖMz*, iv (1949), 180–84
U. Manferrari: *Dizionario universale delle opere melodrammatiche* (Florence, 1954–5)
H. Becker, ed.: *Giacomo Meyerbeer: Briefwechsel und Tagebücher*, i (Berlin, 1960)
H. Bolongaro-Crevenna: *L'arpa festante: die Münchner Oper 1651–1825, von den Anfängen bis zum 'Freyschützen'* (Munich, 1963)
D. G. Henderson: 'The "Magic Flute" of Peter Winter', *ML*, lxiv (1983), 193–205

LINDA TYLER

Winterfeld, Max. *See* GILBERT, JEAN.

Winter's Tale, A. Opera in two acts by JOHN HARBISON to his own libretto after WILLIAM SHAKESPEARE's play; San Francisco Opera (American Opera Project), 20 August 1979.

Leontes, King of Sicily (baritone), becomes mistakenly convinced that his queen, Hermione (soprano), has betrayed him with his friend Polixenes, King of Bohemia (baritone). Leontes rejects his newborn daughter as illegitimate and tries Hermione for her supposed infidelity; she is later reported to have died. Meanwhile, in a dumbshow, a Shepherd (bass) finds the abandoned infant and joyfully takes it home. 16 years later the infant, now a beautiful girl, Perdita (soprano), attracts the love of Polixenes' son Florizel (tenor). Polixenes separates them, but they flee to Leontes, who learns Perdita's identity; Florizel is reconciled with his father, and the two kings revive their friendship. Leontes regrets the death of Hermione, whom he now believes to have been innocent. Her maid Paulina (mezzo-soprano) leads him to a gallery to see a statue of Hermione; at a word from Paulina, the 'statue' comes to life as Hermione herself, and she embraces Leontes.

In adapting Shakespeare's play Harbison eliminated the Autolycus subplot and concentrated on the ritual and lyrical elements. The action moves swiftly, partly through the use of 'dumbshows', six pantomime sequences with music which advance the plot at crucial moments without the need for explanatory recitative. In the original production, music on tape accompanied the dumbshows; Harbison later rewrote those passages for orchestra but only Act 2 of the revised version has been performed, and only in concert.

Much of the stage movement, particularly in the dumbshows, is stylized. The personification of Time (bass) plays a larger role than in the play, appearing in the action and introducing both acts. In Act 1 the music drives the action at a rapid pace, using large intervals and dissonant harmonies to heighten the emotion, especially in the passages associated with Leontes' obsessions. STEVEN LEDBETTER

Winther, Lone Koppel. *See* KOPPEL, LONE.

Wirl, Erik (*b* Ebensee, 1885; *d* Rottach-Egern am Tegernsee, 15 Feb 1954). Austrian tenor. He studied in Munich and made his début in 1906 at Bayreuth as the Young Sailor (*Tristan und Isolde*) and an Esquire (*Parsifal*). Engaged at Frankfurt from 1906 to 1922, he was the first German Pelléas (1907) and created the Chevalier in Schreker's *Der ferne Klang* (1912) and the Jester in that composer's *Der Schatzgräber*(1920). He was a favourite operetta singer in Berlin and Vienna and in 1926 sang Alfred in *Die Fledermaus* at Salzburg. He was engaged at the Kroll Oper, Berlin (1927–31) and the Staatsoper (1928–33), continuing to appear until 1942. ELIZABETH FORBES

Wise, Patricia (*b* Wichita, KS, 31 July 1943). American soprano. She studied in Kansas and New York, making her début in 1966 at Kansas City as Susanna, and then joined the New York City Opera. She made her Covent Garden début as Rosina (1971) and sang her first Zerbinetta at Glyndebourne (1972). She sings regularly in Vienna as Pamina, Konstanze, Gilda, Zdenka, Sophie, Lucia, Musetta and Juliet. She has appeared at San Francisco, Berlin, La Scala, where she sang Nannetta (1980), and Salzburg, where she sang the Protagonist in the première of Berio's *Un re in ascolto* (1984). She sang her first Violetta in Minorca in 1991. The great flexibility of voice and security of technique that she shows in such roles as Lucia and Zerbinetta were displayed to even more dazzling effect as Berg's Lulu, which she first sang in Geneva (1985) and has since repeated in Barcelona, Madrid and Paris.

For illustration *see* RE IN ASCOLTO, UN. ELIZABETH FORBES

Wishart, Peter (Charles Arthur) (*b* Crowborough, 25 June 1921; *d* Frome, 14 Aug 1984). English composer. He studied composition with Hely-Hutchinson at Birmingham University (1938–41) and privately with Boulanger in Paris (1947–8). Later he taught at Birmingham University (1950–59), the GSM (from 1961) and at King's College, London, from 1972 to 1977, when he became professor at Reading University. *Two in the Bush* (1959) was the first of his pieces to attract public attention, and his reputation has remained founded on operatic works. A short comic piece, *Two in the Bush* (for three voices and piano) concerns a girl with two lovers whom she endeavours to keep apart, without success. The music is characterized by alert rhythms and a highly individual use of diatonic dissonance, and at times incorporates witty references to other styles, from early organum to Latin American. A second version, with orchestral accompaniment, was performed in Belfast in 1962. It was followed by *The Captive*, a tragic companion piece written for the same three voices, set in 11th-century Japan; the music is taut and highly condensed, and much of its thematic substance derives from the opening flute phrases. *The Clandestine Marriage*, Wishart's first full-length opera, is a Georgian social satire. All three works have recourse to pastiche, and the music inevitably at times suggests Stravinsky, particularly *The Rake's Progress*. Wishart's last two operas were written for his wife, the mezzo-soprano Maureen Lehane; *Clytemnestra* is elaborately structured and is his only opera to introduce a chorus. *The Lady of the Inn* is set in Turenne in the Middle Ages and is written for orchestra without violins. Wishart's scores are characterized by ostinato figures, motor rhythms and terse orchestration; they also possess a strong and individual lyricism. A talent for imaginative word-setting is evident, perhaps deriving from his studies of vocal ornamentation.

Two in the Bush op.26, 1956 (ob, 1, D. Roberts), Birmingham, Barber Institute, 1959
The Captive op.37 (tragic op, 1, Roberts), Birmingham, Barber Institute, 1960
The Clandestine Marriage op.69 (ob, 3, Roberts, after D. Garrick and G. Colman the elder), Cambridge, Arts, 1 June 1971
Clytemnestra op.72 (tragic op, 2, Roberts), London, Collegiate, 15 Feb 1974
The Lady of the Inn (3, Roberts, after C. Goldoni), Reading University, 17 June 1983

D. J. Roberts: 'Some Recollections of Peter Wishart', *British Music Society Journal*, x (1988), 1–25

Wissmer, Pierre (*b* Geneva, 30 Oct 1915). French composer of Swiss origin. He studied composition under Roger-Ducasse at the Paris Conservatoire (1935–8) and after a period in Switzerland he returned to Paris (1949), taking French nationality in 1958. He is honorary director of the Schola Cantorum, and in 1969 became director of the Ecole Nationale de Musique, Le Mans. Among his works are three operas and three ballets as well as vocal and instrumental pieces; his music has affinities with that of the 'Jeune France' group.

Marion, ou La belle au tricorne, 1945 (oc, 3, J. Goudal), Paris, OC (Favart), 17 Nov 1951
Capitaine Bruno, 1952 (1, G. Hoffmann), Bordeaux, Grand, 4 March 1955
Léonidas, ou La cruauté mentale (opéra bouffe, 1, Wissmer and R. Hofmann, after J. Mardore), Verdun, 3 Nov 1958

ANNE GIRARDOT

Wiszniewski, Zbigniew (*b* Lwów, 30 July 1922). Polish composer. He studied composition with Kazimierz Sikorski at the Łódź Conservatory (1948–52) and later taught at the Warsaw Conservatory. He became known principally for his music for tape, through his work with the Experimental Studio at Polish Radio in Warsaw from 1957. Wiszniewski has also written a number of chamber pieces, but he disappeared from view in the 1980s. His three radio operas belong to a corpus of such works by Polish composers; they are conventionally scored and are of modest length. The best-known is *Neffru* (1959), whose ancient Egyptian setting contrasts with more contemporary subjects in his later radio operas (see E. Derewecka: 'Opery radiowe', *Ruch muzyczny*, 1960, no.21, p.12).

Neffru (radio op, Z. Kopalko), Polish Radio, 6 Oct 1959, unpubd
Tak jakby ... [As Good as ...], 1971 (radio op, B. Wiernik, after R. Gary: *Les racines du ciel*), Wrocław, 21 Feb 1974, unpubd
Paternoster, 1971–4 (radio op, H. Kajzar and Wiszniewski), Cologne, West-Deutscher Rundfunk, 1975, unpubd

ADRIAN THOMAS

Witherspoon, Herbert (*b* Buffalo, NY, 21 July 1873; *d* New York, 10 May 1935). American bass. At Yale he studied both art and music; his singing teacher was Gustav Stoeckel. He continued with MacDowell, among others, and later studied in Paris, London and Berlin. In 1898 he made his début with Savage's Castle Square Opera Company in New York as Ramfis, and was one of the first native singers engaged by the Metropolitan's new manager, Gatti-Casazza. Having made his début as Titurel (1908) he sang, among other roles, Gurnemanz, King Mark, the Landgrave (*Tannhäuser*), Pogner and Sarastro, and took part in the first two American operas given by the Metropolitan, Converse's *The Pipe of Desire* (1910) and Parker's *Mona* (1912). He retired from the Metropolitan in 1916, and was chosen to succeed Gatti-Casazza as general manager but died of a heart attack a month after taking office. He was a distinguished teacher; his writings include *Singing: a Treatise for Teachers and Singers* (1925) and *36 Lessons in Singing for Teacher and Student* (1930).

PHILIP LIESON MILLER

Witkowski, Georges(-Martin) (*b* Mostaganem, Algeria, 6 Jan 1867; *d* Lyons, 12 Aug 1943). French composer. While training at the military establishment of Saint-Cyr he wrote an *opéra comique*, *Le maître à chanter* (1, M. Checzy), performed privately at the chateau of Mme de Trédern in Brissac (1890) and then re-orchestrated for the Grand Théâtre in Nantes (1891). The fine descriptive passages in this work underlined a talent for operatic writing and Witkowski was prompted to study privately with Vincent d'Indy in Paris. He abandoned a military career to settle in Lyons, where he worked as a conductor from 1902; from 1924 to 1941 he was director of the Conservatory. His compositions include several orchestral pieces and one further *opéra comique*, *La princesse lointaine* (4, after E. Rostand), composed between 1929 and 1932 and first performed at the Paris Opéra on 26 March 1934.

Witte, Erich (*b* Bremen, 19 March 1911). German tenor. He studied in Bremen and made his début there in 1930. After engagements in Wiesbaden as Nando (*Tiefland*) and in Breslau, he sang David at Bayreuth (1943–4), returning in 1952 as Loge, a role to which he was particularly suited and which he sang at Covent Garden during the 1950s. He sang regularly at the Berlin Staatsoper and Städtische Oper, where in 1947 he was the first Berlin Grimes. In 1957 at short notice he sang the role of Walther in English in his own production of *Die Meistersinger* at Covent Garden. In 1961 he was appointed chief resident director at Frankfurt and in 1967 resident director at the Berlin Staatsoper. He appeared at the Metropolitan Opera during 1938–9 in roles including Froh, Mime and the Holy Fool in *Boris Godunov*. A highly intelligent singer, he lacked the voice necessary for an international career.

HAROLD ROSENTHAL/R

Wittich, Marie (*b* Giessen, 27 May 1868; *d* Dresden, 4 Aug 1931). German soprano. She studied in Würzburg with Otto-Ubridz and reputedly made her début in 1882, at the age of 14, at Magdeburg as Azucena. After engagements at Basle (1883), Düsseldorf and Schwerin (1886), she joined the Dresden Hofoper, where she sang regularly from 1889 to 1914. Her roles included Leonore (*Fidelio*) and Senta; she took part in the première of Paderewski's *Manru* (1901) and created Strauss's Salome (1905). She appeared at Bayreuth (1901–9) as Sieglinde, Isolde and Kundry. At Covent Garden (1905–6), where she appeared as Elsa, Elisabeth, Isolde, Sieglinde and Brünnhilde, she failed to justify her considerable German reputation because of ill-health. The power of her voice, vibrant in tone and extremely dramatic in character, allowed her to triumph in roles for which she was physically unsuited such as Salome.

HAROLD ROSENTHAL/R

Wittrisch, Marcel (*b* Antwerp, 1 Oct 1901; *d* Stuttgart, 3 June 1955). German tenor. Born of German parents, he was brought up in Belgium and studied in Munich, Leipzig and Milan. He made his début in 1925 at Halle in Marschner's *Hans Heiling* and joined the company at Brunswick the following year. The Berlin Opera engaged him in 1929 and he remained there as principal lyric tenor until 1944, singing a wide range of roles; he gained a special reputation in Mozart. At Covent Garden in 1931 his Eisenstein (*Die Fledermaus*) was admired but he was considered somewhat hard and throaty in *Die Zauberflöte*. In the 1930s his repertory widened to include Lohengrin, which he sang at Bayreuth in 1937. After World War II he was heard as Narraboth (*Salome*) in Paris and as Siegmund and Parsifal at Stuttgart, where he continued to appear until his death. He made many concert tours, sang in operetta and films and, above all, made recordings, in which he was often compared to Richard Tauber. Though less individual in style, he was certainly comparable in timbre and less restricted in the upper register.

J. B. STEANE

Witzthumb, Ignaz. *See* VITZTHUMB, IGNAZ.

Wixell, Ingvar (*b* Luleå, 7 May 1931). Swedish baritone. He studied in Stockholm, making his début there in 1955 as Papageno with the Royal Opera, of which he was a member until 1967. During the company's visit to Covent Garden in 1960 he sang Silvano (*Ballo*) and Ruggiero (Handel's *Alcina*). In 1962 he sang Guglielmo at Glyndebourne, and at the Deutsche Oper, Berlin, where he was subsequently engaged. He made his American début in 1967 at San Francisco as Belcore. At Bayreuth in 1971 he sang the Herald (*Lohengrin*). He made his Covent Garden début in 1972 as Boccanegra and his Metropolitan début in 1973 as Rigoletto, and has sung at Salzburg, Vienna and Munich. His roles include Verdi's Amonasro, Don Carlo (*La forza del destino*), Germont, Luna, Renato and Falstaff, which he sang at Chicago (1988), as well as Count Almaviva (*Le nozze di Figaro*), Rossini's Figaro, Pizarro, Yevgeny Onegin, Mandryka (*Arabella*) and Scarpia, which he sang at Earl's Court, London, in 1991. His dark, firm-toned voice and powerful stage presence combine to make him a highly dramatic interpreter.

ELIZABETH FORBES

Wolanek, Anton. *See* VOLÁNEK, ANTONÍN.

Wolansky, Raymond (*b* Cleveland, OH, 15 Feb 1926). American baritone. After studying in the USA he was engaged in 1952 at Stuttgart, where he sang for over 30 years. He appeared at Hamburg and Frankfurt, sang Olivier (*Capriccio*) in 1963 at Glyndebourne, took the part of Alfred Ill in the American première of Einem's *Besuch der alten Dame* at San Francisco (1972) and made his Covent Garden début (1973) as Mandryka. His roles included Almaviva, Gluck's Orestes, Kurwenal, Rigoletto, Boccanegra, John the Baptist, Háry János and Major Mary (*Die Soldaten*). A very dependable singer, he kept the youthful timbre of his voice throughout a long career. ELIZABETH FORBES

Wolf, Ernst Wilhelm (*b* Grossen Behringen, bap. 25 Feb 1735; *d* Weimar, 29 or 30 Nov 1792). German composer. He studied at the University of Jena and there became director of the Collegium Musicum, for which he composed a number of works including a cantata for the 200th anniversary of the university. When he went to Leipzig in 1758 his reputation increased further in the circle of J. F. Doles and J. A. Hiller. After a period in Naumberg as a music teacher, he became music tutor to Duchess Anna Amalia's sons at Weimar, where he was appointed Konzertmeister (1761), organist (1763) and Kapellmeister (1768), and where he remained until his death, refusing an offer from Frederick the Great of Prussia to succeed C. P. E. Bach.

Throughout his tenure at Weimar Wolf enjoyed the protection of the Duchess; he survived both the artistic rivalry of Anton Schweitzer (exacerbated by the machinations of Wolf's wife, the court singer Maria Karoline Benda) and Goethe's arch dislike. His early comic operas, including *Das Rosenfest*, *Die Dorfdeputierten* and *Die treuen Köhler*, show the influence of Hiller, whose manner he never fully abandoned. Occasionally his sensitivity leads to shallowness. In *Die Dorfdeputierten* folksong elements (as in the trio 'Ein Hund, ein Kätzchen', with its 'Wau, wau' and 'Miau, miau' imitations, and the laughing chorus) are mingled with formulae that anticipate Mozart (e.g. 'Süsse Hoffnung, Tochter des Himmels'). Wolf assisted Anna Amalia in her compositional endeavours; she composed the arias in his melodrama *Polyxena* (published in 1776 under his name only). During the 1780s Wolf sought to reassert himself as a composer of German opera, but without success.

Das Gärtnermädchen (comische Oper, 3, K. A. Musäus), Weimar, Schloss, 1769, vs (Weimar, 1774)
Das Rosenfest (operetta, 3, G. E. Heermann, after C.-S. Favart), Weimar, Schloss, 4 Sept 1770, vs (Berlin, 1771, rev. 2/1775)
Die Dorfdeputierten (komische Oper, 3, Heermann, after C. Goldoni), Weimar, Schloss, 10 Feb 1772, vs (Weimar, 1773)
Die treuen Köhler (comische Oper, 2, Heermann), Weimar, Schloss, 14 July 1772, vs (Weimar, 1774)
Der Abend im Walde (comische Oper, 2, Heermann), Weimar, Schloss, 10 Dec 1773, vs (Riga, 1775)
Das grosse Loos (2, F. J. Bertuch, after Favart), Gotha, Schlosstheater im Rathause, 2 Sept 1774, vs (Berlin, 1776)
Superba (K. A. von Seckendorff), Weimar, 30 Jan 1785
Die Zauberirrungen, oder Die Irrtümer der Zauberei (Schauspiel mit Gesang, 2, F. H. von Einsiedel), Weimar, 24 Oct 1785
Erwin und Elmire (Schauspiel mit Gesang, 2, J. W. von Goethe), Weimar, 1785
Der Eremit auf Formentara (Schauspiel mit Gesang, 2, A. von Kotzebue), Weimar, Hof, 26 Nov 1786
Alceste (5, C. M. Wieland), Weimar, Herzogliches Comödienhaus, 1786
Der Schleier (Spl, 3, C. A. Vulpius), Weimar, 1786
Angelica (Spl, Wieland), Berlin, 1788
Der Papagei (?Kotzebue), *c*1790
Le monde de la lune (komische Oper, 3, after Goldoni), ?unperf., *D-Dlb*

*

J. F. Reichardt: 'E. W. Wolf', *Musikalischer Almanach 1782* (Berlin, 1782), 85
J. N. Forkel: 'E. W. Wolf', *Musikalischer Almanach 1783* (Leipzig, 1782), 70; *1784* (1783), 132–3
J. F. Reichardt: 'E. W. Wolf', *Berlinisches Archiv der Zeit*, i (1795)
F. von Schlichtegroll: *Nekrolog der Teutschen* (Gotha, 1802); ed. R. Schaal (Kassel and Basle, 1954)
M. Friedlaender: *Das deutsche Lied im 18. Jahrhundert* (Stuttgart and Berlin, 1902)
W. Bode: *Die Tonkunst in Goethes Leben*, i (Berlin, 1912)
J. Brockt: *E. W. Wolf: Leben und Werke* (diss., U. of Breslau, 1927)
E. W. Böhme: 'Ernst Wilhelm Wolf, der Weimarische Hofkapellmeister der Goethezeit', *ZMw*, xv (1932–3), 171–2
T. Bauman: *North German Opera in the Age of Goethe* (Cambridge, 1985) G. KRAFT, THOMAS BAUMAN

Wolf, Hugo (Filipp Jakob) (*b* Windischgraz, Styria [now Slovenjgradec, Slovenia], 13 March 1860; *d* Vienna, 22 Feb 1903). Austrian composer. Although he grew up in Lower Styria on the edges of German culture, his first encounter with opera was with an Italian work: his father, a keen musician, took him at the age of eight to see Donizetti's *Belisario* in Klagenfurt. This experience sparked an enthusiasm that lasted for the rest of his life. It was fuelled by his move to Vienna in 1875, where his early love for Italian opera was soon overtaken by an infatuation with Wagner's music dramas. Wagner's visit to the Austrian capital that year proved crucial for Wolf. The young man's restless and passionate musical personality posed many problems for his teachers and he was ousted from the Vienna Academy in 1877; but his personal encounter with Wagner and his music provided a focus for his aspirations and encouraged him to persist in his efforts to become a composer.

Wolf produced sketches for an opera, *König Alboin*, as early as 1875, but there were soon signs that he was inhibited by his admiration for Wagner's achievement. While he developed rapidly as a song composer, his operatic plans remained in limbo. From 1882, when he first sketched the scenario for a comic opera set in Seville, Wolf remained obsessed by thoughts of a Spanish opera. These were given particular impetus by his discovery in 1888 of Alarcón's *El sombrero de tres picos*, the novel that was eventually to form the basis for his opera *Der Corregidor*. Such inspirations were initially directed into songwriting, however; 1888 was the year of the Eichendorff, Mörike and Goethe volumes, Wolf's first mature songbooks. Many of these songs have been compared to miniature dramatic scenes, Wolf picking out the visual details, as well as the emotional content, of each poem. Wagnerian circles in Vienna welcomed the songbooks as a fruitful translation of Wagner's dramatic techniques into a new sphere.

But Wolf was not content to remain merely a songwriter. The flow of songs continued with his Spanish songs of 1889, though Wolf saw these in particular as operatic sketches, preparations for the Spanish opera he was certain must follow. He was fired in his ambitions by Nietzsche's call, 'Il faut méditerraniser la musique!', seeing himself as the composer who would free opera from Wagner's weighty symbolism and re-create the southern lightness of Bizet's *Carmen*. The Italian songs of 1890 and 1891 provided once more an immediate outlet for Wolf's aspirations, but from 1891 the search for an operatic subject became his sole concern. He harboured many different plans (including a setting of Shakespeare's *The Tempest*) and explored a wide variety of dramatic texts without being satisfied by any of them. He was undoubtedly seeking a kind of poetic perfection that was not possible in an operatic libretto. By 1895, after four years of musical inactivity, Wolf was prepared to compromise, returning to Rosa Mayreder's libretto of *El sombrero de tres picos*, which he had rejected in 1890.

Having accepted Mayreder's text, Wolf gave it the respect he accorded to the poems of his songs, despite its dramatic clumsiness. Other features of *Der Corregidor* confirm that Wolf was still rooted in song composition. Many of his characterizations were too subtle for the stage, as with his ambiguous treatment of the servant Repela. The music for the Corregidor himself also lacks consistency, sometimes appearing too grand for the ridiculous figure he cut on stage. At the première it was indeed clear that Wolf was not interested in the stage action; he referred all such matters to Mayreder. He composed the opera as a series of lyrical set pieces, even to the extent of including two songs from the Spanish volume, while cleverly extending the song structure to fit the dramatic action. He also created a kind of overall continuity by bringing back motifs in the Wagnerian fashion, though each motif tends to remain tightly patterned and enclosed in song-like textures. At times *Der Corregidor* gives the impression of moving restlessly between the contrapuntal techniques of Wagner's *Meistersinger* and the set pieces of Bizet's *Carmen*, the two acknowledged models for the opera. The material for Tio Lukas's dramatic monologue in Act 3 is an obvious exception, anticipating the broader, more settled style of Wolf's unfinished opera, *Manuel Venegas*.

Wolf began work on *Manuel Venegas* in 1897, having completed *Der Corregidor* in less than a year. It was also based on a novel by Alarcón, *El niño de la bola*, but its much more tragic content revealed Wolf's wish to break new ground. Although Wolf retained his enthusiasm for *Der Corregidor*, resisting revisions and cuts as much as possible, he eventually admitted some of the limitations of its libretto. Indeed, he decided to bypass Mayreder's adaptation of *Manuel Venegas* in favour of another by his friend Moritz Hoernes. The extant sketch of five scenes from the first act traces a much broader sweep than the music of the earlier opera. Wolf wrote the material continuously, rather than dotting between lyrical numbers as he did when composing *Der Corregidor*. The fragment he completed builds up successfully to the dramatic entry of the hero, returned from exile. As Manuel Venegas (tenor) tells of his sufferings, the tension of the music anticipates his passion for revenge against his faithless beloved, Soledad (soprano), and her husband, Antonio Arregui (baritone). In *Manuel Venegas* Wolf opted for a highly coloured declamatory style, in contrast to the conversational idiom of *Der Corregidor*; he had thus broken away from the condensed lyricism of the Italian songs, to bring in bolder Wagnerian features such as had already been successfully absorbed into some of his other songs. The lyrical style remained, as in the opening hymn to spring, but it now provided strong contrast with the prevailing tone, symbolizing the forces of mercy as against the hero's urge for vengeance.

The *Manuel Venegas* sketch confirms that Wolf had not exhausted his operatic potential with *Der Corregidor*, although it is unlikely he would ever have realized his large-scale operatic ambitions; it may be significant that at the onset of his madness, during the composition of *Manuel Venegas*, Wolf imagined himself to be the head of the Vienna Opera. Perhaps if he had had the chance to complete this second project, he might have gained a more lasting place in the operatic repertory. *Der Corregidor* is valued for its musical invention and for its attempts to regain the lightness of Mozartian comedy, but its lack of stage sense prevents the realization of Wolf's aspirations for the renewal of opera.

See also CORREGIDOR, DER.

Edition: *H. Wolf: Sämtliche Werke*, ed. H. Jancik and others (Vienna, 1960–) [WW]

König Alboin, 1875–7 (4, P. Peitl), frag. *A-Wn* [21 bars]

Der Corregidor, 1895 (4, R. Mayreder, after P. de Alarcón: *El sombrero de tres picos*), Mannheim, National, 7 June 1896 (Leipzig, 1904), WW xii

Manuel Venegas, 1897 (3, M. Hoernes, after Alarcón: *El niño de la bola*), Mannheim, 1 March 1903, vs (Mannheim, 1902) [5 scenes completed], WW xiii

*

E. Hellmer: 'Der Corregidor', *Gesammelte Aufsätze über Hugo Wolf* (Berlin, 1898–1900), 65–73

——, ed.: *'Der Corregidor' von Hugo Wolf: kritische und biographische Beiträge zu seiner Würdigung* (Berlin, 1900)

H. Werner, ed.: *Hugo Wolf: Briefe an Rosa Mayreder, mit einem Nachwort der Dichterin des 'Corregidors'* (Vienna, 1921)

R. Hernried: 'Hugo Wolf's "Corregidor" at Mannheim', *MQ*, xxvi (1940), 19–30

F. Walker: *Hugo Wolf: a Biography* (London, 1951, enlarged 2/1968; Ger. trans., enlarged, 1953 [incl. addl MS facs.])

F. Krieg: 'Gedanken um den "Corregidor"', *ÖMz*, viii (1953), 49–52

I. Fellinger: 'Die Oper im komponistorischen Schaffen von Hugo Wolf', *Jb des Staatlichen Instituts für Musikforschung Preussischer Kulturbesitz 1971*, 87–99

L. Spitzer: 'Rosa Mayreders Textbuch zu Hugo Wolfs "Manuel Venegas"', *ÖMz*, xxviii (1973), 443–51

P. Cook: *Hugo Wolf's Der Corregidor* (London, 1976)

L. Spitzer: 'Hugo Wolfs "Manuel Venegas": ein Beitrag zur Genese', *ÖMz*, xxxii (1977), 68–74

H. Pleasants: 'Wolf among Sheep', *Opera*, xxxi (1980), 883–6

M. Saary: *Persönlichkeit und Musikdramatische Kreativität Hugo Wolfs* (Tutzing, 1984)

S. Youens: 'Hugo Wolf and the Operatic Grail: the Search for a Libretto', *COJ*, i (1989), 277–98

AMANDA GLAUERT

Wolfe, Jacques (Leon) (*b* Botoshan, 29 April 1896; *d* Bradenton, FL, 22 June 1973). American composer of Romanian birth. He went to the USA with his family in 1898. He studied composition with Percy Goetschius at the Institute of Musical Art, and then after World War I taught music in New York public schools, appeared as a concert pianist and served as president of the Composers' and Authors' Guild. He moved to Miami in 1947, where he became chairman of the local Grass Roots Opera Company and a noted photographer. Wolfe is best known for his songs and arrangements in the style of negro spirituals, including 'Short'nin' Bread'. His drama with music *John Henry* (2, R. Bradford; New York, 10 Jan 1940), first performed with Paul Robeson in the title role and a nearly all-black cast, was loosely adapted from folktales of the mythic African American. Wolfe's music was said by Brooks Atkinson to be 'extraordinarily beautiful' and 'eloquent', though static for staged scenes. Wolfe's revision of the work as *Mississippi Legend* (New York, 24 April 1951), performed by the Village Opera Company, received wide attention. While the *New York Times* critic found 'neo-Gershwinesque' or 'trite' harmonies and 'traces of artiness' in the musical settings, he praised the prosody as 'well-nigh perfect' and held that 'this score deserves to be studied by all American operatic composers'. *The*

Trysting Tree (1, I. Roam) was first performed at the University of Florida at Coral Gables on 6 November 1957. DEANE L. ROOT

Wolff, Albert (Louis) (*b* Paris, 19 Jan 1884; *d* Paris, 20 Feb 1970). French composer and conductor. He studied at the Paris Conservatoire with Leroux. In 1906 he joined the staff of the Opéra-Comique, where he was appointed conductor in 1911, making his début with the première of Laparra's *La jota*, and was musical director for three years from 1921, as successor to Messager; from 1945 he was briefly director-general. His other posts included that of conductor at the Opéra (from 1949) and conductor of the French repertory at the Metropolitan (1919–21), including the première of his own *L'oiseau bleu*. Best known as a dedicated exponent of the French music of his time, he gave the first performances of Milhaud's *La brebis égarée* (1923), Ravel's *L'enfant et les sortilèges* and Poulenc's *Les mamelles de Tirésias* (1947).

Soeur Béatrice, 1911 (1, M. Maeterlinck), Nice, 1948
Le marchand de masques (2, L. Merlet and T. Salignac), Nice, 3 April 1914
Lise et Lucas (operetta, 1, F. Lacoste), Amélie-les-bains, 6 Aug 1916
L'oiseau bleu (3, Maeterlinck), New York, Met, 27 Dec 1919

*

S. Wolff: 'Albert Wolff, doyen de l'Opéra-Comique', *Guide du concert* (3 Oct 1958), 62–4

CHRISTIANE SPIETH-WEISSENBACHER/R

Wolff, Beverly (*b* Atlanta, GA, 6 Nov 1928). American mezzo-soprano. She studied in Atlanta and Philadelphia. In 1952 she made her début as Dinah in Bernstein's *Trouble in Tahiti* (CBS TV) and also sang Dinah for her début with New York City Opera (1958). She took part in the première of Menotti's *Labyrinth* (NBC TV, 1963). She created the title role of Douglas Moore's *Carry Nation* at Kansas University, Lawrence (1966), then sang the role in San Francisco (the first professional performance) and for New York City Opera (1968). Other roles included Cherubino, Siébel, Carmen, Sextus (*Giulio Cesare*), Sara (*Roberto Devereux*) and Leona in the première of Menotti's *The Most Important Man* (1971). She also appeared in Chicago, San Diego and Cincinnati, in a repertory that included Desideria (*Saint of Bleecker Street*), Radamistus, Ulrica, Adalgisa, Delilah, Erika (Barber's *Vanessa*) and Kabanicha, which she sang at San Francisco in 1978. Her superb musicianship, sense of style and dramatic involvement can be admired in *Carry Nation*, recorded live from New York City Opera.

RICHARD LeSUEUR/ELIZABETH FORBES

Wolff, Fritz (*b* Munich, 28 Oct 1894; *d* Munich, 18 Jan 1957). German tenor. He studied in Würzburg and made his début as Loge at Bayreuth in 1925, returning regularly until 1941 as Loge, Walther and Parsifal. After engagements in Hagen and Chemnitz, in 1928 he took part in the première of Schreker's *Der singende Teufel* at the Berlin Staatsoper, where he remained until 1943 and, in addition to his Wagner roles, sang the title role in Pfitzner's *Palestrina*. He appeared regularly at Covent Garden (1929–38) in Wagner roles and as Aegisthus (*Elektra*). He also sang in Vienna, Paris, Prague and other European cities, and as Walther in Cleveland (1934–5). His beautiful voice and dignity of bearing admirably suited him to such roles as Lohengrin and Parsifal. HAROLD ROSENTHAL/R

Wolff, Hellmuth Christian (*b* Zürich, 23 May 1906; *d* Leipzig, 1 July 1988). German musicologist and composer. He studied with Abert and others at Berlin University, where he took the doctorate in 1932; he completed his *Habilitation* at Kiel in 1942. He was professor at the musicology institute of Leipzig University from 1954 to 1971, but in 1967 he was banned from teaching or publishing his work there after submitting an article to a Berlin newspaper implicitly criticizing the East German Communist authorities. In 1992, four years after his death, he was officially rehabilitated in the wake of German unification. His reputation rests on his many publications rather than on his operas, none of which has been performed. He wrote extensively about the history of opera, particularly Baroque opera in Venice, Naples and Hamburg; he edited three volumes of excerpts from operas of the 17th, 18th and 19th centuries respectively, for the series Das Musikwerk (xxxviii, xxxix, both 1971, Eng. trans. 1971; xl, 1972, Eng. trans. 1975). His interest in the visual aspects of music culminated in his edition of the volume on opera in the series Musikgeschichte in Bildern (1968). In addition to his operas, he wrote a ballet, incidental music and chamber music. In later years he became known as a painter.

all to librettos by the composer

Der kleine und der grosse Klaus op.27, 1931 (chamber op, 1, after H. C. Andersen), rev. 1940
Die törichten Wünsche [Das kalte Herz] op.35, 1942–4 (3, after W. Hauff)
Esther op.40, 1945 (szenisches Oratorium, 2)
Der Tod des Orpheus op.50, 1947 (3)
Ich lass' mich scheiden op.59, 1950 (heitere Kammeroper, 2)

WRITINGS

Die Venezianische Oper in der zweiten Hälfte des 17. Jahrhunderts (Berlin, 1937, 2/1975)
Agrippina, eine italienische Jugendoper von G. Fr. Händel (Wolfenbüttel and Berlin, 1943)
Die Barockoper in Hamburg 1678–1738 (Wolfenbüttel, 1957)
Die Händel-Oper auf der modernen Bühne (Leipzig, 1957)
Oper: Szene und Darstellung von 1600 bis 1900, Musikgeschichte in Bildern, iv (Leipzig, 1968)

*

'Hellmuth Christian Wolff 65', *Musik und Gesellschaft*, xxi (1971), 340

HORST SEEGER, ANDREW CLARK

Wolf-Ferrari [Wolf], **Ermanno** (*b* Venice, 12 Jan 1876; *d* Venice, 21 Jan 1948). Italian composer. (He added his mother's maiden name, Ferrari, to his surname about 1895.) Although he learnt the piano and was profoundly affected by music from an early age, he also showed signs of having inherited the talents of his father, a painter of Bavarian origin. He therefore studied at the Accademia di Belle Arti, Rome (1891–2), keeping music as a spare-time activity. In 1892, however, after he had moved to Munich to continue his art studies, he entered the Munich Akademie der Tonkunst, where he was a counterpoint pupil of Rheinberger. In 1895, without having completed his final examination, he returned to Venice. He also spent some time in the late 1890s in Milan, where he became a protégé of Boito and met Giulio Ricordi, who did not, however, accept his music for publication. Thus began the long period in which his music repeatedly proved more acceptable in Germany than in Italy.

During 1900–03 Wolf-Ferrari was again in Munich, after the failure in Venice of *Cenerentola*. But the successes in Germany of the opera's revised version, and of his cantata *La vita nuova* (1901), resulted in his being appointed director of the Liceo Musicale, Venice

(1903–9). After resigning from that post, he devoted himself almost entirely to composition, living near Munich but regularly visiting Venice. In 1911–12 he visited the USA. The 1914–18 war (during which he took refuge in Zürich) inevitably came as a severe shock, in view of his mixed blood and background and his hypersensitive yet child-like temperament: he composed little during the conflict or the years immediately thereafter. Having become more active again from the mid-1920s, he was in 1939 appointed professor of composition at the Salzburg Mozarteum. In 1946 he moved to Zürich once more, but returned to Venice for the last year of his life.

Taken as a whole, Wolf-Ferrari's output is strangely heterogeneous. Although best known for his comic operas of 1902–9, in which he revealed a special flair for graceful semi-pastiches of 18th-century music, he had first come to prominence, around 1900, as a composer of high seriousness, writing numerous rather rhapsodic chamber works indebted to the Mendelssohn-Schumann-Brahms tradition, and showing occasional signs of Wagner's influence.

Even *Cenerentola* only intermittently anticipates the *opera buffa* qualities of Wolf-Ferrari's next few operas. This extremely eclectic score is notable, rather, for the delicate yet sometimes surprisingly dissonant chromaticism of some passages: the very first bars repeatedly sound D, D♯ and E simultaneously. Then, in 1902–6, the combined impacts of Mascagni's *commedia dell'arte* opera *Le maschere* (about which Wolf-Ferrari had mixed feelings, but which evidently set him thinking) and of Goldoni's famous comedies led to the composition of *Le donne curiose* and *I quatro rusteghi*. The latter is a particularly successful free evocation of the world of *opera buffa*, especially of the Venetian variety, in a style flexible enough to admit many romantic touches (some of them relatable to the Verdi of *Falstaff*) and even a few gently ironic 'modernisms' where the dramatic situation warrants them – for instance at the beginning of Act 3. *Il segreto di Susanna*, though even more popular than *I quatro rusteghi*, is less sure-footed in its mingling of 18th-century idioms with others of more recent origin. This opera's shortcomings are, however, negligible compared with those of *I gioielli della Madonna*, in which Wolf-Ferrari suddenly – perhaps in an attempt to break down Italian resistance to his music – jumped on to the bandwagon of post-Mascagnian *verismo*, with results which, though uninhibitedly colourful (pseudo-Neapolitan), are often of a vulgarity that had hitherto seemed foreign to him. The return of his better qualities in *L'amore medico* confirms that even to attempt a crude melodrama like *I gioielli* was a betrayal of his true nature.

The psychological crisis aroused by World War I inevitably left its mark on Wolf-Ferrari's few works of those years. The little-known, problematic *Gli amanti sposi* is particularly interesting in this respect. Although it too is based, freely and not altogether satisfactorily, on a Goldoni comedy, much of the music has an expressive complexity far removed from the simpleheartedness of *I quatro rusteghi*. In these passages free pastiche tends again to yield place (as in parts of *L'amore medico*, but more so) to a chromaticism relatable to, but more purposefully deployed than, that of *Cenerentola*. A disturbed state of mind is even more directly evident in *Sly*, notably in the central character's intense monologue in Act 3: recent revivals in Germany have demonstrated that, for all its eclecticism, this is the most genuinely powerful of Wolf-Ferrari's few serious operas. In *La vedova scaltra* and *Il campiello* he returned yet again to Goldoni, and this time reverted, for much of the time, to a style very close to that of the pre-war comedies. Neither of these later Goldoni operas achieved the worldwide fame of *I quatro rusteghi* and *Il segreto di Susanna*; but *Il campiello* in particular contains scenes in which the earlier operas' sparkle is fully rekindled, and others which show that Wolf-Ferrari was still capable of striking new departures: the formidable quarrel scene in Act 3 is probably the most 'modernistic' passage in any of his works.

Wolf-Ferrari edited Mozart's *Idomeneo* (for performance at Munich in 1931), and Galuppi's *Il filosofo di campagna*: his edition of the latter was eventually performed in Venice in 1954.

See also AMORE MEDICO, L'; CAMPIELLO, IL; DONNE CURIOSE, LE; GIOIELLI DELLA MADONNA, I; QUATRO RUSTEGHI, I; SEGRETO DI SUSANNA, IL; SLY; and VEDOVA SCALTRA, LA.

Irene, 1895–6 (Wolf-Ferrari), unpubd, unperf.

La Camargo, *c*1897 (M. Pezzè-Pascolato, after A. de Musset), inc., unpubd

Cenerentola, 1897–1900 (fiaba musicale, 3, Pezzè-Pascolato, after C. Perrault), Venice, Fenice, 22 Feb 1900; rev., Bremen, 31 Jan 1902

Le donne curiose (3, L. Sugana, after C. Goldoni), Munich, Residenz, 27 Nov 1903, as Die neugierigen Frauen (musikalische Komödie)

I quatro rusteghi (3, Sugana, G. Pizzolato, after Goldoni), Munich, Hof, 19 March 1906, as Die vier Grobiane

Il segreto di Susanna (int, 1, E. Golisciani), Munich, Hof, 4 Dec 1909, as Susannens Geheimnis

I gioielli della Madonna (3, Golisciani and C. Zangarini), Berlin, Kurfürstenoper, 23 Dec 1911, as Der Schmuck der Madonna

L'amore medico (2, Golisciani, after Molière: *L'amour médecin*), Dresden, Hof, 4 Dec 1913, as Der Liebhaber als Arzt (musikalisches Lustspiel)

Gli amanti sposi [La gabbia dorata, ovvero Il legame d'amore], lib. begun 1904, music mainly *c*1916 (opera giocosa, 3, Sugana, Pizzolato, Golisciani and G. Forzano, after Goldoni: *Il ventaglio*), Venice, Fenice, 19 Feb 1925

Das Himmelskleid [La veste di cielo], *c*1917–25 (Legende, 3, Wolf-Ferrari, after Perrault), Munich, National, 21 April 1927

Sly, ovvero La leggenda del dormiente risvegliato (3, Forzano, partly after W. Shakespeare: *The Taming of the Shrew*), Milan, Scala, 29 Dec 1927

La vedova scaltra (3, M. Ghisalberti, after Goldoni), Rome, Opera, 5 March 1931

Il campiello (commedia lirica, 3, Ghisalberti, after Goldoni), Milan, Scala, 12 Feb 1936

La dama boba (commedia lirica, 3, Ghisalberti, after F. Lope de Vega), Milan, Scala, 1 Feb 1939

Gli dei a Tebe (3, L. Andersen [L. Strecker] and Ghisalberti), Hanover, Oper, 4 June 1943, as Der Kuckuck von Theben

*

W. Mauke: 'Le donne curiose', *RMI*, xi (1904), 366–70

——: 'I quattro rusteghi', *RMI*, xiii (1906), 315–20

——: 'Ermanno Wolf-Ferrari', *Die Musik*, viii (1908–9), 142–51

L. Schmidt: 'Die neugierigen Frauen'; 'Die vier Grobiane', *Aus dem Musikleben der Gegenwart* (Berlin, 1909), 140–42; 143–6

E. Bontempelli: 'Il segreto di Susanna', *RMI*, xviii (1911), 839–53

J. Korngold: *Die romanische Oper der Gegenwart* (Vienna, Leipzig and Munich, 1922), 40–55

G. M. Gatti: '"Sly" von Wolff Ferrari, und einige allgemeine Bemerkungen', *Melos*, vii (1928), 537–9

A. Lualdi: '*Sly*, opera in tre atti di E. Wolf-Ferrari', *Musica d'oggi*, 1st ser., x (1928), 8–11

E. L. Stahl, ed.: *Ermanno Wolf-Ferrari* (Salzburg, 1936)

R. de Rensis: *Ermanno Wolf-Ferrari: la sua vita d'artista* (Milan, 1937)

A. Gasco: *Da Cimarosa a Strawinsky* (Rome, 1939) [incl. 'Un veneziano a Roma: chiacchierando con Ermanno Wolf-Ferrari', 385–91; '*I quattro rusteghi* al Costanzi (1923)', 392–7; '*La vedova scaltra* e un musicista più scaltra di lei (1931)', 398–405]

G. Gavazzeni: 'Lettera da Milano: *La dama boba* di Wolf-Ferrari alla Scala', *RaM*, xii (1939), 78–81

A. C. Grisson: *Ermanno Wolf-Ferrari: autorisierte Lebensbeschreibung* (Regensburg, 1941, enlarged 2/1958)
W. Zentner: 'Zum Opernschaffen Ermanno Wolf-Ferraris', *ZfM*, Jg.108 (1941), 13–16
A. Berrsche: *Trösterin Musika: gesammelte Aufsätze und Kritiken* (Munich, 1942), 98–9, 493–501
J. Ringo: 'Ermanno Wolf-Ferrari: an Appreciation of his Work', *RMI*, li (1949), 224–47
C. Smith: 'City Opera Presents *I quattro rusteghi*', *MusAm*, lxxi/14 (1951), 5, 23
W. Pfannkuch: *Das Opernschaffen Ermanno Wolf-Ferraris* (diss., U. of Kiel, 1952)
A. Lualdi: 'Saluto a Ermanno Wolf-Ferrari'; 'Il mio maestro', *Tutti vivi* (Milan, 1955), 253–78; 377–426
H. Rebois: *Des rustres de Goldoni aux quatre rustres de Wolf-Ferrari* (Nice, 1960)
G. Vigolo: 'Pudori perduti' [on *I gioielli della Madonna*]; 'Gusto e grazia di Wolf-Ferrari', *Mille e una sera all'opera e al concerto* (Florence, 1971), 225–7; 397–9
A. L. Suder, ed.: *Ermanno Wolf-Ferrari* (Tutzing, 1986)

JOHN C. G. WATERHOUSE

Wölfl [Wölffl, Woelfl], **Joseph** (*b* Salzburg, 24 Dec 1773; *d* London, 21 May 1812). Austrian composer and pianist. As a chorister at Salzburg Cathedral, he received his first musical training from Leopold Mozart and Michael Haydn. He was already appearing in public as a violinist at the age of seven. In 1790 he went to Vienna to see Mozart; after Mozart's death but nevertheless through his influence, Wölfl took up residence as composer to Count Ogiński in Warsaw. He returned in 1795 to Vienna, winning considerable recognition as a composer, and especially as a pianist: he was frequently compared with Beethoven. After a two-year tour, he lived in Paris (from 1801) and London (1805), and continued to gain attention for his piano sonatas, concertos and chamber music. His most important success was his opera *Der Höllenberg*, written to a libretto by Schikaneder. Wölfl's compositions show an unpretentious melodic gift, but also plaintive early Romantic touches.

published as vocal scores

Der Höllenberg (heroic-comic op, 2, E. Schikaneder), Vienna, Wieden, 21 Nov 1795, arr. for pf (Vienna and Brunswick, n.d.)
Das schöne Milchmädchen, oder Der Guckkasten (comic operetta, 1, J. Richter), Vienna, Kärntnertor, 5 Jan 1797
Der Kopf ohne Mann (heroic-comic op, 2, J. Perinet), Vienna, Wieden, 3 Dec 1798, excerpts arr. for pf in *Leipziger Zeitung*, i/30
Das trojanische Pferd (comic op, Schmieder), 1799, ?inc.
L'amour romanesque [Die romanhafte Liebe] (oc, 1, A. Charlemagne), Paris, OC (Feydeau), 3 March 1804, excerpts arr. for pf (Leipzig, 1804)
Fernando, ou Les maures (heroic op, 3), Paris, Feydeau, 11 Feb 1805

Music in: Die Liebe macht kurzen Prozess, oder Die Heirat auf gewisse Art, 1798

HEINZ WOLFGANG HAMANN, PETER BRANSCOMBE

Wolf Trap. National park in Vienna, Virginia, USA, devoted to the performing arts. In 1971 the US Department of the Interior opened the park on land about 32km west of Washington, DC, which had been received five years earlier from Catherine Filene Shouse; Julius Rudel was appointed music director. Shouse also financed the construction of the park's first amphitheatre and sought the formation (1971) of the Wolf Trap Opera Company, a summer artistic residence for singers running from May to September each year, which quickly attained national stature. Singers who made their débuts with the company include Chris Merritt (1973), Rockwell Blake (1974), Dawn Upshaw (1985) and Alan Held (1987).

In 1973 John Moriarty became music director, conducting the première of Pasatieri's *Signor Deluso* the following season. In 1976 Frank Corsaro staged the American première of Busoni's *Doktor Faust* in a controversial production that portrayed Faust as Busoni himself. In 1978 Christopher Keene conducted the première of Stephen Douglas Burton's *The Duchess of Malfi*, and in 1980 Sarah Caldwell led a rare American production of Marschner's *Der Vampyr*. Throughout the 1970s the company gave some performances at the Filene Center, an amphitheatre (6800 seats) that dwarfed many productions. In January 1982 the park opened a small opera house, The Barns at Wolf Trap (cap. 350), more congenial to the company's purpose. In April 1982 the Filene Center was completely destroyed by fire, although The Barns were not damaged. The Center was rebuilt, and opened again in August 1984.

'Wolf Trap Burns but Show goes on', *MadAminA!*, iii/2 (1982), 1–2

NANCY MALITZ

Wollank, (Johann Ernst) Friedrich (*b* Berlin, 3 Nov 1781; *d* Berlin, 6 Sept 1831). German composer. A lawyer by profession, he studied music in his youth with J. A. Gürlich and at the Singakademie with C. F. C. Fasch. He was a founder-member of Zelter's Liedertafel (1808), and was one of Weber's circle of Berlin friends. His music was on the whole modest in aim, consisting chiefly of vocal works and chamber music for strings; but he also wrote a three-act opera *Die Alpenhirten* to a libretto by H. W. Loess, a work in Singspiel manner which Max Maria von Weber described as 'Romantic through and through'. It had some success at its Berlin première on 19 February 1811; however, when Weber gave it in Prague in 1815 (with Caroline Brandt as Betty), it was considered too long and after the first performance (7 May) was cut by five numbers, still leaving the public cold. In 1826 Wollank was one of the founders of the Berlin Philharmonic Society.

J. P. Schmidt: Obituary, *AMZ*, xxxiii (1831), 727
C. von Ledebur: *Tonkünstler-Lexicon Berlins* (Berlin, 1861)
M. M. von Weber: *Carl Maria von Weber* (Leipzig, 1864–6)
Z. Němec: *Weberova pražská léta* [Weber's Prague Years] (Prague, 1944)

JOHN WARRACK

Wolpe, Stefan (*b* Berlin, 25 Aug 1902; *d* New York, 4 April 1972). American composer of German birth. At the Berlin Hochschule für Musik, he studied with Juon and others and received advice from Busoni; he was also influenced by the music of Skryabin and Schoenberg. He was briefly involved with the Berlin dadaists and influenced by the ideas of the Bauhaus at Weimar, and until 1933 gave himself to the cause of radical socialism. He joined the Arbeitertheater Bund, conducted performances at demonstrations and rallies, and composed many pieces on populist and political themes. In 1931 he became composer and pianist for Die Truppe 31, a theatre collective directed by Gustav von Wangenheim. Their first production, *Die Mausefalle*, was a great success and had over 300 performances in Germany and Switzerland. In the music of this period Wolpe struggled to achieve a simple yet forceful tonal idiom for his proletarian revolutionary music while developing a free 12-note idiom in several songs and instrumental works. After 1926 he drew on popular jazz and dance styles in compositions for Berlin cabarets and Communist rallies.

Between 1927 and 1929 he composed two chamber operas and a dramatic setting of Schwitters's dada poem *Anna Blume*. The two operas are burlesques with political overtones. *Zeus und Elida* is a *Zeitoper* in one act to a libretto written by friends of Wolpe. Set in the Potsdamer Platz of Berlin, it satirizes bourgeois attitudes in sophisticated jazz dance style. The influence of Berg's *Wozzeck* can be heard in the extensive use of Sprechstimme and in the extravagant range and angularity of the vocal and instrumental lines. *Schöne Geschichten* is a series of seven short scenes on the topics of Science, Religion, Law, Education, Love, Philosophy and Patriotism that may have been modelled on Lev Tolstoy's *The Wisdom of Children*. Wolpe selected the farcical texts from jokes and Yiddish stories and set them for two male singers and male chorus accompanied by a jazz band. The scenic projections were designed by Frida Dicker, a painter from the Bauhaus. While the voices are mainly in Sprechstimme, the instrumental setting achieves an atonal idiom that verges on free 12-note. The *Anna Blume* scene for 'musical clown' and pianist, who at one point joins the singer in a patter duet, is a hilarious setting using a fully 12-note technique.

In March 1933 Wolpe left Berlin for Vienna, where he studied orchestration with Webern. He then taught in Palestine (until 1938) and in 1936 attended a conducting course with Scherchen at Brussels. In 1938 he settled in the USA, where he taught at a number of institutions; among his pupils were Feldman, Shapey, Tudor and several prominent jazz composers. Among his later compositions are a ballet and incidental music as well as many instrumental works. After the complexities of the scores of the fifties, he pared his musical thought to essentials for the music of his last period.

Schöne Geschichten op.5B, 1927–9 (1), ? Berlin, Cabaret Anti, ?*c*1929, *US-NYp**

Zeus und Elida: Musikalische Groteske op.5A, 1928 (1, K. Wickerhauser and O. Hahn), ? Berlin, Cabaret Anti, ?*c*1928, *NYp**

Anna Blume, 1929 (lyric scene, K. Schwitters), ? Berlin, Cabaret Anti, ?*c*1929; New York, 1983

*

A. Clarkson: 'Stefan Wolpe's Berlin Years', *Music and Civilization: Essays Presented to Paul Henry Lang*, ed. M. R. Maniates and E. Strainchamps (New York, 1983), 371–93

B. Northcott: 'Catching up on Wolpe', *Tempo*, cliv (1985), 11–14

H. Vogt. ed.: *Stefan Wolpe: von Berlin nach New York* (Cologne, 1988)

E. Klemm: 'Zwischen Dadaismus und Agitprop: der Komponist Stefan Wolpe', *Musik und Gesellschaft*, xxxix (1989), 12–17

A. Clarkson: 'The Fantasy can be Critically Examined: Composition and Theory in the Thought of Stefan Wolpe', *Music Theory and the Exploration of the Past*, ed. C. Hatch and D. Bernstein (Chicago, 1992), 375–90

T. Phleps: 'An "Anna Blume": ein vollchromatisiertes Liebesgedicht von Kurt Schwitters und Stefan Wolpe', *Festschrift für Georg Knepler* (forthcoming)

AUSTIN CLARKSON

Wolpert, Franz Alphons (*b* Wiesentheid, 11 Oct 1917; *d* Wiesentheid, 7 Aug 1978). German composer. He was educated in Regensburg from 1928 until 1937, when he was appointed assistant chorus master at the Stadttheater. Two years later, he attended masterclasses given by Wolf-Ferrari, Clemens Krauss and Walter Lampe at the Salzburg Mozarteum, where he then taught (1941–4). After World War II he returned to Bavaria before moving to Überlingen on Lake Constance, where he became a music teacher. Two of Wolpert's operas were performed during his lifetime. In *Pechvogel* and *Der eingebildete Kranke* he attempted to revive the traditions of German Singspiel within a contemporary idiom influenced by Wolf-Ferrari and Puccini rather than later composers. *Der eingebildete Kranke* had a mixed reception at its first performance; critics admired the technical competence and directness of expression of the music, but suggested a lack of dramatic tension.

Der goldene Schuh (op ballet, 4), 1956

Der eingebildete Kranke, 1963 (comic op, 3, Wolpert, after Molière: *Le malade imaginaire*), Vienna, Volksoper, 26 April 1975

Pechvogel (television Spl, 2, Wolpert, after Volkmann-Leander), Austrian TV, 26 Dec 1967

Unperf., dates of composition unknown: Der Gang zum Jahrmarkt; Haiti 1803; Hero und Leander; Tilman Riemenschneider

*

T. Rossnagel: *Franz Alfons Wolpert: sein Leben, seine Arbeit und seine Werke für die Schulen Schloss Salem am Beispiel des Singspiels Der Pechvogel* (diss., Pädagogische Hochschule, Reutlingen, 1967)

E. Valentin: *Der eingebildete Kranke* [Vienna Volksoper programme book, 1974–5]

ERIK LEVI

Wolzogen, Hans (Paul) Freiherr von (*b* Potsdam, 13 Nov 1848; *d* Bayreuth, 2 June 1938). German writer on music and librettist. He was the son of Alfred von Wolzogen (1823–83), Intendant of the Schwerin court theatre. His mother was a daughter of the architect K. F. Schinkel, and it was in the Schinkel residence in Berlin that he received a grounding in the classics. From 1868 to 1870 he studied comparative philology, mythology and history in Berlin. His lack of musical training did not prevent him from writing a series of 'Thematic Guides' on Wagner's *Ring*, *Tristan* and *Parsifal* which, with their simplistic and inaccurate labelling of leitmotifs, have bedevilled a century or more of Wagnerian scholarship.

Wolzogen was introduced to Wagner in 1875; in 1877 he was invited to become editor of the *Bayreuther Blätter*. He established a record of sorts by remaining its editor throughout the 60 years of its existence, superintending its transformation from an in-house journal designed to acquaint members of the Society of Patrons with the ideological background to *Parsifal* to an openly nationalistic organ.

Under Cosima Wagner's watchful eye he edited (and censored) Wagner's correspondence with Theodor Uhlig, Wilhelm Fischer and Ferdinand Heine (Leipzig, 1888) and with Minna Wagner (Berlin, 1908). He wrote extensively on Wagnerian and philological matters, and also wrote the librettos for Hans Sommer's *Das Schloss der Herzen* (1891) and *Augustin* (1898), and d'Albert's *Flauto solo* (1905), as well as revising the text of E. T. A. Hoffmann's *Undine* (1922).

His half-brother Ernst von Wolzogen (1855–1934) wrote the libretto for Strauss's *Feuersnot* (1901) and, together with Otto Julius Bierbaum and Frank Wedekind, founded the satirical 'Überbrettl' Cabaret in Berlin, for which Oscar Straus and Schoenberg, among others, wrote music.

Richard Wagners Tannhäuser und Lohengrin nach Sage, Dichtung und Musik (Berlin, 1873)

Der Nibelungenmythos in Sage und Literatur (Berlin, 1876, 3/1890)

Die Tragödie in Bayreuth und ihr Satyrspiel (Leipzig, 1876, 12/1899) [from 4th edn onwards retitled *Erläuterungen zu R. Wagner's Nibelungendrama für alle Leser und Hörer des Werkes*]

Thematischer Leitfaden durch die Musik zu Richard Wagners Festspiel 'Der Ring des Nibelungen' (Leipzig, 1876; Eng. trans., 1882, 3/1888) [later retitled *Führer durch die Musik zu Richard Wagners Festspiel Der Ring des Nibelungen* and *Der Ring des*

Nibelungen: ein thematischer Leitfaden durch Dichtung und Musik]
Die Sprache in R. Wagner's Dichtungen (Leipzig, 1878, 3/1889)
'The Work and Mission of my Life', *North American Review*, cxxix (1879), 107–24 [pubd under Wagner's name]; Ger. trans. (1879)
Thematischer Leitfaden durch die Musik zu R. Wagner's Tristan und Isolde (Leipzig, 1880, 14/1911; Eng. trans., 1884)
Thematischer Leitfaden durch die Musik zu R. Wagner's Parsifal (Leipzig, 1882, 21/1914; Eng. trans., 1889)
Richard Wagner und die deutsche Kultur (Leipzig, 1883)
Erinnerungen an Richard Wagner (Vienna, 1883, enlarged 2/1891; Eng. trans., 1894)
Zur Einführung in die Bayreuther Festspieldramen 1886: 'Tristan' und 'Parsifal', ihre Entstehung und ihre Bedeutung (Leipzig, 1886)
Wagneriana: gesammelte Aufsätze über R. Wagner's Werke vom Ring bis zum Gral (Leipzig, 1888)
Richard Wagner und die Tierwelt: auch eine Biographie (Leipzig, 1890, 3/1910)
Grossmeister deutscher Musik (Hanover, 1897, enlarged 2/1924)
Aus deutscher Welt: gesammelte Aufsätze über deutsche Art und Kultur (Berlin, 1905, 2/1910)
Aus Richard Wagners Geisteswelt: neue Wagneriana und Verwandtes (Berlin and Leipzig, 1908)
Wagner und seine Werke: ausgewählte Aufsätze (Regensburg, 1924)
Musik und Theater (Regensburg, 1929)

STEWART SPENCER

Wood, Charles (*b* Armagh, 15 June 1866; *d* Cambridge, 12 July 1926). Irish composer and teacher. His career shadowed that of his compatriot Stanford, who taught him composition at the RCM (1883–7). Like Stanford, he conducted the University Musical Society as an organ scholar at Cambridge (1888–94), and was later elected to a fellowship. He taught harmony at the RCM from 1888, became university lecturer in harmony and counterpoint at Cambridge (1897), and was appointed to the Cambridge professorship at Stanford's death in 1924. Wood's unambitious personality was often reflected in the style and modest destiny of his music, yet he enjoyed a lively sense of humour, as evinced in his unpublished one-act chamber operas, both after Dickens: *A Scene from Pickwick*, composed in 1921 (RCM, 20 June 1922; *GB-Lcm*), is a setting of the conversation between Mr and Mrs Pott and Mr Winkle in *Pickwick Papers* (chapter 18); *The Family Party*, composed in 1923 (RCM, 12 Feb 1924; *GB-Lcm*), is based on *Martin Chuzzlewit* (chapter 4). The stage works are discussed in I. Copley, *The Music of Charles Wood* (London, 1978, pp.75–90).

STEPHEN BANFIELD

Wood, Sir **Henry J(oseph)** (*b* London, 3 March 1869; *d* Hitchin, 19 Aug 1944). English conductor. He had given public organ recitals before studying at the RAM, where his teachers included Ebenezer Prout and Manuel García (whose accompanist he became), between 1886 and 1888. Subsequently he worked as a choirmaster and organist, making his début as conductor in 1888. He also gave singing lessons and continued to do so for the rest of his career. Much of Wood's early experience was gained in the theatre, with touring opera companies and West End musicals. He helped Sullivan with the preparation of *The Yeomen of the Guard* (1888) and *Ivanhoe* (1891); he conducted a run of Thomas' *Mignon* (Royalty Theatre, 1889), some opera performances at the Crystal Palace, *Carmen* during Marie Roze's farewell tour (Carl Rosa Company, 1891) and the first English performance of *Yevgeny Onegin* (Olympic Theatre, 1892). In 1896 he conducted Stanford's new *Shamus O'Brien* for a run at the (London) Opera-Comique Theatre and, at the Coliseum in 1913, tableaux from *Parsifal* (without singers). Wood himself wrote four light operas, of which three were given in London: *Daisy* and *Returning the Compliment* in 1890, and *A Hundred Years Ago* in 1892. *Zuleika, or The Turkish Slave*, announced in 1890, was never performed.

The manager of the recently (1893) opened Queen's Hall, Robert Newman, asked Wood to form a new permanent orchestra and with it to give Promenade Concerts there. These concerts, which started in 1895, became the backbone of Wood's, and an essential ingredient in London's, musical life: he remained in charge until 1944. His tastes were as eclectic as they were enterprising. He favoured, as well as the standard classics, Russian music and British composers, the younger generation included, but he found room for operatic solos and regularly and impenitently performed excerpts from Wagner.

Wood wrote a manual, *The Gentle Art of Singing* (London, 1927–8). Further lively observations on singing occur in his autobiography, *My Life of Music* (London, 1938). He was knighted in 1911 and made Companion of Honour in 1944.

R. Pound: *Sir Henry Wood: a Biography* (London, 1969)
A. Jacobs: 'Henry Wood's Operatic Baptism', *Opera*, xlii (1991), 894–8

RONALD CRICHTON

Wood [née Paton], **Mary Anne** (*b* Edinburgh, Oct 1802; *d* Chapelthorpe, nr Wakefield, 21 July 1864). Scottish soprano. A successful performer on the English stage from October 1822, she made her début as Susanna; in 1824 she sang Agathe in the first English production of *Der Freischütz*, and in 1826 she created the role of Reiza in *Oberon*. She married the English tenor Joseph Wood (*b* Bretton, nr Wakefield, 7 March 1801; *d* Harrogate, 6 Sept 1890), and in the midst of her triumphant career at Covent Garden and the Italian Opera in London, they travelled to the USA; their joint début was in New York (9 September 1833) in Michael Rophino Lacy's *Cinderella* (an adaptation of *Cenerentola* with additions from other Rossini operas). On two separate tours, often travelling in small troupes with other singers, they appeared in New York, Boston, Philadelphia and elsewhere (September 1833–May 1836, September 1840–January 1841). Their repertory ranged from 18th-century ballad operas to contemporary English adaptations of Italian works; the two singers contributed greatly to a general American preference (begun by Elizabeth Austin) for Italian bel canto melody, in particular by introducing the works of Bellini (*La sonnambula*, 13 November 1835 and *Norma*, 11 January 1841, both in New York). Mary Anne, whose voice had an extensive compass (*a* to *d'''*/*e'''*), was acclaimed as an actress and as the finest singer of her day; Joseph was generally recognized as an excellent actor, a passable singer, and a shrewd businessman. In 1843 they retired and settled in Yorkshire.

J. Wood: *Memoir of Mr. and Mrs. Wood* (New York, 1840)
F. C. Wemyss: *Twenty-Six Years of the Life of an Actor and Manager* (New York, 1847)
W. W. Clapp: *A Record of the Boston Stage* (Boston, 1853)
J. Warrack: *Carl Maria von Weber* (London, 1968), 334
K. K. Preston: *Travelling Opera Troupes in the United States, 1825–1860* (diss., City U., New York, 1989)

WILLIAM BROOKS, KATHERINE K. PRESTON

Woollam, Kenneth (Geoffrey) (*b* Chester, 16 Jan 1937). English tenor. He was educated at Chester Cathedral Choir School, becoming head chorister, then studied at the RCM. After singing with the Glyndebourne Festival chorus, 1962–4, he joined the BBC Singers in 1964 and the ENO in 1972, making a notable début as Pierre Bezukhov in *War and Peace* (Prokofiev). He spent 12 years with the ENO as principal tenor, his roles there and elsewhere including Calaf, Radames, Siegfried, Rienzi, Bacchus and Herod. He has sung in several Janáček and contemporary operas, including *Owen Wingrave* (Britten) and *The Bassarids* (Henze). He created roles in *The Royal Hunt of the Sun* (Hamilton), *Toussaint* (Blake) and *A Gentle Spirit* (Tavener), and his Covent Garden début was in 1988 as Aegisthus (*Elektra*). Abroad he has sung in most continental and Scandinavian countries, and with the ENO at the Metropolitan in 1984 (*War and Peace*). On film he has appeared as Alfredo, Canio and Hoffmann, on television in Bernstein's *Songfest* conducted by the composer, and on disc in *Margot la Rouge* (Delius). A spinto tenor with a firm, grainy tone, he combines well-paced stamina with poetic feeling. Since 1985 he has been professor of singing at the RCM. NOËL GOODWIN

Wooster. American city, in Ohio. The Ohio Light Opera, the resident professional company of the College of Wooster, was founded there in 1979 by James Stuart, the artistic director, to explore neglected operetta repertory in English translation with young American actors and singers. Stuart has directed most productions and provided translations. In 1979 and 1980 the company performed without orchestra or conductor, using a set built around a piano at centre stage. In 1981 an orchestra was added, and a succession of music directors included William Conable (1981–2), James Paul (1983–4), J. Lynn Thompson (1985–8) and Evan Whallon (appointed 1988). The company maintains a nine-week summer season, the Light Opera Festival, from June to August, giving 69 performances of between seven and nine productions; operas are generally performed six times a week in nightly rotation.

Revivals of works rarely staged in America have included company premières, or premières in English, of Offenbach's *Les brigands* (W. S. Gilbert's translation) in 1983; Edward German's *Merrie England* in 1984; Auber's *Fra Diavolo* (Stuart's translation) in 1988; Lecocq's *La fille de Madame Angot* (as *Clairette*, Stuart's translation) in 1989; Heuberger's *Der Opernball*, Chabrier's *L'étoile* and Hahn's *Ciboulette* (Stuart's translation) in 1990; and Oscar Straus's *Ein Walzertraum* (original version) in 1991. Other rarely performed works have included Sullivan's *The Grand Duke* in 1981, Suppé's *Boccaccio* in 1983, Kálmán's *Die Csárdásfürstin* in 1986, Offenbach's *Barbe-bleue* and Millöcker's *Der Bettelstudent* in 1987, and Suppé's *Die schöne Galatea* in 1990. The Ohio Light Opera has produced all the Gilbert and Sullivan comic operas and the popular works of Johann Strauss, Lehár, Kálmán and Oscar Straus. American operetta has been represented by Romberg's *The Student Prince* (1982, 1985), *The Desert Song* (1986) and *The New Moon* (1991), Friml's *The Vagabond King* (1987) and Herbert's *Naughty Marietta* (1989). The company performs in the Freedlander Theatre (396 seats), an intimate proscenium house built in 1974 on the college campus. In 1990, 25 700 people attended productions.

NANCY MALITZ

Woyrsch, Felix (*b* Troppau, Austrian Silesia, 8 Oct 1860; *d* Altona, 20 March 1944). German composer and choral conductor. He grew up in Dresden and in early youth moved to Hamburg to study with E. A. H. Chevallier, also gaining the approval of Brahms; in Altona he held various posts as a choral conductor and church organist, becoming professor in the court administration in 1901, and from 1903 conducted or directed all concerts in the city. Elected to the Prussian Academy of Arts in 1917, he received the Goethe Medal in 1936; in 1937 he retired from public musical life.

He composed mainly vocal music, and his operas, which were among his earliest works, contain fresh, expressive writing for voices, while structure and orchestration show the stylistic influences of Wagner and Brahms.

Der Pfarrer von Meudon op.20 (komische Oper, 1, Woyrsch), Hamburg, 23 Nov 1886
Der Weiberkrieg op.27 (komische Oper, 3, Woyrsch), Hamburg, Stadt, 12 April 1890
Wikingerfahrt (2, Woyrsch), Nuremberg, 26 Jan 1896
Faust, unpubd

*

StiegerO
F. Pfohl: 'Felix Woyrsch: eine Skizze seines Lebens und Schaffens', *ZfM*, ci (1934), 1197–202
Verzeichnis der Tonwerke von Felix Woyrsch (Hamburg, n.d.)
C. M. Gruber: *Opern Uraufführungen*, ii (Vienna, 1987)

HELMUT WIRTH

Wozzeck. Opera in three acts by ALBAN BERG to his own libretto, after GEORG BÜCHNER's play *Woyzeck*; Berlin, Staatsoper, 14 December 1925.

Wozzeck	baritone*
Marie *his common-law wife*	soprano
Marie's son	treble
Captain	buffo tenor
Doctor	buffo bass
Drum Major	heroic tenor
Andres *Wozzeck's friend*	lyric tenor*
Margret *Marie's neighbour*	contralto
First Apprentice	deep bass*
Second Apprentice	high baritone
Madman	high tenor

Soldiers, apprentices, women, children

Setting A garrison town and the neighbouring countryside, *c*1830

*Sprechstimme roles

Berg began work on an operatic treatment of Büchner's play in 1914, after he had attended its first Viennese performance at the Residenzebühne on 5 May. It had been given in Landau's revision of K. E. Franzos's 1879 edition of the text and entitled *Wozzeck* because of a misreading of the almost illegible manuscript; Berg prepared his libretto from the Landau edition and hence preserved the misspelling in the opera. By the end of 1914 he had prepared a draft libretto and made some musical sketches, but he then set it aside to finish the Three Orchestral Pieces op.6. Conscription and subsequent service in the Austrian War Ministry prevented his returning to work on *Wozzeck* until 1917; he reported progress by autumn the following year, but even after the end of World War I it remained slow. Act 1 was completed by July 1919, Act 2 not until August 1921, and the entire work was finished in short score by October that year. The full score occupied Berg until April 1922; his pupil Fritz Heinrich Klein prepared the piano reduction.

Schoenberg had recommended that Universal Edition take on publication, but Berg initially published the vocal score privately in December 1922; although he signed a contract with Universal the following April no staging was immediately forthcoming. At the suggestion of Hermann Scherchen he prepared for concert performance the *Drei Bruchstücke aus 'Wozzeck'*, consisting of part of Act 1 scene iii, Act 3 scene i and the orchestral interlude between Act 3 scenes iv and v, leading into scene v itself; Scherchen conducted the first performance in Frankfurt in 1924. By then, however, Erich Kleiber had accepted the opera for production at the Berlin Staatsoper; he conducted the première, with Leo Schützendorf in the title role, Sigrid Johanson as Marie and Fritz Soot as the Drum Major in a staging by Franz Ludwig Horth.

Performances in Prague (1926) and Leningrad (1927) followed; the first German production since the première took place at Oldenburg in 1929, conducted by Johannes Schüler, and demonstrated that *Wozzeck* was not beyond the capabilities of provincial houses. The following year seven other German houses included it in their repertories; the Viennese première took place on 30 March 1930. Stokowski conducted the American première in Philadelphia in March 1931. Kleiber's second production, in Berlin in 1932, was the last occasion on which *Wozzeck* was seen in a German house until 1948: Berg was to be officially proscribed by the Nazi regime. Adrian Boult conducted a concert performance with Richard Bitterauf in the title role in the Queen's Hall, London, in 1934; the British stage première took place at Covent Garden in January 1952 conducted by Kleiber, with Marko Rothmüller as Wozzeck and Christel Goltz as Marie. In the same year the French stage première was given, at the Théâtre des Champs-Elysées, Paris. The first commercial recording was of a concert performance in Carnegie Hall, New York, in 1951, conducted by Dimitri Mitropoulos with Mack Harrell and Eileen Farrell; the first studio recording was conducted by Karl Böhm in 1965, with Dietrich Fischer-Dieskau and Evelyn Lear.

Berg himself characterized the large-scale dramatic and musical planning of *Wozzeck* as a ternary *ABA* structure in which the highly wrought 'symphonic' central act was flanked by the more loosely constructed outer acts. But the self-contained musical structure of each scene is precisely tied to its dramatic function. Thus the five scenes of Act 1, an exposition that introduces the five main characters in turn and delineates Wozzeck's relationship to them, are designated as a series of five character-pieces; Act 2, the opera's dramatic development, is a symphony in five movements, while the five scenes and final orchestral interlude of Act 3 ('catastrophe and epilogue') are a sequence of six inventions on single musical ideas.

ACT 1.i (Suite) *The Captain's room, early morning* After a brief introduction (Prelude: obbligato wind quintet), three bars in which the english horn introduces the Captain's theme, Wozzeck is seen shaving the Captain. He urges Wozzeck to work more slowly, and his words 'Langsam, Wozzeck, langsam!' define the tritone motif B–F that permeates the opera. After Wozzeck's numbed response on a single pitch the Captain continues with his lecture (Pavane: obbligato timpani and harp), but despite his enthusiastic contemplation of eternity Wozzeck is unmoved. 'A good man doesn't rush about', he is counselled (Cadenza 1: obbligato viola), and his refusal to react leads the Captain into derision (Gigue: obbligato flutes and celesta); Wozzeck agrees with everything he says. The Captain is delighted with his teasing and continues (Cadenza 2: obbligato double bass, leading to Gavotte: obbligato brass): Wozzeck has no moral sense because he has an illegitimate child (the Captain quotes the regimental chaplain in a parody falsetto). Wozzeck is finally provoked into a lyrical response: 'the Lord will think no less of him because of it' (Double 1: obbligato horns), and the Captain is confounded (Double 2: obbligato trombones). Wozzeck then expands on his theme (Air: obbligato strings) 'Poor folk like us, who have no money', and his first phrase, 'Wir arme Leut!', introduces the opera's most significant motif. The Captain tries to calm him (postlude) and the remainder of the scene then recapitulates the earlier conversation and its associated obbligatos. The following orchestral interlude continues to review the material of the suite and builds to a *fortissimo* climax.

1.ii (Rhapsody) *An open field outside the town, late afternoon* Andres and Wozzeck are cutting sticks, but Wozzeck is disturbed both by the brooding atmosphere, represented musically by the sequence of three chromatic chords on which the scene is based, and by what he perceives as the threatening natural world. Andres is untroubled and sings a folksong, 'Das ist die schöne Jägerei', to counteract Wozzeck's paranoia, but the scene ends with Wozzeck hearing noises under the ground and seeing the sinking sun as engulfing the world in flames. The orchestral interlude gradually dispels the atmosphere of menace with the first stirrings of the military band.

1.iii (Military March and Lullaby) *Marie's house, evening* Marie, her child in her arms, is watching the military band march by. The Drum Major acknowledges her, and the march provides the background to a conversation between Marie and Margret in which the neighbour remarks on Marie's interest in him. Marie slams shut her window and the march is replaced by a lullaby, 'Mädel, was fangst Du jetzt an?', as Marie sings of her life to her child. Wozzeck interrupts them. Ignoring the child, he tries to articulate the fears he experienced in the fields, as the music quotes altered motifs from Act 1 scene ii; Marie is terrified, quoting Wozzeck's own 'Wir arme Leut!' (but to a different figure), and rushes out. The interlude portrays her agitation by developing material from scenes ii and iii into a 12-note figure.

1.iv (Passacaglia) *The Doctor's study, a sunny afternoon* The 12-note theme of the passacaglia is heard as a cello recitative as the Doctor accuses Wozzeck of coughing in the street ('pissing' in Büchner's original) and goes on to question him about his diet (variations 1–5). The Doctor feels betrayed by Wozzeck's behaviour but calms himself, since anger is unscientific. Wozzeck remembers Marie and recounts his visions in the fields (variations 6–12) to music derived from scene ii; the Doctor seizes on an insight into Wozzeck's mental state (variations 13–21) and pronounces his diagnosis, 'eine schöne fixe Idee', to a slow waltz introduced by the first appearance of the Doctor's motif in the violins. As the tempo quickens he becomes more and more carried away with his dreams of scientific immortality. In the subsequent interlude fragments of the passacaglia are gradually replaced by music associated with the following scene.

1.v (Rondo) *The street outside Marie's house, twilight* Marie continues to admire the Drum Major from her doorway. The ritornello theme, related to the opening of the march, represents Marie's desire both for the soldier and for a new, better life; the Drum Major's boasting occupies the first episode, his attempts at seduction the following two sections. The curtain falls as they rush into the house.

ACT 2.i (Sonata) *Marie's room, a sunny morning* Marie is admiring the earrings the Drum Major has given her (exposition). When the child stirs Marie sings him back to sleep with a song about a gypsy who will take her back to his native land: the two themes of her guilt (heard in the orchestra) and her slightly sinister lullaby (derived from Act 1 scene iii) form the subjects of the sonata movement. Wozzeck enters, and Marie tries to hide the earrings (development): she says she found them in the street. He is unconvinced and leaves after briefly contemplating the child. Marie is overtaken by remorse (recapitulation). The interlude, framed by a pair of harp glissandos, is a violent development of the themes of the sonata movement.

2.ii (Fantasia and Fugue) *A street, daytime* The Captain and the Doctor, Wozzeck's two exploiters, meet. The Captain now counsels the Doctor not to rush; the latter (to the same waltz theme as in Act 1 scene iv) diagnoses the Captain's breathing difficulties as symptoms of 'apoplexia cerebria' and gives him four weeks to live. When Wozzeck appears they turn their attention to him and in a triple fugue – its first subject the Captain's theme, its second the Doctor's, its third (representing Wozzeck) derived from the preceding scene – begin to taunt him about Marie and the Drum Major. Deathly pale, Wozzeck rushes off. An interlude for chamber orchestra introduces the material of the following scene.

2.iii (Largo) *The street outside Marie's house, a gloomy day* To chamber-orchestral accompaniment (precisely the scoring of Schoenberg's First Chamber Symphony) Wozzeck confronts Marie with his suspicions. The music is derived almost entirely from reminiscences of previous scenes, especially Act 1 scenes iii and v. This slow movement at the centre of the opera is in three sections, the first devoted to Wozzeck's accusations, the second (as Wozzeck's jealous rage almost boils over in a knife attack) to Marie's defiance: here the chamber orchestra and the full orchestra are cross-cut, and a descending series of chromatic chords represents the knife. She leaves, and in the last part of the Largo Wozzeck is left to reflect on his existence: 'Der Mensch ist ein Abgrund' ('Man is an abyss'). The music that introduces the scene returns and is gradually transformed into a slow Ländler that forms the main material for the next scene.

2.iv (Scherzo with two trios) *A tavern garden, late evening* Soldiers, apprentices and local girls are dancing to the accompaniment of a stage band. Two apprentices deliver drunken soliloquies (Trio 1), and when the scherzo is resumed (with fleeting references to earlier motifs) the company is joined by Marie and the Drum Major. Wozzeck watches them and is about to launch an attack when the dancing is interrupted by an unaccompanied six-part Hunting Chorus in 7/4 (Trio 2), itself interrupted by another folksong from Andres. When the Scherzo is resumed, a madman observes to Wozzeck: 'Everybody is happy, but it smells of blood!' Wozzeck begins to see the scene swallowed up in blood-red mist. The dance music continues, increasingly grotesque, through the interlude, until it is abruptly cut short.

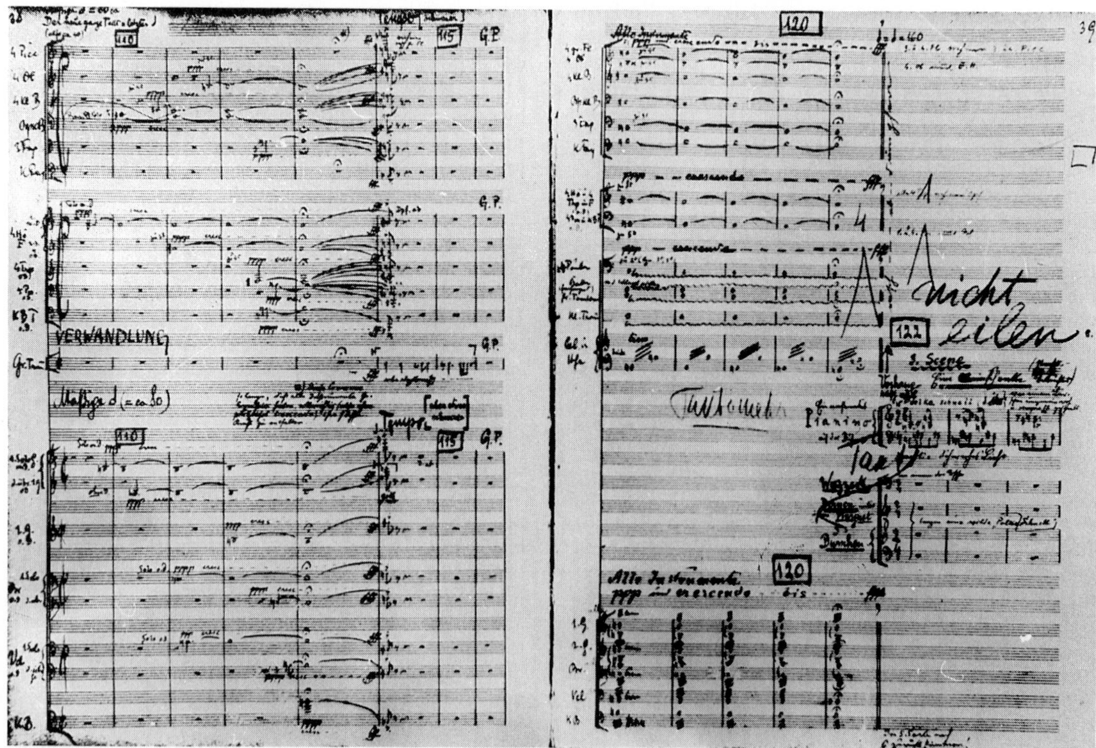

1. Two pages of autograph score from Act 3 of Berg's 'Wozzeck', showing the climax at the end of scene ii and the honky-tonk piano polka at the beginning of scene iii

2. 'Wozzeck' (Berg): Act 3 scene ii (a forest path by a pool, dusk) from the British stage première at Covent Garden, London, 1952, with Marko Rothmüller as Wozzeck and Cristel Goltz as Marie (designed by Caspar Neher)

2.v (Introduction and Rondo) *A guardroom in the barracks, night* To the sounds of snoring soldiers Wozzeck wakes to nightmarish memories of the scene in the tavern. He hears voices, as material from Act 1 scene ii is recalled, and tries to pray. The rondo begins with the arrival of the drunken Drum Major, boasting of his conquest; with each statement of the ritornello he drinks from his bottle. He and Wozzeck fight (to music first heard during Marie's struggles in Act 1 scene v); Wozzeck is knocked down, and when he struggles up he quotes Marie's 'Einer nach dem Andern!' to a whole-tone phrase from Act 2 scene iii. The two alternating chords that closed Act 1 and opened Act 2 fade away to leave an isolated B.

Act 3.i (Invention on a theme) *Marie's room, night, candlelight* Still plagued by guilt, Marie is reading in her Bible the story of the woman taken in adultery. The music unfolds in a series of seven variations on the theme heard in the opening bars as she comforts her child by telling him a fairy story and returns to the Bible to find the passage about Mary Magdalen. Marie's prayer for mercy is accompanied by a three-part fugue, which continues into the interlude, dying away in subdued orchestral colours and arpeggios for harp and celesta.

3.ii (Invention on a note) *A forest path by a pool, dusk* Marie and Wozzeck are walking together. The music of the scene unfolds freely over reiterated B's, sometimes heard as a pedal or in inner parts, sometimes in the high treble. Wozzeck first talks with heavy irony of beauty and fidelity, then tells Marie that he loves her. As the blood-red moon rises, over muted brass Wozzeck draws his knife. To a prolonged crescendo on B he stabs Marie. Images from her life are swiftly recalled in the orchestra – the seduction, lullaby, earrings, march – and as Wozzeck leaves, the opera's fateful tritone is heard. The following interlude builds up to a huge climax on B, cut off by a *fortissimo* chord (which will form the basis of Act 3 scene iv), the opera's *Hauptrhythmus* hammered out by the bass drum.

3.iii (Invention on a rhythm) *A low tavern, dimly lit, night* The rhythm of the polka, heard first on a honky-tonk piano, dominates the scene. Wozzeck is trying to bury his crime in drink. He attempts to silence the pianist by singing a folksong (to a variant of the Act 1 lullaby) but it serves only to remind him of Marie. He persuades Margret to sing, but that also is too painful; Margret notices blood on Wozzeck's hands and goes to tell the other customers. Wozzeck rushes out. The interlude is built from the rhythm of the previous scene.

3.iv (Invention on a six-note chord) *The forest path by the pool, night* Wozzeck has returned to the pool to try to recover his knife. As the orchestral hexachord is put through a spectrum of changes he falls against Marie's corpse, and as the moon rises again, blood-red, he finally loses all reason. Imagining himself covered in Marie's blood he wades ever deeper into the pool to wash himself clean, until he drowns. The Doctor and the Captain pass by hurriedly, scared and not wishing to concern themselves with others' misfortunes, while the scene returns to unearthly calm, with wind instruments simulating the sound of croaking frogs and toads. The final interlude, an invention on a key (D minor), now recapitulates the work's main themes and characters (except Marie); it builds massively on the 'Wir arme Leut!' motif, and its climactic 12-note chord resolves into unambiguous D minor for the Epilogue.

3.v (Invention on a regular quaver movement) *Outside Marie's house, bright morning sunshine* Over a *perpetuum mobile* symbolizing the continuity of normal life, Marie's child is playing on an imaginary hobby-horse, unaware of what has happened. Another child brings news of the discovery of Marie's body, and after a moment's pause her child follows his friends to see it, as the orchestra recalls fragments of themes associated with her. The opera ends on the pair of alternating chords that closed Acts 1 and 2.

* * *

Wozzeck is a work of immense structural complexity in which musical devices and dramatic constructs are tightly integrated. Its composition marked the culmination of the first phase of Berg's development; the initial sketches were made while he was completing the Three Orchestral Pieces op.6, and the opera deploys the same language and even some of the same material: elements of the march from op.6 are quoted in Act 1 scene iii. In its use of atonality, whole-tone writing and other devices alongside passages of Mahlerian diatonicism, as well as in the vocal writing (which moves between speech, parlando, Sprechgesang and arioso), *Wozzeck* represents the most substantial achievement of Schoenberg and his followers in their pre-serial years.

ANDREW CLEMENTS

Wranitzky [Vranický, Wraniczky, Wranizky], **Paul** [Pavel] (*b* Nová Říše, Moravia, 30 Dec 1756; *d* Vienna, 26 Sept 1808). Czech composer and conductor active in Vienna. After early study of singing, the organ and the violin, he entered the theological seminary in Vienna and became its choirmaster. He continued his musical studies, probably with J. M. Kraus and Haydn. He began a career in music, and in about 1785 was appointed music director to Count Johann Nepomuk Esterházy. From about 1790 he was the head orchestra director ('Director bei der Violine') of the Viennese court theatres (i.e. the Burgtheater and the Kärntnertortheater), and was active first at the Italian Opera and later at the German. He conducted a gala performance of his Singspiel *Oberon* during the coronation festivities of Leopold II at Frankfurt (15 October 1790).

Wranitzky played a prominent role in the musical life of Vienna. Both Haydn and Beethoven preferred him as a conductor of their works. From 1805 he alternated with Gyrowetz as head of the Adelige Liebhaber- oder Cavalier-Konzerte of Vienna. Wranitzky was a member of the same freemasons' lodge as Mozart, 'Zur gekrönten Hoffnung'. As secretary of the Viennese Tonkünstler-Sozietät he succeeded in settling Haydn's lengthy quarrel with the society in December 1797.

Wranitzky's best-known stage work, the Singspiel *Oberon*, was received enthusiastically in Vienna and elsewhere. Several of its features figure in Schikaneder's *Die Zauberflöte* and Mozart's setting shows certain resemblances to Wranitzky's work. Goethe considered Wranitzky the most appropriate composer to set his *Zauberflöte zweiter Teil*, and sought his collaboration (letter, 1796). *Oberon* was eclipsed in popularity only in 1826 by Weber's opera of the same name. Even more popular in their day were Wranitzky's ballets, particularly *Das Waldmädchen* (1796).

His brother Anton (1761–1820), active in Vienna as composer and violin virtuoso, had two daughters, Katharina Kraus-Wranitzky (1801–51) and Karoline Seidler-Wranitzky (1790–1872), who were well-known singers. Karoline was engaged at Berlin where she was admired as Rosina, Susanna and Jessonda, and created Agathe in *Der Freischütz*; contemporary critics praised the power and range of her voice and the grace of her appearance.

See also OBERON, KÖNIG DER ELFEN.

MSS in CS-Pnm unless otherwise stated

Oberon, König der Elfen (romantisches Spl, 3, S. Seyler adapted J. G. C. L. Gieseke, after C. M. Wieland: *Oberon*), Vienna, Wiedner, 7 Nov 1789, vs (?Berlin, 1791)
Der dreifache Liebhaber [L'amant de trois jeunes filles] (Spl), Berlin, Königliches, 3 Feb 1791, lost
Walmir und Gertraud, oder Man kann es ja probieren (operetta, 3, J. B. Michaelis), ? Vienna, 1791
Rudolf von Felseck [Die Schwarzthaler Mühle; La tempesta] (Spl, J. Korompay), Vienna, Burg, 6 Oct 1792, lost
Merkur, der Heiratsstifter, oder Der Geiz im Geldkasten (Spl, 2), Vienna, Leopoldstadt, 21 Feb 1793, lost except 1 aria *CS-K*
Die Post-Station (Spl, 2, S. F. Küstner), Vienna, 1793, only lib. extant
Das Fest der Lazaronen (operetta, 2, J. Perinet), Vienna, Leopoldstadt, 4 Feb 1794, vs (Offenbach, 1795)
Das Maroccanische Reich, ?Vienna, *c*1794–5, selections (Offenbach, 1797)
Die gute Mutter (2, J. B. von Alxinger), Vienna, Kärntnertor, 11 May 1795, *A-Wn*
Der Schreiner (Spl, 1, A. von Kotzebue), Vienna, Kärntnertor, 18 July 1799, *Wn*, *B-Bc*
Das Mitgefühl (Liederspiel, 1, F. Treitschke), Vienna, Kärntnertor, 21 April 1804, *A-Wn*

StiegerO
Musikalische Real-Zeitung, ii (1790), 173
G. J. Dlabacž: 'Versuch eines Verzeichnisses der vorzüglichern Tonkünstler in oder aus Böhmen', *Materialien zur alten und neuen Statistik von Böhmen*, ed. J. A. Riegger, xii (Leipzig and Prague, 1794), 295–6
Jb der Tonkunst von Wien und Prag (Vienna, 1796), 67–8, 82ff, 92
G. J. Dlabacž: *Allgemeines historisches Künstler-Lexikon* (Prague, 1815), i, col.538; ii, col.268; iii, cols.413ff
V. Blažek: *Bohemica v lobkovském zámeckém archivu v Roudnici n. L.* [Bohemica in the Lobkowitz Castle Archives in Roudnice nad Labem] (Prague, 1936)
E. Komorzynski: '"Zauberflöte" und "Oberon"', *MJb 1953*, 150–61
J. Pešková: *Vranického Oberon a jeho vliv na rozvoj singspielu* [Wranitzky's *Oberon* and its Influence on the Development of the Singspiel] (diss., U. of Prague, 1955)
C. Schoenbaum: 'Die böhmischen Musiker in der Musikgeschichte Wiens', *SMw*, xxv (1962), 475–95, esp. 488
S. Tesař: 'Nová Říše', *OM*, ii (1970), 88–9
P. Heerenová: 'Zpěvohra Oberon Pavla Vranického a její libreto', *OM*, iv (1972), 73–8
B. Paumgartner: 'Von Mozarts "Zauberflöte" zu Goethes "Faust II"', *Vorträge und Essays* (Salzburg, 1972), 101–13

MILAN POŠTOLKA

Wreckers, The [*Les naufrageurs*; *Strandrecht*]. Lyrical drama in three acts by ETHEL SMYTH to a libretto in French by Henry Brewster and Smyth; Leipzig, Neues Theater, 11 November 1906.

Set in Cornwall at the time of John Wesley's travels (mid-18th century), the plot concerns a poor, isolated community and the tragic struggle of two of its members to escape its oppressive values. Mark (tenor), a young fisherman, is in love with Thirza (mezzo-soprano), who has come to the village from elsewhere and is alienated from her older husband Pascoe (bass-baritone). Pascoe is the village headman and preacher, who condones the practice (source of the local livelihood) of putting the lighthouse out of action on stormy nights, thereby luring ships on to the rocks for plunder; indeed, in Act 1, he attributes the current dearth of wrecks to the villagers' sinfulness. Avis (soprano), however, daughter of the lighthouse-keeper Lawrence (baritone), knows better: someone is lighting a beacon on the cliffs to warn the ships. Herself in love with Mark, who has cast her off, she also knows about Mark's involvement with Thirza and hints about it to Pascoe. A ship is driving on to the rocks, and in Act 2, set on the cliffs, Mark is about to light the warning beacon when Thirza enters and implores him not to because the cliffs are being watched. They sing a passionate duet and decide to run away together, but Thirza lights the torch and Pascoe sees them departing. He faints by the fire, where he is discovered by the villagers who, believing him the culprit, haul him off for trial in a sea cave which is the setting for Act 3. He refuses to betray his wife, but when Avis's attempts first to accuse Thirza of bewitching Pascoe and then to save Mark (when he owns up) are unsuccessful, the lovers are left to die together in the cave as the rising tide engulfs them.

Smyth's virile music, while resting firmly on the *topoi* of German Romanticism from *Der fliegende Holländer* to Wolf and Mahler, also echoes the unpredictability of Bizet and espouses French elements such as whole-tone aggregates that make the style difficult to pin down. It is impressive when depicting the sea (the opening of Act 2, 'On the Cliffs of Cornwall', and the overture have enjoyed success as independent orchestral items), less so in its lyrical solos. But the opera's greatest strength is its dramatic strategy, strikingly prophetic of *Peter Grimes* in details such as the offstage church service set against the foreground confrontation in Act 1.

STEPHEN BANFIELD

Wright, Mrs (*fl* 1727–50). English soprano. In the 1727–8 season she sang Orindo in Handel's *Admeto* and in 1733 was one of the singers the composer brought to Oxford to perform in his oratorios. From 1729 she was at Lincoln's Inn Fields, where she sang Galatea in the first public performance of *Acis and Galatea* (1731). She remained on stage until November 1750, mainly playing goddesses in John Rich's pantomimes.

*

BDA; *LS*

W. Dean: *Handel's Dramatic Oratorios and Masques* (London, 1959)

OLIVE BALDWIN, THELMA WILSON

Wright, Maurice (Willis) (*b* Front Royal, VA, 17 Oct 1949). American composer. He studied composition at Duke University and at Columbia University. He taught at Columbia and at Boston University before joining the composition faculty at Temple University in Philadelphia, where he began teaching in 1980. Wright is a prolific composer with more than 50 works to his credit. His music, often serial and electronic in earlier years, has become increasingly lyrical and tonally orientated in more recent works.

Wright's two-act opera *The Trojan Conflict* was commissioned by the Philadelphia Network for New Music and first performed at the Painted Bride Arts Center in Philadelphia on 2 April 1989. The libretto, written by the composer, relates the major events of the Trojan War through slyly comic 20th-century television news reports. Zeus plays the cello in an instrumental quartet (with oboe, horn and viola) of gods and goddesses who watch the war unfold on their television screen. Balancing the four acoustic instruments is a quartet of synthesizers whose loosely tonal droning dominates the work's soundscape and provides the basic background for madrigal-like choruses and arias in various styles for Paris, Aphrodite, Achilles and the other major characters of the *Iliad*.

Wright's earlier opera, *The Fifth String* (composed 1985), to his own libretto after the novel by John Philip Sousa, and scored for a more traditional chamber orchestra, has not been performed.

JAMES FREEMAN

Wrighten [Pownall; née Matthews], **Mary Ann** (*b* *c*1751; *d* Charleston, SC, 12 Aug 1796). English soprano. She made her début as Diana in *Lionel and Clarissa* (February 1770, Drury Lane), when the prompter Hopkins noted: 'A very fine Voice – Aukward & Clumsy figure – Well faced'. She played some romantic leads at first but soon became established as Lucy rather than Polly in *The Beggar's Opera*, specializing in lively second-woman parts. She was popular for her singing of spirited songs like 'A soldier for me' and 'Tally ho!'. She last appeared at Drury Lane in December 1786, leaving her children and husband (recently appointed the company's prompter) to go to North America, where she acted as Mrs Pownall.

*

BDA; *LS*

A. Pasquin [pseud. of J. Williams]: *The Children of Thespis*, i (London, 1786, 13/1792)

T. Gilliland: *The Dramatic Mirror*, ii (London, 1808)

OLIVE BALDWIN, THELMA WILSON

Wrocław (Ger. Breslau). Polish city, capital of Lower Silesia. It was under Habsburg rule until 1742, when it became part of Prussia; after World War II it became part of Poland. Its operatic traditions go back to the middle of the 17th century, when the Singspiels *Majuma* and *Piastus*, to texts of the Silesian poet Andreas Gryphius (1616–64), were performed in the school theatres (1653, 1660). Some years later, works by J. C. Hallmann (1640–1704) were given with musical interludes from Singspiels and Italian operas. Between 1725 and 1734 an Italian company directed by Antonio Bioni and D. G. Treu performed 42 operas, among them 24 by Bioni, four by Treu, three by F. B. Conti, one each by Albinoni (*Didone abbandonata*, 1726) and Astorga (*Dafnida*, 1726), and the rest adapted from works by Caldara, Orlandini, Porta, Vinci and Vivaldi; the company's favourite prima donna was Anna Maria Giusti. In 1770 Gluck's *Orfeo* was given in concert performance in the Zwinger.

In 1782 the theatre was reconstructed to hold 700 spectators. Singspiels and German and Italian operas were performed, including works by Dittersdorf and Mozart. From 1800 the opera was then directed by V. Tuček, J. L. Dussek, H. C. Ebell, J. Janeczek and, in 1804–6, Weber, who produced *La clemenza di Tito* and *Così fan tutte* besides his own *Peter Schmoll*, raising the standard of the theatre's orchestra and chorus (in the 1805–6 season alone 173 performances were given of works by Cherubini, Hiller, Paer, Salieri and others). Between 1808 and 1828 the opera flourished under the direction of Gottlob Bierey (1772–1840), who succeeded in producing Gluck's *Iphigénie en Tauride* (1810), Weber's *Der Freischütz* (1821) and *Preciosa* (1823), *Fidelio* (1816) and works by Auber, Boieldieu, Cherubini, Méhul, Rossini and Spontini, as well as a popular vaudeville by Carl Holtei, *Der alte Feldherr* (1826), about the Polish national hero Kościuszko. After 1828 the repertory was enlarged with works by Bellini, Donizetti, Lortzing, Meyerbeer and Spohr. Many famous prima donnas appeared, among them Karoline Seidler-Wranitzky (1822), Henriette Sontag (1827) and Wilhelmine Schröder-Devrient (1836 and 1842).

In 1841 the city built a new municipal theatre (cap. *c*1600), to a design by C. F. Langhans. Under the direction of Eugen Seidelmann (1806–64), the company gave up to 150 opera performances a year. Verdi's and Wagner's works were produced comparatively early: *Nabucco* (1847), *Tannhäuser* (1852), *Der fliegende Holländer* (1853), *Lohengrin* (1854), *Il trovatore*, *Ernani* and *Rigoletto* (1858–9). From 1858 to 1871 the music director was Leopold Damrosch. Wagner's dominance continued; a quarter of the opera performances in 1896–7 were of his works, and there had been over 200 performances of *Lohengrin* by 1897. Also in this period there were frequent guest appearances by famous Polish singers, such as Władysław Mierzwiński (1885–90) and Marcella Sembrich (1887–98). The first Polish opera produced was Różycki's *Eros i Psyche* in 1917. German operatic activities continued without interruption until 1944.

When the city became Polish after World War II, a performance of Moniuszko's *Halka* on 8 September 1945 in the old (now rebuilt) theatre (cap. *c*800) initiated the Polish opera. In 1949 the Opera Dolnośląska (Lower Silesian Opera) was nationalized. Its company and repertory were enlarged and a high artistic standard reached, notably under such directors and conductors as Kazimierz Wiłkomirski (1947–52, 1957–61), Jerzy Sillich (1953–7), Adam Kopyciński (1951–3, 1961–71), Robert Satanowski (1976–81) and the outstanding director Lia Rotbaum (1958–70). Beyond the standard repertory, special emphasis has been laid on Polish operas and ballets by Moniuszko, Żeleński, Paderewski, Statkowski, Różycki, Rytel, Szeligowski and contemporary Wrocław composers, as well as on Russian and Czech operas. Szeligowski's *Bunt żaków* ('The Revolt of the Goliards') was staged here in 1951, as was his last opera, *Teodor Gentleman* (1963), as well as the Polish premières of Britten's *Albert Herring* (1972) and Gershwin's *Porgy and Bess* (1973). A second music theatre in Wrocław, the Operetka Dolnośląska (Lower Silesian Operetta), now Operetka Wrocławska, was founded in 1955.

M. Schlesinger: *Geschichte des Breslauer Theaters*, i: *1522–1841* (Breslau, 1897)
L. Sittenfeld: *Geschichte des Breslauer Theaters von 1841 bis 1900* (Breslau, 1909)
J. Hübner: *Bibliographie des schlesischen Musik- und Theaterwesens* (Breslau, 1934)
E. Kurowski, ed.: *Opera Wrocławska 1945–1965* (Wrocław, 1965)
B. Jankowski and M. Misiorny: *Muzyka i życie muzyczne na ziemiach zachodnich i północnych 1945–1965* [Music and Musical Life in Western and Northern Poland] (Poznań, 1968)
W. Roszkowska: 'Opera włoska we Wrocławiu (1725–1734)' [The Italian Opera in Wrocław], *Studia śląskie*, x (1969), 195–210
M. Zduniak: *Muzyka i muzycy polscy w dziewiętnastowiecznym Wrocławiu* [Polish Music and Musicians in 19th-Century Wrocław] (Wrocław, 1984) KORNEL MICHAŁOWSKI

Wüllner, Franz (*b* Münster, 28 Jan 1832; *d* Braunfels, 7 Sept 1902). German conductor, father of the singer Ludwig Wüllner. He studied with Carol Arnold and Anton Schindler before embarking on concert tours as a pianist. From 1856 he held various posts in Munich (apart from a period as director at Aachen) culminating in his appointment as principal Kapellmeister of the court opera in 1871, following his success as conductor of the first performances of *Das Rheingold* (1869) and *Die Walküre* (1870). In 1877 he succeeded Julius Rietz as director of the Dresden Conservatory. Because of increasing difficulties and intrigues, which had forced him to relinquish his direction of the opera to Ernst von Schuch, he left Dresden in 1883 and turned to teaching and orchestral conducting. He composed a recitative arrangement of the dialogue of Weber's *Oberon* for the 1881 production in Vienna. GAYNOR G. JONES

Wunderlich, Fritz (*b* Kusel, Rheinland-Pfalz, 26 Sept 1930; *d* Heidelberg, 17 Sept 1966). German tenor. During his short career Wunderlich was Germany's leading lyric tenor. He studied at the Freiburg Musikhochschule, sang Tamino there in 1954, and was engaged by the Stuttgart Opera in 1955, making his début (apart from some appearances in small parts) in the same role. In 1958 he joined the Frankfurt company, and at the Salzburg Festival in 1959 he sang Henry in Strauss's *Die schweigsame Frau*. In 1960 he joined the Munich Opera and from 1962 also spent part of the year with the Vienna Staatsoper.

Fritz Wunderlich as Don Ottavio in Mozart's 'Don Giovanni' at Covent Garden, London, 1965

Wunderlich's voice was well formed, clear and firm of timbre; his style was unaffected, manly and sensitive. At the time of his death Wagnerian roles were on the horizon; his singing of Mozart was internationally famous (he sang Don Ottavio at Covent Garden, 1965; see illustration); in Munich he undertook such parts as Alfredo and Lensky, and in Vienna the title role in *Palestrina*. His last appearance was as Tamino during the Stuttgart Opera's visit to the Edinburgh Festival; a Metropolitan début was planned for October 1966.

J. B. Steane: *The Grand Tradition* (London, 1974), 545–6
H. Canning: 'Fritz Wunderlich: Unforgettable, Unforgotten', *Opera*, xli (1990), 1048–55 ANDREW PORTER

Wundersame Schustersfrau, Die ('The Wonderful Wife of the Cobbler'). Opera in two acts by UDO ZIMMERMANN to a libretto by Eberhard Schmidt and the composer after Federico García Lorca's play; Schwetzingen, 25 April 1982.

Following the success of *Der Schuhu* at the 1977 Schwetzingen Festival, the Süddeutscher Rundfunk commissioned Zimmermann to write a fifth opera for the 1981 festival: *Die wundersame Schustersfrau* was first performed, in a German translation by E. Beck, in 1982 by a company from the Hamburg Staatsoper and has since been staged at Leipzig, Berlin and Munich.

In its criticism of utopian ideas, the subject appears related to that of *Der Schuhu*. The cobbler's wife (soprano), wrote Lorca,

> is constantly at odds with real ideas and things because she lives in a world of her own where all ideas and objects have a mysterious significance which she does not perceive. She has never lived any-

where else nor had any other love except on the other bank, where she neither can nor will go.

Zimmermann's melodic writing uses the *cante hondo* of the Andalusian Moorish tradition as a basis for improvisation. Major and minor are not resolved, and the rhythms are free of conventional stress patterns. The characterization reveals the influence of light music.

DETLEF GOJOWY

Wuorinen, Charles (*b* New York, 9 June 1938). American composer. He studied composition with Luening, Beeson and Ussachevsky at Columbia University (BA 1961, MA 1963) and taught at Columbia (1964–71) and at the Manhattan School of Music (from 1971). He has been visiting lecturer at several institutions including Princeton University (1967–8) and the New England Conservatory (1968–71), and composer-in-residence at the Universities of Iowa, South Florida and California (San Diego). In 1985 he became composer-in-residence with the San Francisco SO.

Wuorinen has written two operas, *The Politics of Harmony*, a one-act masque performed at Columbia in 1968, and *The W. of Babylon, or The Triumph of Love over Moral Depravity*, a two-act 'Baroque burlesque' given at the Manhattan School in 1975. The first, to a libretto by Richard Monaco, has been described by critics as a 'cleverly crafted work that can be enjoyed on several levels'. The scenario, based on an ancient Chinese tale from the writings of Ssu-ma Ch'ien, tells the story of a ceremonial visit of one monarch to another. The visiting monarch plays a seductive tune for his host, the continuation of which is hailed by the host's music master as evil. The host, oblivious to the threat of this tune, commands it to be played in its entirety. On the tune's completion, a great storm arises in which the host is crushed and the visiting monarch and his entourage make their escape. Parallels have been drawn between the work's plot and various world events of the 1960s, most notably student unrest at Columbia in 1968 and American involvement in Vietnam. The music is serially derived and symmetrically arranged into vocal and instrumental sections – arias for bass and alto soloists, six narrations and four dialogues, an instrumental prelude, postlude, seven *ch'in* tunes (sets of variations) and seven symphonies. Pitch material is taken from two 'type A' hexachords, with transformations of these accomplished by derived set extension. The text-setting exhibits a close relationship between pitch-class and phonemic content, and vocal register is correlated to programmatic aspects of the text – low registers for the supernatural, higher registers for the concepts of sky and light. Extremes of range are used in all sections of the orchestra. Clearly concerned with the beauty of serially derived form, Wuorinen has also created in this work an opera with a profound effect on its audience.

The W. of Babylon, commissioned by the National Opera Institute for the Light Fantastic Players and written to a libretto by R. C. Bruce, is clearly intended to entertain. The composer has stated that the work's 'greatest virtue may be that it is finally about nothing at all'. The scenario involves a lewd Marquise, her club-footed cousin, a pretty boy, four homosexuals and a Chinese princess. The libretto has been described as 'offensive', including several 'racial indiscretions' and the use of 'lamentable metaphors'.

*

M. Hibberd: 'The Politics of Harmony', *PNM*, vii/2 (1969), 155–66

I. Kolodin: 'Music to my Ears', *Saturday Review* (16 Oct 1971), 38 [*The Politics of Harmony*]

J. Hiemenz: 'Debuts & Reappearances', *HiFi/MusAm*, xxii/1 (1972), MA18–19 [*The Politics of Harmony*]

S. Wadsworth: 'Report: U. S.', *ON*, xl/14 (1975–6), 46–8 [*The W. of Babylon*]

JAMES P. CASSARO

Wuppertal. City in western Germany, in North Rhine-Westphalia. It was formed in 1929 through the amalgamation of Barmen, Elberfeld and four other towns.

Theatre companies first visited Elberfeld in 1798. The town had its first theatre in 1806, the Theater an der Hofaue, but the building was soon commandeered for other uses, including as a prison, and performances had to be given on improvised stages and in inns until the Reiterbahnbühne opened in 1835. In 1842 the newly founded Theaterverein built a brick theatre on the site of the original one of 1806, using some of its materials; the new building became the centre of theatrical life in Elberfeld until the 1880s. Important events of the period were a visit from an Italian touring company under Rossini in 1852 and, later, guest performances by the tenors Theodor Wachtel and Albert Niemann. The theatre had to be closed in 1882 because it contravened the safety regulations introduced after the theatrical disasters of 1881. The new civic theatre was opened on 6 September 1888, and its first operatic production, *Fidelio*, took place the next day.

The people of Barmen went to Elberfeld until they built a theatre of their own, opened in 1874. This burnt down several times and was eventually replaced by a new building in 1905. In 1919 the two civic theatres were finally amalgamated, and the merging of the towns in 1929 brought the Städtische Bühnen Wuppertal into being. After the destruction of the theatre in 1943 performances continued in Wuppertal town hall. The new theatre (845 seats) was opened on 14 October 1956, with a production of *Mathis der Maler*.

Intendanten of the Wuppertal theatre have been Grischa Barfuss (1958–64), Arno Wüstenhöfer (1964–75) and Hellmuth Matiasek (1979–83), followed by Holk Freytag. Among other outstanding figures were the stage designer Heinrich Wendel, in charge of the sets from 1941 to 1943 and from 1951 to 1964; Janos Kulka, who became Generalmusikdirektor in 1964; and Kurt Horres who, as opera director between 1964 and 1975, gave special encouragement to modern music drama.

Important events since the war – premières and first West German performances – have included productions of Sutermeister's *Raskolnikoff* (1950), Martin's *Le mystère de la Nativité du Christ* (1961), Rossini's *Le comte Ory* (1963), Massenet's *Don Quichotte* (1964), Dessau's *Puntila* (1967), Milhaud's *Médée* (1972), Blacher's *Yvonne, Prinzessin von Burgund* (1973, première), Udo Zimmermann's *Levins Mühle* (1975), Klebe's *Ein wahrer Held* (1975), Volker David Kirchner's *Die fünf Minuten des Isaak Babel* (1980, première), the revival of Wagner's *Die Feen* (1981) and the first staged performance of Shostakovich's *The Gamblers*, completed by Krzysztof Meyer (1983).

SABINE SONNTAG

Würfel, Václav Vilém [Werfel, Wenzel Wilhelm] (*b* Plaňany, 6 May 1790; *d* Vienna, 23 March 1832). Czech composer. After several years of successful touring in central Europe as a pianist, from 1815 he worked in Warsaw as a music teacher, where his pupils included Chopin. Afterwards he lived for a short while in Prague, where his first opera, *Rübezahl* (3, W. Marsano, after a fairy-tale by J. K. A. Musäus), was given a successful première on 7 October 1824. It was performed in Czech on 7 November 1830. In 1824 he moved to Vienna, where he was appointed Kapellmeister and music director of the Kärntnertortheater. On 31 March 1830 the overture of his second opera, *Der Rotmantel* (4, after Musäus and A. von Kotzebue), was performed there, though the opera was never given complete. Würfel wrote several Singspiels, including the fairy-tale opera *Finetta Aschenbrödel, oder Rose und Schuh* (3, A. Schreiber, 15 April 1830) and the Posse *Der Naturmensch, oder Der Zweikampf im Schublad[en]kasten* (3, F. X. Told, 13 March 1832). Performances of *Rübezahl* were given in Vienna, Leipzig and Budapest, but it did not remain in the repertory: it was for his piano music (which includes some didactic works) that he was best appreciated.

MICHAELA FREEMANOVÁ

Würzburg. City in Germany, capital of Lower Franconia. Until 1802 it was ruled by prince-bishops, and sacred and choral music predominated. In the later 18th century, when secular music in the Italian style flourished at the episcopal court, operas and ballets were performed in the Weisser Saal of the Residenz Palace (*c*1768–1778); the court ensemble reached its peak under Bishop Adam Friedrich von Seinsheim (1755–79). After secularization the size of the ensemble was decreased and the city's first public theatre was built, opening on 3 August 1804. Designed by the court architect J. A. Gärtner in a former religious foundation, the theatre was at first used for plays, but operatic performances soon followed, including Mozart's *Don Giovanni* and *Die Entführung aus dem Serail.* When Würzburg became part of Bavaria in 1814 the theatre lost its royal status and became a provincial theatre, suffering frequent financial difficulty. In 1833 Richard Wagner became chorus master (his brother Albert, a tenor, had been engaged there since 1830). Wagner's early opera *Die Feen* was completed in Würzburg, and parts of it were performed at concerts. In 1843 the theatre was bought by the city and became known as the Stadttheater, although it continued to be run as a private enterprise. During World War I it maintained a complete programme of activity, performing *Spielopern* and operettas as well as plays.

The Würzburg Mozart Festival was inaugurated in 1921 with a production of *La finta giardiniera* that is still staged today. In 1926 Richard Strauss conducted his *Ariadne auf Naxos.* In the economic crisis up to 1930 financial support was drastically reduced and no opera or operetta was produced. Most of the city, including the theatre, was destroyed by an air raid in March 1945. A completely new building (756 seats) opened on 4 December 1966 with *Die Meistersinger.* The Städtisches Philharmonisches Orchester is affiliated to the theatre, which since 1988 has been administered by Tebbe Harms Kleen, presenting the German and Italian operatic repertory, as well as operettas, ballet and drama. The season runs from September to July. The Würzburg Festival, inaugurated in 1985, takes place in September.

KLAUS J. SEIDEL

Wüste Insel, Die (i) ('The Desert Island'). Singspiel in one act by JOSEPH SCHUSTER to a libretto by AUGUST GOTTLIEB MEISSNER after PIETRO METASTASIO's *L'isola disabitata* (1753); Leipzig, Theater am Rannstädter Tor, 30 September 1779.

Meissner made his translation of Metastasio's *azione teatrale* after tiring of adapting French comic opera texts for German composers. As with other German operas of a Metastasian stamp, the recitative is kept as verse (rather than turned into spoken dialogue), but Meissner rewrote several arias that he felt had been written with the composer rather than poetic style in mind. Schuster's through-composed setting may have been the one used at a performance in German at Pressburg (24 April 1780) usually attributed to Haydn, whose music to Metastasio's Italian text had its première at Eszterháza on 6 December 1779, just over two months after Schuster's.

THOMAS BAUMAN

Wüste Insel, Die (ii). Opera by Joseph Haydn; *see ISOLA DISABITATA, L'* (ii).

Wynne, David [Thomas, David Wynne] (*b* Penderyn, Glam., 2 June 1900; *d* Pencoed, South Glam., 23 March 1983). Welsh composer. When he was 14 he left school to work in the coal-mines, but at the age of 20 he began to study music and in 1925 went to University College, Cardiff (BMus, 1928). He became a schoolteacher, and after retiring in 1961 he taught composition at the Welsh College of Music and Drama and at University College, Cardiff.

For one who started late as a composer and who gave much of his time to teaching and administration, Wynne's list of works is impressive. It includes three one-act theatre pieces to his own librettos: *Jack and Jill* (1975), *Night and Cold Peace* (1977–8) and *Cain* (1981). They skilfully combine a predominantly arioso vocal style with more angular and dissonant orchestral writing. Despite the modest resources necessary to stage them, they have remained unperformed.

*

R. Elfyn Jones: *David Wynne* (Cardiff, 1979)

MALCOLM BOYD

Xacarilla, La. Opera in one act by MARCO AURELIO MARLIANI to a libretto by EUGÈNE SCRIBE; Paris, Opéra, 28 October 1839.

The title is a Gallic version of the Spanish *jácara* (diminutive *jácarilla*), a *villancico* or romance about disreputable characters. Louis Véron, from 1831 to 1835 director of the Paris Opéra, claimed that Scribe altered the spelling so that his libretto titles would begin with each letter of the alphabet. In Marliani's opera, situated in Cádiz, the *xacarilla* is a smugglers' chorus with several reprises at key moments in the drama. When the ruffians first sing it, their accomplice, the innkeeper Cojuelo (bass-baritone), opens his doors to admit them. Witnessing this occurrence and misconstruing it as magic, the penniless and hungry young sailor Lazarillo (mezzo-soprano) tries singing the chorus from memory. The doors swing open. Incorrectly assuming him to be one of the brigands, Cojuelo invites him to join the others for dinner. Thus admitted, Lazarillo is astonished to find his mistress Ritta (soprano) within, not realizing that she is Cojuelo's daughter. The lovers reaffirm their commitment, interrupted by Cojuelo, who attempts to deter Lazarillo's courtship by offering him a greater share of the contraband. The Corrégidor (bass-baritone), to whom Ritta is promised, arrives to investigate rumours of smuggling. Faced with incrimination by Lazarillo, Cojuelo saves his neck only by agreeing to let his daughter marry the sailor. The hapless Corrégidor is duped out of both criminals and fiancée, and the lovers are united.

La xacarilla is principally important because of its small dimensions; one-act operas were rare at the Opéra. The work remained in the repertory because its manageable proportions made for easy pairings with ballets or acts excerpted from other operas, and because its graceful music flattered the singers. The trouser role of Lazarillo was an important vehicle for its creator, Rosine Stoltz, when her star at the Opéra was in the ascendant. *La xacarilla* had been performed 100 times in Paris by 1862, and was produced successfully under the title *Lazarillo* in Vienna, Milan and Venice.

LAURIE C. SHULMAN

Xaintonge, Louise-Geneviève Gillot. *See* SAINTONGE, LOUISE-GENEVIÈVE GILLOT.

***Xerse* (i)** ('Xerxes'). *Dramma per musica* in a prologue and three acts by FRANCESCO CAVALLI to a libretto by NICOLÒ MINATO based on Herodotus's *History* (book 7); Venice, Teatro SS Giovanni e Paolo, 12 January 1654.

Xerxes (alto), King of Persia, moves his army to Abydos in order to prepare for an invasion of Athens. While waiting for his engineers to complete a bridge across the Hellespont, he and his brother Arsamene (alto) compete for the love of Romilda (soprano), daughter of Ariodate (tenor), Prince of Abydos. Romilda prefers Arsamene but Xerxes is determined to marry her himself. He tells Ariodate that, as a reward for his alliance with the Persians in their victory over the Moors, he shall have a royal son-in-law. Meanwhile, Amastre (soprano), Princess of Susa, disguises herself as a soldier and arrives in search of Xerxes, to whom she is betrothed. Further complications are caused by the ineptness of Elviro (alto), Arsamene's comic servant, and by the neurotic ploys of Romilda's sister, Adelanta (soprano), who also loves Arsamene. Xerxes' eunuch commander, Eumene (soprano), summarizes the vanity of everyone's behaviour in his sardonic aria 'La bellezza è un don fugace'.

The action in the second and third acts revolves around a love letter written by Arsamene to Romilda. This letter causes a series of misunderstandings as it falls into the hands of virtually every principal character except the woman for whom it was intended. Amastre eventually resolves the tangled plot with her own poignant letter of explanation to Xerxes. Upon reading it, the contrite king sings a wonderful lament, 'Lasciatemi morir, stelle spietate', and announces that Amastre shall become his bride. Romilda and Arsamene joyfully celebrate their own marriage.

Xerse was one of Cavalli's most popular operas; it was revived at least nine times in various Italian cities during his lifetime. In 1660 he produced this opera with ballets by Lully for the wedding of Louis XIV in Paris. The libretto was later set by Giovanni Bononcini, Förtsch and Handel. Handel's famous setting of 'Ombra mai fù', Xerxes' homage to the sacred plane tree, is neither more poignant nor more mellifluous than Cavalli's.

MARTHA NOVAK CLINKSCALE

***Xerse* (ii)** ('Xerxes'). *Dramma per musica* in three acts by GIOVANNI BONONCINI to a libretto by SILVIO STAMPIGLIA after NICOLÒ MINATO's libretto (Venice, 1654); Rome, Teatro di Tordinona, 25 January 1694.

Minato is still named as librettist on the title-page of the 1694 edition, and Stampiglia did retain his plot. King Xerxes (soprano) falls in love with Romilda (soprano), who loves and is loved by his brother Arsamene (contralto). Her sister Adelanta (soprano) also loves Arsamene, and tries to obtain him by various ruses. Princess Amastre (contralto), who loves Xerxes even though he abandoned her, comes to the court disguised as a warrior. These five young lovers are joined by three of an older generation (contralto, tenor and bass) and two comic servants (soprano and tenor). Misunderstood orders and a misdirected letter set the plot spinning comically out of control until the very end, when Xerxes is finally reunited with Amastre and accepts the marriage of Arsamene to Romilda.

Stampiglia changed the focus by trimming Minato's recitative (cutting four characters, 11 scenes, and lines from every remaining scene), by rewriting and doubling the number of arias (from about 35 to about 70), and by altering the function of most arias (from non-exit lyrical interludes to dramatic exit pieces). His changes 'bring out the differences between an opera in which the formal music is primarily part of the decor and an opera in which the formal music is primarily part of a musico-dramatic structure' (Powers 1961).

Stampiglia's text was in turn reworked by an anonymous librettist for a London production set by Handel as *Serse* in 1738. The text was cut somewhat, but relatively little was rewritten, allowing Handel to borrow and rework many items, including 'Ombra mai fù', known widely as 'Handel's Largo'. He had in fact already reworked music from Bononcini's *Xerse* in nine of his earlier dramatic works. The expressiveness of Bononcini's brief and often bel canto arias in da capo form is confirmed by Handel's fondness for them when they were exceedingly antiquated by 18th-century standards. LOWELL LINDGREN

Xyndas [Xyntas, Xinda(s), Xinta(s)], **Spyridon** (*b* Corfu, 8 June 1812 or 1814; *d* Athens, 11 Nov 1896). Greek composer. He studied in Corfu with Nikolaos Mantzaros and in Naples at the Conservatory of S Pietro a Majella with Nicolò Zingarelli (1834–7); on his return to Corfu he taught singing at the Philharmonic Society for nearly 20 years. As a virtuoso guitarist he toured extensively in Italy and around the eastern Mediterranean. He died blind and in dire poverty. Since so few of his operas have survived, it is difficult to get the full measure of Xyndas's achievements. In his lifetime he was one of the most popular composers of the Ionian school founded by Mantzaros. His extant songs and arias show a gift for unaffected melodic invention, some with a flavour of Ionian folk music, others in bel canto style. His most notable work and the only one surviving, *O ypopsifios vouleftis* ('The Parliamentary Candidate'), is the first Greek opera to a Greek libretto. It is a fresh work revealing the dichotomy between corrupt politicians and destitute peasants at the time of the union of the Ionian Islands with Greece (1864). Musically, the obvious model is the Italian *buffo* style, which is happily blended with echoes of southern Italian folklore and distinct references to Ionian and mainland Greek folk elements, heralding the national school. The opera's performance in Athens at the Bourouras Theatre on 14 March 1888 is considered the 'birthday' of Greek lyric theatre.

Anna Winter (4, after A. Dumas *père*: *Les trois mousquetaires*), Corfu, S Giacomo, carn. 1855; as I tris somotofylakes [The Three Musketeers], Corfu, S Giacomo, ?1885, lost

Il conte Giuliano (3, G. Markoras), Corfu, S Giacomo, carn. 1857, *GR-An*, Motsenigos archive (without vocal pts)

O ypopsifios [The Candidate] (1, N. Makris or ?Xyndas), 1857, lost

O odyrmos tou Kerkyraeou horikou [Woes of a Corfu Peasant] (1, Makris or ? Xyndas), 1857, lost

O ypopsifios vouleftis [The Parliamentary Candidate] (3, I. Rinopoulos, after *O ypopsifios* and *O odyrmos tou Kerkyraeou horikou*), Corfu, S Giacomo, Oct 1867; perhaps also as O kyr Yangos ke i kori tou [Old Yangos and his Daughter], Constantinople, Odeon, 1905

Arkadion, Corfu, *c*1867, lost

O neogambros [The Bridegroom] (comic op), 1877, lost

I due pretendenti, Milan, 1878, lost

Galatea, ?1887–96 (5, after S. Vassiliadis), inc., lost

O prikothiras [The Dowry Hunter] (1, after A. Nikolaras), Athens, Omonoia, 9 Aug 1890, collab. D. Rhodhios, lost

To filima (To filaki) [The Kiss], Athens, Tsoha, 22 Sept 1893, lost

*

'S. Xyntas', *Asty*, no.105 (1887), 4

'O melopoios tou *Ypopsifiou*' [The Composer of *The Candidate*], *Hestia* (22–4 Feb, 12, 14 Nov 1896)

T. Hadjipandazis: *To komidhyllio* [The Greek Vaudeville] (Athens, 1981)

G. Leotsakos: 'Xyndas, Spyridon', *Pangosmio viografiko lexiko* (Athens, 1987) GEORGE LEOTSAKOS

Y

Yakar, Rachel (*b* Lyons, 3 March 1938). French soprano. She studied at the Paris Conservatoire and with Germaine Lubin, making her début in 1963 at Strasbourg. In 1964 she joined the Deutsche Oper am Rhein, Düsseldorf, which remained her base for over 20 years. She has sung in Paris, Munich, Vienna, Zürich, Brussels, San Francisco, Chicago, Dallas and Aix-en-Provence. She sang Freia and Gerhilde at Bayreuth (1976), Donna Elvira at Glyndebourne (1977), First Lady (*Zauberflöte*) at Salzburg and Monteverdi's Poppaea in Edinburgh (1978), and made her Covent Garden début as Freia. Her wide repertory includes Rameau's Aricia, Handel's Cleopatra, Celia (*Lucio Silla*), Ilia, Fiordiligi, Tatyana, Mimì, Málinka/Etherea/Kunka (*Excursions of Mr Brouček*), and the Marschallin, which she sang at Glyndebourne in 1980. An extremely musical as well as dramatic singer, she is particularly fine in roles such as Mélisande and Jenůfa.

ELIZABETH FORBES

Yakovlev, Leonid Georgiyevich (*b* Kherson province, 31 March/12 April 1858; *d* Petrograd [now St Petersburg], 2 June 1919). Russian baritone. Some authorities give his birthplace as St Petersburg. He abandoned a career in the army, took singing lessons with Ryadnov in Kiev and decided on an operatic career. After further study in Italy he joined a company in Tbilisi, where Tchaikovsky heard him and recommended him to Kondrat'yev at the Mariinsky Theatre. Yakovlev appeared there as a guest artist in Gounod's *Faust* in April 1887 and was offered a permanent contract; he soon became popular with St Petersburg audiences, singing Wolfram (*Tannhäuser*), Nevers (*Les Huguenots*) and Escamillo (*Carmen*) with great success. He was famous as Yevgeny Onegin, and created Yeletsky in *The Queen of Spades* and the title role in Rubinstein's *The Demon*. His voice was full and resonant throughout the range, with no forcing of high notes; he was excellent in bel canto, and his acting and stage presence were outstanding. He failed to recover his voice after a severe attack of catarrh in 1905, and retired from the stage the next year. For a time he supervised provincial companies and taught in St Petersburg. In 1918 he became a producer at the Mariinsky Theatre.

*

Biryuch petrogradskikh gosudarstvennïkh teatrov [Herald of the Petrograd State Theatres] (1918), no.5

E. Stark: *Peterburgskaya opera i eyo mastera, 1890–1910* (Leningrad, 1940)

D. I. Pokhitonov: *Iz proshlogo russkoy operï* [From the Past of Russian Opera] (Leningrad, 1949), 135ff

Yamada, Kósçak [Kōsaku] (*b* Tokyo, 9 June 1886; *d* Tokyo, 29 Dec 1965). Japanese composer. After graduating from the Tokyo Music School in 1908, he went to the Berlin Hochschule, where he studied composition with Bruch and Karl Leopold Wolf. While still a student he distinguished himself as a composer of symphonic and chamber music, and in 1913 completed his first opera, *Ochitaru tennyo* ('The Depraved Heavenly Maiden'). To prepare for its performance he returned to Tokyo in January 1914; the outbreak of World War I prevented him from going back to Germany. He formed the Tokyo PO (not identical with the later organization) under the patronage of Baron Koyata Iwasaki, and conducted its first concert, the first ever by a Japanese orchestra, in May 1915. By this time he was composing prolifically. Some works, like the opera *Alladine et Palomides*, were planned and never composed. In December 1917 he went to the USA for the first time; he remained there until May 1919, while American publishers began to publish his music. On his return to Japan Yamada began to promote performances of dramatic music, organizing the Nihon Gakugeki Kyōkai (Japanese Association for Music Drama) in September 1920 and conducting Act 3 of Wagner's *Tannhäuser* and Debussy's *L'enfant prodigue* three months later. By this time he had established his own musical style, which clearly shows the influence of Wagner and Strauss, with occasional characteristics of French impressionism; yet Yamada never lost his identity as a Japanese composer.

In 1929 *The Depraved Heavenly Maiden* was finally staged in Tokyo, and two years later Yamada was invited to Paris to write a new opera for the Théâtre Pigalle. He promptly fulfilled the commission with *Ayame* ('The Sweet Flag'), based on a *kiyomoto* play, but the work was not staged until much later. While in France he was made a Chevalier of the Légion d'honneur. His most successful opera, *Kurofune* ('The Black Ships'), was completed in 1939 and staged a year later. He became less active after World War II, and his last opera, *Hsiang Fei* (composed 1946–7), which tells of the tragic love of a Chinese emperor and Turkish empress in the 18th century, was left unfinished; it was later completed by Ikuma Dan and staged in 1981.

Yamada's operas are characterized by rich and colourful orchestral sonorities, flowing vocal melodies and frequent modulations, and are emotionally dramatic. While he frequently uses Japanese elements, such as pentatonic scales, 4ths or 2nds as chordal elements and Japanese folk or popular tunes, these merge into the European vocabulary quite naturally. Yamada was truly the first opera composer in Japan, and the only one to write successfully in a fully Romantic tradition.

See also KUROFUNE.

Reishō, 1909 (1, C. Kobayashi), inc.
Ochitaru tennyo [The Depraved Heavenly Maiden], 1913 (1, S. Tsubouchi), Tokyo, Kabuki-za, 3 Dec 1929
Shichinin no oujo [Seven Princesses], 1913–16 (1, F. von Oppeln-Bronikowski, after M. Maeterlinck: *La Pléiade*), inc., frag. perf. Tokyo, Tsukiji Seiyōken, 13 Feb 1914
Ayame [The Sweet Flag], 1931 (opera-ballet, 1, P. Noël, after *Akegarasu hana no nureginu*), concert perf., Hibiya Public Hall, 9 Oct 1931; stage, Osaka, 24 April 1971
Kurofune [The Black Ships] (3, Yamada and A. Ōki, after Noël), as Yoake [The Dawn], Tokyo, Takarazuka, 28 Nov 1940, vs (Tokyo, 1940)
Hsiang Fei, 1946–7 (4, Yamada and Ōki, after Y. Nagayo), inc., frag. perf. Tokyo, May 1954, vs (Tokyo, ?1961); completed by I. Dan, Tokyo, Dec 1981 MASAKATA KANAZAWA

Yamshchiki na podstave ('Postal Coachmen at the Relay Station'). Comic opera in one act by YEVSTIGNEY IPAT'YEVICH FOMIN to a libretto by NIKOLAY ALEXANDROVICH L'VOV; possibly Tambov, Municipal Theatre, 1788.

The trifling plot concerns a postal coachman who evades an unjust conscription thanks to the kind intercession of the Empress Catherine II. Though almost unknown until the 1940s, the opera is now considered one of the masterpieces of 18th-century Russian music. The autograph score (in *RU-SPtob*) is dated 1787, at St Petersburg, but there is no record of a performance in either Russian capital. The libretto was published in Tambov in 1788, during the term of the poet Gavriil Derzhavin as provincial governor there, and an autograph of the text survives in Derzhavin's archive in St Petersburg. It has therefore been suggested that the opera was intended by Derzhavin as a greeting for Catherine II during her extended tour of the southern provinces in 1787. However, the empress did not visit Tambov, and the opera was not performed in her presence.

The Russian post-driver was known for his singing, and the significance of the L'vov-Fomin opera – its pretext, in fact – lies in its original and multi-faceted adaptation of appropriate folk material. As in many Russian Singspiels of the day, the vocal numbers are mostly written to pre-existing tunes (*na golosï*), after the manner of the *comédie en vaudevilles*. Besides the usual popular fare, however, this work features elaborate stylizations of melismatic choral songs (*protyazhnïye*: literally, 'drawn-out' songs), in imitation of the performances of S. M. Mitrofanov, a singer and choral director to whom L'vov dedicated the libretto. Fomin's magnificent arrangements – particularly the second choral song, 'Vïsoko sokol letayet' ('The hawk soars aloft') – place him among the great Russian composers. Of an unprecedented authenticity, they preserve the responsorial and heterophonic aspects of improvised folk rendition, while at the same time showing how Fomin's contrapuntal mastery enabled him to achieve an exceptional fullness of texture and formal breadth. Also noteworthy is his setting of the dance-song 'Vo pole beryoza stoyala' ('In the field a birch tree stood') – later used by Balakirev and Tchaikovsky (Symphony no.4) – which anticipates Glinka in the hocket-like use of pizzicato strings to imitate the balalaika. Known in its day only to the small literary circle around Derzhavin and L'vov, and in the 19th century only to a handful of local initiates (Alexander Serov wrote enthusiastically about the 'hawk' chorus), *Postal Coachmen at the Relay Station* was rediscovered and publicized by Alexander Rabinovich in his book *Russkaya opera do Glinki* (Moscow, 1948). The full score, edited by Irina Vetlivtsïna, was published in 1977. RICHARD TARUSKIN

Yanovs'ky, Borys Karlovych (*b* Moscow, 19/31 Dec 1875; *d* Kharkiv, 19 Jan 1933). Ukrainian composer of German descent. He studied and initially worked in Kiev, then in St Petersburg and in Moscow (where he was conductor of the Zimin Opera Theatre, 1916–17). From 1918 he worked in Kharkiv as critic, conductor and teacher at the Music Dramatic Institute. He composed ten operas, among them *Sorochyns'ky yarmarok* ('The Fair at Sorochins'ky', 1899, after Gogol), *Sestra Beatrysa* ('Sister Beatrice', 1907, after Maeterlinck, first performed in Kiev), *Ved'ma* ('The Witch', 1916, after Chekhov, given at the Zimin theatre), *Vybukh* ('Explosion', 1927, Kharkiv) and *Duma Chornomors'ka* or *Samiylo Kishka* ('Duma of the Black Sea', 1929, Kiev), this last a grand opera in four acts based on Ukrainian folk dumas and dedicated to Verdi's memory.

*

L. Arkhimovych: 'Nova lyudyna v umovakh novoho zhyttya' [A New Man in Conditions of a New Life], *Ukraïns'ke muzykoznavstvo*, no.3 (1968), 3–17 VIRKO BALEY

Yaw, Ellen Beach (*b* Boston, nr Buffalo, NY, 14 Sept 1869; *d* Covina, CA, 9 Sept 1947). American soprano. She studied in New York with Theodore Björkston and his wife, who discovered a phenomenal upward range touching *e‴*. Further study with Mathilde Marchesi in Paris brought introductions to Saint-Saëns and Massenet, both of whom admired her art, and in 1899 Sullivan composed the role of the Sultana in *The Rose of Persia* with her in mind. Otherwise the climax of her limited operatic career was a single appearance as Lucia at the Metropolitan in 1908, received with enthusiasm and astonishment. With proceeds from concerts she founded the 'Lark Ellen Home for Boys'. Recordings show something of her range and brilliance, the first being made in 1899 and the last some six months before her death.

*

A. Altamirano: 'Ellen Beach Yaw', *Record Collector*, x (1955–6), 149–60 [with discography] J. B. STEANE

Yeend, Frances (*b* Vancouver, WA, 28 Jan 1918). American soprano. She made her début in Spokane as Nedda. In the early 1940s she was occupied with operetta, radio work and concert tours, becoming one of America's foremost concert soloists. She sang Ellen Orford in the American première of *Peter Grimes* at Tanglewood in 1946, and the following year embarked on a world tour with the Bel Canto Trio (also including Mario Lanza and George London). She first sang at the New York City Opera in 1948 as Violetta and remained with the company until 1959, singing roles including Countess Almaviva, Eva, Marguerite and Micaëla. In the 1950s she made débuts in Barcelona, Edinburgh,

London (as Mimì at Covent Garden in 1953), Munich, Verona and Vienna. Her Metropolitan début was in 1961 as Chrysothemis, and she remained with the company for three seasons, also singing Gutrune and Violetta. CORI ELLISON

Yekaterina II. *See* CATHERINE II.

Yekaterinburg. City in western central Russia, on the eastern slope of the Ural mountains; it was known as Sverdlovsk from 1924 to 1991. The city's operatic history began in 1843, when a combined dramatic and musical troupe led by P. A. Sokolov performed several operas in a converted factory hospital after an unsuccessful run in Perm'. From 1847 the 800-seat Gorodskoy Teatr (City Theatre) housed performances of Russian and European operas by local and touring troupes, arranged by numerous entrepreneurs, until P. M. Medvedev opened a fully-fledged operatic season in 1879 with *A Life for the Tsar*. Opera and drama performances then regularly alternated on this stage, with year-long opera seasons established under the successive direction of A. A. Levitsky (1907–9), A. Ia. Al'tshuler (1909–11) and I. P. Paliyev (1911–12). In 1912 a new 1200-seat hall designed by V. I. Simyonov became the home of the Gorodskoy Opernïy Teatr (City Opera Theatre), also known as the Yekaterinburgskiy Opernïy Teatr, which was under the management of the local theatre directorate until becoming independent in 1914. A new opera troupe, formed as a Soviet company in 1918, formally reopened the theatre in 1919 with a performance of *Faust*. In 1924 it was renamed the Gosudarstvennïy Opernïy Teatr imeni A. V. Lunacharskogo (Lunacharsky State Opera Theatre) and became one of the principal operatic centres in the Soviet Union. In 1931 it became the Sverdlovskiy Gosudarstvennïy Teatr Operï i Baleta imeni A. V. Lunacharskogo (Lunacharsky Sverdlovsk State Theatre of Opera and Ballet), in 1966 'Academic' being added to the name. The Teatr Muzïkal'noy Komedii became independent in 1933. Since then the Lunacharsky theatre has concentrated mainly on operas by Soviet composers and has become a centre for productions of works by composers from the Urals, including Trambitsky and Spadavecchia.

*

ME (B. S. Shteynpress; also 'Sverdlovskiy teatr operï i baleta', M. N. Khlyostkina)

Iu. Kurochkin: *Iz teatral'nogo proshlogo Urala* [From the Theatrical Past of the Urals] (Sverdlovsk, 1957)

I. A. Rif: *Sverdlovskiy teatr muzïkal'noy komedii* (Sverdlovsk, 1959)

B. S. Shteynpress, ed.: *Iz muzïkal'nogo proshlogo* [From the Musical Past] (Moscow, 1960–65) [incl. E. V. Mayburova: 'Muzïkal'naya zhizn' Yekaterinburga' [The Musical Life of Yekaterinburg], i, 22–71; B. S. Shteynpress: 'Muzïkal'naya zhizn' Sverdlovska v 1917–1941 gg' [The Musical Life of Sverdlovsk, 1917–41], ii, 5–71; M. N. Khlyostkina: '"Dvadtsat'" dva sezona Sverdlovskoy operï (1919–41)' [Twenty-two Seasons of Sverdlovsk Opera, 1919–41], ii, 72–114]

G. Bernandt: *Slovar' oper vpervïye postavlennïkh ili izdannïkh v dorevolyutsionnoy Rossii i v SSSR 1736–1959* [Dictionary of Operas First Performed or Published in Pre-revolutionary Russia and in the USSR 1736–1959] (Moscow, 1962), 550

GREGORY SALMON

Yellin, Victor (Fell) (*b* Boston, 14 Dec 1924). American musicologist. He studied at Harvard, with Irving Fine, Piston, Milhaud, Otto Gombosi, John M. Ward and others. From 1958 to 1960 he taught at Williams College, where he also directed the glee club; after a year on the faculty of Ohio State University he joined the music department of New York University in 1961. A specialist in American music, Yellin has done research on musical activities in the colonial period (particularly in 17th-century Virginia), analysed the works of contemporary American composers and written surveys of the musical development of the USA; his studies of American opera have centred on the works of George Chadwick, Virgil Thomson and Raynor Taylor.

PAULA MORGAN

Yeomen of the Guard, The [*The Yeomen of the Guard; or, The Merryman and his Maid*]. Operetta in two acts by ARTHUR SULLIVAN to a libretto by W. S. GILBERT; London, Savoy Theatre, 3 October 1888.

For Gilbert this essentially romantic rather than comic libretto represented a new departure, and one which satisfied Sullivan's desire to set what he had called 'a story of human interest and probability'. The story, similar to that of Wallace's *Maritana*, is set within the Tower of London during the 16th century. Falsely accused, Colonel Fairfax (tenor) eludes the headsman through the intervention of Sergeant Meryll (baritone) and his daughter Phoebe (mezzo-soprano). Eventually reprieved, Fairfax finds happiness with his new-found love, the strolling player Elsie Maynard (soprano), but at tragic cost to her devoted jester partner Jack Point (baritone), whose collapse at his rejection is treated with tragic simplicity.

Sullivan's setting is notably more serious and operatic than those of his other Gilbert collaborations. Although there are fine individual numbers, including the ballad 'Is life a boon?', Phoebe's 'When maiden loves' and 'Were I thy bride', the quartet 'When a wooer goes a-wooing' and the celebrated duet 'I have a song to sing, O!' (the setting of whose successively lengthening stanzas caused Sullivan much trouble), the work impresses most by its unity of musical style and atmosphere for, as Gervase Hughes observed, 'the spirit of the grim old Tower indefinably pervades the music from the first bar of the overture to the final *dénouement*' (*The Music of Arthur Sullivan*, 1960). Sullivan lavished his mature creative powers on the operetta, even composing an overture of symphonic cast, albeit on a miniature scale, and was disappointed that Gilbert felt the public response insufficiently enthusiastic to warrant further exploration of similar territory. Retaining a special affection for the work, Sullivan regarded it as his finest operetta. For many it is his finest work of all, with a strong claim to rank among the masterpieces of English opera. DAVID RUSSELL HULME

Yerevan. EREVAN.

Yerma. Opera in three acts by HEITOR VILLA-LOBOS after FEDERICO GARCÍA LORCA's play; Santa Fe, 12 August 1971.

Yerma (soprano) lives in a rural Spanish community where the primary occupation is shepherding. She laments her apparent infertility, for which she receives no sympathy from her husband Juan (tenor), who has no interest in children. Yerma's despair increases as, all around her, she sees signs of fecundity and child-bearing, particularly in the pregnancy of her friend Maria (mezzo-soprano). Yerma's disapproving sisters-in-law confine her both mentally and physically, and she secretly pays a nocturnal visit to a Sorceress (contralto), having been briefly tempted to return to the love of her youth, Victor (baritone). Magic failing, Yerma prays for a child at a religious shrine, but is confronted there with the ironic spectacle of a pagan fertility rite. Juan, outraged that Yerma should be out alone, comes to find her, and in a fit of passionate frustration at Juan's indifference to her need for a child Yerma strangles him, realizing then that her dream of motherhood has now vanished forever. The opera closes with pilgrims singing at the shrine.

Villa-Lobos wrote *Yerma* in 1955 to a commission from John Blankenship, director of drama at St Lawrence College in New York. The orchestration was completed in 1956, but plans by Blankenship for a production shortly thereafter with an all-black cast were inexplicably abandoned. *Yerma* had to wait until after Villa-Lobos's death for its première which, despite playing only two nights, was a success. The opera has since been given in Rio de Janeiro and in London. Lorca's raw vision of female repression in rural Spain, his declamatory, earthy, yet gentle prose, and the play's Hispanic folkloric elements all appealed to Villa-Lobos, who set the play (of 1934) almost verbatim; he provided a score of searing lyricism, coloured by large and exotic orchestral resources. SIMON WRIGHT

Yermolenko-Yuzhina [Ermolenko-Yushina; Plugovskaya], **Nataliya (Stepanovna)** (*b* Kiev, 1881; *d* after 1924). Russian soprano. She studied in Kiev and Paris and made her début under the name of Yermolenko as Lisa in *The Queen of Spades* at Kiev in 1900. She went to St Petersburg in 1901 and to the Bol'shoy in 1905. There she met the tenor David Yuzhin, whom she married, adding his name to her own professional name. For two seasons both singers joined Sergey Zimin's Private Opera in Moscow. Yermolenko was also among the most admired members of the distinguished company from Russia that performed in Paris in 1908, introducing *Boris Godunov* to the West. From 1915 to 1920 she was with the Mariinsky Theatre opera company, and in 1924 emigrated to Paris, where all traces of her appear to have been lost. She was considered the leading Russian lyric-dramatic soprano of her time, with a repertory that included Brünnhilde, Norma, Violetta and Carmen as well as many Russian operas; among these, one of her greatest successes was in Serov's *Judith*. Her rare recordings show clearly the impressive volume and quality of her voice and the authority of her style and technique. J. B. STEANE

Yershov [Ershov, Erschoff], **Ivan Vasil'yevich** (*b* Maliy Nesvetay, nr Novocherkassk, 8/20 Nov 1867; *d* Leningrad [now St Petersburg], 21 Nov 1943). Russian tenor. He studied in Moscow and with S. W. Gabel in St Petersburg, where he made his début as Faust in 1893. There followed a period of training in Italy, with performances at Turin and Reggio Emilia. Back in Russia, he sang for a season at Kharkiv, then in 1895 rejoined the Mariinsky at St Petersburg where he remained until 1929. There he became known as 'the Russian Tamagno', specializing in heroic parts such as Otello, Florestan and the heroes of Meyerbeer's *Les Huguenots* and *Le prophète*, as well as in a comprehensive Wagnerian repertory in which his Tannhäuser was particularly admired. In 1907 he appeared as Grishka Kuter'ma in the première of Rimsky-Korsakov's *Legend of the Invisible City of Kitezh*. After retirement from opera he continued to sing in concerts and taught at the Leningrad Conservatory until his death. His recordings, rare in original form, show an imaginative artist whose voice was impressive not simply for its volume, range and ringing quality but also for the elegance of its management and its mastery of light and shade. J. B. STEANE

Yevgeny Onegin ('Eugene Onegin'). Lyric scenes in three acts by PYOTR IL'YICH TCHAIKOVSKY to a libretto by the composer and KONSTANTIN STEPANOVICH SHILOVSKY after ALEXANDER SERGEYEVICH PUSHKIN's novel in verse (1833); Moscow, Maliy Theatre, 17/29 March 1879 [students of the Moscow Conservatory]; professional première, Moscow, Bol'shoy Theatre, 11/23 January 1881.

Larina *a landowner*	mezzo-soprano
Tat'yana [Tatyana] } *her daughters*	soprano
Ol'ga [Olga] } *her daughters*	contralto
Filipp'yevna [Filipyevna] *an old nurse-maid*	mezzo-soprano
Yevgeny Onegin	baritone
Lensky	tenor
Prince Gremin	bass
A Company Commander	bass
Zaretsky	bass
Triquet *a Frenchman*	tenor
Guillot *valet de chambre*	silent role

Peasants, ballroom guests, landowners, officers

Setting A country estate and St Petersburg, 1820s

The idea of transposing the most beloved work of Russian fiction to the musical stage was not Tchaikovsky's to begin with. It was proposed to him, during a social call on 25 May/6 June 1877, by the contralto Yelizaveta Lavrovskaya (1845–1919), and, according to an oft-cited letter to his brother Modest, at first it struck the composer as 'wild'. The drawbacks were obvious: Pushkin's novel was loved for the telling, not the tale. The plot as such was slender and banal: a dreamy country girl falls in love with a young fop from the big city; she impulsively pours out her feelings to him in a letter; she is rebuffed and humiliated; five years later the two encounter one another again and fop is smitten; by now country girl has become a society matron who will not abandon her husband for her old love. There is also a subplot involving fop's friend, a provincial poetaster, and country girl's vacuous sister, over whom the two young men duel needlessly and the friend is meaninglessly slain. The book was loved for its divine details: the verbal dazzle, the wry social commentary, the perfectly exact descriptions, the endlessly subtle and nuanced characterizations, the ironized interrelationship of literary and social conventions – all that comes under the heading of narrative quality.

What Tchaikovsky shortly perceived – and what critics (not audiences) have failed to perceive for over a century – was that music of a sort he was uniquely inclined and equipped to write could perform exactly those functions for which Pushkin's narrative voice was prized. The result was a chef d'oeuvre of stylized operatic realism: the Russian counterpart to *Traviata* or *Manon*, except that it stands higher in its national tradition than they in theirs, and its realism more fundamentally determined its style.

Tchaikovsky spent a sleepless night after his visit to Lavrovskaya's, at the end of which he had a scenario in hand that differs only slightly from that of the finished opera. On 27 May he sought out his friend Konstantin Shilovsky, who had been pestering him with ideas for biblical and historical grand operas, and persuaded the latter to focus with him on *Onegin*. Together the two of them worked out a text that preserves a maximum of Pushkin's original verses. Shilovsky's major contribution to the libretto consisted of Monsieur Triquet's couplets (both French and ruptured-Russian versions) in Act 2 scene i; the composer was responsible for Lensky's (i.e. the poet's) arioso in 1.i and that of Prince Gremin (Tatyana's – the country girl's – eventual husband, an unnamed general in Pushkin) in 3.i.

1. Maria Klimentova as Tatyana in the Letter Scene from Act 1 of Tchaikovsky's 'Yevgeny Onegin', the role she created in the original production by students of the Moscow Conservatory at the Malïy Theatre, Moscow, 17/29 March 1879

He began composing straight away with Tatyana's letter (1.ii), on Pushkin's unaltered text. This self-contained passage, which all educated Russians know by heart, was something Tchaikovsky had planned to set long before conceiving the operatic project. (During this initial period of ardent imaginative work, identifying strongly with Tatyana and full of indignation at the title character, her unworthy love object, the composer unexpectedly found himself the recipient of a similar confessional letter from an unremembered former pupil named Antonina Milyukova; this suggestive coincidence set in motion the chain of events that led to Tchaikovsky's brief marriage.) The first four scenes of the opera were written during the month of June (Old Style) on Shilovsky's country estate. Then followed the calamitous events connected with the composer's wedding and its aftermath; he returned to *Onegin* during his extended recuperative stay in Western Europe, and only after embarking upon the Fourth Symphony, which would compete for his time for the rest of the year. Act 1 was fully scored by the end of October (in Clarens, Switzerland, where 36 years later Stravinsky composed *The Rite of Spring*). By 13/25 January 1878, all of the opera was complete in score except for the duel scene (2.ii). This, the last vocal music in the opera to be composed, was written in the hills outside San Remo, Italy. The orchestral introduction followed. The whole work was completed in full score on 20 January/1 February. Even with the distractions of personal disaster and major competing projects, it had taken only eight months to write.

The première of the opera was given by students, under Nikolay Rubinstein; at the professional première the conductor was Enrico Bevignani and Onegin was sung by Pavel Khokhlov. Tchaikovsky later revised the third act and this version was first given at the Mariinsky Theatre, St Petersburg, on 19 September/1 October 1885; Eduard Nápravník conducted, with Emiliya Pavlovskaya the sensational Tatyana, Mariya Slavina as Olga, Ippolit Pryanishnikov as Onegin and Mikhail Koryakin as Gremin. The schottisches (écossaises) in Act 3 were added for this production at the request of Ivan Vsevolozhsky, Intendant of the Imperial Theatres.

In the following synopsis, numbers in parentheses refer to Pushkin's novel (chapter and stanza); direct quotations from the novel are from Vladimir Nabokov's translation (1963).

The introduction is based on Tatyana's main leitmotif, establishing her as the opera's central character.

ACT 1.i *The garden of the Larin estate* To the strains of a duet based on Pushkin's early verse *The Poet* ('Slïkhalil' vï ... vdokhnulil' vï': 'Have you not heard ... have you not sighed'), sung by Olga and Tatyana, wafting out from the house like an invocation to the muse, Mme Larina reminisces with Filipyevna about her courtship and marriage, and the relationship of literature to her emotional life, concluding with a maxim paraphrased from Chateaubriand (ii.29–36). The chorus and Dance of the Peasants that follow are a decorative insertion of Tchaikovsky's devising: Mme Larina's serfs return singing from the field bearing the last sheaf, and sing and dance for her to celebrate the harvest. Tchaikovsky did not take these songs from printed anthologies; the second (dance song, 'Uzh kak po mostu-mostochku': 'Across the little bridge') has been identified in oral tradition, but the first (*protyazhnaya*, 'drawn-out song', 'Bolyat moi skorï nozhen'ki so pokhodushki': 'My nimble feet are sore from walking') is evidently original. Attempts have been made to invest the song texts with portent, but unconvincingly. For the *scena* and aria that follow, the librettists extracted a characterization of the two Larin sisters from the verses in which Pushkin contrasted them (ii.23–8) and put it all in Olga's mouth ('Ya ne sposobna k grusti tomnoy': 'I am no good at languid melancholy'). The peasants take their leave. Mme Larina expresses concern at Tatyana's bookish pensiveness; Filipyevna announces Lensky's approach with a stranger.

Lensky and Onegin are introduced; in the quartet, which Tchaikovsky compared to the quartet in Act 2 of Gounod's *Faust*, the men and the Larin sisters stand in respective pairs and sing a skilful concatenation of phrases from the novel (iii.5–8), the men casually appraising the girls and the entranced Tatyana recognizing in Onegin the 'somebody' for whom her soul had been waiting. Thereupon they form two couples; On-

2. *'Yevgeny Onegin' (Tchaikovsky), Act 2 scene i (the ball for Tatyana's name-day) of the original production by students of the Moscow Conservatory at the Maliy Theatre, Moscow, 17/29 March 1879*

egin and Tatyana stroll off. In an arioso Lensky confesses his feelings for Olga, not for the first time ('Ya lyublyu vas, Ol'ga': 'I love you, Olga'). Onegin and Tatyana, the latter now clearly enamoured, stroll back on stage, the former regaling the company with the famous opening stanza of the novel, in which the young rake cynically recalls the uncle whose timely death had brought him into ownership of the estate bordering on the Larins'.

1.ii *Tatyana's bedroom* The introduction is based on an extended version of Tatyana's leitmotif. Tatyana interrogates the uncomprehending Filipyevna about love and asks her to recount her own courtship and marriage; the nursemaid's story, about ancient and unromantic peasant rituals, strikes no chord within the infatuated girl (iii.17–21). She asks Filipyevna to arrange her writing-desk with pen and paper and sends her away. Tatyana composes her letter to Onegin in a huge (12-minute) aria, the Letter Scene ('Puskay pogibnu ya': 'Even if it means I perish'), described below (its text corresponds to iii.31). Dawn breaks, and a shepherd's pipe is heard (the oboe melody here is in the manner of documented Russian shepherd tunes). Filipyevna comes to wake Tatyana and is surprised to find her up; Tatyana asks her old nanny to send her grandson with the letter to Onegin (iii.32–5).

1.iii *Another part of the Larin estate* Berry-picking peasant girls, singing an imitation folksong drawn from the novel (iii.39) and overheard by Tatyana as she waits for Onegin's response, act in the opera as a frame to the action of this scene, returning at the end. Onegin shows up and reproves Tatyana as gently as he can for her lack of self-control, meanwhile confessing himself incapable of anything more than a brother's love (iv.12–17). Tatyana is stunned into silence.

Act 2.i *A brightly lit room in the Larin house* The entr'acte is based on the central theme of the Letter Scene. To the strains of a waltz, played by a military band courtesy of the Company Commander with whom the ladies flirt, the guests assembled for Tatyana's name-day chatter and gossip (v.25–6, 28). Onegin, bored, flirts and dances with Olga (v.41). Lensky jealously confronts Olga but is rebuffed (v.44–5). Monsieur Triquet, a local Frenchman, sings some name-day doggerel he has composed (v.27, 33: the tune, Pushkin notes, is that of 'Réveillez-vous, belle endormie'; Nabokov, having identified the incipit with a melody published by Julien Tiersot, comments, 'It is typical of Chaykovski's slapdash opera *Eugene Onegin* that *his* Triquet sings a totally different tune'). Shilovsky's text begins 'A cette fête conviée', or, in 'Russian', 'Kakoy prekrasnïy etot den'' ('What fine today!'). Olga having promised the cotillon to Onegin, Lensky confronts his rival, forswears their friendship and challenges him to a duel; the latter accepts (v.42; vi.8–12: in the novel, Lensky leaves the ball at the cotillon and issues his challenge the next day through Zaretsky, his second). In the largest ensemble in the opera, the quintet (Tatyana, Olga, Larina, Lensky, Onegin) with chorus, the assembled company express their horror at what has happened (this scene departs the furthest from Pushkin's plot, since the novel contains no public scandal at the ball; even so, many of the principals' repliques do roughly correspond to thoughts and expressions in the novel, especially vi.1–3).

2.ii *A rustic watermill in the countryside at dawn; winter* The introduction is based on the first section of Lensky's aria. Lensky and his second Zaretsky impatiently await their tardy opponent at the appointed duelling place. Zaretsky stomps off to scout for Onegin, while Lensky sings a farewell to Olga (vi.21–6, a letter-in-verse in the novel, meant as a parody: 'Kuda, kuda vï udalilis': 'Whither, ah! whither are ye fled'). Onegin arrives, casually apologizes for the delay, but insults Zaretsky by presenting his valet as his second. The paces are marked off, Onegin fires and, to his horror and remorse, kills Lensky with the first shot (vi.26–31, 35).

Act 3.i *A side room of a rich noble house in St Petersburg* A polonaise is in progress. Onegin, having returned from a long sojourn abroad where he had tried without success to forget the tragic consequences of his ennui, and bored as ever, encounters the Princess Gremina, a celebrated beauty, at a fancy-dress ball and is astounded to recognize Tatyana (viii.13–20). A schottische is danced. Tatyana's husband, Prince

Gremin, confides to Onegin, an old acquaintance, what happiness his marriage has brought him and how gratefully he loves his wife ('Lyubvi vse vozrastï pokornï': 'To love all ages are obedient', words by Tchaikovsky except for the incipit, which comes from viii.29). Tatyana has pleaded fatigue and left with the Prince, and Onegin realizes that he is now in love with her (viii.21–2, 30). His aria ('Uvï, somnen'ya net': 'Alas, there is no doubt') is an ironic recapitulation in music, and partly in words, of the rapturous opening section of Tatyana's Letter Scene. A further schottische is danced. (In place of the foregoing scene Tchaikovsky's original draft scenario had one roughly based on the concluding section of Pushkin's chapter vii, in which, shepherded by her mother through the Moscow 'marriage market', Tatyana meets her unnamed general and receives his proposal.)

3.ii *A reception room in Prince Gremin's house* Tatyana has received a confession from Onegin and does not know how to deal with it. Suddenly Onegin bursts in and confronts her with his newly kindled passion. He forces from her the admission that she loves him still, but cannot shake her resolve to stay with her husband. She rushes tearfully away, leaving him behind, shattered (viii.32, including Onegin's letter to Tatyana, 42–8). (In the original version of this scene Tatyana's exit was preceded by an embrace on which Gremin unexpectedly enters; in removing this melodramatic conclusion, Tchaikovsky made only textual, not musical, alterations.)

* * *

Of all the supreme repertory operas, *Yevgeny Onegin* has surely been treated with the most condescension. In part this has merely reflected general condescension towards Tchaikovsky, typically regarded as a wholly naive, spontaneous creator who could not function vis-à-vis his subjects and tasks except on the basis of infantile personal identification. True, his endlessly quoted letters to his brother and his patron contain a mountain of material for such a reading, and nowhere more so than in those relating to *Yevgeny Onegin*, full of seemingly ingenuous mooning over Tatyana. Such were the conventions by which 19th-century composers presented themselves to the non-musical; and a calculated artlessness was particularly of the essence in an opera that celebrated the triumph of innocence over guile. To the perceptive musician, meanwhile, the self-concealing sophistication of Tchaikovsky's technique is a miracle every bit as bracing and shaming as Pushkin's to the literary.

Beyond the general, two special problems have attended the opera. It has always disconcerted those for whom the value of Russian music can only inhere in an aura of 'Russianness' and who can discern Russianness only in the presence of folksongs. By that standard Tchaikovsky has been irrelevantly dismissed, and just as irrelevantly vindicated, many times over. In *Yevgeny Onegin*, where the folkish is obviously nothing more than an aspect of decor, 'Russianness' is nevertheless especially crucial, forming the basis of the opera's essential realism and therefore pervasive. But it is Russianness of an urbane sort most Western ears cannot descry as such.

The other problem, perhaps the chief one, involves the opera's relationship to its literary source. The solecism according to which an opera derived from pre-existing literature is judged by a simple yardstick of fidelity – correspondingly exigent as the source is valued – has happily been losing ground (in the case of Russian works partly through a timely dissemination of Bakhtin's ideas); but in the case of *Yevgeny Onegin*, the most revered source of all, it adamantly persists. The opera has been the bane of Pushkin-lovers from the beginning (Turgenev to Tolstoy: 'Undeniably notable music...But what a libretto!'). By now, on the authority of the militantly tone-deaf Vladimir Nabokov, denigration of Tchaikovsky's work is literary dogma. The novel's greatness is assumed to lie in its irony, vouchsafed by the intrusive narrative voice – 'a kind of spiritual air conditioner', as McLean (1971) has put it. When that machine is turned off, as it is assumed to be in the opera, 'the atmosphere becomes sticky, the underpinnings of the wonderfully delicate, intricate, balanced structure rot, and it collapses. You are left with a banal, trite, and sentimental bore – which may nevertheless be a vehicle for some delightful music'.

This formulation shows magnificent incomprehension of what the music in an opera does – but particularly in this opera, where the music, quite simply, is the narrator. From the very first notes sung, Olga's and Tatyana's duet to the harp, the music acts as a very busy and detached mediator of situations and feelings. As Asaf'yev was the first to demonstrate in detail, Tchaikovsky 'sings' his opera in an idiom intensely redolent of the domestic, theatrical and ballroom music of its time and place – its, not his – and in so doing he situates it, just as Pushkin situates the literary prototype, in the years 1819–25. And just as Pushkin's characters achieve their 'reality' by virtue of a multitude of precisely manipulated codes, so Tchaikovsky's express themselves through a finely calculated filter of musical genres and conventions.

Moreover, where the novelist must arrange things in a temporal sequence, the musician can simultaneously present and comment without recourse to digression. To pick one example, the comically exaggerated courtly flourishes in the orchestra that accompany Lensky and Onegin on their first appearance instantly sketch their foppish histories, accomplishing much of the work of Pushkin's chapter i, the absence of which is so often and so severely held against the opera's libretto. In their startling anticipation of *Pulcinella*, these '18th-century' curlicues also call attention to Tchaikovsky's under-appreciated mastery of the grotesque.

These points apply not only to the characters' public behaviour and to the obviously 'generic' ballroom scenes, but even, or especially, to their most private and personal utterances. Tatyana's Letter Scene, the most private and personal in the opera, is in effect a string of romances linked by recitatives:

1 'Puskay pogibnu ya' ('Even if it means I perish'): Allegro non troppo, D♭, 4/4, da capo form (18 bars)
2 'Ya k vam pishu' ('I write to you'): Moderato assai quasi Andante, D minor, 4/4, strophic form (56 bars, including recits.)
3 'Net, nikomu na svete ne otdala bï serdtsa ya!' ('No, there is no one else on earth to whom I'd give my heart'): Moderato, C, 2/4 (accompaniment in 6/8), da capo form (80 bars, including recits. and transition)
4 'Kto tï: moy angel-li khranitel'' ('Who art thou – my guardian angel?'): Andante, D♭, 2/4, da capo form (75 bars, 129 with orchestral introduction and orchestral/vocal coda).

The resonances between the music of this scene and the opening duet-romance are many, conspicuous and calculated: they are the resonances between Tatyana's inner and outer worlds. The most obvious is the fact that both incorporate Tatyana's leitmotif (it is the last line of each strophe in the duet, the middle section of the last romance in the Letter Scene). But the leitmotif is itself a bearer of the generic resonance. It begins on the sixth degree of the minor scale, and initiates a descent to the tonic, thus describing the interval that more than any other defines the idiom of the Russian domestic or household romance of the early 19th century: Russian scholars have gone so far as to coin the term *sekstovïy* ('sixthy') to denote that defining quality. Tatyana's part, saturated with 6ths encompassing degrees 1–6 or 6–1, or (more characteristically) 5–3 or 3–5, is, with Lensky's, surely the 'sixthiest' in all of opera (ex.1).

In ex.1*f* melodic 6ths are nested within a harmonic idiom that shows a semiotically marked 'sixthiness' of its own: the constant use of the minor submediant (the 'flattened sixth' in the major) as alternate harmonic root or tone centre. This alternation can take the form of an immediate local progression, as shown, or it can be projected in the form of a subsidiary key governing large spans within the tonal structure. Again, the introduction sets the precedent: its development section is all within the key of the submediant, which resolves to the dominant by way of retransition. In the Letter Scene, the whole vocal coda ('Konchayu! strashno perechest'': 'Finished! I dare not reread') is cast within the key of the starred chord, there spelt enharmonically as A major.

The melodic-harmonic idiom is only one of many genre resonances that tie Tatyana's Letter Scene to the opening duet and thence to the whole world of the domestic romance. The harp-heavy orchestration of the first two sections is no less potent. But the harp does more than evoke the sounds of domestic music-making. The inspired chords (non-arpeggiato) that punctuate the woodwind phrases in the actual letter-writing music (second romance as listed above) take their place within a marvellously detailed sound-portrait of the lovesick girl, in which Tchaikovsky shows himself to be an adept practitioner of Mozart's iconic methods (or 'body portraiture') as outlined in the famous letter to his father about *Die Entführung aus dem Serail*. As in the case of Mozart's Belmonte or Osmin, we can 'see' and 'feel' Tatyana – her movements, her breathing, her heartbeat – in her music. This, too, comes under the heading of narration, and shows off music's advantages: what the novelist must describe, the composer can actually present. (It is notorious, of course, that Tchaikovsky was a confessed Mozartian; for most Western writers the idea that Mozart could have a legitimate Russian heir has seemed an impertinence.)

As to irony, did Pushkin ever make more trenchant comment than Tchaikovsky, when he mocks Onegin's passionate confession to Tatyana in Act 3 with a fleeting reference to the music by which he had rejected her in Act 1? It is not simply a matter of showing that the boot is on the other foot: that much had already been accomplished by setting Onegin's arioso at the end of Act 3 scene i to the melody of the first romance in the Letter Scene (equally ironic in that Onegin, not having 'heard' that music on its earlier appearance, cannot be 'quoting' it now; the reference is entirely a narrator's aside). The allusion to the rejection music shows him fickle and erratic; it takes the place of the lengthy passage in the novel (vii.19–24) in which Tatyana visits the absent Onegin's library and discovers, by peeking at the annotations in his books, the shallowness of his soul.

The concluding confrontation between Onegin and Tatyana has been described as 'a duet in the grand style' (Dahlhaus), but even here the method of construction remains that of stringing romances (a technique Tchaikovsky evidently picked up from his teacher Anton Rubinstein: compare the third act of the latter's *Demon*). Tatyana's chief melody apes her husband's aria in the preceding scene, thus telegraphing her answer to Onegin. Only twice, fleetingly, do the two voices mingle. It is hardly a duet at all. Like Tatyana's total silence in response to rejection (1.iii, and except for her participation in ensembles, in 2.i as well) the scene flies in the face of operatic convention, underscoring by omission – another ironic narrator's aside – the futility of the dramatic situation.

The fact that *Yevgeny Onegin* contains no love duets testifies to its singular affinity with Pushkin's novel. This is not to say that there are no divergences between Tchaikovsky's treatment and Pushkin's: in the case of Lensky, in particular, whose Act 2 aria is a very serious moment, the opera does reflect a later, more sentimental age. But even with Lensky, the use of the modest romance form is more than just evocative; it sets distinct limits on his emotional scale. All the characters in the opera remain denizens of a novel (one of the very earliest to be given operatic treatment), not a historical romance or a well-made play.

In choosing such a source, and matching his musical means to its ambit, Tchaikovsky went in some ways even further than Dargomïzhsky ever did along the path of realism. It is in any case striking to find Tchaikovsky, who professed to despise *The Stone Guest* for its literalistic pretension to 'truth', virtually parroting some of Dargomïzhsky's pronouncements when it came to describing his own equally eccentric work. 'Its content is very unsophisticated', he wrote of his opera to Mme von Meck, 'there are no scenic effects, the music lacks brilliance and rhetorical effectiveness'. That – not, as often supposed, the fact that it consists of extracts from a larger story, still less that he modelled his work on the as yet unchristened *drame lyrique* of Massenet and others – is why Tchaikovsky preferred the term 'lyric scenes' to 'opera' in subtitling the score. The most he could hope for, he thought, were 'a few *chosen* listeners', who would discover *Onegin* for themselves at home, and who would create demand for it 'from below'. That certainly happened; within decades of the composer's death his lyric scenes played on all the biggest operatic stages of the world. He even adapted them somewhat to make this possible. But, like *The Stone Guest*, *Yevgeny Onegin* makes its strongest impression in plainer surroundings.

RICHARD TARUSKIN

Yoake. Opera by Kósçak Yamada; *see* KUROFUNE.

Youmans, Vincent (Millie) (*b* New York, 27 Sept 1898; *d* Denver, 5 April 1946). American composer. He worked as a piano salesman and music-roll maker, and later as a song plugger for the publishers Remick and Harms. He began composing while in the navy in World War I. Between 1921 and 1932 he wrote the scores for 12 musicals, the most successful of which were *Wildflower* (1923, with Herbert Stothart), *No, No, Nanette* (1925, including 'Tea for two') and *Hit the Deck!* (1927); *No, No, Nanette* was the biggest musical comedy success of the 1920s in Europe as well as the USA. His last score, before tuberculosis and other problems led to early retirement and death, was for the film *Flying Down to Rio* (1933). Many of Youmans's early songs consist of two-, three- or four-note phrases repeated over ever-changing harmonies; in later years he turned to longer, more curvilinear melodies.

musicals; dates are of first New York performance unless otherwise stated (librettists and lyricists are listed in that order: where names are separated by a comma, authors collaborated)

Two Little Girls in Blue (A. Francis [I. Gershwin]), collab. P. Lannin, Cohan, 3 May 1921; Wildflower (O. Harbach, O. Hammerstein II), collab. H. Stothart, Casino, 7 Feb 1923; Mary Jane McKane (W. C. Duncan, Hammerstein), collab. Stothart, Imperial, 25 Dec 1923; Lollipop (Z. Sears), Knickerbocker, 21 Jan 1924; A Night Out (G. Grossmith, A. Miller; C. Grey, I. Caesar), Philadelphia, Sept 1925; No, No, Nanette (Harbach, F. Mandel; Caesar, Harbach), Globe, 16 Sept 1925

Oh, Please! (Harbach, A. Caldwell), Fulton, 17 Dec 1926; Hit the Deck! (H. Fields; L. Robin, Grey), Belasco, 25 April 1927; Rainbow (L. Stallings, Hammerstein), Gallo, 21 Nov 1928; Great Day (Duncan, J. Wells; E. Eliscu, W. Rose), Cosmopolitan, 17 Oct 1929; Smiles (W. A. McGuire; Grey, H. Adamson, R. Lardner), Ziegfeld, 18 Nov 1930; Through the Years (B. Hooker; E. Heyman), Manhattan, 28 Jan 1932; Take a Chance (B. G. DeSylva, L. Schwab), collab. R. Whiting, N. H. Brown, Apollo, 26 Nov 1932

*

S. Green: *The World of Musical Comedy* (New York, 1960, 4/1980)
D. Dunn: *The Making of No, No, Nanette* (Secaucus, NJ, 1972)
G. Bordman: *Days to be Happy, Years to be Sad: the Life and Music of Vincent Youmans* (New York, 1982)

GERALD BORDMAN

Young. English family of singers. Cecilia, Isabella (i) and Esther were daughters of Charles Young, organist of All Hallows, Barking. Isabella (ii), Elizabeth and Polly were daughters of his son Charles, a clerk in the Treasury.

(1) **Cecilia Young** [Mrs Arne] (*b* London, bap. 7 Feb 1712; *d* London, 6 Oct 1789). Soprano. A pupil of Geminiani, she sang in concerts from March 1730 and first appeared on stage in English operas by Lampe and Smith in 1732–3. She sang in the premières of Handel's *Ariodante* and *Alcina* (1735). After marrying Thomas Arne in 1737 she appeared in his stage works (notably *Comus*, *Rosamond* and *Alfred*) in London and for two seasons in Dublin (1742–4). Her marriage proved unhappy and she was often ill, making only occasional appearances after 1746; her last new Arne role was in *Eliza* (1754). She sang in the Dublin winter concert season in 1748–9 and returned there with Arne in 1755 to perform in his works at Smock Alley Theatre. Arne returned to London, leaving her in Ireland with her young niece Polly, and in 1758 Mrs Delany found her employed as a singing teacher by a charitable Irish family. She returned to London with Polly in 1762 and was reconciled with Arne shortly before his death. Burney, a pupil of Arne's, remembered her with affection, and Dibdin wrote: 'Mrs Arne was deliciously captivating. She knew nothing in singing or in nature but sweetness and simplicity'.

(2) **Isabella Young (i)** [Mrs Lampe] (*d* London, will proved 12 March 1795). Soprano, sister of (1) Cecilia. She had small singing roles at Drury Lane in 1733–4 but otherwise appeared only in concerts until she sang the heroine Margery in Lampe's burlesque opera *The Dragon of Wantley* in 1737. In the middle of its long run she married the composer and subsequently created roles in all his stage works, including Thisbe in *Pyramus and Thisbe* (1745). The Lampes had two seasons at Smock Alley Theatre, Dublin, from 1748 and then moved to Edinburgh. Lampe died there in July 1751 and she returned to Covent Garden to sing her old roles and some new ones in musical afterpieces. She remained in the company until the 1775–6 season, often singing with her sister Esther, although in the later years they were only members of the chorus. Her daughter-in-law sang for a time as Mrs Lampe at the pleasure gardens and Sadler's Wells.

(3) **Esther** [Hester] **Young** [Mrs Jones] (*b* London, 14 Feb 1717; *d* London, bur. 6 June 1795). Contralto, sister of (1) Cecilia. She appeared in concerts from 1736 and created the role of Mauxalinda in Lampe's *The Dragon of Wantley*. She had other Lampe roles, sang Juno and Ino in the première of Handel's *Semele* in 1744 and played Lucy in *The Beggar's Opera* for many years. She sang in London, mainly at Covent Garden, in every season until 1775–6. Her husband was the music seller and publisher Charles Jones.

(4) **Isabella Young (ii)** [Mrs Scott] (*d* London, 17 Aug 1791). Mezzo-soprano, niece of (1) Cecilia. She studied with the bass Waltz, first appearing in a concert with him in March 1751, and sang in Arne's *Alfred*, *Rosamond* and *Eliza* in 1754. She became a distinguished concert and oratorio singer in London and the provincial festivals, singing for Handel from 1756 until his death, and was a regular performer at Drury Lane every season from 1755 to 1777. Her début there was as Titania in J. C. Smith's opera *The Fairies*. She sang between the acts, in musical interludes and after-

pieces and created roles in George Rush's English operas *The Royal Shepherd* and *The Capricious Lovers*. For several years after her marriage in 1757 to the Hon. John Scott she continued to sing as Miss Young.

(5) **Elizabeth Young** [Mrs Dorman] (*d* London, 12 April 1773). Contralto, sister of (4) Isabella (ii). She appears to have travelled to Ireland with the Arnes in 1755 and returned with Dr Arne in 1756, since she sang his music in Dublin early in 1756 and was in his *Eliza* in London that December. After playing Lucy in *The Beggar's Opera* in June 1758 she appeared regularly at Drury Lane until 1772; her lower voice meant she was given male or older women's parts. She created the roles of Agenor in Rush's *The Royal Shepherd* (1764) and Ursula in Dibdin's *The Padlock* (1768). She married the violinist Ridley Dorman in 1762.

(6) **Polly** [Mary, Maria] **Young** [Mrs Barthélemon] (*b* London, *c*1749; *d* London, 20 Sept 1799). Soprano, sister of (4) Isabella (ii). She went with the Arnes to Ireland and impressed audiences in Dublin by singing 'perfectly in Time and Tune' in Arne's *Eliza* at the age of six. In 1758, after hearing her play the harpsichord, Mrs Delaney wrote: 'the race of Youngs are *born* songsters and musicians'. She appeared on stage in Dublin, where O'Keeffe admired her 'charming face and small figure' as Ariel in *The Tempest* and she created the role of Nysa in O'Hara's burletta *Midas* (1762). She then returned to London and, after two seasons at Covent Garden, moved to the King's Theatre to sing minor roles with the Italian opera. After marrying the violinist and composer Barthélemon in 1766 she usually appeared with him, in London and on visits to Ireland and the Continent. After 1778 they were sometimes joined by their daughter Cecilia Maria, a singer, pianist and composer. Polly sang at the pleasure gardens and appeared again with the Italian opera in 1771 and the early 1780s.

BDA; *BurneyH*; *DNB* (W. B. Squire); *LS*
C. Dibdin: *A Complete History of the English Stage*, v (London, 1800)
M. Delany: *Autobiography and Correspondence*, ed. Lady Llanover (London, 1861)
W. H. Cummings: *Dr Arne and Rule Britannia* (London, 1912)
H. Langley: *Dr Arne* (Cambridge, 1938)
P. Lord: 'The English-Italian Opera Companies 1732–3', *ML*, xlv (1964), 239–51
R. Fiske: *English Theatre Music in the Eighteenth Century* (London, 1973, 2/1986)
T. J. Walsh: *Opera in Dublin 1705–1797* (Dublin, 1973)
B. Boydell: *A Dublin Musical Calendar 1700–1760* (Dublin, 1988)

OLIVE BALDWIN, THELMA WILSON

Young [Youngs], **(Basil) Alexander** (*b* London, 18 Oct 1920). English tenor. He studied at the RCM with Steffan Pollmann and made his début as Scaramuccio (*Ariadne auf Naxos*) at the 1950 Edinburgh Festival. In 1953 he sang Tom Rakewell in the English première of *The Rake's Progress*, the BBC studio production; he recorded it in 1964 under Stravinsky's direction. He created Charles Darnay in Benjamin's *A Tale of Two Cities* (1953, BBC) and Philippe in *A Dinner Engagement* (1954, Aldeburgh), and sang in the British premières of Searle's *The Diary of a Madman* (1960, Sadler's Wells) as Poprichin and *The Bassarids* (1968, BBC) as Dionysus. He appeared at Covent Garden (1955–70), notably as Matteo (*Arabella*) and Britten's Lysander; at Sadler's Wells, where his roles included Count Ory, Almaviva, Gluck's and Monteverdi's Orpheus, Belmonte and Handel's Jupiter and Xerxes; and with the WNO and Scottish Opera, creating Cicero in Hamilton's *The Catiline Conspiracy* (1974, Stirling). Although his voice was not large, Young's fine musicianship and wide repertory brought him great success.

HAROLD ROSENTHAL/R

Young Caeser. Puppet opera in 14 scenes by LOU HARRISON to a libretto by Robert Gordon; Pasadena, California, 5 November 1971.

Harrison claims that his is the only opera with an overtly presented gay subject from history. The action, more described by a narrator than portrayed by actors, seems archaic, formal, stylized, dispassionate. It concerns the coming of age of Gaius Julius Caesar (tenor), from his patrician adolescence in Rome to his first conquest – military and amorous – in the Turkish province of Bithynia, where King Nicomedes (baritone) takes him to heart and bed with detailed pomp and circumstance. The first production used singers sitting in the pit; the orchestra consisted of instruments invented and built by Harrison's companion, William Colvig, besides instruments imported from Korea, Japan and other points east. Lasting around 90 minutes, the work has nine singing and four speaking roles.

The sonic language is of extravagant simplicity. Decades before Philip Glass launched his reiterated diatonic ostinatos, Harrison was preparing 'canvases' of identical ostinatos, upon which he etched ravishing melodic streams. *Young Caeser* [*sic*] emerges from this tradition, albeit with random-sounding vocal lines. Like Britten's *Death in Venice*, it uses stemless neume-like notes in the extended recitatives. The piece was transferred in 1988 to a big stage with live interpreters from the Gay Men's Chorus of Portland; this performance convinced the composer that more arias should interrupt the constant chatter and that cuts and shifts of location were in order. Kerry G. Lewis has made a viable transcription of the opera using Western instruments including a troubador harp, a small electric organ and a 'tack piano', one of Harrison's adapted instruments.

NED ROREM

Ysaÿe, Eugène(-Auguste) (*b* Liège, 16 July 1858; *d* Brussels, 12 May 1931). Belgian composer and violinist. He studied the violin at the conservatories of Liège and Brussels and from 1876 continued his training in Paris. Achieving increasing success as a soloist, he came to be recognized as the outstanding violinist of his generation; in Paris between 1883 and 1886 he formed close ties with Franck, Fauré and Debussy among others, and eventually began to compose, chiefly for violin, in a post-Romantic style. Later in life, due to ill-health, he mainly conducted, and towards the end of his life, while recuperating from an operation, wrote his one opera, *Piére li houïeu* ('Peter the Miner'). A *drame lyrique* in one act, to a Walloon libretto of his own, it is based on an episode in a miners' strike that he had witnessed in his youth. Ysaÿe wished to conduct the work himself, but was too ill to do so, when the first performance took place in Liège on 4 March 1931, though he was able to attend a second one in Brussels on 25 April. He died a few weeks later and the work has remained unpublished.

BORIS SCHWARZ/R

Yudif' ('Judith'). Opera in five acts by ALEXANDER NIKOLAYEVICH SEROV to a libretto based on the composer's scenario after Paolo Giacometti's *Giuditta* (originally written in Italian by Ivan Antonovich

Giustiniani), with textual accretions (mostly to already-composed music) by Konstantin Zvantsov, Dmitry Lobanov and Apollon Maykov, inspired in part by Friedrich Hebbel's tragedy; St Petersburg, Mariinsky Theatre, 16/28 May 1863.

Richard Wagner accurately guessed the way his Russian friend served up the bloody Apocryphal perennial about the Judean heroine who rescues her besieged people by seducing and beheading the Assyrian commander Holofernes: 'In five acts, isn't it? First, populace; then, Judith alone; after that, in the camp, the murder, and triumphant return'. Although by 1863 Serov had long since declared himself Wagner's disciple (and his evident attempt to cast his musical drama in the form of a 'continuous finale' testifies to his sincerity), he remained true to the conventional format of grand 'historical' opera. The outer acts are vast choral tableaux: the first ends with an effectively pessimistic fade out, the last with a grand apotheosis crowned by the heroine's coloratura. The Assyrian acts (3 and 4) contain exotic 'oriental' songs and dances, a procession with onstage *orchestre d'harmonie*, and a telling hallucination scena for the intoxicated Holofernes that would find echo a decade later in *Boris Godunov*. Act 2, with its grandiose five-part soliloquy for the heroine, 'Ya odenus' v visson' ('I will deck myself in purple'), provided the pre-revolutionary Russian operatic stage with its most testing dramatic-soprano showpiece; the culminating section was recorded, magnificently, by Nataliya Yermolenko-Yuzhina (the original singer was Valentina Bianchi). Shalyapin's portrayal of Holofernes (from 1898), a role first sung by Mikhail Sariotti, gave the opera a new lease of life. Dyagilev's presentation of the fourth act in Paris in June 1909 as a vehicle for Shalyapin and Litvinne was the only major professional staging a Serov opera ever received abroad. At home *Judith* was not only extremely popular, it was admired by connoisseurs as distinguished as Grigor'yev, Odoyevsky and even Tchaikovsky. A complete recording, by Bol'shoy Theatre forces under Andrey Chistyakov, was unexpectedly issued in 1991.

RICHARD TARUSKIN

Yugoslavia. Federation in south-eastern Europe, created in 1918 and dissolved in 1992. For discussion of operatic activity *see* CROATIA, SERBIA and SLOVENIA; *see also* under the following cities: BELGRADE, DUBROVNIK, LJUBLJANA, MARIBOR, NOVI SAD, OSIJEK, SARAJEVO, SKOPJE, SPLIT and ZAGREB.

Yun, Isang (*b* Tongyong [now Chung Mu], 17 Sept 1917). Korean-German composer. A son of the court poet Ki-Hyon Yun, he studied composition in Japan, returning to Korea at Japan's entry into World War II, but in 1943 was imprisoned by the Japanese for underground political resistance. He studied with Pierre Revel and Tony Aubin in Paris (1956) and with Boris Blacher and Josef Rufer in Berlin (1957–9). After attending the Darmstadt summer music course in 1958, he played an increasingly important part in the European avant garde. In 1967 Yun was imprisoned by the Park regime for alleged crimes against the state and sentenced to death, but was released after international pressure. The comic opera *Die Witwe des Schmetterlings* (1969) was completed during his imprisonment. Together with his first opera, the Confucian Lehrstück *Der Traum des Liu-Tung* (1965), *Die Witwe* has often been performed under the title *Träume*.

In Yun's music Asian sensibility and performance technique derived from traditional Korean instruments are assimilated into a contemporary European context. It is the use of a rigorous compositional logic, which stems from the post-Darmstadt period, that prevents the music from becoming merely decorative or exotic. A thorough-going dialectic of yin (nostalgic, dark, feminine) and yang (positive, bright, masculine) ensures a wide range of expression.

Although both the above-mentioned operas are for modest forces, a large-scale apparatus is found in the atmospheric *Geisterliebe* (1971). Based on a short story from the Chinese Ming dynasty, it utilizes primitive shamanistic rhythmic devices. The larger and more sophisticated *Sim Tjong* (1972) was written for the full Munich opera ensemble (the Sea Dragon's part is sung simultaneously by five baritones) to coincide with the 1972 Olympiad.

Der Traum des Liu-Tung (1, H. Rudelsberger and W. Bauernfeind, after Ma Chi-Yuan), Berlin, Akademie der Künste, 25 Sept 1965, vs (Berlin and Wiesbaden, 1965)

Die Witwe des Schmetterlings (1, H. Kunz), Nuremberg,

Scene from the original production of Yun's 'Sim Tjong' at the Bayerische Staatsoper, Munich, 1 August 1972, designed by Jürgen Rose

Opernhaus, 23 Feb 1969, vs (Berlin and Wiesbaden, 1968)
Geisterliebe (2, Kunz), Kiel, Landes, 20 June 1971, vs (Berlin and Wiesbaden, 1971)
Sim Tjong (prol., 2, epilogue, Kunz), Munich, Staatsoper, 1 Aug 1972, vs (Berlin and Wiesbaden, 1972)

*

R. Gay: *East Meets West in 'The Butterfly Widow'* (diss., Northwestern U., 1971)
L. Rinser and I. Yun: *Der verwunderte Drache* (Frankfurt, 1977)
H. Heister and W. Sparrer: *Der Komponist Isang Yun* (Munich, 1987)

KEITH GIFFORD

Yurisich, Gregory (*b* Mount Lawley, Western Australia, 13 Oct 1951). Australian baritone. He studied in Perth and made his début in Sydney in 1976 as Paolo (*Simon Boccanegra*) with Australian Opera, for whom he also sang Masetto, Sharpless, Germont, Don Pasquale, Alberich, Yeletsky, Don Alfonso, Sulpice, Varlaam, Grigory (*The Bear*), Michonnet and Melitone; at Melbourne he sang Pizarro and the Dutchman. He made his European début at Frankfurt in 1989 as Bottom (*A Midsummer Night's Dream*), and for the ENO he has sung Escamillo, Mozart's Figaro, Alcibiades, which he created in Stephen Oliver's *Timon of Athens* (1991), and Cadmus in the première of John Buller's *Bakxai* (1992). After his Covent Garden début (1990) as William Tell, he returned as Rossini's Dr Bartolo and the four villains in *Les contes d'Hoffmann* (1992). He also sang Leporello at Glyndebourne (1991), and has appeared in Canada and the USA; his repertory includes Marcello, Macbeth, Iago and Henry VIII (*Anna Bolena*). He has a strong, flexible voice and is a fine actor, particularly in comedy.

ELIZABETH FORBES

Yūzuru ('The Twilight Heron'). Opera in one act by IKUMA DAN, to a libretto which is the unchanged text of Junji Kinoshita's play based on a Japanese folktale; Osaka, Asahi Hall, 30 January 1952 (revised version, Zürich, 27 June 1957).

In a snowy village lives Yohyō (tenor), a farmer, with his new wife Tsū (soprano), who is popular among the village children. Yohyō is an honest and simple young man, but recently he has become lazy, while Tsū supports him by weaving a luxurious fabric made of heron feathers. Two sly villagers, Unzu (baritone) and Sōdo (bass), suspect that Tsū may be a heron which has taken human form, and find out that Yohyō did once help a heron hurt by an arrow; they persuade him to go to the capital to sell the fabric for a very high price. Meanwhile Tsū appears with the village children and laments the change in Yohyō's character. Yohyō asks Tsū to weave the fabric once more, and she finally agrees on condition that he will not look into her room while she is weaving. The temptation, however, is too strong and he peeps in only to find a heron working on the loom. Tsū appears with the newly woven fabric, confesses that she is the bird Yohyō once helped, and disappears. As Yohyō desperately holds the fabric in his arms, the village children notice a heron disappearing in the evening sky.

The work successfully combines Japanese elements with the vocabulary of European music; particularly commendable are the natural way in which the composer treats the Japanese text and the depth of feeling he brings to it. *Yūzuru* is arguably the most popular of Japanese operas, both in Japan and abroad; it has been performed more than 550 times.

MASAKATA KANAZAWA

Z

Zabela(-Vrubel), Nadeshda [Nadezhda] (*b* Kaunas, 1 April 1868; *d* St Petersburg, 21 June/4 July 1913). Lithuanian soprano. She studied at St Petersburg and made her début in 1893 at Kiev, then sang at Tbilisi and St Petersburg. She was engaged by the Mamontov opera company, Moscow (1897–1904), where she sang in the first performances of Rimsky-Korsakov's *The Tsar's Bride* (1899) and *The Tale of Tsar Saltan* (1900). An engagement at the Bol'shoy (1904–11) followed. Her roles included Micaëla, Nedda, Desdemona, Marguerite, Elsa and Elisabeth, as well as Tatyana, Rimsky-Korsakov's Volkhova (*Sadko*) and Snow Maiden. In 1907 she sang in the première of that composer's *Legend of the Invisible City of Kitezh* at the Mariinsky Theatre, St Petersburg. Married to the painter Mikhail Vrubel, a stage designer for the Mamontov company, she had a full, vibrant voice that was particularly suited to Russian music. ELIZABETH FORBES

Zaccaria, Nicola (Angelo) (*b* Piraeus, 9 March 1923). Greek bass. He studied in Athens, where he made his début in 1949 as Raimondo (*Lucia di Lammermoor*). In 1953 he made his début at La Scala as Sparafucile (*Rigoletto*). He sang there regularly in the Italian bass repertory, took part in the first Milan performance of Milhaud's *David* and created the Third Tempter in Pizzetti's *Assassinio nella cattedrale* (1958). He sang in Rome (from 1956) and Vienna, and at Covent Garden in 1957 as Oroveso (*Norma*) and in 1959 as Creon (*Médée*), on both occasions opposite Callas. He first sang at the Salzburg Festival in 1957 as Don Fernando (*Fidelio*) and returned as the Monk (*Don Carlos*), the Commendatore and Ferrando (*Il trovatore*). Zaccaria also appeared regularly at Dallas, where in 1976 he sang his first King Mark. In 1982 he sang Colline at Macerata. His mellow, well-produced voice was always used with intelligence and discretion. HAROLD ROSENTHAL/R

Zadek, Hilde (*b* Bromberg, 15 Dec 1917). German soprano. A refugee from Nazi Germany in 1934, she went to Palestine and worked as a nurse in Jerusalem; she studied singing there with Rose Pauly and, from 1945, in Zürich with Ria Ginster. Her début as Aida at the Vienna Staatsoper in 1947 began her international career. She sang in the première of *Antigonae* (Orff) at the 1949 Salzburg Festival, and the next year made her British début at the Edinburgh Festival with Glyndebourne Opera under Beecham as Ariadne in Strauss's first version of the opera. Later that year she sang at Covent Garden as Aida, Tosca and Lisa in quick succession, and during the early 1950s she was engaged at the Colón, Buenos Aires, the Metropolitan and San Francisco as well as in major European centres. A dark-toned and deeply musical dramatic soprano, she has recorded a notable Donna Anna under Moralt (1955) with Jurinac and London. From 1967 she taught at the Vienna Academy. NOËL GOODWIN

Zádor, Desző (*b* Horna Krupa, 8 March 1873; *d* Berlin, 24 April 1931). Hungarian baritone. He studied in Budapest with Adele Passy-Cornet and made his début at Czernowitz (now Chernovtsy) in 1898, as Count Almaviva in *Figaro*. He sang at Elberfeld, Prague and the Komische Oper, Berlin, until 1911, appearing at Dresden from 1911 to 1916. Between 1906 and 1910 he was heard at Covent Garden as Alberich in the *Ring* cycles conducted by Richter, and as the Father in *Hänsel und Gretel*. He conducted as well as sang at the Budapest National Opera (1916–19) and appeared in North America with the German Opera Company (1922–4). Further engagements took him to Paris, Milan, Vienna and the Wagner festival at Zoppot (now Sopot). In 1908 he recorded Valentin's music in *Faust*. DAVID CUMMINGS

Zador, Eugene [Zádor, Jenő] (*b* Bátaszék, 5 Nov 1894; *d* Hollywood, CA, 4 April 1977). American composer of Hungarian birth. He studied with Richard Heuberger at the Vienna Conservatory (1911), with Max Reger in Leipzig (1912–14) and with Fritz Volbach at Münster University (1920–21). From 1921 he taught at the New Vienna Conservatory, and in 1934 became an honorary teacher at the Budapest Academy of Music. He left Hungary in 1939 and finally settled in Hollywood. Besides orchestrating film scores, Zador composed orchestral pieces and 11 stage works. Stylistically he did not move beyond the innovations of Strauss and Reger; his own view was that he occupied a position midway between Verdi's *La traviata* and Berg's *Lulu*, which can be seen even in his earlier works. His operas show a flair for characterization, with atmospheric music skilfully orchestrated. *Forever Rembrandt* refers to the many copies of Rembrandt self-portraits; *The Scarlet Mill* is an amusing parable about a machine invented by a professor in hell to corrupt a virtuous young man. In this work Zador made extensive use of Hungarian idioms and colours, incorporating Hungarian folk instruments into the score.

Diana (1, J. Mohácsi), Budapest, 22 Dec 1923
A holtak szigete [The Isle of Death] (1, K. G. Zwerenz, after A. Böcklin), Budapest, 29 March 1928
Der Revisor [The Inspector General], 1928 (3, Zador, after N. V. Gogol), Los Angeles, El Camino College, 11 June 1971
X-mal Rembrandt [Forever Rembrandt] (1, K. Pálffy-Waniek), Gera, 24 May 1930, vs (Vienna, 1930)
Dornröschens Erwachen (2, Pálffy-Waniek), Saarbrücken, 18 April 1931
Asra (3, E. Szép), Budapest, 15 Feb 1936
Christoph Columbus (op-oratorio, 1, Mohácsi), New York, 8 Oct 1939; rev. Los Angeles, 12 Oct 1971
The Virgin and the Fawn (1, L. Zilahy), Los Angeles, 24 Oct 1964
The Magic Chair (1, G. Jellinek, after F. Karinthy), Baton Rouge, LA, 14 May 1966
Vörös malom [The Scarlet Mill] (2, Jellinek, after F. Molnár), New York, Brooklyn College, 26 Oct 1968
Yehu, a Christmas Legend (A. Együd, after the Bible), Los Angeles, Bureau of Music, 21 Dec 1974

*

EwenD
R. H. Kornick: *Recent American Opera: a Production Guide* (New York, 1991), 338–40 JÁNOS DEMÉNY

Zafred, Mario (*b* Trieste, 2 March 1922; *d* Rome, 22 May 1987). Italian composer. A pupil of Malipiero in Venice, he graduated in composition at the Rome Conservatory in 1944 and then studied with Pizzetti. He was music critic of *L'Unità* (1949–56). In 1966 he became artistic director of the Teatro Verdi, Trieste, later filling the same post at the Rome Opera (1968–74). Zafred's musical language, while eschewing neo-classicism, remains accessible. He rejects elaboration so contrapuntal as to be atonal, and pursues the ideal of a conservative plot, formal clarity and organically coherent structure, exhibiting what D'Amico has called 'absolute thematicism'. His stage works reveal a musico-dramatic style influenced by Pizzetti.

Amleto (3, L. and M. Zafred, after W. Shakespeare), Rome, 1961
Wallenstein (L. and M. Zafred, after F. von Schiller), Rome, 1965
Kean, Catania, 1981

*

G. Viozzi: 'Mario Zafred', *Il diapason* (1951)
F. D'Amico: 'Un premio a Zafred', *I casi della musica* (Milan, 1962), 122–5
J. S. Weissmann: 'Zafred e il problema dell'accessibilità', *Musica d'oggi*, new ser., vi (1963), 6–17 RAFFAELE POZZI

Zagreb (Ger. Agram). Capital of Croatia. Liturgical dramas and Jesuit plays with music were the precursors of later operatic activity. The first opera staged in Zagreb, Paisiello's *I filosofi immaginari*, was given in 1799 by Barbara Krapf's company from Graz. Subsequently operas were performed in the palace of Count Amadéus de Várkony by touring Italian and German companies. In the 19th century the city gained in economic and political importance and became the principal cultural centre of Croatia. Sources for the years 1827–33 mention works by Mozart, Cherubini, Boieldieu, Hérold, Bellini, Donizetti, Auber, Weber and Rossini. The city owes its first theatre, built in 1834 in Markus Square in the Upper Town, to the merchant Kristofor Stanković. The first Croatian opera, Lisinski's *Ljubav i zloba* ('Love and Malice'), was given in 1846; it was the climax of the national 'Illyrian' movement (1835–48). Until 1860, however, performances were sporadic and given by Italian troupes.

From 1860 Zagreb was the home of the Hrvatsko Narodno Kazalište (Croatian National Theatre), which at first concentrated on spoken drama. Performances of operetta began in 1863, and a permanent opera company was founded in 1870. Its early history was tied to the work of Ivan Zajc, who served as director and conductor of the opera and head of the music school at the Glazbeni Zavod (Institute of Music). Between 1870 and 1889 he directed some 50 operas and 10 operettas, including important works of the international and particularly the Italian repertory, staging some not long after their world premières. Although operatic activities were interrupted in 1889–94 and in 1902–9, operas were still performed from time to time. In 1895 the company moved to the new building of the National Theatre, designed in the neo-Baroque style by Hermann Helmer and Ferdinand Fellner. Drama and ballet as well as opera are still performed there, from October to June.

Since 1909 the Zagreb Opera has become increasingly international in its standards; Richard Strauss conducted the Croatian première of *Der Rosenkavalier* there in 1916. The most important period in the history of the company is that between the two world wars, when many works by Slavonic composers enriched its repertory, and guest performances in Yugoslavia and abroad were arranged with artists of international standing. In later years, particularly since the founding of the Zagreb Biennale of Contemporary Music in 1961, many 20th-century operas have been given at the Zagreb Opera. Operetta is performed at the National Theatre as well as at the Komedija Theatre.

*

Sto godina opera 1870/71 do 1970/71 [100 Years of Opera] (Zagreb, 1971) [pubn of the Hrvatsko Narodno Kazalište]
J. Andreis: *Music in Croatia* (Zagreb, 1974)
Hrvatsko narodno kazalište u Zagrebu 1860–1985 [The Croatian National Theatre at Zagreb] (Zagreb, 1985) KORALJKA KOS

Zagrosek, Lothar (*b* Waging, 13 Nov 1942). German conductor. He was a member of the Regensburg Boys' Choir, and studied conducting in Munich and Essen and with Swarowsky in Vienna, as well as with Kertész, Karajan and Maderna. He won international prizes in Rome and Milan and worked at opera houses in Salzburg, Kiel and Darmstadt, 1967–73. After working as chief conductor of the Austrian RSO, 1982–5, he was music director at the Paris Opéra, 1986–8, where he conducted the première of Höller's *Der Meister und Margarita* (1989), in which his expert direction of a complex score was much admired. He is also noted for Berg's *Wozzeck* and *Lulu*, and his close connection with contemporary works (including Zimmermann's *Die Soldaten*) extends to the Ensemble InterContemporain in Paris and the London Sinfonietta. His British opera début was with the Glyndebourne Touring Opera's *Le nozze di Figaro* (1984). He conducted *Così fan tutte* at Glyndebourne in 1987 and Sellars's *Die Zauberflöte* there in 1990, following the ENO production of that work in 1989. He was chief guest conductor of the BBC SO from 1988, and in 1990 became general music director for Leipzig City Opera. He made the first recording of Kienzl's *Der Evangelimann* (1982) and of von Einem's *Dantons Tod* (1985) in a performance from the 1983 Salzburg Festival. NOËL GOODWIN

Zahortsev, Volodymyr Mykolayovych (*b* Kiev, 27 Oct 1944). Ukrainian composer. He studied composition with Borys Lyatoshyns'ky and Andry Shtoharenko at the Tchaikovsky Conservatory in Kiev, graduating in 1968. He is the youngest member of a group of composers, most of them pupils of Lyatoshyns'ky, which in the early 1960s became known as the 'Kiev avant garde'. Part of a movement which began in the Soviet Union about 1959, this group, very much a product of the post-Stalinist thaw, represented a radical departure from tradition and had affinities with composers such as Boulez, Stockhausen, Cage and Penderecki. Zahortsev's music resembles, in spirit, that of Lyatoshyns'ky in its commitment to the exploration of structural and emotional extremes. The former is seen in his desire to organize pitch, rhythms, dynamics and timbre, the latter in his fondness for aleatory devices that create an ecstatic and transcendental effect, undermining the formalistic elements. This tension is at the root of his opera *Maty* ('Mother'; 2, V. Kuryans'ky, after K. Čapek; 1985, L'viv), a dramatic and explosive work that has something in common with the operas of Henze in its expressionistic devices and heightened emotionalism. Zahortsev explores with originality and technical skill the lyrico-dramatic aspects of his style.

*

V. Baley: 'Die Avantgarde von Kiew: ein Retrospective auf halbem Weg', *Melos/NZM*, ii (1976), 185–92 VIRKO BALEY

Zaide [*Das Serail*]. Singspiel in two acts, K344/336*b*, by WOLFGANG AMADEUS MOZART to a libretto by Johann Andreas Schachtner after Franz Josef Sebastiani's *Das Serail*; Frankfurt, 27 January 1866.

Mozart wrote *Zaide* in Salzburg between autumn 1779 and mid-1780, perhaps for J. H. Böhm's touring company or Schikaneder's, but surely with the National Singspiel in mind. In April 1781 Stephanie rejected it as too serious for Vienna. The autograph is untitled. The source, a Singspiel by Sebastiani, is called *Das Serail*; '*Zaide*' was chosen by Johann Anton André for his 1838 publication, and avoids confusion with *Die Entführung aus dem Serail*. Schachtner's libretto was evidently more than a revision, but it is lost apart from incipits in the autograph score. *Zaide* was first performed at Frankfurt (Mozart's birthday, 1866), as completed by André, who had added an overture and finale, and with new text by Friedrich Carl Gollmick. Other versions followed, in German, French and English, often with additional music from *Thamos, König in Ägypten*, K345/336*a*. There is no evidence for the missing overture being the G major Symphony K318; D is a more likely tonic for the opera, the instrumentation does not correspond, and Mozart is unlikely to have written the overture first.

Act 1 begins with the slaves (tenor solo and unison chorus) cheerfully finishing work for the day ('Brüder, lasst uns lustig sein'). Gomatz (tenor), exiled and enslaved, laments his bitter fate in what is Mozart's greatest melodrama ('Unerforschliche Fügung!'): the opening Adagio anticipates Mendelssohn, and other passages are of unusual enharmonic daring. Gomatz sleeps, watched by Zaide (soprano), the beautiful favourite of the Sultan. Her aria ('Ruhe sanft') is an image of peacefulness, a floating J. C. Bachian melody recurring after each episode. She leaves her portrait, which inspires Gomatz to defy the ragings of fate ('Rase, Schicksal'). Zaide reveals herself and they declare mutual love (duet, 'Meine Seele hüpft von Freuden') in a short and gentle Allegretto.

Allazim (bass), betraying the Sultan, helps prepare their escape. Gomatz ('Herr und Freund') is almost embarrassingly grateful; he returns during the exit-ritornello offering further thanks. Allazim bids his heart take courage ('Nur mutig, mein Herze'). They set out (trio, 'O selige Wonne', in E major): the sea is calm at sunrise, though Zaide imagines thunder; in a final Allegro they pray for future happiness.

Act 2 begins as the Sultan Soliman (tenor), assisted by the only appearance of trumpets and drums, fumes, in a melodrama: Zaide has spurned his love to fly with a Christian slave. An officer tells him that their recapture is imminent. Soliman rails against all women. In his huge aria ('Der stolze Löw' ', 246 bars) his anger twice boils over into a headlong Presto. A proud lion may be tamed, but treat him shamefully and he becomes a tyrant. There follows a comic scene for the overseer Osmin (bass) with a laughing aria ('Wer hungrig bei der Tafel sitzt').

Soliman tells the captives that he rewards service but punishes defiance ('Ich bin so bös' als gut'). Zaide acknowledges his bounty, but he did not offer freedom ('Trostlos schluchzet Philomele'); the caged nightingale sings only of her sorrow. This melting rondo fails to move him, and she turns to attack ('Tiger! wetze nur die Klauen') in a G minor aria of splendid fury. The contrasting middle section ('Ach, mein Gomatz') looks forward to release through death; but her anger extends to the last bar, with its final cry of 'Tiger!'.

Allazim (whose life is spared) lectures Soliman ('Ihr Mächtigen seht ungerührt'): the mighty should recognize slaves as brothers. In the quartet ('Freundin, stille deine Tränen') Gomatz asks Zaide to calm her tears; death will crown their love. Allazim's heart is breaking. Taking the blame (like Konstanze in *Die Entführung*), Zaide pleads for Gomatz's life; Soliman remains vindictive. This resourceful ensemble worthily anticipates the *Idomeneo* and *Entführung* quartets.

Zaide herself is Mozart's first three-dimensional character. In *Das Serail* Zaide and Gomatz are revealed as siblings, children of Renegat (Allazim); Soliman forgives them (Renegat once saved his life). Despite its origins in Voltaire, Mozart may have planned a less perfunctory denouement. With the quartet as finale the two acts are of equivalent length, and conceivably a third was intended. In *Das Serail* Soliman is a spoken role, like Selim in *Die Entführung*; here parts of his arias imply a more compassionate personality, suppressed in the quartet. Although not viable as it stands, *Zaide* marks a striking advance and at its best reaches the level of Mozart's maturity. JULIAN RUSHTON

Zaïde, reine de Grenade ('Zaide, Queen of Granada'). *Ballet-héroïque* in a prologue and three acts by JOSEPH-NICOLAS-PANCRACE ROYER to a libretto by the Abbé de La Marre; Paris, Opéra, 3 September 1739.

First performed as part of the festivities surrounding the wedding of Louis XV's daughter in 1739, *Zaïde* initially ran for 44 performances (the *divertissement*, *Momus amoureux*, was added on 27 October 1739 after the first 31 performances but later dropped; a copy of the opera in *F-Po* includes substantial autograph revisions made before the première). The work was revived for the dauphin's wedding in 1745, first at Versailles on 10 March of that year, and then at the Paris Opéra on 13 May (the prologue, with an added scene not included in later revivals, was omitted at Versailles). It remained in the Opéra repertory until 1770. La Marre's libretto, based on the same quasi-historical material from Moorish Spain as earlier works by Quinault (*La généreuse ingratitude*), Lafayette and La Chapelle, is a *ballet-héroïque* of the type in which a continuous plot links the acts, following an allegorical prologue.

The rival Moorish houses, the Zégris and the Abencerages, each furnish warrior suitors for the hand of Zaïde (soprano), who reveals in the monologue 'Témoins de mon indifférence' her secret passion for Almanzor (*haute-contre*) of the Abencerages. In a fête for the queen's birthday, the people of Granada urge her to choose a husband. Zuléma (bass), head of Zégris, reveals his jealousy of Almanzor and his desire for Zaïde's love. He reminds her how he has risked his life for her, but her indifference torments him the more. Isabelle (soprano) and Octave (*haute-contre*), Neapolitan slaves to Zaïde, express their fear of what Zuléma may do; Zaïde herself is terrified of him. As tensions mount, the queen calls for the diversion of a hunt, but in an impressive vengeance aria, 'Cruelle affreuse préférence', Zuléma reveals his decision to kill his rival. Zaïde, fearing for her own life, implores Almanzor's help. When he departs to do battle, she pleads with the 'god of faithful lovers' to protect her hero. Before long, trumpets announce Almanzor's victory, and the people rejoice. Zaïde announces her choice of her hero as king. For the final *divertissement*, Royer reserved some of his most felicitous music, notably the *air tendrement* (and the quartet 'Ah, quel bien suprême' that forms its conclusion), and the *rondeau pour les turcs*, both of which the composer transcribed in his *Pièces de clavecin* (Paris, 1746).

Tautly constructed, the well-paced narrative produced a colourful and variegated response from the composer. At dramatic moments, Royer's music in both prologue and drama is distinguished by his fondness for repeated semiquaver chords and *tirades* in the orchestra. In the celebrated hunting scene of Act 2 – 'the masterpiece of music in this genre' (*Affiches* of Lyons, 1765) – his use of horns in F antedates Rameau's by six years, while his writing for voices, often virtuoso in its demands, includes both recitative and air in the frequent monologues by the principal characters. Royer also demonstrates skilful integration of the *divertissement* into the plot; the jubilant crowd choruses were much admired by contemporaries. The première of *Zaïde* (and of Rameau's *Les fêtes d'Hébé* which immediately preceded it) was also notable for the inclusion of pantomime by the dancers Barbarina and Rinaldi – an innovation for Parisian opera. The music for some of these dances was published as *Airs italiens de la 2ème [3ème] pantomime dansée par Mr Ribaldini* [sic] *et Mlle Barbarini dans l'opéra de Zaïde* (Paris, n.d.).

LIONEL SAWKINS

Zaira. *Tragedia lirica* in two acts by VINCENZO BELLINI to a libretto by FELICE ROMANI after VOLTAIRE's tragedy *Zaïre*; Parma, Teatro Ducale, 16 May 1829.

Composed for the inauguration of the Teatro Ducale, *Zaira* represents the only lasting failure of Bellini's career. Bellini was second choice of the commissioners, who had wanted Rossini (living in Paris) to compose an opera for the occasion. Bellini refused to set *Cesare in Egitto*, a text by Luigi Torrigiani, controller of theatrical spectacles in Parma; instead he persuaded Romani to adapt Voltaire's *Zaïre*. Composer and librettist arrived in Parma on 17 March, from Milan, where they had successfully staged *La straniera* at La Scala the previous month, but did not start serious work on their opera until mid-April. There were further delays, and the Parmigiani discerned a lack of enthusiasm in Bellini, whose sights were firmly fixed on more important theatres in order to advance his career.

The first performance, attended by the Grand Duchess Marie-Louise, was not a success, despite a cast including Henriette Méric-Lalande in the title role, Luigi Lablache as the Sultan Orosmane and Teresa Cecconi as Nerestano, whose rondò was one of the few numbers to receive warm applause. Only parts of the trio 'Cari oggetti' and the Act 2 duet 'Io troverò nell'Asia' were printed. The opera was revived only once (after Bellini's death), at Florence in 1836, when Cecconi again sang Nerestano. Romani's libretto however was set by Mercadante (1831, Naples) and others.

There is a brief introduction but no overture. The action takes place in the harem at Jerusalem during the Crusades. The Christian captive Zaira (soprano) is about to marry Sultan Orosmane (bass); she is unaware that she is in fact the daughter of another captive, Lusignano (bass), a prince descended from the ancient Christian kings of Jerusalem. Opposed to the marriage are the fanatical vizier, Corasmino (tenor), and the French knight, Nerestano (contralto), Zaira's long-lost brother. Zaira herself, however, is only too happy to marry Orosmane (aria, 'Non è, non è tormento'), despite the doubts of her fellow slave, Fatima (soprano). Nerestano arrives to seek the freedom of ten French knights. Orosmane agrees to free them, except for his enemy, Lusignano, as well as Zaira herself.

In the dungeons Nerestano tells the French captives that Lusignano is not to be freed; accordingly, they all agree to stay. Zaira appears, followed by the ailing Lusignano, whose freedom she has finally won from Orosmane. Lusignano recognizes Nerestano and Zaira as his children in the trio 'Cari oggetti! in seno a voi'; however, he is aghast to find that Zaira has converted to Mohammedanism. As Zaira is summoned by Orosmane, all three express their despair, in the trio 'Non si pianga, si nasconda'. In the harem, Orosmane gives permission for Lusignano to leave with the other captives, against the advice of Corasmino. Zaira is left alone to say farewell to Nerestano, who tries to persuade his sister to reject Orosmane. Zaira's request to Orosmane to delay the wedding leads, at the end of Act 1, to his suspecting that Nerestano is her lover.

In Zaira's quarters, Orosmane threatens to reject her ('Io troverò nell'Asia'), but she reasserts her love for him and asks for one day's grace. In a remote place near the French quarters, Nerestano learns of his father's death, which he laments in a rondò, 'O Zaira! in quel momento'. Back at the harem, Corasmino tells Orosmane that a letter from Nerestano, asking Zaira to join him, has been intercepted; they agree to let Zaira receive the letter where they can watch her. Zaira is torn between love for Orosmane and Christian duty ('Che non tentai per vincere'); and when she sees her father's funeral cortège she collapses. She then meets Nerestano in the harem gardens and prepares to leave. Believing them to be lovers, Orosmane falls on Zaira and kills her. On learning that Nerestano is her brother, he stabs himself over her corpse.

Zaira represents a first step away from the melodic austerity of *La straniera* towards the characteristic *morbidezza* of Bellini's mature style (see Pastura 1959, pp.196–213). Continuing this development, Bellini thoroughly reworked ten sections of *Zaira* for *I Capuleti e i Montecchi* and two each for *Norma* and *Beatrice di Tenda*. 'Non è, non è tormento' was adapted as Romeo's lament over Giulietta's body in *I Capuleti e i*

Montecchi and the Act 1 trio became 'Se ogni speme è a noi rapita'. About half the opera was not used again.

SIMON MAGUIRE, ELIZABETH FORBES

Zaïs. *Pastorale-héroïque* in a prologue and four acts by JEAN-PHILIPPE RAMEAU to a libretto by LOUIS DE CAHUSAC; Paris, Opéra, 29 February 1748.

A vogue for the enchanted world of Middle Eastern myth had been created by such works as Duval's *Les génies* (1736) and Rebel and Francoeur's *Zélindor, roi des sylphes* (1745). Elements of 'la féerie', as it was known, may be found in many of Rameau's later operas, including *Zoroastre*, *La guirlande* and *Les Paladins*, but only *Acante et Céphise* and the present work devote themselves entirely to the genre.

Zaïs (*haute-contre*) is a 'génie de l'air', an elemental being who has fallen in love with Zélide (soprano), a shepherdess. Disguised as a shepherd, he gains Zélide's love, but is commanded by L'Amour [Cupid] (soprano) to prove her constancy. From the various trials by ordeal that she is forced to undergo, Zélide emerges undaunted. She is nevertheless upset to learn of Zaïs's noble lineage. The genie decides to sacrifice all for his love, and breaks the magic ring that is the token of his supernatural power. His temple collapses, and the lovers find themselves alone in a terrifying desert. Touched by this sacrifice, Oromasès (bass), the benevolent king of the genies, restores to Zaïs his power and grants immortality to Zélide.

For a four-act work this plot is insubstantial, yet it provided the composer with outstanding opportunities. Much of the score, in particular the superbly languorous pastoral music of Acts 1 and 5, is thoroughly diverting, while occasionally, as in Zélide's fine monologue 'Coulez mes pleurs', it proves unexpectedly moving for a work of its type. Rameau makes interesting use of thematic cross-references, a technique only hinted at in his earlier scores but more in evidence during the next decade. The prologue, which represents the formation of the universe and the awakening of the elemental spirits, is introduced by an astonishingly bold overture: its first section, depicting the distillation of the elements from primordial chaos, begins with an unaccompanied kettledrum followed by dislocated harmonic progressions that anticipate Beethoven. It proved too bold and was soon replaced. The original overture is included in Gustav Leonhardt's fine recording (Stil, 1979).

GRAHAM SADLER

Zajc, Ivan [Zaytz, Giovanni von] (*b* Rijeka, 3 Aug 1832; *d* Zagreb, 16 Dec 1914). Croatian composer and conductor. He studied at the Milan Conservatory (1850–55) with Stefano Ronchetti-Monteviti, Alberto Mazzucato and Lauro Rossi, and received first prize for his opera *La tirolese*. After working as a conductor in Rijeka (1855–62) he lived in Vienna, where he composed mainly operettas, several of which were successfully performed. In 1870 he moved to Zagreb, remaining there until his death. Zajc was director and conductor of the first permanent Croatian Opera (1870–89) and director, conductor and teacher at the music school of the Croatian Music Institute (1870–1908). His first Croatian opera, *Mislav*, had its première at the opening of the Opera in 1870. This was soon followed by *Nikola Šubić Zrinjski* (1876), still the most popular Croatian opera. His choice of repertory for the opera company was conservative and largely Italian-based.

Zajc was a prolific composer. His musical language, in the tradition of Italian Romantic opera (particularly that of early Verdi), is characterized by a genuine melodic inspiration and a sure dramatic instinct. The attractiveness of his music and his many-sided activity in Zagreb for over 40 years make him the central personality in an important period of Croatian music history, one that is known as 'Zajc's era'.

La tirolese (op lirica, 3, F. Guidi), Milan, Conservatory, 4 May 1855
Adelia, 1858 (grand op, 4), unperf.
Amelia, ossia Il bandito (tragic op, 4, after F. von Schiller), Rijeka, Comunale, 14 April 1860
Braut von Messina [Romilda di Messina; Romilda di Sicilia], before 1862 (grand op, 4), unperf.
I funerali del Carnavale (vaudeville, 1, I. Prodan), Rijeka, Comunale, 1862
La festa da ballo, 1863 (operetta), unperf.
Mannschaft an Bord (operetta, 1, J. L. Harisch), Vienna, Carl, 15 Dec 1863
Fitzliputzli, oder Die Teufelchen der Ehe (operetta, 1, K. Juin), Vienna, Carl, 5 Nov 1864
Die Lazzaroni von Neapel [Stanzel] (operetta, 1, H. Max), Vienna, Carl, 4 May 1865
Die Hexe von Boissy (komische Oper, 3, K. Costa), Vienna, Carl, 24 April 1866
Nachtschwärmer (operetta, 1, E. Nessel), Vienna, Carl, 10 Nov 1866
Zwei Paar Geschwister, 1866 (operetta, 1, I. Skuhra), unperf.
Ein Rendezvous in der Schweiz (operetta, 1, G. Neuhaus), Vienna, Carl, 3 April 1867
Das Gaugericht (operetta, 1, I. C. Folnes), Vienna, Carl, 14 Sept 1867
In der neuen Welt, 1867 (operetta, 1, Skuhra), unperf.
Eine Nacht in Kairo, 1867 (operetta, 1, C. Arnold), Zagreb, 27 April 1904, as Noć u Kairu
Des Teufels Vergnügungsfahrt, ?1867–8 (operetta, 3), lost
Nach Mekka (operetta, 1, Nessel), Vienna, Harmonie, 11 Jan 1868
Somnambule (operetta, 1, B. Young), Vienna, Harmonie, 25 Jan 1868
Meisterschuss von Pottenstein (operetta, 1, A. Langer), Vienna, Carl, 25 July 1868 [as pt 2 of play Schützen von Einst und Heute]
Meister Puff (operetta, 1, Nessel), Vienna, An der Wien, 22 May 1869
Der Raub der Sabinerinnen (operetta, 3, Young), Berlin, Friedrich-Wilhelmstadt, 6 Aug 1870
Mislav (folk op, 3, F. Marković), Zagreb, National, 2 Oct 1870
Mädchenträume, *c*1870 (Liederspiel, 1 scene, Young)
Ban Leget (folk op, 3, I. Dežman), Zagreb, National, 16 March 1872
Der gefangene Amor (operetta, 1, J. Rosen, after C. M. Wieland), Vienna, Vaudeville, 12 Sept 1874
Nikola Šubić Zrinjski (tragic op, 3, H. Badalić, after T. Körner), Zagreb, National, 4 Nov 1876
Lizinka (romantic light op, 3, J. E. Tomić, after A. S. Pushkin), Zagreb, National, 12 Nov 1878
Pan Tvardovski (grand op, 5, Tomić), Zagreb, National, 11 May 1880
Der Hofconditor, 1880 (operetta, 3, H. Bohrmann), unperf.
Zlatka (Croatian folk op, 3, A. Harambašić), Zagreb, National, 7 March 1885
Gospođe i husari [Ladies and Hussars] (comic op, 3, Tomić, after A. Fredro), Zagreb, National, 13 Oct 1886
Afrodita (mythological operetta, 3, N. Milan), Zagreb, National, 3 Jan 1888
Kraljev hir [The King's Fancy] (operetta, 1, Harambašić and S. Miletić), Zagreb, National, 13 May 1889
Armida (4, Harambašić and Miletić, after Tasso: *Gerusalemme liberata*), Zagreb, National, 21 Nov 1896
La dea della montagna, ovvero I minatori, 1899 (leggenda, 3, J. Fontana), unperf.
Primorka [Utopljenica] (glazbo-pjevana drama, 2, I. Trnski), Zagreb, 5 Oct 1901
Postolar i Vrag, [The Shoemaker and the Devil], 1901 (concert op, 2/3, after A. Šenoa)
Der Wildling [Mali divljan] (operetta, 3, R. Genée), Zagreb, National, 23 Sept 1905
John Bull (operetta, 3, E. Generini), Zagreb, 22 Sept 1906
Nihilistica [Die Nihilistin] (operetta, 3, V. Otto), Zagreb, National, 12 Dec 1906

Ženidba na prošćenju [Wedding at the Church Feast], 1907 (operetta, 1, L. Varjačić)
Seoski plemić [The Village Nobleman] (3, S. Širola), Zagreb, National, 3 Oct 1908
Krasuljica [Gänseblümchen] (musikalische Feerie, 4 scenes, epilogue, A. Kassowitz-Cvijić), Zagreb, National, 7 April 1911
Oče naš [Das Vaterunser] (1, J. Benešić, after F. Coppé), Zagreb, 16 Dec 1911
Prvi grijeh [Original Sin] (allegorical op, 3, S. S. Kranjčević), 18 Sept 1912 [orig. perf. as oratorio, 25 April 1907]

Incomplete: Maria Teresia, 1849; Die Wirthin in der Au (2), Princessin Tausendschön (3, Max), Ein Polterabend (1, Nessel), Der Flötenspieler (1), Krampusinerl (2, Young) and Die junge Garde (1), all operettas, ?1867–8; Branković [Čengić aga] (3, Gjorgjević), ?1871; Master John (3, Dežman), ?1873–4; Il bugiardo [Der Lügner] (operetta); Galileo Galilei; Još jedan harambaša; Salvatore Rosa

*

K. Kovačević: *Hrvatski kompozitori i njihova djela* [Croatian Composers and their Works] (Zagreb, 1960), 500–11
H. Pettan: 'Stogodišnjica praizvedbe prve Zajčeve hrvatske opere' [On the Centenary of Zajc's First Croatian Opera], *Sveta Cecilija*, new ser., iii (1971), 1–3
K. Kos: 'Mjesto solo-pjesme u stvaralaštvu Ivana Zajca' [The Place of Solo Song in the Work of Ivan Zajc], *Arti musices*, iii (1972), 85–97
J. Andreis: *Music in Croatia* (Zagreb, 1974)
Zbornik radova sa znanstvenog skupa održanog u povodu 150. obljetnice rođenja Ivana Zajca (1832–1914) [Proceedings of a Symposium to Mark the 150th Anniversary of Zajc's Birth], *Rad JAZU* (Zagreb, 1982)
H. Pettan: *Hrvatska opera: Ivan Zajc (Opere iz doba ravnateljstva, 1870–1889)* [Croatian Opera: Ivan Zajc (The Operas composed during his Directorship, 1870–1889)] (Zagreb, 1983)

KORALJKA KOS

Zambello, Francesca (*b* New York, 24 Aug 1956). American director. After graduating from Colgate University she studied with Ponnelle, with whom she collaborated on Rossini's *L'occasione fa il ladro* (1987, Pesaro, repeated at La Scala in 1989). From 1985 to 1990 she was co-artistic director of the Skylight Opera Theater in Milwaukee, where she directed the American première of Stephen Oliver's *Mario and the Magician* (1989). She has worked extensively in Europe and the USA on productions including *The Devil and Kate* and *Der Templer und die Jüdin* (1988 and 1989, Wexford), Cimarosa's *Gli Orazi ed i Curiazi* (1988, Rome) and *Beatrice di Tenda* (1987, La Fenice) and the American premières of operas by Cesti and Rossini. In 1990 she won international acclaim for her Seattle production of *War and Peace*, which exemplified the fluid grace and style of her work at its best; the next year she directed *Les Troyens* to open the season at Los Angeles and, with *Turandot*, became the first American to direct at the Bol'shoy Opera, Moscow. Her work, including a spectacular *Benvenuto Cellini* at Geneva in 1992, is marked by visual brilliance and fine acting. PATRICK J. SMITH

Zamboni, Gioseffo. *See* ZAMPONI, GIOSEFFO.

Zamboni, Luigi (*b* Bologna, 1767; *d* Florence, 28 Feb 1837). Italian bass-baritone. He made his début in 1791 at Bologna in Cimarosa's *Il fanatico burlato*. He sang in Naples, Venice, Parma, at La Scala and at the Teatro Argentina, Rome, where in 1816 he created Figaro in *Il barbiere di Siviglia*, a role which Rossini, whose father was a family friend, had written specially for him. For two seasons from 1829 he directed an Italian company at St Petersburg, performing 19 Rossini operas (and other works) in Italian, with recitatives intact.

ELIZABETH FORBES

Zamboni, Maria (*b* Peschiera, 25 July 1895; *d* Verona, 25 March 1976). Italian soprano. She studied at the Parma Conservatory and in Milan. Following her début in 1921 as Marguerite in *Faust* at Piacenza, she sang in many leading Italian houses, including La Scala from 1924 to 1931, missing only the 1928 season. In 1926 she sang Liù in the première of *Turandot* under Toscanini, and in 1930 created the part of Maria in Pizzetti's *Lo straniero*. She was also a favourite in South America. Her repertory included the roles of Elsa and Eva, Desdemona, and Manon in the operas of both Massenet and Puccini. The latter she recorded complete in 1930. She retired in 1936, shortly after appearing at the S Carlo, Naples, in her original role of Liù and in the title role of Mario Persico's *Morenita*. As heard on records, her vibrato is too prominent for comfort, but she sings with lively temperament and characterizes vividly. J. B. STEANE

Zámečník, Evžen (*b* Frýdek Místek, 5 Feb 1939). Czech composer. He studied in Brno, with Blažek at the conservatory, then at the Janáček Academy of Musical Arts (1963–8), in Munich with Bialas at the Hochschule (1968–70) and in Prague with Dvořáček at the Academy of Musical Arts. From 1963 to 1981 he worked as a violinist. In his operas he combines simple structures and an economical, neo-classical style with elements from Bohemian and Moravian folklore. Humour is an important element, as in the *opera buffa Fraška o kádi* ('A Farce about the Tub'), about a hen-pecked husband who finally frees himself from his lazy, arrogant wife and domineering mother-in-law. Zámečník also wrote a two-part opera serial (its parts may be performed separately), based on a popular book by O. Sekora about the lives of insects. *Ferda Mravenec* ('Ferda the Ant') and *Brouk Pytlík* ('Baggy the Beetle') concern the humorous adventures of the clever, cheerful Ferda, initially a sermonizing loser, then leader of a children's orchestra, and Baggy the Beetle, the pampered Ladybird, the boastful Bumblebee, the vengeful Meal-beetle and others. Witty musical citations as well as an underlying didacticism characterize both works.

Fraška o kádi [A Farce about the Tub] (ob, 1, Zámečník, after an anonymous French farce), Brno, 29 Jan 1968
Ferda Mravenec [Ferda the Ant] (op for children and adults, Zámečník, after O. Sekora), Brno, Janáček, 3 June 1977
Brouk Pytlík [Baggy the Beetle], 1982 (ob for children and adults, R. Žák, after Sekora), Prague, Smetana, 8 April 1988

*

E. Herrmannová: 'Ferda Mravenec v operních službách' [Ferda the Ant in Operatic Service], *Scéna*, ii/2 (1977), 4
V. Pospíšil: 'Zámečníkův Brouk Pytlík' [Zámečník's Baggy the Beetle], *HRo*, xli (1988), 318–19 HELENA HAVLÍKOVÁ

Zampa [*Zampa, ou La fiancée de marbre* ('Zampa, or The Marble Fiancée')]. *Opéra comique* in three acts by FERDINAND HÉROLD to a libretto by MÉLESVILLE [Anne-Honoré-Joseph Duveyrier]; Paris, Opéra-Comique (Salle Ventadour), 3 May 1831.

In a castle in Sicily Alphonse de Monza (tenor) and his fiancée Camille (soprano) are about to be married. As they await her father, the rich merchant Lugano, Camille sings the ballad of Alice Manfredi, who was betrayed by her lover and now adorns the castle as a statue. A stranger arrives; it is Zampa (tenor), a proscribed pirate sought by the authorities, who is, in fact, the Count de Monza, Alphonse's elder brother and the seducer of Alice. Zampa reveals his identity only to Camille; he has taken her father hostage and desires to marry her. Zampa and his pirates celebrate noisily; in jest he places a ring on the statue's finger, but then cannot remove it.

In the second act Zampa expresses his passionate love for Camille in 'Il faut céder à mes lois'. A letter arrives from the viceroy promising to pardon Zampa if he leads the fleet in battle. As Zampa and Camille enter the chapel, the pirate feels the marble hand of Alice on his shoulder. Camille, waiting in terror for Zampa to come to her, hears the voice of Alphonse from the garden singing a barcarolle. In vain she begs for pity from Zampa, then escapes as the pirate is confronted with the statue of Alice, which crushes him to death in its arms; they are engulfed as Etna erupts in flames. Alphonse, Camille and her father are reunited.

Extremely popular in France, Italy and Germany throughout the 19th century, *Zampa* offered a most effective part to the heroic tenor capable of singing the title role. At the King's Theatre, London, in 1833 it was transposed for baritone. When performed in Italian translation the opera, written with spoken dialogue, was usually provided with sung recitatives. Hérold's beautifully crafted score contains many fine ensemble numbers, such as the quartet on Zampa's first entry, 'Le voilà, que mon âme est émue', the first-act finale for the pirates as they express superstitious horror at the statue's refusal to part with Zampa's ring, the charming love duets for Alphonse and Camille and the final trio. All the music is perfectly suited to its subject, while the portions devoted to Zampa and the statue are highly dramatic as well as melodious. ELIZABETH FORBES

Zampieri, Mara (*b* Padua, 24 May 1941). Italian soprano. She studied in Padua and made her début in 1972 at Pavia as Nedda. After singing at various Italian theatres, in 1978 she appeared at La Scala in three Verdi roles: Elisabeth de Valois (*Don Carlos*), Amelia (*Ballo*) and Amalia (*I masnadieri*). Having made her British début in 1983 at Newcastle as Tosca, she sang the role at Covent Garden a year later. She has appeared in Zürich, Berlin, Hamburg, Munich, Bonn, Vienna, Frankfurt and Lisbon, where she sang Donizetti's Anne Boleyn, Mary Stuart and Elizabeth (*Roberto Devereux*). Her repertory includes Norma, Maddalena (*Andrea Chénier*), Zandonai's Francesca, Puccini's Minnie and Manon Lescaut; but Verdi's Lady Macbeth, Odabella (*Attila*), Elvira (*Ernani*), Leonora (*Il trovatore*), Aida and Amelia (*Simon Boccanegra*) are among her finest roles. She sang Katerina Izmaylova at La Scala in 1992. The dramatic intensity of her performances and the magnetism of her appearance easily compensate for an occasional lack of vocal smoothness.

ELIZABETH FORBES

Zamponi [Zamboni, Samponi], **Gioseffo** [Giuseppe] (*b* ?Rome, 1610–20; *d* Brussels, Feb 1662). Italian composer resident in the south Netherlands. He was invited to Brussels in 1648; in 1661 he was director of music to the Elector of Cologne. On 24 February 1650 his Venetian-style *Ulisse nell'isola di Circe* (*A-Wn*; copy by Wotquenne in *B-Bc*) was presented at court in honour of the marriage of Philip IV of Spain and Maria Anna of Austria. The first opera to be performed in the south Netherlands, it was staged at Brussels by G. B. Angelini with the *Ballet du monde* of Giambattista Balbi performed between the acts. Two further performances took place in 1655 during Queen Christina of Sweden's visit to Brussels.

E. vander Straeten: *La musique aux Pays-Bas avant le XIXe siècle*, i (Brussels, 1867), 216, 269ff; ii (Brussels, 1872), 143ff

R. Haas: 'Gioseppe Zamponis *Ulisse nell'isola di Circe*', *ZMw*, iii (1920–21), 385–405; v (1922–3), 63–4

H. Liebrecht: 'Les origines de l'opéra à Bruxelles', *Le flambeau* (31 Dec 1921)

C. van den Borren: *Geschiedenis van de muziek in de Nederlanden*, ii (Antwerp, 1951), 59ff MARY ARMSTRONG FERRARD

Zanardi, Carlo Antonio ['Il Carlino di Ratta'] (*b* ?Bologna, 15 Oct 1657; *d* Bologna, 22 May 1704). Italian soprano castrato. The son of a city land-surveyor, he became a member of the Bologna Accademia Filarmonica in 1681 and sang in the S Petronio choir (1682–8). His first documented operatic appearance was at Pratolino in 1684; he later claimed to have been in the service of Ferdinando de' Medici there for 19 years (he was a *virtuoso familiare*) and to have sung in the leading Venetian and Roman theatres, as well as in Livorno during 12 carnivals. He is known to have sung in Reggio Emilia and Genoa in the 1680s and at the Capranica, Rome, in 1695–6 in works by Mancia and Stradella. His nickname refers to his patron, senator Francesco Ratta.

He should not be confused with the Bolognese contralto Carlo Antonio Zanatti or Zanatta, a member of the Accademia Filarmonica and also active somewhat later at S Petronio and at the Teatro del Cocomero, Florence, nor with the soprano castrato and composer Nicolò Giovanardi (1661–1729), often known as Zanardi. CARLO VITALI

Zanardi, Nicolò ['Lo Zanardino']. *See* GIOVANARDI, NICOLÒ.

Zancanaro, Giorgio (*b* Verona, 9 May 1939). Italian baritone. He studied in Verona and after winning the 1970 Voci Verdiane competition made his début at the Teatro Nuovo, Milan, as Riccardo (*I puritani*). He appeared at Parma, Bologna, Florence and Venice, then launched an international career singing Luna at Hamburg (1977). He has sung in Vienna, Munich, Zürich, Paris, Frankfurt and Lisbon. He sang Ford at La Scala (1981), and made his Metropolitan début (1982) as Renato and his Covent Garden début (1985) as Gérard (*Andrea Chénier*). His repertory includes Enrico Ashton, Escamillo, Albert (*Werther*), Scarpia and many Verdi roles: Nabucco, Macbeth, Ezio (*Attila*), Miller, Germont and Posa. He has a powerful voice, particularly strong in the upper register, and though not a subtle singer or actor he can portray a character on stage with great conviction. ELIZABETH FORBES

Zander, Johan David (*b* Stockholm, 1753; *d* Stockholm, 21 Feb 1796). Swedish composer and conductor. The son of the violinist Johan David Zander, he joined the Stockholm *hovkapell* as a violinist in 1771, eventually achieving the rank of Konzertmeister in 1788. In 1781 he was engaged by Carl Stenborg to arrange *opéra comique* pasticcios for his private theatre, and he became musical director at Stenborg's Munkbro Theatre in 1784. During this period he also participated as conductor and soloist in the public concerts in Stockholm and taught the violin from 1786 at the Royal Opera School. Zander's musical style owes much to the influence of the German Singspiel and French *opéra comique* in its succinct melodic lines and simple harmonic structure. His orchestration, particularly in

Njugg spar och fan tar ('Thrift Saves and the Devil Takes', 1784) and the 'dramatic divertissement' *Herrgårds högtid* ('The Manor Feast', 1784), displays the colours and textures of such Viennese composers as Haydn. His popularity with Swedish audiences can be attributed to his use of familiar folktunes.

all first performed in Stockholm

Kopparslagaren [The Coppersmith] (comic op, 1, C. Envallsson), Eriksberg, 8 Dec 1781, *S-St*

Njugg spar och fan tar, eller Åldrarnes dårskap [Thrift Saves and the Devil Takes, or The Folly of Age] (comic op, 2, Envallsson), Eriksberg, 17 Feb 1784

Herrgårds högtid [The Manor Feast] (dramatic divertissement, 1, Envallsson), Eriksberg, 4 Aug 1784, *Skma*

Lisette (comic op, 3, N. B. Sparrschöld), Munkbro, 25 Jan 1789, *St*

Den tokroliga natten, eller Lyckan står de djärfve bi [The Ludicrous Night, or Fortune Stands by the Bold] (comic op, 4, Envallsson, after G. Stephanie: *Doktor und Apotheker*), Munkbro, 28 Oct 1791, *St*

Qvinnorna och förtroendet [Women and Trust] (comic op, 1, J. M. Lannerstierna, after A.-F. Quétant: *Les femmes et le secret*), Munkbro, 11 June 1792, *St*

*

F. Dahlgren: *Anteckningar om Stockholms teatrar* (Stockholm, 1866)

J. Flodmark: *Stenborgska skådebanorna* [Stenborg's Theatres] (Stockholm, 1893)

S. Lindström: '"Vermländingarne"' och det svensk-folkliga sångspelet intill 19: de seklets mitt', *STMf*, viii (1926), 94–111

BERTIL H. VAN BOER

Zandonai, Riccardo [Antonio Francesco] (*b* Sacco di Rovereto, Trentino, 28 May 1883; *d* Pesaro, 5 June 1944). Italian composer. He studied at Rovereto and under Mascagni at the Liceo Musicale, Pesaro (1898–1901). In 1907 Boito introduced him to Giulio Ricordi, who launched him as an opera composer: after the success of *Il grillo del focolare* the Ricordis regarded him as Puccini's natural successor and even sent him to Spain to 'collect material' for *Conchita*. After a troubled period during World War I, when the Austrian government condemned him for his irredentist activities, Zandonai married the singer Tarquinia Tarquini and settled in Pesaro, where he directed the Conservatory (formerly Liceo Musicale), 1940–43. Between the wars he was widely active as a conductor.

Although an uneven, often rather superficial composer, Zandonai was the most important of those Italians of his generation who, unlike Pizzetti, G. F. Malipiero and even to some extent Alfano, remained content to modify rather than reject the operatic tradition of Mascagni and Puccini. Not that he was ever a mere imitator of these older composers: even in the unpretentious, homely *Il grillo del focolare* the orchestral part is more 'symphonically' conceived than in most Mascagni, though neither here nor in his later operas could Zandonai match his teacher's melodic spontaneity. In *Conchita* the true nature of his talent was becoming clear: the piquant harmonies and colourful orchestration, with judicious borrowings from Strauss and Debussy comparable to those in *La fanciulla del West*, seemed bold to Italian audiences of the time; yet the result is an eclectic amalgam whose greatest virtue is its strong sense of atmosphere and the picturesque, with many Spanish touches. The prelude and ensuing 'Notte a Siviglia' that open Act 3 are especially effective, and there is abundant vitality in the ensemble scenes, notably the first scene of all. By comparison, the more passionate music can seem self-conscious and overemphatic, though the Carmen-like heroine is forcefully portrayed.

Similar qualities and defects recur in *Francesca da Rimini*, which has had many productions internationally and remains Zandonai's most popular work in Italy. In parts of Acts 1 and 3 (especially those dominated by female voices) his flair for the colourful and decorative is seen at its very best, clearly stimulated by the rich imagery of D'Annunzio's words. Archaic, modal outlines are backed up by 'antique' touches of instrumentation (including a lute), the results having at times an unforgettable radiance and charm, as in the beautiful ensemble sung by Francesca and offstage female chorus at her first entry, or the justly famous 'silent love duet' (again with offstage voices) which ends Act 1. But just as D'Annunzio's opulent poetry of the senses went hand in hand with something more barbarous and sinister, so Zandonai also indulged, especially in the Act 2 battle scene, in orgies of crude orchestral rhetoric. Moreover, in the more dramatic solo music, hardly less than in the comparable parts of *Conchita*, he too often seems to have been affecting more emotion than he felt.

Zandonai's postwar operas on the whole show little fundamental advance on *Francesca*, despite incidental new departures: *Giulietta e Romeo* is an especially direct, though inferior, successor to the earlier work. In *I cavalieri di Ekebù*, however, the strange libretto served both as a safeguard against the worst sort of rhetoric and as an intermittent stimulus to break new ground: the 'theatre band' music in Act 2 even introduces stark parallel minor 2nds, minor 9ths etc. comparable with those in Puccini's *Turandot*. Such harmonic explorations were not developed further in Zandonai's last operas, which show signs, rather, of a return to simplicity: *Giuliano*, with its Oedipus-like plot and its 'mystical' prologue and epilogue, adapts the manner of *Francesca* in more subdued and contemplative terms; while *La farsa amorosa* attempts, entertainingly though not altogether convincingly, to revive something of the spirit (rather than the letter) of *opera buffa*.

See also CAVALIERI DI EKEBÙ, I; CONCHITA; FRANCESCA DA RIMINI (ii); and GIULIETTA E ROMEO (iii).

La coppa del re, 1906 or earlier (1, G. Chiesa, after F. von Schiller), unperf., unpubd

L'uccellino d'oro (children's op, 3, G. Chelodi, after J. L. and W. C. Grimm), Sacco di Rovereto, spr. 1907, unpubd

Il grillo del focolare, begun 1905 (3, C. Hanau, after C. Dickens), Turin, Politeama Chiarella, 28 Nov 1908

Conchita (4, M. Vaucaire and C. Zangarini, after P. Louÿs), Milan, Dal Verme, 14 Oct 1911

Melenis, begun 1908 (3, M. Spiritini and Zangarini, after L. Bouillet), Milan, Dal Verme, 13 Nov 1912

Francesca da Rimini (4, G. D'Annunzio, cut by T. Ricordi, after Dante: *Inferno*), Turin, Regio, 19 Feb 1914

La via della finestra (3, G. Adami, after E. Scribe), Pesaro, Rossini, 27 July 1919; rev. in 2 acts, Trieste, Verdi, 18 Jan 1923

Giulietta e Romeo (3, A. Rossato and M. Bandello, after L. da Porto and N. d'Atri), Rome, Costanzi, 14 Feb 1922

I cavalieri di Ekebù (4, Rossato, after S. Lagerlöf), Milan, Scala, 7 March 1925

Giuliano (prol., 2, epilogue, Rossato, after J. da Varagine and Flaubert), Naples, S Carlo, 4 Feb 1928

Una partita (1, Rossato, after Dumas *père*), Milan, Scala, 19 Jan 1933

La farsa amorosa (3, Rossato, after P. A. de Alarcón), Rome, Opera, 22 Feb 1933

Il bacio, 1940–44 (3, Rossato and E. Mucci, after G. Keller) inc., 2 completed acts perf. RAI, 10 March 1954

*

G. Barini: '*Conchita* di Riccardo Zandonai', *Nuova antologia*, ccxlii (1912), 714–19

A. d'Angeli: '*Francesca da Rimini* di R. Zandonai', *Cronaca musicale* [Pesaro], xviii (1914), 136–55

G. Monaldi: 'La *Francesca da Rimini* di Riccardo Zandonai', *Nuova antologia*, ccliv (1914), 322–5
G. Bastianelli: 'Riccardo Zandonai', *Il convegno* [Milan], ii (1921), 522–32; repr. in *NRMI*, vi (1972), 409–18
G. Cesari: '*Giulietta e Romeo* di Arturo Rossato e Riccardo Zandonai', *RMI*, xxix (1922), 113–28
A. Della Corte: 'Giulietta e Romeo', *Arte e vita* [Turin], iii (1922), 149–56
F. B. Pratella: '*Giulietta e Romeo* di Riccardo Zandonai', *Pensiero musicale* [Bologna], ii (1922), 64–8
B. Ziliotto: *Francesca da Rimini: guida attraverso il poema e la musica* (Milan, 1923)
A. Lualdi: '*I cavalieri di Ekebù* di R. Zandonai alla Scala', *Serate musicali* (Milan, 1928), 171–9
F. M. Napolitano: 'Lettera da Napoli', *RaM*, i (1928), 192–4 [on *Giuliano*]
G. Pannain: 'Le prime esecuzioni: Zandonai: *Giuliano*', *RMI*, xxxv (1928), 161–2
G. Rossi-Doria: 'Lettera da Roma', *RaM*, vi (1933), 117–19 [on *La farsa amorosa*]
——: 'Musica: novità teatrali di Zandonai e Malipiero', *Nuova antologia*, ccclxvi (1933), 310–12 [on *La farsa amorosa*]
A. Gasco: 'Zandonai e *Giulietta e Romeo*', 'I sorrisi della *Farsa amorosa*', *Da Cimarosa a Strawinsky* (Rome, 1939), 258–67, 268–76
L. Tomelleri: 'Francesca da Rimini: D'Annunzio e Zandonai', in L. Tomelleri, I. Pizzetti and others: *Gabriele d'Annunzio e la musica* (Milan, 1939), 28–34; repr. in *RMI*, xliii (1939), 188–94
G. Cetrangolo: *Lo 'Stabat mater' di Jacopone da Todi e il prologo del 'Giuliano' di Arturo Rossato, nei riferimenti delle rispettive composizioni di G. Rossini e R. Zandonai* (Pesaro, 1941)
V. Bonajuti Tarquini: *Riccardo Zandonai nel ricordo dei suoi intimi* (Milan, 1951)
G. Barblan, R. Mariani and others: *A Riccardo Zandonai* (Trent, 1952)
T. Zandonai Tarquini: *Da 'Vita del paradiso' al n.1 (ricordi vicini e lontani)* (Rovereto, 1955)
G. Barblan: 'Riccardo Zandonai e la fede nel melodramma', *Ricordiana* [Milan], new ser., ii (1956), 422–5; Eng. trans. in *Ricordiana* [London], vii/1 (1962), 8–9, 13
D. de' Paoli: 'Gabriele d'Annunzio, la musica e i musicisti', *Nel centenario di Gabriele d'Annunzio* (Turin, 1963) [RAI pubn], 41–118, esp. 98–103 [on *Francesca da Rimini*]
R. Chiesa: 'La *Francesca da Rimini* di d'Annunzio nella musica di Riccardo Zandonai', *Quaderni dannunziani* [Brescia] (1965), nos.32–3, pp.320–54
J. C. G. Waterhouse: *The Emergence of Modern Italian Music (up to 1940)* (diss., U. of Oxford, 1968), 523–8
G. Vigolo: 'Zandonai con d'Annunzio', *Mille e una sera all'opera e al concerto* (Florence, 1971), 484–5
'Zandonai, Riccardo', *Rizzoli-Ricordi: Enciclopedia della musica* (Milan, 1972)
A. Porter: 'Musical Events: Wagnerismo', *New Yorker* (31 March 1973); repr. in *A Musical Season* (New York and London, 1974), 209–13 [on *Francesca da Rimini*]
B. Cagnoli: *Riccardo Zandonai* (Trent, 1978, 2/1983)
R. Chiesa, ed.: *Riccardo Zandonai* (Milan, 1984)
R. A. Zondergeld: 'Riccardo Zandonai: the Master of Fake Emotion', *Opera*, xxxv (1984), 1191–6 JOHN C. G. WATERHOUSE

Zandt, Marie van. *See* VAN ZANDT, MARIE.

Zanella, (Castore) Amilcare (*b* Monticelli d'Ongina, Piacenza, 26 Sept 1873; *d* Pesaro, 9 Jan 1949). Italian composer. He studied under Bottesini and others at the Parma Conservatory. In 1890 he first conducted the orchestra of the Teatro Regio di Parma. From 1893 to 1900 he was in South America, at first as substitute conductor in Marino Mancinelli's opera company, then independently as a pianist. He directed the Parma Conservatory (1903–5) and the Liceo Musicale, Pesaro (1905–40).

Some of Zanella's earlier instrumental pieces were considered adventurous in their day, especially in their rhythmic freedom: a few were deliberately freakish, with nonsense titles paralleling those of Satie. Later he became, on the whole, more staid and conformist – overproductive and often lapsing into a rather prolix academicism. Only three of his eight or nine operas ever reached the stage; and even *Aura* and *La sulamita*, though not wholly unsuccessful when new, suffer from unconvincing librettos (as, it seems, do most of the unperformed operas). The text of *La sulamita* adapts elements from the *Song of Songs* in would-be D'Annunzian terms which now seem dated, and the music lacks dramatic tension, despite a certain lyrical fluency and orchestral resourcefulness which may owe something to Zandonai. Only in *Il revisore* did Zanella create something with real theatrical vitality, showing clear signs of the bizarre sense of humour that had been evident in some of his early piano pieces. Though conservative – in some ways neo-Rossinian – in its basic idiom, and somewhat uneven in quality, the opera won success (albeit ephemerally) in Germany as well as in Italy.

Early operas, unperf., ?uncompleted: Adolfo, ?lost [existence has been doubted]; Osanna!, *c*1901–3; I due sergenti, ?lost

Aura (3, Haydée [I. Finzi]), Pesaro, Rossini, 27 Aug 1910, only lib. pubd
Aeternitas, 1913–14 (4, G. Borelli), unperf., unpubd
La sulamita (3, A. Lega, after *Song of Songs*), Piacenza, Municipale, 11 Feb 1926
Domenico Santorno, 1932 (3, G. Fara, after V. Bersazio), unperf., unpubd
Il revisore [Il trappolone], 1936–8 (3, Lega, after N. V. Gogol: *The Inspector General*), Trieste, Verdi, 20 Feb 1940
Notte d'incanti, completed 1940 [? drafted 1921 as La morte di Euridice] (1, A. Ninchi), unperf.

*

La sulamita: opera in tre atti di Amilcare Zanella (Cremona, 1927)
Amilcare Zanella: artista, uomo, educatore (Ferrara, 1932)
A. Dioli and M. F. Nobili: *La vita e l'arte di Amilcare Zanella* (Bergamo, 1941)
Cronaca musicale [Pesaro], new ser., i/1 (1963) [Zanella issue]
J. C. G. Waterhouse: *The Emergence of Modern Italian Music (up to 1940)* (diss., U. of Oxford, 1968), 620–24, esp. 623–4
F. Bussi: 'Amilcare Zanella musicista piacentino (1873–1949) emulo di Busoni e Paladino di Rossini, vent'anni dopo', *Studi storici in onore di Emilio Nasalli Rocca* (Piacenza, 1971), 83–121, esp. 105–17 JOHN C. G. WATERHOUSE

Zanelli (Morales), Renato (*b* Valparaiso, 1 April 1892; *d* Santiago, 25 March 1935). Chilean baritone, later tenor. He studied in Santiago as a baritone and made his début there in 1916 as Valentin (*Faust*). He was engaged by the Metropolitan in 1919, making his début as Amonasro. In 1923 he went to Italy and was advised to change his voice to tenor; after a year's intensive study he made his tenor début at Naples as Raoul (*Les Huguenots*), following it with Alfredo (*La traviata*) and other lyric parts. He found, however, that the timbre of his voice was better suited to heavy dramatic roles, and in 1926 he sang Otello for the first time in Turin, following it with Lohengrin. In 1928 he made his Covent Garden début as Otello, an interpretation generally considered the finest since Tamagno's. In the next few years he became the leading Wagnerian tenor in Italy and sang Tristan, Lohengrin and Siegmund. In 1930 he created the leading tenor role in Pizzetti's *Lo straniero* in Rome.

*

R. Saavedra and W. R. Moran: 'Renato Zanelli', *Record Collector*, vii (1952), 197–207 [with discography]
HAROLD ROSENTHAL/R

Zanetti, Antonio Maria (*b* Venice, 1706; *d* Venice, 1778). Italian librettist. He and his brother Girolamo (*b* *c*1710; *d* 1782) were literati with expertise in widely diverse fields; they published extensively on the history of Venetian art, and their commentaries on the history and criticism of painting, sculpture and architecture are widely recognized as both discerning and informed. Antonio served for many years until his death as the curator of the library of S Marco. The brothers collaborated on the libretto for Jommelli's early Venetian *dramma per musica Sofonisba* (1746), using a popular subject of the day. It treats the story of intrigue and conquering virtue in a traditional manner, with the normal distribution of recitatives and arias and alternation of scene types.

Antonio also wrote the text for the intermezzo *Li birbi*, first performed at S Angelo, Venice, in 1732 with music by Michele Fini, later reset by Fiorillo and carried by Nicolini's 'Piccoli Hollandesi' to Hamburg, Brunswick, Neumarkt and Prague. Girolamo has been credited with the libretto of Hasse's *Eurimedonte e Timocleone, ovvero I rivali delusi*, a puppet opera performed in the private theatre of the Abate Angelo Labia in Venice in 1746 (probably a pasticcio).

DALE E. MONSON

Zanetti, Francesco. *See* ZANNETTI, FRANCESCO.

Zangarini, Carlo (*b* Bologna, 9 Dec 1874; *d* Bologna, 19 July 1943). Italian librettist. As the son of an American mother he was indicated by Tito Ricordi as the ideal librettist for Puccini's *La fanciulla del West* (1910), on which he worked with the poet Guelfo Civinini. In 1911 he collaborated with Enrico Golisciani on Wolf-Ferrari's *I gioielli della Madonna* and with Maurice Vaucaire on Zandonai's *Conchita*. He was also the Italian translator of Debussy's *Pelléas et Mélisande*. From 1934 he held the chair of poetic and dramatic literature at the Liceo Musicale, Bologna.

JULIAN BUDDEN

Zaniboni, Antonio (*b* Bologna; *d* 6 Aug 1767). Italian librettist. A Bolognese nobleman active as poet and orator, he was a member of the Arcadian Academy, in which he used the pseudonym Esterio, and founded his own called the Accademia de' Nascosti. In addition to at least ten opera librettos for various theatres in Venice and Bologna, he wrote several oratorios and prose translations of a number of French plays, printed variously by Longhi or Pisarri in Bologna between 1712 and 1724. His broad literary background influenced his librettos. *Le gare generose* is based on Jean de Campistron's *Arminius*, and *Il vincitor di se stesso* on Racine's *Mithridate*. The preface to *Anagilda* claims that it is based on a tragedy called *Don Sancio*, which it attributes to Calderón de la Barca, but the work is more probably based on Corneille's *Don Sanche d'Aragon*. Zaniboni's librettos adhere to the elevated tone cultivated by contemporary academic librettists, such as Apostolo Zeno.

Le gare generose, Albinoni, 1712; *Il mago deluso dalla magia*, G. M. Buini, 1718 (various, 1735, as Il destino trionfante e la magia delusa); *Arsacide*, Chelleri, 1721; *Cleofile*, Buini, 1721; *Pithonessa sul Monte Olimpo*, Buini, 1722; *Amor nato tra l'ombre*, G. M. Nelvi and A. Caroli, 1723; *L'odio redivivo*, Nelvi, 1723; *L'amante ravveduto* (pastorale), F. Ciampi, 1725; *Anagilda*, A. G. Pampani, 1735; *Il vincitor di se stesso*, I. Fiorillo, 1741

*

C. Ricci: *I teatri di Bologna* (Bologna, 1888)

HARRIS S. SAUNDERS

Zannetti [Zanetti], **Francesco** (*b* Volterra, 27 March 1737; *d* Perugia, 31 Jan 1788). Italian composer. He studied composition with G. C. M. Clari in Pisa from 1750 to 1754, at the same time performing as a violinist and tenor in Lucca. In 1757 his training in opera began at the Conservatorio della Pietà dei Turchini in Naples, but he abandoned his studies after two years. His subsequent admission to the Accademia Filarmonica in Bologna (1760) indicates his preference for sacred and instrumental music over opera. From 1756 to 1762 he was *maestro di cappella* at Volterra and from 1762 to 1788 at Perugia, where he composed most of his operas; he also worked as music director at the Teatro del Pavone and the Teatro dell'Aquila and occasionally acted as impresario at the Pavone in the 1770s, for works including Sacchini's *Alessandro nell'Indie*, Anfossi's *Quinto Fabio* and *L'incognita perseguitata* and Mysliveček's *Adriano in Siria*. Generally he adopted a strict style, attentive to the innovations introduced by Gluck and completely freed from the Neapolitan school.

L'Antigono (os, P. Metastasio), Livorno, 1765

La Didone abbandonata (os, 2, Metastasio), Livorno, 1766

La contadina fortunata (farsetta, 2), Rome, Capranica, carn. 1771, *I-Rdp*

Le lavanderine (int, 2, F. Mari), Rome, Capranica, carn. 1772, *D-Dlb*, *F-Pn*; as Die Wascherinnen, Dresden, 1779, *D-B*, 3 songs (Leipzig, 1780)

Sismano nel Mogol (os, 2, G. De Gamerra), Livorno, S Sebastiano, 27 Dec 1775

Le cognate in contesa (dg, 2, E. Argolide), Venice, Giustiniani, aut. 1780, *Dlb*, *I-Fc*, *Tf* (as Le due cognate in contesa)

Artaserse (os, 2, A. Zeno and P. Pariati), Treviso, Onigo, aut. 1782

Gismondo da Mendrisio, aria *Nc*

Il figlio del Signor Padre, ?unperf.

*

G. Giustiniani: *Francesco Zannetti: musicista italiano del XVIII secolo* (diss., U. of Florence, 1972)

O. Landmann: 'Die Dresdner italienische Oper zwischen Hasse und Weber', *Studien und Materialen zur Musikgeschichte Dresden*, ii (Dresden, 1976), 44, 80

B. Brumana and M. Pascale: 'Il teatro musicale a Perugia nel settecento: una cronologia dai libretti', *Esercizi arte musica spettacolo*, vi (1983), 71–134

B. Brumana: 'Note a margine delle prime rappresentazioni perugine del *Medonte re di Epiro*', *Giuseppe Sarti musicista faentino* (Modena, 1986), 37–53

GALLIANO CILIBERTI

Zannettini [Zanettini], **Antonio.** *See* GIANNETTINI, ANTONIO.

Zannoni [Zanoni], **Angelo Maria** (*b* Venice; *fl* 1713–32). Italian bass. He was for some years in the service of the Landgrave of Hesse-Darmstadt. He sang at Ferrara in 1713 in Albinoni's *Lucio Vero*. In 1714–15 he was in London; he made his début at the King's Theatre as Argante in Handel's *Rinaldo* and appeared in the pasticcios *Lucio Vero* and *Arminio* (1715). He sang in Venice in two operas by Vivaldi and one by Chelleri in 1716, reappearing in 1719–21, 1726 and 1732 (nine operas in all). In 1718 he sang in Orlandini's *Lucio Papirio* in Bologna and Padua, and in 1723 in Florence. He may also have worked in Vienna, Germany and France.

WINTON DEAN

Zanten, Cornelie van (*b* Dordrecht, 2 Aug 1855; *d* The Hague, 10 Jan 1946). Dutch mezzo-soprano. She studied in Cologne with Carl Schneider and in Milan with Francesco Lamperti. After her début in Turin as Léonor in *La favorite* (1875), she appeared in Breslau and at Kassel during Mahler's season there (1884). She toured North America with Theodore Thomas's American Opera Company (1886–7) and during the 1890s appeared in the first Russian performances of the

Ring. Among her best roles were Fidès (*Le prophète*), Sextus (*La clemenza di Tito*), Azucena and Amneris; she was also successful in the soprano repertory. From 1914 she taught at the Hague Conservatory; Jacques Urlus was among her pupils. DAVID CUMMINGS

Zaporozhets za Dunayem ('A Cossack beyond the Danube'). 'Original little-Russian opera' (i.e. Ukrainian-style Singspiel) in three acts by SEMYON STEPANOVICH GULAK-ARTEMOVSKY to his own libretto; St Petersburg, Mariinsky Theatre, 14/26 April 1863.

The opera is set in 18th-century Turkey (on territory now belonging to Romania). The plot, a thin thread on which to string various sorts of song, dance and stage business, revolves around a chance encounter between Ivan Karas (bass), an old Dnepr cossack (*Zaporozhets*), and the Turkish Sultan (baritone) travelling incognito, resulting in permission for all the cossacks beyond the Danube (that is, on Turkish territory) to resettle on Russian land. It has been suggested that the immediate inspiration for the opera was the mass repatriation of Ukrainian cossacks (many of them runaway serfs) following the emancipation in 1861. In any case, the work is in no sense an expression of Ukrainian ('Little Russian') nationalism. The composer, though Ukrainian-born, was a thoroughly Russified inhabitant of St Petersburg, and the opera glorifies Russian patriotism and benign authority (personified by the magnanimous sultan, reminiscent of Mozart's Pasha Selim).

Gulak-Artemovsky's music resonates with 18th-century 'Turkish' effects and with the Italian opera that was his stock-in-trade as performer (for example, the Donizettian quintet in Act 3). Like any number of contemporary vaudevilles (a genre in which Gulak-Artemovsky was experienced as both singer and composer), it abounds in entertaining folklike songs and dances. The long quarrel duet for Karas and his wife Odarka (soprano) in Act 1 evidently furnished Musorgsky with a model when it came to writing his own 'Little Russian' opera, *Sorochinskaya yarmarka* ('The Fair at Sorochintsï').

A slight thing, little more than a vehicle for its composer-star (who created the leading role), *A Cossack beyond the Danube* had 14 performances in its first season, after which Gulak-Artemovsky retired from the St Petersburg stage. The next year he was engaged by the Moscow Bol'shoy Theatre for a farewell season and brought his Singspiel with him; after this it disappeared from the Imperial Theatres' repertory, but was taken up by amateur and travelling troupes. In Soviet times the work was refurbished and officially established as the cornerstone of the 'Ukrainian national school'. Its libretto was rewritten and translated into Ukrainian by Maxim Rylsky and the music reorchestrated and augmented by Vladimir Yorish. In this form the opera was given at the Bol'shoy Theatre in 1936, thereafter entering the repertory of every Soviet Ukrainian theatre. Gulak-Artemovsky was turned by historians into a Ukrainian Glinka, and the role of Ivan Karas, now an emblem of Ukrainian nationality, became a showpiece role for Ukrainian singing actors, notably Ivan Patorzhinsky, who recorded it. RICHARD TARUSKIN

Zarewitsch, Der ('The Tsarevich'). *Operette* in three acts by FRANZ LEHÁR to a libretto by HEINZ REICHERT and BÉLA JENBACH, after the play by Gabriele Zapolska; Berlin, Deutsches Künstlertheater, 16 February 1927.

Written for Richard Tauber, with Rita Georg as his partner, the work is in the more serious style of Lehár's later works, with an unhappy ending. The music is dramatic for the leading couple, offset with lighthearted dance numbers for the subsidiary couple. It is set at the end of the 19th century, and opens in St Petersburg, where the Tsarevich (tenor) is an austere, isolated and lonely young man (Volga Song: 'Allein! wieder allein!'). His antagonism towards women is so great that even his valet Iwan (*buffo*) has to conceal the existence of a wife, Mascha (soprano). The Tsarevich's lack of interest in women worries his uncle, the Grand Duke (spoken), who wishes to see him marry. To break down his reserve, a plan is hatched whereby Sonja (soprano), a dancer in a Cossack troupe, is brought to him disguised as a boy to join him in a gymnastic work-out. She agrees to the plan with some trepidation ('Einer wird kommen'). By the end of Act 1 the Tsarevich has discovered her true sex, but already she has begun to break down his isolation. By Act 2, indeed, the relationship has developed into genuine love ('Hab' nur dich allein'), much to the concern of the Grand Duke, who has a royal bride in mind. Thus, in order to dispel the Tsarevich's interest, Sonja is persuaded to tell him of a supposed string of previous lovers. However, she cannot maintain the deception, and they fall afresh into each other's arms. By Act 3 they have escaped to Naples together, where they enjoy a bliss they sense may be all too short (Napolitana: 'Warum hat jeder Frühling, ach, nur einen Mai?'). News comes of the Tsar's death, and the Tsarevich realises that he must leave the heartbroken Sonja, to do his duty in St Petersburg. ANDREW LAMB

Zariņš, Marģers [Marģeris] (*b* Jaunpiebalga, 24 May 1910). Latvian composer. He studied composition at the Latvian State Conservatory (1928–33) and was director of music at the Latvian State Art Theatre (1940–50) and Chairman of the Latvian Composers' Union (1951–2, 1956–68). Although his early output includes more than 50 incidental scores and an opera, *Kungs un spēlmanītis* ('The King and the Little Minstrel', 1939), his first success came only with the oratorio *Valmieras varoņi* ('Heroes of Valmiera', 1951). Of his five later operas, showing a veristic influence, the comical *Zaļās dzirnavas* ('The Green Mill', 1958) displays neo-classical elements; *Nabagu opera* ('Beggars' Opera', 1965), set in modern Turkey, depicts a psychological drama; and *Svētā Maurīcija brīnumdarbi* ('The Miracle of St Mauritius', 1974), based on the events of the Reformation in Riga, has a sharp satirical vein. The events of the Russian Revolution form the basis of his *Opera uz laukuma* ('Opera on the Square', 1970), intended to be performed in the open air with audience participation.

Kungs un spēlmanītis [The King and the Little Minstrel], 1939
Uz jauno krastu [Towards the New Shore] (4, after V. Lācis), Riga, 9 March 1954, vs (Leningrad, 1960; in Russ. and Latvian)
Zaļās dzirnavas [The Green Mill] (comic op, 3, after J. Janševskis), Riga, 28 June 1958, vs (Leningrad, 1961; in Russ.)
Nabagu opera [Beggars' Opera] (3, Zariņš, after Ž. Grīva), Riga, 5 Dec 1965, vs (Leningrad, 1977; in Russ.)
Opera uz laukuma [Opera on the Square] (4, J. Vanags and Zariņš, after V. Majakovskij and J. Reed), 1970
Svētā Maurīcija brīnumdarbi [The Miracle of St Mauritius] (comic op-ballet, 2, Zariņš), Riga, 28 Dec 1974, vs (Leningrad, 1979; in Russ.)

*

L. Krasinska: *Marģeris Zariņš* (Riga, 1960)

'Marģeris Zariņš', *Padomju Latvijas mūzikas darbinieki* [The Music Workers of Soviet Latvia] (Riga, 1965), 624–8
L. Viduleja: *Latviešu padomju opera* [Latvian Soviet Operas] (Riga, 1973)
V. Briede-Bulavinova: *Opernoye tvorchestvo latishskiy Kompozitorov* [Operas of Latvian Composers] (Leningrad, 1979)
T. Kuryševa: *Marger Zarin* (Moscow, 1980)

JOACHIM BRAUN, ARNOLDS KLOTIŅŠ

Zar lässt sich photographieren, Der ('The Tsar Has his Photograph Taken'). *Opera buffa* in one act, op.21, by KURT WEILL to a libretto by Georg Kaiser; Leipzig, Neues Theater, 18 February 1928.

In the Studio Angèle, Paris, the telephone rings. The Tsar (baritone) is in town and would like to have his photograph taken by the fashionable photographer Angèle (soprano). But before he arrives, terrorists burst in and take the place of the photographer and her assistants, who are gagged and bound. The 'shooting' of the Tsar turns into a pun around which the rest of the plot revolves: the camera is loaded with a pistol. The Tsar wants a picture of himself as an ordinary citizen. The terrorists want his life. To emphasize his undespotic urbanity he appears in a light suit (with the orchestra playing foxtrot rhythms). His response to the charms of his would-be assassin, the False Angèle (soprano), is also thoroughly human. Rather than be 'shot' by her, he wants to switch roles just as she is about to release the shutter. Cliff-hanging horseplay ensues, with the Tsar trying to photograph the False Angèle instead. Eventually she manages to reassume the photographer's role, but is again interrupted on the count of three. It is the Equerry (bass), who briefly appears to warn of a plot against the Tsar. Just as the False Angèle seems to be warming to the Tsar's advances, there is a further interruption and warning from the Equerry. With a view to escaping, the False Angèle places a recording of the seductive 'Tango Angèle' on the gramophone, requesting that the Tsar avert his gaze while she undresses. The kidnappers take flight just before the real Angèle and her assistants enter, followed by the police. The chorus, which has been commenting on the action all along and sharing the False Angèle's secret with the audience, announces the final event just as it had done at the beginning: 'The Tsar has his photograph taken'.

After the failure of *Royal Palace* to form a worthy companion to *DER PROTAGONIST*, Weill intended that *Der Zar lässt sich photographieren* should take its place, although the new pair was not presented as such until the production in Altenburg on 25 March 1928. At its première, *Der Zar* was given with Nicola Spinelli's *A basso porto* (first performed in 1894). Composition of the new work took from March to August 1927 (it was temporarily set aside for the Songspiel *Mahagonny* in April and May). There was also some hesitation about its title. The initial *Photographie und Liebe* was replaced by the provocatively ambiguous *Der Zar lässt sich* .... The publishers (Universal Edition), however, were perturbed. Perhaps all too readily suggesting the vulgar idiom formerly censored from school editions of Goethe's *Goetz von Berlichingen*, the ellipsis was eventually filled in. Like Weill's earlier one-act operas, *Der Zar lässt sich photographieren* feeds on the audacious mingling of antitheses: chromatic *espressivo* and jaunty jazz rhythms, the old aristocratic order and the new modern world, illusion and reality. According to Weill, it was he who thought of the 'epic' chorus and wrote its impassively commenting texts. He also composed the 'Tango Angèle', which was specially recorded for the première and subsequently included with hire materials supplied by the publishers.

STEPHEN HINTON

Zar und Zimmermann [*Czaar und Zimmermann, oder Die zwei* [*beiden*] *Peter* ('Tsar and Carpenter, or The Two Peters')]. *Komische Oper* in three acts by ALBERT LORTZING to his own libretto after Georg Christian Römer's comedy *Der Bürgermeister von Saardam, oder Die zwei Peter*, itself based on Mélesville, E. C. de Boirie and J. T. Merle's *comédie-héroïque Le bourgmestre de Sardam, ou Les deux Pierres*; Leipzig, Stadttheater, 22 December 1837.

Peter the Great *Tsar of Russia*	baritone
Peter Ivanov *a young Russian carpenter*	tenor
Marie *his niece*	soprano
General Lefort *Russian ambassador*	bass
Van Bett *burgomaster of Saardam*	bass
Widow Browe *master carpenter*	contralto
Lord Syndham *English ambassador*	bass
Marquis de Chateauneuf *French ambassador*	tenor

Inhabitants of Saardam, Dutch officers, carpenters, town officials, sailors

Setting Saardam in the Netherlands, 1698

In the wake of his first success as a theatrical composer – *Die beiden Schützen*, given in February 1837 – Lortzing worked enthusiastically to complete another comic opera. Before the end of the year he had finished and mounted *Zar und Zimmermann*, in which he himself sang the part of Peter Ivanov, gaining a measure of acclaim and confirming his position as the leading German comic-opera composer. The principal factor in Lortzing's success was his perfect matching of libretto and music; indeed, it was his carefully crafted librettos that were seen by contemporaries as his great strength. As the reviewer for the *Allgemeine musikalische Zeitung* remarked of the première:

> At a time when murder, plague, horror and misery of all kinds have to be served up to us from the stage as the piquant fare of opera lovers, often in outrageous dissonances so that we will actually feel something, a comic opera is on the one hand very welcome; on the other, though, it is difficult for it not to disappear without trace. The difficulty lies more in the text than in the music. If there were more well-made comic opera texts there would be more good comic operas.

Zar und Zimmermann was rapidly taken up by other theatres and has retained to the present day a leading place in the German repertory.

ACT 1 *A shipyard in Saardam* Tsar Peter the Great is seen disguised as a carpenter under the name Peter Michaelov to learn the art of shipbuilding. Peter Ivanov, a fellow Russian working in the shipyard who has made friends with the Tsar (unaware of his real identity), is in love with the burgomaster's niece, Marie. In the arietta 'Die Eifersucht ist eine Plage' Marie tries to quiet Ivanov's jealousy of other admirers; her charming song is punctuated by short spoken interjections from him. In the following dialogue, the Tsar is informed by Lefort that there is unrest in Moscow led by his sister. He instructs Lefort to return immediately and gives vent to his anger in the recitative and aria 'Verrathen! von euch Verrathen!', which Lortzing, to underline the Tsar's superior status, treats as an extended number including, unusually, recitative. Van Bett, the burgomaster, arrives and establishes himself as a figure of fun in the aria 'O sancta justitia, ich möchte rasen', which contains prominent solo passages for a bassoon (which has also to supply Van Bett's inaudible bottom F in a cadenza). The burgomaster has received instructions to discover the whereabouts of a foreigner called Peter who is working in the shipyard; he asks to see all Widow Browe's workers, and discovers that though many of them are called Peter, only Michaelov and Ivanov are foreigners; he settles his suspicions on Ivanov. When in the following dialogue Lord Syndham, the English ambassador, offers him £2000 to find out what Peter's plans are in respect of England, Van Bett begins to suspect that Peter must be a man of some importance, and when Ivanov reappears the burgomaster begins, to Ivanov's astonishment, to treat him with exaggerated respect: in the duet 'Darf ich wohl den Worten trauen' Van Bett goes so far as to offer Ivanov his niece's hand in marriage if he will give him information about his plans. The French ambassador, Chateauneuf, arrives on the scene, and in the finale, during preparations for the marriage feast of Widow Browe's son, he quickly decides that Peter Michaelov is the Tsar and makes contact with him.

ACT 2 *An inn* The feast is in full swing. Lefort and Chateauneuf, disguised as sailors, meet with the Tsar to make plans. To distract attention from them Chateauneuf entertains the guests with a song, 'Lebe wohl, mein flandrisch Mädchen'; there is effective participation of Marie and the chorus at the end of each verse. Syndham appears, dressed as a Dutch sailor, and approaches Van Bett to ask whether he has discovered anything. In the following sextet, 'Zum Werk das wir beginnen', Van Bett and Syndham are occupied in making approaches to Ivanov, while at another table Chateauneuf, deep in discussion with the Tsar and Lafort, is on the verge of accomplishing his diplomatic triumph. As in other ensembles Lortzing shows his skill in deriving comic effect from sharp contrast of characters and situations. The wedding feast proceeds with Marie's bridal song 'Lieblich röthen sich die Wangen', but is suddenly interrupted by the arrival of a Dutch officer and soldiers with orders to inspect the credentials of all foreigners; this leads to the unmasking, in the finale, of the three ambassadors and to Van Bett's further confusion as Syndham and Chateauneuf each identify their own Peter as the Tsar. The act ends in general tumult.

ACT 3 *The great hall of the town hall* Van Bett, who still believes Ivanov to be the real Tsar, has assembled a choir to practise a cantata in his honour. In 'Den hohen Herrscher würdig zu empfangen' Lortzing achieves a splendid union between a humorous text and lively music. Marie is unhappy with the idea that Ivanov is the Tsar, since she is convinced that marriage with him will be impossible; the real Tsar promises her that everything will be all right. Left alone, the Tsar reflects on his high position, in the simple and appealing 'Sonst spielt' ich mit Scepter, mit Krone und Stern' (which has now almost gained folksong status in Germany). In the duet 'Darf eine nied're Magd es wagen' Marie begins by treating the bewildered Ivanov as the Tsar, but they end by declaring their love for each other. After she has left, the Tsar returns, cursing the fact that the harbour has been blockaded. Ivanov, however, produces a pass, given to him by Syndham, which guarantees him safe conduct, and explains that the English ambassador has also furnished him with a yacht, sailors and money. The Tsar takes the pass and gives Ivanov a document, which he makes him promise not to open for an hour. Chateauneuf and Lefort arrive and the finale begins. The Tsar and the two ambassadors hasten to the harbour, leaving the confused Ivanov to receive the advancing deputation of honour led by Van Bett. Still believing that Ivanov is the Tsar, Van Bett again addresses him with comic deference and treats him to an extended clog dance (for which Lortzing provides a charming waltz). Cannon fire and shouting eventually interrupt the celebration; the main doors of the hall are opened, revealing the Tsar in uniform on a ship leaving harbour. Ivanov opens his document and reads that he has been made Imperial Overseer, with the Tsar's permission to marry Marie. The opera ends with a gracious farewell from the Tsar and a chorus of general rejoicing.

* * *

In several respects *Zar und Zimmermann* marks an advance on *Die beiden Schützen*. The earlier opera had to some extent lacked homogeneity; the contrast in style between the song-like numbers and comic ensembles, and the more formal arias and duets derived from German Romantic opera, had been noted by contemporary critics. In *Zar und Zimmermann*, the Tsar's aria is the only one which looks back to the other tradition, but it is justified as a piece of characterization, and in the opera as a whole Lortzing achieved a much more consistent style. CLIVE BROWN

Zarzuela (i) (Sp., from *zarza*: 'bramble bush'). A Spanish dramatic form characterized by the alternation of singing and dancing with spoken dialogue.

1. To 1800. 2. The 19th century and the *género chico*. 3. The 20th century.

1. TO 1800. The origin of the zarzuela is closely linked to the early development of opera in Spain. During the 1630s, and especially after 1640, Philip IV developed a particular taste for theatrical music, and attempts were made to perform operas at his hunting-lodge near Madrid, known as La Zarzuela (perhaps because of the brambles that surrounded it). Genuine Italian operas could not be performed because no Italian troupe would risk travelling so far for a bankrupt king in a country where the theatre was constantly threatened with extinction by the Church and where the nearest court (except for Lisbon) was more than a thousand miles away.

Some of the earliest performances at La Zarzuela mixed singing and dialogue, but others were through-composed in imitation of Italian opera. A few of these have been identified, among them *La púrpura de la rosa* and *Celos aun del aire matan*, two Calderón pieces from 1660 with music by Juan Hidalgo. However, to stage such operas was a difficult enterprise, since it meant robbing the Teatro del Buen Retiro in Madrid of almost all its singers and musicians simply for the king's pleasure. Preference was therefore given to a lighter type of musical theatre in which musical numbers alternated with spoken dialogue, and this soon came to be called a 'fiesta de La Zarzuela' and by the end of the century simply 'zarzuela'. Calderón de la Barca's *El jardín de Falerina* (1648) is usually mentioned as the first zarzuela, but the new genre did not become established until his *El golfo de las sirenas* and *El laurel de Apolo* were performed, both in 1657.

Besides Calderón, other playwrights such as Antonio de Solís (*Triunfos de Amor y Fortuna*, 1658) and Juan

Vélez de Guevara provided zarzuela texts. The music was usually by Juan Hidalgo, but much of it is lost; only his *Celos hacen estrellas*, with text by Vélez de Guevara, has been published (see Sage 1970). Calderón's main successor was Juan Bautista Diamante, and composers, besides the prolific Hidalgo, included Cristóbal Galán, a priest. Many of the few remaining early scores are anonymous. The subjects are usually mythological or pastoral. The music, a mixture of monodies, duets and homophonic choruses in four parts, imitates Italian opera, but has a perceptibly French flavour. After a while zarzuelas were given also in Madrid at the Teatro del Buen Retiro, and during the reign of Charles II (1665–1700) they became common fare at the playhouse. The Comtesse d'Aulnoy, who visited Madrid in the 1670s and published an unreliable but widely read account of her visit, mistook the zarzuelas she mentioned for operas.

Foreign companies still refrained from touring in Spain, for Charles II's finances were no better than his father's, and zarzuelas at the Buen Retiro were performed with local singers. The ablest composer in the 1690s and early 18th century was Sebastián Durón. His two-act *Salir el amor del mundo* (1696) was written to a text by José de Cañizares (1676–1750), who became the most important zarzuela librettist in the following 50 years. Durón later wrote *La guerra de los gigantes* (*c*1700–07), the first Spanish piece to be termed 'opera' in its score, though its arias are still called 'tonadas'; the word 'aria' occurs instead in his zarzuela *La nuevas armas de amor* (1711), to a libretto by Cañizares.

By this time Italian opera had finally entered Spain with the advent of the Bourbon Philip V in Madrid and the Catalan king, Charles of Austria, in Barcelona. The zarzuela speedily became thoroughly italianate, throwing off the influence of French models. Many zarzuelas were billed as 'zarzuelas a la italiana' but continued to be based on mythological subjects. Among the main composers to follow this trend were the Majorcan Antonio de Literes (whose *Acis y Galatea*, written for the Madrid court in 1708, contains more music than usual in relation to speech), José San Juan (composer of *Eurotas y Diana*, one of the most successful zarzuelas 'a la italiana' towards 1720), José Nebra and Joaquín Martínez de la Roca (the score of whose *Los desagravios de Troya* (Saragossa, 1712) was the only zarzuela printed in the 18th century).

The success of Italian opera was overwhelming; the zarzuela, however italianate in conception, soon began to lose ground and many composers abandoned it for the simpler TONADILLA. In the meantime some Italian composers, such as Antonio Duni and Francesco Corradini, tried their luck in Spain with the zarzuela. Towards the middle of the century, however, there was a locally based revival, and hopes were set on a kind of rural comedy with texts by the popular playwright Don Ramón de la Cruz, who played an important role in trying to hispanicize opera (he translated several Italian operas into Spanish) and zarzuela. Composers who worked in this genre included Antonio Rodríguez de Hita (1724–87), the Catalan Luís Misón, Pablo Esteve y Grimau (another Catalan, who wrote *Los jardineros de Aranjuez* (1768), but whose main interest was in the *tonadilla*), Ventura Galván (whose greatest success was *Las foncarraleras*, 1772), Fabian García Pacheco (*c*1725–95, a particularly italianate composer), Antonio Rosales (whose *El licenciado Farfulla*, 1776, was a great but short-lived success) and Blas de Laserna.

Among the last important zarzuelas of the 18th century were two with librettos by Luciano F. Comella: Laserna's *Los esclavos felices* (the text was later set as an opera by Arriaga) and the anonymous *La Isabella* (1794), which was still being performed 20 years after its première. Virtually the last 18th-century zarzuela to hold the stage, it was sometimes billed as an opera.

2. THE 19TH CENTURY AND THE 'GÉNERO CHICO'. In the early 1800s the zarzuela was virtually forgotten; Italian opera had taken its place. When in 1832 Ramón Carnicer, Mateo Albéniz and the proto-musicologist Baltasar Saldoni wrote a little opera in Spanish, *Los enredos de un curioso*, for the Madrid Conservatory, Saldoni insisted on calling it a zarzuela since it had spoken parts in Spanish; but the revival of the genre would have to wait until the mid-19th century. Among the first to try his hand at it was the Italian Basilio Basili, whose one-act pieces *El novio y el concierto* (1839) and *El ventorillo de Crespo* (1842) were billed as zarzuelas and show some Andalusian influence. While musical circles in Madrid were trying to create a truly 'national opera' in Spanish, other less ambitious composers revived the zarzuela tradition, especially after Rafael Hernando won great success with *Colegiales y soldados* at the Teatro del Instituto, Madrid, in 1849. This is usually considered the first modern zarzuela, but other pieces by Cristóbal Oudrid, Augustín Azcona, Mariano Soriano Fuertes, Sebastián Iradier and Hernando himself had already been performed with some success.

Hernando's *El duende* (libretto by Luis de Olona) had over a hundred performances after its première at the Teatro de Variedades, Madrid, in 1849 and encouraged other composers, including Joaquín Gaztambide, José Inzenga and Francisco Asenjo Barbieri to compose zarzuelas. These three, together with Hernando, Oudrid, Luis de Olona and the baritone Francisco L. Salas, formed in 1851 a Sociedad Artística which hired the Teatro de Circo for a season of zarzuelas. Their first production, Gaztambide's *Tribulaciones*, was unsuccessful, but the venture was saved by Barbieri's *Jugar con fuego*, which enhanced the composer's standing as leader of the group. Under Barbieri's influence the zarzuela was italianate in musical style but took the outward form of the French *opéra comique*. Many librettos follow the French genre closely, including those of Gaztambide's *El valle de Andorra* (1852, based on Halévy's opera) and *Catalina* (1854, on Meyerbeer's *L'étoile du nord*), Barbieri's *Los diamantes de la corona* (1854, on Auber's opera), Inzenga's *¡Si yo fuera rey!* (1862, on Adam's *Si j'étais roi*) and Martín Sánchez-Allú's *Fra Diavolo* (1857). Some also use plots derived from Italian opera, such as Gaztambide's *Un día de reinado* (1854, following Verdi's *Un giorno di regno*) and his *El juramento* (1858, following Mercadante's opera).

The effectiveness of these zarzuelas attracted composers who had at first snubbed them, the most remarkable being Pascual Emilio Arrieta, who had been working on Italian opera in Spanish for Queen Isabella II at her private theatre in the royal palace (closed after the public Teatro Real was opened in November 1850). With *El dominó azul* (1853, after Auber) Arrieta followed the trend of imitating French *opéra comique* and had great success with *El grumete* (1853), but it was his *Marina* (1855, libretto by Francisco Camprodón) which was to prove his masterpiece after being made into a Spanish opera in 1871 at the request of the Italian tenor Enrico Tamberlik.

The Sociedad Artística's success was so great that its members (Arrieta was admitted, while Inzenga and Oudrid left when more money was required) decided to build a new theatre, the Teatro de la Zarzuela (which still exists). It opened in October 1856 but had to face a severe crisis almost immediately and was always on the brink of bankruptcy, from which it was saved by occasional long-running works such as Gaztambide's *Los Magyares* (1857) and Barbieri's *Pan y toros* (1864).

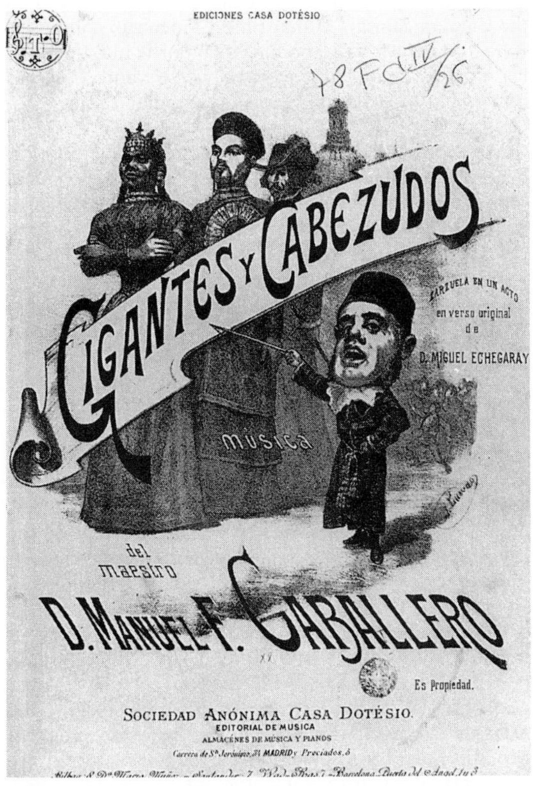

Title-page of Fernández Caballero's 'Gigantes y cabezudos' (1898)

Other composers who took up the genre were Manuel Fernández Caballero (not well known until many years later), Dionisio Scarlatti (a great-grandson of Domenico Scarlatti) and Joaquín Espín y Guillén (1812–81), whose main work was *Carlos Broschi* (1854, Seville). In Barcelona the composers in what was there a new genre included Francesc Porcell and the Minorcan Nicolau Manent, whose *La tapada del Retiro*, given in 1853 at the Gran Teatre del Liceu, was a lasting success. Josep Pujadas (with *Setze jutges*, 1858) and José Anselmo Clavé (with *L'aplec del Remei*, 1858) started a new brand of zarzuela in Catalan, while Manent, the Austrian composer Demay de Schönbrunn and Gabriel Balart (1824–93) usually composed theirs to Spanish librettos.

During the early 1860s the zarzuela attracted a large following, and troupes of singers and musicians travelled throughout the former Spanish dominions in South and Central America and Mexico. Gaztambide, Arrieta and Barbieri were the most popular composers, and Gaztambide's *Una vieja* (1860) and *La conquista de Madrid* (1863), together with Barbieri's *Pan y toros*, the main landmarks in the zarzuela's progress.

Zarzuelas in *opéra comique* style were not to everyone's taste, however, and when the impresario Francisco Arderíus had the idea of imitating Offenbach, offering *buffo* zarzuelas on non-mythological subjects (beginning with *El joven Telémaco*, with music by José Rogel, in 1866), it met with instant approval. At the Teatro de Variedades in Madrid Arderíus's troupe, the Bufos Madrileños, almost ousted the regular zarzuela company and spread the newer style to other cities (they visited Barcelona in the 1870s and 80s). One consequence was the introduction of translated French operetta; Offenbach's works at first, but then Audran's *La mascotte* and Lecocq's popular pieces (especially *La fille de Madame Angot*) began to rival the prestige of the zarzuela.

A type of shorter zarzuela, usually in one act – the so-called *género chico* – developed after the revolution of 1868. Its main characteristics were extended dialogue and a relatively small amount of music; the plots were mostly set in the working-class districts of Madrid, and composers drew on such popular music as the schottische and the mazurka, which the madrileños had come to regard as part of their folklore. Against this trend some composers, notably Fernández Caballero (who scored a political and musical success with *La Marsellesa* in 1876) and the Valencian Ruperto Chapí, maintained the standards of the traditional 'zarzuela grande', even though some of their works (such as Fernández Caballero's *El dúo de la africana* and *Gigantes y cabezudos*, set in Aragón) belong to the *género chico*. A Majorcan composer, Pere Miquel Marquès (1843–1918), wrote a few works remarkable for their robust, almost operatic orchestration, among them *El anillo de hierro* (1878), which is still fairly well known.

The *género chico*'s success, however, was unparalleled and the demand for it so great that in the 1890s no fewer than 11 theatres in Madrid were entirely given over to it and more than 1500 examples were produced. Federico Chueca, Joaquín Valverde, Manuel Nieto (1844–1915) and Tomás Bretón were among the best-received composers in the *género chico*. Some of their works have remained popular, especially Bretón's *La verbena de la paloma* (1894) and Chapí's *La revoltosa* (1897), both of which are set in a typical Madrid district. Chueca and Valverde usually worked together (Valverde for the most part scoring Chueca's musical ideas) and they wrote extremely popular works such as *La gran vía* (1886) and *El año pasado por agua* (1889). After parting with Valverde, Chueca wrote *Agua, azucarillos y aguardiente* (1897) and *El bateo* (1901), delightful sketches of lower middle-class life in old Madrid. In the same vein Tomás López Torregrosa composed *El santo de la Isidra* and *La fiesta de San Antón* (both 1898), while Jerónimo Giménez set his short and tuneful sketches *El baile de Luis Alonso* (1896) and *La boda de Luis Alonso* (1897) in a romanticized Andalusia of the 1840s. Giménez was popular because of his elegant dance music and his interest in genuine folklore and gypsy music, evident in, for example, *La tempranica* (1900).

In Barcelona the zarzuela in Catalan thrived, especially with Urbano Fando, whose *Lo somni de l'Ignoscencia* (1895) was performed more than 3000 times in its first 25 years. A more intellectual approach was taken by the *modernista* generation, with composers such as Enric Morera (1865–1942), who fought to create a renewed Teatre Líric Català excluding the Spanish zarzuela. In Valencia Salvador Giner and Vicent Díez-Peydró (1861–1938) wrote zarzuelas in their Valencian brand of the Catalan language.

3. The 20th century. The turn of the century almost coincided with a renewal in the ranks of zarzuela composers. The elder ones were almost all gone by 1910 and the *género chico* started a speedy decline, despite some late landmarks such as Chapí's *El puña de rosas* (1902). The influence of Lehár and his operettas, especially *Die lustige Witwe*, made itself felt at once, and the waltz soon replaced the schottische and the mazurka in a series of longer works which set typical operetta stories to lilting, delightful tunes. The first in this field, *El rey que rabió*, was written by Chapí as early as 1891, but the influence of the foreign operetta was mainly felt from about 1910, when Vicente Lleó scored a triumph with his suggestive and amusing *La corte de faraón*, while Pablo Luna started his career with *Molinos de viento* (1910) and confirmed it with *Los cadetes de la reina* (1913) and *El asombro de Damasco* (1916). Luna then took a somewhat different path with *El niño jurío* (1918), which started a fashion for including a patriotic song in every zarzuela.

Several younger composers excelled in this new type of operetta-zarzuela, especially Amadeo Vives, who also showed a bent towards opera with *Euda d'Uriac* (1900) and *Bohemios* (1904, based on Murger's famous novel). In *Maruxa* (1914) he made something worthwhile of an unpromising libretto set in Galicia. His remarkable operetta *La generala* (1912) retains its place in the repertory, as does *Doña Francisquita* (1923), his most popular work. José Maria Usandizaga moved further away from operetta in his *verista* zarzuela *Las golondrinas* (1914); after his death his brother transformed it into an opera.

The Valencian José Serrano was among the few composers of this period who remained faithful to some extent to the *género chico*. His keen feeling for Spanish folklore is evident in his most popular works, such as *La reina mora* (1903), *Moros y cristianos* (1905), *La alegría del batallón* (1909), *La canción del olvidó* (1916) and, in the last years of his career, *Los claveles* (1929) and *La dolorosa* (1930). Another Valencian, Manuel Penella, was most successful in his operettas, including *El gato montés* (1916). He often wrote his own librettos: *Don Gíl de Alcalà* (1932) is set in 18th-century Mexico.

Of the composers who came to the fore in the 1920s and 30s, many chose to work in the more lengthy type of zarzuela, among them Jacinto Guerrero, whose *Los gavilanes* (1923) and *La rosa del azafrán* (1930) are influenced by operatic *verismo*. At the same time, some composers were trying to update the zarzuela by including new dances or dance rhythms such as the tango and the foxtrot. Francisco Alonso was able enough to succeed with mainly short zarzuelas, most of which might be counted as *género chico*, although they lack many of the features usually associated with that genre. Among other composers of this period were Jesús Guridi, whose Basque zarzuela *El caserío* (1926) shows a keen theatrical sense and who also wrote some successful operas; the Galician composer Reveriano Soutullo, whose tuneful and attractive zarzuelas, including *La leyenda del beso* (1924), *La del soto del Parral* (1927) and *El último romántico* (1928) were written in collaboration with Joan Vert Carbonell (1890–1931); and José Padilla, whose songs include the well-known 'València' from his *La bien amada* (1925).

Madrid had been losing its hold on the zarzuela. For a number of years Barcelona became a more active centre, and some important premières took place there, including those of Rafael Millán's *La dogaresa* (1920, set in medieval Venice) and *El pájaro azul* (1921), Fernando Díaz Giles's *El cantar del arriero* (1930) and Penella's *Don Gíl de Alcalà*. The great baritone Marcos Redondo settled in Barcelona in the 1920s and the finest productions and most interesting premières were to be seen in the Catalan capital. At that time a Valencian composer, Rafael Martínez Valls, became a favourite in Barcelona; his *Cançó d'amor i de guerra* (1926) and *La legió d'honor* (1930) are still the most popular zarzuelas in Catalan.

Madrid soon had a new and remarkable composer in Federico Moreno Torroba, whose *Luisa Fernanda* (1932), set in the Madrid of the last years of Isabella II, revived interest in Madrid stories. Moreno Torroba repeated his success with *La chulapona* (1934) and wrote many other zarzuelas, several of which remain in the repertory. The Basque composer Pablo Sorozábal started his long career in the 1920s; his first great success came with *Katiuska* (1931), and just before the Spanish Civil War he scored an even bigger one in Barcelona with *La tabernera del puerto* (1936).

Zarzuela suffered severely from the restrictions of the civil war and never fully adapted itself to changing times. Some composers tried to follow new trends; in Sorozábal's *Don Manolito* (1942) a football match is described on the radio. Before the war several of the leading Spanish composers had tried their hands at writing zarzuelas, including Falla, Albéniz, Granados and Conrado del Campo, but after their deaths the prestige of the zarzuela declined, and among composers of quality only Sorozábal and Moreno Torroba still sought to keep the genre alive. With Moreno Torroba's *María Manuela* (1957) the last chapter in the history of the zarzuela seems to have been written; only Manuel Moreno-Buendía, Manuel Parada and a few others have since made the occasional attempt to compose new works of this kind.

The preservation of the repertory owes much to the conductor Ataúlfo Argenta, who in the 1950s began recording many of the finest zarzuelas. His example was followed by others, and today the music of almost a hundred zarzuelas is available on disc. Since the 1960s the Spanish government has tried to protect the zarzuela through publicity and radio broadcasts of the most important recordings, but the Teatro de la Zarzuela, refurbished and reopened in 1956, is now the only subsidized house in Spain which regularly includes zarzuelas in its repertory.

*

LaborD

A. Peña y Goñi: *La ópera española y la música dramática en España en el siglo XIX* (Madrid, 1881, 2/1967 as *España desde la ópera la zarzuela*)

F. A. Barbieri: *La zarzuela: carta a D. Pascual Millán* (Madrid, 1887)

F. Pedrell: *Teatro lirico español anterior al siglo XIX*, iv–v (La Coruña, 1897–8)

E. Cotarelo y Mori: 'Ensayo histórico sobre la zarzuela, ó sea el drama lirico español desde su origen a fines del siglo XIX', *Boletín de la Real academia española*, xix–xxiii (1932–6); pubd separately as *Historía de la zarzuela, ó sea el drama lirico* (Madrid, 1934)

G. Chase: 'Barbieri and the Spanish Zarzuela', *ML*, xx (1939), 32–9

——: 'Origins of the Lyric Theater in Spain', *MQ*, xxv (1939),

292–305
——: *The Music of Spain* (New York, 1941, 2/1959)
J. Subirá: *Historia de la música teatral en España* (Barcelona, 1945)
M. Muñoz: *Historia de la zarzuela y el género chico* (Madrid, 1946)
J. Deleito y Piñuela: *Origen y apogeo del 'género chico'* (Madrid, 1949)
R. Mindin: *Die Zarzuela* (Zürich, 1965)
J. Subirá: 'La ópera "castellana" en los siglos XVII y XVIII', *Segismundo*, i (1965), 23–42
J. Sage: 'La música de Juan Hidalgo para *Los celos hacen estrellas*', in J. Vélez de Guevara: *Los celos hacen estrellas*, ed. J. E. Varey and N. D. Shergold (London, 1970), 169–273
——: 'Nouvelles lumières sur la genèse de l'opéra et la zarzuela en Espagne', *Journées internationales d'étude du Baroque IV: Montauban 1970*, 107–14
A. Fernández Cid: *Cien años de teatro musical en España (1875–1975)* (Madrid, 1975)
A. Martín Moreno: *Salir el amor del mundo: transcripción y estudio de la zarzuela (1696) de S. Durón* (Malaga, 1979)
J. Arnau and C. M. Gómez: *Historia de la zarzuela* (Madrid, 1980–81)
R. Alier and others, eds.: *El libro de la zarzuela* (Madrid, 1982)
A. Martín Moreno: *Historia de la música española*, v: *Siglo XVIII* (Madrid, 1986)

ROGER ALIER

Zarzuela (ii). Theatre in Madrid, active chiefly in the 19th century and since 1955; it has been the only one providing opera while other houses were under renovation. *See* MADRID, §3.

Zauberflöte, Die ('The Magic Flute'). Singspiel in two acts, K620, by WOLFGANG AMADEUS MOZART to a libretto by EMANUEL SCHIKANEDER; Vienna, Theater auf der Wieden, 30 September 1791.

Sarastro *Priest of the Sun*	bass
Tamino *a Javanese Prince*	tenor
An Elderly Priest ['Sprecher'; Orator, Speaker]	bass
Three Priests	bass, tenor, spoken role
The Queen of Night	coloratura soprano
Pamina *her daughter*	soprano
Three Ladies *attendants to the Queen*	2 sopranos, mezzo-soprano
Three Boys	2 sopranos, mezzo-soprano
Papagena	soprano
Papageno *a birdcatcher, employed by the Queen*	baritone
Monostatos *a Moor, overseer at the Temple*	tenor
Two Men in Armour	tenor, bass
Three Slaves	spoken roles

Priests, Attendants, Acolytes, Slaves

Die Zauberflöte is an allegory set in no real locality or historical period. Ancient Egypt is evoked by the mysteries, but early productions also showed Islamic influence on costumes and neo-classical architecture appropriate to the Enlightenment. The exotic costumes and setting (and Tamino's nationality) are a mask; Mozart and Schikaneder intended a coded representation of Freemasonry.

Carl Ludwig Gieseke (who originally played the First Slave) said many years later that he had contributed as much as Schikaneder to the libretto, but his claims are now generally discredited. The sources of the libretto are diverse. Wieland provided the title (*Lulu, oder Die Zauberflöte* from *Dschinnistan*) and the source of Gieseke and Wranitzky's opera *Oberon* (both 1789). Egyptological sources include Gebler's *Thamos, König in Ägypten*, for which Mozart had written incidental music anticipating the style of *Die Zauberflöte*. But in the main the libretto is original and contemporary in its significance.

It has been suggested that the Queen represents Maria Theresa, Sarastro Ignaz von Born (formerly Master of the masonic lodge *Zur wahren Eintracht*) and Tamino Joseph II. Fortunately there is no reason for different significations not to coexist. The masonic allegory (evident in the Egyptian/mystic devices which illustrate the printed libretto) is transparent except for the role of Pamina (see below), and in the rapidity of Tamino's rise from initiate to ruler-designate.

Die Zauberflöte was mostly composed before *La clemenza di Tito* which, however, was performed first. Mozart entered the 'Introduction' [*sic*] in his catalogue in July, but the March of Priests and Overture are dated 28 September, two days before the première. Schikaneder had successfully presented popular 'machine-comedies' at the out-of-town Theater an der Wieden since 1789. Although it was not a fashionable venue, audiences were good and included all ranks; Salieri attended a performance and complimented Mozart warmly. Schikaneder himself played Papageno, and Mozart tested his nerve and improvisatory powers by fooling with the glockenspiel part in his Act 2 aria. Benedikt Schack (Tamino) himself played the flute in the finales. Franz Gerl (Sarastro) and Schack composed for some of Schikaneder's shows, supplying the theme of Mozart's last keyboard variations, K613. The Queen was Mozart's sister-in-law Josepha Hofer; Pamina was Anna Gottlieb (the first Barbarina, still only 17); Monostatos was Johann Joseph Nouseul. Other parts were taken by members of the company including Schikaneder's brother and the wives of Schack and Gerl.

In Vienna, there were 20 performances in the first month, and publication of extracts began in November; Schikaneder had given over 200 performances by 1800. The first Hoftheater performance was in 1801. Soon after Mozart's death *Die Zauberflöte* was given in Prague and in all other centres of German opera (including Warsaw and St Petersburg) before 1798. Goethe projected a sequel; one by Schikaneder, *Das Labyrinth*, was set by Peter Winter (1798). Translations followed apace, beginning with Dutch (1799, Amsterdam), Russian and French (1801, the latter much altered by Lachnith under the title *Les mystères d'Isis*). The first British performances were in Italian (1811), and it was frequently played as *Il flauto magico*. English versions reached London and New York in 1833. No major operatic centre was without a production in the 19th century and, while understanding of it may alter, the popularity of *Die Zauberflöte* has never waned. Among recent presentations Ingmar Bergman's sensitive film, sung in Swedish, has reached an international audience.

Overture: three chords (a masonic number: five if the short upbeats are counted) establish and question the tonic E♭, before a deliberate but mysterious progression to the dominant. The Allegro is monothematic, its principal idea (taken from a piano sonata by Clementi) presented in fugue and (in the dominant) as a counterpoint to smoother wind phrases. The B♭ cadence is marked by three times three tutti chords, the 'dreimalige Akkord'. The development is a tour de force and the recapitulation miraculously transforms elements by new dynamics and counterpoint.

ACT 1 *Rocky country, with trees and mountains; in the foreground a temple* Tamino is pursued by a monstrous serpent, his terror evoked by *Sturm und*

Drang gestures (Introduction, 'Zu hilfe! sonst bin ich verloren': C minor, rapid scales, opposing dynamics). The Three Ladies kill the monster and triumph in the first of many delectable multi-sectioned ensembles. In C major (no change of tempo) they take stock of the unconscious Prince and quarrel over which will guard him while the others tell the Queen. Spitefully (a skipping 6/8) they all decide to go, and make a lingering farewell.

Papageno punctuates a folk-like song about his métier with high-pitched piping ('Der Vogelfänger bin ich ja', in three strophes). In the first extended dialogue Tamino asks who he is. His answer hints at one of the work's themes: 'a man, like you'. He lives by eating and drinking; he catches birds for the starry Queen. Papageno happily accepts responsibility for killing the serpent, whereupon the Ladies bring water and a stone instead of wine and bread, and padlock his mouth. They give Tamino Pamina's portrait. He contemplates its beauty and falls in love; can he be destined for her (aria, 'Dies Bildnis ist bezaubernd schön')? The tender appoggiaturas and pulsations bespeak his wonder and his racing heart. He learns that Pamina has been kidnapped by the tyrant Sarastro. The mountains are sundered, revealing a sumptuous chamber; the Queen is discovered on a starry throne ('O zitt're nicht, mein lieber Sohn!'). Turbulent transformation music introduces the recitative 'Do not fear, dear son'; the aria is a melting G minor Larghetto, the first music in triple time ('Zum Leiden bin ich auserkoren': her daughter's loss torments her), and a fiery Allegro ending in giddy coloratura ascending to f''' ('Du, du, du wirst sie zu befreien gehen'). It forms Tamino's commission to rescue her daughter; its passion and brilliance leave him no room to suspect ulterior motives. The finale to the first scene is a quintet ('Hm hm hm hm'), another blend of comedy and numinous beauty. Papageno can only grunt until the Ladies unlock his mouth. All sing the moral: if liars were gagged brotherly love would prevail. Tamino receives a magic flute, which protects him and can change sorrow to joy. Papageno is horrified at the thought of accompanying Tamino, in whom he has no confidence; Sarastro will surely eat them. He receives silver bells for his protection. To a final Andante of transcendent simplicity, they are told that three wise and lovely boys will guide them.

A fine Egyptian-style chamber in Sarastro's apartment Slaves discuss Pamina's escape from the lust of Monostatos; but he has caught her (trio, 'Du feines Täubchen, nur herein!'). In the brisk *buffo* style which characterizes him throughout, the Moor has the protesting maiden bound. As she faints, Papageno appears; he and Monostatos terrify each other and run away. Papageno recovers (if birds are black, why not a man?), identifies and frees Pamina, and tells her of the Prince who loves her. He, alas, has no mate. Princess and birdcatcher reflect on the mutual dependence of wife and man: united by love, they approach the divine (duet, 'Bei Männern, welche Liebe'). This duet epitomizes the opera's moral, as well as its musical directness. With the simplest accompaniment, it consists of no more than two almost identical 16-bar strophes (each lightly touching on the dominant) and a coda of the same length. The pastoral 6/8 nevertheless brings E♭, the 'Masonic' tonic, also the key of love (compare Tamino's first aria). Only Pamina's serene ornamentation differentiates the voices: it is a vision of classless, as well as domestic and sexual, harmony.

A grove, with three beautiful temples: at the back, 'Wisdom'; on the right, 'Reason'; on the left, 'Nature' The holiness of the place is evoked by the sturdy rhythms of the trombones, silent since the overture, at the opening of the finale. The Three Boys leave Tamino, urging him to be steadfast, patient and silent – the first clear hint of masonic practice. Tamino, in a recitative, assimilates his surroundings: surely a place of virtue. His purpose is honest; let the tyrant tremble! But his approaches to Reason and Nature (to music reminiscent of the Priest's speech in *Idomeneo*) are rebuffed by unseen voices. The old Priest (Orator, sometimes rendered as 'Speaker') emerges from the temple of Wisdom and in an awe-inspiring dialogue finds Tamino's sentiments worthy but his mind clouded by prejudice; he should not trust a woman's tears. He can say nothing of Pamina 'Sobald dich führt der Freundschaft Hand / Ins Heiligtum zum ew'gen Band' ('Until sacred friendship leads you by the hand to join the eternal Order'). Tamino asks when light will come to him; the unseen chorus, while the cellos repeat the Orator's arioso cadence, replies: 'Soon, or never'. But Pamina is alive. In an outburst of gratitude he plays the magic flute: wild animals come to listen, but not Pamina. Then he hears Papageno's pipe, answers it, and runs after the sound. Pamina and Papageno are caught by Monostatos (sarcastically completing their cadence). As the slaves bring chains, Papageno sets them dancing with his bells, and they celebrate freedom with the folk-like 'Könnte jeder brave Mann' (remembered by Schubert in 'Heidenröslein'). Trumpets announce Sarastro, in a chariot drawn by lions, acclaimed in the first substantial chorus. Papageno trembles but Pamina tells the truth: her flight was not from him but from the Moor. Sarastro reassures her, but her mother's pride is beyond forgiveness, and Pamina must stay to learn the ways of virtue from men. Monostatos brings in Tamino; he and Pamina embrace, to the chorus's surprise and Monostatos's fury. Sarastro rewards the Moor with a beating (the chorus again sings his praise, but *sotto voce*) and orders the strangers to be veiled and led to the temple for purification. The act ends with a masonic chorus ('Wenn Tugend und Gerechtigkeit') which anticipates the end of *Fidelio*: virtue and justice will make a paradise on earth.

ACT 2 *A palm grove, with 18 seats: on each, a pyramid and a horn* The priests enter bearing palm-fronds, to strains of a solemn march, coloured by flutes, basset horns and trombones. Punctuated by the 'dreimalige Akkord', Sarastro tells the Priests that Tamino awaits their consent to undergo the ordeals. Pamina is his destined bride and their union a defence against the malice of Night. The Orator inquires whether Tamino will endure the trial: he is, after all, a prince. More, replies Sarastro: he is a man. The scene closes with a noble invocation by Sarastro of the Egyptian gods ('O Isis und Osiris, schenket der Weisheit Geist').

A small forecourt, in darkness: thunder The Orator tells Tamino he can still withdraw, but he is determined to seek the light. Papageno, terrified of the dark, is told he will find no wife without undergoing the trials ('I'll stay single'). But he agrees to try when he learns that Papagena is his reward. The piquant contrast of Tamino's quest through obedience to priestly instruction, and the popular-theatre gags of Schikaneder as Papageno, continues throughout the trials. They are warned by the two priests to mistrust women's arts, and

'Die Zauberflöte' (Mozart): scene from Act 2, one of a series of engravings by J. and P. Schaffer from the Brno monthly magazine 'Allgemeines Europäisches Journal' (1795). The designer has closely followed the stage directions: 'the scene changes to two great mountains; in one of them is a waterfall from which the sounds of roaring water can be heard; the other spits out fire; in front of the mountains is a grille through which the fire and water can be seen; where the fire is burning the backcloth must be bright red, and where the water is a black mist lies; the sets are rocks, each closed off by an iron door'.

meet them with silence ('Bewahret euch vor Weibertücken'). The Three Ladies ask why they are in this place of death; they are lost if they disobey the Queen, who is already within the sacred precinct (quintet, 'Wie? wie? wie? Ihr an diesem Schreckensort?'). Papageno believes everything, but Tamino silences him. The Ladies try a softer approach, but admit defeat and vanish (thunder and offstage chorus), leaving Papageno fainting to a minor-mode cadence. After the threefold chords they are led to new trials.

A garden The Moor prepares to rape the sleeping Pamina (aria, 'Alles fühlt der Liebe Freuden'). Mozart asked the orchestra to sound remote; the piccolo and lightning tempo suggest Turkish music. Why cannot a black slave share the delights of love? but the moon can close its eyes. The Queen exposes her true motivation. She wants the power conferred by the sevenfold circle of the Sun, which her dying husband confided to the initiates. Tamino and Pamina will both be cursed unless hell's fury is assuaged by Sarastro's blood (aria, 'Der Hölle Rache'). Surpassing her Act 1 aria in brilliance (though not in difficulty), this Allegro reaches *f'''* four times, and adds a flood of triplet figuration; yet in addition to agility it demands the passion of a Donna Anna, with similar chromatic harmony in a vengeful D minor. Monostatos has overheard, and offers Pamina death or submission; but Sarastro intervenes. Pamina begs mercy for her mother who, he says, is punished by her own actions. His aria ('In diesen heil'gen Hallen') expresses his humanistic creed; the two verses, in E major, have the purity of folksong, the authority of wisdom. In these sacred halls, they govern not by vengeance but by love, which alone can overcome tyranny.

A large hall The candidates are left alone, bound to silence. Papageno grumbles; his desire for a drink is answered by a very old lady bringing water. She is 18 (not 80) and her boyfriend is ... Papageno! A thunderclap covers the sound of her own name. The Three Boys bring real refreshments ('Seid uns zum zweiten Mal willkommen'). Their exquisite E major trio is a warning of imminent crisis. Tamino plays the flute, leaving Papageno to eat. Pamina enters joyfully; Tamino turns away. Her hurt is palpable in Mozart's most haunting G minor aria ('Ach, ich fühl's'), its ornate melody arched over the simplest accompaniment so that every note bears its weight of pathos. The threefold chord summons them; Papageno remains behind to continue eating. Lions surround him; Tamino's flute calms them.

The vault of a pyramid. Two priests carry an illuminated pyramid; others hold pyramidal lamps The happy outcome of Tamino's trials is anticipated in radiant D major chorus ('O Isis und Osiris, welche Wonne!'). Sarastro brings Pamina to him; they must say a last farewell before the greater trials (trio, 'Soll ich dich, Teurer, nicht mehr sehn?'). Sarastro is reassuring; Tamino expresses confidence, but Pamina is full of fears, for him rather than herself. Papageno comes running but the Orator tells him he will never reach enlightenment; he would settle for a drink, and is given wine. Ringing the bells (their part more elaborate with each of the three verses), he sings his second Volkslied: all he wants is a little wife ('Ein Mädchen oder Weibchen'). She dances in, still looking 80, but when he promises to be true she is revealed as the lovely Papagena and whisked away.

A small garden The finale is preceded by an introduction for *Harmonie*. The Three Boys evoke sunrise, which banishes darkness and death; without change of tempo, the homophonic trio develops into a dramatic quartet. The boys watch the grief-stricken Pamina greet her mother's dagger as bridegroom. At the last moment they intervene (Allegro, 3/4), restoring E♭, and with affectionate assurances lead her to Tamino.

Rocky landscape with two mountains, one gushing forth water, the other fire After a solemn introduction two Men in Armour sing a penitential chorale melody ('Ach Gott, vom Himmel sieh' darein') over nervous counterpoint, but the text foretells the triumph of the brave. Tamino, in ritual garb (shoeless), declares himself ready. Pamina calls; they respond with rapture; even death cannot separate them now. The tonality having settled into A♭, F major has the luminosity of a much sharper key, and it brings Pamina ('Tamino mein! o welch'ein Glück') with the rising major 6th which seems especially significant in Mozart (as at the Count's plea for forgiveness in *Figaro*). She takes Tamino's hand: he must play the flute, which her father carved in a magic hour of violent storm, deep in an ancient wood. The disarmingly simple C major of the slow march for flute, brass, and timpani forms a complement to what should be magnificent scenic effects. Tamino plays them through fire and water; the chorus acclaims their triumph.

The small garden Papageno blows his pipe but cannot bring back Papagena. His agitated rondo in G major with minor-key episodes seizes the attention despite the preceding sublimity. He is about to hang himself when the boys remind him of the bells; the magic brings Papagena in feathered youthfulness, and their duet (stammering over) is an excited hymn to domesticity and children. Monostatos leads the Queen and Ladies beneath the temple ('Nur stille, stille', a sinister little march). The Queen, bereft of high notes, stoops to offering the defector her daughter. But the sun beams forth, Sarastro appears on high with Tamino and Pamina in priestly robes. At this transfiguration the demons are exorcised. The Armed Men's introduction recurs, radiant in the E♭ major Andante 'Heil sei euch Geweihten!': 'Hail chosen ones, who have overcome Night ... [Allegro] Steadfastness conquers and grants the crown to beauty and wisdom'.

* * *

For the allegory, the end is strikingly unorthodox. Masons left their wives at home, whereas Pamina undergoes tests of constancy (the Queen's temptation; Tamino's rejection) equal to the man's, before joining him in trials by fire and water. Like *Così*, *Die Zauberflöte* has been accused of hostility to women. This is to confuse the attitudes of characters, including the absurdly misogynist priests in their duet at the beginning of Act 2 (itself a stage in Tamino's trials rather than dogma), with the meaning of the drama. If the Queen is the source of evil, Pamina is the strongest force for good and a necessary complement to Tamino: their union is divinely ordained. However alien to Freemasonry, the implication that women should become initiates is the opera's title to true Enlightenment.

There is no evidence to support the often-reiterated claim that the authors changed the plot, and that the Queen was originally good and Sarastro evil. If even Mozart's music cannot unequivocally distinguish hypocrisy from sincerity it is a condition (not a deficiency) of the art. That the flute and bells come from the Queen is a problem more apparent than real. By tradition such objects are neutral, or can only help the righteous; but the Queen believes in the justice of her cause. She takes a greater risk in offering the guidance of the wise Boys, but it is the Orator who begins the process of enlightenment. Monostatos, the untrustworthy servant, represents ordinary nature going bad; as cowardly as Papageno, the other representative of Everyman, he chooses evil and seeks power (over Pamina, by misused sexuality and by joining the Queen). He is punished, whereas Papageno, falling short of enlightenment, is good-hearted and achieves domestic contentment.

Die Zauberflöte possesses attributes of pantomime, but is not ramshackle. It unfolds in many short scenes, a Shakespearian dramaturgy which effectively contrasts the grave with the comical, the austerely hieratic with the earthily improvisational. The only possible weakness is Tamino's second rejection of Pamina. This scene may be an addition to the original plan, and was perhaps misplaced from earlier in Act 2; even disguised as a formal farewell ('Soll ich dich, Teurer') it appears redundant, coming between 'Ach, ich fühl's' and Pamina's attempted suicide.

The full dialogue should be retained; even the slaves' scene adds to our understanding, and the priestly debates are indispensable (Mozart snubbed a booby who seemed to find them funny). The musical numbers function by contrast, employing an unprecedented stylistic range. Yet interconnections exist (such as the echo of the Queen's 'O zitt're nicht' in Tamino's 'O ew'ge Nacht', first finale) as does architecture through distinctive instrumentation (emblematic flute, bells, trombones) and tonality (the E♭/C axis which gives unusual prominence to C minor). Diversity and discontinuity do not deprive the score of the right to be considered as an entity, the masterpiece of Mozart's late style.

For further illustration *see* PRODUCTION, fig.12; QUAGLIO; SCHINKEL, KARL FRIEDRICH; and WEIMAR, fig.1. JULIAN RUSHTON

Zaubergeige, Die ('The Magic Violin'). Opera in three acts (six scenes) by WERNER EGK to a libretto by the composer and LUDWIG ANDERSEN after FRANZ POCCI's fairy drama of 1868; Frankfurt, Städtische Bühnen, 22 May 1935 (revised Stuttgart, Württembergische Staatstheater, 2 May 1954).

Act 1 opens in a peasant's hut. Kaspar (baritone), a farm-servant, is fed up with life. He leaves his fiancée Gretl (soprano) to seek fame and fortune in the outside world. On his journey through the forest Kaspar gives his last three coins to a Beggar (low bass), who is instantaneously transformed into Cuperus, ruler of the elemental spirits. In return for such generosity Cuperus grants Kaspar his wish to own a magic violin on the condition that he renounces love and conceals the pact from anyone else. After Cuperus disappears Kaspar has the opportunity to demonstrate the powers of his magic violin when he encounters the shady merchant Guldensack (bass) and hypnotizes him with the beauty of his playing. Two vagabonds, Fangauf (tenor) and Schnapper (bass), take advantage of the situation and rob the unconscious Guldensack of all his money. But when the merchant awakens he believes that Kaspar was the culprit.

Time passes and Kaspar pursues a successful career as the virtuoso violinist Spagatini. Meanwhile, Gretl has become servant to the beautiful noblewoman Ninabella (soprano). In Act 2 Ninabella, entranced by Spagatini's playing, dispatches both Gretl and her marshal Guldensack to the guest house with the offer of jewellery and a thousand ducats if he should perform in front of her. Guldensack, recognizing the violinist as the person he encountered in the forest, plans his revenge, while Gretl becomes distraught when Kaspar evades her advances.

In Act 3 Kaspar plays the violin for Ninabella. He is so overcome by her beauty that he kisses her passionately and thus breaks the spell of the magic violin. Guldensack appears with the guards and demands Kaspar's immediate arrest; Kaspar is then taken to the gallows and sentenced to death. The two vagabonds Fangauf and Schnapper appear with Guldensack's money bags and attest to Kaspar's innocence. After Kaspar is released, Cuperus offers him the return of the instrument on the same conditions as before. But Kaspar, reunited with Gretl, declines the offer, claiming that a faithful heart is worth more than all the valuables in the world.

Die Zaubergeige, Egk's second opera, became one of the most successful and frequently performed contemporary operas written during the Third Reich. It still features regularly in the repertory of many smaller German opera houses. Musically, it is conservative, using traditional methods and a certain would-be naivety of manner manifested through the use of Bavarian folksong, in much modified form, and simple diatonic melody (hailed as 'healthy' by some writers of the time and conforming in essence to Goebbels's prescription that National Socialism should express a 'romanticism of steel'); for Gretl and Kaspar, Egk favours dance-like treatment, for Ninabella a more sophisticated idiom and for the villains and Cuperus (in his beggar's guise) there are hints of the street ballad. ERIK LEVI

Zauberoper (Ger.: 'magic opera'). A term now applied to a category of German opera with spoken dialogue, cultivated largely at Vienna's suburban theatres from the late 1780s into the 19th century, in which magical elements and spectacular stage effects play a central role. The plots were frequently derived from or inspired by the world of the German Märchen or folktale. The genre's theatrical roots lie deep in the tradition of Viennese popular comedy stretching back to the improvisations of the famous Hanswurst J. A. Stranitzky at the beginning of the 18th century.

An early example of the enduring popular appeal in Vienna of operas mixing farce, the supernatural and spectacle was provided by Philipp Hafner's Zauberlustspiel ('magic comedy') *Megära, die förchterliche Hexe* (1764). Paul Wranitzky's *Oberon, König der Elfen* (1789) put the fully developed resources of Austro-Italian comic opera at the service of Wieland's classic tale, whose exotic setting and theme of rescue proved important for later works. The genre's most famous example, Mozart's *Die Zauberflöte* (1791), drew together both popular and literary strands, to which it added a novel musical and visual layer of hieratic solemnity much imitated in the profusion of magic operas that followed it. Another high point in the genre's history was Ferdinand Kauer's *Das Donauweibchen* (1798), which held the stage at the Leopoldstadt theatre for over 40 years. The most popular magic operas invariably occasioned sequels, both within the Viennese tradition proper and on the other German stages that eagerly adopted them.

See also MÄRCHENOPER.

*

G. Weisstein: 'Geschichte der Zauberpossen', *Goldenes Buch des Theaters* (Berlin, 1902)
O. Rommel, ed.: *Barocktradition im österreichisch-bayrischen Volkstheater*, i: *Die Maschinenkomödie* (Leipzig, 1935); ii: *Die romantisch-komischen Volksmärchen* (Leipzig, 1936)
O. Rommel: *Die Alt-Wiener Volkskomödie* (Vienna, 1952)
E. M. Batley: *A Preface to The Magic Flute* (London, 1969)
P. Branscombe: *W. A. Mozart: Die Zauberflöte* (Cambridge, 1991)
THOMAS BAUMAN

Zavertal, Ladislao (Joseph Philip Paul) [Zavrtal, Ladislav (Josef Filip Pavel)] (*b* Milan, 29 Sept 1849; *d* Cadenabbia, 29 Jan 1942). Czech-Italian conductor and composer. His father, Václav Hugo Zavrtal, followed a varied career conducting and teaching at theatres and musical institutions in Ljubljana, Prague, Budapest, Barcelona, Treviso and Modena, and his mother, Carlotta Maironi da Ponte, was an operatic soprano. For a short time he studied at the Naples Conservatory, but he acquired his main musical education from his father, with whose assistance he composed the opera *Tita* (1870, later revised). After a year as chorus master under his father in Modena, in 1871 he became music director of the Teatro Milanese, Milan, where his second opera, *I tre perucchi*, was produced (1872). In 1873 he left for Britain, where he worked for 25 years as master of the Royal Artillery Band; his one-act opera *A Lesson in Magic* was staged in 1883. In Prague Zavertal was known mainly as an operatic composer, and his most important works received their premières there: the *opera tragica Una notte a Firenze* (1880, nine performances) and the *dramma lirico Mirra*, written for the National Theatre (1886, three performances). Zavertal had a well-developed sense of drama in opera; these two works follow the vocal concept of Italian opera while at the same time exploiting the theatrical appeal of certain effects in French grand opera.

Tita (ob, 3, G. Pasetti), Treviso, Garibaldi, 29 May 1870, orchd V. H. Zavrtal; rev. 1880 as Adriana, ovvero il Burattinaro di Venezia (op comica, 3, Pasetti and A. Zanardini), vs (Griante, 1930)
I tre perucchi (commedia musicale, 5, C. Arrighi), Milan, Milanese, 1872
La sura palmira sposa (commedia musicale, 5, Arrighi), Milan, Milanese, 1872
Una notte a Firenze, 1872–3 (op tragica, 4, S. Interdonato); as Noc ve Florencii, Prague, Provisional, 20 March 1880, vs (Milan, 1886)
A Lesson in Magic, 1880 (operetta, 1, T. M. Watson), Woolwich, 27 April 1883; rev. as Love's Magic (J. R. I. Jocelyn), Woolwich, 18 Feb 1890, vs (London, n.d.)
Mirra, 1882–3 (dramma lirico, 4, Interdonato); as Myrrha, Prague, National, 7 Nov 1886, *CS-Pnm* (Cz. and It.), vs (Milan, 1882)

*

[V. J. Novotný]: 'Noc ve Florencii', *Dalibor*, ii (1880), 67–8
V. V. Zelený: 'Národní divadlo: ... Myrrha' [The National Theatre: ... *Mirra*], *Dalibor*, viii (1886), 417–18
Z. Nejedlý: *Dějiny Národního divadla*, iii: *Opera Národního divadla do roku 1900* [History of the National Theatre, iii: Opera at the National Theatre up to 1900] (Prague, 1935, 2/1949)
J. Bartoš: *Prozatímní divadlo a jeho opera* [The Provisional Theatre and its Opera] (Prague, 1938)
H. G. Farmer: *Ladislao Zavertal: his Life and Work* (London, 1949)
MARTA OTTLOVÁ, MILAN POSPÍŠIL

Zaytz, Giovanni von. *See* ZAJC, IVAN.

Zazà. *Commedia lirica* in four acts by RUGGERO LEONCAVALLO to his own libretto after the play by Pierre Berton and Charles Simon; Milan, Teatro Lirico, 10 November 1900.

The première of *Zazà* was conducted by Arturo Toscanini, with a cast including Rosina Storchio (Zazà), Edoardo Garbin (Dufresne) and Mario Sammarco (Cascart). Later the opera became a favourite with star sopranos such as Emma Carelli and Geraldine Farrar. In 1947 the conductor Renzo Bianchi made a reduced version of the score which subsequently became the standard version. More recently, however, *Zazà* has been successfully revived more or less in its entirety.

The action takes place in St Etienne and Paris during the 1890s. After a prelude based on a swirling, heavily charged 'kiss' motif, the curtain rises on the backstage of a sleazy music hall, the Alcazar de St Etienne, during an evening's performance. A stage band is intermittently heard accompanying the various turns in a diversity of styles – Hungarian, Spanish, French *café-chantant* – breaking into dissonance when a couple of clowns appear. A scherzo-like ritornello functions as background for the dialogue. The star of the show is Zazà (soprano), bitterly hated by her rival Floriana (soprano), with whom she comes to blows. Visitors to Zazà's dressing room include her partner and ex-lover Cascart (baritone), her drunken scrounger of a mother Anaide (mezzo-soprano), and the journalist Bussy (baritone), in whose friend Dufresne (tenor) Zazà is very much interested. The attraction is mutual, but Dufresne is determined to avoid an involvement ('È un riso gentil'). However, during the course of a long, apparently casual duet in waltz rhythm (culminating in the 'kiss' motif) Zazà succeeds in overcoming his resistance.

In Act 2, set in Zazà's house, Dufresne is preparing her for his forthcoming departure for America. Their dreamy duet in berceuse rhythm ('E deciso: tu parti') is punctuated by recurrences of the scherzo-like music from Act 1 as well as the 'kiss' motif. Cascart begs Zazà, in the soulful manner of Silvio (*Pagliacci*), to break off her affair with Dufresne ('Buona Zazà del mio buon tempo, ascolta'). When she refuses, Cascart drops his bombshell: he has seen Dufresne at the Variétés in Paris with a young woman. Zazà at once sets off with her maid Natalia (mezzo-soprano) to track him down.

At the beginning of Act 3, Dufresne sits alone in his Parisian house sadly musing on his imminent separation from Zazà ('Mai più, Zazà, raggiar vedrò'). In his absence Zazà arrives with Natalia, having given a false name. They are greeted by Dufresne's small daughter Totò (spoken). From the child's artless prattling (a unique instance of 'melologo' in Italian opera of the time) Zazà realizes that her lover is a happily married man. Totò plays her visitors an 'Ave Maria' by Cherubini, around which Zazà weaves descants of sad lyricism, after which she and Natalia leave.

In Act 4 Zazà returns home in deep dejection, to be confronted by Cascart ('Zazà, piccola zingara'). When Dufresne arrives Zazà confesses that she has visited his home, and claims to have told his wife about their relationship; he denounces her as a slut, but becomes duly contrite when he learns the truth. Regretfully Zazà dismisses him from her life.

The opera's musical style combines the impassioned idiom of the Giovane Scuola with elements of Parisian café music, especially in the diverse styles of the stage band, heard accompanying the various acts. Both this music and the intense motif of the prelude recur in the duet between Zazà and Dufresne in Act 2. There are also moments of period pastiche, as in Zazà's embellishment of Cherubini's 'Ave Maria' and in the scene between Anaide and Cascart. The world of *Pagliacci* is rarely far away. JULIAN BUDDEN

Zbruyeva, Yevgeniya (Ivanovna) (*b* Moscow, 24 or 26 Dec 1867/5 or 7 Jan 1868; *d* Moscow, 20 Oct 1936). Russian contralto. She was the daughter of the singer and composer Pyotr Bulakhov. She graduated from Yelisaveta Lavrovskaya's class at the Moscow Conservatory in 1893 and joined the Bol'shoy the following year. In 1905 she joined the Mariinsky Theatre in St Petersburg and taught at the conservatory (1915–17). Zbruyeva's voice was deep, rich and smooth, powerful and beautiful throughout its wide range. Her clear diction, precise intonation and keen, subtle phrasing made her a finished performer. Her great roles were Glinka's Vanya and Ratmir, and Marfa in *Khovanshchina* (which she sang at the 1911 Mariinsky première), but she was also extraordinarily successful in such character parts as Solokha (Rimsky-Korsakov's *Christmas Eve*) and the Innkeeper (*Boris*). Her memoirs are published in the collection *Muzïkal'noye nasledstvo* ('Musical Heritage', i, Moscow, 1962). I. M. YAMPOL'SKY

Zeani [Zehan], Virginia (*b* Solovastru, 21 Oct 1928). Italian soprano of Romanian birth. After studying in Bucharest and with Pertile in Milan, she made her début at Bologna in 1948 as Violetta, which she also sang at her London (Stoll Theatre, 1953), Vienna (1957), Paris (1957), Metropolitan (1966) and Bol'shoy (1969) débuts and at Covent Garden (1959). She made her Scala début in 1956 as Handel's Cleopatra opposite Nicòla Rossi-Lemeni (whom she married) as Julius Caesar. In 1957 she created Blanche in *Dialogues des Carmélites* at La Scala. She participated in important revivals of *Maria di Rohan* (1965, Naples), Rossini's *Otello* (1968, Rome) and Verdi's *Alzira* (1970, Rome). Originally a specialist in coloratura parts including Lucia, Elvira (*I puritani*) and Adèle (*Le comte Ory*), she began in 1970 to undertake more dramatic roles, notably Aida, Manon Lescaut, Tosca, Magda Sorel (*The Consul*) and Giordano's Fedora (1977–8, Barcelona). A handsome woman with a naturally beautiful voice, she performed with dramatic conviction and great intensity. After retirement from the stage she taught in the USA, at Bloomington, Indiana, and Urbana-Champaign, Illinois.

GV (G. Gualerzi; C. Williams) HAROLD ROSENTHAL/R

Zedda, Alberto (*b* Milan, 2 Jan 1928). Italian conductor and musicologist. He studied at the Milan Conservatory with Votto and Giulini and made his conducting début in 1956. He worked in the USA, 1959–61, teaching and coaching the winners in American vocal competitions. He then took charge of the Italian repertory at the Deutsche Oper, Berlin (1961–3), worked with the New York City Opera in a similar capacity from 1963 and began guest conducting more widely. In 1969 he published (in Milan) a critical edition of *Il barbiere di Siviglia*, which was taken up by several companies and recorded under Abbado (1972); Zedda used it for his Covent Garden début in 1975, and in 1989 with the Cologne Opera in the Far East.

This publication heralded much scholarly research for the Fondazione Rossini at Pesaro, of whose complete edition of Rossini Zedda is joint general editor, with Philip Gossett. Zedda conducted numerous performances in Europe and America of familiar and less familiar Rossini works such as *Adelaide di Borgogna, Ermione* and *Maometto II*; his edition of *La Cenerentola* was also recorded by Abbado (1971). Zedda's editorial attention extended to Monteverdi, whose *L'incoronazione di Poppea* he recorded in his own version; to Bellini, in a recording of *Beatrice di Tenda* (1986) and the revision of the vocal parts for *I Capuleti e i Montecchi*; and to Donizetti, for whose *L'elisir d'amore* he discovered (in Paris) and restored an aria for Adina (1987, Bergamo). In 1992 he was named artistic director of La Scala, Milan.

PIERO RATTALINO, NOËL GOODWIN

Zednik, Heinz (*b* Vienna, 21 Feb 1940). Austrian tenor. After studying in Vienna, he made his début in 1964 at Graz as Trabuco (*Forza*). Engaged at the Vienna Staatsoper since 1965, he created Kalb in von Einem's *Kabale und Liebe* (1976). He sang David, Mime and Loge at Bayreuth (1970–80) and made his Metropolitan début in 1981 as Mime and Loge. He has sung at

Frankfurt, Zürich and Salzburg, where he created the Producer in Berio's *Un re in ascolto* (1984), repeating it at La Scala (1986). He also took part in the première of Krenek's *Kehraus um St Stephan* at Vienna (1990). An excellent actor with a strong voice, he has a repertory of some 140 roles, ranging from Monostatos, Pedrillo and Jaquino to Vašek, Remendado, Valzacchi and the Captain (*Wozzeck*). ELIZABETH FORBES

Zeffirelli, Franco [Corsi, Gian Franco] (*b* Florence, 12 Feb 1923). Italian director and designer. After working for the spoken theatre and in films, he turned to opera in 1948. His early stagings in Italy were of Rossini and Donizetti operas, including *La Cenerentola* at La Scala in 1953. He gave new life to Italian Romantic opera with his production of *Lucia di Lammermoor* (with Joan Sutherland) at Covent Garden in 1959, and later that year he turned to *verismo* with *Cavalleria rusticana* and *Pagliacci*, also at Covent Garden. Both productions were still running 25 years later. In 1963 he collaborated with Karajan on an opulent, Romantic staging of *La bohème* at La Scala, which established him as one of the leading Italian opera directors of his generation. His production of *Falstaff* for the Metropolitan in 1964 was criticized as fussy and un-Shakespearean. In 1965 he worked with Maria Callas on her *Tosca* at Covent Garden and *Norma* at the Paris Opéra. In 1966 he staged the première of Samuel Barber's *Antony and Cleopatra* at the opening of the new Metropolitan Opera building. His *Otello* at La Scala in 1976 and *Carmen* at the Vienna Staatsoper in 1978, both conducted by Carlos Kleiber, were widely recognized as exemplary in their lyrico-dramatic power. His *Turandot* at La Scala in 1983 and *La traviata* in New York, Florence and Paris (1985–6) were the culmination of a growing trend in his work towards spectacular opulence, thought by many to be over-elaborate and prohibitively expensive for most opera houses. He has made films of *La traviata* (1983) and *Otello* (1986), in both of which a number of controversial cuts were made. Zeffirelli accepts all the conventions of grand opera, and matches the lyrical spirit of the music with visual beauty and a feeling for broad dramatic contours.

For illustration *see* ANTONY AND CLEOPATRA; FILM, fig.4; and PRODUCTION, fig.26. ANDREW CLARK

Zeitoper (Ger.: 'opera of the times'). Term for a type of opera current in Germany especially during the 1920s and 30s, dealing with issues 'of the times', usually socio-political ones. It is applied to such works as Krenek's *Jonny spielt auf* (1927), which deals with the claims of pleasure-seeking as opposed to intellectual pursuits, Hindemith's *Neues vom Tage* (1929), a satire on social behaviour, and Weill's *Die Bürgschaft* (1932), a wide-ranging commentary on current civilization and its values.

*

L. Knossl: 'Das dunkle Wasser: Krenek zwischen "Jonny" und Zeitfragen', *NZM*, Jg.125 (1964), 553–4

S. C. Cook: *Opera for a New Republic: the 'Zeitopern' of Krenek, Weill and Hindemith* (Ann Arbor, 1988)

Zeitz. German town, near Leipzig. The Archdukes Moritz of Sachsen-Zeitz resided there between 1663 and 1717. The first musical stage work performed at the court was *Camilla, Königin der Volsker*, by an unknown composer and librettist, on 3 February 1699. After deciding to introduce more such works Archduke Moritz Wilhelm had a special hall built in the palace, where on 28 November 1701 a musical drama (title and composer unknown) was staged in honour of the Archduchess's birthday. In subsequent years operas were put on only as part of birthday celebrations, including *Cupido und Psyche* by Johann Magnus Knüpffer in 1705 and *Lucius Verus* by J. F. Fasch in 1711. Opera did not become a regular event, however, because of its expense and the necessity of bringing in singers from outside Zeitz. In 1713 *Berenice* was given; it is uncertain whether this was also by Fasch, but in any event it was the last operatic performance at the Zeitz court, where all musical activity came to an abrupt end in 1717 when the Archduke moved to Weida.

*

A. Werner: *Städtische und fürstliche Musikpflege in Zeitz* (Bückeburg and Leipzig, 1922)

A. Schmiedecke: 'Aufführungen von Opern, Operetten, Serenaden und Kantaten am Zeitzer Herzogshof', *Mf*, xxi (1972), 168–74

Żeleński, Władysław (*b* Grodkowice, nr Kraków, 6 July 1837; *d* Kraków, 23 Jan 1921). Polish composer. He studied composition with Mirecki in Kraków, Joseph Krejčí in Prague and, from 1866 to 1871, Reber at the Paris Conservatoire. On his return to Poland he was made professor at the Warsaw Music Institute (1872–7), then director of the Warsaw Music Society. In 1881 he moved to Kraków, where six years later he was appointed director of the conservatory. In comparison with the music of his European contemporaries Żeleński's is conservative and retrospective, yet his works occupy an important position in the history of Polish music. Although he was not connected directly with the theatre, his four operas were very successful and nationally his reputation ranks second only to Moniuszko's. He is representative of a nationalist trend in Polish music, and much of his melodic and rhythmic material derives from folk music.

Żeleński's first opera, *Konrad Wallenrod* (1885, Lwów), shows the influence of French grand opera in its extended finales at the ends of acts, its ballet scenes, its use of two orchestras (one on stage) and its oratorio-like choruses, which are not bound up with the action but increase the work's monumental quality. The opera is organized into separate numbers and Żeleński uses leitmotifs for the principal characters. The later operas show a development towards a more integrated structure: there are no more set-piece finales, choruses are more closely linked to the action and the boundaries between individual numbers are blurred until they disappear altogether in his last opera, *Stara baśń* ('Old Fable'; 1907, Lwów). However, these structural innovations are not accompanied by textural ones. The use of contrapuntal techniques and of leitmotifs diminishes, and the 'monumental' style gives way to a more romantic lyricism. *Janek* (1900, Lwów), based on music from the Tatra mountains region, is Żeleński's most folkloristic opera. *Old Fable*, which dates from a period when interest in Wagner was increasing in Poland, comes closest to being a music drama. The orchestra plays an important role, and harmonies are sometimes – uncharacteristically for Żeleński – used coloristically, as in the Prelude to Act 4. In general the musical language remains traditional here, though it is more advanced than in his earlier operas.

Konrad Wallenrod (4, Z. Sarnecki and W. Noskowski, after A. Mickiewicz), Lwów, Hrabiego Fryderyka Skarbka, 26 Feb 1885 (Kraków, 1886)

Goplana, ?1891 (3, L. German, after J. Słowacki), Kraków, Miejski, 23 July 1896 (Kraków, 1899)
Janek (2, German), Lwów, Miejski, 4 Oct 1900, *PL-Kj*, vs (Kraków, 1901)
Stara baśń [Old Fable] (4, A. Bandrowski-Sas, after J. I. Kraszewski), Lwów, Miejski, 14 March 1907, *Kj*, vs (Kraków, 1910)

*

B. Liszczynski: *'Konrad Wallenrod' Władysława Żeleńskiego* (diss., Jagiellonian U., 1933)
I. Moskalik: *'Stara baśń' Władysława Żeleńskiego* (diss., Jagiellonian U., 1950)
Z. Jachimecki: *Władysław Żeleński: życie i twórczość* [Life and Work], Rocznik Krakowski, xxxii/5 (Kraków, 1952, enlarged 2/1959)
J. Gałecka: *Opera 'Janek' Władysława Żeleńskiego: środki dramaturgii operowej* [The Opera 'Janek' by W. Żeleński: the Devices of Opera Dramaturgy] (diss., Jagiellonian U., 1965)

ZOFIA CHECHLIŃSKA

Zelinka, Jan Evangelista (*b* Prague, 13 Feb 1893; *d* Prague, 30 June 1969). Czech composer. He studied music with his father, a composer, and also took advice from Ostrčil. While working as a clerk he was active as a pianist and writer. He was a prolific composer in all genres: besides 14 operas he wrote melodramas and music for pantomimes, plays, films and radio programmes. An eclectic late Romantic with inclinations to sentimentality, he made use of traditional folk elements in the 1950s. *Dceruška hostinského* ('The Innkeeper's Daughter'), based on an old Prague legend in a Romantic occult setting, uses vocal recitation and unvarying, heavy instrumentation. The lyrical musical comedy *Devátá louka* ('The Ninth Meadow') is about the first erotic experience of a naive girl; the folk opera *Paličatý švec* ('The Pigheaded Shoemaker') concerns a good-humoured craftsman who prefers his handicraft to the machine production of shoes. *Meluzína* ('The Wailing Wind') is based on a fairy-tale drawn from folk tradition.

Dceruška hostinského [The Innkeeper's Daughter], 1921 (1, K. Mašek), Prague, National, 24 Feb 1925
Červen [June], 1924 (F. Šrámek)
Kokokodák (satirical op, 3, L. Blatný)
Devátá louka [The Ninth Meadow], 1929 (3, R. Jesenská), Prague, National, 19 Sept 1931
Odchod dona Quijota, 1935 [The Departure of Don Quixote] (chamber op, 1, Zelinka)
Srdce na udici [Heart on Hooks] (opera-groteska, 9 scenes, J. Mařánek, after E. Zola), Brno, National, 28 Jan 1938
Paličatý švec [The Pigheaded Shoemaker], 1940 (2, Zelinka, after J. Kopta), Prague, National, 28 March 1944
Meluzína [The Wailing Wind] (radio op, 5, F. Kožík), Czechoslovak Radio, 31 Jan 1949; stage, Plzeň, 15 April 1950
Námluvy bez konce [Endless Wooing] (radio op, J. F. Mölzer), Czechoslovak Radio, 27 Jan 1950
Čaroděj Žito, 1950 (3, Zelinka)
Jaro u Shakespearů [Spring in Shakespeare], 1955 (musical comedy, P. Kosta)
Masopustní noc [Carnival Night], 1956 (Č. Studna, after L. Holberg: *Mascarade*)
Blouznivé jaro [Spring Fever], 1957 (folk op, 3, F. Doubrava)
Lásky žal i smích [Love's Woe and Laughter], 1958 (3, Doubrava, after C. Goldoni), Czechoslovak Radio, 2 April 1960
Škola pro ženy [School for Wives], 1959 (I. Z. Novák, after Molière)
Dřevěný kůň [The Wooden Horse], 1962–3 (after Erskine)

*

ČSHS
J. Hutter and Z. Chalabala, eds.: *České umění dramatické*, ii: *Zpěvohra* [Czech Dramatic Art: Opera] (Prague, 1941), 363–5
B. Karásek: 'Nová česká opera (K premiéře opery "Meluzína" od J. Ev. Zelinky)', *Divadlo*, i (1949–50), 487–9
F. Pala and V. Pospíšil: *Opera Národního divadla v období O. Ostrčila* [The National Theatre Opera in Ostrčil's Time] (Prague, 1965–89)

HELENA HAVLÍKOVÁ

Zell, F. [Walzel, Camillo] (*b* Magdeburg, 11 Feb 1829; *d* Vienna, 17 March 1895). Austrian librettist and theatre director. At 16 he joined his father's lithographic company in Budapest, and in 1847 he attended the Wiener Akademie der bildenden Künste. During the civil war of 1848–9 he joined a Tyrolean regiment, became an officer, and in 1851, on account of his artistic ability, was taken into the Military Geographical Institute. He then became a newspaper editor and in 1856 joined the Danube Steamship Company in Pest. As captain of the *Mathjas Király* he performed a heroic river rescue at Linz in 1868. He meanwhile indulged his interest in writing and translating, before retiring from the river in 1873. His first original theatrical work was a comedy for Carl Anton Friese (the first Frank in *Die Fledermaus*), after which he teamed up with Richard Genée for the writing of operetta librettos. From 1884 to 1889 he was artistic director of the Theater an der Wien.

Zell and Genée produced the librettos for the most successful Viennese operettas of the 1870s and 80s, including Suppé's *Fatinitza* (1876) and *Boccaccio* (1879), Johann Strauss's *Der lustige Krieg* (1881) and *Eine Nacht in Venedig* (1883), and Millöcker's *Der Bettelstudent* (1882) and *Gasparone* (1884), as well as for Genée's own operettas. Zell was responsible primarily for shaping the plots (many of which used French sources) and the dialogue, while Genée concentrated on the lyrics. Though they rarely matched the wit and structural ingenuity of Meilhac and Halévy or W. S. Gilbert, they nevertheless towered over their contemporary Viennese rivals in their ability to inspire classic Viennese operetta scores. Zell's translations of foreign operettas include works by Offenbach and Sullivan.

Operetten unless otherwise stated

Die Schwaben in Wien (Zeitbild, with ?J. Mery), A. Müller, 1863; *Die Federschlange*, C. de Barbieri, 1867; *Angot an der blauen Donau* (Parodie), K. Pleininger, 1874; *Cagliostro in Wien* (with Genée), J. Strauss, 1875; *Fatinitza* (komische Operette, with Genée), Suppé, 1876; *Der Seekadett* (komische Operette), Genée, 1876; *Die Porträt-Dame* [Die Prophezeiungen des Quiribi] (komische Operette, with Genée), M. Wolf, 1876
Nanon, die Wirtin vom goldenen Lamm, Genée, 1877; *Im Wunderland der Pyramiden* (Spl, with Genée), Genée, 1877; *Vom Touristenkränzchen* (Schwank), F. Roth, 1878; *Die letzten Mohikaner* (komische Operette, with Genée), Genée, 1878; *Die Fornarina* (with Genée and M. West), C. Zeller, 1878; *Boccaccio* (with Genée), Suppé, 1879; *Gräfin Dubarry* (komische Operette, with Genée), C. Millöcker, 1879
Nisida (komische Operette, with West), Genée, 1880; *Donna Juanita* (komische Operette, with Genée), Suppé, 1880; *Capitän Nicoll* [Die Carbonari] (komische Operette, with West), Zeller, 1880; *Apajune, der Wassermann* (with Genée), Millöcker, 1880; *Der Gascogner* (with Genée), Suppé, 1881; *Die Jungfrau von Belleville* (with Genée), Millöcker, 1881; *Der lustige Krieg* (with Genée), J. Strauss, 1881; *Der Bettelstudent* (komische Operette, with Genée), Millöcker, 1882
Königin Mariette (with Genée), I. Brüll, 1883; *Eine Nacht in Venedig* (komische Operette, with Genée), J. Strauss, 1883; *Gasparone* (with Genée), Millöcker, 1884; *Die Holländer*, J. Bayer, 1884; *Die Zwillinge* (with Genée), Genée and L. Roth, 1885; *Die Kindsfrau* (Posse), J. Stern, 1885; *Der Jagdjunker der Kaiserin* (komische Operette, with Genée), A. Czibulka, 1885; *Die Novize* (Vaudeville), W. Rab, 1886; *Der Nachtwandler* (with Genée), L. Roth, 1886
Der Vizeadmiral (komische Operette, with Genée), Millöcker, 1886; *Die Dreizehn* (komische Operette), Genée, 1887; *Die Hochzeit der Reservisten* (Posse), Stern, 1888; *Wolf und Lamperl* (Posse), Stern, 1888; *Die indische Witwe* (with Genée), G. Geiringer, 1889; *Gil Blas von Santillana* (with West), Czibulka, 1889; *Der schöne Kaspar*, J. Bayer, 1889; *Kapitän Fracassa* (komische Operette, with Genée), R. Dellinger, 1889

Wiener Ausstellungsgeschichten [Das Rendezvous der Strohwitwen] (Posse), F. Lehner, 1892; *Der Millionenonkel* (with Genée), A. Müller jr, 1892; *Der Schwiegerpapa* (with Genée), M. von Weinzierl and A. Zamara, 1893; *Das Mädchen von Mirano* [La stupida] (with Genée), A. Neumann, 1893; *Fürst Malachoff* (Spl), Stern, 1894

*

R. Holzer: *Die Wiener Vorstadtbühnen* (Vienna, 1951)

ANDREW LAMB

Zellbell, Ferdinand (*b* Stockholm, 3 Sept 1719; *d* Stockholm, 21 April 1780). Swedish composer. After early musical education with his father Ferdinand Zellbell and J. H. Roman, he continued his studies with Telemann (1741–2). He was then appointed organist at the Storkyrka in Stockholm and in 1750 *hovkapellmästare*. In 1758 he travelled to St Petersburg to write the *opera seria Il giudizio d'Aminta* (2, L. Lazaroni; *S-Skma*) for Tsarina Elisabeth; it was staged there on 17 December. After his return the next year he worked as a conductor and was one of the founders of the Royal Swedish Academy of Music. The style of his opera is almost purely Italian, though his later stage works (insertion arias, ballet movements and choruses) show some influence from Gluck in their orchestration and dynamic contrasts. An opera-ballet, *Sveas högtid, eller Fria Konsternas vördnadsoffer åt Dygderna* ('The Festival of Svea, or Free Art's Homage to the Virtues'; 2, G. F. Gyllenborg), staged at the Bollhus Theatre, Stockholm, on 23 June 1774, is lost.

*

F. Dahlgren: *Anteckningar om Stockholms teatrar* (Stockholm, 1866)

E. Sundström: 'Ferdinand Zellbell den yngre och hans opera *Il giudizio d'Aminta*', *STMf*, i (1919), 58–69

E. Haeger: 'Anteckningar om Ferdinand Zellbell den yngre och hans vokalmusik', *STMf*, xxxiv (1952), 60–83

BERTIL H. VAN BOER

Zeller, Carl (Johann Adam) (*b* St Peter in der Au, 19 June 1842; *d* Baden, nr Vienna, 17 Aug 1898). Austrian composer. As a boy he had a fine soprano voice; at the age of 11 he joined the boys' choir of the court chapel in Vienna, the Wiener Sängerknaben. He studied law at Vienna University, at the same time studying composition with Simon Sechter, and in 1869 took the doctorate in law at Graz University. After practising as a solicitor with the land tribunal he entered the Ministry of Education and Culture in 1873. In 1876 his comic opera *Joconde*, set in Scotland in Cromwell's time, was produced; it was followed by further similar works. His greatest success was achieved with the operetta *Der Vogelhändler* (1891), a work of considerable charm that revived the fortunes of Viennese operetta during the 1890s. Supported by a richness of melodic invention and fine handling of the voice and ensemble numbers, it has remained one of the classics of the genre. *Der Obersteiger* (1894) was also a success and is scarcely inferior in invention, though it is perhaps too similar in style; it has been largely eclipsed by the earlier work, yet remains familiar through the tenor solo 'Sei nicht bös' which, since Elisabeth Schumann, has frequently been appropriated by sopranos. Illness prevented Zeller from completing further operettas, and *Der Kellermeister* (1901), from which the tenor's 'Lass dir Zeit' is sometimes heard, was finished by Johann Brandl. Zeller also composed ballad plays, songs and choral works.

His last years were unhappy. By 1895 he had risen to a high position in the ministry, with the title of 'Hofrat' (court councillor). But signs of nervous disorder appeared; he was retired and involved in legal proceedings.

See also VOGELHÄNDLER, DER.

Operetten, first performed in Vienna, unless otherwise stated

Joconde (komische Oper, 3, M. West and Moret), An der Wien, 18 March 1876, vs (Vienna, 1877)

Die Fornarina (komische Oper, 3, West and R. Genée), Munich, 1878

Capitän Nicoll, oder Die Carbonari (3, West and F. Zell), Carl, 27 Oct 1880

Der Vagabund (3, West and L. Held), Carl, 30 Oct 1886

Der Vogelhändler (3, West and Held, after Varin and Biéville: *Ce que deviennent les roses*), An der Wien, 10 Jan 1891, vs (Vienna, 1891)

Der Obersteiger (3, West and Held), An der Wien, 5 Jan 1894, vs (Vienna, 1894)

Der Kellermeister (3, West), Raimund, 21 Dec 1901, completed by J. Brandl, vs (Vienna, 1902)

*

C. W. Zeller: *Mein Vater Carl Zeller* (St Pölten, 1942)

R. Holzer: *Die Wiener Vorstadtbühnen: Alexander Girardi und das Theater an der Wien* (Vienna, 1951)

R. Traubner: *Operetta: a Theatrical History* (New York, 1983)

ANDREW LAMB

Zeller, Heinrich (*b* Voitswinkel, Laufen, 7 June 1856; *d* Weimar, 9 Aug 1934). German tenor. His voice was discovered by Richard Strauss, who arranged for him to study in Munich. He was then engaged at Weimar, making his début in 1888 as Lohengrin. At Bayreuth (1891–2) he sang Tannhäuser, Heinrich der Schreiber, Melot and an Esquire in *Parsifal*. His repertory also included John of Leyden, Florestan, Mathias (*Der Evangelimann*) and Canio. In 1894 he repaid his debt to Strauss by creating the title role of *Guntram*, a part considered unsingable by most other tenors. Among his later appearances, at Berlin, Munich, Hamburg and London, was a Tannhäuser at Covent Garden in 1907. He retired in 1917. ELIZABETH FORBES

Zelmira. *Dramma* in two acts by GIOACHINO ROSSINI to a libretto by ANDREA LEONE TOTTOLA after Dormont de Belloy's *Zelmire*; Naples, Teatro di S Carlo, 16 February 1822.

Rossini's final Neapolitan opera, a vocally alluring showcase written with an eye to international audiences in Vienna and beyond, is set on the island of Lesbos in ancient times. Old King Polidoro (bass) has ruled over the island peaceably with his daughter Zelmira (soprano) and her husband, the Trojan prince Ilo (tenor). But Polidoro has been deposed in Ilo's absence by an adventurer who has in turn been murdered by Antenore (tenor). Zelmira has hidden the old king and is guarding his and her son's safety with the help of Emma (contralto); but Antenore, having been proclaimed King of Lesbos, institutes various calumnies against Zelmira. Ilo, returning, is led to believe that she has murdered Polidoro. Even when he himself is saved by her from an assassination attempt, his would-be assassin Leucippo (bass) attaches the blame to Zelmira, who is then arrested. In Act 2 Zelmira is released in the hope that she will lead them to the old king. This duly happens and they are thrown into prison to await execution; but Ilo, by now reassured of his wife's good faith, is able to save them from the cruel fate awaiting them at the hands of Antenore.

Despite this primitive and outwardly violent plot, the opera, beautifully laid out for the solo voices, is essentially benign and classical in temper with the stress on the familial bonds between Zelmira, Ilo and Polidoro. There are many distinguishing touches in the orchestration and in the accompanied recitatives. For the Viennese première (13 April 1822) Rossini added a chorus and an aria for Emma at the start of Act 2; these are usually included in modern revivals. RICHARD OSBORNE

Zemira. *Opera seria* in three acts by FRANCESCO BIANCHI to a libretto by GAETANO SERTOR; Naples, Teatro di S Carlo, 4 November 1781 (revised version, Padua, Teatro Nuovo, *fiera del santo* [? 13 June], 1786).

Sarabes (tenor), principal rajah of India, refuses to give his daughter Zemira (soprano) in marriage to Akbar (soprano castrato), emperor of the Mogols. She is betrothed to Gandarte (soprano castrato), another rajah. Fearing for her father's life, she goes to Akbar's tent. Gandarte and Sarabes believe she has betrayed them and rush to avenge themselves. Akbar intercepts them, but Zemira draws a dagger and threatens to kill herself if her father is harmed. Akbar ultimately orders his rival to be put to death, and only after Sarabes has stabbed his own daughter does he relent, declaring that with her noble action Zemira has saved her beloved.

Unusual components in this work are the opening trio with storm music, the short duet for two men, the programmatic battle music, the extensive quartet and the stabbing. The death of Zemira is cut in Anfossi's setting (1782, Venice), and Morandi's setting (1782, Florence) omits the *introduzione*; Bianchi's revised version of 1786 omits both. The version for Naples features extensive use of clarinets, which were generally available there some ten years earlier than in other Italian cities. MARITA P. McCLYMONDS

Zémire et Azor ('Zémire and Azor'). *Comédie-ballet mêlée de chants et de danses* in four acts by ANDRÉ-ERNEST-MODESTE GRÉTRY to a libretto by JEAN FRANÇOIS MARMONTEL; Fontainebleau, 9 November 1771.

This version of the Beauty and the Beast story was created from two literary sources: the substance of the story is from *La belle et la bête* by Jeanne Marie Le Prince de Beaumont, and the names and the setting from *Amour pour amour*, a verse play by P. C. Nivelle de La Chaussée (1742). The precedent of a long *opéra comique* using the supernatural and dances existed in Duni and Favart's *La fée Urgèle*.

The final part of the overture paints a storm, after which we see Sander (baritone), a Persian merchant, and his servant Ali (tenor) sheltering in a deserted palace; it is night. Ali is scared, but induced to stay by food and wine that appear magically. Sander has lost his worldly goods in a shipwreck; for his third daughter, Zémire (soprano), he cuts a rose from an arbour. Azor (tenor) appears in anger. He, a Persian prince, has been given a beast-like countenance by a vengeful Fairy. Insulted by the theft of the rose, Azor demands Sander's life; Sander successfully pleads to see his daughters once more. Azor proposes the life of one daughter instead, then transports Ali and Sander home on a cloud.

In Act 2 Zémire and her sisters are seen in Sander's house at Ormuz. He and Ali arrive and announce the news of the shipwreck. Zémire realizes something graver is wrong. Sander, alone, writes a farewell letter to his daughters, then retires. Offstage, Zémire has forced the truth from Ali. She resolves to give her own life and commands the terrified servant to lead her to Azor. At the opening of Act 3 Azor, in his palace, explains the spell that condemns him to ugliness until he can inspire love (aria, 'Ah! quel tourment'). He retires. Zémire and Ali appear, and as Ali seeks escape, dancers appear as 'Genies of the Arts', paying court to Zémire. She faints on seeing Azor. Soon, however, she realizes his character is noble, and even sings for him ('La fauvette avec ses petits'). Since she misses her family, Azor allows her to see and hear them mourning her in an illuminated magic 'picture' (trio, 'Ah! laissez-moi la pleurer'; *see* OPÉRA COMIQUE fig.1). He declares his love for Zémire. She is permitted to return to Ormuz for a last hour, but is also given a ring that could set her free.

Act 4 finds Zémire trying unsuccessfully to assure her family of her faith in Azor: in a powerful ensemble they oppose her. But she casts away the ring and vanishes. In a grotto of his palace, Azor gives way to despair. Zémire is heard (in an extended solo with echoing horn-calls) searching for him offstage. As she avows her love, the scene is transformed into another palace. The Fairy (spoken) restores Azor's natural beauty and presides over the couple's nuptials.

Zémire et Azor was first performed at the Comédie-Italienne on 16 December 1771. Recognized immediately as Grétry's best as well as largest work to date, it had immense international success (it was given at the King's Theatre, London, in 1779). The text was also used in settings by Linley the elder (1776), Gotthilf von Baumgarten (1776) and Spohr (1819). Grétry's music ranges widely in character and function, and uses special instrumental effects in Acts 3 and 4. Mozart owned a copy of the score. DAVID CHARLTON

Zemire und Azor ('Zemire and Azor'). *Romantische Oper* in two acts by LOUIS SPOHR to a libretto by Johann Jakob Ihlée after JEAN FRANÇOIS MARMONTEL's *comédie-ballet Zémire et Azor*; Frankfurt, 4 April 1819.

After accepting the post of director of the Frankfurt opera in 1817, Spohr considered a number of possible opera projects. He began work on a version of Apel's tale *Der schwarze Jäger* but abandoned it when he heard that Weber was writing an opera (*Der Freischütz*) on the same story. He then accepted the libretto of *Zemire und Azor*, adapted from the French original (*see* ZÉMIRE ET AZOR above) by the director of the Frankfurt theatre. Spohr began work on the music in September 1818 and completed it in February 1819.

In this version of the old story of Beauty and the Beast, Sander (bass) and his servant Ali (tenor) find themselves in a magic garden. By plucking a rose they arouse the wrath of Prince Azor (tenor), who has been changed into a monster and can be redeemed only by the selfless love of a pure maiden. Sander's youngest daughter, Zemire (soprano), goes to try to break the spell on Azor, and eventually comes to love him. When she leaves to visit her family, Azor gives her a magic ring without which she cannot return. Her sisters Lisbe (soprano) and Fatme (soprano) steal the ring, but she is miraculously transported back. The Fairy (speaking role) who had placed the enchantment on Azor releases him from it, and everything ends happily with the union of Zemire and Azor.

The opera contains some of Spohr's most charming melodic writing and some effective coloratura, influenced, Spohr admitted, by the popularity of Rossini. *Zemire und Azor* held a small place in the 19th-century German repertory, and individual numbers were frequently performed in the concert hall. The popularity of Zemire's *Romanze*, 'Rose wie bist du reizend und mild' ('Rose softly blooming') continued into the 20th century. As in Spohr's *Faust*, but less pervasively, musical motifs are used. Both operas have a supernatural element, but *Zemire und Azor* is an altogether lighter piece, engaging rather than gripping. It was revived in Kassel in 1984. CLIVE BROWN

Zemlinsky [Zemlinszky], **Alexander (von)** (*b* Vienna, 14 Oct 1871; *d* Larchmont, NY, 15 March 1942). Austrian composer and conductor. He received his musical training at the Vienna Conservatory (1884–92), where he studied the piano with Anton Door and composition with Robert and J. N. Fuchs. Most of his early chamber and orchestral works take their bearings from Brahms, who discussed some of them with Zemlinsky and recommended the Clarinet Trio op.3 to his publisher Simrock. The Trio and the Second Symphony (1897) were among several early works to be awarded prizes. However, Zemlinsky, as Schoenberg later testified, was equally enthralled by Wagner, and he transmitted this enthusiasm to his pupil (who was also to become his brother-in-law). In 1896 Zemlinsky's first opera, *Sarema*, was one of the winning entries in the Bavarian opera competition named after the Prince Regent, Luitpold. The first performance was given at the Munich Hoftheater on 10 October 1897, with Milka Ternina creating the role of the tragic Circassian heroine torn between her love for a Russian officer and that for her native land.

While *Sarema* still owed something to the grand opera model, Zemlinsky's second opera, *Es war einmal*, was a fairy-tale comedy based on a play by the Danish playwright Holger Drachmann. The genre may have been suggested by the success of Goldmark's *Das Heimchen am Herd*, which Zemlinsky is said to have greeted 'with sheer delight'. The opera was accepted for the Vienna Hofoper by Mahler, who insisted on numerous changes to the libretto and music before conducting the first performance on 22 January 1900. The main roles were created by Selma Kurz (Princess) and Erik Schmedes (Prince). Eduard Hanslick criticized Zemlinsky's obvious debt to Wagner and his use of folksong. Mahler also had reservations about the opera, which he thought lacked originality. He refused to accept Zemlinsky's next work for the stage, a ballet by Hugo von Hofmannsthal, *Das gläserne Herz* (1901).

In 1900 Zemlinsky embarked on a career as a Kapellmeister that took him from the Carltheater, Vienna (where he conducted such works as Heinrich Reinhardt's immensely popular operetta *Das süsse Mädel*), to the Theater an der Wien, where he worked with the famous actor Alexander Girardi in 1903. At this time he was also involved in Ernst von Wolzogen's Überbrettl cabaret, for which he wrote some songs and a mimodrama, *Ein Lichtstrahl*. In 1904 he was appointed principal conductor at the newly founded Volksoper, where, apart from a season at the Hofoper under the tutelage of Mahler, he remained until 1911, conducting the first performance by a Viennese company of *Salome* and the Viennese premières of Dukas' *Ariane et Barbe-bleue* and Puccini's *Tosca*.

Many of Zemlinsky's works after the turn of the century have an autobiographical element. Thus the tone poem *Die Seejungfrau* (1902–3), based on Hans Christian Andersen's fairy-tale, may well have had its origins in the composer's thwarted love for his pupil Alma Schindler. Zemlinsky's third opera, *Der Traumgörge* (1904–6), was a musical offering to his first wife, Ida, whom he married in 1907. However, because of various difficulties, the work was not staged until 1980. Zemlinsky conducted the first performance of his fourth opera, *Kleider machen Leute* (1907–9), at the Volksoper on 2 December 1910; the revised version of 1921 was first performed in Prague in 1922.

In 1911 Zemlinsky moved to Prague to become principal conductor at the Neues Deutsches Theater, where, as Stravinsky, Schoenberg and others testified, his Mozart and Wagner performances and his empathetic conducting of contemporary works became legendary. Perhaps his greatest achievement in this regard was the first performance in 1924 of Schoenberg's *Erwartung*. The Prague years witnessed the composition of a number of important works. In 1915, shortly after completing his most substantial chamber work, String Quartet no.2, Zemlinsky began work on *Eine florentinische Tragödie*, a one-act opera that sought to emulate the success of such 'Renaissance' operas as Schreker's *Die Gezeichneten*, Korngold's *Violanta* and Schillings's *Mona Lisa*. In *Der Zwerg* (1919–21) Zemlinsky returned to the 'tragedy of the ugly man', a subject that had already obsessed him ten years earlier. As Franz Werfel noted, he was moving away from music drama towards opera. This is borne out not only by the excruciating *verismo* ending but also by the prevalence of what Alban Berg called 'the wonderful flow of glorious melody'. The *Lyrische Symphonie* (1922–3) was the last of the major works written in the decade that saw Zemlinsky at the height of his powers.

In 1927 Zemlinsky joined Klemperer at the Krolloper in Berlin. Here he composed his next opera, *Der Kreidekreis* (1930–31), which mingles Chinese elements (the pentatonic scale) with devices that had recently become popular (jazz, spoken dialogue and melodrama). In 1927 he conducted Krenek's *Jonny spielt auf*, and in 1931 the Berlin première of Weill's *Aufstieg und Fall der Stadt Mahagonny*.

In 1931 Zemlinsky left the Krolloper and in 1933, after the advent of the Nazis in Germany, he returned to Vienna. In 1935 he completed the short score and much of the orchestration of *Der König Kandaules*, an opera based on André Gide's play. After the Anschluss Zemlinsky and his family fled to the USA. He had hopes of completing *Der König Kandaules*, a work he termed 'ultra-modern'; however, the bedroom scene militated against its acceptance by the Metropolitan Opera, and the orchestration was never completed. Early in 1939 he began work on another opera, *Circe*, to a libretto by Irma Stein-Firner, but it remained unfinished at his death.

Despite his close ties with the Second Viennese School, Zemlinsky did not explore atonality and serialism. His pupil E. W. Korngold recalled that he found it impossible 'to repress the active inner tonal feeling'. Thus his operas must be seen in the context of contemporaries such as Schreker, Strauss and d'Albert, whose success he sought to emulate. At their best they bear out Schoenberg's remark that his 'ideas, his forms, his sonorities and every turn of the music sprang directly from the action, from the scenery, and from the singers' voices with a naturalness and distinction of supreme quality'.

See also FLORENTINISCHE TRAGÖDIE, EINE; KLEIDER MACHEN LEUTE; KREIDEKREIS, DER; TRAUMGÖRGE, DER; and ZWERG, DER.

Sarema, 1893–5 (3, Adolf von Zemlinsky, after R. von Gottschall: *Die Rose vom Kaukasus*), Munich, Hof, 10 Oct 1897, *D-Mbs*, *US-Wc*, vs (Vienna, 1899)

Es war einmal, 1897–9 (Vorspiel, 3, M. Singer, after H. Drachmann), Vienna, Hof, 22 Jan 1900, *A-Wn*, *US-Wc*
Malwa, 1902 (?Hülschenreiter, after M. Gor'kiy), inc., *Wc*
Der Traumgörge, 1904–6 (2, Nachspiel, L. Feld), Nuremberg, Opernhaus, 11 Oct 1980, *A-Wn*, *US-Wc*, vs (Vienna, 1906)
Kleider machen Leute, 1907–9 (musikalische Komödie, Vorspiel, 3, Feld, after G. Keller), Vienna, Volksoper, 2 Dec 1910, *A-Wn*, *US-Wc*; rev. (Vorspiel, 2), Prague, Neues Deutsches, 22 April 1922, *Wc*, vs (Vienna, 1922)
Eine florentinische Tragödie, op.16 (1, O. Wilde: *A Florentine Tragedy*, trans. M. Meyerfeld), Stuttgart, Hof, 30 Jan 1917, *Wc*, vs (Vienna, 1916)
Herrn Arnes Schatz, 1917 (after S. Lagerlöf), inc., *Wc*
Raphael, ?1918 (G. Klaren, after H. de Balzac: *Le peau de chagrin*), inc., *Wc*
Der Zwerg, op.17, 1919–21 (1, Klaren, after Wilde: *The Birthday of the Infanta*), Cologne, Neues Theater, 28 May 1922, *Wc* (Vienna, 1923)
Vitalis, 1926 (after Keller: *Der schlim-heilige Vitalis*), inc., *Wc*
Der Kreidekreis, 1930–31 (3, after Klabund), Zürich, Stadt, 14 Oct 1933, *Wc* (Vienna, 1933)
Der König Kandaules, 1935–6 (3, A. Gide: *Le roi Candaule*, trans. F. Blei), inc., *Wc*
Circe, 1939 (5, I. Stein-Firner), orchestration inc., *Wc*

*

E. Hanslick: 'Es war einmal', *Aus neuer und neuester Zeit* (Berlin, 1900), 44–50
R. S. Hoffmann: 'Alexander von Zemlinsky', *Der Merker*, ii (1911), 193–7
F. Adler: *Eine florentinische Tragödie: Einführung* (Vienna, ?1917)
G. Klaren: 'Zur Technik des Opernbuches', *Musikblätter des Anbruch*, ii (1920), 215–21
Der Auftakt, i (1921) [Zemlinsky issue, incl.: R. S. Hoffmann: 'Zemlinskys Opern', 211–16; G. Klaren: 'Zemlinsky, vom psychologischen Standpunkt', 204–7; E. W. Korngold: 'Erinnerungen an Zemlinsky aus meiner Lehrzeit', 230–32; L. Laber: 'Zemlinsky auf dem Theater', 223–4; A. Schoenberg: 'Gedanken über Zemlinsky', 228–30, Eng. trans. in *Style and Idea*, 1975; F. Werfel: 'Zemlinsky', 197–200]
J. Korngold: 'Kleider machen Leute', 'Eine florentinische Tragödie', *Deutsches Opernschaffen der Gegenwart* (Leipzig and Vienna, 1921), 240–47, 247–53
H. Teweles: *Theater und Publikum: Erinnerungen und Erfahrungen* (Prague, 1927)
P. W. Jacob: 'Alexander Zemlinsky: zur Wiederaufführung seiner Oper Der Kreidekreis', *Blätter der Städtischen Bühnen Dortmund*, xix (1954–5)
T. W. Adorno: 'Zemlinsky', *Quasi una fantasia* (Frankfurt, 1963), 155–80
A. Mahler: 'Alexander Zemlinsky', *Mf*, xxiv (1971), 250–60
H. Weber: 'Zemlinsky in Wien 1871–1911', *AMw*, xxviii (1971), 77–96
A. Mahler: 'Alexander Zemlinskys Prager Jahre', *HV*, ix (1972), 237–47
S. Stompor: 'Alexander Zemlinsky v Praze', *HRo*, xxvi (1973), 271–8
H. Curjel: *Experiment Krolloper 1927–1931* (Munich, 1975)
L. Oncley: *The Published Works of Alexander Zemlinsky* (diss., Indiana U, 1975)
O. Kolleritsch, ed.: *Alexander Zemlinsky: Tradition im Umkreis der Wiener Schule* (Graz, 1976) [incl. G. Gruber: 'Klangkomposition in den Opern Zemlinskys', 93–100]
H. Weber: *Alexander Zemlinsky: eine Studie*, Österreichische Komponisten des 20. Jahrhunderts, xxiii (Vienna, 1977)
R. Stephan: 'Alexander Zemlinsky: ein unbekannter Meister der Wiener Schule', *Kieler Vorträge zum Theater*, iv (Kiel, 1978)
A. Partsch: *Das Opernschaffen Zemlinskys* (diss., U. of Vienna, 1979)
H. Weber: 'Stil: Allegorie und Secession: zu Zemlinsky's Ballettmusik nach Hofmannsthals "Der Triumph der Zeit"', *Art Nouveau: Jugendstil und Musik*, ed. J. Stenzl (Zürich, 1980), 135–50
A. Clayton: *The Operas of Alexander Zemlinsky* (diss., U. of Cambridge, 1983)
——: 'Zemlinsky's One-act Operas', *MT*, cxxiv (1983), 474–7
S. B. Würffel: ' "... und sage deine letzten Worte in Schweigen": Anmerkungen zur gegenwärtigen Zemlinsky-Renaissance', *Mf*, xxxvii (1984), 191–206
A. Clayton: 'Weitere Anmerkungen zur Zemlinsky-Renaissance', *Mf*, xxxviii (1985), 155–7

ALFRED CLAYTON

Zenatello, Giovanni (*b* Verona, 22 Feb 1876; *d* New York, 11 Feb 1949). Italian tenor. He studied as a baritone at Verona with Zannoni and Moretti and made his début at Belluno in 1898 as Silvio in *Pagliacci*; the next year, at the Fondo, Naples, he sang Canio in the same opera. After a period in minor theatres, he appeared at Lisbon (1902) and during the 1902–3 season at La Scala (*La damnation de Faust* and *Un ballo in maschera*). He sang at La Scala until 1907, taking the leading tenor roles in many premières there, notably of Giordano's *Siberia* (1903) and *Madama Butterfly* (1904). He was frequently engaged at Buenos Aires (1903–10) and was first heard at Covent Garden in 1905 as Riccardo, returning until 1909. He made his New York début in 1907 at the Manhattan Opera House and until 1916 sang mostly in the USA (particularly Boston and Chicago), where his career ended in 1928. Two years previously he had reappeared at Covent Garden as Otello. When he retired he directed a school of singing (among the pupils was Lily Pons), and for several seasons he was manager of the Verona Arena, where he had inaugurated the opera performances as Radames. Among his qualities were a warm and resonant baritonal timbre, and a clear, easily produced top register. A vigorous and passionate interpreter of Don José, Canio and Puccini's Des Grieux, he was also much admired in Verdi (especially as Radames and Otello), although his style sometimes showed the coarsening influence of *verismo*.

For illustration *see* MADAMA BUTTERFLY, fig.2.

*

T. Hutchinson and C. W. Williams: 'Giovanni Zenatello', *Record Collector*, xiv (1961–2), 101–43, 170–1; xv (1963–4), 18–20 [with discography]

RODOLFO CELLETTI

Zender, Hans (*b* Wiesbaden, 22 Nov 1936). German composer and conductor. He studied in Frankfurt, Freiburg and Rome, and was music director of the Bonn Opera (1964–8), at Kiel (1969–71) and at the Hamburg Staatsoper (1984–7). His international career developed after he conducted *Parsifal* at Bayreuth in 1975, and in the late 1980s he became a regular guest conductor at the Théâtre Royal de la Monnaie in Brussels. Zender's intricate and complex style of composition shows the influence of his teacher, B. A. Zimmermann, with strong emphasis on serial and electronic music. His opera *Stephen Climax*, for which Zender wrote his own libretto, was first performed in Frankfurt in 1986. Lasting 130 minutes without a break, it calls for two orchestras and consists of two parallel tales. One is a generalized evocation of an early Christian saint, Simeon the Stylite, and his followers in the Syrian desert; the other, drawn from Joyce's *Ulysses*, follows a specific train of events involving Stephen, an aspiring poet and intellectual, in Dublin in 1904. Simeon and Stephen are both searching for the meaning and purpose of existence, one in a mystical way, the other through experience of the world. Zender offers no conclusions; the opera's raison d'être is simply the creative friction of opposites, a theatrical parallel to musical counterpoint, an acknowledgment that art works on different levels and can express contrasting emotions at one and the same time.

ANDREW CLARK

Zeno, Apostolo (*b* Venice, 11 Dec 1668; *d* Venice, 11 Nov 1750). Italian poet and librettist. His life was essentially a literary one little affected by external events, and followed two distinct directions that he kept separate and valued very differently. Educated in the elegant classicism of Venice, he was an enthusiastic student of history, philology, antiquities and numismatics. With Scipione Maffei, Antonio Vallisnieri and his brother Pier Caterino Zeno he founded the *Giornale de' letterati d'Italia* (Verona, 1710). He was a founder member of the Accademia degli Animosi, which, like the more famous Accademia dell'Arcadia, had as its aim the restoration of 'good taste' and adherence to tradition. He corresponded assiduously with distinguished men of letters (G. G. Orsi, L. A. Muratori, G. Fontanini, G. Gigli, A. Magliabechi, F. Marmi and the brothers A. M. and S. Salvini), and considered his learned studies more important that the theatrical activity on which he embarked at an early age.

His first libretto, set by C. F. Pollarolo in 1696, was *Gli inganni felici*, with a plot full of mistaken identities, disguises and comic interludes in the Baroque fashion; from this time onwards he was constantly engaged in working for theatres in Venice, Milan and the Medici theatre at Pratolino. A frequent collaborator was PIETRO PARIATI, who versified the dramas while Zeno devised the plots and wrote the scenarios. The authorship of certain of the librettos traditionally attributed to both men is still a matter of controversy. Giovanna Gronda (1990), for example, has shown convincingly that two such works, *La Svanvita* (set by Fiorè, 1707) and *Sesostri* (Gasparini, 1710), are by Pariati alone. In the absence of contrary evidence for others, however (notably *Artaserse*, *Anfitrione*, *Il falso Tiberino* and *Costantino*), Zeno's own catalogue of works, published in a literary annual for 1735 and indicating clearly the texts he wrote in collaboration with Pariati, may be taken as authoritative. In spite of his copious libretto production, Zeno always felt constrained by the requirements of opera as a spectacle: content and form were heavily conditioned by the need to entertain – 'if one does not allow oneself many extravagances, the main purpose of such compositions, which is enjoyment, is lost' (letter to Muratori of August 1701) – as well as by an impresario's need to please the audience in order to balance the books. Any ambition for moral aims or classical regularity was impeded by the conventions differentiating tragedy (which Zeno would have liked to restore) from opera, in which 'something has to be conceded to the indulgences of the age, to decoration, to music' (letter to P. C. Zeno of 6 January 1720, on the Venetian production of *Lucio Papirio*).

Though invited to Vienna to become *poeta cesareo* (poet to the Emperor) in 1705, he refused because he had recently married. In 1709–10 he was commissioned by the Hapsburg pretenders to the Spanish throne to write *Atenaide* and *Scipione nelle Spagne*, significant dramas delineating the monarch's role as servant of the state, concerned with respect for the law and the virtues of justice and clemency. He thus showed himself adept in the functions of court poet, and was again invited to take the post when he became a widower. Negotiations were protracted because of his financial requirements and because in addition to being imperial poet he also wished to be known as imperial historian, a title he considered more honourable. He moved to Vienna in 1718 and carried out his duties there until 1729 when Pietro Metastasio was summoned, ostensibly to help the older poet but in effect to replace him. Zeno returned to Venice in the same year and sent one more libretto, *Enone*, to his former patrons. In the latter years of his residence in Vienna he had turned towards scholarly matters, organizing the numismatic collections of Charles VI, and when he returned to Italy he concerned himself exclusively with study.

Some critics have questioned the value of the aims and results of Zeno's 'reform' of opera. It must be understood that he was almost entirely concerned with the literary quality of the text, since he did not feel competent to deal with its transformation into spectacle, from the point of view either of staging or of music. His frequent use of the word *riforma* in discussing his own work should not be overlooked, however. In a letter to Giuseppe Gravisi of 3 November 1730, immediately after he had left the service of the court, he stressed as intrinsic limitations to the verisimilitude of opera 'the need to sing all the little arias from beginning to end, and all those changes of scene'. The first of these caused him special difficulties in sacred dramas, where he found it unseemly to provide dignified personages with trifling passages; and the second prevented exact observance of the rule of unity of place, which he had to relax, though he kept the action within a single town.

As for the unities of time and action Zeno observed these, as well as coherence of character, to the extent allowed by the *liaison des scènes* (elision of scenes), which he considered essential to preserve verisimilitude. In the same letter to Gravisi, he condemned the negligence of writers, including their lack of moral purpose, who did not seek 'to purge the emotions or move to pity and terror. These evils can and should be removed from musical drama, and these writers must be provided with the remedy through praiseworthy reform [*lodevol riforma*]'. In pursuit of this objective Zeno progressively eliminated the comic elements present in his *Griselda* (1701), *Venceslao* (1703) and *Aminta* (1703). He increasingly placed arias at the ends of scenes and organized them into more regular verse, eliminating polymetry.

He also maintained a strong respect for history, punctiliously citing his sources, both classical and medieval, in his plot summaries. His directions for scene changes (few in number) reveal his care for historical evidence, whether the subject was Greek, Roman or Byzantine, medieval or Nordic; the adventurous aspect of a story interested him as much as the investigation of little-known historical incidents. He paid particular attention to the scenic atmosphere of exotic subjects – Chinese (*Teuzzone*, 1706), Persian (*Ormisda*, 1721; *Ornospade*, 1727) and Indian (*Gianguir*, 1724).

The traditional view that Zeno intended to replace mythological subjects with historical ones has been too readily accepted, however; it is only partly true. He often treated mythological subjects interestingly as tragicomedies or pastorales, as suggested by G. B. Guarini: the characters are of noble condition, as they were in tragedies, but the emotional orientation is towards pathos, not terror, and the sadness of the audience is assuaged with a happy ending. He wrote works of this kind in Vienna (*Meride e Selinunte*, 1721; *Euristeo*, 1724; *Imeneo*, 1727) which can be called comedies in the archetypal sense of the genre since they culminate in the marriage of young lovers, opposed in vain by the guardians of the old order. Such happy endings mirrored parallel festivities of the commissioning patrons: celebrating through marriage the cyclical return of spring, the work represented metaphorically an eternal renewing of the dynasty in whose honour the opera was performed. In this way, Zeno contrived to redeem from being exclusively entertainment a type of spectacle in which the audience, especially the female audience, required the presence of the 'effeminate passion' of love.

Zeno dedicated to his imperial patrons his *Poesie sacre drammatiche* (Venice, 1734), which he thought could be performed even without music, or at least defined as 'sacred musical tragedies'. On this occasion he traced an outline of his own activities, in which his move from the commercial theatres of Venice to the Viennese court theatre marked a turning-point in the ethical aspect of his *lodevol riforma*; freed from the constraints of pecuniary success, conscious that his patrons were concerned with the more enduring profits of praise and prestige, he could put forward on the imperial stage models of human perfection. These, according to his assertion in the dedication, would be directly inspired by the imperial pair themselves, and the coherence of artistic imitation would provide the audience with a pleasure that was not only sensual but nobly intellectual. Zeno thus renounced the moral benefit of Aristotelian purgation in favour of the idea, already elaborated by Corneille, of catharsis through admiration, which would produce virtue by example. He therefore fulfilled his duty as court poet with the maximum of moral nobility.

It should not however be thought that Zeno had any deep and lasting faith even in the poetic results of his reform. A letter of 1735 to Gravisi, long after Zeno had ceased to work for the theatre, sounds like a recantation, an extreme condemnation of his dramatic works: 'Save for a few of them, I consider them as failures and monstrosities'. Yet many were remarkable successes, produced often in a variety of theatres and set to music by diverse composers.

See also EUMENE and LUCIO VERO.

drammi per musica unless otherwise stated; selective list of settings

Gli inganni felici, C. F. Pollarolo, 1696 (A. Scarlatti, 1699; Buini, 1722); *Il Tirsi* (dramma pastorale), Lotti, Caldara and Ariosti, 1696; *Il Narciso* (pastorale), Pistocchi, 1697 (Sarti, 1763); *I rivali generosi*, M. A. Ziani, 1697 (Monari, Pistocchi and Capelli, 1710; Albinoni, 1725; Vignati, 1726); *Eumene*, Ziani, 1697 (Gasparini, 1714; Torri, 1720; Porpora, 1721; Albinoni, 1723; Giai, 1737; Jommelli, 1742; Manna, 1750; Aurisicchio, 1754; Mazzoni, 1759; Sacchini, 1763; De Majo, Insanguine and Errichelli, 1771; Carvalho, 1773; Insanguine, 1778; Borghi, 1777; Bertoni, 1783); *Odoardo*, Ziani, 1698; *Faramondo*, Pollarolo, 1698 (Porpora, 1719; Gasparini, 1720; Handel, 1738)

Lucio Vero, Pollarolo, 1700 (Albinoni, 1713; Gasparini, 1719; Torri, 1720; Sarro, 1722; Ciampi, 1726; Ariosti, 1727; Keiser, 1728, as Lucius Verus; Araia, 1735; Sala, 1737, as Vologeso; Di Capua, 1739, as Vologeso re de' Parti; Pulli, 1741, as Vologeso, re de' Parti; Manna, 1745; Galuppi, 1748, as Vologeso; Jommelli, 1754; Perez, 1754; Sarti, 1754, as Vologeso; Bertoni, 1757; Perez, 1762, as Berenice; Fischietti, 1764, as Vologeso; Sacchini, 1764; Jommelli, 1766, as Vologeso; Colla, 1770, as Vologeso; Sacchini, 1772, as Vologeso; Traetta, 1774; Guglielmi, 1775, as Vologeso; Rutini, 1775, as Vologeso; Masi, 1776, as Vologeso; Rust, 1778, as Vologeso; Martín y Soler, 1783, as Vologeso; Brunetti, 1789, as Vologeso, re de' Parti)

Temistocle (azione scenica), Ziani, 1701 (Porpora, 1718; Chelleri, 1721); *Griselda*, A. Pollarolo, 1701 (Albinoni, 1703; Chelleri, 1707; Predieri, 1711, as La virtù in trionfo, o sia La Griselda; Orlandini, 1716; A. M. Bononcini, 1718; G. Bononcini, 1722; A. Scarlatti, 1721; Torri, 1723; Conti, 1725; Ciocchetti, 1728; Vivaldi, 1735; Latilla, 1751); *Il Venceslao*, C. F. Pollarolo, 1703 (Perti, 1708; Mancini, 1714, as Il Vincislao; Boniventi, 1720; Capelli, 1724; Caldara, 1725; Torri, 1725; Porta, 1726, as La Lucinda fedele; Scalabrini, 1744; Pampani, 1752; Latilla, 1754); *Aminta* (dramma regio pastorale), Albinoni, 1703; *Pirro*, Aldrovandini, 1704 (Gasparini, 1717)

Antioco (with P. Pariati), Gasparini, 1705 (Hasse, 1721; Gurecký, 1729); *Artaserse* (with Pariati), Giannettini, 1705 (Orlandini, 1706; Sandoni, 1709; Ariosti, 1724); *Ambleto* (with Pariati), Gasparini, 1706 (D. Scarlatti, 1715; Vignati, 1719; Carcani, 1742); *Statira* (with Pariati), Gasparini, 1706 (Albinoni, 1726); *Il Teuzzone*, Magni and Monari, 1706 (Lotti, 1707; Orlandini and others, 1712; G. Casanova and Fiorè, 1716; Feo, 1720; Ariosti, 1727; Nicolini, 1825); *L'amor generoso*, Gasparini, 1707 (Orlandini and Ceruti, 1708; Costanzi, 1727; Vivaldi, 1731, as Alvilda regina de' Goti; Galuppi, 1737, as L'Alvilda); *Anfitrione* (tragicommedia, with Pariati), Gasparini, 1707

Flavio Anicio Olibrio (with Pariati), Gasparini, 1708 (Porpora, 1711; Porta, 1726, as Il trionfo di Flavio Olibrio; Vinci, 1728; E. Duni, 1736, as La tirannide debellata; Jommelli, 1740, as Ricimero re de' Goti); *Engelberta* (with Pariati), Fiorè, 1708 (Albinoni and Gasparini, 1709; Orefice and Mancini, 1709; C. F. Pollarolo, 1711; Bioni, 1729; Paganelli, 1743); *Astarto* (with Pariati), Albinoni, 1708 (Fago, 1709; G. Bononcini, 1715; Predieri, 1715, as Astarte; Conti, 1718; Caldara, 1725; Hasse, 1726; Galuppi, 1736, as Elisa regina di Tiro; Terradellas, 1739); *Il falso Tiberino* (with Pariati), C. F. Pollarolo, 1709; *Atenaide*, Fiorè, Caldara and Gasparini, 1709 (Ziani, A. Negri and Caldara, 1714; Vivaldi, 1728); *Zenobia in Palmira* (with Pariati), Chelleri, 1709 (Leo, 1725; Brusa, 1725, as L'amore eroico)

Scipione nelle Spagne, comp. unknown, 1710 (A. Scarlatti, 1714; Caldara, 1722; Albinoni, 1724; Ferrandini, 1732; Arrigoni, 1739; Leo, 1740; Bertoni, 1768); *Costantino* (with Pariati), Gasparini, 1711 (Lotti and Caldara, 1716; Orlandini, 1731, as Massimiano); *Merope*, Gasparini, 1712 (Fiorè, 1716; Orlandini, 1717; Predieri, 1718; Torri, 1719; Broschi, 1732; Giacomelli, 1734; Vivaldi, 1737, as L'oracolo in Messenia; Brivio, 1738; G. Scarlatti, 1740; Jommelli, 1741; Terradellas, 1743; Cocchi, 1748; Perez, 1750; Capranica, 1751; Gassmann, 1757; Sciroli, 1761; Latilla, 1763; Sala, 1769; Insanguine, 1772; Guglielmi, 1775; Traetta, 1776)

Alessandro Severo, Lotti, 1717 (Mancini, 1718; Chelleri, 1718; Sarro, 1719; Orlandini, 1723; Giacomelli, 1732; Handel, 1738; Bernasconi, 1738; Sacchini, 1763); *Ifigenia in Aulide*, Caldara, 1718 (Orlandini, 1732; Porpora, 1735; Porta, 1738; Salari, 1776); *Sirita*, Caldara, 1719; *Lucio Papirio dittatore*, Caldara, 1719 (A. Pollarolo, 1721; Giacomelli, 1729; Porta, 1732; Holzbauer, 1737; Hasse, 1742; Graun, 1745, as Quinto Fabio; Manna, 1748; Galupi, 1751; Paisiello, 1767; Anfossi, 1771, as Quinto Fabio; Bertoni, 1778, as Quinto Fabio; Bortnyansky, 1778, as Quinto Fabio; Cherubini, 1779, as Quinto Fabio; Borghi, 1781, as Quinto Fabio; Marinelli, 1791; Zingarelli, 1794)

Don Chisciotte in Sierra Morena (tragicommedia per musica, with Pariati), Conti, 1719; *Alessandro in Sidone* (with Pariati), Conti, 1721 (G. Bononcini, 1737); *Meride e Selinunte*, Porsile, 1721 (Porpora, 1726; Chiarini, 1744); *Ormisda*, Caldara, 1721 (Orlandini, 1723; A. Pollarolo, 1723, as Cosroë; Cordans, 1728; Handel, 1730); *Nitocri*, Caldara, 1722 (Sellitto, 1733; Leo, 1733; Giacomelli, 1736; Cocchi, 1751; Agnesi-Pinottini, 1771; Mercadante, 1824); *Euristeo*, Caldara, 1724 (Hasse, 1732); *Andromaca*, Caldara, 1724 (Feo, 1730); *Gianguir*, Caldara, 1724 (Giacomelli, 1729; Porta, 1732; Giai, 1738; V. Ciampi, 1759); *Semiramide in Ascalona*, Caldara, 1725; *I due dittatori*, Caldara, 1726; *Imeneo*, Caldara, 1727; *Ornospade*, Caldara, 1727; *Mitridate*, Caldara, 1728 (Giai, 1730; Porpora, 1730); *Caio Fabbrizio*, Caldara, 1729 (Hasse, 1732; Scalabrini, 1743; Auletta, 1743; Graun, 1746; Scolari, 1755; De Majo, 1760); *Enone*, Caldara, 1734

Incomplete, in *I-Vnm*: *Antiochide*; *Caio Mario in Minturno*

*

ES (A. Basso); *MGG* (A. A. Abert)

A. Zeno: 'Catalogo dei drammi composti dal signor Apostolo Zeno con la dichiarazione de' luoghi e de'tempi in cui l'autore stesso li la pubblicati', *Novelle della Repubblica Letteraria per l'anno MDCCXXXV*, no.46 (1735), 361–4

——: *Poesie drammatiche*, ed. G. Gozzi (Venice, 1744)

J. Morelli, ed.: *Lettere di Apostolo Zeno Cittadino veneziano istorico e poeta cesareo* (Venice, 1785)

F. Negri: *Vita di A. Zeno* (Venice, 1816)

L. Pistorelli: *Il melodrammi di A. Zeno* (Padua, 1894)

——: 'Due melodrammi inediti di A. Zeno', *RMI*, iii (1896), 261–4

A. Menghi: *Lo Zeno e la critica letteraria* (Camerino, 1901)

A. Wotquenne: *Liste alphabétique des pièces en vers des ouvrages dramatiques de Zeno, Métastase et Goldoni* (Leipzig, 1905)

A. Pietzsch: *A. Zeno in seiner Abhängigkeit von der französischen Tragödie* (Leipzig, 1907)

M. Fehr: *A. Zeno und seine Reform des Operntextes* (Zürich, 1912)

A. Michieli: 'Le poesie sacre drammatiche di A. Zeno', *Giornale storico della letteratura italiana*, xcv (1930), 1–33

R. Giazotto: *Poesia melodrammatica e pensiero critico nel settecento* (Milan, 1952)
R. Freeman: 'Apostolo Zeno's Reform of the Libretto', *JAMS*, xxi (1968), 321–41
D. J. Grout: 'La "Griselda" di Zeno e il libretto dell'opera di Scarlatti', *NRMI*, ii (1968), 207–25
H. E. Smither: *A History of the Oratorio*, i: *The Oratorio in the Baroque Era: Italy, Vienna, Paris* (Chapel Hill, 1977)
R. Freeman: *Opera without Drama: Currents of Change in Italian Opera, 1675–1725* (Ann Arbor, 1981)
P. Gallarati: *Musica e maschera: il libretto italiano del settecento* (Turin, 1984), 7–18
——: 'Zeno e Metastasio', *Metastasio e il melodramma*, ed. E. Sala Di Felice and L. Sannia Nowè (Padua, 1985), 89–104
E. Sala Di Felice: 'Virtù e felicità alla corte di Vienna', ibid, 55–88
——: 'Alla vigilia di Metastasio: Zeno', *Metastasio: Atti del convegno dell'Accademia nazionale dei Lincei: Rome 1985*, 79–110
E. Kanduth: 'Das Libretto im Zeichen der Arcadia, Paradigmatisches in den Musikdramen Zenos (Pariatis) und Metastasios', *Oper als Text: romanistische Beiträge zur Libretto-Forschung*, ed. A. Gier (Heidelberg, 1986), 33–53
F. Della Seta: 'Il librettista', *SOI*, iv, 246–9
G. Gronda: *La carriera di un librettista: Pietro Pariati da Reggio in Lombardia* (Bologna, 1990)
E. Sala Di Felice: 'Zeno: dal teatro impresariale al teatro di corte', *L'opera italiana a Vienna prima di Metastasio*, ed. M. T. Muraro, (Florence, 1990), 65–114
M. Viale Ferrero: 'Le didascalie sceniche nei drammi per musica di Zeno', ibid, 271–85 ELENA SALA DI FELICE

Zenobia [*Tiridate*]. Libretto by PIETRO METASTASIO, first set by Luca Antonio Predieri (1740, Vienna).

ACT 1 Zenobia, daughter of Mitridate, King of Armenia, has married Radamisto, Prince of Iberia, for political reasons. When Mitridate is assassinated, Radamisto, falsely accused, flees with Zenobia. A Parthian army, led by Tiridate, with whom Zenobia had previously been in love, pursues them. Weakened by the flight, Zenobia begs Radamisto to end her life rather than let her fall victim to the Parthians; jealous of the previous love between his wife and Tiridate, Radamisto attempts to comply. The wounded Zenobia, however, is soon discovered by Egle, a shepherdess, and nursed back to health. While searching for Radamisto, Zenobia overhears Tiridate learn of her apparent death from Mitrane, his confidant, and is thus able to save her anguished lover from suicide.

ACT 2 Tiridate tries to persuade Zenobia to marry him, but she refuses. Zopiro, a false friend of Radamisto and also in love with Zenobia, plans to create such enmity between Radamisto and Tiridate that one will kill the other in a contrived confrontation, the victor then falling prey to Zopiro's followers. He suggests to Zenobia that he has the power to save one of the two contestants and invites her to choose which. She names her husband, but secretly prays for Tiridate.

ACT 3 Egle foils the plan, and Radamisto, who pursues and mortally wounds Zopiro, is imprisoned by Tiridate. On his deathbed, Zopiro produces papers that exonerate Radamisto from the murder of Mitridate. Zenobia explains to Tiridate the political necessity for her marriage and offers him the kingdom of Armenia in exchange for her husband's life. Reunited with Radamisto, she bids Tiridate marry Egle who has not only confessed her love for him but is also proved to be Zenobia's sister.

* * *

Like the *Zénobie reyne d'Arménie* of Jacques de Montauban (published 1653) and the *Rhadamiste et Zénobie* of Crébillon (1711), Metastasio's drama about Zenobia, wife of Rhadamistus, King of Armenia, has its classical origin in the Tacitus *Annalium* (book 12). A more common subject for *Zenobia* dramas was the Queen of Palmyra, the title role in such works as Calderón's *La gran Cenobia* (1625), François d'Aubignac's *Zénobie* (1647), Jean Magnon's *Zénobie reyne de Palmire* (1660) and the librettos of Antonio Marchi (1694) and Gaetano Sertor (1789). Pierre Corneille's *Polyeucte* (1641) provided Metastasio with an early model for a plot involving a married woman and a previous lover, but there are also several librettos from which ideas could have been drawn. These include the *Radamisto* texts of Giovanni Moniglia and Pietro Trecchi (both 1695), Marchi (1698), Nicolò Giuvo (1707) and Domenico Lalli (as *L'amor tirannico*, 1710), as well as the *Tiridate* of Ippolito Bentivoglio and Nicolò Minato (1668). In Vienna, Metastasio could also have seen *Zenobia*, a *festa teatrale* written by Giovanni Pasquini and performed with music by the younger Georg Reutter in 1732, and *Radamisto*, a *Zwischenspiel* (librettist and composer unknown), in 1734. Metastasio wrote his drama to be set as part of the birthday celebrations, in 1740, for the Empress Elizabeth, consort to the Austrian Emperor, Charles VI; for this occasion Giuseppe Galli-Bibiena was the stage engineer. *Zenobia*, with just over 20 settings, did not prove a particularly popular libretto. Niccolò Piccinni, however, achieved his first significant success in Naples in 1756 with his setting.

For a list of settings *see* METASTASIO, PIETRO. DON NEVILLE

Zenobia, regina de' Palmireni ('Zenobia, Queen of the Palmyrans'). *Dramma per musica* in three acts by TOMASO GIOVANNI ALBINONI to a libretto by ANTONIO MARCHI; Venice, Teatro SS Giovanni e Paolo, Carnival 1694.

The Palmyran queen Zenobia (soprano) has been defeated by the Roman emperor Aurelian (alto) through the treachery of the governor of Palmyra, Ormonte (tenor), who hopes to wed his daughter Filidea (soprano) to the emperor. Zenobia refuses to submit to her conqueror, even when he falls in love with her and offers marriage. Furious at her resistance, Aurelian resolves to put Zenobia and her son to death, but refrains when he overhears Zenobia refuse Ormonte's offer to assassinate him. The plot takes a historically inaccurate turn when Aurelian rewards Zenobia by restoring her to the Palmyran throne. Through Filidea's pleas, Ormonte's sentence of death is commuted to one of exile, and the opera ends with universal rejoicing.

Zenobia was Albinoni's first opera. Its recitatives lack assurance, but many of its arias already show the simple tunefulness and idiomatic instrumental writing that are the hallmark of his mature style. The surviving score (in *US-Wc*) is of a heavily cut version that perhaps reflects changes made during the original production.

MICHAEL TALBOT

Zenobia di Palmira ('Zenobia of Palmyra'). *Dramma per musica* in three acts by PASQUALE ANFOSSI to a libretto by GAETANO SERTOR; Venice, Teatro S Benedetto, 26 December 1789.

The libretto, by the innovative Sertor, has a different plot from that of Metastasio's *Zenobia*. Publia, daughter of the Roman Emperor Gallieno, has fallen in love with Arsace, Prince of Persia, who is a prisoner of Aureliano [Aurelian], Emperor of Rome, and betrothed to Zenobia, Queen of the Palmyrans. Zenobia arrives to negotiate for Arsace's release, and Aurelian falls in love with her, but she refuses to renounce Arsace. As the Romans rout the Palmyrans, Arsace escapes from prison, joins Zenobia, and leads the Palmyrans in successful retaliation. They are recaptured, and Arsace is condemned to death; but when Zenobia threatens to follow him in death and draws a dagger, Aurelian spares him.

A mature work, *Zenobia* was Anfossi's most successful *opera seria*; Sartori's libretto catalogue lists 11 productions in ten years. The work contains two duets and a trio for the principals and a short third act of four scenes, the last including an aria-length cavatina, and it offers several opportunities for lavish military display.

MARITA P. MCCLYMONDS

Zéphyre ('Zephirus'). *Acte de ballet* by JEAN-PHILIPPE RAMEAU to an anonymous libretto; no known performance in Rameau's time.

Originally entitled 'Les nymphes de Diane', this was probably intended as part of an *opéra-ballet*, possibly the aborted *Les beaux jours de l'Amour* (*see* NAISSANCE D'OSIRIS, LA). It presents the wooing of the nymph Cloris (soprano) by the God of the West Wind, Zephirus (*haute-contre*). While the plot allows little scope for drama, it forms the pretext for much charmingly evocative and descriptive music, notably that depicting the various effects of Zephirus's breezes. The score contains cross-references to a motif derived from Rameau's harpsichord piece *Les niais de Sologne*.

GRAHAM SADLER

Zeppili [Zeppilli], **Alice** (*b* Monte Carlo, 1885; *d* ?Monte Carlo, after 1920). Italian soprano. She sang in Venice from 1902, notably in *Chopin* by Giacomo Orefice and in the title role of Massenet's *Cendrillon* (1905). In 1907 she appeared at the Teatro Regio, Parma, and at Covent Garden as Musetta and in Giordano's *Fedora*. She appeared at the Manhattan Opera House from 1907 (début as Olympia in *Les contes d'Hoffmann*) and sang at the Chicago Opera (1910–14). Guest appearances took her to Egypt, Greece, Bucharest, Buenos Aires and Paris. She returned to Covent Garden in 1914, singing Nannetta, Susanna, Musetta and Oscar. After her retirement from the stage she taught in Monte Carlo. DAVID CUMMINGS

Zerr, Anna (*b* Baden-Baden, 26 July 1822; *d* Winterbach, 14 Dec 1881). German soprano. She studied in Paris and made her début in 1839 in Karlsruhe as Amina (*La sonnambula*). In 1846 she was engaged at the Vienna Hofoper, making her début as Lucia and creating the title role of Flotow's *Martha* (1847). Dismissed from Vienna in 1848 for announcing her intention of singing in a concert for Hungarian refugees in London, she sang at Covent Garden as the Queen of Night (1851), Röschen in Spohr's *Faust* and Catherine in Jullien's *Pietro il grande* (1852). She retired in 1858. ELIZABETH FORBES

Zhelobinsky, Valery Viktorovich (*b* Tambov, 14/27 Jan 1913; *d* Leningrad, 13 Aug 1946). Russian composer. He studied at the Leningrad Conservatory (1928–32) and from the late 1920s was active as a concert pianist. In 1942 he taught at the College of Music in Tambov, where until 1943 he was chairman of the Composers' Union. He wrote five operas, all staged in Leningrad or Moscow in the 1930s.

Pod steklyannïm kolpakom [Beneath the Glass Bubble] (operetta, V. Voinov), Leningrad, 1932

Kamarinskiy muzhik [The Kamarino Peasant] (O. Brik), Leningrad, 15 Sept 1933

Imeninï [Name-day], 1933–4 (Brik, after N. Pavlov), Leningrad, 26 March 1935

Mat' [Mother] (A. Preys and B. Gusman, after M. Gor'kiy), Moscow, Bol'shoy, 1938

Posledniy bal [The Last Ball] (operetta, L. Zeltser and V. Vladimirov), Leningrad, 30 March 1939 DETLEF GOJOWY

Zhenit'ba. Experimental opera by Modest Musorgsky; *see* MARRIAGE.

Zhiganov, Nazib Gayazovich (*b* Uralsk, 2/15 Jan 1911; *d* Kazan, 2 June 1988). Tatar composer. Orphaned at an early age, he studied with G. A. Litinsky at the Moscow Conservatory, graduating in 1938. He held various posts, among them the rectorship of the new Kazan' State Conservatory, from 1945, and the presidency of the governing body of the Composers' Union of the Tatar Autonomous Republic from 1939 for nearly 40 years. His diploma work, the opera *Kachkïn* ('The Fugitive'), was chosen by the Tatar Theatre of Opera and Ballet, Kazan', for its opening in 1939, and all his subsequent operas had their first performances there. His historical-legendary opera *Altïnohach* won a USSR State Prize in 1948. *Dzhalil* was praised for its novel treatment of the idea of the 'positive hero'; based on events in World War II, it has as central figure Zhiganov's friend, the Tatar poet Musa Dzhalil. Zhiganov's use of folk elements in his operas gives the music a distinctive national flavour, though its roots are recognizably in the classical Russian operatic tradition.

first performed at the Tatar Theatre of Opera and Ballet, Kazan'

Kachkïn [The Fugitive], 1939

Irek [Freedom], 1940

Altïnohach [Golden-haired] (M. Dzhalil), 1941

Il'dar, 1942 (Dzhalil), rev. as Doroga pobedï [The Path of Victory], 1954

Tyulyak, 1945, rev. as Tyulyak i Susyilu [Tyulyak and Susyilu], 1967

Poet, 1947

Namus [Honour], 1950

Dzhalil (monologic opera-poem), 1957

*

Y. Girshman: *Nazib Zhiganov* (Moscow, 1957)

STEPHEN JOHNSON

Zhizn' za tsarya. Opera by Mikhail Glinka; *see* LIFE FOR THE TSAR, A.

Zhukovsky, German Leont'yevich (*b* Radziwiłłowo [now Chervonoarmiysk], Volhynia, 29 Oct/11 Nov 1913; *d* Kiev, 15 March 1976). Ukrainian composer. He studied the piano and composition at the Kiev Conservatory, returning there to teach theory (1951–8). In 1950 he was awarded a Stalin Prize, but his opera *Ot vsego serdtsa* ('From the Whole Heart') of the same year was officially banned for ideological deviation.

Marina (V. Dyachenko, after T. H. Shevchenko), Kiev, 12 March 1939

Chest' [Honour] (G. Plotkin), 1943

Ot vsego serdtsa [From the Whole Heart] (V. Bagmet and A. Kovalenko, after E. Mal'tsev), Saratov, 1950; rev., Moscow, Bol'shoy, 16 Jan 1951

Pervaya vesna [First Spring], 1960 (Kiev, 1959)

Andante patetico (opera-ballet), 1960

Kontrastï vekov [Contrasts of Epochs], 1960–67 (3 two-act operas)

Volzhskaya ballada [Volga Ballad] (monodrama), Kiev, 1968; also known as Zhena soldata [The Soldier's Wife]

K. Dankevich: 'G. L. Zhukovsky', *SovM* (1963), no.11, pp.146–7
DETLEF GOJOWY

Zhukovsky, Vasily Andreyevich (*b* Mishenskoye, Belev district, Tula province, 29 Jan/9 Feb 1783; *d* Baden-Baden, 24 April 1852). Russian poet and translator. He was a highly placed official in the government of Tsar Nicholas I. As one of the prime representatives of the Romantic movement in Russia he cast a long shadow over Russian opera in the 19th century. A friend of Glinka, he steered the latter towards writing the opera that won him immortality, *A Life for the Tsar*; Zhukovsky contributed the text of the famous (or infamous) patriotic epilogue-apotheosis that became an alternative tsarist anthem. Earlier, his ballad *Gromoboy* had formed the basis for Alexey Verstovsky's magic-romantic opera *Vadim* (1832), as well as its much later sequel *Gromoboy* (grand fantastic opera, 1854). His translations (which include the standard Russian singing text for Haydn's *The Seasons*) formed the basis for librettos to the operas *Undina* (A. F. L'vov, after La Motte Fouqué, 1848), *The Maid of Orléans* (Tchaikovsky, after Schiller, *Die Jungfrau von Orleans*, 1881) and *Nal' i Damayanti* (Arensky, after the Mahābharata, 1904). RICHARD TARUSKIN

Ziani, Marc'Antonio (*b* Venice, *c*1653; *d* Vienna, 22 Jan 1715). Italian composer, nephew of Pietro Andrea Ziani. In the course of his career he contributed to two distinctly different operatic traditions: from 1674 to 1699 he wrote operas for commercial theatres in and around Venice; from 1700 to 1714 he wrote operas and other dramatic works for the Habsburg court in Vienna.

Ziani presumably studied with his uncle, who may have facilitated his connections with Mantua and Vienna. (In Vienna, Pietro Andrea had served the dowager empress Eleonora (née Gonzaga), of the ruling family of Mantua; he may also have facilitated the Neapolitan restaging of Marc'Antonio's *Alessandro Magno in Sidone*, his first entirely original opera, within a year of its Venetian première.) In 1686 Marc'Antonio became *maestro di cappella* at S Barbara in Mantua, but it is uncertain whether he ever resided there. Between 1687 and 1691 four librettos refer to him as *maestro di cappella* to Ferdinando Carlo Gonzaga, Duke of Mantua. In the 1680s and 90s Ferdinando Carlo was a frequent visitor to Venice, and Ziani wrote for many singers in the duke's employ in his Venetian operas. On 1 April 1700 Ziani was called to Vienna as vice-Kapellmeister to Emperor Leopold I. He was promoted to Kapellmeister in 1712 after the accession of Charles VI, who held him in high esteem.

Ziani's first task as an opera composer was to provide arrangements of older works for the Teatro S Moisè in 1674 and 1676. This activity coincided with the tenure of Francesco Santurini (ii) as impresario at the theatre, a small one, where he reduced the ticket price from four lire to a quarter ducat, an innovation that most other Venetian theatres were forced to adopt within a decade. In 1680 Ziani provided his last arrangement for this theatre – of one of his uncle's most popular operas, *Le fortune di Rodope e Damira*; it was performed with marionettes. From 1679 onwards he wrote for the large Venetian theatres: SS Giovanni e Paolo, S Salvatore, S Angelo and S Cassiano. The only important Venetian theatre he did not work for was S Giovanni Grisostomo, the luxurious theatre owned by the Grimani family which retained the high ticket price. He wrote 24 original operas for Venice, and was one of the most active opera composers from 1687 to 1699, although full scores are extant only for the earlier period of 1674 to 1685. In 1695 he supervised a production of *Alessandro amante eroe* in Turin.

In the course of Ziani's career libretto style changed strikingly from that of such *seicento* librettists as Aurelio Aureli and Giulio Cesare Corradi, focussing on lively character interaction, to that of librettists identified with reform such as Silvani and Zeno, aiming at a consistently elevated style in plot and diction. In addition, Ziani's contrapuntal skill enabled him to negotiate with ease the shift from Venetian commercial theatre, with its focus on the voice, to the Viennese court with its appreciation of counterpoint. Early Venetian scores already demonstrate his preference for continuo parts that maintain their interest and integrity during vocal passages. As in the operas of his contemporaries, Ziani's arias are nearly always in da capo form. His early Venetian scores call for four- or five-part strings with continuo, and occasionally trumpet, while the Viennese operas reflect the varied instrumental forces available at the Habsburg court. In his Viennese scores, two oboes usually double the violins; oboes also have obbligato parts, as do flutes, bassoons, trumpets and viole da gamba. Ziani was among the first to use the chalumeau, in *Caio Popilio* (1704), and he used the lute as a concerting instrument in *Ercole vincitor dell'Invidia*. In his Viennese scores Ziani sometimes contrasted different instrumental forces; for example, a concerto grosso of strings may alternate with a concertino of oboes and bassoon.

In the late 1680s and 1690s Ziani's output for the Venetian stage was surpassed only by C. F. Pollarolo's. Several operas initially set for Venice were restaged in other Italian cities, although it is difficult to ascertain exactly how many later productions retained Ziani's music. The operas he composed for Vienna were tailored to the specific tastes and resources of the Habsburg court, and were only rarely restaged elsewhere.

drammi per musica in three acts, first performed in Venice, unless otherwise stated

La schiava fortunata (G. A. Moniglia and C. G. Corradi), S Moisè, carn. 1674, *I-Vnm*; adaptation of A. Cesti's setting

Leonida in Tegea (N. Minato), S Moisè, carn. 1676, *Vnm*, arias *Vqs*; adaptation of A. Draghi's setting

Alessandro Magno in Sidone (A. Aureli), SS Giovanni e Paolo, carn. 1679; rev. 1683 as La virtù sublimata dal grande, ovvero Il Macedone continente, *Nc*, *Vnm*, arias *Nc*, *Rvat* and *Vqs*; aria ed. M. Zanon, *36 Arie italiane di 36 diversi autori dei secoli XVII e XVIII* (Milan, 1959)

Alcibiade (Aureli), SS Giovanni e Paolo, carn. 1680, *MOe*, *Vnm*, arias *Vqs*

Damira placata (Aureli, rev. F. Acciajuoli), S Moisè, carn. 1680, *Vnm*

Flora (N. Bonis), S Angelo, carn. 1681, *Vnm*, arias *Bca*, *Rvat* and *Vqs*, collab. A. Sartorio

Tullo Ostilio [Alba soggiogata da' romani] (A. Morselli), S Salvatore, carn. 1685, *D-Mbs*, *F-Pc*

L'inganno regnante, ovvero L'Atanagilda regina di Gottia (Corradi), SS Giovanni e Paolo, 26 Dec 1687, arias *GB-Lbl* and *I-Rvat*

Il gran Tamerlano (Corradi), SS Giovanni e Paolo, 1689, arias *F-Pn* and *I-MOe*

Creonte (R. Cialli), S Angelo, aut. 1690, arias *F-Pn* and *I-Rvat*

Falsirena (Cialli), S Angelo, carn. 1690; carn. 1691 as Marte deluso, arias *GB-Lbl*, *I-MOe* and *Rvat*

L'amante eroe (D. David), S Salvatore, carn. 1691; rev. Ferrara, 1695; Turin, carn. 1695, as Alessandro amante eroe, arias *D-MÜs*

La virtù trionfante dell'amore e dell'odio (F. Silvani), S Salvatore, aut. 1691; Milan, Regio Ducal, 1694, as Gli amori ministri della fortuna, arias *GB-Lam* and *I-Rvat*

Rosalinda (A. Marchi), S Angelo, aut. 1692, arias *Rvat*
La moglie nemica (Silvani), S Salvatore, 11 Jan 1694, arias *PAc* and *Rvat*
L'Amore figlio del Merito (M. Noris), S Angelo, carn. 1694, arias *PAc* and *Rvat*
La finta pazzia d'Ulisse (Noris), S Salvatore, carn. 1696, arias *Rvat*
Domizio (Corradi), S Angelo, carn. 1696, arias *Rvat* and *F-Pn*
La costanza in trionfo (Silvani), S Angelo, 5 Nov 1696, arias *B-Bc* and *I-Vc*
I rivali generosi (A. Zeno), S Salvatore, carn. 1697; Florence, 1698, as Belisario in Ravenna, ovvero I rivali generosi, arias *A-Wn*, *F-Pn* and *GB-Ob*
La ninfa bizarra (dramma pastorale, Aureli), Teatro eretto al Dolo sovra la Brenta, nr Venice, Oct 1697
Eumene (Zeno), S Angelo, aut. 1697
Odoardo (Zeno), S Angelo, carn. 1698, arias *Ob*
Egisto re di Cipro (Corradi), S Cassiano, aut. 1698, arias *B-Bc*
Gl'amori tra gli odii, ossia Ramiro in Norvegia (M. A. Rimena), S Cassiano, carn. 1699
Teodosio, S Cassiano, carn. 1699 [lib. not by V. Grimani]
Il duello d'amore e di vendetta (Silvani), S Salvatore, week before 2 Jan 1700
La pace generosa (Silvani, after L. A. Seneca: *Troades*), S Salvatore, 10 Feb 1700
Gordiano Pio (D. Cupeda), Vienna, Wiener Neustadt, 26 July 1700, *D-BB*, *I-Vgc*
Temistocle (azione scenica, Zeno), Vienna, Favorita, 27 June 1701
Gli ossequi della notte (Cupeda), Vienna, Favorita, 25 July 1701
La fuga dell'Invidia (poemetto drammatico, 1), Vienna, Hof, 15 Nov 1701
Romolo (Cupeda), Vienna, Hof, 20 Aug 1702
Esopo (tragicommedia per musica), Vienna, Hof, carn. 1703, *A-Wn* (Act 3)
Caio Popilio (trattenimento musicale, Cupeda), Vienna, Hof, 9 June 1704, *Wn*
Ercole vincitor dell'Invidia (D. Mazza), Vienna, Hof, 19 March 1706, *Wn*
Flora (poemetto drammatico pastorale, P. A. Bernardoni), Vienna, 12 April 1706, with arias by Joseph I, *Wn*, *D-Dlb*
Meleagro (Bernardoni), Vienna, Hof, 16 Aug 1706, *A-Wn*
Introduzione per musica al problema della prima accademia ... se si possi trovare un'amore senza speranza (Bernardoni), Vienna, Hof, 1706, *Wn*
Introduzione per musica al problema della seconda accademia ... se più innamori bella donna che pianga, overo bella donna che canti (Bernardoni), Vienna, Hof, 1706, *Wn*
Introduzione per musica per una altra accademia (Bernardoni), Vienna, Hof, 1707
Alboino, Vienna, Hof, carn. 1707, *Wn* (Act 3) [lib. not by Corradi]
Il campidoglio ricuperato (festa per musica, S. Stampiglia), Vienna, Hof, 26 July 1709, *Wn*
Chilonida (Minato), Vienna, Hof, carn. 1710 (possibly earlier, on 21 April 1709), *Wn*
Atenaide [Act 1] (Zeno), Vienna, Hof, 19 Nov 1714, *Wn*, *D-W* [Act 2 by A. Negri, Act 3 by Caldara]
Amor tra nemici, Vienna, 1714
Andromeda (poemetto drammatico, P. Pariati), Vienna, Hof, 1714, *Wn*

*

A. von Weilen: *Zur Wiener Theatergeschichte: die vom Jahre 1629 bis zum Jahre 1740 am Wiener Hofe zur Aufführung gelangten Werke theatralischen Charackters und Oratorien* (Vienna, 1901)
E. Wellesz: 'Die Opern und Oratorien in Wien von 1660–1708', *SMw*, vi (1919), 5–138
H. C. Wolff: *Die venezianische Oper in der zweiten Hälfte des 17. Jahrhunderts* (Berlin, 1937, 2/1975)
F. Hadamowsky: 'Barocktheater am Wiener Kaiserhof: mit einem Spielplan (1625–1740)', *Jb der Gesellschaft für Wiener Theaterforschung 1951–2*, 7–117
T. Antonicek: 'Die *Damira*-Opern der beiden Ziani', *AnMc*, no.14 (1974), 176–207
H. C. Wolff: 'Italian Opera 1700–1750', NOHM, v (1975), 73–168

HARRIS S. SAUNDERS

Ziani, Pietro Andrea (*b* Venice, probably before 21 Dec 1616; *d* Naples, 12 Feb 1684). Italian composer, uncle of Marc'Antonio Ziani. He became a deacon on 19 March 1639 and a priest on 22 December 1640. In the preface to his op.2 motets (1640) he styles himself canon regular and organist at the convent of S Salvatore in Venice, but he may have already left the congregation by 1641, since his op.3 canzonettas of that year make reference only to his being organist there. During most of the 1650s he was employed at St Mark's, but in what capacity is unclear. In 1657 he succeeded Cazzati as *maestro di cappella* at S Maria Maggiore in Bergamo, which he left two years later to return to St Mark's. In autumn 1662 he went to Innsbruck and, later that year, to Vienna to serve as vice-Kapellmeister to the dowager empress Eleonora. (In winter 1666–7 he was in Dresden to direct music he had composed for the wedding of the Electoral Prince Johann Georg III and Princess Anna Sophia of Denmark.) Ziani left the service of the dowager empress after he was appointed first organist at St Mark's on 20 January 1669, succeeding Cavalli, who had recently been promoted to *maestro di cappella*. In 1673 he was on hand in Naples when two of his works were performed. Four years later he again visited Naples, never to return to his post at St Mark's. (He had failed to obtain the position of *maestro di cappella* on Cavalli's death in April 1676.) Ziani held an honorary position as court organist in Naples until 1680, when he was officially appointed *maestro di cappella*. From 1678 to 1680 he also taught at the conservatory of S Onofrio.

Ziani wrote his first three operas for the short-lived Teatro S Apollinare, a small Venetian theatre that opened in 1651. His *Fortune di Rodope e Damira*, the only opera staged in Venice during the 1657 carnival, proved to be the last opera presented there. Marco Faustini was the impresario at this theatre, having assumed control after his brother Giovanni's death in 1651. After 1657 Faustini left to reopen the Teatro S Cassiano, which he in turn left in 1660 to manage the Teatro SS Giovanni e Paolo. Faustini engaged Ziani for all the theatres he managed. Among Faustini's papers (in *I-Vas*) are 12 letters that Ziani sent from Vienna and Innsbruck in 1665 and 1666, documenting the process involved in arranging a Venetian opera production. These reveal the remarkable speed at which some operas were composed; for example, Ziani claims to have written *Annibale in Capua* in five days. After Ziani's return to Venice in 1669, he wrote for the Teatro SS Giovanni e Paolo for three more seasons, when the theatre was under the management of the owner, Giovanni Grimani; even after settling in Naples, he provided two more scores for S Cassiano.

The librettos Ziani set for the commercial theatres of Venice combine serious and comic elements; few adopt the heroic stance and historical subject matter that prevailed later in the century. The dramatic texts he set for Vienna were sometimes on a smaller scale than opera. Several of these were for court occasions, such as the birthday of Emperor Leopold I or of the dowager empress Eleonora. In the course of Ziani's career, Cavalli, the dominant figure in Venetian opera to the 1660s, was superseded by the younger generation of Antonio Sartorio, Carlo Pallavicino and Giovanni Legrenzi. Along with Cesti, Ziani was important in the transition from Cavalli's style to that of the younger generation, chiefly by responding to the mid-17th-century audience's desire for easily accessible lyricism. In one of his letters, he claims that the public has lost interest in long soliloquies (characteristic of Cavalli), preferring canzonettas. The contrast between the 38 arias of *Le fortune di Rodope e Damira* and the 63 of his last opera, *L'innocenza risorta* (1683), illustrates the change that took place during his career.

Formal variety and smooth transition from one declamatory style to another characterize Ziani's operas. Up to the early 1670s he used a variety of aria forms, any of which could be strophic: bipartite arias, arias in *ABB′* form and arias with refrains, including arias in incipient da capo form. By the late 1670s, da capo form predominates. He often used ostinatos and walking basses for situations in which a character confronts implacable forces. Arioso passages, often in triple metre, are smoothly integrated into recitative. Ziani's instrumental forces respond flexibly to the voice. Most of the arias, like recitative, are accompanied by continuo alone. Detachable ritornellos sometimes follow or, less often, precede continuo arias. In the accompanied arias, upper melodic instruments usually alternate with the voice. The little documentation that survives suggests that the forces for Ziani's Venetian operas were small – 10 to 15 players, on strings, continuo and sometimes one or two trumpets.

See also INNOCENZA RISORTA, L'.

drammi per musica in three acts unless otherwise stated

La guerriera spartana (prol., 3, G. Castoreo), Venice, S Apollinare, carn. 1654

Eupatra (prol., 3, G. Faustini), Venice, S Apollinare, carn. 1655

Le fortune di Rodope e Damira (prol., 3, A. Aureli), Venice, S Apollinare, carn. 1657, *I-IBborromeo*, *MOe*, *Nc*, *Vnm*

L'incostanza trionfante, ovvero Il Theseo (prol., 3, F. M. Piccioli, after Plutarch), Venice, S Cassiano, carn. 1658

Antigona delusa da Alceste (prol., 3, Aureli), Venice, SS Giovanni e Paolo, carn. 1660, *Vnm*

Annibale in Capua (prol., 3, N. Beregan), Venice, SS Giovanni e Paolo, carn. 1661, *D-AN*, *I-Nc* (arias), *Rvat*, *Vnm*; sections ed. in Wolff 1937

Gli scherzi di Fortuna subordinato al Pirro (prol., 3, Aureli), Venice, SS Giovanni e Paolo, carn. 1662, *Vnm*

Le fatiche d'Ercole per Deianira (prol., 3, Aureli), Venice, SS Giovanni e Paolo, carn. 1662, *Vnm*; rev. A. Perruccio, Naples, S Bartolomeo, carn. 1679, *Nc*

L'amor guerriero (prol., 3, C. Ivanovich), Venice, SS Giovanni e Paolo, carn. 1663, *Vnm*; sections ed. in Wolff 1937

Oronisbe (componimento drammatico in musica, 3, A. Draghi), Vienna, 9 June 1663

La congiura del vizio contro la virtù (scherzo musicale, 1, D. Cupeda), Vienna, 15 Nov 1663

La ricreazione burlesca (1), Vienna, 1663 or 1668, *A-Wn*

L'invidia conculcata dalla Virtù, Merito, Valore della S. C. Mta di Leopoldo imperatore (componimento drammatico, Draghi), Vienna, 1664, *Wgm* (1 dance), *Wn*, *I-Vgc*

Circe (Ivanovich), Vienna, 9 June 1665, *Vnm*

Cloridea (Draghi), Vienna, 1665, *Vnm*

Doriclea (prol., 3, G. Faustini), composed for Venice, SS Giovanni e Paolo, carn. 1666, but only prol. perf. as prol. to Cesti: Orontea

L'onore trionfante (D. Federici), Vienna, Favorita, 9 June 1666

Elice (introduzione ad un regio balletto, Federici), Vienna, 18 Nov 1666, *A-Wgm*, *Wn*

Galatea (favola pastorale per musica, 3, Draghi), Vienna, 19 Feb 1667, *Wgm* (sections), *Wn*

Alciade (prol., 3, Faustini), Venice, SS Giovanni e Paolo, carn. 1667

Semiramide (G. A. Moniglia, rev. M. Noris), Venice, SS Giovanni e Paolo, aut. 1670, *D-AN*, *I-Vnm*; sections ed. in Wolff 1937

Ippolita reina delle amazzoni [Act 3] (C. M. Maggi), Milan, Ducale, 1670, *I-Nc*; Act 1 and arias added to Act 2 by L. Busca, Act 2 by P. S. Agostini

Heraclio (Beregan), Venice, SS Giovanni e Paolo, carn. 1671; with prol. (G. Cicinelli), Naples, S Bartolomeo, Dec 1673; *Nc*, *Vnm*, *Vqs* (arias)

Attila (Noris), Venice, SS Giovanni e Paolo, carn. 1672, *IBborromeo*, *Vnm*, *Vqs* (arias)

Chi tal nasce tal vive, ovvero L'Alessandro Bala (A. Perruccio), Naples, S Bartolomeo, Dec 1678, *MC*, *Nc*, arias in *Gl* and *Nc*

Candaule (A. Morselli), Venice, S Cassiano, week before 9 Dec 1679; as Candaule re di Lidia, Naples, Real Palazzo, ded. 21 Dec 1679; *D-AN*, *I-Vnm*, arias in *B-Bc*, *GB-Ob*, *I-MOe*, *Tn* and *Vqs*; sections ed. in Wolff 1937

Enea in Cartagine (M. A. Catania), Palermo, 1680

L'innocenza risorta, ovvero Etio (Morselli), Venice, S Cassiano, week before 6 Feb 1683; as Il talamo preservato dalla fedeltà di Eudossa, Reggio Emilia, 1–11 May 1683, *MOe* (*R*1978: IOB, xii)

Prol. (Cicinelli) to G. A. Boretti: Marcello in Siracusa, Naples, 1673; rev. of A. Sartorio: Orfeo, Naples, 1682, *Nc*

Doubtful: Cleandra (N. Minato), Bologna, 1678 [adaptation of Draghi: Chilonida]

*

A. von Weilen: *Zur Wiener Theatergeschichte: die vom Jahre 1629 bis zum Jahre 1740 am Wiener Hofe zur Aufführung gelangten Werke theatralischen Charakters und Oratorien* (Vienna, 1901)

H. Kretzschmar: 'Weitere Beiträge zur Geschichte der venetianischen Oper', *Jb der Musikbibliothek Peters*, xvii (1910), 61–71

H. C. Wolff: *Die venezianische Oper in der zweiten Hälfte des 17. Jahrhunderts* (Berlin, 1937, 2/1975)

F. Hadamowsky: 'Barocktheater am Wiener Kaiserhof: mit einem Spielplan (1625–1740)', *Jb der Gesellschaft für Wiener Theaterforschung 1951–2*, 7-117

R. Giazotto: 'La guerra dei palchi', *NRMI*, i (1967), 245–86, 465–508; iii (1969), 906–33

T. Antonicek: 'Die *Damira*-Opern der beiden Ziani', *AnMc*, no.14 (1974), 176–207

L. Bianconi: 'Funktionen des Operntheaters in Neapel bis 1700 und die Rolle Alessandro Scarlattis', *Colloquium Alessandro Scarlattis: Würzburg 1975*, 13–116

E. Selfridge-Field: *Venetian Instrumental Music from Gabrieli to Vivaldi* (Oxford, 1975)

H. C. Wolff: 'Italian Opera from the Later Monteverdi to Scarlatti', NOHM, v (1975), 1-72, esp. 39–42

C. B. Schmidt: 'An Episode in the History of Venetian Opera: the *Tito* Commission (1665–66)', *JAMS*, xxxi (1978), 442–66

L. Bianconi and T. Walker: 'Production, Consumption and Political Function of Seventeenth-Century Opera', *Early Music History*, iv (1984), 211–99

P. Fabbri and R. Verti: *Due secoli di teatro per musica a Reggio Emilia: Repertorio cronologico delle opere e dei balli 1645–1857* (Reggio Emilia, 1987)

E. Rosand: *Opera in Seventeenth-Century Venice: the Creation of a Genre* (Berkeley and Los Angeles, 1991)

HARRIS S. SAUNDERS

Zich, Otakar (*b* Králové Městec, 25 March 1879; *d* Ouběnice, nr Benešov, 9 July 1934). Czech composer. While studying mathematics at Prague University (doctorate 1901) he also studied musicology and aesthetics, and later attended a course in composition. From 1901 he taught mathematics and physics at a school in south-west Bohemia and while there collected folksongs and dances, which in turn influenced his own compositions. In 1906 he returned to Prague and completed his *Habilitation* dissertation (1911) on the aesthetic apperception of music. In 1919 he became professor of philosophy at the newly established university in Brno, but in 1924 returned to Prague to become professor of aesthetics.

Zich was essentially a self-taught composer, finding his models in 19th-century Czech national music, particularly that of Smetana and Fibich. Because of his close relation to folk art, he stood apart from the mainstream of early 20th-century Czech music (which tended to follow western European trends). He seldom took his inspiration from modern sources, the most significant exception being his opera *Vina* ('The Sin', composed 1911–15), where following the expressionist plot he showed a fine sense for dramatic musical effect. His compositions are mostly vocal, including three operas and the melodrama *Romance o Černém jezeře* op.6 ('Romance of the Black Lake', 1907). His music has never gained public response and much of it remains unpublished.

Zich's scholarly heritage is more important. Together with his teacher Otakar Hostinský he is considered the founder of Czech musicology, particularly its aesthetics, and a founder of specific semantic theory in music. Among his many writings his studies of Smetana, Dvořák and Berlioz occupy a special place; his *Estetika dramatického umění* ('Aesthetics of Dramatic Art') was published in Prague in 1931.

Malířský nápad [A Painter's Whim] op.7, 1908 (1, Zich, after S. Čech), Prague, National, 11 March 1910
Vina [The Sin] op.10, 1911–15 (3, J. Hilbert), Prague, National, 14 March 1922
Preciézky op.12, 1924 (1, Zich, after Molière: *Les précieuses ridicules*), Prague, National, 21 May 1926

*

Z. Negedlý: 'Otakar Zich: Malířský nápad' [Zich's *A Painter's Whim*], *Směr*, i (1932), 95
J. Mukařovský: 'Otakar Zich: estetika dramatického umění' [Aesthetician of Dramatic Art], *Časopis pro moderní filologii a literaturu*, xix (1933), 318–26
J. Hutter and Z. Chalabala, eds.: *České umění dramatické*, ii: *Zpěvohra* [Czech Dramatic Art: Opera] (Prague, 1941), 301–8

JOSEF BEK

Zichy, Count **Géza** (*b* Sztára, Hungary [now in Slovakia], 23 July 1849; *d* Budapest, 14 Jan 1924). Hungarian composer and poet. He lost his right arm in a hunting accident when he was 14, but became a celebrated piano virtuoso thanks to the instruction and friendship of Liszt. He was director of the National Conservatory in Budapest (1875–1918), Intendant of the Royal Hungarian Opera House (1891–4) and an honorary member of the Hungarian Academy of Sciences (from 1911). Because of his various activities, he began to write operas relatively late, all of them to his own librettos. *A vár története* ('History of the Castle') and *Tündérek tava* ('Fairy Lake'), both performed in the Budapest opera house on 16 May 1888, are not strictly operas. The first, described as '12 orchestral pieces with characteristic poems', is a series of acted tableaux, which are not linked by dramatic content or musical style. The second (orchestrated by Liszt in 1884 and first performed in Vienna in 1885 under the title *Zaubersee*) has a cast of two water nymphs and one man and lacks any real plot.

Alár (1896) is a true opera, with a romantic plot set during the crusades in Hungary and in the Holy Land, describing the adventures of the knight Alár and the tragedy of his lady. The music is mosaic-like, combining Wagnerian declamation with set numbers and a ballet. His next opera, *Roland mester* ('Master Roland', 1899), is closer to the Italian *verismo* style. Its story too is tragic, but is set in a circus on the Champs-Elysées in Paris. The music consists of continuous arioso, alternating between gaiety, sentimentality and tragedy, sometimes with elegant dance rhythms. Zichy's ballet *Gemma* (7 March 1903, Prague), set in the Transylvanian Alps, represents an interesting experiment to revive the melodrama; the action is conveyed by means of recitation and dance, and the composer succeeds in aligning the rhythms of the two elements. His Hungarian historical opera *Nemo* (1905) centres on an imaginary poet and musician from the Rákóczi War of Independence in 1709, the supposed composer of the Rákóczi March. Zichy's setting draws on all elements of Hungarian music, including popular tunes of the time and the rhythmic and melodic patterns of folk music and the Rákóczi March. It became his most frequently performed opera, and he later used it as the second part of a trilogy about Prince Rákóczi. The first part, *II Rákóczi Ferenc* ('Ferenc Rákóczi II', 1909), deals with the leader's childhood and the third, *Rodostó* (1912), portrays him as an old man in exile. This order of composition was not ideal, since in the earlier *Nemo*, when Rákóczi would have been at the height of his power, he has only a supporting role. In all three operas the music remains overtly Hungarian, enriched in melody and harmony by the 'Hungarian' or 'gypsy' scale and by the church modes, which occur often in Hungarian folk music.

all to librettos by Zichy and first performed at the Royal Hungarian Opera House, Budapest; all MSS in H-Bn

Alár (prol., 4), 11 April 1896
Roland mester [Master Roland] (3), 10 Jan 1899
Nemo (prol., 3), 30 March 1905 [pt 2 of trilogy]
II Rákóczi Ferenc [Ferenc Rákóczi II] (prol., 3), 30 Jan 1909 [pt 1 of trilogy]
Rodostó (3), 20 March 1912 [pt 3 of trilogy]

*

LoewenbergA; *StiegerO*
N. N.: *Album gróf Zichy Géza 25 éves működése alkalmából* [Album on the Occasion of Count Géza Zichy's 25 Years of Activity] (Debrecen, 1891)
G. Zichy: *Emlékeim* (Budapest, 1912–13; Ger. trans. as *Aus meinem Leben*, 1913–20)
D. Legány: *Franz Liszt: unbekannte Presse und Briefe aus Wien 1822–1886* (Budapest and Vienna, 1984)

DEZSŐ LEGÁNY

Žídek, Ivo (*b* Kravaře, nr Opava, 4 June 1926). Czechoslovak tenor. He studied in Ostrava, where he made his début as Werther (1944), then joined the Prague Opera in 1948, his roles including Tamino, Don Carlos, Siegmund, Hoffmann, Tom Rakewell and Peter Grimes. Many of his greatest successes were in Janáček operas, most notably as Gregor in *The Makropulos Affair*, Števa and Laca in *Jenůfa* and Skuratov in *From the House of the Dead*. In 1966 he sang the Inventor in the première of Kašlík's *Krakatit*. He also appeared in Vienna, Wexford, Germany, South America and at the Edinburgh Festival (1964 and 1970 as Dalibor and as Mazal in the English première of Janáček's *The Excursions of Mr Brouček*). Though occasionally reported as sounding strained or coarse, he was widely acclaimed for the commanding style of his acting and the clear-cut intensity of his singing. Recordings include ardent performances as Jeník in *The Bartered Bride* and Števa in *Jenůfa*. He became Intendant of the Prague National Opera in 1989.

J. B. STEANE

Ziegler, Delores (*b* Atlanta, 4 Sept 1951). American mezzo-soprano. She took part in the Santa Fe Apprentice Program (1978–9), then sang Maddalena at St Louis and Meg Page at Washington, DC. She made her European début in 1981 at Bonn as Dorabella, then sang Octavian, Cherubino, Berlioz's Marguerite and Adalgisa. In 1984 she sang Dorabella at Glyndebourne and created Teresa in Jens-Peter Ostendorf's *Murieta* at Cologne. She has appeared in Florence, Munich, Vienna, Hamburg, Toronto, Seattle, San Diego and Salzburg, where she sang Sextus in 1988, as well as at the Metropolitan, where she made her début in 1990 as Siébel. Her roles include Idamantes, which she sang at La Scala (1990), Rosina, Carmen, the Composer, Orlofsky and Charlotte. She has a warm, vibrant voice and a handsome figure perfect for trouser roles such as Bellini's Romeo (1991, San Francisco).

ELIZABETH FORBES

Ziehrer, C(arl) M(ichael) (*b* Vienna, 2 May 1843; *d* Vienna, 14 Nov 1922). Austrian composer. He took piano and theory lessons and acted as pianist in the dancing school of Josef Hassreiter. With the backing of the publisher Carl Haslinger, he made his début as conductor of a dance orchestra in 1863. He was bandmaster of the 55th Austro-Hungarian infantry regiment from 1870 to 1873, founded and edited the *Deutsche Musik-Zeitung*, and from 1875 to 1878 was bandmaster of the 76th infantry regiment. At the same time he was giving popular concerts, and in 1878 he formed a civilian orchestra and took over many of Eduard Strauss's musicians. From 1885 to 1894 he was bandmaster of the leading regimental band Hoch und Deutschmeister Nr.4, bringing it to the height of its prestige and taking it to Chicago for the 1893 World's Fair. He had great success with his dance and march compositions, and in 1908 he was named fourth and last holder of the official title 'k. u. k. Hofballmusikdirektor' in succession to three Strausses. In the operetta field his greatest success was with *Die Landstreicher* (1899), but this has since been eclipsed by that of *Der Fremdenführer* (1902), revived at the Raimundtheater in 1943 and the Volksoper in 1978 with great success as an evocation of turn-of-the-century Vienna. Ziehrer wrote homely, tuneful music, highly popular in Vienna; his operettas have retained their popularity mainly because of their stirring marches and dances.

unless otherwise stated, Operetten, first performed in Vienna, and published in Vienna or Leipzig

Mahomed's Paradies (Burleske-Operette, 1, Ziehrer), Harmonie, 26 Feb 1866, unpubd; Das Orakel zu Delfi (Burleske-Operette, 2, C. Costa), Linz, Landes, 21 Sept 1872, unpubd; Cleopatra [Durch drei Jahrtausende] (fantastic burlesque, 3), Komische Oper, 13 Nov 1875, collab. R. Genée and M. von Weinzierl, unpubd; König Jérôme [Immer lustick!] (5, A. Schirmer), Ring, 28 Nov 1878, 2 nos. and various dance arrs. (1879–81); Der kleine Don Juan (L. E. Pohlhammer), Pest, Deutsche, Nov 1879, unpubd; Wiener Kinder (3, L. Krenn and C. Wolff), Carl, 19 Feb 1881, arrs. only

Ein Deutschmeister [Schloss Malakulci] (3, R. Genée and B. Zappert), Carl, 30 Nov 1888, dance arrs. (1888); Wiener Luft (Posse mit Gesang, 3, B. Rauchenegger, C. Lindau and H. Thalboth), An der Wien, 10 May 1889, dance arr. only (1889); Der bleiche Zauberer (indianisches Lagerbild, 1, I. Fuchs, after J. F. Cooper), An der Wien, 20 Sept 1890, unpubd; Der schöne Rigo (2, Krenn and Lindau), Venedig in Wien, 24 May 1898, vs (?1898) [using themes from Ein Deutschmeister]; Die Landstreicher (prelude, 2, Krenn and Lindau), Venedig in Wien, 26 July 1899, vs (1899)

Die drei Wünsche (prelude, 2, Krenn and Lindau), Carl, 9 March 1901, vs (1901); Der Fremdenführer (prelude, 3, Krenn and Lindau), An der Wien, 11 Oct 1902, vs (1902); Der Schätzmeister (3, A. Engel and J. Horst), Carl, 10 Dec 1904, vs (1905); Fesche Geister (prelude, 2, Krenn and Lindau), Venedig in Wien, 7 July 1905, vs (1905); Über'n grossen Teich! (A. Philipp and F. Antony), An der Wien, 2 Sept 1906, collab. E. Eysler, B. von Ujj and F. Ziegler, 1 no. only pubd; Ein tolles Mädel (Vaudeville-Operette, prelude, 2, W. Sterk, after C. Kraatz and H. Stobitzer), Wiesbaden, 24 Aug 1907, vs (1907)

Am Lido (1, O. Tann-Bergler and A. Deutsch-German), Colosseum, 31 Aug 1907, unpubd; Der Liebeswalzer (3, R. Bodanzky and F. Grünbaum), Raimund, 24 Oct 1908 (1908); Herr und Frau Biedermeier (Spl, 1, W. Sterk), Munich, Lustspiel, 9 Jan 1909, vs (1909); Die Gaukler (1, E. and A. Golz), Apollo, 6 Sept 1909, unpubd; In fünfzig Jahren (Burleske-Operette,, 2, Krenn and Lindau), Ronacher, 13 Jan 1911, unpubd; Ball bei Hof (3, Sterk, after T. von Trotha: *Hofgunst*), Stettin, Stadt, 22 Jan 1911, vs (1911); Manöverkinder (3, O. Friedmann and F. Lunzer), Kaisergarten, 22 June 1912, vs (1912)

Fürst Casimir (3, M. Neal and M. Ferner), Carl, 13 Sept 1913, vs (1913); Der Husarengeneral (3, Friedmann and Lunzer), Raimund, 3 Oct 1913, vs (1913); Das dumme Herz (3, R. Oesterreicher and Sterk), Johann-Strauss, 27 Feb 1914, vs (1914); Der Kriegsberichterstatter (8 scenes, Oesterreicher and Sterk), collab. Eysler, B. Granichstaedten, O. Nedbal and C. Weinberger, 1 song (1914); Im siebenten Himmel (3, Neal and Ferner), Munich, Gärtnerplatz, 26 Feb 1916, unpubd

Posthumous arrangements: Die verliebte Eskadron (Operette, 3, Sterk, after B. Buchbinder), Vienna, Johann-Strauss, 11 July 1930, arr. K. Pauspertl, vs (1930); Deutschmeisterkapelle (H. Marischka and Oesterreicher), Vienna, Raimund, 30 May 1958, arr. M. Schönherr, vs (1958)

*

A. Ullrich: 'Carl Michael Ziehrer', *Jahresbericht 1956/57 des Landstrasser Gymnasiums* (Vienna, 1957)

O. Schneidereit: *Operette von Abraham bis Ziehrer* (Vienna, 1966)

M. Schönherr: *Carl Michael Ziehrer: sein Werk, sein Leben, seine Zeit* (Vienna, 1975)

R. Traubner: *Operetta: a Theatrical History* (New York, 1983)

ANDREW LAMB

Zigeunerbaron, Der ('The Gypsy Baron'). *Operette* in three acts by JOHANN STRAUSS to a libretto by IGNAZ SCHNITZER after the novel by Mór Jókai; Vienna, Theater an der Wien, 24 October 1885.

The action takes place in the mid-18th century. Sándor Barinkay (tenor) returns to his native Temesvár after 20 years' exile due to his father's associations with the former Turkish rulers. He has meanwhile followed a catalogue of unlikely occupations ('Als flotter Geist'). The Royal Commissioner, Conte Carnero (baritone), calls the local pig-farmer Zsupán (tenor *buffo*) to witness the deed that will restore Barinkay's lands to him, but Zsupán has been too busy with his pigs to learn to read or write ('Ja, das Schreiben und das Lesen'). Zsupán is anyway none too pleased at Barinkay's return, since he has been making free use of Barinkay's land for farming. Still, in the interest of getting his hands on the treasure reputedly buried on the land, he is happy to encourage Barinkay's interest in his daughter Arsena (soprano). Arsena nevertheless declares that she will marry nobody lower than a baron. Barinkay is now attracted by the singing of the gypsy girl Sáffi (soprano) ('So elend und so treu'), and he is welcomed by a bunch of gypsies as their lost leader. When he thus presents himself to Arsena as a 'gypsy baron', she rejects him afresh, and he immediately pledges allegiance to Sáffi.

In Act 2, with the help of Sáffi and her mother Czipra (mezzo-soprano), Barinkay finds his father's hidden treasure ('Ha, seht es winkt'). However, as a member of the morality commission, Carnero is concerned about the legal status of the relationship between Barinkay and Sáffi. He is unimpressed by Barinkay's assurance that they were married according to gypsy law in a ceremony performed by a bullfinch, with a nightingale singing and two storks as witnesses ('Wer uns getraut'). Just then Count Homonay, governor of the province (light baritone), comes recruiting for the war against Spain ('Her die Hand, es muss ja sein'). Barinkay and (unwittingly) Zsupán enrol, and in Act 3 Zsupán is among the Hungarian troops arriving back in Vienna from the Tagus ('Von des Tajo Strand'). When the main body of troops then marches in ('Hurra, die Schlacht mitgemacht'), Barinkay is a hero at their head, and his properties and Sáffi are formally restored to him.

Produced on the eve of the composer's 60th birthday, the work has a more serious tinge than the normal operetta, representing a step in Strauss's quest for the composition of a genuine opera. The original cast included Alexander Girardi as Zsupán, Carl Streitmann as Barinkay and Ottilie Collin as Sáffi. Modern performances generally give a misleading impression of the original balance of voices, the parts of Zsupán and Homonay customarily being transposed downwards.

ANDREW LAMB

Zilcher, Hermann (Karl Josef) (*b* Frankfurt, 18 Aug 1881; *d* Würzburg, 1 Jan 1948). German composer. Born into a family of musicians, he studied at the Hoch Conservatory in Frankfurt and then embarked on a career as a pianist. He taught from 1908 in Munich, and from 1920 to 1944 was principal of the Würzburg conservatory. As a composer he represented a current of south German traditionalism that was heavily indebted to Schumann and Brahms and sometimes inclined to a popular style. Zilcher employed impressionist harmonies on occasion, and also drew on Baroque music and on folksong. His large output includes incidental music for plays and the operas *Fitzebutze* (Traumspiel, R. Dehmel; 1903, Mannheim) and *Dr Eisenbart* (opera comica, 3, O. Falckenberg; 1922, Mannheim); his music is not always strikingly individual, but gives an impression of vivid inventiveness, with convincing contrapuntal thematic development.

KLAUS KIRCHBERG

Ziliani, Alessandro (*b* Bussetto, 3 June 1906; *d* Milan, 18 Feb 1977). Italian tenor. He studied with Alfredo Cechi in Milan and in 1928 made his début there at the Dal Verme in *Madama Butterfly*. At Rome he sang in the première of Wolf-Ferrari's *La vedova scaltra* (1931) and Mascagni's *Pinotta* (1932). 1932 also brought his début at La Scala, where he continued to appear until 1946. His roles there included Dmitry in *Boris Godunov*, Enzo in *La Gioconda* and Des Grieux in *Manon Lescaut*, in which he was widely considered to be the best of his generation. He made guest appearances at San Francisco in 1938 and travelled extensively in Europe. When Busoni's *Turandot* had its Italian première in 1940 he sang the role of Calaf. He also appeared with Maria Callas in the revival of Rossini's *Armida* at the Florence Festival of 1952. In later years he turned to operetta, films and concert work; he then established himself as an agent, promoting, among others, the career of Luciano Pavarotti. His recordings include the part of Alfredo in the first electrical recording of *La traviata* and display a resonant lyric voice and pleasing style.

J. B. STEANE

Zilioli, Francesco Poncini. *See* PONCINI ZILIOLI, FRANCESCO.

Zilli, Emma (*b* Fagnano, Udine, 11 Nov 1864; *d* Havana, Jan 1901). Italian soprano. She made her début in 1887 at Ferrara as Paolina (*Poliuto*) and in 1889 first sang at La Scala as Camille (*Zampa*). There she created Alice Ford in Verdi's *Falstaff* (1893), repeating the role at Covent Garden in the British première of the opera (1894). A powerful singing actress, she was partial to such roles as Puccini's Manon Lescaut and Fidelia (*Edgar*). She contracted yellow fever while touring South America and died at the height of her career.

ELIZABETH FORBES

Zillig, Winfried (Petrus Ignatius) (*b* Würzburg, 1 April 1905; *d* Hamburg, 18 Dec 1963). German composer and conductor. After preliminary studies in law and music in Würzburg, he became a pupil of Schoenberg in Vienna in 1925, following his teacher to Berlin, 1926–8. In Berlin he also acted as musical assistant to Erich Kleiber at the Staatsoper during the 1927–8 season before securing a position as répétiteur at Oldenburg, where he was involved in the first provincial production of *Wozzeck*. From 1932 to 1937 he was engaged as conductor and theatre composer in Düsseldorf, then moving to Essen. During the war he served as musical director of the Poznán Opera (1940–43). After 1945, he returned briefly to Düsseldorf before becoming principal conductor for Hesse Radio in Frankfurt (1947–51). From 1959 until shortly before his death he was director of the music division of North German Radio in Hamburg.

Although Zillig is principally remembered for his reconstruction of Schoenberg's oratorio *Die Jakobsleiter* and preparation of the vocal score for *Moses und Aron*, he was a prolific opera composer in his own right. As one of the earliest of German composers to employ 12-note procedures, he had the misfortune to achieve wider public attention at a time of great political unrest. Indeed, his opera *Rosse* was given its first performance under Jascha Horenstein only weeks after the Nazis came to power. Based on a play by Billinger in which a mysterious knight murders a tractor dealer as a protest against the mechanization of the land, it embodies an ideological attack on the evils of an industrialized society that might have appealed to certain factions in the new regime. Nevertheless, the highly expressionist and rhythmically frenzied score, which demonstrates the strong influence of Berg, could not be tolerated and the opera was quickly withdrawn.

Subsequently the composer moved towards a more austere style that generated stronger tonal centres. In his second opera, *Das Opfer* (1937), a 12-note row is still employed, but it is cunningly disguised through the use of a cycle of four triads. The work depicts an episode of self-sacrifice and heroism during Scott's expedition to the Antarctic and employs a chorus of penguins to provide a somewhat implausible commentary on the action, much in the manner of a Greek tragedy. It received a cool reception from the critics and survived only four performances. By contrast, the more lyrical and neo-romantic manner of *Die Windsbraut* (1941), the composer's first full-length opera, provoked little opposition. Both this and *Troilus und Cressida* originally commissioned during the war by Rosbaud and the Strasbourg Opera but not performed until 1951, lack the vitality and rhythmic intricacy of the earlier compositions. To some extent, this was recaptured in his later operas, which return to a more complex idiom. Certainly *Die Verlobung in St Domingo* (1957) offers marvellous opportunities for exotic instrumentation. Yet its original conception, as a radio play which juxtaposes a narrator reading an abbreviated form of Kleist's story with more active dialogue for the singers, fails to generate real dramatic tension on the stage.

Rosse (1, R. Billinger), Düsseldorf, 11 Feb 1933 (Kassel, 1959)

Das Opfer (1, R. Goering), Hamburg, Staatsoper, 12 Nov 1937 (Vienna, 1937)

Die Windsbraut (3, Billinger), Leipzig, Neues, 12 May 1941 (Mainz, 1941)

Troilus und Cressida, 1944–9 (3, Zillig, after W. Shakespeare), Düsseldorf, 3 Feb 1951 (Wiesbaden, 1950); rev. 1963

Bauernpassion (television op, Billinger), Munich Radio, 1955

Die Verlobung in St Domingo (radio op, 1, Zillig, after H. von Kleist), North German Radio, 26 May 1957; Bielefeld, 25 Feb 1961 (Kassel, 1960)

Das Verlöbnis (1, Billinger), Linz, 23 Nov 1963 (Kassel, 1963)

*

H. Führmann: '"Das Opfer"', *ZfM*, civ (1937), 1395–6

W. Stärk: '"Die Windsbraut"', *ZfM*, cviii (1941), 410–11

C. Niessen: *Die deutsche Oper der Gegenwart* (Regensburg, 1944)

U. Dibelius: 'Winfried Zillig', *Musica*, xii (1958) 651–5

S. Günther: 'Der Opernkomponist Winfried Zillig', *Das Orchester*, ix (1961), 364–7

——: 'Winfried Zillig: Komponist und Dirigent neuer Musik', *NZM*, Jg.122 (1961), 446–7
C. Orff: 'Nachruf für Winfried Zillig', *Musica*, xviii (1964), 66–7
G. Schumacher: 'Fortschritt, hist. betrachtet: zu einigen Schriften aus der Nachlass von Winfried Zillig', *Musica*, xxvi (1972), 126–30
H. Federhofer: 'Winfried Zilligs Einführung in der Zwölftonmusik', *10 Jahre Hochschule für Musik Graz* (Vienna, 1973)
H.-G. Klein: 'Atonalität in den Opern von Paul von Klenau und Winfried Zillig – zur Duldung einer im Nationalsozialismus verfemten Kompositionstechnik', *GfMKB: Bayreuth 1981*, 490–94 ERIK LEVI

Zimin, Sergey Ivanovich (*b* Orekhovo-Zuyevo, 21 June/3 July 1875; *d* Moscow, 26 Aug 1942). Russian impresario, director of a private opera company in MOSCOW.

Zimmermann, (Johann) Anton (*b* Breitenau [now Široká Niva], bap. 27 Dec 1741; *d* Pressburg [now Bratislava], between 8 and 14 Oct 1781). Austrian composer. By 1772, the year in which his Singspiel *Narcisse et Pierre* is reported to have been performed, he was active at Pressburg. In 1776 he was appointed Kapellmeister and court composer to Prince Joseph Batthyány, the Archbishop of Hungary, and soon developed the orchestra into an outstanding ensemble. Zimmermann's works, mainly symphonies and chamber music, are virtually unexplored; some works attributed to him may not be his, as he has often been confused with like-named contemporaries. Most of his stage works are melodramas. After Georg Benda he was one of the first composers of melodrama who was capable of dramatic characterization in music. *Zelmor und Ermide*, one of the few to survive, consists of music interwoven with spoken text, accompanied recitative, arias and duets.

Narcisse et Pierre (Spl, A. Berger), Pressburg, 1772
Die Wilden (melodrama, J. Schilson), Pressburg, 13 Dec 1777
Andromeda und Perseus (melodrama, 1, A. Cremery), Vienna, Hofburg, 23 April 1781, *CS-Pnm**, vs (Vienna, 1781)
Zelmor und Ermide (melodrama), ?unperf., *D-DO*

Doubtful: Leonardo und Blandine (melodrama, 1), vs (Vienna, ?*c*1808)

*

ČSHS; *WurzbachL*; *ZL*
C. F. Cramer, ed.: *Magazin der Musik*, i (Hamburg, 1783), 190, 276, 480
G. J. Dlabacž: *Allgemeines historisches Künstler-Lexikon* (Prague, 1815), i, 151; iii, 304, 441
Y. Lacroix: 'Un mélodrame du xviiie siècle', *ReM*, v/9 (1924), 1–12
P. Polák: 'Beiträge zur Biographie von A. Zimmermann', *SMw*, xxx (1979), 61–89 MILAN POŠTOLKA

Zimmermann, Bernd Alois (*b* Bliesheim, nr Cologne, 20 March 1918; *d* Königsdorf, nr Cologne, 10 Aug 1970). German composer. Remaining independent of the various fashionable schools of the 1950s and 60s, he developed an individual style in which quotations, carefully woven into a colourful atonal fabric, often played an important part. His single opera, *Die Soldaten*, is sometimes regarded as the most important in German since those of Berg.

Zimmermann's studies at the Cologne Musikhochschule and the universities of Cologne and Bonn were interrupted by military service; but while serving in France he encountered scores by Stravinsky and Milhaud, both formative influences on his music. He resumed studies in 1942, taking lessons from Lemacher and Jarnach, and attended the courses given by Fortner and Leibowitz at Darmstadt, 1948–50. From 1950 to 1952 Zimmermann lectured in music at Cologne University, and from 1957 until his death he taught at the Cologne Musikhochschule. Besides serving as professor of composition he was in charge of the department of radio, film and stage music, genres in which he was himself very active.

Although Zimmermann was not associated with the leaders of new music in the early 1950s, he drew on their innovations; but he had his roots firmly in history, applying his knowledge of historical compositional techniques and ways of establishing contrasts and connections. He drew in particular on medieval Catholic philosophy, on literature from Aeschylus and Dante to Dostoyevsky and Mayakovsky, Pound and Joyce, and on music from the Renaissance to the 20th century (Bach, Mozart and Debussy above all). One of his most characteristic later techniques was quotation. This he referred to as 'collage'; by incorporating melodic elements from both European and non-European music he was able to assimilate a variety of styles. A quotation, in Zimmermann's view, was no mere ornament but could symbolize simultaneous musical gestures on different planes. He did not expect the listener to recognize his quotations, which often appear only fleetingly (though their sources are marked in his scores). In a stylistically alien environment, in music as in history, a quotation loses its innate specific qualities and becomes merely a single ingredient in a 'pluralist' structure akin to the mental filing cabinet of the cultured man. When the work concerned is an opera, *Die Soldaten* (four acts, composed 1957–64), the idea of pluralism can extend to visual as well as musical materials. The Intermezzo from Act 2 exemplifies pluralism in sound: the organ plays the *Dies irae* chant; trombones and tubas join in with the Bach chorale *Wenn ich einmal soll scheiden*; two marches in different tempos are played by the stage ensemble; and four high trumpets give out another chorale, *Komm, Schöpfer Geist*. Scenically the opera uses five planes of action, the end of Act 2 combining three scenes on three planes at the same time. To the composer's own libretto based on J. M. R. Lenz's play, the opera was first performed at the Cologne Opera on 15 February 1965.

Apart from his 'serious' works, Zimmermann composed numerous scores for radio and the theatre, and arrangements for the light orchestras of radio stations; this gave him valuable experience in matters of concern to him – the spoken word, drama and ensemble activity, as well as opportunities to explore the capabilities of instruments and combinations. At the time of his death he was working on a second opera, *Medea*, to a libretto by H. H. Jahnn.

See also SOLDATEN, DIE.

*

M. Lichtenfeld: 'Zimmermann, Bernd Alois', *Rheinische Musiker*, v, ed. K. G. Fellerer (Cologne, 1967), 136–8
M. Rothärmel: 'Der pluralistische Zimmermann', *Melos*, xxxv (1968), 97–102
H. Bienek: 'Kommen wird der Tod', *Melos*, xxxvii (1970), 427–8
H. Krellmann: 'Bernd Alois Zimmermann', *Musica*, xxiv (1970), 485–7
H. H. Stuckenschmidt: 'Ein starker, ein freier Geist', *Melos*, xxxvii (1970), 349
A. Seipt: 'Die Soldaten', *Neue Musik seit 1945* (Stuttgart, 1972), 360–70
H. Halbreich: 'Bernd Alois Zimmermann', *Festschrift für einen Verleger: Ludwig Strecker* (Mainz, 1973), 242–58
K. Kirchberg: 'Omnia tempus habent: ein Rückblick auf Leben und Werk Bernd Alois Zimmermanns', *Neue Musik in der Bundesrepublik Deutschland* (Cologne, 1974), 35–51

M. Karbaum: 'Zur Verfahrensweise im Werk Bernd Alois Zimmermanns', *De ratione in musica: Festschrift Erich Schenk* (Kassel, 1975), 275–85
P. Becker: 'Aspekte der Lenz-Rezeption in Bernd Alois Zimmermanns Oper *Die Soldaten*', *Musiktheater heute: Darmstadt 1982*, 94–104
E. Fischer: 'Bernd Alois Zimmermanns Oper *Die Soldaten*: zur Deutung der musikalischdramatischen Struktur', *Festschrift Heinz Becker* (Laaber, 1982), 268–89
W. Gruhn: 'Die Entstehungsgeschichte von Bernd Alois Zimmermanns Oper *Die Soldaten*', *Mf*, xxxviii (1985), 8–15
N. Tschulik: *Musiktheater in Deutschland: die Oper im 20. Jahrhundert* (Vienna, 1987) MARION ROTHÄRMEL

Zimmermann, Erich (*b* Meissen, 29 Nov 1892; *d* Berlin, 24 Feb 1968). German tenor. He studied in Dresden, where he made his début in 1918. Engagements in Dortmund, Brunswick and Leipzig followed; from 1925 to 1931 he was a member of the Staatsoper in Munich, and from 1931 to 1934 sang in Vienna. After a season in Hamburg he joined the Berlin Staatsoper, where he sang from 1935 to 1944. He rejoined the Dresden company in 1946 and ended his career at the Berlin Städtische Oper. He first sang at Bayreuth in 1925 as David and an Esquire (*Parsifal*), and returned regularly until 1944 as Mime and David. He made his first appearances at Covent Garden in 1934 as Jaquino and Mime. He sang Mozart's Don Basilio at Salzburg, (1930–32) and also appeared there as Monostatos and Valzacchi.

HAROLD ROSENTHAL/R

Zimmermann, Johann Heinrich F. (*b* Hamburg, *c*1742; *d* Brunswick, 1792). German stage designer. He studied painting and architecture in Italy and was in Rome in 1785. After working in Hamburg as a set designer, he served the Duke of Brunswick from 1788 until his death. The few extant designs in his hand are in the Berlin Kunstbibliothek. One, typical of an *opera seria*, depicts a partial arcade in an open courtyard of a palace with several military characters; to the left on a richly decorated throne sits a crowned female figure. Zimmermann's work appears to have been influenced by J. O. Harms and members of the Galli-Bibiena family, his predecessors of some 80 years earlier.

*

U. Thieme and F. Becker, eds.: *Lexikon der bildenden Künstler* (Leipzig, 1907–50), xxxvi, 513
E. Berckenhagen: *Bretter die die Welt bedeuten: Entwürfe zum Theaterdekor und zum Bühnenkostüm in fünf Jahrhunderten* (Berlin, 1978), 127–8 EVAN BAKER

Zimmermann, Margarita (*b* Buenos Aires, Aug 1942). Argentine mezzo-soprano. She studied in Buenos Aires, making her début in 1977 at the Teatro Colón as Gluck's Orpheus, then singing Carmen and Ulrica at the Landestheater, Salzburg. She made her American début at Miami in 1979 as Delilah and her Covent Garden début in 1980 as Cherubino, and sang Rosina at San Francisco (1982). She has sung in Brussels, Naples, Madrid, Bologna, Venice, Geneva, Rome, Lyons and Paris. Her repertory includes Juno (Cavalli's *Ercole amante*), Purcell's Dido, Handel's Agrippina and Julius Caesar, Dorabella, Idamantes, Zerlina, Sextus, Rosina (Haydn's *La vera costanza*), Andromache (*Ermione*), Fricka and Lola. She created the title role of Piazzolla's *Maria di Buenos Aires* (1987, Turcoing). Her beautiful, warm-toned voice, not large but well-projected, is particularly effective in French music: Berlioz's Marguerite and Dido, and Massenet's Charlotte, Dulcinée and Thérèse are among her finest roles, while she sang the Old Prioress (*Dialogues des Carmélites*) in Rome in 1991.

ELIZABETH FORBES

Zimmermann, Udo (*b* Dresden, 6 Oct 1943). German composer. He was encouraged to compose by his choirmaster at the Dresden Kreuzchor, Rudolf Mauersberger, and by the theorist Iwan Schönebaum. His first works (motets) were performed by the choir in 1960. He had planned to become a singer but in 1962 went to the Dresden Hochschule für Musik to study composition (with Johannes Paul Thilman), conducting and singing. From 1968 to 1970 he studied with Günter Kochan at the Akademie der Künste der DDR, where he received the Felix Mendelssohn-Bartholdy scholarship three times and was awarded the Karl Marx Students' Prize in 1968. His *Sonetti amorosi* won distinguished mention at the International Composers' Tribune in Paris in 1971, and in 1972 and 1973 he was awarded the Hanns Eisler Prize by Radio DDR as well as national prizes in 1975 and 1987. In 1970 he was engaged by the Dresden Staatsoper as adviser on contemporary music theatre, and in 1976 he was appointed professor of composition at the Dresden Hochschule für Musik. Since 1978 he has directed the Studio Neue Musik performances given at the Dresden music festivals at which Stockhausen, Ligeti and Kagel made their first appearances in East Germany; and in 1986 he became director of the newly founded Dresden Zentrum für Zeitgenössische Musik. He became artistic adviser to the opera workshop at Bonn Opera in the same year, and was appointed Intendant of Leipzig Opera in 1990.

Zimmermann is a rare example of a composer who has been recognized and valued equally in East and West Germany; he is also noted as a conductor of his own and other composers' works, in which capacity he has appeared in North America and Japan. However, his work developed outside the conventions of the post-war serialist avant garde of the Darmstadt school, going its own way in the rhetorical, laconic, linear and theatrical style of 'new simplicity'. He counts Hans Werner Henze and the Polish school of composers such as Witold Lutosławski among his sources of inspiration; as an opera composer he acknowledges the influence of Mozart and Verdi, and to a lesser extent Wagner. The operatic public owes to Zimmermann the revival of the supposedly extinct genre of *Literaturoper*, to which he has brought fresh ideas, particularly in his use of monody and his raising of relevant humanitarian questions. He is among the most frequently performed operatic composers in Germany in the early 1990s and has embarked on three further operatic projects, on *Gantenbein* (from Max Frisch's novel *Mein Name sei Gantenbein*), *Don Quichotte* and *Die Sündflut* (after Ernst Barlach).

See also LEVINS MÜHLE; SCHUHU UND DIE FLIEGENDE PRINZESSIN, DER; WEISSE ROSE, DIE; and WUNDERSAME SCHUSTERSFRAU, DIE.

Die weisse Rose (8 scenes, I. Zimmermann), Dresden, Staats, Oper Studio, 17 June 1967; rev. version (W. Willaschek, after I. Zimmermann), Hamburg, Staats, 27 Feb 1986
Die zweite Entscheidung (7 scenes, 3 interludes, I. Zimmermann), Magdeburg, 10 March 1971
Levins Mühle (9 scenes, I. Zimmermann, after J. Bobrowski), Dresden, Staats, 27 March 1973
Der Schuhu und die fliegende Prinzessin (E. Schmidt and U. Zimmermann, after P. Hacks), Dresden, Staats, 30 Dec 1976
Die wundersame Schustersfrau (2, Schmidt and U. Zimmermann, after F. G. Lorca), Schwetzingen, 25 April 1982

E. Schwinger: 'Die Oper "Levins Mühle"', *Musica*, xxvii (1973), 268–9
F. Hennenberg: *Udo Zimmermann für Sie porträtiert* (Leipzig, 1983)
W. Lange: 'Udo Zimmermanns fünfte Oper: *Die wundersame Schustersfrau*', *Oper heute*, vii (1984), 90–109

DETLEF GOJOWY

Zingara, La ('The Gypsy Girl'). Intermezzo in two acts by RINALDO DI CAPUA; Paris, Opéra, 19 June 1753.

Nisa (soprano), a gypsy girl, with the connivance of her brother Tagliaborsi (tenor), tricks the old miser Calcante (bass) into parting with his purse and finally into marrying her. Tagliaborsi appears in disguise first as a bear and then as a devil. Calcante has a mute servant, Taddeo, and there is a chorus of gypsies in the finale.

Rinaldo's lively intermezzo played nearly as large a role in the Querelle des Bouffons as Pergolesi's *La serva padrona*. It shows a remarkable variety of resources for a comic opera of this date, including both comic and serious arias, accompanied recitatives and a concluding trio with chorus. Its history is complicated. Six of the arias were taken from Rinaldo's *Il cavalier Mignatta* (1751), which employs similar stock characters. The first Paris production and a revision given at Pesaro in 1755, *Il vecchio amante e la zingara* (*dramma giocoso* in two acts), were mounted by Eustachio Bambini's troupe; possibly Bambini, or his tenor Cosimi, had a hand in the work's genesis. Later in 1755 it was revised and translated into French by C.-S. Favart as *La bohémienne* (*opéra comique* in two acts) and performed at the Comédie-Italienne, Paris. The first Paris production may not have been the original version, and no personal connection with Rinaldo has been established for any of the known productions. Some later versions incorporate numbers by other composers, not all of whom have been identified. STEPHEN C. FISHER

Zingarelli, Niccolò Antonio (*b* Naples, 4 April 1752; *d* Torre del Greco, 5 April 1837). Italian composer. At the age of seven he entered the Conservatorio di S Maria di Loreto in Naples, where Cimarosa was a fellow pupil. His teachers included Fenaroli, Anfossi and Sacchini, and when he left the conservatory in 1769 he may also have studied with Speranza. He worked as an organist and violinist at Torre Annunziata until the Duchess of Castelpagano rescued him from the drudgery of his duties. In 1781 his first opera *Montezuma* was performed at the Teatro S Carlo, Naples; critical opinion varied, but Haydn evidently thought it worth revising for the court theatre at Eszterháza. With the influential support of his patron, Zingarelli began an extremely successful theatrical career, working mostly in northern Italy – Milan, Venice, Genoa, Turin, Modena, Mantua and Trieste – and also in Florence and Rome.

In 1790, at the height of the Revolution, Zingarelli visited Paris, where his opera *Antigone* was performed without success. He probably composed two other operas during his visit: *Les Hespérides* and *Pharamond* were accepted but not produced at the Opéra. From 1792 to 1794 he was *maestro di cappella* of Milan Cathedral, where he succeeded Monza, and from 1794 to 1804 he held a similar post at the Santa Casa in Loreto. After P. A. Guglielmi's death in 1804 Zingarelli became *maestro di cappella* at St Peter's, Rome. As a result of his refusal to conduct the Te Deum for Napoleon's infant son, who was crowned King of Rome, he was arrested and sent to France. But Napoleon was fond of his music; he was soon repatriated, and in 1813 on the Emperor's recommendation he was appointed director of the Royal Conservatory of Naples in place of Paisiello, Fenaroli and Tritto, a controversial appointment that led to the resignation of the rector, Marcello Parrino. After Paisiello's death in 1816 Zingarelli was also appointed *maestro di cappella* of Naples Cathedral. He had a busy teaching career (Mercadante, Michael Costa and Bellini were among his pupils) and he received many academic honours. He became known as a zealous defender of the Neapolitan musical tradition, and was fiercely opposed to innovation, to Rossini and to Romanticism.

Zingarelli was a prolific composer in all vocal and many instrumental genres. Many of his best works – *Artaserse*, *Pirro*, *Giulietta e Romeo*, *Ines de Castro* and *Edipo a Colono* – were revised by his contemporaries. Although he was not temperamentally inclined to comedy, he wrote at least two successful comic operas, *Il mercato di Monfregoso* and *Il ritratto*. His most famous opera, *Giulietta e Romeo*, was performed for several decades (often as a pasticcio, with additional music by other composers to suit different circumstances). Celebrated interpreters of Romeo include Girolamo Crescentini, Giuditta Pasta and Maria Malibran. *Pirro* was part of the repertory of Luigi Marchesi (who published variations on the rondo 'Cara, negli occhi tuoi'). Other successful operas were *Apelle*, *Il conte di Saldagna*, *Il ratto delle Sabine* (influenced by Cimarosa's *Gli Orazi ed i Curiazi*) and *Berenice*.

Zingarelli's style is characterized by thin textures, with prominent vocal lines and an almost obsessive striving for naturalness and simplicity that hovers between a tender, moving pathos and a restricting banality of invention. His arias benefited from their association with such singers as Crescentini, Josephina Grassini, Marchesi, Angelica Catalani, G. B. Rubini, Pasta and Malibran, for whom the simplicity of his writing left ample room for improvisation. His orchestration, rooted in classic Neapolitan models of the 1770s and enriched by his study of Haydn and Mozart, came under other improving influences during the 1780s and 90s. Along with Cimarosa and Guglielmi, Zingarelli moved towards the exploitation of instrumental timbres for expressive purposes. His tendency to extend conventional forms led to elaborate ensemble scenes, producing various schemes: simple or accompanied recitative; solo rondo or cabaletta; choral intervention; intervention of other soloists and duet or trio, with chorus; and ensemble with solos (or double duet or double trio) and chorus. But the centre of Zingarelli's interest remained the expression of tenderness and emotion in a solo, especially in arias for secondary characters accompanied by strings, the evocation of pathos and the development of a lyrical vein which, though sentimental, is often effective. Some of his arias remained popular with distinguished singers until well into the 1820s and 30s, when the advent of Rossini, Bellini and Donizetti effectively consigned the descendants of the Neapolitan school to oblivion.

After 1811 Zingarelli retired from the theatre and returned to composing or reworking stage oratorios. These provide interesting evidence for the way in which an aging composer, standing for an intolerant adherence to the legendary Neapolitan tradition, attempted to adapt his style to new tastes, through more complex scene structure, a richer choral element and the abandonment of writing for castratos.

In his long career Zingarelli collaborated with the best librettists of his day: Foppa, Moretti, Sertor, Ferretti, Sografi, De Gamerra, Rossi, Romanelli and, in France, Marmontel. He favoured plots drawn from the best literary sources and only rarely set librettos containing references to contemporary political problems; when he did set these his music exploited only the possibilities offered by situations: the 'prayer' aria, the love duet, the complications of plot in a first-act finale, the oracular or nocturnal scene, the secret meeting of characters (often a pivotal scene, at the beginning of Act 2 or 3), and the choral finale.

Variously judged by critics and quickly overtaken by changes in musical taste, Zingarelli was both extolled and denigrated as a teacher and as guardian of the conservatory tradition. He was the last major composer of *opera seria*. Much of his large output, in the hands of competent and sensitive performers, provides valuable evidence of the vitality of the 'Neapolitan' tradition.

See also GIULIETTA E ROMEO (i); INES DE CASTRO (i); and PIRRO, RE D'EPIRO.

opere serie unless otherwise stated

I quattro pazzi (int), ?Naples, Conservatory S Maria di Loreto, 1768
Montezuma (3, V. A. Cigna-Santi), Naples, S Carlo, 13 Aug 1781, *A-Ee, I-Nc, P-La*
Alsinda (3, F. Moretti), Milan, Scala, 22 Feb 1785, *A-Wgm, H-Bn* (addns by Haydn), *I-Mc, US-Wc*
Ricimero (3, F. Silvani), Venice, S Benedetto, 5 May 1785
Armida (3, J. Durandi), Rome, Dame, Feb 1786, arias *I-Bsf* and *Rsc*
Antigono (2, after P. Metastasio), Mantua, Ducale, 13 April 1786, *F-Pn, I-PAc*
Ifigenia in Aulide (3, Moretti), Milan, Scala, 27 Jan 1787, *F-Pn, I-Mc, US-Wc*
Artaserse (3, after Metastasio), Trieste, Regio, 19 March 1789, *F-Pn, US-Wc*
Antigone (3, J. F. Marmontel), Paris, Opéra, 30 April 1790, *B-Bc, F-Pn, Po**
La morte di Cesare (3, G. Sertor), Milan, Scala, 26 Dec 1790, *GB-Lbl*
Pirro, re d'Epiro (3, G. De Gamerra), Milan, Scala, 25 Dec 1791, *D-DS, Dlb, F-Pn, I-Bc, Fc, Mc, Nc, PAc, US-Wc*
Annibale in Torino (2 or 3, Durandi), Turin, Regio, carn. 1792, *I-MOe, Mr*
Atalanta (?3, C. Olivieri), Turin, Regio, carn. 1792
L'oracolo sannita (3, D. Del Tufo), Milan, Scala, carn. 1792, *Nc*
Il mercato di Monfregoso (ob, 2, after Goldoni: *Il mercato di Malmantile*), Milan, Scala, 22 Sept 1792, *D-DS, F-Pn*, I-Fc, Nc*
La Rossana (3, P. Calvi), Genoa, S Agostino, carn. 1793, arias *Mc*
La secchia rapita (ob, 2, A. Anelli), Milan, Scala, 7 Sept 1793, *IBborromeo, Mc*
Apelle (2, A. S. Sografi), Venice, Fenice, 18 Nov 1793, *D-Mbs, I-Fc, Mc* (as Apelle e Campaspe, 3), *US-Wc*
Alzira (3, ?G. Rossi, after Voltaire), Florence, Pergola, 7 Sept 1794, duet *I-Mc* and *Rsc*, arias *FAN, Fc, Gl, Mc, Nc* and *PAc*
Quinto Fabio (2, after Zeno: *Lucio Papirio dittatore*), Livorno, Accademia degli Avvalorati, aut. 1794, *Fc*
Il conte di Saldagna (3, Moretti), Venice, Fenice, 24 Dec 1794, *A-Wgm, F-Pn*, I-Fc, Mc, MOe, Nc, OS, US-Bp*
Gli Orazi e i Curiazi (2, G. Sernicola), Naples, S Carlo, 4 Nov 1795, *I-Nc*
Giulietta e Romeo [Romeo e Giulietta] (3, G. Foppa), Milan, Scala, 30 Jan 1796, *D-DS, Hs, Mbs, Sl, F-Pn, GB-Lbl, I-Bc, BZtoggenburg, Fc, Mc, Mr, Nc, US-Bp, Wc*
Andromeda (2, G. Bertati), private perf., Venice, 1796, *I-Mc* (orch. parts only)
La morte di Mitridate [Il Mitridate] (2, Sografi), Venice, Fenice, 27 May 1797, *Mr*
Meleagro (3, G. Schmidt), Milan, Scala, Jan 1798, *Mr*
Carolina e Mexicow (3, G. Rossi), Venice, Fenice, carn. 1798, aria *Mc*
Ines de Castro (2, A. Gasperini), Milan, Carcano, 11 Oct 1798, *A-Wgm, D-DS, Sl, F-Pn, I-Fc, FZc* (Act 2)
I veri amici repubblicani (3, G. Boggio), Turin, Regio, 26 Dec 1798
Il ritratto (ob, 2, L. Romanelli), Milan, Scala, 12 Oct 1799, *F-Pn, I-Fc*
Il ratto delle Sabine (2, Rossi), Venice, Fenice, 26 Dec 1799, *F-Pn, I-Fc, Mr*
Clitennestra (2, F. Salfi), Milan, Scala, 26 Dec 1800, *Mr*
La notte dell'amicizia (G. Foppa), Venice, Fenice, carn. 1802
Edipo a Colono (2, Sografi), Venice, Fenice, 26 Dec 1802, *Mr*
Il bevitore fortunato (ob, 2, Romanelli), Milan, Scala, Nov 1803, *Mr*
Il ritorno di Serse (G. De Ferrari), Modena, Ducale, 8 July 1808
Baldovino (2, J. Ferretti), Rome, Argentina, 11 Feb 1811, *Rdp*
Berenice, regina d'Armenia (2, Ferretti, after Zeno: *Lucio Vero*), Rome, Valle, 12 Nov 1811, duet *Rsc*, finale *Fc* and *Mc*, arias *Fc, Rc* and *Rsc*
Malvina, Naples, S Carlo, carn. 1829, collab. M. Costa

Undated, lost, only frags. extant: Alessandro nelle Indie; Adriano in Siria; Attilio Regolo; Catone in Utica; Castore e Polluce; Ciro riconosciuto; Demetrio; Enea e Lavinia; L'eroe cinese; Ipermestra; Irene; Nitteti; Le nozze di Dorina; Olimpiade; Partenope; Il re pastore

*

ES (U. Prota Giurleo); *FlorimoN*
G. Carpani: *Le Haydine* (Milan, 1812, 2/1823)
——: *Le rossiniane ossia Lettere musico-teatrali* (Padua, 1824)
F. Costabile: 'Niccolò Zingarelli', *Poliorama pittoresco*, i (1836–7), 357–9
R. Liberatore: 'Necrologia di Niccolò Zingarelli', *Gli annali civili del regno delle Due Sicilie*, xxviii (Naples, 1837), 3–56
E. de Tipaldo: *Biografia degli italiani illustri* (Venice, 1837), 475–6
A. de la Fage: 'Nicolas Zingarelli', *Miscellanées musicales* (Paris, 1844), 222–51
Stendhal: 'Notes d'un dilettante', *Mélanges d'art et de littérature* (Paris, 1867), 285–91
O. Chilesotti: *I nostri maestri del passato* (Milan, 1882), 255–67
N. Manferrari: *Dizionario universale delle opere melodrammatiche* (Florence, 1954), 435–8
D. Bartha and L. Somfai: *Haydn als Opernkapellmeister* (Budapest, 1960), 290–94
F. Lippmann: 'Vincenzo Bellini und die italienische Opera Seria seines Zeit: Studien über Libretto, Arienform und Melodik', *AnMc*, no.6 (1969), 70–74
W. Witzenmann: 'Grundzüge des Instrumentation in italienischen Opern von 1770 bis 1839', *AnMc*, no.21 (1982), 276–331
M. Caraci: 'Niccolò Zingarelli tra mito e critica', *NRMI*, xxii (1988), 375–422
S. Balthazar: 'Mayr, Rossini, and the Development of the Early *concertato* Finale', *JRMA*, cxvi (1991), 236–66

MARIA CARACI VELA

Zini, Francesco Saverio (*fl* Naples, *c*1770–1803). Italian librettist. He worked almost exclusively in Naples, and is known particularly for his connection with P. A. Guglielmi. His librettos, all comic or semi-serious, are often set in or around Naples, and sometimes include dialect roles. He seemed particularly fond of comedies of disguise and mistaken identity; the disguise often involves a change of class and provides opportunities for the depiction of inept attempts to be noble, or true nobility shining through humble circumstances: both are found, for example, in *La villanella ingentilita*, set by Guglielmi in 1779.

commedie per musica unless otherwise stated

L'amante confuso, P. Anfossi, 1772; *Dal finto il vero*, G. Paisiello, 1776; *La villanella ingentilita*, P. A. Guglielmi, 1779; *La viaggiatrice* (dg), G. Gazzaniga, 1780; *La stravagante*, Gazzaniga, 1781; *I mietitori*, Guglielmi, 1781; *L'impegno*, G. Furno, 1783; *Lo studente*, G. Monti, 1783; *La donna fedele*, Monti, 1784; *La virtuosa in Mergellina*, Guglielmi, 1785; *Il fanatico burlato*, D. Cimarosa, 1787; *La molinarella spiritosa*, G. Tritto, 1787; *Il ritratto*, F. Bianchi, 1787

La pastorella nobile, Guglielmi, 1788; *La bella pescatrice*, Guglielmi, 1789; *L'ultima che si perde è la speranza*, M. Bernardini, 1790; *Gli amante della dote* (dg), S. Palma, 1791 (Guglielmi, 1791, as La sposa contrastata); *Il poeta di campagna*, Guglielmi, 1792; *Gli accidenti della villa*, P. Dutillieu, 1794; *Liretta e Giannino*, Valentino Fioravanti, 1795; *L'inganno poco dura*, M. A. Portugal, 1796; *Il nemico delle donne*, Dutillieu, 1797; *Gli sposi in cimento*, L. Mosca, 1800; *Le stravaganze d'amore*, Mosca, 1800; *Il ritorno impensato*, Mosca, 1802; *L'amante astuto*, C. Jannoni, 1802; *La donna di bell'umore*, G. Elia, 1803 MARY HUNTER

Zirkusprinzessin, Die ('The Circus Princess'). *Operette* in three acts by EMMERICH KÁLMÁN to a libretto by JULIUS BRAMMER and ALFRED GRÜNWALD; Vienna, Theater an der Wien, 26 March 1926.

At the Stanislavsky Circus in St Petersburg, the mysterious, masked 'Mister X' (tenor) creates a sensation with his daredevil act. In the audience is Princess Fedora Palinska (soprano), who has recently rejected the attentions of Prince Sergius Vladimir (baritone). To avenge himself the Prince hires 'Mister X' to pose as an aristocrat and woo and marry her. 'Mister X' turns out to be Baron Korosov, a young hussar officer disinherited for falling in love with his uncle's fiancée. The latter was none other than Fedora, and the two are only too happy to be reunited. First produced with Hubert Marischka and Betty Fischer in the leading roles, the work has as its principal numbers the tenor solo 'Zwei Märchenaugen' and the *buffo* song 'Die kleinen Mäderln im Trikot'.

ANDREW LAMB

Zirra, Alexandru (*b* Roman, 14 July 1883; *d* Sibiu, 23 March 1946). Romanian composer. He studied at the Iaşi Conservatory (1902–5), then took composition lessons with Gatti at the Milan Conservatory (1905–7, 1909–11). Returning to Romania, he taught at the conservatories in Iaşi and Cernăuţi, and was briefly director of the Romanian Opera House in Bucharest (1940–41).

Zirra was above all attracted to the theatre. Most of his six stage works are based on episodes in Romanian history, and all attest to his supreme handling of the national dramatic-lyrical genre of which, with Caudella, Stephănescu, Drăgoi and Nottara, he was an originator. His greatest achievements were the opera *Alexandru Lăpuşneanu* (1935) and the musical fairy-tale for children *Capra cu trei iezi* ('The Goat with Three Kids', 1939). Zirra's operas give pride of place to the choruses and vocal lines, and there is extensive use of ideas from folk music: recitatives in folk style, melodies built of motifs from the largely improvised genre *doina*, modal harmonies and orchestration influenced by folk instruments. Occasionally Zirra drew on Byzantine chant, as in the friars' chorus in the third act of *Alexandru Lăpuşneanu*. He had a gift for treating powerful dramatic conflicts, despite his essentially lyrical temperament, and this predilection may explain the large number of programmatic orchestral works in his output.

all to librettos by the composer

Luceafărul, 1912 (musical fairy-tale, after M. Eminescu)

Alexandru Lăpuşneanu, 1930–35 (3 acts, 4 tableaux, after C. Negruzzi), Bucharest, Romanian Opera, 6 March 1941; rev. 1944

O făclie de Paşti [An Easter Torch], 1937 (3, after I. L. Caragiale)

Capra cu trei iezi [The Goat with Three Kids], 1939 (children's fairy-tale op, 2, after I. Creangă), Bucharest, Romanian Opera, 23 Dec 1941

Furtuna [The Tempest], 1941 (3, after G. Ureche)

Ion Vodă Potcoavă, 1943 (3) VIOREL COSMA

Zítek, Vilém (*b* Prague, 9 Sept 1890; *d* Prague, 11 Aug 1956). Czech bass. He trained as a mechanic, but at 18 he joined a choral society and then studied singing with Alois Vávra (1909–11). In 1911 he joined the Prague National Theatre. In the 1920s and 30s he was the company's leading member and was given many opportunities by Ostrčil, then head of opera, with whom Zítek maintained a close friendship. Zítek studied with Giovanni Binetti in Milan in 1925 and then took short engagements in Turin, Copenhagen, Milan (singing Hunding, among other roles, under Toscanini), Stockholm, Paris, Berlin, Florence, Yugoslavia and the USSR; his career was cut short by a heart attack in 1947.

Zítek had a sonorous, controlled voice of wide compass and with rich possibilities of expression and timbre, an outstanding ability as an actor and a feeling for the heroic. Among his most remarkable dramatic roles were Vodník in *Rusalka* (Dvořák), Kecal, the Devil in *The Devil's Wall* and Chrudoš in *Libuše*, Boris, Figaro, Don Giovanni, Pizarro, Don Quichotte and Philip II in *Don Carlos*. His performances were often compared with Shalyapin's, whom as a singing actor he much resembled.

*

H. Thein: *Vilém Zítek* (Prague, 1947) [incl. summary of repertory and his autobiography 'How I Began and Continued']

A. Rektorys: *Korespondence Otakara Ostrčila s Vilémem Zítkem* (Prague, 1951) [incl. detailed account of activities at the National Theatre]

C. Sychra: 'Národní umělec Vilém Zítek' [Vilém Zítek, National Artist], *Divadlo*, v (1954), 317–20

F. Pujman: 'Vilému Zítkovi na rozloučenou' [Farewell to Zítek], *HRo*, ix (1956), 643–4 [obituary]

Národní divadlo a jeho předchůdci [The National Theatre and its Predecessors] (Prague, 1988), 594ff [incl. list of repertory and discography]

ALENA NĚMCOVÁ

Zite 'ngalera, Li ('The Lovers on the Galley'). *Commedia per musica* in three acts by LEONARDO VINCI to a libretto by BERNARDO SADDUMENE; Naples, Teatro dei Fiorentini, 3 January 1722.

Carlo (soprano) has deserted Belluccia (soprano) in Sorrento and run off to Naples, where he has fallen in love with Ciomma (soprano). Belluccia disguises herself as a man and goes to Naples in search of Carlo. Her disguise is so successful that both Ciomma and Meneca (tenor) fall in love with her. The *capa y spada* intrigue (Saddumene's phrase for 'cloak and dagger') develops at length until it is resolved with the appearance of the galley captain Federico Mariano (bass), Belluccia's father, who threatens to kill Carlo for betraying his daughter. Tragedy is prevented only by the magnanimous intercession of Belluccia. The appearance of Federico, a serious character who speaks in standard Tuscan, is typical of second-generation *commedia per musica*, which saw a gradual introduction of serious characters and Tuscan speech into the Neapolitan dialect comedy.

Li zite 'ngalera has the double distinction of being the first surviving score of a Neapolitan *commedia per musica* and the first surviving opera by Vinci. The arias differ from those in the contemporary *dramma per musica* in their lack of coloratura and their simple accompaniments; Federico's aria 'Or più non mi fa guerra', a heroic coloratura aria with trumpets and oboes, is an exception. Although many arias are in a declamatory style, some with a pronounced gestic quality, others are in a more tuneful, dance-like style. The opening arietta 'Vorria reventare sorecillo' is frequently cited as an example of the influence of Neapolitan folksong on the music of the *commedia per musica*. *Li zite* also contains some of the earliest known examples of the comic finale, which in spite of their brevity employ the same basic ingredients as the classical *buffo* finale. KURT MARKSTROM

Z mrtvého domu. Opera by Leoš Janáček; *see* *FROM THE HOUSE OF THE DEAD.*

Zoghby, Linda (*b* Mobile, AL, 17 Aug 1949). American soprano. She studied with Elena Nikolaidi at Florida State University and made her début at the Houston Opera in 1975, as Donna Elvira. She has appeared widely in North America as Fiordiligi and Pamina, and as Giulietta in *I Capuleti e i Montecchi* (1976, Dallas). She sang Mimì at the Glyndebourne Festival in 1978 and returned in 1980 for Haydn's *La fedeltà premiata*. At the Metropolitan she has sung Mimì (1982) and Ilia in *Idomeneo* (1986). Among her recordings are Haydn's operas *L'isola disabitata* and *L'incontro improvviso*.

DAVID CUMMINGS

Zola, Emile (*b* Paris, 2 April 1840; *d* Paris, 29 Sept 1902). French writer. Brought up in Aix-en-Provence, he became a leading man of letters in the latter years of the 19th century, having a profound effect on the arts reaching far beyond the boundaries of his own work. He is celebrated as the leading figure in French *naturalisme*. His many expositions of his aesthetic emphasize that his accurate observation of real-life events was not an end in itself but rather a scientific basis underlying the creative nature of his art. 'J'observe pour créer, non pour copier', he stressed, in the belief that he could penetrate the depths of human nature only by seeing man acting in the society in which he lived. His concept of a series of linked novels – the Rougon-Macquart novels – was his major literary contribution in this respect.

His credo affected not only much other writing, visual art and theatre but also opera, providing a French alternative to Italian *verismo*. In the latter part of his life he collaborated on several operas with ALFRED BRUNEAU, of which *Messidor* (1897) is the most celebrated. After Zola's death Bruneau continued to fashion librettos from his novels. Although few other composers have used his material directly as the basis of their operas, it was perhaps his influence that gave rise to the tradition of naturalist operas produced in the early years of the 20th century by composers such as Charpentier, Dupont, Erlanger, Leroux, Widor and, in certain works, Massenet.

*

E. Zola: 'Le drame lyrique', *Le journal* (22 Nov 1893)
——: 'A propos du Messidor', *Le gaulois* (23 Feb 1897)
Carol-Bérard: 'L'intelligence musicale d'Emile Zola', *Revue mondiale* (15 Sept 1923), 187–92
A. Bruneau: *A l'ombre d'un grand coeur: souvenirs d'une collaboration* (Paris, 1932)
C. S. Brown: 'Music in Zola's Fiction, especially Wagner's Music', *Publications of the Modern Language Association of America*, lxxi (1956), 84–96; lxxiii (1958), 448–52
J. Combarieu and R. Dumesnil: 'Réalistes et naturalistes', *Histoire de la musique des origines à nos jours*, iv (Paris, 1958), 84–110
J. Frichet: 'Le théâtre lyrique d'Emile Zola', *Cahiers naturalistes*, xlii (1971), 171–80
J.-M. Guieu: 'Zola et le drame lyrique', *Aux sources de la vérité du théâtre*, ed. J. B. Sanders (Paris, 1974), 63–83
——: 'Lazarus, a Lyrical Drama by Emile Zola', *French American Review*, ii (1977–8), 135–46
G. Favre: *Musique et naturalisme: Alfred Bruneau et Emile Zola* (Paris, 1982)
J.-M. Guieu: *Le théâtre lyrique d'Emile Zola* (Paris, 1983)
M. Kelkel: *Naturalisme, vérisme et réalisme dans l'opéra d'1890 à 1930* (Paris, 1984)

RICHARD LANGHAM SMITH

Zöllner, Heinrich (*b* Leipzig, 4 July 1854; *d* Freiburg, 8 May 1941). German composer and conductor. He studied at the Leipzig Conservatory (1875–7) under Reinecke, Jadassohn and E. F. Richter, and in 1878 was appointed director of music at the University of Dorpat (now Tartu, Estonia). In 1885 he joined the staff of the Cologne Conservatory. From 1890 to 1898 he lived in the USA. On his return to Leipzig, he succeeded Kretzschmar as director of music at the university; in 1902 he was Reinecke's successor as professor of composition, and from 1903 music editor of the *Leipziger Tageblatt*. He resigned his Leipzig positions in 1906, and from 1907 to 1914 was the first Kapellmeister of the newly organized Vlaamse Opera in Antwerp. From 1914 he lived in Freiburg, in retirement except for his duties as opera critic for the *Breisgauer Zeitung*.

Zöllner's extensive output includes ten operas, as well as choral, orchestral and smaller vocal works. His most successful opera, *Die versunkene Glocke*, was revived frequently up to 1939.

Frithjof, 1882 (3, Zöllner), Antwerp, Vlaamsch Lyrisch, 6 Oct 1910
Die lustigen Chinesinnen (komische Oper, 1), Cologne, Stadt, 1885
Faust op.40 (Musikdrama, prol., 4, Zöllner, after J. W. von Goethe), Munich, Hof, 19 Oct 1887, vs (Leipzig, 1887)
Matteo Falcone (1, Zöllner), New York, Irving Place, 18 Dec 1893
Bei Sedan (2, Zöllner), Leipzig, Neues, 1 Sept 1895
Der Überfall op.65 (2, Zöllner, after E. von Wildenbruch: *Die Danaide*), Dresden, Hof, 7 Sept 1895, vs (Berlin, 1903)
Das hölzerne Schwert op.76 (2 scenes, Zöllner), Kassel, Hof, 24 Nov 1897, vs (Leipzig, 1897)
Die versunkene Glocke op.80 (5, Zöllner, after G. Hauptmann: *Märchendichtung*), Berlin, Westens, 8 July 1899, vs (Leipzig, 1899)
Zigeuner (2, Zöllner), Stuttgart, Hof, 15 March 1912
Der Schützenkönig (Spieloper, 3, J. Kulenkampff), Elberfeld-Barmen, Stadt, 18 Dec 1913

*

MGG (P. Hauschild); *StiegerO*
E. Segnitz: 'Heinrich Zöllner', *20 Biographien zeitgenössischer Tonsetzer* (Leipzig, 1907), 267ff
T. Kroyer: 'Die circumpolare Oper', *JbMP 1919*, 16–33
C. Gruber: *Opern Uraufführungen*, ii (Vienna, 1987)

DEANE L. ROOT

Zolotoy petushok. Opera by N. A. Rimsky-Korsakov; *see* *GOLDEN COCKEREL, THE.*

Zolotyy obruch ('The Golden Ring'). Opera-drama in four acts by BORYS MYKOLAYOVYCH LYATOSHYNS'KY to a libretto by Yakiv Mamontov after Ivan Franko's novel *Zakhar Berkut*; Odessa, 28 March 1930 (revised version, L'viv, 29 April 1970).

The opera is set in the Carpathian mountains, where the Tukholtsi live. The son Maxym (tenor) of their leader Zakhar Berkut (bass) rescues, during a hunting expedition, Myroslava (soprano), daughter of the boyar Tuhar Vovk (baritone). The two fall in love. Vovk attempts to take over some public lands and is condemned and banished by the Tukholtsi; he sides with an invading Tatar horde, but is drowned when the Tukholtsi destroy a river barrier and cause a flood. Maxym, their prisoner at the time, perishes too, but is acclaimed as a hero for sacrificing his life for his country.

One of the most significant operas to come out of the Soviet Union in its time, *Zolotyy obruch* (sometimes known as *Berkuty*) was composed under the impact of operatic development in central Europe, and in particular of Berg's *Wozzeck* (which Lyatoshyns'ky had attempted to have performed in Kiev). The style is typical of the composer's early middle period, volatile and unpredictable, the music often beginning as if startled out of deep slumber. The melodic structure is dominated by tritones and minor 2nds; the melodies are brief, often ecstatic in feeling, and seemingly cut short. The opera shows Lyatoshyns'ky's capacity to unify and transform diverse musical structures and at the same time to demonstrate their laconic, restless sensibility in a way that provokes continual development. This is further focussed by his reliance on folk motifs, notably in the monologue for the Tukholtsi leader Berkut, a bass aria of great power based on a Galician folksong (Lyatoshyns'ky re-used the theme in his Symphony no.3, 1951). The composer revised the opera in three acts in the 1960s; when it was given at L'viv in 1970, it won the Shevchenko Prize.

A vocal score of the opera was published in 1931, under the title *Zheleznyy obruch*; the second version appeared in 1973. VIRKO BALEY

Zonca [Zonka, Zonga], **Giovanni Battista** [Johann Baptist] (*b* Brescia, 1728; *d* Gámbara, nr Brescia, 1809). Italian bass, brother or nephew of Giuseppe Zonca. A successful singer in Italian opera houses, he was engaged in 1763 at the Mannheim court of the Elector Carl Theodor, where he excelled in serious roles and also sang well in *opera buffa*. His roles at Mannheim included Thoas in Majo's *Ifigenia in Tauride* (1764) and Xerxes in J. C. Bach's *Temistocle* (1772). In 1771 he was a guest performer at the Teatro S Benedetto in Venice and in 1778 he moved with the court to Munich, where his roles included Mopso in Grua's *Telemaco* (1780), Argeo in Holzbauer's *Tancredi* (1783) and Jupiter in Vogler's *Castore e Polluce* (1787); in 1788 he retired to Gámbara. Mozart commented favourably on his expressive singing (letter of 27 December 1780) and wished that he had been able to write the role of Idomeneus for him. ROBERT MÜNSTER

Zonca [Zonka, Zonga], **Giuseppe** [Joseph] (*b* Brescia, 1715; *d* Munich, 4 Jan 1772). Italian composer active in Germany. Ordained a priest, he dedicated himself to music and was hired as a bass singer in the Munich Hofkapelle in 1752. His serenata *L'Angelica* (2, P. Metastasio; *D-Mbs*) was given on 28 August 1758 and his *opera seria Il re pastore* (3, Metastasio; lost) was performed at the Hoftheater on 15 June 1760. In his other works to texts by Metastasio (among them a serenata, *La partenza*, composed with Jommelli), he followed the methods of Italian *opera seria* without originality. Some of the music attributed to him may have been composed by his brother (or nephew) Giovanni Battista Zonca.

*

F. J. Lipowsky: *Baierisches Musik-Lexicon* (Munich, 1811)
F. M. Rudhart: *Geschichte der Oper am Hofe zu München* (Freising, 1865)
F. Walter: *Geschichte des Theaters und der Musik am kurpfälzischen Hofe* (Leipzig, 1898) ROBERT MÜNSTER

Zopff, Hermann (*b* Glogau [now Głogów], Silesia, 1 June 1826; *d* Leipzig, 12 July 1883). German critic, teacher and composer. At his father's wish he studied agriculture, but after the successful performance of an overture in 1850 he studied with A. B. Marx and Theodor Kullak at the Stern Conservatory in Berlin, where he later joined the staff to teach music theory. In Berlin he also founded an opera academy and an orchestra. He moved to Leipzig in 1864 to become an editor of the *Neue Zeitschrift für Musik*; four years later he was appointed editor-in-chief and continued his advocacy of the New German School. He was also active as a writer (notably of *Grundzüge einer Theorie der Oper*, i, Leipzig, 1868), choral director, and teacher of singing and music theory. None of his operas appears to have been performed in its entirety. Zopff also wrote numerous choral works and songs, the symphonic poem *Wilhelm Tell*, and several chamber pieces, all in a conservative, tasteful but rather superficial style.

Mohamed (5, H. P. Wolff), Weimar, 1856 (frags. only), vs (1863)

Unperf.: Jery und Bätely, *c*1870 (1, J. W. von Goethe); Maccabäus, 1874 (heroische Oper, 4, Wolff); Tell, *c*1876; Karaman, 1878

*

C. Gruber: *Opern Uraufführungen*, ii (Vienna, 1987)

Zoppot [now Sopot]. Resort near GDAŃSK; from 1922 to 1934 it was the site of a summer Wagner festival.

Zoraide di Grenata ('Zoraide of Grenada'). *Melodramma eroico* in two acts by GAETANO DONIZETTI to a libretto by BARTOLOMEO MERELLI after J.-P.-C. de Florian's *Gonsalve de Cordove, ou Grenade reconquise*; Rome, Teatro Argentina, 28 January 1822 (revised version, Rome, Teatro Argentina, 7 January 1824).

The plot deals with the machinations of Almuzir (tenor) to marry Zoraide (soprano), the daughter of the king he has murdered and whose throne he has usurped. His attempts to dispose of his rival Abenamet (contralto *en travesti*), whom Zoraide truly loves, are ultimately foiled when Abenamet, as an unknown knight, wins a single combat to defend her, whereupon he forces Almuzir to confess his perfidy and then defends the usurper against the wrath of the populace. The grateful Almuzir permits Abenamet to marry Zoraide.

Abenamet was to have been a tenor role, but the singer assigned the part died during rehearsals and Donizetti was forced to recast the part as a *musico* role and cut some of the music. The Roman public sympathized with the promising young composer's plight and gave the work a warm reception. In 1824 at the same theatre Donizetti presented a revised version, the text reworked by Ferretti with a new, florid aria-finale for Benedetta Pisaroni as Abenamet. But what the fickle Romans had found acceptable in 1822 left them cold two years later. WILLIAM ASHBROOK

Zoraqi, Nikolla (*b* Korcë, 24 Jan 1929; *d* Tirana, 9 Nov 1991). Albanian composer. He studied the violin and music theory in Tirana (1946–51), became leader of the Tirana PO, then decided to study composition at the Moscow Conservatory (1958–61), where his teacher was Shaporin. On returning to Albania he worked for Albanian Radio (1961–75), concurrently teaching at the Tirana Conservatory. From 1975 he received a regular stipend as *kompozitor profesionist i lir* ('free professional composer') from the Union of Writers and Artists of Albania, as well as continuing with his teaching.

Zoraqi was active in all genres; his music is characterized by clear-cut themes of immediate appeal and elegantly balanced forms. In the opera *Komisari* ('The Commissar'), composed in 1974 and based on a modern classic of Albanian literature dealing with the Albanian uprising against the Germans, he underlined the importance of education in transforming primitive instincts into creative and socially beneficial forces; he interpolated folksongs, popular songs and partisan songs into a musical structure which alternates arioso and recitative with distinct vocal numbers. The work, although considered a novelty in Albania on account of its epic-heroic character, is at the same time one of the most representative operas of an era in which eminent writers such as Dritëro Agolli, Ismail Kadare and Naoum Prifti were becoming attracted to the lyric stage, and encouraged composers towards a more subtle handling of stage action and dramatic conflict.

Përtacet [The Lazy Ones], 1956 (children's operetta, 1, K. Jakova)
Fundi i Golemve [The Extinction of the Golemi Family], 1965–6 (3, Jakova, after D. Shuteriqi: *Ditët e sprasme te Gjërgj Golemit* [The Last Days of Gjërgj Golemi]); Prince's aria, chorus from Act 1, vs, in Sokoli, 134–52
Vjollca e Skënderbeut [The Violet of Scanderbeg], *c*1966 (musical revue, L. Siliqi)
Komisari [The Commissar] (3, D. Agolli, after Agolli: *Komisari Memo*), Tirana, Opera and Ballet Theatre, 23 Feb 1975
Karikaturat [Caricatures], 1986–7 (children's operetta, 3, A. Mamaqi)
Paja [The Dowry] (operetta, 3, S. Mato, after G. Schiro di Maggio), Tirana, Opera and Ballet Theatre, 7 March 1989

*

R. Sokoli: *Figura e Skënderbeut në muzikë* [The Figure of Scanderbeg in Music] (Tirana, 1978), 57, 134–52
S. Vani: *Kur dëgjojmë operën* [Listening to Opera] (Tirana, 1979), 222–31
S. Kalemi: *Arritjet e artit tonë muzikor: vepra dhe krijues të muzikës Shqiptare* [Achievements of our Musical Art: Creations and Creators of Albanian Music] (Tirana, 1982), 119–36
Historia e muzikës Shqiptare [History of Albanian Music], ed. Instituti i Lartë i Artëve (Tirana), ii, 300–14 [on *Komisari]*
G. Leotsakos: 'Alvaniki moussiki', *Moussikologia*, no.1 (1985), 53–4
'A New Comic Opera', *New Albania*, no.3 (1989), 22 [on *Paja*]

GEORGE LEOTSAKOS

Zorin, Dementy Alexeyevich (*b c*1755; *fl* 1777). Russian composer. He wrote the earliest Russian opera (i.e. Singspiel) to survive in its entirety. *Pererozhdeniye* ('The Rebirth'), concerning an old woman who is magically transformed into a young beauty, was given for the first time in Moscow (Theatre on the Znamenka) on 8/19 January 1777. The St Petersburg première took place in 1779, and it is to this production, for which the music may have been revised, that the extant score pertains (in *RU-SPtob*; chorus and aria in Ginzburg, other excerpts in Rabinovich). The author of the libretto, translated by Zakhar Krïzhanovsky (from a language unspecified but almost certainly French), is unknown. For the most part the music is written *na golosï*, that is, to the tunes of existing folksongs and popular songs.

*

A. S. Rabinovich: *Russkaya opera do Glinki* [Russian Opera before Glinka] (Moscow, 1948)
R.-A. Mooser: *Annales de la musique et des musiciens en Russie au XVIIIme siècle*, ii (Geneva, 1951)
A. A. Gozenpud: *Muzïkal'nïy teatr v Rossii ot istokov do Glinki: ocherk* [The Musical Theatre in Russia from its Origins to Glinka: a Study] (Leningrad, 1959)
Yu. V. Keldïsh: *Russkaya muzïka XVIII veka* [Russian Music of the 18th Century] (Moscow, 1965)
S. L. Ginzburg: IRMO, i, 60–64, 452–5

RICHARD TARUSKIN

Zoroastre. *Tragédie en musique* in five acts by JEAN-PHILIPPE RAMEAU to a libretto by LOUIS DE CAHUSAC; Paris, Opéra, 5 December 1749.

Though produced with more than usual magnificence and a cast including Jélyotte (Zoroastre), *Chassé* (Abramane) and Fel (Amélite), *Zoroastre* had initially only limited success. Despite 25 performances it proved far less popular than Mondonville's *Le carnaval du Parnasse*, staged during the same period. By May 1752 Rameau and Cahusac had begun an extensive reworking affecting the whole character of the work. This version, first given on 19 January 1756, was much more successful. It was revived with minor modifications on 26 January 1770 to inaugurate the Opéra's Palais Royal theatre, rebuilt after the fire of 1763. The earlier version was staged at Dresden on 17 January 1752 in an Italian translation by Casanova, music by Johann Adam replacing most of Rameau's.

Zoroastre *founder of the Magi*	haute-contre
Abramane *High Priest of Arimane*	bass
Amélite *heiress to the throne of Bactria*	soprano
Erinice *a Bactrian princess*	soprano
Zopire } *priests of Arimane*	bass
Narbanor† } *priests of Arimane*	bass
Oromasès† *King of the Genii*	bass
Zélize* *a Bactrian woman at Amélitès court*	soprano
Céphie *the same*	soprano
Abénis* *an Indian savage*	haute-contre
Cénide* *the same*	soprano
Orosmade* *a voice from a cloud of fire*	haute-contre
A Salamander*	baritone
A Silphide*	soprano
La Vengeance [Vengeance]	bass
Arimane *a subterranean voice*	bass
Three Furies*	soprano, two haute-contre
Five Furies†	three sopranos, two haute-contres

Bactrian people, Indians, Magi, Elemental Beings, priests of the false gods, demons, Vengeance's retinue, shepherds, herdsmen

Setting Bactria and neighbouring Hindustan in the 6th century BC

* – original version only † – 1756 version only

As Cahusac pointed out, *Zoroastre* represents a deliberate break with the classical legend and medieval romance that formed the conventional material of the *tragédie en musique*. Its theme, derived from Persian sources, is the struggle between Good and Evil – between, on the one hand, the great religious reformer Zoroastre, representative of Orosmade, the Supreme Being and God of Light, and, on the other, an ambitious sorcerer Abramane, servant of Arimane, Spirit of Darkness. Abramane, characterized as 'inventor of the cult of false gods', was created by Cahusac to counterbalance the figure of Zoroastre, who was believed to have instituted a priestly caste – the Magi – and to have discovered white magic. This dualist theme allowed Cahusac to introduce masonic elements (he was secretary to the Grand Master of the French Grande Loge), notably in the worship of the God of Light, the messianic mission, talismans and the temple decor of Act 5; in 1756 further symbols were introduced, together with an initiation ceremony.

With *Zoroastre* the traditional French prologue was abandoned. The overture, designed to replace it, is the first in which Rameau (anticipating Gluck) prepared the audience fot the drama as a whole: its three sections dipict, in turn, Abramane's barbarous rule, the renewal of hope and the rejoicing of the people free from oppression.

In the 1756 version, Acts 1 and 4 remained essentially unchanged; the revised Acts 2, 3 and 5 are shown in brackets.

ACT 1 *Devastated countryside near the city of Bactra* Abramane has exploited the Bactrian king's untimely death to cause Zoroastre's exile. He nevertheless yearns for the Bactrian crown. In 'Non, je ne puis assez punir', an *air* with two obbligato bassoons, the sorcerer dreams of revenge. He woos Erinice who, though scorning his advances, accepts Abramane's offer of help in seizing power: she promises to share the throne with him and thus take revenge on Zoroastre for spurning her. Abramane gives her half his wand, conferring on her a power equal to his own. As Amélite grieves for Zoroastre, her companions try to distract her. Their dances (which include a reworking of the harpsichord piece 'Les tendres plaintes') are interrupted by subterranean noises. Erinice appears and summons tormenting spirits, who drag Amélite away.

ACT 2 *A Hindustani valley near Mount Taurus; in the distance a temple and Magi's dwellings* At dawn, Zoroastre's Indian converts begin their devotions to Orosmade ('Sommeil, fuis de ce séjour', the first of several movements based on the same material, the last of them a version of the keyboard piece 'L'agaçante'). Zoroastre calls upon the god to reveal himself to the converts. As the sun's rays appear, he and the Magi unite Indian couples in marriage and Zoroastre praises eternal love in a virtuoso *ariette*, 'Aimez-vous sans cesse'. Flames emerge from the temple. From a fiery cloud the voice of Orosmade exhorts Zoroastre to victory. Zoroastre is transported upwards, to the acclamation of his people ('Zoroastre, vole à la gloire').

[(1756 version) ACT 2.i *Oromasès's palace* Zoroastre is bemoaning his separation from Amélite when Oromasès apppears. Describing her plight, Oromasès orders Zoroastre to rescue her; in doing so, he will rid the world of evil. To prepare him for his mission, Elemental Spirits perform incantations. Zoroastre is elevated to a higher state of awareness ('Où suis-je? Un nouveau jour m'éclaire') and collapses. To complete the initiation he receives the Book of Life.

2.ii *Inside the Bactrian kings' stronghold* As demons torment Amélite, Erinice demands that she renounce the throne. The gates burst open and Zoroastre appears; Erinice departs, threatening vengeance. Reunited, the lovers reaffirm their love. Zoroastre, recalling his mission, commands the walls to collapse, and a city square is revealed. He presents Amélite to the citizens, who celebrate deliverance of the rightful heir.]

ACT 3 *The walls of Bactra, near Erinice's palace; thick darkness* The townspeople's lamentations are heard in the distance. Surveying the devastation, Zoroastre learns of Amélite's fate; when he prays to Orosmade ('Dieu bienfaisant, Etre suprême') a ray of light appears. Summoning his followers, Zoroastre exhorts them to break their chains. At his command the walls collapse, revealing Amélite threatened by Erinice and the demons. Taken by surprise, Amélite's oppressors flee. Zoroastre and Amélite, overjoyed, sing of their love ('Je vous revois'). But as the people celebrate their deliverance, thick fumes arise and Abramane plunges them into darkness. Zoroastre, now deserted, summons the Elemental Beings. During their *airs* and dances (including reworkings of two keyboard pieces, the E major Sarabande and 'La Livri'), they give Zoroastre talismans and a book of spells, while a salamander gives him a magic wand. Zoroastre places Amélite under their protection.

[(1756 version) ACT 3 *Outside the city walls* Before daybreak, Abramane and Erinice quarrel. Fearing she might jeopardize their cause, Abramane revokes her powers and envelops her in a cloud. He broods on his plans (in 'Osons achever', bassoons darkly sustaining against urgently syncopated strings) and prepares an ambush.

At dawn, Zoroastre, Amélite and the people arrive to perform their devotions to the Supreme Being. They sing an ethereal Hymn to the Sun ('O lumière vive et pure') and celebrate with dances the return of light. Zoroastre and Amélite are about to take marriage vows when the skies darken and Abramane descends in a blazing chariot. As the people scatter, Zoroastre summons the Benevolent Spirits and hastens in pursuit of Abramane. The spirits bear Amélite away unconscious as fire engulfs the city.]

ACT 4 *A vault in Arimane's temple* Beside a bloodstained altar, Abramane expresses his agitation ('Cruels tyrans qui regnez dans mon coeur', a monologue characterized by agitated syncopations). News arrives that the forces of darkness have been humiliated, whereupon Erinice describes the odious spectacle of the happy lovers. Abramane begins an occult ceremony ('Suprême auteur des maux'). While priests perform dances of expiation, Abramane undertakes a sacrifice. Encouraged by the auguries, he summons evil spirits. Led by Hate, Jealousy, Despair and Vengeance, they perform a *ballet figuré*, during which Vengeance is presented with serpents and a bloodstained dagger. When a statue of Zoroastre appears on the altar, the priests cast spells and it vanishes in flames. Abramane takes this as a good omen. The voice of Arimane is heard summoning them to arms. During a series of powerful *airs* and choruses, the priests prepare for battle.

ACT 5 *Amélite's gardens* Alone, Amélite is filled with hope. Zoroastre arrives with news of success. But when the people implore Amélite to rule over them, Abramane and his priests rush in and declare that an oracle has named Erinice queen. As the forces of Light and Darkness confront each other, Abramane and the priests are suddenly engulfed in flames and swallowed by the earth. A brilliant light appears, after which a temple arises filled with Elemental Beings. Amélite, now queen, celebrates with Zoroastre the immortal flame ('Présent des cieux, divine flamme'). Amid general rejoicing they announce their wedding.

[(1756 version) ACT 5.i *The Bactrians' coronation site* Remorseful, Erinice warns Zoroastre of Abramane's impending onslaught. When Zoroastre is unmoved by her pleas, she departs dejectedly. News arrives that Amélite has been abducted during her coronation. Abramane, on a cloud of flames, commands Zoroastre to surrender. The cloud divides to reveal Amélite in chains. But Zoroastre appeals to the heavens, whereupon thunderbolts descend and the earth swallows Abramane and his supporters.

5.ii *The first temple erected to Light* Oromasès, on a brilliant cloud and surrounded by Elemental Spirits, presents the rescued Amélite. Amid general rejoicing, he ordains the coronation of the happy couple.]

* * *

The 1756 version is more conventional in placing greater emphasis on Zoroastre's love for Amélite, undermining his religious stature. As if aware of this, Cahusac elevates the hero's mission from the liberation of Bactria to the more momentous one of freeing the whole world from evil. More stress is laid on Zoroastre's preparation. The initiation ceremony in Act 2 contains some of Rameau's most ecstatic, spiritually elevated music; so too does the mystical sun worship of Act 3, with its serene Hymn to the Light. Moreover, Oromasès's other-worldly character is conveyed (like Christ's in Bach's St Matthew Passion) by the halo of sustained double-stopped strings that surround his utterances. The increased emphasis on Zoroastre's religious observance now creates a better foil for Abramane's colossal occult sacrifice; this occupies virtually the whole of Act 4 and works itself gradually into a frenzy, culminating in a series of astonishingly forceful ensembles and choruses.

Many other changes in the 1756 version prove positive dramatic gains, and the work is richer and more tautly constructed. Certain incidents such as Zoroastre's rescue of Amélite are handled more skilfully, while the long, irrelevant episode in the original Act 2 involving the marriage of Hindustani disciples is removed. Yet the authors never managed to cure the principal defect of the work, an over-reliance on arbitrary supernatural interventions. While the characters – Abramane in particular – are not without interest, the frequent trials of strength between Good and Evil and the resulting reversals of fortune take on something of the nature of second-rate science fiction.

Although Charles Bordes organized a concert performance at the Schola Cantorum, Paris, in November 1903, *Zoroastre* had to wait until 7 June 1964 for its first modern staging (at the Paris Opéra). Most performances today, including Sigiswald Kuijken's fine recording (Deutsche Harmonia Mundi, 1983), present the 1756 version which, unlike the original, involves fewer problems of reconstruction. The only published full score (Paris, 1964) is of the revised version, though this is transposed down a tone and all ornaments are editorially realized on the staff.

GRAHAM SADLER

Zorzisto, Luigi. *See* STROZZI, GIULIO.

Zottmayr, Georg (*b* Munich, 24 Jan 1869; *d* Dresden, 11 Dec 1941). German bass. The son of the bass-baritone Ludwig Zottmayr, he studied in Munich and began his career as a concert singer. After stage appearances in Vienna (1906) and in Prague (1908, Deutsches Theater), he was engaged at Dresden from 1910 to 1927. A true *basso profondo*, he sang Gurnemanz, Daland, Pogner, King Mark and Hunding, as well as the Commendatore, Sarastro, the Hermit (*Der Freischütz*) and Stadinger (*Der Waffenschmied*).

ELIZABETH FORBES

Zottmayr, Ludwig (*b* Amberg, Bavaria, 31 March 1828; *d* Weimar, 16 Oct 1899). German bass-baritone. He made his début in 1855 at Nuremberg and was then engaged at Hamburg, Hanover and, in 1865, at the Munich Hofoper, where he remained until 1880. He sang King Mark in the first performance of *Tristan und Isolde* (1865) and his repertory included Mozart's Figaro, Don Giovanni, Hans Heiling, William Tell and Luna, as well as bass and baritone Wagner roles.

ELIZABETH FORBES

Zouhar, Zdeněk (*b* Kotvrdovice, 8 Feb 1927). Czech composer. He studied at Brno University (PhD 1962) and was a composition pupil of Theodor Schaefer at the Brno Academy, where he later taught. He was head of the music section of the Brno University Library, 1953–61, then an editor for Czech Radio, 1961–70. Thereafter he devoted himself mainly to composition, but continued to teach at the Brno Academy. His early works show the influence of Janáček and Martinů; he corresponded with the latter and did much to promote his music. Later Zouhar made greater use of modality in his music, with loose rhythm and an emphasis on horizontal relationships, eventually becoming more markedly up to date in his resources. His one-act radio opera *Proměna* ('Transformation'; K. Tachovský, after Ovid: *Metamorphoses*) was composed in 1971 and first broadcast by Czechoslovak Radio in Brno in 1975; the music is neo-classical in derivation. The comic opera *Velká láska* ('A Great Love'; 1, Tachovský, after H. Sachs) was first performed by the Chamber Opera of the Brno Academy in 1986. Its musical characterizations are carefully thought out, using a declamatory style and modal harmonies.

JAN TROJAN

Zschiesche, August (*b* Berlin, 29 March 1800; *d* Berlin, 7 July 1876). German bass. He sang in the children's chorus of the Berlin Hofoper, then in the regular chorus and in 1819 took on small parts there. After an engagement in Budapest, in 1826 he joined the Königstädtisches Theater, Berlin, making his début as Gaveston (*La dame blanche*). In 1829 he returned to the Hofoper as Mafaru in Winter's *Das unterbrochene Opferfest* and remained there for the rest of his career. He created Falstaff in *Die lustigen Weiber von Windsor* (1849) and sang a wide variety of roles, including Sarastro, Osmin, Rocco, the High Priest in *Fernand Cortez* and Pontifex Maximus in *La vestale*. He retired in 1861, 52 years after his first stage appearance.

ELIZABETH FORBES

Zubiaurre (y Urionabarrenechea), Valentín María de (*b* Garay, Vizcaya, 13 Feb 1837; *d* Madrid, 13 Jan 1914). Spanish composer of Basque descent. He received his initial musical training in Bilbao, where he was a choirboy in the basilica of Santiago. In 1852 he was appointed organist in the parish church of Santurce, and the following year left Spain for South America, where he was widely acclaimed. He returned in 1866 and began studies in harmony and composition with Hilarión Eslava at the conservatory in Madrid. In 1873 he was the first recipient of a scholarship for the newly created Spanish Academy of Fine Arts in Rome. After his stay in Rome, he returned to Spain through Germany and France, his travels increasing his awareness of European musical trends. In 1875 he was appointed second *maestro* to the royal chapel in Madrid; three years later he succeeded Eslava as first *maestro*, and also began teaching at the conservatory. He continued to teach and compose until his death in 1914.

Although Zubiaurre was a prolific composer of religious music, he is perhaps best known for his operas. The first, *Luis Camoens*, a student work, was never produced. *Don Fernando el emplazado*, composed in 1869, shared first prize (with Barrera Gómez's *Atahualpa*) in a national composition contest to promote Spanish opera. First performed on 12 May 1871 at the Teatro de la Alhambra in Madrid, it was revived in Italian translation in April 1874 at the Teatro Real. A third opera, *Ledia* (also known as *Leda*), with a libretto by José de Cárdenas, was staged at the Teatro Real on 22 April 1877. Set in Basque country, it features a charming *zortzico* (a lively Basque folk dance in 5/8) and is an important precursor of Basque opera. According to Sagardía, Zubiaurre also wrote two zarzuelas: one, to a text by Antonio Arnao, was produced at the Teatro de la Zarzuela, Madrid. Sometimes criticized in Spain for the predominance of italianate melody in his stage works, Zubiaurre nevertheless made an important contribution to the move towards national opera in that country in the latter half of the 19th century.

*

J. García Marcellán: *Catálogo del Archivo de música del Palacio nacional* (Madrid, 1938), 238–9
A Miró Bachs: *Clen músicos célebres españoles* (Barcelona, 1942), 114
J. Subirá: *Historia de la música teatral en España* (Barcelona, 1945), 192–3
A. Fernández-Cid: *Cien años de teatro musical en España (1875–1975)* (Madrid, 1975), 31, 48
A. Sagardía: *Músicos vascos*, iii (San Sebastian, 1972), 137–40
C. Gómez Amat: *Historia de la música española en el siglo XIX* (Madrid, 1984), 115 WALTER AARON CLARK

Zucchelli, Carlo (*b* London, 28 Jan 1793; *d* Bologna, Feb 1879). Italian bass. The son of an Italian father and an English mother, he accompanied his family to Italy in 1803 and for a time studied painting. He eventually studied singing with Crescentini in Bologna, and in 1816 made his début at Ferrara, going in the same year to Munich, where he was engaged at the Hoftheater. In 1819 he sang in operas by Rossini and Guglielmi at the Kärntnertortheater, Vienna, returning to La Scala for Rossini's *La pietra del paragone*, *L'italiana in Algeri* and *La Cenerentola*, in which Rossini thought him the best Don Magnifico he had heard. On 26 December 1820 Zucchelli sang in the Rome première of Pacini's *La gioventù di Enrico V*. In 1821–2 he appeared in Trieste and in the following season he went to London, where he performed in the English première of Rossini's *Mosè in Egitto* (under the title *Pietro l'eremita*). For the next 12 years he divided his time between the King's Theatre in London and the Théâtre Italien in Paris. Thereafter he sang at Bologna, Rome, Livorno and elsewhere in Italy, finally retiring from the stage in 1842.

Zuffi, Giulia Francesca (*fl* 1678–85). Italian soprano. She sang in Venice in 1678 in Carlo Pallavicino's *Vespasiano* for the opening of the Teatro S Giovanni Grisostomo. Thereafter her name appears only in librettos of Neapolitan productions, including the first performances of Alessandro Scarlatti's *Aldimiro, o vero Favor per favore* and *Psiche, o vero Amore innamorato* (1683); the next year she sang in the revivals of his *Pompeo* and Legrenzi's *Giustino* and in the first performance of De Luca's *Epaminonda*. In 1685 she was in the company that revived Pallavicino's *Galieno*.

SERGIO DURANTE

Zumaya [Sumaya], **Manuel de** (*b* Mexico, *c*1678; *d* Oaxaca, between 12 March and 6 May 1756). Mexican composer. As a choirboy at Mexico City Cathedral, he was a pupil of the *maestro de capilla* Antonio Salazar. About 1700 he became a priest. A play, *El Rodrigo*, for which he provided music, was performed in the vice-regal palace; the libretto, in Italian and Spanish on facing pages, was printed in 1711 (copy in the Mexican National Library), but the music is lost. Zumaya's talents were recognized by the Duke of Linares, a devotee of Italian opera who arrived as viceroy in 1711. On 1 May 1711 the composer's three-act opera *La Partenope*, to Stampiglia's libretto, was performed at the palace, the earliest known full opera produced in North America. According to Beristain, Zumaya pleased the duke by translating and setting various other Italian librettos. The remainder of his career was spent as *maestro de capilla* at Mexico City Cathedral and Oaxaca, where his output comprised mostly sacred music.

*

J. M. Beristain y Souza: *Biblioteca hispano-americana setentrional*, iii (Amecameca, 2/1883), 325
R. Stevenson: 'Opera Beginnings in the New World', *MQ*, xiv (1959), 8–25 ALICE RAY CATALYNE

Zumpe, Herman (*b* Oppach, Saxony, 9 April 1850; *d* Munich, 4 Sept 1903). German conductor and composer. He studied at the teacher's seminary at Bautzen (where he also received a thorough musical education) and taught in the local school at Weigsdorf in 1870–71; he then went as a teacher to Leipzig, where he also furthered his musical studies. He turned to music completely when Wagner called him to Bayreuth in 1872 to assist with the copying of parts for the *Ring*. As a conductor he travelled widely throughout Germany and held important positions in Stuttgart (1891), Schwerin (1897) and Munich (1895 and 1900). He also visited London (conducting Wagner at Covent Garden in 1898), Odessa, Madrid and St Petersburg. An energetic and intelligent conductor, he was regarded in his day, especially in Wagner's music, as comparable to Richter, Mottl and Levi. As a composer he was strongly influenced by Wagner; his operas and operettas enjoyed a certain measure of success during his lifetime. At his death he left an unfinished opera, *Sâwitri* (based on the episode of the Mahābharata that also inspired Holst), which was expected to be his masterpiece.

Die verwünschte Prinzess, 1871–8 (romantische komische Oper, 3, F. Hoffmann), unperf.
Fontana, inc.
Anahna (phantastische Oper, 5, Witte), Berlin, Residenz, 1881
Farinelli (Operette, 3, F. W. Wulff and C. Cassmann), Hamburg, Carl-Schulze, 27 Nov 1886, vs (Hamburg, 1887)
Karin (Operette, 3, Wulff and E. Pochmann), Hamburg, Carl-Schulze, 1 Dec 1888, vs (Hamburg, 1889)
Polnische Wirtschaft (Operette, 3, F. Zell and R. Genée), Hamburg, Carl-Schulze, 1889, vs (Hamburg, 1890)
Sâwitri, die Königstochter, 1896–1903 (3, F. Sporck), Schwerin, Hof, 8 Nov 1907, vs (Leipzig, 1908) [completed by G. Rössler]
Das Gespenst von Herodin (komische Oper, 3, H. Hermann), Hamburg, 1910

*

E. von Possart and others: *Herman Zumpe: persönliche Erinnerungen* (Munich, 1905) HANS-HUBERT SCHÖNZELER

Zumsteeg [Zum Steeg], **Johann Rudolf** (*b* Sachsenflur, nr Mergentheim, 10 Jan 1760; *d* Stuttgart, 27 Jan 1802). German composer and conductor. He was originally intended for a career as a sculptor, but his musical talent showed itself early. He studied the cello with the chamber virtuoso Eberhard Malterre and from 1775 with the cello soloist and Kapellmeister at the ducal court of Württemberg, Agostino Poli, who also taught him composition. Among the works of Zumsteeg's student days is his first stage work, *Das tartarische Gesetz* (1780).

From 1781 Zumsteeg held the post of solo cellist in the orchestra of the Württemberg court, and wrote mostly operas, incidental music and cantatas for festival occasions in the ducal family, and numerous songs. From 1785 to 1794 he worked as a music master at the

Carlsschule in Stuttgart, and in 1791, after the death of C. F. D. Schubart, he took over the direction of German music at the court theatre. Finally, in 1793, on Poli's retirement, he was promoted to the post of court Konzertmeister. In contrast to Poli, who in the spirit of Jommelli had maintained the Italian tradition in Stuttgart, Zumsteeg came out unreservedly for the hitherto neglected works of Mozart, and gave the first Stuttgart performances of *Die Zauberflöte*, *Don Giovanni* and *Così fan tutte*. His own greatest success as opera composer came with *Die Geisterinsel* to Gotter's adaptation of Shakespeare's *The Tempest*.

Vocal music occupies the dominant position in Zumsteeg's output. In particular his lieder and ballads (about 300 altogether) are historically significant for their mid-way position between the Berlin song school and Schubert. Initially Zumsteeg's operas were still clearly under the influence of Jommelli, but the technique of melodrama, after the style of Benda's *Ariadne*, became increasingly important and found its purest expression in the duodrama *Tamira* (1788), Zumsteeg's only dramatic work in this genre. His last three operas, composed ten years later, actually abandon the dependence on melodrama, but reveal how his art was enriched by his close preoccupation with this form. The subject matter of these operas was taken from the world of magic (*Die Geisterinsel*), medieval chivalry (*Das Pfauenfest*) and oriental fairy-tale (*Elbondocani*). His knowledge of Mozart's operas reveals itself in his characterization, his ensemble technique and instrumentation and, not least, in his melodic style.

See also PFAUENFEST, DAS.

all first performed in Stuttgart; MSS in D-Sl

Das tartarische Gesetz (Spl, 2, F. W. Gotter), 28 March 1780
Der Schuss von Gänsewiz, oder Der Betrug aus Liebe (Spl, 3), 2 Feb 1781
Le feste della Tessaglia (allegorische Oper, M. Verazi), 17 Sept 1782, collab. A. Poli, C. L. Dieter, J. F. Gauss
Le delizie campestri, o Ippolito e Aricia (Verazi), 22 Sept 1782
Armide (3, J. C. Bock, after G. Bertati), 24 May 1785
Zalaor (3, de la Veaux), 2 March 1787, ov., songs, vs (Leipzig, 1806)
Tamira (Melodram, J. L. Huber), 13 June 1788
Airs du divertissement (Operette, Wargemont), 1796, vs (Stuttgart, 1796)
Le chant des parens éloignés de leurs enfans (Operette, Wargemont), 1796
Die Geisterinsel (Spl, 3, Gotter, after W. Shakespeare: *The Tempest*), 7 Nov 1798, vs (Leipzig, 1799)
Das Pfauenfest (Spl, 2, F. A. C. Werthes), 24 Feb 1801, vs (Leipzig, 1801)
Elbondocani (Spl, 1, J. C. F. Haug), 8 Dec 1803, vs (Leipzig, 1803)

*

L. Landshoff: *Johann Rudolph Zumsteeg (1760–1802): ein Beitrag zur Geschichte des Liedes und der Ballade* (Berlin, 1902)
H. Abert: 'Die dramatische Musik', *Herzog Karl Eugen von Württemberg und seine Zeit*, ed. Württembergischer Geschichts- und Altertums-Verein, i (Esslingen, 1907), 555–611
K. Haering: 'Johann Rudolph Zumsteeg: Opern-, Balladen- und Liederkomponist, Konzertmeister, 1760–1802', *Schwäbische Lebensbilder*, ii (Stuttgart, 1941), 545–55
J. Völckers: *Johann Rudolph Zumsteeg als Opernkomponist: ein Beitrag zur Geschichte des deutschen Singspiels und der Musik am Württembergischen Hofe um die Wende des 18. Jahrhunderts* (Erfurt, 1944)
GUNTER MAIER

Züngel, Emanuel (František) (*b* Prague, 21 June 1840; *d* Prague, 22 April 1894). Czech translator and librettist. He made a living for himself through journalism and translating plays (over a hundred), operas and operettas (about 60). He also wrote original plays himself and some opera librettos, mostly adaptations of foreign sources. His best-known libretto, *The Two Widows*, was the most professional libretto Smetana ever set. It is basically trochaic (ideal for the polka metres used in the opera) with plenty of contrasting metrical variation. Züngel was poorly paid for his pains, though this did not stand in the way of his providing 28 more pages of additional text when Smetana turned the work into a continuously-sung opera.

Dvě vdovy [The Two Widows], Smetana, 1874, rev. 1878, 1882; *Natalie* (after W. A. Gerle), J. Hartl, 1885; *Cesta oknem* [The Way through the Window], Kovařovic, 1886

*

ČSHS [lists further translations and bibliography]
L. Zelenka-Lerando: *B. Smetana a E. Züngel* (Nymburk, 1903) [correspondence]
L. K. Žižka: *Mistři a mistříčkové* [Masters and Small Masters] (Prague, 1939, 2/1947), 117–18 [personal description]
M. Očadlík: *Smetanovi libretisté* [Smetana's Librettists] (Prague, 1948), 18–24
——, ed.: *Emanuel Züngel: Dvě vdovy* [The Two Widows] (Prague, 1962) [critical edn with introduction; further bibliography on pp.33–4]
J. Tyrrell: *Czech Opera* (Cambridge, 1988), 101–4
J. Jiránek: *Smetanova operní tvorba* [Smetana's Operatic Works], ii (Prague, 1989), 9–10
JOHN TYRRELL

Zupan [Suppan], **Jakob** (*b* Schrötten, nr Hengsberg, 27 July 1734; *d* Kamnik, 11 April 1810). Slovene composer. He spent most of his career in Kamnik, near Ljubljana, where he was a music teacher and where he founded the Accademische Confoederation Sanctae Caeciliae. Between 1780 and 1782 he wrote the opera *Belin*, to the libretto of J. D. Dev. The opera, now lost, was the first of its kind in Slovene and among the first to be written in any Slavonic language. He also composed sacred choral works.
BOJAN BUJIĆ

Zürich. The largest city in Switzerland. It is the cultural centre of the German-speaking population. The privately run Aktientheater, which opened in 1833 with *Die Zauberflöte*, was the first established theatre in Zürich to present opera performances. Wilhelmine Schröder-Devrient, Beethoven's first Leonore, was a prominent guest in 1843. Wagner, exiled to Zürich in 1849, conducted a series of performances there between October 1850 and March 1851, including *Der Freischütz*, *Norma*, *Fidelio* and *Don Giovanni*. On 25 April 1852 he conducted the first Zürich performance of *Der fliegende Holländer*, followed in 1855 by *Tannhäuser*. In 1884 the theatre's 50th anniversary was celebrated with *Lohengrin*, but five years later the building was destroyed by a fire on New Year's Eve. The present Opernhaus (cap. 1200), known until the mid-1960s as the Stadttheater, opened on 1 October 1891 with *Lohengrin*. The building, situated in Falkenstrasse parallel to the lakeside, is one of several in Europe based on a design by the Viennese architectural team of Ferdinand Fellner and Hermann Helmer.

Wagner's music dramas continued to play an important part in the Zürich repertory. *Der Ring des Nibelungen* received its Zürich première in April 1900, and on 13 April 1913 the city mounted the first legitimate performance outside Bayreuth of *Parsifal*. Busoni's *Turandot* received its première on 11 May 1917, the composer conducting. In the same year, Arthur Nikisch conducted a series of Wagner performances, and Bruno Walter conducted Pfitzner's *Palestrina* in a staging by the composer. In 1917 and 1918 Richard Strauss was guest conductor for performances of *Elektra* and *Der Rosenkavalier*, as well as for works by Mozart and Wagner. Since 1921 the theatre has devoted itself entirely to opera and ballet.

Zürich held its first international opera festival in May 1909; succeeding the Italienische Gastspiele (from 1916), the Internationale Festspiele (1921–6) and the Jahrhundert-Festspiele (1934), the Junifestspiele (later renamed Juni-Festwochen) became an event of high artistic standard under Karl Schmid-Bloss (1931–47). *Lulu* received its première at Zürich on 2 June 1937, and *Mathis der Maler* on 28 May 1938, both conducted by Robert Denzler. In the postwar period the company's international reputation developed under Hans Zimmermann (director from 1947 to 1956), who helped further the annual June Festival; also at this time Lisa della Casa began her career as a member of the Zürich ensemble (1943–50). Hans Rosbaud, music director from 1955 to 1958, conducted the first stage performance of *Moses und Aron* on 6 June 1957. Other works given their first performance here were Martinů's *The Greek Passion* (9 June 1961), Rudolf Kelterborn's *Die Errettung Thebens* (23 June 1963) and Heinrich Sutermeister's *Madame Bovary* (26 May 1967). Christian Vöchting succeeded Rosbaud as music director (1958–64), and Ferdinand Leitner (1969–86) revived the Zürich tradition of fine Wagner and Strauss conducting. He was briefly succeeded by Ralf Weikert. In the 1970s and 80s, under Nello Santi, the company also became noted for its interpretation of Italian repertory. Zimmermann was succeeded as theatre director by Karl-Heinz Krahl (1956–60), Herbert Graf (1960–62) and Hermann Juch (1964–74). Under Claus Helmut Drese (1976–86) the Opernhaus enjoyed a new era of international prominence, with cycles of Monteverdi and Mozart operas staged and designed by Jean-Pierre Ponnelle and conducted by Nikolaus Harnoncourt.

Plans to renovate and modernize the theatre using public money sparked a wave of riots in 1980, the worst civil unrest known in Switzerland in modern times. The renovation, during which the company put on a limited programme in other premises between 1982 and 1984, preserved the elegant detail and atmosphere of the auditorium, modernized the public areas and created a new rehearsal and administration block. Kelterborn's *Der Kirschgarten* received its première during the reopening celebrations in December 1984. Drese was briefly succeeded by Christoph Groszer, and Alexander Pereira was appointed director from 1991.

The theatre is open on most nights of the season from early September to early July; there are usually six new productions a year, with another 10 or 11 operas in repertory and at least one musical. The company maintains its own ensemble of singers, liberally supplemented by guests, and has traditionally adopted a conservative staging policy, always preserving a sense of musical values. The orchestra was drawn from a pool of musicians administered by the Tonhalle-Gesellschaft until 1985, when the Zürich Opera House Orchestra was formally constituted. The International Opera Studio attached to the company has been the training ground for several notable postwar singers, including Gwyneth Jones and Edith Mathis.

*

M. Hurlimann and E. Jucker: *Theater in Zürich: 125 Jahre Stadttheater* (Zürich, 1959)
150 Jahre Theater in Zürich (Zürich, 1984)

ANDREW CLARK

Zuzana Vojířová. Opera in five acts by JIŘÍ PAUER to his own libretto after Jan Bor's play of the same name; Prague, National Theatre, 30 December 1958.

The opera, set during the years 1587–1620, deals with the love between Petr Vok (baritone), head of the powerful Rožmberk family, and the lowly country girl Zuzana (dramatic soprano). Refusing to be bound by convention, Zuzana gives Petr an heir. Vok's wife (contralto) secretly kidnaps the child; meanwhile the situation has angered and alienated Zuzana's former lover and betrothed, Ondrej (tenor). After Vok's death Zuzana is driven out of the castle, but at the end of her life she sees Ondrej and her son again and finds lasting peace.

Composed between 1954 and 1957, *Zuzana Vojířová* is based on a highly successful historical play written during the German occupation. Pauer completely revised the work in 1978, and it was one of the most frequently performed Czech operas until the end of the 1970s. Pauer viewed opera within a socialist culture as a means to provide a social forum and platform on which to play out the ethical and ideological struggle for the improvement of humanity. In this sense, *Zuzana Vojířová* is a national folk opera intended for the widest of audiences. With its set pieces and its emphasis on the voice – using long cantabile melodies and broadly conceived choruses – it follows closely Smetana's type of romantic opera. Its traditional form and economy of means (the recurrence of a number of motifs works in conjunction with the dramatic development of the opera) make it a readily accessible work.

HELENA HAVLÍKOVÁ

Zvonař, Josef Leopold (*b* Kublov, nr Beroun, Bohemia, 22 Jan 1824; *d* Prague, 23 Nov 1865). Czech composer. He is chiefly remembered as a national pioneer in music teaching. He studied at the Prague Organ School, becoming an assistant there, and later served briefly as its director. In 1860 he became director of the Žofínská Akademie, where he founded courses for women singers. He gave private composition lessons, with Bendl and probably Dvořák among his pupils. He devoted a great deal of attention to church music, and the church style also influenced his opera, the three-act *Záboj* (1859–62, G. Pfleger-Moravský or A. V. Šmilovský, *CS-Pnm**); this deals with the conflict between the Czechs and Germans in Bohemia in the 9th century, a pseudo-historical subject taken from the Dvůr Králové manuscript (presumed to be a medieval text but actually a pastiche dating from 1817). *Záboj* was the first Czech opera based on it. The work was never performed as a whole, but parts were given in a concert performance in 1863.

*

E. Axman: 'Josef Leopold Zvonař', *Časopis Moravského musea zemského*, xv (1916), 11–16
J. Tyrrell: *Czech Opera* (Cambridge, 1988)

MIROSLAV K. ČERNÝ, JITKA LUDVOVÁ

Zween Anton, Die. Singspiel by Benedikt Schack and F. X. Gerl; *see* *DUMME GÄRTNER AUS DEM GEBIRGE, DER*.

Zweerts, Kornelis. *See* SWEERTS, CORNELIS.

Zweig, Stefan (*b* Vienna, 28 Nov 1881; *d* Petrópolis, Brazil, 22 Feb 1942). Austrian writer. In his day a leading European literary figure, he was exceptionally cultivated and had deep humanistic sympathies. His writings include several on musicians – Busoni, Toscanini and Bruno Walter, who were his close friends (Berg was another), as well as Handel, Mahler and Richard Strauss. His autobiography, *Die Welt von Gestern* (Stockholm, 1942; Eng. trans., 1943), includes a lively social and cultural portrait of Vienna during his youth and the early part of the 20th century.

Zweig's significance for music history lies above all in his collaboration with Strauss, which began in 1932 and lasted four years (much earlier he had offered a libretto to Reger who, though interested in it, was not inclined to try his hand at writing for the stage). Only one work was produced, the comic opera *Die schweigsame Frau*, after Ben Jonson's *Epicoene, or The Silent Woman*, although 18 different subjects were discussed, most of them in the collaboration's last year and a half and most proposed by Zweig. Strauss considered that in Zweig he had at last found a partner equal to Hofmannsthal: 'None of my earlier operas was so easy to compose or gave me such lighthearted pleasure'. Zweig was less satisfied: 'a terribly difficult work and thus the very opposite of my original conception of it'.

As Zweig was Jewish, the opera's première at Dresden in 1935 was attended by a political scandal, which led to its cancellation after the fourth performance. Eventually he refused to continue the working relationship even secretly, wishing neither to be made a privileged exception by the Nazi regime nor to see Strauss compromised by their association. At his suggestion, Strauss had the far less gifted Joseph Gregor rework a sketch by Zweig into the libretto of *Friedenstag*. Another Zweig idea later became the basis of *Capriccio*. Texts by him have been used by other composers: by A. E. Spadavecchia in *Pis'mo nyeznakomki* ('The Letter of an Unknown Woman', after *Brief einer Unbekannten*; 1975, Kislovodsk) and S. M. Slonimsky in *Mariya Styuart* (1981, Kuybïshev).

Zweig's large collection of musical and other autograph manuscripts included material from Handel's *Floridante*; arias from Gluck's *Alceste* and Mozart's *Le nozze di Figaro* and *La clemenza di Tito*; sketches for Weber's *Oberon*; material by most of the leading Italian opera composers, including a sketch for the bridal procession in Act 3 of Verdi's *Falstaff*; the full score of Offenbach's *La belle Hélène*; sketches by Wagner; a score of the prologue to *Lulu*, copied by Berg for Schoenberg's 60th birthday; a complete draft of *Die schweigsame Frau*; and writings by Goethe, Nietzsche and Hofmannsthal. In May 1986 the collection was donated to the British Library by Zweig's heirs.

*

A. Mathis: 'Stefan Zweig as Librettist and Richard Strauss', *ML*, xxv (1944), 163–76, 226–45

F. M. Zweig: *Stefan Zweig* (Eng. trans., London, 1946; Ger. orig., Stockholm, Zürich, London and New York, 1947)

H. Arens: 'Stefan Zweig und die Musik', *Neue Musik-Zeitschrift*, iv (1950), 249–53; also pubd in *Musica*, vi (1952), 59–62; and *Acta Mozartiana*, v (1958), 2–5; enlarged as 'Stefan Zweig zum Gedenken', *Acta Mozartiana*, viii (1961), 62–8

H. Zohn: 'Stefan Zweig as a Collector of Manuscripts', *German Quarterly*, xxv (1952), 182

R. Strauss and S. Zweig: *Briefwechsel*, ed. W. Schuh (Frankfurt, 1957; Eng. trans., 1977)

L. Truding: 'Stefan Zweig und die Musik', *NZM*, Jg.119 (1958), 136–9

A. A. Abert: 'Stefan Zweigs Bedeutung für das Alterswerk von Richard Strauss', *Festschrift Friedrich Blume* (Kassel, 1963), 7–15

R. J. Klawiter: *Stefan Zweig: a Bibliography* (Chapel Hill, 1964)

H. Oesterheld: 'Max Reger und Stefan Zweig', *Neue Beiträge zur Regerforschung und Musikgeschichte Meiningens* (Meiningen, 1970)

E. Allday: *Stefan Zweig: a Critical Biography* (London, 1972)

K. W. Birkin: 'Strauss, Zweig and Gregor: Unpublished Letters', *ML*, lvi (1975), 180–95

P. M. Potter: 'Strauss's *Friedenstag*: a Pacifist Attempt at Political Resistance', *MQ*, lxxix (1983), 408–24

O. Neighbour: 'The Stefan Zweig Collection', *MT*, cxxvii (1986), 331–2

RICHARD EVIDON

Zwei Komtessen, Die. Intermezzo by Giovanni Paisiello; *see* DUE CONTESSE, LE.

Zwerenz, Mizzi [Mariel] (*b* Pistyán, Hungary, 13 July 1876; *d* Vienna, 14/15 June 1947). Austro-Hungarian soprano. She sang soubrette roles at the Carltheater in Vienna from 1901 to 1920, also appearing at the summer theatre in the Prater, the Raimundtheater and the Theater an der Wien. She was the original Franzi in Straus's *Ein Walzertraum* (1907) and also created principal soubrette roles in Ziehrer's *Fesche Geister* (1905) and *Fürst Casimir* (1913), Fall's *Die geschiedene Frau* (1908) and Eysler's *Die gold'ne Meisterin* (1926). At the Carltheater she formed a partnership with the *buffo* bass Arthur Guttmann (*b* Vienna, 1 July 1877; *d* Vienna, 12 July 1952), whom she married in 1905. She possessed a well-produced, expressive soprano voice.

ANDREW LAMB

Zwerg, Der ('The Dwarf'). Opera in one act, op.17, by ALEXANDER ZEMLINSKY to a libretto by Georg Klaren after OSCAR WILDE's novel *The Birthday of the Infanta*; Cologne, Neues Theater, 28 May 1922.

The origins of *Der Zwerg* lie in Zemlinsky's obsession with ugliness. Significantly, Alma Mahler referred to Zemlinsky himself in her memoirs as 'a horrible dwarf'. He may first have come across Wilde's story in 1908, when Schreker's pantomime *Der Geburtstag der Infantin* was first performed in Vienna. Three years later Zemlinsky commissioned Schreker to write a libretto on the subject of 'the tragedy of the ugly man'. This crystallized in *Die Gezeichneten*, which Schreker decided to set himself; its principal character, Alviano, bears a striking resemblance to the Dwarf. Zemlinsky's involvement in the origins of *Die Gezeichneten* goes some way towards explaining why Klaren's libretto differs significantly from Wilde's story. In Klaren's version the Infanta is no longer a girl but a young woman whose cruelty is premeditated. The Dwarf is no longer a charming natural monster but a much more complex and indeed civilized being. Zemlinsky's emotional identification with the hero also suggests why the work seems so highly charged. In a letter to his publisher Emil Hertzka he confessed that it differed from *Eine florentinische Tragödie* on account of the greater degree of sectionalization and the emphasis on orchestral colour and melody. Zemlinsky composed *Der Zwerg* between 1919 and 1921. The first performance was conducted by Otto Klemperer, with the principal parts created by Erna Schröder (Infanta), Käthe Herwig (Ghita) and Karl Schröder (Dwarf).

The curtain rises to reveal Don Estoban, the Court Chamberlain (bass-baritone) and the maids preparing for the Infanta's birthday. Musically, the Baroque quality is sketched in by the prevalent use of an inverted mordent. This is contrasted with the soaring, waltz-like lyricism that characterizes the humanity of Ghita, the Infanta's favourite maid (soprano). In the ensuing, delicately scored passage the Infanta and her companions enter, her companions praising her beauty and joining her in a dance. A merry battle develops

'Der Zwerg' (Zemlinsky): costume design by August Haag for the Dwarf for the original production, at the Neues Theater, Cologne, 28 May 1922

when the Infanta, Donna Clara (soprano), insists on seeing her presents, though eventually Don Estoban persuades her to leave. He then reveals that the Sultan has sent the Infanta a dwarf. Zemlinsky uses this opportunity to present the musical material associated with the Dwarf: a haunting english horn theme underpinned by a variation on Wagner's Tarnhelm chords, an apt reference in the context of this drama of delusion; an ascending chain of 4ths, rhythmicized by the bassoon and capped by string glissandos, which mirror his ungainly gait; and mock-heroic music, which epitomizes the fact that the Dwarf, who believes he is a nobleman, is ignorant of his condition.

The birthday festivities begin with a march and courtly dance. The Dwarf (tenor) is then carried in on a sedan chair, to a musical recapitulation. Another chordal idea based on the Tarnhelm 3rds symbolizes that he is entranced by the Infanta. At her request he agrees to sing, though after a few bars of a merry song he sings a melancholy one, the precious imagery of which emphasizes the nature of his delusion. Having been given a new 'toy', the Infanta proceeds to play with it. She asks him to choose a wife from among her companions. Predictably, he chooses the Infanta herself. She dismisses her companions. In the ensuing dialogue he describes his past life, portraying himself in heroic terms. She eventually tells him that she loves him, and lists a number of things he must do in order to be worthy of her love. Unaware that the Infanta is merely toying with him, the Dwarf becomes ever more passionate and finally attempts to kiss her. She is saved by the timely arrival of Ghita, to whom she reveals that the Dwarf is wholly ignorant of his ugliness. Ghita is given orders to show him a mirror. They all go off into the ballroom. Ghita and the maids return, and see the Infanta giving the Dwarf a white rose and permitting him to kiss her. Clutching the flower, which is characterized by a new motif, the Dwarf joins Ghita, who now proceeds to carry out the Infanta's orders. In a passacaglia-like passage Ghita tries to explain to him what a mirror is, but cannot bring herself to show him one. Warning him to beware of the Infanta's throne, she leaves. He thinks longingly of the Infanta (the music recapitulates part of their earlier dialogue), and kisses the cushion on the throne. In so doing he dislodges the curtain draped over a large mirror, and, on seeing the reflection of himself, utters a piercing scream. The ominous trills, triplet runs and violent dynamic contrasts in the ensuing passage, in which he tries to come to terms with his mirror image, tellingly create an impression of near-hysteria.

When the Infanta reappears, the Dwarf begs her to tell him that he is not ugly, working himself up into a frenzy to utter: 'I am a dwarf and I love you'. The Infanta replies that one can only love human beings, 'and you', she sings, 'are like an animal'. The Dwarf sinks to the ground in despair. When Ghita arrives in search of the Infanta she immediately rushes to comfort him. The Infanta, however, bewails the fact that her new toy is already broken and returns to the ballroom. Ghita remains with the Dwarf, who kisses the white rose one last time and dies. The music of the ballroom where the Infanta is enjoying herself is briefly heard in the distance, and the opera ends with a final lurid wrench, a massive C minor chord in place of the D minor that might have been expected.

ALFRED CLAYTON

Zwillingsbrüder, Die ('The Twin Brothers'). Posse in one act by FRANZ SCHUBERT to a libretto by Georg von Hofmann after a French vaudeville *Les deux Valentins*; Vienna, Kärntnertortheater, 14 June 1820.

Schubert received this, his first theatrical commission, at the end of 1818 and completed the work in January 1819. The naive plot is a love story in a pastoral setting complicated by problems of mistaken identity: twin brothers, Franz and Friedrich (played by the one baritone soloist), return separately to their village, the first of them expecting to marry Lieschen (soprano), who is already betrothed to Anton (tenor). Schubert was surely incapable of composing the simple, tuneful melodies and light accompaniments customary in the artless verse patterns of plays of this type. He adopted instead the romantic Singspiel style of such composers as Weigl and Gyrowetz, responding more to the love interest than to the farcical element, thus creating an imbalance between text and music. The rhapsodical sentiments of the young lovers drew him to add new if not entirely appropriate dimensions to the play: tender, lyrical melodies, fine tone-painting which includes nature imagery of great charm, and ensembles in which he used some of the techniques of Rossini, whose operas were becoming increasingly popular in Vienna. The finest music comes in Lieschen's aria (no.3) 'Der Vater mag wohl immer Kind mich nennen', in the brilliant little quartet (no.5) 'Zu rechter Zeit bin ich gekommen', and in the energetic quintet with chorus (no.9) 'Packt ihn, führt ihn vor Gericht'.

ELIZABETH NORMAN McKAY

Zwischenspiel (Ger.). INTERLUDE.

Żyliński, Faustyn (*b* Żary or Laskowiec, 13 Feb 1796 or 1793; *d* Warsaw, 19 June 1867). Polish tenor and conductor. He studied the violin and then made his début as a singer in Paisiello's *La frascatana* at Minsk (1814). He sang at Vilnius (1815–23, 1838 and 1851) and, until 1840, at Warsaw, where he performed in operas by Boieldieu, Hérold, Weber, Meyerbeer, Auber and Kurpiński. He also coached the orchestra and deputized for Kurpiński as conductor. Żyliński taught singing at the Institute of Music and Dramatic Art and, from 1825 to 1827, at the School of Drama and Singing. He composed a number of choral works.

*

Obituary, *Tygodnik ilustrowany*, no. 407 (1867), 19
J. Heppen: 'Żyliński Faustyn', *Kłosy*, no.931 (1883), 284

IRENA PONIATOWSKA

Zylis-Gara, Teresa (*b* Landvarov, nr Vilnius, 23 Jan 1935). Polish soprano. She studied at Łódź and made her début in 1957 at Kraków as Halka. After winning the 1960 Munich radio prize she sang at Oberhausen, Dortmund (1962) and Düsseldorf (1965–70). She appeared as Octavian at Glyndebourne (1965), made her Covent Garden début in 1968 as Violetta, then sang Countess Almaviva, Donna Elvira and Desdemona, a role she took to La Scala in 1977. She made her Metropolitan début in 1968 as Donna Elvira; later roles there included Tatyana, Suor Angelica, Fiordiligi, Elsa, Elisabeth, Marguerite, the Marschallin, Mimì, Tosca, Butterfly and Manon Lescaut. She sang throughout Europe and the USA, her repertory including Adriana Lecouvreur, Amelia (*Ballo*), Leonora (*Il trovatore*), Liù, Lisa (*The Queen of Spades*), Maddalena de Coigny and Ariadne. She was a dignified yet impassioned actress, and had a fresh, creamy-toned voice, notable for its smoothness of production. ALAN BLYTH

Appendices

Appendix A

INDEX OF ROLE NAMES

This appendix is an index of names of the principal roles in some 850 operas. Shown against each name is the voice type for which the role is written, the title (sometimes short title) of the opera and the name of the composer; where the same role name appears in several operas, the operas are listed successively, in alphabetical sequence of titles (chronological where two or more are identical; where an opera exists in more than one language version, e.g. *La favorite*, only the title of the original is given). Role name forms in general reflect the usage within articles throughout the dictionary.

Two procedures are particular to this appendix. First, names with prefatory titles (King, Princess, Countess, Sir, Lady, Bishop, Don, Rev., Mr, Dr, Madame, Captain etc.) are given inverted, under the name or place rather than the title, thus: 'Ruritania, Queen of', 'Ethelred, King', 'Smith, Sir John', 'Clement VII, Pope'. 'Smith, Sir John' might however appear as 'John Smith, Sir', if in the opera concerned he is normally known by his given name rather than his surname. That principle applies too to untitled persons; 'Mary Brown' will appear in that form, under M, rather than as 'Brown, Mary', under B, if in the opera she is normally spoken of as Mary rather than Miss or Mrs Brown (if she is regularly referred to there as 'Mrs Brown', she will be entered, under B, as 'Brown, Mrs'). Prefatory titles are generally given in English. Where it seems helpful, for example where roles are known equally in one form or another, a cross-reference is supplied (full dual role names are entered in special circumstances, twice over: for example Renato/Anckarstroem). We have endeavoured to enter each name in the form that the user is most likely to seek it first of all, but he or she should be prepared to try an alternative in cases where our selection differs from his or hers. The exigencies of operatic usage demand that no overriding consistency be applied, and will even dictate on occasion the alphabetical splitting of families: husband and wife, such as the Pinkertons (Pinkerton, Lieutenant; Kate Pinkerton), mother and son, as with the Herrings (Herring, Mrs; Albert Herring), father and son, with the Germonts (Germont; Alfredo Germont), father, mother and daughter with the Fords (Ford; Alice Ford; Nannetta) and uncle and nephew with the Morosuses (Morosus, Sir; Henry Morosus) – to cite only a few.

Secondly, with classical and some historical names, an established English form (as discussed in the Preface, Volume 1) is given as the principal one. Applicable alternative forms are shown, in alphabetical sequence, separated by oblique strokes: Admetus/Admète/Admeto, Hippolytus/Hippolyte/Ippolito. Where (as in the latter instance) alternative forms do not fall close to the principal one, they are separately entered as cross-references. The form of the name particular to each opera in a sequence is not indicated but should not be difficult to infer (or to ascertain by reference to the entry on the opera concerned). Parentheses are used to indicate the name under which a character is for a time disguised.

This is an index of names, not of people: an entry may be shared by two or more characters bearing the same name, though in the case of bearers of alternative name forms (such as Helen/Elena/Helena/Hélène of Troy) a separate entry is given where one (or more) of those names applies to a quite different fictional character. The oblique stroke is occasionally used for characters appearing under two names and for doubled roles; in such cases a cross-reference from the secondary form may be supplied, especially if it would not have been a neighbouring entry.

Abbreviations: **a** – alto; **b** – bass; **bb** – bass-baritone; **bt** – baritone; **ct** – countertenor; **hc** – haute-contre; **ms** – mezzo-soprano; **s** – soprano; **sp** – spoken role; **t** – tenor; **x** – silent role

A

Aaron/Aronne/Aron/Eliéser/Elisero **t** *Moïse et Pharaon* Rossini; **t** *Mosè in Egitto* Rossini; **t** *Moses und Aron* Schoenberg
Abaris **hc** *Les boréades* Rameau
Abayaldos **bt** *Dom Sébastien* Donizetti
Abbé **t** *Andrea Chénier* Giordano
Abbess **ms** *Suor Angelica* Puccini
Abbot **b** *Curlew River* Britten
Abbot/Astrologer **b** *The Burning Fiery Furnace* Britten
Abbot/Tempter **t** *The Prodigal Son* Britten
Abenamet **a** *Zoraide di Grenata* Donizetti
Abigail **s** *Lucrezia Borgia* Donizetti
Abigail/Abbie **s** *Lizzie Borden* Beeson
Abigaille **s** *Nabucco* Verdi
Abimelech/Abimélech **b** *Samson et Dalila* Saint-Saëns
Abisaj/Abishai **s** *Saul og David* Nielsen
Abner **b** *Saul og David* Nielsen
Abramane **b** *Zoroastre* Rameau
Abu Hassan **t** *Abu Hassan* Weber
Abul Hassan/Barber **b** *Der Barbier von Bagdad* Cornelius
Acciano **b** *I Lombardi* Verdi
Aceste **t** *Ascanio in Alba* Mozart
Achillas/Achilla **b** *Giulio Cesare in Egitto* Handel
Achilles/Achille **t/bt** *La belle Hélène* Offenbach; **s** *Deidamia* Handel; **s** *La finta pazza* Sacrati; **t** *Iphigénie en Aulide* Gluck; **t** *King Priam* Tippett; **bt** *Penthesilea* Schoeck
Acis **t** *Acis and Galatea* Handel; **hc** *Acis et Galatée* Lully
Actaeon/Actéon **hc** *Actéon* Charpentier, M.-A.
Actor **bt** *Der ferne Klang* Schreker
Ada **ms** *Il diluvio universale* Donizetti; **s** *Die Feen* Wagner; **ms** *La vera storia* Berio
Adalberto **a** *Ottone* Handel
Adalgisa **s** *Norma* Bellini
Adam **t** *The Devils of Loudun* Penderecki
Adam Brant **bt** *Mourning Becomes Electra* Levy
Adamas **bt** *Les boréades* Rameau
Adario **t** *Les Indes galantes* Rameau
Addie **a** *Regina* Blitzstein
Adelaida/Adelaide **s** *Adelaide di Borgogna* Rossini; **s** *Lotario* Handel
Adelaide **ms** *Arabella* Strauss
Adelanta **s** *Xerse* Cavalli; **a** *Xerse* Bononcini, G.
Adelberto **t** *Adelaide di Borgogna* Rossini
Adele **s** *Die Fledermaus* Strauss, J.
Adèle, Countess **s** *Le comte Ory* Rossini
Adelia **s** *Ugo conte di Parigi* Donizetti
Adelma **s** *Turandot* Busoni
Adelson, Lord **b** *Adelson e Salvini* Bellini
Adhemar de Monteil **b** *Jérusalem* Verdi
Adina **s** *Adina* Rossini; **s** *L'elisir d'amore* Donizetti
Admetus/Admète/Admeto **a** *Admeto* Handel; **hc** *Alceste* Lully; **t** *Alceste* Gluck
Adolar, Count of **t** *Euryanthe* Weber
Adolf of Harasov **bt** *The Jacobin* Dvořák
Adolfine **ms** *Tintomara* Werle
Adolfo **b** *Alfonso und Estrella* Schubert; **s** *Faramondo* Handel
Adolphe **hc** *Les fêtes vénitiennes* Campra
Adoniram **t** *La reine de Saba* Gounod
Adonis: *see* Captain of the Royal Guard
Adorno, Duke **b** *Die Gezeichneten* Schreker
Adorno, Gabriele: *see* Gabriele Adorno
Adrasto **a** *Il pomo d'oro* Cesti
Adriana Lecouvreur **s** *Adriana Lecouvreur* Cilea
Adriano Colonna **ms** *Rienzi* Wagner
Adriano de Montfort **t** *Il crociato in Egitto* Meyerbeer
Aegeus/Egée/Egeo **t** *Giasone* Cavalli; **a** *Teseo* Handel; **bt** *Thésée* Lully
Aegisthus/Aegisth **t** *Elektra* Strauss
Aegle/Eglé **s** *Thésée* Lully
Aegon **bt** *Gli equivoci* Storace
Aeneas/Enée **bt** *Dido and Aeneas* Purcell; **t** *Les Troyens* Berlioz
Aennchen **ms** *Der Freischütz* Weber
Aeolus/Eolo **t** *Le nozze di Teti e di Peleo* Cavalli; **b** *Il pomo d'oro* Cesti
Aetius/Ezio **a** *Ezio* Handel
Afanasy Ivanovich **t** *The Fair at Sorochintsï* Musorgsky
Afanasy Vyazemsky, Prince **b** *The Maid of Pskov* Rimsky-Korsakov
Afra **ms** *La Wally* Catalani
Afron, Prince **bt** *The Golden Cockerel* Rimsky-Korsakov
Agamemnon **bt** *La belle Hélène* Offenbach; **bt** *Iphigénie en Aulide* Gluck
Agathe **s** *La fausse esclave* Gluck; **s** *Der Freischütz* Weber
Agathe Coquenard **s** *Véronique* Messager
Agathis **t** *Les mariages samnites* Grétry
Agave **ms** *The Bassarids* Henze
Agenor/Agenore **t** *Astarto* Bononcini, G.; **t** *Il re pastore* Mozart
Agilea **s** *Teseo* Handel
Aglaé **s** *Echo et Narcisse* Gluck
Agnes **s** *Agnes von Hohenstaufen* Spontini; **s** *Der arme Heinrich* Pfitzner
Agnès **s** *La nonne sanglante* Gounod
Agnès Sorel **s** *The Maid of Orléans* Tchaikovsky
Agnese del Maino **ms** *Beatrice di Tenda* Bellini
Agnese: *see* Alaide
Agorante **t** *Ricciardo e Zoraide* Rossini
Agrippa, Dr **t** *The Fiery Angel* Prokofiev
Agrippina **s** *Agrippina* Handel
Aida **s** *Aida* Verdi
Airfield Director **bb** *Volo di notte* Dallapiccola
Aithra **s** *Die ägyptische Helena* Strauss, R.
Ajax I **t/bt** *La belle Hélène* Offenbach
Ajax II **t/bt** *La belle Hélène* Offenbach
Akhnaten **ct** *Akhnaten* Glass
Akhrosimova, Mariya **ms** *War and Peace* Prokofiev
Aksin'ya **s** *Lady Macbeth of the Mtsensk District* Shostakovich; **ms** *Quiet Flows the Don* Dzerzhinsky
Aladdin/Alaouddin **bt** *Padmâvatî* Roussel
Aladino **b** *Il crociato in Egitto* Meyerbeer
Alaide/Agnese **s** *La straniera* Bellini
Alain **t** *Grisélidis* Massenet
Alamir **b** *Les fêtes vénitiennes* Campra
Alamiro/Alessi **t** *Belisario* Donizetti
Alaskawolfjoe: *see* Joe
Alba, Duke of **bt** *Il duca d'Alba* Donizetti
Albano **b** *I lituani* Ponchielli
Albany, Duke of **bt** *Lear* Reimann
Alberich **bb** *Götterdämmerung* Wagner; **bb** *Das Rheingold* Wagner; **bb** *Siegfried* Wagner
Albert **b** *Robert le diable* Meyerbeer; **bt** *Werther* Massenet
Albert Herring **t** *Albert Herring* Britten
Albertine **s** *Die Brautwahl* Busoni
Alberto **t** *La gazzetta* Rossini
Alberto, Count **t** *L'occasione fa il ladro* Rossini
Albiani, Paolo: *see* Paolo Albiani
Albine **ms** *Thaïs* Massenet
Albrecht, Cardinal **t** *Mathis der Maler* Hindemith
Albrigòr **bt** *La donna serpente* Casella
Alcade **t** *Il barbiere di Siviglia* Paisiello
Alcaeus/Alcée **b** *Les fêtes d'Hébé* Rameau; **t** *Sapho* Gounod
Alcesta **a/t** *Erismena* Cavalli
Alcestes/Alceste **ms** *Arianna in Creta* Handel
Alcestis/Alceste **s** *Admeto* Handel; **s** *Alceste* Lully; **s** *Alceste* Gluck; **a** *Il pomo d'oro* Cesti
Alcides/Alcide: *see* Hercules
Alcina **s** *Alcina* Handel; **s** *Orlando paladino* Haydn
Alcindoro **b** *La bohème* Puccini
Alcinous/Alcinoo, King **bb** *Ulisse* Dallapiccola
Alcyone **s** *Alcyone* Marais
Aldimira **s** *Erismena* Cavalli; **s** *Sigismondo* Rossini
Alditrúf **t** *La donna serpente* Casella
Aldobrandino **b** *Parisina* Mascagni
Aldona **s** *I lituani* Ponchielli
Aleko **bb** *Aleko* Rakhmaninov
Alessandro **s** *Berenice* Handel; **a** *Tolomeo* Handel
Alessandro Magno: *see* Alexander (the Great)
Alessi: *see* Alamiro
Alessio **b** *La sonnambula* Bellini; *see also* Alexis

Alexander (the Great)/Alessandro (Magno) **a** *Alessandro* Handel; **t** *Poro* Handel; **t** *Il re pastore* Mozart; **s** *Statira* Scarlatti
Alexandr Petrovič Gorjančikov **bt** *From the House of the Dead* Janáček
Alexandra **s** *Regina* Blitzstein
Alexey **b** *Askold's Grave* Verstovsky; **t** *The Gambler* Prokofiev
Alexina **s** *Le roi malgré lui* Chabrier
Alexis **bt** *Le déserteur* Monsigny; **t** *The Sorcerer* Sullivan
Alexis, Prince **t** *Siberia* Giordano
Alexis/Alessio **s** *Il Sant'Alessio* Landi
Alfio **bt** *Cavalleria rusticana* Mascagni
Alfonso **t** *Alfonso und Estrella* Schubert; **t** *Violanta* Korngold
Alfonso, Don **b** *Così fan tutte* Mozart
Alfonso, Duke **bb** *Lucrezia Borgia* Donizetti
Alfonso XI: *see* Alphonse XI
Alfred **t** *Die Fledermaus* Strauss, J.; **bt** *La vie parisienne* Offenbach
Alfred, King **b** *Alfred* Dvořák
Alfredo Germont **t** *La traviata* Verdi
Alhambra del Bolero: *see* Grand Inquisitor
Ali **t** *L'incontro improvviso* Haydn; **b** *Les Indes galantes* Rameau; **t** *La rencontre imprévue* Gluck; **t** *Zémire et Azor* Grétry; *see also* Dori, Princess of Nicaea
Alice **ms** *Arden must Die* Goehr; **s** *Le comte Ory* Rossini; **s** *Robert le diable* Meyerbeer
Alice Ford, Mrs **s** *Falstaff* Verdi
Alidoro **b** *La Cenerentola* Rossini; **t** *Orontea* Cesti
Alim **t** *Le roi de Lahore* Massenet
Alina **s** *Alina, regina di Golconda* Donizetti
Alinda **s** *Giasone* Cavalli
Aline **s** *Drottningen av Golconda* Berwald; **s** *The Sorcerer* Sullivan
Alisa **ms** *Lucia di Lammermoor* Donizetti
Alison **s** *The Wandering Scholar* Holst
Aljeja **ms** *From the House of the Dead* Janáček
Alkonost **a** *Legend of the Invisible City of Kitezh* Rimsky-Korsakov
Alladine **x** *Ariane et Barbe-bleue* Dukas
Allan **t** *Le roi Arthus* Chausson
Allazim **b** *Zaide* Mozart
Allworthy **bt** *Tom Jones* Philidor
Alma **s** *Il crociato in Egitto* Meyerbeer
Almahide **s** *Almahide* [pasticcio]
Almaïde **s** *La caravane du Caire* Grétry
Almanzor **a** *Almahide* [pasticcio]
Almaviva, Count (Lindoro) **t** *Il barbiere di Siviglia* Paisiello; **t** *Il barbiere di Siviglia* Rossini
Almaviva/Almaviva, Count **bt** *La mère coupable* Milhaud; **bt** *Le nozze di Figaro* Mozart
Almaviva, Countess **s** *Le nozze di Figaro* Mozart
Alméric **t** *Iolanta* Tchaikovsky
Almira **s** *Almira* Handel
Almirena **s** *Griselda* Bononcini, G.; **s** *Rinaldo* Handel
Almiro **a** *Almahide* [pasticcio]
Almuzir **t** *Zoraide di Grenata* Donizetti
Aloes **ms** *L'étoile* Chabrier
Aloysia **s** *Masagniello* Keiser
Alpheius/Alphée **hc** *Proserpine* Lully
Alphise **s** *Les boréades* Rameau
Alphonse **t** *La muette de Portici* Auber
Alphonse, Don **hc** *La caverne* Le Sueur
Alphonse de Monza **t** *Zampa* Hérold
Alphonse XI/Alfonso XI, King **bt** *La favorite* Donizetti
Alquif **bt** *Amadis* Lully
Altair **bt** *Die ägyptische Helena* Strauss, R.
Altamort **b** *Tarare* Salieri
Altidòr **t** *La donna serpente* Casella
Altomaro **b** *Sosarme* Handel
Altoum, Emperor **b** *Turandot* Busoni; **t** *Turandot* Puccini
Alvar **t** *Fernand Cortez* Spontini
Alvar, Don **t** *L'Africaine* Meyerbeer; **b** *Les Indes galantes* Rameau
Alvar Fanez **t** *Der Cid* Cornelius
Alvaro **b** *Alzira* Verdi
Alvaro, Don **t** *La forza del destino* Verdi; **t** *Il Guarany* Gomes; **b** *Il viaggio a Reims* Rossini
Alviano Salvago **t** *Die Gezeichneten* Schreker
Alvise Badoero **b** *La Gioconda* Ponchielli
Alwa **t** *Lulu* Berg
Alwina **s** *Alfred* Dvořák
Alzaga **t** *The Magic Opal* Albéniz
Alzira **s** *Alzira* Verdi
Amadis/Amadigi **ms** *Amadigi di Gaula* Handel; **hc** *Amadis* Lully
Amahl **tr** *Amahl and the Night Visitors* Menotti
Amalia **s** *I masnadieri* Verdi
Amaltea: *see* Sinais
Amanda **s** *Le Grand Macabre* Ligeti; **s** *Tintomara* Werle
Amando **ms** *Le Grand Macabre* Ligeti
Amantio, Ser **bt** *Gianni Schicchi* Puccini
Amantius/Amanzio **a** *Giustino* Handel
Amaranta **ms** *La fedeltà premiata* Haydn
Amarilli **s** *Il pastor fido* Handel
Amastre **a** *Serse* Handel; **s** *Xerse* Cavalli; **a** *Xerse* Bononcini, G.
Amazili **s** *Jessonda* Spohr
Amazily **s** *Fernand Cortez* Spontini
Ambrogio **b** *Il barbiere di Siviglia* Rossini
Ambroise, Maître **b** *Mireille* Gounod
Ambrosio **b** *Die drei Pintos* Weber
Ambulance Man **b** *Hin und zurück* Hindemith
Amelfa **a** *The Golden Cockerel* Rimsky-Korsakov
Amelia **s** *Amelia al ballo* Menotti; **s** *Un ballo in maschera* Verdi; **s** *I briganti* Mercadante; **s** *Simon Boccanegra* Verdi
Amelia/Hélène **s** *Il duca d'Alba* Donizetti
Amélie **s** *Gustave III* Auber
Amélite **s** *Zoroastre* Rameau
Amenaide **s** *Tancredi* Rossini
Aménaïs (Olympia/Olympie) **s** *Olimpie* Spontini
Amenophis/Aménophis **t** *Moïse et Pharaon* Rossini
Amenophis/Osiride **t** *Mosè in Egitto* Rossini
Amfortas **bt** *Parsifal* Wagner
Amida **a** *Ormindo* Cavalli
Amina **s** *La sonnambula* Bellini
Amine **s** *La rencontre imprévue* Gluck
Aminta **s** *Die schweigsame Frau* Strauss, R.; *see also* Amyntas
Amira **s** *Ciro in Babilonia* Rossini
Amitta **s** *Der geduldige Socrates* Telemann
Amneris **ms** *Aida* Verdi
Amonasro **bt** *Aida* Verdi
Amor, Amore, Amour: *see* Cupid
Amorveno **t** *L'amor coniugale* Mayr
Amphinomous/Anfinomo **a** *Il ritorno d'Ulisse in patria* Monteverdi
Amyntas/Aminta **t** *Atalanta* Handel; **t** *Euridice* Peri; **s** *Il re pastore* Mozart
Anacoana **ms** *Cristoforo Colombo*
Anaide **a** *Il cappello di paglia di Firenze* Rota; **ms** *Zazà* Leoncavallo
Anaïs/Anaï/Elcia **s** *Moïse et Pharaon* Rossini; **s** *Mosè in Egitto* Rossini
Anastasius/Anastasio **s** *Giustino* Handel
Anatol **t** *Vanessa* Barber
Anatol Kuragin **t** *War and Peace* Prokofiev
Anchise, Don: *see* Podestà
Anckarstroem/Renato **bt** *Un ballo in maschera* Verdi
André **t** *L'étranger* d'Indy
Andrea: *see* Fiesco, Jacopo
Andrea Chénier **t** *Andrea Chénier* Giordano
Andreloux **a** *Mireille* Gounod
Andres **t** *Wozzeck* Berg
Andrès **t** *Carmen* Bizet; **t** *Les contes d'Hoffmann* Offenbach
Andrès del Ribeira **bt** *La Périchole* Offenbach
Andrew Borden **bb** *Lizzie Borden* Beeson
Andrey **t** *Mazepa* Tchaikovsky
Andrey Bolkonsky, Prince **bt** *War and Peace* Prokofiev
Andrey Degtyarenko **b** *The Story of a Real Man* Prokofiev
Andrey Khovansky, Prince **t** *Khovanshchina* Musorgsky
Andrey Morozov **t** *Oprichnik* Tchaikovsky
Andromache/Andromaca/Andromaque **s** *Astianatte* Bononcini, G.; **a** *Ermione* Rossini; **s** *King Priam* Tippett; **s** *Persée* Lully; **x** *Les Troyens* Berlioz

Andronico, Don **b** *Don Procopio* Bizet
Andronicus/Andronico **a** *Tamerlano* Handel
Anežka **s** *The Two Widows* Smetana
Anfinomo: *see* Amphinomous
Ange-Pitou **t** *La fille de Madame Angot* Lecocq
Angel **tr** *The Burning Fiery Furnace* Britten; **s** *Saint François d'Assise* Messiaen; **s** *Il Sant'Alessio Landi*
Angel More **s** *The Mother of Us All* Thomson
Angèle **ms** *Le domino noir* Auber; **s** *Der Zar lässt sich photographieren* Weill
Angèle Aubier **s** *Der Opernball* Heuberger
Angèle Didier **s** *Der Graf von Luxemburg* Lehár
Angelica **s** *Orlando* Handel; **s** *Orlando paladino* Haydn
Angelica, Sister **s** *Suor Angelica* Puccini
Angelina **s** *Trial by Jury* Sullivan; *see also* Cenerentola
Angélique **s** *Angélique* Ibert; **s** *Roland* Lully; **s** *Roland* Piccinni
Angelo **x** *Genoveva* Schumann; **bt** *Gli equivoci* Storace
Angelo custode/Guardian Angel **s** *Rappresentatione di Anima, et di Corpo* Cavalieri
Angelotti, Cesare **b** *Tosca* Puccini
Anichino **t** *Beatrice di Tenda* Bellini
Anima/Soul **s** *Rappresentatione di Anima, et di Corpo* Cavalieri
Animal Tamer/Athlete **b** *Lulu* Berg
Anita **s** *Giuditta* Lehár; **s** *Jonny spielt auf* Krenek; **s/ms** *La Navarraise* Massenet; **a** *West Side Story* Bernstein
Ankastrom, Count **b** *Gustave III* Auber
Anna **ms** *L'Africaine* Meyerbeer; **ms** *Die Bürgschaft* Weill; **s** *I cavalieri di Ekebù* Zandonai; **s** *La dame blanche* Boieldieu **s** *Hans Heiling* Marschner; **s** *Intermezzo* Strauss, R.; **s** *Maometto II* Rossini; **s** *Die sieben Todsünden* Weill; **a** *Les Troyens* Berlioz; **s** *Le villi* Puccini
Anna, Donna **s** *Don Giovanni* Gazzaniga; **s** *Don Giovanni* Mozart; **s** *The Stone Guest* Dargomïzhsky
Annabella Millbank *Lord Byron* Thomson
Anna von Rehberg **s** *Loreley* Catalani
Anne **a** *The Mother of Us All* Thomson
Anne Boleyn/Anna Bolena **s** *Anna Bolena* Donizetti; **ms** *Henry VIII* Saint-Saëns
Anne Page/Anna Reich **s** *Die lustigen Weiber von Windsor* Nicolai
Anne Trulove **s** *The Rake's Progress* Stravinsky
Annetta **s** *Crispino e la comare* Ricci, L. and F.
Annibale Pistacchio, Don **b** *Il campanello di notte* Donizetti
Annina **s** *Eine Nacht in Venedig* Strauss, J.; **a** *Der Rosenkavalier* Strauss, R.; **s** *The Saint of Bleecker Street* Menotti; **s** *La traviata* Verdi
Annius/Annio **s** *La clemenza di Tito* Mozart; **s** *Giulio Sabino* Sarti
Ann Shute **s** *The Lily of Killarney* Benedict
Annunziata **x** *Arlecchino* Busoni
Anselm **t** *Christophorus* Schreker
Anselme **b** *Les Paladins* Rameau
Anselmo **b** *La gazzetta* Rossini
Antenor/Anténor **t** *Dardanus* Rameau; **bt** *Troilus and Cressida* Walton
Antenore **t** *Zelmira* Rossini
Anticlea **s** *Ulisse* Dallapiccola
Antigona/Antigonae/Antigone **s** *Admeto* Handel; **s** *Antigonae* Orff; **s** *Oedipe* Enescu; **s** *Oedipe à Colone* Sacchini
Antigonus/Antigone **b** *Olimpie* Spontini
Antilochus: *see* Ulysses
Antinous/Antinoo **t** *Pénélope* Fauré; **b** *Il ritorno d'Ulisse in patria* Monteverdi; **bt** *Ulisse* Dallapiccola
Antippo **a** *Der geduldige Socrates* Telemann
Anton **t** *Die Zwillingsbrüder* Schubert
Antonia **s** *Les contes d'Hoffmann* Offenbach
Antonida **s** *A Life for the Tsar* Glinka
Antonina **s** *Belisario* Donizetti
Antonio **t** *Les deux journées* Cherubini; **t** *The Duenna* Linley; **t** *La gazza ladra* Rossini; **b** *Masagniello* Keiser; **b** *Mignon* Thomas; **b** *Le nozze di Figaro* Mozart; **s** *Richard Coeur-de-lion* Grétry
Antonio, Dom **t** *Dom Sébastien* Donizetti
Antonio, Don **t** *Betrothal in a Monastery* Prokofiev
Antonio de Mariz, Don **b** *Il Guarany* Gomes
Antonio Loustolot **bt** *Linda di Chamounix* Donizetti
Antoñona **ms** *Pepita Jiménez* Albéniz
Antony **bb** *Antony and Cleopatra* Barber
Anzoleto **b** *Il campiello* Wolf-Ferrari
Apelles/Apelle **t** *Statira* Scarlatti
Apollo/Apollon **hc** *Alceste* Lully; **bt** *Alceste* Gluck; **tr** *Apollo et Hyacinthus* Mozart; **bt** *Les boréades* Rameau; **t** *Dafne* Gagliano; **t** *Daphne* Strauss; **a** *Egisto* Cavalli; **t** *Orfeo* Monteverdi; **ms** *Il pastor fido* Handel
Apollo (Philemon) **hc** *Issé* Destouches
Apollonia **s** *La canterina* Haydn
Apollyon **b** *The Pilgrim's Progress* Vaughan Williams
Arabella **s** *Arabella* Strauss
Araquil, Sergeant **t** *La Navarraise* Massenet
Araspe **b** *Tolomeo* Handel
Arasse **b** *Siroe* Handel
Arbaces/Arbace **s** *Artaxerxes* Arne; **t** *Idomeneo* Mozart
Arbas **b** *Cadmus et Hermione* Lully
Arbates/Arbate **s** *Mitridate* Mozart
Arcabonne **s** *Amadis* Lully
Arcalaus **bt** *Amadis* Lully
Arcanes **a** *Teseo* Handel
Arcas **t** *Dardanus* Rameau; **hc** *Hippolyte et Aricie* Rameau; **b** *Iphigénie en Aulide* Gluck
Arcesius **bt** *Die toten Augen* d'Albert
Arcetrus/Arcetro **a** *Euridice* Peri
Archangel Gabriel **t** *Taverner* Maxwell Davies
Archbishop **b** *King Roger* Szymanowski; **b** *The Maid of Orléans* Tchaikovsky; *see also* Cardinal
Archibaldo, Baron **b** *L'amore dei tre re* Montemezzi
Archibius **bt** *Cleopatra* Mattheson
Arco, Contessa d' **ms** *Matilde di Shabran* Rossini
Arcos, Duke of **a** *Masagniello* Keiser
Ardan Canile, Ghost of **bt** *Amadis* Lully
Ardelao **t** *L'amor coniugale* Mayr
Arden **b** *Arden must Die* Goehr
Aremberg, Countess of **x** *Don Carlos* Verdi
Arespingh, Milord **bt** *L'italiana in Londra* Cimarosa
Aret **t** *Philemon und Baucis* Haydn
Arethusa/Aréthuse **s** *Proserpine* Lully
Arfagard **bt** *Fervaal* d'Indy
Argante **b** *Rinaldo* Handel; **b** *Tancrède* Campra
Argelia **s** *Esule di Roma* Donizetti
Argene **s** *Ciro in Babilonia* Rossini
Argenius/Argenio **b** *Imeneo* Handel
Argie **s** *Les Paladins* Rameau
Argippo **bt/a** *Erismena* Cavalli
Argirio **t** *Tancredi* Rossini
Argone **a** *Sosarme* Handel
Argus **bt** *Isis* Lully
Ariadne/Arianna **s** *Arianna in Creta* Handel; **s** *Giustino* Handel
Ariadne/Prima Donna **s** *Ariadne auf Naxos* Strauss, R.
Ariane **ms** *Ariane et Barbe-bleue* Dukas
Aricia/Aricie **s** *Hippolyte et Aricie* Rameau; **s** *Ippolito ed Aricia* Traetta
Arindal, Prince of Tramond **t** *Die Feen* Wagner
Ariodante/Ariodant **hc** *Ariodant* Méhul; **ms** *Ariodante* Handel; **s** *Ginevra di Scozia* Mayr
Ariodate **b** *Serse* Handel; **t** *Xerse* Cavalli
Aristaeus/Aristée **t** *The Mask of Orpheus* Birtwistle; **t** *Orphée aux enfers* Offenbach
Aristea **a** *Orontea* Cesti
Aristobolo **b** *Berenice* Handel
Aristophanes **t** *Der geduldige Socrates* Telemann
Arjuna, Prince **bt** *Satyagraha* Glass
Arkel, King **b** *Pelléas et Mélisande* Debussy
Arlecchino **sp** *Arlecchino* Busoni; **b** *Le donne curiose* Wolf-Ferrari; *see also* Beppe
Arline **s** *The Bohemian Girl* Balfe
Armand **t** *Les deux journées* Cherubini
Armand Brissard **t** *Der Graf von Luxemburg* Lehár
Armand de Clerval **t** *Thérèse* Massenet
Armand des Grieux **t** *Boulevard Solitude* Henze
Armando D'Orville (Elmireno) **s** *Il crociato in Egitto* Meyerbeer
Armchair **b** *L'enfant et les sortilèges* Ravel

Armel **t** *Gwendoline* Chabrier
Armfelt/Judge **t** *Un ballo in maschera* Verdi
Armida **s** *Armida* Haydn; **s** *Armida* Rossini; **s** *Armida* Dvořák; **s** *Armida abbandonata* Jommelli; **s** *Rinaldo* Handel
Armide **s** *Armide* Lully; **s** *Armide* Gluck
Armidoro **t** *La buona figliuola* Piccinni
Arminda **s** *La finta giardiniera* Mozart
Armindo **t** *Gli equivoci nel sembiante* Scarlatti; **a** *Partenope* Handel
Arminio **t** *I masnadieri* Verdi
Arminius/Arminio **a** *Arminio* Handel
Armira **s** *Scipione* Handel
Arnalta **a** *L'incoronazione di Poppea* Monteverdi
Arnheim, Count **bt** *The Bohemian Girl* Balfe
Arnold **b** *The English Cat* Henze
Arnold Melcthal **t** *Guillaume Tell* Rossini
Arnoldo **bt** *I lituani* Ponchielli
Arnolfo **bt** *L'amore medico* Wolf-Ferrari
Aroldo **t** *Aroldo* Verdi
Aron, Aronne: *see* Aaron
Aronte **t** *Armide* Lully; **b** *Armide* Gluck
Arrigo **t** *La battaglia di Legnano* Verdi; *see also* Henri
Arristippus **b** *The Magic Opal* Albéniz
Arsace **s** *Aureliano in Palmira* Rossini; **a** *Berenice* Handel; **a** *Partenope* Handel; **a** *Semiramide* Rossini
Arsamene **ms** *Serse* Handel; **a** *Xerse* Cavalli; **ct** *Xerse* Bononcini, G.
Arsena **s** *Der Zigeunerbaron* Strauss, J.
Arsete **t** *Dori* Cesti
Arsinda **s** *La clemenza di Scipione* Bach, J. C.
Arsinoe **s** *Dori* Cesti; **ms** *Die toten Augen* d'Albert
Arsinoe, Queen **s** *Arsinoe* Clayton
Artabanes **t** *Artaxerxes* Arne
Artaxerxes **a** *Artaxerxes* Arne
Artémidore **t** *Armide* Lully; **t** *Armide* Gluck
Arthénée **b** *Tarare* Salieri
Arthur, President **t** *The Ballad of Baby Doe* Moore
Arthur/Arthus **bt** *Le roi Arthus* Chausson
Arthur Jones **bt** *Billy Budd* Britten
Artists' Manager **t** *Jonny spielt auf* Krenek
Arturo, Count of Ravenstal **t** *La straniera* Bellini
Arturo Bucklaw, Lord **t** *Lucia di Lammermoor* Donizetti
Arturo Talbo, Lord **t** *I puritani* Bellini
Arv **t** *Maskarade* Nielsen
Arvedson **ms** *Gustave III* Auber
Arvidson/Ulrica **a** *Un ballo in maschera* Verdi
Arvino **t** *I Lombardi* Verdi
Ascanio **s** *Ascanio in Alba* Mozart; **ms/s** *Benvenuto Cellini* Berlioz
Ascanius/Ascagne **s** *Les Troyens* Berlioz
Aschenbach **t** *Death in Venice* Britten
Asdrubale: *see* Hasdrubal
Asdrubale, Count **b** *Emilia di Liverpool* Donizetti; **b** *La pietra del paragone* Rossini
Asdrubale, Don **t** *Lo sposo deluso* Mozart
Ashby **b** *La fanciulla del West* Puccini
Ashton: *see* Enrico Ashton
Aslak **b** *Hulda* Franck
Asnois, Duke of **t** *Colas Breugnon* Kabalevsky
Aspasia **s** *Alceste* Gluck; **s** *Axur, re d'Ormus* Salieri; **s** *Mitridate* Mozart
Aspasia, Baroness **s** *La pietra del paragone* Rossini
Aspern **t** *The Aspern Papers* Argento
Assad **t** *Die Königin von Saba* Goldmark
Assan **bt** *The Consul* Menotti
Assur **b** *Semiramide* Rossini
Astaroth **s** *Die Königin von Saba* Goldmark
Astarotte **b** *Armida* Rossini
Astarto (Clearco) **a** *Astarto* Bononcini, G.
Astasie **s** *Tarare* Salieri
Asteria **s** *Nerone* Boito; **s** *Tamerlano* Handel; **s** *Telemaco* Gluck
Asterion/Astérion **hc** *Naïs* Rameau
Astolfe **hc** *Roland* Lully; **t** *Roland* Piccinni
Astolfi, Cavaliere **bt** *Il campiello* Wolf-Ferrari
Astradamors **b** *Le Grand Macabre* Ligeti
Astraea/Astrée **s** *Phaëton* Lully
Astrologer **b** *L'étoile* Chabrier; **t** *The Golden Cockerel* Rimsky-Korsakov; *see also* Abbot
Astron **ct** *The Ice Break* Tippett
Astyanax/Astianatte **x** *Astianatte* Bononcini, G.; **x** *Les Troyens* Berlioz
Atalanta **s** *Atalanta* Handel; **s** *Serse* Handel
Ataliba **b** *Alzira* Verdi
Atalide **s** *Les Indes galantes* Rameau
Atar **t** *Axur, re d'Ormus* Salieri
Atar, King of Hormuz **b** *Tarare* Salieri
Athamas **ct** *Semele* Handel
Athanaël **bt** *Thaïs* Massenet
Athar **b** *Nurmahal* Spontini
Athlete: *see* Animal Tamer
Atis **hc** *Les Paladins* Rameau
Attalus/Attalo **t** *Ermione* Rossini
Attila **b** *Attila* Verdi
Attis/Atys **hc** *Atys* Lully
Aubry **t** *Maria di Rohan* Donizetti
Aubry, Edgar **t** *Der Vampyr* Marschner
Aufidius/Aufidio **t** *Lucio Silla* Mozart
Augusta **ms** *The Ballad of Baby Doe* Moore
Aunt **s** *Madama Butterfly* Puccini
Aunt Jane **a** *Hugh the Drover* Vaughan Williams
Auntie **a** *Peter Grimes* Britten
Auphis/Mambre **t** *Mosè in Egitto* Rossini
Aurelia **s** *L'oca del Cairo* Mozart
Aurelianus/Aureliano **t** *Aureliano in Palmira* Rossini
Aurelio **ms** *L'assedio di Calais* Donizetti
Aurelius Galba **t** *Die toten Augen* d'Albert
Aurindo **a** *Il pomo d'oro* Cesti
Autonoe **s** *The Bassarids* Henze
Avis **s** *The Wreckers* Smyth
Avito **t** *L'amore dei tre re* Montemezzi
Axur **b** *Axur, re d'Ormus* Salieri
Azema **s** *Semiramide* Rossini
Azor **t** *Zémire et Azor* Grétry
Azucena **ms** *Il trovatore* Verdi
Azzo, Duke of Ferrara **bt** *Parisina* Donizetti

B

Baba/Flora, Mme **a** *The Medium* Menotti
Baba Mustapha **t** *Der Barbier von Bagdad* Cornelius
Baba the Turk **ms** *The Rake's Progress* Stravinsky
Babarikha **a** *The Tale of Tsar Saltan* Rimsky-Korsakov
Babekan **a** *Die Verlobung in San Domingo* Egk
Babekan **sp** *Oberon* Weber
Babette **ms** *The English Cat* Henze
Babinski **t** *Švanda the Bagpiper* Weinberger
Babulen'ka, Granny **ms** *The Gambler* Prokofiev
Baby Doe **s** *The Ballad of Baby Doe* Moore
Bacchis **s** *La belle Hélène* Offenbach
Bacchus **t** *The Olympians* Bliss; **sp** *Orphée aux enfers* Offenbach
Bacchus/Tenor **t** *Ariadne auf Naxos* Strauss, R.
Baculus **b** *Der Wildschütz* Lortzing
Badger **b** *The Cunning Little Vixen* Janáček
Baggot, Mrs **a** *The Little Sweep* Britten
Baghdad, Caliph of **b** *Adina* Rossini
Bailli **bb** *Werther* Massenet
Bajazet/Bajazete **t** *Tamerlano* Handel
Baldad **a** *Job* Dallapiccola
Baldassare **bt** *L'arlesiana* Cilea; *see also* Belshazzar
Baldo **t** *Belfagor* Respighi
Balducci **b** *Benvenuto Cellini* Berlioz
Balkis **s** *L'incontro improvviso* Haydn; **s** *La rencontre imprévue* Gluck
Balkis, Queen of Sheba **s** *La reine de Saba* Gounod
Ballad-Singer **b** *Gloriana* Britten
Balstrode, Captain **bt** *Peter Grimes* Britten
Balthazar **b** *Amahl and the Night Visitors* Menotti; **b** *La favorite* Donizetti

Bánk bán **t** *Bánk bán* Erkel
Banker: *see* Professor of Medicine
Banquo/Banco **b** *Macbeth* Verdi
Baptista **b** *Der widerspänstigen Zähmung* Goetz
Barak **bb** *Die Frau ohne Schatten* Strauss, R.; **bt** *Turandot* Busoni
Barak's Wife/Dyer's Wife **s** *Die Frau ohne Schatten* Strauss, R.
Barbara **ms** *Eine Nacht in Venedig* Strauss, J.
Barbarin **bt** *Cythère assiégée* Gluck
Barbarina **s** *Le nozze di Figaro* Mozart
Barbarino **t** *Alessandro Stradella* Flotow
Barbarossa **b** *La battaglia di Legnano* Verdi
Barbe-bleue: *see* Bluebeard
Barbemuche **b** *La bohème* Leoncavallo
Barber: *see* Abu Hassan, Schneidebart
Barče **s** *The Kiss* Smetana
Bard **hc** *Ariodant* Méhul
Bardolph/Bardolfo **bt** *At the Boar's Head* Holst; **t** *Falstaff* Verdi
Barena **s** *Jenůfa* Janáček
Barnaba **bt** *La Gioconda* Ponchielli
Baron **b** *Der ferne Klang* Schreker
Baroncelli **t** *Rienzi* Wagner
Baroness **ms** *Chérubin* Massenet; **a** *Vanessa* Barber
Barrat, Lord **t** *Der junge Lord* Henze
Barré **b** *The Devils of Loudun* Penderecki
Bartley **bt** *Riders to the Sea* Vaughan Williams
Bartolo/Bartolo, Dr **b** *Il barbiere di Siviglia* Paisiello; **bt** *Il barbiere di Siviglia* Rossini; **b** *Le nozze di Figaro* Mozart
Basil Basilowitsch, Prince **bt** *Der Graf von Luxemburg* Lehár
Basilio, Don **b** *Il barbiere di Siviglia* Paisiello; **b** *Il barbiere di Siviglia* Rossini; **t** *Le nozze di Figaro* Mozart
Basmanov **a** *Oprichnik* Tchaikovsky
Basmanov, Petr Fedorovič **b** *Dimitrij* Dvořák
Bassi **b** *Alessandro Stradella* Flotow
Bassian **t** *Masagniello* Keiser
Bastien **t** *Bastien und Bastienne* Mozart
Bastienne **s** *Bastien und Bastienne* Mozart
Batone **b** *L'inganno felice* Rossini
Baucis **s** *Philémon et Baucis* Gounod; **s** *Philemon und Baucis* Haydn
Bayan **t** *Ruslan and Lyudmila* Glinka
Beatrice **s** *Boccaccio* Suppé; **ms** *Le donne curiose* Wolf-Ferrari
Beatrice/Béatrice **s** *Béatrice et Bénédict* Berlioz
Beatrice di Tenda **s** *Beatrice di Tenda* Bellini
Béatrix **s** *Etienne Marcel* Saint-Saëns
Beaumanoir, Lucas de **b** *Der Templer und die Jüdin* Marschner
Beaupertuis **b** *Il cappello di paglia di Firenze* Rota
Beauty/Bellezza **s** *Egisto* Cavalli
Becket: *see* Thomas Becket
Beckmesser, Sixtus **b** *Die Meistersinger von Nürnberg* Wagner
Begaers **bt** *La mère coupable* Milhaud
Begbick, Leokadja: *see* Leokadja Begbick
Beggar **sp** *The Beggar's Opera*
Begonia **ms** *Der junge Lord* Henze
Belcore **bt** *L'elisir d'amore* Donizetti
Belfagor **bt** *Belfagor* Respighi
Belfiore **b** *Alina, regina di Golconda* Donizetti
Belfiore, Cavalier **t** *Il viaggio a Reims* Rossini
Belfiore, Count **t** *La finta giardiniera* Mozart; **bt** *Fra i due litiganti il terzo gode* Sarti
Belfiore, Countess **s** *Fra i due litiganti il terzo gode* Sarti
Belfiore/Stanislaus of Poland, King **bt** *Un giorno di regno* Verdi
Belinda **s** *Dido and Aeneas* Purcell
Belisarius/Belisario **bt** *Belisario* Donizetti
Belise/Bélise **s** *Roland* Lully; **s** *Roland* Piccinni
Bella **s** *The Midsummer Marriage* Tippett
Bellangère **s** *Ariane et Barbe-bleue* Dukas
Bellante **s** *Almira* Handel
Bellaston, Lady **ms** *Tom Jones* German
Bellezza: *see* Beauty
Belmonte **t** *Die Entführung aus dem Serail* Mozart
Belshazzar/Baldassare **t** *Ciro in Babilonia* Rossini
Belville, Captain **t** *Rosina* Shield
Belville, Mr **t** *Rosina* Shield
Ben **bt** *The Telephone* Menotti
Ben Hubbard **bt** *Regina* Blitzstein
Ben-Selim **b** *Dom Sébastien* Donizetti
Benda **t** *The Jacobin* Dvořák
Benedick/Bénédict **t** *Béatrice et Bénédict* Berlioz
Beneš **b** *Dalibor* Smetana; **b** *The Devil's Wall* Smetana
Benjamin **s** *Joseph* Méhul
Benkendorf, Count **b** *The Decembrists* Shaporin
Benoit **b** *La bohème* Puccini
Bensch, Baron **t** *Die Brautwahl* Busoni
Bentson, Mistress **ms** *Lakmé* Delibes
Benvolio **t** *Roméo et Juliette* Gounod
Beppe **ms** *L'amico Fritz* Mascagni
Beppe/Arlecchino **t** *Pagliacci* Leoncavallo
Beppo **t** *Fra Diavolo* Auber
Berardo **b** *Riccardo Primo* Handel
Berendey, Tsar **t** *The Snow Maiden* Rimsky-Korsakov
Berengario **b** *Adelaide di Borgogna* Rossini; **t** *Lotario* Handel
Berenice **s** *Berenice* Handel; **s** *L'occasione fa il ladro* Rossini; **s** *Scipione* Handel
Bergère: *see* Louis XV Chair
Berkenfeld, Marquise/Marchesa **ms** *La fille du régiment* Donizetti
Berkley, Sir John **b** *Der Vampyr* Marschner
Bernardo **bt** *West Side Story* Bernstein
Beroe **ms** *The Bassarids* Henze; **s** *Fausta* Donizetti
Bersi **ms** *Andrea Chénier* Giordano
Berta **ms** *Il barbiere di Siviglia* Rossini
Bertalda **s** *Undine* Lortzing
Bertarido **a** *Rodelinda* Handel
Berthalda **s** *Undine* Hoffmann
Berthe **s** *Le prophète* Meyerbeer
Bertram **b** *Robert le diable* Meyerbeer
Bertrand **t** *Le déserteur* Monsigny; **b** *Iolanta* Tchaikovsky
Bertrando, Duke **t** *L'inganno felice* Rossini
Bess **s** *Porgy and Bess* Gershwin
Bessie Throckmorton **s** *Merrie England* German
Besso **b** *Giasone* Cavalli
Bestuzhev **b** *The Decembrists* Shaporin
Béthune, Sire de **b** *Les vêpres siciliennes* Verdi
Betly **s** *Betly* Donizetti
Bettina **s** *Don Procopio* Bizet; **s** *Lo sposo deluso* Mozart
Betto di Signa **b** *Gianni Schicchi* Puccini
Bětuška **s** *The Cunning Peasant* Dvořák
Biagio **b** *Don Giovanni* Gazzaniga; **bt** *Nozze istriane* Smareglia
Bianca **s** *Bianca e Falliero* Rossini; **s** *Bianca e Fernando* Bellini; **s** *Eine florentinische Tragödie* Zemlinsky; **a** *Il giuramento* Mercadante; **ms** *The Rape of Lucretia* Britten; **s** *Ugo conte di Parigi* Donizetti; **s** *Der widerspänstigen Zähmung* Goetz
Biancafiore **s** *Francesca da Rimini* Zandonai
Biberach **bt** *Bánk bán* Erkel
Biberich, Margrave of **b** *Loreley* Catalani
Bide-the-Bent: *see* Raimondo Bidebent
Big Prisoner/Nikita **t** *From the House of the Dead* Janáček
Bijou **b** *Le postillon de Lonjumeau* Adam
Bill Bobstay **b** *HMS Pinafore* Sullivan
Billows, Lady **s** *Albert Herring* Britten
Bill/Sparbüchsenbill **bt** *Aufstieg und Fall der Stadt Mahagonny* Weill
Billy Budd **bt** *Billy Budd* Britten
Billy Jackrabbit **b** *La fanciulla del West* Puccini
Biondello **t** *L'oca del Cairo* Mozart
Birdie **s** *Regina* Blitzstein
Biscroma **t** *Axur, re d'Ormus* Salieri
Biterolf **b** *Tannhäuser* Wagner
Black Bob **b** *The Little Sweep* Britten
Black Knight: *see* Richard I
Black Man **t** *Die Verlobung in San Domingo* Egk
Black Will **b** *Arden must Die* Goehr
Blaise **bt** *Lucile* Grétry
Blanche **a** *The Gambler* Prokofiev
Blanche, Lady **a** *Princess Ida* Sullivan
Blanche de la Force **s** *Dialogues des Carmélites* Poulenc
Blansac **b** *La scala di seta* Rossini
Blaženka **s** *The Secret* Smetana
Blifil **t** *Tom Jones* Philidor

Blind, Dr **t** *Die Fledermaus* Strauss, J.
Blind Poetess **s** *Aniara* Blomdahl
Blitch, Olin **bb** *Susannah* Floyd
Blois, Bishop of **bt** *Esclarmonde* Massenet
Blonde **s** *Die Entführung aus dem Serail* Mozart
Blondel **bt** *Richard Coeur-de-lion* Grétry
Bluebeard/Barbe-bleue **b** *Ariane et Barbe-bleue* Dukas; **t** *Barbe-bleue* Offenbach; **bt** *Bluebeard's Castle* Bartók
Blunt, Toms **b** *Der Vampyr* Marschner
Bob **bt** *The Old Maid and the Thief* Menotti
Bob: *see* Tristan Mickleford, Lord
Bobadilla **b** *Cristoforo Colombo* Franchetti
Bobèche **bt** *Barbe-bleue* Offenbach
Bobïl'-Bakula **t** *The Snow Maiden* Rimsky-Korsakov
Bobïlikha **ms** *The Snow Maiden* Rimsky-Korsakov
Bobinet **bt** *La vie parisienne* Offenbach
Boccaccio **ms** *Boccaccio* Suppé
Boccanegra, Simon **bt** *Simon Boccanegra* Verdi
Bocconio **b** *Lo sposo deluso* Mozart
Body: *see* Corpo
Böhni **bt** *Kleider machen Leute* Zemlinsky
Bohuš of Harasov **bt** *The Jacobin* Dvořák
Bois-Guilbert, Brian de **bt** *Der Templer und die Jüdin* Marschner
Bois-Rosé **t** *Les Huguenots* Meyerbeer
Boland **b** *Fierrabras* Schubert
Boles, Bob **t** *Peter Grimes* Britten
Bolkonsky: *see* Andrey Bolkonsky
Bolkonsky, Prince Nikolay **b** *War and Peace* Prokofiev
Bombasto, Dr **b** *Arlecchino* Busoni
Bomelius, Elisa **t** *The Tsar's Bride* Rimsky-Korsakov
Boni Káncsiánu, Count **t/bt** *Die Csárdásfürstin* Kálmán
Bonifác **bt** *The Secret* Smetana
Boniface **bt** *Angélique* Ibert
Boniface, Brother **bt** *Le jongleur de Nôtre-Dame* Massenet
Bonifacio **b** *Adelson e Salvini* Bellini
Bonny Spring/Spring Fairy/Vesna-Krasna **ms** *The Snow Maiden* Rimsky-Korsakov
Bonze **b** *Madama Butterfly* Puccini; **b** *The Nightingale* Stravinsky
Boreas/Boréas **b** *Les boréades* Rameau
Borella **b** *La muette de Portici* Auber
Borilée **bt** *Les boréades* Rameau
Boris Godunov **bt/b** *Boris Godunov* Musorgsky
Boris Grigorjevič **t** *Kát'a Kabanová* Janáček
Boris Izmaylov **b** *Katerina Izmaylova/Lady Macbeth of the Mtsensk District* Shostakovich
Borov **bt** *Fedora* Giordano
Borromeo, Cardinal Carlo **bt** *Palestrina* Pfitzner
Borromeo, Cardinal Federico **b** *I promessi sposi* Ponchielli
Borsa **t** *Rigoletto* Verdi
Bostana **ms** *Der Barbier von Bagdad* Cornelius
Bosun **bt** *Billy Budd* Britten
Bottom **bb** *A Midsummer Night's Dream* Britten
Bouillon, Prince of **b** *Adriana Lecouvreur* Cilea
Bouillon, Princess of **ms** *Adriana Lecouvreur* Cilea
Boulotte **s** *Barbe-bleue* Offenbach
Boum, General **bt** *La Grande-Duchesse de Gérolstein* Offenbach
Bouncer **bt** *Cox and Box* Sullivan
Box **bt** *Cox and Box* Sullivan
Boy **tr** *Der Jasager* Weill
Brack **t/bt** *Down in the Valley* Weill
Bradamante **a** *Alcina* Handel
Bradshaw, Mrs **a** *Arden must Die* Goehr
Brahmin **t** *Padmâvatî* Roussel
Brander **b** *La damnation de Faust* Berlioz
Brangäne **s/ms** *Tristan und Isolde* Wagner
Bravo **t** *Il bravo* Mercadante
Brazilian **bt** *La vie parisienne* Offenbach
Brétigny **bt** *Manon* Massenet
Briano **b** *Aroldo* Verdi
Bride **s** *Blood Wedding* Szokolay; *see also* Young Girl
Bridegroom **t** *Blood Wedding* Szokolay; **sp** *Die Bluthochzeit* Fortner
Bridegroom's Mother **s** *Die Bluthochzeit* Fortner
Brighella **t** *Ariadne auf Naxos* Strauss, R.
Brigitta **a** *Die tote Stadt* Korngold
Brigitte **s** *Le domino noir* Auber
Brillante, Madama **s** *L'italiana in Londra* Cimarosa
Britomarte **s** *Arbore di Diana* Martín y Soler
Brogni, Cardinal **b** *La Juive* Halévy
Bronislawa **s** *Der Bettelstudent* Millöcker
Brontès **bt** *Cythère assiégée* Gluck
Broom-Maker **t** *Die Königskinder* Humperdinck
Brouček, Mr **t** *The Excursions of Mr Brouček* Janáček
Brown **bt** *Die Dreigroschenoper* Weill
Brunehild **s** *Sigurd* Reyer
Brünnhilde **s** *Götterdämmerung* Wagner; **s** *Siegfried* Wagner; **s** *Die Walküre* Wagner
Bruno Robertson, Sir **t** *I puritani* Bellini
Brunoro **t** *Il giuramento* Mercadante
Bruschino (father) **b** *Il Signor Bruschino* Rossini
Bruschino (son) **t** *Il Signor Bruschino* Rossini
Brutamonte **b** *Fierrabras* Schubert
Bubble, Madam **ms** *The Pilgrim's Progress* Vaughan Williams
Budd, Superintendent **b** *Albert Herring* Britten
Budivoj **bt** *Dalibor* Smetana
Bunthorne **bt** *Patience* Sullivan
Bunyan **bb** *The Pilgrim's Progress* Vaughan Williams
Bunyan, Paul **sp** *Paul Bunyan* Britten
Buonafede **bt** *Il mondo della luna* Haydn
Buralicchio **b** *L'equivoco stravagante* Rossini
Burgomaster **t** *Feuersnot* Strauss, R.; **t** *Friedenstag* Strauss, R.; **t** *Lanzelot* Dessau
Burlotto **t** *Le pescatrici* Haydn
Bürstner, Fräulein **s** *Der Prozess* von Einem
Business Acquaintance **bt** *Der Prozess* von Einem
Bussy **bt** *Zazà* Leoncavallo
Bustamento **bt** *La Navarraise* Massenet
Butterfly/Cio-Cio-San **s** *Madama Butterfly* Puccini
By-Ends, Madam **a** *The Pilgrim's Progress* Vaughan Williams
By-Ends, Mister **t** *The Pilgrim's Progress* Vaughan Williams
Byron **t** *Lord Byron* Thomson
Bystrouška/Vixen **s** *The Cunning Little Vixen* Janáček

C

Cacico, Aymoré Chief **bt/b** *Il Guarnay* Gomes
Cacique **b** *Cristoforo Colombo* Franchetti
Cadmus **b** *The Bassarids* Henze; **bt** *Cadmus et Hermione* Lully; **b** *Semele* Handel
Caesar: *see* Julius Caesar, Octavius Caesar
Caesar Augustus **bt** *Cleopatra* Mattheson
Caesar de Bazan, Don **t** *Maritana* Wallace
Caius, Dr **t** *Falstaff* Verdi; **b** *Die lustigen Weiber von Windsor* Nicolai
Calaf **t** *Turandot* Puccini
Calandrino **t** *L'oca del Cairo* Mozart
Calatrava, Marchese di **b** *La forza del destino* Verdi
Calbo, General **a** *Maometto II* Rossini
Calcante **b** *La zingara* Rinaldo da Capua
Calchas **bt** *La belle Hélène* Offenbach; **b** *Iphigénie en Aulide* Gluck
Calender **b** *La rencontre imprévue* Gluck
Calender/Dervish **b** *L'incontro improvviso* Haydn
Caliph **sp** *Abu Hassan* Weber; **bt** *Der Barbier von Bagdad* Cornelius
Calisis **hc** *Les boréades* Rameau
Calkas **b** *Troilus and Cressida* Walton
Callisthènes/Callistene **b** *Les martyrs/Poliuto* Donizetti
Callisto/Calisto **s** *Calisto* Cavalli
Calloandro, Don **t** *La molinara* Paisiello
Calpigi **t** *Tarare* Salieri
Calverley, Colonel **bt** *Patience* Sullivan
Calypso **s** *Ulisse* Dallapiccola
Cam **t** *Il diluvio universale* Donizetti
Camilla **s** *Il trionfo di Camilla* Bononcini, G.
Camille **s** *Zampa* Hérold
Camille de Rosillon **t** *Die lustige Witwe* Lehár

Camille Desmoulins **t** *Dantons Tod* von Einem
Camillo **ms/t** *Olivo e Pasquale* Donizetti
Camoëns **bt** *Dom Sébastien* Donizetti
Campaspe **s** *Statira* Scarlatti
Cancian **b** *I quatro rusteghi* Wolf-Ferrari
Candace **s** *Cleopatra* Mattheson
Candida **s** *Belfagor* Respighi
Candide **t** *Candide* Bernstein
Canio/Pagliaccio **t** *Pagliacci* Leoncavallo
Cantarelli **t** *Le pré aux Clercs* Hérold
Cantatore **t** *Giulietta e Romeo* Zandonai
Capellio **b** *Bianca e Falliero* Rossini; **b** *I Capuleti e i Montecchi* Bellini; **t** *Giulietta e Romeo* Vaccai
Capito **t** *Mathis der Maler* Hindemith
Capocchio **t** *Il filosofo di campagna* Galuppi
Capraja **b** *Massimilla Doni* Schoeck
Captain **bt** *Maritana* Wallace; **t** *Wozzeck* Berg
Captain of the Royal Guard/Adonis **bt** *The Bassarids* Henze
Capulet **b** *Roméo et Juliette* Gounod
Carambollas **b** *The Magic Opal* Albéniz
Caramello **t** *Eine Nacht in Venedig* Strauss, J.
Cardenio **bt** *Il furioso nell'isola di S Domingo* Donizetti
Cardillac **bt** *Cardillac* Hindemith
Cardinal/Archbishop **t** *Taverner* Maxwell Davies
Carilda **a** *Arianna in Creta* Handel
Carite **s** *Cythère assiégée* Gluck
Carl, Prince **t** *Tintomara* Werle
Carlo **t** *Armida* Rossini; **b** *Bianca e Fernando* Bellini; **t** *I masnadieri* Verdi
Carlo, Don **bt** *Ernani* Verdi
Carlo, Viscount de Sirval **t** *Linda di Chamounix* Donizetti
Carlo di Vargas, Don **bt** *La forza del destino* Verdi
Carlo Gérard: *see* Gérard
Carlos, Don **bt** *Betrothal in a Monastery* Prokofiev; **hc** *Les Indes galantes* Rameau; **bt** *The Stone Guest* Dargomïzhsky
Carlos/Carlo, Don **t** *Don Carlos* Verdi
Carlo VII: *see* Charles
Carlotta **ms** *Die schweigsame Frau* Strauss, R.; **ms** *Torvaldo e Dorliska* Rossini
Carlotta Nardi **s** *Die Gezeichneten* Schreker
Carmela **ms** *I gioielli della Madonna* Wolf-Ferrari; **s** *The Saint of Bleecker Street* Menotti; **ms** *La vida breve* Falla
Carmen **ms** *Carmen* Bizet
Carnero, Conte **bt** *Der Zigeunerbaron* Strauss, J.
Carolina **s** *Il matrimonio segreto* Cimarosa
Carolina, Countess of Kirchstetten **a** *Elegy for Young Lovers* Henze
Carolina, Queen of Naples **s** *Madame Sans-Gêne* Giordano
Caronte: *see* Charon
Čaroskvoucí: *see* Würfl
Carpenter **bt** *Il piccolo Marat* Mascagni
Carruthers, Dame **a** *The Yeomen of the Guard* Sullivan
Cascada, Vicomte **bt** *Die lustige Witwe* Lehár
Cascart **bt** *Zazà* Leoncavallo
Casilda **s** *The Gondoliers* Sullivan
Caspar **b** *Der Freischütz* Weber
Cassander/Cassandre **t** *Olimpie* Spontini
Cassandra/Cassandre **ms** *Les Troyens* Berlioz
Cassandre **t** *Le tableau parlant* Grétry
Cassandro **b** *La finta semplice* Mozart
Cassio **t** *Otello* Verdi
Castor **hc** *Castor et Pollux* Rameau
Cat **b** *Renard* Stravinsky
Catarina Cornaro **a** *La reine de Chypre* Halévy
Cate Panciana, Dona **t** *Il campiello* Wolf-Ferrari
Caterina **s** *Caterina Cornaro* Donizetti
Caterina Hubscher/Sans-Gêne, Mme **s** *Madame Sans-Gêne* Giordano
Catharine/Catherine **s** *La jolie fille de Perth* Bizet
Catherine **s** *L'étoile du Nord* Meyerbeer
Catherine of Aragon **s** *Henry VIII* Saint-Saëns
Catherine the Great **x** *The Queen of Spades* Tchaikovsky
Cathleen **s** *Riders to the Sea* Vaughan Williams
Cattaneo, Duke **t** *Massimilla Doni* Schoeck
Cavalier **t** *Cardillac* Hindemith
Cavaradossi, Mario **t** *Tosca* Puccini
Cecchina **s** *La buona figliuola* Piccinni
Cecco **t** *Il mondo della luna* Haydn
Cecco del Vecchio **b** *Rienzi* Wagner
Cecil **b** *Maria Stuarda* Donizetti; **b** *Roberto Devereux* Donizetti
Cecil, Sir Robert **bt** *Gloriana* Britten
Cecilia **s** *Il Guarany* Gomes
Cecilia, St **s** *Four Saints in Three Acts* Thomson
Cecilius/Cecilio **s** *Lucio Silla* Mozart
Cecrops/Cecrope **b** *Il pomo d'oro* Cesti
Cedric of Rotherwood **b** *Der Templer und die Jüdin* Marschner
Ceix: *see* Ceyx
Čekunov **b** *From the House of the Dead* Janáček
Celaenus/Celenus **bt** *Atys* Lully
Celestial Messenger **t** *The Pilgrim's Progress* Vaughan Williams
Celia **s** *Lucio Silla* Mozart; **s** *Silla* Handel; *see also* Fillide
Celidora **s** *L'oca del Cairo* Mozart
Celinda **s** *Almahide* [pasticcio]
Celinda: *see* Tolomeo
Celio **b** *The Love for Three Oranges* Prokofiev
Cellini **t** *Benvenuto Cellini* Berlioz
Cendrillon/Lucette **s** *Cendrillon* Massenet
Cenerentola/Angelina **a** *La Cenerentola* Rossini
Céphalide **s** *Les mariages samnites* Grétry
Céphise **s** *Alceste* Lully
Ceprano, Count **b** *Rigoletto* Verdi
Ceprano, Countess **ms** *Rigoletto* Verdi
Cerberus/Cerbère **barked** *Orphée aux enfers* Offenbach
Ceres/Cérés **s** *Proserpine* Lully
Čerevin **t** *From the House of the Dead* Janáček
Césaire b *Sapho* Massenet
Ceyx/Ceix **hc** *Alcyone* Marais
Chalais, Count de: *see* Riccardo, Count de Chalais
Chamaille **b** *Colas Breugnon* Kabalevsky
Chamberlain **b** *The Nightingale* Stravinsky
Champigny, Baroness **s** *Il cappello di paglia di Firenze* Rota
Chapelou/Saint-Phar **t** *Le postillon de Lonjumeau* Adam
Chaplitsky **t** *The Queen of Spades* Tchaikovsky
Charcoal Burner **bt/b** *May Night* Rimsky-Korsakov
Charlemagne/Karl, King **b** *Fierrabras* Schubert
Charles/Carlo VII **t** *Giovanna d'Arco* Verdi
Charles II **b** *Maritana* Wallace
Charles VII **t** *The Maid of Orléans* Tchaikovsky
Charles X **b** *Il viaggio a Reims* Rossini
Charlie Johnson **bt** *Lady in the Dark* Weill
Charlot **bt** *Angélique* Ibert
Charlotte **ms** *Die Soldaten* Zimmermann; **ms** *Werther* Massenet
Charmeuse, La **s** *Thaïs* Massenet
Charmian **ms** *Antony and Cleopatra* Barber
Charon/Caronte **bt** *Alceste* Lully; **t** *Euridice* Peri; **b** *Orfeo* Monteverdi; **b** *Orlando paladino* Haydn; **a** *Il pomo d'oro* Cesti
Chateauneuf, Marquis de **t** *Zar und Zimmermann* Lortzing
Chavez, St **t** *Four Saints in Three Acts* Thomson
Chazeuil, Abbé of **t** *Adriana Lecouvreur* Cilea
Checco **t** *König Hirsch* Henze
Chefone, Commander **bt** *Aniara* Blomdahl
Chekalinsky **t** *The Queen of Spades* Tchaikovsky
Chénier: *see* Andrea Chénier
Cherevik, Solopy **b** *The Fair at Sorochintsï* Musorgsky
Chérubin **s** *Chérubin* Massenet
Cherubino **ms** *Le nozze di Figaro* Mozart
Chevalier **t** *Der ferne Klang* Schreker
Chevreuse, Duke de **bt** *Maria di Rohan* Donizetti
Chiang Ch'ing **s** *Nixon in China* Adams
Chichibeo **b** *L'oca del Cairo* Mozart
Chief of Police **b** *Amelia al ballo* Menotti
Chief of Secret Police: *see* Gepopo
Chief Technician **t** *Aniara* Blomdahl
Child **ms** *L'enfant et les sortilèges* Ravel
Chimene/Chimène **s** *Der Cid* Cornelius; **s** *Le Cid* Massenet
China, Emperor of **bt** *The Nightingale* Stravinsky
Chocholka **s** *The Cunning Little Vixen* Janáček
Chorèbe: *see* Coroebus
Choregos **bt** *Punch and Judy* Birtwistle
Chou En-lai **bt** *Nixon in China* Adams

Chrisante **bt** *La fausse esclave* Gluck
Chris the Citizen **bt** *The Mother of Us All* Thomson
Christian/Silvano **b** *Un ballo in maschera* Verdi
Christina: *see* Cristina
Christine Mannon **s** *Mourning Becomes Electra* Levy
Christine: *see* Storch, Christine
Christoph **bt** *Christophorus* Schreker
Christoph von Ried **t** *Die Verlobung in San Domingo* Egk
Christopher Sly **t** *Sly* Wolf-Ferrari
Chrudoš od Otavy **b** *Libuše* Smetana
Chrysothemis **s** *Elektra* Strauss
Chub **b** *Cherevichki* Tchaikovsky
Ciboletta **s** *Eine Nacht in Venedig* Strauss, J.
Cid: *see* Rodrigue
Cieca, La **a** *La Gioconda* Ponchielli
Ciesca, La **ms** *Gianni Schicchi* Puccini
Cigolotti **sp** *König Hirsch* Henze
Cinna **s** *Lucio Silla* Mozart; **t** *La vestale* Spontini
Cio-Cio-San: *see* Butterfly
Circe/Circé **s** *Scylla et Glaucus* Leclair; **s** *Telemaco* Gluck; **ms** *Ulisse* Dallapiccola
Circus Director: *see* La Rocca
Circus Master **t** *The Bartered Bride* Smetana
Cirillo **bt** *Fedora* Giordano
Cis **s** *Albert Herring* Britten
Cithaeron/Cithéron **b** *Platée* Rameau
City Crier **bt** *Gloriana* Britten
Claes-Henrik **t** *Tintomara* Werle
Claggart **b** *Billy Budd* Britten
Claire Zachanassian **ms** *Der Besuch der alten Dame* von Einem
Clairette **s** *La fille de Madame Angot* Lecocq
Clairon **a** *Capriccio* Strauss
Clara **s** *The Duenna* Linley; **s** *Porgy and Bess* Gershwin
Clara, Donna (Infanta) **ms** *Betrothal in a Monastery* Prokofiev; **s** *Der Zwerg* Zemlinsky
Clarice **s** *Il mondo della luna* Haydn
Clarice, Marchesina **a** *La pietra del paragone* Rossini
Clarice, Princess **a** *The Love for Three Oranges* Prokofiev
Clarina **ms** *La cambiale di matrimonio* Rossini
Clarine **s** *Platée* Rameau
Clarissa **s** *Die drei Pintos* Weber
Claudia **a** *Doktor und Apotheker* Dittersdorf
Claudio **bt** *Béatrice et Bénédict* Berlioz; **t** *Das Liebesverbot* Wagner
Claudio di Liverpool **bt** *Emilia di Liverpool* Donizetti
Claudius/Claudio **b** *Agrippina* Handel; **a** *Silla* Handel
Claudius, King of Denmark **b** *Hamlet* Thomas
Clelia: *see* Cloelia
Clem **t** *The Little Sweep* Britten
Clémence **s** *Mireille* Gounod
Clement VII, Pope (Salviati, Cardinal) **b** *Benvenuto Cellini* Berlioz; **sp** *Karl V* Krenek
Clemente **b** *Bianca e Fernando* Bellini
Cléomène **t** *Le siège de Corinthe* Rossini
Cleon/Cleone **a** *Alessandro* Handel
Cléon **t** *L'ivrogne corrigé* Gluck
Cléone **s** *Médée* Charpentier, M.-A.
Cleopatra **s** *Antony and Cleopatra* Barber; **s** *Cleopatra* Mattheson; **s** *Giulio Cesare in Egitto* Handel
Cléophas: *see* Joseph
Cleophis/Cleofide **s** *Poro* Handel
Clever Girl **s** *Die Kluge* Orff
Climene, Climène: *see* Clymene
Clitandro **t** *L'amore medico* Wolf-Ferrari
Clitemnestre: *see* Clytemnestra
Clitus/Clito **b** *Alessandro* Handel
Clizia *Teseo* Handel
Clodomiro **b** *Lotario* Handel
Cloé **s** *Cythère assiégée* Gluck
Cloelia/Clelia **a** *Costanza e Fortezza* Fux; **s** *Muzio Scevola* Handel
Clomiris/Clomiri **s** *Imeneo* Handel
Clori **s** *Egisto* Cavalli; **s** *Gli equivoci nel sembiante* Scarlatti
Clorinda **s** *La Cenerentola* Rossini
Clorinde **a** *Tancrède* Campra
Clotarco **t** *Armida* Haydn
Clotilda **a** *Koanga* Delius
Clotilde **s** *Faramondo* Handel; **ms** *Norma* Bellini; **s** *La rosa bianca e la rosa rossa* Mayr
Clubs, King of **b** *The Love for Three Oranges* Prokofiev
Clymene/Climene/Climène **s** *Egisto* Cavalli; **s** *Fetonte* Jommelli; **s** *Phaëton* Lully
Clytemnestra/Clitemnestre/Klytemnästra **ms** *Elektra* Strauss; **s** *Iphigénie en Aulide* Gluck
Coachman **b** *The Nose* Shostakovich
Cobweb **tr** *A Midsummer Night's Dream* Britten
Cochenille **t** *Les contes d'Hoffmann* Offenbach
Cock **s** *The Cunning Little Vixen* Janáček; **t** *Renard* Stravinsky
Cockburn, Lord: *see* Kokbourg
Coigny, Contessa de **ms** *Andrea Chénier* Giordano
Colas **b** *Bastien und Bastienne* Mozart
Colas Breugnon **bt** *Colas Breugnon* Kabalevsky
Colette **s** *Le devin du village* Rousseau; **s** *L'ivrogne corrigé* Gluck
Colin **t** *Le devin du village* Rousseau
Collatinus **b** *The Rape of Lucretia* Britten
Colline **b** *La bohème* Puccini; **bt** *La bohème* Leoncavallo
Colombel **t** *Drömmen om Thérèse* Werle
Colombina **ms** *Arlecchino* Busoni; **s** *Le donne curiose* Wolf-Ferrari; **s** *Die Feuersbrunst* Haydn
Colonna, Steffano **b** *Rienzi* Wagner; *see also* Adriano Colonna
Coltellino **t** *König Hirsch* Henze
Columbina: *see* Nedda
Columbine **s** *Le tableau parlant* Grétry
Columbus **bt** *Christophe Colomb* Milhaud; **bt** *Cristoforo Colombo* Franchetti
Comare **ms** *Crispino e la comare* Ricci, L. and F.
Commandant **bt** *Friedenstag* Strauss, R.
Commandant's Wife: *see* Maria
Commandante **ms** *I cavalieri di Ekebù* Zandonai
Commander: *see* Chefone
Commendatore **b** *Don Giovanni* Gazzaniga; **b** *Don Giovanni* Mozart
Commère **ms** *Four Saints in Three Acts* Thomson
Comminge **bt** *Le pré aux Clercs* Hérold
Commissar **t** *Die Bürgschaft* Weill; **b** *The Story of a Real Man* Prokofiev
Composer **ms** *Ariadne auf Naxos* Strauss, R.
Concepcion **s** *L'heure espagnole* Ravel
Conchiglia, Marchese della **t** *La buona figliuola* Piccinni
Condulmiero, General **t** *Maometto II* Rossini
Conrad **t** *Ein Feldlager in Schlesien* Meyerbeer; **t** *Hans Heiling* Marschner; *see also* Liebenau, Count von
Consalvo **b** *Almira* Handel
Consiglio/Good Counsel **t** *Rappresentatione di Anima, et di Corpo* Cavalieri
Constable **b** *Hugh the Drover* Vaughan Williams
Constance **s** *Les deux journées* Cherubini
Constance Fletcher **ms** *The Mother of Us All* Thomson
Constance of St Denis, Sister **s** *Dialogues des Carmélites* Poulenc
Constancy/Constanza **s** *Il sogno di Scipione* Mozart
Constantine, Emperor **bt** *Fausta* Donizetti
Constanze: *see* Konstanze
Contareno **t** *Bianca e Falliero* Rossini
Cook **b** *The Love for Three Oranges* Prokofiev; **s** *The Nightingale* Stravinsky
Coppélius **b/bt** *Les contes d'Hoffmann* Offenbach
Coralbo **b** *Floridante* Handel
Corasmino **t** *Zaira* Bellini
Corcoran, Captain **bt** *HMS Pinafore* Sullivan
Corcy, Marquis de **t** *Le postillon de Lonjumeau* Adam
Cordelia **s** *Lear* Reimann
Corentin **t** *Dinorah* Meyerbeer
Coridon **t** *Acis and Galatea* Handel; **hc** *Roland* Lully; **t** *Roland* Piccinni
Corilla **s** *Le convenienze teatrali* Donizetti
Corindo **a** *Orontea* Cesti
Corinna **s** *Il viaggio a Reims* Rossini

Corisande **s** *Amadis* Lully
Cornelia **a** *Giulio Cesare in Egitto* Handel; **t** *Il trionfo dell'onore* Scarlatti
Cornwall, Duke of **t** *Lear* Reimann
Coroebus/Chorèbe **bt** *Les Troyens* Berlioz
Corpo/Body **t** *Rappresentatione di Anima, et di Corpo* Cavalieri
Corradino **t** *Matilde di Shabran* Rossini
Corrado **b** *I briganti* Mercadante; **t** *Il corsaro* Verdi; **t** *Una cosa rara* Martín y Soler; **t** *Griselda* Scarlatti; **a** *Griselda* Vivaldi; **bt** *Maria de Rudenz* Donizetti
Corregidor: *see* Eugenio de Zuniga, Don
Corrigan, Mr **b** *The Lily of Killarney* Benedict
Cortese, Madama **s** *Il viaggio a Reims* Rossini
Cortez/Cortes **t** *Fernand Cortez* Spontini; **s** *Montezuma* Graun
Cospicuo, Abbate **bt** *Arlecchino* Busoni
Cosroe **b** *Siroe* Handel
Costanza **s** *Griselda* Scarlatti; **s** *Griselda* Vivaldi; **s** *L'isola disabitata* Haydn; **s** *König Hirsch* Henze; **s** *Riccardo Primo* Handel
Count **bt** *Capriccio* Strauss; **b** *Ein Feldlager in Schlesien* Meyerbeer; **bt** *Der ferne Klang* Schreker; **bt** *Nina* Paisiello; **b** *Die Verschworenen* Schubert
Countess **s** *Chérubin* Massenet; **s** *A Dinner Engagement* Berkeley; **ms** *The Queen of Spades* Tchaikovsky; **s** *Die Verschworenen* Schubert
Courchemin **bt** *Le déserteur* Monsigny
Courtier **x** *Le devin du village* Rousseau
Cox **t** *Cox and Box* Sullivan
Coyle, Mrs **s** *Owen Wingrave* Britten
Coyle, Spencer **bb** *Owen Wingrave* Britten
Crackentorp, Duchesse/Duchessa **sp** *La fille du régiment* Donizetti
Cregan, Mrs **a** *The Lily of Killarney* Benedict
Creon/Créon/Creonte **bt** *L'anima del filosofo* Haydn; **bt** *Antigonae* Orff; **b** *Astianatte* Bononcini, G.; **b** *Médée* Charpentier, M.-A.; **b** *Médée* Cherubini; **bt** *Oedipe* Enescu; **bb** *Oedipus rex* Stravinsky; **bt** *Orontea* Cesti
Crespel **b/bt** *Les contes d'Hoffmann* Offenbach
Cressida **ms** *Troilus and Cressida* Walton
Creusa/Créuse **s** *Médée* Charpentier, M.-A.
Cricket **tr** *The Cunning Little Vixen* Janáček; **s** *Das Heimchen am Herd* Goldmark
Crispino **bt** *Crispino e la comare* Ricci, L. and F.
Crispus/Crispo **t** *Fausta* Donizetti
Cristina **s** *Eduardo e Cristina* Rossini
Cristoforo, Fra **b** *I promessi sposi* Ponchielli
Croissy, Madame de/Old Prioress **a** *Dialogues des Carmélites* Poulenc
Crown **bt** *Porgy and Bess* Gershwin
Ctesippus/Ctésippe **bt** *Pénélope* Fauré
Ctirad **t** *Šárka* Fibich
Cunegonde **s** *Candide* Bernstein
Cuniza **ms** *Oberto* Verdi
Cuno **b** *Der Freischütz* Weber
Cupid/Cupidon/Amor/Amore/Amour **s** *Arbore di Diana* Martín y Soler; **s** *Les boréades* Rameau; **s** *Cadmus et Hermione* Lully; **s** *Dafne* Gagliano; **s** *Dardanus* Rameau; **s** *Echo et Narcisse* Gluck; **s** *Egisto* Cavalli; **hc** *Les fêtes vénitiennes* Campra; **s** *L'incoronazione di Poppea* Monteverdi; **s** *Les Indes galantes* Rameau; **s** *Orfeo ed Euridice* Gluck; **s** *Orontea* Cesti; **ms** *Orphée aux enfers* Offenbach; **s** *Orphée et Eurydice* Gluck; **s** *Paride ed Elena* Gluck; **s** *Pigmalion* Rameau; **s** *Platée* Rameau; **s** *Scylla et Glaucus* Leclair; **s** *Zaïs* Rameau
Curé **t** *The Olympians* Bliss
Curiatius/Curiazio **s** *Gli Orazi ed i Curiazi* Cimarosa
Curius/Curio **b** *Giulio Cesarein Egitto* Handel
Curra **ms** *La forza del destino* Verdi
Curro **bt** *The Magic Opal* Albéniz
Curtio **s** *Il Sant'Alessio* Landi
Curzio, Don **t** *Le nozze di Figaro* Mozart
Cybele/Cybèle **s** *Atys* Lully
Cynire **t** *Echo et Narcisse* Gluck
Cyril **t** *Princess Ida* Sullivan
Cyrus **a** *Ciro in Babilonia* Rossini
Czesnikowa **ms** *The Haunted Manor* Moniuszko
Czipra **ms** *Der Zigeunerbaron* Strauss, J.

D

Da-ud **t** *Die ägyptische Helena* Strauss, R.
Dafne: *see* Daphne
Daisy Dodd **s** *Aniara* Blomdahl
Daland **b** *Der fliegende Holländer* Wagner
Dalibor **t** *Dalibor* Smetana
Dalila: *see* Delilah
Dalinda **s** *Ariodant* Méhul; **s** *Ariodante* Handel; **s** *Ginevra di Scozia* Mayr
Dalua **bt** *The Immortal Hour* Boughton
Daly, Dr **bt** *The Sorcerer* Sullivan
Damazy **t** *The Haunted Manor* Moniuszko
Damigella **s** *L'incoronazione di Poppea* Monteverdi
Damire **b** *Les fêtes vénitiennes* Campra
Damon **t** *Acis and Galatea* Handel; **hc** *Les Indes galantes* Rameau
Danae **s** *Die Liebe der Danae* Strauss, R.
Danaus **bt** *Les Danaïdes* Salieri
Dancaïre **t/bt** *Carmen* Bizet
Dancing-Master **t** *Ariadne auf Naxos* Strauss, R.
Dandau **b** *Jessonda* Spohr
Dandini **b** *La Cenerentola* Rossini
Dangeville, Mlle **ms** *Adriana Lecouvreur* Cilea
Daniel **bt** *Ciro in Babilonia* Rossini; **b** *Les deux journées* Cherubini
Daniel Buchanan **t** *Street Scene* Weill
Daniel Webster **bt** *The Devil and Daniel Webster* Moore; **b** *The Mother of Us All* Thomson
Daniele **t** *Betly* Donizetti
Danieli **t** *Les vêpres siciliennes* Verdi
Daniello **bt** *Jonny spielt auf* Krenek
Danilo, Count Danilowitsch **t** *Die lustige Witwe* Lehár
Danilowitz **t** *L'étoile du Nord* Meyerbeer
Danish Knight **hc** *Armide* Lully; **t** *Armide* Gluck
Danny Mann **bt** *The Lily of Killarney* Benedict
Dansker **b** *Billy Budd* Britten
Dante **t** *Francesca da Rimini* Rakhmaninov
Danton **bt** *Dantons Tod* von Einem
Dapertutto **b/bt** *Les contes d'Hoffmann* Offenbach
Daphné **s** *Cythère assiégée* Gluck
Daphne/Dafne **s** *Dafne* Gagliano; **s** *Daphne* Strauss; **s** *Euridice* Peri
Dardane **s** *L'incontro improvviso* Haydn
Dardano, Prince of Thrace **a** *Amadigi di Gaula* Handel
Dardanus **a** *Dardanus* Rameau
Dark Fiddler **bt** *A Village Romeo and Juliet* Delius
Daughter **s** *Cardillac* Hindemith
Dauphin **a** *Etienne Marcel* Saint-Saëns
Davenaut, Sir Humphrey **b** *Der Vampyr* Marschner
David **t** *Die Meistersinger von Nürnberg* Wagner; **t** *Saul og David* Nielsen
David, Rabbi **bt** *L'amico Fritz* Mascagni
Deacon **t** *Cherevichki* Tchaikovsky
Deaconess **a** *King Roger* Szymanowski
Death **a** *Blood Wedding* Szokolay; **bb** *Der Kaiser von Atlantis* Ullmann; **ms** *The Nightingale* Stravinsky; **b** *Sāvitri* Holst
Deborah/Dèbora **ms** *Dèbora e Jaéle* Pizzetti
De Bracy, Maurice **t** *Der Templer und die Jüdin* Marschner
Děčana **a** *The Brandenburgers in Bohemia* Smetana
Decius/Decio **a** *Tito Manlio* Vivaldi
Dede **s** *A Quiet Place* Bernstein
Ded Moroz: *see* Grandfather Frost
Defence Counsel **t** *The English Cat* Henze
Dehorn, Count **bt** *Gustave III* Auber
Deidamia **s** *Deidamia* Handel; **s** *La finta pazza* Sacrati
Dejanira/Deianira/Déjanire **s** *Déjanire* Saint-Saëns; **s** *Ercole amante* Cavalli; **ms** *Hercules* Handel
Delacqua, Senator **bt** *Eine Nacht in Venedig* Strauss, J.
De Laubardemont **t** *The Devils of Loudun* Penderecki
Delbo **b** *Arsinoe* Clayton
Delfa **a** *Giasone* Cavalli

Delil t *Giovanna d'Arco* Verdi
Delilah/Dalila ms *Samson et Dalila* Saint-Saëns
Dema a *Egisto* Cavalli
Demetrius/Demetrio a *Berenice* Handel; t *Demetrio e Polibio* Rossini; b *Statira* Scarlatti
Demetrius bt *A Midsummer Night's Dream* Britten
Demo t *Giasone* Cavalli
Demodocus/Demodoco t *Ulisse* Dallapiccola
Demogorgon bt *Roland* Lully
Demon bt *The Demon* Rubinstein
Demon (Lucinde) s *Armide* Lully; s *Armide* Gluck
Demon (Mélisse) s *Armide* Lully; s *Armide* Gluck
Demon (Water Nymph) s *Armide* Lully
De Nangis, Count t *Le roi malgré lui* Chabrier
Denise s *The Knot Garden* Tippett
Denisov bb *War and Peace* Prokofiev
Dercetaeus t *Cleopatra* Mattheson
Des Grieux, Armand: *see* Armand des Grieux
Des Grieux, Chevalier t *Manon* Massenet; t *Manon Lescaut* Puccini
Des Grieux, Count b *Manon* Massenet
Desdemona s *Otello* Rossini; s *Otello* Verdi
Deserter t *We Come to the River* Henze
Desideria ms *The Saint of Bleecker Street* Menotti
De Siriex bt *Fedora* Giordano
Despina s *Così fan tutte* Mozart
Desportes t *Die Soldaten* Zimmermann
Devil bt *Cherevichki* Tchaikovsky; t *Christmas Eve* Rimsky-Korsakov; b *Grisélidis* Massenet; b *Il Sant'Alessio* Landi; b *Švanda the Bagpiper* Weinberger; *see also* Rarach
Devil's Wife ms *Grisélidis* Massenet
Devilshoof b *The Bohemian Girl* Balfe
Dew Fairy s *Hänsel und Gretel* Humperdinck
Di Fiesco b *Maria di Rohan* Donizetti
Diana/Diane s *Actéon* Charpentier, M.-A.; s *Arbore di Diana* Martín y Soler; s *Calisto* Cavalli; s *Hippolyte et Aricie* Rameau; s *Ippolito ed Aricia* Traetta; s *Orphée aux enfers* Offenbach; s *The Olympians* Bliss; s *Statira* Scarlatti
Diana Orsini a *Bomarzo* Ginastera
Diana Trapes s *The Beggar's Opera*
Diarte bt *Erismena* Cavalli
Dibdin, George t *Der Vampyr* Marschner
Dickson t *La dame blanche* Boieldieu
Dido/Didon/Didone s *Dido and Aeneas* Purcell; a *Egisto* Cavalli; ms *Les Troyens* Berlioz
Diégo, Don b *L'Africaine* Meyerbeer
Diègue, Don b *Le Cid* Massenet
Diemut s *Feuersnot* Strauss, R.
Dietrich bt *Der arme Heinrich* Pfitzner
Dikoj, Savël Prokofjevič b *Kát'a Kabanová* Janáček
Dimitrij Ivanovič t *Dimitrij* Dvořák
Dinorah s *Dinorah* Meyerbeer
Diomedes/Diomede t *La finta pazza* Sacrati; bt *Troilus and Cressida* Walton
Dionysus/Voice/Stranger t *The Bassarids* Henze
Dirce/Dircé/Glaucus a *Dori* Cesti; s *Médée* Cherubini
Discord/Discordia a *Le nozze di Teti e di Peleo* Cavalli
Distiller t *May Night* Rimsky-Korsakov
Djamileh ms *Djamileh* Bizet
Djura sp *Arabella* Strauss
Dmitri Nekludov t *Risurrezione* Alfano
Dmitry a *Fedora* Giordano; *see also* Pretender
Dmitry, Prince t *The Decembrists* Shaporin
D'Obigny, Marchese b *La traviata* Verdi
Doctor bt *Der Besuch der alten Dame* von Einem; b *The Nose* Shostakovich; bt *Pelléas et Mélisande* Debussy; b *Punch and Judy* Birtwistle; bt *Vanessa* Barber; bb *We Come to the River* Henze; b *Wozzeck* Berg
Dodon, King b *The Golden Cockerel* Rimsky-Korsakov
Doge t *Otello* Rossini; *see also* Francesco Foscari
Doktor Faust: *see* Faust
Dolcina, Sister s *Suor Angelica* Puccini
Doll Tearsheet ms *At the Boar's Head* Holst
Dolly s *Sly* Wolf-Ferrari
Dolokhov b *War and Peace* Prokofiev
Dolore: *see* Trouble
Dominik, Count bt *Arabella* Strauss
Domšík: *see* Sacristan
Donald bt *Billy Budd* Britten
Donner bb *Das Rheingold* Wagner
Donny bt *New Year* Tippett
Dorabella s *Così fan tutte* Mozart
Doralice ms *La gazzetta* Rossini; s *Il trionfo dell'onore* Scarlatti
Doraspe, King of Damascus t *Tigrane* Scarlatti
Dörfling, Field Marshal bt *Der Prinz von Homburg* Henze
Dori, Princess of Nicaea (Ali) s *Dori* Cesti
Dorilla a *Tigrane* Scarlatti
Dorina s *Fra i due litiganti il terzo gode* Sarti
Dorinda s *Orlando* Handel; a *Il pastor fido* Handel
Dorine s *Scylla et Glaucus* Leclair
Doris s *Atys* Lully; s *Issé* Destouches
Dorisbe s *Arsinoe* Clayton
Doristo bt *Arbore di Diana* Martín y Soler
Dorliska s *Torvaldo e Dorliska* Rossini
Dormont t *La scala di seta* Rossini
Dorota s *Švanda the Bagpiper* Weinberger
Dorotea ms *Stiffelio* Verdi
Dorothée ms *Cendrillon* Massenet
Dorset t *Alfred* Dvořák
Dorval (father) b *Lucile* Grétry
Dorval (son) t *Lucile* Grétry
Dorvil t *La scala di seta* Rossini
Dosifey b *Khovanshchina* Musorgsky
Dot s *Das Heimchen am Herd* Goldmark
Doubek t/tr *Osud* Janáček
Double-Bass Player b/bt *Il contrabbasso* Bucchi
Douglas b *La donna del lago* Rossini; t *William Ratcliff* Cui
Douglas, Count bt *Guglielmo Ratcliff* Mascagni
Douphol, Baron bt *La traviata* Verdi
Dourlinski, Baron b *Lodoïska* Cherubini
Dov t *The Knot Garden* Tippett
Doyen de la Faculté t *Cendrillon* Massenet
Draco bt *Cadmus et Hermione* Lully
Drago b *Genoveva* Schumann
Dragon b *Lanzelot* Dessau
Dreieinigkeitsmoses: *see* Trinity Moses
Dromio bt *Gli equivoci* Storace
Drum Major t *Wozzeck* Berg
Drummer ms *Der Kaiser von Atlantis* Ullmann
Drunk Prisoner t *From the House of the Dead* Janáček
Drusilla s *L'incoronazione di Poppea* Monteverdi
Dsheangir: *see* Jehanguire
Duda b *Sadko* Rimsky-Korsakov
Duenna a *Betrothal in a Monastery* Prokofiev
Dufresne t *Zazà* Leoncavallo
Duke: *see* Mantua, Duke of
Dulcamara, Dr b *L'elisir d'amore* Donizetti
Dulcinée ms *Don Quichotte* Massenet
Duncan/Duncano x *Macbeth* Verdi
Dunmow, Earl of bt *A Dinner Engagement* Berkeley
Dunois bt *The Maid of Orléans* Tchaikovsky
Dunyasha a *The Tsar's Bride* Rimsky-Korsakov
Dutchman bb *Der fliegende Holländer* Wagner
Dwarf t *Der Zwerg* Zemlinsky
Dyer's Wife: *see* Barak's Wife
Dziemba b *Halka* Moniuszko

E

Eberbach, Count of bt *Der Wildschütz* Lortzing
Eberbach, Countess of ms *Der Wildschütz* Lortzing
Eboli, Princess ms *Don Carlos* Verdi
Ecclitico t *Il mondo della luna* Haydn
Echo s *Echo et Narcisse* Gluck
Edgar t *Edgar* Puccini; t/ct *Lear* Reimann
Edgar, Sir x *Der junge Lord* Henze
Edgard, King t *Ariodant* Méhul
Edgardo t *Lucia di Lammermoor* Donizetti
Edilia s *Almira* Handel

Edmondo **t** *Manon Lescaut* Puccini
Edmund **t** *Lear* Reimann
Edmund Lehsen **t** *Die Brautwahl* Busoni
Edoardo **t** *Un giorno di regno* Verdi; **a** *Matilde di Shabran* Rossini
Edrisi **t** *King Roger* Szymanowski
Edronica **s** *Der geduldige Socrates* Telemann
Eduard **bt** *Neues vom Tage* Hindemith
Eduardo **a** *Eduardo e Cristina* Rossini
Eduige **s** *Rodelinda* Handel
Edward **b** *L'assedio di Calais* Donizetti; **t** *Das Heimchen am Herd* Goldmark
Edward Milfort **t** *La cambiale di matrimonio* Rossini
Edwige **s** *Robinson Crusoé* Offenbach
Edwin **t** *Trial by Jury* Sullivan
Edwin von und zu Lippert-Weylersheim, Prince **t** *Die Csárdásfürstin* Kálmán
Egberto **bt** *Aroldo* Verdi
Egée, Egeo: *see* Aegeus
Eginhard **s** *Fierrabras* Schubert
Egisto **t** *Egisto* Cavalli
Eglantine **s** *Euryanthe* Weber
Eglé **s** *Echo et Narcisse* Gluck; **s** *Les fêtes d'Hébé* Rameau; *see also* Aegle
Egypt, King of **b** *Aida* Verdi
Egypt, Sultan of **b** *L'incontro improvviso* Haydn
Eily O'Connor **s** *The Lily of Killarney* Benedict
Eino **t** *Puntila* Dessau
Eioff **t** *Hulda* Franck
Eisenhardt **bt** *Die Soldaten* Zimmermann
Eisenstein, Gabriel von **t** *Die Fledermaus* Strauss, J.
Eisslinger, Ulrich **t** *Die Meistersinger von Nürnberg* Wagner
Elaisa **s** *Il giuramento* Mercadante
Elcia: *see* Anaïs
Elder **b** *The Brandenburgers in Bohemia* Smetana
Elderly Prisoner **t** *From the House of the Dead* Janáček
Elder Son **b** *The Prodigal Son* Britten
Eleanor/English Queen **s** *L'assedio di Calais* Donizetti
Eléazar **t** *La Juive* Halévy
Electra/Elektra/Elettra **s** *Elektra* Strauss; **s** *Idomeneo* Mozart
Electress **a** *Der Prinz von Homburg* Henze
Elemer, Count **t** *Arabella* Strauss
Elena **s** *Aroldo* Verdi; **s** *Il cappello di paglia di Firenze* Rota; **s** *Marino Faliero* Donizetti; *see also* Ellen, Helen, Helen of Troy
Eleonora **s** *Le donne curiose* Wolf-Ferrari; **s** *Il furioso nell'isola di S Domingo* Donizetti; **s** *Prima la musica e poi le parole* Salieri
Eleonora d'Este **s** *Torquato Tasso* Donizetti
Eliane **s** *Les mariages samnites* Grétry
Eliéser, Elisero: *see* Aaron
Elifàz **s** *Job* Dallapiccola
Elis **t** *Der Schatzgräber* Schreker
Elisa **s** *Astarto* Bononcini, G.; **s** *Il re pastore* Mozart; **s** *Tolomeo* Handel
Elisa Bacocchi, Grand Duchess of Lucca **s** *Madame Sans-Gêne* Giordano
Elisabeth **s** *Tannhäuser* Wagner
Elisabeth de/Elisabetta di Valois **s** *Don Carlos* Verdi
Elisetta **s** *Il matrimonio segreto* Cimarosa
Elizabeth I/Elisabetta, Queen **s** *Elisabetta, regina d'Inghilterra* Rossini; **s** *Gloriana* Britten; **s** *Maria Stuarda* Donizetti; **a** *Merrie England* German; **s** *Roberto Devereux* Donizetti
Elizabeth Zimmer **s** *Elegy for Young Lovers* Henze
Elle **s** *La voix humaine* Poulenc
Ellen/Elena **s** *La donna del lago* Rossini
Ellen, Miss **s** *Lakmé* Delibes
Ellen Orford **s** *Peter Grimes* Britten
Elmira **a** *Floridante* Handel; **ms** *Ricciardo e Zoraide* Rossini; **s** *Sosarme* Handel
Elmireno: *see* Armando D'Orville
Elmiro **b** *Otello* Rossini
Eloisa **s** *Bianca e Fernando* Bellini
Els **s** *Der Schatzgräber* Schreker
Elsa **s** *Lanzelot* Dessau
Elsa of Brabant **s** *Lohengrin* Wagner
Elsie Maynard **s** *The Yeomen of the Guard* Sullivan
Elvino **t** *Il pirata* Bellini; **t** *La sonnambula* Bellini
Elvira **s** *Ernani* Verdi; **s** *L'italiana in Algeri* Rossini; **s** *I puritani* Bellini
Elvira, Donna **s** *Don Giovanni* Gazzaniga; **s** *Don Giovanni* Mozart
Elvire **s** *La muette de Portici* Auber
Elviro **b** *Serse* Handel; **a** *Xerse* Cavalli
Emilia **s** *Emilia di Liverpool* Donizetti; **s** *Flavio* Handel; **s** *Otello* Rossini; **ms** *Otello* Verdi
Emilia Marty **s** *The Makropulos Affair* Janáček
Emilie **s** *Les Indes galantes* Rameau
Emilio **t** *Partenope* Handel
Emilio, Lieutenant **t** *Il cappello di paglia di Firenze* Rota
Emilio Memmi **t** *Massimilla Doni* Schoeck
Emilius/Emilio **t** *Il sogno di Scipione* Mozart
Emily **s** *Help, Help, the Globolinks!* Menotti
Emira **s** *Siroe*
Emireno **b** *Ottone* Handel
Emma **s** *Fierrabras* Schubert; **s** *Khovanshchina* Musorgsky; **a** *Zelmira* Rossini; *see also* Hamilton, Lady Emma
Emmie **s** *Albert Herring* Britten
Emmy **s** *Der Vampyr* Marschner
Emperor **t** *Die Frau ohne Schatten* Strauss, R.; **ms** *We Come to the River* Henze
Employee **bt** *Volo di notte* Dallapiccola
Empress **s** *Die Frau ohne Schatten* Strauss, R.
Enchantress: *see* Nastas'ya
Endre II **bt** *Bánk bán* Erkel
Endymion/Endimione **t** *Arbore di Diana* Martín y Soler; **a** *Calisto* Cavalli
Enéas **t** *Esclarmonde* Massenet
Enée: *see* Aeneas
English Queen: *see* Eleanor
Englishman **t** *Angélique* Ibert
Ennone: *see* Oenone
Enobarbus **b** *Antony and Cleopatra* Barber
Enone: *see* Oenone
Enrichetta di Francia: *see* Henrietta, Queen
Enrico **t** *Aroldo* Verdi
Enrico **bt** *Il campanello di notte* Donizetti; **t** *L'ajo nell'imbarazzo* Donizetti; **b** *L'isola disabitata* Haydn; **t** *Maria de Rudenz* Donizetti; **s** *La rosa bianca e la rosa rossa* Mayr; *see also* Henry, Henry VIII
Enrico Ashton **bt** *Lucia di Lammermoor* Donizetti
Ensoleillad **s** *Chérubin* Massenet
Enzo Grimaldi **t** *La Gioconda* Ponchielli
Eochaidh **bt** *The Immortal Hour* Boughton
Eolo: *see* Aeolus
Epaphus/Epafo **a** *Fetonte* Jommelli; **bt** *Phaëton* Lully
Ephraimite **bt** *Moses und Aron* Schoenberg
Epponina **s** *Giulio Sabino* Sarti
Equerry **b** *Der Zar lässt sich photographieren* Weill
Eraste **hc** *Les fêtes vénitiennes* Campra
Erato **s** *Il pastor fido* Handel
Ercole: *see* Hercules
Erda **a** *Das Rheingold* Wagner; **a** *Siegfried* Wagner
Erenice **a** *Sosarme* Handel
Erice **t** *Ormindo* Cavalli
Ericlea **s** *Scipione affricano* Cavalli; *see also* Eurycleia
Erik **t** *Der fliegende Holländer* Wagner
Erik Refstrup **t** *Fennimore and Gerda* Delius
Erika **ms** *Vanessa* Barber
Erimante **b/a** *Erismena* Cavalli
Erineo/Idraspe **a/s** *Erismena* Cavalli
Erinice **s** *Zoroastre* Rameau
Eriphyle/Erifile **s** *Oedipe à Colone* Sacchini
Erisbe **s** *Ormindo* Cavalli
Erismena **s** *Erismena* Cavalli
Erissena: *see* Eryxene
Erisso, Paolo **t** *Maometto II* Rossini
Ermanno **t** *I briganti* Mercadante; **t** *L'equivoco stravagante* Rossini
Ermerance (Estelle) **ms** *Véronique* Messager

Erminio **s** *Il trionfo dell'onore* Scarlatti; *see also* Herminius
Ermione: *see* Hermione
Ernando **b** *Scipione* Handel
Ernani **t** *Ernani* Verdi
Ernelinde **s** *Ernelinde* Philidor
Ernestina **a** *L'equivoco stravagante* Rossini; **s** *L'occasione fa il ladro* Rossini
Ernesto **t** *Don Pasquale* Donizetti; **bt** *Don Procopio* Bizet; **s** *Griselda* Bononcini, G.; **a** *Il mondo della luna* Haydn; **b** *Parisina* Donizetti; **t** *Ricciardo e Zoraide* Rossini
Ernesto, Duke of Caldora **b** *Il pirata* Bellini
Ernesto, Marquis **t** *La vera costanza* Haydn
Errico, Count **t** *La vera costanza* Haydn
Eryxene/Erissena **ms** *Poro* Handel
Erzsébet Szilágyi **s** *Hunyadi László* Erkel
Escamillo **bb** *Carmen* Bizet
Esclarmonde **s** *Esclarmonde* Massenet
Esilena **s** *Rodrigo* Handel
Esmeralda **s** *The Bartered Bride* Smetana
Essex, Earl of, Robert/Roberto Devereux **t** *Gloriana* Britten; **bt** *Merrie England* German; **t** *Roberto Devereux* Donizetti
Essex, Countess of, Frances **ms** *Gloriana* Britten
Estelle: *see* Ermerance
Estoban, Don **bb** *Der Zwerg* Zemlinsky
Estrella **s** *Alfonso und Estrella* Schubert
Etain **s** *The Immortal Hour* Boughton
Etherea: *see* Málinka
Ettore, Don **s** *La canterina* Haydn
Eudoxie, Princess **s** *La Juive* Halévy
Eufemiano **t** *Il Sant'Alessio* Landi
Eufemio of Ephesus **t** *Gli equivoci* Storace
Eufemio of Syracuse **t** *Gli equivoci* Storace
Eufrosine: *see* Euphrosyne
Eugene Onegin: *see* Yevgeny Onegin
Eugenia **s** *Il filosofo di campagna* Galuppi; **s** *La molinara* Paisiello; **s** *Lo sposo deluso* Mozart
Eugenio de Zuniga, Don **t** *Der Corregidor* Wolf
Eumaeus/Eumée/Eumeo/Eumete **bt** *Pénélope* Fauré; **t** *Il ritorno d'Ulisse in patria* Monteverdi; **t** *Ulisse* Dallapiccola
Eumelus/Eumelo **s** *Alceste* Gluck
Eumene **b** *Les mariages samnites* Grétry; **s** *Xerse* Cavalli
Eupaforice **s** *Montezuma* Graun
Euphémie **s** *Les mariages samnites* Grétry
Euphrosyne/Eufrosine **s** *Il pomo d'oro* Cesti
Eurice **ms** *Adelaide di Borgogna* Rossini
Eurilda **a** *Le pescatrici* Haydn
Eurilla **s** *Orlando paladino* Haydn; **s** *Il pastor fido* Handel
Eurillo **t** *Gli equivoci nel sembiante* Scarlatti
Eurus/Euro **t** *Il pomo d'oro* Cesti
Euryanthe **s** *Euryanthe* Weber
Eurycleia/Ericlea/Euryclée **ms** *Pénélope* Fauré; **ms** *Il ritorno d'Ulisse in patria* Monteverdi
Eurydice/Euridice **s** *L'anima del filosofo* Haydn; **a** *Antigonae* Orff; **s** *Euridice* Peri; **s** *Euridice* Caccini; **s** *Les malheurs d'Orphée* Milhaud; **ms** *The Mask of Orpheus* Birtwistle; **s** *Orfeo* Monteverdi; **s** *Orfeo ed Euridice* Gluck; **s** *Orfeo ed Euridice* Bertoni; **s** *Orphée aux enfers* Offenbach; **s** *Orphée et Eurydice* Gluck
Eurymachus/Eurimaco/Eurymaque **bt** *Pénélope* Fauré; **t** *Il ritorno d'Ulisse in patria* Monteverdi; **t** *Ulisse* Dallapiccola
Eurytus/Euryto **b** *Ercole amante* Cavalli
Eustazio **a** *Rinaldo* Handel
Euterpova, Mme **s** *Help, Help, the Globolinks!* Menotti
Eutropio **t** *Belisario* Donizetti
Eva **s** *Die Meistersinger von Nürnberg* Wagner; **s** *Puntila* Dessau
Evadne/Maid **ms** *Troilus and Cressida* Walton
Evanco **s** *Rodrigo* Handel
Evander/Evandre **t** *Alceste* Gluck
Evangelist **b** *The Pilgrim's Progress* Vaughan Williams
Eve/Mondeva **s** *Donnerstag aus Licht* Stockhausen; **s** *Montag aus Licht* Stockhausen
Everardo Cappello **t** *Giulietta e Romeo* Zingarelli
Ezio **bt** *Attila* Verdi; *see also* Aetius
Ezra **b** *Mourning Becomes Electra* Levy

F

Faber **bt** *The Knot Garden* Tippett
Fabio **t** *Berenice* Handel
Fabrizio **b** *La pietra del paragone* Rossini
Fabrizio Vingradito **b** *La gazza ladra* Rossini
Fadinard **t** *Il cappello di paglia di Firenze* Rota
Fafner **b** *Das Rheingold* Wagner; **b** *Siegfried* Wagner
Fairfax, Colonel **t** *The Yeomen of the Guard* Sullivan
Fairy Godmother: *see* Fée
Fairy Queen **a** *Iolanthe* Sullivan
Falcon **s** *Die Frau ohne Schatten* Strauss, R.
Falke, Dr **bt** *Die Fledermaus* Strauss, J.
Falliero **ms** *Bianca e Falliero* Rossini
False Angèle **s** *Der Zar lässt sich photographieren* Weill
Falstaff **b** *At the Boar's Head* Holst; **bt** *Falstaff* Verdi; **b** *Die lustigen Weiber von Windsor* Nicolai
Faninal **bt** *Der Rosenkavalier* Strauss, R.
Fanny **s** *La cambiale di matrimonio* Rossini
Fanny Legrand/Sapho **s** *Sapho* Massenet
Fanuèl **bt** *Nerone* Boito
Faramondo **ms** *Faramondo* Handel
Faraone: *see* Pharaoh
Farasmane **b** *Radamisto* Handel
Farfallo **b** *Die schweigsame Frau* Strauss, R.
Farfarello **b** *The Love for Three Oranges* Prokofiev
Farlaf **b** *Ruslan and Lyudmila* Glinka
Farnace: *see* Pharnaces
Fasolt **bb** *Das Rheingold* Wagner
Fata Morgana **s** *The Love for Three Oranges* Prokofiev
Father **b** *Louise* Charpentier, G.; **bt** *The Prodigal Son* Britten
Father Confessor **bt** *Dialogues des Carmélites* Poulenc
Father/Peter **bt** *Hänsel und Gretel* Humperdinck
Father Philippe **b** *The Wandering Scholar* Holst
Fatima **s** *Les Indes galantes* Rameau; **ms** *Oberon* Weber; **s** *Zaira* Bellini
Fatime **s** *Abu Hassan* Weber
Fatty/Willy **t** *Aufstieg und Fall der Stadt Mahagonny* Weill
Fauno **s** *Ascanio in Alba* Mozart
Faust, Dr **t** *La damnation de Faust* Berlioz; **bt** *Doktor Faust* Busoni; **bt** *Faust* Spohr; **t** *Faust* Gounod; **b** *The Fiery Angel* Prokofiev; **t** *Mefistofele* Boito;
Fausta **s** *Fausta* Donizetti
Fayel **t/bt** *Gabriella di Vergy* Donizetti
Fé-an-nich-ton **s** *Ba-ta-clan* Offenbach
Fé-ni-han, Emperor **t** *Ba-ta-clan* Offenbach
Federica, Duchess **a** *Luisa Miller* Verdi
Federico **t** *L'arlesiana* Cilea; **t** *Emilia di Liverpool* Donizetti
Federico di Frengel **t** *Stiffelio* Verdi
Fedora Palinska, Princess **s** *Die Zirkusprinzessin* Kálmán
Fedora Romazov, Princess **s** *Fedora* Giordano
Fedra **s** *Egisto* Cavalli; *see also* Phaedra
Fée/Fairy Godmother **s** *Cendrillon* Massenet
Fekluša **ms** *Kát'a Kabanová* Janáček
Felice **s** *I quatro rusteghi* Wolf-Ferrari
Felicia **a** *Il crociato in Egitto* Meyerbeer
Félix/Felice **t/b** *Les martyrs/Poliuto* Donizetti
Female Cat **ms** *L'enfant et les sortilèges* Ravel
Female Chorus **ms** *The Rape of Lucretia* Britten
Fenena **s** *Nabucco* Verdi
Fenice: *see* Phoenix
Fenicio **a** *Astarto* Bononcini, G.; *see also* Phoenicius
Fennimore **s** *Fennimore and Gerda* Delius; **s** *Der Silbersee* Weill
Fenton **t** *Falstaff* Verdi; **t** *Die lustigen Weiber von Windsor* Nicolai
Feraspe **b** *Arsinoe* Clayton
Ferdinand **bt** *Betrothal in a Monastery* Prokofiev; **t** *The Duenna* Linley; **bt** *Tintomara* Werle
Ferdinand II: *see* Rudolf II
Feri von Kerekes **t/bt** *Die Csárdásfürstin* Kálmán
Fernand/Fernando **t** *La favorite* Donizetti
Fernando **t** *Der Cid* Cornelius; **t** *Goyescas* Granados; **t** *Marino*

Faliero Donizetti; **a** *Rodrigo* Handel
Fernando, Don **b** *Fidelio* Beethoven
Fernando/Floralbo **t** *Almira* Handel
Fernando/Gernando **t** *Bianca e Fernando* Bellini
Fernando Guevara **t** *Cristoforo Colombo* Franchetti
Fernando Villabella **bb** *La gazza ladra* Rossini
Ferrando **t** *Così fan tutte* Mozart; **t** *Il furioso nell'isola di S Domingo* Donizetti; **b** *Il trovatore* Verdi
Ferrara, Duke of **b** *Torquato Tasso* Donizetti
Ferryman **bt** *Curlew River* Britten
Fervaal **t** *Fervaal* d'Indy
Fetonte: *see* Phaethon
Fevroniya **s** *Legend of the Invisible City of Kitezh* Rimsky-Korsakov
Fiakermilli **s** *Arabella* Strauss
Fiametta **s** *Boccaccio* Suppé
Fiancé **t** *Il contrabbasso* Bucchi
Fidalma **s** *Il matrimonio segreto* Cimarosa; **s** *Muzio Scevola* Handel
Fiddler **sp** *The Devil and Daniel Webster* Moore; **bt** *Die Königskinder* Humperdinck
Fidelia **s** *Edgar* Puccini
Fidès **ms** *Le prophète* Meyerbeer
Fieramosca **bt/t** *Benvenuto Cellini* Berlioz
Fierrabras **t** *Fierrabras* Schubert
Fiesco, Jacopo (Andrea) **b** *Simon Boccanegra* Verdi
Figaro **bt** *Il barbiere di Siviglia* Paisiello; **bt** *Il barbiere di Siviglia* Rossini; **bt** *La mère coupable* Milhaud; **b** *Le nozze di Figaro* Mozart
Filaura **t** *Il pomo d'oro* Cesti
Filch **t** *The Beggar's Opera*
Fileno **t** *La fedeltà premiata* Haydn
Filiberto **b** *Il Signor Bruschino* Rossini
Filindo **b** *Les fêtes vénitiennes* Campra
Filip **b** *The Jacobin* Dvořák
Filipp'yevna/Filipyevna **ms** *Yevgeny Onegin* Tchaikovsky
Filipeto **t** *I quatro rusteghi* Wolf-Ferrari
Filippo **b** *Bianca e Fernando* Bellini; **bt** *La gazzetta* Rossini; **t** *L'infedeltà delusa* Haydn; *see also* Philip II
Filippo Maria Visconti, Duke **bt** *Beatrice di Tenda* Bellini
Filka Morozov: *see* Luka Kuzmič
Fillide/Celia **ms** *La fedeltà premiata* Haydn
Finn **t** *Ruslan and Lyudmila* Glinka
Fiora **s** *L'amore dei tre re* Montemezzi
Fiordiligi **s** *Così fan tutte* Mozart
Fiorello **b** *Il barbiere di Siviglia* Rossini
Fiorilla **s** *Il turco in Italia* Rossini
Fiorina **s** *Alina, regina di Golconda* Donizetti
Fish **b** *Vom Fischer un syner Fru* Schoeck
Fisherman **t** *The Nightingale* Stravinsky; **b** *Undine* Hoffmann; **t** *Vom Fischer un syner Fru* Schoeck
Fisherman's Wife **ms** *Undine* Hoffmann
Fisherman's Wife/Ilsebill **s** *Vom Fischer un syner Fru* Schoeck
Fishwife **ms** *Die Verurteilung des Lukullus* Dessau
Flamand **t** *Capriccio* Strauss
Flaminia **s** *Il mondo della luna* Haydn
Flaminio **t** *Il trionfo dell'onore* Scarlatti
Flavia **s** *Silla* Handel
Flavio **a** *Flavio* Handel; **t** *Norma* Bellini
Fleance/Fleanzio **x** *Macbeth* Verdi
Fleury, Prince of/Piccolo Marat **t** *Il piccolo Marat* Mascagni
Fléville: *see* Pietro Fléville
Flint, Mr **bb** *Billy Budd* Britten
Flora **s** *The Knot Garden* Tippett; **s** *The Turn of the Screw* Britten
Flora, Mme: *see* Baba
Flora Bervoix **ms** *La traviata* Verdi
Flora/Flore **s** *Atys* Lully
Floralbo: *see* Fernando
Florence Pike **a** *Albert Herring* Britten
Floreska **s** *L'amor coniugale* Mayr
Floreski, Count **t** *Lodoïska* Cherubini
Florestan **bt** *Amadis* Lully; **b** *La caravane du Caire* Grétry; **t** *Fidelio* Beethoven; **bt** *Richard Coeur-de-lion* Grétry
Florestan, Viscount de Valincourt **bt** *Véronique* Messager
Florestein **t** *The Bohemian Girl* Balfe
Florestine **s** *La mère coupable* Milhaud
Florian **bt** *Princess Ida* Sullivan
Floriana **s** *Zazà* Leoncavallo
Floridano: *see* Alidoro
Floridante **a** *Floridante* Handel
Florinda **s** *Don Rodrigo* Ginastera; **s** *Fierrabras* Schubert; **s** *Rodrigo* Handel
Florindo **t** *Le donne curiose* Wolf-Ferrari
Florville **t** *Il Signor Bruschino* Rossini
Flosshilde **ms** *Götterdämmerung* Wagner; **ms** *Das Rheingold* Wagner
Flute **t** *A Midsummer Night's Dream* Britten
Fluth, Frau: *see* Ford, Mrs
Fluth: *see* Ford
Foleville, Contessa di **s** *Il viaggio a Reims* Rossini
Folle Verdure, Madame de **s** *La vie parisienne* Offenbach
Folly/Folie, La **s** *Platée* Rameau
Foltz, Hans **b** *Die Meistersinger von Nürnberg* Wagner
Fool **sp** *Lear* Reimann
Footman to the Countess **bt** *The Nose* Shostakovich
Ford **bt** *Falstaff* Verdi
Ford/Fluth **bt** *Die lustigen Weiber von Windsor* Nicolai
Ford, Mrs/Fluth, Frau **s** *Die lustigen Weiber von Windsor* Nicolai; *see also* Alice Ford
Foreign Princess **s** *Rusalka* Dvořák
Foreman **bt** *Jenůfa* Janáček
Forest Sprite/Leshiy **bt** *Cherevichki* Tchaikovsky; **t** *The Snow Maiden* Rimsky-Korsakov
Forester **bt** *The Cunning Little Vixen* Janáček
Forester's Wife **a** *The Cunning Little Vixen* Janáček
Foresto **t** *Attila* Verdi
Fortune **s** *Giustino* Handel
Fortune/Fortuna **s** *Il sogno di Scipione* Mozart
Fortune-Teller **s** *Arabella* Strauss
Fotis **bb** *The Greek Passion* Martinů
Fouché **bt** *Madame Sans-Gêne* Giordano
Fouquier Tinville **bb** *Andrea Chénier* Giordano
Four Villains: *see* Coppélius, Dapertutto, Lindorf and Miracle
Fox/Golden-Back **s** *The Cunning Little Vixen* Janáček
Fra Diavolo **t** *Fra Diavolo* Auber
Fraarte **s** *Radamisto* Handel
Fracasso **t** *La finta semplice* Mozart
France, King of **bb** *Lear* Reimann
Frances: *see* Essex, Countess of
Francesca **s** *Francesca da Rimini* Rakhmaninov; **s** *Francesca da Rimini* Zandonai
Francesco **bt** *I masnadieri* Verdi
Francesco Foscari/Doge **bt** *I due Foscari* Verdi
Francis **bt** *Boulevard Solitude* Henze; **bt** *Saint François d'Assise* Messiaen
François **t** *A Quiet Place* Bernstein
Frank **bt** *Edgar* Puccini; **bt** *Die tote Stadt* Korngold
Frank/Warden **bt** *Die Fledermaus* Strauss, J.
Frantík **s** *The Cunning Little Vixen* Janáček
Frantz **t** *Les contes d'Hoffmann* Offenbach
Franz **bt** *Die Zwillingsbrüder* Schubert
Franz I **t** *Karl V* Krenek
Franz Kaiser **bt** *Háry János* Kodály
Frasquita **s** *Carmen* Bizet; **ms** *Der Corregidor* Wolf
Frederic **t** *The Pirates of Penzance* Sullivan
Frédéric **bt** *Lakmé* Delibes; **t/a** *Mignon* Thomas
Frederick the Great, King **sp** *Ein Feldlager in Schlesien* Meyerbeer
Freia **s** *Das Rheingold* Wagner
Freimann, Baroness **s** *Der Wildschütz* Lortzing
French Abbé **t** *War and Peace* Prokofiev
Frick **bt** *La vie parisienne* Offenbach
Fricka **ms** *Das Rheingold* Wagner; **ms** *Die Walküre* Wagner
Friedrich **bt** *Die Zwillingsbrüder* Schubert
Friedrich, Regent **b** *Das Liebesverbot* Wagner
Friedrich Engel **b** *Der Evangelimann* Kienzl
Friedrich Wilhelm, Elector **t** *Der Prinz von Homburg* Henze
Friend **s** *Von heute auf morgen* Schoenberg
Frisellino **t** *Le pescatrici* Haydn

Fritelli, Duke **bt** *Le roi malgré lui* Chabrier
Fritz **t** *Der ferne Klang* Schreker; **t** *La Grande-Duchesse de Gérolstein* Offenbach; **bt** *Die tote Stadt* Korngold
Fritz Kobus **t** *L'amico Fritz* Mascagni
Frog **tr** *The Cunning Little Vixen* Janáček; **t** *L'enfant et les sortilèges* Ravel
Froh **t** *Das Rheingold* Wagner
Froila **bt** *Alfonso und Estrella* Schubert
Frosch **sp** *Die Fledermaus* Strauss, J.
Frosya **s** *Semyon Kotko* Prokofiev
Frugola **ms** *Il tabarro* Puccini
Fulvia **s** *Ezio* Handel
Fulvia, Donna **ms** *La pietra del paragone* Rossini
Fusako Kuroda **s** *Das verratene Meer* Henze
Fyodor **ms** *Boris Godunov* Musorgsky

G

Gabriele Adorno **t** *Simon Boccanegra* Verdi
Gabriella **s** *Gabriella di Vergy* Donizetti
Gabrielle **s** *La vie parisienne* Offenbach
Gabriello **t** *La cena delle beffe* Giordano
Gaea **a** *Daphne* Strauss
Galatea/Galatée/Galathea **s** *Acis and Galatea* Handel; **s** *Acis et Galatée* Lully; **s** *Die schöne Galathée* Suppé
Galitsky, Vladimir **b** *Prince Igor* Borodin
Gama, King **bt** *Princess Ida* Sullivan
Gamberotto **b** *L'equivoco stravagante* Rossini
Gamekeeper **t** *Rusalka* Dvořák
Gandartes/Gandarte **a** *Poro* Handel
Gandhi **t** *Satyagraha* Glass
Ganymede **ms** *Die schöne Galathée* Suppé
Gaoler **t** *Il prigioniero* Dallapiccola
Gara **bt** *Hunyadi László* Erkel
Garcias **s** *Don Quichotte* Massenet
Gardefeu, Raoul de **t** *La vie parisienne* Offenbach
Garibaldo **b** *Rodelinda* Handel
Garrido, General **bt** *La Navarraise* Massenet
Garzia **ms** *Sancia di Castiglia* Donizetti
Gaspar **bt** *Rita* Donizetti
Gaspar, Don **t** *La favorite* Donizetti
Gasparina **s** *Il campiello* Wolf-Ferrari; **s** *La canterina* Haydn
Gaston **t** *Jérusalem* Verdi
Gaston, Don **t** *Die drei Pintos* Weber
Gastone, Vicomte de Letorières **t** *La traviata* Verdi
Gaudenzio **t** *La bohème* Leoncavallo
Gaudenzio Strappapuppole **b** *Il Signor Bruschino* Rossini
Gaveston **bt** *La dame blanche* Boieldieu
Gayle **s** *The Ice Break* Tippett
Gedge, Mr **bt** *Albert Herring* Britten
Gellner **bt** *La Wally* Catalani
Gelone **b** *Orontea* Cesti
Geminius/Geminio **t** *Tito Manlio* Vivaldi
Gemma **s** *Gemma di Vergy* Donizetti
Genaro **t** *Maddalena* Prokofiev
Genazahar, Count **bt** *Pepita Jiménez* Albéniz
Gendarme **b** *Il contrabbasso* Bucchi
General **b** *The Gambler* Prokofiev; **bt** *We Come to the River* Henze
Geneviève **a** *Pelléas et Mélisande* Debussy
Genièvre: *see* Guinevere
Genio: *see* Sibyl
Gennaro **t** *I gioielli della Madonna* Wolf-Ferrari; **t** *Lucrezia Borgia* Donizetti
Genovese **t** *Massimilla Doni* Schoeck
Genoveva **s** *Genoveva* Schumann
Genovieffa, Sister **s** *Suor Angelica* Puccini
Georg **t** *Der Waffenschmied* Lortzing
George **t** *L'étoile du Nord* Meyerbeer
Georges **t** *Der Opernball* Heuberger
Georges/George Brown **t** *La dame blanche* Boieldieu
Gepopo, Chief of the Secret Police **s** *Le Grand Macabre* Ligeti
Gérald **t** *Lakmé* Delibes
Gérard **bt** *Andrea Chénier* Giordano; **t** *La reine de Chypre* Halévy
Gerardo **t** *Caterina Cornaro* Donizetti
Gerda **s** *Fennimore and Gerda* Delius
Gerhilde **s** *Die Walküre* Wagner
German Tenor **t** *Le convenienze teatrali* Donizetti
Germano **b** *La scala di seta* Rossini
Germont: *see* Alfredo Germont
Germont, Giorgio **bt** *La traviata* Verdi
Gernando **t** *Armida* Rossini; **a** *Faramondo* Handel; **t** *L'isola disabitata* Haydn; *see also* Fernando
Geronimo, Don **b** *Il matrimonio segreto* Cimarosa
Geronio, Don **b** *Il turco in Italia* Rossini
Géronte **b** *Le médecin malgré lui* Gounod
Geronte de Revoir **b** *Manon Lescaut* Puccini
Gertrud **a** *Bánk bán* Erkel; *see also* Mother
Gertrude **a** *Hans Heiling* Marschner; **ms** *Roméo et Juliette* Gounod
Gertrude, Queen **ms** *Hamlet* Thomas
Gertrude Stein **s** *The Mother of Us All* Thomson
Geschwitz, Countess **ms** *Lulu* Berg
Gesler **b** *Guillaume Tell* Rossini
Gherardino **a** *Gianni Schicchi* Puccini
Gherardo **t** *Gianni Schicchi* Puccini
Ghino **t** *Pia de' Tolomei* Donizetti
Ghita **s** *Una cosa rara* Martín y Soler; **s** *Der Zwerg* Zemlinsky
Ghost **b** *Hamlet* Thomas
Giacinta **s** *La finta semplice* Mozart
Giacinta (Ismero) **s** *Orontea* Cesti
Giacomo **b** *Fra Diavolo* Auber; **bt** *Giovanna d'Arco* Verdi; *see also* James
Gian Conrado Orsini **b** *Bomarzo* Ginastera
Gianciotto: *see* Malatesta, Giovanni
Gianetta **s** *The Gondoliers* Sullivan
Giannetta **s** *L'elisir d'amore* Donizetti
Giannetto **t** *La gazza ladra* Rossini
Giannetto Malaspini **t** *La cena delle beffe* Giordano
Gianni Schicchi **bt** *Gianni Schicchi* Puccini
Giasone: *see* Jason
Gifflard **b** *Colas Breugnon* Kabalevsky
Gil Blas **t** *La caverne* Le Sueur
Gil, Count **bt** *Il segreto di Susanna* Wolf-Ferrari
Gil-Perez **b** *Le domino noir* Auber
Gilberto **s** *Giulietta e Romeo* Zingarelli
Gilda **s** *L'ajo nell'imbarazzo* Donizetti; **s** *Rigoletto* Verdi
Gilfen **bt** *Die Abreise* d'Albert
Ginevra **s** *Ariodante* Handel; **s** *La cena delle beffe* Giordano; **s** *Ginevra di Scozia* Mayr
Gioconda, La **s** *La Gioconda* Ponchielli
Giocondo **t** *La pietra del paragone* Rossini
Giorgetta **s** *Il tabarro* Puccini
Giorgio **b** *La gazza ladra* Rossini; **t** *Nina* Paisiello; **bt** *Torvaldo e Dorliska* Rossini
Giorgio, Sir **b** *I puritani* Bellini
Giosta **t** *I cavalieri di Ekebù* Zandonai
Giovanna **s** *Ernani* Verdi; *see also* Joan of Arc
Giovanna Seymour: *see* Jane Seymour
Giovanni **b** *Il corsaro* Verdi
Giovanni, Don **t** *Don Giovanni* Gazzaniga; **bt** *Don Giovanni* Mozart
Giovanni, Prince **t** *Una cosa rara* Martín y Soler
Giove: *see* Jupiter
Giovinetto **t** *Il barbiere di Siviglia* Paisiello
Girl **s** *Der Kaiser von Atlantis* Ullmann
Girolamo **bt** *Bomarzo* Ginastera
Girot **t** *Le pré aux Clercs* Hérold
Giselda **s** *I Lombardi* Verdi
Gismonda **s** *Ottone* Handel
Giuditta **s** *Giuditta* Lehár
Giulia **s** *La scala di seta* Rossini
Giuliano **t** *Rodrigo* Handel
Giulietta **s** *I Capuleti e i Montecchi* Bellini; **s** *Les contes d'Hoffmann* Offenbach; **s** *Un giorno di regno* Verdi; **s** *Giulietta e Romeo* Zingarelli; **s** *Giulietta e Romeo* Vaccai; **s** *Giulietta e Romeo* Zandonai; *see also* Juliet
Giulio Cesare: *see* Julius Caesar

Giulio, Marchese **bt** *L'ajo nell'imbarazzo* Donizetti
Giunone: *see* Juno
Giuseppe **bt** *The Gondoliers* Sullivan
Giustino: *see* Justin
Glaša **ms** *Kát'a Kabanová* Janáček
Glaucus **hc** *Scylla et Glaucus* Leclair; *see also* Dirce
Gleby **bt** *Siberia* Giordano
Gloriana: *see* Elizabeth I
Gloucester, Earl of **bb** *Lear* Reimann
Glycère **s** *Sapho* Gounod
Gnese **s** *Il campiello* Wolf-Ferrari
Gobineau, Mr **bt** *The Medium* Menotti
Gobineau, Mrs **s** *The Medium* Menotti
Gobrias **t** *Nerone* Boito
Godvino **t** *Aroldo* Verdi
Goffredo **t** *Armida* Rossini; **a** *Rinaldo* Handel
Go-Go, Prince **tr/s/ct** *Le Grand Macabre* Ligeti
Golaud **bt** *Pelléas et Mélisande* Debussy
Gold Dealer **b** *Cardillac* Hindemith
Golden Cockerel **s** *The Golden Cockerel* Rimsky-Korsakov
Golden-Back: *see* Fox
Golitsïn, Prince Vasily **t** *Khovanshchina* Musorgsky
Golo **b** *Dori* Cesti; **t** *Genoveva* Schumann
Golovan: *see* Toropka Golovan
Gomatz **t** *Zaide* Mozart
Gomez, Don **t** *Die drei Pintos* Weber; **t** *Henry VIII* Saint-Saëns
Gondì, Armando **ms** *Maria di Rohan* Donizetti
Gondremarck, Baron de **bt** *La vie parisienne* Offenbach
Gondremarck, Baroness de **s** *La vie parisienne* Offenbach
Goneril **s** *Lear* Reimann
Gonzales **bt** *Il Guarany* Gomes
Gonzalve **t** *L'heure espagnole* Ravel
Good Counsel: *see* Consiglio
Goose Girl **s** *Die Königskinder* Humperdinck
Gorislava **s** *Ruslan and Lyudmila* Glinka
Gormas, Count of **b** *Le Cid* Massenet
Goro **t** *Madama Butterfly* Puccini
Gothron **bt** *Alfred* Dvořák
Gottardo/Podestà **bb** *La gazza ladra* Rossini
Gotthold **t** *Doktor und Apotheker* Dittersdorf
Governess **s** *The Turn of the Screw* Britten
Governor **t** *Simplicius Simplicissimus* Hartmann; **bt** *We Come to the River* Henze
Governor-General **b** *The Decembrists* Shaporin
Grand Brahmin: *see* High Priest of Brahma
Grand Inquisitor **b** *Don Carlos* Verdi; **bt** *The Gondoliers* Sullivan; **t** *Il prigioniero* Dallapiccola
Grand Inquisitor of Lisbon **b** *L'Africaine* Meyerbeer
Grand-Duchess **s** *La Grande-Duchesse de Gérolstein* Offenbach
Grandfather Frost/Ded Moroz **b** *The Snow Maiden* Rimsky-Korsakov
Grandier, Father **bt** *The Devils of Loudun* Penderecki
Grandmother **ms** *La vida breve* Falla
Grandmother Buryjovka **a** *Jenůfa* Janáček
Grasshopper **tr** *The Cunning Little Vixen* Janáček
Graumann **b** *Der ferne Klang* Schreker
Graumann's Wife **ms** *Der ferne Klang* Schreker
Grech **b** *Fedora* Giordano
Greene **bt** *Arden must Die* Goehr
Gregor, Albert **t** *The Makropulos Affair* Janáček
Gregorio, Don **b** *L'ajo nell'imbarazzo* Donizetti
Gregory/Grégorio **bt** *Roméo et Juliette* Gounod
Gremin, Prince **b** *Yevgeny Onegin* Tchaikovsky
Gretchen **s** *The Grand Duke* Sullivan; **s** *Der Wildschütz* Lortzing
Gretchen's Brother **bt** *Doktor Faust* Busoni
Grete/Greta Graumann **s** *Der ferne Klang* Schreker
Gretel **s** *Hänsel und Gretel* Humperdinck
Grieux, Marquis de **t** *The Gambler* Prokofiev
Grigoris **bt** *The Greek Passion* Martinů
Grigory **bt** *The Bear* Walton; **t** *Quiet Flows the Don* Dzerzhinsky; *see also* Pretender
Grilletta **s** *Lo speziale* Haydn
Grimes, Peter **t** *Peter Grimes* Britten
Grimgerde **a** *Die Walküre* Wagner
Grimoaldo **t** *Rodelinda* Handel
Griselda **s** *Griselda* Scarlatti; **a** *Griselda* Bononcini, G.; **a** *Griselda* Vivaldi
Grisélidis **s** *Grisélidis* Massenet
Grishka Kuter'ma **t** *Legend of the Invisible City of Kitezh* Rimsky-Korsakov
Griso **b** *I promessi sposi* Ponchielli
Grits'ko **t** *The Fair at Sorochintsï* Musorgsky
Grog, Baron **bt** *La Grande-Duchesse de Gérolstein* Offenbach
Grose, Mrs **s** *The Turn of the Screw* Britten
Grosvenor **bt** *Patience* Sullivan
Grumio **b** *Der widerspänstigen Zähmung* Goetz
Grünwiesel, Baroness **ms** *Der junge Lord* Henze
Grüsser **t** *Die Harmonie der Welt* Hindemith
Gryaznoy, Grigory **bt** *The Tsar's Bride* Rimsky-Korsakov
Günther **bb** *Götterdämmerung* Wagner
Gualtiero **b** *Edgar* Puccini; **a** *Griselda* Scarlatti; **ms** *Griselda* Bononcini, G.; **t** *Griselda* Vivaldi; **t** *Il pirata* Bellini; *see also* Raleigh, Sir Walter
Guardian Angel: *see* Angelo custode
Guardiano: *see* Padre Guardiano
Guccio **b** *Gianni Schicchi* Puccini
Gudal, Prince **b** *The Demon* Rubinstein
Gudleik **bt** *Hulda* Franck
Guglielmo **b** *Così fan tutte* Mozart; **bt** *Le villi* Puccini
Guiccioli, Contessa **s** *Lord Byron* Thomson
Guido **a** *Flavio* Handel; **b** *Gemma di Vergy* Donizetti
Guido, Prince of Florence **t** *Eine florentinische Tragödie* Zemlinsky
Guidon, Prince **t** *The Golden Cockerel* Rimsky-Korsakov
Guidon, Tsarevich **t** *The Tale of Tsar Saltan* Rimsky-Korsakov
Guilhen **ms** *Fervaal* d'Indy
Guillot de Morfontaine **t** *Manon* Massenet
Guinevere/Geniѐvre **ms** *Le roi Arthus* Chausson
Gulf, Sir **b** *Faust* Spohr
Gulnara **s** *Il corsaro* Verdi
Gunther **bt** *Götterdämmerung* Wagner; **bt** *Sigurd* Reyer
Gurnemanz **b** *Parsifal* Wagner
Gusmano **bt** *Alzira* Verdi
Gustavo **b** *Faramondo* Handel
Gustavus III/Gustave III **t** *Gustave III* Auber; **t** *Tintomara* Werle
Gustavus III/Riccardo **t** *Un ballo in maschera* Verdi
Gutrune **s** *Götterdämmerung* Wagner
Gwendoline **s** *Gwendoline* Chabrier
Gypsy **b** *The Fair at Sorochintsï* Musorgsky
Gypsy Lover **t** *Aleko* Rakhmaninov

H

Hadji **t** *Lakmé* Delibes
Haemon **t** *Antigonae* Orff
Hagen **b** *Götterdämmerung* Wagner; **bb** *Sigurd* Reyer
Haghenbach **t** *La Wally* Catalani
Haitang **s** *Der Kreidekreis* Zemlinsky
Hal, Prince **t** *At the Boar's Head* Holst
Haliate **t** *Sosarme* Handel
Halka **s** *Halka* Moniuszko
Haly **b** *L'italiana in Algeri* Rossini
Hamilton, Lady Emma **s** *Nelson* Berkeley
Hamlet, Prince **bt** *Hamlet* Thomas
Hanna **s** *The Haunted Manor* Moniuszko; **ms** *May Night* Rimsky-Korsakov
Hanna Glawari **s** *Die lustige Witwe* Lehár
Hannah **ms** *The Ice Break* Tippett
Hannah, Dame **a** *Ruddigore* Sullivan
Hans **b** *Undine* Lortzing
Hans Heiling **bt** *Hans Heiling* Marschner
Hans Sachs **bb** *Die Meistersinger von Nürnberg* Wagner
Hans: *see* Jeník, Jim Mahoney
Hänsel **ms** *Hänsel und Gretel* Humperdinck
Hanswurst **b** *Die Feuersbrunst* Haydn
Harald **t** *Alfred* Dvořák; **bt** *Gwendoline* Chabrier
Harašta/Poacher **b** *The Cunning Little Vixen* Janáček
Hardress Cregan **t** *The Lily of Killarney* Benedict

Hardy **b** *Nelson* Berkeley
Hariadeno **b** *Ormindo* Cavalli
Harlequin **bt** *Ariadne auf Naxos* Strauss, R.
Haroun **t** *Djamileh* Bizet
Harriet Durham, Lady (Martha) **s** *Martha* Flotow
Harrington, Rev. **t** *Lizzie Borden* Beeson
Harry **tr** *Albert Herring* Britten
Harry Benn **t** *The Boatswain's Mate* Smyth
Hasdrubal/Asdrubale **t** *Scipione affricano* Cavalli
Háta **ms** *The Bartered Bride* Smetana
Hate-Good, Lord **b** *The Pilgrim's Progress* Vaughan Williams
Haudy, Major **bt** *Die Soldaten* Zimmermann
Hauk-Šendorf **t** *The Makropulos Affair* Janáček
He-Ancient **b** *The Midsummer Marriage* Tippett
Hebe/Hébé **s** *Les fêtes d'Hébé* Rameau; **s** *Les Indes galantes* Rameau
Hecate/Hécate **hc** *Scylla et Glaucus* Leclair; **b** *Silla* Handel; *see also* Oracle of the Dead
Hector **bt** *King Priam* Tippett
Hector de Florac **t** *The Olympians* Bliss
Hector's Ghost **b** *Les Troyens* Berlioz
Hecuba/Hécube **s** *King Priam* Tippett; **s** *Les Troyens* Berlioz
Hedvika **s** *The Devil's Wall* Smetana
Hedwige **ms** *Guillaume Tell* Rossini
Heilmann **bt** *Undine* Hoffmann
Heinrich **t** *Agnes von Hohenstaufen* Spontini; **t** *Der arme Heinrich* Pfitzner
Heinrich der Schreiber **t** *Tannhäuser* Wagner
Heinrich der Vogler **b** *Lohengrin* Wagner
Heinz/Sparbüchsenheinrich **bt** *Aufstieg und Fall der Stadt Mahagonny* Weill
Helen **s** *Mourning Becomes Electra* Levy
Helena **s** *A Midsummer Night's Dream* Britten
Helene **s** *Hin und zurück* Hindemith; **ms** *Die Verschworenen* Schubert
Helen/Elena/Helena/Hélène of Troy **s** *Die ägyptische Helena* Strauss, R.; **s** *La belle Hélène* Offenbach; **ms** *King Priam* Tippett; **s** *Mefistofele* Boito; **s** *Paride ed Elena* Gluck
Hélène **s** *Jérusalem* Verdi; *see also* Amelia
Hélène Bezukhova **a** *War and Peace* Prokofiev
Hélène de Solanges (Véronique) **s** *Véronique* Messager
Hélène/Helena, Duchess **s** *Les vêpres siciliennes* Verdi
Helenus **t** *Les Troyens* Berlioz
Helfenstein, Countess **a** *Mathis der Maler* Hindemith
Helmwige **s** *Die Walküre* Wagner
Helson, Hel **bt** *Paul Bunyan* Britten
Henri **ms** *Der Opernball* Heuberger; *see also* Marcello di Bruges
Henri/Arrigo **t** *Les vêpres siciliennes* Verdi
Henri de Valois **bt** *Le roi malgré lui* Chabrier
Henrietta, Queen/Enrichetta di Francia **ms** *I puritani* Bellini
Henrik **bb** *Maskarade* Nielsen
Henrique, Dom **b** *Dom Sébastien* Donizetti
Henry Davis **bt** *Street Scene* Weill
Henry/Enrico **ms** *Elisabetta, regina d'Inghilterra* Rossini
Henry/Henri Smith **t** *La jolie fille de Perth* Bizet
Henry Morosus **t** *Die schweigsame Frau* Strauss, R.
Henry the Fowler, King: *see* Heinrich der Vogler
Henry the Lion **b** *Agnes von Hohenstaufen* Spontini
Henry VI, Emperor **bt** *Agnes von Hohenstaufen* Spontini
Henry VIII/Enrico **b** *Anna Bolena* Donizetti; **bt** *Henry VIII* Saint-Saëns
Herald **bt** *The Burning Fiery Furnace* Britten; **b** *Lohengrin* Wagner
Hercules/Ercole/Hercule/Alcides/Alcide **b** *Admeto* Handel; **bt** *Alceste* Lully; **b** *Alceste* Gluck; **t** *Déjanire* Saint-Saëns; **b** *Ercole amante* Cavalli; **b** *Giasone* Cavalli; **b** *Hercules* Handel
Herdswoman **ms** *Jenůfa* Janáček
Hérisson de Porc-Epic **bt** *L'étoile* Chabrier
Hermann **t** *Neues vom Tage* Hindemith; **t** *The Queen of Spades* Tchaikovsky
Hermann, Baron **bt** *Loreley* Catalani
Hermes **t** *King Priam* Tippett
Hermia **s** *Barbe-bleue* Offenbach; **ms** *A Midsummer Night's Dream* Britten
Herminie **s** *Tancrède* Campra
Herminius/Erminio **s** *Costanza e Fortezza* Fux
Hermione/Ermione **s** *Die ägyptische Helena* Strauss, R.; **s** *Astianatte* Bononcini, G.; **s** *Cadmus et Hermione* Lully; **s** *Ermione* Rossini
Hermit **b** *Der Freischütz* Weber; **t** *Simplicius Simplicissimus* Hartmann
Hero/Héro **s** *Béatrice et Bénédict* Berlioz; **s** *Egisto* Cavalli
Herod/Hérod/Herodes **bt** *Hérodiade* Massenet; **t** *Salome* Strauss, R.
Herodias/Hérodiade **ms** *Hérodiade* Massenet; **ms** *Salome* Strauss, R.
Herring, Mrs **ms** *Albert Herring* Britten
Herrmann, Landgrave **b** *Tannhäuser* Wagner
Herz, Mme **s** *Der Schauspieldirektor* Mozart
Hidraot/Hydraot **b** *Armida* Dvořák; **bt** *Armide* Lully; **bt** *Armide* Gluck
Hidulphus, Bishop of Trier **bt** *Genoveva* Schumann
Hierax/Hiérax **bt** *Isis* Lully
Hiérophante **b** *Olimpie* Spontini
High Priest **b** *Fernand Cortez* Spontini; **bt** *Hérodiade* Massenet; **b** *Die Königin von Saba* Goldmark; **b** *Salammbô* Musorgsky
High Priest of Baal **b** *Nabucco* Verdi
High Priest of Brahma/Grand Brahmin **bb** *L'Africaine* Meyerbeer
High Priest of Dagon **bt** *Samson et Dalila* Saint-Saëns
High Priest of Neptune **t** *Idomeneo* Mozart
High Priestess **s** *Aida* Verdi; **ms** *La vestale* Spontini;
High Priestess of Diana **s** *Penthesilea* Schoeck
Hilarion **t** *Princess Ida* Sullivan
Hilda **s** *Sigurd* Reyer
Hilda Mack **s** *Elegy for Young Lovers* Henze
Hilde **s** *Der arme Heinrich* Pfitzner
Hildebrand, King **bt** *Princess Ida* Sullivan
Himeneo: *see* Hymen
Hindu **t** *Sadko* Rimsky-Korsakov
Hippolyta **a** *A Midsummer Night's Dream* Britten
Hippolytus/Hippolyte/Ippolito **t** *Fedra* Pizzetti; **hc** *Hippolyte et Aricie* Rameau; **s** *Ippolito ed Aricia* Traetta
Hirsch, König: *see* Leandro, King
Hizler **b** *Die Harmonie der Welt* Hindemith
Hoango **bt** *Die Verlobung in San Domingo* Egk
Hobhouse, John **bb** *Lord Byron* Thomson
Hobson **b** *Peter Grimes* Britten
Hoël **bt** *Dinorah* Meyerbeer
Hoffmann **t** *Les contes d'Hoffmann* Offenbach
Hohenzollern, Count **t** *Der Prinz von Homburg* Henze
Holsteiner **b** *Friedenstag* Strauss, R.
Holy Fool: *see* Yurodivïy
Homburg, Friedrich Artur, Prince of **bt** *Der Prinz von Homburg* Henze
Homonay, Count **bt** *Der Zigeunerbaron* Strauss, J.
Honoria/Onoria **a** *Ezio* Handel
Honour, Mrs **s** *Tom Jones* Philidor
Horace Adams, Rev. **t** *Peter Grimes* Britten
Horace de Massarena **t** *Le domino noir* Auber
Horace Giddens **b** *Regina* Blitzstein
Horace Tabor **bt** *The Ballad of Baby Doe* Moore
Horatia/Orazia **a** *Gli Orazi ed i Curiazi* Cimarosa
Horatius Cocles/Orazio **s** *Muzio Scevola* Handel; **t** *Costanza e Fortezza* Fux
Horatius, Marcus/Orazio, Marco **t** *Gli Orazi ed i Curiazi* Cimarosa
Horatius, Publius/Orazio, Publio **t** *Gli Orazi ed i Curiazi* Cimarosa
Horn/Tom **b** *Un ballo in maschera* Verdi
Hortense **s** *Der Opernball* Heuberger
Hortensio **b** *Der widerspänstigen Zähmung* Goetz
Hortensius/Ortensio **b** *La fille du régiment* Donizetti
Hostess **s** *At the Boar's Head* Holst
Houdoux, Baron d' **b** *Neues vom Tage* Hindemith
Huascar **b** *Les Indes galantes* Rameau
Hugh the Drover **t** *Hugh the Drover* Vaughan Williams
Hugo, Count **t** *Faust* Spohr
Hugo von Ringstetten **t** *Undine* Lortzing
Hugues Capet: *see* Ugo

Hulda ms *Hulda* Franck
Huldbrand bt *Undine* Hoffmann
Hunding b *Die Walküre* Wagner
Huon of Bordeaux, Sir t *Oberon* Weber
Husband bt *Amelia al ballo* Menotti; bt *Les mamelles de Tirésias* Poulenc; *Von heute auf morgen* bb Schoenberg
Husca bt *La caravane du Caire* Grétry
Hyacinthus tr *Apollo et Hyacinthus* Mozart
Hydraot: *see* Hidraot
Hylas t/a *Les Troyens* Berlioz
Hyllus/Hyllo t *Ercole amante* Cavalli; t *Hercules* Handel
Hymas, King of Lesbos b *Les fêtes d'Hébé* Rameau
Hymen/Hymenaeus/Himeneo/Imene/Imeneo t *Imeneo* Handel; s *Le nozze di Teti e di Peleo* Cavalli; t *Orfeo ed Euridice* Bertoni
Hypermnestra/Hypermnestre s *Les Danaïdes* Salieri
Hypsicrateia/Issicratea a *Mitridate Eupatore* Scarlatti
Hypsipyle/Isifile s *Giasone* Cavalli

I

Iago t *Otello* Rossini; bt *Otello* Verdi
Ibn-Hakia bt *Iolanta* Tchaikovsky
Ida s *Gemma di Vergy* Donizetti; s *Princess Ida* Sullivan
Idalba s *La clemenza di Scipione* Bach, J. C.
Idamantes/Idamante s *Idomeneo* Mozart
Idas b *Atys* Lully
Idelberto a *Lotario* Handel
Idomeneus/Idomeneo t *Idomeneo* Mozart
Idraote b *Armida* Rossini
Idraspe: *see* Erineo
Idreno b *Armida* Haydn; t *Semiramide* Rossini
Ighino s *Palestrina* Pfitzner
Ignatius, St bt *Four Saints in Three Acts* Thomson
Igor, Prince bt *Prince Igor* Borodin
Ilia s *Idomeneo* Mozart
Ill, Alfred bt *Der Besuch der alten Dame* von Einem
Ilo, Prince t *Zelmira* Rossini
Ilsebill: *see* Fisherman's Wife
Imelda ms *La battaglia di Legnano* Verdi
Imene/Imeneo: *see* Hymen
Imogene s *Il pirata* Bellini
Impresario b *Le convenienze teatrali* Donizetti
Ina s *Ariodant* Méhul
Incroyable/Spy t *Andrea Chénier* Giordano
Indian b *The Bartered Bride* Smetana
Indiana Elliot a *The Mother of Us All* Thomson
Indra b *Le roi de Lahore* Massenet
Ines/Inès/Inez s *L'Africaine* Meyerbeer; s *Die drei Pintos* Weber; s *La favorite* Donizetti; ms *Maria Padilla* Donizetti; s *Il trovatore* Verdi
Infanta s *Le Cid* Massenet; *see also* Clara, Donna
Inigo Gomez, Don b *L'heure espagnole* Ravel
Inkslinger, Johnny t *Paul Bunyan* Britten
Innkeeper t *Benvenuto Cellini* Berlioz; ms *Boris Godunov* Musorgsky; b *Der ferne Klang* Schreker; b *Die Königskinder* Humperdinck; bt *Manon* Massenet
Innocente ms *L'arlesiana* Cilea
Innominato, L' t *I promessi sposi* Ponchielli
Ino a *Semele* Handel
Intelleto/Intellect a *Rappresentatione di Anima, et di Corpo* Cavalieri
Interpreter t *The Pilgrim's Progress* Vaughan Williams
Io s *Isis* Lully
Iolanta s *Iolanta* Tchaikovsky
Iolanthe ms *Iolanthe* Sullivan
Iole s *Déjanire* Saint-Saëns; s *Ercole amante* Cavalli; s *Hercules* Handel
Iopas t *Les Troyens* Berlioz
Iphigenia/Ifigenia/Iphigénie s *Iphigénie en Aulide* Gluck; s *Iphigénie en Tauride* Gluck; s *Ifigenia in Tauride* Traetta
Iphise s *Dardanus* Rameau; s *Les fêtes d'Hébé* Rameau; s *Les fêtes vénitiennes* Campra
Ipparco t *Egisto* Cavalli
Ippolito: *see* Hippolytus
Ircano b *Ricciardo e Zoraide* Rossini; b *Sancia di Castiglia* Donizetti
Irene/Irène a *Atalanta* Handel; ms *Belisario* Donizetti; s *Les fêtes vénitiennes* Campra; a *Muzio Scevola* Handel; s *Rienzi* Wagner; a *Tamerlano* Handel
Irene, Baroness s *La vera costanza* Haydn
Iris s *Atys* Lully; s *Iris* Mascagni; s *Semele* Handel
Irmelin s *Irmelin* Delius
Irmengard s *Agnes von Hohenstaufen* Spontini
Irmentraut ms *Der Waffenschmied* Lortzing
Irus/Iro t *Il ritorno d'Ulisse in patria* Monteverdi
Isaac Mendoza b *Betrothal in a Monastery* Prokofiev; t *The Duenna* Linley
Isabella a *Boccaccio* Suppé; s *Christophe Colomb* Milhaud; s *L'inganno felice* Rossini; a *L'italiana in Algeri* Rossini; s *Karl V* Krenek; s *Das Liebesverbot* Wagner; s *Olivo e Pasquale* Donizetti
Isabella, Queen s *Una cosa rara* Martín y Soler; s *Cristoforo Colombo* Franchetti
Isabelle s *Les fêtes vénitiennes* Campra; s *Le pré aux Clercs* Hérold; s *Robert le diable* Meyerbeer; s *Le tableau parlant* Grétry
Isacco t *La gazza ladra* Rossini
Isacio/Isaac b *Riccardo Primo* Handel
Isaoun t *Le calife de Bagdad* Boieldieu
Isaura ms *Tancredi* Rossini
Isaure s *Jérusalem* Verdi
Isella s *Die Verschworenen* Schubert
Isèpo t *La Gioconda* Ponchielli
Isidoro b *Matilde di Shabran* Rossini
Isifile: *see* Hypsipyle
Iskra t *Mazepa* Tchaikovsky
Ismaele t *Nabucco* Verdi
Ismaele, Captain bt *Marino Faliero* Donizetti
Ismen bt *Armida* Dvořák
Ismene s *Alceste* Gluck; s *Antigonae* Orff; s *Mitridate* Mozart
Ismenor/Isménor b *Dardanus* Rameau; b *Tancrède* Campra
Isolde s *Tristan und Isolde* Wagner
Isoletta s *La straniera* Bellini
Isolier ms *Le comte Ory* Rossini
Isotta s *Die schweigsame Frau* Strauss, R.
Issac: *see* Isacio
Issé s *Issé* Destouches
Issicratea: *see* Hypsicrateia
Italian t *Angélique* Ibert
Italian Singer t *Der Rosenkavalier* Strauss, R.
Itulbo t *Il pirata* Bellini
Ivan b *The Nose* Shostakovich
Ivan Khovansky, Prince b *Khovanshchina* Musorgsky
Ivan the Terrible/Ivan IV bt *Ivan IV* Bizet; b *The Maid of Pskov* Rimsky-Korsakov
Ivanhoe, Wilfred of t *Der Templer und die Jüdin* Marschner
Ivasenko b *Semyon Kotko* Prokofiev
Ivo bt *La vera storia* Berio
Iwan bt *Der Zarewitsch* Lehár

J

Jabez Stone b *The Devil and Daniel Webster* Moore
Jacinthe s *Le domino noir* Auber
Jack t *The Midsummer Marriage* Tippett
Jack O'Brien/Jake t *Aufstieg und Fall der Stadt Mahagonny* Weill
Jack the Ripper: *see* Schön, Dr
Jacob bt *Joseph* Méhul
Jacopo Foscari t *I due Foscari* Verdi
Jacopo Loredano b *I due Foscari* Verdi
Jacqueline s *Colas Breugnon* Kabalevsky
Jadwiga ms *The Haunted Manor* Moniuszko
Jael/Jaéle s *Dèbora e Jaéle* Pizzetti
Jago b *Ernani* Verdi
Jake Wallace bt *La fanciulla del West* Puccini
Jake: *see* Jack O'Brien

Jakob **t** *Die Bürgschaft* Weill
James/Giacomo (Uberto) **t** *La donna del lago* Rossini
Jan Janicki **bt** *Der Bettelstudent* Millöcker
Jane/Giovanna Seymour **ms** *Anna Bolena* Donizetti
Janek **t** *The Makropulos Affair* Janáček
Jankel **sp** *Arabella* Strauss
Jano **s** *Jenůfa* Janáček
János, Háry **bt** *Háry János* Kodály
Janthe **s** *Der Vampyr* Marschner
Janusz **bt** *Halka* Moniuszko
Jaquino **t** *Fidelio* Beethoven
Jarek **t** *The Devil's Wall* Smetana
Jarno **b** *Mignon* Thomas
Jaschiu **dancer** *Death in Venice* Britten
Jason/Giasone **a** *Giasone* Cavalli; **hc** *Médée* Charpentier, M.-A.; **t** *Médée* Cherubini
Javelinot, M **bt** *Dialogues des Carmélites* Poulenc
Javier **bt** *María del Carmen* Granados
Javotte **ms** *Manon* Massenet
Jay **s** *The Cunning Little Vixen* Janáček
Jean: *see* John the Baptist
Jean, Frère: *see* John, Friar
Jean Gaussin **t** *Sapho* Massenet
Jean/Juggler **t** *Le jongleur de Nôtre-Dame* Massenet
Jeanne **s** *Die Verlobung in San Domingo* Egk
Jeanne, Sister **s** *The Devils of Loudun* Penderecki
Jeanne of the Child Jesus, Mother **a** *Dialogues des Carmélites* Poulenc
Jehanguire/Dsheangir **t** *Nurmahal* Spontini
Jemmy Tell **s** *Guillaume Tell* Rossini
Jenifer **s** *The Midsummer Marriage* Tippett
Jeník **t** *The Bartered Bride* Smetana; **t** *The Cunning Peasant* Dvořák; **t** *King and Charcoal Burner* Dvořák
Jennie **s** *Down in the Valley* Weill
Jenny **ms** *La dame blanche* Boieldieu; **s** *Die Dreigroschenoper* Weill
Jenny Diver **s** *The Beggar's Opera*
Jenny Hill **s** *Aufstieg und Fall der Stadt Mahagonny* Weill
Jenny Reefer **ms** *The Mother of Us All* Thomson
Jenůfa **s** *Jenůfa* Janáček
Jeremy **x** *Der junge Lord* Henze
Jerome, Don **t** *Betrothal in a Monastery* Prokofiev; **b** *The Duenna* Linley
Jeronimus **b** *Maskarade* Nielsen
Jessel, Miss **s** *The Turn of the Screw* Britten
Jessonda **s** *Jessonda* Spohr
Jester **b** *The Tale of Tsar Saltan* Rimsky-Korsakov; **bt** *Taverner* Maxwell Davies
Jesus **t** *Die toten Augen* d'Albert
Ježibaba/Witch **ms** *Rusalka* Dvořák
Jill-All-Alone **ms** *Merrie England* German
Jim Cocks **bt** *Robinson Crusoé* Offenbach
Jim Mahoney/Johann Ackerman/Hans **t** *Aufstieg und Fall der Stadt Mahagonny* Weill
Jíra **t** *The Brandenburgers in Bohemia* Smetana
Jiří **t** *The Jacobin* Dvořák
Jirka **t** *The Devil and Kate* Dvořák; **t** *The Secret* Smetana
Jitka **s** *Dalibor* Smetana
Jo Ann **s** *New Year* Tippett
Jo the Loiterer **t** *The Mother of Us All* Thomson
Joan of Arc/Giovanna **s** *Giovanna d'Arco* Verdi; **s/ms** *The Maid of Orléans* Tchaikovsky
Job **bb** *Job* Dallapiccola
Jocasta/Jocaste **ms** *Oedipe* Enescu; **ms** *Oedipus rex* Stravinsky
Jochanaan: *see* John the Baptist
Joe, Uncle **b** *Koanga* Delius
Joe/Josef Lettner/Alaskawolfjoe **b** *Aufstieg und Fall der Stadt Mahagonny* Weill
Johann **b/bt** *Werther* Massenet
Johann Ackerman: *see* Jim Mahoney
Johannes Freudhofer **bt** *Der Evangelimann* Kienzl
John **bt** *Das Heimchen am Herd* Goldmark; **bb** *Hugh the Drover* Vaughan Williams
John Adams **t** *The Mother of Us All* Thomson
John, Friar/Jean, Frère **b** *Roméo et Juliette* Gounod
John of Leyden **t** *Le prophète* Meyerbeer
John Sorel **bt** *The Consul* Menotti
John Styx **t** *Orphée aux enfers* Offenbach
John the Baptist/Jean/Jochanaan/Jokanaan **t** *Hérodiade* Massenet; **bt** *Salome* Strauss, R.
John Wellington Wells **bt** *The Sorcerer* Sullivan
Johnson, Dick/Ramerrez **t** *La fanciulla del West* Puccini
Jokanaan: *see* John the Baptist
Jonas **t** *Le prophète* Meyerbeer
Jonathan **t** *Saul og David* Nielsen
Jonny **bt** *Jonny spielt auf* Krenek
Jontek **t** *Halka* Moniuszko
Jorg **b** *Stiffelio* Verdi
José, Don **t** *Carmen* Bizet
José Castro **b** *La fanciulla del West* Puccini
José de Santarem, Don **bt** *Maritana* Wallace
José Martinez, Don **b** *Koanga* Delius
Josef K. **t** *Der Prozess* von Einem
Josef Lettner: *see* Joe
Josef Mauer **sp** *Elegy for Young Lovers* Henze
Joseph/Cléophas **hc** *Joseph* Méhul
Joseph Porter, Sir **bt** *HMS Pinafore* Sullivan
Josephine **s** *HMS Pinafore* Sullivan
Journalist **t** *Les mamelles de Tirésias* Poulenc
Journeyman **t** *Cardillac* Hindemith
Jouvenot, Mlle **s** *Adriana Lecouvreur* Cilea
Jov **b** *Dimitrij* Dvořák
Juam de Sylva, Dom **b** *Dom Sébastien* Donizetti
Juan **t** *Don Quichotte* Massenet
Juan, Don **t** *The Stone Guest* Dargomïzhsky
Juan de Regla **sp** *Karl V* Krenek
Juan Lopez **b** *Der Corregidor* Wolf
Juana **a** *Karl V* Krenek
Juba **t** *Cleopatra* Mattheson
Judge **t** *Die Bürgschaft* Weill; **bb** *The English Cat* Henze; **bt** *Trial by Jury* Sullivan
Judge/Armfelt **t** *Un ballo in maschera* Verdi
Judith/Judit **ms/s** *Bluebeard's Castle* Bartók
Judy **ms** *Punch and Judy* Birtwistle
Juggler: *see* Jean
Julia **s** *La vestale* Spontini; *see also* Nancy
Julia Farnese **s** *Bomarzo* Ginastera
Julián, Don **bt** *Don Rodrigo* Ginastera
Julian, Mrs **s** *Owen Wingrave* Britten
Juliana Bordereau **s** *The Aspern Papers* Argento
Juliano, Count **t** *Le domino noir* Auber
Julie **s** *The Jacobin* Dvořák; **s** *Lucile* Grétry
Julien **bt** *Drömmen om Thérèse* Werle; **t** *Julien* Charpentier, G.; **t** *Louise* Charpentier, G.
Juliet **s** *The Little Sweep* Britten
Juliet/Juliette **s** *Roméo et Juliette* Gounod
Juliette **s** *Der Graf von Luxemburg* Lehár; **s** *Julietta* Martinů
Julius Caesar/Giulio Cesare **a** *Giulio Cesare in Egitto* Handel
Junia/Giunia **s** *Lucio Silla* Mozart
Junior **bt** *A Quiet Place* Bernstein
Junius **bt** *The Rape of Lucretia* Britten
Juno/Giunone/Junon **ms** *Actéon* Charpentier, M.-A.; **a** *Agrippina* Handel; **s** *Cadmus et Hermione* Lully; **s** *Calisto* Cavalli; **s** *Ercole amante* Cavalli; **s** *La finta pazza* Sacrati **s** *Isis* Lully; **s** *The Judgment of Paris* Eccles, D. Purcell, Weldon; **s** *Orphée aux enfers* Offenbach; **s** *Platée* Rameau; **s** *Il pomo d'oro* Cesti; **a** *Semele* Handel
Junoš **t** *The Brandenburgers in Bohemia* Smetana
Jupiter/Giove **b** *Cadmus et Hermione* Lully; **b** *Calisto* Cavalli; **b** *Castor et Pollux* Rameau; **b** *La finta pazza* Sacrati; **bt** *Isis* Lully; **bt** *Die Liebe der Danae* Strauss, R.; **b** *Naïs* Rameau; **b** *Le nozze di Teti e di Peleo* Cavalli; **bt** *The Olympians* Bliss; **bt** *Orphée aux enfers* Offenbach; **bt** *Phaëton* Lully; **bt** *Philémon et Baucis* Gounod; **b** *Platée* Rameau; **b** *Il pomo d'oro* Cesti; **bt** *Proserpine* Lully; **t** *Semele* Handel
Justin/Giustino **a** *Giustino* Handel
Justinian **b** *Belisario* Donizetti

K

Kabanicha/Marfa Ignatevna Kabanova **a** *Káťa Kabanová* Janáček
Káča/Kate **ms** *The Devil and Kate* Dvořák
Kachovsky, Pyotr **t** *The Decembrists* Shaporin
Kadoor, Prince **bt** *Si j'étais roi* Adam
Kaidamà **b** *Il furioso nell'isola di S Domingo* Donizetti
Kaito **a** *Fervaal* d'Indy
Kalaf **t** *Turandot* Busoni
Kalina **bt** *The Secret* Smetana
Karl, King: *see* Charlemagne
Karl V **bt** *Karl V* Krenek
Karnac **bt** *Le roi d'Ys* Lalo
Karolina **s** *The Two Widows* Smetana
Karolka **ms** *Jenůfa* Janáček
Kaspar **t** *Amahl and the Night Visitors* Menotti
Kate **ms** *Owen Wingrave* Britten; **a** *The Pirates of Penzance* Sullivan; *see also* Káča
Kate Pinkerton **ms** *Madama Butterfly* Puccini
Káťa/Katya/Katěrina **s** *Káťa Kabanová* Janáček
Katerina **s** *The Greek Passion* Martinů
Katerina Izmaylova **s** *Katerina Izmaylova/Lady Macbeth of the Mtsensk District* Shostakovich
Katharina **a** *Die Harmonie der Welt* Hindemith
Katharine **s** *Der widerspänstigen Zähmung* Goetz
Kathinka **flautist** *Samstag aus Licht* Stockhausen
Katisha **a** *The Mikado* Sullivan
Katiusha **s** *Risurrezione* Alfano
Katrena **s** *The Whirlpool* Suchoň
Katuška **s** *The Devil's Wall* Smetana
Katya: *see* Káťa
Ké-ki-ka-ko **t** *Ba-ta-clan* Offenbach
Kecal **b** *The Bartered Bride* Smetana
Kedruta **a** *The Excursions of Mr Brouček* Janáček
Kelbar, Baron **b** *Un giorno di regno* Verdi
Kent, Earl of **t** *Lear* Reimann
Kepler, Johannes **bt** *Die Harmonie der Welt* Hindemith
Khan Konchak: *see* Konchak, Khan
Khivrya **ms** *The Fair at Sorochintsï* Musorgsky
Khovansky: *see* Andrey Khovansky, Ivan Khovansky
Khrushchyov **t** *Boris Godunov* Musorgsky
Kilian **bt** *Der Freischütz* Weber
King **bt** *Cendrillon* Massenet; **t** *Hunyadi László* Erkel; **b** *Irmelin* Delius; **bt** *Die Kluge* Orff; **bt** *Si j'étais roi* Adam; **b** *Taverner* Maxwell Davies; **b** *Die Verurteilung des Lukullus* Dessau
King Fisher **bt** *The Midsummer Marriage* Tippett
King's Fool **t** *Der Schatzgräber* Schreker
King's Son **t** *Die Königskinder* Humperdinck
Kissinger, Henry **b** *Nixon in China* Adams
Kitty **s** *Le dernier sauvage* Menotti
Klingsor **b** *Parsifal* Wagner
Klytemnästra: *see* Clytemnestra
Kneebone, Mrs **a** *A Dinner Engagement* Berkeley
Ko-Ko **bt** *The Mikado* Sullivan
Ko-ko-ri-ko **bt** *Ba-ta-clan* Offenbach
Koanga **bt** *Koanga* Delius
Kochubey, Vasily **bt** *Mazepa* Tchaikovsky
Kodana **t** *Le dernier sauvage* Menotti
Kokbourg/Cockburn, Lord **t** *Fra Diavolo* Auber
Kolenatý, Dr **bb** *The Makropulos Affair* Janáček
Konchak, Khan **x** *Prince Igor* Borodin
Konchakovna **a** *Prince Igor* Borodin
Konstanze **s** *Die Entführung aus dem Serail* Mozart
Kornélis **t** *La princesse jaune* Saint-Saëns
Korosov, Baron **t** *Die Zirkusprinzessin* Kálmán
Kostelnička Buryjovka **s** *Jenůfa* Janáček
Kothner, Fritz **b** *Die Meistersinger von Nürnberg* Wagner
Kottwitz, Colonel **b** *Der Prinz von Homburg* Henze
Kovalyov, Major Platon Kuz'mich **bt** *The Nose* Shostakovich
Krasava **s** *Libuše* Smetana
Krautmann, Dr *Doktor und Apotheker* Dittersdorf
Krishna, Lord **b** *Satyagraha* Glass
Kristina/Krista **s** *The Makropulos Affair* Janáček
Kronthal, Baron **t** *Der Wildschütz* Lortzing
Krušina **bt** *The Bartered Bride* Smetana
Krúťňava: *see* Katrena
Ktesiphar **t** *Die toten Augen* d'Albert
Kudrjáš, Váňa **t** *Káťa Kabanová* Janáček
Kühleborn **b** *Undine* Hoffmann; **bt** *Undine* Lortzing
Kuligin **bt** *Káťa Kabanová* Janáček
Kum **bt** *The Fair at Sorochintsï* Musorgsky
Kuma: *see* Nastas'ya
Kundry **ms** *Parsifal* Wagner
Kunigunde **s** *Faust* Spohr
Kunka: *see* Málinka
Kunrad **bt** *Feuersnot* Strauss, R.
Kupava **s** *The Snow Maiden* Rimsky-Korsakov
Kurlyatev, Prince Nikita **bt** *The Enchantress* Tchaikovsky
Kurlyateva, Princess **ms** *The Enchantress* Tchaikovsky
Kurwenal **bt** *Tristan und Isolde* Wagner
Kutuzov, Field Marshal **b** *War and Peace* Prokofiev
Kuz'ka **bt** *Khovanshchina* Musorgsky
Kyoto **bt** *Iris* Mascagni

L

Laca Kleme **t** *Jenůfa* Janáček
Lacouf **t** *Les mamelles de Tirésias* Poulenc
Ladas **sp** *The Greek Passion* Martinů
Ladislao **t** *Sigismondo* Rossini
Ladislav Podhajský **t** *The Two Widows* Smetana
Lady **s** *Cardillac* Hindemith
Lady Jane **a** *Patience* Sullivan
Laelius/Lelio **t** *Scipione* Handel
Laertes/Laerte **t** *Hamlet* Thomas; **t** *Mignon* Thomas
Laertes/Léodès **t** *Pénélope* Fauré
Laetitia **s** *The Old Maid and the Thief* Menotti
La Force, Chevalier de **t** *Dialogues des Carmélites* Poulenc
La Force, Marquis de **bt** *Dialogues des Carmélites* Poulenc
La Haltière, Madame de **ms** *Cendrillon* Massenet
Lahore, King of **t** *Le roi de Lahore* Massenet
Laius/Laïos **t** *Oedipe* Enescu
Lakmé **s** *Lakmé* Delibes
Lambertuccio **bt** *Boccaccio* Suppé
Lamoral, Count **b** *Arabella* Strauss
Lamplighter **bt** *Der junge Lord* Henze
Lancelot **t** *Le roi Arthus* Chausson
Landgrave: *see* Herrmann
Lange, Mlle **s** *La fille de Madame Angot* Lecocq
Lanterna **t** *Don Giovanni* Gazzaniga
Lanzelot **bt** *Lanzelot* Dessau
Laodice **s** *Mitridate Eupatore* Scarlatti; **s** *Siroe* Handel
Laoula, Princess **s** *L'étoile* Chabrier
Lapák **ms** *The Cunning Little Vixen* Janáček
Larina, Madame **ms** *Yevgeny Onegin* Tchaikovsky
Larkens **b** *La fanciulla del West* Puccini
Larmor, King **bt** *Uthal* Méhul
La Rocca **b** *Un giorno di regno* Verdi
La Rocca/Circus Director **t** *Der junge Lord* Henze
La Roche **b** *Capriccio* Strauss
La Roche, Countess de **ms** *Die Soldaten* Zimmermann
La Rose, Madama **ms** *La gazzetta* Rossini
Laroux **b** *Volo di notte* Dallapiccola
Laski, Count **b** *Le roi malgré lui* Chabrier
László **t** *Hunyadi László* Erkel
Latino **t** *Il trionfo di Camilla* Bononcini, G.
Latour, Mme de: *see* Madeleine
Laura **s** *Die drei Pintos* Weber; **ms** *Luisa Miller* Verdi; **s** *Neues vom Tage* Hindemith; **ms** *The Stone Guest* Dargomïzhsky
Laura Adorno **ms** *La Gioconda* Ponchielli
Laura Nowalska, Countess **s** *Der Bettelstudent* Millöcker
Laurence, Friar/Laurent, Frère **b** *Roméo et Juliette* Gounod
Lauret **b** *The Maid of Orléans* Tchaikovsky
Lauretta **s** *Gianni Schicchi* Puccini
Laurette **s** *Le docteur Miracle* Bizet; **s** *Richard Coeur-de-lion* Grétry
Laurie **s** *The Tender Land* Copland

Lavatte b *The Olympians* Bliss
Lavina s *L'oca del Cairo* Mozart
Lavinia s *Mourning Becomes Electra* Levy; s *Il trionfo di Camilla* Bononcini, G.
Lawrence bt *The Wreckers* Smyth
Lawyer t *Punch and Judy* Birtwistle
Lazarillo ms *Maritana* Wallace
Lazuli ms *L'étoile* Chabrier
Leader bt *Down in the Valley* Weill
Leander t *Die Feuersbrunst* Haydn; bt *The Love for Three Oranges* Prokofiev; t *Maskarade* Nielsen
Léandre b *Les fêtes vénitiennes* Campra; t *Le médecin malgré lui* Gounod; t *Le tableau parlant* Grétry
Leandro t *Arlecchino* Busoni
Leandro, King t *König Hirsch* Henze
Lear, King bt *Lear* Reimann
Le Bross t *Olivo e Pasquale* Donizetti
Lechery, Lord t *The Pilgrim's Progress* Vaughan Williams
Lechmere t *Owen Wingrave* Britten
Lefèbvre, Sergeant t *Madame Sans-Gêne* Giordano
Lefort, General b *Zar und Zimmermann* Lortzing
Leicester t *Elisabetta, regina d'Inghilterra* Rossini; t *Maria Stuarda* Donizetti
Leigh, Mrs s *Lord Byron* Thomson
Leïla s *Les pêcheurs de perles* Bizet
Lel' a *The Snow Maiden* Rimsky-Korsakov
Lelio: *see* Laelius
Lena s *Il filosofo di campagna* Galuppi
Léna s *La princesse jaune* Saint-Saëns
Lenio s *The Greek Passion* Martinů
Lenka s *The Stubborn Lovers* Dvořák
Lensky t *Yevgeny Onegin* Tchaikovsky
Leo t *Regina* Blitzstein
Leo, Brother bt *Saint François d'Assise* Messiaen
Leo/Leone b *Tamerlano* Handel
Leocasta a *Giustino* Handel
Léodès: *see* Laertes
Leokadja Begbick a/ms *Aufstieg und Fall der Stadt Mahagonny* Weill
Léon *La mère coupable* Milhaud
Leonard t/bt *Maskarade* Nielsen
Leonarda ms *L'ajo nell'imbarazzo* Donizetti
Léonarde s *La caverne* Le Sueur
Leonardo bt *Blood Wedding* Szokolay; bt *Die Bluthochzeit* Fortner
Leonato/Léonato sp *Béatrice et Bénédict* Berlioz
Leone b *Attila* Verdi
Leonello bt *Boccaccio* Suppé
Leonnatus/Leonato t *Alessandro* Handel
Léonor/Leonora di Gusmann ms *La favorite* Donizetti
Leonora s *La forza del destino* Verdi; s *Maskarade* Nielsen; s *Oberto* Verdi; a *Il trionfo dell'onore* Scarlatti; s *Il trovatore* Verdi; s *La vera storia* Berio
Leonore s *Alessandro Stradella* Flotow; s *Doktor und Apotheker* Dittersdorf; s *Fidelio* Beethoven
Léonore s *Les fêtes vénitiennes* Campra
Léontine s *Les fêtes vénitiennes* Campra
Léopold, Prince t *La Juive* Halévy
Leper t *Saint François d'Assise* Messiaen
Lepidus/Lepido s *Silla* Handel
Leporello b *Don Giovanni* Mozart; b *The Stone Guest* Dargomïzhsky
Lerma, Count of t *Don Carlos* Verdi
Lesbina s *Il filosofo di campagna* Galuppi; s *Le pescatrici* Haydn
Lesbo b *Agrippina* Handel
Lescaut bt *Boulevard Solitude* Henze; bt *Manon* Massenet; bt *Manon Lescaut* Puccini
Leshiy: *see* Forest Sprite
Leucippo b *Zelmira* Rossini
Leukippos t *Daphne* Strauss
Leuthold bt *Guillaume Tell* Rossini
Lev b *The Ice Break* Tippett
Levko t *May Night* Rimsky-Korsakov
Lhotský b *Osud* Janáček
Li x *Der Kreidekreis* Zemlinsky
Libenskof, Conte di t *Il viaggio a Reims* Rossini
Liberto t *L'incoronazione di Poppea* Monteverdi
Libuše s *Libuše* Smetana
Libya/Libia/Libie s *Fetonte* Jommelli; s *Phaëton* Lully
Libyna s *Šárka* Fibich
Lichas a *Hercules* Handel
Licinius t *La vestale* Spontini
Licomede: *see* Lycomedes
Licone t *Orlando paladino* Haydn
Licoris: *see* Sivene
Lictor/Littore b *L'incoronazione di Poppea* Monteverdi
Lida s *La battaglia di Legnano* Verdi
Lidio a *Egisto* Cavalli
Lidoine, Madame/New Prioress s *Dialogues des Carmélites* Poulenc
Lidunka s *The Two Widows* Smetana
Liduška s *King and Charcoal Burner* Dvořák
Liebenau, Count von/Conrad bt *Der Waffenschmied* Lortzing
Lieschen s *Die Zwillingsbrüder* Schubert
Lïkov, Ivan t *The Tsar's Bride* Rimsky-Korsakov
Lilaque (father) t *Boulevard Solitude* Henze
Lilaque (son) bt *Boulevard Solitude* Henze
Lilla s *Una cosa rara* Martín y Soler
Lillas Pastia sp *Carmen* Bizet
Lillian Russell s *The Mother of Us All* Thomson
Lina s *Stiffelio* Verdi
Linco b *Il trionfo di Camilla* Bononcini, G.
Linda s *Linda di Chamounix* Donizetti
Lindorf b/bt *Les contes d'Hoffmann* Offenbach
Lindoro t *La fedeltà premiata* Haydn; t *L'italiana in Algeri* Rossini; t *Nina* Paisiello; b *Le pescatrici* Haydn; *see also* Almaviva
Lindus/Lindo b *Tito Manlio* Vivaldi
Linetta a *The Love for Three Oranges* Prokofiev
Linfea s *Calisto* Cavalli
Lionel bt *The Maid of Orléans* Tchaikovsky; *see also* Lyonel
Lisa/Liza s *Das Land des Lächelns* Lehár; s *The Queen of Spades* Tchaikovsky; s *La sonnambula* Bellini
Lisabetta s *La cena delle beffe* Giordano
Lisargo b *Una cosa rara* Martín y Soler
Lisaura s *Alessandro* Handel
Lisetta s *L'amore medico* Wolf-Ferrari; s *Gli equivoci nel sembiante* Scarlatti; s *La gazzetta* Rossini; a *Il mondo della luna* Haydn; s *La vera costanza* Haydn
Lisette s *La fausse esclave* Gluck; s *La Rondine* Puccini
Lisinga a *Le cinesi* Gluck; s *Demetrio e Polibio* Rossini
Listnitsky, General b *Quiet Flows the Don* Dzerzhinsky
Little Bat McLean t *Susannah* Floyd
Little Buttercup a *HMS Pinafore* Sullivan
Littore: *see* Lictor
Liù s *Turandot* Puccini
Liverotto t *Lucrezia Borgia* Donizetti
Livia s *L'italiana in Londra* Cimarosa
Livietta s *Fra i due litiganti il terzo gode* Sarti; s *Livietta e Tracollo* Pergolesi
Liza: *see* Lisa
Liza Elliott ms *Lady in the Dark* Weill
Lizzie Borden ms *Lizzie Borden* Beeson
Lockit b/bt *The Beggar's Opera*
Locksley bt *Der Templer und die Jüdin* Marschner
Lodger bt *The Aspern Papers* Argento
Lodoïska s *Lodoïska* Cherubini
Lodovico b *Otello* Verdi
Loge t *Das Rheingold* Wagner
Logistille s *Roland* Lully; s *Roland* Piccinni
Lohengrin t *Lohengrin* Wagner
Lola ms *Cavalleria rusticana* Mascagni
Lolika s *The Magic Opal* Albéniz
Lord Chancellor bt *Iolanthe* Sullivan
Lord Mayor t *Der Besuch der alten Dame* von Einem
Loreley s *Loreley* Catalani
Lorenzo t *I Capuleti e i Montecchi* Bellini; t *Fra Diavolo* Auber; t *La muette de Portici* Auber; t *Nozze istriane* Smareglia
Loris Ipanov, Count t *Fedora* Giordano

Lotario **b** *Flavio* Handel; **a** *Lotario* Handel
Lothario **b** *Mignon* Thomas
Lotinka **a** *The Jacobin* Dvořák
Lotteringhi **bt** *Boccaccio* Suppé
Loudspeaker **bb** *Der Kaiser von Atlantis* Ullmann
Louis **bt** *The Wandering Scholar* Holst
Louis V, King **a** *Ugo conte di Parigi* Donizetti
Louis VI, King **b** *Euryanthe* Weber
Louis XV Chair/Bergère **s** *L'enfant et les sortilèges* Ravel
Louisa **s** *Betrothal in a Monastery* Prokofiev; **s** *The Duenna* Linley
Louise **s** *Le déserteur* Monsigny; **s** *The English Cat* Henze; **s** *Julien* Charpentier, G.; **s** *Louise* Charpentier, G.
Lover **t** *Amelia al ballo* Menotti
Loÿs **x** *Grisélidis* Massenet
Luber, Frau von **ms** *Der Silbersee* Weill
Lubino **b** *Una cosa rara* Martín y Soler
Luca **t** *La vera storia* Berio
Lucan/Lucano **t** *L'incoronazione di Poppea* Monteverdi
Lucas **bt** *L'ivrogne corrigé* Gluck
Luceius/Luceio **s** *La clemenza di Scipione* Bach, J. C.; **a** *Scipione* Handel; **s** *Scipione affricano* Cavalli
Lucentio **t** *Der widerspänstigen Zähmung* Goetz
Lucette: *see* Cendrillon
Lucia **ms** *La gazza ladra* Rossini; **s** *Lucia di Lammermoor* Donizetti; **s** *I promessi sposi* Ponchielli; **s** *The Rape of Lucretia* Britten
Lucia, Mamma **a** *Cavalleria rusticana* Mascagni
Lucieta **s** *Il campiello* Wolf-Ferrari; **s** *I quatro rusteghi* Wolf-Ferrari
Lucifer **b** *The Devil and Kate* Dvořák; **b** *Montag aus Licht* Stockhausen; **b** *Samstag aus Licht* Stockhausen; *see also* Luzimon
Lucile **s** *Dantons Tod* von Einem; **s** *Les fêtes vénitiennes* Campra; **s** *Lucile* Grétry
Lucilla **ms** *La scala di seta* Rossini
Lucinda **s** *L'amore medico* Wolf-Ferrari
Lucinda, Marchesa **s** *La buona figliuola* Piccinni
Lucinde **s** *Le médecin malgré lui* Gounod; *see also* Demon (Lucinde)
Lucio Silla: *see* Sulla, Lucius
Lucius/Lucio **s** *Tito Manlio* Vivaldi
Lucretia **a** *The Rape of Lucretia* Britten
Lucrezia **a** *Palestrina* Pfitzner
Lucrezia Borgia **s** *Lucrezia Borgia* Donizetti
Lucrezia Contarini **s** *I due Foscari* Verdi
Lucullus/Lukullus **t** *Die Verurteilung des Lukullus* Dessau
Lucy **s** *The Beggar's Opera*; **s** *Die Dreigroschenoper* Weill; **s** *The Telephone* Menotti; *see also* Lucia
Ludiše **s** *The Brandenburgers in Bohemia* Smetana
Ludmila **s** *The Bartered Bride* Smetana; *see also* Lyudmila
Ludorf **b** *La nonne sanglante* Gounod
Ludwig **bt** *The Grand Duke* Sullivan
Luigi **t** *Il tabarro* Puccini
Luigia **s** *Le convenienze teatrali* Donizetti
Luigino, Don **b** *La molinara* Paisiello
Luis, Don **t** *Pepita Jiménez* Albéniz
Luisa **s** *Luisa Miller* Verdi
Luise **s** *Die Abreise* d'Albert; **s** *Die Bürgschaft* Weill; **s** *Der junge Lord* Henze
Luiz **bt** *The Gondoliers* Sullivan
Luka **b** *The Bear* Walton
Luka Kuzmič/Filka Morozov **t** *From the House of the Dead* Janáček
Lukáš **t** *The Kiss* Smetana
Lukas, Tio **bt** *Der Corregidor* Wolf
Luke **t** *The Ice Break* Tippett
Lukullus: *see* Lucullus
Lulu **s** *Lulu* Berg
Lummer, Baron **t** *Intermezzo* Strauss, R.
Luna, Count di **bt** *Il trovatore* Verdi
Lunardo **b** *I quatro rusteghi* Wolf-Ferrari
Lunobor: *see* Sacristan
Lurcanio **t** *Ariodante* Handel; **s** *Ginevra di Scozia* Mayr
Lusignan **bt** *La reine de Chypre* Halévy
Lusignano **bt** *Caterina Cornaro* Donizetti; **b** *Zaira* Bellini
Luther **bt** *Les contes d'Hoffmann* Offenbach; **bt** *Karl V* Krenek
Lutobor **b** *Libuše* Smetana
Lutomíra **s** *Svätopluk* Suchoň
Luxembourg, René, Count of **t** *Der Graf von Luxemburg* Lehár
Luyn Calvo **b** *Der Cid* Cornelius
Luze **a** *Nozze istriane* Smareglia
Luzimon/Lucifer **b** *Donnerstag aus Licht* Stockhausen
Lycomedes/Licomede **b** *Deidamia* Handel; **b** *La finta pazza* Sacrati
Lynceus/Lyncée **t** *Les Danaïdes* Salieri
Lyonel **t** *Martha* Flotow
Lyonnel **t** *Le roi Arthus* Chausson
Lysander **t** *A Midsummer Night's Dream* Britten
Lysiart, Count of **b** *Euryanthe* Weber
Lyubasha **ms** *The Tsar's Bride* Rimsky-Korsakov
Lyubava Buslayevna **ms** *Sadko* Rimsky-Korsakov
Lyubov' **ms** *Mazepa* Tchaikovsky
Lyudmila **s** *Ruslan and Lyudmila* Glinka

M

M., Frau **ms** *Neues vom Tage* Hindemith
M., Herr **t** *Neues vom Tage* Hindemith
Ma **bt** *Der Kreidekreis* Zemlinsky
Mab **s** *La jolie fille de Perth* Bizet
Mabel **s** *The Pirates of Penzance* Sullivan
Mac the Knife: *see* Macheath
Macbeth **bt** *Macbeth* Verdi
Macbeth, Lady **s** *Macbeth* Verdi
Macduff **t** *Macbeth* Verdi
MacFarlane, Captain Jason **bt** *Lizzie Borden* Beeson
MacGregor **b** *Guglielmo Ratcliff* Mascagni; **b** *William Ratcliff* Cui
Macheath, Captain **t/bt** *The Beggar's Opera*
Macheath/Mac the Knife **t** *Die Dreigroschenoper* Weill
Maciej **bt** *The Haunted Manor* Moniuszko
Macrobio **bt** *La pietra del paragone* Rossini
Mad Margaret **ms** *Ruddigore* Sullivan
Maddalena **s** *Linda di Chamounix* Donizetti; **s** *Maddalena* Prokofiev; **a** *Rigoletto* Verdi
Maddalena de Coigny **s** *Andrea Chénier* Giordano
Madeleine **s** *The Olympians* Bliss
Madeleine, Countess **s** *Capriccio* Strauss
Madeleine/Latour, Mme de **s** *Le postillon de Lonjumeau* Adam
Madelon **ms** *Andrea Chénier* Giordano
Madruscht/Madruzzo, Cardinal Christoph **b** *Palestrina* Pfitzner
Madwoman **t** *Curlew River* Britten
Maerbale **bt** *Bomarzo* Ginastera
Maffio Orsini **ms** *Lucrezia Borgia* Donizetti
Magda de Civry **s** *La Rondine* Puccini
Magdalena **a** *Der Evangelimann* Kienzl
Magdalene **s** *Die Meistersinger von Nürnberg* Wagner
Magda Sorel **s** *The Consul* Menotti
Magdelone **ms** *Maskarade* Nielsen
Magician **b** *Švanda the Bagpiper* Weinberger
Magician/Nika Magadoff **t** *The Consul* Menotti
Magistrate **bt** *Der Prozess* von Einem
Magnifico, Don **bt** *La Cenerentola* Rossini
Mahomet **b** *Maometto II* Rossini
Mahomet II **b** *Le siège de Corinthe* Rossini
Maid: *see* Evadne
Mainfroid/Manfredo **t** *Les vêpres siciliennes* Verdi
Major-Domo **b** *Capriccio* Strauss
Malatesta, Dr **bt** *Don Pasquale* Donizetti
Malatesta, Giovanni/Gianciotto **bt** *Francesca da Rimini* Zandonai
Malatesta, Lanceotto **bt** *Francesca da Rimini* Rakhmaninov
Malatesta, Paolo **t** *Francesca da Rimini* Rakhmaninov
Malatestino **t** *Francesca da Rimini* Zandonai
Malcolm **ms** *La donna del lago* Rossini; **t** *Macbeth* Verdi
Male Chorus **t** *The Rape of Lucretia* Britten
Maliella **s** *I gioielli della Madonna* Wolf-Ferrari
Malina **b** *The Secret* Smetana

Málinka/Etherea/Kunka **s** *The Excursions of Mr Brouček* Janáček
Mallika **ms** *Lakmé* Delibes
Malvina **s** *Uthal* Méhul
Malvino: *see* Zeliska
Malvolino **b** *Alessandro Stradella* Flotow
Malwina **s** *Der Vampyr* Marschner
Malyuta-Skuratov, Grigory **b** *The Tsar's Bride* Rimsky-Korsakov
Mama McCourt **a** *The Ballad of Baby Doe* Moore
Mambre: *see* Auphis
Mamïrov **b** *The Enchantress* Tchaikovsky
Mamm'Agata **bt** *Le convenienze teatrali* Donizetti
Mamma Lucia: *see* Lucia, Mamma
Man Friday/Vendredi **ms** *Robinson Crusoé* Offenbach
Man with Donkey **t** *Die Kluge* Orff
Man with Mule **bt** *Die Kluge* Orff
Manasse **b** *Die Brautwahl* Busoni
Mandane **s** *Artaxerxes* Arne; **s** *Cleopatra* Mattheson
Mandryka **bt** *Arabella* Strauss
Manfredo **bt** *L'amore dei tre re* Montemezzi
Manfredo, Count of Syracuse **b** *Il giuramento* Mercadante; *see also* Mainfroid
Mangus **t/bt** *The Knot Garden* Tippett
Manlius/Manlio **s** *Tito Manlio* Vivaldi
Mannoury **bt** *The Devils of Loudun* Penderecki
Manolios **t** *The Greek Passion* Martinů
Manon Lescaut **s** *Boulevard Solitude* Henze; **s** *Manon* Massenet; **s** *Manon Lescaut* Puccini
Manrico **t** *Il trovatore* Verdi
Manservant: *see* Prince
Manto **hc** *Les Paladins* Rameau
Mantua, Duke of **t** *Rigoletto* Verdi
Manuel **bt** *La vida breve* Falla
Manuela **ms** *Der Corregidor* Wolf
Manuele **bt** *Giuditta* Lehár
Manz **bt** *A Village Romeo and Juliet* Delius
Mao Tse-tung **t** *Nixon in China* Adams
Maragond **ms** *Fierrabras* Schubert
Marbuel **b** *The Devil and Kate* Dvořák
Marcel **bt** *Etienne Marcel* Saint-Saëns
Marcel **b** *Les Huguenots* Meyerbeer
Marcélina **s** *Les deux journées* Cherubini
Marcellina **s** *Le nozze di Figaro* Mozart
Marcello **bt** *La bohème* Puccini; **t** *La bohème* Leoncavallo
Marcello di Bruges/Henri **t** *Il duca d'Alba* Donizetti
Marchesa del Poggio **ms** *Un giorno di regno* Verdi
Marcius/Marzio **s** *La clemenza di Scipione* Bach, J. C.; **t** *Mitridate* Mozart
Marco **b** *L'arlesiana* Cilea; **bt** *Gianni Schicchi* Puccini; **t** *The Gondoliers* Sullivan
Marcovaldo **bt** *La battaglia di Legnano* Verdi
Marcus Antonius: *see* Mark Antony
Mařenka **s** *The Bartered Bride* Smetana
Marfa **ms** *Khovanshchina* Musorgsky; **s** *The Tsar's Bride* Rimsky-Korsakov
Marfa Kabanova: *see* Kabanicha
Marfa Ivanovna **a** *Dimitrij* Dvořák
Margared **ms** *Le roi d'Ys* Lalo
Margaret **ms** *The Duenna* Linley; **ms** *William Ratcliff* Cui
Margaretha **s** *Genoveva* Schumann
Margaret/Margherita **ms** *Guglielmo Ratcliff* Mascagni
Margherita **s** *Mefistofele* Boito
Margiana **s** *Der Barbier von Bagdad* Cornelius
Margret **a** *Wozzeck* Berg
Margret Borden **s** *Lizzie Borden* Beeson
Marguerite **ms** *La dame blanche* Boieldieu; **ms** *La damnation de Faust* Berlioz; **s** *Faust* Gounod
Marguerite de Valois **s** *Les Huguenots* Meyerbeer; **s** *Le pré aux Clercs* Hérold
Marguerite Duménil **s** *Der Opernball* Heuberger
Marguerite of Flanders **s** *Richard Coeur-de-lion* Grétry
Mária **s** *Hunyadi László* Erkel
Maria **s** *Maria de Rudenz* Donizetti; **s** *Maria di Rohan* Donizetti; **s** *West Side Story* Bernstein; *see also* Marie
Maria/Commandant's Wife **s** *Friedenstag* Strauss, R.
María del Carmen **s** *María del Carmen* Granados
Maria Luisa **ms** *Háry János* Kodály
Maria Padilla **s** *Maria Padilla* Donizetti
Mariana **s** *Das Liebesverbot* Wagner
Marianna **s** *Il Signor Bruschino* Rossini
Marianne **s** *Masagniello* Keiser; **s** *Der Rosenkavalier* Strauss, R.
Maria Stuarda: *see* Mary Stuart
Marie **s** *Ivan IV* Bizet; **ms** *Moïse et Pharaon* Rossini; **s** *Die Soldaten* Zimmermann; **s** *Der Waffenschmied* Lortzing; **s** *Wozzeck* Berg; **s** *Zar und Zimmermann* Lortzing
Marie/Maria **s** *La fille du régiment* Donizetti
Marie of the Incarnation, Mother **ms** *Dialogues des Carmélites* Poulenc
Marie's Son **tr** *Wozzeck* Berg
Mariella **s** *Il piccolo Marat* Mascagni
Marietta/Marie **s** *Die tote Stadt* Korngold
Marina Mníškova/Mniszek **ms/s** *Boris Godunov* Musorgsky; **s** *Dimitrij* Dvořák;
Marino Faliero **b** *Marino Faliero* Donizetti
Maritana **s** *Maritana* Wallace
Mariya **s** *Mazepa* Tchaikovsky
Mariya Bolkonskaya **ms** *War and Peace* Prokofiev
Mariya Timofeyevna **s** *The Decembrists* Shaporin
Mark **t** *The Midsummer Marriage* Tippett; **t** *The Wreckers* Smyth
Mark Antony/Marcus Antonius **t** *Cleopatra* Mattheson
Mark, King/König Marke **b** *Tristan und Isolde* Wagner
Marmaduke Pointdextre, Sir **bt** *The Sorcerer* Sullivan
Marquis **x** Cardillac Hindemith; **b** *Linda di Chamounix* Donizetti; *see also* Prince
Mars **bb** *The Olympians* Bliss; **bt** *Orphée aux enfers* Offenbach
Mars/Marte **t** *Il pomo d'oro* Cesti
Marschallin **s** *Der Rosenkavalier* Strauss, R.
Marschallin's Major-Domo **t** *Der Rosenkavalier* Strauss, R.
Marshall, William **t** *Regina* Blitzstein
Marta **ms** *Mefistofele* Boito; **s** *Tiefland* d'Albert
Martha **s** *Der Evangelimann* Kienzl; *see also* Harriet Durham, Lady
Marthe **s** *Faust* Gounod
Marti **bt** *A Village Romeo and Juliet* Delius
Martin **b** *The Cunning Peasant* Dvořák; **t** *The Tender Land* Copland
Martina **a** *The Magic Opal* Albéniz
Martinka **a** *The Kiss* Smetana
Martino **bt** *L'occasione fa il ladro* Rossini
Martio **s** *Il Sant'Alessio* Landi
Marullo **bt** *Rigoletto* Verdi
Marussa **s** *Nozze istriane* Smareglia
Mary **ms** *The Devil and Daniel Webster* Moore; **a** *Der fliegende Holländer* Wagner; **s** *Hugh the Drover* Vaughan Williams; **s** *William Ratcliff* Cui
Mary, Major **bt** *Die Soldaten* Zimmermann
Mary Magdalen **a** *Die toten Augen* d'Albert
Mary/Maria **s** *Guglielmo Ratcliff* Mascagni
Mary Stuart/Maria Stuarda **s** *Maria Stuarda* Donizetti
Marzelline **s** *Fidelio* Beethoven
Masagniello/Masaniello **b** *Masagniello* Keiser; **t** *La muette de Portici* Auber
Mascha **s** *Der Zarewitsch* Lehár
Masetto **b** *Don Giovanni* Mozart
Masinissa/Massanissa **b** *Scipione affricano* Cavalli
Masino **t** *La vera costanza* Haydn
Masotto **t** *Fra i due litiganti il terzo gode* Sarti
Masseo, Brother **t** *Saint François d'Assise* Messiaen
Massimiano: *see* Maximian
Massimiliano, Count Moor **b** *I briganti* Mercadante; **b** *I masnadieri* Verdi
Massimilla Doni **s** *Massimilla Doni* Schoeck
Master of Ceremonies **t** *The Love for Three Oranges* Prokofiev
Mastricco **b** *Le pescatrici* Haydn
Matěj **bt** *King and Charcoal Burner* Dvořák
Mathias **t** *Der Evangelimann* Kienzl
Mathieu **bt** *Andrea Chénier* Giordano
Mathilde **s** *Guillaume Tell* Rossini
Mathilde, Sister **ms** *Dialogues des Carmélites* Poulenc

Mathis **bt** *Mathis der Maler* Hindemith
Mathisen **bb** *Le prophète* Meyerbeer
Mathô **t** *Salammbô* Musorgsky
Mathurin **t** *L'ivrogne corrigé* Gluck
Mathurine **s** *L'ivrogne corrigé* Gluck
Matilda **a** *Lotario* Handel; **a** *Ottone* Handel
Matilde **s** *Elisabetta, regina d'Inghilterra* Rossini; **s** *Giulietta e Romeo* Zingarelli; **s** *Maria de Rudenz* Donizetti; **s** *Matilde di Shabran* Rossini
Matouš **b** *The Kiss* Smetana
Matt of the Mint **bb** *The Beggar's Opera*
Matteo **t** *Arabella* Strauss
Matteo del Sarto, Ser **bb** *Arlecchino* Busoni
Mattes **bt** *Die Bürgschaft* Weill
Matti **bt** *Puntila* Dessau
Maturina **s** *Don Giovanni* Gazzaniga
Matuta, Nikita **t** *The Maid of Pskov* Rimsky-Korsakov
Matyáš, King **bt** *King and Charcoal Burner* Dvořák
Mátyás **s** *Hunyadi László* Erkel
Mauregato **bt** *Alfonso und Estrella* Schubert
Maurizio **t** *Adriana Lecouvreur* Cilea; **b** *I quatro rusteghi* Wolf-Ferrari
Maurrant, Ann **s** *Street Scene* Weill
Maurrant, Frank **bb** *Street Scene* Weill
Maurya **a** *Riders to the Sea* Vaughan Williams
Max **bt** *Betly* Donizetti; **t** *Der Freischütz* Weber; **t** *Jonny spielt auf* Krenek
Maximian/Massimiano **b** *Fausta* Donizetti
Maximilian **bt** *Candide* Bernstein
May **s** *Das Heimchen am Herd* Goldmark
Mayor **bt** *L'assedio di Calais* Donizetti; **bb** *Der junge Lord* Henze; *see also* Podestat
Mazal/Blankytný/Petřík **t** *The Excursions of Mr Brouček* Janáček
Mazeppa/Mazepa **bt** *Mazepa* Tchaikovsky
Medea/Médée **s** *Giasone* Cavalli; **s** *Médée* Charpentier, M.-A.; **s** *Médée* Cherubini; **s** *Teseo* Handel; **s** *Thésée* Lully
Médor/Medoro **a** *Orlando* Handel; **t** *Orlando paladino* Haydn; **hc** *Roland* Lully; **t** *Roland* Piccinni
Medora **s** *Il corsaro* Verdi
Medusa/Méduse **t** *Persée* Lully
Mefistofele **b** *Mefistofele* Boito
Meg Page, Mrs **ms** *Falstaff* Verdi
Mel **bb** *The Knot Garden* Tippett
Melanto **s** *Il ritorno d'Ulisse in patria* Monteverdi; **ms** *Ulisse* Dallapiccola
Melbourne, Lady **s** *Lord Byron* Thomson
Melchior **bt** *Amahl and the Night Visitors* Menotti
Melcthal **b** *Guillaume Tell* Rossini; *see also* Arnold Melcthal
Meleager/Meleagro **s** *Atalanta* Handel
Melia **tr** *Apollo et Hyacinthus* Mozart
Melibea, Marchesa **a** *Il viaggio a Reims* Rossini
Melibeo **b** *La fedeltà premiata* Haydn
Melide **s** *Ormindo* Cavalli
Melinda **s** *Bánk bán* Erkel
Mélisande **s** *Ariane et Barbe-bleue* Dukas; **s** *Pelléas et Mélisande* Debussy
Melissa **s** *Amadigi di Gaula* Handel; **ms** *Princess Ida* Sullivan
Mélisse **s** *Atys* Lully; *see also* Demon (Mélisse)
Melisso **b** *Alcina* Handel
Melito **t** *Der geduldige Socrates* Telemann
Melitone, Fra **b** *La forza del destino* Verdi
Melo **a** *Sosarme* Handel
Melot **t** *Tristan und Isolde* Wagner
Melpomene/Melpomène **s** *Atys* Lully
Mendarse **a** *Siroe* Handel
Mendoza: *see* Isaac Mendoza
Menelaus/Ménélas/Menelas **t** *Die ägyptische Helena* Strauss, R.; **t** *La belle Hélène* Offenbach
Mengone **t** *Lo speziale* Haydn
Mengotto **b** *La buona figliuola* Piccinni
Menico **b** *Nozze istriane* Smareglia
Mephistopheles/Méphistophélès **bt/b** *La damnation de Faust* Berlioz; **b** *Faust* Spohr; **b** *Faust* Gounod; **t** *The Fiery Angel* Prokofiev; *see also* Mefistofele
Meraspes/Meraspe **b** *Admeto* Handel
Mercedes, Donna **a** *Der Corregidor* Wolf
Mercédès **s** *Carmen* Bizet
Mercenary **bt** *Simplicius Simplicissimus* Hartmann
Mercury/Mercure/Mercurio/Merkur **b** *Atalanta* Handel; **t** *Calisto* Cavalli; **t** *Ercole amante* Cavalli; **hc** *Les fêtes d'Hébé* Rameau; **hc** *Isis* Lully; **t** *Die Liebe der Danae* Strauss, R.; **t** *Le nozze di Teti e di Peleo* Cavalli; **t** *Orphée aux enfers* Offenbach; **hc** *Platée* Rameau; **hc** *Proserpine* Lully; **bb** *Les Troyens* Berlioz
Mercutio **bt** *Roméo et Juliette* Gounod
Meres'yov, Alexey **bt** *The Story of a Real Man* Prokofiev
Mergy, Baron de **t** *Le pré aux Clercs* Hérold
Meriones **s** *Telemaco* Gluck
Merkur: *see* Mercury
Merlin **bt** *New Year* Tippett; **bt** *Le roi Arthus* Chausson
Meroe **s** *Penthesilea* Schoeck; **s** *Tigrane* Scarlatti
Merope/Mérope **ms** *Oedipe* Enescu; **s** *Persée* Lully
Meryll, Leonard **t** *The Yeomen of the Guard* Sullivan
Meryll, Sergeant **bt** *The Yeomen of the Guard* Sullivan
Mescalina **ms** *Le Grand Macabre* Ligeti
Messenger **bb** *Oedipus rex* Stravinsky
Metella **s** *Silla* Handel
Métella **ms** *La vie parisienne* Offenbach
Metifio **bt** *L'arlesiana* Cilea
Mezio **t** *Il trionfo di Camilla* Bononcini, G.
Mi **s** *Das Land des Lächelns* Lehár
Micaëla **s** *Carmen* Bizet
Mícha **b** *The Bartered Bride* Smetana
Michael **t** *Arden must Die* Goehr; **t** *Donnerstag aus Licht* Stockhausen; *see also* Mikal
Míchálek **t** *The Devil's Wall* Smetana
Michel **t** *Julietta* Martinů
Michele **t** *The Saint of Bleecker Street* Menotti; **bt** *Il tabarro* Puccini
Michonnet **bt** *Adriana Lecouvreur* Cilea
Midas, King **t** *Die Liebe der Danae* Strauss, R.
Midir **t** *The Immortal Hour* Boughton
Miecznik **bt** *The Haunted Manor* Moniuszko
Mignon **t** *The Devils of Loudun* Penderecki; **ms** *Mignon* Thomas
Miguel de Panatellas, Comte **bt** *La Périchole* Offenbach
Mikado **b** *The Mikado* Sullivan
Mikal/Michael **s** *Saul og David* Nielsen
Mikéli **bt** *Les deux journées* Cherubini
Míla Válková **s** *Osud* Janáček
Míla's Mother **a** *Osud* Janáček
Milada **s** *Dalibor* Smetana
Milan, Prior of **t** *I Lombardi* Verdi
Miles **tr** *The Turn of the Screw* Britten
Militrisa, Tsarina **s** *The Tale of Tsar Saltan* Rimsky-Korsakov
Milkwoman **s** *Louise* Charpentier, G.
Miller **bt** *Luisa Miller* Verdi; **b** *Rusalka* Dargomïzhsky
Mima **Tape** *Aniara* Blomdahl
Mimaroben **bb** *Aniara* Blomdahl
Mime **t** *Das Rheingold* Wagner; **t** *Siegfried* Wagner
Mimì **s** *La bohème* Puccini; **s** *La bohème* Leoncavallo
Mina **s** *Aroldo* Verdi
Minerva/Minerve **s** *La finta pazza* Sacrati; **s** *Orphée aux enfers* Offenbach; **s** *Il ritorno d'Ulisse in patria* Monteverdi; **s** *Thésée* Lully
Minette **s** *The English Cat* Henze
Mingone **t** *Fra i due litiganti il terzo gode* Sarti
Minka **s** *Le roi malgré lui* Chabrier
Minnie **s** *La fanciulla del West* Puccini
Minos, King **b** *Arianna in Creta* Handel
Minto, Lord **bb** *Nelson* Berkeley
Miracle, Dr **b/bt** *Les contes d'Hoffmann* Offenbach
Mireille **s** *Mireille* Gounod
Mirinda **s** *Ormindo* Cavalli
Mirocleto **b** *Belfagor* Respighi
Mirtillo **s** *Il pastor fido* Handel
Mirva **x** *Il crociato in Egitto* Meyerbeer
Missail **t** *Boris Godunov* Musorgsky
Mithridates/Mitridate **t** *Mitridate* Mozart; **s** *Mitridate Eupatore* Scarlatti

Mitrane t *Semiramide* Rossini
Mittenhofer, Gregor bt *Elegy for Young Lovers* Henze
Mizgir' bt *The Snow Maiden* Rimsky-Korsakov
Mlada, Princess x *Mlada* Rimsky-Korsakov
Mocenigo b *Caterina Cornaro* Donizetti; bt *La reine de Chypre* Halévy
Mojmír bt *Svätopluk* Suchoň
Momus/Momo t *Le nozze di Teti e di Peleo* Cavalli; bt *Platée* Rameau; b *Il pomo d'oro* Cesti
Mondeva: *see* Eve
Mondo/World t *Rappresentatione di Anima, et di Corpo* Cavalieri
Monica s *The Medium* Menotti
Monisha ms *Treemonisha* Joplin
Monitress ms *Suor Angelica* Puccini
Monk b *Don Carlos* Verdi
Monostatos t *Die Zauberflöte* Mozart
Montano b *Otello* Verdi
Montauciel t *Le déserteur* Monsigny
Monteblanco, Grand Duchess of a *A Dinner Engagement* Berkeley
Montefiori, Marchioness de ms *Maritana* Wallace
Montefiori, Marquis de b *Maritana* Wallace
Monterone, Count b *Rigoletto* Verdi
Montezuma/Montézuma b *Fernand Cortez* Spontini; s *Montezuma* Graun
Montforte/Montfort, Guy de bt *Les vêpres siciliennes* Verdi
Moore, Thomas bt *Lord Byron* Thomson
Moralès bt *Carmen* Bizet
Morbio bt *Die schweigsame Frau* Strauss, R.
Mordred bt *Le roi Arthus* Chausson
Morena/Svyatokhna ms *Mlada* Rimsky-Korsakov
Moreno b *La muette de Portici* Auber
Morgana s *Alcina* Handel
Morone, Cardinal Giovanni bt *Palestrina* Pfitzner
Moroski b *L'amor coniugale* Mayr
Morosus, Sir b *Die schweigsame Frau* Strauss, R.
Morozova a *Oprichnik* Tchaikovsky
Morpheus/Morphée hc *Atys* Lully; bt *Orphée aux enfers* Offenbach
Moruccio bt *Tiefland* d'Albert
Mosbie t *Arden must Die* Goehr
Moser b *I masnadieri* Verdi
Moser, Augustin b *Die Meistersinger von Nürnberg* Wagner
Moses/Moïse/Mosè b *Moïse et Pharaon* Rossini; *Mosè in Egitto* Rossini; sp *Moses und Aron* Schoenberg
Mosquito t *The Cunning Little Vixen* Janáček
Moss, Grandpa b *The Tender Land* Copland
Moss, Ma a *The Tender Land* Copland
Moth tr *A Midsummer Night's Dream* Britten
Mother s *Amahl and the Night Visitors* Menotti; a *Blood Wedding* Szokolay; a *The Consul* Menotti; a *L'enfant et les sortilèges* Ravel; ms *Der Jasager* Weill; a *Louise* Charpentier, G.; a *Mavra* Stravinsky; ms *Il piccolo Marat* Mascagni; s *Il prigioniero* Dallapiccola; ms *Sapho* Massenet; *see also* Carmela
Mother Gerald *Dialogues des Carmélites* Poulenc
Mother/Gertrud ms *Hänsel und Gretel* Humperdinck
Mother Goose ms *The Rake's Progress* Stravinsky
Mother-in-law a *Blood Wedding* Szokolay
Mountararat, Lord bt *Iolanthe* Sullivan
Mountjoy, Lord bt *Gloriana* Britten
Mozart t *Mozart and Salieri* Rimsky-Korsakov
Mstivoy b *Mlada* Rimsky-Korsakov
Mucius [Mutius] Scaevola/Muzio Scevola a *Muzio Scevola* Handel; a *Costanza e Fortezza* Fux
Mumlal bt *The Two Widows* Smetana
Murena b *Esule di Roma* Donizetti
Murgatroyd, Sir Despard bt *Ruddigore* Sullivan
Murgatroyd, Sir Roderic bt *Ruddigore* Sullivan
Muse ms *Les contes d'Hoffmann* Offenbach
Musetta s *La bohème* Puccini; ms *La bohème* Leoncavallo
Music Director b *Prima la musica e poi le parole* Salieri
Music-Master bt *Ariadne auf Naxos* Strauss, R.
Mustafà b *Adina* Rossini; b *L'italiana in Algeri* Rossini
Mustardseed tr *A Midsummer Night's Dream* Britten
Mutius Scaevola/Muzio Scevola: *see* Mucius
Mydas bt *Die schöne Galathée* Suppé
Myles na Coppaleen t *The Lily of Killarney* Benedict
Mylio t *Le roi d'Ys* Lalo
Myrtocle s *Die toten Augen* d'Albert

N

Nabucco: *see* Nebuchadnezzar
Nachtigal, Konrad b *Die Meistersinger von Nürnberg* Wagner
Nadezhda s *Askold's Grave* Verstovsky
Nadia s *The Ice Break* Tippett
Nadir t *Drottningen av Golconda* Berwald; t *Les pêcheurs de perles* Bizet
Nadori t *Jessonda* Spohr
Naiad s *Armide* Gluck
Naina ms *Ruslan and Lyudmila* Glinka
Naïs/Neis s *Naïs* Rameau
Namouna/Namuna s *Nurmahal* Spontini
Nan ms *New Year* Tippett
Nancy ms *Albert Herring* Britten
Nancy (Julia) ms *Martha* Flotow
Nando t *Tiefland* d'Albert
Nanki-Poo t *The Mikado* Sullivan
Nannetta s *Falstaff* Verdi
Nanni b *L'infedeltà delusa* Haydn
Napoleon bt *Háry János* Kodály; bt *Madame Sans-Gêne* Giordano; bt *War and Peace* Prokofiev
Narbal b *Les Troyens* Berlioz
Narciso, Don t *Il turco in Italia* Rossini
Narcissa s *Philemon und Baucis* Haydn
Narcissus/Narciso/Narcisse a *Agrippina* Handel; t *Echo et Narcisse* Gluck
Nardo t *Il filosofo di campagna* Galuppi; *see also* Roberto
Narraboth t *Salome* Strauss, R.
Nastas'ya/Kuma s *The Enchantress* Tchaikovsky
Natal'ya s *Oprichnik* Tchaikovsky; s *Quiet Flows the Don* Dzerzhinsky
Natalia ms *Zazà* Leoncavallo
Natalie, Princess of Orange s *Der Prinz von Homburg* Henze
Natasha s *Rusalka* Dargomïzhsky
Natasha Rostova s *War and Peace* Prokofiev
Nausicaa s *Ulisse* Dallapiccola
Navrès s *Montezuma* Graun
Néarque/Nearco t *Les martyrs*/*Poliuto* Donizetti
Nebuchadnezzar/Nabucco t *The Burning Fiery Furnace* Britten; bt *Nabucco* Verdi
Ned b *Treemonisha* Joplin
Ned Keene bt *Peter Grimes* Britten
Ned Travers bt *The Boatswain's Mate* Smyth
Nedda/Columbina s *Pagliacci* Leoncavallo
Nefertiti ms *Akhnaten* Glass
Negro b *Angélique* Ibert; *see also* Painter
Neighbour ms *Mavra* Stravinsky
Neipperg, Count of t *Madame Sans-Gêne* Giordano
Neis: *see* Naïs
Neizvestnïy b *Askold's Grave* Verstovsky
Nekrotzar bt *Le Grand Macabre* Ligeti
Nella s *Gianni Schicchi* Puccini
Nello bt *Pia de' Tolomei* Donizetti
Nelly ms *Adelson e Salvini* Bellini
Nelson, Lady ms *Nelson* Berkeley
Nelson, Lord t *Nelson* Berkeley
Nélusko bt *L'Africaine* Meyerbeer
Nemea, Princess s *Si j'étais roi* Adam
Nemesis s *Cleopatra* Mattheson
Nemorino t *L'elisir d'amore* Donizetti
Nencio t *L'infedeltà delusa* Haydn
Néocles t *Le siège de Corinthe* Rossini
Neptune/Nettuno bt *Acis et Galatée* Lully; bt *Alcyone* Marais; b *Hippolyte et Aricie* Rameau; hc *Naïs* Rameau; b *Il pomo d'oro* Cesti; b *Il ritorno d'Ulisse* Monteverdi
Neraea s *Deidamia* Handel
Nereo t *Mefistofele* Boito

Nerestano **a** *Zaira* Bellini
Neri Chiaramantesi **bt** *La cena delle beffe* Giordano
Nerillo **s** *Ormindo* Cavalli
Nerina **s** *La fedeltà premiata* Haydn; **s** *Le pescatrici* Haydn
Nérine **hc** *Les fêtes vénitiennes* Campra
Neris/Néris **ms** *Médée* Cherubini
Nero/Nerone **s** *Agrippina* Handel; **s** *L'incoronazione di Poppea* Monteverdi; **t** *Nerone* Boito; **t** *Nerone* Mascagni; **b** *Octavia* Keiser
Nettchen **s** *Kleider machen Leute* Zemlinsky
Nettuno: *see* Neptune
Nevers, Count **bt** *Les Huguenots* Meyerbeer
New Prioress: *see* Lidoine, Madame
Newspaper Clerk **b** *The Nose* Shostakovich
Nezhata **a** *Sadko* Rimsky-Korsakov
Nicander/Nicandro **b** *Atalanta* Handel
Niccolò d'Este **bt** *Parisina* Mascagni
Nicette **s** *Le pré aux Clercs* Hérold
Nicholas I, Tsar **b** *The Decembrists* Shaporin
Nicia **b** *Der geduldige Socrates* Telemann
Nicias **t** *Thaïs* Massenet
Nick **t** *La fanciulla del West* Puccini
Nick Shadow **bt** *The Rake's Progress* Stravinsky
Nicklausse **ms** *Les contes d'Hoffmann* Offenbach
Nicola **bt** *Nozze istriane* Smareglia
Nicolas **a/t** *Bomarzo* Ginastera
Nicoletta **ms** *The Love for Three Oranges* Prokofiev
Nicomedes/Nicomede **s** *Mitridate Eupatore* Scarlatti
Niels Lyhne **bt** *Fennimore and Gerda* Delius
Nightingale **s** *The Nightingale* Stravinsky
Nightwatchman **b** *Maskarade* Nielsen; **b** *Die Meistersinger von Nürnberg* Wagner
Nika Magadoff: *see* Magician
Nikita: *see* Big Prisoner
Niklas **sp** *Hans Heiling* Marschner
Nikona **ms** *Siberia* Giordano
Nilakantha **bb** *Lakmé* Delibes
Nils **t** *Irmelin* Delius
Nina **s** *Chérubin* Massenet; **s** *Nina* Paisiello
Ninetta **s** *La finta semplice* Mozart; **s** *La gazza ladra* Rossini; **s** *The Love for Three Oranges* Prokofiev; **a** *Les vêpres siciliennes* Verdi
Nino **s** *Astarto* Bononcini, G.
Ninon **a** *The Devils of Loudun* Penderecki
Nirenus/Nireno **a** *Giulio Cesare in Egitto* Handel
Nisa **s** *La zingara* Rinaldo da Capua
Nixon **bt** *Nixon in China* Adams
Nixon, Pat **s** *Nixon in China* Adams
Njegus **sp** *Die lustige Witwe* Lehár
Noboru **t** *Das verratene Meer* Henze
Noctambulist **t** *Louise* Charpentier, G.
Noémie **s** *Cendrillon* Massenet
Nolan, Mrs **ms** *The Medium* Menotti
Nonancourt **b** *Il cappello di paglia di Firenze* Rota
Nora **s** *Riders to the Sea* Vaughan Williams
Norfolk **t** *Elisabetta, regina d'Inghilterra* Rossini
Norina **s** *Don Pasquale* Donizetti
Norma **s** *Norma* Bellini
Normanno **t** *Lucia di Lammermoor* Donizetti
Norns **a** *Götterdämmerung* Wagner
Norton **b** *La cambiale di matrimonio* Rossini
Norwich, Recorder of **b** *Gloriana* Britten
Nose **t** *The Nose* Shostakovich
Notary **b** *Don Pasquale* Donizetti
Nottingham, Duke of **bt** *Roberto Devereux* Donizetti
Nottingham, Sara/Sarah, Duchess of **ms** *Roberto Devereux* Donizetti
Nourabad **b** *Les pêcheurs de perles* Bizet
Nourmahal/Nurmahal **s** *Nurmahal* Spontini
Novice **t** *Billy Budd* Britten
Nun of Monza **ms** *I promessi sposi* Ponchielli
Nureddin **t** *Der Barbier von Bagdad* Cornelius
Nuri **s** *Tiefland* d'Albert
Nurmahal: *see* Nourmahal
Nurse/Nutrice **ms** *Boris Godunov* Musorgsky; **t** *La finta pazza* Sacrati; **ms** *Die Frau ohne Schatten* Strauss, R.; **a** *L'incoronazione di Poppea* Monteverdi; **a** *Violanta* Korngold

O

Oberon **ct** *A Midsummer Night's Dream* Britten; **t** *Oberon* Weber
Oberthal, Count **b** *Le prophète* Meyerbeer
Oberto **tr** *Alcina* Handel; **b** *Oberto* Verdi
Obrist **b** *Die Soldaten* Zimmermann
Ochs auf Lerchanau, Baron **b** *Der Rosenkavalier* Strauss, R.
Octavia/Ottavia **s** *L'incoronazione di Poppea* Monteverdi; **s** *Octavia* Keiser
Octavian, Count Rofrano **s/ms** *Der Rosenkavalier* Strauss, R.
Octavio **t** *Giuditta* Lehár
Octavius Caesar **t** *Antony and Cleopatra* Barber
Odabella **s** *Attila* Verdi
Odoardo **t** *Ariodante* Handel; **t** *Die Feuersbrunst* Haydn; **t** *Don Procopio* Bizet
Oebalus **t** *Apollo et Hyacinthus* Mozart
Oedipus/Oedipe **bb** *Oedipe* Enescu; **b** *Oedipe à Colone* Sacchini; **t** *Oedipus rex* Stravinsky
Oenone/Ennone/Enone **s** *Hippolyte et Aricie* Rameau; **s** *Ippolito ed Aricia* Traetta; **s** *Il pomo d'oro* Cesti
Officer **t** *Cardillac* Hindemith
Okean-More/Sea King **b** *Sadko* Rimsky-Korsakov
Old Convict **b** *Lady Macbeth of the Mtsensk District* Shostakovich
Old Hebrew **b** *Samson et Dalila* Saint-Saëns
Old Lady **ms** *Candide* Bernstein
Old Prioress: *see* Croissy, Madame de
Old Woman **ms/a** *Der ferne Klang* Schreker; **ms** *We Come to the River* Henze
Oldřich Rokycanský **bt** *The Brandenburgers in Bohemia* Smetana
Olga **s** *Rusalka* Dargomïzhsky; **s** *The Story of a Real Man* Prokofiev; **a** *Yevgeny Onegin* Tchaikovsky
Olga Mirnova, Princess **ms** *The Decembrists* Shaporin
Olga Sukarov, Countess **s** *Fedora* Giordano
Olga Yur'yevna Tokmakova, Princess **s** *The Maid of Pskov* Rimsky-Korsakov
Olgar **t/hc** *Cythère assiégée* Gluck
Olim **bt** *Der Silbersee* Weill
Olimpia **ms** *Belfagor* Respighi
Olivier **bt** *Capriccio* Strauss
Olivo **bt** *Olivo e Pasquale* Donizetti
Ollendorf, Colonel **bb** *Der Bettelstudent* Millöcker
Olympia **s** *Les contes d'Hoffmann* Offenbach; **ms** *The Magic Opal* Albéniz
Olympia/Olimpie: *see* Aménaïs
Olympion **t** *The Ice Break* Tippett
Omar **b** *Abu Hassan* Weber
Omniscient Seashell **a** *Die ägyptische Helena* Strauss, R.
Ondrej **t** *The Whirlpool* Suchoň
Onoria: *see* Honoria
Opera Singer **s** *Cardillac* Hindemith
Ophelia/Ophélie **s** *Hamlet* Thomas
Opinion Publique **ms** *Orphée aux enfers* Offenbach
Oracle **b** *Idomeneo* Mozart
Oracle of the Dead/Hecate **s** *The Mask of Orpheus* Birtwistle
Orator: *see* Speaker
Orazia: *see* Horatia
Orazio: *see* Horatius
Orbazzano **b** *Tancredi* Rossini
Orcan **b** *Les Paladins* Rameau
Orcane **t** *Fetonte* Jommelli
Orco/Ogre **b** *Il piccolo Marat* Mascagni
Orcone **b** *Tigrane* Scarlatti
Ordow, Duke of **b** *Torvaldo e Dorliska* Rossini
Orestes/Orest/Oreste **a** *Astianatte* Bononcini, G.; **ms** *La belle Hélène* Offenbach; **bt** *Elektra* Strauss; **t** *Ermione* Rossini; **b** *Giasone* Cavalli; *Ifigenia in Tauride* Traetta; **bt** *Iphigénie en Tauride* Gluck
Orestes' Tutor **b** *Elektra* Strauss

Orfeo: *see* Orpheus
Orgando **s** *Amadigi di Gaula* Handel
Oriana **s** *Amadigi di Gaula* Handel
Oriane **s** *Amadis* Lully
Orimeno, Prince **s/ms** *Erismena* Cavalli
Orin **bt** *Mourning Becomes Electra* Levy
Orindo **a** *Admeto* Handel
Orlando **a** *Orlando* Handel; **t** *Orlando paladino* Haydn
Orlik **b** *Mazepa* Tchaikovsky
Orlofsky, Prince **ms** *Die Fledermaus* Strauss, J.
Orlova, Madame **ms** *The Decembrists* Shaporin
Ormindo **t** *Ormindo* Cavalli
Ormoena **s** *Octavia* Keiser
Ormondo **ct** *Arsinoe* Clayton; **b** *L'inganno felice* Rossini; **b** *Torvaldo e Dorliska* Rossini
Ormonte **b** *Partenope* Handel
Oroe **b** *Semiramide* Rossini
Oromasès **b** *Zaïs* Rameau; **b** *Zoroastre* Rameau
Orombello **t** *Beatrice di Tenda* Bellini
Oronte **t** *Alcina* Handel; **a** *Dori* Cesti; **b** *Floridante* Handel; **t** *I Lombardi* Verdi; **bt** *Médée* Charpentier, M.-A.; **a** *Riccardo Primo* Handel; **t** *Statira* Scarlatti
Orontea **s** *Orontea* Cesti
Orosmade **hc** *Zoroastre* Rameau
Orosmane, Sultan **b** *Zaira* Bellini
Oroveso **b** *Norma* Bellini
Orpheus/Orfeo/Orphée **t** *L'anima del filosofo* Haydn; **t** *Euridice* Peri; **t** *Euridice* Caccini; **bt** *Les malheurs d'Orphée* Milhaud; **bt** *The Mask of Orpheus* Birtwistle; **t** *Orfeo* Monteverdi; **a** *Orfeo ed Euridice* Gluck; **a** *Orfeo ed Euridice* Bertoni; **t** *Orphée aux enfers* Offenbach; **t** *Orphée et Eurydice* Gluck
Orsini, Gian Conrado: *see* Gian Conrado Orsini
Orsini, Maffio: *see* Maffio Orsini
Orsini, Paolo **b** *Rienzi* Wagner
Orsini, Pier Francesco: *see* Pier Francesco Orsini
Orsola **s** *Il campiello* Wolf-Ferrari
Ortel, Hermann **b** *Die Meistersinger von Nürnberg* Wagner
Ortensia **ms** *La pietra del paragone* Rossini
Ortensio: *see* Hortensius
Orth **b** *Die Bürgschaft* Weill
Ortlinde **s** *Die Walküre* Wagner
Ortrud **ms** *Lohengrin* Wagner
Ory, Count **t** *Le comte Ory* Rossini
Örzse **ms** *Háry János* Kodály
Osaka **t** *Iris* Mascagni
Oscar **s** *Un ballo in maschera* Verdi; **bt** *Barbe-bleue* Offenbach
Oscar Hubbard **bt** *Regina* Blitzstein
Osiride: *see* Amenophis
Osiris/Osiride **b** *Moïse et Pharaon* Rossini
Osman **t** *Almira* Handel; **b** *Les Indes galantes* Rameau; **t** *Ormindo* Cavalli
Osmin **b** *La caravane du Caire* Grétry; **b** *Die Entführung aus dem Serail* Mozart; **t** *L'incontro improvviso* Haydn; **t** *La rencontre imprévue* Gluck; **b** *Zaide* Mozart
Osmina, Sister **s** *Suor Angelica* Puccini
Osmino **t** *Il crociato in Egitto* Meyerbeer
Ostasio **bt** *Francesca da Rimini* Zandonai
Otello/Othello **t** *Otello* Rossini; **t** *Otello* Verdi
Otho/Ottone **a** *Agrippina* Handel; **ms** *L'incoronazione di Poppea* Monteverdi
Othon **hc/t** *Ariodant* Méhul
Ottavia: *see* Octavia
Ottavio, Don **t** *Don Giovanni* Mozart
Ottavio, Duca **t** *Don Giovanni* Gazzaniga
Otto **t** *Bánk bán* Erkel
Ottokar **bt** *Der Freischütz* Weber
Ottone **a** *Adelaide di Borgogna* Rossini; **a** *Griselda* Scarlatti; **s** *Griselda* Vivaldi; **a** *Ottone* Handel; *see also* Otho
Otumbo **t** *Alzira* Verdi
Ouf I, King **t** *L'étoile* Chabrier
Ourrias **bt** *Mireille* Gounod
Ovando **t** *Alzira* Verdi
Ovid **t** *Dafne* Gagliano
Ovlur **t** *Prince Igor* Borodin
Owen Wingrave: *see* Wingrave, Owen
Owl **a** *The Cunning Little Vixen* Janáček
Oxana **s** *Cherevichki* Tchaikovsky; **s** *Christmas Eve* Rimsky-Korsakov

P

Paco **t** *La vida breve* Falla
Pacuvio **bt** *La pietra del paragone* Rossini
Padmâvatî **a** *Padmâvatî* Roussel
Padre Guardiano **b** *La forza del destino* Verdi
Pagano **b** *I Lombardi* Verdi
Page **bt** *Amahl and the Night Visitors* Menotti
Page, Mrs/Reich, Frau **ms** *Die lustigen Weiber von Windsor* Nicolai
Page/Reich **b** *Die lustigen Weiber von Windsor* Nicolai
Pagliaccio: *see* Canio
Painter/Negro **t** *Lulu* Berg
Palémon **b** *Thaïs* Massenet
Palestrina, Giovanni Pierluigi da **t** *Palestrina* Pfitzner
Pallas/Pallade/Athena/Athene **s** *Cadmus et Hermione* Lully; **s** *The Judgment of Paris* Eccles, D. Purcell, Weldon; **s** *Paride ed Elena* Gluck; **s** *Il pomo d'oro* Cesti
Pallas/Pallante **b** *Agrippina* Handel
Palmatica **ms** *Der Bettelstudent* Millöcker
Palmide **s** *Il crociato in Egitto* Meyerbeer
Palmyra **s** *Koanga* Delius
Paloucký, Father **b** *The Kiss* Smetana
Pamela, Lady **ms** *Fra Diavolo* Auber
Pamina **s** *Die Zauberflöte* Mozart
Pamyre **s** *Le siège de Corinthe* Rossini
Pan **b** *Isis* Lully; **b** *Issé* Destouches
Panais **t** *The Greek Passion* Martinů
Panas **b** *Christmas Eve* Rimsky-Korsakov
Pancratius **b** *Der Wildschütz* Lortzing
Pandarus **t** *Troilus and Cressida* Walton
Pandolfe **b** *Cendrillon* Massenet
Pang **t** *Turandot* Puccini
Pangloss **bt** *Candide* Bernstein
Pan Golova/Village Head **b** *Cherevichki* Tchaikovsky
Pantaleon de Pachero, Don **b** *Die drei Pintos* Weber
Pantalis **ms** *Mefistofele* Boito
Pantalone **bt** *Le donne curiose* Wolf-Ferrari; **bt** *The Love for Three Oranges* Prokofiev; **b** *Turandot* Busoni
Pantasilea **ms** *Bomarzo* Ginastera
Panteley Melekhov **t** *Quiet Flows the Don* Dzerzhinsky
Panthous/Panthée **b** *Les Troyens* Berlioz
Pantúl **bt** *La donna serpente* Casella
Pao **t** *Der Kreidekreis* Zemlinsky
Paolino **t** *Il matrimonio segreto* Cimarosa
Paolo Albiani **b** *Simon Boccanegra* Verdi
Paolo il Bello **t** *Francesca da Rimini* Zandonai
Paolo, Viscount **bt** *La bohème* Leoncavallo
Paoluccia **s** *La buona figliuola* Piccinni
Papagena **s** *Die Zauberflöte* Mozart
Papageno **bt** *Die Zauberflöte* Mozart
Pappacoda **bt** *Eine Nacht in Venedig* Strauss, J.
Paquette **ms** *Candide* Bernstein
Paquiro **bt** *Goyescas* Granados
Parasha **s** *Mavra* Stravinsky
Parasya **s** *The Fair at Sorochintsï* Musorgsky
Paris/Paride/Pâris **t** *La belle Hélène* Offenbach; **a/b** *The Judgment of Paris* Eccles, D. Purcell, Weldon; **tr/t** *King Priam* Tippett; **s** *Paride ed Elena* Gluck; **t** *Il pomo d'oro* Cesti; **bt** *Roméo et Juliette* Gounod
Parisina **s** *Parisina* Donizetti
Parisina Malatesta **s** *Parisina* Mascagni
Parma, Duchess of **s** *Doktor Faust* Busoni
Parma, Duke of **t** *Doktor Faust* Busoni
Parmenione, Don **bt** *L'occasione fa il ladro* Rossini
Parmenon **t** *Les mariages samnites* Grétry
Parpignol **t** *La bohème* Puccini
Parséis **ms** *Esclarmonde* Massenet
Parsifal **t** *Parsifal* Wagner
Partenope **s** *Partenope* Handel

Pascoe **bb** *The Wreckers* Smyth
Pásek **t** *The Cunning Little Vixen* Janáček
Pasha **b** *La caravane du Caire* Grétry
Pasha Seid: *see* Seid, Pasha
Pasithea: *see* Thalia
Pásková, Mrs **s** *The Cunning Little Vixen* Janáček
Pasqua Polegana, Dona **t** *Il campiello* Wolf-Ferrari
Pasquale **t** *Olivo e Pasquale* Donizetti; **bt** *Orlando paladino* Haydn
Pasquale, Don **b** *Don Pasquale* Donizetti
Pasquariello **b** *Don Giovanni* Gazzaniga
Pastor **b** *Khovanshchina* Musorgsky
Patience **s** *Patience* Sullivan
Patroclus/Patrocle **b** *Iphigénie en Aulide* Gluck; **bt** *King Priam* Tippett
Paul **t** *Der Opernball* Heuberger; **t** *Die tote Stadt* Korngold
Paul, Prince **t** *La Grande-Duchesse de Gérolstein* Offenbach
Pauline **s** *The Gambler* Prokofiev; **a** *The Queen of Spades* Tchaikovsky; **s** *La vie parisienne* Offenbach
Pauline/Paolina **s** *Les martyrs/Poliuto* Donizetti
Peachum **b** *The Beggar's Opera*; **bt** *Die Dreigroschenoper* Weill
Peachum, Mrs **s** *The Beggar's Opera*; **a** *Die Dreigroschenoper* Weill
Peasant **b** *Die Kluge* Orff
Peaseblossom **tr** *A Midsummer Night's Dream* Britten
Pedrillo **t** *Die Entführung aus dem Serail* Mozart
Pedro **t** *Der Corregidor* Wolf; **s** *Don Quichotte* Massenet; **t** *Tiefland* d'Albert
Pedro, Don **b** *Béatrice et Bénédict* Berlioz; *Masagniello* Keiser
Pédro, Don **b** *L'Africaine* Meyerbeer
Pedro de Vargas, Don **bt** *Pepita Jiménez* Albéniz
Pedro Lopes **t** *Jessonda* Spohr
Pedro the Cruel, King **bt** *Maria Padilla* Donizetti
Peisander/Pisandre/Pisandro **bt** *Pénélope* Fauré; **t** *Il ritorno d'Ulisse in patria* Monteverdi; **bt** *Ulisse* Dallapiccola
Pelagio, Don **t** *La canterina* Haydn
Pelegrin **t** *New Year* Tippett
Peleus/Pelée/Peleo **bt** *Alcyone* Marais; **t** *Le nozze di Teti e di Peleo* Cavalli
Pelléas **bt** *Pelléas et Mélisande* Debussy
Pellerin **t** *Volo di notte* Dallapiccola
Pencho **t** *María del Carmen* Granados
Peneios **b** *Daphne* Strauss
Penelope/Pénélope **s** *Pénélope* Fauré; **s** *Il ritorno d'Ulisse in patria* Monteverdi; **s** *Ulisse* Dallapiccola
Penelope, Lady Rich **s** *Gloriana* Britten
Pennybank Bill: *see* Bill
Penthesilea, Queen **ms** *Penthesilea* Schoeck
Pentheus **bt** *The Bassarids* Henze
Pepa **ms** *Goyescas* Granados
Pepík **s** *The Cunning Little Vixen* Janáček
Pepita Jiménez **s** *Pepita Jiménez* Albéniz
Peppe **t** *Rita* Donizetti
Percy **t** *Anna Bolena* Donizetti
Perez, Simon **t** *Koanga* Delius
Perfil'yevna **ms** *The Maid of Pskov* Rimsky-Korsakov
Peri **t** *Il Guarany* Gomes
Périchole **s** *La Périchole* Offenbach
Pernille **s** *Maskarade* Nielsen
Perrucchetto, Count **bt** *La fedeltà premiata* Haydn
Persephone **s** *Alceste* Lully; **s** *Euridice* Peri; **s** *Orfeo* Monteverdi; **s** *Il pomo d'oro* Cesti; **s** *Proserpine* Lully
Perseus/Persée **hc** *Persée* Lully
Pestel', Pavel **b** *The Decembrists* Shaporin
Peter Ivanov **t** *Zar und Zimmermann* Lortzing
Peter Niles **bt** *Mourning Becomes Electra* Levy
Peter Schlemil **bt** *Les contes d'Hoffmann* Offenbach
Peter the Great **b** *L'étoile du Nord* Meyerbeer; **bt** *Zar und Zimmermann* Lortzing
Peter: *see* Father
Peters **b** *L'amor coniugale* Mayr
Petr **b** *Armida* Dvořák
Petruchio **bt** *Der widerspänstigen Zähmung* Goetz
Petur bán **bb** *Bánk bán* Erkel
Phaedra/Fedra/Phèdre **ms** *Fedra* Pizzetti; **s** *Hippolyte et Aricie* Rameau; **s** *Ippolito ed Aricia* Traetta
Phaethon/Fetonte/Phaëton **s** *Fetonte* Jommelli; **hc** *Phaëton* Lully
Phani **s** *Les Indes galantes* Rameau
Phantase **t** *Atys* Lully
Phanuel **b** *Hérodiade* Massenet
Phaon **t** *Sapho* Gounod
Pharaoh/Faraone/Pharaon **b** *Moïse et Pharaon* Rossini; **b** *Mosè in Egitto* Rossini
Pharnaces/Farnace **a** *Mitridate* Mozart; **t** *Mitridate Eupatore* Scarlatti
Phébé: *see* Phoebe
Phèdre: *see* Phaedra
Phénice **s** *Armide* Lully; **s** *Armide* Gluck; **a** *Déjanire* Saint-Saëns
Philemon/Philémon **t** *Philémon et Baucis* Gounod; **t** *Philemon und Baucis* Haydn; *see also* Apollo
Philine **s** *Mignon* Thomas
Philip **t** *Agnes von Hohenstaufen* Spontini
Philip, King of France **bt** *Agnes von Hohenstaufen* Spontini
Philip, Sir: *see* Wingrave, Sir Philip
Philip II, King **b** *Don Carlos* Verdi
Philippe **s** *The Devils of Loudun* Penderecki; **t** *A Dinner Engagement* Berkeley
Philoctetes/Philoctète **bt** *Déjanire* Saint-Saëns
Philosophe **b** *Chérubin* Massenet
Phineus/Phinée **bt** *Persée* Lully
Phobétor **b** *Atys* Lully
Phoebe **s** *Rosina* Shield; **ms** *The Yeomen of the Guard* Sullivan
Phoebe/Phébé **s** *Castor et Pollux* Rameau
Phoenicius/Fenicio **b** *Ermione* Rossini
Phoenix/Fenice **b** *Deidamia* Handel
Phorbas **bt** *Alcyone* Marais; **b** *Oedipe* Enescu
Phorcas, Emperor of Byzantium **b** *Esclarmonde* Massenet
Phyllis **s** *Iolanthe* Sullivan
Physician **b** *Der arme Heinrich* Pfitzner
Pia **s** *Pia de' Tolomei* Donizetti
Piacere/Pleasure **a** *Rappresentatione di Anima, et di Corpo* Cavalieri
Piccolo Marat: *see* Fleury, Prince of
Pick, Frau **a** *Neues vom Tage* Hindemith
Piedmontese **t** *Friedenstag* Strauss, R.
Pier Francesco Orsini **t** *Bomarzo* Ginastera
Pierotto **ms** *Linda di Chamounix* Donizetti
Pierre **t** *The Wandering Scholar* Holst
Pierre Bezukhov **t** *War and Peace* Prokofiev
Pierrino **t** *Giuditta* Lehár
Pierrot **t** *Der Kaiser von Atlantis* Ullmann; **t** *Le tableau parlant* Grétry
Piet the Pot **t** *Le Grand Macabre* Ligeti
Pietro **t** *Boccaccio* Suppé; **b** *La muette de Portici* Auber; **bt** *Simon Boccanegra* Verdi
Pietro Fléville **bb** *Andrea Chénier* Giordano
Pigmalion: *see* Pygmalion
Pilade: *see* Pylades
Pilgrim **bt** *The Pilgrim's Progress* Vaughan Williams
Pilpatoè **s** *Montezuma* Graun
Pimen **b** *Boris Godunov* Musorgsky
Pimpinone **b** *Pimpinone* Albinoni; **b** *Pimpinone* Telemann
Pinellino **b** *Gianni Schicchi* Puccini
Ping **bt** *Turandot* Puccini
Pinkerton, Lieutenant **t** *Madama Butterfly* Puccini
Pinkerton, Miss **s** *The Old Maid and the Thief* Menotti
Pinto de Fonseca, Don **b** *Die drei Pintos* Weber
Piper **bt** *Halka* Moniuszko
Pipetto **t** *L'ajo nell'imbarazzo* Donizetti
Pippo **a** *La gazza ladra* Rossini
Piquillo **t** *La Périchole* Offenbach
Pirate **t** *Oberon* Weber
Pirate King **bt** *The Pirates of Penzance* Sullivan
Pirro **b** *I Lombardi* Verdi; *see also* Pyrrhus
Pirzel **t** *Die Soldaten* Zimmermann
Pisandre, Pisandro: *see* Peisander
Pisandro: *see* Peisander
Pisani **t** *Il bravo* Mercadante
Piso **t** *Octavia* Keiser
Pistofolo **b** *La molinara* Paisiello

Pistol/Pistola **bt** *At the Boar's Head* Holst; **b** *Falstaff* Verdi
Pitho **t** *Der geduldige Socrates* Telemann
Pitichinaccio **t** *Les contes d'Hoffmann* Offenbach
Pitti-Sing **ms** *The Mikado* Sullivan
Pius IV, Pope **b** *Palestrina* Pfitzner
Pizarro, Don **bb** *Fidelio* Beethoven
Plataea/Platée **hc** *Platée* Rameau
Platon Karatayev **t** *War and Peace* Prokofiev
Player **sp** *The Beggar's Opera*
Plaza-Toro, Duchess of **a** *The Gondoliers* Sullivan
Plaza-Toro, Duke of **bt** *The Gondoliers* Sullivan
Pleasure: *see* Piacere
Plumkett **b** *Martha* Flotow
Pluto/Pluton/Plutone **b** *Alceste* Lully; **b** *L'anima del filosofo* Haydn; **t** *Euridice* Peri; **b** *Hippolyte et Aricie* Rameau; **b** *Naïs* Rameau; **b** *Le nozze di Teti e di Peleo* Cavalli; **b** *Orfeo* Monteverdi; **t** *Orphée aux enfers* Offenbach; **b** *Il pomo d'oro* Cesti; **bt** *Proserpine* Lully
Poacher: *see* Harašta
Podesta **b** *Die Gezeichneten* Schreker
Podestà: *see* Gottardo
Podestà/Anchise, Don **t** *La finta giardiniera* Mozart
Podestat/Mayor **bt** *Le docteur Miracle* Bizet
Podtochina, Pelageya **ms** *The Nose* Shostakovich
Poet **b** *Prima la musicae poi le parole* Salieri
Pogner, Veit **b** *Die Meistersinger von Nürnberg* Wagner
Poins **b** *At the Boar's Head* Holst
Point, Jack **bt** *The Yeomen of the Guard* Sullivan
Poisson **t** *Adriana Lecouvreur* Cilea
Policare, King of Lydia **a** *Tigrane* Scarlatti
Police Agent **b** *The Consul* Menotti
Police Chief **bt** *Lady Macbeth of the Mtsensk District* Shostakovich
Police Commissioner **sp** *Lulu* Berg
Police Inspector **t** *The Nose* Shostakovich; **b** *Der Rosenkavalier* Strauss, R.
Police Officer **bb** *Cardillac* Hindemith; **b** *Il Signor Bruschino* Rossini
Policeman **b** *The Boatswain's Mate* Smyth; **bt** *Les mamelles de Tirésias* Poulenc
Polidartes/Polidarte **b** *Giustino* Handel
Polidoro **t** *La finta semplice* Mozart; **b** *L'italiana in Londra* Cimarosa; **b** *Zelmira* Rossini
Polinesso **a** *Ariodante* Handel; **t** *Ginevra di Scozia* Mayr
Polinius/Polinio **s** *Scipione affricano* Cavalli
Polissena **s** *Radamisto* Handel
Polkan, Commander **b** *The Golden Cockerel* Rimsky-Korsakov
Pollione **t** *Norma* Bellini
Pollux **b** *Castor et Pollux* Rameau; **t** *Die Liebe der Danae* Strauss, R.
Polly **s** *The Beggar's Opera*; **s** *Die Dreigroschenoper* Weill
Polonius **b** *Hamlet* Thomas
Polybius/Polibio **b** *Demetrio e Polibio* Rossini
Polyeucte/Poliuto **t** *Les martyrs/Poliuto* Donizetti
Polyhymnia/Polymnie **s** *Les boréades* Rameau
Polynices/Polynice **t** *Oedipe à Colone* Sacchini
Polyphemus/Poliphème **b** *Acis and Galatea* Handel; **bt** *Acis et Galatée* Lully
Polyxena/Polyxène **s** *Les Troyens* Berlioz
Pommersfelden **b** *Mathis der Maler* Hindemith
Pompeo **bt** *Benvenuto Cellini* Berlioz
Pomponio Storione, Don **b** *La gazzetta* Rossini
Pomponnet **t** *La fille de Madame Angot* Lecocq
Pong **t** *Turandot* Puccini
Pontifex Maximus **b** *La vestale* Spontini
Pooh-Bah **bt** *The Mikado* Sullivan
Popolani **bt** *Barbe-bleue* Offenbach
Popova **ms** *The Bear* Walton
Poppaea/Poppea **s** *Agrippina* Handel; **s** *L'incoronazione di Poppea* Monteverdi
Porgy **bb** *Porgy and Bess* Gershwin
Porsena/Porsenna **a** *Costanza e Fortezza* Fux; **b** *Muzio Scevola* Handel
Porus/Poro **a** *Poro* Handel
Posa, Marquis of/Rodrigo/Rodrigue **bt** *Don Carlos* Verdi
Pöschel **bb** *Feuersnot* Strauss, R.
Pottenstein, Count Gustl von **t** *Das Land des Lächelns* Lehár
Poussette **s** *Manon* Massenet
Povarikha **s** *The Tale of Tsar Saltan* Rimsky-Korsakov
Poyarok, Fyodor **bt** *Legend of the Invisible City of Kitezh* Rimsky-Korsakov
Přmysl ze Stadic **t** *Libuše* Smetana
Přmysl, Duke **bt** *Šárka* Fibich
Prascovia **s** *L'étoile du Nord* Meyerbeer
Praskov'ya Osipovna **s** *The Nose* Shostakovich
Predslav **t** *Svätopluk* Suchoň
Prefect **b** *Linda di Chamounix* Donizetti
Prelate **bt** *Friedenstag* Strauss, R.
Premier Ministre **b** *Cendrillon* Massenet
Prenesto **s** *Il trionfo di Camilla* Bononcini, G.
Presto **bt** *Les mamelles de Tirésias* Poulenc
Pretender/Grigory/Dmitry **t** *Boris Godunov* Musorgsky
Pretty Polly **s** *Punch and Judy* Birtwistle
Preziosilla **ms** *La forza del destino* Verdi
Priam **bb** *King Priam* Tippett; **b** *Les Troyens* Berlioz
Priest **t** *Il contrabbasso* Bucchi; **b** *The Cunning Little Vixen* Janáček; **bt** *From the House of the Dead* Janáček; **b** *Hercules* Handel; **b** *Moses und Aron* Schoenberg
Priest-Confessor **ct** *Taverner* Maxwell Davies
Prilepa **s** *The Queen of Spades* Tchaikovsky
Prima Donna/Ariadne **s** *Ariadne auf Naxos* Strauss, R.
Prince **bt** *The Cunning Peasant* Dvořák; **t** *The Love for Three Oranges* Prokofiev; **t** *Rusalka* Dargomïzhsky; **t** *Rusalka* Dvořák
Prince Charmant/Charming **s** *Cendrillon* Massenet
Prince/Manservant/Marquis **t** *Lulu* Berg
Princess **s** *Il contrabbasso* Bucchi; **s** *The Cunning Peasant* Dvořák; **s** *The Devil and Kate* Dvořák; **s** *L'enfant et les sortilèges* Ravel; **ms** *Rusalka* Dargomïzhsky; **a** *Suor Angelica* Puccini
Princess's Father **b** *Il contrabbasso* Bucchi
Prior **b** *Le jongleur de Nôtre-Dame* Massenet; **b** *La straniera* Bellini
Prison Chaplain **bt** *Der Prozess* von Einem
Prison Governor **b** *From the House of the Dead* Janáček; **b** *Die Kluge* Orff; **b** *Siberia* Giordano
Prisoner **bt** *Il prigioniero* Dallapiccola
Procida, Jean **b** *Les vêpres siciliennes* Verdi
Proclo **b** *Le convenienze teatrali* Donizetti
Procopio, Don **b** *Don Procopio* Bizet
Proculejus **a** *Cleopatra* Mattheson
Producer **t** *Un re in ascolto* Berio
Professor **bt** *Hin und zurück* Hindemith
Professor of Medicine/Banker/Professor **sp/b/x** *Lulu* Berg
Profondo, Don **b** *Il viaggio a Reims* Rossini
Prosdocimo **b** *Il turco in Italia* Rossini
Prosecuting Counsel **bb** *The English Cat* Henze
Proserpina, Proserpine: *see* Persephone
Prospero **bb** *Un re in ascolto* Berio
Prostitute **ms** *From the House of the Dead* Janáček
Protagonist **s** *Un re in ascolto* Berio
Proteus/Protée **bt** *Phaëton* Lully
Prothoe **s** *Penthesilea* Schoeck
Prunier **t** *La Rondine* Puccini
Prus, Baron **bt** *The Makropulos Affair* Janáček
Psyche, Lady **ms** *Princess Ida* Sullivan
Ptolemy/Ptolemaeus/Tolomeo **a** *Cleopatra* Mattheson; **a** *Giulio Cesarein Egitto* Handel; **a** *Tolomeo* Handel
Publia **ms** *Aureliano in Palmira* Rossini
Publius/Publio **b** *La clemenza di Tito* Mozart; **t** *Il sogno di Scipione* Mozart
Publius Valerius/Publio Valerio **b** *Costanza e Fortezza* Fux
Puck **x** *A Midsummer Night's Dream* Britten; **ms** *Oberon* Weber
Puck, Prince **bt** *La Grande-Duchesse de Gérolstein* Offenbach
Puff, Lord **t** *The English Cat* Henze
Pulcheria **s** *Riccardo Primo* Handel
Pulcherio **t** *Lo sposo deluso* Mozart
Punch **bt** *Punch and Judy* Birtwistle
Puntila **b** *Puntila* Dessau
Puntila, Johannes **b** *Puntila* Dessau

Pygmalion/Pigmalion **hc** *Pigmalion* Rameau; **t** *Die schöne Galathée* Suppé
Pylades/Pilade **a** *Astianatte* Bononcini, G.; **t** *Ermione* Rossini; **s** *Ifigenia in Tauride* Traetta; **t** *Iphigénie en Tauride* Gluck
Pyrrhus/Pirro **ms** *Astianatte* Bononcini, G.; **t** *Ermione* Rossini
Pythéas **b** *Sapho* Gounod

Q

Queen **ms** *Švanda the Bagpiper* Weinberger; *see also* Gertrude, Queen
Queen of Night **s** *Die Zauberflöte* Mozart
Queen of the Earth Spirits **s** *Hans Heiling* Marschner
Queen of the Gypsies **s** *The Bohemian Girl* Balfe
Quichotte, Don **b** *Don Quichotte* Massenet
Quickly, Mistress **ms** *Falstaff* Verdi
Quimper-Karadec, Madame de **ms** *La vie parisienne* Offenbach
Quinault **b** *Adriana Lecouvreur* Cilea
Quince **b** *A Midsummer Night's Dream* Britten
Quinquin: *see* Octavian
Quint, Peter **t** *The Turn of the Screw* Britten

R

Rachel **s** *La Juive* Halévy; **s** *We Come to the River* Henze
Rachelina **s** *La molinara* Paisiello
Radames **t** *Aida* Verdi
Radamisto **s** *Radamisto* Handel
Radio Operator **t** *Volo di notte* Dallapiccola
Radmila **a** *Libuše* Smetana
Radovan **bt** *Libuše* Smetana
Rafaele **bt** *I gioielli della Madonna* Wolf-Ferrari
Raffaele von Leuthold **t** *Stiffelio* Verdi
Ragonde **ms** *Le comte Ory* Rossini
Raimbaud **bt** *Le comte Ory* Rossini
Raimbaut **t** *Robert le diable* Meyerbeer
Raimondo **b** *Matilde di Shabran* Rossini
Raimondo Bidebent **b** *Lucia di Lammermoor* Donizetti
Raimondo, Cardinal **b** *Rienzi* Wagner
Rakewell, Tom **t** *The Rake's Progress* Stravinsky
Raleigh, Sir Walter/Gualtiero **b** *Gloriana* Britten; **t** *Merrie England* German; **b** *Roberto Devereux* Donizetti
Ralph **b/bt** *La jolie fille de Perth* Bizet
Ralph Rackstraw **t** *HMS Pinafore* Sullivan
Ram **b** *Renard* Stravinsky
Rambaldo **b** *Griselda* Bononcini, G.
Rambaldo Fernandez **bt** *La Rondine* Puccini
Ramerrez: *see* Johnson, Dick
Ramfis **b** *Aida* Verdi
Ramiro **t** *La Cenerentola* Rossini; **ms** *La finta giardiniera* Mozart; **bt** *L'heure espagnole* Ravel
Ramisa/Ramise **a** *Arminio* Handel
Ramla, Emir of **b** *Jérusalem* Verdi
Ramon, Maître **b** *Mireille* Gounod
Rance, Jack **bt** *La fanciulla del West* Puccini
Randy Curtis **bt** *Lady in the Dark* Weill
Rangier **b** *The Devils of Loudun* Penderecki
Rangoni **b** *Boris Godunov* Musorgsky
Raoul **a/t** *Gabriella di Vergy* Donizetti
Raoul de Nangis **t** *Les Huguenots* Meyerbeer
Rarach **b** *The Devil's Wall* Smetana
Ratan-Sen **t** *Padmâvatî* Roussel
Ratcliffe, Lieutenant **b** *Billy Budd* Britten
Ratmir **a** *Ruslan and Lyudmila* Glinka
Raymond **t** *Jérusalem* Verdi; **t** *The Maid of Orléans* Tchaikovsky
Raymondo **b** *Almira* Handel
Rebecca **s** *Der Templer und die Jüdin* Marschner
Rector: *see* Horace Adams, Rev.
Red Whiskers **t** *Billy Budd* Britten
Redburn, Mr **bt** *Billy Budd* Britten
Reede **b** *Arden must Die* Goehr
Regan **s** *Lear* Reimann; **s** *New Year* Tippett
Regina **s** *Mathis der Maler* Hindemith
Regina Giddens **s** *Regina* Blitzstein
Reich, Frau: *see* Page, Mrs
Reich: *see* Page
Reinmar von Zweter **b** *Tannhäuser* Wagner
Reiza **s** *Oberon* Weber
Remendado **t** *Carmen* Bizet
Remenyuk **b** *Semyon Kotko* Prokofiev
Remigio **b** *La Navarraise* Massenet
Remus **t** *Treemonisha* Joplin
Renata **s** *The Fiery Angel* Prokofiev
Renato/Anckarstroem **bt** *Un ballo in maschera* Verdi
Renaud **hc** *Armide* Lully; **t** *Armide* Gluck
René, King **b** *Iolanta* Tchaikovsky
Renzo **t** *I promessi sposi* Ponchielli
Repela **b** *Der Corregidor* Wolf
Řeřicha **b** *The Stubborn Lovers* Dvořák
Resi **s** *Intermezzo* Strauss, R.
Reuterholm, Baron **b** *Tintomara* Werle
Rezia **s** *L'incontro improvviso* Haydn
Rézia **s** *La rencontre imprévue* Gluck
Ribbing/Samuel **b** *Un ballo in maschera* Verdi
Riccardo **t** *Oberto* Verdi; **s** *Il trionfo dell'onore* Scarlatti
Riccardo, Count de Chalais **t** *Maria di Rohan* Donizetti
Riccardo, Don **t** *Ernani* Verdi
Riccardo, Sir **t** *I quatro rusteghi* Wolf-Ferrari
Riccardo Forth, Sir **b** *I puritani* Bellini
Riccardo/Gustavus III **t** *Un ballo in maschera* Verdi
Ricciardo **t** *Ricciardo e Zoraide* Rossini
Rich, Lady: *see* Penelope
Richard Dauntless **t** *Ruddigore* Sullivan
Richard I/Richard the Lionheart/Black Knight/Riccardo **a** *Riccardo Primo* Handel; **t** *Richard Coeur-de-lion* Grétry; **b** *Der Templer und die Jüdin* Marschner
Richard Taverner **bt** *Taverner* Maxwell Davies
Ricimer **bt** *Ernelinde* Philidor
Riedinger **b** *Mathis der Maler* Hindemith
Rienzi, Cola **t** *Rienzi* Wagner
Riff **bt** *West Side Story* Bernstein
Rigoletto **bt** *Rigoletto* Verdi
Říhová **a** *The Stubborn Lovers* Dvořák
Rïleyev, Kondraty **bt** *The Decembrists* Shaporin
Rimenes **t** *Artaxerxes* Arne
Rinald/Rinaldo **t** *Armida* Haydn; **t** *Armida* Rossini; **t** *Armida* Dvořák; **s** *Armida abbandonata* Jommelli; **s** *Il filosofo di campagna* Galuppi; **ms** *Rinaldo* Handel
Rinuccio **t** *Gianni Schicchi* Puccini
Rita **s** *Rita* Donizetti
Rivière **bb** *Volo di notte* Dallapiccola
Rizzardo del Maino **t** *Beatrice di Tenda* Bellini
Robert **t** *Hin und zurück* Hindemith; **bt** *Iolanta* Tchaikovsky; *see also* Storch, Robert
Robert de Loris **t** *Etienne Marcel* Saint-Saëns
Robert le diable **t** *Robert le diable* Meyerbeer
Roberto **s** *Griselda* Scarlatti; **s** *Griselda* Vivaldi; **t** *Torquato Tasso* Donizetti; **t** *Le villi* Puccini
Roberto/Nardo **bt** *La finta giardiniera* Mozart
Robert/Roberto **bt** *Les vêpres siciliennes* Verdi
Robert/Roberto Devereux: *see* Essex, Earl of
Robespierre **t** *Dantons Tod* von Einem
Robin Oakapple/Ruthven Murgatroyd **bt** *Ruddigore* Sullivan
Robineau **b** *Volo di notte* Dallapiccola
Robinet **t** *Colas Breugnon* Kabalevsky
Robinson **t** *Robinson Crusoé* Offenbach
Robinson, Count **b** *Il matrimonio segreto* Cimarosa
Rocco **b** *Fidelio* Beethoven
Rochefort **b** *Anna Bolena* Donizetti
Rodelinda **s** *Rodelinda* Handel
Roderick Dhu/Rodrigo **t** *La donna del lago* Rossini
Roderigo **t** *Otello* Verdi
Rodimarte **b** *Il trionfo dell'onore* Scarlatti
Rodisette **s** *Der geduldige Socrates* Telemann
Rodoald **b** *Ernelinde* Philidor
Rodolfo **t** *La bohème* Puccini; **bt** *La bohème* Leoncavallo; **t** *Luisa Miller* Verdi; **b** *La rosa bianca e la rosa rossa* Mayr;

b *La sonnambula* Bellini
Rodolphe **b** *Les fêtes vénitiennes* Campra; **t** *Guillaume Tell* Rossini; **t** *La nonne sanglante* Gounod
Rodomonte **b** *Orlando paladino* Haydn
Rodrigo **t** *Otello* Rossini; **ms** *Pia de' Tolomei* Donizetti; **s** *Rodrigo* Handel; **t** *Sancia di Castiglia* Donizetti; *see also* Roderick Dhu
Rodrigo, Don **t** *Don Rodrigo* Ginastera; **bt** *I promessi sposi* Ponchielli
Rodrigue/Cid **t** *Le Cid* Massenet
Rodrigue/Rodrigo: *see* Posa, Marquis of
Rodriguez **t** *Don Quichotte* Massenet
Rofrano, Count: *see* Octavian
Roger **b** *Jérusalem* Verdi
Roger II, King **bt** *King Roger* Szymanowski
Roi: *see* King
Roland **bt** *Fierrabras* Schubert; **bt** *Roland* Lully; **b** *Roland* Piccinni
Roland de Blois **t** *Esclarmonde* Massenet
Rolando **bt** *La battaglia di Legnano* Verdi; **b** *La caverne* Le Sueur; **b** *Gemma di Vergy* Donizetti
Roldano Ximenes **b** *Cristoforo Colombo* Franchetti
Rolf **bb** *Irmelin* Delius
Rolla **t** *I masnadieri* Verdi
Romeo/Roméo **ms** *I Capuleti e i Montecchi* Bellini; **s** *Giulietta e Romeo* Zingarelli; **a** *Giulietta e Romeo* Vaccai; **t** *Giulietta e Romeo* Zandonai; **t** *Roméo et Juliette* Gounod
Romilda **s** *Serse* Handel; **s** *Xerse* Cavalli; **s** *Xerse* Bononcini, G.
Romualdo, Don **b** *Emilia di Liverpool* Donizetti
Rosa Mamai **s** *L'arlesiana* Cilea
Rosalie **s** *Doktor und Apotheker* Dittersdorf
Rosalinde **s** *Die Fledermaus* Strauss, J.
Rosario **s** *Goyescas* Granados
Rosaura **s** *Le donne curiose* Wolf-Ferrari
Röschen **ms** *Faust* Spohr
Rose **s** *Lakmé* Delibes
Rose Maurrant **s** *Street Scene* Weill
Rose Maybud **s** *Ruddigore* Sullivan
Rose Parrowe **ms** *Taverner* Maxwell Davies
Rosette **ms** *Manon* Massenet
Rosimonda **ms** *Faramondo* Handel
Rosina **s** *Il barbiere di Siviglia* Paisiello; **a** *Il barbiere di Siviglia* Rossini; **s** *La finta semplice* Mozart; **s** *Rosina* Shield; **a** *Il trionfo dell'onore* Scarlatti; **s** *La vera costanza* Haydn; *see also* Almaviva, Countess
Rosine **s** *La mère coupable* Milhaud
Rosmene **s** *Imeneo* Handel
Rosmina **s** *Giasone* Cavalli
Rosmira **a** *Partenope* Handel
Rospolone, Don **b** *La molinara* Paisiello
Rossane **s** *Floridante* Handel; *see also* Roxana
Rossweisse **a** *Die Walküre* Wagner
Rostov, Count **bb** *War and Peace* Prokofiev
Rostovtsev **t** *The Decembrists* Shaporin
Rothsay, Duke of **bt** *La jolie fille de Perth* Bizet
Roucher **bb** *Andrea Chénier* Giordano
Rowan **s** *The Little Sweep* Britten
Rowena of Hargottstandstede **s** *Der Templer und die Jüdin* Marschner
Roxana/Rossane **s** *Alessandro* Handel; **s** *King Roger* Szymanowski
Róza, Miss **a** *The Secret* Smetana
Rozenn **s** *Le roi d'Ys* Lalo
Rozgonyi **bt** *Hunyadi László* Erkel
Ruben **t** *Joseph* Méhul
Rubria **ms** *Nerone* Boito
Rudolf **bb** *Der ferne Klang* Schreker
Rudolf II/Ferdinand II **b** *Die Harmonie der Welt* Hindemith
Ruggero Lastouc **t** *La Rondine* Puccini
Ruggiero **a** *Alcina* Handel; **bt** *La Juive* Halévy; **s** *Tancredi* Rossini
Ruiz, Don **t** *Maria Padilla* Donizetti
Ruprecht **bt** *The Fiery Angel* Prokofiev
Rusalka **s** *Rusalka* Dvořák
Ruslan **bt** *Ruslan and Lyudmila* Glinka
Russell Paxton **bt** *Lady in the Dark* Weill
Rustighello **t** *Il pirata* Bellini
Ruth **a** *The Pirates of Penzance* Sullivan
Ruthven, Lord **bt** *Der Vampyr* Marschner
Ruthven Murgatroyd: *see* Robin Oakapple
Ruy Diaz **bt** *Der Cid* Cornelius
Ryuji Tsukazaki **bt** *Das verratene Meer* Henze

S

Saba: *see* Sheba
Sabina **s** *Gli Orazi ed i Curiazi* Cimarosa
Sabinus/Sabino **s** *Giulio Sabino* Sarti
Saburova, Domna **s** *The Tsar's Bride* Rimsky-Korsakov
Sachs: *see* Hans Sachs
Sacristan **b** *Tosca* Puccini
Sacristan/Lunobor/Jan/Domšík **bb** *The Excursions of Mr Brouček* Janáček
Sadko **t** *Sadko* Rimsky-Korsakov
Sadomar **b** *Drottningen av Golconda* Berwald
Sáffi **s** *Der Zigeunerbaron* Strauss, J.
Sailor **s** *Dido and Aeneas* Purcell
St Brioche, Raoul de **bt** *Die lustige Witwe* Lehár
Saint-Bris, Count of **b** *Les Huguenots* Meyerbeer
St Corentin **bb** *Le roi d'Ys* Lalo
Saint-Just **b** *Dantons Tod* von Einem
Saint-Phar **t** *La caravane du Caire* Grétry; **bt** *Drottningen av Golconda* Berwald; *see also* Chapelou
Salammbô **s** *Salammbô* Musorgsky; **s** *Salammbô* Reyer
Sali **t** *A Village Romeo and Juliet* Delius
Salieri **bt** *Mozart and Salieri* Rimsky-Korsakov
Salome/Salomé **s** *Hérodiade* Massenet; **s** *Salome* Strauss, R.
Saltan, Tsar **b** *The Tale of Tsar Saltan* Rimsky-Korsakov
Saluces, Marquis **bt** *Grisélidis* Massenet
Salud **s** *La vida breve* Falla
Salviati: *see* Clement VII, Pope
Salvini **t** *Adelson e Salvini* Bellini
Sam **tr** *The Little Sweep* Britten; **bt** *A Quiet Place* Bernstein; **t** *Susannah* Floyd
Sam Kaplan **t** *Street Scene* Weill
Samaritana **s** *Francesca da Rimini* Zandonai
Samarkand, Queen Mother of **s** *Turandot* Busoni
Samiel **sp** *Der Freischütz* Weber
Samson **t** *Samson et Dalila* Saint-Saëns
Samuel **b** *Saul og David* Nielsen
Samuel/Ribbing **b** *Un ballo in maschera* Verdi
Sancho Panza **bb** *Don Quichotte* Massenet
Sancia **s** *Sancia di Castiglia* Donizetti
Sander **bt** *Zémire et Azor* Grétry
Sandman **s** *Hänsel und Gretel* Humperdinck
Sandomir **t** *Ernelinde* Philidor
Sandon **t** *Aniara* Blomdahl
Sándor Barinkay **t** *Der Zigeunerbaron* Strauss, J.
Sandrina **s** *La buona figliuola* Piccinni; **s** *L'infedeltà delusa* Haydn; *see also* Violante Onesti
Sangaride **s** *Atys* Lully
Sangazure, Lady **a** *The Sorcerer* Sullivan
Sans-Gêne, Mme: *see* Caterina Hubscher
Santuzza **s** *Cavalleria rusticana* Mascagni
Saphir **t** *Barbe-bleue* Offenbach
Sapho/Sappho **s** *Les fêtes d'Hébé* Rameau; **ms** *Sapho* Gounod; **s** *Sapho* Massenet; *see also* Fanny Legrand
Šapkin **t** *From the House of the Dead* Janáček
Sarah, Duchess of Nottingham: *see* Nottingham, Duchess of
Sarastro **b** *Die Zauberflöte* Mozart
Sardula **s** *Le dernier sauvage* Menotti
Šárka **s** *Šárka* Fibich
Sarvaor, Tio **b** *La vida breve* Falla
Sashka **b** *Quiet Flows the Don* Dzerzhinsky
Satyavān **t** *Sāvitri* Holst
Satyr **bt** *Platée* Rameau
Saul, King **bb** *Saul og David* Nielsen
Sāvitri **s** *Sāvitri* Holst
Scaramuccio **t** *Ariadne auf Naxos* Strauss, R.

Scarpia **bt** *Tosca* Puccini
Schaunard **bt** *La bohème* Puccini; **bt** *La bohème* Leoncavallo
Schigolch **b** *Lulu* Berg
Schmidt **b** *Andrea Chénier* Giordano; **t** *Werther* Massenet
Schneidebart/Barber **bt** *Die schweigsame Frau* Strauss, R.
Schön, Dr/Jack the Ripper **bt** *Lulu* Berg
Schoolmaster **t** *The Cunning Little Vixen* Janáček; *see also* Teacher
Schwalb **t** *Mathis der Maler* Hindemith
Schwarz, Hans **b** *Die Meistersinger von Nürnberg* Wagner
Schwertleite **a** *Die Walküre* Wagner
Sciarrone **b** *Tosca* Puccini
Scindia **bt** *Le roi de Lahore* Massenet
Scipio/Scipione **t** *La clemenza di Scipione* Bach, J. C.; **a** *Scipione* Handel; **s** *Scipione affricano* Cavalli; **t** *Il sogno di Scipione* Mozart
Scolatella **s** *König Hirsch* Henze
Scotland, King of **b** *Ariodante* Handel; **t** *Ginevra di Scozia* Mayr
Scratch, Mr **t** *The Devil and Daniel Webster* Moore
Scylla **s** *Scylla et Glaucus* Leclair
Sea King: *see* Okean-More
Seashell: *see* Omniscient Seashell
Sebastiano **bt** *Tiefland* d'Albert
Sébastien, Dom **t** *Dom Sébastien* Donizetti
Secretary **ms** *The Consul* Menotti
Sedley, Mrs **ms** *Peter Grimes* Britten
Segestes/Segeste **b** *Arminio* Handel
Seid, Pasha **bt** *Il corsaro* Verdi
Seide **t** *Alina, regina di Golconda* Donizetti
Sela **s** *Il diluvio universale* Donizetti
Selene **a** *Berenice* Handel
Seleuce **s** *Tolomeo* Handel
Sélika **s** *L'Africaine* Meyerbeer
Selim **b** *Il turco in Italia* Rossini
Selim, Pasha **sp** *Die Entführung aus dem Serail* Mozart
Selimo **t** *Adina* Rossini
Selina **ms** *Colas Breugnon* Kabalevsky
Sellem **t** *The Rake's Progress* Stravinsky
Selva **b** *La muette de Portici* Auber
Sélysette **ms** *Ariane et Barbe-bleue* Dukas
Semele **s** *Egisto* Cavalli; **s** *Semele* Handel
Semira **s** *Artaxerxes* Arne
Semiramide **s** *Semiramide* Rossini
Sémire **s** *Les boréades* Rameau
Sempronio **t** *Lo speziale* Haydn
Semyon **t** *Semyon Kotko* Prokofiev
Seneca **b** *L'incoronazione di Poppea* Monteverdi; **b** *Octavia* Keiser
Senta **s** *Der fliegende Holländer* Wagner
Ser Matteo: *see* Matteo del Sarto
Serafina **s** *Il campanello di notte* Donizetti
Séraphine **s** *La caverne* Le Sueur
Sergeant **bt** *Hugh the Drover* Vaughan Williams; **bt** *Der Prinz von Homburg* Henze
Sergeant of Police **b** *The Pirates of Penzance* Sullivan
Sergeich **b** *The Decembrists* Shaporin
Sergey **t** *Katerina Izmaylova/Lady Macbeth of the Mtsensk District* Shostakovich
Sergius Vladimir, Prince **bt** *Die Zirkusprinzessin* Kálmán
Serpetta **s** *La finta giardiniera* Mozart
Serpina **s** *La serva padrona* Pergolesi
Serse: *see* Xerxes
Servilia **s** *La clemenza di Tito* Mozart; **a** *Tito Manlio* Vivaldi
Sesto: *see* Sextus
Settimio **t** *Esule di Roma* Donizetti
Settlement, St **s** *Four Saints in Three Acts* Thomson
Sévère/Severo **bt** *Les martyrs/Poliuto* Donizetti
Severin **t** *Der Silbersee* Weill
Sextus/Sesto **s** *La clemenza di Tito* Mozart; **s** *Giulio Cesarein Egitto* Handel
Sganarelle **bt** *Le médecin malgré lui* Gounod
Shadbolt, Wilfred **b** *The Yeomen of the Guard* Sullivan
Shakebag **t** *Arden must Die* Goehr
Shaklovity **bt** *Khovanshchina* Musorgsky
Sharpless **bt** *Madama Butterfly* Puccini
Shchelkalov **bt** *Boris Godunov* Musorgsky
She-Ancient **ms** *The Midsummer Marriage* Tippett
Sheba/Saba, Queen of **ms** *Die Königin von Saba* Goldmark
Shelley **bt** *Lord Byron* Thomson
Shemakha, Queen of **s** *The Golden Cockerel* Rimsky-Korsakov
Shepherd **t** *King Roger* Szymanowski; **t** *Oedipe* Enescu; **t** *Oedipus rex* Stravinsky; **bt** *Pelléas et Mélisande* Debussy; **t** *Die toten Augen* d'Albert; **t** *Tristan und Isolde* Wagner
Shepherd-Boy **a** *Tosca* Puccini
Sherasmin **bt** *Oberon* Weber
Sheriff **b** *Martha* Flotow
Shuysky **t** *Boris Godunov* Musorgsky
Sibyl/Genio **s** *L'anima del filosofo* Haydn
Sichel **t** *Doktor und Apotheker* Dittersdorf
Sicle **s** *Ormindo* Cavalli
Sid **bt** *Albert Herring* Britten; **bt** *La fanciulla del West* Puccini
Sidney, Lord **b** *Il viaggio a Reims* Rossini
Sidonia **s** *Astarto* Bononcini, G.
Sidonie **s** *Armide* Lully; **s** *Armide* Gluck
Siébel **s** *Faust* Gounod
Siegfried **t** *Götterdämmerung* Wagner; **t** *Siegfried* Wagner
Siegfried, Count Palatine **bt** *Genoveva* Schumann
Sieglinde **s** *Die Walküre* Wagner
Siegmund **t** *Die Walküre* Wagner
Siegrune **ms** *Die Walküre* Wagner
Sieward **bt** *Alfred* Dvořák
Siface: *see* Syphax
Sifare: *see* Xiphares
Sigismond/Sigismondo **s** *Arminio* Handel
Sigismondo, King of Poland **a** *Sigismondo* Rossini
Sigurd **t** *Sigurd* Reyer
Silandra **s** *Orontea* Cesti
Silango (Tirsis) **t** *Le cinesi* Gluck
Silberklang, Mlle **s** *Der Schauspieldirektor* Mozart
Silla **ms** *Palestrina* Pfitzner; *see also* Sulla, Lucius
Silva, Don Ruy Gomez de **b** *Ernani* Verdi
Silvano/Christian **b** *Un ballo in maschera* Verdi
Silvia/Sylvia **s** *Ascanio in Alba* Mozart; **s** *L'isola disabitata* Haydn; **s** *Orfeo* Monteverdi
Silvio **t** *Arbore di Diana* Martín y Soler; **t** *Le docteur Miracle* Bizet; **bt** *Pagliacci* Leoncavallo; **a** *Il pastor fido* Handel
Silvio de Narni **bt** *Bomarzo* Ginastera
Siméon **t** *Joseph* Méhul
Simon **b** *Dantons Tod* von Einem
Simona Fabien **s** *Volo di notte* Dallapiccola
Simone **b** *La finta semplice* Mozart; **bt** *Eine florentinische Tragödie* Zemlinsky; **b** *Gianni Schicchi* Puccini
Simone Trovai **bt** *Violanta* Korngold
Simon Glover **b** *La jolie fille de Perth* Bizet
Simon Magus/Simon Mago **bt** *Nerone* Boito
Simonson **bt** *Risurrezione* Alfano
Simplicius **s** *Simplicius Simplicissimus* Hartmann
Sinais/Amaltea/Sinaïde **s** *Moïse et Pharaon* Rossini; **s** *Mosè in Egitto* Rossini
Singer **t** *Von heute auf morgen* Schoenberg
Sinodal **t** *The Demon* Rubinstein
Sintram **b** *I cavalieri di Ekebù* Zandonai
Siroco **b** *L'étoile* Chabrier
Siroe **a** *Siroe* Handel
Sirval, Viscount of: *see* Carlo
Sisera **t** *Dèbora e Jaéle* Pizzetti
Šiškov **bt** *From the House of the Dead* Janáček
Sister-in-law of Village Head **a** *May Night* Rimsky-Korsakov
Sitâ **s** *Le roi de Lahore* Massenet
Sivene (Licoris) **s** *Le cinesi* Gluck
Siveno **a** *Demetrio e Polibio* Rossini
Skołuba **b** *The Haunted Manor* Moniuszko
Skřivánek **t** *The Secret* Smetana
Skula **b** *Prince Igor* Borodin
Skuratov **t** *From the House of the Dead* Janáček
Sleep/Sonno **x** *Ercole amante* Cavalli
Slender/Spärlich **t** *Die lustigen Weiber von Windsor* Nicolai
Slim **t** *Paul Bunyan* Britten
Slook, Mr **b** *La cambiale di matrimonio* Rossini
Small Prisoner **bt** *From the House of the Dead* Janáček

Smeraldina **ms** *The Love for Three Oranges* Prokofiev
Smeton **ms** *Anna Bolena* Donizetti
Smirnov **bt** *The Bear* Walton
Snegurochka: *see* Snow Maiden
Snout **t** *A Midsummer Night's Dream* Britten
Snow Maiden/Snegurochka **s** *The Snow Maiden* Rimsky-Korsakov
Snug **b** *A Midsummer Night's Dream* Britten
Sobakin, Vasily **b** *The Tsar's Bride* Rimsky-Korsakov
Sobinin, Bogdan **t** *A Life for the Tsar* Glinka
Socrates **bt** *Der geduldige Socrates* Telemann
Sof'ya **s** *Semyon Kotko* Prokofiev
Sofia **s** *I Lombardi* Verdi; **s** *Il Signor Bruschino* Rossini
Sofonisba: *see* Sophonisba
Sofronia **s** *Gli equivoci* Storace
Soldier **t** *Der Kaiser von Atlantis* Ullmann; **t** *We Come to the River* Henze
Solicitor **bt** *Der Prozess* von Einem
Soliman, Sultan **bt** *Karl V* Krenek; **t** *Zaide* Mozart
Solinus **bt** *Gli equivoci* Storace
Solokha/Sorceress **ms** *Cherevichki* Tchaikovsky; **a** *Christmas Eve* Rimsky-Korsakov
Solomon/Soliman, King **bt** *Die Königin von Saba* Goldmark; **b** *La reine de Saba* Gounod
Somarone **b** *Béatrice et Bénédict* Berlioz
Somnus **b** *Semele* Handel
Sonetka **a** *Lady Macbeth of the Mtsensk District* Shostakovich
Sonia **ms** *The Aspern Papers* Argento
Sonja **s** *Der Zarewitsch* Lehár
Sonno: *see* Sleep
Sonora **bt** *La fanciulla del West* Puccini
Sonya **ms** *War and Peace* Prokofiev
Soothsayer **bt** *Le devin du village* Rousseau
Sophia **s** *Tom Jones* Philidor; **s** *Tom Jones* German
Sophie **s** *Der Rosenkavalier* Strauss, R.; **s** *Werther* Massenet
Sophonisba/Sofonisba **s** *Scipione affricano* Cavalli
Sorceress **bt/ms** *Dido and Aeneas* Purcell; *see also* Solokha
Sorel: *see* John Sorel
Sosarme **a** *Sosarme* Handel
Sosostris **a** *The Midsummer Marriage* Tippett
Sostrata **s** *Gli equivoci* Storace
Sou-Chong, Prince **t** *Das Land des Lächelns* Lehár
Soul: *see* Anima
Spalanzani **t** *Les contes d'Hoffmann* Offenbach
Sparafucile **b** *Rigoletto* Verdi
Sparbüchsenbill: *see* Bill
Sparbüchsenheinrich: *see* Heinz
Spärlich: *see* Slender
Speaker/Orator **b** *Die Zauberflöte* Mozart
Sphinx **a** *Oedipe* Enescu
Spinelloccio, Maestro **b** *Gianni Schicchi* Puccini
Spirit **a** *Dido and Aeneas* Purcell
Spirit Messenger **bt** *Die Frau ohne Schatten* Strauss, R.
Spirit of the Boy **tr** *Curlew River* Britten
Spirit of the Masque **t** *Gloriana* Britten
Splendiano **bt** *Djamileh* Bizet
Spoletta **t** *Tosca* Puccini
Sportin' Life **t** *Porgy and Bess* Gershwin
Spring Fairy: *see* Bonny Spring
Spy: *see* Incroyable
Squeak **t** *Billy Budd* Britten
Squirrel **ms** *L'enfant et les sortilèges* Ravel
Stadinger, Hans **b** *Der Waffenschmied* Lortzing
Stag **sp** *König Hirsch* Henze
Šťáhlav na Radbuze **bt** *Libuše* Smetana
Stanislaus, King of Poland: *see* Belfiore
Stankar **bt** *Stiffelio* Verdi
Stanley, Major-General **bt** *The Pirates of Penzance* Sullivan
Starveling **bt** *A Midsummer Night's Dream* Britten
Stasi, Countess **s** *Die Csárdásfürstin* Kálmán
Statira **ms** *Olimpie* Spontini; **a** *Statira* Scarlatti
Statue **s** *Pigmalion* Rameau
Steersman **t** *Der fliegende Holländer* Wagner; **bt** *Tristan und Isolde* Wagner
Stefan **t** *The Haunted Manor* Moniuszko
Stefana **s** *Siberia* Giordano
Štelina **b** *The Whirlpool* Suchoň
Stella **s** *Les contes d'Hoffmann* Offenbach
Stella de' Tolomei **ms** *Parisina* Mascagni
Stemid **t** *Askold's Grave* Verstovsky
Stenio **bt** *Maddalena* Prokofiev
Steno **b** *Marino Faliero* Donizetti
Stephan **b** *Hans Heiling* Marschner
Stéphano **s** *Roméo et Juliette* Gounod
Stepmother **ms** *May Night* Rimsky-Korsakov
Stesha **ms** *The Decembrists* Shaporin
Števa Buryja **t** *Jenůfa* Janáček
Stiffelio **t** *Stiffelio* Verdi
Stolnik **b** *Halka* Moniuszko
Stolzius **bt** *Die Soldaten* Zimmermann
Stolzius, Madame **a** *Die Soldaten* Zimmermann
Stone, Dr **bt** *Help, Help, the Globolinks!* Menotti
Storch, Christine **s** *Intermezzo* Strauss, R.
Storch, Robert **bt** *Intermezzo* Strauss, R.
Stössel **b** *Doktor und Apotheker* Dittersdorf
Stradella **t** *Alessandro Stradella* Flotow
Stranger **bt** *L'étranger* d'Indy; *see also* Dionysus
Strapinski **t** *Kleider machen Leute* Zemlinsky
Stratonica **s** *Mitridate Eupatore* Scarlatti
Strephon **bt** *Iolanthe* Sullivan
Stroh **t** *Intermezzo* Strauss, R.
Stroh's Wife **s** *Intermezzo* Strauss, R.
Stromminger **b** *La Wally* Catalani
Struley **b** *Adelson e Salvini* Bellini
Student Leader *Maskarade* Nielsen
Sturmwald, Captain **t** *Doktor und Apotheker* Dittersdorf
Suda, Dr **t** *Osud* Janáček
Sulamith **s** *Die Königin von Saba* Goldmark
Sulla, Lucius/Silla, Lucio **t** *Lucio Silla* Mozart; **a** *Silla* Handel
Sulpice Pingot **b** *La fille du régiment* Donizetti
Sultan **t** *La rencontre imprévue* Gluck
Sumers **t** *L'italiana in Londra* Cimarosa
Surin **b** *The Queen of Spades* Tchaikovsky
Surintendant des plaisirs **bt** *Cendrillon* Massenet
Susan **s** *Arden must Die* Goehr; **s** *A Dinner Engagement* Berkeley
Susan B. Anthony **s** *The Mother of Us All* Thomson
Susanin, Ivan **b** *A Life for the Tsar* Glinka
Susanna **s** *Die Harmonie der Welt* Hindemith; **s** *Khovanshchina* Musorgsky; **s** *Nina* Paisiello; **s** *Le nozze di Figaro* Mozart; **ms** *Il segreto di Susanna* Wolf-Ferrari
Susannah Polk **s** *Susannah* Floyd
Suse Blunt **ms** *Der Vampyr* Marschner
Suzanne **ms** *La mère coupable* Milhaud; **s** *Robinson Crusoé* Offenbach
Suzel **s** *L'amico Fritz* Mascagni
Suzuki **ms** *Madama Butterfly* Puccini
Švanda **bt** *Švanda the Bagpiper* Weinberger
Svatava **s** *Šárka* Fibich
Svätopluk, King **b** *Svätopluk* Suchoň
Svatopluk Čech **t** *The Excursions of Mr Brouček* Janáček
Svätopluk the younger **t** *Svätopluk* Suchoň
Sven **t** *Armida* Dvořák
Svetozar **b** *Ruslan and Lyudmila* Glinka
Svyatokhna: *see* Morena
Swallow **b** *Peter Grimes* Britten
Swanhilda **s** *Hulda* Franck
Sycorax **s** *Faust* Spohr
Sylva Varescu **s** *Die Csárdásfürstin* Kálmán
Sylvester **t** *Mathis der Maler* Hindemith
Sylvia *see* Silvia
Symon Rymanovicz **t** *Der Bettelstudent* Millöcker
Syndham, Lord **b** *Zar und Zimmermann* Lortzing
Syphax/Siface **a** *Scipione affricano* Cavalli

T

Tabarco **t** *Almira* Handel
Tackleton **b** *Das Heimchen am Herd* Goldmark

Tacmas **hc** *Les Indes galantes* Rameau
Taddeo **b** *L'italiana in Algeri* Rossini; *see also* Tonio
Tadzio **dancer** *Death in Venice* Britten
Tagliaborsi **t** *La zingara* Rinaldo da Capua
Tagliaferro **b** *La buona figliuola* Piccinni
Talbot **b** *Giovanna d'Arco* Verdi; **b** *Maria Stuarda* Donizetti
Talpa **b** *Il tabarro* Puccini
Tamara **s** *The Demon* Rubinstein
Tamare, Vitelozzo **bt** *Die Gezeichneten* Schreker
Tamas **t** *Gemma di Vergy* Donizetti
Tamerlane/Tamerlano **a** *Tamerlano* Handel
Tamino **t** *Die Zauberflöte* Mozart
Tamorin **t** *La caravane du Caire* Grétry
Tamyris/Tamiri **s** *Il re pastore* Mozart
Tancrède/Tancredi **t** *Armida abbandonata* Jommelli; **bt** *Tancrède* Campra; **a** *Tancredi* Rossini
Tangia **a** *Le cinesi* Gluck
Tannhäuser **t** *Tannhäuser* Wagner
Tansur **b** *Die Harmonie der Welt* Hindemith
Tapioca **bt** *L'étoile* Chabrier
Tarabotta **b** *L'inganno felice* Rossini
Tarare **t** *Tarare* Salieri
Tarquinius/Tarquinio **s** *Muzio Scevola* Handel; **bt** *The Rape of Lucretia* Britten
Tartagíl **t** *La donna serpente* Casella
Tartaglia **bb** *König Hirsch* Henze; **b** *Turandot* Busoni
Tassile: *see* Taxiles
Tasso **bt** *Torquato Tasso* Donizetti
Tatyana **s** *Yevgeny Onegin* Tchaikovsky
Taupe, Monsieur **t** *Capriccio* Strauss
Tauris/Tauride **ms** *Arianna in Creta* Handel
Tausendmark, Jan **bt** *The Brandenburgers in Bohemia* Smetana
Taven **a** *Mireille* Gounod
Taverner **t** *Taverner* Maxwell Davies
Taxiles/Tassile **a** *Alessandro* Handel
Teacher **bt** *Der Besuch der alten Dame* von Einem; **bt** *Der Jasager* Weill
Tebaldo **t** *I Capuleti e i Montecchi* Bellini; **t** *Giulietta e Romeo* Zingarelli; **bt** *Giulietta e Romeo* Vaccai; **bt** *Giulietta e Romeo* Zandonai; *see also* Thibault
Telaira/Télaïre **s** *Castor et Pollux* Rameau
Télasco **t** *Fernand Cortez* Spontini
Telemachus/Telemaco **t** *Il ritorno d'Ulisse in patria* Monteverdi; **a** *Telemaco* Gluck; **ct** *Ulisse* Dallapiccola
Télème: *see* Thelemus
Telenus/Télénus **b** *Naïs* Rameau
Tell, Guillaume/William **bt** *Guillaume Tell* Rossini
Telramund, Friedrich von **b** *Lohengrin* Wagner
Temire/Témire **s** *Roland* Lully; **s** *Scylla et Glaucus* Leclair
Tempter: *see* Abbot
Tenor/Bacchus **t** *Ariadne auf Naxos* Strauss, R.
Teobaldo **b** *Faramondo* Handel
Teodata **a** *Flavio* Handel
Teodora **s** *Il bravo* Mercadante
Teofane **s** *Ottone* Handel
Teresa **s** *Benvenuto Cellini* Berlioz; **ms** *La sonnambula* Bellini
Teresa I, St **s** *Four Saints in Three Acts* Thomson
Teresa II, St **a** *Four Saints in Three Acts* Thomson
Terinka **s** *The Jacobin* Dvořák
Termes, Mlle de **s** *Colas Breugnon* Kabalevsky
Tersandre **t** *Roland* Lully
Teseo: *see* Theseus
Tessa **ms** *The Gondoliers* Sullivan
Teti, Tetide: *see* Thetis
Teucer **b** *Dardanus* Rameau
Thaddeus **t** *The Bohemian Girl* Balfe
Thaddeus Stevens **t** *The Mother of Us All* Thomson
Thaïs **s** *Thaïs* Massenet
Thalia/Pasithea **a** *Il pomo d'oro* Cesti
Thea **m** *The Knot Garden* Tippett
Theatre Director **bt** *Les mamelles de Tirésias* Poulenc
Theban High Priest **b** *Oedipe* Enescu
Thelemus/Télème **hc** *Les fêtes d'Hébé* Rameau
Thémir **hc** *Les fêtes vénitiennes* Campra
Thémire **s** *Roland* Piccinni
Théone **s** *Phaëton* Lully
Thérèse **s** *Drömmen om Thérèse* Werle; **ms** *Thérèse* Massenet
Thérèse/Tirésias **s** *Les mamelles de Tirésias* Poulenc
Theseus/Teseo/Thésée **ms** *Arianna in Creta* Handel; **bt** *Fedra* Pizzetti; **b** *Hippolyte et Aricie* Rameau; **t** *Ippolito ed Aricia* Traetta; **b** *A Midsummer Night's Dream* Britten; **bt** *Oedipe* Enescu; **b** *Oedipe à Colone* Sacchini; **s** *Teseo* Handel; **hc** *Thésée* Lully
Thetis/Teti/Tetide **t** *La finta pazza* Sacrati; **s** *Le nozze di Teti e di Peleo* Cavalli
Thibaut d'Arc **b** *The Maid of Orléans* Tchaikovsky
Thibault/Tebaldo **s** *Don Carlos* Verdi; **t** *Les vêpres siciliennes* Verdi
Third Knight **b** *Irmelin* Delius
Thirza **ms** *The Wreckers* Smyth
Thoas/Toante **t** *Ifigenia in Tauride* Traetta; **b** *Iphigénie en Tauride* Gluck
Thomas Becket **bb** *Assassinio nella cattedrale* Pizzetti
Thomas Bouché **b** *Down in the Valley* Weill
Thomyris/Tomiri **s** *Tigrane* Scarlatti
Thorel, André **bt** *Thérèse* Massenet
Thrasymedes/Trasimede **a** *Admeto* Handel
Thusman **t** *Die Brautwahl* Busoni
Thusnelda/Tusnelda **s** *Arminio* Handel
Tiborc **bt** *Bánk bán* Erkel
Tibrino **s** *Orontea* Cesti
Tichon Kabanov **t** *Kát'a Kabanová* Janáček
Tigellinus/Tigellino **b** *Nerone* Boito
Tigrana **ms** *Edgar* Puccini
Tigranes/Tigrane **s** *Radamisto* Handel; **s** *Tigrane* Scarlatti
Timagenes/Timagene **b** *Poro* Handel
Timante **s** *Floridante* Handel; **t** *Lucile* Grétry
Timur, King **b** *Turandot* Puccini
Tina **ms** *The Aspern Papers* Argento
Tinca **b** *Il tabarro* Puccini
Tinti **s** *Massimilla Doni* Schoeck
Tintomara **ms** *Tintomara* Werle
Tinville: *see* Fouquier Tinville
Tirenio **b** *Il pastor fido* Handel
Tiresias/Tiresia/Tirésias/Tirésie **t** *Antigonae* Orff; **t** *The Bassarids* Henze; **b** *Naïs* Rameau; **b** *Oedipe* Enescu; **b** *Oedipus rex* Stravinsky; **t** *Ulisse* Dallapiccola; *see also* Thérèse
Tiridate/Tiridates **ct** *Octavia* Keiser; **t** *Radamisto* Handel
Tirinthus/Tirinto **ms** *Imeneo* Handel
Tirsi **a** *Dafne* Gagliano; **t** *Euridice* Peri
Tirsis: *see* Silango
Tisbe ms *La Cenerentola* Rossini
Tisiphone **hc** *Hippolyte et Aricie* Rameau
Tita **b** *Una cosa rara* Martín y Soler
Titania/Tytania **s** *A Midsummer Night's Dream* Britten
Titta **bt** *Fra i due litiganti il terzo gode* Sarti
Titurel **b** *Parsifal* Wagner
Titus **t** *New Year* Tippett
Titus Manlius/Tito Manlio **b** *Tito Manlio* Vivaldi
Titus Tarquinius/Tito Tarquinio **s** *Costanza e Fortezza* Fux
Titus/Tito **t** *La clemenza di Tito* Mozart; **t** *Giulio Sabino* Sarti
Titzikan **bt** *Lodoïska* Cherubini
Tkachenko **bb** *Semyon Kotko* Prokofiev
Tkachikha **ms** *The Tale of Tsar Saltan* Rimsky-Korsakov
Tobby Higgins **t** *Aufstieg und Fall der Stadt Mahagonny* Weill
Tobias **b** *Undine* Lortzing
Tobias Mill **b** *La cambiale di matrimonio* Rossini
Toby **t** *Robinson Crusoé* Offenbach
Todd, Miss **a** *The Old Maid and the Thief* Menotti
Tokmakov, Prince Yury **b** *The Maid of Pskov* Rimsky-Korsakov
Tolloller, Lord **t** *Iolanthe* Sullivan
Tolomeo: *see* Ptolemy
Tolomeo (Celinda) **s** *Dori* Cesti
Tom **bt** *The English Cat* Henze
Tom, Father **b** *The Lily of Killarney* Benedict
Tomcat **bt** *L'enfant et les sortilèges* Ravel
Tom/Horn **b** *Un ballo in maschera* Verdi
Tom Jones **t** *Tom Jones* Philidor; **bt** *Tom Jones* German
Tomeš **bt** *The Kiss* Smetana
Tomiri: *see* Thomyris

Tommaso **b** *Tiefland* d'Albert
Tomsky, Count **bt** *The Queen of Spades* Tchaikovsky
Tong **t** *Der Kreidekreis* Zemlinsky
Toni Reischmann **t** *Elegy for Young Lovers* Henze
Toník **t** *The Stubborn Lovers* Dvořák; **t** *The Two Widows* Smetana
Tonina **s** *Prima la musica e poi le parole* Salieri
Tonio **t** *La fille du régiment* Donizetti
Tonio/Taddeo **bt** *Pagliacci* Leoncavallo
Tonuelo **b** *Der Corregidor* Wolf
Tony **t** *West Side Story* Bernstein
Top **bt** *The Tender Land* Copland
Tornaquinci **b** *La cena delle beffe* Giordano
Toropka Golovan **t** *Askold's Grave* Verstovsky
Torquemada **t** *L'heure espagnole* Ravel
Torvaldo **t** *Torvaldo e Dorliska* Rossini
Tosca, Floria **s** *Tosca* Puccini
Toulouse, Count of **bt** *Jérusalem* Verdi
Trabuco, Mastro **t** *La forza del destino* Verdi
Trabucos **bt** *The Magic Opal* Albéniz
Tracollo **b** *Livietta e Tracollo* Pergolesi
Trasimede: *see* Thrasymedes
Traveller **bt** *Curlew River* Britten; **bb** *Death in Venice* Britten
Traversen, Monsù **b** *La gazzetta* Rossini
Treemonisha **s** *Treemonisha* Joplin
Trinity Moses/Dreieinigkeitsmoses **bt** *Aufstieg und Fall der Stadt Mahagonny* Weill
Triquet, Monsieur **t** *Yevgeny Onegin* Tchaikovsky
Tristan **t** *Tristan und Isolde* Wagner
Tristan d'Acunha **bt** *Jessonda* Spohr
Tristan Mickleford, Lord (Bob) **b** *Martha* Flotow
Tritemio, Don **b** *Il filosofo di campagna* Galuppi
Triton **hc** *Phaëton* Lully
Troilus, Prince **t** *Troilus and Cressida* Walton
Trombonok, Barone di **b** *Il viaggio a Reims* Rossini
Trott **t** *Die Abreise* d'Albert
Trouble/Dolore **x** *Madama Butterfly* Puccini
Trubetskoy, Prince **bt** *The Decembrists* Shaporin
Truchsess von Waldburg **b** *Mathis der Maler* Hindemith
Truffaldino **b** *Ariadne auf Naxos* Strauss, R.; **t** *The Love for Three Oranges* Prokofiev; **t** *Turandot* Busoni
Trulove **b** *The Rake's Progress* Stravinsky
Tsar **bt** *Der Zar lässt sich photographieren* Weill
Tsarevich **t** *Der Zarewitsch* Lehár
Tsaryov **bt** *Semyon Kotko* Prokofiev
Tschang **a** *Der Kreidekreis* Zemlinsky; **bt** *Das Land des Lächelns* Lehár
Tschang-Ling **bt** *Der Kreidekreis* Zemlinsky
Tschao **s** *Der Kreidekreis* Zemlinsky
Tschu-Tschu **sp** *Der Kreidekreis* Zemlinsky
Tucha, Mikhail **t** *The Maid of Pskov* Rimsky-Korsakov
Tuck, Friar **b** *Der Templer und die Jüdin* Marschner
Tullia **t** *Il trionfo di Camilla* Bononcini, G.
Tullius/Tullio **a** *Arminio* Handel
Turandot, Princess **s** *Turandot* Busoni; **s** *Turandot* Puccini
Turiddu **t** *Cavalleria rusticana* Mascagni
Turno **s** *Il trionfo di Camilla* Bononcini, G.
Turnspit **s** *Rusalka* Dvořák
Tusnelda: *see* Thusnelda
Tutor **bt** *Le comte Ory* Rossini
Tybalt **t** *Roméo et Juliette* Gounod
Tye, Queen **s** *Akhnaten* Glass
Tyrtaeus/Tyrtée **b** *Les fêtes d'Hébé* Rameau
Tytania: *see* Titania

U

Ubald/Ubalde/Ubaldo **t** *Armida* Haydn; **t** *Armida* Rossini; **b** *Armida* Dvořák; **bt** *Armide* Lully; **bt** *Armide* Gluck
Überall, Emperor **bt** *Der Kaiser von Atlantis* Ullmann
Uberto **b** *La serva padrona* Pergolesi; *see also* James
Udolin **s/t** *Die Verschworenen* Schubert
Ugo **t** *Parisina* Donizetti
Ugo, Commandant **t** *La vera storia* Berio
Ugo/Hugues Capet **t** *Ugo conte di Parigi* Donizetti
Ugone **t** *Flavio* Handel
Uldino **t** *Attila* Verdi
Ulisse: *see* Ulysses
Ulrica/Arvidson **a** *Un ballo in maschera* Verdi
Ulrik Cilley, Count **b** *Hunyadi László* Erkel
Ulysses S. Grant **bb** *The Mother of Us All* Thomson
Ulysses/Ulisse/Ulysse **a** *La finta pazza* Sacrati; **t** *Pénélope* Fauré; **t** *Il ritorno d'Ulisse in patria* Monteverdi; **t** *Telemaco* Gluck; **bt** *Ulisse* Dallapiccola
Ulysses/Ulisse (Antilochus) **ms** *Deidamia* Handel
Undine **s** *Undine* Hoffmann; **s** *Undine* Lortzing
Unulfo **a** *Rodelinda* Handel
Upfold, Mr **t** *Albert Herring* Britten
Urbain **s** *Les Huguenots* Meyerbeer
Urbino, Duke of **t** *Eine Nacht in Venedig* Strauss, J.
Urgande **s** *Amadis* Lully
Ursula **ms** *Béatrice et Bénédict* Berlioz; **s** *Mathis der Maler* Hindemith
Ursule **s** *Le domino noir* Auber
Uthal **hc** *Uthal* Méhul
Utobal **bt** *Joseph* Méhul

V

Vakhrameyevna **a** *Askold's Grave* Verstovsky
Vakula **t** *Cherevichki* Tchaikovsky; **t** *Christmas Eve* Rimsky-Korsakov
Valdeburgo, Baron **b** *La straniera* Bellini
Valencienne **s** *Die lustige Witwe* Lehár
Valentin **bt** *Faust* Gounod
Valentine **s** *Les Huguenots* Meyerbeer
Valère **t** *La fausse esclave* Gluck; **hc** *Les Indes galantes* Rameau
Valeria **s** *Costanza e Fortezza* Fux
Valletto **s** *L'incoronazione di Poppea* Monteverdi
Valzacchi **t** *Der Rosenkavalier* Strauss, R.
Van Bett **b** *Zar und Zimmermann* Lortzing
Vanessa **s** *Vanessa* Barber
Vanoldo **t** *La rosa bianca e la rosa rossa* Mayr
Vanuzzi **b** *Die schweigsame Frau* Strauss, R.
Vanya **a** *A Life for the Tsar* Glinka
Vašek **t** *The Bartered Bride* Smetana
Varlaam **b** *Boris Godunov* Musorgsky
Varneman **t** *The Brandenburgers in Bohemia* Smetana
Varus/Varo **t** *Arminio* Handel; **b** *Ezio* Handel
Varvara **ms** *Kát'a Kabanová* Janáček
Vasco da Gama **t** *L'Africaine* Meyerbeer
Vasilij Šujský, Prince **bt** *Dimitrij* Dvořák
Vasily **t** *Mavra* Stravinsky
Vassili **t** *Siberia* Giordano
Vaudémont **t** *Iolanta* Tchaikovsky
Vaudemont, Count of **b** *Les vêpres siciliennes* Verdi
Vávra **bt** *The Stubborn Lovers* Dvořák
Veit **t** *Undine* Lortzing
Velasco, Don **t** *Masagniello* Keiser
Vendramin **bt** *Massimilla Doni* Schoeck
Vendredi: *see* Man Friday
Vendulka **s** *The Kiss* Smetana
Venetian **bt** *Sadko* Rimsky-Korsakov
Venus/Venere/Vénus **s** *Ascanio in Alba* Mozart; **s** *Cadmus et Hermione* Lully; **s** *Dafne* Gagliano; **s** *Dardanus* Rameau; **s** *Ercole amante* Cavalli; **s** *La finta pazza* Sacrati; **s** *The Judgment of Paris* Eccles, D. Purcell, Weldon; **s** *Orphée aux enfers* Offenbach; **s** *Il pomo d'oro* Cesti; **s** *Scylla et Glaucus* Leclair; **s** *Tannhäuser* Wagner
Vera Boronel **a** *The Consul* Menotti
Vere, Captain **t** *Billy Budd* Britten
Vergy, Count of **bt** *Gemma di Vergy* Donizetti
Véronique: *see* Hélène de Solanges
Vertigo **bt** *La rencontre imprévue* Gluck
Verva **bt** *Osud* Janáček
Vesna-Krasna: *see* Bonny Spring
Vespetta **a** *Pimpinone* Albinoni; **s** *Pimpinone* Telemann
Vespina **s** *L'infedeltà delusa* Haydn

Vespone **x** *La serva padrona* Pergolesi
Vicar **bb** *Der Besuch der alten Dame* von Einem; **b** *Pepita Jiménez* Albéniz
Viceroy: *see* Andrès del Ribeira
Viclinda **s** *I Lombardi* Verdi
Victorin **t** *Die tote Stadt* Korngold
Victory/Vittoria **s** *La finta pazza* Sacrati
Vielka **s** *Ein Feldlager in Schlesien* Meyerbeer
Vigelius, Dr **b** *Der ferne Klang* Schreker
Viking **b** *Sadko* Rimsky-Korsakov
Vilém of Harasov, Count **b** *The Jacobin* Dvořák
Village Clerk **b** *May Night* Rimsky-Korsakov
Village Head **b** *May Night* Rimsky-Korsakov; *see also* Pan Golova
Villager **t** *Halka* Moniuszko
Villars, Colonel **t** *Emilia di Liverpool* Donizetti
Villotto **bt** *La vera costanza* Haydn
Vincenette **s** *Mireille* Gounod
Vincent **t** *Mireille* Gounod
Violanta **s** *Violanta* Korngold
Violante Onesti, Marchioness (Sandrina) **s** *La finta giardiniera* Mozart
Violetta **s** *Il bravo* Mercadante; **s** *La traviata* Verdi
Virgil, Shade of **bt** *Francesca da Rimini* Rakhmaninov
Virgil Thomson **bt** *The Mother of Us All* Thomson
Viscardo **t** *Il giuramento* Mercadante
Vïshata **b** *Askold's Grave* Verstovsky
Vít **t** *The Secret* Smetana
Vita **s** *L'étranger* d'Indy
Vita mondana/Worldly Life **s** *Rappresentatione di Anima, et di Corpo* Cavalieri
Vitalian/Vitaliano **t** *Giustino* Handel
Vítek **t** *Dalibor* Smetana; **t** *The Makropulos Affair* Janáček
Vitellia **s** *La clemenza di Tito* Mozart; **a** *Tito Manlio* Vivaldi
Vitellius **bt** *Hérodiade* Massenet
Vitellozzo **b** *Lucrezia Borgia* Donizetti
Vitige **s** *Flavio* Handel
Vitoldo **b** *I lituani* Ponchielli
Vitoraz **b** *Šárka* Fibich
Vittoria: *see* Victory
Vivetta **s** *L'arlesiana* Cilea
Vixen **t** *Renard* Stravinsky; *see also* Bystrouška
Vladimir Igorevich **t** *Prince Igor* Borodin
Vladislav **bt** *Dalibor* Smetana
Vlas'yevna **a** *The Maid of Pskov* Rimsky-Korsakov
Vlasta **ms** *Šárka* Fibich
Vlčenka **s** *The Brandenburgers in Bohemia* Smetana
Vodník **b** *Rusalka* Dvořák
Vogelgesang, Kunz **t** *Die Meistersinger von Nürnberg* Wagner
Vogelsang **t** *Der Schauspieldirektor* Mozart
Vogt **bt** *Der Schatzgräber* Schreker
Voice: *see* Dionysus
Voice from Above **a** *Parsifal* Wagner
Voice from Heaven **s** *Don Carlos* Verdi
Voice of Apollo **ct** *Death in Venice* Britten
Vok Vítkovic **bt** *The Devil's Wall* Smetana
Volàno **t** *Giasone* Cavalli
Volfram Olbramovič **b** *The Brandenburgers in Bohemia* Smetana
Volkhova **s** *Sadko* Rimsky-Korsakov
Volmar **bt** *Alina, regina di Golconda* Donizetti
Volpino **s** *Lo speziale* Haydn
Voluptuousness/Volupia **s** *Egisto* Cavalli
Voswinkel **bt** *Die Brautwahl* Busoni
Voyslava **s** *Mlada* Rimsky-Korsakov
Vreli **s** *A Village Romeo and Juliet* Delius
Vseslav **t** *Askold's Grave* Verstovsky
Vsevolod, Princeling **t** *Legend of the Invisible City of Kitezh* Rimsky-Korsakov
Vulcan/Vulcain/Vulcano **b** *La finta pazza* Sacrati; **b** *Philémon et Baucis* Gounod
Vyazminsky **bt** *Oprichnik* Tchaikovsky

W

Wagner **b** *Doktor Faust* Busoni; **bt** *Faust* Gounod; **t** *Mefistofele* Boito
Waldner, Count **b** *Arabella* Strauss
Wallenstein **t** *Die Harmonie der Welt* Hindemith
Wally **s** *La Wally* Catalani
Walter **s** *La Wally* Catalani
Walter, Count **b** *Luisa Miller* Verdi
Walter Furst **b** *Guillaume Tell* Rossini
Walter von Oberwesel **t** *Loreley* Catalani
Walther von der Vogelweide **t** *Tannhäuser* Wagner
Walther von Stolzing **t** *Die Meistersinger von Nürnberg* Wagner
Walton, Lord Gualtiero **b** *I puritani* Bellini
Waltraute **ms** *Götterdämmerung* Wagner; **a** *Die Walküre* Wagner
Wamba **t** *Der Templer und die Jüdin* Marschner
Wanda **s** *La Grande-Duchesse de Gérolstein* Offenbach
Wanderer: *see* Wotan
Wanton, Madam **s** *The Pilgrim's Progress* Vaughan Williams
Warden: *see* Frank
Watchful **bt** *The Pilgrim's Progress* Vaughan Williams
Water Nymph: *see* Demon (Water Nymph)
Waters, Mrs **s** *The Boatswain's Mate* Smyth
Welko **sp** *Arabella* Strauss
Wellgunde **s** *Götterdämmerung* Wagner; **s** *Das Rheingold* Wagner
Werther **t** *Werther* Massenet
Wesener **b** *Die Soldaten* Zimmermann
Western, Mrs **ms** *Tom Jones* Philidor
Western, Squire **b** *Tom Jones* Philidor
Westmoreland, Conte di **bt** *Sly* Wolf-Ferrari
Weston, Squire **bt** *Tom Jones* German
White Abbot **bt** *Taverner* Maxwell Davies
White Man **bt** *Die Verlobung in San Domingo* Egk
Widow Browe **a** *Zar und Zimmermann* Lortzing
Wife **s** *Blood Wedding* Szokolay; **s** *Von heute auf morgen* Schoenberg
Wigmaker **bt** *Ariadne auf Naxos* Strauss, R.
Wilhelm **t** *Der junge Lord* Henze
Wilhelm Meister **t** *Mignon* Thomas
Wilhelm Reischmann, Dr **b** *Elegy for Young Lovers* Henze
William **ms** *Rosina* Shield
William, Sir **bt** *Nelson* Berkeley
William Jennings Bryan **bb** *The Ballad of Baby Doe* Moore
William Ratcliff **t** *Guglielmo Ratcliff* Mascagni; **bt** *William Ratcliff* Cui
Williams **b** *Richard Coeur-de-lion* Grétry
William Tell: *see* Tell, Guillaume
Willis, Private **b** *Iolanthe* Sullivan
Willy: *see* Fatty
Wingrave, Miss **s** *Owen Wingrave* Britten
Wingrave, Owen **bt** *Owen Wingrave* Britten
Wingrave, Sir Philip **t** *Owen Wingrave* Britten
Wise Man **t** *Hin und zurück* Hindemith
Witch **ms** *Hänsel und Gretel* Humperdinck; **a** *Die Königskinder* Humperdinck; *see also* Ježibaba
Witch of Endor **a** *Saul og David* Nielsen
Woglinde **s** *Götterdämmerung* Wagner; **s** *Das Rheingold* Wagner
Wolfram von Eschinbach **bt** *Tannhäuser* Wagner
Woman **s** *Erwartung* Schoenberg
Woodbird **s** *Siegfried* Wagner
Woodcutter **b** *Die Königskinder* Humperdinck
Woodcutter's Boy **s/tr** *The Pilgrim's Progress* Vaughan Williams
Woodpecker **a** *The Cunning Little Vixen* Janáček
Wordsworth, Miss **s** *Albert Herring* Britten
World: *see* Mondo
Worldly Life: *see* Vita mondana
Wotan **bb** *Das Rheingold* Wagner; **bb** *Siegfried* (Wanderer); **bb** *Die Walküre* Wagner
Wowkle **ms** *La fanciulla del West* Puccini
Wozzeck **bt** *Wozzeck* Berg
Würfl/Čaroskvoucí/Alderman **b** *The Excursions of Mr Brouček*

Janáček
Wurm **b** *Luisa Miller* Verdi
Wurmerhelm, Baroness **x** *The Gambler* Prokofiev

X

Xanthe **s** *Die Liebe der Danae* Strauss, R.
Xantippe **s** *Der geduldige Socrates* Telemann
Xenia **s** *Boris Godunov* Musorgsky
Xenie Borisovna **s** *Dimitrij* Dvořák
Xerxes/Serse/Xerse **ms** *Serse* Handel; **a** *Xerse* Cavalli; **s** *Xerse* Bononcini, G.
Ximena, Donna **s** *Don Giovanni* Gazzaniga
Xiphares/Sifare **s** *Mitridate* Mozart

Y

Yakubovich **b** *The Decembrists* Shaporin
Yakuside **b** *Madama Butterfly* Puccini
Yamadori, Prince **t** *Madama Butterfly* Puccini
Yanika **ms** *Cristoforo Colombo* Franchetti
Yannakos **t** *The Greek Passion* Martinů
Yarïzhkin **t** *The Nose* Shostakovich
Yaromir **t** *Mlada* Rimsky-Korsakov
Yaroslavna **s** *Prince Igor* Borodin
Yelena **s** *The Decembrists* Shaporin
Yeletsky, Prince **bt** *The Queen of Spades* Tchaikovsky
Yeroshka **t** *Prince Igor* Borodin
Yevgeny **bt** *Quiet Flows the Don* Dzerzhinsky
Yevgeny Onegin **bt** *Yevgeny Onegin* Tchaikovsky
Ygraine **s** *Ariane et Barbe-bleue* Dukas
Yniold **tr/s** *Pelléas et Mélisande* Debussy
Young Cadet **sp** *Die Soldaten* Zimmermann
Young Count **t** *Die Soldaten* Zimmermann
Young Girl/Bride **s** *Die Bluthochzeit* Fortner
Young Huntsman **sp** *Die Soldaten* Zimmermann
Young Prisoner **t** *From the House of the Dead* Janáček
Young Woman **s** *We Come to the River* Henze
Younger Son **t** *The Prodigal Son* Britten
Ys, King of **b** *Le roi d'Ys* Lalo
Yü-Pei **s** *Der Kreidekreis* Zemlinsky
Yum-Yum **s** *The Mikado* Sullivan
Yuri **bt** *The Ice Break* Tippett
Yurodivïy/Holy Fool **t** *Boris Godunov* Musorgsky
Yury **t** *The Enchantress* Tchaikovsky
Yury Vsevolodovich, Prince **b** *Legend of the Invisible City of Kitezh* Rimsky-Korsakov
Yvonne **s** *Jonny spielt auf* Krenek

Z

Záboj **t** *Svätopluk* Suchoň
Zaccaria **b** *Nabucco* Verdi
Zacharie **b** *Le prophète* Meyerbeer
Zaida **s** *Il turco in Italia* Rossini
Zaide **s** *Zaide* Mozart
Zaira **s** *Zaira* Bellini
Zaïre **s** *Les Indes galantes* Rameau
Zaïs **hc** *Zaïs* Rameau
Zamoro **t** *Alzira* Verdi
Zampa **t** *Zampa* Hérold
Záviš **a** *The Devil's Wall* Smetana
Zayda **ms** *Dom Sébastien* Donizetti
Zazà **s** *Zazà* Leoncavallo
Zbigniew **b** *The Haunted Manor* Moniuszko
Zdeněk **x** *Dalibor* Smetana
Zdenka **s** *Arabella* Strauss
Zélide **s** *Zaïs* Rameau
Zélie **ms** *Drottningen av Golconda* Berwald; **s** *Les fêtes vénitiennes* Campra
Zélime **s** *La caravane du Caire* Grétry
Zeliska/Malvino **s** *L'amor coniugale* Mayr
Zelmira **s** *Armida* Haydn; **s** *Zelmira* Rossini
Zémaïde **ms** *Le calife de Bagdad* Boieldieu
Zemfira **s** *Aleko* Rakhmaninov
Zémire **s** *Zémire et Azor* Grétry
Zenobia **s** *Aureliano in Palmira* Rossini; **a** *Radamisto* Handel
Zéphoris **t** *Si j'étais roi* Adam
Zephyrus **tr** *Apollo et Hyacinthus* Mozart
Zerbinetta **s** *Ariadne auf Naxos* Strauss, R.
Zerlina **s** *Don Giovanni* Mozart
Zerline **s** *Fra Diavolo* Auber
Zeta, Baron Mirko **bt** *Die lustige Witwe* Lehár
Zétulbe **s** *Le calife de Bagdad* Boieldieu
Zhemchuznïy, Prince **b** *Oprichnik* Tchaikovsky
Ziliante **bt** *Roland* Lully
Zima **s** *Les Indes galantes* Rameau
Zimmerlein, Widow **a** *Die schweigsame Frau* Strauss, R.
Zinovy Izmaylov **t** *Lady Macbeth of the Mtsensk District* Shostakovich
Zita **a** *Gianni Schicchi* Puccini
Zivný **t** *Osud* Janáček
Zobeide **sp** *Abu Hassan* Weber
Zofàr **t** *Job* Dallapiccola
Zofia **s** *Halka* Moniuszko
Zomira **a** *Ricciardo e Zoraide* Rossini
Zoraide **s** *Ricciardo e Zoraide* Rossini; **s** *Zoraide di Grenata* Donizetti
Zorn, Balthasar **t** *Die Meistersinger von Nürnberg* Wagner
Zoroastre **hc** *Zoroastre* Rameau
Zoroastro **b** *Orlando* Handel
Zorzeto **t** *Il campiello* Wolf-Ferrari
Zsupán **t** *Der Zigeunerbaron* Strauss, J.
Zuàne **b** *La Gioconda* Ponchielli
Zulma **ms** *L'italiana in Algeri* Rossini
Zuma **ms** *Alzira* Verdi
Zuniga **b** *Carmen* Bizet
Zurga **bt** *Les pêcheurs de perles* Bizet
Zuzka **a** *The Whirlpool* Suchoň

Appendix B

INDEX OF INCIPITS OF ARIAS, ENSEMBLES ETC.

This appendix is an index of first lines of arias, duets and other ensembles and choruses, designed to enable the user to look up the opening words of any item from an opera and find its source. Each entry gives the singer (or singers, for an ensemble), the short title of the opera, the act (if an opera with scene numbers but not acts, the number is in small roman type) and the composer. The arrangement is strictly alphabetical, including the definite or indefinite article and disregarding any punctuation; where two numbers have the same incipit they are alphabetized by the titles of the operas they come from.

This index is inevitably highly selective. Were it to include all significant arias (etc.) from all the operas entered in the dictionary, it would occupy more than 100 pages. The objective here has been to include well-known 'detachable' numbers from the basic repertory operas and a generous selection of the more significant items from fringe-repertory works, including Baroque operas. For arias (or duets etc.) comprising more than one section, first lines may be given of later sections (such as cabalettas) where these are familiar; so may the first lines of introductory recitatives. Numbers known by titles (Bell Song, Anvil Chorus) are also included, usually as cross-references. Numbers are normally cited in their original language but a few familiar translated first lines are also given.

With minor exceptions, the list is confined to English, French, German and Italian, with a small number of entries in Czech; no transliterated Russian, nor other Slavonic works, are included, though – bearing in mind that this list is intended primarily for the English-speaking reader – a selection of well-known items from this repertory is included where a familiar English translation exists.

A

A, B, C, D (Baculus, Gretchen) *Der Wildschütz* 1 Lortzing
Abendlich strahlt der Sonne Auge (Wotan) *Das Rheingold* Wagner
Abends will ich schlafen gehn (Gretel, Hänsel) *Hänsel und Gretel* 2 Humperdinck
Aber der Richtige (Arabella, Zdenka) *Arabella* 1 Strauss
Above measure is the pleasure (Juno) *Semele* 3 Handel
A brani, a brani, o perfido (Luisa) *Luisa Miller* 2 Verdi
Abscheulicher! ... Komm Hoffnung ... Ich folg' dem innern Triebe (Leonore) *Fidelio* 1 Beethoven
Abuso forse ... Mira, di acerbe lagrime ... Vivrà! Contende il giubilo (Leonora, Luna) *Il trovatore* 4 Verdi
Accablé de regrets (Orpheus) *Orphée et Eurydice* 1 Gluck
Accogli, oh re del mar (Idomeneus, chorus) *Idomeneo* 3 Mozart
A celui que jamais (Elvire) *La muette de Portici* 1 Auber
A ce mot seul s'anime (Marguerite de Valois) *Les Huguenots* 2 Meyerbeer
Acerba voluttà, dolce tortura (Princess of Bouillon) *Adriana Lecouvreur* 2 Cilea
A cette fête conviée (Monsieur Triquet) *Yevgeny Onegin* 2 Tchaikovsky
A cette heure suprême (Werther, Charlotte) *Werther* 4 Massenet
Ach Belmonte! ach mein Leben (Konstanze, Belmonte, Blonde, Pedrillo) *Die Entführung aus dem Serail* 2 Mozart
Ach, das Leid hab' ich getragen (Nureddin) *Der Barbier von Bagdad* 1 Cornelius
Ach! du bist wieder da (Marschallin, Octavian) *Der Rosenkavalier* 1 Strauss
A che smarriti e pallidi (Federico Barbarossa, ensemble) *La battaglia di Legnano* 2 Verdi
Ach Herr, dass ich es offen sag (Aminta) *Die schweigsame Frau* 2 Strauss
Ach, ich fühl's (Pamina) *Die Zauberflöte* 2 Mozart
Ach, ich liebte (Konstanze) *Die Entführung aus dem Serail* 1 Mozart
Ach, so fromm (Lyonel) *Martha* 3 Flotow
Ach wir armen, armen Leute (Peter) *Hänsel und Gretel* 1 Humperdinck
Ach! wo war ich? (Ariadne, Nymphs) *Ariadne auf Naxos* Strauss
A consolarmi affrettati (Linda, Pierotto) *Linda di Chamounix* 2 Donizetti
Adamastor, roi des vagues profondes (Nélusko) *L'Africaine* 3 Meyerbeer
Addio, del passato (Violetta) *La traviata* 3 Verdi
Addio, dolce svegliare (Mimì, Rodolfo, Marcello, Musetta) *La bohème* 3 Puccini
Addio, fiorito asil (Pinkerton) *Madama Butterfly* 2 Puccini
Addio Firenze, addio, cielo divino (Gianni Schicchi, ensemble) *Gianni Schicchi* Puccini
Addio, mia vita (Italian Singers) *Capriccio* Strauss
Addio, mio dolce amor (Fidelia) *Edgar* 3 Puccini
Addio, speranza ed anima (Duke, Gilda) *Rigoletto* 1 Verdi
Adieu, conservez dans votre âme (Iphigenia) *Iphigénie en Aulide* 3 Gluck
Adieu, fière cité (Dido) *Les Troyens* 5 Berlioz
Adieu, Mignon (Wilhelm Meister) *Mignon* 2 Thomas
Adieu mon beau rivage (Inès) *L'Africaine* 1 Meyerbeer

Adieu, notre petite table (Manon) *Manon* 2 Massenet
Adina, credimi (Nemorino, Adina, Belcore) *L'elisir d'amore* 1 Donizetti
A Dio Roma (Octavia) *L'incoronazione di Poppea* 3 Monteverdi
A dispetto d'un volto ingrato (Tamerlane) *Tamerlano* 3 Handel
Aer tranquillo (Amyntas) *Il re pastore* 1 Mozart
Affanni del pensier (Teofane) *Ottone* 1 Handel
A garden by a river (Mountjoy) *Gloriana* 2 Britten
A girl went out walking (Marfa) *Khovanshchina* iii Musorgsky
Agitata da due venti (Costanza) *Griselda* 2 Vivaldi
Agitato da fiere tempeste (Richard) *Riccardo* 1 Handel
Agitato da fiere tempeste (Sosarme) *Sosarme* 1 Handel
Ah! ah! tout va bien (Golaud, Mélisande) *Pelléas et Mélisande* 2 Debussy
Ah! Belinda (Dido) *Dido and Aeneas* 1 Purcell
Ah! bello, a me ritorna (Norma) *Norma* 1 Bellini
Ah, bitterly I weep (Yaroslavna) *Prince Igor* 4 Borodin
Ah! cedi, cedi (Raimondo) *Lucia di Lammermoor* 2 Donizetti
Ah, ces cris d'allégresse (Alphonse) *La muette de Portici* 1 Auber
Ah! che scordar non so (Tancredi) *Tancredi* 2 Rossini
Ah, chi m'accusa (Gemma, ensemble) *Gemma di Vergy* 2 Donizetti
Ah, chi mi dice mai (Donna Elvira) *Don Giovanni* 1 Mozart
Ah! chi sa quale e dove la vita (Carlo, Prefect) *Linda di Chamounix* 3 Donizetti
Ah come il core (Celia) *La fedeltà premiata* 2 Haydn
Ah! così nei di ridenti (Percy) *Anna Bolena* 1 Donizetti
Ah! crudel d'onor ragioni (Romeo, Giulietta) *I Capuleti e i Montecchi* 1 Bellini
Ah! crudel, il pianto mio (Armida) *Rinaldo* 2 Handel
Ah dal ciel discenda un raggio (Elizabeth, ensemble) *Maria Stuarda* 1 Donizetti
Ah! Deh! per pietà sospendi ... Vanne indegno (Leicester, Elizabeth, Cecil) *Maria Stuarda* 2/3 Donizetti
Ah! del Tebro al giogo indegno (Oroveso) *Norma* 2 Bellini
Ah! d'immenso, estremo affetto (Orombello, Beatrice) *Beatrice di Tenda* 1 Bellini
Ah! dimmi ... dimmi io t'amo (Carlo, Linda) *Linda di Chamounix* 2 Donizetti
Ah dov'è, dov'è il cimento (Idreno) *Semiramide* 1 Rossini
Ah! du moins à Médée (Medea, Creon) *Médée* 2 Cherubini
Ah! d'un consorte, o perfidi (Lida, Arrigo, Rolando) *La battaglia di Legnano* 3 Verdi
Ah, du wolltest mich nicht (Salome) *Salome* Strauss
Ah! ella è mia madre (Arsace) *Semiramide* 2 Rossini
Ah! faut-il, en un jour (Hippolytus) *Hippolyte et Aricie* 4 Rameau
Ah! faut-il me venger (Medea) *Thésée* 5 Lully
Ah fors'è lui ... Sempre libera degg'io (Violetta) *La traviata* 1 Verdi
Ah! fuggi il traditor! (Donna Elvira) *Don Giovanni* 1 Mozart
Ah! fu guisto il mio sospetto (Miller) *Luisa Miller* 1 Verdi
Ah! fuyez, douce image (Des Grieux) *Manon* 3 Massenet
Ah! gran Dio! morir sì giovane (Alfredo, Violetta) *La traviata* 3 Verdi
Ah guarda sorella (Fiordiligi, Dorabella) *Così fan tutte* 1 Mozart
Ah, I am worn out by grief (Lisa) *Queen of Spades* 3 Tchaikovsky
Ahi caso acerbo (chorus) *Orfeo* 2 Monteverdi
Ah il più lieto (Almaviva) *Il barbiere di Siviglia* 2 Rossini
Ah! je ris de me voir (Marguerite) *Faust* 3 Gounod
Ah, je vais l'aimer (Benedick) *Béatrice et Bénédict* 1 Berlioz
Ah! la flamme (Orpheus) *Orphée et Eurydice* 2 Gluck
Ah! laissez-moi la pleurer (trio) *Zémire et Azor* 3 Grétry
Ah la morte (Beatrice) *Beatrice di Tenda* 2 Bellini
Ah, la paterna mano (Macduff) *Macbeth* 4 Verdi
Ah, la sorte ci tradì ... Deh! ti ferma (Assur, soldiers) *Semiramide* 2 Rossini
Ah! le carnaval apporte (Catharine) *La jolie fille de Perth* 1 Bizet
Ah! le rire est béni (Sophie) *Werther* 3 Massenet
Ah! lève-toi, soleil! (Romeo) *Roméo et Juliette* 2 Gounod
Ah! l'honnête homme! (Raimbaut, Bertram) *Robert le diable* 3 Meyerbeer
Ah! Life is tedious ... My Dimitry (Marina) *Boris Godunov* 3 Musorgsky
Ah lo veggio quell'anima bella (Ferrando) *Così fan tutte* 2 Mozart
Ah! ma femme! (Blaise) *Lucile* 1 Grétry
Ah! malgré moi (Alcestis) *Alceste* 2 Gluck
Ah, Mimì, tu più non torni (Rodolfo, Marcello) *La bohème* 4 Puccini
Ah mio cor! schernito sei (Alcina) *Alcina* 2 Handel
Ah! mon ami (Pylades, Orestes) *Iphigénie en Tauride* 3 Gluck
Ah! mon fils, sois béni (Fidès) *Le prophète* 2 Meyerbeer
Ah! mon remords te venge (Hoël) *Dinorah* 3 Meyerbeer
Ah! ne fuis pas encore (Romeo, Juliet) *Roméo et Juliette* 2 Gounod
Ah! non credea mirarti (Amina) *La sonnambula* 2 Bellini
Ah! non giunge uman pensiero (Amina, ensemble) *La sonnambula* 2 Bellini
Ah! nos peines seront communes (Neris) *Médée* 2 Cherubini
Ah, parea che per incanto (Smeton) *Anna Bolena* 1 Donizetti
Ah paventa il furor d'un Dio vendicatore (Baldassare) *La favorita* 2 Donizetti
Ah! perchè non posso odiarti? (Elvino) *La sonnambula* 2 Bellini
Ah perdona al primo affetto (Annius, Servilia) *La clemenza di Tito* 1 Mozart
Ah! per sempre io ti perderi ... Bel sogno beato (Riccardo) *I puritani* 1 Bellini
Ah, per sempre ... Pronti destrieri ... Ah! seguirti fino agl'ultimi confini (Don Alvaro, Leonora) *La forza del destino* 1 Verdi
Ah pietà, signori miei (Leporello) *Don Giovanni* 2 Mozart
Ah! più non vedrò ... O don fatale (Eboli) *Don Carlo* 3/4 Verdi
Ah! qual colpo ... Zitti zitti, piano piano (Rosina, Almaviva, Figaro) *Il barbiere di Siviglia* 2 Rossini
Ah! quando all'ara scorgemi ... Ah dal ciel discenda un raggio (Elizabeth, ensemble) *Maria Stuarda* 1 Donizetti
Ah! quand viendra l'instant (Aeneas) *Les Troyens* 5 Berlioz
Ah! quel giorno ognor rammento (Arsace) *Semiramide* 1 Rossini
Ah! qu'elle est belle! (Robert) *Robert le diable* 4 Meyerbeer
Ah! quel plaisir d'être soldat (George Brown) *La dame blanche* 1 Boieldieu
Ah quel respect madame (Ory, Adèle) *Le comte Ory* 2 Rossini
Ah! quel tourment (Médor) *Roland* 1 Lully
Ah! qui me donnera comme à la colombe (Salammbô) *Salammbô* 3 Reyer
Ah! qu'il est loin mon pays (Jean) *Sapho* 1 Massenet
Ah, scostati! ... Smanie implacabili (Dorabella) *Così fan tutte* 1 Mozart
Ah se a morir mi chiama (Cecilius) *Lucio Silla* 2 Mozart
Ah, se fosse intorno (Titus) *La clemenza di Tito* 1 Mozart
Ah! segnar invano io tento (Argirio) *Tancredi* 2 Rossini
Ah, segnasti la tua sorte (Don Carlo, Don Alvaro) *La forza del destino* 4 Verdi
Ah! segnata è la mia sorte (Anne Boleyn, ensemble) *Anna Bolena* 1 Donizetti
Ah! seguirti fino agl'ultimi confini (Don Alvaro, Leonora) *La forza del destino* 1 Verdi
Ah se il crudel periglio (Junia) *Lucio Silla* 2 Mozart
Ah! se la speme ... Figlia! a tal nome io palpito (Amelia, Boccanegra) *Simon Boccanegra* 1 Verdi
Ah! se tu vuoi fuggir (Arturo, Alaide) *La straniera* 1 Bellini
Ah! se un giorno (Mary, Leicester, ensemble) *Maria Stuarda* 2/3 Donizetti
Ah! se un'urna è a me concessa ... Ah la morte (Beatrice) *Beatrice di Tenda* 2 Bellini
Ah sì, ben mio, coll'essere ... Di quella pira (Manrico) *Il trovatore* 3 Verdi
Ah! sì, fa core e abbracciami (Adalgisa, Norma) *Norma* 1 Bellini
Ah! si la liberté me doit être ravie (Armide) *Armide* 3 Gluck
Ah! si maledetto, sospetto fatale (Philip II, Posa, Eboli, Elisabetta di Valois) *Don Carlo* 3/4 Verdi
Ah! speranza dolce ancora (Lucrezia Contarini, Jacopo Foscari) *I due Foscari* 2 Verdi
Ah! spietato! e non ti muove (Melissa) *Amadigi* 1 Handel
Ah taci, ingiusto core (Don Giovanni, Leporello, Donna Elvira) *Don Giovanni* 2 Mozart
Ah! tardai troppo ... O luce di quest'anima (Linda) *Linda di Chamounix* 1 Donizetti
Ah! the world's not what it was ... Je crains de lui parler (Countess) *Queen of Spades* 2 Tchaikovsky
Ah! veglia o donna (Rigoletto, Gilda) *Rigoletto* 1 Verdi
Ah, viens dans la forêt profonde (Gérald) *Lakmé* 3 Delibes

Ah! vivre deux (Hoffmann) *Les contes d'Hoffmann* 2 Offenbach
Ai Greci questa spada (Achilles) *Deidamia* 3 Handel
Ai-je dit vrai ... Ah! qu'il est loin (Werther, Charlotte) *Werther* 2 Massenet
Aimez-vous sans cesse (Zoroastre) *Zoroastre* 2 Rameau
Ai nostri monti (Azucena, Manrico) *Il trovatore* 4 Verdi
Air des larmes: *see* Va! laisse couler mes larmes
Alabama Song: *see* O moon of Alabama
A la faveur de cette nuit (Ory, Adèle, Isolier) *Le comte Ory* 2 Rossini
A la fleur du bel âge (Nicette) *Le Pré aux Clercs* 3 Hérold
A la noblesse je m'allie (Chapelou) *Le postillon de Lonjumeau* 3 Adam
A l'aspect de ce nuage (Plataea) *Platée* 2 Rameau
A l'autel j'allais rayonnant (Rozenn, Mylio) *Le roi d'Ys* 3 Lalo
A la voix d'un amant fidèle (Henry Smith) *La jolie fille de Perth* 2 Bizet
Al bel destin che attendevi (Pierotto, Linda) *Linda di Chamounix* 2 Donizetti
Albert the Good (ensemble) *Albert Herring* 2 Britten
Alcide est vainqueur du trépas (chorus) *Alceste* 5 Lully
Alcides' name in latest story (Hercules) *Hercules* 2 Handel
Al dolce guidami castel natio ... Cielo, a miei lunghi spasimi ... Coppia iniqua (Anne Boleyn, ensemble) *Anna Bolena* 2 Donizetti
Alessio, che farai? (Alexis) *Sant'Alessio* 2 Landi
Alfin son tua ... Spargi d'amaro pianto (Lucia, ensemble) *Lucia di Lammermoor* 3 Donizetti
Alla fama, dimmi il vero (Teofane) *Ottone* 2 Handel
All'afflitto è dolce il pianto (Sarah) *Roberto Devereux* 1 Donizetti
Al lampo dell'armi (Julius Caesar) *Giulio Cesare* 3 Handel
Alla vita che t'arride (Renato [Captain Anckarstroem]) *Un ballo in maschera* 1 Verdi
Allein! Weh, ganz allein (Electra) *Elektra* Strauss
Alle più calde immagini (Arsace, Semiramide) *Semiramide* 1 Rossini
Allez dans un cloître, Ophélie (Hamlet, Ophelia, Gertrude) *Hamlet* 3 Thomas
All'idea di qual metallo (Figaro, Almaviva) *Il barbiere di Siviglia* 1 Rossini
Allmächt'ge Jungfrau (Elisabeth) *Tannhäuser* 3 Wagner
Allmächt'ger Vater (Rienzi) *Rienzi* 5 Wagner
Allons, allons, accourez tous (Attis, chorus) *Atys* 1 Lully
Allor che i forti corrono ... Da te questo (Odabella) *Attila* prol. Verdi
Alma soave e cara (Count de Chalais) *Maria di Rohan* 2 Donizetti
Al mio piè, perchè ... Di qual amor (Don Carlo, Elisabetta di Valois) *Don Carlo* 1 Verdi
Al mio pregar t'arrendi (Semiramide) *Semiramide* 2 Rossini
A lonely Arab maid (Fatima) *Oberon* 2 Weber
Als Büblein klein (Falstaff) *Die lustigen Weiber von Windsor* 2 Nicolai
Als du in kühnem Sange ... War's Zauber, war es reine Macht (Wolfram) *Tannhäuser* 1 Wagner
Als ein Gott kam Jeder gegangen (Zerbinetta) *Ariadne auf Naxos* Strauss
Als junger Liebe Lust mir verblich (Wotan, Brünnhilde) *Die Walküre* 2 Wagner
Al suon del tamburo (Preziosilla) *La forza del destino* 2 Verdi
Als zullendes Kind (Mime) *Siegfried* 1 Wagner
Al tuo seno fortunato (Sibyl) *L'anima del filosofo* 3 Haydn
Alzati ... Eri tu (Renato [Captain Anckarstroem]) *Un ballo in maschera* 3 Verdi
Amai, ma un solo istante ... Or del padre benedetta (Joan of Arc, Giacomo) *Giovanna d'Arco* 3 Verdi
Amami, Alfredo (Violetta) *La traviata* 2 Verdi
Ama, sospira, mà non ti offende (Morgana) *Alcina* 2 Handel
Ambo nati in questa valle (Antonio Loustolot) *Linda di Chamounix* 1 Donizetti
Amenaide ... serbami tua fé (Tancredi) *Tancredi* 2 Rossini
Ami! ... le coeur d'Hélène (Hélène) *Les vêpres siciliennes* 4 Verdi
Amis, la matinée est belle (Masaniello) *La muette de Portici* 2 Auber
Amis, l'amour tendre et rêveur, erreur! (Hoffmann) *Les contes d'Hoffmann* 3 Offenbach
Am Jordan Sankt Johannes stand (David) *Die Meistersinger* 3 Wagner
Amo, amas, I love a lass (Lingo) *The Agreeable Surprise* Arnold
A moi les plaisirs (Faust, Méphistophélès) *Faust* 1 Gounod
Amore misterio celeste (Faust, Helen of Troy) *Mefistofele* 4 Boito
Amore o grillo (Pinkerton, Sharpless) *Madama Butterfly* 1 Puccini
Amor è qual vento (Dorinda) *Orlando* 3 Handel
Amore, vieni a me (Glaucus) *Medea* 1 Cherubini
Amor nel mio penar (Guido) *Flavio* 3 Handel
Amor ti vieta (Loris) *Fedora* 2 Giordano
Amour, lance tes traits (Folly) *Platée* 3 Rameau
Amour que veux-tu de moi? (Arcabonne) *Amadis* 2 Lully
Amour! viens aider ma faiblesse (Delilah) *Samson et Dalila* 2 Saint-Saëns
Am stillen Herd (Walther, ensemble) *Die Meistersinger* 1 Wagner
Anch'io dischiuso un giorno ... Salgo già del trono aurato (Abigaille) *Nabucco* 2 Verdi
Ancor non giunse? ... Regnava nel silenzio ... Quando rapito in estasi (Lucia) *Lucia di Lammermoor* 1 Donizetti
And do you prefer the storm to Auntie's parlour (Balstrode, Peter Grimes) *Peter Grimes* 1 Britten
And now we summon from this leafy bower (Spirit of the Masque, chorus) *Gloriana* 2 Britten
Andrem, raminghi e poveri (Luisa, Miller) *Luisa Miller* 3 Verdi
Andrò, ramingo e solo (Ilia, Electra, Idamantes, Idomeneus) *Idomeneo* 3 Mozart
Ange adorable (Romeo, Juliet) *Roméo et Juliette* 1 Gounod
Ange adoré (Marguerite, Faust) *La damnation de Faust* 3 Berlioz
Angelo casto e bel (Marcello di Bruges) *Il duca d'Alba* 4 Donizetti
Anges du paradis (Vincent) *Mireille* 5 Gounod
Ange si pur (Fernand) *La favorite* 4 Donizetti
Anges purs, anges radieux (Marguerite, Faust, Méphistophélès) *Faust* 5 Gounod
A nous les amours et les roses (Manon) *Manon* 4 Massenet
Answer me, bright orb (Queen of Shemakha) *The Golden Cockerel* 2 Rimsky-Korsakov
Anvil Chorus: *see* Vedi! le fosche notturne
A peine aux autels d'Hymenée (Lynceus) *Les Danaïdes* 4 Salieri
Apparvi alla luce (Maria, Sulpizio) *La figlia del reggimento* 1 Donizetti
Apri la tua finestra! (Osaka) *Iris* 1 Mascagni
Aprite, presto aprite (Susanna, Cherubino) *Le nozze di Figaro* 2 Mozart
Aprite un po' quegl'occhi (Figaro) *Le nozze di Figaro* 4 Mozart
A quanto peni! ma pur fa core (ensemble) *La traviata* 2 Verdi
A quoi bon l'économie ... O Rosalinde (Lescaut) *Manon* 3 Massenet
Arbitre d'une vie (Elvire) *La muette de Portici* 4 Auber
Arbitre suprême du ciel et de la terre (Moses) *Moïse et Pharaon* 2 Rossini
Ardon gl'incensi ... splendon le sacre faci ... Alfin son tua ... Spargi d'amaro pianto (Lucia, ensemble) *Lucia di Lammermoor* 3 Donizetti
Ardo, sospiro e piango (Diana) *Calisto* 1 Cavalli
Ariadne's lament: *see* Lasciatemi morire
Armide est encore plus aimable (Hidraot, chorus) *Armide* 1 Lully
Arrêtez, ô mes frères (Samson) *Samson et Dalila* 1 Saint-Saëns
Arrigo! ah parli a un core ... È dolce raggio (Arrigo, Elena) *I vespri siciliani* 4 Verdi
Art thou troubled: *see* Dove sei, amato bene
Ascolta o figlio quell'augellino (Andromache) *Astianatte* 3 Bononcini
Asile héréditaire (Arnold Melcthal) *Guillaume Tell* 4 Rossini
As I said to you [Jak vám pravím pane kmotře] (Kecal, Ludmila, Krušina) *The Bartered Bride* 1 Smetana
Aspetta, aspetta, cara sposina (Malatesta, Don Pasquale) *Don Pasquale* 3 Donizetti
Assassini! (Enzo) *La Gioconda* 1 Ponchielli
Assisa a piè d'un salice (Desdemona) *Otello* 3 Rossini
Assis au pied d'un hêtre (Chapelou) *Le postillon de Lonjumeau* 2 Adam
Astres étincelants (Phanuel) *Hérodiade* 3 Massenet
As-tu souffert? As-tu pleuré (Lothario, Mignon) *Mignon* 2 Thomas

A suoi piedi, padre essangue (Bajazet) *Tamerlano* 2 Handel
As when the dove laments her love (Galatea) *Acis and Galatea* 1 Handel
A tanto amor (Alfonso XI) *La favorita* 3 Donizetti
A te Furie, volate a me (Medea) *Medea* 3 Cherubini
A te grave cagion m'adduce ... Rivedrai le foreste imbalsamate ... Su dunque! ... Padre! a costoro (Amonasro, Aida) *Aida* 3 Verdi
A te, o cara (Arturo, Elvira, ensemble) *I puritani* 1 Bellini
A terra ... sì ... nel livido fango (Desdemona, ensemble) *Otello* 3 Verdi
A te sarà (Otello, Desdemona) *Otello* 3 Rossini
A tes lois je souscris d'avance (Robert, Alice, Bertram) *Robert le diable* 5 Meyerbeer
Atys est trop heureux! (Sangaride) *Atys* 1 Lully
Au bonheur dont mon âme est pleine ... Mais celle qui devint ma femme (Albert, Werther) *Werther* 2 Massenet
Au bruit de la guerre (Marie, Sulpice Pingot) *La fille du régiment* 1 Donizetti
Auch ich war ein Jüngling (Hans Stadinger) *Der Waffenschmied* 3 Lortzing
Auf, Gesellen, greift zur Axt (Peter the Great) *Zar und Zimmermann* 1 Lortzing
Auf hohem Felsen (Erik) *Der fliegende Holländer* 2 Wagner
Au fond du temple saint (Nadir, Zurga) *Les pêcheurs de perles* 1 Bizet
Augelletti che cantate (Almirena) *Rinaldo* 1 Handel
Augelletti, ruscelletti (Mirtillo) *Il pastor fido* 1 Handel
A un dottor della mia sorte (Bartolo) *Il barbiere diSiviglia* 1 Rossini
Au palais des fées (Eboli) *Don Carlos* 2 Verdi
Aure chete (Angelica) *Orlando paladino* 2 Haydn
Aure, deh, per pietà (Julius Caesar) *Giulio Cesare* 3 Handel
Aure trecce (Erisbe, Mirinda) *Ormindo* 2 Cavalli
Au revoir dans un monde (Elisabeth de Valois, Don Carlos) *Don Carlos* 5 Verdi
Au sein de la puissance (Montfort) *Les vêpres siciliennes* 3 Verdi
Aussi nombreux que les étoiles (Zacharie) *Le prophète* 3 Meyerbeer
Autrefois un roi de Thulé (Marguerite) *La damnation de Faust* 3 Berlioz
Aux langueurs d'Apollon (Folly) *Platée* 2 Rameau
Aux troupes du Sultan ... Promesse de mon avenir (Scindia) *Le roi de Lahore* 4 Massenet
Avant de quitter ces lieux (Valentin) *Faust* 2 Gounod
Avec bonté voyez ma peine (Isabelle, Robert) *Robert le diable* 2 Meyerbeer
Ave Maria (Desdemona) *Otello* 4 Verdi
Ave signor (Mefistofele, chorus) *Mefistofele* prol. Boito
Avete torto ... Firenze è come un albero fiorito (Rinuccio) *Gianni Schicchi* Puccini
A vos jeux ... Partagez-vous mes fleurs ... Pâle et blonde, dort sous l'eau (Ophelia) *Hamlet* 4 Thomas
A voti così ardente (Maria, Tonio) *La figlia del reggimento* 1 Donizetti
Avvezza al contento (Orpheus, Eurydice) *Orfeo ed Euridice* 3 Gluck
A woman is a sometime thing (Jake) *Porgy and Bess* 1 Gershwin

B

Bacia per me la mano (Costanza) *Riccardo* 3 Handel
Bagnato dalle lagrime (Gualtiero, Imogene) *Il pirata* 1 Bellini
Bambina, non ti crucciar (Michonnet, Adriana) *Adriana Lecouvreur* 4 Cilea
Bannis la crainte (Admetus) *Alceste* 2 Gluck
Barbara! io ben lo sò (Oberto) *Alcina* 3 Handel
Barbaro! partirò (Polissena) *Radamisto* 3 Handel
Barcarolle: *see* Belle nuit, ô nuit d'amour
Basta che sol tu chieda (Claudius) *Agrippina* 2 Handel
Basta che sol tu chieda (Argante) *Rinaldo* 2 Handel
Batti, batti (Zerlina) *Don Giovanni* 1 Mozart
Beauté divine, enchanteresse (Raoul, Marguerite de Valois) *Les Huguenots* 2 Meyerbeer
Beckmesser's Serenade: *see* Den Tag seh' ich erscheinen
Begone, my fears (Dejanira) *Hercules* 2 Handel
Behold on Lethe's dismal strand (Artaxerxes) *Artaxerxes* 1 Arne
Bei jener Nacht (Helen, Menelaus) *Die ägyptische Helena* 1 Strauss
Bei Männern (Pamina, Papageno) *Die Zauberflöte* 1 Mozart
Bel inconnu (Balkis) *La rencontre imprévue* 1 Gluck
Bella Asteria, il tuo cor (Andronicus) *Tamerlano* 1 Handel
Bella figlia dell'amore (Duke, Gilda, Maddalena, Rigoletto) *Rigoletto* 3 Verdi
Bella Italia (Selim) *Il turco in Italia* 1 Rossini
Bell'alme generose (Elizabeth, ensemble) *Elisabetta, regina d'Inghilterra* 2 Rossini
Bella siccome un angelo (Dr Malatesta) *Don Pasquale* 1 Donizetti
Belle Hermione, Hélas (Cadmus) *Cadmus et Hermione* 5 Lully
Belle nuit, ô nuit d'amour (Giulietta, Nicklausse) *Les contes d'Hoffmann* 4 Offenbach
Bell Song: *see* Où va la jeune Hindoue
Bel piacere e godere (Poppaea) *Agrippina* 3 Handel
Bel piacere e godere (Almirena) *Rinaldo* 3 Handel
Bel raggio lusinghier (Semiramide) *Semiramide* 1 Rossini
Bel sogno beato (Riccardo) *I puritani* 1 Bellini
Benchè mi sia crudele (Teofane) *Ottone* 3 Handel
Benchè mi sprezzi (Andronicus) *Tamerlano* 1 Handel
Ben io t'invenni ... Anch'io dischiuso un giorno ... Salgo già del trono aurato (Abigaille) *Nabucco* 2 Verdi
Bess, you is my woman (Porgy, Bess) *Porgy and Bess* 2 Gershwin
Bester Jüngling (Mlle Silberklang) *Der Schauspieldirektor* Mozart
Bethörte! (Eglantine) *Euryanthe* 1 Weber
Bimba dagli occhi pieni di malià (Pinkerton, Butterfly) *Madama Butterfly* 1 Puccini
Bin Akademiker (Barber, Nureddin) *Der Barbier von Bagdad* 1 Cornelius
Birdcatcher's Song: *see* Der Vogelfänger bin ich ja
Bleib und wache bis sie dich ruft (Emperor, Nurse) *Die Frau ohne Schatten* 1 Strauss
Blick' ich umher (Wolfram) *Tannhäuser* 2 Wagner
Blickt sein Auge doch so ehrlich (Lady Harriet, Lyonel) *Martha* 2 Flotow
Blühenden Lebens labendes Blut (Siegfried, Gunther) *Götterdämmerung* 1 Wagner
Bois épais (Amadis) *Amadis* 2 Lully
Bolero: *see* Mercè, dilette amiche/Merci, jeunes amies
Bramo di trionfar (Ruggiero) *Alcina* 1 Handel
Brangäne's Watch: *see* Einsam wachend in der Nacht
Bridal March: *see* Treulich geführt
Brillant auteur de la lumière (Agamemnon) *Iphigénie en Aulide* 1 Gluck
Brillant soleil (Huascar) *Les Indes galantes* 2 Rameau
Brillez, astres nouveaux (Planet) *Castor et Pollux* 5 Rameau
Brindisi: *see* Libiamo ne' lieti calici; Viva il vino spumeggiante
Brisons tous nos fers (chorus) *Castor et Pollux* 3 Rameau
Brothers, into the storm (Sobinin) *A Life for the Tsar* 4 Glinka
Brüderchen komm tanz mit mir (Gretel, Hänsel) *Hänsel und Gretel* 1 Humperdinck
Brünnhilde's Immolation: *see* Starke Scheite
Buona sera, mio signore (Rosina, Almaviva, Figaro, Don Basilio, Bartolo) *Il barbiere di Siviglia* 2 Rossini
But hark! the heavenly sphere turns round (Ino) *Semele* 2 Handel
By the croaking of the toad (Ismeron) *The Indian Queen* 3 Purcell
By the walls of Kazan (Varlaam) *Boris Godunov* iv/1 Musorgsky

C

Cade il mondo soggiogato (Claudius) *Agrippina* 2 Handel
Caduto è il reprobo! (Amalia, Carlo, Massimiliano) *I masnadieri* 4 Verdi
Calchas, d'un trait mortel percé (Achilles) *Iphigénie en Aulide* 3 Gluck
Calore! Luce! Amor! (chorus) *Iris* 1 Mascagni
Cangiò d'aspetto il crudo fato (Admetus) *Admeto* 1 Handel
Cara è vero (Rinaldo) *Armida* 2 Haydn
Cara non dubitar ... Io ti lascio (Carolina, Paolino) *Il matrimonio segreto* 1 Cimarosa
Cara patria, già madre (Foresto) *Attila* prol. Verdi

Cara sposa, amante cara (Rinaldo) *Rinaldo* 1 Handel
Cara sposa, amato bene (Radamisto) *Radamisto* 1 Handel
Cara tomba del mio diletto (Laodice) *Mitridate Eupatore* 3 Scarlatti
Care selve, ombre beate (Meleager) *Atalanta* 1 Handel
Cari luoghi (Pierotto) *Linda di Chamounix* 1 Donizetti
Carlo! io muoio (Amalia, Massimiliano) *I masnadieri* 1 Verdi
Carlo vive? (Amalia) *I masnadieri* 2 Verdi
Caro! bella! più amabile beltà (Cleopatra, Julius Caesar) *Giulio Cesare* 3 Handel
Caro nome (Gilda) *Rigoletto* 1 Verdi
Cassio's Dream: *see* Era la notte
Casta diva ... Ah! bello, a me ritorna (Norma) *Norma* 1 Bellini
Catalogue aria: *see* Madamina, il catalogo è questo
Cease, ruler of the day (Dejanira) *Hercules* 2 Handel
Cease to beauty to be suing (Polyphemus) *Acis and Galatea* 2 Handel
Cease your funning (Polly) *Beggar's Opera* 2
C'è a Windsor una dama (Ford, Falstaff) *Falstaff* 2 Verdi
Cedo al destin orribile (Imogene, Gualtiero, Ernesto) *Il pirata* 2 Bellini
Cedo a Roma, e cedo a te (Luceius) *Scipione* 2 Handel
Ce domaine est celui des contes d'Avenel (Anna, George Brown) *La dame blanche* 2 Boieldieu
Ce fauteuil (King Ouf I) *L'étoile* 1 Chabrier
Celeste Aida (Radames) *Aida* 1 Verdi
C'en est fait! Le ciel même (Baron de Mergy, Isabelle, Marguerite) *Le Pré aux Clercs* 3 Hérold
Ce que j'appelle le beau (Fanny) *Sapho* 2 Massenet
Cercherò lontana terra (Ernesto) *Don Pasquale* 2 Donizetti
Cerco il mio ben così (Orpheus) *Orfeo ed Euridice* 1 Gluck
Cerco in vano di placare (Andronicus) *Tamerlano* 2 Handel
Ces lettres! (Charlotte) *Werther* 3 Massenet
Ce soir j'arrive donc (Baron de Mergy) *Le Pré aux Clercs* 1 Hérold
Cessa di più resistere ... Ah il più lieto (Almaviva) *Il barbiere di Siviglia* 2 Rossini
Cessa omai di sospirare (Cornelia) *Giulio Cesare* 2 Handel
Cesse, cruel Amour (Iphise) *Dardanus* 1 Rameau
Cessez mes yeux (Herminie) *Tancrède* 3 Campra
C'est à toi de trembler (Licinius, Pontifex Maximus) *La vestale* 3 Spontini
C'est le dieu de la jeunesse (Lakmé, Gerald) *Lakmé* 1 Delibes
C'est mon jour suprême ... Carlos, écoute (Posa) *Don Carlos* 4 Verdi
C'est sur ce banc (Penelope, Eumaeus) *Pénélope* 2 Fauré
C'est toi! C'est moi! (Don José, Carmen) *Carmen* 4 Bizet
C'est une chanson d'amour (Hoffmann, Antonia) *Les contes d'Hoffmann* 3 Offenbach
C'est un torrent impétueux (Vertigo) *La rencontre imprévue* 3 Gluck
C'était bien gentil autrefois (Irène, Jean) *Sapho* 2 Massenet
Cet asile aimable et tranquille (Eurydice) *Orphée et Eurydice* 2 Gluck
Cette nuit j'ai revu (Iphigenia) *Iphigénie en Tauride* 1 Gluck
Chacun le sait (Marie) *La fille du régiment* 1 Donizetti
Champagne aria: *see* Fin ch'han dal vino
Chanson de Magali: *see* La brise est douce et parfumée
Chantons, célébrons en ce jour (chorus) *Platée* 3 Rameau
Chantons Platée, égayons-nous (chorus) *Platée* 3 Rameau
Charmes trop dangereux (Abaris) *Les Boréades* 2 Rameau
Che bel contento sarebbe amore (Vitige) *Flavio* 1 Handel
Che colpa è la mia (Teodata) *Flavio* 3 Handel
Che farò senza Euridice? (Orpheus) *Orfeo ed Euridice* 3 Gluck
Che far vuoi tu? ... Qual sarà dolor che uccide (Alaide, Isoletta, Arturo, Valdeburgo) *La straniera* 2 Bellini
Che fiero momento! (Eurydice) *Orfeo ed Euridice* 3 Gluck
Che gelida manina (Rodolfo) *La bohème* 1 Puccini
Ch'ella mi creda libero e lontano (Dick Johnson) *La fanciulla del West* 3 Puccini
Che maestà, che brio (septet) *Eraclea* 1 Scarlatti
Che non avrebbe il misero (Foresto) *Attila* 3 Verdi
Che puro ciel (Orpheus) *Orfeo ed Euridice* 2 Gluck
Chère enfant! (Antonia, Antonia's mother, Dr Miracle) *Les contes d'Hoffmann* 3 Offenbach
Cherry duet: *see* Suzel, buon dì
Chers enfants (Medea, Jason) *Médée* 2 Cherubini
Chers Tyriens (Dido) *Les Troyens* 3 Berlioz
Che soave zeffiretto (Countess Almaviva, Susanna) *Le nozze di Figaro* 3 Mozart
Che sorda al mesto pianto (Orestes, Pylades) *Ermione* 1 Rossini
Cheti, cheti, immantinente ... Aspetta, aspetta, cara sposina (Dr Malatesta, Don Pasquale) *Don Pasquale* 3 Donizetti
Chiamo il mio ben così (Orpheus) *Orfeo ed Euridice* 1 Gluck
Chi cede al furore (Romilda) *Serse* 2 Handel
Chi del gitano (chorus) *Il trovatore* 2 Verdi
Chiedi all'aura lusinghiera (Nemorino, Adina) *L'elisir d'amore* 1 Donizetti
Chi il bel sogno di Doretta (Magda de Civry) *La rondine* 1 Puccini
Chi mi frena in tal momento (Lucia, Alisa, Edgardo, Arturo, Enrico, Raimondo) *Lucia di Lammermoor* 2 Donizetti
Chi m'insegna il caro padre (Oberto) *Alcina* 2 Handel
Chi nacque al rimbombo (Maria, ensemble) *La figlia del reggimento* 2 Donizetti
Ch'io lasci mai d'amare (Melissa) *Amadigi* 2 Handel
Ch'io parta? sì, crudele (Arsace) *Partenope* 3 Handel
Chi scherza colle rose (Hymen) *Imeneo* 2 Handel
Chiudetevi, miei lumi (Admetus) *Admeto* 1 Handel
Chorus of the Hebrew Slaves: *see* Va pensiero
Ciascun lo dice (Maria) *La figlia del reggimento* 1 Donizetti
Cieca notte, infidi sguardi (Ariodante) *Ariodante* 3 Handel
Ciel che feci! (Riccardo) *Oberto, conte di San Bonifacio* 2 Verdi
Ciel e terra armi di sdegno (Bajazet) *Tamerlano* 1 Handel
Cielo, a miei lunghi spasimi ... Coppia iniqua (Anne Boleyn, ensemble) *Anna Bolena* 2 Donizetti
Ciel, O ciel! le fleuve agite (chorus) *Les fêtes d'Hébé* 1 Rameau
Cielo e mar (Enzo) *La Gioconda* 2 Ponchielli
Cielo! se tu il consenti (Orlando) *Orlando* 2 Handel
Ciel pietoso, in si crudo momento ... Or sei pago, o ciel tremendo (Alaide, ensemble) *La straniera* 2 Bellini
Ciel, sei tu che in tal momento ... Ugo è spento (Parisina, ensemble) *Parisina* 3 Donizetti
Cingetemi il crine (Venus) *Il pomo d'oro* 1 Cesti
Cinque ... dieci ... venti (Figaro, Susanna) *Le nozze di Figaro* 1 Mozart
Cinta di fiori (Giorgio) *I puritani* 2 Bellini
Clock Scene: *see* Give me air, I suffocate
Coat Song: *see* Vecchia zimarra
Colma il tuo cor d'un palpito (Faust) *Mefistofele* 2 Boito
Col raggio placido (Pallas) *Agrippina* 2 Handel
Col sangue sol cancellasi ... Le minaccie, i fieri accenti ... Ah, segnasti la tua sorte (Don Carlo, Don Alvaro) *La forza del destino* 4 Verdi
Col sorriso d'innocenza ... Oh sole ti vela (Imogene) *Il pirata* 2 Bellini
Combatti da forte (Almirena) *Rinaldo* 1 Handel
Come all ye songsters (tenor) *The Fairy-Queen* 2 Purcell
Come away, fellow sailors (Sailor, chorus) *Dido and Aeneas* 3 Purcell
Com'è bello (Lucrezia) *Lucrezia Borgia* prol. Donizetti
Come dal ciel precipita (Banquo) *Macbeth* 2 Verdi
Come due tizzi accessi (Baldassare) *L'Arlesiane* 1 Cilea
Come frenar il pianto! (Ninetta, Fernando Villabella) *La gazza ladra* 1 Rossini
Com'è gentil (Ernesto) *Don Pasquale* 3 Donizetti
Come if you dare (British Warrior) *King Arthur* 1 Purcell
Come il bacio d'un padre amoroso (Carlo, Massimiliano) *I masnadieri* 4 Verdi
Come innocente giovane ... Non v'ha sguardo (Anne) *Anna Bolena* 1 Donizetti
Come in quest'ora bruna (Amelia) *Simon Boccanegra* 1 Verdi
Come notte al sol fulgente (Zaccaria) *Nabucco* 1 Verdi
Come nube che fugge dal vento (Nero) *Agrippina* 3 Handel
Come Paride vezzoso (Belcore) *L'elisir d'amore* 1 Donizetti
Come per me sereno ... Sovra il sen la man mi posa (Amina) *La sonnambula* 1 Bellini
Come poteva un angelo (Oronte) *I Lombardi* 2 Verdi
Come rugiada al cespite ... O tu, che l'alma adora (Ernani) *Ernani* 1 Verdi

Come scoglio (Fiordiligi) *Così fan tutte* 1 Mozart
Come un'ape ne' giorni d'aprile (Dandini) *La Cenerentola* 1 Rossini
Come un bel dì di maggio (Andrea Chénier) *Andrea Chénier* 4 Giordano
Come uno spirto angelico (Robert) *Roberto Devereux* 3 Donizetti
Comme autrefois dans la nuit sombre (Leïla) *Les pêcheurs de perles* 2 Bizet
Comment le Dédain pourrait il mourir? (Benedick, Beatrice) *Béatrice et Bénédict* 1 Berlioz
Comment peut-on penser du bien (Sancho Panza) *Don Quichotte* 2 Massenet
Comme une pâle fleur (Hamlet) *Hamlet* 4 Thomas
Complices de sa gloire (Cassandra) *Les Troyens* 2 Berlioz
Confusa smarrita (Marcia) *Catone in Utica* 3 J. C. Bach
Con l'ali di costanza (Alexander) *Alessandro Severo* 3 Handel
Con l'ali di costanza (Ariodante) *Ariodante* 1 Handel
Connais-tu le pays? (Mignon) *Mignon* 1 Thomas
Con rauco mormorio (Bertarido) *Rodelinda* 2 Handel
Consider, fond shepherd (Damon) *Acis and Galatea* 2 Handel
Consolati, o bella (Dorinda, Angelica, Medoro) *Orlando* 1 Handel
Contente-toi d'une victime (Theseus, Tisiphone) *Hippolyte et Aricie* 2 Rameau
Contro un cor (Rosina) *Il barbiere di Siviglia* 2 Rossini
Con un' vezzo, con un' riso (Teodata) *Flavio* 2 Handel
Con un' vezzo, con un' riso (Armira) *Scipione* 2 Handel
Convien partir (Maria) *La figlia del reggimento* 1 Donizetti
Coperta la frode di lana servile (Polinesso) *Ariodante* 1 Handel
Coppia iniqua (Anne Boleyn, ensemble) *Anna Bolena* 2 Donizetti
Coraggio, su, coraggio (Elena) *I vespri siciliani* 1 Verdi
Cor di padre e cor d'amante (Asteria) *Tamerlano* 3 Handel
Cor ingrato, ti rammembri (Rinaldo) *Rinaldo* 1 Handel
Cortigiani, vil razza dannata (Rigoletto) *Rigoletto* 2 Verdi
Cosa sento (Count Almaviva, Susanna, Don Basilio) *Le nozze di Figaro* 1 Mozart
Could it then have been known (Anne, Tom, Baba) *The Rake's Progress* 2 Stravinsky
Coulez mes pleurs (Zélide) *Zaïs* 3 Rameau
Couplets du pal: *see* Ce fauteuil
Courage! ... du courage (Hélène) *Les vêpres siciliennes* 1 Verdi
Credeasi, misera (Arturo, Elvira, ensemble) *I puritani* 3 Bellini
Credete alle femmine (Fiorilla, Selim) *Il turco in Italia* 2 Rossini
Credete al mio dolore (Morgana) *Alcina* 3 Handel
Credo a una possanza arcana (Andrea Chénier) *Andrea Chénier* 2 Giordano
Credo in un Dio crudel (Iago) *Otello* 2 Verdi
Crown with festal pomp (chorus) *Hercules* 1 Handel
Cruda, funesta smania ... La pietade in suo favore (Enrico) *Lucia di Lammermoor* 1 Donizetti
Cruda sorte! (Isabella) *L'italiana in Algeri* 1 Rossini
Crude furie degl'orridi abissi (Xerxes) *Serse* 3 Handel
Crudele? ... Non mi dir (Donna Anna) *Don Giovanni* 2 Mozart
Crudeli, fermate (Sandrina) *La finta giardiniera* 2 Mozart
Crudel! perchè finora (Count Almaviva, Susanna) *Le nozze di Figaro* 3 Mozart
Cruelle mère des amours (Phaedra) *Hippolyte et Aricie* 3 Rameau
Cruels tyrans qui regnez (Abramane) *Zoroastre* 4 Rameau
Csárdás: *see* Klänge der Heimat

D

Da geht er hin (Marschallin) *Der Rosenkavalier* 1 Strauss
Dagl'immortali vertici ... È gettata la mia sorte (Ezio) *Attila* 2 Verdi
Da Gusman, su fragil barca ... Nell'astro che piu fulgido (Alzira) *Alzira* 1 Verdi
Dai campi, dai prati (Faust) *Mefistofele* 1 Boito
Dai più remoto esilio ... Odio solo, ed odio atroce (Jacopo Foscari) *I due Foscari* 1 Verdi
Dal crudel che m'ha tradita (Irene) *Tamerlano* 1 Handel
Dal fulgor di questa spada (Achillas) *Giulio Cesare* 3 Handel
Da lieg' ich! Was einem Kavalier (Ochs, Annina, Servants) *Der Rosenkavalier* 2 Strauss
Dal labbro il canto (Fenton) *Falstaff* 3 Verdi
Dalla sponda tenebrosa (Junia) *Lucio Silla* 1 Mozart
Dalla sua pace (Don Ottavio) *Don Giovanni* 1 Mozart
Dall'aule raggianti ... Deh! la parola amara (Federica, Rodolfo) *Luisa Miller* 1 Verdi
Dalle basse e dall'alte regioni (Macbeth, Witches) *Macbeth* 3 Verdi
Dalle stanze ove Lucia (Raimondo) *Lucia di Lammermoor* 3 Donizetti
Dall'orror di notte cieca (chorus) *Alcina* 3 Handel
Dal tuo stellato soglio (Moses) *Mosè in Egitto* 3 Rossini
Dammi la dolce e lieta parole (Desdemona, Emilia, Otello, Iago) *Otello* 2 Verdi
D'amore al dolce impero (Armida) *Armida* ? Rossini
D'amor sull'ali rosee (Leonora) *Il trovatore* 4 Verdi
D'amour l'ardente flamme (Marguerite) *La damnation de Faust* 4 Berlioz
Dans ce beau pays, pur d'hérétique levain (Grand Inquisitor, Philip II) *Don Carlos* 4 Verdi
Dans ce lieu solitaire (Raimbaud, chorus) *Le comte Ory* 2 Rossini
Dans ce séjour (Adèle, Ragonde) *Le comte Ory* 2 Rossini
Dans l'ombre et le silence (Procida) *Les vêpres siciliennes* 2 Verdi
Dans ma cabane obscure (Colin) *Le devin du village* 1 Rousseau
Dans son regard plus sombre (Gertrude) *Hamlet* 2 Thomas
Da quel dì che lei perduta (Percy) *Anna Bolena* 1 Donizetti
Da qual dì che t'ho veduta (Don Carlo, Elvira) *Ernani* 1 Verdi
Da quel dì che t'incontrai (Carlo) *Linda di Chamounix* 1 Donizetti
Da quel dì ... Vieni fra queste braccia (Arturo, Elvira) *I puritani* 3 Bellini
Da schlägt des Abschieds Stunde (Mme Herz) *Der Schauspieldirektor* Mozart
Das Essen ist da (Marta, Pedro) *Tiefland* 2 D'Albert
Das süsse Lied verhallt (Lohengrin, Elsa) *Lohengrin* 3 Wagner
Das Tor ist zu. Wir sind allein (Pedro, Marta) *Tiefland* 1 D'Albert
Das war sehr gut, Mandryka (Arabella, Mandryka) *Arabella* 3 Strauss
Date almen per pieta (Medea, Creon) *Medea* 2 Cherubini
Da tempeste il legno infranto (Cleopatra) *Giulio Cesare* 3 Handel
Da te questo (Odabella) *Attila* prol. Verdi
Da tutti abbandonata (Mary, Leicester) *Maria Stuarda* 1/2 Donizetti
Daughter of gods, bright liberty (Iole) *Hercules* 1 Handel
Daylight is fading (Vladimir) *Prince Igor* 2 Borodin
Dear children (Susanin, Antonida, Vanya, Sobinin) *A Life for the Tsar* 3 Glinka
De cet aveu si tendre (Marie, Tonio) *La fille du régiment* 1 Donizetti
Deggio dunque, o Dio, lasciarti (Zenobia) *Radamisto* 3 Handel
D'Egitto là sui lidi ... Come notte al sol fulgente (Zaccaria) *Nabucco* 1 Verdi
Deh! fuggi un traditore (Tigrane) *Radamisto* 1 Handel
Deh! la parola amara (Federica, Rodolfo) *Luisa Miller* 1 Verdi
Deh! lascia o core di sospirar (Andromache) *Astinatte* 2 Bononcini
Deh non parlare al misero ... Ah! veglia o donna (Rigoletto, Gilda) *Rigoletto* 1 Verdi
Deh, non turbare (Laura, Enzo) *La Gioconda* 2 Ponchielli
Deh! non voler costringere (Smeton) *Anna Bolena* 1 Donizetti
Deh! non volerli vittime (Norma, Pollione, Oroveso) *Norma* 2 Bellini
Deh per questo istante solo (Sextus) *La clemenza di Tito* 2 Mozart
Deh prendi un dolce amplesso (Sextus, Annius) *La clemenza di Tito* 1 Mozart
Deh! proteggimi, o Dio! (Adalgisa) *Norma* 1 Bellini
Deh! rallentate, o barbari (Azucena, ensemble) *Il trovatore* 3 Verdi
Deh, scusa i trasporti (Leicester, Norfolk) *Elisabetta, regina d'Inghilterra* 2 Rossini
Deh se piacer mi vuoi (Vitellia) *La clemenza di Tito* 1 Mozart
Deh soccorri un infelice (Celia) *La fedeltà premiata* 1 Haydn
Deh! ti ferma (Assur, soldiers) *Semiramide* 2 Rossini
Deh! tu calma, o Dio possente ... Coraggio, su, coraggio (Elena) *I vespri siciliani* 1 Verdi

Deh! tu, deh! tu bell'anima (Romeo, Giulietta, ensemble) *I Capuleti e i Montecchi* 2 Bellini
Deh vieni alla finestra (Don Giovanni) *Don Giovanni* 2 Mozart
Deh vieni non tardar (Susanna) *Le nozze di Figaro* 4 Mozart
Dei pietosi (Rinaldo) *Armida* 3 Haydn
Dei tuoi figli (Medea) *Medea* 1 Cherubini
Del fiero duol (Medea) *Medea* 3 Cherubini
Del futuro nel buio (Zaccaria) *Nabucco* 3 Verdi
Della crudele Isotta (Adina) *L'elisir d'amore* 1 Donizetti
Della Duchessa ai prieghi ... Guai se ti sfugge un moto (Alfonso, Lucrezia, Gennaro) *Lucrezia Borgia* 1 Donizetti
Dell'antro magico (Medea) *Giasone* 1 Cavalli
Delle faci festante al barlume ... Piango, perchè mi parla (Fiesco, Boccanegra) *Simon Boccanegra* 3 Verdi
Del mar sul lido (Fiesco, Boccanegra) *Simon Boccanegra* prol. Verdi
Del minacciar del vento (Emireno) *Ottone* 1 Handel
Del più sublime soglio (Titus) *La clemenza di Tito* 1 Mozart
Demain je partirai ... Faut-il avoir aimé (Fanny) *Sapho* 5 Massenet
De' miei bollenti spiriti ... Oh mio rimorso! (Alfredo) *La traviata* 2 Verdi
De mon amie fleur endormie (Nadir) *Les pêcheurs de perles* 2 Bizet
Den Bronnen, den uns wolfram nannte (Walther) *Tannhäuser* 2 Wagner
Denn wie man sich bettet (Jimmy, ensemble) *Aufstieg und Fall der Stadt Mahagonny* 1 Weill
De noirs pressentiments (Thoas) *Iphigénie en Tauride* 1 Gluck
Den Tag seh' ich erscheinen (Beckmesser) *Die Meistersinger* 2 Wagner
Dépit mortel (Medea) *Thésée* 2 Lully
Depuis le jour (Louise) *Louise* 3 Charpentier
Depuis longtemps j'habitais (Julien, Louise) *Louise* 1 Charpentier
De quels transports ... Toujours unis par la serment (Elisabeth de Valois, Don Carlos) *Don Carlos* 1 Verdi
Der heilige Michael (Nuri) *Tiefland* 2 D'Albert
Der Hölle Rache (Queen of Night) *Die Zauberflöte* 2 Mozart
Der kleine Sandmann bin ich (Sandman) *Hänsel und Gretel* 2 Humperdinck
Der kleine Taumann heiss' ich (Dew Fairy) *Hänsel und Gretel* 3 Humperdinck
Der Lenz ist gekommen (Lady Harriet, Lyonel) *Martha* 4 Flotow
Der Männer Sippe (Sieglinde) *Die Walküre* 1 Wagner
Derrière ce pilier (Marcel, Valentine) *Les Huguenots* 3 Meyerbeer
Der Unglücksel'ge ... Ich fleh' für ihn (Elisabeth) *Tannhäuser* 2 Wagner
Der Vogelfänger bin ich ja (Papageno) *Die Zauberflöte* 1 Mozart
Des chevaliers de ma patrie (Robert, Bertram) *Robert le diable* 3 Meyerbeer
Des cieux où tu résides grand Dieu (Moses) *Moïse et Pharaon* 4 Rossini
Deserto sulla terra (Manrico) *Il trovatore* 1 Verdi
De son coeur j'ai calmé la fièvre (Lothario) *Mignon* 3 Thomas
Desterò dall'empia Dite (Melissa) *Amadigi* 2 Handel
Devant la maison (Méphistophélès) *La danmation de Faust* 3 Berlioz
Dì ad Irene, tiranna, infedele (Amintas) *Atalanta* 2 Handel
Diane impitoyable! ... Brillant auteur de la lumière (Agamemnon) *Iphigénie en Aulide* 1 Gluck
Dica il falso, dica il vero (Roxana) *Alessandro* 2 Handel
Di che fulgor (Oscar, Amelia, Renato, Samuel, Tom) *Un ballo in maschera* 3 Verdi
Dich, teure Halle (Elisabeth) *Tannhäuser* 2 Wagner
D'ici je vois la mer (Sélika) *L'Africaine* 5 Meyerbeer
D'ici voyez ce beau domaine (Jenny) *La dame blanche* 1 Boieldieu
Dì, cor mio, quanto t'amai (Alcina) *Alcina* 1 Handel
Di Cupido, impiego i vanni (Garibaldo) *Rodelinda* 1 Handel
Dido's Lament: *see* When I am laid in earth
Did thou not see my lady?: *see* Non lo dirò col labbro
Die Freiheit Roms (Rienzi) *Rienzi* 1 Wagner
Die Frist ist um (Dutchman) *Der fliegende Holländer* 1 Wagner
Die Kinder sind's (Paul, Marietta) *Die tote Stadt* 3 Korngold
Die Kraft versagt (Katharine) *Die widerspenstigen Zahmung* 4 Goetz
Diese Liebe, plötzlich geboren (Flamand, Countess) *Capriccio* Strauss
Dieu bienfaisant (Zoroastre) *Zoroastre* 3 Rameau
Dieux et déesses tutélaires (Creon, Dirce, Jason) *Médée* 1 Cherubini
Dieux qui me poursuivez (Orestes) *Iphigénie en Tauride* 2 Gluck
Die Zeit, die ist ein sonderbar Ding (Marschallin) *Der Rosenkavalier* 1 Strauss
Digli ch'è sangue italico (Lida, Rolando) *La battaglia di Legnano* 3 Verdi
Di ladroni attorniato (Carlo) *I masnadieri* 2 Verdi
Di misera regina (Penelope) *Il ritorno d'Ulisse* 1 Monteverdi
Dimitry! Tsarevich! (Marina, Dimitry) *Boris Godunov* 3 Musorgsky
Dimmi cara: tu dei morir (Lucius) *Scipione* 1 Handel
Dinnè, perchè in quest'eremo ... Orfanella il tetto umile ... Ah! se la speme ... Figlia! a tal nome io palpito (Amelia, Boccanegra) *Simon Boccanegra* 1 Verdi
Dio, che mi vedi in core ... Va, infelice (Anne Boleyn, Jane Seymour) *Anna Bolena* 2 Donizetti
Dio, che nell'alma infondere (Don Carlo, Posa) *Don Carlo* 1/2 Verdi
Dio di Giuda (Nabucco) *Nabucco* 4 Verdi
Dio di giustizia (Fedora) *Fedora* 3 Giordano
Diomede! Father (Cressida) *Troilus and Cressida* 3 Walton
Dio! mi potevi scagliar (Otello) *Otello* 3 Verdi
Dio pietoso (Katiusha) *Risurrezione* 2 Alfano
Dio ti giocondi, o sposo (Desdemona, Otello) *Otello* 3 Verdi
Di pescatore ignobile (Gennaro, Lucrezia) *Lucrezia Borgia* prol. Donizetti
Di piacer mi balza il cor (Ninetta) *La gazza ladra* 1 Rossini
Di Provenza il mar, il suol ... No, non udrai rimproveri (Germont) *La traviata* 2 Verdi
Di qual amor (Don Carlo, Elisabetta di Valois) *Don Carlo* 1 Verdi
Di quella pira (Manrico) *Il trovatore* 3 Verdi
Diresti poi così? (Matilda) *Ottone* 1 Handel
Di rigori armato il seno (Italian Singer) *Der Rosenkavalier* 1 Strauss
Dir töne Lob! (Tannhäuser) *Tannhäuser* 1 Wagner
Di rughe il volta ... Andrem, raminghi e poveri (Luisa, Miller) *Luisa Miller* 3 Verdi
Di scrivermi ogni giorno (Fiordiligi, Dorabella, Ferrando, Guglielmo, Don Alfonso) *Così fan tutte* 1 Mozart
Dis-moi que je suis belle (Thaïs) *Thaïs* 2 Massenet
Disprezzata regina (Octavia) *L'incoronazione di Poppea* 1 Monteverdi
Di tale amor (Leonora) *Il trovatore* 1 Verdi
Di tanti palpiti (Tancredi) *Tancredi* 1 Rossini
Dite alla giovine ... Morrò! la mia memoria (Germont, Violetta) *La traviata* 2 Verdi
Dite, che fà, dov'è (Seleuce, Ptolemy) *Tolomeo* 2 Handel
Di te mi rido, semplice stolto (Ruggiero) *Alcina* 1 Handel
Dite pace, e fulminate (Hermione) *Oreste* 1 Handel
Dite pace, e fulminate (Elmira) *Sosarme* 1 Handel
Di te sordarmi, e viver! (Paris) *Paride ed Elena* 4 Gluck
Di tue pene sparve il sogno (Carlo, Linda) *Linda di Chamounix* 3 Donizetti
Di' tu se fedele (Riccardo [Gustavus III]) *Un ballo in maschera* 1 Verdi
Di un cor che muore (Mary, ladies) *Maria Stuarda* 2/3 Donizetti
Divinités des grandes âmes (Pylades) *Iphigénie en Tauride* 3 Gluck
Divinités du Styx (Alcestis) *Alceste* 1 Gluck
Dolce Amor! (Aminta, Henry Morosus) *Die schweigsame Frau* 3 Strauss
Dolce sogno, deh la porta (Gualtiero) *Griselda* G. Bononcini
Dolce sonno, amor pietoso (Selim) *La schiava liberata* Jommelli
Dolci aurette che spirate (Berenice) *Scipione* 1 Handel
Doll's song: *see* Les oiseaux dans la charmille
Dôme épais, le jasmin (Lakmé, Mallika) *Lakmé* 1 Delibes
Domerò la tua fierezza (Ptolemy) *Giulio Cesare* 3 Handel
Don Basilio (quintet) *Il barbiere di Siviglia* 3 Paisiello
Donc, le Pape est hostile ... Qui donc commande (Henry) *Henry VIII* 1 Saint-Saëns

Donde lieta usci (Mimì) *La bohème* 3 Puccini
Donna, chi sei? (Nabucco, Abigaille) *Nabucco* 3 Verdi
Donna non vidi mai (Des Grieux) *Manon Lescaut* 1 Puccini
Donne mie la fate a tanti (Guglielmo) *Così fan tutte* 2 Mozart
Donne, passe (Charon) *Alceste* 4 Lully
Donnez pour une pauvre âme (Fidès) *Le prophète* 4 Meyerbeer
Don Ottavio, son morta! ... Or sai chi l'onore (Donna Anna) *Don Giovanni* 1 Mozart
Dopo l'orrore d'un ciel turbato (Ottone) *Ottone* 2 Handel
Dopo notte atra e funesta (Ariodante) *Ariodante* 3 Handel
Dopo notte atra e funesta (Alexander) *Poro* 3 Handel
Dopo torbide procelle (Polissena) *Radamisto* 1 Handel
D'Oreste, d'Ajace (Electra) *Idomeneo* 3 Mozart
Dormi, dormi (Jason, Medea) *Giasone* 3 Cavalli
Dormons tous (Sleep, Sons) *Atys* 3 Lully
Dors, petite, dors tranquille (Dinorah) *Dinorah* 1 Meyerbeer
Doute de la lumière (Ophelia, Hamlet) *Hamlet* 2 Thomas
D'où viens-tu? (Penelope, Ulysses) *Pénélope* 2 Fauré
Doux repos (Medea) *Thésée* 2 Lully
Dove sei, amato bene? (Bertarido) *Rodelinda* 1 Handel
Dove son (Ubaldo) *Armida* 1 Haydn
Dove sono i bei momenti (Countess Almaviva) *Le nozze di Figaro* 3 Mozart
Dovunque al mondo ... Amore o grillo (Pinkerton, Sharpless) *Madama Butterfly* 1 Puccini
Du bist der Lenz (Sieglinde) *Die Walküre* 1 Wagner
Du! denn du bist stark (Electra, Chrysothemis) *Elektra* Strauss
Du Destin le vouloir suprême (Three Fates) *Hippolyte et Aricie* 2 Rameau
Due bell'alme inamorate (Deidamia) *Deidamia* 1 Handel
Duetto de la chartreuse verte: *see* Je me sens, hélas, tout chose
Due vaticini (Macbeth, Banquo) *Macbeth* 1 Verdi
Du gai soleil (Sophie) *Werther* 2 Massenet
D'un cerf dix cors (Squire Western) *Tom Jones* 1 Philidor
D'une image, hélas! (Iphigenia) *Iphigénie en Tauride* 3 Gluck
D'un pensiero e d'un accento (Amina, ensemble) *La sonnambula* 1 Bellini
Dunque io son (Rosina, Figaro) *Il barbiere di Siviglia* 1 Rossini
Dunque, o cruda, e gloria e trono ... Vieni al tempio (Charles VII, Joan of Arc) *Giovanna d'Arco* 1 Verdi
D'un tenero amore (Assur, Arsace) *Semiramide* 1 Rossini
Du pauvre seul ami fidèle (Masaniello) *La muette de Portici* 4 Auber
Durch dich musst' ich verlieren (Telramund) *Lohengrin* 2 Wagner
Durch die Wälder (Max) *Der Freischütz* 1 Weber
Durch Zärtlichkeit und Schmeicheln (Blonde) *Die Entführung aus dem Serail* 2 Mozart
Duri e penosi (Melanto) *Il ritorno d'Ulisse* 1 Monteverdi
Dutchman's Monologue: *see* Die Frist ist um
Du trouble affreux (Medea) *Médée* 3 Cherubini
Du Venussohn (Composer) *Ariadne auf Naxos* prol. Strauss

E

E allor perchè, di', tu m'hai stregato (Nedda, Silvio) *Pagliacci* 1 Leoncavallo
È amore un ladroncello (Dorabella) *Così fan tutte* 2 Mozart
Easter hymn: *see* Inneggiamo, il Signor non è morto
Ebben, a te, ferisci ... Giorno d'orrore (Semiramide, Arsace) *Semiramide* 2 Rossini
Ebben ... ne andrò lontana (Wally) *La Wally* 1 Catalani
È ben altro il mio sogno (Giorgetta, Luigi) *Il tabarro* Puccini
E ben, per mia memoria (Ninetta, Pippo) *La gazza ladra* 2 Rossini
Ecco alle mie catene (Aetius) *Ezio* 2 Handel
Ecco il mondo (Mefistofele) *Mefistofele* 2 Boito
Ecco il monologo (Michonnet) *Adriana Lecouvreur* 1 Cilea
Ecco il punto, oh Vitellia ... Non più di fiori (Vitellia) *La clemenza di Tito* 2 Mozart
Ecco l'indegno ... Un perfido, un vile, un mentitore tu sei (Nottingham, Robert, Elizabeth) *Roberto Devereux* 2 Donizetti
Ecco l'orrido campo ... Ma dall'arido stelo divulsa (Amelia) *Un ballo in maschera* 2 Verdi
Eccomi giunto inosservato e solo ... A te sarà (Otello, Desdemona) *Otello* 3 Rossini
Ecco ridente in cielo (Almaviva) *Il barbiere di Siviglia* 1 Rossini
Ecco spiano (Pasquale) *Orlando paladino* 2 Haydn
Echo, viens sur l'air embaumé (Catharine) *La jolie fille de Perth* 4 Bizet
Eclatante trompette (Iphise) *Les fêtes d'Hébé* 2 Rameau
Eclate, mon amour (Chimène) *Le Cid* 4 Massenet
E così sia! quest'ultimo (Laura, Enzo, La Gioconda) *La Gioconda* 4 Ponchielli
Ecoute-moi bien (Valentin, ensemble) *Faust* 4 Gounod
Ecoutez-moi (Elvire, Alphonse) *La muette de Portici* 3 Auber
Ed ancor la tremenda porta ... Come uno spirto angelico (Robert) *Roberto Devereux* 3 Donizetti
È dolce raggio (Arrigo, Elena) *I vespri siciliani* 4 Verdi
È gelosia, forza e d'amore (Bradamante) *Alcina* 1 Handel
È gettata la mia sorte (Ezio) *Attila* 2 Verdi
Egli è salvo (Don Carlo) *La forza del destino* 3 Verdi
Egli riede (Gemma) *Gemma di Vergy* 1 Donizetti
Eia popeia (Marie) *Wozzock* 1 Berg
È il sol dell'anima ... Addio, speranza ed anima (Duke, Gilda) *Rigoletto* 1 Verdi
Ein Augenblick ist wenig (Zerbinetta, Composer) *Ariadne auf Naxos* prol. Strauss
Ein Mädchen oder Weibchen (Papageno) *Die Zauberflöte* 2 Mozart
Ein Männlein steht in Walde (Gretel, Hänsel) *Hänsel und Gretel* 2 Humperdinck
Ein Rinderhirt bin ich (Apollo) *Daphne* Strauss
Einsam in trüben Tagen (Elsa) *Lohengrin* 1 Wagner
Einsam wachend in der Nacht (Brangäne) *Tristan und Isolde* 2 Wagner
Ein Schönes war (Ariadne) *Ariadne auf Naxos* Strauss
Ein schwert verhiess mir der Vater (Siegmund) *Die Walküre* 1 Wagner
Einst träumte ... Trübe Augen (Aennchen) *Der Freischütz* 3 Weber
È la solita storia del pastore (Federico) *L'arlesiana* 2 Cilea
È la voce che primiera (Carlo) *Linda di Chamounix* 3 Donizetti
Elektra! Schwester! komm mit uns! (Chrysothemis, Electra) *Elektra* Strauss
Elena! oh tu, che chiamo! (Malcolm) *La donna del lago* 1 Rossini
Elisabeth's Greeting: *see* Dich, teure Halle
Ella è morta, o sciagurato (Romeo, Tebaldo) *I Capuleti e i Montecchi* 2 Bellini
Ella giammai m'amò (Philip II) *Don Carlo* 3/4 Verdi
Ella in poter del barbaro ... Cara patria, già madre (Foresto) *Attila* prol. Verdi
Ella mi fu rapita! ... Parmi veder le lagrime ... Possente amor (Duke) *Rigoletto* 2 Verdi
Ella verrà (Scarpia) *Tosca* 2 Puccini
Elle a fui, la tourterelle (Antonia) *Les contes d'Hoffmann* 3 Offenbach
Elle est là, près de lui? (Mignon) *Mignon* 2 Thomas
Elle ne croyait pas (Wilhelm Meister) *Mignon* 3 Thomas
Elle ne m'aime pas (Philip II) *Don Carlos* 4 Verdi
Eloigné pour jamais (Jason) *Médée* 1 Cherubini
E lucevan le stelle (Cavaradossi) *Tosca* 3 Puccini
È lui, è lui ne palpiti (Ulrica [Mam'zelle Arvidson]) *Un ballo in maschera* 1 Verdi
Embroidery in childhood (Ellen) *Peter Grimes* 3 Britten
Empio, dirò, tu sei (Julius Caesar) *Giulio Cesare* 1 Handel
Empio, per farti guerra (Bajazet) *Tamerlano* 3 Handel
En ces lieux ... Samson, ô toi mon bien-aimé (Samson, Delilah) *Samson et Dalila* 2 Saint-Saëns
Endless pleasure, endless love (Semele) *Semele* 1 Handel
En fermant les yeux (Des Grieux) *Manon* 2 Massenet
Enfin, il est en ma puissance (Armide) *Armide* 2 Gluck
Enfin, il est en ma puissance (Armide) *Armide* 2 Lully
Enfin, je me sens mieux! (Lazuli) *L'étoile* 2 Chabrier
En marche (Mireille) *Mireille* 4 Gounod
En mon bon droit j'ai confiance (Raoul, ensemble) *Les Huguenots* 3 Meyerbeer
En proie à la tristesse (Adèle, Isolier, Ory) *Le comte Ory* 1 Rossini
Entre l'amour et le devoir (Teresa) *Benvenuto Cellini* 1 Berlioz

En vain j'espère (Isabelle) *Robert le diable* 2 Meyerbeer
En vain pour éviter les réponses amères (Carmen) *Carmen* 3 Bizet
Enzo Grimaldi, Principe di Santafiore (Barnaba, Enzo) *La Gioconda* 1 Ponchielli
Epouse chérie (Ulysses) *Pénélope* 1 Fauré
Epouse quelque brave fille (Des Grieux) *Manon* 3 Massenet
E pure io torno (Otho) *L'incoronazione di Poppea* 1 Monteverdi
Era d'amor l'immagine ... Sul crin la rivale (Leicester, Elizabeth) *Maria Stuarda* 1 Donizetti
Era la notte (Iago) *Otello* 2 Verdi
Era più calmo? ... Piangea cantando ... Ave Maria (Emilia, Desdemona) *Otello* 4 Verdi
Er geht ... Ja eine Welt voll Leiden (Adriano, Irene) *Rienzi* 1 Wagner
Erhebe dich ... Durch dich musst' ich verlieren (Telramund) *Lohengrin* 2 Wagner
Erik's Dream Narration: *see* Auf hohem Felsen
Eri tu (Renato [Captain Anckarstroem]) *Un ballo in maschera* 3 Verdi
Eri tu dunque un tempo (Arturo) *La straniera* 1 Bellini
Er kommt! Er kommt! (Margiana, Bostana, Baba Mustapha) *Der Barbier von Bagdad* 2 Cornelius
Ernani! ... Ernani, involami ... Tutto sprezzo che d'Ernani (Elvira) *Ernani* 1 Verdi
Errante sur tes pas (Dido, Aeneas) *Les Troyens* 5 Berlioz
È scherzo od è follia (Riccardo [Gustavus III], Samuel, Tom, Oscar, Ulrica [Mam'zelle Arvidson]) *Un ballo in maschera* 1 Verdi
Esci omai garzon malnato (finale) *Le nozze di Figaro* 2 Mozart
È sempre la stessa (Elizabeth, Mary, Talbot, Anna, Leicester, Cecil) *Maria Stuarda* 1/2 Donizetti
E serbato a questo acciaro ... L'amo, l'amo, e m'è più cara (Tebaldo) *I Capuleti e i Montecchi* 1 Bellini
Es gibt ein Reich (Ariadne) *Ariadne auf Naxos* Strauss
È si dolce il mio contento (Amadigi) *Amadigi* 1 Handel
Es ist kein Laut zu vernehmen ... Ah, du wolltest mich nicht (Salome) *Salome* Strauss
È sogno? O realtà? (Ford) *Falstaff* 2 Verdi
Espoir si cher et si doux (Cybele) *Atys* 3 Lully
Esprits de haine et de rage (Armide, Hidraot) *Armide* 2 Lully
Essa corre al trionfo (Hermione, ensemble) *Ermione* 2 Rossini
Esser madre è un inferno (Rosa Mamai) *L'arlesiana* 3 Cilea
Est-ce la paix que vous donnez au monde? (Posa, Philip II) *Don Carlos* 2 Verdi
È strano! è strano! ... Ah fors'è lui ... Sempre libera degg'io (Violetta) *La traviata* 1 Verdi
Esultate! (Otello) *Otello* 1 Verdi
E Susanna non vien! ... Dove sono i bei momenti (Countess Almaviva) *Le nozze di Figaro* 3 Mozart
Eterno! immenso! incomprensibil Dio (Moses) *Mosè in Egitto* 1 Rossini
Et je sais votre nom (Des Grieux, Manon) *Manon* 1 Massenet
Et toi, Palerme ... Dans l'ombre et le silence (Procida) *Les vêpres siciliennes* 2 Verdi
È un folle, è un vile affetto (Oronte) *Alcina* 2 Handel
Evviva la Francia (Maria, ensemble) *La figlia del reggimento* 2 Donizetti
Ewig war ich (Brünnhilde) *Siegfried* 3 Wagner

F

Fabliau: *see* Oui, dans les bois
Fairest isle (Venus) *King Arthur* 5 Purcell
Faites-lui mes aveux (Siébel) *Faust* 3 Gounod
Falke, Falke, du wiedergefundener (Emperor) *Die Frau ohne Schatten* 2 Strauss
Falsa immagine, m'ingannasti (Teofane) *Ottone* 1 Handel
Fama! si: l'avrete (Jane Seymour, Henry VIII) *Anna Bolena* 1 Donizetti
Fammi combattere (Orlando) *Orlando* 1 Handel
Fanget an! So rief der Lenz in den Wald (Walther, ensemble) *Die Meistersinger* 1 Wagner
Fantaisie aux divins mensonges (Gérald) *Lakmé* 1 Delibes
Farewell my son, I am dying (Boris, Fyodor) *Boris Godunov* vii/4 Musorgsky
Farewell, O forests (Joan of Arc) *The Maid of Orleans* 1 Tchaikovsky
Farewell to Arms: *see* Ora e per sempre addio
Far from my beloved and constrained (Lyudmila) *Ruslan and Lyudmila* 4 Glinka
Fatal Amour (Pygmalion) *Pigmalion* 1 Rameau
Fatal Goffredo! ... Trono e corona (Eleonora d'Este) *Torquato Tasso* 1 Donizetti
Fatal mia donna! un murmure (Macbeth, Lady Macbeth) *Macbeth* 1 Verdi
Fatal vow (Oberon) *Oberon* 1 Weber
Fatto è Amor un dio d'inferno (Arsace) *Partenope* 3 Handel
Fear no danger (Belinda, Second Woman) *Dido and Aeneas* 1 Purcell
Felice cor mio (Drusilla) *L'incoronazione di Poppea* 2 Monteverdi
Ferma, crudel, estinguere (Elvira, Ernani, Silva) *Ernani* 4 Verdi
Fernand, imite la clémence du ciel (Léonor, Fernand) *La favorite* 4 Donizetti
Figlia! a tal nome io palpito (Amelia, Boccanegra) *Simon Boccanegra* 1 Verdi
Figlia che reggi il tremulo piè (La Gioconda, La Cieca, Barnaba) *La Gioconda* 1 Ponchielli
Figlia! ... Deh non parlare al misero ... Ah! veglia o donna (Rigoletto, Gilda) *Rigoletto* 1 Verdi
Figlia mia, non pianger, nò (Bajazet) *Tamerlano* 3 Handel
Figli miei, miei tesori (Medea, Jason) *Medea* 2 Cherubini
Fille des rois (Nélusko) *L'Africaine* 2 Meyerbeer
Fin ch'han dal vino (Don Giovanni) *Don Giovanni* 1 Mozart
Fin dall'età più tenera (Anne Boleyn, Percy, Henry VIII) *Anna Bolena* 2 Donizetti
Fleurissait une rose (Brother Boniface) *Le jongleur de Notre-Dame* 2 Massenet
Flieder Monologue: *see* Was duftet doch der Flieder
Flower Duet: *see* Sous le dôme épais; Tutti i fior
Flower Song: *see* La fleur que tu m'avais jetée
Fly, soft ideas fly (Mandane) *Artaxerxes* 1 Arne
Fontainebleau! foresta immensa e solitaria ... Io la vidi (Don Carlo) *Don Carlo* 1 Verdi
Fontainebleau! forêt immense et solitaire ... Je l'ai vue (Don Carlos) *Don Carlos* 1 Verdi
Forging Song: *see* Nothung! Nothung! Neidliches Schwert
Forgive me, my angel sent from Heaven (Hermann) *Queen of Spades* 2 Tchaikovsky
Forma ideal purissima ... Amore misterio celeste (Faust, Helen of Troy) *Mefistofele* 4 Boito
Forse in quel cor sensibile (Nottingham) *Roberto Devereux* 1 Donizetti
Forse la soglia attinse ... Ma se m'è forza perderti (Riccardo [Gustavus III]) *Un ballo in maschera* 3 Verdi
Forse un dì conoscerete (Ninetta, Giannetto) *La gazza ladra* 2 Rossini
Forte e lieto a morte andrei (Bajazet) *Tamerlano* 1 Handel
Fortune ennemie (Eurydice) *Orphée et Eurydice* 3 Gluck
Foudre céleste je t'appelle (Hypermnestra) *Les Danaïdes* 2 Salieri
Fountain Aria: *see* Regnava nel silenzio
Fra gli amplessi (Fiordiligi, Ferrando) *Così fan tutte* 2 Mozart
Fra i pensier (Junia) *Lucio Silla* 3 Mozart
Fra le tue braccia amore (Manon Lescaut, Des Grieux) *Manon Lescaut* 4 Puccini
Frà l'ombre e gl'orrori (Altomaro) *Sosarme* 1 Handel
Franco son io ... So che per via di trioli (Giacomo) *Giovanna d'Arco* 1 Verdi
Fra poco a me ricovero ... Tu che a Dio spiegasti l'ali (Edgardo) *Lucia di Lammermoor* 3 Donizetti
Frà tempeste funeste a quest'alma (Grimoaldo) *Rodelinda* 3 Handel
Fratricidi!!! Plebe! Patrizi! (Boccanegra, ensemble) *Simon Boccanegra* 1 Verdi
Fredda ed immobile (Rosina, ensemble) *Il barbiere di Siviglia* 1 Rossini
Frisch zum Kampfe (Pedrillo) *Die Entführung aus dem Serail* 2 Mozart
From boyhood trained (Huon) *Oberon* 1 Weber
From the gutter, why should we trouble (Nieces, Ellen, Auntie)

Peter Grimes 2 Britten
Fuggiam gli ardori inospiti ... La tra foreste vergini ... Sì: fuggiam da queste mura (Aida, Radames) *Aida* 3 Verdi
Fuggi, crudele, fuggi! (Donna Anna, Don Ottavio) *Don Giovanni* 1 Mozart
Fugitif et tremblant (Lothario) *Mignon* 1 Thomas
Fu la sorte dell'armi (Amneris, Aida) *Aida* 2 Verdi
Fünftausend Thaler (Baculus) *Der Wildschütz* 2 Lortzing
Fuoco di gioia! (chorus) *Otello* 1 Verdi
Fuor del mar (Idomeneus) *Idomeneo* 2 Mozart
Fuor di queste urne dolenti (chorus) *Lucio Silla* 1 Mozart
Furibondo spira il vento (Arsace) *Partenope* 2 Handel

G

Galatea, dry thy tears (chorus) *Acis and Galatea* 2 Handel
Galenus und Hippocrates (Stössel) *Doktor und Apotheker* 1 Dittersdorf
Gavotte: *see* Obéissons quand leur voix appelle
Gelido in ogni vena (Timagenes) *Poro* 3 Handel
Gelido in ogni vena (Cosroe) *Siroe* 3 Handel
Geme la tortorella (Sandrina) *La finta giardiniera* 1 Mozart
Gently, little boat (Anne) *The Rake's Progress* 3 Stravinsky
Gerechter Gott! (Adriano) *Rienzi* 3 Wagner
Già dagli occhi (Pharnaces) *Mitridate* 3 Mozart
Già d'insolito ardore (Mustafà) *L'italiana in Algeri* 1 Rossini
Già il mandorlo vicino (Fidelia) *Edgar* 1 Puccini
Già il sol si cela (Shepherd) *Nina* 1 Paisiello
Già i sacerdoti adunansi (Amneris, Radames) *Aida* 4 Verdi
Già la mensa è preparata (finale) *Don Giovanni* 2 Mozart
Già l'ebro mio ciglio (Orlando) *Orlando* 3 Handel
Già lo stringo, già l'abbraccio (Orlando) *Orlando* 3 Handel
Già, mi dicon venal (Scarpia) *Tosca* 2 Puccini
Già nella notte densa (Otello, Desdemona) *Otello* 1 Verdi
Già risonar d'intorno (Varus) *Ezio* 3 Handel
Giorni poveri vivea ... Deh! rallentate, o barbari (Azucena, ensemble) *Il trovatore* 3 Verdi
Giorno di pianto (Arrigo) *I vespri siciliani* 4 Verdi
Giorno d'orrore (Semiramide, Arsace) *Semiramide* 2 Rossini
Giudici! ad Anna ... Ah! segnata è la mia sorte (Anne Boleyn, ensemble) *Anna Bolena* 1 Donizetti
Giunse alfin il momento ... Deh vieni non tardar (Susanna) *Le nozze di Figaro* 4 Mozart
Giunto sul passo estremo (Faust) *Mefistofele* epilogue Boito
Giuriam d'Italia por fini ai danni (chorus) *La battaglia di Legnano* 3 Verdi
Giusto ciel in tal periglio (Anna) *Maometto II* 1 Rossini
Giusto Cielo! che feci in tal giorno? (Adriana Lecouvreur) *Adriana Lecouvreur* 3 Cilea
Giusto Dio che umile adoro (Amenaide) *Tancredi* 2 Rossini
Give me air, I suffocate (Boris) *Boris Godunov* v/2 Musorgsky
Gli sguardi trattieni (Cupid) *Orfeo ed Euridice* 1 Gluck
Glöcklein im Thale (Euryanthe) *Euryanthe* 1 Weber
Gloire immortelle de nos aïeux (chorus) *Faust* 4 Gounod
Gloria all'Egitto (ensemble) *Aida* 2 Verdi
Glück, das mir verlieb (Paul, Marietta) *Die tote Stadt* 1 Korngold
Gode l'alma consolata (Teofane) *Ottone* 3 Handel
Godiam la pace (chorus) *Idomeneo* 1 Mozart
Go there! Here's your sea boots! (Peter Grimes) *Peter Grimes* 2 Britten
Gott! welch' Dunkel hier ... In des Lebens Frühlingstagen ... Und spür' ich nicht linde, sanftsäuselnde Luft (Florestan) *Fidelio* 2 Beethoven
Grâce au hazard (Madeleine, Chapelou) *Le postillon de Lonjumeau* 2 Adam
Grand Dieu que j'implorai (Anna) *La dame blanche* 3 Boieldieu
Grand dieux! Que vois-je? ... Ange adoré (Marguerite, Faust) *La damnation de Faust* 3 Berlioz
Grands dieux (Alcestis) *Alceste* 1 Gluck
Grands dieux! ... Ah! malgré moi (Alcestis) *Alceste* 2 Gluck
Grands dieux! que viens-je d'entendre (Jenny, Dickson, George Brown) *La dame blanche* 1 Boieldieu
Gross Glück und Heil (chorus) *Götterdämmerung* 2 Wagner
Grossmächtige Prinzessin! ... Als ein Gott kam Jeder gegangen (Zerbinetta) *Ariadne auf Naxos* Strauss
Guai se ti sfugge un moto (Alfonso, Lucrezia, Gennaro) *Lucrezia Borgia* 1 Donizetti
Gualtier Maldè! ... Caro nome (Gilda) *Rigoletto* 1 Verdi
Guardate, pazzo son (Des Grieux) *Manon Lescaut* 3 Puccini
Gurnemanz's Narration: *see* Titurel, der fromme Held
Gut, Söhnchen, gut (Leonore, Marzelline, Rocco) *Fidelio* 1 Beethoven

H

Habanera: *see* L'amour est un oiseau rebelle
Hab' ich nur deine Liebe (Fiametta) *Boccaccio* 1 Suppé
Hab' mir's gelobt (Sophie, Marschallin, Octavian) *Der Rosenkavalier* 3 Strauss
Ha! du solltest für mich sterben (Konstanze, Belmonte) *Die Entführung aus dem Serail* 3 Mozart
Hagen's Watch: *see* Hier sitz' ich zur Wacht
Hai ben raggione (Luigi) *Il tabarro* Puccini
Happy we (Acis, Galatea) *Acis and Galatea* 1 Handel
Happy were he (Essex, Elizabeth I) *Gloriana* 1 Britten
Hâtez-vous de vous embarquer (Valère) *Les Indes galantes* 1 Rameau
Hat man nicht auch Gold beineben (Rocco) *Fidelio* 1 Beethoven
Ha! welch' ein Augenblick (Pizarro) *Fidelio* 1 Beethoven
Heart, the seat of soft delight (Galatea) *Acis and Galatea* 2 Handel
Heil dir, Sonne! (Brünnhilde, Siegfried) *Siegfried* 3 Wagner
Heil dir, weiser Schmied! (Wanderer, Mime) *Siegfried* 1 Wagner
Heil sei dem Tag (Van Bett) *Zar und Zimmermann* 3 Lortzing
Heil sei dem Tag (chorus) *Fidelio* 2 Beethoven
Hélas! d'une si pure flamme (Polynices) *Oedipe à Colone* 2 Sacchini
Hélas, hélas! quel bruit (Pan) *Isis* 3 Lully
Hélas! mon coeur s'égare encore (Hoffmann, ensemble) *Les contes d'Hoffmann* 4 Offenbach
Hélas! mon coeur sensible (Iphigenia) *Iphigénie en Aulide* 1 Gluck
Hence, Iris, hence away (Juno) *Semele* 2 Handel
Here I stand ... Since it is not by merit (Tom Rakewell) *The Rake's Progress* 1 Stravinsky
Here upon this spot, the world (Dosifey) *Khovanshchina* 5 Musorgsky
Herz, verzage nicht geschwind (Corregidor) *Der Corregidor* 2 Wolf
Heureux petit berger (Mireille) *Mireille* 4 Gounod
Hier im ird'schen Jammerthal (Caspar) *Der Freischütz* 1 Weber
Hier in stillen Schatten gründen (Lady Harriet, Lyonel) *Martha* 3 Flotow
Hier sitz' ich zur Wacht (Hagen) *Götterdämmerung* 1 Wagner
Hier soll ich dich denn sehen (Belmonte) *Die Entführung aus dem Serail* 1 Mozart
Hier weilest du? ... Wie liebt' ich dich (Adolar, Euryanthe) *Euryanthe* 3 Weber
Hin nimm die Seele mein (Euryanthe, Adolar) *Euryanthe* 2 Weber
Hither, dear husband (Polly, Lucy) *Beggar's Opera* 3
Ho capito (Masetto) *Don Giovanni* 1 Mozart
Hoiho! Ihr Gibichsmannen (Hagen, Vassals) *Götterdämmerung* 2 Wagner
Ho il cor già lacero (Griselda) *Griselda* 1 Vivaldi
Hojotoho (Brünnhilde) *Die Walküre* 2 Wagner
Hola! ihr Streiter in Apoll! (La Roche) *Capriccio* Strauss
Ho perduto il caro sposo (Rodelinda) *Rodelinda* 1 Handel
Horch, die Lerche singt im Hain! (Fenton) *Die lustigen Weiber von Windsor* 2 Nicolai
Ho un non so che nel cor (Agrippina) *Agrippina* 1 Handel
Ho un non so che nel cor (Eurilla) *Il pastor fido* 2 Handel
Ho un non so che nel cor (Dorinda) *Il pastor fido* 3 Handel
Ho un tumore (Vespina) *L'infedeltà delusa* 2 Haydn
Ho viaggiato in Francia (Pasquale) *Orlando paladino* 1 Haydn
How can he believe [Jak možná věřit] (Jeník) *The Bartered Bride* 2 Smetana
How can I sleep? (Cressida) *Troilus and Cressida* 2 Walton
How goes it, Prince? (Konchak) *Prince Igor* 2 Borodin
How happy could I be with either (Macheath) *Beggar's Opera* 2

How in the world did I meet Brudeus (Khivrya) *Fair at Sorochintsï* 2 Musorgsky
How unhappy's the nymph (Laura) *The Chaplet* 2 Boyce
Hüll in die Mantille dich (Sebastiano) *Tiefland* 2 D'Albert
Humming chorus *Madama Butterfly* 2 Puccini
Huntsmen's chorus: *see* Was gleicht wohl auf Erden
Hurr hopp hopp hopp (Witch) *Hänsel und Gretel* 3 Humperdinck
Hush, ye pretty warbling quire (Galatea) *Acis and Galatea* 1 Handel
Hymen, viens dissiper une vaine frayeur (Dirce) *Médée* 1 Cherubini
Hymn to the Sun: *see* Answer me, bright orb; Calore! Luce! Amor!

I

Iago's Creed: *see* Credo in un Dio crudel
I am sad, dear father (Lyudmila) *Ruslan and Lyudmila* 1 Glinka
I can't remember everything (Albert, ensemble) *Albert Herring* 3 Britten
Ich baue ganz (Belmonte) *Die Entführung aus dem Serail* 3 Mozart
Ich bin die erste Sängerin (Mme Herz, Mlle Silberklang, Vogelsang) *Der Schauspieldirektor* Mozart
Ich fleh' für ihn (Elisabeth) *Tannhäuser* 2 Wagner
Ich grüsse dich, du Bote (Ariadne, Bacchus, Nymphs) *Ariadne auf Naxos* Strauss
Ich grüss' noch einmal meine Berge (Pedro) *Tiefland* prol. D'Albert
Ich kann nicht sitzen und ins Dunkel starren (Chrysothemis) *Elektra* Strauss
Ich kenn' Ihn schon recht wohl (Sophie, Octavian) *Der Rosenkavalier* 2 Strauss
Ich komme, grünende Brüder (Daphne) *Daphne* Strauss
Ich sah das Kind (Kundry) *Parsifal* 2 Wagner
Ich weiss nicht, wer mein Vater war (Marta) *Tiefland* 2 D'Albert
Ich will mich Keinem geben (Katharine) *Die Widerspenstigen Zähmung* 2 Goetz
Ich will nichts hören ... Träumst du Mutter? (Clytemnestra, Electra) *Elektra* Strauss
I desideri sono i fiori dei vivi (Sister Angelica) *Suor Angelica* Puccini
Idol mio, se ritroso (Electra) *Idomeneo* 2 Mozart
Idolo del cor mio (Poppaea, Nero) *L'incoronazione di Poppea* 3 Monteverdi
I do not know her name and fortune (Hermann) *Queen of Spades* 1 Tchaikovsky
I don't know who they really are (Mark) *The Midsummer Marriage* 1 Tippett
I dreamt that I dwelt in marble halls (Arline) *The Bohemian Girl* 2 Balfe
If I had a hoard of gold (Sadko) *Sadko* i Rimsky-Korsakov
If love's a sweet passion (soprano, chorus) *The Fairy-Queen* 3 Purcell
If one last doubt (Troilus, Cressida) *Troilus and Cressida* 2 Walton
I gaze over the broad field (Antonida) *A Life for the Tsar* 1 Glinka
I go to him (Anne Trulove) *The Rake's Progress* 1 Stravinsky
I got plenty o' nuttin' (Porgy) *Porgy and Bess* 2 Gershwin
I have attained the highest power (Boris) *Boris Godunov* v/2 Musorgsky
I know a bank where the wild thyme blows (Oberon) *A Midsummer Night's Dream* 1 Britten
I know a girl who burns for you [Známt' já jednu dívčinu] (Mařenka, Vasek) *The Bartered Bride* 2 Smetana
Il balen del suo sorriso ... Per me ora fatale (Count di Luna) *Il trovatore* 2 Verdi
Il capro e la capretta (Marcellina) *Le nozze di Figaro* 4 Mozart
Il cavallo scalpita (Alfio) *Cavalleria rusticana* Mascagni
Il core vi dono (Guglielmo, Dorabella) *Così fan tutte* 2 Mozart
Il cor mio, ch'è già per te (Alexander) *Alessandro* 2 Handel
Il dolce idillio (Count Gil) *Il segreto di Susanna* Wolf- Ferrari
Il dolce suono ... Ardon gl'incensi ... splendon le sacre faci ... Alfin son tua ... Spargi d'amaro pianto (Lucia, ensemble) *Lucia di Lammermoor* 3 Donizetti
Il est doux, il est bon (Salome) *Hérodiade* 1 Massenet
Il était une fois à la cour d'Eisenach (Hoffmann) *Les contes d'Hoffmann* 1 Offenbach
Il était un roi de Thulé (Marguerite) *Faust* 3 Gounod
Il faut nous séparer (Charlotte, Werther) *Werther* 1 Massenet
Il faut partir (Marie) *La fille du regiment* 1 Donizetti
Il faut partir (Romeo, Juliet) *Roméo et Juliette* 4 Gounod
Il faut passer tôt ou tard (Charon) *Alceste* 4 Lully
Il lacerato spirito (Fiesco) *Simon Boccanegra* prol. Verdi
Il meglio mio carattere (Merlina) *L'impresario in angustie* 1 Cimarosa
Il m'en souvient ... Je l'aime donc? (Beatrice) *Béatrice et Bénédict* 2 Berlioz
Il me revient fidèle (Hero) *Béatrice et Bénédict* 1 Berlioz
Il mio ben quando (Nina) *Nina* 1 Paisiello
Il mio crudel martoro (Ginevra) *Ariodante* 2 Handel
Il mio piano è preparato (Gottardo) *La gazza ladra* 1 Rossini
Il mio sangue, la vita darei (Count Walter) *Luisa Miller* 1 Verdi
Il mio tesoro (Don Ottavio) *Don Giovanni* 2 Mozart
Il nous frappait dans sa colère (Old Hebrew) *Samson et Dalila* 1 Saint-Saëns
I love you beyond measure (Yeletsky) *Queen of Spades* 2 Tchaikovsky
I love you, I adore you (Lensky) *Yevgeny Onegin* 1 Tchaikovsky
Il padre adorato (Idamantes) *Idomeneo* 1 Mozart
Il pallor funesto ... Soffriva nel pianto languia (Enrico, Lucia) *Lucia di Lammermoor* 2 Donizetti
Il pensier sta negli oggetti (Creon) *L'anima del filosofo* 1 Haydn
Il reviendra, j'en suis certaine (Penelope, ensemble) *Pénélope* 1 Fauré
Il rival salvar tu dêi ... Suoni la tromba, e intrepido (Giorgio, Riccardo) *I puritani* 2 Bellini
Il russo Mencikoff (Maurizio) *Adriana Lecouvreur* 3 Cilea
Il santo nome di Dio ... La Vergine degli angeli (Leonora, Padre Guardiano, Franciscan friars) *La forza del destino* 2 Verdi
Il segreto per esser felici (Maffio Orsini) *Lucrezia Borgia* 2 Donizetti
Ils s'en vont, c'est la solitude (Jean) *Sapho* 2 Massenet
Il sonne et résonne (Catherine) *L'étoile du nord* 1 Meyerbeer
Ils sont rudes (Gwendoline) *Gwendoline* 1 Chabrier
Il Tricerbero umiliato (Rinaldo) *Rinaldo* 2 Handel
Il va venir! et d'effroi je me sens frémir (Rachel) *La Juive* 2 Halévy
Il vecchiotto cerca moglie (Berta) *Il barbiere di Siviglia* 2 Rossini
Il vostro maggio (Siren) *Rinaldo* 2 Handel
I'm like a skiff on the ocean tost (Lucy) *Beggar's Opera* 3
Immolation: *see* Starke Scheite
I'm not disposed to meditation (Olga) *Yevgeny Onegin* 1 Tchaikovsky
Improvviso: *see* Un dì, all'azzurro spazio
Im Walde entschlief ich (Grete) *Der ferne Klang* 2 Schreker
Inaffia l'ugola (Iago) *Otello* 1 Verdi
In braccio alle dovizie (Montforte) *I vespri siciliani* 3 Verdi
Inbrunst im Herzen (Tannhäuser) *Tannhäuser* 3 Wagner
Incauta, che festi! (Leicester, Matilde) *Elisabetta, regina d'Inghilterra* 1 Rossini
In cielo benedetto (Oronte) *I Lombardi* 4 Verdi
In dem Schatten meiner Locken (Frasquita) *Der Corregidor* 1 Wolf
In diesen heil'gen Hallen (Sarastro) *Die Zauberflöte* 2 Mozart
Infelice, che ascolto (Hypsipyle) *Giasone* 3 Cavalli
Infelice, delusa, rejetta ... Venite fidente alla croce (Leonora, Padre Guardiano) *La forza del destino* 2 Verdi
Infelice! e tu credevi (Silva) *Ernani* 1 Verdi
In fernem Land (Lohengrin) *Lohengrin* 3 Wagner
In Früh'n versammelt uns der Ruf (chorus) *Lohengrin* 2 Wagner
In mia man alfin tu sei (Norma, Pollione) *Norma* 2 Bellini
In mille dolci modi (Sosarme) *Sosarme* 2 Handel
In Mohrenland gefangen war (Pedrillo) *Die Entführung aus dem Serail* 3 Mozart
Inneggiamo, il Signor non è morto (Santuzza, chorus) *Cavalleria rusticana* Mascagni
Inosservata, penetrava ... Angelo casto e bel (Marcello di Bruges)

Il duca d'Alba 4 Donizetti
In pure stille (Iris) *Iris* 1 Mascagni
In qual fiero contrasto ... Tradito, schernito (Ferrando) *Così fan tutte* 2 Mozart
In quali eccessi ... Mi tradì (Donna Elvira) *Don Giovanni* 2 Mozart
In quelle trine morbide (Manon Lescaut) *Manon Lescaut* 2 Puccini
In questa reggia (Turandot) *Turandot* 2 Puccini
In si barbara sciagura ... Ah! ella è mia madre (Arsaces) *Semiramide* 2 Rossini
Inspirez-moi, race divine (Adoniram) *La reine de Saba* 2 Gounod
In Syriens Glut (Midas) *Die Liebe der Danae* 3 Strauss
In the gypsy's life (chorus) *The Bohemian Girl* 1 Balfe
Intorno all'idol mio (Orontea) *Orontea* 2 Cesti
In uomini (Despina) *Così fan tutte* 1 Mozart
Inutiles regrets! ... Ah! quand viendra l'instant (Aeneas) *Les Troyens* 5 Berlioz
Invano Alvaro! ti celasti al mondo ... Col sangue sol cancellasi ... Le minaccie, i fieri accenti ... Ah, segnasti la tua sorte (Don Carlo, Don Alvaro) *La forza del destino* 4 Verdi
In veder l'amata stanza (Frédéric) *Mignon* 2 Thomas
Io di Roma il Giove sono (Claudius) *Agrippina* 3 Handel
Io già t'amai, ritrosa (Grimoaldo) *Rodelinda* 1 Handel
Io già t'amai, ritrosa (Araspe) *Tolomeo* 2 Handel
Io la vidi (Don Carlo) *Don Carlo* 1 Verdi
Io l'ho perduta (Don Carlo) *Don Carlo* 1 Verdi
Io non chiedo (Alcestis, Eumelus, Aspasia) *Alceste* 1 Gluck
Io no son che una povera fanciulla (Minnie, Dick Johnson) *La fanciulla del West* 1 Puccini
Io seguo sol fiero (Rosmira) *Partenope* 1 Handel
Io so che alle sue pene (Sharpless, Suzuki, Pinkerton) *Madama Butterfly* 2 Puccini
Io son l'umile ancella (Adriana) *Adriana Lecouvreur* 1 Cilea
Io son quella navicella (Rosmene) *Imeneo* 3 Handel
Io son ricco e tu sei bella (Dulcamara, Adina) *L'elisir d'amore* 2 Donizetti
Io son sua per l'amor (Adriana, Princess of Bouillon) *Adriana Lecouvreur* 2 Cilea
Io sposar l'empio tiranno? (Don Pelagio) *La canterina* Haydn
Io t'abbraccio; è più che morte (Rodelinda, Bertarido) *Rodelinda* 2 Handel
Io t'abbraccio; è più che morte (Seleuca, Ptolemy) *Tolomeo* 2 Handel
Io t'amo Amalia ... Ti scosta, o malnato (Francesco, Amalia) *I masnadieri* 2 Verdi
Io ti levo l'impero dell'armi (Partenope) *Partenope* 1 Handel
Io ti rivedo ... Ah! se un giorno (Mary, Leicester, ensemble) *Maria Stuarda* 2/3 Donizetti
Io vengo a domandar ... Perduto ben ... Qual voce a me dal ciel ... Sotto al mio piè (Don Carlo, Elisabetta di Valois) *Don Carlo* 1/2 Verdi
I revel in hope and joy (Huon) *Oberon* 3 Weber
Irne lungi ancor dovrei ... Non di codarde lagrime (Zamoro) *Alzira* 2 Verdi
Irritons notre barbarie (Arcabonne, Arcalaus) *Amadis* 2 Lully
I sacri nomi ... Numi, pietà (Aida) *Aida* 1 Verdi
Is Cressida a slave? (Troilus) *Troilus and Cressida* 1 Walton
Is it so strange if I resent (Jenifer) *The Midsummer Marriage* 1 Tippett
Is it you, Vladimir mine (Konchakovna, Vladimir) *Prince Igor* 2 Borodin
Is this the very same Tatyana (Yevgeny Onegin) *Yevgeny Onegin* 3 Tchaikovsky
Ist mein Liebster dahin (Empress, Falcon) *Die Frau ohne Schatten* 1 Strauss
It ain't necessarily so (Sportin' Life, chorus) *Porgy and Bess* 2 Gershwin
Ite sul colle, o Druidi! (Oroveso) *Norma* 1 Bellini
It happened long ago (Levko) *A May Night* 1 Rimsky-Korsakov
It is he, my bright falcon (Yaroslavna, Igor) *Prince Igor* 4 Borodin
I've found out everything (Igor, Konchakovna, Vladimir) *Prince Igor* 3 Borodin
I was born in a big town (Dov) *The Knot Garden* 2 Tippett

J

Jägerin, schlau im Sinn (Nancy) *Martha* 3 Flotow
J'ai des yeux (Coppélius) *Le contes d'Hoffmann* 2 Offenbach
J'ai gravi la montagne ... La victoire facile (High Priest, Delilah) *Samson et Dalila* 2 Saint-Saëns
J'ai perdu mon Eurydice (Orpheus) *Orphée et Eurydice* 3 Gluck
Jak možná věřit: *see* How can he believe
Jako matka: *see* Like a mother
Jak vám pravím pane kmotre: *see* As I said to you
Ja, seit früher Kindheit Tagen (Lyonel, Plumkett) *Martha* 1 Flotow
J'avais fait un beau rêve ... Oui, voilà l'héroisme ... Au revoir dans un monde (Elisabeth de Valois, Don Carlos) *Don Carlos* 5 Verdi
Je cherche à vous faire (Amine) *La rencontre imprévue* 2 Gluck
Je comprends que la belle aime le militaire (Drum-Major) *Le caïd* 1 Thomas
Je connais un pauvre enfant (Mignon) *Mignon* 2 Thomas
Je crains de lui parler (Countess) *Queen of Spades* 2 Tchaikovsky
Je crains de lui parler (Laurette) *Richard Coeur-de-lion* 1 Grétry
Je crois entendre encore (Nadir) *Les pêcheurs de perles* 1 Bizet
Je crois entendre les doux compliments (Philine, Wilhelm Meister) *Mignon* 2 Thomas
Jeden heiligen Morgen (Apollo) *Daphne* Strauss
Je dis que rien ne m'épouvante (Micaëla) *Carmen* 3 Bizet
Je goûtais les charmes (Orpheus, Eurydice) *Orphée et Eurydice* 3 Gluck
Je l'aime donc (Beatrice) *Béatrice et Bénédict* 2 Berlioz
Je l'ai vue (Don Carlos) *Don Carlos* 1 Verdi
Je marche sur tous les chemins (Manon) *Manon* 3 Massenet
Je me sens, hélas, tout chose (King Ouf I, Siroco) *L'étoile* 3 Chabrier
Je ne pourrai plus sortir (Golaud, Mélisande) *Pelléas et Mélisande* 1 Debussy
Je ne suis plus ce dieu volage (Neptune) *Naïs* 2 Rameau
Je ne te verrai plus (Theseus) *Hippolyte et Aricie* 5 Rameau
Jenifer, Jenifer, my darling (Mark, Jenifer) *The Midsummer Marriage* 1 Tippett
Jerum! Jerum! (Hans Sachs, Beckmesser) *Die Meistersinger* 2 Wagner
Je suis du pays des gondoles (Duke Fritelli) *Le roi malgré lui* 3 Chabrier
Je suis encore toute étourdie (Manon) *Manon* 1 Massenet
Je suis heureuse! l'air m'enivre (Mignon, Wilhelm Meister) *Mignon* 2 Thomas
Je suis Lazuli! (Lazuli) *L'étoile* 1 Chabrier
Je suis le roi (De Nangis, ensemble) *Le roi malgré lui* 2 Chabrier
Je suis Titania (Philine) *Mignon* 2 Thomas
Je t'ai trompé, je fus coupable (Bertram) *Robert le diable* 5 Meyerbeer
Je t'implore et je tremble (Iphigenia) *Iphigénie en Tauride* 4 Gluck
Jetzt, Schätzchen (Jaquino, Marzelline) *Fidelio* 1 Beethoven
Je vais le voir! ... Il me revient fidèle (Hero) *Béatrice et Bénédict* 1 Berlioz
Je vais mourir ... Adieu, fière cité (Dido) *Les Troyens* 5 Berlioz
Je vais revoir (Isolier, Ory) *Le comte Ory* 1 Rossini
Je veux vivre dans ce rêve (Juliet) *Roméo et Juliette* 1 Gounod
Je viens célébrer la victoire (Delilah, Samson, Old Hebrew) *Samson et Dalila* 1 Saint-Saëns
Je viens solliciter ... O bien perdu ... Par quelle douce voix ... Que sous mes pieds (Don Carlos, Elisabeth de Valois) *Don Carlos* 2 Verdi
Je vous revois (Zoroastre, Amélite) *Zoroastre* 3 Rameau
Jewel Song: *see* Ah! je ris de me voir
Jochanaan, ich bin verliebt (Salome, Jochanaan) *Salome* Strauss
Johohoe! (Senta) *Der fliegende Holländer* 2 Wagner
Joignons nos voix (trio) *Le carnaval de Venise* prol. Campra
Jour et nuit je me mets en quatre (Frantz) *Les contes d'Hoffmann* 3 Offenbach
Juliet's Waltz Song: *see* Je veux vivre dans ce rêve
Jungfrau Maria! (Stradella) *Alessandro Stradella* 3 Flotow
Jupiter, lance la foudre (Clytemnestra) *Iphigénie en Aulide* 3 Gluck

Jurons, jurons par nos dangers (William Tell, ensemble) *Guillaume Tell* 2 Rossini
Justes dépits, brisez ma chaîne (Oriane) *Amadis* 1 Lully
Just think, my son, about the tsars (Pimen, Grigory) *Boris Godunov* iii/1 Musorgsky

K

Kein Andres, das mir so im Herzen loht (Count, Clairon) *Capriccio* Strauss
Kick on the back-side (Moore) *The Dragon of Wantley* 3 Lampe
Klänge der Heimat Rosalinde *Die Fledermaus* 2 Strauss
Komm denn (Eglantine, Lysiart) *Euryanthe* 2 Weber
Komm, mein Bub ... Eia popeia (Marie) *Wozzeck* 1 Berg
Kommt ein schlanker Bursch' gegangen (Aennchen) *Der Freischütz* 2 Weber
Konstanze, dich wiederzusehen ... O wie ängstlich (Belmonte) *Die Entführung aus dem Serail* 1 Mozart

L

Là bas, là bas dans la montagne (Carmen, Don José) *Carmen* 2 Bizet
Labbro di foco! (Nannetta, Fenton) *Falstaff* 1 Verdi
La belle immagini (Paris) *Paride ed Elena* 2 Gluck
La bocca vaga: quell'occhio nero (Ruggiero) *Alcina* 1 Handel
La brise et douce et parfumée (Mireille, Vincent) *Mireille* 2 Gounod
La calunnia è un venticello (Don Basilio) *Il barbiere di Siviglia* 1 Rossini
Lachst du mich aus? (Marschallin, Octavian) *Der Rosenkavalier* 1 Strauss
Là ci darem la mano (Don Giovanni, Zerlina) *Don Giovanni* 1 Mozart
Là dal Gange, a te primiero (Idreno) *Semiramide* 1 Rossini
La dolcissima effigie sorridente (Maurizio) *Adriana Lecouvreur* 1 Cilea
La donna è mobile (Duke) *Rigoletto* 3 Verdi
La farfalla (Irène) *Les fêtes vénitiennes* 5 Campra
La fatal pietra ... Morir! sì pura e bella ... Vedi? di morte l'angelo ... O terra addio (Aida, Radames) *Aida* 4 Verdi
La fauvette avec ses petits (Zémire) *Zémire et Azor* 3 Grétry
La fleur que tu m'avais jetée (Don José) *Carmen* 2 Bizet
Laggiù nel Soledad, ero piccina (Minnie) *La fanciulla del West* 1 Puccini
La gloire était ma seule idole (Cellini) *Benvenuto Cellini* 2 Berlioz
L'ai-je bien entendu? ... Hélas! mon coeur sensible (Iphigenia) *Iphigénie en Aulide* 1 Gluck
Laisse-moi, laisse-moi contempler ton visage ... O nuit d'amour (Faust, Marguerite) *Faust* 3 Gounod
Lakmé! c'est toi (Gérald, Lakmé) *Lakmé* 2 Delibes
Lakmé, ton doux regard se voile (Nilakantha) *Lakmé* 2 Delibes
L'alma mia fra le tempeste (Agrippina) *Agrippina* 1 Handel
L'alto retaggio non ho bramato ... O meco incolume (Wurm, Count Walter) *Luisa Miller* 2 Verdi
L'altra notte (Margherita) *Mefistofele* 3 Boito
La luce langue (Lady Macbeth) *Macbeth* 2 Verdi
La luna immobile innonda l'etere (Helen of Troy) *Mefistofele* 4 Boito
La mamma morta (Maddalena de Coigny) *Andrea Chénier* 3 Giordano
Lament of Ariadne: *see* Lasciatemi morire
L'amerò, sarò costante (Amyntas) *Il re pastore* 2 Mozart
La mia letizia infondere ... Come poteva un angelo (Oronte) *I Lombardi* 2 Verdi
La mia sorte fortunata (Pallas) *Agrippina* 1 Handel
L'amo come il fulgor del creato (La Gioconda, Laura) *La Gioconda* 2 Ponchielli
L'amo, l'amo, e m'è più cara (Tebaldo) *I Capuleti e i Montecchi* 1 Bellini
L'amor suo mi fe' beata (Elizabeth) *Roberto Devereux* 1 Donizetti
L'amour, ce divin maître (Minka) *Le roi malgré lui* 1 Chabrier
L'amour est une vertu rare (Thaïs) *Thaïs* 2 Massenet
L'amour est un flambeau (Beatrice, Benedick) *Béatrice et Bénédict* 2 Berlioz
L'amour est un monstre barbare (High Priestess) *La vestale* 1 Spontini
L'amour est un oiseau rebelle (Carmen) *Carmen* 1 Bizet
L'amour qui brûle dans notre âme (Julia, Licinius) *La vestale* 2 Spontini
L'angue offeso mai riposa (Sextus) *Giulio Cesare* 2 Handel
Languir per una bella (Lindoro) *L'italiana in Algeri* 1 Rossini
La nostra morte (Andrea Chénier, Maddalena de Coigny) *Andrea Chénier* 4 Giordano
La pia materna mano (Arrigo) *La battaglia di Legnano* 1 Verdi
La pietade in suo favore (Enrico) *Lucia di Lammermoor* 1 Donizetti
L'ara, o l'avello apprestami (Rodolfo) *Luisa Miller* 2 Verdi
Largo: *see* Ombra mai fù
Largo al factotum della città (Figaro) *Il barbiere di Siviglia* 1 Rossini
La rivedrà nell estasi (Riccardo [Gustavus III], Oscar, ensemble) *Un ballo in maschera* 1 Verdi
L'armellin vita non cura (Guido) *Flavio* 1 Handel
L'art accord avec la nature (Nymph of the Tuileries) *Alceste* prol. Lully
Lascia Amor e segui Marte (Zoroastro) *Orlando* 1 Handel
Lascia ch'io pianga (Almirena) *Rinaldo* 2 Handel
Lasciami! non t'ascolto (Tancredi, Amenaide) *Tancredi* 2 Rossini
Lasciate i monti (chorus) *Orfeo* 1 Monteverdi
Lasciatemi morire (Ariadne) *Arianna* 1 Monteverdi
La sorte mia tiranna (Siroes) *Siroe* 1 Handel
La speranza è giunta in porto (Gismonda) *Ottone* 1 Handel
Lassa ch'io t'ho perduta (Atalanta) *Atalanta* 2 Handel
Lass dir zu Füssen wonnesam mich liegen (Barber, Nureddin) *Der Barbier von Bagdad* 1 Cornelius
Lass mich euch fragen (Plunkett) *Martha* 3 Flotow
Lasso, io vivo (Egisto) *Egisto* 2 Cavalli
Lassù, in cielo (Gilda, Rigoletto) *Rigoletto* 3 Verdi
Lassù risplendere (Amalia, Carlo) *I masnadieri* 3 Verdi
Last Rose of Summer: *see* Letzte Rose
La sua lampada vitale ... Tremate, o miseri! (Francesco) *I masnadieri* 1 Verdi
La tendresse (Orpheus) *Orphée et Eurydice* 2 Gluck
La tigre arde di sdegno (Admetus) *Admeto* 3 Handel
La tomba è un letto ... Di rughe il volto ... Andrem, raminghi e poveri (Luisa, Miller) *Luisa Miller* 3 Verdi
La tra foreste vergini ... Sì: fuggiam da queste mura (Aida, Radames) *Aida* 3 Verdi
La tremenda ultrice spada (Romeo, ensemble) *I Capuleti e i Montecchi* 1 Bellini
La turba adulatrice (Haliate) *Sosarme* 1 Handel
L'aura che intorno spira (Amenaide, Tancredi) *Tancredi* 1 Rossini
L'aura che spira (Julius Caesar) *Giulio Cesare* 3 Handel
La vendetta (Bartolo) *Le nozze di Figaro* 1 Mozart
La Vergine degli angeli (Leonora, Franciscan friars) *La forza del destino* 2 Verdi
La vita è inferno all'infelice ... Oh, tu che in seno agli angeli (Don Alvaro) *La forza del destino* 3 Verdi
L'avoir tant adorée (Nélusko) *L'Africaine* 4 Meyerbeer
Leave me, loathsome light (Somnus) *Semele* 3 Handel
Lebe wohl mein flandrisch' Mädchen (Marquis de Chateauneuf) *Zar und Zimmermann* 2 Lortzing
Le bruit des chants (Sigurd) *Sigurd* 2 Reyer
Leb' wohl (Wotan) *Die Walküre* 3 Wagner
Le calme rentre dans mon coeur (Orestes) *Iphigénie en Tauride* 2 Gluck
Le faccio un inchino (Carolina, Elisetta, Fidalma) *Il matrimonio segreto* 1 Cimarosa
Legend of the Sage: *see* Fleurissait une rose
Légères hirondelles (Mignon, Lothario) *Mignon* 1 Thomas
Le héros que j'attens (Nymph of the Seine) *Alceste* prol. Lully
Le jour se lève (Andreloux) *Mireille* 4 Gounod
Le minaccie, i fieri accenti ... Ah, segnasti la tua sorte (Don Carlo, Don Alvaro) *La forza del destino* 4 Verdi

L'empio rigor del fato (Rodelinda) *Rodelinda* 1 Handel
L'empio, sleale, indegno (Ptolemy) *Giulio Cesare* 1 Handel
Lensky's Aria: *see* Shall I survive the day that's dawning
Léonor, viens (Alphonse XI) *La favorite* 2 Donizetti
Le perfide Renaud me fuit (Armide) *Armide* 5 Gluck
Le perfide Renaud me fuit (Armide) *Armide* 5 Lully
Le Polonais est triste et grave (Duke Fritelli) *Le roi malgré lui* 1 Chabrier
Les cieux s'emplissent d'étincelles (Balthazar) *La favorite* 4 Donizetti
Les dieux prendront pitié (Licinius) *La vestale* 2 Spontini
Les Grecs ont disparu ... Malheurex Roi (Cassandra) *Les Troyens* 1 Berlioz
Les loups croient le berger bien loin (Ulysses, ensemble) *Pénélope* 3 Fauré
Les oiseaux dans la charmille (Olympia) *Les contes d'Hoffmann* 2 Offenbach
Les pauvres gens (Father) *Louise* 4 Charpentier
L'esperto nocchiero (Nino) *Astarto* 3 Bononcini
L'espoir renaît dans mon âme (Orpheus) *Orphée et Eurydice* 1 Gluck
Les tringles des sistres tintaient (Carmen) *Carmen* 2 Bizet
Let's go to Benares (Jenny, ensemble) *Aufstieg und Fall der Stadt Mahagonny* 3 Weill
Let us take the road (Matt of the Mint, chorus) *Beggar's Opera* 2
Letzte Rose (Lady Harriet) *Martha* 2 Flotow
Le veau d'or (Méphistophélès) *Faust* 2 Gounod
Le vieil hiver (Faust) *La damnation de Faust* 1 Berlioz
Le vieux sorcier de la montagne (Dinorah) *Dinorah* 2 Meyerbeer
Le voilà, c'est l'Infant ... Toi! mon Rodrigue! c'est toi (Posa, Don Carlos) *Don Carlos* 2 Verdi
L'ho perduta (Barbarina) *Le nozze di Figaro* 4 Mozart
Libiamo ne' lieti calici (Alfredo, Violetta) *La traviata* 1 Verdi
Licinius je vais donc te revoir (Julia) *La vestale* 1 Spontini
Liebestod: *see* Mild und leise
Lieto cammino dolce viaggio (Telemachus) *Il ritorno d'Ulisse* 2 Monteverdi
Lieux désolés (Abaris) *Les Boréades* 4 Rameau
Lieux funestes (Dardanus) *Dardanus* 4 Rameau
Like a mother [Jako matka] (Mařenka, Jeník) *The Bartered Bride* 1 Smetana
L'Infant Carlos, notre espérance (Posa) *Don Carlos* 2 Verdi
L'insana parola ... I sacri nomi ... Numi, pietà (Aida) *Aida* 1 Verdi
L'objet qui règne dans mon âme (Terpsichore) *Les fêtes d'Hébé* 3 Rameau
Lo farò; dirò spietato (Eduige) *Rodelinda* 1 Handel
Lohengrin's Narration: *see* In fernem Land
L'onore! Ladri (Falstaff) *Falstaff* 1 Verdi
Lontano, lontano (Margherita, Faust) *Mefistofele* 3 Boito
Look! through the port comes the moonshine (Billy) *Billy Budd* 2 Britten
L'ora, o Tirsi, è vaga e bella (Manon Lescaut) *Manon Lescaut* 2 Puccini
Lorsque je t'ai vu soudain reparaître (Margared) *Le roi d'Ys* 2 Lalo
Lorsque l'enfant revient d'un voyage (Werther) *Werther* 2 Massenet
Lorsque le temps d'amour a fui (Dulcinée) *Don Quichotte* 4 Massenet
Lo sguardo avea degli angeli (Amalia) *I masnadieri* 1 Verdi
Lo sognai ferito, esangue ... Sventurata, anch'io deliro (Imogene) *Il pirata* 1 Bellini
Lo vedremo (Don Carlo, Silva) *Ernani* 2 Verdi
Love in her eyes sits playing (Acis) *Acis and Galatea* 1 Handel
Love sounds th'alarm (Acis) *Acis and Galatea* 2 Handel
Love, too frequently betrayed (Tom Rakewell) *The Rake's Progress* 1 Stravinsky
Lo vidi e 'l primo palpito (Luisa) *Luisa Miller* 1 Verdi
Lunge da lei ... De' miei bollenti spiriti ... Oh mio rimorso! (Alfredo) *La traviata* 2 Verdi
Lungi da te, mio bene (Xiphares) *Mitridate* 2 Mozart
Lusinghe più care (Roxana) *Alessandro* 1 Handel
Lusinghe più care (Armira) *Scipione* 1 Handel

M

Mab, reine des mensonges (Mercutio) *Roméo et Juliette* 1 Gounod
Ma dall'arido stelo divulsa (Amelia) *Un ballo in maschera* 2 Verdi
Madamina, il catalogo è questo (Leporello) *Don Giovanni* 1 Mozart
Ma di' l'amato giovane ... Oh non tremare (Norma, Adalgisa, Pollione) *Norma* 1 Bellini
Madre, pietosa vergine (Leonora, Franciscan friars) *La forza del destino* 2 Verdi
Mai non si vide ancor (Turno) *Il trionfo di Camilla* 1 Bononcini
M'ai resa infelice (Deidamia) *Deidamia* 3 Handel
Mais Alice, qu'as tu donc? (Bertram, Alice) *Robert le diable* 3 Meyerbeer
Mais celle qui devint ma femme (Albert, Werther) *Werther* 2 Massenet
Mai volsi ch'il mio core (Erice) *Ormindo* 1 Cavalli
Ma la sola, ohimè! son io (Beatrice) *Beatrice di Tenda* 1 Bellini
Ma lassù ci vedremo (Elisabetta di Valois, Don Carlo) *Don Carlo* 4/5 Verdi
Malheureux et non coupable (Henri, Hélène) *Les vêpres siciliennes* 4 Verdi
Malheureux Roi (Cassandra) *Les Troyens* 1 Berlioz
Malheur sur toi, fils adultère (Eboli, Don Carlos, Posa) *Don Carlos* 3 Verdi
Mal reggendo (Manrico, Azucena) *Il trovatore* 2 Verdi
Má ma-ma-ma-tič-ka po-po-povída la: *see* My m-m-mother s-s-said
Mamma, quel vino è generoso (Turiddu) *Cavalleria rusticana* Mascagni
Mânes plaintifs (Teucer, Antenor) *Dardanus* 1 Rameau
Ma non fia sempre odiata (Gualtiero) *Il pirata* 2 Bellini
M'apparì tutt'amor: *see* Ach, so fromm
Ma quando tornerai (Alcina) *Alcina* 3 Handel
Ma quel piacer che adesso (Giannetto) *La gazza ladra* 1 Rossini
Marie, dein Atem ... Nein, sie lebt (Paul) *Die tote Stadt* 1 Korngold
Mars, Bellone, guidez nos coups (Teucer, Antenor, chorus) *Dardanus* 1 Rameau
Marsch, marsch, marsch (Belmonte, Pedrillo, Osmin) *Die Entführung aus dem Serail* 1 Mozart
Mars und Merkur (Abul, Nureddin) *Der Barbier von Bagdad* 1 Cornelius
Marta! ... Tu mit mir, was du willst (Sebastiano, Marta) *Tiefland* 1 D'Albert
Martern aller Arten (Konstanze) *Die Entführung aus dem Serail* 2 Mozart
Ma se m'è forza perderti (Riccardo [Gustavus III]) *Un ballo in maschera* 3 Verdi
Maudite à jamais (High Priest) *Samson et Dalila* 1 Saint-Saëns
Maudit soit le soupçon infâme (Philip II, Posa, Eboli, Elisabeth de Valois) *Don Carlos* 4 Verdi
Meco all'altar ... Me protegge! (Pollione) *Norma* 1 Bellini
Meco tu vieni, o misera (Valdeburgo) *La straniera* 2 Bellini
Meine Herren (Jenny) *Aufstieg und Fall der Stadt Mahagonny* 2 Weill
Mein Elemer! (Arabella) *Arabella* 1 Strauss
Meinetwegen sollst du sterben (Belmonte, Konstanze) *Die Entführung aus dem Serail* 3 Mozart
Mein Gott! Es war nicht mehr ... Hab' mir's gelobt (Sophie, Marschallin, Octavian) *Der Rosenkavalier* 3 Strauss
Mein Herr! Der Singer Meisterschlag (David, Walther) *Die Meistersinger* 1 Wagner
Mein Herr und Gott (King Henry the Fowler) *Lohengrin* 1 Wagner
Mein Herz voll Treue bis zum Sterben (Erik, Senta) *Der fliegende Holländer* 2 Wagner
Mein Sehnen, mein Wähnen (Fritz) *Die tote Stadt* 2 Korngold
Mêlons! Coupons! ... En vain pour éviter les réponses amères (Frasquita, Mercédès, Carmen) *Carmen* 3 Bizet
Men fedele e men costante (Alexander) *Alessandro* 1 Handel

Men tiranne (Orpheus) *Orfeo ed Euridice* 2 Gluck
Mentre gonfiarsi l'anima ... Oltre quel limite (Attila) *Attila* 1 Verdi
Me pellegrina ed orfana (Leonora) *La forza del destino* 1 Verdi
Me protegge! (Pollione) *Norma* 1 Bellini
Mercè, dilette amiche (Elena) *I vespri siciliani* 5 Verdi
Merci, doux crépuscule! (Faust) *La damnation de Faust* 3 Berlioz
Merci, jeunes amies (Hélène) *Les vêpres siciliennes* 5 Verdi
Mes amis écoutez ... O qu'il était beau (Chapelou) *Le postillon de Lonjumeau* 1 Adam
Mesíčku na nebi hlubokém: *see* O silver moon
Mes longs cheveux descendent (Mélisande, Pelléas) *Pelléas et Mélisande* 3 Debussy
Metà di voi (Don Giovanni) *Don Giovanni* 2 Mozart
Me voici dans son boudoir (Frédéric) *Mignon* 2 Thomas
Mia madre, la mia vecchia madre (Loris) *Fedora* 2 Giordano
Mi chiamano Mimì (Mimì) *La bohème* 1 Puccini
Miei rampolli femminini (Don Magnifico) *La Cenerentola* 1 Rossini
Mieux vaut mourir que rester miserable! (Masaniello, Pietro) *La muette de Portici* 2 Auber
Mi lagnerò tacendo (Iphigenia) *Oreste* 3 Handel
Mi lagnerò tacendo (Laodice) *Siroe* 2 Handel
Mild und leise (Isolde) *Tristan und Isolde* 3 Wagner
Mille pene (Orpheus) *Orfeo ed Euridice* 2 Gluck
Mi lusinga il dolce affetto (Ruggiero) *Alcina* 2 Handel
Mi lusingo e l'alma spera (Camilla) *Il trionfo di Camilla* 1 Bononcini
Mime hiess ein mürrischer Zwerg (Siegfried, ensemble) *Götterdämmerung* 3 Wagner
Mime's Starling Song: *see* Als zullendes Kind
Mimì's Farewell: *see* Donde lieta usci
Ministres saints (Alphise) *Les Boréades* 2 Rameau
Minnie, dalla mia casa (Jack Rance) *La fanciulla del West* 1 Puccini
Mio bel tesoro, fedel son io (Ruggiero) *Alcina* 2 Handel
Mio caro bene (Rodelinda) *Rodelinda* 3 Handel
Mio caro ben non sospirar (Nino, Sidonia) *Astarto* 1 Bononcini
Mio cor, che mi sai dir? (Goffredo) *Rinaldo* 2 Handel
Mio dolce amato sposo (Ariadne) *Giustino* 1 Handel
Mio fiore! (Calaf, Turandot) *Turandot* 3 Puccini
Mira, di acerbe lagrime ... Vivra! Contende il giubilo (Leonora, Luna) *Il trovatore* 4 Verdi
Mir anvertraut (Barak, Barak's Wife) *Die Frau ohne Schatten* 3 Strauss
Mira, o Norma ... Sì, fino all'ore estreme (Adalgisa, Norma) *Norma* 2 Bellini
Mir dies? (King Mark) *Tristan und Isolde* 2 Wagner
Mi restano le lagrime (Alcina) *Alcina* 3 Handel
Mir ist die Ehre widerfahren (Octavian, Sophie) *Der Rosenkavalier* 2 Strauss
Mir ist so wunderbar (Marzelline, Leonore, Rocco, Jaquino) *Fidelio* 1 Beethoven
Mi sembra un sogno (Rezia, Balkis, Dardane) *L'incontro improvviso* 1 Haydn
Miserere d'un alma ... Tu vedrai che amore in terra (Manrico, Leonora) *Il trovatore* 4 Verdi
Mit Gewitter und Sturm (Steersman) *Der fliegende Holländer* 1 Wagner
Mit Ihren Augen (Octavian, Sophie) *Der Rosenkavalier* 2 Strauss
Mi tradì (Donna Elvira) *Don Giovanni* 2 Mozart
Mögst du mein Kind (Daland) *Der fliegende Holländer* 2 Wagner
Moi, je n'ai pas une âme ingrate (Princess Laoula) *L'étoile* 2 Chabrier
Molto voglio, molto spero (Armida) *Rinaldo* 1 Handel
Mon coeur ne saurait contenir (Iphigenia, Clytemnestra, Achilles, Agamemnon) *Iphigénie en Aulide* 3 Gluck
Mon coeur s'élance et palpite (Berthe) *Le prophète* 1 Meyerbeer
Mon coeur s'ouvre à ta voix (Delilah, Samson) *Samson et Dalila* 2 Saint-Saëns
Mondo ladro, mondo rubaldo (Falstaff) *Falstaff* 3 Verdi
Mon petit mari (Madeleine) *Le postillon de Lonjumeau* 1 Adam
Monstre affreux! (Antenor) *Dardanus* 4 Rameau
Morgenlich leuchtend in rosigem Schein (Walter, ensemble) *Die Meistersinger* 3 Wagner
Morgen mittag um elf (Countess, Major-Domo) *Capriccio* Strauss
Morir! sì pura e bella ... Vedi? di morte l'angelo ... O terra addio (Aida, Radames) *Aida* 4 Verdi
Morning and evening (Cressida) *Troilus and Cressida* 1 Walton
Morrai, sì; l'empia tua testa (Rodelinda) *Rodelinda* 1 Handel
Morrò! la mia memoria (Germont, Violetta) *La traviata* 2 Verdi
Morrò, ma prima in grazia (Amelia) *Un ballo in maschera* 3 Verdi
Morta al mondo (Elizabeth, Mary, ensemble) *Maria Stuarda* 1/2 Donizetti
Morte io non temo, il sai (Giulietta) *I Capuleti e i Montecchi* 2 Bellini
Mortels, pour être heureux (Tyrtaeus) *Les fêtes d'Hébé* 2 Rameau
Mourn, all ye muses (chorus) *Acis and Galatea* 2 Handel
Mourn thou poor heart (Reiza) *Oberon* 3 Weber
Musetta's Waltz Song: *see* Quando m'en vo'
Music is bitter-sweet (Denise, Mel) *The Knot Garden* 2 Tippett
Musik ist eine heilige Kunst (Composer, Music-Master) *Ariadne auf Naxos* prol. Strauss
Must I my Acis still bemoan (Galatea) *Acis and Galatea* 2 Handel
My breast with tender pity swells (Iole) *Hercules* 3 Handel
My dear companions (Pauline) *Queen of Spades* 2 Tchaikovsky
My Dimitry (Marina) *Boris Godunov* 3 Musorgsky
My hour of triumph is near (Farlaf) *Ruslan and Lyudmila* 2 Glinka
My lord was early and abrupt (Lady-in-waiting, Ladies) *Gloriana* 3 Britten
My love is all madness and folly (Lucy) *Beggar's Opera* 3
My man's gone now (Serena) *Porgy and Bess* 1 Gershwin
My m-m-mother s-s-said [Má ma-ma-ma-tič-ka po-po-povídala] (Vasek) *The Bartered Bride* 2 Smetana
My poor horse has fallen in the field (Vanya) *A Life for the Tsar* 4 Glinka
Myself I shall adore (Semele) *Semele* 3 Handel

N

N'achevez pas ... ce premier baiser (Charlotte, Werther) *Werther* 3 Massenet
Nacque al bosco, nacque al prato (Leocasta) *Giustino* 1 Handel
Nacqui all'affanno e al pianto ... Non più mesta (Cenerentola) *La Cenerentola* 2 Rossini
Nasce al bosco in rozza cuna (Marcianus) *Alessandro Severo* 2 Handel
Nasce al bosco in rozza cuna (Varus) *Ezio* 2 Handel
Nature, Amour, qui partage mon coeur (Pollux) *Castor et Pollux* 2 Rameau
Nature immense (Faust) *La damnation de Faust* 4 Berlioz
Ne bronchez pas (Lescaut) *Manon* 1 Massenet
Nè gustare m'è dato ... Voi che sì larghe cure ... Sleale! Il segreto fu dunque violato? (Don Alvaro, Don Carlo) *La forza del destino* 3 Verdi
Nein, nein! I' trink' kein Wein (Octavian, Ochs) *Der Rosenkavalier* 3 Strauss
Nel fragor della festa ... Alma soave e cara (Count de Chalais) *Maria di Rohan* 2 Donizetti
Nel furor delle tempeste ... Per te di vane lagrime (Gualtiero) *Il pirata* 1 Bellini
Nel giardin del bello (Eboli) *Don Carlo* 1/2 Verdi
Nella pace nel mesto riposo (Mary) *Maria Stuarda* 1/2 Donizetti
Nell'argilla maledetta (Carlo) *I masnadieri* 1 Verdi
Nell'astro che piu fulgido (Alzira) *Alzira* 1 Verdi
Nell'ispano suol mai l'eresia domino (Grand Inquisitor, Philip II) *Don Carlo* 3/4 Verdi
Nell'ombra e nel silenzio (Procida) *I vespri siciliani* 2 Verdi
Nel mio core ritorna il contento (Mirtillo) *Il pastor fido* 2 Handel
Nel mirarti un sol istante ... Da quel dì ... Vieni fra queste braccia (Arturo, Elvira) *I puritani* 3 Bellini
Nel mondo e nell'abisso (Isaac) *Riccardo* 3 Handel
Nel mondo e nell'abisso (Leo) *Tamerlano* 3 Handel
Nel sen mi palpita (Aspasia) *Mitridate* 1 Mozart
Ne m'en veux pas d'être venue (Fanny, Jean) *Sapho* 4 Massenet
Ne me refuse pas (Herodias) *Hérodiade* 1 Massenet
Nemici senza cor (Medea, Jason) *Medea* 1 Cherubini

Nemico della patria (Gérard) *Andrea Chénier* 3 Giordano
N'espérez pas me fuir ... Ecoutez-moi (Elvire, Alphonse) *La muette de Portici* 3 Auber
Nessun dorma (Calaf) *Turandot* 3 Puccini
N'est-ce plus ma main (Manon, Des Grieux) *Manon* 3 Massenet
Nettuno s'onori (chorus) *Idomeneo* 1 Mozart
Nicht wollen die Götter (Daphne, Apollo) *Daphne* Strauss
Noble châtelaine (Ory, Cavalier, Raimbaud, Tutor) *Le comte Ory* 2 Rossini
Nobles seigneurs, salut ... Une dame noble et sage (Urbain) *Les Huguenots* 1 Meyerbeer
No! che giova? (Maurizio, Adriana) *Adriana Lecouvreur* 2 Cilea
No, che il morir non è (Amenaide) *Tancredi* 2 Rossini
No! forme d'angelo (Charles VII, Giacomo, Joan of Arc, ensemble) *Giovanna d'Arco* 2 Verdi
No! giusta causa non è d'Iddio (Giselda) *I Lombardi* 2 Verdi
Nò, la morte (Idamantes) *Idomeneo* 3 Mozart
No little time has passed (Yaroslavna) *Prince Igor* 1 Borodin
Non! ce n'est point un sacrifice (Alcestis) *Alceste* 1 Gluck
Non di codarde lagrime (Zamoro) *Alzira* 2 Verdi
Non disperar, chi sà? (Cleopatra) *Giulio Cesare* 1 Handel
Non è amor nè gelosia (Alcina, Bradamante, Ruggiero) *Alcina* 3 Handel
Non è più tempo, nò (Asteria) *Tamerlano* 2 Handel
None Shall Sleep: *see* Nessun dorma
Non è si vago e bello (Julius Caesar) *Giulio Cesare* 1 Handel
Non fù già men forte Alcide (Orlando) *Orlando* 1 Handel
Non fu sogno (Giselda) *I Lombardi* 4 Verdi
Non hàn calma (Eupaforice) *Montezuma* 1 Graun
Non ha più che temere (Cornelia) *Giulio Cesare* 3 Handel
Non ho colpa (Idamantes) *Idomeneo* 1 Mozart
Non imprecare, umiliati (Padre Guardiano, Leonora, Don Alvaro) *La forza del destino* 4 Verdi
Non, je ne puis assez punir (Zoroastre) *Zoroastre* 1 Rameau
Non la sospiri la nostra casetta (Tosca) *Tosca* 1 Puccini
Non lo dirò col labbro (Alessandro) *Tolomeo* 1 Handel
Non maledirmi, o prode (Jacopo Foscari) *I due Foscari* 2 Verdi
Non me resta che il pianto (Suzel) *L'amico Fritz* 3 Mascagni
Non mi dir (Donna Anna) *Don Giovanni* 2 Mozart
Non morir Seneca (Seneca's pupils) *L'incoronazione di Poppea* 2 Monteverdi
Non, non, je vis encore (Licinius) *La vestale* 3 Spontini
Non! – non, non, non, non, non! Vous n'avez jamais, je gage (Urbain) *Les Huguenots* 2 Meyerbeer
No, no, I'll take no less (Semele) *Semele* 3 Handel
No! non è sogno ... Spirti, fermate (Attila, ensemble) *Attila* 1 Verdi
No, non morrai, chè i perfidi ... Ah! speranza dolce ancora (Lucrezia Contarini, Jacopo Foscari) *I due Foscari* 2 Verdi
No, non temere, o bella (Emireno) *Ottone* 3 Handel
No, non temer ... Se uniti negli affanni (Iago, Rodrigo) *Otello* 1 Rossini
No, non udrai rimproveri (Germont) *La traviata* 2 Verdi
No, no Turiddu, rimani (Santuzza, Turiddu) *Cavalleria rusticana* Mascagni
Non partir, mia bella face (Angelica) *Orlando paladino* 1 Haydn
Non piangere, Liù (Calaf) *Turandot* 1 Puccini
Non pianger, mia compagna (Elisabetta de Valois) *Don Carlo* 1/2 Verdi
Non più andrai (Figaro) *Le nozze di Figaro* 1 Mozart
Non più di fiori (Vitellia) *La clemenza di Tito* 2 Mozart
Non più mesta (Cenerentola) *La Cenerentola* 2 Rossini
Non prosegui! comprendo (Hermione, Pyrrhus) *Ermione* 1 Rossini
Non sai tu che se l'anima mia ... Oh qual soave brivido (Riccardo [Gustavus III], Amelia) *Un ballo in maschera* 2 Verdi
Non sembra un angelo (chorus) *Giovanna d'Arco* 3 Verdi
Non siate ritrosi (Guglielmo) *Così fan tutte* 1 Mozart
Non si dà follia maggiore (Fiorilla) *Il turco in Italia* 1 Rossini
Non so più (Cherubino) *Le nozze di Figaro* 1 Mozart
Non temer, amato bene (Idamantes) *Idomeneo* 2 Mozart
Non ti fidar, o misera (Donna Elvira, Donna Anna, Don Ottavio, Don Giovanni) *Don Giovanni* 1 Mozart
Non t'inganni la speranza (Clodomiro) *Lotario* 2 Handel
Non, tu ne m'aimes pas ... Là bas, là bas dans la montagne (Carmen, Don José) *Carmen* 2 Bizet
Non v'è chi me aiuta (Gasparina) *La canterina* Haydn
Non v'è rimedio (Nanni) *L'infedeltà delusa* 1 Haydn
Non v'ha sguardo (Anne Boleyn) *Anna Bolena* 1 Donizetti
No! Pagliaccio non son! (Canio) *Pagliacci* 2 Leoncavallo
No pow'r on earth (Polly) *Beggar's Opera* 2
Nor sleep, nor rest of any kind (Igor) *Prince Igor* 2 Borodin
Not for that do I grieve, dear friends (Antonida) *A Life for the Tsar* 3 Glinka
Nothung! Nothung! Neidliches Schwert (Siegfried, Mime) *Siegfried* 1 Wagner
Notte e giorno faticar (Leporello, Donna Anna, Don Giovanni, Commendatore) *Don Giovanni* 1 Mozart
Nous avons en tête une affaire (Frasquita, Mercédès, Carmen, Le Dancaïre, Le Remendado) *Carmen* 2 Bizet
Nous avons vu finir ... Chers Tyriens (Dido) *Les Troyens* 3 Berlioz
Nouvelle Hébé, charmante Lycoris (Anacréon) *Les surprises de l'Amour* 3 Rameau
Now close your arms (Troilus, Cressida) *Troilus and Cressida* 2 Walton
Now, dear young fellow [Nuže, milý chasníku] (Kecal, Jeník) *The Bartered Bride* 2 Smetana
Now if pretty girls had wings (Tomsky) *Queen of Spades* 3 Tchaikovsky
No word from Tom ... Quietly, night ... I go to him (Anne Trulove) *The Rake's Progress* 1 Stravinsky
Now the Great Bear and Pleiades (Peter Grimes, ensemble) *Peter Grimes* 1 Britten
Nuit d'hyménée ... Il faut partir (Romeo, Juliet) *Roméo et Juliette* 4 Gounod
Nuit d'ivresse (Dido, Aeneas) *Les Troyens* 4 Berlioz
Nuit paisible et sereine (Hero, Ursula) *Béatrice et Bénédict* 1 Berlioz
Nulla! Silenzio (Michele) *Il tabarro* Puccini
Numi, pietà (Aida) *Aida* 1 Verdi
Nun eilt herbei ... Verführer! Warum stellt ihr so (Mrs Ford) *Die lustigen Weiber von Windsor* 1 Nicolai
Nun hört, und versteht mich recht! (Pogner) *Die Meistersinger* 1 Wagner
Nun sei bedankt, mein lieber Schwan! (Lohengrin) *Lohengrin* 1 Wagner
Nur das Eine lasst Euch bitten (Schneidebart) *Die schweigsame Frau* 1 Strauss
Nur eine Waffe taugt (Parsifal) *Parsifal* 3 Wagner
Nuže, milý chasníku: *see* Now, dear young fellow

O

O amore, o bella luce (Fritz Kobus) *L'amico Fritz* 3 Mascagni
Obbligato, ah, sì! obbligato (Nemorino, Dulcamara) *L'elisir d'amore* 1 Donizetti
O beau pays de la Touraine ... A ce mot seul s'anime (Marguerite de Valois) *Les Huguenots* 2 Meyerbeer
O beauty, o handsomeness, goodness! (Claggart) *Billy Budd* 1 Britten
Obéis aux lois des enfers (chorus) *Dardanus* 2 Rameau
Obéissons quand leur voix appelle (Manon) *Manon* 3 Massenet
O bien perdu ... Par quelle douce voix ... Que sous mes pieds (Don Carlos, Elisabeth de Valois) *Don Carlos* 2 Verdi
Objet de mon amour (Orpheus) *Orphée et Eurydice* 1 Gluck
O bleib, geliebter Tag! (Daphne) *Daphne* Strauss
Oblivion soave (Arnalta) *L'incoronazione di Poppea* 2 Monteverdi
O blonde Cérès (Iopas) *Les Troyens* 4 Berlioz
O care parolette, o dolci sguardi (Sallustia) *Alessandro Severo* 3 Handel
O care parolette, o dolci sguardi (Dorinda) *Orlando* 1 Handel
O Carlo, ascolta (Posa) *Don Carlo* 3/4 Verdi
Ocean! thou mighty monster (Reiza) *Oberon* 2 Weber
O cessate di piagarmi Sextus *Pompeo* 2 Scarlatti
O che muso, che figura! (Isabella, Mustafà, ensemble) *L'italiana in Algeri* 1 Rossini
Och, jaký žal ... Ten lásky sen: *see* Oh what pain ... That dream

of love
O coeur ami! O coeur promis! (Julien) *Louise* 1 Charpentier
O, Colombina, il tenero fido Arlecchin (Beppe) *Pagliacci* 2 Leoncavallo
O del ben', che acquistero (Paris) *Il pomo d'oro* 2 Cesti
O del mio dolce ardor (Paris) *Paride ed Elena* 1 Gluck
O des infortunés, déesse tutélaire (Julia) *La vestale* 2 Spontini
O dieu Brahma! (Leïla, Nadir) *Les pêcheurs de perles* 1 Bizet
O Dieu de nos pères (Elèazar) *La Juive* 2 Halévy
O Dieu! de quelle ivresse (Hoffmann) *Les contes d'Hoffmann* 4 Offenbach
Odio, furor, dispetto, dolor (Armida) *Armida* 2 Haydn
Odio solo, ed odio atroce (Jacopo Foscari) *I due Foscari* 1 Verdi
O disgrace cruelle (Phaedra) *Hippolyte et Aricie* 4 Rameau
O dolci mani (Cavaradossi) *Tosca* 3 Puccini
O don fatal (Eboli) *Don Carlos* 4 Verdi
O don fatale (Eboli) *Don Carlo* 3/4 Verdi
O du, mein holder Abendstern (Wolfram) *Tannhäuser* 3 Wagner
O fatidica foresta (Joan of Arc) *Giovanna d'Arco* 1 Verdi
O field, who has bestrewn thee with dead bones (Ruslan) *Ruslan and Lyudmila* 2 Glinka
O fior del giorno (Fidelia) *Edgar* 1 Puccini
Oft she visits (Second Woman) *Dido and Aeneas* 2 Purcell
O gioia, la nube leggera (Susanna) *Il segreto di Susanna* Wolf-Ferrari
Ogni vento ch'al porto lo spinga (Agrippina) *Agrippina* 2 Handel
O Gott! O welch' ein Augenblick (Leonore, Florestan, ensemble) *Fidelio* 2 Beethoven
Oh che gusto, che piacere (Don Polidoro) *L'italiana in Londra* 2 Cimarosa
Oh chi piange? ... Del futuro nel buio (Zaccaria) *Nabucco* 3 Verdi
Oh ciel! Où courez-vous? ... Tu l'as dit (Valentine, Raoul) *Les Huguenots* 4 Meyerbeer
Oh come il cor di giubilo (Lindoro) *L'italiana in Algeri* 2 Rossini
Oh Dei, che sania è questa (Sextus) *La clemenza di Tito* 1 Mozart
Oh de'verd'anni miei (Don Carlo) *Ernani* 3 Verdi
Oh, dischiuso è il firmamento (Fenena) *Nabucco* 4 Verdi
Oh! Fanny ma maîtresse ... Nous irons en rêvant (Jean, Fanny) *Sapho* 3 Massenet
Oh fiamma soave (James) *La donna del lago* 2 Rossini
Oh! guardate che accidente (Fiorilla, Zaida, Narciso, Geronio, Selim) *Il turco in Italia* 2 Rossini
Oh, il Signore vi manda (Alfio, Santuzza) *Cavalleria rusticana* Mascagni
Ohimé, ch'un'hora sola (Wife, Mother, Eufemiano) *Sant'Alessio* 3 Landi
Oh! la pitoyable aventure (Concepcion) *L'heure espagnole* Ravel
Oh Luigi! Luigi! Bada a te! (Giorgetta, Luigi) *Il tabarro* Puccini
Oh mio rimorso! (Alfredo) *La traviata* 2 Verdi
Oh! nel fuggente nuvolo (Odabella) *Attila* 1 Verdi
Oh non tremare (Norma, Adalgisa, Pollione) *Norma* 1 Bellini
O, holdes Bild in Engelschöne (Nureddin, Margiana) *Der Barbier von Bagdad* 2 Cornelius
Oh qual soave brivido (Riccardo [Gustavus III], Amelia) *Un ballo in maschera* 2 Verdi
Oh! quante volte, oh! quante (Giulietta) *I Capuleti e i Montecchi* 1 Bellini
Oh, se sapeste (Minnie) *La fanciulla del West* 2 Puccini
Oh sole ti vela (Imogene) *Il pirata* 2 Bellini
Oh sommo Carlo (Don Carlo, ensemble) *Ernani* 3 Verdi
Oh the pleasure of the plains (chorus) *Acis and Galatea* 1 Handel
Oh, tu che in seno agli angeli (Don Alvaro) *La forza del destino* 3 Verdi
Oh what pain it is to part (Polly) *Beggar's Opera* 1
Oh what pain ... That dream of love [Och, jaký žal ... Ten lásky sen] (Mařenka) *The Bartered Bride* 3 Smetana
Oh, you dark forest (Sadko) *Sadko* 2 Rimsky-Korsakov
Oh, you may stare in horror (Denise) *The Knot Garden* 1 Tippett
O inferno! ... Sento avvampar nell'anima (Gabriele) *Simon Boccanegra* 2 Verdi
O Isis und Osiris, schenket der Weisheit Geist (Sarastro) *Die Zauberflöte* 2 Mozart
O jour affreux (Iphise) *Dardanus* 3 Rameau
O jour de peine (Henri) *Les vêpres siciliennes* 4 Verdi
O jours d'innocence! (Isabelle) *Le Pré aux Clercs* 2 Hérold
O lebbra, sozzura del mondo (Edgar) *Edgar* 3 Puccini
O légère hirondelle (Mireille) *Mireille* 1 Gounod
O Lisbonne (Camoëns) *Dom Sébastien, roi de Portugal* Donizetti
O Lola, ch'ai di latti (Turiddu) *Cavalleria rusticana* Mascagni
O Lord, if I have sinned (René) *Iolanta* Tchaikovsky
Oltre quel limite (Attila) *Attila* 1 Verdi
O luce di quest'anima (Linda) *Linda di Chamounix* 1 Donizetti
O lumière sainte (Leïla, Nadir) *Les pêcheurs de perles* 3 Bizet
O lumière vive et pure (Amélite, chorus) *Zoroastre* 3 Rameau
O ma chère compagne (Elisabeth de Valois) *Don Carlos* 2 Verdi
O ma Fanny que j'aime (Jean, Fanny) *Sapho* 2 Massenet
O ma femme! ô ma bien aimée (Romeo) *Roméo et Juliette* 5 Gounod
O malheureuse Iphigénie (Iphigenia) *Iphigénie en Tauride* 2 Gluck
O mattutini albori! (Ellen) *La donna del lago* 1 Rossini
Ombra cara di mia sposa (Radamisto) *Radamisto* 2 Handel
Ombra leggiera: *see* Ombre légère
Ombra mai fù (Xerxes) *Serse* 1 Handel
Ombre, larve (Alcestis) *Alceste* 1 Gluck
Ombre légère (Dinorah) *Dinorah* 2 Meyerbeer
Ombre pallide, lo so, mi udite (Alcina) *Alcina* 2 Handel
Ombre, piante, urne funeste (Rodelinda) *Rodelinda* 1 Handel
O meco incolume (Wurm, Count Walter) *Luisa Miller* 2 Verdi
O mein Leid (Eglantine) *Euryanthe* 1 Weber
O messager de Dieu ... Baigne d'eau mes mains (Thaïs, Athanaël) *Thaïs* 3 Massenet
O mia vita! (Oenone, Paris) *Il pomo d'oro* 1 Cesti
O mio babbino caro (Lauretta) *Gianni Schicchi* Puccini
O mio castel paterno ... Nell'argilla maledetta (Carlo) *I masnadieri* 1 Verdi
O mio Fernando (Leonora) *La favorita* 3 Donizetti
O mon Fernand (Léonor) *La favorite* 3 Donizetti
O monumento (Barnaba) *La Gioconda* 1 Ponchielli
O moon of Alabama (Jenny, Girls) *Aufstieg und Fall der Stadt Mahagonny* 1 Weill
O muto asil: *see* Asile héréditaire
O My Beloved Father: *see* O mio babbino caro
O Nadir, tendre ami de mon jeune âge (Zurga) *Les pêcheurs de perles* 3 Bizet
O namenlose Freude (Leonore, Florestan) *Fidelio* 2 Beethoven
O Nature, pleine de grâce (Werther) *Werther* 1 Massenet
Once a gnat was cutting wood (Nurse) *Boris Godunov* 2 Musorgsky
One fine day: *see* Un bel dì
Onegin, I was then far younger (Tatyana, Yevgeny Onegin) *Yevgeny Onegin* 3 Tchaikovsky
On l'appelle Manon (Des Grieux, Manon) *Manon* 2 Massenet
O noble lame étincelante (Rodrigue) *Le Cid* 1 Massenet
On our street (Olga) *Rusalka* 3 Dargomïzhsky
On rivalries 'tis safe for kings (Elizabeth I) *Gloriana* 1 Britten
On the banks of the sweet Garonne (Sherasmin, Fatima) *Oberon* 3 Weber
O nube! che lieve per l'aria ... Nella pace nel mesto riposo (Mary) *Maria Stuarda* 1/2 Donizetti
O Nuit (Angélique) *Roland* 4 Lully
O nuit d'amour (Faust, Marguerite) *Faust* 3 Gounod
O nume benfico (Ninetta, Fernando Villabella, Gottardo) *La gazza ladra* 1 Rossini
On with the motley: *see* Vesti la giubba
O paradis sorti de l'onde (Vasco da Gama) *L'Africaine* 4 Meyerbeer
O patria mia (Aida) *Aida* 3 Verdi
O patrizi, tremate L'Eterno (Lucrezia Contarini) *I due Foscari* 1 Verdi
O prêtres de Baal (Fidès) *Le prophète* 5 Meyerbeer
O qu'il est beau (Chapelou) *Le postillon de Lonjumeau* 1 Adam
Ora a noi (Sharpless, Butterfly) *Madama Butterfly* 2 Puccini
Ora di morte e di vendetta (Macbeth, Lady Macbeth) *Macbeth* 3 Verdi
Ora e per sempre addio (Otello) *Otello* 2 Verdi
Ora soave (Maddalena de Coigny, Andrea Chénier) *Andrea Chenier* 2 Giordano
Or che più non vedrò (Jason) *Medea* 1 Cherubini
Or che siete speranze tradite (Amastre) *Serse* 2 Handel

Or dammi il braccio tuo (Osaka, Iris) *Iris* 2 Mascagni
Or del padre benedetta (Joan of Arc, Giacomo) *Giovanna d'Arco* 3 Verdi
Ore dolci e divine (Magda de Civry) *La rondine* 1 Puccini
O rendetemi la speme ... Qui la voce sua soave ... Vien, diletto (Elvira) *I puritani* 3 Bellini
Orest! Orest! Orest! (Electra, Orestes) *Elektra* Strauss
Orfanella il tetto umile ... Ah! se la speme ... Figlia! a tal nome io palpito (Amelia, Boccanegra) *Simon Boccanegra* 1 Verdi
Orgia, chimera dall'occhio vitreo (Edgar) *Edgar* 2 Puccini
O Richard! ô mon Roi! (Blondel) *Richard Coeur-de-lion* 1 Grétry
O rich-soiled land, O land of Phthia (Achilles) *King Priam* 2 Tippett
Or la tromba in suon festante (Rinaldo) *Rinaldo* 3 Handel
O Roi! j'arrive de Flandre ... Est-ce la paix que vous donnez au monde? (Posa, Philip II) *Don Carlos* 2 Verdi
O Rosalinde (Lescaut) *Manon* 3 Massenet
Orrida a gl'occhi miei (Ginevra) *Ariodante* 1 Handel
Or sai chi l'onore (Donna Anna) *Don Giovanni* 1 Mozart
Or sei pago, o ciel tremendo (Alaide, ensemble) *La straniera* 2 Bellini
Or son sei mesi (Dick Johnson) *La fanciulla del West* 2 Puccini
Or tutti sorgete (Lady Macbeth) *Macbeth* 1 Verdi
O ruddier than the cherry (Polyphemus) *Acis and Galatea* 2 Handel
Or vicina a te, mio cuore (Rezia) *L'incontro improvviso* 2 Haydn
O sancta justitia, ich möchte rasen (Van Bett) *Zar und Zimmermann* 1 Lortzing
O s'apre al riso (Morgana) *Alcina* 1 Handel
O Schwester, sprich (Rienzi, Adriano, Irene) *Rienzi* 1 Wagner
O sdegni miei ... Se sincero è quell'accento ... Arrigo! ah parli a un core ... È dolce raggio (Arrigo, Elena) *I vespri siciliani* 4 Verdi
O signor, di Fiandra arrivo (Posa, Philip II) *Don Carlo* 1/2 Verdi
O Signore, dal tetto natio (chorus) *I Lombardi* 4 Verdi
O silver moon [Měsíčku na nebi hlubokém] (Rusalka) *Rusalka* 1 Dvořák
O sink' herneider, Nacht der Liebe (Isolde, Tristan) *Tristan und Isolde* 2 Wagner
O sleep, why dost thou leave me? (Semele) *Semele* 2 Handel
O soave fanciulla (Rodolfo, Mimì) *La bohème* 1 Puccini
Osons achever (Abramane) *Zoroastre* 3 Rameau
O souverain, ô juge, ô père! (Rodrigue) *Le Cid* 3 Massenet
O splendid star of love (Gorislava) *Ruslan and Lyudmila* 3 Glinka
O statua gentilissima (Leporello, Don Giovanni) *Don Giovanni* 2 Mozart
O Tanz, o Rausch (Marietta, Paul) *Die tote Stadt* 1 Korngold
O Teresa, vous que j'aime plus que ma vie (Cellini, Teresa, Fieramosca) *Benvenuto Cellini* 1 Berlioz
O terra addio (Aida, Radames) *Aida* 4 Verdi
O Tisiphone, implacable déesse (Medea) *Médée* 3 Cherubini
O toi, l'objet le plus aimable (Agamemnon) *Iphigénie en Aulide* 2 Gluck
O toi qui prolongeas mes jours (Iphigenia) *Iphigénie en Tauride* 1 Gluck
O transports, o douce extase (Vasco da Gama, Sélika) *L'Africaine* 4 Meyerbeer
O tu, che l'alma adora (Ernani) *Ernani* 1 Verdi
O tu, Palermo ... Nell'ombra e nel silenzio (Procida) *I vespri siciliani* 2 Verdi
Oui, c'est moi (Charlotte, Werther) *Werther* 3 Massenet
Oui, dans les bois (Manon) *Manon* 3 Massenet
Oui, des choristes du théâtre (Bijou) *Le postillon de Lonjumeau* 2 Adam
Oui, je souffre votre tristesse (Dulcinée, Don Quichotte) *Don Quichotte* 4 Massenet
Oui, je vous hais (Alexina, Henri de Valois) *Le roi malgré lui* 2 Chabrier
Oui, ta voix m'inspire (Fernand) *La favorite* 1 Donizetti
Oui, voilà l'héroisme ... Au revoir dans un monde (Elisabeth de Valois, Don Carlos) *Don Carlos* 5 Verdi
Oui, vous l'arrachez à mon âme (Mathilde, Arnold Melchthal) *Guillaume Tell* 2 Rossini
Où peut-on être mieux (Lucile, Timante, Dorval *père* and *fils*) *Lucile* 1 Grétry
Our sword has given us victory (Konchak) *Prince Igor* 3 Borodin
Où suis-je? Mes enfants! (Antigone, Polynices, Oedipus) *Oedipe à Colone* 3 Sacchini
Où va la jeune Hindoue (Lakmé) *Lakmé* 2 Delibes
Où vas-tu? (Arnold, Melithal, William Tell) *Guillaume Tell* 1 Rossini
O vecchio cor, che batte (Francesco Foscari) *I due Foscari* 1 Verdi
Over the dark blue waters (Reiza, Huon, Fatima, Sherasmin) *Oberon* 2 Weber
O vin, dissipe la tristesse (Hamlet) *Hamlet* 1 Thomas
O voto tremendo (High Priest) *Idomeneo* 3 Mozart
O wär ich schon mit dir vereint (Marzelline) *Fidelio* 1 Beethoven
O, was klag' ich um Ehre und Eid (Fricka) *Die Walküre* 2 Wagner
O welche Lust! (chorus) *Fidelio* 1 Beethoven
O why should I be weeping (Lisa) *Queen of Spades* 2 Tchaikovsky
O wie ängstlich (Belmonte) *Die Entführung aus dem Serail* 1 Mozart
O, wie will ich triumphieren (Osmin) *Die Entführung aus dem Serail* 3 Mozart
Ozean, du Ungeheuer (Reiza) *Oberon* 2 Weber
O zitt're nicht, mein lieber Sohn ... Zum Leiden bin ich auserkoren (Queen of Night) *Die Zauberflöte* 1 Mozart

P

Pace, pace, mio Dio (Leonora) *La forza del destino* 4 Verdi
Padre! a costoro (Amonasro, Aida) *Aida* 3 Verdi
Padre, germani, addio (Ilia) *Idomeneo* 1 Mozart
Padre, ricevi l'estremo addio (Luisa, Rodolfo, Miller) *Luisa Miller* 3 Verdi
Pâle et blonde, dort sous l'eau (Ophelia) *Hamlet* 4 Thomas
Palpito incerta l'alma (Desdemona) *Otello* 1 Rossini
Papillons inconstants (Fatima) *Les Indes galantes* 3 Rameau
Pappataci! che mai sento! (Lindoro, Isabella, Mustafà) *L'italiana in Algeri* 2 Rossini
Parasya's Dumka (Parasya) *Fair at Sorochintsï* 3 Musorgsky
Par che mi nasca in seno (Irene) *Tamerlano* 2 Handel
Par ici, mes amis ... Ecoute-moi bien (Valentin, ensemble) *Faust* 4 Gounod
Parigi, o cara ... Ah! gran Dio! morir sì giovane (Alfredo, Violetta) *La traviata* 3 Verdi
Pari siamo (Rigoletto) *Rigoletto* 1 Verdi
Par la crainte et par l'espérance (Iphigenia) *Iphigénie en Aulide* 2 Gluck
Parle-moi de ma mère (Don José, Micaëla) *Carmen* 1 Bizet
Parmi les pleurs (Valentine) *Le Huguenots* 4 Meyerbeer
Parmi veder le lagrime ... Possente amor (Duke) *Rigoletto* 2 Verdi
Par quelle douce voix ... Que sous mes pieds (Don Carlos, Elisabeth de Valois) *Don Carlos* 2 Verdi
Partagez-vous mes fleurs ... Pâle et blonde, dort sous l'eau (Ophelia) *Hamlet* 4 Thomas
Parto, m'affretto (Junia) *Lucio Silla* 2 Mozart
Parto, parto (Sextus) *La clemenza di Tito* 1 Mozart
Par une châine trop forte (Rozenn) *Le roi d'Ys* 1 Lalo
Par un sommeil agréable (First, Second and Third Dreams, chorus) *Dardanus* 4 Rameau
Pastorello d'un povero armento (Grimoaldo) *Rodelinda* 3 Handel
Patria oppressa (chorus) *Macbeth* 4 Verdi
Pays merveilleux ... O paradis sorti de l'onde (Vasco da Gama) *L'Africaine* 4 Meyerbeer
Pearlfishers' Duet: *see* Au fond du temple saint
Peasant Lad's Dumka (Grits'ko) *Fair at Sorochintsï* 1 Musorgsky
Pegno adorato e caro (Don Ramiro) *La Cenerentola* 2 Rossini
Pena tiranna io sento al core (Dardano) *Amadigi* 2 Handel
Pendu! (Chapelou, Biju, Marquis Corcy) *Le postillon de Lonjumeau* 3 Adam
Pensa a chi geme d'amor piagata (Melisso) *Alcina* 2 Handel
Pensa alla patria (Isabella) *L'italiana in Algeri* 2 Rossini
Pensa che sei mia figlia (Argirio) *Tancredi* 1 Rossini
Pensa che sol per poco sospendo l'ira mia (Elizabeth, Matilda) *Elisabetta, regina d'Inghilterra* 2 Rossini

Pensieri, voi mi tormentate (Agrippina) *Agrippina* 2 Handel
Pensieri, voi mi tormentate (Orestes) *Oreste* 1 Handel
Perche mai, destin crudel (Elizabeth, Norfolk) *Elisabetta, regina d'Inghilterra* 1 Rossini
Perchè, perchè non m'ami più? ... Resta vicino a me (Michele, Giorgetta) *Il tabarro* Puccini
Per darvi alcun pegno (Cato) *Catone in Utica* 3 J. C. Bach
Perdona! perdona ... No, più nobile sei (Maurizio, Adriana) *Adriana Lecouvreur* 4 Cilea
Perdon, perdon, Amelia (Gabriele, Amelia, Boccanegra) *Simon Boccanegra* 2 Verdi
Perduto ben ... Qual voce a me dal ciel ... Sotto al mio piè (Don Carlo, Elisabetta di Valois) *Don Carlo* 1/2 Verdi
Perfides ennemis (Medea, Jason) *Médée* 1 Cherubini
Perfido! di a quell'empio tiranno (Radamisto) *Radamisto* 1 Handel
Per la gloria d'adorarvi (Ernesto) *Griselda* G. Bononcini
Per le porte del tormento (Rosmene, Tirinthus) *Imeneo* 3 Handel
Per le porte del tormento (Elmira, Sosarme) *Sosarme* 2 Handel
Per lui che adoro (Isabella) *L'italiana in Algeri* 2 Rossini
Per me giunto è il dì supremo ... O Carlo, ascolta (Posa) *Don Carlo* 3/4 Verdi
Per me ora fatale (Count di Luna) *Il trovatore* 2 Verdi
Permettez astre du jour (Huascar) *Les Indes galantes* 2 Rameau
Per piacere alla Signora (Geronio, Fiorilla) *Il turco in Italia* 1 Rossini
Per pietà, ben mio, perdona (Fiordiligi) *Così fan tutte* 2 Mozart
Per rendermi beato (Xerxes) *Serse* 3 Handel
Per sua madre (Pierotto) *Linda di Chamounix* 1 Donizetti
Per te di vane lagrime (Gualtiero) *Il pirata* 1 Bellini
Per viver vicino a Maria (Tonio) *La figlia del reggimento* 2 Donizetti
Pescator, affonda l'esca (Barnaba) *La Gioconda* 2 Ponchielli
Peut-être l'heure était venue (Harald) *Gwendoline* 1 Chabrier
Peuvent-ils ordonner qu'un père (Agamemnon) *Iphigénie en Aulide* 1 Gluck
Piangea cantando ... Ave Maria (Desdemona) *Otello* 4 Verdi
Piangerò la sorte mia (Cleopatra) *Giulio Cesare* 3 Handel
Piangete, occhi dolente (Climene) *Egisto* 2 Cavalli
Piangete voi? ... Al dolce guidami castel natio ... Cielo, a miei lunghi spasimi ... Coppia iniqua (Anne Boleyn, ensemble) *Anna Bolena* 2 Donizetti
Piangi o figlia (Giorgio, Elvira) *I puritani* 1 Bellini
Piango il mio ben così (Orpheus) *Orfeo ed Euridice* 1 Gluck
Piango, perchè mi parla (Fiesco, Boccanegra) *Simon Boccanegra* 3 Verdi
Pian, pianin (finale) *Le nozze di Figaro* 4 Mozart
Pietà, rispetto, amore (Macbeth) *Macbeth* 4 Verdi
Pietoso al lungo pianto (Edoardo) *Un giorno di regno* 2 Verdi
Pietoso al par del nume (Leonora, Fernando) *La favorita* 4 Donizetti
Piff, paff, piff, paff (Marcel) *Les Huguenots* 1 Meyerbeer
Pigeon's Song: *see* Spera sì, mi dice il core
Più che penso alle fiamme del core (Xerxes) *Serse* 1 Handel
Più non vive (Lucrezia Contarini) *I due Foscari* 3 Verdi
Placido è il mar (chorus) *Idomeneo* 2 Mozart
Plaisirs du rang suprême ... A celui que jamais (Elvire) *La muette de Portici* 1 Auber
Plauso! Voci di gioia! ... Sin la tomba è a me negata (Antonina, Eutopio) *Belisario* 1 Donizetti
Plein de trouble (Orpheus) *Orphée et Eurydice* 1 Gluck
Pleurez, pleurez mes yeux (Chimène) *Le Cid* 3 Massenet
Plus blanche que la blanche hermine (Raoul) *Les Huguenots* 1 Meyerbeer
Plus j'observe ces lieux (Renaud) *Armide* 2 Gluck
Plus j'observe ces lieux (Renaud) *Armide* 2 Lully
Plus on connaît l'amour (Hatred) *Armide* 3 Gluck
Pondo è letal, martiro (Charles VII) *Giovanna d'Arco* prol. Verdi
Porgi, Amor (Countess Almaviva) *Le nozze di Figaro* 2 Mozart
Porté au vent, tombant au loin (Fisherman) *The Nightingale* 1 Stravinsky
Portrait Aria: *see* Dies Bildnis ist bezaubernd schön
Possente amor (Duke) *Rigoletto* 2 Verdi
Pour cette cause sainte (Count of Saint-Bris, ensemble) *Les Huguenots* 4 Meyerbeer
Pour la Vierge (Brother Boniface) *Le jongleur de Notre-Dame* 1 Massenet
Pour me rapprocher de Marie (Tonio) *La fille du régiment* 2 Donizetti
Pour moi, je ne crains rien (Leïla, Zurga) *Les pêcheurs de perles* 3 Bizet
Pour notre amour plus d'espérance ... Sur la rive etrangère (Mathilde, Arnold Melcthal) *Guillaume Tell* 3 Rossini
Pourquoi me reveiller (Werther) *Werther* 3 Massenet
Pour tant d'amour (Alphonse XI) *La favorite* 3 Donizetti
Pour toujours (Lorenzo) *Fra Diavolo* 3 Auber
Poveri fiori (Adriana) *Adriana Lecouvreur* 4 Cilea
Povero Ernesto! ... Cercherò lontana terra (Ernesto) *Don Pasquale* 2 Donizetti
Powers mysterious, powers invincible (Marfa) *Khovanshchina* ii Musorgsky
Prender moglie! (Don Pasquale, Ernesto) *Don Pasquale* 1 Donizetti
Prendi, l'anel ti dono (Elvino, Amina) *La sonnambula* 1 Bellini
Prendi; prendi, per me sei libero (Adina) *L'elisir d'amore* 2 Donizetti
Prendi, quest'è l'immagine (Violetta, ensemble) *La traviata* 3 Verdi
Prenez mon bras (Faust, Marguerite, Méphistophélès, Marthe) *Faust* 3 Gounod
Près des ramparts de Séville (Carmen) *Carmen* 1 Bizet
Presentation of the Rose: *see* Mir ist die Ehre widerfahren
Présent des cieux (Amélite, Zoroastre) *Zoroastre* 5 Rameau
Presti omai l'Egizia terra (Julius Caesar) *Giulio Cesare* 1 Handel
Pretty Polly, say (Macheath, Polly) *Beggar's Opera* 1
Pria che spunti (Paolino) *Il matrimonio segreto* 2 Cimarosa
Pria di partir, o Dio! (Idamantes, Electra, Idomeneus) *Idomeneo* 2 Mozart
Prigioniera ho l'alma in pena (Grimoaldo) *Rodelinda* 2 Handel
Prigioniera ho l'alma in pena (Araspe) *Tolomeo* 1 Handel
Principessa di morte! ... Mio fiore! (Calaf, Turandot) *Turandot* 3 Puccini
Printemps qui commence (Delilah) *Samson et Dalila* 1 Saint-Saëns
Prisoners' chorus: *see* O welche Lust
Priva son d'ogni conforto (Cornelia) *Giulio Cesare* 1 Handel
Prize Song: *see* Morgenlich leuchtend in rosigem Schein
Profonds abîmes du Ténare (Envy) *Le temple de la Gloire* prol. Rameau
Prologue: *see* Si può? Si può?
Pronta io son (Norina, Dr Malatesta) *Don Pasquale* 1 Donizetti
Pronti destrieri ... Ah! seguirti fino agl'ultimi confini (Don Alvaro, Leonora) *La forza del destino* 1 Verdi
Pronube dive, dei custodi (Creon, Glaucus, Jason) *Medea* 1 Cherubini
Psyche wandelt durch Säulenhallen (Myrtocle) *Die toten Augen* 1 D'Albert
Pugneremo, vinceremo (Cecrops) *Il pomo d'oro* 2 Cesti
Puisque Pluton est inflexible (Theseus) *Hippolyte et Aricie* 2 Rameau
Puissant maître des flots (Theseus) *Hippolyte et Aricie* 3 Rameau
Pupille amate (Cecilius) *Lucio Silla* 3 Mozart
Pura siccome un angelo ... Dite alla giovine ... Morrò! la mia memoria (Germont, Violetta) *La traviata* 2 Verdi
Pursue thy conquest (Belinda) *Dido and Aeneas* 1 Purcell
Pur ti miro (Poppaea, Nero) *L'incoronazione di Poppea* 3 Monteverdi
Pur ti riveggo ... Fuggiam gli ardori inospiti ... La tra foreste vergini ... Sì: fuggiam da queste mura (Aida, Radames) *Aida* 3 Verdi

Q

Qual cieco fato ... Del mar sul lido (Fiesco, Boccanegra) *Simon Boccanegra* prol. Verdi
Qual cor tradisti (Norma, Pollione) *Norma* 2 Bellini
Qual destino, qual favor (Tonio) *La figlia del reggimento* 1 or 2 Donizetti
Quale più fido amico (Charles VII) *Giovanna d'Arco* 3 Verdi
Qual mare, qual terra ... Lassù risplendere (Amalia, Carlo) *I*

masnadieri 3 Verdi
Qual nuovo terrore (chorus) *Idomeneo* 2 Mozart
Qual'occhio al mondo (Cavaradossi) *Tosca* 1 Puccini
Qual sarà dolor che uccide (Alaide, Isoletta, Arturo, Valdeburgo) *La straniera* 2 Bellini
Qualunque sia l'evento (Alfonso) *Lucrezia Borgia* 1 Donizetti
Qual voce a me dal ciel ... Sotto al mio piè (Don Carlo, Elisabetta di Valois) *Don Carlo* 1/2 Verdi
Qual voluttà trascorrere (Oronte, Giselda, Pagano) *I Lombardi* 3 Verdi
Quand apparaissent les étoiles (Don Quichotte) *Don Quichotte* 1 Massenet
Quand des sommets de la montagne (Cellini, Teresa) *Benvenuto Cellini* 3 Berlioz
Quand'ero paggio del Duca di Norfolk (Falstaff) *Falstaff* 2 Verdi
Quand je quittais la Normandie (Alice) *Robert le diable* 3 Meyerbeer
Quand la flamme de l'amour (Ralph) *La jolie fille de Perth* 2 Bizet
Quand l'Helvétie est un champ de supplices (William Tell, Arnold Melcthal, Walter Furst) *Guillaume Tell* 2 Rossini
Quand ma bonté toujours nouvelle (Montfort, Henri) *Les vêpres siciliennes* 3 Verdi
Quand nos jours s'éteindront (Salome, John the Baptist) *Hérodiade* 4 Massenet
Quando al mio sen (Montforte, Arrigo) *I vespri siciliani* 3 Verdi
Quando di luce rosea (Mary, Talbot) *Maria Stuarda* 2/3 Donizetti
Quando le sere al placido ... L'ara, o l'avello apprestami (Rodolfo) *Luisa Miller* 2 Verdi
Quando m'en vo' (Musetta) *La bohème* 2 Puccini
Quando rapito in estasi (Lucia) *Lucia di Lammermoor* 1 Donizetti
Quand une femme est si jolie (Miss Ellen, Rose, Mistress Bentson, Gérald, Frédéric) *Lakmé* 1 Delibes
Quanto amore (Adina, Dulcamara) *L'elisir d'amore* 2 Donizetti
Quanto a quest'alma amante (Roderick Dhu) *La donna del lago* 1 Rossini
Quanto è bella (Nemorino) *L'elisir d'amore* 1 Donizetti
Quanto godrà, allor che mi vedrà (Alcestis) *Admeto* 2 Handel
Quanto più fiera (Eduige) *Rodelinda* 3 Handel
Qu'as-tu donc fait de ton mâle courage (Atar) *Tarare* 1 Salieri
Que ce rivage retentisse (chorus) *Hippolyte et Aricie* 3 Rameau
Que ces moments sont doux (Alphise, Abaris) *Les Boréades* 5 Rameau
Que d'un objet aimé (Abaris) *Les Boréades* 3 Rameau
Que fais-tu, blanche tourterelle? (Stéphano) *Roméo et Juliette* 3 Gounod
Que faites-vous donc? ... De quels transports ... Toujours unis par la serment (Elisabeth de Valois, Don Carlos) *Don Carlos* 1 Verdi
Que je puis respirer ... Quand nos jours s'éteindront (Salomé, John the Baptist) *Hérodiade* 4 Massenet
Que l'amour embellit la vie (Abaris) *Les Boréades* 5 Rameau
Que l'Averne (Pluto) *Hippolyte et Aricie* 2 Rameau
Quel bronzo feral (Francesco Foscari) *I due Foscari* 3 Verdi
Quel cor che mi donasti (Adelaida) *Lotario* 1 Handel
Quel cor che mi donasti (Almirena) *Rinaldo* 1 Handel
Que l'Enfer applaudisse (chorus) *Castor et Pollux* 1 Rameau
Que les destins prospères (Ory) *Le comte Ory* 1 Rossini
Que le Sultan Saladin (Blondel) *Richard Coeur-de-lion* 1 Grétry
Quel guardo il cavaliere ... So anch'io la virtù magica (Norina) *Don Pasquale* 1 Donizetti
Quella, che tutta fè (Arsamene) *Serse* 2 Handel
Quelle est aima-a-a-able (chorus) *Platée* 2 Rameau
Qu'elle gémisse (chorus) *Les Boréades* 5 Rameau
Quelle prière de reconnaissance (Albert) *Werther* 1 Massenet
Quelle pupille tenere (Curiatius) *Gli Orazi ed i Curiazi* 1 Cimarosa
Quelle soudaine horreur (Three Fates) *Hippolyte et Aricie* 2 Rameau
Quelle surprise, ma beauté de Venise (Henri de Valois, Alexina, Duke Fritelli) *Le roi malgré lui* 2 Chabrier
Quel nouveau ciel (Orpheus) *Orphée et Eurydice* 2 Gluck
Quel ribelle e quell'ingrato (Mithridates) *Mitridate* 1 Mozart
Quel torrente che cada dal monte (Julius Caesar) *Giulio Cesare* 3 Handel
Quel vecchio maledivami! (Rigoletto, Sparafucile) *Rigoletto* 1 Verdi
Que sous mes pieds (Don Carlos, Elisabeth de Valois) *Don Carlos* 2 Verdi
Questa o quella (Duke of Mantua) *Rigoletto* 1 Verdi
Queste innocenti lagrime (Jacopo Foscari, ensemble) *I due Foscari* 2 Verdi
Questo è il cielo di contenti (chorus) *Alcina* 1 Handel
Que tout gémisse (chorus) *Castor et Pollux* 1 Rameau
Qui chiamata m'avete? (Laura, Alvise Badoero) *La Gioconda* 3 Ponchielli
Quick music is best (Essex) *Gloriana* 1 Britten
Qui dolcemente spira soave zeffiretto (Filandro) *Le astuzie femminili* 1 Cimarosa
Quietly, night ... I go to him (Anne Trulove) *The Rake's Progress* 1 Stravinsky
Qui la voce sua soave ... Vien, diletto (Elvira) *I puritani* 2 Bellini
Qui m'accolse opresso, errante (Filippo) *Beatrice di Tenda* 2 Bellini
Qui Radames verrà ... O patria mia (Aida) *Aida* 3 Verdi
Qui te fait si sévère (Thaïs) *Thaïs* 1 Massenet
Quittez, nymphes (Plataea) *Platée* 1 Rameau
Quoi? quoi? (chorus) *Platée* 1 Rameau
Quoi tous les deux (Madeleine, Chapelou) *Le postillon de Lonjumeau* 1 Adam
Qu'une première amour est belle (Sangaride, Doris, Idas) *Atys* 4 Lully

R

Rachel, quand du Seigneur (Eléazar) *La Juive* 4 Halévy
Rataplan (Preziosilla, chorus) *La forza del destino* 3 Verdi
Recondita armonia (Cavaradossi, Sacristan) *Tosca* 1 Puccini
Re dell'abisso ... È lui, è lui ne palpiti (Ulrica [Mam'zelle Arvidson]) *Un ballo in maschera* 1 Verdi
Redoutez la fureur d'un Dieu (Balthazar) *La favorite* 2 Donizetti
Regardez-moi bien dans les yeux (Lescaut) *Manon* 1 Massenet
Regnava nel silenzio ... Quando rapito in estasi (Lucia) *Lucia di Lammermoor* 1 Donizetti
Régnez, Amours (Emilie) *Les Indes galantes* 1 Rameau
Reine, je suis Enée (Aeneas, ensemble) *Les Troyens* 3 Berlioz
Rendi'l sereno al ciglio (Elmira) *Sosarme* 1 Handel
Resign thy club (Dejanira) *Hercules* 2 Handel
Resta immobile: *see* Sois immobile
Resta vicino a me (Michele, Giorgetta) *Il tabarro* Puccini
Reste au foyer, petit grillon (Cendrillon) *Cendrillon* 1 Massenet
Reverenza! ... Buon giorno buona donna (Mistress Quickly, Falstaff) *Falstaff* 2 Verdi
Reviens à toi, vierge adorée (Coroebus, Cassandra) *Les Troyens* 1 Berlioz
Riconosci in questo amplesso (Susanna, Marcellina, Don Curzio, Count Almaviva, Figaro, Bartolo) *Le nozze di Figaro* 3 Mozart
Riddle scene: *see* Heil dir, weiser Schmied!
Rien! en vain j'interroge (Faust) *Faust* 1 Gounod
Rienzi's Prayer: *see* Allmächt'ger Vater
Riot Scene: *see* Zum Teufel mit dir
Ritorna, oh caro e dolce mio tesoro (Rodelinda) *Rodelinda* 2 Handel
Ritorna vincitor! ... L'insana parola ... I sacri nomi ... Numi, pietà (Aida) *Aida* 1 Verdi
Rivages du Jourdain (Jephtha) *Jephté* 1 Montéclair
Rivedrai le foreste imbalsamate ... Su dunque! ... Padre! a costoro (Amonasro, Aida) *Aida* 3 Verdi
Robert, toi que j'aime (Isabelle) *Robert le diable* 4 Meyerbeer
Roi du Ciel et des anges (John of Leyden) *Le prophète* 3 Meyerbeer
Roland courez aux armes (chorus) *Roland* 5 Lully
Rome Narration: *see* Inbrunst im Herzen
Rosa del ciel (Orpheus) *Orfeo* 1 Monteverdi
Rossignols amoureux (Shepherdess) *Hippolyte et Aricie* 5 Rameau

Rozmysli si, Mařenko!: *see* Think it over, Mařenka
Ruhe sanft (Zaide) *Zaide* 1 Mozart
Ruler of this awful hour (Huon) *Oberon* 2 Weber

S

Sacra la scelta è d'un consorte ... Ah! fu giusto il mio sospetto (Miller) *Luisa Miller* 1 Verdi
Sai com'arde in petto mio ... Piangi o figlia (Giorgio, Elvira) *I puritani* 1 Bellini
Salgo già del trono aurato (Abigaille) *Nabucco* 2 Verdi
S'altro che lacrime (Servilia) *La clemenza di Tito* 2 Mozart
Salut à la France (Marie, ensemble) *La fille du régiment* 2 Donizetti
Salut! demeure chaste et pure (Faust) *Faust* 3 Gounod
Salve Maria! (Giselda) *I Lombardi* 1 Verdi
Salvezza a la Francia (Maria, ensemble) *La figlia del reggimento* 2 Donizetti
Samson, ô toi mon bien-aimé (Samson, Delilah) *Samson et Dalila* 2 Saint-Saëns
Sangue a me (Macbeth, ensemble) *Macbeth* 2 Verdi
Sans regrets j'ai quitté les riantes campagnes (Faust) *La damnation de Faust* 2 Berlioz
Saper vorreste (Oscar) *Un ballo in maschera* 3 Verdi
Sarebbe bella questa (Livietta) *Livietta e Tracollo* 1 Pergolesi
Saria possibile (chorus) *L'elisir d'amore* 2 Donizetti
Sa voix fait naître dans mon sein (Dido, Anna) *Les Troyens* 3 Berlioz
Scacciata dal suo nido (Bertarido) *Rodelinda* 2 Handel
Schelm, halt fest (Aennchen, Agathe) *Der Freischütz* 2 Weber
Scherza infida, in grembo al drudo (Ariodante) *Ariodante* 2 Handel
Scherza in mar la navicella (Adelaida) *Lotario* 1 Handel
Scherza in mar la navicella (Amarillis) *Il pastor fido* 2 Handel
Schiudi, inferno (ensemble) *Macbeth* 1 Verdi
Schläfst du, Hagen, mein Sohn? (Alberich, Hagen) *Götterdämmerung* 2 Wagner
Schweig, schweig (Caspar) *Der Freischütz* 1 Weber
Schweigt doch, ihr Stimmen (Barak's Wife) *Die Frau ohne Schatten* 3 Strauss
Schwüles Gedünst (Donner) *Das Rheingold* Wagner
Scintille, diamant (Dapertutto) *Les contes d'Hoffmann* 4 Offenbach
Scocca dardi l'altero suo ciglio (Ottone) *Griselda* 2 Vivaldi
Scoglio d'immota fronte (Berenice) *Scipione* 2 Handel
Scuoti quella fronda di ciliegio ... Tutti i fior (Butterfly, Suzuki) *Madama Butterfly* 2 Puccini
Se a caso Madama (Figaro, Susanna) *Le nozze di Figaro* 1 Mozart
Se all'impero, amici dei (Titus) *La clemenza di Tito* 2 Mozart
Se bramate d'amar chi vi sdegna (Xerxes) *Serse* 2 Handel
Se di lauri (Mithridates) *Mitridate* 2 Mozart
Sediziose voci ... Casta diva ... Ah! bello, a me ritorna (Norma) *Norma* 1 Bellini
See, the dreadful sisters rise (Dejanira) *Hercules* 3 Handel
Se fiato in corpo avete (Geronimo, Count Robinson) *Il matrimonio segreto* 2 Cimarosa
Seguidilla: *see* Près des ramparts de Séville
Seid uns zum zweiten Mal wilkommen (Three Boys) *Die Zauberflöte* 2 Mozart
Seigneur Dieu! (Charlotte) *Werther* 3 Massenet
Seigneur, rempart et seul soutien (Marcel) *Les Huguenots* 1 Meyerbeer
Se il mio nome (Almaviva) *Il barbiere di Siviglia* 1 Rossini
Se il mio valor (Selim) *La schiava liberata* Jommelli
Se il padre perdei (Ilia) *Idomeneo* 2 Mozart
Se il zefiro si posa (Fiorilla) *Il turco in Italia* 2 Rossini
Sein bin ich, sein (Marta) *Tiefland* 1 D'Albert
Se in fiorito ameno prato (Julius Caesar) *Giulio Cesare* 2 Handel
Se i padroni fra lor fanno l'amore (Laura) *L'Arcadia in Brenta* 2 Galuppi
Seit er von dir geschieden (Waltraute) *Gotterdämmerung* 1 Wagner
Séjour de l'éternelle paix (Castor) *Castor et Pollux* 4 Rameau
Se l'arco avessi e i strali (Thrasymedes) *Admeto* 1 Handel
Se la vita ancor t'è cara (Arsaces, Semiramis) *Semiramide* 2 Rossini
Se l'idol mio rapir mi vuoi (Romilda) *Serse* 1 Handel
Selig sind, die Verfolgung leiden (Mathias, Children) *Der Evangelimann* 2 Kienzl
Selig, wie die Sonne (Eva, Magdalene, David, Walther, Hans Sachs) *Die Meistersinger* 3 Wagner
Se'l mio duol non è si forte (Rodelinda) *Rodelinda* 3 Handel
Selva opaca: *see* Sombre forêt
Se mai senti (Sextus) *La clemenza di Tito* 1 Gluck
Semplicetto! a donna credi? (Oronte) *Alcina* 1 Handel
Sempre all'alba ed alla sera (Joan of Arc) *Giovanna d'Arco* prol. Verdi
Sempre in contrasti (Uberto) *La serva padrona* 1 Pergolesi
Sempre libera degg'io (Violetta) *La traviata* 1 Verdi
Senta's Ballad: *see* Johohoe!
Sento avvampar nell'anima (Gabriele) *Simon Boccanegra* 2 Verdi
Sento la gioja (Amadigi) *Amadigi* 3 Handel
Sento, o Dio (Fiordiligi, Dorabella, Ferrando, Guglielmo, Don Alfonso) *Così fan tutte* 1 Mozart
Sento un certo ... Dolce amor! (Aminta, Henry Morosus) *Die schweigsame Frau* 3 Strauss
Sento un certo non so che (Page) *L'incoronazione di Poppea* 2 Monteverdi
Sento un'interna voce (Matilde) *Elisabetta, regina d'Inghilterra* 1 Rossini
Senza mamma, bimbo, tu sei morto (Sister Angelica) *Suor Angelica* Puccini
Senza procelle ancora (Porus) *Poro* 2 Handel
Se per voi (Clarice) *La pietra del paragone* Rossini
Se pietade avete o Numi (Armida) *Armida* 1 Haydn
Se pietà di me non senti (Cleopatra) *Giulio Cesare* 2 Handel
Se quel guerrier io fossi ... Celeste Aida (Radames) *Aida* 1 Verdi
Serbami ognor sì fido ... Alle più calde immagini (Arsace, Semiramide) *Semiramide* 1 Rossini
Serba, serba i tuoi segreti ... Ah! se tu vuoi fuggir (Arturo, Alaide) *La straniera* 1 Bellini
Se risolvi abbandonarmi (Rossane) *Floridante* 3 Handel
Se Romeo t'uccise un figlio ... La tremenda ultrice spada (Romeo, ensemble) *I Capuleti e i Montecchi* 1 Bellini
Se sincero è quell'accento ... Arrigo! ah parli a un core ... È dolce raggio (Arrigo, Elena) *I vespri siciliani* 4 Verdi
S'estinto è l'idol mio (Oriana) *Amadigi* 2 Handel
Se tanto in ira (Carlo) *Linda di Chamounix* 2 Donizetti
Se tu mi doni un'ora (Faust, Mefistofele) *Mefistofele* 1 Boito
Seul pour lutter ... Sur les monts les plus sauvages (Cellini) *Benvenuto Cellini* 3 Berlioz
Se un bell'ardire (Varus) *Ezio* 1 Handel
Se uniti negli affanni (Iago, Rodrigo) *Otello* 1 Rossini
Se vano è il pregare ... No! giusta causa non è d'Iddio (Giselda) *I Lombardi* 2 Verdi
Se viver non degg'io (Xiphares, Aspasia) *Mitridate* 2 Mozart
Se vuoi pace, o volto amato (Agrippina) *Agrippina* 3 Handel
Se vuol ballare (Figaro) *Le nozze di Figaro* 1 Mozart
Sgombra è la sacra selva ... Deh! proteggimi, o Dio! (Adalgisa) *Norma* 1 Bellini
Shadow Song: *see* Ombre légère qui suis mes pas
Shall I survive the day that's dawning (Lensky) *Yevgeny Onegin* 2 Tchaikovsky
She is life and joy to me (Ratmir) *Ruslan and Lyudmila* 5 Glinka
Shepherd, what art thou pursuing (Damon) *Acis and Galatea* 1 Handel
Sia qualunque delle figlie (Don Magnifico) *La Cenerentola* 2 Rossini
Sibillar gli angui d'Aletto (Argante) *Rinaldo* 1 Handel
Sì, caro, sì, ti stringo (Alcestis) *Admeto* 3 Handel
Sì, caro, sì, ti stringo (Almirena) *Rinaldo* 3 Handel
Si, che un tuo solo accento (Fernando) *La favorita* 1 Donizetti
Si colmi il calice (Lady Macbeth) *Macbeth* 2 Verdi
Siegmund! Sieh' auf mich (Brünnhilde, Siegmund) *Die Walküre* 2 Wagner
Siegmund's Narration: *see* Der Männer Sippe
Sieh jene Kraniche in grossen Bogen (Jenny, Jimmy) *Aufstieg und Fall der Stadt Mahagonny* 2 Weill
Sie ist ein Weib, für solchen Mann geschaffen (Petruchio) *Die Widerspenstigen Zähmung* 1 Goetz
Sie woll'n mich heiraten (Arabella, Mandryka) *Arabella* 2 Strauss
Sì, fino all'ore estreme (Adalgisa, Norma) *Norma* 2 Bellini
Sì: fuggiam da queste mura (Aida, Radames) *Aida* 3 Verdi
Sì, fuggire a noi non resta ... Ah crudel d'onor ragioni (Romeo,

Giulietta) *I Capuleti e i Montecchi* 1 Bellini
Si, fui soldato (Andrea Chénier) *Andrea Chénier* 3 Giordano
Signore, ascolta (Liù) *Turandot* 1 Puccini
Signor, una parola (Cenerentola, Dandini, Don Ramiro, Alidoro, Don Magnifico) *La Cenerentola* 1 Rossini
Sì, il patto mantengo (La Gioconda, Barnaba) *La Gioconda* 4 Ponchielli
Si la rigueur ou la vengeance (Brogni) *La Juive* 1 Halévy
Si, la stanchezza m'opprime ... Ai nostri monti (Azucena, Manrico) *Il trovatore* 4 Verdi
Si le bonheur à sourire t'invite (Siébel) *Faust* 4 Gounod
Silent Worship: *see* Non lo dirò col labbro
Sì l'eroismo è questo ... Ma lassù ci vedremo (Elisabetta di Valois, Don Carlo) *Don Carlo* 4/5 Verdi
Si les doux accords (Cupid) *Orphée et Eurydice* 1 Gluck
Si les filles d'Arles (Ourrias) *Mireille* 2 Gounod
Si, li sciogliete ... Meco tu vieni, o misera (Valdeburgo) *La straniera* 2 Bellini
Si l'univers entier (Richard) *Richard Coeur-de-lion* 2 Grétry
Si, mi chiamano Mimì (Mimì) *La bohème* 1 Puccini
Si, morir ella de'! (Alvise Badoero) *La Gioconda* 3 Ponchielli
Since it is not by merit (Tom Rakewell) *The Rake's Progress* 1 Stravinsky
Sin la tomba è me negata (Antonina, Eutopio) *Belisario* 1 Donizetti
S'io non moro (Ilia, Idamantes) *Idomeneo* 3 Mozart
Sì, pel ciel (Otello, Iago) *Otello* 2 Verdi
Si può? Si può? (Tonio) *Pagliacci* prol. Leoncavallo
Sì, quello io son, ravvisami (Odabella, Foresto) *Attila* 1 Verdi
Si ridesti il Leon di Castiglia (chorus) *Ernani* 3 Verdi
Sirius rising as the sun's wheel (Mark, Jenifer) *The Midsummer Marriage* 3 Tippett
Sì: son quella (Alcina) *Alcina* 1 Handel
Si, sperate (Assur) *Semiramide* 1 Rossini
Sì, spietata, il tuo rigore (Ptolemy) *Giulio Cesare* 2 Handel
Sì ... sulla salma del fratello (Valdeburgo, Arturo) *La straniera* 2 Bellini
Sì, tra i ceppi e le ritorte (Demetrio) *Berenice* 2 Handel
Si tu m'aimes, Carmen (Escamillo, Carmen) *Carmen* 4 Bizet
Sì, vendetta (Gilda, Rigoletto) *Rigoletto* 2 Verdi
Sì, vincemmo (Ernesto) *Il pirata* 1 Bellini
Si vous le permettiez, princes ... Ulysse! (Ulysses, Penelope, ensemble) *Pénélope* 3 Fauré
Sleale! Il segreto fu dunque violato? (Don Alvaro, Don Carlo) *La forza del destino* 3 Verdi
Sleep my beauty, sleep (Levko) *A May Night* 3 Rimsky- Korsakov
Sleepwalking Scene: *see* Una macchia è qui tuttora!
Slowly it all comes back (Cressida) *Troilus and Cressida* 1 Walton
Smanie implacabili (Dorabella) *Così fan tutte* 1 Mozart
So anch'io la virtù magica (Norina) *Don Pasquale* 1 Donizetti
Soave sia il vento (Fiordiligi, Dorabella, Don Alfonso) *Così fan tutte* 1 Mozart
So ben che difforme (Nedda, Tonio) *Pagliacci* 1 Leoncavallo
So bin ich nun verlassen (Euryanthe) *Euryanthe* 3 Weber
Soccorso, sostegno accordate ... Non si pianga (Giulietta, Romeo, ensemble) *I Capuleti e i Montecchi* 1 Bellini
So che per via di trioli (Giacomo) *Giovanna d'Arco* 1 Verdi
So che pietosa sei (Selim) *La schiava liberata* Jommelli
Soffriva nel pianto languia (Enrico, Lucia) *Lucia di Lammermoor* 2 Donizetti
Sois immobile (William Tell) *Guillaume Tell* 3 Rossini
Sola, furtiva, al tempio ... Ah! sì, fa core e abbracciami (Adalgisa, Norma) *Norma* 1 Bellini
Sola, perduta, abbandonata (Manon Lescaut) *Manon Lescaut* 4 Puccini
Sola sola in buio loco (sextet) *Don Giovanni* 2 Mozart
Solche hergelauf'ne Laffen (Osmin) *Die Entführung aus dem Serail* 1 Mozart
Sol da te mio dolce amore (Ruggiero) *Orlando* 2 Vivaldi
Soldiers' chorus: *see* Gloire immortelle de nos aïeux
Solenne in quest'ora (Don Alvaro, Don Carlo) *La forza del destino* 3 Verdi
Soll ich dich, Teurer, nicht mehr sehn (Pamina, Tamino, Sarastro) *Die Zauberflöte* 2 Mozart
Solo un pianto (Neris) *Medea* 2 Cherubini
Sombre forêt (Mathilde) *Guillaume Tell* 2 Rossini
Sombres forêts (Tancrède) *Tancrède* 4 Campra
Son confusa pastorella (Eryxene) *Poro* 3 Handel
Songe affreux (Alphise) *Les Boréades* 3 Rameau
Son geloso del zeffiro errante (Elvino, Amina) *La sonnambula* 1 Bellini
Son giunta! ... Madre, pietosa vergine (Leonora, Franciscan friars) *La forza del destino* 2 Verdi
Son gobbo, son Demo (Demo, Orestes) *Giasone* 1 Cavalli
Song of the Coat: *see* Vecchia zimarra
Song of the Gnat: *see* Once a gnat was cutting wood
Song of the Hindu Guest (Hindu) *Sadko* iv Rimsky-Korsakov
Song of the Venetian Guest (Venetian) *Sadko* iv Rimsky-Korsakov
Song of the Viking Guest (Viking) *Sadko* iv Rimsky-Korsakov
Song to the moon: *see* O silver moon
Son guerriera che a gloria t'invita (Joan of Arc, Charles VII, Giacomo) *Giovanna d'Arco* prol. Verdi
Son ìo dinanzi al rè? ... Nell'ispano suol mai l'eresia dominò (Grand Inquisitor, Philip) *Don Carlo* 3/4 Verdi
Son lo spirto che nega sempre (Mefistofele) *Mefistofele* 1 Boito
Son nata a lagrimar (Sextus, Cornelia) *Giulio Cesare* 1 Handel
Sono andati? (Mimì, Rodolfo) *La bohème* 4 Puccini
Son Pereda, son ricco d'onore (Don Carlo) *La forza del destino* 2 Verdi
Son pochi fiori (Suzel) *L'amico Fritz* 1 Mascagni
Son sessant'anni (Gérard) *Andrea Chénier* 1 Giordano
Sonst spielt' ich mit Scepter, mit Krone und Stern (Peter the Great) *Zar und Zimmermann* 3 Lortzing
Son vergin vezzosa (Elvira) *I puritani* 1 Bellini
Sorge infausta una procella (Zoroastro) *Orlando* 3 Handel
Sorge nell'alma mia (Tirinthus) *Imeneo* 2 Handel
Sorgete ... Lo sognai ferito, esangue ... Sventurata, anch'io deliro (Imogene) *Il pirata* 1 Bellini
Sortez de l'esclavage (Pollux, Telaira) *Castor et Pollux* 3 Rameau
Sortez, Ombres (Medea) *Thésée* 3 Lully
Sotto al mio piè (Don Carlo, Elisabetta di Valois) *Don Carlo* 1/2 Verdi
Sotto uno quercia parvemi ... Pondo è letal, martiro (Charles VII) *Giovanna d'Arco* prol. Verdi
Soulevons tous les Dieux (Phoebe) *Castor et Pollux* 5 Rameau
Soumis au silence (Cupid) *Orphée et Eurydice* 1 Gluck
Sound fame (countertenor) *Dioclesian* 4 Purcell
Sous le beau ciel (Raoul) *Les Huguenots* 1 Meyerbeer
Sous le ciel tout étoilé (Lakmé) *Lakmé* 3 Delibes
Sous le dôme épais (Lakmé, Mallika) *Lakmé* 1 Delibes
Sous les vastes arceaux ... Pour Berthe, moi je soupire (John of Leyden) *Le prophète* 2 Meyerbeer
Souvenirs du jeune âge (Isabelle) *Le Pré aux Clercs* 1 Hérold
Sovra il sen la man mi posa (Amina) *La sonnambula* 1 Bellini
So weih' ich mich den Rach' gewalten (Lysiart) *Euryanthe* 2 Weber
So weit Leben und Weben (Loge) *Das Rheingold* Wagner
Spargi d'amaro pianto (Lucia, ensemble) *Lucia di Lammermoor* 3 Donizetti
Spectacle affreux! O Dieu! toi qui m'as destiné ... Du pauvre seul ami fidèle (Masaniello) *La muette de Portici* 4 Auber
Spectre infernal! (Hamlet) *Hamlet* 1 Thomas
Spera sì, mi dice il core (Teofane) *Ottone* 2 Handel
Sperate, o figli ... D'Egitto là sui lidi ... Come notte al sol fulgente (Zaccaria) *Nabucco* 1 Verdi
Spiagge amate (Paris) *Paride ed Elena* 1 Gluck
Spiegarti non poss'io (Ilia, Idamantes) *Idomeneo* 3 Mozart
Spietati, io vi giurai (Rodelinda) *Rodelinda* 2 Handel
Spinning chorus: *see* Summ und brumm
Spirti, fermate (Attila, ensemble) *Attila* 1 Verdi
Spirto gentil (Fernando) *La favorita* 4 Donizetti
Splendon più belle in ciel le stelle (Baldassare) *La favorita* 4 Donizetti
Spunta l'aurora pallida (Margherita) *Mefistofele* 3 Boito
Squilli, echeggi la tromba guerriera (chorus) *Il trovatore* 3 Verdi
Sta nell'Ircana pietrosa tana (Ruggiero) *Alcina* 3 Handel
Starke Scheite (Brünnhilde) *Götterdämmerung* 3 Wagner
Starling Song: *see* Als zullendes Kind
Steady! There you are! Nearly home! (Peter Grimes) *Peter Grimes* 3 Britten
Stella del marinar (Laura) *La Gioconda* 2 Ponchielli
Stelle! Che ardir ... Come scoglio (Fiordiligi) *Così fan tutte* 1

Mozart
Steuermann! Lass die Wacht! (chorus) *Der fliegende Holländer* 3 Wagner
Stille amare, già vi sento (Ptolemy) *Tolomeo* 3 Handel
Stolto! a un sol mio grido (Tebaldo, Romeo) *I Capuleti e i Montecchi* 2 Bellini
Stragi, morti, sangue ed armi (Tiridate) *Radamisto* 1 Handel
Stragi, morti, sangue ed armi (Giuliano) *Rodrigo* 1 Handel
Stride la vampa (Azucena) *Il trovatore* 2 Verdi
Stridono lassù (Nedda) *Pagliacci* 1 Leoncavallo
Su dunque! ... Padre! a costoro (Amonasro, Aida) *Aida* 3 Verdi
Suicidio! (La Gioconda) *La Gioconda* 4 Ponchielli
Suis-je devant le Roi? ... Dans ce beau pays, pur d'hérétique levain (Grand Inquisitor, Philip II) *Don Carlos* 4 Verdi
Suivons la fureur (Argante, Ismenor) *Tancrède* 1 Campra
Sul crin la rivale (Leicester, Elizabeth) *Maria Stuarda* 1 Donizetti
Sul fil d'un soffio etesio (Nannetta) *Falstaff* 3 Verdi
Sulla tomba che rinserra (Edgardo, Lucia) *Lucia di Lammermoor* 1 Donizetti
Sultry heat has supplanted shade of night (Ratmir) *Ruslan and Lyudmila* 3 Glinka
Summertime (Clara) *Porgy and Bess* 1 Gershwin
Summ und brumm (chorus) *Der fliegende Holländer* 2 Wagner
Suoni la tromba, e intrepido (Giorgio, Riccardo) *I puritani* 2 Bellini
Suprême auteur des maux (Abramane) *Zoroastre* 4 Rameau
Sur cet autel sacré (Julia, Licinius) *La vestale* 3 Spontini
Sur la rive etrangère (Mathilde, Arnold Melcthal) *Guillaume Tell* 3 Rossini
Sur les monts les plus sauvages (Cellini) *Benvenuto Cellini* 3 Berlioz
Sur mes genoux, fils du soleil (Sélika) *L'Africaine* 2 Meyerbeer
Susanna or via sortite (Count Almaviva, Countess Almaviva, Susanna) *Le nozze di Figaro* 2 Mozart
Suse, liebe Suse (Gretel, Hänsel) *Hänsel und Gretel* 1 Humperdink
Suspendez à ces murs (Almanzor) *Les abencérages* 1 Cherubini
Suspendez la vengeance (Julia) *La vestale* 2 Spontini
Suspends ta brillante carrière (Ismenor) *Dardanus* 2 Rameau
Sussurrando il venticello (Meroe) *Tigrane* 3 Scarlatti
Su, su dunque su al'armi (Adrasto) *Il pomo d'oro* 4 Cesti
Suzel, buon dì (Fritz Kobus, Suzel) *L'amico Fritz* 2 Mascagni
Svegliatevi nel core (Sextus) *Giulio Cesare* 1 Handel
Sventurata, anch'io deliro (Imogene) *Il pirata* 1 Bellini
Sventurato il cor che fida (Alaide) *La straniera* 1 Bellini
Swearing of Blood Brotherhood: *see* Blühenden Lebens labendes Blut

T

T'abbraccio ... Qual mare, qual terra ... Lassù risplendere (Amalia, Carlo) *I masnadieri* 3 Verdi
Tacea la notte placida ... Di tale amor (Leonora) *Il trovatore* 1 Verdi
Taci, lo voglio (Douglas) *La donna del lago* 1 Rossini
Taci, taci: rimorsi amari (Gualtiero, Imogene) *Il pirata* 2 Bellini
Tanti affanni ho nel core (Ottone) *Ottone* 3 Handel
Tanti affetti (Ellen, ensemble) *La donna del lago* 2 Rossini
Tanto amore segreto (Liù) *Turandot* 3 Puccini
Tardo per gli anni, e tremulo ... Vanitosi che abbietti e dormenti (Ezio, Attila) *Attila* prol. Verdi
Tarquinius does not wait (Male chorus) *The Rape of Lucretia* 1 Britten
Tatyana's Letter Scene: *see* To write is foolishness, I know it
Teco io sto ... Non sai tu che se l'anima mia ... Oh qual soave brivido (Riccardo [Gustavus III], Amelia) *Un ballo in maschera* 2 Verdi
Temple sacré (Aricia) *Hippolyte et Aricie* 1 Rameau
Tendre amour (Orpheus, Eurydice, Cupid) *Orphée et Eurydice* 3 Gluck
Tergi l'ingiuste lagrime (Massimo) *Ezio* 3 Handel
Terminez mes tourments (Io) *Isis* 5 Lully
Te souvient-il du lumineux voyage (Thaïs, Athanaël) *Thaïs* 3 Massenet
Thanks to these lonesome vales (Belinda) *Dido and Aeneas* 2 Purcell
The daylight dies (Konchakovna) *Prince Igor* 2 Borodin
The echoing horn (Squire) *Thomas and Sally* 1 Arne
The fatal blessing I resign (Jupiter) *Peleus and Thetis* Boyce
The flocks shall leave the mountains (Acis, Galatea, Polyphemus) *Acis and Galatea* 2 Handel
The gift of love is rightly treasured (Gremin) *Yevgeny Onegin* 3 Tchaikovsky
The heart bowed down (Count Arnheim) *The Bohemian Girl* 2 Balfe
The moon is high in the sky (Aleko) *Aleko* Rakhmaninov
The nest of *streltsii* sleeps (Shaklovtïy) *Khovanshchina* iii Musorgsky
There is a desert land (Bayan) *Ruslan and Lyudmila* 1 Glinka
The soldier tir'd of war's alarms (Mandane) *Artaxerxes* 3 Arne
The summer morning dances in my heart (Mark) *The Midsummer Marriage* 1 Tippett
The turtle thus, with plaintive crying (Polly) *Beggar's Opera* 1
The world, when day's career is run (Dejanira) *Hercules* 1 Handel
Think it over, Mařenka [Rozmysli si, Mařenko!] (Kecal, ensemble) *The Bartered Bride* 3 Smetana
Tief in Alaskas schneeweissen Wäldern (Jimmy) *Aufstieg und Fall der Stadt Mahagonny* 1 Weill
Tiger! wetze nur die Klauen (Zaide) *Zaide* 2 Mozart
Timor di me? ... D'amor sull'ali rosee (Leonora) *Il trovatore* 4 Verdi
Tiranna gelosia (Turno) *Il trionfo di Camilla* 2 Bononcini
Tirannia gli diede il regno (Garibaldo) *Rodelinda* 2 Handel
Tiranni miei pensieri (Ptolemy) *Tolomeo* 1 Handel
Ti scosta, o malnato (Francesco, Amalia) *I masnadieri* 2 Verdi
'Tis sad to leave our fatherland (Thaddeus) *The Bohemian Girl* 1 Balfe
Titurel, der fromme Held (Gurnemanz) *Parsifal* 1 Wagner
To bind by force, to bolt with bars (Blind Ballad-singer) *Gloriana* 3 Britten
Todesverkündigung: *see* Siegmund! Sieh' auf mich
Toh, toh, poffare il mondo! (Melitone) *La forza del destino* 3 Verdi
Toi, le coeur de la rose (Child) *L'enfant et les sortilèges* 1 Ravel
Toi! mon Rodrigue! c'est toi (Posa, Don Carlos) *Don Carlos* 2 Verdi
Toi que je laisse sur la terre (Julia) *La vestale* 3 Spontini
Toi, que j'implore ... Impitoyables dieux (Julia) *La vestale* 2 Spontini
Toi qui n'as pas rougi (Mâtho) *Salammbô* 4 Reyer
Toi qui sus le néant (Elisabeth de Valois) *Don Carlos* 5 Verdi
Tombe degl'avi miei ... Fra poco a me ricovero ... Tu che a Dio spiegasti l'ali (Edgardo) *Lucia di Lammermoor* 3 Donizetti
Ton coeur n'as pas compris le mien (Nadir, Leïla) *Les pêcheurs de perles* 2 Bizet
Toreador's Song: *see* Votre toast, je peux vous le rendre
Torna la pace (Idomeneus) *Idomeneo* 3 Mozart
Tornami a dir che m'ami (Norina, Ernesto) *Don Pasquale* 3 Donizetti
Tornami a vagheggiar (Morgana/Alcina) *Alcina* 1 Handel
Torna pure al caro bene (Zelmira) *Armida* 3 Haydn
Torna sol per un momento (Ptolemy) *Tolomeo* 1 Handel
Torno di Tito a lato (Annius) *La clemenza di Tito* 2 Mozart
Torture Aria: *see* Martern aller Arten
Tosca è un buon falco ... Ella verrà (Scarpia) *Tosca* 2 Puccini
Toujours unis par la serment (Elisabeth de Valois, Don Carlos) *Don Carlos* 1 Verdi
Tout conspire à vaincre mes remords (Dido, Aeneas, Anna, Iopas, Narbal) *Les Troyens* 4 Berlioz
Toute la nuit (Ulysses) *Pénélope* 3 Fauré
Tout être a le droit (Father) *Louise* 4 Charpentier
Tout tremble devant le Seigneur (chorus) *Jephté* 1 Montéclair
To write is foolishness, I know it (Tatyana) *Yevgeny Onegin* 1 Tchaikovsky
Tra caligini profonde (Zoroastro) *Orlando* 2 Handel
Tradito, schernito (Ferrando) *Così fan tutte* 2 Mozart
Traft Ihr das Schiff (Senta) *Der fliegende Holländer* 2 Wagner
Tra-la-la ... mais qu'ai-je donc? (Ascanio) *Benvenuto Cellini* 3 Berlioz
Tranquillo ei posa! ... Com'è bello (Lucrezia) *Lucrezia Borgia* prol. Donizetti
Tra sospetti, affetti e timori (Grimoaldo) *Rodelinda* 3 Handel
Tra tante smanie (Otello, Rodrigo, Desdemona) *Otello* 2 Rossini
Träumst du Mutter (Clytemnestra, Electra) *Elektra* Strauss
Traure, mein Herz (Reiza) *Oberon* 3 Weber
Traurigkeit ward mir zum Lose (Konstanze) *Die Entführung aus dem Serail* 2 *Mozart*

Tra voi belle, brune o bionde (Des Grieux) *Manon Lescaut* 1 Puccini
Trema per te, falso figliuolo (Eboli, Don Carlo, Posa) *Don Carlo* 2/3 Verdi
Tremate, o miseri! (Francesco) *I masnadieri* 1 Verdi
Tre sbirri, una carrozza ... Va, Tosca! (Scarpia) *Tosca* 1 Puccini
Treulich geführt (chorus) *Lohengrin* 3 Wagner
Trinche vaine allegramente (Vespina) *L'infedeltà delusa* 2 Haydn
Triumph, victorious love (finale) *Dioclesian* 5 Purcell
Trono e corona (Eleonora d'Este) *Torquato Tasso* 1 Donizetti
Troppo Pallade pretende (Venus) *Il pomo d'oro* 3 Cesti
Troppo soavi i gusti (Delfa) *Giasone* 1 Cavalli
Trostlos schluchzet Philomele (Zaide) *Zaide* 2 Mozart
Trotze nicht! (Adolar, Lysiart) *Euryanthe* 3 Weber
Trübe Augen (Aennchen) *Der Freischütz* 3 Weber
Tu al cui sguardo onnipossente ... O patrizi, tremate l'Eterno (Lucrezia Contarini) *I due Foscari* 1 Verdi
Tu caro sei il dolce mio tesoro (Elmira, Sosarme) *Sosarme* 3 Handel
Tu che a Dio spiegasti l'ali (Edgardo) *Lucia di Lammermoor* 3 Donizetti
Tu che di gel sei cinta (Liù) *Turandot* 3 Puccini
Tu, che le vanità (Elisabetta di Valois) *Don Carlo* 4/5 Verdi
Tu del mio Carlo al seno ... Carlo vive? (Amalia) *I masnadieri* 2 Verdi
Tu la mia stella sei (Cleopatra) *Giulio Cesare* 1 Handel
Tu l'as dit (Raoul) *Les Hugenots* 4 Meyerbeer
Tu m'apristi in cor ferita (Imogene, Ernesto) *Il pirata* 2 Bellini
Tu m'as donné le plus doux rêve (Gérald, Lakmé) *Lakmé* 3 Delibes
Tu mi lasci? (Sandrina, Count Belfiore) *La finta giardiniera* 3 Mozart
Tuo drudo è mio rivale (Grimoaldo) *Rodelinda* 2 Handel
Tu preparati a morire (Ariodante) *Ariodante* 2 Handel
Tu puniscimi, o Signore ... A brani, a brani, o perfido (Luisa) *Luisa Miller* 2 Verdi
Tu pur lo sai, che giudice (Lucrezia Contarini, Francesco Foscari) *I due Foscari* 1 Verdi
Tu qui, Santuzza? (Turiddu, Santuzza) *Cavalleria rusticana* Mascagni
Tu, rea donna (Attila, Odabella, Foresto, Ezio) *Attila* 3 Verdi
Tu sciagurato! ah! fuggi ... Bagnato dalle lagrime (Gualtiero, Imogene) *Il pirata* 1 Bellini
Tu sei il cor di questo core (Achillas) *Giulio Cesare* 1 Handel
Tu sei la mia vittoria (Maurizio, Adriana Lecouvreur) *Adriana Lecouvreur* 2 Cilea
Tu sul labbro (Zaccaria) *Nabucco* 2 Verdi
Tutta raccolta ancor (Berenice) *Scipione* 2 Handel
Tutte armate di flagelli (Prenesto) *Il trionfo di Camilla* 3 Bononcini
Tutte le feste al tempio ... Sì, vendetta (Gilda, Rigoletto) *Rigoletto* 2 Verdi
Tutte nel cor vi sento (Electra) *Idomeneo* 1 Mozart
Tutti i fior (Butterfly, Suzuki) *Madama Butterfly* 2 Puccini
Tutto è disposto ... Aprite un po' quegl'occhi (Figaro) *Le nozze di Figaro* 4 Mozart
Tutto nel mondo è burla (Falstaff, ensemble) *Falstaff* 3 Verdi
Tutto sprezzo che d'Ernani (Elvira) *Ernani* 1 Verdi
Tu, tu, amore (Manon Lescaut, Des Grieux) *Manon Lescaut* 2 Puccini
Tu? tu? piccolo iddio (Butterfly) *Madama Butterfly* 2 Puccini
Tu vedi in un bel ciel (Don Juan) *Don Juan de la Mañara* 2 Alfano
Tu vedrai che amore in terra (Leonora) *Il trovatore* 4 Verdi
Tu vedrai che amore in terra (Manrico, Leonora) *Il trovatore* 4 Verdi
Tu vedrai la sventurata ... Ma non fia sempre odiata (Gualtiero) *Il pirata* 2 Bellini
Tu vuoi ch'io parta; io parto (Polissena) *Radamisto* 1 Handel

U

Udite tutti, udite (Geronimo) *Il matrimonio segreto* 1 Cimarosa
Udite, udite, o rustici (Dulcamara) *L'elisir d'amore* 1 Donizetti
Ugo è spento (Parisina, ensemble) *Parisina* 3 Donizetti
Ulysse! Fier époux! (Penelope) *Pénélope* 1 Fauré
Una donna a quindici anni (Despina) *Così fan tutte* 2 Mozart
Una furtiva lagrima (Nemorino) *L'elisir d'amore* 2 Donizetti
Un altare ed una benda ... Ah, chi m'accusa (Gemma, ensemble) *Gemma di Vergy* 2 Donizetti
Una macchia è qui tuttora! (Lady Macbeth) *Macbeth* 4 Verdi
Un ange, une femme inconnue (Fernand) *La favorite* 1 Donizetti
Una parola, o Adina ... Chiedi all'aura lusinghiera (Nemorino, Adina) *L'elisir d'amore* 1 Donizetti
Una povera ragazza (Cecchina) *La buona figliuola* 1 Piccinni
Un'aura amorosa (Ferrando) *Così fan tutte* 1 Mozart
Un autre est son époux ... J'aurais sur ma poitrine (Werther) *Werther* 2 Massenet
Una vergine, un angiol di Dio (Fernando) *La favorita* 1 Donizetti
Una voce al cor ... Egli riede (Gemma) *Gemma di Vergy* 1 Donizetti
Una voce poco fa (Rosina) *Il barbiere di Siviglia* 1 Rossini
Una volta c'era un rè (Cenerentola) *La Cenerentola* 1 Rossini
Un bandeau couvre les yeux (Blondel) *Richard Coeur-de-lion* 1 Grétry
Un bel dì (Butterfly) *Madama Butterfly* 2 Puccini
Un buon servo del visconte (Antonio Loustolot, Linda) *Linda di Chamounix* 2 Donizetti
Un cenno leggiadretto (Atalanta) *Serse* 1 Handel
Un detto, un sol ... Vago sogno m'arrise ... Sì l'eroismo è questo ... Ma lassù ci vedremo (Elisabetta di Valois, Don Carlo) *Don Carlo* 4/5 Verdi
Und glaubst du, Elende (Paul, Marietta) *Die tote Stadt* 2 Korngold
Un dì, all'azzurro spazio (Andrea Chénier) *Andrea Chénier* 1 Giordano
Un dì (ero piccina) al tempio (Iris) *Iris* 2 Mascagni
Un dì felice, eterea (Alfredo, Violetta) *La traviata* 1 Verdi
Un dì, se ben rammentomi ... Bella figlia dell'amore (Duke of Mantua, Gilda, Maddalena, Rigoletto) *Rigoletto* 3 Verdi
Und ist kein Betrug ... Es war einmal (Marie) *Wozzeck* 3 Berg
Und jetzt sag' ich adieu (Arabella, Dominik, Elemer, Lamoral) *Arabella* 2 Strauss
Und ob die Wolke (Agathe) *Der Freischütz* 3 Weber
Une dame noble et sage (Urbain) *Les Huguenots* 1 Meyerbeer
Une fièvre brûlante (Blondel) *Richard Coeur-de-lion* 1 Grétry
Une grande innocence! (Golaud) *Pelléas et Mélisande* 4 Debussy
Une heure encore ... La gloire était ma seule idole (Cellini) *Benvenuto Cellini* 2 Berlioz
Une poupée aux yeux d'émail (Nicklausse) *Les contes d'Hoffmann* 1 Offenbach
Une puce gentille (Méphistophélès) *La damnation de Faust* 2 Berlioz
Unheilvolle Daphne (Apollo, Daphne) *Daphne* Strauss
Un horizon serein (Alphise) *Les Boréades* 1 Rameau
Unis dès la plus tendre enfance (Pylades) *Iphigénie en Tauride* 2 Gluck
Un jour, dans les flots de la Meuse (Fidès, Berthe) *Le prophète* 1 Meyerbeer
Un momento di contento (Oronte) *Alcina* 2 Handel
Un mot, un seul ... J'avais fait un beau rêve ... Oui, voilà l'héroïsme ... Au revoir dans un monde (Elisabeth de Valois, Don Carlos) *Don Carlos* 5 Verdi
Un orage affreux vous emporte (Penelope, ensemble) *Pénélope* 3 Fauré
Un perfido, un vile, un mentitore tu sei (Nottingham, Robert, Elizabeth) *Roberto Devereux* 2 Donizetti
Un ruisselet bien clair (Vertigo) *La rencontre imprévue* 3 Gluck
Un segreto d'importanza (Don Magnifico, Dandini) *La Cenerentola* 2 Rossini
Un soave non so che (Don Ramiro, Cenerentola) *La Cenerentola* 1 Rossini
Un tal gioco, credetemi (Canio) *Pagliacci* 1 Leoncavallo
Unter blüh'nden Mandelbäumen (Adolar) *Euryanthe* 1 Weber
Un vago sembiante di gioia (Narciso) *Il turco in Italia* 1 Rossini
Urna fatale ... Egli è salvo (Don Carlo) *La forza del destino* 3 Verdi

V

Va crudele, al Dio spietato ... Vieni in Roma (Adalgisa, Pollione) *Norma* 1 Bellini
Va, dal furor portata (Maximus) *Ezio* 2 Handel
Vado al campo (Erenice) *Sosarme* 2 Handel
Vado a morir, vi lascio (Arminius) *Arminio* 2 Handel
Vado a pugnar contento (Rinaldo) *Armida* 1 Haydn
Vado, e giro nei palchetti (Don Crisobolo) *L'impresario in angustie*

1 Cimarosa
V'adoro, pupille (Cleopatra) *Giulio Cesare* 2 Handel
Vaghe fonti, che mormorando (Otho) *Agrippina* 2 Handel
Vaghe pupille, non piangete (Orlando) *Orlando* 2 Handel
Va godendo, vezzoso e bello (Romilda) *Serse* 1 Handel
Vago sogno m'arrise ... Sì l'eroismo è questo ... Ma lassù ci vedremo (Elisabetta di Valois, Don Carlo) *Don Carlo* 4/5 Verdi
Vainement j'ai parlé ... Par une chaîne trop forte (Rozenn) *Le roi d'Ys* 1 Lalo
Vainement, ma bien aimée (Mylio) *Le roi d'Ys* 3 Lalo
Va, infelice (Anne Boleyn, Jane Seymour) *Anna Bolena* 2 Donizetti
Va! laisse couler mes larmes (Charlotte) *Werther* 3 Massenet
Vallon sonore (Hylas) *Les Troyens* 5 Berlioz
Vanitosi che abbietti e dormenti (Ezio, Attila) *Attila* prol. Verdi
Vanne indegno (Leicester, Elizabeth, Cecil) *Maria Stuarda* 2/3 Donizetti
Va, pensiero (chorus) *Nabucco* 3 Verdi
Va, preparati (Elizabeth, ensemble) *Maria Stuarda* 1/2 Donizetti
Va! Spirto d'abisso ... Sangue a me (Macbeth, ensemble) *Macbeth* 2 Verdi
Vaste empire des mers (Emilie) *Les Indes galantes* 1 Rameau
Va tacito e nascosto (Julius Caesar) *Giulio Cesare* 1 Handel
Vater! hör mich flehn zu Dir (Huon) *Oberon* 2 Weber
Va, Tosca! (Scarpia) *Tosca* 2 Puccini
Va! va! dit-elle (Alice) *Robert le diable* 1 Meyerbeer
Vecchia zimarra (Colline) *La bohème* 4 Puccini
Ve' come gli astri stessi (Ernani, Elvira) *Ernani* 4 Verdi
Vedete? io son fedele (Manon Lescaut, Des Grieux) *Manon Lescaut* 1 Puccini
Vedi? di morte l'angelo ... O terra addio (Aida, Radames) *Aida* 4 Verdi
Vedi! le fosche notturne ... Chi del gitano (chorus) *Il trovatore* 2 Verdi
Vedrai, carino (Zerlina) *Don Giovanni* 2 Mozart
Vedrò mentre io sospiro (Count Almaviva) *Le nozze di Figaro* 3 Mozart
Vedrommi intorno (Idomeneus) *Idomeneo* 1 Mozart
Veil Song: *see* Au palais des fées/Nel giardin del bello
Vendicata! e di qual sangue (Hermione, Orestes) *Ermione* 2 Rossini
Venere bella (Cleopatra) *Giulio Cesare* 2 Handel
Venez, venez, Haine implacable (Armide) *Armide* 3 Lully
Venga pur fiera tempest (Momo) *Il pomo d'oro* 5 Cesti
Vengo! ... aspettate (Vitellia, Annius, Publius) *La clemenza di Tito* 1 Mozart
Venite fidente alla croce (Leonora, Padre Guardiano) *La forza del destino* 2 Verdi
Venite inginocchiatevi (Susanna) *Le nozze di Figaro* 2 Mozart
Venti scudi (Nemorino, Belcore) *L'elisir d'amore* 2 Donizetti
Venti, turbini, prestate (Rinaldo) *Rinaldo* 1 Handel
Verachtet mir die Meister nicht (Hans Sachs, ensemble) *Die Meistersinger* 3 Wagner
Verdi allori sempre unito (Medoro) *Orlando* 2 Handel
Verdi pianti, erbette liete (Angelica) *Orlando* 2 Handel
Verdi prati e selve amene (Ruggiero) *Alcina* 2 Handel
Verdorben! Gestorben (Fiddler) *Königskinder* 3 Humperdinck
Verführer! Warum stellt ihr so (Mrs Ford) *Die lustigen Weiber von Windsor* 1 Nicolai
Verlässt die Kirche mich ... Wohl liebst auch ich (Rienzi, Irene) *Rienzi* 5 Wagner
Verliebte brauchen keine Zeugen (Rosalie) *Doktor und Apotheker* 1 Dittersdorf
Verloren! Verloren! (Dutchman, Senta, Erik) *Der fliegende Holländer* 3 Wagner
Verranno a te sull'aure (Edgardo, Lucia) *Lucia di Lammermoor* 1 Donizetti
Versez! que tout respire l'ivresse (John of Leyden) *Le prophète* 5 Meyerbeer
Vesti la giubba (Canio) *Pagliacci* 1 Leoncavallo
Vezzosetta mia diletta (finale) *L'Arcadia in Brenta* 2 Galuppi
V'ho ingannato! ... Lassù, in cielo (Gilda, Rigoletto) *Rigoletto* 3 Verdi
Via resti servita (Susanna, Marcellina) *Le nozze di Figaro* 1 Mozart
Vicino a te s'acqueta ... La nostra morte (Andrea Chénier, Maddalena de Coigny) *Andrea Chénier* 4 Giordano
Vien, diletto (Elvira) *I puritani* 2 Bellini
Viene la sera (Pinkerton, Butterfly) *Madama Butterfly* 1 Puccini
Vieni al tempio (Charles VII, Joan of Arc) *Giovanna d'Arco* 1 Verdi
Vieni, appage il tuo consorte (Orpheus, Eurydice) *Orfeo ed Euridice* 3 Gluck
Vieni, cerchiam pe' mari ... Taci, taci: rimorsi amari (Gualtiero, Imogene) *Il pirata* 2 Bellini
Vieni fra queste braccia (Arturo, Elvira) *I puritani* 3 Bellini
Vieni fra queste braccia ... Ma quel piacer che adesso (Giannetto) *La gazza ladra* 1 Rossini
Vieni Imeneo deh vieni (chorus) *Orfeo* 1 Monteverdi
Vieni in Roma (Adalgisa, Pollione) *Norma* 1 Bellini
Vieni, la mia vendetta ... Qualunque sia l'evento (Alfonso) *Lucrezia Borgia* 1 Donizetti
Vieni, o cara, a consolarmi (Argante) *Rinaldo* 1 Handel
Vieni, o cara, ch'in lacci stretto (Claudius) *Agrippina* 1 Handel
Vieni, o figlio, e mi consola (Gismonda) *Ottone* 2 Handel
Vieni, o Levita! ... Tu sul labbro (Zaccaria) *Nabucco* 2 Verdi
Vieni t'affretta ... Or tutti sorgete (Lady Macbeth) *Macbeth* 1 Verdi
Vieni, torna, idolo mio (Agilea) *Teseo* 3 Handel
Vien, Leonora (Alfonso XI) *La favorita* 2 Donizetti
Viens à nous, Dieu tutélaire ... Courage! ... du courage (Hélène) *Les vêpres siciliennes* 1 Verdi
Viens! fuyons au bout du monde (Romeo, Juliet) *Roméo et Juliette* 5 Gounod
Viens, gentille dame (George Brown) *La dame blanche* 2 Boieldieu
Viens, Hymen (Phani) *Les Indes galantes* 2 Rameau
Viens, suis un époux (Orpheus, Eurydice) *Orphée et Eurydice* 3 Gluck
Vil trofeo d'un alma imbelle (Porus) *Poro* 1 Handel
Vinto è l'amor da sdegno e gelosia (Matilda) *Ottone* 1 Handel
Vi parlo all'olandese (Sumers) *L'italiana in Londra* 2 Cimarosa
Vi ravviso, o luoghi ameni (Rodolfo) *La sonnambula* 1 Bellini
Virgins are like the fair flower (Polly) *Beggar's Opera* 1
Vi ricorda o bosch'ombrosi (Orpheus) *Orfeo* 2 Monteverdi
Vision fugitive (Herod) *Hérodiade* 2 Massenet
Vissi d'arte (Tosca) *Tosca* 2 Puccini
Viva il vino spumeggiante (Turiddu) *Cavalleria rusticana* Mascagni
Vivat Bacchus (Pedrillo, Osmin) *Die Entführung aus dem Serail* 2 Mozart
Vivere io non potrò (Malcolm, Ellen) *La donna del lago* 1 Rossini
Vivi, ingrato (Elizabeth) *Roberto Devereux* 3 Donizetti
Vivi, tiranno! io t'ho scampato (Bertarido) *Rodelinda* 3 Handel
Vivi tu (Percy) *Anna Bolena* 2 Donizetti
Vivrà! Contende il giubilo (Leonora, Luna) *Il trovatore* 4 Verdi
Voce di donna o d'angelo (La Cieca) *La Gioconda* 1 Ponchielli
Vo' far guerra, e vincer voglio (Armida) *Rinaldo* 2 Handel
Voglio passar! ... In lei tanta pietà? (Tigrana, Edgar, Frank) *Edgar* 3 Puccini
Voi che sapete (Cherubino) *Le nozze di Figaro* 2 Mozart
Voi che sì larghe cure ... Sleale! Il segreto fu dunque violato? (Don Alvaro, Don Carlo) *La forza del destino* 3 Verdi
Voi che udite il mio lamento (Otho) *Agrippina* 2 Handel
Voici ce qu'il écrit à son frère (Geneviève, Arkel) *Pelléas et Mélisande* 1 Debussy
Voici des roses (Méphistophélès) *La damnation de Faust* 2 Berlioz
Voici la vaste plaine ... En marche (Mireille) *Mireille* 4 Gounod
Voi lo sapete (Santuzza) *Cavalleria rusticana* Mascagni
Vois ma misère, hélas! (Samson) *Samson et Dalila* 3 Saint-Saëns
Volate, amori (Ginevra) *Ariodante* 1 Handel
Volgendo a me lo sguardo (Gualtiero) *Griselda* G. Bononcini
Vollendet das ewige Werk! (Wotan) *Das Rheingold* Wagner
Volta la terrea (Oscar) *Un ballo in maschera* 1 Verdi
Von den edlen Kavalieren (Nancy, Lady Harriet) *Martha* 1 Flotow
Von Jugend auf in dem Kampfgefild (Huon) *Oberon* 1 Weber
Vor deinem Fenster (Nureddin) *Der Barbier von Bagdad* 1 Cornelius
Vorrei vendicarmi del perfido cor (Bradamante) *Alcina* 2 Handel
Votre toast, je peux vous le rendre ... Toréador, en garde (Escamillo) *Carmen* 2 Bizet
Vous devez vous animer (Cybele, chorus) *Atys* 1 Lully
Vous êtes mon Prince Charmant (Cendrillon, Prince Charmant) *Cendrillon* 2 Massenet
Vous me disiez sans cesse (Isabelle, Marguerite de Valois, Cantarelli) *Le pré aux Clercs* 2 Hérold

Vous qui du Dieu vivant (Brogni) *La Juive* 3 Halévy
Vous qui faites l'endormie (Méphistophélès) *Faust* 4 Gounod
Vous voulez que je vous oublie? (Tom) *Tom Jones* 2 Philidor
Vous voyez de vos fils la mère infortunée (Medea) *Médée* 1 Cherubini
Voyez du haut de ces rivages (Pietro) *La muette de Portici* 5 Auber
Voyons, Manon, plus de chimères (Manon) *Manon* 1 Massenet

W

Wach auf, es nahet gen den Tag (ensemble) *Die Meistersinger* 3 Wagner
Wache, Wala! (Wanderer, Erda) *Siegfried* 3 Wagner
Wahn! Wahn! Überall Wahn (Hans Sachs) *Die Meistersinger* 3 Wagner
Walther's Trial Song: *see* Fanget an! So rief der Lenz in dem Wald
Waltraute's Narration: *see* Seit er von dir geschieden
War es so schmählich (Brünnhilde, Wotan) *Die Walküre* 3 Wagner
Was die Steine glänzen? (Marie) *Wozzeck* 2 Berg
Was duftet doch der Flieder (Hans Sachs) *Die Meistersinger* 2 Wagner
Was gleicht wohl auf Erden (chorus) *Der Freischütz* 3 Weber
Was musst' ich hören, Gott (Erik, Senta) *Der fliegende Holländer* 3 Wagner
Was seh ich? ... Nicht wollen die Götter (Daphne, Apollo) *Daphne* Strauss
Was soll ich dazu sagen (Lady Harriet, Nancy, Lyonel, Plunkett) *Martha* 2 Flotow
Was ward aus mir? (Paul) *Die tote Stadt* 2 Korngold
Was willst du, fremder Mensch? (Electra, Orestes) *Elektra* Strauss
Water parted from the sea (Artaxerxes) *Artaxerxes* 3 Arne
Wayward sisters (Sorceress) *Dido and Aeneas* 1 Purcell
Wehe, mein Mann! Welchen Weg (Empress) *Die Frau ohne Schatten* 2 Strauss
Wehen mir Lüfte Ruh (Adolar) *Euryanthe* 2 Weber
Wehvolles Erbe (Amfortas) *Parsifal* 1 Wagner
Weia! Waga! Woge, du Welle (Rhinemaidens, Alberich) *Das Rheingold* Wagner
Weiche, Wotan! weiche! (Erda, Wotan) *Das Rheingold* Wagner
Welch ein Geschick! ... Ha! du solltest für mich sterben (Konstanze, Belmonte) *Die Entführung aus dem Serail* 3 Mozart
Welcher Kummer ... Traurigkeit (Konstanze) *Die Entführung aus dem Serail* 2 Mozart
Welches Unholds List (Brünnhilde, Hagen, Gunther) *Götterdämmerung* 2 Wagner
Welche Wonne, welche Lust (Blonde) *Die Entführung aus dem Serail* 2 Mozart
Welko! das Bild! (Mandryka, Waldner) *Arabella* 1 Strauss
Well met, pretty maid (Sally, Squire) *Thomas and Sally* 2 Arne
Wenn der Freude Tränen fliessen (Belmonte) *Die Entführung aus dem Serail* 2 Mozart
Wenn der Himmel hell wird (Jimmy) *Aufstieg und Fall der Stadt Mahagonny* 2 Weill
Wenn sie sich verirrten im Walde dort (Peter, Gertrud) *Hänsel und Gretel* 1 Humperdinck
Wenn zum Gebet (Bostana, Nureddin) *Der Barbier von Bagdad* 1 Cornelius
Wer ein Liebchen hat gefunden (Osmin) *Die Entführung aus dem Serail* 1 Mozart
Westwärts schweift der Blick (Young Sailor) *Tristan und Isolde* 1 Wagner
What flatt'ring noise is this (Envy, Attendants) *The Indian Queen* 2 Purcell
What is life? (Hermann) *Queen of Spades* 3 Tchaikovsky
What shall I do to show (Maximian) *Dioclesian* 3 Purcell
When I am laid in earth (Dido) *Dido and Aeneas* 3 Purcell
When monarchs unite (chorus) *Dido and Aeneas* 1 Purcell
When other lips (Thaddeus) *The Bohemian Girl* 3 Balfe
When young the Countess used to live in Paris (Tomsky) *Queen of Spades* 1 Tchaikovsky
Where art thou, where? ... Daylight is fading (Vladimir) *Prince Igor* 2 Borodin
Where congeal'd the northern streams (Hyllus) *Hercules* 1 Handel
Where'er you walk (Jupiter) *Semele* 2 Handel
Where shall I fly ... See, the dreadful sisters rise (Dejanira) *Hercules* 3 Handel
Where shall I seek the charming fair (Acis) *Acis and Galatea* 1 Handel
Who hopes to conjure with the world of dreams (Sosostris) *The Midsummer Marriage* 3 Tippett
Who may compare with my Mathilde (Robert) *Iolanta* Tchaikovsky
Why did I not know this before (Iolanta) *Iolanta* Tchaikovsky
Why dost thou untimely grieve (Ino, Athamas, Cadmus, Semele) *Semele* 1 Handel
Wie aus der Ferne längst vergang'n Zeiten (Dutchman, Senta) *Der fliegende Holländer* 2 Wagner
Wie dünkt mich doch die Aue heut' so schön (Gurnemanz, Parsifal) *Parsifal* 3 Wagner
Wie du warst! Wie du bist! (Marschallin, Octavian) *Der Rosenkavalier* 1 Strauss
Wie freu' ich mich (Falstaff, Ford) *Die lustigen Weiber von Windsor* 2 Nicolai
Wie? Hör' ich recht? (Doland, Dutchman) *Der fliegende Holländer* 1 Wagner
Wie liebt' ich dich (Adolar, Euryanthe) *Euryanthe* 3 Weber
Wie nahte mir der Schlummer ... Leise, leise (Agathe) *Der Freischütz* 2 Weber
Wie? was? Entsetzen! (Agathe, Aennchen, Max) *Der Freischütz* 2 Weber
Willow song: *see* Assisa a piè d'un salice; Piangea cantando
Willst jenes Tag's (Erik) *Der fliegende Holländer* 3 Wagner
Winterstürme wichen dem Wonnemond (Siegmund) *Die Walküre* 1 Wagner
With solemn pomp (Venus, chorus) *Venus and Adonis* Blow
Wo ist mein Bruder? ... Morgen mittag um elf (Countess, Major-Domo) *Capriccio* Strauss
Wondrous firstling of creation (Iolanta, Vaudémont) *Iolanta* Tchaikovsky
Wo nicht dem Knaben Cupido (Ochs, Marschallin, Octavian) *Der Rosenkavalier* 1 Strauss
Would you gain the tender creature (Coridon/Damon) *Acis and Galatea* 2 Handel
Wretched lovers (chorus) *Acis and Galatea* 2 Handel
Wunderbar! Ja, wunderbar ... Glück, das mir verlieb (Paul, Marietta) *Die tote Stadt* 1 Korngold

Y

Yaroslavna's lament: *see* Ah, bitterly I weep
Ye blust'ring brethren (Aeolus) *King Arthur* 5 Purcell
Yes, they call me Mimì: *see* Si, mi chiamano Mimì
You appeared to me like a heavenly vision (Vaudémont) *Iolanta* Tchaikovsky
Your tiny hand is frozen: *see* Che gelida manina
Youth's the Season Made for Joys (chorus) *Beggar's Opera* 2
You will come, my dawn (Susanin) *A Life for the Tsar* 4 Glinka
You wrote a letter, do not deny it (Yevgeny Onegin) *Yevgeny Onegin* 1 Tchaikovsky

Z

Zauberfest ... bezähmt ein Schlaf (Siegmund) *Die Walküre* 2 Wagner
Zeffiretti lusinghieri (Ilia) *Idomeneo* 3 Mozart
Zitti zitti, piano piano (Rosina, Almaviva, Figaro) *Il barbiere di Siviglia* 2 Rossini
Zitto, zitto (Don Ramiro, Dandini) *La Cenerentola* 1 Rossini
Známt' já jednu dívčinu: *see* I know a girl who burns for you

Zu Magdeburg (Commandant) *Friedenstag* Strauss
Zum Leiden bin ich auserkoren (Queen of Night) *Die Zum letzen Lievesmahle (Chorus) Parsifal* 1 Wagner
Zum letzten Liebesmahle (chorus) *Parsifal* 1 Wagner
Zum Teufel mit dir (David, ensemble) *Die Meistersinger* 2 Wagner
Zu neuen Thaten (Brünnhilde, Siegfried) *Götterdämmerung* prol. Wagner
Zur Ruhe! ist dies die Achtung (Rienzi) *Rienzi* 1 Wagner
Zweite Brautnacht! (Helen) *Die ägyptische Helena* 2 Strauss
Zwei Vaterunser bet' ich (Pedro) *Tiefland* prol. D'Albert

Appendix C

LIST OF CONTRIBUTORS

The list below includes the names of all those whose work appears in the dictionary. For living contributors, the name is followed by his/her last known place of work or residence.

Abbate, Carolyn (Princeton, NJ, USA)
Aber-Count, Alice Lawson (Walnut Creek, CA, USA)
Abert, Anna Amalie (Kiel, Germany)
Accorsi, Maria Grazia (Bologna, Italy)
Adams, Stephen J. (London, Ont., Canada)
Albrecht, Otto E.
Albright, William (Ann Arbor, MI, USA)
Aldrich, Richard
Alen, M. Pilar (Santiago de Compostela, Spain)
Alexander, J. Heywood (Cleveland, OH, USA)
Alier, Roger (Barcelona, Spain)
Allan, Jean Mary
Allen, Ross C. (Bloomington, IN, USA)
Allroggen, Gerhard (Detmold, Germany)
Alm, Irene (Los Angeles, CA, USA)
Anderson, Nicholas (London, UK)
Anderson, Robert (London, UK)
Andrewes, Richard (Cambridge, UK)
Angermüller, Rudolph (Salzburg, Austria)
Annaheim, Ellwood J. (Washington, DC, USA)
Anthony, James R. (Tucson, AZ, USA)
Antolini, Bianca Maria (Rome, Italy)
Aranovsky, M. (St Petersburg, Russia)
Archibald, Bruce (Philadelphia, PA, USA)
Arfanis, Stathis (Athens, Greece)
Ariuli, Rosella (Bologna, Italy)
Arni, Erkki (London, UK)
Arnold, Denis
Ashbrook, William (Terre Haute, IN, USA)
Ashman, Mike (Cardiff, UK)
Åstrand, Hans (Stockholm, Sweden)

Backus, Joan (Victoria, BC, Canada)
Badura-Skoda, Eva (Vienna, Austria)
Baggiani, Franco (Pisa, Italy)
Bagüés, Jon (Rentería, Spain)
Bailey, Robert (New York City, NY, USA)
Baily, Dee (Menlo Park, CA, USA)
Baker, Evan (New York City, NY, USA)
Baker, Nicole (Santa Monica, CA, USA)
Bakounakis, Nikos (Athens, Greece)
Baldwin, Olive (Brentwood, Essex, UK)
Baley, Virko (Las Vegas, NV, USA)
Ballerini, Graziano (Bologna, Italy)
Ballola, Giovanni Carli (Rome, Italy)
Balthazar, Scott L. (West Chester, PA, USA)
Banfield, Stephen (Birmingham, UK)
Barkin, Elaine (North Hollywood, CA, USA)
Barnard, Michael (Chappaqua, NY, USA)
Barnes, Harold (Paris, France)
Baron, John H. (New Orleans, LA, USA)
Barr, Raymond A. (Coral Gables, FL, USA)
Barrière, Mireille (Sainte-Foy, Quebec Province, Canada)
Barsova, Inna (Moscow, Russia)
Bartlet, M. Elizabeth C. (Durham, NC, USA)
Bartlett, Ian (London, UK)
Barulich, Frances (New York City, NY, USA)
Basart, Ann P. (Berkeley, CA, USA)
Baselt, Bernd (Halle, Germany)
Baser, Friedrich (Baden-Baden, Germany)
Bashford, Christina (London, UK)
Bauman, Thomas (Seattle, WA, USA)
Beaumont, Antony (Bremen, Germany)
Becker, Heinz (Reinbek-Krabbenkamp, Germany)
Becker-Weidmann, Gudrun (Reinbek-Krabbenkamp, Germany)
Beckwith, John (Toronto, Ont., Canada)
Beechey, Gwilym (Hull, UK)
Béhague, Gerard (Austin, TX, USA)
Bek, Josef (Prague, Czechoslovakia)
Belsom, Jack (New Orleans, LA, USA)
Belza, Igor (Moscow, Russia)
Benestad, Finn (Oslo, Norway)
Benjamin, Gerald R. (San Antonio, TX, USA)
Bennett, Lawrence E. (New York City, NY, USA)
Benoit, Marcelle (Paris, France)
Benson, Robert (Seattle, WA, USA)
Benson, Robert E. (Glen Burnie, MD, USA)
Bent, Caroline (New York City, NY, USA)
Benton, Rita
Berg, Sigurd (Copenhagen, Denmark)
Bergsagel, John (Copenhagen, Denmark)
Bernard, Elisabeth (St Pierre-en-Port, France)
Bernas, Richard (London, UK)
Bernheimer, Martin (Los Angeles, CA, USA)
Bertini, Argia (Rome, Italy)
Besutti, Paola (Virgilio, Mantua, Italy)
Bianconi, Lorenzo (Bologna, Italy)

Bijvoet, Ellinor (Utrecht, Netherlands)
Billeter, Bernhard (Zürich, Switzerland)
Binns, Georgina (Ivanhoe, Victoria, Australia)
Bisogni, Fabio (Florence, Italy)
Black, John (Pyrton, nr Watlington, Oxon., UK)
Blair, Ted M. (San Rafael, CA, USA)
Blake, David (York, UK)
Bledsoe, Robert (El Paso, TX, USA)
Bloch, David (Tel-Aviv, Israel)
Block, Adrienne Fried (New York City, NY, USA)
Blom, Eric
Blomster, Wes (Boulder, CO, USA)
Blyth, Alan (Lavenham, Suffolk, UK)
Bodley, Seóirse (Dublin, Ireland)
Boer, Bertil H. van (Wichita, KS, USA)
Boetzkes, Manfred (Hildesheim, Germany)
Bonaventura, Sam di (Fairfax, VA, USA)
Boneau, Denise (Chicago, IL, USA)
Bongiovanni, Carmela (Genoa, Italy)
Bónis, Ferenc (Budapest, Hungary)
Boomgaarden, Donald R. (St Mary's City, MD, USA)
Bordman, Gerald (Nottingham, PA, USA)
Borroff, Edith (Binghamton, NY, USA)
Bosonnet, F. R. (Basle, Switzerland)
Bossa, Renato (Rome, Italy)
Bosseur, Jean-Yves (Neuilly, France)
Bouquet-Boyer, Marie-Thérèse (Auffargis, France)
Bourligueux, Guy (Orvault, France)
Bouws, Jan (Stellenbosch, Cape Province, South Africa)
Bowen, Jean (New York City, NY, USA)
Bowen, William R. (North York, Ont., Canada)
Boyd, Malcolm (Cardiff, UK)
Boydell, Brian (Dublin, Ireland)
Brabbins, Martyn (Marshfield, nr Chippenham, Wilts., UK)
Bracanin, Philip K. (St Lucia, Queensland, Australia)
Bradbury, Ernest (Bradford, UK)
Bradshaw, Susan (London, UK)
Branscombe, Peter (St Andrews, Fife, UK)
Brashovanova, Lada (Sofia, Bulgaria)
Braun, Joachim (Ramat-Gan, Israel)
Brereton, Joy (London, UK)
Brett, Philip (Riverside, CA, USA)
Brewer, Charles E. (Tuscaloosa, AL, USA)
Brincker, Jens (Copenhagen, Denmark)
Briner, Andres (Zürich, Switzerland)
Briquet, Marie
Brody, Elaine
Brody, Martin (Wellesley, MA, USA)
Brofsky, Howard (Flushing, NY, USA)
Brook, Barry S. (New York City, NY, USA)
Brooks, William (Urbana, IL, USA)
Brown, A. Peter (Bloomington, IN, USA)
Brown, Bruce Alan (Los Angeles, CA, USA)
Brown, Clive (Wakefield, UK)
Brown, Howard Mayer (Chicago, IL, USA)
Brown, Leslie Ellen (Monaca, PA, USA)
Brown, Malcolm H. (Bloomington, IN, USA)
Brown, Maurice J. E.
Bruce, Phyllis (Ann Arbor, MI, USA)
Brumana, Biancamaria (Perugia, Italy)
Brunner, Gerhard (Graz, Austria)
Bruun, Carl L.
Bryant, David (Venice, Italy)
Budden, Julian (London, UK)
Buelow, George J. (Bloomington, IN, USA)
Bujić, Bojan (Oxford, UK)
Burchi, Guido (Siena, Italy)
Burden, Michael (Oxford, UK)
Burk, James M. (Columbia, MD, USA)
Burlas, Ladislav (Bratislava, Czechoslovakia)
Burrows, David L. (Riverdale, NY, USA)
Burton, Nigel (Reading, UK)
Bush, Geoffrey (London, UK)
Busk, Gorm (Virum, Denmark)
Bussi, Francesco (Piacenza, Italy)
Butir, L. M. (Petrozavodsk, Russia)
Buyssens, Marie-Thérèse (Antwerp, Belgium)
Byers, David (Belfast, UK)
Byrnside, Ronald (Decatur, GA, USA)

Cafiero, Rosa (Salerno, Italy)
Cagli, Bruno (Rome, Italy)
Cairns, David (London, UK)
Caluori, Eleanor (New Paltz, NY, USA)
Camajani, Giovanni (San Francisco, CA, USA)
Campbell, David E. (New York City, NY, USA)
Campbell, Jennet (Gerrans, Cornwall, UK)
Canning, Hugh (London, UK)
Capell, Richard
Caraci Vela, Maria (Milan, Italy)
Carapezza, Paolo Emilio (Palermo, Italy)
Cardell, Karen (Houston, TX, USA)
Careri, Enrico (Rome, Italy)
Carnegy, Patrick (London, UK)
Carner, Mosco
Carr, Bruce (Pittsburgh, PA, USA)
Carr-Boyd, Ann (Northwood, NSW, Australia)
Carreira, Xoán M. (La Coruña, Spain)
Carroll, Charles Michael (St Petersburg, FL, USA)
Carter, Tim (Egham, Surrey, UK)
Casares, Emilio (Madrid, Spain)
Casella, Alfredo
Casini, Claudio (Rome, Italy)
Cassaro, James P. (Ithaca, NY, USA)
Catalyne, Alice Ray (Laguna Hills, CA, USA)
Cattelan, P. (Venice, Italy)
Cauthen, Paul (Cincinnati, OH, USA)
Çelletti, Rodolfo (Milan, Italy)
Černý, Miroslav K. (Prague, Czechoslovakia)
Chan, Mary (Kensington, NSW, Australia)
Chapman, Clive (Winchester, Hants., UK)
Charlton, David (Norwich, UK)
Charters, Murray R. (St John's, Newfoundland, Canada)
Chase, Gilbert
Chechlińska, Zofia (Warsaw, Poland)
Cheke, D. J. (Bramley, Hants., UK)
Cherney, Brian (Montreal, Quebec Province, Canada)
Chew, Geoffrey (Egham, Surrey, UK)
Chiesa, Renato (Rome, Italy)
Chiti, Rossana (Livorno, Italy)
Chmara-Żaczkiewicz, Barbara (Warsaw, Poland)
Cholij, Irena (Birmingham, UK)
Chylińska, Teresa (Kraków, Poland)
Ciliberti, Galliano (Perugia, Italy)
Clark, Andrew (Berne, Switzerland)
Clark, Caryl (Oakville, Ont., Canada)
Clark, J. Bunker (Lawrence, KS, USA)
Clark, Joseph (New York City, NY, USA)
Clark, Walter Aaron (Calabasas, CA, USA)
Clarke, F. R. C. (Kingston, Ont., Canada)

Clarkson, Austin (Toronto, Ont., Canada)
Claro-Valdés, Samuel (Santiago, Chile)
Clayton, Alfred (Hamburg, Germany)
Clements, Andrew (Milton Keynes, Bucks., UK)
Clercx-Lejeune, Suzanne
Clinkscale, Martha Novak (Riverside, CA, USA)
Cobbe, Hugh (London, UK)
Cockrell, Dale (Williamsburg, VA, USA)
Coelho, Victor A. (Calgary, Alta., Canada)
Coeyman, Barbara (Morgantown, WV, USA)
Cohen, Albert (Stanford, CA, USA)
Cohen, Peter (Hamburg, Germany)
Cole, Hugo (London, UK)
Commanday, Robert (San Francisco, CA, USA)
Cone, John Frederick (Highlands, NJ, USA)
Conrad, Jon Alan (Newark, DE, USA)
Cook, D. F. (St John's, Newfoundland, Canada)
Cook, Elisabeth (London, UK)
Cooke, Deryck
Cooper, Jeffrey (Ann Arbor, MI, USA)
Cooper, Martin
Cooper, Paul (Houston, TX, USA)
Cope, David (Santa Cruz, CA, USA)
Corneilson, Paul (Chapel Hill, NC, USA)
Corrêa de Azevedo, Luis Heitor (Paris, France)
Corti, Sandro (Pisa, Italy)
Cosma, Viorel (Bucharest, Romania)
Costonis, Maureen Needham (Nashville, TN, USA)
Cotte, Roger J. V. (São Paulo, Brazil)
Covell, Roger (Kensington, NSW, Australia)
Cox, David (London, UK)
Cox, John (London, UK)
Crane, Frederick (Iowa City, IA, USA)
Cranmer, David (Lisbon, Portugal)
Crawford, Richard (Ann Arbor, MI, USA)
Crichton, Ronald (Eastbourne, E. Sussex, UK)
Croll, Gerhard (Salzburg, Austria)
Cross, Eric (Newcastle upon Tyne, UK)
Crossley-Holland, Peter
Crutchfield, Will (New York City, NY, USA)
Cudworth, Charles
Cumming, Julie E. (Wellesley, MA, USA)
Cummings, David (Harrow, Middx., UK)
Cusick, Suzanne G. (Seneca Falls, NY, USA)
Cvetko, Dragotin (Ljubljana, Slovenia)
Cymbron, Luisa (Lisbon, Portugal)
Cyr, Mary (Montreal, Quebec Province, Canada)

Dahms, Sibylle (Salzburg, Austria)
Daitz, Mimi Segal (New York City, NY, USA)
Daniel, Oliver (New York City, NY, USA)
Davidson, Michael (Amsterdam, Netherlands)
Davis, Peter G. (New York City, NY, USA)
Davis, Shelley (College Park, MD, USA)
Davis-Millis, Nina (Cambridge, MI, USA)
Davison, Dennis (Melbourne, Victoria, Australia)
Dean, Susan Thach (South Bend, IN, USA)
Dean, Winton (Godalming, Surrey, UK)
Deathridge, John (Cambridge, UK)
Deaville, James A. (Hamilton, Ont., Canada)
De Brito, Manuel Carlos (Lisbon, Portugal)
Deguire, William W. (Annandale, NJ, USA)
De Lerma, Dominique-René (Chicago, IL, USA)
De Leur, Truus (Amsterdam, Netherlands)
Demény, János (Budapest, Hungary)
Derr, Ellwood (Ann Arbor, MI, USA)
Derra de Moroda, Friderica
DeVal, Dorothy (London, UK)
DeVos, Bradford R. (Huntingdon, WV, USA)
Di Benedetto, Renato (Parma, Italy)
DiChiera, David (Detroit, MA, USA)
Dietz, Hanns-Bertold (Austin, TX, USA)
Dixon, Graham (London, UK)
Dobbins, Frank (London, UK)
Dobbs Mackenzie, Barbara (Stanford, CT, USA)
Doctor, Jennifer R. (Evanston, IL, USA)
Dolmetsch, Carl (Williamsburg, VA, USA)
Donà, Mariangela (Milan, Italy)
Donaldson, Frances (London, UK)
Dowling, John (Athens, GA, USA)
Downes, Peter (Wellington, New Zealand)
Drew, David (London, UK)
Dreyer, Martin (York, UK)
Dreyfus, Kay (Camberwell, Victoria, Australia)
Druilhe, Paule (Paris, France)
Dubiaga, Michael jr (Corpus Christi, TX, USA)
Dubowy, Norbert (Rome, Italy)
Duckworth, William (Lewisburg, PA, USA)
Dufourcq, Norbert (Paris, France)
Durante, Sergio (Padua, Italy)
Đurić-Klajn, Stana
Duron, Jean (Paris, France)
Dyer, Karen M. (Lincoln, NE, USA)
Dyer, Richard (Dorchester, MA, USA)
Dzięgbowska, Elżbieta (Warsaw, Poland)

East, Leslie (London, UK)
Echols, Paul C. (New York City, NY, USA)
Eckert, Thor jr (New York City, NY, USA)
Edwards, Owain (Ås, Norway)
Eekeren, Michael van (Utrecht, Netherlands)
Eggebrecht, Hans Heinrich (Ehrenkirchen, Germany)
Eive, Gloria (El Cerrito, CA, USA)
Elias, William Y. (Tel-Aviv, Israel)
El-Kholy, Samha (Cairo, Egypt)
Elliott, Susan (New York City, NY, USA)
Ellison, Cori (New York City, NY, USA)
Elste, Martin (Berlin, Germany)
Emerson, John A. (Richmond, CA, USA)
Emerson, June (Ampleforth, N. Yorks., UK)
Ermen, Reinhard (Cologne, Germany)
Erwin, Charlotte (Glendale, CA, USA)
Everist, Mark (London, UK)
Evidon, Richard (Hamburg, Germany)

Fabbri, Paolo (Udine, Italy)
Fabian, Imre (Zürich, Switzerland)
Fabio Ivaldi, Armando (Genoa, Italy)
Fallows, David (Manchester, UK)
Fanning, David (Manchester, UK)
Fay, Laurel E. (Staten Island, NY, USA)
Fearn, Raymond (Keele, Staffs., UK)
Feder, Susan (Irvington, NY, USA)
Feldman, Mary Ann (Minneapolis, MN, USA)
Feldmann, Fritz
Fellinger, Imogen (Berlin, Germany)
Fend, Michael (Aberdeen, UK)
Fenlon, Iain (Cambridge, UK)
Fenner, Theodore (Potsdam, NY, USA)
Ferchault, Guy (Paris, France)

Ferrard, Mary Armstrong (Moustier, Belgium)
Ferraro, Giuseppe (Messina, Italy)
Fifield, Christopher (London, UK)
Fillion, Michelle (Oakland, CA, USA)
Finch, Hilary (London, UK)
Finn, Robert (Cleveland, OH, USA)
Fisher, Stephen C. (Philadelphia, PA, USA)
Fiske, Roger
FitzLyon, April (London, UK)
Fleischmann, Aloys
Fleming, Michael (St Petersburg, FL, USA)
Fletcher, Richard D. (Landorer Hills, MD, USA)
Flotzinger, Rudolf (Graz, Austria)
Forbes, Anne-Marie H. (St Lucia, Queensland, Australia)
Forbes, Elizabeth (London, UK)
Forbes, Elliot (Cambridge, MA, USA)
Fortune, Nigel (Birmingham, UK)
Fox, Leland (Oxford, MS, USA)
Franco, Enrique (Madrid, Spain)
Franklin, Peter (Leeds, UK)
Franze, Juan Pedro (Buenos Aires, Argentina)
Freeman, Daniel (Minneapolis, MN, USA)
Freeman, James (Swarthmore, PA, USA)
Freeman, Robert (Rochester, NY, USA)
Freeman, Robert N. (Santa Barbara, CA, USA)
Freemanová, Michaela (Prague, Czechoslovakia)
Freitas Branco, João de (Lisbon, Portugal)
Frémiot, Marcel (Aix-en-Provence, France)
Fukač, Jiří (Brno, Czechoslovakia)
Fuller, David (Buffalo, NY, USA)
Fuller Maitland, J. A.
Furnari, Antonello (Rome, Italy)

Gabay, Yury (Baku, Azerbaijan)
Galkin, Elliott W.
Gallarati, Paolo (Turin, Italy)
Gallico, Claudio (Mantua, Italy)
Gann, Kyle (New York City, NY, USA)
Gänzl, Kurt (St Paul de Vence, France)
Garofalo, Robert (Washington, DC, USA)
Gatti, Guido M.
Gehring, Franz
Gerhard, Anselm (Münster, Germany)
Gianturco, Carolyn (Pisa, Italy)
Gibbs, Gary (Houston, TX, USA)
Gibney, Wendy N. (San Francisco, CA, USA)
Gibson, Elizabeth (London, UK)
Giffin, Glenn (Denver, CO, USA)
Gifford, Keith (London, UK)
Gilbert, Steven E. (Fresno, CA, USA)
Gilson, Philippe (Liège, Belgium)
Girardi, Michele (Parma, Italy)
Girardot, Anne (Paris, France)
Girdham, Jane (Brunswick, ME, USA)
Giuntini, Francesco (Pisa, Italy)
Glackin, William (Sacramento, CA, USA)
Glauert, Amanda (St Albans, Herts., UK)
Glixon, Beth L. (Lexington, KY, USA)
Gmeinwieser, Siegfried (Munich, Germany)
Goertz, Harald (Vienna, Austria)
Gojowy, Detlef (Unkel am Rhein, Germany)
Gómez Amat, Carlos (Madrid, Spain)
González, Jorge Antonio (Havana, Cuba)
Goodman, Alfred (Munich, Germany)
Goodwin, Noël (London, UK)
Gordon, Eric A. (Venice, CA, USA)
Gossett, Philip (Chicago, IL, USA)
Grant, Kerry S. (Lincoln, NE, USA)
Gray, Maxine Cushing
Graziano, John (New York City, NY, USA)
Green, Rebecca (Toronto, Ont., Canada)
Green, Richard D. (Evanston, IL, USA)
Greenfield, Edward (London, UK)
Greenslade, David (London, Ont., Canada)
Gribenski, Jean (Paris, France)
Griesbach, Jennifer (Toronto, Ont., Canada)
Griffin, Julia Ann (Paris, France)
Griffioen, David (Bloomington, IN, USA)
Griffiths, Paul (Lower Heyford, Oxon., UK)
Grigor'yeva, Galina (Moscow, Russia)
Gronda, Giovanna (Bologna, Italy)
Gruber, Gernot (Vaterstetten, Germany)
Grünzweig, Werner (Berlin, Germany)
Gudger, William D. (Charleston, SC, USA)
Guest, Ivor (London, UK)
Gyger, A. I. (Greenwich, NSW, Australia)

Haefliger, Kathleen (State College, PA, USA)
Hagberg, Karen A. (Rochester, NY, USA)
Haglund, Rolf (Brämhult, Sweden)
Halász, Gábor (Ludwigshafen, Germany)
Hamann, Heinz Wolfgang (Osnabrück, Germany)
Hammond, Frederick (Germantown, NY, USA)
Hannan, Michael (Lismore, NSW, Australia)
Hanning, Barbara R. (New York City, NY, USA)
Hansell, Kathleen Kuzmick (Chicago, IL, USA)
Hansell, Sven (Iowa City, IA, USA)
Hanuszewska, Mieczysława (Kraków, Poland)
Hardeman, Anita (London, Ont., Canada)
Harden, Jean (Syracuse, NY, USA)
Hardie, Graham (Sydney, NSW, Australia)
Harewood, Earl of (London, UK)
Hargot, Jean (Dhuy, Belgium)
Harper, John (Bangor, UK)
Harris, Laughton (Clayton, Victoria, Australia)
Harris-Warrick, Rebecca (Ithaca, NY, USA)
Hart, Philip (Santa Fe, NM, USA)
Hartford, Robert (London, UK)
Härtwig, Dieter (Dresden, Germany)
Haskell, Diana (Chicago, IL, USA)
Haskell, Harry (New Haven, CT, USA)
Hassan, Tarek (Cairo, Egypt)
Häusler, Josef (Baden-Baden, Germany)
Havlíková, Helena (Prague, Czechoslovakia)
Hayes, Jeremy (Birmingham, UK)
Hays, William (Princeton, NJ, USA)
Healy, James N. (Cork, Ireland)
Heartz, Daniel (Berkeley, CA, USA)
Hellyer, Roger (Stratford-on-Avon, Warwicks., UK)
Helm, E. Eugene (College Park, MD, USA)
Helmer, Axel (Stockholm, Sweden)
Henderson, Marina (London, UK)
Henderson, Robert (London, UK)
Hennenberg, Fritz (Leipzig, Germany)
Henry, Derrick (Smyrna, GA, USA)
Herbage, Julian
Herrmannová, Eva (Prague, Czechoslovakia)
Hertelendy, Paul (Berkeley, CA, USA)
Heyman, Barbara B. (New York City, NY, USA)
Heyworth, Peter
Hicks, Anthony (London, UK)

Higginbottom, Edward (Oxford, UK)
Highstein, Ellen (New York City, NY, USA)
Hill, Cecil
Hill, John Walter (Urbana, IL, USA)
Hines, James R. (Newport News, VA, USA)
Hintermaier, Ernst (Salzburg, Austria)
Hinton, Stephen (New Haven, CT, USA)
Hitchcock, H. Wiley (New York City, NY, USA)
Ho, Allan B. (Edwardsville, IL, USA)
Hoérée, Arthur
Hoffmann-Erbrecht, Lothar (Langen-Oberlinden, Germany)
Hogwood, Christopher (Cambridge, UK)
Hollingdale, R. J. (London, UK)
Hollis, George Truett (Pasadena, CA, USA)
Holman, Peter (Colchester, Essex, UK)
Holmes, James (New York City, NY, USA)
Holmes, William C. (Irvine, CA, USA)
Holoman, D. Kern (Davis, CA, USA)
Holzer, Robert R. (New York City, NY, USA)
Honegger, Marc (Lauzes, France)
Hopkins, Robert (Youngstown, OH, USA)
Horner, Keith (Toronto, Ont., Canada)
Horowitz, Joseph (New York City, NY, USA)
Hoskins, Robert (Palmerston North, New Zealand)
Höslinger, Clemens (Vienna, Austria)
Hough, David J. (Swanbourne, Western Australia)
Hovland, Michael (Iowa City, IA, USA)
Howard, Patricia (Guildford, Surrey, UK)
Howes, Frank
Hübsch-Pfleger, Lini (Heidelberg, Germany)
Hucke, Helmut (Friedrichsdorf, Germany)
Hudec, Vladimír (Olomouc, Czechoslovakia)
Huebner, Steven (Montreal, Quebec Province, Canada)
Hughes, Anthony (Dublin, Ireland)
Hughes, Robert (Emeryville, CA, USA)
Hume, Robert D. (State College, PA, USA)
Humphrey, Mary Lou (New York City, NY, USA)
Hunter, Mary (Research Triangle Park, NC, USA)
Huot, Cécile (Montreal, Quebec Province, Canada)
Hurd, Michael (West Liss, Hants., UK)
Hutchings, Arthur
Hüttel, Walter (Glauchau, Germany)

Ingles, Elisabeth (London, UK)
Irwin, Carol O. (Grand Forks, ND, USA)

Jackman, James L. (San Francisco, CA, USA)
Jackson, Paul J. (Randolph Center, VT, USA)
Jacobs, Arthur (Oxford, UK)
Jacobson, Bernard (The Hague, Netherlands)
Jahant, Charles (Hyattsville, MD, USA)
James, Richard S. (Bowling Green, OH, USA)
Jameux, Dominique (Paris, France)
Jamieson, Alasdair (Buckland, nr Faringdon, Oxon., UK)
Jander, Owen (Wellesley, MA, USA)
Jefferson, Alan (Deviock, Torpoint, Cornwall, UK)
Jenkins, Newell (Hillside, NY, USA)
Jensen, Niels Martin (Copenhagen, Denmark)
Jerger, Wilhelm (Salzburg, Austria)
John, Nicholas (London, UK)
Johnson, Anna (Uppsala, Sweden)
Johnson, Douglas (New Brunswick, NJ, USA)
Johnson, Janet (Los Angeles, CA, USA)
Johnson, Jennifer E. (Cambridge, UK)
Johnson, Stephen (London, UK)
Johnstone, H. Diack (Oxford, UK)
Jolly, James (Harrow, Middx., UK)
Jones, Andrew V. (Cambridge, UK)
Jones, Gaynor G. (Toronto, Ont., Canada)
Jones, Richard (Abingdon, Oxon., UK)
Jowers, Sidney Jackson (Canterbury, Kent, UK)
Joyce, John (New Orleans, LA, USA)

Kagan, Susan (Riverdale, NY, USA)
Kallmann, Helmut (Nepean, Ont., Canada)
Kanazawa, Masakata (Tokyo, Japan)
Kantner, Leopold M. (Vienna, Austria)
Károlyi, Melinda Berlász (Budapest, Hungary)
Kárpáti, János (Budapest, Hungary)
Karstädt, Georg
Kaufman, Tom (Boonton, NJ, USA)
Kaye, Nicholas (London, UK)
Keller, Michael A. (New Haven, CT, USA)
Kemp, Ian (London, UK)
Kennedy, Michael (Sale, Cheshire, UK)
Kerman, Judith (Edinboro, PA, USA)
Kernfeld, Barry (Pennsylvania, PA, USA)
Kidd, Ronald R. (West Lafayette, IN, USA)
King, Alec Hyatt (Southwold, Suffolk, UK)
King, Richard G. (Stanford, CA, USA)
Kirchberg, Klaus (Oberhausen, Germany)
Kirk, Elise K. (Washington, DC, USA)
Kjeldsberg, Peter Andreas (Trondheim, Norway)
Kjellberg, Erik (Uppsala, Sweden)
Klein, Deanne Arkus
Klein, Herman
Klein, Rudolf (Vienna, Austria)
Klimovitsky, Abraham I. (St Petersburg, Russia)
Klotiņš, Arnolds (Riga, Latvia)
Knapp, J. Merrill (Princeton, NJ, USA)
Knight, Ellen (Winchester, MA, USA)
Knittel, Kristin M. (Princeton, NJ, USA)
Knowles, Christopher (Whitwell, nr Hitchin, Herts., UK)
Koegler, Horst (Stuttgart, Germany)
Konold, Wulf (Hamburg, Germany)
Koole, Arend (Cape Town, South Africa)
Korda, Marion (Louisville, KY, USA)
Kos, Koraljka (Zagreb, Croatia)
Kosman, Joshua (San Francisco, CA, USA)
Kostakeva, Maria (Bochum, Germany)
Kovačević, Krešimir (Zagreb, Croatia)
Kozinn, Allan (New York City, NY, USA)
Kraft, G.
Krasner, Orly Leah (Long Island City, NY, USA)
Kravitt, Edward F. (New York City, NY, USA)
Krehbiel, H. E.
Krellmann, Hanspeter (Munich, Germany)
Krummacher, Friedhelm (Kiel, Germany)
Kucaba, John (Geneseo, NY, USA)
Kühn, Hellmut (Berlin, Germany)
Kuna, Milan (Prague, Czechoslovakia)
Küntzel, Gottfried (Lüneburg, Germany)
Kunzmann, Vladia (Holliswood, NY, USA)
Kushner, David Z. (Gainesville, FL, USA)
Kuss, Malena (Denton, TX, USA)

Ladell, Madeleine (London, UK)
La Gorce, Jérôme de (Paris, France)
Laini, Marinella (Venice, Italy)
La May, Thomasin (Baltimore, MD, USA)
Lamb, Andrew (Croydon, Surrey, UK)
Lampert, Vera (Framingham, MA, USA)
Lampila, Hannu Ilari (Helsinki, Finland)
Landon, Brooks (Iowa City, IA, USA)
Langevin, Kenneth (Pittsburgh, PA, USA)
Langham Smith, Richard (London, UK)
Langhans, Edward A. (Honolulu, HI, USA)
Langley, Leanne (London, UK)
Langner, Thomas-M.
Lanza, Andrea (Pecetto Torinese, Italy)
Large, Brian (Whyteleafe, Surrey, UK)
Larner, Gerald (Alderley Edge, Cheshire, UK)
Larrad, Mark (Liverpool, UK)
Latino, Adriana (Lisbon, Portugal)
Lattes, Sergio (Milan, Italy)
Laudon, Robert T. (Minneapolis, MN, USA)
Laurie, Margaret (Reading, UK)
Lawford, Irene (Harrow, Middx., UK)
Layer, Adolf
Layng, Judith (Oberlin, OH, USA)
Layton, Robert (London, UK)
Lazarevich, Gordana (Victoria, BC, Canada)
Lebeau, Elisabeth (Paris, France)
Leclercq, Fernand (Mons, Belgium)
Ledbetter, Steven (Boston, MA, USA)
Lederer, Josef-Horst (Graz, Austria)
Leedy, Douglas (Oceanside, OR, USA)
Legány, Dezső (Budapest, Hungary)
Leich, Karl (Recklingshausen, Germany)
Leotsakos, George (Athens, Greece)
LeSueur, Richard (Ann Arbor, MI, USA)
Letailleur, Paulette (Paris, France)
Leuchtmann, Horst (Munich, Germany)
Levarie, Siegmund (Brooklyn, NY, USA)
Leverett, Adelyn Peck (Ann Arbor, MI, USA)
Levi, Erik (Egham, Surrey, UK)
Lewis, Anthony
Lewis, Geraint (Cardiff, UK)
Lewis-Griffith, Dorothy (Cunover, NC, USA)
Lewy Gidwitz, Patricia (Baltimore, MD, USA)
Libby, Dennis
Lichtenfeld, Monika (Cologne, Germany)
Liebscher, Julia (Munich, Germany)
Lindgren, Lowell (Cambridge, MA, USA)
Lindsay, Maurice (Milton, Dumbarton, UK)
Link, Dorothea (Toronto, Ont., Canada)
Lippman, Martin S. (Milford, CT, USA)
Lippmann, Friedrich (Rome, Italy)
Lo, Vivien (Wellesley, MA, USA)
Locke, Ralph P. (Rochester, NY, USA)
Loewenberg, Alfred
Longyear, Katherine E. (Lexington, KY, USA)
Loomis, George W. (Larchmont, NY, USA)
López-Calo, José (Santiago de Compostela, Spain)
Loppert, Max (London, UK)
Lott, R. Allen (Fort Worth, TX, USA)
Louvier, Alain (Boulogne, France)
Love, Harold (Clayton, Victoria, Australia)
Loveland, Kenneth (Cwmbran, Gwent, UK)
Lucarelli, Nicola (Umbertide, Italy)
Lück, Rudolf (Cologne, Germany)
Ludvová, Jitka (Prague, Czechoslovakia)
Luening, Otto (New York City, NY, USA)
Lukanyuk, Bogdan (St Petersburg, Russia)
Lyne, Peter H. (Wellingborough, Northants., UK)

McAllister, Rita (Glasgow, UK)
McClatchie, Stephen (London, Ont., Canada)
McClellan, William (Champaign, IL, USA)
McClymonds, Marita P. (Charlottesville, VA, USA)
McCredie, Andrew D. (Adelaide, Southern Australia)
Macdonald, Hugh (St Louis, MO, USA)
MacDonald, Malcolm (London, UK)
McGairl, Pamela (Bromley, Kent, UK)
MacGregor, Lynda (Murthly, Perthshire, UK)
Machavariani, Yevgeny (Tbilisi, Georgia)
McIntire, Dennis K. (Indianapolis, IN, USA)
McKay, Elizabeth Norman (Long Hanborough, Oxon., UK)
Mackay, Neil (Edinburgh, UK)
Mackay-Shapiro, Marjorie (New York City, NY, USA)
Mackenzie, Kirk (Dayton, KY, USA)
Mackey, Jocelyn (Muncie, IN, USA)
McLean, Eric (Montreal, Quebec Province, Canada)
McMahan, Robert Young (Towson, MD, USA)
McMahon, Melody Layton (Cleveland Heights, OH, USA)
MacMillan, Keith
McMillin, Arnold (Liverpool, UK)
Macnutt, Richard (Hartfield, Sussex, UK)
McVeigh, Simon (London, UK)
Maehder, Jürgen (Berlin, Germany)
Maffei, Fabiola (Milan, Italy)
Maguire, Simon (London, UK)
Maier, Gunter (Fellbach, Germany)
Major, Norma (London, UK)
Malitz, Nancy (Detroit, MI, USA)
Mancini, Franco (Naples, Italy)
Mann, William S.
Manolova, Magdalena (Sofia, Bulgaria)
Marchesi, Gustavo (Parma, Italy)
Marco, Tomás (Madrid, Spain)
Mark, Jeffry
Markstrom, Kurt (Toronto, Ont., Canada)
Marretta-Schär, Luise (Berne, Switzerland)
Marsh, Robert C. (New Glarus, WI, USA)
Martin, Bryan (Toronto, Ont., Canada)
Martinotti, Sergio (Milan, Italy)
Marvin, Roberta Montemorra (Medford, MA, USA)
Marx, Hans Joachim (Hamburg, Germany)
Matthews, Betty (Wimborne Minster, Dorset, UK)
Matthews, Colin (London, UK)
Matthews, David (London, UK)
Matz, Mary Jane Phillips (Venice, Italy)
May, James (Cape Town, South Africa)
Mears, Caroline (Tokai, Cape Province, South Africa)
Meckna, Michael (Fort Worth, TX, USA)
Medek, Tilo (Remagen-Oberwinter, Germany)
Medina, Angel (Oviedo, Spain)
Mell, Albert (Flushing, NY, USA)
Mellers, Wilfrid (York, UK)
Meloncelli, Raoul (Rome, Italy)
Mercer, Ruby (Toronto, Ont., Canada)
Mercier, Philippe (Louvain, Belgium)
Merkling, Frank (New Milford, CT, USA)
Mertens, Corneel

Metcalf, Steven P. (West Hartford, CT, USA)
Meyer, Eve R. (Havertown, PA, USA)
Meylan, Pierre
Michaels, Amanda (London, UK)
Michałowski, Kornel (Poznań, Poland)
Michelsen, Kari (Trondheim, Norway)
Mikhashoff, Yvar (Buffalo, NY, USA)
Milhous, Judith (New York City, NY, USA)
Miller, Franklin S. (Milwaukee, WI, USA)
Miller, Malcolm (London, UK)
Miller, Philip Lieson (New York City, NY, USA)
Millington, Barry (London, UK)
Milnes, Rodney (London, UK)
Minardi, Gian Paolo (Parma, Italy)
Minko, Anne (Champaign, IL, USA)
Minniear, John Mohr (Oshkosh, WI, USA)
Miranda-Pérez, Ricardo (San Jerónimo Lídice, Mexico)
Moens-Haenen, Greta (Mechelen, Belgium)
Moliterni, Pierfranco (Bari, Italy)
Monastra, Margaret (Rochester, NY, USA)
Mongrédien, Jean (Nogent-sur-Marne, France)
Monson, Dale E. (State College, PA, USA)
Monson, Karen (Baltimore, MD, USA)
Montecchi, Giordano (Bologna, Italy)
Moore, Gerald
Morawska, Katarzyna (Warsaw, Poland)
Morawski, Jerzy (Warsaw, Poland)
Morey, Carl (Toronto, Ont., Canada)
Morgan, John (Atlanta, GA, USA)
Morgan, Paula (Princeton, NJ, USA)
Morgan, Robert P. (New Haven, CT, USA)
Morreau, Annette (London, UK)
Morris, Mitchell (Berkeley, CA, USA)
Muggler, Fritz (Zürich, Switzerland)
Mulard, Eric (Paris, France)
Müller, Karl-Josef (Mainz, Germany)
Münster, Robert (Munich, Germany)
Murata, Margaret (Irvine, CA, USA)
Murray, David (London, UK)

Neff, Jerome P. (Canterbury, Kent, UK)
Neff, Severine (New York City, NY, USA)
Neighbour, O. W. (London, UK)
Neiiendam, Klaus (Copenhagen, Denmark)
Němcová, Alena (Brno, Czechoslovakia)
Nest'yeva, Marina (Moscow, Russia)
Neuls-Bates, Carol (New York City, NY, USA)
Neumann, Klaus L. (Bensberg, Germany)
Neville, Don (London, Ont., Canada)
Newsom, Jon (Washington, DC, USA)
Nichols, Roger (Leominster, Hereford and Worcester, UK)
Niemöller, Klaus Wolfgang (Cologne, Germany)
Nisbett, Robert F. (Fort Collins, CO, USA)
Noack, Elisabeth
Noble, Jeremy (Buffalo, NY, USA)
Noiray, Michel (Paris, France)
Norderval, Haakon (Trondheim, Norway)
Norris, Geoffrey (London, UK)
Northcott, Bayan (London, UK)
Nowak-Romanowicz, Alina (Katowice, Poland)

O'Connor, Patrick (Richmond, Surrey, UK)
Oehlschlägel, Reinhard (Cologne, Germany)
Oja, Carol J. (New York City, NY, USA)
Oliver, A. Richard (Washington, PA, USA)
Olnick, Harvey (Toronto, Ont., Canada)
O'Loughlin, Niall (Loughborough, Leics., UK)
Olt, Harry (Södertälje, Sweden)
Oramo, Ilkka (Helsinki, Finland)
Orledge, Robert (Liverpool, UK)
Orlov, Genrikh (Middletown, CT, USA)
Orrego-Salas, Juan A. (Bloomington, IN, USA)
Ortakov, Dragoslav (Skopje, Macedonia)
Osborne, Richard (Bradfield, Berks., UK)
Osmond-Smith, David (Brighton, UK)
Ottlová, Marta (Prague, Czechoslovakia)

Pachl, Peter P. (Rudolstadt, Germany)
Paddison, Max (Totnes, Devon, UK)
Pagano, Roberto (Palermo, Italy)
Page, Frederick
Page, Tim (New York City, NY, USA)
Palmer, A. Dean (Chatsworth, CA, USA)
Palmer, Christopher (London, UK)
Palmer, Larry (Dallas, TX, USA)
Palmer, Robert V. (Rochester, NY, USA)
Pampaloni, Caterina (Pisa, Italy)
Pampolini, Angela (Ferrara, Italy)
Parisi, Susan (Urbana, IL, USA)
Parker, Mary Ann (Toronto, Ont., Canada)
Parker, Roger (Ithaca, NY, USA)
Parkinson, John A. (Selsdon, S. Croydon, Surrey, UK)
Parr, Anthony (London, UK)
Parsons, Michael (London, UK)
Pascall, Robert J. (Nottingham, UK)
Pasler, Jann (La Jolla, CA, USA)
Patton, Faye E. (Camberwell, Victoria, Australia)
Pauly, Reinhard G. (Portland, OR, USA)
Peduzzi, Lubomír (Brno, Czechoslovakia)
Peire, Patrick (Assebroeck, Belgium)
Pejović, Roksanda (Belgrade, Serbia)
Pendle, Karin (Cincinnati, OH, USA)
Pereyra, Marie Louise
Perlis, Vivian (New Haven, CT, USA)
Perry, Martha (Washington, DC, USA)
Pestelli, Giorgio (Turin, Italy)
Petazzi, Paolo (Milan, Italy)
Petersen, Barbara A. (New York City, NY, USA)
Petrobelli, Pierluigi (Rome, Italy)
Petty, Frederick (Carlisle, PA, USA)
Philip, Robert (Ashwell, Herts., UK)
Pigozzi, Marinella (Bologna, Italy)
Pincoe, Ruth (Toronto, Ont., Canada)
Pines, Roger (San Diego, CA, USA)
Pinzauti, Leonardo (Florence, Italy)
Piperno, Franco (Rome, Italy)
Pitt, Charles (Nogent-sur-Marne, France)
Platoff, John (Hartford, CT, USA)
Platt, Peter (Pymble, NSW, Australia)
Platt, Richard (Falmouth, Cornwall, UK)
Pogue, Samuel F. (Cincinnati, OH, USA)
Polacek, J. (Jerusalem, Israel)
Pollin, Burton R. (Bronxville, NY, USA)
Poniatowska, Irena (Warsaw, Poland)
Porter, Andrew (London, UK)
Porter, Susan L. (Lima, OH, USA)
Pospíšil, Milan (Prague, Czechoslovakia)
Poštolka, Milan (Prague, Czechoslovakia)
Potvin, Gilles (Outrement, Quebec Province, Canada)

Powell, John S. (Tulsa, OK, USA)
Pozzi, Raffaele (Rome, Italy)
Preston, Katherine K. (Williamsburg, VA, USA)
Price, Curtis (London, UK)
Primmer, Brian (Capelgarmon, Gwynedd, UK)
Pritchard, Brian W. (Christchurch, New Zealand)
Przybylski, Tadeusz (Kraków, Poland)
Pukl, Oldřich (Prague, Czechoslovakia)
Purkis, Charlotte (Southampton, UK)

Quattrocchi, Arrigo (Rome, Italy)

Radic, Thérèse (Clayton, Victoria, Australia)
Radomski, James (Los Angeles, CA, USA)
Rae, Caroline A. (Cardiff, UK)
Raeburn, Christopher (London, UK)
Rainbow, Bernarr (Richmond, Surrey, UK)
Ralston, Jack L. (Virginia Beach, VA, USA)
Rasch, Rudolf A. (Utrecht, Netherlands)
Raspé, Paul (Brussels, Belgium)
Rattalino, Piero (Milan, Italy)
Ravenni, Gabriella Biagi (Pisa, Italy)
Reed, Ida (Chapel Hill, NC, USA)
Rehbach, Jeffrey R. (Middlebury, VT, USA)
Reissinger, Marianne (Frankfurt, Germany)
Rex, Walter (Berkeley, CA, USA)
Reynolds, Barbara (Cambridge, UK)
Reynolds, William H. (Riverside, CA, USA)
Rice, John A. (Houston, TX, USA)
Richardson, Cynthia S. (Seattle, WA, USA)
Ricketts, Carolyn V. (London, Ont., Canada)
Ridgway, Ronald S. (Saskatoon, Sask., Canada)
Ridout, Godfrey
Riedel, Friedrich W. (Mainz, Germany)
Riemens, Leo
Riepe, Juliane (Mechernich, Germany)
Riessauw, Anne-Marie (Ghent, Belgium)
Rigoli, Paolo (Verona, Italy)
Riis, Thomas (Athens, GA, USA)
Rijavec, Andrej (Ljubljana, Slovenia)
Riva, Douglas (Brooklyn, NY, USA)
Robert, Frédéric (Paris, France)
Roberts, John H. (Berkeley, CA, USA)
Roberts, Sarah (London, UK)
Robinson, Michael F. (Cardiff, UK)
Robinson, Philip (Hatfield, Herts., UK)
Robinson, Philip E. J. (Canterbury, Kent, UK)
Roccatagliati, Alessandro (Reggio Emilia, Italy)
Roche, Elizabeth (Durham, UK)
Rockwell, John (Paris, France)
Rolf, Marie (Rochester, NY, USA)
Røllum-Larsen, Claus (Roskilde, Denmark)
Rönnau, Klaus
Root, Deane L. (Pittsburgh, PA, USA)
Rorem, Ned (Nantucket, MA, USA)
Rosand, Ellen (New Haven, CT, USA)
Rose, Michael (London, UK)
Roseman, Ulysses jr
Rosen, Jerome (Davis, CA, USA)
Rosenberg, Jesse (New York City, NY, USA)
Rosenfeld, Sybil (London, UK)
Rosenthal, Harold
Rosner, Arnold (Brooklyn, NY, USA)
Rosow, Lois (Columbus, OH, USA)
Ross, Peter (Stuttgart, Germany)
Rosselli, John (Cambridge, UK)
Rossi, Nick (Columbia, SC, USA)
Rothärmel, Marion (Plittersdorf, Germany)
Roy, James G. (New York City, NY, USA)
Rumessen, Vardo (Tallin, Estonia)
Rushton, Julian (Leeds, UK)
Russell, Eleanor (Northridge, CA, USA)
Russell Hulme, David (Aberystwyth, UK)
Rutter, John (Duxford, Cambs., UK)

Sabol, Andrew J. (Providence, RI, USA)
Sachs, Harvey (Loro Ciuffenna, Italy)
Sadie, Julie Anne (London, UK)
Sadie, Stanley (London, UK)
Sadler, Graham (Hull, UK)
Sage, Jack (London, UK)
Sala di Felice, Elena (Cagliari, Italy)
Salgado, Susana (Alexandria, VA, USA)
Salmenhaara, Erkki (Helsinki, Finland)
Salmon, Gregory
Saloman, Ora Frishberg (New York City, NY, USA)
Salter, Lionel (London, UK)
Samama, Leo (Hilversum, Netherlands)
Sams, Eric (Sanderstead, Croydon, Surrey, UK)
Sams, Jeremy (London, UK)
Samson, Jim (Exeter, UK)
Samuel, Harold E. (New Haven, CT, USA)
Sandow, Gregory (New York City, NY, USA)
Sansone, Matteo (Florence, Italy)
Santiago, Antón de (La Coruña, Spain)
Sarkisyan, Svetlana (Erevan, Armenia)
Sarnaker, Benedict (London, UK)
Saunders, Harris S. (Los Angeles, CA, USA)
Savage, Roger (Edinburgh, UK)
Sawer, David (London, UK)
Sawkins, Lionel (Beckenham, Kent, UK)
Saya, Virginia (Los Angeles, CA, USA)
Saylor, Bruce (New York City, NY, USA)
Schabas, Ezra (Toronto, Ont., Canada)
Schäffer, Bogusław (Kraków, Poland)
Scharnagl, August (Straubing, Germany)
Schauensee, Max de
Schiørring, Nils (Frederiksberg, Denmark)
Schlotel, Brian (Woking, Surrey, UK)
Schmid, Hans (Munich, Germany)
Schmidt, Carl B. (Philadelphia, PA, USA)
Schneider, Herbert (Heidelberg, Germany)
Schnitzler, Rudolf (Kingston, Ont., Canada)
Schnoebelen, Anne (Houston, TX, USA)
Schönleber, Jochen (Tübingen, Germany)
Schönzeler, Hans-Hubert (London, UK)
Schousboe, Torben (Copenhagen, Denmark)
Schröder, Dorothea (Hamburg, Germany)
Schuller, Gunther (Newton Center, MA, USA)
Schwartz, Deborah (Arcata, CA, USA)
Schwarz, Boris
Schwinger, Wolfram (Stuttgart, Germany)
Scott, David (London, UK)
Searle, Humphrey
Seeger, Horst (Dresden, Germany)
Sehnal, Jiří (Brno, Czechoslovakia)
Seidel, Klaus J. (Munich, Germany)
Seifert, Herbert (Vienna, Austria)
Selfridge-Field, Eleanor (Sunnyvale, CA, USA)
Sellors, Anthony (London, UK)
Semeonoff, Boris (Edinburgh, UK)

Senn, Walter
Šerých, Anna (Prague, Czechoslovakia)
Shaheen, Ronald (Los Angeles, CA, USA)
Shanet, Howard (New York City, NY, USA)
Shapiro, Anne Dhu (Newton, MA, USA)
Sharp, G. B.
Shawe-Taylor, Desmond (Wimborne Minster, Dorset, UK)
Shearon, Stephen (Raleigh, NC, USA)
Shelpuk, Natalie (Charlotte, NC, USA)
Shepard, John (New York City, NY, USA)
Shere, Charles (Berkeley, CA, USA)
Sheren, Paul (New York City, NY, USA)
Short, Bradley H. (Waltham, MA, USA)
Shulman, Laurie C. (Dallas, TX, USA)
Sietz, Reinhold
Sievers, Heinrich (Hanover, Germany)
Simeone, Nigel (Histon, Cambs., UK)
Simmons, Walter (Crompond, NY, USA)
Simon, Delbert R. (Rockford, IL, USA)
Simpson, Adrienne (Wellington, New Zealand)
Simpson, Helen (London, UK)
Sjoerdsma, R. D. (Kenosha, WI, USA)
Skelton, Geoffrey (Shoreham by Sea, Sussex, UK)
Slatford, Rodney (London, UK)
Slim, H. Colin (Irvine, CA, USA)
Smaczny, Jan (Birmingham, UK)
Smet, Monique de (Auderghem, Brussels, Belgium)
Smith, Catherine Parsons (Reno, NV, USA)
Smith, Christopher (Norwich, UK)
Smith, Dean (Charlotte, NC, USA)
Smith, Kent M. (Edina, MN, USA)
Smith, Patrick J. (New York City, NY, USA)
Smith, Peter (London, Ont., Canada)
Smither, Howard E. (Chapel Hill, NC, USA)
Snyder, Kerala Johnson (Rochester, NY, USA)
Sommer, Susan T. (New York City, NY, USA)
Sonntag, Sabine (Hanover, Germany)
Soumagnac, Myriam (Courbevoie, France)
Southern, Eileen (Cambridge, MA, USA)
Spencer, Jennifer (Wymondham, Norfolk, UK)
Spencer, Stewart (London, UK)
Špendal, Manica (Maribor, Slovenia)
Spiegl, Fritz (Liverpool, UK)
Spieth-Weissenbacher, Christiane
Spitzer, John (Baltimore, MD, USA)
Spratt, Geoffrey K. (Cork, Ireland)
Starr, Lawrence (Seattle, WA, USA)
Starreveld, Rogier (Amsterdam, Netherlands)
Steane, J. B. (Coventry, UK)
Stedman, Jane W. (Chicago, IL, USA)
Stefanović, Dimitrije (Belgrade, Serbia)
Stein, Louise K. (Ann Arbor, MI, USA)
Steinbeck, Dietrich (Berlin, Germany)
Steinberg, Michael (Edina, MA, USA)
Stenzl, Jürg (Neyruz, Switzerland)
Stephenson, Kurt (Bad Bramstedt, Germany)
Stern, Kenneth (New York City, NY, USA)
Sternfeld, Frederick W. (Oxford, UK)
Steude, Wolfram (Dresden, Germany)
Stevenson, Robert (Los Angeles, CA, USA)
Stewart, Brian D. (Hamburg, Germany)
Stiller, Andrew (Philadelphia, PA, USA)
Stone, Peter Eliot (New York City, NY, USA)
Stonehouse, Alison (London, Ont., Canada)
Suarez Pajares, Javier (Madrid, Spain)
Suffern, Carlos (Buenos Aires, Argentina)
Surian, Elvidio (Pesaro, Italy)
Suskin, Sylvan (Oberlin, OH, USA)
Sutcliffe, Bob (Gernika, Spain)
Suttoni, Charles (New York City, NY, USA)
Swift, Richard (Davis, CA, USA)
Symons, Christopher (Belgrave, Victoria, Australia)
Szeker-Madden, Lisa (London, Ont., Canada)
Szweykowska, Anna (Kraków, Poland)

Taïeb, Patrick (Paris, France)
Talbot, Michael (Liverpool, UK)
Tallián, Tibor (Budapest, Hungary)
Tammaro, Ferruccio (Turin, Italy)
Tanenbaum, Faun (Evanston, IL, USA)
Tarr, Edward H. (Basle, Switzerland)
Tartak, Marvin (San Francisco, CA, USA)
Taruskin, Richard (Berkeley, CA, USA)
Tauragis, Adeodatas (Vilnius, Lithuania)
Tawa, Nicholas E. (Boston, MA, USA)
Taylor, Carole (London, UK)
Teal, Mary D. (Ypsilanti, MI, USA)
Tegen, Martin (Stockholm, Sweden)
Temperley, Nicholas (Urbana, IL, USA)
Termini, Olga (Los Angeles, CA, USA)
Thériault, Jacques (Montreal, Quebec Province, Canada)
Thomas, Adrian (London, UK)
Thomas, Ernst (Darmstadt, Germany)
Thompson, Donald (Rio Piedras, Puerto Rico)
Thompson, Kenneth (St Albans, Herts., UK)
Thompson, Wendy (Moreton Morrell, Warwicks., UK)
Thomson, J. M. (Wellington, New Zealand)
Thorne, Francis (New York City, NY, USA)
Tilmouth, Michael
Timms, Colin (Birmingham, UK)
Tonini, Giuliano (Bolzano, Italy)
Toop, Richard (Sydney, NSW, Australia)
Torres Mulas, Jacinto (Madrid, Spain)
Toscani, Claudio (Casalmaggiore, Italy)
Townend, Richard (London, UK)
Trevitt, John (Athens, Greece)
Trojan, Jan (Brno, Czechoslovakia)
Troost, Linda V. (Washington, PA, USA)
Trotter, Herman (Buffalo, NY, USA)
Trowell, Brian (Oxford, UK)
Troy, Charles E.
Trudu, Antonio (Cagliari, Italy)
Tsou, Judy (Berkeley, CA, USA)
Tubeuf, André (Strasbourg, France)
Tucker, Mark (New York City, NY, USA)
Tunley, David (Nedlands, Western Australia)
Turchin, Barbara (Merrick, NY, USA)
Turnbull, Michael T. R. B. (Longniddry, E. Lothian, UK)
Turnbull, T. Michael (Edinburgh, UK)
Tyler, Linda (Princeton, NJ, USA)
Tyrrell, John (Nottingham, UK)

Ulrich, Allan (Oakland, CA, USA)
Unverricht, Hubert (Mainz, Germany)

Vajda, Igor (Bratislava, Czechoslovakia)
Van Deun, Jacques (Antwerp, Belgium)

Vanhulst, Henri (Brussels, Belgium)
Várnai, Péter P.
Vázquez, Roland J. (Medford, MA, USA)
Vázsonyi, Bálint (Bloomington, IN, USA)
Vendrix, Philippe (Liège, Belgium)
Veniard, Juan María (Buenos Aires, Argentina)
Vernaz, Fannie (Paris, France)
Viale Ferrero, Mercedes (Turin, Italy)
Viano, Richard (Hackensack, NJ, USA)
Vicini, Sara (Funo di Argelato, Bologna, Italy)
Vitali, Carlo (Bologna, Italy)
Vītoliņš, Jēkabs
Volborth-Danys, Diana von (Brussels, Belgium)
Volek, Tomislav (Prague, Czechoslovakia)
Vollsnes, Arvid (Oslo, Norway)
Vratislavský, Jan
Vysloužil, Jiří (Brno, Czechoslovakia)

Wade, Mara R. (Urbana, IL, USA)
Wagner, John W. (Newberry, SC, USA)
Wagstaff, John (Oxford, UK)
Wahlström, Erik (Helsinki, Finland)
Walker, Evan
Walker, Thomas (Princeton, NJ, USA)
Walsh, Michael (New York City, NY, USA)
Walter, Horst (Bergisch Gladbach, Germany)
Walton, Robin (Johannesburg, South Africa)
Wangermee, Robert (Brussels, Belgium)
Warburton, Ernest (London, UK)
Warburton, Thomas (Chapel Hill, NC, USA)
Ward Jones, Peter (Oxford, UK)
Warrack, John (Oxford, UK)
Watanabe, Ruth T. (Rochester, NY, USA)
Waterhouse, John C. G. (Birmingham, UK)
Waters, Edward N.
Watson, Derek (West Linton, Peeblesshire, UK)
Weaver, Robert Lamar (Louisville, KY, USA)
Weaver, William (Arezzo, Italy)
Weimer, Eric D. (Chicago, IL, USA)
Weiss, Piero (Baltimore, MD, USA)
Weller, Philip (Nottingham, UK)
Wells, Walter (State College, PA, USA)
Wessely, Helene (Vienna, Austria)
Wessely, Othmar (Vienna, Austria)
Westrup, Jack
Whenham, John (Birmingham, UK)
Whisler, Bruce A. (Orlando, FL, USA)
White, A. Duane (Milledgeville, GA, USA)
White, Chappell (Manhattan, KS, USA)
Whitesitt, Linda (Rock Hill, SC, USA)
Whittall, Arnold (London, UK)
Wierzbicki, James (St Louis, MO, USA)
Wignall, Harrison James (Mount Holly, NJ, USA)
Wiklund, Anders (Göteborg, Sweden)
Wild, Nicole (Paris, France)
Wiley, Roland J. (Ann Arbor, MI, USA)
Will, Ethyl L.
Willaert, Saskia (London, UK)
Williams, A. Glyn (Birkenhead, UK)
Williams, Bernard (Oxford, UK)
Williams, Cedric (Norwich, UK)
Williams, Hermine W. (Clinton, NJ, USA)
Williams, Nicholas (London, UK)
Willier, Stephen A. (Philadelphia, PA, USA)
Willis, Stephen C. (Ottawa, Ont., Canada)
Wilson, Charles A. (Bournemouth, Dorset, UK)
Wilson, Christopher R. (Reading, UK)
Wilson, Fredric Woodbridge (New York City, NY, USA)
Wilson, Thelma (Brentwood, Essex, UK)
Wingrove, Susan (Anchorage, AK, USA)
Wintle, Christopher (London, UK)
Wirsta, Aristide (Bourg-la-Reine, France)
Wirth, Helmut
Wollenberg, Susan (Oxford, UK)
Wood, Caroline (Hull, UK)
Wood, Elizabeth (Staten Island, NY, USA)
Woodward, Julie (Croton-on-Hudson, NY, USA)
Worbs, Hans Christoph (Hamburg, Germany)
Wouters, Jos
Wright, David (New York City, NY, USA)
Wright, Elizabeth A. (Brooklyn, NY, USA)
Wright, Josephine (Wooster, OH, USA)
Wright, Lesley A. (Honolulu, HI, USA)
Wright, Simon (Moreton-in-Marsh, Gloucs., UK)
Wright, Stella J. (London, UK)
Würtz, Roland (Weisenheim am Berg, Germany)
Würz, Anton (Munich, Germany)

Yampol'sky, I. M.
Yellin, Victor Fell (New York City, NY, USA)
Yener, Faruk (Istanbul, Turkey)
Young, Percy M. (Wolverhampton, UK)

Zanetti, Emilia (Rome, Italy)
Zaslaw, Neal (Ithaca, NY, USA)
Zoppelli, Luca (Venice, Italy)
Županović, Lovro (Zagreb, Croatia)

Appendix D

ILLUSTRATION ACKNOWLEDGMENTS

We are grateful to those listed below for permission to reproduce illustrative material, and those contributors who supplied or helped us obtain it. Every effort has been made to contact copyright holders; we apologize to anyone who may have been omitted.

VOLUME ONE

Ackté, Aino Stuart-Liff Collection, Port Erin, Isle of Man
Admeto British Library, London
Adriana Lecouvreur Giancarlo Costa, Milan
Africaine, L' Mary Evans Picture Library, London
Ägyptische Helena, Die Bildarchiv, Österreichische Nationalbibliothek, Vienna
Aida Bibliothèque et Musée de l'Opéra/photo Bibliothèque Nationale, Paris
Albani, Emma Theatre Museum/Board of Trustees of the Victoria and Albert Museum, London
Albert Herring Hulton-Deutsch Collection, London
Alboni, Marietta Elizabeth Forbes Collection, London
Alceste (i) *1* Musée du Louvre, Paris/photo Réunion des Musées Nationaux; *2* Bibliothèque Nationale, Paris
Alceste (ii) Bibliothèque et Musée de l'Opéra/photo Bibliothèque Nationale, Paris
Alceste (iv) Museum der Bildenden Künste, Leipzig
Al gran sole carico d'amore Teatro alla Scala, Milan/photo Lelli and Masotti
Amadis Bibliothèque Nationale, Paris
Amahl and the Night Visitors Collection Robert L. B. Tobin, San Antonio, Texas
Amsterdam Richard Macnutt, Withyham, Sussex
Andrea Chénier photo Giancarlo Costa, Milan
Anisfeld, Boris Izrayelevich The Art Institute of Chicago (Friends of American Art Collection, 1922–85)/photo © 1992
Anna Bolena Museo Teatrale alla Scala, Milan
Antony and Cleopatra Metropolitan Opera Archives, New York
Arabella Theatermuseum, University of Cologne
Ariadne auf Naxos (ii) *1* Archives of the Staatstheater, Stuttgart; *2* Bildarchiv, Österreichische Nationalbibliothek, Vienna
Armide (i) Bibliothèque Nationale, Paris
Arsinoe Board of Trustees of the Victoria and Albert Museum, London
Artaxerxes Theatre Museum/Board of Trustees of the Victoria and Albert Museum, London
Attilio Regolo Kupferstichkabinett, Dresden/photo Deutsche Fotothek, Sächsische Landesbibliothek, Dresden
Atys (i) Bibliothèque Nationale, Paris
Aufstieg und Fall der Stadt Mahagonny Weill-Lenya Research Center, Kurt Weill Foundation for Music, New York

Baccaloni, Salvatore Stuart-Liff Collection, Port Erin, Isle of Man
Bach, Johann Christian Museo Civico, Turin
Bahr-Mildenburg, Anna Stuart-Liff Collection, Port Erin, Isle of Man
Balbi, Giovan Battista Fototeca dell'Istituto per le Lettere, il Teatro e il Melodramma, Fondazione Giorgio Cini, Venice
Balfe, Michael William Elizabeth Forbes Collection, London
Ballet de Cour The National Trust, Waddesdon Manor/photo Courtauld Institute of Art, University of London
Barbiere di Siviglia, Il (ii) Fondazione G. Rossini, Pesaro/photo Comune de Pesaro
Bartered Bride, The Národní Muzeum (Muzeum České Hudby), Prague
Bassarids, The Max-Reinhardt-Forschungs- und Gedenkstätte, Salzburg/photo Madner
Bassi, Luigi Mary Evans Picture Library, London
Battistini, Maria Stuart-Liff Collection, Port Erin, Isle of Man
Bayreuth *1* Callwey Verlag, Munich/photo Helga Schmidt-Glassner (for M. Baur-Heinhold, *Theater des Barock*, Munich, 1966; Eng. trans., 1967); *2*, *4* Nationalarchiv der Richard-Wagner-Stiftung/ Richard-Wagner-Gedenkstätte, Bayreuth; *3* Methuen London Ltd: from R. Leacroft and H. Leacroft, *Theatre and Playhouse* (London, 1984)
Beatrice di Tenda Museo Correr, Venice/photo Civici Musei Veneziani d'Arte e di Storia
Beggar's Opera, The Kunstbibliothek, Staatliche Museen, Berlin
Bellavite, Innocente Museo Civico, Turin
Belle Hélène, La Bibliothèque et Musée de l'Opéra/ photo Bibliothèque Nationale, Paris
Bellini, Vincenzo Conservatorio di Musica S

Cecilia, Rome

Benefit *1* Richard Macnutt, Withyham, Sussex; *2* Theatre Museum/Board of Trustees of the Victoria and Albert Museum, London

Benois, Nicola Teatro alla Scala, Milan/photo Erio Piccagliani

Benvenuto Cellini Bibliothèque et Musée de l'Opéra/photo Bibliothèque Nationale, Paris

Berlin *1* from Ernst Bücken, *Die Musik des Rokokos und der Klassik* (Wildpark-Potsdam, 1927); 2 Staatliche Schlösser und Gärten, Potsdam Sans Souci, Berlin/photo Herrmann; *3*, *4* Archiv für Kunst und Geschichte, Berlin; *5* © Hartmut Henning/Archiv Komische Oper, Berlin

Berlioz, Hector *1* Nationale Forschungs- und Gedenkstätten der klassischen deutschen Literatur, Weimar; 2 Bibliothèque Nationale, Paris

Bernacchi, Antonio Maria Istituto di Storia dell'Arte, Fondazione Giorgio Cini, Venice

Berthélémy, Jean-Simon Bibliothèque et Musée de l'Opéra/photo Bibliothèque Nationale, Paris

Bertin, Louise Bibliothèque et Musée de l'Opéra/photo Bibliothèque Nationale, Paris

Beuther, Friedrich Christian Kunstbibliothek, Staatliche Museen, Berlin

Billy Budd photo Roger Wood, Deal, Kent

Bizet, Georges Stiftelsen Musikkulturens Främjande, Stockholm

Björling, Jussi Opera News, Metropolitan Opera Guild Inc., New York

Bluebeard's Castle *1* Universal Edition, Vienna; *2* Bartók Archívum, Magyar Tudományos Akadémia, Budapest

Bohème, La (i) *1* Ricordi Historical Archive, Milan; 2 Biblioteca Braidense, Milan/photo Giancarlo Costa

Bohème, La (ii) Biblioteca Braidense, Milan/photo Giancarlo Costa

Bologna Teatro Comunale, Bologna

Bomarzo Collection Robert L. B. Tobin, San Antonio, Texas

Bordeaux Bibliothèque et Musée de l'Opéra/photo Bibliothèque Nationale, Paris

Bordoni, Faustina Kupferstichkabinett, Dresden/Deutsche Fotothek, Sächsische Landesbibliothek, Dresden

Boris Godunov *1* Society for Co-operation in Russian and Soviet Studies, London; 2 Muzïka, Moscow: from R. Shirinian, *M. P. Musorgsky* (Moscow, 1987)

Boulevard Solitude Niedersächsische Staatstheater, Hanover/photo Kurt Julius

Bregenz Bregenzer Festspiel

Britten, Benjamin The Hulton-Deutsch Collection, London; ex.1, Faber Music Ltd, London (© 1973)

Brouwenstijn, Gré photo Reg Wilson, London

Brussels Bibliothèque Royale, Brussels

Buenos Aires Teatro Colón, Buenos Aires

Buona figliuola, La Motley Books Ltd

Bürgschaft, Die Deutsche Oper Berlin/photo Heinz Köster

Bury, John photo Guy Gravett, Hurstpierpoint, Sussex

Caldara, Antonio *1* Biblioteca Apostolicana Vaticana (Fondo Ruspoli, vol.B51, 1711); 2 Österreichische Nationalbibliothek (MS.17160), Vienna

Calvé, Emma Stuart-Liff Collection, Port Erin, Isle of Man

Cambon, Charles-Antoine Bibliothèque et Musée de l'Opéra/photo Bibliothèque Nationale, Paris

Capriccio Deutsches Theatermuseum, Munich

Capuleti e i Montecchi, I Museo Correr, Venice/photo Civici Musei Veneziani d'Arte e di Storia

Cardillac Theatermuseum, University of Cologne

Carmen Editions Choudens, Paris/photo Evan Baker, New York

Carnaval de Venise, Le Bibliothèque et Musée de l'Opéra/photo Bibliothèque Nationale, Paris

Caron, Rose Bibliothèque et Musée de l'Opéra/photo Bibliothèque Nationale, Paris

Caruso, Enrico Stuart-Liff Collection, Port Erin, Isle of Man

Castelli, Ottaviano Biblioteca Apostolica Vaticana, Rome

Castor et Pollux English Bach Festival/photo Chris Davies

Catalani, Angelica Theatre Museum/Board of Trustees of the Victoria and Albert Museum, London

Catel, Charles-Simon Bibliothèque et Musée de l'Opéra/photo Bibliothèque Nationale, Paris

Cavalleria rusticana (i) photo Giancarlo Costa, Milan

Cavalli, Francesco Biblioteca Nazionale Marciana, Venice/photo Toso

Cendrillon (ii) Motley Books Ltd

Chicago Chicago Historical Society

Christoff, Boris Stuart-Liff Collection, Port Erin, Isle of Man

Cigoli Galleria degli Uffizi, Florence/Fototeca dell'Istituto per le Lettere, il Teatro e il Melodramma, Fondazione Giorgio Cini, Venice

Cinti-Damoreau, Laure Opera Rara Collection, London

Clemenza di Tito, La Theatermuseum, University of Cologne

Colas Breugnon Society for Co-operation in Russian and Soviet Studies, London

Colbran, Isabella Museo Teatrale alla Scala, Milan/photo Giancarlo Costa

Colonello, Attilio Arena di Verona, Press Office Archive/photo Franco Fainello

Commedia dell'Arte Galleria degli Uffizi, Florence/Fototeca dell'Istituto per le Lettere, il Teatro e il Melodramma, Fondazione Giorgio Cini, Venice

Comte Ory, Le Bibliothèque et Musée de l'Opéra/photo Bibliothèque Nationale, Paris

Contes d'Hoffmann, Les Bibliothèque et Musée de l'Opéra/photo Bibliothèque Nationale, Paris

Continuo Deutsches Theatermuseum, Munich

Corigliano, John Metropolitan Opera Association Inc., Lincoln Center, New York/photo Winnie Klotz

Corregidor, Der from H. Werner, ed., *Hugo Wolf: Briefe an Rosa Mayreder* (Vienna, 1921)

Così fan tutte Biblioteka Jagiellońska, Kraków/photo Janusz Podlecki

Costume *1* Biblioteca Nazionale Centrale, Florence; *2* private collection/photo Jim Styles, Canterbury, Kent; *3* Trustees of the British Museum (Department of Prints and Drawings), London; *4a* Nationalmuseum/photo Statens Konstmuseer, Stockholm; *4b* Musée du Louvre (Collection Rothschild)/photo Réunion des Musées Nationaux, Paris; *5a* Motley Books Ltd; *5b* Marina Henderson Gallery, London; 6 Bibliothèque et Musée de l'Opéra/photo Bibliothèque Nationale, Paris; *7*, *8*, *10* Bibliothèque Nationale, Paris; *9*, *12*, *14* Royal Opera House Archives, Covent Garden, London; *11* Bayerische Verwaltung der Staatlichen Schlösser, Gärten und Seen, Munich; *13* Board of Trustees of the Victoria and Albert Museum, London/Boosey & Hawkes Music Publishers Ltd; *15* Drottningholms Teatermuseum, Stockholm; *16* © Irene Sharaff: from I. Sharaff, *Broadway and Hollywood* (New York, 1976); *17* Theatre Museum (Messel Collection)/Board of Trustees of the Victoria and Albert Museum, London (by permission of the Earl of Snowdon); *18* © Maurizio Chiari/photo Royal Opera House Archives, Covent Garden, London; *19a* © Marcel Escoffier/photo Royal Opera House Archives, Covent Garden, London; *19b* photo Zoë Dominic, London; *20*, *26* (left) Collection Robert L. B. Tobin, San Antonio, Texas; *21* © Julia Trevelyan Oman/photo Donald Southern, London; *22* Oper der Stadt Köln; *23a* Nationalarchiv der Richard-Wagner-Stiftung / Richard-Wagner-Gedenkstätte, Bayreuth; *23b* Theatre Museum/Board of Trustees of the Victoria and Albert Museum, London; *23c* © Peter Sykora/Deutsche Oper Berlin: from G. Friedrich and others, *Der Ring des Nibelungen: Die Walküre* (Berlin, 1984–8); *24* Pet Halmen, Munich; *25* Maria Bjornson, London/photo David Crossthwaite; *26* (right) San Francisco Opera

Craig, Edward Gordon Motley Books Ltd

Crociato in Egitto, Il Museo Teatrale alla Scala, Milan/photo Giancarlo Costa

Crosato, Giambattista Museo Civico, Turin

Cunning Little Vixen, The *1*, *2* Moravské Muzeum, Brno

Curtain drawing by Alan Forster

Daguerre, Louis-Jacques-Monde Bibliothèque et Musée de l'Opéra/photo Bibliothèque Nationale, Paris

Dalibor Národní Muzeum (Muzeum České Hudby), Prague

Dance *1* Archives Nationales, Paris; *2* Bibliothèque Nationale, Paris; *3* Bibliothèque et Musée de l'Opéra/photo Bibliothèque Nationale, Paris; *4* Deutsches Theatermuseum, Munich; *5* Britten-Pears Library, Aldeburgh/photo John Garner

Dardanus (i) *1* Bibliothèque et Musée de l'Opéra/photo Bibliothèque Nationale, Paris; *2* Caisse Nationale des Monuments Historiques et des Sites, Paris/photo Jérôme de La Gorce

Del Monaco, Mario Stuart-Liff Collection, Port Erin, Isle of Man

De Luca, Giuseppe Opera News, Metropolitan Opera Guild Inc., New York

De Nobili, Lila Teatro alla Scala, Milan/photo Erio Piccagliani

De Reszke Bibliothèque et Musée de l'Opéra/photo Bibliothèque Nationale, Paris

Déserteur, Le formerly Collection Musicale André Meyer, Paris/photo J. P. Ziolo

Desprez, Louis-Jean Drottningholms Teatermuseum, Stockholm

Devils of Loudun, The Staatsoper, Hamburg/photo Peyer

Devin du village, Le Bibliothèque Nationale, Paris

Devoto, John Trustees of the British Museum (Department of Prints and Drawings), London

Dialogues des Carmélites Teatro alla Scala, Milan/photo Erio Piccagliani

Dibdin, Charles Harvard Theater Collection, Harvard University, Cambridge, Massachusetts

Dido and Aeneas Royal College of Music, London

Didon (i) Motley Books Ltd

Dimitrij Theatre Collection, Národní Muzeum, Prague/photo Olga Hilmerová

Divertissement Bulloz, Paris

Doktor Faust (ii) Theatermuseum, University of Cologne

Doktor Faustus Teatro alla Scala, Milan/photo Lelli and Masotti

Dom Sébastien, roi de Portugal Mary Evans Picture Library, London

Don Carlos Bibliothèque et Musée de l'Opéra/photo Bibliothèque Nationale, Paris

Don Giovanni (ii) private collection/photo Národní Muzeum, Prague

Donizetti, Gaetano Comune di Bergamo: from facsimile of *Lucia di Lammermoor* (Milan: Bestetti, 1941)

Donnerstag aus Licht Teatro alla Scala, Milan/photo Lelli and Masotti

Don Pasquale Royal Opera House Archives, Covent Garden, London

Don Quichotte Motley Books Ltd

Dorus-Gras, Julie Bibliothèque et Musée de l'Opéra/photo Bibliothèque Nationale, Paris

Dreigroschenoper, Die Theatermuseum, University of Cologne

Dresden *1* Fototeca dell'Istituto per le Lettere, il Teatro e il Melodramma, Fondazione Giorgio Cini, Venice; *2* Kupferstichkabinett, Dresden/Deutsche Fotothek, Sächsische Landesbibliothek, Dresden; *3* Deutsches Theatermuseum, Munich; *4*, *8* Deutsche Fotothek, Sächsische Landesbibliothek, Dresden; *5* Mary Evans Picture Library, London; *6* Archiv für Kunst und Geschichte, Berlin; *7* Staatsoper, Dresden

Drottningholm *1–3*, Drottningholms Teatermuseum, Stockholm

Dugazon, Louise-Rosalie Motley Books Ltd

Duni, Egidio Bibliothèque Nationale, Paris

VOLUME TWO

Eames, Emma Stuart-Liff Collection, Port Erin, Isle of Man

Egk, Werner B. Schott's Söhne, Mainz/photo Helmuth von Kujawa

Einstein on the Beach Byrd Hoffman Foundation Inc., New York

Elegy for Young Lovers photo Sabine Toepffer, Munich

Elektra British Library Newspaper Library, Colindale, London

Elisir d'amore, L' Theatre Museum/Board of Trustees of the Victoria and Albert Museum, London

Enfant et les sortilèges, L' Société de Bains de Mer, Monte Carlo

English Cat, The B. Schott's Söhne, Mainz/photo Joachim Schmidtmann

Entführung aus dem Serail, Die from

Neujahrsgeschenk an die Zürcherische Jugend, new ser., xxi (1833)
Ernelinde, princesse de Norvège Bibliothèque et Musée de l'Opéra/photo Bibliothèque Nationale, Paris
Esclarmonde Bibliothèque et Musée de l'Opéra/photo Bibliothèque Nationale, Paris
Eszterháza Bartók Archívum, Magyar Tudományos Akadémia, Budapest
Euridice (ii) Österreichische Nationalbibliothek, Vienna
Euryanthe Bildarchiv der Preussischer Kulturbesitz, Berlin
Excursions of Mr Brouček, The Moravské Muzeum, Brno

Falcon, Cornélie Bibliothèque et Musée de l'Opéra/photo Bibliothèque Nationale, Paris
Falstaff (ii) *1* photo Giancarlo Costa, Milan; *2* Ricordi Historical Archive, Milan
Fanciulla del West, La Metropolitan Opera Archives, New York
Farinelli National Gallery of Victoria (Felton Bequest), Melbourne, Australia
Faure, Jean-Baptiste Kunsthalle, Hamburg
Faust (ii) *1* Elizabeth Forbes Collection, London; *2* photo Harlingue-Viollet, Roger Viollet, Paris
Favart, Marie-Justine-Benoîte Bibliothèque et Musée de l'Opéra/photo Bibliothèque Nationale, Paris
Favorite, La Richard Macnutt, Withyham, Sussex
Fedra (ii) Biblioteca Braidense, Milan/photo Giancarlo Costa
Ferne Klang, Der © Dietrich Alfred Roller, Vienna/Musiksammlung, Österreichische Nationalbibliothek
Ferrara Biblioteca Comunale Ariostea, Ferrara
Ferrario, Carlo private collection
Fetonte Museu Nacional de Arte Antiga, Lisbon
Feuersnot British Library Newspaper Library, Colindale, London
Fidelio Stadtbibliothek Winterthur
Fiery Angel, The Archivio Storico delle Arti Contemporanee della Biennale di Venezia
Fille du régiment, La photo Giancarlo Costa, Milan
Film *1, 2, 4, 5* photo BFI Stills, Posters and Designs, London; *3* Movie Acquisitions Film Library, Pinewood Studios, Iver, Bucks./photo BFI Stills, Posters and designs, London; 6 Betafilm, Munich/photo BFI Stills, Posters and Designs, London
Finta pazza, La Biblioteca Apostolica Vaticana, Rome
Flagstad, Kirsten Stuart-Liff Collection, Port Erin, Isle of Man
Fledermaus, Die Johann Strauss Society/photo Royal Opera House Archives, Covent Garden, London
Fliegende Holländer, Der Mary Evans Picture Library, London
Florence *1* Kunstbibliothek, Staatliche Museen, Berlin; *2* Civico Museo Bibliografico Musicale, Bologna; *3, 4* Biblioteca Nazionale Centrale, Florence
Fontana, Girolamo Motley Books Ltd
Fontanesi, Francesco Fototeca dell'Istituto per le Lettere, il Teatro e il Melodramma, Fondazione Giorgio Cini, Venice
Forza del destino, La Kirov Theatre, St Petersburg
Four Saints in Three Acts Bettmann Archive, New York
Francesca da Rimini (ii) Museo Teatrale alla Scala, Milan/photo Giancarlo Costa
Frau ohne Schatten, Die Deutsches Theatermuseum, Munich
Freischütz, Der *1* Kunstbibliothek, Staatliche Museen, Berlin; 2 from Julius Kapp, *Geschichte des Staatsoper Berlin* (Berlin, 1937)
Friedenstag Archiv für Kunst und Geschichte, Berlin
Frigerio, Ezio Staatsoper, Hamburg/photo Joachim Thode
From the House of the Dead Moravské Muzeum, Brno

Galliari Museo Civico, Turin
Galli-Bibiena *1* Fototeca dell'Istituto per le Lettere, il Teatro e il Melodramma, Fondazione Giorgio Cini, Venice; *2* Národní Muzeum, Prague/photo Olga Hilmerová; *3* British Architectural Library, Royal Institute of British Architects, London; *4* Drottningholms Teatermuseum, Stockholm
Galli-Curci, Amelita Stuart-Liff Collection, Port Erin, Isle of Man
Galli-Marié, Célestine Bibliothèque et Musée de l'Opéra/photo Bibliothèque Nationale, Paris
Galuppi, Baldassare Motley Books Ltd
Gambling Mary Evans Picture Library, London
García, Manuel Bibliothèque et Musée de l'Opéra/photo Bibliothèque Nationale, Paris
Garden, Mary Stuart-Liff Collection, Port Erin, Isle of Man
Gaspari, Giovanni Paolo Staatliche Graphische Sammlung, Munich
Genoa Armando Fabio Ivaldi
Georgiadis, Nicholas Nicholas Georgiadis/photo Richard Holltum
Gérard, Rolf Metropolitan Opera Archives, New York
Ghighlia, Lorenzo Teatro alla Scala, Milan/photo Erio Piccagliani
Gianni Schicchi Metropolitan Opera Archives, New York
Gigli, Beniamino Opera News, Metropolitan Opera Guild Inc., New York
Gioconda, La Mary Evans Picture Library, London
Girardi, Alexander Historisches Museum der Stadt Wien
Giulio Sabino Civica Raccolta delle Stampe Achille Bertarelli, Castello Sforzesco, Milan
Gluck, Christoph Willibald *1* Bibliothèque et Musée de l'Opéra/photo Bibliothèque Nationale, Paris; *2* Bibliothèque Municipale, Nantes
Glyndebourne Glyndebourne Festival Opera
Gobbi, Tito Stuart-Liff Collection, Port Erin, Isle of Man
Golden Cockerel, The *1* All-Union Pushkin Museum, St Petersburg/Muzïka, Moscow; *2* Central A. A. Bakhrushin State Theatrical Museum, Moscow/Muzïka, Moscow (both from A. Kruchinina and I. Obraztsova, *N. A. Rimsky-Korsakov*, 1988)
Gondoliers, The Raymond Mander and Joe Mitchenson Theatre Collection, Beckenham, Kent
Gonzaga, Pietro Hermitage Museum, St Petersburg/Fototeca dell'Istituto per le Lettere, il Teatro e il Melodramma, Fondazione Giorgio Cini, Venice
Götterdämmerung Nationalarchiv der Richard-Wagner-Stiftung / Richard-Wagner-Gedenkstätte, Bayreuth
Goyescas Metropolitan Opera Archives, New York
Grand Macabre, Le Kungliga Teatern, Stockholm/

photo Enar Rydberg
Grand opéra *1, 4* Bibliothèque et Musée de l'Opéra/photo Bibliothèque Nationale, Paris; *2* Bibliothèque Historique de la Ville de Paris; *3* Elizabeth Forbes Collection, London; *5* Civica Raccolta delle Stampe Achille Bertarelli, Castello Sforzesco, Milan
Greek Passion, The Universal Edition, Vienna
Greenwood, Thomas Motley Books Ltd
Griselda private collection/Fototeca dell'Istituto per le Lettere, il Teatro e il Melodramma, Fondazione Giorgio Cini, Venice
Grisi, Giulia Elizabeth Forbes Collection, London
Guillaume Tell Bibliothèque et Musée de l'Opéra/photo Bibliothèque Nationale, Paris
Guitti, Francesco Fototeca dell'Istituto per le Lettere, il Teatro e il Melodramma, Fondazione Giorgio Cini, Venice
Gustaf Wasa National Museum, Stockholm/Statens Konstmuseer
Gustave III Bibliothèque et Musée de l'Opéra/photo Bibliothèque Nationale, Paris
Gwendoline Mary Evans Picture Library, London

Halka Museum of the Wielki Theatre, Warsaw/photo Tadeusz Kazimierski
Hamburg *1* Staats- und Universitätsbibliothek/Freie und Hansestadt Hamburg; *2* Landesbibliothek, Weimar/Fototeca dell'Istituto per le Lettere, il Teatro e il Melodramma, Fondazione Giorgio Cini, Venice; *3* Kurpfälzisches Museum der Stadt Hamburg
Hamlet Theatermuseum, University of Cologne
Handel, George Frideric *1, 2* British Library, London; *3* Kungliga Teatern, Stockholm/photo Enar Rydberg; *4* Archiv Komische Oper, Berlin/photo Arwid Lagenpusch; *5* Boston Early Music Festival/photo Peter Schweitzer
Hänsel und Gretel Archiv für Kunst und Geschichte, Berlin
Harms, Johann Oswald Herzog Anton Ulrich-Museum, Brunswick
Hasse, Johann Adolf Conservatorio di Musica Giuseppe Verdi, Milan
Haydn, Joseph Széchényi Nationalbibliothek, Budapest
Heinrich, Rudolf Archiv Komische Oper, Berlin/photo Jürgen Simon
Hempel, Frieda Stuart-Liff Collection, Port Erin, Isle of Man
Hidalgo, Juan Houghton Library, Harvard University, Cambridge, Massachusetts
Hockney, David photo Guy Gravett, Hurstpierpoint, Sussex
Hong Kong Charles Pitt
Hotter, Hans Theatre Museum/Board of Trustees of the Victoria and Albert Museum, London
Huguenots, Les Bibliothèque et Musée de l'Opéra/photo Bibliothèque Nationale, Paris
Hurry, Leslie Royal Opera House Archives, Covent Garden, London/photo Baron

Intermedio Board of Trustees of the Victoria and Albert Museum, London
Intermezzo Museo Teatrale alla Scala, Milan
Intermezzo Sabine Toepffer, Munich
Intolleranza 1960 Josef Svoboda, Prague
Iphigénie en Aulide Musée du Louvre, Paris/Réunion des Musées Nationaux
Iphigénie en Tauride Kungliga Biblioteket, Stockholm
Italiana in Algeri, L' Richard Macnutt, Withyham, Sussex

Janáček, Leoš *1, 2* Moravské Muzeum, Brno
Jasager, Der Weill-Lenya Research Center, Kurt Weill Foundation for Music, New York
Jenůfa Moravské Muzeum, Brno
Jessonda Kunstbibliothek, Staatliche Museen, Berlin
Jolli, Antonio Staatlichen Kunstsammlungen Dresden
Jommelli, Niccolò Biblioteca Nazionale, Naples/Fototeca dell'Istituto per le Lettere, il Teatro e il Melodramma, Fondazione Giorgio Cini, Venice
Jones, Inigo Trustees of the Chatsworth Settlement (Devonshire Collection, Chatsworth)/photo Courtauld Institute of Art, University of London
Jones, Robert Edmond Collection Robert L. B. Tobin, San Antonio, Texas
Jonny spielt auf Theatermuseum, University of Cologne
Joseph Marina Henderson Gallery, London
Journet, Marcel Stuart-Liff Collection, Port Erin, Isle of Man
Juive, La Bibliothèque et Musée de l'Opéra/photo Bibliothèque Nationale, Paris
Julietta Theatre Collection, Národní Muzeum, Prague/photo Olga Hilmerová
Junge Lord, Der B. Schott's Söhne, Mainz/photo Heinz Köster
Jurinac, Sena Stuart-Liff Collection, Port Erin, Isle of Man
Juvarra, Filippo Board of Trustees of the Victoria and Albert Museum, London

Kagel, Mauricio Staatsoper, Hamburg/photo Fritz Peyer
Kát'a Kabanová Moravské Muzeum, Brno
Keiser, Reinhard Staats- und Universitätsbibliothek Hamburg/Freie und Hansestadt Hamburg
Khovanshchina Muzïka, Moscow: from R. Shirinian, *M. P. Musorgsky* (Moscow, 1987)
King Priam Theatre Museum/Board of Trustees of the Victoria and Albert Museum, London/photo Houston Rogers
King Roger Museum of the Wielki Theatre, Warsaw/photo Tadeusz Kazimierski
Kiss, The Theatre Collection, Národní Muzeum (Muzeum Český Hudby), Prague
König Hirsch B. Schott's Söhne, Mainz/photo Jlse Buhs
Königin von Saba, Die Bildarchiv, Österreichische Nationalbibliothek, Vienna
Königskinder Metropolitan Opera Archives, New York
Krenek, Ernst Universal Edition, Vienna
Krusceniski, Salomea Stuart-Liff Collection, Port Erin, Isle of Man
Kurz, Selma Stuart-Liff Collection, Port Erin, Isle of Man

Lady Macbeth of the Mtsensk District Novosti Photo Library, London
Lakmé Mary Evans Picture Library, London
Lazaridis, Stefanos English National Opera/photo Clive Barda

Legend of the Invisible City of Kitezh and the Maiden Fevroniya Muzïka, Moscow: from A. Kruchinina and I. Obraztsova, *N. A. Rimsky-Korsakov* (Moscow, 1988)

Lehmann, Lilli Bibliothèque et Musée de l'Opéra/ photo Bibliothèque Nationale, Paris

Lehmann, Lotte Stuart-Liff Collection, Port Erin, Isle of Man

Leider, Frida Stuart-Liff Collection, Port Erin, Isle of Man

Leipzig *2* Museum für Geschichte der Stadt Leipzig

Lenya, Lotte National Portrait Gallery, Smithsonian Institution, Washington DC

Libretto (i) *1–5* Richard Macnutt, Withyham, Sussex

Libuše Archive of the National Theatre, Prague/photo Olga Hilmerová

Liebe der Danae, Die Max-Reinhardt-Forschungs- und Gedenkstätte, Salzburg

Life for the Tsar, A Muzïka, Moscow: from A. Rozanov, *M. I. Glinka* (Moscow, 1983)

Lighting *1a* Suffolk County Council, Arts and Libraries Department, Ipswich; *1b* Drottningholms Teatermuseum, Stockholm; *2* Muzeum Narodowe, Warsaw; *3b*, *5b*, *5c* Mary Evans Picture Library, London; *3c*, *4*, *5a*, *6* Motley Books Ltd; *7* Metropolitan Opera Association Inc., Lincoln Center, New York/photo Winnie Klotz; *8* Royal Opera House, Covent Garden, London/photo Richard Holltum; *9* Sipa Press, Paris/photo Kleinefenn and Moatti; *10* Electronic Theater Controls, Middleton, Wisconsin; *12* (above) Nationalarchiv der Richard-Wagner-Stiftung/ Richard-Wagner-Gedenkstätte, Bayreuth; *12* (lower) Bibliothèque et Musée de l'Opéra/photo Bibliothèque Nationale, Paris; *13* © Gunther Schneider-Siemssen/William Morrow & Co. Inc., New York: from R. Hartmann, *Opera* (New York, 1977)

Lind, Jenny Elizabeth Forbes Collection, London

Lingwood, Tom The Australian Opera

Lisbon *1* Richard Macnutt, Withyham, Sussex; *2* Museu Nacional de Arte Antiga, Lisbon

Lohengrin (i) Raymond Mander and Joe Mitchenson Theatre Collection, Beckenham, Kent

Lombardi alla prima crociata, I Museo Correr/ photo Civici Musei Veneziani d'Arte e di Storia, Venice

VOLUME THREE

London *1* Bodleian Library, Oxford; *2*, *4* Trustees of the British Museum (Department of Prints and Drawings), London/photo Fotomas Index, Beckenham, Kent; *3* Royal Library, Windsor Castle (© Her Majesty the Queen); *5*, *8*, *14*, *17* Theatre Museum/Board of Trustees of the Victoria and Albert Museum, London; *7* Pennsylvania State University Library (Winston Papers); *9* Elizabeth Forbes Collection, London; *10* Raymond Mander and Joe Mitchenson Theatre Collection, Beckenham, Kent; *11* Hulton-Deutsch Collection, London; *12* English National Opera, London/photo Clive Barda; *13* The London Museum; *15* Motley Books Ltd

Lorenzaccio Ricordi Historical Archive, Milan

Los Angeles, Victoria de Stuart-Liff Collection, Port Erin, Isle of Man

Love for Three Oranges, The Muzïka, Moscow: from M. Nest'yeva, *Serge Prokofyev* (Moscow, 1981)

Love in a Village Board of Trustees of the Victoria and Albert Museum, London

Lubin, Germaine Bibliothèque et Musée de l'Opéra/ photo Bibliothèque Nationale, Paris

Lucca Museo Civico, Turin

Lucca, Pauline Stuart-Liff Collection, Port Erin, Isle of Man

Lucia di Lammermoor Opera Rara Collection, London

Lucio Silla (i) Pinacoteca di Brera, Milan

Lulu (ii) Universal Edition, Vienna

Lustige Witwe, Die Bildarchiv, Österreichische Nationalbibliothek, Vienna

Macbeth (ii) Collection Carrara-Verdi, Sant'Agata, nr Busseto/photo Giancarlo Costa, Milan

Machinery *1* Callwey Verlag, Munich/photo Helga Schmidt-Glassner (for M. Baur-Heinhold, *Theater des Barock*, Munich, 1966; Eng. trans., 1967); *2*, *5* Gustaf Kull; *3*, *6*, *13* drawings by Alan Forster; *4*, *8* Archives Nationales, Paris; *7* Bibliothèque et Musée de l'Opéra/photo Bibliothèque Nationale, Paris; *9* Explorer, Paris/photo Jacques Moatti, Paris; *10* Methuen London Ltd: from Richard Leacroft, *The Development of the English Playhouse* (London, 1973, 2/1988); *11* Theatre Museum/Board of Trustees of the Victoria and Albert Museum, London; *12*, *18* Motley Books Ltd; *14* from E. O. Sachs and A. E. Woodrow, *Modern Opera Houses and Theatres*, iii (London, 1898); *15a* photo Roger Wood, Deal, Kent; *15b* Bayreuther Festspiele; *19a* Mary Evans Picture Library, London

Madama Butterfly *1* Ricordi Historical Archive, Milan; *2* Stuart-Liff Collection, Port Erin, Isle of Man

Madrid *1* Österreichische Nationalbibliothek, Vienna/ Fototeca dell'Istituto per le Lettere, il Teatro e il Melodramma, Fondazione Giorgio Cini, Venice; *2* Museo del Prado, Madrid

Maid of Orléans, The Muzïka, Moscow: from G. Pribegina, *P. I. Chaykovsky* (Moscow, 1984)

Makropulos Affair, The Moravské Muzeum, Brno

Malibran, Maria Opera Rara Archives, London

Mamelles de Tirésias, Les private collection (heirs of Francis Poulenc)

Mannheim Städtisches Reiss Museum, Mannheim

Manon Bibliothèque et Musée de l'Opéra/photo Bibliothèque Nationale, Paris

Manon Lescaut (ii) Biblioteca Braidense, Milan/photo Giancarlo Costa

Manzuoli, Giovanni Civica Raccolta delle Stampe Achille Bertarelli, Castello Sforzesco, Milan

Marazzoli, Marco Kungliga Biblioteket Stockholm

Marchisio Elizabeth Forbes Collection, London

Maria di Rohan Opera Rara Collection, London

Marini, Leonardo Mercedes Viale Ferrero, Turin

Martha Bildarchiv, Österreichische Nationalbibliothek, Vienna

Martinelli, Giovanni Stuart-Liff Collection, Port Erin, Isle of Man

Maschinist Hopkins Theatermuseum, University of Cologne

Mask of Orpheus, The photo Zoë Dominic, London

Masnadieri, I Theatre Museum/Board of Trustees of the Victoria and Albert Museum, London
Masque Trustees of the Chatsworth Settlement (Devonshire Collection, Chatsworth)/photo Courtauld Institute of Art, University of London
Maurel, Victor Museo Teatrale alla Scala, Milan
Mauro Fototeca dell'Istituto per le Lettere, il Teatro e il Melodramma, Fondazione Giorgio Cini, Venice
Mavra Bibliothèque et Musée de l'Opéra/photo Bibliothèque Nationale, Paris
Maximowna, Ita Teatro La Fenice, Venice
May Night Muzïka, Moscow: from A. Kruchinina and I. Obraztsova, *N. A. Rimsky-Korsakov* (Moscow, 1988)
Mayr, Richard Bildarchiv, Österreichische Nationalbibliothek, Vienna
Medea in Corinto Opera Rara Collection, London
Medée (i) Archives Nationales, Paris
Medium, The Playpont Films Ltd, London/photo BFI Stills, Posters and Designs, London
Mefistofele Motley Books Ltd/from V. Bignami, *Cinquecento bozzetti di scenografia di Carlo Ferrario* (Milan, 1919)
Meistersinger von Nürnberg, Die Bayerisches Verwaltung der Staatliches Schlösser, Gärten und Seen, Munich
Melchior, Lauritz Royal Opera House Archives, Covent Garden, London
Melodrama Nationale Forschungs- und Gedenkstätten der klassischen deutschen Literatur, Weimar
Messidor Editions Choudens, Paris
Midsummer Marriage, The Theatre Museum/Board of Trustees of the Victoria and Albert Museum, London/photo Houston Rogers
Midsummer Night's Dream, A Particam Foundation, Amsterdam/photo Maria Austria
Mignon Bibliothèque et Musée de l'Opéra/photo Bibliothèque Nationale, Paris
Milan *1*, *2*, *3* Civica Raccolta delle Stampe Achille Bertarelli, Castello Sforzesco, Milan; *4* photo Giancarlo Costa, Milan; *5* Trustees of the British Museum (Department of Prints and Drawings), London; *6* Biblioteca Braidense, Milan/photo Giancarlo Costa; *7* Teatro alla Scala, Milan/photo Lelli and Masotti
Milwaukee Franklin S. Miller
Mireille Bibliothèque et Musée de l'Opéra/photo Bibliothèque Nationale, Paris
Mlada (ii) Muzïka, Moscow: from A. Kruchinina and I. Obraztsova, *N. A. Rimsky-Korsakov* (Moscow, 1988)
Mödl, Martha photo Siegfried Lauterwasser, Überlingen
Molinara, La Akademie für Bildenden Künste, Vienna
Mondo della luna, Il Motley Books Ltd
Montag aus Licht Teatro alla Scala, Milan/photo Lelli and Masotti
Monte Carlo Mary Evans Picture Library, London
Montresor, Beni Collection Robert L. B. Tobin, San Antonio, Texas
Moscow photo Giancarlo Costa, Milan
Moses und Aron Opernhaus, Zürich/photo Susann Schimert-Ramme
Mozart, Wolfgang Amadeus Deutsche Staatsbibliothek, Berlin
Muette de Portici, La *1* Theatre Museum/Board of Trustees of the Victoria and Albert Museum, London; *2* Bibliothèque et Musée de l'Opéra/photo Bibliothèque Nationale, Paris
Munich *1*, *2* Deutsches Theatermuseum, Munich; *3* Stadtmuseum, Munich; *4* Bayerische Verwaltung der Staatlichen Schlösser, Gärten und Seen, Munich; *5* Motley Books Ltd
Muzio, Claudia Stuart-Liff Collection, Port Erin, Isle of Man

Nabucco Ricordi Historical Archive, Milan
Naples *1* Bibliothèque et Musée de l'Opéra/photo Bibliothèque Nationale, Paris; *2* Fototeca dell'Istituto per le Lettere, il Teatro e il Melodramma, Fondazione Giorgio Cini, Venice; *3* Harvard Theater Collection, Harvard University, Cambridge, Massachusetts
Nerone (ii) Biblioteca Braidense, Milan/photo Giancarlo Costa
Neumann-Spallart, Gottfried private collection
New Year photo Guy Gravett, Hurstpierpoint, Sussex
New York *1* Library of Congress, Washington DC; *2* Mary Evans Picture Library, London; *3* Bettmann Archive, New York; *4 Opera*, London; *5* Metropolitan Opera House, New York; *6*, *7* Lincoln Center for the Performing Arts Inc./Metropolitan Opera Association Inc., New York/US Postal Service, Washington DC; *8* Irene Lawford
Nicolini Istituto di Storia dell'arte, Fondazione Giorgio Cini, Venice
Niemann, Albert Nationalarchiv der Richard-Wagner-Stiftung / Richard-Wagner-Gedenkstätte, Bayreuth
Nilsson, Birgit Stuart-Liff Collection, Port Erin, Isle of Man
Nilsson, Christine Elizabeth Forbes Collection, London
Nina Bildarchiv, Österreichische Nationalbibliothek, Vienna
Nixon in China Houston Grand Opera Archives, Houston, Texas/photo Jim Caldwell
Nordica, Lillian Stuart-Liff Collection, Port Erin, Isle of Man
Norma Elizabeth Forbes Collection, London
Nourrit, Adolphe Bibliothèque et Musée de l'Opéra/photo Bibliothèque Nationale, Paris
Nozze di Figaro, Le Bibliothèque Nationale, Paris

Oberon *1* Royal Opera House Archives, Covent Garden, London; *2* Board of Trustees of the Victoria and Albert Museum, London/photo Fotomas Index, Beckenham, Kent
Oedipe à Colone Motley Books Ltd
Oedipus rex Boosey & Hawkes Music Publishers Ltd, London
Oenslager, Donald private collection/Patton Campbell/photo Jeffrey S. Koger
Olimpie Bibliothèque et Musée de l'Opéra/photo Bibliothèque Nationale, Paris
Opéra comique *1*, *2*, *3* Bibliothèque et Musée de l'Opéra/photo Bibliothèque Nationale, Paris
Opera glasses *1* Henry E. Huntington Library and Art Gallery, San Marino, California
Opera seria *1* Museo Civico d'Arte Antica, Turin; *3* Deutsches Theatermuseum, Munich; *4* Museo Teatrale alla Scala, Milan/Fototeca dell'Istituto per le Lettere, il Teatro e il Melodramma, Fondazione

Giorgio Cini, Venice; *5* Music Library, University of California, Berkeley

Operetta *1*, *2*, *6* Bibliothèque et Musée de l'Opéra/photo Bibliothèque Nationale, Paris; *3* Pierpont Morgan Library, New York

Orchestra *1* Civica Raccolta delle Stampe Achille Bertarelli, Castello Sforzesco, Milan; *2* Fototeca dell'Istituto per le Lettere, il Teatro e il Melodramma, Fondazione Giorgio Cini, Venice; *3* Museo Correr, Venice/photo Civici Musei Veneziani d'Arte e di Storia; *4* Theatre Collection, Národní Muzeum, Prague/photo Olga Hilmerová; *5* Bibliothèque Nationale, Paris; *6* Bibliothèque et Musée de l'Opéra/photo Bibliothèque Nationale, Paris; *7* Museo Civico d'Arte Antica, Turin; *8* Bildarchiv, Österreichische Nationalbibliothek, Vienna; *9* Royal College of Music, London; *10* Bibliothèque Municipale, Versailles; *11*, *12*, *13* drawings by Alan Forster; *14* photo Siegfried Lauterwasser, Überlingen; *16* Frank Spooner Pictures, London/photo Laurie Lewis; *17* Teatro alla Scala, Milan/photo Lelli and Masotti; *18* photo Carl Machover

Orfeo (i) *1* Early Opera Project/Historic Arts; *2* Biblioteca Nazionale Centrale, Florence

Orfeo ed Euridice (i) Kungliga Teatern, Stockholm/photo Enar Rydberg

Orff, Carl Staatstheater, Stuttgart/photo Hannes Kilian

Orlando paladino Széchényi Nationalbibliothek, Budapest

Orphée aux enfers Bulloz, Paris

Ossian, ou Les bardes Bibliothèque et Musée de l'Opéra/photo Bibliothèque Nationale, Paris

Osud John Tyrrell, University of Nottingham

Otello (ii) *1* Ricordi Historical Archive, Milan; *2*, *3* Biblioteca Braidense, Milan

Padmâvatî Bibliothèque et Musée de l'Opéra/photo Bibliothèque Nationale, Paris

Padua photo Giancarlo Costa, Milan

Pagliacci photo Giancarlo Costa, Milan

Paisiello, Giovanni Mercedes Viale Ferrero, Turin

Paladins, Les Caisse Nationale des Monuments Historiques et des Sites, Paris/photo Jérôme de La Gorce

Palestrina Theatermuseum, University of Cologne

Parigi, Giulio Board of Trustees of the Victoria and Albert Museum, London

Paris *1*, *4*, *7*, *8* Bibliothèque Nationale, Paris; *2*, *12–15*, *17*, *20–22* Bibliothèque et Musée de l'Opéra/photo Bibliothèque Nationale, Paris; *3* Museo Teatrale alla Scala, Milan; *5* Musée Carnavalet, Paris/photo Bulloz; *6* Archives Nationales, Paris; *10* Kunstbibliothek, Staatliche Museen, Berlin; *11* Motley Books Ltd; *16* Giraudon, Paris; *18* Mary Evans Picture Library, London; *19* Musée de Luxembourg/photo Roger-Viollet, Paris; *23* Opera Rara Collection, London; *24*, *25* Sipa Press, Paris/photo Kleinefenn and Moatti

Parma *1* Archivi Alinari, Florence; *2* Teatro Regio/Archivio Storico Comunale, Parma

Parsifal from F. Kranich, *Bühnentechnik der Gegenwart*, i (Munich, 1929)

Pasqualini, Marc'Antonio The Metropolitan Museum of Art (Enid A. Haupt Gift; Gwynne Andrews Fund and purchase, 1871, by exchange, 1981), New York

Pasta, Giuditta Museo Teatrale alla Scala, Milan

Pasticcio private collection

Pastoral *2* Civica Raccolta della Stampe Achille Bertarelli, Castello Sforzesco, Milan

Patzak, Julius Stuart-Liff Collection, Port Erin, Isle of Man

Pêcheurs de perles, Les Bibliothèque et Musée de l'Opéra/photo Bibliothèque Nationale, Paris

Pénélope Société des Bains de Mer, Monte Carlo

Peter Grimes Collection Robert L. B. Tobin, San Antonio, Texas

Petrov, Osip Society for Co-operation in Russian and Soviet Studies, London

Philadelphia Library of Congress, Washington DC

Pilgrim's Progress, The Harvard Theater Collection, Harvard University, Cambridge, Massachusetts/photo Angus McBean

Pinza, Ezio Stuart-Liff Collection, Port Erin, Isle of Man

Pirata, Il Opera Rara Collection, London

Plançon, Pol Stuart-Liff Collection, Port Erin, Isle of Man

Platée Musée du Louvre, Paris/photo Réunion des Musées Nationaux

Platzer, Joseph Akademie der Bildenden Künste, Vienna

Playbill *1*, *2* Richard Macnutt, Withyham, Sussex; *3* Theatre Museum/Board of Trustees of the Victoria and Albert Museum, London; *4* Bibliothèque et Musée de l'Opéra/photo Bibliothèque Nationale, Paris

Pomo d'oro, Il Bildarchiv, Österreichische Nationalbibliothek, Vienna

Ponnelle, Jean-Pierre Royal Opera House, Covent Garden, London/photo Donald Southern

Ponselle, Rosa Stuart-Liff Collection, Port Erin, Isle of Man

Porgy and Bess Collection Robert L. B. Tobin, San Antonio, Texas

Prague *1–4* Theatre Collection, Národní Muzeum, Prague/photo Olga Hilmerová

Price, Leontyne Stuart-Liff Collection, Port Erin, Isle of Man

Prigioniero, Il Teatro Comunale, Florence

Prinz von Homburg, Der Staatsoper, Hamburg

Prodigal Son, The Britten-Pears Library, Aldeburgh/photo Clive Strutt

Production *1* Azienda di Promozione Turistica, Vicenza; *2*, *18* Board of Trustees of the Victoria and Albert Museum, London; *3* Fototeca dell'Istituto per le Lettere, il Teatro e il Melodramma, Fondazione Giorgio Cini, Venice; *4*, *19*, *20* Theatermuseum, University of Cologne; *5* Verwaltung der Staatlichen Schlösser und Gärten, Schloss Charlottenburg, Berlin/photo Jörg P. Anders; *6* Museum of Fine Arts (Gift of Elizabeth Paine Cardin), Boston; *7* Theatre Museum/Board of Trustees of the Victoria and Albert Museum, London; *9* Museo Teatrale alla Scala, Milan; *10* Trustees of the British Museum (Department of Prints and Drawings), London; *11* Bibliothèque et Musée de l'Opéra/photo Bibliothèque Nationale, Paris; *12a* Schloss Tiefurt/photo Nationalen Forschungs- und Gedenkstätten der klassischen deutschen Literatur, Weimar; *12b* Städtische Reiss Museum, Mannheim; *14* Harvard Theater Collection, Harvard University, Cambridge, Massachusetts; *15*, *17* Bibliothèque de la Ville de Paris; *16* Biblioteca Nazionale (Lucchesi-Palli Collection), Naples; *21* Nationalarchiv der Richard-Wagner-Stiftung/Richard-Wagner-Gedenkstätte, Bayreuth/photo Raymond Mander and Joe Mitchenson Theatre Collection, Beckenham, Kent; *22* photo Siegfried Lauterwasser, Überlingen; *23* photo Stuart Robinson, Redruth, Cornwall; *24* Bildarchiv, Bayreuther Festspiele/photo Jean-Marie Bottaquin; *25* photo Mara Eggert, Frankfurt; *26* Metropolitan Opera Association Inc./Lincoln Center, New York/photo Winnie Klotz

Programme *1*, *3*, *4* Richard Macnutt, Withyham, Sussex; *2* Pierpont Morgan Library (Gilbert and Sullivan Collection), New York

Prophète, Le Mary Evans Picture Library, London

Publishing *2*, *4–8*, *10–13* Richard Macnutt, Withyham, Sussex

Puccini, Giacomo *2* Ricordi Historical Archive, Milan

Punch and Judy photo Zoë Dominic, London

Puppet opera Salzburger Marionettentheater

Puritani, I Bibliothèque et Musée de l'Opéra/photo Bibliothèque de l'Opéra, Paris

Pyne, Louisa Elizabeth Forbes Collection, London

Pyotr I Novosti Photo Library, London

Quaglio Theatermuseum, University of Cologne

Queen of Spades, The Theatre and Music Museum, St Petersburg

Quiet Place, A Houston Grand Opera Archives, Houston, Texas/photo Jim Caldwell

Raaff, Anton Deutsches Theatermuseum, Munich

Rake's Progress, The Archivio Storico delle Arti Contemporanee della Biennale di Venezia/photo Giacomelli

Rape of Lucretia, The Raymond Mander and Joe Mitchenson Theatre Collection, Beckenham, Kent

Rauzzini, Venanzio Trustees of the British Museum, (Department of Prints and Drawings), London

Re, Vincenzo British Architectural Library, Royal Institute of British Architects, London

Recording Metropolitan Opera Archives, New York

Rehearsal *1* private collection/photo Colnaghi, London; *2* Bibliothèque et Musée de l'Opéra/photo Bibliothèque Nationale, Paris; *3* Music Division, New York Public Library at Lincoln Center (Astor, Lenox and Tilden Foundations), New York; *4* Royal Opera House, Covent Garden, London/Boosey & Hawkes Music Publishers Ltd

Reichmann, Theodor Nationalarchiv der Richard-Wagner-Stiftung / Richard-Wagner-Gedenkstätte, Bayreuth

Reimann, Aribert photo Sabine Toepffer, Munich

Re in ascolto, Un Universal Edition, Vienna

Re pastore, Il Fototeca dell'Istituto per le Lettere, il Teatro e il Melodramma, Fondazione Giorgio Cini, Venice

Rheingold, Das Nationalarchiv der Richard-Wagner-Stiftung/Richard-Wagner-Gedenkstätte, Bayreuth

Richard Coeur-de-lion Bibliothèque Nationale, Paris

Richards, John Inigo Yale Center for British Art (Paul Mellon Collection), New Haven, Connecticut

Rienzi Deutsches Theatermuseum, Munich

Righini, Pietro Fototeca dell'Istituto per le Lettere, il Teatro e il Melodramma, Fondazione Giorgio Cini, Venice

Rigoletto *1* Museo Correr, Venice/Civici Musei Veneziani d'Arte e di Storia; *2* Richard Macnutt, Withyham, Sussex

Rivarola, Alfonso Conservatorio di Musica S Cecilia, Rome/Fototeca dell'Istituto per le Lettere, il Teatro e il Melodramma, Fondazione Giorgio Cini, Venice

Robert le diable Conservatoire de Musique, Paris/photo Réunion des Musées Nationaux

VOLUME FOUR

Roi Arthus, Le Motley Books Ltd

Roi d'Ys, Le Bibliothèque et Musée de l'Opéra/photo Bibliothèque Nationale, Paris

Roi malgré lui, Le Bibliothèque et Musée de l'Opéra/photo Bibliothèque Nationale, Paris

Roland (i) Bibliothèque Nationale, Paris

Roland (ii) Motley Books Ltd

Rome *1* Biblioteca Apostolica Vaticana, Rome; *2* Biblioteca Nazionale Universitaria, Turin; *3* Musée du Louvre, Paris/photo Réunion des Musées Nationaux: *4* Biblioteca Braidense, Milan/photo Giancarlo Costa

Roméo et Juliette (ii) Theatre Museum (Guy Little Collection)/Board of Trustees of the Victoria and Albert Museum, London

Rooker, Michael Angelo Trustees of the British Museum (Department of Prints and Drawings), London

Rosenkavalier, Der *1*, *2* Marina Henderson Gallery, London

Rossini, Gioachino *1* Harry Ransom Humanities Research Center (Gernsheim Collection), University of Texas, Austin; *2* Civico Museo Bibliografico Musicale, Bologna; *3* Museo Teatrale alla Scala, Milan

Rubini, Giovanni Battista Opera Rara Collection, London

Rusalka (iii) Národní Technické Muzeum, Prague/photo Olga Hilmerová

Ruslan and Lyudmila Muzïka, Moscow: from A. Rozanov, *M. I. Glinka* (Moscow, 1983)

Russia Society for Co-operation in Russian and Soviet Studies, London

Sacred opera Nationalarchiv der Richard-Wagner-Stiftung/Richard-Wagner-Gedenkstätte, Bayreuth

Sadko Muzïka, Moscow: from A. Kruchinina and I. Obraztsova, *N. A. Rimsky-Korsakov* (Moscow, 1988)

Saint François d'Assise Bibliothèque Nationale, Paris/photo Jacques Moatti

St Petersburg *1* Robert Harding Picture Library, London/photo Victor Kennett; *2* Mary Evans Picture Library, London; *3* Muzïka, Moscow: from A. Rozanov, *M. I. Glinka* (Moscow, 1983); *4* Novosti Photo Library, London

Saint-Saëns, Camille Bibliothèque et Musée de l'Opéra/photo Bibliothèque Nationale, Paris

Salome Archiv für Kunst und Geschichte, Berlin

Salzburg photo Max-Reinhardt-Forschungs- und Gedenkstätte, Salzburg

Samson et Dalila Mary Evans Picture Library, London

San Francisco Performing Arts Library and Museum, San Francisco
Sanquirico, Alessandro Kunstbibliothek, Staatliche Museen, Berlin
Santa Fe Santa Fe Opera, Santa Fe, New Mexico/ photo David Stein
Sant'Alessio Innsbruck Festival of Early Music/photo Egon Wurm
Santurini, Francesco (i) Fototeca dell'Istituto per le Lettere, il Teatro e il Melodramma, Fondazione Giorgio Cini, Venice
Šárka Theatre Collection, Národní Muzeum, Prague/ photo Olga Hilmerová
Satyagraha Staatstheater, Stuttgart
Scalzi, Carl The Wadsworth Atheneum (Sumner Collection), Hartford, Connecticut
Scarlatti Board of Trustees of the Victoria and Albert Museum, London
Schikaneder, Emanuel Internationale Stiftung Mozarteum, Salzburg
Schipa, Tito Stuart-Liff Collection, Port Erin, Isle of Man
Schneider-Siemssen, Günther Metropolitan Opera Association Inc., Lincoln Center, New York/photo Winnie Klotz
Schnorr von Carolsfeld, Ludwig Stuart-Liff Collection, Port Erin, Isle of Man
Schorr, Friedrich Stuart-Liff Collection, Port Erin, Isle of Man
Schröder-Devrient, Wilhelmine Bildarchiv, Österreichische Nationalbibliothek, Vienna
Schubert, Franz Landesbibliothek, Vienna
Schumann, Elisabeth Gerhard Puritz, London
Schumann-Heink, Ernestine Stuart-Liff Collection, Port Erin, Isle of Man
Schwarze Maske, Die B. Schott's Söhne, Mainz
Schwarzkopf, Elisabeth Stuart-Liff Collection, Port Erin, Isle of Man
Scotti, Antonio Stuart-Liff Collection, Port Erin, Isle of Man
Scribe, Eugène Bibliothèque et Musée de l'Opéra/ photo Bibliothèque Nationale, Paris
Seating *1* Museum des Kunsthandwerks, Leipzig; *2* Methuen London Ltd: from R. Leacroft and H. Leacroft, *Theatre and Playhouse* (London, 1984); *3* Motley Books Ltd; *4* Royal Opera House, Covent Garden, London; *5* Deutsche Oper Berlin; *6* Staatsoper, Vienna; *7* Paris Opéra (Garnier); *8* Metropolitan Opera House, New York; *9* Paris Opéra (Bastille); *10* Bayreuther Festspiele; *11* British Architectural Library, Royal Institute of British Architects, London; *13* Bibliothèque Nationale, Paris; *14* Drottningholms Teatermuseum
Secret, The Theatre Collection, Národní Muzeum, Prague
Seelewig Stadtbibliothek, Nuremberg
Semiramide Board of Trustees of the Victoria and Albert Museum, London
Semyon Kotko Muzïka, Moscow: from M. Nest'yeva, *Sergey Prokofiev* (Moscow, 1981)
Senesino Raymond Mander and Joe Mitchenson Theatre Collection, Beckenham, Kent
Serenata *1* Biblioteca Museo Correr, Venice/photo Giacomelli; *2* Kupferstichkabinett, Dresden/ Deutsche Fotothek, Sächsische Landesbibliothek, Dresden
Serva padrona, La formerly Collection Musicale André Meyer, Paris/photo J. P. Ziolo
Shalyapin, Fyodor Theatre Museum/Board of Trustees of the Victoria and Albert Museum, London
Siège de Corinthe, Le Bibliothèque et Musée de l'Opéra/photo Bibliothèque Nationale, Paris
Siege of Rhodes, The Trustees of the Chatsworth Settlement (Devonshire Collection, Chatsworth)/ photo Courtauld Institute of Art, University of London
Siegfried Nationalarchiv der Richard-Wagner-Stiftung/Richard-Wagner-Gedenkstätte, Bayreuth
Sievert, Ludwig Theatermuseum (Niessen Collection), University of Cologne
Silbersee, Der Weill-Lenya Research Center, Kurt Weill Foundation for Music, New York
Simon Boccanegra Biblioteca Braidense, Milan
Singspiel Bildarchiv, Österreichische Nationalbibliothek, Vienna
Siroe re di Persia Museo Civico, Turin
Slezak, Leo Stuart-Liff Collection, Port Erin, Isle of Man
Sociology of opera *1* Staatliche Kunstsammlungen, Dresden; *2* Civica Raccolta delle Stampe Achille Bertarelli, Castello Sforzesco, Milan; *3* photo Giancarlo Costa, Milan; *4* photo Bill Cooper, London
Soldaten, Die Theatermuseum, University of Cologne
Sonnambula, La *1* Museo Teatrale alla Scala, Milan; *2* Motley Books Ltd
Sontag, Henriette Theatre Museum/Board of Trustees of the Victoria and Albert Museum, London
Stabile, Mariano Stuart-Liff Collection, Port Erin, Isle of Man
Stage design *1* Metropolitan Museum of Art (Harris Brisbane Dick Fund, 1931, 31.72.5 pl.15), New York; *2, 4, 10, 23* Board of Trustees of the Victoria and Albert Museum, London; *3* Drottningholms Teatermuseum, Stockholm/photo Statens Konstmuseer; *5* Herzog Anton Ulrich-Museum, Brunswick; *6* Theatermuseum, University of Cologne (Niessen Collection); *7* Museo Teatrale alla Scala, Milan/Fototeca dell'Istituto per le Lettere, il Teatro e il Melodramma, Fondazione Giorgio Cini, Venice; *8* Österreichisches TheaterMuseum, Vienna; *9* Bibliothèque Municipale, Besançon; *11, 18* Bibliothèque et Musée de l'Opéra/photo Bibliothèque Nationale, Paris; *12* from *Decorationen auf den beiden königlichen Theatern in Berlin* (Berlin, 1819–24); *13* Kunstbibliothek, Staatliche Museen, Berlin; *14* Motley Books Ltd: from V. Bignami, *Cinquecento bozzetti di scenografia di Carlo Ferrario* (Milan, 1919); *15* Bayerisches Verwaltung der Staatliche Schlösser, Gärten und Seen, Munich; *16* Motley Books Ltd; *17* © Dietrich Alfred Roller/Österreichisches TheaterMuseum, Vienna; *19, 21* Theatermuseum, University of Cologne; *20* from A. Kruchenykh, *Victory over the Sun* (St Petersburg, 1913); *22* photo Weill-Lenya Research Center, Kurt Weill Foundation for Music, New York; *23* Theatre Museum (Messel Collection)/Board of Trustees of the Victoria and Albert Museum, London (by permission of the Earl of Snowdon); *24* The Norman Bel Geddes Collection, Theatre Arts Collection, Harry Ransom Humanities Research Center, University of Texas, Austin (by permission of Edith Lutyens Bel Geddes, executrix); *25* photo Siegfried

Lauterwasser, Überlingen; *26* photo Stuart Robinson, Redruth, Cornwall; *27* Staatstheater, Stuttgart/photo Horst Huber; *28* Théâtre de la Monnaie, Brussels/photo Oliver Herrmann

Stamps Irene Lawford

Storace, Nancy Opera Rara Collection, London

Strauss, Richard *1*, *2* Strauss Archive, Garmisch-Partenkirchen

Street Scene Weill-Lenya Research Center, Kurt Weill Foundation for Music, New York

Suor Angelica Metropolitan Opera Archives, New York

Supervia, Conchita Bibliothèque et Musée de l'Opéra/photo Bibliothèque Nationale, Paris

Sutherland, Joan Stuart-Liff Collection, Port Erin, Isle of Man

Svoboda, Josef Bildarchiv, Staatsoper, Hamburg/photo Fritz Peyer

Sydney *1* photo Kurt Muller, Wayne, New Jersey; *2* Sydney Opera House Trust

Tabarro, Il Metropolitan Opera Archives, New York

Tacca, Ferdinando Deutsches Theatermuseum, Munich

Taglioni, Filippo Marina Henderson Gallery, London

Tale of Tsar Saltan, The Muzïka, Moscow: from A. Kruchinina and I. Obraztsova, *N. A. Rimsky-Korsakov* (Moscow, 1988)

Tamagno, Francesco Stuart-Liff Collection, Port Erin, Isle of Man

Tamburini, Antonio Royal Opera House Archives, Covent Garden, London

Tannhäuser *1* Theatre Collection, Hessischen Landesbibliothek, Darmstadt; *2* Bibliothèque et Musée de l'Opéra/photo Bibliothèque Nationale, Paris

Taverner Royal Opera House Archives, Covent Garden, London/photo Stuart Robinson, Redruth, Cornwall

Television Copyright © BBC

Teofane Kupferstichkabinett, Dresden/Deutsche Fotothek, Sächsische Landesbibliothek, Dresden

Ternina, Milka Stuart-Liff Collection, Port Erin, Isle of Man

Tesi, Vittoria Istituto di Storia d'Arte, Fondazione Giorgio Cini, Venice

Tetrazzini, Luisa Stuart-Liff Collection, Port Erin, Isle of Man

Teyte, Maggie Stuart-Liff Collection, Port Erin, Isle of Man

Thaïs Bibliothèque et Musée de l'Opéra/photo Bibliothèque Nationale, Paris

Theatre architecture *1* Methuen London Ltd: from R. Leacroft and H. Leacroft, *Theatre and Playhouse* (London, 1984); *2*, *6* Methuen London Ltd: from R. Leacroft, *The Development of the English Playhouse* (London, 1973, 2/1988); *3* Deutsches Theatermuseum, Munich; *4* Biblioteca Braidense, Milan/photo Giancarlo Costa; *5* Callwey Verlag, Munich/photo Helga Schmidt-Glassner (for M. Baur-Heinhold, *Theater des Barock*, Munich, 1966; Eng. trans., 1967); *7*, *9* McGraw-Hill Inc., New York: from G. C. Izenour, *Theater Design* (New York, 1977); *8* Deutsche Oper Berlin; *10* photo Giancarlo Costa, Milan; *11* Bibliothèque et Musée de l'Opéra/photo Bibliothèque Nationale, Paris; *12* © 1966 Donald A Mackay/The New York Times

Thomson, Brian State Theatre Company of South Australia, Adelaide

Thornhill, James The Art Institute of Chicago/photo © 1992

Tichatschek, Joseph Royal Opera House Archives, Covent Garden, London

Ticket *a* Trustees of the British Museum (Department of Prints and Drawings, Banks Collection), London; *b*, *h* Theatre Museum/Board of Trustees of the Victoria and Albert Museum, London; *c*, *d*, *e*, *f*, *g*, *i* Richard Macnutt, Withyham, Sussex

Todi, Luisa Civica Raccolta delle Stampe Achille Bertarelli, Castello Sforzesco, Milan

Tom Jones (i) formerly Collection Musicale André Meyer, Paris/photo J. P. Ziolo

Torelli, Giacomo Motley Books Ltd

Tosca Biblioteca Braidense, Milan/photo Giancarlo Costa

Tragédie en musique *1* Bibliothèque Nationale, Paris; *2*, *3* Bibliothèque et Musée de l'Opéra/photo Bibliothèque Nationale, Paris; *4* Drottningholms Teatermuseum

Traviata, La Museo Correr, Venice

Treemonisha Bettmann Archive, New York

Tricarico, Nicolò Istituto di Storia dell'Arte, Fondazione Giorgio Cini, Venice

Tristan und Isolde Bayerische Verwaltung der Staatlichen Schlösser, Gärten und Seen, Munich

Troilus and Cressida Royal Opera House Archives, Covent Garden, London/photo Wilfred Newton

Trovatore, Il Museo Correr, Venice/photo Civici Musei Veneziani d'Arte e di Storia

Troyens, Les *1* Bibliothèque et Musée de l'Opéra/photo Bibliothèque Nationale, Paris; *2* Musée du Louvre, Paris/photo Réunion des Musées Nationaux

Turandot (ii) Biblioteca Braidense, Milan/photo Giancarlo Costa

Turcotti, Maria Giustina Istituto di Storia dell'Arte, Fondazione Giorgio Cini, Venice

Turin *1* Biblioteca Nazionale Universitaria, Turin; *2* Biblioteca Reale, Turin

Turner, Eva Royal Opera House Archives, Covent Garden, London

Turn of the Screw, The Archivio Storico delle Arti Contemporanee della Biennale di Venezia/photo Giacomelli

Two Widows, The Národní Muzeum (Muzeum České Hudby), Prague

Ulisse Deutsche Oper Berlin/photo Harry Croner

Undine (i) Kupferstichkabinett, Staatliche Museen, Berlin

Ursuleac, Viorica Stuart-Liff Collection, Port Erin, Isle of Man

Vampyr, Der (i) A. Dean Palmer, Chatsworth, California

Vanessa Metropolitan Opera Archives, New York

Vanni-Marcoux Bibliothèque et Musée de l'Opéra/photo Bibliothèque Nationale, Paris

Vanvitelli, Luigi Metropolitan Museum of Art (the Elisha Wittelsey Fund, 1964, 64.669.4), New York

Varesi, Felice Museo Teatrale alla Scala, Milan/photo Giancarlo Costa

Vaudeville Bibliothèque Nationale, Paris

Venice *1* Trustees of Sir John Soane's Museum, London; *2*, *3*, *4* Museo Correr, Venice/photo Civici Musei Veneziani d'Arte e di Storia; *5* Metropolitan

Museum of Art (Rogers Fund, 1937, 37.165.73), New York; 6 Nuovo Editoriale SpA, Venice; 7 Teatro La Fenice, Venice/photo Arici and Smith

Vêpres siciliennes, Les from C. Gatti, *Verdi nelle immagini* (Milan, 1941)

Vera storia, La Universal Edition, Vienna

Verdi, Giuseppe *1* from C. Gatti, *Verdi nelle immagini* (Milan, 1941); *2* Carrara-Verdi Collection, Sant'Agata, nr Busseto/photo Giancarlo Costa, Milan; *4* Pierpont Morgan Library (Mary Flagler Cary Collection), New York

Verismo Biblioteca Braidense, Milan/photo Giancarlo Costa

Verona, *1* Royal Library, Windsor Castle (© Her Majesty the Queen); *2* Arena di Verona, Press Office Archive

Verona, Bartolomeo Kunstbibliothek, Staatliche Museen, Berlin

Vestale, La (i) Elizabeth Forbes Collection, London

Vestris, Lucia Elizabeth Theatre Museum/Board of Trustees of the Victoria and Albert Museum, London

Vicenza *1* Mansell Collection, London, and Archivi Alinari, Florence; *2* Theatre Museum/Board of Trustees of the Victoria and Albert Museum, London

Vickers, Jon Metropolitan Opera Archives, New York

Vienna, *1*, *7* Bildarchiv, Österreichische Nationalbibliothek, Vienna; *2* Civica Raccolta delle Stampe Achille Bertarelli, Castello Sforzesco, Milan; *3* Deutsches Theatermuseum, Munich; *4* Hofburg, Vienna/Bildarchiv, Österreichische Nationalbibliothek; *6* Historisches Museum der Stadt Wien; *8* © Dietrich Alfred Roller/Österreichisches TheaterMuseum, Vienna/Bildarchiv, Österreichische Nationalbibliothek

Vie parisienne, La Bibliothèque et Musée de l'Opéra, Paris/photo Giraudon

Village Romeo and Juliet, A Bradford Grammar School/photo Royal Opera House Archives, Covent Garden, London

Von Stade, Frederica The Dallas Opera/photo © 1988 Phil Scheknyder

Wagner *1* Bildarchiv, Österreichische Nationalbibliothek, Vienna; *2* Nationalarchiv der Richard-Wagner-Stiftung / Richard-Wagner-Gedenkstätte, Bayreuth; *3* photo Siegfried Lauterwasser, Überlingen

Wakhévitch, Georges Board of Trustees of the Victoria and Albert Museum, London

Walküre, Die Raymond Mander and Joe Mitchenson Theatre Collection, Beckenham, Kent

War and Peace Novosti Photo Library, London

Weber, Carl Maria von *1* Staatliche Kunstsammlungen, Weimar; *2* Deutsche Staatsbibliothek, Berlin

Weber, Ludwig Stuart-Liff Collection, Port Erin, Isle of Man

We Come to the River B. Schott's Söhne, Mainz/photo Stuart Robinson, Redruth, Cornwall

Weill, Kurt Weill-Lenya Research Center, Kurt Weill Foundation for Music, New York

Weimar Goethemuseum, Weimar/Nationale Forschungs- und Gedenkstätten der klassischen deutschen Literatur, Weimar

Werther Bildarchiv, Österreichische Nationalbibliothek, Vienna

Windgassen, Wolfgang Oper der Stadt Köln

Wozzeck *1* Universal Edition, Vienna; *2* Harvard Theater Collection, Harvard University, Cambridge, Massachusetts/photo Angus McBean

Wunderlich, Fritz photo Reg Wilson, London

Yevgeny Onegin *1* Muzïka, Moscow/VEB Deutscher Verlag für Musik, Leipzig: from K. Yu. Davïdova, I. G. Sokolinskaya and P. E. Vaidman, *P. I. Chaykovsky* (Moscow and Leipzig, 1978); *2* Muzïka, Moscow: from G. Pribegina, *P. I. Chaykovsky* (Moscow, 1984)

Yun, Isang photo Sabine Toepffer, Munich

Zarzuela Biblioteca Catalana, Barcelona

Zauberflöte, Die Historisches Museum der Stadt Wien

Zwerg, Der Theatermuseum, University of Cologne